Reverse
Acronyms, Initialisms &
Abbreviations Dictionary

Explore your options!

Gale databases are offered in a variety of formats

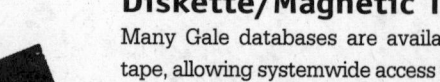

ISSN 0270-4404

Reverse Acronyms, Initialisms & Abbreviations Dictionary

A Companion Volume to *Acronyms, Initialisms & Abbreviations Dictionary*, with Terms Arranged Alphabetically by Meaning of Acronym, Initialism, or Abbreviation

Covering: Aerospace, Associations, Banking, Biochemistry, Business, Data Processing, Domestic and International Affairs, Economics, Education, Electronics, Genetics, Government, Information Technology, Internet, Investment, Labor, Law, Medicine, Military Affairs, Pharmacy, Physiology, Politics, Religion, Science, Societies, Sports, Technical Drawings and Specifications, Telecommunications, Trade, Transportation, and Other Fields

25th Edition

Volume 3

Part 1
A-F

Mary Rose Bonk,
Editor

Pamela Dear,
Associate Editor

GALE

DETROIT • LONDON

Editor:	Mary Rose Bonk
Associate Editor:	Pamela Dear
Contributing Editor:	Mildred Hunt
Data Entry Manager:	Eleanor M. Allison
Data Entry Coordinator:	Kenneth Benson
Production Director:	Mary Beth Trimper
Production Assistant:	Deborah Milliken
Graphic Services Manager:	Barbara J. Yarrow
Macintosh Artist:	Gary Leach
Manager, Technical Support Services:	Theresa A. Rocklin
Programmer:	Charles Beaumont

Library of Congress Catalog Card Number 84-643188
ISBN 0-7876-2455-1 (Volume 1 Complete)
ISBN 0-7876-2456-X (Part 1: A-F only)
ISBN 0-7876-2457-8 (Part 2: G-O only)
ISBN 0-7876-2458-6 (Part 3: P-Z only)
ISSN 0270-4404

Printed in the United States of America

Contents

Volume 1
Part 1 A-F

Volume 1
Part 2 G-O

Volume 1
Part 3 P-Z

Gale's publications in the acronyms and abbreviations field include:

Acronyms, Initialisms & Abbreviations Dictionary series:

Acronyms, Initialisms & Abbreviations Dictionary (Volume 1). A guide to acronyms, initialisms, abbreviations, and similar contractions, arranged alphabetically by abbreviation.

Acronyms, Initialisms & Abbreviations Dictionary Supplement (Volume 2). An interedition supplement in which terms are arranged alphabetically both by abbreviation and by meaning.

Reverse Acronyms, Initialisms & Abbreviations Dictionary (Volume 3). A companion to Volume 1 in which terms are arranged alphabetically by meaning of the acronym, initialism, or abbreviation.

Acronyms, Initialisms & Abbreviations Dictionary Subject Guide series:

Computer & Telecommunications Acronyms (Volume 1). A guide to acronyms, initialisms, abbreviations, and similar contractions used in the field of computers and telecommunications in which terms are arranged alphabetically both by abbreviation and by meaning.

Business Acronyms (Volume 2). A guide to business-oriented acronyms, initialisms, abbreviations, and similar contractions in which terms are arranged alphabetically both by abbreviation and by meaning.

International Acronyms, Initialisms & Abbreviations Dictionary series:

International Acronyms, Initialisms & Abbreviations Dictionary (Volume 1). A guide to foreign and international acronyms, initialisms, abbreviations, and similar contractions, arranged alphabetically by abbreviation.

Reverse International Acronyms, Initialisms & Abbreviations Dictionary (Volume 2). A companion to Volume 1, in which terms are arranged alphabetically by meaning of the acronym, initialism, or abbreviation.

Periodical Title Abbreviations series:

Periodical Title Abbreviations: By Abbreviation (Volume 1). A guide to abbreviations commonly used for periodical titles, arranged alphabetically by abbreviation.

Periodical Title Abbreviations: By Title (Volume 2). A guide to abbreviations commonly used for periodical titles, arranged alphabetically by title.

New Periodical Title Abbreviations (Volume 3). An interedition supplement in which terms are arranged alphabetically both by abbreviation and by title.

Highlights

Over 15,000 New Terms
Arrangement by Meaning
Comprehensive Coverage
Subject Categories
Source Citations

Reverse Acronyms, Initialisms, and Abbreviations Dictionary (RAIAD) enables you to determine the generally accepted short forms of organization names and technical terms in hundreds of fields. It contains essentially the same entries as its companion volume *(Acronyms, Initialisms, and Abbreviations Dictionary)* but arranges these entries alphabetically by meaning, rather than by acronym or initialism. The twenty-fifth edition offers increased coverage in all fields of human endeavor. Many of the 15,000 new terms are from the subject areas of:

- Arts
- Associations
- Business
- Education
- Internet
- Medicine
- Military affairs

Of major value to librarians and researchers is the inclusion of:

- airlines/airports
- information systems
- library symbols
- organizations
- radio/television station call letters
- research centers
- stock exchange symbols

Subject Categories Provided

Where possible, and if not already implied in the entry itself, a category or identifier follows many terms. It provides a subject context for those entries that require clarification.

Major Sources Cited

Codes are provided to indicate the source from which the information was obtained. This feature allows you to verify the entries and may, in some instances, lead to additional information. Complete bibliographic data about the publications cited can be found in the List of Selected Sources following the acknowledgments. Terms that are obtained from miscellaneous newspapers and newsmagazines, are provided by outside contributors, or are discovered through independent research by the editorial staff remain uncoded.

Reverse Acronyms,
Initialisms &
Abbreviations
Dictionary
was named an
***"Outstanding
Reference Source,"***
*the highest honor
given by the
American Library
Association Reference
and Adult Services
Division.*

Preface

Acronyms, initialisms, and other abbreviated letter symbols make up what is perhaps the fastest growing "language" in contemporary society. Whether one views the phenomenon with disdain or delight, it is apparent that the abbreviated form has established a lasting and ever-widening influence on both written and spoken communication.

For over thirty years, Gale's *Acronyms, Initialisms, and Abbreviations Dictionary (AIAD)* has served as a reliable and up-to-date reference, guiding librarians, businesspeople, technical writers, and other researchers through this alphabetical maze. Its scope has been broadened by publication of this companion volume, *Reverse Acronyms, Initialisms, and Abbreviations Dictionary (RAIAD),* which is Volume 3 of the *AIAD* series.

Useful in Sorting Out Inconsistencies

If all abbreviated terms were as logically formed as Royal Artillery-RA, there would be little need for a tool such as *RAIAD*. The countless exceptions to this generalized formation, however, make a guide essential. Receipt Acknowledged, for instance, is not necessarily shortened to RA, but often to REACK; Sisters of the Most Holy Sacrament is abbreviated as MHS, not SMHS; and the military designation for First Available Air Transportation is not FAAT, but FAIRTRANS.

Sometimes, *all* words in a term are represented in the initialism, including articles, prepositions, etc.:

Radiation, Detection, and Computation .... RADIAC

Or, the first syllables or a part of each word, rather than initial letters, are used to form the acronym:

Quick FORTRAN .... QWIKTRAN

Often, terms that are particularly long are shortened by representing only the first several words:

Easter Seal Research Foundation of the National Easter Seal Society .... ESRF

Yet another method uses only *selected* words to create a telescoped form:

International Information Centre for Terminology .... INFOTERM

Another popular practice is to tack on a stray letter that has no connection with the acronym's translation, but that renders it pronounceable or gives it an appropriate meaning:

Greater Underwater Propulsive Power [*Type of submarine*] .... GUPPY

It is obvious from these cited examples that *RAIAD* can take the guesswork out of acronym and initialism formation and usage.

Mistaken Identity Avoided

An incorrect initialism can not only cause confusion, but may even change the meaning of a term. A Bachelor of Interior Architecture is designated BI Arch. Abbreviating it as BIA confers on the subject a Bachelor of Industrial Arts degree.

Some commercial firms and associations use their entire corporate name in their initials: Cancer Care, Inc.-CCI; while others use only the principal part of their name: American Airlines, Inc.-AA. If Cancer Care, Inc., is abbreviated to CC, it may indicate Chrysler Corporation; lengthening the initialism for American Airlines, Inc., to AAI may result in translation as Alliance of American Insurers. Even terms in the same subject field are not always shortened the same way. The abbreviation for Luggage and Leather Goods Manufacturers of America is formed as one might expect-LLGMA; however, the Luggage and Leather Goods Salesman's Association of America is shortened simply to LLG.

A Valuable Key to Abbreviations and Symbols

Because simple abbreviations are also included in the *AIAD* series, a user will be able to find in *RAIAD* that the common abbreviated forms for Commission include CMSN, COM, COMM, COMMN, and COMSN. This type of information is often sought by users of data processing systems, where limited space makes the use of abbreviated terms necessary.

Both *AIAD* and *RAIAD* contain a number of letter symbols as well. These do not meet the criteria for being acronyms, initialisms, or abbreviations, but are included as an important part of an alphabetical reference. *Reverse Acronyms, Initialisms, and Abbreviations Dictionary* is especially valuable in assigning correct symbols to given terms, since the symbol often bears little or no resemblance to what it represents. For example, the meteorological symbol for Hail is A; the Navy symbol for a Cruiser Submarine is SSC; the New York Stock Exchange symbol for Borden, Inc. is BN; the research code symbol for Travenol Laboratories is BAX.

Airport code names may also seem baffling. A few are apparent, such as the symbol for Denver-DEN. But in many cases the connection between subject and symbol seems remote at best; Michigan's Willow Run Airport is represented by YIP, illogical unless one realizes the airport's proximity to the city of Ypsilanti; the giant Chicago O'Hare Airport is represented by ORD-few remember that this is because its original name was Orchard Field.

Available in Electronic Format

RAIAD is available for licensing on magnetic tape or diskette in a fielded format. Either the complete database or a custom selection of entries may be ordered. The database is available for internal data processing and nonpublishing purposes only. For more information, call 800-877-GALE.

Suggestions Are Welcome

Many suggestions concerning individual terms to be included or subjects to be covered have been received from individual users and have been most helpful. The editors invite all such comments and will make every effort to incorporate them in future editions.

Acknowledgments

For suggestions, contributions of terms, permission to take material from personal or published sources, and for other courtesies extended during the preparation of previous editions and the present one, the editors are indebted to the following:

James Aguirre, former staff writer and editor, Quality Evaluation Laboratory, United States Naval Weapons Station, Concord, California

O.T. Albertini, Plans and Policy Directorate, Joint Chiefs of Staff, Department of Defense (retired)

Irving Allen, Professor of Sociology, University of Connecticut

American Library Association (publisher of *Pugh's Dictionary of Acronyms & Abbreviations*)

Associated Press

Associated Spring Corp., B-G-R Division (publisher of *Civilian's Dictionary,* a dictionary of wartime abbreviations)

Association of American Railroads

Paul Axel-Lute

Janice Badash

Burroughs Corp. (publisher of *Computer Acronyms and Abbreviations Handbook*)

Butterworth & Co. (Publishers) Ltd. (publisher of *Index to Legal Citations and Abbreviations*)

Ethel M. Fair

John Fobian

David Glagovsky

Jack Gordon

Hoyt Hammer, Jr.

Hanley & Belfus Inc. (publisher of *Dictionary of Medical Acronyms & Abbreviations*)

William S. Hein Co. (publisher of *Bieber's Dictionary of Legal Abbreviations*)

Charles C. Hinckley, executive vice president, Union Central Life Insurance Co.

Roy Hubbard

Mildred Hunt, editorial consultant

International Business Machines Corp., Data Processing Division (publisher of *IBM Glossary for Information Processing*)

David J. Jones, compiler of *Australian Dictionary of Acronyms and Abbreviations* and *Australian Periodical Title Abbreviations*

Kogan Page Ltd. (publisher of *Dictionary of British Qualifications*)

Steven C. Krems, computer specialist, Internal Revenue Service

Ktav Publishing House, Inc. (publisher of *Biblical and Judaic Acronyms*)

Robert E. Lacey, journalist

Lund Humphries Publishers Ltd. (publisher of *Dictionary of Graphic Arts Abbreviations*)

David MacLaren

Lawrence Marwick, late editor of *Biblical and Judaic Acronyms*

David Mattison

Mamie Meredith, late Professor of English, University of Nebraska

National Association of Securities Dealers (publisher of the *NASDAQ Company Directory*)

National Library of Canada

National Library of Medicine

Morgan Oates, late librarian, *Detroit Free Press*

Charles Parsons, formerly of Translation Research Institute

Eric Partridge, late author of *A Dictionary of Slang and Unconventional English; A Dictionary of Abbreviations, with Especial Attention to War-Time Abbreviations;* and other books

James U. Rose

Janet I. Rose

Rynd Communications (publisher of *Dictionary of Health Services Management*)

Harry Schechter, late chairman, Government Printing Office Style Board

Edward A. Schmerler

Brian Scott, editor of *Dictionary of Military Abbreviations*

Peter Sikli

Standard & Poor's Corporation (publisher of *Security Owner's Stock Guide*)

Edwin B. Steen, professor emeritus of biology, Western Michigan University, author of *Abbreviations in Medicine and Dictionary of Biology*

Miriam M. Steinert, editorial consultant

A. Marjorie Taylor, editor, *Language of World War II*

Edith Thompson

Toronto Stock Exchange

David J. Trotz, editor of *Defense Weapon Systems Glossary*

Tracey Head Turbett

The University Press of Virginia (publisher of *Dictionary of Sigla and Abbreviations to and in Law Books before 1607*)

U.S. Air Force, Translation Section HQ

VCH Publishers (publisher of *Index of Acronyms and Abbreviations in Electrical and Electronic Engineering*)

Donald Weeks

Witherby & Co. Ltd. (publisher of *Aviation Insurance Abbreviations, Organisations, and Institutions; Dictionary of Commercial Terms and Abbreviations; Dictionary of Shipping International Trade Terms and Abbreviations*)

Harvey J. Wolf

User's Guide

The following examples illustrate possible elements of entries in *RAIAD:*

① ② ③ ④

Force Aerienne Tactique [*Tactical Air Force*] [*French*] (NATG) ....FATAC

⑤ ⑥

Multiple-Mirror Telescope [*Mount Hopkins, AZ*] [*Jointly operated by
Smithsonian Institution and the University of Arizona*] [*Astronomy*].......................MMT

⑦ ⑧

①   Meaning or Phrase

②   English Translation

③   Language (for non-English entries)

④   Source code (Allows you to verify entries or find additional information. Decoded in the List of Selected Sources)

⑤   Location or Country of origin (Provides geographic identifiers for airports, colleges and universities, libraries, military bases, political parties, radio and television stations, and others)

⑥   Sponsoring organization

⑦   Subject category (Clarifies entries by providing appropriate context)

⑧   Acronym, Initialism, or Abbreviation

The completeness of a listing is dependent upon both the nature of the term and the amount of information provided by the source. If additional information becomes available during future research, an entry is revised.

Arrangement of Entries

Terms are arranged in alphabetical order, according to the meaning of the acronym, initialism, or abbreviation. If a particular translation has more than one initialism representing it, the various choices are then arranged alphabetically. Thus:

Liquid Nitrogen...LIN
Liquid Nitrogen..LN

Articles, conjunctions, prepositions, etc., generally are not considered in the alphabetizing:

Master Switch..MS
Master *of* Textile Chemistry...MTC
Not Less Than...NLT
Not *in* Line *of* Duty...NLD

List of Selected Sources

Each of the sources included in the following list contributed at least 50 terms. It would be impossible to cite a source for every entry because the majority of terms are sent by outside contributors, are uncovered through independent research by the editorial staff, or surface as miscellaneous broadcast or print media references.

For sources used on an ongoing basis, only the latest edition is listed. For most of the remaining sources, the edition that was used is cited. The editors will provide further information about these sources upon request.

Unless further described in an annotation, the publications listed here contain no additional information about the acronym, initialism, or abbreviation cited.

(AABC) *Catalog of Abbreviations and Brevity Codes.* Washington, DC: U.S. Department of the Army, 1981. [Use of source began in 1969]

(AAG) *Aerospace Abbreviations Glossary.* Report Number AG60-0014. Prepared by General Dynamics/Astronautics. San Diego, CA: 1962.

(AAGC) *Acronyms and Abbreviations in Government Contracting.* 2d ed. By Patricia A. Tobin and Joan Nelson Phillips. Washington, DC: George Washington University, 1997.

(AAMN) *Abbreviations and Acronyms in Medicine and Nursing.* By Solomon Garb, Eleanor Krakauer, and Carson Justice. New York, NY: Springer Publishing Co., 1976.

(ABBR) *Abbreviations: The Comprehensive Dictionary of Abbreviations and Letter Symbols.* Vol. 1 C. By Edward Wall. Ann Arbor, MI: The Pierian Press, 1984.

(AC) *Associations Canada 1995/96.* Edited by Ward McBurney. Toronto, Canada: Canadian Almanac & Directory Publishing Co. Ltd., 1995.

(ACII) *"Acronym and Initials Index."* 7 February 1996. <http://www.ioi.ie/~readout/cl.html> (7 November 1996).

(AD) *Abbreviations Dictionary.* 8thed. By Ralph De Sola. Boca Raton, FL: CRC Press, 1992.

(ADA) *The Australian Dictionary of Acronyms and Abbreviations.* 2nd ed. Compiled by David J. Jones. Leura, NSW, Australia: Second Back Row Press Pty. Ltd., 1981.

(ADDR) *Army Dictionary and Desk Reference.* By Tim Zurick. Harrisburg, PA: Stackpole Books, 1992.

(AEBS) *Acronyms in Education and the Behavioral Sciences.* By Toyo S. Kawakami. Chicago, IL: American Library Association, 1971.

(AEE) *American Educators' Encyclopedia.* By Edward L. Dejnozka and David E. Kapel. Westport, CT: Greenwood Press, 1991.

(AF) *Reference Aid: Abbreviations in the African Press.* Arlington, VA: Joint Publications Research Service, 1979.

(AFIT) *Compendium of Authenticated Systems and Logistics.* Washington, DC: Air Force Institute of Technology, 1984.

(AFM) *Air Force Manual of Abbreviations.* Washington, DC: U.S. Department of the Air Force, 1975. [Use of source began in 1969]

(AIA) *Aviation Insurance Abbreviations, Organisations and Institutions.* By M.J. Spurway. London, England: Witherby & Co. Ltd., 1983.

(AIE) *Acronyms and Initialisms in Education.* 6th ed. Compiled by John Hutchins. Norwich, England: Librarians of Institutes and Schools of Education, 1995.

(ANA) *"Abbreviations" - U.S. Navy Dictionary.* 3rd revision. Washington DC: DCP, 1989.

(APTA) *Australian Periodical Title Abbreviations.* Compiled by David J. Jones. Leura, NSW, Australia: Second Back Row Press Pty. Ltd., 1985.

(ARC) *Agricultural Research Centres: A World Directory of Organizations and Programmes.* 2 vols. Edited by Nigel Harvey. Harlow, Essex, England: Longman Group, 1983.
> A world guide to official, educational, industrial, and independent research centers which support research in the fields of agriculture, veterinary medicine, horticulture, aquaculture, food science, forestry, zoology, and botany.

(ARCH) *Dictionary of Architecture and Construction.* Edited by Cyril M. Harris. New York, NY: McGraw-Hill, Inc., 1975.

(ASF) *Guide to Names and Acronyms of Organizations, Activities, and Projects.* By Food and Agriculture Organization of the United Nations. Fishery Information, Data, and Statistics Service and U.S. National Oceanic and Atmospheric Administration. Aquatic Sciences and Fisheries Information System Reference Series, Number 10, 1982. n.p.

(BABM) *Bailliere's Abbreviations in Medicine.* 5th ed. By Edwin B. Steen. London, England: Bailliere Tindall, 1984.

(BARN) *The Barnhart Abbreviations Dictionary.* Edited by Robert K. Barnhart. New York, NY: John Wiley & Sons, Inc., 1995.

(BI) *British Initials and Abbreviations.* 3rd ed. By Ian H. Wilkes. London, England: Leonard Hill Books, 1971.

(BIB) *Bibliotech.* Ottawa, Canada: National Library of Canada, 1988-89.

(BJA) *Biblical and Judaic Acronyms.* By Lawrence Marwick. New York, NY: Ktav Publishing House, Inc., 1979.

(BRI) *Book Review Index.* 1997 Cumulation. Edited by Beverly Baer. Detroit, MI: Gale Research, 1998.

(BROA) *Broadcasting and Cable Yearbook 1997.* 2 vol. New Providence, NJ: R.R. Bowker, 1997.

(BTTJ) *Breaking Through Technical Jargon: A Dictionary of Computer and Automation Acronyms.* By Mark S. Merkow. New York, NY: Van Nostrand Reinhold, 1990.

(BUR) *Computer Acronyms and Abbreviations Handbook.* Tokyo, Japan: Burroughs Co. Ltd., 1978.

(BYTE)   *Byte: The Small Systems Journal.* Peterborough, NH: McGraw-Hill Information Systems, Inc., 1987-89.

(CAAL)   *CAAL COMOPTEVFOR Acronym and Abbreviation List.* Norfolk, VA: (CAAL-U) Operational Test and Evaluation Force, 1981.

(CB)   *Centres & Bureaux: A Directory of Concentrations of Effort, Information and Expertise.* Edited by Lindsay Sellar. Beckenham, Kent, England: CBD Research Ltd., 1987.
           A guide to British organizations which include the words "centre" or "bureau" in their names. Entries include name and address; telephone and telex numbers; chief official; and a description of the purposes, activities, and services of the organization.

(CDAI)   *Concise Dictionary of Acronyms and Initialisms.* By Stuart W. Miller. New York, NY: Facts on File Publications, 1988.

(CDE)   *The Computer Desktop Encyclopedia.* By Alan Freedman. New York, NY: AMACOM, 1996.

(CDI)   *The Cancer Dictionary.* By Roberta Altman and Michael Sarg, M.D. New York, NY: Facts on File, 1992.

(CED)   *Current European Directories.* 2nd ed. Edited by G.P. Henderson. Beckenham, Kent, England: CBD Research, 1981.

(CET)   *Communications-Electronics Terminology.* AFM 11-1. Vol. 3. U.S. Department of the Air Force, 1973.

(CINC)   *A CINCPAC Glossary of Commonly Used Abbreviations and Short Titles.* By Ltc. J.R. Johnson. Washington, DC: 1968.

(CMD)   *Complete Multilingual Dictionary of Computer Terminology.* Compiled by Georges Nania. Chicago, IL: National Textbook Co., 1984.
           Computer-related terms in Spanish, French, Italian, Portuguese, and English. Indexes in French, Italian, Spanish, and Portuguese are also provided.

(CNC)   *American National Standard Codes for the Representation of Names of Countries, Dependencies, and Areas of Special Sovereignty for Information Interchange.* U.S. National Bureau of Standards. Washington, DC: Government Printing Office, 1986. [Use of source began in 1977]
           These standard codes, approved by the International Organization for Standardization and the American National Standards Institute, are used in the international interchange of data in many fields.

(CPH)   *The Charles Press Handbook of Current Medical Abbreviations.* 3rd ed. Philadelphia, PA: The Charles Press Publishers, Inc., 1991.

(CRD)   *Computer-Readable Databases: A Directory and Data Sourcebook.* 6th ed. Edited by Kathleen Young Marcaccio. Detroit, MI: Gale Research, 1990.
           A guide to online databases, offline files available in various magnetic formats, and CD-ROM files. Entries include producer name, address, telephone number, description of coverage, vendors, and contact person.

(CROSS)   *Cross-Border Links: A Directory of Organizations in Canada, Mexico, and the United States.* Edited by Ricardo Hernandez and Edith Sanchez. Albuquerque, NM: Inter-Hemispheric Education Resource Center, 1992.

(CSR)   *Computer Science Resources: A Guide to Professional Literature.* Edited by Darlene Myers. White Plains, NY: Knowledge Industry Publications, Inc., 1981.
> Covers several types of computer-related literature including journals, technical reports, directories, dictionaries, handbooks, and university computer center newsletters. Five appendices cover career and salary trends in the computer industry, user group acronyms, university computer libraries, and trade fairs and shows.

(CTT)   *Corporate TrendTrac.* Edited by A. Dale Timpe. Detroit, MI: Gale Research, 1988-89.
> Covers mergers and acquisitions, stock exchange listings and suspensions, company name changes, bankruptcies, liquidations, and reorganizations.

(DA)   *Dictionary of Aviation.* By R. J. Hall and R. D. Campbell. Chicago, IL: St. James Press, 1991.

(DAS)   *Dictionary of Abbreviations and Symbols.* By Edward Frank Allen. London, England: Cassell and Co. Ltd., 1949.

(DAVI)   *The Davis Book of Medical Abbreviations: A Deciphering Guide.* By Sarah Lu Mitchell-Hatton. Philadelphia, PA: F. A. Davis Co., 1991.

(DBA)   *Directory of British Associations.* Edited by G. P. Henderson and S. P. A. Henderson. Beckenham, Kent, England: CBD Research, Ltd., 1990.

(DBQ)   *A Dictionary of British Qualifications.* London, England: Kogan Page Ltd., 1985.

(DCTA)   *Dictionary of Commercial Terms and Abbreviations.* By Alan E. Branch. London, England: Witherby & Co. Ltd., 1984.

(DD)   *The Financial Post Directory of Directors 1997.* Toronto, Canada: The Financial Post, 1996.

(DEN)   *Dictionary of Electronics and Nucleonics.* By L.E.C. Hughes, R. W. B. Stephens and L. D. Brown. New York, NY: Barnes & Noble, 1969.

(DFIT)   *Dictionary of Finance and Investment Terms.* 4th ed. Edited by John Downes and Jordan Elliot Goodman. Hauppauge, NY: Barron's Educational Series, 1995.

(DGA)   *Dictionary of Graphic Arts Abbreviations.* By L. W. Wallis. Rockport, MA: Rockport Publishers, Inc., 1986.

(DHSM)   *Dictionary of Health Services Management.* 2nd ed. By Thomas C. Timmreck. Owings Mills, MD: Rynd Communications, 1987.

(DI)   *The Dictionary of Initials-What They Mean.* Compiled and edited by Harriette Lewis. Kingswood, Surrey, England: Paper Fronts Elliot Right Way Books, 1983.

(DICI)   *The Dictionary of Initials.* By Betsy M. Parks. Secaucus, NJ: Citadel Press, 1981.

(DIT)   *Dictionary of Informatics Terms in Russian and English.* By G. S. Zhdanov, E. S. Kolobrodov, V. A. Polushkin, and A. I. Cherny. Moscow: Nauka, 1971.

(DLA)   *Bieber's Dictionary of Legal Abbreviations.* 3rd ed. By Mary Miles Prince. Buffalo, NY: William S. Hein & Co., 1988.

(DMA)   *Dictionary of Military Abbreviations: British, Empire, Commonwealth.* By B. K. C. Scott. Hastings, East Sussex, England: Tamarisk Books, 1982.

(DMAA)   *Dictionary of Medical Acronyms and Abbreviations.* 3rd ed. Edited by Stanley Jablonski. Philadelphia, PA: Hanley & Belfus, Inc., 1998.

(DMC)   *Webster's New World Dictionary of Media and Communications.* Revised ed. By Richard Weiner. New York, NY: Macmillan, 1996.

(DNAB)   *Dictionary of Naval Abbreviations.* 3rd ed. Compiled and edited by Bill Wedertz. Annapolis, MD: Naval Institute Press, 1984.

(DOAD)   *The Dictionary of Advertising.* Edited by Laurence Urdang. Lincolnwood, IL: NTC Business Books, 1986.

(DOG)   *A Dictionary of Genetics.* 5th ed. By Robert C. King and William D. Stansfield. New York, NY: Oxford University Press, 1997.

(DOGT)   *"List of Acronyms."* <http://www.em.doe.gov/rtc1994/loa.html> (5 March 1997).

(DOM)   *The Dictionary of Multimedia: Terms & Acronyms.* By Brad Hansen. Wilsonvillee, OR: Franklin, Beedle & Associates, 1997.

(DOMA)   *Dictionary of Military Abbreviations.* By Norman Polmar, Mark Warren, and Eric Wertheim. Annapolis, MD: Naval Institute Press, 1994.

(DS)   *Dictionary of Shipping International Trade Terms and Abbreviations.* 3rd ed. By Alan E. Branch. London, England: Witherby & Co. Ltd., 1986.

(DSA)   *Dictionary of Sigla and Abbreviations to and in Law Books before 1607.* By William Hamilton Bryson. Charlottesville, VA: University Press of Virginia, 1975.

(DSUE)   *A Dictionary of Slang and Unconventional English.* 8th ed. By Eric Partridge. New York, NY: Macmillan Publishing Co., 1984.

(DUND)   *Directory of United Nations Databases and Information Services.* 4th ed. Compiled by the Advisory Committee for the Coordination of Information Systems. New York, NY: United Nations, 1990.
        A guide to computerized databases and information systems/services. Entries include sponsoring organization, year established, type, scope, coverage, timespan, and contact information.

(DWSG)   *Defense Weapon Systems Glossary.* By David Trotz. Piscataway, NJ: Target Marketing, 1992.

(EA)   *Encyclopedia of Associations.* 29th ed. Vol. 1, National Organizations of the U.S. Edited by Carol A. Schwartz and Rebecca L. Turner. Detroit, MI: Gale Research, 1995 (and supplement 1995) [Use of source began in 1960]
        A guide to trade, professional, and other nonprofit associations that are national and international in scope and membership and that are headquartered in the United States. Entries include name and address; telephone and telex number; chief official; and a description of the purpose, activities, and structure of the organization.

(EAAP)   *Encyclopedia of Associations: Association Periodicals*. 3 vols. Edited by Denise M. Allard and Robert C. Thomas. Detroit, MI: Gale Research, 1987.
> A directory of publications issued by all types of national nonprofit organizations in the United States. Entries include title and organization name, address, telephone number; description of periodical, frequency of publication, and price.

(EAIO)   *Encyclopedia of Associations: International Organizations*. 29th ed. Edited by Linda Irvin. Detroit, MI: Gale Research, 1995. [Use of source began in 1985]
> A guide to trade, professional, and other nonprofit associations that are national or international in scope and membership and that are headquartered outside the United States. Entries include name and address; principal foreign language name; telephone and telex number; chief official; and a description of the purpose, activities, and structure of the organization.

(ECED)   *The European Communities Encyclopedia and Directory 1992*. London, England: Europa Publications Ltd., 1991; distributed in U.S. by Gale Research, Detroit, MI.
> A comprehensive guide to the European Communities. Entries explain widely-used acronyms and include address, telephone, telex, fax numbers and chief officers for EC-level organizations.

(ECII)   *Electronics, Computers and Industrial Instrumentation Abbreviations and Acronyms.* Edited by Sergio Sobredo. Miami, FL: Sergio Sobredo Technical Services, 1986.

(ECON)   *The Economist*. London, England: The Economist Newspaper Ltd., 1997. [Use of source began in 1988]

(EDAC)   *Dictionary of Educational Acronyms, Abbreviations, and Initialisms.* 2nd ed. Edited by James C. Palmer and Anita Y. Colby. Phoenix, AZ: Oryx Press, 1985.

(EE)   *Eastern Europe and the Commonwealth of Independent States 1992*. London, England: Europa Publications Ltd., 1992; distributed in U.S. by Gale Research, Detroit, MI.

(EECA)   *Dictionary of Electrical, Electronics, and Computer Abbreviations.* By Phil Brown. London, England: Buttersworth, 1985.

(EG)   *Environmental Glossary*. 4th ed. Edited by G. William Frick and Thomas F.P. Sullivan. Rockville, MD: Government Institutes, Inc., 1986.

(EGAO)   *Encyclopedia of Governmental Advisory Organizations*. 9th ed. Edited by Donna Batten. Detroit, MI: Gale Research, 1994-95 (and supplement, 1995). [Use of source began in 1975]
> A reference guide to permanent, continuing, and ad hoc U.S. presidential advisory committees, interagency committees, and other government-related boards, panels, task forces, commissions, conferences, and other similar bodies serving in a consultative, coordinating, advisory, research, or investigative capacity. Entries include name and address, telephone number, designated federal employee, history, recommendation and findings of the committee, staff size, publications, and subsidiaries. Also includes indexes to personnel, reports, federal agencies, presidential administration, and an alphabetical and keyword index.

(EMRF)   *The St. James Encyclopedia of Mortgage & Real Estate Finance*. By James Newell, Albert Santi, and Chip Mitchell. Chicago, IL: St. James Press, 1991.

(EPA)   *Glossary of EPA Acronyms*. Washington, DC: Environmental Protection Agency, 1987.

(ERG)   *Environmental Regulatory Glossary*. 5th ed. Edited by G. William Frick and Thomas F. P. Sullivan. Rockville, MD: Government Institutes, Inc., 1990.

(EY)   *The Europa World Year Book 1992*. London: Europa Publications Ltd., 1992. distributed in U.S. by Gale Research, Detroit, MI.
> An annual survey containing detailed information about the political, economic, statistical, and commercial situation of the regions and countries covered.

(FAAC)   *Contractions Handbook*. Changes. U.S. Department of Transportation. Federal Aviation Administration, 1993. [Use of source began in 1969]

(FAAL)   *Location Identifiers*. U.S. Department of Transportation. Federal Aviation Administration. Air Traffic Service, 1982.

(FEA)   *The Far East and Australasia 1987*. 18th ed. London, England: Europa Publications Ltd., 1986; distributed in U.S. by Gale Research, Detroit, MI.
> An annual survey containing detailed information about the political, economic, statistical, and commercial situation of the regions and countries covered.

(FFDE)   *The Facts on File Dictionary of Environmental Science*. By L. Harold Stevenson and Bruce Wyman. New York, NY: Facts on File, 1991.
> Defines terms from disciplines as diverse as biology, chemistry, geology, physics, engineering, meteorology, social science, medicine, and economics.

(GAAI)   *"Glossary of Abbreviations, Acronyms, and Initialisms."* 17 February 1998.
       <http://www.em.doe.gov/idb97/acropdf.html

(GAVI)   *"Glossary of Aviation Acronyms and Abbreviations."*
       <http://olias.arc.nasa.gov/AFO_Acronyms_.html> (5 March 1997).

(GEA)   *Government Economic Agencies of the World: An International Directory of Governmental Organisations Concerned with Economic Development and Planning*. A Keesing's Reference Publication. Edited by Alan J. Day. Harlow, Essex, England: Longman Group Ltd., 1985.
> Covers over 170 countries and territories. Two introductory sections for each area cover economic data and prevailing economic and political conditions. Individual entries provide title, address, and names of chief officials of each agency. Current activities and financial structure of each agency are also detailed. An index of agency officials is provided.

(GFGA)   *Guide to Federal Government Acronyms*. Edited by William R. Evinger. Phoenix, AZ: The Oryx Press, 1989.

(GNE)   *The Green Encyclopedia.* By Irene Franck and David Brownstone. New York, NY: Prentice Hall General Reference, 1992.

(GPO)   *Style Manual*. Washington, DC: Government Printing Office, 1984. Terms are included in Chapter 24, Foreign Languages.

(GRD)   *Government Research Directory*. 8th ed. Edited by Joseph M. Palmisano. Detroit, MI: Gale Research, 1994. (and supplement, 1994).
> A descriptive guide to U.S. government research and development centers, institutes, laboratories, bureaus, test facilities, experiment stations, data collection and analysis centers, and grants management and research coordinating offices in agriculture, business, education, energy, engineering, environment, the humanities, medicine, military science, and basic applied sciences.

(HCT)   *Health Care Terms.* 2nd ed. By Vergil N. and Debora A. Slee. St. Paul, MN: Tringa Press, 1991.

(HGAA)   *The Handy Guide to Abbreviations and Acronyms for the Automated Office.* By Mark W. Greenia. Seattle, WA: Self-Counsel Press Inc., 1986.

(IAA)   *Index of Acronyms and Abbreviations in Electrical and Electronic Engineering.* Compiled by Buro Scientia. New York, NY: VCH Publishers, 1989.

(IBMDP)   *IBM Data Processing Glossary.* 6th ed. White Plains, NY: IBM Corp., 1977.

(ICAO)   *Aircraft Type Designators.* 13th ed. International Civil Aviation Organization, August, 1981.

(ICDA)   *Designators for Aircraft Operating Agencies, Aeronautical Authorities and Services.* 49th ed. International Civil Aviation Organization, June, 1982.
           Document also includes telephony designators and postal and telegraphic addresses of government civil aviation authorities.

(ICLI)   *Location Indicators.* 51st ed. International Civil Aviation Organization, February, 1987.
           Document also contains addresses of flight information centers.

(IDOE)   *The Illustrated Dictionary of Electronics.* 6th ed. By Stan Gibilisco. New York, NY: TAB Books, 1994.

(IEEE)   *IEEE Standard Dictionary of Electrical and Electronics Terms.* Edited by Frank Jay. New York, NY: The Institute of Electrical and Electronics Engineers, Inc., 1977, 1984.
           Includes definitions for thousands of electrical and electronics terms. Each entry includes a numeric source code.

(IIA)   *Index of Initials and Acronyms.* Compiled by Richard Kleiner. New York, NY: Auerbach Publishers, 1971.

(IID)   *Information Industry Directory.* 15th ed. Edited by Annette Novallo. Detroit, MI: Gale Research, 1995. (and supplement, 1995).
           An international guide to computer-readable databases, database producers, and publishers, online vendors and time-sharing companies, telecommunications networks, and many other information systems and services. Entries include name and address, telephone number, chief official, and a detailed description of the purpose and function of the system or service.

(ILCA)   *Index to Legal Citations and Abbreviations.* By Donald Raistrick. Abingdon, Oxfordshire, England: Professional Books Ltd., 1981.

(IMH)   *International Marketing Handbook.* 2nd ed. Edited by Frank Bair. Detroit, MI: Gale Research, 1985.
           An in-depth guide to commercial and trade data on 142 countries of the world. Features include a list of European trade fairs and a report on growth markets in Western Europe.

(INF)   *Infantry.* Fort Benning, GA: U.S. Army Infantry Training School, 1996. [Use of source began in 1983]

(IRC)   *International Research Centers Directory 1992-93.* 6th ed. Edited by Annette Piccirelli. Detroit, MI: Gale Research, 1991.
           A world guide to government, university, independent, nonprofit, and commercial research and development centers, institutes, laboratories, bureaus, test facilities,

experiment stations, and data collection and analysis centers, as well as foundations, councils, and other organizations which support research.

(IRUK) *Industrial Research in the United Kingdom*. 12th ed. Harlow, Essex, England: Longman Group UK Ltd., 1987.
A guide to all groups conducting or funding research relevant to British industrial development. Entries include name, address, telephone and telex numbers; chief officials; and scope of activities.

(IT) *Information Today: The Newspaper for Users and Producers of Electronic Information Services*. Medford, NJ: Learned Information Inc., 1988-89.

(ITD) *International Tradeshow Directory*. 5th ed. Frankfurt, Germany: M + A Publishers for Fairs, Exhibitions and Conventions Ltd., 1989.
A guide to trade fairs and exhibitions throughout the world. Entries include event name, dates, frequency, location, description of purpose, profile of exhibitors and attendees.

(IYR) *The 1989-92 International Yacht Racing Rules*. London, England: International Yacht Racing Union, 1989.

(KSC) *A Selective List of Acronyms and Abbreviations*. Compiled by the Documents Department, Kennedy Space Center Library, 1971, 1973.

(LAIN) *Latest Intelligence: An International Directory of Codes Used by Government, Law Enforcement, Military, and Surveillance Agencies*. By James E. Tunnell. Blue Ridge Summit, PA: TAB BOOKS, 1990.

(LCCP) *MARC Formats for Bibliographic Data*. Appendix II. Washington, DC: Library of Congress, 1982.

(LCLS) *Symbols of American Libraries*. 14th ed. Edited by the Enhanced Cataloging Division. Washington, DC: Library of Congress, 1992. [Use of source began in 1980]

(LWAP) *Legal Words and Phrases: Speed Abbreviations*. By Joel Larus. Boston, MA: Aurico Publishing, 1965.

(MAE) *Medical Abbreviations and Eponyms*. By Sheila B. Sloane. Philadelphia, PA: W.B. Saunders Co., 1985.

(MAH) *Medical Abbreviations Handbook*. 2nd ed. Oradell, NJ: Medical Economics Co., Inc., 1983.

(MCD) *Acronyms, Abbreviations, and Initialisms*. Compiled by Carl Lauer. St. Louis, MO: McDonnell Douglas Corp., 1989. [Use of source began in 1969]

(MDG) *Microcomputer Dictionary and Guide*. By Charles J. Sippl. Champaign, IL: Matrix Publishers, Inc., 1975.
A listing of definitions for over 5,000 microelectronics terms. Seven appendices.

(MEDA) *Medical Acronyms*. 2nd ed. By Marilyn Fuller Delong. Oradell, NJ: Medical Economic Books, 1989.

(MENA) *The Middle East and North Africa 1987*. 33rd ed. London, England: Europa Publications Ltd., 1986; distributed in U.S. by Gale Research, Detroit, MI.
An annual survey containing detailed information about the political, economic, statistical, and commercial situation of the regions and countries covered.

(MHDB)   *McGraw-Hill Dictionary of Business Acronyms, Initials, and Abbreviations.* By Jerry M. Rosenberg. New York, NY: McGraw-Hill, Inc., 1992.

(MHDI)   *McGraw-Hill Dictionary of Information Technology and Computer Acronyms, Initials, and Abbreviations.* By Jerry M. Rosenberg. New York, NY: McGraw-Hill, Inc., 1992.

(MHDW)   *McGraw-Hill Dictionary of Wall Street Acronyms, Initials, and Abbreviations.* By Jerry M. Rosenberg. New York, NY: McGraw-Hill, Inc., 1992.

(MSA)   *Military Standard Abbreviations for Use on Drawings, and in Specifications, Standards, and Technical Documents.* MIL-STD-12D. U.S. Department of Defense, 1981. [Use of source began in 1975]

(MSC)   *Annotated Acronyms and Abbreviations of Marine Science Related Activities.* 3rd ed. Revised by Charlotte M. Ashby and Alan R. Flesh. Washington, DC: U.S. Department of Commerce. National Oceanographic and Atmospheric Administration. Environmental Data Service. National Oceanographic Data Center, 1976, 1981.

(MUGU)   *The Mugu Book of Acronyms and Abbreviations.* Missile Range, California: Management Engineering Office, 1963, 1964.

(NADA)   *The New American Dictionary of Abbreviations.* By Mary A. De Vries. New York, NY: Signet, 1991.

(NASA)   *Space Transportation System and Associated Payloads: Glossary, Acronyms, and Abbreviations.* Washington, DC: U.S. National Aeronautics and Space Administration, 1985.

(NATG)   *Glossary of Abbreviations Used in NATO Documents.* AAP 15(B), n.p., 1979. [Use of source began in 1976]

(NCC)   *NCC The National Centre for Information Technology. Guide to Computer Aided Engineering, Manufacturing and Construction Software.* Manchester, England: NCC Publications. The National Computing Centre Ltd., 1985.
   Includes software classifications and descriptions, names and addresses of suppliers, processor manufacturers, and operating systems.

(NFD)   *The NSFRE Fund-Raising Dictionary.* Edited by Barbara R. Levy. New York, NY: John Wiley & Sons, Inc., 1996.

(NFPA)   *Standard for Fire Safety Symbols/NFPA170.* Quincy, MA: National Fire Protection Association, 1994.

(NG)   *NAVAIR Glossary of Unclassified Common-Use Abbreviated Titles and Phrases.* NAVAIRNOTE 5216 AIR-6031, n.p., July, 1969.

(NGC)   *Catalogue of the National Gallery of Canada.* Compiled by National Gallery of Canada. Ottawa, Canada: National Gallery of Canada, 1998.

(NHD)   *The New Hacker's Dictionary.* Edited by Eric Raymond. Cambridge, MA: MIT Press, 1991.

(NITA)   *Dictionary of New Information Technology Acronyms.* 2nd ed. By Michael Gordon, Alan Singleton, and Clarence Rickards. London, England: Kogan Page, Ltd., 1986.

(NLC)   *Symbols of Canadian Libraries.* 12th ed. National Library of Canada. Minister of Supply and Services Canada, 1987.

(NOAA) *NOAA Directives Manual.* 66-13 Acronyms. 1977.

(NQ) *NASDAQ Company Directory.* New York, NY: National Association of Securities Dealers, Inc., 1990. [Use of source began in 1983]
> Entries include company name, SIC code, contact person's name, title, address, and telephone number.

(NRCH) *A Handbook of Acronyms and Initialisms.* Washington, DC: U.S. Nuclear Regulatory Commission. Division of Technical Information and Document Control, 1985.

(NTCM) *NTC's Mass Media Dictionary.* R. Terry Ellmore. Lincolnwood, IL: National Textbook Co., 1991.

(NUCP) *A Dictionary of Nuclear Power and Waste Management with Abbreviations and Acronyms.* Foo-Sun Lau. Letchworth, England: Research Studies Press, Ltd., 1987.

(NVT) *Naval Terminology.* NWP3. Rev. B. U.S. Department of the Navy. Office of the Chief of Naval Operations, 1980. [Use of source began in 1974]
> Includes a section on definitions of naval terminology.

(OA) *Ocran's Acronyms: A Dictionary of Abbreviations and Acronyms Used in Scientific and Technical Writing.* By Emanuel Benjamin Ocran. London, England: Routledge & Kegan Paul Ltd., 1978.

(OAG) *Official Airline Guide Worldwide Edition.* Oak Brook, IL: Official Airlines Guide, Inc., 1984. [Use of source began in 1975]

(OCD) *Oxford Classical Dictionary.* 2nd ed. Edited by N.G. Hammond and H.H. Scullard. London, England: Oxford University Press, 1970.

(OCLC) *OCLC Participating Institutions Arranged by OCLC Symbol.* Dublin, OH: OCLC, 1981.

(ODBW) *The Oxford Dictionary for the Business World.* New York, NY: Oxford University Press, Inc., 1993.

(OICC) *Abbreviations and Acronyms.* Des Moines, IA: Iowa State Occupational Information Coordinating Committee, 1986.

(OLDSS) *Online Database Search Services Directory.* 2nd ed. Edited by Doris Morris Maxfield. Detroit, MI: Gale Research, 1988.
> Provides detailed descriptions of the online information retrieval services offered by libraries, private information firms, and other organizations in the United States and Canada. Entries include name and address, telephone number, and key contact, as well as online systems accessed, frequently searched databases, and access hardware.

(OPSA) *"Official Postal Service Abbreviations."* <http://www.usps.gov/ncsc/lookups/abbr_suffix.txt> (17 December 1996).

(OSI) *OSI Standards and Acronyms.* 3rd ed. Compiled by Adrian V. Stokes. United Kingdom: Stokes, 1991.

(PAZ) *Parenting A to Z.* By Irene M. Franck and David M. Brownstone. New York, NY: HarperCollins Publishers, Inc., 1996.

(PCM) *PC Magazine.* New York, NY: Ziff-Davis Publishing Co., 1997. [Use of source began in 1987]

(PD)   *Political Dissent: An International Guide to Dissident, Extra-Parliamentary, Guerrilla and Illegal Political Movements*. A Keesing's Reference Publication. Compiled by Henry W. Degenhardt. Edited by Alan J. Day. Harlow, Essex, England: Longman Group, 1983.
> Includes the history and aims of approximately 1,000 organizations, with details of their leaderships.

(PDAA)   *Pugh's Dictionary of Acronyms and Abbreviations: Abbreviations in Management, Technology and Information Science*. 5th ed. By Eric Pugh. Chicago, IL: American Library Association, 1987.

(PGP)   *Peterson's Graduate Programs in the Humanities, Arts & Social Sciences*. 31st ed. Princeton, NJ: Peterson's 1997.

(PPE)   *Political Parties of Europe*. 2 vols. Edited by Vincent E. McHale. The Greenwood Historical Encyclopedia of the World's Political Parties. Westport, CT: Greenwood Press, 1983.
> One of a series of reference guides to the world's significant political parties. Each guide provides concise histories of the political parties of a region and attempts to detail the evolution of ideology, changes in organization, membership, leadership, and each party's impact upon society.

(PPW)   *Political Parties of the World*. 2nd ed. A Keesing's Reference Publication. Compiled and edited by Alan J. Day and Henry W. Degenhardt. Harlow, Essex, England: Longman Group, 1980, 1984.
> Covers historical development, structure, leadership, membership, policy, publications, and international affiliations. For each country, an overview of the current political situation and constitutional structure is provided.

(PS)   *Popular Science*. New York, NY: Times-Mirror Magazines, Inc., 1995. [Use of source began in 1992]

(RCD)   *Research Centers Directory*. 19th ed. Edited by Thomas J. Cichonski. Detroit, MI: Gale Research, 1994. [Use of source began in 1986]
> A guide to university-related and other nonprofit research organizations carrying on research in agriculture, astronomy and space sciences, behavioral and social sciences, computers and mathematics, engineering and technology, physical and earth sciences and regional and area studies.

(RDA)   *Army RD and A Magazine*. Alexandria, VA: Development, Engineering, and Acquisition Directorate, Army Materiel Command, 1997. [Use of source began in 1979]

(ROG)   *Dictionary of Abbreviations*. By Walter T. Rogers. London, England: George Allen & Co. Ltd., 1913; reprinted by Gale Research, 1969.

(SAA)   *Space-Age Acronyms, Abbreviations and Designations*. 2nd ed. By Reta C. Moser. New York, NY: IFI/Plenum, 1969.

(SAG)   *Stock Abbreviation Guide*. New York, NY: Associated Press. [Database]

(SDI)   *Report to the Congress on the Strategic Defense Initiative*. U.S. Department of Defense. Strategic Defense Initiative Organization, April, 1987.

(SEIS)   *Seismograph Station Codes and Characteristics*. Geological Survey. Circular 791. By Barbara B. Poppe, Debbi A. Naab, and John S. Derr. Washington, DC: U.S. Department of the Interior, 1978.

(SLS)   *World Guide to Scientific Associations and Learned Societies/Internationales Verzeichnis Wissenschaftlicher Verbande und Gesellschaften.* 4th ed. Edited by Barbara Verrel. New York, NY: K.G. Saur, 1984.
> A directory of more than 22,000 societies and associations in all fields of science, culture, and technology. International, national, and regional organizations from 150 countries are also included.

(SPSG)   *Security Owner's Stock Guide.* New York, NY: Standard & Poor's Corp., 1994. [Use of source began in 1988]

(SRA)   *State and Regional Associations of the United States.* 9th ed. Edited by Tracey E. Chirico, Buck J. Downs and John J. Russell. Washington, DC: Columbia Books, Inc., 1997.

(SSD)   *Space Station Directory and Program Guide.* Edited and compiled by Melinda Gipson, Jane Glass, and Mary Linden. Arlington, VA: Pasha Publications Inc., 1988.

(TAG)   *Transportation Acronym Guide 1996.* U.S. Department of Transportation. Washington, DC: Bureau of Transportation Statistics, 1996.

(TDOB)   *The Dictionary of Banking.* By Charles J. Woelfel. Chicago, IL: Probus Publishing Company, 1994.

(TEL)   *Telephony's Dictionary.* 2nd ed. By Graham Langley. Chicago, IL: Telephony Publishing Corp., 1986.
> Includes definitions for U.S. and international telecommunications terms. Ten appendices.

(TNIG)   *Telecommunications, Networking and Internet Glossary.* By George S. Machovec. Chicago, IL: American Library Association, 1993.

(TOCD)   *The Official Catholic Directory 1997.* New Providence, NJ: P.J. Kenedy & Sons, 1997.

(TSPED)   *Trade Shows and Professional Exhibits Directory.* 2nd ed. Edited by Robert J. Elster. Detroit, MI: Gale Research, 1987. [Use of source began in 1986]
> A guide to scheduled events providing commercial display facilities including conferences, conventions, meetings, fairs and festivals, etc. Entries include name of trade show; sponsor name, address, and telephone number; attendance figures; principal exhibits; special features; publications; and date and location of shows.

(TSSD)   *Telecommunications Systems and Services Directory.* 4th ed. (and supplement). Edited by John Krol. Detroit, MI: Gale Research, 1989. [Use of source began in 1985]
> An international descriptive guide to telecommunications organizations, systems, and services. Entries include name and address, telephone number, chief official, and a description of the purposes, technical structure, and background of the service or system.

(USDC)   *"Glossary of Acronyms".* U.S. Department of Commerce. <http://www.pmel.noaa.gov/pubs/acronym.html> (5 March 1997).

(USGC)   *"U.S. Government Commonly Used Abbreviations and Acronyms."* <http://www.fed.gov/hptext/infohwy/gov_acro.html> (5 March 1997).

(VNW)   *Words of the Vietnam War.* By Gregory R. Clark. Jefferson, NC: McFarland and Co., Inc., 1990.

(VRA)   *VRA Special Bulletin. No. 2, 1987: Standard Abbreviaitons for Image Descriptions for Use in Fine Arts Visual Resources Collections.* Compiled by Nancy S. Schuller. Austin, TX: Visual Resources Association, 1987.

(WDAA)   *Webster's New World Dictionary of Acronyms and Abbreviations.* By Auriel Douglas and Michael Strumpf. New York, NY: Webster's New World, 1989.

(WDMC)   *Webster's New World Dictionary of Media and Communications.* Revised and updated ed. By Richard Weiner. New York, NY: Webster's New World, 1996.

(WGA)   *Webster's Guide to Abbreviations.* Springfield, MA: Merriam-Webster Inc., 1985.

(WYGK)   *HR Words you Gotta Know!* By William R. Tracey. New York, NY: AMACOM, 1994.

Reverse
Acronyms, Initialisms &
Abbreviations Dictionary

A-F

Numerics
By Meaning

A
By Meaning

A. A. Weinman [*Designer's mark, when appearing on US coins*] .... AW
A & A Foods Ltd. [*Associated Press*] (SAG) .... A & A Fd
A & A Foods Ltd. [*Vancouver Stock Exchange symbol*] .... AA
A & A Foods Ltd. [*NASDAQ symbol*] (SAG) .... ANAF
A & A Foods Ltd [*NASDAQ symbol*] (TTSB) .... ANAFF
A/B Astra [*Sweden*] [*Research code symbol*] .... A
A/B Rederi Transatlantic [*Pacific Australia Direct Line*] (MHDB) .... ABRT
A. Barton Hepburn Hospital, Ogdensburg, NY [*Library symbol Library of Congress*] (LCLS) .... NOgH
A Battuta [*Music*] .... A Batt
A. C. Dougherty Memorial Township Library, Dupo, IL [*Library symbol Library of Congress*] (LCLS) .... IDup
A. C. Owners Club - American Centre (EA) .... ACOC
A Cappella [*Unaccompanied*] [*Music*] .... A Capp
A Capriccio [*At One's Fancy*] [*Music*] (ROG) .... A CAPO
A Cembalo [*Music*] .... A Cemb
A. Christiaens [*Belgium*] [*Research code symbol*] .... AC
A Classification of Residential Neighborhoods [*Database CACI*] [*Information service or system*] (CRD) .... ACORN
A Coeur Joie International [*An association*] (EAIO) .... ACJI
A Computer Series [*Nippon Electric Co. Japan*] .... ACOS
A Computerised London Information Service [*Greater London Council Research Library*] [*British*] .... ACOMPLIS
A Computerised London Information System Online [*Greater London Council Research Library Bibliographic database*] [*British*] .... ACOMPLINE
A Data Management System (NITA) .... ADAM
A. de Lara Limited Edition Recordings [*Now Orfeo with same numbers*] [*Record label Great Britain*] .... AdL
A Destra [*To the Right*] [*Italian*] (ADA) .... A DES
A Direction Finder .... ADF
A Drink .... AD
A. E. Lepage Capital Prop. [*Limited Partnership Units*] [*Toronto Stock Exchange symbol*] .... AEP
A Favor [*In Favor*] [*Spanish*] .... AF
A Fortiori [*With More Reason*] [*Latin*] (ROG) .... A FORT
A. H. Brown Public Library, Mobridge, SD [*Library symbol Library of Congress*] (LCLS) .... SdMo
A. H. Robins Co. [*Research code symbol*] .... AHR
A. H. Robins Co., Richmond, VA [*OCLC symbol*] (OCLC) .... VIR
A. H. Robins Co., Richmond, VA [*Library symbol Library of Congress*] (LCLS) .... ViRRob
A. J. Hurley Ltd., London, United Kingdom [*Library symbol Library of Congress*] (LCLS) .... UkLHu
A. K. Smiley Public Library, Redlands, CA [*Library symbol Library of Congress*] (LCLS) .... CRedl
A Kinder and Gentler America .... AKAGA
A la Carte [*According to the Menu, each item ordered individually*] [*French*] (ADA) .... ALC
A la Gloire du Grand Architecte de l'Univers [*Freemasonry*] [*French*] (ROG) .... ALGDGADLU
A l'Orient [*At the East*] [*Freemasonry*] [*French*] .... A l'OR
A l'Orient [*At the East*] [*Freemasonry*] [*French*] (ROG) .... Al'O
A Lover's Complaint [*Poem usually attributed to Shakespeare*] (BARN) .... Compl
A. M. Best Electronic Retrieval Services [*A. M. Best Co.*] [*Database*] .... AMBERS
A Mind Forever Voyaging [*Infocom Computer gaming*] .... AMFV
A Mon Ordre [*To My Order*] [*French Business term*] (ROG) .... AM/O
A. N. Tupolev [*Initialism used as designation for Russian aircraft designed by Tupolev*] .... ANT
A. Nattermann & Cie [*Germany*] [*Research code symbol*] .... CH
A+ Network [*NASDAQ symbol*] (TTSB) .... ACOM
A New Genesis (TOCD) .... ANG
A. Philip Randolph Educational Fund (EA) .... APREF
A. Philip Randolph Institute (EA) .... APRI
A Plus Communications, Inc. [*NASDAQ symbol*] (SAG) .... ACOM
A Plus Network, Inc. [*Associated Press*] (SAG) .... A Plus
A Posteriori Probability (MCD) .... APP
A Posteriori Probability Distribution [*Mathematics*] .... PPD
A Protester [*To Be Protested*] [*French Business term*] .... AP
A Public Library/Community Access Tool [*Acronym used by Community Information Database Dallas Public Library Texas*] [*Information service or system*] (IID) .... APL/CAT
A Rat in the House May Eat the Ice Cream [*Mnemonic guide for spelling "arithmetic"*] .... ARITHMETIC
A/S Eksportcinans 8.70% Pfd [*NYSE symbol*] (TTSB) .... EKPPr
A/S Eksportfinans [*Export Finance*] [*NYSE symbol*] (SPSG) .... EKP
A/S Eksportfinans [*Export Finance*] **Capital Securities** [*Associated Press*] (SAG) .... Eksprt
A S V Inc. [*NASDAQ symbol*] (TTSB) .... ASVI
A Search Tree Underlying the Experiment [*University of Michigan's experimental online catalog*] .... ASTUTE
A Selective Strategy for Utilization Review Effectiveness [*Health insurance*] (GHCT) .... ASSURE
A Severity Characterization of Trauma [*Medicine*] (DMAA) .... ASCOT
A Spolecnost [*and Company*] [*Czech*] (BARN) .... A spol
A Tempo [*In Strict Time*] [*Music*] .... A Tem
A Tempo [*In Strict Time*] [*Music*] .... A TEMP
A Tempo [*In Strict Time*] [*Music*] .... AT
A. V. Roe & Co. Ltd. [*Acronym used as designation for a British aircraft and is formed from the name of the aircraft's manufacturer*] .... AVRO
A. W. Wright Nuclear Structure Laboratory [*Yale University*] [*Research center*] (RCD) .... WNSL
A. Y. Jackson High School, Kanata, Ontario [*Library symbol National Library of Canada*] (BIB) .... OKAYJ
AAA Stamp & Coin [*Vancouver Stock Exchange symbol*] .... ASJ
AABBAX International Financial [*Vancouver Stock Exchange symbol*] .... AXF
AABCO Ventures, Inc. [*Vancouver Stock Exchange symbol*] .... AAB
Aachen [*Federal Republic of Germany*] [*Seismograph station code, US Geological Survey Closed*] (SEIS) .... AAC
Aachen Aphasia Test [*Medicine*] (DMAA) .... AAT
Aachen/Merzbruck [*Germany ICAO location identifier*] (ICLI) .... EDCM
Aaland Islands .... AI
Aalborg [*Denmark*] [*Airport symbol*] (OAG) .... AAL
Aalborg Airtaxi [*Denmark ICAO designator*] (FAAC) .... DAX
Aalen-Heidenheim/Elchingen [*Germany ICAO location identifier*] (ICLI) .... EDTA
Aalenian [*Geology*] .... Aal
Aalesund [*Norway*] [*Airport symbol*] (OAG) .... AES
Aalst [*Belgium ICAO location identifier*] (ICLI) .... EBAL
Aames Financial [*NYSE symbol*] (TTSB) .... AAM
Aames Financial Corp. [*NYSE symbol*] (SAG) .... AAM
Aames Financial Corp. [*Associated Press*] (SAG) .... Aames
Aantekening [*Note*] [*Netherlands*] (ILCA) .... aant
AAO Aquaculture [*Vancouver Stock Exchange symbol*] .... AAO
AAON, Inc. [*NASDAQ symbol*] (SAG) .... AAON
AAR Corp. [*Associated Press*] (SAG) .... AAR
AAR Corp. [*NYSE symbol*] (SPSG) .... AIR
Aargang [*Annual Volume*] [*Sweden*] (BARN) .... aarg
Aarhus [*Denmark*] [*Airport symbol*] (OAG) .... AAR
Aaron Burr Association (EA) .... ABA
Aaron Diamond AIDS Research Center .... ADARC
Aaron Mining Ltd. [*Vancouver Stock Exchange symbol*] .... AOM
Aaron Rents [*NASDAQ symbol*] (TTSB) .... ARON
Aaron Rents Cl'A' [*NASDAQ symbol*] (TTSB) .... ARONA
Aaron Rents, Inc. [*Associated Press*] (SAG) .... AarnRt
Aaron Rents, Inc. [*Associated Press*] (APAG) .... AaronRt
Aaron Rents, Inc. [*NASDAQ symbol*] (NQ) .... ARON
Aaronson, Huchra, and Moruld [*Method of determining age of the universe*] .... AHM
Aasche Transport Svcs Wrrt [*NASDAQ symbol*] (TTSB) .... ASHEW
Aasche Transportation [*NASDAQ symbol*] (TTSB) .... ASHE
Aasche Transportation Services [*Associated Press*] (SAG) .... Aasche
Aasche Transportation Services [*Associated Press*] (SAG) .... AascheT
Aasche Transportation Services [*NASDAQ symbol*] (SAG) .... ASHE
AASL [*American Association of School Librarians*] **Non-Public Schools Section** .... AASL NPSS
AASL [*American Association of School Librarians*] **School Library Media Educators Section** .... AASL SLMES
AASL [*American Association of School Librarians*] **Supervisors Section** .... AASL SS
A-Associate Response [*Computer science*] (TNIG) .... AARE
AASTRA Aerospace, Inc., Downsview, Ontario [*Library symbol National Library of Canada*] (BIB) .... OTAA
AAU [*Amateur Athletic Union of the United States*]/USA Junior Olympics (EA) .... AAU/USA JO
Aavahelukka [*Finland ICAO location identifier*] (ICLI) .... EFAA
Aavid Thermal Technologies [*NASDAQ symbol*] (TTSB) .... AATT
Aavid Thermal Technologies, Inc. [*NASDAQ symbol*] (SAG) .... AATT
Aavid Thermal Technologies, Inc. [*Associated Press*] (SAG) .... AavidTh
Aaxico Air Lines .... AXO
Ab Abraham [*The chronological reckoning from the first year of Abraham; St. Jerome's translation and enlargement of Eusebius' Chronicle*] [*Classical studies*] (OCD) .... ab Abr
AB Bofors [*Sweden*] [*Research code symbol*] .... LAC

AB Bookman's Weekly [*A publication*] (BRI) ... AB
Ab Extra [*From Without*] [*Latin*] ... ABEX
Ab Initio [*From the Beginning*] [*Latin*] ... AB INIT
A.B. Middle School, International Falls, MN [*Library symbol*] [*Library of Congress*] (LCLS) ... MnIfM
AB Nyge Aero [*Sweden*] [*FAA designator*] (FAAC) ... TGT
AB Svensk Exp Cap Sec [*NYSE symbol*] (TTSB) ... SEPPr
Ab Urbe Condite [*From the Year of the Founding*] [*Latin*] ... AUC
Aba [*Zaire*] [*ICAO location identifier*] (ICLI) ... FZJF
ABA [*American Bar Association*] **Center on Children and the Law** (EA) ... ABACCL
ABA Journal [*A publication*] (BRI) ... ABA Jour
Ababa [*Ethiopia*] [*Airport symbol*] (AD) ... ABA
ABAC Resources [*Vancouver Stock Exchange symbol*] ... ABS
Abacan Resource [*NASDAQ symbol*] (TTSB) ... ABACE
Abacan Resource Corp. [*NASDAQ symbol*] (SAG) ... ABAC
Abacan Resource Corp. [*Associated Press*] (SAG) ... Abacan
Abacus ... ABCS
Abacus Direct Corp. [*Associated Press*] (SAG) ... AbacDir
Abacus Direct Corp. [*NASDAQ symbol*] (SAG) ... ABDR
Abacus Programming Corp. ... APC
Abadan [*Iran*] [*Airport symbol*] (OAG) ... ABD
Abadan [*Iran*] [*ICAO location identifier*] (ICLI) ... OIAT
Abadan/International [*Iran*] [*ICAO location identifier*] (ICLI) ... OIAA
Abadeh [*Iran*] [*ICAO location identifier*] (ICLI) ... OISA
Abaiang [*Kiribati*] [*Airport symbol*] (OAG) ... ABF
Abaiang [*Kiribati*] [*ICAO location identifier*] (ICLI) ... NGAB
Abakan [*Former USSR ICAO location identifier*] (ICLI) ... UNKA
Abakan-Avia [*Former USSR*] [*FAA designator*] (FAAC) ... ABG
Abalone (VRA) ... abal
Abalone Management Advisory Committee [*Australia*] ... ABMAC
Abampere [*Also, Bi*] [*Unit of electric current*] ... aA
Abandon [*Legal shorthand*] (LWAP) ... ABAN
Abandon Call and Retry [*Telecommunications*] ... ACR
Abandon Ship (MSA) ... ABDNSHP
Abandoned ... ABAND
Abandoned (ABBR) ... ABDND
Abandoned Lighthouse ... ABAND LT HO
Abandoned Military Reservations Act [*1884*] ... AMRA
Abandoned Mine Land [*Department of the Interior*] ... AML
Abandoned Mine Land Reclamation [*Department of the Interior*] ... AMLR
Abandoned Police Post [*Board on Geographic Names*] ... PPQ
Abandoned Private Property ... APP
Abandoned Property Collection Act [*1863*] ... APCA
Abandoner (ABBR) ... ABDNR
Abandonment (ABBR) ... ABANDMT
Abandonment ... ABANDT
Abandonment [*Legal shorthand*] (LWAP) ... ABANM
Abandonment (ABBR) ... ABDMT
Abandonment (ABBR) ... ABDNNT
Abandonment [*Insurance*] ... Abdnt
Abandonment (ABBR) ... ABNDMNT
Abarghou [*Iran*] [*ICAO location identifier*] (ICLI) ... OISU
Abarth Register, USA (EA) ... ARUSA
Abasement (ABBR) ... ABASNT
Abasement (ABBR) ... ABAST
Abashiri [*Japan*] [*Seismograph station code, US Geological Survey*] ... ABJ
Abasing (ABBR) ... ABASG
Abastumani [*Former USSR Seismograph station code, US Geological Survey Closed*] ... ABS
Abatable (ABBR) ... ABATB
Abatement [*Legal term*] (DLA) ... ABAT
Abatement (ABBR) ... ABATMT
Abatement (ABBR) ... ABATNT
Abatement and Control [*Environmental Protection Agency*] (GFGA) ... A & C
Abatement Council of the Midwest (SRA) ... ACM
Abatement of Nuisances Caused by Air Transport ... ANCAT
Abaterra Energy Ltd. [*Toronto Stock Exchange symbol Vancouver Stock Exchange symbol*] ... ABR
Abating (ABBR) ... ABATG
Abatix Environmental [*NASDAQ symbol*] (TTSB) ... ABIX
Abatix Environmental Corp. [*Associated Press*] (SAG) ... Abatix
Abatix Environmental Corp. [*NASDAQ symbol*] (NQ) ... ABIX
Abaton Resources Ltd. [*Vancouver Stock Exchange symbol*] ... AAT
Abau [*Papua*] [*Airport symbol*] (AD) ... ABW
Abaxial (MSA) ... ABXL
Abaxial Leaflet Pubescence - Curly [*Botany*] ... ABPC
Abaxis, Inc. [*NASDAQ symbol*] (SAG) ... ABAX
Abaxis, Inc. [*Associated Press*] (SAG) ... Abaxis
ABB AB [*NASDAQ symbol*] (SAG) ... ABB AB
ABB AB [*Associated Press*] (SAG) ... ABB AB
ABB AB [*NASDAQ symbol*] (SAG) ... ABBB
ABB AB ADR [*NASDAQ symbol*] (TTSB) ... ABBBY
Abbas Air Ltd. [*British ICAO designator*] (FAAC) ... ABA
Abbas Antiquus [*Deceased, 1296*] [*Authority cited in pre-1607 legal work*] (DSA) ... Ab
Abbas Siculus [*Deceased, 1445*] [*Authority cited in pre-1607 legal work*] (DSA) ... Sicu Ab
Abbassamento [*Music*] ... Abb
Abbaye de Saint-Benoit-Du-Lac, Comte De Brome, PQ, Canada [*Library symbol Library of Congress*] (LCLS) ... CaQStBL
Abbaye de Saint-Benoit-Du-Lac, Comte De Brome, Quebec [*Library symbol National Library of Canada*] (NLC) ... QSTBL
Abbe Sine Condition ... ASC
Abberrant (ABBR) ... ABER
Abbe's Sine Law ... ASL
Abbess ... ABS
Abbeville [*France ICAO location identifier*] (ICLI) ... LFOI
Abbeville, AL [*AM radio station call letters*] (RBYB) ... WARI
Abbeville, AL [*FM radio station call letters*] (RBYB) ... WIZB
Abbeville, LA [*AM radio station call letters*] ... KROF
Abbeville, LA [*FM radio station call letters*] ... KROF-FM
Abbeville, SC [*FM radio station call letters*] ... WZLA
Abbeville-Greenwood Regional Library, Greenwood, SC [*Library symbol Library of Congress*] (LCLS) ... ScGrw
Abbey ... A
Abbey [*or Abbot*] ... AB
Abbey [*Record label*] ... Abb
Abbey ... ABB
Abbey Exploration, Inc. [*Toronto Stock Exchange symbol*] ... ABB
Abbey Lane Elementary School, Levittown, NY [*Library symbol*] [*Library of Congress*] (LCLS) ... NLevAE
Abbey Natl. [*Associated Press*] (SAG) ... AbbyNtl
Abbey Natl. [*NYSE symbol*] (SAG) ... ANB
Abbey of Gethsemani, Trappist, KY [*Library symbol Library of Congress*] (LCLS) ... KyTrA
Abbey Woods Development [*Vancouver Stock Exchange symbol*] ... AWD
Abbie J. Lane Memorial Hospital, Halifax, NS, Canada [*Library symbol Library of Congress*] (LCLS) ... CaNSHALMH
Abbildungen [*Illustration, Figure*] [*German*] (BJA) ... Abb
Abbot Energy Corp. [*Vancouver Stock Exchange symbol*] ... ABT
Abbot Public Library Marblehead, Ma [*Library symbol*] [*Library of Congress*] (LCLS) ... MMh
Abbotsbury [*England*] ... ABBOTSB
Abbotsford [*Canada Airport symbol*] ... YXX
Abbotsford Air Services [*Canada ICAO designator*] (FAAC) ... ABE
Abbotsford, BC [*ICAO location identifier*] (ICLI) ... CYXX
Abbotsford-Matsqui, AB [*FM radio station call letters*] ... CFSR
Abbotsford-Matsqui, BC [*AM radio station call letters*] ... CKMA
Abbott and Costello Fan Club (EA) ... ACFC
Abbott Laboratories [*Research code symbol*] ... A
Abbott Laboratories ... Abb
Abbott Laboratories [*NYSE symbol*] (SPSG) ... ABT
Abbott Laboratories [*Research code symbol*] ... AG
Abbott Laboratories [*Research code symbol*] ... MO
Abbott Laboratories [*Research code symbol*] ... PR
Abbott Laboratories [*Research code symbol*] ... PS
Abbott Laboratories Ltd. [*Associated Press*] (SAG) ... AbtLab
Abbott Laboratories Ltd. [*Great Britain*] [*Research code symbol*] ... ES
Abbott Laboratories Ltd., Montreal, PQ, Canada [*Library symbol Library of Congress*] (LCLS) ... CaQMALL
Abbott Laboratories Ltd., Montreal, Quebec [*Library symbol National Library of Canada*] (NLC) ... QMALL
Abbott Laboratories, North Chicago, IL [*Library symbol Library of Congress*] (LCLS) ... INcA
Abbott Laboratories, North Chicago, IL [*OCLC symbol*] (OCLC) ... ITB
Abbott Mead Vickers [*Commercial firm British*] ... AMV
Abbott Memorial Library, Pomfret, VT [*Library symbol Library of Congress*] (LCLS) ... VtPom
Abbott on Civil Jury Trials [*A publication*] (ILCA) ... Abbott Civ Jur Tr
Abbott on Civil Jury Trials [*A publication*] (DLA) ... Abbott Civ Jury Trials
Abbott on Criminal Trial Practice [*A publication*] (DLA) ... Abbott Crim Tr Pr
Abbott on Merchant Ships and Seaman [*1802-1901*] [*A publication*] (DLA) ... Abbott
Abbott on Shipping [*A publication*] (DLA) ... Abb Sh
Abbott on Shipping [*A publication*] (DLA) ... Abb Ship
Abbott. United States Circuit and District Court Reports [*A publication*] (DLA) ... Abb
Abbottabad [*Pakistan*] [*Airport symbol*] (AD) ... AOT
Abbottabad [*Pakistan*] [*ICAO location identifier*] (ICLI) ... OPAB
Abbott-Northwestern Hospitals, Inc., Minneapolis, MN [*Library symbol Library of Congress*] (LCLS) ... MnMAb
Abbott's Admiralty Reports [*United States*] [*A publication*] (DLA) ... Abb Ad
Abbott's Admiralty Reports [*United States*] [*A publication*] (DLA) ... Abb Ad R
Abbott's Admiralty Reports [*United States*] [*A publication*] (DLA) ... Abb Adm
Abbott's Admiralty Reports [*United States*] [*A publication*] (DLA) ... Abbott's Ad Rep
Abbott's Admiralty Reports [*United States*] [*A publication*] (DLA) ... Abbott's Adm
Abbott's Circuit Court Reports [*United States*] [*A publication*] (DLA) ... Abb CC
Abbott's Circuit Court Reports [*United States*] [*A publication*] (DLA) ... Abb US
Abbott's Clerks and Conveyancers' Assistant [*A publication*] (DLA) ... Abb Cl Ass
Abbott's Court of Appeals Decisions [*New York*] [*A publication*] (DLA) ... Abb Ap Dec
Abbott's Court of Appeals Decisions [*New York*] [*A publication*] (DLA) ... Abb App Dec
Abbott's Court of Appeals Decisions [*New York*] [*A publication*] (DLA) ... Abb Ct App
Abbott's Court of Appeals Decisions [*New York*] [*A publication*] (DLA) ... Abb Ct of App Dec
Abbott's Court of Appeals Decisions [*New York*] [*A publication*] (DLA) ... Abb NY App
Abbott's Decisions [*A publication*] (DLA) ... Abb Dec
Abbott's Dictionary [*A publication*] (DLA) ... Abb Dict
Abbott's Dictionary [*A publication*] (DLA) ... Abbott
Abbott's Digest of the Law of Corporations [*A publication*] (DLA) ... Abb Dig Corp
Abbott's Forms of Pleading [*A publication*] (DLA) ... Abb F
Abbott's Forms of Pleading, Supplement [*A publication*] (DLA) ... Abb F Sup
Abbott's Indiana Digest [*A publication*] (DLA) ... Abb Ind Dig
Abbott's Introduction to Practice under the Codes [*A publication*] (DLA) ... Abb Int
Abbott's Law Dictionary [*1879*] [*A publication*] (DLA) ... Abb L Dic

Abbott's Law Dictionary [*1879*] [*A publication*] (DLA) ... Abb Law Dict
Abbott's Legal Remembrancer [*A publication*] (DLA) ... Abb Leg Rem
Abbott's Merchant Ships and Seamen, by Story [*A publication*] (DLA) ... Story Merchants
Abbott's Monthly Index [*A publication*] (DLA) ... Abb Mo Ind
Abbott's National Digest [*A publication*] (DLA) ... Abb Nat Dig
Abbott's New Cases [*New York*] [*A publication*] (DLA) ... Abb N Cas
Abbott's New Cases [*New York*] [*A publication*] (DLA) ... Abb NC
Abbott's New Cases [*New York*] [*A publication*] (DLA) ... Abb New Cas
Abbott's New Cases [*New York*] [*A publication*] (DLA) ... Abbott's NC
Abbott's New Cases [*New York*] [*A publication*] (DLA) ... AN
Abbott's New Cases [*New York*] [*A publication*] (DLA) ... ANC
Abbott's New York Digest [*A publication*] (DLA) ... Abb Dig
Abbott's New York Digest [*A publication*] (DLA) ... Abb NY Dig
Abbott's New York Digest, Second [*A publication*] (DLA) ... Abb NY Dig 2d
Abbott's Pleadings under the Code [*A publication*] (DLA) ... Abb Pl
Abbott's Practice in the United States Courts [*A publication*] (DLA) ... Abb US Pr
Abbott's Practice Reports [*New York*] [*A publication*] (DLA) ... Abb PR
Abbott's Practice Reports [*New York*] [*A publication*] (DLA) ... Abb Pr Rep
Abbott's Practice Reports [*New York*] [*A publication*] (DLA) ... Abb Prac
Abbott's Practice Reports [*New York*] [*A publication*] (DLA) ... Abbott PR
Abbott's Practice Reports [*New York*] [*A publication*] (DLA) ... Abbott Pr Rep
Abbott's Practice Reports [*New York*] [*A publication*] (DLA) ... Abbott Pract Cas
Abbott's Practice Reports [*New York*] [*A publication*] (DLA) ... Abbott's Pr Rep
Abbott's Practice Reports [*New York*] [*A publication*] (DLA) ... Abbott's Prac Rep
Abbott's Practice Reports, New Series [*New York*] [*A publication*] (DLA) ... Abb NS
Abbott's Practice Reports, New Series [*New York*] [*A publication*] (DLA) ... Abb Pr NS
Abbott's Practice Reports, New Series [*New York*] [*A publication*] (DLA) ... Abb Prac NS
Abbott's Real Property Statutes [*A publication*] (DLA) ... Abb RPS
Abbott's Reports of the Beecher Trial [*A publication*] (DLA) ... Abb Beech Tr
Abbott's Trial Evidence [*A publication*] (DLA) ... Abb Tr Ev
Abbott's United States Circuit and District Courts Reports [*A publication*] (DLA) ... Abb USCC
Abbott's United States Circuit and District Courts Reports [*A publication*] (DLA) ... Abbott US Rep
Abbott's United States Circuit and District Courts Reports [*A publication*] (DLA) ... Abbott USR
Abbott's Year Book of Jurisprudence [*A publication*] (DLA) ... Abb Y Bk
Abbreviated (ABBR) ... ABBRD
Abbreviated (DAVI) ... abbrev
Abbreviated Analysis [*Military*] ... AA
Abbreviated Antibiotic Drug Application [*Food and Drug Administration*] ... AADA
Abbreviated COBOL Preprocessor [*Computer science*] (IEEE) ... ACOPP
Abbreviated Conners Parent/Teacher Rating Scale (EDAC) ... ACRS
Abbreviated Cost Form (MCD) ... ACF
Abbreviated Dial (DNAB) ... ABD
Abbreviated Effectiveness Report [*Air Force*] ... AER
Abbreviated Injury Scale [*Medicine*] (PDAA) ... AIS
Abbreviated Item Description (NASA) ... AID
Abbreviated New Drug Application [*FDA*] ... ANDA
Abbreviated Operational Evaluation (MCD) ... AOE
Abbreviated Outline Test Plan [*DoD*] ... AOTP
Abbreviated Parent Symptom Questionnaire [*Medicine*] (DMAA) ... APSQ
Abbreviated Performance Characteristics [*Army*] ... APC
Abbreviated Precision Approach Path Indicator [*Aviation*] (DA) ... APAPI
Abbreviated Purchase Order ... ABBR PO
Abbreviated Registered Address ... ARA
Abbreviated Symptom Questionnaire [*Medicine*] (AAMN) ... ASQ
Abbreviated Test Language for Avionics Systems ... ATLAS
Abbreviated Transportation Accounting Classification [*Army*] ... ATAC
Abbreviated Visual Approach Slope Indicator [*Aviation*] ... AVASI
Abbreviated Visual Approach Slope Indicator System [*Aviation*] (DA) ... AV
Abbreviated Visual Approach Slope Indicator System [*Aviation*] ... AVASIS
Abbreviating (ABBR) ... ABBRG
Abbreviation (IAA) ... A
Abbreviation (ROG) ... AB
Abbreviation (ROG) ... ABB
Abbreviation (AFM) ... ABBR
Abbreviation (DMAA) ... abbr
Abbreviation (EY) ... ABBREV
Abbreviation (ABBR) ... ABBRN
Abbreviation (ROG) ... ABBRON
Abbreviation (IAA) ... ABR
Abbreviations and Related Acronyms Associated with Defense, Astronautics, Business, and Radio-Electronics [*Raytheon Co. publication*] ... ABRACADABRA
Abbreviator (ABBR) ... ABBRR
Abbreviomania (ABBR) ... ABBREVIO
Abbs [*Yemen*] [*ICAO location identifier*] (ICLI) ... OYAS
Abbse [*Yemen Arab Republic*] [*Airport symbol*] (OAG) ... EAB
Abby Investment [*Vancouver Stock Exchange symbol*] ... ABY
ABC [*Air Business Contact*] [*France ICAO designator*] (FAAC) ... ACB
ABC Bancorp [*Associated Press*] (SAG) ... ABC Bc
ABC Bancorp [*NASDAQ symbol*] (SAG) ... ABCB
ABC Dispensing Technologies, Inc. [*NASDAQ symbol*] (SAG) ... ABC Dsp
ABC Dispensing Technologies, Inc. [*Associated Press*] (SAG) ... ABC Dsp
ABC Dispensing Technologies, Inc. [*NASDAQ symbol*] (SAG) ... ABCC
ABC Rail Products [*Associated Press*] (SAG) ... ABC Rail
ABC Rail Products [*NASDAQ symbol*] (SAG) ... ABCR
ABC Rail Products [*NASDAQ symbol*] (TTSB) ... ABCR
ABC Technology, Inc. [*Vancouver Stock Exchange symbol*] ... ABW
ABC World Airways Guide [*ICAO designator*] (FAAC) ... ABC
Abcoulomb (IDOE) ... abC
Abcoulomb [*Unit of electric charge*] ... aC
Abdanan [*Iran*] [*ICAO location identifier*] (ICLI) ... OICD
Abdicate (ABBR) ... ABDI
Abdicated (ROG) ... ABD
Abdicated (ABBR) ... ABDID
Abdication (ABBR) ... ABDIN
Abdomen [*Medicine*] ... AB
Abdomen [*or Abdominal*] ... ABD
Abdomen (ABBR) ... ABDM
Abdomen ... ABDOM
Abdomen (DMAA) ... abdom
Abdominal (ABBR) ... ABDML
Abdominal Aortic Aneurysm [*or Aneurismectomy*] [*Medicine*] ... AAA
Abdominal Circumference [*Neonatology and pediatrics*] (DAVI) ... AC
Abdominal Diameter [*Roentgenology*] ... AD
Abdominal Fluid [*Medicine*] (DAVI) ... ABD
Abdominal Hysterectomy [*Gynecology*] (CPH) ... Abd Hyst
Abdominal Hysterectomy [*Medicine*] ... AH
Abdominal Muscles ... AB's
Abdominal Pad [*Orthopedics*] (DAVI) ... ABD
Abdominal Perineal [*Medicine*] (CPH) ... A-P
Abdominal Surgery [*Medical specialty*] (DHSM) ... ABS
Abdominal Trauma Index [*Medicine*] (DMAA) ... ATI
Abdominal Tympany [*Medicine*] (AAMN) ... AT
Abdominal Vena Cava [*Medicine*] ... AVC
Abdominal X-Ray [*Medicine*] ... AXR
Abdominally (ABBR) ... ABDMLY
Abdominally (ABBR) ... ABDMY
Abdominojugular Reflux Maneuver [*Medicine*] (DMAA) ... AJR
Abdominoperineal Resection [*Medicine*] ... APR
Abducens Motoneuron [*Neuroanatomy*] ... ABM
Abduct [*or Abductor*] [*Neurology and orthopedics*] (DAVI) ... abd
Abduct [*or Abduction*] [*Neurology and orthopedics*] (DAVI) ... abdc
Abducted (ABBR) ... ABDCD
Abducting (ABBR) ... ABDCG
Abduction [*FBI standardized term*] ... ABD
Abduction (ABBR) ... ABDCN
Abduction ... ABDUC
Abduction, External Rotation [*Physiology*] ... ABDER
Abduction, Internal Rotation [*Physiology*] ... ABDIR
Abductor (ABBR) ... ABDCR
Abductor Digiti Minimi [*Muscles of Hands or Feet*] [*Anatomy*] (DAVI) ... ADM
Abductor Digiti Quinti [*Muscles of Hands or Feet*] [*Anatomy*] (DAVI) ... ADQ
Abductor Pollicis [*Muscle*] [*Anatomy*] (DAVI) ... abd poll
Abductor Pollicis Brevis [*Muscle*] [*Anatomy*] (DAVI) ... APB
Abductor Pollicis Longus [*Medicine*] (DMAA) ... APL
Abdy and Walker's Gaius and Ulpian [*A publication*] (DLA) ... A & W Gai
Abdy and Walker's Gaius and Ulpian [*A publication*] (DLA) ... Abdy & W Gai
Abdy and Walker's Justinian [*A publication*] (DLA) ... A & W Just
Abdy and Walker's Justinian [*A publication*] (DLA) ... Abdy & W Just
Abdy's Roman Civil Procedure [*A publication*] (DLA) ... Ab Rom Proc
Abdy's Roman Civil Procedure [*A publication*] (DLA) ... Abdy R Pr
Abe-Ali [*Iran*] [*ICAO location identifier*] (ICLI) ... OIIA
Abeam ... ABM
Abeche [*Chad*] [*Seismograph station code, US Geological Survey Closed*] ... ABC
Abeche [*Chad*] [*ICAO location identifier*] (ICLI) ... FTTC
Abecher [*Chad*] [*Airport symbol*] (AD) ... AEH
A'Beckett's Comic Blackstone [*A publication*] (DLA) ... Com Black
A'Beckett's Reserved Judgements [*A publication*] (ILCA) ... A'Beck Res Judg
A'Beckett's Reserved Judgements [*Victoria*] [*A publication*] (ILCA) ... A'Beckett Res Judg
A'Beckett's Reserved Judgements [*Port Phillip*] [*A publication*] (ILCA) ... RJ
Abelag Airways [*Belgium ICAO designator*] (ICDA) ... VY
Abelag Aviation [*Belgium ICAO designator*] (FAAC) ... AAB
Abell Cluster Inertial Frame [*Cosmology*] ... ACIF
Abell-Corwin-Olowin Clusters [*Galaxy cluster*] ... ACO
Abelson Leukemia Virus ... ALV
Abelson Lymphosarcoma [*Oncology*] ... ABLS
Abelson Plasmacytoid Lymphosarcoma [*Oncology*] ... ABPL
Abelson Plasmacytoma [*Oncology*] ... ABPC
Abelson Virus Transformed [*Medicine*] (DMAA) ... ATV
Abelson-Murine Leukemia [*Virus*] ... AbL
Abelson-Murine Leukemia Virus ... A-MuLV
Abemama [*Kiribati*] [*Airport symbol*] (OAG) ... AEA
Abemama [*Kiribati*] [*ICAO location identifier*] (ICLI) ... NGTB
Abengourou [*Ivory Coast*] [*ICAO location identifier*] (ICLI) ... DIAU
Abengourou [*Ivory Coast*] [*Airport symbol*] (OAG) ... OGO
Abequose Residue [*Medicine*] (BABM) ... abe
Aber Resource Ltd. [*NASDAQ symbol*] (TTSB) ... ABERE
Aber Resources Ltd. [*NASDAQ symbol*] (NQ) ... ABER
Aber Resources Ltd. [*Associated Press*] (SAG) ... AberRs
Aber Resources Ltd. [*Toronto Stock Exchange symbol*] ... ABZ
Aberbeeg [*Welsh depot code*] ... ABEEG
Abercrombie & Fitch [*Retail stores*] ... A & F
Abercrombie & Fitch Co. [*Associated Press*] (SAG) ... AberFit
Abercrombie & Fitch Co. [*NYSE symbol*] (SAG) ... ANF
Abercynon [*Cardiff*] [*Welsh depot code*] ... AYN
Aberdare [*Welsh depot code*] ... ABDR
Aberdeen [*City and county in Scotland*] (ROG) ... ABD
Aberdeen [*Scotland*] [*Seismograph station code, US Geological Survey*] (SEIS) ... ABE
Aberdeen [*City and county in Scotland*] (ROG) ... ABER
Aberdeen [*City and county in Scotland*] ... ABERD
Aberdeen [*South Dakota*] [*Airport symbol*] (OAG) ... ABR

Aberdeen [*Scotland*] [*Airport symbol*] (OAG) .... ABZ
Aberdeen Airways [*British ICAO designator*] (FAAC) .... AAW
Aberdeen Airways [*Airline flight code*] (ODBW) .... SM
Aberdeen Airways Ltd. .... AAW
Aberdeen/Amory, MS [*Location identifier FAA*] (FAAL) .... HWF
Aberdeen and North Scotland Library and Information Cooperative Services (NITA) .... ANSLICS
Aberdeen & Rockfish Railroad Co. [*AAR code*] .... AR
Aberdeen Cable Services [*Cable TV*] (NITA) .... ACS
Aberdeen/Dyce [*British ICAO location identifier*] (ICLI) .... EGPD
Aberdeen Ground/Materiel Testing Directorate [*Maryland*] [*Army*] .... APG/MT
Aberdeen Hospital, New Glasgow, Nova Scotia [*Library symbol National Library of Canada*] (NLC) .... NSNGA
Aberdeen Marine Laboratory .... AML
Aberdeen, MD [*Location identifier FAA*] (FAAL) .... APG
Aberdeen, MD [*Location identifier FAA*] (FAAL) .... PPM
Aberdeen, MD [*AM radio station call letters*] .... WAMD
Aberdeen, MS [*AM radio station call letters*] .... WWZQ
Aberdeen, MS [*FM radio station call letters*] .... WWZQ-FM
Aberdeen, NC [*AM radio station call letters*] .... WQNX
Aberdeen Proving Ground [*Maryland*] [*Army*] .... APG
Aberdeen Proving Ground/Ballistics Research Laboratory [*Army*] .... APGBRL
Aberdeen Proving Ground/Human Engineering Laboratory [*Army*] .... APG/HEL
Aberdeen Proving Ground/Ordnance Bomb Disposal Center [*Army*] (KSC) .... APG/OBDC
Aberdeen Proving Ground/Ordnance Training Command [*Army*] (KSC) .... APG/OTC
Aberdeen Public Library, Aberdeen, ID [*Library symbol*] [*Library of Congress*] (LCLS) .... IdAb
Aberdeen Public Library, Aberdeen, WA [*Library symbol Library of Congress*] (LCLS) .... WaA
Aberdeen Pulsed Reactor Facility .... APRF
Aberdeen Research and Development Center (MCD) .... ARDC
Aberdeen, SD [*Television station call letters*] .... KABY
Aberdeen, SD [*Television station call letters*] .... KDSD
Aberdeen, SD [*AM radio station call letters*] .... KGIM
Aberdeen, SD [*AM radio station call letters*] .... KKAA
Aberdeen, SD [*FM radio station call letters*] .... KQAA
Aberdeen, SD [*AM radio station call letters*] .... KSDN
Aberdeen, SD [*FM radio station call letters*] .... KSDN-FM
Aberdeen University Research and Industrial Services (AIE) .... AURIS
Aberdeen University Research & Industrial Services Ltd. [*British Research center*] (IRUK) .... AURIS
Aberdeen, WA [*FM radio station call letters*] .... KAYO-FM
Aberdeen, WA [*AM radio station call letters*] (RBYB) .... KBKW
Aberdeen, WA [*FM radio station call letters*] .... KDUX
Aberdeen, WA [*AM radio station call letters*] .... KXRO
Aberdeen-Angus Journal, Webster City, IA [*Library symbol Library of Congress*] (LCLS) .... IaWecAJ
Aberford Resources Ltd. [*Toronto Stock Exchange symbol*] .... ABC
Aberfoyle [*Scotland*] [*Seismograph station code, US Geological Survey*] (SEIS) .... EAB
Abermarle County Historical Society, Charlottesville, VA [*Library symbol Library of Congress*] (LCLS) .... ViCAHi
Abermin Corp. [*Toronto Stock Exchange symbol*] .... ABM
Aberporth [*British ICAO location identifier*] (ICLI) .... EGUC
Aberrance (ABBR) .... ABRN
Aberrancy (ABBR) .... ABRNC
Aberrant (DMAA) .... aber
Aberrant (ABBR) .... ABRNT
Aberrant Banding Region [*Genetics*] .... ABR
Aberrant Behavior Checklist [*Treatment effectiveness test*] [*Psychology*] .... ABC
Aberrantly (ABBR) .... ABRNTY
Aberration (IAA) .... ABER
Aberration (ABBR) .... ABERN
Aberration (ABBR) .... ABRAN
Aberrational (ABBR) .... ABERNL
Aberrational (ABBR) .... ABRANL
Aberration-Compensated Input Lens [*Optics*] .... ACIL
Aberystwyth [*Borough in Wales*] .... ABERY
Aberystwyth [*Welsh depot code*] .... ABH
Abetalipoproteinemia [*Medicine*] (MAE) .... ABL
A-Beta-Lipoproteinemia [*Medicine*] (MAH) .... ABL
Abetment (ABBR) .... ABETMT
Abetment (ABBR) .... ABETNT
Abetted (ABBR) .... ABETD
Abetting (ABBR) .... ABETG
Abettor (ABBR) .... ABETR
Abex, Inc. [*NYSE symbol*] (SPSG) .... ABE
Abeyance (ABBR) .... ABYNC
Abeyant (ABBR) .... ABYNT
Abfarad (IDOE) .... abF
Abfarad [*Unit of capacitance*] .... aF
Abgekuerzt [*Abbreviated*] [*German*] .... ABGK
Abgeordneter [*Member of Parliament*] [*German*] (BARN) .... Abg
Abha [*Saudi Arabia*] [*Airport symbol*] (OAG) .... AHB
Abha [*Saudi Arabia*] [*ICAO location identifier*] (ICLI) .... OEAB
Abhandlungen [*Transactions*] [*German Business term*] .... ABH
Abhandlungen der Preussische Akademie der Wissenschaften zu Berlin [*A publication*] (OCD) .... Berl Abh
Abhandlungen. Saechsische Gesellschaft der Wissenschaften [*A publication*] (OCD) .... Abh Sachs Ges Wiss
Abhandlungen zur Geschichte der Mathematischen Wissenschaften [*A publication*] (OCD) .... Abh zu Gesch d Math
Abhandlungen zur Geschichte der Naturwissenschaften und der Medizin [*A publication*] (OCD) .... Abh zu Gesch d Med
Abhenry (IDOE) .... abH
Abhenry [*Unit of inductance*] .... aH
Abhorred (ABBR) .... ABHRD
Abhorrence (ABBR) .... ABHRNC
Abhorrent (ABBR) .... ABHRNT
Abhorrent (ABBR) .... ABHRT
Abhorrently (ABBR) .... ABHRNTY
Abhorrently (ABBR) .... ABHRTY
Abhorrer (ABBR) .... ABHRR
Abhorring (ABBR) .... ABHRG
[*The*] **Abibi Jazz Artists** [*British*] .... TAJA
Abidance (ABBR) .... ABIDNC
Abiding (ABBR) .... ABIDG
Abidingly (ABBR) .... ABIDGY
Abidjan [*Ivory Coast*] [*Airport symbol*] (OAG) .... ABJ
Abidjan [*Ivory Coast*] [*ICAO location identifier*] (ICLI) .... DIAV
Abidjan [*Ivory Coast*] [*ICAO location identifier*] (ICLI) .... DIII
Abidjan/Port Bouet [*Ivory Coast*] [*ICAO location identifier*] (ICLI) .... DIAP
Abigail Adams Historical Society (EA) .... AAHS
Abigail Adams Historical Society, Weymouth, MA [*Library symbol Library of Congress*] (LCLS) .... MWeyAA
Abigail Adams National Bancorp, Inc. [*NASDAQ symbol*] (SAG) .... AANB
Abigail Adams National Bancorp, Inc. [*Associated Press*] (SAG) .... AbigAd
Abilene [*Texas*] [*Airport symbol*] (OAG) .... ABI
Abilene & Southern Railway Co. [*AAR code*] .... AS
Abilene Christian University, Abilene, TX [*Library symbol Library of Congress*] (LCLS) .... TxAbC
Abilene Christian University, Abilene, TX [*OCLC symbol*] (OCLC) .... TXC
Abilene/Dyess Air Force Base [*Texas*] [*ICAO location identifier*] (ICLI) .... KDYS
Abilene Free Public Library, Abilene, KS [*Library symbol Library of Congress*] (LCLS) .... KAb
Abilene, KS [*AM radio station call letters*] .... KABI
Abilene, KS [*FM radio station call letters*] .... KSAJ
Abilene/Municipal [*Texas*] [*ICAO location identifier*] (ICLI) .... KABI
Abilene Public Library, Abilene, TX [*Library symbol Library of Congress*] (LCLS) .... TxAb
Abilene Public Library, Abilene, TX [*OCLC symbol*] (OCLC) .... TXB
Abilene, TX [*Location identifier FAA*] (FAAL) .... DYS
Abilene, TX [*FM radio station call letters*] .... KACU
Abilene, TX [*FM radio station call letters*] (RBYB) .... KAQD-FM
Abilene, TX [*AM radio station call letters*] .... KBBA
Abilene, TX [*AM radio station call letters*] .... KEAN
Abilene, TX [*FM radio station call letters*] .... KEAN-FM
Abilene, TX [*FM radio station call letters*] .... KEYJ
Abilene, TX [*FM radio station call letters*] .... KFXJ
Abilene, TX [*FM radio station call letters*] .... KGNZ
Abilene, TX [*FM radio station call letters*] .... KHXS
Abilene, TX [*AM radio station call letters*] .... KNTS
Abilene, TX [*FM radio station call letters*] .... KORQ-FM
Abilene, TX [*Television station call letters*] .... KRBC
Abilene, TX [*Television station call letters*] .... KTAB
Abilene, TX [*AM radio station call letters*] .... KYYD
Abilene, TX [*Location identifier FAA*] (FAAL) .... TQA
Abilene, TX [*Location identifier FAA*] (FAAL) .... TYY
Ability (ABBR) .... ABIL
Ability (ABBR) .... ABLT
Ability Based on Long Experience .... ABLE
Ability Grouped Active Teaching (EDAC) .... AGAT
Abingdon [*Australia Airport symbol*] (OAG) .... ABG
Abingdon [*England*] .... ABING
Abingdon [*British ICAO location identifier*] (ICLI) .... EGUD
Abingdon Mile [*Newmarket Racecourse*] [*Horseracing*] [*British*] .... ABM
Abingdon Pottery Club (EA) .... APC
Abingdon Press [*Publisher*] .... AP
Abingdon, VA [*Location identifier FAA*] (FAAL) .... ATX
Abingdon, VA [*AM radio station call letters*] .... WABN
Abingdon, VA [*FM radio station call letters*] .... WABN-FM
Abinger [*United Kingdom*] [*Later, HAD*] [*Geomagnetic observatory code*] .... ABN
Abington Free Library, Abington, PA [*Library symbol Library of Congress*] (LCLS) .... PAb
Abington Library Society, Jenkintown, PA [*Library symbol Library of Congress Obsolete*] (LCLS) .... PJA
Abington Savings Bank [*NASDAQ symbol*] (NQ) .... ABBK
Abington Savings Bank [*Associated Press*] (SAG) .... AbingSB
Abington Township Public Library, Abington, PA [*OCLC symbol*] (OCLC) .... ABG
Abiomed, Inc. [*Associated Press*] (SAG) .... Abiomd
Abiomed, Inc. [*NASDAQ symbol*] (SAG) .... ABMD
Abisko [*Sweden*] [*Seismograph station code, US Geological Survey Closed*] .... ABK
Abisko [*Sweden ICAO location identifier*] (ICLI) .... ESHA
Abitibi Asbestos Mining Co. Ltd. [*Vancouver Stock Exchange symbol*] .... ABS
Abitibi Resources Ltd. [*Vancouver Stock Exchange symbol*] .... AIR
Abitibi-Price [*NYSE symbol*] (TTSB) .... ABY
Abitibi-Price, Inc. [*Toronto Stock Exchange symbol Vancouver Stock Exchange symbol*] .... A
Abitibi-Price, Inc. [*Associated Press*] (SAG) .... Abitibi
Abitibi-Price, Inc. [*NYSE symbol*] (SPSG) .... ABY
Abitibi-Price, Inc., Mississauga, ON, Canada [*Library symbol Library of Congress*] (LCLS) .... CaOMABP
Abitibi-Price, Inc., Mississauga, Ontario [*Library symbol National Library of Canada*] (NLC) .... OMABP
Abitur [*School Exit Examination*] [*German*] .... Abit
Abject (ABBR) .... ABJT
Abjection (ABBR) .... ABJTN

Abjectly (ABBR) ... ABJTY
Abjectness (ABBR) ... ABJTNS
Abjuration (ABBR) ... ABJRN
Abjure (ABBR) ... ABJR
Abjured (ABBR) ... ABJRD
Abjurer (ABBR) ... ABJRR
Abjuring (ABBR) ... ABJRG
Abkuerzungsfimmel [*Abbreviation Craze*] ... ABKUFI
Abkurzung [*Abbreviation*] [*German*] (BARN) ... Abk
Ablating Blunt Body ... ABB
Ablating Inner Surface ... AIS
Ablative [*Grammar*] (ROG) ... A
Ablative ... ABL
Ablative (KSC) ... ABLAT
Ablative (ABBR) ... ABLTV
Ablative Heat Rate (MCD) ... AHR
Ablative Heat Shield ... AHS
Ablative Insulative Plastic ... AIP
Ablative Photo Decomposition [*Physics*] ... APD
Ablative Thrust Chamber [*NASA*] ... ATC
Ablative Thrust Chamber Engine [*NASA*] ... ATCE
Ablative Thrust Control (MCD) ... ATC
Ablative Toroidal Compressor ... ATC
Ablator Insulated Ramjet Study [*NASA*] (KSC) ... AIRS
Ablaze (ABBR) ... ABLZ
Able [*Phonetic alphabet*] [*World War II*] (DSUE) ... A
Able (ABBR) ... ABL
Able and Available [*Unemployment insurance*] (OICC) ... AA
Able Chief (MCD) ... AC
Able Seaman [*Navy*] ... AB
Able Seaman Clearance Diver ... ABCD
Able Telcom Holding Corp. [*Associated Press*] (SAG) ... AbleTel
Able Telcom Holding Corp. [*NASDAQ symbol*] (SAG) ... ABTE
Able Telecom Holding [*NASDAQ symbol*] (TTSB) ... ABTE
Able-Bodied Seaman ... AB
Able-Bodied Seaman ... ABS
Able-Bodied Seaman, Air Technical Aircraft [*Navy*] ... ABATA
Able-Bodied Seaman, Air Technical Communications [*Navy*] ... ABATC
Able-Bodied Seaman, Air Technical Weapons Electrical [*Navy*] ... ABATWL
Able-Bodied Seaman Cook [*Navy*] ... ABCK
Able-bodied Seaman Coxswain [*Navy*] ... ABCOX
Able-Bodied Seaman Dental, NV ... ABDEN
Able-Bodied Seaman Electrical Technical Power [*Navy*] ... ABETP
Able-Bodied Seaman Electrical Technical Weapons [*Navy*] ... ABETW
Able-Bodied Seaman Electronic Technical Communications [*Navy*] ... ABETC
Able-Bodied Seaman Electronic Warfare [*Navy*] ... ABEW
Able-Bodied Seaman Fire Control [*Navy*] ... ABFC
Able-Bodied Seaman Firefighter [*Navy*] ... ABFF
Able-Bodied Seaman Marine Technical Hull [*Navy*] ... ABMTH
Able-Bodied Seaman Marine Technical Propulsion [*Navy*] ... ABMTP
Able-Bodied Seaman Medical [*Navy*] ... ABMED
Able-Bodied Seaman Meteorology [*Navy*] ... ABMET
Able-Bodied Seaman Mine Warfare [*Navy*] ... ABMW
Able-Bodied Seaman Motor Transport Driver [*Navy*] ... ABMTD
Able-Bodied Seaman Musician [*Navy*] ... ABMUSN
Able-Bodied Seaman Photography [*Navy*] ... ABPH
Able-Bodied Seaman Physical Training [*Navy*] ... ABPT
Able-Bodied Seaman Quartermaster Gunner [*Navy*] ... ABQMG
Able-Bodied Seaman RADAR Plotter [*Navy*] ... ABRP
Able-Bodied Seaman Radio Operator [*Navy*] ... ABRO
Able-Bodied Seaman Signalman [*Navy*] ... ABSIG
Able-Bodied Seaman Steward [*Navy*] ... ABSTD
Able-Bodied Seaman Stores Naval [*Navy*] ... ABSN
Able-Bodied Seaman Stores Victualling [*Navy*] ... ABSV
Able-Bodied Seaman Survival Equipment [*Navy*] ... ABSE
Able-Bodied Seaman Underwater Control [*Navy*] ... ABUC
Able-bodied Seaman Work Study [*Navy*] ... ABWS
Able-Bodied Seaman Writer [*Navy*] ... ABWTR
Able-Bodied Sick Bay Attendant [*Navy*] ... ABBA
Abler (ABBR) ... ABLR
Ablest (ABBR) ... ABLT
Abloom (ABBR) ... ABLM
Ablow [*Vanuatu*] [*ICAO location identifier*] (ICLI) ... NVSA
Ablution (ABBR) ... ABLUN
Ablutionary (ABBR) ... ABLUNRY
Ablutionary (ABBR) ... ABLUNY
ABM Industries, Inc. [*Associated Press*] (SAG) ... ABM
ABN AMRO Holdings N.V. [*AM Symbol*] (TTSB) ... ALGEE
Abnegate (ABBR) ... ABNG
Abnegate (ABBR) ... ABNGA
Abnegated (ABBR) ... ABNGAD
Abnegated (ABBR) ... ABNGD
Abnegates (ABBR) ... ABNGS
Abnegating (ABBR) ... ABNGAG
Abnegating (ABBR) ... ABNGG
Abnegation (ABBR) ... ABNGN
Abnegator (ABBR) ... ABNGR
Abnormal [*Medicine*] (AAMN) ... A
Abnormal (MAE) ... AB
Abnormal [*or Abnormality*] [*Medicine*] (AAMN) ... ABN
Abnormal (MSA) ... ABNL
Abnormal [*or Abnormality*] ... ABNOR
Abnormal [*Medicine*] (AAMN) ... ABNORM
Abnormal Banding Region [*Genetics*] ... ABR
Abnormal Blood Gas ... ABG
Abnormal Control Plasma [*Clinical chemistry*] ... ACP
Abnormal Curve [*Biochemistry*] (DAVI) ... ABNC
Abnormal End [*Computer science*] ... ABEND
Abnormal End [*Computer science*] (IAA) ... ABNED
Abnormal Fluctuation in the Economy (MCD) ... AFIE
Abnormal Forms Percent [*Sperm count*] [*Urology*] (DAVI) ... ABN F%
Abnormal Frequency ... AF
Abnormal Glucose Tolerance Test [*Medicine*] ... AGTT
Abnormal Involuntary Movement Disorder [*Medicine*] (DMAA) ... AIMD
Abnormal Involuntary Movement Scale [*Medicine*] ... AIMS
Abnormal Left Axis Deviation (MAE) ... ALAD
Abnormal Liver Function Test [*Medicine*] (DMAA) ... ALFT
Abnormal Localization of Immature P recursors [*Clinical hematology*] ... ALIP
Abnormal Lungs [*Medicine*] ... AL
Abnormal Mission Routine ... AMR
Abnormal Mucopolysacchariduria [*Medicine*] (MAE) ... AMPS
Abnormal Occurrence (NRCH) ... AO
Abnormal Occurrence Report ... AOR
Abnormal Occurrence Reporting System (MHDB) ... AORS
Abnormal Operating Condition (GFGA) ... AOC
Abnormal Operating Procedure (NRCH) ... AOP
Abnormal Oxygen Affinity [*Hematology*] (DAVI) ... AOA
Abnormal Posterior Vector [*Medicine*] (DMAA) ... APV
Abnormal Record Compatible with Myocardial Disease [*Lower-case c in acronym means "with"*] [*Cardiology*] ... ARCcMD
Abnormal Record Compatible with Myocardial Drug Effect [*Lowercase c in acronym means "with"*] [*Cardiology*] ... ARCcMDE
Abnormal [*or Anomalous*] **Retinal Correspondence** [*Ophthalmology*] ... ARC
Abnormal Skin Reflex [*Medicine*] (DMAA) ... AbSR
Abnormal Steady State Limits (MCD) ... ASSL
Abnormal Transient Operational Guidelines [*Nuclear energy*] (NRCH) ... ATOG
Abnormal Uterine Bleeding [*Gynecology*] (DMAA) ... AUB
Abnormal Voltage ... AV
Abnormal Wall Motion [*Medicine*] (DMAA) ... AWM
Abnormal Xylem Elements [*Botany*] ... AX
Abnormality (ABBR) ... ABNMT
Abnormally (ABBR) ... ABNMY
Abo Akademi [*Swedish University of Abo*], Turku, Finland [*Library symbol Library of Congress*] (LCLS) ... FiTA
ABO Resource Corp. [*Vancouver Stock Exchange symbol*] ... ABU
Aboard (BARN) ... abd
Aboard (ABBR) ... ABRD
Aboda Zara (BJA) ... AbZ
Aboda Zara (BJA) ... AbZar
Aboda Zara (BJA) ... AZ
Abode (ABBR) ... ABOD
Abogada Internacional [*A publication*] (DLA) ... Abogada Int'l
Abohoy [*Indonesia*] [*ICAO location identifier*] (ICLI) ... WAKH
Aboisso [*Ivory Coast*] [*ICAO location identifier*] (ICLI) ... DIAO
Aboitiz Air Transport Corp. [*Philippines*] [*ICAO designator*] (FAAC) ... BOI
Abolish (ABBR) ... ABLH
Abolishable (ABBR) ... ABLHB
Abolished ... ABOL
Abolished (ABBR) ... ABOLD
Abolisher (ABBR) ... ABLHR
Abolishing (ABBR) ... ABOLG
Abolishment (ABBR) ... ABLHNT
Abolishment (ABBR) ... ABOLT
Abolition (ABBR) ... ABOLN
Abolitionism (ABBR) ... ABOLNM
Abolitionist ... abol
Abolitionist (ABBR) ... ABOLNST
Abolitionist (ABBR) ... ABOLNT
Abominable (ABBR) ... ABMNB
Abominable (ABBR) ... ABOML
Abominably (ABBR) ... ABMNBY
Abominate (ABBR) ... ABMNA
Abominate (ABBR) ... ABOM
Abominated (ABBR) ... ABOMD
Abominating (ABBR) ... ABMNAG
Abominating (ABBR) ... ABOMG
Abomination (ABBR) ... ABMNAN
Abomination (ABBR) ... ABOMN
Abong-M'Bang [*Cameroon*] [*ICAO location identifier*] (ICLI) ... FKAG
Abonminated (ABBR) ... ABMNAD
Abopo [*Bolivia*] [*ICAO location identifier*] (ICLI) ... SLAB
Aboriginal (ABBR) ... ABO
Aboriginal (ABBR) ... ABORL
Aboriginal (ABBR) ... ABRGNL
Aboriginal Advancement Trust Account [*Australia*] ... AATA
Aboriginal Affairs Foundation [*Australia*] ... AAF
Aboriginal and Islander Child Care Agencies [*Australia*] ... AICCA
Aboriginal and Islander Forum [*A publication*] ... Abo Island Forum
Aboriginal and Islander Teacher Education Program [*Australia*] ... AITEP
Aboriginal and Torres Strait Islander Commission Regional Information Syste ... ARIS
Aboriginal and Torres Strait Islander Legal Service [*Australia*] ... ATSILS
Aboriginal and Torres Strait Islander Library and Resource Network [*Australia*] ... ATSILRN
Aboriginal Areas Protection Authority [*Northern Territory, Australia*] ... AAPA
Aboriginal Child at School [*A publication*] ... Abo Child School
Aboriginal Children's Services [*Australia*] ... ACS
Aboriginal Community Affairs Panel [*Australia*] ... ACAP
Aboriginal Community Liaison Officer [*Australia*] ... ACLO
Aboriginal Community Recreation Health Services Centre [*Australia*] ... ACRHSC

Aboriginal Community Recreation Health Services Centre of South Australia ... ACRHSCSA
Aboriginal Coordinating Council [*Australia*] ... ACC
Aboriginal Cultural Centre and Keeping Place [*University of New England*] [*Australia*] ... ACCKP
Aboriginal Cultural Foundation [*Australia*] ... ACF
Aboriginal Development Assistance Association [*Australia*] ... ADAA
Aboriginal Economic and Employment Development Officer [*Australia*] ... AEEDO
Aboriginal Education Council (New South Wales) [*Australia*] ... AEC(NSW)
Aboriginal Education Direct Assistance Program [*Australia*] ... AEDAP
Aboriginal Education Foundation of South Australia ... AEFSA
Aboriginal Education Worker [*Australia*] ... AEW
Aboriginal Electoral Assistant [*Australia*] ... AEA
Aboriginal Electoral Information Service [*Australia*] ... AEIS
Aboriginal Environmental Health Worker [*Australia*] ... AEHW
Aboriginal Evangelical Fellowship of Australia ... AEFA
Aboriginal Health Development Group [*Australia*] ... AHDG
Aboriginal Health Policy Review Team [*Australia*] ... AHPRT
Aboriginal Health Service [*Australia*] ... AHS
Aboriginal Health Worker Education Program [*Australia*] ... AHWEP
Aboriginal Heritage Branch [*South Australia*] ... AHB
Aboriginal Home Care Service [*Australia*] ... AHCS
Aboriginal Housing Development Committee [*Australia*] ... AHDC
Aboriginal Independent Community Schools [*Australia*] ... AICS
Aboriginal Issues Unit [*Australia*] ... AIU
Aboriginal Land Fund Commission [*Australia*] ... ALFC
Aboriginal Lands Council [*Australia*] ... ALC
Aboriginal Lands of Hawaiian Ancestry [*Hawaiian group seeking compensation for land*] ... ALOHA
Aboriginal Language Maintenance Project [*Australia*] ... ALMP
Aboriginal Languages Education Strategy [*Australia*] ... ALES
Aboriginal Legal Service of Western Australia ... ALSWA
Aboriginal Loans Commission [*Australia*] ... ALC
Aboriginal Mental Health Network [*Western Australia*] ... AMHN
Aboriginal Middle Management Program [*Australia*] ... AMMP
Aboriginal Multi-Media Society of Alberta (AC) ... AMMSA
Aboriginal National Theatre Trust [*Australia*] ... ANTT
Aboriginal Nurses Association of Canada [*Association des Infirmieres et Infirmiers Autochtones du Canada*] [*Indian & Inuit Nurses of Canada*] (AC) ... ANAC
Aboriginal People's Business Association (AC) ... APBA
Aboriginal Programs Management Information System [*Australia*] ... APMIS
Aboriginal Protection Board [*Australia*] ... APB
Aboriginal Reconciliation Unit [*Australia*] ... ARU
Aboriginal Research Club (EA) ... ARC
Aboriginal Resource and Development Services [*Australia*] ... ARDS
Aboriginal Resource Unit [*University of New England*] [*Australia*] ... ARU
Aboriginal Rights Coalition [*Coalition pour les Droits des Autochtones*] [*Project North*] (AC) ... ARC
Aboriginal Sacred Sites Protection Authority [*Northern Territory, Australia*] ... ASSPA
Aboriginal Staff Cadetship Program [*Australia*] ... ASCP
Aboriginal Teaching Assistant [*Australia*] ... ATA
Aboriginal Trappers Federation of Canada (AC) ... ATFC
Aboriginal Visitors' Scheme [*Australia*] ... AVS
Aboriginal Welfare Board [*New South Wales, Australia*] ... AWB
Aboriginal Work Experience Program [*Australia*] ... AWEP
Aboriginally (ABBR) ... ABORLY
Aborigine (ABBR) ... ABO
Aborigine ... ABOR
Aborigine (ABBR) ... ABRGN
Aborigines Inland Mission of Australia ... AIMA
Aborigines Protection Society [*Later, Anti-Slavery Society for the Protection of Human Rights*] ... APS
Abort (MCD) ... ABRT
Abort ... ABT
Abort Accept [*Telecommunications*] (OSI) ... AA
Abort Advisory Channel [*NASA*] (KSC) ... AAC
Abort Advisory Equipment [*NASA*] (KSC) ... AAE
Abort Advisory System [*NASA*] ... AAS
Abort Electronics [*Apollo*] [*NASA*] ... AE
Abort Electronics Assembly [*Apollo*] [*NASA*] ... AEA
Abort Guidance Section [*NASA*] (KSC) ... AGS
Abort Guidance System [*or Subsystem*] [*Apollo*] [*NASA*] ... AGS
Abort/Hold/Orbit [*NASA*] ... A/H/O
Abort Inertial Digital System [*NASA*] (KSC) ... AIDS
Abort Interface Unit [*NASA*] ... AIU
Abort Motor Facility [*NASA*] (NASA) ... AMF
Abort Once Around [*NASA*] ... AOA
Abort Once around Cutoff (MCD) ... ACO
Abort Programmer Assembly [*NASA*] (KSC) ... APA
Abort Request (MCD) ... ABRTREQ
Abort Sensing and Implementation System ... ASIS
Abort Sensing Control Unit ... ASCO
Abort Sensor Assembly [*Apollo*] [*NASA*] ... ASA
Abort Solid Rocket Motor [*NASA*] (NASA) ... ASRM
Abort Time Assembly [*NASA*] (NASA) ... ATA
Abort Timer (HGAA) ... ABT
Aborted (ABBR) ... ABRTD
Aborting (ABBR) ... ABRTG
Abortion [*Medicine*] (DMAA) ... ab
Abortion [*Obstetrics*] (DAVI) ... ABO
Abortion [*Medicine*] ... ABOR
Abortion (DMAA) ... Abor
Abortion (ABBR) ... ABRTN
Abortion Fund (EA) ... AF
Abortion Information Data Bank [*of Zero Population Growth, Inc.*] [*Defunct*] ... AID
Abortion Law Reform Association (EAIO) ... ALRA
Abortion Law Reform Association. News Letter [*A publication*] (DLA) ... ALRANL
Abortion Law Reporter [*A publication*] (DLA) ... Abortion L Rep
Abortion Patient [*Medicine*] ... AB
Abortion Sydney [*An association Australia*] ... AS
Abortionist (ABBR) ... ABRTNST
Abortionist (ABBR) ... ABRTNT
Abortive (ABBR) ... ABRTV
Abortively (ABBR) ... ABRTVY
Abortiveness (ABBR) ... ABRTVNS
Abort-Scan Table [*NASA*] ... AST
Abort-to-Orbit [*NASA*] (NASA) ... ATO
Abortus Bang Ringprobe [*Test*] [*Medicine*] ... ABR
Abortus, Militensis, Suis [*Microbiology*] ... AMS
Aboth (BJA) ... Ab
Aboth [*or Avot*] **d'Rabbi Nathan** (BJA) ... ARN
Abou Deia [*Chad*] [*Airport symbol*] (AD) ... AOD
Abound (ABBR) ... ABND
About ... A
About (WDMC) ... a
About ... AB
About (MUGU) ... ABT
About [*Internet language*] [*Computer science*] ... abt
About Books, Inc. [*An association*] (EA) ... ABI
About Buttonhooks, Spoons, and Patents [*An association Defunct*] (EA) ... ABSP
About Face [*An association*] (EAIO) ... AF
About Face/Let's Face It (EA) ... AFLFI
About or On (MCD) ... A/O
About Proof (WDAA) ... AP
About-Face (ABBR) ... ABT-FC
Above (MSA) ... ABV
Above ... ABV
Above Aerodrome Level ... AAL
Above Baseline ... ABL
Above Burst Height (DNAB) ... ABH
Above Client Expectations [*Program*] ... ACE
Above Clouds [*Aviation*] (FAAC) ... ACLD
Above Core Load Pad [*Nuclear energy*] (NRCH) ... ACLP
Above Core Load Plane [*Nuclear energy*] (NRCH) ... ACLP
Above Deck [*of a ship*] (DS) ... AD
Above Elbow [*Amputation*] [*Medicine*] (DMAA) ... A/E
Above Elbow [*Medicine*] ... AE
Above Field Level [*Aerospace*] (AAG) ... AFL
Above Finished Floor [*Technical drawings*] ... AFF
Above Grade (DAC) ... AG
Above Ground Level ... AGL
Above Ground Net Primary Production [*Ecology*] ... ANPP
Above Ground Storage Tank ... AST
Above Ground Test [*Defense Nuclear Agency*] ... AGT
Above Knee [*Amputation*] [*Medicine*] (DMAA) ... A/K
Above Knee [*Medicine*] ... AK
Above Knee Amputation [*Medicine*] ... AKA
Above Local Terrain (MCD) ... ALT
Above Mean Sea Level [*Navigation*] ... AMSL
Above Mentioned ... AM
Above Modern River Level [*Geology*] ... AMRL
Above Mountains [*ICAO*] (FAAC) ... MON
Above Normal Loss [*Insurance*] ... ANL
Above Ordnance Datum [*Military*] (DA) ... AOD
Above Proof ... AP
Above Scale [*Laboratory*] (DAVI) ... AS
Above Sea Level ... ASL
Above Suspended Ceiling [*Technical drawings*] ... ASC
Above Target Elevation (MCD) ... ATE
Above the Horizon ... ATH
Above Transmitted as Received (FAAC) ... ATAR
Above Upper Limit (MHDB) ... AUL
Above Waist [*Medicine*] ... AW
Above Water ... AW
Above Water Thrown Torpedo [*Navy*] (CAAL) ... AWTT
Above Water Torpedo Tube [*Navy*] (NVT) ... AWTT
Above Water Warfare [*Navy*] (NVT) ... AWW
Above-Board (ABBR) ... ABV-BRD
Above-Elbow Amputation [*Orthopedics*] (DAVI) ... AEA
Aboveground Biomass [*Of vegetation*] ... AGB
Aboveground Net Primary Production [*Of biomass*] ... AGNPP
Above-Knee Amputation [*Orthopedics*] (DAVI) ... AK Amp
Above-Named ... AN
Above-Named Officer [*Army orders*] ... ANO
Above-Threshold Ionization (MCD) ... ATI
ABR Information Services [*NASDAQ symbol*] (TTSB) ... ABRX
ABR Information Services, Inc. [*Associated Press*] (SAG) ... ABR Inf
ABR Information Services, Inc. [*NASDAQ symbol*] (SAG) ... ABRX
Abra De Llog [*Philippines*] [*Seismograph station code, US Geological Survey Closed*] ... ABP
Abracadabra (DSUE) ... ABRAC
Abrade (ABBR) ... ABRAD
Abrade (ABBR) ... ABRD
Abraded (ABBR) ... ABRADD
Abraded (ABBR) ... ABRDD
Abrading (ABBR) ... ABRADG
Abrading (ABBR) ... ABRDG
Abraham (ABBR) ... ABR

Abraham (ABBR)	ABRA
Abraham (ABBR)	ABRAM
Abraham & Straus [Retail store]	A & S
Abraham Baldwin Agricultural College [Tifton, GA]	ABAC
Abraham Baldwin Agricultural College, Tifton, GA [Library symbol Library of Congress] (LCLS)	GTiA
Abraham Baldwin Agricultural College, Tifton, GA [OCLC symbol] (OCLC)	GTM
Abraham Lincoln [US president, 1809-1865]	AL
Abraham Lincoln Association (EA)	ALA
Abraham Lincoln Birthplace National Monument	ABLI
Abrams Industries [NASDAQ symbol] (TTSB)	ABRI
Abrams Industries, Inc. [Associated Press] (SAG)	Abrams
Abrams Industries, Inc. [NASDAQ symbol] (NQ)	ABRI
Abrams Power Train Evolution	APTE
Abrasion (DAVI)	ABR
Abrasion (ABBR)	ABRAN
Abrasion (ABBR)	ABRAS
Abrasion (ABBR)	ABRSN
Abrasion-Resistant Print Coating [for plastic laminates] [Nevamar]	ARP
Abrasive (ABBR)	ABR
Abrasive	ABR
Abrasive (ABBR)	ABRAV
Abrasive (MSA)	ABRSV
Abrasive Ceramic Mosaic (DICI)	ACM
Abrasive Engineering Society (EA)	AES
Abrasive Flow Machining [Mechanical engineering]	AFM
Abrasive Grain Association (EA)	AGA
Abrasive Industries Association (MHDB)	AIA
Abrasive Jet Machining (PDAA)	AJM
Abrasive Machining (IAA)	AM
Abrasive Paver (DICI)	AP
Abrasive Water Jet Machining [Factory automation] (BTTJ)	AWJM
Abraxas Petroleum [NASDAQ symbol] (TTSB)	AXAS
Abraxas Petroleum Corp. [Associated Press] (SAG)	Abraxas
Abraxas Petroleum Corp. [NASDAQ symbol] (SAG)	AXAS
Abreast (ABBR)	ABRST
ABRES [Advanced Ballistic Reentry System] Instrumentation Range Safety Systems [Air Force] (MCD)	AIRSS
Abridge (ABBR)	ABRG
Abridgeable (ABBR)	ABRGB
Abridged	ABR
Abridged (WDMC)	abr
Abridged (ABBR)	ABRGD
Abridged (ABBR)	ABRID
Abridged Arrival Report [Navy] (NVT)	HAVREP
Abridged Building Classification for Architects, Builders, and Civil Engineers	ABC
Abridged Index Medicus Accessed by Teletypewriter Exchange Service [National Library of Medicine]	AIM-TWX
Abridged Ocular Chart [Ophthalmology] (DAVI)	AOC
Abridger (ABBR)	ABRGR
Abridging (ABBR)	ABRGG
Abridgment (DLA)	Ab
Abridgment (WDMC)	abr
Abridgment (ABBR)	ABRGNT
Abridgment (ABBR)	ABRGT
Abridgment of Cases in Equity [1667-1744] [A publication] (DLA)	Abr Ca Eq
Abridgment of Cases in Equity [1667-1744] [A publication] (DLA)	Eq Ab
Abridgment of Cases in Equity [1667-1744] [A publication] (DLA)	Eq Ca Abr
Abril [April] [Spanish] (BARN)	Abl
Abr-Nahrain (BJA)	AbN
Abr-Nahrain (BJA)	AN
Abroad (ABBR)	ABRD
Abroad	ABRD
Abroad (ABBR)	ABROD
Abrogate (ABBR)	ABRGA
Abrogate (ABBR)	ABROG
Abrogated (ABBR)	ABRGAD
Abrogated (ABBR)	ABROGD
Abrogating (ABBR)	ABROGAG
Abrogating (ABBR)	ABROGG
Abrogation (ABBR)	ABRGAN
Abrogation (ABBR)	ABROGN
Abrupt (ABBR)	ABRP
Abrupt Junction Varactor Doubler	AJVD
Abrupt Space Charge Edge [Algorithm]	ASCE
Abrupt Symmetrical Pull Up (MCD)	ASPU
Abruptness (ABBR)	ABRPNS
ABS Industries [Associated Press] (SAG)	ABS
ABS Industries, Inc. [NASDAQ symbol] (NQ)	ABSI
ABS Resources Ltd. [Vancouver Stock Exchange symbol]	ABL
ABS [Australian Bureau of Statistics] Time-Series Database [Information service or system] (CRD)	ABSTD
Absatz [Paragraph] [German] (ILCA)	Abs
Absatzwirtschaft Data Bank [Dusseldorf, Federal Republic of Germany] [Database producer Information service or system] (IID)	ASW
Abscess (ABBR)	AB
Abscess (ABBR)	ABCS
Abscessed (ABBR)	ABCSD
Abscesses (ABBR)	ABS
Abscessing (ABBR)	ABCSG
Abschnitt [Section, Part, Chapter, or Division] [German] (BARN)	Abs
Abschnitt [Paragraph, Chapter] [German] (ILCA)	Abschn
Abschnittsbevollmaechtiger [Section Deputy] [German]	ABV

Abscisic Acid [Biochemistry]	ABA
Abscissa [Mathematics] (AAMN)	ABSC
Abscissa (IDOE)	x
Abscissa of a Coordinate (BARN)	X
Abscission Zone [Botany]	AZ
Abscond (ABBR)	ABSC
Abscond (ABBR)	ABSCD
Absence (ABBR)	ABSC
Absence (ABBR)	ABSNC
Absence and Turnover Rates [Database]	ABSTURN
Absence of Immunoglobulin [Immunology] (DAVI)	AIGA
Absence of Immunoglobulin G [Biochemistry] (DAVI)	ABIG
Absence of Immunoglobulin M [Immunology] (DAVI)	AIGM
Absence of Sex Chromosome (DAVI)	O
Absent	A
Absent (ROG)	AB
Absent (AFM)	ABS
Absent (ABBR)	ABSNT
Absent Bed Occupancy [Medicine]	ABO
Absent by Reason of Being Held by Civil Authorities [Military]	HCA
Absent On Duty [Military]	AOD
Absent on Temporary Additional Duty [Navy]	ATAD
Absent on Temporary Duty [Navy]	ATD
Absent over Leave [Navy]	AOL
Absent Sick in Hospital (DAVI)	ASIH
Absent Subscriber, Office Closed (WDMC)	ABS
Absent With Leave [Military]	AWL
Absent Without Leave [Military British]	AWL
Absent without Official Leave [Military]	AWOL
Absent without Pay (MCD)	AWOP
Absente Febre [In the Absence of Fever] [Pharmacy]	ABS FEB
Absente Febre [In the Absence of Fever] [Pharmacy] (ROG)	ABS FEBR
Absente Reo [The Defendant Being Absent] [Legal term Latin] (ADA)	ABS RE
Absente Reo [The Defendant Being Absent] [Legal term Latin] (ADA)	ABSE RE
Absented (ABBR)	ABSD
Absentee (ABBR)	ABSNTE
Absentee (ABBR)	ABST
Absentee	ABSTEE
Absenteeism (ABBR)	ABSNTEM
Absenteeism (ABBR)	ABSTM
Absenting (ABBR)	ABSG
Absently (ABBR)	ABSY
Absent-Minded Club [Defunct] (EA)	AMC
Absiemens (IDOE)	abS
Absiemens [Unit of conductance]	aS
Absolute [Temperature in Fahrenheit degrees]	A
Absolute [Flowchart]	ABS
Absolute (ABBR)	ABSLT
Absolute	ABSLT
Absolute	ABSOL
Absolute Address (AAG)	AA
Absolute Altitude [Navigation]	AA
Absolute Ampere	ABAMP
Absolute Assembly Language [Programming language] (BUR)	AAL
Absolute Average Percent Deviation [Mathematics]	AAPD
Absolute Band Count [Biochemistry] (DAVI)	ABC
Absolute Basophil Count [Hematology] (MAE)	ABC
Absolute Bed Rest [Medicine]	ABR
Absolute Boiling Point	ABP
Absolute Cardiac Dullness [Medicine]	ACD
Absolute Catabolic Rate [Medicine] (DMAA)	ACR
Absolute Ceiling	ABCLG
Absolute Ceiling [Aviation]	ABS CLG
Absolute Ceiling [Aviation]	AC
Absolute Coefficient of Yawing Moments	CN
Absolute Dullness [on Auscultation] [Medicine] (DAVI)	M_3
Absolute Electrical Unit Scale	AEUS
Absolute Electrostatic Unit (IAA)	AESU
Absolute Error (IAA)	ABSE
Absolute Error	AE
Absolute Essential Equipment	AEE
Absolute Filtration Rating	AFR
Absolute Granulocyte Count [Medicine] (DMAA)	AGC
Absolute Ground Level (MCD)	AGL
Absolute Interferometric LASER (SAA)	AIL
Absolute Iodine Uptake [Medicine]	AIU
Absolute Limen [Psychophysics]	AL
Absolute Loader [Computer science]	ABSLDR
Absolute Lymphocyte Count [Medicine]	ALC
Absolute Magnitude [Astronomy]	M
Absolute Magnitude Difference Function (PDAA)	AMDF
Absolute Maximum Loss	AML
Absolute Memory Image (MCD)	AMI
Absolute Neutrophil Count [Hematology]	ANC
Absolute Output [Computer science]	AO
Absolute Pardon (ADA)	AP
Absolute Pitch [Physiology]	AP
Absolute Plate Motion [Geophysics]	APM
Absolute Position Indication [Nuclear energy] (NRCH)	API
Absolute Pressure Control	APC
Absolute Pressure Sensor [Automotive engineering]	APS
Absolute Proximal Reabsorption [Medicine] (DMAA)	APR
Absolute Radiation Scale (PDAA)	ARS
Absolute Rate Theory [Statistics]	ART
Absolute Reaction of Degeneration	ARD

Absolute Reaction Rate Theory [*Physical chemistry*] .... ARRT
Absolute Refractory Period .... ARP
Absolute Retention Time (MAE) .... ART
Absolute Rod Position Indication [*Nuclear energy*] (NRCH) .... ARPI
Absolute Sensation Threshold .... AST
Absolute Space-Time .... AST
Absolute Specular Reflectance [*Spectroscopy*] .... ASR
Absolute Temperature [*Symbol*] [*IUPAC*] .... T
Absolute Temperature Scale .... ATS
Absolute Term (IAA) .... AT
Absolute Terminal Innervation Ratio [*Psychiatry*] .... ATIR
Absolute Threshold .... AT
Absolute Time Base Error [*Computer science*] (IAA) .... ATBE
Absolute Title [*Business term*] .... AT
Absolute Total and Complete Camouflage [*Hunting*] .... ATACC
[*The*] Absolute Truth [*In Julian Barnes' novel "Staring at the Sun"*] .... TAT
Absolute Value (IAA) .... ABSV
Absolute Value (BUR) .... ABV
Absolute Value BIT [*Binary Digit*] Synchronizer .... AVBS
Absolute Virtual Address [*Computer science*] .... AVA
Absolute Voltmeter (IAA) .... ABSVM
Absolute Worst Case .... AWC
Absolute Zero [*Temperature*] (MAE) .... K
Absolutely (ABBR) .... ABSLTY
Absolutely (ROG) .... ABSLY
Absolutely (ABBR) .... ABSOLY
Absolutely Bloody Final [*Especially with reference to a drink*] .... ABF
Absolutely Fabulous (DSUE) .... ABFAB
Absolutely to Die [*Slang*] .... ATD
Absoluteness (ABBR) .... ABSOLNS
Absolution (ABBR) .... ABSLTN
Absolution (ABBR) .... ABSOLN
Absolution (BARN) .... Absoluo
Absolutism (ABBR) .... ABSLTM
Absolutist (ABBR) .... ABSLTST
Absolutus Iuris [*Absolute Jurisdiction*] [*Latin*] .... Abs Iur
Absolvable (ABBR) .... ABSLVB
Absolve (ABBR) .... ABSLV
Absolved (ABBR) .... ABSLVD
Absolver (ABBR) .... ABSLVR
Absolving (ABBR) .... ABSLVG
Absolvo [*I Acquit*] [*Used by Romans in criminal trials*] [*Latin*] .... A
Absonant (ABBR) .... ABS
Absorb [*or Absorption*] .... ABS
Absorb (ABBR) .... ABSB
Absorbability (ABBR) .... ABSBBT
Absorbable (ABBR) .... ABSBB
Absorbance [*Internal transmission density*] [*Symbol IUPAC*] .... A
Absorbance (ABBR) .... ABSBNC
Absorbance Expanded [*Spectroscopy*] .... ABEXed
Absorbance Unit [*Physical chemistry*] .... AU
Absorbance Units Full Scale [*Physical chemistry*] .... AUFS
Absorbance-Detected Magnetic Resonance [*Physics*] .... ADMR
Absorbed (ABBR) .... ABSBD
Absorbency (ABBR) .... ABSBCY
Absorbency (ABBR) .... ABSBNC
Absorbent (ABBR) .... ABSBT
Absorbent Paper Manufacturers Association [*Defunct*] .... APMA
Absorber (ABBR) .... ABSBR
Absorber Open Test Assembly [*Nuclear energy*] (NRCH) .... AOTA
Absorbing (ABBR) .... ABSBG
Absorbtion Heat Transformer .... AHT
Absorption (DMAA) .... Abs
Absorption (ABBR) .... ABSBN
Absorption .... ABSORB
Absorption (DMAA) .... absorp
Absorption (ABBR) .... ABSPN
Absorption Coefficient, Linear [*Symbol*] [*IUPAC*] .... a
Absorption, Distribution, Metabolism, Excretion [*Medicine*] .... ADME
Absorption Equivalent Thickness .... AET
Absorption Heat Pumping [*Engineering*] .... AHP
Absorption Limiting Frequency (DEN) .... ALF
Absorption of Conversion Electrons (IAA) .... ACE
Absorptive (ABBR) .... ABSPV
Absorptive Hypercalciuria [*Medicine*] (DMAA) .... AH
Absorptive Technology, Inc. [*Vancouver Stock Exchange symbol*] .... ABV
Absorptivity .... A
Absorptivity (ABBR) .... ABSPT
Absorptivity-Emissivity [*Ratio*] .... A/E
Absque Ulla Nota [*Without Any Marking or Note*] [*Latin*] (ROG) .... ABS U N
Absque Ulla Nota [*Without Any Marking or Note*] [*Latin*] .... AUN
Abstain (ILCA) .... Abs
Abstain (ABBR) .... ABSTA
Abstained (ABBR) .... ABSTAD
Abstaining (ABBR) .... ABSTAG
Abstaining Motorists' Association (EA) .... AMA
Abstemious (ABBR) .... ABSTMS
Abstemiously (ABBR) .... ABSTMSY
Abstemiousness (ABBR) .... ABSTMSNS
Abstention (ABBR) .... ABSTN
Abstinence (ABBR) .... ABSTNC
Abstinent (ABBR) .... ABSTNT
Abstract [*Online database field identifier*] .... AB
Abstract .... ABS
Abstract .... ABST

Abstract .... ABSTR
Abstract .... ABSTRCT
Abstract [*Legal*] [*British*] (ROG) .... ABSTT
Abstract and Book Title Index Card Service [*United Kingdom*] .... ABTICS
Abstract Data Type [*Computer science*] .... ADT
Abstract Enterprise [*Vancouver Stock Exchange symbol*] .... AEP
Abstract Evolution Equation (PDAA) .... AEE
Abstract Expressionism (BARN) .... Ab Ex
Abstract Family of Deterministic Languages (PDAA) .... AFDL
Abstract Family of Languages [*Computer science*] .... AFL
Abstract Family of Processors [*Computer science*] (PDAA) .... AFP
Abstract Family of Relations (PDAA) .... AFR
Abstract Information Digest Service [*Forest Products Research Society*]
   [*Information service or system*] (IID) .... AIDS
Abstract Machine Description Language [*1977*] [*Computer science*]
   (CSR) .... AMDL
Abstract Number [*Database terminology*] (NITA) .... AN
Abstract Planning Tool .... ABT
Abstract Service Primitive [*Telecommunications*] (OSI) .... ASP
Abstract Syntax [*Data structure*] [*Computer science*] (TNIG) .... AS
Abstract Syntax Notation (CDE) .... ASN
Abstract Syntax Notation [*Computer science*] .... ASN
Abstract Test Method [*Telecommunications*] (OSI) .... ATM
Abstract Test Suite [*Telecommunications*] (OSI) .... ATS
Abstract Window Toolkit [*Computer science*] .... AWT
Abstract Windowing Toolkit [*Computer science*] .... AWT
Abstract Windowing Toolkit [*Computer science*] .... AWT
Abstracted (ABBR) .... ABSTRD
Abstracted Business Information, Inc. .... ABI
Abstracted Reappraisal Decisions [*A publication*] (DLA) .... R
Abstracted Valuation Decisions [*A publication*] (DLA) V
Abstracter (ABBR) .... ABSTRR
Abstracting and Indexing .... A & I
Abstracting and Indexing Services Directory [*A publication*] .... AISD
Abstracting Board [*International Council of Scientific Unions*] [*Information
   service or system*] (IID) .... AB
Abstraction (ABBR) .... ABSTRN
Abstractly (ABBR) .... ABSTRY
Abstractness (ABBR) .... ABSTRNS
Abstracts .... A
Abstracts of Bioanalytic Technology [*Council of American Bioanalysts*]
   [*A publication*] (AEBS) .... ABT
Abstracts of Classified Reports [*A publication*] .... ACR
Abstracts of Declassified Documents [*A publication*] .... ADD
Abstracts of Instructional Materials/Abstracts of Research Materials .... AIM/ARM
Abstracts of Instructional Materials in Vocational and Technical
   Education (OICC) .... AIMVTE
Abstracts of New World Archaeology [*A publication*] .... ANWA
Abstracts of North American Geology [*A publication*] .... ANAG
Abstracts of Photographic Science and Engineering Literature
   [*A publication*] .... APSE
Abstracts of Star Chamber Proceedings [*1550-58*] [*A publication*] (DLA) .... Mundy
Abstracts of Title [*A publication*] (DLA) .... Abstr T
Abstracts of Treasury Decisions [*United States*] [*A publication*] (DLA) .... Ab
Abstracts of Treasury Decisions [*A publication*] (DLA) .... Abs
Abstracts of Treasury Decisions, New Series [*A publication*] (DLA) .... Ab N
Abstracts of Treasury Decisions, New Series [*A publication*] (DLA) .... Ab NS
Abstracts of Treasury Decisions, New Series [*A publication*] (DLA) .... Abs (NS)
Abstracts of Working Papers in Economics [*Cambridge University Press*]
   [*Information service or system*] (IID) .... AWPE
Abstrene (ABBR) .... ABS
Abstruse (ABBR) .... ABSTRS
Abstruse (ABBR) .... ABSTRU
Abstrusely (ABBR) .... ABSTRUY
Abstruseness (ABBR) .... ABSTRUNS
Absurd (ABBR) .... ABSRD
Absurd Special Interest Group (EA) .... ASIG
Absurdity (ABBR) .... ABSDT
Absurdity (ABBR) .... ABSRDT
Absurdly (ABBR) .... ABSRDY
Absurdness (ABBR) .... ABSRDNS
ABT Building Products [*NASDAQ symbol*] (TTSB) .... ABTC
ABT Building Products Corp. [*Associated Press*] (SAG) .... ABT Bld
ABT Building Products Corp. [*NASDAQ symbol*] (SAG) .... ABTC
Abteilung [*Department, Division, Section*] [*German*] .... ABT
Abtesia [*Unit of magnetic induction*] .... abT
Abu Dhabi [*United Arab Emirates*] [*Airport symbol*] (OAG) .... AUH
Abu Dhabi/Al Dhafra [*United Arab Emirates*] [*ICAO location identifier*]
   (ICLI) .... OMAM
Abu Dhabi/Bateen [*United Arab Emirates*] [*ICAO location identifier*] (ICLI) .... OMAD
Abu Dhabi/International [*United Arab Emirates*] [*ICAO location identifier*]
   (ICLI) .... OMAA
Abu Dhabi International Bank, Inc. .... ADIB
Abu Dhabi National Oil Co. (ODBW) .... ADNOC
Abu Dhabi Oil Co. [*United Arab Emirates*] (EY) .... ADOC
Abu Simbel [*Egypt*] [*Airport symbol*] (OAG) .... ABS
Abu Simbel [*Egypt*] [*ICAO location identifier*] (ICLI) .... HEBL
Abuja [*Nigeria*] [*Airport symbol*] (OAG) .... ABV
Abuja [*Nigeria*] [*ICAO location identifier*] (ICLI) .... DNBJ
Abuja/International [*Nigeria*] [*ICAO location identifier*] (ICLI) .... DNAA
Abulia (ABBR) .... ABUL
Abuliomania (ABBR) .... ABUL
Abumumbazi [*Zaire*] [*ICAO location identifier*] (ICLI) .... FZFE
Abumusa Island [*Iran*] [*ICAO location identifier*] (ICLI) .... OIBA
Abundance (ABBR) .... ABNDNC

Abundance (ABBR) ... ABUNDNC
Abundant [*With respect to occurrence of species*] ... A
Abundant (ABBR) ... ABNDNT
Abundant (ABBR) ... ABT
Abundant (BARN) ... abund
Abundant (ABBR) ... ABUNDT
Abundant Life Seed Foundation (EA) ... ALSF
Abundant Wildlife Society of North America (EA) ... AWS
Abundantly (ABBR) ... ABNDNTY
Abundantly (ABBR) ... ABUNDTY
Abundantly Yours (EA) ... AY
Aburra (VRA) ... abu
Abuse (ABBR) ... ABS
Abuse (ABBR) ... ABUS
Abused (ABBR) ... ABSD
Abused (ABBR) ... ABUSD
Abused Women's Aid in Crisis (EA) ... AWAIC
Abuser (ABBR) ... ABSR
Abuser (ABBR) ... ABUSR
Abusing (ABBR) ... ABSG
Abusing (ABBR) ... ABUSG
Abusive (ABBR) ... ABSV
Abusive (ABBR) ... ABUSV
Abusive Men Exploring New Directions [*In association name AMEND Network*] ... AMEND
Abusively (ABBR) ... ABSVY
Abusively (ABBR) ... ABUSVY
Abusiveness (ABBR) ... ABSVNS
Abusiveness (ABBR) ... ABUSVNS
Abutment (ABBR) ... ABTNT
Abutment (ABBR) ... ABUT
Abutment (ABBR) ... ABUTMT
Abutted (ABBR) ... ABTD
Abutted (ABBR) ... ABUTD
Abutting (ABBR) ... ABTG
Abutting (ABBR) ... ABUTG
Abuyama [*Japan*] [*Seismograph station code, US Geological Survey*] ... ABU
Abvolt (IDOE) ... abV
Abvolt [*Unit of electromotive force*] ... aV
Abwatt (IDOE) ... abW
Abweber [*Also, Mx*] [*Unit of magnetic flux*] ... abWb
Abwehrdienst [*Counterintelligence Service*] [*German military - World War II*] ... AD
Abwehroffizier [*Counterintelligence Officer*] [*German military - World War II*] ... AO
Abyek [*Iran*] [*ICAO location identifier*] (ICLI) ... OIIE
Abysmal (ABBR) ... ABSML
Abysmal (ABBR) ... ABYSM
Abyss (ABBR) ... ABYS
Abyssinia ... AB
Abyssinia ... Aby
Abyssinia ... ABYSS
Abyssinian [*Cat species*] ... ABY
Abzahlungsgesetz [*Law on hire purchase agreements*] [*German*] (ILCA) ... AbzG
AC [*Alternating Current*] **Amperometric** [*Electromagnetics*] ... ACAmp
AC [*Alternating Current*] **Control Unit** ... ACU
AC Network (MCD) ... ACNET
AC Resistance (IDOE) ... R_{ac}
AC Spark Plug Co., Electronics Division, Milwaukee, WI [*Library symbol Library of Congress*] (LCLS) ... WMACS
AC Spark Plug Co., General Motors Corp., Flint, MI [*Library symbol Library of Congress*] (LCLS) ... MiFliACS
AC [*Alternating Current*] **Voltage** (ACII) ... VAC
Acacia [*Gum Arabic*] [*Chemistry*] (ROG) ... ACAC
Acacia Confusa Trypsin Inhibitor [*Biochemistry*] ... ACTI
Acacia Mineral [*Vancouver Stock Exchange symbol*] ... AMD
Acacia Research Corp. [*Associated Press*] (SAG) ... AcaciaR
Acacia Research Corp. [*NASDAQ symbol*] (SAG) ... ACRI
Academe (ABBR) ... ACDM
Academia Brasileira de Ciencias [*Brazil*] (MCD) ... ABC
Academia Cosmologica Nova [*International Free Academy of New Cosmology - IFANC*] (EAIO) ... ACN
Academia Europaea ... AE
Academia Maria Reina, Rio Piedras, PR [*Library symbol Library of Congress*] (LCLS) ... PrRA
Academia Mexicana de Derechos Humanos [*The Mexican Academy for Human Rights*] (CROSS) ... AMDH
Academia Ophthalmologica Internationalis (EAIO) ... AOI
Academia R.S. Romania [*Academy of Romania*], Bucharest, Romania [*Library symbol Library of Congress*] (LCLS) ... RoBA
Academiae Americanae Socius [*Fellow of the American Academy (Academy of Arts and Sciences)*] [*Latin*] (GPO) ... AAS
Academiae Antiquarinae Societales Socius ... AASS
Academic (ABBR) ... ACAD
Academic (ABBR) ... ACADC
Academic ... ACDMC
Academic (ABBR) ... ACDMK
Academic Administration Internship Program [*Later, AFP*] (EA) ... AAIP
Academic Alertness Test [*Education*] (AEBS) ... AA
Academic Alliances (EA) ... AA
Academic and Creative Thinking Skills ... ACTS
Academic and Social Anxiety Program [*Cornell University*] ... ASAP
Academic Aptitude Test [*Vocational guidance test*] ... AAT
Academic Book Center, Portland, OR [*Library symbol*] [*Library of Congress*] (LCLS) ... OrPAB
Academic Class Year (DNAB) ... ACAD CL YR
Academic Clinical Laboratory Physicians and Scientists ... ACLPS
Academic Collective Bargaining Information Service (EA) ... ACBIS
Academic Committee on Soviet Jewry (EA) ... ACSJ
Academic Computation Center [*Georgetown University*] [*Research center*] (RCD) ... ACC
Academic Computer Center [*University of Washington*] [*Research center*] (RCD) ... ACC
Academic Computer Facility [*Roosevelt University*] [*Research center*] (RCD) ... ACF
Academic Computer Service [*Generic*] [*Research center*] (RCD) ... ACS
Academic Computer Services Division [*Milwaukee School of Engineering*] [*Research center*] (RCD) ... ACSD
Academic Computing and Network Services [*Northwestern University*] [*Information service or system*] (IID) ... ACNS
Academic Computing Center [*University of California, Riverside*] [*Research center*] (RCD) ... ACC
Academic Computing Center [*University of Vermont*] [*Research center*] (RCD) ... ACC
Academic Computing Group ... ACCOMP
Academic Consortium for Economic and Social Surveys [*Australia*] ... ACCESS
Academic Council on the United Nations System ... ACUNS
Academic Courseware Exchange [*Combined Apple University Consortium and Kinko's project*] [*Software distributor*] ... ACE
Academic English ... AE
Academic Evaluation Report [*Military*] (INF) ... AER
Academic Health Center ... AHC
Academic Health Center ... AHC
Academic Individual Advanced Development [*Military*] (RDA) ... AIAD
Academic Information Management Center (NITA) ... AIMC
Academic Instructional Measurement System [*Academic achievement and aptitude test*] ... AIMS
Academic Instructor and Allied Officer School [*Military*] (AFM) ... AIAOS
Academic Instructor and Foreign Officer School [*Military*] ... AIFOS
Academic Instructors School [*Air Force*] ... AIS
Academic Librarians Assisting the Disabled Discussion Group [*Association of Specialized and Cooperative Library Agencies*] ... ALAD
Academic Libraries of Brooklyn [*Library network*] ... ALB
Academic Library Book Review [*A publication*] (BRI) ... ALBR
Academic Nursing Home (DMAA) ... ANH
Academic Potential Coding [*Military*] (DNAB) ... APC
Academic Press (DGA) ... ACAD PR
Academic Press, Inc. [*Publishers*] ... AP
Academic Press, Inc. [*Publishers*] (MCD) ... API
Academic Profile Code [*Military*] (DNAB) ... APC
Academic Program Evaluation Project (EDAC) ... APEP
Academic Promise Test [*Psychology*] (AEBS) ... APT
Academic Ranking (EDAC) ... AR
Academic Remedial Training [*Navy*] ... ART
Academic Research Enhancement Award [*NIH*] ... AREA
Academic Self-Concept Scale (EDAC) ... ASCS
Academic Senate for California Community Colleges (EDAC) ... ASCCC
Academic Staff Association of Curtin University of Technology [*Australia*] ... ASACUT
Academic Staff Association of University College, University of New South Wales [*Australia*] ... ASAUCUNSW
Academic Staff Training and Development Programme [*British*] (AIE) ... ASTDP
Academic Strategic Alliances Program ... ASAP
Academic Strategic Alliances Program ... ASAP
Academic Training Division [*Military*] (DNAB) ... ATD
Academic Travel Abroad (EA) ... ATA
Academic Year (MCD) ... AY
Academic Year Institute [*National Science Foundation*] ... AYI
Academica Posteriora [*of Cicero*] [*Classical studies*] (OCD) ... Acad Post
Academica Priora [*of Cicero*] [*Classical studies*] (OCD) ... Acad Pr
Academicae Quaestiones [*of Cicero*] [*Classical studies*] (OCD) ... Acad
Academical (ABBR) ... ACADL
Academical (ABBR) ... ACDMKL
Academical Rank of Civil Engineers ... ARCE
Academically (ABBR) ... ACADCLY
Academically (ABBR) ... ACDMKY
Academically Talented (DAVI) ... AT
Academically Talented Student ... ATS
Academically-Related Research ... ARR
Academically-Separated Budgeted Research ... ASBR
Academician [*or Academy*] ... A
Academician [*or Academy*] (EY) ... ACAD
Academician (ABBR) ... ACADCN
Academician (ABBR) ... ACDMN
Academician of the National Academy of Design, New York [*1825*] (NGC) ... NA
Academics for the Second Amendment ... A2A
Academie Canadienne de Medecine Sportive (AC) ... ACMS
Academie Canadienne d'Endodontie [*Canadian Academy of Endodontics*] (EAIO) ... ACE
Academie Canadienne des Arts et des Sciences de l'Enregistrement (AC) ... ACASE
Academie Canadienne du Genie [*Canadian Academy of Engineering*] (EAIO) ... ACG
Academie Canadienne Francaise [*French-Canadian Academy*] [*French*] (BARN) ... ACF
Academie de Musique du Quebec (AC) ... AMQ
Academie des Sciences [*Academy of Science*] [*French*] ... ADS
Academie Europeenne des Sciences, des Arts, et des Lettres [*European Academy of Arts, Sciences, and Humanities*] (EAIO) ... AESAL
Academie Europeenne d'Histoire [*European Academy of History - EAH*] (EAIO) ... AEH
Academie Internationale d'Astronautique [*France*] (EAIO) ... AIA

Academie Internationale de Droit et de Sante Mentale (AC) ...... AIDSM
Academie Internationale de la Ceramique [*International Academy of Ceramics - IAC*] (EAIO) ...... AIC
Academie Internationale de Medecine Aeronautique et Spatiale [*International Academy of Aviation and Space Medicine IAASM*] [*Canada*] (EA) ...... AIMAS
Academie Internationale d'Heraldique [*Bridel, Luxembourg*] (EAIO) ...... AIH
Academie Internationale d'Histoire de la Pharmacie [*International Academy of the History of Pharmacy*] (EAIO) ...... AIHP
Academie Internationale du Tourisme [*International Academy of Tourism*] (EAIO) ...... AcIT
Academie Internationale Olympique [*International Olympic Academy*] [*Athens, Greece*] (EAIO) ...... AIO
Academie Royale des Arts du Canada [*Royal Canadian Academy of Arts - RCA*] ...... ARAC
Academy (VRA) ...... acad
Academy [*Record label*] ...... Acad
Academy (ABBR) ...... ACDMY
Academy ...... ACDMY
Academy Award [*Academy of Motion Picture Arts and Sciences film award*] ...... AA
Academy Board (VRA) ...... acad bd
Academy for Catholic Health Care Leadership [*Defunct*] (EA) ...... ACHCL
Academy for Educational Development (EA) ...... AED
Academy for Friends of Secretarial Arts and Sciences [*Defunct*] (EA) ...... AFSAS
Academy for Health Services Marketing [*Chicago, IL*] (EA) ...... AHSM
Academy for Implants and Transplants (EA) ...... AIT
Academy for Interscience Methodology (EA) ...... AIM
Academy for Peace Research (EA) ...... APR
Academy for Sports Dentistry (EA) ...... ASD
Academy for State and Local Government (EA) ...... ASLG
Academy for the Psychology of Sports International [*Later, ASPI*] (EA) ...... APSI
Academy Introduction Mission [*Military*] ...... AIM
Academy of Accounting Historians (EA) ...... AAH
Academy of Air Traffic Control Medicine ...... AATCM
Academy of Ambulatory Foot Surgery (EA) ...... AAFS
Academy of American Franciscan History (EA) ...... AAFH
Academy of American Poets (EA) ...... AAP
Academy of Aphasia (EA) ...... AA
Academy of Applied Science (EA) ...... AAS
Academy of Art and Literature [*British*] ...... AAL
Academy of Arts and Sciences of the Americas (EA) ...... AASA
Academy of Behavioral Medicine Research (EA) ...... ABMR
Academy of Canadian Cinema [*Academie du Cinema Canadien*] ...... ACC
Academy of Canadian Cinema & Television [*Academie Canadienne du Cinema et de la Television*] (AC) ...... ACCT
Academy of Canadian Cinema and Television [*Canada*] (WWLA) ...... ACCTV
Academy of Certified Social Workers (EA) ...... ACSW
Academy of Chief Executive Nurses of Teaching Hospitals (AC) ...... ACEN
Academy of Comic Book Artists ...... ACBA
Academy of Comic-Book Fans and Collectors [*Defunct*] ...... ACBFC
Academy of Country Music (EA) ...... ACM
Academy of Country Music Entertainment [*Canada*] ...... ACME
Academy of Criminal Justice Sciences (EA) ...... ACJS
Academy of Dental Materials (EA) ...... ADM
Academy of Dentistry for the Handicapped (EA) ...... ADH
Academy of Dentistry International (EA) ...... ADI
Academy of Denture [*or Dental*] Prosthetics (EA) ...... ADP
Academy of Dispensing Audiologists (EA) ...... ADA
Academy of Electrical Contracting (EA) ...... AEC
Academy of Family Films and Family Television (EA) ...... AFFFT
Academy of Family Mediators (EA) ...... AFM
Academy of Florida Trial Lawyers (SRA) ...... AFTL
Academy of General Dentistry (EA) ...... AGD
Academy of Hazard Control Management (EA) ...... AHCM
Academy of Health Care Consultants [*Defunct*] (EA) ...... AHCC
Academy of Health Sciences [*Health Services Command*] [*Fort Sam Houston, TX*] [*Army*] ...... AHS
Academy of Homiletics (EA) ...... AH
Academy of Hospital Counselors [*Later, AHCC*] (EA) ...... AHC
Academy of Hospital Public Relations [*Later, Hospital Academy - HA*] ...... AHPR
Academy of Human Rights (EA) ...... AHR
Academy of Independent Scholars [*Defunct*] (EA) ...... AIS
Academy of International Business [*Cleveland, OH*] (EA) ...... AIB
Academy of International Dental Studies (EAIO) ...... AIDS
Academy of International Military History [*Later, IMA*] (EA) ...... AIMH
Academy of Irish Art ...... AIA
Academy of Lighting Arts ...... ALA
Academy of Live and Recorded Arts [*British*] ...... ALRA
Academy of Management [*Mississippi State, MS*] (EA) ...... AM
Academy of Marketing Science [*Coral Gables, FL*] (EA) ...... AMS
Academy of Master Wine Growers (EA) ...... AMWG
Academy of Medicine of New Jersey (SRA) ...... AMNJ
Academy of Medicine of New Jersey, Bloomfield, NJ [*Library symbol Library of Congress*] (LCLS) ...... NjBIM
Academy of Medicine, Toronto, ON, Canada [*Library symbol Library of Congress*] (LCLS) ...... CaOTA
Academy of Medicine, Toronto, Ontario [*Library symbol National Library of Canada*] (NLC) ...... OTA
Academy of Model Aeronautics (EA) ...... AMA
Academy of Motion Picture Arts and Sciences (EA) ...... AMPAS
Academy of Motion Picture Arts and Sciences, Los Angeles, CA [*Library symbol Library of Congress*] (LCLS) ...... CLAc
Academy of Natural Science (BARN) ...... Acad Nat Sci
Academy of Natural Sciences [*Academy of Natural Sciences of Philadelphia*] [*Acronym is based on former name,*] (EA) ...... ANSP

Academy of Natural Sciences of Philadelphia, Philadelphia, PA [*OCLC symbol*] (OCLC) ...... ANS
Academy of Natural Sciences of Philadelphia, Philadelphia, PA [*Library symbol Library of Congress*] (LCLS) ...... PPAN
Academy of Operative Dentistry (EA) ...... AOD
Academy of Oral Diagnosis, Radiology, and Medicine (EA) ...... AODRM
Academy of Oral Dynamics (EA) ...... AOD
Academy of Orthomolecular Medicine (EA) ...... AOM
Academy of Orthomolecular Psychiatry [*Later, AOM*] (EA) ...... AOP
Academy of Osteopathic Directors of Medical Education (EA) ...... AODME
Academy of Parapsychology and Medicine [*Defunct*] (EA) ...... APM
Academy of Parish Clergy (EA) ...... APC
Academy of Pharmaceutical Sciences (EA) ...... APS
Academy of Pharmacy Practice (EA) ...... APP
Academy of Political Science (EA) ...... APS
Academy of Product Safety Management [*Defunct*] (EA) ...... APSM
Academy of Psychic Arts and Sciences (EA) ...... APAS
Academy of Psychologists in Marital Counseling [*Later, APMSFT*] ...... APMC
Academy of Psychologists in Marital Sex and Family Therapy (EA) ...... APMSFT
Academy of Psychosomatic Medicine (EA) ...... APM
Academy of Rehabilitative Audiology (EA) ...... ARA
Academy of Religion and Mental Health [*Later, Institutes of Religion and Health*] ...... ARMH
Academy of Religion and Psychical Research (EA) ...... ARPR
Academy of Richmond County, Augusta, GA [*Library symbol Library of Congress*] (LCLS) ...... GAuAR
Academy of Roofing Contractors [*Defunct*] (EA) ...... ARC
Academy of Science Fiction, Fantasy, and Horror Films (EA) ...... ASFFHF
Academy of Science (Union of Soviet Socialist Republics) ...... ASUSSR
Academy of Sciences ...... AS
Academy of Scientific Hypno Therapy (EA) ...... ASH
Academy of Screen Printing Technology (EA) ...... ASPT
Academy of Security Educators and Trainees (EA) ...... ASET
Academy of Sports Psychology International (EA) ...... ASPI
Academy of Stress and Chronic Disease (EA) ...... ASCD
Academy of Teachers of Occupations [*Defunct*] (EA) ...... ATO
Academy of Television Arts and Sciences (EA) ...... ATAS
Academy of the New Church ...... ANC
Academy of the New Church, Bryn Athyn, PA [*Library symbol Library of Congress*] (LCLS) ...... PBa
Academy of the Street of Puerto Rican Congress (EA) ...... ASPRC
Academy of Underwater Arts and Sciences [*Defunct*] (EA) ...... AUAS
Academy of Veterinary Allergy (EA) ...... AVA
Academy of Veterinary Cardiology (EA) ...... AVC
Academy of Wind and Percussion Arts (EA) ...... AWAPA
Academy of Zoology [*Uttar Pradesh, India*] (EA) ...... AZ
Academy on Human Rights and Peace (EA) ...... AHRP
Academy Resources Ltd. [*Vancouver Stock Exchange symbol*] ...... AMY
Academy Sergeant-Major [*British military*] (DMA) ...... AcSM
Acadia (ABBR) ...... ACAD
Acadia Health Education Coalition (SRA) ...... AHEC
Acadia Mineral Ventures Ltd. [*Toronto Stock Exchange symbol*] ...... ALV
Acadia National Park ...... ACAD
Acadia Parish Library, Crowley, LA [*Library symbol Library of Congress*] (LCLS) ...... LCrA
Acadia University, Department of Geography, Wolfville, NS, Canada [*Library symbol Library of Congress*] (LCLS) ...... CaNSWAG
Acadia University, Wolfville, Nova Scotia [*Library symbol National Library of Canada*] (NLC) ...... NSWA
Acadia University, Wolfville, NS, Canada [*Library symbol Library of Congress*] (LCLS) ...... CaNSWA
Acadian Friendship Committee [*See also CAA*] (EAIO) ...... AFC
Acadian Genealogical and Historical Association [*Defunct*] (EA) ...... AGHA
Acadian Home Builders Association (SRA) ...... AHBA
Acadiana Bancshares, Inc. [*Associated Press*] (SAG) ...... Acadiana
Acadiana Bancshares, Inc. [*AMEX symbol*] (SAG) ...... ANA
Acandi [*Colombia*] [*Airport symbol*] (OAG) ...... ACD
Acanthiomeatal Line [*Medicine*] (MEDA) ...... AML
Acanthosis Nigricans [*Medicine*] ...... AN
Acanthrocytes [*Hematology*] (DAVI) ...... ACAN
Acanthrocytes [*Hematology*] (DAVI) ...... ACANTH
Acanthus (VRA) ...... acant
Acao Libertadora National [*Brazilian Action for National Liberation*] [*Political party*] (LAIN) ...... ALN
Acapulco [*Mexico*] [*Airport symbol*] ...... ACA
Acapulco [*Mexico*] (ABBR) ...... ACAP
Acapulco/General Juan N. Alvarez Internacional [*Mexico ICAO location identifier*] (ICLI) ...... MMAA
Acarigua [*Venezuela*] [*Airport symbol*] (OAG) ...... AGV
Acarigua, Portuguesa [*Venezuela ICAO location identifier*] (ICLI) ...... SVAC
ACARS [*ARINC Communications and Address Reporting System*] Management Unit (GAVI) ...... ACARS MU
ACB [*American Council of the Blind*] Radio Amateurs [*An association*] (EA) ...... ACBRA
ACC Consumer Finance [*NASDAQ symbol*] (TTSB) ...... ACCI
ACC Consumer Finance Corp. [*NASDAQ symbol*] (SAG) ...... ACC Cns
ACC Consumer Finance Corp. [*Associated Press*] (SAG) ...... ACC Cns
ACC Consumer Finance Corp. [*NASDAQ symbol*] (SAG) ...... ACCI
ACC Corp. [*Associated Press*] (SAG) ...... ACC
ACC Corp. [*Associated Press*] (SAG) ...... ACC Cp
ACC Corp. [*NASDAQ symbol*] (NQ) ...... ACCC
Accademia [*Academy*] [*Italian*] (BJA) ...... Acc
Accademia ...... ACCAD
Accao Nacional Popular [*National Popular Action*] [*Angola*] [*Political party*] (AF) ...... ANP

Accao Social Democratica [Social Democratic Action] [Portugal Political party] (PPE) .... ASD
Accao Socialista Portugues [Portuguese Socialist Action] (PPE) .... ASP
Accede (ABBR) .... ACD
Accede (ABBR) .... ACED
Acceded (ABBR) .... ACDD
Acceded to Throne (ROG) .... AC
Accedence (ABBR) .... ACDNC
Acceder (ABBR) .... ACDR
Acceding (ABBR) .... ACDG
Accel International Corp. [Associated Press] (SAG) .... Accel
Accel International Corp. [Formerly, Acceleration Corp.] [NASDAQ symbol] (NQ) .... ACLE
Accel International Corp. Productivity Interface [Computer science] (BYTE) .... API
Accel Intl. [NASDAQ symbol] (TTSB) .... ACLE
Accelerando [Quickening the Pace] [Music] .... ACC
Accelerando [Quickening the Pace] [Music] .... ACCEL
Accelerando [Quickening the Pace] [Music] (ROG) .... ACCELO
Accelerate (AABC) .... ACCEL
Accelerate (ABBR) .... ACEL
Accelerate (ABBR) .... ACLRA
Accelerate (BARN) .... ACLT
Accelerated (ABBR) .... ACELD
Accelerated (ABBR) .... ACLRAD
Accelerated Accounting and Reporting System .... AARS
Accelerated Acquisition Approach [Pronounced "a-cubed"] [Air Force] .... A³
Accelerated Active Search System (CAAL) .... A²S²
Accelerated Apprenticeship Training (ADA) .... AAT
Accelerated Assemblies (NASA) .... AA
Accelerated Business Collection and Delivery [Postal Service] .... ABCD
Accelerated Capabilities Initiative [Office of naval research] .... ACI
Accelerated Capital Cost Allowance [Accounting] .... ACCA
Accelerated Capital Recovery System [Accounting] .... ACRS
Accelerated Cathode Excitation [Electricity] (IAA) .... ACE
Accelerated Christian Education [An association] .... ACE
Accelerated Claimant Match .... ACM
Accelerated Climatic Simulator (PDAA) .... ACS
Accelerated College Examination Board (PAZ) .... ACE
Accelerated Constrained Simplex Technique (PDAA) .... ACSIM
Accelerated Construction Completion Date (NATG) .... ACCD
Accelerated Co-Pilot Enrichment [Program] .... ACE
Accelerated Cost Recovery [Accounting] (ADA) .... ACR
Accelerated Cost Recovery Schedule [Accounting] .... ACRS
Accelerated Cost Recovery System [Accounting] .... ACRS
Accelerated Deactivation Test [Chemistry] .... ADT
Accelerated Declassification System (NVT) .... ADS
Accelerated Development Test (MUGU) .... ADT
Accelerated Development Test Program (AAG) .... ADTP
Accelerated Evaluation Method .... AEM
Accelerated Freeze-Drying [Food processing] .... AFD
Accelerated Graphics Port [Computer science] .... AGP
Accelerated Graphics Port [Computer science] .... AGP
Accelerated Growth Area [Embryology] .... AGA
Accelerated Hypertension [Medicine] .... AH
Accelerated Idioventricular Rhythm [Cardiology] (DAVI) .... AIR
Accelerated Idioventricular Rhythm [Cardiology] .... AIVR
Accelerated Individual and Company Development (PDAA) .... AICD
Accelerated Inspection System (DNAB) .... AIS
Accelerated Intelligence Report (NATG) .... CELINTREP
Accelerated Inverse Voltage .... AIV
Accelerated Investment Mortgage .... AIM
Accelerated Item Reduction [Military] .... AIR
Accelerated Learning of Logic .... ALL
Accelerated Life Testing .... ALT
Accelerated Loading Facility (ADA) .... ALF
Accelerated Mental Process (MEDA) .... AMP
Accelerated Mission Endurance Test (MCD) .... AMET
Accelerated Mission Testing (IEEE) .... AMT
Accelerated Pacification Campaign [South Vietnam] .... APC
Accelerated Pacification Program [Vietnam, 1968] (VNW) .... APP
Accelerated Painless Labor (MAE) .... APL
Accelerated Pavement Testing [FHWA] (TAG) .... APT
Accelerated Photosynthetic System [Sewage purification] .... APS
Accelerated Project to Automate Critical Hardware Hardcore Systems .... APACHE
Accelerated Propagation System [Gardening] .... APS
Accelerated Public Works [Program] [Department of the Interior] .... APW
Accelerated Public Works Program [Department of the Interior] .... APWP
Accelerated Random Search (MCD) .... ARS
Accelerated Readiness Analysis (NG) .... ARA
Accelerated Reeducation of Emotions, Behavior, and Attitudes [Rehabilitation program] .... AREBA
Accelerated Refuge Maintenance Management [Department of the Interior] .... ARMM
Accelerated Relaxation Method (PDAA) .... ARM
Accelerated Remittance Cycle [Business term] (EMRF) .... ARC
Accelerated Research Initiative [Marine science] (OSRA) .... ART
Accelerated Retirement of Vehicles Program [Air quality implementation plans] .... ARVP
Accelerated Rural Development .... ARD
Accelerated Service Test .... AST
Accelerated Service Test Program (SAA) .... ASTP
Accelerated Simulated Mission Endurance Test (MCD) .... ASMET
Accelerated Solicitation to Award Process [National Institutes of Health] .... ASAP

Accelerated Specialized Inspection Sites [Customs inspection at airports] .... ASIST
Accelerated Storage Adapter (IAA) .... ASA
Accelerated Strike Aircraft Program Requirement [DoD] (MCD) .... ASAPR
Accelerated Surface Post [British] (DCTA) .... ASP
Accelerated Take-Off [British military] (DMA) .... ATO
Accelerated Test Technology .... ATT
Accelerated Turn-Over to Vietnamese [Military] .... ACTOV
Accelerated Ventricular Rhythm [Cardiology] (DMAA) .... AVR
Accelerated View of Input Data .... AVOID
Accelerates (ABBR) .... ACELS
Accelerate-Stop Distance Available [FAA] (TAG) .... ASDA
Accelerate-Stop Distance Available [Aviation] (FAAC) .... ASDA
Accelerating (ABBR) .... ACELG
Accelerating (ABBR) .... ACLRAG
Accelerating Contactor or Relay (IEEE) .... A
Accelerating Rate Calorimeter [Instrumentation] .... ARC
Acceleration [or Accelerator] .... A
Acceleration (IDOE) .... a
Acceleration (IDOE) .... acc
Acceleration .... ACC
Acceleration (ABBR) .... ACELN
Acceleration (ABBR) .... ACLRAN
Acceleration [Symbol] (DEN) .... f
Acceleration Command .... AC
Acceleration Compensation [or Control] Unit [Aviation] .... ACU
Acceleration Correction C
Acceleration, Cruising, Idling, Deceleration (MHDI) .... ACID
Acceleration Curve Restraint Seat [Automotive safety systems] .... ACRS
Acceleration Enrichment [Automotive fuel systems] .... AE
Acceleration Force (DMAA) .... G
Acceleration Monitoring Guidance System (MCD) .... AMGS
Acceleration Position Sensor [Diesel engines] .... APS
Acceleration Restraint Curve [Automotive engineering] .... ARC
Acceleration Slip Regulation [Automotive engineering] .... ASR
Acceleration Spectral Density (PDAA) .... ASD
Acceleration Switching Valve .... ASV
Acceleration Time .... ACT
Acceleration Vector Control .... AVC
Acceleration-Deceleration Unit .... ADU
Acceleration-Type Control Law .... ATCL
Accelerative (ABBR) .... ACELV
Accelerative (ABBR) .... ACLRAV
Accelerator (AAG) .... AC
Accelerator [Automotive engineering] .... ACCEL
Accelerator (ABBR) .... ACELR
Accelerator (ABBR) .... ACLRTR
Accelerator (MSA) .... ACLTR
Accelerator and Reactor Improvement and Modification .... ARIM
Accelerator for Physics and Chemistry of Heavy Metals .... APACHE
Accelerator Free Fall [Parachuting] .... AFF
Accelerator Globulin [Medicine] .... AcG
Accelerator Heel Point [Automotive engineering] .... AHP
Accelerator Heel Point .... AHP
Accelerator, High Voltage (SAA) .... AHV
Accelerator Information Center [ORNL] .... AIC
Accelerator Mass Spectrometry .... AMS
Accelerator Pedal Position Sensor [Automotive engineering] .... APS
Accelerator Pedal with Idler [Automotive engineering] .... API
Accelerator Production of Tritium [Physics] .... APT
Accelerator Pulsed Fast Assembly .... APFA
Accelerator Transmutation of Waste [Nuclear waste] .... ATW
Accelerator-Tritium Producer [Nuclear physics] .... ATP
Accelerometer .... ACCEL
Accelerometer .... ACCLRM
Accelerometer Assembly [NASA] .... AA
Accelerometer Calibration Vibration Exciter .... ACVE
Accelerometer Monitoring Program [NASA] (KSC) .... AMP
Accelerometer Package (KSC) .... AP
Accelerometer Package (KSC) .... APK
Accelerometer Parameter Shift .... APS
Accelerometer Pulse Converter .... APC
Accelerometer Scale Factor Error .... ASFE
Accelerometer Scale Factor Input Panel .... ASFIP
Accelerometer Signal Conditioner (KSC) .... ASC
Accelerometer-Timer (SAA) .... AT
Accelerometer-Timer Switch (IAA) .... ATS
Accelr8 Technology Corp. [Associated Press] (SAG) Accelr8
Accelr8 Technology Corp. [NASDAQ symbol] (SAG) .... ACLY
Accent (NTCM) .... A
Accent .... ACCT
Accent (ABBR) .... ACNT
Accent before Cooking [Advertising slogan] .... ABC
Accent Color Sciences, Inc. [Associated Press] (SAG) .... AccCSci
Accent Color Sciences, Inc. [NASDAQ symbol] (SAG) .... ACLR
Accent on Developing Abstract Processes of Thought .... ADAPT
Accent on Information (EA) .... AI
Accent on Information [Databank for the handicapped and rehabilitation professionals] [Accent on Living] (IID) .... AOI
Accent Software International Inc. [Associated Press] (SAG) .... AccentS
Accent Software International Ltd. [Associated Press] (SAG) .... Accent
Accent Software International Ltd. [NASDAQ symbol] (SAG) .... ACNW
Accent Software International Ltd. [NASDAQ symbol] (SAG) .... ACNW
Accent Software Intl. [NASDAQ symbol] (TTSB) .... ACNTF
Accent Software Intl. Ltd. [Associated Press] (SAG) .... AccSftI

Accent Software Intl. Ltd. [*NASDAQ symbol*] (SAG) .... ACNU
Accented (WDAA) .... ACCTD
Accented (ABBR) .... ACNTD
Accenting (ABBR) .... ACNTG
Accentual (ABBR) .... ACNTL
Accentuate (ABBR) .... ACNTU
Accentuated (ABBR) .... ACNTUD
Accentuating (ABBR) .... ACNTUG
Accentuation (ABBR) .... ACNTUN
Accept [*or Acceptance*] [*Banking*] (KSC) .... ACCPT
Accept (AABC) .... ACPT
Accept Data State [*Computer science*] (IAA) .... ACDS
Accept No Verbal Orders .... ANVO
Accept Request (IAA) .... ARQ
Accept Response (IAA) .... ARP
Acceptability (ABBR) .... ACPTBT
Acceptability (ABBR) .... ACPTBY
Acceptable (ABBR) .... ACPTB
Acceptable Biological Catch [*Fishery management*] (MSC) .... ABC
Acceptable Biological Removal [*Fishery management*] .... ABR
Acceptable Container Condition [*Shipping*] (DS) .... ACC
Acceptable Daily Intake [*Toxicology*] .... ADI
Acceptable Defect Level .... ADL
Acceptable Environmental Range Test .... AERT
Acceptable Failure Rate .... AFR
Acceptable Hazard Rate (IEEE) .... AHR
Acceptable Hazard Rate (ODBW) .... ahr
Acceptable Intake Daily [*of foods and additives*] .... AID
Acceptable Level (GNE) .... AL
Acceptable Limit for Dispersion .... ALD
Acceptable Means of Compliance (DA) .... AMC
Acceptable Periodic Inspection .... API
Acceptable Process Level .... APL
Acceptable Productivity Level [*Quality control*] .... APL
Acceptable Quality Level [*Quality control*] .... AQL
Acceptable Quality Rate [*Quality control*] .... AQR
Acceptable Quality Test [*Quality control*] (MSA) .... AQT
Acceptable Reliability Level [*Quality control*] .... ARL
Acceptable Supplier List .... ASL
Acceptable Use Policy .... AUP
Acceptable Workload Factor [*Management*] .... AWF
Acceptableness (ABBR) .... ACPTNS
Acceptably (ABBR) .... ACPTY
Acceptance [*Banking*] .... ACC
Acceptance [*Banking*] .... ACCE
Acceptance [*Banking*] (ROG) .... ACCEPTCE
Acceptance .... ACCEPTN
Acceptance (WDMC) .... acpt
Acceptance (ABBR) .... ACPTNC
Acceptance Advice Form .... AAF
Acceptance and Certification Branch [*Social Security Administration*] .... ACB
Acceptance and Checkout / Maintenance Ground Equipment (SAA) .... ACO/MGE
Acceptance and Ferry Flight [*NASA*] (NASA) .... AFF
Acceptance and Operational Checkout Requirements Document [*NASA*] (NASA) .... AOCRD
Acceptance and Takeover Date [*Telecommunications*] (TEL) .... ATD
Acceptance and Transfer .... A & T
Acceptance Checkout [*NASA*] (NASA) .... ACO
Acceptance Checkout and Evaluation System [*NASA*] (NASA) .... ACES
Acceptance Checkout Equipment [*NASA*] .... ACE
Acceptance Checkout Equipment - Spacecraft [*NASA*] (KSC) .... ACE-S/C
Acceptance Checkout Procedure (KSC) .... ACP
Acceptance, Conforming, and Qualification Test .... AC & QT
Acceptance Control Equipment Section [*or System*] [*NASA*] (NASA) .... ACES
Acceptance Data Package (KSC) .... ADP
Acceptance for Honor [*Business term*] .... AFH
Acceptance Functional Test Procedure [*NASA*] (KSC) .... A/FTP
Acceptance Inspection Equipment [*Army*] (AABC) .... AIE
Acceptance Inspection Instruction .... AII
Acceptance Inspection Package (KSC) .... AIP
Acceptance Insurance Companies [*NYSE symbol*] (SPSG) .... AIF
Acceptance Insurance Companies, Inc. [*Associated Press*] (SAG) .... Acpt Ins
Acceptance Message [*Aviation code*] .... ACP
Acceptance Number [*Business term*] .... Ac
Acceptance of Others Scale [*Psychology*] (EDAC) .... AOS
Acceptance Readiness (NASA) .... AR
Acceptance Requirement .... AR
Acceptance Review (NASA) .... AR
Acceptance Summary Report .... ASR
Acceptance Tag (NRCH) .... AT
Acceptance Test (NRCH) .... AT
Acceptance Test and Launch Operations [*NASA*] (MCD) .... ATLO
Acceptance Test Equipment (MCD) .... ATE
Acceptance Test Facility [*Nuclear energy*] .... ATF
Acceptance Test of Launch Language [*NASA*] .... ATOLL
Acceptance Test Plan [*or Procedure*] .... ATP
Acceptance Test Report (MCD) .... ATR
Acceptance Test Specification [*DoD*] .... ATS
Acceptance Thermal Test [*or Testing*] [*NASA*] (NASA) .... ATT
Acceptance Trials [*Shipbuilding*] .... AT
Acceptance Vibration Testing [*NASA*] (NASA) .... AVT
Acceptation [*Acceptance*] [*French Banking*] (ROG) .... ACCEPN
Accepte sous Protet pour Compte [*Accepted under Protest for Account*] [*French*] .... ASPC
Accepted .... A
Accepted (ROG) .... AC
Accepted (ABBR) .... ACPTD
Accepted Alternative Designation Of .... AADO
Accepted Batch Listing [*Accounting*] .... ABL
Accepted Dental Remedies [*A publication*] .... ADR
Accepted Dental Remedy (DAVI) .... ADR
Accepted Dental Therapeutics .... ADT
Accepted on Hire .... AOH
Accepted Weight/Estimate [*Ships*] .... AWE
Accepting (ABBR) .... ACPTG
Accepting Houses Committee [*Banking*] [*British*] .... AHC
Accepting Individual Differences Curriculum (EDAC) .... AID
Acceptor [*Physiology*] .... A
Acceptor (MSA) .... ACPTR
Acceptor Energy Level .... AEL
Acceptor Handshake (MHDI) .... AH
Accept-Reject Rule [*Statistics*] .... AR
Accepts Transfer as Offered (NOAA) .... ATRSO
Access [*Credit card*] [*British*] .... A
Access [*Telecommunications*] (TEL) .... AC
Access .... ACC
Access .... ACCSS
Access [*Telecommunications*] (MSA) .... ACS
Access .... AXS
Access America [*Commercial firm*] (EA) .... AA
Access and Amendment Refusal Authority [*Army*] (AABC) .... AARA
Access and Control Point [*Telecommunications*] (TEL) .... A & CP
Access Anytime Bancorp, Inc. [*NASDAQ symbol*] (SAG) .... AABC
Access Anytime Bancorp, Inc. [*Associated Press*] (SAG) .... AccessAny
Access Area Digital Switching System (MCD) .... AADS
Access ATM Network, Inc. [*Toronto Stock Exchange symbol*] .... ATM
Access Authorization [*Nuclear energy*] .... AA
Access Beyond, Inc. [*NASDAQ symbol*] (SAG) .... ACCB
Access Beyond, Inc. [*Associated Press*] (SAG) .... AccBynd
Access Block Diagram .... ABD
Access Characteristics Estimation System [*Computer science*] (MHDI) .... ACCESS
Access Committee Centre on Environment for the Handicapped [*British*] .... ACCEH
Access Control (SAA) .... AC
Access Control Committee .... ACC
Access Control Document [*NASA*] (NASA) .... ACD
Access Control Facility .... ACF
Access Control Field [*Computer science*] (ACRL) .... ACF
Access Control List [*Computer science*] (HGAA) .... ACL
Access Control Register [*Computer science*] .... ACR
Access Control Verification [*Computer science*] (HGAA) .... ACV
Access Control Word [*Computer science*] (MHDI) .... ACW
Access Control-Logging and Reporting [*Computer science*] (MHDI) .... ACLR
Access Cost Factor [*Telecommunications*] (TEL) .... ACF
Access Cycle (IAA) .... AC
Access Decision Binding Time (MHDI) .... ADBT
Access Developer's Toolkit [*Microsoft Corp.*] (PCM) .... ADT
Access Door .... AD
Access Electronic Payment Terminals [*for credit cards*] [*British*] .... ACCEPT
Access Floor [*Technical drawings*] .... ACFL
Access Floor Manufacturing Association (EA) .... AFMA
Access Flooring Association [*British*] (DBA) .... AFA
Access for the Handicapped [*Defunct*] (EA) .... AH
Access Function Register .... AFR
Access Health [*NASDAQ symbol*] (TTSB) .... ACCS
Access Health, Inc. [*Associated Press*] (SAG) .... AccesHlt
Access Health Marketing, Inc. [*NASDAQ symbol*] (SAG) .... ACCS
Access Health Marketing, Inc. [*Associated Press*] (SAG) .... AcesHlt
Access HealthNet, Inc. [*Associated Press*] (SAG) .... AccesH
Access HealthNet, Inc. [*NASDAQ symbol*] (SAG) .... AHNT
Access/Information [*Information service or system*] (IID) .... AI
Access Isolation Mechanism [*Computer science*] (NITA) .... AIM
Access Manager [*Computer science*] .... AM
Access Method [*Computer science*] .... AM
[*The*] **Access Method** (IAA) .... TAM
Access Method Control Block [*Computer science*] (BUR) .... ACB
Access Method for Indexed Data Generalized for Operating System [*Computer science*] .... AMIGOS
Access Method Service [*Computer science*] (BUR) .... AMS
Access Method Services Cryptographic Option (MHDI) .... AMSCO
Access Methods, Inc. (NITA) .... AMI
Access Methods Service Macros [*Computer science*] (HGAA) .... AMSM
Access Methods Services Utilities [*Computer science*] (HGAA) .... AMSU
Access Network, Media Resource Center [*UTLAS symbol*] .... ACN
Access Now for Gay and Lesbian Equality [*An association*] .... ANGLE
Access Opening (AAG) .... ACS-O
Access Opening [*Technical drawings*] .... AO
Access Panel [*Technical drawings*] (IAA) .... ACSPNL
Access Panel [*Technical drawings*] .... AP
Access Permit [*or Permittee*] [*Nuclear energy*] .... AP
Access Permit Holder .... APH
Access Point [*Telecommunications*] (TEL) .... AP
Access Point Pace (KSC) .... APP
[*The*] **Access Program for the CompuServe Information Service** (PCM) .... TAPCIS
Access Refusal and Barrier Interface Terminal [*Hardware-based security device from Computer Security Systems*] .... ARBITER
Access Solutions International, Inc. [*Associated Press*] (SAG) .... AccSol
Access Solutions International, Inc. [*NASDAQ symbol*] (SAG) .... ASIC
Access Tandem .... AT

Access Time	ACST
Access Time	AT
Access to Information and Reading Service (AIE)	AIRS
Access to Information for Medicine [Allegheny General Hospital, Health Sciences Library] [Information service or system] (IID)	AIM
Access to Information on Multicultural Educational Resources (AIE)	AIMER
Access to Learning for Adults (AIE)	ALFA
Access Type BIT [Binary Digit] [Computer science]	ATB
Access Unit [Computer science] (TNIG)	AU
Access Upsizing Tools [Microsoft Corp.] (PCM)	AUT
ACCESS.bus Industry Group [Computer science] (PCM)	ABIG
Accessed BIT [Binary Digit] [Computer science]	A
Accessibility (ABBR)	ACSBT
Accessibility to Gate Arrays through Technology and Engineering (PDAA)	AGATE
Accessible (ABBR)	ACSB
Accessibleness (ABBR)	ACSBNS
Accessibly (ABBR)	ACSBY
Accession (ABBR)	ACSN
Accession Compensatory Account (DCTA)	ACA
Accession Designation Number [Military]	ADN
Accession List	AL
Accession Number [Online database field identifier]	ACN
Accession Number [Online database field identifier]	AN
Accession Treaty and Decision Concerning the European Coal and Steel Community [A publication] (DLA)	ATD
Accessional (ABBR)	ACSNL
Accessioned (ABBR)	ACSND
Accessioning (ABBR)	ACSNG
Accessions Document [Air Force]	AD
Accessorial (AABC)	ACCSL
Accessories Bulletin (MCD)	AB
Accessory [Protein synthesis]	A
Accessory	ACC
Accessory	ACC
Accessory	ACCES
Accessory (KSC)	ACCESS
Accessory (KSC)	ACCRY
Accessory (AFM)	ACCY
Accessory (IAA)	ACESS
Accessory (ABBR)	ACSRY
Accessory and Equipment Technical Committee (KSC)	AETC
Accessory Boring Organ [of a gastropod]	ABO
Accessory Bulletin (MCD)	AYB
Accessory Cells [Histology]	AC
Accessory Change (MCD)	AYC
Accessory Clinical Findings [Medicine]	ACF
Accessory Conduction Pathway [Medicine] (DMAA)	ACP
Accessory Drive Gear Box (MCD)	ADG
Accessory Drive Gear Box (MCD)	ADGB
Accessory Drive System (NG)	ADS
Accessory Gear Box	AGB
Accessory Gland	AG
Accessory Manufacturers Racing Association [British] (BI)	AMRA
Accessory Meningeal Artery [Anatomy]	AMA
Accessory Olfactory Bulb [Anatomy]	AOB
Accessory Optic Nucleus [Neuroanatomy]	AON
Accessory Optic System [Neuroanatomy]	AOS
Accessory Pathway [Medicine] (DMAA)	AP
Accessory Pedal Ganglia	APG
Accessory Power Supply (AABC)	APS
Accessory Power Unit (MUGU)	APU
Accessory Record Card (DNAB)	ARC
Accessory Sex Organ [Anatomy]	ASO
Accessory Supply System	ASS
Accident	Ac
Accident	ACC
Accident	ACCD
Accident (AAMN)	ACCID
Accident (AFM)	ACDNT
Accident	ACDNT
Accident (AABC)	ACDT
Accident Anatomy Method [Engineering]	AAM
Accident and Emergency [Ward, Department, or Services] [Medicine]	A & E
Accident and Health Insurance	A & H
Accident and Indemnity [Insurance]	A & I
Accident and Sickness Insurance	A & S
Accident Benefits [Insurance]	AB
Accident Compensation Commission (BARN)	ACC
Accident Compensation Journal [Madhya Pradesh, India] [A publication] (DLA)	ACJ (Mad Pr)
Accident Cost Indicator Model [US Bureau of Mines]	ACIM
Accident Data Recorder [Aviation] (AIA)	ADR
Accident Dispensary [Medicine]	AD
Accident Documentation System [Safety research] [Automotive engineering]	ADS
Accident Evolution and Barrier [Engineering]	AEB
Accident Frequency Rate [Employment] (ODBW)	AFR
Accident/Incident	A/I
Accident/Incident [FRA] (TAG)	ACC/INC
Accident/Incident Analysis (PDAA)	AIA
Accident/Incident Data System [Database] [FAA]	AIDS
Accident, Incident, Deficiencies (AFM)	AID
Accident/Incident Reporting System [National Transportation Safety Board] [Information service or system] (IID)	AIRS

Accident Information Retrieval System (RDA)	AIRS
Accident Injury	ACCI
Accident/Injury/Damages (DLA)	AID
Accident Insurance Policy (MHDB)	AIP
Accident Intelligence [British police term]	AI
Accident Investigation [Aviation]	AIG
Accident Investigation Methodology [Engineering]	AIM
Accident Legal Advise Service [British]	ALAS
Accident Mitigation System [Industrial engineering]	AMS
Accident Model Document [NASA] (KSC)	AMD
Accident Officers Association (AIE)	AOA
Accident Offices Association [British] (BI)	AOA
Accident Prevention Plan	APP
Accident Reconstruction Criminology (LAIN)	ACC
Accident Response Group [Department of Energy]	ARG
Accident Sequence Evaluation Program [Nuclear energy] (NRCH)	ASEP
Accident Sequence Precursor Study [Nuclear Regulatory Commission]	ASP
Accident Source Term Program Office [Nuclear energy] (NRCH)	ASTPO
Accidental [Injury Insurance] (BARN)	Acc
Accidental (ABBR)	ACDNTL
Accidental (ABBR)	ACDTL
Accidental Damage (WDAA)	AD
Accidental Death and Disability [Insurance]	ADD
Accidental Death and Dismemberment [Insurance]	AD and D
Accidental Death Benefit [Insurance]	ADB
Accidental Discharge [Firearms]	AD
Accidental Hypothermia [Medicine]	AH
Accidental Incident Sabotage Assistance Request (MCD)	AISAR
Accidental Injury	AI
Accidental Launch Prevention System (DOMA)	ALPS
Accidental Launch Protection System [Military]	ALPS
Accidental Loss [Nuclear energy]	AL
Accidental Nuclear War Prevention Project [Nuclear Age Peace Foundation] (EA)	ANWPP
Accidentally (ABBR)	ACDNTLY
Accidentally Incurred	AI
Accident-Experience Learning Curve (PDAA)	AELC
Accidents and Road Safety [British]	ARS
Accidents Investigation Branch [Air Force British]	AIB
Accion Chilena Anticomunista [Chilean Anticommunist Action] [Political party] (EY)	ACHA
Accion Ciudadana Liberal [Liberal Citizens' Action] [Spain Political party] (PPE)	ACL
Accion del Pueblo [Costa Rica] [Political party] (EY)	AP
Accion Democratica [Democratic Action] [Venezuela Political party] (PPW)	AD
Accion Democratica [Democratic Action] [El Salvador] [Political party] (PD)	AD
Accion Democratica 86 [Democratic Action 1986] [Aruba] [Political party] (EY)	AD 86
Accion Democratica Ecuatoriana [Ecuadorean Democratic Action] [Political party] (PPW)	ADE
Accion Democratica Nacionalista [Nationalist Democratic Action] [Bolivia] [Political party] (PPW)	ADN
Accion Democratica Popular [Popular Democratic Action] [Costa Rica] [Political party]	ACP
Accion Democratico Nacional [National Democratic Action] [Aruba] [Political party] (EY)	ADN
Accion Espanola [Spanish Action] [Political party] (PPE)	AE
ACCION International (EA)	AI
Accion Nacional [National Action] [Spain Political party] (PPE)	AN
Accion Nacional Vasca [Basque National Action] [Spain Political party] (PPE)	ANV
Accion Politica Progresista [Progressive Political Action] [Ecuador] [Political party] (PPW)	APP
Accion Politica Socialista [Socialist Political Action] [Peru] [Political party] (PPW)	APS
Accion Popular [Popular Action] [Peru] [Political party] (PPW)	AP
Accion Popular [Popular Action] [Spain Political party] (PPE)	AP
Accion Revolucionaria Nacional Ecuatoriana [National Revolutionary Action] [Ecuador] [Political party]	ARNE
Accion Revolucionaria Socialista [Socialist Revolutionary Action] [Peru] [Political party] (PPW)	ARS
Accion Socialista Revolucionaria [Peru] [Political party] (EY)	ASR
Acclaim (ABBR)	ACLM
Acclaim Entertainment [NASDAQ symbol] (TTSB)	AKLM
Acclaim Entertainment, Inc. [Associated Press] (SAG)	Acclaim
Acclaim Entertainment, Inc. [NASDAQ symbol] (NQ)	AKLM
Acclamation (ABBR)	ACLMAN
Acclamation (ABBR)	ACLMN
Acclamatory (ABBR)	ACLMY
Acclimate (ABBR)	ACLIM
Acclimate (ABBR)	ACLMA
Acclimated (ABBR)	ACLIMD
Acclimated (ABBR)	ACLMAD
Acclimating (ABBR)	ACLIMG
Acclimating (ABBR)	ACLMAG
Acclimation (ABBR)	ACLIMN
Acclimatization (ABBR)	ACLMZN
Acclimatization (ABBR)	ACLMATZN
Acclimatization Experiences Institute [Later, IEE] (EA)	AEI
Acclimatize (ABBR)	ACLIMZ
Acclimatize (ABBR)	ACLMATZ
Acclimatized (ABBR)	ACLIMZD
Acclimatized (ABBR)	ACLMATZD
Acclimatizing (ABBR)	ACLIMZG
Acclimatizing (ABBR)	ACLMATZG

Accokeek Foundation (EA) .... AF
Accolade (ABBR) .... ACLD
Accom, Inc. [*Associated Press*] (SAG) .... Accom
Accom, Inc. [*NASDAQ symbol*] (SAG) .... ACMM
Accomac, VA [*FM radio station call letters*] .... WVES
Accommodate [*or Accommodation*] (AFM) .... ACCOM
Accommodate (ABBR) .... ACMD
Accommodated (ABBR) .... ACMDD
Accommodating (ABBR) .... ACMDG
Accommodation .... A
Accommodation .... ACC
Accommodation .... ACCN
Accommodation (ROG) .... ACCOMMODON
Accommodation (ABBR) .... ACMDN
Accommodation Address (LAIN) .... AA
Accommodation and Messenger Service, Admiralty [*Obsolete British*] .... AMS
Accommodation Convergence [*Ophthalmology*] .... AC
Accommodation Endorsement [*Banking*] .... AE
Accommodation Sales Authorization (MCD) .... ASA
Accommodation Sales Order .... ASO
Accommodation Sales Requisition .... ASR
Accommodation Weight Investigation (KSC) .... AWI
Accommodative (ABBR) .... ACMDV
Accomodative Convergence/Accomodation (Ratio) [*Ophthalmology*] .... AC/A
Accompagnamento [*Accompaniment*] [*Music*] .... ACC
Accompanied .... ACC
Accompanied (ABBR) .... ACMPD
Accompanied (ABBR) .... ACMPYD
Accompanied by Adult [*British Board of Film Censors*] .... AA
Accompaniment [*Music*] .... ACCOM
Accompaniment [*Music*] .... ACCOMP
Accompaniment (WGA) .... ACCPT
Accompaniment [*Music*] .... ACCT
Accompaniment (ABBR) .... ACMPNT
Accompaniment (ABBR) .... ACMPT
Accompaniment (ABBR) .... ACOMP
Accompaniment ad Libitum [*Music*] .... Accom ad Lib
Accompaniment Obligato [*Music*] .... Accom Oblto
Accompanist (ABBR) .... ACMPST
Accompany (AFM) .... ACCOM
Accompany (ROG) .... ACCOY
Accompany (AABC) .... ACMP
Accompany (ABBR) .... ACMPY
Accompany (ABBR) .... ACOMP
Accompany (FAAC) .... ACPY
Accompanying (ABBR) .... ACMPG
Accompanying Spare Parts Kit [*Navy*] .... ASPK
Accomplice [*FBI standardized term*] .... ACCPL
Accomplice (ABBR) .... ACMPL
Accomplice (ABBR) .... ACMPLS
Accomplish (AFM) .... ACCOMP
Accomplish (MUGU) .... ACCOMPL
Accomplish (ABBR) .... ACMPLH
Accomplish (ABBR) .... ACOMP
Accomplishable (ABBR) .... ACMPLHB
Accomplishable (ABBR) .... ACOMPB
Accomplished (ABBR) .... ACMPLHD
Accomplished (ABBR) .... ACOMPD
Accomplisher (ABBR) .... ACOMPR
Accomplishing (ABBR) .... ACOMPG
Accomplishment .... ACCMPLSMNT
Accomplishment (ABBR) .... ACMPLHNT
Accomplishment (ABBR) .... ACOMPT
Accomplishment/Cost Procedure .... ACP
Accomplishment of Assigned Mission Impeded by Deadline [*Army*] (AABC) .... AAMID
Accomplishment Quotient .... AQ
Accomplishment Ratio (ADA) .... AR
Accomplishment Utilization Report .... AUR
Accord (DLA) .... Acc
Accord (AABC) .... ACD
Accord (ABBR) .... ACRD
Accord Dangereuse Routier [*European agreement on the carriage of dangerous goods by road*] .... ADR
Accord European Relative au Transport International par Route des Marchandises Dangereuses par Route [*European Agreement on the International Transport of Dangerous Goods by Road*] (PDAA) .... ADR
Accord General sur les Tarifs Douaniers et le Commerce [*General Agreement on Tariffs and Trade*] [*Switzerland*] (EAIO) .... AGTDC
Accord Transports Permissables [*European agreement on the transport of perishable foodstuffs*] .... ATP
Accordance (ROG) .... ACCDCE
Accordance (ROG) .... ACCORDCE
Accordance (ABBR) .... ACRDNC
Accordance With (MSA) .... A/W
Accordant (ABBR) .... ACRDT
Accorded (ABBR) .... ACRDD
According .... ACCORD
According (ROG) .... ACCORDG
According (ABBR) .... ACRDG
According (To) .... ACC
Accordingly (ABBR) .... ACRDGY
Accordion [*Music*] .... Accord
Accordion Federation of North America (EA) .... AFNA
Accordion for All International [*An association*] (EAIO) .... AAI
Accordion Teachers' Guild (EA) .... ATG
Accost (ABBR) .... ACOS
Accost (ABBR) .... ACST
Accosted (ABBR) .... ACOSD
Accosting (ABBR) .... ACOSG
Account .... A
Account .... AC
Account [*Internet language*] [*Computer science*] .... acc
Account (EY) .... ACC
Account [*or Accountant*] (AFM) .... ACCT
Account .... ACCT
Account (WDMC) .... acct
Account (ABBR) .... ACONT
Account Access Layer [*Computer science*] .... AAL
Account and Risk [*Investment term*] .... A & R
Account Balance Pension (WYGK) .... ABP
Account Book (DGA) .... A/C BK
Account Control (AFM) .... AC
Account Current [*Business term*] .... A/C
Account Directory [*Computer science*] (OA) .... AD
Account Executive [*Advertising, securities*] .... AE
Account Identification and Description Services [*Dun & Bradstreet*] (IID) .... AIDS
Account Identifier [*Computer science*] .... ACCTID
Account Manager Code (TEL) .... AMC
Account Mechanical (FAAC) .... AMECH
Account Number .... AN
Account Number Change File [*IRS*] .... ANCF
Account Number File [*Integrated Data Retrieval System*] [*IRS*] .... ANF
Account Number Update File [*IRS*] .... ANUF
Account Of [*Business term*] .... AO
Account Paid .... AP
Account Reconciliation Plan .... ARP
Account Resources Manager .... ARM
Account Sales .... AS
Account Sales .... ASLE
Account Traffic [*Aviation*] (FAAC) .... ATFC
Accountability (ABBR) .... ACCTBT
Accountability (ABBR) .... ACONTBT
Accountability Data Package (MCD) .... ADP
Accountable (ABBR) .... ACCTB
Accountable (ABBR) .... ACONTB
Accountable Activity .... AA
Accountable Entertainment Allowance [*British*] .... AEA
Accountable Health Partnership [*Medicine*] .... AHP
Accountable Health Plan [*Medicine*] .... AHP
Accountable Indirect Representational Supplement [*British*] .... AIR
Accountable Property Officer [*Military*] (AABC) .... ACTPO
Accountable Property Officer [*Military*] .... APO
Accountable Strength (AABC) .... ACCTSTR
Accountable Supply Distribution Activity (MCD) .... ASDA
Accountableness (ABBR) .... ACCTBNS
Accountably (ABBR) .... ACCTBY
Accountably (ABBR) .... ACONTBLY
Accountancy .... ACCT
Accountancy .... ACCTCY
Accountancy .... ACCTNCY
Accountancy (ABBR) .... ACCTY
Accountancy (AFM) .... ACCY
Accountancy (ABBR) .... ACONTNC
Accountancy & Legal Professions Selection Ltd. [*British*] (ECON) .... ALPS
Accountancy Law Reporter [*A publication*] (DLA) .... Accountancy L Rep
Accountant .... ACCNT
Accountant (ABBR) .... ACCT
Accountant (DLA) .... ACCTANT
Accountant (ABBR) .... ACCTNT
Accountant (MUGU) .... ACTNT
Accountant (ABBR) .... ACTT
Accountant General .... AG
Accountant Law Reports [*England*] [*A publication*] (DLA) .... Acct L Rep
Accountant [*or Accounting*] **Officer** .... AO
Accountants and Controllers .... AC
Accountants Association of Iowa (SRA) .... AAI
Accountants Computer Users Technical Exchange (EA) .... ACUTE
Accountants' Fellowship of New South Wales [*Australia*] .... ACFNSW
Accountants for the Public Interest [*Washington, DC*] .... API
Accountants International Study Group [*Later, International Federation of Accountants*] .... AISG
Accountant's Resource Network [*Information service or system*] (IID) .... ARNE
Accounted (ABBR) .... ACCTD
Accounting .... ACCTG
Accounting (DD) .... acctg
Accounting .... ACCTG
Accounting .... ACCTNG
Accounting (ABBR) .... ACONTG
Accounting .... ACTNG
Accounting and Auditing Enforcement Releases (TDOB) .... AAER
Accounting and Budget Distribution System [*Air Force*] .... ABDS
Accounting and Budgetary Control (DNAB) .... ABC
Accounting and Disbursing (MCD) .... A & D
Accounting and Disbursing (MCD) .... AD
Accounting and Disbursing Station Number [*Air Force*] (AFM) .... ADSN
Accounting and Finance (AFM) .... A & F
Accounting and Finance (AFIT) .... AAF
Accounting and Finance Office [*or Officer*] .... AFO
Accounting and Finance Officer [*Air Force*] .... ACCTG & FINO

Accounting and Financial Management Division [*GAO*] (AAGC) .... AFMD
Accounting and Reporting Management Improvement Program [*Army*] (AABC) .... ARMIP
Accounting Careers Council [*Later, AICPA*] .... ACC
Accounting Classification Code (AFM) .... ACC
Accounting Classification Reference Number (MCD) .... ACRN
Accounting Code Reference Number .... ACRN
Accounting Computer (IAA) .... AC
Accounting Computer System [*Burroughs Corp.*] .... ACSYS
Accounting Control System .... ACS
Accounting Control Table (CMD) .... ACT
Accounting Controllers Committee .... ACC
Accounting, Cost, Estimating .... ACE
Accounting Data System .... ADS
Accounting Department Instructions .... ADI
Accounting Incomplete Records System [*Software package*] (NCC) .... AIRS
Accounting Information System (BUR) .... AIS
Accounting Line Number (CINC) .... ALN
Accounting Master of Business Administration (GAGS) .... AMBA
Accounting Point (GFGA) .... AP
Accounting Policy Division (AAGC) .... PACO
Accounting Policy Division (AAGC) .... PAD
Accounting Principles Board [*Later, Financial Accounting Standards Board*] [*American Institute of Certified Public Accountants*] .... APB
Accounting Principles Board Opinions [*A publication*] (DLA) .... APB Op
Accounting Processing Code (AABC) .... APC
Accounting Program [*Association of Independent Colleges and Schools specialization code*] .... AC
Accounting Property Officer .... APO
Accounting Rate of Return (ADA) .... ARR
Accounting Requirements Code [*Military*] (AABC) .... ARC
Accounting Research and Education Centre [*McMaster University*] [*Canada Research center*] (RCD) .... ARC
Accounting Research Board Opinion [*A publication*] (DLA) .... ARB
Accounting Research Bulletin [*A publication*] .... ARB
Accounting Research Centre [*University of Sydney*] [*Australia*] .... ARC
Accounting Research Study .... ARS
Accounting Researchers International Association [*Defunct*] (EA) .... ARIA
Accounting Review [*A publication*] (BRI) .... AR
Accounting Series Release [*Securities and Exchange Commission*] .... ASR
Accounting Series Releases (TDOB) .... ASR
Accounting Standards Board [*British*] (ECON) .... ASB
Accounting Standards Committee [*British*] .... ASC
Accounting Standards Executive Committee .... AccSEC
Accounting Standards Executive Committee (TDOB) .... AcSEC
Accounting Standards Steering Committee (ODBW) .... ASSC
Accounting Systems International World Group [*Consortium of resellers*] (PCM) .... ASI
Accounting Tabulating [*Card*] (AAG) .... AT
Accounting Tabulating Form (AAG) .... ATF
Accounting Unit (NATG) .... AU
Accounting Work Order .... AWO
Account-Purchase (ADA) .... A/P
Accounts [*Secondary school course*] [*British*] .... ACCTS
Accounts and Collection Unit Circulars [*A publication*] (DLA) .... A & C Cir
Accounts, Collection, and Taxpayer Service [*Internal Revenue Service*] ...... ACTS
Accounts Control Area (AFM) .... ACA
Accounts Enquiry Sales and Order Processing (ADA) .... AESOP
Accounts Maintenance [*IRS*] .... AM
Accounts Office [*Army*] (AABC) .... AO
Accounts Payable (HGAA) .... A/csPay
Accounts Payable .... AP
Accounts Receivable [*Business term*] (MHDB) .... A/C Rec
Accounts Receivable [*Accounting*] .... A/CS REC
Accounts Receivable [*Accounting*] .... AR
Accounts Register [*Computer science*] .... AR
Accoustic Information Processing System [*Navy*] (DOMA) .... ACIPS
Accra [*Ghana*] [*Airport symbol*] (OAG) .... ACC
Accra [*Ghana*] [*ICAO location identifier*] (ICLI) .... DGAC
Accra [*Ghana*] [*ICAO location identifier*] (ICLI) .... DGFC
Accra/Kotoka International [*Ghana*] [*ICAO location identifier*] (ICLI) .... DGAA
Accredit (ABBR) .... ACRD
Accredit (ABBR) .... ACRT
Accreditation .... ACCRDTN
Accreditation .... acred
Accreditation and Institutional Eligibility Staff [*Office of Education*] .... AIES
Accreditation Association for Ambulatory Health Care (EA) .... AAAHC
Accreditation Board for Engineering and Technology (EA) .... ABET
Accreditation Council for Accountancy [*Later, ACAT*] (EA) .... ACA
Accreditation Council for Accountancy and Taxation (EA) .... ACAT
Accreditation Council for Continuing Medical Education (EA) .... ACCME
Accreditation Council for Facilities for the Mentally Retarded .... ACF-MR
Accreditation Council for Graduate Medical Education [*American Medical Association*] .... ACGME
Accreditation Council for Services for Mentally Retarded and Other Developmentally Disabled Persons [*Later, ACDD*] (EA) .... AC/MRDD
Accreditation Council on Services for People with Developmental Disabilities (EA) .... ACDD
Accreditation of Prior Achievement [*Education*] (AIE) .... APA
Accreditation of Prior Learning (AIE) .... APL
Accreditation Program / Ambulatory Health Care (MEDA) .... AP/AHC
Accreditation Program / Home Health Care (MEDA) .... AP/HHC
Accreditation Program / Hospice (MEDA) .... AP/HC
Accreditation Program / Long Term Care [*Medicine*] (MEDA) .... AP/LTC
Accreditation Program / Psychiatric Facilities (MEDA) .... AP/PF

Accreditation Review Committee on Education for Physicians Assistants (EA) .... ARC-PA
Accreditation Review Council for Educational Programs in Surgical Technology (HCT) .... ARC-ST
Accredited .... ACCRDTRD
Accredited (EY) .... ACCRED
Accredited (ABBR) .... ACRTD
Accredited Agents Scheme .... AAS
Accredited Airport Executive [*American Association of Airport Executives*] [*Designation awarded by*] .... AAE
Accredited Appraiser, Canadian Institute .... AACI
Accredited Center [*Youth Training Scheme*] [*British*] (AIE) .... AC
Accredited Dosimetry Calibration Laboratories .... ADCL
Accredited Farm Manager [*Designation given by American Society of Farm Managers and Rural Appraisers*] .... AFM
Accredited Financial Examiner [*Society of Financial Examiners*] [*Designation awarded by*] .... AFE
Accredited Gemologists Association (EA) .... AGA
Accredited Home Newspapers of America [*Later, SNA*] .... AHNA
Accredited in Public Relations .... APR
Accredited in Public Relations [*Canadian Public Relations Society, Inc.*] (DD) .... APR
Accredited Leasing Officer [*Canada*] (DD) .... ALO
Accredited Management Organization [*Institute of Real Estate Management*] [*Designation awarded by*] .... AMO
Accredited Off-Campus Instruction .... AOCI
Accredited Pet Cemetary Society .... APCS
Accredited Quality Assurance .... AQA
Accredited Record Technician [*American Medical Record Association*] .... ART
Accredited Resident Manager [*Institute of Real Estate Management of the National Association of Realtors*] [*Designation awarded by*] .... ARM
Accredited Review Appraisers Council (EA) .... ARAC
Accredited Rural Appraiser [*American Society of Farm Managers and Rural Appraisers*] [*Designation awarded by*] .... ARA
Accredited Standards Committee (AAGC) .... ASC
Accredited Training Centre [*Education*] [*British*] (AIE) .... ATC
Accrediting (ABBR) .... ACRTG
Accrediting and Recording Centralized System (MCD) .... ARCS
Accrediting Association of Bible Colleges [*Later, American Association of Bible Colleges*] (EA) .... AABC
Accrediting Bureau of Health Education Schools (EA) .... ABHES
Accrediting Bureau of Medical Laboratory Schools [*Later, ABHES*] .... ABMLS
Accrediting Commission for Business Schools (EA) .... ACBS
Accrediting Commission for Specialized Colleges [*Defunct*] (EA) .... ACSC
Accrediting Commission on Education for Health Services Administration (EA) .... ACEHSA
Accrediting Council for Independent Colleges and Schools (PGP) .... ACICS
Accrediting Council for Theological Education in Africa [*of the Association of Evangelicals of Africa and Madagascar*] [*See also COHETA*] (EAIO) .... ACTEA
Accrediting Council on Education in Journalism and Mass Communications (EA) .... ACEJMC
Accrescinto [*Increased*] [*Music*] (ROG) .... ACCRES
Accrete (ABBR) .... ACCR
Accreted (ABBR) .... ACCRD
Accreted Crystaline Anthropoid Homologue .... ACAH
Accreting (ABBR) .... ACCRG
Accretion (ABBR) .... ACCRN
Accretion (ABBR) .... ACRN
Accretion Disk Corona [*Astrophysics*] .... ADC
Accretion-Induced Collapse [*Astrophysics*] .... AIC
Accretion-Induced Rotational Fragmentation [*Astrophysics*] .... ARF
Accretive (ABBR) .... ACCRV
Accretive (ABBR) .... ACRV
Accretive Industrial Development Syndrome [*Real estate phenomenon*] ...... AIDS
Accrington Public Library, Accrington, United Kingdom [*Library symbol Library of Congress*] (LCLS) .... UkAc
Accrual Accounting and Reporting System .... AARS
Accrue (ABBR) .... ACRU
Accrued (AFM) .... ACCR
Accrued .... Accrd
Accrued (ABBR) .... ACRD
Accrued (ABBR) .... ACRUD
Accrued Comprehensive Income (DICI) .... ACI
Accrued Dividend .... AD
Accrued Expenditure [*Accounting*] (AFM) .... AE
Accrued Expenditure Paid [*Accounting*] (AFM) .... AEP
Accrued Expenditure Unpaid [*Accounting*] (AFM) .... AEU
Accrued Interest [*Finance*] (BARN) .... accrd int
Accrued Interest [*Investment term*] .... AI
Accrued Leave [*Military*] .... ACLV
Accrued Liability [*Accounting*] .... AL
Accrued Military Pay System (AFM) .... AMPS
Accruement (ABBR) .... ACRUT
Accruing (ABBR) .... ACRUG
Accruing Return Investments [*Business term*] .... ARI
Acctex Information Systems (NITA) .... AIS
Accugraph Corp. [*NASDAQ symbol*] (SAG) .... ACCU
Accugraph Corp. [*NASDAQ symbol*] (TTSB) .... ACCUF
Accugraph Corp. [*Associated Press*] (SAG) .... Accugph
Accugraph Corp. [*Associated Press*] (SAG) .... Accugrph
Accugraph Corp. [*Toronto Stock Exchange symbol*] .... ACU
Accumaster Consolidated Workstation [*Computer science*] (TNIG) .... ACW
AccuMed International, Inc. [*Associated Press*] (SAG) .... AccuM
AccuMed International, Inc. [*Associated Press*] (SAG) .... AccuMed
AccuMed International, Inc. [*NASDAQ symbol*] (SAG) .... ACMI

AccuMed Intl. [*NASDAQ symbol*] (TTSB) .... ACMI
AccuMed Intl. Wrrt [*NASDAQ symbol*] (TTSB) .... ACMIW
Accumulable (ABBR) .... ACUMB
Accumulate (KSC) .... ACCUM
Accumulate (ABBR) .... ACMLA
Accumulate (ABBR) .... ACUM
Accumulated (ABBR) .... ACMLAD
Accumulated (ABBR) .... ACUMD
Accumulated Alveolar Ventilatory Volume [*Respiratory testing*] (DAVI) .... AAVV
Accumulated Benefit Obligation (TDOB) .... ABO
Accumulated Heat Unit (OA) .... AHU
Accumulated Interest [*Banking*] .... AI
Accumulated Leading (DGA) .... ACL
Accumulated Operating Results .... AOR
Accumulated Surplus [*Profit margin*] .... AS
Accumulating (ABBR) .... ACMLAG
Accumulating (ABBR) .... ACUMG
Accumulation (ROG) .... ACCUMULON
Accumulation (ABBR) .... ACMLAN
Accumulation (ABBR) .... ACUMN
Accumulation Area Ratio .... AAR
Accumulation Distribution Unit [*Computer science*] .... ADU
Accumulation Factor (DEN) .... AF
Accumulation Mode Charge Injection Device (MCD) .... AMCID
Accumulation Time .... ACT
Accumulations [*Finance*] .... ACCUM
Accumulative (ABBR) .... ACMLAV
Accumulative (ABBR) .... ACUMV
Accumulator [*Computer science*] (MDG) .... A
Accumulator [*Computer science*] .... AC
Accumulator [*Flowchart*] (MSA) .... ACC
Accumulator [*Computer science*] .... ACCUM
Accumulator (DNAB) .... ACM
Accumulator (ABBR) .... ACMLATR
Accumulator (ABBR) .... ACUMR
Accumulator and Buffer [*Computer science*] (IAA) .... AB
Accumulator Buffer Register [*Computer science*] (MHDI) .... ACBR
Accumulator Gating [*Naval Space Surveillance System*] (DNAB) .... ACCGAT
Accumulator High [*Computer science*] .... AH
Accumulator High-Pressure Air .... AHPA
Accumulator Injection System [*Nuclear energy*] (NRCH) .... AIS
Accumulator Left Shift (SAA) .... ALS
Accumulator Low [*Computer science*] .... AL
Accumulator Makers' Association [*British*] (BI) .... AMA
Accumulator Read-In Module (OA) .... ARM
Accumulator Register [*Computer science*] (IAA) .... ACR
Accumulator Register [*Computer science*] .... AR
Accumulator Register [*Computer science*] (IAA) .... AREG
Accumulator/Reservoir (MCD) .... A/R
Accumulator Reservoir Manifold Assembly .... ARMA
Accumulator Right Shift (SAA) .... ARS
Accumulator Switch [*Computer science*] .... ACS
Accumulator, Temporary .... ACT
Accumulators Shift Right [*Computer science*] (BUR) .... ASR
Accura Resources [*Vancouver Stock Exchange symbol*] .... ACR
Accuracy .... ACCRCY
Accuracy (AFM) .... ACCRY
Accuracy (ABBR) .... ACRCY
Accuracy (ABBR) .... ACURC
Accuracy Control Document (NASA) .... ACD
Accuracy Control Document (NASA) .... ACD
Accuracy Figure [*British and Canadian*] [*World War II*] .... AF
Accuracy in Academia (EA) .... AA
Accuracy in Academia .... AIA
Accuracy in Media (EA) .... AIM
Accuracy of Position (MCD) .... AOP
Accurate .... ACCRT
Accurate [*or Accurately*] (MSA) .... ACCUR
Accurate (ABBR) .... ACRA
Accurate (ABBR) .... ACUR
Accurate and Reliable Prototype Earth Sensor Head [*NASA*] .... ARPESH
Accurate Position Finder .... APF
Accurate Position Indicator .... API
Accurate Surgical and Scientific Instruments Corp. (DAVI) .... ASSI
Accurate Tracking (MUGU) .... ACTRAC
Accurate Traffic Volume [*BTS*] (TAG) .... ATV
Accurately (ABBR) .... ACRAY
Accurately (ABBR) .... ACURY
Accurately Defined System [*Computer science*] .... ADS
Accurateness (ABBR) .... ACRANS
Accurateness (ABBR) .... ACURNS
Accuratissime [*Most Carefully*] [*Pharmacy*] (DAVI) .... accur
Accursed (ABBR) .... ACRSD
Accursedly (ABBR) .... ACRSDY
Accursedness (ABBR) .... ACRSDNS
Accursius [*Deceased, 1263*] [*Authority cited in pre-1607 legal work*] (DSA) .... A
Accursius [*Deceased, 1263*] [*Authority cited in pre-1607 legal work*] (DSA) .... Ac
Accursius [*Deceased, 1263*] [*Authority cited in pre-1607 legal work*] (DSA) .... Acc
Accursius [*Deceased, 1263*] [*Authority cited in pre-1607 legal work*] (DSA) .... Accur
Accursius [*Deceased, 1263*] [*Authority cited in pre-1607 legal work*]
(DSA) .... Acsius
Accursius [*Deceased, 1263*] [*Authority cited in pre-1607 legal work*] (DSA) .... Acu
Accurst (ABBR) .... ACRST
Accusation (ABBR) .... ACUSN
Accusative [*Grammar*] (ROG) .... A

Accusative .... ACC
Accusative .... ACCUS
Accusative (ABBR) .... ACSTV
Accusative (ABBR) .... ACUSV
Accusatorial (ABBR) .... ACUSTL
Accusatory (ABBR) .... ACUSTRY
Accusatory (ABBR) .... ACUSTY
Accuse (ABBR) .... ACUS
Accused (ABBR) .... ACUSD
Accuser (ABBR) .... ACUSR
Accusing (ABBR) .... ACUSG
Accusingly (ABBR) .... ACUSGY
AccuStaff, Inc. [*Associated Press*] (SAG) .... AccuStff
AccuStaff, Inc. [*NYSE symbol*] (SAG) .... ASI
AccuStaff, Inc. [*NASDAQ symbol*] (SAG) .... ASTF
Accustom (ABBR) .... ACSTM
Accustomed (ABBR) .... ACSTMD
Accustoming (ABBR) .... ACSTMG
Ace .... A
Ace Air Cargo Express, Inc. [*ICAO designator*] (FAAC) .... AER
Ace Bandage (HGAA) .... ab
Ace Cash Express [*NASDAQ symbol*] (SAG) .... AACE
Ace Cash Express [*Associated Press*] (SAG) .... AceCsh
ACE [*Allied Command Europe*] **Communication Management Organization** [*NATO*] (NATG) .... ACMO
ACE Developments [*Vancouver Stock Exchange symbol*] .... AE
ACE [*American Council on Education*] **Fellows Program** (EA) .... AFP
ACE Ltd. [*Associated Press*] (SAG) .... ACE Ltd.
ACE Ltd. [*NYSE symbol*] (SPSG) .... ACL
ACE Limited [*NYSE symbol*] (TTSB) .... ACL
ACE [*Allied Command Europe*] **Mobile Force** [*NATO*] .... AMF
ACE Operational Telegraph Network (MCD) .... AOTN
ACE Target Data Base (MCD) .... ATDB
ACEC [*American Consulting Engineers Council*] **Research and Management Foundation** (EA) .... ACEC/RMF
Aceglutamide Aluminum [*Biochemistry*] .... AGA
Aceite [*Acceptance*] [*Portuguese Business term*] .... A.
Acellular Vaccine [*Medicine*] .... ACV
Acepromazine .... ACP
Acerbity (ABBR) .... ACRBT
Aces [*ICAO designator*] (AD) VX
Acetaldehyde Monoperacetate (PDAA) .... AMP
Acetaldehyde Oxime [*Organic chemistry*] .... AAO
(Acetamidol)Aminoethanesulfonic Acid [*A buffer*] .... ACES
(Acetamidol)Iminodiacetic Acid [*A buffer*] .... ADA
Acetaminophen [*Medicine*] (DMAA) .... APAP
Acetate [*Also, ACTT*] [*Organic chemistry*] .... AC
Acetate (VRA) .... acet
Acetate (ABBR) .... ACTA
Acetate [*Also, AC*] [*Organic chemistry*] (MSA) .... ACTT
Acetate Cloth Tape .... ACT
Acetate Film Tape .... AFT
Acetate Halftone Litho [*Du Pont*] .... AHL
Acetazolamide-Responsive Familial Paroxysmal Ataxia [*Medicine*]
(DMAA) .... AREPA
Acetic (ABBR) .... ACE
Acetic Acid [*Organic chemistry*] (MAE) .... AA
Acetic Acid [*Organic chemistry*] (OA) .... AC
Acetic Acid, Alcohol, Formalin [*Biology*] .... AAF
Aceto Corp. [*NASDAQ symbol*] (NQ) .... ACET
Aceto Corp. [*Associated Press*] (SAG) .... Aceto
Acetoacetanilide [*Organic chemistry*] .... AAA
Acetoacetate Decarboxylase [*An enzyme*] .... AAD
Acetoacetic Acid [*Biochemistry*] (DAVI) .... AcAcOH
Acetoacet-m-xylidide [*Organic chemistry*] .... AAMX
Acetoacet-o-anisidide [*Organic chemistry*] .... AAOA
Acetoacet-o-chloroanilide [*Organic chemistry*] .... AAOC
Acetoacet-o-toluidide [*Organic chemistry*] .... AAOT
Acetoacetoxyethyl Methacrylate [*Organic chemistry*] .... AAEM
Acetocoenzyme A Acetyltransferase (DMAA) .... ACAT
Acetohexamide [*Pharmacology*] (DAVI) .... AH
Acetohydroxamic Acid [*Medicine*] (DMAA) .... AHA
Acetohydroxyacidsynthase [*An enzyme*] .... AHAS
Acetolactate Decarboxylase [*An enzyme*] .... ALDC
Acetolactate Synthase [*An enzyme*] .... ALS
Acetone [*Medicine*] .... Acet
Acetone (ABBR) .... ACTNE
Acetone, Butanol, and Ethanol [*Fermentation products*] .... ABE
Acetone Cyanohydrin [*Organic chemistry*] (PDAA) .... ACH
Acetone Cyanohydrin [*Organic chemistry*] .... ACN
Acetone Powder Extract (MAE) .... APE
Acetone Producers Association [*Belgium*] (EAIO) .... APA
Acetone/Water [*Medicine*] (AAMN) .... AC/W
Acetone-Dicarboxylic Acid (WDAA) .... ADA
Acetonitrile [*Organic chemistry*] (BABM) .... ACE
Acetonitrile [*Organic chemistry*] .... ACN
Acetonitrile [*Organic chemistry*] .... AN
Acetophenone [*Organic chemistry*] .... ACP
Acetosyringone [*Organic chemistry*] .... AS
Acetoxy [*Biochemistry*] .... AcO
(Acetoxyacetylamino)fluorene [*Organic chemistry*] .... AAAF
Acetoxycycloheximide [*Biochemistry*] .... AXM
Acetoxycyclopentenone [*Organic chemistry*] .... ACP
Acetoxymethyl Ester .... AM
Acetoxy-N-trimethylanilinium Iodide [*Organic chemistry*] .... ANTI

Acetoxypregnenolone [*Pharmacology*] .... AOP
Acetum [*Medicine*] (DMAA) .... A
Acetyl [*As substituent on nucleoside*] [*Biochemistry*] .... ac
Acetyl Benzoyl Peroxide [*Organic chemistry*] .... ABP
Acetyl Coenzyme A [*Biochemistry*] .... AcCoA
Acetyl Ethyl Tetramethyl Tetralin [*Musk fragrance, neuro-toxic compound*] .... AETT
Acetyl Levo-Carnitine Chloride [*Biochemistry*] .... ALCC
Acetyl Tributylcitrate [*Organic chemistry*] .... ATBC
Acetyl Xylan Esterase [*An enzyme*] .... AXE
Acetylacetonate [*Organic chemistry*] .... Acac
Acetylacetone [*Organic chemistry*] .... ACAC
Acetylacrolein [*Organic chemistry*] .... AA
(Acetylalanyl)histidine Aluminum [*Biochemistry*] .... AAHA
Acetyl(alanyl)phenylalanylchloromethyl Ketone [*Biochemistry*] .... AAPCK
Acetylaminobiphenyl [*Biochemistry*] (OA) .... AABP
Acetylaminofluorene [*Also, AcAF, AcNHFln, FAA*] [*Organic chemistry*] .... AAF
Acetylaminofluorene [*Also, AAF, AcNHFln, FAA*] [*Organic chemistry*] .... AcAF
Acetylaminofluorene [*Also, AAF, AcAF, FAA*] [*Organic chemistry*] .... AcNHFln
Acetylamino(formylamino)methyluracil [*Biochemistry*] .... AFMU
Acetylarginine Methyl Ester [*Biochemistry*] (AAMN) .... AAME
Acetylated Low-Density Lipoprotein [*Biochemistry*] .... AcLDL
Acetylbutyrolactone [*Organic chemistry*] .... ABL
Acetylcholine [*Biochemistry*] (IIA) .... AC
Acetylcholine [*Biochemistry*] (AAMN) .... AcCh
Acetylcholine [*Biochemistry*] .... ACh
Acetylcholine Receptor [*Also, AChR*] [*Biochemistry*] .... AcChR
Acetylcholine Receptor [*Also, AcChR*] [*Biochemistry*] .... AChR
Acetylcholine Receptor Antibody [*Immunology*] .... AChRAb
Acetylcholine Receptor-Inducing Activity [*Biochemistry*] .... ARIA
Acetylcholinesterase [*An enzyme*] (MAE) .... AcCHS
Acetylcholinesterase [*An enzyme*] (PDAA) .... ACH
Acetylcholinesterase [*An enzyme*] (OA) .... AChE
Acetyl-CoA Carboxylase [*An enzyme*] .... ACC
Acetyl-CoA Carboxylase [*An enzyme*] .... ACCase
Acetylcoenzyme A [*Biochemistry*] (DAVI) .... acetyl-CoA
Acetylcysteine [*Biochemistry*] (AAMN) .... AC
Acetylcysteine [*Biochemistry*] .... ACC
Acetylene (MSA) .... ACET
Acetylene (ABBR) .... ACETL
Acetylene (ABBR) .... ACTYLN
Acetylene Reduction Assay [*Botany*] .... ARA
Acetylene-Terminated Bisphel [*Organic chemistry*] .... ATB
Acetylene-Terminated Imide [*Polymer technology*] .... ATI
Acetylene-Terminated Phenylquinoxaline [*Polymer technology*] .... ATPQ
Acetylene-Terminated Sulfone [*Organic chemistry*] .... ATS
Acetyl-Glyceryl-Ether Phosphorylcholine .... AGEPC
(Acetylglycyl)lysine Methyl Ester Acetate [*Biochemistry*] .... AGLME
Acetylhomocysteinethiolactone [*Citiolone*] [*Organic chemistry*] .... AHCTL
Acetyl-L-Tyrosine Ethyl Ester [*Biochemistry*] (MAE) .... ALTEE
Acetyllysine Methyl Ester [*Biochemistry*] .... ALME
Acetylneuraminic Acid [*Also, NAN, NANA*] [*Biochemistry*] .... AcNeu
Acetylneuraminic Acid [*Biochemistry*] (MAE) .... ANA
Acetyl-para-aminophenol [*Pharmacology*] .... APAP
Acetyl(p-nitrophenyl)sulfanilamide [*Pharmacology*] .... APNPS
Acetylpyridineadenine Dinucleotide [*Biochemistry*] .... APAD
Acetylsalicylic Acid [*Aspirin*] .... ASA
Acetylsalicylic Acid [*Aspirin*], Phenacetin, and Caffeine Compound [*Slang translation is, "All Purpose Capsules"*] [*Pharmacy*] .... APC
Acetylstrophanthidin [*Organic chemistry*] .... ACS
Acetylstrophanthidin [*Organic chemistry*] (MAE) .... AS
Acetylsulfanilyl Chloride [*Organic chemistry*] .... ASC
Acetyltyrosine Ethyl Ester [*Biochemistry*] .... ATEE
Acetyltyrosine Hydrazide (MAE) .... ATH
ACF Industries, Inc., Albuquerque, NM [*Library symbol Library of Congress*] (LCLS) .... NmAACF
Achaete-Scute Homologue [*Genetics*] .... ASH
Achaguas, Apure [*Venezuela ICAO location identifier*] (ICLI) .... SVCH
Achard-Thiers Syndrome [*Medicine*] (DMAA) .... ATS
Acharnenses [*Acharnians*] [*of Aristophanes*] [*Classical studies*] (OCD) .... Ach
Achates Resources Ltd. [*Vancouver Stock Exchange symbol*] .... ATR
Ached (ABBR) .... ACHD
Achenbach Child Behavior Checklist (EDAC) .... ACBC
Acheron Resources Ltd. [*Vancouver Stock Exchange symbol*] .... ACZ
Aches (ABBR) .... ACHS
Achiasaph (BJA) .... Ach
Achievable (ABBR) .... ACHVB
Achievable Benefit Achieved .... ABA
Achievable Benefit Not Achieved .... ABNA
Achievable Data Rate (MCD) .... ADR
Achieve (ABBR) .... ACHV
Achieve (ABBR) .... ACHVE
Achieve Successful Performance, Intensify Reliability Effort .... ASPIRE
Achieved (ABBR) .... ACHVD
Achieved Availability (MCD) .... AA
Achieved Availability (AAGC) .... Aa
Achievement (ABBR) .... ACHIEV
Achievement .... ACHVIT
Achievement .... ACHVMNT
Achievement (ABBR) .... ACHVNT
Achievement (ABBR) .... ACHVT
Achievement Age [*Psychology*] .... AA
Achievement Anxiety Scale [*Psychology*] .... AAS
Achievement Anxiety Text [*Psychology*] (EDAC) .... AAT
Achievement Drive [*Psychology*] (AAMN) .... AD
Achievement Identification Measure [*Educational test*] .... AIM
Achievement Orientation [*Psychology*] (AAMN) .... AO
Achievement Quotient .... AQ
Achievement Ratio .... AR
Achievement Rewards for College Scientists [*Foundation*] .... ARCS
Achievement Test .... AT
Achievement through Counselling and Treatment .... ACT
Achiever (ABBR) .... ACHVR
Achieving (ABBR) .... ACHVG
Achilleis [*of Statius*] [*Classical studies*] (OCD) .... Achil
Achilles Heel Cleavage (DOG) .... AHC
Achilles Resources [*Vancouver Stock Exchange symbol*] .... ACL
Achilles Tectonic Exhibit .... ATE
Achilles Tendon [*Anatomy*] .... AT
Achilles Tendon Lengthening [*Medicine*] .... ATL
Achilles Tendon Reflex [*Neurology*] .... ATR
Achilles Tendon Reflex Test [*Neurology and orthopedics*] (DAVI) .... ART
Achilles Track Club (EA) .... ATC
Aching (ABBR) .... ACHG
Acholi [*MARC language code Library of Congress*] (LCCP) .... ach
Achondroplasia [*Medicine*] .... ACH
Achromatic (ABBR) .... ACHR
Achromatic (ABBR) .... ACHRMTK
Achromatic Color Removal (DGA) .... ACR
Achromatically (ABBR) .... ACHRY
Achromaticity (ABBR) .... ACHRT
Achromatism (ABBR) .... ACHRM
Achromatism (ABBR) .... ACHROM
Achutupo [*Panama*] [*Airport symbol*] (OAG) .... ACU
ACI Telecentrics, Inc. [*Associated Press*] (SAG) .... ACI Tlcn
ACI Telecentrics, Inc. [*NASDAQ symbol*] (SAG) .... ACIT
Acicular (ABBR) .... ACIC
Acid [*or Acidity*] .... A
Acid (AAMN) .... AC
Acid [*Pharmacy*] (ROG) .... ACI
Acid and Base Washed and Silanized (SAA) .... ABS
Acid/Base [*Ratio*] (AAMN) .... A/B
Acid/Base Electrolyte [*Disorder diagnosed by an experimental medical system of the same name*] .... ABEL
Acid/Base Electrolyte Disorders (MHDB) .... ABED
Acid Bismuth Yeast [*Agar*] (MAE) .... ABY
Acid Cholesteryl Ester Hydrolase [*An enzyme*] .... ACEH
Acid Concentrator Feed [*Nuclear energy*] (NRCH) .... ACF
Acid Copper Chromate [*Wood preservative*] .... ACC
Acid Degree Value [*Food technology*] .... ADV
Acid Deposition and Atmospheric Research Division [*Environmental Protection Agency*] (GFGAG) .... ADARD
Acid Deposition and Oxidant Model [*for acid rain*] [*Canada and Federal Republic of Germany*] .... ADOM
Acid Deposition Assessment Staff [*Environmental Protection Agency*] (GFGA) .... ADAS
Acid Deposition Planning Staff [*Environmental Protection Agency*] (GFGA) .... ADPS
Acid Detergent Fiber Nitrogen [*Organic chemistry*] (DICI) .... ADF-N
Acid Dew Point .... ADP
Acid Equivalent (GNE) .... AE
Acid Fractionator Distillate (GFGA) .... AFD
Acid Fractionator Off-Gas [*Nuclear energy*] (NRCH) .... AOG
Acid Fractionator Recycle [*Nuclear energy*] (NRCH) .... AFR
Acid Gas Removal System [*Chemical engineering*] .... AGRS
Acid Generator [*Chemistry*] .... AG
Acid Glycoprotein [*Biochemistry*] .... AGP
Acid Ionization Constant [*Physics*] (DAVI) .... K_a
Acid Mine Drainage [*Mining technology*] .... AMD
Acid Mucopolysaccharide [*Biochemistry*] .... AMP
Acid Mucopolysaccharide [*Biochemistry*] .... AMPS
Acid Number [*Chemistry*] .... AN
Acid Open Hearth (PDAA) .... AOH
Acid Output [*Physiology*] .... AO
Acid Phosphatase [*An enzyme*] (CPH) .... ac phos
Acid Phosphatase [*Also, ACPH, AP*] [*An enzyme*] .... ACP
Acid Phosphatase [*Also, ACP, AP*] [*An enzyme*] .... ACPH
Acid Phosphatase [*Also, ACP, ACPH*] [*An enzyme*] .... AP
Acid Phosphatase Prostatic Fluid [*Biochemistry*] (DAVI) .... ACPP PF
Acid Phosphatase with Tartrate [*Clinical chemistry*] .... ACPT
Acid Precipitation Experiment .... APEX
[*The*] **Acid Rain Foundation** (EA) .... TARF
Acid Rain Information Clearinghouse (GNE) .... ARIC
Acid Rain Mitigation Strategies .... ARMS
Acid Rain Policy Office [*Environmental Protection Agency*] (GFGA) .... ARPO
Acid Rain Research Program [*Environmental Protection Agency*] (GFGA) .... ARRP
Acid Resistant Cement .... ARC
Acid Resisting [*Technical drawings*] .... AR
Acid Rock Draining [*Mining technology*] .... ARD
Acid Value [*Chemistry*] .... AV
Acid Waste .... AW
Acid-Citrate-Dextrose [*Hematology*] .... ACD
Acid-Detergent Fiber [*Food analysis*] .... ADF
Acid-Detergent Lignin [*Food analysis*] .... ADL
Acid-Detergent Residue [*Food analysis*] .... ADR
Acide Nucleique [*French Medicine*] .... AN
Acid-Fast [*Microbiology*] .... AF
Acid-Fast Bacillus [*Microbiology*] .... AFB
Acid-Fast Culture [*Biochemistry*] (DAVI) .... ACF
Acid-Fast Smear [*Biochemistry*] (DAVI) .... AFS
Acidic and Neutral [*Chemical analysis*] .... A/N

Acidic Fibroblast Growth Factor [*Biochemistry*] ... AFGF
Acidic Glycoaminoglycan [*Biochemistry*] ... AGAG
Acidic Gneisses and Schists [*Agronomy*] ... AC GN SCH
Acidic Proline-Rich Protein [*Medicine*] (DMAA) ... APRP
Acidified Glycerol Lysis Test [*Clinical chemistry*] ... AGLT
Acidified Potato-Dextrose Agar [*Microbiology*] ... APDA
Acidity Oxidation Potential [*Chemistry*] ... AOP
Acid-Modified Flour (OA) ... AMF
Acid-Neutralizing Capacity [*Chemistry*] ... ANC
Acidophil [*Medicine*] (DMAA) ... A
Acid-Precipitable Globulin [*Clinical chemistry*] ... APG
Acid-Precipitable Material [*Antiviral agent*] ... APM
Acid-Precipitated Protein [*Food analysis*] ... APP
Acid-Prepared Mesostructure [*Inorganic chemistry*] ... APM
Acidproof ... AP
Acidproof Cement Manufacturers Association [*Defunct*] (EA) ... ACMA
Acidproof Floor [*Technical drawings*] ... APF
Acid-Rinsing Solution [*Clinical chemistry*] ... ARS
Acid-Soluble Collagen [*Biochemistry*] ... ASC
Acid-Soluble Oil [*Petroleum refining*] ... ASO
Acidulated Phosphofluoride ... APF
Acidus [*Acid*] [*Latin*] (ROG) ... AC
Acidus [*Acid*] [*Latin*] (ROG) ... ACID
Acid-Volatile Sulfide [*Chemistry*] ... AVS
Acier Haut Resistance [*Bicycling*] (DICI) ... AHR
Acinetobacter Calcoaceticus Varanitratus [*Microbiology*] ... ACV
Acinic Cell Carcinoma [*Medicine*] ... ACC
Aciodistoincisal [*Medicine*] (MEDA) ... ADI
Ack [*Phonetic alphabet*] [*Pre-World War II*] (DSUE) ... A
Ackerley Communications [*AMEX symbol*] (TTSB) ... AK
Ackerley Communications, Inc. [*Associated Press*] (SAG) ... AckCom
Ackerley Communications, Inc. [*AMEX symbol*] (SPSG) ... AK
Ackerley Group [*Associated Press*] (SAG) ... AckGrp
Ackerman Institute for Family Therapy (EA) ... AIFT
Ackerman, MS [*FM radio station call letters*] ... WFCA
Acklands Ltd. [*Toronto Stock Exchange symbol*] ... ACK
Ackley Public Library, Ackley, IA [*Library symbol Library of Congress*] (LCLS) ... IaAc
Acknowledge (AFM) ... ACK
Acknowledge ... ACKNE
Acknowledge (ABBR) ... ACNWLG
Acknowledge Control (IAA) ... ACC
Acknowledge Enable [*Computer science*] (IAA) ... ACE
Acknowledge Hold [*Computer science*] (IAA) ... ACH
Acknowledge Input [*Computer science*] (IAA) ... ACKI
Acknowledge Output [*Computer science*] (IAA) ... ACKO
Acknowledge Receipt Of [*Telecommunications*] (TEL) ... AKRO
Acknowledgeable (ABBR) ... ACKB
Acknowledgeable (ABBR) ... ACNWLGB
Acknowledged [*Business term*] ... ACK'D
Acknowledged (ABBR) ... ACNWLGD
Acknowledged (ROG) ... AKGD
Acknowledged Information Transfer Service [*Telecommunications*] (ACRL) ... AITS
Acknowledgement (WDMC) ... ack
Acknowledgement [*Telecommunications*] (OSI) ... ACK
Acknowledgement (WDMC) ... ackl
Acknowledgement (DLA) ... ACKNOWL
Acknowledgement Signal Unit [*Telecommunications*] (TEL) ... ASU
Acknowledgement Unit [*Telecommunications*] (TEL) ... ACU
Acknowledger (ABBR) ... ACNWLGR
Acknowledging (ABBR) ... ACKG
Acknowledging (ABBR) ... ACNWLGG
Acknowledgment ... ACKGT
Acknowledgment (ROG) ... ACKNT
Acknowledgment (ABBR) ... ACKT
Acknowledgment (ABBR) ... ACNWLGNT
Acknowledgment Character [*Keyboard*] [*Computer science*] ... ACK
Acknowledgment Due ... AD
Acknowledgment of Receipt [*Message handling*] [*Telecommunications*] ... AR
Acknowledgment of Receipt [*Message handling*] [*Telecommunications*] ... R
ACLANT [*Allied Command, Atlantic*] **Planning Guidance** [*NATO*] ... APG
ACM [*Association for Computing Machinery*] **Accreditation Committee** ... ACMAC
ACM Government Income Fund [*NYSE symbol*] (SPSG) ... ACG
ACM Government Income Fund, Inc. [*Associated Press*] (SAG) ... ACMIn
ACM Government Opportunity Fund [*NYSE symbol*] (SAG) ... ACF
ACM Government Opportunity Fund, Inc. [*Associated Press*] (SAG) ... ACM Op
ACM Government Opportunity Fund, Inc. [*NYSE symbol*] (CTT) ... AOF
ACM Government Securities [*NYSE symbol*] (SPSG) ... GSF
ACM Government Securities Fund, Inc. [*Associated Press*] (SAG) ... ACM Sc
ACM Government Spectrum Fund [*NYSE symbol*] (SPSG) ... SI
ACM Government Spectrum Fund, Inc. [*Associated Press*] (SAG) ... ACMSp
ACM Gvt Income Fund [*NYSE symbol*] (TTSB) ... ACG
ACM Gvt Opportunity Fd [*NYSE symbol*] (TTSB) ... AOE
ACM Gvt Securities [*NYSE symbol*] (TTSB) ... GSF
ACM Gvt Spectrum Fund [*NYSE symbol*] (TTSB) ... SI
ACM Managed Dollar Income [*NYSE symbol*] (TTSB) ... ADF
ACM Managed Dollar Income Fund [*NYSE symbol*] (SPSG) ... ADF
ACM Managed Dollar Income Fund, Inc. [*Associated Press*] (SAG) ... ACMMD
ACM Managed Income Fund [*NYSE symbol*] (TTSB) ... AMF
ACM Managed Income Fund, Inc. [*Associated Press*] (SAG) ... ACM MI
ACM Managed Income Fund, Inc. [*NYSE symbol*] (CTT) ... AMF
ACM Muni Securities Income [*NYSE symbol*] (TTSB) ... AMU
ACM Municipal Securities Income [*Associated Press*] (SAG) ... ACMMu
ACM [*Association for Computing Machinery*] **Municipal Securities Income** [*NYSE symbol*] (SPSG) ... AMU
ACM [*Association for Computing Machinery*] **Standards Committee** ... ACMSC
ACMAT Corp'A' [*NASDAQ symbol*] (TTSB) ... ACMTA
ACMAT Corp. [*NASDAQ symbol*] (NQ) ... ACMT
ACMD [*Advanced Concepts and Missions Division*] **Combined Control and EnergyStorage System** (SSD) ... ACCESS
Acme [*Spain ICAO designator*] (FAAC) ... AKM
Acme Aviation Ltd. [*British ICAO designator*] (FAAC) ... ADP
Acme Electric [*NYSE symbol*] (TTSB) ... ACE
Acme Electric Corp. [*NYSE symbol*] (SPSG) ... ACE
Acme Electric Corp. [*Associated Press*] (SAG) ... AcmeE
Acme Metals [*NASDAQ symbol*] (SAG) ... ACME
Acme Metals [*Associated Press*] (SAG) ... AcmeMet
Acme Metals [*Associated Press*] (SAG) ... AcmeMt
Acme Metals [*NYSE symbol*] (SAG) ... AMI
Acme Metals [*NYSE symbol*] (TTSB) ... AMI
Acme Municipal Library, Acme, AB, Canada [*Library symbol Library of Congress*] (LCLS) ... CaAAM
Acme Municipal Library, Alberta [*Library symbol National Library of Canada*] (NLC) ... AAM
Acme Steel Co., Chicago, IL [*Library symbol Library of Congress*] (LCLS) ... ICAS
Acme Steel Co., Chicago, IL [*Library symbol*] [*Library of Congress*] (LCLS) ... ICASC
Acme United [*AMEX symbol*] (TTSB) ... ACU
Acme United Corp. [*Associated Press*] (SAG) ... AcmeU
Acme United Corp. [*AMEX symbol*] (SPSG) ... ACU
Acme-Cleveland [*NYSE symbol*] (TTSB) ... AMT
Acme-Cleveland Corp. [*Associated Press*] (SAG) ... AcmeC
Acme-Cleveland Corp. [*NYSE symbol*] (SPSG) ... AMT
Acmite [*CIPW classification*] [*Geology*] ... ac
Acne Neonatorum [*Medicine*] (DMAA) ... AN
Acne Research Institute (EA) ... ARI
ACNielsen Corp. [*NYSE symbol*] (SAG) ... ART
ACOA [*Administrative and Clerical Officers Association*] **Journal** [*A publication*] ... ACOA Jl
Acolyte (ABBR) ... ACLYT
Aconite, Belladonna, and Chloroform [*Liniment compound*] ... ABC
Acordia, Inc. [*NYSE symbol*] (SPSG) ... ACO
Acordia, Inc. [*Associated Press*] (SAG) ... Acordia
Acorn Interactive System [*Videodisc control system*] (NITA) ... AIS
Acorn Library District, Oak Forest, IL [*Library symbol Library of Congress*] (LCLS) ... IOf
Acorn Resources Ltd. [*Vancouver Stock Exchange symbol*] ... ARN
Acorn RISC Machine [*Acorn Computers*] [*Reduced instruction set computer*] (NITA) ... ARM
Acorn Venture Cap [*NASDAQ symbol*] (TTSB) ... AVCC
Acorn Venture Capital Corp. [*Associated Press*] (SAG) ... AcrnVn
Acorn Venture Capital Corp. [*NASDAQ symbol*] (NQ) ... AVCC
Acoustic (IAA) ... A
Acoustic [*or Acoustical*] (KSC) ... ACOUS
Acoustic (ABBR) ... ACOUST
Acoustic (MSA) ... ACST
Acoustic ... ACSTC
Acoustic Add-On Unit (MCD) ... AAU
Acoustic Artillery Location System (DNAB) ... AALS
Acoustic Beacon Ranging and Location (PDAA) ... ABRALOC
Acoustic Bullet Detector [*Military*] (VNW) ... ABD
Acoustic Charge Transport [*Computer science*] ... ACT
Acoustic Comfort Index ... ACI
Acoustic Communication Program ... ACP
Acoustic Containerless Experiment System [*Materials processing*] ... ACES
Acoustic Containerless Processing Facility ... ACPF
Acoustic Containerless Processing Module (MCD) ... ACPM
Acoustic Control (NVT) ... ACCON
Acoustic Control and Telemetry System ... ACTS
Acoustic Control Induction System [*Automotive engineering*] ... ACIS
Acoustic Control Induction System ... ACIS
Acoustic Correlation and Detection System ... ACCORDS
Acoustic Counter-Countermeasures [*Navy*] (NG) ... ACCM
Acoustic Countermeasures [*Navy*] (NG) ... ACM
Acoustic Coupler [*Computer MODEM*] ... AC
Acoustic Data Analysis Center ... ADAC
Acoustic Data Capsule [*Oceanography*] (MSC) ... ACODAC
Acoustic Data Processor (MCD) ... ADP
Acoustic Data Reduction Program (CAAL) ... ADRP
Acoustic Deception Device (CAAL) ... ADD
Acoustic Decoupler (DNAB) ... AD
Acoustic Delay Line ... ADL
Acoustic Depth Finder ... ADF
Acoustic Detection and Ranging [*Geophysics*] ... ACDAR
Acoustic Detection Device (MCD) ... ADD
Acoustic Detection Range Prediction Model (MCD) ... ADRPM
Acoustic Device, Countermeasure (CAAL) ... ADC
Acoustic Digital Memory ... ADM
Acoustic Directed Energy Pulse Train (BARN) ... ADEPT
Acoustic Discrimination of Decoys ... ADD
Acoustic Distribution Box (CAAL) ... ADB
Acoustic Doppler Current Profiler [*Oceanography*] ... ADCP
Acoustic Doppler Sounder (MCD) ... ADS
Acoustic Doppler Velocimeter [*Instrumentation*] ... ADV
Acoustic Emission ... AE
Acoustic Emission Testing (MHDB) ... AET
Acoustic Emission Weld Monitor (PDAA) ... AEWM

Acoustic Environmental Support Detachment [*Office of Naval Research*] [*Arlington, VA*] .... AESD
Acoustic Evoked Potential [*Physiology*] .... AEP
Acoustic Evoked Response [*Neurophysiology*] (DMAA) .... AER
Acoustic Fatigue Test Article (NASA) .... AFTA
Acoustic Firing Device (CAAL) .... AFD
Acoustic Guidance SONAR (HGAA) .... AGS
Acoustic Helicopter Overflight Detector (MCD) .... ACHOD
Acoustic Homing Torpedo .... AHT
Acoustic Impact Technique [*Test*] (PDAA) .... AIT
Acoustic Intelligence [*Military*] (NG) .... ACINT
Acoustic Intelligence Data System [*Navy*] .... AIDS
Acoustic Intelligence Gathering System [*Military*] (CAAL) .... AIGS
Acoustic Intercept Receiver [*Navy*] .... AIR
Acoustic Intercept Receiver/Multimode Hydrophone System [*Navy*] ..... AIR/MMH
Acoustic Isolation Chamber .... AIC
Acoustic Lens SONAR System (MCD) .... ALSS
Acoustic Locating Device (SAA) .... ALD
Acoustic Low-Flying-Aircraft Detector (MCD) .... ALFAD
Acoustic Match Filter .... AMF
Acoustic Material Signature (MCD) .... AMS
Acoustic Measurement System (KSC) .... AMS
Acoustic, Meteorological, and Oceanographic Survey .... AMOS
Acoustic Minesweeping .... AMNSWP
Acoustic Miss Distance Indicator (PDAA) .... AMDI
Acoustic Model Evaluation Committee [*Woods Hole Oceanographic Institution*] (MSC) .... AMEC
Acoustic Model Test Facility [*NASA*] (NASA) .... AMTF
Acoustic Myography [*Otorhinolaryngology*] (DAVI) .... AMG
Acoustic Neuroma [*Medicine*] (DMAA) .... AN
Acoustic Neuroma Association (EA) .... ANA
Acoustic Neuroma Association of Australasia .... ANAA
Acoustic Neuroma Association of Canada [*Association pour les Neurinomes Acoustiques du Canada*] (AC) .... ANAC
Acoustic Noise Canceling [*Headsets*] [*Bose Corp.*] .... ANC
Acoustic Noise Environment .... ANE
Acoustic Noise Generator .... ANG
Acoustic Noise Making (CAAL) .... ANM
Acoustic Noise Test .... ANT
Acoustic Optical RADAR Classification System (CAAL) .... ARCS
Acoustic Paramagnetic Resonance [*Physics*] .... APR
Acoustic Performance Monitor .... APM
Acoustic Performance Prediction [*Navy*] (MSC) .... APP
Acoustic Playback System [*Army*] .... APS
Acoustic Radiation Element .... ARE
Acoustic Range-Finder (MCD) .... ARF
Acoustic Rate Sensor (PDAA) .... ARS
Acoustic Ray Trace Indicator (PDAA) .... ARTI
Acoustic Reflex .... AR
Acoustic Reflex Ear Defender .... ARED
Acoustic Reflex Ear Defender System (RDA) .... AREDS
Acoustic Reflex Test [*Audiology*] .... ART
Acoustic Research Center (MCD) .... ARC
Acoustic Resistance Unit .... ARU
Acoustic Response of Reusable Shuttle Tiles (MCD) .... ARREST
Acoustic Sensor Operator .... ASO
Acoustic Sensor Pattern Assessment System (MCD) .... ASPAS
Acoustic Sensor [*or SONAR*] Range Prediction (NVT) .... ASRAP
Acoustic Sensor [*or SONAR*] Range Prediction System (NVT) .... ASRAPS
Acoustic Sensor Training Aids Program [*Navy*] (CAAL) .... ASTAP
Acoustic Sensor Unit [*Navy*] (CAAL) .... ASU
Acoustic Shield Thermal/Variable Cycle Engine (MCD) .... AST/VCE
Acoustic Ship Positioning - Advanced (MCD) .... ASPA
Acoustic Ship Positioning System .... ASPS
Acoustic Short-Pulse Echo Classification Technique (NVT) .... ASPECT
Acoustic Signal Data Analysis and Conversion System [*Navy*] .... ASDACS
Acoustic Signal Generator System .... ASGE
Acoustic Signal Processor (MHDB) .... ASP
Acoustic Sound Intrusion Device [*Military*] (VNW) .... ACOU-SID
Acoustic Stapedius Reflex [*Medicine*] .... ASR
Acoustic Surface Analysis Technology .... ASAT
Acoustic Surface Wave .... ASW
Acoustic Target Generator .... ATG
Acoustic Target Sensor .... ATS
Acoustic Telemetry Bathythermometer .... ATBT
Acoustic Telemetry Subsystem (MCD) .... ATS
Acoustic Telephone Interface [*Telecommunications*] .... ATI
Acoustic Test Laboratory .... ATL
Acoustic Test Signal Generator (CAAL) .... ATSG
Acoustic Thermometry of Ocean Climate [*International oceanographic project*] .... ATOC
Acoustic Thermometry of Ocean Climate .... ATOC
Acoustic Thermometry of Ocean Climate .... ATOC
Acoustic Transmission System .... ATS
Acoustic Transponder Navigation (PDAA) .... ATNAV
Acoustic Traveling Wave Lens .... ATWL
Acoustic Trials (NVT) .... ACTRL
Acoustic Underwater Range Determination Systems .... ACURAD
Acoustic Underwater Sound Experiment (MCD) .... AUSEX
Acoustic Valve Leak Detector (DNAB) .... AVLD
Acoustic Valve Operating System (PDAA) .... AVOS
Acoustic Velocity Meter (NOAA) .... AVM
Acoustic Video Processor (DWSG) .... AVP
Acoustic Video Processor Integrated Display Station .... AVPIDS
Acoustic Warfare (NVT) .... AW

Acoustic Warfare Support Measures (NVT) .... ACSM
Acoustic Warfare Support Measures (NVT) .... AWSM
Acoustic Warfare System [*Navy*] (MCD) .... AWS
Acoustic Wave .... AW
Acoustic Wave Analysis .... AWA
Acoustic Wave Analysis System .... AWAS
Acoustical [*Technical drawings*] .... AC
Acoustical (ABBR) .... ACSTL
Acoustical Absorption Coefficient .... AAC
Acoustical Absorption Loss .... AAL
Acoustical Analysis Memo [*Navy*] (MCD) .... AAM
Acoustical and Board Products Association .... ABPA
Acoustical and Insulating Materials Association [*Later, ABPA*] (EA) .... AIMA
Acoustical Attenuation Constant .... AAC
Acoustical Displacement (BARN) .... W
Acoustical Door Institute [*Defunct*] (EA) .... ADI
Acoustical Emission Monitoring (NASA) .... AEM
Acoustical Intelligence [*Military*] (AABC) .... ACOUSTINT
Acoustical Materials Association [*Later, ABPA*] (EA) .... AMA
Acoustical Phase Constant .... APC
Acoustical Plaster [*Technical drawings*] .... ACPL
Acoustical Plaster Ceiling [*Technical drawings*] .... APC
Acoustical Propagation Constant .... APC
Acoustical Signal Classification and Analysis Center [*Navy*] (CAAL) .... ASCAC
Acoustical Society of America .... ACSA
Acoustical Society of America .... ACSOC
Acoustical Society of America (EA) .... ASA
Acoustical Society of Scandinavia [*Formerly, Nordic Acoustics Society*] (EA) .... ASS
Acoustical Standards Board (MUGU) .... ASB
Acoustical Standards Management Board .... ASMB
Acoustical Test Chamber .... ATC
Acoustical Tile [*Technical drawings*] .... ACT
Acoustical Tile Ceiling [*Technical drawings*] .... ATC
Acoustically (ABBR) .... ACSTLY
Acoustically Navigated Geological Underwater Survey [*Unmanned vehicle*] .... ANGUS
Acoustic-Daylight, Ambient-Noise Imaging System .... ADONIS
Acoustic-Gravity Wave .... AGW
Acoustic-Magnetic (NVT) .... AM
Acoustic-Magneto-Electric (PDAA) .... AME
Acoustic-Optic [*Ophthalmology and otorhinolaryngology*] (DAVI) .... A-O
Acoustic-Pressure (NVT) .... AP
Acoustics (ROG) .... ACOUST
Acoustics and Vibration Data Center (MCD) .... AVDC
Acoustics Associates (AAG) .... AA
Acoustics Laboratory .... AL
Acoustics of the Target .... ACTAR
Acoustics Propellant Utilization .... APU
Acoustics, Speech, and Signal Processing (MCD) .... ASSP
Acoustic-Seismic Intrusion Detector (MCD) .... ACOUSID
Acousto-Electric (PDAA) .... AE
Acoustoelectric Oscillator (IEEE) .... AEO
Acoustographic Imaging System (PDAA) .... AGIS
Acousto-Optic (MCD) .... A-O
Acousto-Optic Beam Deflector [*Instrumentation*] .... AOBD
Acousto-Optic Mode Locker and Frequency Doubler (MCD) .... AMOL-FD
Acousto-Optic Mode-Locker / Frequency Doubles (PDAA) .... AOML/FD
Acousto-Optic Modulator .... AOM
Acousto-Optic Tunable Filter [*Instrumentation*] .... AOTF
Acousto-Optic Tunable Scanning [*Instrumentation*] .... AOTS
Acousto-Optical Imaging .... AOI
Acousto-Optical Spectrograph (ADA) .... AOS
Acousto-Optics Device .... AOD
Acoyapa [*Nicaragua*] [*Seismograph station code, US Geological Survey*] (SEIS) .... ACY
ACPA [*Affiliated Conference of Practicing Accountants*] International (EA) ..... ACPA
Acquaint (ABBR) .... ACQNT
Acquaintance (ABBR) .... ACQNTNC
Acquaintanceship (ABBR) .... ACQNTNCSP
Acquainted (ABBR) .... ACQNTD
Acquainting (ABBR) .... ACQNTG
Acqualin Resources Ltd. [*Vancouver Stock Exchange symbol*] .... AQU
Acquest Enterprises Ltd. [*Vancouver Stock Exchange symbol*] .... ACQ
Acquiesce (ABBR) .... ACQS
Acquiesced (ABBR) .... ACQSD
Acquiescence (DLA) .... A
Acquiescence (ABBR) .... ACQSNC
Acquiescent (ABBR) .... ACQSNT
Acquiescently (ABBR) .... ACQSNTY
Acquiescing (ABBR) .... ACQSG
Acquirable (ABBR) .... ACQRB
Acquire (ROG) .... ACQ
Acquire (ABBR) .... ACQR
Acquire on Jam .... AOJ
Acquired (ABBR) .... ACQRD
Acquired Aplastic Anemia [*Medicine*] (DMAA) .... AAA
Acquired Artery Immune Augmentation [*Cardiology*] (DAVI) .... AAIA
Acquired Artery Immune Augmentation [*Medicine*] (DAVI) .... AIA
Acquired Cystic Kidney Disease [*Medicine*] (DMAA) .... ACKD
Acquired Epidermolysis Bullosa [*Medicine*] .... AEB
Acquired Hemolytic Anemia [*Medicine*] (MAE) .... AHA
Acquired Hepatocellular Degeneration [*Medicine*] (DMAA) .... AHCD
Acquired Idiopathic Sideroblastic Anemia [*Medicine*] (DMAA) .... AISA

Acquired Immune Deficiency Syndrome [*Internet language*] [*Computer science*] .... AIDS
Acquired Immune Deficiency Syndrome [*Medicine*] (ODBW) .... Aids
Acquired Immune Deficiency Syndrome [*Also, AID, GRID*] [*Medicine*] .... AIDS
Acquired Immune Deficiency Syndrome with Kaposi's Sarcoma [*Medicine*] .... AIDS-KS
Acquired Immune Hemolytic Disease [*Medicine*] (DMAA) .... AIHD
Acquired Immunodeficiency [*Also, AIDS, GRID*] [*Medicine*] .... AID
Acquired Immunodeficiency Syndrome [*Medicine*] (DAVI) .... AIDS
Acquired Immunodeficiency Syndrome Self-Help and Care [*Medicine*] (DMAA) .... ASHAC
Acquired Intelligence, Inc. [*Information service or system*] (IID) .... AII
Acquired Monosaccharide Intolerance [*Medicine*] (DMAA) .... AMI
Acquired Pattern Addiction [*Telecommunications*] (PCM) .... APA
Acquired Red Cell Aplasia [*Medicine*] (DMAA) .... ARCA
Acquired Red Cell Aplasia [*Hematology*] .... ARCA
Acquired Severe Aplastic Anemia [*Hematology*] (DAVI) .... ASAA
Acquirement (ABBR) .... ACQRNT
Acquirement (ABBR) .... ACQRT
Acquirer (ABBR) .... ACQRR
Acquiring (ABBR) .... ACQRG
Acquisicorp Capital [*Vancouver Stock Exchange symbol*] .... AQ
Acquisition (AFM) .... ACQ
Acquisition (ABBR) .... ACQIS
Acquisition (IAA) .... ACQN
Acquisition (ABBR) .... ACQSN
Acquisition .... ACQSTN
Acquisition .... ACQUIS
Acquisition (KSC) .... AQUIS
Acquisition Adjustment (IAA) .... ACQADJ
Acquisition Advice Code [*NASA*] (KSC) .... AAC
Acquisition Advisory Board (MCD) .... AAB
Acquisition Advisory Group [*Business term*] .... AAG
Acquisition Aid .... AQUAID
Acquisition Aid Vehicle [*Army*] (AABC) .... AADV
Acquisition and Command Support (MCD) .... ACS
Acquisition and Control Module (MCD) .... ACM
Acquisition and Control Query Executive [*Programming language*] .... ACQE
Acquisition and Distribution of Commercial Products [*Also, ADCP*] [*Department of Defense program*] .... ADCOP
Acquisition and Distribution of Commercial Products [*Also, ADCOP*] [*Department of Defense program*] (MCD) .... ADCP
Acquisition and Inoculation Access Period [*Immunology*] .... AAP
Acquisition and Logistics (MCD) .... AL
Acquisition and Synchronization Unit (LAIN) .... ASU
Acquisition and Technology .... A & T
Acquisition and Tracking Electronics (MCD) .... A & TE
Acquisition and Tracking Electronics (MCD) .... ATE
Acquisition and Tracking Subsystem (MUGU) .... ATSS
Acquisition and Tracking System .... ATS
Acquisition Based on Consideration of Logistic Effects [*Air Force*] .... ABLE
Acquisition Basic Course [*DSMC*] (AAGC) .... ABC
Acquisition Beacon .... AB
Acquisition Bus Monitor [*Computer science*] (MCD) .... ABM
Acquisition Career Enhancement .... ACE
Acquisition Career Field [*Army*] (RDA) .... ACF
Acquisition Career Management Advocate [*Army*] (RDA) .... ACMA
Acquisition, Cataloguing, and Circulation Working Party of the Aslib Computer Applications Group [*Banking*] (NITA) .... ACCWP
Acquisition Category (AAGC) .... ACAT
Acquisition Category (CAAL) .... ACAT
Acquisition Circular (AAGC) .... AC
Acquisition Command Headquarters (AFIT) .... ACH
Acquisition, Construction, and Improvement (DNAB) .... AC & I
Acquisition, Control of Test [*Units*] (NASA) .... ACT
Acquisition Costs .... AC
Acquisition Data Facility (MCD) .... ADF
Acquisition Data Input Equipment (AABC) .... ADIE
Acquisition Decision Memorandum (MCD) .... ADM
Acquisition, Development, and Construction [*Real estate loan*] .... ADC
Acquisition Director .... AD
Acquisition Education Learning Center [*Army*] .... AELC
Acquisition Enhancement [*Program*] (DOMA) .... ACE
Acquisition Executive [*Military*] (DOMA) .... AE
Acquisition Information Management Program [*Army*] .... AIM
Acquisition Institute [*Defunct*] (EA) .... AI
Acquisition Integrated Data Base [*Army*] (RDA) .... AID
Acquisition Law Specialist (AAGC) .... ALS
Acquisition Lead Time .... ALT
Acquisition Letter [*Replaced PIL*] (AAGC) .... AL
Acquisition Life Cycle .... ALC
Acquisition Logistician (NG) .... AL
Acquisition Management Guide [*Military*] (AFIT) .... AMG
Acquisition Management Information System [*Air Force*] .... AMIS
Acquisition Management Milestone System [*DoD*] .... AMMS
Acquisition Management Mission Cluster Group [*Army*] (RDA) .... AMMCG
Acquisition Management Plan [*Navy*] .... AMP
Acquisition Management System Control (AAGC) .... AMSC
Acquisition Management System Control Officer (MCD) .... AMSCO
Acquisition Management System Data List [*Military*] (DOMA) .... AMSDL
Acquisition Management System List (MCD) .... AMSL
Acquisition Management Systems and Data Control List .... AMSDCL
Acquisition Management Systems and Data Control List .... AMSDL
Acquisition Management Systems and Data Requirements Control List [*A publication*] (AAGC) .... AMSDL

Acquisition Management Systems and Data Requirements Control Program [*Navy*] .... AMSDRP
Acquisition Management Systems Control Aviation Structural Mechanic, Structures,Chief [*Navy rating*] (DNAB) .... AMSC
Acquisition Manager .... AM
Acquisition Material List (MCD) .... AML
Acquisition Message .... AQ
Acquisition Method Coding (MCD) .... AMC
Acquisition Method Suffix Code (AAGC) .... AMSC
Acquisition of Land Act [*Town planning*] [*British*] .... AL
Acquisition of Monographs and Bibliographical Enquiry Remotely [*Computer software*] (NITA) .... AMBER
Acquisition of Satellite [*Telecommunications*] .... AOS
Acquisition of Signal [*Telecommunications*] .... AOS
Acquisition Officer Selection Board [*Army*] (INF) .... AOSB
Acquisition on Target .... AOT
Acquisition Orbit Determination Program Assembly [*Space Flight Operations Facility, NASA*] .... AODP
Acquisition Plan .... AP
Acquisition Plan (Procurement) .... APP
Acquisition Plan Review Board [*Army*] .... APRB
Acquisition Planning and Tracking System .... APATS
Acquisition Planning Executive Council (AAGC) .... APEC
Acquisition Point (MUGU) .... AP
Acquisition Policy .... AP
Acquisition Professional Development Program [*DoD*] .... APDP
Acquisition Program Baseline (DOMA) .... APB
Acquisition Program Office [*DoD*] .... APO
Acquisition Project Manager .... APM
Acquisition RADAR .... AR
Acquisition RADAR and Control System .... ARCS
Acquisition RADAR Jamming .... ARJ
Acquisition Reform Working Group [*Coalition of nine industry groups*] (AAGC) .... ARWG
Acquisition Requirements Tracking System (MCD) .... ARTS
Acquisition Review Board [*Military*] (CAAL) .... ARB
Acquisition Review Committee [*Navy*] (CAAL) .... ARC
Acquisition Review Quarterly [*A publication*] (AAGC) .... ARQ
Acquisition Select Switch (MCD) .... ACQSEL
Acquisition Sponsor Project Officer [*USMC*] (AAGC) .... ASPO
Acquisition Strategy (AAGC) .... Acq/Strat
Acquisition Strategy [*Army*] (RDA) .... AS
Acquisition Strategy Comparison Model (MCD) .... ASCM
Acquisition Strategy Meeting (AAGC) .... ASM
Acquisition Strategy/Plan [*Military*] (CAAL) .... AS/P
Acquisition Strategy Report [*Military*] (DOMA) .... ASR
Acquisition Streamlining and Standardization Electronic Transfer System (AAGC) .... ASSETS
Acquisition Streamlining and Standardization Information System (AAGC) .... ASSIST
Acquisition Sun Sensor (MCD) .... ASS
Acquisition System Integration Program (DWSG) .... ASIP
Acquisition Systems Protection Office [*DoD*] (RDA) .... ASPO
Acquisition Target and Search .... ATS
Acquisition Task Force on Modeling and Simulation [*Army*] .... ATFM & S
Acquisition Team [*Army*] (RDA) .... A-TEAM
Acquisition, Tracking, and Pointing [*Military*] (SDI) .... ATP
Acquisition Tracking and Recognition [*Aviation*] .... ATAR
Acquisition, Tracking, Pointing, and Fire Control [*Military*] (SDI) .... ATP-FC
Acquisition Trigger at Zero Beat .... ATZ
Acquisitions, Cataloguing, Technical Systems [*Library service*] .... ACTS
Acquisitions Section [*Resources and Technical Services Division of ALA*] .... AS
Acquisitor Mines Ltd. [*Vancouver Stock Exchange symbol*] .... AQT
Acquit (ABBR) .... ACQT
Acquittal (AFM) .... ACQ
Acquittal (ABBR) .... ACQTL
Acquittance (ABBR) .... ACQTNC
Acquitted (ABBR) .... ACQTD
Acquitting (ABBR) .... ACQTG
ACR Group [*Associated Press*] (SAG) .... ACR
ACR Group [*NASDAQ symbol*] (SAG) .... ACRG
Acral Lentiginous Melanoma [*Medicine*] .... ALM
Acral Lick Dermatitis [*Medicine*] .... ALD
Acre .... A
Acre (IDOE) .... a
Acre (ABBR) .... AC
Acre Foot (ABBR) .... AC FT
Acreage (ABBR) .... ACRG
Acreage Conservation Reserve .... ACR
Acreage Diversion [*Agriculture*] .... ADV
Acreage Marketing Guide .... AMG
Acreage Reduction Program [*Department of Agriculture*] (GFGA) .... ARP
Acre-Feet per Day .... ACRE-FT/D
Acre-Foot .... AF
Acres American, Inc., Buffalo, NY [*Library symbol Library of Congress*] (LCLS) .... NBuAA
Acres Consulting Services Ltd., Niagara Falls, ON, Canada [*Library symbol Library of Congress*] (LCLS) .... CaONfA
Acres Consulting Services Ltd., Niagara Falls, Ontario [*Library symbol National Library of Canada*] (NLC) .... ONFA
Acres Consulting Services Ltd., Toronto, ON, Canada [*Library symbol Library of Congress*] (LCLS) .... CaOTAC
Acres Consulting Services Ltd., Toronto, Ontario [*Library symbol National Library of Canada*] (NLC) .... OTAC
Acres Gaming [*NASDAQ symbol*] (TTSB) .... AGAM

Acres Gaming, Inc. [*Associated Press*] (SAG) .... AcreG
Acres Gaming, Inc. [*Associated Press*] (SAG) .... AcresGm
Acres Gaming, Inc. [*NASDAQ symbol*] (SAG) .... AGAM
Acres Gaming Wrrt [*NASDAQ symbol*] (TTSB) .... AGAMW
Acres, Roods, Perches [*Land measurement*] [*British*] (ROG) .... ARP
Acrid (ABBR) .... ACRI
Acridine Orange [*Dye*] .... AO
Acridinyl Ansidide [*Antineoplastic drug*] (DAVI) .... m-AMSA
(Acridinylamino)methanesulfon-m-anisidide [*Antineoplastic drug regimen*] .... AMSA
Acridity (ABBR) .... ACRDT
Acridity (ABBR) .... ACRIT
Acriflavine [*Anti-infective mixture*] .... Acr
Acrimonious (ABBR) .... ACRMNIS
Acrimonious (ABBR) .... ACRMS
Acrimony (ABBR) .... ACRM
Acrimony (ABBR) .... ACRMNY
ACRL [*Association of College and Research Libraries*] **Anthropology and Sociology Section** .... ACRL ANSS
ACRL [*Association of College and Research Libraries*] **Anthropology and Sociology Section** .... ACRL ASS
ACRL [*Association of College and Research Libraries*] **Art Section** .... ACRL ARTS
ACRL [*Association of College and Research Libraries*] **Art Section** .... ACRL AS
ACRL [*Association of College and Research Libraries*] **Asian and African Section** .... ACRL AAS
ACRL [*Association of College and Research Libraries*] **Bibliographic Instruction Section** .... ACRL BIS
ACRL [*Association of College and Research Libraries*] **College Libraries Section** .... ACRL CLS
ACRL [*Association of College and Research Libraries*] **Community and Junior College and Research Libraries** .... ACRL CJCLS
ACRL [*Association of College and Research Libraries*] **Education and Behavioral Sciences Section** .... ACRL EBSS
ACRL [*Association of College and Research Libraries*] **Law and Political Science Section** .... ACRL LPSS
ACRL [*Association of College and Research Libraries*] **Rare Books and Manuscripts Section** .... ACRL RBMS
ACRL [*Association of College and Research Libraries*] **Science and Technology Section** .... ACRL STS
ACRL [*Association of College and Research Libraries*] **Slavic and East European Section** .... ACRL SEES
ACRL [*Association of College and Research Libraries*] **University Libraries Section** .... ACRL ULS
ACRL [*Association of College and Research Libraries*] **Western European Specialists Section** .... ACRL WESS
ACRL [*Association of College and Research Libraries*] **Women's Studies Section** .... ACRL WSS
Acrobat (DSUE) .... ACRO
Acrobatic (FAAC) .... ACRBT
Acrobatic (ABBR) .... ACRBTC
Acrobatically (ABBR) .... ACRBTCY
Acrocephalopolysyndactyly (DMAA) .... ACPS
Acrocephalosyndactyly [*Medicine*] (DMAA) .... ACS
Acrodermatitis Enteropathica [*Medicine*] .... AE
Acrodyne Communications [*NASDAQ symbol*] (TTSB) .... ACRO
Acrodyne Communications, Inc. [*NASDAQ symbol*] (SAG) .... ACRO
Acrodyne Communications, Inc. [*Associated Press*] (SAG) .... Acrodyne
Acrodyne Communicns Wrrt [*NASDAQ symbol*] (TTSB) .... ACROW
Acrodyne Holdings, Inc. [*NASDAQ symbol*] (SAG) .... ACRO
Acrodyne Holdings, Inc. [*Associated Press*] (SAG) .... Acrody
Acrokeratoelastoidosis (DMAA) .... AKE
Acrolect (ABBR) .... ACROL
Acromioclavicular [*Joint*] [*Medicine*] (DHSM) .... AC
Acromioclavicular Joint [*Anatomy*] (DAVI) .... ACJ
Acromioclavicular Line [*Anatomy*] (DAVI) .... ACL
Acronym (ABBR) .... ACRNM
Acronym (WDAA) .... ACRON
Acronym Data Base [*Defunct*] .... ACRODABA
[*The*] **Acronym Generator** [*An RCA computer program*] .... TAG
[*The*] **Acronym Generator Converter Program** [*RCA computer program*] (IAA) .... TCP
[*The*] **Acronym Generator Reference** [*RCA computer program*] (IAA) .... TAREF
Acronym May Be Ignored Totally [*Computer science*] (CSR) .... AMBIT/L
Acronym Production Particularly at Lavish Level Is No Good [*Term coined by Theodore M. Bernstein*] .... APPALLING
Acronym-Oriented Nut .... ACORN
Acronyms and Initialisms Dictionary [*Later, AIAD*] [*A publication*] .... AID
Acronyms in Moderation [*Term coined by Ralph Slovenko*] .... AIM
Acronyms, Initialisms, and Abbreviations Dictionary [*Formerly, AID*] [*A publication*] .... AIAD
Acronyms, Initials, and Abbreviations (DAVI) .... AIA
Acro-Osteolysis [*Medicine*] .... AOL
Acrophobe [*or Acrophobia*] (ABBR) .... ACRO
Acrophobia (ABBR) .... ACPHOB
Acropolis (VRA) .... acrpl
Acrorenal Field Defect, Ectodermal Dysplasia, Lipoatrophic Diabetes [*Medicine*] (DMAA) .... AREDYLD
Across .... ACR
Across (MSA) .... ACR
Across (BARN) .... acrs
Across Data Systems [*NASDAQ symbol*] (TTSB) .... ACRS
Across Data Systems, Inc. [*Associated Press*] (SAG) .... Across
Across Data Systems, Inc. [*NASDAQ symbol*] (SAG) .... ACRS
Across Flats .... ACRFLT
Across Flats .... AF
Across Shoulder (WDMC) .... XS
Across Tape [*Curve*] .... AT
Across the Board .... ATB
Across the Fence [*Real estate*] (DICI) .... ATF
Acrostic (ABBR) .... ACROS
Acroteria (VRA) .... acrt
Acryl Group [*Organic chemistry*] (DAVI) .... Ac
Acrylamide Bis-Acrylamide .... ACRYL-BIS
Acrylamide Gel Electrophoresis (MAE) .... AGE
Acrylamide Producers Association (EA) .... APA
Acrylamidomethylbutyl Trimethylammonium Chloride [*Organic chemistry*] .... AMBTAC
(Acrylamido)methylpropanesulfonic Acid [*Trademark of Lubrizol*] [*Organic chemistry*] .... AMPS
Acrylate-Butadiene Rubber .... ABR
Acrylic [*Organic chemistry*] .... Acr
Acrylic .... ACRY
Acrylic (MSA) .... ACRYL
Acrylic Acid [*Organic chemistry*] .... AA
Acrylic Eye Illustrator [*Medicine*] .... AEI
Acrylic on Canvas (VRA) .... ac/c
Acrylic Styrene [*Plastics technology*] .... AS
Acrylic-Styrene-Acrylonitrile [*Organic chemistry*] .... ASA
Acrylonitrile [*Organic chemistry*] .... ACN
Acrylonitrile [*Organic chemistry*] .... AN
Acrylonitrile/Butadiene [*Organic chemistry*] .... AC/BD
Acrylonitrile Butadiene Alternating Copolymer Rubber (PDAA) .... ABACR
Acrylonitrile Ethylene Styrene [*Organic chemistry*] .... AES
[*The*] **Acrylonitrile Group** (EA) .... TAG
Acrylonitrile Methyl Methacrylate [*Organic chemistry*] .... AMMA
Acrylonitrile Styrene Acrylate [*Plastics*] [*Organic chemistry*] .... ASA
Acrylonitrile-Butadiene [*Organic chemistry*] .... AB
Acrylonitrile-Butadiene-Acrylate [*Organic chemistry*] .... ABA
Acrylonitrile-Butadiene-Styrene [*Organic chemistry*] .... ABS
Acrylonitrile-Butadiene-Styrene and Styrene-Acrylonitrile [*Organic chemistry*] (ERG) .... ABS/SAN
Acrylonitrile-Styrene-Acrylate .... ASA
Acryloyloxyethyl N-Methylcarbamate [*Organic chemistry*] .... AEMC
ACS Biblio-information, Inc., Brossard, Quebec [*Library symbol National Library of Canada*] (BIB) .... QBRA
ACSE [*Association Control Service Element*]-Associate-Request [*Telecommunications*] (OSI) .... AARE
ACSE [*Association Control Service Element*]-Associate-Request [*Telecommunications*] (OSI) .... AARQ
Act Day [*Financial Services*] [*British*] .... A-(Day)
Act Environment Protection [*Alligator Rivers Region*] [*Act 1978*] [*Commonwealth*] (EERA) .... EP (ARR)
Act for Better Child Care Services .... ABC
Act in Crisis Today [*Fund sponsored by the Lutheran Church in America*] .... ACT
Act Inside the Army [*European antiwar group*] .... AITA
ACT Manufacturing [*NASDAQ symbol*] (TTSB) .... ACTM
ACT Manufacturing, Inc. [*Associated Press*] (SAG) .... ACT Mf
ACT Manufacturing, Inc. [*NASDAQ symbol*] (SAG) .... ACTM
ACT Networks [*NASDAQ symbol*] (TTSB) .... ANET
ACT Networks, Inc. [*Associated Press*] (SAG) .... ACT Net
ACT Networks, Inc. [*NASDAQ symbol*] (SAG) .... ANET
Act of Sederunt (DLA) .... Act of Sed
Act of Sederunt (DLA) .... AS
Act Teleconferencing [*NASDAQ symbol*] (TTSB) .... ACTT
Act Teleconferencing, Inc. [*NASDAQ symbol*] (SAG) .... ACTT
Act Teleconferencing, Inc. [*Associated Press*] (SAG) .... ActTele
Act Teleconferencing Unit [*NASDAQ symbol*] (TTSB) .... ACTTU
Act Teleconferencing Wrrt [*NASDAQ symbol*] (TTSB) .... ACTTW
Act Together [*Defunct*] (EA) .... AT
Acta Cancellariae [*England*] [*A publication*] (DLA) .... Monro
Acta Cancellariae, by Monroe [*England*] [*A publication*] (DLA) .... Act Can
Acta Dominorum Concilii [*3 vols.*] [*1839-1943 Scotland*] [*A publication*] (DLA) .... ADC
Acta Juridica [*South Africa*] [*A publication*] (ILCA) .... AJ
Acta Sanctorum [*Acts of the Saints*] [*Latin*] .... ASS
Acted (ABBR) .... ACTD
Actel Corp. [*Associated Press*] (SAG) .... Actel
Actel Corp. [*NASDAQ symbol*] (SAG) .... ACTL
Actifed [*Burroughs-Wellness, Inc.*] [*Pharmacology*] (DAVI) .... ACTIFD
Actin [*Muscle physiology*] .... A
Actin-Binding Protein [*Cytology*] .... ABP
Acting .... A
Acting (ROG) .... AC
Acting .... ACT
Acting (AFM) .... ACTG
Acting (ADA) .... AG
Acting Air Vice-Marshal [*British*] (DAS) .... AAVM
Acting Air-Marshal [*British*] .... AAM
Acting Appointment .... AA
Acting Assistant Adjutant-General [*Military British*] (ROG) .... AAAG
Acting Assistant Quartermaster [*Marine Corps*] .... AAQM
Acting Commissary General of Subsistence [*Army*] .... ACGS
Acting Commissary of Subsistence .... ACS
Acting Fort Major [*Military British*] (ROG) .... AFM
Acting Grand Master [*Freemasonry*] .... AGM
Acting Judge (ADA) .... AJ
Acting Justice (ADA) .... AJ
Acting Lieutenant [*Navy British*] .... A/L
Acting Pay Clerk [*Navy*] .... ACTPC
Acting Paymaster Sub-Lieutenant [*Navy British*] .... APSL

Acting Petty Officer Air Mechanic [*British military*] (DMA) .... APOAM
Acting Pilot Officer [*British*] .... APO
Acting Secretary (BARN) .... Actg Sec
Acting Secretary of Defense (SAA) .... ACTSECDEF
Acting Secretary of the Navy .... ACTSECNAV
Acting Sergeant-Major [*Military*] (WDAA) .... ASM
Acting Sub-Lieutenant [*Navy British*] .... ASL
Acting Sub-Lieutenant [*Canadian*] .... ASLT
Acting Transportation Officer .... ATRO
Acting Wing-Commander [*British*] .... AWC
Actinic Keratosis [*Ophthalmology*] (DAVI) .... AK
Actinic Reticuloid Syndrome [*Medicine*] (DMAA) .... AR
Actinide Nitride-Fueled Reactor (NRCH) .... ANF
Actinidin .... ACT
Actinium [*Chemical element*] .... Ac
Actinium Emanation [*Chemistry*] (MAE) .... ACE
Actinium Emanation [*Chemistry*] (IAA) .... ACEM
Actinomyces (MAE) .... A
Actinomycin [*Also, act*] [*Antibiotic compound*] .... A
Actinomycin [*Also, A*] [*Generic form Antibiotic compounds*] .... act
Actinomycin D [*Medicine*] (DMAA) .... ACD
Actinomycin D, Bleomycin, Vincristine [*Antineoplastic drug regimen*] .... ABV
Actinomycin D, Fluorouracil, Cyclophosphamide [*Antineoplastic drug regimen*] .... ACFUCY
Actinomycin D, Vincristine, Cisplatin [*Antineoplastic drug regimen*] (DAVI) .... AVP-II
Actinomycin D, Vincristine, Platinol [*Cisplatin*] [*Antineoplastic drug regimen*] .... AVP
Actinomycin Dactinomycin [*Antineoplastic drug regimen*] (DAVI) .... ACTIN-D
Actinomycin-C [*Antineoplastic drug*] .... act-C
Actinomycin-D [*Also, AMD, DACT*] [*Antineoplastic drug*] .... act-D
Actinomycin-D [*Also, act-D, DACT*] [*Antineoplastic drug*] .... AMD
Actinomycin-D [*Also, act-D, DACT*] [*Antineoplastic drug*] .... AMD
Actinomycin-D, Dacarbazine, Vincristine [*Antineoplastic drug regimen*] .... ADV
Actinon (MAE) .... An
Action .... A
Action [*NATO*] .... ACT
Action .... ACTN
Action .... ACTN
Action Against Allergy [*British*] (EAIO) .... AAA
Action Against Armageddon Project [*Defunct*] (EA) .... AAAP
Action Against Burns [*Formerly, APBIC*] (EA) .... AAB
Action and/or Reply [*Control system*] .... A/R
Action and Reply Notice (SAA) .... ARN
Action Bell Canada .... ABC
Action by Christians Against Torture (EAIO) .... ACT
Action by the Community Relating to the Environment [*EC*] (ECED) .... ACE
Action Canada Network [*Coalition formed in 1987 opposed to free trade*] (CROSS) .... ACN
Action Center for Educational Service and Scholarships .... ACCESS
Action Change Card .... ACC
Action Chretienne pour l'Eglise du Silence [*Belgium*] .... ACES
Action Civile [*Civil Action*] [*French*] (ILCA) .... AC
Action Committee Against Narcotics .... ACAN
Action Committee for a United States of Europe [*EC*] (ECED) .... ACUSE
Action Committee for Higher Education [*Defunct*] (EA) .... ACHE
Action Committee for Narcotics Education and Enforcement .... ACNEE
Action Committee for Rural Electrification (EA) .... ACRE
Action Committee of Public Transport of the European Communities GG2 [*See also CATPCE*] (EAIO) .... ACPTEC
Action Committee on American-Arab Relations [*Later, AARC*] .... ACAAR
Action Congress Party [*Ghana*] [*Political party*] (PPW) .... ACP
Action Control Number [*Army*] (MCD) .... ACN
Action Control Point [*Telecommunications*] .... ACP
ACTION Cooperative Volunteer Program .... ACV
Action Coordinating Committee to End Segregation in the Suburbs .... ACCESS
Action Coordinating Council for Comprehensive Child Care .... ACC-CCC
Action Council of Regional Dissemination Directors .... ACORDD
Action Current Potential (IAA) .... ACP
Action Cut-Out .... ACO
Action Data Automation [*British*] (NATG) .... ADA
Action Data Automation Language [*Computer science*] (MHDB) .... ADAL
Action Data Automation - Small (SAA) .... ADA-S
Action Data Automation Weapons System (MCD) .... ADAWS
Action Data Network (MCD) .... ADNET
Action Decision [*or Determination*] **Taken** .... ADTAKE
Action Democratique Guyanaise [*French Guiana*] [*Political party*] (EY) .... ADG
Action des Chretiens pour l'Abolition de la Torture [*Action by Christians for the Abolition of Torture*] (EAIO) .... ACAT
Action Directe [*Direct Action*] [*Terrorist group*] [*French*] (PD) .... AD
Action Driver [*Computer science*] .... AD
ACTION Drug Prevention Program .... ADPP
Action d'Urgence Internationale [*International Emergency Action - IEA*] [*Paris, France*] (EAIO) .... AUI
Action Error Analysis [*Engineering*] .... AEA
Action for Better Living [*Defunct*] (EA) .... ABL
Action for Brain-Handicapped Children [*Defunct*] (EA) .... ABC
Action for Child Protection (EA) .... ACP
Action for Child Transportation Safety [*Defunct*] (EA) .... ACTS
Action for Children in Trouble (EA) .... ACT
Action for Children's Television [*Defunct*] (EA) .... ACT
Action for Children's Television .... AFCTV
Action for Development [*FAO*] [*United Nations*] .... AD
Action for Disabled Customers [*British Telecom*] .... ADC
Action for Dysphasic Adults [*British*] .... ADA
Action for Former Military Wives [*Later, NAFMW*] [*An association*] (EA) .... AFMW
Action for Independent Maturity [*Later, AARP*] .... AIM
Action for Industrial Recycling [*An association*] .... AIR
Action for Interracial Understanding [*Defunct*] (EA) .... AIU
Action for Life (EA) .... AL
Action for Non-Violence in Learning [*British*] (DI) .... ANVIL
Action for Nuclear Disarmament Education Fund (EA) .... ANDEF
Action for Prevention of Burn Injuries to Children [*Later, AAB*] (EA) .... APBIC
Action for Soviet Jewry (EA) .... ASJ
Action for Victims of Medical Accidents [*British*] [*An association*] (DBA) .... AVMA
Action from Ireland [*An association*] (EAIO) .... AFRI
Action Group [*United National Independence Party Alliance of Nigeria*] [*Political party*] .... AG
Action Group Against Harassment & Discrimination in the Workplace [*Groupe d'Action Contre le Harcelement et Discrimination au Travail*] [*Action Against Harassment*] (AC) .... AGAHD
Action Group on Immigration and Nationality [*British*] (DI) .... AGIN
Action in Distress [*British*] (DI) .... AID
Action Indus [*AMEX symbol*] (TTSB) .... ACZ
Action Industries [*AMEX symbol*] (SAG) .... ACZ
Action Industries, Inc. [*Associated Press*] (SAG) .... Action
Action Industries, Inc. [*AMEX symbol*] (SPSG) .... ACX
Action Information Control Officer [*Navy*] .... AICO
Action Information Display System .... AIDS
Action Information Operations Tactical Trainer (ADA) .... AIOTT
Action Information Organization .... AIO
Action Information Training Center .... AITC
Action International Ministries (EAIO) .... ACTION
Action Internationale Contre la Faim [*International Action Against Hunger*] [*Paris, France*] (EAIO) .... AICF
Action Internationale pour les Droits de l'Enfant [*International Action for the Rights of the Child - IARC*] [*Paris, France*] (EAIO) .... AIDE
Action Item (NASA) .... AI
Action Item Assignment (DNAB) .... AIA
Action Item Closeout Sheet (MCD) .... AICS
Action Item Control Card (MCD) .... AICC
Action Item Directive (AAG) .... AID
Action Item List (MCD) .... AIL
Action Item Report (NASA) .... AIR
Action Item Sheet (MCD) .... AIS
Action Item Tracking System [*Radiation measurement*] (NRCH) .... AITS
Action League of Physically Handicapped Adults [*Canada*] .... ALPHA
Action Learning (PDAA) .... AL
Action [*Indicator*] **Level** [*Radiation measurement*] (NRCH) .... AL
Action Library, Washington, DC [*OCLC symbol*] (OCLC) .... ACT
Action Linkage [*An association*] (EA) .... AL
Action Monegasque [*Monegasque Action*] [*Political party*] (PPE) .... AM
Action Nationale [*National Action for People and Homeland*] [*Switzerland Political party*] (PPE) .... AN
Action of Instant Recording [*Video technology*] .... AIR
Action Officer [*Army*] (AABC) .... ACTO
Action Officer [*Air Force*] (AFM) .... AO
Action on Alcohol Abuse [*British*] .... AAA
Action on Smoking and Health (EA) .... ASH
Action on Smoking and Health in Wales (EAIO) .... ASHW
Action on Smoking and Health - Northern Ireland (EAIO) .... ASH-NI
Action on Smoking and Health - Scotland (EAIO) .... ASH-S
Action Performance Companies [*NASDAQ symbol*] (SAG) .... ACTN
Action Performance Companies [*Associated Press*] (SAG) .... ActPerf
Action Performance Cos. [*NASDAQ symbol*] (TTSB) .... ACTN
Action Potential [*of auditory nerve*] .... AP
Action Potential Amplitude [*Physiology*] .... APA
Action Potential Duration [*Electrophysiology*] .... APD
Action pour la Renaissance de Corse [*Action for the Rebirth of Corsica*] [*French*] .... ARC
Action Print Only [*Cinematography*] (WDMC) .... APO
Action Products International, Inc. [*Associated Press*] (SAG) .... ActnPr
Action Products International, Inc. [*NASDAQ symbol*] (NQ) .... APII
Action Products Intl. [*NASDAQ symbol*] (TTSB) .... APII
Action Program for Women .... APW
Action Public Library, Action, ON, Canada [*Library symbol Library of Congress*] (LCLS) .... CaOAc
Action Register .... AR
Action Republicaine et Sociale [*Republican and Social Action*] [*France Political party*] (PPE) .... ARS
Action Research into Multiple Sclerosis [*See also Arms of America - AA*] [*British*] .... ARMS
Action Research Model [*Program of Keep America Beautiful, Inc.*] .... ARM
Action Resource Centre [*British*] (CB) .... ARC
Action Revolutionnaire Corse [*Corsican Revolutionary Action*] (PD) .... ARC
Action Sociale Tchadienne [*Chadian Social Action*] .... AST
Action Socialiste [*Socialist Action*] [*Congo*] .... AS
Action Socialiste Congolaise [*Congolese Socialist Action*] .... ASC
Action Speed Tactical .... AST
Action Speed Tactical Trainer (SAA) .... ASTT
Action Sports Entertainment Cable [*Cable TV programming service*] .... ASEC
Action Surveys, Inc. [*Information service or system*] (IID) .... ASI
Action Table Print (SAA) .... ATP
Action Taken .... AT
Action Taken Code (MCD) .... ATC
Action Technical Order .... ATO
Action through Creative Organization, Research, and Discussion [*An association*] (EA) .... ACORD
Action Time [*Air Force*] .... A/T
Action Tracking System [*Environmental Protection Agency*] (GFGA) .... ATS

Action Training Coalition [*Defunct*] (EA) ... ATC
Action Variable [*Physics*] (BARN) ... J
Action Volunteers for Animals (AC) ... AVA
Action Will Be Cancelled (NOAA) ... ACWCN
Actionable (ABBR) ... ACTNB
ActionAid [*British*] (EAIO) ... AA
Action-Centered Leadership [*Management term*] ... ACL
Action-Chart Diagramer [*Computer science*] ... ACD
Actions Having Significant Personnel Implications (MCD) ... AHSPI
Actions per Time Interval ... APTI
Action-Study Center for a Governed World [*Defunct*] (EA) ... ASCGW
Activate (AFM) ... ACTV
Activate (ABBR) ... ACTVA
Activate (MSA) ... ACTVT
Activate Logical Unit [*IBM Co.*] (ACRL) ... ACTLU
Activate Physical Unit [*IBM Co.*] (ACRL) ... ACTPU
Activate Test Article [*Military*] (NASA) ... ACTA
Activated (ABBR) ... ACTVAD
Activated (ABBR) ... ACTVTD
Activated Carbon ... AC
Activated Carbon Fiber ... ACF
Activated Carbon Treatment System (MCD) ... ACTS
Activated Carbons Producers' Association [*European Council of Chemical Manufacturers Federations*] [*Brussels, Belgium*] (EAIO) ... ACPA
Activated Charcoal Granule (PDAA) ... ACG
Activated Clotting [*or Coagulation*] **Time** [*Medicine*] ... ACT
Activated Clotting Time for Dactinomycin [*Clinical medicine*] ... ACT-D
Activated Dough Development (OA) ... ADD
Activated/Non-Activated [*Cytology*] ... A/NA
Activated Partial Thromboplastin Time [*Hematology*] ... APTT
Activated Partial Thromboplastin Time, Control [*Hematology*] (DAVI) ... PTT-CT
Activated Protein C ... APC
Activated Reactive Evaporation [*Coating technology*] ... ARE
Activated Sludge Process ... ASP
Activated Thymus Cell [*s*] [*Immunochemistry*] ... ATC
Activating (ABBR) ... ACTVAG
Activating (ABBR) ... ACTVTG
Activating Event [*or Experience*], Belief System, Consequence [*Irrational behavior theory*] [*Psychotherapy*] ... ABC
Activating Factor [*Biochemistry*] ... AF
Activating Transcription Factors [*Genetics*] ... ATF
Activation (NVT) ... ACT
Activation (NASA) ... ACTIV
Activation (ABBR) ... ACTVAN
Activation (ABBR) ... ACTVTN
Activation Acceptance Team [*NASA*] (NASA) ... AAT
Activation Analysis [*Chemistry*] ... AA
Activation Analysis (MSA) ... ACTVNANAL
Activation Analysis Unit [*British*] ... AAU
Activation Ballistic Missile Site (SAA) ... ABMS
Activation Coefficient ... AC
Activation/Conversion (DNAB) ... ACT/CONV
Activation Domain [*Biochemistry*] ... AD
Activation Energy (MAE) ... AE
Activation Engineering Information Bulletin (AAG) ... AEIB
Activation Management Group [*NASA*] (NASA) ... AMG
Activation Project Control Plan ... APCP
Activation Sequence Factor [*Genetics*] ... ASF
Activation Test Program (MCD) ... ATP
Activation Work Notice ... AWN
Activation Working Group [*Military*] (MCD) ... AWG
Activation-Induced Cell Death [*Immunology*] ... AICD
Activator [*Genetics*] ... AC
Activator (ABBR) ... ACTVOR
Activator (MSA) ... ACTVTR
Activator Protein ... AP
Activator-Dissociation System (DOG) ... Ac Ds System
Active (VRA) ... act
Active (AFM) ... ACT
Active (FAAC) ... ACTV
Active Acoustic Device ... AAD
Active Acquisition Aid ... AAA
Active Aero Charter [*FAA designator*] (FAAC) ... JUS
Active Air Defence [*British World War II*] ... AA
Active Air Target Fuse (MCD) ... AATF
Active Airborne Expendable Decoy ... AAED
Active Aircraft Plume Suppression (MCD) ... AAPS
Active Alkali [*Chemistry*] ... AA
Active Antenna Array (MCD) ... AAA
Active Apparel Group [*NASDAQ symbol*] (TTSB) ... AAGP
Active Apparel Group, Inc. [*NASDAQ symbol*] (SAG) ... AAGP
Active Apparel Group, Inc. [*Associated Press*] (SAG) ... ActApp
Active Arm External Load Stabilization System [*Army*] ... AAELSS
Active Army ... AA
Active Army Locator System (AABC) ... AALS
Active Army Military Manpower Program ... AAMMP
Active Army Personnel Reporting System [*Europe*] (MCD) ... AAPERS
Active Assertive Range of Motion [*Medicine*] (DMAA) ... AAROM
Active Assets ... AA
Active Assisted (HGAA) ... AA
Active Assistive Exercise [*Medicine*] ... AAE
Active Assistive Range of Motion [*Medicine*] ... AAROM
Active Attached Reserve [*Military*] ... AA
Active Attached Reserve [*Royal Australian Naval Reserve*] ... AAR
Active Avoidance [*Medicine*] (DMAA) ... AA
Active Avoidance Reaction [*Medicine*] (DMAA) ... AAR
Active Band-Pass [*Electronics*] (IAA) ... ABP
Active Beacon Collision Avoidance System [*Aviation*] (DA) ... A-BCAS
Active Bilaterally (HGAA) ... ab
Active Bioprosthetic Composition [*Artificial ligament*] ... ABC
Active Body Control [*Automotive engineering*] ... ABC
Active Body Control ... ABC
Active Boom Suspension [*Engineering*] ... ABS
Active Business Records [*Bell & Howell Co.*] ... ABR
Active Capital [*Investment term*] ... AC
Active Cavity Radiometer ... ACR
Active Cavity Radiometer Irradiance Monitor ... ACRIM
Active Certificate Information Program [*for stock certificates*] [*Computer science*] ... ACIP
Active Chronic Hepatitis [*Medicine*] (DMAA) ... ACH
Active Cirrhosis [*Medicine*] ... AC
Active Citizen Force [*British military*] (DMA) ... ACF
Active Citizenship Campaign ... ACC
Active Cleaning Technique [*Optical surface*] ... ACT
Active Clearance Control (PDAA) ... ACC
Active Color Enhancement [*Proxima Corp.*] [*Computer science*] (PCM) ... ACE
Active Commission Base Date [*Military*] ... ACBD
Active Communications Satellite ... ACS
Active Component ... AC
Active Components and Reserve Components ... AC & RC
Active Contamination Control Subsystem (SSD) ... ACCS
Active Contract Data Review Board [*Air Force*] (AFIT) ... ACDRB
Active Contract File [*DoD*] ... ACF
Active Contrast Reduction System (MCD) ... ACRS
Active Control Device (SSD) ... ACD
Active Control for Total In-Flight Simulator (MCD) ... ACTIFS
Active Control of Space Structures ... ACOSS
Active Control Technique [*or Technology*] ... ACT
Active Control Torque System [*Automotive engineering*] (PS) ... ACTS
Active Corps of Executives [*Maintained by the Service Corps of Retired Executives Association*] ... ACE
Active Correlation Track-on-Jam ... ACTOJ
Active Countermeasures ... ACM
Active Deferral Service (MCD) ... ADS
Active Delayed Phase Shift (IAA) ... ADPS
Active Diffusion Control (MCD) ... ADC
Active Directory Service Interface [*Computer science*] ... ADSI
Active Disk Table [*Computer science*] (IBMDP) ... ADT
Active Dosimeter ... AD
Active Duty ... ACDU
Active Duty (DNAB) ... ACTDU
Active Duty ... AD
Active Duty Agreement ... ADA
Active Duty Assistance Program (DNAB) ... ADAP
Active Duty Assistance Program Team ... ADAPT
Active Duty Base Date [*Later, PSD*] [*Navy*] ... ADBD
Active Duty Commitment ... ADC
Active Duty Dates of Rank [*Army*] (INF) ... ADOR
Active Duty for Training [*Army*] (MCD) ... ACDUTRA
Active Duty for Training [*Army*] (AABC) ... ADT
Active Duty in a Flying Status, Involving Operational or Training Flights [*Navy*] (DNAB) ... ACDIFOPS
Active Duty in a Flying Status, Involving Proficiency in Flying [*Navy*] (DNAB) ... ACDIFPRO
Active Duty in a Flying Status, Not Involving Flying [*Navy*] (DNAB) ... ACDIFDEN
Active Duty in a Flying Status, Operational and Training Flights [*Navy*] ... ACDIFOT
Active Duty in a Flying Status, Operational and Training Flights as Crewmember [*Navy*] ... ACDIFOTCREW
Active Duty in a Flying Status, Operational and Training Flights as Noncrewmember [*Navy*] ... ACDIFOTNONCREW
Active Duty List [*Army*] (INF) ... ADL
Active Duty Nondisability Retirement Branch [*BUPERS*] [*Navy*] ... ANDRB
Active Duty Obligation [*DoD*] ... ACDUOBLI
Active Duty Service Commitment [*Military*] (AFM) ... ADSC
Active Duty Service Date [*Military*] (DNAB) ... ADSD
Active Duty under Instruction [*Navy*] ... ACDUINS
Active Duty under Instruction in a Flying Status, Involving Operational or Training Flights [*Navy*] (DNAB) ... ACDIFINOPS
Active Duty under Instruction in a Flying Status, Involving Proficiency Flying [*Navy*] (DNAB) ... ACDIFINSPRO
Active Duty under Instruction in a Flying Status, Not Involving Flying [*Navy*] (DNAB) ... ACDIFDENIS
Active Duty under Instruction in a Flying Status, Operational and Training Flights [*Navy*] ... ACDIFOTINS
Active Duty under Instruction in a Flying Status, Operational and Training Flights as Crewmember [*Navy*] ... ACDIFOTINSCREW
Active Duty under Instruction in a Flying Status, Operational and Training Flights as Noncrewmember [*Navy*] ... ACDIFOTINSNONCREW
Active Electromagnetic System [*Electronics*] (IAA) ... AES
Active Electronic Buoy (DWSG) ... AEB
Active Electronic Counter-Measure (PDAA) ... AECM
Active Electronic Decoy (CAAL) ... AED
Active Electronic Gimballess Inertial System ... AEGIS
Active Element Array ... AEA
Active Element Group [*QCR*] ... AEG
Active Employment Strategy ... AES
Active Employment Training Organization ... AETO
Active Engine Mount [*Automotive engineering*] ... AEM
Active Enhancement (MCD) ... AE

Active Enlisted Plans Branch [BUPERS] .... AEPB
Active Exercise [Rehabilitation] (DAVI) .... Act Ex
Active Federal Commissioned Service .... AFCS
Active Federal Service (DOMA) .... AFS
Active File Table [Computer science] (IBMDP) .... AFT
Active Filter Design .... AFD
Active Filter Network .... AFN
Active Flight Load System (MCD) .... AFLS
Active Fuel Length [Nuclear energy] (NRCH) .... AFL
Active Fuzing System .... AFS
Active Galactic Nucleus [Astronomy] .... AGN
Active Guard and Reserve [Military] (DOMA) .... AGR
Active Guard Reserve [DoD] .... AGR
Active High Resolution (MCD) .... AHR
Active History File [Army] .... AHF
Active Hostility Index [Psychology] .... AHI
Active Imaging Pointer-Tracker System (MCD) .... AIPTS
Active in Commission [Vessel status] [Navy] .... ACT/IC
Active in Service [Vessel status] [Navy] .... ACT/IS
Active Inert Missile .... AIM
Active Ingredient .... AI
Active Integral Defense (AFM) .... AID
Active Integrated Module .... AIM
Active Isolation/Balance System [for aircraft] (RDA) .... AIBS
Active Lane Control [Image control and lane positioning] [Automotive engineering] .... ALC
Active LASER Seeker (MCD) .... ALS
Active Lift Distribution Control System [Aerospace] .... ALDCS
Active Line Rotation [Telecommunications] (TEL) .... ALR
Active Low-Light-Level Television [Night vision device] [Air Force] (MCD) .... ALLTV
Active Magnetic Bearing [Mechanical engineering] .... AMB
Active Magnetospheric Particle Tracer Explorer [Project] [NASA/West Germany] .... AMPTE
Active Maintenance Downtime .... AMDT
Active Maintenance Time .... AMT
Active Maintenance Training Simulator [Military] .... AMTS
Active Mariner Program [Military] (DNAB) .... A-M
Active Market [Investment term] .... AM
Active Matrix Electroluminescent (RDA) .... AMEL
Active Matrix Liquid Crystal Display .... AMLCD
Active Medium Propagation [Amplifier] .... AMP
Active Memory Technology (ECON) .... AMT
Active Mesospheric Particle Tracer Explorer (MCD) .... AMPTE
Active Microwave Instrument .... AMI
Active Microwave Workshop .... AMW
Active Monitor [Telecommunications] .... AM
Active Monitor Present (ACRL) .... AMP
Active Name Table (HGAA) .... ANT
Active Network Synthesis .... ANS
Active Night Covert Viewing [or Vision] System .... ANCOVS
Active Noise Control [Noise pollution technique] .... ANC
Active Noise Control .... ANC
Active Noise Reduction (MCD) .... ANR
Active Nutation Control .... ANC
Active Nutation Damper .... AND
Active Nutation Damper Electronics .... ANDE
Active Officer Promotion Branch [BUPERS] .... AOPB
Active on Target .... AOT
Active Optical Fuze .... AOF
Active Optical Fuzing System .... AOFS
Active Optical Sensor (MCD) .... AOS
Active Optical Target Detector (NVT) .... AOTD
Active Optical Target Housing (MCD) .... AOTH
Active Optics Simulation Program [NASA] (KSC) .... AOSP
Active Optics Simulation System [NASA] .... AOSS
Active out of Commission [Vessel status] [Navy] .... ACT/OC
Active out of Service [Vessel status] [Navy] .... ACT/OS
Active Oxygen Method [Food fat stability test] .... AOM
Active Oxygen Species [Biochemistry] .... AOS
Active Page Register [Computer science] (MHDI) .... APR
Active Participation Rental Real Estate [IRS] .... APRRE
Active Pass, BC [ICAO location identifier] (ICLI) .... CUAP
Active/Passive Reliable Acoustic Path SONAR (MCD) .... APRAPS
Active Personnel Dosimeter .... APD
Active Protection System [Military] (INF) .... APS
Active Pulse Compression Network .... APCN
Active Purchase Request File [DoD] .... APRF
Active RADAR Augmentor Beacon System (MCD) .... ARABS
Active RADAR Seeker .... ARS
Active RADAR Test System (MCD) .... ARTS
Active Range (MCD) .... AR
Active Range of Motion [Medicine] .... AROM
Active Range of the Day (MCD) .... ARD
Active Reconnaissance Zone .... ARZ
Active Recording Program (SAA) .... ARP
Active Records/Fiche-Oriented Retrieval (DNAB) .... AR/FOR
Active Reduction of Contrast .... ARC
Active Reference Table (HGAA) .... ART
Active Relaxed Static Stability (MCD) .... ARSS
Active Repeater Satellite [Air Force] .... ARS
Active Requisition Control and Status File [DoD] .... ARCSF
Active Resistance [Occupational therapy] .... AR
Active Resistive Exercise .... ARE
Active Responsive Factor [Biochemistry] .... ARF

Active Rest Point (IAA) .... ARP
Active Retirees in Israel [An association] .... ARI
Active Retrodirective Array (MCD) .... ARA
Active Roll Stabilization [Automotive suspension] .... ARS
Active Satellite Attitude Control .... ASAC
Active Scattering Aerosol Spectrometer [Aerosol measurement device] .... ASAS
Active Scattering Aerosol Spectrometer Probe (MCD) .... ASASP
Active Security [Investment term] .... AS
Active Segment Field [Computer science] (MHDI) .... ASF
Active Segment Table (HGAA) .... AST
Active Seismic Experiment [NASA] (MCD) .... ASE
Active Server Page [Computer science] .... ASP
Active Server Page [Microsoft Corp.] .... ASP
Active Service Base Date (DNAB) .... ASBD
Active Service Career for Reserve Officers .... ASCRO
Active Service Unit [Irish Republican Army] [Northern Ireland] .... ASU
Active Signal Correction [Video technology] .... ASC
Active Singles Quest [Technique] [In book title] .... ASQ
Active Site Peptide [Immunochemistry] .... ASP
Active Sleep [Physiology] .... AS
Active Sodium Transport Inhibitor [Biochemistry] .... ASTI
Active SONAR Frequency Analysis and Recording .... ASFAR
Active SONAR Processor .... ASP
Active Spacecraft Potential Control [Instrumentation] .... ASPOC
Active Status Register .... ASR
Active Streaming Format [Computer science] .... ASF
Active Surface Area (MCD) .... ASA
Active Swept-Frequency Interferometer RADAR [RADC] .... ASFIR
Active Task List [Computer science] (MHDI) .... ATL
Active Television System (MCD) .... ATS
Active Test Article (MCD) .... ACTA
Active Thermal Control .... ATC
Active Thermal Control Subsystem [NASA] (MCD) .... ATCS
Active Thermal Control System [NASA] (MCD) .... ACTCS
Active Thermal Feedback (PCM) .... ATF
Active Thermal Protection for Avionics Crew and Heat-Sensitive Equipment [Air Force] (MCD) .... APACHE
Active Thermo-Atmosphere Combustion (PDAA) .... ATAC
Active Thermo-Atmosphere Combustion .... ATAC
Active Time List [Computer science] .... ATL
Active Token Collectors Organization (EA) .... ATCO
Active Torque Transfer System .... ATTS
Active Training [Army] .... AT
Active Transfer and Conversion, Army .... ATCAR
Active Transfer Command .... ATC
Active Tuition Assistance Plan [UAW-General Motors Corp.] .... ATAP
Active Unattached Reserve [Royal Australian Navy] .... AUR
Active Universal Joints .... AUJ
Active Valve Train [Automotive engineering] .... AVT
Active Vibration Isolation System .... AVIS
Active Vibration Isolator (MCD) .... AVI
Active Voice [NASDAQ symbol] (TTSB) .... ACVC
Active Voice Corp. [Associated Press] (SAG) .... ActVoic
Active Voice Corp. [NASDAQ symbol] (SAG) .... ACVC
Active Well Coincidence Counter [Nuclear energy] (NRCH) .... AWCC
Active Work Space [Computer science] (NITA) .... AWS
Active Zone .... AZ
Active-Assistive [Range of motion] [Orthopedics] (DAVI) .... AA
Active-Gated Television (PDAA) .... AGTV
Actively (ABBR) .... ACTVY
Actively Shared Knowledge [Data processing system] .... ASK
Activeness (ABBR) .... ACTVNS
Active-Retired Lighthouse Service Employees' Association (EA) .... ARLSEA
ActiveX Data Objects [Computer science] .... ADO
ActiveX Data Objects [Computer science] .... ADO
Activin [Biochemistry] .... ATV
Activin Responsive Element [Biochemistry] .... ARE
Activision, Inc. [Associated Press] (SAG) .... Activisn
Activision, Inc. [NASDAQ symbol] (SAG) .... ATVI
Activists for Protective Animal Legislation (EA) .... A-PAL
Activities Committee on New Directions for ALA [American Library Association] .... ACONDA
Activities File [CSIRO database] (ADA) .... ACTF
Activities Implemented Jointly [Between nations] .... AIJ
Activities Integrating Math and Science .... AIMS
Activities of Daily Living (WYGK) .... ADL
Activities of Daily Living .... ADL
Activities of Daily Living [Medicine] .... ADL
Activities Report [Shipping] .... ACTREP
Activity .... A
Activity (WDAA) .... AC
Activity (MSA) .... ACT
Activity (ABBR) .... ACTIV
Activity (AABC) .... ACTV
Activity .... ACTVTY
Activity .... ACTVTY
Activity (AFM) .... ACTY
Activity Account .... AA
Activity Accreditation Schedule (MCD) .... AAS
Activity Address Code [DoD] .... AAC
Activity Automatic Data Process Security Plan (MCD) .... AADPSP
Activity Balance Line Evaluation [PERT] .... ABLE
Activity Based Costing [Financial management] .... ABC
Activity Captain (MCD) .... AC
Activity Career Program Manager [Military] .... ACPM

Activity Characteristics Sheet [*Agency for International Development*] ... ACS

Activity Civil Engineer (DNAB) ... ACE

Activity Classification Number [*NASA*] (GFGA) ... ACN

Activity Code [*DoD*] ... AC

Activity Completion Technique [*Personality development test*] [*Psychology*] ... ACT

Activity Control Number ... ACM

Activity Control Number [*Navy*] ... ACN

Activity Credit Unit (DNAB) ... ACU

Activity Data Method (IEEE) ... ADM

Activity Data Sheet (IEEE) ... ADS

Activity Elements (MCD) ... A/E

Activity Identification Code [*Navy*] ... AIC

Activity Index ... AI

Activity, Interest, and Opinion [*Factor scores*] [*Marketing*] ... AIO

Activity Level Dependent (KSC) ... ALD

Activity Level Dependent Operations (NASA) ... ALDO

Activity Level Independent (KSC) ... ALI

Activity Level Independent Operations (NASA) ... ALIO

Activity Median Aerodynamic Diameter ... AMAD

Activity Metabolic Rate ... AMR

Activity Mission Code (DNAB) ... AMC

Activity Operating Schedule ... AOS

Activity Order and Shipping Quantity (AFIT) ... AOSQ

Activity Performing Inspection (SAA) ... API

Activity Processing Code ... APC

Activity Providing Telephone Service (DNAB) ... APTS

Activity Readiness Code (DNAB) ... ARC

Activity Reorder Point [*Military*] (AFIT) ... AROP

Activity Report (MCD) ... AR

Activity Reporting Information System (PDAA) ... ARIS

Activity Routing Indicator (MCD) ... ARI

Activity Safety Level (AFIT) ... ASL

Activity Scheduling Processor [*NASA*] ... ASP

Activity Scheduling Program [*NASA*] ... ASP

Activity Sections Council [*Association of College and Research Libraries*] ... ASC

Activity Support File (DNAB) ... ASF

Activity Test ... AT

Activity Therapy center ... ATC

Activity Time Status Report (MCD) ... ATSR

Activity Vector Analysis [*Psychology*] ... AVA

Activity-Based Cost [*Management accounting system*] ... ABC

Actoma Resources Ltd. [*Vancouver Stock Exchange symbol*] ... ATA

Actomyosin [*Biochemistry*] ... AM

Acton High School, Acton, ON, Canada [*Library symbol Library of Congress*] (LCLS) ... CaOAcH

Acton High School, Ontario [*Library symbol National Library of Canada*] (NLC) ... OACH

Acton, MA [*FM radio station call letters*] (RBYB) ... WHAB

Acton Public Library, Ontario [*Library symbol National Library of Canada*] (NLC) ... OAC

Acton Society [*British*] (EAIO) ... AS

Acton, TX [*Location identifier FAA*] (FAAL) ... AQN

Acton's Prize Cases, Privy Council [*A publication*] (DLA) ... Act

Acton's Prize Cases, Privy Council [*A publication*] (DLA) ... Acton

Acton's Reports, Prize Cases [*England*] [*A publication*] (DLA) ... Act Pr C

Actor ... ACTR

Actors and Others for Animals (EA) ... A & O

Actors' Benevolent Fund [*Australia*] ... ABF

Actors' Church Union [*Episcopalian*] ... ACU

Actor's Conservatory Theater ... ACT

Actors' Equity Association (EA) ... AEA

Actors' Equity of Australia ... AEA

Actors' Feature Film Award [*Australia*] ... AFFA

Actors' Fund of America (EA) ... AFA

Actors Studio (EA) ... AS

Actors Working for an Actors Guild (EA) ... AWAG

Actrade International Ltd. [*NASDAQ symbol*] (SAG) ... ACRT

Actrade International Ltd. [*Associated Press*] (SAG) ... Actrade

Actrade Intl Ltd. [*NASDAQ symbol*] (TTSB) ... ACRT

Actress (ABBR) ... ACTRE

Actress (ABBR) ... ACTRS

Actresses' Franchise League [*British*] ... AFL

Actron Microprocessor Softwear Support System (MCD) ... AMSSS

Acts and Joint Resolutions of the State of Iowa [*A publication*] (DLA) ... Iowa Acts

Acts and Joint Resolutions of the State of South Carolina [*A publication*] (DLA) ... SC Acts

Acts and Ordinances of the Interregnum [*1642-60*] [*British A publication*] (ILCA) ... Acts & Ords Interreg

Acts and Ordinances of the Interregnum [*1642-60*] [*United Kingdom*] [*A publication*] (DLA) ... Acts & Ords Interregnum

Acts and Resolves of Massachusetts [*A publication*] (DLA) ... Mass Acts

Acts of Alabama [*A publication*] (DLA) ... Ala Acts

Acts of Andrew (BJA) ... ActAndr

Acts of Indiana [*A publication*] (DLA) ... Ind Acts

Acts of John (BJA) ... ActJn

Acts of Lawting Court [*Scotland*] [*A publication*] (DLA) ... Act Lawt Ct

Acts of Lords Auditors of Causes [*Scotland*] [*A publication*] (DLA) ... Act Ld Aud C

Acts of Lords of Council in Civil Causes [*1478-1501*] [*Scotland*] [*A publication*] (DLA) ... Act Ld Co CC

Acts of Lords of Council in Public Affairs [*Scotland*] [*A publication*] (DLA) ... Act Ld Co Pub Aff

Acts of Paul (BJA) ... ActPaul

Acts of Peter (BJA) ... ActPet

Acts of the Apostles [*New Testament book*] (BJA) ... AA

Acts of the Apostles [*New Testament book*] (BJA) ... Ac

Acts of the Apostolic See ... AAS

Acts of the Australian Parliament [*A publication*] (ILCA) ... Acts Austl Parl

Acts of the Australian Parliament [*A publication*] (DLA) ... Austl Acts

Acts of the General Assembly, Church of Scotland [*1638-1842*] [*A publication*] (DLA) ... Act Ass

Acts of the General Assembly, Commonwealth of Virginia [*A publication*] (DLA) ... VA Acts

Acts of the Gods (BJA) ... AG

Acts of the Legislature of West Virginia [*A publication*] (DLA) ... W Va Acts

Acts of the Parliaments of Scotland ... APS

Acts of the Parliaments of Scotland (DLA) ... Scot Parl Acts

Acts of the Privy Council [*England*] [*A publication*] (DLA) ... PCA

Acts of the Privy Council, Colonial Series [*England*] [*A publication*] (DLA) ... Act Pr C Col S

Acts of the Privy Council, Colonial Series [*A publication*] (DLA) ... PCC

Acts of the Privy Council (Dasent) [*England*] [*A publication*] (DLA) ... Act PC

Acts of the Privy Council (Dasent) [*England*] [*A publication*] (DLA) ... Dasent

Acts of the Privy Council, New Series (Dasent) [*England*] [*A publication*] (DLA) ... Act PC NS

Acts, Resolves, and Constitutional Resolutions of the State of Maine [*A publication*] (DLA) ... ME Acts

Actual (ADA) ... A

Actual (KSC) ... ACT

Actual (MSA) ... ACTL

Actual Acquisition Cost ... AAC

Actual Availability (MCD) ... AA

Actual Block Processor [*IBM Corp.*] [*Computer science*] (BUR) ... ABP

Actual Body Weight (DAVI) ... ABW

Actual Bottom Time ... ABT

Actual Calculated Landing Time [*FAA*] (TAG) ... ACLT

Actual Cash Value [*Accounting*] ... ACV

Actual Completion Date of Activity [*Business term*] ... AA

Actual Cost [*Accounting*] ... AC

Actual Cost for Work Performed [*Accounting*] ... ACWP

Actual Cost Incurred [*Accounting*] (MCD) ... ACI

Actual Cost of Work Flow [*Accounting*] ... ACWF

Actual Cost Report (NASA) ... ACR

Actual Count (MHDI) ... AC

Actual Cubic Feet per Minute (NRCH) ... ACFM

Actual Current on Board (DNAB) ... ACOB

Actual Departure Time (CINC) ... ADT

Actual Development Cost Certification [*HUD*] ... ADCC

Actual Dive Time ... ADT

Actual Elapsed Time ... AET

Actual Equipment Trainer (MCD) ... AET

Actual Evapotranspiration [*Biology*] ... AET

Actual Expenses Allowable [*Military*] (AFM) ... AEA

Actual Exposure Time (MUGU) ... AET

Actual Gross Weight [*Railroads*] ... AGW

Actual Gross Weight (ODBW) ... agw

Actual Ground Zero [*Nuclear explosions*] ... AGZ

Actual Ground Zone (MUGU) ... AGZ

Actual Leaf Area [*Botany*] ... ALA

Actual Loss Ratio [*Insurance*] ... ALR

Actual Loss Sustained - No Specified Daily Indemnity [*Insurance*] ... ALS-NSDI

Actual Measured Loss [*Telecommunications*] (TEL) ... AML

Actual Measurement Weight [*Railroads*] ... AMW

Actual Mechanical Advantage [*Physics*] ... AMA

Actual Miss [*Distance*] ... AM

Actual Operating Time (MCD) ... AOT

Actual Production History Program ... APH

Actual Projected on Board [*Allowance*] (DNAB) ... APOB

Actual Range (IAA) ... AR

Actual Range Angle (IAA) ... ARA

Actual Ship Position ... ASP

Actual Test Number [*NASA*] ... ATN

Actual Time of Arrival ... ATA

Actual Time of Departure ... ATD

Actual Time of Fall ... ATF

Actual Time of Interception ... ATI

Actual Time of Penetration [*Aviation*] (FAAC) ... ATP

Actual Time of Refueling (SAA) ... ATR

Actual Time of Release [*Aviation*] ... ATRLS

Actual Time of Return to Operation (AFM) ... ATRO

Actual Time Over (MCD) ... ATO

Actual Time over Target (AFM) ... ATOT

Actual Total Loss ... ATL

Actual Unit Price [*Billing*] (MCD) ... AUP

Actual Value [*Business term*] (MHDB) ... Act Val

Actual Value ... AV

Actual Velocity ... AV

Actual Volume of the Lung [*Medicine*] (DAVI) ... V_L

Actual Weight [*Business term*] ... AW

Actual Weight [*Business term*] (ODBW) ... aw

Actual Weight Report ... AWR

Actual Wind Factor [*NWS*] (FAAC) ... ALWF

Actual Work Time [*Bell System*] ... AWT

Actual Working Pressure ... AWP

Actualite Juridique [*A publication*] (ILCA) ... AJ

Actuality (ABBR) ... ACTLT

Actualization (ABBR) ... ACTLZAN

Actualization (ABBR) ... ACTLZN

Actualize (ABBR) ... ACTLZ

Actualized (ABBR) ... ACTLZD
Actualizing (ABBR) ... ACTLZG
Actualizing Assessment Battery [*Personality development test*] [*Psychology*] ... AAB
Actually (ABBR) ... ACTLY
Actuarial ... ACTRL
Actuarial Common Claims File [*Health insurance*] (GHCT) ... ACCF
Actuarial Data Base [*I. P. Sharp Associates*] [*Database*] ... ACT
Actuarial Engine Life (AFIT) ... AEL
Actuarial Life Expectancy (AFIT) ... ALE
Actuarial Mail File [*IRS*] ... AMF
Actuarial Removal Interval (AFIT) ... ARI
Actuarial Science (DD) ... ActSc
Actuarial Society of America [*Later, SA*] ... ASA
Actuarial Studies in Non-Life Insurance [*of the International Actuarial Association*] [*Brussels, Belgium*] (EA) ... ASTIN
Actuary [*Insurance*] ... ACT
Actuary (ABBR) ... ACTRY
Actuary ... ACTRY
Actuary (ABBR) ... ACTUR
Actuary (ROG) ... ACTY
Actuate (KSC) ... ACT
Actuate ... ACTE
Actuate (ABBR) ... ACTU
Actuated (ABBR) ... ACTAD
Actuated (ABBR) ... ACTUD
Actuating (ABBR) ... ACTAG
Actuating (KSC) ... ACTG
Actuating (ABBR) ... ACTUG
Actuating Transfer Function (SAA) ... ATF
Actuation (ABBR) ... ACTAN
Actuation (ABBR) ... ACTUN
Actuation Data Communication [*Naval Ordnance Laboratory*] ... ADC
Actuation Mechanism Subsystem (MCD) ... AMS
Actuation Mine Simulator (MCD) ... AMS
Actuation Test Mode [*Automotive service*] ... ATM
Actuator (ABBR) ... ACTAR
Actuator (KSC) ... ACTR
Actuator Drive (SAA) ... AD
Actuator/Indicator ... AI
Actuator Mechanism (NASA) ... AM
Actuator Selection Logic (SAA) ... ASL
Actuator Sensor Interface (ACII) ... ASI
Actum Fide [*Done in Faith*] [*Latin*] (WGA) ... AF
Actum ut Supra [*Done as Above*] [*Latin*] ... AUS
ACTV, Inc. [*Associated Press*] (SAG) ... ACTV
ACTV, Inc. [*NASDAQ symbol*] (SAG) ... IATV
Acuerdo Nacional [*Paraguay*] [*Political party*] (EY) ... AN
Acuity of Color Vision [*Ophthalmology*] (DAVI) ... VC
Acumen (ABBR) ... ACMN
Acupuncture ... ACPNCTR
Acupuncture (ABBR) ... ACUP
Acupuncture Analgesia [*Medicine*] (DMAA) ... AA
Acupuncture and Transcutaneous Electrical Nerve Stimulation [*Orthopedics and neurology*] (DAVI) ... ACUTENS
Acupuncture Association and Register Ltd. [*British*] ... AAR
Acupuncture Association of Minnesota (SRA) ... AAM
Acupuncture Association of South Australia ... AASA
Acupuncture Clinic [*British*] ... AC
Acupuncture Foundation of Canada ... AFC
Acupuncture International Association (EA) ... AIA
Acupuncture Research Institute (EA) ... ARI
Acupuncture Society of Virginia (SRA) ... ASVA
Acuson Corp. [*NYSE symbol*] (CTT) ... ACN
Acuson Corp. [*Associated Press*] (SAG) ... Acuson
Acute ... A
Acute [*Medicine*] ... AC
Acute Abdominal Series [*Medicine*] (MEDA) ... AAS
Acute Abdominal Tympany [*Medicine*] (AAMN) ... AAT
Acute Allergic Encephalitis [*Medicine*] (MAE) ... AAE
Acute Alveolar Respiratory Failure [*Medicine*] (CPH) ... AARF
Acute Angle Closure Glaucoma [*Ophthalmology*] ... AACG
Acute Anterior Uveitis [*Medicine*] (MEDA) ... AAU
Acute Anxiety Attack [*Medicine*] ... AAA
Acute Appendicitis [*Medicine*] ... AA
Acute Articular Rheumatism [*Medicine*] (DMAA) ... AAR
Acute Aseptic Meningitis Syndrome [*Medicine*] (DMAA) ... AAMS
Acute Atrophic Spinal Paralysis [*Medicine*] (DMAA) ... AASP
Acute Bacterial Endocarditis [*Medicine*] ... ABE
Acute Bacterial Exacerbation of Chronic Bronchitis [*Medicine*] ... ABECB
Acute Bacterial Meningitis [*Medicine*] ... ABM
Acute Bisectrix [*Crystallography*] ... AB
Acute Bovine Pulmonary Emphysema [*Cattle disease*] ... ABPE
Acute Brain Syndrome [*Medicine*] ... ABS
Acute Bronchopulmonary Asthma [*Medicine*] (MEDA) ... ABPA
Acute Canine Idiopathic Polyneuropathy [*Veterinary science*] (DMAA) ... ACIP
Acute Cardiovascular Disease [*Medicine*] (AAMN) ... ACVD
Acute Care Admission [*Medicine*] ... ACA
Acute Care Bed Need Methodology [*Hospital management*] ... ACBNM
Acute Care Center [*Medicine*] (DAVI) ... ACC
Acute Care Facility [*Medicine*] ... ACF
Acute Care Unit [*Medicine*] ... ACU
Acute Cerebrospinal Meningitis [*Medicine*] (DMAA) ... ACM
Acute Conditioned Neurosis ... ACN
Acute Confusional State [*Medicine*] (MEDA) ... ACS
Acute Coronary Disease [*Medicine*] (PDAA) ... ACD
Acute Coronary Insufficiency (HGAA) ... ACI
Acute Coronary Occlusion [*Medicine*] (DMAA) ... ACO
Acute Diarrheal Syndrome [*Medicine*] (DMAA) ... ADS
Acute Disseminated Encephalitis [*Neurology*] (DAVI) ... ADE
Acute Disseminated Encephalomyelitis [*Medicine*] ... ADE
Acute Disseminated [*or Disseminating*] **Encephalomyelitis** [*Medicine*] ... ADEM
Acute Dystonic Reaction [*Neurology*] (DAVI) ... ADR
Acute Emergency Guideline Levels [*EPA*] ... AEGL
Acute Encephalography and Fatty Degeneration of the Viscera [*Reye's syndrome*] [*Medicine*] ... AEFDV
Acute Erosion Gastritis [*Medicine*] ... AEG
Acute Erythroleukemia [*Oncology*] ... AEL
Acute Extrapyramidal Syndrome [*Medicine*] ... EPS
Acute Fatty Liver of Pregnancy [*Medicine*] ... AFLP
Acute Fear Regarding AIDS ... AFRAIDS
Acute Febrile Neutrophilic Dermatosis [*Medicine*] (DMAA) ... AFND
Acute Febrile Respiratory Disease [*Medicine*] ... AFRD
Acute Febrile Respiratory Illness [*Medicine*] ... AFRI
Acute Fibrinopurulent Pneumonia [*Medicine*] ... AFPP
Acute Fibrinoserous Pneumonia [*Medicine*] ... AFSP
Acute Flaccid Paralysis [*Medicine*] ... AFP
Acute Focal Appendicitis [*Medicine*] ... AFA
Acute Focal Cerebral Ischemia [*Medicine*] (DMAA) ... AFCI
Acute Gastroenteritis [*Medicine*] (DAVI) ... AGE
Acute Glomerulonephritis [*Medicine*] ... AGN
Acute Gonococcal Arthritis [*Medicine*] (CPH) ... AGA
Acute Granulocytic Leukemia [*Medicine*] ... AGL
Acute Heart Failure [*Medicine*] ... AHF
Acute Hemolytic Transfusion Reaction [*Medicine*] ... AHTR
Acute Hemorrhagic Conjunctivitis [*Ophthalmology*] (AAMN) ... AHC
Acute Hemorrhagic Cystitis [*Urology*] (AAMN) ... AHC
Acute Hemorrhagic Encephalomyelitis [*Medicine*] (MAE) ... AHE
Acute Hemorrhagic Leukoencephalitis [*Medicine*] (MAE) ... AHLE
Acute Hemorrhagic Pancreatitis [*Medicine*] (MAE) ... AHP
Acute Herpetic Gingival Stomatitis [*Dentistry*] ... AHGS
Acute Hospital Syndrome [*Used facetiously to explain the popularity of a West German soap opera*] ... AHS
Acute Idiopathic Demyelinating Polyneuropathy [*Medicine*] (DMAA) ... AIDP
Acute Idiopathic Pericarditis [*Medicine*] (DMAA) ... AIP
Acute Inclusion Body Encephalitis [*Medicine*] (DMAA) ... AIE
Acute Infarction Ramipril Efficacy [*Cardiology study*] ... AIRE
Acute Infectious Disease [*Medicine*] ... AID
Acute Infectious Disease Series [*Medicine*] (DAVI) ... AIDS
Acute Infectious Endocarditis [*Medicine*] (DMAA) ... AIE
Acute Infectious Lymphocytosis [*Medicine*] (DMAA) ... AIL
Acute Infectious Polyneuritis [*Medicine*] (DMAA) ... AIP
Acute Infero-Posterior Myocardial Infarction [*Medicine*] ... AIPMI
Acute Insulin Response [*Endocrinology*] ... AIR
Acute Intensive Treatment [*Medicine*] (DMAA) ... AIT
Acute Intermittent Porphyria [*Medicine*] ... AIP
Acute Interstitial Nephritide [*or Nephritis*] [*Medicine*] (MAE) ... AIN
Acute Intestinal Infection [*Medicine*] (DMAA) ... AII
Acute Ionization Detector [*Medicine*] (DMAA) ... AID
Acute Joint Syndrome [*Medicine*] (DMAA) ... AJS
Acute Laryngotracheobronchitis [*Virus*] ... ALTB
Acute Laryngotracheobronchitis [*Commonly known as croup*] (PAZ) ... LTB
Acute Lateral Sclerosis [*Medicine*] ... ALS
Acute Launch Emergency Reliability Tip [*NASA*] (KSC) ... ALERT
Acute Left Ventricular Failure [*Cardiology*] (DMAA) ... ALVF
Acute Lethal Catatonia [*Neurology and psychiatry*] (DAVI) ... ALC
Acute Leukemia [*Medicine*] ... AL
Acute Lower Repiratory Infection [*Medicine*] (CPH) ... ALRI
Acute Lumbar Traumatic Sprain (HGAA) ... ALTS
Acute Lung Injury [*Medicine*] (DMAA) ... ALI
Acute Lupus Pericarditis [*Medicine*] (AAMN) ... ALP
Acute Lymphatic [*or Lymphoblastic or Lymphocytic*] **Leukemia** [*Medicine*] ... ALL
Acute Lymphocytic Leukemia Antigen [*Medicine*] (DMAA) ... ALLA
Acute Megakaryoblastic Leukemia [*Medicine*] (DMAA) ... AMEGL
Acute Mesenteric Ischemia [*Medicine*] ... AMI
Acute Mesenteric Vascular Insufficiency [*Medicine*] (AAMN) ... AMVI
Acute Mesenteric Venous Thrombosis [*Medicine*] ... AMVT
Acute Military Tuberculosis [*Medicine*] (DMAA) ... AMT
Acute Monoblastic Leukaemia [*Medicine*] (BABM) ... AMOL
Acute Monoblastic Leukemia [*Also, AMoL*] [*Medicine*] ... AMonoL
Acute Monocytic Leukemia [*Medicine*] (DAVI) ... AML
Acute Monocytic Leukemia [*Also, AMonoL*] [*Medicine*] ... AMoL
Acute Mountain Sickness ... AMS
Acute Multifocal Placoid Pigment Epitheliopathy [*Ophthalmology*] ... AMPPE
Acute Multifocal Posterior Placoid Pigment Epitheliopathy [*Dermatology*] (DAVI) ... AMPPPE
Acute Myeloblastic Leukemia [*Hematology and oncology*] (DAVI) ... AMBL
Acute Myelogenous Leukemia [*Medicine*] ... AML
Acute Myeloid [*or Myeloblastic or Myelocytic*] **Leukemia** [*Medicine*] ... AML
Acute Myelomonoblastic Leukemia [*Medicine*] ... AMMOL
Acute Myelomonocytic Leukemia [*Medicine*] ... AMML
Acute Myocardial Infarction [*Medicine*] ... AMI
Acute Narrow Angle Glaucoma [*Opthamology*] (DMAA) ... ANAG
Acute Necrosis of Intestinal Mucosa [*Gastroenterology*] ... ANIM
Acute Necrotic Myelopathy [*Medicine*] ... ANM
Acute Necrotizing Ulcerative Gingivitis [*Dentistry*] ... ANUG
Acute Nerve Irritation (HGAA) ... ANI
Acute Nerve Root Irritation (HGAA) ... ANRI
Acute Nonlymphoblastic Leukemia [*Medicine*] ... ANL
Acute Nonlymphoblastic Leukemia [*Medicine*] (DAVI) ... ANLL

Acute Nonlymphocytic Leukemia [*Medicine*] ... ANLL
Acute Organic Brain Syndrome [*Medicine*] (DMAA) ... AOBS
Acute Otitis Media [*Medicine*] ... AOM
Acute Pernicious Beriberi [*Medicine*] (PDAA) ... APB
Acute Pharyngoconjunctival Fever [*Medicine*] (MEDA) ... APC
Acute Pharyngo-Conjunctival Fever [*Medicine*] ... APCF
Acute Phase [*Laboratory*] (DAVI) ... ACUT
Acute Phase Reactant [*Medicine*] ... APR
Acute Phase Reactant Protein [*Medicine*] (DMAA) ... APRP
Acute Phase Response [*Medicine*] ... APR
Acute Physiology and Chronic Health Evaluation ... APACHE
Acute Physiology Score [*In evaluating impact of intensive care*] ... APS
Acute Posterior Multifocal Placoid Pigment Epitheliopathy [*Ophthalmology*] ... APMPPE
Acute Postoperative Renal Failure [*Medicine*] (AAMN) ... APORF
Acute Poststreptococcal Glomerulonephritis [*Immunology*] ... APSGN
Acute Progranulocytic [*or Promyelocytic*] **Leukemia** [*Hematology*] ... APL
Acute Progranulocytic Leukemia [*Hematology*] (DAVI) ... AProL
Acute Proliferative [*or Proliferation*] (MAE) ... AP
Acute Promyelocytic Leukemia [*Medicine*] ... APL
Acute Promyelocytic Leukemia [*Hematology*] (MAE) ... AProL
Acute Psychotic Episode ... APE
Acute Pulmonary Edema (DAVI) ... APE
Acute Pyelonephritis [*Medicine*] (MAE) ... APN
Acute Radiation Syndrome [*Medicine*] ... ARS
Acute Renal Failure [*Medicine*] ... ARF
Acute Renal Failure and Chronic Renal Failure [*Nephrology*] (DAVI) ... ARF/CRF
Acute Respiratory Disease [*Medicine*] ... ARD
Acute Respiratory Distress Syndrome [*Medicine*] ... ARDS
Acute Respiratory Failure [*Medicine*] ... ARF
Acute Respiratory Illness [*Medicine*] (DMAA) ... ARI
Acute Respiratory System Malfunction [*Medicine*] ... ARSM
Acute Respiratory Tract Illness ... ARTI
Acute Rheumatic Fever [*Medicine*] ... ARF
Acute Salpingitis [*Medicine*] (MEDA) ... AS
Acute Sclerosing Hyaline Necrosis [*Medicine*] (MAE) ... ASHN
Acute Serum Sickness [*Medicine*] (DMAA) ... ASS
Acute Spinal Cord Injury (DMAA) ... ASCI
Acute Splenic Sequestration Crisis [*Medicine*] (DMAA) ... ASSC
Acute Stress Erosion [*Gastroenterology*] (DAVI) ... ASE
Acute Stroke Unit [*Medicine*] (DAVI) ... ASU
Acute Subdural Hematoma [*Medicine*] ... ASDH
Acute Suppurative Parotitis [*Otorhinolaryngology*] (DAVI) ... ASP
Acute Transient Radiation Myelopathy [*Oncology*] ... ATRM
Acute Transverse Myelopathy [*Medicine*] (DMAA) ... ATM
Acute Tubular Necrosis [*Nephrology*] ... ATN
Acute Undifferentiated Leukemia [*Hematology*] ... AUL
Acute Variceal Haemorrhage [*Medicine*] (PDAA) ... AVH
Acute Vasomotor Nephropathy [*Medicine*] (DAVI) ... AVN
Acute Vertebral Collapse [*Medicine*] ... AVC
Acute Viral Hepatitis [*Medicine*] ... AVH
Acute Viral Meningitis [*Medicine*] ... AVM
Acute Viral Respiratory Infection [*Medicine*] (DMAA) ... AVRI
Acute Yellow Atrophy [*Medicine*] (DMAA) ... AYA
Acutely (ABBR) ... ACTY
Acutely Hazardous Material ... AHM
Acuteness (ABBR) ... ACTNS
Acuteness (ABBR) ... ACUTNS
Acute-Phase Response Element [*Biochemistry*] ... APRE
Acute-Phase Response Factor [*Biochemistry*] ... APRF
Acuvision Systems, Inc. [*Vancouver Stock Exchange symbol*] ... AVI
Acvila Air-Romanian Carrier [*FAA designator*] (FAAC) ... RRM
ACX Technologies [*NYSE symbol*] (TTSB) ... ACX
ACX Technologies [*NYSE symbol*] (SAG) ... ACX
ACX Technologies [*Associated Press*] (SAG) ... ACX Tc
ACX Technologies [*NASDAQ symbol*] (SAG) ... ACXT
Acxiom Corp. [*Associated Press*] (SAG) ... Acxiom
Acxiom Corp. [*NASDAQ symbol*] (NQ) ... ACXM
Acycloguanosine [*Also, ACV, Acyclovir*] [*Antiviral compound*] ... ACG
Acyclovir [*Pharmacology*] (DAVI) ... ACA
Acyclovir [*Also, ACG, Acycloguanosine*] [*Antiviral compound*] ... ACV
Acyclovir Diphosphate [*Antiviral compound*] ... ACV-DP
Acyclovir Monophosphate [*Antiviral compound*] ... ACV-MP
Acyclovir Triphosphate [*Antiviral compound*] ... ACVTP
Acyl [*Organic chemistry*] ... Ac
Acyl Carrier Protein [*Biochemistry*] ... ACP
Acyl Coenzyme A Oxidase (DMAA) ... ACAO
Acyl Coenzyme A: Retinal Acyltransferase [*An enzyme*] ... ARAT
Acylaminocephalosporanic Acid [*Medicine*] (DMAA) ... AACA
Acylated Octapeptide [*Biochemistry*] ... A-OP
Acylated Plasminogen-Streptokinase Activator Complex [*Anticlotting agent*] ... APSAC
Acylcholine Acyl-Hydrolase [*Same as PCE*] [*An enzyme*] ... ACAH
Acyltransferase [*An enzyme*] ... AT
Ad [*To or At*] [*Latin*] (ROG) ... A
AD 2000: a Journal of Religious Opinion [*A publication*] (APTA) ... AD
Ad Annum [*Up to the Year*] [*Latin*] ... AD AN
Ad Aperturam Libri [*As the Book Opens*] [*Latin*] (BARN) ... AA
Ad Captandum [*For the Purpose of Captivating*] [*Latin*] ... Ad Capt
Ad Com Marketing, Inc. [*Vancouver Stock Exchange symbol*] ... ADO
Ad Defectionem Animi [*To the Point of Fainting*] [*Pharmacy*] ... AD DEF AN
Ad Deliquium [*To Fainting*] [*Pharmacy*] (DAVI) ... ad Deliq
Ad Duas Vices [*For Two Doses*] [*Pharmacy*] ... AD 2 VIC
Ad Effectum [*Until Effectual*] [*Pharmacy*] ... AD EFFECT
Ad Eundem Gradum [*To the Same Degree*] [*Of the admission of a graduate of one university to the same degree at another without examination*] [*Latin*] ... AD EUND
Ad Eundem Gradum [*To the Same Degree*] [*Of the admission of a graduate of one university to the same degree at another without examination*] [*Latin*] ... AEG
Ad Extremum [*To the Extreme, To the End*] [*Latin*] ... AD EX
Ad Finem [*At or To the End*] [*Latin*] ... AD FIN
Ad Finem [*At or To the End*] [*Latin*] ... AF
Ad Finem [*At or To the End*] [*Latin*] (ADA) ... FIN
Ad Gentes [*Decree on the Church's Missionary Activity*] [*Vatican II document*] ... AG
Ad Gratum Aciditatem [*To an Agreeable Sourness*] [*Pharmacy*] ... AD GR ACID
Ad Gratum Aciditatem [*To an Agreeable Sourness*] [*Pharmacy*] ... Ad Grat Acid
Ad Gratum Gustum [*To an Agreeable Taste*] [*Pharmacy*] ... AD GR GUST
Ad Hanc Vocem [*At This Word*] [*Latin*] ... AHV
Ad Helviam [*of Seneca the Younger*] [*Classical studies*] (OCD) ... Helv
Ad Hoc Advisory Group on Science Programs [*Terminated, 1976*] [*National Science Foundation*] (EGAO) ... AGOSP
Ad Hoc Committee for American Silver (EA) ... AHCAS
Ad Hoc Committee for Lebanese Freedom [*Defunct*] (EA) ... AHCLF
Ad Hoc Committee on Copyright Law (EA) ... AHCCL
Ad Hoc Committee on Equipment Interoperability [*NATO*] (NATG) ... AHCEI
Ad Hoc Committee on Freedom of Scholarly Inquiry [*Defunct*] (EA) ... AHCFSI
Ad Hoc Committee on New Directions of the Research and Technical Services Division of the ALA [*American Library Association*] (NITA) ... AHONDA
Ad Hoc Committee on the Baltic States and the Ukraine (EA) ... AHCBSU
Ad Hoc Committee on the Cumulative Regulatory Effects on the Cost of Automotive Transportation [*Terminated, 1972*] (EGAO) ... RECAT
Ad Hoc Congressional Committee for Irish Affairs (EA) ... AHCCIA
Ad Hoc Congressional Committee on the Baltic States and the Ukraine (EA) ... AHCCBSU
Ad Hoc Crypto-Coordination Agency (MUGU) ... ACCA
Ad Hoc Group for Medical Research Funding (EA) ... AHGMRF
Ad Hoc Group on Missile Reliability (SAA) ... AHGMR
Ad Hoc Group on US Policy toward the UN [*Defunct*] (EA) ... AHGUSPTUN
Ad Hoc Mixed Working Group (SAA) ... AHMWG
Ad Hoc Monitoring Group on Southern Africa [*Defunct*] (EA) ... AHMGSA
Ad Hoc Requirements Committee [*Later, COMOR*] ... ARC
Ad Hoc Schedule Message (DA) ... ASM
Ad Hoc Working Group [*Army*] ... AHWG
Ad Hominem [*To the man*] [*A debating technique that attacks the person not his ideas*] [*Latin*] (BARN) ... ad hom
Ad Hunc Locum [*To (or At) This Place*] [*Latin*] ... AD HL
Ad Hunc Locum [*To (or At) This Place*] [*Latin*] ... AHL
Ad Infinitum [*To Infinity*] [*Latin*] ... AD INF
Ad Initium [*At the Beginning*] [*Latin*] ... AD INIT
Ad Interim [*In the Meantime*] [*Latin*] ... AD INT
Ad Interim [*In the Meantime*] [*Latin*] (EY) ... AI
Ad Interim Specification [*Navy*] ... INT
Ad Jesum per Mariam [*To Jesus through Mary*] [*Latin*] ... AJPM
Ad Libitum [*At Pleasure, As Desired*] [*Music*] (ROG) ... AD L
Ad Libitum [*At Pleasure, As Desired*] [*Music*] ... AD LIB
Ad Libitum [*At Pleasure, As Desired*] [*Music*] ... AD LIBIT
Ad Locum [*To (or At) the Place*] [*Latin*] ... AD LOC
Ad Majorem Dei Gloriam [*To the Greater Glory of God*] [*Latin*] (WGA) ... AMDG
Ad Manus Medici [*To Be Delivered into the Hands of the Physician*] [*Pharmacy*] ... AD MAN MED
Ad Nationes [*of Tertullian*] [*Classical studies*] (OCD) ... Ad Nat
Ad Nauseum [*To the Extent of Producing Nausea*] [*Latin*] ... AD NAUS
Ad Neutralizandum [*To Neutralization*] [*Pharmacy*] ... AD NEUT
Ad Partes Dolentes [*To the Painful Parts*] [*Pharmacy*] ... Ad Part Dol
Ad Partes Dolentes [*To the Painful Parts*] [*Pharmacy*] ... ad part dolent
Ad Pondus Omnium [*To the Weight of the Whole*] [*Pharmacy*] ... AD POND OM
Ad Saeculum [*To the Century*] [*Latin*] (ADA) ... AD SAEC
Ad Saturandum [*To Saturation*] [*Pharmacy*] ... AD SAT
Ad Saturandum [*To Saturation*] [*Pharmacy*] ... AD SATUR
Ad Sectam [*At the Suit Of*] [*Legal term Latin*] ... Ads
Ad Tertiam Vicem [*Three Times*] [*Pharmacy*] ... AD TERT VIC
Ad Universiterrarum Orbis Summi Architecti Gloriam [*To the Glory of the GrandArchitect of the Universe*] [*Freemasonry*] [*Latin*] ... AUTOSAG
Ad Usum [*According to Custom*] [*Pharmacy*] ... Ad Us
Ad Usum [*According to Custom*] [*Pharmacy*] ... AU
Ad Usum Externum [*For External Use*] [*Pharmacy*] ... AD US EXTER
Ad Valorem [*According to the Value*] [*Latin Business term*] ... AD VAL
Ad Valorem [*According to the Value*] [*Latin Business term*] ... ADV
Ad Valorem [*According to the Value*] [*Latin Business term*] ... AV
Ad Valorem [*According to the Value*] **Equivalent** ... AVE
Ad Valorem Tax [*Added Value Tax*] ... AVT
Ada [*Byron*] [*The name of a computer language*] (BARN) ... Ada
Ada [*Oklahoma*] [*Airport symbol*] (AD) ... ADH
Ada [*Ghana*] [*ICAO location identifier*] (ICLI) ... DGAD
ADA Air [*Albania*] [*FAA designator*] (FAAC) ... ADE
ADA and Software Engineering Technology [*British*] (NITA) ... ASET
Ada Compiler Validation Capacity [*Computer science*] ... ACVC
Ada County District Library, Boise, ID [*Library symbol*] [*Library of Congress*] (LCLS) ... IdBC
ADA Design and Coping Standards [*DoD*] ... ADCS
Ada Design Language [*Computer science*] (ODBW) ... ADL
Ada Development Environment (SSD) ... ADVENT
ADA Development Environment Portable Tools [*A programming language*] (NITA) ... ADEPT
Ada Elementary School, Ada, MN [*Library symbol*] [*Library of Congress*] (LCLS) ... MNAdaE

Ada High School, Ada, MN [*Library symbol*] [*Library of Congress*]
(LCLS) .... MnAdaH
ADA Integrated Methodology (MCD) .... AIM
Ada Joint Program Office [*Later, Ada Board*] [*DoD*] (RDA) .... AJPO
ADA Language System (MCD) .... ALS
Ada Language System/Navy (SSD) .... ALS/N
Ada/Lattice ICE [*Integrated Conceptual Environment*] [*Computer science*] ..... ALICE
Ada, MN [*FM radio station call letters*] .... KRJB
Ada, OH [*FM radio station call letters*] .... WONB
Ada, OK [*Location identifier FAA*] (FAAL) .... ADH
Ada, OK [*Location identifier FAA*] (FAAL) .... AMR
Ada, OK [*AM radio station call letters*] .... KADA
Ada, OK [*AM radio station call letters*] .... KADA-FM
Ada, OK [*Television station call letters*] .... KTEN
Ada, OK [*FM radio station call letters*] .... KTLS
Ada Programming Support Environments [*Computer science*] (RDA) .... APSE
[*The*] Ada Project [*World Wide Web*] .... TAP
Ada Public Library, Ada, MN [*Library symbol*] [*Library of Congress*]
(LCLS) .... MnAda
Ada Public Library, Ada, OK [*Library symbol Library of Congress*] (LCLS) ..... OkAd
Ada Software Repository .... ASR
Adaba [*Ethiopia*] [*ICAO location identifier*] (ICLI) .... HAAD
ADABAS [*Adaptable Database System*] **network software** [*Computer*]
(NITA) .... ADANET
ADAC Laboratories [*NASDAQ symbol*] (NQ) .... ADAC
ADAC Laboratories [*Associated Press*] (SAG) .... AdacLb
Adagdak [*Alaska*] [*Seismograph station code, US Geological Survey*] (SEIS) AD8
Adage (ABBR) .... ADG
Adage Graphics Terminal .... AGT
Adage, Inc. [*Associated Press*] (SAG) .... Adage
Adage, Inc. [*NASDAQ symbol*] (NQ) .... ADGE
Adagio [*Slow*] [*Music*] .... ADAG
Adagio [*Slow*] [*Music*] (ROG) .... ADAGO
Adagio [*Slow*] [*Music*] .... ADGO
Adagio [*Slow*] [*Music*] .... ADO
Adair County Free Press, Greenfield, IA [*Library symbol Library of
Congress*] (LCLS) .... IaGrefFP
Adair News, Adair, IA [*Library symbol Library of Congress*] (LCLS) .... IaAdN
Adair on Law Libels [*A publication*] (DLA) .... Adair Lib
Adair on Libels [*A publication*] (DLA) .... Ad Lib
Adair-Koshland-Nemethy-Filmer [*Enzyme model*] .... AKNF
Adak, AK [*Location identifier FAA*] (FAAL) .... NUD
Adak/Davis [*Alaska*] [*ICAO location identifier*] (ICLI) .... PADK
Adak Island [*Alaska*] [*Seismograph station code, US Geological Survey
Closed*] (SEIS) .... ADA
Adak Island [*Alaska*] [*Airport symbol*] (OAG) .... ADK
Adak Island [*Alaska*] [*Seismograph station code, US Geological Survey*]
(SEIS) .... ADK
Adak [*Alaska*] **Search and Rescue Coordinator** [*Coast Guard*]
(DNAB) .... ADAKSARCOORD
Adam and Eve (EA) .... AE
Adam, Harding & Lueck [*Commercial firm British*] .... AHL
Adam on the Law of Slavery in British India [*A publication*] (DLA) .... Adam Sl
Adam on Trial by Jury [*A publication*] (DLA) .... Adam Jur Tr
Adam Smith Institute (EA) .... ASI
A.D.A.M. Software [*NASDAQ symbol*] (TTSB) .... ADAM
ADAM Software, Inc. [*NASDAQ symbol*] (SAG) .... ADAM
ADAM Software, Inc. [*Associated Press*] (SAG) .... AdamSft
Adam Walsh Child Resource Center (EA) .... AWCRC
Adamant (ABBR) .... ADAMT
Adamant (ABBR) .... ADMNT
Adamantane [*Organic chemistry*] .... AD
Adamantine (ABBR) .... ADAM
Adamantly (ABBR) .... ADAMTY
Adamantly (ABBR) .... ADMNTY
Adams [*New York*] [*Seismograph station code, US Geological Survey Closed*]
(SEIS) .... ADN
Adams and Durham on Real Property [*A publication*] (DLA) .... AD & Dur RP
Adams & Rountree Technology, Inc. [*Information service or system*]
(IID) .... A & RT
Adams County Free Press, Corning, IA [*Library symbol Library of
Congress*] (LCLS) .... IaCornFP
Adams County Juvenile Detention Center, Brighton, CO [*Library symbol
Library of Congress*] (LCLS) .... CoBriJ
Adams County Legal Journal [*Pennsylvania*] [*A publication*] (DLA) .... Adams
Adams County Legal Journal [*Pennsylvania*] [*A publication*] (DLA) .... Adams LJ
Adams County Public Library, Bennett, CO [*Library symbol Library of
Congress*] (LCLS) .... CoBen
Adams County Public Library, Brighton, CO [*Library symbol Library of
Congress*] (LCLS) .... CoBri
Adams County Public Library, Northglenn, CO [*Library symbol Library of
Congress*] (LCLS) .... CoNgA
Adams County School District No. 12, Northglenn, CO [*Library symbol
Library of Congress*] (LCLS) .... CoNgSD
Adams County School District No. 12, Northglenn, CO [*OCLC symbol*]
(OCLC) .... DVA
Adams Elementary School, Fergus Falls, MN [*Library symbol*] [*Library of
Congress*] (LCLS) .... MnEfAE
Adams' Equity [*A publication*] (DLA) .... Ad Eq
Adams' Equity [*A publication*] (DLA) .... Adams Eq
Adams' Essay on Anglo-Saxon Law [*A publication*] (DLA) .... Ad Ang Sax L
Adams Exploration Ltd. [*Vancouver Stock Exchange symbol*] .... ADM
Adams Express [*NYSE symbol*] (TTSB) .... ADX
[*The*] Adams Express Co. [*Associated Press*] (SAG) .... AdaEx
[*The*] Adams Express Co. [*NYSE symbol*] (SPSG) .... ADX

Adams Family Association (EA) .... AFA
Adams Field [*FAA*] (TAG) .... LIT
Adams International Ltd. .... AIL
Adam's Justiciary Reports [*1893-1906*] [*Scotland*] [*A publication*] (ILCA) .... A
Adams' Justiciary Reports [*Scotland*] [*A publication*] (DLA) .... Ad Jus
Adams' Legal Journal [*Pennsylvania*] [*A publication*] (DLA) .... Adams Leg J (PA)
Adams Library (Chelmsford Public Library), Chelmsford, MA [*Library
symbol Library of Congress*] (LCLS) .... MChelm
Adams, MA [*Television station call letters*] .... WCDC
Adams Mansion, Quincy, MA [*Library symbol Library of Congress*] (LCLS) .... MQA
Adams National Historic Site .... ADAM
Adams on Ejectment [*A publication*] (DLA) .... Ad Ej
Adams on the Education Act [*A publication*] (DLA) .... Ad Ed Act
Adams on Trade Marks [*A publication*] (DLA) .... Ad Tr M
Adams Public Library, Adams, OR [*Library symbol*] [*Library of Congress*]
(LCLS) .... OrAd
Adams' Reports [*41, 42 Maine*] [*A publication*] (DLA) .... Adams
Adams' Reports [*1 New Hampshire*] [*A publication*] (DLA) .... Adams
Adams Res & Energy [*AMEX symbol*] (TTSB) .... AE
Adams Resources & Energy, Inc. [*Associated Press*] (SAG) .... AdmRsc
Adams Resources & Energy, Inc. [*AMEX symbol*] (SPSG) .... AE
Adams' Roman Antiquities [*A publication*] (DLA) .... Ad Rom Ant
Adams' Roman Antiquities [*A publication*] (DLA) .... Adams Rom Ant
Adams State College (GAGS) .... Adams St C
Adams State College [*Alamosa, CO*] .... ASC
Adams State College, Alamosa, CO [*Library symbol Library of Congress*]
(LCLS) .... CoAlC
Adams, WI [*FM radio station call letters*] .... WDKM
Adams-Brown County Bookmobile, Winchester, OH [*Library symbol Library
of Congress*] (LCLS) .... OWin
Adams-Stokes [*Cardiology*] .... A-S
Adams-Stokes Attack [*Cardiology*] (MAE) .... ASA
Adamsville, TN [*AM radio station call letters*] .... WEAB
Adana [*Turkey*] [*Airport symbol*] (OAG) .... ADA
Adana/Incirlik [*Turkey ICAO location identifier*] (ICLI) .... LTAG
Adana/Sakirpasa [*Turkey ICAO location identifier*] (ICLI) .... LTAF
Adanac Mining & Exploration Ltd. [*Toronto Stock Exchange symbol
Vancouver Stock Exchange symbol*] .... ADN
Adapt .... AD
Adaptability (ABBR) .... ADPBT
Adaptability, Partnership, Growth, Affection, and Resolve [*Family Therapy
Questionnaire*] .... APGAR
Adaptable .... A
Adaptable (ABBR) .... ADAPB
Adaptable (ABBR) .... ADPB
Adaptable Board Computer [*Signetics*] .... ABC
Adaptable Data Manager [*Hitachi Ltd.*] [*Japan*] .... ADM
Adaptable Database System [*Database management system*] [*Registered
trademark of Software AG, Darmstadt, Germany*] .... ADABAS
Adaptable Space Propulsion System [*Military*] .... ASPS
Adaptable Surface Interface Terminal (MCD) .... ASIT
Adaptable Terminal Interface Configuration [*Military*] (MCD) .... ATIC
Adaptable-Programmable Assembly System [*Computer science*] (PDAA) .... APAS
Adaptably (ABBR) .... ADAPY
Adaptation (ABBR) .... ADAPN
Adaptation .... ADAPT
Adaptation (ABBR) .... ADAPTTN
Adaptation Level .... AL
Adaptation Mathematical Processor .... AMP
Adaptation Of [*Etymology*] .... AD
Adaptation to Premises and Equipment Scheme [*Education*] (AIE) .... APE
Adaptec, Inc. [*Associated Press*] (SAG) .... Adaptec
Adaptec, Inc. [*NASDAQ symbol*] (NQ) .... ADPT
Adaptec RAIDport Option [*Computer science*] .... ARO
Adapted (ABBR) .... ADAPD
Adapted Delivered Source Instruction .... ADSI
Adapted Identification Decision Equipment .... AIDE
Adapted Swimming-Pool Tank Reactor, Austria .... ASTRA
Adapted Uzgiris-Hunt Scales (EDAC) .... AUHS
Adapter (ABBR) .... ADAPR
Adapter .... ADAPT
Adapter [*MARC relator code*] [*Library of Congress*] (LCCP) .... adp
Adapter (KSC) .... ADPT
Adapter (MSA) .... ADPTR
Adapter, Binding Post .... ABP
Adapter Booster .... AB
Adapter, Bulkhead .... AB
Adapter Cable .... AC
Adapter Control Block [*Computer science*] (IBMDP) .... ACB
Adapter Control Detector [*Computer science*] .... ACD
Adapter Definition File (BYTE) .... ADF
Adapter Description File [*Computer science*] (PCM) .... ADF
Adapter Fault Tolerance [*Intel*] [*Computer science*] .... AFT
Adapter Kit (MCD) .... AK
Adapter Panel .... AP
Adapter, Right Angle .... ARA
Adapter Section [*NASA*] (KSC) .... AS
Adapter Service Area (MCD) .... ASA
Adapter, Straight .... AS
Adapter Subunit Tester .... ASUT
Adapter, Tee .... AT
Adapter Unit (NG) .... ADU
Adapting (ABBR) .... ADAPG
Adaption (ABBR) .... ADAPN
Adaption Binary Load [*Program*] (CET) .... ABL

Adaption Error Note ... AEN
Adaption Kit ... AK
Adaptive (ABBR) ... ADAPTV
Adaptive (ABBR) ... ADAPV
Adaptive Agile RADAR ECCM [*Electronic Counter-Countermeasures*] (MCD) ... AAREC
Adaptive and Integrated Decision Expeditor (MCD) ... AIDE
Adaptive Angle Bias ... AAB
Adaptive Antenna Control (MCD) ... AAC
Adaptive Antenna Receiver System ... ADARS
Adaptive Arithmetical Method ... ADAM
Adaptive Beam Forming (NVT) ... ABF
Adaptive Behavior [*Psychology*] ... AB
Adaptive Behavior Inventory for Children [*Psychology*] ... ABIC
Adaptive Behavior Scale [*American Association on Mental Deficiency*] [*Psychology*] ... ABS
Adaptive Behavior Scale for Infants and Early Childhood [*Child development test*] ... ABSI
Adaptive Behavior Scale, School Edition [*Child development test*] ... ABS-SE
Adaptive Communication (MHDB) ... ADAPTICOM
Adaptive Communication Live Controller (MCD) ... ACLC
Adaptive Computer Technologies [*San Jose, CA*] ... ACT
Adaptive Control [*Manufacturing term*] ... AC
Adaptive Control Constrained [*Manufacturing term*] ... ACC
Adaptive Control of Thought [*Psychology*] ... ACT
Adaptive Control Optimized [*Manufacturing term*] ... ACO
Adaptive Control Process ... ACP
Adaptive Control System ... ACS
Adaptive Controlled Phased Array (CAAL) ... ACPA
Adaptive Data Compression [*Computer science*] ... ADC
Adaptive Decision Maker in an Information Retrieval Environment [*Stanford University*] (NITA) ... ADMIRE
Adaptive Delta Modulation [*Electronics*] ... ADM
Adaptive Delta Voice Modulation [*Air Force*] ... ADVM
Adaptive Differential Pulse Code Modulated Transcoder [*Telecommunications*] ... ADPCMT
Adaptive Differential Pulse Code Modulation [*Computer science*] ... ADCPM
Adaptive Differential Pulse Code Modulation [*Telecommunications*] (MCD) ... ADPCM
Adaptive Digital Avionics Module ... ADAM
Adaptive Digital Signal Processor (MCD) ... ADSP
Adaptive Dynamic Analysis and Maintenance (MHDI) ... ADAM
Adaptive Dynamic Decision-Aiding Method ... ADDAM
Adaptive Echo Cancellation [*Navy*] (MCD) ... AEC
Adaptive Environmental Assessment and Management ... AEAM
Adaptive Escalator Predictor (MCD) ... AEP
Adaptive Ferroelectric Transformer (OA) ... AFT
Adaptive Flight Control System ... AFCS
Adaptive Flight Training System (MCD) ... AFTS
Adaptive Ground-Implemented Phased Array [*NASA*] ... AGIPA
Adaptive Head Lamp ... AHL
Adaptive Hough Transform [*Computer science*] ... AHT
Adaptive Inferential Control [*Control technology*] ... AIC
Adaptive Injection Molding [*Engineering*] ... AIM
Adaptive Intelligent Dialog (PDAA) ... AID
Adaptive Intercommunication Requirement (MCD) ... ADAP
Adaptive Intercommunication Requirement ... AICR
Adaptive Intercommunication Requirement (NASA) ... AIR
Adaptive Interference Cancellation System (CAAL) ... AICS
Adaptive Internetwork Management System [*Ungermann-Bass, Inc.*] ... AIM
Adaptive Intrusion Data System (MCD) ... AIDS
Adaptive Iterated Extended Kalman Filtering (MCD) ... AIEKF
Adaptive Jam-Resistant Tranceiver (PDAA) ... AJRT
Adaptive LASER Optics Techniques (MCD) ... ALOT
Adaptive LASER Resonator Technique (MCD) ... ALERT
Adaptive Lattice Linear Prediction (PDAA) ... ALLP
Adaptive Learn Processor [*Fuel systems*] [*Automotive engineering*] ... ADP
Adaptive Learning Environments Model (EDAC) ... ALEM
Adaptive Learning Network [*Computer science*] ... ALN
Adaptive Lens Array (MCD) ... ADLAR
Adaptive Library Management System [*Lipman Management Resources Ltd.*] [*Information service or system*] (IID) ... ADLIB
Adaptive Light Pattern ... ALP
Adaptive Line Canceller and Enhancer (CAAL) ... ALICE
Adaptive Line Enhancer [*Telecommunications*] (CAAL) ... ALE
Adaptive Linear (KSC) ... ADALINE
Adaptive Linear Combiner [*Computer science*] ... ALC
Adaptive Linear Predictive Coding (TEL) ... ALPC
Adaptive Logic Circuit ... ALC
Adaptive Long-Range Infrared Tracker ... ALIRT
Adaptive Man/Machine Non-Numeric Information Processing System [*IBM Corp.*] (NITA) ... AMNIPS
Adaptive Maneuvering Logic (MCD) ... AML
Adaptive Maneuvering Logic Score (MCD) ... AMLS
Adaptive Man-Machine Nonarithmetic Information Processing [*Documentation*] ... AMNIP
Adaptive Mathematical Model ... AMM
Adaptive Microwave Proximity [*Military*] (MCD) ... AMP
Adaptive Mission-Oriented Software System (MCD) ... AMOSS
Adaptive Mobile Access Protocol (MCD) ... AMAP
Adaptive Mobile Torpedo Decoy [*Navy*] (MCD) ... AMTD
Adaptive Mode Planning System [*Computer program*] ... AMPS
Adaptive Mode Planning System Input [*Computer program*] ... AMPSIN
Adaptive Moving Target Indicator [*Military*] ... AMTI
Adaptive Multibeam Experiment for Aeronautical and Maritime Services (MCD) ... AMEAMS
Adaptive Multibeam Phased Array [*RADAR*] (MCD) ... AMPA
Adaptive Multifunction Antenna (MCD) ... AMA
Adaptive Multiplexer (CAAL) ... AM
Adaptive Narrowband FM [*Frequency Modulation*] **MODEM** [*Telecommunications*] (TEL) ... ANBFM
Adaptive Noise Cancelling (MCD) ... ANC
Adaptive Noise Control [*Automotive engineering*] ... ADC
Adaptive Null Antenna ... ANA
Adaptive Pattern-Perceiving Electronic Computer System ... APPECS
Adaptive Phase Array RADAR ... APAR
Adaptive Phase Velocimeter ... APV
Adaptive Planning and Control Sequence [*Marketing*] ... APACS
Adaptive Polarization Electronic Countermeasure (MCD) ... APECM
Adaptive Predictive Coding [*Telecommunications*] (TEL) ... APC
Adaptive Processor, SONAR (CAAL) ... APS
Adaptive Programming Technology ... APT
Adaptive Pulse Code Modulation [*Telecommunications*] (TEL) ... APCM
Adaptive Random Search Technique [*Computer science*] (MHDI) ... ARSTEC
Adaptive Recognition Technology [*Calera Recognition Systems, Inc.*] [*Computer science*] (PCM) ... ART
Adaptive Reliability Control System [*Electronics*] (IAA) ... ARCS
Adaptive Residual Coding (MCD) ... ARC
Adaptive Resonance Theory [*Computer science*] ... ART
Adaptive Seating Device [*Occupational therapy*] ... ASD
Adaptive Sensing Vehicle [*Robot*] ... ASV
Adaptive Side-Lobe Canceller [*RADAR*] (MCD) ... ASLC
Adaptive Signal Control Optimization Techniques ... ASCOT
Adaptive Signal Correction (IAA) ... ASC
Adaptive Solution Domain ... ASD
Adaptive Solutions [*NASDAQ symbol*] (TTSB) ... ADSO
Adaptive Solutions, Inc. [*Associated Press*] (SAG) ... AdapSl
Adaptive Solutions, Inc. [*Associated Press*] (SAG) ... AdapSol
Adaptive Solutions, Inc. [*NASDAQ symbol*] (SAG) ... ADSO
Adaptive Solutions Wrrt [*NASDAQ symbol*] (TTSB) ... ADSOW
Adaptive Source Routing Transparent [*Computer science*] (PCM) ... ASRT
Adaptive Speed Control (PDAA) ... ASC
Adaptive Static Margin Controller (MCD) ... ASMC
Adaptive Statistical Processor [*Computer science*] (MHDI) ... APROC
Adaptive Step-Size Random Search [*Computer science*] (IAA) ... ASSRS
Adaptive Subbands Excited Transform [*Telecommunications*] (OSI) ... ACIT
Adaptive Subbands Excited Transform [*Computer science*] ... ASET
Adaptive Surface-Signal Recognition and Direction Indicator [*Navy*] ... ASRADI
Adaptive System (IAA) ... ASM
Adaptive Tactical Navigation (MCD) ... ATN
Adaptive Technologies (Canada) [*Vancouver Stock Exchange symbol*] ... ADT
Adaptive Threshold Detection with Estimated Sequence (LAIN) ... ATDES
Adaptive Threshold Gate (PDAA) ... ATG
Adaptive Traffic Control [*Automotive engineering*] ... ATC
Adaptive Transform Coding (PDAA) ... ATC
Adaptive Video Guidance System (MCD) ... AVGS
Adaptive Video Processor ... AVP
Adaptive Wafer Scale Integration (MCD) ... AWSI
Adaptive Waveform Recognition ... AWR
Adaptively Data Equalized MODEM ... ADEM
Adaptor (KSC) ... ADAP
Adaptronics, Inc. ... ADI
Adas [*or Adath*] **Israel** (BJA) ... AI
Adas Israel Congregation, Washington, DC [*Library symbol Library of Congress*] (LCLS) ... DAdI
Adas [*or Adath*] **Jeshurun** (BJA) ... AJ
Adastra Aviation Ltd. [*Canada ICAO designator*] (FAAC) ... ADD
Adastral Resources Ltd. [*Vancouver Stock Exchange symbol*] ... ASA
Adaxial Leaflet Pubescence - Curly [*Botany*] ... ADPC
Adbuct (ABBR) ... ABDC
ADC Telecommunications [*NASDAQ symbol*] (TTSB) ... ADCT
ADC Telecommunications, Inc. [*NASDAQ symbol*] (NQ) ... ADCT
ADC Telecommunications, Inc. [*Associated Press*] (SAG) ... ADCTel
ADCC [*Air Defense Command Computer*] **Programming and System Training Office** (SAA) ... APASTO
Adco Technologies [*NASDAQ symbol*] (TTSB) ... ADCO
Adco Technologies, Inc. [*NASDAQ symbol*] (SAG) ... ADCO
ADCOM [*Air Defense Command*] **Intelligence Memorandum** (MCD) ... AIM
Adcom Technologies, Inc. [*Associated Press*] (SAG) ... AdcoTc
ADCOM Weekly Intelligence Review Support (MCD) ... AWIR
Add [*Computer science*] [*Telecommunications*] ... a
Add and Carry Logical Word (SAA) ... ACL
Add BCD [*Binary Coded Decimal*] **Number with Extend** [*Computer science*] ... ABCD
Add/Drop Multiplexer [*Telecommunications*] (ACRL) ... ADM
Add Index Register [*Computer science*] (IAA) ... ADX
Add, Initial, Multiprecision ... AIM
Add Magnitude [*Computer science*] (IAA) ... ADM
Add, Multiprecision ... AMP
Add One to Memory [*Computer science*] ... AOM
Add One to the Right (SAA) ... AOR
Add or Subtract ... AOS
Add Packed [*Computer science*] ... AP
Add with Carry ... ADC
Addams' Ecclesiastical Reports [*A publication*] (DLA) ... Ad
Addams' Ecclesiastical Reports [*A publication*] (DLA) ... Add
Addams' Ecclesiastical Reports [*A publication*] (DLA) ... Add Ecc
Addams' Ecclesiastical Reports [*A publication*] (DLA) ... Add Eccl
Addams' Ecclesiastical Reports [*A publication*] (DLA) ... Add Eccl Rep

Addams' Ecclesiastical Reports [*A publication*] (DLA) .... Add ER
Addams' Ecclesiastical Reports [*A publication*] (DLA) .... Addams
Addams' Ecclesiastical Reports [*A publication*] (DLA) .... Addams Ecc (Eng)
Addantur [*Let Them Be Added*] [*Latin*] .... add
Adde [*Add or Up To*] [*Pharmacy*] .... AD
Adde [*Add or Up To*] [*Pharmacy*] .... ADD
Adde cum Tritu [*Add Trituration*] [*Pharmacy*] .... ADD c TRIT
Adde Cum Tritu [*Add Triturition*] [*Pharmacology*] (DAVI) .... add C Trit
Added Belly Band [*Military*] (CAAL) .... ABB
Added Entry [*Online database field identifier*] .... AE
Added Thermal Barrier (CAAL) .... ATB
Addend (ABBR) .... ADND
Addenda (ABBR) .... ADNDA
Addenda and Corrigenda (ADA) .... A & C
Addendum .... AD
Addendum (KSC) .... ADD
Addendum (WDMC) .... add
Addendum (ABBR) .... ADDNDM
Addendum (ABBR) .... ADNDM
Addendum to Monthly Collection [*IRS*] .... ADDM
Addendus [*To Be Added*] [*Pharmacy*] .... ADDEND
Adder [*Computer device*] .... A
Adder [*Computer device*] .... ADDR
Adder [*Computer device*] (MDG) .... ADR
Adder, Logical, and Transfer Unit [*Computer*] .... ALTU
ADD-H [*Attention Deficit Disorder with Hyperactivity*] **Comprehensive Teachers Rating Scale** .... ACTERS
Addict [*Drug*] [*Slang*] .... AD
Addict (ABBR) .... ADDC
Addict Rehabilitation Counselor .... ARC
Addicted (ABBR) .... ADDCD
Addicting (ABBR) .... ADDCG
Addiction (ABBR) .... ADDCN
Addiction [*Chemical dependency*] (DAVI) .... Addict
Addiction Research and Treatment Corp. (EA) .... ARTC
Addiction Research Center [*Baltimore, MD*] [*Department of Health and Human Services*] .... ARC
Addiction Research Center Inventory [*Psychology*] .... ARCI
Addiction Research Foundation [*Fondation de la Recherche sur la Toxicomanie*] [*Formerly, Alcoholism & Drug Addiction Research Foundation*] (AC) .... ARF
Addiction Research Foundation Library [*Canada*] (DI) .... ARFL
Addiction Research Foundation of Ontario Library [*UTLAS symbol*] .... ARF
Addiction Research Foundation, Toronto, ON, Canada [*Library symbol*] [*Library of Congress*] (LCLS) .... CaOTAD
Addiction Research Foundation, Toronto, Ontario [*Library symbol National Library of Canada*] (NLC) .... OTAD
Addictions Community Centres for Education, Prevention, Treatment, and Research [*British*] (AIE) .... ACCEPT
Addictive Behavior Group [*Psychology*] (DAVI) .... abg
Addicts Anonymous (EA) .... AA
Adding (ABBR) .... ADDG
Addington Resources [*NASDAQ symbol*] (TTSB) .... ADDR
Addington Resources, Inc. [*NASDAQ symbol*] (NQ) .... ADDR
Addington Resources, Inc. [*Associated Press*] (SAG) .... Adingtn
Addington's Abridgment of Penal Statutes [*A publication*] (DLA) .... Add Abr
Addis Ababa [*Ethiopia*] [*Seismograph station code, US Geological Survey*] .... AAE
Addis Ababa [*Ethiopia*] [*Airport symbol*] (OAG) .... ADD
Addis Ababa [*Ethiopia*] [*ICAO location identifier*] (ICLI) .... HAAA
Addis Ababa/Bole International [*Ethiopia*] [*ICAO location identifier*] (ICLI) .... HAAB
Addis Ababa/Liddetta [*Ethiopia*] [*ICAO location identifier*] (ICLI) .... HAAL
Addison Charges [*Addison's Pennsylvania Reports*] [*A publication*] (DLA) .... Add Ch
Addison Foster [*Record label*] .... AF
Addison on Contract [*A publication*] (ILCA) .... Ad Cont
Addison on Contracts [*A publication*] (DLA) .... Ad Con
Addison on Contracts [*A publication*] (DLA) .... Add C
Addison on Contracts [*A publication*] (DLA) .... Add Con
Addison on Contracts [*A publication*] (DLA) .... Add Cont
Addison on the Agricultural Holdings Act [*A publication*] (DLA) .... Add Agr Act
Addison on Torts [*A publication*] (DLA) .... Ad Torts
Addison on Torts [*A publication*] (DLA) .... Add T
Addison on Torts [*A publication*] (DLA) .... Add Tor
Addison on Torts [*A publication*] (DLA) .... Add Torts
Addison on Torts, Abridged [*A publication*] (DLA) .... Add Torts Abr
Addison on Torts, Dudley and Baylies' Edition [*A publication*] (DLA) .... Add Torts D & B
Addison on Torts, Woods Edition [*A publication*] (DLA) .... Add Torts Woods
Addison Public Library, Addison, NY [*Library symbol Library of Congress*] (LCLS) .... NAd
Addison, TX [*Location identifier FAA*] (FAAL) .... TBQ
Addison's County Court Reports [*Pennsylvania*] [*A publication*] (DLA) .... Add PA
Addison's County Court Reports [*Pennsylvania*] [*A publication*] (DLA) .... Add Rep
Addison's County Court Reports [*Pennsylvania*] [*A publication*] (DLA) .... Addis
Addison's County Court Reports [*Pennsylvania*] [*A publication*] (DLA) .... Addison (PA)
Addison's Pennsylvania Supreme Court Reports [*A publication*] (DLA) .... Add
Addison-Wesley [*Publisher*] .... A-W
Addition (AABC) .... ADD
Addition .... ADDN
Addition .... ADDTN
Addition (ABBR) .... ADTN
Addition Nucleophile Ring Opening Ring Closure [*Organic chemistry*] .... ANRORC
Addition, Subtraction, Timing, and Ratio .... ASTR
Additional (DLA) .... addit
Additional (KSC) .... ADDL
Additional .... ADDNL
Additional .... ADDTL
Additional (DA) .... ADNI
Additional (ABBR) .... ADTNL
Additional Air Force Specialty Code (AFM) .... AAFSC
Additional Authorization Item [*Military*] (INF) .... AAI
Additional Authorization List [*Army*] (AABC) .... AAL
Additional Benefits [*Unemployment insurance*] .... AB
Additional Billet Requirements [*Military*] .... ABR
Additional Budget Submissions [*DoD*] .... ABS
Additional Claim [*Unemployment insurance*] (OICC) .... AC
Additional Conditional Purchase [*Business term*] (ADA) .... ACP
Additional Crew Member [*Military*] (AFM) .... ACM
Additional Curates' Society [*British*] .... ACS
Additional Day Off .... ADO
Additional Dealer Markup [*Automobile retailing*] .... ADM
Additional Dealer Profit [*Automobile retailing*] .... ADP
Additional Delay in Reporting [*Military*] (DNAB) .... ADDELREP
Additional Dialogue Replacement .... ADR
Additional Duty .... ADDU
Additional Duty (AABC) .... ADY
Additional Education .... ADDED
Additional Expediting Expense [*Insurance*] .... AEE
Additional Expenses .... AE
Additional Extended Coverage [*Insurance*] .... AEC
Additional Fiscal Year Money Is Authorized by the Secretary of the Army (AABC) .... AFYMOSAP
Additional Flight Training Period (AABC) .... AFTP
Additional Government Requirement (AAGC) .... AGR
Additional Gunner Training (MCD) .... AGT
Additional Information Form .... AIF
Additional Information Request (MCD) .... AIR
Additional Listing [*Telecommunications*] (TEL) .... AL
Additional Living Expense [*Insurance*] .... ALE
Additional Material Required to Complete Fabrication Order .... AMRCFO
Additional Member System [*Electoral reform*] [*British*] .... AMS
Additional Memory Module .... AMM
Additional Military Production .... AMP
Additional Mobile SAM [*Surface-to-Air Missile*] **Site** (NATG) .... AMOSS
Additional Nonresidential Conditional Purchase (ADA) .... ANRCP
Additional Pension/Benefit .... AP/B
Additional Personal Allowance (DLA) .... APA
Additional Personal Injury Protection [*Insurance*] .... APIP
Additional Places .... ADDPLA
Additional Planning Capability (SAA) .... APC
Additional Premium [*Insurance*] .... AP
Additional Programming Language (IAA) .... APL
Additional Qualification Designation/Utilization (DNAB) .... AQD/U
Additional Qualification Designator (NVT) .... AQD
Additional Qualifying Symptom [*Medicine*] (MAE) .... AQS
Additional Reference Carrier Transmission [*Telecommunications*] (TEL) .... ART
Additional Reference Number [*NASA*] (NASA) .... ARN
Additional Requirements (DLA) .... AR
Additional Secondary Phase [*Navigation*] .... ASP
Additional Selection Factor .... ASF
Additional Skill Identifier [*Army*] (INF) .... ASI
Additional Sources .... AS
Additional Specialty [*Military*] (INF) .... ADSPEC
Additional Specialty Training [*Military*] .... AST
Additional Traffic [*Air Traffic Control*] (FAAC) .... ADNL TFC
Additional Training Assemblies .... ATA
Additional Uniform Allowance [*Military*] .... ADDUNIFALW
Additional Voluntary Contribution [*Employee's wage contribution toward a company pension plan*] .... AVC
Additionally (ABBR) .... ADDNLY
Additionally (ABBR) .... ADTNLY
Additionally Awarded Military Occupational Specialty .... AMOS
Additions (WDMC) .... adds
Additions and Amendments (ADA) .... A & A
Additions to Esther [*Apocrypha*] (BJA) .... AddEsther
Additive (MSA) .... ADDT
Additive (ABBR) .... ADDV
Additive (ABBR) .... ADTV
Additive Color Process .... ACP
Additive Color Viewer Printer .... ACVP
Additive Delivery System .... ADS
Additive Full-Time Manning (MCD) .... AFTM
Additive Gaussian Noise .... AGN
Additive Histologic Assessment [*Medicine*] .... AHA
Additive Noise Linear Sequential Circuit .... ANLSC
Additive Operational Project [*Army*] .... ADOP
Additive Operational Project [*Army*] (MCD) .... AOP
Additive System of Photographic Exposure (DICI) .... APEX
Additive Voice Gaussian Noise [*Telecommunications*] (NITA) .... AWGN
Additive White Gaussian Noise [*Telecommunications*] (TEL) .... AWGN
Additive-Free Hard Gold [*Metallurgy*] .... AFHG
Additives and Containments Committee [*British*] .... ACC
Ad-Dome International Ltd. [*Vancouver Stock Exchange symbol*] .... ADI
Add-On Audio Unit (MCD) .... AAU
Add-On Conference Call [*Telecommunications*] (DOM) .... CONF
Add-On Non-Stop Reliability (PDAA) .... ANSR
Add-On Stabilization (MCD) .... AOS
Address [*Computer character*] [*Computer science*] .... A
Address (IAA) .... AD

Address ... ADD
Address [*Computer character*] [*Computer science*] ... ADDR
Address ... ADDR
Address (ECII) ... ADDSS
Address [*Computer character*] [*Computer science*] ... ADR
Address [*Computer character*] [*Computer science*] (AFM) ... ADRS
Address (FAAC) ... ADS
Address Adder [*Computer science*] (IAA) ... AAD
Address Adder (IAA) ... ADA
Address Arithmetic Unit [*Computer science*] ... AAU
Address Buffer (MCD) ... AB
Address Bus [*Computer science*] ... AB
Address Calculation Machine [*Compagnie Honeywell Bull*] (NITA) ... ACM
Address Carry [*Computer science*] (IAA) ... AC
Address Census [*or Control*] **File** [*Bureau of the Census*] (GFGA) ... ACF
Address Change Service [*Postal Service*] [*United States*] (WDMC) ... ACS
Address Coding [*Business term*] ... AC
Address Coding Guide ... ACG
Address Complete, Charge [*Telecommunications*] (TEL) ... ADC
Address Complete, Coin-Box [*Telecommunications*] (TEL) ... ADX
Address Complete Message [*Telecommunications*] (ACRL) ... ACM
Address Complete, No-Charge [*Telecommunications*] (TEL) ... ADN
Address Complete, Subscriber Free, Coin-Box [*Telecommunications*] (TEL) ... AFX
Address Complete, Subscriber Free, No-Charge [*Telecommunications*] (TEL) ... AFN
Address Constant [*Computer science*] ... ADCON
Address Control File [*US Census Bureau*] ... ACF
Address Control Register [*Computer science*] (MHDI) ... ACR
Address Control Unit [*Computer science*] (MDG) ... ACU
Address Correction Requested ... ACR
Address Counter [*Computer science*] (MHDI) ... AC
Address Data ... AD
Address Data Strobe [*Electronics*] ... ADS
Address Decoding [*Computer science*] (IAA) ... ADEC
Address Display System [*or Subsystem*] ... ADS
Address Effective [*Computer science*] (IAA) ... AE
Address Enable [*Computer science*] (IAA) ... ADE
Address Enable [*Computer science*] ... AEN
Address Error (NITA) ... ADE
Address Extension Register [*Computer science*] (IAA) ... AER
Address Generation/Execute Cycle [*Computer science*] ... AGEX
Address Generator ... ADGEN
Address Generator Module ... ADGM
Address Incomplete [*Telecommunications*] (TEL) ... ADI
Address Incomplete [*Telecommunications*] (TEL) ... AI
Address Indicating Group [*Computer science*] ... AIG
Address Information Center [*Memphis, TN*] [*US Postal Service*] ... AIC
Address Key Register ... AKR
Address Latch Enable [*Computer science*] ... ALE
Address Locator Logic [*Computer science*] ... ALL
Address Mark [*Microprocessors*] ... AM
Address Matching Software Package [*Bureau of the Census*] (GFGA) ... ADMATCH
Address Mode [*Computer science*] ... AM
Address Modifier ... AM
Address Out [*Computer science*] (IAA) ... ADO
Address Plate Cabinet ... APC
Address Recognition Unit ... ARU
Address Register ... ADDR
Address Register (BUR) ... ADR
Address Register (CMD) ... AR
Address Register Area [*Bureau of the Census*] (GFGA) ... ARA
Address Resolution Protocol [*Telecommunications*] (BYTE) ... ARP
Address Shift Register [*Computer science*] (NITA) ... ASR
Address Space Control Block [*Computer science*] (MHDI) ... ASCB
Address Space Control Task [*Fujitsu*] (NITA) ... ASCT
Address Space Identifier (BUR) ... ASID
Address Space Manager [*Computer software*] (NITA) ... ASM
Address Start Register [*Computer science*] (IAA) ... ASR
Address Strobe [*Signal*] [*Computer science*] ... AS
Address Syllable (IAA) ... AS
Address to Index, True ... AXT
Address Translation Buffer [*Telecommunications*] (TEL) ... ATB
Address Translation Cache [*Motorola, Inc.*] [*Computer science*] ... ATC
Address Translation Chip ... ATC
Address Translation Memory [*Computer science*] (IAA) ... ATM
Address Translation Unit (NITA) ... ATU
Address Translator [*Computer science*] ... AT
Address Unit [*Computer science*] ... AU
Address Validity (MCD) ... AVL
Address Verification Pulse (KSC) ... AVP
Address Verification System Plus [*Information Design, Inc.*] [*Information service or system*] (IID) ... AVS+
Addressable Asynchronous Receiver Transmitter ... AART
Addressable Remote Multiplexer Unit (MCD) ... ARMU
Addressed (ABBR) ... ADDRD
Addressed (ABBR) ... ADDSD
Addressed [*Computer science*] (IAA) ... ADSD
Addressed Cable Delivery (IAA) ... ACD
Addressee (NVT) ... ADDEE
Addressee (ABBR) ... ADDRE
Addressee (ECII) ... ADDSSEE
Addressee (CINC) ... ADEE
Addressee (ABBR) ... ADRSE
Addressee ... ADSE
Address-Generation Unit [*Computer science*] ... AGU
Addressing (ABBR) ... ADDRG
Addressing Systems International (NITA) ... ASI
Addressograph Multigraph [*Later, AM International*] (DGA) ... AM
Addressograph-Multigraph Copier Duplicator ... AMCD
Address-Selective [*British*] (MCD) ... ADSEL
Add-Subtract ... AS
Add-Subtract Time ... AST
Adducable (ABBR) ... ADUCB
Adduce (ABBR) ... ADC
Adduce (ABBR) ... ADUC
Adduced (ABBR) ... ADUCD
Adducing (ABBR) ... ADUCG
Adduct (ABBR) ... ADCT
Adducted (ABBR) ... ADUCTD
Adducting (ABBR) ... ADUCTG
Adduction (ABBR) ... ADCTN
Adduction [*or Adductor*] [*Medicine*] ... ADD
Adduction [*Neurophysiology*] (DAVI) ... A-D-Duct
Adduction (ABBR) ... ADUCTN
Adductive (ABBR) ... ADCTV
Adductive (ABBR) ... ADUCTV
Adductor Longus [*Anatomy*] ... AL
Adductor Pollicis [*Muscle*] [*Antomy*] (DAVI) ... Add Poll
AddValue Communications [*Telecommunications service*] (TSSD) ... AVC
ADE Corp. [*Associated Press*] (SAG) ... ADECp
ADE Corp. [*NASDAQ symbol*] (SAG) ... ADEX
Adecco SA [*Associated Press*] (SAG) ... AdccoSA
Adecco SA [*NASDAQ symbol*] (SAG) ... ADEC
Adel, GA [*AM radio station call letters*] ... WBIT
Adel, GA [*FM radio station call letters*] ... WDDQ
Adelaide [*Mount Bonython*] [*Australia Seismograph station code, US Geological Survey*] (SEIS) ... ADE
Adelaide [*South Australia*] (BARN) ... Adel
Adelaide [*Australia Airport symbol*] (OAG) ... ADL
Adelaide [*Australia ICAO location identifier*] (ICLI) ... APAA
Adelaide [*Australia ICAO location identifier*] (ICLI) ... APAD
Adelaide [*Australia ICAO location identifier*] (ICLI) ... APAR
Adelaide [*Australia ICAO location identifier*] (ICLI) ... APAX
Adelaide [*Australia ICAO location identifier*] (ICLI) ... APRM
Adelaide [*South Africa*] [*ICAO location identifier*] (ICLI) ... FAAD
Adelaide Airways Ltd. [*Australia*] ... AAL
Adelaide College of Divinity ... ACD
Adelaide Convention and Tourism Authority [*Australia*] ... ACTA
Adelaide Entertainment Centre [*Australia*] ... AEC
Adelaide Festival of Arts [*Australia*] ... AFA
Adelaide Gem and Mineral Club [*Australia*] ... AGMC
Adelaide Harriers Athletic Club [*Australia*] ... AHAC
Adelaide Historical Bottle Club [*Australia*] ... AHBC
Adelaide Junior Chamber of Commerce [*Australia*] ... AJCC
Adelaide Medical Centre for Women and Children [*Australia*] ... AMCWC
Adelaide/Parafield [*Australia ICAO location identifier*] (ICLI) ... APPF
Adelaide Pistol Shooting Club [*Australia*] ... APSC
Adelaide Potters' Club [*Australia*] ... APC
Adelaide Produce Market [*Australia*] ... APM
Adelaide Review [*A publication*] ... Adel R
Adelaide Steamship Co. (MHDB) ... ASC
Adelaide University Hockey Club [*Australia*] ... AUHC
Adelaide Wool Brokers' Association [*Australia*] ... AWB
Adelanto, CA [*Location identifier FAA*] (FAAL) ... HAK
Adelphi Parent Administered Readiness Test [*Educational development test*] ... APART
Adelphi University (GAGS) ... Adelphi U
Adelphi University, Garden City, NY [*Library symbol Library of Congress*] (LCLS) ... NGcA
Adelphi University, Garden City, NY [*OCLC symbol*] (OCLC) ... VJA
Adelphia Communic'A' [*NASDAQ symbol*] (TTSB) ... ADLAC
Adelphia Communications Corp. [*Associated Press*] (SAG) ... Adelph
Adelphia Communications Corp. [*NASDAQ symbol*] (SAG) ... ADLAC
Adelphoe [*of Terence*] [*Classical studies*] (OCD) ... Ad
Adelson-Velskii and Landis Trees [*Computer science*] ... AVL
Aden [*People's Democratic Republic of Yemen*] [*Airport symbol*] (OAG) ... ADE
Aden [*People's Democratic Republic of Yemen*] ... ADN
Aden [*People's Democratic Republic of Yemen*] [*ICAO location identifier*] (ICLI) ... ODAF
Aden Airways ... AD
Aden/International [*People's Democratic Republic of Yemen*] [*ICAO location identifier*] (ICLI) ... ODAA
Aden Law Reports [*A publication*] (ILCA) ... Aden LR
Aden News Agency [*People's Democratic Republic of Yemen*] (MENA) ... ANA
Aden Protectorate Levies [*British military*] (DMA) ... APL
Aden Trade Union Congress ... ATUC
Adenin, Thymine, Guanine [*Medicine*] (BABM) ... ATG
Adenine [*Also, Ade*] [*Biochemistry*] ... A
Adenine [*Also, A*] [*Biochemistry*] ... Ade
Adenine and Thymine [*Genetics*] (DAVI) ... AT
Adenine Arabinoside [*Medicine*] (DMAA) ... AA
Adenine Arabinoside [*Also called vidarabine*] [*Antineoplastic drug*] (DAVI) ... ARA-A
Adenine Arabinoside Monophosphate [*Biochemistry*] ... ara-AMP
Adenine Arabinoside Triphosphate [*Biochemistry*] ... ara-ATP
Adenine Nucleotide Translocator [*Genetics*] ... ANT
Adenine Phosphoribosyltransferase [*An enzyme*] ... APRT
Adenine Phosphoribosyltransferase [*An enzyme*] ... APRT
Adenine Ribose Naphthaline Imide [*Genetics*] ... ARNI
Adenine Ribose Thymine [*Genetics*] ... ART

Adenine, Thymine, Guanine [*Genetics*] (DAVI) ATG
Adenine, Uracil, Guanine [*Biochemistry*] AUG
Adenine-D-ribose-phosphate-phosphate-D-ribose-nicotinamide [*Also, NAD, DPN*] [*Biochemistry*] ARPPRN
Adenine-Guanine-Cytosine-Thymine (PDAA) AGCT
(Adeninyl)hydroxypropanoic Acid [*Antiviral*] AHPA
Adeno-Associated Virus AAV
Adenocarcinoma [*Medicine*] (MAE) ACA
Adenocarcinoma [*Medicine*] adenoca
Adenocarcinoma-Squamous Cell Carcinoma [*Oncology*] Adeno-SCC
Adenoid [*Otorhinolaryngology*] (DAVI) adn
Adenoid Cystic Carcinoma [*Medicine*] ACC
Adenoid Degenerative [*Viruses*] AD
Adenoidal-Pharyngeal-Conjunctival [*Virus*] [*Obsolete usage*] APC
Adenoidectomy [*Otorhinolaryngology*] (DAVI) adn
Adeno-Like Virus [*Medicine*] (DMAA) ALV
Adenoma Malignum of the Cervix [*Oncology*] AMC
Adenomatosis of the Colon and Rectum [*Medicine*] ACR
Adenomatous Hyperplasia [*Medicine*] AH
Adenomatous Polyposis Coli [*Genetics*] APC
Adenomatous Polyposis Coli [*Medicine*] APE
Adenosine [*One-letter symbol; see Ado*] [*A nucleoside*] A
Adenosine [*Also, A*] [*A nucleoside*] Ado
Adenosine Deaminase [*An enzyme*] ADA
Adenosine Deaminase [*An enzyme*] (DMAA) ADD
Adenosine Deaminase Complexing Protein (DMAA) ADCP
Adenosine Deaminase Inhibitor (PDAA) ADAI
Adenosine Deceminase Binding Protein [*Biochemistry*] ADABP
Adenosine Deminase [*An enzyme*] (DMAA) ADase
Adenosine Diphosphatase [*An enzyme*] ADPase
Adenosine Diphosphate [*Biochemistry*] ADP
Adenosine Diphosphate Ribosyltransferase [*An enzyme*] ADPRT
Adenosine Kinase (DMAA) ADK
Adenosine Kinase [*An enzyme*] AK
Adenosine Monophosphate [*Biochemistry*] AMP
Adenosine Monophosphate Deaminase [*An enzyme*] AMPDA
Adenosine Monophosphate Succinate [*Biochemistry*] AMPS
Adenosine Phosphate [*Pharmacology*] (DAVI) B_8
Adenosine Phosphate Phosphosulfate [*Also, PAPS*] [*Biochemistry*] APPS
Adenosine Phosphoribosyltransferase [*An enzyme*] ADPT
Adenosine Phosphosulfate [*Biochemistry*] APS
Adenosine Tetraphosphate [*Biochemistry*] Atetra P
Adenosine Triphosphatase [*An enzyme*] ATPase
Adenosine Triphosphatase (Na, K-Activated) [*An enzyme*] Na K-ATPase
Adenosine Triphosphate [*Biochemistry*] (AAMN) ADT
Adenosine Triphosphate [*Biochemistry*] ATP
Adenosis Pattern [*Medicine*] AP
Adenosyl Homocysteine (DMAA) AHCy
Adenosylcobalamin [*A vitamin*] (BABM) Abe Cbl
Adenosylcobalamin [*Biochemistry*] (DAVI) Ade Cbl
Adenosylcobalamin [*Also, DBC*] [*A vitamin*] ADOCBL
Adenosylhomocysteine [*Biochemistry*] AdoHcy
Adenosylmethionine [*Also, SAM, SAMe*] [*Biochemistry*] AdoMet
Adenovirus [*Also, ADV*] AD
Adenovirus [*Also, AD*] ADV
Adenovirus Major Late [*Medicine*] ADML
Adenovirus Major Late Promoter [*Genetics*] ADMLP
Adenovirus Respiratory Disease [*Medicine*] (PDAA) ARD
Adenylate Cyclase [*An enzyme*] AC
Adenylate Cyclase (DMAA) AdC
Adenylate Cyclase Inhibitor [*Biochemistry*] ACI
Adenylate Cyclase-Stimulating Activity [*Medicine*] (DMAA) ACSA
Adenylate Energy Charge (BARN) AEC
Adenylate Kinase [*An enzyme*] ADK
Adenylate Kinase [*An enzyme*] AK
Adenylic Acid [*Biochemistry*] AA
Adept (ABBR) ADPT
Adept Technology [*NASDAQ symbol*] (TTSB) ADTK
Adept Technology, Inc. [*Associated Press*] (SAG) AdeptT
Adept Technology, Inc. [*NASDAQ symbol*] (SAG) ADTK
Adeptly (ABBR) ADPY
Adeptness (ABBR) ADEPNS
Adeptness (ABBR) ADPNS
Adequacy (ABBR) ADQC
Adequacy (ABBR) ADQCY
Adequate A
Adequate (DMAA) adeq
Adequate (DAVI) ADEQ
Adequate (ABBR) ADQA
Adequate (FAAC) ADQT
Adequately (ABBR) ADQAY
Adequately (ABBR) ADQTY
Adequateness (ABBR) ADQTNS
Adera Financial Corp. Ltd. [*Vancouver Stock Exchange symbol*] ADF
ADFlex Solutions [*Associated Press*] (SAG) ADFlex
ADFlex Solutions [*NASDAQ symbol*] (SAG) AFLX
Adhere (MSA) ADH
Adhere (ABBR) ADHR
Adhered (ABBR) ADHRD
Adherence (ABBR) ADHRNC
Adherence Ratio [*Medicine*] (DMAA) AR
Adherens Junction [*Cytology*] AJ
Adherent (ABBR) ADHRNT
Adherent (ABBR) ADHRT
Adherent Cell (AAMN) AC
Adherently (ABBR) ADHRTY
Adhering (ABBR) ADHRG
Adhesion [*Medicine*] (DMAA) adh
Adhesion (ABBR) ADHN
Adhesion Molecule on Glia (DMAA) AMOG
Adhesion Proteoglycan [*Biochemistry*] AP
Adhesion Society (EA) AS
Adhesive (KSC) ADH
Adhesive (ROG) ADHEVE
Adhesive (ABBR) ADHSV
Adhesive ADHSV
Adhesive (ABBR) ADNV
Adhesive Active [*Tire manufacturing*] AA
Adhesive and Sealant Council (EA) ASC
Adhesive Bonding [*Welding*] ABD
Adhesive Bonding Repair ABR
Adhesive Component System (PDAA) ACS
Adhesive Film Mechanism AFM
Adhesive Insulation Material AIM
Adhesive Tape Manufacturers Association (EAIO) ATMA
Adhesively (ABBR) ADHSVY
Adhesively Bonded Joint [*or Junction*] ABJ
Adhesiveness (ABBR) ADHSVNS
Adhesiveness (ABBR) ADHVNS
Adhesives Manufacturers Association (EA) AMA
Adhesives Manufacturers Association of America [*Later, AMA*] (EA) AMAA
Adhibendus [*To Be Used*] [*Pharmacy*] (ROG) A
Adhibendus [*To Be Used*] [*Pharmacy*] (ROG) ADH
Adhibendus [*To Be Administered*] [*Pharmacy*] (DAVI) ADHIB
Adhibendus [*To Be Used*] [*Pharmacy*] ADHIBEND
Ad-Hoc Committee AHC
Adi Dassler [*Founder of German sporting goods company; acronym used as brand name of shoes manufactured by the firm*] ADIDAS
Adia SA [*Associated Press*] (SAG) AdiaSA
Adia S.A. ADS [*NASDAQ symbol*] (TTSB) ADIAY
Adia Services, Inc. [*NASDAQ symbol*] (NQ) ADIA
Adiabatic Fast Passage (OA) AFP
Adiabatic Film Cooling ADFC
Adiabatic Low-Energy Injection and Capture Experiment ALICE
Adiabatic Rapid Passage [*Physics*] ARP
Adiabatic Storage Test [*For hazardous chemicals*] AST
Adiabatic Toroidal Compressor [*Nuclear energy*] ATC
Adiake [*Ivory Coast*] [*ICAO location identifier*] (ICLI) DIAD
Adipic, Glutaric, and Succinic [*Acids for flue-gas cleaning*] AGS
Adipocyte Lipid-Binding Protein ALBP
Adipokinetic Hormone [*Endocrinology*] AKH
Adiponitrile [*Organic chemistry*] ADN
Adipose Differentiation-Related Protein [*Medicine*] (DMAA) ADRP
Adipose Fin [*Fish anatomy*] AD
Adipose Fin and Left Pectoral Fin Clips [*Pisciculture*] ADLP
Adipose Fin and Left Ventral Fin Clips [*Pisciculture*] ADLV
Adipose Fin and Right Pectoral Fin Clips [*Pisciculture*] ADRP
Adipose Fin and Right Ventral Fin Clips [*Pisciculture*] ADRV
Adipose Fin Clip with Coded Wire Tag [*Pisciculture*] ADCWT
Adipose Tissue Extract [*Biochemistry*] (MAE) ATE
Adirondack (FAAC) ADRNDCK
Adirondack Community College, Glens Falls, NY [*Library symbol Library of Congress*] (LCLS) NGlfAC
Adirondack Council (EA) AC
Adirondack Forty-Sixers (EA) AFS
Adirondack Historical Association (EA) AHA
Adirondack Historical Association Museum Library, Blue Mountain Lake, NY [*Library symbol Library of Congress*] (LCLS) NBmlA
Adirondack Mountain Club (EA) ADK
Adirondack Trail Improvement Society (EA) ATIS
Adirondack World Affairs Resources for Education AWARE
ADIS [*Australasian Drug Information Services*] **Drug Information Retrieval System** [*ADIS Press Ltd.*] [*Auckland, New Zealand*] ADIRS
Adizes Network International [*Santa Monica, CA*] (EA) ANI
Adjacency (ABBR) ADJC
Adjacency (ABBR) ADJCNC
Adjacens [*Adjacent*] [*Pharmacy*] (ROG) ADJAC
Adjacent ADJ
Adjacent (ABBR) ADJA
Adjacent (ABBR) ADJCNT
Adjacent (AFM) AJA
Adjacent Channel (IAA) AC
Adjacent Channel Attenuation ACA
Adjacent Channel Interference ACI
Adjacent Channel Rejection ACR
Adjacent Charging Group [*Telecommunications*] (TEL) ACG
Adjacent Fire Platoon [*Army*] ADJFP
Adjacent Phase Pulse Generator [*Electronics*] (OA) APPG
Adjacent Tone (IAA) AT
Adjacent Tone-Reference Phase-Shift Keying [*Computer science*] (IAA) ATPSK
Adjacently (ABBR) ADJAY
Adjacently (ABBR) ADJCNTY
Adjal [*Former USSR*] [*FAA designator*] (FAAC) ADJ
Adjectival (ABBR) ADJVL
Adjective A
Adjective (ROG) AD
Adjective ADJ
Adjective (ABBR) ADJV
Adjective Check List [*Psychology*] ACL
Adjective Noun [*Used in correcting manuscripts, etc.*] AjN

Adjective Phrase [*Linguistics*] ... AP
Adjoin (ABBR) ... ADJN
Adjoining ... ADJ
Adjoining (ABBR) ... ADJNG
Adjoining (ROG) ... ADJOING
Adjoining Landowner (DLA) ... ADJ L
Adjoint (ABBR) ... ADJ
Adjoint Gamma-Ray Moments [*Computer code*] ... ADJMOM
Adjoint Neutron Transport Equation (PDAA) ... ANTE
Adjoint Wave Function ... AWF
Adjornator [*British*] ... ADJ
Adjourn (ROG) ... ADJN
Adjourn (ABBR) ... ADJRN
Adjourned ... ADJ
Adjourned (ROG) ... ADJD
Adjourned (ABBR) ... ADJRND
Adjourned Session (DLA) ... Adj Sess
Adjourned Summons (BARN) ... adjd sumns
Adjourning (ABBR) ... ADJRNG
Adjournment (ABBR) ... ADJRNNT
Adjournment (ABBR) ... ADJRNT
Adjournment in Contemplation of Dismissal [*Law*] ... ACD
Adjournment in Contemplation of Dismissal [*Law*] ... ACOD
Adjudge (ABBR) ... ADJDG
Adjudged (ROG) ... ADJ
Adjudged (ABBR) ... ADJDGD
Adjudging (ABBR) ... ADJDGG
Adjudicate (ABBR) ... ADJDCA
Adjudicate (ABBR) ... ADJUD
Adjudicated (ADA) ... ADJD
Adjudicated (ABBR) ... ADJDCAD
Adjudicated (ABBR) ... ADJUDD
Adjudicating (ABBR) ... ADJDCAG
Adjudicating (ABBR) ... ADJUDG
Adjudication (ABBR) ... ADJDCAN
Adjudication (ABBR) ... ADJUDN
Adjudication (ROG) ... ADJUN
Adjudicator (ABBR) ... ADJDCR
Adjudicator (ABBR) ... ADJUDR
Adjudicatory (ABBR) ... ADJUDRY
Adjunct [*Linguistics*] ... A
Adjunct ... ADJ
Adjunct (ABBR) ... ADJNC
Adjunct in Arts ... Adj A
Adjunct/Switch Applications Interface [*Tekelec*] ... ASAI
Adjunctive (ABBR) ... ADJNCV
Adjunctive Therapy [*Medicine*] ... AT
Adjuntas, PR [*AM radio station call letters*] ... WPJC
Adjunto [*Enclosure*] [*Spanish Business term*] ... adj
Adjuration (ABBR) ... ADJRAN
Adjuratory (ABBR) ... ADJRAY
Adjure (ABBR) ... ADJR
Adjured (ABBR) ... ADJRD
Adjurer (ABBR) ... ADJRR
Adjuring (ABBR) ... ADJRG
Adjust ... ADJ
Adjust (ABBR) ... ADJS
Adjust Mode [*Computer science*] ... ADMD
Adjustable ... ADJ
Adjustable ... ADJBLE
Adjustable (ABBR) ... ADJSB
Adjustable [*Technical drawings*] ... ADJT
Adjustable Buoyancy Jacket ... ABJ
Adjustable Buoyancy Life Jacket ... ABLJ
Adjustable Chain Clutch (PDAA) ... ACC
Adjustable Focus Control (MCD) ... AFC
Adjustable Leg and Ankle Repositioning Mechanism (DMAA) ... ALARM
Adjustable Mortgage Loan [*Business term*] (EMRF) ... AML
Adjustable Multi-Class Organizing System (MHDI) ... AMOS
Adjustable Muzzle Stabilizer [*Rifles*] [*Army*] (INF) ... AMS
Adjustable Pawl Fastener ... APF
Adjustable Pitch Device ... APD
Adjustable Pressure Conveyor ... APC
Adjustable Ranging Telescope [*Army*] (MCD) ... ART
Adjustable Rate Mortgage ... ARM
Adjustable Rate Preferred Stock ... ARPS
Adjustable Rear Plate [*Air conditioning systems*] [*Automotive engineering*] ... ARP
Adjustable Shock Absorber ... ASA
Adjustable Speed (IAA) ... ADJSPD
Adjustable Speed Drive ... ASD
Adjustable Stroke Kit ... ASK
Adjustable Thermal Wire Stripper ... ATWS
Adjustable Thigh Antiembolism Stockings [*Cardiology*] (DAVI) ... ATS
Adjustable Voltage Inverter (PDAA) ... AVI
Adjustable Voltage Rectifier (IAA) ... AVR
Adjustable Voltage Screwdown ... AVS
Adjustable Wire Stripper ... AWS
Adjustable Zero, Adjustable Range ... AZAR
Adjustable Zero, Adjustable Span (IAA) ... AZAS
Adjustable-Rate Preferred Stock (MHDB) ... ARP
Adjustably (ABBR) ... ADJSBY
Adjusted (ABBR) ... ADJSD
Adjusted Agreement Index (EDAC) ... AAI
Adjusted Air Speed [*Navigation*] ... AAS
Adjusted Average per Capita Cost ... AAPC
Adjusted Average per Capita Cost ... AAPCC
Adjusted Balance Method ... ABM
Adjusted Calving Interval [*Dairy science*] (OA) ... ACI
Adjusted Compensation Payment Act [*1936*] ... ACPA
Adjusted Current Earnings ... ACE
Adjusted Daily Average (ADA) ... ADA
Adjusted Debit Balance [*Accounting*] ... ADB
Adjusted Family Income (GFGA) ... AFI
Adjusted Gross Income [*Income taxes*] ... AGI
Adjusted Gross Weight (MCD) ... AGW
Adjusted Insured Unemployment Rate ... AIUR
Adjusted Liquid Capital ... ALC
Adjusted Market Value [*Automobile retailing*] ... AMV
Adjusted Maximum Dive Time ... AMDT
Adjusted Megaton Equivalent (MCD) ... AMTE
Adjusted Monetary Base [*Economics*] ... AMB
Adjusted Net Present Value (MCD) ... ANPV
Adjusted on Basis of Photostat or Reviewed Copy of Temporary Pay Record from Finance Center, United States Army (AABC) ... ADJFCUSA
Adjusted Output [*Computer science*] ... AO
Adjusted Performance Percentile (DNAB) ... APP
Adjusted Permanent Pay Record [*Military*] (DNAB) ... ADJ/PPR
Adjusted Reviewed Copy of Temporary Pay Record [*Military*] (DNAB) ... ADJ/RCT
Adjusted Sequential Probability Ratio Test [*Statistics*] ... ASPRT
Adjusted Service Rating Score [*Military*] ... ASRS
Adjusted Total Financial Assistance Requirement ... ATFAR
Adjusted Transcript Deserter's Account [*Military*] (DNAB) ... ADJ/TDA
Adjusted Transcript Deserter's Account [*Military*] (DNAB) ... ADJ/TDA
Adjuster [*Finance*] ... ADJ
Adjuster (ABBR) ... ADJSR
Adjuster ... ADJSTER
Adjuster (ABBR) ... ADJSTR
Adjusting (ABBR) ... ADJSG
Adjusting Journal Entry [*Accounting*] ... AJE
Adjustment (IAA) ... A
Adjustment (AFM) ... ADJ
Adjustment ... ADJMT
Adjustment (ABBR) ... ADJSNT
Adjustment (ABBR) ... ADJST
Adjustment [*Accounting*] ... AJ
Adjustment and Preventative (MCD) ... AP
Adjustment Assistance ... AA
Adjustment Bond [*Investment term*] ... AB
Adjustment File [*IRS*] ... ADJF
Adjustment Inventory [*Psychology*] ... AI
Adjustment of Scheduled Maintenance Requirements through Analysis (MCD) ... ASMRA
Adjustment Payment Level [*Social Security Administration*] ... APL
Adjustment Reaction to Adult Life [*Medicine*] (DMAA) ... ARAL
Adjustment With a Human Face [*UNICEF phrase to describe African adjustment programs*] ... AWAHF
Adjustment-Calibration ... AC
Adjustor ... ADJTOR
Adjutancy (ABBR) ... ADJTNC
Adjutant ... A
Adjutant (AFM) ... ADJ
Adjutant ... ADJT
Adjutant ... ADJT
Adjutant General (DNAB) ... ADJG
Adjutant General ... AG
[*The*] **Adjutant General** [*Army*] ... TAG
[*The*] **Adjutant General Center** [*Army*] (AABC) ... TAGCEN
Adjutant General Inspection (DNAB) ... AGI
Adjutant General Management Information System ... AGMIS
Adjutant General Pool [*for Army officers*] ... AGP
Adjutant General Publications Center [*Army*] ... AGPC
Adjutant General, War Department [*Obsolete*] ... AGWAR
[*The*] **Adjutant General's Board, United States Army** ... TAGBDUSA
Adjutant General's Corps (AAGC) ... AG Corps
Adjutant General's Corps ... AGC
Adjutant General's Department [*Army*] ... AGD
Adjutant General's Office [*Washington, DC*] [*Army*] ... AGO
[*The*] **Adjutant General's Office** [*Army*] ... TAGO
[*The*] **Adjutant General's Research and Development Command, United States Army** ... TAGRDCUSA
[*The*] **Adjutant General's School** [*United States*], Army ... TAGSUSA
Adjutant Inspector General [*Military*] ... AIG
Adjutant-General (DAS) ... Adj-Gen
Adjutant-General [*British military*] (DMA) ... Adjt-Gen
Adjutant-General and Quartermaster-General [*British*] ... AG & QMG
Adjutant-General of the Royal Marines [*British*] ... AGRM
Adjutant-General to the Forces [*British*] ... AGF
Adjutants (ABBR) ... ADJTS
Adjutants General Association of the United States [*Later, AGAUS*] (EA) ... AGA
Adjutants General Association of the United States (EA) ... AGAUS
Adjuvant Arthritis ... AA
Adjuvant Chemotherapy [*Oncology*] ... ACT
Adjuvant Therapy [*Antineoplastic drug regimen*] (DAVI) ... AT
Adkins Life Skills Program (EDAC) ... ALSP
Adkinson on Township and Town Law in Indiana [*A publication*] (DLA) ... Adk Town
ADL [*Avionics Development Laboratory*] **Master Control Program** [*NASA*] (NASA) ... AMCP
Adler. Handbuch der Musikgeschichte [*A publication*] ... AdHM
Adler/Sochi [*Former USSR Airport symbol*] (OAG) ... AER

Adlerian Psychological Association of British Columbia (AC) .... APABC
Adlerian Society of Great Britain (BI) .... ASGB
ADM Tronics Unlimited [*Associated Press*] (SAG) .... ADM Tr
ADM Tronics Unlimited [*NASDAQ symbol*] (TTSB) .... ADMT
ADM Tronics Unltd. [*NASDAQ symbol*] (SAG) .... ADMT
Admar Group, Inc. [*Associated Press*] (SAG) .... Admar
[*The*] **Admar Group, Inc.** [*NASDAQ symbol*] (NQ) .... ADMR
Administer (CPH) .... admin
Administer (ABBR) .... ADMN
Administer (ABBR) .... ADMSTR
Administered (ABBR) .... ADMND
Administering (ABBR) .... ADMNG
Administracion de Aeropuertos [*Bolivia*] [*ICAO designator*] (FAAC) XXV
Administradora de Fondos ADS [*NYSE symbol*] (TTSB) .... PVD
Administradora de Fondos de Pensiones Provida SA [*Associated Press*] (SAG) .... AFProv
Administradora de Fondos de Pensiones Provida SA [*NYSE symbol*] (SAG) .... PVD
Administradoras de Fondos de Pensione [*Chile*] (ECON) .... AFP
Administrate (ABBR) .... ADMNT
Administrate (ABBR) .... ADMSTRA
Administrated (ABBR) .... ADMNTD
Administrates (ABBR) .... ADMNTS
Administrateur Agree [*Canada*] (DD) .... AdmA
Administrating (ABBR) .... ADMNTG
Administration .... A
Administration (DLA) .... Ad
Administration [*or Administrator*] (EY) .... ADM
Administration [*or Administrator*] (EY) .... ADMIN
Administration (DD) .... admin
Administration (DMAA) .... Admin
Administration (DLA) .... Administrn
Administration .... ADMN
Administration .... ADMN
Administration (ABBR) .... ADMNTN
Administration (ROG) .... ADMON
Administration (ABBR) .... ADMSTRAN
Administration .... ADOM
Administration above the Company (MCD) .... AAC
Administration and Logistics [*Military*] (INF) .... A & L
Administration and Management Operations [*Kennedy Space Center*] [*NASA*] (NASA) .... AM
Administration and Program Support [*George C. Marshall Space Flight Center Directorate*] [*NASA*] (NASA) .... A & PS
Administration and Storage Building .... ASB
Administration Branch, Manitoba Department of Municipal Affairs, Winnipeg, Manitoba [*Library symbol National Library of Canada*] (NLC) .... MWAMA
Administration Building Library, Canada Institute for Scientific and Technical Information [*Bibliotheque de l'Edifice de l'Administration, Institut Canadien de l'Information Scientifique et Technique*] **Ottawa, Ontario** [*Library symbol National Library of Canada*] (NLC) .... OONAB
Administration by Competency [*Business term*] .... ABC
Administration by Objectives .... ABO
Administration Center .... ADMCEN
Administration de la Voie Maritime du Saint-Laurent [*St. Lawrence Seaway Authority - SLSA*] [*Canada*] .... AVMS
Administration de l'Assistance Technique des Nations Unies [*United Nations Technical Assistance Administration*] .... AATNU
Administration des Mesures d'Encouragement du Secteur Petrolier [*Petroleum Incentives Administration*] [*Canada*] .... AMESP
Administration du Petrole et du Gaz des Terres du Canada [*Canada Oil and Gas Lands Administration*] .... APGTC
Administration du Pipeline du Nord Canada [*Northern Pipeline Agency Canada - NPAC*] .... APNC
Administration du Retablissement Agricole des Prairies [*Prairie Farm Rehabilitation Administration - PFRA*] .... ARAP
Administration Duty Officer (NATG) .... ADO
Administration for Children and Families [*Department of Health and Human Services*] .... ACF
Administration for Children, Youth, and Families [*Office of Human Development Services*] .... ACYF
Administration for Civil Affairs in Liberated Areas [*World War II*] .... ACALA
Administration for Native Americans [*Office of Human Development Services*] .... ANA
Administration for Native Americans Research Analysis Project (EDAC) .... ANARAP
Administration for Public Services [*Office of Human Development Services*] .... APS
Administration Group Office .... AGO
Administration Laboratory Project File [*University of Alberta*] [*Canada Information service or system*] (CRD) .... ALP
Administration/Logistics (INF) .... A/L
Administration Management Domain [*Telecommunications*] (TEL) .... ADMD
Administration Module (MCD) .... ADMIN MOD
Administration of Designed Services (TEL) .... ADS
Administration of Justice Branch [*US Military Government, Germany*] .... AJB
Administration of Territories Committee (Balkans) [*World War II*] .... AT(B)
Administration of Territories Committee (Europe) [*World War II*] .... AT(E)
Administration of Territories Committee (Europe), Shipping and Supply Subcommittee [*World War II*] .... AT(E)SSS
Administration of the Customs Union [*EEC*] (DS) .... ACU
Administration of Veterans Affairs [*Army*] .... AVA
Administration Office .... AO
Administration on Aging [*HEW*] [*Defunct*] .... AA
Administration on Aging [*Defunct Department of Health and Human Services*] .... AOA
Administration on Developmental Disabilities [*Human Development Services*] .... ADD
Administration Publique [*A publication*] (ILCA) .... Admin pub
Administration, Ryukyu Islands, Army (AABC) .... ARIA
Administration Sciences Research Centre [*University of Moncton*] [*Canada Research center*] (RCD) .... CRSA
Administration Support Equipment (MCD) .... ASE
Administration-Logistics [*Military*] (INF) .... ALOG
Administrative (DLA) .... Ad
Administrative (DLA) .... Adminstrv
Administrative .... ADMINV
Administrative (FAAC) .... ADMIV
Administrative .... ADMNSTRV
Administrative (ABBR) .... ADMNTV
Administrative (ABBR) .... ADMSTRAV
Administrative Adjustment Report [*Supply*] [*Military*] .... AAR
Administrative Agreement .... AA
Administrative Aircraft [*When a suffix to Navy plane designation*] .... Z
Administrative Aircraft Standardization Office [*NASA*] .... AASO
Administrative Analysis, Information, and Statistics [*Red Cross*] .... AAIS
Administrative and Accounting Purposes .... ADANDAC
Administrative and Clerical (ADA) .... A & C
Administrative and Direct Support Logistics [*Company*] [*Army*] .... A & DSL
Administrative and Logistics Delay [*or Down*] **Time** (MCD) .... ALDT
Administrative and Logistics Operations Center [*Military*] (INF) .... ALOC
Administrative and Management Services (OICC) .... AMS
Administrative and Management Services [*DoD*] (GFGA) .... AMSD
Administrative and Miscellaneous Duties [*RAF*] [*British*] .... AMD
Administrative and Operational Procedure (MCD) .... AOP
Administrative and Overhead [*Costs*] (KSC) .... AO
Administrative Appeals Reports [*Australia A publication*] .... AAR
Administrative Appeals Tribunal (ADA) .... AAT
Administrative Appeals Tribunal Decisions [*Australia A publication*] .... ADMN
Administrative Area Control Centre [*Military British*] .... AACC
Administrative Area Unit [*Army*] .... AAU
Administrative Arrangements Order (ADA) .... AAO
Administrative Assistant .... AA
Administrative Assistant to the Secretary of the Army .... AASA
Administrative Base Unit [*British military*] (DMA) .... ABU
Administrative Battalion [*British military*] (DMA) .... AB
Administrative Board - Dress Industry (EA) .... ABDI
Administrative Bulletin (MCD) .... AB
Administrative, Business, and Commercial (AIE) .... ABC
Administrative, Business, and Commercial Training Group (AIE) .... ABCTG
Administrative Circular .... ADCIR
Administrative Clerical and Technical Programs [*Department of Labor*] .... ACT
Administrative Code [*A publication*] (DLA) .... Admin Cd
Administrative Command .... ADCOM
Administrative Command [*Navy British*] .... ADCOMD
Administrative Command, Amphibious Forces, Pacific Fleet .... ADCOMPHIBSPAC
Administrative Command, Amphibious Forces, Pacific Fleet, Subordinate Command .... ADCOMSUBORDCOMPHIBSPAC
Administrative Command, Minecraft, Pacific Fleet .... ADCOMINPAC
Administrative Commitment Document .... ACD
Administrative Committee on Administration [*United Nations*] .... ACA
Administrative Committee on Coordination [*of the United Nations*] [*Aviation*] .... ACC
Administrative Committee on Coordination - Subcommittee on Nutrition [*United Nations*] (EAIO) .... ACC/SCN
Administrative Communications Distribution Center [*Air Force*] (AFM) .... ACDC
Administrative Communications Requirement (IAA) .... ACR
Administrative Computing Service .... ACS
Administrative Conference of the United States [*Independent government agency*] [*Washington, DC*] .... ACUS
Administrative Consent Order [*Environmental Protection Agency*] .... ACO
Administrative Contract Document (MCD) .... ACD
Administrative Contracting Office [*or Officer*] .... ACO
Administrative Control .... ADCON
Administrative Control System [*Telecommunications*] (TEL) .... ACS
Administrative Court Digest [*A publication*] (DLA) .... Ad Ct Dig
Administrative Data Processing (KSC) .... ADP
Administrative Data Systems .... ADS
Administrative Data Systems - Teleprocessing (IEEE) .... ADS-TP
Administrative Decisions [*A publication*] (DLA) .... Admin Dec
Administrative Decisions under Immigration and Nationality Laws of the United States [*A publication*] (DLA) .... BIA
Administrative Department (ADA) .... AD
Administrative Determination of Fault .... ADF
Administrative Directive (MCD) .... AD
Administrative Discharge [*Military*] (VNW) .... AD
Administrative Dispute Resolution Act (AAGC) .... ADRA
Administrative Dispute Resolution Act of 1996 (AAGC) .... ADRA
Administrative Distributed Network (GFGA) .... ADNET
Administrative District (ADA) .... AD
Administrative Division [*Municipality*] [*Board on Geographic Names*] .... ADMD
Administrative Engineering Information Management System .... AEIMS
Administrative Entity [*Job Training and Partnership Act*] (OICC) .... AE
Administrative Fact Sheet [*Vocational education*] (OICC) .... AFS
Administrative Flagship [*Navy symbol Obsolete*] .... APF
Administrative Identification (MHDI) .... ADMINID
Administrative Information Data System (AFM) .... AIDS
Administrative Inspection [*Military*] (NVT) .... ADINSP
Administrative Inspection [*Military*] (NVT) .... ADMININSP

Administrative Instructions ... ADMINI
Administrative Instructions ... ADMININST
Administrative Instructions ... AI
Administrative/Intelligence/Logistics [*Military*] ... AIL
Administrative Interpretations [*A publication*] (DLA) ... Adm Interp
Administrative Law (DLA) ... Ad L
Administrative Law (DLA) ... ADMIN L
Administrative Law Bulletin [*A publication*] (ILCA) ... Ad L Bull
Administrative Law Bulletin [*A publication*] (DLA) ... Ad LB
[*The*] **Administrative Law Journal of The American University** [*A publication*] (AAGC) ... Admin LJ
Administrative Law Judge [*Also, HE*] [*Federal trial examiner*] ... ALJ
Administrative Law Judge of the Department [*Department of Labor*] (OICC) ... ALJD
Administrative Law News [*A publication*] (DLA) ... Ad L News
Administrative Law Newsletter [*A publication*] (DLA) ... Ad L Newsl
Administrative Law Notes [*Australia A publication*] ... ALN
Administrative Law Reporter, Second (Pike and Fischer) [*A publication*] (DLA) ... Ad L Rep 2d (P & F)
Administrative Law Review [*A publication*] [*ABA*] (AAGC) ... Admin L Rev
Administrative Lead Time ... ALT
Administrative Leave (GFGA) ... AL
Administrative Liaison Officer ... ALO
Administrative License Revocation [*Laws*] ... ALR
Administrative/Logistics Center [*Military*] (INF) ... ALC
Administrative Machine Branch [*Army*] (AABC) ... AMB
Administrative Machine Division [*Army*] (AABC) ... AMD
Administrative Management by Objectives Appraisal System (EDAC) ... AMOAS
Administrative Management Division [*Coast Guard*] ... CAM
Administrative Management Society [*Willow Grove, PA*] (EA) ... AMS
Administrative Management Staff [*Environmental Protection Agency*] (GFGA) ... AMS
Administrative Manual ... AM
Administrative Medical Officer [*British*] ... AMO
Administrative Medicine (AAMN) ... ADM
Administrative Memo (NATG) ... ADMM
Administrative Module [*AT&T*] (ACRL) ... AM
Administrative Module Processor (ACRL) ... AMP
Administrative Motor Vehicle Management ... AMVM
Administrative Note ... AN
Administrative Office [*or Officer*] (CINC) ... ADMINO
Administrative Office Instruction ... AOINST
Administrative Office - Navy ... AO-N
Administrative Office, Navy Department ... AOND
Administrative Office of the Courts. Newsletter [*A publication*] (DLA) ... AOC Newsl
Administrative Office of United States Courts ... AOUSC
Administrative Officer [*Army*] ... Admo
Administrative Officer (GFGA) ... AO
Administrative Officer of the Day (DAVI) ... AOD
Administrative Officer on Duty ... AOD
Administrative Operation and Support Services [*Kennedy Space Center*] [*NASA*] (NASA) ... AD
Administrative Operations ... AO
Administrative Operations Branch [*NTIS*] ... AOB
Administrative Order ... ADMINO
Administrative Order (NVT) ... ADMINORD
Administrative Order [*Army*] ... Admo
Administrative Order (DLA) ... AO
Administrative Order on Consent [*Environmental Protection Agency*] (ERG) ... AOC
Administrative Organs Department (LAIN) ... AOD
Administrative Plan (NVT) ... ADMINPLAN
Administrative Procedure (NRCH) ... AP
Administrative Procedures Act [*1946*] ... APA
Administrative Processor (TEL) ... AP
Administrative Professional and Technical Evaluation System (DNAB) ... APTES
Administrative, Professional, Technical, and Clerical Grades [*Education*] (AIE) ... APT&C
Administrative Protective Order [*Department of Commerce*] (GFGA) ... APO
Administrative Publication [*Navy*] ... AP
Administrative Radio Conference [*International Telecommunications Union*] ... ARC
Administrative Real Time Express Mortgage and Investment System (MHDB) ... ARTEMIS
Administrative Reform Unit ... ARU
Administrative Report (NVT) ... ADMINREP
Administrative Research Bulletin ... ARB
Administrative Review [*A publication*] ... Admin Rev
Administrative Rules and Regulations of the Government of Guam [*A publication*] (DLA) ... Guam Admin R
Administrative Rules of Montana [*A publication*] (AAGC) ... ARM
Administrative Rules of Montana [*A publication*] (DLA) ... Mont Admin R
Administrative Rules of South Dakota [*A publication*] (AAGC) ... ARSD
Administrative Rules of South Dakota [*A publication*] (DLA) ... SD Admin R
Administrative Rules of Utah [*A publication*] (DLA) ... Utah Admin R
Administrative Ruling [*US*] ... AR
Administrative Science (DD) ... AdminSc
Administrative Sciences Association of Canada [*Association des Sciences Administratives du Canada*] ... ASAC
Administrative Sciences Corp. ... ASC
Administrative Section for Technical Cooperation [*United Nations*] ... ASTC
Administrative Service Centers (AABC) ... ASC
Administrative Service Office ... ASO
Administrative Service Officer Class ... ASOC
Administrative Service Officer Structure ... ASOS
Administrative Service Only ... ASO
Administrative Service Test ... AST
Administrative Service Unit ... ASU
Administrative Services Contract [*Health insurance*] (GHCT) ... ASC
Administrative Services Department [*Queensland, Australia*] ... ASD
Administrative Services Division [*Census*] (OICC) ... ASD
Administrative Site Procedures [*Nuclear energy*] (NRCH) ... ASP
Administrative, Staff, and Technical [*Budget term*] ... AS & T
Administrative Staff College [*British*] (DI) ... ASC
Administrative Staff Officer ... Admin SO
Administrative Support (NVT) ... ADMINSUP
Administrative Support (MCD) ... ADMSPT
Administrative Support ... AS
Administrative Support Airlift (MCD) ... ASA
Administrative Support and Logistic Company [*Military*] ... AS & L
Administrative Support Center [*Marine science*] (OSRA) ... ASC
Administrative Support Group [*Army*] ... ASG
Administrative Support Manual (DNAB) ... ASM
Administrative Support Operations Center [*Army*] ... ADSOC
[*The*] **Administrative Support Theaters Army** ... TASTA
Administrative Support Unit (DNAB) ... ADMINSUPP
Administrative Support Unit ... ASU
Administrative Survey Detachment [*Army*] (LAIN) ... ASD
Administrative Systems Testing Section [*Social Security Administration*] ... ASTS
Administrative Telecommunications Agency [*Canada*] ... ATA
Administrative Terminal Management System [*Computer science*] (HGAA) ... ATMS
Administrative Terminal System [*IBM Corp.*] ... ATS
Administrative Trainee [*Civil Service*] [*British*] ... AT
Administrative Transport Management Survey (MCD) ... ATMS
Administrative Use Vehicle [*Military*] (AABC) ... AUV
Administrative Use Vehicle Management Information System [*Military*] (MCD) ... AUVMIS
Administrative Veterinary Officer [*British military*] (DMA) ... AVO
Administrative Vice President (HGAA) ... AVP
Administrative Watch Officer (DNAB) ... AWO
Administrative Weight Limitation [*Military*] (AABC) ... AWL
Administratively (ABBR) ... ADMNTVY
Administratively Uncontrollable Overtime ... AUO
Administrative-Material Inspection [*Military*] (NVT) ... ADMAT
Administrative-Supply Technician [*Army*] (AABC) ... AST
Administrator (DLA) ... Ad
Administrator ... ADMINR
Administrator (DLA) ... Adminstr
Administrator ... ADMNSTR
Administrator (ABBR) ... ADMNTR
Administrator (ROG) ... ADMOR
Administrator ... ADMR
Administrator (WGA) ... ADMS
Administrator ... ADMSTR
Administrator (ABBR) ... ADMSTRATR
Administrator ... ADMTR
Administrator, Deputy (SAA) ... AD
Administrator Professional Leadership Scale ... APLS
Administrators' Bulletin [*A publication*] ... Admin Bull
Administrator's Discretionary Fund [*Marine science*] (OSRA) ... ADF
Administrators of Medium Public Libraries of Ontario (AC) ... AMPLO
Administrator's Pesticide Advisory Committee [*Terminated, 1985*] [*Environmental Protection Agency*] ... APAC
Administrator's Tracking System [*Environmental Protection Agency*] (GFGA) ... ATS
Administrators's Discretionary Fund (USDC) ... ADF
Administratrices [*Legal shorthand*] (LWAP) ... ADMRCS
Administratrix [*Business term*] (ADA) ... ADMIN
Administratrix [*Business term*] (ROG) ... ADMIX
Administratrix (ABBR) ... ADMNTX
Administratrix [*Business term*] (ROG) ... ADMRX
Administratrix [*Business term*] (ROG) ... ADMTRX
Administratrix [*Business term*] (ROG) ... ADMX
Adminstrative Data Transmission Network [*FAA*] (TAG) ... ADTN
Admirable (ABBR) ... ADMRB
Admirably (ABBR) ... ADMRY
Admirably (ABBR) ... ADMRY
Admiral ... A
Admiral ... ADM
Admiral (EY) ... ADM
Admiral (BARN) ... Adml
Admiral [*Navy*] ... O10
Admiral Commanding ... AC
Admiral Commanding Aircraft-Carriers [*Navy British*] ... ACAC
Admiral Commanding Battlecruisers [*Obsolete Navy British*] ... ACQ
Admiral Commanding North Atlantic Station [*Navy British*] (DMA) ... ACNAS
Admiral Commanding Reserves [*Navy British*] ... ACR
Admiral of the Fleet [*British*] ... AF
Admiral of the Ocean Sea [*Annual award of US Merchant Marine; title originally bestowed on Christopher Columbus by the Spanish government*] ... AOTOS
Admiral Superintendent [*Obsolete British*] ... AS
Admiral's Club [*American Airlines' club for frequent flyers*] [*Dallas/Ft. Worth Airport Texas*] (EA) ... AC
Admiralty [*British*] ... ADM
Admiralty (ABBR) ... ADMLT
Admiralty (ABBR) ... ADMRLT
Admiralty (NATG) ... ADMTY

Admiralty [*British*] ... ADMY
Admiralty and Ecclesiastical (DLA) ... A & E
Admiralty Berthing Officer [*British*] ... ABQ
Admiralty Board [*British*] ... AB
Admiralty Centre for Scientific Information and Liaison [*British*] ... ACSIL
Admiralty Chart Datum (PDAA) ... ACD
Admiralty Civilian Shore Wireless Service [*British*] (IAA) ... ACSWS
Admiralty Compass Observatory [*British*] (DEN) ... ACO
Admiralty Computing Service [*British*] (SAA) ... ACS
Admiralty Corrosion Committee [*British*] (KSC) ... ACC
Admiralty Court (BARN) ... Adm Ct
Admiralty Decisions of Hopkinson in Gilpin's Reports [*A publication*] (DLA) ... Hopk Adm Dec
Admiralty Decisions Tempore Hay and Marriott [*England*] [*A publication*] (DLA) ... Dec T H & M
Admiralty Division (DLA) ... Admir
Admiralty Engineering Laboratory [*British*] (MCD) ... AEL
Admiralty Experiment Works [*British*] ... AEW
Admiralty Experimental Diving Unit [*British*] ... AEDU
Admiralty Fleet Confidential Order [*British*] (DMA) ... AFCO
Admiralty Fleet Order [*Obsolete British*] ... AFO
Admiralty Floating Dock [*British*] ... AFD
Admiralty Fuel Experimental Station [*British*] ... AFES
Admiralty General Message [*Obsolete British*] ... AGM
Admiralty Gunnery Establishment [*British*] ... AGE
Admiralty Instruction [*A publication*] (DLA) ... AI
Admiralty Interview Board [*British*] ... AIB
Admiralty Islands ... AI
Admiralty Letter [*British military*] (DMA) ... AL
Admiralty Liaison Officer [*British*] ... ALO
Admiralty List of Lights [*British*] ... ALL
Admiralty List of Radio Signals [*British*] ... ALRS
Admiralty Marine Engineering Establishment [*British*] ... AMEE
Admiralty Marine Technology Establishment [*Research center British*] (IRC) ... AMTE
Admiralty Marine Training Establishment (Physiological Laboratory) [*Research center British*] ... AMTE(PL)
Admiralty Materials Laboratory [*British*] ... AML
Admiralty Medical Board [*British military*] (DMA) ... AMB
Admiralty Merchant Ship Defense Instructions [*British*] ... AMDI
Admiralty Merchant Shipping Instructions [*British*] ... AMSI
Admiralty Mining Establishment [*British*] (MCD) ... AME
Admiralty Monthly Order [*British military*] (DMA) ... AMO
Admiralty Naval Staff [*British*] ... ANS
Admiralty Net Defence [*Antitorpedo nets*] [*British World War II*] ... AND
Admiralty Notice to Mariners [*British*] (DI) ... ANM
Admiralty Office [*Navy British*] (ROG) ... AO
Admiralty Office, London (ROG) ... AOL
Admiralty Oil Laboratory [*British*] ... AOL
Admiralty Pattern [*The right procedure, the correct thing to do*] [*British*] ... AP
Admiralty Press Division [*British military*] (DMA) ... APD
Admiralty Reactor Test Establishment (MCD) ... ARTE
Admiralty Recruiting Service [*British*] ... ARS
Admiralty Regional Electrical Engineer [*British*] (IAA) ... AREE
Admiralty Research Establishment [*British*] (IRUK) ... ARE
Admiralty Research Laboratory [*British*] ... ARL
Admiralty Research Laboratory Extension [*British*] ... ARLE
Admiralty Sailing Directions for the World (BARN) ... ASDW
Admiralty Salvage Department [*British military*] (DMA) ... ASD
Admiralty Signal and RADAR Establishment [*British*] ... ASRE
Admiralty Signal Establishment [*British*] ... ASE
Admiralty Standard Stockless [*Anchor*] (PDAA) ... ASS
Admiralty Supply Item ... ASI
Admiralty Surface Weapons Establishment [*British Ministry of Defense*] [*Research center*] ... ASWE
Admiralty Weekly Order [*British military*] (DMA) ... AWO
Admiralty Works Department Employees Association [*A union*] [*British*] ... AWDEA
Admiration (ABBR) ... ADMRAN
Admiration (ABBR) ... ADMRN
Admire (ABBR) ... ADMR
Admired (ABBR) ... ADMRD
Admirer (ABBR) ... ADMRR
Admiring (ABBR) ... ADMRG
Admiringly (ABBR) ... ADMRGY
Admissibility (ABBR) ... ADMSBLT
Admissibility (ABBR) ... ADMSBT
Admissible (ABBR) ... ADMSB
Admissible Linear Unbiased Estimator [*Statistics*] ... ALUE
Admissible Rank Test [*Statistics*] ... ART
Admission ... ADM
Admission [*Medicine*] (DAVI) ... admit
Admission (ROG) ... ADMON
Admission (AFM) ... ADMSN
Admission and Discharge ... A & D
Admission and Disposition [*Medicine*] (DAVI) ... A & D
Admission and Disposition [*Military*] (AABC) ... AAD
Admission and Dispositions Section [*Field or evacuation hospital*] (VNW) ... A & D
Admission/Discharge/Transfer [*Hospital records*] (DHSM) ... ADT
Admission Multiphasic Screening [*Medicine*] (CPH) ... AMS
Admission Pattern Monitoring [*Medicine*] (HCT) ... APM
Admission Referral and Information Center [*Commission on Independent Colleges and Universities*] ... ARIC
Admission Scheduling and Control System [*Hospital management*] ... ASCS
Admission Test for Graduate Study in Business ... ATGSB
Admissions ... ADMIS
Admissions Testing Program ... ATP
Admissive (ABBR) ... ADMSV
Admit (WGA) ... ADM
Admit (ABBR) ... ADMT
Admittance (MAE) ... A
Admittance (ABBR) ... ADMTNC
Admittance [*Symbol*] [*IUPAC*] ... Y
Admitted [*Medicine*] (DAVI) ... Adm
Admitted (ABBR) ... ADMTD
Admittedly (ABBR) ... ADMTDY
Admitting (MSA) ... ADMG
Admitting (ABBR) ... ADMTG
Admitting Blood Sugar [*Medicine*] ... ABS
Admitting Diagnosis [*Medicine*] (MAE) ... AD
Admixture (ABBR) ... ADMXR
Admixture-Lathe-Cut + Eutectic [*Dental alloy*] ... ALE
Admixture-Lathe-Cut + Single Composition Spherical [*Dental alloy*] ... ALSCS
Admonish (ABBR) ... ADMNH
Admonish (ABBR) ... ADMON
Admonished (ABBR) ... ADMOND
Admonisher (ABBR) ... ADMNHR
Admonisher (ABBR) ... ADMONR
Admonishing (ABBR) ... ADMONG
Admonishingly (ABBR) ... ADMONGY
Admonishment (ABBR) ... ADMONT
Admonition (ABBR) ... ADMNN
Admonition (ABBR) ... ADMONTN
Admonitions (ABBR) ... ADMNTNS
Admove [*Apply*] [*Pharmacy*] ... ADM
Admove [*Apply*] [*Pharmacy*] ... ADMOV
Adnexa [*Medicine*] (CPH) ... ad
Adobe (VRA) ... adb
Adobe Font Metrics File (CDE) ... AFM File
Adobe Illustrator [*Computer science*] (PCM) ... AI
Adobe Systems [*NASDAQ symbol*] (TTSB) ... ADBE
Adobe Systems [*Associated Press*] (SAG) ... AdobeSy
Adobe Systems, Inc. [*NASDAQ symbol*] (NQ) ... ADBE
Adobe Type Manager [*Computer software*] [*Adobe Systems, Inc.*] (PCM) ... ATM
Adola Mining Corp. [*Vancouver Stock Exchange symbol*] ... ADA
Adolescence (ABBR) ... ADLSNC
Adolescence (DMAA) ... adol
Adolescence [*A publication*] (BRI) ... Adoles
Adolescent (ABBR) ... ADLSNT
Adolescent (ABBR) ... ADLST
Adolescent ... ADOL
Adolescent Abuse Inventory (EDAC) ... AAI
Adolescent Alienation Index [*Personality development test*] [*Psychology*] ... AAI
Adolescent and Adult Psychoeducational Profile [*Educational testing*] ... AAPEP
Adolescent Behavior Rating Scale [*Devereaux*] [*Also, DAB*] [*Psychology*] ... ABRS
Adolescent Drug Abuse Unit [*Medicine*] (DMAA) ... ADAU
Adolescent Family Life Act [*of 1981*] ... AFLA
Adolescent Family Life Program [*Department of Health and Human Services*] ... AFL
Adolescent Language Quotient (PAZ) ... ALQ
Adolescent Language Screening Test [*Speech development test*] ... ALST
Adolescent Medicine [*Medical specialty*] (DHSM) ... ADL
Adolescent Medicine [*Medicine*] (DMAA) ... ADO
Adolescent Multiphasic Personality Inventory [*Personality development test*] [*Psychology*] ... AMPI
Adolescent-Coping Orientation for Problem Experiences [*Psychology*] ... A-COPE
Adolescent-Family Inventory of Life Events and Changes [*Psychology*] ... A-FILE
Adolfo [*Couturier*] ... A
Adolph Meyer Mental Health Center, Decatur, IL [*Library symbol Library of Congress*] (LCLS) ... IDecM
Adolphus and Ellis' English King's Bench Reports [*A publication*] (DLA) ... Ad & E
Adolphus and Ellis' English King's Bench Reports [*A publication*] (DLA) ... Ad & El
Adolphus and Ellis' English King's Bench Reports [*A publication*] (DLA) ... Ad & El (Eng)
Adolphus and Ellis' English King's Bench Reports [*A publication*] (DLA) ... Adol & El
Adolphus and Ellis' English King's Bench Reports [*A publication*] (DLA) ... Adolph & E
Adolphus and Ellis' English Queen's Bench Reports [*A publication*] (DLA) ... A & E
Adolphus and Ellis' English Queen's Bench Reports, New Series [*A publication*] (DLA) ... A & E (NS)
Adolphus and Ellis' English Queen's Bench Reports, New Series [*A publication*] (DLA) ... Ad & Ell NS
Adolphus and Ellis' English Queen's Bench Reports, New Series [*A publication*] (DLA) ... Adol & El NS
Adolphus and Ellis' Reports, New Series [*A publication*] (ILCA) ... Ad & El NS
Adopt a Special Kid (PAZ) ... AASK
Adoptable (ABBR) ... ADOPB
Adopted (ABBR) ... ADOPD
Adopted By ... AD
Adopted Child ... AC
Adopted Child [*Legal shorthand*] (LWAP) ... ADC
Adopted From [*or Adoption Of*] [*Etymology*] ... A
Adoptee/Natural Parent Locators [*Later, ANPLI*] (EA) ... ANPL
Adoptee/Natural Parent Locators - International [*Formerly, ANPL*] [*Later, MPI*] (EA) ... ANPLI

Adoptee-Birthparent Center [*An association*] (EA) ... ABC
Adoptee-Birthparent Support Network (EA) ... ABSN
Adoptees and Natural Parents Organization (EA) ... ANPO
Adoptees in Search [*An association*] (EA) ... AIS
Adoptees Liberty Movement Association (EA) ... ALMA
Adoptees' Liberty Movement Association (PAZ) ... ALMA Society
Adopter (ABBR) ... ADOPR
Adopting (ABBR) ... ADOPG
Adoption (ABBR) ... ADOP
Adoption (ABBR) ... ADOPN
Adoption (DLA) ... ADOPT
Adoption ... ADPTN
Adoption Act [*British*] ... AA
Adoption and Family Reunion Center (EA) ... AFRC
Adoption Directory [*A publication*] ... AD
Adoption Identity Movement (EA) ... AIM
Adoption of Automatically Programmed Tools [*Computer science*] (IEEE) ... ADAPT
Adoption Resource Exchange [*British*] (DI) ... ARE
Adoption Resource Exchange of North America [*Later, NAIES*] (EA) ... ARENA
Adoption Search Institute [*Inactive*] (EA) ... ASI
Adoption Taxpayer Identification Number ... ATIN
Adoption Triangle Ministries [*Later, AFRC*] (EA) ... ATM
Adoptive (ABBR) ... ADOPV
Adoptive Bit Rate Encoding [*Computer science*] ... ABRE
Adoptive Families of America [*An association*] ... AFA
Adoptive Families of America [*Formerly, OURS (Organization for United Response)*] (PAZ) ... AFA
Adoptive Family Network [*Formerly, Families Adopting Children Everywhere (FACE)*] (PAZ) ... AFN
Adoptive Triangle New South Wales [*Australia An association*] ... ATNSW
Adorability (ABBR) ... ADORBT
Adorable (ABBR) ... ADORB
Adorableness (ABBR) ... ADORBNS
Adorably (ABBR) ... ADORBL
Adorably (ABBR) ... ADORBY
Adoration (ABBR) ... ADORAN
Adoration (ABBR) ... ADORTN
Adoratrici Perpetuae del Santissimo Sacramento [*Nuns of the Perpetual Adoration of the Blessed Sacrament*] [*Roman Catholic religious order*] ... AP
Adored (ABBR) ... ADORD
Adorers of the Blood of Christ [*Roman Catholic women's religious order*] ... ASC
Adorers of the Precious Blood (TOCD) ... APB
Adoring (ABBR) ... ADORG
Adoringly (ABBR) ... ADORGY
Adornment (ABBR) ... ADORNT
Adornment (ABBR) ... ADRNT
Adorno Fathers (TOCD) ... CRM
Adorno Fathers (TOCD) ... crm
ADP [*Automatic Data Processing, Inc.*] **Brokerage Information Services Group** [*Also, an information service or system*] (IID) ... ADP/BISG
ADP [*Automatic Data Processing, Inc.*] **Electronic Financial Services** [*Telecommunications service*] (TSSD) ... ADP-EFS
ADP [*American Defense Preparedness*] **Equipment** (DOMA) ... ADPE
ADP [*Automatic Data Processing, Inc.*] **Financial Information Services, Inc.** [*Later, ADP/BISG*] [*Information service or system*] (IID) ... ADP/FIS
ADP [*Adenosine Diphosphate*] **Ribosylated Enzyme** ... ADPR
ADP [*Adenosine Diphosphate*]-Ribosylation Factor [*Biochemistry*] ... ARF
ADP [*Automatic Data Processing*] **Systems Resources Analysis** ... ASRA
ADP [*Automatic Data Processing, Inc.*] **Telephone Computing Services, Inc.** [*Telecommunications service*] (TSSD) ... ADP/TCS
Ad-Page Exposure (NTCM) ... APX
ADPE [*Automatic Data Processing Equipment*] **Resources Management System** (AFM) ... ARMS
Ad-Print, Belleville, NJ [*Library symbol Library of Congress*] (LCLS) ... NjBeA
Adrar [*Algeria*] [*Airport symbol*] (OAG) ... AZR
Adrar/Touat [*Algeria*] [*ICAO location identifier*] (ICLI) ... DAUA
Adrenal [*Medicine*] ... Ad
Adrenal [*Gland*] (ABBR) ... ADREN
Adrenal Androgen [*Medicine*] (DMAA) ... AA
Adrenal Androgen Corticotropic Stimulating Hormone [*Medicine*] (DMAA) ... AACSH
Adrenal Androgen Stimulating Hormone [*Medicine*] ... AASH
Adrenal [*or Adrenocortical*] **Autoantibody** ... AA
Adrenal Cortex [*Medicine*] ... AC
Adrenal Cortex [*Medicine*] ... AdC
Adrenal Cortical Extract [*Endocrinology*] ... ACE
Adrenal Cortical Hormone [*Endocrinology*] ... ACH
Adrenal Cortical Insufficiency [*Endocrinology*] (MAE) ... ACI
Adrenal Gland [*Anatomy*] ... ADGL
Adrenal Hypoplasia Congenita [*Metabolic disease*] ... AHC
Adrenal Hypoplasia Congenita [*Medicine*] ... AHC
Adrenal Medulla [*Anatomy*] ... AdM
Adrenal Medulla [*Anatomy*] ... AM
Adrenal Metabolic Research Society of the Hypoglycemia Foundation (EA) ... AMRSHF
Adrenal Weight Factor [*Endocrinology*] ... AWF
Adrenalectomized [*Medicine*] ... ADX
Adrenalectomy [*Medicine*] (DAVI) ... Adrenex
Adrenaline [*Endocrinology*] (MAE) ... A
Adrenaline [*Endocrinology*] ... Adr
Adrenaline (ABBR) ... ADRN
Adrenergic Receptor [*Physiology*] ... AR
Adrenergic Receptor Binder [*Physiology*] (DMAA) ... ARB
Adrenergic Receptor Material [*Physiology*] (DMAA) ... ARM
Adrenocortical Carcinoma [*Medicine*] ... ACC
Adrenocortical Renin Inhibitory Peptide [*Biochemistry*] ... ACRIP
Adrenocorticoid [*Medicine*] ... AC
Adrenocorticopolypeptide [*Endocrinology*] ... ACPP
Adrenocorticosteroid [*Medicine*] (OA) ... ACS
Adrenocorticotrophic Hormone [*Endocrinology*] ... ACTH
Adrenocorticotrophic Polypeptide [*Endocrinology*] ... ACTP
Adrenocorticotrophin (PDAA) ... ACT
Adrenocorticotrophin-Like Immunoreactivity [*Immunochemistry*] ... ACTH-LI
Adrenocorticotropic Hormone Receptor [*Medicine*] (DMAA) ... ACTHR
Adrenocorticotropic Hormone-Releasing Factor [*Endocrinology*] (MAE) ... ACTH-RF
Adrenocorticotropin [*Endocrinology*] (MAE) ... ACTN
Adrenogenital Syndrome [*Medicine*] ... AGS
Adrenoglomerulotrophin [*Medicine*] (MEDA) ... AGT
Adrenoglomerulotrophin [*Also, ASH*] [*Endocrinology*] ... AGTr
Adrenoglomerulotropin Hormone [*Endocrinology*] (MAE) ... AGTH
Adrenoleukodystrophy [*Medicine*] ... ALD
Adrenoleukodystrophy Protein [*Biochemistry*] ... ALDP
Adrenomyeloneuropathy [*Neurology*] ... AMN
Adria Airways [*Yugoslavia*] [*ICAO designator*] (FAAC) ... ADR
Adria Airways [*Airline flight code*] (ODBW) ... JP
Adria Laboratories, Inc., Columbus, OH [*OCLC symbol*] (OCLC) ... OAD
Adriamcin, Cyclophosphamide, Cisplatin [*Antineoplastic drug regimen*] (DAVI) ... CAD-I
Adriamycin [*Also, ADM, ADR, D, H*] [*Antineoplastic drug*] ... A
Adriamycin [*Also, A, ADR, D, H*] [*Antineoplastic drug*] ... ADM
Adriamycin [*Also, A, ADM, D, H*] [*Antineoplastic drug*] ... ADR
Adriamycin (DMAA) ... Adr
Adriamycin [*Also called doxorubicin*] [*Antineoplastic drug*] (DAVI) ... ADRIA
Adriamycin, ARA-C [*Cytosine Arabinoside*] [*Antineoplastic drug*] (CDI) ... AA
Adriamycin, ARA-C [*Cytarabine*] [*Antineoplastic drug*] (CDI) ... AA
Adriamycin, BCNU [*Carmustine*], Cyclophosphamide [*Antineoplastic drug regimen*] ... ABC
Adriamycin, Bleomycin, CCNU [*Lomustine*], Dacarbazine [*Antineoplastic drug regimen*] ... ABCD
Adriamycin, Bleomycin, Cisplatin, Radiation Therapy [*Antineoplastic drug regimen*] (DAVI) ... ABCX
Adriamycin, Bleomycin, Cyclophosphamide, Mitomycin C [*Antineoplastic drug regimen*] ... ABCM
Adriamycin, Bleomycin, Dacarbazine [*Antineoplastic drug regimen*] ... ABD
Adriamycin, Bleomycin, Dacarbazine, CCNU [*Lomustine*] [*Antineoplastic drug regimen*] ... ABDIC
Adriamycin, Bleomycin, Dacarbazine, Vinblastine [*Antineoplastic drug regimen*] ... ABDV
Adriamycin, Bleomycin, Prednisone [*Antineoplastic drug regimen*] ... ABP
Adriamycin, Bleomycin, Vinblastine [*Antineoplastic drug regimen*] ... ABV
Adriamycin, Bleomycin, Vinblastine [*Oncovin*], Dacarbazine [*Antineoplastic drug regimen*] ... ABVD
Adriamycin, Carmustine [*Antineoplastic drug*] (CDI) ... AC
Adriamycin, CCNU [*Lomustine*] [*Antineoplastic drug regimen*] ... AC
Adriamycin Cisplatin [*Antineoplastic drug*] (CDI) ... AP
Adriamycin, Cisplatin, Arabinosylcytosine, Adrenocorticoid [*Antineoplastic drug*] (CDI) ... ASHAP
Adriamycin, Cyclophosphamide [*Antineoplastic drug regimen*] ... AC
Adriamycin, Cyclophosphamide [*Antineoplastic drug regimen*] ... ACe
Adriamycin, Cyclophosphamide, 5-Fluorouracil, Actinomycin D [*Antineoplastic drug regimen*] (DAVI) ... ADCONFU
Adriamycin, Cyclophosphamide, Dacarbazine [*Antineoplastic drug regimen*] ... A-CY-DIC
Adriamycin, Cyclophosphamide, Dacrabazine [*DTIC*], Actinomycin D [*Antineoplastic drug regimen*] (DAVI) ... ACID
Adriamycin [*Doxorubicin*], Cyclophosphamide, Etoposide [*VP-16*] [*Antineoplastic drug regimen*] (DAVI) ... ACE
Adriamycin, Cyclophosphamide, Methotrexate [*Antineoplastic drug regimen*] ... ACM
Adriamycin, Cyclophosphamide, Oncovin [*Vincristine*], Prednisone [*Antineoplastic drug regimen*] ... ACOP
Adriamycin, Cyclophosphamide, Oncovin [*Vincristine*], Procarbazine, Prednisone [*Antineoplastic drug regimen*] ... ACOPP
Adriamycin, Cyclophosphamide, Vincristine, 5-Fluorouracil, [*Antineoplastic drug regimen*] (DAVI) ... ADCONFU
Adriamycin, Cyclophosphamide, Vincristine, Cytosine Arabinoside, Prednisone [*Antineoplastic drug regimen*] (DAVI) ... ACOAP
Adriamycin, Cyclophosphamide/X-Ray Therapy [*Antineoplastic drug regimen*] ... AC/XRT
Adriamycin [*Doxorubicin*], Cyclophosphanide, and Etoposide in High Dose Infusion [*Vepeside*] [*Antineoplastic drug regimen*] (DAVI) ... ACE-11
Adriamycin [*Doxorubicin*], Cytosine Arabinoside , Vincristine, Prednisone [*Cytarabine*] [*Antineoplastic drug regimen*] (DAVI) ... ADOAP
Adriamycin, Dacarbazine [*Antineoplastic drug regimen*] ... A-DIC
Adriamycin, Dacarbazine, Bleomycin, CCNU [*Lomustine*] [*Antineoplastic drug regimen*] ... ADBC
Adriamycin, Dacarbazine, Dactinomycin [*Antineoplastic drug regimen*] ... A-DIC-DACT
Adriamycin, Dactinomycin [*Antineoplastic drug regimen*] ... A-DACT
Adriamycin, Ifosfamide, Dacarbazine [*Antineoplastic drug regimen*] ... AID
Adriamycin, Leukeran [*Chlorambucil*], Oncovin , Methotrexate, Actinomycin D, Dacarbazine [*Vincristine*] [*Antineoplastic drug regimen*] ... ALOMAD
Adriamycin, L-Phenylalanine Mustard [*Antineoplastic drug regimen*] ... Adria-L-PAM
Adriamycin, Oncovin, ara-C, Prednisone [*Antineoplastic drug regimen*] ... ADOAP
Adriamycin, Oncovin [*Vincristine*], Prednisone [*Antineoplastic drug regimen*] ... ADOP

Adriamycin, Prednisone, Oncovin [*Vincristine*] [*Antineoplastic drug regimen*] .... APO
Adriamycin, Vinblastine, Methotrexate [*Antineoplastic drug regimen*] (DAVI) .... AVM
Adriamycin, Vincristine [*Antineoplastic drug regimen*] .... AV
Adriamycin, Vincristine, Cyclophosphamide [*Antineoplastic drug regimen*]..... AVC
Adriamycin, Vincristine, Procarbazine [*Antineoplastic drug regimen*] (DAVI) .... AVP
Adrian C. and Leon Israel [*in company name "ACLI International"*] .... ACLI
Adrian College, Adrian, MI [*OCLC symbol*] (OCLC) .... EEA
Adrian College, Adrian, MI [*Library symbol Library of Congress*] (LCLS) ...... MiAdC
Adrian, MI [*Location identifier FAA*] (FAAL) .... ADG
Adrian, MI [*AM radio station call letters*] .... WABJ
Adrian, MI [*FM radio station call letters*] .... WLEN
Adrian, MI [*FM radio station call letters*] .... WQTE
Adrian, MI [*FM radio station call letters*] .... WVAC
Adrian Public Library, Adrian, MI [*Library symbol Library of Congress*] (LCLS) .... MiAd
Adrian Resources [*Vancouver Stock Exchange symbol*] .... ADL
Adrian Resources [*NASDAQ symbol*] (TTSB) .... ADLRF
Adrian Resources Ltd. [*NASDAQ symbol*] (SAG) .... ADLR
Adrian Resources Ltd. [*Associated Press*] (SAG) .... AdrianR
Adrian Van Reypen Egerton [*Near-acronym used as shortened first name of detective-story character Average Jones, in stories by Samuel Hopkins Adams*] .... AVERAGE
Adriance Memorial Library, Poughkeepsie, NY [*Library symbol Library of Congress*] (LCLS) .... NP
Adriatic (ABBR) .... ADR
Adriatic Base Command [*Military*] .... ABC
Adriatic Force [*Military*] .... ADFOR
Adriatic Resources Corp. [*Vancouver Stock Exchange symbol*] .... AIC
Adroit (ABBR) .... ADRT
Adroit .... ADRT
Adroitly (ABBR) .... ADRTY
Adroitness (ABBR) .... ADRTNS
Adsorb (ABBR) .... ADSB
Adsorbed Normal Pool Plasma [*Clinical chemistry*] .... A-NPP
Adsorbent (ABBR) .... ADSBNT
Adsorbent (ABBR) .... ADSBT
Adsorbent (ABBR) .... ADSORB
Adsorption .... Ads
Adsorption (ABBR) .... ADSPN
Adsorption Isotherm Test [*Environmental chemistry*] (FFDE) .... AI
Adsorption Layer Open Tubular Column [*Chromatography*] .... ALOT
Adsorption Wall Open Tubular Column [*Chromatography*] .... AWOT
Adsorptive Heat Recovery [*Chemical engineering*] .... AHR
Adstante Febre [*When Fever Is Present*] [*Pharmacy*] .... AD FEB
Adstante Febre [*When Fever Is Present*] [*Pharmacy*] .... ADST FEB
ADT Aviation Ltd. [*British ICAO designator*] (FAAC) .... AUC
ADT Limited [*NYSE symbol*] (TTSB) .... ADT
ADT Ltd. [*NYSE symbol*] (SPSG) .... ADT
Adtran, Inc. [*NASDAQ symbol*] (SAG) .... ADTN
Adtran, Inc. [*Associated Press*] (SAG) .... Adtran
Adulate (ABBR) .... ADLA
Adulate (ABBR) .... ADUL
Adulated (ABBR) .... ADLAD
Adulated (ABBR) .... ADULD
Adulating (ABBR) .... ADLAG
Adulating (ABBR) .... ADULG
Adulation (ABBR) .... ADLAN
Adulation (ABBR) .... ADULN
Adulator (ABBR) .... ADLAR
Adulator (ABBR) .... ADULR
Adulatory (ABBR) .... ADLARY
Adulatory (ABBR) .... ADULY
Adult [*Film certificate*] [*British*] .... A
Adult (WGA) .... AD
Adult (ABBR) .... ADLT
Adult (ABBR) .... ADLT
Adult Accompaniment [*Restricted to age 14 and up unless accompanied by an adult*] [*Movie rating Canadian*] .... AA
Adult Acquired Immunodeficiency Syndrome [*Medicine*] (DAVI) .... AAIDS
Adult Adrenogenital Syndrome [*Medicine*] (DAVI) .... AAGS
Adult Album Alternative [*Radio broadcasting*] .... AAA
Adult Alternative Album [*Radio stations*] .... Triple-A
Adult and Community Education .... ACE
Adult and Vocational Educational Electronic Mail Network [*National Center for Research in Vocational Education*] [*Columbus, OH*] [*Telecommunications*] (TSSD) .... ADVOCNET
Adult Assessment and Coordination Team .... AACT
Adult Authority (OICC) .... AA
Adult Basic and Continuing Education (EDAC) .... ABCE
Adult Basic Education .... ABE
Adult Basic Education Resource and Information Service [*Australia*] .... ARIS
Adult Basic Learning Examination (NVT) .... ABLE
Adult Basic Skill Training (NVT) .... ABST
Adult Bovine Serum [*Medicine*] (DMAA) .... ABS
Adult, Career, and Vocational Education [*Educational Resources Information Center (ERIC) Clearinghouse*] [*Ohio State University*] (PAZ) .... CE
Adult Career Concerns Inventory [*Test*] .... ACCI
Adult Celiac Disease [*Medicine*] (CPH) .... ACD
Adult Certificate [*Board of Film Censors*] [*British*] (WDMC) .... A certificate
Adult Child of a Dysfunctional Family [*Psychology*] (DAVI) .... ACDF
Adult Child of Alcoholic [*Psychology*] (DAVI) .... ACOA
Adult Children Anonymous (EA) .... ACA

Adult Children Educational Foundation (EA) .... ACEF
Adult Children of Alcoholics [*Support group*] .... ACA
Adult Children of Alcoholics [*Bestseller by Janet Geringer Woititz*] .... ACoA
Adult Children of Alcoholics .... ACOA
Adult Children of Alcoholics [*Chemical dependency*] [*Psychology*] (DAVI) .... ADA
Adult Christian Education Foundation (EA) .... ACEF
Adult Community Movement for Equality [*Civil rights*] .... ACME
Adult Congregate Living Facilities [*Military*] .... ACLF
Adult Continuing Education (OICC) .... ACE
Adult Cost per Entered Employment [*Job Training and Partnership Act*] (OICC) .... ACEE
Adult Daily Minimum Requirement (HGAA) .... ADMR
Adult Day Health Care (GFGA) .... ADHC
Adult Diabetes Education Program and Training .... ADEPT
Adult Diphtheria and Tetanus Virus .... ADT
Adult Education .... AE
Adult Education and Lifelong Learning .... ADELL
Adult Education Association of the USA (EA) .... AEA
Adult Education Association of Victoria [*Australia*] .... AEAV
Adult Education Centre [*British*] .... AEC
Adult Education Institute (AIE) .... AEI
Adult Education Journal Review [*A publication*] (ADA) .... AEJR
Adult Education Program .... AEP
Adult Education Quarterly [*A publication*] (BRI) .... AE
Adult Education Tutors' Association [*Australia*] .... AETA
Adult Emergency Service [*In TV series "A.E.S. Hudson Street"*] .... AES
Adult Employment Training Programme [*British*] (AIE) .... ATP
Adult Entered Employment Rate [*Job Training and Partnership Act*] (OICC) .... AEER
Adult Erythrocyte [*Medicine*] (DMAA) .... AE
Adult Female (HGAA) .... AF
Adult Females, Density Of [*Ecology*] .... AFDEN
Adult Film Association of America (EA) .... AFAA
Adult Foster Care .... AFC
Adult Growth Examination [*Test*] .... AGE
Adult Heart .... AH
Adult Information on Drugs [*Referral service*] .... AID
Adult Inventory of Reading Interests and Attitudes (EDAC) .... AIRIA
Adult Jewish Education .... AJE
Adult Language Use Survey (AIE) .... ALUS
Adult Learning [*A publication*] (BRI) .... Adult L
Adult Learning Association (EA) .... ALA
Adult Learning Satellite Service [*Public Broadcasting Service*] [*Telecommunications service*] (TSSD) .... ALSS
Adult Life Long Learning Section [*Public Library Association*] .... ALLS
Adult Literacy and Basic Education .... ALBE
Adult Literacy and Basic Skills Action Coalition [*Australia*] .... ALBSAC
Adult Literacy and Basic Skills Unit [*British*] .... ALBSU
Adult Literacy and Numeracy Scale .... ALAN
Adult Literacy Support Services Fund (AIE) .... ALSSF
Adult Literacy Unit [*British*] .... ALU
Adult Males, Density Of [*Ecology*] .... AMDEN
Adult Migrant Education [*Department of Labor*] .... AME
Adult Migrant Education Home Tutor Scheme .... AMEHTS
Adult Migrant English Services [*New South Wales, Australia*] .... AMES
Adult Migrant Information System [*Australia*] .... AMIS
Adult Normal [*Medicine*] (DMAA) .... AN
Adult Nurse Practitioner (DAVI) .... ANP
Adult Onset Diabetes [*Medicine*] (DMAA) .... AOD
Adult Operculum .... AO
Adult Opportunity Center [*State employment service*] .... AOC
Adult Oriented Rock [*Music*] .... AOR
Adult Outpatient Psychotherapy Clinic (DMAA) .... AOPC
Adult Performance Level Project [*Defunct*] (EA) .... APL
Adult Personal Data Inventory [*Medicine*] (DMAA) .... APDI
Adult Polycystic Disease [*Nephrology*] (DAVI) .... APCD
Adult Polycystic Disease [*Medicine*] .... APD
Adult Protective Services .... APS
Adult Rat Growth Hormone [*Endocrinology*] .... ARGH
Adult Reading Improvement Association .... ARIA
Adult Recovery Services [*Chemical dependency and rehabilitation*] (DAVI) .... ARS
Adult Rehabilitation Centre [*Canada*] .... ARC
Adult Residential Colleges Association [*British*] (DBA) .... ARCA
Adult Respiratory Distress [*Medicine*] .... ARD
Adult Respiratory Distress Syndrome [*Medicine*] .... ARDS
Adult Retraining Program .... ARP
Adult Services Division [*American Library Association*] [*Later, RASD*] (EA)..... ASD
Adult Situation Stress Reaction [*Psychology*] (DAVI) .... ASSR
Adult T-Cell Leukemia [*Medicine*] (DMAA) .... ATCI
Adult T-Cell Leukemia [*Medicine*] .... ATL
Adult T-Cell Leukemia Antigen [*Medicine*] .... ATLA
Adult T-Cell Leukemia Virus [*Medicine*] .... ATLV
Adult T-Cell Leukemia-Lymphoma [*Medicine*] .... ATLL
Adult Training Strategy (AIE) .... ATS
Adult Unemployed Project [*Department of Education and Science*] [*British*] (AIE) .... AUP
Adult Use of Tobacco Survey [*1986*] .... AUTS
Adult Video Association (EA) .... AVA
Adult, Vocational, and Technical Education .... AVTE
Adult Vocational Training [*HEW*] .... AVT
Adult Vocational Training Program [*HEW*] .... AVTP
Adult Xanthogranuloma [*Medicine*] (DMAA) .... AXG
Adult-Child Interaction [*Test*] .... ACI
Adult-Contemporary [*Music*] .... AC
Adulterant (ABBR) .... ADLTNT

Adulterant (ABBR) ... ADLTRNT
Adulterant (ABBR) ... ADULT
Adulterate (ABBR) ... ADLTA
Adulterate (ABBR) ... ADLTRA
Adulterate (ABBR) ... ADULT
Adulterated (ABBR) ... ADLTAD
Adulterated (ABBR) ... ADLTRAD
Adulterating (ABBR) ... ADLTAG
Adulterating (ABBR) ... ADLTRAG
Adulteration (ABBR) ... ADLTRAN
Adulteration (ABBR) ... ADULT
Adulterer (ABBR) ... ADLTR
Adulterer (ABBR) ... ADLTRR
Adulteress [*Letter embroidered on Hester Prynne's dress in Nathaniel Hawthorne's "The Scarlet Letter"*] ... A
Adulteress (ABBR) ... ADLTRES
Adulteress (ABBR) ... ADLTRS
Adulterous (ABBR) ... ADLTRU
Adulterous (ABBR) ... ADLTUS
Adulterously (ABBR) ... ADLTUSY
Adultery (ABBR) ... ADLTRY
Adultery [*FBI standardized term*] ... ADLTY
Adultery (DLA) ... ADULT
Adulthood (ABBR) ... ADLTHD
Adult-Onset Diabetes Mellitus [*Medicine*] (DAVI) ... ADODM
Adult-Onset Diabetes Mellitus [*Endocrinology*] ... AODM
Adult-Onset Polycystic Kidney Disease [*Medicine*] ... APCKD
Adult-Onset Polycystic Kidney Disease [*Medicine*] ... APKD
Adult-Onset Still's Disease [*Medicine*] (DAVI) ... AOSD
Adults Molested as Children United (EA) ... AMACU
Adults Molested as Children United (EA) ... AMCU
Adults Only (ADA) ... AO
Adult-Versus-Child [*Medicine*] (DMAA) ... A-C
Adumbrate (ABBR) ... ADMB
Adumbrate (ABBR) ... ADMBRA
Adumbrated (ABBR) ... ADMBD
Adumbrated (ABBR) ... ADMBRAD
Adumbrating (ABBR) ... ADMBG
Adumbrating (ABBR) ... ADMBRAG
Advance [*Wire service code*] (NTCM) ... A
Advance [*Flowchart*] (AFM) ... ADV
Advance (FAAC) ... ADVN
Advance ... ADVNC
Advance (ABBR) ... ADVNC
Advance Acquisition Planning (AAGC) ... AAP
Advance Air Charters [*Canada ICAO designator*] (FAAC) ... ADV
Advance Airlines [*Australia*] ... AA
Advance Airlines [*ICAO designator*] (AD) ... DR
Advance Alteration Notice (MSA) ... AAN
Advance Antitank Weapon System - Medium (DWSG) ... AAWS-M
Advance Australia [*A publication*] ... Advance Aust
Advance Australia Party [*Political party*] ... AAP
Advance Aviation Services, Inc. [*ICAO designator*] (FAAC) ... XTJ
Advance Base Components [*Military*] (AFIT) ... ABC
Advance Base Section Dock [*Floating drydock, first used in World War II*] ... ABSD
Advance Baseline Configuration (MCD) ... ABC
Advance Book Information [*Publishing*] ... ABI
Advance Booking Charter [*Airline fare*] ... ABC
Advance Booking Fare [*Airlines*] ... ABF
Advance Boundary Information (DA) ... ABI
Advance Capability (MCD) ... ADVCAP
Advance Carrier Training Group [*Navy*] ... ACTG
Advance Cash Allowance Authorized ... ADCASHAL
Advance Change (DNAB) ... ADVCHG
Advance Change Authorization (SAA) ... ACA
Advance Change Notice (AAG) ... ACN
Advance Circuit Order and Layout Information [*Telecommunications*] (TEL) ... ACOLI
Advance Command ... ADCOM
Advance Command Post (NATG) ... ACP
Advance Components through Increased Volumetric Efficiency (SAA) ... ACTIVE
Advance Concepts for Terrain Avoidance ... ADCON
Advance Contracting Officer (AAG) ... ACO
Advance Corporate Contract Directive (MCD) ... ACCD
Advance Corporation Tax [*British*] ... ACT
Advance Count Switch ... ACS
Advance/Decline (MCD) ... A/D
Advance Decoy Missile (MCD) ... ADM
Advance Delivery of Correspondence [*Military*] ... ADC
Advance Development Engineering Order ... ADEO
Advance Development Group [*Army*] (AABC) ... ADG
Advance Deviations Report (AAG) ... ADR
Advance Devices and Material Committee [*British*] ... ADMG
Advance Discontinuance of Allotment ... ADVDISC
Advance Document Storage and Retrieval ... ADSTAR
Advance Drawing Release Notice (KSC) ... ADRN
Advance Electronic Diagnostics [*Automotive industry supplier*] ... AED
Advance Engineering Change Proposal (MSA) ... AECP
Advance Engineering Material Order ... AEMO
Advance Engineering Memorandum (AAGC) ... AE
Advance Engineering Memorandum ... AEM
Advance Engineering Order ... AEO
Advance Evaluation Note ... AEN
Advance Financial Bancorp [*Associated Press*] (SAG) ... AdvFnlB
Advance Financial Bancorp [*NASDAQ symbol*] (SAG) ... AFBC
Advance Freight [*Shipping*] (MHDW) ... Adv Frt
Advance Freight [*Shipping*] ... AF
Advance in Schedule (KSC) ... AIS
Advance in Schedule (KSC) ... AVS
Advance Information Document (MCD) ... AID
Advance Information Letter [*Military*] (AABC) ... AIL
Advance Information Memo (MCD) ... AIM
Advance Leave [*Military*] ... ADV/L
Advance Light Imaging with Computer Enhancement [*First projection television that houses a computer system*] ... ALICE
Advance List of Oversea-Returnees for Reassignment [*Army*] ... AOR
Advance Logistical Command [*Army*] ... ADLOG
Advance Manned Mission (SAA) ... AMM
Advance Manufacturing Directive ... AMD
Advance Market Protection (MCD) ... AMP
Advance Master Schedule Change Notice (SAA) ... AMSCN
Advance Material List (DNAB) ... AML
Advance Material Order [*Manufacturing*] ... AMO
Advance Material Request ... AMR
Advance Materials Process Program [*Department of Energy*] ... AMPP
Advance Missile Deviation Report ... AMDR
Advance Murgor [*Vancouver Stock Exchange symbol*] ... AVR
Advance Notice of Proposed Rulemaking [*Also, ANPRM*] [*US Government agencies*] ... ANPR
Advance Notice of Proposed Rulemaking [*Also, ANPR*] [*US Government agencies*] ... ANPRM
Advance of Pay and Allowances (AABC) ... APA
Advance Opinions [*A publication*] (DLA) ... Adv Ops
Advance Opinions in Lawyers' Edition of United States Reports [*A publication*] (DLA) ... Adv O
Advance Ordering Information ... AOI
Advance Paradigm, Inc. [*NASDAQ symbol*] (SAG) ... ADVP
Advance Paradigm, Inc. [*Associated Press*] (SAG) ... AdvPara
Advance Pay (MCD) ... AP
Advance Payment [*Finance*] ... ADVPMT
Advance Payment of Dislocation Allowance to Dependents [*Air Force*] (AFM) ... ADVDLA-DEP
Advance Payment of Mileage Authorized [*Army*] ... APMA
Advance Payment of Monetary Allowance in Lieu of Transportation Is Authorized [*Army*] ... APMALTA
Advance Payment of Subsistence and Quarters ... APSQ
Advance Payment of Travel per Diem Authorized [*Army*] ... APTPDA
Advance Payment Plan [*Airlines*] ... APX
Advance Personnel Requirements Research Note ... APRRN
Advance Planning Procedure Change (SAA) ... APPC
Advance Planning Procurement Information [*Army*] (MCD) ... APPI
Advance Port Purchase [*Investment term*] (ECON) ... APP
Advance Post Office Check [*Bureau of the Census*] (GFGA) ... APOC
Advance Prediction Computer Program ... APCP
Advance Process Engineering Order [*Manufacturing*] (MCD) ... APEO
Advance Procurement Data Worksheets [*Air Force*] (AFIT) ... APDW
Advance Procurement List (MCD) ... APL
Advance Procurement Plan (AAGC) ... AP Plan
Advance Procurement Plan [*Navy*] ... APP
Advance Procurement Planning Council [*DoD*] (PDAA) ... APPC
Advance Production Release (NRCH) ... APR
Advance Programming and Proposal Operations (MCD) ... AP & PO
Advance Purchase Excursion Fare [*Aviation*] (DA) ... APEX
Advance Purchase Required [*Also, AP*] [*Airline fare code*] ... AB
Advance Purchase Required [*Also, AB*] [*Airline fare code*] ... AP
Advance RADAR Maintenance Target Set (DWSG) ... ARMTS
Advance Reading Copy [*Publishing*] (WDMC) ... ARC
Advance Release [*Military*] ... ADVR
Advance Release Record (AAG) ... ARR
Advance Remote Display System [*Computer science*] (PDAA) ... ARDS
Advance Research Projects Agency Network [*Australia*] ... ARPNET
Advance Ross Corp. [*Associated Press*] (SAG) ... AdvRoss
Advance Ross Corp. [*NASDAQ symbol*] (NQ) ... AROS
Advance Sciences, Inc. (GAAI) ... ASI
Advance Section [*Military*] ... AD SEC
Advance Sensor Development Program [*Military*] (MCD) ... ASDP
Advance Services of Supply [*Army*] ... ADSOS
Advance Sheet (DLA) ... Ad Sh
Advance Sheet (DLA) ... Adv Sh
Advance Simulation Facility Interconnection and Setup System [*or Subsystem*] [*Air Force*] ... ASFISS
Advance Space System Hardening (MCD) ... ASSH
Advance STOL [*Short Takeoff and Landing*] **Transport (Medium)** [*Aviation*] (MCD) ... ASTM
Advance Stoppage (MUGU) ... ADVST
Advance Strike Gully [*Mining engineering*] ... ASG
Advance Surface-to-Air Weapons System ... ASAWS
Advance Synthetic Aperture RADAR System (MCD) ... ASARS
Advance Tax Rulings [*Also, Tax Advance Rulings*] [*Database*] (IID) ... ATR
Advance Technical Requirements (MCD) ... ATR
Advance Technology Alert System [*United Nations*] (DUND) ... ATAS
Advance Test Plant (AAG) ... ATP
Advance Transportation Control and Movement Document ... ATCMD
Advance Weapon Ammunition Support Point ... AWASP
Advanced ... ADV
Advanced (ABBR) ... ADVNCD
Advanced ... ADVNCD
Advanced Academic Degree (AFM) ... AAD
Advanced Academic Degree Management System (AFM) ... AADMS
Advanced Accounting System ... AAS

Advanced Acoustic Search Sensors (MCD) .... AASS
Advanced Acquisition Plan (MCD) .... AAP
Advanced Action Manipulator System .... ADAMS
Advanced Active Sonobuoy (MCD) .... AAS
Advanced Adaptive Control (SSD) .... AAC
Advanced Administrative System [IBM Corp.] .... AAS
Advanced AERA Concepts [FAA] (TAG) .... AAC
Advanced Aerial Fire Support System [Army] .... AAFSS
Advanced Aerial Fire Support System Office [Army] (MCD) ..... AAFSSO
Advanced Aerial Gunnery TOW Target System .... AAGTTS
Advanced Aerodynamics & Structures, Inc. [Associated Press] (SAG) .... AA&S
Advanced Aerodynamics and Structures, Inc. (ECON) ..... AASI
Advanced Aerodynamics & Structures, Inc. [Associated Press] (SAG) ...... AdA&S
Advanced Aerodynamics & Structures, Inc. [Associated Press] (SAG) ...... AdvA&S
Advanced Aerospace Vehicle (MCD) .... AAV
Advanced Aero-Wing Systems Corp. [Vancouver Stock Exchange symbol] ..... AAS
Advanced Air Cycle Machine (MCD) .... AACM
Advanced Air Defense Electro-Optic Sensor [Army] ..... AADEOS
Advanced Air Defense System .... AADS
Advanced Air Defense Weapon .... AADW
Advanced Air Depot Area [Air Force] .... AADA
Advanced Air Refueling Boom [Air Force] (MCD) .... AARB
Advanced Air Station (DAS) .... AAS
Advanced Air Striking Force [British] .... AASF
Advanced Air Traffic Management System [Department of Transportation] .... AATMS
Advanced Air Training Command [Military] .... AATC
Advanced Airborne Command Post (MCD) .... AABCP
Advanced Airborne Command Post .... AACP
Advanced Airborne Demonstrator .... AAD
Advanced Airborne Expendable Decoy and Launcher Control (DWSG) .... AED & LC
Advanced Airborne Launch Center (MCD) .... AALC
Advanced Airborne National Command Post (MCD) .... AABNCP
Advanced Airborne National Command Post (DOMA) ... AABNCP
Advanced Airborne National Command Post [Air Force] (PDAA) ...... AANCP
Advanced Airborne RADAR System (MCD) .... AARS
Advanced Airborne Radio Position Location System [Army] (MCD) ...... AARPLS
Advanced Airborne Surveillance Sensor (MCD) .... AASS
Advanced Aircraft Early Warning RADAR (MCD) ...... AAEWR
Advanced Aircraft Electrical System [Navy] .... AAES
Advanced Aircraft Programs Office .... AAPO
Advanced Airframe Assembly Program [Aviation] ...... AAAP
Advanced Air-Launched Missile (MCD) .... AALM
Advanced Air-Launched Motor (MCD) .... AALM
Advanced Air-to-Air Missile [Military] .... AAAM
Advanced Air-to-Surface Missile (MCD) .... AASM
Advanced Air-to-Surface Missile Seeker [Navy] (MCD) ..... AASMS
Advanced Allied Headquarters [World War II] .... AAHQ
Advanced Alternative Minuteman Defense Study [Military] .... AAMDS
Advanced Ammunition Depot .... AAD
Advanced Amphibious Assault [Marine Corps] (DOMA) ..... AAA
Advanced Amphibious Assault Vehicle [Marine Corps] ..... AAAV
Advanced Amphibious Training Base [Navy] .... AATB
Advanced and Applied Concepts Office [MERDC] [Army] ...... AACO
Advanced Antenna System [Air Force] .... AAS
Advanced Anti-Aircraft and Anti-Tank Guided-Missile System (ECON) ..... ADATS
Advanced Antiarmor Missile Systems (MCD) .... AAAMS
Advanced Antiarmor Vehicle Evaluation Test (RDA) .... ARMVAL
Advanced Antiarmor Weapon System, Medium [Army] (INF) ..... AAWS-M
Advanced Antiradiation Missile (MCD) .... AARM
Advanced Antisubmarine Rocket (SAA) .... AASROC
Advanced Antisubmarine Warfare Exercise (NVT) ..... ADEX
Advanced Antitank Missile System (MCD) .... AAMS
Advanced Antitank Weapon [Army] (MCD) .... AATW
Advanced Antitank Weapon System - Heavy .... AAWS-H
Advanced Antitank Weapon System - Medium [Pronounced "awesome"] (RDA) ...... AAWS-M
Advanced Application Rotary Launcher (DWSG) .... AARL
Advanced Applications Flight Equipment (MCD) .... AAFE
Advanced Applications Flight Experiment Radiometer-Scatterometer Sensor [Aviation] (PDAA) .... AAFE RADSCAT
Advanced Applications Flight Experiments [NASA] (MCD) ...... AAFE
Advanced Architecture Microprocessor (MCD) .... AAMP
Advanced Army Aircraft Instrument System (MCD) .... AAAIS
Advanced Army System Requirements .... AASR
Advanced Assembly Outline (MCD) .... AAO
Advanced Assembly Sequence Record Sheet (MCD) ... ASRS
Advanced Atmospheric Burst Location (MCD) .... AABL
Advanced Atmospheric Sounder and Imaging Radiometer [NASA] (NASA) ...... AAIR
Advanced Atmospheric Sounder and Imaging Radiometer [NASA] (MCD) ...... AASIR
Advanced Attack Aircraft (CAAL) .... AAA
Advanced Attack Helicopter [Army] .... AAH
Advanced Automated Directional Solidification Furnace [Materials processing] .... AADSF
Advanced Automated Sample Processor .... AASP
Advanced Automated System .... AAS
Advanced Automatic Compilation System [Computer science] (MHDI) ..... AACS
Advanced Automatic Film Titles System (MCD) .... AAFTS
Advanced Automatic Flight Control System (MCD) .... AAFCS
Advanced Automation [FAA] (TAG) .... AAP
Advanced Automation Research Laboratory [Purdue University] ...... AARL
Advanced Automation System .... AAS

Advanced Automotive Power Systems .... AAPS
Advanced Aviation Base Ship [Navy symbol Obsolete] ..... AVB
Advanced Aviation Transportation Technology (GAVI) ..... AATT
Advanced Avionic Display Processor (MCD) .... AADP
Advanced Avionic Fault Isolation System [Navy] (MCD) ..... AAFIS
Advanced Avionic System (MCD) .... AAS
Advanced Avionic System for Multi-Mission Application (MCD) ...... AASMMA
Advanced Avionic Systems for Multi-Mission Application (PDAA) ...... AASMA
Advanced Avionics Data Handling System [Air Force] (MCD) ..... AADHS
Advanced Avionics Digital Computer [Naval Air Systems Command] ..... AADC
Advanced Avionics Integration Program (MCD) .... AAIP
Advanced Avionics Test Bed [The Boeing Co.] .... AAT
Advanced Ballistic Missile Defense [Army] .... ABMD
Advanced Ballistic Missile Defense Agency [Alexandria, VA] [Army] ...... ABMDA
Advanced Ballistic Missile Systems (KSC) .... ABMS
Advanced Ballistic Reentry System .... ABRES
Advanced Ballistic Reentry Vehicle (MCD) .... ABRV
Advanced Ballistics Concepts [Air Force] (MCD) ...... ABC
Advanced Ballistic-Type Logistic Spacecraft System (MCD) ...... ABLSS
Advanced Banking On-Line System (BUR) .... ABOS
Advanced Base Aviation Training Unit [Navy] .... ABATU
Advanced Base Combat Communication Training Center [Pearl Harbor] .... ABCCTC
Advanced Base Components [Military] .... ABCO
Advanced Base Construction Depot .... ABCD
Advanced Base Depot [or Dock] [Obsolete Navy] ...... ABD
Advanced Base Depot Area Command .... ABDACOM
Advanced Base Functional Component [Military] ...... ABFC
Advanced Base Functional Component System [Military] ..... ABFCS
Advanced Base Hospital [British] .... ABH
Advanced Base Initial Outfitting List [Military] .... ABIOL
Advanced Base Initial Support Lists [Navy] (AFIT) .... ABISL
Advanced Base Personnel Administration .... ABPA
Advanced Base Personnel Officer .... ABPO
Advanced Base Personnel Unit .... ABPU
Advanced Base Proving Ground .... ABPG
Advanced Base Receiving Barracks .... ABRB
Advanced Base Receiving Depot .... ABRD
Advanced Base Repair Depot .... ABRD
Advanced Base Reshipment Depot .... ABRD
Advanced Base Supply Depot .... ABSD
Advanced Base Torpedo Unit [Navy] .... ABTU
Advanced Base Training Unit [Navy] .... ABTU
Advanced Basic Input/Output System [Computer science] (DOM) ...... ABIOS
Advanced [or Alternate] Battery Acquisition RADAR ..... ABAR
Advanced Battlefield Simulation (RDA) .... ABS
Advanced Beach Signal Station (IAA) .... ABSS
Advanced Beamformer (MCD) .... ABF
Advanced Beef Breeds Federation (EA) .... ABBF
Advanced Bill of Material [Accounting] (AAG) .... ABM
Advanced Bio-Mechanical Linkage Enablement [Rehabilitation technology] .... ABLE
Advanced Biomedical Capsule .... ABC
Advanced Biophysical Research Accelerator (BARN) .... ABRA
Advanced Biotechnologies, Inc. .... ABI
Advanced Blown Lift Enhancement (MCD) .... ABLE
Advanced Boiling Water Reactor .... ABWR
Advanced Bomb Family [Navy] (DOMA) .... ABF
Advanced Bombardment System .... ABOSS
Advanced Boost Phase Track Satellite .... ABPTS
Advanced Booster Technology (MCD) .... ABT
Advanced Boresight Equipment [Army] .... ABE
Advanced Brake Control System (MCD) .... ABCS
Advanced Branch [Training] [Military] (DNAB) .... ADV-BR
Advanced Business Communications, Inc. [McLean, VA] [Telecommunications] (TSSD) ...... ABCI
Advanced Business Processor [Datapoint Corp.] ...... ABP
Advanced Byte-Oriented [Computer science] (HGAA) .... ABO
Advanced Cab and Visual System [Army] (RDA) ...... ACAVS
Advanced Cabin Entertainment and Services System [Aircraft] ...... ACESS
Advanced Cableship Navigation Aid System (TEL) .... ACNAS
Advanced Capabilities RADAR .... ACR
Advanced Capability .... ADCAP
Advanced Capability Tanker (MCD) .... ACT
Advanced Carbon-Carbon (MCD) .... ACC
Advanced Card Technology Association of Canada (AC) ..... ACT Canada
Advanced Cardiac Life Support System .... ACLS
Advanced Cardiovascular Systems .... ACS
Advanced Career Training .... ACT
Advanced Cargo Aircraft .... ACA
Advanced Cargo Rotorcraft [Later, Advanced Cargo Aircraft - ACA] ...... ACR
Advanced Cargo/Tanker Aircraft .... ACTA
Advanced Cartographic Data Digitizing System (MCD) ..... ACDDS
Advanced Ceramic System .... ACS
Advanced Certificate (PGP) .... AC
Advanced Certificate (PGP) .... Adv C
Advanced Certificate .... AdvCert
Advanced Certificate in Applied Management Communication .... AdvCertApplMgtComm
Advanced Certificate in Banking and Finance .... AdvCertBankFin
Advanced Certificate in Building Construction .... AdvCertBuildCons
Advanced Certificate in Building Inspection .... AdvCertBuildInsp
Advanced Certificate in Customs Agent Procedures ..... AdvCertCustomsAgProc
Advanced Certificate in Education (GAGS) .... ACE
Advanced Certificate in Education .... Adv Cert in Ed

Advanced Certificate in Estate Agency	AdvCertEstateAg
Advanced Certificate in Furniture Production	AdvCertFurnProd
Advanced Certificate in Management	AdvCertMgt
Advanced Certificate in Music Education	Adv Cert in Mus Ed
Advanced Certificate in Office Management	AdvCertOffMgt
Advanced Certificate in Personnel	AdvCertPers
Advanced Certificate in Sales Management	AdvCertSalesMgt
Advanced Certificate of Education (AIE)	ACE
Advanced Certificate of the Welsh College of Music and Drama [British] (DBQ)	WCMD
Advanced Certification [Canadian Society of Radiological Technicians]	AC
Advanced Certified Fund Raising Executive [National Society of Fund Raising Executives]	ACFRE
Advanced Certified Fund-Raising Executive (NFD)	ACFRE
Advanced Chain Home [RADAR]	ACH
Advanced Change Study Notice [Aerospace]	ACSN
Advanced Chassis Technology [Automotive engineering]	ACT
Advanced Chemical Agent Detector Alarm (MCD)	ACADA
Advanced Chemical Rocket Engine [Air Force]	ACRE
Advanced Chemistry Development	ACD
Advanced Chip Interconnect [Computer science]	ACI
Advanced Circuit Module	ACM
Advanced Circular Scan Thermal Imaging System (MCD)	ACSTIS
Advanced Circular Scan Thermal Imaging System (MCD)	ACTIS
Advanced Civil/Military Aircraft (MCD)	ACMA
Advanced Civil Schooling [Army] (INF)	ACS
Advanced Civilian Technology Agency (AAGC)	ACTA
Advanced Clean Emission [Automotive engineering]	ACE
Advanced Clothing Subsystem [SIPE] [Military] (RDA)	ACS
Advanced CMOS Logic [Texas Instruments, Inc.]	ACL
Advanced Coastal Zone Color Scanner	ACZCS
Advanced Coherent Deception Countermeasure (MCD)	ACDC
Advanced Collaborative Filtering [Firefly Network] [Computer science]	ACF
Advanced Color Technology, Inc. [Chelmsford, MA] [Printer manufacturer]	ACT
Advanced Combat Air Patrol (MCD)	ACAP
Advanced Combat Aircraft (MCD)	ACA
Advanced Combat Direction System (MCD)	ACDS
Advanced Combat Optical Gunsight [Military] (INF)	ACOG
Advanced Combat Rifle [Military] (INF)	ACR
Advanced Combat Surveillance RADAR	ACSR
Advanced Combat Training Academy [Army] (AABC)	ACTA
Advanced Combustion Engineering	ACE
Advanced Command and Control Architectural Testbed (MCD)	ACCAT
Advanced Command Data System (NG)	ACDS
Advanced Common Intercept Missile (MCD)	ACIM
Advanced Common Intercept Missile Demonstration (MCD)	ACIMD
Advanced Communication and Timekeeping Technology [Seiko Telecommunications Systems] [FM data receiver chip set] (PCM)	ACTT
Advanced Communication Enhancement [Multimedia modem] [Telecommunications] (PCM)	ACE
Advanced Communication Facility	ACF
Advanced Communication System [Computer science] (TNIG)	ACS
Advanced Communication Technology Satellite Program [Office of Space Scie nce and Applications] [Washington, DC NASA] (GRD)	ACTS
Advanced Communications (DNAB)	ADCOM
Advanced Communications Control System (CAAL)	ACCS
Advanced Communications Equipment Depot (NATG)	ACED
Advanced Communications Function [IBM Corp.] [Computer science]	ACF
Advanced Communications Interface [Computer science] (DGA)	ACI
Advanced Communications Network Service (MHDI)	ACNS
Advanced Communications Service [Later, AIS] [AT & T]	ACS
Advanced Communications Support System [Sytek, Inc.] [Computer science] (TNIG)	ACSS
Advanced Communications Technology [Tymshare, Inc.]	ACT
Advanced Communications-Electronics Requirements Plan [Air Force]	ACERP
Advanced Compatible Television [Wide-screen, high-resolution system utilizing standard broadcast channels] [RCA Corp.]	ACTV
Advanced Compilation Equipment (MCD)	ACE
Advanced Composite Airframe Program [Air Force]	ACAP
Advanced Composite Cost Estimating Model (MCD)	ACCEM
Advanced Composite Products, Inc.	ACP
Advanced Composite Technology [Materials science]	ACT
Advanced Composite Vertical Fin (MCD)	ACVF
Advanced Composite Wing Cover-to-Substructure Attachment (MCD)	CTSA
Advanced Composites Technology Transfer Consortium	ACTTC
Advanced Composition Explorer [Satellite] [NASA] (USDC)	ACE
Advanced Composition Explorer	ACE
Advanced Composition Explorer [Satellite] [Marine science] (OSRA)	ACE
Advanced Compound Engine	ACE
Advanced Computational Element (MCD)	ACE
Advanced Computational Processor	ACP
Advanced Computer Audit Techniques [Arthur Andersen & Co.]	ACAT
Advanced Computer Communications [Santa Barbara, CA]	ACC
Advanced Computer Flight Plan [Air Force] (GFGA)	ACFP
Advanced Computer for Array Processing	ACAP
Advanced Computer for Medical Research [Stanford University]	ACME
Advanced Computer Image Generator (MCD)	ACIG
Advanced Computer Oriented System (BUR)	ACOS
Advanced Computer Program Multiple Array Processor System	ACMAPS
Advanced Computer Services [Honeywell Information Systems] (IEEE)	ACS
Advanced Computer System [IBM Corp.] (IEEE)	ACS
Advanced Computer Techniques (MCD)	ACT
Advanced Computer Techniques Project (KSC)	ACTP
Advanced Computer Technology Project [British] (EECA)	ACTP
Advanced Computer Training Institute [Springfield, VA]	ACTI

Advanced Computer-Aided Design	ACAD
Advanced Computing Center for the Arts and Design [Ohio State University] [Research center] (RCD)	ACCAD
Advanced Computing Environment [Personal computer standard] (ECON)	ACE
Advanced Computing Environment (CDE)	ACE
Advanced Computing Group (USDC)	ACG
Advanced Computing Group [Marine science] (OSRA)	ACG
Advanced Concept and Technology Demonstration [Military] (RDA)	ACTD
Advanced Concept Cost Model	ACCM
Advanced Concept Ejection Seat [Aviation] (MCD)	ACES
Advanced Concept Escape System (MCD)	ACES
Advanced Concept Technology Demonstration	ACTD
Advanced Concept Technology Demonstration [DoD]	ATCD
Advanced Concept Tire [Firestone Tire & Rubber Co.]	ACT
Advanced Concept Train [Aerospace]	ACT
Advanced Concepts and Missions Division [NASA]	ACMD
Advanced Concepts and Technology Demonstration [Military] (INF)	ACTD
Advanced Concepts and Technology Program [Army] (RDA)	ACT
Advanced Concepts Center [General Motors Corp.] [Automotive engineering]	ACC
Advanced Concepts Flight Simulator (GAVI)	ACFS
Advanced Concepts for Ordnance	ACORD
Advanced Concepts Group	ACG
Advanced Concepts Missile (MCD)	ACM
Advanced Concepts Team [Army] (RDA)	ACT
Advanced Concepts Test (MCD)	ACT
Advanced Confidential Report (MCD)	ACR
Advanced Configuration and Power Interface (PCM)	ACPI
Advanced Configuration Management System	ACMS
Advanced Conformal Antenna Technique	ACAT
Advanced Conformal Submarine Acoustic Sensor	ACSAS
Advanced Connector Unit [Telecommunications] (TSSD)	ACU
[The] Advanced Construction Technology Show [British] (ITD)	ACTS
Advanced Consumer Marketing	ACM
Advanced Contingency Theater Sensor [Military] (DOMA)	ACTS
Advanced Continuous Simulation Language [Pronounced "axle"] [Computer science] (CSR)	ACSL
Advanced Continuous System Language (MCD)	ACSL
Advanced Contract Administrator	ACA
Advanced Control Experiments (MCD)	ACE
Advanced Control Function/Virtual Telecommunications Access Method [IBM Corp.] (NITA)	ACF/Vtam
Advanced [Flight] Control Programmer	ADCP
Advanced Control Signal Processor [For spacecraft]	ACSP
Advanced Control System [IBM Corp.] (NITA)	ACS
Advanced Control Technology Program [Oak Ridge National Laboratory]	ACTP
Advanced Control Test Operation [Oak Ridge National Laboratory]	ACTO
Advanced Conventional Munitions	ACM
Advanced Conventional Standoff Missile (MCD)	ACSM
Advanced Conventional Standoff Weapon	ACSW
Advanced Conversion Technology (MCD)	ACT
Advanced Converter Reactor [Atomic energy]	ACR
Advanced Cooperative Countermeasure (MCD)	ADCCM
Advanced Cooperative Countermeasure (MCD)	ADCOM
Advanced Cooperative Project [NASA]	ACP
Advanced Copies Delivered	ACD
Advanced Core Performance Reactor (NRCH)	ACPR
Advanced Core Pulsed Reactor (NRCH)	ACPR
Advanced Core Test [Nuclear energy]	ACT
Advanced Coronary Treatment [Cardiology] (DAVI)	ACT
Advanced Coronary Treatment Foundation	ACT
Advanced Corporation Tax Act [British] (ECON)	ACT
Advanced Cost Management System (AAGC)	ACMS
Advanced CounterMeasure Systems [Commercial firm] (RDA)	ACMS
Advanced Course Studentships [British]	ACS
Advanced Cracking Reactor [Fuel technology]	ACR
Advanced Credit Information System	ACIS
Advanced Crew-Served Weapon [Army] (INF)	ACSW
Advanced Critical Pulse Reactor [Nuclear energy]	ACPR
Advanced CRT Controller [Computer chip]	ACRTC
Advanced Cruise Missile	ACM
Advanced Cruise Missile Combustor (MCD)	ACMC
Advanced Cruise Missile Program [Navy]	ACMP
Advanced Cruise Missile Technology (MCD)	ACMT
Advanced Cryogenic Rocket Engineering (PDAA)	ACRE
Advanced Cryptographic System [Air Force] (MCD)	ACS
Advanced Data Access Method [Computer science] (IAA)	ADAM
Advanced Data Acquisition Routine [Computer science] (OA)	ADAR
Advanced Data Collection and Location System	ADCLS
Advanced Data Collection - Position Location (MCD)	ADC/PL
Advanced Data Communication Protocol [Computer science]	ADCP
Advanced Data Communications [Computer science] (ECII)	ADC
Advanced Data Communications Control Procedure [American National Standards Institute]	ADCCP
Advanced Data Connector [Computer science]	ADC
Advanced Data Display System (DNAB)	ADDS
Advanced Data Entry	ADE
Advanced Data Link Control [Computer science]	ADLC
Advanced Data Management	ADAM
Advanced Data Management [Information service or system] (IID)	ADM
Advanced Data Processing (NITA)	ADP
Advanced Data Scalar	ADS
Advanced Data System [DoD]	ADS
Advanced Database System	ADBS
Advanced Dated Remittances [IRS]	ADR

Advanced Debugging System ... ADS
Advanced Deck-Launched Interceptor (MCD) ... ADLI
Advanced Declassification Schedule (MCD) ... ADS
Advanced Decoy Technology (SAA) ... ADTEC
Advanced Decoy Technology (MCD) ... ADTECH
Advanced Deep Diving Submersible ... ADDS
Advanced Deep-Dive System (NVT) ... ADS
Advanced Deep-Running Acoustic Torpedo (MCD) ... ADRAT
Advanced Defense Communications Satellite [*Air Force*] (AFM) ... ADCS
Advanced Defense Communications Satellite Program [*Air Force*] ... ADCSP
Advanced Defense Intelligence Support System (MCD) ... ADISS
Advanced Defense Suppression Antiradiation Missile ... ADSARM
Advanced Defense Suppression Weapon ... ADSW
Advanced Degree in Education ... Ed A2
Advanced Degree in Education (GAGS) ... EdA
Advanced Degree Program for ROTC Instructor Duty (MCD) ... ADPRID
Advanced Deployability Posture [*Military*] (DOMA) ... AD
Advanced Deployable Digital Imagery Support System [*Military*] (DOMA) ... ADDISS
Advanced Deployment Model (MCD) ... ADM
Advanced Deposition Tech [*NASDAQ symbol*] (TTSB) ... ADTC
Advanced Deposition Tech Wrrt [*NASDAQ symbol*] (TTSB) ... ADTCW
Advanced Deposition Technologies [*NASDAQ symbol*] (SAG) ... ADTC
Advanced Deposition Technologies [*Associated Press*] (SAG) ... AdvD
Advanced Deposition Technologies [*Associated Press*] (SAG) ... AdvDep
Advanced Deposition Technologies [*Associated Press*] (SAG) ... AdvDp
Advanced Design (IEEE) ... AD
Advanced Design Aluminum Metal Shelter [*A prefabricated building known as an ADAMS hut*] ... ADAMS
Advanced Design Array RADAR ... ADAR
Advanced Design [*or Drawing*] **Change** ... ADC
Advanced Design [*or Drawing*] **Change Notice** ... ADCN
Advanced Design Composite Aircraft (MCD) ... ADCA
Advanced Design Electronic Key System [*Telecommunications*] ... ADEKS
Advanced Design Methods Laboratory [*Ohio State University*] [*Research center*] (RCD) ... ADML
Advanced Design Special Processor (LAIN) ... ADSP
Advanced Design Team ... ADT
Advanced Destroyer/Aircraft Lightweight Torpedo (MCD) ... AD/ALT
Advanced Developing Institutions Program ... ADIP
Advanced Development ... AD
Advanced Development [*Army*] (AABC) ... ADDEV
Advanced Development [*Army*] ... ADV DEV
Advanced Development Aims Processor Transponder [*Military*] (MCD) ... ADAPT
Advanced Development Analysis ... ADA
Advanced Development Concept (CAAL) ... ADC
Advanced Development Design (CAAL) ... ADD
Advanced Development Experimental [*Army*] (AABC) ... ADX
Advanced Development Facility [*Branch*] [*Marine science*] (OSRA) ... ADF
Advanced Development Facility Branch [*Forecast Systems Laboratory*] (USDC) ... ADF
Advanced Development Hardware (SSD) ... ADH
Advanced Development Memory (MCD) ... ADM
Advanced Development Model ... ADM
Advanced Development Objective [*Military*] ... ADO
Advanced Development Plan [*Air Force*] (MCD) ... ADP
Advanced Development Plan (System) ... ADP(S)
Advanced Development Program Office ... ADPO
Advanced Development Prototype (MHDI) ... ADEPT
Advanced Development Report [*NASA*] (KSC) ... ADR
Advanced Development Technology (KSC) ... ADT
Advanced Development Unit Test [*Army*] ... ADUT
Advanced Development Vehicle ... ADV
Advanced Development Verification Test (RDA) ... ADVT
Advanced Development Verification Test - Coordinator (MCD) ... ADVT-C
Advanced Development Verification Test - Government (MCD) ... ADVT-G
Advanced Diagnostic Engine Monitoring System [*Air Force*] ... ADEMS
Advanced Diagnostic Executive System ... ADES
Advanced Digital Avionics System (MCD) ... ADAS
Advanced Digital Electronic Displays ... ADEDS
Advanced Digital Inertial Optical Sensor ... ADIOS
Advanced Digital Information Corp. (PCM) ... ADIC
Advanced Digital Information Corp. [*Associated Press*] (SAG) ... AdvDIn
Advanced Digital/Optical Control System ... ADOCS
Advanced Digital Processing System ... ADPS
Advanced Digital RADAR Imagery Exploitation System ... ADRIES
Advanced Digital Ranging System [*NASA*] (KSC) ... ADRAN
Advanced Digital SAR Processor (MCD) ... ADSP
Advanced Digital Signal Processor ... ADSP
Advanced Digital Simulation System (MCD) ... ADSS
Advanced Digital Systems [*Commercial firm*] (NITA) ... ADS
Advanced Digital Systems, Inc. [*NASDAQ symbol*] ... ADVA
Advanced Digital Television Service ... ACATS
Advanced Diploma ... AdvDip
Advanced Diploma, Australian Risk Management ... A Dip ARM
Advanced Diploma in Art Education [*British*] ... ADAE
Advanced Diploma in Education (ADA) ... AdvDipEd
Advanced Diploma in Midwifery [*British*] ... ADM
Advanced Diploma in Teaching ... AdvDipT
Advanced Direct Memory Access [*Siemens Corp.*] (NITA) ... ADMA
Advanced Direct Support Unit (NATG) ... ADSU
Advanced Directional Warhead (MCD) ... ADWAR
Advanced Direct-Landing Apollo Mission [*NASA*] (IEEE) ... ADAM
Advanced Disk Array [*Computer science*] ... ADA
Advanced Diskette Operating System ... ADOS
Advanced Dispenser Technology (MCD) ... ADT
Advanced Display and Debriefing Subsystem (DWSG) ... ADDS
Advanced Display System ... ADS
Advanced Disposal Fee ... ADF
Advanced Distributed Onboard Processor (SDI) ... ADOP
Advanced Distributed Simulation [*Army*] ... ADS
Advanced Distributed Simulation Technology [*Army*] (RDA) ... ADST
Advanced Diving System ... ADS
Advanced Document Revision Notice [*NASA*] (KSC) ... ADRN
Advanced Dosimetry System (PDAA) ... ADS
Advanced Dressing Station [*British*] ... ADS
Advanced Driver and Vehicle Advisory Navigation Concept ... ADVANC
Advanced Driver And Vehicle Advisory Navigation Concept [*FHWA*] (TAG) ... ADVANCE
Advanced Driver and Vehicle Navigation Concept ... ADVANCE
Advanced Driver and Vehicle Navigation Concept ... ADVANCE
Advanced Driver Information System [*Automotive engineering*] ... ADIS
Advanced Driver Training [*British military*] (DMA) ... ADT
Advanced Dungeons and Dragons ... AD & D
Advanced Dynamic Anthropomorphic Manikin [*Air Force*] ... ADAM
Advanced Earned Income Credit [*IRS*] ... AEIC
Advanced Earth Observation Satellite ... AEOS
Advanced Earth Observing Satellite [*Japan*] ... ADEOS
Advanced Earth Resources Observation System ... AEROS
Advanced Earth Satellite Weapon System [*Air Force*] ... AEWS
Advanced Echelon [*Marine Corps*] ... ADVON
Advanced Education Institution ... AEI
Advanced Electric Distribution System ... AEDS
Advanced Electrical Development Package (MCD) ... AEDP
Advanced Electrochemical Depolarized Concentrator Module [*NASA*] ... AEDCM
Advanced Electronic and Digital Sensor Technology ... AEADST
Advanced Electronic Design ... AED
Advanced Electronic Display System [*FAA*] ... ADEDS
Advanced Electronic Publishing System (NITA) ... AEPS
Advanced Electronic Warfare System (MCD) ... AEWS
Advanced Electronic Warfare Test Set (MCD) ... AEWTS
Advanced Electronically Tuned Radio [*Automotive accessory*] ... AETR
Advanced Electronics Design [*Commercial firm*] [*British*] (NITA) ... AED
Advanced Electronics Field ... AEF
Advanced Electronics Network [*British*] (NITA) ... AEON
Advanced Electro-Optical Sensor Simulation ... AEOSS
Advanced Electro-Optical Tracker/Ranger (MCD) ... AEOTR
Advanced Emergency Medical Technician (HCT) ... A-EMT
Advanced Energy Industries [*NASDAQ symbol*] (TTSB) ... AEIS
Advanced Energy Industries, Inc. [*Associated Press*] (SAG) ... AdvEnld
Advanced Energy Industries, Inc. [*NASDAQ symbol*] (SAG) ... AEIS
Advanced Energy Projects [*Department of Energy*] ... AEP
Advanced Energy Technology ... AET
Advanced Engine Aerospace ... AEA
Advanced Engine Bell ... AEB
Advanced Engine Development [*Automotive industry supplier*] ... AED
Advanced Engine Overhaul Base ... AEOB
Advanced Engineering Services [*General Motors Corp.*] [*Automotive engineering*] ... AES
Advanced Engineering Test Reactor ... AETR
Advanced Entry Control System [*Air Force*] ... AECS
Advanced Envirn Recycl Tech [*NASDAQ symbol*] (TTSB) ... AERTA
Advanced Environ Recycling Technologies, Inc. [*Associated Press*] (SAG) ... AdvEnv
Advanced Environ Recycling Technologies, Inc. [*NASDAQ symbol*] (SAG) ... AERT
Advanced Environmental Control System (MCD) ... AECS
Advanced Environmental Control Technology Research Center [*University of Illinois*] [*Environmental Protection Agency Research center*] (RCD) ... AECTRC
Advanced Environmental Recycling Technology, Inc. [*NASDAQ symbol*] (NQ) ... AERT
Advanced Environmental Research and Technology (MCD) ... AERT
Advanced Environmental Research Group [*Commercial firm*] ... AERG
Advanced Environm'l Recyclg Wrrt [*NASDAQ symbol*] (TTSB) ... AERTZ
Advanced Epithermal Thorium Reactor ... AETR
Advanced Equipment Repair Program [*Military*] (DNAB) ... AERP
Advanced [*or Aircrew*] **Escape/Rescue Capability** [*Navy - Air Force*] ... AERCAB
Advanced Executive Master of Business (PGP) ... AEMBA
Advanced Experimental Vehicle - 5th Generation [*Toyota*] ... AXV-V
Advanced Extravehicular Protective System [*NASA*] ... AEPS
Advanced Extravehicular Suit [*NASA*] ... AES
Advanced Facility Intrusion Detection System (DWSG) ... AFIDS
Advanced - Far Infrared Search/Track ... A-FIRST
Advanced Fast Time Acoustic Analysis System (MCD) ... AFTAAS
Advanced Fault Recognition [*Computer science*] (NITA) ... AFR
Advanced Fault Tree Analysis Program [*SIA Computer Services*] [*Software package*] (NCC) ... AFTP
Advanced Fermentation System ... AFS
Advanced Fiber Optic Digital Autopilot [*Military*] ... AFDAP
Advanced Fibre Communications [*Associated Press*] (SAG) ... AdvFCm
Advanced Fibre Communications [*NASDAQ symbol*] (SAG) ... AFCI
Advanced Field Array RADAR ... AFAR
Advanced Field Artillery System ... AFAS
Advanced Field Artillery System - Armaments [*Army*] (RDA) ... AFAS-ARM
Advanced Field Artillery System - Cannon ... AFAS-C
Advanced Field Artillery System - Future Armored Resupply Vehicle [*Army*] (RDA) ... AFAS-FARV
Advanced Field Artillery System - Mobility [*Army*] (RDA) ... AFAS-MOB
Advanced Field Artillery Tactical Data System [*Army*] ... AFADS
Advanced Field Artillery Tactical Data System ... AFATDS

Advanced Field Operating System [*National Weather Service*] ... AFOS
Advanced Field Site Facility ... AFSF
Advanced Fighter Capability (MCD) ... AFC
Advanced Fighter Capability Demonstrator (MCD) ... AFCD
Advanced Fighter Control Flight Simulator [*Military*] (PDAA) ... AFCFS
Advanced Fighter Diagnostic System (MCD) ... AFDS
Advanced Fighter RADAR System ... AFRS
Advanced Fighter Technology Integration [*Air Force*] ... AFTI
Advanced Figure Sensor (KSC) ... AFS
Advanced Filament Wound Structure ... AFWS
Advanced File Organization ... AFO
Advanced Fileable Processor ... AFP
Advanced Financial [*AMEX symbol*] (TTSB) ... AVF
Advanced Financial, Inc. [*Associated Press*] (SAG) ... AdvFin
Advanced Financial, Inc. [*Associated Press*] (SAG) ... AdvFn
Advanced Financial, Inc. [*AMEX symbol*] (SPSG) ... AVF
Advanced Financial, Inc. [*NASDAQ symbol*] (SAG) ... AVFI
Advanced Finl 10.50% Cv'B' Pfd [*NASDAQ symbol*] (TTSB) ... AVFIP
Advanced Fire Control (MCD) ... AFC
Advanced Fire Control RADAR System (MCD) ... AFCORS
Advanced Fire/Flight Control System (MCD) ... AFFC
Advanced Fire Support Avionics System ... AFSAS
Advanced Firefighter [*Military*] ... AFF
Advanced Firing Systems (MSA) ... AFS
Advanced First-Term Avionics (DNAB) ... AFTA
Advanced Flash X-Ray Facility ... AFXF
Advanced Fleet Reactor [*Navy*] (DOMA) ... AFR
Advanced Flexible Processor (MCD) ... AFP
Advanced Flexible Reusable Surface Insulation [*For space shuttles*] ... AFRSI
Advanced Flight Control Actuation System [*Navy*] (MCD) ... AFCAS
Advanced Flight Control Actuation System - All Electric (MCD) ... AFCAS-AE
Advanced Flight Control Programmer ... AFCP
Advanced Flight Control System (MCD) ... AFCS
Advanced Flight Deck Simulator [*Aviation*] (PDAA) ... AFDS
Advanced Flight Management System (DA) ... AFMS
Advanced Flight Research Model (SAA) ... AFRM
Advanced Flow LASER (MCD) ... AFL
Advanced Flying School [*British military*] (DMA) ... AFS
Advanced Flying Unit [*Air Force*] ... AFU
Advanced Foreign System Requirements ... AFSR
Advanced Forward Air Defense System [*Missiles*] (IEEE) ... AFADS
Advanced Forward Area Air Defense System ... AFAADS
Advanced Forward Area Air Defense Weapon ... AFAADW
Advanced Forward-Looking Infrared ... AFLIR
Advanced Fuel Accessories Test System (DWSG) ... AFATS
Advanced Fuel Assembly [*Nuclear energy*] (NUCP) ... AFA
Advanced Fuel Electronics [*Automotive engineering*] ... AFE
Advanced Function Printing (IAA) ... AFP
Advanced Fuze Function Control System (MCD) ... AFFCS
Advanced Gas Centrifuge ... AGC
Advanced Gas Turbine ... AGT
Advanced Gas-Cooled Reactor [*British*] ... AGR
Advanced General Aviation Transport Experiments (GAVI) ... AGATE
Advanced General Purpose Bomb (MCD) ... AGPB
Advanced Genetic Sciences, Inc. ... AGS
Advanced Geometry Blade [*Military*] (RDA) ... AGB
Advanced Geosynchronous Observation Environment Satellite [*NASA*] (NASA) ... AGOES
Advanced Glass Melter ... AGM
Advanced Glycosylated End-Product [*Biochemistry*] ... AGE
Advanced GPS/Inertial Integration (MCD) ... ADGINT
Advanced Graduate Certificate ... AGC
Advanced Graduate Specialist (GAGS) ... AGS
Advanced Graduate Specialist Certificate (PGP) ... AGSC
Advanced Graphics Avionics Display System (MCD) ... AGADS
Advanced Graphics Port [*Intel*] [*Computer science*] ... AGP
Advanced Graphics Software, Inc. (PCM) ... AGS
Advanced Graphics Workstation [*Auto-trol Technology Corp.*] (NITA) ... AGW
Advanced Graphite Experiments Testing [*Military*] ... AGENT
Advanced Gravis [*Vancouver Stock Exchange symbol*] ... AED
Advanced Ground Receiving Equipment Experiment [*NASA*] (PDAA) ... AGREE
Advanced Ground Segment Design (SSD) ... AGSD
Advanced Ground Surveillance RADAR (MCD) ... AGSR
Advanced Ground Transport ... AGT
Advanced Ground Transportation Vehicle (PDAA) ... AGTV
Advanced Ground Vehicle Technology Project [*Army*] ... AGVT
Advanced Growth Systems, Inc. [*Vancouver Stock Exchange symbol*] ... AVG
Advanced Guard [*British military*] (DMA) ... Adv Gd
Advanced Guard ... AG
Advanced Guidance and Control System (MCD) ... AGCS
Advanced Guidance System ... AGS
Advanced Guidance Technology [*SAMSO*] [*Air Force*] (MCD) ... AGT
Advanced Guided Projectile (MCD) ... AGP
Advanced Gun Technology (DOMA) ... AGT
Advanced Gun Weapon System (MCD) ... AGWS
Advanced Gunnery Target Systems (MCD) ... AGTS
Advanced Hardened Guidance Computer (MCD) ... AHGC
Advanced Harpoon Guidance System (MCD) ... AHGS
Advanced Headquarters (MUGU) ... ADVHED
Advanced Health Corp. [*Associated Press*] (SAG) ... AdHlthC
Advanced Health Corp. [*NASDAQ symbol*] (SAG) ... ADVH
Advanced Heavy Antitank Missile System [*Army*] (MCD) ... AHAMS
Advanced Heavy Antitank Weapon System (MCD) ... AHAWS
Advanced Helicopter Development (DNAB) ... AHD
Advanced Helicopter Improvement Program [*Army*] (RDA) ... AHIP
Advanced Helmet Sight Reticle Assembly [*Air Force*] (MCD) ... AHRA
Advanced High-Performance Nuclear Attack Submarine ... AHPNAS
Advanced Highway Advisory Radio [*FHWA*] (TAG) ... AHAR
Advanced Homing Sensor ... AHS
Advanced Human Systems Institute [*San Jose State University*] [*Research center*] (RCD) ... AHSI
Advanced Hybrid Computer System ... AHCS
Advanced Hypersonic Manned Aircraft ... AHMA
Advanced Icing Severity Indication System [*Military*] (RDA) ... AISIS
Advanced Identification Techniques (MCD) ... AIT
Advanced Image Compression (MCD) ... AIC
Advanced Image Management Software [*Computer science*] ... AIMS
Advanced Imagery Manipulation System ... AIMS
Advanced Imagery Requirements and Exploitation System (MCD) ... AIRES
Advanced Imaging Communications System (MCD) ... AICS
Advanced Imaging Software (DGA) ... AIS
Advanced Impact Drilling System (HGAA) ... AIDS
Advanced Impact Location System (SAA) ... AILS
Advanced Impact Management System [*Padding for sportswear*] ... AIMS
Advanced Indication Technology Experiment (MCD) ... AITE
Advanced Indications Structure (MCD) ... AIS
Advanced Indications System (MCD) ... AIS
Advanced Indirect Fire System ... AIFS
Advanced Individual Combat Weapon [*Army*] (INF) ... AICW
Advanced Individual Training [*Army*] ... AIT
Advanced Individual Training Attrition Analysis (MCD) ... AITAA
Advanced Individual Training Available [*Military*] ... AITA
Advanced Industrial Management ... AIM
Advanced Inert Missile Simulator (DWSG) ... AIMS
Advanced Inertial Measurement System ... AIMS
Advanced Inertial Navigation System (MCD) ... AINS
Advanced Inertial Reference Sphere [*ICBM technology*] ... AIRS
Advanced Infantry Training ... AIT
Advanced Informatics in Medicine [*British*] ... AIM
Advanced Information and Management Systems (NITA) ... AIMS
Advanced Information in Medicine ... AIM
Advanced Information Management [*Information service or system*] (IID) ... AIM
Advanced Information Manager [*Fujitsu Ltd.*] [*Japan*] ... AIM
Advanced Information System/Net 1 Service [*Formerly, ACS*] [*American Bell, Inc.*] ... AIS
Advanced Information Technology (NITA) ... AIT
Advanced Infrared Imaging Seeker (MCD) ... AIRIS
Advanced Infrared Sounder (GAVI) ... AIRS
Advanced/Innovative Wind Energy Concept (MCD) ... AIWEC
Advanced Institutional Development Program [*Under Title III of the Higher Education Act*] ... AIDP
Advanced Instruction Flying School ... AIFS
Advanced Instruction Technique (DA) ... AIT
Advanced Instructional System (MCD) ... AIS
Advanced Instrumentation and Data Analysis System ... AIDAS
Advanced Instrumentation for Reflood Studies [*Nuclear energy*] (NRCH) ... AIRS
Advanced Instrumentation Unit [*National Physical Laboratory*] (PDAA) ... AIU
Advanced Integrated Circuit Design Aids [*ESPRIT*] (NITA) ... AIDA
Advanced Integrated Data System (AFM) ... AIDS
Advanced Integrated Diagnostics (BUR) ... AID
Advanced Integrated Display System [*Military*] ... AIDS
Advanced Integrated Flight System (MCD) ... AIFS
Advanced Integrated Landing System ... AILS
Advanced Integrated Life-Support System ... AILSS
Advanced Integrated Magnetic Anomaly Detection System (MCD) ... AIMS
Advanced Integrated Modular Instrumentation System (MCD) ... AIMIS
Advanced Integrated Power Supply ... AIPS
Advanced Integrated Propulsion System [*Aerospace*] ... AIPS
Advanced Integrated Safety and Optimizing Computer ... ADVISOR
Advanced Integration Research [*PC motherboard*] [*Computer science*] (PCM) ... AIR
Advanced Intelligence Center [*Navy*] ... ADINTELCEN
Advanced Intelligence Center [*Navy*] ... ADV INTEL CEN
Advanced Intelligence Center [*Navy*] ... AIC
Advanced Intelligence Center, Pacific Ocean Areas [*Navy*] ... AICPOA
Advanced Intelligent Network ... AIN
Advanced Intelligent Network [*Computer science*] (ACRL) ... AIN
Advanced Intelligent Tape [*Sony Corp.*] (PCM) ... AIT
Advanced Interactive Data Entry / Transaction Processing System [*Computer science*] (PDAA) ... AIDE/TPS
Advanced Interactive Debugging System ... AIDS
Advanced Interactive Draughting [*McGrane Computer Systems Ltd.*] [*Software package*] (NCC) ... AID
Advanced Interactive Executive [*IBM RT Personal Computer*] (BYTE) ... AIX
Advanced Interactive Presentation System ... AIPS
Advanced Interactive Software (DGA) ... AIS
Advanced Interactive Video ... AIV
Advanced Intercept Missile ... AIM
Advanced Interceptor Air-to-Air Missile (MCD) ... AIAAM
Advanced Interceptor Missile Subsystem [*Military*] ... AIMS
Advanced Interceptor Propulsion (MCD) ... AIP
Advanced Interceptor Technology (MCD) ... AIT
Advanced Intercontinental Missile System ... AIMS
Advanced Interdiction Weapon System [*Military*] ... AIWS
Advanced Interior Communication System ... AICS
Advanced Internally Blown Jet Flag (MCD) ... AIBF
Advanced International Studies Institute (EA) ... AISI
Advanced Ion Exchange Cellulose [*Analytical biochemistry*] ... AIEC
Advanced Ionization Detector ... AID
Advanced Ionization Development (MCD) ... AID

Advanced Ionospheric Sounder [*A ground-based instrument*] .... AIS
Advanced IR Imaging Seeker (MCD) .... AIIS
Advanced Isotope Separation [*Process*] [*Nuclear energy*] .... AIS
Advanced IT [*Information Technology*] **Transfer** [*British*] .... AIT^3
Advanced Jaguar [*Jaguar PLC*] [*Automotive engineering*] .... AJ
Advanced Jet Trainer .... AJT
Advanced Kick Stage [*Missile launching*] (MCD) .... AKS
Advanced Kinematic Bombing System .... AKBS
Advanced Land Combat Systems [*Army*] (RDA) .... ALCOS
Advanced Land Navigation (MCD) .... ALN
Advanced Landing Ground [*Air Force*] .... ALG
Advanced Landing System .... ALS
Advanced Language Program [*Institute for Defense Analysis*] .... ALP
Advanced LASER Designator .... ALD
Advanced LASER Flow Analysis (MCD) .... ALFA
Advanced LASER Intercept Receiver (MCD) .... ALIR
Advanced LASER Requirements Assessment (MCD) .... ALRA
Advanced LASER Spot Tracker (MCD) .... ALAST
Advanced LASER System Study .... ALSS
Advanced LASER-Aided Defect Inspection in Nondestructive Testing (IAA) .... ALADIN
Advanced Launch System [*Rocketry*] .... ALS
Advanced Legal Education, Hamline University School of Law (DLA) .... ALEHU
Advanced Legal Software [*Computer science*] (HGAA) .... ALS
Advanced Level [*School graduating grade*] [*British*] .... A
Advanced Level (ODBW) .... A level
Advanced Levitation Unit [*Materials processing*] .... ALU
Advanced Liaison Forward Area (MCD) .... ALFA
Advanced Libraries & Information, Inc. [*Information service or system*] (IID) .... ALII
Advanced Library Concepts, Inc. [*Later, ALI'I*] [*Information service or system*] (IID) .... ALC
Advanced Library Systems, Inc. [*Information service or system*] (IID) .... ALS
Advanced Life Information System [*Computer science*] .... ALIS
Advanced Life Support [*System*] .... ALS
Advanced Life Support System (MCD) .... ALSS
Advanced Light Antitank Weapon (RDA) .... ALAW
Advanced Light Helicopter [*Air Force*] (PDAA) .... ALH
Advanced Light Rapid Transit .... ALRT
Advanced Light Source [*For Synchrotron radiation*] [*High-energy physics*] .... ALS
Advanced Lighting Technol [*NASDAQ symbol*] (TTSB) .... ADLT
Advanced Lighting Technologies, Inc. [*NASDAQ symbol*] (SAG) .... ADLT
Advanced Lighting Technologies, Inc. [*Associated Press*] (SAG) .... AdvLight
Advanced Lightweight SONAR [*Military*] .... ALWS
Advanced Lightweight Torpedo [*Navy*] .... ALWT
Advanced Limb Scanner (MCD) .... ALS
Advanced Linear Programming System [*Operational research technique*] .... ALPS
Advanced Liquid Metal Reactors [*Nuclear energy*] .... ALMR
Advanced Liquid Propulsion System [*NASA*] .... ALPS
Advanced List of Materials .... ALM
Advanced Lithography Research Initiative [*British*] .... ALRI
Advanced Location Strike System [*Formerly, Airborne Location and Strike System*] [*Air Force*] .... ALSS
Advanced Logic Design (MHDB) .... ALD
Advanced Logic Research [*NASDAQ symbol*] (SAG) .... AALR
Advanced Logic Research Access 386 [*Microcomputer*] .... ALR
Advanced Logic Research, Inc. [*Associated Press*] (SAG) .... AdvLog
Advanced Logic Research, Inc. (PCM) .... ALR
Advanced Logical Programming Environments Support [*ESPRIT project*] (NITA) .... ALPES
Advanced Logical Utility (PDAA) .... ALU
Advanced Logistic System (AFM) .... ALS
Advanced Logistics Development .... ALD
Advanced Logistics Information and Control System [*Air Force*] .... ALICS
Advanced Logistics Spacecraft .... ALS
Advanced Logistics Support Base [*Navy*] .... ALSB
Advanced Logistics System Project Advisory Committee [*Terminated, 1977*] [*DoD*] (EGAO) .... ALSPAC
Advanced Logistics Systems Center [*Air Force*] .... ADVLOGSYSCEN
Advanced Long-Range All-Weather Interceptor (MCD) .... ALRAWI
Advanced Long-Range Interceptor .... ALRI
Advanced Long-Wave IR Circuit and Array Technology (MCD) .... ALICAT
Advanced Low Altitude Terrain [*Missile*] (DOMA) .... ADLAT
Advanced Low-Altitude Infrared Reconnaissance Sensor .... ALAIRS
Advanced Low-Altitude RADAR Model (MCD) .... ALARM
Advanced Low-Altitude SAM (MCD) .... ALASAM
Advanced Low-Altitude Technique .... ADLAT
Advanced Low-Altitude Terrain System (MCD) .... ADLAT
Advanced Low-Cost G-Cueing System .... ALCOGS
Advanced Low-Power Schottky (MCD) .... ALS
Advanced Low-Volume Ramjet .... ALVRJ
Advanced Lunar Operation .... ALO
Advanced Lunar Orbital Rendezvous (IEEE) .... ALOR
Advanced Lunar Projects .... ALP
Advanced Lunar Projects Laboratory .... ALPL
Advanced Lunar Studies .... ALS
Advanced Lunar Transportation Systems .... ALTS
Advanced Magnetic Minesweeping (MCD) .... AMMS
Advanced Magnetic Silencing Project [*Military*] (DNAB) .... AMSP
Advanced Magnetics [*Associated Press*] (SAG) .... AdvMag
Advanced Magnetics [*AMEX symbol*] (SAG) .... AVM
Advanced Mail Coding System (MCD) .... AMCS
Advanced Mammography Sys [*NASDAQ symbol*] (TTSB) .... MAMO
Advanced Mammography Systems [*Associated Press*] (SAG) .... AdvMam
Advanced Mammography Systems [*NASDAQ symbol*] (SAG) .... MAMO
Advanced Management Information Service [*or System*] [*Air Force*] .... AMIS
Advanced Management Program .... AMP
Advanced Management Program for Clinician (PGP) .... AMPC
Advanced Management Research [*A publication*] (DLA) .... AMR
Advanced Maneuvering Demonstrator Aircraft (MCD) .... AMDA
Advanced Maneuvering FLAP [*Flight Application Software*] (MCD) .... AMF
Advanced Maneuvering Orbit-to-Orbit Shuttle [*NASA*] (NASA) .... AMOOS
Advanced Maneuvering Propulsion System .... AMPS
Advanced Maneuvering Propulsion Technology [*NASA*] (KSC) .... AMPT
Advanced Maneuvering Reentry Vehicle (MCD) .... AMARV
Advanced Manned Interceptor [*US Air Force Artillery Spotting Division interceptor*] .... AMI
Advanced Manned Launch System [*NASA*] .... AMLS
Advanced Manned Missions Program [*NASA*] (MCD) .... AMMP
Advanced Manned Penetrator .... AMP
Advanced Manned Penetrator System .... AMPS
Advanced Manned Precision Strike System [*Proposed Air Force plane*] .... AMPSS
Advanced Manned Space Simulator .... AMSS
Advanced Manned Spacecraft .... AMS
Advanced Manned Strategic Aircraft [*Facetious translation: "America's Most Studied Aircraft"*] [*Air Force*] .... AMSA
Advanced Manportable Weapons System (Provisional) [*Army*] (RDA) .... AMWS
Advanced Manufacturing, Accounting, and Production System (MCD) .... AMAPS
Advanced Manufacturing, Accounting, and Production System for Government Contractors (MCD) .... AMAPS/G
Advanced Manufacturing Engineering Council .... AMEC
Advanced Manufacturing Initiative [*Department of Energy*] .... AMI
Advanced Manufacturing Methods (MHDB) .... AMM
Advanced Manufacturing System (MCD) .... AMS
Advanced Manufacturing Systems Exposition and Conference (ITD) .... AMS
Advanced Manufacturing Techniques (NITA) .... AMT
Advanced Manufacturing Technology [*Technical Insights, Inc.*] [*Information service or system*] (CRD) .... AMT
Advanced Manufacturing Technology Centre [*University of Manchester*] [*British*] (NITA) .... AMTC
Advanced Manufacturing Technology Centre [*Research center British*] (CB) .... AMTeC
Advanced Manufacturing Technology Research Institute [*Research center British*] (IRC) .... AMTRI
Advanced Mapping and Surveying Equipment (IIA) .... AMASE
Advanced Mapping System [*Geography*] .... AMS
Advanced Maritime Patrol Aircraft (PDAA) .... AMPA
Advanced Marketing Services [*Book supplier*] .... AMS
Advanced Marketing Services, Inc. [*NASDAQ symbol*] (NQ) .... ADMS
Advanced Marketing Svcs [*NASDAQ symbol*] (TTSB) .... ADMS
Advanced Marketing Systems [*Associated Press*] (SAG) .... AdMkSv
Advanced Masking Systems [*Automotive engineering*] [*3M Co.*] .... AMS
Advanced Master (PGP) .... Adv M
Advanced Master of Education (GAGS) .... AdMEd
Advanced Master of Education .... AME
Advanced Master of Library Science (GAGS) .... AdMLS
Advanced Materials at Tuskegee University (RDA) .... CEAM-TU
Advanced Materials Cargo Sling System (MCD) .... AMCSS
Advanced Materials Fabrication Facility [*Manufacturing*] (MCD) .... AMFF
Advanced Materials Group, Inc. [*NASDAQ symbol*] (SAG) .... ADMG
Advanced Materials Group, Inc. [*Associated Press*] (SAG) .... AdvMat
Advanced Materials Technology [*Information service or system*] (IID) .... AMT
Advanced Materiel Concepts Agency [*Alexandria, VA*] [*Army*] .... AMCA
Advanced Math Library [*Computer science*] (MHDI) .... AML
Advanced Matts Group [*NASDAQ symbol*] (TTSB) .... ADMG
Advanced Meat Recovery [*Food Technology*] .... AMR
Advanced Medical Communications [*Commercial firm*] [*British*] (NITA) .... AMC
Advanced Medical, Inc. [*Associated Press*] (SAG) .... AdMd
Advanced Medical, Inc. [*Associated Press*] (SAG) .... AdvMed
Advanced Medical, Inc. [*AMEX symbol*] (SPSG) .... AMA
Advanced Medium Antitank Missile (MCD) .... AMAMS
Advanced Medium Antitank Weapon (MCD) .... AMAW
Advanced Medium Rocket (MCD) .... AMR
Advanced Medium STOL [*Short Takeoff and Landing*] **Transport** .... AMST
Advanced Medium-Caliber Aircraft Weapon System (MCD) .... AMCAWS
Advanced Medium-Range Air-to-Air Missile (MCD) .... AMRAAM
Advanced Medium-Resolution Imaging Radiometer .... AMRIR
Advanced Med'l 10% cm Pfd [*AMEX symbol*] (TTSB) .... AMAPr
Advanced Memory Concepts (MCD) .... AMC
Advanced Memory Management Architecture [*Computer science*] (BYTE) .... AMMA
Advanced Memory Specification [*Computer science*] .... AMS
Advanced Memory Systems, Inc. (IEEE) .... AMS
Advanced Metallic Air Vehicle Structure (MCD) .... AMAVS
Advanced Metallic Structures [*Program*] [*Air Force*] .... AMS
Advanced Metals Research Corp. .... AMRC
Advanced Meteorological Sounding System .... AMSS
Advanced Meteorological System (MCD) .... AMS
Advanced Meteorological Temperature Sounder (MCD) .... AMTS
Advanced Micro Dev [*NYSE symbol*] (TTSB) .... AMD
Advanced Micro Devices, Inc. .... ADV
Advanced Micro Devices, Inc. [*NYSE symbol*] (SPSG) .... AMD
Advanced Microdevices, Inc. (NITA) .... ADM
Advanced Microprocessor Programming Language [*Texas Instruments, Inc.*] .... AMPL
Advanced Microprocessor Prototyping Laboratory [*Texas Instruments, Inc.*] .... AMPL
Advanced Microprogrammable Processors (MCD) .... AMPP
Advanced Microstructure Profiler [*Instrumentation, oceanography*] .... AMP
Advanced Microwave Circuit Analysis Programme (HGAA) .... AMCAP

Advanced Microwave Moisture Sensor (MCD) .... AMMS
Advanced Microwave Radiometer (SSD) .... AMR
Advanced Microwave Scanning Radiometer (MCD) .... AMSR
Advanced Microwave Sounding Unit [*Satellite instrument for meteorology*] .... AMSU
Advanced Midcourse Active System (MCD) .... AMAS
Advanced Military Occupational Specialty [*Army*] (AABC) .... ADVMOS
Advanced Military Spaceflight Capability .... AMSC
Advanced Military Spaceflight Technology (MCD) .... AMST
Advanced Military Studies Program [*DoD*] .... AMSP
Advanced Millimeter Wave Device .... AMWD
Advanced Mine Countermeasures (MCD) .... AMCM
Advanced Mine Detection System [*Navy*] (DOMA) .... AMDS
Advanced Mine-Hunting SONAR System (MCD) .... AMSS
Advanced Minuteman Accelerometer .... AMA
Advanced Minuteman Computer .... AMC
Advanced Minuteman Platform .... AMP
Advanced Minuteman System .... AMS
Advanced Missile Control System (SAA) .... AMCS
Advanced Missile Materials Research Technical Advisory Group [*Terminated, 1975*] [*DoD*] (EGAO) .... AMMRES
Advanced Missile Propulsion Definition Study [*NASA*] (KSC) .... AMPDS
Advanced Missile Receiver (MCD) .... AMR
Advanced Missile System .... AMS
Advanced Missile System - Heavy (MCD) .... AMS-H
Advanced Mission Studies [*NASA*] (KSC) .... AMS
Advanced Missions Docking System [*or Subsystem*] [*NASA*] (NASA) .... AMDS
Advanced Mobile Phone Service [*Bell System*] .... AMPS
Advanced Mobile Phone System .... AMPS
Advanced Mobile Phone System (ACRL) .... AMPS
Advanced Mobile Telephone System (MCD) .... AMTS
Advanced Mobile Traffic Information and Communications System [*Automotive engineering*] .... AMTICS
Advanced Mobile-Phone System .... AMPS
Advanced Model Builder Shell [*Programming language*] [*1970*] (CSR) .... AMBUSH
Advanced Modeling Extension [*Computer science*] (PCM) .... AME
Advanced Modular Audio Visual Unit (MHDI) .... AMAVU
Advanced Modular RADAR (MCD) .... AMR
Advanced Monopulse Seeker .... AMS
Advanced Mortgage Online System [*Computer science*] (HGAA) .... AMOS
Advanced Motor Case (MCD) .... AMC
Advanced Moving Target Indicator, RADAR .... AMTIR
Advanced Multimission RADAR .... AMMR
Advanced Multimission Reconnaissance System [*Military*] (MCD) .... AMMRS
Advanced Multimission Remotely Piloted Vehicle (MCD) .... AMRPV
Advanced Multimission Sensor System .... AMSS
Advanced Multimission Torpedo (MCD) .... AMMT
Advanced Multiplatform Navy Computer System (MCD) .... AMNCS
Advanced Multiple-Beam Equalization Radiography [*Medicine*] (DMAA) .... AMBER
Advanced Multipurpose Gas Turbine Program .... AMPGATP
Advanced Multipurpose Large Launch Vehicle (MCD) .... AMLLV
Advanced Multipurpose Missile (MCD) .... AMM
Advanced Multipurpose Surfacing System (MCD) .... AMSS
Advanced Multispectral Image Descriptor System [*Photography*] .... AMIDS
Advanced Multi-Stage Axial-Flow Compresor Program [*NASA*] (PDAA) .... AMSAC
Advanced Mutual Security Act .... AMSA
Advanced Narrowband Digital Voice Terminal (MCD) .... ANDVT
Advanced National Radio Data Service [*Joint venture of IBM and Motorola*] (CDE) .... Ardis
Advanced Natural Gas Vehicle .... ANGV
Advanced Naval Gun Weapon System (MCD) .... ANGWS
Advanced Naval System Requirements .... ANSR
Advanced Naval Training School .... ANTS
Advanced Naval Vehicle (CAAL) .... ANV
Advanced Naval Vehicle Concepts Evaluation (MCD) .... ANVCE
Advanced Navigation School [*British military*] (DMA) .... ANS
Advanced Navigator [*Air Force*] .... AN
Advanced Navy Display System .... ANDS
Advanced Navy Tactical Command and Control System (NG) .... ANTACCS
Advanced Negative Resist [*Materials science*] .... ANR
Advanced Network & Services, Inc. [*Nonprofit company formed to manage the National Science Foundation Network*] (IID) .... ANS
Advanced Network Design and Management System [*Computer science*] (MHDB) .... ANDMS
Advanced Network Integration (TEL) .... ANI
Advanced Network Support System [*Computer science*] (PCM) .... ANSS
Advanced Network System [*Computer science*] (ECON) .... ANS
Advanced Network System Architecture (BUR) .... ANSA
Advanced Neutron Source [*Proposed nuclear reactor*] .... ANS
Advanced Night Viewer Subsystem (MCD) .... ANVS
Advanced Night Vision [*Goggles*] .... ANVIS
Advanced NMR Sys Wrrt [*NASDAQ symbol*] (TTSB) .... ANMRW
Advanced NMR Systems [*Associated Press*] (SAG) .... AdNMR
Advanced NMR Systems [*Associated Press*] (SAG) .... ANMR
Advanced NMR Systems, Inc. [*NASDAQ symbol*] (NQ) .... ANMR
Advanced Noncommissioned Officer Course [*Army*] (INF) .... ANCOC
Advanced Noncommissioned Officer Course [*Army*] .... ANOC
Advanced Noncommissioned Officer Education System (MCD) .... ANCOES
Advanced Non-Rigid Airship [*British*] .... ANR
Advanced Nosetip Test [*AEC*] (MCD) .... ANT
Advanced Nozzle Concepts (MCD) .... ANC
Advanced Nuclear Attack Submarine Program (MCD) .... ANASP
Advanced Nurse Practitioner (MEDA) .... ANP
Advanced Ocean Drilling Program [*National Science Foundation*] .... AODP
Advanced Ocean Engineering Laboratory [*Scripps Institution of Oceanography*] .... AOEL
Advanced Office Computer [*Northern Telecom, Inc.*] (NITA) .... AOC
Advanced Office Concepts Corp. [*Defunct Information service or system*] (IID) .... AOC
Advanced Office Concepts Corp. [*Defunct*] (TSSD) .... AOCC
Advanced Officer's Course [*Army*] .... AOC
Advanced On-Board Processor [*Computer*] .... AOP
Advanced On-the-Job Training System (MCD) .... AOTS
Advanced Operating Facility [*Computer Technology, Inc.*] .... AOF
Advanced Operating System [*Data General Corp.*] .... AOS
Advanced Operating System/Virtual Storage [*Data General Corp.*] .... AOS/VS
Advanced Operational Base [*Navy*] .... AOB
Advanced Operations Unit [*Navy*] .... ADVON
Advanced Optical Adjunct (LAIN) .... AOA
Advanced Optical Character Reader .... AOCR
Advanced Optical Countermeasures (MCD) .... AOCM
Advanced Optical Power Spectrum Analyzer (MCD) .... AOPSA
Advanced Optical Rate Sensor .... AORS
Advanced Optics Technology (MCD) .... ADOPT
Advanced Orbit/Ephemeris Subsystem .... AOES
Advanced Orbital Launch Operations .... AOLO
Advanced Orbital Test Satellite [*European Space Agency*] .... AOTS
Advanced Orbiting Astronautical Observatory .... AOAO
Advanced Orbiting Geophysical Observatory .... AOGO
Advanced Orbiting Solar Observatory [*NASA*] .... AOSO
Advanced Order Entry [*Investment system*] (ECON) .... AOE
Advanced Ordnance Department [*British*] .... AOD
Advanced Ordnance Depot .... AOD
Advanced Orthopedic Tech [*NASDAQ symbol*] (TTSB) .... AOTI
Advanced Orthopedic Technologies, Inc. [*Associated Press*] (SAG) .... AdvOrtho
Advanced Orthopedic Techs [*NASDAQ symbol*] (SAG) .... AOTI
Advanced Oxidation Process [*Chemistry*] .... AOP
Advanced Papyrological Information System .... APIS
Advanced Parts List (SAA) .... APL
Advanced Parts Procurement (MCD) .... APP
Advanced Parts Release (NASA) .... APR
Advanced Passenger Train [*British*] .... ADP
Advanced Passenger Train [*British*] .... APT
Advanced Passenger Transport (OA) .... APT
Advanced Passive Array Sonobuoy [*Navy*] (CAAL) .... APAS
Advanced Passive Light Water Reactor [*Nuclear energy*] .... APLWR
Advanced Patent Technique .... APT
Advanced Patrol Sensor System (MCD) .... ADPASS
Advanced Pay .... ADV/P
Advanced Pay Grade (DNAB) .... APG
Advanced Peer-to-Peer Networking [*Computer science*] .... APPN
Advanced Penetration Model (MCD) .... APM
Advanced Performance Computer .... APC
Advanced Performance Interceptor .... API
Advanced Personal Computer (NITA) .... APC
Advanced Personal Defense Weapon [*Army*] (INF) .... APDW
Advanced Personnel Data System (MCD) .... APDS
Advanced Personnel System .... APS
Advanced Photo System [*Camera and film system introduced in 1996*] [*Eastman Kodak Co.*] .... APS
Advanced Photo System .... APS
Advanced Photo System .... APS
Advanced Photon Research Facility [*Proposed, 1986, for high-energy physics*] .... APRF
Advanced Photon Source [*Particle accelerator*] [*Argonne National Laboratory*] .... APS
Advanced Photonix, Inc. [*Associated Press*] (SAG) .... AdvPhot
Advanced Photonix, Inc. [*AMEX symbol*] (SPSG) .... API
Advanced Photonix'A' [*AMEX symbol*] (TTSB) .... API
Advanced Photoscale Technology (PCM) .... APT
Advanced Photosynthetic System .... APS
Advanced Physical Fitness Test (INF) .... APFT
Advanced Pilot Training (PDAA) .... APT
Advanced Pioneering Performance by Leading Engineering .... APPLE
Advanced Piston Coring [*Drilling technology*] .... APC
Advanced Placement [*Education*] .... AP
Advanced Placement Program .... APP
Advanced Planetary Mission Technology [*NASA*] .... APMT
Advanced Planetary Probe .... APP
Advanced Planetary Spacecraft System .... APSS
Advanced Planning (ODBW) .... ADPLAN
Advanced Planning Acquisition Information (AAGC) .... APAI
Advanced Planning and Design [*NASA*] (KSC) .... AP & D
Advanced Planning and Technology Office [*Kennedy Space Center Directorate*] (NASA) .... PT
Advanced Planning Briefing [*Program*] [*DoD*] (RDA) .... APB
Advanced Planning Briefs [*or Briefings*] **for Industry** (MCD) .... APBI
Advanced Planning Data Sheet .... APDS
Advanced Planning Document [*DoD*] (AABC) .... APD
Advanced Planning Program Scheduling .... APPS
Advanced Point Defense Missile System [*Navy*] .... APDMS
Advanced Point Defense Surface Missile System [*Navy*] .... APDSMS
Advanced Pointing Tracking (MCD) .... APT
Advanced Polar Orbiting Satellite .... APOS
Advanced Polaris Guidance Information .... APOGI
Advanced Polymer Composite [*Materials science*] .... APC
Advanced Polymer Sys [*NASDAQ symbol*] (TTSB) .... APOS
Advanced Polymer Systems, Inc. [*Associated Press*] (SAG) .... AdvPoly
Advanced Polymer Systems, Inc. [*NASDAQ symbol*] (NQ) .... APOS

Advanced Pork Technology Association (AC) .... APTA
Advanced Post [*Military*] .... AP
Advanced Post Boost System [*Military*] .... APBS
Advanced Post Boost Vehicle (MCD) .... APBV
Advanced Post Office [*Military*] .... APO
Advanced Power Conversion Experimental Facility .... APCEF
Advanced Power Management [*Computer science*] (PCM) .... APM
Advanced Power Management System [*Jammer*] (MCD) .... APMS
Advanced Power System .... APS
Advanced Power Technology [*Army*] .... APT
Advanced Power Train Electronic Controller [*Automotive engineering*] .... APTEC
Advanced Pressure Tube Reactor [*Nuclear energy*] .... APTR
Advanced Pressurized [*In name of nuclear reactor, AP 600, developed by Westinghouse Electric Corp.*] .... AP
Advanced Pressurized-Water Reactor [*Nuclear energy*] .... APWR
Advanced Processing Science Center [*Oak Ridge National Laboratory*] .... APSC
Advanced Processor [*Honeywell, Inc.*] (NITA) .... AP
Advanced Procurement (NG) .... AP
Advanced Procurement Change [*or Check*] (MCD) .... APC
Advanced Procurement Engineering (MCD) .... APE
Advanced Procurement Funding (MCD) .... APF
Advanced Procurement Information (MCD) .... API
Advanced Procurement Package (MCD) .... APP
Advanced Procurement Plan [*Navy British*] .... APP
Advanced Procurement Planning Program .... APPP
Advanced Procurement Planning System for Security Assistance .... APPSSA
Advanced Product Change Notice .... APCN
Advanced Product Evaluation Laboratory .... APEL
Advanced Product Line (IAA) .... APL
Advanced Product Planning Operation (MUGU) .... APPO
Advanced Production Engineering .... APE
Advanced Productivity Research and Technology (MCD) .... APRT
Advanced Professional Certificate (PGP) .... APC
Advanced Professional Computer (HGAA) .... APC
Advanced Professional Programs, University of Southern California Law Center (DLA) .... USCAPP
Advanced Program Development .... APD
Advanced Program Weight Control System .... APWCS
Advanced Programmable Interrupt Controller .... AIPC
Advanced Programmable Interrupt Controller [*Computer science*] .... APIC
Advanced Programming Course [*Computer science*] .... APC
Advanced Programming Language [*Computer science*] .... APL
Advanced Programming Language Statistical Package (MCD) .... APLSTATPACK
Advanced Programs Authorization .... APA
Advanced Program-to-Program Communication [*Computer science*] .... APPC
Advanced Program-to-Program Communication/Personal Computer [*IBM Corp.*] (BYTE) .... APPC/PC
Advanced Progressive Matrices [*Intelligence test*] .... APM
Advanced Project Planning .... APP
Advanced Promotion Technologies, Inc. [*Associated Press*] (SAG) .... AdvPro
Advanced Promotion Technology [*NASDAQ symbol*] (SPSG) .... APTV
Advanced Propellant System .... APS
Advanced Propulsion Comparison Study [*NASA*] (NASA) .... APC
Advanced Propulsion Cooling .... APC
Advanced Propulsion Payload Effects [*NASA*] (NASA) .... APPLE
Advanced Propulsion Subsystem Integration [*Air Force*] .... APSI
Advanced Propulsion Test (SSD) .... APT
Advanced Protein Crystal Growth Facility (SSD) .... APCGF
Advanced Protein Purification System .... APPS
Advanced Protocol Controller [*Adax, Inc.*] .... APC
Advanced Proton Source [*Physics*] .... APS
Advanced Public Transportation Systems .... APTS
Advanced Purification [*Chromatography*] .... AP
Advanced PVO [*Protivo-Vozdushnaia Oborona*] **Intercepter** [*Military*] (MCD) .... APVOI
Advanced Qualification Program [*FAA*] (TAG) .... AQP
Advanced Qualification Program (GAVI) .... AQP
Advanced Qualitative and Quantitative Personnel Requirements Information [*Army*] .... AQQPRI
Advanced Quick Look [*Army*] .... AQL
Advanced Quickfix [*Military*] .... AQF
Advanced RADAR Experimental Systems Technology [*Army*] .... AREST
Advanced RADAR Information Evaluation System .... ARIES
Advanced RADAR Pattern Recognition .... ARPR
Advanced RADAR Processing System .... ARPS
Advanced RADAR Terminal System (IEEE) .... ARTS
Advanced Radar Test-Bed [*Military*] (DOMA) .... ARTB
Advanced RADAR Traffic Control System [*Air Force*] (AFM) .... ARTCS
Advanced RADAR Traffic Control System [*Air Force*] .... ARTS
Advanced RADAR Warning Receiver (MCD) .... ARWR
Advanced RADAR Warning System (MCD) .... ARWS
Advanced Radiation Effects Simulation .... ARES
Advanced Radiation Space Defense Application (MCD) .... ARSDA
Advanced Radiation Technology Office [*Military*] .... ARTO
Advanced Radio Astronomy Explorer (PDAA) .... ARAE
Advanced Radio Data Information Service [*IBM Corp., Motorola, Inc.*] .... ARDIS
Advanced Radio Telecom Corp. [*Associated Press*] (SAG) .... AdvRdio
Advanced Radio Telecom Corp. [*NASDAQ symbol*] (SAG) .... ARTT
Advanced Railroad Electronics System [*A space guidance system made by Collins Air Transport*] .... ARES
Advanced Range Data System [*Air Force*] .... ARDS
Advanced Range Instrumentation Aircraft .... ARIA
Advanced Range Instrumentation Ship [*Navy symbol*] .... ARIS
Advanced Range Instrumentation Systems (MCD) .... ARIS
Advanced Range Testing, Reporting, and Control .... ARTRAC
Advanced Raster-Graphics System (MHDB) .... ARGS
Advanced Reactivity Measurement Facility [*Idaho Falls, ID*] [*Department of Energy*] .... ARMF
Advanced Reactor (KSC) .... AR
Advanced Reactor Development Associates .... ARDA
Advanced Reactor Technology (IEEE) .... ART
Advanced Reactors Division [*of the Nuclear Regulatory Commission*] (NRCH) .... ARD
Advanced Readiness (MCD) .... AR
Advanced Real-Time Executive (BUR) .... ARE
Advanced Real-Time Processing System (PDAA) .... ARPS
Advanced Real-Time Range Control (IEEE) .... ARTRAC
Advanced Real-Time Simulation (MCD) .... ARTS
Advanced Real-Time System (MCD) .... ARTS
Advanced Receiver Model System .... ARMS
Advanced Recoilless Weapon (MCD) .... ARW
Advanced Reconfigurable Computer System .... ARCS
Advanced Reconnaissance and Target Acquisition Capabilities .... ARTAC
Advanced Reconnaissance Electrically-Propelled Spacecraft [*Military*] (PDAA) .... AREPS
Advanced Reconnaissance Helicopter .... ARH
Advanced Reconnaissance Satellite .... ARS
Advanced Reconnaissance System (MUGU) .... ARS
Advanced Record System [*Air Force*] .... ARS
Advanced Recovery Mode [*Computer science*] .... ARM
Advanced Recovery Sequencer (DWSG) .... ARS
Advanced Recovery System (MCD) .... ADRECS
Advanced Reentry Concepts [*Aerospace*] .... ARC
Advanced Reentry Program [*Aerospace*] .... ARP
Advanced Reentry System [*Aerospace*] .... ARS
Advanced Regional Prediction System [*Marine science*] (OSRA) .... ARPS
Advanced Regional Prediction System (USDC) .... ARPS
Advanced Registered Nurse Practitioner .... ARNP
Advanced Regulating Station [*British military*] (DMA) .... ARS
Advanced Remote Display Station (IAA) .... ARDS
Advanced Remote Node [*Bay Networks*] [*Computer science*] .... ARN
Advanced Remote Tracking Station (MCD) .... ARTS
Advanced Remotely Piloted Modular Aircraft (MCD) .... ARPMA
Advanced Remotely Piloted Vehicle [*Aviation*] (AIA) .... ARPV
Advanced Reproductive Technology [*Medicine*] .... ART
Advanced Requirements Tasking Information and Support System (MCD) .... ARTISS
Advanced Rescue and Recovery System [*Proposed VTOL aircraft*] [*Also, ARS*] (MCD) .... ARRS
Advanced Rescue System [*Proposed VTOL aircraft*] [*Also, ARRS*] .... ARS
Advanced Reseach and Development Agency .... ARDA
Advanced Research Agency Project Tempo (MCD) .... ARAPT
Advanced Research and Development .... AR & D
Advanced Research and Technology (MUGU) .... AR & T
Advanced Research and Technology .... ART
Advanced Research and Technology Development Program [*Department of Energy*] .... AR & TD
Advanced Research Center [*Aerospace*] .... ARC
Advanced Research Consultants (MCD) .... ARCON
Advanced Research Craft Hydrokeel (MCD) .... ARCK
Advanced Research Division .... ARD
Advanced Research EMP [*Electromagnetic Pulse*] **Simulator** .... ARES
Advanced Research Engine (MCD) .... ARE
Advanced Research Geophysical Observatory (IAA) .... ARGO
Advanced Research Instrument System, Inc. .... ARIS
Advanced Research Objective (MCD) .... ARO
Advanced Research Planning Document .... ARPD
Advanced Research Program Directive (MCD) .... ARPD
Advanced Research Projects .... ARP
Advanced Research Projects Agency [*Later, DARPA*] [*DoD*] .... ARPA
Advanced Research Projects Agency Network [*DoD*] .... ARPANET
Advanced Research Projects Agency Research Center [*DoD*] (DNAB) .... ARPARSCHCEN
Advanced Research Projects Agency Terminal [*DoD*] .... ARPAT
Advanced Research Workshop .... ARW
Advanced Resident Training Plan [*Military*] (AABC) .... ARTP
Advanced Resource Tracking Spreadsheet [*Scitor Corp.*] [*Computer science*] (PCM) .... ARTS
Advanced Restricted Report .... ARR
Advanced Rifle Grenade Munition [*Army*] (INF) .... ARGM
Advanced Rifle Marksmanship [*Military*] (INF) .... ARM
Advanced RISC [*Reduced Instruction Set Computer*] **Computing** (CDE) .... ARC
Advanced RISC [*Reduced Instruction-Set Computerizing*] **Machine** (ECON) .... ARM
Advanced Road Profile Measurement Vehicle [*Suspension design and testing*] [*Automotive engineering*] .... ARPMV
Advanced Robotics Research .... ARR
Advanced Rocket Engine Storable (MCD) .... ARES
Advanced Rocket Ramjet (MCD) .... ARR
Advanced Rocket Ramjet .... ARRJ
Advanced Rocket System [*Military*] (DOMA) .... ARS
Advanced Rotorcraft Technology Integration (MCD) .... ARTI
Advanced Ruling Expiration Date [*IRS*] .... AD
Advanced Run Length Limited [*Computer science*] .... ARLL
Advanced Rural Transportation Systems [*FHWA*] (TAG) .... ARTS
Advanced Safety Vehicle [*Automotive engineering*] .... ASV
Advanced SAGE [*Semiautomatic Ground Environment*] **Tracking Study** [*Military*] (IAA) .... ASTS
Advanced Sales Index [*LIMRA*] .... ASI
Advanced Salvo Rifle (MCD) .... ASR
Advanced Satellite .... ASAT

Advanced Satellite for Cosmology and Astrophysics [*Japanese spacecraft*] .... ASCA
Advanced Satellite Products Project [*Madison, WI*] [*NOAA/NESDIS*] (GRD) .... ASPP
Advanced Satellite Tracking Center .... ASTC
Advanced Scatterable Mine [*Air Force*] (MCD) .... ASM
Advanced Schools (MUGU) .... ADVSCOL
Advanced Science Education Program [*National Science Foundation*] .... ASEP
Advanced Sciences Research Group (SAA) .... ASRG
Advanced Scientific Computer [*Texas Instruments, Inc.*] .... ASC
Advanced Scientific Instrument (IAA) .... ASIS
Advanced Scientific Instruments [*AMR, Inc.*] .... ASI
Advanced Scientific Instruments Symbolic Translator [*Assembly program*] (DEN) .... ASIST
Advanced Scout Helicopter [*Military*] .... ASH
Advanced Scout Helicopter Task Force [*Army*] (RDA) .... ASH-TF
Advanced SCSI [*Small Computer System Interface*] **Programming Interface** (PCM) .... ASPI
Advanced Sea-Based Deterrent [*Navy*] .... ASBD
Advanced Seal Delivery System [*Formerly, Advanced Swimmer Delivery System*] [*Navy*] (DOMA) .... ASDS
Advanced Sea-Launched Cruise Missile (MCD) .... ASLCM
Advanced Secretarial Language Certificate [*British*] (DI) .... ASLC
Advanced Section Communication Zone [*World War II*] .... ADSC
Advanced Self-Protection [*Jammer*] (MCD) .... ASP
Advanced Self-Protection Integrated Suite [*Military*] (DOMA) .... ASPIS
Advanced Self-Protection Jammer .... ASPJ
Advanced Semi Mat's [*NASDAQ symbol*] (TTSB) .... ASMIF
Advanced Semiconductor Equipment Exposition (TSPED) .... ASEE
Advanced Semiconductor Materials .... ASM
Advanced Semiconductor Materials International (MHDW) .... ASMIF
Advanced Semiconductor Materials International NV [*Associated Press*] (SAG) .... AdvSem
Advanced Semiconductor Materials International NV [*NASDAQ symbol*] (NQ) .... ASMI
Advanced Sensor Analog Relay System [*Army*] (MCD) .... ASARS
Advanced Sensor Evaluation and Test [*NASA*] .... ASET
Advanced Servomanipulator .... ASM
Advanced Ship Concept Development .... ASCD
Advanced Ship Concepts .... ASC
Advanced Ship Development .... ASD
Advanced Ship Types and Combatant Craft (MCD) .... ASTACC
Advanced Shipboard Command Communications System (SAA) .... ASCCS
Advanced Shipboard Communications (MCD) .... ADSCOM
Advanced Shipboard Satellite Communications (DNAB) .... ASSC
Advanced Shipment Notification [*Inventory control*] [*Automotive manufacturing*] .... ASN
Advanced Short Takeoff and Vertical Landing [*Military*] .... ASTOVL
Advanced Short-Range Air Defense System (MCD) .... ASHORAD
Advanced Short-Range Air-to-Air Missile (MCD) .... ASRAA
Advanced Short-Range Air-to-Air Missile (RDA) .... ASRAAM
Advanced Short-to-Medium Range .... ASMR
Advanced Signal Processor [*Computer science*] .... ASP
Advanced Simulation [*Missions project*] .... ADSIM
Advanced Simulation Center [*Army*] (MCD) .... ASC
Advanced Simulation Facility [*Army*] (MCD) .... ASF
Advanced Simulation Technology [*DoD*] (IEEE) .... AST
Advanced Simulator for Pilot Training (MCD) .... ASPT
Advanced Simulator for Undergraduate Pilot Training [*Air Force*] .... ASUPT
Advanced Size Reduction Facility .... ASRF
Advanced Skewed Sensory Electronic Triad [*Navy*] .... ASSET
Advanced Skills Education Program [*Army*] .... ASEP
Advanced Sleep Phase Syndrome [*Medicine*] (DMAA) .... ASPS
Advanced Small Axial Turbine Technology (RDA) .... ASATT
Advanced Small Launch Vehicle .... ASLV
Advanced Smokeless Technology Demonstration Motor (MCD) .... ASTDM
Advanced Sodium-Cooled Reactor .... ASCR
Advanced Solar Observatory (DEN) .... ASO
Advanced Solar Turbo-Electric Conversion .... ASTEC
Advanced Solid Logic Technology [*Computer science*] .... ASLT
Advanced Solid Rocket Motor [*Proposed*] [*NASA*] .... ASRM
Advanced Sonobuoy Communications Link [*Navy*] (MCD) .... ASC
Advanced Sonobuoy Communications Link [*Navy*] (MCD) .... ASCL
Advanced Soviet [*Combined with GENS to form A Group*] [*Division of National Security Agency*] .... ADVA
Advanced Space Applications Program [*Military*] .... ASAP
Advanced Space Engine (NASA) .... ASE
Advanced Space Ground Link Subsystem (MCD) .... ASGLS
Advanced Space Guidance System (IIA) .... ASGS
Advanced Space Propellant Demonstration (MCD) .... ASPD
Advanced Space Station .... ASS
Advanced Space Structure Technology Research Experiments (MCD) .... ASTREX
Advanced Space Technology Division [*NASA*] (NASA) .... ASTD
Advanced Space Technology Program [*Military*] (DOMA) .... ASTP
Advanced Spacecraft Subsystem Cost Analysis Structure (MCD) .... ASSCAS
Advanced Spacecraft Trainer [*or Transport or Truck*] **Reusable Orbiter** [*NASA*] (MCD) .... ASTRO
Advanced Special Projects in Radiation Effects .... ASPIRE
Advanced Specialist in Education Certificate (GAGS) .... ASEdCert
Advanced Speech Processor (ACRL) .... ASP
Advanced Standard Buried Collector .... ASBC
Advanced STANO [*Surveillance, Target Acquisition, and Night Observation*] **Data Link** [*Military*] (MCD) .... ASDL
Advanced Star/Target Reference Optical Sensor (SSD) .... ASTROS

Advanced Static Test Recording Apparatus .... ASTRA
Advanced Station (MHDI) .... ADVAST
Advanced Statistical Analysis Program [*Computer science*] (MCD) .... ASTAP
Advanced Status Threat Generator (DWSG) .... ASTG
Advanced Stirling Conversion System [*Mechanical engineering*] .... ASCS
Advanced Strategic Aerodynamic Configuration Technology (MCD) .... ASACT
Advanced Strategic Air Defense .... ASAD
Advanced Strategic Airborne RADAR System .... ASARS
Advanced Strategic Air-Launched Missile (MCD) .... ASALM
Advanced Strategic Missile System [*DoD*] .... ASM
Advanced Strategic Missile System [*DoD*] (MCD) .... ASMS
Advanced Strategic Missile Systems [*Air Force*] (DOMA) .... ASMS
Advanced Strategic Penetrator Aircraft (MCD) .... ASPA
Advanced Strategic Reconnaissance System [*Air Force*] .... ASRS
Advanced Strategic Standoff Aircraft (MCD) .... ASSA
Advanced Strategic Standoff Attack Missile (MCD) .... ASSAM
Advanced Strategic Transport Aircraft .... ASTA
Advanced Strike Weapon System (MCD) .... ASWS
Advanced Structural Analyser (IAA) .... ASTRA
Advanced Structural Concept and Evaluation Program [*Military*] (DNAB) .... ADCEP
Advanced Structures Technology Demonstration .... ASTD
Advanced Student in Law [*British*] (ROG) .... ASL
Advanced Studies Group [*Air Force*] .... ASG
Advanced Study Institutes (NATG) .... ASI
Advanced Study Program .... ASP
Advanced Submarine Control Program (MCD) .... ASCOP
Advanced Submarine Detection (MCD) .... ASD
Advanced Submarine Weapon Handling System (MCD) .... ASWHS
Advanced Supersonic All-Purpose Dispenser (MCD) .... ASAP
Advanced Supersonic Technology .... AST
Advanced Supersonic Transport .... ASST
Advanced Supersonic Transport .... AST
Advanced Supplementary [*Education level*] [*British*] .... AS
Advanced Support Processor [*Computer science*] (IAA) .... ASP
Advanced Surface Engineering Technologies .... ASET
Advanced Surface Missile .... ASM
Advanced Surface Missile System .... ASMS
Advanced Surface-to-Air Ramjet [*Navy*] .... ASAR
Advanced Surface-to-Air Ramjet, Extended Range (MCD) .... ASAR-ER
Advanced Surface-to-Air Ramjet, Medium Range (MCD) .... ASAR-MR
Advanced Surface-to-Air Rocket Ramjet (MCD) .... ASARR
Advanced Surgical Centre [*British and Canadian*] [*World War II*] .... ASC
Advanced Surgical, Inc. [*Associated Press*] (SAG) .... AdvSu
Advanced Surgical, Inc. [*Associated Press*] (SAG) .... AdvSurg
Advanced Surgical, Inc. [*NASDAQ symbol*] (SAG) .... ASUR
Advanced Surveillance Aircraft (MCD) .... ASA
Advanced Surveillance and Reconnaissance Systems .... ASURS
Advanced Surveillance and Target Acquisition RADAR .... ASTAR
Advanced Surveillance Drone (MCD) .... ASD
Advanced Surveillance RADAR .... ASR
Advanced Survivability Test Bed [*Military*] (INF) .... ASTB
Advanced Survival Avionics Program (MCD) .... ASAP
Advanced Symbolic Artwork Preparation (MCD) .... ASAP
Advanced Synchronous Meteorological Satellite .... ASMS
Advanced Synthetic Aperture RADER [*Marine science*] (OSRA) .... ASAR
Advanced System [*NAS*] .... AS
Advanced System Architecture for Postscript [*Printer technology*] [*QMS, Inc.*] [*Computer science*] (PCM) .... ASAP
Advanced System Avionics [*Air Force*] .... ASA
Advanced System Concept (MCD) .... ASC
Advanced System Concepts Laboratory [*Army*] .... ASCL
Advanced System Data Processing Simulation (AABC) .... ASDPSIM
Advanced System Environment and Threat Simulation .... ASETS
Advanced System for Communications and Education in National Development (MCD) .... ASCEND
Advanced System for Process Engineering .... ASPEN
Advanced System Integration Demonstration [*Military*] .... ASID
Advanced System Planning [*Air Force*] (MCD) .... ASP
Advanced System Synthesis and Evaluation Technique [*Lockheed Aircraft*] .... ASSET
Advanced System Technology .... AST
Advanced System Time Domain .... ASYSTD
Advanced Systematic Techniques for Reliable Operational Software [*Computer science*] (MHDI) .... ASTROS
Advanced Systems and Design .... ASD
Advanced Systems and Technology (MCD) .... AS & T
Advanced Systems and Technology Programme [*European Space Agency*] .... ASTP
Advanced Systems Buying .... ASB
Advanced Systems Concepts Office [*Army*] (RDA) .... ASCO
Advanced Systems Division [*IBM Corp.*] .... ASD
Advanced Systems Engineering .... ASE
Advanced Systems Laboratory .... ASL
Advanced Systems Planning, Research, Development, and Engineering Course [*Army*] .... ASPRDEC
Advanced Systems Project Office (SAA) .... ASPO
Advanced Systems Requirements .... ASR
Advanced Systems Research and Analysis Office [*Army and NASA joint operation*] (RDA) .... ASRAO
Advanced Systems Research Department .... ASRD
Advanced Systems Technology (IEEE) .... ASTEC
Advanced Systems Technology and Integration Office [*Army*] .... ASTIO
Advanced Tactical .... ATAC

Advanced Tactical Aerial Reconnaissance System [*Cancelled 1993*] [*Air Force*] (DOMA) ... ATARS
Advanced Tactical Air Combat Simulation ... ATACS
Advanced Tactical Air Command and Control System (MCD) ... ATACCS
Advanced Tactical Air Command Center [*Marine Corps*] (DOMA) ... ATACC
Advanced Tactical Air Command Central (AAGC) ... ATACC
Advanced Tactical Air Command Missile Systems (AAGC) ... ATACMS
Advanced Tactical Air Control Central ... ATACC
Advanced Tactical Air Reconnaissance System (AAGC) ... ATARS
Advanced Tactical Airborne Reconnaissance System [*Air Force*] (MCD) ... ATARS
Advanced Tactical Aircraft [*Army*] ... ATA
Advanced Tactical Aircraft Launch and Recovery System (MCD) ... ATALARS
Advanced Tactical Aircraft Program System ... ATAPS
Advanced Tactical Air-to-Air Missile (MCD) ... ATAAM
Advanced Tactical Assault Weapon ... ATAW
Advanced Tactical Attack System (MCD) ... ATAS
Advanced Tactical Attack System Mission Analysis (MCD) ... ATASMA
Advanced Tactical Attacks/Manned System (IEEE) ... ATAMS
Advanced Tactical Avionics RADAR ... ATAR
Advanced Tactical Ballistic Missile [*AMC - Missile*] ... ATBM
Advanced Tactical Command and Control Capabilities ... ATCCC
Advanced Tactical Control System (MCD) ... ATCS
Advanced Tactical Electronic Warfare System (AFM) ... ATEWS
Advanced Tactical Fighter [*Air Force*] (MCD) ... ATF
Advanced Tactical Fighter Mission Analysis (MCD) ... ATFMA
Advanced Tactical Inertial Guidance System [*Navy*] ... ATIGS
Advanced Tactical Jamming System [*Aircraft*] ... ATJS
Advanced Tactical Lightweight Air Superiority [*RADAR*] [*Air Force*] (MCD) ... ATLAS
Advanced Tactical Lightweight Avionics System ... ATLAS
Advanced Tactical Processor ... ATP
Advanced Tactical Prototype (DOMA) ... ATP
Advanced Tactical RADAR [*Army*] (MCD) ... ATR
Advanced Tactical Reconnaissance System (MCD) ... ATRS
Advanced Tactical Stand-Off Missile (MCD) ... ATSM
Advanced Tactical Strike (MCD) ... ATS
Advanced Tactical Support [*Aircraft*] [*Navy*] (DOMA) ... ATS
Advanced Tactical Support Aircraft [*Navy*] (DOMA) ... ATSA
Advanced Tactical Support Base [*Navy*] (NVT) ... ATSB
Advanced Tactical Support System (DOMA) ... ATSS
Advanced Takeoff and Landing System (MCD) ... ATOLS
Advanced Tank Cannon (DOMA) ... ATAC
Advanced Tank Cannon System [*Army*] ... ATACS
Advanced Tanker Cargo [*Aircraft*] (MCD) ... ATAC
Advanced Tanker Cargo Aircraft ... ATCA
Advanced Target Acquisition Sensor [*Air Force*] (MCD) ... ATAS
Advanced Target Acquisition System [*Air Force*] ... ATAS
Advanced Target Location and Strike ... ATLAS
Advanced Technical Education Program ... ATEP
Advanced Technical Engagement Model (MCD) ... ATEM
Advanced Technical Experimental Transportation (MCD) ... ATET
Advanced Technical Objective Working Group ... ATOWG
Advanced Technical Payload (SAA) ... ATP
Advanced Technical Requirements [*DoD*] ... ATR
Advanced Technical Training Center [*Military*] (MUGU) ... ATTC
Advanced Technical Training Facility [*Military*] ... ATTF
Advanced Technician's Test (MCD) ... ATT
Advanced Techniques for Electrical Power Management, Control, and Distribution Systems [*Army*] (RDA) ... ATEPS
Advanced Techniques for Imagery Interpretation (AABC) ... ATII
Advanced Techniques Integration into Efficient Scientific Application Software [*ESPRIT project*] (NITA) ... ATES
Advanced Technologies for Tactical Aircraft (MCD) ... ATTAC
Advanced Technologies Testing Aircraft System [*NASA*] ... ATTAS
Advanced Technology [*In PC AT, model name of a computer*] [*IBM Corp.*] ... AT
Advanced Technology Airfoil Tests (MCD) ... ATAT
Advanced Technology Applications Facility [*UNCHS*] [*United Nations*] (DUND) ... ATAF
Advanced Technology Attachment [*Hard disk interface*] [*Computer science*] ... ATA
Advanced Technology Bomber [*Air Force*] ... ATB
Advanced Technology Center [*Aerospace*] ... ATC
Advanced Technology Centre, Honeywell Ltd., Willowdale, Ontario [*Library symbol National Library of Canada*] (NLC) ... OTHL
Advanced Technology Components [*Program*] [*Army, Navy*] (RDA) ... ATC
Advanced Technology Crew Protection (MCD) ... ATCP
Advanced Technology Cruise Missile (MCD) ... ATCM
Advanced Technology Demonstration ... ATD
Advanced Technology Demonstration Aircraft ... ATDA
Advanced Technology Demonstration LASER Gyro (MCD) ... ATDLG
Advanced Technology Demonstration Network [*Telecommunications*] ... ATDNet
Advanced Technology Demonstrator Engine ... ATDE
Advanced Technology Developments (MCD) ... ATD
Advanced Technology Directorate [*Army Strategic Defense Command*] [*Huntsville, AL*] ... ATD
Advanced Technology Energy Efficient Demonstrator (MCD) ... ATEED
Advanced Technology Engine (MCD) ... ATE
Advanced Technology Fighter ... ATF
Advanced Technology for Large Structural Systems [*National Science Foundation*] ... ATLASS
Advanced Technology Ground Attack Fighter [*Air Force*] ... ATGAF
Advanced Technology Group [*Navy*] ... ATG
Advanced Technology Innovation [*Computer science*] ... ATI
Advanced Technology Laboratories, Inc. [*Associated Press*] (SAG) ... AdvTLb
Advanced Technology Laboratories, Inc. [*Formerly, Westmark International, Inc.*] [*NASDAQ symbol*] (SPSG) ... ATLI
Advanced Technology Laboratory [*Navy*] (MCD) ... ATL
Advanced Technology Labortories, Inc. (DAVI) ... ATL
Advanced Technology Labs [*NASDAQ symbol*] (TTSB) ... ATLI
Advanced Technology Large Aircraft System [*Air Force*] (MCD) ... ATLAS
Advanced Technology/Libraries [*Information service*] ... AT/L
Advanced Technology Light Twin Engine Aircraft (MCD) ... ATLIT
Advanced Technology Light Twin Engine Research Aircraft [*Air Force*] (MCD) ... ATLIT
Advanced Technology Maintenance [*British*] (NITA) ... ATM
Advanced Technology Materials [*Commercial firm Associated Press*] (SAG) ... AdvTch
Advanced Technology Materials [*NASDAQ symbol*] (SAG) ... ATMI
Advanced Technology Matr'l [*NASDAQ symbol*] (TTSB) ... ATMI
Advanced Technology Microelectronic Array Computer (MCD) ... ATMAC
Advanced Technology Multimedia Communications (MCD) ... ATMC
Advanced Technology of Management (SAA) ... ATOM
Advanced Technology Park ... ATP
Advanced Technology Program [*Department of Commerce*] ... ATP
Advanced Technology Pultrusion ... ATP
Advanced Technology Rotor System (MCD) ... ATRS
Advanced Technology Satellite ... ATS
Advanced Technology Spacecraft [*NASA*] (MCD) ... ATS
Advanced Technology Systems, Inc. [*Arlington, VA*] [*Telecommunications*] (TSSD) ... ATS
Advanced Technology Tactical Transport [*Proposed low-altitude long-range airlifter*] [*Military*] ... AT^3
Advanced Technology Tactical Transport [*Proposed low-altitude long-range airlifter*] [*Military*] (MCD) ... ATTT
Advanced Technology Training [*Army*] (VNW) ... ATT
Advanced Technology Transition Demonstration [*Army*] (INF) ... ATTD
Advanced Technology Transport ... ATT
Advanced Technology Upper Stage (MCD) ... ATUS
Advanced Technology Vehicle ... ATV
Advanced Technology Workstation [*Computer system*] ... ATW
Advanced Telecommunication Research ... ATR
Advanced Telecommunications Corp. [*Atlanta, GA*] (TSSD) ... ATC
Advanced Telecommunications Sciences Office [*STRATCOM*] [*Army*] (RDA) ... ATSO
Advanced Teleprocessing System (IAA) ... ATS
Advanced Telescope Mission [*Skylab*] [*NASA*] ... ATM
Advanced Telescopes Project [*University of Colorado*] [*Research center*] (RCD) ... ATP
Advanced Television [*See also HDTV*] ... ATV
Advanced Television Research Consortium (PS) ... ATRC
Advanced Television Seeker (MCD) ... ATVS
Advanced Television Services [*FCC*] (NTCM) ... ATS
Advanced Television Systems Committee [*FCC*] (NTCM) ... ATSC
Advanced Television Test Center [*Telecommunications*] (TSSD) ... ATTC
Advanced Terminal Aerial Weapon Delivery Simulation (MCD) ... ATAWDS
Advanced Terminal Defense Interceptor (MCD) ... ATDI
Advanced Terminal Guidance System ... ATGS
Advanced Terminal Interceptor ... ATI
Advanced Terminal Interceptor Technology ... ATIT
Advanced Terminal Interceptor Technology Program ... ATITP
Advanced Test Accelerator [*Lawrence Livermore National Laboratory*] ... ATA
Advanced Test Battery [*Aptitude and skills test*] ... ATB
Advanced Test in Psychology ... ATP
Advanced Test Reactor [*Nuclear energy*] ... ATR
Advanced Test Reactor Critical Experiment [*Nuclear energy*] ... ATRCE
Advanced Test Reactor Critical Facility [*Nuclear energy*] ... ATRC
Advanced Test Reactor Critical Facility [*Nuclear energy*] (GFGA) ... ATRCF
Advanced Test Vehicle (MCD) ... ATV
Advanced Tethered Vehicle [*Navy*] ... ATV
Advanced Text Management System [*IBM Corp.*] ... ATMS
Advanced Therapeutic Sys [*AMEX symbol*] (TTSB) ... ATH
Advanced Therapeutic Systems Ltd. [*Associated Press*] (SAG) ... AdvThr
Advanced Therapeutic Systems Ltd. [*AMEX symbol*] (SAG) ... ATH
Advanced Thermal Analysis (MCD) ... ATHAS
Advanced Thermal Flight Experiment (MCD) ... ATFE
Advanced Thermal Imaging Scanner [*or System*] ... ATIS
Advanced Thermal Reactor ... ATR
Advanced Threat Infrared Countermeasures Program (DWSG) ... ATIRCM
Advanced Threat Radar Jammer [*DoD*] ... ATRJ
Advanced Throttling Slurry Engine (KSC) ... ATSE
Advanced Time-Division Multiple Access (IEEE) ... ATDMA
Advanced TIROS [*Television Infrared Observation Satellite*] **Operational Vertical Sounder** ... ATOVS
Advanced Tissue Sci [*NASDAQ symbol*] (TTSB) ... ATIS
Advanced Tissue Sciences, Inc. [*Associated Press*] (SAG) ... AdvTiss
Advanced Tissue Sciences, Inc. [*NASDAQ symbol*] (SAG) ... ATIS
Advanced Toroidal Facility [*Oak Ridge National Laboratory*] ... ATF
Advanced Torpedo Decoy (CAAL) ... ATD
Advanced Torsion Bar (MCD) ... ATB
Advanced Total Traction Engineering System for All-Terrain [*Automotive engineering*] ... ATTESA
Advanced Tracking Program (MCD) ... ATP
Advanced Traffic Information Supply System [*Highway traffic management*] ... ATISS
Advanced Traffic Management [*FAA*] (GFGA) ... ATF
Advanced Traffic Management System ... ATMS
Advanced Traffic Signal System ... ATSS
Advanced Train Control System [*Union Pacific Railroad Co.*] ... ATCS
Advanced Trainer [*Air Force*] ... AT

Advanced Training [*Military*] (NVT) ... ADVTNG
Advanced Training Command (MCD) ... ATC
Advanced Training System [*Air Force*] ... ATS
Advanced Training Technology Associates [*Commercial firm British*] ... ATTA
Advanced Training Unit ... ATU
Advanced Transit Association (EA) ... ATRA
Advanced Transonic Technology (MCD) ... ATT
Advanced Transport Aircraft (MCD) ... ATA
Advanced Transport Operating System (MCD) ... ATOPS
Advanced Transport Technology Mission Analysis (MCD) ... ATTMA
Advanced Transport Technology Program [*NASA*] (OA) ... ATTP
Advanced Transport Technology Program Office [*NASA*] ... ATTPO
Advanced Transport Telematics [*Traffic management*] (ECON) ... ATT
Advanced Trauma Life Support System ... ATLS
Advanced Travel Information Systems [*Formerly, ADI*] [*Highway safety research*] ... ATIS
Advanced Treatment (GNE) ... AT
Advanced Triga Prototype Reactor ... ATPR
Advanced Turbine Engine Gas Generator [*Air Force*] ... ATEGG
Advanced Turbo Systems [*Automotive industry supplier*] ... ATS
Advanced Turbocharged Intercooled [*Truck engineering*] ... ATi
Advanced Turbofan Engine ... ATE
Advanced Turboprop [*Aeronautics*] ... ATP
Advanced TV Systems Committee (EA) ... ATSC
Advanced TV Systems Committee (EA) ... ATVSC
Advanced UHF Communication System (MCD) ... AUCS
Advanced Underseas Weapons [*Army*] ... AUW
Advanced Underseas Weapons Circuitry ... AUWC
Advanced Underwater Missile ... AUM
Advanced Underwater Search System (MCD) ... AUSS
Advanced Underwater Warfare [*Navy*] ... AUW
Advanced Underwriting Service [*Database*] [*R & R Newkirk*] [*Information service or system*] (CRD) ... AUS
Advanced Unit Training [*Army*] ... AUT
Advanced Universal Jamming System ... AUJS
Advanced Upper Stage Motor (MCD) ... AUSM
Advanced User Terminal [*Navy*] (MCD) ... AUT
Advanced Utility Simulation Model [*Environmental Protection Agency*] (GFGA) ... AUSM
Advanced V/STOL [*Vertical/Short Takeoff and Landing*] **Weapon System** (MCD) ... AVS
Advanced Vehicle Control System [*Automotive engineering*] ... AVCS
Advanced Vehicle Design Department ... AVDD
Advanced Vehicle Highway System [*Automotive engineering*] ... AVHS
Advanced Vehicle Identification ... AVI
Advanced Vehicle Simulation Technique ... AVST
Advanced Vehicle System [*Automotive engineering*] ... AVS
Advanced Vehicle Technologies [*Military*] (RDA) ... AVT
Advanced Vertical Speed Indicator ... AVSI
Advanced Vertical Strike Fighter (MCD) ... AVS
Advanced Vertical Strike Fighter ... AVSF
Advanced Very-High-Resolution Radiometer [*NASA*] ... AVHRR
Advanced Very-Large-Scale Integration [*Electronics*] ... AVLSI
Advanced Video Imaging [*Zenith Electronics Corp.*] ... AVI
Advanced Video Tape Recorder ... AVTR
Advanced Video Terminal ... AVT
Advanced Vidicon Camera System ... AVCS
Advanced Virtual Machine (IAA) ... AVM
Advanced Visible and Near-Infrared Radiometer [*Instrumentation*] ... AVNIR
Advanced Visual [*Near Visual*] **Electro-Optic Sensor** [*Simulator*] (MCD) ... AVEOS
Advanced Visual Extension (PCM) ... AVE
Advanced Visual Information Display ... AVID
Advanced Visual System ... AVS
Advanced Visual Target Acquisition System (MCD) ... AVTAS
Advanced Visual Technology System [*NASA*] ... AVTS
Advanced VLF/LF [*Very Low Frequency/Low Frequency*] **Receiver** (DWSG) ... AVR
Advanced Voice Technol Wrrt [*NASDAQ symbol*] (TTSB) ... HMWKW
Advanced Voice Technologies [*NASDAQ symbol*] (TTSB) ... HMWK
Advanced Voice Technologies, Inc. [*Associated Press*] (SAG) ... AdVoic
Advanced Voice Technologies, Inc. [*Associated Press*] (SAG) ... AdvVoic
Advanced Voice Technologies, Inc. [*NASDAQ symbol*] (SAG) ... HMWK
Advanced Voice Tehcnol's 'Unit' [*NASDAQ symbol*] (TTSB) ... HMWKU
Advanced Vortex System (MCD) ... AVS
Advanced Voyager ... AV
Advanced Vulcan Air Defense System (MCD) ... AVADS
Advanced Warfighter [*or Warfighting*] **Experiment** [*Military*] (RDA) ... AWE
Advanced Warfighting Experiment [*Military*] (INF) ... AWE
Advanced Warfighting Experiment ... AWE
Advanced Warning Airborne Command System ... AWACS
Advanced Warning and Control System (IEEE) ... AWACS
Advanced Warning and Control System/Combat Air Patrol [*Air Force*] ... AWACS/CAP
Advanced Warning System ... AWS
Advanced Waste Treatment [*of water*] ... AWT
Advanced Waste Treatment Laboratory [*National Environmental Research Center*] ... AWTL
Advanced Waste Treatment Processes (PDAA) ... AWTR
Advanced Wave Effects [*Sound synthesis*] (DOM) ... AWE
Advanced Weapon/Aircraft Requirements Evaluation (MCD) ... AWARE
Advanced Weapon Carriage Integration Technology (MCD) ... AWCIT
Advanced Weapon Delivery RADAR ... AWDR
Advanced Weapons Carriage Configured Vehicle (MCD) ... AWCCV
Advanced Weapons Support Command [*Army*] (AABC) ... AWSCOM
Advanced Weapons System (MCD) ... AWS
Advanced Weather Interactive Processing System [*National Oceanic and Atmospheric Administration*] ... AWIPS
Advanced Weather Interactive Processing System of the 1990's [*National Oceanic and Atmospheric Administration*] ... AWIPS-90
Advanced Weather RADAR (MCD) ... AWR
Advanced WESTAR (MCD) ... AW
Advanced Wide Area Defense Missile (MCD) ... AWADM
Advanced Wide-Area Antipersonnel Mine (MCD) ... AWAAPM
Advanced Wide-Area Missile (MCD) ... AWAM
Advanced Wild Weasel [*RADAR warning system*] ... AWW
Advanced Wind Energy Conversion System (MCD) ... AWECS
Advanced Windowing Toolkit (PCM) ... AWT
Advanced Workshop Detachment [*British and Canadian*] [*World War II*] ... AWD
Advanced Workstation Products [*El Segundo, CA*] (ECON) ... AWP
Advanced X-Ray Astrophysics Facility [*Great Observatory Program*] [*NASA*] ... AXAF
Advanced X-Ray Facility ... AXF
Advanced X-Ray System (DWSG) ... AXS
Advanced-Booking Charter (PDAA) ... ABC
Advanced-Composite Thermoplastic [*Materials engineering*] ... ACTP
Advance-Decline Line [*Investment term*] ... A-D
Advanced-Level Examination [*Education*] (AIE) ... A
Advanced-Technology Medium-Range Transport ... ATMR
Advancement (DLA) ... ADVANCEM
Advancement ... ADVMNT
Advancement (ABBR) ... ADVNCNT
Advancement (ABBR) ... ADVNCT
Advancement of Computing in Education ... AACE
Advancement of Management (SAA) ... AM
Advancement, Strength, and Training Plan System ... ADSTAP
Advance-Purchase Excursion [*Airline fare code*] ... APEX
Advance-Purchase Excursion Fare [*Airline fare code*] (ADA) ... APEF
Advances for Mutual Defense Assistance ... AMDA
Advancing (IAA) ... ADVG
Advancing (ABBR) ... ADVNCG
Advancing Blade Concept [*Helicopter*] ... ABC
Advancing Careers in Engineering ... ACE
Advancing Developing Countries [*Economics*] ... ADC
Advancing the Consumer Interest [*A publication*] ... ACI
Advanta Corp. [*Associated Press*] (SAG) ... Advant
ADVANTA Corp. [*Associated Press*] (SAG) ... Advanta
Advanta Corp. [*Associated Press*] (SAG) ... AdvantB
Advanta Corp. [*NASDAQ symbol*] (SAG) ... ADVN
ADVANTA Corp. Cl'A' [*NASDAQ symbol*] (TTSB) ... ADVNA
ADVANTA Corp. Cl'B' [*NASDAQ symbol*] (TTSB) ... ADVNB
ADVANTA Corp. Dep Shrs [*NASDAQ symbol*] (TTSB) ... ADVNZ
Advantage (WGA) ... AD
Advantage ... ADV
Advantage (ABBR) ... ADVATG
Advantage (MSA) ... ADVG
Advantage (ABBR) ... ADVNTG
Advantage ... ADVTG
Advantage (ROG) ... ADVTGE
Advantage [*Tennis*] (BARN) ... van
Advantage Bancorp [*NASDAQ symbol*] (TTSB) ... AADV
Advantage Bancorp, Inc. [*NASDAQ symbol*] (SAG) ... AADV
Advantage Bancorp, Inc. [*Associated Press*] (SAG) ... AdvBcp
Advantage Companies, Inc. [*NASDAQ symbol*] (SAG) ... ADVG
Advantage Companies, Inc. [*Associated Press*] (SAG) ... AdvntCos
Advantage Enterprises, Inc. [*Vancouver Stock Exchange symbol*] ... ADG
Advantage Health Corp. [*NASDAQ symbol*] (SAG) ... ADHC
Advantage Health Corp. [*Associated Press*] (SAG) ... AdvHlt
Advantage Life Products [*Associated Press*] (SAG) ... AdvLfe
Advantage Life Products [*NASDAQ symbol*] (NQ) ... ADVT
Advantaged (ABBR) ... ADVNTGD
Advantageous (ABBR) ... ADVATGUS
Advantageous (ABBR) ... ADVNTGU
Advantageously (ABBR) ... ADVATGUSY
Advantageously (ABBR) ... ADVNTGUY
Advantaging (ABBR) ... ADVNTGG
Advection [*NWS*] (FAAC) ... ADVCTN
Advection (ABBR) ... ADVEC
Advection (ABBR) ... ADVECT
Advection-Dominated Accretion Flow [*Planetary science*] ... ADAF
Advent ... ADV
Advent (ABBR) ... ADVNT
Advent Christian General Conference of America (EA) ... ACGCA
Advent Orbital Test and Operation Plan (SAA) ... AOTOP
Advent Software [*NASDAQ symbol*] (TTSB) ... ADVS
Advent Software, Inc. [*Associated Press*] (SAG) ... Advent
Advent Software, Inc. [*NASDAQ symbol*] (SAG) ... ADVS
Adventist Community Services (EA) ... CS
Adventist Development and Relief Agency, International (EA) ... ADRA
Adventist Health Network of North America [*Defunct*] (EA) ... AHN
Adventist Language Teachers Association [*Defunct*] (EA) ... ALTA
Adventist Network of Georgia, Cumberland Elementary Library, Collegedale, TN [*OCLC symbol*] (OCLC) ... TCA
Adventist Radio Television Services [*Canada*] ... ARTS
Adventist World Radio (NTCM) ... AWR
Adventitious Root Formation [*Botany*] ... ARF
Adventura Energy [*Vancouver Stock Exchange symbol*] ... AVU
Adventure ... ADVNTR
Adventure (ABBR) ... ADVNTR
Adventure Unlimited Retail Association [*Commercial firm*] (EA) ... AURA
Adventure Vehicle [*Vancouver Stock Exchange symbol*] ... AVH

Adventured (ABBR) ... ADVNTRD
Adventurer ... adven
Adventurer (ABBR) ... ADVNTRR
Adventurers Club of New York [*Defunct*] (EA) ... ACNY
Adventurers' Guild [*British*] (DBA) ... AG
Adventures in Movement for the Handicapped (EA) ... AIM
Adventures in Travel [*Oakland, CA*] [*Information service or system*] (IID) ... AIT
[*The*] **Adventures of Buckaroo Banzai across the Eighth Dimension** [*1984 movie title*] ... TAOBBATED
Adventuresome (ABBR) ... ADVNTRSM
Adventuress (ABBR) ... ADVNTRES
Adventuring (ABBR) ... ADVNTRG
Adventurous (ABBR) ... ADVNTRU
Adventurous (ABBR) ... ADVNTRUS
Adventurously (ABBR) ... ADVNTRUSY
Adverb (ROG) ... AD
Adverb [*or Adverbial*] ... ADV
Adverbial ... ADVB
Adverbial (ABBR) ... ADVBL
Adverbial (ABBR) ... ADVL
Adverbs (ADA) ... ADVV
Adversary (ABBR) ... ADVRSRY
Adversary (ABBR) ... ADVSY
Adversary Information System [*Military*] (RDA) ... AIS
Adversary Threat Training Group [*Military*] ... ATTG
Adversative (ABBR) ... ADVERSAT
Adverse (ABBR) ... ADVRS
Adverse Channel Enhancement ... ACE
Adverse Drug Event [*Food and Drug Administration*] ... ADE
Adverse Drug Event [*Medicine*] ... ADE
Adverse Drug Event ... ADEs
Adverse Drug Reaction [*Medicine*] ... ADR
Adverse Effect Wage Rate (GFGA) ... AEWR
Adverse Effects [*Medicine*] ... AE
Adverse Environment Effect ... AEE
Adverse Patient Occurence [*Medicine*] (HCT) ... APO
Adverse Patient Occurrences [*Medicine*] (MEDA) ... APO
Adverse Possession [*Legal term*] (DLA) ... ADV POSS
Adverse Reaction Monitoring System [*Food and Drug Administration*] (PAZ) ... ARMS
Adverse Reactions Reporting System [*FDA*] ... ARRS
Adverse Weather [*or All-Weather*] **Aerial Delivery System** [*Ordnance delivery method*] ... AWADS
Adverse Weather Close Air Support [*Military*] (MCD) ... AWCAS
Adverse Weather Precision Guided Munition [*Air Force*] (DOMA) ... AWPGM
Adversely (ABBR) ... ADVRSY
Adverseness (ABBR) ... ADVRSNS
Adversity (ABBR) ... ADVRST
Adversity Quotient [*Psychology*] ... AQ
Adversus [*Against*] [*Latin*] (ROG) ... ADS
Adversus [*or Adversum*] [*Against*] [*Latin*] ... ADV
Adversus Indoctum [*of Lucian*] [*Classical studies*] (OCD) ... Ind
Adversus Iovinianum [*of St. Jerome*] [*Classical studies*] (OCD) ... Adv Iovinian
Adversus Mathematicos [*of Sextus Empiricus*] [*Classical studies*] (OCD) ... Math
Adversus Valentinianos [*of Tertullian*] [*Classical studies*] (OCD) ... Adv Valent
Advertence (ABBR) ... ADVERTNC
Advertent (ABBR) ... ADVRTNT
Advertise ... ADVT
Advertise and Award (KSC) ... A & A
Advertised (ABBR) ... ADVTD
Advertised Computer Technologies [*Data Courier, Inc.*] [*Information service or system Defunct*] (IID) ... ACT
Advertisement ... AD
Advertisement ... AD
Advertisement (WDMC) ... ad
Advertisement ... ADV
Advertisement (BARN) ... advers
Advertisement ... ADVERT
Advertisement (ABBR) ... ADVRTZNT
Advertisement (AABC) ... ADVT
Advertisement (WDMC) ... advt
Advertisement (ODBW) ... advt
Advertisement (VRA) ... advt
Advertisement (ABBR) ... ADVTMT
Advertisement Contractors' Association [*British*] (BI) ... ACA
Advertisement Digest [*A publication*] ... AD
Advertisement Format Selection [*Marketing*] ... ADFORS
Advertiser (ABBR) ... ADVRTZR
Advertiser ... ADVT
Advertiser (ABBR) ... ADVTR
Advertiser (Adelaide) [*A publication*] ... Adv (Adel)
Advertiser, Franklinville, NJ [*Library symbol Library of Congress*] (LCLS) ... NjFrvA
Advertiser Syndicated Television Association (NTCM) ... ASTA
Advertisers Casting Service ... ACS
Advertising (WDMC) ... ad
Advertising (WDMC) ... adv
Advertising (DLA) ... ADVERTIS
Advertising ... advg
Advertising (ABBR) ... ADVRTZG
Advertising (WDMC) ... advt
Advertising (DD) ... advtg
Advertising (ABBR) ... ADVTG
Advertising ... ADVTSNG
Advertising Advisory Board of the Canadian Advertising Foundation ... AAB
Advertising Agency (NTCM) ... AA
Advertising Agency Association of British Columbia (AC) ... AAABC
Advertising Agency Print Production Association (AC) ... AAPPA
Advertising Agency Production Association (DGA) ... AAPA
Advertising Agency Production Club of New York [*Later, APC*] (EA) ... AAPC
Advertising Agency Service Interchange [*Defunct*] (EA) ... AASI
Advertising and Marketing Association ... A & MA
Advertising and Marketing Intelligence [*The New York Times Co.*] [*Information service or system*] (CRD) ... AMI
Advertising and Marketing International Network [*Stamford, CT*] (EA) ... AMIN
Advertising and Marketing Law Bulletin [*Australia A publication*] ... AMLB
Advertising and Publicity (WDMC) ... ADPUB
Advertising and Publicity [*Theater*] (WDMC) ... ad-pub
Advertising Association (EAIO) ... AA
Advertising Association of the West [*Later, AAF*] (EA) ... AAW
Advertising Checking Bureau ... ACB
Advertising Club of New York [*New York, NY*] (EA) ... ACNY
Advertising Club of New York (SRA) ... ACNY
Advertising Club of Victoria [*Australia*] ... ACV
Advertising Control for Television [*Advertising testing service*] (WDMC) ... ACT
Advertising Council (EA) ... AC
[*The*] **Advertising Council, Inc.** (NTCM) ... ACI
Advertising Council of America, Inc. (NTCM) ... ACA
Advertising Creative Circle (DGA) ... ACC
Advertising Dimensions Standards [*American Newspaper Publishers Association*] ... ADS
Advertising Educational Foundation (EA) ... AEF
Advertising Federation of America [*Later, AAF*] ... AFA
Advertising Federation of Minnesota (SRA) ... Ad-Fed
Advertising Film and Videotape Producers' Association [*British*] ... AFVPA
Advertising Film Producers Association [*British*] (BI) ... AFPA
Advertising Information Services ... AIS
Advertising Inquiry Council (DGA) ... AIC
Advertising Investigation Department [*British*] ... AID
Advertising Law Anthology [*A publication*] (ILCA) ... Advert L Anth
Advertising Manager (DGA) ... AD MAN
Advertising Matter [*Freight*] ... ADV MTR
Advertising Media Credit Executives Association [*Toledo, OH*] (EA) ... AMCEA
Advertising Media Representation Agency (DGA) ... AMRA
Advertising Photographers of America (EA) ... APA
Advertising Production Club of New York (EA) ... APC
Advertising Provider (WDMC) ... AP
Advertising Research Foundation (EA) ... ARF
Advertising/Sales Ratio (WDMC) ... A/S
Advertising Specialty Guild of America ... ASGA
Advertising Specialty Institute (WDMC) ... ASI
Advertising Standards Authority [*British*] ... ASA
Advertising Standards Council [*Canada Australia*] ... ASC
Advertising Training Center [*New York, NY*] ... ATC
Advertising, Typesetting and Foundry Employers Federation (DGA) ... ATFEF
Advertising Typographers Association (EA) ... ATA
Advertising Typographers Association of America (DGA) ... ATAA
Advertising Video (WDMC) ... advid
Advertising Videotape ... ADVID
Advertising Women of New York [*New York, NY*] (EA) ... AWNY
Advertising-Press Club [*Republic of Ireland*] (BI) ... APC
Advest Group [*NYSE symbol*] (TTSB) ... ADV
[*The*] **Advest Group, Inc.** [*NYSE symbol*] (SPSG) ... ADV
[*The*] **Advest Group, Inc.** [*Associated Press*] (SAG) ... Advest
Advice (AABC) ... AD
Advice (ROG) ... ADV
Advice Decision [*or Determination*] **Taken** ... ADTAKE
Advice Note (ADA) ... AN
Advice of Allotment (AFM) ... A/A
Advice of Charge [*Telecommunications*] (TEL) ... AC
Advice of Charge [*Telecommunications*] (DOM) ... AOC
Advice of Duration and Charge (ODBW) ... ADC
Advice of Payment ... AP
Advice of Receipt ... AR
Advice of Rights [*Legal term*] (BARN) ... AOR
Advice Services Alliance [*British*] (DBA) ... ASA
Advieskomitee vir Internasionale Samewerking op Wetenskaplike Gebied [*International Council of Scientific Unions*] ... AISWG
Advisability (ABBR) ... ADVSBT
Advisable (ABBR) ... ADVSB
Advisably (ABBR) ... ADVSBY
Advise [*Legal term*] ... ADV
Advise (AFM) ... ADVS
Advise ... ADZ
Advise Acceptance (NOAA) ... ADVAC
Advise Action Taken (NOAA) ... ADACT
Advise Action to Be Taken by This Office (NOAA) ... ADATT
Advise All Concerned ... ADALCON
Advise [*or Issue Instructions to*] **All Concerned** ... ADCON
Advise Appropriate Command Having Cognizance of Transportation when Available for Transportation [*Military*] (DNAB) ... ADVAILTRANS
Advise Appropriate Command Having Cognizance of Transportation when Available for Transportation to Continental United States [*Military*] ... ADVAILTRANSCONUS
Advise Approximate Date (NOAA) ... ADADA
Advise Arrival [*Aviation*] (FAAC) ... ADZAR
Advise as Soon as Possible (NOAA) ... ADSAP
Advise at What Time Able [*Aviation*] (FAAC) ... AAWTA
Advise Availability [*Army*] ... ADAVAL
Advise Availability [*Army*] ... ADVAL
Advise by Air Mail as Soon as Possible (FAAC) ... ADMAP

Advise by Airmail [*Army*] ADAML
Advise by [*Electronically Transmitted*] **Message** [*Army*] (AABC) ADMSG
Advise by Message of Action the Following Individual Is Taking [*Military*] ADPERSACT
Advise by Message Reduction Current Period of Active Duty [*Military*] ADREDPRED
Advise by Message Why Individual Is Being Reduced [*Military*] ADPRORED
Advise by Wire (MHDB) ABW
Advise Customs [*Aviation*] (FAAC) ADCUS
Advise [*Command Designated*] **Date Available for Transportation from Port ofEmbarkation** [*Military*] ADVAILTRANSPOE
Advise Date of Receipt (NOAA) ADARE
Advise Date of Reporting in Compliance with Orders [*Navy*] ADARCO
Advise Date of Shipment (NOAA) ADASH
Advise Disposition [*Aviation*] (FAAC) ADSPN
Advise Duration and Charge [*British telephone term*] AD and C
Advise Earliest Date (NOAA) ADSDA
Advise Effective Date (NOAA) ADEDA
Advise if Able [*Aviation*] (FAAC) AIA
Advise if Able to Proceed [*Aviation*] (FAAC) AAP
Advise if Not Correct [*Aviation*] (FAAC) ADNOK
Advise Immediately by Dispatch (NOAA) ADIMD
Advise Individual Concerned of Change of Assignment [*Military*] CHASG
Advise Intentions [*Aviation*] (FAAC) ADZI
Advise Latest Address [*Military*] (AABC) ADLATAD
Advise Method and Date of Shipment (NOAA) ADMAD
Advise Method, Bill of Lading, and Date Shipped AMBLADS
Advise Present Grade, Status, Physical Condition, and Mailing Address of Following Named [*Military*] STATREP
Advise Present Position and Altitude [*Aviation*] (FAAC) APPA
Advise Reason for Delay [*Aviation*] (FAAC) ADRDE
Advise [*names of*] **Representatives, Accommodations, and Transportation** [*desired*] [*Army*] (AABC) ARAT
Advise Shipping Data (AABC) ADSHIPDA
Advise Shipping Date ADSHIPDA
Advise Shipping Date ADSHPDAT
Advise Soldier Write Home ASWH
Advise Status and/or Disposition [*Army*] ADSTADIS
Advise Status and/or Disposition [*Army*] (DNAB) ASTADIS
Advise Stock on Hand [*Army*] ADSTKOH
Advise This Headquarters of Complete Action [*Army*] ADHCA
Advise This Office (NOAA) ADVOF
Advise This Office (FAAC) ADZOF
Advise What Action Has Been Taken [*Military*] (NVT) ADTAKE
Advise When Able [*Aviation*] (FAAC) AWA
Advise When Established [*Aviation*] (FAAC) AWE
Advise Whether Individual May Be Properly Utilized in Your Installation [*Army*] (AABC) ADIPU
Advised (ABBR) ADVSD
Advised and Released [*Medicine*] A & R
Advised Not to Move Dependents until Suitable Quarters Located [*Military*] ADNOMOVPEN
Advisedly (ABBR) ADVSDY
Advisement (ABBR) ADVSNT
Advisement (ABBR) ADVST
Adviser Business Oriented Language [*Programming language*] ABOL
Adviser on Combined Operations [*British*] ACO
Advising (ABBR) ADVSG
Advisor (AABC) ADVR
Advisor (AFM) ADVSR
Advisor ADVSR
Advisor, Middletown, NJ [*Library symbol Library of Congress*] (LCLS) NjMiA
Advisor Virtual Memory Operating System [*Computer science*] (MHDI) AVOS
Advisory (DD) adv
Advisory ADV
Advisory ADVRY
Advisory (ABBR) ADVSRY
Advisory (AFM) ADVSY
Advisory [*NWS*] (FAAC) ADVY
Advisory (FAAC) ADZY
Advisory Agricultural Meteorologist (NOAA) AAM
Advisory and Coordinating Committee on Child Abuse [*Western Australia*] ACCCA
Advisory Board AB
Advisory Board for Cooperative Systems [*of ICIREPAT*] ABCS
Advisory Board for Medical Specialties (DAVI) ABMS
[*The*] **Advisory Board for the Research Councils** [*British*] ABRC
Advisory Board on the Built Environment [*Formerly, BRAB*] (EA) ABBE
Advisory Board on Veterinary Specialties (EA) ABVS
Advisory Caution Panel (MCD) ACP
Advisory Centre for Education [*British*] ACE
Advisory Centre on Technology for Industry in Victoria [*Australia*] ACTIV
Advisory Circular AC
Advisory Commission on Intergovernmental Relations [*Washington, DC*] ACIR
Advisory Commission on Parliamentary Accommodation [*Canada*] ACPA
Advisory Commission on Textbook Specifications ACTS
Advisory Committee (NRCH) AC
Advisory Committee for Biology and Medicine [*AEC*] ACBM
Advisory Committee for Chemical, Biochemical, and Thermal Engineering [*Washington, DC*] [*National Science Foundation*] (EGAO) CBTE
Advisory Committee for Civil and Environmental Engineering [*Terminated, 1 985*] [*National Science Foundation*] (EGAO) CEE
Advisory Committee for Earthquake Hazard Mitigation [*Washington, DC*] [*National Science Foundation*] (EGAO) EHM
Advisory Committee for Electrical, Computer, and Systems Engineering [*Terminated, 1985*] (EGAO) ECSE
Advisory Committee for Innovation and Technology Transfer [*EC*] (ECED) CIT
Advisory Committee for Land-Mobile Radio Services (NTCM) ACLMRS
Advisory Committee for Mechanical Engineering and Applied Mechanics [*Washington, DC*] [*Terminated, 1985*] [*National Science Foundation*] (EGAO) MEAM
Advisory Committee for Operational Hydrology [*WMO*] (MSC) ACOH
Advisory Committee for Research on Information Transfer [*Netherlands*] (NITA) ACRIT
Advisory Committee for Scientific and Technical Information [*British*] ACSTI
Advisory Committee for Scientific, Technological, and International Affairs [*National Science Foundation*] (EGAO) ACSTIA
Advisory Committee for Teacher Education in the Mid-South (AIE) ACTEMS
Advisory Committee for the Co-Ordination of Information Systems [*Database producer*] [*Geneva, Switzerland*] [*United Nations*] ACCIS
Advisory Committee for the Education of Romany and Other Travellers ACERT
Advisory Committee for the Research and Development Department [*British Library*] (AIE) ACORDD
Advisory Committee for the Supply and Education of Teachers, Further Education Sub-Committee (AIE) ACSET(FE)
Advisory Committee for the US Meat Animal Research Center [*Terminated, 1977*] (EGAO) USMARC
Advisory Committee for Trade Policy and Negotiations [*US Trade Representative*] (EGAO) ACTPN
Advisory Committee for Vocational Training (AIE) ACVT
Advisory Committee of Experts on Marine Resources Research [*Marine science*] (OSRA) ACMRR
Advisory Committee of the Supply and Training of Teachers [*British*] ACSTT
Advisory Committee on Administrative and Budgetary Questions [*United Nations*] ACABQ
Advisory Committee on Advanced Television Service [*FCC high-definition television*] (NTCM) ACATS
Advisory Committee on Air Quality [*Australia*] ACAQ
Advisory Committee on Allotments [*New Deal*] ACA
Advisory Committee on Antarctic Feature Names [*Board on Geographic Names*] (NOAA) ACAN
Advisory Committee on Chemicals in the Environment [*Australia*] ACCE
Advisory Committee on Civilian Policy [*World War II*] ACCP
Advisory Committee on Climate Applications and Data [*Marine science*] (OSRA) ACCAD
Advisory Committee on Dangerous Pathogens [*British*] ACDP
Advisory Committee on Dangerous Substances [*British*] ACDS
Advisory Committee on Electrical Appliances and Accessories ACEAA
Advisory Committee on Electronics and Telecommunications [*International Electrotechnical Commission*] [*ISO*] (DS) ACET
Advisory Committee on Energy Research and Development [*British government*] ACORD
Advisory Committee on Export Policy [*Department of Commerce*] ACEP
Advisory Committee on Fisheries Applications of Remote Sensing [*Australia*] ACFARS
Advisory Committee on Flight Information [*FAA*] ACFI
Advisory Committee on Genetic Manipulation [*Health and Safety Executive*] [*British*] ACGM
Advisory Committee On Highway Policy [*MTMC*] (TAG) ACHP
Advisory Committee on Human Radiation Experiments ACHRE
Advisory Committee on Immunization Practices [*Public Health Service*] ACIP
Advisory Committee on Immunization Practices ACIP
Advisory Committee on Information Dissemination in Science and Technology CIDST
Advisory Committee on Information Technology Standardization [*Commission of the European*] (NITA) ACITS
Advisory Committee on International Oceanographic Affairs [*British*] ACIOA
Advisory Committee on Irradiated and Novel Foods [*Government body*] [*British*] ACINF
Advisory Committee on Live Fish [*Australia*] ACLF
Advisory Committee on Major Hazards [*British*] ACMH
Advisory Committee on Marine Resources Research (USDC) ACMR
Advisory Committee on Marine Resources Research ACMRR
Advisory Committee on Medical Uses of Isotopes [*Nuclear energy*] (NRCH) ACMI
Advisory Committee on Northern Development [*Canada*] ACND
Advisory Committee on Novel Foods and Processes [*British*] ACNFP
Advisory Committee on Nuclear Materials Safeguards ACNMS
Advisory Committee on Nuclear Safety [*Canada*] ACNS
Advisory Committee on Nuclear Waste [*United States Nuclear Regulatory Commission*] ACNW
Advisory Committee on Oceanic Meteorological Research (USDC) ACOMR
Advisory Committee on Oceanic Meteorological Research [*Marine science*] (OSRA) ACOMR
Advisory Committee on Personal Dosimetry Services [*National Science Foundation*] (NRCH) ACPDS
Advisory Committee on Pesticides [*British*] ACP
Advisory Committee on Polar Programs [*National Science Foundation*] (MSC) ACPP
Advisory Committee on Pollution of the Sea (EAIO) ACOPS
Advisory Committee on Program Management (MHDB) ACPM
Advisory Committee on Protection of the Sea [*Marine science*] (OSRA) ACOPS
Advisory Committee on Radiological Protection [*Canada*] ACRP
Advisory Committee on Reactor Safeguards [*Nuclear Regulatory Commission*] ACRS
Advisory Committee on Releases to the Environment [*British*] ACRE

Advisory Committee on Safety [*International Electrotechnical Commission*] [*ISO*] (DS) .... ACOS

Advisory Committee on Science and Technology [*British*] .... ACOST

Advisory Committee on Science and Technology and Foreign Affairs [*Terminated, 1975*] [*Department of State*] (EGAO) .... ACSTFA

Advisory Committee on Technology Innovation [*Board on Science and Technology for International Development*] [*Office of International Affairs National Research Council*] (EGAO) .... ACTI

Advisory Committee on the Application of Science and Technology to Development [*Also, ACASTD, ACST*] [*United Nations*] .... ACAST

Advisory Committee on the Application of Science and Technology to Development [*Also, ACAST, ACST*] [*United Nations*] .... ACASTD

Advisory Committee on the Application of Science and Technology to Development [*Also, ACAST, ACASTD*] [*United Nations*] .... ACST

Advisory Committee on the Arts [*Terminated, 1973*] (EGAO) .... ACA

Advisory Committee on the Law of the Sea [*Department of State*] [*Terminated, 1983*] (NOAA) .... ACLOS

Advisory Committee on the Marine Environment [*Marine science*] (OSRA) .... ACME

Advisory Committee on the NAIC [*National Astronomy and Ionosphere Center*] Nation-Wide Marine Definition (EA) .... COI

Advisory Committee on the Safety of Nuclear Installations [*British*] (NUCP) .... ACSNI

Advisory Committee on the Supply and Education of Teachers [*British*] .... ACSET

Advisory Committee on the Transport of Radioactive Materials [*British*] .... ACTRAM

Advisory Committee on Toxic Substances [*British*] .... ACTS

Advisory Committee on Undersea Feature Names [*Board on Geographic Names*] (NOAA) .... ACUF

Advisory Committee on Voluntary Foreign Aid [*Department of State*] .... ACVA

Advisory Committee on Voluntary Foreign Aid [*Department of State*] .... ACVFA

Advisory Committee on Voter Education [*Defunct*] (EA) .... ACVE

Advisory Committee on Weather Control [*Terminated, 1957*] .... ACWC

Advisory Committee, Statistics [*British*] .... AC(S)

Advisory Committee to the Board and to the Committee on Commodities [*UNCTAD*] .... ACBCC

Advisory Committee to the Canada Centre for Inland Waters (PDAA) .... ACCC

Advisory Committee to the Department of Housing and Urban Development .... ACHUD

Advisory, Conciliation, and Arbitration Service [*London, England*] .... ACAS

Advisory Council, Allied Control Commission [*Italy*] [*World War II*] .... ACACC

Advisory Council for Adult and Continuing Education [*British*] .... ACACE

Advisory Council for Applied Research and Development [*British government*] .... ACARD

Advisory Council for Minority Enterprise [*Department of Commerce*] .... ACME

Advisory Council for Orthopaedic Resident Education (EA) .... ACORE

Advisory Council for the Church's Ministry [*Church of England*] .... ACCM

Advisory Council for the Elimination of Tuberculosis .... ACET

Advisory Council of National Organizations [*Corporation for Public Broadcasting*] (NTCM) .... ACNO

Advisory Council of the International Geophysical Year .... ACIGY

Advisory Council on Australia's Languages Policy .... ACALP

Advisory Council on Calibration and Measurement (ACII) .... ACCM

Advisory Council on Camps (EA) .... ACC

Advisory Council on Clean Air Compliance Analysis [*Environmental Protection Agency*] .... ACCACA

Advisory Council on College Chemistry .... ACCC

Advisory Council on Education and Training (AIE) .... ACET

Advisory Council on Education Statistics [*Department of Education*] (GFGA) .... ACES

Advisory Council on Energy Conservation [*British*] .... ACEC

Advisory Council on Exhibition Birds [*Australia*] .... ACEB

Advisory Council on Federal Reports .... ACFR

Advisory Council on Historic Preservation (NRCH) .... ACHP

Advisory Council on Medical Education .... ACME

Advisory Council on Naval Affairs .... ACNA

Advisory Council on Naval Affairs of the Navy League .... ACONA

Advisory Council on Personnel Policy [*Canada*] .... ACPP

Advisory Council on Research and Redevelopment for Fuel and Power (NUCP) .... ACORD

Advisory Council on Scientific Policy .... ACSP

Advisory Council on Scientific Research and Technical Development [*British*] .... AC

Advisory Council on Technology [*British*] .... ACT

Advisory Council on the Status of Women [*Canada*] .... ACSW

Advisory Defense Committee .... ADC

Advisory Direction (NATG) .... AD

Advisory Group [*Military*] .... ADGRU

Advisory Group .... ADVGP

Advisory Group [*Military*] .... AG

Advisory Group for Aerospace Research and Development [*NATO*] .... AGARD

Advisory Group for Ocean Engineering [*Society of Naval Architects and Marine Engineers*] (DNAB) .... AGOE

Advisory Group on Electron Devices [*Army Washington, DC*] .... AGED

Advisory Group on Electron Tubes .... AGET

Advisory Group on Electronic Parts [*Military*] .... AGEP

Advisory Group on Energy [*Army*] (RDA) .... AGE

Advisory Group on Greenhouse Gases [*Australia*] .... AGGG

Advisory Group on Management of Electronic Parts Specifications .... AGMEPS

Advisory Group on National Bibliographic Control .... AGNBC

Advisory Group on Reliability of Electronic Equipment [*Military*] .... AGREE

Advisory Leaflet .... AL

Advisory Light Panel (MCD) .... ALP

Advisory Panel for Oceanography [*National Science Foundation*] (MSC) .... APO

Advisory Panel for Operations Research .... APOR

Advisory Panel of Alternative Means of Financing and Managing Radioactive Waste Facilities [*Terminated, 1984*] [*Department of Energy*] (EGAO) .... AMFM

Advisory Panel on Safeguarding Special Nuclear Material .... APSSNM

Advisory Route [*Aviation*] (FAAC) .... ADR

Advisory Rule (DA) .... ADR

Advisory Support Force [*Military*] .... ASF

Advisory Tax Board Recommendation [*Internal Revenue Bureau*] [*United States*] [*A publication*] (DLA) .... TBR

Advisory Team .... ADVTM

Advisory, Training, and Operaions Mission (VNW) .... ATOM

Advisory Unit for Computer Based Education [*Hatfield, England*] [*Information service or system Telecommunications*] (TSSD) .... AUCBE

ADVO Inc. [*NYSE symbol*] (TTSB) .... AD

Advo, Inc. [*NYSE symbol*] (SAG) .... AD

Advo, Inc. [*Associated Press*] (SAG) .... Advo Inc

Advocaat [*Barrister*] [*Netherlands*] (ILCA) .... adv

Advocacy (ABBR) .... ADVCY

Advocacy Centre for the Elderly (AC) .... ACE

Advocacy Group for the Environmentally Sensitive [*Association Groupant les Malades de l'Environnement*] (AC) .... AGES

Advocacy Institute (EA) .... AI

Advocacy Resource Centre for the Handicapped [*Canada*] .... ARCH

Advocat, Inc. [*Associated Press*] (SAG) .... Advocat

Advocat, Inc. [*NYSE symbol*] (SAG) .... AVC

Advocate [*Ife, Nigeria*] [*1968*] [*A publication*] (ILCA) .... Adv

Advocate [*Cleveland*] [*1929*] [*A publication*] (ILCA) .... Adv

Advocate [*Canada*] [*1943*] [*A publication*] (ILCA) .... Adv

Advocate (ABBR) .... ADVCA

Advocate (ABBR) .... ADVO

Advocate (DLA) .... ADVOC

Advocate, East Orange, NJ [*Library symbol Library of Congress*] (LCLS) .... NjEoA

Advocate, Pictou, Nova Scotia [*Library symbol National Library of Canada*] (NLC) .... NSPA

Advocated (ABBR) .... ADVCAD

Advocated (ABBR) .... ADVOD

Advocates (ABBR) .... ADVOS

Advocates Against Psychic Abuse [*Defunct*] (EA) .... AAPA

Advocates' Chronicle [*India*] [*A publication*] (DLA) .... Adv Chron

Advocates for a Safe Vaccine (EA) .... ASV

Advocates for Better Communication [*An association*] .... ABC

Advocates for Communication Technology for Deaf/Blind People .... ACT

Advocates for Community Based Training & Education for Women (AC) .... ACTEW

Advocates for Library Outreach [*Office for Literacy and Outreach*] [*American Library Association*] .... AFLO

Advocates for Self-Government (EA) .... ASG

Advocates for Women [*Defunct*] (EA) .... AFW

Advocates of International Trade and Comity [*Defunct*] (EA) .... AITC

Advocates to Save Legal Services [*Inactive Defunct*] (EA) .... ASLS

Advocating (ABBR) .... ADVCAG

Advocating (ABBR) .... ADVOG

Advocation (ABBR) .... ADVCAN

Advocation (ABBR) .... ADVON

Advocator (ABBR) .... ADVOR

Advokatbladet [*Denmark*] [*1921-*] [*A publication*] (ILCA) .... Adv Bl

Adye on Courts-Martial [*A publication*] (DLA) .... Adye CM

AE Developments Ltd. [*Research center British*] .... AED

A.E. Staley Manufacturing Co., Decatur, IL [*Library symbol*] [*Library of Congress*] (LCLS) .... IDecS

AECL International, Mississauga, ON, Canada [*Library symbol Library of Congress*] (LCLS) .... CaOMAECL

AECL International, Mississauga, Ontario [*Library symbol National Library of Canada*] (NLC) .... OMAECL

Aedicula (VRA) .... aed

AEELS [*Airborne ELINT Emitter Location System*] **Fixed Downlink Terminal** (MCD) .... AFDT

Aegean Aviation [*Greece*] [*ICAO designator*] (FAAC) .... AEE

Aegean Sea .... AEG S

Aegis Combat System [*Navy*] (LAIN) .... ACS

Aegis Consumer Funding [*NASDAQ symbol*] (TTSB) .... ACAR

Aegis Consumer Funding Group [*NASDAQ symbol*] (SAG) .... ACAR

Aegis Consumer Funding Group [*Associated Press*] (SAG) .... Aegis

AEGIS Display System (DNAB) .... ADS

Aegis Surface Action Group [*Military*] (DOMA) .... ASAG

AEGIS [*Airborne Early Warning Ground Environment Integrated Segment*] **Tactical Executive Program** .... ATEP

AEGON N.V. [*NYSE symbol*] (SPSG) .... AEG

AEGON NV [*Associated Press*] (SAG) .... Aegon

Aegrus [*or Aegra*] [*The Patient*] [*Medicine*] .... AEG

AEL Industries, Inc. [*Associated Press*] (SAG) .... AEL

AEL Industries, Inc. [*NASDAQ symbol*] (NQ) .... AELN

Aelianus [*c. 170-235AD*] [*Classical studies*] (OCD) .... Ael

Aelius Donatus [*Fourth century AD*] [*Classical studies*] (OCD) .... Donat

Aemilius Ferretus [*Deceased, 1552*] [*Authority cited in pre-1607 legal work*] (DSA) .... Aemil Ferret

Aemilius Papinianus [*Deceased, 212*] [*Authority cited in pre-1607 legal work*] (DSA) .... Aemil Pap

Aemilius Paulus [*of Plutarch*] [*Classical studies*] (OCD) .... Aem

Aeneid [*of Vergil*] [*Classical studies*] (OCD) .... Aen

Aeolian-Skinner Organ Co. [*Record label*] .... ASK

Aeon [*10⁹ years*] [*Geology*] .... AE

AEP Industries [*Associated Press*] (SAG) .... AEP Ind

AEP Industries [*NASDAQ symbol*] (TTSB) .... AEPI

AEP Industries, Inc. [*Moonachie, NJ*] [*NASDAQ symbol*] (NQ) .... AEPI
Aequales [*Equal*] [*Latin*] .... AEQ
Aequitron Medical [*NASDAQ symbol*] (TTSB) .... AQTN
Aequitron Medical, Inc. [*Associated Press*] (SAG) .... Aequtrn
Aequitron Medical, Inc. [*Minneapolis, MN*] [*NASDAQ symbol*] (NQ) .... AQTN
Aer Arann Teo [*ICAO designator*] (AD) .... RE
Aer Arann Teoranta [*Ireland*] [*ICAO designator*] (ICDA) II
Aer Arann Teoranta [*Ireland*] [*ICAO designator*] (FAAC) .... REA
AER Energy Resources [*Associated Press*] (SAG) .... AER En
AER Energy Resources [*NASDAQ symbol*] (SAG) .... AERN
Aer Lingus Teoranta [*Ireland*] .... ALT
Aer Lingus Teoranta [*Ireland*] [*ICAO designator*] (FAAC) .... EIN
Aer Turas Teoranta [*Republic of Ireland*] [*ICAO designator*] (FAAC) .... ATT
Aerated Autoclaved Concrete .... AAC
Aerated Bread Co. [*Chain of restaurants in London*] .... ABC
Aerated Drain Tank [*Nuclear energy*] (NRCH) .... ADT
Aerated Stabilization Basin [*For water purification*] .... ASB
Aeration (ABBR) .... AERA
Aeration Test Burner [*Heating*] .... ATB
Aereo Postal de Mexico SA de CV [*ICAO designator*] (FAAC) .... PTX
Aereo Taxi de Leon SA de CV [*Mexico ICAO designator*] (FAAC) .... TXL
Aereotaxis SA de CV [*Mexico ICAO designator*] (FAAC) .... TXI
Aerial (IAA) .... A
Aerial (IAA) .... ADX
Aerial (IAA) .... AER
Aerial (AFM) .... AERL
Aerial .... ARL
Aerial Ambulance Co. [*Army*] (AABC) .... AAC
Aerial Armored Reconnaissance Vehicle .... AARV
Aerial Biosensing Association (EA) .... ABA
Aerial Bulk Fuel Delivery System [*Military*] (AFIT) .... ABFDS
Aerial Burst Bombs .... AB
Aerial Cartographic and Geodetic Squadron [*Air Force*] (AFM) .... ACGSq
Aerial Color Infrared Management System (MCD) .... ACIMS
Aerial Combat and Surveillance System (SAA) .... AC & SS
Aerial Combat Evaluator (MCD) .... ACE
Aerial Combat Maneuvering Training (MCD) .... ACMT
Aerial Combat Reconnaissance .... ACR
Aerial Combat Tactics (SAA) .... ACT
Aerial Common Sensor [*Military*] (RDA) .... ACS
Aerial Communications, Inc. [*Associated Press*] (SAG) .... AerialC
Aerial Communications, Inc. [*NASDAQ symbol*] (SAG) .... AERL
Aerial Communications Point [*Military*] (DOMA) .... ACP
Aerial Control Display (IAA) .... ACD
Aerial Control Point [*Military*] (DOMA) .... ACP
Aerial Current (IAA) .... AC
Aerial Delivered Land Mine (AFM) .... ADLM
Aerial Delivery (MCD) .... AD
Aerial Delivery Equipment (MCD) .... ADE
Aerial Delivery System .... ADS
Aerial Demonstration Squadron (MCD) .... ADS
Aerial Demonstration Team (MCD) .... ADT
Aerial Direction Finding .... ADF
Aerial Distribution Wire [*Telecommunications*] (TEL) .... ADW
Aerial Enterprises Ltd. [*British ICAO designator*] (FAAC) .... AEG
Aerial Exploitation Battalion (MCD) .... AEB
Aerial Exposure Index .... AEI
Aerial Field Artillery (MCD) .... AFA
Aerial Field Artillery Multi-Mode (MCD) .... AFAMM
Aerial Film Speed .... AFS
Aerial Fire Support .... AFS
Aerial Fire Support Officer [*Army*] (INF) .... AFSO
Aerial Free Gunnery Instructions School [*Obsolete*] .... AFGIS
Aerial Free Gunnery Unit .... AFGU
Aerial Geological and Geophysical Survey of Northern Australia. Report [*A publication*] .... AGGSNA Rept
Aerial Gunnery Part Task Trainer (MCD) .... AGPTT
Aerial Gunnery Target System (MCD) .... AGTS
Aerial Gunnery TOW Target (MCD) .... AGTT
Aerial Independent Model (OA) .... AIM
Aerial Inspection Instrument .... AII
Aerial Intercept Missile .... AIM
Aerial Lentiginous Melanoma [*Medicine*] (DMAA) .... ALM
Aerial Mail Terminal (AFM) .... AMT
Aerial Manufacturers Association [*British*] (DBA) .... AMA
Aerial Mission Photographic Indoctrination (MCD) .... AMPHI
Aerial Monitoring System [*Nuclear energy*] (NRCH) .... AMS
Aerial Nurse Corps of America .... ANCOA
Aerial Observer [*Military*] (NVT) .... AO
Aerial Phenomena Research Organization [*Defunct*] (EA) .... APRO
Aerial Phenomena Research Organization, Inc., Information Services Division, Tucson, AZ [*Library symbol Library of Congress*] (LCLS) .... AzTAP
Aerial Photographic Analysis Center .... APAC
Aerial Photographic Reconnaissance .... APR
Aerial Photography Field Office [*Department of Agriculture*] (GFGA) .... APFO
Aerial Port .... AP
Aerial Port Detachment .... APD
Aerial Port Documentation and Management System .... ADAM II
Aerial Port Flight [*Air Force*] .... APF
Aerial Port Group [*Air Force*] (AFM) .... APG
Aerial Port Group [*Air Force*] .... APGp
Aerial Port Group [*Air Force*] (AFM) .... APOG
Aerial Port Liaison Office [*or Officer*] [*Air Force*] (AFM) .... APLO
Aerial Port Logistics Office [*Air Force*] .... APLO
Aerial Port of Debarkation [*Military*] .... APOD
Aerial Port of Embarkation [*Military*] .... APE
Aerial Port of Embarkation [*Military*] .... APOE
Aerial Port Operations Center .... APOC
Aerial Port Squadron [*Air Force*] .... APS
Aerial Port Squadron [*Air Force*] (AFM) .... APSq
Aerial Ports [*And Air Operating Base File*] [*Military*] (DOMA) .... APORTS
Aerial Profiling of Terrain [*System*] [*Department of the Interior*] .... APT
Aerial RADIAC Instrument .... ARI
Aerial RADIAC Instrument System .... ARIS
Aerial Radiological Measurement and Survey [*Program*] .... ARMS
Aerial Radiological Measurements System [*Nuclear energy*] (NRCH) .... ARMS
Aerial Reconnaissance and Security .... ARS
Aerial Reconnaissance and Security Troop .... ARST
Aerial Reconnaissance and Surveillance Penetration Analysis [*Army*] .... ARSPA
Aerial Reconnaissance and Surveillance Survivability Analysis [*Army*] .... ARSSA
Aerial Reconnaissance Camera [*Military*] (PDAA) .... ARC
Aerial Reconnaissance Helicopter [*Army*] .... ARH
Aerial Reconnaissance Laboratory .... ARL
Aerial Reconnaissance Surveillance (MCD) .... ARS
Aerial [*In-Flight*] **Refueling** .... AR
Aerial Refueling Area .... ARA
Aerial Refueling Operator (MCD) .... ARO
Aerial Refueling Receptacle (MCD) .... ARR
Aerial Refueling Squadron (DNAB) .... AERREFRON
Aerial Refueling Squadron (SAA) .... ARS
Aerial Refueling Squadron [*Navy symbol*] (DNAB) .... VAK
Aerial Refueling Systems Advisory Group [*Military*] (CAAL) .... ARSAG
Aerial Refueling Wing [*Aeronautics*] .... ARW
Aerial Relay Transportation System (MCD) .... ARTS
Aerial Resupply and Communications [*Air Force*] (LAIN) .... ARC
Aerial Rocket Antitank Program (MCD) .... ARAT
Aerial Rocket Artillery .... ARA
Aerial Rocket Control System [*or Subsystem*] (MCD) .... ARCS
Aerial Ropeways Association [*British*] (BI) .... ARA
Aerial Scout Helicopter (MCD) .... ASH
Aerial Sensor .... AS
Aerial Stores Lift Truck (MCD) .... ASLT
Aerial Surveillance (MCD) .... AS
Aerial Survey and Target Acquisition [*Military*] .... ASTA
Aerial Survey Team (AFM) .... AST
Aerial Surveys (1980) Ltd. [*New Zealand*] [*ICAO designator*] (FAAC) .... SUY
Aerial Survival Equipment .... ASE
Aerial Tape Armor [*Telecommunications*] (TEL) .... AT
Aerial Target .... AT
Aerial Target Control Central (NG) .... ATCC
Aerial Torpedo .... AT
Aerial Transit Co. [*ICAO designator*] (FAAC) .... AEZ
Aerial Tuning Condenser .... ATC
Aerial Tuning Inductance .... ATI
Aerial Tuning Unit [*Telecommunications*] (OA) .... ATU
Aerial Unmanned Vehicle [*Military*] .... AUV
Aerial View (VRA) .... arl vw
Aerial Weapons Company [*Military*] (VNW) .... AWC
Aerialift Industries Association [*Defunct*] (EA) .... AIA
Aerialist (ABBR) .... AERLT
Aeriantur-M Airlines [*Moldova*] [*FAA designator*] (FAAC) .... TUM
Aeritalia SpA [*Italy ICAO aircraft manufacturer identifier*] (ICAO) .... AY
Aerlinte Eireann Teoranta [*Irish Air Lines*] .... AET
Aermacchi SpA [*Italy ICAO aircraft manufacturer identifier*] (ICAO) .... MC
Aero [*Denmark ICAO location identifier*] (ICLI) .... EKAE
Aero 1 Prop-Jet, Inc. [*Canada ICAO designator*] (FAAC) .... SSM
Aero/Acoustic Detection System [*Army*] (MCD) .... AADS
Aero/Acoustic Rotor (RDA) .... A/AR
Aero Albatros [*Mexico ICAO designator*] (FAAC) .... ALB
Aero Algarve Lda. [*Portugal*] [*FAA designator*] (FAAC) .... DSK
Aero America, Inc. [*ICAO designator*] (ICDA) .... EO
Aero Asia [*Pakistan*] [*ICAO designator*] (FAAC) .... RSO
Aero Astra [*Mexico ICAO designator*] (FAAC) .... OSA
Aero Aviation Centre Ltd. [*Canada ICAO designator*] (FAAC) .... AAD
Aero Barloz SA de CV [*Mexico ICAO designator*] (FAAC) .... BLZ
Aero Belize Ltd. [*FAA designator*] (FAAC) .... ABZ
Aero Campeche SA de CV [*Mexico ICAO designator*] (FAAC) .... CPC
Aero Car (SAA) .... ACAR
Aero Chasqui SA [*Peru*] [*ICAO designator*] (FAAC) .... XYC
Aero Chombo SA [*Mexico ICAO designator*] (FAAC) .... CHM
Aero Club of America [*Later, National Aeronautic Association of the USA*] .... ACA
Aero Coach Aviation International, Inc. [*ICAO designator*] (FAAC) .... DFA
Aero Continente [*Peru*] [*ICAO designator*] (FAAC) .... ACQ
Aero Contractors Company of Nigeria Ltd. [*ICAO designator*] (FAAC) .... NIG
Aero Control Air Ltd. [*Canada ICAO designator*] (FAAC) .... LFC
Aero Costa Rica [*ICAO designator*] (FAAC) .... AEK
Aero Ejecutiva SA [*Mexico ICAO designator*] (FAAC) .... EJT
Aero Ejecutivo de Baja California SA de CV [*Mexico ICAO designator*] (FAAC) .... EBC
Aero Ejecutivo SA de CV [*Mexico ICAO designator*] (FAAC) .... AJO
Aero Ejecutivos CA [*Venezuela*] [*ICAO designator*] (FAAC) .... VEJ
Aero Empresa Mexicana SA [*Mexico ICAO designator*] (FAAC) .... AFO
Aero Energy Ltd. [*Toronto Stock Exchange symbol*] .... AEY
Aero Fe SA [*Mexico ICAO designator*] (FAAC) .... RFE
Aero Fiesta Mexicana SA de CV [*Mexico*] [*FAA designator*] (FAAC) .... FIT
Aero Filipanas Ltd. [*Philippines*] [*ICAO designator*] (FAAC) .... AFI
Aero Flight Service, Inc. [*FAA designator*] (FAAC) .... AGY
Aero Flotilla [*Airline*] [*Former USSR*] .... AEROFLOT
Aero Flugzeugbau [*Germany ICAO aircraft manufacturer identifier*] (ICAO) .... AE
Aero Geo Astro Corp. .... AGAC

Aero Gun Sights .... AGS
Aero Industries, Inc. [*ICAO designator*] (FAAC) .... WAB
Aero Industries Technical Institute .... AITI
Aero Insurance Underwriters .... AIU
Aero Jalisco SA de CV [*Mexico ICAO designator*] (FAAC) .... AJL
Aero Jets Corporativos, SA de C.V. [*Mexico*] [*FAA designator*] (FAAC) .... AJP
Aero Leasing Italiana SpA [*Italy ICAO designator*] (FAAC) .... ALJ
Aero Lider SA de CV [*Mexico ICAO designator*] (FAAC) .... LDR
Aero Lloyd Flugreisen GmbH [*Germany ICAO designator*] (FAAC) .... AEF
Aero Madrid [*Spain ICAO designator*] (FAAC) .... AEM
Aero North Aviation Services [*Canada ICAO designator*] (FAAC) .... SKP
Aero North Icelandic, Inc. [*ICAO designator*] (FAAC) .... ANF
Aero O/Y [*Finnish airline*] .... FINNAIR
Aero Personal SA de CV [*Mexico ICAO designator*] (FAAC) .... PNL
Aero Peru [*ICAO designator*] (AD) .... PL
Aero Premier de Mexico, SA de CV [*Mexico*] [*FAA designator*] (FAAC) .... MIE
Aero Quick [*Mexico ICAO designator*] (FAAC) .... QIC
Aero Quimmco SA de CV [*Mexico ICAO designator*] (FAAC) .... QUI
Aero Renta de Coahuila SA de CV [*Mexico ICAO designator*] (FAAC) .... RCO
Aero Repair (MCD) .... AR
Aero Rifle Platoon [*Military*] (VNW) .... ARP
Aero Sami SA de CV [*Mexico ICAO designator*] (FAAC) .... SMI
Aero Santos SA de CV [*Mexico ICAO designator*] (FAAC) .... STO
Aero Scout Platoon [*Military*] (VNW) .... ASP
Aero Service Bolivia [*ICAO designator*] (FAAC) .... GHM
Aero Services [*Barbados*] [*ICAO designator*] (FAAC) .... BAS
Aero Services Executive [*France ICAO designator*] (FAAC) .... BES
Aero Servicio de Carga Mexicana SA de CV [*Mexico ICAO designator*] (FAAC) .... SCM
Aero Servicio del Norte SA de CV [*Mexico ICAO designator*] (FAAC) .... SNV
Aero Servicios Ejecutivas del Pacifico, SA de CV [*Mexico*] [*FAA designator*] (FAAC) .... SEF
Aero Servicios Especializados SA de CV [*Mexico ICAO designator*] (FAAC) .... SVE
Aero Servicios Pro-Bajio, SA de CV [*Mexico*] [*FAA designator*] (FAAC) .... PRJ
Aero Sierra Eco SA de CV [*Mexico ICAO designator*] (FAAC) .... ACO
Aero Sierra Eco, SA de CV [*Mexico*] [*FAA designator*] (FAAC) .... ECO
Aero Slovakia [*FAA designator*] (FAAC) .... ASO
Aero Sonora SA de CV [*Mexico ICAO designator*] (FAAC) .... SNR
Aero Spacelines [*Air carrier designation symbol*] .... AERX
Aero Spacelines [*ICAO aircraft manufacturer identifier*] (ICAO) .... AP
Aero Sudpacifico SA [*Mexico ICAO designator*] (FAAC) .... SDP
Aero Sys Engr [*NASDAQ symbol*] (TTSB) .... AERS
Aero Systems Engineering, Inc. [*NASDAQ symbol*] (NQ) .... AERS
Aero Systems Engineering, Inc. [*Associated Press*] (SAG) .... AerSyE
Aero Talleres Boero SRL [*Argentina ICAO aircraft manufacturer identifier*] (ICAO) .... AB
Aero Taxi [*Canada ICAO designator*] (FAAC) .... QAT
Aero Taxi Aviation, Inc. [*ICAO designator*] (FAAC) .... QKC
Aero Toluca Internacional, SA de CV [*Mexico*] [*FAA designator*] (FAAC) .... TUL
Aero Tonala [*Mexico ICAO designator*] (FAAC) .... TON
Aero Top SRL Societa [*Italy ICAO designator*] (FAAC) .... TOP
Aero Trade International [*Romania*] [*ICAO designator*] (FAAC) .... AON
Aero Trades (Western) Ltd. [*Canada ICAO designator*] (FAAC) .... ATW
Aero Transporte SA [*Peru*] [*ICAO designator*] (FAAC) .... AMP
Aero Transportes Sociedad Anonima [*Mexican airline*] .... ATSA
Aero Transporti Italiani [*ICAO designator*] (AD) .... BM
Aero Transporti Italiani SpA [*Italy ICAO designator*] (FAAC) .... ATI
Aero Veracruz SA de CV [*Mexico ICAO designator*] (FAAC) .... VRZ
Aero Vics SA de CV [*Mexico ICAO designator*] (FAAC) .... ARI
Aero Virgin Islands [*ICAO designator*] (AD) .... QY
Aero Weapons Platoon (VNW) .... AWP
Aero West Airlines, Inc. [*ICAO designator*] (FAAC) .... RWE
Aero Zambia Ltd. [*FAA designator*] (FAAC) .... RZI
Aero-Alentejo, Servicos Aereos Lda. [*Portugal ICAO designator*] (FAAC) .... ANJ
Aeroamerica [*ICAO designator*] (AD) .... EO
Aeroamerica, Inc. [*Air carrier designation symbol*] .... AAIX
Aeroamistad SA de CV [*Mexico ICAO designator*] (FAAC) .... MST
Aeroassisted Orbital Transfer Vehicle .... AOTV
Aerobacter [*Microbiology*] .... Aero
Aeroballistic Reentry Vehicle .... ARV
Aeroballistics (SAA) .... AERO
Aeroballistics - Aerodynamics Analysis (SAA) .... AERO-A
Aeroballistics - Director (SAA) .... AERO-DIR
Aeroballistics - Dynamics Analysis (SAA) .... AERO-D
Aeroballistics - Experimental Aerodynamics (SAA) .... AERO-E
Aeroballistics - Flight Evaluation (SAA) .... AERO-F
Aeroballistics - Future Projects (SAA) .... AERO-P
Aeroballistics - Program Coordination and Administration (SAA) .... AERO-PCA
Aeroballistics - Project Staff (SAA) .... AERO-PS
Aeroballistics - Technical and Scientific Staff (SAA) .... AERO-TS
Aerobeira, Sociedade de Transportes Aeros [*Portugal ICAO designator*] (FAAC) .... ARA
Aerobic Chair Exercise (MEDA) .... ACE
Aerobic Dive Limit [*Psysiology*] .... ADL
Aerobic Plate Count [*Microbiology*] .... APC
Aerobic Way Association [*Defunct*] (EA) .... AWA
Aerobically Thioglycolate Broth Disk (PDAA) .... AeTBD
Aerobic-Media Trickling Filter (PDAA) .... AMTF
Aerobics and Fitness Association of America (EA) .... AFAA
Aerobics and Fitness Foundation of America (EA) .... AFFA
Aerobics International Research Society (EA) .... AIRS
Aerobiology and Evaluation Laboratory [*Army*] (KSC) .... AEL
Aerocalifornia SA [*Mexico ICAO designator*] (FAAC) .... SER
Aerocancun [*Mexico ICAO designator*] (FAAC) .... ACU
Aerocardal [*Chile*] [*FAA designator*] (FAAC) .... CDA
Aerocer SA [*Mexico ICAO designator*] (FAAC) .... RCE
Aerocesar, Aerovias del Cesar [*Colombia*] [*ICAO designator*] (FAAC) .... AEC
Aero-Chaco [*ICAO designator*] (AD) .... CQ
Aerochago [*Dominican Republic*] [*ICAO designator*] (FAAC) .... AHG
Aerocharter [*Czechoslovakia*] [*ICAO designator*] (FAAC) .... STX
Aerocharter GmbH [*Austria ICAO designator*] (FAAC) .... MOZ
Aerocharter, Inc. [*Canada ICAO designator*] (FAAC) .... MRM
Aerocharter Midlands Ltd. [*British ICAO designator*] (FAAC) .... ACC
Aero-Chem Research Laboratories, Inc. (KSC) .... ACRL
Aerochemical Metal-Oxide Kinetics [*Program*] (MCD) .... AMOK
Aerochiapas SA de CV [*Mexico ICAO designator*] (FAAC) .... AHP
Aerocombi SA [*Spain ICAO designator*] (FAAC) .... HSW
Aerocomponentes Internacionales, SA de CV [*Mexico*] [*FAA designator*] (FAAC) .... CPE
Aerocontrol Electronics Unit [*NASA*] (NASA) .... ACEU
Aerocozumel SA [*Mexico ICAO designator*] (FAAC) .... AZM
Aerodan, SA de CV [*Mexico*] [*FAA designator*] (FAAC) .... ROD
Aerodespachos de El Salvador [*ICAO designator*] (FAAC) .... DNA
Aerodienst GmbH [*Germany ICAO designator*] (FAAC) .... ADN
Aerodin SA de CV [*Mexico ICAO designator*] (FAAC) .... DIN
Aerodrome .... AD
Aerodrome .... ADRM
Aerodrome (IAA) .... AER
Aerodrome Beacon (IAA) .... ABCN
Aerodrome Beacon (DA) .... ABE
Aerodrome Beacon [*ICAO*] (FAAC) .... ABN
Aerodrome Control [*British*] .... ADC
Aerodrome Control RADAR (IAA) .... ACR
Aerodrome Control Service .... ACS
Aerodrome Control Tower [*ICAO designator*] (ICDA) .... ZT
Aerodrome Control Tower [*FAA designator*] (FAAC) .... ZTZ
Aerodrome Damage Repair [*NATO*] .... ADR
Aerodrome Defence Corps [*British*] .... ADC
Aerodrome Emergency Service (DA) .... AES
Aerodrome Fire Service [*British*] (AIA) .... AFS
Aerodrome Flight Information Service .... AFIS
Aerodrome Flight Information Service (Officer) (DA) .... AFIS(O)
Aerodrome Flight Information Service Officer's Licence [*British*] (DBQ) .... AFISOL
Aerodrome Obstruction Chart .... AOC
Aerodrome [*or Airport*] **of Entry** .... AOE
Aerodrome Officer-of-the-Day (DNAB) .... AOD
Aerodrome Operation (DA) .... AOP
Aerodrome Owners Association [*British*] (BI) .... AOA
Aerodrome RADAR/Radio Approach Aid .... ARAA
Aerodrome Reference Code Panel [*ICAO*] (DA) .... ARCP
Aerodrome Report [*Aviation*] (DA) .... Ae
Aerodrome Security Services [*FAA designator*] (FAAC) .... ZYZ
Aerodrome Surface Movement Control .... AMC
Aerodrome Surface Movement Indicator (SAA) .... ASMI
Aerodrome to Aerodrome .... A/A
Aerodrome Traffic Zone .... ATZ
Aerodrome Warning (DA) .... AW
Aerodromes, Air Routes, and Ground Aid (DA) .... AGA
Aerodromes, Air Routes, and Ground Aids [*Aviation*] .... AGA
Aerodynamic (IAA) .... AER
Aerodynamic (ABBR) .... AERDYN
Aerodynamic (NASA) .... AERO
Aerodynamic (KSC) .... AERODYN
Aerodynamic Accounting Technique (MCD) .... AAT
Aerodynamic and Propulsion Test Unit .... APTU
Aerodynamic Center (IDOE) .... ac
Aerodynamic Coefficient Identification Package (NASA) .... ACIP
Aerodynamic Coefficient Instrumentation Package (NASA) .... ACIP
Aerodynamic Configuration Drivers (MCD) .... ACD
Aerodynamic Configured Missile (MCD) .... ACM
Aerodynamic Damping Moment in Pitch [*Helicopter rotor*] .... ADMP
Aerodynamic Data Analysis and Integration System [*Computer science*] .... ADAIS
Aerodynamic Data Analysis Program [*Computer science*] (SSD) .... ADAP
Aerodynamic Data Book (NASA) .... ADB
Aerodynamic Data Correlation (MCD) .... ADC
Aerodynamic Decelerator (AAG) .... AD
Aerodynamic Deployable Decelerator Performance Evaluation Program .... ADDPEP
Aerodynamic Design and Analysis System for Supersonic Aircraft (MCD) .... ADASSA
Aerodynamic Equivalent Diameter (PDAA) .... AED
Aerodynamic Flight Control (MCD) .... AFC
Aerodynamic Flight Test (NASA) .... AFT
Aerodynamic Heat Test Plans .... AHTP
Aerodynamic Heating (NG) .... AEROHEAT
Aerodynamic Heating Indicator (MCD) .... AHI
Aerodynamic Influence Coefficients with Interference (PDAA) .... AIC/INT
Aerodynamic Load Balanced Elliptical Nozzle (MCD) .... ALBEN
Aerodynamic Maneuver Capability (SAA) .... AMC
Aerodynamic Mean Chord (DA) .... AMC
Aerodynamic Model Test Plan (SAA) .... AMTP
Aerodynamic Model Test Report (SAA) .... AMTR
Aerodynamic Modeling [*Module*] .... AEROMOD
Aerodynamic Post-Processing [*Module*] .... AEROPOST
Aerodynamic Propulsive Interactive Force [*Air Force*] .... APIF
Aerodynamic Report .... AR
Aerodynamic Spacecraft Two-Stage Reusable Orbiter [*NASA*] .... ASTRO

Aerodynamic Stability Augmentation System [*or Subsystem*] [*NASA*] (NASA) ... ASAS
Aerodynamic Surface Assembly and Checkout [*NASA*] (NASA) ... ASAC
Aerodynamic Test Vehicle (MCD) ... ATV
Aerodynamic Yaw Coupling ... AYC
Aerodynamic Yaw Coupling Parameters ... AYCP
Aerodynamically Neutral Spin-Stabilized Rocket (MCD) ... ANSSR
Aerodynamically Neutral Spin-Stabilized Rocket Artillery System [*Army*] (MCD) ... ANSSRAS
Aerodynamically Regenerated Trap ... ART
Aerodynamic-Influence Coefficient ... AIC
Aerodynamics ... ARODYN
Aerodynamics Advisory Panel [*AEC*] (MCD) ... AAP
Aerodynamics Center [*NASA*] ... AC
Aerodynamics Laboratory [*Naval Ship Research and Development Center*] ... AL
Aerodynamics Note ... AN
Aerodynamics Surface Control (MCD) ... ASC
Aerodynamics-Thermodynamics-Acoustic Wind Tunnel [*Automotive research*] ... ATAWT
Aerodyne Charter [*ICAO designator*] (FAAC) ... AQZ
Aerodyne Executive Aviation Services [*ICAO designator*] (FAAC) ... ADY
Aerodyne Research, Inc. ... ARI
Aeroejecutivos, Aeroservicios Ejecutivos [*Colombia*] [*ICAO designator*] (FAAC) ... AJS
Aeroel Airways Ltd. [*Israel*] [*FAA designator*] (FAAC) ... ROL
Aeroelastic and Structures Research Laboratory [*Massachusetts Institute of Technology*] ... ASRL
Aero-Elastic Research Laboratory [*MIT*] (MCD) ... AERL
Aeroelastic Research Wing (MCD) ... ARW
Aeroelastic Rotor Experimental System (MCD) ... ARES
Aeroelastic Wind Tunnel ... AWT
Aeroelastically Conformable Rotor (RDA) ... ACR
Aeroelectronic (IEEE) ... AE
Aero-Electronic Technology Department [*Navy*] (MCD) ... AETD
Aeroexpreso Bogota [*Colombia*] [*ICAO designator*] (FAAC) ... ABO
Aeroexpreso Interamerican [*Colombia*] [*ICAO designator*] (FAAC) ... AEI
Aerofer, SL [*Spain ICAO designator*] (FAAC) ... ARF
Aeroflex, Inc. [*Associated Press*] (SAG) ... Aeroflex
Aeroflex, Inc. [*NYSE symbol*] (SAG) ... ARX
Aeroflightdynamics Directorate [*Army and NASA joint operation*] (RDA) ... AFDD
Aeroflot - Russian International Airlines [*Russian Federation*] [*ICAO designator*] (FAAC) ... AFL
Aerofrance [*France ICAO designator*] (FAAC) ... ROF
Aerofrisco [*Mexico ICAO designator*] (FAAC) ... FCO
Aerographer ... AERO
Aerographer's Mate [*Navy rating*] ... AERM
Aerographer's Mate [*Navy rating*] ... AG
Aerographer's Mate, Chief [*Navy rating*] ... AGC
Aerographer's Mate, First Class [*Navy rating*] ... AG1
Aerographer's Mate, Master Chief [*Navy rating*] ... AGCM
Aerographer's Mate, Second Class [*Navy rating*] ... AG2
Aerographer's Mate, Senior Chief [*Navy rating*] ... AGCS
Aerographer's Mate, Third Class [*Navy rating*] ... AG3
Aeroguayacan [*Chile*] [*ICAO designator*] (FAAC) ... AGY
Aerojelk, SA de CV [*Mexico*] [*FAA designator*] (FAAC) ... JEL
Aerojet/Bumblebee [*Navy missile*] ... AEROBEE
Aerojet de Costa Rica SA [*ICAO designator*] (FAAC) ... ARJ
Aerojet Differential Analyzer ... ADA
Aerojet Electrosystems Co. (MCD) ... AESC
Aerojet Electrosystems Co., Azusa, CA [*Library symbol Library of Congress*] (LCLS) ... CAzA
Aerojet Liquid Rocket Co. (KSC) ... ALRC
Aerojet Manufacturing Co. ... AMCO
Aerojet Mass Analyzer Program (MCD) ... AMAP
Aerojet Network Analyzer ... ANA
Aerojet Nuclear Co., Idaho Falls, ID [*Library symbol Library of Congress*] (LCLS) ... IdIfA
Aero-Jet SA [*Switzerland ICAO designator*] (FAAC) ... AOJ
Aerojet Services Co. ... ASC
Aerojet Solid Propulsion Co. ... ASPC
Aerojet-General Corp. ... AG
Aerojet-General Corp. ... AGC
Aerojet-General Nucleonics [*of Aerojet-General Corp.*] ... AGN
Aerojobeni SA de CV [*Mexico ICAO designator*] (FAAC) ... JOB
Aerokuznetsk, Joint Stock Company [*Former USSR*] [*FAA designator*] (FAAC) ... AKZ
Aerolastic and Structures Research Laboratory (SAA) ... ASRL
Aeroleasing SA [*Switzerland ICAO designator*] (FAAC) ... FPG
Aerolift, Inc. [*Vancouver Stock Exchange symbol*] ... AER
Aerolift Philippines Corp. [*ICAO designator*] (FAAC) ... LFT
Aerolik [*Former USSR*] [*FAA designator*] (FAAC) ... AKR
Aerolinas Nacionales del Ecuador SA [*ICAO designator*] (FAAC) ... EDA
Aerolinas Uruguayas SA [*Uruguay*] [*ICAO designator*] (FAAC) ... AUY
Aerolinea Federal Argentina [*Argentine Federal Airline*] (EY) ... ALFA
Aerolinea Federal Argentina [*ICAO designator*] (AD) ... CQ
Aerolinea Muri [*Mexico ICAO designator*] (FAAC) ... MUR
Aerolineas Argentinas [*Argentina ICAO designator*] (FAAC) ... ARG
Aerolineas Centrales de Colombia [*Airline*] [*Colombia*] ... ACES
Aerolineas Centrales de Colombia [*ICAO designator*] (FAAC) ... AES
Aerolineas Centroamericanas SA [*Central American Airlines*] [*Nicaragua*] [*ICAO designator*] (FAAC) ... ACN
Aerolineas Coco Club Hoteles de Mexico SA de CV [*ICAO designator*] (FAAC) ... CCO
Aerolineas Colonia SA [*Airline*] [*Uruguay*] ... ARCO
Aerolineas Cordillera Ltda. [*Chile*] [*ICAO designator*] (FAAC) ... AEROCOR
Aerolineas Cordillera Ltda. [*Chile*] [*ICAO designator*] (FAAC) ... CRD
Aerolineas de El Salvador [*Airline*] [*El Salvador*] ... AESA
Aerolineas de El Salvador SA [*ICAO designator*] (FAAC) ... SZA
Aerolineas de Honduras, SA [*Honduras*] [*FAA designator*] (FAAC) ... AHB
Aerolineas de Michoacan [*Mexico ICAO designator*] (FAAC) ... MIC
Aerolineas Del Mayab, SA de CV [*Mexico*] [*FAA designator*] (FAAC) ... MYB
Aerolineas del Oeste SA de CV [*Mexico ICAO designator*] (FAAC) ... AST
Aerolineas del Sol, SA de CV [*Mexico*] [*FAA designator*] (FAAC) ... LSO
Aerolineas del Sureste SA [*Mexico ICAO designator*] (FAAC) ... SUE
Aerolineas Dominicanas [*ICAO designator*] (AD) ... YU
Aerolineas Dominicanas SA [*Dominican Republic*] [*ICAO designator*] (FAAC) ... ADM
Aerolineas Ejecutivas de San Luis Potosi SA de CV [*Mexico ICAO designator*] (FAAC) ... ELP
Aerolineas Ejecutivas SA [*Mexico ICAO designator*] (FAAC) ... LET
Aerolineas Especiales de Colombia [*ICAO designator*] (FAAC) ... ALE
Aerolineas Internacionales, SA de CV [*Mexico*] [*FAA designator*] (FAAC) ... LNT
Aerolineas Latinas CA [*Venezuela*] [*ICAO designator*] (FAAC) ... LTN
Aerolineas Marcos SA de CV [*Mexico ICAO designator*] (FAAC) ... MCO
Aerolineas Medellin [*Colombia*] [*ICAO designator*] (FAAC) ... AMD
Aerolineas Mexicanas JS SA de CV [*Mexico ICAO designator*] (FAAC) ... LMX
Aerolineas Nacionales del Ecuador [*Airline*] ... ANDES
Aerolineas Nicaraguenses [*Nicaragua Airlines*] (EY) ... AERONICA
Aerolineas Nicaraguenses [*ICAO designator*] (AD) ... RL
Aerolineas Pacifico Atlantico SA [*Spain ICAO designator*] (FAAC) ... APP
Aerolineas Peruanas Sociedad Anonima [*Peruvian Air Lines*] ... APSA
Aerolineas Yasi, SA de CV [*Mexico*] [*FAA designator*] (FAAC) ... RLY
Aerolinee Italiane Internazionali [*Italian International Airline*] [*Facetious translation: Always Late in Takeoffs, Always Late in Arrivals*] ... ALITALIA
Aerological ... AEROL
Aerological Officer ... AER OF
Aerologist ... AEROG
Aerology [*NAO code*] (DNAB) ... A
Aeromak [*Yugoslavia*] [*ICAO designator*] (FAAC) ... AMK
Aeromaritime (CAAA) [*France ICAO designator*] (FAAC) ... QKL
Aeromarket Express [*Spain ICAO designator*] (FAAC) ... ARM
Aero-Mechanical Engineering Laboratory [*Army*] (RDA) ... AMEL
Aero-Mechanics Department [*Navy*] (MCD) ... AMD
Aeromechanics Laboratory [*Army*] (GRD) ... AL
Aeromedical ... AEROMED
Aero-Medical Acceleration Laboratory (DMAA) ... AMAL
Aeromedical Airlift Group [*Air Force*] ... AAG
Aeromedical Airlift Group [*Air Force*] (AFM) ... AAGp
Aeromedical Airlift Squadron [*Air Force*] ... AAS
Aeromedical Airlift Squadron [*Air Force*] (AFM) ... AASq
Aeromedical Airlift Wing [*Air Force*] (MCD) ... AAW
Aeromedical Airlift Wing [*Air Force*] (AFM) ... AAWg
Aeromedical Data ... AMD
Aeromedical Education Division [*FAA*] ... AED
Aeromedical Equipment Laboratory ... AMEL
Aeromedical Evacuation [*Later, AME*] (AFM) ... AE
Aeromedical Evacuation [*Later, AME*] ... AMDLEVAC
Aeromedical Evacuation [*Formerly, AE, AMDLEVAC*] (AABC) ... AME
Aeromedical Evacuation Control Center [*Military*] (MCD) ... AECC
Aeromedical Evacuation Control Officer [*Military*] (AABC) ... AECO
Aeromedical Evacuation Flight [*Air Force*] ... AEF
Aeromedical Evacuation Group [*Air Force*] ... AEG
Aeromedical Evacuation Group [*Air Force*] (AFM) ... AEGp
Aeromedical Evacuation Liaison Officer [*Air Force*] (AFM) ... AELO
Aeromedical Evacuation Operations Office [*or Officer*] [*Military*] (MCD) ... AEOO
Aeromedical Evacuation Squadron [*Air Force*] ... AES
Aeromedical Evacuation Squadron [*Air Force*] (DAVI) ... AESQ
Aeromedical Evacuation Support Team ... AEST
Aeromedical Evacuation System [*Air Force*] (AFM) ... AMES
Aeromedical Evacuation Technician ... AET
Aeromedical Laboratory ... AML
Aeromedical Liaison Office [*or Officer*] [*Air Force*] (AFM) ... AMLO
Aeromedical Library, 6571st Aeromedical Research Laboratory, Holloman AFB, NM [*Library symbol Library of Congress*] (LCLS) ... NmHARL
Aeromedical Monitor (SAA) ... AM
Aeromedical Monitor Console ... AMC
Aeromedical Research Laboratory [*Army*] (KSC) ... ARL
Aeromedical Research Unit [*Army*] (MCD) ... ARU
Aeromedical Staging Facility ... ASF
Aeromedical Staging Flight [*Air Force*] ... ASF
Aeromedical Staging Unit (AFM) ... ASU
Aeromedicare Ltd. [*British ICAO designator*] (FAAC) ... AMQ
Aeromega Ltd. [*British ICAO designator*] (FAAC) ... OMG
Aeromere SpA [*Italy ICAO aircraft manufacturer identifier*] (ICAO) ... AO
Aerometric and Emissions Reporting System [*Environmental Protection Agency*] ... AEROS
Aerometric Information Retrieval System [*Environmental Protection Agency Information service or system*] (CRD) ... AIRS
Aeromexico [*Airline*] (DS) ... AM
Aeromexpress, SA de CV [*Mexico*] [*FAA designator*] (FAAC) ... MPX
Aeromonterrey SA [*Mexico ICAO designator*] (FAAC) ... MOT
Aeromorelos SA de CV [*Mexico ICAO designator*] (FAAC) ... MRL
Aeromundo Ejecutivo, SA de CV [*Mexico*] [*FAA designator*] (FAAC) ... MUN
Aeromyl SA de CV [*Mexico ICAO designator*] (FAAC) ... MYL
Aeron International Airlines, Inc. [*ICAO designator*] (FAAC) ... AXI
Aeronardi SpA [*Italy ICAO designator*] (FAAC) ... NRD
Aeronaut (ABBR) ... AERN
Aeronaut Society (EA) ... AS
Aeronautica and Air Label Collectors Club (EA) ... AAL
Aeronautica and Air Label Collectors Club (EA) ... AALCC

Aeronautica Industrial SA [*Spain ICAO aircraft manufacturer identifier*] (ICAO) .... AI
Aeronautica Interespacial SA de CV [*Mexico ICAO designator*] (FAAC) .... ITS
Aeronautica Venezolana CA [*Venezuela*] [*ICAO designator*] (FAAC) .... AEROVENCA
Aeronautica Venezolana, CA [*Venezuela*] [*ICAO designator*] (FAAC) .... AVC
Aeronautical (ABBR) .... AE
Aeronautical (ABBR) .... AERNL
Aeronautical .... AERON
Aeronautical .... AERONL
Aeronautical .... ARNTCL
Aeronautical Administration Communication [*A class of communication which supports administrative communication*] (GAVI) .... AAC
Aeronautical Advisory Council .... AAC
Aeronautical and Astronautical Engineering (MCD) .... AAE
Aeronautical and Mechanical Engineering Branch, Canada Institute for Scientific and Technical Information [*Division du Genie Aeronautique et Mecanique, Institut Canadien de l'Information Scientifique et Technique*] **Ottawa, Ontario** [*Library symbol National Library of Canada*] (NLC) .... OONAM
Aeronautical and Navigational Electronics (MCD) .... ANE
Aeronautical Approach Chart [*Air Force*] .... AAC
Aeronautical Approach Chart [*Air Force*] .... AC
Aeronautical Army and Navy (AAG) .... AAN
Aeronautical Board [*Air Force*] .... AB
Aeronautical Broadcast Station [*ITU designation*] (CET) .... FAB
Aeronautical Center [*FAA*] .... AC
Aeronautical Chamber of Commerce of America [*Later, AIA*] .... ACCA
Aeronautical Chart and Information Center [*St. Louis, MO*] [*Later, DMAAC*] [*Air Force*] .... ACIC
Aeronautical Chart and Information Center Technical Translation Section [*Air Force*] .... ACIC-TC
Aeronautical Chart and Information Office [*Air Force*] (SAA) .... ACIO
Aeronautical Chart and Information Squadron [*Air Force*] (DNAB) .... ACIS
Aeronautical Chart and Information Squadron [*Air Force*] .... ACISQ
Aeronautical Chart Automation Project [*Military*] (DA) .... ACAP
Aeronautical Charting and Information Center [*Marine science*] (OSRA) .... ACIC
Aeronautical Command Systems [*Air Force*] .... ACS
Aeronautical Communications Equipment Corp. .... AEROCOM
Aeronautical Communications Satellite System .... AEROSAT
Aeronautical Computers Laboratory [*Johnsville, PA*] [*Navy*] .... ACL
Aeronautical Data .... AD
Aeronautical Data Communication Network (DA) .... ADCN
Aeronautical Data Interchange System Panel (OA) .... ADISP
Aeronautical Data Report [*Navy*] .... ADR
Aeronautical Data-Link [*FAA*] (TAG) .... ADL
Aeronautical Depot Maintenance Industrial Technology [*Navy*] (AFIT) .... ADMIT
Aeronautical Design Standard [*Army*] .... ADS
Aeronautical Development Group [*Military*] (AFIT) .... ADG
Aeronautical Digital Information Display System (DA) .... ADIDS
Aeronautical Earth Station (DA) .... AES
Aeronautical Engine Laboratory [*Later, NAPC*] [*Navy*] .... AEL
Aeronautical Engineer .... AE
Aeronautical Engineer .... AeE
Aeronautical Engineer (IEEE) .... AeEng
Aeronautical Engineer (ADA) .... AerE
Aeronautical Engineering and Electronic Laboratory [*Johnsville, PA*] [*Navy*] .... AEEL
Aeronautical Engineering Department [*NASA*] (KSC) .... AED
Aeronautical Engineering Division [*Air Force*] (DOMA) .... AED
Aeronautical Engineering Duty [*Navy*] .... AED
Aeronautical Engineering Duty Officer [*Navy*] (DOMA) .... AEDO
Aeronautical Engineering Laboratory [*NASA*] (KSC) .... AEL
Aeronautical Engineering Report .... AER
Aeronautical Enroute Information Service (DA) .... AEIS
Aeronautical Equipment Reference (SAA) .... AER
Aeronautical Equipment Reference Number [*Military*] .... AERNO
Aeronautical Equipment Service Record (MCD) .... AESR
Aeronautical Fixed Service .... AFS
Aeronautical Fixed Station [*ITU designation*] (CET) .... FAX
Aeronautical Fixed Station [*ICAO designator*] (ICDA) .... YF
Aeronautical Fixed Systems Planning for Data Interchange Panel [*ICAO*] (DA) .... ASPP
Aeronautical Fixed Telecommunication Network [*United Kingdom*] .... AFTN
Aeronautical Fixed Telecommunications Service .... AFTS
Aeronautical Frequency Management Committee [*British*] (DA) .... AFMLC
Aeronautical Icing Research Laboratory .... AIRL
Aeronautical Information Circular (FAAC) .... AIC
Aeronautical Information Manual [*FAA*] (TAG) .... AIM
Aeronautical Information Publication [*FAA*] (TAG) .... AIP
Aeronautical Information Publication (FAAC) .... AIP
Aeronautical Information Regulation and Control .... AIRAC
Aeronautical [*or Aerospace*] **Information Report** (MCD) .... AIR
Aeronautical Information Section .... AIS
Aeronautical Information Service .... AIS
Aeronautical Information Service Automation Group [*ICAO*] (DA) .... AAG
Aeronautical Information Service Automation Group [*ICAO*] (DA) .... AISAG
Aeronautical Information Service Automation Specialist Panel [*ICAO*] (DA) .... AISAP
Aeronautical Information Service Unit [*ICAO designator*] (ICDA) .... YO
Aeronautical Information Specialist (FAAC) .... AIS
Aeronautical Inspection Directorate [*British*] (MCD) .... AID
Aeronautical Instruments Laboratory [*Military*] .... AIL
Aeronautical Laboratory .... AL
Aeronautical Maintenance Duty Officer .... AMDO
Aeronautical Maintenance Support Equipment List [*Military*] (AFIT) .... AMSEL
Aeronautical Manufacturers' Planning Report [*NASA*] .... AMPR
Aeronautical Manufacturers Planning Report (AAGC) .... AMPR
Aeronautical Manufacturers Progress Report [*NASA*] .... AMPR
Aeronautical Marker Beacon [*ITU designation*] (CET) .... RLA
Aeronautical Material Screening Unit (AFIT) .... AMSU
Aeronautical [*or Aerospace*] **Material Specification** .... AMS
Aeronautical Material Support Equipment (DNAB) .... AMSE
Aeronautical Materials Laboratory .... AML
Aeronautical Medical Acceleration Laboratory [*Air Force*] .... AMAL
Aeronautical Military Standards .... AMS
Aeronautical Mobile .... AEM
Aeronautical Mobile Satellite Service [*ICAO designator*] (FAAC) .... AMSS
Aeronautical Mobile Satellite Service Panel [*ICAO*] (DA) .... AMSSP
Aeronautical National Taper Pipe Threads .... ANPT
Aeronautical Operating Systems Division [*NASA*] .... AOSD
Aeronautical Operation Control [*Communications which support safety and regularity of flight that normally take place between aircraft and the operator*] (GAVI) .... AOC
Aeronautical Operational Control .... AOC
Aeronautical Order (AFM) .... AO
Aeronautical Passenger Communication [*A class of communication which supports passenger communication*] (GAVI) .... APC
Aeronautical Photographic Experimental Laboratory [*Johnsville, PA*] [*Navy*] .... APEL
Aeronautical Planning Chart [*Military*] .... APC
Aeronautical Production Control System .... APCS
Aeronautical Propulsion Division [*NASA*] .... APD
Aeronautical Public Correspondence (DA) .... APC
Aeronautical Quality Assurance Directorate [*British*] (PDAA) .... AQAD
Aeronautical Quality Assurance Directorate [*British*] .... AQD
Aeronautical RADAR Research Complex .... ARRC
Aeronautical Radio (IAA) .... AR
Aeronautical Radio and RADAR Laboratory [*Navy*] .... ARRL
Aeronautical Radio, Inc. (KSC) .... ARI
Aeronautical Radio, Inc. .... ARINC
Aeronautical Radio, Inc. .... ARINCO
Aeronautical Radio, Inc. [*ICAO designator*] (FAAC) .... XAA
Aeronautical Radio of Canada .... ARCAN
Aeronautical Radio Range [*Nautical charts*] .... AERO R Rge
Aeronautical Radiobeacon [*Nautical charts*] .... AERO R Bn
Aeronautical Radionavigation Glide Path (IAA) .... ARGP
Aeronautical Radionavigation Land Station [*ITU designation*] .... AL
Aeronautical Radionavigation Mobile Station [*ITU designation*] .... AM
Aeronautical Radionavigation RADAR .... ARR
Aeronautical [*or Aerospace*] **Recommended Practice** .... ARP
Aeronautical Repair Station Association (EA) .... ARSA
Aeronautical [*or Aircraft*] **Requirement** [*Military*] (MCD) .... AR
Aeronautical Research (IAA) .... AR
Aeronautical Research Associates of Princeton (MCD) .... ARAP
Aeronautical Research Council [*British*] .... ARC
Aeronautical Research Division [*NASA*] .... ARD
Aeronautical Research Foundation .... ARF
Aeronautical Research, Inc. (MCD) .... ARINC
Aeronautical Research Institute of Sweden (MCD) .... ARIS
Aeronautical Research Scientist .... ARS
Aeronautical Satellite .... AEROSAT
Aeronautical Satellite Communications Center (NITA) .... ASCC
Aeronautical Satellite Communications Processor (DA) .... ASCAP
Aeronautical Satellite Datalink System [*Mitre Corp.*] (NITA) .... ASDL
Aeronautical Services Communication Center [*Great Britain*] .... ASCC
Aeronautical Services Earth Terminal (OA) .... ASET
Aeronautical Shipboard Installation Representative (NVT) .... ASIR
Aeronautical Society of Great Britain (BI) .... ASGB
Aeronautical Specifications .... AS
Aeronautical Staging Flight (DNAB) .... ASF
Aeronautical Standards .... AS
Aeronautical Standards Group [*Military*] .... AG
Aeronautical Standards Group [*Military*] .... ASG
Aeronautical Standards Group [*Military*] (AFIT) .... ASGP
Aeronautical Station [*ITU designation*] (CET) .... FA
Aeronautical Station [*ICAO designator*] (ICDA) .... YS
Aeronautical Station [*FAA designator*] (FAAC) .... YSY
Aeronautical Structures Laboratory [*Navy*] .... ASL
Aeronautical Support Equipment Type Designation System .... ASETDS
Aeronautical System Development (NG) .... ASD
Aeronautical System Training Equipment (SAA) .... ASTE
Aeronautical Systems Center [*Air Force*] .... ASC
Aeronautical Systems Division [*Wright-Patterson Air Force Base, OH*] [*Air Force*] .... ASD
Aeronautical Systems Division A-10 System Program Office [*Wright-Patterson Air Force Base, OH*] ASD/A-10-SPO
Aeronautical Systems Division Form .... ASDF
Aeronautical Systems Division Manual .... ASDM
Aeronautical Systems Division Regulation .... ASDR
Aeronautical Technical Directive Requirement [*Obsolete*] .... ATDR
Aeronautical Telecommunications Network .... ATN
Aeronautical Telecommunications Officers (ADA) .... ATO
Aeronautical Telecommunications Operator .... ATO
Aeronautical Training Society .... ATS
Aeronautical Turbine Laboratory [*Navy*] .... ATL
Aeronautical Video Charts (MCD) .... AVC
Aeronautical Video Plates (MCD) .... AVP
Aeronautically (ABBR) .... AERNLY
Aeronautically Fixed .... AF
Aeronautics (IAA) .... A

Aeronautics (MCD) ... AER
Aeronautics (ABBR) ... AERNC
Aeronautics (AFM) ... AERO
Aeronautics (DD) ... Aero
Aeronautics and Astronautics Coordinating Board [*NASA*] ... AACB
Aeronautics and Astronautics, University of Southampton [*British*] (SAA) ... AASU
Aeronautics and Space ... AEROSPACE
Aeronautics and Space Engineering Board [*National Academy of Engineering*] ... ASEB
Aeronautics and Space Historical Center (EA) ... ASHC
Aeronautics Supply Officer (MUGU) ... ASO
Aeronautics Upper Atmosphere Impact Program [*NASA*] ... AUAIP
Aeronave Militar Espanola, Ministerio de Defensa [*Spain*] [*FAA designator*] (FAAC) ... AME
Aeronaves de Mexico SA [*Mexican airline*] (MCD) ... ADM
Aeronaves de Mexico SA [*Mexico ICAO designator*] (ICDA) ... AM
Aeronaves del Centro [*Venezuela*] [*ICAO designator*] (FAAC) ... AGA
Aeronaves del Peru SA [*ICAO designator*] (FAAC) ... WPL
Aeronavs La Dprada SA [*Spain ICAO designator*] (FAAC) ... ALD
Aeronca Aviators Club (EA) ... AAC
Aeronca Club (EA) ... AC
Aeronca Lovers Club (EA) ... ALC
Aeronca Manufacturing [*ICAO aircraft manufacturer identifier*] (ICAO) ... AR
Aeronca Sedan Club (EA) ... ASC
Aeronias Nacionales de Honduras Sociedad Anonima [*Airline*] [*Honduras*] ... ANHSA
Aeronoleggi e Lavoro Aereo (AERAL) [*Italy ICAO designator*] (ICDA) ... HS
Aeronomic South Hemisphere and Antarctic Year (PDAA) ... ASHAY
Aeronomy and Space Data Center [*Later, NGSDC*] [*National Oceanic and Atmospheric Administration*] ... ASDC
Aeronomy Laboratory [*National Institute of Standards and Technology*] ... AL
Aeronomy Satellite - Neutral Atmosphere Temperature Experiment ... AEROS-NATE
Aeronorte SA [*Colombia*] [*ICAO designator*] (FAAC) ... ANR
Aeronorte - Transportes Aereos Lda. [*Portugal ICAO designator*] (FAAC) ... RTE
Aeronutronic Ford Corp., Newport Beach, CA [*Library symbol Library of Congress*] (LCLS) ... CNbAF
Aeronutronic General Perturbations Differential Correction Program ... AGPDC
Aeronutronics Division, Ford Motor Co. (AAG) ... ADF
Aero-Palma SA [*Spain ICAO designator*] (FAAC) ... AET
Aeropelican ... AP
Aeropelican Air Services Pty Ltd. [*Australia ICAO designator*] (FAAC) ... PEL
Aeropelican Intercity Commuter Air Services [*ICAO designator*] (AD) ... PO
Aeropeninsular, SA de CV [*Mexico*] [*FAA designator*] (FAAC) ... PSU
Aeropesca [*ICAO designator*] (AD) ... RS
Aeropetrel [*Chile*] [*ICAO designator*] (FAAC) ... PET
Aerophilatelic Federation of the Americas (EA) ... AFA
Aerophysics - Curtiss-Wright (SAA) ... A-CW
Aerophysics Development Corp. ... ADC
Aerophysics Laboratory (MCD) ... AL
Aerophysics Laboratory Memorandum [*NASA*] (KSC) ... ALM
Aerophysics Research Corp. ... ARC
Aeropiloto-Sociedade Exploradora de Servicos Aereos Lda. [*Portugal ICAO designator*] (FAAC) ... AOP
Aeroplane (ADA) ... AER
Aeroplane and Armament Experimental Establishment [*British*] ... AAEE
[*The*] **Aeroplane Collection** [*British*] ... TAC
Aeroplane Flag [*Navy British*] ... AP
Aeroposta SA [*Argentina ICAO designator*] (FAAC) ... POS
Aeroposta, SA [*Argentina*] [*FAA designator*] (FAAC) ... RPO
Aeropro [*Canada ICAO designator*] (FAAC) ... APO
Aero-Propulsion Fuels Laboratory [*Air Force*] ... APFL
Aero-Propulsion Laboratory [*Air Force*] ... APL
Aeropropulsion Systems Test Facility [*Arnold Air Force Station, TN*] [*Air Force*] (MCD) ... ASTF
Aeropuerto del Norte [*Mexico ICAO location identifier*] (ICLI) ... MMAN
Aeropuma SA [*El Salvador*] [*ICAO designator*] (FAAC) ... APU
Aeroput [*Yugoslavia*] [*ICAO designator*] (FAAC) ... PUT
Aeropycsa SA de CV [*Mexico ICAO designator*] (FAAC) ... PYC
Aeroquetzal [*ICAO designator*] (AD) ... AW
Aerora SA [*Mexico ICAO designator*] (FAAC) ... ARR
Aero-Rent SA de CV [*Mexico ICAO designator*] (FAAC) ... REN
Aerorepresentaciones Tupac Amaru [*Peru*] [*ICAO designator*] (ICDA) ... XU
Aerorepresentaciones Tupac Amaru [*Peru*] [*ICAO designator*] (FAAC) ... XUT
Aerorepublica [*Columbia*] [*FAA designator*] (FAAC) ... RPB
Aero-Rey SA de CV [*Mexico ICAO designator*] (FAAC) ... REY
Aerosaba SA de CV [*Mexico*] [*FAA designator*] (FAAC) ... ESB
Aeroservice [*Kazakhstan*] [*FAA designator*] (FAAC) ... AVZ
Aeroservicio Sipse SA de CV [*Mexico ICAO designator*] (FAAC) ... PSE
Aeroservicios Carabobo CA [*Venezuela*] [*ICAO designator*] (FAAC) ... ASERCA
Aeroservicios Carabobo CA (ASERCA) [*Venzuela*] [*ICAO designator*] (FAAC) ... OCA
Aeroservicios del Bajio, SA de CV [*Mexico*] [*FAA designator*] (FAAC) ... RBJ
Aeroservicios Ejecutivos del Occidente SA de CV [*Mexico ICAO designator*] (FAAC) ... AEO
Aeroservicios Ejecutivos del Pacifico SA [*Mexico ICAO designator*] (FAAC) ... SPO
Aeroservicios Ejecutivos Sinaloenses SA [*Mexico ICAO designator*] (FAAC) ... SLS
Aeroservicios Monterrey SA de CV [*Mexico ICAO designator*] (FAAC) ... SVM
Aerosevicios Ecuatorianos CA [*Ecuador*] [*ICAO designator*] (FAAC) ... EAE
Aerosi SA de CV [*Mexico ICAO designator*] (FAAC) ... OSI
Aerosierra de Durango [*Mexico ICAO designator*] (FAAC) ... SDG
Aerosiyusa, SA [*Mexico*] [*FAA designator*] (FAAC) ... SIY
Aerosol (ABBR) ... AERSL
Aerosol Analyzer (KSC) ... AA
Aerosol Characterization Experiment [*Marine science*] (OSRA) ... ACE
Aerosol Characterization Experiment (USDC) ... ACE
Aerosol Characterization Experiment (PDAA) ... ACHEX
Aerosol Climatic Effects [*NASA*] ... ACE
Aerosol Inhalation Measurement [*Medicine*] ... AIM
Aerosol Mask [*Medicine*] (DAVI) ... Aer M
Aerosol Obscurant (MCD) ... AO
Aerosol Optical Depth (USDC) ... AOD
Aerosol Optical Depth (OSRA) ... AOD
Aerosol Optical Thickness [*Climatology factor*] ... AOT
Aerosol Physical Properties of the Stratosphere [*NASA*] (MCD) ... APPS
Aerosol Protective (DICI) ... AP
Aerosol Release and Transport [*Nuclear energy*] (NRCH) ... ART
Aerosol Sampling System ... ASS
Aerosol Scattering Coefficient [*Climatology factor*] ... ASC
Aerosol Scattering Spectrometer Probe (USDC) ... ASSP
Aerosol Scattering Spectrometer Probe [*Marine science*] (OSRA) ... ASSP
Aerosol Techniques, Inc. ... ATI
Aerosol Tent [*Medicine*] (DAVI) ... Aer T
Aerosol Time-of-Flight Mass Spectrometer ... ATOFMS
Aerosonic Corp. [*Associated Press*] (SAG) ... Aeroson
Aerosonic Corp. [*AMEX symbol*] (SPSG) ... AIM
Aerososel [*Chile*] [*FAA designator*] (FAAC) ... AOE
Aerospace (MCD) ... A
Aerospace ... AERO
Aerospace (MSA) ... AEROSP
Aerospace (ABBR) ... AERSPC
Aerospace ... ARSPC
Aerospace (IEEE) ... AS
Aerospace Amplifier (MCD) ... ASA
Aerospace and Electronic Systems Society (NITA) ... AESC
Aerospace and Electronics Systems (IEEE) ... AESS
Aerospace and Environmental Medicine Information System (IID) ... AEMIS
Aerospace and Flight Test Radio Coordinating Council (MCD) ... AFTRCC
Aerospace and Navigational Electronics (MCD) ... ANE
Aerospace Applications Studies Committee [*NATO*] (PDAA) ... AASC
Aerospace Audiovisual Service [*Air Force*] (MCD) ... AAVS
Aerospace Auxiliary Equipment [*NASA*] ... AAE
Aerospace Business Environment Simulator [*Computer-programmed management game*] ... ABES
Aerospace Cartographic and Geodetic Service ... ACGS
Aerospace Catalog Automated Microfilm, Inc. (MCD) ... ASCAM
Aerospace Center [*Defense Mapping Agency*] ... AC
Aerospace Command and Control System (SAA) ... ACCS
Aerospace Communication and Controls Division [*NASA*] (KSC) ... ACCD
Aerospace Communications ... AEROSPACECOM
Aerospace Communications Complex [*Air Force*] ... AIRCOM
Aerospace Communications Wing [*Air Force*] ... ACOMMW
Aerospace Computer Program [*Air Force*] ... ACP
Aerospace Computer Program Model [*Air Force*] (IAA) ... ACPM
Aerospace Contract Engineers (MCD) ... ACE
Aerospace Control [*Air Force*] (MCD) ... ASC
Aerospace Control Environment [*Air Force*] ... ACE
Aerospace Control Squadron [*Air Force*] ... ACONS
Aerospace Corp. (AAG) ... AC
Aerospace Corp., El Segundo, CA [*Library symbol Library of Congress*] (LCLS) ... CEsA
Aerospace Crew Equipment Development ... ACED
Aerospace Crew Equipment Laboratory [*Philadelphia, PA*] (MCD) ... ACEL
Aerospace Data Systems (MCD) ... ADS
Aerospace Data Systems Standard (SSD) ... ADSS
Aerospace Defense Command [*Formerly, Air Defense Command*] [*Air Force*] ... ADC
Aerospace Defense Command Region [*Military*] ... ADCOMR
Aerospace Defense Division [*Air Force*] ... ADD
Aerospace Defense Flight [*Air Force*] ... AERODF
Aerospace Defense Squadron [*Air Force*] ... AERODS
Aerospace Defense Systems Officer [*Air Force*] (AFM) ... ADSO
Aerospace Defense Wing [*Air Force*] ... AERODW
Aerospace Department Chairmen's Association (EA) ... ADCA
Aerospace Design and Development, Inc. (AAGC) ... ADD
Aerospace Digital Development ... ADD
Aerospace Division Commitment Record (SAA) ... ADCR
Aerospace Draftsman's Education and Proficiency Training (MCD) ... ADEPT
Aerospace Driver (GFGA) ... ASDE
Aerospace Education ... AE
Aerospace Education Association (EA) ... AEA
Aerospace Education Foundation (EA) ... AEF
Aerospace Education Instructor (AFM) ... AEI
Aerospace Education Workshop Project ... AEWP
Aerospace Electrical Division (SAA) ... AED
Aerospace Electrical Society (EA) ... AES
Aerospace Electronics Laboratories (MCD) ... AEL
Aerospace Electronics System (IAA) ... AES
Aerospace Engine Life Committee [*Air Force*] (AFIT) ... AELC
Aerospace Engineer (PGP) ... AE
Aerospace Engineering Process Institute ... AEPI
Aerospace Engineering Test Establishment [*Canada*] ... AETE
Aerospace Engineering Test Establishment, Canadian Forces Base Coal Lake, Medley, Alberta [*Library symbol National Library of Canada*] (NLC) ... AMECFA
Aerospace Environment (MCD) ... AE
Aerospace Environment Simulation System ... ASESS

Aerospace Environmental Support Unit [*Air Weather Service*] (IID) .... AESU
Aerospace Facilities Engineer .... AFE
Aerospace Flight Vehicle .... AFV
Aerospace Ground Equipment [*NASA*] .... AGE
Aerospace Ground Equipment Department .... AGED
Aerospace Ground Equipment Illustration [*Air Force*] (SAA) .... AGEI
Aerospace Ground Equipment Installation .... AGEI
Aerospace Ground Equipment Out of Commission for Parts [*Air Force*] .... AGEOCP
Aerospace Ground Equipment Out of Commission for Parts [*Air Force*] (SAA) .... AGEOP
Aerospace Ground Equipment Requirements Data .... AGERD
Aerospace Ground Equipment/Support Equipment (MCD) .... AGE/SE
Aerospace Ground Support Equipment .... AGSE
Aerospace Ground Unit .... AGU
Aerospace Group .... AG
Aerospace Guidance and Metrology Center [*Air Force*] (AFIT) .... AG
Aerospace Guidance and Metrology Center [*Newark Air Force Station, OH*] .... AG & MC
Aerospace Guidance and Metrology Center [*Air Force*] .... AGE
Aerospace Guidance and Metrology Center [*Newark Air Force Station, OH*] (AFM) .... AGMC
Aerospace Industrial Life Sciences Association [*of Aerospace Medical Association*] (MCD) .... AILSA
Aerospace Industrial Modernization .... AIM
Aerospace Industries Association of America (EA) .... AIA
Aerospace [*formerly, Aircraft*] **Industries Association of America** (MCD) .... AIAA
Aerospace Industries Association of Canada [*Association des Industries Aerospatiales du Canada*] [*Formerly, Air Industries Association of Canada*] (AC) .... AIAC
Aerospace Information Division [*Library of Congress*] .... AID
Aerospace Information Report [*SAE*] (AAGC) .... AIR
Aerospace [*or Aircraft*] **Installation Diagnostic Equipment** (KSC) .... AIDE
Aerospace Instrumentation Laboratory [*Air Force*] (MCD) .... AIL
Aerospace Instrumentation Range Station .... AESIR
Aerospace Intelligence Data System [*IBM Corp.*] (DIT) .... AIDS
Aerospace Intelligence File (CINC) .... AIF
Aerospace Intelligence Squadron [*Air Force*] .... AEROIS
Aerospace Intelligence Squadron [*Air Force*] .... AISq
Aerospace Internal Data Report [*Air Force*] (MCD) .... AIDR
Aerospace Maintenance and Development Unit (MCD) .... AMDU
Aerospace Maintenance and Operational Status (AFM) .... AMOS
Aerospace Maintenance and Regeneration Center [*Air Force*] .... AMARC
Aerospace Manufacturers Council [*Defunct*] (EA) .... AMC
Aerospace Material Specification (MCD) .... AMS
Aerospace Materials Document (MCD) .... AMD
Aerospace Materials Information .... AMI
Aerospace Materials Information Center [*Air Force*] (MCD) .... AMIC
Aerospace Materials Specifications (AAGC) .... AMS
Aerospace Mechanical Fastening Requirements (MCD) .... AMFR
Aerospace Medical Association (MCD) .... AMA
Aerospace Medical Association (EA) .... AsMA
Aerospace Medical Command [*Air Force*] .... AMC
Aerospace Medical Division [*Brooks Air Force Base, TX*] [*Air Force*] .... AMD
Aerospace Medical Laboratory (Clinical) [*Lackland Air Force Base, TX*] (MCD) .... AMLC
Aerospace Medical Operations Office [*NASA*] (KSC) .... AMOO
Aerospace Medical Research .... AMR
Aerospace Medical Research Laboratory [*Later, MRL*] [*Wright-Patterson Air Force Base, OH*] .... AMRL
Aerospace Medicine (MCD) .... AM
Aerospace Medicine and Biology .... AMB
Aerospace Multiple Station Analysis (MCD) .... AMSA
Aerospace Nuclear Safety Information Center (MCD) .... ANSIC
Aerospace Observation Platform .... AOP
Aerospace Photographic Reconnaissance Equipment .... APRE
Aerospace Plane .... ASP
Aerospace Planning Charts .... ASC
Aerospace Power Division [*Air Force*] .... APD
Aerospace Primus Club .... APC
Aerospace Products Division, SED Systems Ltd., Saskatoon, Saskatchewan [*Library symbol National Library of Canada*] (NLC) .... SSSEDA
Aerospace Program-Oriented Language [*Computer science*] (PDAA) .... APOL
Aerospace Radioisotope Power Information Center (KSC) .... ARPIC
Aerospace Recommended Practice (MCD) .... ARP
Aerospace Reconnaissance Technical Squadron [*Air Force*] .... ARTSq
Aerospace Reconnaissance Technical Wing (MCD) .... ARTW
Aerospace Recovery Facility (MCD) .... ARF
Aerospace Reference Project [*Formerly, ATP*] [*Library of Congress*] .... ARP
Aerospace Remote Calculator (MCD) .... ARC
Aerospace Rescue and Recovery .... ARR
Aerospace Rescue and Recovery Center [*Air Force*] (AFM) .... ARRC
Aerospace Rescue and Recovery Group [*Air Force*] .... ARRG
Aerospace Rescue and Recovery Group [*Air Force*] (AFM) .... ARRGp
Aerospace Rescue and Recovery Service [*Air Force*] (PDAA) .... AARS
Aerospace Rescue and Recovery Service [*Scott Air Force Base, IL*] (MCD) .... ARRS
Aerospace Rescue and Recovery Squadron [*Air Force*] .... AR & RSq
Aerospace Rescue and Recovery Squadron [*Air Force*] (AFM) .... ARRSq
Aerospace Rescue and Recovery Training Center [*Air Force*] (AFM) .... ARRTC
Aerospace Rescue and Recovery Wing [*Air Force*] (MCD) .... ARRW
Aerospace Rescue and Recovery Wing [*Air Force*] (AFM) .... ARRWg
Aerospace Research and Testing Committee (SAA) .... ARTC
Aerospace Research Applications Center [*Indiana University*] [*NASA*] .... ARAC
Aerospace Research Association (MCD) .... ARA
Aerospace Research Chamber .... ARC
Aerospace Research Laboratory [*Wright-Patterson Air Force Base, OH*] (AFM) .... ARL
Aerospace Research Pilot School [*Air Force*] .... ARPS
Aerospace Research Pilot School - Edwards Air Force Base [*Air Force*] .... ARPSE
Aerospace Research Satellite .... ARS
Aerospace Research Support Program [*Air Force*] .... ARSP
Aerospace Research USAF Test Pilot School [*Later, USAFTESTPLTSCH*] .... AEROSPRSCHPLTSCH
Aerospace Research Vehicle .... ARV
[*The*] **Aerospace Safety Advisory Panel** [*NASA/Air Force*] (NASA) .... ASAP
Aerospace Safety Research and Data Institute [*Lewis Research Center*] [*NASA*] .... ASRDI
Aerospace Security Force (AFM) .... ASF
Aerospace Services Division [*NASA*] (KSC) .... ASD
Aerospace Spin-Off Laboratory .... AEROSOL
Aerospace Standards .... AS
Aerospace Static Converter .... ASC
Aerospace Static Inverter .... ASI
Aerospace Structural Material .... ASM
Aerospace Structures Information and Analysis Center [*Wright-Patterson Ai r Force Base, OH*] [*Air Force*] (MCD) .... ASIAC
Aerospace Structures Test Facility [*Air Force*] .... ASTF
Aerospace Studies [*AFROTC*] (AFM) .... AS
Aerospace Studies Institute [*Air Force*] (MCD) .... ASI
Aerospace Support Equipment .... ASE
Aerospace Support Group [*Air Force*] .... AEROSG
Aerospace Support Squadron [*Air Force*] .... AEROSS
Aerospace Support Squadron [*Air Force*] .... AEROSSq
Aerospace Support Systems (MCD) .... ASS
Aerospace Surveillance and Control [*Air Force*] (AFM) .... AS & C
Aerospace Surveillance and Control Squadron [*Air Force*] .... ASCS
Aerospace Surveillance and Warning .... ASSAW
Aerospace Surveillance System .... ASS
Aerospace Surveillance Warning System (MCD) .... ASWS
Aerospace System Test and Evaluation Complex (KSC) .... ASTEC
Aerospace Systems Center [*Dayton, OH*] [*Air Force*] (MCD) .... ASC
Aerospace Systems, Inc. .... ASI
Aerospace Systems Safety Society (MCD) .... ASSS
Aerospace Systems Security Program (AFM) .... ASSP
Aerospace Systems Test Environment .... ASTE
Aerospace Systems Test Reactor [*Formerly, Aircraft Shield Test Reactor*] .... ASTR
Aerospace Technical Intelligence Center .... ATIC
Aerospace Technologist [*or Technology*] [*NASA*] .... AST
Aerospace Technology Division [*Formerly, Aerospace Information Division; later, ARP*] [*Library of Congress*] .... ATD
Aerospace Technology Division [*Formerly, Aerospace Information Division; later, ARP*]/Library of Congress (AFM) .... ATD/LC
Aerospace Test Equipment .... ATE
Aerospace Test Group (NASA) .... ASTG
Aerospace Test System (MCD) .... ATS
Aerospace Test Wing [*Air Force*] .... ASTW
Aerospace Test Wing [*Air Force*] (AFM) .... ASTWg
Aerospace Test Wing [*Air Force*] .... ATW
Aerospace Traffic Control Center .... ATCC
Aerospace Vehicle (KSC) .... ASV
Aerospace Vehicle (AFM) .... AV
Aerospace Vehicle Detection .... AVD
Aerospace Vehicle Distribution Office [*or Officer*] [*Air Force*] (AFM) .... AVDO
Aerospace Vehicle Electronics (MCD) .... AVE
Aerospace [*or Airborne*] **Vehicle Equipment** .... AVE
Aerospace Vehicle Interactive Design (MCD) .... AVID
Aerospace Vehicle Inventory, Status, and Utilization Reporting System .... AVISURS
Aerospace Vehicle Simulation (PDAA) .... AVS
Aerospace Vehicle System (MCD) .... AVS
Aerospace Warning and Control (MCD) .... ASWAC
Aerospatiale [*Societe Nationale Industrielle Aerospatiale*] [*France ICAO aircraft manufacturer identifier*] (ICAO) .... ND
Aerospatiale (SOCATA) Stark KG [*Germany ICAO aircraft manufacturer identifier*] (ICAO) .... TB
Aerospatiale [*Societe Nationale Industrielle Aerospatiale*] **(Sud Aviation)** [*France ICAO aircraft manufacturer identifier*] (ICAO) .... S
Aerospray [*Ionization*] [*Physics*] .... AS
Aerospun Cluster Munitions (MCD) .... ACM
Aerostar Airlines, Inc. [*ICAO designator*] (FAAC) .... FNT
Aerostar Owners Association (EA) .... AOA
Aerostat .... ARSTT
Aerosucre SA [*Colombia*] [*ICAO designator*] (FAAC) .... HRE
Aerosucre, SA [*Colombia*] [*FAA designator*] (FAAC) .... KRE
AeroSun International, Inc. [*ICAO designator*] (FAAC) .... ASI
Aerosuper AS de CV [*Mexico ICAO designator*] (FAAC) .... SUP
Aerosurface Amplifier (NASA) .... ASA
Aerosurface Control [*NASA*] (NASA) .... ASC
Aerosurface Driver/Monitor [*NASA*] (MCD) .... ASDM
Aerosurface End-to-End Test (MCD) .... AET
Aerosurface Position (NASA) .... ASP
Aerosurface Position Indicator (MCD) .... ASPI
Aerosurface Servo Amplifier [*NASA*] (NASA) .... ASA
Aerosurfaces (NASA) .... AERO
Aerotal Aerolineas Territoriales de Colombia Ltd. [*ICAO designator*] (FAAC) .... ART
Aerotamatan SA de CV [*Mexico ICAO designator*] (FAAC) .... TAA
Aerotaxi Casanare Ltda. [*Colombia*] [*ICAO designator*] (FAAC) .... ATK

Aerotaxi del Valle [Colombia] [ICAO designator] (FAAC) .... AOX
Aerotaxi Villa Rica, SA de CV [Mexico] [FAA designator] (FAAC) .... VRI
Aerotaxis Calzada SA de CV [Mexico ICAO designator] (FAAC) .... CLZ
Aerotaxis Corporativo SA de CV [Mexico ICAO designator] (FAAC) .... CRP
Aerotaxis de Aguascalientes SA de CV [Mexico ICAO designator] (FAAC) ..... GUA
Aerotaxis del Centro SA [Mexico ICAO designator] (FAAC) .... CTO
Aerotaxis del Golfo, SA de CV [Mexico] [FAA designator] (FAAC) ...... TGF
Aerotaxis Latinoamericanos SA de CV [Mexico ICAO designator] (FAAC) ...... LTI
Aerotaxis Pegaso SA de CV [Mexico ICAO designator] (FAAC) .... APG
Aerotec [Sociedade Aerotec Ltda.] [Brazil ICAO aircraft manufacturer identifier] (ICAO) .... T
Aerotherm Axisymmetric Transient Heating and Material Ablation [Program] .... ASTHMA
Aerotherm Prediction Procedure for LASER Effects (MCD) .... APPLE
Aerothermal Re-Entry Experiment (MCD) .... ARE
Aerothermodynamic Data Book [NASA] (NASA) .... ATDB
Aerothermodynamic Duct .... ATHODYD
Aerothermodynamic Elastic Vehicle .... AEV
Aerothermodynamic Integration Model .... AIM
Aerothermodynamic Structural Systems Environmental Test [Military] ..... ASSET
Aerothermodynamic Structural Vehicle [Air Force] .... ASV
Aerotours Dominican, C por A [Dominican Republic] [ICAO designator] (FAAC) .... ATD
Aerotranscolombiana de Carga Ltda. [Columbia] [FAA designator] (FAAC) .... TCO
Aerotransporte Peruanos Internacionales SA [Peru] [ICAO designator] (FAAC) .... APS
Aerotransportes Barlovento SA de CV [Mexico ICAO designator] (FAAC) ...... BLO
Aerotransportes Entre Rios SRL [Argentina ICAO designator] (FAAC) .... SFA
Aerotransportes Especiales Ltda. [Colombia] [ICAO designator] (FAAC) .... ATP
Aerotransportes Mas de Carga SA de CV [Mexico ICAO designator] (FAAC) .... MAA
Aerotransportes Privados SA de CV [Mexico ICAO designator] (FAAC) ...... PVA
Aerotronic Associate (IAA) .... AA
Aerotur SA [Mexico ICAO designator] (FAAC) .... TUR
Aerovaradero SA [Cuba] [FAA designator] (FAAC) .... AVY
Aerovekel SA [Mexico ICAO designator] (FAAC) .... VKL
Aeroventas SA [Mexico ICAO designator] (FAAC) .... AEV
Aerovia del Altiplano SA de CV [Mexico ICAO designator] (FAAC) .... APN
Aerovia Sud Americana .... ASUD
Aeroviajes Ejecuitvos SA de CV [Mexico ICAO designator] (FAAC) .... AVJ
Aerovial [Chile] [ICAO designator] (FAAC) .... AVL
Aerovias Bueno Ltd. [Colombia] [ICAO designator] (FAAC) .... ABU
Aerovias Caribe SA [Mexico ICAO designator] (FAAC) .... CBE
Aerovias Castillo SA [Mexico ICAO designator] (FAAC) CLL
Aerovias Condor de Colombia Ltda. [Condor Airlines of Colombia Ltd.] .... AEROCONDOR
Aerovias Condor de Colombia Ltda. (AEROCONDOR) [Colorado ICAO designator] (ICDA) .... OD
Aerovias Dap [Chile] [ICAO designator] (FAAC) .... DAP
Aerovias de Lagos SA de CV [Mexico ICAO designator] (FAAC) .... LAG
Aerovias de Mexico SA de CV [ICAO designator] (FAAC) .... AMX
Aerovias de Poniente SA de CV [Mexico ICAO designator] (FAAC) .... PNI
Aerovias del Atlantico Ltd. [Colombia] [ICAO designator] (FAAC) .... AOK
Aerovias Ecuatoriana SA .... AREA
Aerovias Especiales de Carga Ltda. [Colombia] [ICAO designator] (FAAC) .... AVESCA
Aerovias Especiales de Carga Ltda. [Colombia] [ICAO designator] (FAAC) .... VSC
Aerovias Interamericanas de Panama SA .... AVISPA
Aerovias Las Amricas, SA [Panama] [FAA designator] (FAAC) .... AVL
Aerovias Montes Azules, SA de CV [Mexico] [FAA designator] (FAAC) ...... MZL
Aerovias Nacionales de Colombia [Colombian National Airways] .... AVIANCA
Aerovias Oaxaquenas SA [Mexico ICAO designator] (FAAC) .... AVO
Aerovias Panama Airways .... APA
Aerovias Quisqueyana [Airlines] [Dominican Republic] [ICAO designator] (OAG) .... QQ
Aerovias Venezolanas Sociedad Anonima [Airline] [Venezuela] .... AVENSA
Aerovias Xalitic SA de CV [Mexico ICAO designator] (FAAC) .... XAL
Aerovilla Ltda. [Columbia] [FAA designator] (FAAC) .... VVG
Aerovironment, Inc. .... AV
Aerovitro SA de CV [Mexico ICAO designator] (FAAC) .... VRO
Aerovox, Inc. [Associated Press] (SAG) .... Aerovx
Aerovox, Inc. [NASDAQ symbol] (SAG) .... ARVX
Aes [Obverse] [Numismatics] .... AE
AES China Generating Co. [Associated Press] (SAG) ...... AES Chn
AES China Generating Co. [NASDAQ symbol] (SAG) .... CHGN
AES China Generating Co. [NASDAQ symbol] (SAG) .... CHGN
AES China Generating'A' [NASDAQ symbol] (TTSB) .... CHGNF
AES Corp. [NYSE symbol] (SAG) .... AES
AES Corp. [Associated Press] (SAG) .... AES Cp
AES Corp. [NASDAQ symbol] (SAG) .... AESC
AES Regina Weather Office, Environment Canada [Bureau Meteorologique du SEA de Regina, Environnement Canada] Saskatchewan [Library symbol National Library of Canada] (NLC) .... SREAE
Aeschines [c. 397-322BC] [Classical studies] (OCD) .... Aeschin
Aeschylus [Greek poet, 525-456BC] [Classical studies] (ROG) .... AESCH
Aesculapian Club (EA) .... AC
Aesculapius International Medicine (EA) .... AIM
Aesop (BARN) .... Aes
Aesthete (ABBR) .... AESTH
Aesthetic .... ASTHTC
Aesthetic Realism Foundation (EA) .... ARF
Aesthetically (ABBR) .... AESTHY
Aestheticians International Association (EA) .... AIA
Aesthetics .... AESTH
Aesthetics and Visual Literacy Council [Australia] .... AVLC

Aetas [or Aetatis] [Age or Aged] [Latin] .... aet
Aetatis [Age] [Latin] .... AE
Aetatis [Age] [Latin] .... AETAT
Aethelred [King of England] (ILCA) .... Athlr
Aether [Ether] (ROG) .... AETH
Aetherius Society (EA) .... AS
Aethestan [King of England, 895-940] (ILCA) .... As
Aetia [of Callimachus] [Classical studies] (OCD) .... Aet
Aetiology [or Etiology] [Medicine] (DAVI) .... Aet
Aetiology [or Etiology] [Medicine] (DAVI) .... aetiol
Aetna Capital 9.50%'MIPS' [NYSE symbol] (TTSB) .... AETPrA
Aetna Capital LLC [NYSE symbol] (SAG) .... AET
Aetna Capital LLC, Inc. [Associated Press] (SAG) .... AetnaC
Aetna, Inc. [NYSE symbol] (SAG) .... AET
Aetna, Inc. [Associated Press] (SAG) .... Aetna Inc
Aetna Life & Casualty [NYSE symbol] (TTSB) .... AET
Aetna Life & Casualty Co. [NYSE symbol] (SAG) .... AET
Aetna Life & Casualty Co. [Associated Press] (SAG) ...... AetnLf
Aetna Life Insurance Co. of Canada [Toronto Stock Exchange symbol] .... ALI
Aetna Telecommunications Consultants [Centerville, MA] [Telecommunications] (TSSD) .... ATC
Aetrium, Inc. [Associated Press] (SAG) .... Aetrium
Aetrium, Inc. [NASDAQ symbol] (SAG) .... ATRM
Afan Cooperative Development Agency [British] .... ACDA
Afar Liberation Front [Ethiopia] (PD) .... ALF
Afar Locality [Paleoanthropology] .... AL
Afareaitu [Society Islands] [Seismograph station code, US Geological Survey] (SEIS) .... AFR
AFC Cable Systems [Associated Press] (SAG) .... AFC Cbl
AFC Cable Systems [NASDAQ symbol] (SAG) .... AFCX
Afebrile [Free from fever] [Medicine] (DAVI) .... afeb
Afebrile, Vital Signs Stable [Medicine] (DAVI) .... AFVSS
Afebrile, Vital Signs Stable [Medicine] (DAVI) .... AVSS
Affability (ABBR) .... AFBT
Affable (ABBR) .... AFB
Affably (ABBR) .... AFBY
Affair .... AFFR
Affair .... AFFR
Affaires des Anciens Combattants du Canada [Department of Canadian Veterans Affairs - DVA] .... AACC
Affaires Exterieures Canada [External Affairs Canada] ...... AEC
Affairs (AFM) .... AFF
Affect .... A
Affect .... AFCT
Affect Adjective Check List [Psychology] .... AACL
Affect Elaboration [Scale] [Psychology] .... AE
Affectation (ABBR) .... AFCTAN
Affected (ABBR) .... AFCTD
Affected Areas .... AA
Affected Pair Method [Statistics] .... APM
Affectedly (ABBR) .... AFCTDY
Affected-Pedigree-Member [Technique for genetic study] .... APM
Affecting (ABBR) .... AFCTG
Affecting (ROG) .... AFF
Affectingly (ABBR) .... AFCTGY
Affection (ABBR) .... AFCTN
Affectionate (ABBR) .... AFCTNA
Affectionate (ABBR) .... AFCTNT
Affectionate (ADA) .... AFFEC
Affectionate [Correspondence] (ROG) .... AFFTE
Affectionately (ABBR) .... AFCTNAY
Affectionately (ABBR) .... AFCTNTY
Affectionately [Correspondence] .... AFF
Affectionately [Correspondence] (ROG) .... AFFECTLY
Affectionately [Correspondence] (ROG) .... AFFLY
Affectionately [Correspondence] (ROG) .... AFFY
Affective Perception Inventory [Student personality test] ...... API
Affective Sensitivity Scale .... ASS
Affective Spectrum Disorder [Psychiatry] (ECON) .... ASD
Affective System .... AS
Affective Work Competencies Inventory (EDAC) .... AWCI
Affects Balance Scale [Personality development test] [Psychology] ...... ABS
Affenpinscher Club of America [Later, AAA] .... ACA
Afferent [Medicine] .... AFF
Afferent Pupillary Defect [Ophthalmology] (DAVI) .... APD
Affettuoso [With Expression] [Music] .... AFFET
Affettuoso [With Expression] [Music] .... AFFETT
Affettuoso [With Expression] [Music] .... AFFETTO
Affezionatissimo [Very Tenderly, Pathetically] [Music] (ROG) .... AFFMO
Affidavit .... AFDVT
Affidavit [Legal term] (DLA) .... AFFI
Affidavit .... AFFT
Affiliate .... AFFIL
Affiliate (MUGU) .... AFFL
Affiliate .... AFFLT
Affiliate Artists (EA) .... AA
Affiliate Assembly [American Association of School Librarians] .... AA
Affiliate, Association of Medical Secretaries, Practice Administrators, and Receptionists [British] (DBQ) .... AMS(Aff)
Affiliate of the Company Directors' Association of Australia ...... ACDA
Affiliate of the Institute of Plumbing [British] (DBQ) .... AffIP
Affiliate of the Institute of Sales Management [British] (DI) .... AffInstSM
Affiliate of the Institution of Works and Highways Technician Engineers [British] (DBQ) .... AffIWHTE
Affiliate of the Royal Society of Health [British] .... Affil RSH

Affiliate of the Society of Licensed Aircraft Engineers and Technologists [*British*] (DBQ) .... AffilSLAET
Affiliated (ADA) .... AFF
Affiliated .... AFFLTD
Affiliated Advertising Agencies International (EA) 3AI
Affiliated Advertising Agencies International [*Aurora, CO*] (EA) .... AAAI
Affiliated Boards of Officials (EA) .... ABO
Affiliated Chiropodists-Podiatrists of America (EA) .... ACPA
Affiliated Community Bancorp [*NASDAQ symbol*] (TTSB) .... AFCB
Affiliated Community Bancorp, Inc. [*NASDAQ symbol*] (SAG) .... AFCB
Affiliated Community Bancorp, Inc. [*Associated Press*] (SAG) .... AffCom
Affiliated Computer Services, Inc. [*NASDAQ symbol*] (SAG) .... ACSA
Affiliated Computer Services, Inc. [*Associated Press*] (SAG) .... AffCmpS
Affiliated Computer Services'A' [*NASDAQ symbol*] (TTSB) .... ACSA
Affiliated Computer Systems [*Later, MPEC Co.*] [*Telecommunications*] (TSSD) .... ACS
Affiliated Conference of Practicing Accountants International [*Later, ACPA*] (EA) .... ACPAI
Affiliated Dress Manufacturers (EA) .... ADM
Affiliated Drug Stores (EA) .... ADS
Affiliated Employers of California (SRA) .... AEC
Affiliated Government Employees' Distributing Co. [*California*] .... AGE
Affiliated Inventors Foundation (EA) .... AIF
Affiliated Leadership League of and for the Blind of America (EA) .... ALL
Affiliated Medical Research, Inc. [*Research code symbol*] .... AMR
Affiliated National Coaches Council (EA) .... ANCC
Affiliated National Riding Commission (EA) .... ANRC
Affiliated Nutritional Retailers Association [*Commercial firm*] (EA) .... ANRA
Affiliated Warehouse Companies (EA) .... AWC
Affiliated Woodcarvers Ltd. (EA) .... AFWC
Affiliation .... AFFILTN
Affiliation Code [*IRS*] .... AFC
Affiliation of Author [*Online database field identifier*] .... AF
Affiliation of First Author [*Used to define searchable field*] (NITA) .... AF
Affiliation of Multicultural Societies & Service Agencies of BC (AC) .... AMSSA
Affiliation Officer [*British*] .... AO
Affiliation Testing Program [*for Catholic secondary schools*] (AEBS) .... ATP
Affinely Connected Space .... ACS
Affinis [*Having an Affinity with but Not Identical To*] [*Latin*] (MAE) .... aff
Affinity Teleproductions, Inc. [*Associated Press*] (SAG) .... AffinTel
Affinity [*Laboratory analysis*] .... Affin
Affinity Capillary Electrophoresis [*An enzyme*] .... ACE
Affinity Chromatography [*Biopharmaceutical Purification*] .... AC
Affinity Column [*Chromatography*] .... Aff
Affinity Cross-Flow Filtration .... ACFF
Affinity Entertainment, Inc. [*Associated Press*] (SAG) .... AffinEnt
Affinity Entertainment, Inc. [*NASDAQ symbol*] (SAG) .... AFTY
Affinity Technology Gp [*NASDAQ symbol*] (TTSB) .... AFFI
Affinity Technology Group, Inc. [*NASDAQ symbol*] (SAG) .... AFFI
Affinity Technology Group, Inc. [*Associated Press*] (SAG) .... AffTech
Affinity Teleproductions, Inc. [*NASDAQ symbol*] (SAG) .... AFTY
Affinity-Based-Collection [*Immunoassay*] .... ABC
Affirmation [*Linguistics*] .... A
Affirmation (ROG) .... AFFRMN
Affirmation Book [*Self-help advice*] .... AFFIE
Affirmation: United Methodists for Lesbian/Gay Concerns (EA) .... AUMLGC
Affirmative .... AFF
Affirmative (AABC) .... AFIRM
Affirmative [*ICAO designator*] (FAAC) .... AFM
Affirmative Acknowledge [*Computer Science*] (NITA) .... ACK
Affirmative Action [*Employment policies for minorities*] .... AA
Affirmative Action Compliance Manual [*BNA*] [*A publication*] (AAGC) .... AACM
Affirmative Action Coordinating Center [*Defunct*] (EA) .... AACC
Affirmative Action Employer (MEDA) .... AAE
Affirmative Action Plan [*or Program*] [*Equal opportunity employment*] .... AAP
Affirmative Action Planning Guide [*Executive Telecom System, Inc.*] [*Information service or system*] (CRD) .... AAPG
Affirmative Action Program Plans [*DoD*] .... AAPP
Affirmative Fair Housing Marketing Regulations [*Department of Housing and Urban Development*] (GFGA) .... AFHM
Affirmative Flag [*Navy British*] .... AF
Affirmative Marketing Agreement [*Business term*] (EMRF) .... AMA
Affirmative Poll Response State (IAA) .... APRS
Affirmative Replies Neither Required nor Desired (MUGU) .... NOAFIRM
Affirmed (DLA) .... A
Affirmed .... AFFD
Affirmed [*or Affirming*] **on Rehearing** [*Legal term*] (DLA) .... Aff Reh
Affirming (ROG) .... AFF
Affirming .... AFFG
Affirmist Society [*Defunct*] (EA) .... AS
Affix [*Linguistics*] .... A
Affix [*Linguistics*] .... AF
Afflizione [*Afflictedly*] [*Music*] (ROG) .... AFFLIZ
Affluent .... AFFL
Afford Service Member Opportunity to Apply for Ordinary Leave [*Army*] (AABC) .... ASMOLV
Affordable Basic Floppy Disk [*Computer science*] (MHDI) .... ABFD
Affordable Housing Action Group (AC) .... AHAG
Affordable Housing Management Association - Pacific Southwest (SRA) .... AHMA-PSW
Affordable Housing Program [*Federal Home Loan Bank*] .... AHP
Affray [*FBI standardized term*] .... AFFR
Affretair [*Zimbabwe*] [*ICAO designator*] (FAAC) .... AFM
Affrettando [*Hurrying the Pace*] [*Music*] .... AFFRET
Affrettando [*Tenderly*] [*Music*] [*Italian*] [*Music*] (BARN) .... affrett

Affrettando [*Hurrying the Pace*] [*Music*] .... AFFRETTO
Affymetrix, Inc. [*NASDAQ symbol*] (SAG) .... AFFX
Affymetrix, Inc. [*Associated Press*] (SAG) .... Affymet
Afghan Border Crusade [*Later, NWFF*] (EA) .... ABC
Afghan Community in America (EA) .... ACA
Afghan Hound Club of America (EA) .... AHCA
Afghan National Movement Party [*Political party*] (EY) .... ANMP
Afghan Refugee Aid Committee (AC) .... ARAC
Afghan Refugee Fund (EA) .... ARF
Afghan Refugee Information Network [*British Defunct*] .... ARIN
Afghan Tourist Organization (MENA) .... ATO
Afghan Youth Council in America (EA) .... AYCA
Afghani [*Monetary unit*] [*Afghanistan*] .... AF
Afghani .... AFG
Afghanistan [*MARC geographic area code Library of Congress*] (LCCP) .... a-af--
Afghanistan [*ANSI two-letter standard code*] (CNC) .... AF
Afghanistan [*MARC country of publication code Library of Congress*] (LCCP) .... af
Afghanistan [*ANSI three-letter standard code*] (CNC) .... AFG
Afghanistan .... AFGH
Afghanistan (VRA) .... Afgh
Afghanistan Information Center [*Later, ASAP*] (EA) .... AIC
Afghanistan National Liberation Front .... ANLF
Afghanistan Relief Committee (EA) .... ARC
Afghanistan Studies Association (EA) .... ASA
Afghanite [*A zeolite*] .... AFG
AFGL International, Inc. [*NASDAQ symbol*] (SAG) .... AFGL
AFGL Intl. [*NASDAQ symbol*] (TTSB) .... AFGL
Afiamalu [*Samoa Islands*] [*Seismograph station code, US Geological Survey*] (SEIS) .... AFI
AFLAC, Inc. [*NYSE symbol*] (SPSG) .... AFL
AFLAC, Inc. [*Associated Press*] (SAG) .... AFLAC
Aflatoxicol [*Metabolite of AFB*] [*Biochemistry*] .... AFL
Aflatoxin [*A toxic factor*] [*Biochemistry*] (DAVI) .... AF
Aflatoxin [*Mycotoxin*] [*Generic form*] .... AFT
Aflatoxin B [*Mycotoxin*] .... AFB
Aflatoxin G [*Mycotoxin*] .... AFG
Aflatoxin M [*Mycotoxin*] .... AFM
Aflatoxin P [*Mycotoxin*] .... AFP
Aflatoxin Q [*Mycotoxin*] .... AFQ
Afloat Command and Control System (CAAL) .... ACCS
Afloat Communications Management Office [*Naval Ship Engineering Center*] (IEEE) .... ACMO
Afloat Consumption Cost and Effectiveness Surveillance System [*Navy*] .... ACCESS
Afloat Correlation System [*Navy*] .... ACS
Afloat Intelligence System Manager Overview (DOMA) .... AISMO
Afloat Planning System [*Navy*] (DOMA) .... APS
Afloat Prepositioned Ship [*Navy*] (DOMA) .... APS
Afloat Prepositioning Force (DOMA) .... APF
AFloat Prepositioning Ship (DOMA) .... AFS
Afloat Supply Systems Improvement and Support Team (MCD) .... ASSIST
Afluidal Variant [*Bacteriology*] .... AFV
Afobaka [*Surinam*] [*ICAO location identifier*] (ICLI) .... SMAF
Afore [*Papua New Guinea*] [*Airport symbol*] (OAG) .... AFR
Aforesaid .... AFSD
AFOS [*Automation of Field Operations and Services*] **Regional Representative** [*National Weather Service*] (NOAA) .... ARR
AFP Imaging [*NASDAQ symbol*] (TTSB) .... AFPC
AFP Imaging Corp. [*Associated Press*] (SAG) .... AFP
AFP Imaging Corp. [*NASDAQ symbol*] (NQ) .... AFPC
AFPS Forecast Working Group (USDC) .... AFWG
Africa .... AA
Africa .... AF
Africa .... AFR
Africa (VRA) .... Afr
Africa [*MARC geographic area code Library of Congress*] (LCCP) .... f-----
Africa Air Links [*Sierra Leone*] [*ICAO designator*] (FAAC) .... AFK
Africa and Asia .... AFRASIA
Africa, Central [*MARC geographic area code Library of Congress*] (LCCP) .... fc----
Africa Church Information Service (EAIO) .... ACIS
Africa Circle and Correspondence Association for Thematicists (EAIO) .... AC & CAT
Africa Committee [*British World War II*] .... A
Africa Community Technical Service [*Formerly, Red Sea Desert Development*] (AC) .... ACTS
Africa Diary [*A publication*] .... AD
Africa, East [*MARC geographic area code Library of Congress*] (LCCP) .... fe----
Africa Educational Trust [*British*] .... AET
Africa, Equatorial [*MARC geographic area code Library of Congress*] (LCCP) .... fq----
Africa (Ethiopia) Committee [*British World War II*] .... A(E)
Africa Evangelical Fellowship (EA) .... AEF
Africa Faith and Justice Network (EA) .... AFJN
[*The*] Africa Fund (EA) .... AF
Africa Guild [*Defunct*] (EA) .... AG
Africa Inland Mission International (EAIO) .... AIM
Africa Inland Transport [*British World War II*] .... A(IT)
Africa - Middle East Theater [*World War II*] .... AMET
Africa Music International [*Lorient, France*] (EAIO) .... AMI
Africa Network [*An association*] (EA) .... AN
Africa News Service (EA) .... AFRICA NEWS
Africa, North [*MARC geographic area code Library of Congress*] (LCCP) .... ff----
Africa Project Development Facility [*United Nations*] (EY) .... APDF
Africa Publications Trust [*British*] .... APT
Africa Report [*A publication*] (BRI) .... Afr Rep

Africa Report [*A publication*] ..... Afr Rpt
Africa Research and Publications Project (EA) ..... ARPP
Africa Research Bulletin [*A publication*] ..... ARB
Africa Resources Trust ..... ART
Africa Service Institute of New York [*Defunct*] ..... ASI
Africa South of the Sahara [*A publication*] ..... AFSS
Africa South of the Sahara [*Military*] (EA) ..... ASOTS
Africa, Southern [*MARC geographic area code Library of Congress*] (LCCP) ..... fs----
Africa, Sub-Saharan [*MARC geographic area code Library of Congress*] (LCCP) ..... fb----
Africa Today [*A publication*] (BRI) ..... Africa T
Africa Travel Association (EA) ..... ATA
Africa Watch [*An association*] (EA) ..... AW
Africa, West [*MARC geographic area code Library of Congress*] (LCCP) ..... fw----
Africair Service [*Senegal*] [*ICAO designator*] (FAAC) ..... FFB
African [*Derogatory nickname for blacks in Zimbabwe and South Africa*] ..... Af
African ..... AFRCN
African Adult Education Association [*Later, AALAE*] (EAIO) ..... AAEA
African Affairs [*A publication*] ..... AA
African Airlines Association [*Kenya*] (AF) ..... AFRAA
African Airlines International Ltd. [*Kenya*] [*ICAO designator*] (FAAC) ..... AIK
African American Family History Association (EA) ..... AAFHA
African American Museums Association (EA) ..... AAMA
African American Review [*A publication*] (BRI) ..... Afr Am R
African American Study of Kidney Diseases and Hypertension Pilot Study (DMAA) ..... AASK
African and Mauritian Union of Development Banks (EAIO) ..... AMUDB
African Anti-Colonial Movement of Kenya ..... AACM
African Association for Biological Nitrogen-Fixation [*Egypt*] (EAIO) ..... AABNF
African Association for Literacy and Adult Education (EA) ..... AALAE
African Association for the Study of Liver Diseases (EAIO) ..... AASLD
African Association of Cartography (EA) ..... AAC
African Association of Education for Development (EAIO) ..... AFASED
African Association of Tax Administrators (EAIO) ..... AATA
African Bank [*South Africa*] ..... AFBANK
African Bar Association (EAIO) ..... ABA
African Bibliographic Center (EA) ..... ABC
African Bibliographic Center, Washington, DC [*Library symbol Library of Congress*] (LCLS) ..... DABC
African Biosciences Network [*International Council of Scientific Unions*] ..... ABN
African Capacity Building Foundation (ECON) ..... ACBF
African, Caribbean, and Pacific Countries [*Associated with the EEC*] (AF) ..... ACP
African Cassanova Mosaic Disease [*Botany*] ..... ACMD
African Cavalry Guard [*British military*] (DMA) ..... ACG
African Centre for Applied Research and Training in Social Development (EAIO) ..... ACARTSD
African Centre for Technology Studies [*Kenya*] (EAIO) ..... ACTS
African Civil Aviation Commission [*See also CAFAC*] (EAIO) ..... AFCAC
African Coastal Security (DOMA) ..... ACS
African Coasters [*Steamship*] (MHDB) ..... AC
African Colonial Forces [*British military*] (DMA) ..... ACF
African Commission on Agricultural Statistics (EA) ..... ACAS
African Commission on Agricultural Statistics [*Ghana*] (EAIO) ..... AFCAS
African Commune of Bad Relevant Artists [*Chicago*] ..... AFRICOBRA
African Communications Liaison Service (EA) ..... ACLS
African Comprehensive Party [*Jamaica*] [*Political party*] (EY) ..... ACP
African Confederation of Cooperative Savings and Credit Associations [*See also ACECA*] [*Nairobi, Kenya*] (EAIO) ..... ACCOSCA
African Continental Bank Ltd. ..... ACB
African Cooperative Savings and Credit Association [*See also ACECA*] [*Later, ACCOSCA*] (EAIO) ..... ACOSCA
African Cultural Foundation (EA) ..... ACF
African Curriculum Organisation (AIE) ..... ACO
African Democratic Party [*Political party*] ..... ADP
African Development [*A publication*] ..... AFD
African Development Bank [*Also, AfDB*] ..... ADB
African Development Bank [*Also, ADB*] (EY) ..... AfDB
African Development Bank (USGC) ..... AFDB
African Development Foundation (EGAO) ..... ADF
African Development Fund ..... AFDF
African Economic Affairs Committee [*London*] [*World War II*] ..... AEA
African Economic Development News [*Kenya*] [*A publication*] (EY) ..... AEDN
African Economic Research Consortium ..... AERC
African Economic Research Consortium ..... AERC
African Elected Members Organization ..... AEMO
African Elephant and Rhino Specialist Group [*of the International Union for Conservation of Nature and Natural Resources*] (EA) ..... AERSG
African Elephant Conservation Coordinating Group ..... AECCG
African Export Import Bank ..... AFREXIMBANK
African Farmers Committee [*See also CPA*] (EAIO) ..... AFC
African Football Confederation (EAIO) ..... AFC
African Force Headquarters [*World War II*] ..... AFHQ
African Forestry Commission [*UN Food and Agriculture Organization*] ..... AFC
African Graduate Fellowship Program [*African-American Institute*] (AEBS) ..... AFGRAD
African Green Monkey Immunodeficiency Virus ..... AGMIV
African Green Monkey Kidney [*Type of cell line*] ..... AGMK
African Green Monkey Kidney [*Type of cell line*] [*Medicine*] (DMAA) ..... AGMkK
African Green Monkeys [*Virology*] ..... AGM
African Groundnut Council [*See also CAA*] [*Nigeria*] ..... AGC
African Heritage Center for African Dance and Music (EA) ..... AHCADM
African Heritage Federation of the Americas [*Defunct*] (EA) ..... AHFA
African Heritage Studies Association (EA) ..... AHSA
African Horse Sickness [*Medicine*] (DMAA) ..... AHS
African Horsesickness Virus [*Veterinary medicine*] ..... AHSV
African Household Survey Capability Programme [*United Nations*] (EY) ..... AHSCP
African Human Rights Research Association [*Formerly, African Human Rights Study Group*] (EA) ..... AHRA
African Imprint Library Services, Bedford, NY [*Library symbol Library of Congress*] (LCLS) ..... Afrl
African India Ocean Region [*USTTA*] (TAG) ..... AFI
African/Indian Ocean [*Aviation*] ..... AFI
African Institute of Human Rights (EAIO) ..... AIHR
African International Airlines [*Lesotho*] [*ICAO designator*] (FAAC) ..... AFN
African International Airways [*Swaziland*] [*ICAO designator*] (FAAC) ..... AIN
African International Airways (West Africa) Ltd. [*Nigeria*] [*FAA designator*] (FAAC) ..... ROB
African International Movement of Catholic Students (EA) ..... AIMCS
African International Reservation System (PDAA) ..... AIRS
African Jazz Art Society Studios ..... AJASS
African Journal of Medical Practice [*A publication*] ..... AJMP
African Journal of the Health Sciences [*A publication*] ..... AJHS
African Language Review [*A publication*] ..... ALR
African Law Association in America [*Later, INTWORLSA*] (EA) ..... ALAA
African Law Digest [*A publication*] (ILCA) ..... African LD
African Law Reports [*A publication*] (DLA) ..... Afr LR
African Law Reports, Appellate Division [*A publication*] (DLA) ..... AD
African Law Reports, Commercial Series [*A publication*] (DLA) ..... African LR Comm
African Law Reports, Malawi Series [*A publication*] (DLA) ..... Afr LR Mal Ser
African Law Reports, Malawi Series [*A publication*] (DLA) ..... African LR Mal
African Law Reports, Malawi Series [*A publication*] (DLA) ..... ALR Mal
African Law Reports, Malawi Series [*A publication*] (DLA) ..... ALR (Malawi Ser)
African Law Reports, Sierra Leone Series [*A publication*] (DLA) ..... Afr LR Sierre L Ser
African Law Reports, Sierra Leone Series [*A publication*] (DLA) ..... African LRSL
African Law Reports, Sierra Leone Series [*A publication*] (DLA) ..... ALR (Sierra L Ser)
African Law Reports, Sierra Leone Series [*A publication*] (DLA) ..... ALRSL
African Law Studies [*A publication*] (DLA) ..... Af L Studies
African Library [*Belgium Ministry of Foreign Affairs*] [*Information service or system*] (CRD) ..... AFLI
African Literature Association (EA) ..... ALA
African Love Bird Society (EA) ..... ALBS
African Mathematical Union (EA) ..... AMU
African Medical and Research Foundation (EA) ..... AMRF
African Medical and Research Foundation, USA (EA) ..... AMREF
African Methodist Episcopal [*Church*] ..... AME
African Methodist Episcopal Mission ..... AMEM
African Methodist Episcopal Zion [*Church*] ..... AMEZ
African National Congress [*South Africa*] (PD) ..... ANC
African National Congress of South Africa ..... ANCSA
African National Congress Youth League [*South Africa*] (PD) ..... ANCYL
African National Council [*Later, UANC*] [*Zimbabwe*] [*Political party*] (PPW) ..... ANC
African National People's Empire Re-Established (EA) ..... AFANPERA
African Nationalist Pioneer Movement [*Defunct*] ..... ANPM
African Nations' Cup [*Soccer*] ..... ANC
African Network of Administrative Information [*Information service or system*] (IID) ..... ANAI
African Network of Scientific and Technological Institutes [*Kenya*] [*Research center*] ..... ANSTI
African NGOs [*Nongovernmental Organizations*] **Environment Network** (EAIO) ..... ANEN
African Notes [*Ibadan*] [*A publication*] ..... AN
African Organization of Supreme Audit Institutions [*Lome, Togo*] (EAIO) ..... AFROSAI
African Peanut (Groundnut) Council ..... APC
African People's Democratic Union of South Africa (PD) ..... Apdusa
African People's Movement [*British*] ..... APM
African People's Organization (WDAA) ..... APO
African People's Party [*Kenya*] (AF) ..... APP
African Refugee Housing Action Group [*British*] ..... ARHAG
African Region Traffic Analysis Forecasting Group [*ICAO*] (DA) ..... ATAFG
African Regional Agricultural Credit Association (EAIO) ..... AFRACA
African Regional Centre for Engineering Design and Manufacturing (EA) ..... ARCEDEM
African Regional Centre for Technology [*See also CRAT*] (EA) ..... ARCT
African Regional Organization for Standardization [*Kenya*] ..... ARSO
African Regional Trade Information System [*ECA*] [*United Nations*] (DUND) ..... ARTIS
African Research Foundation (EA) ..... ARF
African Research Institute [*La Trobe University*] [*Australia*] ..... ARI
African Resistance Movement [*South Africa*] (PD) ..... ARM
African Rhino Group (EA) ..... ARG
African Safari Airways Ltd. [*Kenya*] [*ICAO designator*] (FAAC) ..... QSC
African Safari Club of Philadelphia (EA) ..... ASCP
African Satellite ..... AFROSAT
African Scholarship Program of American Universities [*Joint undertaking, headquartered in Cambridge, MA, to provide aid to African applicants for admission to American universities*] ..... ASPAU
African Scientific Institute (EA) ..... ASI
African Social and Environmental Studies Programme [*Formerly, African Social Studies Programme*] [*Kenya*] (EAIO) ..... ASSP
African Social Studies Programme (EA) ..... ASSP
African Society for Human Rights [*Defunct*] (EA) ..... ASHR
African Star [*Decoration*] [*British*] ..... AS
African Starvation and Hunger Relief Fund (EA) ..... ASHRF
African Studies [*Johannesburg*] [*A publication*] ..... AFS

African Studies and Research Program [*Howard University*] [*Research center*] (RCD) ..... ASRP
African Studies Association (EA) ..... ASA
African Studies Association, Brandeis University, Waltham, MA [*Library symbol Library of Congress*] (LCLS) ..... MWalAF
African Studies Association United Kingdom ..... ASAUK
African Studies Center [*Michigan State University*] [*Research center*] (RCD) ..... ASC
African Succulent Plant Society [*Defunct*] (EA) ..... ASPS
African Swine Fever [*Veterinary medicine*] ..... ASF
African Swine Pox [*Medicine*] (DMAA) ..... ASP
African Timber Organization (EAIO) ..... ATO
African Trade Union Confederation [*Later, OATUU*] ..... ATUC
African Trades Union Congress of Southern Rhodesia ..... ATUC(SR)
African Transair [*Nigeria*] [*FAA designator*] (FAAC) ..... FTS
African Union of Physics [*See also UAP*] (EAIO) ..... AUP
African Violet Association of Australia ..... AVAA
African Violet Society of America (EA) ..... AVSA
African West Air [*Senegal*] [*ICAO designator*] (FAAC) ..... AFC
African West Air [*Senegal*] [*ICAO designator*] (FAAC) ..... AWA
African Wildlife Foundation (EA) ..... AWF
African Wildlife Leadership Foundation ..... AWLF
African Workers Federation [*Kenya*] (AF) ..... AWF
African Writers Series [*A publication*] ..... AWS
Africana Bulletin [*Warsaw*] [*A publication*] ..... AB
Africana Bulletin [*Warsaw*] [*A publication*] ..... Africana
African-American Almanac [*A publication*] ..... AAA
African-American English [*A dialect*] ..... AAE
African-American Historical and Cultural Society (EA) ..... AAHCS
African-American Institute (EA) ..... AAI
African-American Labor Center (EA) ..... AALC
African-American Library and Information Science Association ..... AALISA
African-American Natural Foods Association (EA) ..... AANFA
African-American Reference Library [*A publication*] ..... AARL
African-American Scholars Conference [*Defunct*] (EA) ..... AASC
African-Atlantic Coast Association of Round Tables ..... AACART
African-Canadian Council (AC) ..... ACC
Africanized Honey Bee ..... AHB
Afrihili [*MARC language code Library of Congress*] (LCCP) ..... afh
Afrikaans [*MARC language code Library of Congress*] (LCCP) ..... afr
Afrikaans ..... AFRIK
Afrikaner Volkfront [*An association*] ..... AVF
Afrikaner Weerstandsbeweging [*Afrikaner Resistance Movement*] [*South Africa*] [*Political party*] (ECON) ..... AWB
Afrique Equatoriale Francaise [*French Equatorial Africa*] [*French*] (AF) ..... AEF
Afrique Occidentale Francaise [*French West Africa*] [*French*] ..... AOF
Afriwest Airlines Ltd. [*Nigeria*] [*FAA designator*] (FAAC) ..... AFW
Afro International Ent. Ltd. [*Nigeria*] [*FAA designator*] (FAAC) ..... AOR
Afro Unity Airways [*Benin*] [*ICAO designator*] (FAAC) ..... AFU
Afro-American Art Institute ..... AAAI
Afro-American Association of Performing Artists (EA) ..... AAAPA
Afro-American Cultural and Historical Society [*Later, AACHSM*] ..... AACHS
Afro-American Cultural and Historical Society Museum (EA) ..... AACHSM
Afro-American Cultural Foundation (EA) ..... AACF
Afro-American Cultural Technological Scientific Olympics ..... ACT-SO
Afro-American Historical and Genealogical Society (EA) ..... AAHGS
Afro-American Museum of Detroit ..... AAM
Afro-American Music Foundation (EA) ..... AAMF
Afro-American Music Opportunities Association (EA) ..... AAMOA
Afro-American Police League (EA) ..... AAPL
Afro-American Purchasing Center (PDAA) ..... AAPC
Afro-American Resources and Library Manpower Project [*Columbia University*] (NITA) ..... AARLMP
Afro-American Society for International Relations (EA) ..... AASIR
Afro-American Student Association (EA) ..... AASA
Afro-American Studies Librarians Section [*Association of College and Research Libraries*] ..... AASLS
Afro-American Studies Librarians Section [*Association of College and Research Libraries*] ..... AFAS
Afro-Asian Center (EA) ..... AAC
Afro-Asian Housing Organization [*Cairo, Egypt*] (EAIO) ..... AAHO
Afro-Asian Journalists' Association (NATG) ..... AAJA
Afro-Asian Latin American People's Solidarity Organization ..... AALAPSO
Afro-Asian Latin-American Students' Organization (NATG) ..... AALASO
Afro-Asian Lawyers' Conference (NATG) ..... AALC
Afro-Asian Organization for Economic Cooperation ..... AFRASEC
Afro-Asian People's Solidarity Organization [*Cairo, Egypt*] (EAIO) ..... AAPSO
Afro-Asian Rural Reconstruction Organization [*New Delhi, India*] ..... AARRO
Afro-Asian Rural Reconstruction Organization (EAIO) ..... ARRO
Afro-Asian Solidarity Organization (NATG) ..... AASO
Afro-Asian Solidarity Secretariat (NATG) ..... AASS
Afro-Asian Workers' Organization (NATG) ..... AAWO
Afro-Asian Writers' Permanent Bureau (NATG) ..... AAWPB
Afro-Asian Youth Solidarity Organization (NATG) ..... AAYSO
Afro-Asiatic [*MARC language code Library of Congress*] (LCCP) ..... afa
Afro-Caribbean Action Group [*British*] ..... ACAG
Afro-Caribbean Alliance [*British*] ..... ACA
Afro-Caribbean Educational Resource Centre [*British*] ..... ACER
Afro-Caribbean Educational Resource Project (AIE) ..... ACER
Afro-Hispanic Institute (EA) ..... AHI
Afrolit Society [*Defunct*] (EAIO) ..... AS
Afro-Mauritian Common Organization ..... AMCO
Afro-Mediterranean Orbital System [*Israel*] ..... AMOS
Afro-Shirazi Party [*Tanzania*] (AF) ..... ASP
Afro-Shirazi Party [*Zanzibar*] ..... ASP

Afro-Shirazi Youth League [*Tanzania*] (AF) ..... ASYL
AFS [*American Field Service*] International-Intercultural Programs (CDAI) ..... AFSIIP
Afsala Bancorp, Inc. [*NASDAQ symbol*] (SAG) ..... AFED
Afsala Bancorp, Inc. [*Associated Press*] (SAG) ..... AfsalaBc
AFSC Technical Information Center, Washington, DC [*OCLC symbol*] (OCLC) ..... SCH
Aft ..... A
Aft Across the Hatch [*Stowage*] (DNAB) ..... A/AC
Aft Cargo Carrier (IEEE) ..... ACC
Aft Cargo Compartment (MCD) ..... ACC
Aft Crew Station [*NASA*] (MCD) ..... ACS
Aft End Assembly ..... AEA
Aft End Cone [*NASA*] (NASA) ..... AEC
Aft Engineering Operating Station (DNAB) ..... AEOS
Aft Equipment Bay [*NASA*] (KSC) ..... AEB
Aft Events Controller [*NASA*] (MCD) ..... AEC
Aft Flight Deck (NASA) ..... AFD
Aft Flight Deck Control Panel (MCD) ..... AFDCP
Aft Flight Deck Operator (MCD) ..... AFDO
Aft Flight Deck Power Distribution Box (MCD) ..... AFDPDB
Aft Frame Tilt Actuator [*Aviation*] (NASA) ..... AFTA
Aft Fuselage (NASA) ..... AF
Aft Left (MCD) ..... AL
Aft Load Control Assembly (MCD) ..... ALCA
Aft Load Controller (MCD) ..... ALC
Aft Master Events Controller [*NASA*] (NASA) ..... AMEC
Aft Motor Control Assembly (NASA) ..... AMCA
Aft Peak Tank [*Shipping*] ..... APT
Aft Perpendicular [*Naval engineering*] ..... AP
Aft Power Controller (MCD) ..... APC
Aft Power Controller Assembly [*NASA*] (MCD) ..... APCA
Aft Propulsion System [*or Subsystem*] [*NASA*] (NASA) ..... APS
Aft Reaction Control System [*or Subsystem*] [*NASA*] (NASA) ..... ARCS
Aft Right (MCD) ..... AR
Aft Utility Bridge (NASA) ..... AUB
After ..... A
After (VRA) ..... aft
After (KSC) ..... AFT
After Action Report [*Military*] ..... AAR
After Action Review [*Military*] (MCD) ..... AAR
After All [*Message handling*] ..... AA
After Arrival ..... AA
After Body ..... AB
After Bottom Center [*Valve position*] ..... ABC
After Bottom Dead Center [*Valve position*] ..... ABDC
After Bulkhead in Hatch [*Stowage*] (DNAB) ..... AF/B
After Care Association of New South Wales [*Australia*] ..... ACANSW
After Christ ..... AC
After Conning Position [*British military*] (DMA) ..... ACP
After Cooler ..... AFTCLR
After Dark [*NWS*] (FAAC) ..... AFDK
After Date [*Business term*] ..... AD
After Date of Award (MCD) ..... ADAD
After Date of Award of Contract [*Telecommunications*] (TEL) ..... ADA
After Deducting Freight [*Billing*] ..... ADF
After Delivery Economies ..... ADE
After Diastase Digestion [*Biochemistry*] (DAVI) ..... PASD
After Digital [*Post-computer revolution*] ..... AD
After Dinner Opera Co. ..... ADOCo
After Diversity Demand (IAA) ..... ADD
After End [*Naval engineering*] (DAS) ..... AE
After End of the Hatch [*Stowage*] (DNAB) ..... AF/E
After Engine Room ..... AER
After Engineering Operating Station (CAAL) ..... AEOS
After England Failed [*Soldier slang for American Expeditionary Force in World War I*] ..... AEF
After Ford [*Calendar used in Aldous Huxley's novel, "Brave New World;" refers to Henry Ford*] ..... AF
After Full Moon [*Freemasonry*] (ROG) ..... AFM
After Glucose Infusion Started [*Biochemistry*] (DAVI) ..... POSG
After Goetz [*A reference to "vigilante" Bernhard Goetz, who shot four youths on a New York subway in 1984 after allegedly being threatened by them*] [*See also BG*] ..... AG
After Hatch [*Shipping*] ..... AH
After Hours (ADA) ..... AH
After Image [*Psychology*] ..... AI
After Initial Release (MCD) ..... AIR
After Japan [*Industry*] ..... AJ
After Market [*Investment term*] ..... AM
After New Moon [*Freemasonry*] (ROG) ..... ANM
After Orders (MCD) ..... AO
After Overhaul Inspection ..... AOHI
After Passing [*ICAO*] (FAAC) ..... APSG
After Peak (MSA) ..... AP
After Peak Bulkhead [*Shipping*] (DS) ..... APBH
After Puparium Formation [*Entomology*] ..... APF
After Quarter Day [*Freemasonry*] (ROG) ..... A Qr D
After Receipt of Order ..... ARO
After Receipt of Proposal ..... ARP
After Sale Assurance Program ..... ASAP
After Sale Price ..... ASP
After Sales Manager (DCTA) ..... ASM
After Tax Cash Flow ..... ATCF
After the Christian Era (BJA) ..... ACE

After the Dish [*Description of TV viewing via satellite transmission vs traditional or cable TV*] (PS) .... AD
After the Fact (MCD) .... ATF
After Top Center [*Valve position*] .... ATC
After Top Dead Center [*Valve position*] .... ATDC
After Torpedo Room .... ATRM
After Women or Liquor [*Slang*] .... AWOL
Afterburner (AFIT) A3
Afterburner [*on jet engines*] .... AB
Afterburner [*on jet engines*] .... AFTB
After-Care Instructions [*Medicine*] (DAVI) .... ACI
Aftercoming Head [*Obstetrics*] .... ACH
Aftercooled [*Automotive engineering*] .... A
After-Depolarization [*Neurophysiology*] .... ADP
Afterdischarge [*Electrophysiology*] .... AD
After-Hyperpolarization [*Also, AHP*] [*Neurophysiology*] .... AH
Afterhyperpolarization [*Also, AH*] [*Neurophysiology*] .... AHP
Afterloaded Quick Release [*Physiology*] .... AQR
Aftermarket Body Parts Association (EA) .... ABPA
Aftermarket Body Parts Distributors Association [*Later, ABPA*] (EA) .... ABPDA
Aftermarket Technology Corp. [*Associated Press*] (SAG) .... Aftmarkt
Aftermarket Technology Corp. [*NASDAQ symbol*] (SAG) .... ATAC
Afternoon .... A
Afternoon (WDMC) .... aft
Afternoon .... AFT
Afternoon (FAAC) .... AFTN
Afternoon (ROG) .... ARNOON
Afterpiece Kisser [*Slang Bowdlerized version*] .... AK
Aftersight [*Billing*] .... AS
Afterwards (ROG) .... AFTWDS
Afterwards (ROG) .... ARWDS
Afton, OK [*Location identifier FAA*] (FAAL) .... AGB
Afton Star-Enterprise, Afton, IA [*Library symbol Library of Congress*] (LCLS) .... IaAfSE
Afton, WY [*Location identifier FAA*] (FAAL) .... AFO
Afton, WY [*AM radio station call letters*] .... KRSV
Afton, WY [*FM radio station call letters*] .... KRSV-FM
Afunctional Neutrophil (DMAA) .... AFN
Afwaj al-Muqawimah al-Lubnaniyah [*Lebanese Resistance Battalions*] .... AMAL
AFWAL [*Air Force Wright Aeronautical Laboratories*] **Technical Information Center, Wright-Patterson AFB, OH** [*OCLC symbol*] (OCLC) .... SCW
AFWL [*Air Force Weapons Laboratory*] **LASER Engineering and Applications to Prototype Systems** (MCD) .... AFWL/LEAPS
Afyon [*Turkey*] [*Airport symbol*] (AD) .... AFY
Afyon [*Turkey ICAO location identifier*] (ICLI) .... LTAH
AG Associates [*NASDAQ symbol*] (TTSB) .... AGAI
AG Associates, Inc. [*Associated Press*] (SAG) .... AG Asc
AG Associates, Inc. [*NASDAQ symbol*] (SAG) .... AGAI
Ag Services of America, Inc. [*NASDAQ symbol*] (SAG) .... AGSV
Ag Services of America, Inc. [*Associated Press*] (SAG) .... AgSvcs
Ag Services of America, Inc. [*NYSE symbol*] (SAG) .... ASV
Aga Khan Foundation [*Switzerland*] (EAIO) .... AKF
Aga Khan Fund for Economic Development .... AKFED
Aga Khan University [*Karachi, Pakistan*] .... AKU
Agada (BJA) .... Ag
Agades [*Niger*] [*Airport symbol*] (OAG) .... AJY
Agades-Sud [*Niger*] [*ICAO location identifier*] (ICLI) .... DRZA
Agadir [*Morocco*] [*Airport symbol*] (OAG) .... AGA
Agadir/Inezgane [*Morocco*] [*ICAO location identifier*] (ICLI) .... GMAA
Again [*Telecommunications*] (TEL) .... AG
Again .... AGN
Against (ROG) .... AG
Against (ROG) .... AGNST
Against .... AGST
Against .... AGT
Against All Risks [*Insurance*] .... AAR
Against Apion [*Josephus*] (BJA) .... AgAp
Against Apion [*Josephus*] (BJA) .... JAp
Against Apion [*Josephus*] (BJA) .... JosApion
Against Drunk Driving [*Also, The Neil Gray Memorial Fund*] (AC) .... ADD
Against Grain .... AG
Against Gravity (HGAA) .... AG
Against Leocrates [*of Lycurgus*] [*Classical studies*] (OCD) .... Leoc
Against Leptines [*of Demosthenes*] [*Classical studies*] (OCD) .... Lept
Against Manufacturing Defects [*Automotive engineering*] .... AMD
Against Medical Advice .... AMA
Against Meidias [*of Demosthenes*] [*Classical studies*] (OCD) .... Meid
Against Testing on Mururoa [*An association Australia*] .... ATOM
Agamemnon [*of Aeschylus*] [*Classical studies*] (OCD) .... Ag
Agammaglobulinemia [*Medicine*] .... AGG
Agammaglobulinemia Leukemia [*Medicine*] (DAVI) .... AGG
Agana [*Diocesan abbreviation*] [*Guam*] (TOCD) .... AGN
Agana, GU [*Television station call letters*] .... KGTF
Agana, GU [*AM radio station call letters*] .... KGUM
Agana, GU [*FM radio station call letters*] .... KOKU
Agana, GU [*FM radio station call letters*] (RBYB) .... KPRG
Agana, GU [*FM radio station call letters*] .... KSTO
Agana, GU [*AM radio station call letters*] .... KTWG
Agana, GU [*AM radio station call letters*] .... KUAM
Agana, GU [*FM radio station call letters*] .... KUAM-FM
Agana, GU [*Television station call letters*] .... KUAM-TV
Agana, GU [*FM radio station call letters*] .... KZGZ
Agana, GU [*Location identifier FAA*] (FAAL) .... ZUA
Agana Naval Air Station [*FAA*] (TAG) .... NGM

Agana Naval Air Station, Guam Island [*Mariana Islands*] [*ICAO location identifier*] (ICLI) .... PGUM
Agape Force (EA) .... AF
Agar [*Biochemistry*] (DAVI) .... a
Agar Gel Double Diffusion [*Medicine*] (DMAA) .... AGDD
Agar Gel Precipitation [*Biochemistry*] (DMAA) .... AGP
Agar Gel Precipitin Inhibition (DMAA) .... AGPI
Agar Gell Immunodiffusion [*Veterinary medicine*] .... AGID
Agar Immersion, Plating, and Contact (PDAA) .... AIPC
Agar-Gel Diffusion [*Clinical chemistry*] .... AGD
Agar-Gel Diffusion Test [*Clinical chemistry*] (MAE) .... ADT
Agar-Gel Precipitation Test [*Clinical chemistry*] .... AGPT
Agarose Diffusion [*Method*] [*Cardiology*] (DAVI) .... AGD
Agarose Diffusion Method [*Medical device safety test*] .... ADM
Agarose Gel Zone Electrophoresis .... AGE
Agartala [*India*] [*Airport symbol*] (OAG) .... IXA
Agartala [*India*] [*ICAO location identifier*] (ICLI) .... VEAT
Agarwal Resources Ltd. [*Vancouver Stock Exchange symbol*] .... AWL
Agassiz Resources Ltd. [*Toronto Stock Exchange symbol*] .... AGZ
Agassiz-Harrison Historical Society, Agassiz, British Columbia [*Library symbol National Library of Canada*] (BIB) .... BHLH
Agat, GU [*FM radio station call letters*] .... KSDA
Agate (VRA) .... ag
Agate [*Typography*] (DGA) .... AG
Agateware (VRA) .... agwr
Agatha Christie Appreciation Society: Postern of Murder (EA) .... ACAS
Agathon Publication Services, Inc. [*Later, APS Publications*] .... APS
Agats [*Indonesia*] [*ICAO location identifier*] (ICLI) .... WAKG
AG-Bag International Ltd. [*Associated Press*] (SAG) .... AGBag
AG-Bag International Ltd. [*NASDAQ symbol*] (SAG) .... AGBG
Ag-Bag Intl. Ltd. [*NASDAQ symbol*] (TTSB) .... AGBG
Agboville [*Ivory Coast*] [*ICAO location identifier*] (ICLI) .... DIAE
AG-Chem Equipment [*NASDAQ symbol*] (TTSB) .... AGCH
Ag-Chem Equipment Co., Inc. [*NASDAQ symbol*] (SAG) .... AGCH
Ag-Chem Equipment Co. Inc. [*Associated Press*] (SAG) .... Ag-Chm
AGCO Corp. [*NYSE symbol*] (SAG) .... AG
AGCO Corp. [*Associated Press*] (SAG) .... AGCO
Agderfly AS [*Norway ICAO designator*] (FAAC) .... AGD
Age .... A
Age Action Year [*1976*] (DI) .... AAY
Age at Time of Bomb [*Of survivors at Hiroshima*] .... ATB
Age Concern England [*An association British*] .... ACE
Age Concern Scotland [*An association*] (EAIO) .... ACS
Age Controlled Item (NASA) .... ACI
Age Discrimination Claims Assistance Act [*1988*] .... ADCAA
Age Discrimination in Employment Act [*1967*] [*Department of Labor*] .... ADEA
Age Equivalent [*Development level*] [*Education*] .... AE
Age Equivalent (MAE) .... AEq
Age Exemption (WDAA) .... AE
AGE [*Air-Ground Equipment*] **Module Test Set** (MCD) .... AMTS
Age Monthly Review [*A publication*] .... Age MR
Age of Date, Clock (SSD) .... AODC
Age of Date, Ephermis (SSD) .... AODE
Age of Primary Taxpayer [*IRS*] .... AG
Age; Prior Service; Physical, Legal, Educational, and Marital Status; and Dependents [*Army recruiting questionnaire*] .... APPLE-MD
Age Progression Technique [*Criminology*] (LAIN) .... APT
Age Replacement .... AR
Age Replacement Policy (PDAA) .... ARP
Age Run Length .... ARL
Age/Sex Rate .... ASR
Age Standardized Mortality Ratio .... ASMR
Age Weighted Pupil Unit [*Education*] (AIE) .... AWPU
Age-Appropriately Immunized [*Children*] .... AAI
Age-Associated Memory Disorder [*Medicine*] (CPH) .... AAMD
Age-Associated Memory Impairment [*Medicine*] .... AAMI
Aged, Adrenalectomized Animals [*Endocrinology*] .... AX
Aged and Invalid Pensioners' Association of South Australia .... AIPASA
Aged and Invalid Pensioners' Home .... AIPH
Aged, Blind, or Disabled [*HEW*] .... ABD
Aged Care Australia [*An association*] .... ACA
Aged Care Support Program [*Australia*] .... ACSP
Aged Individual [*Title XVI*] [*Social Security Administration*] (OICC) .... AI
Aged Intact Animal [*Endocrinology*] .... AI
Aged Persons Homes Act [*Australia*] .... APHA
Aged Persons' Residential Program [*Australia*] .... APRP
Aged Services Association [*Australia*] .... ASA
Aged Spouse [*Social Security Administration*] (OICC) .... AS
Age-Dependent Epileptic Encephalopathy [*Medicine*] (DMAA) .... ADEE
Aged-Related Eye Disease Study [*National Eye Institute*] .... AREDS
Agen [*France*] [*Airport symbol*] (OAG) .... AGF
Agen/La Garenne [*France ICAO location identifier*] (ICLI) .... LFBA
Agena Class Lunar Orbiter [*NASA*] .... ACLO
Agena Control System [*NASA*] .... ACS
Agena Detailed Maneuver Table [*NASA*] (SAA) .... ADMT
Agena Ephemeris Data [*NASA*] (SAA) .... AED
Agena Systems/Power-On Test [*NASA*] (KSC) .... AS/POT
Agena Target Vehicle [*NASA*] (KSC) .... ATV
Agenahambo [*Papua New Guinea*] [*Seismograph station code, US Geological Survey Closed*] (SEIS) .... AGE
Agence Africaine d'Information [*African Information Agency*] [*Zaire*] .... AAI
Agence Africaine d'Information et de Documentation [*African Information and Documentation Agency*] .... AAID
Agence Angolaise de Presse et d'Information [*Angolan Press and Information Agency*] .... API

Agence Camerounaise de Presse [*Cameroon Press Agency*] ACAP
Agence Canadienne de Developpement International [*Canadian International Development Agency - CIDA*] ACDI
Agence Centrafricaine des Communications Fluviales [*Central African Agency for River Communications*] (AF) ACCF
Agence Centrale des Approvisionnements [*Central Supplies Agency*] (NATG) ACA
Agence Centrale Parisienne de Presse [*Parisian Central Press Agency*] [*French*] (AF) ACP
Agence Civile OTAN [*Organisation du Traite de l'Atlantique Nord*] **du Temps de Guerre** [*NATO Civil Wartime Agency*] (NATG) ACOG
Agence Congolaise de Presse [*Congolese Press Agency*] ACP
Agence Congolaise d'Information [*Congolese Information Agency*] (AF) ACI
Agence Dahomeene de Presse [*Dahomean Press Agency*] ADP
Agence Dahomeenne de Presse [*Dahomean Press Agency*] ADP
Agence de Cooperation Culturelle et Technique [*Agency for Cultural and Technical Cooperation*] (EAIO) ACCT
Agence de Cooperation Internationale Pour l'Integration Economique et Sociale des Personnes Handicapees (AC) ACIPH
Agence de l'OCDE pour l'Energie Nucleaire [*OECD Nuclear Energy Agency - NEA*] (EAIO) AEN
Agence de Presse de l'OPEC [*OPEC News Agency - OPECNA*] [*Vienna, Austria*] (EAIO) APOPEC
Agence de Presse Ivoirienne [*Ivorian Press Agency*] API
Agence de Presse Libre du Quebec [*Free Press Agency of Quebec*] [*Canada*] APLQ
Agence de Presse Senegalaise [*Senegalese Press Agency*] APS
Agence de Surveillance du Secteur Petrolier [*Petroleum Monitoring Agency, Energy, Mines & Resources, Canada*] ASSP
Agence des Telecommunications Administratives [*Administrative Telecommunications Agency*] [*Canada*] ATA
Agence des Telecommunications Gouvernementales [*Government Telecommunications Agency*] [*Canada*] ATG
[*French Rating Agency*] **Agence d'Evaluation Financiere** (ODBW) ADEF
Agence d'Examen de l'Investissement Etranger [*Foreign Investment Review Agency - FIRA*] [*Canada*] AEIE
Agence d'Illustrations pour la Presse [*Press Illustrations Agency*] [*French*] (AF) AGIP
Agence Djiboutienne de Presse (EY) ADP
Agence Europeenne d'Approvisionnement AEA
Agence Europeenne pour l'Energie Nucleaire [*France*] (NUCP) AEEN
Agence France-Presse [*French Press Agency*] (IID) AFP
Agence Gabonaise de Presse [*Gabonese Press Agency*] (AF) AGP
Agence Gabonaise d'Information [*Gabonese Information Agency*] (AF) AGI
Agence Generale de Transit en Afrique [*General Transit Agency in Afica*] [*Congo*] AGTA
Agence Generale d'Editions Professionnelles [*Agency General of Professional Publishing*] [*Canada*] AGEP
Agence Guineenne de Presse [*Guinean Press Agency*] (AF) AGP
Agence Internationale de l'Energie Atomique AIEA
Agence Internationale d'Information du Mali [*Press agency*] [*Mali*] ANIM
Agence Internationale pour le Developpement [*Paris, France*] (EAIO) AIDE
Agence Ivoirienne de Presse [*Ivory Coast*] (AF) AIP
Agence Khmere de Presse [*Cambodian Press Agency*] AKP
Agence Lao Presse [*Laos Press Agency*] ALP
Agence Madagascar - Presse [*Press agency*] [*Malagasy Republic*] AMP
Agence Malgache de Presse [*Malagasy Press Agency*] (AF) AMP
Agence Maritime Internationale [*International Maritime Agency*] AMI
Agence Mauritanienne de l'Information [*News Agency*] (EY) AMI
Agence Nationale de Valorisation de la Recherche [*National Agency for the Promotion of Research*] [*Information service or system*] (IID) ANVAR
Agence Nationale d'Edition et de Publicite [*National Publication and Advertising Agency*] [*Algeria*] (AF) ANEP
Agence Nationale des Aerodromes et de la Meteorologie [*Ivory Coast*] [*ICAO designator*] (FAAC) ZZM
Agence Nationale d'Information Malienne [*Malian National Information Agency*] (AF) ANIM
Agence Nigerienne de Presse [*News Agency*] [*Niger*] (EY) ANP
Agence Parisienne de Presse [*Parisian Press Agency*] [*French*] (AF) APP
Agence pour la Securite de la Navigation Aerienne en Afrique et a Madagascar (ASECNA) [*ICAO designator*] (ICDA) XK
Agence pour la Securite de la Navigation Aerienne en Afrique et Madagascar [*Agency for Air Navigation Safety in Africa and Madagascar*] (AF) ASECNA
Agence pour la Securite de la Navigation Afrique-Madagascar [*France*] [*FAA designator*] (FAAC) XKX
Agence Presse Voltaique [*Upper Voltan Press Agency*] (AF) APV
Agence Spatiale Europeenne [*European Space Agency*] (EAIO) ASE
Agence Tchadienne de Presse [*Chadian Press Agency*] (AF) ATP
Agence Telegraphique Suisse [*Swiss News Agency*] [*Berne, Switzerland*] ATS
Agence Transcongolaise des Communications [*Trans-Congolese Communications Agency*] (AF) ATC
Agence Transcontinentale de Presse [*Transcontinental Press Agency*] [*France*] (AF) ATP
Agence Transequatoriale des Communications [*Trans-Equatorial Communications Agency*] [*Africa*] (AF) ATEC
Agence Zaire-Presse [*Zaire Press Agency*] AZAP
Agencement en Rames Automatisees de Modules Independants dans les Stations [*Arrangement in automated trains of independent modules in stations*] [*A satirical novel by Bruno Latour*] [*Based on an actual Personal Rapid Transit program pursued by the French government*] ARAMIS
Agencia Centroamericana de Noticias SA [*Press agency*] [*Panama*] ACAN
Agencia Latinoamericana de Informacion [*Latin American Information Agency*] [*Canada*] ALAI
Agencia Mexicana de Noticias SA [*Press agency*] [*Mexico*] AMEX
Agencia Nacional [*National Agency*] [*Press agency*] [*Brazil*] AN
Agencia Nacionale de Informacoes [*National Information Agency*] [*Portugal*] ANI
Agencia Nicaraguense de Noticias [*News agency*] (EY) ANN
Agencia Noticiosa Corporacion de Periodistas [*Press agency*] [*Chile*] COPER
Agencia Noticiosa Saporiti [*Press agency*] [*Argentina*] ANS
Agencies (EY) AGS
Agencja Robotricza [*Press agency*] [*Poland*] AR
Agency A
Agency (EY) AG
Agency (AFM) AGCY
Agency AGCY
Agency (WDMC) agcy
Agency AGNCY
Agency (ADA) AGY
Agency AY
Agency Activity Analysis [*LIMRA*] AAA
Agency Broadcast Producers Workshop [*Defunct*] (EA) ABPW
Agency Coordinating Body for Afghan Relief [*Afghanistan/Pakistan*] (ECON) ACBAR
Agency for Business and Career Development (EA) ABCD
Agency for Cooperation and Research in Development [*International consortium on Africa*] (ECON) ACORD
Agency for Health Care Policy and Research [*Department of Health and Human Services*] AHCPR
Agency for Industrial Mission [*Canada*] AIM
Agency for Instructional Technology (EA) AIT
Agency for Instructional Television (NTCM) AIT
Agency for International Development [*State Department*] [*Also, USAID US International Development Cooperation Agency*] AID
Agency for International Development Acquisition Regulation [*A publication*] (AAGC) AIDAR
Agency for International Development, Bureau for Technical Assistance [*Department of State*] AID/TA
Agency for International Development/Private Enterprise Promotion AID/PEP
Agency for International Development, Procurement Regulations AIDPR
Agency for International Development, Washington, DC [*OCLC symbol*] (OCLC) AID
Agency for Navigation on the Rhine and the Moselle (NATG) RHIMO
Agency for Tele-Education in Canada ATEC
Agency for the Coordination of Transport in the Mediterranean [*NATO*] (MCD) ACTIME
Agency for the Coordination of Transport in the Mediterranean [*NATO*] (NATG) ACTIMED
Agency for the Security of Air Navigation (AFM) ASECNA
Agency for Toxic Substances and Disease Registry [*Atlanta, GA*] [*Department of Health and Human Services*] ATSDR
Agency for Toxic Substances and Emergency Response ATSER
Agency Investigation Board AIB
Agency Management Conference [*LIMRA*] AMC
Agency Management Information Systems [*DCAA*] (AAGC) AMIS
Agency Manager Survey [*LIMRA*] AMS
Agency Name [*Database terminology*] (NITA) AN
Agency of Industrial Science and Technology AIST
Agency of Record [*An advertising agency*] (WDMC) AOR
Agency Officers School [*Formerly, FOS*] [*LIMRA*] AOS
Agency Owners Roundtable [*Formerly, Canadian Association of Professional Advertising Agencies*] (AC) AOR
Agency Procedure AP
Agency Procurement Request APR
Agency Progress Report APR
Agency Ranking Committee [*Environmental Protection Agency*] (GFGA) ARC
Agency Sales Magazine [*Manufacturers' Agents National Association*] [*A publication*] ASM
Agency State [*Database Terminology*] (NITA) AS
Agency to Prevent Evil [*Organization in TV series "Lancelot Link"*] APE
Agency-Wide Coding Structure [*Military*] AWCS
Agency-Wide Information Management System [*Department of Agriculture*] (GFGA) AIMS
Agenda Item (MCD) AI
Agent (ODBW) ag
Agent AGNT
Agent (WDMC) agt
Agent (AABC) AGT
Agent Collaboration Language [*Computer science*] (RDA) ACL
Agent Development Program [*LIMRA*] ADP
Agent Distributor Service [*Departments of State and Commerce*] ADS
Agent General AG
Agent in Charge [*Criminology*] (LAIN) AIC
Agent Job Review [*LIMRA*] AJR
Agent Orange Victims International [*Later, VVAOVI*] (EA) AOVI
Agent Orange Working Group [*Cabinet Council on Human Resources*] AOWG
Agent Reference Material [*Used by airline agents*] ARM
Agent Report (MCD) AR
Agent Report [*Army*] (AABC) AREPT
Agent Selection Kit [*LIMRA*] ASK
Agent to the Governor-General [*British*] AGG
Agents and Brokers Automated Computer Users System (MHDI) ABACUS
Agents' Association, Totalizator Agency Board, New South Wales AATAB
Agents Master File [*IRS*] AGMF
Agents of Biological Origin [*Military*] ABO
Agent's Vehicle Record (DS) AVR
Agentstvo Pechati Novosti [*News agency*] [*Former USSR*] APN
Agenzia Europea per L'Energia Nucleare (NUCP) AEEN
Agenzia Giornalistica Italia [*Press agency*] [*Italy*] AGI

Agenzia Internazionale Fides [*News agency*] [*Vatican City*] (EY) .... AIF
Agenzia Nationale Stampa Associata [*Associated National Press Agency*] [*Italy*] .... ANSA
Age-Related Macular Degeneration [*Ophthalmology*] .... AMD
Age-Related Macular Degeneration [*Ophthalmology*] (CPH) .... ARMD
Agesilaus [*of Plutarch*] [*Classical studies*] (OCD) .... Ages
Agesilaus [*of Xenophon*] [*Classical studies*] (OCD) .... Ages
Age-Specific Fertility Rate .... ASFR
Age-Specific Mortality Rate .... ASMR
AGF Management Ltd. [*Toronto Stock Exchange symbol*] .... AGF
Aggadah (BJA) .... Agg
Aggadic (BJA) .... Agg
Aggeneys [*South Africa*] [*Airport symbol*] (OAG) .... AGZ
Aggeneys [*South Africa*] [*ICAO location identifier*] (ICLI) .... FAAG
Agglomerate [*Geology*] .... A
Agglutination [*Immunology*] .... AGG
Agglutination [*Immunology*] .... AGGL
Agglutination (DMAA) .... aggl
Agglutination (DMAA) .... agglut
Agglutination [*Immunology*] (AAMN) .... AGGLUT
Agglutination Activating Factor [*Medicine*] .... AAF
Agglutination Negative, Absorption Positive [*Medicine*] (MAE) .... ANAP
Agglutination Test for Brucellosis [*Immunology*] (DMAA) .... ABr
Agglutination-Flocculation Test [*Immunology*] (DMAA) .... AFT
Agglutination-Inhibition Test [*Clinical chemistry*] .... AIT
Aggravated (MAE) .... agg
Aggravated in Military Service (MAE) .... AMS
Aggravation (DSUE) .... AGGRO
Aggrediente Febre [*When the Fever Increases*] [*Pharmacy*] .... AG FEB
Aggrediente Febre [*When the Fever Increases*] [*Pharmacy*] .... Aggred Feb
Aggregate .... AGG
Aggregate (AABC) .... AGGR
Aggregate .... AGGRGT
Aggregate (VRA) .... agr
Aggregate Base Course (DAC) .... ABC
Aggregate Concrete Block Association [*British*] (DBA) .... ACBA
Aggregate Demand .... AD
Aggregate Demand Potential (PDAA) .... ADP
Aggregate Estimated Net Pool Return [*Business term*] .... AENPR
Aggregate Exercise Price [*Investment term*] .... AEP
Aggregate Expenditure [*Economics*] .... AE
Aggregate Expense Analysis [*Insurance*] .... AEA
Aggregate Field Expense Study [*LIMRA*] .... AFES
Aggregate Level Simulation Protocol .... ALSP
Aggregate Measure of Support [*International trade*] (ECON) .... AMS
Aggregate Producers Association of Ontario (AC) .... APAO
Aggregate Production Planning (PDAA) .... APP
Aggregate Ready-Mix of Minnesota (SRA) .... ARM
Aggregate Supply .... AS
Aggregated Albumin (MAE) .... AA
Aggregated Human Globulin [*Biochemistry*] (DAVI) .... AHG
Aggregated School Budget (AIE) .... ASB
Aggregated Switch Procurement Program [*General Services Administration*] (GFGA) .... ASP
Aggregates of P-Protein [*Botany*] .... AgPp
Aggregation [*Medicine*] (AAMN) .... AGGREG
Aggregation Factor [*Biochemistry*] .... AF
Aggregation Half Time [*Medicine*] (DMAA) .... AHT
Aggregation of Red Blood Cells [*Hematology*] .... ARC
Aggregation-Attachment Pheromone [*Entomology*] .... AAP
Aggressive Behavioral Disturbance [*Medicine*] (DMAA) .... ABD
Aggressive Growth [*Investment term*] .... AG
Aggressor Squadron [*Air Force*] .... AS
Aghajari [*Iran*] [*ICAO location identifier*] (ICLI) .... OIAG
Agile Combat Aircraft [*Proposed*] .... ACA
AGILE [*Autonetics General Information Learning Equipment*] **Homing Interceptor Simulation** .... AHIS
Agile Intelligent Manufacturing [*Computer-assisted manufacturing*] .... AIM
AGILE [*Autonetics General Information Learning Equipment*] **Interceptor** .... AI
AGILE [*Autonetics General Information Learning Equipment*] **Interceptor Defense** .... AID
AGILE [*Autonetics General Information Learning Equipment*] **Responsive Effective Support** [*Army/Air Force*] .... ARES
Agile-Beam Illuminator (MCD) .... ABI
Agility Excellent .... AX
Agincourt [*Canada*] [*Later, OTT*] [*Geomagnetic observatory code*] .... AGN
Agincourt Exploration, Inc. [*Vancouver Stock Exchange symbol*] .... AGX
Aging .... AGNG
Aging Aircraft Nondestructive Inspection Development and Demonstration Center [*Federal Aviation Administration*] .... AANC
Aging Aircraft Program [*FAA*] (DA) .... AAP
Aging, Federal Council (OICC) .... AC
Aging Health Policy Center [*Research center*] (RCD) .... AHPC
Aging in America (EA) .... AIA
Aging Research Institute [*Defunct*] (EA) .... ARI
Agio Resources Corp. [*Vancouver Stock Exchange symbol*] .... AGI
Agita [*Shake*] [*Pharmacy*] .... AGIT
Agita Ante Sumendum [*Shake Before Taking*] [*Latin Pharmacy*] (WDAA) .... AGIT ANTE SU
Agita ante Usum [*Shake before Using*] [*Pharmacy*] .... AGIT A US
Agita Bene [*Shake Well*] [*Pharmacy*] .... AGIT BENE
Agitate (MSA) .... AG
Agitation and Propaganda [*Military*] .... AGIT-PROP
Agitato [*Agitatedly*] [*Music*] .... Agit
Agitato [*Agitatedly*] [*Music*] .... AGITO
Agitato [*Agitatedly*] [*Music*] (ROG) .... AGO
Agitato Vase [*The Vessel Being Shaken*] [*Pharmacy*] .... Agit Vas
Agitator [*FBI standardized term*] .... AGTR
Agkistrodon Contortrix Thrombin-Like Enzyme .... ACTE
AGL Resources [*NYSE symbol*] (TTSB) .... ATG
AGL Resources, Inc. [*NYSE symbol*] (SAG) .... ATG
AGLA [*Australian Government Lawyers' Association*] **Bulletin** [*A publication*] .... AGLA
Agmatine Iminohydrolase [*An enzyme*] .... AIH
Agnes Etherington Art Centre, Queen's University, Kingston, Ontario [*Library symbol National Library of Canada*] (NLC) .... OKQA
Agnes Scott College [*Decatur, GA*] .... ASC
Agnes Scott College, Decatur, GA [*OCLC symbol*] (OCLC) .... EGA
Agnes Scott College, Decatur, GA [*Library symbol Library of Congress*] (LCLS) .... GDS
Agness Community Library, Agness, OR [*Library symbol Library of Congress*] (LCLS) .... OrAg
Agnetha Faltskog, Bjorn Ulvaeus, Benny Andersson, Anni-Frid Lyngstad [*Swedish singing group; acronym formed from first letters of their first names*] .... ABBA
Agnew Association of America (EA) .... AAA
Agnew on Patents [*A publication*] (DLA) .... Agn Pat
Agnew on the Statute of Frauds [*A publication*] (DLA) .... Agn Fr
Agni Yoga Society (EA) .... AYS
Agnico Eagle Mines [*NASDAQ symbol*] (TTSB) .... AEM
Agnico-Eagle Mines, Inc. [*NYSE symbol*] (SAG) .... AEM
Agnico-Eagle Mines, Inc. [*Associated Press*] (SAG) .... Agnico
Agnico-Eagle Mines Ltd. [*Toronto Stock Exchange symbol*] .... AGE
Agnogenic Myeloid Metaplasia [*Medicine*] .... AMM
Agnosia [*Medicine*] .... AGN
Agnostic .... AGNOS
Agnostic Christians for Equality for Dignity (EA) .... ACED
Agnostics' Adoption Society [*British*] (BI) .... AAS
Agnus Dei [*Lamb of God*] [*Latin*] .... AD
Agnus Dei [*Lamb of God*] [*Latin*] .... Ag
AGOR [*Auxiliary General Oceanographic Research*] **Oceanographic Digital DataSystem** (MCD) .... AGODDS
Agora/Documentaire [*Agence France-Presse*] [*French Information service or system*] (CRD) .... ADOC
Agora-Economie [*Agence France-Presse*] [*French Information service or system*] (CRD) .... AECO
AGORA-GENERAL [*Agence France-Presse*] [*Information service or system*] (CRD) .... AGRA
Agoraphobic Foundation of Canada Inc. [*Fondation Canadienne pour les Agoraphobes Inc.*] (AC) .... AFC
Agoraphobics Anonymous (EA) .... AA
Agoraphobics in Motion [*An association*] (EA) .... AIM
AGORA-SPORTS [*Agence France-Presse*] [*Information service or system*] (CRD) .... ASPO
Agordat [*Ethiopia*] [*ICAO location identifier*] (ICLI) .... HAAG
Agorot [*Monetary unit*] [*Israel*] .... AG
Agostiniani Secolari Agustinos Seculares [*Order Secular of St. Augustine - OSSA*] [*Rome, Italy*] (EAIO) .... ASAS
Agouron Pharmaceuticals, Inc. [*Associated Press*] (SAG) .... Agourn
Agouron Pharmaceuticals, Inc. [*NASDAQ symbol*] (NQ) .... AGPH
AGP & Company, Inc. [*Associated Press*] (SAG) .... AGP & Co
AGP & Co., Inc. [*NASDAQ symbol*] (SAG) .... AGPC
Agra [*India*] [*Airport symbol*] (OAG) .... AGR
Agra [*India*] [*Seismograph station code, US Geological Survey Closed*] (SEIS) .... AGR
Agra [*India*] [*ICAO location identifier*] (ICLI) .... VIAG
Agra Full Bench Rulings [*India*] [*A publication*] (ILCA) .... Agra FB
Agra High Court Reports [*India*] [*A publication*] (ILCA) .... Agra
Agra High Court Reports [*India*] [*A publication*] (DLA) .... Agra HC
Agra Industries Ltd. [*Toronto Stock Exchange symbol*] .... AGR
Agranulocytic Angina [*Medicine*] (DMAA) .... AA
Agrar-Aviacion SA [*Spain ICAO designator*] (FAAC) .... AGI
Agrarian Party [*Albania*] [*Political party*] (EY) .... AP
Agrartudomanyi Egyetem, Keszthely, Hungary [*Library symbol Library of Congress*] (LCLS) .... HuKeAgE
Agrartudomanyi Egyetem Koezlemenyei [*A publication*] .... Agrartud Egy Kozl
Agree (ILCA) .... Ag
Agree (FAAC) .... AGR
Agree en Relations Publiques [*Canada*] (DD) .... ARP
Agree Reality Corp. [*NYSE symbol*] (SAG) .... ADC
Agree Realty [*NYSE symbol*] (TTSB) .... ADC
Agree Realty Corp. [*Associated Press*] (SAG) .... AgreeRlt
Agreed .... AGD
Agreed Case [*Legal term*] (DLA) .... AGR C
Agreed, Cease Fire Line [*Military*] (INF) .... AFCL
Agreed Medical examiner (DAVI) .... AME
Agreed Operational Characteristics (DNAB) .... AOC
Agreed Syllabus Conference [*Education*] (AIE) .... ASC
Agreement (ODBW) .... ag
Agreement (ADA) .... AG
Agreement (ROG) .... AGMT
Agreement (ROG) .... AGREET
Agreement (AABC) .... AGRM
Agreement (FAAC) .... AGRMT
Agreement .... AGRT
Agreement .... AGT
Agreement (WDMC) .... agt
Agreement and Account of Crew (ADA) .... AAC
Agreement for Fighter Interceptor Operations .... AFIO
Agreement for the International Transport of Perishable Products .... ATP

Agreement Item (MCD) .... AGI
Agreement on Government Procurement (AAGC) .... AGP
Agreement to Extend Enlistment [*Military*] .... AEX
Agreement to Remain on Active Duty Until Date Specified (DNAB) ..... GREEMAIN
Agreements for Recreation and Conservation [*Canada*] .... ARC
Agree-Undecided-Disagree [*Multiple choice test*] (BARN) .... AUD
Agrement Dangereuse Routier [*Agreement on the International Carriage of Dangerous Goods by Road*] [*1968*] .... ADR
Agri [*Turkey*] [*Airport symbol*] (AD) .... AGZ
Agri [*Turkey ICAO location identifier*] (ICLI) .... LTCB
AgriBioTech, Inc. [*NASDAQ symbol*] (SAG) .... ABTX
AgriBioTech, Inc. [*Associated Press*] (SAG) .... AgriBio
Agribusiness Accountability Project [*Public interest research group*] [*Defunct*] .... AAP
Agribusiness Association of Australia and New Zealand ...... AAANZ
Agribusiness Association of Iowa (SRA) .... AAI
Agribusiness Council (EA) .... AC
Agri-Business Council of Arizona (SRA) .... ABC
Agri-Business Council of Oregon (SRA) .... ABC
Agribusiness Foundation of Australia .... AFA
Agribusiness Information [*G. V. Olsen Associates*] [*Information service or system*] (CRD) .... AGBIZ
Agrico Chemical Co., Memphis, TN [*Library symbol Library of Congress*] (LCLS) .... TMAC
Agricola [*of Tacitus*] [*Classical studies*] (OCD) .... Agr
Agricultural .... ACRCLTL
Agricultural (ROG) .... AGL
Agricultural [*or Agriculture*] .... AGR
Agricultural (DD) .... Agr
Agricultural .... AGRL
Agricultural Adjustment Act [*1933, 1938, 1980*] [*Department of Agriculture*] .... AAA
Agricultural Adjustment Administration [*or Agency*] [*Production and Marketing Administration*] [*Department of Agriculture*] .... AAA
Agricultural Advisory Council for England and Wales (BI) ...... AAC
Agricultural Advisory Meteorologist (NOAA) .... AAM
Agricultural Aids Foundation .... AAF
Agricultural Aircraft Association [*Later, CAAA*] (EA) ...... AAA
Agricultural Ammonia Institute [*Later, The Fertilizer Institute*] (EA) ...... AAI
Agricultural and Allied Workers' National Trade Group [*British*] ...... AAWTG
Agricultural and Dairy Educational Political Trust .... ADEPT
Agricultural and Food Policy Center [*Texas A & M University*] [*Research center*] (RCD) .... AFPC
Agricultural and Food Products Market Development Assistance Program [*Canada*] .... AGMAP
Agricultural and Food Research Council [*Research center British*] (IRC) ..... AFRC
Agricultural and Food Research Service [*Ministry of Agriculture, Fisheries, and Food*] [*British*] (IRUK) .... AFRS
Agricultural and Horticultural .... A & H
Agricultural and Horticultural Engineering Abstracts [*A publication*] ...... AHA
Agricultural and Industrial [*In a college name*] .... A & I
Agricultural and Industrial Manufacturers' Representatives Association (EA) .... AIMRA
Agricultural and Industrial Process Heat (MCD) .... AIPH
Agricultural and Mechanical [*In a college name*] .... A & M
Agricultural and Natural Resources .... ANR
Agricultural and Pastoral (ADA) .... A & P
Agricultural and Rural Development Act [*Canada*] .... ARDA
Agricultural and Technical [*In a college name*] .... A & T
Agricultural and Veterinary Chemical .... AVC
Agricultural and Veterinary Chemicals Association of Australia ...... AVCAA
Agricultural and Veterinary Chemicals Unit .... AVCU
Agricultural and Veterinary Products Index [*A publication*] ...... AVPI
Agricultural Automation .... AGRIMATION
Agricultural Aviation Research Unit [*British*] (ARC) ...... AARU
Agricultural Bank of China .... ABoC
Agricultural Biotechnology Center [*University of Maryland*] [*Research center*] .... ABC
Agricultural Bureau of New South Wales [*Australia*] ...... ABNSW
Agricultural Bureau of South Australia .... ABSA
Agricultural Business and Commerce .... ABC
Agricultural Central Cooperative Association Ltd. [*British*] (BI) ...... ACCA
Agricultural Central Trading [*British*] .... ACT
Agricultural Chemicals Consultative Group [*Australia*] ...... ACCG
Agricultural Climatological Office [*Department of Commerce*] ...... ACO
Agricultural Code [*A publication*] (DLA) .... Agric C
Agricultural Commodities Data Base [*Alberta Department of Agriculture*] [*Information service or system*] (IID) .... AGDATA
Agricultural Communications Network [*Purdue University*] [*Telecommunications service*] (TSSD) .... ACN
Agricultural Communicators in Education (EA) .... ACE
Agricultural Computer Association [*Defunct*] (EA) .... ACA
Agricultural Conservation and Adjustment Administration [*New Deal*] ..... ACAA
Agricultural Conservation Program [*Department of Agriculture*] ...... ACP
Agricultural, Construction, and Earthmoving Equipment [*Acronym is the name of a metal coating painting product*] [*Imperial Chemical Industries Ltd.*] [*British*] .... ACE
Agricultural Construction Industry Association [*British*] (EAIO) ...... ACIA
Agricultural Cooperative Council of Oregon (SRA) .... ACCO
Agricultural Cooperative Development International (EA) ...... ACDI
Agricultural Cooperative Service [*Washington, DC Department of Agriculture*] (GRD) .... ACS
Agricultural Council of Arkansas (SRA) .... ACA
Agricultural Council of California (SRA) .... ACC
Agricultural Credit Corp. Act [*1932*] .... ACCA

Agricultural Credit Corp. Ltd. [*British*] (BI) .... ACC
Agricultural Decisions [*A publication*] .... AD
Agricultural Decisions [*A publication*] (DLA) .... Agric Dec
Agricultural Development and Advisory Service [*British*] (ARC) ...... ADAS
Agricultural Development and Marketing Authority [*Northern Territory, Australia*] .... ADMA
Agricultural Development and Marketing Board [*Northern Territory Australia*] .... ADMB
Agricultural Development Branch, Agriculture Canada [*Direction Generale du Developpement Agricole, Agriculture Canada*], New Westminster, British Columbia [*Library symbol National Library of Canada Obsolete*] (BIB) .... BNWAG
Agricultural Development Council [*Later, WIIAD*] (EA) ...... ADC
Agricultural Development Planning Center [*ASEAN*] [*Thailand*] [*Research center*] (IRC) .... ADPC
Agricultural Development Project [*London, England*] ...... ADP
Agricultural, Ecological, and Geographical Information System ...... AEGIS
Agricultural Economic Reports .... AER
Agricultural Economics [*Database*] [*Department of Agriculture Washington, DC*] .... AGECON
Agricultural Economics Bulletin for Africa [*A publication*] ...... AEBA
Agricultural Economics Division [*of AMS, Department of Agriculture*] ...... AEC
Agricultural Economics Research Institution [*British*] ...... AERI
Agricultural Economics Society (EAIO) .... AES
Agricultural Education Association [*British*] .... AEA
Agricultural Engineer .... AE
Agricultural Engineer .... AgE
Agricultural Engineering (DD) .... AgrEng
Agricultural Engineering Research and Development [*Canada*] ...... AERD
Agricultural Engineering Research Division [*of ARS, Department of Agriculture*] .... AE
Agricultural Engineers Association [*British*] (DS) .... AEA
Agricultural Environmental Quality Institute [*Department of Agriculture*] [*Beltsville, MD*] .... AEQI
Agricultural Equipment Advisory Committee [*Australia*] ...... AEAC
Agricultural Equipment Liaison Committee [*Victoria, Australia*] ...... AELC
Agricultural Estimates Division [*of AMS, Department of Agriculture*] ...... AES
Agricultural Executive Council [*British*] .... AEC
Agricultural Extension and Research Liaison Service [*Nigeria*] (IRC) ...... AERLS
Agricultural Extension and Rural Development Centre [*University of Reading*] [*British*] (CB) .... AERDC
Agricultural Extension Service (OICC) .... AES
Agricultural Fair Practices Act of 1967 .... AFPA
Agricultural Forecaster (NOAA) .... AF
Agricultural Foreign Investment Disclosure Act [*1978*] ...... AFIDA
Agricultural Futures Exchange [*London, England*] .... AFE
Agricultural Genetics Co. Ltd. [*British*] (IRUK) .... AGC
Agricultural History Society (EA) .... AHS
Agricultural Implements Hand [*Freight*] .... AG IMPS HND
Agricultural Implements Other Than Hand [*Freight*] ...... AG IMPS O T HND
Agricultural Improvement Council [*British*] .... AIC
Agricultural Index [*Edinburgh School of Agriculture*] [*Information service or system*] [*British*] (NITA) .... AGDEX
Agricultural Index .... AI
Agricultural, Industrial, and Development [*Bank*] [*Dominica*] (EY) ...... AID
Agricultural Industry Development Advisory Service (ODBW) ...... AIDAS
Agricultural Information and Documentation Section [*Royal Tropical Institute*] [*Netherlands Information service or system*] (IID) ...... AIDS
Agricultural Information and Marketing Services [*Department of Agriculture*] [*Information service or system*] (IID) .... AIMS
Agricultural Information Association for Australasia .... AIAA
Agricultural Information Bank for Asia [*Southeast Asian Regional Center for Graduate Study and Research in Agriculture*] [*Information service or system*] (IID) .... AIBA
Agricultural Information Bulletin .... AIB
Agricultural Information Development Scheme (EAIO) ...... AIDS
Agricultural Information Services [*HUD Information service or system*] (IID) .... AGROINFORM
Agricultural Information System (NITA) .... ARIS
Agricultural Institute of Canada .... AIC
Agricultural Laboratory Technology .... ALT
Agricultural Labourer .... AL
Agricultural Land Commission [*British*] (BI) .... ALC
Agricultural Land Service [*Later, ADAS*] [*British*] ...... ALS
Agricultural Librarians in Colleges and Universities (AIE) ...... ALCU
Agricultural Libraries Information Network [*Department of Agriculture*] [*Library network*] .... AGLINET
Agricultural Libraries Information Network [*Department of Agriculture*] [*Library network*] .... ALIN
Agricultural Library Networks [*IAALD*] [*United Kingdom*] ...... AGLINET
Agricultural Limestone Institute .... ALI
Agricultural Machinery and Tractor Dealers Association (HGAA) ...... AMTDA
Agricultural Management Information System [*European Economic Community*] (ADA) .... AMIS
Agricultural Manpower Society [*British*] (EAIO) .... AMS
Agricultural Manufacturers' Association [*Australia*] ...... AMA
Agricultural Marketing .... AM
Agricultural Marketing Administration [*World War II*] ...... AMA
Agricultural Marketing Project [*Defunct*] (EA) .... AMP
Agricultural Marketing Service [*Formerly, CMS*] [*Washington, DC Department of Agriculture*] .... AMS
Agricultural Marketing Service, P and S Docket [*United States*] [*A publication*] (DLA) .... AMS P & S
Agricultural Materials Analysis Information Service [*Laboratory of the Government Chemist*] [*British*] (NITA) .... AMAIS

Agricultural Materials in Libraries [*Later, Agriculture Library*] [*Online Computer Library Center, Inc.*] [*Information service or system*] (CRD) ...... AgMIL
Agricultural Meteorological Data Logging System (NOAA) ...... AMDLS
Agricultural Missions (EA) ...... AM
Agricultural Mortgage Corp. [*Finance British*] ...... AMC
Agricultural Network Serving Extension and Research [*University of Kentucky*] [*Lexington*] [*Information service or system*] [*Research center*] (IID) ...... ANSER
Agricultural On-Line Access [*Formerly, CAIN*] [*National Agricultural Library, Information Systems Division Bibliographic database*] [*Information service or system*] (IID) ...... AGRICOLA
Agricultural Pilots Association [*Defunct*] (EA) ...... APA
Agricultural Pipe Drain ...... APD
Agricultural Procurement Regulations ...... AGPR
Agricultural Production and Management ...... APM
Agricultural Program (NTCM) ...... A
Agricultural Property Management Regulations ...... AGPMR
Agricultural Publishers Association (EA) ...... APA
Agricultural Real Time Imaging Satellite System (PDAA) ...... ARTISS
Agricultural Relations Council (EA) ...... ARC
Agricultural Representative [*Canada*] ...... Ag Rep
Agricultural Requirements Board [*Queensland, Australia*] ...... ARB
Agricultural Research ...... AR
Agricultural Research Administration [*Superseded by ARS, 1953*] [*Department of Agriculture*] ...... ARA
Agricultural Research and Advisory Station [*New South Wales, Australia*] ...... ARAS
Agricultural Research and Education Center, Belle Glade [*University of Florida*] [*Research center*] (RCD) ...... AREC
Agricultural Research and Education Center, Fort Lauderdale [*University of Florida*] [*Research center*] (RCD) ...... AREC
Agricultural Research and Educational Center [*American University of Beirut*] ...... AREC
Agricultural Research and Veterinary Centre [*New South Wales, Australia*] ...... ARVC
Agricultural Research Center [*of ARS, Department of Agriculture*] ...... ARC
Agricultural Research Center Operations [*of ARS, Department of Agriculture*] ...... ARCO
Agricultural Research Council [*Research center British*] (IRC) ...... ARC
Agricultural Research Council Radiological Laboratory [*British*] ...... ARCRL
Agricultural Research Council Unit of Statistics [*British*] (ARC) ...... ARCUS
Agricultural Research Council Weed Research Organization [*British*] .... ARCWRO
Agricultural Research Foundation [*Oregon State University*] [*Research center*] (RCD) ...... ARF
Agricultural Research Information Centre [*Indian Council of Agricultural Research*] (IID) ...... ARIC
Agricultural Research Information Index [*United Nations*] ...... AGRINDEX
Agricultural Research Institute (EA) ...... ARI
Agricultural Research Policy Advisory Committee [*Terminated, 1977*] [*Department of Agriculture*] ...... ARPAC
Agricultural Research Service [*Washington, DC Department of Agriculture Also, an information service or system*] ...... ARS
Agricultural Research Service Water Conservation Laboratory [*Tempe, AZ*] ...... WCL-ARS
Agricultural Research Services, Animal Health Division [*Department of Agriculture ICAO designator*] (FAAC) ...... AGR
Agricultural Research Station (ADA) ...... ARS
Agricultural Resources Conservation Program [*Department of Agriculture*] ...... ARCP
Agricultural Science Review [*A publication*] ...... ASR
Agricultural Sciences Information Network [*National Agricultural Library*] [*Beltsville, MD*] ...... ASIN
Agricultural Service Information Network [*Database producer*] (NITA) ...... ASIN
Agricultural Show Council of Tasmania [*Australia*] ...... ASCT
Agricultural Show Exhibitors' Association [*British*] (BI) ...... ASEA
Agricultural Societies Council of New South Wales [*Australia*] ...... ASCNSW
Agricultural Society of Nigeria. Proceedings [*A publication*] ...... ASNP
Agricultural Soil Moisture Estimation (MCD) ...... ASME
Agricultural Special Fund [*Asian Development Bank*] [*United Nations*] (EY) ..... ASF
Agricultural Stabilization and Conservation ...... ASC
Agricultural Stabilization and Conservation Service [*Department of Agriculture*] ...... ASCS
Agricultural Statistics Board [*Department of Agriculture*] [*Information service or system*] (IID) ...... ASB
Agricultural Subterminal Facilities Act of 1980 ...... ASFA
Agricultural System for Storage and Subsequent Selection of Information [*British*] [*Information service or system*] (NITA) ...... ASSASSIN
Agricultural Systems Research Institute [*Beltsville, MD*] [*Department of Agriculture*] (GRD) ...... ASRI
Agricultural Teachers' Association of the Australian Capital Territory .... ATAACT
Agricultural Technical Assistance Foundation [*Defunct*] (EA) ...... ATAF
Agricultural Technologist [*A publication*] ...... Agric Tech
Agricultural Trade Council (EA) ...... ATC
Agricultural Trade Office [*Foreign Agricultural Service*] ...... ATO
Agricultural Wages Board [*British*] ...... AWB
Agricultural Wages Committee [*British*] (DAS) ...... AWC
Agricultural Water Quality Protection Program [*Department of Agriculture*] ...... AWQPP
Agricultural Weather Service Center [*National Oceanic and Atmospheric Administration*] ...... AWSC
Agricultural Workers' Organization ...... AWO
Agricultural Workers Organizing Committee [*Later, UFWA*] [*AFL-CIO*] ...... AWOC
Agricultural Workers' Union (DAS) ...... AWU
Agricultural-Biological Literature Exploitation [*Systems study of National Agricultural Library*] ...... ABLE
Agriculture ...... AG
Agriculture (DD) ...... Agr
Agriculture ...... AGRCLT
Agriculture (DLA) ...... AGRI
Agriculture ...... AGRIC
Agriculture and Consumer Protection Act of 1973 ...... ACPA
Agriculture and Fishery Development Corp. [*South Korea*] ...... AFDC
Agriculture and Forestry Committee [*US Senate*] ...... A & F
Agriculture and Forestry Secretariat ...... AFS
Agriculture and Livestock Professional Photographers Association (EA) ...... ALPPA
Agriculture and Markets [*A publication*] (DLA) ...... Agric & Mkts
Agriculture and Resource Management Council of Australia and New Zealand ...... ARMCANZ
Agriculture and Resources Inventory Survey through Aerospace Remote Sensing ...... AgRISTARS
Agriculture and Resources Inventory Surveys through Aerospace (MCD) ...... AGRISTARS
Agriculture and Rural Development Subsidiary Agreement [*Canada*] ...... ARDSA
Agriculture Biotechnology Research Advisory Committee [*Department of Agriculture*] (EGAO) ...... ABRAC
Agriculture Board of Contract Appeals (AAGC) ...... AGBCA
Agriculture Canada ...... AGC
Agriculture Canada ...... AGRIC
Agriculture Canada, Lethbridge, Alberta [*Library symbol National Library of Canada*] (NLC) ...... ALAG
Agriculture Canada Library [*UTLAS symbol*] ...... DAG
Agriculture Canada, Montreal, Quebec [*Library symbol National Library of Canada*] (NLC) ...... QMPCA
Agriculture Canada, Saint Hyacinthe Food Research Centre, Saint Hyacinthe, PQ, Canada [*Library symbol*] [*Library of Congress*] (LCLS) ...... CaQStHAG
Agriculture Canada, Vancouver, British Columbia [*Library symbol National Library of Canada*] (NLC) ...... BVAAG
Agriculture Council of America (EA) ...... ACA
Agriculture Department [*US government*] ...... A
Agriculture Department (US) (AAGC) ...... Ag
Agriculture Department's Automated Manpower ...... ADAM
Agriculture Division [*Census*] (OICC) ...... AGR
Agriculture, Forestry, Fishing [*Department of Employment*] [*British*] ...... AFF
Agriculture (Great Britain). Ministry of Agriculture, Fisheries, and Food [*A publication*] ...... A/GB
Agriculture Handbook ...... AH
Agriculture, Nutrition, and Forestry (DLA) ...... ANF
Agriculture Online [*Doane Western, Inc.*] (NITA) ...... AGLINE
Agriculture Working Group ...... AWG
AgriData Network [*AgriData Resources, Inc.*] [*Milwaukee, WI*] [*Telecommunications service*] (TSSD) ...... ADN
AgriDyne Technologies, Inc. [*NASDAQ symbol*] (SAG) ...... AGRI
AgriDyne Technologies, Inc. [*Associated Press*] (SAG) ...... AgriDyn
Agri-Energy Roundtable (EA) ...... AER
Agri-Markets Data Service [*Capitol Publications, Inc.*] [*Database*] [*Defunct*] ...... AMDS
Agrinion [*Greece*] [*Airport symbol*] (AD) ...... AGQ
Agrinion [*Greece*] [*ICAO location identifier*] (ICLI) ...... LGAG
Agri-Nutrition Group [*Associated Press*] (SAG) ...... AgriNutr
Agri-Nutrition Group Ltd. [*NASDAQ symbol*] (SAG) ...... AGNU
Agri-Products Exporters Association (EA) ...... APEA
Agriservices Foundation (EA) ...... AF
Agri-Silviculture Institute (EA) ...... ASI
Agrium, Inc. [*Associated Press*] (SAG) ...... Agrium
Agrium, Inc. [*NYSE symbol*] (SAG) ...... AGU
Agro-Environmental Monitoring System [*Computerized Data Collection*] ..... AEMS
Agrolet-Mci Ltd. [*Slovakia*] [*FAA designator*] (FAAC) ...... AGZ
Agronomy ...... AGRON
Agronomy Research Center [*Southern Illinois University at Carbondale*] [*Research center*] (RCD) ...... ARC
Agrophysics Breeding Control Device [*Birth-control device for dogs*] ...... ABCD
Agropyron Mosaic Virus [*Plant pathology*] ...... AGMV
Agrotikon Komma [*Agrarian Party*] [*Greek Political party*] (PPE) ...... AGROT
Agrotikon Komma Ellados [*Agrarian Party of Greece*] [*Political party*] ...... AKE
Agrupacion de Exportadores del Centro de Espana [*Trade association*] [*Spain*] (EY) ...... AGRECE
Agrupacion Herrena Independiente [*Spain Political party*] (EY) ...... AHI
Agrupaciones Independientes de Canarias [*Spain Political party*] (EY) ...... AIC
Agrupament Democratic d'Andorra [*Andorran Democratic Association*] [*Political party*] (PPW) ...... ADA
Aguada, PR [*FM radio station call letters*] ...... WNNV
Aguadilla [*Puerto Rico*] [*Airport symbol*] (OAG) ...... BQN
Aguadilla/Borinquen [*Puerto Rico*] [*ICAO location identifier*] (ICLI) ...... TJBQ
Aguadilla, PR [*Location identifier FAA*] (FAAL) ...... JFF
Aguadilla, PR [*AM radio station call letters*] ...... WABA
Aguadilla, PR [*Television station call letters*] ...... WELU
Aguadilla, PR [*FM radio station call letters*] ...... WIVA
Aguadilla, PR [*AM radio station call letters*] ...... WNOZ
Aguadilla, PR [*Television station call letters*] ...... WOLE
Aguadilla, PR [*FM radio station call letters*] ...... WTPM
Aguadilla, PR [*Television station call letters*] ...... WVEO
Aguan [*Papua New Guinea*] [*Airport symbol*] (OAG) ...... AUP
Aguarico [*Ecuador*] [*ICAO location identifier*] (ICLI) ...... SERI
Aguas Blancas [*Peru*] [*ICAO location identifier*] (ICLI) ...... SPCB
Aguas Calientes [*Peru*] [*ICAO location identifier*] (ICLI) ...... SPAT
Aguascalientes [*Mexico*] [*Airport symbol*] (OAG) ...... AGU
Aguascalientes [*Mexico ICAO location identifier*] (ICLI) ...... MMAS

Agudas Harabonim [*Union of Orthodox Rabbis of the United States and Canada*] .... AH
Agudas Israel World Organization [*Jerusalem, Israel*] .... AIWO
Agudath Israel [*Union of Israel*] [*World organization of Orthodox Jews*] .... AI
Agudath Israel of America (EA) .... AIA
Agudath Shofte ha-Hakhra'ah ha-Yehudit (BJA) .... ASHY
Aguelhoc [*Mali*] [*ICAO location identifier*] (ICLI) .... GAGL
Aguilar Public Library, Aguilar, CO [*Library symbol Library of Congress*] (LCLS) .... CoAg
Aguni [*Japan*] [*Airport symbol*] (OAG) .... AGJ
Aguni [*Ryukyu Islands*] [*ICAO location identifier*] (ICLI) .... RORA
Agusta [*Construzioni Aeronautiche Giovanni Agusta SpA*] [*Italy ICAO aircraft manufacturer identifier*] (ICAO) .... A
Agway, Inc., Library, Syracuse, NY [*OCLC symbol*] (OCLC) .... ZUL
Agway, Inc., Syracuse, NY [*Library symbol Library of Congress*] (LCLS) ...... NSyAg
AHA Automotive Technologies Corp. [*Toronto Stock Exchange symbol*] .... AHA
Ah-Ah [*Lava-Flow*] [*Hawaiian*] .... AA
Ahar [*Iran*] [*ICAO location identifier*] (ICLI) .... OITQ
Aharonov-Bohm [*Physics*] .... AB
Ahavah, Zedakah, Ahdut (BJA) .... AZA
Ahead (FAAC) .... AHD
Ahead Flag [*Navy British*] .... AD
Ahead-Throwing Weapon [*Antisubmarine*] .... ATW
AHI Healthcare Systems, Inc. [*Associated Press*] (SAG) .... AHIHlth
AHI Healthcare Systems, Inc. [*NASDAQ symbol*] (SAG) .... AHIS
Ahikar (BJA) .... Ah
Ahilot (BJA) .... Ah
AHL Group [*Formerly, Automotive Hardware Ltd.*] [*Toronto Stock Exchange symbol*] .... AHL
Ahlhorn [*Germany ICAO location identifier*] (ICLI) .... EDNA
Ahmadabad [*India*] [*ICAO location identifier*] (ICLI) .... VAAH
Ahmadiyya Muslim Association (EAIO) .... AMA
Ahmanson [*H. F.*] & Co. [*NYSE symbol*] (SPSG) .... AHM
Ahmanson [*H.F.*] & Co. [*Associated Press*] (SAG) .... Ahmans
Ahmanson [*H.F.*] & Co. [*Associated Press*] (SAG) .... Ahmn
Ahmedabad [*India*] [*Airport symbol*] (OAG) .... AMD
[*The*] Ahnapee & Western Railway Co. [*Formerly, AW*] [*AAR code*] .... AHW
[*The*] Ahnapee & Western Railway Co. [*Later, AHW*] [*AAR code*] .... AW
Aho Weinberger Kernighan (CDE) .... awk
Ahold Ltd. [*NYSE symbol*] (SAG) .... AHO
Ahold Ltd. [*Associated Press*] (SAG) .... Ahold
Ahoskie, NC [*Location identifier FAA*] (FAAL) .... ASJ
Ahoskie, NC [*FM radio station call letters*] .... WQDK
Ahoskie, NC [*AM radio station call letters*] .... WRCS
Ahoskie Public Library, Ahoskie, NC [*Library symbol Library of Congress*] (LCLS) .... NcAh
Ahoy [*Slang*] (DNAB) .... AY
Ahrens-Fox Fire Buffs Club [*Defunct*] (EA) .... AFFBC
Ahtari [*Finland ICAO location identifier*] (ICLI) .... EFHT
Ahua [*Hawaii*] [*Seismograph station code, US Geological Survey*] (SEIS) ...... AHA
Ahuachapan [*El Salvador*] [*Seismograph station code, US Geological Survey*] (SEIS) .... AHU
Ahvenanmaan Kokoomus; Alaendsk Samling [*Aland Coalition*] [*Finland*] (PPE) .... ALSAML
Ahwaz [*Iran*] [*Airport symbol Obsolete*] (OAG) .... AWZ
Ahwaz [*Iran*] [*ICAO location identifier*] (ICLI) .... OIAW
Aid and Attendance (MAE) .... A & A
Aid and Trade Provision [*Shipping*] (DS) .... ATP
Aid Association for Lutherans (EA) .... AAL
Aid Auto Stores, Inc. [*NASDAQ symbol*] (SAG) .... AIDA
Aid Auto Stores, Inc. [*Associated Press*] (SAG) .... AidAut
Aid Auto Stores, Inc. [*Associated Press*] (SAG) .... AidAuto
AID [*Agency for International Development*] Consultant Registry Information System (IID) .... ACRIS
Aid for Afghan Refugees [*An association*] (EA) .... AAR
Aid for Afghan Refugees [*An association*] (EA) .... AFAR
Aid for Commonwealth English Scheme [*British*] .... ACE
Aid for Commonwealth Teaching of Science Scheme [*British*] .... ACTS
Aid for India [*An association British*] (EAIO) .... AFI
Aid for International Medicine (EA) .... AIM
Aid for the Elderly in Government Institutions [*British*] .... AEGIS
Aid Refugee Chinese Intellectuals [*Defunct*] (EA) .... ARCI
Aid to Adoption of Special Kids [*An association*] (EA) .... AASK
Aid to Artisans (EA) .... ATA
Aid to Believers in the Soviet Union [*See also ACU*] [*Paris, France*] (EAIO) .... ABSU
Aid to Children with Tracheostomies [*British*] [*An association*] (DBA) .... ACT
Aid to Dependent Children .... ADC
Aid to Displaced Persons and Its European Villages (EAIO) .... ADPEV
Aid to Families with Dependent Children .... AFDC
Aid to Families with Dependent Children of Unemployed Fathers .... AFDCUF
Aid to Families with Dependent Children - Unemployed Parents .... AFDC-UP
Aid to Improved Marksmanship [*Army training aid*] (INF) .... AIM
Aid to Incarcerated Mothers (EA) .... AIM
Aid to the Aged, Blind, or Disabled [*Department of Health and Human Services*] .... AABD
Aid to the Blind .... AB
Aid to the Church in Need (EA) .... ACN
Aid to the Disabled .... AD
Aid to the Permanently and Totally Disabled [*HEW*] .... APTD
Aid to the Potentially Self-Supporting Blind (IIA) .... APSB
Aid to the Totally and Permanently Disabled [*Social Security Administration*] (OICC) .... ATPD
Aid to the Totally Disabled (IIA) .... ATD

Aide aux Personnes Deplacees et Ses Villages Europeens [*Aid to Displaced Persons and Its European Villages*] (EAIO) .... APDVE
Aide Informatisee pour le Developpement des Entreprises [*Automated Information for Management - AIM*] .... AIDE
Aided .... AID
Aided Card (LAIN) .... AC
Aided Display Submarine Control System [*Navy*] (MCD) .... ADSCS
Aided LASER Tracking System (RDA) .... ALTS
Aided School [*British*] .... A
Aided Target Detection / Classification [*Military*] .... ATD/C
Aided Target Recognition [*Army*] .... ATR
Aided Tracking .... ADT
Aided Tracking System (IAA) .... ATS
Aided Visual Development Program .... AVDP
Aided Visual Homing Missile (MCD) .... AVHOM
Aided Visual Sensor System .... AVSS
Aided Visual System .... AVS
Aide-de-Camp [*Military French*] .... ADC
Aide-de-Camp General [*Appointment to the Queen*] [*British*] .... ADCGEN
Aide-de-Camp Personal [*Appointment to the Queen*] [*British*] .... ADC(P)
Aiding Leukemia Stricken American Children [*Later, ALSAC - St. Jude Children's Research Hospital*] [*Fund-raising organization*] .... ALSAC
Aiding Mothers Experienceing Neonatal Death [*Medicine*] (MEDA) .... AMEND
AIDS [*Acquired Immune Deficiency Syndrome*]-Associated Retrovirus .... ARV
AIDS [*Acquired Immune Deficiency Syndrome*] Clinical Trials Group (EA) ...... ACTG
AIDS [*Acquired Immune Deficiency Syndrome*] Clinical Trials Information Service (IID) .... ACTIS
AIDS [*Acquired Immune Deficiency Syndrome*] Coalition to Unleash Power .... ACT UP
AIDS Committee of Cambridge, Kitchener/Waterloo & Area (AC) .... ACCKWA
AIDS Committee of Guelph & Wellington County (AC) .... ACGWC
AIDS Committee of London (AC) .... ACOL
AIDS Committee of North Bay & Area [*Comite du Sida de North Bay et de la Region*] (AC) .... ACNBA
AIDS Committee of Simcoe County (AC) .... ACSC
AIDS Committee of Thunder Bay (AC) .... ACT-B
AIDS Committee of Toronto (AC) .... ACT
AIDS Committee of Windsor (AC) .... ACW
AIDS Community Care Montreal [*Sida Benevoles Montreal*] (AC) .... ACCM
AIDS [*Acquired Immune Deficiency Syndrome*] Council of Central Australia .... ACOA
AIDS [*Acquired Immune Deficiency Syndrome*] Council of South Australia .... ACOSA
AIDS [*Acquired Immune Deficiency Syndrome*] Dementia Complex [*Medicine*] .... ADC
Aids Distribution List [*Military*] (SAA) .... ADL
AIDS [*Acquired Immuno-Deficiency Syndrome*] Drug Assistance Program ..... ADAP
AIDS Education/Services for the Deaf [*An association*] .... AESD
AIDS Follow-Up Assessment Questionnaire [*Department of Health and Human Services*] (GFGA) .... AFA
AIDS Housing Group of Ottawa (AC) .... AHGO
AIDS Initial Assessment Questionnaire [*Department of Health and Human Services*] (GFGA) .... AIA
AIDS Malignancy Bank [*National Cancer Institute*] .... AMB
AIDS [*Acquired Immune Deficiency Syndrome*] Prevention League (EA) .... APPLE
Aids Production and Distribution List (SAA) .... APDL
AIDS [*Acquired Immune Deficiency Syndrome*]-Related Complex [*Medicine*] ... ARC
AIDS [*Acquired Immune Deficiency Syndrome*] Related Virus [*Immunology*] (DAVI) .... ARV
AIDS Research Advisory Committee [*National Institutes of Health*] (EGAO) .... ARAC
AIDS Resource Foundation for Children (EA) .... ARFC
AIDS Saint John (AC) .... ASJ
AIDS Services and Prevention Coalition (EA) .... ASAP
AIDS Society for Asia and the Pacific .... ASFAP
AIDS [*Acquired Immune Deficiency Syndrome*] Targeted Information Newsletter [*Williams & Wilkins*] [*A publication*] .... ATIN
Aids to Communication in Education (AIE) .... ACE
Aids to Navigation .... A to N
Aids to Navigation .... AN
Aids to Navigation .... ATON
Aids to Navigation Boat .... ANB
Aids to Navigation Radio Control [*Military*] .... ANRAC
Aids Vaccine Advocacy Coalition .... AVAC
AIDS Vancouver Island [*Also Vancouver Island AIDS Society*] (AC) .... AVI
AIDS Virus Education and Research Trust [*British*] .... AVERT
Aidu [*Inawashiro*] [*Seismograph station code, US Geological Survey Closed*] (SEIS) .... AID
Aiea, HI [*FM radio station call letters*] .... KGMZ
Aigen/Ennstal [*Austria ICAO location identifier*] (ICLI) .... LOXA
Aigle Azur [*France ICAO designator*] (FAAC) .... AAF
Aigner Holdings [*Vancouver Stock Exchange symbol*] .... AHS
Aikawa [*Japan*] [*Seismograph station code, US Geological Survey*] (SEIS) .... AIK
Aiken Dahlgren Electronic Calculator (MCD) .... ADEC
Aiken Dynamic Algebra (MCD) .... ADA
Aiken Relay Calculator .... ARC
Aiken, SC [*Location identifier FAA*] (FAAL) .... AIK
Aiken, SC [*FM radio station call letters*] .... WKXC
Aiken, SC [*FM radio station call letters*] .... WLJK
Aiken, SC [*FM radio station call letters*] .... WRXR
Aiken Technical College, Aiken, SC [*Library symbol*] [*Library of Congress*] (LCLS) .... ScAiTC
Aiken-Bamberg-Barnwell-Edgefield Regional Library, Aiken, SC [*Library symbol Library of Congress*] (LCLS) .... ScAi
Aiken's Digest of Alabama Statutes [*A publication*] (DLA) .... Aik Dig

Aiken's Digest of Alabama Statutes [*A publication*] (DLA) .... Aik Stat
Aikens, Macaulay & Thorauldson Law Firm, Winnipeg, MB, Canada [*Library symbol Library of Congress*] (LCLS) .... CaMWAMT
Aikens' Vermont Reports [*A publication*] (DLA) .... Aik Rep
Aikens' Vermont Reports [*A publication*] (DLA) .... Aik (VT) Rep
Aikens' Vermont Reports [*A publication*] (DLA) .... Aikens' Rep
Aikens' Vermont Reports [*A publication*] (DLA) .... Aikens (VT)
Aikens' Vermont Supreme Court Reports [*1825-28*] [*A publication*] (DLA) .... Aik
Aikins, MacAulay, and Thorvaldson Law Firm, Winnipeg, Manitoba [*Library symbol National Library of Canada*] (NLC) .... MWAMT
AIL Absorbent Industry [*Vancouver Stock Exchange symbol*] .... AIJ
Aileen, Inc. [*NYSE symbol*] (SPSG) .... AEE
Aileen, Inc. (IIA) .... AIL
Aileen, Inc. [*Associated Press*] (SAG) .... Aileen
Aileron [*Aviation*] .... AIL
Aileron [*Martinique*] [*Seismograph station code, US Geological Survey*] (SEIS) .... AIL
Aileron Rudder Interconnect (MCD) .... ARI
Aileron Station (MCD) .... AS
Ailing-In Difficulty .... AID
Ailuk [*Marshall Islands*] [*Airport symbol*] (OAG) .... AIM
Aim Point Bias [*Military*] .... APB
Aim Safety Co. [*Vancouver Stock Exchange symbol*] .... ASF
AIM Strategic Income Fd [*AMEX symbol*] (TTSB) .... AST
AIM Strategic Income Fund [*Associated Press*] (SAG) .... AIM Str
AIM Strategic Income Fund [*AMEX symbol*] (SPSG) .... AST
Aiming Point .... AP
Aiming Point Determination .... APD
Aiming Symbol (DNAB) .... AS
Aimpoint Correlator [*Weaponry*] (MCD) .... APC
Aim-Point-Miss .... APM
Aims College, Greeley, CO [*Library symbol Library of Congress*] (LCLS) .... CoGrA
Ain Oussera [*Algeria*] [*ICAO location identifier*] (ICLI) .... DAAQ
Ain Shems (BJA) .... AS
Ain Zalah [*Iraq*] [*ICAO location identifier*] (ICLI) .... ORBZ
Ainahou [*Hawaii*] [*Seismograph station code, US Geological Survey*] (SEIS) .... AIN
Ainsworth, NE [*Location identifier FAA*] (FAAL) .... ANW
Ainsworth, NE [*AM radio station call letters*] .... KBRB
Ainsworth, NE [*FM radio station call letters*] .... KBRB-FM
Ainsworth's Latin-English Dictionary [*1837*] [*A publication*] (DLA) .... Ainsworth Lex
Ainsworth's Lexicon [*A publication*] (DLA) .... Ainsw
Aintree Resources [*Vancouver Stock Exchange symbol*] .... ANJ
Aiome [*Papua New Guinea*] [*Airport symbol*] (OAG) .... AIE
Aioun El Atrouss [*Mauritania*] [*Airport symbol*] (OAG) .... AEO
Aioun El Atrouss [*Mauritania*] [*ICAO location identifier*] (ICLI) .... GQNA
Aiquile [*Bolivia*] [*ICAO location identifier*] (ICLI) .... SLAQ
Air .... A
Air 21, Inc. [*FAA designator*] (FAAC) .... RKT
Air 500 Ltd. [*Canada ICAO designator*] (FAAC) .... BRM
Air 2000 Airlines Ltd. [*Canada ICAO designator*] (FAAC) .... CMM
Air 2000, Ltd, [*British ICAO designator*] (FAAC) .... AMM
Air Abort (SAA) .... A/A
Air Abrasive Trimming (PDAA) .... AAT
Air Accident .... AIRACCDT
Air Accounting and Finance Center [*Air Force*] .... AAFC
Air Acetylene Welding .... AAW
Air ACG [*France*] [*FAA designator*] (FAAC) .... QSP
Air Acoustic Echo Ranging System [*Automotive safety systems*] .... AAERS
Air Activities Logistic Information System (MCD) .... AIRACLIS
Air Adjutant-General [*Military*] .... AAG
Air Administrative Net [*Army*] (AABC) .... AIRAD
Air Affaires EJA France [*ICAO designator*] (FAAC) .... AEJ
Air Afrique (MCD) .... AFQ
Air Afrique [*Ivory Coast*] [*ICAO designator*] (ICDA) .... RK
Air Afrique [*Ivory Coast*] [*ICAO designator*] (FAAC) .... RKA
Air Afrique Vacances [*Ivory Coast*] [*FAA designator*] (FAAC) .... AFV
Air Aide-de-Camp [*RAF*] [*British*] .... AADC
Air Alba Ltd. [*British ICAO designator*] (FAAC) .... RLB
Air Alfa Hava Yollari Ve Tec, AS [*Turkey*] [*FAA designator*] (FAAC) .... LFA
Air Algerie [*ICAO designator*] (AD) .... AH
Air Algerie [*Algeria*] [*ICAO designator*] (FAAC) .... DAH
Air Alliance, Inc. [*Canada ICAO designator*] (FAAC) .... AAQ
Air Alma, Inc. [*Canada ICAO designator*] (FAAC) .... AAJ
Air Alpes [*ICAO designator*] (AD) .... LP
Air Alpha, AS [*Denmark*] [*ICAO designator*] (FAAC) .... AHA
Air Alpha, Inc. [*ICAO designator*] (FAAC) .... DBA
Air Alsace [*ICAO designator*] (AD) .... SY
Air Alsie, AS [*Denmark ICAO designator*] (FAAC) .... ALS
Air Ambulance Network [*MTMC*] (TAG) .... AAN
Air America [*ICAO designator*] (AD) .... GM
Air America, Inc. (CINC) .... AA
Air America, Inc. [*Air carrier designation symbol*] .... AAMX
Air and Earth Shock (MCD) .... AES
Air and Energy Engineering Research Laboratory [*Research Triangle Park, NC*] [*Environmental Protection Agency*] (GRD) .... AEERL
Air and Energy Staff [*Environmental Protection Agency*] (GFGA) .... AES
Air and Expedited Motor Carriers Conference (EA) .... AEMCC
Air and Ground Forces Resources and Technical Staff [*Army*] .... AGFRTS
Air and Naval Gunfire Liaison Company [*Military*] .... ANGLICO
Air and Radiation Division [*Environmental Protection Agency*] (GFGA) .... AR
Air and Radiation Division [*Environmental Protection Agency*] (GFGA) .... ARD
Air and Rail [*Shipping*] .... A & R
Air and Space Lawyer [*A publication*] (DLA) .... Air & Space Law
Air & Space/Smithsonian [*A publication*] (BRI) .... A & S Sm
Air and Toxics Division [*Environmental Protection Agency*] (GFGA) .... ATD
Air and Waste Management (OICC) .... AWM
Air and Waste Management Association (FFDE) .... AWMA
Air and Waste Management Division [*Environmental Protection Agency*] (GFGA) .... AWMD
Air & Water Tech'A' [*AMEX symbol*] (TTSB) .... AWT
Air & Water Technologies Corp. [*Associated Press*] (SAG) .... AirWat
Air & Water Technologies Corp. [*AMEX symbol*] (SPSG) .... AWT
Air Anglia [*ICAO designator*] (AD) .... AQ
Air Angouleme [*France ICAO designator*] (FAAC) .... AGL
Air Antares Ltd. [*Romania*] [*ICAO designator*] (FAAC) .... AAY
Air Antilles [*Airline*] (MHDB) .... GD
Air Antisubmarine Squadron [*Navy*] .... AIRANTISUBRON
Air Antisubmarine Squadron [*Navy*] .... VS
Air [*Defense*] **Anti-Tank System** (DOMA) .... ATATS
Air Approach Control (MCD) .... AAC
Air Aquitaine [*France ICAO designator*] (FAAC) .... AQE
Air Arc Heater .... AAH
Air Arc Heater Housing .... AAHH
Air [*Traffic*] **Area Control** (DOMA) .... AAC
Air Armament (NATG) .... AA
Air Armament School [*British military*] (DMA) .... AAS
Air Armorique [*France*] [*FAA designator*] (FAAC) .... RMQ
Air Aruba [*ICAO designator*] (FAAC) .... ARU
Air Aruba [*ICAO designator*] (AD) .... FQ
Air Assault [*Military*] (DOMA) .... AA
Air Assault [*Army*] (AABC) .... AASLT
Air Assault Badge [*Military decoration*] (GFGA) .... AIRASLT
Air Assault Brigade (MCD) .... AAB
Air Assault Division [*Army*] .... AAD
Air Assault Task Force [*Army*] (ADDR) .... AATF
Air Assault Task Force [*Army*] (INF) .... AATFC
Air at Atmospheric Pressure (MAE) .... AAP
Air Atlantic [*Canada ICAO designator*] (FAAC) .... ATL
Air Atlantic Airlines [*ICAO designator*] (AD) .... OX
Air Atlantic Uruguay [*ICAO designator*] (FAAC) .... AUM
Air Atlantique [*British ICAO designator*] (FAAC) .... AAG
Air Atlantique [*ICAO designator*] (AD) .... ES
Air Atlantique [*ICAO designator*] (AD) .... KL
Air Atlantique Air Publicite [*France ICAO designator*] (FAAC) .... APB
Air Atlas/Air Maroc .... ATM
Air Atonabee Ltd. [*Canada ICAO designator*] (FAAC) .... OUL
Air Attache [*British*] .... AA
Air Attache [*Air Force*] .... AIRA
Air Attack RADAR .... AAR
Air Aurora, Inc. [*ICAO designator*] (FAAC) .... AAI
Air Austral [*France*] [*FAA designator*] (FAAC) .... REU
Air Bag Impact Attentuation System (MCD) .... ABIAS
Air Bag Skid System (MCD) .... ABSS
Air Bag System Diagnostic Module [*Automotive engineering*] .... ASDM
Air Bags .... AB
Air Balance Consultants (EA) .... ABC
Air Balear [*ICAO designator*] (ICDA) .... JI
Air Ballistics Missile Division [*Air Force*] .... ABMD
Air Ban Ltd. [*Bulgaria*] [*FAA designator*] (FAAC) .... BAN
Air Barrier Exercise [*Military*] (NVT) .... AIRBAREX
Air Base .... AB
Air Base Advisory Team (CINC) .... ABAT
Air Base Air Defense [*Air Force*] (MCD) .... ABAD
Air Base Augmentation Support Set [*Air Force*] (AFM) .... ABASS
Air Base Commander .... AIRBASECOM
Air Base Damage Assessment Model (MCD) .... ADAM
Air Base Damage Assessment Model (MCD) .... AIDA
Air Base Defense/Sensor Communications and Display System [*Air Force*] (MCD) .... ABD/SCADS
Air Base Flight [*Air Force*] .... ABF
Air Base Group [*Obsolete Navy*] .... ABG
Air Base Group [*Air Force*] .... ABGP
Air Base Simulator [*Air Force*] .... ABS
Air Base Squadron [*Air Force*] .... ABS
Air Base Squadron [*Air Force*] .... ABSq
Air Base Survivability .... ABS
Air Base Wing [*Air Force*] (MCD) .... ABW
Air Base Wing [*Air Force*] .... ABWG
Air Bases Command, 1st Naval District .... AB ONE
Air Bath Chamber .... ABC
Air Battalion Royal Engineers [*Later, Royal Aircraft Establishment*] [*British*] .... ABRE
Air Battle Analysis Center Utility System [*Air Force*] .... ABACUS
Air Battle Analysis Division [*Air Force*] .... ABAD
Air Battle Captain (INF) .... ABC
Air Battle Captain (DOMA) .... ABC
Air Battle Management [*Military*] .... ABM
Air Battle Net [*Military*] (INF) .... ABN
Air BC Ltd. [*Canada ICAO designator*] (FAAC) .... ABL
Air Bearing (KSC) .... AB
Air Bearing Lift Pad (KSC) .... ABLP
Air Bearing Platform .... ABP
Air Belgium [*ICAO designator*] (FAAC) .... ABB
Air Berlin USA [*ICAO designator*] (ICDA) .... AB
Air Berlin, USA [*Germany ICAO designator*] (FAAC) .... BER
Air Blast (MSA) .... AB
Air Blast Circuit Breaker .... ABCB
Air Blast Cooled (IAA) .... ABC
Air Blast Heat Exchanger [*Nuclear energy*] (NRCH) .... ABHX
Air Blast Loading .... ABL

Air Blast Time-of-Arrival Detector (PDAA) .... ABTOAD
Air Blast Transformer (MSA) .... ABT
Air Blast Valve .... ABV
Air Bleed Actuator Valve [Automotive engineering] .... ABAV
Air Board [RAF] [British] .... AB
Air Board Order .... ABO
Air Bomber .... AB
Air Bombers Training Unit [Navy] .... ABTU
Air Botnia OY, AB, Finland [FAA designator] (FAAC) .... KFB
Air Botswana [ICAO designator] (AD) .... BP
Air Botswana (Pty) Ltd. [ICAO designator] (FAAC) .... BOT
Air Brake [Automotive engineering] .... AB
Air Brake Association (EA) .... ABA
Air Bras d'Or [Canada ICAO designator] (FAAC) .... BRL
Air Bravo [Uganda] [ICAO designator] (FAAC) .... BRF
Air Break [Mechanical engineering] (IAA) .... AB
Air Breather [Aerospace] .... A/B
Air Breathing Missile [Military] (LAIN) .... ABM
Air Bremen [ICAO designator] (AD) .... HR
Air Brick .... AB
Air Bridge Carriers [ICAO designator] (AD) .... AG
Air Bristol, Ltd. [British] [FAA designator] (FAAC) .... AZX
Air Brousse, Inc. [Canada ICAO designator] (FAAC) .... ABT
Air Bubble Craft .... ABC
Air Bubble Vehicle .... ABV
Air Budapest Club Ltd. [Hungary ICAO designator] (FAAC) .... BUD
Air Burkina [Burkina Faso] [ICAO designator] (FAAC) .... VBW
Air Burkina [ICAO designator] (AD) .... VH
Air Burst Contact Maker .... ABCM
Air Burst Effect .... ABE
Air Burst Fuze .... ABF
Air Burst/Surface Burst (MCD) .... ABSB
Air Burundi [ICAO designator] (AD) .... PB
Air Business Contact [France ICAO designator] (FAAC) .... ABC
Air Busol [Ukraine] [FAA designator] (FAAC) .... BUA
Air BVI [ICAO designator] (AD) .... BL
Air Bypass Valve [Automotive engineering] .... ABV
Air Cadet Central Gliding School [British] .... ACCGS
Air Cadet League of Canada [World War II] .... ACLC
Air Cadets School [RAF] [British ICAO designator] (FAAC) .... ACW
Air Caledonia, Inc. [Canada ICAO designator] (FAAC) .... ACM
Air Caledonie [France ICAO designator] (FAAC) .... TPC
Air Caledonie [ICAO designator] (AD) .... TY
Air Caledonie International [France ICAO designator] (FAAC) .... ACI
Air Caledonie International [ICAO designator] (AD) .... SB
Air California [Air carrier designation symbol] .... ACAX
Air California (MCD) .... ACF
Air California [Air carrier designation symbol] (AD) .... OC
Air Call Medical Services [British] .... ACMS
Air Canada [ICAO designator] (OAG) .... AC
Air Canada [ICAO designator] (FAAC) .... ACA
Air Canada (MHDW) .... AIR CAN
Air Canada Corp. [Vancouver Stock Exchange symbol Toronto Stock Exchange symbol] .... AC
Air Canada Corp. [NASDAQ symbol] (SAG) .... ACNA
Air Canada Corp. [Associated Press] (SAG) .... AirCan
Air Canada Library [UTLAS symbol] .... ACA
Air Canada, Montreal, PQ, Canada [Library symbol Library of Congress] (LCLS) .... CaQMTC
Air Canada, Montreal, Quebec [Library symbol National Library of Canada] (NLC) .... QMTC
Air Canada'A' [NASDAQ symbol] (TTSB) .... ACNAF
Air Canarias S. Coop Ltd. [Spain ICAO designator] (FAAC) .... CAN
Air Capable Ship (MCD) .... ACS
Air Cape [ICAO designator] (FAAC) .... ACK
Air Cape [South Africa ICAO designator] (FAAC) .... ACP
Air Capitol [Italy ICAO designator] (FAAC) .... ACL
Air Caravane [ICAO designator] (AD) .... EN
Air Carbon Arc Cutting [Welding] .... AAC
Air Carcinogen Policy [Environmental Protection Agency] (GFGA) .... ACP
Air Cargo America, Inc. [ICAO designator] (FAAC) .... MVM
Air Cargo Belize Ltd. [FAA designator] (FAAC) .... CGB
Air Cargo Carriers, Inc. [ICAO designator] (FAAC) .... PRT
Air Cargo Carriers, Inc. [ICAO designator] (FAAC) .... SNC
Air Cargo Exhibition [British] (ITD) .... ACE
Air Cargo Express, Inc. .... ACG
Air Cargo Fast Flow (DA) .... ACFF
Air Cargo Glider .... ACG
Air Cargo Integrated System (MCD) .... ACIS
Air Cargo Processing in the 80's [British Telecom] .... ACP 80
Air Caribe [ICAO designator] (AD) .... QA
Air Caribe International [ICAO designator] (AD) .... ZE
Air Carolina [ICAO designator] (AD) .... FN
Air Carrier Activity Information System [BTS] [FAA] (TAG) .... ACAIS
Air Carrier Contract Personnel .... AACP
Air Carrier District Office .... ACDO
Air Carrier Economic Regulation Act .... ACERA
Air Carrier Engineering Service .... ACES
Air Carrier Flight Engineers Association .... ACFEA
Air Carrier Mechanic Association .... ACMA
Air Carrier Safety District Office .... ACSDO
Air Carrier Service Corp. .... ACSC
Air Carrier Standard Security Programs [FAA] (TAG) .... ACSSP
Air Cavalry (BARN) .... Aircav
Air Cavalry Attack Brigade (MCD) .... ACAB

Air Cavalry Combat Brigade [Army] .... ACCB
Air Cavalry Combat Brigade/Triple Capability Division [Army] (MCD) .... ACCB/TRICAP
Air Cavalry Division [Army] .... ACD
Air Cavalry Regiment .... ACR
Air Cavalry Troop (DOMA) .... ACT
Air Center Commander .... ACC
Air Central [ICAO designator] (AD) .... HV
Air Ceylon Ltd. .... AIRCEY
Air Change per Hour [Ventilation and infiltration rates] .... ACH
Air Change per Hour [Ventilation and infiltration rates] .... ACPH
Air Characteristic Improvement Board [Navy] (DOMA) .... ACIB
Air Charter [France ICAO designator] (FAAC) .... ACF
Air Charter Carriers Association (MHDB) .... ACCA
Air Charter Express [France ICAO designator] (FAAC) .... CHX
Air Charter Express AS [Norway ICAO designator] (FAAC) .... ECR
Air Charter Ltd. (Leiguflug Isleifs Ottesen) [Iceland] [FAA designator] (FAAC) .... LIO
Air Charter Services [Zaire] [ICAO designator] (FAAC) .... CHR
Air Charter Services (Pty) Ltd. South Africa [ICAO designator] (FAAC) .... IPL
Air Charter World [ICAO designator] (FAAC) .... XAC
Air Charters [Senegal] [ICAO designator] (ICDA) .... JV
Air Charters, Inc. [Canada ICAO designator] (FAAC) .... ACX
Air Chathams [Airline code] [Australia] CV
Air Chico [ICAO designator] (AD) .... FZ
Air Chief Commandant [British] .... ACC
Air Chief Marshal [RAF] [British] .... ACM
Air China [ICAO designator] (FAAC) .... CCA
Air Circuit Breaker .... ACB
Air Circulating .... ACIRC
Air City SA [Switzerland ICAO designator] (FAAC) .... ACY
Air Cleaner [Automotive engineering] .... A/CLNR
Air Cleaner .... AIRCLNR
Air Cleaner Bi-Metal Sensor [Automotive engineering] .... ACLBIMET
Air Cleaner Cold Weather Modulator [Automotive engineering] .... ACCWM
Air Cleaner Duct and Valve [Automotive engineering] .... ACLDV
Air Cleaner Gasket [Automotive engineering] .... ACL
Air Cleaner Housing [Automotive engineering] .... ACH
Air Cleanup Unit [Nuclear energy] (NRCH) .... ACU
Air Clearance Authority .... ACA
Air Club International [Canada] [FAA designator] (FAAC) CLI
Air Clutch Antislack Device (CAAL) .... ACASD
Air Coach Transport Association .... ACTA
Air Coating System (PDAA) .... ACS
Air Collection and Enrichment .... ACE
Air Collection and Enrichment System .... ACES
Air Collection Engine System .... ACES
Air Colombia [ICAO designator] (FAAC) .... ACO
Air Columbus SA [Portugal ICAO designator] (FAAC) .... CNB
Air Combat Analysis .... ACA
Air Combat and Surveillance System (MCD) .... ACSS
Air Combat Command [Air Force] .... ACC
Air Combat Element (MCD) .... ACE
Air Combat Emulator [Computer game] .... ACE
Air Combat Engagement (MCD) .... ACE
Air Combat Engagement Experiment .... ACEE
Air Combat Evaluation (MCD) .... ACEVAL
Air Combat Evaluation / Air Intercept Missile Evaluation (PDAA) .... ACEVAL/AIMVAL
Air Combat Expert Simulation [Military] (RDA) .... ACES
Air Combat Fighter (MCD) .... ACF
Air Combat Information .... ACI
Air Combat Intelligence [Obsolete Navy] .... ACI
Air Combat Intelligence Office [or Officer] [Navy] .... ACIO
Air Combat Maneuvering (AFM) .... ACM
Air Combat Maneuvering Instrumentation System [Air Force] (DWSG) .... ACMIS
Air Combat Maneuvering Performance Measurement (MCD) .... ACMPM
Air Combat Maneuvering Range .... ACMR
Air Combat Maneuvering Range (DOMA) .... ACMR
Air Combat Maneuvering Simulator (MCD) .... ACMS
Air Combat Maneuvering Visual System (MCD) .... ACMVS
Air Combat Part Task Trainer .... ACPTT
Air Combat Tactics (AFM) .... ACT
Air Combat Tactics Instructor (DOMA) .... ACTI
Air Combat Training System [Army] .... ACTS
Air Command (ADA) .... AC
Air Command (MCD) .... AIRCOM
Air Command and Control Improvement System [NATO] .... ACCIS
Air Command and Control System [NATO] .... ACCS
Air Command and Staff College [Maxwell AFB, AL] [Air Force] .... AC & SC
Air Command and Staff College [Maxwell AFB, AL] [Air Force] (MCD) .... ACSC
Air Command and Staff College [Air Force] .... AIRCSC
Air Command and Staff School [Air Force] .... AC & SS
Air Command and Staff School [Air Force] .... ACSS
Air Command Headquarters, Canadian Forces Base, Westwin, Manitoba [Library symbol National Library of Canada] (NLC) .... MWAC
Air Command Net [Army] (AABC) .... AIRCOMD
Air Command Operations Center [NATO] (NATG) .... ACOC
Air Command Post [Military] .... ACPT
Air Command, Southeast Asia .... ACSEA
Air Commandant [British] .... A CDT
Air Commandant [British] (DMA) .... A Ct
Air Commander, Canadian Atlantic Subarea .... COMAIRCANLANT
Air Commander, Central Atlantic Subarea .... COMAIRCENTLANT
Air Commander, North Norway [NATO] (NATG) .... ACNN

Air Commander, Northeast Subarea Channel .... COMAIRNORECHAN
Air Commander, Northern Atlantic Subarea .... COMAIRNORLANT
Air Commander, Norway [*NATO*] (NATG) .... ACN
Air Commander, Plymouth Subarea Channel .... COMAIRPLYMCHAN
Air Commander-in-Chief, Eastern Atlantic Area .... CINCAIREASTLANT
Air Commando Association (EA) .... ACA
Air Commando Squadron [*Air Force*] .... ACMDOSq
Air Commando Squadron (CINC) .... ACS
Air Commerce [*Yugoslavia*] [*ICAO designator*] (FAAC) .... ACS
Air Commerce Manual .... ACM
Air Commodore [*RAF, RCAF*] .... A/C
Air Commodore [*RAF, RCAF*] .... A CDE
Air Commodore [*RAF, RCAF*] (DMA) .... A Cdre
Air Commodore [*RAF, RCAF*] (DAS) .... A Comm
Air Communication Officer [*Military*] (IAA) .... ACO
Air Communications and Weather [*Group*] [*Navy*] .... AC & W
Air Communications and Weather Group [*Navy*] (IAA) .... ACAW
Air Communications Network .... AIRCOMNET
Air Comores [*ICAO designator*] (AD) .... OR
Air Co. Ltd. [*Romania*] [*FAA designator*] (FAAC) .... RMR
Air Component Command [*Military*] (MCD) .... ACC
Air Component Commander [*Air Force*] (DOMA) .... ACC
Air Component Commander, Southeast Asia Treaty Organization (CINC) .... ACCSEATO
Air Compressor (AAG) .... AC
Air Compressor Research Council [*Defunct*] .... ACRC
Air Concept [*Germany ICAO aircraft manufacturer identifier*] (ICAO) .... VW
Air Condal SA [*Spain ICAO designator*] (FAAC) .... JID
Air Condensate Drain [*Aerospace*] (AAG) .... ACD
Air Condition [*Technical drawings*] (DAC) .... AIR COND
Air Conditioned Microclimate System [*Army*] (RDA) .... ACMS
Air Conditioner Air Transportable (MCD) .... ACAT
Air Conditioner Technical Data Package (DWSG) .... ACTDP
Air Conditioning (IDOE) .... a/c
Air Conditioning [*Automotive engineering*] .... A/COND
Air Conditioning .... AC
Air Conditioning (KSC) .... AC
Air Conditioning Analytical Simulation Package (PDAA) .... A/CASP
Air Conditioning and Mechanical Contractors' Association of Queensland [*Australia*] .... ACMCAQ
Air Conditioning and Mechanical Contractors' Association of South Australia .... ACMCASA
Air Conditioning and Mechanical Contractors' Association of Victoria [*Australia*] .... ACMCAV
Air Conditioning and Refrigeration Contractors Association of New Jersey (SRA) .... ARCA
Air Conditioning & Refrigeration Industry Association of British Columbia (AC) .... ARIA
Air Conditioning and Refrigeration Program [*Association of Independent Colleges and Schools specialization code*] .... AR
Air Conditioning and Temperature Control System [*Aerospace*] .... ACTCS
Air Conditioning Clutch Compressor [*Automotive engineering*] .... ACC
Air Conditioning Contractors of America (EA) .... ACCA
Air Conditioning Equipment Room [*NFPA pre-fire planning symbol*] (NFPA) .... AC
Air Conditioning Sensor [*Automotive engineering*] .... ACS
Air Conditioning System .... ACS
Air Conditioning Trade Association of California (SRA) .... ACCACA
Air Conduction .... AC
Air Conduction and Bone Conduction [*Otorhinolaryngology*] (DAVI) .... AC & BC
Air Congo [*Zaire*] .... AC
Air Consignment Note (ADA) .... ACN
Air Containment Atmosphere Dilution [*Nuclear energy*] (NRCH) .... ACAD
Air Continental, Inc. [*ICAO designator*] (FAAC) .... NAR
Air Contrast Barium Enema [*Medicine*] .... ACBE
Air Control and Reporting (NATG) .... ACR
Air [*or Aircraft*] **Control and Warning** [*Military*] .... AC & W
Air [*or Aircraft*] **Control and Warning** [*Military*] .... ACW
Air Control Area Commander (NVT) .... ACAC
Air Control Center [*Military*] .... ACC
Air Control Commission (AAG) .... ACC
Air Control Component .... ACPC
Air Control Intercept .... ACI
Air [*or Airborne*] **Control Officer** [*or Contract*] [*Military British*] .... ACO
Air Control Officer [*Navy*] (DOMA) .... ACO
Air Control Point .... ACP
Air Control RADAR .... ACR
Air Control Room (MUGU) .... ACR
Air Control Team [*Air Force*] .... ACT
Air Control Valve (MCD) .... ACV
Air Controller (NVT) .... AC
Air Controlman [*Navy rating*] .... AC
Air Controlman, Chief [*Navy rating*] .... ACC
Air Controlman, First Class [*Navy rating*] AC1
Air Controlman, Master Chief [*Navy rating*] .... ACCM
Air Controlman, Second Class [*Navy rating*] AC2
Air Controlman, Senior Chief [*Navy rating*] .... ACCS
Air Controlman, Third Class [*Navy rating*] AC3
Air Cooled (IAA) .... AC
Air Cooled Heat Exchanger Manufacturers Association [*Defunct*] (EA) .... ACHEMA
Air Cooled Triode [*Chemistry*] (IAA) .... ACT
Air Cooperation Command [*RAF*] [*British*] .... AC/OC
Air Coordinating Committee [*Governmental policy body for civil aviation in US; terminated, 1960*] .... ACC
Air Coordinating Committee [*Terminated*] **Airspace Subcommittee** .... ACCASP
Air Coordinating Committee [*Terminated*] **Communications Subcommittee** .... ACC/COM
Air Coordinating Committee [*Terminated*] **Meteorological Subcommittee** .... ACC/MET
Air Coordinator [*Air Force*] .... AIRCO
Air Corps [*Obsolete*] .... AC
Air Corps Board [*Obsolete*] (MCD) .... ACB
Air Corps Information Circular [*Obsolete*] .... ACIC
Air Corps Medical Forces [*Obsolete*] .... ACMF
Air Corps Reserve [*Obsolete*] .... ACR
Air Corps Tactical School [*Obsolete*] .... ACTS
Air Corps Technical Report [*Obsolete*] .... ACTR
Air Correction Jet [*Automotive engineering*] .... ACJ
Air Correction Jet-Primary [*Automotive engineering*] .... ACJP
Air Correction Jet-Secondary [*Automotive engineering*] .... ACJS
Air Corse [*France ICAO designator*] (FAAC) .... ARK
Air Cote d'Opale [*France ICAO designator*] (FAAC) .... OPL
Air Council (ADA) .... AC
Air Council for Training [*British*] (DAS) .... ACT
Air Council Instruction [*World War II*] .... ACI
Air Courier Conference of America (EA) .... ACCA
Air Couriers International, Inc. [*Defunct*] (TSSD) .... ACI
Air Courses of Action Assessment Model [*Navy*] .... ACAAM
Air Court-Martial .... ACM
Air Craft Energy Efficiency .... ACEE
Air Creebec [*Canada ICAO designator*] (FAAC) .... CRQ
Air Crew Association Canada .... ACAC
Air Crew Change .... ACC
Air Crew Equipment Laboratory (MCD) .... ACEL
Air Crew Error (MCD) .... ACE
Air Crew Rescue (CINC) .... ACR
Air Crew System Bulletin (MCD) .... ACB
Air Crew Training System .... ACTS
Air Curtain Incinerator (MCD) .... ACI
Air Cushion Equipment (MHDB) .... ACE
Air Cushion Launch Platform (MCD) .... ACLP
Air Cushion Recovery System (MCD) .... ACRS
Air Cushion Relief Equipment (PDAA) .... ACRE
Air Cushion Restraint System Module .... ACRSM
Air Cushion Rig Mover (PDAA) .... ACRM
Air Cushion Take-Off and Landing [*Aviation*] (PDAA) .... ACTOL
Air Cycle Air-Conditioning System (MCD) .... ACACS
Air Cycle Air-Conditioning System (MCD) .... ACAS
Air Cycle Engine / Liquid Air Cycle Engine (SAA) .... ACE/LACE
Air Cycle Machine [*Aerospace*] .... ACM
Air Dan [*Nigeria*] [*FAA designator*] (FAAC) .... DMT
Air Data (MCD) .... AD
Air Data Assembly (NASA) .... ADA
Air Data Computer [*or Computing*] (MCD) .... ADC
Air Data Computer Set .... ADCS
Air Data Computer Static Pressure Compensator (MCD) .... ADCSPC
Air Data Computing System .... ADCS
Air Data Converter .... ADC
Air Data Inertial Reference System (DA) .... ADIRS
Air Data Inertial Reference Unit .... ADIRU
Air Data Ltd. [*British*] [*FAA designator*] (FAAC) .... AFS
Air Data Measuring Unit (NATG) .... ADMU
Air Data Package .... ADP
Air Data Probe [*Aerospace*] (MCD) .... ADP
Air Data Probe Assemblies [*Aerospace*] (NASA) .... ADPA
Air Data Screening System [*Environmental Protection Agency*] (GFGA) .... ADSS
Air Data Sensor [*Aerospace*] (MCD) .... ADS
Air Data Sensor Unit (MCD) .... ADSU
Air Data System [*or Subsystem*] (RDA) .... ADS
Air Data Test System .... ADTS
Air Data Transducer [*Aerospace*] (MCD) .... ADT
Air Data Transducer Assembly [*Aerospace*] (NASA) .... ADTA
Air Decoy Missile (AFM) .... ADM
Air Defence Artillery Commander [*Military British*] .... ADAC
Air Defence Cadet Corps [*Military British*] .... ADCC
Air Defence Experimental Establishment [*Later, ADRDE, RRE*] [*British*] .... ADEE
Air Defence Officer [*Navy British*] .... ADO
Air Defence Research and Development Establishment [*Later, RRE*] [*British*] .... ADRDE
Air Defences, Eastern Mediterranean [*British military*] (DMA) .... ADEM
Air Defense [*Air Force*] .... AD
Air Defense Action Area [*Military*] .... ADAA
Air Defense Aircraft (MCD) .... AD/AC
Air Defense Air-to-Ground Engagement [*Simulation*] .... ADAGE
Air Defense Alerting Device [*Military*] .... ADAD
Air Defense Annual Service Practice (AABC) .... ADASP
Air Defense Antimissile .... ADAM
Air Defense Antitank System .... ADATS
Air Defense Area [*Army*] .... ADA
Air Defense Area [*Army*] .... ADAR
Air Defense Area Monthly Report [*Army*] .... ADAM
Air Defense Artillery [*Military*] .... ADA
Air Defense Artillery Board [*Army*] .... ADABD
Air Defense Artillery Complex (MCD) .... ADAC
Air Defense Artillery Control Station [*Army*] .... ADACS
Air Defense Artillery, Director [*Air Force*] .... ADAD
Air Defense Artillery Officer (SAA) .... ADAO
Air Defense Artillery Operations Detachment .... ADAOD
Air Defense Artillery Operations Office [*or Officer*] .... ADAOO
Air Defense Artillery Threat Simulator (MCD) .... ADATS

Air Defense Board [*Army*] (AAG) .... ADB
Air Defense Center (AAG) .... ADC
Air Defense Combined Arms Tactical Trainer [*Army*] .... ADCATT
Air Defense Command [*Peterson Air Force Base, CO*] .... ADC
Air Defense Command [*Army*] .... ADCOM
Air Defense Command and Control [*MICOM*] (RDA) .... ADCC
Air Defense Command and Control System (MCD) .... ADCCS
Air Defense Command Center .... ADCC
Air Defense Command Commendation Certificate .... ADCCC
Air Defense Command Communications Network [*Military*] (IAA) .... ADCCOMNET
Air Defense Command Computer [*Military*] (IAA) .... ADCC
Air Defense Command, Control, and Coordination System (AABC) .... ADCCCS
Air Defense Command Headquarters, St. Hubert, Province of Quebec, Canada .... CANAIRDEF
Air Defense Command Interoperability System [*Army*] .... ADCOINS
Air Defense Command Manual (SAA) .... ADCM
Air Defense Command Post .... ADCOP
Air Defense Command Post (AABC) .... ADCP
Air Defense Command Regulation (SAA) .... ADCR
Air Defense Commander .... AIRDEFCOM
Air Defense Command-Office of Operations Analysis [*Peterson Air Force Base, CO*] .... ADC-OA
Air Defense Communication Equipment [*Military*] .... ADCE
Air Defense Communications Jammer [*Military*] (PDAA) .... ADCJ
Air Defense Communications Office (AABC) .... ADCO
Air Defense Computer (AAG) .... ADC
Air Defense Control and Targets Office [*Army*] .... ADCAT
Air Defense Control Center [*Air Force*] .... ADCC
Air Defense Control Facility (FAAC) .... ADCF
Air Defense Control System [*Military*] .... ADCS
Air Defense Defended Area [*Army*] .... ADDA
Air Defense Defended Point [*Army*] .... ADDP
Air Defense Demonstration System (MCD) .... ADDS
Air Defense Development .... ADD
Air Defense Direction Center [*Air Force*] .... ADDC
Air Defense District (NATG) .... ADD
Air Defense Division [*NATO*] (SAA) .... ADD
Air Defense Division [*NATO*] (NATG) .... AIRDEF
Air Defense Early Warning (NATG) .... ADEW
Air Defense Effectiveness Demonstration [*Army*] (MCD) .... ADED
Air Defense Electronic Environment (SAA) .... ADEE
Air Defense Electronic Warfare System (MCD) .... ADEWS
Air Defense Element (AABC) .... ADE
Air Defense Emergency [*Military*] (AABC) .... ADE
Air Defense Engagement System (MCD) .... ADES
Air Defense Engineering Service (MCD) .... ADES
Air Defense Evaluation .... ADE
Air Defense Evaluation Tests (MCD) .... ADVAL
Air Defense Exercise (NVT) .... ADEX
Air Defense Exercise [*Army/Air Force*] (AABC) .... ADX
Air Defense Fighter (DOMA) .... ADF
Air Defense Filter Center [*Military*] .... ADFC
Air Defense Firing Unit (MCD) .... ADFU
Air Defense Force .... ADF
Air Defense Force Headquarters (SAA) .... ADFHQ
Air Defense Ground Environment [*NATO*] (MCD) .... ADGE
Air Defense Group [*Air Force*] (MCD) .... ADG
Air Defense Group [*Air Force*] (AFM) .... ADGp
Air Defense Guard [*Military*] .... ADG
Air Defense Gun Missile Experiment [*Army*] .... ADGILE
Air Defense Hardware Committee [*NATO*] (NATG) .... ADHC
Air Defense High Energy LASER (MCD) .... ADHEL
Air Defense Identification Line [*Air Force*] .... ADIL
Air Defense Identification Zone [*Air Force, FAA*] .... ADIZ
Air Defense Initiative [*DoD*] .... ADI
Air Defense Inspector Provost Marshall (SAA) .... ADIPM
Air Defense Institute .... ADI
Air Defense Integrated System [*Military*] .... ADIS
Air Defense Intercept [*Air Force*] .... ADI
Air Defense, Interdiction, and Photographic .... ADIP
Air Defense Liaison Officer .... ADLO
Air Defense Machine Gun (MCD) .... ADMG
Air Defense Management Office (MCD) .... ADMO
Air Defense Missile .... ADM
Air Defense Missile Base (SAA) .... ADMB
Air Defense Missile Battalion [*Army*] (AABC) .... ADMSLBN
Air Defense Missile Command (AABC) .... ADMC
Air Defense Missile Squadron [*Air Force*] .... ADMS
Air Defense Mission [*Army*] .... ADM
Air Defense National Center (NATG) .... ADNC
Air Defense Notification Center (NATG) .... ADNC
Air Defense of Great Britain .... ADGB
Air Defense of North American Continent [*Army*] (AABC) .... ADNAC
Air Defense of the Division (MCD) .... ADDIV
Air Defense Operations (NATG) .... ADO
Air Defense Operations Area [*Army*] (ADDR) .... ADDA
Air Defense Operations Center [*Air Force*] .... ADOC
Air Defense Planning Board (MCD) .... ADPB
Air Defense Planning Group (MCD) .... ADPG
Air Defense Position [*Military*] .... ADP
Air Defense Region (NATG) .... ADR
Air Defense Requirement (SAA) .... ADR
Air Defense Sector [*Air Force*] .... ADS
Air Defense Service Medal [*Military decoration*] (GFGA) .... ADSM
Air Defense Ship (NATG) .... ADS
Air Defense Simulator Evaluation (MCD) .... ADSVAL
Air Defense Software Committee (NATG) .... ADSC
Air Defense Special Weapons Support Organization .... ADSWSO
Air Defense Squadron [*Air Force*] .... ADEFSq
Air Defense Squadron [*Air Force*] .... ADS
Air Defense Squadron [*Vietnam*] [*Air Force*] (AFM) .... ADSq
Air Defense Suppression Missile (AABC) .... ADSM
Air Defense Suppression System (MCD) .... ADSS
Air Defense - Surface-to-Air Missile .... AD/SAM
Air Defense System .... ADS
Air Defense System Engineering Committee .... ADSEC
Air Defense System Management Office [*Air Force*] .... ADSMO
Air Defense Systems Command .... ADSC
Air Defense Systems Directorate (NATG) .... ADSD
Air Defense Systems Integration Division [*Air Force*] .... ADSID
Air Defense Systems Operation Division (SAA) .... ADSOD
Air Defense Tactical Air Commander [*Air Force*] .... ADTAC
Air Defense Tactical Data Systems [*Missile minder*] (RDA) .... ADTDS
Air Defense Technical Center (NATG) .... ADTC
Air Defense/Theater Missile Defense .... AD/TMD
Air Defense Variant .... ADV
Air Defense Vulnerability Simulation [*Simulation game*] .... ADVUL
Air Defense Warning [*Air Force*] .... ADW
Air Defense Warning Key Point [*Air Force*] .... ADWKP
Air Defense Weapon .... ADW
Air Defense Weapon Simulation System (MCD) .... ADWSS
Air Defense Weapon System (MCD) .... ADWS
Air Defense Weapons Center [*Tyndall Air Force Base, FL*] (MCD) .... ADWC
Air Defense Weapons Center Regulation (MCD) .... ADWCR
Air Defense Weapons Cost Effectiveness Study (AABC) .... ADWEPS
Air Defense Wing [*Air Force*] .... ADW
Air Defense Zone [*Army/Airforce*] (NATG) .... ADZ
Air Deflection and Modification [*NASA*] (KSC) .... ADAM
Air Deflection and Modulation [*Air Force*] (MCD) .... ADAM
Air Delivery Equipment Division [*Natick Laboratories*] [*Army*] .... ADED
Air Delivery Operations [*Aerial resupply*] [*Military*] (NVT) .... AIRDELOPS
Air Delivery Platoon (DNAB) .... ADP
Air Delivery Platoon .... AIRDELPLT
Air Density [*Explorer satellite*] [*NASA*] .... AD
Air Density [*Explorer satellite*] [*NASA*] .... ADE
Air Density A [*Explorer satellite*] [*NASA*] .... AD-A
Air Density Gauge [*Aviation*] .... ADG
Air Density/Injun [*Explorer satellite*] .... AD/I
Air Department of the Admiralty [*British*] .... AD
Air Deployable Active Reservoir [*Military*] (DOMA) .... ADAR
Air Deployable Airborne Deception Device System .... ADS
Air Deployable Drifting Linear Array SONAR System (MCD) .... ADDLASS
Air Deployed Oceanographic Mooring (PDAA) .... ADOM
Air Deployment Delivery System [*Military*] (NVT) .... ADDS
Air Depot .... AD
Air Depot [*Army*] .... ADEP
Air Deputy [*NATO*] (NATG) .... AIRDEP
Air Deputy [*NATO*] (NATG) .... DEPAIR
Air Design Review (MCD) .... ADR
Air Despatch [*British military*] (DMA) .... AD
Air Detector/Tracker (CAAL) .... AD/T
Air Development Center [*Air Force*] .... ADC
Air Development Delivery System (DNAB) .... ADDS
Air Development Force .... ADF
Air Development Service (MCD) .... ADS
Air Development Squadron [*Navy*] .... AIRDEVRON
Air Development Squadron [*Navy*] VX
Air Development Station [*Navy*] .... ADS
Air Device Systems [*Honda Motor Co.*] [*Automotive air conditioning*] .... ADSYS
Air Diffusion and Components Council of South Australia .... ADCCSA
Air Diffusion Council (EA) .... ADC
Air Diffusion Perfomance Index [*Of room ventilation*] .... ADPI
Air Direct Ltd. [*British ICAO designator*] (FAAC) .... DFT
Air Direction Center .... ADC
Air Direction Finder .... ADF
Air Director (DAS) .... AD
Air Dispatch Letter Service [*Navy*] .... ADLS
Air Distance (SAA) .... AD
Air Distribution Institute (EA) .... ADI
Air Distribution Unit [*Portable cooling system*] [*Air Force*] .... ADU
Air Diverter Valve [*Automotive engineering*] .... ADV
Air Division [*Air Force*] .... A DIV
Air Division [*Air Force*] .... AD
Air Division [*Air Force*] .... AIRDIV
Air Division Advisor [*Air Force*] (SAA) .... ADA
Air Division Defense [*Air Force*] (MUGU) .... AIRDIVDEF
Air Djibouti [*ICAO designator*] (AD) .... DJ
Air Djibouti [*ICAO designator*] (FAAC) .... DJB
Air Dolomiti [*Italy ICAO designator*] (FAAC) .... DLA
Air Dorval Ltd. [*Canada ICAO designator*] (FAAC) .... ADT
Air Dose [*Also called air exposure, referring to radiation exposure*] (DAVI) .... E
Air Driven Pump .... ADP
Air Drop Operator .... ADO
Air Drop System [*Army*] .... ADS
Air Droppable, Expendable Ocean Sensor [*Oceanography*] (MSC) .... ADEOS
Air Droppable Measurement System [*Oceanography*] (MSC) .... ADRAMS
Air Duct (MSA) .... AD
Air East Africa Ltd. [*Kenya*] [*FAA designator*] (FAAC) .... JND
Air Economy [*Ukraine*] [*FAA designator*] (FAAC) .... AYY
Air Ecosse [*ICAO designator*] (AD) .... EC

Air Ecosse Ltd. [*British*] ... AE
Air Education and Training Command [*Air Force*] (DOMA) ... AETC
Air Education Recreation Organization [*British*] (DA) ... AERO
Air Education Section of the Irish Aviation Council (EAIO) ... AESIAC
Air Efficiency Award [*RAF*] [*British*] (DMA) ... AE
Air Efficiency Award [*RAF*] [*British*] ... AEA
Air Efficiency Medal [*RAF*] [*British*] ... AEM
Air Ejection Off Gas (IEEE) ... AEOG
Air Ejector ... AE
Air Electrical [*NATO*] (NATG) ... AE
Air Electrical [*Special duties officer*] [*Military British*] ... AL
Air Electrical Officer ... AIRELO
Air Electrical Officer's Writer [*British military*] (DMA) ... ALOW
Air Electronics Officer [*British*] ... AEO
Air Element Coordinator [*Military*] (CAAL) ... AREC
Air Eligibility Code ... AEC
Air, Emergency Breathing System (DNAB) ... AEB
Air Emplaced Classifier (MCD) ... AEC
Air Encephalogram [*Medicine*] ... AEG
Air Enforcement Division [*Office of Enforcement and Compliance Monitoring*] [*Environmental Protection Agency*] (EPA) ... AED
Air Engiadina [*Switzerland ICAO designator*] (FAAC) ... RQX
Air Engineer Officer ... AEO
Air Engineer Officer ... AIREO
Air Engineer Officer's Writer [*British military*] (DMA) ... AEOW
Air Engineering [*British*] ... AE
Air Engineering Development Division [*Air Force*] ... AEDD
Air Enterprise [*France ICAO designator*] (FAAC) ... AEN
Air Entraining Agent [*Freight*] ... AEA
Air Entry [*Respiration*] (DAVI) ... AE
Air Equipment and Support [*Army*] (AABC) ... AE & S
Air Equipment and Support [*Army*] (AFIT) ... AEAS
Air Equipment Department [*British military*] (DMA) ... AED
Air Equivalence Ratio [*For hydrocarbon combustion*] ... AER
Air Escape [*Technical drawings*] ... AE
Air Europa [*Spain ICAO designator*] (FAAC) ... AEA
Air Europe [*ICAO designator*] (AD) ... AE
Air Europe SpA [*Italy ICAO designator*] (FAAC) ... AEL
Air Evacuation ... AEVAC
Air Evacuation ... AIREVAC
Air Evacuation Patients (AFIT) ... AEP
Air Evacuation Unit [*Military*] ... AEU
Air Evacuation Wing ... AIREVACWING
Air Evasion [*France ICAO designator*] (FAAC) ... IVS
Air Evex GmbH [*Germany ICAO designator*] (FAAC) ... EVE
Air Exchange, Inc. [*ICAO designator*] (FAAC) ... EXG
Air Exel [*France ICAO designator*] (FAAC) ... RXL
Air Exel Belgique [*Belgium ICAO designator*] (FAAC) ... BXL
Air Exel Executive [*France ICAO designator*] (FAAC) ... AOL
Air Exel Netherlands BV [*ICAO designator*] (FAAC) ... AXL
Air Experienc Flight [*British ICAO designator*] (FAAC) ... AED
Air Experience Flight [*British military*] (DMA) ... AEF
Air Explorer Squadron ... AESQ
Air Express ... AXPS
Air Express AS [*Norway ICAO designator*] (FAAC) ... AXP
Air Express Division of the Railway Express Agency ... AIRYX
Air Express in Norrkoping AB [*Sweden ICAO designator*] (FAAC) ... GOT
Air Express, Inc. [*ICAO designator*] (FAAC) ... ARX
Air Express International Corp. ... AEI
Air Express International Corp. [*NASDAQ symbol*] (SAG) ... AEIC
Air Express International Corp. [*Associated Press*] (SAG) ... AirExp
Air Express Intl. [*NASDAQ symbol*] (TTSB) ... AEIC
Air Facility (DNAB) ... AFY
Air Fecteau Ltd. [*Canada ICAO designator*] (FAAC) ... AFH
Air Ferry Squadron [*Navy*] ... AIRFERRON
Air Field Attack Munition (MCD) ... AFAM
Air Fighting Development Unit [*British*] ... AFDU
Air Filter ... AF
Air Filter [*Freight*] ... AIR FIL
Air Filter Institute [*Later, ARI*] (EA) ... AFI
Air Fleet Marine Force ... AFMF
Air Fleet Marine Force (AFIT) ... AIRFMF
Air Florida [*Air carrier designation symbol*] ... AFLX
Air Florida [*ICAO designator*] (FAAC) ... FLA
Air Flow Actuated Switch ... AFAS
Air Flow Control [*Automotive engineering*] ... AFC
Air Flow Indicator ... AFI
Air Flow Meter [*Automotive engineering*] ... AFM
Air Flow Sensor [*Automotive engineering*] ... AFS
Air Flow Thermal Balance Calorimeter ... AFTBC
Air Foil Design System [*Automotive engineering*] ... AFDS
Air Forager [*Ornithology*] ... AF
Air Force ... AF
Air Force Academy ... AFA
Air Force Academy and Aircrew Examining Center ... AFAAEC
Air Force Academy Board ... AFAB
Air Force Acceptance Team (MCD) ... AFAT
Air Force Accountable Property Officer (AAG) ... AFAPO
Air Force Accounting and Finance Center ... AFAFC
Air Force Achievement Medal [*Military decoration*] ... AFAM
Air Force Acquisition Circular (MCD) ... AFAC
Air Force Acquisition Document (MCD) ... AFAD
Air Force Acquisition Executive (MCD) ... AFAE
Air Force Acquisition Executive System (AAGC) ... AFAES
Air Force Acquisition Logistics Center (MCD) ... AFALC
Air Force Acquisition Logistics Division [*Wright Patterson Air Force Base*] (MCD) ... AFALD
Air Force Acquisition Logistics Division (AAGC) ... AFLD
Air Force Acquisition Model (AAGC) ... AFAM
Air Force Act [*British military*] (DMA) ... AFA
Air Force Administrative Order [*Canada, 1946-1964*] ... AFAO
Air Force Advanced Management Class ... AFADVMC
Air Force Advisory ... AFA
Air Force Advisory Group (CINC) ... AFADGRU
Air Force Advisory Group ... AFAG
Air Force Advisory Group ... AFGP
Air Force Advisory Team ... AFAT
Air Force Aeronautical Chart and Information Center (MUGU) ... AFAC & IC
Air Force Aeronautical Systems Command ... AFASC
Air Force Aeronautical Systems Division ... AFASD
Air Force Aero-Propulsion Laboratory [*Wright-Patterson Air Force Base, OH*] (AFM) ... AFAPL
Air Force Aerospace Fuel Petroleum Supply Office ... AFAFPSO
Air Force Aerospace Fuels Field Office (AFM) ... AFAFFO
Air Force Aerospace Medical Research Laboratory [*Wright-Patterson Air Force Base, OH*] ... AFAMRL
Air Force Aerospace Rescue and Recovery Service (SAA) ... AARRS
Air Force Aerospace Rescue and Recovery Service (MCD) ... AARS
Air Force Agent Installation (AFM) ... AFAI
Air Force Aid Society (EA) ... AFAS
Air Force Air Base ... AAB
Air Force Air Materiel Area ... AFAMA
Air Force Air Pictorial Service (SAA) ... AFAPS
Air Force Alaskan Long Line System [*Communications*] (MCD) ... AFALLS
Air Force Alternate Headquarters ... AFALT
Air Force Arctic Broadcasting Squadron [*New York, NY*] (EY) ... AFABS
Air Force Armament Center [*Eglin Air Force Base, FL*] ... AFAC
Air Force Armament Development and Test Center (MCD) ... AFADTC
Air Force Armament Museum ... AFAM
Air Force Armament Technology Laboratory [*Eglin Air Force Base, FL*] (AFM) ... AFATL
Air Force Armament Testing Laboratory (DOMA) ... AFATL
Air Force/Armed Service Procurement Regulation ... AF/ASPR
Air Force Assistance Fund ... AFAF
Air Force Association (EA) ... AFA
Air Force Association - Space Education Foundation ... AFA-SEF
Air Force Astronautics Laboratory [*Edwards Air Force Base, CA*] (GRD) ... AFAL
Air Force Atlantic Test Range (SAA) ... AFATR
Air Force Audit Agency ... AFAA
Air Force Audit Branch (AFM) ... AFAB
Air Force Auditor General ... AFAUD
Air Force Authorization Document (MCD) ... AFAD
Air Force Automated Systems Project Office ... AFASPO
Air Force Auxiliary [*British*] ... AFA
Air Force Auxiliary Field ... AFAF
Air Force Auxiliary Field ... AFAUX
Air Force Avionics Laboratory [*Wright-Patterson Air Force Base, OH*] ... AFAL
Air Force Bailment Property ... AFBP
Air Force Ballistic Missile (KSC) ... AFBM
Air Force Ballistic Missile Arsenal ... AFBMA
Air Force Ballistic Missile Center ... AFBMC
Air Force Ballistic Missile Committee ... AFBMC
Air Force Ballistic Missile Division [*Inglewood, CA*] ... AFBMD
Air Force Ballistic Missile Division - Field Operations (SAA) ... AFBMD-FO
Air Force Ballistic Missile Installation Regulation ... AFBMIR
Air Force Ballistic Missile Training Center ... AFBMTC
Air Force Ballistic Systems Division [*Later, Space and Missile Systems Operations*] ... AFBSD
Air Force Base ... AFB
Air Force Base Disposal Agency (DOMA) ... AFBDA
Air Force Base Information Transfer System (MCD) ... AFBITS
Air Force Base Unit ... AFBU
Air Force Bent Fin Artillery Rocket (MCD) ... AFBFAR
Air Force Board for Correction of Military Records (GFGA) ... AFBCMR
Air Force Board of Review ... AFBR
Air Force Board Structure (MCD) ... AFBS
Air Force Broadcasting Service (DOMA) ... AFBS
Air Force Bulletin ... AFB
Air Force Business Research Management Center [*Wright-Patterson Air Force Base, OH*] ... AFBRMC
Air Force Cambridge Research Center [*Obsolete*] ... AFCRC
Air Force Cambridge Research Laboratories [*Later, AFGL*] [*Hanscom Air Force Base, MA*] ... AFCRL
Air Force Cambridge Research Library (MCD) ... AFCRL
Air Force Capability Assessment Program (GFGA) ... AFCAP
Air Force Center for Environmental Excellence (DOMA) ... AFCEE
Air Force Center for International Programs ... AFCIP
Air Force Center for Studies and Analyses [*Washington, DC*] ... AFCSA
Air Force Central Notice to Airmen Facility ... AFCNF
Air Force Central Review Board (AAG) ... AFCRB
Air Force Change (AAGC) ... AFC
Air Force Chaplain School [*Maxwell Air Force Base, AL*] ... AF Ch Sch
Air Force Chief of Operations Analysis (MUGU) ... AFCOA
Air Force Chief of Staff (SAA) ... AFCS
Air Force Chief of Staff, Studies and Analysis (SAA) ... AFCSA
Air Force Circulars ... AFC
Air Force Civil Engineering Center [*Tyndall Air Force Base, FL*] ... AFCEC
Air Force Civil Engineering Support Agency (DOMA) ... AFCESA
Air Force Civil Engineering Unit (MCD) ... AFCE
Air Force Civilian Appellate Review Agency ... AFCARA

Air Force Civilian Appellate Review Agency (DOMA) .... AFCARA
Air Force Civilian Automated Pay System (GFGA) .... AFCAPS
Air Force Civilian Personnel Management Center .... AFCPMC
Air Force Civilian Welfare Fund (AFM) .... AFCWF
Air Force Clothing and Textile Office (AFIT) .... AFC & TO
Air Force Coated Aluminum Metal (MCD) .... AFCAM
Air Force Coding System (SAA) .... AFCS
Air Force Combat Ammunitions Center .... AFCOMAC
Air Force Combat Command .... AFCC
Air Force Combat Operations Staff .... AFCOS
Air Force Combat Theater Communications Program (AFIT) .... AFCTCP
Air Force Combined Tomography System (MCD) .... AFCTS
Air Force Command and Control Development Center .... AFCCDC
Air Force Command and Control Development Division [Bedford, MA]
(AAG) .... AFCCDD
Air Force Command and Control Post .... AFCCP
Air Force Command and Control System .... AFCCS
Air Force Command and Control System Graphic Operator Macros
(MCD) .... AFGOM
Air Force Command and Staff College .... AFCSC
Air Force Command Post .... AFCP
Air Force Commendation Medal [Military decoration] (AFM) .... AFCM
Air Force Commendation Medal [Military decoration] .... AFCOM
Air Force Commissary Service .... AFCOMS
Air Force Communication Center .... AFCC
Air Force Communications [Satellite] .... AFCOM
Air Force Communications Command .... AFCC
Air Force Communications Computer Programming Center .... AFCCPC
Air Force Communications Program .... AIRCOM
Air Force Communications Security .... AFCOMSEC
Air Force Communications Security Center (AFM) .... AFCOMSECCEN
Air Force Communications Security Letter .... AFCSL
Air Force Communications Security Manual .... AFCOMSECM
Air Force Communications Security Manual .... AFCSM
Air Force Communications Security Pamphlet (MCD) .... AFCSP
Air Force Communications Service [or System] [Scott Air Force Base, IL] .... AFCS
Air Force Communications Service, Engineering and Installation
(CET) .... AFCS E & I
Air Force Communications Service Manual .... AFCSM
Air Force Communications Service, Scott AFB, IL [OCLC symbol]
(OCLC) .... ACS
Air Force Communications Squadron (MCD) .... AFCS
Air Force Communications Station .... AFCOMMSTA
Air Force Communications Support System .... AFCSS
Air Force Communications-Computer Systems Doctrine Office .... AFCSDO
Air Force Component .... AFC
Air Force Component Command Post (AFM) .... AFCCP
Air Force Component Commander (AFM) .... AFCC
Air Force Component Headquarters .... AFCH
Air Force Comptroller .... AFAAC
Air Force Comptroller (AAG) .... AFC
Air Force Comptroller .... AFOC
Air Force Comptroller Management Engineering Team .... AFCOMPMET
Air Force Computer Acquisition Center .... AFCAC
Air Force Computer Acquisition Office .... AFCAO
Air Force Computer Program Library (SAA) .... AFCPL
Air Force Configuration Control Board (AAG) .... AFCCB
Air Force Consolidation and Containerization Point (DOMA) .... AF-CCP
Air Force Container System Development Group .... AFCSDG
Air Force Contract Adjustment Board (AAGC) .... AFCAB
Air Force Contract Law Center .... AFCLC
Air Force Contract Maintenance Center (AFM) .... AFCMC
Air Force Contract Management Division [Los Angeles, CA] .... AFCMD
Air Force Contract Management Division Directorate of Quality Assurance
[Los Angeles, CA] .... AFCMD/QA
Air Force Contract Management Office .... AFCMO
Air Force Contracting Office Approval .... AFCOA
Air Force Contracting Officer .... AFCO
Air Force Contractor (SAA) .... AFCON
Air Force Contractor Experience List (AFM) .... AFCEL
Air Force Control Office (AAG) .... AFCO
Air Force Controlled [Units] .... AFCON
Air Force Coordinating Office for Logistics Research (MCD) .... AFCOLR
Air Force Coronary Atherosclerosis Prevention Study .... AFCAPS
Air Force Cost Analysis Agency (DOMA) .... AFCAA
Air Force Cost Center .... AFCCE
Air Force Cost Reduction Program (AFM) .... AFCRP
Air Force Council [Advisory board to Air Force] .... AFC
Air Force Cross [US and British] [Military decoration] .... AFC
Air Force Cryptographic Aid, General .... AFKAG
Air Force Cryptographic Aid, Recognition and Identification Systems
(CET) .... AFKAI
Air Force Cryptographic Code System (CET) .... AFKAC
Air Force Cryptographic Maintenance Manual (CET) .... AFKAM
Air Force Cryptographic One Time Pads (CET) .... AFKAP
Air Force Cryptologic Depot (AFM) .... AFCD
Air Force Cryptologic Support Center .... AFCSC
Air Force Data Automation Agency (AFM) .... AFDAA
Air Force Data Automation Management Ergineering Team .... AFDAMET
Air Force Data Automation Planning Concepts [Manual] .... AFDAP
Air Force Data Communications System .... AFDATACOM
Air Force Data Services Center .... AFDSC
Air Force Data Station .... AFDASTA
Air Force Data Station (CET) .... AFDATASTA

Air Force Data Systems Design Center [Gunter Air Force Station, AL]
(AFM) .... AFDSDC
Air Force Data Systems Evaluation Center .... AFDSEC
Air Force Decision Coordinating Paper (MCD) .... AFDCP
Air Force Decorations Board .... AFDB
Air Force Defense Acquisition Regulation Supplement [Superseded by
AFFARS in 1984] (AAGC) .... AFDARS
Air Force Defense Acquisition Regulations (MCD) .... AFDAR
Air Force Department Constabulary [British military] (DMA) .... AFDC
Air Force Department Fire Service [British military] (DMA) .... AFDFS
Air Force Departmental Catalog Coordinating Office .... AFDCCO
Air Force Departmental Industrial Equipment Reserve (SAA) .... AFDIER
Air Force Departmental Industrial Equipment Reserve Storage Site .... AFDIERSS
Air Force Depot .... AFD
Air Force Depot Equipment Performance Tester (AAG) .... ADEPT
Air Force Designated Acquisition Program .... AFDAP
Air Force Detachment .... AFD
Air Force Development Field Representative (AAG) .... AFDFR
Air Force Development Test Center (DOMA) .... AFDTC
Air Force Directive (AAG) .... AFD
Air Force Director of Accounting and Financing (AAG) .... AFAF
Air Force Director of Command Control and Communications .... AFOCC
Air Force Director of Data Automation (IEEE) .... AFDDA
Air Force Director of Development and Planning (SAA) .... AFDAP
Air Force Director of Inspection Services (MUGU) .... AFDIS
Air Force Director of Personnel Planning (SAA) .... AFDPP
Air Force Director of Reconnaissance and Electronic Warfare (IEEE) ...... AFDRR
Air Force Director of Requirements .... AFDRQ
Air Force Director [or Directorate] of Research and Development .... AFDRD
Air Force Director of Research and Technology (SAA) .... AFDRT
Air Force Director of Special Investigations (SAA) .... AFDSI
Air Force Directorate of Advanced Technology .... AFDAT
Air Force Directorate of Materials and Processes (KSC) .... AFDMP
Air Force Directorate of Requirement (AAG) .... AFDR
Air Force Directory of Resident Inspection Facilities (AAG) .... AFDRIF
Air Force Disability Review Board .... AFDRB
Air Force Disaster Preparedness Resource Center .... AFDPRC
Air Force Discharge Review Board .... AFDRB
Air Force Distribution Agency .... AFDA
Air Force Distribution Control Office .... AFDCO
Air Force District of Washington .... AFDW
Air Force District of Washington Accounting and Finance Office .... AFDWAFO
Air Force Drug Testing Laboratory [Brooks Air Force Base, TX] (GRD) ...... AFDTL
Air Force Duty Officer .... AFDO
Air Force Eastern Test Range [Later, ESMC] [Patrick Air Force Base,
FL] .... AFETR
Air Force Eastern Test Range Manual [A publication] (MCD) .... AFETRM
Air Force Educational Requirements Board (AFM) .... AFERB
Air Force Edwards Research Center .... AFERC
Air Force Electronic Data Processing Center (AAG) .... AFEDPC
Air Force Electronic Failure Report (SAA) .... AFEFR
Air Force Electronic Properties Information Center (PDAA) .... AFEPIC
Air Force Electronic Security Command .... AFESC
Air Force Electronic Systems Division .... AFESD
Air Force Electronic Warfare Center (CAAL) .... AFEWC
Air Force Electronic Warfare Evaluation Simulator .... AFEWES
Air Force Electro-Optical Site (CET) .... AFEOS
Air Force Emergency Force .... AFEF
Air Force Emergency Operations Center (CET) .... AFEOC
Air Force Engineering and Logistics Information System (IEEE) .... AFELIS
Air Force Engineering and Services Center [Tyndall Air Force Base, FL] .... AFESC
Air Force Engineering and Services Center/Engineering and Services
Laboratory [Tyndall Air Force Base, FL] .... AFESC/ESL
Air Force Engineering and Services Management Engineering
Team .... AFESMET
Air Force Engineering and Technical Service (AFM) .... AFETS
Air Force Engineering Responsibility (CET) .... AFER
Air Force Engineering Technology Office [Tyndall Air Force Base, FL] ...... AFETO
Air Force Environmental Rocket-Sounding System [Meteorology] .... AFERSS
Air Force Environmental Technical Applications Center (MCD) .... AFETAC
Air Force Equipment Maintenance Management Information System
(MCD) .... AFEMMIS
Air Force Equipment Management Survey Team .... AFEMST
Air Force Equipment Management System (AFM) .... AFEMS
Air Force Equipment Management Team (AFIT) .... AFEMT
Air Force Equipment Procurement Instruction .... AFEPI
Air Force European Broadcasting Squadron .... AFEBS
Air Force European Office of Aerospace Research (KSC) .... AFEOAR
Air Force Exchange Service (AFM) .... AFES
Air Force Experiment .... AFE
Air Force Far East .... AFFE
Air Force Federal Acquisition Regulation Supplement [Replaced AFDARS in
1984] (AAGC) .... AFFARS
Air Force Field Office Manager (AAG) .... AFFOM
Air Force Field Technical Center [Edwards Air Force Base, CA] (MCD) .... AFFTC
Air Force Film Library Center .... AFFLC
Air Force Finance Center .... AFFC
Air Force Finance Center .... AFN
Air Force Financial Postal Clerk (AFM) .... AFFPC
Air Force Flight Dynamics Laboratory [Wright-Patterson Air Force Base,
OH] (AFM) .... AFFDL
Air Force Flight Standards Agency (DOMA) .... AFFSA
Air Force Flight Test Center [Edwards Air Force Base, CA] .... AFFTC
Air Force Flight Test Center [Edwards Air Force Base, CA] (MCD) .... AFTEC
Air Force Flight Test Instrumentation System .... AFFTIS

Air Force Flight Training Command ... AFTC
Air Force Forces [*Element of a joint task force*] ... AFFOR
Air Force Forces Deputy [*or Director*] **Communications-Electronics** (AFIT) ... AFFOR/DC
Air Force Foreign Technology Division (KSC) ... AFFTD
Air Force Frequency Management Agency (DOMA) ... AFFMA
Air Force General Order ... AFGO
Air Force Geophysics Laboratory [*Formerly, AFCRL*] [*Hanscom Air Force Base, MA*] ... AFGL
Air Force Geophysics Laboratory Research Library, Hanscom AFB, MA [*OCLC symbol*] (OCLC) ... SCG
Air Force Global Weather Center (DOMA) ... AFGWC
Air Force Global Weather Central [*or Control*] [*Offutt Air Force Base, NE*] ... AFGWC
Air Force Global Weather Reconnaissance Program ... AFGWRP
Air Force Good Conduct Medal [*Military decoration*] (AFM) ... AFGCM
Air Force Guide for Writing ... GW
Air Force Guide Specification (MCD) ... AFGS
Air Force Headquarters ... AFHQ
Air Force Headquarters Command ... AFHC
Air Force Headquarters, Ottawa, Ontario, Canada ... CANAIRHED
Air Force Health Professions Scholarship Program ... AFHPSP
Air Force Historical Foundation (EA) ... AFHF
Air Force Historical Research Agency (DOMA) ... AFHRA
Air Force Hospital ... AFH
Air Force Human Resources Laboratory [*Brooks Air Force Base, TX*] (AFM) ... AFHRL
Air Force Human Resources Laboratory/Flying Training Division [*Williams Air Force Base, AZ*] ... AFHRL/FT
Air Force Human Resources Laboratory/Manpower Development Division [*Alexandria, VA*] ... AFHRL/MD
Air Force in Europe ... AFE
Air Force Industrial Fund (AFM) ... AFIF
Air Force Industrial Security Regulations ... AFISR
Air Force Information for Industry Office (DOMA) ... AFIFIO
Air Force Information Management Study ... AFIMS
Air Force Information Program (SAA) ... AFIP
Air Force Inspection Agency (DOMA) ... AFIA
Air Force Inspection and Safety Center ... AFISC
Air Force Inspector General (SAA) ... AFIG
Air Force Inspector General Activities Center ... AFIGAC
Air Force Installation Representative ... AFIR
Air Force Installation Representative Officer ... AFIRO
Air Force Institute of Pathology (DAVI) ... AFIP
Air Force Institute of Technology (GAGS) ... AF Inst
Air Force Institute of Technology [*Wright-Patterson Air Force Base, OH*] ... AFIT
Air Force Institute of Technology, Residence School ... AFIT(RS)
Air Force Institute of Technology School of Systems and Logistics [*Wright-Patterson Air Force Base, OH*] ... AFIT/SL
Air Force Institute of Technology, Wright-Patterson AFB, OH [*OCLC symbol*] (OCLC) ... SCT
Air Force Integrated Command and Control System (AFM) ... AFICCS
Air Force Intelligence Center ... AFIC
Air Force Intelligence Command [*Established 1991*] (DOMA) ... AFIC
Air Force Intelligence Data Handling System [*ESD*] ... AIDS
Air Force Intelligence Management Engineering Team ... AFINTELMET
Air Force Intelligence Publication (SAA) ... AFIP
Air Force Intelligence Service ... AFIS
Air Force Intelligence Study ... AFIS
Air Force Intelligence Support Agency (DOMA) ... AFISA
Air Force International Standard ... AIR-STD
Air Force Inventory Manager ... AFIM
Air Force JAG Bulletin [*A publication*] (AAGC) ... AF JAG Bull
Air Force Jet ... AFJ
Air Force Job Knowledge Test ... AFJKT
Air Force Joint Project Office (SAA) ... AFJPO
Air Force Judge Advocate General ... AFJAG
Air Force Judge Advocate General School ... AFJAGS
Air Force Junior Reserve Officers Training Corps (AFM) ... AFJROTC
Air Force Justification for Major System New Start (MCD) ... AFJMSNS
Air Force Knowledge Test (SAA) ... AFKT
Air Force Language Aptitude Test ... AFLAT
Air Force Law Enforcement Terminal System ... AFLETS
Air Force Legal Services Agency (DOMA) ... AFLSA
Air Force Legal Services Center ... AFLSC
Air Force Legislative Item ... AFLI
Air Force Letter ... AFL
Air Force Liaison ... AFL
Air Force List [*British military*] (DMA) ... AFL
Air Force, Logistics and Engineering (DOMA) ... AF/LE
Air Force Logistics Center (MCD) ... AFLC
Air Force Logistics Command [*Formerly, Air Materiel Command*] [*Wright-Patterson Air Force Base, OH*] ... AFLC
Air Force Logistics Command Form ... AFLCF
Air Force Logistics Command Letter (MCD) ... AFLCL
Air Force Logistics Command Manual (MCD) ... AFLCM
Air Force Logistics Command Operations Analysis Office [*Wright-Patterson Air Force Base, OH*] ... AFLC-OA
Air Force Logistics Command Operations Network (MCD) ... AFLCON
Air Force Logistics Command Pamphlets ... AFLCP
Air Force Logistics Command Regulations ... AFLCR
Air Force Logistics Communications Network (AFM) ... AFLCON
Air Force Logistics Control Group ... AFLCG
Air Force Logistics Management Center [*Gunter Air Force Station, AL*] (AFM) ... AFLMC
Air Force Logistics Management Engineering Team ... AFLOGMET
Air Force Longevity Service Award [*Military decoration*] (AFM) ... AFLSA
Air Force - Los Alamos EMP [*Electromagnetic Pulse*] **Calibration Simulator** ... ALECS
Air Force Machinability Data Center (MCD) ... AFMDC
Air Force Maintenance and Supply Management Engineering Team [*Wright-Patterson Air Force Base, OH*] ... AFMSMET
Air Force Maintenance Management Engineering Team ... AFMAINMET
Air Force Management Analysis Group (MCD) ... AFMAG
Air Force Management Engineering Agency ... AFMEA
Air Force Manpower and Personnel Center (MCD) ... AFMPC
Air Force Manpower and Personnel Management Engineering Team ... AFMPMET
Air Force Manpower Standards ... AFMS
Air Force Manual [*A publication*] ... AFM
Air Force Manual of Procurement and Productions [*A publication*] (AAGC) ... AFMPP
Air Force Manufacturing Technology ... AFMT
Air Force Material Command ... AFMC
Air Force Material Review Board (MCD) ... AFMRB
Air Force Material Supply and Services (SAA) ... AFMSS
Air Force Materials Information Center (DIT) ... AFMIC
Air Force Materials Laboratory [*Wright-Patterson Air Force Base, OH*] ... AFML
Air Force Maui Optical Station ... AMOS
Air Force Measurement Standards Laboratories (AFIT) ... AFMSL
Air Force Medal [*British*] ... AFM
Air Force Medical Logistics Office ... AFMLO
Air Force Medical Management Engineering Team ... AFMEDMET
Air Force Medical Materiel Field Office (AFM) ... AFMMFO
Air Force Medical Materiel Letter ... AFMML
Air Force Medical Operations Agency (DOMA) ... AFMOA
Air Force Medical Publications Agency ... AFMPA
Air Force Medical Service ... AFMS
Air Force Medical Service Center (MCD) ... AFMSC
Air Force Medical Specialist Corps ... AFMSC
Air Force Medical Support Agency (DOMA) ... AFMSA
Air Force Meteorological Satellite Program (NOAA) ... AFMSP
Air Force - Military Interdepartmental Purchase Requests ... AF-MIPR
Air Force Military Personnel Center [*Randolph Air Force Base, TX*] ... AFMPC
Air Force Military Training Center (AFM) ... AFMTC
Air Force MIPR [*Military Interdepartmental Purchase Request*] **Management Office** (AFIT) ... AFMMO
Air Force Missile Development Center [*AFSC*] ... AFMDC
Air Force Missile Division (SAA) ... AFMD
Air Force Missile Test Center [*Later, AFETR*] [*Patrick Air Force Base, FL*] ... AFMTC
Air Force Mission Element Need Statement ... AFMENS
Air Force Mission Support System (DOMA) ... AFMSS
Air Force Morale, Welfare, and Recreation Agency (DOMA) ... AFMWRA
Air Force Mortuary Services Office ... AFMSO
Air Force Museum ... AFM
Air Force National Range Division ... AFNRD
Air Force NATO Agreement (MCD) ... AFNAG
Air Force/Navy (AAG) ... AF/N
Air Force - Navy ... AFNA
Air Force - Navy ... AN
Air Force/Navy Aeronautical ... AF/NA
Air Force - Navy Aeronautical ... ANA
Air Force - Navy Aeronautical Bulletin ... AFNAB
Air Force - Navy Aeronautical Bulletin (NASA) ... ANA
Air Force - Navy Aeronautical Standard ... AFNAS
Air Force - Navy Standard (SAA) ... AFNS
Air Force Negotiation Team (AAGC) ... AFNT
Air Force Networks Station ... AFNETSTA
Air Force News Agency (DOMA) ... AFNEWS
Air Force News Service ... AFNS
Air Force Noncommissioned Officer Academy [*Graduate*] **Ribbon** [*Military decoration*] (AFM) ... AFNCOAR
Air Force NOTAM [*Notice to Airmen*] **Exchange Area** ... AFNEA
Air Force NOTAM [*Notice to Airmen*] **Exchange Office** ... AFNEO
Air Force Nuclear Engineering Test Facility [*Reactor*] ... AF NETF
Air Force Nuclear Engineering Test Reactor (SAA) ... AFNETR
Air Force Nurse Corps ... AFNC
Air Force Objective Series [*Papers*] ... AFOS
Air Force Occupational and Environmental Health Lab ... AFOEHL
Air Force Occupational Safety and Health [*Standards*] ... AFOSH
Air Force of the People Chinese Liberation Army ... AFPCA
Air Force of the United States ... AFUS
Air Force Office of Aerospace Research [*AFSC*] ... AFOAR
Air Force Office of Aerospace Sciences [*AFOAR*] ... AFOAS
Air Force Office of Atomic Energy ... AFOAT
Air Force Office of Civil Engineering (SAA) ... AFOCE
Air Force Office of Manpower and Organization ... AFOMO
Air Force Office of Medical Support ... AFOMS
Air Force Office of Medical Support (DOMA) ... AFOMS
Air Force Office of Public Affairs ... AFOPA
Air Force Office of Research Analysis (AFM) ... AFORA
Air Force Office of Scientific Research [*Bolling Air Force Base*] [*Washington, DC*] ... AFOSR
Air Force Office of Security Police ... AFOSP
Air Force Office of Special Investigation ... AFOSI
Air Force Officer Education Program (AFM) ... AFOEP
Air Force Officer in Charge ... AFOIC
Air Force Officer Qualifying Test ... AFOQT
Air Force On-Line Data System ... AFOLDS

Air Force Operational Report (AFM) .... AFOREP
Air Force Operational Service (SAA) .... AFOS
Air Force Operational Test and Evaluation Center [Kirtland Air Force Base, NM] .... AFOTEC
Air Force Operational Test Center (MCD) .... AFOTC
Air Force Operations Analysis Office (KSC) .... AFOAO
Air Force Operations Base .... AFOB
Air Force Operations Center .... AFOC
Air Force Operations Resource Management Systems .... AFORMS
Air Force Operations Room [British military] (DMA) .... AFOR
Air Force Organization Status Change Report .... AFOSCR
Air Force Outstanding Unit Award [Military decoration] (AFM) .... AFOUA
Air Force Outstanding Unit Award Ribbon [Military decoration] .... AFOUAR
Air Force Outstanding Unit Emblem [Military decoration] .... AFOUE
Air Force Overseas Replacement Depot [World War II] .... AFORD
Air Force Overseas Replacement Group [World War II] .... AFORG
Air Force Pacific Broadcasting Squadron .... AFPBS
Air Force Packaging Evaluation Agency (MCD) .... AFPEA
Air Force Packaging Laboratory .... AFPL
Air Force Pamphlet .... AFP
Air Force Pamphlet .... AFPAM
Air Force Personnel and Training Research Center [Later, Air Force Personnel Research Laboratory] [Lackland Air Force Base, TX] .... AFPTRC
Air Force Personnel Board .... AFPB
Air Force Personnel Council .... AFPC
Air Force Personnel on Duty with Army .... AFWAR
Air Force Personnel on Duty with Navy .... AFWN
Air Force Personnel Processing Group .... AFPG
Air Force Personnel Research Lab (MCD) .... AFPRL
Air Force Personnel Test (AFM) .... AFPT
Air Force Petroleum Retail Distribution Station (AFM) .... AFPRDS
Air Force Physical Disability Appeal Board .... AFPDAB
Air Force Plan (MCD) .... AFP
Air Force Planning Element .... AFPE
Air Force Planning Guide .... AFPG
Air Force Plant Representative .... AFPR
Air Force Plant Representative Office .... AFPRO
Air Force Polaris Material Office .... AFPMO
Air Force Police (NATG) .... AFP
Air Force Policy Council (AAG) .... AFPC
Air Force Policy Letter for Commanders .... AFPLC
Air Force Policy on Disclosure of Classified Military Information (SAA) .... AFDCMI
Air Force Post Office .... APO
Air Force Postal Clerk (AFM) .... AFPC
Air Force Postal Unit .... AFPU
Air Force Potential Contractor Program (MCD) .... AFPCP
Air Force Preliminary Evaluation (MCD) .... AFPE
Air Force Procurement Circulars .... AFPC
Air Force Procurement Instructions .... AFPI
Air Force Procurement Officer (AAGC) .... APO
Air Force Procurement Procedures .... AFPP
Air Force Procurement Regulation .... AFPR
Air Force Procurement Representative .... AFPR
Air Force Production Reserve Policy .... AFPRP
Air Force Professional Entertainment Branch .... AFPEB
Air Force Professional Manpower and Personnel Management School .... AFPMPMS
Air Force Program Executive Office (DOMA) .... AFPEO
Air Force Program Executive Offices (BARN) .... AFPEO
Air Force Program Objectives Memorandum (MCD) .... AFPOM
Air Force Program Representative Office (MCD) .... AFPRO
Air Force, Programs and Evaluation (DOMA) .... AF/PR
Air Force Project Representative .... AFPR
Air Force Property Officer (MCD) .... AFPO
Air Force Purchase Item Description .... AFPID
Air Force Purchasing Office (MUGU) .... AFPO
Air Force Quality Assurance (KSC) .... AFQA
Air Force Quality Assurance Representative .... AFQAR
Air Force Quality Control .... AFQC
Air Force Quality Control Representative .... AFQCR
Air Force Range Support Facility .... AFRSF
Air Force Records Center .... AFRC
Air Force Recoverable Assembly Management (PDAA) .... AFRAM
Air Force Recoverable Assembly Management System (AFM) .... AFRAMS
Air Force Recruiter Assistance Program (MCD) .... AFRAP
Air Force Recurring Publication (AFM) .... AFRP
Air Force Regional Civil Engineers .... AFRCE
Air Force Regulation .... AFR
Air Force Rescue Coordination Center .... AFRCC
Air Force Rescue Service .... AFRS
Air Force Research and Development Branch .... AFRDB
Air Force Research and Technology Division .... AFRTD
Air Force Research Directorate (KSC) .... AFRD
Air Force Research Division .... AFRD
Air Force Research in Aircraft Propulsion Technology Program [West Lafayette, IN] (GRD) .... AFRAPT
Air Force Research Objectives .... AFRO
Air Force Research Training Center .... AFRTC
Air Force Reserve .... AFR
Air Force Reserve (DOMA) .... AFR
Air Force Reserve .... AFRES
Air Force Reserve Base Support Group .... AFRBSGP
Air Force Reserve Combat Support Training Center .... AFRCSTC
Air Force Reserve Combat Training Center .... AFRCTC

Air Force Reserve Coordination Center (AFM) .... AFRCC
Air Force Reserve Division .... AFRD
Air Force Reserve Flying Training Center .... AFRFTC
Air Force Reserve Navigation Squadron .... AFRESNAVSQ
Air Force Reserve Officers Training Corps [Washington, DC] .... AFROTC
Air Force Reserve Orders .... AFRO
Air Force Reserve Policy Committee .... AFRPC
Air Force Reserve Recovery Group (AFM) .... AFRRGp
Air Force Reserve Regions .... AFRESR
Air Force Reserve Regions (AFM) .... AFRR
Air Force Reserve Regions Base Support Group .... AFRESBSGP
Air Force Reserve Regions Group .... AFRESRGP
Air Force Reserve Sectors .... AFRESS
Air Force Reserve Sectors (AFM) .... AFRS
Air Force Reserve Specialist Training Center .... AFRSTC
Air Force Reserve Training Center .... AFRTC
Air Force Resident Officer in Charge .... AFROIC
Air Force Resident Representative (AAG) .... AFRR
Air Force Retired Officer's Community .... AFROC
Air Force Retiring Board .... AFRB
Air Force Review Boards Agency (DOMA) .... AFRBA
Air Force Review Boards Office .... AFRBO
Air Force Rocket Propulsion Laboratory [Later, AFAL] [Edwards Air Force Base, CA] .... AFRPL
Air Force Rome Air Development Center .... AF/RADC
Air Force Route (DA) .... AFR
Air Force Routine Order [Canada, 1920-1945] .... AFRO
Air Force Safety Agency (DOMA) .... AFSA
Air Force Salary Impact Report .... AFSIR
Air Force Satellite Communications System (AFM) .... AFSATCOM
Air Force Satellite Communications System (MCD) .... AFSCS
Air Force Satellite Control Center (CET) .... AFSCC
Air Force Satellite Control Facility .... AFSATLCF
Air Force Satellite [or Spacecraft] Control Facility [Sunnyvale Air Force Station, CA] .... AFSCF
Air Force Satellite Control Network (MCD) .... AFSCN
Air Force Satellite Facility .... AFSF
Air Force Satellite Test Center (MCD) .... AFSTC
Air Force School of Aviation Medicine .... AFSAM
Air Force Scientific Advisory Board (MCD) .... AFSAB
Air Force Section (AFTer) .... AFSec
Air Force Section, Military Assistance Advisory Group .... AFSMAAG
Air Force Security Clearance Office .... AFSCO
Air Force Security Communications Center (MCD) .... AFSCC
Air Force Security Police (VNW) .... AFSP
Air Force Security Police Agency (DOMA) .... AFSPA
Air Force Security Policy Management Engineering Team .... AFSPMET
Air Force Security Service [Later, AFESC] (AFM) .... AFSS
Air Force Security Service Office of Production .... AFSSOP
Air Force Senior Advisory .... AFSA
Air Force Senior Advisory - Jefferson Barracks .... AFSA-JB
Air Force Senior Noncommissioned Officers' Academy (AFM) .... AFSNCOA
Air Force Sergeants Association (EA) .... AFSN
Air Force Serial Number [or Command] .... AFSN
Air Force Service Center [or Command] .... AFSC
Air Force Service Contract Advisory Group (MCD) .... AFSCAG
Air Force Service Information and News Center .... AFSINC
Air Force Service Number .... AFSN
Air Force Service Office (AFM) .... AFSO
Air Force Service Statement .... AFSS
Air Force Skill Code .... AFSC
Air Force Solar Observing Optical Network (MCD) .... AFSOON
Air Force Space and Missile Systems Organization (KSC) .... AFSAMSO
Air Force Space Command (DOMA) .... AFSC
Air Force Space Command (DOMA) .... AFSPACECOM
Air Force Space Division (MCD) .... AFSD
Air Force Space Plane (AAG) .... AFSP
Air Force Space Program .... AFSP
Air Force Space Systems Division .... AFSSD
Air Force Space Technology Center [Kirtland Air Force Base, NM] (MCD) .... AFSTC
Air Force Space Test Center [Later, Western Test Range] .... AFSTC
Air Force Spare (SAA) .... AFSP
Air Force Special Activities Center .... AFSAC
Air Force Special Activities Wing .... AFSAW
Air Force Special Air Warfare Center (MCD) .... AFSAWC
Air Force Special Communications Center (CET) .... AFSCC
Air Force Special Communications Center (AFM) .... AFSPCOMMCEN
Air Force Special Elements Activity [American Embassy security] (VNW) .... AFSEA
Air Force Special Operation Base (MCD) .... AFSOB
Air Force Special Operations Command .... AFSOC
Air Force Special Operations Command (DOMA) .... AFSOC
Air Force Special Security Office [or Officer] (AFM) .... AFSSO
Air Force Special Staff Management Engineering Team .... AFSSMET
Air Force Special Weapons Center [AFSC] [Kirtland Air Force Base, NM] .... AFSWC
Air Force Specialty .... AFS
Air Force Specialty Code .... AFSC
Air Force Specification Bulletin .... AFSB
Air Force Staff Requirement .... AFSR
Air Force Standard (NASA) .... AFS
Air Force Standard Intelligence Publication (AFM) .... AFSIP
Air Force Standard Items and Equipment (SAA) .... AFSIE
Air Force Standard Practice .... AFSP
Air Force Station .... AFS

Air Force Stock (AAG) ... AFS
Air Force Stock Data (SAA) ... AFSD
Air Force Stock Fund ... AFSF
Air Force Stock Number ... AFSN
Air Force Stock Record Account Number (AAG) ... AFSRAN
Air Force Strike Command (MCD) ... AFSTRIKE
Air Force Studies and Analyses Agency (DOMA) ... AFSAA
Air Force Supply ... AFS
Air Force Supply Catalog ... AFSC
Air Force Supply Code ... AFSC
Air Force Supply Date ... AFSD
Air Force Supply Depot ... AFSD
Air Force Supply Directive (MCD) ... AFSD
Air Force Supply Force ... AFSF
Air Force Supply Services System ... AFSS
Air Force Support Base (SAA) ... AFSB
Air Force System Acquisition Review Council ... AFSARC
Air Force Systems Command [*Andrews Air Force Base, MD*] ... AFSC
Air Force Systems Command Design Handbooks ... AFSC-DH
Air Force Systems Command Director of Laboratories ... AFSC/DL
Air Force Systems Command Form ... AFSCF
Air Force Systems Command Inspection Center ... AFSCIC
Air Force Systems Command Letter ... AFSCL
Air Force Systems Command Manual ... AFSCM
Air Force Systems Command Pamphlet ... AFSCP
Air Force Systems Command Procurement Production (MCD) ... AFSCPP
Air Force Systems Command Regulation ... AFSCR
Air Force Systems Command, Scientific Technical Liaison Office (MUGU) ... AFSC/STLO
Air Force Systems Command Space Systems Division ... AFSC/SSD
Air Force Systems Concept Paper (MCD) ... AFSCP
Air Force Systems Project Division (MCD) ... AFSPD
Air Force Tactical Air Command (MCD) ... AFTAC
Air Force Tactical Exploitation of National Capability [*Air Force*] ... AFTENCAP
Air Force Tactical Fighter Weapons Center (MCD) ... AFTFWC
Air Force Tactical Shelter (MCD) ... AFTS
Air Force Task Force (AFM) ... AFTF
Air Force Technical Applications Center [*Patrick Air Force Base, FL*] ... AFTAC
Air Force Technical Approval Team (AAG) ... AFTAT
Air Force Technical Intelligence Center ... AFTIC
Air Force Technical Objectives Documents ... AFTOD
Air Force Technical Order ... AFTO
Air Force Technical Order Management Center (MCD) ... AFTOC
Air Force Technical Order Standardization Board ... AFTOSB
Air Force Technical Report ... AFTR
Air Force Technical Service Command ... AFTSC
Air Force Technical Training Headquarters ... AFTTH
Air Force Telecom Association (AC) ... AFTA
Air Force Test and Evaluation Center [*Kirtland Air Force Base, NM*] (AFM) ... AFTEC
Air Force Test Base ... AFTB
Air Force Test Director (MCD) ... AFTD
Air Force Test Pilot School (MCD) ... AFTPS
Air Force Test Unit (MCD) ... AFTU
Air Force Test Unit, Vietnam ... AFTU-V
Air Force Thermionic Engineering and Research [*Stanford University*] (PDAA) ... AFTER
Air Force Training Auxiliary [*British*] ... ATA
Air Force Training Category [*48 inactive duty training periods and 15 days active duty training per year*] ... A
Air Force Training Category [*24 inactive duty training periods and 15 days active duty training per year*] ... B
Air Force Training Category [*Inactive duty training periods and 15 days active duty training per year*] ... D
Air Force Training Category [*Inactive duty training periods and 30 days active duty training per year*] ... E
Air Force Training Category [*No inactive duty periods and 4 months minimum initial active duty training per year*] ... F
Air Force Training Category [*12 training periods and zero days active duty training per year*] ... G
Air Force Training Category ... H
Air Force Training Category [*No training*] ... I
Air Force Training Category [*Officer training program*] ... J
Air Force Training Command ... AFTRC
Air Force Transportation Management Engineering Team ... AFTRANSMET
Air Force Troop Carrier Command [*British military*] (DMA) ... AFTCC
Air Force Unit Post Office ... AFUPO
Air Force Units ... AFU
Air Force Visual Aid ... AFVA
Air Force Weapon ... AFW
Air Force Weapon Supply [*or System*] (SAA) ... AFWS
Air Force Weapons Effectiveness Testing (AFM) ... AFWET
Air Force Weapons Effectiveness Testing System ... AFWETS
Air Force Weapons Laboratory [*Kirtland Air Force Base, NM*] ... AFWL
Air Force Weapons Laboratory, Kirtland AFB, NM [*OCLC symbol*] (OCLC) ... SCK
Air Force Weather Observing and Forecasting System ... AFWOFS
Air Force Weather Wing (SAA) ... AFWW
Air Force Welfare Board (AFM) ... AFWB
Air Force Western Test Range [*Later, Space and Missile Test Center*] [*Vandenberg Air Force Base, CA*] ... AFWTR
Air Force Western Test Range Manual (MCD) ... AFWTRM
Air Force Wide Mission Area Analysis (MCD) ... AFWMAA
Air Force with Army ... AFWA
Air Force World Wide Military Command and Control System (MCD) ... AFWWMCCS
Air Force Wright Aeronautical Laboratories [*Wright-Patterson Air Force Base, OH*] ... AFWAL
Air Force Wright Aeronautical Laboratories Materials Laboratory [*Wright-Patterson Air Force Base, OH*] ... AFWAL/ML
Air Force WWMCCS [*Worldwide Military Command and Control System*] **Information System** (GFGA) ... AFWIS
Air Force-Navy Design ... AND
Air Force-Navy Ground RADAR (SAA) ... AN/GRA
Air Force-Navy-Civil Committee on Aircraft Requirements ... ANC
Air Forces, Arabian Peninsula [*British military*] (DMA) ... AFAP
Air Forces, Atlantic ... AFLANT
Air Forces, Atlantic Fleet [*Navy*] ... AIRLANT
Air Forces, [*US*] Central Command (DOMA) ... AIRCENT
Air Forces Escape and Evasion Society (EA) ... AFEES
Air Forces Europe Exchange ... AFEX
Air Forces Ferry Command ... AFFC
Air Forces, Iceland (MCD) ... AFI
Air Forces, Iceland ... AFICE
Air Forces Pacific Advanced ... AIRPAC(ADV)
Air Forces, Pacific Fleet ... AIRPAC
Air Forces Pacific, Pearl Harbor ... AIRPAC(PEARL)
Air Forces Southern Europe Command [*NATO*] ... AFSOUTHCOM
Air Forces Subordinate Command, Forward Area ... AIRPACSUBCOMFORD
Air Forces Tactical Center ... AFTAC
Air Forces, Western Europe [*NATO*] (NATG) ... AFWE
Air Foundation ... AF
Air Foyle Airways Ltd. [*British*] [*FAA designator*] (FAAC) ... UPC
Air Foyle Charter Airways Ltd. [*British*] [*FAA designator*] (FAAC) ... UPD
Air Foyle (Executive) Ltd. [*British ICAO designator*] (FAAC) ... AFY
Air Foyle Ltd. [*British ICAO designator*] (FAAC) ... UPA
Air Frame (MCD) ... AF
Air Frame Assembly (MCD) ... AFA
Air France [*ICAO designator*] ... AF
Air France [*ICAO designator*] (FAAC) ... AFR
Air Freight [*Air carrier designation symbol*] ... AFFX
Air Freight (FAAC) ... AFRT
Air Freight Association of America (EA) ... AFA
Air Freight Bill [*Shipping*] ... AFB
Air Freight Decision Tool (MCD) ... AFDT
Air Freight Express, Inc. [*ICAO designator*] (FAAC) ... AFX
Air Freight Forwarders Association of America [*Later, AFA*] (EA) ... AFFA
Air Freight Motor Carriers Conference [*Later, AEMCC*] (EA) ... AFMCC
Air Freight Motor Carriers Conference, Inc., Arlington VA [*STAC*] ... AFM
Air Freight Terminal ... AFT
Air Freighters [*Air carrier designation symbol*] ... AFIX
Air Fret Senegal [*FAA designator*] (FAAC) ... ABN
Air/Fuel [*Mixture ratio*] ... A/F
Air Gabon [*ICAO designator*] (AD) ... GN
Air Gambia [*ICAO designator*] (FAAC) ... AGS
Air Gambia [*Airline flight code*] (ODBW) ... iv
Air Gap ... AG
Air Gap Width ... AGW
Air Gauge ... AG
Air GEFCO [*France ICAO designator*] (FAAC) ... GEF
Air Georgia [*Former USSR*] [*FAA designator*] (FAAC) ... GEO
Air Georgian [*Canada*] [*FAA designator*] (FAAC) ... GGN
Air Glaciers SA [*Switzerland ICAO designator*] (FAAC) ... AGV
Air Goyle Charter Ltd. [*British*] [*FAA designator*] (FAAC) ... UPB
Air Grease System (PDAA) ... AGS
Air Great Lakes [*ICAO designator*] (AD) ... BB
Air Great Wall [*CHINA*] [*FAA designator*] (FAAC) ... CGW
Air Greece SA [*FAA designator*] (FAAC) ... AGJ
Air Ground Engagement [*Military*] (DOMA) ... AGE
Air Group ... AG
Air Group ... AIRGRP
Air Guadeloupe [*ICAO designator*] (AD) ... OG
Air Guam [*ICAO designator*] (FAAC) ... AGM
Air Guinea [*Guinea*] [*ICAO designator*] (FAAC) ... GIB
Air Guinee [*ICAO designator*] (AD) ... GI
Air Gunner [*British*] ... AG
Air Gunnery Instructor [*British military*] (DMA) ... AGI
Air Gunnery Officer ... AGO
Air Gunnery School [*British*] (OA) ... AGS
Air Guyane [*France ICAO designator*] (FAAC) ... GUY
Air Guyane [*ICAO designator*] (AD) ... KJ
Air Hainaut [*France ICAO designator*] (FAAC) ... AHN
Air Haiti [*ICAO designator*] (FAAC) ... HJA
Air Handling [*Nuclear energy*] (NRCH) ... A/H
Air Hanson Ltd. [*British ICAO designator*] (FAAC) ... AHL
Air Hawaii [*ICAO designator*] (AD) ... HP
Air Header ... AHDR
Air Headquarters ... AHQ
Air Heater Blower ... AHB
Air Height Surveillance RADAR ... AHSR
Air, High Pressure (DNAB) ... AHP
Air Historical Branch [*Air Ministry*] [*British*] ... AHB
Air Holland Regional (AHR) [*ICAO designator*] (FAAC) ... AHR
Air Hong Kong Ltd. [*ICAO designator*] (FAAC) ... AHK
Air Horsepower [*Air Force*] ... AHP
Air Ile de France [*ICAO designator*] (FAAC) ... AIF
Air Iliria [*Yugoslavia*] [*ICAO designator*] (FAAC) ... ILR
Air Illinois [*ICAO designator*] (AD) ... UX
Air Illinois, Inc. [*ICAO designator*] (FAAC) ... AIL
Air Illinois, Inc. [*Air carrier designation symbol*] ... AILX
Air Images [*British*] [*FAA designator*] (FAAC) ... IMS

Air Incident Message ... AIM
Air Incident Report ... AIR
Air Independent Propulsion [*Submarine*] (DOMA) ... AIP
Air India [*ICAO designator*] (AD) ... AI
Air India [*ICAO designator*] (FAAC) ... AIC
Air India International ... AII
Air Induction ... AINDTN
Air Induction Control System [*Air Force*] ... AICS
Air Industries and Transports Association (MCD) ... AITA
Air Infiltration Measurement Service [*National Association of Home Builders National Research Center*] ... AIMS
Air Inflatable Retarder [*for bombs*] (MCD) ... AIR
Air Information Center (NATG) ... AIC
Air Information Codification (NATG) ... AIC
Air Information Division [*Library of Congress*] (MCD) ... AID
Air Injection [*Automotive engineering*] ... AI
Air Injection Reactor ... AIR
Air Injection Relief Valve [*Automotive engineering*] ... AIRV
Air Injection Tube [*Automotive engineering*] ... AIT
Air Inlet [*Automotive engineering*] ... A/INL
Air Inlet Control System ... AICS
Air Inlet Control System Test Set ... AICSTS
Air Inlet Controller (MCD) ... AIC
Air Inlet Damper (NRCH) ... AID
Air Inspection Directorate [*British*] ... AID
Air Inspector ... AI
Air Inspector General (MCD) ... AIG
Air Installation Compatible Use Zoning [*Air Force*] ... AICUZ
Air Installation Office ... AIO
Air Installations ... AI
Air Intake Duct (DNAB) ... AID
Air Intake Panel ... AIP
Air Integra, Inc. [*Canada ICAO designator*] (FAAC) ... AII
Air Intelligence (NVT) ... AI
Air Intelligence Agency [*Air Force*] ... AIA
Air Intelligence Command (SAA) ... AIC
Air Intelligence Duty Officer (DNAB) ... AIDO
Air Intelligence Force ... AIF
Air Intelligence Group [*Military*] (MCD) ... AIG
Air Intelligence Group [*Military*] (MCD) ... AINTELG
Air Intelligence Liaison [*British*] ... AIL
Air Intelligence Liaison Officer [*British*] ... AILO
Air Intelligence Officer [*Air Force*] ... AINTELO
Air Intelligence Officer [*Navy*] (NVT) ... AIO
Air Intelligence Organization (NATG) ... AIO
Air Intelligence Section [*Army*] ... AINTSEC
Air Intelligence Service ... AIS
Air Intelligence Services Squadron [*Defunct Air Force*] ... AISS
Air Intelligence Squadron [*Air Force*] ... AINTELS
Air Intelligence Training Center (MCD) ... AITC
Air Inter [*ICAO designator*] (AD) ... IT
Air Inter Gabon [*ICAO designator*] (FAAC) ... AIG
Air Inter Gabon [*ICAO designator*] (AD) ... GB
Air Inter, Societe [*France ICAO designator*] (ICDA) ... IT
Air Inter, Societe [*France ICAO designator*] (FAAC) ... ITF
Air Intercept Battle Analysis ... AIBA
Air Intercept [*or Interception*] **Control** [*or Controller*] ... AIC
Air Intercept Control Command (SAA) ... AICC
Air Intercept Control School ... AICS
Air Intercept Controller Supervisor (NVT) ... AICS
Air Intercept Missile (AFM) ... AIM
Air Intercept Missile Evaluation (MCD) ... AIMVAL
Air Intercept Missile Package ... AIMP
Air Intercept Officer (MCD) ... AIO
Air Intercept Rocket (IEEE) ... AIR
Air Interception Committee [*Air Ministry*] [*British*] ... AIC
Air Interceptor Fuze ... AIF
Air Interdiction (MCD) ... AI
Air Interface Sub-Working Group [*NATO*] (NATG) ... AISWG
Air International [*British ICAO designator*] (FAAC) ... AIX
Air International (Holdings) PLC [*British ICAO designator*] (FAAC) ... JPR
Air Inuit Ltd. [*Canada ICAO designator*] (FAAC) ... AIE
Air Isolated Monolithic [*Circuit*] ... AIM
Air Ivoire [*ICAO designator*] (AD) ... VU
Air Ivoire Societe [*Ivory Coast*] [*ICAO designator*] (FAAC) ... VUN
Air Jamaica [*ICAO designator*] (FAAC) ... AJM
Air Jamaica Ltd. [*ICAO designator*] (OAG) ... JM
Air Jet [*ICAO designator*] (FAAC) ... AIJ
Air Jet Control Unit ... AJCU
Air Jet Distortion Generator (MCD) ... AJDG
Air Jordan [*Airline*] ... AJ
Air Kangaroo Island [*Airline code*] [*Australia*] ... UV
Air Kentucky [*ICAO designator*] (AD) ... KN
Air Kiev [*Ukraine*] [*FAA designator*] (FAAC) ... KIV
Air Kilroe Ltd. [*British ICAO designator*] (FAAC) ... AKL
Air Korea Co. Ltd. [*South Korea*] [*ICAO designator*] (FAAC) ... AKA
Air Koryo [*North Korea*] [*ICAO designator*] (FAAC) ... KOR
Air La [*ICAO designator*] (AD) ... UE
Air LA, Inc. [*ICAO designator*] (FAAC) ... UED
Air/Land Battlefield Environment [*Army*] (RDA) ... ALBE
Air Landing Exercise [*Military*] (NVT) ... AIRLEX
Air Lanka [*Sri Lanka*] [*ICAO designator*] (FAAC) ... ALK
Air Lanka [*ICAO designator*] (AD) ... UL
Air Launch [*or Lift*] (SAA) ... A/L
Air Launch Sounding Rocket ... ALSOR
Air Launchable Concept ... ALC
Air League [*An association*] (EAIO) ... AL
Air Letter ... AL
Air Liaison ... AL
Air Liaison Officer [*Air Force*] ... AIRLO
Air Liaison Officer ... ALO
Air Liaison Officer Net (NATG) ... ALON
Air Liaison Party ... ALP
Air Liaison Section [*British and Canadian*] [*World War II*] ... AL Sec
Air Liberia [*ICAO designator*] (FAAC) ... ALI
Air Liberia [*ICAO designator*] (AD) ... NL
Air Liberte [*France ICAO designator*] (FAAC) ... LIB
Air Liberte Tunisie [*Tunisia*] [*ICAO designator*] (FAAC) ... LBT
Air Lietuva [*Lithuania*] [*ICAO designator*] (FAAC) ... KLA
Air Limousin TA [*France ICAO designator*] (FAAC) ... LMT
Air Lincoln, Inc. [*ICAO designator*] (FAAC) ... ALN
Air Line Communication Employees Association ... ACEA
Air Line Communication Employees Association ... ALCEA
Air Line Dispatchers Association [*Defunct*] ... ALDA
Air Line Employees Association, International (EA) ... ALEA
Air Line of Communication [*Air Force*] ... ALOC
Air Line Pilots Association, International (EA) ... ALPA
Air Line Pilots Association, International (EA) ... ALPAI
Air Line Stewards and Stewardesses Association (EA) ... ALSSA
Air Lines Circuit (SAA) ... ALC
Air Lines of Communication ... AIRLOC
Air Lingus [*ICAO designator*] (AD) ... EI
Air Link [*ICAO designator*] (AD) ... FF
Air Link Charters [*Canada*] (FAAC) ... FSR
Air Liquide Canada Ltee., Montreal, Quebec [*Library symbol National Library of Canada*] (NLC) ... QMAL
Air Liquide, Montreal, PQ, Canada [*Library symbol Library of Congress*] (LCLS) ... CaQMAL
Air Littoral [*ICAO designator*] (AD) ... FU
Air Littoral [*France ICAO designator*] (FAAC) ... LIT
Air Lock [*Technical drawings*] ... AL
Air Lock System (MCD) ... ALS
Air Logistic Coordination Center ... ALCORCEN
Air Logistics Center [*McClellan Air Force Base, CA*] (MCD) ... ALC
Air Logistics Center Augmentation Squadron [*Air Force*] ... ALCAS
Air Logistics Chain (MCD) ... ALOC
Air Logistics Command [*Air Force*] ... ALC
Air Logistics Command Local Area Network ... ALCLAN
Air Logistics Officer (AAGC) ... ALO
Air Logistics Pipeline Study (MCD) ... ALP
Air Logistics Service [*or System*] [*Military*] ... ALS
Air London [*British ICAO designator*] (FAAC) ... ACG
Air, Low Pressure (DNAB) ... ALP
Air Lubricated Free Attitude [*NASA*] (KSC) ... ALFA
Air Madagascar [*ICAO designator*] (AD) ... MD
Air Madagascar, Societe Nationale Malgache de Transports Aeriens [*ICAO designator*] (FAAC) ... MDG
Air Mahe [*ICAO designator*] (AD) ... HM
Air Mail Center ... AMC
Air Mail Facility [*Post Office*] ... AMF
Air Mail Field ... AMF
Air Mail Pioneers (EA) ... AMP
Air Mail Route Number 2 ... AM2
Air Mail Service ... AMS
Air Mail Transfer (ADA) ... AMT
Air Mail Transfer (ODBW) ... amt
Air Mail Transmission ... AMT
Air Malawi [*ICAO designator*] (FAAC) ... AML
Air Malawi [*ICAO designator*] (AD) ... QM
Air Maldives [*ICAO designator*] (FAAC) ... AMI
Air Mali [*ICAO designator*] (AD) ... MY
Air Malta [*ICAO designator*] (AD) ... KM
Air Malta Co. Ltd. [*ICAO designator*] (FAAC) ... AMC
Air Management Division [*Environmental Protection Agency*] (GFGA) ... AMD
Air Management Station ... AMS
AIR [*All India Law Reporter*] **Manual: Unrepealed Central Acts** [*2nd ed.*] [*India*] [*A publication*] (DLA) ... India AIR Manual
Air Margarita [*Venezuela*] [*ICAO designator*] (FAAC) ... MAG
Air Marshal [*British*] ... AM
Air Marshall Islands [*Airline code*] [*Australia*] ... CW
Air Martinique (Satair) [*ICAO designator*] (AD) ... BT
Air Mass [*Solar energy research*] ... AM
Air Mass (FAAC) ... AMS
Air Mass and Frontal Analysis [*Meteorology*] ... AMAFA
Air Mass Transportation Experiment [*Global Atmospheric Research Program*] (USDC) ... AMTEX
Air Mass Zero ... AMO
Air Material AG [*Switzerland ICAO designator*] (FAAC) ... AMG
Air Material Area Stock Control Point (NG) ... AMASCP
Air Material Armament Test Center ... AMATC
Air Material Armament Test Center [*Air Force*] (MCD) ... AMTC
Air Material Command [*Later, Air Force Logistics Command*] [*Air Force*] ... AIMACO
Air Material Command [*later, Air Force Logistics Command*] **Compiling** [*System*] ... AIMACC
Air Material Command Headquarters, Ottawa, Ontario, Canada ... CANAIRMAT
Air Material Computer (MCD) ... AIMACO
Air Material Office [*Military*] (DNAB) ... AMO
Air Material Proving Ground ... AMPG
Air Materiel Area [*Later, Air Logistics Centers*] [*Air Force*] ... AMA
Air Materiel Area System Management [*Air Force*] ... AMASM

Air Materiel Command [*Later, Air Force Logistics Command*] ... AMC
Air Materiel Command [*later, Air Force Logistics Command*] **- Air Force** ... AMC-AF
Air Materiel Command [*later, Air Force Logistics Command*] **Ballistic Missile Center** (IEEE) ... AMCBMC
Air Materiel Command [*later, Air Force Logistics Command*] **Forms** ... AMCF
Air Materiel Command [*later, Air Force Logistics Command*] **Headquarters** ... AMCHQ
Air Materiel Command [*later, Air Force Logistics Command*] **Letter** ... AMCL
Air Materiel Command [*later, Air Force Logistics Command*] **Liaison Office** [*or Officer*] ... AMCLO
Air Materiel Command [*later, Air Force Logistics Command*] **Logistics Office** [*or Officer*] ... AMCLO
Air Materiel Command [*later, Air Force Logistics Command*] **Manual** ... AMCM
Air Materiel Command [*later, Air Force Logistics Command*] **Missile Field Office** ... AMCMFO
Air Materiel Command [*later, Air Force Logistics Command*] **Regulations** ... AMCR
Air Materiel Command [*later, Air Force Logistics Command*] **Test Site Office** ... AMCTSO
Air Materiel Force ... AMF
Air Materiel Force, European Area ... AMFEA
Air Materiel Force, Pacific Area ... AMFPA
Air Mattress [*Medicine*] ... AM
Air Mauritanie [*Mauritania*] [*ICAO designator*] (ICDA) ... MR
Air Mauritanie [*Mauritania*] [*ICAO designator*] (FAAC) ... MRT
Air Mauritius [*ICAO designator*] (AD) ... MK
Air Mauritius [*Airline flight code*] (ODBW) ... MK
Air Mauritius Ltd. [*ICAO designator*] (FAAC) ... MAU
Air Mechanic (Engines) [*British military*] (DMA) ... AE
Air Mechanician ... AM
Air Med Jetoperations [*Austria ICAO designator*] (FAAC) ... JDE
Air Medal [*Military decoration*] ... AM
Air Medical Ltd. [*British ICAO designator*] (FAAC) ... MCD
Air Medical Research Laboratory [*Later, MRL*] (MCD) ... AMRL
Air Melanesiae [*ICAO designator*] (AD) ... HB
Air Member, Canadian Joint Staff, London, England ... CANAIRLON
Air Member, Canadian Joint Staff, Washington, DC ... CANAIRWASH
Air Member for Accounts and Finance [*British and Canadian*] [*World War II*] ... AMAF
Air Member for Aeronautical Engineering [*British and Canadian*] [*World War II*] ... AMAE
Air Member for Air Staff [*British and Canadian*] [*World War II*] ... AMAS
Air Member for Development and Production [*Air Ministry*] [*British*] ... AMDP
Air Member for Engineering and Supply [*British and Canadian*] [*World War II*] ... AMES
Air Member for Organization [*British and Canadian*] [*World War II*] ... AMO
Air Member for Organization and Training [*British and Canadian*] [*World War II*] ... AMOT
Air Member for Personnel [*Air Ministry*] [*British*] ... AMP
Air Member for Research and Development [*Later, TRE*] [*Air Ministry*] [*British*] ... AMRD
Air Member for Supply [*British and Canadian*] [*World War II*] ... AMS
Air Member for Supply and Organisation [*Air Ministry*] [*British*] ... AMSO
Air Member for Supply and Research [*Air Ministry*] [*British*] ... AMSR
Air Member for Training [*British and Canadian*] [*World War II*] ... AMT
Air Mercury International [*Belgium ICAO designator*] (FAAC) ... AMI
Air Methods [*NASDAQ symbol*] (TTSB) ... AIRM
Air Methods Corp. [*NASDAQ symbol*] (SAG) ... AIRM
Air Methods Corp. [*Associated Press*] (SAG) ... AirMeth
Air Meuse - Dat Wallonie [*Belgium ICAO designator*] (FAAC) ... AMZ
Air Midwest [*ICAO designator*] (AD) ... ZV
Air Midwest, Inc. [*ICAO designator*] (FAAC) ... AMW
Air Mileage Indicator [*Navigation*] ... AMI
Air Mileage Unit [*Navigation*] ... AMU
Air Ministry [*British*] ... AM
Air Ministry Bulletin [*British military*] (DMA) ... AMB
Air Ministry Constabulary [*British military*] (DMA) ... AMC
Air Ministry Experimental Station [*British*] ... AMES
Air Ministry Local Staff Union [*Singapore*] ... AMLSU
Air Ministry Order [*British*] ... AMO
Air Ministry Reconnaissance Department [*British*] (DAS) ... AMRE
Air Ministry Research Establishment [*British military*] (DMA) ... AMRE
Air Ministry Secret Intelligence Summary [*British military*] (DMA) ... AMSIS
Air Ministry War Room [*British World War II*] ... AMWR
Air Ministry Warden [*British military*] (DMA) ... AMW
Air Ministry's Accident Branch [*British*] ... AMAB
Air Missile System (NG) ... AMS
Air Mission [*Air Force*] ... AIRMSN
Air Mission Brief [*Air Force*] (INF) ... AMB
Air Mission Commander [*Military*] (INF) ... AMC
Air Mission Unit [*Air Force*] ... AMU
Air Mobile ... AM
Air Mobile Aircraft Refueling System ... AMARS
Air Mobile Assault Brigade (MCD) ... AMAB
Air Mobile Ground Security and Surveillance System [*Army*] ... AMGSSS
Air Mobile, Light Helicopter [*Army*] (VNW) ... AML
Air Mobile Refueling Equipment ... ARE
Air Mobile Task Force ... AMTF
Air Mobile Van [*Trailer unit for use on ground or in air*] [*Military*] ... AIRVAN
Air Mobility Command [*Air Force*] ... AMC
Air Mobility Research and Development Laboratory [*Also, USAMR & DL*] [*Army*] ... AMR & DL
Air Mobility Research and Development Laboratory [*Also, AMR & DL, USAMR & DL*] [*Army*] (MCD) ... AMRD
Air Moldova [*ICAO designator*] (FAAC) ... MLD
Air Moldova International, SA [*FAA designator*] (FAAC) ... MLV
Air Molokai-Tropic Airlines [*ICAO designator*] (FAAC) ... TRO
Air Mongol [*ICAO designator*] (AD) ... OM
Air Monitoring Analysis and Prediction [*System*] ... AIRMAP
Air Monitoring Center [*Rockwell International Corp.*] ... AMC
Air Monitoring Center [*Rockwell International Corp.*] ... AMC
Air Montenegro [*Yugoslavia*] [*ICAO designator*] (FAAC) ... AMN
Air Montreal, Inc. [*Canada ICAO designator*] (FAAC) ... AMO
Air Moorea [*France ICAO designator*] (FAAC) ... TAH
Air Moravia [*Czechoslovakia*] [*ICAO designator*] (FAAC) ... MAI
Air Motor Servo Unit (MCD) ... AMSU
Air Mounting Centre [*British military*] (DMA) ... AMC
Air Movement [*Message*] (NVT) ... AIRMOVE
Air Movement and Control Association (EA) ... AM & CA
Air Movement and Control Association (EA) ... AMCA
Air Movement Data [*Air Force*] ... AMD
Air Movement Designator [*Army*] ... AMD
Air Movement Exercise [*Military*] (NVT) ... AIRMOVEX
Air Movement Information Center [*NATO*] (NATG) ... AMIC
Air Movement Institute (EA) ... AMI
Air Movement Officer [*Military*] ... AMO
Air Movement Recorder ... AMR
Air Movements (SAA) ... AM
Air Movements Information Section ... AMIS
Air Movements Talker (SAA) ... AMT
Air Movements Training Flight ... AMTF
Air Moving and Conditioning Association (SAA) ... AMCA
Air Munitions ... AMUN
Air Munitions Development Laboratory (MUGU) ... AMDL
Air Munitions Requirements and Development Committee [*DoD*] (MCD) ... AMRAD
Air Muskoka [*Canada ICAO designator*] (FAAC) ... AMS
Air National Guard ... ANG
Air National Guard Base ... ANGB
Air National Guard Fighter Weapons Office [*Tucson, AZ*] ... ANG-FWO
Air National Guard of the United States ... ANGUS
Air National Guard Operational Support Aircraft [*Air Force*] (DOMA) ... ANGOSA
Air National Guard Optometric Society (EA) ... ANGOS
Air National Guard Policy Council ... ANGPC
Air National Guard Support Center ... ANGSC
Air Nauru [*ICAO designator*] (AD) ... ON
Air Nauru [*ICAO designator*] (FAAC) ... RON
Air Navigation ... AN
Air Navigation Act [*British*] ... ANA
Air Navigation and Bombing School ... ANBS
Air Navigation and Tactical Control ... ANTAC
Air Navigation & Trading Co. Ltd. [*British ICAO designator*] (FAAC) ... ANB
Air Navigation and Traffic Control ... ANATC
Air Navigation Board [*Military*] (SAA) ... ANB
Air Navigation Bureau [*British*] (AIA) ... ANB
Air Navigation Charge (ADA) ... ANC
Air Navigation Committee [*NATO*] (NATG) ... ANC
Air Navigation Computer Unit (MCD) ... ANCU
Air Navigation Conference [*ICAO*] ... ANC
Air Navigation Data Center (SAA) ... ANDAC
Air Navigation Development Board [*Functions absorbed by the FAA*] ... ANDB
Air Navigation Device ... AND
Air Navigation Directions ... AND
Air Navigation Facility ... ANF
Air Navigation (General) Regulation [*British*] (DA) ... ANGR
Air Navigation Multiple Indicator (PDAA) ... ANMI
Air Navigation Office [*Navy*] ... AIRNAVO
Air Navigation Office [*Navy*] ... ANO
Air Navigation Order ... ANO
Air Navigation Plan (DA) ... ANP
Air Navigation Radio Aids ... ANRA
Air Navigation Regulations (ADA) ... ANR
Air Navigation School [*British*] ... ANS
Air Navigation Technical Committee (SAA) ... ANTC
Air Navigation Traffic Control ... ANTC
Air Navigation Training Unit ... ANTU
Air Navigational Aid [*Navy*] (NG) ... AIRNAVAID
Air Nebraska [*ICAO designator*] (AD) ... DF
Air Nelson Ltd. [*New Zealand*] [*ICAO designator*] (FAAC) ... RLK
Air Nevada [*ICAO designator*] (AD) ... LW
Air Nevada Airlines, Inc. [*ICAO designator*] (FAAC) ... ANV
Air New England [*ICAO designator*] (AD) ... NE
Air New Zealand Ltd. [*Airline*] ... Air NZ
Air New Zealand Ltd. [*ICAO designator*] (FAAC) ... ANZ
Air New Zealand Ltd. (Domestic Division) [*ICAO designator*] (ICDA) ... NZ
Air Newark, Inc. [*ICAO designator*] (FAAC) ... NER
Air Niagara Express, Inc. [*Canada ICAO designator*] (FAAC) ... DBD
Air Niger [*ICAO designator*] (FAAC) ... AWN
Air Nippon Co. Ltd. [*Japan ICAO designator*] (FAAC) ... ANK
Air Niugini [*Papua New Guinea*] [*ICAO designator*] (FAAC) ... ANG
Air Niugini [*Air New Guinea*] [*ICAO designator*] (AD) ... PX
Air, Noise, and Radiation Health Research Division [*Environmental Protection Agency*] (GFGA) ... ANRHRD
Air Nordic in Vasteras AB [*Sweden ICAO designator*] (FAAC) ... NOX
Air Nordic SWE Aviation, AB [*Sweden*] [*FAA designator*] (FAAC) ... NDC
Air Nordic Sweden [*ICAO designator*] (AD) ... EO
Air Normandie [*France ICAO designator*] (FAAC) ... RNO
Air North [*ICAO designator*] (AD) ... GD
Air North [*ICAO designator*] (AD) ... NO
Air North [*ICAO designator*] (AD) ... XG
Air North Charter [*Canada ICAO designator*] (FAAC) ... ANT

Air North Ltd. [*Australia ICAO designator*] (FAAC) ... ANO
Air Nova [*British ICAO designator*] (FAAC) ... HMT
Air Nova, Inc. [*Canada ICAO designator*] (FAAC) ... ARN
Air Objective Folder (SAA) ... AOF
Air Observation Post ... AOP
Air Observation Post Flight [*British military*] (DMA) ... AOPF
Air Observer [*Military British*] ... AO
Air Observer [*Military*] (AFM) ... AOBSR
Air Observer School [*British*] ... AOS
Air Observers Navigation School [*Military*] (OA) ... AONS
Air Officer [*RAF*] [*British*] ... AO
Air Officer Commanding [*RAF*] [*British*] ... AOC
Air Officer Commanding Base Air Forces [*RAF*] [*British*] ... AOCBAF
Air Officer Commanding-in-Chief [*RAF*] [*British*] ... AOCIC
Air Officer Commanding-in-Chief [*RAF*] [*British*] (NATG) ... AOCINC
Air Officer Commanding-in-Chief [*RAF*] [*British*] ... AOC-in-C
Air Officer Commanding-in-Chief British Air Force Occupation [*RAF*] ... AOC in CBAFO
Air Officer in Charge of Administration [*RAF*] [*British*] ... AOA
Air Officer of the Day [*Air Force*] (AFM) ... AOD
Air Oil Cooler ... AOC
Air Oil Separator ... AOS
Air Ontario Ltd. [*Canada ICAO designator*] (FAAC) ... ONT
Air Operational Network [*Air Force*] ... AIROPNET
Air Operational Training ... APTRA
Air Operations [*Military*] ... AIROPS
Air Operations [*Military*] (NVT) ... AOPS
Air Operations Center [*Air Force*] ... AOC
Air Operations Officer [*Air Force*] ... AIROPNSO
Air Operations Room ... AOR
Air Operations Specialist ... AOS
Air Operator (NRCH) ... AO
Air Operators Certificate [*British*] (AIA) ... AOC
Air Order of Battle (AFM) ... AOB
Air Order of Battle Textual Summary (MCD) ... AOBTS
Air Ordnance [*Special duties officer*] [*British*] ... AO
Air Organisation and Training Division [*British military*] (DMA) ... AOTD
Air Orkney [*British ICAO designator*] (FAAC) ... ORK
Air Ostravia Ltd. [*Czechoslovakia*] [*FAA designator*] (FAAC) ... VTR
Air Outlet [*Automotive engineering*] ... A/OUT
Air Over (MSA) ... AO
Air Over Hydraulic (AAG) ... A/H
Air Over Hydraulic [*Automotive engineering*] ... AOH
Air Pacific [*ICAO designator*] (AD) ... AIRPAC
Air Pacific [*ICAO designator*] (AD) ... FJ
Air Pacific Airlines [*ICAO designator*] (FAAC) ... APM
Air Pacific Crake [*Philippines*] [*ICAO designator*] (FAAC) ... CRK
Air Pacific Ltd. [*Fiji*] [*ICAO designator*] (FAAC) ... FJI
Air Panama Internacional [*ICAO designator*] (FAAC) ... API
Air Panama Internacional [*ICAO designator*] (AD) ... OP
Air Parcel Express [*ICAO designator*] (FAAC) ... APE
Air Parcel Post [*Shipping*] (AABC) ... APP
Air Paris [*ICAO designator*] (AD) ... IO
Air Park ... APRK
Air Park Aviation Ltd. [*Canada ICAO designator*] (FAAC) ... APA
Air Particulate Detector (IEEE) ... APD
Air Particulate Matter [*Environmental science*] ... APM
Air Particulate Monitor [*Nuclear energy*] (NRCH) ... APM
Air Passage (MSA) ... AP
Air Pathway Analyses [*Environmental chemistry*] ... APA
Air Patrol (DNAB) ... AP
Air Patrol Area (NVT) ... APA
Air Patrol Zone (NVT) ... APZ
Air Pennsylvania [*ICAO designator*] (AD) ... ZY
Air Permeability Meter ... APM
Air, Pesticides, and Toxics Management Division [*Environmental Protection Agency*] (GFGA) ... APTMD
Air Philippines Corporation, Inc. [*ICAO designator*] (FAAC) ... APQ
Air Photo Production Unit [*Canada*] ... APPU
Air Photographic and Charting Service ... APCS
Air Pictorial Service ... APS
Air Pilot ... AP
Air Plan International [*Zaire*] [*FAA designator*] (FAAC) ... APV
Air Plot (DNAB) ... AP
Air Police [*By extension, a person who is a member of the Air Police*] ... AP
Air Pollutant Emissions Report [*Environmental Protection Agency*] ... APER
Air Pollution (KSC) ... AP
Air Pollution Control ... APC
Air Pollution Control Association (EA) ... APCA
Air Pollution Control Code (SAA) ... APCC
Air Pollution Control District ... APCD
Air Pollution Control Equipment Manufacturers' Association ... APCEMA
Air Pollution Control Office [*Obsolete Environmental Protection Agency*] ... APCO
Air Pollution Control Regulation (MCD) ... APCR
Air Pollution Exercise ... APEX
Air Pollution Information and Computation System ... APICS
Air Pollution Meteorologist (NOAA) ... APM
Air Pollution Potential ... APP
Air Pollution Research Advisory Committee ... APRAC
Air Pollution Syndrome ... APS
Air Pollution Technical Data [*Series*] [*A publication*] ... APTD
Air Pollution Technical Information Center [*Also, NAPTIC*] [*Bibliographic database*] [*Environmental Protection Agency*] ... APTIC
Air Pollution Training Institute [*Environmental Protection Agency*] (GFGA) ... APTI
Air Polynesie [*ICAO designator*] (AD) ... VT
Air Portable Bridge (PDAA) ... APB
Air Position ... AP
Air Position Indicating Station [*Air Force*] (IAA) ... APIS
Air Position Indicator [*Air Force*] ... API
Air Post Office (MCD) ... APO
Air Postal Squadron [*Air Force*] ... AIRPS
Air Power History [*A publication*] ... APH
Air Pressure (MCD) ... AP
Air Pressure Analysis Program [*Bell System*] ... AIRPAP
Air Pressure Switch ... APS
Air Primary Training ... PRIMTRA
Air Priority ... APRI
Air Priority Rating ... APR
Air Prisoner of War Interrogation ... APWI
Air Processing Subsystem (MCD) ... AP
Air Procurement Directive (MCD) ... APD
Air Procurement District [*Air Force*] ... APD
Air Procurement District Commander [*Air Force*] ... APDC
Air Procurement Office ... APO
Air Procurement Region, Europe (AFM) ... APRE
Air Procurement Region, Far East (AFM) ... APRFE
Air Products & Chem [*NYSE symbol*] (TTSB) ... APD
Air Products & Chemicals, Inc. [*Associated Press*] (SAG) ... AirProd
Air Products & Chemicals, Inc. [*NYSE symbol*] (SPSG) ... APD
Air Products & Chemicals, Inc., Allentown, PA [*OCLC symbol*] (OCLC) ... APA
Air Products & Chemicals, Inc., Allentown, PA [*Library symbol Library of Congress*] (LCLS) ... PAtA
Air Programs Office [*Environmental Protection Agency*] ... APO
Air Project Coordinator [*Military*] (DNAB) ... APC
Air Proving Ground ... APG
Air Proving Ground Center [*or Command*] [*Eglin Air Force Base, FL*] ... APGC
Air Proving Ground Center - Eglin Air Force Base ... APGCE
Air Provost Marshal ... APM
Air Public Relations Association [*British*] (BI) ... APRA
Air Publication [*Navy*] ... AP
Air Pump Diverter Valve [*Automotive engineering*] ... APDV
Air Quality Act ... AQA
Air Quality Advisory Board ... AQAB
Air Quality Assessment Model [*Air Force*] ... AQAM
Air Quality Control Region [*Environmental Protection Agency*] ... AQCR
Air Quality Criteria and Control Techniques [*Environmental Protection Agency*] (GFGA) ... AQCCT
Air Quality Data Handling System [*or Subsystem*] [*Environmental Protection Agency*] ... AQDHS
Air Quality Display Model ... AQDM
Air Quality Forecast ... AQF
Air Quality Guideline Values [*World Health Organization*] ... AQGV
Air Quality Improvement Research Program [*Automotive industry, research consortium*] ... AQIRP
Air Quality Index ... AQI
Air Quality Maintenance Area [*Environmental Protection Agency*] (GFGA) ... AQMA
Air Quality Maintenance Plan [*Environmental Protection Agency*] (GFGA) ... AQMP
Air Quality Management ... AQM
Air Quality Management District ... AQMD
Air Quality Region ... AQR
Air Quality Related Values/Visibility Test [*Environmental Protection Agency*] ... AQRV
Air Quality Simulation Model [*Environmental Protection Agency*] ... AQSM
Air Quality Standard ... AQS
Air Quality Technical Assistance Demonstration [*Environmental Protection Agency*] (GFGA) ... AQTAD
Air Queensland [*Australia*] ... AQ
Air Queensland [*Australia ICAO designator*] (FAAC) ... AQN
Air Quenched (IAA) ... AQ
Air Radio [*Special duties officer*] [*British*] ... AR
Air Radio Officer ... ARO
Air Raid Precautions [*British World War II*] ... ARP
Air Raid Precautions Controller [*British World War II*] ... ARPC
Air Raid Precautions Officer [*British World War II*] ... ARPO
Air Raid Protection (NATG) ... ARP
Air Raid Reporting Control Ship [*Navy*] (NVT) ... ARRCS
Air Raid Warden ... ARW
Air Raid Warning [*Air Force*] ... ARW
Air Rarotonga [*ICAO designator*] (AD) ... GZ
Air Reactor Experiment ... ARE
Air Receive ... AR
Air Reconnaissance (IAA) ... AR
Air Reconnaissance Detection Force (CINC) ... ARDF
Air Reconnaissance Liaison Officer ... ARLO
Air Reconnaissance Low [*Army*] (RDA) ... ARL
Air Reconnaissance Support (AABC) ... ARSPT
Air Reconnaissance Support Battalion ... ARSB
Air Recovery and Rescue Service (NASA) ... ARRS
Air Recreational Vehicle ... ARV
Air Reduction Center [*NASA*] (KSC) ... ARC
Air Reduction Co., Inc., Central Research Department Library, Murray Hill, NJ [*Library symbol Library of Congress*] (LCLS) ... NjMuA
Air Refueling [*Aviation*] (FAAC) ... AIRFL
Air Refueling ... AR
Air Refueling Boom (MCD) ... ARB
Air Refueling Control Point (AFM) ... ARCP
Air Refueling Control Time (AFM) ... ARCT
Air Refueling Egress Point [*Aviation*] (FAAC) ... AREP
Air Refueling Exit [*Aviation*] (FAAC) ... AREX
Air Refueling Facility [*Military*] (DOMA) ... ARF

Air Refueling Group [*Air Force*] (DOMA) ... ARG
Air Refueling Initial Point [*Air Force*] (AFM) ... ARIP
Air Refueling Part Task Trainer ... ARPTT
Air Refueling Probe ... ARP
Air Refueling Squadron ... AREFS
Air Refueling Squadron ... AREFSQ
Air Refueling Wing ... AREFW
Air Regenerative Exhaust ... ARX
Air Regional Library (PGSL), Transport Canada [*Bibliotheque Regionale de l'Air (PGSL), Transports Canada*] **Vancouver, British Columbia** [*Library symbol National Library of Canada*] (NLC) ... BVATCA
Air Regional Representative ... ARR
Air Register [*Combustion emission control*] ... AR
Air Registration Board [*British*] ... ARB
Air Regulating Squadron ... ARS
Air Regulator ... AR
Air Release Capacity [*Aviation*] ... ARC
Air Report [*Aviation ICAO designator*] (FAAC) ... AIREP
Air Report [*Aviation*] ... ARP
Air Reporting Control (NVT) ... ARC
Air Reporting Net (NATG) ... ARN
Air Rescue (CINC) ... AIRRES
Air Rescue ... AR
Air Rescue and Recovery Squadron ... ARRS
Air Rescue Operations Center [*Air Force*] ... AROC
Air Rescue Science (NASA) ... ARS
Air Rescue Service [*Air Force*] ... ARS
Air Rescue Ship ... ARS
Air Research and Development ... AR & D
Air Research and Development Center [*Later, Air Force Systems Command*] ... ARDC
Air Research and Development Command [*Washington, DC Air Force*] ... ARDC
Air Research and Development Command - Andrews Air Force Base ... ARDCA
Air Research and Development Command Forms ... ARDCF
Air Research and Development Command Manual [*Air Force*] ... ARDCM
Air Research and Development Command Regulations ... ARDCR
Air Research and Development Council [*NATO*] (NATG) ... ARDC
Air Research and Testing Committee (MUGU) ... ARTC
Air Research Bureau ... ARB
Air Research Organization (SAA) ... ARO
Air Research Vehicle (MCD) ... ARV
Air Reservations Interline Message Procedure ... AIRIMP
Air Reserve ... AR
Air Reserve Association [*Later, Air Force Association*] ... ARA
Air Reserve Base ... ARB
Air Reserve Center ... ARC
Air Reserve Components [*Military*] ... ARC
Air Reserve District ... ARD
Air Reserve Flying Center [*Air Force*] ... ARFC
Air Reserve Forces ... ARF
Air Reserve Forces Facility [*Military*] ... ARFF
Air Reserve Forces Meritorious Service Award [*Military decoration*] ... ARFMSA
Air Reserve Forces Meritorious Service Medal [*Military decoration*] (GFGA) ... ARFMS
Air Reserve Forces Meritorious Service Ribbon [*Military decoration*] (AFM) ... ARFMSR
Air Reserve Forces Personnel Data System (AFM) ... ARFPDS
Air Reserve Forces Policy Committee ... ARFPC
Air Reserve Officers' Training Corps [*Air Force*] ... AROTC
Air Reserve Pay and Allowance System ... ARPAS
Air Reserve Pay System (AFM) ... ARPS
Air Reserve Personnel Center [*Air Force*] ... ARPC
Air Reserve Records Center ... ARRC
Air Reserve Specialist Training Squadron ... ARSTS
Air Reserve Squadron [*Air Force*] ... ARS
Air Reserve Technician [*Air Force*] ... ART
Air Reserve Technician Program [*Air Force*] ... ARTP
Air Reserve Unit ... ARU
Air Reserve Unit (General Training) ... ARUG
Air Reserve Unit (General Training, Nonpay) ... ARUSNP
Air Reserve Unit (General Training, Pay) ... ARUSP
Air Reserve Volunteer Support Group ... ARVSG
Air Reserve Wing [*Canada*] (DD) ... ARW
Air Resistance ... AR
Air Resorts [*ICAO designator*] (FAAC) ... ARZ
Air Resorts Airlines [*ICAO designator*] (AD) ... UZ
Air Resources Atmospheric Turbulence and Diffusion Laboratory [*National Oceanic and Atmospheric Administration*] (NOAA) ... ARATDL
Air Resources Board [*California*] ... ARB
Air Resources Environmental Research Laboratory [*National Oceanic and Atmospheric Administration*] (NOAA) ... AREL
Air Resources Information Clearinghouse [*Also, an information service or system*] (EA) ... ARIC
Air Resources Laboratory [*Silver Spring, MD*] [*National Oceanic and Atmospheric Administration*] ... ARL
Air Resources Laboratory - Field Research Office [*National Oceanic and Atmospheric Administration*] (NOAA) ... ARL-FRO
Air Resources Management [*Environmental Protection Agency*] (GFGA) ... ARM
Air Resources Regional Pollution Assessment Model [*Environmental Protection Agency*] (GFGA) ... ARRPA
Air Resources Solar Radiation Laboratory [*National Oceanic and Atmospheric Administration*] (NOAA) ... ARRL
Air Resupply and Communication Service ... ARCS
Air Reunion [*France ICAO designator*] (FAAC) ... REU
Air Revitalization System (MCD) ... ARS
Air Roberval [*Canada ICAO designator*] (FAAC) ... RBV
Air Route Surveillance RADAR ... ARSR
Air Route Surveillance RADAR (FAAC) ... ARSR
Air Route Traffic Control [*Aviation*] ... ARTC
Air Route Traffic Control Center [*Aviation*] ... ARTCC
Air Routes and Ground Aids (SAA) ... AGA
Air Routing International Corp. [*ICAO designator*] (FAAC) ... ARC
Air Royal [*France ICAO designator*] (FAAC) ... RFO
Air Russia Airlines [*Russian Federation*] [*ICAO designator*] (FAAC) ... RUS
Air Rwanda [*ICAO designator*] (FAAC) ... RWD
Air Rwanda [*ICAO designator*] (AD) ... RY
Air Rwanda [*Rwanda*] [*ICAO designator*] (ICDA) ... UW
Air Sacculitis [*Avian pathology*] ... AS
Air Safaris & Services (NZ) Ltd. [*New Zealand*] [*ICAO designator*] (FAAC) ... SRI
Air Safety Board ... ASB
Air Safety Group [*British*] ... ASG
Air Safety Incident Reporting ... ASIR
Air Safety Reporting System [*NASA*] ... ASRS
Air Saigon [*Vietnam*] [*ICAO designator*] (FAAC) ... SGA
Air St. Pierre [*ICAO designator*] (AD) ... PJ
Air St. Thomas [*ICAO designator*] (FAAC) ... STT
Air Saint-Pierre SA [*France ICAO designator*] (FAAC) ... SPM
Air Sampling System ... ASS
Air Sandy, Inc. [*Canada ICAO designator*] (FAAC) ... SNY
Air Sardinia International [*ICAO designator*] (FAAC) ... ARS
Air Sardinia SpA [*Italy ICAO designator*] (FAAC) ... ASZ
Air Sarthe Organisation - Societe [*France ICAO designator*] (FAAC) ... ASO
Air Satellite [*ICAO designator*] (AD) ... QR
Air Satellite, Inc. [*Canada ICAO designator*] (FAAC) ... ASJ
Air Savoie [*France ICAO designator*] (FAAC) ... ASV
Air Scatterable Antipersonnel Mine (MCD) ... ASPM
Air Schefferville, Inc. [*Canada ICAO designator*] (FAAC) ... ASF
Air Screw ... AS
Air, Sea, and Space Club (EA) ... ASSC
Air Sea International [*British*] ... ASI
Air Sea Rescue Kit [*Military*] ... ASRK
Air Search Acquisition RADAR (CAAL) ... ASAR
Air Search Attack Team [*Military*] ... ASAT
Air Search Attack Unit [*Military*] ... ASAU
Air Search RADAR ... ASR
Air Search RADAR Receiver [*Shipborne*] ... SR
Air Seasoned (IAA) ... AS
Air Section ... AS
Air Security Agency (MCD) ... ASA
Air Sedona [*ICAO designator*] (AD) ... UJ
Air Self-Defense Force [*Japan*] (CINC) ... ASDF
Air Senegal [*ICAO designator*] (AD) ... DS
Air Senegal, Societe Nationational de Transport Aerien [*ICAO designator*] (FAAC) ... DSB
Air Sensors, Inc. [*Associated Press*] (SAG) ... AirSen
Air Sensors, Inc. [*NASDAQ symbol*] (SAG) ... ARSN
Air Separation Unit [*For oxygen production*] ... ASU
Air Service ... A/Svc
Air Service ... AS
Air Service [*Poland ICAO designator*] (FAAC) ... ASQ
Air Service [*Mali*] [*ICAO designator*] (FAAC) ... ODB
Air Service Affaires [*France ICAO designator*] (FAAC) ... RSA
Air Service Area Command ... ASAC
Air Service Command ... ASC
Air Service Command Advisory Team ... ASCAT
Air Service Coordination Office [*Military*] (DNAB) ... ASCO
Air Service Coordination Office, Mediterranean [*Military*] (DNAB) ... ASCOMED
Air Service Force (IIA) ... ASF
Air Service Group [*Air Force*] ... ASG
Air Service Information Circular ... ASIC
Air Service Signal Corps ... ASSC
Air Service State Co. [*Hungary ICAO designator*] (FAAC) ... RSZ
Air Service Support Squadron [*Army*] ... ASSRON
Air Service Training Ltd. [*British ICAO designator*] (FAAC) ... ATZ
Air Service Vosges [*France ICAO designator*] (FAAC) ... VGE
Air Services [*Military*] (NVT) ... AIRSVC
Air Services Agreement (DA) ... ASA
Air Services Ltd. [*Czechoslovakia*] [*ICAO designator*] (FAAC) ... RIS
Air Services Nantes [*France ICAO designator*] (FAAC) ... ASN
Air Seychelles [*ICAO designator*] (FAAC) ... SEY
Air Shutoff ... ASHOF
Air Shutoff Valve ... ASV
Air Shutter ... AIRSHTR
Air Shuttle (CDAI) ... A-S
Air Sicilia, SRL [*Italy*] [*FAA designator*] (FAAC) ... SIC
Air Sierra [*ICAO designator*] (AD) ... SI
Air Signal Officer ... ASO
Air Sinai [*Egypt*] [*ICAO designator*] (FAAC) ... ASD
Air Sinclair Ltd. [*British ICAO designator*] (FAAC) ... SCK
Air Situation Coordinator (SAA) ... ASC
Air Situation Display (SAA) ... ASD
Air Slovakia BWJ Ltd. [*FAA designator*] (FAAC) ... SVK
Air Society, International (EA) ... ASI
Air Sofia [*Bulgaria*] [*ICAO designator*] (FAAC) ... SFB
Air Solenoid Valve ... ASV
Air Solomons Command [*US*] ... AIRSOLS
Air Sorel Ltd. [*Canada ICAO designator*] (FAAC) ... WHY
Air South Australia ... AirSA
Air South, Inc. [*Airline code*] ... KQ
Air South, Inc. [*ICAO designator*] (FAAC) ... SHW

Air South West [*British*] [*FAA designator*] (FAAC) ... PIE
Air Southwest [*Canada ICAO designator*] (FAAC) ... ASW
Air Space ... ASPA
Air Space Paper Core ... ASPC
Air Space Transportation ... ASTRA
Air Space Travel Research Organization ... ASTRO
Air Special [*Czechoslovakia*] [*ICAO designator*] (FAAC) ... ASX
Air Specialties Corp. [*ICAO designator*] (FAAC) ... AMR
Air Specification (NG) ... AS
Air Spirit, Inc. [*ICAO designator*] (FAAC) ... SIP
Air Staff [*Air Force*] ... AS
Air Staff Board [*Air Force*] (AFM) ... ASB
Air Staff Defense Force (CINC) ... ASDF
Air Staff Office Automation System [*Air Force*] (GFGA) ... ASOAS
Air Staff Officer ... ASO
Air Staff Orientation (AFM) ... ASO
Air Staff Requirement ... ASR
Air Staff Target [*Royal Air Force*] [*British*] ... AST
Air Staff Trainee [*or Training*] [*Air Force*] ... ASTRA
Air Stagnation Advisories [*National Weather Service*] ... ASA
Air Stagnation Model ... ASM
Air Standard Efficiency ... ASE
Air Standardization Coordinating Committee ... ASCC
Air Standardization Coordination Program [*NATO*] ... ASCP
Air Star Corp. [*Canada ICAO designator*] (FAAC) ... ASC
Air Star Zanzibar [*Tanzania*] [*ICAO designator*] (FAAC) ... AZU
Air Starline AG [*Switzerland ICAO designator*] (FAAC) ... ASA
Air Starting ... ASTRG
Air Station ... AS
Air Station [*Air Force*] ... ASTN
Air Stations Weekly Orders [*Navy*] ... ASWO
Air Steward [*British military*] (DMA) ... AS
Air Stord AS [*Norway ICAO designator*] (FAAC) ... SOR
Air Store Issuing Ship ... AIRIS
Air Stores Depot [*Navy*] ... AIRSTORDEP
Air Stores Park [*British military*] (DMA) ... ASP
Air Straubing Luftfahrtgesellschaft MbH, Atting [*Germany*] [*FAA designator*] (FAAC) ... ASN
Air Strike ... A/S
Air Suction Valve [*Automotive engineering*] ... ASV
Air Sunshine, Inc. [*ICAO designator*] (FAAC) ... RSI
Air Superiority (MCD) ... AS
Air Superiority Fighter ... ASF
Air Superiority Program ... ASP
Air Supplemented Solid Rocket Motor (MCD) ... ASSRM
Air Supply (NRCH) ... AS
Air Supply ... ASUP
Air Supply Board [*Ministry of Aircraft Production*] [*British*] ... ASB
Air Supply Fan Club (EA) ... ASFC
Air Support ... AS
Air Support Command ... ASC
Air Support Control ... ASC
Air Support Control Units ... ASCU
Air Support Coordination and Control (MCD) ... ASCC
Air Support Coordinator (MCD) ... ASC
Air Support Director [*Military*] (NVT) ... ASD
Air Support Officer [*Military*] ... ASO
Air Support Operations (CAAL) ... ASO
Air Support Operations Center [*Air Force*] ... ASOC
Air Support Operations Center Squadron [*Air Force*] ... ASOCS
Air Support Operations Group [*Air Force*] ... ASOG
Air Support RADAR Team [*Marine Corps*] ... ASRT
Air Support Signal Unit (NATG) ... ASSU
Air Support Tactics ... AST
Air Support Test Unit ... ASTU
Air Support Training Units ... ASTU
Air Sur [*Spain ICAO designator*] (FAAC) ... NCR
Air, Surface, and Electronic Warfare Division [*Navy*] (MCD) ... AS & EWD
[*The*] **Air Surgeon** [*Army*] ... TAS
Air Surveillance [*Air Force*] ... AS
Air Surveillance and Airspace Control (MCD) ... ASAC
Air Surveillance Broadcast (MCD) ... ASB
Air Surveillance Evaluation (SAA) ... ASE
Air Surveillance Group (SAA) ... ASG
Air Surveillance Officer [*Air Force*] ... ASO
Air Surveillance RADAR (AFM) ... ASR
Air Surveillance RADAR/Operations Center System ... ASR/OPS
Air Surveillance Subsystem Evaluation and Training [*Air Force*] (IAA) ... ASSET
Air Surveillance System ... ASS
Air Surveillance Technician [*Air Force*] ... AST
Air Suspension [*Automotive engineering*] ... A/SUSP
Air Swazi Cargo (Pty) Ltd. [*Swaziland*] [*ICAO designator*] (FAAC) ... CWS
Air Swift [*British ICAO designator*] (FAAC) ... SWF
Air Systems Command [*Navy*] ... AIRSYSCOM
Air Systems Command [*Navy*] ... ASC
Air Tactical Communications [*FAA*] (TAG) ... ATC
Air Tactical Control Officer (NVT) ... ATACO
Air Tactical Control Operator ... ATACO
Air Tactical Data System (MCD) ... ATDS
Air Tactical Operations Center [*Military*] ... ATOC
Air Tactical Publication ... ATP
Air Tactical School [*Air Force*] ... ATS
Air Tactics Officer [*Air Force*] ... ATO
Air Tahiti [*France ICAO designator*] (FAAC) ... VTA
Air Tanzania [*ICAO designator*] (FAAC) ... ATC
Air Tanzania [*ICAO designator*] (AD) ... TC
Air Tara Ltd. [*Republic of Ireland*] [*ICAO designator*] (FAAC) ... AGP
Air Target Chart (CINC) ... ATC
Air Target Indicator ... ATI
Air Target Intelligence Liaison Program [*Air Force*] ... ATIL
Air Target Materials [*Military*] ... ATM
Air Target Materials Program [*Military*] (AFM) ... ATMP
Air Target Mosaic (MCD) ... ATM
Air Targets Officer ... ATO
Air Task Force ... ATF
Air Task Force Commander (MUGU) ... ATFC
Air Tasking Order ... ATO
Air Tasmania [*ICAO designator*] (AD) ... XZ
Air Taxi and Commercial Pilots Association [*Defunct*] (EA) ... ATCPA
Air Taxi-Commercial Operator ... ATCO
Air Tchad [*ICAO designator*] (AD) ... HT
Air Tchad, Societe de Transport Aeriens [*Chad*] [*ICAO designator*] (FAAC) ... HTT
Air Team, AS [*Norway*] [*FAA designator*] (FAAC) ... TTX
Air Technical Analysis Division (SAA) ... ATAD
Air Technical Battalion (MCD) ... ATB
Air Technical Index [*Air Force*] ... ATI
Air Technical Information [*Used by Armed Services Technical Information Agency - later, Defense Documentation Center - to accession and identify documents*] ... ATI
Air Technical Intelligence [*Air Force*] ... ATI
Air Technical Intelligence Center ... ATIC
Air Technical Intelligence Services Command [*Air Force*] ... ATISC
Air Technical Intelligence Study [*Air Force*] ... ATIS
Air Technical Library, Department of National Defence [*Bibliotheque Techniquede l'Aviation, Ministere de la Defense Nationale*] **Ottawa, Ontario** [*Library symbol National Library of Canada*] (NLC) ... OONDAT
Air Technical Service (IAA) ... ATS
Air Technical Service Command [*Air Force*] ... ATSC
Air Technical Training [*Navy*] ... TECHTRA
Air Technician [*Air National Guard*] (AFM) ... AT
Air Temperature ... AT
Air Temperature Control (IEEE) ... ATC
Air Temperature Correction ... T
Air Temperature Sensor [*Automotive engineering*] ... ATS
Air Tenglong [*China*] [*ICAO designator*] (FAAC) ... CTE
Air Terminal ... ATERM
Air Terminal Identifier Code ... ATIC
Air Terminal Officer [*Air Force*] ... ATO
Air Terminal Team ... ATT
Air Terrex [*Czechoslovakia*] [*ICAO designator*] (FAAC) ... TRX
Air Test Vehicle ... ATV
Air Texana [*ICAO designator*] (AD) ... OJ
Air Thanet [*British ICAO designator*] (FAAC) ... THL
Air Threat to Central Europe ... ATCE
Air to Heat Exchanger [*Aerospace*] (AAG) ... AHE
Air to Pneumatic Distribution [*Aerospace*] ... APD
Air to Underwater (SAA) ... AU
Air Today, Inc. [*ICAO designator*] (FAAC) ... TDY
Air Tonga [*ICAO designator*] (FAAC) ... ATO
Air Toronto [*ICAO designator*] (AD) ... CS
Air Toronto, Inc. [*Canada ICAO designator*] (FAAC) ... CNE
Air Torpedo-Firing (DNAB) ... ATF
Air Toulon [*France ICAO designator*] (FAAC) ... ATU
Air Toulouse [*France ICAO designator*] (FAAC) ... TLE
Air Toxics and Radiation Monitoring Research Division [*Environmental Protection Agency*] (EPA) ... ATRMRD
Air, Toxics, and Radiation Staff [*Environmental Protection Agency*] (GFGA) ... ATRS
Air Toxics Exposure & Risk Information System (ACII) ... ATERIS
Air Toxics Exposure and Risk Information System (GNE) ... ATERIS
Air Toxics Task Force [*Environmental Protection Agency*] (GFGA) ... ATTF
Air Tracker (DNAB) ... A/T
Air Tracker/Long-Range (DNAB) ... AT/LR
Air Tracker/Short-Range (DNAB) ... AT/SR
Air Traffic [*FAA*] (TAG) ... AT
Air Traffic Communication System [*NASA*] (KSC) ... ATCS
Air Traffic Communications (MCD) ... ATCOM
Air Traffic Communications Service (MCD) ... ATCS
Air Traffic Communications Station ... ATCS
Air Traffic Conference of America [*Defunct*] (EA) ... ATC
Air Traffic Conference of America [*Defunct*] (EA) ... ATCA
Air Traffic Control [*or Controller*] ... ATC
Air Traffic Control [*ICAO designator*] (ICDA) ... ZG
Air Traffic Control [*FAA designator*] (FAAC) ... ZGZ
Air Traffic Control Advises (FAAC) ... ATCA
Air Traffic Control Advisory Committee [*Department of Transportation*] ... ATCAC
Air Traffic Control and Landing System [*DoD*] ... ATCALS
Air Traffic Control and Navigation Board ... ATCNB
Air Traffic Control and Warning (IAA) ... ATCW
Air Traffic Control Assigned Airspace [*FAA*] (TAG) ... ATCAA
Air Traffic Control Assistant (DA) ... ATCA
Air Traffic Control Association (EA) ... ATCA
Air Traffic Control Automatic System [*Sweden*] ... ATCAS
Air Traffic Control Automation Panel [*International Civil Aviation Organization*] ... ATCAP
Air Traffic Control Beacon Ground Station ... ATCBGS
Air Traffic Control Beacon Interrogator ... ATCBI
Air Traffic Control Center [*Air Force*] ... ATCC
Air Traffic Control Clears (FAAC) ... ATCC
Air Traffic Control Command Center [*FAA*] (TAG) ... ATCCC

Air Traffic Control Communication	ATCC
Air Traffic Control Coordination Center (IAA)	ATCCC
Air Traffic Control Evaluation Unit [British]	ATCEU
Air Traffic Control Facility	ATCF
Air Traffic Control Flight	ATCF
Air Traffic Control Flight Advisory Service (MCD)	ATCFAS
Air Traffic Control Line (AFM)	ATCL
Air Traffic Control Office [or Operations] [Air Force]	ATCO
Air Traffic Control Procedures	ATCP
Air Traffic Control Product [Army]	ATCP
Air Traffic Control Proficiency Training System [Navy]	APTS
Air Traffic Control Project for Satellite (DA)	ATCPROSAT
Air Traffic Control RADAR Beacon	ATCRB
Air Traffic Control RADAR Beacon/Identification Friend or Foe/Mark XII/ System	AIMS
Air Traffic Control RADAR Beacon System	ATCRBS
Air Traffic Control RADAR System	ATCRS
Air Traffic Control RADAR Unit (AFM)	ATCRU
Air Traffic Control Request (FAAC)	ATCR
Air Traffic Control Satellite (IIA)	ATCS
Air Traffic Control Service (OA)	ATCS
Air Traffic Control Signaling System	ATCSS
Air Traffic Control Simulation Facility	ATCSF
Air Traffic Control System Command Center (GAVI)	ATCSCC
Air [or Airport] Traffic Control Tower	ATCT
Air Traffic Control Transponder	ATCT
Air Traffic Coordinating Officer	ATCO
Air Traffic Coordinator	ATCOR
Air Traffic Coordinator Europe	ATCOREU
Air Traffic Data Processor	ATDP
Air Traffic Delay	ATD
Air Traffic Division [Air Traffic Control] (FAAC)	ATD
Air Traffic Engineer [British] (DA)	ATE
Air Traffic Flow [Later, ATIF] (MCD)	ATF
Air Traffic Flow Control Unit [ICAO designator] (ICDA)	ZD
Air Traffic Flow Control Unit [FAA designator] (FAAC)	ZDZ
Air Traffic Flow Management [ICAO designator] (FAAC)	ATEM
Air Traffic Flow Management (DA)	ATFM
Air Traffic Flow Management Unit (DA)	ATFMU
Air Traffic GmbH [Germany ICAO designator] (FAAC)	ATJ
Air Traffic Information Service (DA)	ATIS
Air Traffic Management	ATM
Air Traffic Management Automated Center (AABC)	ATMAC
Air Traffic Management System [Army] (AABC)	ATMS
Air Traffic Operations Management System [FAA] (TAG)	ATOMS
Air Traffic Operations Service [FAA] (TAG)	ATO
Air Traffic Procedures	ATP
Air Traffic Procedures Advisory Committee [FAA] (TAG)	ATPAC
Air Traffic Regulation Center (AFM)	ATRC
Air Traffic Regulation Identification System [Army]	ATRIS
Air Traffic Regulations	ATR
Air Traffic Representative (FAAC)	ATREP
Air Traffic Section (AFM)	ATS
Air Traffic Service [of FAA] [Also known as AAT, AT]	ATS
Air Traffic Service Communications [Communications related to air traffic services.] (GAVI)	ATSC
Air Traffic Service Contingency Command Post (FAAC)	ATSCCP
Air Traffic Service Flight Services Division [of FAA]	ATSFSD
Air Traffic Service System Error Analysis (SAA)	ATESSEA
Air Traffic Service Unit (OA)	ATSU
Air Traffic Services Organization [Military] (DOMA)	ATSO
Air Traffic Services Outside Regulated Airspace [British] (DA)	ATSORA
Air Traffic Services Planning Manual (DA)	ATSPM
Air Traffic Services Reporting Office [Aviation]	ARO
Air Traffic Services Reporting Office [ICAO designator] (ICDA)	ZP
Air Traffic Services Reporting Office [FAA designator] (FAAC)	ZPZ
Air Traffic Transponder	ATT
Air Trails [ICAO designator] (AD)	NN
Air Training Advisor (NATG)	ATA
Air Training Advisory Group	ATAG
Air Training Association [British] (DA)	ATA
Air Training Command [Randolph Air Force Base, TX]	ATC
Air Training Command [Air Force]	ATRC
Air Training Command Manual [Air Force]	ATCM
Air Training Command Pamphlet [Air Force]	ATCP
Air Training Command Regulation [Air Force]	ATCR
Air Training Communications Division [Air Force]	ATCD
Air Training Corps [RAF] [British]	ATC
Air Training Corps Cadet [British]	ATCC
Air Training Corps of America	ATCA
Air Training Officer [Air Force]	ATO
Air Training Squadron (MUGU)	AIRTRAINRON
Air Training Squadron	AIRTRARON
Air Training Team (NATG)	ATT
Air Tranport School [Former USSR ICAO designator] (FAAC)	AIS
Air Trans NG Group Moldova [FAA designator] (FAAC)	NGG
Air Transafrik Ltd. [Ghana] [ICAO designator] (FAAC)	TRF
Air Transat [Canada ICAO designator] (FAAC)	TSC
Air Transfer Order	ATO
Air Transmit	AT
Air Transn Hldgs [NASDAQ symbol] (TTSB)	AIRT
Air Transport [Military]	AT
Air Transport Advisory Council [British]	ATAC
Air Transport and Travel Industry Training Board [British] (AIA)	ATTITB
Air Transport Association	ATA
Air Transport Association of America (EA)	ATA
Air Transport Association of America	ATAA
Air Transport Association of Canada	ATAC
Air Transport Auxiliary [British World War II]	ATA
Air Transport Auxiliary Association (DA)	ATAA
Air Transport Auxiliary Service [British World War II]	ATAS
Air Transport Bureau [ICAO]	ATB
Air Transport (Chatham Island) Ltd. [New Zealand] [ICAO designator] (FAAC)	CVA
Air Transport Command [Air Force]	ATC
Air Transport Command Headquarters, Rockcliffe, Ontario, Canada	CANAIRLIFT
Air Transport Committee [ICAO]	ATC
Air Transport Coordinator for the United States	ATCORUS
Air Transport Council [New South Wales, Australia]	ATC
Air Transport Development Unit [British]	ATDU
Air Transport Force	ATF
Air Transport Industry Training Association (DA)	ATITA
Air Transport International [ICAO designator] (FAAC)	ATN
Air Transport Liaison [Military British]	ATL
Air Transport Liaison Officer [British]	ATLO
Air Transport Licensing Authority [British]	ATLA
Air Transport Licensing Board	ATLB
Air Transport Ltd. [Slovakia] [ICAO designator] (FAAC)	EAT
Air Transport Movement Control Center	ATMC
Air Transport Movement Control Center [Military]	ATMCC
Air Transport of Radiation	ATR
Air Transport Operation Centre [Military British]	ATOC
Air Transport Operators Association (EAIO)	ATOA
Air Transport Pressurizing Unit	ATPU
Air Transport Pyrenees [France ICAO designator] (FAAC)	TPR
Air Transport Radio [NASA] (NASA)	ATR
Air Transport Regulation Panel [ICAO] (DA)	ATRP
Air Transport Schiphol [Netherlands ICAO designator] (FAAC)	ATQ
Air Transport Service [Zaire] [ICAO designator] (FAAC)	ATS
Air Transport Service [Navy]	ATS
Air Transport Squadron	AIRTRANSRON
Air Transport Squadron [Air Force] (MCD)	ATS
Air Transport Squadron [Air Force]	ATSq
Air Transport Squadron, Atlantic	AIRTRANSRONLANT
Air Transport Squadron, Pacific	AIRTRANSRONPAC
Air Transport Squadron, West Coast	AIRTRANSRONWESTCOAST
Air Transport Statistical Programme [International Civil Aviation Authority] [Canada] (NITA)	ATSP
Air Transport Statistics	ATS
Air Transport Users' Association [British] (DA)	ATUA
Air Transport Wing [Air Force]	ATW
Air Transport Wing [Air Force] (AFM)	ATWg
Air Transportability Test Loading Agency	ATTLA
Air Transportable Acoustic Communications (CAAL)	ATAC
Air Transportable Buffet Lab (DWSG)	ATBL
Air Transportable Clinic (MCD)	ATC
Air Transportable Communications Complex	ATRAX
Air Transportable Communications Unit (NVT)	ATCU
Air Transportable Dispensary (AFM)	ATD
Air Transportable Earth Station (IAA)	ATES
Air Transportable Hospital (AFM)	ATH
Air Transportable Loading Dock (AFM)	ATLD
Air Transportable Pantograph Fueling System (MCD)	ATPFS
Air Transportable Radio Installations	ATRI
Air Transportable SONAR	ATS
Air Transportable SONAR Surveillance System	ATSSS
Air Transportable Telecommunications Unit	ATTU
Air Transportation Association (AAGC)	ATA
Air Transportation Board	ATB
Air Transportation Coordination Office (CINC)	ATCO
Air Transportation Exercise [Military] (NVT)	AIRTRANSEX
Air Transportation Holding Co., Inc. [NASDAQ symbol] (NQ)	AIRT
Air Transportation Holding Co., Inc. [Associated Press] (SAG)	AirTrans
Air Transportation Hydrant Refueling System (AFIT)	ATHRS
Air Transportation Management (GAVI)	ATM
Air Transportation Rack [NASA] (NASA)	ATR
Air Transportation Research Information Service [National Academy of Sciences] [Information service or system]	ATRIS
Air Transportation Research International Forum (MCD)	ATRIF
Air Transportation Squadron (Medium)	ATS(M)
Air Transportation Training Flight [Military]	ATTF
Air Travel Card [Airline notation]	ATC
Air Travel Card of High Credit [Airline notation]	ATCQ
Air Travel Corp. [ICAO designator] (FAAC)	ATH
Air Travel Organisers Licence [British]	ATOL
Air Travel Plan (IIA)	ATP
Air Travel Security Unit	ATSU
Air Troika [Russian Federation] [ICAO designator] (FAAC)	TKA
Air Truck [Spain ICAO designator] (FAAC)	TRK
Air Tungaru [British ICAO designator] (FAAC)	TUN
Air Tungaru [ICAO designator] (AD)	VK
Air Tungaru (Gilbert Islands) [British ICAO designator] (ICDA)	RT
Air Turbine Alternator	ATA
Air Turbine Drive (NG)	ATD
Air Turbine Generator	ATG
Air Turbine Motor	ATM
Air Turbine Starter (NG)	ATS
Air Turbine Starter/Accessory Drive (MCD)	ATS/AD
Air Turbine Starter, Cartridge (MCD)	ATSC

Air Turbine Starter Control Value (MCD) ... ATSCV
Air Turbo Exchanger ... ATE
Air Turbo Rocket ... ATR
Air Turks and Caicos [*ICAO designator*] (AD) ... QW
Air UK (Leisure) Ltd. [*British ICAO designator*] (FAAC) ... LEI
Air UK Ltd. [*British ICAO designator*] (FAAC) ... UKA
Air Ukraine [*ICAO designator*] (FAAC) ... UKR
Air Ukraine Cargo [*FAA designator*] (FAAC) ... UKC
Air Ukraine International [*ICAO designator*] (FAAC) ... AUI
Air University (MCD) ... AIRU
Air University [*Maxwell Air Force Base, AL*] ... AU
Air University Board of Visitors ... AUBV
Air University Center for Professional Development [*Military*] ... AUCPD
Air University Library ... AUL
Air University Press ... AUP
Air University. Review [*A publication*] (DLA) ... Air U Rev
Air University-Airpower Research Institute [*Maxwell Air Force Base, AL*] ... AU-ARI
Air Urga [*Ukraine*] [*FAA designator*] (FAAC) ... URG
Air Users' Committee [*British*] ... AUC
Air Valve Silencer ... AVS
Air Vane Erection System (MCD) ... AVES
Air Vanuatu [*ICAO designator*] (FAAC) ... AVN
Air Vanuatu [*Airline code*] [*Australia*] ... NF
Air Varna Co. [*Bulgaria*] [*ICAO designator*] (FAAC) ... BAV
Air Vectors [*ICAO designator*] (AD) ... ZB
Air Vegas Airlines, Inc. [*FAA designator*] (FAAC) ... VGA
Air Vehicle Detection (MCD) ... AVD
Air Vehicle Digital Computer Unit ... ADCU
Air Vehicle Field Maintenance Evaluation Requirement (MCD) ... AVFMER
Air Vehicle Functional Group [*Military*] ... AVFG
Air Vehicle/Jet Vane ... AV/JV
Air Vehicle/Launch Module ... AV/LM
Air Vehicle Nuclear Radiation ... AVNR
Air Vehicle Specification (MCD) ... AVS
Air Vehicle / Swivel Nozzle [*Military*] ... AV/SN
Air Vehicle Synthesis [*Program*] ... AVSYN
Air Velocity Detector ... AVD
Air Velocity Index ... AVI
Air Velocity Meter ... AVM
Air Velocity Transducer ... AVT
Air Vendee [*France ICAO designator*] (FAAC) ... AVD
Air Vent ... AV
Air Ventilation Garment [*NASA*] ... AVG
Air Vibrating Table ... AVT
Air Vice-Marshal [*British*] ... AVM
Air Viet-Nam ... VNA
Air Virginia [*ICAO designator*] (AD) ... CE
Air Volta [*ICAO designator*] (AD) ... VH
Air Volume Totalizer [*Navy*] ... AVT
Air War College [*Air Force*] ... AIRWC
Air War College [*Maxwell Air Force Base, AL*] ... AWC
Air War College Associate Program (AFM) ... AWCAP
Air Warfare Analysis Section [*British*] ... AWA
Air Warfare Analysis Section [*British*] ... AWAS
Air Warfare Center [*Air Force*] (DOMA) ... AWC
Air Warfare Control (MCD) ... AWC
Air Warfare Control Officer ... AWCO
Air Warfare Co-Ordination [*British military*] (DMA) ... AWC
Air Warfare Division [*Navy*] ... AWD
Air Warfare Instructor [*Navy British*] ... AWI
Air Warfare Research Department [*Navy*] (MCD) ... AWRD
Air Warfare Simulation [*Military*] ... ACOSIM
Air Warfare Simulation Complex (MCD) ... AWSC
Air Warfare Systems Analysis ... AWSA
Air Warfare Systems Development (DNAB) ... AWSD
Air Warfare Training Division [*Navy British*] ... AWTD
Air Warning ... AW
Air Warning Service (IAA) ... AWSVC
Air Warning Squadron [*Marine Corps*] ... AWS
Air Warning System ... AWS
Air/Water Pollution Report [*Business Publishers, Inc.*] [*Information service or system*] (CRD) ... A/WPR
Air Waybill [*Shipping*] ... AWB
Air Weapon [*British military*] (DMA) ... AW
Air Weapon Systems [*Air Force*] ... AWS
Air Weapons Control System [*Air Force*] ... AWCS
Air Weapons Controller ... AWC
Air Weapons Systems Management ... AWSM
Air Weapons Systems Plan ... AWSP
Air Weapons Training Installation (NATG) ... AWTI
Air Weather Association (EA) ... AWA
Air Weather Flight [*Military*] ... AWF
Air Weather Network ... AWN
Air Weather Service [*Scott Air Force Base, IL*] (IAA) ... AWEASVC
Air Weather Service [*Scott Air Force Base, IL*] ... AWS
Air Weather Service [*AEC*] (DOMA) ... AWS
Air Weather Service Manual ... AWSM
Air Weather Service Office ... AWSWO
Air Weather Service Technical Library [*Air Force Information service or system*] (IID) ... AWSTL
Air Weather Service, Technical Library, Scott AFB, IL [*OCLC symbol*] (OCLC) ... SCA
Air Weather Service Training Guide ... AWSTG
Air West [*Canada ICAO designator*] (FAAC) ... AWT
Air West Airlines [*ICAO designator*] (AD) ... ZX
Air West Airlines, Inc. [*ICAO designator*] (FAAC) ... LEP
Air Whitsunday [*Australia ICAO designator*] (FAAC) ... RWS
Air Wing Commander ... AWC
Air Wing Duty Officer (DNAB) ... AWDO
Air Wing Staff [*Air Force*] ... AWS
Air Wisconsin [*ICAO designator*] (FAAC) ... AWI
Air Wisconsin [*ICAO designator*] (AD) ... ZW
Air Wisconsin [*Airline code*] ... ZW
Air World Ltd. [*British*] [*FAA designator*] (FAAC) ... AWD
Air Yendis Ltd. [*Zambia*] [*FAA designator*] (FAAC) ... SYD
Air Yugoslavia [*ICAO designator*] (FAAC) ... YRG
Air Zaire SA [*Zaire*] [*ICAO designator*] (ICDA) ... QC
Air Zaire, Societe [*ICAO designator*] (FAAC) ... AZR
Air Zanzibar [*Tanzania*] [*ICAO designator*] (FAAC) ... AZL
Air Zero ... AZ
Air Zero Gas ... AZG
Air Zimbabwe [*ICAO designator*] (FAAC) ... AZW
Air Zimbabwe [*Zimbabwe*] [*ICAO designator*] (ICDA) ... RH
Air Zimbabwe [*ICAO designator*] (AD) ... UM
Air Zory [*Bulgaria*] [*FAA designator*] (FAAC) ... MZA
Air-Assisted Fuel Injection [*Automotive engineering*] ... AAFI
Air-Augmented Propulsion for Short-Range Air Defense (MCD) ... AAP/SHORAD
Air-Augmented Rocket ... AAR
Air-Augmented Rocket Propulsion System ... AARPS
Airavia [*France ICAO designator*] (FAAC) ... IAV
Airbag Central Sensor [*Automotive safety*] ... ACS
Air-Based Electronics (MCD) ... ABE
Airblast Fuel Injection Tube [*Gas turbine engine*] ... AFIT
Airborne (IAA) ... A
Airborne [*ICAO designator*] (FAAC) ... AB
Airborne (AFM) ... ABN
Airborne Acoustic Information System (Intelligence) ... ACINF
Airborne Activity Monitor [*Nuclear energy*] (NRCH) ... AAM
Airborne Advanced Reconfigurable Computer System (PDAA) ... ARCS
Airborne Adverse Weather Weapons System (MCD) ... AAWWS
Airborne Alert (AFM) ... AA
Airborne Alert (IIA) ... ABA
Airborne Alert Indoctrination (AFM) ... AAI
Airborne Alert Weapon System ... AAWS
Airborne Alternate Command Echelon [*NATO*] (NATG) ... AACE
Airborne and Communications-Electronics Board [*Army*] (RDA) ... ACEBD
Airborne and Electronics Board [*Army*] (MCD) ... AEB
Airborne and Ground Communications Central (MCD) ... AGCC
Airborne and Helicopter Division [*Aeroplane and Armament Experimental Establishment*] [*British*] ... AHD
Airborne and Surface Early Warning ... ASEW
Airborne Angular Position Sensor ... AAPS
Airborne Antarctic Ozone Experiment ... AAOE
Airborne Antarctic Ozone Experiment [*Marine science*] (OSRA) ... AAOE
Airborne Antenna System ... AAS
Airborne Antiarmor Defense Concept (MCD) ... AADC
Airborne Antiballistic Missiles (MCD) ... AABM
Airborne Antiship Missile Defense (MCD) ... AASMD
Airborne Antisubmarine Warfare ... AASW
Airborne Antitank Armor Air Defense (MCD) ... AAAD
Airborne Arctic Stratospheric Expedition ... AASE
Airborne Arctic Stratospheric Experiment [*Marine science*] (OSRA) ... AASE
Airborne Argon Ion LASER ... AAIL
Airborne Armament Control [*Air Force*] (MCD) ... AAC
Airborne Assault (CINC) ... ABA
Airborne Assault Division (MCD) ... AAD
Airborne [*or Amphibious or Armored*] **Assault Vehicle** ... AAV
Airborne Associative Array Processor ... AAAP
Airborne Astrographic Camera System [*Air Force*] (MCD) ... AACS
Airborne Attack Recorder (MCD) ... AAR
Airborne Audio Frequency Coder ... AAFC
Airborne Automatic Voice Communications System (MCD) ... AAVCRS
Airborne Auxiliary Memory System ... AAMS
Airborne Auxiliary Power Unit ... AAPU
Airborne Backing Store ... ABS
Airborne Ballistic Missile Intercept System ... ABMIS
Airborne Ballistics Division [*NASA*] (KSC) ... ABD
Airborne Battlefield Command and Control Center (SAA) ... ABC3
Airborne Battlefield Command and Control Center (MCD) ... ABCC
Airborne Battlefield Command and Control Center [*Air Force*] (AFM) ... ABCCC
Airborne Battlefield Light Equipment System [*Army*] ... ABLES
Airborne Beacon Electronic Test Set ... ABETS
Airborne Beacon Interference Locator (MCD) ... ABIL
Airborne Beacon Processing System ... ABPS
Airborne Beacon Processor ... ABP
Airborne Bombing Evaluation ... ABE
Airborne Central Data Tape Recorder (MCD) ... ACDTR
Airborne Chromatograph for Atmospheric Trace Species [*Instrumentation*] ... ACATS
Airborne Collision Warning ... ACW
Airborne Collision-Avoidance System [*Later, TCAS*] ... ACAS
Airborne Command and Control System ... ACCS
Airborne Command Center ... ABCC
Airborne Command Control Squadron [*Air Force*] (CINC) ... ACCS
Airborne Command Control Squadron [*Air Force*] (AFM) ... ACCSq
Airborne Command Element [*Air Force*] (DOMA) ... ACE
Airborne Command Post (MCD) ... ABCP
Airborne Command Post [*Air Force*] ... ABNCP
Airborne Command Post [*Air Force*] ... ACP

Airborne Command-Launch Control Subsystem (CAAL) ... ACLCS
Airborne Communication Relay Station [*Air Force*] ... ACRES
Airborne Communications and Electronics (MCD) ... ACE
Airborne Communications Center [*Military*] ... ABCC
Airborne Communications Location Identification and Collection System ... ACLICS
Airborne Communications Reconnaissance Platform ... ACRP
Airborne Communications Reconnaissance Program (AFM) ... ACRP
Airborne Communications Squadron [*Air Force*] ... ACSQ
Airborne Control [*System*] ... ABC
Airborne Control Computer ... ACC
Airborne Control Unit [*Telecommunications*] (TSSD) ... ACU
Airborne Controlled Intercept [*Air Force*] ... ACI
Airborne Cooperational Equipment ... ACE
Airborne Coordinating Group ... ACG
Airborne Corps Operation Plan [*Military*] (AABC) ... ACOP
Airborne Countermeasures Environment and RADAR Target Simulation ... ACEARTS
Airborne Data Acquisition and Recording System ... ADARS
Airborne Data Acquisition Multifunction System (MCD) ... ADAMS
Airborne Data Acquisition Registration [*Digital mapping*] ... ADAR
Airborne Data Acquisition System ... ADAS
Airborne Data Analysis and Monitoring System (MCD) ... ADAMS
Airborne Data Automation (AFM) ... ADA
Airborne Data Insertion Unit (DNAB) ... ADIU
Airborne Data Link ... ADL
Airborne Data Link System ... ADLS
Airborne Data Loader [*Aviation*] ... ADL
Airborne Data Marketing Ltd. [*Vancouver Stock Exchange symbol*] ... ABD
Airborne Data Processor [*Air Force*] ... ADP
Airborne Data Recorder (MCD) ... ADR
Airborne Data Requisition Center (SAA) ... ADAC
Airborne Data Terminal (MCD) ... ADT
Airborne Data Transfer System (MCD) ... ADTS
Airborne Deception Device ... ADD
Airborne Designator (MCD) ... AD
Airborne Detection Discrimination Sensor ... ADDS
Airborne Digital Computer [*Air Force*] ... ADC
Airborne Digital Instrumentation System ... ADIS
Airborne Digital Processing Unit ... ADPU
Airborne Digital Recorder ... ADR
Airborne Digital Recording System ... ADRS
Airborne Digital Timer ... ADT
Airborne Digital Voltmeter ... ADV
Airborne Direct Air Support Center ... ABNDASC
Airborne Direction Finder (MCD) ... ADF
Airborne Display Electrical Management System (MCD) ... ADEMS
Airborne Doppler Velocity Altitude Navigation Compass Equipment (MCD) ... ADVANCE
Airborne Drone Missile Target [*DOD missile designation*] (MCD) ... BQM
Airborne Dual Detector Indicator (MCD) ... ADDI
Airborne Dual-Channel Variable Input Severe Environmental Recorder/Reproducer [*Air Force*] (MCD) ... ADVISER
Airborne Dynamic Alignment System (MCD) ... ADAS
Airborne Early Warning Aircraft ... AEWA
Airborne Early Warning and Control [*Army*] (AFM) ... AEW & C
Airborne Early Warning and Control [*Army*] (AABC) ... AEWC
Airborne Early Warning and Control [*Air Force*] (IAA) ... AEWCON
Airborne Early Warning and Control Squadron [*Air Force*] ... AEW & CSq
Airborne Early Warning and Interceptor Control System ... AEWICS
Airborne Early Warning Combat Air Patrol (NVT) ... AEWCAP
Airborne Early Warning Fighter ... AEWF
Airborne Early Warning/Ground Integration Segment ... AEGIS
Airborne Early Warning RADAR [*Air Force*] (IAA) ... AEWRADAR
Airborne Early Warning Squadron ... AEWRON
Airborne [*or Aircraft*] **Early Warning Station** ... AEW
Airborne Early Warning Training Unit ... AEWTU
Airborne Early Warning Wing (MUGU) ... AEWW
Airborne Electromechanical Bombing ... AEMB
Airborne Electron Beam Recorder ... AEBR
Airborne Electronic Equipment Modification ... AEEM
Airborne Electronic LASER System ... AELS
Airborne Electronic Ranging Instrumentation System ... AERIS
Airborne Electronic Sensor Operator [*Canadian Navy*] ... AESO
Airborne Electronic Terrain Map System (MCD) ... AETMS
Airborne Electronic Warfare (NG) ... AEW
Airborne Electronics (MCD) ... AE
Airborne Electronics Operator (IAA) ... AEO
Airborne Electronics Research Activity [*Lakehurst, NJ*] [*United States Army Communications-Electronics Command*] (GRD) ... AERA
Airborne Electronics Warfare Course (DNAB) ... AELW
Airborne ELINT Emitter Location System (MCD) ... AEELS
Airborne Emergency Actions Officer [*SAC*] ... AEAO
Airborne Emergency Alternate Command Post (CINC) ... AEACP
Airborne Emergency Reaction Unit ... ABERU
Airborne Engineer Contraction Equipment (MCD) ... AECE
Airborne Environmental Reporting System ... AERS
Airborne Equipment (AAG) ... A/BE
Airborne Equipment Division [*Bureau of Aeronautics; later, NASC*] [*Navy*] ... AE
Airborne Equipment Failure [*Air Force*] ... AEF
Airborne Equipment Repair Squadron (MCD) ... AERS
Airborne Evaluation Equipment (IEEE) ... AEE
Airborne Expendable Bathythermograph ... AXBT
Airborne Expendable Current Profiler [*Marine science*] (OSRA) ... AXCP
Airborne Expendable Current Profiler (USDC) ... AXCP
Airborne Expendable Rocket System (MCD) ... AERS
Airborne Experiment to Study Ozone Production (USDC) ... AESOP
Airborne Experiment to Study Ozone Production [*Marine science*] (OSRA) ... AESOP
Airborne Express, Inc. [*ICAO designator*] (FAAC) ... ABX
Airborne Extended Range ... AER
Airborne Fill-and-Drain (AAG) ... A/B F & D
Airborne Fire Control RADAR Set (MCD) ... AFCRS
Airborne Fire Fighting Equipment [*Air Force*] (MCD) ... AFFE
Airborne Fixed Array RADAR (MSA) ... AFAR
Airborne Flat Plate Array ... AFPA
Airborne Flight Detection Measurement System (MCD) ... AFDMS
Airborne Flight Test System (MCD) ... AFTS
Airborne Formation Flight Simulator (MCD) ... AFFSIM
Airborne Forward Air Controller ... AFAC
Airborne Forward Delivery Airfield Group ... AFDAG
Airborne Fraunhofer Line Discriminator ... AFLD
Airborne Freight [*NYSE symbol*] (TTSB) ... ABF
Airborne Freight Corp. [*NYSE symbol*] (SPSG) ... ABF
Airborne Freight Corp. [*Associated Press*] (SAG) ... AirFrt
Airborne Frequency Doubler ... AFD
Airborne Frequency Multiplexing System ... AFMS
Airborne Fuze Test Jammer (CAAL) ... AFTJ
Airborne General Illumination Light ... AGIL
Airborne Ground Fire Locating System ... AGFLS
Airborne Ground Fire Locator ... AGFL
Airborne Gun-Laying ... AGL
Airborne Gun-Laying for Turrets ... AGLT
Airborne Gun-Laying RADAR (AFM) ... AGLR
Airborne Gunsight ... AGS
Airborne Hardware Simulator (MCD) ... AHS
Airborne Height-Surveillance RADAR (IAA) ... AHSR
Airborne Helmet Mounted Display ... AHMD
Airborne Identification Kit (DEN) ... ABK
Airborne Identification, Mark XII System ... AIMS
Airborne Identification, Mobile System [*Military*] (NVT) ... AIMS
Airborne Imaging Spectrometer ... AIS
Airborne Infantry [*Military*] (SAA) ... ABINF
Airborne Infantry [*Military*] ... ABNINF
Airborne Information Correlation (MCD) ... AIC
Airborne Infrared Decoy Evaluation System (MCD) ... AIDES
Airborne Infrared Early Warning ... AIREW
Airborne Infrared Equipment for Target Analysis ... AIETA
Airborne Infrared Gunfire Locator ... AIRGLO
Airborne Infrared Live Scanner ... AILS
Airborne Infrared Mapper ... AIM
Airborne Infrared Mapper ... AIRM
Airborne Infrared Measurement Instrument ... AIMI
Airborne Infrared Observatory [*NASA*] ... AIO
Airborne Infrared Radiometer System ... AIRS
Airborne Infrared Spectrometer ... AIS
Airborne Infrared Surveillance Set ... AISS
Airborne Initiation System ... AIS
Airborne Insertion Display Equipment ... AIDE
Airborne Institute Laboratories, Melville, NY [*Library symbol Library of Congress*] (LCLS) ... NMelA
Airborne Instrumentation Platform ... AIP
Airborne Instrumentation Subsystem (MCD) ... AIS
Airborne Instrumentation Subsystem Internal (MCD) ... AISI
Airborne Instruments Laboratory [*Mineola, NY*] ... AIL
Airborne Instruments Laboratory Approach ... AILA
Airborne Integrated Data System ... AIDS
Airborne Integrated Flight Test Data System [*NASA*] ... AIFTDS
Airborne Integrated Light Avionics System ... AILAS
Airborne Integrated Maintenance System ... AIMS
Airborne Integrated Reconnaissance System (MCD) ... AIRS
Airborne Integration Area (MCD) ... AIA
Airborne Intelligent Display (MCD) ... AID
Airborne Intercept [*RADAR*] [*Air Force*] (AFM) ... AI
Airborne Intercept Missile Evaluation (MCD) ... AIMEVAL
Airborne Interception Fire Control System [*Air Force*] ... AIFCS
Airborne Interception RADAR and Pilot's Attack Sight System ... AIRPASS
Airborne Interceptor Equipment ... AIE
Airborne Interceptor Missile (SAA) ... AIM
Airborne Interceptor Officer (MCD) ... AIO
Airborne Interceptor RADAR ... AIR
Airborne Interceptor Rocket (AFM) ... AIR
Airborne Ionospheric Observatory (MCD) ... AIO
Airborne LASER (MCD) ... ABL
Airborne LASER Bathymeter (PDAA) ... ALB
Airborne LASER Equipment Real-Time Surveillance ... ALERTS
Airborne LASER Experiment [*Strategic Defense Initiative*] ... ALE
Airborne LASER Illuminator ... ALI
Airborne LASER Illuminator Ranging and Tracking System ... ALIRATS
Airborne LASER Laboratory [*Air Force*] ... ALL
Airborne LASER Locator Designator (MCD) ... ALLD
Airborne LASER Propagation Experiment (MCD) ... ALPE
Airborne LASER Range-Finder ... ALR
Airborne LASER Receiver Module (MCD) ... ALARM
Airborne LASER System ... ALS
Airborne LASER Tracker [*System*] ... ALT
Airborne Launch Control and Recovery System (MCD) ... ALCARS
Airborne Launch Control Center ... ALCC
Airborne Launch Control System [*Air Force*] (MCD) ... ALCS
Airborne Launching [*Aviation*] (FAAC) ... ABLCHG

Airborne Law Enforcement Association (EA) .... ALEA
Airborne Lidar Bathymetry Technical Center of Expertise [US Army Corps of Engineers] .... ALBTCX
Airborne LIDAR [Light Detection and Ranging] Oceanographic Probing Experiment [NASA] .... ALOPE
Airborne Light Optical Fiber Technology .... ALOFT
Airborne Lighting System [Air Force] (MCD) .... AIRLIGHT
Airborne Lightweight Optical Tracking [Air Force] .... ALOT
Airborne Lightweight Optical Tracking System [Air Force] .... ALOTS
Airborne Line Discriminator .... ALD
Airborne Line Printer .... ALP
Airborne Live Scanner .... ALS
Airborne Location and Strike System (MCD) .... ALSS
Airborne Long-Range Input (KSC) .... ALRI
Airborne Long-Range Input System (SAA) .... ALRIS
Airborne Long-Range Intercept .... ALRI
Airborne Long-Range RADAR Input (MUGU) .... ALRRI
Airborne Low-Frequency SONAR [Sound Navigation and Ranging] [Navy].... ALFS
Airborne Magnetic Recorder .... AMR
Airborne Maintenance System .... AMS
Airborne Mechanical Special Mission System (MCD) .... AMSMS
Airborne Microwave Refractometer (CAAL) .... AMR
Airborne Microwave Scatterometer [For measuring wind speed and direction] .... AMSCAT
Airborne Mine Countermeasure Equipment .... AMCM
Airborne Mine Countermeasure System (NG) .... AMCMS
Airborne Mine Detection and Surveillance System [Navy] (DOMA) .... AMDAS
Airborne Mine Detection System (MCD) .... AMDS
Airborne Mine Neutralization Equipment (DWSG) .... AMNE
Airborne Mine Neutralization System (DOMA) .... AMNSYS
Airborne Minefield Detector System (MCD) .... AMIDS
Airborne Missile Control Subsystem .... AMCSS
Airborne Missile Control System .... AMCS
Airborne Missile Maintenance Squadron [Air Force] .... AMMSq
Airborne Mode Control .... AMC
Airborne Modular Integrated System (MCD) .... AMIS
Airborne Moving Attack Target (SAA) .... AMAT
Airborne Moving Target Attack .... AMTA
Airborne Moving Target Indicator (CAAL) .... AMTI
Airborne National Command Force [DoD] .... ABNCP
Airborne Navigation Computer .... ANC
Airborne Navigation Sensor .... ANS
Airborne Navigational Multiple Indicators (MCD) .... ANMI
Airborne Night Classification System (MCD) .... ANCS
Airborne Night Observation Device (MCD) .... ANOD
Airborne Night Television System [Obsolete Army] (MCD) .... ANTS
Airborne Observer [Military] (VNW) .... AO
Airborne Oceanographic LIDAR [Light Detection and Ranging] (PDAA) .... AOL
Airborne of Sweden AB [ICAO designator] (FAAC) .... MIW
Airborne Oil Surveillance System .... AOSS
Airborne Operational Computer Program (MCD) .... AOCP
Airborne Operational Equipment .... AOE
Airborne Operations Center [NATO] (NATG) .... ABNOC
Airborne Optical Adjunct [Army] (RDA) .... AOA
Airborne Optical Beacon .... AOB
Airborne Optical Platform .... AOP
Airborne Optical Sensor [Military] (SDI) .... AOS
Airborne Optical Surveillance (MCD) .... AOS
Airborne Optical System (LAIN) .... AOS
Airborne Overland RADAR .... AOR
Airborne Parabolic Arc Computer .... APAC
Airborne Particle Monitoring System (MCD) .... APMS
Airborne Photography of the Eclipse of the Quiet Sun .... APEQS
Airborne Platform (DWSG) .... AP
Airborne Platform Versus Airbreathing Strategic Threats (MCD) .... APVAST
Airborne Pointer and Tracker .... APT
Airborne Position and Altitude Camera System (OA) .... APACS
Airborne Power Adapter .... APA
Airborne Power Supply (KSC) .... APS
Airborne Power System (IAA) .... APS
Airborne Power Unit (IAA) .... APU
Airborne Precision Emitter Location System (MCD) .... APELS
Airborne Processing Unit .... APU
Airborne Profile Recorder .... APR
Airborne Propellant System (AAG) .... A/BPS
Airborne Provisioning Parts Breakdown .... APPB
Airborne Proximity Warning Indicator (DA) .... APWI
Airborne Pulse Search RADAR after Passing [Aviation] (FAAC) .... APS
Airborne RADAR and Doppler .... ARAD
Airborne RADAR Approach (AFM) .... ARA
Airborne RADAR Approach Control (DNAB) .... ARAC
Airborne RADAR Inflight Monitoring System .... ARIMS
Airborne RADAR Jamming System (MCD) .... ARJS
Airborne RADAR Navigational Aid (MCD) .... ARN
Airborne RADAR Orbital Determination System .... ARODS
Airborne RADAR Platform [Air Force] .... ARP
Airborne RADAR Target Simulator .... ARTS
Airborne RADAR Unit [Aviation] (FAAC) .... ARU
Airborne Radiation Detection and Fixing [Military] .... ARDF
Airborne Radiation Thermometer .... ART
Airborne Radio Communicating .... ARC
Airborne Radio Control .... ARC
Airborne Radio Direction Finding (AFM) .... ARDF
Airborne Radio Installation [RADAR] .... ARI
Airborne Radio Instrument .... ARI

Airborne Radio Navigation .... ARN
Airborne Radio Receiver .... ARR
Airborne Radioactivity Removal System (NRCH) .... ARRS
Airborne Range Instrumentation Station .... ARIS
Airborne Range Only [RADAR ranging set for use with various gun computers] .... ARO
Airborne Ranging and Orbit Determination System .... AROD
Airborne Ranging System .... ARS
Airborne Rapid-Blooming Off-Board Chaff (DOMA) .... AIRBOC
Airborne Rapid-Scan Spectrometer .... ARS
Airborne Real-Time Instrumentation System (MCD) .... ARTIS
Airborne Recce Low (DOMA) .... ARL
Airborne Receiver .... AR
Airborne Receiving Antenna .... ARA
Airborne Reconnaissance Integrated Electronic System (MCD) .... ARIES
Airborne Reference Noise Source (MCD) .... ARNS
Airborne Reference RADAR (PDAA) .... ARR
Airborne Refrigeration System .... ARS
Airborne Relay Facility (MCD) .... ARF
Airborne Relay Stations (MCD) .... ARS
Airborne Relay Vehicle .... ARV
Airborne Remote Control Operator (DNAB) .... ARCO
Airborne Remote Sensing Oceanography Project .... ARSOP
Airborne Remote Sensing System [Coast Guard] (MCD) .... ARSS
Airborne Remotely Operated Device [Marine Corps] .... AROD
Airborne Research Australia .... ARA
Airborne Research Capsule .... ARC
Airborne Research Integration Engineering Support (MCD) .... ARIES
Airborne Resupply (CINC) .... ABR
Airborne Satellite Receiving Station .... ASRS
Airborne Scanning Radiometer .... ASR
Airborne Science Program [NASA] (NASA) .... ASP
Airborne Science Shuttle [or Spacelab] Experiment System Simulation [NASA] (MCD) .... ASSESS
Airborne Science Shuttle Experiments System Simulation [NASA] (NASA) .... ASSESS
Airborne Sea/Swell Recorder [Oceanography] (MSC) .... ASSR
Airborne Search and Attack Plotter .... ABSAP
Airborne Search Equipment .... ASE
Airborne Search Target Attack RADAR (MCD) .... ASTAR
Airborne Seeker Evaluation Test System [Air Force] .... ASETS
Airborne Self-Propelled Gun .... ASU
Airborne Self-Protection Jammer (MCD) .... ASPJ
Airborne Self-Protection Jammer Rack Assembly (DWSG) .... ASPJRA
Airborne Sensor Platform (MCD) .... ASP
Airborne SIGINT Reconnaissance Program (MCD) .... ASRP
Airborne Signal Battalion (IAA) .... ABNSIGBN
Airborne Software Change (MCD) .... ASC
Airborne Sonobuoy Communications Center .... ASCC
Airborne Sonobuoy Communications Link .... ASCL
Airborne Southern Hemisphere Ozone Expedition [Marine science] (OSRA) .... ASHOE
Airborne Southern Hemisphere Ozone Expedition (USDC) .... ASHOE
Airborne Special Bombing .... ASB
Airborne Special-Type Auxiliary Assembly (MCD) .... ASTAA
Airborne Special-Type Navigational Aid (MCD) .... ASN
Airborne Stabilized Viewing System .... ASVS
Airborne Standoff Minefield Detection System [Military] (RDA) .... ASTAMIDS
Airborne Support Equipment (MCD) .... ASE
Airborne Support Platform [Army] .... ASP
Airborne Surface Vessel Detection [RADAR device] .... ASV
Airborne Surveillance and Control System [ASD] .... ASACS
Airborne Surveillance and Intercept Defense System .... ASIDS
Airborne Surveillance and Target Acquisition (SAA) .... AS & TA
Airborne Surveillance RADAR (IEEE) .... ASR
Airborne Surveillance Set .... ASS
Airborne Surveillance Testbed [Army] .... AST
Airborne Surveillance Warning and Control RADAR [ASD/ADC] .... ASWCR
Airborne Synthetic Aperture RADAR [Instrumentation] .... AIRSAR
Airborne Systems Functional Test Stand (IAA) .... ASFTS
Airborne Systems Support Center .... ASSC
Airborne Tactical Air Battle Control System .... ATABCS
Airborne Tactical Air Control Capability [Air Force] (AFM) .... ATACC
Airborne Tactical Air Coordinator [Navy] (NVT) .... ATAC
Airborne Tactical Command System [Formerly, ATDS] (MCD) .... ATCS
Airborne Tactical Data Processing System .... ATDPS
Airborne Tactical Data System [Later, ATCS] .... ATDS
Airborne Tactical Jamming System [Air Force] .... ATJS
Airborne Tanker, Boom (NVT) .... TAB
Airborne Tanker, Drogue (NVT) .... TAD
Airborne Tanker, General (NVT) .... TAG
Airborne Target Acquisition and Fire Control System (MCD) .... ATAFCS
Airborne Target Acquisition Control System (MCD) .... ATACS
Airborne Target Augmenter .... ATA
Airborne Target Handover System [Military] (DOMA) .... ATHS
Airborne Task Force .... ABTF
Airborne Teletypewriter Equipment .... ATE
Airborne Test Bed .... ATB
Airborne Test Bed Mode Control .... ATBMC
Airborne Test Bed Turret .... ATBT
Airborne Test Conductor (MUGU) .... ATC
Airborne Test Equipment (MCD) .... ATE
Airborne Test Instrumentation System [Air Force] (MCD) .... ATIS
Airborne Test Reactor (SAA) .... ATR
Airborne Test Safety Board (MCD) .... ATSB

Airborne Time/Frequency Range/Altitude Monitor (MCD) .... ATFRAM
Airborne TOW [*Tube-Launched, Optically Tracked, Wire-Guided Weapon*]
   USAREUR Repair Facility [*United States Army, Europe*] (MCD) .... ATURF
Airborne Towed Array SONAR System (MCD) .... AIRTASS
Airborne Toxic Control Measure .... ATCM
Airborne Toxic Elements and Organic Species .... ATEOS
Airborne Track Illuminator [*Military*] (DOMA) .... ATI
Airborne Tracking (MCD) .... ABT
Airborne Tracking, Acquisition, and Recognition .... ATAR
Airborne Tracking LASER Identification System .... ATLIS
Airborne Traffic Situation Display [*FAA*] .... ATSD
Airborne Transponder Subsystem .... ABTSS
Airborne Troops [*British and Canadian*] [*World War II*] .... airtps
Airborne Two-Way Acoustic and Control System (MCD) .... ATAC
Airborne Ultraviolet LASER .... AUVL
Airborne Unit .... AU
Airborne V/STOL [*Vertical/Short Takeoff and Landing*] Simulator (MCD) .... AVS
Airborne Vehicle Equipment (MCD) .... AVE
Airborne Vehicle Identification .... AVI
Airborne Vehicle Identification (AABC) .... AVID
Airborne Very-Low-Frequency (NG) .... AVLF
Airborne Vibration Monitor (NG) .... AVM
Airborne Video Recorder [*Automotive engineering*] .... AVR
Airborne Video Tape Recorder (MCD) .... AVTR
Airborne Viewing System .... AVS
Airborne Visible-Infrared Imaging Spectrometer .... AVIRIS
Airborne Visible-LASER Optical-Communications .... AVLOC
Airborne Warning and Control Group [*Air Force*] .... AWACG
Airborne Warning and Control Squadron [*Air Force*] .... AWACS
Airborne Warning and Control Squadron [*Air Force*] .... AWCSq
Airborne [*or Aircraft*] Warning and Control System [*Air Force*] .... AWACS
Airborne Warning and Control Training Squadron [*Air Force*] .... AWACTS
Airborne Warning and Control Wing [*Air Force*] .... AWACW
Airborne Warning and Recording Equipment .... AWARE
Airborne Waveguide Slotted Array .... AWSA
Airborne Waveguide Slotted Array Antenna .... AWSAA
Airborne Weapon and Control .... AWAC
Airborne Weapon Control System (MCD) .... AWCS
Airborne Weapons Control .... AWC
Airborne Weapons Corrective Action Program (MCD) .... AWCAP
Airborne Weather and Reconnaissance System (MCD) .... AWARS
Airborne Weather and Reconnaissance System (MCD) .... AWRS
Airborne Weather RADAR System .... AWRS
Airborne Wind-Shear Alert Sensor (PDAA) .... AWAS
Airborne XBT [*Expendable Bathythermograph*] (USDC) .... AXBT
Airborne-Delivered Multipurpose Submunition (MCD) .... ARDEMS
Airbourne School of Flying [*British*] [*FAA designator*] (FAAC) .... RGT
Air-Brake Switch .... ABS
Air-Brake Switch .... ABSW
Air-Breathing Electric LASER (MCD) .... ABEL
Air-Breathing Engine (KSC) .... ABE
Air-Breathing Engine System .... ABES
Air-Breathing Launch Vehicle [*Military*] (PDAA) .... ABLV
Air-Breathing Propulsion System [*or Subsystem*] [*NASA*] .... ABPS
Air-Breathing Propulsion System [*or Subsystem*] [*NASA*] (NASA) .... APS
Air-Breathing System .... ABS
Air-Breathing Target [*Military*] .... ABT
Air-Breathing Threat [*Military*] .... ABT
Air-Britain Historians [*An association*] (EAIO) .... ABH
Airbrush (VRA) .... airbr
Air-Burundi [*ICAO designator*] (FAAC) .... PBU
Airbus Industrie [*France ICAO designator*] (FAAC) .... AIB
Airbus Industrie [*France ICAO aircraft manufacturer identifier*] (ICAO) .... EA
Airbus Industries Group [*FAA*] (TAG) .... AIG
Aircam Aviation Ltd. [*British ICAO designator*] (FAAC) .... RCM
Aircarrier (DA) .... AC
Air-Charged Temperature [*Automotive engineering*] .... ACT
Airco Speer Research & Development Laboratories, Niagara Falls, NY
   [*Library symbol Library of Congress*] (LCLS) .... NNiaA
AIRCOA Hotel Ltd. [*AMEX symbol*] (SPSG) .... AHT
Aircoa Hotel Partners Ltd. [*Associated Press*] (SAG) .... Aircoa
Air-Commodore-in-Chief [*RAF, RCAF*] (DAS) .... A-Com-in-C
Aircompany Karat [*Former USSR*] [*FAA designator*] (FAAC) .... AKT
Aircompany Liana JSA [*Ukraine*] [*FAA designator*] (FAAC) .... NSG
Air-Conditioning and Pneumatic System (MCD) .... ACPS
Air-Conditioning and Refrigerating Machinery Association [*Later, ARI*]
   (KSC) .... ACRMA
Air-Conditioning and Refrigeration Institute (MSA) .... ACRI
Air-Conditioning and Refrigeration Institute (EA) .... ARI
Air-Conditioning and Refrigeration Wholesalers (EA) .... ARW
Air-Conditioning Apparatus [*JETDS nomenclature*] [*Military*] (CET) .... HD
Air-Conditioning Equipment (AAG) .... ACE
Air-Conditioning Pack .... ACP
Air-Conditioning Power Panel (DAC) .... PP-AC
Air-conditioning Protection and Diagnostic System [*Automotive electronics*] .... APADS
Air-Conditioning Room (AAG) .... AC/RM
Air-Conditioning Unit .... ACU
Aircooled (MSA) .... ACLD
Aircooled Beryllium Oxide with Integrated Gas Turbine .... ABORIGINE
Air-Cooled Compact Reactor (SAA) .... ACR
Aircooled Fluidized Bed [*Chemical engineering*] .... AFB
Aircooled Motor .... AM
Air-Core Gauge (RDA) .... ACG
Aircorp Airlines, Inc. [*Canada ICAO designator*] (FAAC) .... BBJ

Aircraft [*or Airplane*] .... A
Aircraft [*FAA*] (TAG) .... A/C
Aircraft (IDOE) .... a/c
Aircraft [*Public-performance tariff class*] [*British*] .... AC
Aircraft (AFM) .... ACFT
Aircraft .... ACRFT
Aircraft .... Aircft
Aircraft .... ARCRFT
Aircraft [*Wind triangle problems*] .... P
Aircraft Accident Authority [*ICAO designator*] (ICDA) .... YL
Aircraft Accident Authority [*FAA designator*] (FAAC) .... YLY
Aircraft Accident Board .... AAB
Aircraft Accident/Incident Reporting System [*International Civil Aviation Organization*] [*Information service or system*] (IID) .... ADREP
Aircraft Accident Investigation (DNAB) .... AAI
Aircraft Accident Investigation Board .... AAIB
Aircraft Accident Investigation System .... AAIS
Aircraft Accident Record [*Obsolete Military*] .... AAR
Aircraft Accident Report [*Military*] .... AAR
Aircraft Acquisition and Support (NG) .... AIRACS
Aircraft Actually Possessed [*Air Force*] (AFIT) .... AAP
Aircraft Adapter Group (DWSG) .... AAG
Aircraft Airworthiness Certification Authority (DA) .... AACA
Aircraft Airworthiness Section .... AAS
Aircraft Alerting Cockpit Equipment (DWSG) .... AACE
Aircraft Alerting Communications Electromagnetic Pulse (MCD) .... AACE
Aircraft Alerting Communications Electromagnetic Pulse .... AACEP
Aircraft and Adventure Factory [*Mallard*] .... AAF
Aircraft and Armament Development .... AAD
Aircraft and Armament Experimental Establishment [*British*] .... A & AEE
Aircraft and Engine Mechanic .... AEM
Aircraft and Engineering (MCD) .... A & E
Aircraft and Engines (AAG) .... A & E
Aircraft and Equipment Configuration List (MCD) .... AECL
Aircraft and Facilities [*Navy appropriation*] .... A & F
Aircraft & Instrument Demisting Ltd. [*British*] .... AID
Aircraft and Related Procurement, Navy .... ARPN
Aircraft and Rocket Design Engineers .... ARDE
Aircraft and Weapons Control Interceptor .... AWCI
Aircraft and Weapons Control Interceptor System .... AWCIS
Aircraft Anticollision Beacon System High-Intensity Light [*Army*]
   (PDAA) .... AABSHIL
Aircraft Anticollision Beacon System High-Intensity Light [*Army*]
   (MCD) .... AABSHILL
Aircraft Antisubmarine Development Detachment, Atlantic
   Fleet .... AIRASDEVLANT
Aircraft Antisubmarine Squadron (DNAB) .... AIRASRON
Aircraft Approach Light (MSA) .... AAL
Aircraft Approach Limitation .... AAL
Aircraft Armament Bulletin [*Navy A publication*] (MCD) .... AAB
Aircraft Armament Change .... AAC
Aircraft Armament Laboratory [*Naval Air Development Center*] .... AAL
Aircraft Armament Unit .... AIRARMUNIT
Aircraft Armaments, Inc. (DNAB) .... AAI
Aircraft Arresting Gear (NG) .... A/G
Aircraft Arresting System .... AAS
Aircraft Artificer [*British*] .... AA
Aircraft, Asiatic Fleet .... AIRAF
Aircraft Assembly Plant .... AAP
Aircraft Assignment Directive .... AAD
Aircraft Assignment Letter .... AAL
Aircraft Attack, Experimental-Light [*Navy*] .... VAX-L
Aircraft Availability Model (MCD) .... AAM
Aircraft Battle Force [*Obsolete Navy*] .... ABF
Aircraft Battle Force, Pacific Fleet [*Navy*] .... AIRBATFORPAC
Aircraft Blast Interaction Tests (MCD) .... ABIT
Aircraft Builders Council [*British*] (AIA) .... ABC
Aircraft Bulletin .... A/B
Aircraft Camera Parameter Control .... ACPC
Aircraft Capable of Satellite Operations .... ACSO
Aircraft Cargo Loader (DWSG) .... ACL
Aircraft Carrier .... A/CC
Aircraft Carrier (ABBR) .... ACFTC
Aircraft Carrier [*Navy symbol*] CV
Aircraft Carrier Firefighting Assistance Team (DNAB) .... ACFAT
Aircraft Carrier Flag [*Navy British*] .... AC
Aircraft Carrier General Memorandum .... ACGM
Aircraft Carrier, Helicopter [*NATO*] .... CVH
Aircraft Carrier Intelligence Center (NVT) CVIC
Aircraft Carrier Landing System (PDAA) .... ACLS
Aircraft Carrier, Medium Sized [*Navy symbol*] CVV
Aircraft Carrier, Nuclear Propulsion [*Navy symbol*] (NVT) .... CVN
Aircraft Carrier Squadron [*British military*] (DMA) .... ACS
Aircraft Catering Equipment [*British airlines*] .... ACE
Aircraft Certification Systems Evaluation Program [*FAA*] (TAG) .... ACSEP
Aircraft Change Analysis (AAG) .... ACA
Aircraft Change Application List (MCD) .... ACAL
Aircraft Change Control Board [*DoD*] .... ACCB
Aircraft Checker's Report (AAG) .... ACR
Aircraft Circular Letter (MCD) .... ACL
Aircraft Classification Number [*Aviation*] (FAAC) .... ACN
Aircraft Classification Number/Pavement Classification Number
   (DA) .... ACN/PCN
Aircraft Collision Avoidance System (PDAA) .... ACAS
Aircraft Coloring and Marking (NATG) .... ACM

Aircraft Combat Maneuvering Instrument (DWSG) .... ACMI
Aircraft Commander .... AC
Aircraft Commander [MTMC] (TAG) .... ACC
Aircraft Commander Time .... ACT
Aircraft Communication Control and Electronic Signaling System [Air Force] .... ACCESS
Aircraft Communication Procedures [Navy] (MCD) .... ACP
Aircraft Communications Addressing and Reporting System (IEEE) .... ACARS
Aircraft Communications System .... ACCS
Aircraft Communications System .... ACS
Aircraft Communicator [Signaling device] [Aviation] (IAA) .... ACCOM
Aircraft Compatibility Control Drawing (MCD) .... ACCD
Aircraft Component Intensive Management System [Military] (AABC) .... ACIMS
Aircraft Component Mating Evaluation (MCD) .... ACME
Aircraft Condition Evaluation [Navy] (MCD) .... ACE
Aircraft Condition Inspection (MCD) .... ACI
Aircraft Condition Monitoring System (GAVI) .... ACMS
Aircraft Configuration Allowance List (DNAB) .... ACAL
Aircraft Configuration Change Board .... ACCB
Aircraft Configuration Control Board [DoD] .... ACCB
Aircraft Control (MUGU) .... AC
Aircraft Control and Surveillance [Air Force] .... ACS
Aircraft Control and Warning (MCD) .... ACAW
Aircraft Control and Warning (SAA) .... ACW
Aircraft Control and Warning Group [Air Force] .... ACWG
Aircraft Control and Warning Officer [Military] .... ACWO
Aircraft Control and Warning Squadron [Air Force] .... AC & WSq
Aircraft Control and Warning Squadron [Military] .... ACWRON
Aircraft Control and Warning Squadron [Air Force] .... ACWS
Aircraft Control and Warning Stations [Military] .... AC & WS
Aircraft Control and Warning System [Military] .... ACWS
Aircraft Control and Warning System Station [Military] (IAA) .... ACWSS
Aircraft Control Link .... ACL
Aircraft Control Operator (MUGU) .... ACO
Aircraft Control Room .... ACR
Aircraft Control Room Officer [British military] (DMA) .... ACRO
Aircraft Control System (MUGU) .... ACS
Aircraft Control Unit (NVT) .... ACU
Aircraft Controlling Custodian (MCD) .... ACC
Aircraft Corp. of Great Britain (OA) .... ACGB
Aircraft Crash Rescue Field Assistance and Evaluation Team [Air Force] (AFM) .... ACRFAET
Aircraft Crashworthiness Program Plan (MCD) .... ACPP
Aircraft Crew Interphone System (MCD) .... ACIS
Aircraft Crewman Badge [Military decoration] (GFGA) .... ACCMB
Aircraft Crewman Badge [Military decoration] (AABC) .... AcftCrmnBad
Aircraft Cross-Servicing Program [Military] .... ACSP
Aircraft Damage (ADA) .... ACD
Aircraft Damage Sensing System .... ADSS
Aircraft Data Entry (DNAB) .... ADE
Aircraft Data Line (MCD) .... ADL
Aircraft Data Link Processor [Mode S subnetwork function onboard the aircraft that implements OSI network layer protocols] (GAVI) .... ADLP
Aircraft Data Recording Evaluation System (PDAA) .... ADRES
Aircraft Decontaminating, Deicing, Cleaning System (MCD) .... ADDCS
Aircraft Defense Analysis (MCD) .... ADA
Aircraft De-Ice and Inhibitor [MTMC] (TAG) .... ADI
Aircraft Delivery Group [Air Force] .... ADG
Aircraft Delivery Unit [Air Force] .... ADU
Aircraft Depot [British military] (DMA) .... AD
Aircraft Depth [Bomb] (DNAB) .... AD
Aircraft Design Research Division [Navy] .... ADR
Aircraft Design-Induced Pilot Error [National Transportation Safety Board] .... ADIPE
Aircraft Destination Record (MCD) .... ADR
Aircraft Development Service [Air Force] .... ADS
Aircraft Development Test Activity [Army] (MCD) .... ADTA
Aircraft Development Test Activity [Army] (MCD) .... ATA
Aircraft Diagnostics and Integrated Test System (MCD) .... ADITS
Aircraft Direction Room [Navy] .... ADR
Aircraft Directives Configuration [Navy] (NG) .... ADC
Aircraft Discrepancy Report .... ADR
Aircraft Division (MCD) .... AD
Aircraft Division/Department List [Air Force] .... AD/DL
Aircraft Dummy Deck Landing [Navy] .... ADDL
Aircraft Earth Station [ICAO designator] (FAAC) .... AES
Aircraft Ejection Kit .... AEK
Aircraft Ejection Seat .... AES
Aircraft Ejection Seat System .... AESS
Aircraft Electrical Power System .... AEPS
Aircraft Electrical Society (SAA) .... AES
Aircraft Electrical System Component Tester (DWSG) .... AESCOT
Aircraft Electronics Association (EA) .... AEA
Aircraft Electronics Warfare Self-Protection System [Army] .... AEWSP
Aircraft Electronics Warfare Self-Protection System [Army] .... AEWSPS
Aircraft Emergency Procedures over Water .... AEPW
Aircraft Emission Estimator (MCD) .... ACEE
Aircraft Energy Efficiency (MCD) .... ACEE
Aircraft Engine Laboratory .... AEL
Aircraft Engine Management System (MCD) .... AEMS
Aircraft Engine Record Card (DNAB) .... AERC
Aircraft Engineering District Office .... AEDO
Aircraft Engineering Foundation .... AEF
Aircraft Engineering Maintenance Co. .... AEMCO
Aircraft Engineering Squadron (SAA) .... AES

Aircraft Engineers Association .... AEA
Aircraft Environmental Support Office [Naval Air Rework Facility] [North Island, CA] .... AESO
Aircraft Equipment .... AE
Aircraft Equipment Failure .... AEF
Aircraft Equipment List (MCD) .... AEL
Aircraft Equipment Procedures (MCD) .... AEP
Aircraft Equipment Requirement Schedule .... AERS
Aircraft Equipment Trainer (MCD) .... AET
Aircraft Escape System Maintenance Data (MCD) .... AESMD
Aircraft Escort Vessel [Navy symbol Obsolete] .... AVG
Aircraft Evaluation Group [FAA] (TAG) .... AEG
Aircraft Expendable Bathythermograph Program in the Pacific [National Science Foundation] (MSC) .... AIRPAX
Aircraft Explosive Device (MCD) .... AED
Aircraft Familiarization .... AIRFAM
Aircraft Fatigue Data Analysis System (ADA) .... AFDAS
Aircraft Fault Indentification System [Aviation] (PDAA) .... AFIS
Aircraft Ferry Squadron [Navy] .... VRF
Aircraft Finance Association [Later, NAFA] (EA) .... AFA
Aircraft, Fleet Marine Force, Atlantic [Obsolete] .... AIRFMFLANT
Aircraft, Fleet Marine Force, Pacific [Obsolete] .... AFMFP
Aircraft, Fleet Marine Force, Pacific [Obsolete] .... AIRFMFPAC
Aircraft Flight Report (AAG) .... AFR
Aircraft Flying Training .... ACFT
Aircraft Force Projection Model [Computer] [Navy] .... AFPM
Aircraft Gas and Turbine .... AGT
Aircraft General Standards [British] .... AGS
Aircraft Generation Squadron (MCD) .... AGS
Aircraft Generation Squadron [Air Force] .... AGSq
Aircraft Ground Fire Suppression and Rescue [Air Force] (MCD) .... AGFSR
Aircraft Ground Fire Suppression and Rescue Systems [Wright-Patterson Air Force Base, OH] [Air Force] .... AGFSRS
Aircraft Ground Mishap (DOMA) .... AGM
Aircraft Ground Mobility System (MCD) .... AGMS
Aircraft Ground Support Equipment (MCD) .... AGSE
Aircraft Grounded for Lack of Parts .... AGP
Aircraft Gun Pod (NG) .... AGP
Aircraft Gunfire Detector .... AGD
Aircraft Handler [British] .... AH
Aircraft Handling Vehicle (MCD) .... AHV
Aircraft Hangar (MCD) .... ACH
Aircraft Identification (KSC) .... ACID
Aircraft Identification (AAG) .... AI
Aircraft Identification Control (SAA) .... AIC
Aircraft Identification Determination (SAA) .... AID
Aircraft IFF [Identification, Friend or Foe] Mark XII System (AABC) .... AIMXS
Aircraft in Commission .... AIC
Aircraft in Flight [ICAO designator] (ICDA) .... ZZ
Aircraft in Flight [FAA designator] (FAAC) .... ZZZ
Aircraft Incident Report [Navy] (NG) .... AIR
Aircraft Industries Association (BARN) .... AIA
Aircraft Industries Center (AAG) .... AIC
Aircraft Industry (AAG) .... AI
Aircraft Industry Conference [Navy] .... AIC
Aircraft Inflight Monitoring System (MCD) .... AIMS
Aircraft Information Correlator (CAAL) .... AIC
Aircraft Inspection System .... AIS
Aircraft Inspections and Repair .... AIR
Aircraft Installation Delay (DA) .... AID
Aircraft Installation Diagnostic Equipment (MCD) .... AIDE
Aircraft Instrument Bulletin [Navy] (NG) .... AIB
Aircraft Instrument Laboratory [Navy] (AAG) .... AIL
Aircraft Instrument Repair Facility .... AIRF
Aircraft Instrument Subsystem [Navy] (MCD) .... AIS
Aircraft Instruments and Aircrew Stations [NATO] (NATG) .... AI
Aircraft Integrated Crew Station Concepts (MCD) .... AICSC
Aircraft Integrated Data System (MCD) .... AIDS
Aircraft Integrated Design System (MCD) .... AIDS
Aircraft Integrated Munition System (MCD) .... AIMS
Aircraft Integrated Test Equipment .... AITE
Aircraft Intensively Managed Items .... AIMI
Aircraft Interceptor (MCD) .... AI
Aircraft Interface Data Summaries (MCD) .... AIDS
Aircraft Interface Device (DWSG) .... AID
Aircraft Intermediate Maintenance [Detachment] [Navy] [Marine Corps] (DOMA) .... AIM
Aircraft Intermediate Maintenance Department [Navy] (NVT) .... AIMD
Aircraft Intermediate Maintenance Support Office (DNAB) .... AIMSO
Aircraft Intrusion Detection System [RADAR] .... AIDS
Aircraft Inventory Management Group [Military] (AFIT) .... AIM
Aircraft Inventory Record (NVT) .... AIR
Aircraft Inventory Reporting System (AABC) .... AIRS
Aircraft Kill Indicator .... AKI
Aircraft Landing Gear .... ALG
Aircraft Landing Lamp .... ALL
Aircraft Landing Measurement System (MCD) .... ALMS
Aircraft Landing System .... ALS
Aircraft Latitude (MCD) .... ALAT
Aircraft Launch and Recovery Equipment [Navy] (MCD) .... ALRE
Aircraft Launch and Recovery Equipment Maintenance Program [Navy] (NG) .... ALREMP
Aircraft Launching Accessory Service Change (MCD) .... ALASC
Aircraft Launching Bulletin .... ACLB
Aircraft Launching Bulletin (MCD) .... ALB

Aircraft Life Support Equipment [*Military*] (DOMA) ... ALSE
Aircraft Limited Model ... ALM
Aircraft Load ... ACL
Aircraft Loaders Control Assembly ... ALCA
Aircraft Locknut Manufacturers Association (EA) ... ALMA
Aircraft Logistics Division [*Bureau of Aeronautics*] [*Later, NASC*] [*Navy*] ... AL
Aircraft Logistics Planning Board (MCD) ... ALPB
Aircraft Longitude (MCD) ... ALON
Aircraft Loss, Utilization, Combat, and Repair Damage (MCD) ... ALUCARD
Aircraft Machine Gunner ... AIRMG
Aircraft Machine Gunner ... AMG
Aircraft Maintenance and Repair Department [*British military*] (DMA) ... AMRD
Aircraft Maintenance Base ... AMB
Aircraft Maintenance Co. [*Egypt*] [*ICAO designator*] (FAAC) ... AMV
Aircraft Maintenance Delayed for Parts [*Military*] ... AMDP
Aircraft Maintenance Department [*Military*] (AFIT) ... AMD
Aircraft Maintenance Effectiveness Simulation (MCD) ... AMES
Aircraft Maintenance Irregularity Control System (PDAA) ... AMICS
Aircraft Maintenance Management Information System ... AMMIS
Aircraft Maintenance Manpower Information System [*Air Force*] ... AMMIS
Aircraft Maintenance Manpower Requirement [*Air Force*] (AFM) ... AMMR
Aircraft Maintenance Manual ... AMM
Aircraft Maintenance Material Readiness List [*Navy*] (NG) ... AMMRL
Aircraft Maintenance Support Equipment (MCD) ... AMSE
Aircraft Manufacturers Association [*Superseded by MAA*] (EA) ... AMA
Aircraft Manufacturer's Council ... AMC
Aircraft Manufacturing Co. (MCD) ... AMC
Aircraft Material Management Center [*Air Force*] ... AMMC
Aircraft Material Officer ... AMO
Aircraft Material Specifications [*Society of Automotive Engineers*] ... AMS
Aircraft Mechanician [*British military*] (DMA) ... AMN
Aircraft Mechanics Fraternal Association (EA) ... AMFA
Aircraft Meteorological (NATG) ... AC/M
Aircraft Military Mission ... AIRMILMIS
Aircraft Mishap Board (DNAB) ... AMB
Aircraft/Missile Maintenance - Production Compression Report ... AMREP
Aircraft/Missile Project (AFM) ... AMP
Aircraft Mission Equipment (MCD) ... AME
Aircraft Model Change ... AMC
Aircraft Monitor and Control (NG) ... AMAC
Aircraft Motion Compensation ... AMC
Aircraft Mounted Control System ... AMCS
Aircraft Movement Element (MCD) ... AME
Aircraft Movement Information Service [*Air Force*] ... AMIS
Aircraft Multiengine Land [*Pilot rating*] (IEEE) ... AMEL
Aircraft Multiengine Sea [*Pilot rating*] (AIA) ... AMES
Aircraft Multiplex Intercommunications ... AMI
Aircraft Multiplex Intercommunications System ... AMIS
Aircraft Multipurpose Test Inspection and Diagnostic Equipment ... AMTIDE
Aircraft Multispectral Photographic System [*NASA*] ... AMPS
Aircraft Nationality and Registration Marks ... REG
Aircraft Noise Prediction Office [*NASA*] ... ANOPO
Aircraft Noise Prediction Program [*NASA*] ... ANOPP
Aircraft Nonflying-Electronics (CINC) ... ANFE
Aircraft, Northern Solomons [*Military*] ... AIRNORSOLS
Aircraft Not Combat Ready (MCD) ... ANCR
Aircraft Not Fully Equipped ... ANFE
Aircraft Not Operationally Ready Due to Lack of Equipment (SAA) ... ANORE
Aircraft Not Operationally Ready Due to Lack of Parts (SAA) ... ANORP
Aircraft Not Operationally Ready Supply (AFIT) ... ANOPS
Aircraft Nuclear Power [*or Propulsion*] ... ANP
Aircraft Nuclear Power Plant Facility ... ANPPF
Aircraft Nuclear Propulsion Department [*Navy*] ... ANPD
Aircraft Nuclear Propulsion Office [*of AEC*] [*Defunct*] ... ANPO
Aircraft Nuclear Propulsion Program ... ANPP
Aircraft of Bomber Command [*British*] ... ABC
Aircraft on Ground [*Navy*] ... ACOG
Aircraft on Ground [*Navy*] ... AOG
Aircraft Operating Cost Report (NG) ... AOCR
Aircraft Operating Fee (ADA) ... AOF
Aircraft Operating Manual (GAVI) ... AOM
Aircraft Operating Report (MCD) ... AOR
Aircraft Operational Capability (DNAB) ... AOC
Aircraft Operations Center (OSRA) ... AOC
Aircraft Operations Center (USDC) ... AOC
Aircraft Operations Division [*Johnson Space Center*] [*NASA*] (NASA) ... AOD
Aircraft Operations Group Association ... AOGA
Aircraft Operator (DA) ... AO
Aircraft Out for Parts (MCD) ... AOP
Aircraft Out of Commission for Maintenance [*Military*] ... AOCM
Aircraft out of Commission for Parts [*MTMC*] (TAG) ... AOCM
Aircraft Out of Commission for [*Lack of*] **Parts** [*Obsolete Military*] ... AOCP
Aircraft Overhaul Work Stoppage (NG) ... AOWS
Aircraft Owners and Pilots Association (EA) ... AOPA
Aircraft Parachute Flare (SAA) ... APF
Aircraft Penetration Model (MCD) ... ACPEN
Aircraft Performance (SAA) ... ACP
Aircraft Plume Analysis ... APA
Aircraft Position Information Converter [*Air Force*] ... APICON
Aircraft Position Sensor (PDAA) ... APS
Aircraft Precision Position Location Equipment (DA) ... APPL
Aircraft Prepared for Service ... APS
Aircraft Procurement (Appropriations), Army/Navy/Air Force (AAGC) ... AP/A/N/AF
Aircraft Procurement, Army (AABC) ... APA
Aircraft Procurement, Navy (NVT) ... APN
Aircraft Production Resources Agency ... APRA
Aircraft Program Data File ... APDF
Aircraft Propulsion Subsystem Integration ... APSI
Aircraft Propulsion Unit ... APU
Aircraft Proximity Hazard (DA) ... APHAZ
Aircraft Proximity Warning Device ... APWD
Aircraft Proximity Warning System ... APWS
Aircraft Pulse Navigation ... APN
Aircraft Quality (AAG) ... AQ
Aircraft Radio, Inc. (MCD) ... ARINC
Aircraft Radio Laboratory ... ARL
Aircraft Radio Regulations ... ARR
Aircraft Radio Sight (IAA) ... ARS
Aircraft Reactor Equipment ... ARE
Aircraft Reactor Experiment (NUCP) ... ARE
Aircraft Reactor Test (IAA) ... ART
Aircraft Reactors Branch ... ARB
Aircraft Readiness Maintainability Simulator (MCD) ... ARMS
Aircraft Ready (AFIT) ... AR
Aircraft Recommended Practice (DNAB) ... ARP
Aircraft Recording Instrumentation System [*British*] ... ARIS
Aircraft Recovery (CINC) ... AIR
Aircraft Recovery Association (EA) ... ARA
Aircraft Recovery Bulletin (MCD) ... ARB
Aircraft Recovery Equipment ... ARE
Aircraft Reference Point ... ARP
Aircraft Refuel/Rearm Study (MCD) ... ARRS
Aircraft Regression Model (MCD) ... ARM
Aircraft Reliability and Maintainability Simulation ... ARMS
Aircraft Reliability, Maintainability, Availability Design Analysis (PDAA) ... ARMADA
Aircraft Repair and Supply Base (AFIT) ... ARSB
Aircraft Repair and Supply Center ... ARSC
Aircraft Repair Division (SAA) ... AIREDIV
Aircraft Repair Division [*Military*] ... AIREPDIV
Aircraft Repair Division [*Military*] ... AIREPDN
Aircraft Repair Ship [*Navy*] ... ARS
Aircraft Repair Ship [*Navy symbol*] ... ARV
Aircraft Repair Ship (Aircraft) [*Navy symbol*] ... ARVA
Aircraft Repair Ship (Engine) [*Navy symbol*] ... ARVE
Aircraft Repair Ship (Helicopter) [*Navy symbol*] ... ARVH
Aircraft Replaceable Assemblies ... ARA
Aircraft Reply and Interference Environment Simulator (MCD) ... ARIES
Aircraft Report ... AIREP
Aircraft Report, Special (ADA) ... ARS
Aircraft Requirements Computer System ... ARCS
Aircraft Requiring Overhaul (AFIT) ... AOH
Aircraft Rescue and Fire Fighting [*Air Traffic Control*] (FAAC) ... ARFF
Aircraft Rescue and Fire Fighting ... ARFF
Aircraft Rescue and Fire Fighting Vehicle ... ARFFV
Aircraft Rescue Boat [*Navy symbol*] ... AVH
Aircraft Rescue Vessel [*Navy*] (MCD) ... ARV
Aircraft [*or Aviation*] **Rescue Vessel** [*Navy symbol Obsolete*] ... AVR
Aircraft Research and Development Unit [*Australia*] ... ARDU
Aircraft Research and Testing Committee (MCD) ... ARTC
Aircraft Research Association (EAIO) ... ARA
Aircraft Research Instrumentation System ... ARIS
Aircraft Resources Control Office ... ARCO
Aircraft Resources Management System [*Military*] ... ARMS
Aircraft Resources Management System, Pacific [*Military*] (NVT) ... ARMSPAC
Aircraft Response to Wind Spectrum (MCD) ... ARWS
Aircraft Rocket (NVT) ... AR
Aircraft Rocket Subsystem [*Army/Air Force*] ... ARS
Aircraft Safety Beacon ... ASB
Aircraft Salvage-Handling Equipment (DNAB) ... ASHE
Aircraft Sampling Inspection (MCD) ... ASI
Aircraft Schedule for Delivery to Fleet ... AIRSKEDELFLT
Aircraft Scheduling Unit ... ASU
Aircraft Scouting Force, Pacific Fleet ... AIRSCOFORPAC
Aircraft Security System (MCD) ... ASS
Aircraft Security Vessel ... A/CS
Aircraft Sensor Correlation Device (MCD) ... ASCD
[*The*] **Aircraft Service Association** ... TASA
Aircraft Service Change [*Navy*] ... ASC
Aircraft Service Period Adjustments [*Air Force*] (DOMA) ... ASPA
Aircraft Services Base ... ASB
Aircraft Services Facility ... ASF
Aircraft Servicing Platform (DA) ... ASP
Aircraft Shield Test Reactor (SAA) ... ASTR
Aircraft Shipment Readiness Date [*Army*] (AABC) ... ASRD
Aircraft Single Engine Sea [*Pilot rating*] (AIA) ... ASES
Aircraft Situation Display [*FAA*] (TAG) ... ASD
Aircraft Sound Description System [*FAA*] ... ASDS
Aircraft, South Pacific Force [*Navy*] ... AIRSOPAC
Aircraft, Southwest Pacific Force [*Navy*] ... AIRSOWESPAC
Aircraft Space Position Measurement System (MCD) ... ASPMS
Aircraft Specialties Lines ... ASL
Aircraft Specification Forum Committee ... ASFC
Aircraft Stabilization Equipment [*Aviation*] (PDAA) ... ASE
Aircraft Standard Parts (NATG) ... ASP
Aircraft Standards ... AS
Aircraft Starting Unit ... ASU
Aircraft Station Keeper (MCD) ... ASK
Aircraft Stations [*ITU designation*] (CET) ... MA

Aircraft Statistical Data .... ASD
Aircraft Storage and Disposition Group [*Air Force*] .... ASDG
Aircraft Storage Facility (SAA) .... ACSF
Aircraft Storage Unit [*Military British*] .... ASU
Aircraft Stores Establishment [*Navy*] .... ASE
Aircraft Stores Interface Data Systems .... ASIDS
Aircraft Stores Interface Manual (MCD) .... ASIM
Aircraft Structural Integrity Management Information System [*Air Force*]
(AFIT) .... ASIMIS
Aircraft Structural Integrity Program .... ASIP
Aircraft Structural Integrity Program Recorder .... ASPR
Aircraft Summary List .... ASL
Aircraft Supply Council [*Ministry of Aircraft Production*] [*British*] ...... ASC
Aircraft Supply Group .... ASG
Aircraft Support and Service Equipment Tug (PDAA) .... ASSET
Aircraft Surge Launch and Recovery [*FAA*] (TAG) .... ASLAR
Aircraft Survivability Equipment .... ASE
Aircraft Survivability Equipment (DOMA) .... ASE
Aircraft Survivability Equipment - Product Manager .... ASE-PM
Aircraft Survival Measures Programme [*NATO*] .... ASM
Aircraft Synthesis [*Computer science*] .... ACSYNT
Aircraft Synthesis Analysis Program .... ASAP
Aircraft Systems Activation Program [*Military*] .... ASAP
Aircraft Systems Trainer (MCD) .... AST
Aircraft Tactical Control System .... ATCS
Aircraft Tail Warning .... ATW
Aircraft Technical Bulletin .... ATB
Aircraft Technical Committee [*Aerospace Industries Association*] (MCD) .... ATC
Aircraft Technical Order .... ATO
Aircraft Technical Publishers [*Information service or system*] (IID) .... ATP
Aircraft Test Equipment Modification .... ATEM
Aircraft Thermal Management (MCD) .... ATM
Aircraft Time Compliance Technical Manuals .... TCTM
Aircraft to Be Identified [*Aviation*] (AIA) .... ACFTTBI
Aircraft Torpedo Development Unit [*British*] .... ATDU
Aircraft Torpedo Maintenance Unit [*Navy*] .... ATMU
Aircraft Traffic Advisory Resolution System .... ATARS
Aircraft Trailing Vortices .... ATV
Aircraft (Training) [*Navy symbol*] .... VTD
Aircraft Transfer Order .... ATO
Aircraft Transmitter-Receiver (IAA) .... ATR
Aircraft Transportation Lighter [*Navy symbol*] .... YCK
Aircraft Transportation Lighter [*Non-self-propelled*] [*Navy symbol*] ...... YCV
Aircraft Transportation Officer [*Navy*] (DOMA) .... ATO
Aircraft Trouble Report .... ATR
Aircraft Trouble-Shooting System (MCD) .... ATS
Aircraft Tube-Launched Recoilless System (MCD) .... ATLRS
Aircraft Unitized Diagnostic Inspection and Test [*Boeing*] .... AUDIT
Aircraft Utilization Report .... AUR
Aircraft Velocity (MCD) .... AVEL
Aircraft Warning (IAA) .... AW
Aircraft Warning Company [*Army*] .... AWCo
Aircraft Warning Company [*Marine Corps*] .... AWRNCO
Aircraft Warning Service [*Military*] .... AWS
Aircraft Weapons Handling Vehicle .... AWHV
Aircraft Weapons Release Set [*or System*] (NG) .... AWRS
Aircraft Weapons Release Unit [*DoD*] (MCD) .... AWRU
Aircraft Wide-Angle Reflective Display System [*Singer Co., Link Division*] .... AWARDS
Aircraft Wireless Intercom (DWSG) .... AWIC
Aircraft-Based Infrared Detector .... ABIRD
Aircrafthand [*British*] .... ACH
Aircraft-Landing Quality Association Scheme (OA) .... ALQAS
Aircraftman [*British*] .... AC
Aircraftman, First Class [*Canadian*] AC1
Aircraftman, Second Class [*Canadian*] AC2
Aircraft-to-Satellite Data Relay [*Meteorology*] .... ASDAR
Aircraft-to-Surface Vessel [*Navy*] .... ASV
Aircraftwoman [*Military*] .... AC
Aircraftwoman [*British*] .... ACW
Aircraftwoman, First Class [*Canadian*] AW1
Aircraftwoman, Second Class [*Canadian*] AW2
Aircrew .... ACREW
Aircrew (AFM) .... ACRW
Aircrew Association (EAIO) .... ACA
Aircrew Body Armor [*System*] [*Army*] .... ACBA
Aircrew Classification Test (AFM) .... ACT
Aircrew Classification Test Battery .... ACTB
Aircrew Egress Trainer (MCD) .... AET
Aircrew Electronic Warfare Tactics Facility (NATG) .... AEWTF
Aircrew Escape Propulsion System [*Navy*] .... AEPS
Aircrew Eyes Respiratory System (DWSG) .... AERP
Aircrew Flight Training Period (AABC) .... AFTP
Aircrew Gliding Escape System (MCD) .... AGES
Aircrew Holding Unit [*British military*] (DMA) .... ACHU
Aircrew Life Support System (CAAL) .... ALSS
Aircrew Microclimate Cooling System [*Military*] (DOMA) .... AMCS
Aircrew Part Task Trainer (MCD) .... APTT
Aircrew Reception Centre [*British military*] (DMA) .... ARC
Aircrew Respiratory Protection .... ARP
Aircrew Standardization and Evaluation Team [*Military*] .... ASET
Aircrew Station Standardization Panel .... ASSP
Aircrew Survival Equipmentman [*Navy rating*] .... PR
Aircrew Systems Advisory Panel [*NASA, Air Force*] (MCD) .... ASAP
Aircrew Systems Change (MCD) .... ASC

Aircrew Training and Test Squadron [*Air Force*] .... ATTSq
Aircrew Training Device (MCD) .... ATD
Aircrew Training Manual [*A publication*] (MCD) .... ATM
Aircrew Training System (MCD) .... ATS
Aircrew Training Test Wing [*Air Force*] .... ATTW
Aircrew Uniform, Integrated Battlefield [*Army*] .... AUIB
Aircrewman .... AC
Aircrewman [*British military*] (DMA) .... ACMN
Air-Cure Environmental [*NASDAQ symbol*] (SPSG) .... AIRE
Air-Cure Technologies [*NASDAQ symbol*] (TTSB) .... ATSS
Air-Cure Technologies, Inc. [*Associated Press*] (SAG) ...... AirCure
Air-Cure Technologies, Inc. [*AMEX symbol*] (SAG) .... ATS
Air-Cure Technologies, Inc. [*NASDAQ symbol*] (SAG) .... ATSS
Air-Cushion Barge (MCD) .... ACB
Air-Cushion Equipment Transportation System .... ACETS
Air-Cushion Landing Gear .... ACLG
Air-Cushion Landing System .... ACLS
Air-Cushion Logistic Vehicle [*Helicopter*] .... ACLV
Air-Cushion Restraint System [*General Motors*] .... ACRS
Air-Cushion Takeoff System (MCD) .... ACTS
Air-Cushion Trailer [*or Transporter*] .... ACT
Air-Cushion Vehicle .... ACV
Air-Cushion Vehicle built by Air Bearings [*England*] [*Usually used in combination with numerals*] .... AB
Air-Cushion Vehicle built by Air Vehicles [*England*] [*Usually used in combination with numerals*] .... AV
Air-Cushion Vehicle built by Ajax Hovercraft [*England*] [*Usually used in combination with numerals*] .... AH
Air-Cushion Vehicle built by Canadian Cushion Craft [*Usually used in combination with numerals*] [*Canada*] .... CANAIR
Air-Cushion Vehicle built by Commercial Hovercraft Industries [*New Zealand*] [*Usually used in combination with numerals*] .... CH
Air-Cushion Vehicle built by Cushioncraft [*England*] [*Usually used in combination with numerals*] CC
Air-Cushion Vehicle built by DeHavilland Aircraft Co. of Canada [*Usually used in combination with numerals*] [*Canada*] .... DHC
Air-Cushion Vehicle built by Denny Brothers [*England*] [*Usually used in combination with numerals*] .... D
Air-Cushion Vehicle built by Flygtekniska Forsoksanstalen [*Sweden*] [*Usually used in combination with numerals*] .... FFA
Air-Cushion Vehicle built by Hover Vehicles [*New Zealand*] [*Usually used in combination with numerals*] .... HV
Air-Cushion Vehicle built by Hovercraft Development [*England*] [*Usually used in combination with numerals*] .... HD
Air-Cushion Vehicle built by Hoverjak [*England*] [*Usually used in combination with numerals*] .... HJ
Air-Cushion Vehicle built by Hoverjet [*Usually used in combination with numerals*] [*Canada*] .... HJ
Air-Cushion Vehicle Built by Hovermarine [*Usually used in combination with numerals*] .... HM
Air-Cushion Vehicle built by Hoversport [*US*] [*Usually used in combination with numerals*] .... HS
Air-Cushion Vehicle built by Mitsubishi [*Japan*] [*Usually used in combination with numerals*] .... MH
Air-Cushion Vehicle built by Nakamura Seisakusho [*Usually used in combination with numerals*] [*Japan*] .... NAMCO
Air-Cushion Vehicle built by Research Vehicle Department [*Brazil*] [*Usually used in combination with numerals*] .... DEPV
Air-Cushion Vehicle built by Rhein Flugzeugbau [*Usually used in combination with numerals*] [*Germany*] .... RFB
Air-Cushion Vehicle built by Saunders Roe [*England*] [*Usually used in combination with numerals*] .... SR
Air-Cushion Vehicle built by Sealand Air Cushion Vehicles [*US*] [*Usually used in combination with numerals*] .... SAVC
Air-Cushion Vehicle built by Sealand Hovercraft [*England*] [*Usually used in combination with numerals*] .... SH
Air-Cushion Vehicle built by Societe National Industrielle Aerospatiale [*France*] [*Usually used in combination with numerals*] .... SA
Air-Cushion Vehicle built by Universal Hovercraft [*US*] [*Usually used in combination with numerals*] .... UH
Air-Cushion Vehicle built by Vosper Thorneycroft [*England*] [*Usually used in combination with numerals*] .... VT
Aird. Blackstone Economised [*1873*] [*A publication*] (ILCA) .... Aird Black
Air-Dale Ltd. [*Canada ICAO designator*] (FAAC) .... ADL
Air-Deliverable Antipollution Transfer System .... ADAPTS
Air-Delivered Attack Marker [*Air Force*] (MCD) .... ADAM
Air-Delivered Land Mine System [*Military*] .... ADLMS
Air-Delivered Seismic Intrusion Detectors .... ADSID
Air-Delivered Target-Activated Munitions (AFM) .... ADTAM
Air-Deployed Towed-Array Surveillance System (MCD) .... AIRTAS
Air-Derived Separation Assurance [*Aviation*] .... ADSA
Air-Derived Separation Assurance System [*Aviation*] ...... ADSAS
Airdrie Municipal Library, Airdrie, AB, Canada [*Library symbol Library of Congress*] (LCLS) .... CaAAiM
Airdrie Municipal Library, Alberta [*Library symbol National Library of Canada*] (NLC) .... AAIM
Air-Dried [*Lumber*] .... AD
Air-Dried Ton .... ADT
Air-Driven Air Amplifier .... ADAA
Air-Driven Generator (MCD) .... ADG
Airdrome .... AD
Airdrome Battalion .... ADROBN
Airdrome Control [*British*] (SAA) .... AC
Airdrome Defense Corps [*Air Force*] .... ADC
Airdrome Officer .... AO

Airdrop [*Military*] (AABC) ... ADRP
Airdrop by Parachute ... PARADROP
Aird's Civil Laws of France [*A publication*] (DLA) ... Aird Civ Law
Airedale Terrier Association of New South Wales [*Australia*] ... ATANSW
Airedale Terrier Club of America (EA) ... ATCA
Aires, Aerovias de Integracion Regional SA [*Colombia*] [*ICAO designator*] (FAAC) ... ARE
AiResearch Manufacturing Co. ... AMC
Aire-Sur-L'Addour [*France ICAO location identifier*] (ICLI) ... LFDA
Aireworth Volunteer Corps [*British military*] (DMA) ... AVC
Airfast Service Indonesia PT [*ICAO designator*] (FAAC) ... AFE
Airfield (NATG) ... A/F
Airfield (AFM) ... AFLD
Airfield and Carrier Requirements Department (SAA) ... ACRD
Airfield and Seaplane Stations of the World (MUGU) ... ASSOTW
Airfield Construction Branch [*British military*] (DMA) ... ACB
Airfield Control RADAR [*Air Force*] ... ACR
Airfield Damage Repair [*Military*] ... ADR
Airfield Delay Simulation Model [*FAA*] (TAG) ... ADSIM
Airfield Heliport ... AH
Airfield Index ... AI
Airfield Lighting System ... ALS
Airfield Marking and Lighting (NATG) ... AML
Airfield Operations Designator [*Air Force/Army*] ... AOD
Airfield Pavement [*Air Force*] ... AFPAV
Airfield Surface Movement Indicator [*RADAR*] [*Aviation*] (IAA) ... ASM
Airfield Surface Movement Indicator [*RADAR*] [*Aviation*] ... ASMI
Airfield Vehicle Obstacle Indication Device ... AVOID
Airfields Environment Federation (EAIO) ... AEF
Airfields Environment Trust [*British*] ... AET
Air-Filled Cushion [*Medicine*] (DAVI) ... AFC
Airflex Clutch (DS) ... AFC
Airflow Club of America (EA) ... ACA
Airflow per Unit of Time [*Medicine*] (DAVI) ... V_E
Airfoil Design and Analysis Center [*Ohio State University*] (MCD) ... ADAC
Airfoil Leading Edge Separation (MCD) ... ALESEP
Airframe (KSC) ... AF
Airframe ... AFME
Airframe ... AFR
Airframe (AABC) ... AFRM
Airframe and Engine ... A and E
Airframe and Powerplant [*Aviation*] ... A & P
Airframe and System Assembly/Test (MCD) ... ASA/T
Airframe Bulletin (MCD) ... AFB
Airframe Change ... AC
Airframe Change (MCD) ... AFC
Airframe Change Control Board (MCD) ... ACCB
Airframe Design Division [*Bureau of Aeronautics; later, NASC*] [*Navy*] ... AD
Airframe Fatigue Data Analysis System (MCD) ... AFDAS
Airframe Flight Qualification ... AFQ
Airframe Integrated Nozzle (MCD) ... AIN
Airframe Manufacturing Equipment Committee ... AMEC
Airframe Mechanical and Fluid Subsystems (MCD) ... AMFS
Airframe Repair Technician-Repairman (AAG) ... ART/R
Airframe Unit Weight ... AUW
Airframe-Mounted Accessory Drive (MCD) ... AMAD
Airframe-Mounted Accessory Drive System ... AMADS
Airfreight Container [*Shipping*] (DCTA) ... AC
Air-Fuel Ratio (ADA) ... AFR
Air-Fuel Ratio Control Device [*Automotive engineering*] ... AFRCD
Airgas, Inc. [*Associated Press*] (SAG) ... Airgas
Airgas, Inc. [*NYSE symbol*] (SPSG) ... ARG
Airgraph (ADA) ... A/G
Air-Ground Chart (AFM) ... AGC
Air-Ground Communications (CET) ... AGC
Air-Ground Communications Channel ... AGCC
Air-Ground Communications System (SAA) ... AGCS
Air-Ground Cooling Unit (MCD) ... AGCU
Air-Ground Cooperation Officer ... AGCO
Air-Ground Correlation Factor (AABC) ... AGCF
Air-Ground Engagement Simulation (RDA) ... AGES
Air-Ground Equipment ... AGE
Air-Ground Information Center ... AGIC
Air-Ground Integration System ... AGIS
Air-Ground Liaison Officer [*Marine Corps*] ... AGLO
Air-Ground Operations Section [*or School or System*] ... AGOS
Air-Ground System ... AGS
Air-Ground-Air Communications System ... AGACS
Air-Handling Unit [*Mechanical engineering*] (OA) ... AHU
Airhead [*Army*] (AABC) ... AHD
Airhead Air Traffic Coordination Center [*Army*] (AFIT) ... AATCC
Airhead Maintenance Area [*Military British*] ... AMA
Air-Independent Propulsion System [*Navy*] ... AIP
Air-Land Assault (CINC) ... ALA
Air-Land Battle (MCD) ... ALB
Air-Land Battle Management ... ALBM
Air-Land Battle-Future [*Army*] (INF) ... ALB-F
Air-Land Forces Agency [*Air Force Army*] (MCD) ... ALFA
Air-Land Forces Applications ... ALFA
Air-Land Forces Applications Agency [*TAC-TRADOC*] (MCD) ... ALFAA
Air-Land Forces Integration (MCD) ... ALFI
Air-Land Forces Interface ... ALFI
Air-Land Operations Manual (MCD) ... ALOM
Air-Land Programs Office ... ALPO
Air-Land Resupply (CINC) ... ALR
Air-Landing [*British military*] (DMA) ... A/L
Airlantic Transport [*Air carrier designation symbol*] ... ATIX
Air-Launched [*Missile launch environment symbol*] ... A
Air-Launched Advanced Ramjet Missile (KSC) ... ALARM
Air-Launched, Air-Recoverable Rocket ... ALARR
Air-Launched Antiballistic Missile ... ALABM
Air-Launched Antiradiation Missile ... ALARM
Air-Launched Ballistic Intercept ... ALBI
Air-Launched Ballistic Intercept System (MCD) ... ALBIS
Air-Launched Ballistic Missile ... ALBM
Air-Launched Balloon System (MCD) ... ALBS
Air-Launched Boost Intercept (MSA) ... ALBI
Air-Launched Booster (MCD) ... ALB
Air-Launched Cruise Missile ... ALCM
Air-Launched Cruise Missile Guidance Set (MCD) ... ALCMGS
Air-Launched Guided Missile [*Military*] ... ALGM
Air-Launched High-Altitude Reconnaissance Drone (MCD) ... ALHARD
Air-Launched Instrumented Vehicle Evaluation (MCD) ... ALIVE
Air-Launched Intercept Missile ... ALIM
Air-Launched Intercept Missile Record System ... AIMS
Air-Launched Interceptor Missile (MCD) ... AIM
Air-Launched Long-Range Air-to-Air Missile (MCD) ... ALRAAM
Air-Launched Low-Altitude Cruise Missile (MCD) ... ALLACM
Air-Launched Low-Volume Ramjet (MCD) ... ALLVRJ
Air-Launched Low-Volume Ramjet ... ALVRJ
Air-Launched Medium-Intermediate Range Ballistic Missile (MCD) ... ALMIRBM
Air-Launched Miniature Vehicle ... ALMV
Air-Launched Missile ... ALM
Air-Launched Missile Ballistics (MCD) ... ALMB
Air-Launched Missile Bulletin (MCD) ... AMB
Air-Launched Missile Change (DNAB) ... ALMC
Air-Launched Missile Change (MCD) ... AMC
Air-Launched Missile Intermediate Maintenance System Program [*Navy*] (MCD) ... ALMIMSIP
Air-Launched Missile Inventory Objectives Study (MCD) ... ALMIOS
Air-Launched Missile Propulsion Technology (MCD) ... ALMPT
Air-Launched Missile System ... ALMS
Air-Launched Nonnuclear Ordnance (DNAB) ... ALNN
Air-Launched Nonnuclear Ordnance ... ALNNO
Air-Launched Nuclear Weapon (DNAB) ... ALNW
Air-Launched Platform (NVT) ... ALP
Air-Launched Probe System (MCD) ... ALPS
Air-Launched Projected Sonobuoy (MCD) ... ALPS
Air-Launched Report [*Navy*] (NG) ... ALREP
Air-Launched Ship-Attack Missile ... ALSAM
Air-Launched Sortie Vehicle [*Aviation*] (AIA) ... ALSV
Air-Launched Strategic Missile ... ALSM
Air-Launched Surface Attack Missile ... ALSAM
Air-Launched Trainer Rocket (AFM) ... ATR
Air-Launched Unit ... ALU
Air-Launched Vehicle (AFM) ... ALV
Air-Launched Weapon ... ALW
Airlease Ltd. [*Associated Press*] (SAG) ... Airlease
Airlease Ltd. [*NYSE symbol*] (SPSG) ... FLY
Airlease Ltd L.P. [*NYSE symbol*] (TTSB) ... FLY
Airlec [*France ICAO designator*] (FAAC) ... ARL
Airlen [*Russian Federation*] [*ICAO designator*] (FAAC) ... LNA
Airletter Mail Express [*American Express Co.*] ... AMEX
Airlie Beach [*Australia Airport symbol*] ... WSY
AirLifeLine (EA) ... ALL
Airlift (AABC) ... AL
Airlift [*International*] ... ALF
Airlift ... ALFT
Airlift ... ARLFT
Airlift and Training Division [*Air Force*] (MCD) ... ATD
Air-Lift Associates, Inc. [*ICAO designator*] (FAAC) ... WPK
Airlift Association (EA) ... AA
Airlift Center [*Air Force*] (MCD) ... ALCENT
Airlift Clearance Authority (AFM) ... ACA
Airlift Command Post (AFM) ... ACP
Airlift Communications Division [*Military*] ... ACD
Airlift Concepts and Requirements Agency ... ACRA
Airlift Contingency Battalion Landing Team (NVT) ... ACBLT
Airlift Contingency Forces [*Marine Corps*] (DOMA) ... ACF
Airlift Control Center (AFM) ... ALCC
Airlift Control Element (AFM) ... ALCE
Airlift Coordinating Office [*or Officer*] (AFIT) ... ALCO
Airlift Coordination Center [*Air Force*] (DOMA) ... ACC
Airlift Division [*Air Force*] ... ALD
Airlift Field Maintenance Section ... AFMS
Airlift Group [*Military*] ... ALG
Airlift Industrial Services Flight [*Military*] ... AISF
Airlift International, Inc. [*ICAO designator*] (FAAC) ... AIR
Airlift International, Inc. (IIA) ... ALI
Airlift International, Inc. [*ICAO designator*] ... RD
Airlift International, Inc. [*Air carrier designation symbol*] ... RDLX
Airlift Launch Control Officer [*Air Force*] (AFM) ... ALCO
Airlift Liaison Coordination Officer [*Air Force*] ... ALCO
Airlift Loading Model ... ALM
Air-Lift Management System [*Air Force*] (PDAA) ... ALMS
Airlift Mission Planning and Scheduling System [*Air Force*] (MCD) ... AMPSS
Airlift Operational Report ... ALOREP
Airlift Operations Directive (AFM) ... AOD
Airlift Operations School Library, Scott AFB, IL [*OCLC symbol*] (OCLC) ... AOS
Airlift Service Industrial Fund [*Military*] ... ASIF

Airlift Simulation Model	ASM
Airlift Summary Report [*Air Force*]	LIFSUM
Airlift Task Force [*Air Force*] (AFM)	ALTF
Airline	ARLN
Airline Administrative Message (DA)	AAM
Airline Aviation Academy, Inc. [*ICAO designator*] (FAAC)	ACD
Airline Cargo Services, Inc. [*British*] [*FAA designator*] (FAAC)	ACV
Airline Carriers of Goods	ACG
Airline Carriers of Passengers	ACP
Airline Charter Service	ACS
Airline Control Program Transaction Processing Facility [*IBM Corp.*] (NITA)	ACP/TF
Airline Control Program / Transaction Processing Facility [*Computer science*] (BTTJ)	ACP/TPF
Airline Credit Union Association (EA)	ACUA
Airline Economic Modeling System (HGAA)	AEMS
AirLine Employees Association, International (EA)	ALEA
Airline Feed System	AFS
Airline Flight Attendants Association [*Defunct*] (EA)	AFAA
Airline Ground Transportation Association [*Defunct*] (EA)	AGTA
Airline Group of International Federation of Operational Research Societies [*Denmark*] (MCD)	AGIFORS
Airline Industrial Relations Conference (EA)	AIR
Airline Interline Development	AID
Airline Link Control (HGAA)	ALC
Airline Medical Directors Association (EA)	AMDA
Airline Mutual Insurance [*International Air Transport Association*]	AMI
Airline of Adriatic [*Croatia*] [*ICAO designator*] (FAAC)	ADC
Airline of the Marshall Islands [*ICAO designator*] (FAAC)	MRS
Airline Operational Control Society [*Defunct*] (EA)	AOCS
Airline Operations Planning Model (NASA)	AOPM
Airline Operations Services, Inc. [*ICAO designator*] (FAAC)	XAO
Airline Operations Simulation Model (MCD)	AOSM
Airline Passengers Association of North America (EA)	APANA
Airline Passengers of America [*Defunct*] (EA)	AP/USA
Airline Public Relations Organization [*British*] (DBA)	APRO
Airline Request Communication System (DA)	ARCS
Airline Reservation System [*Aviation*] (ECII)	ARS
Airline Revenue (DA)	ARE
Airline Schedules and Interline Availability Study [*IATA*] (DS)	ASIAS
Airline Service Quality Performance [*FAA*] (TAG)	ASQP
Airline Services Association [*ARSA*] [*Absorbed by*] (EA)	ASA
Airline System Simulator	ALSS
Airline Tariff Analysis (DA)	ATA
Airline Tariff Publishing Co.	ATP
Airline Tariff Publishing Co. (IID)	ATPCO
Airline Traffic Association	ALTA
Airline Transport Pilot [*Certificate*] [*British*] (IEEE)	ATP
Airline Transport Pilot's Licence [*British*] (AIA)	ALTP
Airline Transport Pilot's Licence [*British*] (DBQ)	ATPL
Airline Transport Rating (IIA)	ATR
Airline Travel Clubs (EA)	ATC
Airline Users' Committee [*British*] (DI)	AUC
Airline-Like Maintenance (DNAB)	AIRLMAINT
Airlines Communications Administrative Council	ALCAC
Airlines Computer Tracing System [*Luggage retrieving system*]	ACTS
Airlines Control Program [*IBM Corp.*]	ACP
Airlines Deregulation Act [*1978*]	ADA
Airlines Electronic Engineering Committee	AEEC
Airlines Load Optimization Recording and Display System [*Airport passenger-moving sidewalk*]	AIRLORDS
Airlines of Hainan Province [*China*] [*ICAO designator*] (FAAC)	CHH
Airlines of Tasmania [*Australia ICAO designator*] (FAAC)	ATM
Airlines of Tasmania [*ICAO designator*] (AD)	IP
Airlines of Western Australia [*Australia ICAO designator*] (ICDA)	MV
Airlines Sports and Cultural Association (EA)	ASCA
Airlines Staff International Association (EAIO)	ASIA
Airlink Airlines (Pty) Ltd. [*South Africa ICAO designator*] (FAAC)	LNK
Airlink Luftverkehrsgesellschaft GmbH [*Austria ICAO designator*] (FAAC)	JAR
Airlis SA [*Spain ICAO designator*] (FAAC)	LIS
Airlock Adapter Plate (MCD)	AAP
Airlock/Extravehicle Mobility Unit [*NASA*] (MCD)	AL/EMU
Airlock Illumination Subassembly (MCD)	AIS
Airlock Module [*NASA*]	AM
Airlock Module and Multiple Docking Adapter (PDAA)	AM/MDA
Airlock Module Station [*NASA*] (MCD)	AMS
Airlock Multiple Docking Adapter [*NASA*] (MCD)	ALMDA
Airlock Outfitting (SSD)	AO
Airlock Signal Conditioning Electronics (MCD)	ASCE
Airlock Stowage Bag [*NASA*] (MCD)	ASB
Airlock Support Subsystem [*NASA*] (NASA)	ASS
Airlock Support System [*or Subsystem*] [*NASA*] (MCD)	ALSS
Airlock Systems Test [*NASA*] (MCD)	AST
Airlock Wall (MCD)	AW
Airluxor Ltda. [*Portugal ICAO designator*] (FAAC)	LXR
Airmail	AM
Airmail (FAAC)	ARML
Airmailgram	AMGM
Airman	A
Airman (AFM)	AMN
Airman [*Nonrated enlisted man*] [*Navy*]	AN
Airman [*British military*] (DMA)	ARMN
Airman	ARMN
Airman [*Air Force*]	E2
Airman, Aerographer's Mate, Striker [*Navy rating*]	AGAN

Airman, Air Controlman, Striker [*Navy rating*]	ACAN
Airman Apprentice [*Navy rating*]	AA
Airman Apprentice, Aerographer's Mate, Striker [*Navy rating*]	AGAA
Airman Apprentice, Air Controlman, Striker [*Navy rating*]	ACAA
Airman Apprentice, Aviation ASW [*Antisubmarine Warfare*] Operator, Striker [*Navy rating*]	AWAA
Airman Apprentice, Aviation ASW [*Antisubmarine Warfare*] Technician, Striker [*Navy rating*]	AXAA
Airman Apprentice, Aviation Boatswain's Mate, Striker [*Navy rating*]	ABAA
Airman Apprentice, Aviation Electrician, Striker [*Navy rating*]	AEAA
Airman Apprentice, Aviation Fire Control Technician, Striker [*Navy rating*]	AQAA
Airman Apprentice, Aviation Machinist's Mate, Reciprocating Engine Mechanic, Striker [*Navy rating*]	ADRAA
Airman Apprentice, Aviation Maintenance Administrationman, Striker [*Navy rating*]	AZAA
Airman Apprentice, Aviation Storekeeper [*Navy rating*]	AKAA
Airman Apprentice, Aviation Structural Mechanic, Striker [*Navy rating*]	AMAA
Airman Apprentice, Aviation Support Equipment Technician, Striker [*Navy rating*]	ASAA
Airman Apprentice (High School)	AA(HS)
Airman Apprentice, Jet Striker [*Navy rating*]	ADJAA
Airman Apprentice, Parachute Rigger, Striker [*Navy rating*]	PRAA
Airman Apprentice, Photographer's Mate, Striker [*Navy rating*]	PHAA
Airman Apprentice, Photographic Intelligenceman, Striker [*Navy rating*]	PTAA
Airman Apprentice, TRADEVMAN [*Training Devices Man*], Striker [*Navy rating*]	TDAA
Airman, Aviation ASW [*Antisubmarine Warfare*] Operator, Striker [*Navy rating*]	AWAN
Airman, Aviation ASW [*Antisubmarine Warfare*] Technician, Striker [*Navy rating*]	AXAN
Airman, Aviation Boatswain's Mate, Striker [*Navy rating*]	ABAN
Airman, Aviation Electrician, Striker [*Navy rating*]	AEAN
Airman, Aviation Electronics Technician [*Navy rating*]	ATAN
Airman, Aviation Fire Control Technician, Striker [*Navy rating*]	AQAN
Airman, Aviation Machinist's Mate, Reciprocating Engine Mechanic, Striker [*Navy rating*]	ADRAN
Airman, Aviation Maintenance Administrationman, Striker [*Navy rating*]	AZAN
Airman, Aviation Storekeeper [*Navy rating*]	AKAN
Airman, Aviation Structural Mechanic, Striker [*Navy rating*]	AMAN
Airman, Aviation Support Equipment Technician, Striker [*Navy rating*]	ASAN
Airman Basic	AB
Airman Classification Squadron [*Air Force*]	ACS
Airman Commissioning Program [*Air Force*] (AFM)	ACP
Airman Education and Commissioning Program	AECP
Airman Effectiveness Report [*Air Force*]	AER
Airman, First Class	A/1C
Airman, First Class (IIA)	AFC
Airman, First Class	E3
Airman (High School) (DNAB)	AN(HS)
Airman, Jet Striker [*Navy rating*]	ADJAN
Airman Memorial Foundation (EA)	AMF
Airman Military Record [*Air Force*]	AMR
Airman, Parachute Rigger, Striker [*Navy*]	PRAN
Airman Performance Report	APR
Airman Performance Report Review Board (AFM)	APRRB
Airman, Photographer's Mate, Striker [*Navy rating*]	PHAN
Airman, Photographic Intelligenceman, Striker [*Navy rating*]	PTAN
Airman Qualifying Examination	AQE
Airman Records [*Air Force*] (AFM)	AR
Airman Recruit	AR
Airman Recruit (High School) (DNAB)	AR(HS)
Airman, Second Class	A/2C
Airman, Third Class	A/3C
Airman, TRADEVMAN [*Training Devices Man*], Striker [*Navy rating*]	TDAN
Airman's Guide [*A publication*]	AIRGI
Airman's Information Manual [*FAA*]	AIM
Airman's Medal [*Military decoration*] (AFM)	AmnM
Airman's Meteorological Information [*FAA*] (TAG)	AIRMET
Airmanship Training Squadron [*Air Force*]	ATS
Airmark Aviation, Inc. [*ICAO designator*] (FAAC)	TRH
Air-Mass Transformation Experiment [*National Science Foundation/ Japan*]	AMTEX
Airmen Classification Battery [*Military tests*]	ACB
Airmen Proficiency Test	APT
Air-Mining Mission [*Military*]	AMM
Airmobile (AABC)	AMBL
Air-Moving Device [*Technical drawings*] (DAC)	AMD
AirNet Systems [*NASDAQ symbol*] (TTSB)	ANSY
AirNet Systems, Inc. [*Associated Press*] (SAG)	AirNetS
AirNet Systems,Inc. [*NASDAQ symbol*] (SAG)	ANSY
Air-Nitrogen Pressurization Control	ANPC
Air-Ocean Environmental Specialist (DNAB)	AOES
Air-Operated Plastic Valve	AOPV
Air-Operated Unit	AOU
Air-Operated Valve (NRCH)	AOV
Airpac Airlines, Inc. [*ICAO designator*] (FAAC)	APC
Air-Piloted Control Valve	APCV
Air-Piloted Valve	APV
Airplane (ABBR)	A
Airplane [*Freight*]	AIRPL
Airplane	AP
Airplane (KSC)	APL
Airplane Avionics (NASA)	AA
Airplane Avionics/AUTOLAND (NASA)	AA/AL

Airplane Condition Monitoring System [*Aviation*] .... ACMS
Airplane Configuration System .... ACS
Airplane Economic Design Evaluator [*Boeing Co.*] .... AEDE
Airplane Engine, Propeller, and Accessory Overhaul [*Navy*] .... AIRENGPROPACCOVERHAUL
Airplane Flight Manual [*Federal Aviation Administration*] .... AFM
Airplane, General (MCD) .... APG
Airplane Group (MCD) .... AG
Airplane Information Management System [*Honeywell, Inc.*] .... AIMS
Airplane Model List of America .... AMLA
Airplane Nose Down .... AND
Airplane Nose Up (NG) .... ANU
Airplane Operating Empty Weight (OA) .... AOEW
Airplane Pilot .... AP
Airplane Responsive Engine Selection (MCD) .... ARES
Airplane Single-Engine Land [*Aviation rating*] .... ASEL
Airplane Sizing and Mission Performance [*Computer program*] .... ASAMP
Airplanes, Inc. [*ICAO designator*] (FAAC) .... REZ
Airport .... A/P
Airport (VRA) .... airpt
Airport .... AP
Airport (AFM) .... APRT
Airport (AFIT) .... APT
Airport .... ARPRT
Airport .... ARPRT
Airport .... ARPT
Airport Acceptance Rate [*FAA*] (TAG) .... AAR
Airport Acceptance Rate [*Aviation*] (FAAC) .... AARTE
Airport Advisory Service [*FAA*] (TAG) .... AAS
Airport and Airspace Delay Model (PDAA) .... AADM
Airport and Airspace Simulation Model [*FAA*] (TAG) .... SIMMOD
Airport and Airway Improvement Act [*OST*] (TAG) .... AAIA
Airport and Airways (OICC) .... A/A
Airport and Airways Surveillance RADAR [*Air Force*] .... AASR
Airport Associations Coordinating Council [*Geneva Airport, Switzerland*] (EAIO) .... AACC
Airport Bird Detection Equipment .... ABDE
Airport Business Center, Inc. [*Minneapolis, MN*] [*Telecommunications*] (TSSD) .... ABCI
Airport Capacity Enhancement [*FAA*] (TAG) .... ACE
Airport Capital Improvement Program [*OST*] (TAG) .... ACIP
Airport Characteristics Data Bank [*International Civil Aviation Organization*] [*Information service or system*] (IID) .... ACDB
Airport Consultants Council (EA) .... ACC
Airport Control Station [*ITU designation*] (DEN) .... FAC
Airport Control Tower .... ACT
Airport Data Information System (DA) .... ADIS
Airport Data System [*FAA*] .... ADS
Airport Development Aid Program [*FAA*] .... ADAP
Airport Development Program .... ADP
Airport Directory [*FAA*] .... APD
Airport Engineering Data Sheet [*FAA*] (MCD) .... AEDS
Airport Facility Directory [*FAA*] (TAG) .... AFD
Airport Fire Officer (DA) .... AFO
Airport Ground Traffic Control [*Department of Transportation*] .... AGTC
Airport Ground Transportation Association (EA) .... AGTA
Airport Handling Agreements Sub-Committee [*IATA*] (DS) .... AHASC
Airport Handling Committee [*IATA*] (DS) .... AHC
Airport Handling Equipment Sub-Committee [*IATA*] (DS) .... AHESC
Airport Handling Manual [*IATA*] (DS) .... AHM
Airport Handling Procedures Sub-Committee [*IATA*] (DS) .... AHPSC
Airport Hangar [*New York*] [*Seismograph station code, US Geological Survey*] (SEIS) .... APH
Airport Hotel Directory [*National Association of Business Travel Agents*] [*A publication*] .... AHD
Airport Improvement Program [*FAA*] (TAG) .... AIP
Airport in Sight (FAAC) .... AIS
Airport Information Desk .... AID
Airport Information Retrieval System [*FAA*] .... AIRS
Airport Landing Equipment (MCD) .... ALE
Airport Layout Plan [*FAA*] (TAG) .... ALP
Airport Layout Plan (FAAC) .... ALP
Airport Lighting Equipment (NASA) .... ALE
Airport Lights (FAAC) .... APL
Airport Lights [*FAA*] (TAG) .... APL
Airport Mail Facility (AFM) .... AMF
Airport Management and Information Display System (DA) .... AMIDS
Airport Management Information System .... AMIS
Airport Manager (FAAC) .... AMGR
Airport Managers Association of South Dakota (SRA) .... AMASD
Airport Movement Area Safety System [*FAA*] (TAG) .... AMASS
Airport Movement RADAR (DA) .... AMR
Airport Network Flow Simulator (MCD) .... ANFS
Airport Network Simulation Model [*FAA*] (TAG) .... AIRNET
Airport Noise Abatement Plan (PDAA) .... ANAP
Airport Noise Evaluation Process (PDAA) .... ANEP
Airport of Entry (DA) .... AOE
Airport Operation Area (DA) .... AOA
Airport Operators Council [*Later, AOCI*] (EA) .... AOC
Airport Operators Council International (EA) .... AOCI
Airport RADAR Service Area [*Aeronautics*] .... ARSA
Airport Reference Point .... ARP
Airport Rescue and Fire Fighting Alarm Checked (FAAC) .... ARFFOK
Airport Reservation Function [*FAA*] (TAG) .... ARF
Airport Reservation Office [*FAA*] (TAG) .... ARO
Airport Reservations Office (FAAC) .... ARO
Airport Security Council (EA) .... ASC
Airport Surface Detection Equipment [*RADAR*] .... ASDE
Airport Surface Detection Equipment [*RADAR*] (IAA) .... ASE
Airport Surface Detection RADAR .... ASDR
Airport Surface Movement Equipment .... ASME
Airport Surface Surveillance RADAR (DA) .... ASSR
Airport Surface Traffic Automation [*FAA*] (TAG) .... ASTA
Airport Surface Traffic Control (OA) .... ASTC
Airport Surface Traffic RADAR Equipment (MCD) .... ASTRE
Airport Surface Traffic Simulator .... ASTS
Airport Surveillance RADAR (MSA) .... APSR
Airport Surveillance RADAR .... ASR
Airport Systems [*NASDAQ symbol*] (SAG) .... ASII
Airport Systems International, Inc. [*Associated Press*] (SAG) .... AirSys
Airport Systems Intl [*NASDAQ symbol*] (TTSB) .... ASII
Airport Traffic [*ICAO*] [*Information service or system United Nations*] (DUND) .... AT
Airport Traffic Area (MCD) .... ATA
Airport [*or Airway*] **Traffic Control** .... ATC
Airport Traffic Controller (IAA) .... APTC
Airport Trailing Vortex Warning System .... ATVWS
Airport Transportation .... AIRTRANS
Airport Vicinity Air Pollution .... AVAP
Airportable [*British military*] (DMA) .... APT
Airportable Lifting Equipment [*British military*] (PDAA) .... APLE
Airports [*Public-performance tariff class*] [*British*] .... ARP
Airports and Construction Services, Transport Canada [*Service des Aeroports et de la Construction, Transports Canada*] **Ottawa, Ontario** [*Library symbol National Library of Canada*] (NLC) .... OOTAC
Airports Association Council International [*Switzerland*] (EAIO) .... AACI
Airports Authority Group [*Transport Canada*] (DA) .... AAG
Airports Economic Panel [*ICAO*] (DA) .... AEP
Airports Field Office .... AFO
Airports National Network [*British Airports Authority*] (NITA) .... ANN
Airports Program Report (FAAC) .... APR
Airports Service [*of FAA*] .... AS
Airpower Research Institute [*Air University*] [*Research center*] (RCD) .... ARI
Air-Purifying Respirator (FFDE) .... APR
Air-Raid Defence [*British World War II*] .... ARD
Air-Rep [*FAA designator*] (FAAC) .... XPR
Air-Resistance Horsepower [*Automotive engineering*] .... HPAR
AIRS [*Aerometric Information Retrieval System*] **Facility Subsystem** [*Environmental Protection Agency*] (GFGA) .... AFS
AIRS [*Aerometric Information Retrieval System*] **Facility Users Group** [*Environmental Protection Agency*] (GFGA) .... AFUG
Airscoop .... AS
Air-Scooping Orbital Rocket (PDAA) .... A-SCOOR
Air-Sea Rescue .... ASR
Air-Sea Rescue Craft .... ASRC
Air-Sea Rescue Flight [*British military*] (DMA) .... ASRF
Air-Sea Rescue Service [*British military*] (DMA) .... ASRS
Airsearch Manufacturing Co., Los Angeles, CA [*Library symbol Library of Congress*] (LCLS) .... CLAi
AirSensors, Inc. [*NASDAQ symbol*] (NQ) .... ARSN
AirSensors Wrrt [*NASDAQ symbol*] (TTSB) .... ARSNW
Air-Service-Gabon [*ICAO designator*] (FAAC) .... AGB
Airshed Model Data-Handling System [*Environmental Protection Agency*] (GFGA) .... ASMDHS
Airship .... ASHP
Airship, Air-Sea Rescue [*Navy symbol*] .... ZNH
Airship Association [*British*] (EAIO) .... AA
Airship Association - US (EA) .... AA
Airship Experimental Center [*Navy*] .... AEC
Airship Group .... AIRSHIPGR
Airship Group [*Navy symbol*] .... ZPG
Airship Industries Ltd. [*British*] .... AI
Airship (Nonrigid) [*Navy symbol*] .... ZN
Airship Rigger .... AR
Airship Squadron .... AIRSHIPRON
Airship Tender [*Navy symbol Obsolete*] .... AZ
Airship, Utility [*Navy symbol*] .... ZNJ
Airship Utility Squadron [*Navy symbol*] .... ZUTRON
Airspace (IAA) .... AS
Airspace and Traffic Management [*ICAO*] (DA) .... ATM
Airspace and Traffic Management Center (DA) .... ATMC
Airspace Control Authority [*Air Force*] (DOMA) .... ACA
Airspace Control Center (MCD) .... ACC
Airspace Control Command [*South Africa*] [*ICAO location identifier*] (ICLI) .... FAAC
Airspace Control [*or Coordination*] **Element** [*Army*] .... ACE
Airspace Coordination Area (MCD) .... ACA
Airspace Coordination Center [*NATO*] (DOMA) .... ACC
Airspace Flight Inspection Pilot (FAAC) .... ASIP
Airspace Management (DA) .... ASM
Airspace Management (DA) .... ASMT
Airspace Management and Control (MCD) .... AMC
Airspace Management Center (MCD) .... AMC
Airspace Management Element (MCD) .... AME
Airspace Management Element Liaison Officer .... AME LNO
Airspace Management Liaison Section (MCD) .... AMLS
Air-Space Multiple-Twin (IAA) .... ASMT
Airspace Reservation Unit [*Canada*] (FAAC) .... ARU
Airspace Subcommittee [*ACC*] .... ASP
Airspace Surveillance Station .... ASS
Airspace Warning (DNAB) .... AW
Airspeed .... AS

Airspeed	ASP
Airspeed and Altitude Computer Set (CAAL)	AACS
Airspeed and Direction Sensor (PDAA)	AADS
Airspeed Aviation, Inc. [Canada ICAO designator] (FAAC)	SPD
Airspeed Indicator (MSA)	AI
Airspeed Indicator	ASI
Airspeed Indicator Reading	ASIR
Airspeed Mach Indicator (MCD)	AMI
Air-Spray 1967 Ltd. [Canada ICAO designator] (FAAC)	ASB
Air-Start Diesel Engine (DNAB)	AD
Airstream Direction Detector (PDAA)	ADD
Airstream Direction Sensing Unit (MCD)	ADSU
Air-Supported Threat [Army]	AST
Air-Supported Threat Defense [Army] (AABC)	ASTD
Air-Supported Threat Defense System [Army]	ASTDS
Airtaxi Bedarfsluftverkehrsges GmbH [Austria ICAO designator] (FAAC)	JOK
Airtaxi Wings AG [Switzerland ICAO designator] (FAAC)	AWG
Airtight [Technical drawings]	AT
Airtight Containers [Freight]	AT C
Air-to-Air [NASA]	AA
Air-to-Air	ATA
Air-to-Air Aftercooling	AAA
Air-to-Air Aftercooling System [Pronounced "attack"]	ATAAC
Air-to-Air Armament Mission Analyses [Air Force] (MCD)	AAAMA
Air-to-Air Combat Environment (DOMA)	AACE
Air-to-Air Guided Weapons (NATG)	AAGW
Air-to-Air Gunnery Assessment (MCD)	ATAGAS
Air-to-Air Gunnery Range [Army]	AAGR
Air-to-Air Identification [Air Force]	AAI
Air-to-Air Identification Control Panel [Air Force] (MCD)	AAICP
Air-to-Air Identification Friend or Foe [Air Force] (MCD)	AAIFF
Air-to-Air Intercept (MCD)	AAI
Air-to-Air Interrogation (MCD)	AAI
Air-to-Air Missile [Army]	AAM
Air-to-Air Missile (RDA)	ATAM
Air-to-Air Missile Guidance Element	AAMGE
Air-to-Air Missile Weapons System Flight Report (NG)	AAMREP
Air-to-Air Recovery [Air Force] (AFM)	ATAR
Air-to-Air Refueling (MCD)	AAR
Air-to-Air Refueling Squadron	AARS
Air-to-Air Refuelling Area (DA)	AARA
Air-to-Air Stinger (MCD)	ATAS
Air-to-Air Visual Recognition [Aviation]	ATAR
Air-to-Boil Temperature [Mechanical engineering]	ATB
Air-to-Cloth [Air pollution control] (FFDE)	A/C
Air-to-Fuel Ratio (MCD)	AF
Air-to-Ground [FAA] (TAG)	A/G
Air-to-Ground [Photos, missiles, etc.]	AG
Air-to-Ground [Photos, missiles, etc.]	ATG
Air-to-Ground Acquisition and Tracking Equipment	AGATE
Air-to-Ground Engagement System (MCD)	AGES
Air-to-Ground Engagement System - Air Defense (DWSG)	AGES/AD
Air-to-Ground Gunnery (MCD)	ATOG
Air-to-Ground Gunnery Range	AGGR
Air-to-Ground Liaison Code [Air Force]	AGLC
Air-to-Ground Missile	AGM
Air-to-Ground Missile System (RDA)	AGMS
Air-to-Ground Moving Target Indicator	AGMTI
Air-to-Ground Ranging	AGR
Air-to-Ground Rocket (MCD)	AGR
Air-to-Ground Standoff Weapon (MCD)	AGSW
Air-to-Ground Voice System [or Subsystem] (MCD)	AGVS
Air-to-Ground-to-Air	AGA
Air-to-Ship (DNAB)	ATS
Air-to-Ship Launched Ballistic Missile [Navy] (IAA)	ASLBM
Air-to-Surface [Missiles] (NATG)	AS
Air-to-Surface [Missiles] (MCD)	ATS
Air-to-Surface Ballistic Missile	ASBM
Air-to-Surface Missile	ASM
Air-to-Surface Missile Development (MCD)	ASMD
Air-to-Surface Weapon	ASW
AirTouch Communications [Associated Press] (SAG)	AirTch
AirTouch Communications [NYSE symbol] (TTSB)	ATI
AirTouch Communications Co. [Formerly, PacTel Corp.] [Associated Press] (SAG)	AirTouch
Airtouch Communications Co. [Formerly, PacTel Corp.] [NYSE symbol] (SAG)	ATI
Air-to-Umbilical Junction Box	AUJ
Air-to-Underwater Missile [Air Force]	AUM
Air-to-Underwater Missile - Nuclear [Air Force] (IAA)	AUMN
Airtours International Airways Ltd. [British ICAO designator] (FAAC)	AIH
Air-to-Vessel (IAA)	ATV
Air-to-Water	AW
AirTran Airways, Inc. [FAA designator] (FAAC)	MTE
AirTran Corp. [NASDAQ symbol] (SPSG)	ATCC
Airung AEP [Ukraine] [FAA designator] (FAAC)	UNG
Airvallee SpA-Services Aeriens de Val d'Aoste [Italy ICAO designator] (FAAC)	RVL
AirVantage, Inc. [ICAO designator] (FAAC)	AVV
Airventure, BVBD [Belgium] [FAA designator] (FAAC)	RVE
Air-Via [Bulgaria] [ICAO designator] (FAAC)	VIM
Airvias SA Linhas Aereas [Brazil] [FAA designator] (FAAC)	AIV
Airvolga [Former USSR] [FAA designator] (FAAC)	VOG
Airwave Transport, Inc. [Canada ICAO designator] (FAAC)	AWV
Airway	ARWY

Airway	AWY
Airway (IAA)	AY
Airway, Breathing, and Circulation [Medicine] (DAVI)	ABC
Airway, Breathing, Circulation, Cervical Spine, Consciousness Level [Medicine] (MEDA)	ABC & C & C
Airway, Breathing, Circulation, Intravenous Crystalloid [Medicine] (DMAA)	ABCIC
Airway Centre, AES Data Ltd., Mississauga, Ontario [Library symbol National Library of Canada] (NLC)	OMADA
Airway Conductance [Medicine] (DAVI)	Ga
Airway Conductance [The reciprocal of airway resistance] [Medicine] (DAVI)	GAW
Airway Facilities [FAA] (TAG)	AF
Airway Opened, Breathing Restored, and Circulation Restored [Cardiopulmonary resuscitation] [Medicine]	ABC
Airway Opened, Breathing Restored, Circulation Restored, and Definitive Therapy [Cardiopulmonary resuscitation] [Medicine]	ABCD
Airway Operations Specialist [Airport]	AOSAP
Airway Planning Standard [FAA] (TAG)	APS
Airway Pressure [Pulmonary ventilation]	AP
Airway Pressure [Pulmonary ventilation]	AWP
Airway Radio Station (IAA)	ARSTN
Airway Reactivity Index [Physiology]	ARI
Airway Resistance [Medicine] (MAE)	Ra
Airway Resistance [Medicine]	RAW
Airway Traffic Controller (IAA)	AWTC
Airways [Medicine] (DAVI)	aw
Airways	AW
Airways and Air Communications Service [Air Force]	AACS
Airways and Air Communications Service Manual	AACSM
Airways and Air Communications Service Regulation [Air Force] (IAA)	AACSR
Airways and Air Communications Service Squadron [Air Force] (IAA)	AACSRON
Airways and Air Communications Service Wing [Air Force] (IAA)	AACSWG
Airways Communication Station (NATG)	ACS
Airways Communications System	AIRCOM
Airways Corp. [NASDAQ symbol] (SAG)	AAIR
Airways Corp. [Associated Press] (SAG)	Airways
Airways Corp. of New Zealand Ltd. [ICAO designator] (FAAC)	XFX
Airways Data Collection and Distribution [Computer science]	ADCAD
Airways Engineer	AENG
Airways Engineering Society [Defunct] (EA)	AES
Airways Environmental RADAR Information System (IEEE)	AERIS
Airways Facilities Sector Field Office (FAAC)	AFSFO
Airways Facilities Sector Field Office Plus Unit (FAAC)	AFSFOU
Airways Facilities Sector Office (FAAC)	AFSO
Airways Failities Sector (FAAC)	AFS
Airways Flight Inspector	AFINS
Airways Inspector	AI
Airways Integrating and Monitoring System (MCD)	AIMS
Airways International [ICAO designator] (AD)	HO
Airways International, Inc. [ICAO designator] (FAAC)	AWB
Airways Modernization Board [Functions transferred to FAA]	AMB
Airways Operations Evaluation Center	AOEC
Airways Operations Specialist (SAA)	AOS
Airways Operations Specialist	AOSS
Airways Operations Specialist (General)	AOSG
Airways Operations Supervisor	AOSPV
Airways Technical District Office [FAA]	ATDO
Airways Technical District Supervisor [FAA]	ATDS
Airways Technical Field Office [FAA]	ATFO
Airwolf Recovery Team [An association Defunct] (EA)	ART
Airwoman	Awmn
Airwork Ltd. [British]	AW
Airwork Ltd. [British ICAO designator] (FAAC)	HRN
Airwork (New Zealand) Ltd. [ICAO designator] (FAAC)	PST
Airwork Service Training [British ICAO designator] (FAAC)	AWK
Air-World Co.	AW
Airworthiness	AIR
Airworthiness and Flight Characteristics (MCD)	AFC
Airworthiness Certificate (MCD)	AC
Airworthiness Circular (DA)	AC
Airworthiness Committee	AC
Airworthiness Directive	AD
Airworthiness Library, Atlantic Region, Transport Canada [Bibliotheque de la Navigabilite Aerienne, Region de l'Atlantique, Transports Canada], Moncton, New Brunswick [Library symbol National Library of Canada] (NLC)	NBMOTA
Airworthiness Library, Central Region, Transport Canada [Bibliotheque de la Navigabilite Aerienne, Region Centrale, Transports Canada], Winnipeg, Manitoba [Library symbol National Library of Canada] (NLC)	MWTA
Airworthiness Library, Ontario Region, Transport Canada [Bibliotheque de la Navigabilite Aerienne, Region de l'Ontario, Transports Canada], Willowdale, Ontario [Library symbol National Library of Canada] (NLC)	OWTAI
Airworthiness Library, Transport Canada [Bibliotheque de la Navigabilite Aerienne, Transports Canada], Ottawa, Ontario [Library symbol National Library of Canada] (NLC)	OOTA
Airworthiness Qualification Plan	AQP
Airworthiness Qualification Program	AQL
Airworthiness Qualification Program (MCD)	AQP
Airworthiness Qualification Specification	AQS
Airworthiness Qualification Test Directorate [Military] (RDA)	AQTD
Airworthiness Requirements Board [British] (AIA)	ARB
Airworthiness Requirements Committee	ARC
Airworthiness Standards Evaluation Committee [FAA]	ASEC

Airworthiness Substantiation Document [*Army*] (RDA) .... ASD
Airworthy (ADA) .... A/W
Airy Township Public Library, Whitney, Ontario [*Library symbol National Library of Canada*] (NLC) .... OWAIT
AIS Resources Ltd. [*Vancouver Stock Exchange symbol*] .... AIS
Aishalton [*Guyana*] [*ICAO location identifier*] (ICLI) .... SYAH
Aisin Warner [*Automotive industry supplier*] [*Japan*] .... AW
Aitape [*Papua New Guinea*] [*Airport symbol*] (OAG) .... ATP
Aitken Jr.-Sr. High School Media Center, Aitken, MN [*Library symbol*] [*Library of Congress*] (LCLS) .... MnAJ
Aitken Public Library, Aitken, MN [*Library symbol*] [*Library of Congress*] (LCLS) .... MnA
Aitkin, MN [*Location identifier FAA*] (FAAL) .... AIT
Aitkin, MN [*FM radio station call letters*] .... KEZZ
Aitkin, MN [*AM radio station call letters*] .... KKIN
Aitkin, MN [*FM radio station call letters*] (RBYB) .... KKIN-FM
Aitutaki [*Cook Islands*] [*Airport symbol*] (OAG) .... AIT
Aitutaki [*Cook Islands*] [*ICAO location identifier*] (ICLI) .... NCAI
Aix-En-Provence [*France ICAO location identifier*] (ICLI) .... LFMB
Aix-En-Provence [*France ICAO location identifier*] (ICLI) .... LFMM
Aix-Les-Milles [*France ICAO location identifier*] (ICLI) .... LFMA
Aiyar's Company Cases [*India*] [*A publication*] (DLA) .... Aiyar
Aiyar's Company Cases [*India*] [*A publication*] (DLA) .... Aiyar CC
Aiyar's Leading Privy Council Cases [*India*] [*A publication*] (DLA) .... Aiyar LPC
Aiyar's Unreported Decisions [*India*] [*A publication*] (DLA) .... Aiyar Unrep D
Aiyura [*Papua New Guinea*] [*Airport symbol Obsolete*] (OAG) .... AYU
Aizwal [*India*] [*ICAO location identifier*] (ICLI) .... VEAZ
AJ Services Ltd. [*British ICAO designator*] (FAAC) .... AJA
Ajaccio [*Corsica*] [*Airport symbol*] (OAG) .... AJA
Ajaccio/Campo Dell'Oro, Corse [*France ICAO location identifier*] (ICLI) .... LFKJ
Ajax [*of Sophocles*] [*Classical studies*] (OCD) .... Aj
Ajax Magnethermic (IIA) .... AJX
Ajax, ON [*FM radio station call letters*] (RBYB) .... CJKX
Ajax Public Library, Ajax, ON, Canada [*Library symbol Library of Congress*] (LCLS) .... CaOAj
Ajax Public Library, Ontario [*Library symbol National Library of Canada*] (NLC) .... OAJ
Ajax Resources Ltd. [*Vancouver Stock Exchange symbol*] .... AJR
Ajay Resources, Inc. [*Vancouver Stock Exchange symbol*] .... AJY
Ajay Sports [*NASDAQ symbol*] (TTSB) .... AJAY
Ajay Sports 10% Cv Pfd [*NASDAQ symbol*] (TTSB) .... AJAYP
Ajay Sports, Inc. [*NASDAQ symbol*] (NQ) .... AJAY
Ajay Sports Wrrt [*NASDAQ symbol*] (TTSB) .... AJAYW
Ajiro [*Japan*] [*Seismograph station code, US Geological Survey*] (SEIS) .... AJI
AJL Peps Trust [*Associated Press*] (SAG) .... AJL
AJL Peps Trust [*NYSE symbol*] (SAG) .... AJP
Ajmer-Merwara Law Journal [*India*] [*A publication*] (DLA) .... Ajmer-Merwara LJ
Ajmer-Merwara Law Journal [*India*] [*A publication*] (DLA) .... AMLJ
Ajo, AZ [*FM radio station call letters*] .... KTTZ
Ajoutez [*Add*] [*Music*] .... AJ
AJR: American Journalism Review [*A publication*] (BRI) .... AJR
AJS [*Albert John Stevens*] **and Matchless Owners Club** [*Mount Sorrel, Leicestershire, England*] (EAIO) .... AJSMOC
Ajstra Resources Corp. [*Vancouver Stock Exchange symbol*] .... ARC
AJT Air International [*Russian Federation*] [*ICAO designator*] (FAAC) .... TRJ
Ajustable (ABBR) .... ADJSTB
AK Steel Hldg 7%'SAILS' [*NYSE symbol*] (TTSB) .... AKSPr
AK Steel Holding [*NYSE symbol*] (TTSB) .... AKS
AK Steel Holding Corp. [*Associated Press*] (SAG) .... AK Steel
AK Steel Holding Corp. [*Associated Press*] (SAG) .... AK Stl
AK Steel Holding Corp. [*NYSE symbol*] (SAG) .... AKS
Akademie [*Academy*] [*German*] (BJA) .... Ak
Akademiet for de Tekniska Videnskaber [*Academy of Technical Sciences*] [*Denmark*] .... ATV
Akademiia Nauk Belorusskaia SSR, Fundamemtalnaia Biblioteka Imeni Ia. Kolasa [*Academy of Sciences of the Belorussian SSR, J. Kolasa Fundamental Library*], Minsk, Belorussian SSR, Soviet Union [*Library symbol Library of Congress*] (LCLS) .... RuBeMiA
Akademiia Nauk Kirgizskoi SSR, Tsentralnaia Nauchaia Biblioteka [*Academy of Sciences of the Kirghiz SSR, Central Scientific Library*], Frunze, Kirghiz SSR,Soviet Union [*Library symbol Library of Congress*] (LCLS) .... RuKiFrA
Akademiia Nauk Moldavskoi SSR, Tsentralnaia Nauchnaia Biblioteka [*Academy of Sciences of the Moldavian SSR, Central Scientific Library*], Kishivev, Moldavian SSR, Soviet Union [*Library symbol Library of Congress*] (LCLS) .... RuMoKisA
Akademiia Nauk SSSR [*Academy of Sciences of the USSR*], Leningrad, Soviet Union [*Library symbol Library of Congress*] (LCLS) .... RuLA
Akademiia Nauk Turkmenskoi SSR, Tsentralnaia Nauchnaia Biblioteka [*Academy ofSciences of Turkmen SSR, Central Scientific Library*], Ashkhabad, Turkmen, SS R, Soviet Union [*Library symbol Library of Congress*] (LCLS) .... RuTuAsA
Akademio Internacia de la Sciencoj [*International Academy of Sciences - IAS*] (EAIO) .... AIS
Akademisches Computer Netz [*Academic Computer Network*] [*Computer science*] [*Austria*] (TNIG) .... ACONet
Akaflieg Muenchen Mitsubishi Heavy Industries [*Germany Japan ICAO aircraft manufacturer identifier*] (ICAO) .... MU
Akaitcho Yellowknife Gold Mines Ltd. [*Toronto Stock Exchange symbol*] .... AKY
Akatsi [*Ghana*] [*ICAO location identifier*] (ICLI) .... DGAP
Akciova Spolecnost [*Joint-Stock Company*] .... as
Akdeniz Hava Tasimacilik TIC, Ve San A.S. [*Turkey*] [*FAA designator*] (FAAC) .... AKD
Akeley Elementary School, Akeley, MN [*Library symbol*] [*Library of Congress*] (LCLS) .... MnAkE
Akeley High School, Akeley, MN [*Library symbol*] [*Library of Congress*] (LCLS) .... MnAkH
Akeno [*Japan ICAO location identifier*] (ICLI) .... RJOE
Akerman, Senterfitt, Eidson, Law Library, Orlando, FL [*Library symbol*] [*Library of Congress*] (LCLS) .... FOAS
Akers Medical Technology Ltd. [*Vancouver Stock Exchange symbol*] .... AKE
Akersberga [*Sweden ICAO location identifier*] (ICLI) .... ESHR
Aketi [*Zaire*] [*ICAO location identifier*] (ICLI) .... FZKN
Akhal [*Turkmenistan*] [*ICAO designator*] (FAAC) .... AKH
Akhalkalaki [*Former USSR Seismograph station code, US Geological Survey Closed*] (SEIS) .... AKH
Akhal-Teke Registry of America (EA) .... A-TRA
Akhiok [*Alaska*] [*Airport symbol*] (OAG) .... AKK
Akhisar [*Turkey*] [*Airport symbol*] (AD) .... AKH
Akhisar [*Turkey ICAO location identifier*] (ICLI) .... LTBT
Akhmos-I [*Belarus*] [*FAA designator*] (FAAC) .... AKS
Akiachak [*Alaska*] [*Airport symbol*] (OAG) .... KKI
Akiak [*Alaska*] [*Airport symbol*] (OAG) .... AKI
Akieni [*Gabon*] [*Airport symbol*] (OAG) .... AKE
Akieni [*Gabon*] [*ICAO location identifier*] (ICLI) .... FOGA
Akiko-Lori Gold [*Vancouver Stock Exchange symbol*] .... AKI
Akim Oda [*Ghana*] [*ICAO location identifier*] (ICLI) .... DGKA
Akimuga [*Indonesia*] [*ICAO location identifier*] (ICLI) .... WAKA
Akinetic .... A
Akita [*Japan*] [*Seismograph station code, US Geological Survey*] (SEIS) .... AKI
Akita [*Japan*] [*Airport symbol*] (OAG) .... AXT
Akita [*Japan ICAO location identifier*] (ICLI) .... RJSK
Akita Club of America (EA) .... ACA
Akjoujt [*Mauritania*] [*Airport symbol*] (AD) .... AJJ
Akjoujt [*Mauritania*] [*ICAO location identifier*] (ICLI) .... GQNJ
Akkadian [*MARC language code Library of Congress*] (LCCP) .... akk
Akkadian (BJA) .... Akkad
Akkadische Fremdwoerter als Beweis fuer Babylonischen Kultureinfluss [*A publication*] (BJA) .... AFw
Akkadische Goetterepitheta [*A publication*] (BJA) .... AGe
Akkadische Keilschrifttexte [*A publication*] (BJA) .... ASKT
Akkadisches Handwoerterbuch [*A publication*] (BJA) .... AHw
Aklak Air Ltd. [*Canada ICAO designator*] (FAAC) .... AKK
Aklavik [*Canada*] [*Airport symbol*] (OAG) .... LAK
Akobo [*Sudan*] [*ICAO location identifier*] (ICLI) .... HSAK
Akola [*India*] [*ICAO location identifier*] (ICLI) .... VAAK
Akorn, Inc. [*Associated Press*] (SAG) .... Akorn
Akorn, Inc. [*NASDAQ symbol*] (NQ) .... AKRN
Akro Agate Art Association [*Defunct*] (EA) .... AAAA
Akron [*Ohio*] [*ICAO location identifier*] (ICLI) .... KAKR
[*The*] **Akron & Barberton Belt Railroad Co.** [*AAR code*] .... ABB
Akron/Canton [*Ohio*] [*Airport symbol*] .... CAK
[*The*] **Akron, Canton & Youngstown Railroad Co.** (IIA) .... AC & Y
[*The*] **Akron, Canton & Youngstown Railroad Co.** [*AAR code*] .... ACY
Akron Carnegie Public Library, Akron, IN [*Library symbol Library of Congress*] (LCLS) .... InAk
Akron Child Guidance Center, Akron, OH [*Library symbol Library of Congress*] (LCLS) .... OAkCh
Akron, CO [*Location identifier FAA*] (FAAL) .... AKO
Akron, OH [*Location identifier FAA*] (FAAL) .... ACO
Akron, OH [*Location identifier FAA*] (FAAL) .... AKR
Akron, OH [*Location identifier FAA*] (FAAL) .... GGZ
Akron, OH [*Location identifier FAA*] (FAAL) .... RGO
Akron, OH [*Television station call letters*] .... WAKC
Akron, OH [*AM radio station call letters*] .... WAKR
Akron, OH [*FM radio station call letters*] .... WAPS
Akron, OH [*Television station call letters*] .... WBNX
Akron, OH [*Television station call letters*] .... WEAO
Akron, OH [*AM radio station call letters*] .... WHLO
Akron, OH [*FM radio station call letters*] .... WKDD
Akron, OH [*FM radio station call letters*] .... WONE
Akron, OH [*AM radio station call letters*] .... WTOU
Akron, OH [*FM radio station call letters*] .... WZIP
Akron Public Library, Akron, CO [*Library symbol Library of Congress*] (LCLS) .... CoAk
Akron Public Library, Akron, OH [*Library symbol Library of Congress*] (LCLS) .... OAk
Akron Register-Tribune, Akron, IA [*Library symbol Library of Congress*] (LCLS) .... IaAkRT
Akron University College of Engineering [*Ohio*] .... AUE
Akron-Canton, OH [*Location identifier FAA*] (FAAL) .... HJM
Akron-Summit County Public Library, Akron, OH [*OCLC symbol*] (OCLC) .... APL
Akrotiri [*Cyprus*] [*ICAO location identifier*] (ICLI) .... LCRA
Aksjeselskap [*Joint-Stock Company*] [*Norway*] (GPO) .... A/S
Aksu [*China*] [*Airport symbol*] (OAG) .... AKU
Aksu [*China*] [*ICAO location identifier*] (ICLI) .... ZWAK
Aksys Ltd. [*NASDAQ symbol*] (SAG) .... AKSY
Aksys Ltd. [*Associated Press*] (SAG) .... AksysL
AKsys Ltd [*NASDAQ symbol*] (TTSB) .... AKSYS
Aktiebolag [*or Aktiebolaget*] [*Joint-Stock Company*] [*Sweden*] .... AB
Aktiebolaget Aero Transport [*Swedish airline*] .... ABA
Aktiebolaget Atomenergi [*Swedish nuclear development company*] .... ABA
Aktiebolaget Atomenergi Computer-Based User-Oriented Service .... ABACUS
Aktiekomitee Zuidelyk Afrika [*Belgium*] .... AKZA
Aktiengesellschaft [*Corporation*] [*German*] .... AG
Aktiengesellschaft fuer Anilinfabrikaten [*German photographic manufacturer*] .... AGFA
Aktiengesetz [*Law governing public companies*] [*German*] (ILCA) .... AktG
Aktieselskab [*Joint-Stock Company*] [*Sweden*] .... A/S

Aktion Demokratischer Fortschritt [*Action for Democratic Progress*] [*Germany*] (PPE) ... ADF
Aktion Soziale Gemeinschaft, die Partei der Sozialversicherten Arbeitnehmer und Rentner [*Social Community Action (Party of Socially Insured Employees and Pensioners)*] [*Germany Political party*] (PPW) ... ASG
Aktionsgemeinschaft Unabhaengiger Deutscher [*Action Group of Independent Germans*] [*Germany Political party*] (PPE) ... AUD
Aktionsgemeinschaft Vierte Partei [*Fourth Party Action Group*] [*Germany Political party*] (PPW) ... AVP
Aktiv [*Active*] [*German*] ... akt
Aktiv Hinten Kinematik [*Active Rear-Axle Movement*] [*German*] ... AHK
Aktyubinsk [*Former USSR ICAO location identifier*] (ICLI) ... UATT
Akulik, AK [*Location identifier FAA*] (FAAL) ... AKU
Akulivik [*Canada*] [*Airport symbol*] (OAG) ... AKV
Akureyri [*Iceland*] [*Airport symbol*] (OAG) ... AEY
Akureyri [*Iceland*] [*Seismograph station code, US Geological Survey*] (SEIS) ... AKU
Akureyri [*Iceland*] [*ICAO location identifier*] (ICLI) ... BIAR
Akuse [*Ghana*] [*ICAO location identifier*] (ICLI) ... DGAK
Akutan [*Alaska*] [*Airport symbol*] (OAG) ... KQA
Akutan, AK [*Location identifier FAA*] (FAAL) ... KQA
Akwesasne, ON [*FM radio station call letters*] ... CKON
Akyab [*Burma*] [*Airport symbol*] (AD) ... AKY
Akyab [*Myanmar*] [*Airport symbol*] (OAG) ... AKY
Akzo Nobel N.V. ADS [*NASDAQ symbol*] (TTSB) ... AKZOY
Akzo NV [*NASDAQ symbol*] (NQ) ... AKZO
Akzo NV [*Associated Press*] (SAG) ... Akzo
Al Ain [*United Arab Emirates*] [*ICAO location identifier*] (ICLI) ... OMAL
Al Akhawayn University, Ifrane [*Morocco*] ... AUI
Al Arish [*Egypt*] [*Airport symbol*] (OAG) ... AAC
Al Bahrain Arab African Bank ... AL-BAAB
Al Bayda [*Libya*] [*Airport symbol*] (AD) ... LAQ
Al Fine [*To the End*] [*Music*] ... AF
Al Ghaydah [*Aden*] [*Airport symbol*] (AD) ... AAY
Al Hamra [*United Arab Emirates*] [*ICAO location identifier*] (ICLI) ... OMAH
Al Hoceima [*Morocco*] [*Airport symbol*] (OAG) ... AHU
Al Hoceima/Cote Du Rif [*Morocco*] [*ICAO location identifier*] (ICLI) ... GMTA
AL Laboratories, Inc. [*NYSE symbol*] (SPSG) ... BMD
AL Pharmaceuticals, Inc. [*Later, AL Labs*] [*NYSE symbol*] (SAG) ... ALO
AL Pharmaceuticals, Inc. [*Associated Press*] (SAG) ... Alpharma
Al Pharmaceuticals, Inc. [*Associated Press*] (SAG) ... Alphm
Al Segno [*At the Sign*] [*Music*] ... AL SEG
Al Segno [*At the Sign*] [*Music*] (ROG) ... AS
Al Sigl Center Library, Rochester, NY [*OCLC symbol*] (OCLC) ... VQA
Ala Abaete Linhas Aereas, SA [*Brazil*] [*FAA designator*] (FAAC) ... ABJ
Ala Pwr Cap 17.375% Tr Pfd Sec [*NYSE symbol*] (TTSB) ... ALPPrQ
Alabama [*Postal code*] ... AL
Alabama ... ALA
Alabama [*MARC country of publication code Library of Congress*] (LCCP) ... alu
Alabama [*MARC geographic area code Library of Congress*] (LCCP) ... n-us-al
Alabama Acupuncture Council (SRA) ... AAC
Alabama Administrative Monthly [*A publication*] (AAGC) ... Ala Admin Month
Alabama Aggregates Association (SRA) ... AAA
Alabama Agricultural and Mechanical University (GAGS) ... Ala A&M U
Alabama Agricultural and Mechanical University, Normal, AL [*Library symbol Library of Congress*] (LCLS) ... ANA
Alabama Alliance of Business and Industry (SRA) ... AABI
Alabama Appellate Court (DLA) ... Ala A
Alabama Appellate Court Reports [*A publication*] (DLA) ... Ala App
Alabama Army Ammunition Plant (AABC) ... ALAAP
Alabama Asphalt Pavement Association (SRA) ... AAPA
Alabama Association of Credit Executives (SRA) ... AACE
Alabama Association of Health Maintenance Organizations (SRA) ... AAHMO
Alabama Association of Independent Colleges and Universities (SRA) ... AAICU
Alabama Association of Realtors (SRA) ... AAR
Alabama Association of School Boards (SRA) ... AASB
Alabama Automated Clearinghouse Association (SRA) ... ALACHA
Alabama Bankers Association (SRA) ... ABA
Alabama Basic Competency Test (EDAC) ... ABCT
Alabama Cable Telecommunications Association (SRA) ... ACTA
Alabama Cattlemen's Association (SRA) ... ACA
Alabama Central R. R. [*AAR code*] ... ALC
Alabama Chiropractic Association (SRA) ... ASCA
Alabama Christian School of Religion, Montgomery, AL [*Library symbol*] [*Library of Congress*] (LCLS) ... AMAC
Alabama Civil Appeals [*A publication*] (DLA) ... Ala Civ App
Alabama Coal Association (SRA) ... ACA
Alabama Code [*A publication*] (AAGC) ... Ala Code
Alabama Concrete Industries Association (SRA) ... ACIA
Alabama Constitution [*A publication*] (DLA) ... Ala Const
Alabama Council for School Administration and Supervision (SRA) ... ACSAS
Alabama Council of Association Executives (SRA) ... ACAE
Alabama Counseling Association (SRA) ... ALCA
Alabama Court of Appeals (DLA) ... Ala App
Alabama Credit Union League (SRA) ... ACUL
Alabama Criminal Appeals [*A publication*] (DLA) ... Ala Cr App
Alabama Crop Improvement Association (SRA) ... ACIA
Alabama Dental Association (SRA) ... ALDA
Alabama Department of Archives and History, Montgomery, AL [*OCLC symbol*] (OCLC) ... AAR
Alabama Department of Archives and History, Montgomery, AL [*Library symbol Library of Congress*] (LCLS) ... A-Ar
Alabama Department of Archives and History, State Documents, Montgomery, AL [*OCLC symbol*] (OCLC) ... AAS
Alabama District Attorneys Association (SRA) ... ADAA
Alabama Education Association (SRA) ... AEA
Alabama Fan Club (EA) ... AFC
Alabama Farm and Power Equipment Dealers Association (SRA) ... AFPEDA
Alabama Farmers Federation (SRA) ... AFF
Alabama Financial Services Association (SRA) ... AFSA
Alabama Food and Agriculture Council (SRA) ... AFAC
Alabama Forest Owners' Association (SRA) ... AFOA
Alabama Forestry Association (SRA) ... AFA
Alabama Funeral Directors Association (SRA) ... AFDA
[*The*] **Alabama Great Southern Railroad Co.** [*AAR code*] ... AGS
Alabama High School Graduation Examination (EDAC) ... AHSGE
Alabama Home Builders Association (SRA) ... AHBA
Alabama Hospital Association (SRA) ... AlaHA
Alabama Hospitality Association (SRA) ... AHA
Alabama Independent Automobile Dealers Association (SRA) ... AIADA
Alabama Independent Insurance Agents (SRA) ... AIIA
Alabama Independent School Association (SRA) ... AISA
Alabama Initial Teacher Certification Test (EDAC) ... AITCT
Alabama International Trade Center [*University of Alabama*] [*Research center*] (RCD) ... AITC
Alabama League of Municipalities (SRA) ... ALM
Alabama Lenders Association (SRA) ... ALA
Alabama Library Association (SRA) ... AlaLA
Alabama Lutheran College, Selma, AL [*Library symbol Library of Congress*] (LCLS) ... ASeLC
Alabama Manufactured Housing Institute (SRA) ... AMHI
Alabama Marine and Recreation Association (SRA) ... AMRA
Alabama National Bancorporation [*NASDAQ symbol*] (SAG) ... ALAB
Alabama National Bancorporation [*Associated Press*] (SAG) ... AlaNBcp
Alabama Natl Bancorp [*NASDAQ symbol*] (TTSB) ... ALAB
Alabama Nurserymen's Association (SRA) ... ANA
Alabama Nursing Home Association (SRA) ... ANHA
Alabama Oilmen's Association and Alabama Association of Convenience Stores (SRA) ... AOA/AACS
Alabama Optometric Association (SRA) ... ALOA
Alabama Pawnbrokers Association (SRA) ... APA
Alabama Peace Officers Association (SRA) ... APOA
Alabama Peanut Producers Association (SRA) ... APPA
Alabama Petroleum Council (SRA) ... APC
Alabama Pharmacy Association (SRA) ... APA
Alabama Polytechnic Institute (MCD) ... API
Alabama Poultry and Egg Association (SRA) ... AP&EA
Alabama Power Capital Trust I [*Associated Press*] (SAG) ... AlaPC
Alabama Power Capital Trust I [*NYSE symbol*] (SAG) ... ALP
Alabama Power Co. [*Associated Press*] (SAG) ... AlaP
Alabama Power Co. [*NYSE symbol*] (SPSG) ... ALP
Alabama Power Co., Birmingham, AL [*Library symbol Library of Congress*] (LCLS) ... ABAP
Alabama Press Association (SRA) ... APA
Alabama Primary Health Care Association (SRA) ... APHCA
Alabama Propane Gas Association (SRA) ... APGA
Alabama Public Library Service, Montgomery, AL [*Library symbol Library of Congress*] (LCLS) ... A
Alabama Public Library Service, Montgomery, AL [*OCLC symbol*] (OCLC) ... ASL
Alabama Public Service Commission Decisions [*A publication*] (DLA) ... APSC
Alabama Pwr 6.40% 'A'Pfd [*NYSE symbol*] (TTSB) ... ALPPrC
Alabama Pwr 6.80% 'A'Pfd [*NYSE symbol*] (TTSB) ... ALPPrB
Alabama Pwr 7.60% 2nd'A'Pfd [*NYSE symbol*] (TTSB) ... ALPPrH
Alabama Pwr 7.60%'A'Pfd [*NYSE symbol*] (TTSB) ... ALPPrA
Alabama Recreation and Parks Association (SRA) ... ARPA
Alabama Reports [*A publication*] (DLA) ... AL Rep
Alabama Reports [*A publication*] (DLA) ... Ala
Alabama Reports [*A publication*] (DLA) ... Ala R
Alabama Reports [*A publication*] (DLA) ... Ala Rep
Alabama Reports [*A publication*] (DLA) ... Ala Reps
Alabama Reports [*A publication*] (DLA) ... Alab Rep
Alabama Reports [*A publication*] (DLA) ... Alabama Rep
Alabama Reports, New Series [*A publication*] (DLA) ... Ala NS
Alabama Reports, New Series [*A publication*] (DLA) ... Ala Rep NS
Alabama Reports, New Series [*A publication*] (DLA) ... Ala RNS
Alabama Reports, New Series [*A publication*] (DLA) ... Alab (NS)
Alabama Resources Information System [*Auburn University*] [*Information service or system*] (IID) ... ARIS
Alabama Restaurant Association (SRA) ... ARA
Alabama Retail Association (SRA) ... ARA
Alabama Road Builders Association (SRA) ... ARBA
Alabama Roofing, Sheet Metal, Heating and Air Conditioning Contractors Association (SRA) ... ARSM-HACCA
Alabama Rural Electric Association of Cooperatives (SRA) ... AREAC
Alabama Rural Water Association (SRA) ... ARWA
Alabama Select Cases (Supreme Court), by Shepherd [*37, 38, 39*] [*A publication*] (DLA) ... Ala Sel Cas
Alabama Sheriff's Association (SRA) ... ASA
Alabama Society of Professional Engineers (SRA) ... ASPE
Alabama Society of Professional Land Surveyors (SRA) ... ASPLS
Alabama Soft Drink Association (SRA) ... ASDA
Alabama State Bar (SRA) ... ASB
Alabama State Bar Foundation. Bulletin [*A publication*] (DLA) ... Ala St B Found Bull
Alabama State Employees Association (SRA) ... ASEA
Alabama State Foundation Bulletin [*A publication*] (ILCA) ... Ala St Found Bull
Alabama State Normal School, Daphne, AL [*Library symbol Library of Congress Obsolete*] (LCLS) ... ADaN
Alabama State Nurses Association (SRA) ... ASNA

Alabama State Supreme Court Library, Montgomery, AL [*Library symbol Library of Congress*] (LCLS) .... A-SC

Alabama State University, Montgomery, AL [*Library symbol Library of Congress*] (LCLS) .... AMS

Alabama State University, Montgomery, AL [*OCLC symbol*] (OCLC) .... AMU

Alabama Supreme Court and State Law Library, Montgomery, AL [*OCLC symbol*] (OCLC) .... ALS

Alabama Supreme Court Reports [*A publication*] (DLA) .... Ala

Alabama, Tennessee & Northern R. R. [*AAR code*] .... ATN

Alabama Textile Manufacturers Association (SRA) .... ATMA

Alabama Tobacco and Candy Distributors Association (SRA) .... AT&CDA

Alabama Travel Council (SRA) .... ATC

Alabama Trial Lawyers Association (SRA) .... ATLA

Alabama Trucking Association (SRA) .... ATA

Alabama Trucking Association, Montgomery AL [*STAC*] .... ALT

Alabama Vending Association (SRA) .... AVA

Alabama Veterinary Medical Association (SRA) .... AVMA

Alabama Vocational Association (SRA) .... AVA

Alabama Water Resources Research Institute [*Auburn, AL*] [*Department of the Interior*] (GRD) .... WRRI

Alabama Wholesale Beer and Wine Association (SRA) .... AWBWA

Alabama World Trade Association (SRA) .... AWTA

Alabama-Mississippi Telephone Association (SRA) .... AMTA

Alabamine [*Superseded by astatine*] [*Chemical element*] .... Ab

Alabamine [*Chemical element*] (BARN) .... Am

Alabaster, AL [*Location identifier FAA*] (FAAL) .... AOA

Alabaster, AL [*AM radio station call letters*] .... WGTT

Alabaster Cavern State Park [*Oklahoma*] [*Seismograph station code, US Geological Survey*] (SEIS) .... ACO

Alabat, Quezon [*Philippines*] [*ICAO location identifier*] (ICLI) .... RPXT

Alachua, FL [*FM radio station call letters*] (RBYB) .... WNDT-FM

Aladdin Knights of the Mystic Light (EA) .... AKML

Aladdin Knowledge Systems [*Commercial firm Associated Press*] (SAG) .... AladnKn

Aladdin Knowledge Systems [*NASDAQ symbol*] (SAG) .... ALDN

Aladdin Knowledge Systems [*NASDAQ symbol*] (TTSB) .... ALDNF

Alah [*Philippines*] [*Airport symbol*] (OAG) .... AAV

Al-Ahli Bank of Qatar (MENA) .... QSC

Al-Ahsa [*Saudi Arabia*] [*ICAO location identifier*] (ICLI) .... OEAH

Alajuela [*Costa Rica*] [*ICAO location identifier*] (ICLI) .... MRAL

Alak [*Former USSR ICAO designator*] (FAAC) .... LSV

Alakanuk [*Alaska*] [*Airport symbol*] (OAG) .... AUK

[*The*] Alalakh Tablets (BJA) .... AT

Alamar Biosciences, Inc. [*Associated Press*] (SAG) .... Alamar

Alamar Biosciences, Inc. [*Associated Press*] (SAG) .... Alamr

Alamar Biosciences, Inc. [*NASDAQ symbol*] (SAG) .... ALMR

Alamco, Inc. [*Associated Press*] (SAG) .... Alamco

Alamco, Inc. [*AMEX symbol*] (SPSG) .... AXO

Alamdeh [*Iran*] [*ICAO location identifier*] (ICLI) .... OINL

Alameda/Alameda Naval Air Station [*California*] [*ICAO location identifier*] (ICLI) .... KNGZ

Alameda Belt Line [*AAR code*] .... ABL

Alameda, CA [*FM radio station call letters*] (RBYB) .... KZSF

Alameda, CA [*Location identifier FAA*] (FAAL) .... NGZ

Alameda County Health Department, Oakland, CA [*Library symbol Library of Congress*] (LCLS) .... COH

Alameda County Law Library, Oakland, CA [*Library symbol Library of Congress*] (LCLS) .... COAL

Alameda County Library, Fremont, CA [*Library symbol Library of Congress*] (LCLS) .... CFrA

Alameda County Public Library, Hayward, CA [*Library symbol Library of Congress*] (LCLS) .... CHA

Alameda Free Library, Alameda, CA [*Library symbol Library of Congress*] (LCLS) .... CAla

Alameda Naval Air Base [*California*] (SAA) .... ANAB

Alamethicin [*An antibiotic*] .... ALA

Alamo [*Nevada*] [*Seismograph station code, US Geological Survey*] (SEIS) .... ALA

Alamo Community, NM [*AM radio station call letters*] .... KABR

Alamo Commuter Airlines [*ICAO designator*] (AD) .... JZ

Alamo Developments [*Vancouver Stock Exchange symbol*] .... ALO

Alamo Group [*NYSE symbol*] (TTSB) .... ALG

Alamo Group, Inc. [*Associated Press*] (SAG) .... AlamoGp

Alamo Group, Inc. [*NYSE symbol*] (SAG) .... ALG

Alamo Heights, TX [*AM radio station call letters*] .... KDRY

Alamo Personal Computer Organization (PCM) .... APCO

Alamo, TN [*AM radio station call letters*] .... WCTA

Alamo, TN [*FM radio station call letters*] .... WWGM

Alamo, TX [*FM radio station call letters*] .... KJAV

Alamogordo [*New Mexico*] [*Airport symbol*] (OAG) .... ALM

Alamogordo/Holloman Air Force Base [*New Mexico*] [*ICAO location identifier*] (ICLI) .... KHMN

Alamogordo, NM [*Location identifier FAA*] (FAAL) .... HMN

Alamogordo, NM [*AM radio station call letters*] .... KINN

Alamogordo, NM [*FM radio station call letters*] (RBYB) .... KNMZ-FM

Alamogordo, NM [*AM radio station call letters*] .... KPSA

Alamogordo, NM [*FM radio station call letters*] .... KYEE

Alamogordo, NM [*FM radio station call letters*] .... KZZX

Alamogordo, NM [*Location identifier FAA*] (FAAL) .... MUK

Alamogordo Public Library, Alamogordo, NM [*OCLC symbol*] (OCLC) .... AMO

Alamogordo Public Library, Alamogordo, NM [*Library symbol Library of Congress*] (LCLS) .... NmAl

Alamosa [*Colorado*] [*Airport symbol*] (OAG) .... ALS

Alamosa, CO [*FM radio station call letters*] .... KALQ

Alamosa, CO [*FM radio station call letters*] .... KASF

Alamosa, CO [*AM radio station call letters*] .... KGIW

Alamosa, CO [*FM radio station call letters*] .... KRZA

Alan Feinstein Fan Club (EA) .... AFFC

Alan Guttmacher Institute (EA) .... AGI

Alan Hutchison Publishing Ltd. [*British*] .... AH

Alan Mann Helicopters Ltd. [*British*] [*FAA designator*] (FAAC) .... AMH

Alan Pascoe Associates [*British*] .... APA

Alan R. Barton Nuclear Plant (NRCH) .... ABNP

Alan Stratford and Associates [*Aviation consultants*] [*British*] (ECON) .... ASA

Alan Thicke Fan Club (EA) .... ATFC

Alanco Environmental Res [*NASDAQ symbol*] (TTSB) .... ALAN

Alanco Resources Corp. [*NASDAQ symbol*] (SAG) .... ALAN

Alanco Resources Corp. [*Associated Press*] (SAG) .... Alanco

Alanine [*One-letter symbol; see Ala*] .... A

Alanine [*Also, A*] [*An amino acid*] .... Ala

Alanine Aminotransferase [*Also, ALAT, ALT, GPT*] [*An enzyme*] .... AAT

Alanine Aminotransferase [*Formerly, SGPT*] [*Pharmacology*] (DAVI) .... ALAT

Alanine Aminotransferase [*Also, AAT, ALAT, GPT*] [*An enzyme*] .... ALT

Alanine Nitroanilide [*Biochemistry*] .... ANA

Alanine Nitrogen Mustard [*L-PAM*] [*Antineoplastic drug*] .... A

Alanine Transaminase [*Also, AAT, ALT, GPT*] [*An enzyme*] .... ALAT

Alanine Transaminase [*Biochemistry*] (DAVI) .... ALT

Al-Anon Family Group Headquarters (EA) .... AAFGH

ALANON Family Group Headquarters (EA) .... AFG

Alanson Public Library, Alanson, MI [*Library symbol Library of Congress*] (LCLS) .... MiAln

Alantec Corp. [*Associated Press*] (SAG) .... Alantec

Alantec Corp. [*NASDAQ symbol*] (SAG) .... ALTC

Alantic Canada Centre for Environmental Science (AC) .... ACCES

Alanus Anglicus [*Flourished, 1208-10*] [*Authority cited in pre-1607 legal work*] (DSA) .... A

Alanus Anglicus [*Flourished, 1208-10*] [*Authority cited in pre-1607 legal work*] (DSA) .... Al

Alanus Anglicus [*Flourished, 1208-10*] [*Authority cited in pre-1607 legal work*] (DSA) .... Ala

Alarm [*Telecommunications*] (TEL) .... AL

Alarm (MSA) .... ALM

Alarm .... ALRM

Alarm and Control System [*Telecommunications*] (TEL) .... ACS

Alarm and Jettison Panel .... AJP

Alarm and Status Module .... ASM

Alarm Association of Florida (SRA) .... AAF

Alarm Check Valve (MSA) .... ACV

Alarm Communications and Display Segment (MCD) .... ACADS

Alarm Communications and Display System (MCD) .... ACAD

Alarm Control and Display (TEL) .... ACD

Alarm Control Center (NVT) .... ACC

Alarm Control Module [*Telecommunications*] (TEL) .... ACM

Alarm Control Panel .... ACP

Alarm Control Unit [*Bell System*] [*Telecommunications*] .... ACU

Alarm Display and Control Unit [*Telecommunications*] (TEL) .... ADCU

Alarm Identification Reporting System (ACRL) .... AIRS

Alarm Indicating Monitor .... AIM

Alarm Indication Signal [*Telecommunications*] (TEL) .... AIS

Alarm Industry Committee for Combating Crime [*Defunct*] (EA) .... AICCC

Alarm Inhibit Signal [*Telecommunications*] (TEL) .... AIS

Alarm Interface Unit [*Telecommunications*] (TEL) .... AIU

Alarm Monitor Computer .... AMC

Alarm Monitor Group [*Army*] .... AMG

Alarm Monitor Unit [*Telecommunications*] (TEL) .... AMU

Alarm Monitoring System .... AMS

Alarm Network Group .... ANG

Alarm Panel Monitor (AFM) .... APM

Alarm Reaction [*Psychology*] .... AR

Alarm Receiving and Reporting Equipment [*Telecommunications*] (TEL) ..... ARRE

Alarm Reporting Telephone [*Telecommunications*] (TEL) .... ART

Alarm Response Team [*Military*] .... ART

Alarm System [*Automotive advertising*] .... ALRM

Alarm System Control Unit .... ASCU

Alarm System Improvement Guide (MCD) .... ASIG

Alarm System Operation .... ASO

Alarm Termination Subsystem [*Telecommunications*] (TEL) .... ATS

Alarm Valve (DAC) .... ALV

Alarms by Carrier (PDAA) .... ABC

Alas Nacionales SA [*Dominican Republic*] [*ICAO designator*] (FAAC) .... ALW

Alas Panamenas SA [*Panama*] [*ICAO designator*] (FAAC) .... ALPANSA

Alas Panamenas SA [*Panama*] [*ICAO designator*] (FAAC) .... PWI

ALAS, SA [*Uruguay*] [*ICAO designator*] (ICDA) .... HP

Alasehir [*Turkey ICAO location identifier*] (ICLI) .... LTBC

Alaska .... AAA

Alaska [*Postal code*] .... AK

Alaska (ROG) .... AKA

Alaska [*MARC country of publication code Library of Congress*] (LCCP) .... aku

Alaska (AFM) .... ALAS

Alaska [*MARC geographic area code Library of Congress*] (LCCP) .... n-us-ak

Alaska Administrative Code [*A publication*] (AAGC) .... AAC

Alaska Administrative Code [*A publication*] (DLA) .... Alaska Admin Code

Alaska Administrative Journal [*A publication*] (AAGC) .... AAJ

Alaska Aeronautical Industries [*ICAO designator*] (AD) .... YC

Alaska Agricultural Experiment Station, Palmer, AK [*Library symbol Library of Congress*] (LCLS) .... AkPalA

Alaska Air Carriers Association (SRA) .... AACA

Alaska Air Command [*Air Force*] .... ALAC

Alaska Air Group [*NYSE symbol*] (TTSB) .... ALK

Alaska Air Group, Inc. [*NYSE symbol*] (SPSG) .... ALK

Alaska Air Group, Inc. [*Associated Press*] (SAG) .... AlskAir

Alaska Airlines [*ICAO designator*] (AD) .... Alaska
Alaska Airlines, Inc. (IIA) .... ALK
Alaska Airlines, Inc. [*ICAO designator*] (OAG) .... AS
Alaska Airlines, Inc. [*ICAO designator*] (FAAC) .... ASA
Alaska Apollo Gold Mines [*Associated Press*] (SAG) .... AlskAplo
Alaska Apollo Gold Mines [*NASDAQ symbol*] (SAG) .... APLO
Alaska Apollo Gold Mines Ltd. [*Vancouver Stock Exchange symbol*] .... ASK
Alaska Apollo Res Ltd [*NASDAQ symbol*] (TTSB) .... APLOF
Alaska Association of Realtors (SRA) .... AAR
Alaska Bar Association (SRA) .... ABA
Alaska Bar Brief [*A publication*] (DLA) .... Alaska B Brief
Alaska Bar Journal [*A publication*] (DLA) .... Alaska BJ
Alaska British Columbia Transportation Co. [*AAR code*] .... ABCK
Alaska Broadcasters Association (SRA) .... ABA
Alaska, Canada, United States (AABC) .... ALCANUS
Alaska Carriers Association, Inc., Anchorage AK [*STAC*] .... ACA
Alaska Census Data Network [*Alaska State Department of Labor*] [*Juneau*] [*Information service or system*] (IID) .... ACDN
Alaska Coal Association (SRA) .... ACA
Alaska Coalition (EA) .... AC
Alaska Coastal Airlines .... ACA
Alaska Coastal Current [*Marine science*] (OSRA) .... ACC
Alaska Coastal Management Office .... ACMO
Alaska Codes (Carter) [*A publication*] (DLA) .... Alaska Co
Alaska Communication System Industrial Fund (AFM) .... ACSIF
Alaska Conservation Society (EA) .... ACS
Alaska Constitution [*A publication*] (DLA) .... Alaska Const
Alaska Council of School Administrators (SRA) .... ACSA
Alaska Credit Union League (SRA) .... ACUL
Alaska Defense Command [*Known to many of the soldiers who served in it as "All Damn Confusion"*] [*World War II*] .... ADC
Alaska Defense Frontier [*Military*] .... ADF
Alaska Dental Society (SRA) .... ADS
Alaska Department of Environmental Conservation, Juneau, AK [*Library symbol*] [*Library of Congress*] (LCLS) .... AkJEC
Alaska Department of Fish and Game Habitat, Anchorage, AK [*Library symbol*] [*Library of Congress*] (LCLS) .... AkAEG
Alaska Department of Fish and Game, Juneau, AK [*Library symbol Library of Congress*] (LCLS) .... AkJFG
Alaska Detroit Diesel Allison [*Commercial firm*] .... ADDA
Alaska Early Childhood Certification Process (EDAC) .... AECCP
Alaska Engineering Commission [*Later, the Alaska Railroad*] .... AEC
Alaska Eskimo Whaling System (USDC) .... AEWC
Alaska Federal Reports [*A publication*] (DLA) .... AF Rep
Alaska Federal Reports [*A publication*] (DLA) .... Alaska Fed
Alaska Federal Reports [*A publication*] (DLA) .... Alaska Fed Rep
Alaska Federation of Natives (EA) .... AFN
Alaska Field Operations Center [*Anchorage, AK*] [*Department of the Interior*] (GRD) .... AFOC
Alaska Fish and Game Library, Douglas, AK [*Library symbol*] [*Library of Congress*] (LCLS) .... AkDFG
Alaska Forest Association (SRA) .... AFA
Alaska Forest Fire Council .... AFFCO
Alaska Game Commission [*Terminated, 1959*] .... AGC
Alaska Health Sciences Library, Anchorage, AK [*Library symbol Library of Congress*] (LCLS) .... AkAAH
Alaska Historical Library and Museum, Juneau, AK [*Library symbol Library of Congress*] (LCLS) .... AkHi
Alaska Hotel and Motel Association (SRA) .... AKHMA
Alaska Hydro-Train [*AAR code*] .... AHT
Alaska Independent Insurance Agents and Brokers (SRA) .... AIIAB
Alaska Institute for Fisheries Development .... AIFD
Alaska International Air, Inc. [*Air carrier designation symbol*] .... AIAX
Alaska International Rail and Highway Commission [*Terminated, 1961*] .... AIRHC
Alaska Island Air, Inc. [*ICAO designator*] (FAAC) .... AAK
Alaska Juneau Aeronautics, Inc. [*ICAO designator*] (FAAC) .... WAK
Alaska Landscape Flux Study (OSRA) .... ALFS
Alaska Landscape Flux Study (USDC) .... ALFS
Alaska Legislative Affairs Agency, Legislative Reference Library, Juneau, AK [*Library symbol*] [*Library of Congress*] (LCLS) .... AkJL
Alaska Legislative Teleconference Network [*Alaska State Legislative Affairs Agency*] [*Juneau, AK*] [*Telecommunications service*] (TSSD) .... LTN
Alaska Library Association .... AkLA
Alaska Manufactured Housing Association (SRA) .... AMHA
Alaska Methodist University .... AMU
Alaska Methodist University, Anchorage, AK [*Library symbol Library of Congress*] (LCLS) .... AkAM
Alaska Military Highway .... AMH
Alaska Mineral Resource Assessment Program [*Department of the Interior*] .... AMRAP
Alaska Miners Association (SRA) .... AMA
Alaska Municipal League (SRA) .... AML
Alaska National Interest Land Conservation Act [*1980*] .... ANILCA
Alaska Native Arts and Crafts Cooperative Association .... ANAC
Alaska Native Claims Appeals Board (in United States Interior Decisions) [*A publication*] (DLA) .... ANCAB
Alaska Native Claims Settlement Act [*1971*] .... ANCSA
Alaska Native Language Center [*Research center*] (RCD) .... ANLC
Alaska Natural Gas Transportation Act of 1976 .... ANGTA
Alaska Natural Gas Transportation System .... ANGTS
Alaska Nurses Association (SRA) .... AaNA
Alaska Oil and Gas Association (SRA) .... AOGA
Alaska Pacific University, Anchorage, AK [*Library symbol*] [*Library of Congress*] (LCLS) .... AkAAPU
Alaska Power Administration [*Department of Energy*] .... APA
Alaska Public Interest Research Group [*Research center*] (RCD) .... AKPIRG
Alaska Public Lands Information Center .... APLIC
Alaska Public Radio Network .... APRN
Alaska Quaternary Center [*University of Alaska, Fairbanks*] [*Research center*] (RCD) .... AQC
[*The*] **Alaska Railroad** [*AAR code*] .... ARR
Alaska Reporter [*A publication*] (DLA) .... Alaska
Alaska Reports [*A publication*] (AAGC) .... Alaska
Alaska Reports [*A publication*] (DLA) .... Alk
Alaska Resources for the Moderately/Severely Impaired (EDAC) .... ARMSI
Alaska Rural Electric Cooperative Association (SRA) .... ARECA
Alaska Rural Teacher Training Corps (EDAC) .... ARTTC
Alaska Session Laws [*A publication*] (DLA) .... Alaska Sess Laws
Alaska Standard Time .... ALST
Alaska State Chamber of Commerce (SRA) .... ASCC
Alaska State Court System, Law Library, Anchorage, AK [*Library symbol Library of Congress*] (LCLS) .... Ak-L
Alaska State Data Center [*Alaska State Department of Labor*] [*Information service or system*] (IID) .... ASDC
Alaska State District Council of Laborers (SRA) .... ASDCL
Alaska State Homebuilders Association (SRA) .... ASHBA
Alaska State Hospital and Nursing Home Association (SRA) .... ASHNHA
Alaska State Library, Juneau, AK [*Library symbol Library of Congress*] (LCLS) .... Ak
Alaska State Medical Association (SRA) .... ASMA
Alaska Statutes [*A publication*] (DLA) .... Alaska Stat
Alaska Synthetic Aperture RADAR Facility [*NASA*] (GRD) .... ASF
Alaska Telephone Association (SRA) .... ATA
Alaska Trucking Association (SRA) .... ATA
Alaska Tsunami Warning Center [*Army*] (OSRA) .... ATWC
Alaska Tsunami Warning Center (USDC) .... ATWC
Alaska Tsunami Warning System [*National Oceanic and Atmospheric Administration*] (GFGA) .... ATWS
Alaska Village Demonstration Project [*Environmental Protection Agency*] .... AVDP
Alaska Visitors Association (SRA) .... AVA
Alaska Wine and Spirits Wholesalers Association (SRA) .... AWSWA
Alaska Yukon Pioneers (EA) .... AYP
Alaska-Canada [*Highway*] .... ALCAN
Alaskagold Mines Ltd. [*Vancouver Stock Exchange symbol*] .... AKG
Alaska-Hawaii Standard Time (WGA) .... AHST
Alaskan ADCOM Region [*Military*] .... AKADCOMRGN
Alaskan Air Command [*Elmendorf Air Force Base*] .... AAC
Alaskan Air Command [*Elmendorf Air Force Base*] [*Air Force*] .... ALAIRC
Alaskan Collectors Club (EA) .... ACC
Alaskan Command [*Discontinued, 1975*] [*Military*] .... AC
Alaskan Command [*Discontinued, 1975*] [*Military*] .... ALCOM
Alaskan Communications Region [*Air Force*] .... ACR
Alaskan Communications System [*Air Force*] .... ACS
Alaskan Daylight Time .... ADT
Alaskan Integrated Air Defense System .... ALIADS
Alaskan Integrated Communications Exchange .... ALICE
Alaskan Long-Period Array .... ALPA
Alaskan Malamute Club of America (EA) .... AMCA
Alaskan Malamute Protection League (EA) .... AMPL
Alaskan NICS [*FAA*] (TAG) .... ANICS
Alaskan NORAD Region .... ANR
Alaskan Projects Office, Fort Wainwright, AK [*Library symbol Library of Congress*] (LCLS) .... AkFwP
Alaskan Sea Frontier [*Navy*] .... AL SEA FRON
Alaskan Sea Frontier [*Navy*] .... ASF
Alaskan Sector .... AL SEC
Alaskan Standard Time [*Aviation*] (SAA) .... AST
Alaskan Territorial Guard .... ATG
Alaskon Resources [*Vancouver Stock Exchange symbol*] .... AKN
Alatenn Resources, Inc. [*Associated Press*] (SAG) .... Alaten
AlaTenn Resources, Inc. [*NASDAQ symbol*] (NQ) .... ATNG
Alavus [*Finland ICAO location identifier*] (ICLI) .... EFAL
Alawas Gold Corp. [*Vancouver Stock Exchange symbol*] .... ALW
Albacete [*Spain ICAO location identifier*] (ICLI) .... LEAB
Al-Baha [*Saudi Arabia*] [*Airport symbol*] (OAG) .... BBH
Alban Exploration Ltd. [*Vancouver Stock Exchange symbol*] .... ABN
Alban Institute (EA) .... AI
Albania [*MARC country of publication code Library of Congress*] (LCCP) .... aa
Albania [*ANSI two-letter standard code*] (CNC) .... AL
Albania [*ANSI three-letter standard code*] (CNC) .... ALB
Albania (VRA) .... Alb
Albania .... Alban
Albania [*MARC geographic area code Library of Congress*] (LCCP) .... e-aa--
Albania [*License plate code assigned to foreign diplomats in the US*] .... GP
Albania Society of Britain [*British*] (EAIO) .... ASB
Albania Workers' Party [*Political party*] .... AWP
Albanian [*MARC language code Library of Congress*] (LCCP) .... alb
Albanian Airline Co. [*ICAO designator*] (FAAC) .... LBC
Albanian Airways [*ICAO designator*] (FAAC) .... ABW
Albanian Catholic Information Center (EA) .... ACIC
Albanian Communist Party [*Political party*] .... ACP
Albanian Kosovar Youth in the Free World (EA) .... AKYFW
Albanian People's Army .... APA
Albanian Republican Party [*Partia Republikane Shqiptare*] [*Political party*] (EY) .... ARP
Albanian Society (EAIO) .... AS
Albanian Society Jusuf Gervalla (EA) .... ASJG
Albanian Telegraphic Agency [*News agency*] (EY) .... ATA
Albanian-American National Organization .... AANO
Albank Financial Corp. [*Associated Press*] (SAG) .... Albank

Albank Financial Corp. [*NASDAQ symbol*] (SAG) ... ALBK
ALBANK Finl [*NASDAQ symbol*] (TTSB) ... ALBK
Albany [*Georgia*] [*Airport symbol*] (OAG) ... ABY
Albany [*New York*] [*Airport symbol*] (OAG) ... ALB
Albany [*Australia Airport symbol*] (OAG) ... ALH
Albany [*Australia ICAO location identifier*] (ICLI) ... APAL
Albany/Albany [*New York*] [*ICAO location identifier*] (ICLI) ... KALB
Albany/Albany Naval Air Station [*Georgia*] [*ICAO location identifier*] (ICLI) ... KNAB
Albany & Northern Railway Co. (IIA) ... A & N
Albany & Northern Railway Co. [*AAR code*] ... ALN
Albany Area Board of Cooperative Education Services, Colonie, NY [*Library symbol*] [*Library of Congress*] (LCLS) ... NColnA
Albany Avenue Elementary School, North Massapequa, NY [*Library symbol*] [*Library of Congress*] (LCLS) ... NNomAE
Albany Business College, Albany, NY [*Library symbol Library of Congress*] (LCLS) ... NAlBC
Albany College of Pharmacy, Albany, NY [*Library symbol Library of Congress*] (LCLS) ... NAIP
Albany Corp. [*Toronto Stock Exchange symbol*] ... AYO
Albany County Public Library, Laramie, WY [*Library symbol Library of Congress*] (LCLS) ... WyLar
Albany Free Public Library, Albany, CA [*Library symbol Library of Congress*] (LCLS) ... CAlb
Albany, GA [*Location identifier FAA*] (FAAL) ... NHX
Albany, GA [*Television station call letters*] ... WALB
Albany, GA [*AM radio station call letters*] ... WALG
Albany, GA [*AM radio station call letters*] ... WANL
Albany, GA [*Television station call letters*] ... WFXL
Albany, GA [*FM radio station call letters*] ... WGNP
Albany, GA [*AM radio station call letters*] ... WGPC
Albany, GA [*FM radio station call letters*] ... WGPC-FM
Albany, GA [*FM radio station call letters*] ... WJIZ
Albany, GA [*AM radio station call letters*] ... WJYZ
Albany, GA [*FM radio station call letters*] ... WKAK
Albany, GA [*FM radio station call letters*] ... WUNV
Albany General Hospital, Albany, OR [*Library symbol Library of Congress*] (LCLS) ... OrAlH
Albany Institute of History of Art, Albany, NY [*Library symbol Library of Congress*] (LCLS) ... NAII
Albany International Corp. [*NYSE symbol*] (CTT) ... AIN
Albany International Corp. [*Associated Press*] (SAG) ... AlbnyIn
Albany Intl. 'A' [*NYSE symbol*] (TTSB) ... AIN
Albany Junior College, Albany, GA [*Library symbol Library of Congress*] (LCLS) ... GAlJC
Albany Jr. H.S./Elementary Library, Albany, MN [*Library symbol*] [*Library of Congress*] (LCLS) ... MnAlJ
Albany, KY [*AM radio station call letters*] ... WANY
Albany, KY [*FM radio station call letters*] ... WANY-FM
Albany Law Journal [*A publication*] (DLA) ... Alb LJ
Albany Law Journal [*A publication*] (DLA) ... ALJ
Albany Law School, Albany, NY [*Library symbol Library of Congress*] (LCLS) ... NAlLS
Albany Law School, Albany, NY [*OCLC symbol*] (OCLC) ... YZA
Albany Law School Journal [*A publication*] (DLA) ... Alb LS Jour
Albany Medical College (GAGS) ... Albany Med C
Albany Medical College, Albany, NY [*Library symbol Library of Congress*] (LCLS) ... NAIA
Albany Medical College, Schaffer Library of Health Sciences, Albany, NY [*OCLC symbol*] (OCLC) ... VXL
Albany, MN [*AM radio station call letters*] ... KASM
Albany, MN [*FM radio station call letters*] ... KASM-FM
Albany, NY [*Location identifier FAA*] (FAAL) ... DEJ
Albany, NY [*AM radio station call letters*] ... WABY
Albany, NY [*FM radio station call letters*] ... WAMC
Albany, NY [*FM radio station call letters*] ... WCDB
Albany, NY [*AM radio station call letters*] (RBYB) ... WDCD
Albany, NY [*AM radio station call letters*] ... WGNA
Albany, NY [*FM radio station call letters*] ... WGNA-FM
Albany, NY [*FM radio station call letters*] ... WHRL
Albany, NY [*FM radio station call letters*] ... WKLI
Albany, NY [*Television station call letters*] ... WNYT
Albany, NY [*FM radio station call letters*] ... WPYX
Albany, NY [*AM radio station call letters*] ... WROW
Albany, NY [*Television station call letters*] ... WTEN
Albany, NY [*Television station call letters*] ... WXXA
Albany, NY [*FM radio station call letters*] ... WYJB
Albany, OR [*FM radio station call letters*] ... KHPE
Albany, OR [*AM radio station call letters*] ... KRKT
Albany, OR [*FM radio station call letters*] ... KRKT-FM
Albany, OR [*AM radio station call letters*] ... KWIL
Albany Port District [*AAR code*] ... APD
Albany Public Library, Alabany, MN [*Library symbol*] [*Library of Congress*] (LCLS) ... MnAl
Albany Public Library, Albany, GA [*Library symbol Library of Congress*] (LCLS) ... GAl
Albany Public Library, Albany, NY [*Library symbol Library of Congress*] (LCLS) ... NAl
Albany Public Library, Albany, OR [*Library symbol Library of Congress*] (LCLS) ... OrAl
Albany Resources [*Vancouver Stock Exchange symbol*] ... ALX
Albany Senior High School, Albany, MN [*Library symbol*] [*Library of Congress*] (LCLS) ... MnAlS
Albany State College [*Georgia*] ... ASC
Albany State College, Albany, GA [*Library symbol Library of Congress*] (LCLS) ... GAlSC
Albany-Corvallis [*Oregon*] [*Airport symbol*] (AD) ... CVO
Albaraka Algeria Islamic Bank (EY) ... AAIB
Albatros Airline, Inc. [*Turkey*] [*ICAO designator*] (FAAC) ... ABK
Albatrosz Ltd. [*Hungary ICAO designator*] (FAAC) ... ALT
Alba-Waldensian [*AMEX symbol*] (TTSB) ... AWS
Alba-Waldensian, Inc. [*Associated Press*] (SAG) ... AlbaW
Alba-Waldensian, Inc. [*AMEX symbol*] (SPSG) ... AWS
Albedo [*Psychology*] ... A
Al-Beida [*Yemen*] [*ICAO location identifier*] (ICLI) ... OYBI
Albemarle Corp. [*Associated Press*] (SAG) ... Albemr
Albemarle, NC [*Location identifier FAA*] (FAAL) ... SWY
Albemarle, NC [*FM radio station call letters*] ... WABZ
Albemarle, NC [*AM radio station call letters*] ... WSPC
Albemarle, NC [*AM radio station call letters*] ... WZKY
Albemarle-Stanly County Public Library, Albemarle, NC [*Library symbol Library of Congress*] (LCLS) ... NcAlb
Albendazole [*Anthelmintic*] ... ABZ
Albenga [*Italy*] [*Airport symbol*] (AD) ... ALL
Albenga [*Italy ICAO location identifier*] (ICLI) ... LIMG
Albericus de Maletis [*Flourished, 1431-33*] [*Authority cited in pre-1607 legal work*] (DSA) ... Alber de Malet
Albericus de Porta Ravennate [*Flourished, 1165-94*] [*Authority cited in pre-1607 legal work*] (DSA) ... A
Albericus de Porta Ravennate [*Flourished, 1165-94*] [*Authority cited in pre-1607 legal work*] (DSA) ... Al
Albericus de Porta Ravennate [*Flourished, 1165-94*] [*Authority cited in pre-1607 legal work*] (DSA) ... Alb
Albericus de Porta Ravennate [*Flourished, 1165-94*] [*Authority cited in pre-1607 legal work*] (DSA) ... Albri
Albericus de Rosate [*Deceased, 1360*] [*Authority cited in pre-1607 legal work*] (DSA) ... Alb
Albericus de Rosate [*Deceased, 1360*] [*Authority cited in pre-1607 legal work*] (DSA) ... Alb de Ros
Albericus de Rosate [*Deceased, 1360*] [*Authority cited in pre-1607 legal work*] (DSA) ... Albe
Albericus de Rosate [*Deceased, 1360*] [*Authority cited in pre-1607 legal work*] (DSA) ... Alber
Albericus de Rosate [*Deceased, 1360*] [*Authority cited in pre-1607 legal work*] (DSA) ... Alberic de Rosat
Albericus de Rosate [*Deceased, 1360*] [*Authority cited in pre-1607 legal work*] (DSA) ... Albri de Rosa
Albermarle Corp. [*NYSE symbol*] (SAG) ... ALB
Albermarle Corp. [*Associated Press*] (SAG) ... Albemar
Albermarle Regional Library, Winton, NC [*Library symbol Library of Congress*] (LCLS) ... NcWintA
Alberni [*British Columbia*] [*Seismograph station code, US Geological Survey*] (SEIS) ... ALB
Alberni Airway [*Canada ICAO designator*] (FAAC) ... BNI
Alberni District Archives, Port Alberni, British Columbia [*Library symbol National Library of Canada*] (BIB) ... BPADA
Alberni Valley Museum, Port Alberni, BC, Canada [*Library symbol Library of Congress*] (LCLS) ... CaBPaM
Alberni Valley Museum, Port Alberni, British Columbia [*Library symbol National Library of Canada*] (NLC) ... BPAM
Albert Arbitration [*Lord Cairns' Decisions*] [*A publication*] (DLA) ... Alb Arb
Albert/Bray [*France ICAO location identifier*] (ICLI) ... LFAQ
Albert Campbell Branch, Scarborough Public Library, Ontario [*Library symbol National Library of Canada*] (NLC) ... OTSPA
Albert Champion [*Automotive industrialist whose company is now part of General Motors*] ... AC
Albert County Historical Society, Inc., Hopewell Cape, New Brunswick [*Library symbol National Library of Canada*] (NLC) ... NBHCA
Albert Einstein Institution (EA) ... AEI
Albert Einstein International Academy Foundation (EA) ... AEIAF
Albert Einstein Medical Center ... AEMC
Albert Einstein Medical Center, Northern Division, Philadelphia, PA [*Library symbol Library of Congress*] (LCLS) ... PPAEM
Albert Einstein Medical College (DAVI) ... AEMD
Albert Einstein Peace Prize Foundation (EA) ... AEPPF
Albert F. Simpson Historical Research Center (AFM) ... AFSHRC
Albert Kahn Associates [*Founded in 1895, one of the oldest architectural firms in the US*] ... AKA
Albert Lea, MN [*Location identifier FAA*] (FAAL) ... AEL
Albert Lea, MN [*Location identifier FAA*] (FAAL) ... FYB
Albert Lea, MN [*AM radio station call letters*] ... KATE
Albert Lea, MN [*FM radio station call letters*] ... KCPI
Albert Lea, MN [*FM radio station call letters*] ... KQPR
Albert Lea Public Library, Albert Lea, MN [*Library symbol Library of Congress*] (LCLS) ... MnAlb
Albert Medal [*British*] ... AM
Albert Rolland [*France*] [*Research code symbol*] ... ANP
Albert Rolland [*France*] [*Research code symbol*] ... Rd
Albert Schweitzer Fellowship (EA) ... ASF
Albert South Library, Regina, Saskatchewan [*Library symbol National Library of Canada*] (NLC) ... SRAS
Albert South Library, Regina, SK, Canada [*Library symbol*] [*Library of Congress*] (LCLS) ... CaSRAS
Albert W. Thompson Memorial Library, Clayton, NM [*Library symbol Library of Congress*] (LCLS) ... NmCla
Albert W. Thompson Memorial Library, Clayton, NM [*Library symbol*] [*Library of Congress*] (LCLS) ... NmClaP
Alberta [*Canadian province*] [*Postal code*] ... AB
Alberta [*MARC country of publication code Library of Congress*] (LCCP) ... abc

Alberta [*Canadian province*] ... ALB
Alberta [*Canadian province*] ... ALBA
Alberta [*Canadian province*] ... ALTA
Alberta [*Canada*] (DD) ... Alta
Alberta [*MARC geographic area code Library of Congress*] (LCCP) ... n-cn-ab
Alberta 5 Pin Bowlers' Association (AC) ... A5-PBA
Alberta Advanced Education, Edmonton, Alberta [*Library symbol National Library of Canada*] (NLC) ... AEAE
Alberta Agriculture, Edmonton, Alberta [*Library symbol National Library of Canada*] (NLC) ... AEAG
Alberta Agriculture Library [*UTLAS symbol*] ... AAG
Alberta Alcoholism and Drug Abuse Commission Library, Edmonton, AB, Canada [*OCLC symbol*] (OCLC) ... AAD
Alberta Amateur Softball Association [*Also Softball Alberta*] (AC) ... AASA
Alberta & Southern Gas Co. Ltd., Calgary, Alberta [*Library symbol National Library of Canada*] (BIB) ... ACASG
Alberta Arbitration & Mediation Society (AC) ... AAMS
Alberta Association for Community Living [*Alberta Association for the Mentally Handicapped*] (AC) ... AACL
Alberta Association for Marriage & Family Therapy (AC) ... AAMFT
Alberta Association for Multicultural Education [*Association de l'Education Multiculturelle de l'Alberta*] (AC) ... AAME
Alberta Association of Agricultural Fieldmen (AC) ... AAAF
Alberta Association of Agricultural Societies (AC) ... AAAS
[*The*] **Alberta Association of Animal Health Technologists** (AC) ... AAAHT
Alberta Association of Architects (AC) ... AAA
Alberta Association of Architects [*1906*] [*Canada*] (NGC) ... AAA
Alberta Association of College Librarians (AC) ... AACL
Alberta Association of Designers & Architectural Technologists (AC) ... AADAT
Alberta Association of Landscape Architects (AC) ... AALA
Alberta Association of Legal Assistants (AC) ... AALA
Alberta Association of Library Technicians (AC) ... AALT
Alberta Association of Medical Radiation Technologists (AC) ... AAMRT
Alberta Association of Midwives (AC) ... AAM
Alberta Association of Registered Nurses (AC) ... AARN
Alberta Association of Registered Nurses, Edmonton, AB, Canada [*Library symbol*] [*Library of Congress*] (LCLS) ... CaAEARN
Alberta Association of Registered Nurses, Edmonton, Alberta [*Library symbol National Library of Canada*] (NLC) ... AEARN
Alberta Association of Registered Occupational Therapists (AC) ... AAROT
Alberta Association of Rehabilitation Centres (AC) ... AARC
Alberta Association of Services for Children & Families [*Formerly, Alberta Association of Child Care Centres*] (AC) ... AASCF
Alberta Association of the Appraisal Institute of Canada (AC) ... AA-AIC
Alberta Association of the Canadian Institute of Planners (AC) ... AACIP
Alberta Association of Translators & Interpreters [*Association des Traducteurs et Interpretes de l'Alberta*] (AC) ... AATI
Alberta Attorney General, Edmonton, Alberta [*Library symbol National Library of Canada*] (NLC) ... AEATG
Alberta Attorney General, Provincial Court Libraries [*UTLAS symbol*] ... PCL
Alberta Attorney General, Queen's Bench Libraries [*UTLAS symbol*] ... AQB
Alberta Ballet Co. [*Canada*] ... ABC
Alberta Beach Municipal Library, Alberta [*Library symbol National Library of Canada*] (NLC) ... AABM
Alberta Camping Association (AC) ... ACA
Alberta Cancer Clinic, Edmonton, AB, Canada [*Library symbol Library of Congress*] (LCLS) ... CaAECC
Alberta Cancer Clinic, Edmonton, Alberta [*Library symbol National Library of Canada*] (NLC) ... AECC
Alberta Case Locator [*University of Alberta*] [*Canada Information service or system*] (CRD) ... ACL
Alberta Chess Association (AC) ... ACA
Alberta Children's Hospital, Calgary, AB, Canada [*Library symbol*] [*Library of Congress*] (LCLS) ... CaACACH
Alberta Children's Hospital, Calgary, Alberta [*Library symbol National Library of Canada*] (NLC) ... ACACH
Alberta Children's Hospital Research Centre [*Canada*] (IRC) ... ACHRC
Alberta Choral Federation (AC) ... ACF
Alberta College of Art, Calgary, AB, Canada [*Library symbol Library of Congress*] (LCLS) ... CaACSAA
Alberta College of Art, Calgary, Alberta [*Library symbol National Library of Canada*] (NLC) ... ACSAA
Alberta Committee of Citizens with Disabilities (AC) ... ACCD
Alberta Conservation Tillage Society (AC) ... ACTS
Alberta Construction Association (AC) ... ACA
Alberta Consumer and Corporate Affairs, Edmonton, Alberta [*Library symbol National Library of Canada*] (NLC) ... AECA
Alberta Council on Aging (AC) ... ACA
Alberta Craft Council (AC) ... ACC
Alberta Crown Attorneys' Association (AC) ... ACAA
Alberta Culture, Edmonton, AB, Canada [*Library symbol Library of Congress*] (LCLS) ... CaAECL
Alberta Culture, Edmonton, AB, Canada [*Library symbol Library of Congress*] (LCLS) ... CaAECYR
Alberta Culture, Edmonton, Alberta [*Library symbol National Library of Canada*] (NLC) ... AECL
Alberta Culture, Heritage Resources Development, Edmonton, AB, Canada [*Library symbol Library of Congress*] (LCLS) ... CaAECYRH
Alberta Culture Library Services, Edmonton, AB, Canada [*Library symbol Library of Congress*] (LCLS) ... CaAECLS
Alberta Culture Library Services, Edmonton, Alberta [*Library symbol National Library of Canada*] (NLC) ... AECLS
Alberta Curling Federation (AC) ... ACF
Alberta Deaf Sports Association (AC) ... ADSA
Alberta Debate & Speech Association (AC) ... ADSA
Alberta Dental Assistants Association [*Formerly, Alberta Dental Nurses & Assistants Association*] (AC) ... ADAA
Alberta Department of Advanced Education and Manpower, Edmonton, AB, Canada [*Library symbol Library of Congress*] (LCLS) ... CaAEAE
Alberta Department of Agriculture, Dairy Division, Wetaskiwin, AB, Canada [*Library symbol Library of Congress*] (LCLS) ... CaAWAD
Alberta Department of Agriculture, Edmonton, AB, Canada [*Library symbol Library of Congress*] (LCLS) ... CaAEAg
Alberta Department of Agriculture, Farm Business Management Branch, Olds, AB, Canada [*Library symbol Library of Congress*] (LCLS) ... CaAOAF
Alberta Department of Agriculture, Field Crops Branch, Lacombe, AB, Canada [*Library symbol Library of Congress*] (LCLS) ... CaALaAF
Alberta Department of Agriculture, Horse Industry Branch, Calgary, AB, Canada [*Library symbol Library of Congress*] (LCLS) ... CaACAH
Alberta Department of Agriculture, Irrigation Division, Lethbridge, AB, Canada [*Library symbol Library of Congress*] (LCLS) ... CaALAI
Alberta Department of Agriculture, Laboratory, Edmonton, AB, Canada [*Library symbol Library of Congress*] (LCLS) ... CaAEAgL
Alberta Department of Agriculture, O. S. Longman Building, Edmonton, AB, Canada [*Library symbol Library of Congress*] (LCLS) ... CaAEAO
Alberta Department of Agriculture, Regional Office, Airdrie, AB, Canada [*Library symbol Library of Congress*] (LCLS) ... CaAAAR
Alberta Department of Agriculture, Regional Office, Barrhead, AB, Canada [*Library symbol Library of Congress*] (LCLS) ... CaABaAR
Alberta Department of Agriculture, Regional Office, Fairview, AB, Canada [*Library symbol Library of Congress*] (LCLS) ... CaAFAAR
Alberta Department of Agriculture, Regional Office, Lethbridge, AB, Canada [*Library symbol Library of Congress*] (LCLS) ... CaALAR
Alberta Department of Agriculture, Regional Office, Red Deer, AB, Canada [*Library symbol Library of Congress*] (LCLS) ... CaARDAR
Alberta Department of Agriculture, Regional Office, Vermilion, AB, Canada [*Library symbol Library of Congress*] (LCLS) ... CaAVAR
Alberta Department of Agriculture, Veterinary Laboratory, Fairview, AB, Canada [*Library symbol Library of Congress*] (LCLS) ... CaAFAAV
Alberta Department of Business Development and Tourism, Edmonton, AB, Canada [*Library symbol Library of Congress*] (LCLS) ... CaAEIC
Alberta Department of Consumer and Corporate Affairs, Edmonton, AB, Canada [*Library symbol Library of Congress*] (LCLS) ... CaAECA
Alberta Department of Culture Library [*UTLAS symbol*] ... AEC
Alberta Department of Economic Development, Edmonton, AB, Canada [*Library symbol Library of Congress*] (LCLS) ... CaAEEC
Alberta Department of Education, Audio Visual Services Branch, Edmonton, AB, Canada [*Library symbol Library of Congress*] (LCLS) ... CaAEEAV
Alberta Department of Education, Edmonton, AB, Canada [*Library symbol Library of Congress*] (LCLS) ... CaAEE
Alberta Department of Education, Special Education, Materials Resource Centre, Edmonton, AB, Canada [*Library symbol Library of Congress*] (LCLS) ... CaAEESE
Alberta Department of Energy and Natural Resources, Edmonton, AB, Canada [*Library symbol Library of Congress Obsolete*] (LCLS) ... CaAEMM
Alberta Department of Energy and Natural Resources, Edmonton, AB, Canada [*Library symbol Library of Congress*] (LCLS) ... CaAENR
Alberta Department of Energy and Natural Resources, Renewable Resources Division, Edmonton, AB, Canada [*Library symbol Library of Congress Obsolete*] (LCLS) ... CaAELF
Alberta Department of Federal and Intergovernmental Affairs, Edmonton, AB, Canada [*Library symbol Library of Congress*] (LCLS) ... CaAEFIA
Alberta Department of Government Services, Computing and Systems Division, Edmonton, AB, Canada [*Library symbol Library of Congress*] (LCLS) ... CaAEDC
Alberta Department of Government Services, Edmonton, AB, Canada [*Library symbol Library of Congress*] (LCLS) ... CaAEGS
Alberta Department of Housing and Public Works, Edmonton, AB, Canada [*Library symbol Library of Congress*] (LCLS) ... CaAEPW
Alberta Department of Labour, Edmonton, AB, Canada [*Library symbol Library of Congress*] (LCLS) ... CaAEML
Alberta Department of Labour, Occupational Health and Safety Division, Edmonton,AB, Canada [*Library symbol Library of Congress*] (LCLS) ... CaAEMLOH
Alberta Department of Municipal Affairs, Edmonton, AB, Canada [*Library symbol Library of Congress*] (LCLS) ... CaAEMA
Alberta Department of Recreation, Parks, and Wildlife, Edmonton, AB, Canada [*Library symbol Library of Congress*] (LCLS) ... CaAERPW
Alberta Department of Social Services and Community Health, Edmonton, AB, Canada [*Library symbol Library of Congress*] (LCLS) ... CaAEHSD
Alberta Department of the Attorney General, Edmonton, AB, Canada [*Library symbol Library of Congress*] (LCLS) ... CaAEAtG
Alberta Department of the Attorney General, Planning, Research, and Development Division, Edmonton, AB, Canada [*Library symbol Library of Congress*] (LCLS) ... CaAEPRD
Alberta Department of the Environment, Calgary, AB, Canada [*Library symbol Library of Congress*] (LCLS) ... CaACEN
Alberta Department of the Environment, Edmonton, AB, Canada [*Library symbol Library of Congress*] (LCLS) ... CaAEEN
Alberta Department of the Environment, Lethbridge, AB, Canada [*Library symbol Library of Congress*] (LCLS) ... CaALEn
Alberta Department of the Environment, Peace River, AB, Canada [*Library symbol Library of Congress*] (LCLS) ... CaAPrEN
Alberta Department of Transportation, Edmonton, AB, Canada [*Library symbol Library of Congress*] (LCLS) ... CaAEHT
Alberta Department of Transportation, Highways Testing Laboratory, Edmonton, AB,Canada [*Library symbol Library of Congress*] (LCLS) ... CaAEHTT

Alberta Department of Utilities and Telephones, Edmonton, AB, Canada [*Library symbol Library of Congress*] (LCLS) ... CaAEUT
Alberta Economic Development and Trade, Edmonton, Alberta [*Library symbol National Library of Canada*] (NLC) ... AEED
Alberta Education, Edmonton, Alberta [*Library symbol National Library of Canada*] (NLC) ... AEE
Alberta Education Libraries [*Professional collection*] [*UTLAS symbol*] ... ACL
Alberta Education Materials Resource Centre [*UTLAS symbol*] ... AMR
Alberta Education Materials Resource Centre, Edmonton, AB, Canada [*Library symbol Library of Congress*] (LCLS) ... CaAEEM
Alberta Education Materials Resources Centre, Calgary, AB, Canada [*Library symbol Library of Congress*] (LCLS) ... CaACEM
Alberta Energy [*NYSE symbol*] (TTSB) ... AOG
Alberta Energy and Natural Resources, Edmonton, Alberta [*Library symbol National Library of Canada*] (NLC) ... AENR
Alberta Energy and Natural Resources Library [*UTLAS symbol*] ... ANR
Alberta Energy and Natural Resources Library, Edmonton, AB, Canada [*Library symbol Library of Congress*] (LCLS) ... CaAEENR
Alberta Energy Co., Calgary, AB, Canada [*Library symbol Library of Congress*] (LCLS) ... CaACAE
Alberta Energy Co., Calgary, Alberta [*Library symbol National Library of Canada*] (NLC) ... ACAE
Alberta Energy Co. Ltd. [*Toronto Stock Exchange symbol Vancouver Stock Exchange symbol*] ... AEC
Alberta Energy Co. Ltd. [*Associated Press*] (SAG) ... AlbrtE
Alberta Energy Co. Ltd. [*NYSE symbol*] (SAG) ... AOG
Alberta Energy Resources Conservation Board, Calgary, AB, Canada [*Library symbol Library of Congress*] (LCLS) ... CaACER
Alberta Energy Resources Conservation Board, Calgary, Alberta [*Library symbol National Library of Canada*] (NLC) ... ACER
Alberta Environment, Calgary, Alberta [*Library symbol National Library of Canada*] (NLC) ... ACEN
Alberta Environment Centre, Vegreville, Alberta [*Library symbol National Library of Canada*] (NLC) ... AVEE
Alberta Environment, Edmonton, Alberta [*Library symbol National Library of Canada*] (NLC) ... AEEN
Alberta Environment, Lethbridge, Alberta [*Library symbol National Library of Canada*] (NLC) ... ALEN
Alberta Environment Library [*UTLAS symbol*] ... AEL
Alberta Environment, Peace River, Alberta [*Library symbol National Library of Canada*] (NLC) ... APREN
Alberta Environmental Centre Library [*UTLAS symbol*] ... AEN
Alberta Environmental Centre, Vegreville, AB, Canada [*Library symbol Library of Congress*] (LCLS) ... CaAVeE
Alberta Environmental Network (AC) ... AEN
Alberta Equestrian Federation (AC) ... AEF
Alberta Exploration [*Vancouver Stock Exchange symbol*] ... AXO
Alberta Family Histories Society (AC) ... AFHS
Alberta Federal and Intergovernmental Affairs, Edmonton, Alberta [*Library symbol National Library of Canada*] (NLC) ... AEFIA
Alberta Federation of Labour [*Federation du Travail de l'Alberta*] (AC) ... AFL
Alberta Fire Training School, Alberta Labour, Vermilion, Alberta [*Library symbol National Library of Canada*] (NLC) ... AVLF
Alberta Forest Development Research Trust Fund [*Also Forest Research Program - Environmental Protection & Enhancement Fund*] (AC) ... AFDRTF
Alberta Forest Products Association (AC) ... AFPA
Alberta Gas Ethylene Co., Calgary, AB, Canada [*Library symbol Library of Congress*] (LCLS) ... CaACAG
Alberta Gas Ethylene Co., Calgary, Alberta [*Library symbol National Library of Canada*] (NLC) ... ACAG
Alberta Gas Trunk Line Co. Ltd., Calgary, AB, Canada [*Library symbol Library of Congress*] (LCLS) ... CaACGTL
Alberta Gas Trunk Line Co. Ltd., Calgary, Alberta [*Library symbol National Library of Canada*] (NLC) ... ACGTL
Alberta Gazette [*A publication*] (DLA) ... Alta Gaz
Alberta Genealogical Society (AC) ... AGS
Alberta Government [*Canada ICAO designator*] (FAAC) ... GOA
Alberta Government Civil Lawyers Association (AC) ... AGCLA
Alberta Government Libraries' Council (AC) ... AGLC
Alberta Government Libraries Union Catalogue, Edmonton, Alberta [*Library symbol National Library of Canada*] (NLC) ... AEAUC
Alberta Government Services, Operating and Maintenance Division, Edmonton, AB, Canada [*Library symbol*] [*Library of Congress*] (LCLS) ... CaAEAGS
Alberta Government Telephones [*Part of Telecom Canada*] [*Calgary, AB*] [*Telecommunications service*] (TSSD) ... AGT
Alberta Government Telephones Commission, Edmonton, AB, Canada [*Library symbol Library of Congress*] (LCLS) ... CaAEGT
Alberta Government Telephones, Edmonton, Alberta [*Library symbol National Library of Canada*] (NLC) ... AEGT
Alberta Government Union Catalogue, Edmonton Concordia College, Edmonton, AB, Canada [*Library symbol Library of Congress*] (LCLS) ... CaAEAUC
Alberta Health Record Association (AC) ... AHRA
Alberta Healthcare Association [*Formerly, Alberta Hospital Association*] (AC) ... AHA
Alberta Heritage Foundation for Medical Research [*Canada*] ... AHFMR
Alberta Historical Resources, Alberta Culture and Multiculturalism, Edmonton, Alberta [*Library symbol National Library of Canada*] (NLC) ... AEA
Alberta Historical Resources, Edmonton, AB, Canada [*Library symbol Library of Congress*] (LCLS) ... CaAEA
Alberta Historical Resources Foundation (AC) ... AHRF
Alberta Horticultural Research Centre, Brooks, AB, Canada [*Library symbol Library of Congress*] (LCLS) ... CaABAH
Alberta Horticultural Research Centre, Brooks, Alberta [*Library symbol National Library of Canada*] (NLC) ... ABAH
Alberta Hospital Association [*Edmonton*] ... AHA
Alberta Hospital Association, Resource Library, Edmonton, AB, Canada [*Library symbol*] [*Library of Congress*] (LCLS) ... CaAEAHA
Alberta Hospital, Edmonton, AB, Canada [*Library symbol*] [*Library of Congress*] (LCLS) ... CaAEAH
Alberta Hospital, Edmonton, Alberta [*Library symbol National Library of Canada*] (BIB) ... AEAH
Alberta Hospital Library, Oliver, Alberta [*Library symbol National Library of Canada*] (NLC) ... AEHO
Alberta Hospital, Oliver, AB, Canada [*Library symbol Library of Congress*] (LCLS) ... CaAEHO
Alberta Hospital, Ponoka, Alberta [*Library symbol National Library of Canada*] (NLC) ... APH
Alberta Hospital, Staff Library, Ponoka, AB, Canada [*Library symbol Library of Congress*] (LCLS) ... CaAPH
Alberta Hospitals & Medical Care, Edmonton, Alberta [*Library symbol National Library of Canada*] (NLC) ... AEHSC
Alberta Housing Corp., Edmonton, AB, Canada [*Library symbol Library of Congress*] (LCLS) ... CaAEHC
Alberta Human Rights Commission, Edmonton, AB, Canada [*Library symbol Library of Congress*] (LCLS) ... CaAEHR
Alberta Information Retrieval for Health, Physical Education and Recreation (NITA) ... AIRHPER
Alberta Institute of Law Research and Reform [*Canada*] (ILCA) ... Alberta LRR
Alberta Irrigation Projects Association (AC) ... AIPA
Alberta Labour, Alberta Fire Training School, Vermilion, AB, Canada [*Library symbol*] [*Library of Congress*] (LCLS) ... CaAVLF
Alberta Labour, Edmonton, Alberta [*Library symbol National Library of Canada*] (NLC) ... AEML
Alberta Labour-Building Standards Library, Edmonton, AB, Canada [*Library symbol Library of Congress*] (LCLS) ... CaAELBS
Alberta Land Surveyors' Association (AC) ... ALSA
Alberta Land Use Planning Data Bank [*Alberta Municipal Affairs*] [*Information service or system Defunct*] (IID) ... LANDUP
Alberta Law [*A publication*] (DLA) ... Alta L
Alberta Law Foundation (AC) ... ALF
Alberta Law Quarterly [*A publication*] (DLA) ... Alb LQ
Alberta Law Quarterly [*A publication*] (DLA) ... Alta LQ
Alberta League for Environmentally Responsible Tourism (AC) ... ALERT
Alberta Legislation Information [*Alberta Public Affairs Bureau*] [*Canada Information service or system*] (CRD) ... ALI
Alberta Legislature Library, Edmonton, AB, Canada [*Library symbol Library of Congress*] (LCLS) ... CaAEP
Alberta Legislature Library, Edmonton, Alberta [*Library symbol National Library of Canada*] (NLC) ... AEP
Alberta Library Trustees' Association (AC) ... ALTA
Alberta Limousin Association (AC) ... ALA
Alberta Manpower, Edmonton, AB, Canada [*Library symbol*] [*Library of Congress*] (LCLS) ... CaAEMAN
Alberta Manpower, Edmonton, Alberta [*Library symbol National Library of Canada*] (NLC) ... AEMAN
Alberta Marine Trades Association (AC) ... AMTA
Alberta Materials Exchange [*Formerly, Alberta Waste Materials Exchange*] (AC) ... AME
Alberta Medal [*Canada*] (DD) ... AM
Alberta Microelectronic Centre [*University of Alberta*] [*Research center*] (RCD) ... AMC
Alberta Motion Picture Industries Association (AC) ... AMPIA
Alberta Motion Picture Industries Association [*Canada*] (WWLA) ... AMPIA
Alberta Municipal Affairs, Edmonton, Alberta [*Library symbol National Library of Canada*] (NLC) ... AEMA
Alberta Native Plants Council (AC) ... ANPC
Alberta Natural Gas Co. Ltd. [*Toronto Stock Exchange symbol Vancouver Stock Exchange symbol*] ... ANG
Alberta Occupation Health and Safety, Edmonton, Alberta [*Library symbol National Library of Canada*] (NLC) ... AEOH
Alberta Office of the Ombudsman, Edmonton, Alberta [*Library symbol National Library of Canada*] (NLC) ... AEOM
Alberta Oil Sands Index [*Alberta Oil Sands Technology and Research Authority*] [*Information service or system*] ... AOSI
Alberta Oil Sands Information Centre, Edmonton, AB, Canada [*Library symbol Library of Congress*] (LCLS) ... CaAEAOS
Alberta Oil Sands Information Centre, Edmonton, Alberta [*Library symbol National Library of Canada*] (NLC) ... AEAOS
Alberta Oil Sands Technology and Research Authority (IID) ... AOSTRA
Alberta Ombudsman, Edmonton, AB, Canada [*Library symbol Library of Congress*] (LCLS) ... CaAEOM
Alberta Orienteering Association (AC) ... AOA
Alberta Personnel Administration, Edmonton, AB, Canada [*Library symbol Library of Congress*] (LCLS) ... CaAEAPA
Alberta Personnel Administration, Edmonton, Alberta [*Library symbol National Library of Canada*] (NLC) ... AEAPA
Alberta Pesticide Action Network (AC) ... APAN
Alberta Petroleum Marketing Commission, Calgary, AB, Canada [*Library symbol Library of Congress*] (LCLS) ... CaACPMC
Alberta Petroleum Marketing Commission, Calgary, Alberta [*Library symbol National Library of Canada*] (NLC) ... ACPMC
Alberta Pharmaceutical Association (AC) ... APhA
Alberta Plastics Recycling Association (AC) ... APRA
Alberta Provincial Courts, Edmonton, AB, Canada [*Library symbol Library of Congress*] (LCLS) ... CaAEPC
Alberta Provincial Courts, Edmonton, Alberta [*Library symbol National Library of Canada*] (NLC) ... AEPC

Alberta Psychiatric Association (AC) .... APA
Alberta Public Affairs Bureau, Bibliography Section, Edmonton, AB, Canada [*Library symbol*] [*Library of Congress*] (LCLS) .... CaAEPA
Alberta Public Health Association (AC) .... APHA
Alberta Public Utilities Board, Edmonton, AB, Canada [*Library symbol Library of Congress*] (LCLS) .... CaAEPU
Alberta Public Utilities Board, Edmonton, Alberta [*Library symbol National Library of Canada*] (NLC) .... AEPU
Alberta Public Works, Supply and Services, Edmonton, Alberta [*Library symbol National Library of Canada*] (NLC) .... AEGS
Alberta RCMP Century Library, Beaverlodge, AB, Canada [*Library symbol*] [*Library of Congress*] (LCLS) .... CaABeaAr
Alberta RCMP Century Library, Beaverlodge, Alberta [*Library symbol National Library of Canada*] (NLC) .... ABAR
Alberta Real Estate Association (AC) .... AREA
Alberta Recording Industry Association (AC) .... ARIA
Alberta Recreation and Parks, Edmonton, Alberta [*Library symbol National Library of Canada*] (NLC) .... AERPW
Alberta Recreation, Parks & Wildlife Foundation (AC) .... RPW Foundation
Alberta Registered Dietitians Association (AC) .... ARDA
Alberta Registered Music Teachers' Association (AC) .... ARMTA
Alberta Registered Professional Foresters Association (AC) .... ARPFA
Alberta Research Council, Clover Bar Branch, Edmonton, AB, Canada [*Library symbol Library of Congress*] (LCLS) .... CaAERC
Alberta Research Council, Edmonton, Alberta [*Library symbol National Library of Canada*] (NLC) .... AER
Alberta Research Council, Solar and Wind Energy Research Program Information Centre, Edmonton, AB, Canada [*Library symbol Library of Congress*] (LCLS) .... CaAERSWE
Alberta Research Council, Southern Branch Library, Calgary, AB, Canada [*Library symbol*] [*Library of Congress*] (LCLS) .... CaACRS
Alberta Research Council, Terrace Plaza Branch Library, Edmonton, AB, Canada [*Library symbol*] [*Library of Congress*] (LCLS) .... CaAERTP
Alberta Research Council, University Branch, Edmonton, AB, Canada [*Library symbol Library of Congress*] (LCLS) .... CaAERU
Alberta Research, Edmonton, AB, Canada [*Library symbol Library of Congress*] (LCLS) .... CaAER
Alberta Research Network [*Computer science*] [*Canada*] (TNIG) .... ARnet
Alberta Restaurant & Foodservices Association (AC) .... ARFA
Alberta Revised Statutes [*Canada*] [*A publication*] (DLA) .... Alta Rev Stat
Alberta Roofing Contractors Association Ltd. (AC) .... ARCA
Alberta School Boards Association [*Formerly, Alberta School Trustees' Association*] (AC) .... ASBA
Alberta School for the Deaf, Edmonton, AB, Canada [*Library symbol Library of Congress*] (LCLS) .... CaAESD
Alberta School for the Deaf, Edmonton, Alberta [*Library symbol National Library of Canada*] (NLC) .... AESD
Alberta Schools Athletic Association (AC) .... ASAA
Alberta Scuba Divers Council (AC) .... ASDC
Alberta Securities Commission, Edmonton, AB, Canada [*Library symbol Library of Congress*] (LCLS) .... CaAEASC
Alberta Securities Commission, Edmonton, Alberta [*Library symbol National Library of Canada*] (NLC) .... AEASC
Alberta Senior Citizens Sport & Recreation Association (AC) .... ASCSRA
Alberta Sheep Breeders Association (AC) .... ASBA
Alberta Simmental Association (AC) .... ASA
Alberta Snowmobile Association (AC) .... ASA
Alberta Social Services and Community Health, Edmonton, Alberta [*Library symbol National Library of Canada*] (NLC) .... AEHSD
Alberta Society of Artists [*1931*] [*Canada*] (NGC) .... ASA
Alberta Society of Engineering Technologists (AC) .... ASET
Alberta Society of Professional Biologists (AC) .... ASPB
Alberta Solicitor General, Edmonton, Alberta [*Library symbol National Library of Canada*] (NLC) .... AESG
Alberta Solicitor General's Department, Edmonton, AB, Canada [*Library symbol Library of Congress*] (LCLS) .... CaAESG
Alberta Speleological Society (AC) .... ASS
Alberta Sports & Recreation Association for the Blind (AC) .... ASRAB
Alberta Statistical Information System [*Alberta Treasury, Bureau of Statistics*] [*Database*] .... ASIST
Alberta Statutes [*Canada*] [*A publication*] (DLA) .... Alta Stat
Alberta Stock Exchange (HGAA) .... ASE
Alberta Sulphur Research Ltd. (AC) .... ASRL
Alberta Swine Breeders' Association (AC) .... ASBA
Alberta Table Tennis Association (AC) .... ATTA
Alberta Teachers' Association [*Association des Enseignants de l'Alberta*] (AC) .... ATA
Alberta Therapeutic Riding Association (AC) .... ATRA
Alberta Tourism and Small Business, Edmonton, Alberta [*Library symbol National Library of Canada*] (NLC) .... AEIC
Alberta Transportation, Edmonton, Alberta [*Library symbol National Library of Canada*] (NLC) .... AEHT
Alberta Treasury Department, Bureau of Statistics, Edmonton, AB,Canada [*Library symbol Library of Congress*] (LCLS) .... CaAETBS
Alberta Treasury Department, Corporate Tax Administration, Edmonton, AB, Canada [*Library symbol Library of Congress*] (LCLS) .... CaAETCT
Alberta Treasury Department, Edmonton, AB, Canada [*Library symbol Library of Congress*] (LCLS) .... CaAET
Alberta Treasury, Edmonton, Alberta [*Library symbol National Library of Canada*] (NLC) .... AET
Alberta Tree Nursery and Horticultural Centre, Edmonton, Alberta [*Library symbol National Library of Canada*] (BIB) .... AETN
Alberta Union of Civil Service Employees, Edmonton, AB, Canada [*Library symbol Library of Congress*] (LCLS) .... CaAECS
Alberta Union of Provincial Employees [*Canada*] (BARN) .... AUPE
Alberta Union of Provincial Employees, Edmonton, Alberta [*Library symbol National Library of Canada*] (NLC) .... AECS
Alberta Urban Municipalities Association (AC) .... AUMA
Alberta Utilities and Telephones, Edmonton, Alberta [*Library symbol National Library of Canada*] (NLC) .... AEUT
Alberta Veterinary Medical Association (AC) .... AVMA
Alberta Vocational Centre, Calgary, AB, Canada [*Library symbol Library of Congress*] (LCLS) .... CaACVC
Alberta Vocational Centre, Calgary, Albert [*Library symbol National Library of Canada*] (NLC) .... ACVC
Alberta Vocational Centre, Edmonton, AB, Canada [*Library symbol Library of Congress*] (LCLS) .... CaAEVC
Alberta Vocational Centre, Edmonton, Alberta [*Library symbol National Library of Canada*] (NLC) .... AEVC
Alberta Vocational Centre, Grouard, AB, Canada [*Library symbol Library of Congress*] (LCLS) .... CaAGVC
Alberta Vocational Centre, Grouard, Alberta [*Library symbol National Library of Canada*] (NLC) .... AGVC
Alberta Vocational Centre, Lac La Biche, AB, Canada [*Library symbol Library of Congress*] (LCLS) .... CaALLbVC
Alberta Vocational Centre, Lac La Biche, Alberta [*Library symbol National Library of Canada*] (NLC) .... ALLBVC
Alberta Volleyball Association (AC) .... AVA
Alberta Water Polo Association (AC) .... AWPA
Alberta Water Well Drilling Association (AC) .... AWWDA
Alberta Weekly Newspapers Association (AC) .... AWNA
Alberta Wilderness Association (AC) .... AWA
Alberta Women's Institutes (AC) .... AWI
Alberta Worker's Health, Safety, and Compensation, Edmonton, AB, Canada [*Library symbol Library of Congress*] (LCLS) .... CaAEOH
Albertine Sisters (Krakow, Poland) (TOCD) .... CSA
Alberto Culver [*NYSE symbol*] (SAG) .... ACV
Alberto Culver Co. [*Associated Press*] (SAG) .... Alberto
Alberto Culver Co. [*Associated Press*] (SAG) .... AlCulA
Alberto-Culver Cl'A' [*NYSE symbol*] (TTSB) .... ACVA
Alberto-Culver Cl'B' [*NYSE symbol*] (TTSB) .... ACV
Alberto-Culver Co., Melrose Park, IL [*Library symbol Library of Congress*] (LCLS) .... IMelpA
Alberton High School, Alberton, MT [*Library symbol*] [*Library of Congress*] (LCLS) .... MtAHS
Albertson College of Idaho (GAGS) .... Albertson C (ID)
Albertson's, Inc. [*NYSE symbol*] (SPSG) .... ABS
Albertson's, Inc. [*Associated Press*] (SAG) .... Albertsn
Albertus Beneventanus [*Deceased, 1187*] [*Authority cited in pre-1607 legal work*] (DSA) .... A
Albertus Beneventanus [*Deceased, 1187*] [*Authority cited in pre-1607 legal work*] (DSA) .... Al
Albertus Brunus [*Deceased, 1541*] [*Authority cited in pre-1607 legal work*] (DSA) .... Alb Brun
Albertus Brunus [*Deceased, 1541*] [*Authority cited in pre-1607 legal work*] (DSA) .... Alber Bru
Albertus de Saliceto [*Authority cited in pre-1607 legal work*] (DSA) .... Alb
Albertus Denarii de Odofredo [*Deceased, 1300*] [*Authority cited in pre-1607 legal work*] (DSA) .... Alb de Odofre
Albertus Electus Imperator Optimus Vivat [*Inscription used by Albert II, 15th-century German king*] .... AEIOU
Albertus Longobardista [*Flourished, 12th century*] [*Authority cited in pre-1607 legal work*] (DSA) .... a
Albertus Longobardista [*Flourished, 12th century*] [*Authority cited in pre-1607 legal work*] (DSA) .... Al
Albertus Longobardista [*Flourished, 12th century*] [*Authority cited in pre-1607 legal work*] (DSA) .... Alb
Albertus Magnus [*Teutonicus*] [*Deceased, 1280*] [*Authority cited in pre-1607 legal work*] (DSA) .... Al
Albertus Magnus College [*New Haven, CT*] .... AMC
Albertus Magnus College, New Haven, CT [*Library symbol Library of Congress*] (LCLS) .... CtNhA
Albertus Magnus Guild (EA) .... AMG
Albertus Papiensis [*Flourished, 1211-40*] [*Authority cited in pre-1607 legal work*] (DSA) .... Al Pa
Albertus Papiensis [*Flourished, 1211-40*] [*Authority cited in pre-1607 legal work*] (DSA) .... Al Pp
Albertus Papiensis [*Flourished, 1211-40*] [*Authority cited in pre-1607 legal work*] (DSA) .... Alb Pp
Albertus Ranconis [*Flourished, 1369-72*] [*Authority cited in pre-1607 legal work*] (DSA) .... Al
Albertville [*France ICAO location identifier*] (ICLI) .... LFKA
Albertville, AL [*Location identifier FAA*] (FAAL) .... ARF
Albertville, AL [*AM radio station call letters*] .... WAVU
Albertville, AL [*FM radio station call letters*] .... WQSB
Albertville Elementary School, Albertville, MN [*Library symbol*] [*Library of Congress*] (LCLS) .... MnAlvE
Albertville Olympic Organizing Committee [*Albertville, France*] (EAIO) .... AOOC
Albert-Westmorland-Kent Regional Library, Moncton, NB, Canada [*Library symbol Library of Congress*] (LCLS) .... CaNBMoW
Albert-Westmorland-Kent Regional Library, Moncton, New Brunswick [*Library symbol National Library of Canada*] (NLC) .... NBMOW
Albi [*France*] [*Airport symbol*] (OAG) .... LBI
Albi/Le Sequestre [*France ICAO location identifier*] (ICLI) .... LFCI
Albia, IA [*AM radio station call letters*] .... KLBA
Albia, IA [*FM radio station call letters*] .... KLBA-FM
Albia Public Library, Albia, IA [*Library symbol Library of Congress*] (LCLS).... IaAlb
Albia Union-Republican, Albia, IA [*Library symbol Library of Congress*] (LCLS) .... IaAlbUR
Albina [*Surinam*] [*ICAO location identifier*] (ICLI) .... SMBN

Albinism World Alliance ... AWA
Albinism-Deafness [*Syndrome*] [*Medicine*] (DMAA) ... ADFN
Albino Guinea Pig [*Medicine*] (DMAA) ... A
Albion Banc Corp. [*NASDAQ symbol*] (SAG) ... ALBC
Albion Banc Corp. [*Associated Press*] (SAG) ... AlbionBc
Albion College, Albion, MI [*OCLC symbol*] (OCLC) ... EXA
Albion College, Albion, MI [*Library symbol Library of Congress*] (LCLS) ... MiAlbC
Albion Community Library, Albion, ID [*Library symbol*] [*Library of Congress*] (LCLS) ... IdAl
Albion, IL [*FM radio station call letters*] (RBYB) ... WBJW-FM
Albion, MI [*AM radio station call letters*] ... WALM
Albion, MI [*FM radio station call letters*] ... WUFN
Albion, NE [*Television station call letters*] ... KCAN
Albion, NE [*Television station call letters*] (RBYB) ... KLKE
Albion Public Library, Albion, IL [*Library symbol Library of Congress*] (LCLS) ... IAlb
Albion Public Library, Albion, MI [*Library symbol Library of Congress*] (LCLS) ... MiAlb
Albion State Normal School, Albion, ID [*Library symbol Library of Congress*] (LCLS) ... IdAlN
Albion-Bolton Branch, Town of Caledon Public Libraries, Bolton, Ontario [*Library symbol National Library of Canada*] (NLC) ... OBCAB
Albite [*CIPW classification*] [*Geology*] ... ab
Alborg [*Denmark ICAO location identifier*] (ICLI) ... EKYT
Alborn Elementary School, Alborn, MN [*Library symbol*] [*Library of Congress*] (LCLS) ... MnAbnE
Al-Bough [*Yemen*] [*ICAO location identifier*] (ICLI) ... OYBO
Albrecht Durer [*German artist, 1471-1528*] ... AD
Albrecht Durer Study Unit [*American Topical Association*] (EA) ... ADSU
[*Secretary of State Madeleine*] **Albright,** [*National-Security Adviser Sandy*] **Berger,** [*and Defense Secretary William*] **Cohen** [*A troika known in Washington*] ... ABC
Albright College, Reading, PA [*Library symbol Library of Congress*] (LCLS) ... PRA
Albright-Butler-Bloomberg Syndrome [*Medicine*] (DMAA) ... ABB
Albright-Knox Art Gallery [*Buffalo, NY*] ... AK
Albright-Knox Art Gallery Library, Buffalo Fine Arts Academy, Buffalo, NY [*Library symbol Library of Congress*] (LCLS) ... NBuAK
Albright's Hereditary Osteodystrophy [*Medicine*] ... AHO
Albrook High School, Saginaw, MN [*Library symbol*] [*Library of Congress*] (LCLS) ... MnSagHS
Album (VRA) ... alb
Album Adult Alternative [*Music classification*] ... AAA
Album Oriented Rock [*Facetious translation: Another Old Record*] [*Broadcasting*] ... AOR
Albumen (VRA) ... ALPT
Albumin [*Also, ALB*] [*Biochemistry*] ... AL
Albumin [*Also, AL*] [*Biochemistry*] ... ALB
Albumin Clearance (DMAA) ... ALBC
Albumin Clearance [*Biochemistry*] (DAVI) ... C_{alb}
Albumin, Dextrose, Catalase [*Media*] ... ADC
Albumin Excretion Rate [*Physiology*] ... AER
Albumin/Globulin [*Medicine*] ... A/G
Albumin/Globulin Ratio [*Gastroenterology*] (DAVI) ... ALB/GLOB
Albumin-Buffered Saline [*Clinical chemistry*] ... ABS
Albumin-Calcium-Magnesium [*Biochemistry*] (MAE) ... ACM
Albumin-Coagulin Ratio [*Biochemistry*] (MAE) ... A/C
Albumin-Free [*Medicine*] ... AF
Album-Oriented Radio [*Radio station format*] (WDMC) ... AOR
Albuq [*Yemen*] [*Airport symbol*] (OAG) ... BUK
Albuquerque [*New Mexico*] [*Seismograph station code, US Geological Survey*] (SEIS) ... ABQ
Albuquerque [*New Mexico*] [*Airport symbol*] (OAG) ... ABQ
Albuquerque [*New Mexico*] [*Seismograph station code, US Geological Survey*] (SEIS) ... ALQ
Albuquerque [*New Mexico*] [*Seismograph station code, US Geological Survey*] (SEIS) ... ANMO
Albuquerque [*New Mexico*] [*ICAO location identifier*] (ICLI) ... KZAB
Albuquerque Academy, Albuquerque, NM [*Library symbol*] [*Library of Congress*] (LCLS) ... NmAAc
Albuquerque Bar Journal [*A publication*] (DLA) ... Albuquerque BJ
Albuquerque/International [*New Mexico*] [*ICAO location identifier*] (ICLI) ... KABQ
Albuquerque, NM [*Location identifier FAA*] (FAAL) ... ILT
Albuquerque, NM [*AM radio station call letters*] ... KABQ
Albuquerque, NM [*FM radio station call letters*] ... KANW
Albuquerque, NM [*FM radio station call letters*] ... KASY
Albuquerque, NM [*Television station call letters*] ... KASY-TV
Albuquerque, NM [*Television station call letters*] ... KAZQ
Albuquerque, NM [*AM radio station call letters*] ... KDAZ
Albuquerque, NM [*AM radio station call letters*] ... KDEF
Albuquerque, NM [*AM radio station call letters*] ... KDZZ
Albuquerque, NM [*FM radio station call letters*] ... KFLQ
Albuquerque, NM [*FM radio station call letters*] ... KHFM
Albuquerque, NM [*AM radio station call letters*] (RBYB) ... KHTL
Albuquerque, NM [*FM radio station call letters*] (RBYB) ... KHTZ
Albuquerque, NM [*AM radio station call letters*] ... KKIM
Albuquerque, NM [*AM radio station call letters*] ... KKOB
Albuquerque, NM [*FM radio station call letters*] ... KKOB-FM
Albuquerque, NM [*Television station call letters*] ... KLUZ
Albuquerque, NM [*FM radio station call letters*] ... KLYT
Albuquerque, NM [*FM radio station call letters*] ... KMGA
Albuquerque, NM [*Television station call letters*] ... KNAT
Albuquerque, NM [*Television station call letters*] ... KNME
Albuquerque, NM [*AM radio station call letters*] (RBYB) ... KNOS
Albuquerque, NM [*Television station call letters*] ... KOAT
Albuquerque, NM [*Television station call letters*] ... KOB
Albuquerque, NM [*FM radio station call letters*] (RBYB) ... KPEK-FM
Albuquerque, NM [*Television station call letters*] ... KRQE
Albuquerque, NM [*FM radio station call letters*] ... KRST
Albuquerque, NM [*FM radio station call letters*] ... KRZN
Albuquerque, NM [*AM radio station call letters*] ... KRZY
Albuquerque, NM [*FM radio station call letters*] (RBYB) ... KTBL-FM
Albuquerque, NM [*FM radio station call letters*] (RBYB) ... KTEG
Albuquerque, NM [*FM radio station call letters*] ... KUNM
Albuquerque, NM [*AM radio station call letters*] ... KXKS
Albuquerque, NM [*FM radio station call letters*] ... KZRR
Albuquerque, NM [*AM radio station call letters*] ... KZSS
Albuquerque, NM [*Location identifier FAA*] (FAAL) ... SPT
Albuquerque, NM [*Location identifier FAA*] (FAAL) ... ZAB
Albuquerque Operations Office (DOGT) ... AL
Albuquerque Operations Office [*Department of Energy*] ... ALO
Albuquerque Operations Office [*Department of Energy*] (GRD) ... ALOO
Albuquerque Public Library, Albuquerque, NM [*Library symbol Library of Congress*] (LCLS) ... NmA
Albuquerque Public Library, Albuquerque, NM [*OCLC symbol*] (OCLC) ... QUE
Albuquerque Public Library, Ernie Pyle Memorial Branch, Albuquerque, NM [*Library symbol Library of Congress*] (LCLS) ... NmA-EP
Albuquerque Public Library, Los Griegos Branch, Albuquerque, NM [*Library symbol Library of Congress*] (LCLS) ... NmA-LG
Albuquerque Public Library, Prospect Park Branch, Albuquerque, NM [*Library symbol Library of Congress*] (LCLS) ... NmA-PP
Albuquerque Testing Laboratory (AAGC) ... ATL
Albury [*Australia Airport symbol*] (OAG) ... ABX
Albury [*New South Wales*] [*Airport symbol*] (AD) ... ABX
Albury [*Australia ICAO location identifier*] (ICLI) ... AMAY
Albury-Wodonga Environment Center [*Australia*] ... AWEC
Albus [*White*] [*Pharmacy*] ... ALB
Alcadd Test [*Psychology*] ... AT
Alcaeus [*Seventh century BC*] [*Classical studies*] (OCD) ... Alc
ALCAN Aluminium Ltd. [*NYSE symbol Toronto Stock Exchange symbol Vancouver Stock Exchange symbol*] (SPSG) ... AL
Alcan Aluminium Ltd [*NYSE symbol*] (TTSB) ... AL
Alcan Aluminum Co., Cleveland, OH [*Library symbol Library of Congress*] (LCLS) ... OClA
ALCAN Aluminum Ltd. [*Associated Press*] (SAG) ... Alcan
ALCAN International Ltee. [*ALCAN International Ltd.*] **Jonquiere, Quebec** [*Library symbol National Library of Canada*] (NLC) ... QAA
ALCAN Research & Development Ltd., Kingston, ON, Canada [*Library symbol Library of Congress*] (LCLS) ... CaOKA
ALCAN Smelters Chemical Ltd., Technical Library, Kitimat, BC, Canada [*Library symbol Library of Congress*] (LCLS) ... CaBKAS
ALCAN [*Aluminum Co. of Canada Ltd.*] **World Price** [*Obsolete*] (FEA) ... AWP
Alcatel Alsthom ADS [*NYSE symbol*] (TTSB) ... ALA
Alcatel Alsthom Compagnie General d'Electricite [*NYSE symbol*] (SPSG) ... ALA
Alcatel Alsthom Compagnie General d'Electricite [*Associated Press*] (SAG) ... Alcatel
Alcatel Thomson Gigadisc [*Optical disk*] ... ATG
Alcester Public Library, Alcester, SD [*Library symbol Library of Congress*] (LCLS) ... SdAl
Alcestis [*of Euripides*] [*Classical studies*] (OCD) ... Alc
Alchemy ... ALCH
Alchemy (VRA) ... alch
Alcian Blue [*A biological stain*] ... AB
Alcian Blue-Aldehyde Fuchsin [*Dyes*] (OA) ... AB-AF
Alcian Blue-Periodic Acid Schiff-Lead Hematoxylin Procedure [*Biotechnology*] ... AB-PAS-Pbh
Alcibiades [*of Plutarch*] [*Classical studies*] (OCD) ... Alc
Alcibiades [*of Plato*] [*Classical studies*] (OCD) ... Alc
Alcide Corp. [*NASDAQ symbol*] (NQ) ... ALCD
Alcide Corp. [*Associated Press*] (SAG) ... Alcide
Alcina Development Corp. [*Vancouver Stock Exchange symbol*] ... AIV
Alclad [*Metallurgy*] ... ALCD
Alclare Resources [*Vancouver Stock Exchange symbol*] ... ALS
Alclometasone Dipropionate [*Glucocorticoid*] ... ADP
Alcman [*Seventh century BC*] [*Classical studies*] (OCD) ... Alcm
Alco Standard [*NYSE symbol*] (TTSB) ... ASN
Alco Standard Corp. [*Associated Press*] (SAG) ... AlcoSt
Alco Standard Corp. [*NYSE symbol*] (SPSG) ... ASN
Alco Std $5.04 Cv Dep Pfd [*NYSE symbol*] (TTSB) ... ASNPrB
Alcoa Picturephone Remote Information System [*AT&T Co.*] (NITA) ... APRIS
ALCOA Smelting Process ... ASP
Alcoa, TN [*AM radio station call letters*] ... WBCR
Alcoa, TN [*FM radio station call letters*] ... WYLV
Alcobaca [*Brazil*] [*Airport symbol*] (OAG) ... ABC
Alcock and Napier's Irish King's Bench Reports [*A publication*] (DLA) ... A & N
Alcock and Napier's Irish King's Bench Reports [*A publication*] (DLA) ... Al & N
Alcock and Napier's Irish King's Bench Reports [*A publication*] (DLA) ... Al & Nap
Alcock and Napier's Irish King's Bench Reports [*A publication*] (ILCA) ... Alc & N
Alcock and Napier's Irish King's Bench Reports [*A publication*] (DLA) ... Alc & Nap
Alcock and Napier's Irish King's Bench Reports [*A publication*] (DLA) ... Alcock & N
Alcock on Personal Property [*A publication*] (DLA) ... Alc Per Prop
Alcock's Registry Cases [*1832-41*] [*Ireland*] [*A publication*] (DLA) ... Alc
Alcock's Registry Cases [*Ireland*] [*1832-41*] [*A publication*] (ILCA) ... Alc Reg
Alcock's Registry Cases [*1832-41*] [*Ireland*] [*A publication*] (DLA) ... Alc Reg C
Alcock's Registry Cases [*1832-41*] [*Ireland*] [*A publication*] (DLA) ... Alc Reg Cas
Alcohol (ADA) ... A
Alcohol (KSC) ... ALC
Alcohol ... ALCH

Alcohol .... ALCOH
Alcohol .... ALCOL
Alcohol 5%, Dextrose 5% in Water A5D5W
Alcohol and Dependency Intervention Council [*Military*] (AABC) .... ADDIC
Alcohol and Drug [*Type of addiction*] .... A & D
Alcohol and Drug Abuse Education Act (GFGA) .... ADAEA
Alcohol and Drug Abuse Prevention and Control Program [*Military*] (AABC) .... ADAPCP
Alcohol and Drug Abuse Prevention Treatment .... ADAPT
Alcohol and Drug Control Office [*Military*] (AABC) .... ADCO
Alcohol and Drug Dependency Clinic (DAVI) .... ADD
Alcohol and Drug Dependency Unit [*Medicine*] (DAVI) .... ADDU
Alcohol and Drug Education Service, Winnipeg, Manitoba [*Library symbol National Library of Canada*] (NLC) .... MWAD
Alcohol and Drug Foundation of Victoria [*Australia*] .... ADFV
Alcohol and Drug Institute, Seattle, WA [*Library symbol*] [*Library of Congress*] (LCLS) .... WaSAD
Alcohol and Drug Problems Association of North America (EA) .... ADPA
Alcohol and Drug Programs, Vancouver, BC, Canada [*Library symbol Library of Congress*] (LCLS) .... CaBVaADP
Alcohol and Drug Programs, Vancouver, British Columbia [*Library symbol National Library of Canada*] (NLC) .... BVAADP
Alcohol and Drug Programs, Victoria, British Columbia [*Library symbol National Library of Canada*] (BIB) .... BVIADP
Alcohol and Drug Treatment and Rehabilitation Block Grant [*Department of Health and Human Services*] (GFGA) .... ADTR
Alcohol and Tobacco Tax Division [*Internal Revenue Service*] [*United States*] (DLA) .... AT
Alcohol and Tobacco Tax Division [*Internal Revenue Service*] .... ATTD
Alcohol Beverage Legislative Council (EA) .... ABLC
Alcohol, Chloroform, Ether [*An early anesthetic mixture*] .... ACE
Alcohol Community Centre for Education, Prevention, and Treatment [*British*] (DI) .... ACCEPT
Alcohol Concentration (TAG) .... AC
Alcohol Counselling Service [*British*] (DI) .... ACS
Alcohol Dehydrogenase [*Also, ADH*] [*An enzyme*] .... AD
Alcohol Dehydrogenase [*Also, AD*] [*An enzyme*] .... ADH
Alcohol Dependency Treatment Program (DAVI) .... ADTP
Alcohol, Drug Abuse, and Mental Health [*Block grant*] .... ADA/MH
Alcohol, Drug Abuse, and Mental Health Administration [*Formerly, HSMHA*] [*Department of Health and Human Services Rockville, MD*] .... ADAMHA
Alcohol, Drug Abuse, and Mental Health Administration [*Formerly, HSMHA*] [*Department of Health and Human Services*] (OICC) .... ADMHA
Alcohol Drug Motorsensory Impairment Test [*Pharmometrics Corp.*] .... ADMIT
Alcohol, Drug or Mental Disorder .... ADM
Alcohol, Drugs, Driving, and You [*An association*] .... ADDY
Alcohol Education Centre [*British*] (DI) .... AEC
Alcohol Education for Youth (EA) .... AEY
Alcohol Education for Youth [*An association*] .... AYE
Alcohol Education for Youth and Community [*Defunct*] (EA) .... AEYC
Alcohol, Ether, Acetone [*Solvent mixture*] .... AEA
Alcohol Insoluble Solids [*Food analysis*] .... AIS
Alcohol Level Evaluation Road Tester .... ALERT
Alcohol on Breath [*Police term*] .... AOB
Alcohol Policy Council (EA) .... APC
Alcohol Quotient .... AQ
Alcohol Recovery [*or Rehabilitation*] **Drydock** (DNAB) .... ARD
Alcohol Recovery Service (DNAB) .... ARS
Alcohol Rehabilitation Center (NVT) .... ARC
Alcohol Rehabilitation Unit (DNAB) .... ARU
Alcohol Research Group [*Research center*] (RCD) .... ARG
Alcohol Research Information Service (EA) .... ARIS
Alcohol Rub [*Medicine*] .... AlcR
Alcohol Safety Action Project [*Department of Transportation*] .... ASAP
Alcohol Safety Interlock System .... ASIS
Alcohol Sensors International Ltd. [*NASDAQ symbol*] (SAG) .... ASIL
Alcohol Sensors Intl. Ltd. [*Associated Press*] (SAG) .... AlSens
Alcohol Sensors Intl. Ltd. [*Associated Press*] (SAG) .... AlSns
Alcohol Sensors Intl Unit [*NASDAQ symbol*] (TTSB) .... ASILU
Alcohol Soluble Propionate [*Press coating*] (DGA) .... ASP
Alcohol Studies Centre [*British*] (CB) .... ASC
Alcohol Tax Unit [*Department of the Treasury*] .... ATU
Alcohol, Tobacco, and Firearms Cumulative Bulletin [*A publication*] (DLA) .... ATFCB
Alcohol, Tobacco, Firearms Bureau [*Department of the Treasury*] (PDAA) .... ATFB
Alcohol Treatment Program .... ATP
Alcohol Use Disorders Identification Test .... AUDIT
Alcohol Use Inventory [*Medicine*] (DMAA) .... AUI
Alcohol-Drug Education Association in Alberta (AC) .... ADEAA
Alcohol-Formaldehyde-Acetic [*Fixative*] [*Medicine*] (DMAA) .... AFA
Alcoholic .... ALCHLC
Alcoholic [*Freight*] .... ALCOLIC
Alcoholic and Narcotic Addict Rehabilitation Amendments .... ANARA
Alcoholic Beverage (DLA) .... Alco Bev
Alcoholic Beverage Control [*Board*] .... ABC
Alcoholic Beverage Control (DLA) .... Alco Bev Cont
Alcoholic Hepatitis [*Medicine*] .... AH
Alcoholic Ketoacidosis [*Endocrinology and gastroenterology*] (DAVI) .... AKA
Alcoholic Liver Disease [*Medicine*] .... ALD
Alcoholic Onion Extract .... AOE
Alcoholics Anonymous (AC) .... AA
Alcoholics Anonymous Family Groups (ADA) .... ALANON
Alcoholics Anonymous Teens (BARN) .... Alateen
Alcoholics Anonymous World Services (EA) .... AA
Alcoholics Anonymous World Services [*Canada*] .... AAWS
Alcohol-Induced Hyperlipidemia [*Medicine*] (PDAA) .... AHL
Alcoholism [*Chemical dependency and psychiatry*] (DAVI) .... AL
Alcoholism [*Chemical dependency*] (DAVI) .... alc
Alcoholism .... ALCHLSM
Alcoholism and Drug Abuse Commission, Calgary, AB, Canada [*Library symbol Library of Congress*] (LCLS) .... CaACAD
Alcoholism and Drug Abuse Commission, Calgary, Alberta [*Library symbol National Library of Canada*] (NLC) .... ACAD
Alcoholism and Drug Abuse Commission, Edmonton, AB, Canada [*Library symbol Library of Congress*] (LCLS) .... CaAEAD
Alcoholism and Drug Abuse Commission, Edmonton, Alberta [*Library symbol National Library of Canada*] (NLC) .... AEAD
Alcoholism and Drug Abuse Commission, Vancouver, British Columbia [*Library symbol National Library of Canada*] (NLC) .... BVAAD
Alcoholism Center for Women (EA) .... ACW
Alcoholism Commission of Saskatchewan, Regina, Saskatchewan [*Library symbol National Library of Canada*] (NLC) .... SRAC
Alcoholism Commission of Saskatchewan, Regina, SK, Canada [*Library symbol Library of Congress*] (LCLS) .... CaSRAC
Alcoholism Foundation of Manitoba, Winnipeg, Manitoba [*Library symbol National Library of Canada*] (NLC) .... MWAF
Alcohol-Related Brain Damage Association [*Australia*] .... ABDA
Alcohol-Related End-Stage Liver Disease [*Medicine*] .... ARESLD
Alcohol-Related Liver Disease [*Medicine*] .... ARLD
Alcoma Community Library, Rainier, AB, Canada [*Library symbol*] [*Library of Congress*] (LCLS) .... CaARaC
Alcoma Community Library, Rainier, Alberta [*Library symbol National Library of Canada*] (NLC) .... ARAC
Alcon Laboratories, Inc., Fort Worth, TX [*Library symbol Library of Congress*] (LCLS) .... TxFAI
Alcona County Library, Harrisville, MI [*Library symbol Library of Congress*] (LCLS) .... MiHarv
Alconbury [*British ICAO location identifier*] (ICLI) .... EGWZ
Alcor Life Extension Foundation (EA) .... ALEF
Alcorn Agricultural and Mechanical College, Lorman, MS [*Library symbol Library of Congress*] (LCLS) .... MsAM
Alcove (ABBR) .... A
Alcove [*Classified advertising*] (ADA) .... ALC
ALCTS [*Association for Library Collections and Technical Services*] **Cataloging and Classification Section** .... ALCTS CCS
ALCTS [*Association for Library Collections and Technical Services*] **Reproduction of Library Materials Section** .... ALCTS RLMS
ALCTS [*Association for Library Collections and Technical Services*] **Resources Section** .... ALCTS RS
Alcuin Club (EAIO) .... AC
Alcuin Society (EA) .... AS
Aldehyde Dehydrogenase [*An enzyme*] .... ALDH
Aldehyde Ferredoxin Oxidoreductase [*An enzyme*] .... AOR
Aldehyde Fuchsin [*A dye*] .... AF
Aldehyde Oxidase [*An enzyme*] .... AO
Aldehyde Reductase (DMAA) .... ALR
Aldehydes [*Organic chemistry*] .... HCHO
Alden and Van Hoesen's Digest of Mississippi Laws [*A publication*] (DLA) .... Ald & VH
Alden Electronics, Inc. [*NASDAQ symbol*] (NQ) .... ADNE
Alden Electronics, Inc. [*Associated Press*] (SAG) .... Alden
Alden Electronics'A' [*NASDAQ symbol*] (TTSB) .... ADNEA
Alden [*John*] **Financial Corp.** [*Associated Press*] (SAG) .... JAlden
Alden Ocean Shell Association (EA) .... AOSA
Alden Public Library, Alden, IA [*Library symbol Library of Congress*] (LCLS) .... IaAld
Alden Terrace Elementary School, Elmont, NY [*Library symbol*] [*Library of Congress*] (LCLS) .... NElmoAE
Alden Terrace Elementary School, Valley Stream, NY [*Library symbol*] [*Library of Congress*] (LCLS) .... NVsAE
Alden's Abridgment of Law [*A publication*] (DLA) .... Ald Abr
Alden's Condensed Reports [*Pennsylvania*] [*A publication*] (DLA) .... Ald
Alden's Index of United States Reports [*A publication*] (DLA) .... Ald Ind
Alden's Law Reports [*A publication*] (DLA) .... ALR
Alder Flats Public Library, Alberta [*Library symbol National Library of Canada*] (NLC) .... AAF
Alderman .... ALD
Alderman (WGA) .... ALDM
Alderman .... ALDM
Alderman (ROG) .... ALDMN
Aldermaston Mechanised Cataloging and Ordering System [*British*] (DIT) .... AMCOS
Aldermaston Mechanized Cataloguing and Ordering Systems [*British*] .... AMCOS
Aldermaston Project for the Application of Computers to Engineering [*United Kingdom Atomic Energy Authority*] (NITA) .... APACE
Alderney [*United Kingdom*] [*Airport symbol*] (AD) .... ACI
Alderney [*Channel Islands*] [*Airport symbol*] (OAG) .... ACI
Alderney [*International vehicle registration*] (ODBW) .... GBA
Alderney, Channel Islands [*British ICAO location identifier*] (ICLI) .... EGJA
Alderson-Broaddus College, Philippi, WV [*OCLC symbol*] (OCLC) .... WVA
Alderson-Broaddus College, Philippi, WV [*Library symbol Library of Congress*] (LCLS) .... WvPhA
Aldila, Inc. [*NASDAQ symbol*] (SAG) .... ALDA
Aldila, Inc. [*Associated Press*] (SAG) .... Aldila
Aldine [*of Aldus Manutius*] (DGA) .... ALD
Aldo Ray Fan Club (EA) .... ARFC
Aldolase [*An enzyme*] .... ALD
Aldolase [*An enzyme*] (DAVI) .... ALDOL
Aldolase [*An enzyme*] .... ALS
Aldose Reductase Inhibitor [*Organic chemistry*] (DAVI) .... ARI

Aldosterone [*Endocrinology*] .... ALDO
Aldosterone [*Endocrinology*] (DAVI) .... ALDOST
Aldosterone Excretion Rate [*Endocrinology*] .... AER
Aldosterone Secretion Defect [*Endocrinology*] (MAE) .... ASD
Aldosterone Secretion Inhibitory Factor [*Endocrinology*] .... ASIF
Aldosterone Secretion Rate [*Endocrinology*] .... ASR
Aldosterone-Binding Protein [*Endocrinology*] .... ABP
Aldosterone-Induced Protein [*Biochemistry*] .... AIP
Aldosterone-Producing Adenoma [*Clinical chemistry*] .... APA
Aldosterone-Stimulating Hormone [*Also, AGTr*] [*Endocrinology*] .... ASH
Aldracus [*Flourished, 13th century*] [*Authority cited in pre-1607 legal work*] (DSA) .... Aldra
Aldred's Questions on the Law of Property [*A publication*] (DLA) .... Ald Ques
Aldrich's Edition of Ansen on Contracts [*A publication*] (DLA) .... Ald Ans Cont
Aldricus [*Flourished, 1154-72*] [*Authority cited in pre-1607 legal work*] (DSA) .... Ald
Aldricus [*Flourished, 1154-72*] [*Authority cited in pre-1607 legal work*] (DSA) .... Aldri
Aldridge. History and Jurisdiction of the Courts of Law [*1835*] [*A publication*] (ILCA) .... Ald
Aldridge. History and Jurisdiction of the Courts of Law [*A publication*] (DLA) .... Ald Hist
Ale, Bread, and Cheese .... ABC
Ale Firkin [*Unit of measurement*] (ROG) .... AF
Aledo, IL [*FM radio station call letters*] .... WRMJ
Aleg [*Mauritania*] [*Airport symbol*] (AD) .... LEG
Alegrete [*Brazil*] [*Airport symbol Obsolete*] (OAG) .... ALQ
Aleknagik [*Alaska*] [*Airport symbol*] (OAG) .... WKK
Aleknagik, AK [*Location identifier FAA*] (FAAL) .... WKK
Aleksandr Solzhenitsyn Society for Freedom and Justice (EA) .... ASSFJ
Alencon/Valframbert [*France ICAO location identifier*] (ICLI) .... LFOF
Alenquer [*Brazil*] [*Airport symbol*] (AD) .... AQR
Aleph Zadik Aleph [*Society*] .... AZA
Aleppo [*Syria*] [*Airport symbol*] (OAG) .... ALP
Aleppo/Neirab [*Syria*] [*ICAO location identifier*] (ICLI) .... OSAP
Alergic Encephalomyelitis [*Medicine*] (BARN) .... AE
Alert [*Northwest Territories*] [*Seismograph station code, US Geological Survey*] (SEIS) .... ALE
Alert and Oriented (CPH) .... A & O
Alert and Oriented Times Four [*Neurology and psychiatry*] (DAVI) .... A & OX4
Alert and Oriented Times Three [*Neurology and psychiatry*] (DAVI) .... A & OX3
Alert and Oriented to Person, Place, and Time [*Neurology and psychiatry*] (DAVI) .... A & OX3
Alert and Oriented to Person, Place, Time, and Date [*Neurology and psychiatry*] (DAVI) .... A & OX4
Alert Area [*Military*] .... A
Alert Area Supervisor [*Military*] (AFM) .... AAS
Alert Availability (MCD) .... AA
Alert Bay, BC [*ICAO location identifier*] (ICLI) .... CYAL
Alert Bay Public Library and Museum, British Columbia [*Library symbol National Library of Canada*] (NLC) .... BABM
Alert Building (NATG) .... AB
Alert Centre, Inc. [*Associated Press*] (SAG) .... AlertC
Alert Centre, Inc. [*Associated Press*] (SAG) .... AlertCt
Alert Centre, Inc. [*AMEX symbol*] (SAG) .... ALT
Alert Citizens for Environmental Safety [*Formed to protect West Texas and the US/Mexico border region's natural resources*] (CROSS) .... ACES
Alert Condition [*Military*] (AABC) .... LERTCON
Alert Conditions (MCD) .... ALERTCONS
Alert, Cooperative, and Oriented (HGAA) .... ACO
Alert Crew Billet Security (AFM) .... ACBS
Alert Exercise (NATG) .... ALEX
Alert Force Capability Test (MCD) .... AFCAT
Alert Force Capability Test (MCD) .... AFCT
Alert Holding Area [*Military*] (DOMA) .... AHA
Alert Implementation Report (MCD) .... ALIMREP
Alert Implementation Reports (NATG) .... ALIMPREPS
Alert Message (CINC) .... AM
Alert Notice .... ALNOT
Alert, NT [*FM radio station call letters*] .... CHAR
Alert, NT [*ICAO location identifier*] (ICLI) .... CYLT
Alert Phase [*Aviation code*] .... ALERFA
Alert Reaction Time .... ART
Alert Transmit Console (SAA) .... ATC
Alert Transmit Panel (SAA) .... ATP
Alert, Verbal, Painful, Unresponsive [*Neurologic test*] [*Medicine*] (DMAA) ..... AVPU
Alert Weather Watch [*Meteorology*] (DA) .... AWW
Alerta [*Peru*] [*ICAO location identifier*] (ICLI) .... SPAR
Alerting and Status (SAA) .... ALS
Alerting Automatic Telling Status (SAA) .... AAS
Alerting Long-Range Airborne RADAR for MTI [*Moving Target Indicator*] .... ALARM
Alerting Message [*Aviation code*] .... ALR
Alerting Search Service from Kinokuniya [*Kinokuniya Co. Ltd.*] [*Japan Information service or system*] (IID) .... ASK
Alertness, Airway, Breathing, Circulation, Cervical Spine [*Medicine*] (DMAA) .... AABCC
AlertVIEW [*Virtual Interface Environment Workstation*] **Manager** [*Shany, Inc.*] (PCM) .... AVM
AlertVIEW [*Virtual Interface Environment Workstation*] **Station** [*Shany, Inc.*] [*Computer science*] (PCM) .... AVS
Ales/Deaux [*France ICAO location identifier*] (ICLI) .... LFMS
Alesund/Vigra [*Norway ICAO location identifier*] (ICLI) .... ENAL
Aleta Resource Industries [*Vancouver Stock Exchange symbol*] .... ALH
Aleut [*MARC language code Library of Congress*] (LCCP) .... ale
Aleutian (FAAC) .... ALUTN
Aleutian Disease [*of mink*] [*Veterinary medicine*] .... AD
Aleutian Disease Virus [*of mink*] .... ADV
Aleutian Islands .... ALUTS
Alex [*Aarons*] **and Vinton** [*Freedley*] [*Theatrical producers of the 1920's and 1930's, after whom the Alvin Theatre in New York City was named*] .... ALVIN
Alex Brown Inc. [*NYSE symbol*] (TTSB) .... AB
Alex Brown, Inc. [*Associated Press*] (SAG) .... AlexBr
Alex Brown, Inc. [*Associated Press*] (SAG) .... AlexBrn
Alex von Falkenhausen Motorenwerke [*Automobile manufacturer*] .... AFM
Alexa Ventures, Inc. [*Vancouver Stock Exchange symbol*] .... AXA
Alexandair, Inc. [*Canada ICAO designator*] (FAAC) .... JMR
Alexander [*of Plutarch*] [*Classical studies*] (OCD) .... Alex
Alexander [*of Lucian*] [*Classical studies*] (OCD) .... Alex
Alexander & Alex Sv [*NYSE symbol*] (TTSB) .... AAL
Alexander & Alexander Services, Inc. [*NYSE symbol*] (SPSG) .... AAL
Alexander & Alexander Services, Inc. [*Associated Press*] (SAG) .... AlexAlx
Alexander & Baldwin [*NASDAQ symbol*] (TTSB) .... ALEX
Alexander & Baldwin, Inc. [*NASDAQ symbol*] (NQ) .... ALEX
Alexander & Baldwin, Inc. [*Associated Press*] (SAG) .... AlexBld
Alexander Bay [*South Africa*] [*Airport symbol*] (OAG) .... ALJ
Alexander Bay [*New York*] [*Seismograph station code, US Geological Survey*] (SEIS) .... ALX
Alexander Bay [*South Africa*] [*ICAO location identifier*] (ICLI) .... FAAB
Alexander Bonaparte Cust [*Antagonist of Agatha Christie's novel "The ABC Murders"*] .... ABC
Alexander Brown, Inc. [*NYSE symbol*] (SPSG) .... AB
Alexander City, AL [*Location identifier FAA*] (FAAL) .... ALX
Alexander City, AL [*AM radio station call letters*] .... WRFS
Alexander City, AL [*FM radio station call letters*] .... WSTH
Alexander City State Junior College, Alexander City, AL [*Library symbol Library of Congress*] (LCLS) .... AAcC
Alexander County Public Library, Taylorsville, NC [*Library symbol Library of Congress*] (LCLS) .... NcTayA
Alexander Energy [*NASDAQ symbol*] (TTSB) .... AEOK
Alexander Energy Corp. [*NASDAQ symbol*] (NQ) .... AEOK
Alexander Energy Corp. [*Associated Press*] (SAG) .... AlexEng
Alexander Graham Bell Association for the Deaf (EA) .... AGBA
Alexander Graham Bell Association for the Deaf (EA) .... AGBAD
Alexander Haagen Properties [*AMEX symbol*] (TTSB) .... ACH
Alexander Haagen Property, Inc. [*AMEX symbol*] (SPSG) .... ACH
Alexander Haagen Property, Inc. [*Associated Press*] (SAG) .... AHaagen
Alexander M. Poniatoff, Excellence [*Acronym is name of electronics company and brand name of its products; formed from name of firm's founder, plus "excellence"*] .... AMPEX
Alexander Marx Jubilee Volume [*A publication*] (BJA) .... AMJV
Alexander Mitchell Library, Aberdeen, SD [*Library symbol Library of Congress*] (LCLS) .... SdAbA
Alexander on Life Insurance in New York [*A publication*] (DLA) .... Alex Ins
Alexander Railroad Co. [*AAR code*] .... ARC
Alexander Raxlen Memorial Library, Doctors Hospital, Toronto, Ontario [*Library symbol National Library of Canada*] (NLC) .... OTDAR
Alexander Severus [*of Scriptores Historiae Augustae*] [*Classical studies*] (OCD) .... Alex Sev
Alexander Tartagna de Imola [*Deceased, 1477*] [*Authority cited in pre-1607 legal work*] (DSA) .... Alex
Alexander Tartagna de Imola [*Deceased, 1477*] [*Authority cited in pre-1607 legal work*] (DSA) .... Alexan
Alexander Tartagna de Imola [*Deceased, 1477*] [*Authority cited in pre-1607 legal work*] (DSA) .... Alexand
Alexander Zonjic Fan Club (EA) .... AZFC
Alexander's British Statutes in Force in Maryland [*A publication*] (DLA) .... Alex Br Stat
Alexander's Chancery Practice in Maryland [*A publication*] (DLA) .... Alex Ch Pr
Alexander's, Inc. [*Associated Press*] (SAG) .... Alexdr
Alexander's, Inc. [*NYSE symbol*] (SPSG) .... ALX
Alexanders, Laing & Cruickshank [*Broker*] [*British*] .... ALC
Alexander's Practice of the Commissary Courts, Scotland [*A publication*] (DLA) .... Alex Com Pr
Alexander's Reports [*66-72 Mississippi*] [*A publication*] (DLA) .... Alexander
Alexander's Texas Digest [*A publication*] (DLA) .... Alex Dig
Alexandra [*of Lycophron*] [*Classical studies*] (OCD) .... Alex
Alexandra [*New Zealand*] [*Airport symbol*] (OAG) .... ALR
Alexandra [*Newport and South Wales*] **Docks & Railway** [*Wales*] .... AD
Alexandria [*Diocesan abbreviation*] [*Louisiana*] (TOCD) .... ALX
Alexandria [*Egypt*] [*Airport symbol*] (OAG) .... ALY
Alexandria [*Minnesota*] [*Airport symbol Obsolete*] (OAG) .... AXN
Alexandria [*Louisiana*] [*Airport symbol*] (OAG) .... ESF
Alexandria [*Egypt*] [*ICAO location identifier*] (ICLI) .... HEAX
Alexandria [*Greece*] [*ICAO location identifier*] (ICLI) .... LGAX
Alexandria [*Virginia*] [*Airport symbol*] (AD) .... WVA
Alexandria Branch, Stormount, Dundas, and Glengarry County Public Library, Ontario [*Library symbol National Library of Canada*] (NLC) .... OASDG
Alexandria/England Air Force Base [*Louisiana*] [*ICAO location identifier*] (ICLI) .... KAEX
Alexandria/Esler Field [*Louisiana*] [*ICAO location identifier*] (ICLI) .... KESF
Alexandria, IN [*FM radio station call letters*] .... WAXT
Alexandria, LA [*Location identifier FAA*] (FAAL) .... AEX
Alexandria, LA [*Location identifier FAA*] (FAAL) .... ERJ
Alexandria, LA [*Location identifier FAA*] (FAAL) .... ESF
Alexandria, LA [*Television station call letters*] .... KALB-TV
Alexandria, LA [*FM radio station call letters*] (RBYB) .... KAPM-FM
Alexandria, LA [*AM radio station call letters*] (RBYB) .... KDBS-AM
Alexandria, LA [*FM radio station call letters*] .... KFAD
Alexandria, LA [*Television station call letters*] .... KLAX-TV
Alexandria, LA [*AM radio station call letters*] (RBYB) .... KLBG

Alexandria, LA [*Television station call letters*] KLPA

Alexandria, LA [*FM radio station call letters*] KLSA

Alexandria, LA [*FM radio station call letters*] (RBYB) KOUZ

Alexandria, LA [*FM radio station call letters*] KQID

Alexandria, LA [*AM radio station call letters*] KRRV

Alexandria, LA [*FM radio station call letters*] KRRV-FM

Alexandria, LA [*AM radio station call letters*] KSYL

Alexandria, LA [*FM radio station call letters*] KZMZ

Alexandria Library, Alexandria, VA [*Library symbol Library of Congress*] (LCLS) ViAl

Alexandria, MN [*Location identifier FAA*] (FAAL) AJW

Alexandria, MN [*Television station call letters*] KCCO

Alexandria, MN [*FM radio station call letters*] KIKV

Alexandria, MN [*Television station call letters*] KSAX

Alexandria, MN [*FM radio station call letters*] KSTQ

Alexandria, MN [*AM radio station call letters*] KXRA

Alexandria, MN [*FM radio station call letters*] KXRA-FM

Alexandria News, Alexandria, IN [*Library symbol Library of Congress*] (LCLS) InAleN

Alexandria Public Library, Alexandria, IN [*Library symbol Library of Congress*] (LCLS) InAle

Alexandria Public Library, Alexandria, MN [*Library symbol*] [*Library of Congress*] (LCLS) MnAle

Alexandria Public Library, Alexandria, SD [*Library symbol Library of Congress*] (LCLS) SdAle

Alexandria Public Library, Alexandria, VA [*OCLC symbol*] (OCLC) VAX

Alexandria Runestone Museum, Alexandria, MN [*Library symbol*] [*Library of Congress*] (LCLS) MnAleR

Alexandria Shipping & Navigation Co. [*Egypt*] (IMH) ALEXSHIP

Alexandria Technical Institute, Alexandria, MN [*Library symbol*] [*Library of Congress*] (LCLS) MnAleTI

Alexandria Times-Tribune, Alexandria, IN [*Library symbol Library of Congress*] (LCLS) InAleTT

Alexandria, VA [*AM radio station call letters*] (RBYB) WBZS

Alexandrian Free Public Library, Mount Vernon, IN [*Library symbol Library of Congress*] (LCLS) InMtv

Alexandroupolis [*Greece*] [*Airport symbol*] (OAG) AXD

Alexandroupolis [*Greece*] [*ICAO location identifier*] (ICLI) LGAL

Alexian Brothers (TOCD) cfa

Alexian Brothers (TOCD) CFA

Alexion Pharmaceuticals [*NASDAQ symbol*] (TTSB) ALXN

Alexion Pharmaceuticals, Inc. [*Associated Press*] (SAG) Alexion

Alexion Pharmaceuticals, Inc. [*NASDAQ symbol*] (SAG) ALXN

Alexipharmaca [*of Nicander*] [*Classical studies*] (OCD) Alex

Alexis De Tocqueville Society (EA) ATS

Alexis Nihon Finance, Inc. [*Toronto Stock Exchange symbol*] AXN

Alexis Nihon Finance, Inc. [*Vancouver Stock Exchange symbol*] AXV

Aleyn's English King's Bench Reports [*A publication*] (DLA) Al

Aleyn's English King's Bench Reports [*A publication*] (DLA) Allen

Aleyn's Select Cases, English King's Bench [*82 English Reprint*] [*A publication*] (DLA) Aleyn

Aleyn's Select Cases, English King's Bench [*82 English Reprint*] [*A publication*] (DLA) Aleyn (Eng)

Alfa [*Phonetic alphabet*] [*International*] (DSUE) A

Alfa Air [*Czechoslovakia*] [*ICAO designator*] (FAAC) AFA

Alfa Corp. [*NASDAQ symbol*] (NQ) ALFA

Alfa Corp. [*Associated Press*] (SAG) AlfaCp

Alfa Jet [*Spain ICAO designator*] (FAAC) AJE

Alfa Romeo Club of Canada (AC) ARCC

Alfa Romeo Nissan Autoveicoli [*Italian-Japanese alliance for the joint manufacture of automobiles with Alfa engines and Nissan bodies*] ARNA

Alfa Romeo Owners Club (EA) AROC

Alfa Romeo Owners' Club of Australi AROCA

Alfacell Corp. [*NASDAQ symbol*] (SAG) ACEL

Alfacell Corp. [*Associated Press*] (SAG) Alfacell

Alfalfa Club (EA) AC

Alfalfa Cryptic Virus [*Plant pathology*] ACV

Alfalfa Mosaic Virus AMV

Alfalfa Pest Management APM

Alfalfa Temperate Virus [*Plant pathology*] ATEV

Alfarbandishe Gezelshaft far Ainordenen Yidn af Erd in FSSR [*A publication*] (BJA) GEZERD

Alfa-Romeo Distributors of North America ARDONA

Alfin Fragrances, Inc. [*AMEX symbol*] (SPSG) AFN

Alfin Inc. [*AMEX symbol*] (TTSB) AFN

Alfin, Inc. [*Associated Press*] (SAG) Alfin

Alfred [*New York*] [*Seismograph station code, US Geological Survey*] (SEIS) ALF

Alfred Adler Institute (EA) AAI

Alfred C. Kinsey Institute for Sex Research, Bloomington, IN [*Library symbol Library of Congress*] (LCLS) InBloKi

Alfred Dickey Free Library, Jamestown, ND [*Library symbol Library of Congress*] (LCLS) NdJ

Alfred E. Packer Society (EA) AEPS

Alfred Holbrook College, Manchester, OH [*Library symbol Library of Congress Obsolete*] (LCLS) OMancAH

Alfred Holt [*Blue Funnel Line*] [*Steamship*] (MHDB) AH

Alfred, NY [*FM radio station call letters*] WALF

Alfred, NY [*FM radio station call letters*] WETD

Alfred, NY [*FM radio station call letters*] (RBYB) WZKZ-FM

Alfred Township Public Library, Bibliotheque Publique du Canton d'Alfred, Lefaivre, ON, Canada [*Library symbol*] [*Library of Congress*] (LCLS) CaOLAL

Alfred University (GAGS) Alfred U

Alfred University, Alfred, NY [*Library symbol Library of Congress*] (LCLS) NAlf

Alfred University, Alfred, NY [*OCLC symbol*] (OCLC) YAH

Alfred University, School of Theology, Alfred, NY [*Library symbol Library of Congress Obsolete*] (LCLS) NAlf-ST

Alfven Number [*IUPAC*] Al

Alfven Propulsion Engine [*Aerospace*] APE

Algarvilara Transportes Aereos Algarvios SA [*Portugal ICAO designator*] (FAAC) ALR

Algas Resources Ltd., Halifax, Nova Scotia [*Library symbol National Library of Canada*] (NLC) NSHAR

Algas Resources Ltd., Halifax, NS, Canada [*Library symbol Library of Congress*] (LCLS) CaNSHAR

Algebra ALG

Algebra ALGEB

Algebra Package [*Computer science*] ALPAK

Algebraic Automated Digital Iterative Network [*Computer science*] (MHDI) ALADIN

Algebraic Code-Excited Linear Prediction (ACRL) ACELP

Algebraic Compiler [*or Computer*] [*Computer science*] ALCOM

Algebraic Compiler and Translator [*Computer science*] ACT

Algebraic Interpretive Dialogue [*Computer science*] (BUR) AID

Algebraic Logic Investigation of Apollo Systems (MCD) ALIAS

Algebraic Manipulation by Identity Translation AMBIT

Algebraic Multigrid [*Computation method*] AMG

Algebraic Operating System [*Texas Instruments, Inc.*] [*Computer science*] AOS

Algebraic Reconstruction Technique ART

Algebraic Solution for Queues ASQ

Algebraic Stress Model (MCD) ASM

Algebraic Technological Function [*Computer science*] ATF

Algebraic Translator [*Programming language*] [*1969*] ALTRAN

Algebraic Translator and Compiler [*Computer science*] (MCD) ALTAC

Algemeen Nederlandisch Persbureau [*Press agency*] [*Netherlands*] ANP

Algemeen Rijksarchief te s'Gravenhage (Central State Archives), The Hague, Netherlands [*Library symbol Library of Congress*] (LCLS) Ne

Algemeen Vrijzinning Vakverbond in Nederland [*General Liberal Labor Federation*] [*Netherlands*] AVV

Algemene Bond van Rooms Katholieke Kiesverenigingen [*General League of Roman Catholic Election Societies*] [*Netherlands*] (PPE) BRKKV

Algemene Kunstzijde Unie [*Later, AKZO*] [*Netherlands*] [*Commercial firm*] AKU

Algemene Maatregel van Bestuur [*Order in Council*] [*Netherlands*] (ILCA) AMvB

Algemene Spaar- en Lijfrentekas/Caisse Generale d'Espargne et de Retraite [*Commercial bank*] [*Belgium*] (EY) ASLK-CGER

Alger [*Algeria*] [*ICAO location identifier*] (ICLI) DAAA

Alger [*Algeria*] [*ICAO location identifier*] (ICLI) DAAL

Alger [*Algeria*] [*ICAO location identifier*] (ICLI) DAMM

Alger/Houari Boumediene [*Algeria*] [*ICAO location identifier*] (ICLI) DAAG

Alger-Bouzareah [*Algeria*] [*Seismograph station code, US Geological Survey*] ABA

Algeria [*Aircraft nationality and registration mark*] (FAAC) 7T

Algeria [*MARC country of publication code Library of Congress*] (LCCP) ae

Algeria [*IYRU nationality code*] (IYR) AL

Algeria ALG

Algeria (VRA) Alg

Algeria [*ANSI two-letter standard code*] (CNC) DZ

Algeria [*ANSI three-letter standard code*] (CNC) DZA

Algeria [*MARC geographic area code Library of Congress*] (LCCP) f-ae--

Algeria - Palma, Spain [*Submarine cable*] [*Telecommunications*] ALPAL

Algerian-Franc (ABBR) A-FR

Algerie Presse Service [*Algerian Press Service*] (AF) APS

Alger's Law in Relation to Promoters and Promotion of Corporations [*A publication*] (DLA) Alger's Law Promoters & Prom Corp

Algers, Winslow & Western Railway Co. [*AAR code*] AWW

Al-Gheida [*People's Democratic Republic of Yemen*] [*ICAO location identifier*] (ICLI) ODAG

Alghero [*Italy*] [*Airport symbol*] (OAG) AHO

Alghero [*Italy ICAO location identifier*] (ICLI) LIEA

Algiers [*Algeria*] [*Seismograph station code, US Geological Survey*] (SEIS) ALG

Algiers [*Algeria*] [*Airport symbol*] (OAG) ALG

Algo Group, Inc. [*Toronto Stock Exchange symbol*] AO

Algo Resources Ltd. [*Vancouver Stock Exchange symbol*] AGO

ALGOL Compiler [*Computer science*] (DIT) ALCOM

ALGOL Extended for Design [*1967*] [*Computer science*] AED

ALGOL-to-FORTRAN Translator [*Computer science*] (MCD) ALFTRAN

Algoma Airways, Inc. [*Canada ICAO designator*] (FAAC) AGG

Algoma Central & Hudson Bay Railroad (IIA) AC & HB

Algoma Central Railway [*AAR code*] AC

Algoma Central Railway [*Toronto Stock Exchange symbol*] ALC

Algoma College, Sault Ste. Marie, ON, Canada [*Library symbol Library of Congress*] (LCLS) CaOStMA

Algoma College, Sault Ste. Marie, Ontario [*Library symbol National Library of Canada*] (NLC) OSTMA

Algoma Steel [*NASDAQ symbol*] (TTSB) ALGSE

Algoma Steel Corp. Ltd. [*Toronto Stock Exchange symbol Vancouver Stock Exchange symbol*] ALG

Algoma Steel Corp., Quality Control and Research Department, Sault Ste. Marie, ON, Canada [*Library symbol Library of Congress*] (LCLS) CaOStMAS

Algoma Steel, Inc. [*Associated Press*] (SAG) Algma

Algoma Steel, Inc. [*NASDAQ symbol*] (SAG) ALGS

Algoma, WI [*FM radio station call letters*] WBDK

Algona, IA [*Location identifier FAA*] (FAAL) AXA

Algona, IA [*AM radio station call letters*] KLGA

Algona, IA [*FM radio station call letters*] KLGA-FM

Algona Public Library, Algona, IA [*Library symbol Library of Congress*] (LCLS) IaAlg

Algoneurodystrophy [*Medicine*] (DMAA) AND

Algonquian [*MARC language code Library of Congress*] (LCCP) alg

Algonquian Syllabic Texts in Canadian Repositories [*Bibliographic project*] ..... ASTIC
Algonquin Arts Council (AC) ..... AAC
Algonquin College, Colonel By Campus, Ottawa, ON, Canada [*Library symbol*] [*Library of Congress*] (LCLS) ..... CaOOACC
Algonquin College of Applied Arts and Technology, Heron Park Campus, Ottawa, ON,Canada [*Library symbol*] [*Library of Congress*] (LCLS) ..... CaOOACH
Algonquin College of Applied Arts and Technology, Library Technician Program, Ottawa, ON, Canada [*Library symbol*] [*Library of Congress*] (LCLS) ..... CaOOACL
Algonquin College of Applied Arts and Technology, Ottawa, Ontario [*Library symbol National Library of Canada*] (NLC) ..... OOAC
Algonquin College of Applied Arts and Technology, School of Lanark County, Resource Centre, Perth, ON, Canada [*Library symbol*] [*Library of Congress*] (LCLS) ..... CaOPAC
Algonquin College, Ottawa, ON, Canada [*Library symbol Library of Congress*] (LCLS) ..... CaOOAC
Algonquin College, Rideau Campus, Ottawa, ON, Canada [*Library symbol Library of Congress*] (LCLS) ..... CaOOACR
Algonquin College, Upper Ottawa Valley Campus Resource Centre, Pembroke, ON, Canada [*Library symbol Library of Congress*] (LCLS) ..... CaOPemAC
Algonquin Mercantile Corp. [*Toronto Stock Exchange symbol*] ..... AM
Algonquin Minerals [*Vancouver Stock Exchange symbol*] ..... AMF
Algonquin Radio Observatory [*Research center*] (RCD) ..... ARO
Algonquin Regional Library, Parry Sound, ON, Canada [*Library symbol Library of Congress*] (LCLS) ..... CaOPsA
Algonquin Regional Library, Parry Sound, Ontario [*Library symbol Obsolete National Library of Canada*] (NLC) ..... OPSA
Algonquin Regional Library System, Sturgeon Falls Branch, Sturgeon Falls, ON, Canada [*Library symbol Library of Congress*] (LCLS) ..... CaOSfAR
Algood, TN [*AM radio station call letters*] ..... WATX
Algorithm Development Facility [*for spacecraft data*] [*Jet Propulsion Laboratory*] ..... ADF
Algorithm for Non-Synchronized Waveform Error Reduction (MHDB) ..... ANSWER
Algorithm Mass-Factoring Method (MCD) ..... AM-FM
Algorithm Programming Language [*Computer science*] (HGAA) ..... APL
Algorithm Simulation Test and Evaluation Program [*NASA*] ..... ASTEP
Algorithmic and Business Oriented Language [*Computer science*] ..... ALABOL
Algorithmic Language [*1958*] [*Formerly, IAL*] [*Computer science*] ..... ALGOL
Algorithmic Language for Economic Calculations [*Computer science*] ..... ALGEC
Algorithmic Procedural Language [*Computer science*] (IAA) ..... APL
Algorithmic Processor Description Language [*Computer science*] (MHDI) ..... APDL
Algorithmic Remote Manipulation [*Programming language*] ..... ARM
Algorithmic State Machine [*Computer science*] (ODBW) ..... ASM
Algos Pharmaceutical Corp. [*NASDAQ symbol*] (SAG) ..... ALGO
Algos Pharmaceutical Corp. [*Associated Press*] (SAG) ..... AlgosPh
Alhambra (BARN) ..... Alh
Alhambra [*Record label*] [*Spain*] ..... Ambra
Alhambra Public Library, Alhambra, CA [*Library symbol Library of Congress*] (LCLS) ..... CAlh
Al-Hazm [*Yemen*] [*ICAO location identifier*] (ICLI) ..... OYZM
Alia [*Others*] [*Latin*] ..... AL
Alia Editione [*Another Edition*] [*Latin*] (ROG) ..... AL E
Alia Editione [*Another Edition*] [*Latin*] (ADA) ..... AL ED
Alia Lectio [*Another Reading*] [*Latin*] ..... Al L
ALI-ABA [*American Law Instutute - American Bar Association*] **Committee on Continuing Professional Education** (EA) ..... ALI-ABA
Alianca Anticomunista Brasileira [*Brazilian Anti-Communist Alliance*] (PD) ..... AAB
Alianca Democratica [*Democratic Alliance*] [*Brazil Political party*] (EY) ..... AD
Alianca Democratica [*Democratic Alliance*] [*Portugal Political party*] (PPE) ..... AD
Alianca Libertadora Nacional [*National Liberation Alliance*] [*Brazil Political party*] (PD) ..... ALN
Alianca Operaria Camponesa [*Peasants and Workers Alliance*] [*Portugal Political party*] (PPE) ..... AOC
Alianca Popular Unida/Alianca Povo Unido [*United People's Alliance*] [*Portugal Political party*] (PPW) ..... APU
Alianca Renovadora Nacional [*Alliance for National Renewal*] [*Brazil Political party*] (PPW) ..... ARENA
Alianca Socialista de Juventude [*Socialist Youth Alliance*] [*Portugal Political party*] (PPE) ..... ASJ
Aliant Communications, Inc. [*Associated Press*] (SAG) ..... AliantCm
Aliant Communications, Inc. [*NASDAQ symbol*] (SAG) ..... ALNT
Alianza Anticomunista Argentina [*Argentine Anti-Communist Alliance*] (PD) ..... AAA
Alianza Apostolica Anticomunista [*Anti-Communist Apostolic Alliance*] [*Spain*] (PD) ..... AAA
Alianza Apostolica Antigua [*Apostolic Ancient Alliance*] [*Spain Political party*] (EY) ..... AAA
Alianza Campesina de Organizaciones Nacionales de Honduras [*Peasant Alliance of National Organizations of Honduras*] [*Political party*] (PD) ..... ALCONH
Alianza del Movimiento Nacionalista Revolucionario [*Bolivia*] (PPW) ..... A-MNR
Alianza Democratica [*Democratic Alliance*] [*Chile*] [*Political party*] (PPW) ..... AD
Alianza Democratica de Oposicion Civilista [*Panama*] [*Political party*] (EY) ..... ADOC
Alianza Democratica Revolucionaria [*Democratic Revolutionary Alliance*] [*Bolivia*] ..... ADR
Alianza Federal des Pueblos Libres [*An association*] (NTCM) ..... AFPL
Alianza Interamericana [*Defunct*] (EA) ..... AI
Alianza Nacional [*National Alliance*] [*Spain Political party*] (PPE) ..... AN
Alianza Nacional Cristiana [*Costa Rica*] [*Political party*] (EY) ..... ANC
Alianza Nacional Popular [*National Popular Alliance*] [*Colorado*] (PD) ..... ANAPO
Alianza para el Progreso [*Alliance for Progress*] [*Washington, DC*] ..... ALPRO
Alianza para el Progreso [*Alliance for Progress*] [*Washington, DC*] ..... AP
Alianza Patriotica [*Bolivia*] [*Political party*] (EY) ..... AP
Alianza Popular [*Popular Alliance*] [*Madrid, Spain*] (PPW) ..... AP
Alianza Popular Conservadora [*Nicaragua*] [*Political party*] (EY) ..... APC
Alianza Popular de Integracion Nacional [*Bolivia*] [*Political party*] (PPW) ..... APIN
Alianza Popular Revolucionaria Americana [*American Popular Revolutionary Alliance*] [*Peru*] [*Political party*] (PPW) ..... APRA
Alianza Popular Revolucionaria Ecuatoriana [*Ecuadorean Popular Revolutionary Alliance*] [*Political party*] (PPW) ..... APRE
Alianza pour Accion Anticommunista [*Honduras*] [*Political party*] (EY) ..... AAA
Alianza Republicana Nacionalista [*Nationalist Republican Alliance*] [*El Salvador*] [*Political party*] (PPW) ..... ARENA
Alianza Revolucionaria Barrientista [*Bolivia*] [*Political party*] (PPW) ..... ARB
Alianza Revolucionaria Democratica [*Democratic Revolutionary Alliance*] [*Nicaragua*] [*Political party*] (PD) ..... ARDE
Alias [*Computer science*] [*Telecommunications*] ..... a
Alias [*Otherwise*] [*Latin*] ..... AL
Alias [*Otherwise*] [*Latin*] ..... ALS
Alibag [*India*] [*Geomagnetic observatory code*] ..... ABG
Alibi [*Elsewhere*] [*Latin*] (ROG) ..... AL
Alibi [*Elsewhere*] [*Latin*] ..... Ali
ALIBI Fan Club (EA) ..... AFC
Aliblu Airways SpA [*Italy ICAO designator*] (FAAC) ..... KRO
Alicahue [*Chile*] [*Seismograph station code, US Geological Survey*] (SEIS) ..... ALH
Alicante [*Spain*] [*Airport symbol*] (OAG) ..... ALC
Alicante [*Spain*] [*Seismograph station code, US Geological Survey*] (SEIS) ..... ALI
Alicante [*Spain ICAO location identifier*] (ICLI) ..... LEAL
Alice Arm/Kitsault [*Canada*] [*Airport symbol*] (OAG) ..... ZAA
Alice/International [*Texas*] [*ICAO location identifier*] (ICLI) ..... KALI
Alice Lake Mines [*Vancouver Stock Exchange symbol*] ..... ALM
Alice Lloyd College, Pippa Passes, KY [*Library symbol*] [*Library of Congress*] (LCLS) ..... KyPpA
Alice Meynell [*British poet, 1847-1922*] ..... AM
Alice Springs [*Australia ICAO location identifier*] (ICLI) ..... ABAS
Alice Springs [*Australia Seismograph station code, US Geological Survey*] (SEIS) ..... ASP
Alice Town/South Bimini, Bimini Island [*Bahamas*] [*ICAO location identifier*] (ICLI) ..... MYBS
Alice, TX [*Location identifier FAA*] (FAAL) ..... ALI
Alice, TX [*AM radio station call letters*] ..... KDSI
Alice, TX [*FM radio station call letters*] (RBYB) ..... KNDA
Alice, TX [*AM radio station call letters*] (RBYB) ..... KOPY-AM
Alice, TX [*FM radio station call letters*] (RBYB) ..... KOPY-FM
Alice, TX [*FM radio station call letters*] ..... KQNN
Aliceville, AL [*Location identifier FAA*] (FAAL) ..... AIV
Alico, Inc. [*NASDAQ symbol*] (NQ) ..... ALCO
Alico, Inc. [*NASDAQ symbol*] (TTSB) ..... ALCO
Alico, Inc. [*Associated Press*] (SAG) ..... Alico
Alicudi [*Lipari Islands*] [*Seismograph station code, US Geological Survey*] (SEIS) ..... ACL
Alicyclic [*Chemistry*] ..... ac
Alidade [*Engineering*] ..... ALDD
Alidaunia SRL [*Italy ICAO designator*] (FAAC) ..... LID
Alien Cell ..... AC
Alien Declared Intention ..... ADI
Alien Documentation, Identification, and Telecommunications [*Immigration and Naturalization Service*] ..... ADIT
Alien Firearms Act ..... AFA
Alien Grange ..... AGR
Alien Life Force [*Acronym is name of title character in television series*] ..... ALF
Alien, Penumbral, Umbral, Penumbral, Alien ..... APUPA
Alien Priory ..... APR
Alien Property Custodian [*World War II*] ..... APC
Alien Property Division [*Department of Justice*] (DLA) ..... APD
Alien Status Verification Index [*Immigration and Naturalization Service*] (GFGA) ..... ASVI
Aligarh [*India*] [*ICAO location identifier*] (ICLI) ..... VIAH
Alighting Area [*Aviation*] ..... ALA
Aligiulia SpA [*Italy ICAO designator*] (FAAC) ..... RWA
Align ..... ALN
Aligned Short Fiber Sheet Molding Compound (MCD) ..... ASSM
Aligner ..... ALGNR
Aligning ..... ALGNNG
Alignment (KSC) ..... ALGN
Alignment ..... ALIGN
Alignment ..... ALIGN
Alignment (AAG) ..... ALNMT
Alignment and Diagnostic Display Console ..... ADDC
Alignment and Test Facility for Optical Systems [*Navy*] ..... ATFOS
Alignment Control Panel ..... ACP
Alignment Countdown Set [*Aerospace*] (AAG) ..... A-CS
Alignment Countdown Set Inertial Guidance [*Aerospace*] (AAG) ..... ACSIG
Alignment Group ..... AG
Alignment Group Sensing Platform (AAG) ..... AGSP
Alignment Lab ..... AL
Alignment Mark [*On cardiography*] [*Cardiology*] (DAVI) ..... AL
Alignment Optical Telescope ..... AOT
Alignment Periscope ..... AP
Alignment Procedures ..... AP
Alignment Progress Indicator (KSC) ..... API
Alignment Requirements Outline (MCD) ..... ARO
Alignment Unit ..... AU
Alignment Window ..... AW
Alignment-Off-Time [*Instrumentation*] ..... AOT
Align-Rite International, Inc. [*Associated Press*] (SAG) ..... AligrR
Align-Rite International, Inc. [*NASDAQ symbol*] (SAG) ..... MASK

Align-Rite Intl. [*NASDAQ symbol*] (TTSB) ...... MASK
Aligoodarz [*Iran*] [*ICAO location identifier*] (ICLI) ...... OICZ
Alijo [*Portugal ICAO location identifier*] (ICLI) ...... LPJO
Alimentary Sleep [*Medicine*] (BABM) ...... AS
Alimentary System [*Medicine*] ...... AS
Alimentary Toxic Aleukia ...... ATA
Alimentos para Animales, SA [*Feed plant*] [*Guatemala*] ...... ALIANSA
Alimony [*Legal shorthand*] (LWAP) ...... ALI
Alina International Industries [*Vancouver Stock Exchange symbol*] ...... ALA
Alindao [*Central African Republic*] [*ICAO location identifier*] (ICLI) ...... FEFA
Alinea [*Paragraph*] [*Italian*] (ILCA) ...... AI
Alinea [*Paragraph*] [*Dutch*] (ILCA) ...... AI
Alingsas [*Sweden ICAO location identifier*] (ICLI) ...... ESGI
Alinine, Sulphur, and Formaldehyde [*Medicine*] (BABM) ...... ASF
Alinord [*Italy ICAO designator*] (FAAC) ...... DNO
Aliphatic Acyl Radical [*Biochemistry*] (DAVI) ...... RCO
Aliphatic Ammonium Nitrate (MCD) ...... AAN
Aliquippa & Southern Railroad Co. [*AAR code*] ...... ALQS
Alis [*Former USSR*] [*FAA designator*] (FAAC) ...... LSI
Alisarda [*ICAO designator*] (AD) ...... IG
ALISARDA SpA [*Italy ICAO designator*] (ICDA) ...... IG
Aliserio [*Italy ICAO designator*] (FAAC) ...... ALL
Alishan [*Republic of China*] [*Seismograph station code, US Geological Survey*] (SEIS) ...... ALS
Alison's Practice [*Scotland*] [*A publication*] (DLA) ...... Alison Pr
Alison's Principles of the Criminal Law of Scotland [*A publication*] (DLA) .... Al Pr
Alison's Principles of the Criminal Law of Scotland [*A publication*] (DLA) ...... Al Sc CrL
Alison's Principles of the Criminal Law of Scotland [*A publication*] (ILCA) ...... Alis Princ Scot Law
Alison's Principles of the Criminal Law of Scotland [*A publication*] (DLA) ...... Alis Princ Scotch Law
Alister Hardy Research Centre [*Manchester College*] [*British*] (CB) ...... AHRC
Alitak [*Alaska*] [*Airport symbol*] (OAG) ...... ALZ
ALITALIA [*Aerolinee Italiane Internazionali*] [*Italian airline*] (MCD) ...... ALI
ALITALIA [*Aerolinee Italiane Internazionali*] [*Italian airline*] [*ICAO designator*] ...... AZ
ALITALIA, Lufthansa, Air France, Sabena [*Consortium of airlines*] (MCD) ...... ATLAS
Alitalia-Linee Aeree Italiane SpA [*Italy ICAO designator*] (FAAC) ...... AZA
Alitaxi SRL [*Italy ICAO designator*] (FAAC) ...... ALX
Aliter [*Otherwise*] [*Latin*] (ADA) ...... ALR
Alive ...... A
Alive and Well ...... A & W
Alive with Disease [*Medicine*] ...... AWD
Aliwal North [*South Africa*] [*ICAO location identifier*] (ICLI) ...... FAAN
Alix Public Library, Alberta [*Library symbol National Library of Canada*] (NLC) ...... AALI
Alizarin (DMAA) ...... AZR
Alizarin Red S [*An indicator*] [*Chemistry*] ...... ARS
Aljamia [*MARC language code Library of Congress*] (LCCP) ...... ajm
Al-Jouf [*Saudi Arabia*] [*ICAO location identifier*] (ICLI) ...... OESK
Alkair [*Denmark ICAO designator*] (ICDA) ...... KA
Alkair Flight Operations APS [*Denmark ICAO designator*] (FAAC) ...... LKA
Alkali and Clean Air Inspectorate [*British*] (DCTA) ...... ACAI
Alkali and Radiochemical Inspectorate [*British*] (NUCP) ...... ARCI
Alkali Cellulose [*Chemistry*] ...... AC
Alkali Flame Ionization Detector [*Instrumentation*] ...... AFID
Alkali Metal Cleaning Facility [*Nuclear energy*] (NRCH) ...... AMCF
Alkali Metal Thermoelectric Converter [*Power source*] (MCD) ...... AMTEC
Alkali Plasma Hall Accelerator (MCD) ...... ALPHA
Alkali-Extractable Light Chain [*Biochemistry*] ...... ALC
Alkali-Gravity-Viscosity [*Glass technology*] ...... AGV
Alkali-Metal Turbine ...... AMT
Alkaline (KSC) ...... ALK
Alkaline Calcium Petroleum Sulfonate ...... ACPS
Alkaline Contaminant Material [*In used frying oils*] ...... ACM
Alkaline Electrolyte Fuel Cell ...... AEFC
Alkaline Fuel Cell ...... AFC
Alkaline Peptone Water (DMAA) ...... APW
Alkaline Permanganate [*Nuclear energy*] (NUCP) ...... AP
Alkaline Permanganate Ammonium Citrate (OA) ...... APAC
Alkaline Phosphatase (DMAA) ...... AKP
Alkaline Phosphatase [*An enzyme*] (CPH) ...... alk phos
Alkaline Phosphatase [*An enzyme*] (CPH) ...... alk ptase
Alkaline Phosphatase [*An enzyme*] (DAVI) ...... ALK-P
Alkaline Phosphatase [*Also, AP*] [*An enzyme*] ...... ALP
Alkaline Phosphatase [*Also, ALP*] [*An enzyme*] ...... AP
Alkaline Phosphatase [*An enzyme*] (DAVI) ...... KA
Alkaline Phosphatase [*Biochemistry*] (DAVI) ...... p'ase
Alkaline Phosphatase Activity (USDC) ...... APA
Alkaline Phosphatase Activity [*Marine science*] (OSRA) ...... APA
Alkaline Phosphatase Activity, Granular Leukocytes [*Immunochemistry*] (MAE) ...... APGL
Alkaline Phosphatase:Antialkaline Phosphatase [*Immunochemistry*] ...... APAAP
Alkaline Phosphatase Isoenzymes [*Biochemistry*] (DAVI) ...... ALKISO
Alkalinity (MSA) ...... ALKY
Alkali-Refined Linseed Oil [*Organic chemistry*] ...... ARLO
Alkalisilica Reaction [*Chemistry*] ...... ASR
Alkali-Soluble Nitrogen (MAE) ...... ASN
Alkali-Tin-Silicate [*Glass for possible nuclear waste storage*] ...... ATS
Alkali-Treated Straw (PDAA) ...... ATS
Alkalyzing Agent ...... AA
Alkan Air Ltd. [*Canada ICAO designator*] (FAAC) ...... AKN
Alkan Air Ltd. [*ICAO designator*] (AD) ...... TO
Alkan Society [*Surrey, England*] (EAIO) ...... AS

Alkane [*Organic chemistry*] ...... AL
Alkaril Chemicals Ltd., Mississauga, ON, Canada [*Library symbol Library of Congress*] (LCLS) ...... CaOMAC
Alkaril Chemicals Ltd., Mississauga, Ontario [*Library symbol National Library of Canada*] (NLC) ...... OMAC
Alkenyl Succinic Anhydride [*Organic chemistry*] ...... ASA
Alkermes, Inc. [*Associated Press*] (SAG) ...... Alkerm
Alkermes, Inc. [*NASDAQ symbol*] (SPSG) ...... ALKS
Al-Kharj [*Saudi Arabia*] [*ICAO location identifier*] (ICLI) ...... OEKJ
Alkoxyglycerol [*Organic chemistry*] ...... AKG
Alkyd Moulding Compound (PDAA) ...... AMC
Alkyl [*Chemistry*] ...... Alk
Alkyl Amines Council (EA) ...... AAC
Alkyl Benzenesulfonate [*Organic chemistry*] ...... ABS
Alkyl Ketene Dimer [*Organic chemistry*] ...... AKA
Alkyl Lysophospholipid [*Biochemistry*] ...... ALP
Alkyl Polyglycoside [*Organic chemistry*] ...... APG
Alkyl Sulfate [*Surfactant*] [*Organic chemistry*] ...... AS
Alkylated Chlorsulfonated Polyethylene [*Plastics technology*] ...... ACSM
Alkylation Unit Acid [*Petroleum refining*] ...... AUA
Alkyldimethylamine [*Acronym is a trademark of Ethyl Corp. for its brand of alkyldimethylamine products*] ...... ADMA
Alkylethoxylated Sulfate [*Surfactant*] [*Organic chemistry*] ...... AES
Alkylketene Dimer [*Organic chemistry*] ...... AKD
Alkylphenol Ethoxylate [*Organic chemistry*] ...... APE
Alkylphenol Polyethoxylate [*Organic chemistry*] ...... APEO
Alkylsuccinic Anhydride [*Organic chemistry*] ...... ASA
All Ability School [*British*] ...... AA
All Abnormal [*Clinical hematology*] ...... AA
All About Issues American [*An association*] (EA) ...... AAIA
All Accident Notice Offices ...... ALANO
All Africa Students Union [*See also UPE*] (EAIO) ...... AASU
All Africa Teachers' Organization (EAIO) ...... AATO
All After [*Aviation*] (DA) ...... AA
All [*Text*] After [*Specified Point*] [*Message handling*] ...... AA
All Air Carrier Field Offices (FAAC) ...... ALACFO
All Air Defense Liasion Officers in Region (FAAC) ...... ALADLO
All Air Route Traffic Control Centers in Region (FAAC) ...... ALARTC
All Air Traffic (Area) Supervisors in Region (FAAC) ...... ALATAS
All Air Traffic Field Facilities (FAAC) ...... ALATF
All Air Traffic Field Offices (FAAC) ...... ALATFO
All Air Traffic Service Personnel in Region (FAAC) ...... ALAT
All Airway Facilities Sector and Field Offices (FAAC) ...... ALAFFO
All Along (ADA) ...... AA
All Aluminum Alloy Conductor (MCD) ...... AAAC
All Aluminum Conductor ...... AAC
All Amer Communications'B' [*NASDAQ symbol*] (TTSB) ...... AACIB
All Amer Semiconductor [*NASDAQ symbol*] (TTSB) ...... SEMI
All America Girls Professional Baseball League [*In 1992 movie, "A League of Their Own"*] [*Also, GPBL*] ...... AAGPBL
All American Association of Contest Judges (EA) ...... AAACJ
All American Cables & Radio, Inc. ...... AAC & R
All American Commun [*NASDAQ symbol*] (TTSB) ...... AACI
All American Communications, Inc. [*NASDAQ symbol*] (SAG) ...... AACI
All American Communications, Inc. [*Associated Press*] (SAG) ...... AllACm
All American Food Group, Inc. [*NASDAQ symbol*] (SAG) ...... AAFG
All American Food Group, Inc. [*Associated Press*] (SAG) ...... AllAFG
All American Semiconductor, Inc. [*Associated Press*] (SAG) ...... AllASem
All American Semiconductor, Inc. [*NASDAQ symbol*] (NQ) ...... SEMI
All American Target Term Trust [*NYSE symbol*] (SAG) ...... AAT
All American Target Term Trust [*Associated Press*] (SAG) ...... AllAmTar
All Applications Digital Computer [*Navy*] ...... AADC
All Army Activities (AABC) ...... ALARACT
All Aspect Gunsight Evaluation (MCD) ...... AAGE
All [*Text*] Before [*Specified Point*] [*Message handling*] ...... AB
All Body Type [*Army*] (AABC) ...... ABT
All Brit Karate Organisation (DBA) ...... TABKO
All Bureaus [*Navy*] ...... ALBUS
All Busy Low [*AT & T*] ...... ABL
All but Not Only ...... ABNO
All But the Dissertation [*PhD candidates*] ...... ABD
All Canada Insurance Federation ...... ACIF
All Canada Poetry Contests ...... ACPC
All Canadian Congress of Labour ...... ACCL
All Ceylon Federation of Free Trade Unions ...... ACFFTU
All Charter Ltd. [*British ICAO designator*] (FAAC) ...... BLA
All Chiefs, No Indians [*Slang*] (AAG) ...... ACNI
All Commands [*A dispatch to all commands in an area*] [*Navy*] ...... ALCOM
All Commands, [*US*] Atlantic Fleet [*Navy*] (NVT) ...... ALCOMLANT
All Commands, [*US*] Pacific Fleet [*Navy*] (NVT) ...... ALCOMPAC
All Commands Process as Attached [*Army*] (AABC) ...... ACPATT
All Composite Aircraft (MCD) ...... ACA
All Concerned [*Army*] (AABC) ...... ALCON
All Concerned Notified ...... ACN
All Culture [*Broth*] [*Biochemistry*] (DAVI) ...... AC
All Dielectric Filter ...... ADF
All Edges Gilt [*Bookbinding*] (ADA) ...... AEG
All Engines Operating [*Aviation*] ...... AEO
All England ...... AE
All England Law Reports [*A publication*] ...... AER
All England Law Reports (Reprint) [*1558-1935*] [*A publication*] (DLA) ...... AER Rep
All England Law Reports (Reprint) [*1558-1935*] [*A publication*] (DLA) .... All ER Rep
All England Law Reports (Reprint) [*1558-1935*] [*A publication*] (DLA) ...... All ER Repr

All England Law Reports (Reprint) Australian Extension Volumes [*A publication*] (DLA) ... AER Rep Ext
All England Law Reports (Reprint), Australian Extension Volumes [*A publication*] (DLA) ... All ER Rep Ext
All England Lawn Tennis Club ... AELTC
All England Netball Association (EAIO) ... AENA
All England Women's Hockey Association (EAIO) ... AEWHA
All England Women's Lacrosse Association (EAIO) ... AEWLA
All Equipment OK [*Expression meaning "in perfect working order." Popularized during early development of NASA's space program*] ... A-OK
All Equipment Production Reliability Tests (MCD) ... AEPRT
All Faiths for One Race (AIE) ... AFFOR
All Figure Number [*Telecommunications*] (TEL) ... AFN
All Flight Service Stations in Region (FAAC) ... ALFSS
All Flight Standards Field Offices (FAAC) ... ALFSFO
All Food Activities [*DoD*] ... ALFOODACT
All for the Children Foundation [*Defunct*] (EA) ... ACF
All Former Buyers ... AFB
All Fouled-Up [*Bowdlerized version*] (AAG) ... AFU
All Got Up (ADA) ... AGU
All Hope Abandoned [*Union*] [*British*] (DGA) ... AHA
All in Hand (ADA) ... AIH
All in the Family [*TV program*] ... AITF
All India Criminal Decisions [*A publication*] (DLA) ... AI Cr D
All India Criminal Decisions [*A publication*] (ILCA) ... All Ind Crim Dec
All India Criminal Decisions [*A publication*] (DLA) ... All India Crim Dec
All India Criminal Times [*A publication*] (DLA) ... All Ind Cr T
All India Law Reporter [*Usually followed by a province abbreviation*] [*as AIR All., for Allahabad, Bom. for Bombay, Dacca for Dacca, HP for Himachal Pradesh, Hyd. for Hyderabad, etc.*] [*A publication*] (DLA) ... AIR
All India Reporter, Ajmer Series [*A publication*] (ILCA) ... AIR Aj
All India Reporter, Ajmer Series [*A publication*] (ILCA) ... Aj
All India Reporter, Allahabad Series [*A publication*] (ILCA) ... AIR All
All India Reporter, Allahabad Series [*A publication*] (ILCA) ... AIRA
All India Reporter, Andhra Pradesh Series [*A publication*] (ILCA) ... AIR Andh Pra
All India Reporter, Andhra Pradesh Series [*A publication*] (DLA) ... Andh Pra
All India Reporter, Andhra Series [*A publication*] (ILCA) ... AIR And
All India Reporter, Andhra Series [*A publication*] (ILCA) ... AIR Andh
All India Reporter, Andhra Series [*A publication*] (DLA) ... And
All India Reporter, Andhra Series [*A publication*] (DLA) ... Andh
All India Reporter, Assam Series [*A publication*] (ILCA) ... AIR Asm
All India Reporter, Assam Series [*A publication*] (ILCA) ... AIR Assam
All India Reporter, Assam Series [*A publication*] (DLA) ... Asm
All India Reporter, Bhopal Series [*A publication*] (ILCA) ... AIR Bhop
All India Reporter, Bhopal Series [*A publication*] (DLA) ... Bhop
All India Reporter, Bilaspur Series [*A publication*] (ILCA) ... AIR Bilas
All India Reporter, Bilaspur Series [*A publication*] (DLA) ... Bilas
All India Reporter, Bombay Series [*A publication*] (ILCA) ... AIR Bom
All India Reporter, Bombay Series [*A publication*] (ILCA) ... AIRB
All India Reporter, Bombay Series [*A publication*] (DLA) ... B
All India Reporter, Calcutta Series [*A publication*] (ILCA) ... AIR Cal
All India Reporter, Calcutta Series [*A publication*] (ILCA) ... AIRC
All India Reporter, Calcutta Series [*A publication*] (DLA) ... C
All India Reporter, Calcutta Series [*A publication*] (DLA) ... Cal
All India Reporter, Dacca Series [*A publication*] (ILCA) ... AIR Dacca
All India Reporter, Dacca Series [*1949-50*] [*A publication*] (DLA) ... Dacca
All India Reporter, East Punjab [*1948-50*] [*A publication*] (DLA) ... East Punjab
All India Reporter, East Punjab Series [*A publication*] (ILCA) ... AIR East Punjab
All India Reporter, Federal Court [*1947-50*] [*A publication*] (DLA) ... FC
All India Reporter, Federal Court Series [*A publication*] (ILCA) ... AIRFC
All India Reporter, Himachal Pradesh [*A publication*] (DLA) ... Him Pra
All India Reporter, Himachal Pradesh [*A publication*] (DLA) ... HP
All India Reporter, Himachal Pradesh Series [*A publication*] (ILCA) ... AIR Him Pra
All India Reporter, Himachal Pradesh Series [*A publication*] (ILCA) ... AIRHP
All India Reporter, Hyderabad [*A publication*] (DLA) ... Hy
All India Reporter, Hyderabad [*A publication*] (DLA) ... Hyd
All India Reporter, Hyderabad Series [*A publication*] (ILCA) ... AIR Hy
All India Reporter, Hyderabad Series [*A publication*] (ILCA) ... AIR Hyd
All India Reporter, Indian Digest [*A publication*] (ILCA) ... AIR Ind Dig
All India Reporter, Indian Digest [*1946-52*] [*A publication*] (DLA) ... Ind Dig
All India Reporter, Jammu and Kashmir [*A publication*] (DLA) ... J & K
All India Reporter, Jammu and Kashmir Series [*A publication*] (ILCA) ... AIRJ & K
All India Reporter, Kerala Series [*A publication*] (ILCA) ... AIR Kerala
All India Reporter, Kutch [*1949-56*] [*A publication*] (DLA) ... Kutch
All India Reporter, Kutch Series [*A publication*] (ILCA) ... AIR Kutch
All India Reporter, Lahore Series [*A publication*] (ILCA) ... AIR Lahore
All India Reporter, Lahore Series [*A publication*] (ILCA) ... Lahore
All India Reporter, Madhya Bharat [*1950-57*] [*A publication*] (DLA) ... MB
All India Reporter, Madhya Bharat Series [*A publication*] (ILCA) ... AIRMB
All India Reporter, Madhya Pradesh [*A publication*] (DLA) ... Madh Pra
All India Reporter, Madhya Pradesh [*A publication*] (DLA) ... MP
All India Reporter, Madhya Pradesh Series [*A publication*] (ILCA) ... AIR Madh Pra
All India Reporter, Madhya Pradesh Series [*A publication*] (ILCA) ... AIRMP
All India Reporter, Madras [*A publication*] (DLA) ... Mad
All India Reporter, Madras Series [*A publication*] (ILCA) ... AIR Mad
All India Reporter, Madras Series [*A publication*] (ILCA) ... AIRM
All India Reporter, Madras Series [*A publication*] (ILCA) ... M
All India Reporter, Manipur [*A publication*] (DLA) ... Manip
All India Reporter, Manipur Series [*A publication*] (ILCA) ... AIR Manip
All India Reporter, Mysore [*A publication*] (DLA) ... Mys
All India Reporter, Mysore Series [*A publication*] (ILCA) ... AIR My
All India Reporter, Mysore Series [*A publication*] (ILCA) ... My
All India Reporter, Nagpur [*A publication*] (DLA) ... All India Rep
All India Reporter, Nagpur [*A publication*] (DLA) ... Nag
All India Reporter, Nagpur Series [*A publication*] (ILCA) ... AIR Nag
All India Reporter, Nagpur Series [*A publication*] (ILCA) ... AIRN
All India Reporter, Nagpur Series [*A publication*] (ILCA) ... N
All India Reporter, New Series [*A publication*] (DLA) ... All Ind Rep NS
All India Reporter, Orissa [*A publication*] (DLA) ... Oris
All India Reporter, Orissa [*A publication*] (DLA) ... Orissa
All India Reporter, Orissa Series [*A publication*] (ILCA) ... AIR Oris
All India Reporter, Oudh Series [*A publication*] (ILCA) ... AIR Oudh
All India Reporter, Patiala and East Punjab States Union [*1950-57*] [*A publication*] (DLA) ... PEPSU
All India Reporter, Patiala and East Punjab States Union Series [*A publication*] (ILCA) ... AIR PEP
All India Reporter, Patiala and East Punjab States Union Series [*A publication*] (ILCA) ... AIR PEPSU
All India Reporter, Patiala and East Punjab States Union Series [*A publication*] (ILCA) ... PEP
All India Reporter, Patna [*A publication*] (DLA) ... P
All India Reporter, Patna Series [*A publication*] (ILCA) ... AIR Pat
All India Reporter, Patna Series [*A publication*] (ILCA) ... AIRP
All India Reporter, Patna Series [*A publication*] (ILCA) ... Pat
All India Reporter, Peshawar [*1933-50*] [*A publication*] (DLA) ... Peshawar
All India Reporter, Peshawar Series [*A publication*] (ILCA) ... AIR Pesh
All India Reporter, Privy Council [*A publication*] (ILCA) ... AIRPC
All India Reporter, Privy Council [*1914-50*] [*A publication*] (DLA) ... PC
All India Reporter, Punjab [*A publication*] (DLA) ... Pun
All India Reporter, Punjab Series [*A publication*] (ILCA) ... AIR Pun
All India Reporter, Rajasthan [*A publication*] (DLA) ... R
All India Reporter, Rajasthan [*A publication*] (DLA) ... Raj
All India Reporter, Rajasthan Series [*A publication*] (ILCA) ... AIR Raj
All India Reporter, Rajasthan Series [*A publication*] (ILCA) ... AIRR
All India Reporter, Saurashtra [*1950-57*] [*A publication*] (DLA) ... Sau
All India Reporter, Saurashtra Series [*A publication*] (ILCA) ... AIR Sau
All India Reporter, Simla [*1951*] [*A publication*] (DLA) ... Simla
All India Reporter, Simla Series [*A publication*] (ILCA) ... AIR Simla
All India Reporter, Sind [*1914-50*] [*A publication*] (DLA) ... Sind
All India Reporter, Sind Series [*A publication*] (ILCA) ... AIR Sind
All India Reporter, Supreme Court [*A publication*] (ILCA) ... AIRSC
All India Reporter, Supreme Court Reports [*A publication*] (DLA) ... SC
All India Reporter, Travancore-Cochin [*1950-57*] [*A publication*] (DLA) ... TC
All India Reporter, Travancore-Cochin Series [*A publication*] (ILCA) ... AIRTC
All India Reporter, Tripura [*A publication*] (DLA) ... Trip
All India Reporter, Tripura Series [*A publication*] (ILCA) ... AIR Trip
All India Reporter, Vindhya Pradesh [*1951-57*] [*A publication*] (DLA) ... VP
All India Reporter, Vindhya Pradesh Series [*A publication*] (ILCA) ... AIRVP
All India Reports [*A publication*] (DLA) ... All IR
All Indian Criminal Reports [*A publication*] (DLA) ... All ICR
All Indian Criminal Reports [*A publication*] (DLA) ... All Ind Cr R
All Indian Law Reports, Kerala Series [*A publication*] (DLA) ... Kerala
All Indian Pueblo Council (EA) ... AIPC
All Individuals Deserve Support [*Alternative translation of AIDS, Acquired Immune Deficiency Syndrome, used as a slogan by AWARE*] ... AIDS
All Indonesian Labor Federation (IMH) ... FBSI
All Inertial (SAA) ... AI
All Inertial Guidance [*Aerospace*] (AAG) ... AIG
All Inertial Guidance System [*Aerospace*] ... AIGS
All International Air Traffic Communications Stations [*FAA*] ... ALIATCS
All International Air Traffic Switching Centers (FAAC) ... AIATSC
All International Field Offices (FAAC) ... ALIFO
All International Flight Service Stations in Region (FAAC) ... ALIFSS
All Iron ... AI
All Is Well [*Search and rescue symbol that can be stamped in sand or snow*] ... LL
All Island Air [*ICAO designator*] (AD) ... AJ
All Known Allergies [*Medicine*] (DAVI) ... AKA
All Leisure Aviation Ltd. [*British*] [*FAA designator*] (FAAC) ... ALT
All Lengths [*Lumber*] ... AL
All London Parents' Action Group [*British*] (AIE) ... ALPAG
All London Teachers Against Racism and Fascism [*British*] (AIE) ... ALTARF
All Major Commands ... ALMAJCOM
All Major Commands (MCD) ... AMC
All Malignant Neoplasm [*Medicine*] ... AMN
All Marine Corps Activities (NVT) ... ALMAR
All Military Activities (AFM) ... ALMILACT
All Nationals Congress [*Fiji*] [*Political party*] (EY) ... ANC
All Nations Christian College [*British*] ... ANCC
All Nations Women's League (EA) ... ANWL
All Naval Activities Employing Civilians (MCD) ... ANAEC
All Naval Stations [*A dispatch to all Naval stations in an area*] ... ALLNAVSTAS
All Naval Stations [*A dispatch to all Naval stations in an area*] ... ALNAVSTA
All Navy Activities [*A dispatch to all activities in an area*] ... ALNAV
All Navy Activities [*A dispatch to all activities in an area*] ... NAVACT
All Nigeria Law Reports [*A publication*] (DLA) ... All Nig LR
All Nigeria Law Reports [*A publication*] (DLA) ... All NLR
All Nippon [*ICAO designator*] (AD) ... NH
All Nippon Airways Co. Ltd. [*Japan ICAO designator*] (FAAC) ... ANA
All Normal [*Hematology*] ... AN
All Numbers Calling [*Telephone*] ... ANC
All Officers Meeting [*Military*] (DNAB) ... AOM
All Offices Having Send-Receive Teletypewriter Service on Circuit (FAAC) ... ALCKT
All Operator Letter (MCD) ... AOL
All or None [*Investment, securities*] ... AON
All Other Perils [*Insurance*] ... AOP
All Others [*Later, G Group*] [*Division of National Security Agency*] ... ALLO
All Out-of-Kilter [*Slang*] ... AOK
All Over Pattern [*Quilting*] ... AOP
All Over Set [*Quilting*] ... AOS

All Over the Hatch [*or Hold*] [*Stowage*] (DNAB) .... A/O
All Pakistan Legal Decisions [*A publication*] (ILCA) .... PLD
All Party Alliance [*British*] .... APA
All Pass Network .... APN
All Peoples' Republican Party [*Ghana*] (AF) .... APRP
All Personnel Communication [*Military*] (AFM) .... ALPERSCOM
All Pilots Meeting [*Military*] (DNAB) .... APM
All Points Addressable [*Computer science*] .... APA
All Points Bulletin [*Police call*] .... APB
All Points Bulletin [*Law enforcement*] (WDMC) .... APB
All Present or Accounted For .... APOAF
All Propulsive Orbited Transfer Vehicle [*NASA*] .... APOTV
All Purpose Carrier (SSD) .... APC
All Purpose Electronic x Computer [*Early computer*] [*Birkbeck College*] [*British*] .... APExC
All Purpose Paper [*Euphemism for toilet paper*] .... APP
All Purpose Structure Eurocontrol RADAR Information Exchange (DA) .... ASTERIX
All Quadrants (FAAC) .... ALQDS
All Quotes, Inc. [*Associated Press*] (SAG) .... AllQt
All Quotes, Inc. [*Associated Press*] (SAG) .... AllQuote
All Quotes, Inc. [*NASDAQ symbol*] (SAG) .... ALQT
All RADAR Air Traffic Control Facilities in Region [*FAA*] .... ALRAFAC
All Radio Marketing Study [*Business term*] (DOAD) .... ARMS
All Rail [*Railroad*] .... AR
All Red Series [*A publication*] .... ARS
All Regional Offices (FAAC) .... ALRGN
All Returned (DGA) .... A/R
All Right [*From Oll Korrect; or from Old Kinderhook, a political club that supported the 1840 presidential campaign of Martin Van Buren*] .... OK
All Risk Management [*Insurance*] .... ARM
All Risks [*Insurance*] .... AR
All Roads Ministry [*An association*] (EA) .... ARM
All Rock-and-Roll Oldies [*Radio station format*] (WDMC) .... ARRO
All Rods Out [*Nuclear energy*] (NRCH) .... ARO
All Round [*Price*] (ROG) .... A/R
All Routes Busy [*Telecommunications*] (TEL) .... ARB
All Routes Explorer [*Source route bridging*] (ACRL) .... ARE
All Safety Commands [*Air Force*] (AFM) .... ALSAFECOM
All Saints' Day .... ASD
All Savers Certificate [*Banking*] .... ASC
All Seasons Global Fund [*Associated Press*] (SAG) .... AllSeasG
All Seasons Global Fund [*NASDAQ symbol*] (TTSB) .... FUND
All Sectors (FAAC) .... ALSEC
All Service Postal Chess Club (EA) .... ASPCC
All Ships and Stations Letters .... AS & SL
All Source Analysis Center (MCD) .... ASAC
All Source Analysis System [*Military*] (DOMA) .... ASAR
All Source Analysis System [*DoD*] .... ASAS
All Source Analysis System/Software [*Military*] (RDA) .... ASAS/SFT
All Source Document Index [*Army*] .... ASDI
All Source Intelligence Center (MCD) .... ASIC
All South Africa Law Reports [*A publication*] (DLA) .... ASAR
All South Pole (IAA) .... ASP
All Star Airlines, Inc. [*ICAO designator*] (FAAC) .... ASR
All Star Dairy Association (EA) .... ASDA
All Star Resources [*Vancouver Stock Exchange symbol*] .... ASR
All States Hobby Club [*Later, NASHC*] .... ASHC
All Stations (KSC) .... ALSTA
All Stations, Continental United States (MUGU) .... ALSTACON
All Systems Test [*NASA*] (KSC) .... AST
All Systems Test Equipment Group .... ASTEG
All Systems Vehicle .... ASV
All Tariffs Computerized [*Project*] .... ATAC
All Taxa Biodiversity Inventory [*Proposed*] [*National Science Foundation*] .... ATBI
All Terrain Lifter Articulated System [*MTMC*] (TAG) .... ATLAS
All Test Go (MCD) .... ATG
All the Best Dog Poems [*A publication*] .... AIBD
All the Conveniences .... A/C
All Things Considered [*Radio program*] .... ATC
All Thrust Terminate Relay (MUGU) .... ATTR
All Thrust Termination (MUGU) .... ATT
All Together (EA) .... AT
All Transistor (IAA) .... ATR
All Trunks Busy [*Telecommunications*] .... ATB
All Union Central Council of Trade Unions [*Former USSR*] .... AUCCTU
All Up (ADA) .... AU
All Up Round (MCD) .... AUR
All Up Weight (DOMA) .... AUW
All Vehicle Test .... AVT
All Volatile Treatment [*Nuclear energy*] (NRCH) .... AVT
All Wales Ladies Lacrosse Association (BI) .... AWLLA
All Water .... AW
All Wave Antenna .... AWA
All Weather Flying Division [*Air Force*] .... AWAF
All Weather Operations (DA) .... AWO
All Widths [*Lumber*] .... AW
All Women's Archaeological Research Expedition .... AWARE
All Wood Screw (DAC) .... AWS
All Year Round Chrysanthemum Growers' Association (EAIO) .... AYRCGA
Alla Cacia [*In the Hunting Style*] [*Music*] (ROG) .... AL CAC
Alla Capella [*In Church Style*] [*Music*] (ROG) .... AL CAP
Alla Militaire [*In Military Style*] [*Music*] (ROG) .... AL MIL
Alla Moderna [*In Modern Style*] [*Music*] (ROG) .... AL MOD
All-Activity Vehicle .... AAV
All-Africa Conference of Churches [*Nairobi, Kenya*] (AF) .... AACC
All-African People's Revolutionary Party (EA) .... A-APRP
All-African Women's Conference [*or Congress*] .... AAWC
Allagash [*Maine*] [*Seismograph station code, US Geological Survey*] (SEIS) .... AGM
Allahabad [*India*] [*Airport symbol*] (OAG) .... IXD
Allahabad [*India*] [*ICAO location identifier*] (ICLI) .... VIAL
Allahabad Criminal Cases [*India*] [*A publication*] (DLA) .... A Cr C
Allahabad Criminal Cases [*India*] [*A publication*] (DLA) .... ACC
Allahabad Criminal Cases [*India*] [*A publication*] (DLA) .... All Cr Cas
Allahabad Criminal Reports [*India*] [*A publication*] (DLA) .... A Cr R
Allahabad Law Journal [*India*] [*A publication*] (DLA) .... All LJ
Allahabad Law Review [*India*] [*A publication*] (DLA) .... All LR
Allahabad Law Times [*India*] [*A publication*] (DLA) .... All LT
Allahabad Series, Indian Law Reports [*A publication*] (DLA) .... All Ser
Allahabad Weekly Notes [*India*] [*A publication*] (DLA) .... AWN
Allahabad Weekly Notes (and Supplement) [*India*] [*A publication*] (DLA) .... All WN
Allahabad Weekly Reporter [*India*] [*A publication*] (DLA) .... All WR
Allahabad Weekly Reporter [*India*] [*A publication*] (DLA) .... AWR
Allakaket [*Alaska*] [*Airport symbol*] (OAG) .... AET
All-Altitude Air-Bearing Research and Training Simulator .... ARTS
All-Altitude Spin Projected [*Munition*] .... ASP
Allamakee County Courthouse, Waukon, IA [*Library symbol*] [*Library of Congress*] (LCLS) .... IaWaukAC
Allamakee County Courthouse, Waukon, IA [*Library symbol Library of Congress*] (LCLS) .... IaWaukCoC
Allamakee Journal, Lansing, IA [*Library symbol Library of Congress*] (LCLS) .... IaLanJ
All-America Football Conference [*Major league 1946-49, merged with NFL 1950*] .... AAFC
All-America Gladiolus Selections (EA) .... AAGS
All-America Rose Selections [*An association*] (EA) .... AARS
All-America Selections (EA) .... AAS
All-American Amateur Baseball Association (EA) .... AAABA
All-American Boy [*Lifestyle classification*] (ECON) .... AAB
All-American Bronze Club (EA) .... AABC
All-American Challenge [*Auto racing*] .... AAC
All-American Collegiate Golf Foundation (EA) .... AACGF
All-American Conference to Combat Communism (EA) .... AACCC
All-American Girl [*Lifestyle classification*] (ECON) .... AAG
All-American Indian Motorcycle Club (EA) .... AAIMC
All-American Racers [*Automobile racing team*] .... AAR
All-American Target Term Trust [*NYSE symbol*] (SPSG) .... AAT
All-American Term Trust [*NYSE symbol*] (TTSB) .... AAT
All-American Youth Orchestra .... AAYO
Allamin Gorkij Konyvtar, Budapest, Hungary [*Library symbol Library of Congress*] (LCLS) .... HuBG
Allamvedelmi Hivatal [*Hungarian secret police*] .... AVH
Allan Blair Memorial Clinic, Regina, Saskatchewan [*Library symbol National Library of Canada*] (NLC) .... SRAB
Allan Blair Memorial Clinic, Regina, SK, Canada [*Library symbol*] [*Library of Congress*] (LCLS) .... CaSRAB
Allan Hancock College [*Santa Maria, CA*] .... AHC
Allan Hancock College, Santa Maria, CA [*Library symbol Library of Congress*] (LCLS) .... CStmaAH
Allan Hills [*Antarctic meteorology*] .... ALH
Allan Memorial Institute, Montreal, Quebec [*Library symbol National Library of Canada*] (NLC) .... QMAM
Allanco Iolite Monitor Corp. [*Vancouver Stock Exchange symbol*] .... AIT
Allantoin Vaginal Cream [*Gynecology*] (MAE) .... AVC
Allarcom Pay Television Ltd. [*Canada*] .... APT
Allard Owners Club [*British*] (EAIO) .... AOC
Allard Owners Club USA (EA) .... AOC-USA
Allard Register (EA) .... AR
All-Articles Configuration Inspection Log [*Aerospace*] (AAG) .... AACIL
All-Aspect Maneuvering Index (MCD) .... AAMI
Allative (BJA) .... All
All-Attitude Control Capability [*Aerospace*] (AAG) .... AACC
All-Attitude Indicator .... AAI
All-Attitude Indicator Bombing System (MCD) .... AABS
All-Attitude Vertical Reference System [*Aerospace*] .... AAVRS
All-Band Intercept Receiver .... ABIR
All-Breeds Rescue Conservancy (EA) .... ARC
Allcanada Express Ltd. [*Canada ICAO designator*] (FAAC) .... CNX
All-Canada Weekly Summaries [*Canada Law Book Ltd.*] [*Database*] .... ACWS
All-Ceylon Harbor and Dock Workers' Union .... ACHDWU
All-Channel Television Society [*UHF interest group*] (NTCM) .... ACTS
All-China Federation of Trade Unions [*Communist China*] .... ACFTU
Allcity Insurance [*NASDAQ symbol*] (TTSB) .... ALCI
Allcity Insurance Co. [*NASDAQ symbol*] (NQ) .... ALCI
Allcity Insurance Co. [*Associated Press*] (SAG) .... AllCity
All-Comm Media [*NASDAQ symbol*] (TTSB) .... ALCM
All-Comm Media Corp. [*NASDAQ symbol*] (SAG) .... ALCM
All-Comm Media Corp. [*Associated Press*] (SAG) .... AllCom
All-Commodity Volume [*Marketing*] (WDMC) .... ACV
All-Craft Foundation (EA) .... ACF
All-Digital Answering Machine [*PhoneMate, Inc.*] .... ADAM
All-Digital Attack Center (MCD) .... ADAC
All-Digital Data Tape (KSC) .... ADDT
All-Digital Phase-Locked Loop (KSC) .... ADPLL
All-Digital Simulator .... ADS
Alle Macht aan de Arbeiders [*All Power to the Workers*] [*Belgium Political party*] (PPW) .... AMADA
Alleberg [*Sweden ICAO location identifier*] (ICLI) .... ESGC
Allegan, MI [*FM radio station call letters*] (RBYB) .... WNTX

Allegan Public Library, Allegan, MI [*Library symbol Library of Congress*]
(LCLS) .... MiAlle
Allegany Community College, Cumberland, MD [*Library symbol Library of Congress*] (LCLS) .... MdCuAC
Allegany County Library, Cumberland, MD [*Library symbol Library of Congress*] (LCLS) .... MdCu
Allegata [*Schedules, Enclosures*] [*Italian*] (ILCA) .... all
Alleged Discrimination Official (MCD) .... ADO
Alleged Onset Date [*of disability*] [*Social Security Administration*] (OICC) .... AOD
Alleged Quarter [*of the year*] Disability Began [*Social Security Administration*] (OICC) .... AQD
Alleged Year Disability Began [*Social Security Administration*] (OICC) .... AYD
Allegemeine Elektrizitats Gesellschaft [*Federal Republic of Germany*] (NUCP) .... AEG
Alleghany Corp. [*NYSE symbol*] (SPSG) .... Y
Alleghany County Public Library, Sparta, NC [*Library symbol Library of Congress*] (LCLS) .... NcSpa
Allegheny (GAVI) .... AL
Allegheny (FAAC) .... ALGHNY
Allegheny Airlines [*Air carrier designation symbol*] .... AAA
Allegheny Airlines [*ICAO designator*] (AD) .... AL
Allegheny Airlines (IIA) .... ALA
Allegheny Airlines (MCD) .... ALL
Allegheny & South Side [*AAR code*] .... AYSS
Allegheny & Western Energy Corp. [*NASDAQ symbol*] (NQ) .... ALGH
Allegheny Ballistics Laboratory [*Cumberland, MD*] (MCD) .... ABL
Allegheny College (GAGS) .... Allegheny C
Allegheny College, Meadville, PA [*OCLC symbol*] (OCLC) .... AVL
Allegheny College, Meadville, PA [*Library symbol Library of Congress*] (LCLS) .... PMA
Allegheny Corp. [*Associated Press*] (SAG) .... AllegCp
Allegheny Corp. [*Associated Press*] (SAG) .... AllegCp
Allegheny County Law Library, Pittsburgh, PA [*OCLC symbol*] (OCLC) .... PAL
Allegheny County Law Library, Pittsburgh, PA [*Library symbol Library of Congress*] (LCLS) .... PPiAL
Allegheny International, Inc., Brackenridge, PA [*Library symbol Library of Congress*] (LCLS) .... PBracAL
Allegheny Ludlum [*NYSE symbol*] (TTSB) .... ALS
Allegheny Ludlum Corp. [*Associated Press*] (SAG) .... AlgLud
Allegheny Ludlum Corp. [*NYSE symbol*] (SPSG) .... ALS
Allegheny Ludlum Steel Company .... ALS
Allegheny Portage Railroad National Historic Site .... ALPO
Allegheny Power Sys [*NYSE symbol*] (TTSB) .... AYP
Allegheny Power System, Inc. [*Associated Press*] (SAG) .... AllgPow
Allegheny Power System, Inc. .... APS
Allegheny Power System, Inc. [*NYSE symbol*] (SPSG) .... AYP
Allegheny Region .... AR
Allegiance .... ALLEG
Allegiance Banc [*NASDAQ symbol*] (TTSB) .... ALLG
Allegiance Banc Corp. [*Associated Press*] (SAG) .... Allegian
Allegiance Banc Corp. [*NASDAQ symbol*] (SAG) .... ALLG
Allegiance Corp. [*NYSE symbol*] (SAG) .... AEH
Allegiance Corp. [*Associated Press*] (SAG) .... Allegnc
Allegiant Bancorp [*NASDAQ symbol*] (TTSB) .... ALLE
Allegiant Bancorp, Inc. [*NASDAQ symbol*] (SAG) .... ALLE
Allegiant Bancorp, Inc. [*Associated Press*] (SAG) .... Allegiant
Allegiant Physician Services, Inc. [*Associated Press*] (SAG) .... AllegPhy
Allegiant Physician Services, Inc. [*NASDAQ symbol*] (SAG) .... ALPS
Allegory (ADA) .... ALLEG
Allegory (VRA) .... alleg
Allegretto [*Moderately Quick*] [*Music*] (ROG) .... ALLEGTO
Allegretto [*Moderately Quick*] [*Music*] .... Allgett
Allegretto [*Moderately Quick*] [*Music*] (ROG) .... ALLGTTO
Allegretto [*Moderately Quick*] [*Music*] (ROG) .... ALLTO
Allegro [*Quick*] [*Music*] (ROG) .... ALL
Allegro [*Quick*] [*Music*] .... ALLO
Allegro New Media [*NASDAQ symbol*] (TTSB) .... ANMI
Allegro New Media, Inc. [*Associated Press*] (SAG) .... Allegro
Allegro New Media, Inc. [*NASDAQ symbol*] (SAG) .... ANMI
Allegro New Media, Inc. [*NASDAQ symbol*] (SAG) .... SPCO
Allegro-Elite [*Formerly, Allegro*] [*Record label*] .... Allo
Allein bei Christo die Ewige Freude [*With Christ Alone Is Eternal Joy*] [*Motto of Albrecht Gunther, Count Schwarzburg (1582-1634)*] [*German*] .... ABCDEF
Allein Gott Traue Ich [*I Trust in God Alone*] [*Motto of Dorothee, Duchess of Braunschweig-Lunebert (1546-1617)*] [*German*] .... AGTI
Allele [*Genetics*] .... A
All-Electric Aircraft [*Aviation*] (PDAA) .... AEA
Allele-Specific Oligonucleotide [*Genetics*] .... ASO
Allelix, Inc., Mississauga, ON, Canada [*Library symbol Library of Congress*] (LCLS) .... CaOMAI
Allelix, Inc., Mississauga, Ontario [*Library symbol National Library of Canada*] (NLC) .... OMAI
Alleluia [*An old abbreviation, formed from the vowels of the word*] .... AEUIA
Alleluia .... ALL
Allen Academy, Bryan, TX [*Library symbol Library of Congress*] (LCLS) .... TxBryA
Allen & Hanburys [*Great Britain*] [*Research code symbol*] .... AH
Allen & Hanburys [*Great Britain*] [*Research code symbol*] .... CB
Allen and Morris' Trial [*A publication*] (DLA) .... All & Mor Tr
Allen and Wright [*Root beer*] [*Initialism also used as name of franchised drive-in restaurants*] .... A & W
Allen, Brady & Marsh [*British advertising agency*] .... ABM
Allen Cognitive Levels Test .... ACL
Allen County Law Library, Lima, OH [*Library symbol Library of Congress*] (LCLS) .... OLimaAL
Allen County Public Library, Fort Wayne, IN [*OCLC symbol*] (OCLC) .... IMF

Allen County Times, New Haven, IN [*Library symbol Library of Congress*] (LCLS) .... InNhvAT
Allen County-Fort Wayne Historical Society Library, Fort Wayne, IN [*Library symbol Library of Congress*] (LCLS) .... InFwAHi
Allen Group [*NYSE symbol*] (TTSB) .... ALN
[The] Allen Group, Inc. [*Associated Press*] (SAG) .... AllenGp
[The] Allen Group, Inc. [*NYSE symbol*] (SPSG) .... ALN
Allen, KY [*FM radio station call letters*] .... WMDJ
Allen on Sheriffs [*A publication*] (DLA) .... All Sher
Allen Organ Cl'B' [*NASDAQ symbol*] (TTSB) .... AORGB
Allen Organ Co. [*Associated Press*] (SAG) .... AlnOrg
Allen Organ Co. [*NASDAQ symbol*] (NQ) .... AORG
Allen Parish Library, Oberlin, LA [*Library symbol Library of Congress*] (LCLS) .... LObA
Allen Park Public Library, Allen Park, MI [*Library symbol Library of Congress*] (LCLS) .... MiAp
Allen Township Consolidated Community School District 65, Ransom, IL [*Library symbol Library of Congress*] (LCLS) .... IRanASD
Allen University, Columbia, SC [*Library symbol*] [*Library of Congress*] (LCLS) .... ScCoA
Allen Video-Enhanced Contrast [*Microscopy*] .... AVEC
Allen Video-Enhanced Differential Interference Contrast [*Microscopy*] .... AVEC DIC
Allen Vision Test [*Ophthalmology*] (DAVI) .... AVT
Allen-Bradley Co. .... A-B
Allendale, MI [*FM radio station call letters*] .... WGVU
Allendale, SC [*Location identifier FAA*] (FAAL) .... ALD
Allendale, SC [*AM radio station call letters*] .... WDOG
Allendale, SC [*FM radio station call letters*] .... WDOG-FM
Allendale, SC [*Television station call letters*] .... WEBA
Allendale Township Library, Allendale, MI [*Library symbol Library of Congress*] (LCLS) .... MiAll
Allendale-Hampton-Jasper Regional Library, Allendale, SC [*Library symbol*] [*Library of Congress*] (LCLS) .... ScAl
Allendorf/Eder [*Germany ICAO location identifier*] (ICLI) .... EDFQ
Allenford Branch, Bruce County Public Library, Ontario [*Library symbol National Library of Canada*] (NLC) .... OALL
All-England Series .... AES
Allenmore Community Hospital, Tacoma, WA [*Library symbol Library of Congress*] (LCLS) .... WaTAC
Allens Creek [*Nuclear power plant*] (NRCH) .... AC
Allens Creek Nuclear Generating Station (NRCH) .... ACNGS
Allen's Massachusetts Reports [*A publication*] (DLA) .... All
Allen's Massachusetts Supreme Judicial Court Reports [*1861-67*] [*A publication*] (DLA) .... Allen
Allen's New Brunswick Reports [*Canada*] [*A publication*] (DLA) .... All
Allen's New Brunswick Reports [*Canada*] [*A publication*] (DLA) .... All NB
Allen's New Brunswick Reports [*Canada*] [*A publication*] (DLA) .... Allen
Allen's New Brunswick Reports [*Canada A publication*] (DLA) .... Allen NB
Allen's New Brunswick Reports [*Canada A publication*] (DLA) .... NBR All
Allen's Telegraph Cases [*A publication*] (DLA) .... Al Tel Ca
Allen's Telegraph Cases [*A publication*] (DLA) .... All Tel Cas
Allen's Telegraph Cases [*A publication*] (DLA) .... Allen Tel Cas
Allen's Washington Territory Reports [*1854-85*] [*A publication*] (DLA) .... Allen
Allen's Washington Territory Reports, New Series [*A publication*] (DLA) .... Wash Ter NS
Allentown [*Diocesan abbreviation*] [*Pennsylvania*] (TOCD) .... ALN
Allentown/Bethlehem/Easton [*Pennsylvania*] [*Airport symbol*] .... ABE
Allentown Borough Hall, Allentown, NJ [*Library symbol Library of Congress*] (LCLS) .... NjAIB
Allentown College of Saint Francis De Sales, Center Valley, PA [*OCLC symbol*] (OCLC) .... ALL
Allentown College of Saint Francis De Sales, Center Valley, PA [*Library symbol Library of Congress*] (LCLS) .... PCvA
Allentown Historical Society, Allentown, NJ [*Library symbol Library of Congress*] (LCLS) .... NjAIHi
Allentown, PA [*Location identifier FAA*] (FAAL) .... BXY
Allentown, PA [*AM radio station call letters*] .... WAEB
Allentown, PA [*FM radio station call letters*] .... WAEB-FM
Allentown, PA [*FM radio station call letters*] .... WDIY
Allentown, PA [*FM radio station call letters*] .... WFMZ
Allentown, PA [*Television station call letters*] .... WFMZ-TV
Allentown, PA [*AM radio station call letters*] .... WHOL
Allentown, PA [*FM radio station call letters*] (RBYB) .... WJCS-FM
Allentown, PA [*AM radio station call letters*] (RBYB) .... WKAP
Allentown, PA [*Television station call letters*] .... WLVT
Allentown, PA [*FM radio station call letters*] .... WMUH
Allentown, PA [*AM radio station call letters*] .... WTKZ
Allentown Printing Service, Allentown, NJ [*Library symbol Library of Congress*] (LCLS) .... NjAIA
Allentown Public Library, Allentown, NJ [*Library symbol Library of Congress*] (LCLS) .... NjAI
Allentown Public Library, Allentown, PA [*OCLC symbol*] (OCLC) .... AYP
Allentown Public Library, Allentown, PA [*Library symbol Library of Congress*] (LCLS) .... PAt
Allentown State Hospital, Allentown, PA [*OCLC symbol*] (OCLC) .... PHL
Aller Ehren Ist Oesterreich Voll [*Austria Is Crowned with All Honor*] [*Variation of 15th-century inscription*] .... AEIOU
Aller Erst Ist Oesterreich Verdorben [*Variation of 15th-century inscription*] .... AEIOU
Allergan, Inc. [*NYSE symbol*] (SPSG) .... AGN
Allergan, Inc. [*Associated Press*] (SAG) .... Alergn
Allergan Ligand Retinoid Therapeutics [*Associated Press*] (SAG) .... AllLig
Allergan Ligand Retinoid Therapeutics [*NASDAQ symbol*] (SAG) .... ALRI
Allergan Ligand Retinoid (Unit) [*NASDAQ symbol*] (TTSB) .... ALRIZ

Allergen Challenge Test [*Medicine*] (DAVI) ... ACT
Allergen Tachyphylaxis [*Immunology*] ... AT
Allergenic Unit [*Medicine*] (DAVI) ... AU
Allergic Bronchopulmonary Aspergillosis [*Medicine*] ... ABA
Allergic Bronchopulmonary Aspergillosis [*Medicine*] ... ABPA
Allergic Conjunctivitis [*Ophthalmology*] ... AC
Allergic Contact Dermatitis [*Dermatology*] ... ACD
Allergic Disease ... AD
Allergic Eczematous Contact Dermatitis [*Dermatology*] (DMAA) ... AECD
Allergic Reaction [*Immunology*] ... AR
Allergic Rhinitis [*Medicine*] ... AR
Allergic to Combat [*A play on the initialism for the Air Transport Command*]... ATC
Allergist [*Medicine*] (DAVI) ... A
Allergist ... ALLRGST
Allergologist [*Medicine*] (DMAA) ... A
Allergro New Media, Inc. [*Associated Press*] (SAG) ... Allegro
Allergy ... A
Allergy (AAMN) ... ALL
Allergy ... ALLRGY
Allergy and Asthma Network/Mothers of Asthmatics (PAZ) ... AAN/MA
Allergy and Immunology (DMAA) ... A&I
Allergy and Immunology [*Medical specialty*] (DHSM) ... AI
Allergy/Asthma Information Association ... AAIA
Allergy Foundation of America [*Later, A & AFA*] ... AFA
Allergy, Immunology, and Transplantation Program [*NIH*] ... AITP
Allergy Index [*Medicine*] (DAVI) ... AI
Allergy Information Association [*Canada*] ... AIA
Allergy Relief Medicine [*Pharmacology*] (DAVI) ... ARM
Allerton Public Library, Allerton, IA [*Library symbol Library of Congress*] (LCLS) ... IaAll
Allerton Public Library, Monticello, IL [*Library symbol Library of Congress*] (LCLS) ... IMont
Alles Erdreich Ist Oesterreich Unterthan [*Variation of 15th-century inscription*] ... AEIOU
Alles mit Gott [*Everything with God*] [*Motto of Georg Albrecht, Margrave of Brandenburg-Baireuth (1619-66)*] [*German*] ... AMG
Alles nach Gottes Willen [*Everything According to the Will of God*] [*Motto for a number of members of German and Bavarian royalty during the 16th and 17th centuries*] ... ANGW
Alley (WGA) ... AL
Alley ... ALL
Alley [*Commonly used*] (OPSA) ... ALLEE
Alley [*Commonly used*] (OPSA) ... ALLY
Alley ... ALY
Alley (MCD) ... ALY
Alley Cat Allies [*An association*] (EA) ... ACA
Alleyne. Legal Decrees of Marriage [*1810*] [*A publication*] (DLA) ... All LD of Mar
Allgemaine Elektizitaetsgesellschaft [*Automotive industry supplier*] ... AEG
Allgemein [*General*] [*Music*] ... Allgem
Allgemeine Geschaftsbedingungen [*General Conditions of Contracts, Transactions, Etc.*] [*German*] (DLA) ... AGB
Allgemeine Geschaftsbedingungen [*General conditions of contracts, transactions, etc.*] [*German*] (ILCA) ... Allg Gesch Bed
Allgemeine Nahrungs und Genussmittel Ausstellung [*General Food and Delicacies Fair*] [*West Germany*] ... ANUGA
Allgemeine Unabhaengige Juedische Wochenzeitung (BJA) ... AUJW
Allgemeine Versicherungsbedingungen [*General conditions of insurance*] [*German*] (ILCA) ... Allg VersBed
Allgemeine Versicherungsbedingungen [*General conditions of insurance*] [*German*] (ILCA) ... AVB
Allgemeine Verwaltungsvorschrift [*or Vorschrift*] [*General Administrative Regulation*] [*German*] (ILCA) ... AV
Allgemeiner Deutscher Automobil Club [*German Automobile Association*] ... ADAC
Allgemeiner Deutscher Nachrichtendienst [*German General News Service*] [*Germany*] (EG) ... ADN
Allgemeines Bucher-Lexikon [*A publication*] ... ABL
Allgemeines Buergerliches Gesetzbuch [*Austrian Civil Code*] (DLA) ... ABGB
Allgemeines Deutsches Handelsgesetzbuch von 1861 [*German commercial code*] (ILCA) ... ADHGB
Allgemeines Krankenhaus [*Austria*] [*Largest hospital in Europe*] ... AKH
Alliance [*Uganda*] [*FAA designator*] (FAAC) ... AFJ
Alliance [*Nebraska*] [*Airport symbol*] (OAG) ... AIA
Alliance ... ALLNCE
Alliance Against Fraud in Telemarketing (EA) ... AAFT
Alliance Against Intoxicated Motorists [*An association*] ... AAIM
Alliance Against Sexual Coercion (EA) ... AASC
Alliance All Market Advantage Fund, Inc. [*Associated Press*] (SAG) ... AlliAM
Alliance All Market Advantage Fund, Inc. [*Associated Press*] (SAG) ... AlliAMkt
Alliance All Market Advantage Fund, Inc. [*NYSE symbol*] (SAG) ... AMO
Alliance All-Mkt Adv Fd [*NYSE symbol*] (TTSB) ... AMO
Alliance Balkanique [*Balkan Alliance*] ... AB
Alliance Biblique Universelle ... ABU
Alliance Cabinet Makers Association [*A union*] [*British*] ... ACMA
Alliance Canadienne des Responsables et Enseignants en Francais [*Canadian Association for the Teachers of French as a First Language*] (AC) ... ACREF
Alliance Cap Mgmt L.P. [*NYSE symbol*] (TTSB) ... AC
Alliance Capital Management Ltd. [*Associated Press*] (SAG) ... AlnCap
Alliance Capital Management LP [*NYSE symbol*] (SPSG) ... AC
Alliance Carpenters and Joiners Society [*A union*] [*British*] ... ACJS
Alliance Centriste et Democrate [*Algeria*] [*Political party*] (EY) ... ACD
Alliance College, Cambridge Springs, PA [*Library symbol Library of Congress*] (LCLS) ... PCamA
Alliance Communic 'B' [*NASDAQ symbol*] (TTSB) ... ALLIF
Alliance Communications Corp. [*Associated Press*] (SAG) ... AllCom
Alliance Communications Corp. [*NASDAQ symbol*] (SAG) ... ALLI
Alliance Co-Operative Internationale [*International Co-Operative Alliance*] (EAIO) ... ACI
Alliance de Baboma-Bateke du Kwamouth [*Alliance of Baboma-Bateke People of Kwamouth*] ... ABAKWA
Alliance de Jeunesse Angolaise pour la Liberte [*Alliance of Angolan Youth for Freedom*] ... AJEUNAL
Alliance de la Fonction Publique du Canada [*Public Service Alliance of Canada - PSAC*] ... AFPC
Alliance Defense Industry and Technology (NATG) ... ADIT
Alliance Democratique pour le Progres du Cameroun [*Political party*] (EY) ... ADPC
Alliance Democratique pour le Progres et l'Emancipation [*Cameroon*] [*Political party*] (EY) ... ADPE
Alliance Democratique Senegalaise [*Allied Democratic Party of Senegal*] [*Political party*] ... ADS
Alliance des Bahemba au Katanga [*Alliance of the Bahemba in Katanga*] [*Zaire*] ... ALLIBAKAT
Alliance des Bakongo [*Alliance of the Bakongo People*] ... ABAKO
Alliance des Bateke [*Alliance of Bateke*] ... ABATE
Alliance des Bayanzi [*Alliance of Bayanzis*] ... ABAZI
Alliance des Communautes Culturelles pour l'Egalite dans la Sante et les Services Sociaux (AC) ... ACCESS
Alliance des Independants [*Independent Party*] [*Switzerland Political party*] (PPE) ... AdI
Alliance des Jeunes pour le Socialisme [*Alliance of Youth for Socialism*] [*France Political party*] (PPE) ... AJS
Alliance des Moniteurs de Ski du Canada [*Canadian Ski Instructors' Alliance*] ... AMSC
Alliance des Patriotes Independents du Congo [*Alliance of Independent Patriots of the Congo*] ... APIC
Alliance des Pays Producteurs de Cacao [*Cocoa Producers' Alliance*] [*Use COPAL*] (AF) ... APC
Alliance des Professeures et Professeurs de Montreal (AC) ... APPM
Alliance des Proletaires Independents du Congo [*Alliance of Independent Proletarians of the Congo*] ... APIC
Alliance Entertainment [*NYSE symbol*] (TTSB) ... CDS
Alliance Entertainment Corp. [*Associated Press*] (SAG) ... AlnEnt
Alliance Entertainment Corp. [*NYSE symbol*] (SAG) ... CDS
Alliance Europeenne des Agences de Presse ... AEAP
Alliance for a Clean Rural Environment (EA) ... ACRE
Alliance for a Drug-Free Canada [*Alliance pour un Canada sans Drogues*] (AC) ... ADFC
Alliance for a Paving Moratorium (EA) ... APM
Alliance for Acid Rain Control (EA) ... AARC
Alliance for Aging Research (EA) ... AAR
Alliance for Arts Education (EA) ... AAE
Alliance for Balanced Environmental Solutions [*Defunct*] (EA) ... ABES
Alliance for Canadian New Music Projects [*Alliance pour des Projets de Musique Canadienne Nouvell*] [*Also Contemporary Showcase*] (AC) ... ACNMP
Alliance for Cannabis Therapeutics (EA) ... ACT
Alliance for Capital Access [*Defunct*] (EA) ... ACA
Alliance for Chemical Sciences & Technologies in Europe ... AllChemE
[*The*] **Alliance for Children & Television** [*The Children's Broadcast Institute*] (AC) ... ACT
Alliance for Clean Energy [*Defunct*] (EA) ... ACE
Alliance for Coal and Competitive Transportation ... ACCT
Alliance for Communities in Action (EA) ... ACA
Alliance for Consumer Rights (EA) ... ACR
Alliance for Cultural Democracy (EA) ... ACD
Alliance for Democracy [*Malawi*] [*Political party*] (ECON) ... AFORD
Alliance for Democracy in Korea [*Defunct*] (EA) ... ADK
Alliance for Engineering in Medicine and Biology [*Defunct*] (EA) ... AEMB
Alliance for Environmental Education (EA) ... AEE
Alliance for Environmental Technology ... AET
Alliance for Fair Competition [*Falls Church, VA*] (EA) ... AFC
Alliance for Gay and Lesbian Artists in the Entertainment Industry [*Defunct*] (EA) ... AGLA
Alliance for Justice (EA) ... AJ
Alliance for Labor Action [*1968-1971*] ... ALA
Alliance for Leadership Development [*Defunct*] (EA) ... ALD
Alliance for Monetary Education (EA) ... AME
Alliance for Neighborhood Government [*Later, NAN*] (EA) ... ANG
Alliance for Opportunity [*Defunct*] (EA) ... AO
Alliance for Our Common Future (EA) ... AOCF
Alliance for Parental Involvement in Education (PAZ) ... ALLPIE
Alliance for Patriotic Re-Orientation and Construction [*Gambia*] [*Political party*] ... APRC
Alliance for Perinatal Research and Services (EA) ... APRS
Alliance for Philippine Concerns (EA) ... APC
Alliance for Progress [*OAS*] ... AP
Alliance for Rail Commuter Progress [*Later, ARCP*] (EA) ... ARC
Alliance for Responsible CFC [*Chlorofluorocarbon*] **Policy** (EA) ... ARCFCP
Alliance for Simple, Equitable, and Rational Truck Taxation (EA) ... ASERTT
Alliance for Social Security and Disability Recipients (EA) ... ASSDR
Alliance for South Asian AIDS Prevention (AC) ... ASAP
Alliance for Technology Access ... ATA
Alliance for the Preservation of English in Canada ... APEC
Alliance for the Preservation of Religious Liberties (DICI) ... APRL
Alliance for the Prudent Use of Antibiotics (EA) ... APUA
Alliance for Traffic Safety (EA) ... ATS
Alliance for Undesirable but Necessary Tasks [*From book title, "The Woman from AUNT"*] ... AUNT
Alliance for Volunteerism [*Defunct*] (EA) ... AFV

Alliance Francaise de New York [*Later, FIAF*] ... AFNY
Alliance Gaming [*NASDAQ symbol*] (TTSB) ... ALLY
Alliance Gaming Corp. [*Associated Press*] (SAG) ... AlliGam
Alliance Gaming Corp. [*NASDAQ symbol*] (SAG) ... ALLY
Alliance Global Enviro Fd [*NYSE symbol*] (TTSB) ... AEF
Alliance Global Environmental Fund, Inc. [*NYSE symbol*] (SPSG) ... AEF
Alliance Global Environmental Fund, Inc. [*Associated Press*] (SAG) ... AllGlE
Alliance Graphique Internationale [*International League of Graphic Artists*] [*Zurich, Switzerland*] (EAIO) ... AGI
Alliance Imaging [*NASDAQ symbol*] (TTSB) ... SCAN
Alliance Imaging, Inc. [*Associated Press*] (SAG) ... AllnImg
Alliance Imaging, Inc. [*NASDAQ symbol*] (SPSG) ... SCAN
Alliance Internationale de la Distribution par Cable [*International Alliance for Distribution by Cable*] (EAIO) ... AID
Alliance Internationale de la Distribution par Cable [*International Alliance for Distribution by Cable - IADC*] (EAIO) ... AIDC
Alliance Internationale de Tourisme [*International Touring Alliance*] (EAIO) ... AIT
Alliance Internationale des Femmes [*International Alliance of Women - IAW*] [*Valetta, Malta*] (EAIO) ... AIF
Alliance Internationale Jeanne d'Arc [*Saint Joan's International Alliance - SJIA*] (EAIO) ... AIJA
Alliance Internationale pour le Merite (EA) ... AIM
Alliance Israelite Universelle [*Universal Israelite Alliance*] ... AIU
Alliance Libre Europeenne [*European Free Alliance - EFA*] [*Political party Brussels, Belgium*] (EAIO) ... ALE
Alliance Missionnaire Evangelique [*Missionary Evangelical Alliance - MEA*] [*Renens, Switzerland*] (EAIO) ... AME
Alliance Nationale pour la Democratie et le Progres [*Haiti*] [*Political party*] (EY) ... ANDP
Alliance, NE [*Location identifier FAA*] (FAAL) ... AOQ
Alliance, NE [*FM radio station call letters*] ... KAAQ
Alliance, NE [*AM radio station call letters*] ... KCOW
Alliance, NE [*FM radio station call letters*] ... KPNY
Alliance, NE [*FM radio station call letters*] ... KTNE
Alliance, NE [*Television station call letters*] ... KTNE-TV
Alliance of American Insurers [*Schaumburg, IL*] (EA) ... AAI
Alliance of Associations for the Advancement of Education [*Defunct*] (EA) ... AAAE
Alliance of Atomic Veterans [*International Alliance of Atomic Vetrans*] [*Acronym is based on former name,*] (EA) ... IAAV
Alliance of British Clubs (EAIO) ... ABC
Alliance of Canadian Cinema, Television & Radio Artists [*Alliance des Artistes Canadiens du Cinema, de la Television et de la Radio*] [*Formerly, Association of Canadian Television & Radio Artists*] (AC) ... ACTRA
Alliance of Canadian Cinema, Television and Radio Artists [*Canada*] (WWLA) ... ACTRA
Alliance of Canadian Regional Motion Picture Industry Associations ... ACRMPIA
Alliance of Canadian Travel Associations ... ACTA
Alliance of Canadian Travel Associations - Saskatchewan (AC) ... SATA
Alliance of Female Owned Businesses Involved in Construction (EA) ... AFOBIC
Alliance of Free Democrats [*Hungary Political party*] (EY) ... AFD
Alliance of Free Democrats [*Hungary Political party*] ... SZDSZ
Alliance of Gay Artists (EA) ... AGA
Alliance of Genetic Support Groups (EA) ... AGSG
Alliance of Independent Colleges of Art (EA) ... AICA
Alliance of Independent Retailers (EAIO) ... AIR
Alliance of Independent Telephone Unions [*Later, TIU*] (EA) ... AITU
Alliance of Independent Telephone Unions [*Later, TIU*] ... ATU
Alliance of Individual Grocers [*British*] (BI) ... AIG
Alliance of Information and Referral Systems (EA) ... AIRS
Alliance of Latin Artistes Society [*Defunct*] (EA) ... ALAS
Alliance of Manufacturing and Management Organizations (MHDB) ... AMMO
Alliance of Metalworking Industries (EA) ... AMI
Alliance of Minority Women for Business and Political Development (EA) ... AMWBPD
Alliance of Motion Picture and Television Producers (EA) ... AMPTP
Alliance of Natives of Zombo [*Angola*] ... ALIAZO
Alliance of NGOs [*Nongovernmental Organizations*] **on Crime Prevention and Criminal Justice** (EA) ... ANCPCJ
Alliance of Nonprofit Mailers (EA) ... ANM
Alliance of Pan American Round Tables ... APART
Alliance of Poles of America (EA) ... APA
Alliance of Progressive and Left-Wing Forces [*Greek*] (PPE) ... APLF
Alliance of Rail Citizens for Progress (EA) ... ARCP
Alliance of Reform Forces [*Macedonia*] [*Political party*] ... ARF
Alliance of Resident Theatres/New York (EA) ... ART/NY
Alliance of Small Firms and Self Employed People [*British*] (DBA) ... ASP
Alliance of Small Island States ... AOSIS
Alliance of State Aftermarket Associations ... ASAAA
Alliance of State Car and Truck Renting and Leasing Associations [*Defunct*] (EA) ... ASCTRLA
Alliance of States Supporting Indians in Science and Technology [*Montana State Universty*] ... ASSIST
Alliance of Television Film Producers [*Later, Association of Motion Picture andTelevision Producers*] (EA) ... ATFP
Alliance of Transylvanian Saxons [*Cleveland, OH*] (EA) ... ATS
Alliance of Warehouses and Federations [*Defunct*] (EA) ... AWF
Alliance of Women Bikers (EA) ... AWB
Alliance of Women for Equality ... AWE
Alliance of Women in Architecture (EA) ... AWA
Alliance of Women Road Riders and Associates (EA) ... AWRRA
Alliance, OH [*AM radio station call letters*] ... WDPN
Alliance, OH [*Television station call letters*] ... WNEO
Alliance, OH [*FM radio station call letters*] ... WRMU
Alliance, OH [*FM radio station call letters*] ... WZKL
Alliance Party [*Fiji*] [*Political party*] (EY) ... AP
Alliance Party of Northern Ireland [*Political party*] (EAIO) ... APNI
Alliance Pharmaceutical [*NASDAQ symbol*] (TTSB) ... ALLP
Alliance Pharmaceutical Corp. [*Associated Press*] (SAG) ... AlianPh
Alliance Pharmaceutical Corp. [*NASDAQ symbol*] (NQ) ... ALLP
Alliance Pharmaceuticals [*Associated Press*] (SAG) ... AlianPh
Alliance pour la Democratie au Mali - Parti Pan-Africain pour la Liberte, la Solidarite, et la Justice [*Political party*] (EY) ... ADEMA-PPLSJ
Alliance pour la Democratie et la Federation [*Burkina Faso*] [*Political party*] (EY) ... ADF
Alliance pour la Democratie et le Progres [*Benin*] [*Political party*] (EY) ... ADP
Alliance pour la Democratie et l'Emancipation Sociale [*Burkina Faso*] [*Political party*] (EY) ... ADES
Alliance pour la Social-Democratie [*Benin*] [*Political party*] (EY) ... ASD
Alliance pour l'Enfant et la Television [*The Children's Broadcast Institute*] (AC) ... AET
Alliance pour Une Mauritanie Democratique [*Alliance for One Democratic Mauritania*] (PD) ... AMD
Alliance Property and Construction [*Commercial firm British*] ... APC
Alliance Public Library, Alberta [*Library symbol National Library of Canada*] (NLC) ... AAL
Alliance Reformee Mondiale [*World Alliance of Reformed Churches - WARC*] [*Geneva, Switzerland*] (EAIO) ... ARM
Alliance Republicaine pour les Libertes et le Progres [*Republican Alliance for Liberties and Progress*] [*France Political party*] (PPE) ... ARLP
Alliance Research Center [*Nuclear energy*] (NRCH) ... ARC
Alliance Resources Ltd. [*Vancouver Stock Exchange symbol*] ... ALE
Alliance Revolutionnaire Caraibe [*Guadeloupe*] [*Political party*] (EY) ... ARC
Alliance Semiconductor [*NASDAQ symbol*] (TTSB) ... ALSC
Alliance Semiconductor Corp. [*Associated Press*] (SAG) ... AlnSem
Alliance Semiconductor Corp. [*NASDAQ symbol*] (SAG) ... ALSC
Alliance Telecommunications Frequency Management Group [*Telecommunications service*] (TSSD) ... ATFMG
Alliance to End Childhood Lead Poisoning (PAZ) ... AECLP
Alliance to End Repression (EA) ... AER
Alliance to Save Energy (EA) ... ASE
Alliance Universelle des Ouvriers Diamantaires [*Universal Alliance of Diamond Workers - UADW*] [*Antwerp, Belgium*] (EAIO) ... AUOD
Alliance Universelle des Unions Chretiennes de Jeunes Gens [*World Alliance of Young Men's Christian Associations*] ... UCJG
Alliance World Dollar Government Fund [*Associated Press*] (SAG) ... AllWrld
Alliance World Dollar Government Fund [*NYSE symbol*] (SPSG) ... AWF
Alliance World Dollar Government Fund [*NYSE symbol*] (SPSG) ... AWG
Alliance World Dollar Government Fund 2 [*Associated Press*] (SAG) ... AllWrld2
Alliance World Dollar Gvt Fd [*NYSE symbol*] (TTSB) ... AWG
Alliance World Dollar Gvt Fd II [*NYSE symbol*] (TTSB) ... AWF
Alliance World Fellowship (EA) ... AWF
Alliances for Minority Participation [*National Science Foundation*] ... AMP
Alliant Techsystems [*Associated Press*] (SAG) ... AllTch
Alliant Techsystems [*NYSE symbol*] (TTSB) ... ATK
Alliant Techsystems [*NYSE symbol*] (SPSG) ... ATK
Allied ... ALLD
Allied ... ALLD
Allied Administrative Publication [*NATO*] ... AAP
Allied Aerial Photographic Interpretation Unit [*Obsolete*] ... AAPIU
Allied African Economic Affairs Committee [*World War II*] ... AAEA
Allied Agencies Center, Peoria, IL [*Library symbol Library of Congress*] (LCLS) ... IPA
Allied Air Defense Ground Environment (MCD) ... AADGE
Allied Air Forces ... AAF
Allied Air Forces, Baltic Approaches [*NATO*] (NATG) ... AIRBALTAP
Allied Air Forces, Central Europe [*Later, AIRCENT*] [*NATO*] (MCD) ... AAFCE
Allied Air Forces, Central Europe [*Formerly, AAFCE*] [*NATO*] ... AIRCENT
Allied Air Forces in Italy [*World War II*] ... AAFI
Allied Air Forces, North Norway [*NATO*] (NATG) ... AIRNON
Allied Air Forces, Northern Europe [*Later, AIRNORTH*] [*NATO*] ... AAFNE
Allied Air Forces, Northern Europe [*Formerly, AAFNE*] [*NATO*] ... AIRNORTH
Allied Air Forces, South Norway [*NATO*] (NATG) ... AIRSONOR
Allied Air Forces, South West Pacific Area [*NATO*] (ADA) ... AAFSWPA
Allied Air Forces, Southern Europe [*Later, AIRSOUTH*] [*NATO*] ... AAFSE
Allied Air Forces, Southern Europe [*Formerly, AAFSE*] [*NATO*] ... AIRSOUTH
Allied Air Headquarters [*Obsolete*] ... AAHQ
Allied Air Intelligence Center ... AAIC
Allied Air Support Command [*Mediterranean*] ... AASC
Allied Airborne Association (EA) ... AAA
Allied Armies in Italy [*Obsolete*] ... AAI
Allied Army Procedures (NATG) ... AAP
Allied Army Publications (NATG) ... AAP
Allied Artists of America (EA) ... AAA
Allied Authorized Publication ... AAP
Allied Bank Capital, Inc. [*NASDAQ symbol*] (SAG) ... ABCI
Allied Bank Capital, Inc. [*Associated Press*] (SAG) ... AlBCap
Allied Bank of Nigeria Ltd. ... ABN
Allied Bankshares [*Associated Press*] (SAG) ... AlldBksh
Allied Bankshares (GA) [*NASDAQ symbol*] (TTSB) ... ABGA
Allied Bankshares, Inc. [*NASDAQ symbol*] (NQ) ... ABGA
Allied Bankshares, Inc. [*Associated Press*] (SAG) ... AlldBk
Allied Beauty Association (AC) ... ABA
Allied Board of Trade ... ABT
Allied Boating Association of Canada (AC) ... ABC
Allied Brewery Traders' Association [*British*] (DI) ... ABTA
Allied Camouflage and Concealment Publication [*NATO*] (NATG) ... ACAMP
Allied Capital Advisers [*NASDAQ symbol*] (TTSB) ... ALLA
Allied Capital Advisers, Inc. [*Associated Press*] (SAG) ... AldCAdv

Allied Capital Advisers, Inc. [*NASDAQ symbol*] (SAG) .... ALLA
Allied Capital Commercial [*NASDAQ symbol*] (TTSB) .... ALCC
Allied Capital Commercial Corp. [*NASDAQ symbol*] (SAG) .... ALCC
Allied Capital Commercial Corp. [*Associated Press*] (SAG) .... AldCapC
Allied Capital Corp II [*Associated Press*] (SAG) .... AldCaII
Allied Capital Corp II [*NASDAQ symbol*] (TTSB) .... ALII
Allied Capital Corp. [*NASDAQ symbol*] (SAG) .... ALLC
Allied Capital Corp. [*Associated Press*] (SAG) .... AldCap
Allied Capital Corp. II [*NASDAQ symbol*] (SAG) .... ALLI
Allied Capital Lending [*NASDAQ symbol*] (TTSB) .... ALCL
Allied Capital Lending Corp. [*NASDAQ symbol*] (SAG) .... ALCL
Allied Capital Lending Corp. [*Associated Press*] (SAG) .... AldCap
Allied Captured Intelligence Center [*US and Britain*] .... ACIC
Allied Cellular [*Vancouver Stock Exchange symbol*] .... ALY
Allied Central Air Bureau [*World War II*] .... ACAB
Allied Central Interpretation Unit [*World War II*] .... ACIU
Allied Central Mediterranean Force [*Later, AAI*] [*World War II*] .... ACMF
Allied Chemical Corp. [*Later, Allied Corp.*] (MCD) .... ACC
Allied Chemical Corp., Fibers Division, Technical Center Library, Petersburg, VA [*Library symbol Library of Congress*] (LCLS) .... ViPetA
Allied Chemical Corp., Library, Solvay, NY [*OCLC symbol*] (OCLC) .... ZUB
Allied Chemical Technology [*Trademark*] .... ACT
Allied Chief Commissioner [*World War II*] .... ACC
Allied Chiefs of Staff [*World War II*] .... ACS
Allied Civil Affairs Office [*World War II*] .... ACAO
Allied Civil Defense [*World War II*] .... ACD
Allied Collection Point [*World War II*] .... ACP
Allied Command Atlantic (EAIO) .... ACA
Allied Command Atlantic [*NATO*] .... ACLANT
Allied Command Atlantic Frequency Allocation Panel [*Obsolete NATO*] (NATG) .... LANTFAP
Allied Command Atlantic Reporting System [*NATO*] (MCD) .... ACLANTREP
Allied Command Baltic Approaches [*NATO*] .... COMBALTAP
Allied Command Channel [*NATO*] .... ACCHAN
Allied Command Channel Intelligence Plan [*NATO*] (NATG) .... CHIP
Allied Command Europe [*NATO*] .... ACE
Allied Command Europe [*NATO*] .... ACEUR
Allied Command Europe [*ICAO designator*] (FAAC) .... ALF
Allied Command Europe Automated Command Control and Information System [*Proposed*] [*NATO*] .... ACE-ACCIS
Allied Command Europe Communications Network [*NATO*] (NATG) .... ACENET
Allied Command Europe Report (AFM) .... ACEREP
Allied Command Europe Reporting System .... ACERS
Allied Command Operations Center .... ACOC
Allied Command Southeast Asia [*World War II*] .... ACSEA
Allied Commander-in-Chief [*World War II*] .... ACC
Allied Commander-in-Chief, Channel (MCD) .... CINCCHAN
Allied Commission [*World War II*] .... AC
Allied Commission, Agriculture Subcommission [*World War II*] .... ACAGR
Allied Commission, Austria [*World War II*] .... ACA
Allied Commission, Austria, British Element [*World War II*] .... ACABRIT
Allied Commission, Commerce Subcommission, Exports [*World War II*] .... ACCCE
Allied Commission, Economic Section [*World War II*] .... ACECO
Allied Commission, Industry Subcommission [*World War II*] .... ACIDY
Allied Commission, Military Government Subcommission [*World War II*] .... ACMG
Allied Commission, Mining Subcommission [*World War II*] .... ACMNG
Allied Commission on Reparations .... ACR
Allied Commission, Requisitions Subcommittee [*World War II*] .... ACREQ
Allied Communications Publications [*Military*] .... ACP
Allied Communications Security Agency [*Brussels, Belgium*] [*NATO*] .... ACSA
Allied Communications Support Area .... ACSA
Allied Container Advisory Committee [*Obsolete*] .... ACAC
Allied Control Authority [*Allied German Occupation Forces*] .... ACA
Allied Control Center [*NATO*] (NATG) .... ACC
Allied Control Commission [*World War II*] .... ACC
Allied Control Commission for Austria [*World War II*] .... AACA
Allied Control Commission for Bulgaria [*World War II*] .... AACB
Allied Control Commission for Hungary [*World War II*] .... AACH
Allied Control Commission for Italy [*World War II*] .... AACI
Allied Control Commission for Rumania [*World War II*] .... AACR
Allied Control Council [*World War II*] .... ACC
Allied Control Council for Germany [*World War II*] .... AACG
Allied Control Council for Japan [*World War II*] .... AACJ
Allied Corp. [*Initialism is trademark*] .... A-C
Allied Corp., Hopewell, VA [*Library symbol Library of Congress*] (LCLS) .... ViHopA
Allied Corp., Solvay Process Division, Syracuse, NY [*Library symbol Library of Congress*] (LCLS) .... NSyA
Allied Corp., Specialty Chemicals Division, Buffalo, NY [*Library symbol Library of Congress*] (LCLS) .... NBuA
Allied Data Processing Publications (NATG) .... ADatP
Allied Data System Interoperability Agency [*Brussels, Belgium*] [*NATO*] .... ADSIA
Allied Defense Publications (NATG) .... ADP
Allied Demands, Supplies [*World War II*] .... AD(S)
Allied Devices Corp. [*Associated Press*] (SAG) .... AldDevic
Allied Devices Corp. [*NASDAQ symbol*] (SAG) .... ALDV
Allied Digital Tech [*AMEX symbol*] (TTSB) .... ADK
Allied Digital Technologies [*Formerly, AMG Digital Technologies*] [*AMEX symbol*] (SAG) .... ADK
Allied Digital Technologies [*Formerly, AMG Digital Technologies*] [*Associated Press*] (SAG) .... AldD
Allied Digital Technologies [*Formerly, AMG Digital Tchnologies*] [*Associated Press*] (SAG) .... AlldDgtl
Allied Distribution [*An association*] (EA) .... AD
Allied Distribution (EA) .... ADI
Allied Electrical Publication [*Military*] .... AELP
Allied Electrical Publications (NATG) .... AEIP
Allied Electronics Publications (NATG) .... AEtP
Allied Engineering Publications (NATG) .... AEP
Allied Equipment Publications .... AEP
Allied Equipment Publications (NATG) .... AEqP
Allied Exercise Publications [*NATO*] .... AXP
Allied Expeditionary Air Force .... AEAF
Allied Expeditionary Force .... AEF
Allied Expeditionary Force Long Lines Control [*British military*] (DMA) .... AEFLLC
Allied Explosive Ordnance Disposal Publication (MCD) .... AEODP
Allied Explosive Ordnance Disposal Publications (NATG) .... AEoP
Allied Finance Adjusters Conference [*Greensboro, NC*] (EA) .... AFAC
Allied Financial Agency [*World War II*] .... AFA
Allied Fiscal Administration [*World War II*] .... AFA
Allied Forces .... ALFOR
Allied Forces Baltic Approaches [*NATO*] (MCD) .... AFBALTAP
Allied Forces Baltic Approaches [*NATO*] .... BALTAP
Allied Forces Central Europe [*NATO*] (MCD) .... ACE
Allied Forces Central Europe [*NATO*] (MCD) .... AFCE
Allied Forces Central Europe [*NATO*] .... AFCENT
Allied Forces Headquarters [*Might refer to any theater of war*] [*World War II*] .... AFHQ
Allied Forces Headquarters (Counter Intelligence Corps) [*World War II*] .... AFHQ (CIC)
Allied Forces Headquarters Petroleum Section [*World War II*] .... AFHQPS
Allied Forces Local Resources Section [*World War II*] .... AFLRS
Allied Forces Mediterranean [*NATO*] .... AFMED
Allied Forces North Norway [*NATO*] (MCD) .... AFNON
Allied Forces Northern Europe [*NATO*] .... AFNE
Allied Forces Northern Europe [*NATO*] .... AFNORTH
Allied Forces South Norway [*NATO*] (MCD) .... AFSONOR
Allied Forces Southern Europe [*NATO*] (NATG) .... AFSE
Allied Forces Southern Europe [*NATO*] .... AFSOUTH
Allied Freighter Guard (NATG) .... AFG
Allied Geographic Section [*Southwest Pacific*] [*Obsolete*] .... AGS
Allied Group [*NASDAQ symbol*] (SAG) .... ALGR
Allied Group [*Associated Press*] (SAG) .... AlliedGp
Allied Hat Manufacturers Association (EA) .... AHMA
Allied Headquarters .... AHQ
Allied Health Professionals .... AHP
Allied Health Professions Admissions Test [*Admissions and selection test*] .... AHPAT
Allied Health Program [*Association of Independent Colleges and Schools specialization code*] .... AH
Allied Healthcare Products, Inc. [*NASDAQ symbol*] (SAG) .... AHPI
Allied Healthcare Products, Inc. [*Associated Press*] (SAG) .... AldHlPd
Allied High Commission [*Germany*] (NATG) .... AHC
Allied Holdings [*NASDAQ symbol*] (TTSB) .... HAUL
Allied Holdings, Inc. [*Associated Press*] (SAG) .... AlldHldg
Allied Holdings, Inc. [*NASDAQ symbol*] (SAG) .... HAUL
Allied Hydrographic Publication [*NATO*] .... AHP
Allied Independent Unions [*Lebanon*] .... AIU
Allied Indian Metis Society [*Canada*] .... AIMS
Allied Intelligence Bureau (ADA) .... AIB
Allied Intelligence Committee [*London*] .... AIC
Allied Intelligence Publications [*NATO*] (NATG) .... AIP
Allied Interrogating Organization .... AIO
Allied Invasion Forces [*World War II*] .... AIF
Allied Irish Banks ADS [*NYSE symbol*] (SPSG) .... AIB
Allied Irish Banks Ltd. [*Associated Press*] (SAG) .... AldIrish
Allied Irish Banks PLC [*Associated Press*] (SAG) .... AldIrish
Allied Irish Banks PLC [*Associated Press*] (SAG) .... ALIrish
Allied Irish Investment Bank .... AIIB
Allied Kinetic Energy Recovery Rope [*Army*] (INF) .... AKERR
Allied Kommandatura .... AK
Allied Land Forces .... ALF
Allied Land Forces Central Europe [*NATO*] (NATG) .... ALFCE
Allied Land Forces Central Europe [*NATO*] .... LANDCENT
Allied Land Forces Denmark [*NATO*] .... LANDENMARK
Allied Land Forces North Norway [*NATO*] (NATG) .... LANDNON
Allied Land Forces Northern Europe [*NATO*] (NATG) .... LANDNORTH
Allied Land Forces Norway [*NATO*] .... LANDNORWAY
Allied Land Forces Schleswig-Holstein [*NATO*] (NATG) .... ALFSH
Allied Land Forces Schleswig-Holstein and Jutland [*NATO*] (NATG) .... LANDJUT
Allied Land Forces South Norway [*NATO*] (NATG) .... LANDSONOR
Allied Land Forces Southeast Asia [*NATO*] .... ALFSEA
Allied Land Forces Southeastern Europe [*NATO*] .... ALFSEE
Allied Land Forces Southeastern Europe [*NATO*] .... LANDSOUTHEAST
Allied Land Forces Southern Europe [*NATO*] .... ALFSE
Allied Land Forces Southern Europe [*NATO*] .... LANDSOUTH
Allied Land Forces Zealand [*NATO*] (NATG) .... LANDZEALAND
Allied Land Headquarters [*World War II*] .... LHQ
Allied Liaison and Protocol [*Military*] .... ALP
Allied Liaison Office [*Military*] .... ALO
Allied Life Financial [*Commercial firm Associated Press*] (SAG) .... AldLife
Allied Life Financial [*NASDAQ symbol*] (SAG) .... ALFC
Allied Linens and Domestics Association [*Defunct*] (EA) .... ALDA
Allied Logistics Publication [*Military*] .... ALP
Allied Longline Agency [*NATO*] .... ALLA
Allied Longline Agency Annual Conference [*NATO*] (NATG) .... AAC
Allied Maritime Air Commander-in-Chief, Channel .... CINCMAIRCHAN
Allied Masonic Degrees [*Freemasonry*] .... AMD
Allied Medical Group [*British*] .... AMG

Allied Medical Publications (NATG) .... AMed P
Allied Mediterranean Commission [*World War II*] .... AMC
Allied Meteorological Office (NATG) .... AMO
Allied Military Administration Civil Affairs Branch [*World War II*] .... AMACAB
Allied Military Communications Panel .... AMCP
Allied Military Communications-Electronics Committee (AABC) .... AMCEC
Allied Military Financial Agency [*World War II*] .... AMFA
Allied Military Government [*of occupied territory*] [*Formerly, AMGOT Post-World War II*] .... AMG
Allied Military Government of Occupied Territory [*Later, AMG*] [*Post-World War II*] .... AMGOT
Allied Military Liaison [*Balkans*] [*World War II*] .... AML
Allied Military Liaison, Greece [*World War II*] .... AMLG
Allied Military Mission [*World War II*] .... AMM
Allied Military Security Publication .... AMSP
Allied Military Staff Conference [*Quebec, Yalta, etc.*] [*World War II*] .... AMSC
Allied Minimum Imports Program [*World War II*] .... AMIP
Allied Mining and Mine Countermeasures Publications [*NATO*] (NATG) .... AMP
Allied Mobile Force [*NATO*] .... AMF
Allied Mobile Force (Air) [*NATO*] .... AMF(A)
Allied Mobile Force (Land) [*NATO*] .... AMF(L)
Allied Naval Commander Expeditionary Forces .... ANCXF
Allied Naval Commander-in-Chief [*World War II*] .... ANC-in-C
Allied Naval Communications Agency [*London, England*] [*NATO*] .... ANCA
Allied Naval Expeditionary Force [*British military*] (DMA) .... ANXF
Allied Naval Forces [*NATO*] .... ANF
Allied Naval Forces, Baltic Approaches [*NATO*] (NATG) .... NAVBALTAP
Allied Naval Forces Central Europe [*NATO*] .... ANFCE
Allied Naval Forces, Central Europe [*NATO*] .... NAVCENT
Allied Naval Forces, North Norway [*NATO*] (NATG) .... NAVNON
Allied Naval Forces, Northern Europe [*NATO*] .... NAVNORTH
Allied Naval Forces, Scandinavian Approaches [*NATO*] (NATG) .... NAVSCAP
Allied Naval Forces, Southern Europe [*NATO*] (NATG) .... NAVSOUTH
Allied Naval Maneuvering Instructions [*NATO*] (NATG) .... ANMI
Allied Navigation Publications [*NATO*] (NATG) .... ANP
Allied/Neutral [*Military*] .... A/N
Allied Non-Theatrical Film Association (AEBS) .... ANFA
Allied Nuclear Power Program [*Military*] (GFGA) .... ANPP
Allied Ordnance Publications (NATG) .... AOP
Allied Papers .... A/P
Allied Petroleum Service Organization .... APSO
Allied Pilots Association (EA) .... APA
Allied Political and Military Commission [*World War II*] .... APMC
Allied Press Information Center [*NATO*] (NATG) .... APIC
Allied Printing Trades Council (DGA) .... APTC
Allied Procedures Publications (NATG) .... APP
Allied Products [*NYSE symbol*] (TTSB) .... ADP
Allied Products Corp. [*NYSE symbol*] (SPSG) .... ADP
Allied Products Corp. [*Associated Press*] (SAG) .... AlldPd
Allied Provincial Securities [*British*] (ECON) .... APS
Allied Publication (RDA) .... AP
Allied Publications Board [*World War II*] .... APB
Allied Purchasing Co. (EA) .... APC
Allied Quality Assurance Provision [*NATO*] (MCD) .... AQAP
Allied Quality Assurance Publication [*NATO*] (NATG) .... AQAP
Allied Radio Frequency Agency [*Formerly, ERFA*] [*Brussels, Belgium*] [*NATO*] .... ARFA
Allied Railway Supply Association [*Later, RSA*] .... ARSA
Allied Record Sales [*Record label*] .... Ald
Allied Record Sales [*Record label*] .... Alld
Allied Reliability and Maintainability Publication (MCD) .... ARMP
Allied Research Associates, Inc. [*Associated Press*] (SAG) .... AlldRsh
Allied Research Associates, Inc. (MCD) .... ARA
Allied Research Corp. [*AMEX symbol*] (SPSG) .... ALR
Allied Research Institute [*Later, Aluminum Recycling Association*] (EA) .... ARI
Allied Secretariat [*Allied German Occupation Forces*] .... ASEC
Allied Signal, Inc. [*Associated Press*] (SAG) .... Aldsignl
Allied Signal, Inc., Baltimore, MD [*Library symbol*] [*Library of Congress*] (LCLS) .... MdBASI
Allied Signal, Inc., Communications Diviaion, Baltimore, MD [*Library symbol*] [*Library of Congress*] (LCLS) .... MdBASI-C
Allied Signal Training Center [*NATO*] (IAA) .... ASTC
Allied Social Science Associations (EA) .... ASSA
Allied Staff, Berlin [*Post-World War II*] .... ASB
Allied Staff Chiefs [*World War II*] .... ASC
Allied Standing Procedure [*NATO*] (NATG) .... ASP
Allied States Association of Motion Picture Exhibitors [*Later, NATO*] .... ASAMPE
Allied Steel and Wire, Ltd. [*British*] .... ASW
Allied Stone Industries (EA) .... ASI
Allied Supply Executive [*World War II*] .... ASE
Allied Supply Executive, China [*World War II*] .... ASE(C)
Allied Supply Executive, Chinese Oil Supplies [*World War II*] .... ASE(OC)
Allied Supply Executive, Middle East [*World War II*] .... ASE(ME)
Allied Supply Executive, Other Allies [*World War II*] .... ASE(OA)
Allied Supply Executive, Persian Gulf [*World War II*] .... ASE(PG)
Allied Supply Executive, Russia and Persian Gulf [*World War II*] .... ASE(R)
Allied Supply Executive, Transportation [*World War II*] .... ASE(T)
Allied Supreme Council [*World War II*] .... ASC
Allied Tactical Air Force [*NATO*] .... ATAF
Allied Tactical Air Force, Northern Norway [*NATO*] .... TAFNORNOR
Allied Tactical Air Force, South Norway [*NATO*] (NATG) .... TAFSONOR
Allied Tactical Communications Agency [*Brussels, Belgium*] [*NATO*] (NATG) .... ATCA
Allied Tactical Data Systems Interoperability Agency [*NATO*] (NATG) .... ATADSIA
Allied Tactical Operations Center [*Military*] .... ATOC
Allied Tactical Publication [*Army NATO*] .... ATP
Allied Tanker Coordinating Committee in London .... ATCC (L)
Allied Tanker Coordinating Committee in Washington .... ATCC (W)
Allied Task Force Commander, North Norway [*NATO*] (NATG) .... ATFCNN
Allied Task Force, North Norway [*NATO*] (NATG) .... TASKFORNON
Allied Technical Publication [*Navy NATO*] .... ATP
Allied Telecommunications Committee [*Allied Control Commission for Italy*] .... ATC
Allied Textiles Companies [*British*] .... ATC
Allied Trades of the Baking Industry (EA) .... ATBI
Allied Training Publications [*NATO*] (NATG) .... ATrP
Allied Translator and Interpreter Service .... ATIS
Allied Travel Office (NATG) .... ATO
Allied Underwear Association (EA) .... AUA
Allied Vehicle Testing Publication [*Army*] (RDA) .... AVTP
Allied Waste Ind [*NASDAQ symbol*] (TTSB) .... AWIN
Allied Waste Industries [*NASDAQ symbol*] (SPSG) .... AWIN
Allied Waste Industries, Inc. [*Associated Press*] (SAG) .... AldWste
Allied Weather Publications [*NATO*] (NATG) .... AWP
Allied Workers International Union (Independent) .... AWIU(I)
Allied Works Council [*World War II*] .... AWC
Allied Youth [*Later, AYFCC*] .... AY
Allied Youth and Family Counseling Center (EA) .... AYFCC
Allied-General Nuclear Services (NRCH) .... AGNS
Allied-Lyons [*Toronto Stock Exchange symbol*] .... ALD
Allied-Signal, Inc. [*Toronto Stock Exchange symbol*] .... ACD
Allied-Signal, Inc. [*NYSE symbol*] (SPSG) .... ALD
Alligator Rivers Research Institute [*Australia*] .... ARRI
Alligatorweed Stunting Virus [*Plant pathology*] .... AWSV
Allin Communications Corp. [*Associated Press*] (SAG) .... AllinCm
Allin Communications Corp. [*NASDAQ symbol*] (SAG) .... ALLN
All-Inclusive Trust Deed [*Insurance*] .... AITD
All-India Anna Dravida Munnetra Kazhagam [*Political party*] (PPW) .... ADMK
All-India Anna Dravida Munnetra Kazhagam [*Tamil Nadu*] [*Political party*] .... AIADMK
All-India Congress Committee .... AICC
All-India Coordinated Millet Improvement Programme .... AICMIP
All-India Coordinated Rice Improvement Program .... AICRIP
All-India Federation of Electricity Employees .... AIFEE
All-India Institute of Medial Sciences .... AIMS
All-India Insurance Employees' Association .... AIIEA
All-India Jute Textile Workers' Federation .... AIJWF
All-India Port and Dock Workers' Federation .... AIPDWF
All-India Radio .... AIR
All-India Railwaymen's Federation .... AIRF
All-India Trade Union Congress .... AITUC
All-Industry Electronics Conference .... AIEC
All-Industry Radio Music Licensing Committee (NTCM) .... AIRMLC
All-Industry Research Advisory Council [*Later, IRC*] (EA) .... AIRAC
All'Ingrosso [*wholesale*] [*Italian*] (ODBW) .... all'ingr
All-in-One Business Contactbook [*A publication*] .... ABC
Allinson's Pennsylvania Superior and District Court Reports [*A publication*] (DLA) .... Allin
Allinson's Pennsylvania Superior and District Court Reports [*A publication*] (DLA) .... Allinson
All-Ireland Distress (DI) .... AID
Allis-Chalmers Corp. .... AC
Allis-Chalmers Critical Experimental Facility .... AC-CEF
Allison Gas Turbine [*Engine*] .... AGT
Allison Smith Fan Club (EA) .... ASFC
Allison Transmission Electronic Control [*Detroit Diesel Allison*] .... ATEC
Allison's American Dictionary [*A publication*] (DLA) .... Allison's Am Dict
Alliston Memorial Public Library, Ontario [*Library symbol National Library of Canada*] (BIB) .... OAL
Alliston Public Library, Alliston, ON, Canada [*Library symbol Library of Congress*] (LCLS) .... CaOAL
All-Language Services, Inc. .... ALS
Allmerica Financial [*NYSE symbol*] (TTSB) .... AFC
Allmerica Financial Corp. [*NYSE symbol*] (SAG) .... AFC
Allmerica Financial Corp. [*Associated Press*] (SAG) .... AllmrFn
Allmerica Prop & Cas Cos. [*NYSE symbol*] (TTSB) .... APY
Allmerica Property & Casualty [*Associated Press*] (SAG) .... AllmerPr
Allmerica Property & Casualty [*NYSE symbol*] (SAG) .... APY
Allmerica Sec Tr [*NYSE symbol*] (TTSB) .... ALM
Allmerica Securities Trust [*Formerly, State Mutual Securities Trust*] [*Associated Press*] (SAG) .... AllmrST
Allmerica Securities Trust [*Formerly, State Mutual Securities Trust*] [*NYSE symbol*] (SAG) .... ALM
Allmerican Financial Corp. [*Associated Press*] (SAG) .... AllmrFn
Allnat. Law of Partition [*1820*] [*A publication*] (DLA) .... Alln Part
Allnat on Wills [*A publication*] (DLA) .... Alln Wills
All-Navy Message .... ALNAV
All-Nigeria Trade Union Federation .... ANTUF
All-North Resources Ltd. [*Vancouver Stock Exchange symbol*] .... ANH
Allo-Activated Killer [*Medicine*] (DMAA) .... AAK
Allocable Installment Indebtedness (MHDB) .... AII
Allocate .... ALLCT
Allocate [*or Allocation*] (AFM) .... ALLOC
Allocate [*or Allocation*] (AABC) .... ALOC
Allocate on Demand [*Computer science*] (BYTE) .... AOD
Allocated .... ALLOT
Allocated Baseline (MCD) .... ABL
Allocated Configuration Audit (MCD) .... ACA
Allocated Configuration Documentation (AAGC) .... ACD
Allocated Configuration Identification [*NASA*] (KSC) .... ACI

Allocated Configuration Item [Navy] .... ACI
Allocated Configuration Management [NASA] (NASA) .... ACM
Allocated Reserve .... AR
Allocated Transfer Risk Reserve [Banking] .... ATRR
Allocation .... ALLCTN
Allocation Assessment and Analysis [Report] .... AAA
Allocation Counter [Computer science] (IAA) .... AC
Allocation Strategy Module (IAA) .... ASM
Allocations for Budgetary Control .... ABC
Allocator .... A
Allogeneic Effect Factor [Immunochemistry] .... AEF
Allograft-Bound Lymphocytes [Biochemistry] (DAVI) .... ABL
Allophycocyanin [Also, APC] [Biochemistry] .... AP
Allophycocyanin [Also, AP] [Biochemistry] .... APC
All-Optical Towed-Array SONAR [Navy] (DOMA) .... AOTA
Allopurinol Phosphate [Biochemistry] .... APP
Allopurinol Phosphate Ribonucleotide [Biochemistry] .... APPR
All-Ordnance Destruct System .... AODS
All-Ordnance Thrust Termination (KSC) .... AOTT
Allosteric [Biochemistry] .... AI
Alloter Switch (IAA) .... AS
Allotetrahydrocortisol [Organic chemistry] (DAVI) .... ATHC
Allotment (AABC) .... ALOT
Allotment (AFM) .... ALOTM
Allotment (DNAB) .... ALOTMT
Allotment Advice (FAAC) .... ADVALT
Allotment Division [Navy] .... NAVALOT
Allotment Serial Number (AFM) .... ASN
Allotment-of-Probability Shares (PDAA) .... APS
All'Ottava [At the Octave] [Music] .... ALL'OTT
All'Ottava [At the Octave] [Music] .... All'Ova
Allou Health & Beauty Care, Inc. [Associated Press] (SAG) .... AllouH
Allou Health & Beauty Care, Inc. [AMEX symbol] (SPSG) .... ALU
Allou Health&Beauty'A' [AMEX symbol] (TTSB) .... ALU
Allouez, WI [FM radio station call letters] (RBYB) .... WJLW-FM
All-Over Good (IIA) .... AOG
Allow Enable Intercept [Military] (CAAL) .... AEI
Allowable Biological Catch .... ABC
Allowable Cabin Load [in an aircraft] .... ACL
Allowable Cargo Load [Air Force] (AFIT) .... ACL
Allowable Cleanliness Level [Industrial maintenance and engineering] .... ACL
Allowable Container Load [in an aircraft] (NASA) .... ACL
Allowable Cost (OICC) .... AC
Allowable Daily Intake [Toxicology] .... ADI
Allowable Deficiency (MCD) .... AD
Allowable Expense Level [Department of Housing and Urban Development] (GFGA) .... AEL
Allowable [Takeoff] Gross Weight [for an aircraft] .... AGW
Allowable Ship Turn .... AST
Allowable Steering Error .... ASE
Allowable Supply List [Military] (DOMA) .... ASL
Allowable Takeoff Gross [Weight] [for an aircraft] .... ATOG
Allowable Utilities Consumption Level [Department of Housing and Urban Development] (GFGA) .... AUCL
Allowance (ROG) .... ALLCE
Allowance .... ALLOW
Allowance (AFM) .... ALW
Allowance Appendix Package .... AAPG
Allowance Appendix Page .... AAP
Allowance Change Request .... ACR
Allowance Equipage List .... AEL
Allowance for Funds Used during Construction .... AFUDC
Allowance for Loan and Lease Losses (TDOB) .... ALLI
Allowance for Project Adjustment .... APA
Allowance Holder [Environmental Protection Agency] (GFGA) .... AH
Allowance Holder Monthly [Environmental Protection Agency] (GFGA) .... AHM
Allowance in Lieu of Overtime .... AILOT
Allowance Item Code .... AIC
Allowance List .... AL
Allowance Load List (AFIT) .... ALL
Allowance Officer Desk Code (DNAB) .... AODC
Allowance Override Requirement (CAAL) .... AOR
Allowance Parts List .... APL
Allowance Parts List/Component Identification Number .... APL/CID
Allowance Parts List Master Index (MCD) .... APLMI
Allowance Prescribed in Joint Travel Regulations [Military] (AABC) .... AJTR
Allowance Quality (DNAB) .... AQTY
Allowance Race [Horse racing] .... ALW
Allowance Requirement Register (MCD) .... ARR
Allowance Source Code [Military] (AFM) .... ASC
Allowance Summary Code .... ASC
Allowance Type [Military] (AFIT) .... A/T
Allowed .... ALLD
Allowed Failure Effect .... AFE
Allowed Off-Engine Time (AFIT) .... AOET
Allowed-Off Aircraft Time .... AOAT
Alloxazine Adenine Dinucleotide [Biochemistry] .... AAD
Alloxazine Mononucleotide [Pharmacology] .... AMN
Alloy .... ALLY
Alloy (VRA) .... aly
Alloy .... ALY
Alloy Bulk Diffusion (IAA) .... ABD
Alloy Casting Institute [Later, SFSA] (EA) .... ACI
Alloy Container [Shipping] (DCTA) .... A
Alloy Data Center [National Institute of Standards and Technology] .... ADC

Alloy Development for Irradiation Performance (MCD) .... ADIP
Alloy Diffused (IAA) .... AD
Alloy Junction .... AJ
Alloy Phase Diagram .... APD
Alloy Restoration [Medicine] (DMAA) .... AR
Alloy Steel (IAA) .... AS
Alloy-Coated Aluminum (KSC) .... ALCAL
Alloyed Zinc Sheet .... AZS
Alloys Index [METADEX] (NITA) .... AI
Alloy-Steel Protective Plating .... ASPP
All-Party Hill Leaders' Conference [India] [Political party] (PPW) .... APHLC
All-Party Parliamentary Committee for the Release of Soviet Jewry (EAIO) .... PCSJ
All-People's Congress [Sierra Leone] [Political party] (PPW) .... APC
All-Peoples Congress [An association] (EA) .... APC
Allport-Vernon [Psychology] (BARN) .... AV
Allport-Vernon-Lindzey [Study of values] .... AVL
All-Purpose .... AP
All-Purpose Communications System .... ALPURCOMS
All-Purpose Decontaminant (MCD) .... APD
All-Purpose Electronic Computer (IEEE) .... APEC
All-Purpose Interface [Computer science] (HGAA) .... API
All-Purpose Lightweight Individual Carrying Equipment [Army] (RDA) .... ALICE
All-Purpose Lightweight Individual Carrying Equipment [Army] .... ALICW
All-Purpose Linotype (DGA) .... APL
All-Purpose Rocket for Collecting Atmospheric Soundings [Navy] (IAA) .... APRCAS
All-Purpose Rocket for Collecting Atmospheric Soundings [Navy] .... ARCAS
All-Purpose Room .... APR
All-Purpose Terminal [Computer technology] .... APT
All-Purpose Ticket Issuing System (PDAA) .... APTIS
All-Purpose Tween [Microorganism growth medium] .... APT
All-Purpose Vehicle [Automotive engineering] .... APV
All-Radio Methodology Study [Audience ratings] (NTCM) .... ARMS
All-Reflecting Schmidt Telescope (PDAA) .... ARST
All-Russian Cooperative Society [English equivalent of AMTORG] .... ARCOS
All-Russian Monarchist Front [Defunct] (EA) .... ARMF
All's Well That Ends Well [Shakespearean work] .... AWW
All-Season .... AS
All-Season Performance .... ASP
All-Season Touring .... AST
All-Service Close Air Support [Military] .... ASCAS
All-Services Evaluation Group [Military] .... ASEG
All-Sky Camera .... ASC
All-Sky Imaging Photometer .... ASIP
All-Sky Monitor [Optics] .... ASM
Allsopp, Morgan Engineering Ltd., Edmonton, AB, Canada [Library symbol Library of Congress] (LCLS) .... CaAEAME
Allsopp, Morgan Engineering Ltd., Edmonton, Alberta [Library symbol National Library of Canada] (NLC) .... AEAME
All-Source Production [Army] (ADDR) .... ASP
All-Source Production Section [Army] (ADDR) .... ASPS
Allstate Corp. [NYSE symbol] (SPSG) .... ALL
Allstate Corp. [Associated Press] (SAG) Allst98
Allstate Corp. [Associated Press] (SAG) .... Allstate
Allstate Corp. [NYSE symbol] (SAG) .... PME
Allstate Cp 6.76% Exch Nts '98 [NYSE symbol] (TTSB) .... PME
Allstate Financial [NASDAQ symbol] (TTSB) .... ASFN
Allstate Financial Corp. [Associated Press] (SAG) .... AllstFn
Allstate Financial Corp. [NASDAQ symbol] (NQ) .... ASFN
Allstate Insurance Co., Barrington, IL [Library symbol] [Library of Congress] (LCLS) .... IBarAS
Allstate Insurance, Inc., Corporate Library, Northbrook, IL [Library symbol] [Library of Congress] (LCLS) .... INbAS
Allstates-Programming & Systems, Inc. .... APSI
All-Steel Equipment, Inc. .... ASE
ALLTEL Corp. [Formerly, Allied Telephone Co.] [Associated Press] (SAG) .... Alltel
ALLTEL Corp. [Formerly, Allied Telephone Co.] [NYSE symbol] (SPSG) .... AT
ALLTEL Corp. $2.06 Cv Pfd [NYSE symbol] (TTSB) .... ATPr
All-Terrain All-Purpose Cart [Military] (INF) .... ATAC
All-Terrain Bike .... ATB
All-Terrain Carrier [Roscoe Brown Corp.] .... ATC
All-Terrain Cycle .... ATC
All-Terrain Lightweight Articulating Suspension .... ATLAS
All-Terrain Mobile Platform .... ATMP
All-Terrain Racing Association (EA) .... ATRA
All-Terrain Remote Control Vehicle (MCD) .... ATRCV
All-Terrain Vehicle .... ATV
Alltransport International Group .... AIG
All-Trans-Retinoc Acid [Medicine] .... ATRA
Alltrista Corp. [Associated Press] (SAG) .... Alltrista
Alltrista Corp. [NASDAQ symbol] (SAG) .... JARS
All-Ukrainian Evangelical Baptist Fellowship (EA) .... AUEBF
Allure Industries Corp. [Vancouver Stock Exchange symbol] .... ARU
Allusion .... ALLUS
All-Volunteer Force [Army] .... AVF
All-Volunteer Force Program Action Request [Military] (DNAB) .... AVF/PAR
Allwaste, Inc. [Associated Press] (SAG) .... Allwaste
Allwaste, Inc. [NYSE symbol] (SAG) .... ALW
Allwe [Former USSR] [FAA designator] (FAAC) .... LWE
All-Weather [As applied to fighter aircraft, etc.] .... AW
All-Weather Air Delivery System (SAA) .... AWADS
All-Weather Aircraft [Air Force] (NATG) .... AWX
All-Weather Aircraft Guided Missile (MCD) .... AWAG
All-Weather Air-to-Air Missile (MCD) .... AWAAM

All-Weather Attack ... AWA
All-Weather Attack Avionics System (MCD) ... AWAAS
All-Weather Carrier Landing System [*Navy*] ... ACLS
All-Weather Carrier Landing System [*Navy*] ... AWCLS
All-Weather Chassis Dynamometer (PDAA) ... AWCD
All-Weather Electronics ... AWE
All-Weather Fighter ... AWX(F)
All-Weather Flare ... AWF
All-Weather Ground Surveillance RADAR ... AGSR
All-Weather Guidance (MCD) ... AWG
All-Weather Identification Sensor ... AWIS
All-Weather Interceptor ... AWI
All-Weather Intruder ... AWX(I)
All-Weather Landing ... AWL
All-Weather Landing System [*Also, AWLS*] ... ALS
All-Weather Landing System [*Also, ALS*] ... AWLS
All-Weather Long-Range Fighter ... AWLRF
All-Weather Operations Committee [*ATA*] ... AWOC
All-Weather Operations Division [*ICAO*] (MCD) ... AWOD
All-Weather Operations Panel [*International Civil Aviation Organization*] ... AWOP
All-Weather Radial Tire [*Automotive accessory*] ... AWR
All-Weather Reconnaissance System ... AWRS
All-Weather Sea Target Acquisition System [*Navy*] (MCD) ... AWSTAS
All-Weather Short-Range Air Defense Missile System (MCD) ... AW-SHORADS
All-Weather Sleepout (ADA) ... AWSO
All-Weather Standoff Attack Control System (MCD) ... AWSACS
All-Weather Station ... AWSTA
All-Weather Surface Observations [*NASA*] (PDAA) ... AWSO
All-Weather System (MCD) ... AWS
All-Weather Tactical Bombing System ... AWTBS
All-Weather Tactical Strike System [*Air Force*] (MCD) ... AWTSS
All-Weather Test Bed (MCD) ... AWTB
All-Weather Topographic Mapping System [*Army*] ... AWTMS
All-Weather Yaw Damper Computer ... AWYDC
All-Wheel Control [*Mitsubishi*] [*Transmisssion systems*] ... AWC
All-Wheel Drive [*Automotive engineering*] ... AWD
Allwood's Appeal Cases under the Weights and Measures Act [*England*] [*A publication*] (DLA) ... Allwood
Allyl Chloride [*Organic chemistry*] ... AC
Allyl Diglycol Carbonate [*Organic chemistry*] ... ADC
Allyl Elthenesulphonate (PDAA) ... AES
Allyl Glycidyl Ether [*Organic chemistry*] ... AGE
Allyl Isothiocyanate [*Organic chemistry*] ... AITC
Allyl Methacrylate [*Organic chemistry*] ... ALMA
Allyl(dimethyl)chlorosilane [*Organic chemistry*] ... ADMCS
Allylisopropylacetamide [*Biochemistry*] ... AIA
[*The*] **Alma & Jonquieres Railway Co.** [*AAR code*] ... AJ
Alma College, Alma, MI [*OCLC symbol*] (OCLC) ... EZA
Alma College, Alma, MI [*Library symbol Library of Congress*] (LCLS) ... MiAC
Alma, GA [*Location identifier FAA*] (FAAL) ... AMG
Alma, GA [*AM radio station call letters*] ... WAJQ
Alma, GA [*FM radio station call letters*] ... WAJQ-FM
Alma Mater Society [*Canada*] ... AMS
Alma, MI [*Location identifier FAA*] (FAAL) ... AMN
Alma, MI [*Location identifier FAA*] (FAAL) ... GTX
Alma, MI [*AM radio station call letters*] ... WFYC
Alma, MI [*FM radio station call letters*] ... WQAC
Alma, MI [*FM radio station call letters*] (RBYB) ... WQBX
Alma, PQ [*AM radio station call letters*] ... CFGT
Alma, PQ [*FM radio station call letters*] (RBYB) ... CKYK-FM
Alma Public Library, Alma, MI [*Library symbol Library of Congress*] (LCLS) ... MiA
Alma Urbis [*Beloved City*] [*Rome*] ... AU
Alma White College [*New Jersey*] ... AWC
Alma White College, Zarephath, NJ [*Library symbol Library of Congress*] (LCLS) ... NjZaA
Alma-Ata [*Former USSR Seismograph station code, US Geological Survey*] (SEIS) ... AAA
Alma-Ata [*Former USSR Airport symbol*] (OAG) ... ALA
Alma-Ata [*Former USSR ICAO location identifier*] (ICLI) ... UAAA
Almaden [*California*] [*Seismograph station code, US Geological Survey*] (SEIS) ... AMC
Almaden Resources Corp. [*Vancouver Stock Exchange symbol*] ... AMH
Almagest [*of Ptolemy*] [*Classical studies*] (OCD) ... Alm
Almagro [*Spain ICAO location identifier*] (ICLI) ... LEAO
Almaguin Highlands Community Living (AC) ... AHCL
Almanac (ROG) ... ALK
Almanac (ROG) ... ALMC
[*The*] **Almanac of American Politics** [*National Journal Inc.*] [*Database*] [*A publication*] ... AMPOL
Almanor Railroad Co. [*AAR code*] ... AL
Almazy Rossii-Sakha ... ARS
Almenara [*Brazil*] [*Airport symbol Obsolete*] (OAG) ... AMJ
Almeria [*Spain*] [*Seismograph station code, US Geological Survey*] (SEIS) ... ALM
Almeria [*Spain ICAO location identifier*] (ICLI) ... LEAM
Almeria [*Spain*] [*Airport symbol*] (OAG) ... LEI
Almeta Air [*Austria*] [*FAA designator*] (FAAC) ... AAW
Almine Resources [*Vancouver Stock Exchange symbol*] ... ART
Almirall [*Spain*] [*Research code symbol*] ... LAS
Almond Board of California (EA) ... ABC
Almond Hullers and Processors Association (SRA) ... AHPA
Almond Leaf Scorch [*Plant pathology*] ... ALS
Almond Leaf Scorch Bacterium [*Plant pathology*] ... ALSB
Almondsbury [*England*] ... ALMOND
Almonte Public Library, Ontario [*Library symbol National Library of Canada*] (NLC) ... OA
Almost [*Philately*] ... alm
Almost Difference Quasiternary Code (PDAA) ... ADQC
Almost Differential Quasiternary Code [*Telecommunications*] (TEL) ... ADQ
Almost Everywhere ... AE
Almost Ideal Demand System [*Agriculture*] ... AIDS
Almost Letter Quality [*Refers to the quality of print or of a printer*] (NITA) ... ALQ
Almost Ready to Fly [*Remote-control plane*] ... ARF
Almost Uncirculated [*Condition of coins*] [*Numismatics*] ... AU
Almost Verbatim (AAGC) ... AV
Almost-Developed Country ... ADC
Aloe Technology Association (EA) ... ATA
Aloette Cosmetics [*NASDAQ symbol*] (TTSB) ... ALET
Aloette Cosmetics, Inc. [*NASDAQ symbol*] (NQ) ... ALET
Aloette Cosmetics, Inc. [*Associated Press*] (SAG) ... Aloette
Alofi/Niue International [*Niue Island*] [*ICAO location identifier*] (ICLI) ... NIUE
Aloft (FAAC) ... ALF
Aloha Airlines [*ICAO designator*] (FAAC) ... AAH
Aloha Airlines [*ICAO designator*] (AD) ... AQ
Aloha Airlines, Inc. [*Air carrier designation symbol*] ... TSA
Aloha Islandair [*ICAO designator*] (AD) ... WP
Aloha Society of Association Executives - Hawaii (SRA) ... ASAE-HI
Aloin, Extract of Belladonna, and Strychnine Pill [*A laxative*] [*Pharmacology*] (DAVI) ... ABS
Aloin, Strychnine, and Belladonna [*Pharmacy*] ... AS & B
Aloin, Strychnine, Belladonna, and Ipecac [*Pharmacy*] ... ASB & I
Alon, Inc. [*ICAO aircraft manufacturer identifier*] (ICAO) ... FO
Along (FAAC) ... ALG
Along [*India*] [*Airport symbol*] (AD) ... IXV
Along [*India*] [*ICAO location identifier*] (ICLI) ... VEAN
Alongside ... AS
Along-Track Scanning Radiometer ... ATSR
Alopecia Areata [*Medicine*] ... AA
Alor [*Indonesia*] [*Airport symbol*] (OAG) ... ARD
Alor Setar [*Malaysia*] [*Airport symbol*] (OAG) ... AOR
Alor Setar/Sultan Abdul Halim [*Malaysia*] [*ICAO location identifier*] (ICLI) ... WMKA
Alotau [*Papua New Guinea*] [*Airport symbol*] (OAG) ... GUR
Alotta Resources Ltd. [*Vancouver Stock Exchange symbol*] ... AOS
Alouette Topside Sounder Synoptic [*NASA*] ... ALOSYN
Alpavia [*France ICAO aircraft manufacturer identifier*] (ICAO) ... AL
Alpena [*Michigan*] [*Airport symbol*] (OAG) ... APN
Alpena Community College [*Michigan*] ... ACC
Alpena Community College, Alpena, MI [*Library symbol Library of Congress*] (LCLS) ... MiAlpC
Alpena County Library, Alpena, MI [*Library symbol Library of Congress*] (LCLS) ... MiAlp
Alpena, MI [*Location identifier FAA*] (FAAL) ... CLO
Alpena, MI [*AM radio station call letters*] ... WATZ
Alpena, MI [*FM radio station call letters*] ... WATZ-FM
Alpena, MI [*Television station call letters*] ... WBKB
Alpena, MI [*FM radio station call letters*] ... WCML
Alpena, MI [*Television station call letters*] ... WCML-TV
Alpena, MI [*FM radio station call letters*] ... WHSB
Alpenair GmbH & Co. KG [*Austria ICAO designator*] (FAAC) ... LPN
Alperin Jet-Diffuser Ejector (MCD) ... AJDE
Alpes Maritimes [*French*] ... AM
Alpha ... A
Alpha [*Australia Airport symbol*] (OAG) ... ABH
Alpha ... ALPH
Alpha 1-Antitrypsin Deficiency [*Genetic disorder*] (PAZ) ... a1AT
Alpha Activity Median Diameter [*Nuclear energy*] (NRCH) ... AMD
Alpha Antiprotease [*Biochemistry*] ... AAP
Alpha Aviation, Inc. [*ICAO designator*] (FAAC) ... ALH
Alpha Aviation, Inc. [*ICAO designator*] (FAAC) ... APH
Alpha Benzene Hexachloride [*Organic chemistry*] (ADA) ... ABH
Alpha Block Control Number [*Computer science*] ... ABC
Alpha Control Guidance ... ACG
Alpha Counter Tube ... ACT
Alpha Cutoff ... ACO
Alpha Delta [*Society*] ... AD
Alpha Delta Phi [*Fraternity*] ... ADP
Alpha Delta Pi [*Sorority*] ... ADP
Alpha Delta Sigma [*Fraternity*] (NTCM) ... ADS
Alpha Disintegration Energy ... ADE
Alpha Energy Range Discrimination [*Analysis of radioactivity*] ... AERD
Alpha Epsilon (EA) ... AE
Alpha Epsilon Rho [*Also, AERho*] [*Fraternity*] (NTCM) ... AER
Alpha Fetal Globulin [*Biochemistry*] (DAVI) ... AFG
Alpha Hand and Shoe Monitor [*Radiation detection*] ... AHSM
Alpha Hospitality [*NASDAQ symbol*] (TTSB) ... ALHY
Alpha Hospitality Corp. [*NASDAQ symbol*] (SAG) ... ALHY
Alpha Hospitality Corp. [*Associated Press*] (SAG) ... AlphH
Alpha Hospitality Corp. [*Associated Press*] (SAG) ... AlphHsp
Alpha Hospitality Wrrt [*NASDAQ symbol*] (TTSB) ... ALHYW
Alpha Industries, Inc. [*AMEX symbol*] (SPSG) ... AHA
Alpha Industries, Inc. [*Associated Press*] (SAG) ... AlphaIn
Alpha Kappa Kappa [*Fraternity*] ... AKK
Alpha Kappa Psi [*Fraternity*] ... AKP
Alpha/Mach Indicator (NASA) ... AMI
Alpha Magnetic Spectrometer ... AMS
Alpha Meter (MCD) ... AM
Alpha Micro Users Society (EA) ... AMUS
Alpha Microsystems [*NASDAQ symbol*] (NQ) ... ALMI
Alpha Microsystems [*Associated Press*] (SAG) ... AlpMic
Alpha Microsystems Operating System ... AMOS
Alpha Microsystems Wrrt [*NASDAQ symbol*] (TTSB) ... ALMIW

Alpha Omega Computer System (IEEE) .... AOCS
Alpha Park Public Library, Bartonville, IL [Library symbol Library of Congress] (LCLS) .... IBart
Alpha Park Public Library District, Pekin, IL [OCLC symbol] (OCLC) .... ISF
Alpha Particle (ADA) .... A-PART
Alpha Particle Spectrometer (KSC) .... AP
Alpha Proton X-Ray Spectrometer .... APXS
Alpha Ray Spectrometer .... ARS
Alpha Ray Spectrometric Equipment .... ARSE
ALPHA [AMC Logistics Program - Hardcore Automated] Remote Terminal Interactive System .... ARTIS
Alpha Repertory Television Service [Cable-television system] .... ARTS
Alpha Research and Development (KSC) .... ARAD
Alpha Roster Locator List (United States Army Reserve) Colonels .... ARLLUC
Alpha Solar Array Drive (SSD) .... ASAD
Alpha Solarco [NASDAQ symbol] (TTSB) .... ASCO
Alpha Solarco, Inc. [Associated Press] (SAG) .... AlphaSo
Alpha Solarco, Inc. [NASDAQ symbol] (NQ) .... ASCO
Alpha Tau Alpha (EA) .... ATA
Alpha Tau Omega [Fraternity] .... ATO
Alpha Technologies Grp [NASDAQ symbol] (TTSB) .... ATGI
Alpha Technology Group, Inc. [Associated Press] (SAG) .... AlphaTch
Alpha Technology Group, Inc. [NASDAQ symbol] (SAG) .... ATGI
Alpha Temperature Probe Assembly [NASA] (MCD) .... ATPA
Alpha Track (GNE) .... AT
Alpha Trans-Inducing Factor [Genetics] .... ATIF
Alpha Waste Storage Facility [Nuclear energy] .... AWSF
Alpha Xi Delta [Sorority] .... AXD
Alpha Zeta (EA) .... AZ
Alpha Zeta Omega [Fraternity] .... AZO
Alpha-1-Antitrypsin [Protease inhibitor] [Serology] .... A_1AT
Alpha-2HS-Glycoprotein (DMAA) .... AHSG
Alpha-66 (EA) A-66
Alpha-Amino Nitrogen (MAE) .... AAN
Alpha-Aminoisobutyric Acid [Organic chemistry] .... AIBA
Alpha-Antitrypsin [Biochemistry] .... AAT
Alpha-Atrial Natriuretic Polypeptide [Biochemistry] (DAVI) .... ANP
[The] Alphabet (BARN) .... ABC
Alphabeta Pseudocoincidence Discrimination [Analysis of radioactivity] .... ABDP
Alpha-Beta Technology [NASDAQ symbol] (TTSB) .... ABTI
Alpha-Beta Technology, Inc. [NASDAQ symbol] (SAG) .... ABTI
Alpha-Beta Technology, Inc. [Associated Press] (SAG) .... AlphaBta
Alphabetic .... A
Alphabetic Phonogram [Egyptology] (ROG) .... ALPH
Alphabetic Subject Index [A publication] .... ASI
Alphabetical (WDAA) .... ALPH
Alphabetical [Flowchart] .... ALPHA
Alphabetical (WDMC) .... alpha
Alphabetical British [Railway Guide of Timetables] (BARN) .... ABC
Alphabetical Index of Names .... AION
Alpha-Cedrene .... ACDR
Alpha-Comp Simulation Package [Alpha-Comp Ltd.] [Software package] (NCC) .... ASIM
Alpha-Fetoprotein [Clinical chemistry] .... AFP
Alpha-Hydrazine Analogue of Histidine (MAE) .... AHH
Alpha-Hydroxy Acid [Organic chemistry] .... AHA
Alpha-Hydroxybutyric Acid (DMAA) .... AHB
Alpha-Hydroxybutyric Dehydrogenase [An enzyme] (MAH) .... AHB
Alpha-Hydroxybutyric Dehydrogenase [An enzyme] .... AHBD
Alphalytic Protease [An enzyme] .... ALP
Alpha-Macroglobulin [Biochemistry] .... AMG
Alpha-Methyldopa [Also, MD] [Antihypertensive compound] .... AMD
Alpha-Methylmannoside [Biochemistry] .... AMM
Alpha-Methyl-m-tyrosine [Pharmacology] .... MMT
Alpha-Methylphenethylamine [CNS stimulant] .... AMPHETAMINE
Alpha-Methyl-p-tyrosine [Also, MPT] [Pharmacology] .... AMPT
Alpha-Methyl-p-tyrosine [Also, AMPT] [Pharmacology] .... MPT
Alpha-Methylstyrene [Organic chemistry] .... AMS
Alpha-Methyltyrosine [Pharmacology] (MAE) .... AMT
Alpha-Naphthoflavone [Biochemistry] .... ANF
Alpha-Naphthyl Acetate [Organic chemistry] .... ANA
Alpha-Naphthyl Butyrate [Organic chemistry] .... ANB
Alpha-Naphthyl Butyrate Esterase [An enzyme] .... ANBE
Alpha-Naphthylisothiocyanate [Organic chemistry] .... ANIT
Alpha-Naphthylthiourea [Organic chemistry] .... ANTU
AlphaNet Solutions [NASDAQ symbol] (TTSB) .... ALPH
AlphaNet Solutions, Inc. [NASDAQ symbol] (SAG) .... ALPH
AlphaNet Solutions, Inc. [Associated Press] (SAG) .... AlphNet
Alphanumeric .... ALPHANUM
Alphanumeric .... AN
Alpha-Numeric Character Generator [Computer science] (MHDB) .... ANCHOR
Alphanumeric Character Graphic [Computer science] (ECII) .... ACG
Alphanumeric Code for Music Analysis [Input code for music notation] (NITA) .... ALMA
Alphanumeric Digital Display (CAAL) .... ADD
Alphanumeric Display .... AND
Alphanumeric Display Equipment .... ADE
Alphanumeric Display Equipment .... ANDE
Alphanumeric Entry Device .... AED
Alphanumeric Impact Printer .... AIP
Alphanumeric Keyboard .... ANK
Alphanumeric Keyboard .... ANKB
Alphanumeric Language for Music Analysis .... ALMA
Alpha-Numeric Logic Package [Computer science] (MHDI) .... ANLP
Alphanumeric Output .... ANO

Alphanumeric Photocomposer System (IEEE) .... APS
Alphanumeric System for Classification of Recordings .... ANSCR
Alphanumeric Warning Display (MCD) .... ANWD
Alpha-Olefin Sulfonate [Surfactant] [Organic chemistry] .... AOS
Alpha-Omega Industries, Inc. [Vancouver Stock Exchange symbol] .... ALF
Alphaprodine [Anesthesiology] .... AP
Alpharel, Inc. [Associated Press] (SAG) .... Alpharl
Alpharel, Inc. [Associated Press] (SAG) .... Alphr
Alpharel, Inc. [NASDAQ symbol] (SAG) .... AREL
Alpharetta, GA [AM radio station call letters] .... WVNF
Alpharm, Inc. [NYSE symbol] (SAG) .... ALO
Alpharm, Inc. [Associated Press] (SAG) .... Alpharma
Alpharm, Inc. [Associated Press] (SAG) .... Alphm
ALPHARMA INC.'A' [NYSE symbol] (TTSB) .... ALO
ALPHARMA Inc.Wrrt [NYSE symbol] (TTSB) .... ALO WS
Alphonsus College, Woodcliff Lake, NJ [Library symbol Library of Congress] (LCLS) .... NjWolA
Alpi Eagles SpA [Italy ICAO designator] (FAAC) .... ELG
Alpine Aviation [ICAO designator] (AD) .... ZA
Alpine Aviation Inc. [ICAO designator] (FAAC) .... AIP
Alpine Club [British] .... AC
Alpine Club, Banff, AB, Canada [Library symbol Library of Congress] (LCLS) .... CaABAC
Alpine Club, Banff, Alberta [Library symbol National Library of Canada] (NLC) .... ABAC
Alpine Club of Canada (EA) .... ACC
Alpine Experiment [International Council of Scientific Unions] .... ALPEX
Alpine Exploration [Vancouver Stock Exchange symbol] .... AXC
Alpine Garden Society (EA) .... AGS
Alpine Group [Associated Press] (SAG) .... AlpineGr
Alpine Group, Inc. [AMEX symbol] (SPSG) .... AGI
Alpine Group, Inc. [Associated Press] (SAG) .... AlpinGr
Alpine Lace Brands [NASDAQ symbol] (SPSG) .... LACE
Alpine Lace Brands, Inc. [Associated Press] (SAG) .... AlpLce
Alpine Luft-Transport AB [Switzerland ICAO designator] (FAAC) .... ALU
Alpine Science Information Service [Information service or system] (IID) .... ASISS
Alpine Silver Ltd. [Vancouver Stock Exchange symbol] .... ASV
Alpine Tourist Commission [See also TGA] [Switzerland] (EAIO) .... ATC
Alpine, TX [Location identifier FAA] (FAAL) .... BWR
Alpine, TX [FM radio station call letters] .... KALP
Alpine, TX [AM radio station call letters] .... KVLF
Alpines International (EA) .... AI
Alpinopolis/Furnas [Brazil ICAO location identifier] (ICLI) .... SBFU
Alpliner AG [Switzerland ICAO designator] (FAAC) .... ALP
Alpnet, Inc. [NASDAQ symbol] (NQ) .... AILP
Alpnet, Inc. [Associated Press] (SAG) .... Alpnet
Alport Syndrome [Medicine] .... AS
Alprazolam [Tranquilizer] .... ALP
Alps Region [MARC geographic area code Library of Congress] (LCCP) .... ea----
Al-Rajhi Co. for Currency Exchange and Commerce [Saudi Arabia] .... ARCCEC
Already Been Chewed [Gum] .... ABC
Already Been Converted (PDAA) .... ABC
Alrenco, Inc. [Associated Press] (SAG) .... Alrenco
Alrenco Inc. [NASDAQ symbol] (TTSB) .... RNCO
Alrenco, Inc. [NASDAQ symbol] (SAG) .... RNCO
ALS [Amyotrophic Lateral Sclerosis] and Neuromuscular Research Foundation (EA) .... ALSNRF
Alsager's Dictionary of Business Terms (DLA) .... Alsager
Alsair Societe [France ICAO designator] (FAAC) .... LSR
Alsands Energy Ltd., Library and Records Centre, Calgary, AB, Canada [Library symbol Library of Congress] (LCLS) .... CaACAEL
Alsatian Yiddish (BJA) .... AY
Alsavia, Societe [France ICAO designator] (FAAC) .... ALV
Alsip-Merrionette Park Library District, Alsip, IL [Library symbol Library of Congress] (LCLS) .... IAlsA
Also Known As [Pseudonym] (WDMC) .... aka
Also Known As .... AKA
Alston & Bird, Law Library, Atlanta, GA [Library symbol] [Library of Congress] (LCLS) .... GAAB
Alston Wilkes Society (EA) .... AWS
Alt Tuberculin [Old Tuberculin] [German] .... AT
Alta [Utah] [Seismograph station code, US Geological Survey Closed] (SEIS) .... AAU
Alta [Norway] [Airport symbol] (OAG) .... ALF
Alta [Norway ICAO location identifier] (ICLI) .... ENAT
Alta Advertiser, Alta, IA [Library symbol Library of Congress] (LCLS) .... IaAltaA
Alta Flights Ltd. [Canada ICAO designator] (FAAC) .... ALZ
Alta Gold Co. [NASDAQ symbol] (NQ) .... ALTA
Alta Gold Co. [Associated Press] (SAG) .... AltaGld
Alta Public Library, Alta, IA [Library symbol Library of Congress] (LCLS) .... IaAlta
ALTA [American Library Trustee Association] Specialized Outreach Services Committee [American Library Association] .... ALTA SOSC
Alta Velocidad Espanola [Spain] [High speed train] .... AVE
Alta Vista Branch, Ontario Cancer Foundation, Ottawa, Ontario [Library symbol National Library of Canada] (NLC) .... OOACF
Altadena Library District, Altadena, CA [OCLC symbol] (OCLC) .... ALD
Altadena Library District, Altadena, CA [Library symbol Library of Congress] (LCLS) .... CAlt
Altair [Airline] (MHDB) .... AK
Altair Aviation Ltd. [Canada ICAO designator] (FAAC) .... ALQ
Altamira [Brazil] [Airport symbol] (OAG) .... ATM
Altamira [Brazil ICAO location identifier] (ICLI) .... SBHT
Altamira De San Carlos [Costa Rica] [ICAO location identifier] (ICLI) .... MRAT
Altamont, OR [FM radio station call letters] .... KCHQ

Altamont Public Library, Altamont, IL [*Library symbol Library of Congress*] (LCLS) ... IAlta
Altar Gold & Resources [*Vancouver Stock Exchange symbol*] ... ALT
Altaramaeische Urkunden aus Assur [*A publication*] (BJA) ... AaUA
Altarpiece (VRA) ... altpc
Altavista, VA [*AM radio station call letters*] ... WKDE
Altavista, VA [*FM radio station call letters*] ... WKDE-FM
Altay [*China*] [*Airport symbol*] (OAG) ... AAT
Altbabylonische Briefe im Umschrift und Uebersetzung [*A publication*] (BJA) ... AbB
Alte Kaempfer [*Old Fighters*] [*German*] ... AK
Altemaria citri Rough Lemon-specific Toxins ... ACRL
Altena/Hegenscheid [*Germany ICAO location identifier*] (ICLI) ... EDKD
Altenrhein [*Switzerland ICAO location identifier*] (ICLI) ... LSZR
Altenstadt [*Germany ICAO location identifier*] (ICLI) ... EDPL
Altenstadt [*Germany ICAO location identifier*] (ICLI) ... EDZT
Alteon, Inc. [*Associated Press*] (SAG) ... Alteon
Alteon, Inc. [*NASDAQ symbol*] (SPSG) ... ALTN
Alter ... ALTR
Alter Course [*Navigation*] ... A/C
Alter Ego [*My Other Self*] [*Latin*] ... Alt Eg
Alter Heading [*Navigation*] ... AH
Alter Idem [*Another Self*] [*Latin*] ... Alt Id
Alter Orient und Altes Testament [*Kevelaer/Neukirchen*] [*A publication*] (BJA) ... AltOrAT
Alter Orient und Altes Testament. Veroeffentlichungen zur Kultur und Geschichte des Alten Orients und des Alten Testaments [*Kevelaer/Neukirchen/Vluyn*] [*A publication*] (BJA) ... AOAT
Alter Ridge [*Washington*] [*Seismograph station code, US Geological Survey*] (SEIS) ... ALD
Altera Corp. [*Associated Press*] (SAG) ... Altera
Altera Corp. [*NASDAQ symbol*] (NQ) ... ALTR
Alterable Control Memory ... ACM
Alterable Read-Only Memory [*Computer science*] ... AROM
Alterable Read-Only Operating System [*Computer science*] ... AROS
Alteration ... ALT
Alteration (ROG) ... ALTER
Alteration ... ALTERON
Alteration [*Technical drawings*] (DAC) ... ALTN
Alteration (AABC) ... ALTR
Alteration (MSA) ... ALTRN
Alteration ... ALTRN
Alteration (ROG) ... ALTRON
Alteration and Improvement Program [*Navy*] ... A & I
Alteration and Inspection ... A & I
Alteration and Project Report (DNAB) ... APR
Alteration Equivalent to a Repair ... AER
Alteration Identification ... ALTID
Alteration Management System (NVT) ... AMS
Alteration of Instruments [*Legal term*] (DLA) ... ALT INST
Alteration Request Number ... ARN
Alterations (ROG) ... ALTS
Alterations in Respiratory Function [*Medicine*] (DMAA) ... AIRF
Altercate Minimum Tax (TDOB) ... AMT
Altered (DCTA) ... ALT
Altered (MSA) ... ALTRD
Altered Commercial Item (MCD) ... ACI
Altered from a Detail (SAA) ... A/FD
Altered Item Drawing (SSD) ... AID
Altered Mental Status (MEDA) ... AMS
Altered Oceanic Crust [*Geology*] ... AOC
Altered State of Consciousness [*Parapsychology*] ... ASC
Altered State of Consciousness Induction Device [*Parapsychology*] ... ASCID
Altering [*FBI standardized term*] ... ALT
Alterio Resources Ltd. [*Toronto Stock Exchange symbol*] ... AWO
Alterius Diebus [*Every Other Day*] [*Pharmacy*] ... Al Dieb
Alternant Molecular Orbital [*Physical chemistry*] ... AMO
Alternaria [*A fungus*] ... Alt
Alternaria alternata f lycopersici [*A toxin-producing fungus*] ... AL
Alternaria Citri (Lemon race) [*A toxin-producing fungus*] ... ACL
Alternaria citri (Tangerine race) [*A toxin-producing fungus*] ... ACT
Alternaria kikuchiana [*A toxin-producing fungus*] ... AK
Alternaria mali [*A toxin-producing fungus*] ... AM
Alternariol [*Biochemistry*] ... AOH
Alternariol Methyl Ether [*Biochemistry*] ... AME
Alternate [*Approach and landing charts*] [*Aviation*] ... A
Alternate (VRA) ... alt
Alternate ... ALT
Alternate ... ALTER
Alternate (AFM) ... ALTN
Alternate (KSC) ... ALTR
Alternate Acquisition RADAR (MCD) ... AAR
Alternate Aircraft Takeoff System (MCD) ... AATS
Alternate Airport (FAAC) ... ALTPT
Alternate Alerting Network [*Air Force*] ... ALTAN
Alternate Antiair Warfare Commander (NVT) ... AAAWC
Alternate Binaural Loudness Balance [*Otorhinolaryngology*] (DAVI) ... ABLB
Alternate Binaural Loudness Balancing [*Audiometry*] ... ABLB
Alternate Birthing Center [*Obstetrics*] (DAVI) ... ABC
Alternate Call Listing [*Telecommunications*] (TEL) ... AC
Alternate Captain [*Sports*] ... A
Alternate Care Plan [*Health Care Financing Administration*] ... ACP
Alternate Central Computer Complex (MCD) ... ACCC
Alternate Command [*or Commander*] [*Navy*] (NVT) ... ALTCOM
Alternate Command and Control Center [*Air Force*] (MCD) ... ACCC
Alternate Command, Atlantic Fleet (MCD) ... ALTCOM
Alternate Command, Atlantic Fleet ... ALTCOMLANTFLT
Alternate Command Center [*Navy*] (CINC) ... ACC
Alternate Command Center [*Navy*] (NVT) ... ALTCOMCEN
Alternate Command Elements [*Navy*] (CINC) ... ACE
Alternate Command Facility [*Navy*] (NVT) ... ACF
Alternate Command Post [*Military*] (CET) ... ACP
Alternate Command Post [*Military*] (AFM) ... ALCOP
Alternate Command Post ... ALCP
Alternate Commander, Atlantic [*Navy*] (NVT) ... ALTCOMLANT
Alternate Commander, Pacific [*Navy*] (NVT) ... ALTCOMPAC
Alternate Communications Facility [*Military*] ... ACF
Alternate Competition Advocate (AAGC) ... ACA
Alternate Concentration Limit [*Nuclear energy*] (NRCH) ... ACL
Alternate Core Spray [*Nuclear energy*] (NRCH) ... ACS
Alternate CPU [*Central Processing Unit*] **Recovery** [*IBM Corp.*] [*Computer science*] (BUR) ... ACR
Alternate Definition of Accident [*Insurance*] ... A/D
Alternate Delivery System [*Medicine*] (DHSM) ... ADS
Alternate Departure Route [*Air Traffic Control*] (FAAC) ... ADRT
Alternate Detection and Control Unit (MCD) ... ADCU
Alternate Device Support [*NASA*] ... ADS
Alternate Digit Inversion [*Computer science*] (IAA) ... ADI
Alternate Drop [*Electroanalysis*] ... AD
Alternate Emergency Action Center (CINC) ... AEAC
Alternate Energy Institute [*Defunct*] (EA) ... AEI
Alternate Fighter Engine (MCD) ... AFE
Alternate Financial Mechanisms [*Health insurance*] (GHCT) ... AFM
Alternate Flight Plan ... AFP
Alternate Gross Weight (MCD) ... AGW
Alternate Headquarters [*Military*] (NVT) ... AH
Alternate Headquarters [*Military*] (AABC) ... ALTHQ
Alternate Headquarters Command Facility [*Military*] (MCD) ... AHCF
Alternate Health Services ... AHS
Alternate Inspection Policy ... AIP
Alternate Instruction Address Register [*Computer science*] (MHDI) ... ALTINSAR
Alternate Interim Successor [*Military*] (NVT) ... AIS
Alternate Joint Command Center (MCD) ... AJCC
Alternate Joint Communications Center ... AJCC
Alternate Joint Typhoon Warning Center (DNAB) ... AJTWC
Alternate Joint War Room [*Later, ANMCC*] (CINC) ... AJWR
Alternate Landing Site [*NASA*] (NASA) ... ALS
Alternate Launch Officer [*Air Force*] ... ALO
Alternate Launch Officer Console [*Air Force*] ... ALOC
Alternate Liaison Officer ... ALO
Alternate Library [*Computer program*] [*NASA*] ... ALTLIB
Alternate Life Style ... ALS
Alternate Low Energy (CAAL) ... ALE
Alternate Management Summary Report (MCD) ... AMSR
Alternate Mark Inversion [*Telecommunications*] (IEEE) ... AMI
Alternate Master Unit (MCD) ... AMU
Alternate Media Center [*New York University*] [*New York, NY Telecommunications*] ... AMC
Alternate Military Occupational Specialty (MUGU) ... AMOS
Alternate Mission Equipment (MCD) ... AME
Alternate Mode (CAAL) ... AM
Alternate Monoaural Loudness Balance Test [*Medicine*] (DMAA) ... AMLB
Alternate National Military Command Center [*Formerly, AJWR*] (AFM) ... ANMCC
Alternate National Military Intelligence Center (MCD) ... ANMIC
Alternate Net Control Officer [*Navy*] (NVT) ... ANCO
Alternate Net Control Station (CET) ... ANCS
Alternate [*or Alternative*] **News Service** (ADA) ... ANS
Alternate Path Reentry [*Fujitsu Ltd.*] [*Computer science*] (MCD) ... APR
Alternate Postal Delivery [*NASDAQ symbol*] (TTSB) ... ALTD
Alternate Postal Delivery, Inc. [*NASDAQ symbol*] (SAG) ... ALTD
Alternate Postal Delivery, Inc. [*Associated Press*] (SAG) ... AltPosD
Alternate Program (DNAB) ... ALT PROG
Alternate Record-Voice ... ARV
Alternate Reproductive Behavior [*Zoology*] ... ARB
Alternate Rod Insertion [*Nuclear energy*] (NRCH) ... ARI
Alternate Route [*Telecommunications*] (TEL) ... A/R
Alternate Route Cancel [*Telecommunications*] (TEL) ... ARC
Alternate Source Council (MCD) ... ASC
Alternate Source Development ... ASD
Alternate Space Inversion (ACRL) ... ASI
Alternate Squadron Commander [*Air Force*] ... ASC
Alternate Supply Rate (MCD) ... ASR
Alternate Supply Route ... ASR
Alternate Target Docking Adapter [*NASA*] (MCD) ... ATDA
Alternate Target Point ... ATP
Alternate Test Procedure [*for aviation jet fuels*] [*Navy*] ... ATP
Alternate Thermal Protection System (MCD) ... ATPS
Alternate Training Assemby [*Army*] (ADDR) ... ATA
Alternate Uses [*Personality research*] [*Psychology*] ... AU
Alternate Voice Data ... AVD
Alternate Weapon ... AW
Alternate Weeks [*Advertising term*] (WDMC) ... A/W
Alternate-Day Treatment [*Medicine*] ... ADT
Alternate-Top-Bevel Teeth [*Saw blades*] ... ATB
Alternating [*Polymer*] [*Organic chemistry*] ... alt
Alternating Continuous Wave [*Radio*] ... ACW
Alternating Current ... A
Alternating Current ... AC
Alternating Current (IDOE) ... ac
Alternating Current Circuit ... ACC

Alternating Current Continuous Wave ... ACCW
Alternating Current/Direct Current ... A-C/D-C
Alternating Current Dump ... ACD
Alternating Current Electrocoagulation [*Chemical engineering*] ... ACE
Alternating Current Flip-Flop (IAA) ... ACFF
Alternating Current Generator ... ACG
Alternating Current Input (MHDI) ... ACI
Alternating Current Network ... ACNET
Alternating Current Normal Mode Rejection [*Electronics*] (IAA) ... ACNMR
Alternating Current Output (MHDI) ... ACO
Alternating Current Plasma Detector [*Spectrometry*] ... ACPD
Alternating Current Plasma Display Panel [*Electronics*] (IAA) ... ACPDP
Alternating Current Relay [*Electronics*] (IAA) ... ACREL
Alternating Current Signal Generator ... AC-SG
Alternating Current Spark Plug (IAA) ... ACSP
Alternating Current, Synchronous ... ACS
Alternating Current Synthesizer [*Exxon Corp.*] ... ACS
Alternating Current Test Volts (MSA) ... VACT
Alternating Current Thin-Film Electroluminescence (MHDI) ... ACTEL
Alternating Current Vacuum Tube Voltmeter (IAA) ... ACVTVM
Alternating Current Volts ... ACV
Alternating Current Volts ... VAC
Alternating Current Working Volts (MSA) ... VACW
Alternating Direction Implicit [*Algorithm*] ... ADI
Alternating Direction Iterative (PDAA) ... ADI
Alternating Exotropia [*Ophthalmology*] ... AXT
Alternating Field ... AF
Alternating Field Demagnetization ... AFD
Alternating Fixed and Flashing [*Lights*] ... ALTFFL
Alternating Fixed and Group Flashing [*Lights*] ... ALTFGPGL
Alternating, Fixed, and Group-Flashing [*Lights*] (DNAB) ... ALTFGFL
Alternating Flashing [*Lights*] ... ALTFL
Alternating Flow ... AF
Alternating Frequency Rejection [*Automotive technology*] ... AFR
Alternating Gradient ... AG
Alternating Gradient Focusing ... AGF
Alternating Gradient Synchrotron ... AGS
Alternating Group Occulting [*Lights*] ... ALTGPOCC
Alternating Guidance Section ... AGS
Alternating Hamiltonian Path ... AHP
Alternating Light [*Navigation signal*] ... Al
Alternating Light [*Navigation signal*] ... Alt
Alternating Monocular Deprivation [*Optics*] ... AMD
Alternating Motion Rate ... AMR
Alternating Motion Reflex [*Neurology*] (DAVI) ... AMR
Alternating Motion Reflexes [*Medicine*] (BABM) ... AMR
Alternating Occulting [*Lights*] ... ALTOCC
Alternating Pressure Air Mattress [*for prevention of pressure sores*] ... APAM
Alternating Rate of Motion [*Neurophysiology*] (DAVI) ... ARM
Alternativa Revolucionaria del Pueblo [*Bolivia*] [*Political party*] (EY) ... ARP
Alternative (ROG) ... ALT
Alternative (IEEE) ... ALTN
Alternative (MSA) ... ALTNV
Alternative ... ALTRNTV
Alternative Access Vendor [*Telecommunications*] ... AAV
Alternative Antenna Array (MCD) ... AAA
Alternative Automotive Power Systems [*Environmental Protection Agency*] ... AAPS
Alternative Birth Crisis Coalition [*Defunct*] (EA) ... ABCC
Alternative Book Service [*Reference to an edition of the Anglican Book of Common Prayer*] (BARN) ... ASB
Alternative Broadcasting [*An association*] (EA) ... AB
Alternative Carrier Telecommunications Association (EA) ... ACTA
Alternative Center for International Arts (EA) ... ACIA
Alternative Coated Paper ... ACP
Alternative Communities Movement [*British*] ... ACM
Alternative Complement Pathway [*Hematology*] ... ACP
Alternative Concentration Limits [*Environmental Protection Agency*] (EPA) ... ACL
Alternative Control Technology [*Environmental science*] ... ACT
Alternative County Government [*A publication*] (DLA) ... Alt County Gov't
Alternative Criminology Journal [*A publication*] ... Alt Criminol J
Alternative Curriculum Strategies [*Education*] (AIE) ... ACS
Alternative Defense Posture (DNAB) ... ADP
Alternative Delivery and Financing System [*Medicine*] (HCT) ... ADFS
Alternative Delivery Schedule Evaluator (MHDB) ... ADSE
Alternative Delivery System [*Health care service*] ... ADS
Alternative Dispute Resolution ... ADR
Alternative Dispute Resolution (WYGK) ... ADR
Alternative Economic Strategy ... AES
Alternative Education Project (EA) ... AEP
Alternative Energy ... AE
Alternative Energy Resources Organization (EA) ... AERO
Alternative Environmental Futures [*An association*] ... AEF
Alternative Fertility [*Demography*] ... AF
Alternative Fertility Proportion [*Demography*] ... AFP
Alternative Financing System [*Health care*] (HCT) ... AFS
Alternative Fluorocarbon Environmental Acceptability Study [*World Meteorological Organization*] ... AFEAS
Alternative Force Generator (MCD) ... AFG
Alternative Forum [*An association*] (EAIO) ... AF
Alternative Fuel Data Bank [*Bartlesville Energy Technology Center*] [*Database*] ... AFDB
Alternative Fuel Electronics [*Fuel systems*] [*Automotive engineering*] ... AFE
Alternative Fuel Vehicle ... AFV
Alternative Fuels Development Unit [*La Porte, TX*] [*Department of Energy*] ... AFDU
Alternative Generator Model (DNAB) ... AGM
Alternative Health Insurance Services [*An association*] (EA) ... AHIS
Alternative Health Plans [*Department of Health and Human Services*] (GFGA) ... AHP
Alternative Hypothesis (DAVI) ... H_1
Alternative Information Center [*Israeli news organization*] ... AIC
Alternative Information Network (EA) ... AIN
Alternative Intermediate Services for the Mentally Retarded ... AIS/MR
Alternative Land Uses and the Rural Economy [*Ministry of Agriculture*] [*British*] ... ALURE
Alternative Launch-Point System ... ALPS
Alternative Learning Program for High School Age ... ALPHA
Alternative Lengthening of Telomeres [*Genetics*] ... ALT
Alternative Level of Care [*Medicine*] (MEDA) ... ALC
Alternative Lifestyle Checklist ... ALC
Alternative List [*Sweden Political party*] ... AL
Alternative Liste [*Alternative List*] [*Austria Political party*] ... AL
Alternative Liste Oesterreich [*Austrian Alternative List*] [*Political party*] (PPW) ... ALO
Alternative Living Manager's Association [*Defunct*] (EA) ... ALMA
Alternative Living Services [*AMEX symbol*] (SAG) ... ALI
Alternative Living Services [*Associated Press*] (SAG) ... AltLivng
Alternative Loan Program ... ALP
Alternative Local Telephone Company (ECON) ... ALT
Alternative Mark Inversion Signal (NITA) ... AMI
Alternative Marriage and Relationship Council of the United States ... AMRCUS
Alternative Mating Technique [*Zoology*] ... AMT
Alternative Medical Association (EA) ... AMA
Alternative Method of Management (MHDB) ... AMM
Alternative Minimum Tax ... AMT
Alternative Minimum Taxable Income ... AMTI
Alternative Mortgage Instrument ... AMI
Alternative Motor Fuels Act ... AMFA
Alternative Music Market ... AMM
Alternative Operational Concepts in Europe [*Military*] ... AOCEUR
Alternative Operator Services [*Telecommunications*] ... AOS
Alternative Performance Appraisal System (DOMA) ... APAS
Alternative Poland [*Defunct*] (EA) ... AP
Alternative Press Center (EA) ... APC
Alternative Press Centre, Toronto, ON, Canada [*Library symbol Library of Congress*] (LCLS) ... CaOTAP
Alternative Press Centre, Toronto, Ontario [*Library symbol National Library of Canada*] (NLC) ... OTAP
Alternative Press Review [*A publication*] (BRI) ... Alt Pr R
Alternative Press Syndicate [*Defunct*] (EA) ... APS
Alternative Regulatory Option [*Environmental Protection Agency*] (GFGA) ... ARO
Alternative Release Procedures (MCD) ... ARP
Alternative Remedial Contracting Strategy (AAGC) ... ARCS
Alternative Remedial Contracting Systems [*Environmental Protection Agency*] ... ARCS
Alternative Reproduction Vehicle [*Medicine*] ... ARV
Alternative Resource Allocation Priorities [*Military*] ... ARAP
Alternative Resource Center (EA) ... ARC
Alternative Resources [*NASDAQ symbol*] (TTSB) ... ALRC
Alternative Resources Corp. [*NASDAQ symbol*] (SAG) ... ALRC
Alternative Resources Corp. [*Associated Press*] (SAG) ... AltResc
Alternative Route to Ordained Service (DICI) ... ARTOS
Alternative Salient Future (PDAA) ... ASF
Alternative Society [*British*] ... AS
Alternative Sources of Energy (EA) ... ASE
Alternative Splicing Factor [*Genetics*] ... ASF
Alternative System Design Concept ... ASDC
Alternative System Exploration (MCD) ... ASE
Alternative Technologies and Approaches [*Military*] (RDA) ... ATA
Alternative Technology ... AT
Alternative Technology Association [*Australia*] ... ATA
Alternative Technology Information Group (EAIO) ... ATIG
Alternative Term Plan (IAA) ... ATP
Alternative to Amniocentesis [*Medicine*] ... ATA
Alternative to Dedicated Hospital Ship (CAAL) ... ADHOS
Alternative to the New York Times Committee (EA) ... ANYTC
Alternative Type Acceptance [*Model for interference measurement*] (NITA) ... ATA
Alternative Vote ... AV
Alternative Work Schedule (GFGA) ... AWS
Alternatively Refined Carrageenan [*Food grade*] ... ARC
Alternatives for Learning through Educational Research and Technology (DICI) ... ALERT
Alternatives in Higher Education [*Program*] [*National Science Foundation*] ... AHE
Alternatives Loan Program [*Humane Society of the United States*] ... ALP
Alternatives to Abortion International [*Later, AAI/WHEF*] (EA) ... AAI
Alternatives to Abortion International/Women's Health and Education Foundation (EA) ... AAI/WHEF
Alternator (KSC) ... ALT
Alternator ... ALTNR
Alternator (MSA) ... ALTNTR
Alternator [*Automotive engineering*] ... ALTR
Alternator ... ALTRNTR
Alternator Research Package ... ARP
Alternator-Powered Electrically Heated Catalyst [*Automotive engineering*] ... APEHC
Alternis Diebus [*Alternate Days*] [*Pharmacy*] ... AD
Alternis Diebus [*Every Other Day*] [*Pharmacy*] ... ALT DIEB
Alternis Horis [*Every Other Hour*] [*Pharmacy*] ... ALT HOR

Alternis Horis [*Every Other Hour*] [*Pharmacy*] ..... ALTERN HOR
Alternis Nocibus [*Every Other Night*] [*Pharmacy*] (BARN) ..... alt noc
Alternis Nocte [*Every Other Night*] [*Pharmacy*] ..... ALT NOCT
Altero Technology [*Vancouver Stock Exchange symbol*] ..... ALK
Alters- und Hinterlassenen-Versicherung [*Old Age and Dependents Insurance*] [*State insurance company Liechtenstein*] (EY) ..... AHV
Altertext Conversion System (DGA) ..... ACS
Altertumswissenschaft (BJA) ..... AW
Altes Testament [*Old Testament*] [*German*] ..... AT
Altesse [*Highness*] [*French*] ..... ALT
Altesse Imperiale [*Imperial Highness*] [*French*] ..... AI
Altesse Royale [*Royal Highness*] [*French*] ..... AR
Altesses [*Highnesses*] [*French*] ..... AA
Altex Resources Ltd. [*Toronto Stock Exchange symbol*] ..... AX
Altezza [*Highness*] [*Italian*] ..... A
Althaea [*Rose of Sharon*] [*Pharmacology*] (ROG) ..... ALTH
Althemer & Gray, Chicago, IL [*Library symbol*] [*Library of Congress*] (LCLS) ..... ICAG
Althydusamband Islands [*Icelandic Federation of Labor*] ..... ASI
Altimeter (NG) ..... ALT
Altimeter (KSC) ..... ALTM
Altimeter Check Location [*Aviation*] (FAAC) ..... ACL
Altimeter Control Equipment [*Aviation*] ..... ACE
Altimeter Indicator (MCD) ..... AI
Altimeter Setting (FAAC) ..... ALSTG
Altimeter Setting Indicator [*Aviation*] (FAAC) ..... ASI
Altimeter Setting Region [*Aviation*] (AIA) ..... ASR
Altimeter Setting Region [*Aviation*] ..... ASRGN
Altimeter Station [*ITU designation*] (CET) ..... ROA
Altimeter Transmitter Multiplier (DNAB) ..... ATM
Altimeter/Velocity Sensor Antenna ..... A/VSA
Altimeter Vertical Velocity Indicator [*NASA*] (MCD) ..... AVVI
Altimetry System Error [*Aviation*] (DA) ..... ASE
Altintas [*Turkey*] [*Seismograph station code, US Geological Survey*] (SEIS) ..... ALT
Altiranisches Woerterbuch [*A publication*] (BJA) ..... AiWb
Altitude (AFM) ..... ALT
Altitude ..... ALTTD
Altitude ..... H
Altitude and Rate-Indicating System (DNAB) ..... ARIS
Altitude Barometric Switch [*Automotive engineering*] ..... ABS
Altitude Command Indicator ..... ACI
Altitude Compensator [*Automotive engineering*] ..... AC
Altitude Control Electronics ..... ACE
Altitude Control System ..... ACS
Altitude Control Test Facility ..... ACTF
Altitude Controller Assembly (MCD) ..... ACA
Altitude Conversion Kit ..... ACK
Altitude Deviation ..... AD
Altitude Difference [*Navigation*] ..... A
Altitude Direction Indicator (AFM) ..... ADI
Altitude Encoder Unit (MCD) ..... AEU
Altitude Engine Control (AAG) ..... AEC
Altitude Engine Control Panel (AAG) ..... AECP
Altitude Error ..... ALTE
Altitude Error (GAVI) ..... HE
Altitude Gyroscope Control Assembly [*Military*] (CAAL) ..... AGCA
Altitude Heading Reference System (GAVI) ..... AHRS
Altitude Hold Mode (GAVI) ..... ALT HOLD
Altitude Identification Military System (MCD) ..... AIMS
Altitude Indication System ..... AIS
Altitude Indicator [*Aviation*] (DA) ..... AI
Altitude Indoctrination (MCD) ..... AI
Altitude Instrument Flying (DA) ..... AIF
Altitude Layer Surveillance Terminal Area RADAR ..... ALSTAR
Altitude Manned Penetrator (MCD) ..... AMP
Altitude Marking Range (KSC) ..... AMR
Altitude Measurement System ..... AMS
Altitude Proximity Sensor (MCD) ..... APS
Altitude Radial (FAAC) ..... ARAD
Altitude Rate [*Symbol*] (NASA) ..... H
Altitude Rate Command ..... ARC
Altitude Rate Command System (MCD) ..... ARCS
Altitude Reconnaissance Probe (MUGU) ..... ARP
Altitude Referenced Radiometer ..... ARR
Altitude Report Status (SAA) ..... ALRS
Altitude Reporting (DA) ..... A/R
Altitude Reporting Mode of Secondary Radar [*FAA*] (TAG) ..... MODE C
Altitude Reservation [*Air Force*] (AFM) ..... ALTRV
Altitude Reservation Void for Aircraft Not Airborne By [*Aviation*] (FAAC) ..... AVANA
Altitude Sensing System ..... ASS
Altitude Sensing Unit [*Aviation*] (AIA) ..... ASU
Altitude Sensor Bypass (MCD) ..... ASB
Altitude Sounding Projectile (MUGU) ..... ASP
Altitude Transmitting Equipment [*FAA*] (MSA) ..... ALTE
Altitude Transmitting Equipment [*FAA*] ..... ATE
Altitude Variation Rate and Displacement ..... AVRAD
Altitude Velocity Chart ..... AVC
Altitude Warning Signal System (PDAA) ..... AWSS
Altitude Warning System (MCD) ..... AWS
Altitude Wind Tunnel ..... AWT
Altitude-Vertical Scale ..... AVS
Altitude-Vertical Velocity Indicator [*NASA*] (AFM) ..... AVVI
Altman Information Systems, Inc. [*Information service or system*] (IID) ..... AIS
Alto ..... A
Alto ..... ALT
Alto Comisionado de las Naciones Unidas para los Refugiados [*Office of the United Nations High Commissioner for Refugees*] [*Spanish*] (DUND) ..... ACNUR
Alto Exploration [*Vancouver Stock Exchange symbol*] ..... ANE
Alto Palena [*Chile*] [*Airport symbol*] (AD) ..... WAP
Alto Palena/Alto Palena [*Chile*] [*ICAO location identifier*] (ICLI) ..... SCAP
Alto Parnaiba [*Brazil*] [*Airport symbol*] (AD) ..... APY
Alto Rio Senguerr [*Argentina*] [*Airport symbol*] (OAG) ..... ARR
Alto Rio Senguerr [*Argentina ICAO location identifier*] (ICLI) ..... SAVR
Altocumulus [*Cloud*] [*Meteorology*] ..... AC
Altocumulus [*Cloud*] [*Meteorology*] (MUGU) ..... ACU
Altocumulus [*Cloud*] [*Meteorology*] ..... ALCU
Altocumulus Castellanus [*Cloud*] [*Meteorology*] ..... ACC
Altocumulus Castellanus [*NWS*] (FAAC) ..... ACCAS
Altoff High School, Belleville, IL [*Library symbol Library of Congress*] (LCLS) ..... IBelHS
Altogether (ROG) ..... ALTOGR
Altogether Builders, Labourers, and Constructional Workers Society [*A union*] [*British*] ..... ABLCWS
Alton & Southern Railroad ..... A & S
[*The*] **Alton & Southern Railway Co.** [*AAR code*] ..... ALS
[*The*] **Alton & Southern Railway Co.** ..... ALT & S
Alton Community Unit 11, Alton, IL [*Library symbol Library of Congress*] (LCLS) ..... IAlCU
Alton Downs [*Australia Airport symbol Obsolete*] (OAG) ..... AWN
Alton, IL [*Location identifier FAA*] (FAAL) ..... ALN
Alton, IL [*Location identifier FAA*] (FAAL) ..... CVM
Alton, IL [*FM radio station call letters*] ..... KNJZ
Alton, IL [*AM radio station call letters*] ..... WBGZ
Alton Memorial Hospital, Alton, IL [*Library symbol Library of Congress*] (LCLS) ..... IAlH
Alton Mental Health Center, Development and Training Center, Staff Library, Alton, IL [*Library symbol Library of Congress*] (LCLS) ..... IAlMH
Alton Public Library, Alton, IA [*Library symbol Library of Congress*] (LCLS) ..... IaAltn
Altona Community Memorial Health Centre, Altona, MB, Canada [*Library symbol Library of Congress*] (LCLS) ..... CaMACMH
Altona Community Memorial Health Centre, Manitoba [*Library symbol National Library of Canada*] (NLC) ..... MACMH
Altona, MB [*AM radio station call letters*] ..... CFAM
Altona Medical Centre, Altona, MB, Canada [*Library symbol Library of Congress*] (LCLS) ..... CaMAMC
Altona Medical Centre Library, Manitoba [*Library symbol National Library of Canada*] (NLC) ..... MAMC
Altoona [*Pennsylvania*] ..... ALT
Altoona [*Pennsylvania*] [*Airport symbol*] (OAG) ..... AOO
Altoona Area Public Library, Altoona, PA [*OCLC symbol*] (OCLC) ..... AOP
Altoona Area Public Library, Altoona, PA [*Library symbol Library of Congress*] (LCLS) ..... PAlt
Altoona, PA [*Television station call letters*] ..... WATM
Altoona, PA [*AM radio station call letters*] ..... WFBG
Altoona, PA [*FM radio station call letters*] ..... WFGY
Altoona, PA [*Television station call letters*] ..... WKBS
Altoona, PA [*FM radio station call letters*] ..... WPRR
Altoona, PA [*AM radio station call letters*] ..... WRTA
Altoona, PA [*Television station call letters*] ..... WTAJ
Altoona, PA [*AM radio station call letters*] ..... WVAM
Altoona Public Library, Altoona, IA [*Library symbol Library of Congress*] (LCLS) ..... IaAlto
Altoona, WI [*FM radio station call letters*] ..... WISM
Altoona-Johnstown [*Diocesan abbreviation*] [*Pennsylvania*] (TOCD) ..... ALT
Altoona-Martinsburg [*Pennsylvania*] [*Airport symbol*] (AD) ..... AOO
Altorientalische Bilder zum Alten Testament [*A publication*] (BJA) ..... AOBAT
Altos Computer Systems (NITA) ..... ACS
Altos Hornos de Mexico SA de CV [*Associated Press*] (SAG) ..... AltosHrn
Altos Hornos de Mexico SA de CV [*NYSE symbol*] (SAG) ..... IAM
Altos Office Manager [*Altos Computer Systems*] ..... AOM
Altostratus [*Also, AS*] [*Meteorology*] ..... ALST
Altostratus [*Also, ALST*] [*Meteorology*] ..... AS
Altostratus [*Cloud*] [*Meteorology*] (AIA) ..... ASt
Altostratus and Altocumulus [*Meteorology*] ..... ASAC
Altris Software, Inc. [*Associated Press*] (SAG) ..... Altris
Altris Software, Inc. [*NASDAQ symbol*] (SAG) ..... ALTS
Altron, Inc. [*NASDAQ symbol*] (NQ) ..... ALRN
Altron, Inc. [*Associated Press*] (SAG) ..... Altron
Altrusa International (EA) ..... AI
Alturas, CA [*Location identifier FAA*] (FAAL) ..... ARU
Alturas, CA [*AM radio station call letters*] ..... KCNO
Alturas, CA [*FM radio station call letters*] (RBYB) ..... KCNO-FM
Alturas, CA [*AM radio station call letters*] (RBYB) ..... KKFJ-AM
Alturas, CA [*FM radio station call letters*] ..... KYAX
Altus [*Oklahoma*] [*Airport symbol*] (OAG) ..... AXS
Altus Air Force Base [*Oklahoma*] [*ICAO location identifier*] (ICLI) ..... KLTS
Altus Airlines [*ICAO designator*] (FAAC) ..... AXS
Altus Library, Altus, OK [*Library symbol Library of Congress*] (LCLS) ..... OkAl
Altus, OK [*Location identifier FAA*] (FAAL) ..... ALT
Altus, OK [*Location identifier FAA*] (FAAL) ..... AXS
Altus, OK [*Location identifier FAA*] (FAAL) ..... HVU
Altus, OK [*FM radio station call letters*] ..... KEYB
Altus, OK [*FM radio station call letters*] ..... KKVO
Altus, OK [*FM radio station call letters*] ..... KRKZ
Altus, OK [*AM radio station call letters*] ..... KWHW
Altus, OK [*Location identifier FAA*] (FAAL) ..... LTS
Alula [*Somalia*] [*Airport symbol*] (OAG) ..... ALU

Alula [*Somalia*] [*ICAO location identifier*] (ICLI) .... HCMA
Alum, Blood, and Charcoal [*A method of deodorizing by addition of a compound of these*] [*Medicine*] .... ABC
Alum, Blood, Clay Method [*Raw sewage treatment*] [*Organic chemistry*] (DAVI) .... ABC
Alum Co. Amer $3.75 Pfd [*AMEX symbol*] (TTSB) .... AAPr
Alum Precipitated [*Medicine*] .... AP
Alum Precipitated Pyridine [*Medicine*] (MAE) .... APP
Alum Precipitated Toxoid [*Medicine*] .... APT
Alumax, Inc. [*Associated Press*] (SAG) .... Alumax
Alumax Inc. [*NYSE symbol*] (TTSB) .... AMX
Alumax, Inc. [*NYSE symbol*] (SAG) .... AMX
Alumina Ceramic Manufacturers Association [*Defunct*] (EA) .... ACMA
Alumina Ceramic Test .... ACT
Alumina Trihydrate [*Inorganic chemistry*] .... ALTH
Alumina Trihydrate [*Inorganic chemistry*] .... ATH
Alumina-Zirconia-Silica [*Inorganic chemistry*] .... AZS
Aluminium [*British*] (ADA) .... ALU
Aluminium Can Group [*Australia An association*] .... ACG
Aluminium Coatings Association [*British*] (DBA) .... ACA
Aluminium Fabricators' Association of Western Australia .... AAFAWA
Aluminium Federation .... AF
Aluminium Oxide .... ALOX
Aluminium Radiator Manufacturers Association [*British*] (DBA) ...... ARMA
Aluminium Rolled Products Manufacturers Association [*British*] (DBA) .... ARPMA
Aluminium Stockholders' Association [*British*] .... ASA
Aluminium Submarine for Deep-Ocean Research [*Navy symbol British*] .... ALUMINAUT
Aluminium Suisse, SA [*Commercial firm*] .... AS
Aluminium Window Association [*British*] (DBA) .... AWA
Aluminium Window Industry Association of Victoria [*Australia*] ...... AWIAV
Aluminium-Zentrale eV .... AZ
Aluminocalcium Phosphorous Oxide [*Inorganic chemistry*] .... ALCAP
Aluminophosphate [*Inorganic chemistry*] .... ALPO
Aluminosilicate Polyacrylate [*Type of dental cement*] .... ASPA
Aluminum [*Chemical element*] .... Al
Aluminum [*Chemical symbol is Al*] .... ALUM
Aluminum (VRA) .... alum
Aluminum .... ALUMN
Aluminum [*Chemical symbol is Al*] .... ALUMN
Aluminum Alloy (MCD) .... ALALY
Aluminum Alloy Constructor Steel Reinforced (IEEE) .... AACSR
Aluminum and Polyethylene [*Components of a type of telecommunications cable*] .... ALPETH
Aluminum and Steel [*Freight*] .... AS
Aluminum Association (EA) .... AA
Aluminum Association .... AIA
Aluminum Association Aluminum Standards and Data [*Information service or system*] (IID) .... AAASD
Aluminum Association of Florida (SRA) .... AAF
Aluminum Beaker Oxidation Test [*Lubricant testing*] .... ABOT
Aluminum, Brick, and Clay Workers International Union (EA) .... ABCWIU
Aluminum, Brick, and Glass Workers International Union .... ABGW
Aluminum, Brick, and Glass Workers International Union (EA) .... ABGWIU
Aluminum Building Products Credit Association [*Defunct*] .... ABPCA
Aluminum Cable Steel Reinforced .... ACSR
Aluminum Chlorohydrate [*Inorganic chemistry*] .... ACH
Aluminum Chlorohydroxyallantoinate [*Organic chemistry*] .... ALCA
Aluminum Company of America [*Wall Street slang names: "Ack Ack" and "All American"*] [*NYSE symbol*] (SPSG) .... AA
Aluminum Co. of America [*NYSE symbol*] (SAG) .... AA
Aluminum Co. of America [*AMEX symbol*] (SAG) .... AAp
Aluminum Co. of America [*Associated Press*] (SAG) .... Alcoa
Aluminum Co. of America, ALCOA Research Laboratories Library, New Kensington, PA [*Library symbol Library of Congress*] (LCLS) .... PNkA
Aluminum Co. of Canada Ltd. [*Toronto Stock Exchange symbol Vancouver Stock Exchange symbol*] .... ACC
Aluminum Co. of Canada Ltd. .... ALCAN
Aluminum Co. of Canada Ltd., Arvida, PQ, Canada [*Library symbol Library of Congress*] (LCLS) .... CaQAA
Aluminum Co. of Canada Ltd., Kingston, ON, Canada [*Library symbol Library of Congress*] (LCLS) .... CaOKAL
Aluminum Co. of Canada Ltd., Kingston, Ontario [*Library symbol National Library of Canada*] (NLC) .... OKAL
Aluminum Conductor Alloy Reinforced (MCD) .... ACAR
Aluminum Conductor Steel Reinforced .... ACSR
Aluminum Crown [*Dentistry*] .... AL CR
Aluminum Dihydroxyaminoacetate [*Also, ALGLYN*] [*Pharmacology*] ...... ADA
Aluminum Efficient Radiator [*General Motors Corp.*] [*Automotive engineering*] .... AER
Aluminum Electrical Lead .... AEL
Aluminum Extension Jacket .... AEJ
Aluminum Extruders Association (DAC) .... AEA
Aluminum Extruders Council (EA) .... AEC
Aluminum Field Coil .... AFC
Aluminum Foil Container Manufacturers Association (EA) .... AFCMA
Aluminum Foil Field Coil .... AFFC
Aluminum Four Barrel Carburetor [*Automotive engineering*] (DICI) ...... AFB
Aluminum Fracture Toughness Database [*Information service or system*] (IID) .... ALFRAC
Aluminum Gallium Arsenide (IEEE) .... AlGaAs
Aluminum Glycinate [*Also, ADA*] [*Pharmacology*] .... ALGLYN
Aluminum Hydroxide [*Antacid*] [*Pharmacology*] (DAVI) .... $Al(OH)_3$
Aluminum Intensive Vehicle [*Auto industry*] .... AIV
Aluminum Isopropoxide [*or Isopropylate*] [*Organic chemistry*] .... AIP

Aluminum Linear Shaped Charge (PDAA) .... ALSC
Aluminum Manufacturers Credit Bureau [*Defunct*] (EA) .... AMCB
Aluminum Matting [*Military*] .... AM
Aluminum, Nickel, Cobalt [*Alloy*] .... ALNICO
Aluminum Perchlorate (MCD) .... AP
Aluminum Plasma Model (MCD) .... ALPLASMA
Aluminum Powder Metallurgy .... APM
Aluminum Powder Metallurgy Product .... APMP
Aluminum Recycling Association (EA) .... ARA
Aluminum Research Institute .... ARI
Aluminum Secretariat Ltd., Montreal, PQ, Canada [*Library symbol Library of Congress*] (LCLS) .... CaQMA
Aluminum Siding Association [*Later, AAMA*] (EA) .... ASA
Aluminum Silicate Pigment .... ASP
Aluminum Silicon [*An alloy*] .... ALSI
Aluminum, Silicon, Calcium, Magnesium [*Geology*] .... ASCM
Aluminum Smelters Research Institute [*Later, ARA*] (EA) .... ASRI
Aluminum Structured Vehicle [*Automotive engineering*] .... ASV
Aluminum Structured Vehicle Technology [*Automotive engineering*] .... ASVT
Aluminum Tartrate (DMAA) .... AIT
Aluminum Triethyl [*Organic chemistry*] .... ATE
Aluminum Trihydrate .... ATH
Aluminum Trimethyl [*Organic chemistry*] .... ATM
Aluminum Tube Multi-Effect (PDAA) .... ATME
Aluminum Wares Association [*Later, CMA*] .... AWA
Aluminum Window Manufacturers Association [*Later, Architectural Aluminum Manufacturers Association*] .... AWMA
Aluminum Workers International Union [*Later, ABCWIU*] (EA) .... AWIU
Aluminum Workers International Union [*Later, ABCWIU*] .... AWU
Aluminum-Clad (MSA) .... ALCD
Aluminum(dihydroxy)allantoinate [*Organic chemistry*] .... ALDA
Aluminum-Free Inorganic Suspended Material .... AFISM
Aluminum-Oxide Electrolytic Capacitor (MUGU) .... ALOXCON
Alumnae Advisory Center [*Later, CCP*] (EA) .... AAC
Alumni Association of Shriners Hospitals (EA) .... AASH
Alumni Association of the University of New England [*Australia*] .... AAUNE
Alumni Memorial Library, Orchard Lake, MI [*Library symbol Library of Congress*] (LCLS) .... MiOlA
Alumni Presidents' Council of Independent Secondary Schools (EA) ...... APCISS
Alumni Yalensia [*Alumni of Yale College*] [*Latin*] .... Alum Yalen
Alumnus (ROG) .... ALUM
Alum-Precipitated Protein [*Biochemistry*] (DAVI) .... APP
Alure Resource Corp. [*Vancouver Stock Exchange symbol*] .... ARU
Alushta [*Former USSR Seismograph station code, US Geological Survey Closed*] (SEIS) .... ALU
Aluta [*Leather*] [*Pharmacy*] (ROG) .... ALUT
Alva, OK [*Location identifier FAA*] (FAAL) .... AVK
Alva, OK [*AM radio station call letters*] .... KALV
Alva, OK [*FM radio station call letters*] .... KTTL
Alva, OK [*FM radio station call letters*] .... KXLS
Alveolar [*Gas*] [*Medicine*] .... A
Alveolar [*Anatomy*] .... alv
Alveolar Carbon Dioxide Pressure [*in blood gases*] [*Medicine*] (DAVI) .... PA_{CO2}
Alveolar Cell Carcinoma [*Oncology*] (AAMN) .... ACC
Alveolar Dead-space Volume [*Medicine*] (DAVI) .... V_{DA}
Alveolar Duct (MAE) .... AV
Alveolar Gas Volume [*Medicine*] (DAVI) .... V_A
Alveolar Hypoventilation Syndrome [*Medicine*] (DMAA) .... AHS
Alveolar Lining Material [*Medicine*] (DAVI) .... ALM
Alveolar Macrophage [*Hematology*] .... AM
Alveolar Mixing Efficiency [*Physiology*] .... AME
Alveolar Mucosa [*Medicine*] (DMAA) .... ALVM
Alveolar Oxygen Pressure (WDAA) PAO2
Alveolar Oxygen Pressure [*in blood gases*] [*Medicine*] (DAVI) .... PA_{O2}
Alveolar Pressure [*Medicine*] (DAVI) .... P_A
Alveolar Sac (MAE) .... AS
Alveolar Soft Part Sarcoma [*Oncology*] .... ASPS
Alveolar Tidal Volume [*Medicine*] (DAVI) .... V_{TA}
Alveolar Ventilation .... VA
Alveolar Ventilation per Minute [*Medicine*] (DAVI) .... V_A
Alveolar Volume [*Clinical chemistry*] (AAMN) .... VA
Alveolar-Arterial [*Physiology*] (MAE) .... AA
Alveolar-Arterial Carbon Dioxide Difference [*Biochemistry*] (DAVI) .... $(A-A)P\ CO_2$
Alveolar-Arterial Oxygen Difference [*Physiology*] .... $A\text{-}aDO_2$
Alveolar-Arterial Oxygen Gradient [*Biochemistry*] (DAVI) .... $A\text{-}AO_2$
Alveolar-Arterial Pressure Difference [*For A-aDO$_2$*] [*Medicine*] (DAVI) ..... $P(A\text{-}a)O_2$
Alveolar-Capillary Membrane Permeability [*Medicine*] (DMAA) .... ACMP
Alveolar-Macrophage-Derived Growth Factor [*Biochemistry*] .... AMDGF
Alveolectomy [*Dentistry and maxillofacial surgery*] (DAVI) .... Alvx
Alveolectomy [*Medicine*] (DMAA) .... ALVX
Alverca [*Portugal ICAO location identifier*] (ICLI) .... LPAR
Alverno College, Milwaukee, WI [*OCLC symbol*] (OCLC) .... GZA
Alverno College, Milwaukee, WI [*Library symbol Library of Congress*] (LCLS) .... WMA
Alverno College, Milwaukee, WI [*Library symbol*] [*Library of Congress*] (LCLS) .... WMAC
Alverthorpe Gallery, Rosenwald Collection, Jenkintown, PA [*Library symbol Library of Congress*] (LCLS) .... PJAlG
Alvey Research for Insurance Expert Systems (NITA) .... ARIES
Alvi Dejectiones [*Discharge from the Bowels*] [*Pharmacy*] .... ALV DEJECT
Alvin Ailey American Dance Center .... AAADC
Alvin Junior College [*Texas*] .... AJC
Alvin Junior College, Alvin, TX [*Library symbol Library of Congress*] (LCLS) .... TxAlvC
Alvin, Mid-Atlantic Ridge [*Oceanography*] .... AMAR

Alvin, TX [FM radio station call letters]	KACC
Alvin, TX [Television station call letters]	KHSH
Alvin, TX [AM radio station call letters]	KTEK
Alvin W. Vogtle, Jr. Plant [Nuclear energy] (NRCH)	AVP
Alvis Owners Club [North Droitwich, Worcestershire, England] (EAIO)	AOC
Alvo Adstricta [When the Bowels Are Constipated] [Pharmacy]	ALV ADST
Alvo Adstricta [When the Bowels Are Constipated] [Pharmacy]	Alv Adstrict
Alvsbyn [Sweden ICAO location identifier] (ICLI)	ESUV
Alvus [Stomach] [Medicine] (ROG)	ALV
Always Afloat [Ship's charter]	AA
Always Causing Legal Unrest [An association] (EA)	ACLU
Always On/Dynamic ISDN [Integrated Services Digital Network] [Telecommunications]	AO/DI
Aly Aviation [British ICAO designator] (FAAC)	AAV
Alyemda Democratic Yemen [ICAO designator] (AD)	DY
Alyemda-Democratic Yemen Airlines [ICAO designator] (FAAC)	DYA
Alyeska Air Service [ICAO designator] (FAAC)	ALY
Alyn Corp. [NASDAQ symbol] (SAG)	ALYN
Alyn Corp. [Associated Press] (SAG)	AlynCp
ALZA Corp. [Associated Press] (SAG)	ALZA
Alza Corp. [NYSE symbol] (SAG)	AZA
ALZA Corp. [NYSE symbol] (TTSB)	AZA
Alzamento [Raising, Lifting] [Music]	Alz
Alzheimer Society of Canada [Societe Alzheimer du Canada] (AC)	ASC
Alzheimer Society of Oxford County (AC)	ASOC
Alzheimer Type Dementia [Medicine]	ATD
Alzheimer-Like Senile Dementia [Medicine] (DMAA)	ALSD
Alzheimers Association [Australia]	AA
Alzheimer's Disease [Medicine]	AD
Alzheimer's Disease and Related Conditions [Medicine]	ADRC
Alzheimer's Disease and Related Disorders Association (EA)	ADRDA
Alzheimer's Disease Assessment Scale	ADAS
Alzheimer's Disease Assessment Scale Cognitive Subscale	ADAS-Cog
Alzheimers Disease Education and Referral [Center]	ADEAR
Alzheimer's Disease Education Referral Center (BARN)	ADERC
Alzheimer's Disease International (EA)	ADI
Alzheimer's Disease Research	ADR
Alzheimer's Disease Research Center [Bronx, NY] [Department of Health and Human Services] (GRD)	ADRC
Alzheimer's Disease Society [British]	ADS
Alzheimer's Disease-Associated Protein [Medicine]	ADAP
Alzhirskaia Kommunisticheskaia Partia [Albanian Communist Party] [Political party]	AKP
Am Angefuehrten Orte [At the Place Quoted] [German]	AAO
AM International [AMEX symbol] (TTSB)	AM
AM International [Associated Press] (SAG)	AM In
AM International [Associated Press] (SAG)	AM Intl
AM International, Inc. [Formerly, Addressograph-Multigraph Corp.] [AMEX symbol] (SPSG)	AM
AM Intl Wrrt [AMEX symbol] (TTSB)	AM WS
A.M. MacArthur Primary School, Locust Valley, NY [Library symbol] [Library of Congress] (LCLS)	NLvMP
Am Rhein [on the River Rhine] [German] (ODBW)	a Rh
Ama [Papua New Guinea] [Airport symbol] (OAG)	AMF
Ama Air Express [ICAO designator] (AD)	YD
AMA [American Management Association]/International [New York, NY] (EA)	AMA/I
Amacrine Cell [of the retina] [Optics]	AM
Amadeo [Record label] [Austria, etc.]	Ama
Amadeus Global Travel Distrution SA [Spain ICAO designator] (FAAC)	AGT
Amadeusair GmbH [Austria ICAO designator] (FAAC)	AMU
Amador Central Railroad Co. [AAR code]	AMC
Amador County Free Library, Jackson, CA [Library symbol Library of Congress] (LCLS)	CJ
Amador Heritage Center, Almelund, MN [Library symbol] [Library of Congress] (LCLS)	MnAlmA
Ama-Flyg [ICAO designator] (AD)	VW
Amagansett Free Library, Amagansett, NY [Library symbol Library of Congress] (LCLS)	NAma
Amagansett Historical Association, Amagansett, NY [Library symbol Library of Congress] (LCLS)	NAmaHi
Amagat-Leduc Rule [Physics]	ALR
Amahai [Indonesia] [Airport symbol] (OAG)	AHI
Amahai [Indonesia] [ICAO location identifier] (ICLI)	WAPA
Amalagmated Society of Engineers, Machinists, Smiths, Millwrights, and Pattern Makers [A union] [British]	ASEMSMP
Amalfi [Colombia] [Airport symbol] (AD)	AFI
Amalgam [Dentistry]	AM
Amalgam [Metallurgy]	AMLG
Amalgama [Amalgamation] [Pharmacy] (ROG)	AAA
Amalgamate Paper Books [British]	APB
Amalgamated (ADA)	AMAL
Amalgamated (EY)	AMALG
Amalgamated Association of Beamers, Twisters, and Drawers [A union] [British] (DCTA)	AABTD
Amalgamated Association of Brass Founders, Turners, Fitters, and Coppersmiths [A union] [British]	AABFTFC
Amalgamated Association of Felt Hat Trimmers and Wool Formers [A union] [British] (DCTA)	AAFHTWF
Amalgamated Association of Felt Hat Trimmers and Wool Formers [A union] [British] (DCTA)	AFHTWF
Amalgamated Association of Machine Workers [A union] [British]	AAMW
Amalgamated Association of Street, Electric Railway, and Motor Coach Employees of America [Later, ATU]	SERMCE
Amalgamated Association of Wistful War Wives [World War II]	AAWWW
Amalgamated Book Services [British]	ABS
Amalgamated Carriage and Wagon Society [A union] [British]	ACWS
Amalgamated Clothing and Textile Workers Union (EA)	ACTWU
Amalgamated Clothing Workers of America [Later, ACTWU] (EA)	ACWA
Amalgamated Conservation Society (AC)	ACS
Amalgamated Drillers and Hole Cutters Society [A union] [British]	ADHCS
Amalgamated Engineering Union [United Kingdom]	AEU
Amalgamated Engineering Union. Monthly Journal [A publication]	Amal Engng Union Mon J
Amalgamated Flying Saucer Clubs of America (EA)	AFSCA
Amalgamated Footwear and Textile Workers' Union of Australia	AFTWUA
Amalgamated Gas Accumulation [Stove designed by Gustaf Dalen in 1922]	AGA
Amalgamated Hackle Pin Grinders Sick and Mutual Benefit Society [British]	AHPGSMBS
Amalgamated Instrument Makers Society [A union] [British]	AIMS
Amalgamated Lace Operatives of America	ALO
Amalgamated Lace Operatives of America [Defunct] (EA)	ALOA
Amalgamated Lithographers of America [Later, GAIU]	ALA
Amalgamated Lithographers of America (DGA)	ALOA
Amalgamated Machine and General Labourers Union [British]	AMGLU
Amalgamated Meat Cutters and Butcher Workmen of North America [Later, UFCWIU] (EA)	AMCBW
Amalgamated Meat Cutters and Butcher Workmen of North America [Later, UFCWIU]	MCBW
Amalgamated Metal Workers and Shipwrights' Union [Australia]	AMSWU
Amalgamated Military and Technical Improvement Plan (DNAB)	AMI
Amalgamated Military Technical (DNAB)	AMT
Amalgamated Milk Vendors' Association of New South Wales [Australia]	AMVANSW
Amalgamated Mining [Vancouver Stock Exchange symbol]	AMA
Amalgamated Moulders and Kindred Industries Trade Union [British]	AMKITU
Amalgamated National Union of Local Authorities Employees' Federation of Malaya	ANULAE
Amalgamated Picture Frame Trade Union [British]	APFTU
Amalgamated Power Engineering (ODBW)	APE
Amalgamated Printers' Association (EA)	APA
Amalgamated Printing Trades Employees' Union [Australia] (DGA)	APTEU
Amalgamated Publishers, Inc.	API
Amalgamated Scale, Beam, and Weighing Machine Makers Association [A union] [British]	ASBWMMA
Amalgamated Sewing Machine, Cycle, and Tool Makers Association [A union] [British]	ASMCTMA
Amalgamated Shipyard Helpers Association [A union] [British]	ASHA
Amalgamated Slaters, Tilers and Roofing Operatives Society [British] (BI)	ASTRO
Amalgamated Society of Anchorsmiths, Ship Tackle, and Shackle Makers [A union] [British]	ASASTSM
Amalgamated Society of Boilermakers, Shipwrights, Blacksmiths, and Structural Workers [A union] [British] (DCTA)	ASBSBSW
Amalgamated Society of Brass Workers [A union] [British]	ASBW
Amalgamated Society of Casters [A union] [British]	ASC
Amalgamated Society of Coremakers of Great Britain and Ireland [A union]	ASCGBI
Amalgamated Society of Engineers [A union] [British]	ASE
Amalgamated Society of General Tool Makers, Engineers, and Machinists [A union] [British]	ASGTMEM
Amalgamated Society of Journeymen Felt Hatters and Allied Workers [A union] [British] (DCTA)	ASJFHAW
Amalgamated Society of Lithographic Printers (DGA)	ASLP
Amalgamated Society of Metal Workers [A union] [British]	ASMW
Amalgamated Society of Operative Engineers [A union] [British]	ASOE
Amalgamated Society of Plate and Machine Moulders [A union] [British]	ASPMM
Amalgamated Society of Scale Beam and Weighing Machine Makers [A union] [British]	ASSBWMM
Amalgamated Society of Shuttlemakers [A union] [British]	ASS
Amalgamated Society of Telegraph and Telephone Construction Men [A union] [British]	ASTTCM
Amalgamated Society of Telephone Employees [A union] [British]	ASTE
Amalgamated Society of Textile Workers and Kindred Trades [A union] [British] (DCTA)	ASTWKT
Amalgamated Society of Tobacco Manufacturers [A union] [British]	ASTM
Amalgamated Society of Wire Drawers and Kindred Workers [A union] [British] (DCTA)	ASWDKW
Amalgamated Society of Wood Workers [British]	ASWW
Amalgamated Society of Woodcutting Machinists [British] (BI)	ASWM
Amalgamated Society of Woodworkers [British] (BI)	ASW
Amalgamated Textile Workers' Union [British] (DCTA)	ATWU
Amalgamated Tin Mines of Nigeria	ATMN
Amalgamated Transit Union (EA)	ATU
Amalgamated Typefounders Trade Society (DGA)	ATTS
Amalgamated Union of Asphalt Workers [British] (DCTA)	AUAW
Amalgamated Union of Engineering and Foundry Workers [British]	AUEFW
Amalgamated Union of Engineering Workers [British] (DCTA)	AUEW
Amalgamated Union of Engineering Workers - Constructional [British] (DCTA)	AUEW(C)
Amalgamated Union of Engineering Workers - Engineering [British] (DCTA)	AUEW(E)
Amalgamated Union of Engineering Workers - Foundry [British] (DCTA)	AUEW(F)
Amalgamated Union of Engineering Workers - Technical and Supervisory [British] (DCTA)	AUEW-TASS
Amalgamated Union of Foundry Workers [British]	AUFW
Amalgamated Union of Public Employees [Singapore]	AUPE

Amalgamated Welded Boiler Makers Society [*A union*] [*British*] ... AWBMS
Amalgamated Wireless Australasia Computers Division Services (NITA) ... AWACS
Amalgamated Wireless Australasia Ltd. [*Telecommunications service*] ... AWA
Amalvius de Claris Aquis [*Flourished, 14th century*] [*Authority cited in pre-1607 legal work*] (DSA) ... Amal
Amalvius de Claris Aquis [*Flourished, 14th century*] [*Authority cited in pre-1607 legal work*] (DSA) ... Amalvis
Amami [*Japan ICAO location identifier*] (ICLI) ... RJKA
Amami O Shima [*Japan*] [*Airport symbol*] (OAG) ... ASJ
Amana Heritage Society, Middle Amana, IA [*Library symbol*] [*Library of Congress*] (LCLS) ... IaMidaHA
Amanab [*Papua New Guinea*] [*Airport symbol*] (OAG) ... AMU
Amanda Resources Ltd. [*Vancouver Stock Exchange symbol*] ... AAU
(Amanitinylazobenzoyl)glycylglycine ... ABGG
Amanu [*Tuamotu Archipelago*] [*Seismograph station code, US Geological Survey*] (SEIS) ... AMN
Amapa [*Brazil*] [*Airport symbol*] (AD) ... APA
Amapa [*Brazil ICAO location identifier*] (ICLI) ... SBAM
Amapala [*Honduras*] [*ICAO location identifier*] (ICLI) ... MHAM
AMARC [*Automatic Message Accounting Recording Center*] **Protocol Converter** (TEL) ... APC
Amarillo [*Texas*] [*Airport symbol*] (OAG) ... AMA
Amarillo/Amarillo Air Terminal [*Texas*] [*ICAO location identifier*] (ICLI) ... KAMA
Amarillo Biosciences, Inc. [*NASDAQ symbol*] (SAG) ... AMAR
Amarillo Biosciences, Inc. [*Associated Press*] (SAG) ... AmarBio
Amarillo Branch [*Military*] (SAA) ... AB
Amarillo College, Amarillo, TX [*OCLC symbol*] (OCLC) ... ACC
Amarillo College, Amarillo, TX [*Library symbol Library of Congress*] (LCLS) ... TxAmC
Amarillo Grain Exchange (EA) ... AGE
Amarillo Public Library, Amarillo, TX [*OCLC symbol*] (OCLC) ... TAP
Amarillo Public Library, Amarillo, TX [*Library symbol Library of Congress*] (LCLS) ... TxAm
Amarillo, TX [*FM radio station call letters*] ... KACV
Amarillo, TX [*Television station call letters*] ... KACV-TV
Amarillo, TX [*FM radio station call letters*] ... KAEZ
Amarillo, TX [*Television station call letters*] ... KAMR
Amarillo, TX [*FM radio station call letters*] (RBYB) ... KAPU-FM
Amarillo, TX [*FM radio station call letters*] ... KATP
Amarillo, TX [*FM radio station call letters*] ... KBUY-FM
Amarillo, TX [*Television station call letters*] ... KCIT
Amarillo, TX [*AM radio station call letters*] ... KDJW
Amarillo, TX [*Television station call letters*] ... KFDA
Amarillo, TX [*AM radio station call letters*] ... KGNC
Amarillo, TX [*FM radio station call letters*] ... KGNC-FM
Amarillo, TX [*AM radio station call letters*] ... KIXZ
Amarillo, TX [*FM radio station call letters*] ... KJRT
Amarillo, TX [*FM radio station call letters*] (RBYB) ... KLLR
Amarillo, TX [*FM radio station call letters*] ... KLMN
Amarillo, TX [*FM radio station call letters*] ... KMML
Amarillo, TX [*AM radio station call letters*] ... KPUR
Amarillo, TX [*FM radio station call letters*] ... KPVY
Amarillo, TX [*FM radio station call letters*] ... KQAC
Amarillo, TX [*FM radio station call letters*] ... KQIZ
Amarillo, TX [*FM radio station call letters*] ... KRGN
Amarillo, TX [*AM radio station call letters*] (RBYB) ... KTNZ
Amarillo, TX [*Television station call letters*] ... KVII
Amarillo, TX [*FM radio station call letters*] ... KYFA
Amarillo, TX [*AM radio station call letters*] ... KZIP
Amarillo, TX [*Location identifier FAA*] (FAAL) ... TDW
Amark Explorations Ltd. [*Vancouver Stock Exchange symbol*] ... AMK
Amaryllis Research Institute (EA) ... ARI
Amateur ... A
Amateur ... AMTR
Amateur All-Star Baseball [*An association*] (EA) ... AABI
Amateur Artists Association of America [*Defunct*] (EA) ... AAAA
Amateur Astronomers Association [*Later, AAANY*] ... AAA
Amateur Astronomers Association, Brooklyn, NY [*Library symbol Library of Congress*] (LCLS) ... NBA
Amateur Astronomers Association, Brooklyn, NY [*Library symbol*] [*Library of Congress*] (LCLS) ... NBAA
Amateur Astronomers Association of New York [*Formerly, AAA*] (EA) ... AAANY
Amateur Astronomers Association of New York City [*Later, AAA*] (EA) ... AAANYC
Amateur Astronomers, Inc. (EA) ... AAI
Amateur Athletic Association [*British*] ... AAA
Amateur Athletic Club ... AAC
Amateur Athletic Union of the United States (EA) ... AAU
Amateur Basketball Association [*British*] (BI) ... ABBA
Amateur Basketball Association of Scotland (BI) ... ABAS
Amateur Basketball Association of the United States of America [*Later, USA Basketball*] (EA) ... ABAUSA
Amateur Beekeepers' Association of New South Wales [*Australia*] ... ABANSW
Amateur Beekeepers' Society of South Australia ... ABSSA
Amateur Bicycle League of America [*Later, USCF*] ... ABLA
Amateur Boxing Association [*British*] ... ABA
Amateur Boxing Association of England (EAIO) ... ABAE
Amateur Canoe Association of Western Australia ... ACAWA
Amateur Cartoonist Extraordinary [*National Cartoonists' Society award*] ... ACE
Amateur Chamber Music Players (EA) ... ACMP
Amateur Drama League [*Republic of Ireland*] (BI) ... ADL
Amateur Dramatic Club [*British*] ... ADC
Amateur Dramatic Society [*Cambridge, England*] ... ADS
Amateur Entomologists' Society (EA) ... AES
Amateur Fencers League of America [*Later, USFA*] (EA) ... AFLA
Amateur Fencing Association (EAIO) ... AFA
Amateur Field Trial Clubs of America (EA) ... AFTCA
Amateur Fishermen's Association of the Northern Territory ... AFANT
Amateur Football Alliance [*British*] (BI) ... AFA
Amateur Golfers' Association of America (EA) ... AGA
Amateur Golfers' Association of America [*Defunct*] (EA) ... AGAA
Amateur Gymnastics Association (WDAA) ... AGA
Amateur Hockey Association of the United States (EA) ... AHAUS
Amateur Martial Association [*British*] (DBA) ... AMA
Amateur Microprocessor Teleprinter Over Radio ... AMTOR
Amateur Motor Cycle Association [*British*] (DBA) ... AMCA
Amateur Music Association [*British*] (DBA) ... AMA
Amateur Organist Association International (EA) ... AOAI
Amateur Organists and Keyboard Association International (EA) ... AOKAI
Amateur Pistol Shooting Union of Australia ... APSU
Amateur Press Alliance [*Defunct*] (EA) ... APA
Amateur Press Association [*Generic term*] ... APA
Amateur Printers' Association (DGA) ... APA
Amateur Publishers' Association ... APA
Amateur Publishers' Association Magazine [*Generic term for one-person science-fiction fan magazine*] ... APAZINE
Amateur Radio Club (LAIN) ... ARC
Amateur Radio Direction Finding ... ARDF
Amateur Radio Emergency Corps [*of ARPSC*] ... AREC
Amateur Radio Emergency Service ... ARES
Amateur Radio League (SAA) ... ARL
Amateur Radio Monitor ... ARM
Amateur Radio Public Service Corps ... ARPSC
Amateur Radio Research and Development Corp. (IID) ... AMRAD
Amateur Radio Service (ECII) ... ARS
Amateur (Radio) Station [*ITU designation*] (CET) ... AR
Amateur Radio Station (IDOE) ... ARS
Amateur Radio Technical Abstracts ... ARTA
Amateur Riders Association [*British*] (DBA) ... ARA
Amateur Rocketeers of America ... ARA
Amateur Rose Breeders Association [*British*] (DBA) ... ARBA
Amateur Rowing Association [*British*] ... ARA
Amateur Rowing Association of Western Australia ... ARAWA
Amateur Scientist Research Organization (EA) ... ASRO
Amateur Skating Union of the United States (WGA) ... ASUUS
Amateur Skating Union of the United States of America (EA) ... ASU-USA
Amateur Softball Association of America (EA) ... ASA
Amateur Station [*ITU designation*] ... AT
Amateur Swimming Association ... ASA
Amateur Television (MSA) ... ATV
Amateur Television Association (EA) ... ATA
Amateur Traffic Net [*Radio*] ... ATN
Amateur Trapshooting Association (EA) ... ATA
Amateur Volleyball Association [*British*] (BI) ... AVA
Amateur Volume Control ... AVC
Amateur Yacht Research Society [*Turnchapel, Plymouth, England*] (EAIO) ... AYRS
Amatex Export Trade Association [*Defunct*] (EA) ... AETA
Amati Communications [*NASDAQ symbol*] (TTSB) ... AMTX
Amati Communications Corp. [*Associated Press*] (SAG) ... Amati
Amati Communications Corp. [*NASDAQ symbol*] (SAG) ... AMTX
Amatignak Island [*Alaska*] [*Seismograph station code, US Geological Survey Closed*] (SEIS) ... AMA
Amatol [*Materials*] ... AM
Amatorius [*of Plutarch*] [*Classical studies*] (OCD) ... Amat
Amatsia [*Israel*] [*Geomagnetic observatory code*] ... AMT
Amaurosis Fugax [*Medicine*] (DMAA) ... AF
Amaurotic Familial Idiocy ... AFI
Amax Gold [*Associated Press*] (SAG) ... Amax
Amax Gold $3.75 SrB'Cv Pfd [*NYSE symbol*] (TTSB) ... AUPrB
Amax Gold, Inc. [*Associated Press*] (SAG) ... AmaxG
Amax Gold, Inc. [*NYSE symbol*] (SPSG) ... AU
Amax Gold, Inc. [*Toronto Stock Exchange symbol*] ... AXG
AMAX, Inc. [*Formerly, Alumax, Inc., American Metal Climax, Inc.*] [*NYSE symbol Toronto Stock Exchange symbol*] (SPSG) ... AMX
AMAX, Inc., Golden, CO [*Library symbol Library of Congress*] (LCLS) ... CoGA
Amazing Magic Pivot Swing [*Training device for baseball batter's rear foot*] ... AMPS
Amazon Bay [*Papua New Guinea*] [*Airport symbol*] (OAG) ... AZB
Amazon Boundary Layer Experiment (MCD) ... ABLE
Amazon Ground Emissions (MCD) ... AGE
Amazon Petroleum Corp. [*Vancouver Stock Exchange symbol*] ... AMZ
Amazon River and Basin [*MARC geographic area code Library of Congress*] (LCCP) ... sa----
AMB Financial [*NASDAQ symbol*] (TTSB) ... AMFC
AMB Financial Corp. [*Associated Press*] (SAG) ... AMBFinl
AMB Financial Corp. [*NASDAQ symbol*] (SAG) ... AMFC
AMBAC, Inc. [*NYSE symbol*] (SPSG) ... ABK
Ambac, Inc. [*Associated Press*] (SAG) ... Ambac
Ambalavao [*Madagascar*] [*ICAO location identifier*] (ICLI) ... FMSA
Ambanc Corp. [*Associated Press*] (SAG) ... Ambanc
Ambanc Corp. [*NASDAQ symbol*] (SAG) ... AMBK
Ambanc Holding Co., Inc. [*NASDAQ symbol*] (SAG) ... AHCI
Ambanc Holding Co., Inc. [*Associated Press*] (SAG) ... AmbancH
Ambanja [*Madagascar*] [*ICAO location identifier*] (ICLI) ... FMNJ
Ambanja [*Madagascar*] [*Airport symbol*] (OAG) ... IVA
Ambar [*Pakistan*] [*Seismograph station code, US Geological Survey*] (SEIS) ... AMP
Ambar, Inc. [*Associated Press*] (SAG) ... Ambar
Ambar, Inc. [*NASDAQ symbol*] (SAG) ... AMBR

Ambassador ... AMB
Ambassador ... AMB
Ambassador ... Ambass
Ambassador Airways Ltd. [*British ICAO designator*] (FAAC) ... AMY
Ambassador Apartments, Inc. [*NYSE symbol*] (SAG) ... AAH
Ambassador Apartments, Inc. [*Associated Press*] (SAG) ... AmbssApt
Ambassador College, Big Sandy, TX [*Library symbol Library of Congress*] (LCLS) ... TxBsaA
Ambassador College Library, Pasadena, CA [*Library symbol*] [*Library of Congress*] (LCLS) ... CPAC
Ambassador College, Pasadena, CA [*OCLC symbol*] (OCLC) ... ACL
Ambassador College, Pasadena, CA [*Library symbol Library of Congress*] (LCLS) ... CPA
Ambassador Extraordinary and Plenipotentiary [*Diplomacy*] ... AE & P
Ambassador Industries Ltd. [*Vancouver Stock Exchange symbol*] ... AMS
Ambassador of the United States ... AUS
Ambassador's Club [*TWA's club for frequent flyers*] (EA) ... AC
Ambassadors for Friendship (EA) ... AF
Ambassadors in Mission [*Religious organization*] [*Canada*] ... AIM
Ambassadors International, Inc. [*Associated Press*] (SAG) ... AmbIn
Ambassadors International, Inc. [*NASDAQ symbol*] (SAG) ... AMIE
Ambassadors Intl. [*NASDAQ symbol*] (TTSB) ... AMIE
Ambassadors of Mary (EA) ... AM
Ambato [*Ecuador*] [*ICAO location identifier*] (ICLI) ... SEAM
Ambatomainty [*Madagascar*] [*Airport symbol*] (OAG) ... AMY
Ambatondrazaka [*Madagascar*] [*ICAO location identifier*] (ICLI) ... FMMZ
Ambatondrazaka [*Madagascar*] [*Airport symbol*] (OAG) ... WAM
Amber (AAG) ... A
Amber ... AM
Amber (MSA) ... AMB
Amber (VRA) ... amb
Amber (DAVI) ... AMBR
Amber Airways Ltd. [*British ICAO designator*] (FAAC) ... ABM
Amber Boron Nitride (PDAA) ... ABN
Amber Light (MSA) ... AL
Amber Light (IAA) ... ALT
Amber University, Garland, TX [*Library symbol*] [*Library of Congress*] (LCLS) ... TxGarA
Amberg [*Germany ICAO location identifier*] (ICLI) ... EDEA
Ambergate Exploration [*Vancouver Stock Exchange symbol*] ... AGQ
Amberhill Petroleum Ltd. [*Vancouver Stock Exchange symbol*] ... APT
Amberieu [*France ICAO location identifier*] (ICLI) ... LFXA
Amberley [*Australia ICAO location identifier*] (ICLI) ... ABAM
Amberley [*New Zealand*] [*Later, EYR*] [*Geomagnetic observatory code*] ... AML
Amberquest Resources Ltd. [*Vancouver Stock Exchange symbol*] ... AMB
Ambert-Le-Poyet [*France ICAO location identifier*] (ICLI) ... LFHT
AMBI, Inc. [*Associated Press*] (SAG) ... AMBI
AMBI, Inc. [*NASDAQ symbol*] (SAG) ... AMBI
Ambiance ... AMBNC
Ambient [*Electronics*] ... A
Ambient (KSC) ... AM
Ambient (MSA) ... AMB
Ambient Absolute Pressure (PDAA) ... AAP
Ambient Air Control Panel [*Army*] ... AACP
Ambient Air Cooling System [*Military*] ... AACS
Ambient Air Quality Standard (EG) ... AAQS
Ambient Air Ventilation Microclimate System [*Army*] (RDA) ... AVMCS
Ambient Multimedia Environmental Goals [*Environmental Protection Agency*] ... AMEG
Ambient Noise [*Composite of sounds present at a given spot in the ocean*] (NVT) ... AN
Ambient Noise and Data System [*Pacific Missile Range*] (MCD) ... ANADS
Ambient Noise Background ... ANB
Ambient Noise Directionality Estimator (MCD) ... ANODE
Ambient Noise Index (CAAL) ... ANI
Ambient Noise Measurement (CAAL) ... ANM
Ambient Quality Standard [*Environmental science*] (FFDE) ... AQS
Ambient Temperature ... AT
Ambient Temperature and Pressure, Dry [*Medicine*] ... ATPD
Ambient Temperature and Pressure, Saturated [*Medicine*] ... ATPS
Ambient Temperature Observer/Predictor (MCD) ... ATOP
Ambient Temperature Range ... ATR
Ambiguity [*Used in correcting manuscripts, etc.*] ... A
Ambiguity [*or Ambiguous*] (MCD) ... AMBIG
Ambiguity Eliminator [*Electronics*] ... AMBEL
Ambiguity Reference Tone (MCD) ... ART
Ambiguous [*Used in correcting manuscripts, etc.*] ... AMB
Ambiguous Genitalia Support Network (PAZ) ... AGSN
Ambilobe [*Madagascar*] [*Airport symbol*] (OAG) ... AMB
Ambilobe [*Madagascar*] [*ICAO location identifier*] (ICLI) ... FMNE
Ambitendency [*Psychology*] ... A
Ambitious (DSUE) ... AMBI
Amble Resources Ltd. [*Vancouver Stock Exchange symbol*] ... ALU
Ambler [*Alaska*] [*Airport symbol*] (OAG) ... ABL
Ambler, AK [*Location identifier FAA*] (FAAL) ... AMF
Ambler, PA [*Location identifier FAA*] (FAAL) ... ING
Ambler's Reports, Chancery [*27 English Reprint*] [*A publication*] (DLA) ... Amb
Ambler's Reports, Chancery [*27 English Reprint*] [*A publication*] (DLA) ... Ambl
Ambleteuse [*France ICAO location identifier*] (ICLI) ... LFAA
Ambohijanahary [*Madagascar*] [*ICAO location identifier*] (ICLI) ... FMMJ
Amboin [*Papua New Guinea*] [*Airport symbol*] (OAG) ... AMG
Amboina [*Indonesia*] [*Seismograph station code, US Geological Survey*] (SEIS) ... AMO
Amboise/Dierre [*France ICAO location identifier*] (ICLI) ... LFEF
Ambon [*Indonesia*] [*Seismograph station code, US Geological Survey*] ... AAI
Ambon [*Indonesia*] [*Airport symbol*] (OAG) ... AMQ
Ambon/Pattimura [*Indonesia*] [*ICAO location identifier*] (ICLI) ... WAPP
Ambon Sector [*Indonesia*] [*ICAO location identifier*] (ICLI) ... WAPZ
Amboseli [*Kenya*] [*ICAO location identifier*] (ICLI) ... HKAM
Ambridge, PA [*AM radio station call letters*] ... WMBA
Ambriz [*Angola*] [*ICAO location identifier*] (ICLI) ... FNAM
Ambrosius de Vignate [*Flourished, 15th century*] [*Authority cited in pre-1607 legal work*] (DSA) ... Amb de Vig
Ambrosius Opizonus [*Flourished, 15th century*] [*Authority cited in pre-1607 legal work*] (DSA) ... Ambr Opizo
Ambrotype (VRA) ... ATYP
Ambulance (AFM) ... AMB
Ambulance ... AMBL
Ambulance and Medical Service Association of America [*Later, AAA*] (EA) ... AMSAA
Ambulance Association of America [*Later, AAA*] ... AA of A
Ambulance Association of America [*Later, AAA*] (EA) ... AAOA
Ambulance Association of Pennsylvania (SRA) ... AAP
Ambulance Corps (ADA) ... AC
Ambulance Design Criteria [*National Highway Transportation Safety Administration*] ... ADC
Ambulance Driver ... AD
Ambulance Employees' Association of Tasmania [*Australia*] ... AEAT
Ambulance Employees' Association of Victoria [*Australia*] ... AEAV
Ambulance Exchange Point [*Army*] (INF) ... AXP
Ambulance Loading Post [*Military*] ... ALP
Ambulance Manufacturers Association [*Later, TBEA*] (EA) ... AMA
Ambulance Manufacturers Division [*An association*] (EA) ... AMD
Ambulance Officer ... AO
Ambulance Plane [*Navy symbol*] ... VH
Ambulance Service Institute [*British*] (DBA) ... ASI
Ambulance Superintendents' Association of Queensland [*Australia*] ... ASAQ
Ambulances for Nicaragua (EA) ... AN
Ambulancias Insulares SA [*Spain ICAO designator*] (FAAC) ... AIM
Ambulate with Assistance [*Medicine*] ... AWA
Ambulatory [*Medicine*] ... A
Ambulatory [*or Ambulation*] [*Also, AMBUL*] [*Medicine*] ... AMB
Ambulatory (AABC) ... AMBT
Ambulatory [*or Ambulation*] [*Also, AMB*] [*Medicine*] ... AMBUL
Ambulatory (VRA) ... ambul
Ambulatory Blood Pressure Monitoring [*Medicine*] ... ABPM
Ambulatory Care [*Medicine*] (DAVI) ... A/C
Ambulatory Care Clinic [*or Center*] [*Medicine*] ... ACC
Ambulatory Care Research Facility [*Medicine*] (DMAA) ... ACRF
Ambulatory Care Research Facility (DMAA) ... ACRF
Ambulatory Care - Sensitive Condition ... ACSC
Ambulatory Care Utilization Review [*Insurance*] (WYGK) ... ACUR
Ambulatory Diagnostic Group [*Medicine*] (DMAA) ... ADG
Ambulatory Electrocardiogram (MCD) ... AECG
Ambulatory Health Care Information System ... AHCIS
Ambulatory Holter Monitoring [*Medicine*] (CPH) ... AHM
Ambulatory Pediatric Association (EA) ... APA
Ambulatory Peritoneal Dialysis [*Medicine*] (CPH) ... APD
Ambulatory Renal Monitoring [*Medicine*] ... ARM
Ambulatory Surgery Facility [*Health insurance*] (GHCT) ... ASF
Ambulatory Surgery Initiative [*Health insurance*] (GHCT) ... ASI
Ambulatory Surgical Center [*Medicine*] ... ASC
Ambulatory Utilization Review ... AUR
Ambulatory Visit Group [*Patient classification*] [*Medicine*] (DAVI) ... AVG
Ambulong [*Philippines*] [*Seismograph station code, US Geological Survey Closed*] (SEIS) ... AMB
Ambunti [*Papua New Guinea*] [*Airport symbol*] (OAG) ... AUJ
Ambush ... AB
Ambush ... AMB
Ambush Communication Equipment [*Military*] ... ACE
Ambush Patrol ... AP
AMC Entertainment [*AMEX symbol*] (TTSB) ... AEN
AMC Entertainment, Inc. [*AMEX symbol*] (SPSG) ... AEN
AMC Entertainment, Inc. [*Associated Press*] (SAG) ... AMC
AMC Entertain't $1.75 Cv Pfd [*AMEX symbol*] (TTSB) ... AENPr
AMC [*Army Materiel Command*] **Logistics Program - Hardcore Automated** ... ALPHA
AMC [*American Motors Corp.*] **Rambler Club** (EA) ... AMCRC
AMCA International Ltd., Ottawa, ON, Canada [*Library symbol Library of Congress*] (LCLS) ... CaOOAI
AMCA International Ltd., Ottawa, Ontario [*Library symbol National Library of Canada*] (NLC) ... OOAI
AMCA Resources Ltd. [*Vancouver Stock Exchange symbol*] ... AMC
Amcan Cyphermaster Ltd. [*Vancouver Stock Exchange symbol*] ... ACY
Amcast Industrial [*NYSE symbol*] (SPSG) ... AIZ
Amcast Industrial [*Associated Press*] (SAG) ... Amcast
AMCEL Propulsion Co. [*Later, Northrup Caroline Co.*] (KSC) ... APC
Amcel Propulsion Co., Asheville, NC [*Library symbol Library of Congress*] (LCLS) ... NcAAP
Amchitka [*Alaska*] [*Seismograph station code, US Geological Survey Closed*] (SEIS) ... AEB
Amchitka [*Alaska*] [*Seismograph station code, US Geological Survey Closed*] (SEIS) ... ANA
Amchitka [*Alaska*] [*Seismograph station code, US Geological Survey Closed*] (SEIS) ... ANB
Amchitka [*Alaska*] [*Seismograph station code, US Geological Survey Closed*] (SEIS) ... AND
Amchitka [*Alaska*] [*Seismograph station code, US Geological Survey Closed*] (SEIS) ... ASB

Amchitka [*Alaska*] [*Seismograph station code, US Geological Survey Closed*] (SEIS) .... ASC
Amchitka [*Alaska*] [*Seismograph station code, US Geological Survey Closed*] (SEIS) .... ASD
Amchitka [*Alaska*] [*Seismograph station code, US Geological Survey Closed*] (SEIS) .... AWA
Amchitka, AK [*Location identifier FAA*] (FAAL) .... AHT
Amchitka Central A [*Alaska*] [*Seismograph station code, US Geological Survey Closed*] (SEIS) .... ACA
Amchitka Central B [*Alaska*] [*Seismograph station code, US Geological Survey Closed*] (SEIS) .... ACB
Amchitka Central C [*Alaska*] [*Seismograph station code, US Geological Survey Closed*] (SEIS) .... ACC
Amchitka Central D [*Alaska*] [*Seismograph station code, US Geological Survey Closed*] (SEIS) .... ACD
Amchitka Central E [*Alaska*] [*Seismograph station code, US Geological Survey Closed*] (SEIS) .... ACE
Amchitka Central F [*Alaska*] [*Seismograph station code, US Geological Survey Closed*] (SEIS) .... ACF
Amchitka East [*Alaska*] [*Seismograph station code, US Geological Survey Closed*] (SEIS) .... AME
Amco Industrial Holdings Ltd. [*Toronto Stock Exchange symbol*] .... AMO
Amcol International Corp. [*NASDAQ symbol*] (SAG) .... ACOL
Amcol International Corp. [*Associated Press*] (SAG) .... AMCOL
Amcol International Corp. [*Associated Press*] (SAG) .... Amcol Int
AMCOL Intl. [*NASDAQ symbol*] (TTSB) .... ACOL
AMCON Distributing [*Associated Press*] (SAG) .... AMCON
AMCON Distributing [*NASDAQ symbol*] (TTSB) .... DIST
AMCON Distributing [*NASDAQ symbol*] (SAG) .... DIST
Amcor Capital Ltd. [*Associated Press*] (SAG) .... Amcor
Amcor Ltd. [*NASDAQ symbol*] (SAG) .... AMCP
Amcor Ltd. [*NASDAQ symbol*] (SAG) .... AMCR
Amcor Limited ADR [*NASDAQ symbol*] (TTSB) .... AMCRY
Amcore Financial [*Associated Press*] (SAG) .... AmcorFn
Amcore Financial [*NASDAQ symbol*] (SAG) .... AMFI
Amcot, Inc. (EA) .... AI
Amdahl Corp. [*Associated Press*] (SAG) .... AMDHL
Amdahl Corp. [*AMEX symbol*] (SPSG) .... AMH
Amdahl Diagnostics Assistance Center .... AMDAC
Amdahl Internally Developed Software .... AIDS
Amdahl Users Group (EA) .... AUG
Amdar [*Afghanistan*] [*ICAO location identifier*] (ICLI) .... OAAD
Amderma [*Former USSR Seismograph station code, US Geological Survey Closed*] (SEIS) .... AMD
AMDF [*Army Master Data File*] **Positive Improvement Program** (MCD) .... APIP
AMDF [*Army Master Data File*] **Reader Microfilm System** [*Formerly, AMDFRMS*] (AABC) .... ARMS
Amdura Corp. [*Associated Press*] (SAG) .... Amdura
Amebiasis [*Medicine*] (DAVI) .... AMEBIA
Amebic Prevalence Rate (MAE) .... APR
AMEDISYS, Inc. [*Associated Press*] (SAG) .... AMDSYS
AMEDISYS, Inc. [*NASDAQ symbol*] (SAG) .... AMED
Amegroid Society of America (EA) .... ASA
Ameican Medical Technologies, Inc. [*NASDAQ symbol*] (SAG) .... AMTI
Ameland [*Netherlands ICAO location identifier*] (ICLI) .... EHAL
Amelia Earhart Collectors Club (EA) .... AEC
Amelia Earhart Collectors Club (EA) .... AECC
Amelia Earhart Research Consortium (EA) .... AERC
Ameliasburgh Historical Society, Ontario [*Library symbol National Library of Canada*] (BIB) .... OAMHS
Amelioration .... AMLRTN
Amend .... AMD
Amend [*or Amendment*] (AFM) .... AMND
Amend Existing Orders Pertaining To .... AEOP
Amended (DLA) .... A
Amended Basis of Issue Plan [*DoD*] .... ABOIP
Amended Basis of Issue Plan, Feeder Data [*DoD*] .... ABOIPFD
Amended Clearance [*Aviation*] (FAAC) .... AMCL
Amended Operator and Maintenance Decision [*Army*] .... AOMD
Amended Program Decision Memorandum [*Navy*] (NVT) .... APDM
Amended Route of Flight [*Aviation*] .... AMRF
Amended Shipping Instruction [*Military*] .... ASI
Amended Shipping Instrument (MCD) .... ASI
Amendment .... AM
Amendment (AABC) .... AMDT
Amendment .... AMEND
Amendment .... AMENDT
Amendment /Query [*Computer science*] (NITA) .... A/Q
Amendment Request [*Navy*] .... AR
Amendment to the Constitution (DLA) .... Const Amend
Amendment to the Constitution of the United States (DLA) .... ACUS
Amendment to the Constitution of the United States (DLA) .... Const US Amend
Amendment to the Final Qualitative and Quantitative Personnel Requirements Information (MCD) .... AFQQPRI
Amendments and Additions (DLA) .... A & A
Amendola [*Italy ICAO location identifier*] (ICLI) .... LIBA
Amenorrhea and Hirsutism [*Endocrinology*] (MAE) .... AH
Amenorrhea/Hyperprolactinemia [*Endocrinology*] .... A/H
Amer Bancorp Nevada [*NASDAQ symbol*] (TTSB) .... ABCN
Amer Bancorp Ohio [*NASDAQ symbol*] (TTSB) .... AMBC
Amer Bancshares [*NASDAQ symbol*] (TTSB) .... ABAN
Amer Bank, Conn [*AMEX symbol*] (TTSB) .... BKC
Amer Bankers Insur Grp [*NASDAQ symbol*] (TTSB) .... ABIG
Amer Banknote [*NYSE symbol*] (TTSB) .... ABN
Amer Biltrite [*AMEX symbol*] (TTSB) .... ABL

AMER BINGO & GAMING [*NASDAQ symbol*] (TTSB) .... BNGO
Amer Bingo & Gaming Wrrt [*NASDAQ symbol*] (TTSB) .... BNGOW
Amer Biogenetic Sciences'A' [*NASDAQ symbol*] (TTSB) .... MABXA
Amer Body Armor & Equip [*AMEX symbol*] (TTSB) .... ABE
Amer Brands [*AMB*] (TTSB) .... AMEL
AMER BRANDS $2.67 CV Pfd [*NYSE symbol*] (TTSB) .... AMBPrA
Amer Buildings [*NASDAQ symbol*] (TTSB) .... ABCO
Amer Business Computers [*NASDAQ symbol*] (TTSB) .... ABCC
Amer Business Information [*NASDAQ symbol*] (TTSB) .... ABII
Amer Business Prod [*NYSE symbol*] (TTSB) .... ABP
Amer Casino Enterprises [*NASDAQ symbol*] (TTSB) .... ACES
Amer Claims Evaluation [*NASDAQ symbol*] (TTSB) .... AMCE
Amer Classic Voyages [*NASDAQ symbol*] (TTSB) .... AMCV
Amer Coin Merchandising [*NASDAQ symbol*] (TTSB) .... AMCN
Amer Communications Svcs [*NASDAQ symbol*] (TTSB) .... ACNS
Amer Complex Care [*NASDAQ symbol*] (TTSB) .... ACCI
Amer Dental Technologies [*NASDAQ symbol*] (TTSB) .... ADLI
Amer Eagle Outfitters [*NASDAQ symbol*] (TTSB) .... AEOS
Amer Eco Corp. [*NASDAQ symbol*] (TTSB) .... ECGOF
Amer Ecology [*NASDAQ symbol*] (TTSB) .... ECOLE
Amer Educational Prd [*NASDAQ symbol*] (TTSB) .... AMEP
Amer Electric Pwr [*NYSE symbol*] (TTSB) .... AEP
Amer Exp 6.25% 'DECS' '96 [*NYSE symbol*] (TTSB) .... AXD
Amer Explor Cv Dep'C'Pfd [*AMEX symbol*] (TTSB) .... AXPrC
Amer Exploration(New) [*AMEX symbol*] (TTSB) .... AX
Amer Express [*NYSE symbol*] (TTSB) .... AXP
Amer Federal Bank [*NASDAQ symbol*] (TTSB) .... AMER
Amer Filtrona [*NASDAQ symbol*] (TTSB) .... AFIL
Amer Finl Group [*NYSE symbol*] (TTSB) .... AFG
Amer First Finl 1987-A Fd [*NASDAQ symbol*] (TTSB) .... AFFFZ
Amer First Prep Fd 2 L.P. [*AMEX symbol*] (TTSB) .... PF
Amer First Ptc/Pfd Eqty Mtg [*NASDAQ symbol*] (TTSB) .... AFPFZ
Amer First Tax Exempt Mtg 2 [*NASDAQ symbol*] (TTSB) .... ATAXZ
Amer First Tax Exempt Mtg L.P. [*NASDAQ symbol*] (TTSB) .... AFTXZ
Amer Freightways [*NASDAQ symbol*] (TTSB) .... AFWY
Amer Fuel [*NASDAQ symbol*] (TTSB) .... COAL
Amer Fuel Unit [*NASDAQ symbol*] (TTSB) .... COALU
Amer General [*NASDAQ symbol*] (TTSB) .... AGC
Amer Genl 7% Cv Pfd [*NYSE symbol*] (TTSB) .... AGCPrD
Amer Genl 8.45% 'MIPS' [*NYSE symbol*] (TTSB) .... AGCPrM
Amer Genl 8.125% 'MIPS' [*NYSE symbol*] (TTSB) .... AGCPrN
Amer Gen'l Del LLC 6% Cv'MIPS' [*NYSE symbol*] (TTSB) .... AGCPrC
Amer Gvt Income Portfolio [*NYSE symbol*] (TTSB) .... AAF
Amer Healthcorp [*NASDAQ symbol*] (TTSB) .... AMHC
Amer Homestar [*NASDAQ symbol*] (TTSB) .... HSTR
Amer Industrial Prop [*NYSE symbol*] (TTSB) .... IND
Amer Intl. Petroleum [*NASDAQ symbol*] (TTSB) .... AIPN
Amer Israeli Paper Ord [*AMEX symbol*] (TTSB) .... AIP
Amer List [*AMEX symbol*] (TTSB) .... AMZ
Amer Locker Group [*NASDAQ symbol*] (TTSB) .... ALGI
Amer Media CI'A' [*NYSE symbol*] (TTSB) .... ENQ
Amer Media Wrrt [*NYSE symbol*] (TTSB) .... ENQWS
Amer Medical Response [*NYSE symbol*] (TTSB) .... EMT
Amer Mgmt Systems [*NASDAQ symbol*] (TTSB) .... AMSY
Amer Mobile Satellite [*NASDAQ symbol*] (TTSB) .... SKYC
Amer Muni Income Portfolio [*NYSE symbol*] (TTSB) .... XAA
Amer Muni Term Trust [*NYSE symbol*] (TTSB) .... AXT
Amer Muni Term Trust II [*NYSE symbol*] (TTSB) .... BXT
Amer Natl Bancorp [*NASDAQ symbol*] (TTSB) .... ANBK
Amer Natl Insur [*NASDAQ symbol*] (TTSB) .... ANAT
Amer Oilfield Divers [*NASDAQ symbol*] (TTSB) .... DIVE
Amer Oncology Res [*NASDAQ symbol*] (TTSB) .... AORI
Amer Opportunity Income [*NYSE symbol*] (TTSB) .... OIF
Amer Pac Bk Aumsville OR [*NASDAQ symbol*] (TTSB) .... AMPBA
Amer Pacific [*NASDAQ symbol*] (TTSB) .... APFC
Amer Paging [*AMEX symbol*] (TTSB) .... APP
Amer Physicans Svc Gr [*NASDAQ symbol*] (TTSB) .... AMPH
Amer Portable Telecom [*NASDAQ symbol*] (TTSB) .... APTI
Amer Precision Indus [*NYSE symbol*] (TTSB) .... APR
Amer President Cos. [*NYSE symbol*] (TTSB) .... APS
Amer Radio Systems'A' [*NASDAQ symbol*] (TTSB) .... AMRD
Amer Re Capital 8.50% 'QUIPS' [*NYSE symbol*] (TTSB) .... ARNPrA
Amer Re Corp. [*NYSE symbol*] (TTSB) .... ARN
Amer R.E. Ptnrs 5%'PIK'Pfd [*NYSE symbol*] (TTSB) .... ACPPr
Amer Real Estate Investment [*AMEX symbol*] (TTSB) .... REA
Amer Realty Tr SBI [*NYSE symbol*] (TTSB) .... ARB
Amer Recreation Ctrs [*NASDAQ symbol*] (TTSB) .... AMRC
Amer R.E.Ptnrs L.P. [*NYSE symbol*] (TTSB) .... ACP
Amer Res Del Wrrt [*NASDAQ symbol*] (TTSB) .... GASSW
Amer Resource [*NASDAQ symbol*] (TTSB) .... AREE
Amer Resources Del [*NASDAQ symbol*] (TTSB) .... GASS
Amer Restaurant Ptnrs'A' [*AMEX symbol*] (TTSB) .... RMC
Amer Rice [*NASDAQ symbol*] (TTSB) .... RICE
Amer Safety Closure [*NASDAQ symbol*] (TTSB) .... CLOS
Amer Safety Razor [*NASDAQ symbol*] (TTSB) .... RAZR
Amer Science & Engr [*AMEX symbol*] (TTSB) .... ASE
Amer Sensors [*NASDAQ symbol*] (TTSB) .... SNIFF
Amer Service Group [*NASDAQ symbol*] (TTSB) .... ASGR
Amer Shared Hosp Sv [*AMEX symbol*] (TTSB) .... AMS
Amer Software'A' [*NASDAQ symbol*] (TTSB) .... AMSWA
Amer Standard [*NYSE symbol*] (TTSB) .... ASD
Amer States Financial [*NYSE symbol*] (TTSB) .... ASX
Amer Stores [*NYSE symbol*] (TTSB) .... ASC
Amer Strategic Inc. Portfol III [*NYSE symbol*] (TTSB) .... CSP
Amer Strategic Inc. Portfolio [*NYSE symbol*] (TTSB) .... ASP

Amer Strategic Inc. Portfolio II [*NYSE symbol*] (TTSB) .... BSP
Amer Studios [*NASDAQ symbol*] (TTSB) .... AMST
Amer Superconductor [*NASDAQ symbol*] (TTSB) .... AMSC
Amer Techl Ceramics [*AMEX symbol*] (TTSB) .... AMK
Amer Telecasting [*NASDAQ symbol*] (TTSB) .... ATEL
Amer Toys [*NASDAQ symbol*] (TTSB) .... ATOY
Amer Travellers [*NASDAQ symbol*] (TTSB) .... ATVC
Amer United Global [*NASDAQ symbol*] (TTSB) .... AUGI
Amer Vanguard [*NASDAQ symbol*] (TTSB) .... AMGD
Amer Wagering [*NASDAQ symbol*] (TTSB) .... BETM
Amer Waste Svcs'A' [*NYSE symbol*] (TTSB) .... AW
Amer Water Wks 5%Pref [*NYSE symbol*] (TTSB) .... AWKPrA
Amer Water Wks,5% Pfd [*NYSE symbol*] (TTSB) .... AWKPrB
Amer Water Works [*NYSE symbol*] (TTSB) .... AWK
Amer Woodmark [*NASDAQ symbol*] (TTSB) .... AMWD
Amerada Hess Corp. [*NYSE symbol Toronto Stock Exchange symbol*]
    (SPSG) .... AHC
Amerada-Hess Corp. [*Associated Press*] (SAG) .... AmHes
Ameralia Inc. [*NASDAQ symbol*] (TTSB) .... AALA
Ameralia, Inc. [*NASDAQ symbol*] (SAG) .... AALA
Ameralia, Inc. [*Associated Press*] (SAG) .... Ameral
Amerasia Journal [*A publication*] (BRI) .... Amerasia J
Ameravia [*Uruguay*] [*FAA designator*] (FAAC) .... VAM
Amercian League Championship .... ALC
AMERCO [*NYSE symbol*] (SAG) .... ACP
AMERCO [*Associated Press*] (SAG) .... AMERCO
Amerco [*NASDAQ symbol*] (SAG) .... AMOO
AMERCO [*NASDAQ symbol*] (TTSB) .... AMOO
AMERCO [*NYSE symbol*] (SAG) .... AO
AMERCO [*NASDAQ symbol*] (SAG) .... UHAL
Amerco, Inc. [*Associated Press*] (SAG) .... Amerc
AMERCO Sr'A'Pfd [*NYSE symbol*] (TTSB) .... AOPrA
Ameriana Bancorp [*Associated Press*] (SAG) .... Ameriana
Ameriana Bancorp [*Associated Press*] (SAG) .... Amriana
Ameriana Bancorp [*NASDAQ symbol*] (SAG) .... ASBI
America [*A publication*] (BRI) .... Am
America (ROG) .... AM
America [*or American*] .... AMER
America (VRA) .... Amer
America .... AMER
America and West Indies [*Obsolete British*] .... AWI
America, Britain, Canada, Australia (ADA) .... ABCA
America, Britain, China, and Dutch East Indies [*The ABCD Powers*] [*World War II*] .... ABCD
America Defense Society (SAA) .... ADS
America First (EA) .... AF
America First Apartment Investors LP [*Associated Press*] (SAG) .... AFstApt
America First Apartment Investors LP [*NASDAQ symbol*] (SAG) .... APRO
America First Financial Fund 1987 [*NASDAQ symbol*] (NQ) .... AFFF
America First Financial Fund Ltd. [*Associated Press*] (SAG) .... AFFF
America First Part Preferred Equity Mortgage Fund Ltd. [*Associated Press*] (SAG) .... AmFPr
America First Preferred Equity Mortgage Ltd. [*NASDAQ symbol*] (NQ) .... AFPF
America First PREP [*Preferred Real Estate Participation*] **Fund 2 Ltd.** [*Associated Press*] (SAG) AFstP2
America First Tax Exempt Mortgage [*NASDAQ symbol*] (NQ) .... AFTX
America First Tax Exempt Mortgage Fund [*Associated Press*] (SAG) .... AFTxE
America First Tax Exempt Mortgage Fund [*NASDAQ symbol*] (NQ) .... ATAX
America: History and Life [*ABC-Clio Information Services*] [*Database*] [*A publication*] .... AHL
America Israel Friendship League (EA) .... AIFL
America Online [*NASDAQ symbol*] (TTSB) .... AMER
America Online [*Online Service*] (PCM) .... AOL
America Online, Inc. [*NASDAQ symbol*] (SAG) .... AMER
America Online, Inc. [*Associated Press*] (SAG) .... AmerOn
America Remembers (EA) .... AR
America Service Group, Inc. [*Associated Press*] (SAG) .... AmSvce
America Service Group, Inc. [*NASDAQ symbol*] (SAG) .... ASGR
America Sky Broadcasting .... ASkyB
America the Beautiful Fund (EA) .... ABF
America Victory Force (EA) .... AVF
America/West Africa Conference [*Shipping*] .... AMWAC
America West Airlines [*ICAO designator*] (FAAC) .... AWE
America West Airlines [*ICAO designator*] (AD) .... HP
America West Airlines 'B' [*NYSE symbol*] (TTSB) .... AWA
America West Airlines, Inc. [*Associated Press*] (SAG) .... AmWest
America West Airlines, Inc. [*NYSE symbol*] (SAG) .... AWA
America West Airlines Wrrt [*NYSE symbol*] (TTSB) .... AWA.WS
America West Holdings Corp. [*Associated Press*] (SAG) .... AWest
America-Australia Interaction Association (EA) .... AAIA
America-India Dispensary [*Pharmacology*] (DAVI) .... AID
AmericaIntelligent Transportation Society of America [*Formerly, IVHS America*] .... ITS
America-Israel Council for Israeli-Palestinian Peace (EA) .... AICIPP
America-Israel Cultural Foundation (EA) .... AICF
America-Italy Society (EA) .... AIS
Americal Division [*Army*] (VNW) .... AMCAL
Americal Division Veterans Association (EA) .... ADVA
Americam Philatelist [*A publication*] .... Am Phil
America-Mideast Educational and Training Services [*Acronym is now organization's official name*] (EA) .... AMIDEAST
American .... A
American .... AM
American (BARN) .... AME
American .... AMERCN

American Abolitionist Movement (EA) .... AAM
American Abstract Artists (EA) .... AAA
American Academic Environments, Inc. .... AAE
American Academy and Institute of Arts and Letters (EA) .... AAIAL
American Academy for Cerebral Palsy [*Later, AACPDM*] (EA) .... AACP
American Academy for Cerebral Palsy and Developmental Medicine (EA) .... AACPDM
American Academy for Health, Physical Education, and Recreation (DAVI) .... AAHPER
American Academy for Jewish Research (EA) .... AAJR
American Academy for Plastics Research in Dentistry [*Later, Academy of Dental Materials - ADM*] .... AAPRD
American Academy for Professional Law Enforcement [*Defunct*] (EA) .... AAPLE
American Academy in Rome (EA) .... AAR
American Academy of Achievement (EA) .... AAA
American Academy of Actuaries [*Washington, DC*] (EA) .... AAA
American Academy of Addictionology (HCT) .... AAA
American Academy of Advertising [*Charleston, SC*] (EA) .... AAA
American Academy of Allergy [*Later, AAAI*] (EA) .... AAA
American Academy of Allergy and Immunology (EA) .... AAAI
American Academy of Ambulatory Nursing Administration (EA) .... AAANA
American Academy of Anatomists (DAVI) .... AAA
American Academy of Anesthesiologists' Assistants (DAVI) .... AAAA
American Academy of Applied Nutrition [*Later, ICAN*] (EA) .... AAAN
American Academy of Art [*Chicago, IL*] .... AAA
American Academy of Arts and Letters [*Later, AAIAL*] (EA) .... AAA & L
American Academy of Arts and Letters [*Later, AAIAL*] (EA) .... AAAL
American Academy of Arts and Letters, New York, NY [*Library symbol Library of Congress*] (LCLS) .... NNAL
American Academy of Arts and Sciences (EA) .... AAA & S
American Academy of Arts and Sciences (EA) .... AAAS
American Academy of Arts and Sciences, Boston, MA [*Library symbol Library of Congress*] (LCLS) .... MBA
American Academy of Asian Studies (EA) .... AAAS
American Academy of Ballet .... AAB
American Academy of Behavioral Medicine (EA) .... AABM
American Academy of Child and Adolescent Psychiatry (EA) .... AACAP
American Academy of Child Psychiatry [*Later, AACAP*] (EA) .... AACP
American Academy of Clinical Psychiatrists (EA) .... AACP
American Academy of Clinical Toxicology (EA) .... AACT
American Academy of Compensation Medicine [*Later, AALIM*] (EA) .... AACM
American Academy of Cosmetic Surgery (EA) .... AACS
American Academy of Craniomandibular Disorders (EA) .... AACD
American Academy of Criminalistics (EA) .... AAC
American Academy of Crisis Interveners (EA) .... AACI
American Academy of Crown and Bridge Prosthodontics (EA) .... AACBP
American Academy of Dental Electrosurgery (EA) .... AADE
American Academy of Dental Group Practice (EA) .... AADGP
American Academy of Dental Medicine [*Later, AAOM*] (EA) .... AADM
American Academy of Dental Practice Administration (EA) .... AADPA
American Academy of Dental Prosthetics (DAVI) .... AADP
American Academy of Dental Radiology (EA) .... AADR
American Academy of Dental Schools (DAVI) .... AADS
American Academy of Dentists [*Defunct*] (EA) .... AAD
American Academy of Dermatology (EA) .... AAD
American Academy of Diplomacy (EA) .... AAD
American Academy of Disability Evaluating Physicians (EA) .... AADEP
American Academy of Dramatic Arts (NTCM) .... AADA
American Academy of Environmental Engineers (EA) .... AAEE
American Academy of Environmental Medicine (EA) .... AAEM
American Academy of Equine Art (EA) .... AAEA
American Academy of Esthetic Dentistry (EA) .... AAED
American Academy of Facial Plastic and Reconstructive Surgery (EA) .... AAFPRS
American Academy of Family Physicians [*Formerly, AAGP*] (EA) .... AAFP
American Academy of Forensic Psychology (EA) .... AAFP
American Academy of Forensic Sciences (EA) .... AAFS
American Academy of General Practice [*Later, AAFP*] (EA) .... AAGP
American Academy of Gnathologic Orthopedics (EA) .... AAGO
American Academy of Gold Foil Operators (EA) .... AAGFO
American Academy of Gynecologic Laparoscopists (DMAA) .... AAGI
American Academy of Head, Facial, and Neck Pain and TMJ [*Temporomandibular Joint*] Orthopedics (EA) .... AAHFNPTO
American Academy of Health Administration (EA) .... AAHA
American Academy of Homeopathic Medicine (EA) .... AAHM
American Academy of Homiletics [*Later, AH*] (EA) .... AAH
American Academy of Hospital Attorneys (EA) .... AAHA
American Academy of Humor Columnists (DGA) .... AAHC
American Academy of Husband-Coached Childbirth (EA) .... AAHCC
American Academy of Implant Dentistry (EA) .... AAID
American Academy of Implant Prosthodontics (EA) .... AAIP
American Academy of Industrial Hygiene (EA) .... AAIH
American Academy of Judicial Education (DLA) .... AAJE
American Academy of Legal and Industrial Medicine (EA) .... AALIM
American Academy of Matrimonial Lawyers (EA) .... AAML
American Academy of Matrimonial Lawyers. Journal [*A publication*] (DLA) .... Am Acad Matri Law J
American Academy of Maxillofacial Prosthetics (EA) .... AAMP
American Academy of Mechanics (EA) .... AAM
American Academy of Medical Administrators (EA) .... AAMA
American Academy of Medical Administrators Research and Educational Foundation (EA) .... AAMAREF
American Academy of Medical Directors [*American College of Physician Exec utives*] [*Absorbed by*] (EA) .... AAMD
American Academy of Medical Hypnoanalysts (EA) .... AAMH

American Academy of Medical Preventics [*Later, ACAM*] (EA) ... AAMP
American Academy of Medical-Legal Analysis (EA) ... AAMLA
American Academy of Medicine and Science (EA) ... AAMS
American Academy of Microbiology (EA) ... AAM
American Academy of Natural Family Planning (EA) ... AANFP
American Academy of Neurological Surgery (EA) ... AANS
American Academy of Neurology (EA) ... AAN
American Academy of Nursing (EA) ... AAN
American Academy of Nutrition (EA) ... AAN
American Academy of Occupational Medicine (EA) ... AAOM
American Academy of Ophthalmology (EA) ... AAO
American Academy of Ophthalmology and Otolaryngology (EA) ... AAOO
American Academy of Optometry (EA) ... AAO
American Academy of Oral Medicine (EA) ... AAOM
American Academy of Oral Pathology (EA) ... AAOP
American Academy of Oral Pathology (DMAA) ... AAOP
American Academy of Oral Roentgenology [*Later, AADR*] ... AAOR
American Academy of Organ (EA) ... AAO
American Academy of Orthodontics for the General Practitioner (EA) ... AAOGP
American Academy of Orthopaedic Surgeons (EA) ... AAOS
American Academy of Orthotists and Prosthetists (EA) ... AAOP
American Academy of Osteopathy (EA) ... AAO
American Academy of Otolaryngologic Allergy (EA) ... AAOA
American Academy of Otolaryngology (DAVI) ... AAO
American Academy of Otolaryngology - Head and Neck Surgery (EA) ... AAO-HNS
American Academy of Pain Medicine (EA) ... AAPM
American Academy of Pediatric Dentistry (EA) ... AAPD
American Academy of Pediatricians (PAZ) ... AAP
American Academy of Pediatrics (EA) ... AAP
American Academy of Pedodontics [*Later, AAPD*] (EA) ... AAP
American Academy of Periodontology (EA) ... AAP
American Academy of Philately [*Later, APC*] (EA) ... AAP
American Academy of Physical Education (EA) ... AAPE
American Academy of Physical Medicine and Rehabilitation (EA) ... AAPMR
American Academy of Physician Assistants (EA) ... AAPA
American Academy of Physiologic Dentistry (EA) ... AAPD
American Academy of Plastic Surgeons (DAVI) ... AAPS
American Academy of Podiatric Sports Medicine (EA) ... AAPSM
American Academy of Podiatry Administration (EA) ... AAPA
American Academy of Podiatry Administration (EA) ... AAPO
American Academy of Political and Social Science (EA) ... AAPSS
American Academy of Political and Social Science (DLA) ... Am Acad Pol & Soc Sci
American Academy of Political and Social Science. Annals [*A publication*] (BRI) ... AAPSS-A
American Academy of Pro-Life Physicians (EA) ... AAPLP
American Academy of Psychiatrists in Alcoholism and Addictions (EA) ... AAPAA
American Academy of Psychiatry and the Law (EA) ... AAPL
American Academy of Psychiatry and the Law. Bulletin [*A publication*] (DLA) ... Am A Psych L Bull
American Academy of Psychoanalysis (EA) ... AAP
American Academy of Psychotherapists (EA) ... AAP
American Academy of Religion (EA) ... AAR
American Academy of Restorative Dentistry (EA) ... AARD
American Academy of Safety Education (EA) ... AASE
American Academy of Sanitarians (EA) ... AAS
American Academy of Somnology (EA) ... AAS
American Academy of Spinal Surgeons (EA) ... AASS
American Academy of Sports Physicians (EA) ... AASP
American Academy of Stress Disorders (EA) ... AASD
American Academy of Teachers of Singing (EA) ... AATS
American Academy of the History of Dentistry (EA) ... AAHD
American Academy of Thermology (EA) ... AAT
American Academy of Transportation ... AAT
American Academy of Tropical Medicine (EA) ... AATM
American Academy of Tuberculosis Physicians (EA) ... AATP
American Academy of Veterinary and Comparative Toxicology (EA) ... AAVCT
American Academy of Veterinary Dermatology (EA) ... AAVD
American Academy of Veterinary Nutrition (EA) ... AAVN
American Academy of Veterinary Pharmacology and Therapeutics (EA) ... AAVPT
American Academy of Wine [*Defunct*] (EA) ... AAW
American Academy on Mental Retardation (EA) ... AAMR
American Accordion Musicological Society (EA) ... AAMS
American Accordionists' Association (EA) ... AAA
American Accounting Association [*Sarasota, FL*] (EA) ... AAA
American Acupuncture Association (EA) ... AAA
American Adjustable Rate Term Trust 1997 [*NYSE symbol*] (SPSG) ... CDJ
American Adoption Congress [*Later, NAAC*] (EA) ... AAC
American Adventurers Association (DICI) ... AAA
American Advertising Federation [*Washington, DC*] (EA) ... AAF
American Aerobics Association (EA) ... AAA
American Affenpinscher Association (EA) ... AAA
American Affiliation of Visiting Nurses Associations and Services [*Later, VNAA*] (EA) ... AAVNA
American Afghan Action [*Later, FAAA*] (EA) ... AAA
American Afghan Education Fund (EA) ... AAEF
American Afro-Asian Educational Exchange [*Later, AAEE*] (EA) ... AAAEE
American Agents Association [*Indianapolis, IN*] (EA) ... AAA
American Agricultural Economics Association (EA) ... AAEA
American Agricultural Economics Documentation Center [*Department of Agriculture*] (IID) ... AAEDC
American Agricultural Economics Documentation Center, Washington, DC [*OCLC symbol*] (OCLC) ... AGU
American Agricultural Editors' Association (EA) ... AAEA
American Agricultural Law Association (EA) ... AALA
American Agricultural Marketing Association (EA) ... AAMA
American Agriculture Movement (EA) ... AAM
American Agri-Women (EA) ... AAW
American Agri-Women Resource Center (EA) ... AAWRC
American Aid for Afghans (EA) ... AAF
American Aid for Afghans (EA) ... AAFA
American Aid Society for the West Indies (EA) ... AASWI
American Aid Society of Paris [*France*] (EA) ... AASP
American Aid to Ulster (EA) ... AATU
American Aid to Ulster (EA) ... AAU
American Air Export & Import Co. ... AAXICO
American Air Filter Co. (MHDB) ... AAF
American Air Mail Society (EA) ... AAMS
American Air Services, Inc. [*ICAO designator*] (FAAC) ... EJM
American Airforce [*World War II*] ... AAF
American Airlines, Inc. [*ICAO designator*] ... AA
American Airlines, Inc. [*Air carrier designation symbol*] (MCD) ... AAL
American Airlines Technical Training Corp. ... AATTC
American Airship Association [*Later, Airship Association*] (EA) ... AAA
American Albino Association [*Later, WWWCRW*] ... AAA
American Albino Horse Club [*Later, WWWCRW*] (EA) ... AAHC
American Alfalfa Processors Association (EA) ... AAPA
American Allergy Association (EA) ... AAA
American All-Hobbies Association (EA) ... AAHA
American Alliance Against Violence (EA) ... AAAV
American Alliance for Health, Physical Education, and Recreation [*Later, AAHPERD*] ... AAHPER
American Alliance for Health, Physical Education, Recreation, and Dance (EA) ... AAHPERD
American Alligator Council [*Defunct*] (EA) ... AAC
American Alligator Farmers Association (EA) ... AAFA
American All-Terrain Vehicle Association (EA) ... AATVA
American Alpine Club (EA) ... AAC
American Alpine Club, New York, NY [*Library symbol Library of Congress*] (LCLS) ... NNAAI
American Alumni Council [*Later, Council for the Advancement and Support of Education*] (EA) ... AAC
American Amaryllis Society (EA) ... AAS
American Amateur Baseball Congress (EA) ... AABC
American Amateur Inventors Club (EA) ... AAIC
American Amateur Karate Federation (EA) ... AAKF
American Amateur Press Association (EA) ... AAPA
American Amateur Racquetball Association (EA) ... AARA
American Ambulance and Rescue Association [*Defunct*] (EA) ... AARA
American Ambulance Association (EA) ... AAA
American Amputee Foundation (EA) ... AAF
American Amusement Machine Association (EA) ... AAMA
American and Australian Line [*Shipping*] (ROG) ... A & A
American and British Commonwealth Association ... ABC
American and Canadian Connection for Efficient Securities Settlement [*Canada*] ... ACCESS
American and Common Market Club (EAIO) ... ACMC
American and Delaine-Merino Record Association (EA) ... AD-MRA
American and English Annotated Cases [*A publication*] (DLA) ... A & E Ann Cas
American and English Annotated Cases [*A publication*] (DLA) ... A & E Anno
American and English Annotated Cases [*A publication*] (DLA) ... A & E Cas
American and English Annotated Cases [*A publication*] (DLA) ... A & EAC
American and English Annotated Cases [*A publication*] (DLA) ... Am & Eng Ann Cas
American and English Annotated Cases [*A publication*] (DLA) ... Am-Eng Ann Cases
American and English Annotated Cases [*A publication*] (DLA) ... Ann Cas
American and English Corporation Cases [*United States*] [*A publication*] (DLA) ... A & E Cor Cases
American and English Corporation Cases [*A publication*] (DLA) ... A & E Corp Cas
American and English Corporation Cases [*United States*] [*A publication*] (DLA) ... A & ECC
American and English Corporation Cases [*A publication*] (DLA) ... Am & E Corp Cas
American and English Corporation Cases [*A publication*] (DLA) ... Am & Eng Corp Cas
American and English Corporation Cases [*A publication*] (DLA) ... Cor Cas
American and English Corporation Cases, New Series [*A publication*] (DLA) ... A & E Corp Cas NS
American and English Corporation Cases, New Series [*A publication*] (DLA) ... Am & E Corp Cas NS
American and English Decisions in Equity [*A publication*] (DLA) ... Am & E Eq D
American and English Decisions in Equity [*A publication*] (DLA) ... Am & Eng Dec Eq
American and English Decisions in Equity [*A publication*] (DLA) ... Am & Eng Eq D
American and English Encyclopedia of Law [*A publication*] (DLA) ... A & E Enc L
American and English Encyclopedia of Law [*A publication*] (DLA) ... A & E Ency
American and English Encyclopedia of Law [*A publication*] (DLA) ... Am & Eng Enc Law
American and English Encyclopedia of Law [*A publication*] (DLA) ... Am & Eng Ency Law
American and English Encyclopedia of Law [*A publication*] (DLA) ... Amer & Eng Enc Law
American and English Encyclopedia of Law [*A publication*] (DLA) ... Enc Law
American and English Encyclopedia of Law [*A publication*] (DLA) ... Ency Law

American and English Encyclopedia of Law and Practice [*A publication*] (DLA) ... A & E Enc
American and English Encyclopedia of Law and Practice [*A publication*] (DLA) ... A & E Enc L & Pr
American and English Encyclopedia of Law and Practice [*A publication*] (DLA) ... A & E Ency Law
American and English Encyclopedia of Law and Practice [*A publication*] (DLA) ... Am & Eng Enc Law & Pr
American and English Encyclopedia of Law and Practice [*A publication*] (DLA) ... Ency L & P
American and English Encyclopedia of Law. Supplement [*A publication*] (DLA) ... Am & Eng Enc Law Sup
American and English Patent Cases [*A publication*] (DLA) ... A & E Pat Cas
American and English Patent Cases [*A publication*] (DLA) ... Am & Eng Pat Cas
American and English Pleading and Practice [*A publication*] (DLA) ... A & EP & P
American and English Pleading and Practice [*A publication*] (DLA) ... A & EP & Pr
American and English Railroad Cases [*A publication*] (DLA) ... A & E RRC
American and English Railroad Cases [*A publication*] (DLA) ... A & ER Cas
American and English Railroad Cases [*A publication*] (DLA) ... A & ERC
American and English Railroad Cases [*A publication*] (DLA) ... A & ERR Cas
American and English Railroad Cases [*A publication*] (DLA) ... Am & Eng R Cas
American and English Railroad Cases [*A publication*] (DLA) ... Am & Eng RR Ca
American and English Railroad Cases [*A publication*] (DLA) ... Am & Eng RR Cas
American and English Railroad Cases [*A publication*] (DLA) ... Am & Eng RR Cases
American and English Railroad Cases [*A publication*] (DLA) ... Am & ER Cas
American and English Railroad Cases, New Series [*A publication*] (DLA) ... A & ER Cas NS
American and English Railroad Cases, New Series [*A publication*] (DLA) ... A & ERR Cas (NS)
American and English Railroad Cases, New Series [*A publication*] (DLA) ... Am & Eng R Cas NS
American and English Railroad Cases, New Series [*A publication*] (DLA) ... Am & Eng Ry Cas NS
American and English Railroad Cases, New Series [*A publication*] (DLA) ... Am & ER Cas NS
American and English Railway Cases [*A publication*] (DLA) ... Am & Eng Ry Cas
American and English Railway Cases [*A publication*] (DLA) ... Am & Engl RC
American and Foreign Bible Society ... AFBS
American and Foreign Christian Union (EA) ... AFCU
American & Foreign Power Co., Inc. ... A & FP
American and French Research on the Treasury of the French Language [*University of Chicago*] [*Research center*] (RCD) ... ARTFL
American Angora Goat Breeder's Association (EA) ... AAGBA
American Angus Association (EA) ... AAA
American Animal Health Pharmaceutical Association [*Defunct*] ... AAHPhA
American Animal Hospital Association (EA) ... AAHA
American Annotated Cases [*A publication*] (DLA) ... Am Ann Cas
American Annotated Cases [*A publication*] (DLA) ... Ann Cas
American Annotated Cases [*A publication*] (DLA) ... Anno Cases
American Annuity Group [*Formerly, STI Group*] [*NYSE symbol*] (SPSG) ... AAG
American Annuity Group, Inc. [*Associated Press*] (SAG) ... AAnnuity
American Annuity Group, Inc. Capital Trust I [*Associated Press*] (SAG) ... AAnnu
American Anorexia/Bulimia Association (EA) ... AABA
American Anorexia Nervosa Association [*Later, AABA*] (EA) ... AANA
American Antarctic Association (EA) ... AAA
American Antarctic Mountaineering Expedition ... AAME
American Anthology [*A publication*] ... AA
American Anthropological Association (EA) ... AAA
American Anthropologist [*A publication*] (BRI) ... A Anth
American Antiquarian Society (EA) ... AAS
American Antiquarian Society, Worcester, MA [*OCLC symbol*] (OCLC) ... AQM
American Antiquarian Society, Worcester, MA [*Library symbol Library of Congress*] (LCLS) ... MWA
American Antique Graphics Society (EA) ... AAGS
American Antiques and Crafts Society [*Defunct*] (EA) ... AACS
American Antiquity [*A publication*] (BRI) ... Am Ant
American Anti-Terrorism Institute [*Defunct*] (EA) ... AATI
American Anti-Vivisection Society (EA) ... AAVS
American Apartment Communities, Inc. [*Associated Press*] (SAG) ... AmApt
American Apparel Contractors Association (EA) ... AACA
American Apparel Manufacturers Association (EA) ... AAMA
American Aquatech International [*Vancouver Stock Exchange symbol*] ... AAA
American Arab Relief Agency [*Defunct*] ... AARA
American Arabic Association (EA) ... AMERA
American Arbitration Association (EA) ... AAA
American Arbitration Association, New York, NY [*Library symbol Library of Congress*] (LCLS) ... NNAAr
American Archery Council (EA) ... AAC
American Architectural Foundation [*Later, AIAF*] ... AAF
American Architectural Manufacturers Association (EA) ... AAMA
American Archives Association (EA) ... ARA
American Archivist Quarterly [*A publication*] (BRI) ... A Arch
American Armwrestling Association (EA) ... AAA
American Army (DAS) ... AA
American Art Association [*Predecessor of Parke-Bernet, New York*] ... AAA
American Art Pottery Association (EA) ... AAPA
American Art Therapy Association (EA) ... AATA
American Artist [*A publication*] (BRI) ... A Art
American Artists Professional League (EA) ... AAPL
American Artists Series ... AAS
American Arts Alliance (EA) ... AAA
American Arts and Crafts Alliance (EA) ... ARCA
American Arts Documentation Centre (EA) ... AMARTS
American Assembly (EA) ... AA
American Assembly for Men in Nursing (EA) ... AAMN
American Assembly of Collegiate Schools of Business (EA) ... AACSB
American Associates, Ben-Gurion University of the Negev (EA) ... AABGU
American Association [*Baseball league*] ... AA
American Association Against Addiction [*Defunct*] (EA) ... AAAA
American Association - Electronic Voice Phenomena (EA) ... AA-EVP
American Association for Accreditation of Ambulatory Plastic Surgery Facilities (EA) ... AAAAPSF
American Association for Accreditation of Laboratory Animal Care (EA) ... AAALAC
American Association for Acupuncture and Oriental Medicine (EA) ... AAAOM
American Association for Adult and Continuing Education (EA) ... AAACE
American Association for Aerosol Research (EA) ... AAAR
American Association for Affirmative Action (EA) ... AAAA
American Association for Agricultural Education (EA) ... AAAE
American Association for Applied Linguistics (EA) ... AAAL
American Association for Artificial Intelligence (EA) ... AAAI
American Association for Automotive Medicine (DAVI) ... AAAM
American Association for Budget and Program Analysis (EA) ... AABPA
American Association for Cancer Education (EA) ... AACE
American Association for Cancer Research (EA) ... AACR
American Association for Career Education (EA) ... AACE
American Association for Chinese Studies (EA) ... AACS
American Association for Cleft Palate Rehabilitation [*Later, ACPA*] ... AACPR
American Association for Clinical Histocompatibility Testing [*Later, ASHI*] (EA) ... AACHT
American Association for Clinical Immunology and Allergy (EA) ... AACIA
American Association for Comprehensive Health Planning [*Later, AHPA*] ... AACHP
American Association for Conservation Information [*Later, ACI*] (EA) ... AACI
American Association for Consumer Benefits (EA) ... AACB
American Association for Contamination Control [*Later, IES*] (EA) ... AACC
American Association for Continuity of Care (EA) ... AACC
American Association for Corporate Contributions [*Defunct*] (EA) ... AACC
American Association for Correctional Psychology (EA) ... AACP
American Association for Counseling and Development (EA) ... AACD
American Association for Crystal Growth (EA) ... AACG
American Association for Dental Research (EA) ... AADR
American Association for Ethiopian Jews (EA) ... AAEJ
American Association for Functional Orthodontics (EA) ... AAFO
American Association for Geodetic Surveying (EA) ... AAGS
American Association for Geriatric Psychiatry (EA) ... AAGP
American Association for Gifted Children (EA) ... AAGC
American Association for Hand Surgery (EA) ... AAHS
American Association for Health, Physical Education, and Recreation (AEBS) ... AAHPEAR
American Association for Health, Physical Education, and Recreation (DMAA) ... AAHPER
American Association for Higher Education (EA) ... AAHE
American Association for Hospital Planning [*Later, The Forum for Health Care Planning*] (EA) ... AAHP
American Association for Humanistic Psychology [*Later, AHP*] ... AAHP
American Association for International Aging (EA) ... AAIA
American Association for Italian Studies (BARN) ... AAIS
American Association for Jewish Education [*Later, JESNA*] (EA) ... AAJE
American Association for Labor Legislation (DMAA) ... AALL
American Association for Labor Legislation (DMAA) ... AALL
American Association for Laboratory Accreditation (AAGC) ... A2LA
American Association for Laboratory Accreditation (RCD) ... A2LA
American Association for Laboratory Accreditation (EA) ... AALA
American Association for Laboratory Animal Science (EA) ... AALAS
American Association for Legal and Political Philosophy (EA) ... AALPP
American Association for Leisure and Recreation (EA) ... AALR
American Association for Marriage and Family Therapy (EA) ... AAMFT
American Association for Maternal and Child Health [*Defunct*] (EA) ... AAMCH
American Association for Maternal and Infant Health [*Later, AAMCH*] (EA) ... AAMIH
American Association for Medical Systems and Informatics [*Later, AMIA*] (EA) ... AAMSI
American Association for Medical Transcription (EA) ... AAMT
American Association for Middle East Studies [*Defunct*] (EA) ... AAMES
American Association for Museum Volunteers (EA) ... AAMV
American Association for Music Therapy (EA) ... AAMT
American Association for Nurses Practicing Independently (DAVI) ... AANPI
American Association for Paralegal Education (EA) ... AAFPE
American Association for Paralegal Education (EA) ... AAPE
American Association for Parapsychology (EA) ... AAP
American Association for Partial Hospitalization (EA) ... AAPH
American Association for Pediatric Ophthalmology and Strabismus (EA) ... AAPO & S
American Association for Protecting Children (EA) ... AAPC
American Association for Public Information, Education and Research (AEBS) ... AAPIER
American Association for Public Opinion Research (EA) ... AAPOR
American Association for Rehabilitation Therapy [*Defunct*] (EA) ... AART
American Association for Respiratory Care (EA) ... AARC
American Association for Respiratory Therapy [*Later, AARC*] (EA) ... AART
American Association for Small Dredging and Marine Construction Companies (EA) ... AASDMCC
American Association for Social Psychiatry (EA) ... AASP
American Association for Social Security (EA) ... AASS
American Association for State and Local History (EA) ... AASLH
American Association for Study of Neoplastic Diseases (EA) ... AASND
American Association for Study of the United States in World Affairs (EA) ... USWA
American Association for Textile Technology (EA) ... AATT

American Association for the Abolition of Involuntary Mental Hospitalization [*Defunct*] .... AAAIMH
American Association for the Advancement of Atheism [*Later, AA*] (EA) .... AAAA
American Association for the Advancement of Health Education [*Medicine*] (DMAA) .... AAAHE
American Association for the Advancement of Science (EA) .... AAAS
American Association for the Advancement of Science, Washington, DC [*Library symbol*] [*Library of Congress*] (LCLS) .... DAAAS
American Association for the Advancement of Slavic Studies (EA) .... AAASS
American Association for the Advancement of Tension Control [*Later, ISTC*] .... AAATC
American Association for the Advancement of the Humanities .... AAAH
American Association for the Comparative Study of Law (EA) .... AACSL
American Association for the Education of Severely/Profoundly Handicapped (EDAC) .... AAESPH
American Association for the Educational Service Agencies (EDAC) .... AAESA
American Association for the Gifted .... AAG
American Association for the History of Medicine [*University of Rochester Medical Center*] (EA) .... AAHM
American Association for the History of Nursing (EA) .... AAHN
American Association for the Improvement of Boxing (EA) .... AAIB
American Association for the International Commission of Jurists (EA) .... AAICJ
American Association for the Promotion of Science .... AAPS
American Association for the Study of Headache (EA) .... AASH
American Association for the Study of Liver Diseases (EA) .... AASLD
American Association for the Surgery of Trauma (EA) .... AAST
American Association for the United Nations [*Later, United Nations Association of the United States*] (EA) .... AAUN
American Association for Therapeutic Humor (EA) .... AATH
American Association for Thoracic Surgery (EA) .... AATS
American Association for Vital Records and Public Health Statistics [*Later, AVRHS*] (EA) .... AAVRPHS
American Association for Vocational Instructional Materials (EA) .... AAVIM
American Association for Women Podiatrists (EA) .... AAWP
American Association for World Health (EA) .... AAWH
American Association for Zoological Nomenclature (EA) .... AAZN
American Association of Aardvark Aficionados (EA) .... AAAA
American Association of Academic Editors (EA) .... AAAE
American Association of Accompanists and Coaches (EA) .... AAAC
American Association of Advertising Agencies [*New York, NY*] .... 4A's
American Association of Advertising Agencies [*New York, NY*] (EA) .... AAAA
American Association of Advertising Agencies, New York, NY [*Library symbol Library of Congress*] (LCLS) .... NNAdv
American Association of Agricultural College Editors [*Later, ACE*] (EA) .... AAACE
American Association of Agricultural Communicators of Tomorrow (EA) .... ACT
American Association of Airport Executives (EA) .... AAAE
American Association of Aluminum Importers and Warehouse Distributors [*Later, AMIA*] (EA) .... AAAIWD
American Association of Anatomists (EA) .... AAA
American Association of Applied Psychology [*Division of American Psychological Association*] .... AAAP
American Association of Architectural Bibliographers .... AAAB
American Association of Attorney-Certified Public Accountants [*Mission Viejo, CA*] (EA) .... AAA-CPA
American Association of Audio Analgesia [*Defunct*] .... AAAA
American Association of Automatic Door Manufacturers .... AAADM
American Association of Avian Pathologists (EA) .... AAAP
American Association of Backgammon Clubs (EA) .... AABC
American Association of Baggage Traffic Managers [*Defunct*] (EA) .... AABTM
American Association of Behavioral Therapists (EA) .... AABT
American Association of Behavioral Therapists (EA) .... BT
American Association of Bible Colleges (EA) .... AABC
American Association of Bicycle Importers (EA) .... AABI
American Association of Bioanalysts [*or Bioanalysis*] (DAVI) .... AAB
American Association of Biofeedback Clinicians [*Defunct*] (EA) .... AABC
American Association of Black Women Entrepreneurs [*Silver Spring, MD*] (EA) .... AABWE
American Association of Blacks in Energy (EA) .... AABE
American Association of Blood Banks (EA) .... AABB
American Association of Book Wholesalers .... AABW
American Association of Botanical Gardens and Arboreta (EA) .... AABGA
American Association of Bovine Practitioners (EA) .... AABP
American Association of Breeders of Holsteiner Horses (EA) .... AABHH
American Association of Cable TV Owners [*Inactive*] (EA) .... AACTO
American Association of Cable TV Owners (EA) .... AACTVO
American Association of Candy Technologists (EA) .... AACT
American Association of Cardiovascular and Pulmonary Rehabilitation (EA) .... AACVPR
American Association of Ceramic Industries (EA) .... AACI
American Association of Cereal Chemists (EA) .... AACC
American Association of Certified Allergists (EA) .... AACA
American Association of Certified Allied Health Personnel in Ophthalmology (EA) .... AACAHPO
American Association of Certified Appraisers [*Cincinnati, OH*] (EA) .... AACA
American Association of Certified Orthoptists (EA) .... AACO
American Association of Chairmen of Departments of Psychiatry (EA) .... AACDP
American Association of Children's Residential Centers (12L) .... AACRC
American Association of Chiropractors (EA) .... AAC
American Association of Christian Schools (EA) .... AACS
American Association of Classified School Employees (EA) .... AACSE
American Association of Clinic Physicians and Surgeons [*Defunct*] (EA) .... AACPS
American Association of Clinical Chemistry (EA) .... AACC
American Association of Clinical Endocrinologists .... AACE
American Association of Clinical Urologists (EA) .... AACU
American Association of College and University Business Officers [*Defunct*] .... AACUBO
American Association of College Baseball Coaches (EA) .... AACBC
American Association of Colleges for Teacher Education (EA) .... AACTE
American Association of Colleges of Chiropody-Podiatry .... AACCP
American Association of Colleges of Nursing (EA) .... AACN
American Association of Colleges of Osteopathic Medicine (EA) .... AACOM
American Association of Colleges of Pharmacy (EA) .... AACP
American Association of Colleges of Podiatric Medicine (EA) .... AACPM
American Association of Colleges of Podiatry [*Later, AACPM*] (EA) .... AACP
American Association of Collegiate Registrars and Admissions Officers (EA) .... AACRAO
American Association of Commerce Publications [*Later, American Chamber of Commerce Executives Communications Council*] (EA) .... AACP
American Association of Commercial Colleges [*Later, United Business Schools Association*] (AEBS) .... AACC
American Association of Commodity Traders [*Defunct*] (EA) .... AACT
American Association of Community and Junior Colleges (EA) .... AACJC
American Association of Community Colleges (NFD) .... AACC
American Association of Community Psychiatrists (EA) .... AACP
American Association of Community Theatre (EA) .... AACT
American Association of Computer Professionals (EA) .... AACP
American Association of Concerned Engineers (EA) .... AACE
American Association of Conservators and Restorers (EA) .... AACR
American Association of Convention Planners [*Defunct*] (EA) .... AACP
American Association of Correctional Facility Officers [*Later, IACO*] (EA) .... AACFO
American Association of Correctional Officers [*Later, IACO*] (EA) .... AACO
American Association of Correctional Training Personnel (EA) .... AACTP
American Association of Cost Engineers (EA) .... AACE
American Association of Councils of Medical Staffs [*Later, PDA*] (EA) .... CMS
American Association of Creative Artists (EA) .... AACA
American Association of Credit Counselors [*Defunct*] (EA) .... AACC
American Association of Crimean Turks (EA) .... AACT
American Association of Criminology (AEBS) .... AAC
American Association of Critical Care Nurses (DAVI) .... AACCN
American Association of Critical-Care Nurses (EA) .... AACN
American Association of Crop Insurers [*Washington, DC*] (EA) .... AACI
American Association of Dealers in Ancient, Oriental, and Primitive Art (EA) .... AADAOPA
American Association of Dental Consultants [*Bloomington, MN*] (EA) .... AADC
American Association of Dental Editors (EA) .... AADE
American Association of Dental Examiners (EA) .... AADE
American Association of Dental Schools (EA) .... AADS
American Association of Dental Schools Application Service (GAGS) .... AADSAS
American Association of Dental Victims (EA) .... AADV
American Association of Diabetes Educators (EA) .... AADE
American Association of Directors of Psychiatric Residency Training (EA) .... AADPRT
American Association of Disability Communicators [*Defunct*] (EA) .... AADC
American Association of Doctors' Nurses (EA) .... AADN
American Association of Electrodiagnostic Medicine (EA) .... AAEM
American Association of Electromyography and Electrodiagnosis [*Later, AAEM*] (EA) .... AAEE
American Association of Elementary/Kindergarten/Nursery Educators [*Defunct*] .... AAE/K/N/E
American Association of Endodontists (EA) .... AAE
American Association of Engineering Societies (EA) .... AAES
American Association of Engineers [*Later, NSPE*] (EA) .... AAE
American Association of English Jewish Newspapers [*Later, AJPA*] (BJA) .... AAEJN
American Association of Entrepreneurial Dentists (EA) .... AAED
American Association of Equine Practitioners (EA) .... AAEP
American Association of Equipment Lessors (EA) .... AAEL
American Association of Esthetics (EA) .... AAE
American Association of Evangelical Students [*Defunct*] (EA) .... AAES
American Association of Examiners and Administrators of Educational Personnel [*Later, American Association of School Personnel Administrators*] (AEBS) .... AAEAEP
American Association of Exporters and Importers [*New York, NY*] (EA) .... AAEI
American Association of Eye and Ear Hospitals (EA) .... AAEEH
American Association of Family and Consumer Sciences (PAZ) .... AAFCS
American Association of Feed Exporters [*Defunct*] (EA) .... AAFE
American Association of Feed Microscopists (EA) .... AAFM
American Association of Feline Practitioners (EA) .... AAFP
American Association of Financial Professionals [*Defunct*] (EA) .... AAFP
American Association of First Responders [*Later, National Association of First Aid Responders*] (EA) .... AAFAR
American Association of Fitness Directors in Business and Industry (EA) .... AAFDBI
American Association of Food Stamp Directors (EA) .... AAFSD
American Association of Foot Specialists [*Defunct*] (EA) .... AAFS
American Association of Foreign Medical Graduates [*Defunct*] (EA) .... AAFMG
American Association of Forms Executives (EA) .... AAFE
American Association of Foundations for Medical Care [*Later, AMCRA*] (EA) .... AAFMC
American Association of Franchisees and Dealers .... AAFD
American Association of Functional Orthodontists [*Later, American Association for Functional Orthodontics*] (EA) .... AAFO
American Association of Fund-Raising Counsel (EA) .... AAFRC
American Association of Fund-Raising Counsel, Inc. .... AAFRC

American Association of Fund-Raising Counsel, Inc., Trust for Philanthropy (NFD) .... AAFRC Trust for Philanthropy
American Association of Fund-Raising Counsel Trust for Philanthropy (EA) .... AAFRCTP
American Association of Genito-Urinary Surgeons (EA) .... AAGUS
American Association of Grain Inspection and Weighing Agencies (EA) .... AAGIWA
American Association of Gravity Field Energy [*Defunct*] (EA) .... AAGFE
American Association of Gynecological Laparoscopists (EA) .... AAGL
American Association of Handwriting Analysts (EA) .... AAHA
American Association of Health Data Systems [*Defunct*] (EA) .... AAHDS
American Association of Health Plans (DMAA) .... AAHP
American Association of Health Plans .... AAHP
American Association of Healthcare Consultants (EA) .... AAHC
American Association of Hides, Skins, and Leather Merchants [*Later, USHSLA*] .... AAHSLM
American Association of Hispanic CPA's [*Certified Public Accountants*] [*Houston, TX*] (EA) .... AAHCPA
American Association of Homeopathic Pharmacists (EA) .... AAHP
American Association of Homes and Services for the Aging .... AAHSA
American Association of Homes for the Aging (EA) .... AAHA
American Association of Hospital Accountants [*Later, HFMA*] (EA) .... AAHA
American Association of Hospital Consultants [*Later, American Association of Healthcare Consultants*] (EA) .... AAHC
American Association of Hospital Dental Chiefs [*Later, AAHD*] .... AAHDC
American Association of Hospital Dentists [*Formerly, AAHDC*] (EA) .... AAHD
American Association of Hospital Podiatrists (EA) .... AAHP
American Association of Hospital Purchasing Agents (EA) .... AAHPA
American Association of Housing Educators (EA) .... AAHE
American Association of Immunologists (EA) .... AAI
American Association of Imported Car Dealers [*Defunct*] (EA) .... AAICD
American Association of Independent News Distributors (EA) .... AAIND
American Association of Independent Publishers (NTCM) .... AAIP
American Association of Individual Investors [*Chicago, IL*] (EA) .... AAII
American Association of Industrial Dentists [*Defunct*] (EA) .... AAID
American Association of Industrial Editors [*Later, IABC*] (EA) .... AAIE
American Association of Industrial Engineers .... AAIE
American Association of Industrial Management [*Springfield, MA*] (EA) .... AAIM
American Association of Industrial Nurses [*Later, AAOHN*] (EA) .... AAIN
American Association of Industrial Social Workers (EA) .... AAISW
American Association of Industrial Veterinarians (EA) .... AAIV
American Association of Inhalation Therapists [*Later, AART*] (EA) .... AAIT
American Association of Instructors of the Blind [*Later, AEVH*] (EA) .... AAIB
American Association of Insurance Management Consultants [*Houston, TX*] (EA) .... AAIMCo
American Association of Insurance Services [*Bensenville, IL*] (EA) .... AAIS
American Association of Inventors [*Defunct*] (EA) .... AAI
American Association of Inventors .... AAOI
American Association of IV Therapy (EA) .... AAIVT
American Association of Jesuit Scientists [*Defunct*] (EA) .... AAJS
American Association of Journalism School Administrators (EA) .... AAJSA
American Association of Judges (EA) .... AAJ
American Association of Junior Colleges [*Later, AACJC*] (EA) .... AAJC
American Association of Kidney Patients (EA) .... AAKP
American Association of Laban Movement Analysts (EA) .... AALMA
American Association of Language Specialists (BARN) .... AALS
[*The*] **American Association of Language Specialists** (EA) .... TAALS
American Association of Law Libraries (EA) .... AALL
American Association of Library Trustees [*Later, ALTA*] .... AALT
American Association of Limited Partners (EA) .... AALP
American Association of Machinery Importers [*Defunct*] .... AAMI
American Association of Managed Care Nurses .... AAMCN
American Association of Managing General Agents [*Washington, DC*] (EA) .... AAMGA
American Association of Marriage and Family Counselors [*Later, AAMFT*] .... AAMFC
American Association of Marriage Counselors [*Later, AAMFT*] (EA) .... AAMC
American Association of Meat Processors (EA) .... AAMP
American Association of Media Specialists and Librarians [*Defunct*] (EA) .... AAMSL
American Association of Medical Assistants (EA) .... AAMA
American Association of Medical Clinics [*Later, AGPA*] (EA) .... AAMC
American Association of Medical Colleges (DAVI) .... AAMC
American Association of Medical Milk Commissioners (EA) .... AAMMC
American Association of Medical Record Administrators [*Formerly, American Association of Medical Record Librarians*] [*Also, AMRA*] (DAVI) .... AAMRA
American Association of Medical Record Librarians [*Later, AMRA*] (EA) .... AAMRL
American Association of Medical Social Workers [*Later, National Association of Social Workers*] (AEBS) .... AAMSW
American Association of Medical Society Executives (EA) .... AAMSE
American Association of Medico-Legal Consultants (EA) .... AAMC
American Association of Mental Health Professionals in Corrections (EA) .... AAMHPC
American Association of Meta-Science (EA) .... AAMS
American Association of Microcomputer Investors [*Defunct*] (EA) .... AAMI
American Association of Microprocessor Engineers .... AAME
American Association of Minority Enterprise Small Business Investment Companies [*Washington, DC*] (EA) .... AAMESBIC
American Association of Motor Vehicle Administrators (EA) .... AAMVA
American Association of Museums (EA) .... AAM
American Association of Music Festivals [*Defunct*] .... AAMF
American Association of Naturopathic Physicians (EA) .... AANP
American Association of Nephrology Nurses and Technicians [*Later, ANNA*] (EA) .... AANNT
American Association of Neurological Surgeons (EA) .... AANS
American Association of Neuropathologists (DAVI) .... AAN
American Association of Neuropathologists (EA) .... AANP
American Association of Neuroscience Nurses (EA) .... AANN
American Association of Neurosurgical Nurses [*Later, ABNN*] (EA) .... AANN
American Association of Newspaper Representatives [*Later, NASA*] (EA) .... AANR
American Association of Nurse Anesthetists (EA) .... AANA
[*The*] **American Association of Nurse Attorneys** (EA) .... AANA
[*The*] **American Association of Nurse Attorneys** (EA) .... TAANA
American Association of Nurse-Midwives [*Later, ACNM*] .... AANM
American Association of Nurserymen (EA) .... AAN
American Association of Nursing Assistants (EA) .... AANA
American Association of Nutritional Consultants (EA) .... AANC
American Association of Obstetricians and Gynecologists [*Later, AGOS*] (EA) .... AAOG
American Association of Occupational Health Nurses (EA) .... AAOHN
American Association of Office Nurses (EA) .... AAON
American Association of Oilwell Drilling Contractors [*Later, IADC*] (EA) .... AAODC
American Association of Ophthalmology [*Absorbed by American Academy of Ophthalmology - AAO*] .... AAO
American Association of Oral and Maxillofacial Surgeons (EA) .... AAOMS
American Association of Orthodontists (EA) .... AAO
American Association of Orthomolecular Medicine (EA) .... AAOM
American Association of Orthopaedic Medicine (EA) .... AAOM
American Association of Orthopedic Medicine (EA) .... AAOrthMed
American Association of Orthoptic Technicians [*Later, AACO*] (EA) .... AAOT
American Association of Osteopathic Colleges [*Later, AACOM*] (EA) .... AAOC
American Association of Osteopathic Examiners (EA) .... AAOE
American Association of Osteopathic Medical Examiners (EA) .... AAOME
American Association of Osteopathic Specialists (EA) .... AAOS
American Association of Owners and Breeders of Peruvian Paso Horses (EA) .... AAOBPPH
American Association of Passenger Rate Men [*Defunct*] (EA) .... AAPRM
American Association of Passenger Traffic Officers [*Defunct*] (EA) .... AAPTO
American Association of Pastoral Counselors (EA) .... AAPC
American Association of Pathologists (EA) .... AAP
American Association of Pathologists and Bacteriologists [*Later, AAP*] (EA) .... AAPB
American Association of Pathologists' Assistants (EA) .... AAPA
American Association of Personal Financial Planners [*Defunct*] (EA) .... AAPFP
American Association of Petroleum Geologists (EA) .... AAPG
American Association of Petroleum Geologists, Energy Resources Library, Tulsa, OK [*Library symbol*] [*Library of Congress*] (LCLS) .... OkTA
American Association of Petroleum Landmen (EA) .... AAPL
American Association of Pharmaceutical Scientists (EA) .... AAPS
American Association of Philosophy Teachers (EA) .... AAPT
American Association of Phonetic Sciences (EA) .... AAPS
American Association of Physical Anthropologists (EA) .... AAPA
American Association of Physical Medicine and Rehabilitation (DAVI) .... AAPMR
American Association of Physician-Hospital Organization .... AAPHO
American Association of Physicians and Surgeons (DAVI) .... AAPS
American Association of Physicians' Assistants [*Defunct*] (EA) .... AAPA
American Association of Physicians for Human Rights (EA) .... AAPHR
American Association of Physicians Practicing the Transcendental Meditation Program [*Later, WMAFPH*] (EA) .... AAPPTMP
American Association of Physicists in Medicine (EA) .... AAPM
American Association of Physics Teachers (EA) .... AAPT
American Association of Planned Parenthood Physicians [*Later, APPP*] (EA) .... AAPPP
American Association of Plastic Surgeons (EA) .... AAPS
American Association of Podiatric Physicians and Surgeons (EA) .... AAPPS
American Association of Poison Control Centers (EA) .... AAPCC
American Association of Police Polygraphists (EA) .... AAPP
American Association of Political Consultants (EA) .... AAPC
American Association of Port Authorities (EA) .... AAPA
American Association of Preferred Provider Organizations [*Alexandria, VA*] (EA) .... AAPPO
American Association of Presidents of Independent Colleges and Universities (EA) .... AAPICU
American Association of Private Railroad Car Owners (EA) .... AAPRCO
American Association of Pro Life Obstetricians and Gynecologists (EA) .... AAPLOG
American Association of Professional Bridal Consultants (EA) .... AAPBC
American Association of Professional Consultants [*Manchester, NH*] (EA) .... AAPC
American Association of Professional Hypnologists [*Defunct*] (EA) .... AAPH
American Association of Professional Hypnotherapists (EA) .... AAPH
American Association of Professional Standards Review Organizations [*Later, AMPRA*] (EA) .... AAPSRO
American Association of Professors in Sanitary Engineering [*Later, AEEP*] .... AAPSE
American Association of Professors of Yiddish (EA) .... AAPY
American Association of Pro-Life Pediatricians (EA) .... AAPLP
American Association of Psychiatric Administrators (EA) .... AAPA
American Association of Psychiatric Clinics for Children [*Later, AAPSC*] (EA) .... AAPCC
American Association of Psychiatric Services for Children (EA) .... AAPSC
American Association of Psychiatric Technicians .... AAPT
American Association of Psychiatrists (EA) .... AAP
American Association of Public Health Dentistry (EA) .... AAPHD
American Association of Public Health Dentists (DMAA) .... AAPHD

American Association of Public Health Physicians (EA) ... AAPHP
American Association of Public Welfare Attorneys (EA) ... AAPWA
American Association of Public Welfare Information Systems Management (EA) ... AAPWISM
American Association of Publishers' electronic ordering system ... PUBNET
American Association of Rabbis (EA) ... AAR
American Association of Radon Scientists and Technologists (EA) ... AARST
American Association of Railroad Superintendents (EA) ... AARS
American Association of Railroad Ticket Agents [*Defunct*] (EA) ... AARTA
American Association of Railway Surgeons [*Defunct*] (EA) ... AARS
American Association of Religious Therapists (EA) ... AART
American Association of Retired Persons (EA) ... AARP
American Association of Retired Persons, Washington, DC [*Library symbol*] [*Library of Congress*] (LCLS) ... DAARP
American Association of School Administrators (EA) ... AASA
American Association of School Librarians (EA) ... AASL
American Association of School Personnel Administrators (EA) ... AASPA
American Association of Schools and Departments of Journalism (EA) ... AASDJ
American Association of Schools of Religious Education [*Later, ATS*] (EA) ... AASRE
American Association of Scientific Workers [*Later, USFSS*] (EA) ... AASW
American Association of Securities Representatives ... AASR
American Association of Senior Physicians (EA) ... AASP
American Association of Sex Educators and Counselors [*Later, AASECT*] (EA) ... AASEC
American Association of Sex Educators, Counselors, and Therapists (EA) ... AASECT
American Association of Sheep and Goat Practitioners [*Later, AASRP*] (EA) ... AASGP
American Association of Sheriff Posses and Riding Clubs (EA) ... AASPRC
American Association of Shotgunning [*Defunct*] (EA) ... AAS
American Association of Small Business [*Later, NSBU*] ... AASB
American Association of Small Cities (EA) ... AASC
American Association of Small Research Companies (EA) ... AASRC
American Association of Small Ruminant Practitioners (EA) ... AASRP
American Association of Soap and Glycerin Producers [*Later, SDA*] ... AAS & GP
American Association of Social Workers ... AASW
American Association of Special Educators [*Defunct*] (EA) ... AASE
American Association of Specialized Colleges (EA) ... AASC
American Association of Spinal Cord Injury Nurses (EA) ... AASCIN
American Association of State Climatologists (EA) ... AASC
American Association of State Colleges and Universities (EA) ... AASCU
American Association of State Highway and Transportation Officials (EA) ... AASHTO
American Association of State Highway Officials [*Later, AASHTO*] (EA) ... AASHO
American Association of State Libraries [*Later, ASCLA*] ... AASL
American Association of State Libraries [*Later, ASCLA*] (EA) ... ASL
American Association of State Social Work Boards (EA) ... AASSWB
American Association of Stratigraphic Palynologists (EA) ... AASP
American Association of Students of German [*Defunct*] (EA) ... AASG
American Association of Suicidology (EA) ... AAS
American Association of Sunday and Feature Editors (EA) ... AASFE
American Association of Surgeon's Assistants (EA) ... AASA
American Association of Swine Practitioners (EA) ... AASP
American Association of Swiss Alpine Club Members [*Defunct*] (EA) ... AASACM
American Association of Teacher Educators in Agriculture [*Later, AAAE*] (EA) ... AATEA
American Association of Teachers of Arabic (EA) ... AATA
American Association of Teachers of Chinese Language and Culture [*Later, AACS*] (EA) ... AATCLC
American Association of Teachers of English as a Second Language ... AATESL
American Association of Teachers of Esperanto (EA) ... AATE
American Association of Teachers of French (EA) ... AATF
American Association of Teachers of German (EA) ... AATG
American Association of Teachers of Italian (EA) ... AATI
American Association of Teachers of Slavic and East European Languages [*Defunct*] (EA) ... AATSEEL
American Association of Teachers of Spanish and Portuguese (EA) ... AATSP
American Association of Teachers of Turkish (EA) ... AATT
American Association of Temporary and Contract Employees (EA) ... AATCE
American Association of Testifying Physicians (EA) ... AATP
American Association of Textile Chemists and Colorists (EA) ... AATCC
American Association of the Deaf-Blind (EA) ... AADB
American Association of the Professions (EA) ... AAP
American Association of Theatre for Youth (EA) ... AATY
American Association of Theological Schools [*Later, ATS*] (EA) ... AATS
American Association of Tissue Banks (EA) ... AATB
American Association of Trauma Specialists [*Defunct*] (EA) ... AATS
American Association of Traveling Passenger Agents [*Defunct*] ... AATPA
American Association of University Administrators (EA) ... AAUA
American Association of University Affiliated Programs for Persons with Developmental Disabilities (EA) ... AAUAP
American Association of University Affiliated Programs for Persons with Developmental Disabilities [*Later, AAUAP*] (EA) ... AAUAPDD
American Association of University Affiliated Programs for the Developmentally Disabled [*Washington, DC*] ... AAUP
American Association of University Professors (EA) ... AAUP
American Association of University Professors Foundation (EA) ... AAUPF
American Association of University Professors of Italian (EDAC) ... AAUPI
American Association of University Professors of Urban Affairs and EnvironmentalSciences (EA) ... AAUP-UAES
American Association of University Students (EA) ... AAUS
American Association of University Supervisors and Coordinators (BARN) ... AAUSC
American Association of University Teachers of Insurance [*Later, ARIA*] ... AAUTI
American Association of University Women (EA) ... AAUW
American Association of University Women Educational Foundation (EA) ... AAUWEF
American Association of University Women Educational Foundation, Washington, DC [*Library symbol Library of Congress*] (LCLS) ... DAAUW
American Association of Variable Star Observers (EA) ... AAVSO
American Association of Veterinary Anatomists (EA) ... AAVA
American Association of Veterinary Bacteriologists [*Defunct*] (EA) ... AAVB
American Association of Veterinary Laboratory Diagnosticians (EA) ... AAVLD
American Association of Veterinary Parasitologists (EA) ... AAVP
American Association of Veterinary State Boards (EA) ... AAVSB
American Association of Volunteer Services Coordinators [*Later, AVA*] ... AAVSC
American Association of Waterbed Manufacturers [*Later, WMA*] ... AAWM
American Association of Wildlife Veterinarians (EA) ... AAWV
American Association of Women (EA) ... AAW
American Association of Women Dentists (EA) ... AAWD
American Association of Women in Community and Junior Colleges (EA) ... AAWCJC
American Association of Women Ministers [*Later, IAWM*] (EA) ... AAWM
American Association of Women Radiologists (EA) ... AAWR
American Association of Woodturners (EA) ... AAW
American Association of Workers for Children ... AAWC
American Association of Workers for the Blind [*Later, AER*] (EA) ... AAWB
American Association of Working People ... AAWP
American Association of Yellow Pages Publishers [*Defunct*] (EA) ... AAYPP
American Association of Youth Museums (EA) ... AAYM
American Association of Zoo Keepers (EA) ... AAZK
American Association of Zoo Veterinarians (EA) ... AAZV
American Association of Zoological Parks and Aquariums (EA) ... AAZPA
American Association on Emeriti [*Later, NCE*] (EA) ... AAE
American Association on Mental Deficiency [*Later, AAMR*] (EA) ... AAMD
American Association on Mental Retardation (EA) ... AAMR
American Associations of Spanish Speaking CPA's (EA) ... AASSCPA
American Astronautical Federation [*Defunct*] (EA) ... AAF
American Astronautical Society (EA) ... AAS
American Astronomers Association (EA) ... AAA
American Astronomical Society (EA) ... AAS
American Astronomical Society, Tarzana, CA [*Library symbol Library of Congress*] (LCLS) ... CTarA
American Astrophysical Society (USDC) ... AAS
American Atheist Addiction Recovery Groups [*Later, MOM*] (EA) ... AAARG
American Atheist Women (EA) ... AAW
American Athletic Association for the Deaf (EA) ... AAAD
American Athletic Trainers Association and Certification Board (EA) ... AATACB
American Audio Institute ... AAI
American Auditory Society (EA) ... AAS
American Austin/Bantam Club (EA) ... AABC
American Australian Association (EA) ... AAA
American Australian Bicentennial Foundation [*Defunct*] (EA) ... AABF
American Australian Business ... AAB
American Auto Laundry Association [*Later, ICA*] ... AALA
American Auto Racing Writers and Broadcasters Association (EA) ... AARWBA
American Automatic Control Council (EA) ... AACC
American Automobile Association (EA) ... AAA
American Automobile Labeling Act of 1992 ... AALA
American Automobile Manufacturers Association ... AAMA
American Automobile Manufacturers Association [*BTS*] (TAG) ... AAMA
American Automobile Touring Alliance (EA) ... AATA
American Automotive Leasing Association (EA) ... AALA
American Aviation Historical Society (EA) ... AAHS
American Award Manufacturers Association [*Later, TDMA*] (EA) ... AAMA
American Bach Foundation (EA) ... ABF
American Backgammon Players Association [*Defunct*] (EA) ... ABPA
American Backgammon Society ... ABS
American Badminton Association [*Later, USBA*] (EA) ... ABA
American Bail Bondsman Association (EA) ... ABBA
American Bakers Association (EA) ... ABA
American Bakery and Confectionery Workers' International Union [*Later, BCTWIU*] ... ABCW
American Ballads and Folk Songs [*A publication*] ... ABF
American Ballads and Songs [*A publication*] ... ABS
American Ballet Competition (EA) ... ABC
American Ballet Theater ... ABT
American Bamboo Society (EA) ... ABS
American Bancorp [*NASDAQ symbol*] (NQ) ... AMBC
American Bancorp of Nevada [*NASDAQ symbol*] (SAG) ... ABCN
American Bancorp of Nevada [*Associated Press*] (SAG) ... ABcpNV
American Bancorp Ohio [*NASDAQ symbol*] (SAG) ... AMBC
American Bancorp Ohio [*Associated Press*] (SAG) ... AmBcp
American Bancshares, Inc. (FL) [*NASDAQ symbol*] (SAG) ... ABAN
American Bancshares, Inc. (FL) [*Associated Press*] (SAG) ... ABncFL
American Bandmasters Association (EA) ... ABA
American Bandstand Memory Club [*Later, 1950's American Bandstand Fan Club*] (EA) ... ABMC
American Banjo Fraternity (EA) ... ABF
American Bank Note (BARN) ... ABN
American Bank Note Co. (MHDW) ... ABNCO
American Bank Note Holographics, Inc. ... ABNH
American Bank Notes Development Corporation (AAGC) ... ABND
American Bank of Connecticut [*Associated Press*] (SAG) ... ABkCT

American Bank of Connecticut [*AMEX symbol*] (SPSG) .... BKC
American Banker [*A publication*] .... AB
American Bankers Association [*Washington, DC*] (EA) .... ABA
American Bankers Association, New York, NY [*Library symbol Library of Congress*] (LCLS) .... NNABA
American Bankers Insurance Group [*Associated Press*] (SAG) .... ABnkr
American Bankers Insurance Group, Inc. [*NASDAQ symbol*] (NQ) .... ABIG
American Banknote Corp. [*NYSE symbol*] (SAG) .... ABN
American Banknote Corp. [*Associated Press*] (SAG) .... AmBknt
American Bankruptcy [*A publication*] (DLA) .... Am Bankr
American Bankruptcy Institute (EA) .... ABI
American Bankruptcy, New Series [*A publication*] (DLA) .... Am B (NS)
American Bankruptcy, New Series [*A publication*] (DLA) .... Am Bankr NS
American Bankruptcy Register [*A publication*] (DLA) .... Am Bankr Reg
American Bankruptcy Reports [*A publication*] (DLA) .... AB Rep
American Bankruptcy Reports [*A publication*] (DLA) .... ABR
American Bankruptcy Reports [*A publication*] (DLA) .... Am Bank R
American Bankruptcy Reports [*A publication*] (DLA) .... Am Bankr R
American Bankruptcy Reports [*A publication*] (DLA) .... Am Bankruptcy Reps
American Bankruptcy Reports [*A publication*] (DLA) .... Am B'kc'y Rep
American Bankruptcy Reports [*A publication*] (DLA) .... Am BR
American Bankruptcy Reports .... AMBANKRREP
American Bankruptcy Reports, New Series [*A publication*] (DLA) .... ABRNS
American Bankruptcy Reports, New Series [*A publication*] (DLA) .... Am Bankr R (NS)
American Bankruptcy Reports, New Series [*A publication*] (DLA) .... Am Bankr Rep NS
American Bankruptcy Reports, New Series [*A publication*] (DLA) .... Am BR (NS)
American Bankruptcy Review [*A publication*] (DLA) .... AB Rev
American Bankruptcy Review [*A publication*] (DLA) .... Am Bank Rev
American Bankruptcy Review [*A publication*] (DLA) .... Am Bankr Rev
American Bantam Association (EA) .... ABA
American Baptist Association .... ABA
American Baptist Black Caucus (EA) .... ABBC
American Baptist Churches .... ABC
American Baptist Churches of Oregon (SRA) .... ABCO
American Baptist Education Association [*Defunct*] (EA) .... ABEA
American Baptist Extension Corp. .... ABEC
American Baptist Foreign Mission Society [*Congo - Leopoldville*] .... ABFMS
American Baptist Historical Society (EA) .... ABHS
American Baptist Historical Society Library, Rochester, NY [*OCLC symbol*] (OCLC) .... RXP
American Baptist Historical Society, Rochester, NY [*Library symbol Library of Congress*] (LCLS) .... NRAB
American Baptist Home Mission Society [*Later, Board of National Ministries*] (EA) .... ABHMS
American Baptist Homes and Hospitals Association (EA) .... ABHHA
American Baptist Missionary Union [*Later, Board of International Ministries*] .... ABMU
American Baptist Publication Society, Philadelphia, PA [*Library symbol Library of Congress Obsolete*] (LCLS) .... PPABP
American Baptist Publishing Society (BARN) .... ABPS
American Baptist Seminary of the West, Berkeley, CA [*Library symbol Library of Congress*] (LCLS) .... CBGTU-B
American Baptist Theological Seminary, Nashville, TN [*Library symbol Library of Congress*] (LCLS) .... TNBT
American Baptist Women (EA) .... ABW
American Baptists Concerned (EA) .... ABC
American Bar Association (EA) .... ABA
American Bar Association (DLA) .... Am BA
American Bar Association Center for Professional Discipline (DLA) .... ABACPD
American Bar Association Center for Professional Responsibility (EA) .... ABACPR
American Bar Association. Comparative Law Bureau. Bulletin [*A publication*] (DLA) .... Bull Comp L
American Bar Association, Family Law Section, Mediation and Arbitration Committee [*Defunct*] (EA) .... ABAFLSMAC
American Bar Association. International and Comparative Law Section. Reports [*A publication*] (DLA) .... ABA Rep Int'l & Comp L Sec
American Bar Association Model Business Corporation Act, Annotated [*A publication*] (DLA) .... Model Business Corp Act
American Bar Association Model Business Corporation Act, Annotated, Second Series [*A publication*] (DLA) .... Model Bus Corp Act Anno 2d
American Bar Association Model Procurement Code [*A publication*] (AAGC) .... ABA MPC
American Bar Association Reporter [*A publication*] (DLA) .... ABA Rep
American Bar Association Reports [*A publication*] (DLA) .... ABA Rep
American Bar Association Reports [*A publication*] (DLA) .... Am Bar Asso Rep
American Bar Association Representation of the Homeless Project (EA) .... ABARHP
American Bar Association Section of International Law and Practice (EA) .... ABASILP
American Bar Association. Section of Labor Relations Law (DLA) .... ABA Sec Lab Rel L
American Bar Association Special Committee on Dispute Resolution (EA) .... ABASCDR
American Bar Association Young Lawyers Division (EA) .... ABAYLD
American Bar Foundation (EA) .... ABF
American Bar Foundation, Chicago, IL [*Library symbol Library of Congress*] (LCLS) .... ICABF
American Bar Foundation Research Journal [*A publication*] (AAGC) .... Am B Found Res J
American Bar Foundation. Research Newsletter [*A publication*] (DLA) .... ABF Res Newsl
American Bar Foundation. Research Reporter [*A publication*] (DLA) .... ABF Research Reptr
American Bar Foundation. Research Reporter Journal [*A publication*] (DLA) .... ABF Research Reptr J
American Bar News [*A publication*] (DLA) .... Am B News
American Barefoot Club (EA) .... ABC
American Barred Plymouth Rock Bantam Club [*Defunct*] (EA) .... ABPRBC
American Barred Plymouth Rock Club [*Later, Plymouth Rock Fanciers Club*] (EA) .... ABPRC
American Barrick Resources Corp. [*LA Barrick Gold*] [*NYSE symbol Toronto Stock Exchange symbol*] (SPSG) .... ABX
American Bartenders' Association (EA) .... ABA
American Baseball Coaches Association (EA) .... ABCA
American Baseball Fans Association (EA) .... ABFA
American Bashkir Curly Registry (EA) .... ABCR
American Basketball Association [*Later, NBA*] [*League of professional basketball players*] (EA) .... ABA
American Bass Association (EA) .... ABA
American Battle Monuments Commission [*Independent government agency*] .... ABMC
American Battleship Association (EA) .... ABA
American Bay Horse Registry [*Defunct*] (EA) .... ABHR
American Beagle Club (EA) .... ABC
American Beauty Association (EA) .... ABA
American Bed and Breakfast Association (EA) .... ABBA
American Bee Breeders Association (EA) .... ABBA
American Beefalo Association (EA) .... ABA
American Beefalo World Registry (EA) .... ABWR
American Beekeeping Federation (EA) .... ABF
American Beethoven Society (EA) .... ABS
American Begonia Society (EA) .... ABS
American Behcet's Association (EA) .... ABA
American Behcet's Foundation (EA) .... ABF
American Belgian Hare Club (EA) .... ABHC
American Belgian Tervuren Club (EA) .... ABTC
American Bell Association [*Later, ABAI*] (EA) .... ABA
American Bell Association International (EA) .... ABAI
American Bell, Inc. .... ABI
American Belted Galloway Cattle Breeders' Association [*Later, BGS*] (EA) .... BGA
American Benedictine Academy (EA) .... ABA
American Berkshire Association (EA) .... ABA
American Berlin Opera Foundation (EA) .... ABOF
American Beverage Alcohol Association [*Defunct*] (EA) .... ABAA
American Beverage Institute .... ABI
American Beveren Club .... ABC
American Bible Society (EA) .... ABS
American Bible Society, New York, NY [*Library symbol Library of Congress*] (LCLS) .... NNAB
American Biblical Encyclopedia Society (EA) .... ABES
American Bibliographical Center .... ABC
American Bicentennial Commemorative Society [*Defunct*] .... ABCS
American Bicycle Association (EA) .... ABA
American Bike Month Committee [*Defunct*] (EA) .... ABMC
American Bikers Aimed toward Education .... ABATE
American Bikeways Foundation [*Defunct*] (EA) .... ABF
American Bill of Rights Day Association [*Defunct*] (EA) .... ABRDA
American Billiard Association (EA) .... ABA
American Biltrite, Inc. [*AMEX symbol*] (SPSG) .... ABL
American Biltrite, Inc. [*Associated Press*] (SAG) .... AmBiltrt
American Bingo & Gambing Corp. [*NASDAQ symbol*] (SAG) .... BNGO
American Bingo & Gambling Corp. [*Associated Press*] (SAG) .... ABingo
American Biodynamics, Inc. [*Vancouver Stock Exchange symbol*] .... ACB
American Biogenetic Sciences, Inc. [*Associated Press*] (SAG) .... AmBiogn
American Biogenetic Sciences, Inc. [*NASDAQ symbol*] (SAG) .... MABX
American Biographical Institute Research Association (EA) .... ABIRA
American Biological Society (EA) .... ABS
American Bionetics, Inc. .... ABN
American Biotechnology Laboratory [*A publication*] .... ABL
American Birding Association (EA) .... ABA
American Birth Control League .... ABCL
American Black and Tan Coonhound Association (EA) .... ABTCA
American Black Book Writers Association (EA) .... ABBWA
American Black Chiropractors Association (EA) .... ABCA
American Black Maine-Anjou Association (EA) .... ABMAA
American Blade Collectors (EA) .... ABC
American Blade Collectors Association (EA) .... ABCA
American Bladesmith Society (EA) .... ABS
American Blake Foundation (EA) .... ABF
American Bleached Shellac Manufacturers Association (EA) .... ABSMA
American Blind Bowling Association (EA) .... ABBA
American Blind Lawyers Association (EA) .... ABLA
American Blind Skiing Foundation (EA) .... ABSF
American Blonde d'Aquitaine Association (EA) .... ABAA
American Blood Commission (EA) .... ABC
American Blood Resources Association (EA) .... ABRA
American Bloodhound Club (EA) .... ABC
American Blue and White Rabbit Club (EA) .... ABWRC
American Blue Cheese Association [*Defunct*] (EA) .... ABCA
American Board for Certification in Orthotics and Prosthetics (EA) .... ABC
American Board for Occupational Health Nurses (EA) .... ABOHN
American Board of Abdominal Surgery (EA) .... ABAS
American Board of Allergy and Immunology (EA) .... ABAI
American Board of Anesthesiology (EA) .... ABA
American Board of Applied Toxicology (DMAA) .... ABAT

American Board of Bioanalysis (EA) .... ABB
American Board of Bio-Analysis [*No connection with ABB*] [*Defunct*]
(EA) .... ABB-A
American Board of Bionic Rehabilitative Psychology (EA) .... ABBRP
American Board of Bloodless Medicine and Surgery (EA) .... ABBMS
American Board of Cardiovascular Perfusion (EA) .... ABCP
American Board of Certified and Registered Encephalographic
Technicians and Technologists (EA) .... ABCRETT
American Board of Chelation Therapy (EA) .... ABCT
American Board of Clinical Biofeedback [*Defunct*] (EA) .... ABCB
American Board of Clinical Chemistry (EA) .... ABCC
American Board of Clinical Hypnosis (EA) .... ABCH
American Board of Clinical Immunology and Allergy (EA) .... ABCIA
American Board of Colon and Rectal Surgery (EA) .... ABCRS
American Board of Commissioners for Foreign Missions [*Later,*
UCBWM] .... ABCFM
American Board of Commissioners for Foreign Missions, Boston, MA
[*Library symbol Library of Congress*] (LCLS) .... MBACFM
American Board of Cosmetic Surgery (EA) .... ABCS
American Board of Criminal Lawyers (EA) .... ABCL
American Board of Criminalistics (EA) .... ABC
American Board of Dental Medicine and Surgery (EA) .... ABDMS
American Board of Dental Public Health (EA) .... ABDPH
American Board of Dermatology (EA) .... ABD
American Board of Emergency Medicine (EA) .... ABEM
American Board of Endodontics (EA) .... ABE
American Board of Environmental Medicine (EA) .... ABEM
American Board of Examiners in Pastoral Counseling (EA) .... ABEPC
American Board of Examiners in Professional Psychology [*Later,*
ABPP] .... ABEPP
American Board of Examiners in Psychological Hypnosis [*Later, ABPH*]
(EA) .... ABEPH
American Board of Examiners in Psychotherapy (EA) .... ABEP
American Board of Examiners of Psychodrama, Sociometry, and Group
Psychotherapy (EA) .... ABEPSGP
American Board of Family Practice (EA) .... ABFP
American Board of Foreign Missions .... ABFM
American Board of Forensic Anthropology (EA) .... ABFA
American Board of Forensic Psychiatry (EA) .... ABFP
American Board of Forensic Psychology (EA) .... ABFP
American Board of Funeral Service Education (EA) .... ABFSE
American Board of Genetic Counseling .... ABCG
American Board of Hand Surgery (EA) .... ABHS
American Board of Health Physics (EA) .... ABHP
American Board of Homeopathic Medicine (EA) .... ABHM
American Board of Industrial Hygiene (EA) .... ABIH
American Board of Industrial Medicine and Surgery (EA) .... ABIMS
American Board of Internal Medicine (EA) .... ABIM
American Board of International Missions (EA) .... ABIM
American Board of Laser Surgery (EA) .... ABLS
American Board of Master Educators (EA) .... ABME
American Board of Medical Genetics (EA) .... ABMG
American Board of Medical Microbiology (EA) .... ABMM
American Board of Medical Psychotherapists (EA) .... ABMP
American Board of Medical Specialties (EA) .... ABMS
American Board of Medical Toxicology (EA) .... ABMT
American Board of Medical-Legal Analysis in Medicine and Surgery
(EA) .... ABMLAMS
American Board of Missions to the Jews [*Later, CPM*] (EA) .... ABMJ
American Board of National Missions (EA) .... ABNM
American Board of Neurological and Orthopaedic Medicine and Surgery
(EA) .... ABNOMS
American Board of Neurological Microsurgery (EA) .... ABNM
American Board of Neurological Surgery (EA) .... ABNS
American Board of Neuroscience Nursing (EA) .... ABNN
American Board of Nuclear Medicine (EA) .... ABNM
American Board of Nutrition (EA) .... ABN
American Board of Obstetrics and Gynecology (EA) .... ABOG
American Board of Ophthalmology (EA) .... ABO
American Board of Opticianry [*Later, NAO*] (EA) .... ABO
American Board of Oral and Maxillofacial Surgery (EA) .... ABOMS
American Board of Oral Pathology (EA) .... ABOP
American Board of Oral Pathology [*Later, ABOP*] (EA) .... AMBOP
American Board of Oral Surgery [*Later, ABOMS*] (EA) .... ABOS
American Board of Orthodontics (EA) .... ABO
American Board of Orthopaedic Microneurosurgery (EA) .... ABOM
American Board of Orthopedic Surgery (EA) .... ABOS
American Board of Otolaryngology (EA) .... ABO
American Board of Pathology (EA) .... ABP
American Board of Pediatric Dentistry (EA) .... ABPD
American Board of Pediatrics (EA) .... ABP
American Board of Pedodontics [*Later, ABPD*] (EA) .... ABP
American Board of Periodontology (EA) .... ABP
American Board of Physical Medicine and Rehabilitation (EA) .... ABPMR
American Board of Plastic Surgery (EA) .... ABPS
American Board of Podiatric Dermatology [*Defunct*] (EA) .... ABPD
American Board of Podiatric Orthopedics (EA) .... ABPO
American Board of Podiatric Surgery (EA) .... ABPS
American Board of PostAnesthesia Nursing Certification (EA) .... ABPANC
American Board of Preventive Medicine (EA) .... ABPM
American Board of Professional Disability Consultants (EA) .... ABPDC
American Board of Professional Liability Attorneys [*Chicago, IL*] (EA) .... ABPLA
American Board of Professional Psychology (EA) .... ABPP
American Board of Prosthodontics (EA) .... ABP
American Board of Psychiatry and Neurology (EA) .... ABPN

American Board of Psychological Hypnosis (EA) .... ABPH
American Board of Quality Assurance and Utilization Review (EA) .... ABQAUR
American Board of Quality Assurance and Utilization Review Physicians
[*Later, ABQAUR*] (EA) .... ABQAURP
American Board of Radiology (EA) .... ABR
American Board of Registration of EEG [*Electroencephalographic*]
Technologists (EA) .... ABRET
American Board of Ringside Medicine and Surgery (EA) .... ABRMS
American Board of Spinal Surgery (EA) .... ABSS
American Board of Surgery (EA) .... ABS
American Board of Thoracic Neurological Orthopaedic Medicine and
Surgery (EA) .... ABTNOMS
American Board of Thoracic Surgery (EA) .... ABTS
American Board of Toxicology (EA) .... ABT
American Board of Trade .... ABT
American Board of Trial Advocates (EA) .... ABOTA
American Board of Trial Advocates (EA) .... ABTA
American Board of Tropical Medicine [*Inactive*] (EA) .... ABTM
American Board of Urologic Allied Health Professionals (EA) .... ABUAHP
American Board of Urology (EA) .... ABU
American Board of Veterinary Toxicology (EA) .... ABVT
American Board of Vocational Experts (EA) .... ABVE
American Board on Counseling Services [*Later, IACS*] (EA) .... ABCS
American Board Products Association [*Later, AHA*] (EA) .... ABPA
American Boarding Kennels Association (EA) .... ABKA
American Boards of Examiners in Speech Pathology and Audiology [*Later,*
COPS] (EA) .... ABESPA
American Boardsailing Industries Association (EA) .... ABIA
American Boat and Yacht Council (EA) .... ABYC
American Boat Builders and Repairers Association (EA) .... ABBRA
American Boccaccio Association (EA) .... ABA
American Boiler Manufacturers Association (EA) .... ABMA
American Bonanza Society (EA) .... ABS
American Bonsai Society (EA) .... ABS
[*The*] American Book Award [*Later, ABA*] .... TABA
American Book Awards [*Formerly, TABA*] .... ABA
American Book Co. (AEBS) .... ABC
American Book Council [*Defunct*] (EA) .... ABC
American Book Prices Current [*A publication*] .... ABPC
American Book Producers Association (EA) .... ABPA
American Book Publishers Council [*Later, AAP*] .... ABPC
American Book Publishers Political Action Committee (EA) .... ABPPAC
American Book Publishing Record [*A publication*] .... ABPR
American Book Review [*A publication*] (BRI) .... ABR
American Book Trade Directory [*A publication*] .... ABTD
American Book-Prices Current [*A publication*] (DGA) .... ABC
American Booksellers Association (EA) .... ABA
American Border Fancy Canary Club (EA) .... ABFCC
American Bosch Arma Corp. (AAG) .... ABAC
American Bosch Arma Corp. (MCD) .... AMBAC
American Bosch Arma Corp. (AAG) .... ARMA
American Botanical Council (EA) .... ABC
American Bottled Water Association [*Later, IBWA*] (EA) .... ABWA
American Bottlers of Carbonated Beverages [*Later, NSDA*] (EA) .... ABCB
American Bough of the International Society of Shropshires (EA) .... ABISS
American Bouvier des Flandres Club (EA) .... ABDFC
American Bowhunters Association [*Defunct*] (EA) .... ABA
American Bowling Congress (EA) .... ABC
American Boxer Club (EA) .... ABC
American Boxwood Society (EA) .... ABS
American Boys Club in Defense of Errol Flynn [*Facetious*
organization] .... ABCDEF
American Brahma Club (EA) .... ABC
American Brahman Breeders Association (EA) .... ABBA
American Brain Tumor Association [*Formerly Association for Brain Tumor*
Research (AFBTR)] (PAZ) .... ABTA
American Bralers Association (EA) .... ABA
American Brands, Inc. [*Associated Press*] (SAG) .... ABrand
American Brands, Inc. [*Associated Press*] (SAG) .... ABrd
American Brands, Inc. [*NYSE symbol*] (SPSG) .... AMB
American Brazilian Association [*Later, Brazilian American Chamber of*
Commerce] (EA) .... ABA
American Breed Association (EA) .... ABA
American Breeder Service (EA) .... ABS
American Breweriana Association (EA) .... ABA
American Bridge Association (EA) .... ABA
American Bridge Teachers' Association (EA) .... ABTA
American Bridge, Tunnel, and Turnpike Association [*Later, IBTTA*]
(EA) .... ABTTA
American, British, and Canadian .... ABC
American, British, Australian [*Military*] .... ABA
American British Cab Society (EA) .... ABCS
American, British, Canadian, Australian (MHDB) .... ABCA
American, British, Dutch, Australian (ADA) .... ABDA
American British Numismatic Society [*Defunct*] (EA) .... ABNS
American Brittany Club (EA) .... ABC
American Brittle Bone Society [*Defunct*] (EA) .... ABBS
American Broadcasting Companies, Inc. [*Subsidiary of Capital Cities/ABC,*
Inc.] .... ABC
American Broadcasting Co. Contemporary Network (LAIN) .... ABC-C
American Broadcasting Co. Direction Network (LAIN) .... ABC-D
American Broadcasting Co. Entertainment Network (LAIN) .... ABC-E
American Broadcasting Co. FM Network (LAIN) .... ABC-F
American Broadcasting Co. Information Network (LAIN) .... ABC-I
American Broadcasting Co. Rock Radio Network (LAIN) .... ABC-R

American Broadcasting Co. Talkradio Network (LAIN) .... ABC-T
American Broadcasting Co. Television Satellite (NTCM) .... ABSAT
American Broadcasting Station in Europe [*OWI*] .... ABSIE
American Broadcasting System (IAA) .... ABS
American Broadcasting-Paramount Theatres, Inc. (NTCM) .... AB-PT
American Broncho-Esophagological Association (EA) .... ABEA
American Broncho-Esophagological Association (EA) .... ABES
American Brown Leghorn Club (EA) .... ABLC
American Brunswick [*Record label*] .... AmB
American Brush Manufacturers Association (EA) .... ABMA
American Brussels Griffon Association (EA) .... ABGA
American Bryological and Lichenological Society (EA) .... ABLS
American Bryological Society [*Later, ABLS*] (EA) .... ABS
American Buckskin Registry Association (EA) .... ABRA
American Buddhist Academy (EA) .... ABA
American Buddhist Association (EA) .... ABA
American Buddhist Movement (EA) .... ABM
American Budgerigar Society (EA) .... ABS
American Budgetel, Inc. [*Vancouver Stock Exchange symbol*] .... ABG
American Buff Plymouth Rock Club (EA) .... ABPRC
American Buff Wyandotte Club [*Defunct*] (EA) .... ABWC
American Buffalo Association (EA) .... ABA
American Bugatti Club (EA) .... ABC
American Building Contractors Association (EA) .... ABCA
American Building Maintenance Industries [*NYSE symbol*] (SPSG) .... ABM
American Buildings Co. [*NASDAQ symbol*] (SAG) .... ABCO
American Buildings Co. [*Associated Press*] (SAG) .... AmBldg
American Bulgarian League [*Defunct*] (EA) .... ABL
American Bullmastiff Association (EA) .... ABA
American Bureau for Medical Advancement in China (EA) .... ABMAC
American Bureau of Metal Statistics (EA) .... ABMS
American Bureau of Shipping .... AB
American Bureau of Shipping (EA) .... ABS
American Bureau of Shipping (Hellas) (DS) .... ABH
American Bureau of Shipping Information Retrieval System (MSC) .... ABSORS
American Bureau of Shipping Worldwide Technical Services (MHDB) .... ABSTECH
American Burn Association (EA) .... ABA
American Bus Association (EA) .... ABA
American Business Association [*New York, NY*] (EA) .... ABA
American Business Cancer [*in name "ABC Research Foundation"*] .... ABC
American Business Cancer Research Foundation [*Later, ABFCR*] (EA) .... ABCRF
American Business Card Club (EA) .... ABCC
American Business Collaboration for Quality Dependent Care .... ABC
American Business Communication Association [*Later, ABC*] .... ABCA
American Business Communication Association Unification of Engineering Standards (MHDB) .... ABCA/UES
American Business Computers Corp. [*NASDAQ symbol*] (NQ) .... ABCC
American Business Computers Corp. [*Associated Press*] (SAG) .... ABsCpt
American Business Conference [*Washington, DC*] (EA) .... ABC
American Business Council, Malaysia (EA) .... ABC
American Business Council of Singapore (EA) .... ABCS
American Business Foundation for Cancer Research [*Defunct*] (EA) .... ABFCR
American Business History Collection [*Microfiche*] (IID) .... ABHC
American Business Information .... ABI
American Business Information, Inc. [*NASDAQ symbol*] (SAG) .... ABII
American Business Information, Inc. [*Associated Press*] (SAG) .... AmBusn
American Business Law Association (EA) .... ABLA
American Business Media Council [*Defunct*] (EA) .... ABMC
American Business Men's Research Foundation [*Later, ARIS*] (EA) .... ABMRF
American Business Network [*US Chamber of Commerce*] [*Washington, DC Cable-television system*] [*Telecommunications*] (TSSD) .... BIZNET
American Business Press [*Later, American Business Publishers*] .... ABP
American Business Products, Inc. [*NYSE symbol*] (SPSG) .... ABP
American Business Products, Inc. [*Associated Press*] (SAG) .... ABusnP
American Business Products, Inc. [*Associated Press*] (SAG) .... ABusnPd
American Business Women's Association (EA) .... ABWA
American Business Writing Association [*Later, ABCA*] (EA) .... ABWA
American Businessmen of Jeddah (EA) .... ABJ
American Businessmen's Group of Riyadh (EA) .... ABGR
American Butter Institute (EA) .... ABI
American Buyers Federation (EA) .... ABF
American Buyers of Meeting and Incentive Travel (EA) .... ABMIT
American Cable & Radio Corp. .... AC & R
American Cable Network, Inc. (NTCM) .... ACN
American Cadet Alliance (EA) .... ACA
American Camellia Society (EA) .... ACS
American Camp and Hospital Service .... ACHS
American Campaign Medal [*Military decoration*] .... ACM
American Camping Association (EA) .... ACA
American Can Canada [*Toronto Stock Exchange symbol*] .... ACX
American Can Co. (CDAI) .... AC
American Can Co., Barrington, IL [*Library symbol Library of Congress*] (LCLS) .... IBarA
American, Canadian, Australian, British Urban Game [*Computer-assisted simulation wargame*] [*Army*] (INF) .... ACABUG
American Canadian Systems, Inc. [*Vancouver Stock Exchange symbol*] .... ACW
American Canal Society (EA) .... ACS
American Cancer Society (EA) .... ACS
American Cancer Society, New York, NY [*Library symbol Library of Congress*] (LCLS) .... NNACS
American Canine Sports Medicine Association (EA) .... ACSMA
American Cannabis Research Experiment (EA) .... ACRE
American Canoe Association (EA) .... ACA
American Canoe Manufacturers Union [*Defunct*] (EA) .... ACMU
American Canvas Institute .... ACI
American Capital Bond Fund, Inc. [*Associated Press*] (SAG) .... ACapBd
American Capital Bond Fund, Inc. [*NYSE symbol*] (SPSG) .... ACB
American Capital Convertible Securities, Inc. [*Associated Press*] (SAG) .... ACapCv
American Capital Convertible Securities, Inc. [*NYSE symbol*] (SPSG) .... ACS
American Capital Income Trust [*Associated Press*] (SAG) .... ACapIn
American Capital Income Trust [*NYSE symbol*] (SPSG) .... ACD
American Capon Producers Association (EA) .... ACPA
American Car and Foundry .... ACF
American Car and Foundry, Electronics .... ACFE
American Car and Foundry Industries .... ACFI
American Car Rental Association (EA) .... ACRA
American Carbon Society (EA) .... ACS
American Cardiology Technologists Association [*Later, NSCPT*] (EA) .... ACTA
American Cargo War Risk Reinsurance Exchange (EA) .... ACWRRE
American Carnation Society [*Defunct*] (EA) .... ACS
American Carnival Glass Association (EA) .... ACGA
American Carnivals Association (EA) .... ACA
American Carousel Society (EA) .... ACS
American Carpal Tunnel Syndrome Association (EA) .... ACTSA
American Carpet Institute [*Later, CRI*] (EA) .... ACI
American Cartographic Association (EA) .... ACA
American Casino Enterprises, Inc. [*NASDAQ symbol*] (NQ) .... ACES
American Casino Enterprises, Inc. [*Associated Press*] (SAG) .... AmCasn
American Cast Metals Association (EA) .... ACMA
American Casting Association (EA) .... ACA
American Cat Association (EA) .... ACA
American Cat Fanciers Association (EA) .... ACFA
American Catalogue [*A bibliographic publication*] .... AmC
American Catfish Marketing Association (EA) .... ACMA
American Catholic Committee (EA) .... ACC
American Catholic Conference [*Defunct*] (EA) .... ACC
American Catholic Correctional Chaplains Association (EA) .... ACCCA
American Catholic Esperanto Society (EA) .... ACES
American Catholic Historical Association (EA) .... ACHA
American Catholic Historical Society (EA) .... ACHS
American Catholic Historical Society, Philadelphia, PA [*Library symbol Library of Congress*] (LCLS) .... PPACHi
American Catholic Philosophical Association (EA) .... ACPA
American Catholic Psychological Association [*Later, PIRI*] (EA) .... ACPA
American Catholic Sociological Society [*Later, ASR*] (EA) .... ACSS
American Catholic Truth Society [*Defunct*] (EA) .... ACTS
American Catholic Union (EA) .... ACU
American Cause [*An association*] (EA) .... AC
American Cave Conservation Association (EA) .... ACCA
American Cavy Breeders Association (EA) .... ACBA
American CB Radio Association (EA) .... ACBRA
American Celiac Society [*Later, ACS/DSC*] (EA) .... ACS
American Celiac Society/Dietary Support Coalition (EA) .... ACS/DSC
American Cement Alliance (EA) .... ACA
American Cement Trade Alliance [*Later, ACA*] (EA) .... ACTA
American Cemetery Association (EA) .... ACA
American Cemetery-Mortuary Council (EA) .... ACMC
American Center for Chinese Medical Sciences (EA) .... ACCMS
American Center for Design (EA) .... ACD
American Center for Homeopathy (EA) .... ACH
American Center for Immuno-Biology and Metabolism .... ACIBM
American Center for International Leadership (EA) .... ACIL
American Center for Law and Justice [*Located on Pat Robertson's estate*] [*Virginia Beach, VA*] (ECON) .... ACLJ
American Center for Stanislavski Theatre Art (EA) .... ACSTA
American Center for Students and Artists (EA) .... ACSA
American Center for the Alexander Technique (EA) .... ACAT
American Center for the Quality of Work Life (EA) .... ACQWL
American Center of Films for Children (EA) .... ACFC
American Center of Oriental Research .... ACOR
American Center of the Union Internationale de la Marionette (EA) .... UNIMA-USA
American Central European Dental Institute .... ACEDI
American Central NOTAM [*Notice to Airmen*] **Facility** [*Military*] .... ACNF
American Ceramic Society (EA) .... ACerS
American Ceramic Society (EA) .... ACS
American Ceramic Society, Columbus, OH [*Library symbol Library of Congress*] (LCLS) .... OCoAC
American Certified Morticians Association [*Defunct*] (EA) .... ACMA
American Cetacean Society (EA) .... ACS
American Chain Association (EA) .... ACA
American Chain of Warehouses (EA) .... ACW
American Chamber of Commerce (DCTA) .... ACC
American Chamber of Commerce Executives (EA) .... ACCE
American Chamber of Commerce in Australia .... ACCA
American Chamber of Commerce in Australia .... AMCHAM
American Chamber of Commerce in Austria (EA) .... ACCA
American Chamber of Commerce in Hong Kong (EA) .... AmCham HK
American Chamber of Commerce in Japan (EA) .... ACCJ
American Chamber of Commerce in Republic of China (EA) .... ACC-ROC
American Chamber of Commerce in Thailand (EA) .... ACCT
American Chamber of Commerce of Bolivia (EA) .... ACCB
American Chamber of Commerce of El Salvador (EA) .... ACCES
American Chamber of Commerce of Mexico (CROSS) .... AmCham
American Chamber of Commerce of the Philippines (EA) .... ACCP
American Chamber of Commerce Researchers Association (EA) .... ACCRA
American Chancery Digest [*A publication*] (DLA) .... Am Ch Dig
American Chaplain's Association (EA) .... ACA

American Chapter, International Real Estate Federation (EA) ... AC/IREF
American Charbray Breeders Association [Later, AICA] (EA) ... ACBA
American Checker Federation (EA) ... ACF
American Checkered Giant Club [Later, ACGRC] ... ACGC
American Checkered Giant Rabbit Club (EA) ... ACGRC
American Cheerleader Association ... ACA
American Cheese (IIA) ... AC
American Cheese Society (EA) ... ACS
American Chemical Exchange ... ACE
American Chemical Society (EA) ... ACS
American Chemical Society, Washington, DC [Library symbol Library of Congress] (LCLS) ... DACS
American Chesapeake Club (EA) ... ACC
American Chess Academy [Commercial firm] (EA) ... ACA
American Chess Foundation (EA) ... ACF
American Chestnut Foundation (EA) ... ACF
American Cheviot Sheep Society (EA) ... ACSS
American Chianina Association (EA) ... ACA
American Child Care Services [Defunct] (EA) ... ACCS
American Child Custody Alliance (EA) ... ACCA
American Child Guidance Foundation [Defunct] (EA) ... ACGF
American Chinchilla Rabbit Breeders Association (EA) ... ACRBA
American Chinese Medical Society [Later, CAMS] (EA) ... ACMS
American Chiropractic Association (EA) ... ACA
American Chiropractic Registry of Radiologic Technologists (EA) ... ACRRT
American Choral Directors Association (EA) ... ACDA
American Choral Foundation (EA) ... ACF
American Christian Action Council [Later, NCBBC] (EA) ... ACAC
American Christian Association for Israel [Later, American-Israel Cultural Foundation] (EA) ... ACAI
American Christian Committee for Refugees [Post-World War II, Europe] ... ACCR
American Christian Palestine Committee [Defunct] ... ACPC
American Christian Television Service [Cable-television system] ... ACTS
American Christmas Crib Society [Defunct] (EA) ... ACCS
American Chronic Pain Association (EA) ... ACPA
American Church Building Fund Commission [Later, Episcopal Church Building Fund] (EA) ... ACBFC
American Church Union (EA) ... ACU
American Cimflex Corp. [Pittsburgh, PA] ... ACC
American Cinema Editors (EA) ... ACE
American Cinemastores [NASDAQ symbol] (SAG) ... ACSI
American Cinemastores [Associated Press] (SAG) ... AmCin
American Cinemastores [Associated Press] (SAG) ... AmCine
American Cinemastores Wrrt [NASDAQ symbol] (TTSB) ... ACSIW
American Circus Memorial Association (EA) ... ACMA
American Citizens [Military] (ADDR) ... AMCITS
American Citizens Abroad (EA) ... ACA
American Citizens and Lawmen Association (EA) ... ACLA
American Citizens Band Operators Association (EA) ... ACBOA
American Citizens Committee on Reducing Debt (EA) ... ACCORD
American Citizens Concerned for Life Education Fund/ACCL Communications Center [Defunct] (EA) ... ACCL
American Citizens for Honesty in Government [Defunct] (EA) ... ACHG
American Citizens for Justice [An association] (EA) ... ACJ
American Citizens for Political Action (EA) ... ACPA
American Citizens Together [An association] ... ACT
American Citizenship Center (EA) ... ACC
American City Bureau [An association] (EA) ... ACB
American City Planning Institute ... ACPI
American City Racing League [Auto racing] ... ACRC
American City Racing League [Auto racing] ... ACRL
American Civic Association (EA) ... ACA
[The] American Civil Defense Association (EA) ... TACDA
American Civil Law Journal [A publication] (DLA) ... ACLJ
American Civil Law Journal [A publication] (DLA) ... Am CLJ
American Civil Liberties Union (EA) ... ACLU
American Civil Liberties Union Foundation (EA) ... ACLUF
American Civil Liberties Union. Legislative Action Bulletin [A publication] (ILCA) ... ACLU Leg Act Bull
American Civil Liberties Union. Legislative Action Bulletin [A publication] (DLA) ... ACLU Leg Action Bull
American Civil War Association (EA) ... ACWA
American Civil War Bulletin Board System [Information service or system] (IID) ... ACWBBS
American Civil War Round Table (EAIO) ... ACWRT
American Civilian Internee Information Bureau [Army] (AABC) ... ACIIB
American Civilian Internee Information Bureau (Branch) (GFGA) ... ACIIB(Br)
American Claims Evaluation, Inc. [NASDAQ symbol] (NQ) ... AMCE
American Claims Evaluators [Associated Press] (SAG) ... AClaim
American Classic Voyages, Inc. [Associated Press] (SAG) ... AClasVoy
American Classic Voyages, Inc. [NASDAQ symbol] (SAG) ... AMCV
American Classical League (EA) ... ACL
American Clean Water Association (EA) ... ACWA
American Cleft Palate Association [Later, ACPCA] (EA) ... ACPA
American Cleft Palate-Craniofacial Association (EA) ... ACPCA
American Clinical and Climatological Association (EA) ... ACCA
American Clinical Laboratory Association (EA) ... ACLA
American Clipper Owners Club (EA) ... ACOC
American Cloak and Suit Manufacturers Association (EA) ... ACSMA
American Club of Paris (EA) ... ACP
American Coal Ash Association (EA) ... ACAA
American Coal Foundation (EA) ... ACF
American Coalition for Life (EA) ... ACL
American Coalition for Traditional Values (EA) ... ACTV
American Coalition for Traffic Safety (EA) ... ACTS
American Coalition of Citizens with Disabilities [Defunct] (EA) ... ACCD
American Coalition of Patriotic Societies [Defunct] (EA) ... ACPS
American Coalition of Unregistered Churches (EA) ... ACUC
American Coalition on Trade Expansion with Canada (EA) ... ACTEC
American Coaster Enthusiasts (EA) ... ACE
American Cockatiel Society (EA) ... ACS
American Cocker Spaniel Club (EAIO) ... ACSC
American Cocoa Research Institute (EA) ... ACRI
American Coin Merchandising, Inc. [NASDAQ symbol] (SAG) ... AMCN
American Coin Merchandising, Inc. [Associated Press] (SAG) ... AmCoin
American Coke and Coal Chemicals Institute (EA) ... ACCCI
American Collection Association [Orem, UT] (EA) ... ACA
American Collectors Association [Minneapolis, MN] (EA) ... ACA
American Collectors of Infant Feeders (EA) ... ACIF
American College Admissions Advisory and Career Counseling Center (EA) ... ACAACCC
American College Admissions Advisory Center [Later, ACAACCC] (EA) ... ACAAC
American College Admissions Center [Later, ACAAC] ... ACAC
American College, Bryn Mawr, PA [OCLC symbol] (OCLC) ... AMC
American College Dance Festival Association (EA) ... ACDFA
American College for Continuing Education (EA) ... ACCE
American College for the Applied Arts, Los Angeles, CA [Library symbol] [Library of Congress] (LCLS) ... CLACA
American College Health Association (EA) ... ACHA
American College of Addiction Treatment Administrators (EA) ... ACATA
American College of Advancement in Medicine (EA) ... ACAM
American College of Allergists (EA) ... ACA
American College of Allergy, Asthma, and Immunology (DMAA) ... ACAAI
American College of Anesthesiologists (EA) ... ACA
American College of Angiology (EA) ... ACA
American College of Animal Laboratory Medicine (RDA) ... ACALM
American College of Apothecaries (EA) ... ACA
American College of Applied Arts, Atlanta, GA [Library symbol] [Library of Congress] (LCLS) ... GACA
American College of Cardiology (EA) ... ACC
American College of Cardiology Extended Study Services ... ACCESS
American College of Cardiovascular Administrators (EA) ... ACCA
American College of Chemosurgery (EA) ... ACC
American College of Chest Physicians (EA) ... ACCP
American College of Chiropractic Orthopedists (EA) ... ACCO
American College of Clinic Administrators [Defunct] (EA) ... ACCA
American College of Clinic Managers [Later, ACMGA] (EA) ... ACCM
American College of Clinical Hypnosis [Defunct] (EA) ... ACCH
American College of Clinical Pharmacology (EA) ... ACCP
American College of Clinical Pharmacy (EA) ... ACCP
American College of Computer Lawyers [Defunct] (EA) ... ACCL
American College of Counselors (EA) ... ACC
American College of Cryosurgery (EA) ... ACC
American College of Dentists (EA) ... ACD
American College of Ecology [Defunct] (EA) ... ACE
American College of Emergency Physicians (EA) ... ACEP
American College of Epidemiology (EA) ... ACE
American College of Foot and Ankle Orthopedics and Medicine (DMAA) ... ACFAO
American College of Foot and Ankle Surgeons (DMAA) ... ACFAS
American College of Foot Orthopedists (EA) ... ACFO
American College of Foot Roentgenologists [Later, American College of PodiatricRadiologists] (EA) ... ACFR
American College of Foot Specialists [Later, ACCE] (EA) ... ACFS
American College of Foot Surgeons (EA) ... ACFS
American College of Gastroenterology (EA) ... ACG
American College of General Practice [Later, ACM] (EA) ... ACGP
American College of General Practitioners in Osteopathic Medicine and Surgery (EA) ... ACGPOMS
American College of Health Care Administrators (EA) ... ACHCA
American College of Healthcare Executives (EA) ... ACHE
American College of Heraldry (EA) ... ACH
American College of Home Obstetrics (EA) ... ACHO
American College of Hospital Administrators [Later, ACHE] (EA) ... ACHA
American College of International Physicians (EA) ... ACIP
American College of Laboratory Animal Medicine (EA) ... ACLAM
American College of Legal Medicine (EA) ... ACLM
American College of Life Underwriters [Later, The American College] (EA) ... ACLU
American College of Life Underwriters, Bryn Mawr, PA [Library symbol Library of Congress] (LCLS) ... PBmA
American College of Medical Group Administrators (EA) ... ACMGA
American College of Medical Informatics (DMAA) ... ACMI
American College of Medical Technologists (EA) ... ACMT
American College of Medicine (EA) ... ACM
American College of Mental Health Administration (EA) ... ACMHA
American College of Musicians (EA) ... ACM
American College of Neuropsychiatrists (EA) ... ACN
American College of Neuropsychopharmacology (EA) ... ACNP
American College of Nuclear Medicine (EA) ... ACNM
American College of Nuclear Physicians (EA) ... ACNP
American College of Nurse-Midwives (EA) ... ACNM
American College of Nursing Home Administrators [Later, ACHCA] ... ACNHA
American College of Nutrition (EA) ... ACN
American College of Obstetricians and Gynecologists (EA) ... ACOG
American College of Optometric Physicians (EA) ... ACOP
American College of Oral and Maxillofacial Surgeons (EA) ... ACOMS
American College of Orgonomy (EA) ... ACO
American College of Osteopathic Emergency Physicians (EA) ... ACOEP

American College of Osteopathic Hospital Administrators [*Later, COHE*] (EA) ... ACOHA
American College of Osteopathic Internists (EA) ... ACOI
American College of Osteopathic Obstetricians and Gynecologists (EA) ... ACOOG
American College of Osteopathic Pediatricians (EA) ... ACOP
American College of Osteopathic Surgeons (EA) ... ACOS
American College of Otorhinolaryngologists (EA) ... ACO
American College of Pain Medicine ... ACPM
American College of Pathologists (DAVI) ... ACP
American College of Pharmacists (EA) ... ACP
American College of Physician Executives (EA) ... ACPE
American College of Physicians (EA) ... ACP
American College of Physicians Assistants [*Defunct*] (EA) ... ACPA
American College of Podiatric Radiologists (EA) ... ACPR
American College of Podopediatrics (EA) ... ACP
American College of Preventive Medicine (EA) ... ACPM
American College of Probate Counsel [*Later, ACTEC*] (EA) ... ACPC
American College of Prosthodontists (EA) ... ACP
American College of Psychiatrists (EA) ... ACP
American College of Psychoanalysts (EA) ... ACPn
American College of Radiation Oncology ... ACRO
American College of Radio Marketing (EA) ... ACRM
American College of Radiology (EA) ... ACR
American College of Radiology, Reston, VA [*Library symbol*] [*Library of Congress*] (LCLS) ... ViReA
American College of Real Estate Consultants [*Later, RECP*] (EA) ... ACREC
American College of Rheumatology (EA) ... ACR
American College of Sports Medicine (EA) ... ACSM
American College of Surgeons (EA) ... ACS
American College of Surgeons, Chicago, IL [*Library symbol Library of Congress*] (LCLS) ... ICAC
American College of Surgeons Committee on Trauma ... ACSCOT
American College of Switzerland ... ACS
American College of Theriogenologists (EA) ... ACT
American College of Toxicology (EA) ... ACT
American College of Trial Lawyers (EA) ... ACTL
American College of Trust and Estate Counsel (EA) ... ACTEC
American College of Utilization Review Physicians (EA) ... ACURP
American College of Veterinary Dermatology (EA) ... ACVD
American College of Veterinary Internal Medicine (EA) ... ACVIM
American College of Veterinary Microbiologists (EA) ... ACVM
American College of Veterinary Ophthalmologists (EA) ... ACVO
American College of Veterinary Pathologists (EA) ... ACVP
American College of Veterinary Radiology (EA) ... ACVR
American College of Veterinary Surgeons (EA) ... ACVS
American College of Veterinary Toxicologists [*Later, AAVCT*] (EA) ... ACVT
American College Personnel Accreditation (OICC) ... ACPC
American College Personnel Association (EA) ... ACPA
American College Public Relations Association [*Later, Council for the Advancement and Support of Education*] ... ACPRA
American College Testing Program (EA) ... ACT
American College Testing Service (HCT) ... ACTS
American College Theater Festival ... ACTF
American Collegians for Life (EA) ... ACL
American Collegiate Press ... ACP
American Collegiate Retailing Association (EA) ... ACRA
American Colon Therapy Association (EA) ... ACTA
American Colonization Society ... ACS
American Color Association (EA) ... ACA
American Color Print Society (EA) ... ACPS
American Columbia [*Record label*] ... AmC
American Comedy Museum Association [*Defunct*] (EA) ... ACMA
American Comet Club - United Spoilers of America [*Later, MERCPAC*] (EA) ... ACC-USA
American Commercial Barge Lines, Inc. [*AAR code*] ... ACBL
American Commercial Collectors Association (EA) ... ACCA
American Commercial Lines, Inc. ... ACL
American Commercial Rabbit Association [*Defunct*] (EA) ... ACRA
American Commission for Protection and Salvage of Artistic and Historical Monuments in War Areas [*World War II Defunct*] ... ACPSAHMWA
American Commission on Ministerial Training (EA) ... ACMT
American Committee for Aid to Poland (EA) ... ACAP
American Committee for Cultural Freedom ... ACCF
American Committee for Democracy and Freedom in Greece (EA) ... ACDFG
American Committee for Flags of Necessity [*Later, FACS*] (EA) ... ACFN
American Committee for Human Rights (EA) ... ACHR
American Committee for International Conservation (EA) ... ACIC
American Committee for International Wild Life Protection [*Later, ACIC*] (EA) ... ACIWLP
American Committee for Irish Studies (AEBS) ... ACIS
American Committee for KEEP (EA) ... ACK
American Committee for Liberation [*Later, RFE/RL*] ... ACL
American Committee for Rescue and Resettlement of Iraqi Jews (EA) ... AMCORR
American Committee for Shaare Zedek in Jerusalem (EA) ... ACSZJ
American Committee for South Asian Art [*Defunct Defunct*] (EA) ... ACSAA
American Committee for the Advancement of Torah Education in Israel [*Later, OTII*] (EA) ... ACATEI
American Committee for the National Sick Fund of Israel (EA) ... ACNSFI
American Committee for the Weizmann Institute of Science (EA) ... ACWIS
American Committee for Ulster Justice (EA) ... ACUJ
American Committee of OSE [*Defunct*] ... AMEROSE
American Committee of Slavists (EA) ... ACS
American Committee of the Slovak World Congress (EA) ... ACSWC
American Committee of United Europe ... ACUE
American Committee on Africa (EA) ... ACOA
American Committee on East-West Accord [*Later, ACUSSR*] (EA) ... ACEWA
American Committee on Italian Migration (EA) ... ACIM
American Committee on Japan (EA) ... ACJ
American Committee on the History of the Second World War (EA) ... ACHSWW
American Committee on US-Soviet Relations [*Defunct*] (EA) ... ACUSSR
American Committee to Advance the Study of Petroglyphs and Pictographs (EA) ... ACASPP
American Commodity Distribution Association (EA) ... ACDA
American Communication Services [*Evanston, IL*] [*Telecommunications*] (TSSD) ... ACS
American Communication Services, Inc. [*Evanston, IL*] (TSSD) ... ACSI
American Communications Association ... ACA
American Communications Consultants, Inc. [*Telecommunications service*] (TSSD) ... ACC
American Communications Services, Inc. [*NASDAQ symbol*] (SAG) ... ACNS
American Communications Services, Inc. [*Associated Press*] (SAG) ... AComS
American Community Cultural Center Association (EA) ... ACCCA
American Community Gardening Association (EA) ... ACGA
American Community Schools [*In foreign countries*] ... ACS
American Community Theatre Association (EA) ... ACTA
American Commuters Association ... ACA
American Comparative Literature Association (EA) ... ACLA
American Compensation Association (EA) ... ACA
American Component Dealers Association (EA) ... ACDA
American Composers Alliance (EA) ... ACA
American Composers Orchestra ... ACO
American Computer Appraisal Service (MHDI) ... ACAS
American Computer Referral (NITA) ... ACR
American Computer Science League (EA) ... ACSL
American Concert Choir [*Defunct*] (EA) ... ACC
American Concert Choir and Choral Foundation [*Later, ACF*] ... ACCCF
American Concrete Agricultural Pipe Association [*Defunct*] ... ACAPA
American Concrete Institute (EA) ... ACI
American Concrete Institute, Detroit, MI [*Library symbol Library of Congress*] (LCLS) ... MiDACI
American Concrete Pavement Association (EA) ... ACPA
American Concrete Pipe Association (EA) ... ACPA
American Concrete Pressure Pipe Association (EA) ... ACPP
American Concrete Pressure Pipe Association (EA) ... ACPPA
American Concrete Pumping Association (EA) ... ACPA
American Conditions [*Insurance*] ... AC
American Conference for Irish Studies (EA) ... ACIS
American Conference Institute (AAGC) ... ACI
American Conference of Academic Deans (EA) ... ACAD
American Conference of Cantors (EA) ... ACC
American Conference of Governmental Industrial Hygienists (EA) ... ACGIH
American Conference of Real Estate Investment Trusts [*Defunct*] (EA) ... ACREIT
American Conference of Therapeutic Selfhelp/Selfhealth Social Action Clubs [*Defunct*] (EA) ... ACT
American Congregation of Jews from Austria (EA) ... ACJA
American Congregational Association (EA) ... ACA
American Congregational Association, Boston, MA [*Library symbol Library of Congress*] (LCLS) ... MBC
American Congregational Union ... ACU
American Congress of Physical Medicine and Rehabilitation [*Later, ACRM*] (EA) ... ACPMR
American Congress of Rehabilitation Medicine (EA) ... ACRM
American Congress on Surveying and Mapping (EA) ... ACSM
American Conifer Society (EA) ... ACS
American Connemara Pony Society (EA) ... ACPS
American Conservation Association, Inc. (EPA) ... ACA
American Conservative Trust (EA) ... ACT
American Conservative Union (EA) ... ACU
American Conservative Union Education and Research Institute (EA) ... ACU-ERI
American Conservatives for Freedom (EA) ... ACF
American Conservatory of Music [*Chicago, IL*] ... ACM
American Conservatory of Music, Chicago, IL [*Library symbol Library of Congress*] (LCLS) ... ICACMu
American Conservatory of Music, Chicago, IL [*OCLC symbol*] (OCLC) ... IVI
American Conservatory Theatre ... ACT
American Conservatory Theatre Foundation (EA) ... ACTF
American Constitutional and Civil Rights Union [*Defunct*] (EA) ... ACCRU
American Constitutional Rights Association (EA) ... ACRA
American Construction Owners Association [*Defunct*] (EA) ... ACOA
American Consul ... AMCON
American Consular Reporting Officer ... AMCONREPO
American Consulate General (CINC) ... AMCONGEN
American Consultants League (EA) ... ACL
American Consulting Engineers Council (EA) ... ACEC
American Consumers Association [*Chicago, IL*] (EA) ... ACA
American Contemplative Society [*Defunct*] (EA) ... ACS
American Continental Corp. ... ACC
American Contract Bridge League (EA) ... ACBL
American Coon Hunters Association (EA) ... ACHA
American Coordinated Medical Society (EA) ... ACMS
American Coordinating Committee for Equality in Sport and Society (EA) ... ACCESS
American Copper Council (EA) ... ACC
American Coptic Association (EA) ... ACA
American Copyright Council (EA) ... ACC
American Copyright Society [*Defunct*] (EA) ... ACS
American Cordage and Netting Manufacturers (EA) ... ACNM

American Cormo Sheep Association (EA) ... ACSA
American Corn Millers' Federation (EA) ... ACMF
American Corporate Counsel Association (EA) ... ACCA
American Corporate Counsel Institute [*Washington, DC*] (EA) ... ACCI
American Corporation Cases [*A publication*] (DLA) ... Amer Corp Cas
American Corporation Cases, by Withrow [*1868-87*] [*A publication*] (DLA) ... ACC
American Corporation Cases, by Withrow [*A publication*] (DLA) ... Am Corp Cas
American Correctional Association (EA) ... ACA
American Correctional Chaplains Association (EA) ... ACCA
American Correctional Food Service Association (EA) ... ACFSA
American Correctional Health Services Association (EA) ... ACHSA
American Corrective Therapy Association [*Later, AKA*] (EA) ... ACTA
American Corriedale Association (EA) ... ACA
American Cotswold Record Association (EA) ... ACRA
American Cottage Cheese Institute [*Later, ACDPI*] (EA) ... ACCI
American Cotton Cooperative Association (EA) ... ACCA
American Cotton Exporters' Association (EA) ... ACEA
American Cotton Linter Association [*Defunct*] (EA) ... ACLA
American Cotton Manufacturers Institute [*Later, ATMI*] ... ACMI
American Cotton Shippers Association (EA) ... ACSA
American Cotton Waste Exchange [*Defunct*] (EA) ... ACWE
American Council for an Energy Efficient Economy (EA) ... ACEEE
American Council for Better Broadcasts (EA) ... ACBB
American Council for Capital Formation (EA) ... ACCF
American Council for Career Women [*New Orleans, LA*] (EA) ... ACCW
American Council for Competitive Telecommunications [*Formerly, Ad Hoc Committee for Competitive Telecommunications*] (EA) ... ACCT
American Council for Construction Education (EA) ... ACCE
American Council for Coordinated Action [*Defunct*] (EA) ... ACCA
American Council for Drug Education (EA) ... ACDE
American Council for Elementary School Industrial Arts [*Later, TECC*] (EA) ... ACESIA
American Council for Emigres in the Professions [*Defunct*] (EA) ... ACEP
American Council for Free Asia (EA) ... ACFA
American Council for Headache Education [*Medicine*] ... ACHE
American Council for Health Care Reform (EA) ... ACHCR
American Council for Healthful Living (EA) ... ACHL
American Council for International Studies (EA) ... ACIS
American Council for Judaism (EA) ... ACJ
American Council for Nationalities Service (EA) ... ACNS
American Council for Polish Culture (EA) ... ACPC
American Council for Private International Communications, Inc. [*Proposed corporation to replace Radio Free Europe*] ... ACPIC
American Council for Romanians (EA) ... ACR
American Council for the Advancement of Human Rights (EA) ... ACAHR
American Council for the Arts (EA) ... ACA
American Council for the Arts in Education [*Defunct*] (EA) ... ACAE
American Council for Turfgrass [*Defunct*] (EA) ... ACT
American Council for University Planning and Academic Excellence (EA) ... ACUPAE
American Council for World Freedom (EA) ... ACWF
American Council of Applied Clinical Nutrition (EA) ... ACACN
American Council of Blind Lions (EA) ... ACBL
American Council of Christian Churches (EA) ... ACCC
American Council of Christian Laymen [*Later, LCACCC*] (EA) ... ACCL
American Council of Commercial Laboratories [*Later, ACIL*] (KSC) ... ACCL
American Council of Executives in Religion [*Defunct*] (EA) ... ACER
American Council of Highway Advertisers (EA) ... ACHA
American Council of Human Rights [*Later, PHR*] (EA) ... ACHR
American Council of Hypnotist Examiners (EA) ... ACHE
American Council of Independent Laboratories (EA) ... ACIL
American Council of Industrial Arts State Association Officers [*Later, CTEA*] (EA) ... ACIASAO
American Council of Industrial Arts Supervisors (EA) ... ACIAS
American Council of Learned Societies (EA) ... ACLS
American Council of Life Insurance [*Washington, DC*] (EA) ... ACLI
American Council of Nanny Schools (EA) ... ACNS
American Council of Otolaryngology [*Later, ACO-HNS*] (EA) ... ACO
American Council of Otolaryngology - Head and Neck Surgery [*Later, AAO-HNS*] (EA) ... ACO-HNS
American Council of Parent Cooperatives [*Later, PCPI*] (EA) ... ACPC
American Council of Polish Cultural Clubs [*Later, ACPC*] (EA) ... ACPCC
American Council of Railroad Women (EA) ... ACRW
American Council of Spotted Asses (EA) ... ACSA
American Council of Taxpayers [*Formerly, COST*] (EA) ... ACT
American Council of Teachers of Russian (EA) ... ACTR
American Council of Teachers of Uncommonly Taught Asian Languages [*Defunct*] (EA) ... ACTUAL
American Council of the Blind (EA) ... ACB
American Council of the Blind Enterprises and Services (EA) ... ACBES
American Council of the Blind Federal Employees (EA) ... ACBFE
American Council of the Blind Parents [*Later, CFVI*] (EA) ... ACBP
American Council of the International Institute of Welding (EA) ... ACIIW
American Council of the Slovak World Congress [*Defunct*] (EA) ... ACSWC
American Council of Venture Clubs (EA) ... ACVC
American Council of Voluntary Agencies for Foreign Service [*Later, I/ACVIA*] (EA) ... ACVAFS
American Council of Women Chiropractors [*Later, Council of Women Chi ropractors*] (EA) ... ACWC
American Council of Young Political Leaders (EA) ... ACYPL
American Council on Alcohol Problems (EA) ... ACAP
American Council on Alcoholism (EA) ... ACA
American Council on Capital Gains and Estate Taxation [*Later, ACCF*] [*Tax lobbying organization*] ... ACCGET
American Council on Chiropractic Physiotherapy [*Later, CCPT*] (EA) ... ACCP
American Council on Chiropractic Roentgenology [*Later, Council on Roentgenologyof the American Chiropractic Association*] (EA) ... ACCR
American Council on Consumer Interests (EA) ... ACCI
American Council on Cosmetology Education [*Defunct*] (EA) ... ACCE
American Council on Education (EA) ... ACE
American Council on Education for Journalism [*Later, ACEJMC*] (EA) ... ACEJ
American Council on Educational Simulation and Gaming ... ACESG
American Council on German Studies ... ACGS
American Council on Germany (EA) ... ACG
American Council on Gift Annuities (NFD) ... ACGA
American Council on Industrial Arts Teacher Education [*of the International Technology Education Association*] [*Later, CTTE*] (EA) ... ACIATE
American Council on International Personnel [*New York, NY*] (EA) ... ACIP
American Council on International Sports (EA) ... ACIS
American Council on Marijuana and Other Psychoactive Drugs [*Later, ACDE*] (EA) ... ACM
American Council on NATO [*Later, Atlantic Council of the United States*] ... ACN
American Council on Pharmaceutical Education (EA) ... ACPE
American Council on Race Relations ... ACRR
American Council on Rural Special Education (EA) ... ACRSE
American Council on Rural Special Eduction ... ACRES
American Council on Schools and Colleges (EA) ... ACSC
American Council on Science and Health (EA) ... ACSH
American Council on the Environment (EA) ... ACE
American Council on the Middle East [*Defunct*] (EA) ... ACME
American Council on the Teaching of Foreign Languages (EA) ... ACTFL
American Council on Transplantation [*Defunct*] (EA) ... ACT
American Council to Improve Our Neighborhoods [*Later, NUC*] ... ACTION
American Counseling Association [*NACFT*] [*Absorbed by*] (EA) ... ACA
American Counter-Trade Association (EA) ... ACA
American Country Life Association (EA) ... ACLA
American Court and Commercial Newspapers (EA) ... ACCN
American Craft [*A publication*] (BRI) ... Am Craft
American Craft Brewing International [*NASDAQ symbol*] (SAG) ... ABRE
American Craft Brewing International [*NASDAQ symbol*] (SAG) ... ABRW
American Craft Brewing International [*Associated Press*] (SAG) ... AmCraft
American Craft Brewing International [*Associated Press*] (SAG) ... AmCrft
American Craft Council (EA) ... ACC
American Craft Retailers Association (EA) ... ACRA
American Craftsmen's Council (BARN) ... ACC
American Cranberry Growers' Association [*Defunct*] (EA) ... ACGA
American Cream Draft Horse Association (EA) ... ACDHA
American Creativity Association (EA) ... ACA
American Cricket Growers Association [*Defunct*] (EA) ... ACGA
American Crime Fighters (EA) ... ACF
American Crime Writers League [*An association*] ... ACWL
American Criminal Justice Association [*A publication*] (DLA) ... ACJA
American Criminal Justice Association - Lambda Alpha Epsilon (EA) ... ACJA-LAE
American Criminal Reports [*A publication*] (DLA) ... Am Cr
American Criminal Reports [*A publication*] (DLA) ... Am Cr R
American Criminal Reports, Edited by Hawley [*A publication*] (DLA) ... ACR
American Criminal Reports, Edited by Hawley [*A publication*] (DLA) ... Am Cr R (Hawley)
American Criminal Reports, Edited by Hawley [*A publication*] (DLA) ... Am Cr Rep
American Criminal Trials (Chandler) [*A publication*] (DLA) ... Am Cr Tr
American Croatian Academic Club [*Later, ACAS*] ... ACAC
American Croatian Academic Society [*Formerly, ACAC*] (EA) ... ACAS
American Crossbow Association (EA) ... ACA
American Crossbred Pony Registry (EA) ... ACPR
American Crossword Federation (EA) ... ACF
American Cryonics Society (EA) ... ACS
American Cryptogram Association (EA) ... ACA
American Crystal Sugar Co. (MHDW) ... ACS
American Crystallographic Association (EA) ... ACA
American Crystallographic Community ... ACC
American Culinary Federation (EA) ... ACF
American Cultural Resources Association ... ACRA
American Cultural Society [*Defunct*] ... ACS
American Culture Association (EA) ... ACA
American Cultured Dairy Products Institute (EA) ... ACDPI
American Custard Glass Collectors (EA) ... ACGC
American Custom Gunmakers Guild (EA) ... ACGG
American Cut Glass Association (EA) ... ACGA
American Cutlery Manufacturers Association (EA) ... ACMA
American Cyanamid Co. (KSC) ... ACC
American Cyanamid Co. ... ACCO
American Cyanamid Co., Agricultural Division, Princeton, NJ [*Library symbol Library of Congress*] (LCLS) ... NjPA
American Cyanamid Co., Lederle Laboratories, Pearl River, NY [*Library symbol Library of Congress*] (LCLS) ... NPrA
American Cyanamid Co., Organic Chemicals Division, Bound Brook, NJ [*Library symbol Library of Congress*] (LCLS) ... NjBbA
American Cyanamid Co., Pigments Division, Piney River, VA [*Library symbol Library of Congress*] (LCLS) ... ViPrA
American Cyanamid Co., Princeton, NJ [*OCLC symbol*] (OCLC) ... ACA
American Cyanamid Co., Stamford, CT [*Library symbol Library of Congress*] (LCLS) ... CtSA
American Cycling Union (EA) ... ACU
American Czechoslovak Society (EA) ... ACS
American Daffodil Society (EA) ... ADS
American Dahlia Society (EA) ... ADS
American Dairy Association (EA) ... ADA
American Dairy Association and Dairy Council (SRA) ... ADADC
American Dairy Association of Georgia and Alabama (SRA) ... ADAG

American Dairy Association of Virginia (SRA) .... ADAV
American Dairy Goat Association (EA) .... ADGA
American Dairy Goat Products Association (EA) .... ADGPA
American Dairy Products Institute (EA) .... ADPI
American Dairy Science Association (EA) .... ADSA
American Daleco Technologies, Inc. [*Vancouver Stock Exchange symbol*] .... AAD
American Dance Asylum .... ADA
American Dance Ensemble .... ADE
American Dance Festival [*Later, AADF*] (EA) .... ADF
American Dance Guild (EA) .... ADG
American Dance Machine .... ADM
American Dance Therapy Association (EA) .... ADTA
American Dart Association [*Defunct*] (EA) .... ADA
American Darts Organization (EA) .... ADO
American Deaf Volleyball Association (EA) .... ADVA
American Deafness and Rehabilitation Association (EA) .... ADARA
American Decartelization Agency [*Post-World War II*] .... AMDAG
American Decca [*Record label*] .... AmD
American Decisions [*A publication*] (DLA) .... AD
American Decisions [*A publication*] (DLA) .... Am D
American Decisions [*A publication*] (DLA) .... Am Dec's
American Decisions [*A publication*] (DLA) .... Amer Dec
American Decisions, Select Cases [*San Francisco, CA*] [*A publication*] (DLA) .... Am Dec
American Deep Drawing Research Group (DICI) .... ADDRG
American Defenders [*Defunct*] (EA) .... AD
American Defenders Against Animal Mistreatment [*Inactive*] (EA) .... ADAM
American Defenders of Bataan and Corregidor (EA) .... ADBC
American Defense Foundation (EA) .... ADF
American Defense Institute (EA) .... ADI
American Defense Preparedness Association (EA) .... ADPA
American Defense Service Medal (BARN) .... ADSM
American Dehydrated Onion and Garlic Association (EA) .... ADOGA
American Dehydrators Association [*Later, AAPA*] (EA) .... ADA
American Democratic Political Action Committee (EA) .... ADPAC
American Dental Assistants Association (EA) .... ADAA
American Dental Assistant's Program .... ADAP
American Dental Association (EA) .... ADA
American Dental Association, Chicago, IL [*Library symbol Library of Congress*] (LCLS) .... ICADA
American Dental Association, Chicago, IL [*OCLC symbol*] (OCLC) .... JAA
American Dental Association Health Foundation .... ADAHF
American Dental Association Specifications .... ADAS
American Dental Hygienists' Association (EA) .... ADHA
American Dental Interfraternity Council (EA) .... ADIC
American Dental LaserAm [*NASDAQ symbol*] (SAG) .... ADLI
American Dental LaserAm [*Associated Press*] (SAG) .... AmDentl
American Dental Society of Anesthesiology (EA) .... ADSA
American Dental Society of Europe (EA) .... ADSE
American Dental Trade Association (EA) .... ADTA
American Dentists for Foreign Service (EA) .... ADFS
American Denture Society .... ADS
American Depositary Receipt .... ADR
American Depositary Share (ECON) .... ADS
American Dermatologic Society of Allergy and Immunology (EA) .... ADSAI
American Dermatological Association (EA) .... ADA
American Deserters Committee, France (EA) .... ADC
American Design Bicentennial [*An association Defunct*] (EA) .... ADB
American Design Drafting Association (EA) .... ADDA
American Devon Cattle Club [*Later, Devon Cattle Association*] (EA) .... ADCC
American Dexter Cattle Association (EA) .... ADCA
American Diabetes Association (EA) .... ADA
American Diagnostics Corp. .... AmD
American Dialect Society (EA) .... ADS
American Diamond Industry Association (EA) .... ADIA
American Die Casting Institute (EA) .... ADCI
American Die Casting Institute, Inc. .... ADCII
American Dietetic Association (EA) .... ADA
American Digest [*A publication*] (DLA) .... Am Dig
American Digest (Century Edition) [*A publication*] (DLA) .... Am Cent Dig
American Digest (Century Edition) [*A publication*] (DLA) .... Am Dig Cent Ed
American Digest (Decennial Edition) [*A publication*] (ILCA) .... Decen Dig
American Digest (Decennial Edition) (West) [*A publication*] (DLA) .... Am Dig Dec Ed
American Digest (Decennial Edition) (West) [*A publication*] (DLA) .... Am Dig Decen Ed
American Digest (Eighth Decennial Edition) (West) [*A publication*] (DLA) .... Am Dig Eighth Dec Ed
American Digest (Fifth Decennial Edition) (West) [*A publication*] (DLA) .... Am Dig Fifth Dec Ed
American Digest (Fourth Decennial Edition) (West) [*A publication*] (DLA) .... Am Dig Fourth Dec Ed
American Digest (Key Number Series) (West) [*A publication*] (DLA) .... Am Dig Key No Ser
American Digest (Second Decennial Edition) (West) [*A publication*] (DLA) .... Am Dig Secd Dec Ed
American Digest (Seventh Decennial Edition) (West) [*A publication*] (DLA) .... Am Dig Seventh Dec Ed
American Digest (Sixth Decennial Edition) (West) [*A publication*] (DLA) .... Am Dig Sixth Dec Ed
American Digest System, Decennial Digests [*A publication*] (DLA) .... Dec Dig
American Digest (Third Decennial Edition) (West) [*A publication*] (DLA) .... Am Dig Third Dec Ed
American Digestive Disease Society (EA) .... ADDS
American Digital Cartography .... ADC
American Dinner Theatre Institute (EA) .... ADTI
American Diopter and Decibel Society (EA) .... ADDS
American Directors Institute (EA) .... ADI
American Directory of Organized Labor [*A publication*] .... ADOL
American Disability Evaluation Research Institute [*Research center*] (RCD) .... ADERI
American Disabled for Accessible Public Transit (EA) .... ADAPT
American Disposal Services, Inc. [*NASDAQ symbol*] (SAG) .... ADSI
American Disposal Services, Inc. [*Associated Press*] (SAG) .... AmDisp
American District Telegraph .... ADT
American Ditchley Foundation (EA) .... ADF
American Diversified Dog Society [*Defunct*] (EA) .... ADDS
American Divorce Association for Men .... ADAM
American Doctoral Dissertations [*A publication*] .... ADD
American Doctors [*Later, PCOS*] (EA) .... AMDOC
American Documentation Institute [*Later, American Society for Information Science*] .... ADI
American Dog Breeders Association [*Defunct*] (EA) .... ADBA
American Dog Feed Institute [*Defunct*] (EA) .... ADFI
American Dog Owners Association (EA) .... ADOA
American Donkey and Mule Society (EA) .... ADMS
American Double Dutch League (EA) .... ADDL
American Dove Association (EA) .... ADA
American Down Association (EA) .... ADA
American Drag Racing Association [*Commercial firm*] (EA) .... ADRA
American Dressage Institute .... ADI
American Driver and Traffic Safety Education Association (EA) .... ADTSEA
American Driver Education Association [*Later, ADTSEA*] (EA) .... ADEA
American Driving Society (EA) .... ADS
American Drug Manufacturers' Association [*Later, PMA*] .... ADMA
American Druze Public Affairs Committee (EA) .... AD-PAC
American Druze Society (EA) .... ADS
American Dry Milk Institute [*Later, ADPI*] (EA) .... ADMI
American Dutch Rabbit Club (EA) .... ADRC
American Duty Free [*Freight*] .... ADF
American Eagle Group [*Associated Press*] (SAG) .... AEaglG
American Eagle Group [*Associated Press*] (SAG) .... AmEagl
American Eagle Group [*NYSE symbol*] (SAG) .... FLI
American Eagle Outfitters, Inc. [*Associated Press*] (SAG) .... AEagleO
American Eagle Outfitters, Inc. [*NASDAQ symbol*] (SAG) .... AEOS
American Eagle Petroleums Corp. [*Toronto Stock Exchange symbol*] .... AEO
American Ear Association for Research (EA) .... AEAR
American Eco Corp. [*Associated Press*] (SAG) .... AmerEco
American Eco Corp. [*NASDAQ symbol*] (SAG) .... ECGO
American Ecology Corp. [*Associated Press*] (SAG) .... AmEcol
American Ecology Corp. [*NASDAQ symbol*] (SAG) .... ECOL
American Ecology Services (EA) .... AES
American Economic Association (EA) .... AEA
American Economic Council (EA) .... AEC
American Economic Development Council (EA) .... AEDC
American Economic Foundation (EA) .... AEF
American Edge Collectors Association (EA) .... AECA
American Edition (DLA) .... Am Ed
American Education Association (EA) .... AEA
American Education Coalition [*Defunct*] (EA) .... AEC
American Education Fellowship [*Defunct*] (AEBS) .... AEF
American Education Finance Association (EA) .... AEFA
American Education Week .... AEW
American Educational Products [*NASDAQ symbol*] (SAG) .... AMEP
American Educational Products, Inc. [*Associated Press*] (SAG) .... AmEduc
American Educational Publishers Institute [*Later, AAP*] .... AEPI
American Educational Research Association (EA) .... AERA
American Educational Society (EA) .... AES
American Educational Studies Association (EA) .... AESA
American Educational Television Network [*Cable-television system*] .... AETN
American Educational Theatre Association [*Later, ATA*] (EA) .... AETA
American Egg Board (EA) .... AEB
American Egyptian Cooperation Foundation (EA) .... AECF
American Election Commission [*Defunct*] (EA) .... AEC
American Electric Power .... AEP
American Electric Power Co., Inc. [*Associated Press*] (SAG) .... AEIPw
American Electric Power Co., Inc. [*NYSE symbol*] (SAG) .... AEP
American Electric Power Co., Inc. Unified Dial Network (TEL) .... AUDINET
American Electrical Cases [*A publication*] (DLA) .... AEC
American Electrical Cases [*A publication*] (ILCA) .... Am El Ca
American Electrical Cases [*A publication*] (ILCA) .... Am Elec Ca
American Electrical Cases [*A publication*] (DLA) .... Am Elect Cas
American Electrical Cases [*A publication*] (ILCA) .... Am Electl Cas
American Electrical Cases [*A publication*] (DLA) .... Am Electr Cas
American Electrical Cases [*A publication*] (DLA) .... Amer Elec Ca
American Electro Metal Corp. .... AEMC
American Electrochemical Society [*Later, ECS*] .... AES
American Electroencephalographic Society (EA) .... AEEGS
American Electroencephalographic Society (EA) .... AES
American Electrology Association (EA) .... AEA
American Electromechanical Society .... AES
American Electronic Components, Inc. [*NASDAQ symbol*] (SAG) .... AECI
American Electronic Components, Inc. [*Associated Press*] (SAG) .... AEICmp
American Electronic Laboratories, Inc. .... AEL
American Electronical Society .... AES
American Electronics Association (EA) .... AEA
American Electronics Laboratory (AAGC) .... AEL
American Electroplaters & Surface Finishers Society [*Association des Galvanoplastes d'Amerique*] [*Formerly, American Electroplaters Society*] (AC) .... AESF

American Electroplaters' and Surface Finishers Society (EA) ... AESFS
American Electroplaters' and Surface Finishers Society Exposition (ITD) ... SUR/FIN
American Electroplaters' Society (EA) ... AES
American Elsevier Publishing Co. (DGA) ... AEPCO
American Embassy ... AE
American Embassy (DNAB) ... AMEB
American Embassy (AFM) ... AMEMB
American Embryo Transfer Association (EA) ... AETA
American Emergency Committee for Tibetan Refugees [*Defunct*] (EA) ... AECTR
American Emigrants' League (EA) ... AEL
American Encephalographic Society [*Neurophysiology*] (DAVI) ... AES
American Encyclopedic Dictionary [*A publication*] (DLA) ... Am Enc Dict
American Endocrine Society (DAVI) ... AES
American Endodontic Society (EA) ... AES
American Endurance Ride Conference (EA) ... AERC
American Energy Month [*Defunct*] (EA) ... AEM
American Energy Week [*Later, AEM*] [*An association*] (EA) ... AEW
American Engineering Association [*Defunct*] (EA) ... AEA
American Engineering Council ... AEC
American Engineering Model Society (EA) ... AEMS
American Engineering Standards Committee [*Later, ANSI*] ... AESC
American English [*Language*] (WGA) ... AmE
American English Spot Rabbit Club (EA) ... AESRC
American Enka Corp., Enka, NC [*Library symbol Library of Congress*] (LCLS) ... NcEnk
American Enterprise Association [*Later, AEI*] ... AEA
American Enterprise Institute for Public Policy Research (EA) ... AEI
American Enterprise Institute for Public Policy Research (EA) ... AEIPPR
American Entomological Society (EA) ... AES
American Entrepreneurs Association [*Defunct*] (EA) ... AEA
American Epidemiological Society (EA) ... AES
American Epilepsy Society (EA) ... AES
American Equilibration Society (EA) ... AES
American Equine Association (EA) ... AEA
American Eskimo Association (EA) ... AEA
American Esquire [*Record label*] ... AmEsq
American Ethical Union (EA) ... AEU
American Ethnological Society (EA) ... AES
American Ethnologist [*A publication*] (BRI) ... Am Ethnol
American Ethnology Bureau [*British*] (DAS) ... AEB
American Eugenics Society [*Later, SSSB*] (EA) ... AES
American European Foundation [*Later, SFMJF*] (EA) ... AEF
American Euthanasia Foundation (EA) ... AEF
American Evaluation Association (EA) ... AEA
American Excess Insurance Association [*East Hartford, CT*] (EA) ... AEIA
American Executives for Management Excellence [*An association*] (EA) ... AEME
American Exiles ... AMEX
American Exmoor Pony Registry (EA) ... AEPR
American Expeditionary Force [*World War I*] ... AEF
American Exploration Co. [*Associated Press*] (SAG) ... AExpl
American Exploration Co. [*AMEX symbol*] (SPSG) ... AX
American Exploration Co. [*AMEX symbol*] (SAG) ... AXpC
American Export Airlines ... AEA
American Export Isbrandtsen Lines [*Later, American Export Industries Co.*] ... AEIL
American Express Card [*Credit card*] ... AEC
American Express Co. (CDAI) ... AE
American Express Co. [*Associated Press*] (SAG) ... AExp
American Express Co. [*Associated Press*] (SAG) ... AExp 96
American Express Co. ... AMEX
American Express Co. ... AMEXCO
American Express Co. [*Associated Press*] (SAG) ... AmExp
American Express Co. (ADA) ... AX
American Express Co. [*NYSE symbol*] (SAG) ... AXD
American Express Co. [*NYSE symbol Toronto Stock Exchange symbol*] (SPSG) ... AXP
American Express Interactive [*Corporate travel computer site*] ... AXI
American Express International (ODBW) ... AEI
American Ex-Prisoners of War (EA) ... XPW
American Fabricating Institute of Technology [*Defunct*] (EA) ... AFIT
American Facsimile Association [*Later, IFAXA*] (EA) ... AFaxA
American Fair Trade Council [*Sausalito, CA*] (EA) ... AMTC
American Falls District Library, American Falls, ID [*Library symbol*] [*Library of Congress*] (LCLS) ... IdAm
American Falls High School, American Falls, ID [*Library symbol*] [*Library of Congress*] (LCLS) ... IdAmHS
American Falls, ID [*FM radio station call letters*] (RBYB) ... KORR
American Falls, ID [*FM radio station call letters*] ... KOUU
American Family Association (EA) ... AFA
American Family Communiversity (EA) ... AFCO
American Family Farm and Ranch Association (EA) ... AFFRA
American Family Farm Foundation (EA) ... AFFF
American Family Foundation (EA) ... AFF
American Family Heritage Society [*Defunct*] (EA) ... AFHS
American Family Member ... AFM
American Family Records Association (EA) ... AFRA
American Family Restaurants, Inc. [*Associated Press*] (SAG) ... AFamR
American Family Restaurants, Inc. [*AMEX symbol*] (SAG) ... FRI
American Family Society (EA) ... AFS
American Family Therapy Association (EA) ... AFTA
American Fan Association (EA) ... AFA
American Fan Collectors Association (EA) ... AFCA
American Fancy Rat and Mouse Association (EA) ... AFRMA
American Fans of Jon Pertwee (EA) ... AFOJP
American Far Eastern Society (EA) ... AFES
American Farm Bureau ... AFB
American Farm Bureau Federation (EA) ... AFBF
American Farm Bureau Research Foundation (EA) ... AFBRF
American Farm Economic Association [*Later, AAEA*] (EA) ... AFEA
American Farm Foundation [*Defunct*] (EA) ... AFF
American Farm Research Association [*Superseded by AFBRF*] (EA) ... AFRA
American Farmland Trust (EA) ... AFT
American Farriers Association (EA) ... AFA
American Fashion Association (EA) ... AFA
American Fashion Homesewing Council ... AFHSC
American Fastener and Closure Association [*Defunct*] (EA) ... AFCA
American Federal Bank [*NASDAQ symbol*] (CTT) ... AMFB
American Federal Tax Reports [*Prentice-Hall, Inc.*] [*A publication*] (DLA) ... AFTR
American Federal Tax Reports [*Prentice-Hall, Inc.*] [*A publication*] (DLA) ... Am Fed Tax R
American Federal Tax Reports [*Prentice-Hall, Inc.*] [*A publication*] (DLA) ... Amer Fed Tax Rep
American Federal Tax Reports (Prentice-Hall, Inc.) [*A publication*] (DLA) ... P-H Cas
American Federal Tax Reports, Second Series [*Prentice-Hall, Inc.*] [*A publication*] (DLA) ... AFTR2d
American Federal Tax Reports, Second Series [*Prentice-Hall, Inc.*] [*A publication*] (DLA) ... Am Fed Tax R 2d
American Federation for Aging Research (EA) ... AFAR
American Federation for Clinical Research (EA) ... AFCR
American Federation for the Pueri Cantores (EA) ... AFPC
American Federation of Arts (EA) ... AFA
American Federation of Astrologers (EA) ... AFA
American Federation of Aviculture (EA) ... AFA
American Federation of Catholic Workers for the Blind [*Later, CAPVI*] (EA) ... AFCWB
American Federation of Catholic Workers for the Blind and Visually Handicapped [*Later, CAPVI*] (EA) ... AFCWBVH
American Federation of Film Societies [*Defunct*] (EA) ... AFFS
American Federation of Government Employees (EA) ... AFGE
American Federation of Grain Millers (EA) ... AFGM
American Federation of Guards (EA) ... AFG
American Federation of Home Health Agencies (EA) ... AFHHA
American Federation of Hosiery Workers [*Later, ACTWU*] ... AFHW
American Federation of Information Processing [*Formerly, AFIPS*] ... AFIP
American Federation of Information Processing Societies [*Later, AFIP*] (EA) ... AFIPS
American Federation of International Institutes [*Later, ACNS*] ... AFII
American Federation of Italian Evangelicals [*Later, AEIM*] (EA) ... AFIE
American Federation of Jewish Fighters, Camp Inmates and Nazi Victims [*Defunct*] (EA) ... AFJFCINV
American Federation of Jews from Central Europe (EA) ... AFJCE
American Federation of Labor [*Later, AFL-CIO*] ... AF of L
American Federation of Labor [*Later, AFL-CIO*] (GPO) ... AFL
American Federation of Labor and Congress of Industrial Organizations ... AFL-CIO
American Federation of Labor and Congress of Industrial Organizations Library, Washington, DC [*Library symbol Library of Congress*] (LCLS) ... DAFL
American Federation of Labor-Congress of Industrial Organizations (AAGC) ... AFL-CIO
American Federation of Medical Accreditation (EA) ... AFMA
American Federation of Mineralogical Societies (EA) ... AFMS
American Federation of Musicians of the United States and Canada [*Later, THFC*] (EA) ... AFM
American Federation of Musicians of the United States and Canada [*Later, THFC*] ... AFMUSC
American Federation of New Zealand Rabbit Breeders (EA) ... AFNZRB
American Federation of Police (EA) ... AFP
American Federation of Polish Jews (EA) ... AFPJ
American Federation of Poultry Producers Associations [*Defunct*] (EA) ... AFPPA
American Federation of Priests ... AFP
American Federation of Radio Artists ... AFRA
American Federation of Retail Kosher Butchers (EA) ... AFRKB
American Federation of School Administrators (EA) ... AFSA
American Federation of School Administrators and Supervisors [*AFL-CIO*] ... AFSAS
American Federation of Small Business [*Chicago, IL*] (EA) ... AFSB
American Federation of Soroptimist Clubs [*Later, Soroptimist International of the Americas*] ... AFSC
American Federation of State, County, and Municipal Employees (EA) ... AFSCME
American Federation of State, County, and Municipal Employees ... SCME
American Federation of Teachers (EA) ... AFT
American Federation of Teachers in Virginia (SRA) ... AFTVA
American Federation of Technical Engineers [*Later, International Federation of Professional and Technical Engineers*] (EA) ... AFTE
American Federation of Television and Radio Artists (EA) ... AFTRA
American Federation of the Physically Handicapped ... AFPH
American Federation of Violin and Bow Makers (EA) ... AFVBM
American Federation of World Citizens [*Later, Fellowship of World Citizens*] (EA) ... AFWC
American Feed Industry Association (EA) ... AFIA
American Feed Manufacturers Association [*Later, AFIA*] (EA) ... AFMA
American Feline Society (EA) ... AFS
American Female Impersonators Association (EA) ... AFIA
American Fern Society (EA) ... AFS
American Fertility Society (EA) ... AFS
American Fertility Society Classification of Endometriosis ... AFSCE

American Festival Ballet AFB
American Festival of Microtonal Music (EA) AFMM
American Fiber Institute AFI
American Fiber Manufacturers Association (EA) AFMA
American Fiber, Textile, Apparel Coalition (EA) AFTAC
American Fibre Corp. [*Vancouver Stock Exchange symbol*] AFB
American Field Service [*Later, AFSIIP*] AFS
American Fighter Aces Association (EA) AFAA
American Fighter Aces Museum Foundation (EA) AFAMF
American Film and Video Association (EA) AFVA
American Film Export Association (EA) AFEA
American Film Institute (EA) AFI
American Film Institute Alumni Association Writers Workshop (EA) AFIAAWW
American Film Institute, Center for Advanced Film Studies, Beverly Hills, CA [*Library symbol Library of Congress*] (LCLS) CBevA
American Film Marketing Association (EA) AFMA
American Film Theater AFT
American Filtrona Corp. AFC
American Filtrona Corp. [*NASDAQ symbol*] (NQ) AFIL
American Filtrona Corp. [*Associated Press*] (SAG) AFiltrn
American Finance Association (EA) AFA
American Finance Conference [*Later, NCFA*] (EA) AFC
American Financial Group, Inc. [*NYSE symbol*] (SAG) AFG
American Financial Group, Inc. [*Associated Press*] (SAG) AFnclGp
American Financial Services Association [*Washington, DC*] (EA) AFSA
American Fine Arts Society (EA) AFAS
American Fine China Guild (EA) AFCG
American Fire Sprinkler Association (EA) AFSA
American Firearm Association (EA) AFA
American Firearms Industry [*A publication*] (EAAP) AFI
American Firewalking Association (EA) AFA
American First Day Cover Foundation [*Defunct*] (EA) AFDCF
American First Day Cover Society (EA) AFDCS
American First PREP [*Preferred Real Estate Participation*] **Fund 2 Ltd.** [*AMEX symbol*] (SPSG) PF
American Fish Decoy Association (EA) AFDA
American Fish Farmers Federation [*Defunct*] (EA) AFFF
American Fisheries Advisory Committee AFAC
American Fisheries Protection Act AFPA
American Fisheries School (USDC) AFS
American Fisheries Society (EA) AFS
American Fishing Tackle Manufacturers Association (EA) AFTMA
American Fitness Association (EA) AFA
American Flag Association [*Defunct*] (EA) AFA
American Flag Committee (EA) AFC
American Flag Institute [*Defunct*] (EA) AFI
American Flagship Available AFSA
American Flight Service Systems, Inc. [*ICAO designator*] (FAAC) XFS
American Flight Strips Association (EA) AFSA
American Flint Glass Workers Union (EA) AFGWU
American Flint Glass Workers' Union of North America [*Later, AFGWU*] AFGW
American Flock Association (EA) AFA
American Floral Marketing Council (EA) AFMC
American Florists Association (EA) AFA
American Fluid Technology AFT
American Flyers Airline (MCD) AFA
American Flywheel Systems [*Research center*] (ECON) AFS
American Folklife Center [*Library of Congress*] AFC
American Folklife Preservation Act [*1976*] AFPA
American Folklore Society (EA) AFS
American Food for Peace Council [*Defunct*] (EA) AFPC
American Foot Care Institute [*Defunct*] (EA) AFCI
American Foot Health Foundation (EA) AFHF
American Football Coaches Association (EA) AFCA
American Football Conference [*of NFL*] AFC
American Football League [*Reorganized as part of AFC and NFC*] (EA) AFL
American Footwear Industries Association [*Later, FIA*] AFIA
American Footwear Manufacturers' Association [*Later, FIA*] AFMA
American Forage and Grassland Council [*Lexington, KY*] AFGC
American Forces in Action [*Military*] AFA
American Forces Information Council (DOMA) AFIC
American Forces Information Service [*DoD*] AFIS
American Forces Information Service [*DoD*] (AABC) AMFINFOS
American Forces Korea Network [*Military*] (GFGA) AFKN
American Forces Network (AABC) AFN
American Forces Network, Europe (AABC) AFNE
American Forces Press and Publications Service AFPPS
American Forces Press Service [*Formerly, AFNB*] AFPS
American [*formerly, Armed*] **Forces Radio and Television** [*DoD*] AFRT
American [*formerly, Armed*] **Forces Radio and Television Service** [*or System*] AFRTS
American Forces Radio and Television Service [*Network of broadcast stations*] [*United States military*] [*Formerly, Armed Forces Radio Service*] (WDMC) AFRTS
American Forces Radio and Television Service-Programming Center [*See also AFIS*] [*DoD*] (WDMC) AFRTS-PC
American Forces Radio Station [*Vietnam*] (VNW) AFRS
American [*formerly, Armed*] **Forces Vietnam Network** AFVN
American Foreign Insurance Association (EA) AFIA
American Foreign Law Association (EA) AFLA
American Foreign Law Association. Newsletter [*A publication*] (DLA) Am For L Ass'n Newsl
American Foreign Policy Institute [*Defunct*] (EA) AFPI
American Foreign Service Association (EA) AFSA
American Foreign Service Protective Association [*Washington, DC*] (EA) AFSPA
American Forensic Association (EA) AFA
American Forest Adventures [*Defunct*] (EA) AFA
American Forest and Paper Association (ECON) AFPA
American Forest Council (EA) AFC
American Forest Institute [*Later, AFC*] AFI
American Forest Products Industries [*Later, AFC*] AFPI
American Forestry Association (EA) AFA
American Forestry Association, Washington, DC [*Library symbol Library of Congress*] (LCLS) DAFA
American Forests [*A publication*] (BRI) AF
American Forged Fitting and Flange Association [*Defunct*] (EA) AFFFA
American Formalwear Association [*Later, IFA*] (EA) AFA
American Forum for Global Education (IID) AFGE
American Forum for Jewish-Christian Cooperation (EA) AFJCC
American Foster Care Resources (EA) AFCR
American Foulbrood [*Honeybee disease*] AFB
American Foundation for Aging Research (EA) AFAR
American Foundation for AIDS Research (EA) AFAR
American Foundation for AIDS Research [*New York, NY*] (EA) AmFAR
American Foundation for Alternative Health Care [*Later, AFAHCRD*] (EA) AFAHC
American Foundation for Alternative Health Care, Research, and Development (EA) AFAHCRD
American Foundation for Continuing Education (EA) AFCE
American Foundation for Health (EA) AFH
American Foundation for Homeopathy (EA) AFH
American Foundation for Learning Disabilities AFLD
American Foundation for Management Research [*Later, AMA*] (EA) AFMR
American Foundation for Management Research, Hamilton, NY [*Library symbol Library of Congress*] (LCLS) NHA
American Foundation for Management Research, Library, Hamilton, NY [*OCLC symbol*] (OCLC) ZUC
American Foundation for Maternal and Child Health (EA) AFMCH
American Foundation for Mental Hygiene AFMH
American Foundation for Negro Affairs (EA) AFNA
American Foundation for Overseas Blind [*Later, HKI*] (EA) AFOB
American Foundation for Pharmaceutical Education (EA) AFPE
American Foundation for Political Education AFPE
American Foundation for Psychoanalysis and Psychoanalysis in Groups (EA) AFPPG
American Foundation for Resistance International (EA) AFRI
American Foundation for the Blind (EA) AFB
American Foundation for the Blind, New York, NY [*Library symbol Library of Congress*] (LCLS) NNAF
American Foundation for the Prevention of Venereal Disease (EA) AFPVD
American Foundation for the Science of Creative Intelligence (EA) AFSCI
American Foundation for Tropical Medicine (EA) AFTM
American Foundation for Urologic Disease (EA) AFUD
American Foundation for Vision Awareness (EA) AFVA
American Foundation for World Youth Understanding (EA) AFWYU
American Foundation of Religion and Psychiatry [*Later, Institutes of Religion and Health*] (EA) AFRAP
American Foundation of Religion and Psychiatry [*Later, Institutes of Religion and Health*] AFRP
American Foundation of Traditional Chinese Medicine (EA) AFTCM
American Foundation on Automation and Employment [*Later, CNB-TV*] (EA) AFAE
American Foundrymen's Association [*Later, AFS*] AFA
American Foundrymen's Society (EA) AFS
American Foundrymen's Society Archives and Museum, British Columbia Chapter, Delta, BC,Canada [*Library symbol*] [*Library of Congress*] (LCLS) CaBDEAF
American Foundrymen's Society, Des Plaines, IL [*Library symbol Library of Congress*] (LCLS) IDesA
American Fox Terrier Club (EA) AFTC
American Fox Trotting Horse Breed Association (EA) AFTHBA
American Foxhound Club (EA) AFC
American Fracture Association (EA) AFA
American Franchise Association (EA) AFA
American Franciscan Society for Vocations [*Later, FVC*] (EA) AFSV
American Fraternal Snowshoe Union (EA) AFSU
American Fraternal Union [*Ely, MN*] (EA) AFU
American Freedom Association AFA
American Freedom Center (EA) AFC
American Freedom Coalition (EA) AFC
American Freedom from Hunger Foundation [*Later, MFM/FFH*] AFFHF
American Freedom of Residence Fund [*Defunct*] (EA) AFRF
American Freeman Association (EA) AFA
American Freightways Corp. [*NASDAQ symbol*] (NQ) AFWY
American Freightways Corp. [*Associated Press*] (SAG) AmFrght
American Friends of Afghan Refugees (EA) AFAR
American Friends of Anne Frank Center (EA) AFAFC
American Friends of Beit Halochem (EA) AFBH
American Friends of Beth Hatefutsoth (EA) AFBH
American Friends of Boys Town of Jerusalem [*BTJFA*] [*Superseded by*] (EA) BTJ
American Friends of Cambridge University (EA) AFCU
American Friends of Chung-Ang University (EA) AFC-AU
American Friends of Covent Garden and the Royal Ballet (EA) AFCGRB
American Friends of Greece (EA) AFG
American Friends of Israel (EA) AFI
American Friends of Lafayette (EA) AFL
American Friends of Refugees [*Defunct*] AFR

American Friends of Religious Freedom in Israel [*Defunct*] (EAIO) .... AFRFI
American Friends of Romania (EA) .... AFRom
American Friends of Russian Freedom [*Later, AFR*] (EA) .... AFRF
American Friends of Scottish Opera (EA) .... AFSO
American Friends of Scottish War Blinded [*Defunct*] (EA) .... AFSWB
American Friends of the Alliance Israelite Universelle (EA) .... AFAIU
American Friends of the Anti-Bolshevik Bloc of Nations (EA) .... AFABBN
American Friends of the Anti-Bolshevik Bloc of Nations (EA) .... AF-ABN
American Friends of the Association for Welfare of Soldiers in Israel (EA) .... AWSI
American Friends of the Australian National Gallery .... AFANG
American Friends of the Australian National Gallery Foundation (EA) .... AFANG
American Friends of the Captive Nations [*Defunct*] (EA) .... AFCN
American Friends of the Gutenberg Museum (EA) .... AFGM
American Friends of the Haifa Maritime Museum (EA) .... AFHMM
American Friends of the Hebrew University (EA) .... AFHU
American Friends of the Israel Museum (EA) .... AFIM
American Friends of the Jerusalem Institute for Talmudic Research (EA) .... AFJITR
American Friends of the Jerusalem Society for World Fellowship (EA) .... AFJSWF
American Friends of the Jewish Museum of Greece (EA) .... AFJMG
American Friends of the Middle East [*Later, AMIDEAST*] (EA) .... AFME
American Friends of the Paris Opera and Ballet (EA) .... AFPOB
American Friends of the Royal Shakespeare Theatre (EA) .... AFRST
American Friends of the Tel Aviv University (EA) .... AFTAU
American Friends of the Vatican Library (EA) .... AFVL
American Friends of Turkey (EA) .... AFOT
American Friends of Turkey (EA) .... AFT
American Friends of Vietnam (EA) .... AFV
American Friends Service Committee (EA) .... AFSC
American Frozen Food Institute (EA) .... AFFI
American Fuchsia Society (EA) .... AFS
American Fund for Alternatives to Animal Research (EA) .... AFAAR
American Fund for Czechoslovak Refugees (EA) .... AFCR
American Fund for Dental Education [*Later, AFDH*] (EA) .... AFDE
American Fund for Dental Health (EA) .... AFDH
American Fund for Free Jurists (EA) .... AFFJ
American Fund for Slovak Refugees [*Defunct*] (EA) .... AFSR
American Funeral Directors and Embalmers Association (EA) .... AFDEA
American Fur Industry (EA) .... AFI
American Fur Liner Contractors Association (EA) .... AFLCA
American Fur Merchants' Association (EA) .... AFMA
American Fur Resources Institute [*Defunct*] (EA) .... AFRI
American Furniture Manufacturers Association (EA) .... AFMA
American Galloway Breeders' Association (EA) .... AGBA
American Galvanizers Association (EA) .... AGA
American Game Collectors Association (EA) .... AGCA
American Gas and Electric Services .... AGES
American Gas Association (EA) .... AGA
American Gas Association Laboratories .... AGAL
American Gas Association Natural Gas Vehicle Coalition .... AGANGVC
American Gas Association, New York, NY [*Library symbol Library of Congress*] (LCLS) .... NNAG
American Gasoline Dealers Association (EA) .... AGDA
American Gastroenterological Association (EA) .... AGA
American Gathering of Jewish Holocaust Survivors (EA) .... AGJHS
American Gauge Design Committee .... AGD
American Gauge Design Committee (MCD) .... AGDC
American Gauge Design Standard .... AGDS
American Gay Atheists (EA) .... AGA
American Gear Manufacturers Association (EA) .... AGMA
American Gelbvieh Association (EA) .... AGA
American Gem and Mineral Suppliers Association (EA) .... AGMSA
American Gem Market System [*Information service or system*] (IID) .... AGMS
American Gem Society (EA) .... AGS
American Gem Trade Association (EA) .... AGTA
American Genealogical Research Institute .... AGRI
American Genealogist [*A publication*] (BRI) .... Am Geneal
American General Corp. [*Associated Press*] (SAG) .... AGenCp
American General Corp. Capital LLC [*Associated Press*] (SAG) .... AGC
American General Delaware LLC [*Associated Press*] (SAG) .... AGnDE
American General Hospitality Corp. [*Associated Press*] (SAG) .... AGnHosp
American General Hospitality Corp. [*NYSE symbol*] (SAG) .... AGT
American General Life Insurance Co. [*NYSE symbol*] (SPSG) .... AGC
American Genetic Association (EA) .... AGA
American Geographical and Statistical Society .... AGSS
American Geographical Institute .... AGI
American Geographical Society (EA) .... AGS
American Geographical Society, New York, NY [*Library symbol Library of Congress*] (LCLS) .... NNA
American Geological Institute (EA) .... AGI
American Geophysical Union (EA) .... AGU
American Geriatric Research Foundation [*Later, ARI*] .... AGRF
American Geriatrics Association (DAVI) .... AGA
American Geriatrics Society (EA) .... AGS
American Gesneria Society [*Later, GSI*] (EA) .... AGS
American GI Forum (OICC) .... AGIF
American Girl Resources [*Vancouver Stock Exchange symbol*] .... AGA
American Glassware Association [*Defunct*] .... AGA
American Glovebox Society (EA) .... AGS
American Gloxinia and Gesneriad Society (EA) .... AGGS
American Gloxinia Society [*Later, AGGS*] (EA) .... AGS
American Go Association (EA) .... AGA
American Goat Society (EA) .... AGS
American Goiter Association [*Later, American Thyroid Association*] .... AGA
American Gold Association [*Defunct*] (EA) .... AGA
American Gold Star Mothers (EA) .... AGSM
American Golf Sponsors (EA) .... AGS
American Good Government Society [*Defunct*] (EA) .... AGGS
American Gotland Horse Association (EA) .... AGHA
American Gourd Society (EA) .... AGS
American Government Income Fund [*NYSE symbol*] (SPSG) .... AGF
American Government Income Fund [*Associated Press*] (SAG) .... AmGvI
American Government Income Portfolio, Inc. [*NYSE symbol*] (CTT) .... AAF
American Government Income Portfolio, Inc. [*Associated Press*] (SAG) .... AGIP
American Government Term Trust [*NYSE symbol*] (SPSG) .... AGT
American Government Term Trust [*Associated Press*] (SAG) .... AGTT
American Graduate School of International Management [*Formerly, Thunderbird Graduate School of International Management*] [*Glendale, AZ*] .... AGSIM
American Graduate School of International Management, Glendale, AZ [*Library symbol*] [*Library of Congress*] (LCLS) .... AzGAGS
American Grain Products Processing Institute [*Defunct*] (EA) .... AGPPI
American Grand Prix Association (EA) .... AGA
American Graniteware Association (EA) .... AGA
American Grape Growers Alliance for Fair Trade [*Defunct*] (EA) .... AGGAFT
American Graphological Society (EA) .... AGS
American Grassland Council [*Later, AFGC*] (EA) .... AGC
American Graves Registration Command [*Military*] .... AGRC
American Graves Registration Command [*Military*] .... AGRCO
American Graves Registration Service [*Military*] .... AGRS
American Greek Exchange Society (EA) .... AGES
American Green Movement (EA) .... AGM
American Greenhouse Vegetable Growers Association (EA) .... AGVGA
American Greetings Corp. [*NASDAQ symbol*] (NQ) .... AGRE
American Greetings Corp. [*Associated Press*] (SAG) .... AGreet
American Greyhound Track Operators Association (EA) .... AGTOA
American Groomer's Guild (EA) .... AGG
American Grooming Shop Association (EA) .... AGSA
American Ground Flat Stock Association (EA) .... AGFSA
American Ground Water Trust (EA) .... AGWT
American Group of CPA Firms [*Lombard, IL*] (EA) .... TAG
American Group Practice Association (EA) .... AGPA
American Group Psychotherapy Association (EA) .... AGPA
American Guernsey Association (EA) .... AGA
American Guernsey Cattle Club [*Later, AGA*] (EA) .... AGCC
American Guides Association [*Defunct*] (EA) .... AGA
American Guild of Animal Artists (EA) .... AGAA
American Guild of Authors and Composers (EA) .... AGAC
American Guild of English Handbell Ringers (EA) .... AGEHR
American Guild of Hypnotherapists (EA) .... AGH
American Guild of Luthiers (EA) .... AGL
American Guild of Music (EA) .... AGM
American Guild of Musical Artists (EA) .... AGMA
American Guild of Musical Artists Magazine [*A publication*] (EAAP) .... AGMAzine
American Guild of Organists (EA) .... AGO
American Guild of Patient Account Management (EA) .... AGPAM
American Guild of Variety Artists (EA) .... AGVA
American Gulf West Indies Co. .... AGWI
American Gun Dealers Association (EA) .... AGDA
American Guppy Association [*Later, IFGA*] (EA) .... AGA
American Gynecological and Obstetrical Society (EA) .... AGOS
American Gynecological Society [*Later, AGOS*] (EA) .... AGS
American Habonim Association [*Later, Labor Zionist Alliance*] .... AHA
American Hackney Horse Society (EA) .... AHHS
American Hair Loss Council (EA) .... AHLC
American Hair Replacement Association [*Inactive*] (EA) .... AHRA
American Hair Restoration .... AHR
American Half-Paso Association [*Defunct*] (EA) .... AHPA
American Hampshire Sheep Association (EA) .... AHSA
American Handwriting Analysis Foundation (EA) .... AHAF
American Hanoverian Society (EA) .... AHS
American Hardboard Association (EA) .... AHA
American Hardware Manufacturers Association (EA) .... AHMA
American Hardwood Export Council (EA) .... AHEC
American Harlequin Rabbit Club (EA) .... AHRC
American Harp Society (EA) .... AHS
American Hazardous Waste Association (EA) .... AHWA
American Healing Association [*Defunct*] (EA) .... AHA
American Health and Beauty Aids Institute (EA) .... AHBAI
American Health and Temperance Society (EA) .... AHTS
American Health Assistance Foundation (EA) .... AHAF
American Health Association (EA) .... AHA
American Health Care Advisory Association (EA) .... AHCAA
American Health Care Association (EA) .... AHCA
American Health Consultants [*Information service or system*] (IID) .... AHC
American Health Decisions (EA) .... AHD
American Health Foundation (EA) .... AHF
American Health Industries Institute (EA) .... AHII
American Health Planning Association (EA) .... AHPA
American Health Professionals .... AHP
American Health Professions Institute (DAVI) .... AHPI
American Health Properties [*NYSE symbol*] (SPSG) .... AHE
American Health Properties [*NASDAQ symbol*] (SAG) .... AHEP
American Health Properties [*Associated Press*] (SAG) .... AHltPr
American Health Security Act [*Medicine*] .... AHSA
American Healthcare Institute [*Later, AMHS Institute*] (EA) .... AHI
American Healthcare Management, Inc. [*NYSE symbol*] (SPSG) .... AHI
American Healthcare Management, Inc. [*Associated Press*] (SAG) .... AHltMg

American Healthcare Radiology Administrators (EA) .... AHRA
American HealthChoice, Inc. [*NASDAQ symbol*] (SAG) .... AHIC
American HealthChoice, Inc. [*Associated Press*] (SAG) .... AHltCh
American Healthcorp [*NASDAQ symbol*] (SPSG) .... AMHC
American Healthcorp, Inc. [*Associated Press*] (SAG) .... AHlthcp
American Hearing Impaired Hockey Association (EA) .... AHIHA
American Hearing Research Foundation (EA) .... AHRF
American Hearing Society [*Later, NAHSA*] (EA) .... AHS
American Heart Association (EA) .... AHA
American Heartworm Society (EA) .... AHS
American Hebrew (BJA) .... AH
American Helicopter Company [*Air Force*] (MCD) .... AHC
American Helicopter Society (EA) .... AHS
American Hellenic Alliance (EA) .... AHA
American Hellenic Congress [*Defunct*] (EA) .... AHC
American Hellenic Educational Progressive Association .... AHEPA
American Hellenic Institute (EA) .... AHI
American Hellenic Institute Public Affairs Committee (EA) .... AHIPAC
American Helvetia Philatelic Society (EA) .... AHPS
American Hemerocallis Society (EA) .... AHS
American Hepatic Foundation (EA) .... AHF
American Hepatitis Association (EA) .... AHA
American Herb Association (EA) .... AHA
American Herbal Products Association (EA) .... AHPA
American Herbalists Guild (EA) .... AHG
American Hereford Association (EA) .... AHA
American Herens Association (EA) .... AHA
American Heritage [*A publication*] (BRI) .... AH
American Heritage Dictionary [*A publication*] .... AHD
American Heritage Foundation (EA) .... AHF
American Heritage Life Investment Corp. [*Associated Press*] (SAG) .... AHeritge
American Heritage Life Investment Corp. [*NYSE symbol*] (SPSG) .... AHL
American Heritage Society [*Defunct*] (EA) .... AHS
American Hibiscus Society (EA) .... AHS
American High-Density Gradient .... AHG
American Highways and Byways [*A publication*] .... AHB
American Hiking Society (EA) .... AHS
American Himalayan Rabbit Association (EA) .... AHRA
American Histadrut Cultural Exchange Institute [*Defunct*] (EA) .... AHCEI
American Historic and Cultural Society (EA) .... AHCS
American Historic Racing Motorcycle Association (EA) .... AHRMA
American Historical Association (EA) .... AHA
American Historical Philatelic Society [*Formerly, AHPS-CWPS*] (EA) .... AHPS
American Historical Philatelic Society - Civil War Philatelic Society [*Later, AHPS*] .... AHPS-CWPS
American Historical Print Collectors Society (EA) .... AHPCS
American Historical Review [*A publication*] (BRI) .... AHR
American Historical Society of Germans from Russia (EA) .... AHSGR
American History [*A publication*] (BRI) .... Am Hist
American Hitchhiker Association .... AHA
American Hobbit Association (EA) .... AHA
American Hobby Federation [*Defunct*] (EA) .... AHF
American Hockey Coaches Association (EA) .... AHCA
American Hockey League (EA) .... AHL
American Holdings, Inc. [*NASDAQ symbol*] (SAG) .... HOLD
American Holistic Health Sciences Association [*Defunct*] (EA) .... AHHSA
American Holistic Medical Association (EA) .... AHMA
American Holistic Medical Foundation (EA) .... AHMF
American Holistic Medical Institute [*of the American Holistic Medical Association*] [*Formerly, BIA Later, AHMF*] (EA) .... AHMI
American Holistic Nurses Association (EA) .... AHNA
American Holistic Veterinary Medical Association (EA) .... AHVMA
American Holstein Horse Association (EA) .... AHHA
American Home Business Association [*Greenwich, CT*] (EA) .... AHBA
American Home Economics Association (EA) .... AHEA
American Home Laundry Manufacturers Association [*Later, AHAM*] (EA) .... AHLMA
American Home Lighting Institute (EA) .... AHLI
American Home Mission Society .... AHMS
American Home Products Co. [*Associated Press*] (SAG) .... AHome
American Home Products Corp. [*Associated Press*] (SAG) .... AHme
American Home Products Corp. [*NYSE symbol*] (SPSG) .... AHP
American Home Products Corp., Ayerst Medical Library, New York, NY [*Library symbol Library of Congress*] (LCLS) .... NNAy
American Home Satellite Association [*Defunct*] (EA) .... AHSA
American Home Sewing and Craft Association (EA) .... AHSCA
American Home Sewing Association [*Later, AHSCA*] (EA) .... AHSA
American Home Sewing Council [*Later, AHSCA*] (EA) .... AHSC
American Homebrewers Association (EA) .... AHA
American Homeopathic Pharmacopoeia [*Last published in 1920*] .... AHP
American Homeowners Association [*Defunct*] (EA) .... AHA
American Homeowners Foundation (EA) .... AHF
American HomePatient Care [*NASDAQ symbol*] (SAG) .... AHOM
American HomePatient Care [*Associated Press*] (SAG) .... AHomPat
American Homestar Corp. [*Associated Press*] (SAG) .... AHomstr
American Homestar Corp. [*NASDAQ symbol*] (SAG) .... HSTR
American Hominological Association (EA) .... AHA
American Honey Institute [*Later, HICA*] (EA) .... AHI
American Honey Producers Association (EA) .... AHPA
American Hop Latent Virus [*Plant pathology*] .... AHLV
American Horizons [*Defunct*] (EA) .... AH
American Horse Council (EA) .... AHC
American Horse Protection Association (EA) .... AHPA
American Horse Publications (EA) .... AHP
American Horse Shows Association (EA) .... AHSA
American Horticultural Council [*Later, AHS*] .... AHC
American Horticultural Marketing Council (EA) .... AHMC
American Horticultural Society (EA) .... AHS
American Hospital Association (EA) .... AHA
American Hospital Association, Chicago, IL [*Library symbol Library of Congress*] (LCLS) .... ICAH
American Hospital Association Library, Chicago, IL [*OCLC symbol*] (OCLC) .... IHD
American Hospital Corps .... AHC
American Hospital Formulary [*A publication*] .... AHF
American Hospital Formulary Service .... AHFS
American Hospital Radiology Administrators (DAVI) .... AHRA
American Hospital Society .... AHS
American Hospital Supply Corp (BABM) .... AHSC
American Hospital Supply Corp., Evanston, IL [*Library symbol Library of Congress*] (LCLS) .... IEA
American Hospital Supply Corp., Evanston, IL [*Library symbol*] [*Library of Congress*] (LCLS) .... IEAH
American Hospital Supply Corp., Evanston, IL [*OCLC symbol*] (OCLC) .... JAU
American Hospital Video Network [*Satellite television system*] .... AHVN
American Host Foundation (EA) .... AHF
American Hosta Society (EA) .... AHS
American Hostage Committee [*Defunct*] (EA) .... AHC
American Hot Dip Galvanizers Association [*Later, AGA*] (EA) .... AHDGA
American Hot Rod Association (EA) .... AHRA
American Hotel & Motel Association (EA) .... AH & MA
American Hotel and Motel Brokers [*Formerly, MBAA*] (EA) .... AHMB
American Hotel Association [*Later, AH & MA*] .... AHA
American Hotel Trade Association Executives (EA) .... AHTAE
American Hound Association .... AHA
American Housing Survey [*Department of Housing and Urban Development*] (GFGA) .... AHS
American Housing Survey-Metropolitan Sample [*Department of Housing and Urban Development*] (GFGA) .... AHS-MS
American Hovercraft Association [*Superseded by HA*] (EA) .... AHA
American Hull Insurance Syndicate [*New York, NY*] (EA) .... AHIS
American Humane Association (EA) .... AHA
American Humane Association, Denver, CO [*Library symbol Library of Congress*] (LCLS) .... CoDAH
American Humane Education Society (EA) .... AHES
American Humane Society .... AHS
American Humanics (EA) .... AH
American Humanics Foundation [*Later, AH*] (EA) .... AHF
American Humanist Association (EA) .... AHA
American Humor Studies Association (EA) .... AHSA
American Hungarian Catholic Society [*Later, William Penn Association*] (EA) .... AHCS
American Hungarian Educators' Association (EA) .... AHEA
American Hungarian Federation (EA) .... AHF
American Hungarian Folklore Centrum (EA) .... AHFC
American Hungarian Foundation (EA) .... AHF
American Hungarian Library and Historical Society (EA) .... AHLHS
American Hungarian Studies Foundation [*Later, AHF*] (EA) .... AHSF
American Hydrogen Association (EA) .... AHA
American Hypnodontic Society (EA) .... AHS
American Hypnosis Association (EA) .... AHA
American Hypnotists' Association (EA) .... AHA
American Imagery Association [*Defunct*] (EA) .... AIA
American Immigration and Citizenship Conference (EA) .... AICC
American Immigration Control Foundation (EA) .... AICF
American Immigration Lawyers Association (EA) .... AILA
American Importers Association [*Later, AAEI*] .... AIA
American Importers Meat Products Group (EA) .... AIMPG
American Incense Manufacturers Association (EA) .... AIMA
American Income Holding, Inc. [*NYSE symbol*] (SPSG) .... AIH
American Income Holdings, Inc. [*Associated Press*] (SAG) .... AmInc
American Indemnity Financial Corp. [*NASDAQ symbol*] (NQ) .... AIFC
American Indemnity Financial Corp. [*Associated Press*] (SAG) .... AIndF
American Independent Designers and Engineers Society .... AIDES
American Independent Designers Association (EA) .... AIDA
American Independent Oil Co. .... AMINOIL
American Independent Party .... AIP
American Independent Refiners Association (EA) .... AIRA
American Indian .... AI
American Indian .... AMERIND
American Indian .... AMIND
American Indian/Alaska Native Nurses Association (EA) .... AIANNA
American Indian and Alaska Native .... AI/AN
American Indian and Eskimo Cultural Foundation [*Defunct*] .... AIECF
American Indian Archaeological Institute (EA) .... AIAI
American Indian Arts Council (EA) .... AIAC
American Indian Assistance League (OICC) .... AIAL
American Indian Community House .... AICH
American Indian Community House [*An association*] .... ASO
American Indian Council of Architects and Engineers (EA) .... AICAE
American Indian Culture and Research Journal [*A publication*] (BRI) .... Am Ind CRJ
American Indian Culture Research Center (EA) .... AICRC
American Indian Development Association [*Defunct*] (EA) .... AIDA
American Indian Environmental Council (EA) .... AIEC
American Indian Ethnohistorical Conference [*Later, American Society for Ethnohistory*] (EA) .... AIEC
American Indian Film Institute .... AIFI
American Indian Graduate Center (EA) .... AIGC
American Indian Health Care Association (EA) .... AIHCA

American Indian Heritage Foundation (EA) .... AIHF
American Indian Higher Education Consortium (EA) .... AIHEC
American Indian Historical Association (EA) .... AIHA
American Indian Historical Society [Defunct] (EA) .... AIHS
American Indian Horse Registry (EA) .... AIHR
American Indian Institute (EA) .... AII
American Indian Journal [A publication] (DLA) .... Am Ind J
American Indian Law Center (EA) .... AILC
American Indian Law Newsletter [A publication] (DLA) .... Am Ind L Newsl
American Indian Law Review [A publication] (DLA) .... Am Ind L Rev
American Indian Law Students Association [Later, NALSA] (EA) .... AILSA
American Indian Liberation Crusade (EA) .... AILC
American Indian Library Association (EA) .... AILA
American Indian Lore Association (EA) .... AILA
American Indian Movement (EA) .... AIM
American Indian Press Association [Defunct] (EA) .... AIPA
American Indian Projects Foundation [Defunct] (EA) .... AIPF
American Indian Radio on Satellite .... A/ROS
American Indian Refugees (EA) .... AIR
American Indian Registry for the Performing Arts (EA) .... AIRPA
American Indian Religious Freedom Act [1978] .... AIRFA
American Indian Research and Development [An association] (EA) .... AIRD
American Indian Research Center (OICC) .... AIRC
American Indian Scholarships [Later, AIGC] (EA) .... AIS
American Indian Science and Engineering Society (EA) .... AISES
American Indian Sign Language (BYTE) .... AIS
American Indian Studies Center [Research center] (RCD) .... AISC
American Indian Travel Commission [Defunct] (EA) .... AITC
American Indians for Sobriety (EA) .... AIS
American Indicator Digest Average [American Stock Exchange] .... AIDA
American Indonesian Chamber of Commerce (EA) .... AICC
American Indoor Soccer Association (EA) .... AISA
American Industrial Arts Association (EA) .... AIAA
American Industrial Arts Student Association [Later, TSA] (EA) .... AIASA
American Industrial Bankers Association [Later, NCFA] (EA) .... AIBA
American Industrial Development Council [Later, AEDC] (EA) .... AIDC
American Industrial Health Council (EA) .... AIHC
American Industrial Heritage Project .... ATHP
American Industrial Hygiene Association (EA) .... AIHA
American Industrial Music Association (EA) .... AIMA
American Industrial Properties [Formerly, Trammell Crow Real Estate Investment] [NYSE symbol] (SPSG) .... IND
American Industrial Properties Real Estate Investment Trust [Associated Press] (SAG) .... AIndPrp
American Industrial Radium and X-Ray Society [Later, ASNT] .... AIRXRS
American Industrial Real Estate Association (EA) .... AIR
American Industrial Transport, Inc. .... AIT
American Industrial Writing Institute .... AIWI
American Indycar Series [Auto racing] .... AIS
American Information Exchange [Information service or system] (ECON) .... AMIX
American Information Network (EA) .... AIN
American Information Network Ltd. [Information service or system] (IID) .... AIN
American Information Retrieval Service [Document delivery service] (NITA) .... AIRS
American Information Services [Information service or system] (IID) .... AIS
American Information Technologies Corp. [Telecommunications Chicago, IL] .... AMERITECH
American Innerspring Manufacturers (EA) .... AIM
American Inns of Court Foundation (EA) .... AICF
American Insolvency Reports [A publication] (DLA) .... A Ins R
American Insolvency Reports [A publication] (DLA) .... Am Ins Rep
American Insolvency Reports [A publication] (DLA) .... Am Insolv Rep
American Institute .... AI
American Institute for Aerological Research (MCD) .... AIAR
American Institute for Archaeological Research (EA) .... AIAR
American Institute for Cancer Research [Research center] (RCD) .... AICR
American Institute for Certified Public Accountants - Professional Standards (Commerce Clearing House) [A publication] (DLA) .... AICPA-Prof Stand (CCH)
American Institute for Character Education [Later, CEI] (EA) .... AICE
American Institute for Conservation of Historic and Artistic Works (EA) .... AIC
American Institute for Contemporary German Studies (EA) .... AICGS
American Institute for Decision Sciences [Later, DSI] (EA) .... AIDS
American Institute for Design and Drafting [Later, ADDA] (EA) .... AIDD
American Institute for Economic Development (EA) .... AIED
American Institute for Economic Research [Great Barrington, MA] (EA) .... AIER
American Institute for Exploration (EA) .... AIFE
American Institute for Foreign Study (EA) .... AIFS
American Institute for Foreign Study Scholarship Foundation (EA) .... AIFSSF
American Institute for Foreign Trade .... AIFT
American Institute for Free Labor Development (EA) .... AIFLD
American Institute for Hollow Structural Sections (EA) .... AIHSS
American Institute for Human Engineering and Development (EA) .... AIHED
American Institute for Imported Steel (EA) .... AIIS
American Institute for International Steel (EA) .... AIIS
American Institute for Islamic Affairs (EA) .... AIIA
American Institute for Maghrib Studies (EA) .... AIMS
American Institute for Marxist Studies [Defunct] (EA) .... AIMS
American Institute for Mental Studies [Later, AITSV] (EA) .... AIMS
American Institute for Patristic and Byzantine Studies (EA) .... AIPBS
American Institute for Political Communication .... AIPC
American Institute for Professional Education (EA) .... AIPE
American Institute for Property and Liability Underwriters [Malvern, PA] (EA) .... AIPLU
American Institute for Public Service (EA) .... AIPS

American Institute for Research and Education in Naturopathy (EA) .... AIREN
American Institute for Research in the Behavioral Sciences .... AIRBS
American Institute for Shippers' Associations (EA) .... AISA
American Institute for the Medical Research of Trauma (EA) .... AIMRT
American Institute for the Prevention and Eradication of Dental Disease .... AIPEDD
American Institute for Verdi Studies (EA) .... AIVS
American Institute in Taiwan .... AIT
American Institute, Inc. (EA) .... AII
American Institute of Aeronautics and Astronautics (EA) .... AIAA
American Institute of Aeronautics and Astronautics, New York, NY [Library symbol Library of Congress] (LCLS) .... NNIA
American Institute of Aeronautics and Astronautics, Pacific Aerospace Library, Los Angeles, CA [Library symbol Library of Congress] (LCLS) .... CLIA
American Institute of Aeronautics and Astronautics, Technical Information Service, New York, NY [Library symbol] [Library of Congress] (LCLS) .... NNAIAA
American Institute of Architects (EA) .... AIA
American Institute of Architects Foundation (SRA) .... AIAF
American Institute of Architects in Kansas (SRA) .... AIAKS
American Institute of Architects Service Corp. [Information service or system] (IID) .... AIA/SC
American Institute of Architects, Washington, D.C. [1867] (NGC) .... AIA
American Institute of Architects, Washington, DC [Library symbol Library of Congress] (LCLS) .... DAIA
American Institute of Architecture Students (EA) .... AIAS
American Institute of Baking (EA) .... AIB
American Institute of Baking, Chicago, IL [Library symbol Library of Congress] (LCLS) .... ICAI
American Institute of Banking (EA) .... AIB
American Institute of Biological Sciences (EA) .... AIBS
American Institute of Bolt, Nut, and Rivet Manufacturers [Later, Industrial Fasteners Institute] .... AIBNRM
American Institute of Building Design (EA) .... AIBD
American Institute of Certified Planners (EA) .... AICP
American Institute of Certified Public Accountants [New York, NY] (EA) .... AICPA
American Institute of Certified Public Accountants, New York, NY [Library symbol Library of Congress] (LCLS) .... NNAIA
American Institute of Ceylonese Studies (EA) .... AICS
American Institute of Chefs [Later, ACF] .... AIC
American Institute of Chemical Engineers [New York, NY] .... AICE
American Institute of Chemical Engineers (EA) .... AIChE
American Institute of Chemists (EA) .... AIC
American Institute of Child Care Centers [Defunct] .... AICCC
American Institute of Commemorative Art .... AICA
American Institute of Computerized Accounting Professionals [Defunct] (EA) .... AICAP
American Institute of Constructors (EA) .... AIC
American Institute of Consulting Engineers [Later, ACEC] (EA) .... AICE
American Institute of Cooperation [Defunct] (EA) .... AIC
American Institute of Crop Ecology (EA) .... AICE
American Institute of Electrical and Electronics Engineers [Also, IEEE] (NTCM) .... AIEEE
American Institute of Electrical Engineers [Later, IEEE] .... AIEE
American Institute of Electrical Engineers [Later, IEEE] .... AmInstEE
American Institute of Engineers .... AIE
American Institute of Family Relations .... AIFR
American Institute of Fellows in Free Enterprise [Houston, DE] (EA) .... FIFE
American Institute of Financial Brokers (EA) .... AIFB
American Institute of Fishery Research Biologists (EA) .... AIFRB
American Institute of Floral Designers (EA) .... AIFD
American Institute of Food Distribution (EA) .... AIFD
American Institute of France [Defunct] (EA) .... AIF
American Institute of Graphic Arts (EA) .... AIGA
American Institute of Group Counseling [Defunct] (EA) .... AIGC
American Institute of Homeopathy (EA) .... AIH
American Institute of Hydrology (EA) .... AIH
American Institute of Indian Studies (EA) .... AIIS
American Institute of Industrial Engineers [Later, IIE] (EA) .... AIIE
American Institute of Interior Designers [Later, ASID] (EA) .... AID
American Institute of Interior Designers [Later, ASID] (AEBS) .... AIID
American Institute of Iranian Studies (EA) .... AIIS
American Institute of Islamic Studies (EA) .... AIIS
American Institute of Islamic Studies, Denver, CO [Library symbol Library of Congress] (LCLS) .... CoDAmI
American Institute of Kitchen Dealers .... AIKD
American Institute of Landscape Architects [Later, ASLA] (EA) .... AILA
American Institute of Laundering [Later, IFI] (EA) .... AIL
American Institute of Leisuretime (EA) .... AIL
American Institute of Maintenance (EA) .... AIM
American Institute of Management [Quincy, MA] (EA) .... AIM
American Institute of Marine Underwriters [New York, NY] (EA) .... AIMU
American Institute of Maritime Services .... AIMS
American Institute of Medical and Biological Engineering .... AIMBE
American Institute of Medical Climatology (EA) .... AIMC
American Institute of Men's and Boys' Wear [Later, MFA] .... AIMBW
American Institute of Merchant Shipping [Washington, DC] (EA) .... AIMS
American Institute of Mining and Metallurgical Engineers (NUCP) .... AIMME
American Institute of Mining, Metallurgical, and Petroleum Engineers (EA) .... AIME
American Institute of Mining, Metallurgical, and Petroleum Engineers (BARN) .... AIMMPE
American Institute of Mortgage Brokers [Washington, DC] (EA) .... AIMB
American Institute of Musical Studies (EA) .... AIMS

American Institute of Nail and Tack Manufacturers (EA) .... AINTM
American Institute of Nautical Archaeology [*Later, INA*] (EA) .... AINA
American Institute of Nutrition (EA) .... AIN
American Institute of Oral Biology (EA) .... AIOB
American Institute of Organbuilders (EA) .... AIO
American Institute of Pacific Relations [*Defunct*] .... AIPR
American Institute of Park Executives [*Later, APRS*] (EA) .... AIPE
American Institute of Parliamentarians (EA) .... AIP
American Institute of Pathologic Science [*Defunct*] (EA) .... AIPS
American Institute of Physics (EA) .... AIP
American Institute of Physics, New York, NY [*Library symbol Library of Congress*] (LCLS) .... NNAIP
American Institute of Planners [*Later, American Planning Association*] (EA) .... AIP
American Institute of Plant Engineers (EA) .... AIPE
American Institute of Polish Culture (EA) .... AIPC
American Institute of Pollution Prevention .... AIPP
American Institute of Professional Geologists (EA) .... AIPG
American Institute of Public Opinion [*Also, ARI*] (NTCM) .... AIPO
American Institute of Radio Engineers [*Telecommunications*] [*An association*] (ECII) .... AIRE
American Institute of Real Estate Appraisers [*Later, AI*] (EA) .... AIREA
American Institute of Reciprocators [*Defunct*] (EA) .... AIR
American Institute of Refrigeration [*Defunct*] .... AIR
American Institute of Research (OICC) .... AIR
American Institute of Steel Construction (EA) .... AISC
American Institute of Stress (EA) .... AIS
American Institute of Supply Associations [*Later, ASA*] (EA) .... AISA
American Institute of Tax Practice (EA) .... AITP
American Institute of Technical Illustrators Association [*Defunct*] (EA) ...... AITIA
American Institute of Technology (MCD) .... AIT
American Institute of the History of Pharmacy (EA) .... AIHP
American Institute of Timber Construction (EA) .... AITC
American Institute of Ultrasound in Medicine (EA) .... AIUM
American Institute of Urban and Regional Affairs .... AIURA
American Institute of Vocal Pedagogy (EA) .... AIVP
American Institute of Weights and Measures [*Defunct*] (EA) .... AIWM
American Institute of Wholesale Plumbing and Heating Supply Associations [*Later, AISA*] .... AIWPHSA
American Institute of Wine and Food (EA) .... AIWF
American Institute on Problems of European Unity [*Later, AFPI*] (EA) .... AIPEU
American Institute - the Training School at Vineland [*Later, TTS*] (EA) ...... AITSV
American Institutes for Research [*Information service or system*] (IID) .... AIR
American Institutes for Research in the Behavioral Sciences (EA) .... AIR
American Institution in Thailand .... AIT
American Institutions Food Service Association (EA) .... AIFSA
American Instructors of the Deaf [*Also known as CAID*] (EA) .... AID
American Instrument Co. .... AMINCO
American Insulator Corp. .... AICO
American Insurance Association [*New York, NY*] (EA) .... AIA
American Insurance Group [*Commercial firm*] .... AIG
American Insurance Services Group [*New York, NY*] (EA) .... AISG
American Insured Mortgage Investors 1988 [*Associated Press*] (SAG) ...... AIM 88
American Insured Mortgage Investors Ltd. [*Associated Press*] (SAG) ...... AIM 84
American Insured Mortgage Investors. Series 84 Ltd. [*AMEX symbol*] (SPSG) .... AIA
American Insured Mortgage Investors - Series 85 Ltd. [*AMEX symbol*] (SPSG) .... AII
American Insured Mortgage Investors - Series 85 Ltd. [*Associated Press*] (SAG) .... AIM 85
American Insured Mortgage Investors - Series 86 Ltd. [*AMEX symbol*] (SPSG) .... AIJ
American Insured Mortgage Investors - Series 86 Ltd. [*Associated Press*] (SAG) .... AIM 86
American Insured Mortgage Investors - Series 88 Ltd. [*AMEX symbol*] (SPSG) .... AIK
American Insurers Highway Safety Alliance (EA) .... AIHSA
American Intellectual Property Law Association (EA) .... AIPLA
American Interactive Media, Inc. [*Software manufacturer*] .... AIM
American Intercultural Student Exchange (EA) .... AISE
American International Academy [*Defunct*] (EA) .... AIA
American International Airways, Inc. [*ICAO designator*] (FAAC) .... AIT
American International Airways, Inc. [*FAA designator*] (FAAC) .... CKS
American International Association for Economic and Social Development [*Defunct*] (EA) .... AIA
American International Assurance Co., Ltd. [*Commercial firm*] (ECON) .... AIA
American International Automobile Dealers Association (EA) .... AIADA
American International Checkers Society (EA) .... AICS
American International College [*Springfield, MA*] .... AIC
American International College, Springfield, MA [*Library symbol Library of Congress*] (LCLS) .... MSAI
American International Communications Corp. [*Boulder, CO*] .... AIC
American International Data Search, Inc. [*Information service or system Defunct*] (IID) .... AIDSEARCH
American International Dragon Association (EA) .... AIDA
American International Exhibition for Travel (ITD) .... AIET
American International Freight Association .... AIFA
American International Group [*Associated Press*] (SAG) .... AmIntG
American International Group, Inc. [*NYSE symbol*] .... AIG
American International Law Cases [*1783-1968*] [*A publication*] (DLA) .... AILC
American International Managers Society .... AIMS
American International Marchigiana Society (EA) .... AIMS
American International Media [*Joint venture of Philips International and PolyGram BV International*] .... AIM
American International Music Fund [*Defunct*] (EA) .... AIMF
American International Petroleum [*Associated Press*] (SAG) .... AmIntPt
American International Petroleum [*Associated Press*] (SAG) .... AmIntPt
American International Petroleum Corp. [*NASDAQ symbol*] (NQ) .... AIPN
American International Petroleum Corp. [*Associated Press*] (SAG) .... AmInPt
American International Pictures, Inc. .... AIP
American International Travel Service (IIA) .... AITS
American International Underwriters .... AIU
American Interprofessional Institute [*Defunct*] (EA) .... AII
American Intl. Pete Wrrt [*NASDAQ symbol*] (TTSB) .... AIPNW
American Intra-Ocular Implant Society [*Later, ASCRS*] (EA) .... AIOIS
American Inventors Association .... AIA
American Invitational Mathematics Examination [*Educational test*] .... AIME
American In-Vitro Allergy/Immunology Society (EA) .... AIAIS
American Ionospheric Propagation Association .... AIPA
American Ireland Fund (EA) .... AIF
American Iris Society (EA) .... AIS
American Irish Bicentennial Committee (EA) .... AIBC
American Irish Historical Society (EA) .... AIHS
American Irish Historical Society, New York, NY [*Library symbol Library of Congress*] (LCLS) .... NNAI
American Irish Political Education Committee (EA) .... PEC
American Irish Unity Committee (EA) .... AIUC
American Iron and Steel Institute (EA) .... AISI
American Iron and Steel Institute. Statistical Report [*A publication*] (EAAP) .... ASR
American Iron Ore Association (EA) .... AIOA
American Israel Opera Foundation (EA) .... AIOF
American Israel Public Affairs Committee (EA) .... AIPAC
American Israeli Civil Liberties Coalition (EA) .... AICLC
American Israeli Lighthouse (EA) .... AIL
American Israeli Paper Mills Ltd. [*AMEX symbol*] (SPSG) .... AIP
American Israeli Paper Mills Ltd. [*Associated Press*] (SAG) .... AIsrael
American Israelite (BJA) .... AI
American Issues Forum [*American bicentennial project*] .... AIF
American Italian Congress (EA) .... AIC
American Italian Historical Association (EA) .... AIHA
American Ivy Society (EA) .... AIS
American Jail Association (EA) .... AJA
American Japanese Trade Committee (EA) .... AJTC
American Jazz Alliance [*Formerly, CJOA*] (EA) .... AJA
American Jazz Orchestra .... AJO
American Jersey Cattle Club (EA) .... AJCC
American Jesuit Missionary Association [*Later, JM*] (EA) .... AJMA
American Jewelry Marketing Association [*Defunct*] (EA) .... AJMA
American Jewish Alternatives to Zionism (EA) .... AJAZ
American Jewish Archives [*An association*] (EA) .... AJA
American Jewish Archives, Cincinnati, OH [*Library symbol Library of Congress*] (LCLS) .... OCAJA
American Jewish Commission on the Holocaust (EA) .... AJCH
American Jewish Committee (EA) .... AJC
American Jewish Committee, New York, NY [*Library symbol Library of Congress*] (LCLS) .... NNAJ
American Jewish Conference .... AJC
American Jewish Congress (EA) .... AJC
American Jewish Correctional Chaplains Association (EA) .... AJCCA
American Jewish Heritage Committee (EA) .... AJHC
American Jewish Historical Society (EA) .... AJHS
American Jewish Historical Society, Waltham, MA [*Library symbol Library of Congress*] (LCLS) .... MWalA
American Jewish History Center of the Jewish Theological Seminary [*Defunct*] (EA) .... AJHC
American Jewish Institute [*Later, JIB*] (EA) .... AJI
American Jewish Joint Distribution Committee (EA) .... AJJDC
American Jewish Joint Distribution Committee (EA) .... JDC
American Jewish Leadership Conference (EA) .... AJLC
American Jewish League Against Communism (EA) .... AJLAC
American Jewish League for Israel (EA) .... AJLI
American Jewish Periodical Center (EA) .... AJPC
American Jewish Periodical Center, Cincinnati, OH [*Library symbol Library of Congress*] (LCLS) .... OCAJ
American Jewish Philanthropic Fund (EA) .... AJPF
American Jewish Physicians' Committee [*Later, AFHU*] (EA) .... AJPC
American Jewish Press Association (EA) .... AJPA
American Jewish Public Relations Society (EA) .... AJPRS
American Jewish Society for Service (EA) .... AJSS
American Jewish World Service (EA) .... AJWS
American Jews Opposed to Israeli Aggression (EA) .... AJOIA
American Jobs Abroad [*A publication*] .... AJA
American Joint Committee for Cancer Staging and End Results [*Oncology*] (DAVI) .... AJCCS & ER
American Joint Committee for Cancer Staging and End Results Reporting [*Later, AJCC*] (EA) .... AJC
American Joint Committee on Cancer (EA) .... AJCC
American Joint Committee on Cancer Staging [*Oncology*] (DAVI) .... AJCCS
American Joint Distribution Committee .... AJDC
American Journal Law Review [*A publication*] (DLA) .... Am J L Rev
American Journal of Archaeology [*A publication*] (BRI) .... AJA
American Journal of Clinical Hypnosis [*A publication*] .... AJCH
American Journal of Education [*A publication*] (BRI) .... AJE
American Journal of Forensic Psychiatry [*A publication*] (DLA) ..... Am J For Psych
American Journal of International Law [*A publication*] .... AJIL
American Journal of Jurisprudence [*Lawyers Co-op*] [*A publication*] (AAGC) .... Am J Juris
American Journal of Neuroradiology [*A publication*] .... AJNR
American Journal of Nursing (IIA) .... AJN

American Journal of Nursing Co., New York, NY [*Library symbol Library of Congress*] (LCLS) ... NNAJN
American Journal of Philology [*A publication*] (BRI) ... AJP
American Journal of Police Science [*A publication*] (DLA) ... Am J Police Sci
American Journal of Psychiatry [*A publication*] ... AJP
American Journal of Psychiatry [*A publication*] (BRI) ... AJPsych
American Journal of Psychology [*A publication*] (BRI) ... A J Psy
American Journal of Sociology [*A publication*] (BRI) ... AJS
American Journal of Sociology [*A publication*] (DLA) ... Am Jour Soc
American Journal of Tax Policy [*A publication*] (DLA) ... Am J Tax Pol'y
American Journal of Trial Advocacy [*A publication*] (DLA) ... Am J Trial Advoc
American Journal on Mental Retardation [*A publication*] (BRI) ... AJMR
American Journalism Review [*A publication*] [*Formerly, WJR Washington Journalism Review*] (WDMC) ... AJR
American Judges Association (EA) ... AJA
American Judicature Society (EA) ... AJS
American Judo Association (EA) ... AJA
American Junior Academy of Sciences ... AJAS
American Junior Bowling Congress (EA) ... AJBC
American Junior Brahman Association (EA) ... AJBA
American Junior Chianina Association (EA) ... AJCA
American Junior College of Puerto Rico, Bayamon, PR [*Library symbol Library of Congress*] (LCLS) ... PrBayA
American Junior College of Puerto Rico, Bayamon, PR [*OCLC symbol*] (OCLC) ... PRJ
American Junior Golf Association (EA) ... AJGA
American Junior Hereford Association (EA) ... AJHA
American Junior High School National Mathematics Exam ... AJHSNME
American Junior Paint Horse Association (EA) ... AJPHA
American Junior Polled Hereford Association [*Later, NJPHA*] (EA) ... AJPHA
American Junior Quarter Horse Association (EA) ... AJQHA
American Junior Red Cross ... AJRC
American Junior Shorthorn Association (EA) ... AJSA
American Junior Simmental Association [*Later, ASA*] (EA) ... AJSA
American Jurisprudence [*A publication*] (DLA) ... Am Jr
American Jurisprudence [*A publication*] (DLA) ... Am Jur
American Jurisprudence Legal Forms [*A publication*] (DLA) ... Am Jur Legal Forms
American Jurisprudence Legal Forms, Annotated [*A publication*] (DLA) ... Am J Leg Forms Anno
American Jurisprudence Legal Forms, Annotated [*A publication*] (DLA) ... Am Jur Leg Forms Anno
American Jurisprudence Legal Forms, Second Series [*A publication*] (DLA) ... Am Jur Legal Forms 2d
American Jurisprudence Pleading and Practice Forms, Annotated [*A publication*] (DLA) ... Am J Pl & Pr Forms Anno
American Jurisprudence Pleading and Practice Forms, Annotated [*A publication*] (DLA) ... Am Jur Pl & Pr Forms
American Jurisprudence Pleading and Practice Forms, Revised Editions [*A publication*] (DLA) ... Am Jur Pl & Pr Forms (Rev Ed)
American Jurisprudence Proof of Facts [*A publication*] (DLA) ... Am J Proof of Facts
American Jurisprudence Proof of Facts [*A publication*] (DLA) ... Am Jur Proof of Facts
American Jurisprudence Proof of Facts [*A publication*] ... POF
American Jurisprudence Proof of Facts, Annotated [*A publication*] (DLA) ... Am Jur Proof of Facts Anno
American Jurisprudence, Second Series [*A publication*] (DLA) ... Am J 2d
American Jurisprudence, Second Series [*A publication*] (DLA) ... Am Jur 2d
American Jurisprudence Trials [*A publication*] (DLA) ... Am J Trials
American Jurisprudence Trials [*A publication*] (DLA) ... Am Jur Trials
American Jurist [*A publication*] (DLA) ... AJ
American Jurist [*A publication*] (DLA) ... Am Jr
American Jurist [*A publication*] (DLA) ... Am Jur
American Jurist [*A publication*] (DLA) ... Am Jurist
American Jurist [*A publication*] (DLA) ... Amer Jur
American Justice Federation [*An association*] ... AJF
American Justice Institute (EA) ... AJI
American Juvenile Arthritis Organization (EA) ... AJAO
American Karakul Fur Sheep Registry [*Later, AKSR*] (EA) ... AKFSR
American Karakul Sheep Registry (EA) ... AKSR
American Kennel Club (EA) ... AKC
American Kennel Club, New York, NY [*Library symbol Library of Congress*] (LCLS) ... NNAKC
American Kidney Fund (EA) ... AKF
American Killifish Association (EA) ... AKA
American Kinesiotherapy Association (EA) ... AKA
American Kitefliers Association (EA) ... AKA
American Knit Glove Association (EA) ... AKGA
American Labor Arbitration Awards [*Prentice-Hall, Inc.*] [*A publication*] (DLA) ... ALAA
American Labor Arbitration Awards (Prentice-Hall, Inc.) [*A publication*] (DLA) ... Am Lab Arb Awards (P-H)
American Labor Arbitration Awards (Prentice-Hall, Inc.) [*A publication*] (DLA) ... P-H Am Lab Arb Awards
American Labor Arbitration Cases [*Prentice-Hall, Inc.*] [*A publication*] (DLA) ... Am Lab Arb Cas
American Labor Arbitration Services [*A publication*] (DLA) ... Am Lab Arb Serv
American Labor Cases [*Prentice-Hall, Inc.*] [*A publication*] (DLA) ... ALC
American Labor Cases [*Prentice-Hall, Inc.*] [*A publication*] (DLA) ... ALR
American Labor Cases [*Prentice-Hall, Inc.*] [*A publication*] (DLA) ... Am Lab Cas
American Labor Cases (Prentice-Hall, Inc.) [*A publication*] (DLA) ... P-H Am Lab Cas
American Labor Committee for Human Rights in Northern Ireland (EA) ... ALCHRNI
American Labor Education Center (EA) ... ALEC
American Labor Education Service [*Defunct*] ... ALES
American Labor Health Association [*Later, GHAA*] ... ALHA
American Labor Party ... ALP
American Lace Manufacturers Association ... ALMA
American Ladder Institute (EA) ... ALI
American LaMancha Club (EA) ... ALC
American Lamb Council (EA) ... ALC
American Laminators Association (EA) ... ALA
American Lancia Club (EA) ... ALC
American Land Alliance [*Defunct*] (EA) ... ALA
American Land Development Association (EA) ... ALDA
American Land Forum [*Later, ALRA*] (EA) ... ALF
American Land Resource Association [*Defunct*] (EA) ... ALRA
American Land Title Association (EA) ... ALTA
American Landrace Association (EA) ... ALA
American Landscape Horticulture Association (EA) ... ALHA
American Langshan Club (EA) ... ALC
American Language College Placement Test (DNAB) ... ALCPT
American Language Course [*Military*] (DNAB) ... ALC
American Laryngological Association (EA) ... ALA
American Laryngological, Rhinological, and Otological Society (EA) ... ALROS
American Latvian Association in the United States (EA) ... ALA
American Law Enforcement Officers Association (EA) ... ALEOA
American Law Firms for African Relief [*Defunct*] (EA) ... ALFAR
American Law Institute (EA) ... ALI
American Law Institute - American Bar Association Council of Legal Education Review [*A publication*] (DLA) ... ALI-ABA CLE Rev
American Law Institute - American Bar Association. Course Materials Journal [*A publication*] (DLA) ... ALI-ABA Course MJ
American Law Institute Federal Income Tax Project [*A publication*] (DLA) ... ALI Fed Income Tax Project
American Law Institute Model Land Development Code [*A publication*] (DLA) ... Model Land Dev Code
American Law Institute. Restatement of the Law [*A publication*] (DLA) ... Am L Ins
American Law Institute. Restatement of the Law [*A publication*] (DLA) ... Am L Inst
American Law Institute. Restatement of the Law [*A publication*] (DLA) ... Am Law Inst
American Law Magazine [*A publication*] (DLA) ... Am L Mag
American Law Network [*Telecommunications service*] (TSSD) ... ALN
American Law of Elections [*A publication*] (DLA) ... Am L Elec
American Law of Property [*A publication*] (DLA) ... Am Property
American Law of Veterans [*A publication*] (DLA) ... Am Vets
American Law Record [*Cincinnati*] [*A publication*] (DLA) ... AL Rec
American Law Record [*Ohio*] [*A publication*] (DLA) ... Am L Rec
American Law Record [*Cincinnati*] [*A publication*] (DLA) ... Am Law Rec
American Law Record (Reprint) [*Ohio*] [*A publication*] (DLA) ... Am Law Rec
American Law Record (Reprint) [*Ohio*] [*A publication*] (DLA) ... Am Law Record
American Law Record (Reprint) (Ohio) [*A publication*] (DLA) ... Am L Rec (Ohio)
American Law Register [*Philadelphia*] [*A publication*] (DLA) ... AL Reg
American Law Register [*A publication*] (DLA) ... ALR
American Law Register [*Philadelphia*] [*A publication*] (DLA) ... Am L Reg
American Law Register [*Philadelphia*] [*A publication*] (DLA) ... Am Law Reg
American Law Register [*Philadelphia*] [*A publication*] (DLA) ... Law Reg
American Law Register and Review [*A publication*] (DLA) ... Am L Reg & Rev
American Law Register, New Series [*A publication*] (DLA) ... AL Reg (NS)
American Law Register, New Series [*A publication*] (ILCA) ... ALRNS
American Law Register, New Series [*A publication*] (DLA) ... Am L Reg (NS)
American Law Register, New Series [*A publication*] (DLA) ... Am Law Reg NS
American Law Register, New Series [*A publication*] (DLA) ... Amer Law Reg (NS)
American Law Register, Old Series [*A publication*] (DLA) ... AL Reg (OS)
American Law Register, Old Series [*A publication*] (DLA) ... Am L Reg (OS)
American Law Register, Old Series [*A publication*] (DLA) ... Am Law Reg OS
American Law Register, Old Series [*A publication*] (DLA) ... Amer Law Reg (OS)
American Law Register (Reprint) [*Ohio*] [*A publication*] (DLA) ... Am Law Reg (Old Ser)
American Law Register (Reprint) [*Ohio*] [*A publication*] (DLA) ... NS Am Law Register
American Law Reporter [*Davenport, IA*] [*A publication*] (DLA) ... AL Rep
American Law Reporter [*Davenport, IA*] [*A publication*] (DLA) ... Am L Rep
American Law Reports ... ALR
American Law Reports Annotated, 1st-5th Series [*Lawyers Co-op*] [*A publication*] (AAGC) ... ALR
American Law Reports, Annotated, Federal [*A publication*] (DLA) ... ALR Fed
American Law Reports, Annotated, Fourth Series [*A publication*] (DLA) ... ALR 4th
American Law Reports, Annotated, Second Series [*A publication*] (DLA) ... ALR 2d
American Law Reports, Annotated, Third Series [*A publication*] (DLA) ... ALR 3d
American Law Reports Later Case Service [*A publication*] (DLA) ... ALRLCS
American Law School Review [*A publication*] (DLA) ... Am L Sch Rev
American Law School Review [*A publication*] (DLA) ... Am L School Rev
American Law School Review [*A publication*] (DLA) ... Am Law S Rev
American Law School Review [*A publication*] (DLA) ... Am LS Rev
American Law Student Association [*Later, Law Student Division - American Bar Association*] (EA) ... ALSA
American Law Times [*A publication*] (DLA) ... ALT
American Law Times [*A publication*] (DLA) ... Am LT
American Law Times, Bankruptcy Reports [*A publication*] (DLA) ... ALT Bankr
American Law Times, Bankruptcy Reports [*A publication*] (DLA) ... AM LT Bankr
American Law Times, Bankruptcy Reports [*A publication*] (DLA) ... Am LT Bankr Rep
American Law Times, Bankruptcy Reports [*A publication*] (DLA) ... Bank Ct Rep
American Law Times, Bankruptcy Reports [*A publication*] (DLA) ... Bank Rep

American Law Times Reports [*A publication*] (DLA) ... ALTR
American Law Times Reports [*A publication*] (DLA) ... Am Law T Rep
American Law Times Reports [*A publication*] (DLA) ... Am LT Rep
American Law Times Reports [*A publication*] (DLA) ... Am LTR
American Law Times Reports, New Series [*United States*] [*A publication*] (DLA) ... ALTRNS
American Law Times Reports, New Series [*A publication*] (DLA) ... Am LTRNS
American Lawn Bowls Association (EA) ... ALBA
American Lawyers Association [*Later, TAG*] (EA) ... ALA
American Lawyers Auxiliary (EA) ... ALA
American Leadership Forum (EA) ... ALF
American Leading Cases [*A publication*] (DLA) ... ALC
American Leading Cases [*A publication*] (DLA) ... Am L Cas
American Leading Cases [*A publication*] (DLA) ... Am LC
American Leading Cases [*A publication*] (DLA) ... Am Lead Cases
American Leading Cases [*A publication*] (DLA) ... Am Leading Cas
American Leading Cases [*A publication*] (DLA) ... Amer Lea Cas
American Leading Cases, Edited by Hare and Wallace [*A publication*] (DLA) ... Am Lead Cas
American Leading Cases, Edited by Hare and Wallace [*A publication*] (DLA) ... Am Lead Cas (H & W)
American Leading Cases, Edited by Hare and Wallace [*A publication*] (DLA) ... Hare & Wal LC
American Leading Cases, Edited by Hare and Wallace [*A publication*] (DLA) ... Hare & Wallace Amer Leading Cases
American Leading Cases, Edited by Hare and Wallace [*A publication*] (DLA) ... Hare & Wallace Lead Cases (Am)
American Leading Cases, Edited by Hare and Wallace [*A publication*] (DLA) ... Lead Cas Am
American Leading Cases (Edition of 1871) [*A publication*] (DLA) ... Am Lead Ca (Ed of 1871)
American League [*Baseball*] ... A
American League [*Baseball*] ... AL
American League Championship Series [*Baseball*] ... ALCS
American League for Exports and Security Assistance [*Washington, DC*] (EA) ... ALESA
American League of Anglers (EA) ... ALA
American League of Anglers and Boaters (EA) ... ALAB
American League of Financial Institutions [*Washington, DC*] (EA) ... ALFI
American League of Lobbyists (EA) ... ALL
American League of Professional Baseball Clubs (EA) ... ALPBC
American League to Abolish Capital Punishment [*Defunct*] (EA) ... ALACP
American Leather Belting Association [*Later, NIBA*] ... ALBA
American Leather Chemists Association (EA) ... ALCA
American Lebanese League (EA) ... ALL
American Lebanese Syrian Association Charities (EA) ... ALSAC
American Leduc Petroleums Ltd. [*Toronto Stock Exchange symbol*] ... ARL
American Legal Foundation [*WLF*] [*Absorbed by*] (EA) ... ALF
American Legal News [*A publication*] (DLA) ... Am Leg N
American Legal Studies Association (EA) ... ALSA
American Legation, United States Naval Attache (MUGU) ... ALUSNA
American Legation, United States Naval Liaison Officer ... ALUSLO
American Legation, United States Naval Liaison Officer (MCD) ... ALUSNLO
American Legation, United States Naval Observer ... ALUSNOB
American Legend (EA) ... AL
American Legion (EA) ... AL
American Legion Auxiliary (EA) ... ALA
American Legion Auxiliary Library, Cheyenne Wells, CO [*Library symbol Library of Congress*] (LCLS) ... CoChey
American Legion Baseball (EA) ... ALB
American Legion, National Headquarters Library, Indianapolis, IN [*Library symbol Library of Congress*] (LCLS) ... InIAL
American Legion of Honor ... AL of H
American Legion Press Association [*Later, NALPA*] (EA) ... ALPA
American Legion Transportation Post ... ALTP
American Legislative Exchange Council (EA) ... ALEC
American Legislator [*A publication*] (DLA) ... Am Leg
American Leprosy Missions (EA) ... ALM
American Lessing Society [*Later, LS*] (EA) ... ALS
American Lhasa Apso Club (EA) ... ALAC
American Liaison Office ... ALO
American Liberal Association (EA) ... ALA
American Liberation League ... ALL
American Libraries [*A publication*] (BRI) ... A Lib
American Library and Educational Services Co. ... ALESCO
American Library Association (EA) ... ALA
American Library Association, Booklist, Chicago, IL [*OCLC symbol*] (OCLC) ... JAB
American Library Association, Chicago, IL [*Library symbol Library of Congress*] (LCLS) ... ICALA
American Library Association, Chicago, IL [*OCLC symbol*] (OCLC) ... IEH
American Library Association Information Science and Automation Division (NITA) ... ALA/ISAD
American Library Association Office for Library Personnel Resources (EA) ... ALAOLPR
American Library Association/Social Responsibilities Round Table/Gay and LesbianTask Force (EA) ... ALA/SRRT/GLTF
American Library Association's Electronic Information Service ... ALANET
American Library Directory [*R. R. Bowker Co.*] [*Online database*] ... ALD
American Library for Education, Research, and Training ... ALERT
American Library History Round Table ... ALHRT
American Library in Paris, Paris, France [*Library symbol*] [*Library of Congress*] (LCLS) ... FrPALP
American Library Society [*Defunct*] ... ALS
American Library Trustee Association (EA) ... ALTA
American Licensed Practical Nurses Association (EA) ... ALPNA
American Life Convention [*Later, ACLI*] ... ALC
American Life Education and Research Trust (EA) ... ALERT
American Life Foundation [*Press*] ... ALF
American Life Group, Inc. [*NYSE symbol*] (SAG) ... AGP
American Life Group, Inc. [*Associated Press*] (SAG) ... AmLife
American Life Holding Co. [*NASDAQ symbol*] (SAG) ... ALHC
American Life Holding Co. [*Associated Press*] (SAG) ... AmLfe
American Life Insurance Association [*Later, ACLI*] (EA) ... ALIA
American Life Insurance Co. [*Surinam*] (EY) ... ALICO
American Life League (EA) ... ALL
American Life Lobby (EA) ... ALL
American Lifesaving Emergency Response Team (EA) ... ALERT
American Lighting Association (EA) ... ALA
American Lightwave [*Vancouver Stock Exchange symbol*] ... AWV
American List Corp. [*Associated Press*] (SAG) ... AmList
American List Corp. [*AMEX symbol*] (SPSG) ... AMZ
American Liszt Society (EA) ... ALS
American Literary Anthology ... ALA
American Literary Society [*Defunct*] (EA) ... ALS
American Literary Translators Association (EA) ... ALTA
American Literature [*A publication*] (BRI) ... AL
American Lithotripsy Society (EA) ... ALS
American Lithuanian Catholic Federation Ateitis [*Later, LCFA*] (EA) ... ALCFA
American Lithuanian Engineers' and Architects' Association (EA) ... ALEAA
American Lithuanian Musicians Alliance (EA) ... ALMA
American Lithuanian Organist - Musicians Alliance [*Formerly, ALRCOA*] (EA) ... ALOMA
American Lithuanian Press and Radio Association ... ALPRA
American Lithuanian Press and Radio Association - Viltis (EA) ... ALPRA-V
American Lithuanian Roman Catholic Organist Alliance [*Later, ALOMA*] (EA) ... ALRCOA
American Lithuanian Roman Catholic Women's Alliance [*Later, LCW*] (EA) ... ALRCWA
American Lithuanian Workers Literary Association (EA) ... ALWLA
American Littoral Society (EA) ... ALS
American Liver Foundation (EA) ... ALF
American Lives Endowment [*Defunct*] (EA) ... ALE
American Loan Fund ... ALF
American Lobbyists Directory [*A publication*] ... ALD
American Lock Collectors Association (EA) ... ALCA
American Locker Group, Inc. [*NASDAQ symbol*] (NQ) ... ALGI
American Locker Group, Inc. [*Associated Press*] (SAG) ... AmLck
American Locomotive Co. ... ALCO
American Logistics Association (EA) ... ALA
American Longevity Association (EA) ... ALA
American Loudspeaker Manufacturers Association (EA) ... ALMA
American Low Power Television Association [*Defunct*] (EA) ... ALPTA
American Luggage Dealers Association [*Later, ALDC*] (EA) ... ALDA
American Luggage Dealers Cooperative (EA) ... ALDC
American Lumber Standards ... ALS
American Lumber Standards Committee (EA) ... ALSC
American Lumen [*Record label*] ... AmLum
American Lunar Society (EA) ... ALS
American Lung Association (EA) ... ALA
[*The*] **American Lupus Society** (EA) ... TALS
American Lutheran Church [*Later, ELCA*] ... ALC
American Lutheran Church Men (EA) ... ALCM
American Lutheran Church Women [*Defunct*] (EA) ... ALCW
American Lutheran Education Association [*Later, ELEA*] (EA) ... ALEA
American Lutheran Publicity Bureau (EA) ... ALPB
American Luxembourg Society (EA) ... ALS
American Lyric Poems: from Colonial Times to the Present [*A publication*] ... AmLP
American Machine Tool Distributors Association (EA) ... AMTDA
American Machine Tool Export Associates (EA) ... AMTEA
American Machinery Association ... AMA
American Magnetics Corp. (MHDW) ... AMMG
American Magnolia Society [*Later, TMS*] (EA) ... AMS
American Mail Line ... AML
American Mailorder Association (EA) ... AMOA
American Mail-Order Merchants Association (EA) ... AMMA
American Maine-Anjou Association (EA) ... AMAA
American Majority Party (EA) ... AMP
American Malacological Union (EA) ... AMU
American Maltese Association (EA) ... AMA
American Malting Barley Association (EA) ... AMBA
American Managed Care and Review Association (EA) ... AMCRA
American Managed Care Pharmacy Association (EA) ... AMCPA
American Management Association [*New York, NY*] (EA) ... AMA
American Management Associations, New York, NY [*Library symbol Library of Congress*] (LCLS) ... NNAMA
American Management Institute (IIA) ... AMI
American Management Systems [*Associated Press*] (SAG) ... AMS
American Management Systems, Inc. [*Information service or system*] (IID) ... AMS
American Management Systems, Inc. [*NASDAQ symbol*] (NQ) ... AMSY
American Manchester Terrier Club (EA) ... AMTC
American Manganese Producers Association [*Defunct*] (EA) ... AMPA
American Marine Insurance Clearinghouse [*New York, NY*] (EA) ... AMIC
American Marine Insurance Forum [*New York, NY*] (EA) ... AMIF
American Marine Insurance Syndicate for Insurance of Builder's Risks [*Defunct*] (EA) ... AMISIBR
American Maritain Association (EA) ... AMA
American Maritime Association (EA) ... AMA
American Maritime Cases ... AMC

American Maritime Officers Service (EA) ... AMOS
American Market for International Program [*Telecommunications*] ... AMIP
American Market Selection [*Cigars*] ... AMS
American Marketing Association [*Chicago, IL*] (EA) ... AMA
American Massage Therapy Association (EA) ... AMTA
American Material Handling Society [*Later, IMMS*] (EA) ... AMHS
American Materials & Technologies Corp. (The) [*Associated Press*] (SAG) ... AmMatT
American Materials & Technologies Corp. (The) [*NASDAQ symbol*] (SAG) ... AMTK
American Mathematical Association of Two Year Colleges (EA) ... AMATYC
American Mathematical Society (EA) ... AMS
American Mathematical Society, Providence, RI [*Library symbol Library of Congress*] (LCLS) ... RPAM
American Mathematics Project (EA) ... AMP
American Matthay Association (EA) ... AMA
American McAll Association (EA) ... AMA
American Mead Association [*Inactive*] (EA) ... AMA
American Measuring Tool Manufacturers Association [*Defunct*] (EA) ... AMTMA
American Meat Institute (EA) ... AMI
American Meat Institute Foundation (EA) ... AMIF
American Meat Science Association (EA) ... AMSA
American Mechanical Rights Agency ... AMRA
American Med Technologies [*NASDAQ symbol*] (TTSB) ... AMTI
American Medallic Sculpture Association (EA) ... AMSA
American Media, Inc. [*Formerly, Enquirer/Star Group*] [*Associated Press*] (SAG) ... Amdia
American Media, Inc. [*Formerly, Enquirer/Star Group*] [*Associated Press*] (SAG) ... AMedia
American Media, Inc. [*Formerly, Enquirer/Star Group*] [*NYSE symbol*] (SAG) ... ENQ
American Medical Alert Corp. [*NASDAQ symbol*] (NQ) ... AMAC
American Medical Alert Corp. [*Associated Press*] (SAG) ... AMdAlt
American Medical Association (EA) ... AMA
American Medical Association Auxiliary (EA) ... AMAA
American Medical Association, Chicago, IL [*Library symbol Library of Congress*] (LCLS) ... ICAM
American Medical Association Committee on Insurance and Prepayment Plans (EA) ... AMA-CIPP
American Medical Association, Division of Library and Archival Services, Chicago, IL [*OCLC symbol*] (OCLC) ... AMA
American Medical Association Drug Evaluation ... AMA-DE
American Medical Association Education and Research Foundation (EA) ... AMA-ERF
American Medical Association Network (NITA) ... AMA/NET
American Medical Association Political Action Committee ... AMAPAC
American Medical Association, Washington Office, Washington, DC [*Library symbol Library of Congress*] (LCLS) ... DAMA
American Medical Athletic Association (EA) ... AMAA
American Medical Center at Denver (AAMN) ... AMCD
American Medical Center for Burma [*Defunct*] (EA) ... AMCB
American Medical Center, Medical Library, Denver, CO [*Library symbol Library of Congress*] (LCLS) ... CoDAMC-M
American Medical College Application Service ... AMCAS
American Medical Curling Association (EA) ... AMCA
American Medical Directors Association (EA) ... AMDA
American Medical Electroencephalographic Association (DAVI) ... AMEA
American Medical Electroencephalographic Association (EA) ... AMEEGA
American Medical Equestrian Association (EA) ... AMEA
American Medical Fly Fishing Association (EA) ... AMFFA
American Medical Golf Association (EA) ... AMGA
American Medical Holdings, Inc. [*Associated Press*] (SAG) ... AMedH
American Medical Informatics Association (EA) ... AMIA
American Medical Joggers Association [*Later, AMAA*] ... AMJA
American Medical Optics [*Commercial firm*] (DAVI) ... AMO
American Medical Optics Posterior Chamber [*Lens*] [*Ophthalmology*] (DAVI) ... AMO PC
American Medical Peer Review Association (EA) ... AMPRA
American Medical Political Action Committee (EA) ... AMPAC
American Medical Publishers' Association (EA) ... AMPA
American Medical Qualification [*British*] ... AMQ
American Medical Record Association (EA) ... AMRA
American Medical Research Expedition to Mount Everest ... AMREE
American Medical Resources Foundation (DMAA) ... AMRF
American Medical Response [*Associated Press*] (SAG) ... AmMdRs
American Medical Response [*NYSE symbol*] (SPSG) ... EMT
American Medical Security Group, Inc. ... AMS
American Medical Society on Alcoholism ... AMSA
American Medical Society on Alcoholism and Other Drug Dependencies [*Later, ASAM*] (EA) ... AMSAODD
American Medical Student Association (EA) ... AMSA
American Medical Support Flight Team [*Later, Operation Angel Plane*] (EA) ... AMSFT
American Medical Systems [*Commercial firm*] (DAVI) ... AMS
American Medical Systems, Inc., Minneapolis, MN [*Library symbol Library of Congress*] (LCLS) ... MnMAM
American Medical Technologies [*NASDAQ symbol*] (SAG) ... AMTI
American Medical Technologies, Inc. [*Associated Press*] (SAG) ... AmMdTc
American Medical Technologists (EA) ... AMT
American Medical Technology, Inc. [*Vancouver Stock Exchange symbol*] ... AMO
American Medical Television ... AMT
American Medical Tennis Association (EA) ... AMTA
American Medical Women's Association (EA) ... AMWA
American Medical Writers' Association (EA) ... AMWA
American Medserve Corp. [*NASDAQ symbol*] (SAG) ... AMCI
American Medserve Corp. [*Associated Press*] (SAG) ... AmMdsv
American Megatrends, Inc. (PCM) ... AMI
American Melting Point ... AMP
American Men and Women of Science [*R. R. Bowker Co.*] [*Information service or system A publication*] (IID) ... AMWS
American Men and Women of Science [*Database*] [*R. R. Bowker Co.*] [*Information service or system*] (CRD) ... MWSC
American Men of Letters [*A publication*] ... AML
American Mental Health Counselors Association (EA) ... AMHCA
American Mental Health Foundation (EA) ... AMHF
American Mental Health Fund (EA) ... AMHF
American Merchandise Display Osaka [*Department of Commerce Japan*] (IMH) ... AMDO
American Merchant Marine Institute [*Later, AIMS*] (EA) ... AMMI
American Merchant Marine Library Association (EA) ... AMMLA
American Merchant Marine Library Association, New York, NY [*Library symbol Library of Congress*] (LCLS) ... NNAMM
American Merchant Marine Veterans (EA) ... AMMV
American Messianic Fellowship (EA) ... AMF
American Metal Climax, Inc. [*Later, AMAX, Inc.*] ... AMAX
American Metal Detector Manufacturers Association (EA) ... AMDMA
American Metal Importers Association [*Defunct Defunct*] (EA) ... AMIA
American Metal Repair Association [*Defunct*] ... AMRA
American Metal Stamping Association [*Later, PMA*] (EA) ... AMSA
American Metalworking Technology for the European Community (SAA) ... AMTEC
American Metaphysical Association (EA) ... AMA
American Meteor Society (EA) ... AMS
American Meteorite Laboratory ... AML
American Meteorological Observation Station (HGAA) ... AMOS
American Meteorological Society [*Boston, MA*] ... AMS
American Metered Postage Society [*Defunct*] (EA) ... AMPS
American Methanol Institute ... AMI
American Mexican Claims Commission [*Terminated, 1947*] ... AMCC
American MGB Association (EA) ... AMGBA
American MGC Register (EA) ... AMGCR
American Micro Co., Kansas City, MO [*Library symbol Library of Congress*] (LCLS) ... AmCo
American Microchemical Society (EA) ... AMS
American Microcomputer Dealers Association (EA) ... AMDA
American Microfilm Information Society [*An association*] (ECII) ... AMFIS
American Microscopical Society (EA) ... AMS
American Microsystems, Inc. (MCD) ... AMI
American Middle East Rehabilitation (EA) ... AMER
American Military Assistance Staff ... AMAS
American Military Association ... AMA
American Military Government ... AMG
American Military Industrial Complex ... AMERIMIC
American Military Institute (EA) ... AMI
American Military Mission, Delhi [*World War II*] ... AMMDEL
American Military Mission to China [*World War II*] ... AMMISCA
American Military Music Association (EA) ... AMMA
American Military Precision Flying Teams Association (EA) ... AMPFTA
American Military Retirees Association (EA) ... AMRA
American Military Society (EA) ... AMS
American Military University ... AMU
American Milk Goat Record Association [*Later, ADGA*] (EA) ... AMGRA
American Milking Devon Association (EA) ... AMDA
American Milking Shorthorn Junior Society (EA) ... AMSJS
American Milking Shorthorn Society (EA) ... AMSS
American Millinery Manufacturers Association [*Defunct*] ... AMMA
American Mime Theatre (EA) ... AMT
[*The*] **American Mime Theatre** (EA) ... TAMT
American Mineral Spirits Co. ... AMSCO
American Miniature Horse Association (EA) ... AMHA
American Miniature Horse Registry (EA) ... AMHR
American Miniature Racing Car Association ... AMRCA
American Miniature Schnauzer Club (EA) ... AMSC
American Mining Congress (EA) ... AMC
American Ministerial Association (EA) ... AMA
American Minor Breeds Conservancy (EA) ... AMBC
American Miscellaneous Society (EA) ... AMSOC
American Mission for Aid to Greece ... AMAG
American Mission for Aid to Turkey ... AMAT
American Mission for Opening Churches (EA) ... AMOC
American Mission for Opening Closed Churches [*Later, AMOC*] (EA) ... AMOCC
American Mission in Korea ... AMIK
American Mission to Greeks [*Later, AMG International*] (EA) ... AMG
American Mission to the Chinese [*Later, American Mission to the Chinese and Asian*] (EA) ... AMC
American Mission to the Chinese and Asian [*Defunct*] (EA) ... AMCA
American Missionary Association ... AMA
American Missionary Fellowship (EA) ... AMF
American Mizrachi Women [*Formerly, MWOA*] (EA) ... AMW
American Mobile Satellite Corp. [*Associated Press*] (SAG) ... AmMbSat
American Mobile Satellite Corp. [*NASDAQ symbol*] (SAG) ... SKYC
American Mobilehome Association (EA) ... AMA
American Model Yachting Association (EA) ... AMYA
American Modern Dance Caucus (EA) ... AMDC
American Modified Golf Association (EA) ... AMGA
American Mohammedan Society [*Later, MM*] (EA) ... AMS
American Mold Builders Association (EA) ... AMBA
American Money Management Association [*Barrington, IL*] (EA) ... AMM
American Monitor Corp. (MCD) ... AMC
American Montessori Society (EA) ... AMS

American Monument Association (EA) .... AMA
American Morab Horse Association (EA) .... AMHA
American Morgan Horse Association (EA) .... AMHA
American Morgan Horse Institute (EA) .... AMHI
American Mosquito Control Association (EA) .... AMCA
American Motel Association (EA) .... AMA
American Mothers Committee (EA) .... AMC
American Mothers, Inc. (EA) .... AMI
American Mothers of Korean Orphans (EA) .... AMKO
American Motility Society (EA) .... AMS
American Motion Picture Export Co. (EA) .... AMPEC
American Motion Picture Export Co./Africa [Later, AMPEC] [An
    association] (EA) .... AMPECA
American Motivational Association (EA) .... AMA
American Motor Hotel Association (EA) .... AMHA
American Motorcycle Drag Racing Association [of the National Hot Rod
    Association] [Later, NMRA] (EA) .... AMDRA
American Motorcycle Heritage Foundation (EA) ..... AMHF
American Motorcyclist Association (EA) .... AMA
American Motorcyclist Political Action Committee .... AMPAC
American Motors Corp. (EA) .... AM
American Motors Corp. .... AMC
American Motors Owners Association (EA) .... AMO
American Motorsport International (EA) .... AMI
American Movement for World Government (EA) .... AMWG
American Movers Conference (EA) .... AMC
American Movie Classics [Cable-television network] ... AMC
American Mule Association (EA) .... AMA
American Multi Cinema [Third largest theatre chain in America] ... AMC
American Municipal Association [Later, NLC] (EA) ... AMA
American Municipal Bond Assurance Corp. .... AMBAC
American Municipal Income Portfolio [NYSE symbol] (SPSG) ... XAA
American Municipal Income Portfolio, Inc. [Associated Press] (SAG) ... AMunInc
American Municipal Term Trust [Associated Press] (SAG) ... AmMuTr
American Municipal Term Trust [NYSE symbol] (SPSG) ... AXT
American Municipal Term Trust II [Associated Press] (SAG) ... AmMuT2
American Municipal Term Trust II [NYSE symbol] (SAG) ... BXT
American Municipal Term Trust III [Associated Press] (SAG) ... AmMuT3
American Municipal Term Trust III [NYSE symbol] (SPSG) ... CXT
American Murray Grey Association (EA) .... AMGA
American Museum of Immigration (EA) .... AMI
American Museum of Marine Archaeology .... AMMA
American Museum of Natural History, New York, NY [Library symbol Library
    of Congress] (LCLS) .... NNM
American Museum of Natural History, New York, NY [OCLC symbol]
    (OCLC) .... YAM
American Museum of Safety (EA) .... AMS
American Museum of the Moving Image [New York City] (ECON) ... AMMI
American Mushroom Institute (EA) .... AMI
American Music [A publication] .... Am M
American Music [A publication] (BRI) .... Am M
American Music Center (EA) .... AMC
American Music Conference (EA) .... AMC
American Music Festival Association (EA) .... AMFA
American Music Scholarship Association (EA) .... AMSA
American Music Teacher [A publication] (BRI) ...... Am MT
American Music Theater Festival .... AMTF
American Musical Instrument Society (EA) .... AMIS
American Musicians Union (EA) .... AMU
American Musicological Society (EA) .... AMS
American Mustang and Burro Association (EA) ...... AMBA
American Mustang Association (EA) .... AMA
American Mutual Alliance [Insurance association] [Later, Alliance of American
    Insurers] (EA) .... AMA
American Mutual Insurance Alliance [Later, Alliance of American Insurers]
    (EA) .... AMIA
American Mutual Life Association (EA) .... AMLA
American Nail Producers Council .... ANPC
American Name Society (EA) .... ANS
American Naprapathic Association (EA) .... ANA
American Narcolepsy Association (EA) .... ANA
American National Archives (DIT) .... ANA
American National Bancorp [Associated Press] (SAG) ... ANatBc
American National Bancorp [NASDAQ symbol] (SAG) ... ANBK
American National Bank & Trust Co. (MHDB) .... ANB & TC
American National Cattle Women (EA) .... ANCW
American National Cattlemen's Association [Later, NCA] (EA) ... ANCA
American National Commission for the Accreditation of Colleges and
    Universities (EA) .... ANCACU
American National Committee to Aid Homeless Armenians (EA) ... ANCHA
American National Council for Health Education of the Public (EA) ... ANCHEP
American National Cowbelles [Later, ANCW] (EA) ... ANC
American National Cowbelles [Later, ANCW] (EA) ... ANCB
American National Dictionary for Information Processing Systems
    [A publication] .... ANDIPS
American National Heritage Association (EA) .... ANHA
American National Insurance Co. [NASDAQ symbol] (NQ) ... ANAT
American National Insurance Co. .... ANI
American National Insurance Co. .... ANICO
American National Insurance Co. [Associated Press] (SAG) ... ANtlns
American National Metric Council (EA) .... ANMC
American National Postal Employees Retirees Association (EA) ... ANPERA
American National Red Cross [Later, ARC] .... ANRC
American National Red Cross, Washington, DC [Library symbol Library of
    Congress] (LCLS) .... DARC

American National Savings Bank [NASDAQ symbol] (SAG) ... ANBK
American National Standard [ANSI] (MCD) .... ANS
American National Standard Character Set for Optical Character
    Recognition (MCD) .... ANSCS OCR
American National Standard Code for Information Interchange (MCD) ... ANSCII
American National Standard Labels (BUR) .... ANL
American National Standard Vocabulary for Information Processing ... ANSVIP
American National Standards Institute (EA) .... ANSI
American National Standards Institute/American Society for Quality
    Control (RDA) .... ANSI/ASQC
American National Standards (Institute) Committee [Later, NISO] ... ANSC
American National Standards Institute, New York, NY [Library symbol Library
    of Congress] (LCLS) .... NNASA
American National Theater [Kennedy Center for the Performing Arts] ... ANT
American National Theatre and Academy [Defunct] (EA) ... ANTA
American Nationalities Council (EA) .... ANC
American Native Press Research Association [Defunct] (EA) ... ANPRA
American Natural Energy Corp. [Associated Press] (SAG) ... AmNtEn
American Natural Energy Corp. [NASDAQ symbol] (SAG) ... ANEC
American Natural Hygiene Society (EA) .... ANHS
American Natural Soda Ash Corp. (EA) .... ANSAC
American Naturalized Citizen Welfare Association [Later, US Naturalized
    CitizenAssociation] (EA) .... ANCWA
American Nature Association [Defunct] .... ANA
American Nature Study Society (EA) .... ANSS
American Naturopathic Medical Association (EA) ... ANMA
American Navion Society (EA) .... ANS
American NAZI Party [Later, NSWWP] .... ANP
American Near East Refugee Aid (EA) .... ANERA
American Needlepoint Guild (EA) .... ANG
American Negligence Cases [A publication] (DLA) ... Am Neg Ca
American Negligence Cases [A publication] (DLA) ... Am Neg Cas
American Negligence Cases [A publication] (DLA) ... Am Neg Cases
American Negligence Cases [A publication] (DLA) ... Am Negl Cas
American Negligence Cases [A publication] (DLA) ... ANC
American Negligence Digest [A publication] (DLA) ... Am Neg Dig
American Negligence Reports [A publication] (DLA) ... Am Neg Rep
American Negligence Reports [A publication] (DLA) ... Am Negl R
American Negligence Reports [A publication] (DLA) ... Am Negl Rep
American Negligence Reports, Current Series [A publication] (DLA) ... ANR
American Negro Poetry [A publication] .... AmNP
American Nephrology Nurses' Association (EA) ..... ANNA
American Neturei Karta [Friends of Jerusalem] (EA) ... ANK
American Network, Inc. [Portland, OR] (TSSD) ...... AMNET
American Neurological Association (EA) .... ANA
American Neurotology Society (EA) .... ANS
American Newcomen Society .... ANS
American News Co. (DGA) .... ANC
American News Women's Club (EA) .... ANWC
American Newspaper Association .... ANA
American Newspaper Guild [Later, TNG] (EA) .... ANG
American Newspaper Publishers Abstracting Technique ... ANPAT
American Newspaper Publishers Association (EA) ... ANPA
American Newspaper Publishers Association Foundation (EA) ... ANPAF
American Newspaper Publishers' Association/Research Institute
    (DGA) .... ANPA/RI
American Newspaper Publishers' Association Technical Exposition and
    Conference (ITD) .... ANPA/TEC
American Newspapers, 1821-1936 [A bibliographic publication] ... AN
American Nickel Collectors' Association (EA) .... ANCA
American Nobel Anniversary Committee (EA) .... ANAC
American Nominalist Group (EA) .... ANG
American Normande Association (EA) .... ANA
American North Country Cheviot Sheep Association (EA) ... ANCCSA
American Norwich Society [Defunct] (EA) .... ANS
American Notary [A publication] (DLA) .... Am Notary
American Nuclear Energy Council (EA) .... ANEC
American Nuclear Insurers [Farmington, CT] (EA) ... ANI
American Nuclear Science Corp. (MCD) .... ANSC
American Nuclear Society (EA) .... ANS
American Nuclear Standards Institute .... ANSI
American Numismatic Association (EA) .... ANA
American Numismatic Association Certification Service ... ANACS
American Numismatic Association, Colorado Springs, CO [Library symbol
    Library of Congress] (LCLS) .... CoCAN
American Numismatic Society (EA) .... ANS
American Numismatic Society, New York, NY [Library symbol Library of
    Congress] (LCLS) .... NNAN
American Nurses' Association (EA) .... ANA
American Nurses' Association, Kansas City, MO [Library symbol Library of
    Congress] (LCLS) .... MoKA
American Nurses' Foundation (EA) .... ANF
American Nursing Assistants' Association (EA) ..... ANAA
American Nursing Home Association [Later, AHCA] (EA) ... ANHA
American Nutrition Society (EA) .... ANS
American Nutritionists Association (EA) .... ANA
American Occupational Medical Association (EA) ... AOMA
American Occupational Therapy Association (EA) ... AOTA
American Occupational Therapy Certification Board [AOTA] ... AOTCB
American Occupational Therapy Foundation (MEDA) ... AOTF
American Occupational Therapy Political Action Committee [AOTA] ... AOTPAC
American Oceanic Organization (EA) .... AOO
American Oceans Campaign [An association] (EA) ... AOC
American Office Supply Exporters Association [Defunct] (EA) ... AOSEA
American Oil Chemists' Society (EA) .... AOCS

American Oil Co. [*Later, Amoco Oil Co.*] ... AMOCO
American Oil Co. [*Later, Amoco Oil Co.*], Texas City, TX [*Library symbol Library of Congress*] (LCLS) ... TxTA
American Oilfield Divers, Inc. [*Associated Press*] (SAG) ... AmOilfDv
American Oilfield Divers, Inc. [*NASDAQ symbol*] (SAG) ... DIVE
American Old Time Fiddlers Association (EA) ... AOTFA
American Oncology Resources, Inc. [*Associated Press*] (SAG) ... AOncol
American Oncology Resources, Inc. [*NASDAQ symbol*] (SAG) ... AORI
American Ontoanalytic Association (EA) ... AOA
American Open University [*Computer science*] ... AOU
American Ophthalmological Color [*Chart*] ... AOC
American Ophthalmological Society (EA) ... AOS
American Opportunity Foundation [*Washington, DC*] (EA) ... AOF
American Opportunity Income [*NYSE symbol*] (SPSG) ... OIF
American Opportunity Income Fund, Inc. [*Associated Press*] (SAG) ... AOIF
American Optical Corp. ... AO
American Optical Corp. (DAVI) ... AOC
American Optical Corp., Southbridge, MA [*Library symbol Library of Congress*] (LCLS) ... MSbrA
American Optometric Association (EA) ... AOA
American Optometric Foundation (EA) ... AOF
American Optometric Student Association (EA) ... AOSA
American Orchid Society (EA) ... AOS
American Order of Stationary Engineers ... AOSE
American Order of the French Croix de Guerre (EA) ... AOFCG
American [*or Army*] **Ordnance Association** [*Later, ADPA*] (EA) ... AOA
American Orff-Schulwerk Association (EA) ... AOSA
American Organization for the Education of the Hearing Impaired [*Later, IOEHI*] (EA) ... AOEHI
American Organization of Nurse Executives (EA) ... AONE
American Organization of Tour Operators to Israel [*Defunct*] (EA) ... AOTOI
American Oriental Society (EA) ... AOS
American Ornithologists' Union (EA) ... AOU
American Orthodontic Society (EA) ... AOS
American Orthopaedic Society for Sports Medicine (EA) ... AOSSM
American Orthopedic Association (EA) ... AOA
American Orthopedic Foot and Ankle Society (EA) ... AOFAS
American Orthopedic Foot Society [*Later, AOFAS*] (EA) ... AOFS
American Orthopsychiatric Association (EA) ... AOA
American Orthopsychiatric Association (EA) ... ORTHO
American Orthoptic Council (EA) ... AOC
American Orthotic and Prosthetic Association (EA) ... AOPA
American Osler Society (EA) ... AOS
American Osteopathic Academy of Orthopedics (EA) ... AOAO
American Osteopathic Academy of Sclerotherapy (EA) ... AOAS
American Osteopathic Academy of Sports Medicine (EA) ... AOASM
American Osteopathic Association (EA) ... AOA
American Osteopathic Association, Chicago, IL [*Library symbol Library of Congress*] (LCLS) ... ICAO
American Osteopathic Board of Emergency Medicine (EA) ... AOBEM
American Osteopathic Board of General Practice (EA) ... AOBGP
American Osteopathic Board of Pediatrics (EA) ... AOBP
American Osteopathic College of Allergy and Immunology (EA) ... AOCAI
American Osteopathic College of Anesthesiologists (EA) ... AOCA
American Osteopathic College of Dermatology (EA) ... AOCD
American Osteopathic College of Nuclear Medicine [*Defunct*] (EA) ... AOCNM
American Osteopathic College of Pathologists (EA) ... AOCP
American Osteopathic College of Pathologists ... AOCPA
American Osteopathic College of Physical Medicine and Rehabilitation [*Later, AOCRM*] (EA) ... AOCPMR
American Osteopathic College of Preventive Medicine (EA) ... AOCPM
American Osteopathic College of Proctology (EA) ... AOCP
American Osteopathic College of Proctology ... AOCPR
American Osteopathic College of Radiology (EA) ... AOCR
American Osteopathic College of Rehabilitation Medicine (EA) ... AOCRM
American Osteopathic College of Rheumatology (EA) ... AOCR
American Osteopathic Historical Society [*Defunct*] (EA) ... AOHS
American Osteopathic Hospital Association (EA) ... AOHA
American Osteopathic Hospital Research and Education Foundation (EA) ... AOHREF
American Osteopathic Network [*American Osteopathic Association*] [*Information service or system*] (IID) ... AONET
American Ostrich Association (EA) ... AOA
American Otological Society (EA) ... AOS
American Otorhinologic Society for Plastic Surgery [*Later, AAFPRS*] (EA) ... AOSPS
American Outreach Association (EA) ... AOA
American Overseas Airlines ... AOA
American Overseas Association [*Later, ARCOA*] (EA) ... AOA
American Overseas Book Co. ... AOBC
American Overseas Educators Organization [*Later, Association of Overseas Educators*] (AEBS) ... AOEO
American Oxford Down Record Association [*Later, AOSA*] (EA) ... AODRA
American Oxford Sheep Association (EA) ... AOSA
American Pacific Bank [*NASDAQ symbol*] (SAG) ... AMPB
American Pacific Bank [*Associated Press*] (SAG) ... APacBk
American Pacific Bank [*Vancouver Stock Exchange symbol*] ... APB
American Pacific Corp. [*Associated Press*] (SAG) ... AmPac
American Pacific Corp. [*NASDAQ symbol*] (NQ) ... APFC
American Pacific Minerals Ltd. [*Associated Press*] (SAG) ... APacMin
American Pacific Minerals Ltd. [*NASDAQ symbol*] (SAG) ... APML
American Package Express Carriers Association (EA) ... APECA
American Pad & Paper [*Stock exchange term*] ... AGP
American Pad & Paper [*NYSE symbol*] (SAG) ... AGP
American Pad & Paper [*Associated Press*] (SAG) ... APadP
American Paging, Inc. [*Associated Press*] (SAG) ... AmerPag
American Paging, Inc. [*AMEX symbol*] (SAG) ... APP
American Pain Society (EA) ... APS
American Paint Horse Association (EA) ... APHA
American Palestine Committee [*Defunct*] (EA) ... APC
American Pancreatic Association (EA) ... APA
American Paper and Pulp Association [*Later, API*] ... APPA
American Paper and Pulp Mills Superintendents' Association (DGA) ... APPMSA
American Paper Co. ... AP
American Paper Exchange Club [*Later, PIR*] (EA) ... APEC
American Paper Institute (EA) ... API
American Paper Machinery Association (EA) ... APMA
American Paralysis Association (EA) ... APA
American Paramedical Institute [*Hawaii*] ... API
American Paraplegia Society (EA) ... APS
American Parapsychological Research Foundation [*Later, AAP*] (EA) ... APRF
American Parents Committee (EA) ... APC
American Park and Recreation Society (EA) ... APRS
American Park Rangers Association (EA) ... APRA
American Parkinson Disease Association (EA) ... APDA
American Parquet Association [*Defunct*] (EA) ... APA
American Part-Blooded Horse Registry (EA) ... APB
American Partridge Plymouth Rock Club (EA) ... APPRC
American Paso Fino Horse Association (EA) ... APFHA
American Patent Law Association [*Later, AIPLA*] (EA) ... APLA
American Patent Law Association. Bulletin [*A publication*] (DLA) ... Am Pat L Assoc Bull
American Patent Law Association. Bulletin [*A publication*] (DLA) ... Am Pat LA Bull
American Pathology Foundation (EA) ... APF
American Patients Association (EA) ... APA
American Pawnbrokers Association (EA) ... APA
American Pax Association [*Later, PC-USA*] (EA) ... APA
American Payroll Association (EA) ... APA
American Peace Society (EA) ... APS
American Peace Test (EA) ... APT
American Peanut Product Manufacturers, Inc. (EA) ... APPMI
American Peanut Research and Education Association [*Later, APRES*] (EA) ... APREA
American Peanut Research and Education Society (EA) ... APRES
American Pedestrian Association (EA) ... APA
American Pediatric Gastroesophageal Reflux Association (EA) ... APGRA
American Pediatric Gross Assessment Record ... APGAR
American Pediatric Society (EA) ... APS
American Pediatric Surgical Association (EA) ... APSA
American Pencil Collectors Society (EA) ... APCS
American Penstemon Society (EA) ... APS
American Peony Society (EA) ... APS
American People for American Prisoners (EA) ... APAP
American People/Link [*American Design and Communication*] [*Information service or system*] (IID) ... PLINK
American People's Mobilization [*Formerly, American Peace Mobilization*] [*World War II*] ... APM
American Performance Horse Association (EA) ... APHA
American Performing-Rights Society ... APRS
American Personnel and Guidance Association [*Later, AACD*] (EA) ... APGA
American Peruvian Paso Horse Registry (EA) ... APPHR
American Pet Boarding Association (EA) ... APBA
American Pet Products Manufacturers Association (EA) ... APPMA
American Pet Society (EA) ... APS
American Petanque Association USA (EA) ... APA
American Petroleum Credit Association [*Minneapolis, MN*] (EA) ... APCA
American Petroleum Institute (EA) ... API
American Petroleum Institute Patents (NITA) ... APIPAT
American Petroleum Institute Research (MCD) ... APIR
American Petroleum Institute Research Project ... APIRP
American Petroleum Institute, Washington, DC [*Library symbol Library of Congress*] (LCLS) ... DAPI
American Petroleum Refiners Association [*Later, AIRA*] (EA) ... APRA
American Pewter Guild (EA) ... APG
American Pharmaceutical Association ... APA
American Pharmaceutical Association (EA) ... APhA
American Pharmaceutical Association, Washington, DC [*Library symbol Library of Congress*] (LCLS) ... DAPh
American Pharmacopeia ... AP
American Pheasant and Waterfowl Society (EA) ... AP & WS
American Pheasant Society [*Later, AP & WS*] (EA) ... APS
American Phenolic Corp. (KSC) ... AMPHENOL
American Philatelic Congress (EA) ... APC
American Philatelic Research Library (EA) ... APRL
American Philatelic Research Library, State College, PA [*Library symbol Library of Congress*] (LCLS) ... PStcA
American Philatelic Society (EA) ... APS
American Philatelic Society Writers Unit (EA) ... APSWU
American Philatelist [*A publication*] (BRI) ... Am Phil
American Philological Association (EA) ... APA
American Philosophical Association (EA) ... APA
American Philosophical Society (EA) ... APS
American Philosophical Society, Philadelphia, PA [*Library symbol Library of Congress*] (LCLS) ... PPAmP
American Phoenix Group, Inc. [*Associated Press*] (SAG) ... AmPhoeG
American Phoenix Group, Inc. [*Associated Press*] (SAG) ... APhoe
American Phoenix Group, Inc. [*NASDAQ symbol*] (SAG) ... APHX
American Photo-Engravers Association (DGA) ... APEA
American Photograph Equipment Co. ... APECO
American Photographic Artisans Guild (EA) ... APAG

American Photographic Book Publishing Co.	AMPHOTO
American Photographic Historical Society (EA)	APHS
American Photonics, Inc. [*Brookfield Center, CT*] (TSSD)	API
American Photoplatemakers Association [*Later, IAP*]	APA
American Physical Fitness Research Institute [*Defunct*] (EA)	APFRI
American Physical Society (EA)	APS
American Physical Therapy Association (EA)	APTA
American Physical Therapy Association, Arkansas Chapter (SRA)	ArPTA
American Physical Therapy Foundation (DMAA)	APTF
American Physicians Art Association	APAA
American Physicians Association of Computer Medicine (EA)	APACM
American Physicians Fellowship for Medicine in Israel (EA)	APF
American Physicians Poetry Association (EA)	APPA
American Physicians Service Group, Inc. [*NASDAQ symbol*] (NQ)	AMPH
American Physicians Service Group, Inc. [*Associated Press*] (SAG)	APhyG
American Physiological Society (EA)	APS
American Physiotherapy Association [*Later, APTA*]	APA
American Phytopathological Society (EA)	APS
American Piedmontese Association (EA)	APA
American Pigeon Racing Association (EA)	APRA
American Pilots' Association (EA)	APA
American Pinto Horse Association (EA)	APHA
American Pinzgauer Association (EA)	APA
American Pioneer Lines [*Steamship*] (MHDW)	AP
American Pioneer Trails Association	APTA
American Pipe Fittings Association (EA)	APFA
American Pistol and Revolver Association [*Defunct*] (EA)	APRA
American Pistol Institute (EA)	API
American Place Theatre (EA)	APT
American Plan [*Hotel room rate*]	AP
American Planning Association (EAIO)	APA
American Planning Civic Association [*Later, NUC*] (EA)	APCA
American Plant Life Society (EA)	APLS
American Plant Selections [*An association Defunct*] (EA)	APS
American Plate Number Single Society (EA)	APNSS
American Platform Tennis Association (EA)	APTA
American Platinum, Inc. [*Vancouver Stock Exchange symbol*]	AP
American Playwrights Theatre [*Defunct*]	APT
American Pleader's Assistant [*A publication*] (DLA)	Am Pl Ass
American Plum Line Pattern Virus [*Plant pathology*]	APLPV
American Plywood Association (EA)	APA
American Podiatric Circulatory Society (EA)	APCS
American Podiatric Medical Association (EA)	APMA
American Podiatric Medical Association Auxiliary (EA)	APMAA
American Podiatric Medical Students Association (EA)	APMA
American Podiatric Medical Writers Association (EA)	APMWA
American Podiatry Association [*Later, APMA*]	APA
American Podiatry Association Auxiliary [*Later, APMAA*] (EA)	APAA
American Poems; a Contemporary Collection [*A publication*]	AmPC
American Poetry [*A publication*]	AmP
American Poetry [*A publication*]	AmPo
American Poetry [*A publication*]	AP
American Poetry [*A publication*]	APA
American Poetry and Prose [*A publication*]	AmPP
American Poetry Association (EA)	APA
American Poetry League	APL
American Poetry Review [*A publication*] (BRI)	APR
American Poinsettia Society [*Defunct*] (EA)	APS
American Point System [*Typography*] (DGA)	APS
American Pointer Club (EA)	APC
American Polar Society (EA)	APS
American Police Academy (EA)	APA
American Polish War Relief [*Post-World War II*]	APWR
American Political Items Collectors (EA)	APIC
American Political Science Association (EA)	APSA
American Political Science Association. Quarterly [*A publication*]	PS
American Political Science Review [*A publication*] (BRI)	APSR
American Polled Hereford Association (EA)	APHA
American Polled Shorthorn Society (EA)	APSS
American Polygraph Association (EA)	APA
American Polypay Sheep Association (EA)	APSA
American Pomeranian Club (EA)	APC
American Pomological Society (EA)	APS
American Poolplayers Association (EA)	APA
American Popular Revolutionary Alliance [*Peru*] [*Political party*]	APRA
American Porphyria Foundation (EA)	APF
American Portrait Society (EA)	APS
American Portuguese Cultural Society [*Later, APS*] (EA)	APCS
American Portuguese Society (EA)	APS
American Postal Chess League [*Defunct*] (EA)	APCL
American Postal Chess Tournaments (EA)	APCT
American Postal Workers Union (EA)	APWU
American Potash & Chemical Corp., Whittier, CA [*Library symbol Library of Congress*] (LCLS)	CWhA
American Potash Institute [*Later, PPI*] (EA)	API
American Poultry and Hatchery Federation [*Later, PEIA*] (EA)	APHF
American Poultry Association (EA)	APA
American Poultry Historical Society (EA)	APHS
American Poultry International (EA)	API
American Powder Metallurgy Institute (EA)	APMI
American Power Boat Association (EA)	APBA
American Power Committee [*Defunct*]	APC
American Power Conversion [*NASDAQ symbol*] (SAG)	APCC
American Power Conversion [*Associated Press*] (SAG)	APwrCnv
American Power Conversion Co. (PCM)	APC
American Power Drinkers Association	APDA
American Power Jet Co.	APJ
American Power Net Association [*Later, EFMCNTA*] (EA)	APNA
American Practice [*A publication*] (DLA)	Am Pr
American Practice Reports [*Washington, DC*] [*A publication*] (DLA)	Am Pr Rep
American Practice Reports, New Series [*A publication*] (DLA)	Am Pr Rep NS
American Precision Industries, Inc. [*NYSE symbol*] (SPSG)	APR
American Precision Industries, Inc. [*Associated Press*] (SAG)	APrec
American Precision Optics Manufacturers Association (EA)	APOMA
American Prepaid Legal Services Institute (EA)	API
American Presbyterian Congo Mission	APCM
American President Companies Ltd.	APC
American President Companies Ltd. [*Associated Press*] (SAG)	APresid
American President Companies Ltd. [*NYSE symbol*] (SPSG)	APS
American President Lines	APL
American Press Institute (EA)	API
American Primrose Society (EA)	APS
American Printed Fabrics Council (EA)	APFC
American Printing History Association (EA)	APHA
American Printing House for the Blind (EA)	APH
American Printing House for the Blind	APHB
American Printing House for the Blind Central Automated Resource List [*Information service or system*] (CRD)	APH-CARL
American Printing Technologies (DGA)	APT
American Prison Ministry [*An association*] (EA)	APM
American Prisoner of War (AABC)	APW
American Prisoner of War Information Bureau (AABC)	APWIB
American Private Line Services, Inc. [*Newton, MA*] [*Telecommunications*] (TSSD)	APLS
American Pro Life Council (EA)	APLC
American Probate, New Series [*A publication*] (DLA)	Am Prob NS
American Probate Reports [*A publication*] (DLA)	Am Pro Rep
American Probate Reports [*A publication*] (DLA)	Am Prob
American Probate Reports [*A publication*] (DLA)	Am Prob Rep
American Probation and Parole Association (EA)	APPA
American Proctologic Society [*Later, ASCRS*] (EA)	APS
American Produce Association (EA)	APA
American Producers of Italian Type Cheese Association (EA)	APITCA
American Production and Inventory Control Society (EA)	APICS
American Productivity Center [*Houston, TX*] (EA)	APC
American Productivity Management Association [*Skokie, IL*] (EA)	APMA
American Professional Basketball Association [*Game*] [*Pronounced "apbah"*]	APBA
American Professional Faceters Association [*Defunct*] (EA)	APFA
American Professional Needlework Retailers (EA)	APNR
American Professional Pet Distributors, Inc. [*An association*] (EA)	APPDI
American Professional Practice Association (EA)	APPA
American Professional Racquetball Organization (EA)	APRO
American Professional Society of the Deaf (EA)	APSD
American Professional Society on the Abuse of Children	Apsac
American Professional Surfing Association (EA)	APSA
American Professors for Peace in the Middle East [*Defunct*] (EA)	APPME
American Program Bureau [*Lectures*]	APB
American Programmers Guild	APG
American Progress Foundation	APF
American Prosecutors Research Institute (EA)	APRI
American Prospect Research Association (EA)	APRA
American Prosthetic Research Laboratory (DAVI)	APRL
American Prosthodontic Society (EA)	APS
American Protective Association [*Late-19th-century organization opposed to so-called encroachments of the Catholic Church in the US*]	APA
American Protestant Association	APA
American Protestant Correctional Chaplains Association (EA)	APCCA
American Protestant Defense League (EA)	APDL
American Protestant Health Association (EA)	APHA
American Protestant Hospital Association (DAVI)	APHA
American Protestant Society	APS
American Protestants for Truth about Ireland (EA)	APTI
American Psychiatric Association (EA)	APA
American Psychiatric Nurses Association (EA)	APNA
American Psychical Institute	API
[*The*] American Psycho/Info Exchange [*Information service or system*] (IID)	AMPIE
American Psychoanalytic Association (EA)	APA
American Psychoanalytic Association (EA)	APsaA
American Psychological Association (EA)	APA
[*Division of Child and Youth Services*] American Psychological Association (PAZ)	APA
American Psychological Foundation	APF
American Psychological Practitioners Association (EA)	APPA
American Psychological Society (DAVI)	APS
American Psychologists for Social Action [*Later, PSA*]	APSA
American Psychology-Law Society (EA)	AP-LS
American Psychopathological Association	APA
American Psychopathological Association (EA)	APS
American Psychosomatic Society (EA)	APS
American Psychotherapy Association [*Inactive*] (EA)	APA
American Public Communications Council (EA)	APCC
American Public Gas Association (EA)	APGA
American Public Health Association (EA)	APHA
American Public Power Association (EA)	APPA
American Public Radio	APR
American Public Relations Association [*Later, PRSA*]	APRA
American Public Transit Association (EA)	APTA
American Public Welfare Association (EA)	APWA

American Public Works Association (EA) ... APWA
American Publicists Guild [*Defunct*] (EA) ... APG
American Publishing Co. [*NASDAQ symbol*] (SAG) ... AMPC
American Puerto-Rican Action League ... APAL
American Puffer Alliance [*An association*] (EA) ... APA
American Pulpwood Association (EA) ... APA
American Puppet Arts Council [*Defunct*] ... APAC
American Purchasing Society (EA) ... APS
American Puritan Ethic ... APE
American Pyramid Resources, Inc. [*Vancouver Stock Exchange symbol*] ... APE
American Pyrotechnics Association (EA) ... APA
American Quarter Horse Association (EA) ... AQHA
American Quarter Horse Racing Council (EA) ... AQHRC
American Quarter Pony Association (EA) ... AQPA
American Quarterly [*A publication*] (BRI) ... Am Q
American Quaternary Association (EA) ... AMQUA
American Quick Printing Association [*Defunct*] (EA) ... AQPA
American Quicksilver Institute [*Defunct*] (EA) ... AQI
American Quilt Study Group (EA) ... AQSG
American Quilter's Society (EA) ... AQS
American Rabbit Breeders Association (EA) ... ARBA
American Racing Driver's Club (EA) ... ARDC
American Racing Pigeon Union (EA) ... ARPU
American Racing Series ... ARS
American Radiator & Standard Sanitary Corp. [*Later, American Standard, Inc.*] ... AMSTAN
American Radiator & Standard Sanitary Corp. [*Later, American Standard, Inc.*] ... ARSS
American Radio Association (EA) ... ARA
American Radio Co. of the Air [*Radio program*] ... ARC
American Radio Council [*Later, PRO-IF*] (EA) ... ARC
American Radio Importers Association (EA) ... ARIA
American Radio Relay League (EA) ... ARRL
American Radio Systems Corp. [*NASDAQ symbol*] (SAG) ... AMRD
American Radio Systems Corp. [*Associated Press*] (SAG) ... ARadio
American Radio Telephone System (TEL) ... ARTS
American Radiography Technologists (EA) ... ART
American Radiological Nurses Association (EA) ... ARNA
American Radium Society (EA) ... ARS
American Rafting Association [*Defunct*] (EA) ... ARA
American Railroad and Corporation Reports [*A publication*] (DLA) ... Am R & C Rep
American Railroad and Corporation Reports [*A publication*] (DLA) ... Am R & Corp
American Railroad and Corporation Reports [*A publication*] (DLA) ... Am RR & C Rep
American Railroad Foundation [*Defunct*] (EA) ... ARF
American Railway and Airline Supervisors Association (EA) ... RSA
American Railway Association [*Later, AAR*] ... ARA
American Railway Bridge and Building Association (EA) ... ARBBA
American Railway Car Export Association (EA) ... ARCEA
American Railway Car Institute (EA) ... ARCI
American Railway Cases [*A publication*] (DLA) ... Am R Ca
American Railway Cases [*A publication*] (DLA) ... Am Rail Cas
American Railway Cases [*A publication*] (DLA) ... Am Railw Cas
American Railway Cases [*A publication*] (DLA) ... Am RR Ca
American Railway Cases [*A publication*] (DLA) ... Am RR Cas
American Railway Cases [*A publication*] (DLA) ... Am Ry Ca
American Railway Cases [*A publication*] (DLA) ... Am Ry Cases
American Railway Cases [*Legal*] ... ARC
American Railway Development Association (EA) ... ARDA
American Railway Engineering Association (EA) ... AREA
American Railway Magazine Editors Association [*Later, Association of Railroad Editors*] (EA) ... ARMEA
American Railway Master Mechanics' Association ... ARMMA
American Railway Reports [*A publication*] (DLA) ... Am R Rep
American Railway Reports [*A publication*] (DLA) ... Am Rail R
American Railway Reports [*A publication*] (DLA) ... Am RR Rep
American Railway Reports [*A publication*] (DLA) ... Am Ry Rep
American Railway Reports [*A publication*] (DLA) ... Amer R'y Rep
American Railway Reports [*A publication*] (DLA) ... ARR
American Railway Reports [*A publication*] (DLA) ... ARRR
American Railway Union ... ARU
American Rambouillet Sheep Breeders Association (EA) ... ARSBA
American Rape Prevention Association (EA) ... ARPA
American Rat, Mouse, and Hamster Society (EA) ... ARMHS
American Rationalist Federation (EA) ... ARF
American Rayon Institute [*Defunct*] ... ARI
American Re Corp. [*Associated Press*] (SAG) ... AmReCp
American Re Corp. Capital [*Associated Press*] (SAG) ... AmReC
American Re Corp. Capital [*NYSE symbol*] (SAG) ... ARN
American Reading Council [*Defunct*] (EA) ... ARC
American Real Estate and Urban Economics Association (EA) ... AREUEA
American Real Estate Exchange ... AMREX
American Real Estate Investment Corp. [*Associated Press*] (SAG) ... AREInv
American Real Estate Investment Corp. [*AMEX symbol*] (SAG) ... REA
American Real Estate Partners Ltd. [*Associated Press*] (SAG) ... AREst
American Real Estate Partnership [*NYSE symbol*] (SPSG) ... ACP
American Real Estate Society (EA) ... ARES
American Realty Corp. [*NYSE symbol*] (SPSG) ... ARN
American Realty Trust [*Associated Press*] (SAG) ... AmRlt
American Realty Trust SBI [*NYSE symbol*] (SPSG) ... ARB
American Record Merchandisers and Distributors Association [*Defunct*] (EA) ... ARMADA
American Recorder Society (EA) ... ARS
American Records Management Association (NITA) ... ARMA
American Recovery Association (EA) ... ARA
American Recreation Centers, Inc. [*NASDAQ symbol*] (NQ) ... AMRC
American Recreation Centers, Inc. [*Associated Press*] (SAG) ... ARecr
American Recreation Coalition (EA) ... ARC
American Recreation Co. Holdings [*NASDAQ symbol*] (SAG) ... AMRE
American Recreation Society [*Later, APRS*] (EA) ... ARS
American Recreational Activities ... ARA
American Recreational Equipment Association (EA) ... AREA
American Recreational Golf Association (EA) ... ARGA
American Recreational Racket Sports Association (EA) ... ARRSA
American Recreational Vehicle Living Association [*Defunct*] (EA) ... ARVLA
American Red Brangus Association (EA) ... ARBA
American Red Cross ... AMCROSS
American Red Cross (EA) ... ARC
American Red Cross Children's Fund ... ARCCF
American Red Cross Overseas Association (EA) ... ARCOA
American Red Magen David for Israel [*An association*] ... ARMD
American Red Magen David for Israel (EA) ... ARMDI
American Red Poll Association (EA) ... ARPA
American Reference Books Annual [*A publication*] (BRI) ... ARBA
American Refrigeration Transit Co. [*AAR code*] ... ART
American Refugee Committee (EA) ... ARC
American Registered Inhalation Therapist [*Academic degree*] ... ARIT
American Registered Respiratory Therapist ... ARRT
American Registry of Architectural Antiquities (EA) ... ARAA
American Registry of Certified Professionals in Agronomy, Crops, and Soils (EA) ... ARCPACS
American Registry of Clinical Radiography Technologists (EA) ... ARCRT
American Registry of Diagnostic Medical Sonographers (EA) ... ARDMS
American Registry of Inhalation Therapists [*Later, NBRT*] (EA) ... ARIT
American Registry of Medical Assistants (EA) ... ARMA
American Registry of Pathologists ... ARP
American Registry of Pathology (EA) ... ARP
American Registry of Physical Therapists [*Defunct*] (EA) ... ARPT
American Registry of Professional Entomologists (EA) ... ARPE
American Registry of Radiologic [*or Radiology*] **Technologists** (EA) ... ARRT
American Rehabilitation Committee [*FEGS*] [*Absorbed by*] (EA) ... ARC
American Rehabilitation Counseling Association (EA) ... ARCA
American Rehabilitation Educational Network [*Pittsburgh, PA*] [*Telecommunications service*] (TSSD) ... AREN
American Rehabilitation Foundation [*Later, SKI*] (EA) ... ARF
American Rehabilitation Foundation Minneapolis, MN [*Library symbol Library of Congress*] (LCLS) ... MnMAR
American Relief Administration Association ... ARA
American Relief for Poland [*Defunct*] (EA) ... ARP
American Reloaders Association (EA) ... ARA
American Remount Association (EA) ... ARA
American Rental Association (EA) ... ARA
American Repair Service ... ARS
American Reperatory Ballet Company [*Formerly, Princeton Ballet*] ... ARBC
American Repertory Theatre ... ART
American Reports [*A publication*] (DLA) ... A Rep
American Reports [*A publication*] (DLA) ... Am R
American Reports [*A publication*] (DLA) ... Am Rep
American Reports [*A publication*] (DLA) ... Am Reports
American Reports [*A publication*] (GFGA) ... Am Repts
American Reports [*A publication*] (DLA) ... Amer Rep
American Reports [*A publication*] (DLA) ... Amer Reports
American Reports [*A publication*] (DLA) ... Amer Reps
American Reports [*A publication*] (DLA) ... American Repts
American Reports [*A publication*] (DLA) ... AR
American Republics Area [*Department of State*] ... ARA
American Rescue Dog Association (EA) ... ARDA
American Rescue Workers (EA) ... ARW
American Research Bureau ... ARB
American Research Institute for Community Development (EA) ... ARICD
American Research Institute of Turkey [*University of Pennsylvania*] [*Research center*] (RCD) ... ARIT
American Research Merchandising Institute [*Later, NASM*] (EA) ... ARMI
American Reserve Mining Corp. [*Vancouver Stock Exchange symbol*] ... AMI
American Residential Services, Inc. [*Associated Press*] (SAG) ... AResidS
American Residential Services, Inc. [*NYSE symbol*] (SAG) ... ARS
American Resort and Residential Development Association (EA) ... ARRDA
American Resource [*Vancouver Stock Exchange symbol*] ... AXE
American Resource Corp., Inc. [*Associated Press*] (SAG) ... AmResCp
American Resources Corp, Inc. [*NASDAQ symbol*] (SAG) ... AREE
American Resources Group (EA) ... ARG
American Resources, Inc. [*Associated Press*] (SAG) ... AmResc
American Resources, Inc. [*Associated Press*] (SAG) ... AmRsc
American Resources, Inc. [*NASDAQ symbol*] (SAG) ... GASS
American Restaurant China Council (EA) ... ARCC
American Restaurant Partners Ltd. [*Associated Press*] (SAG) ... ARestr
American Restaurant Partners Ltd. [*AMEX symbol*] (SPSG) ... RMC
American Restitution Association (EA) ... ARA
American Retail Association Executives [*Defunct*] (EA) ... ARAE
American Retail Coal Association (EA) ... ARCA
American Retail Federation [*Later, NRF*] (EA) ... ARF
American Retiree Association [*An association*] ... ARA
American Retreaders Association (EA) ... ARA
American Reuseable Textile Association (EA) ... ARTA
American Revenue Association (EA) ... ARA
American Review of East-West Trade [*A publication*] (DLA) ... Amer Rev E-W Tr
American Review of Soviet and Eastern European Foreign Trade [*A publication*] (DLA) ... Sov & E Eur For Tr
American Revised Version [*of the Bible*] ... ARV

American Revised Version [*of the Bible*], Margin ... ARVm
American Revolution Bicentennial Administration [*Formerly, ARBC*] [*Disbanded, 1977*] ... ARBA
American Revolution Bicentennial Advisory Council [*American Revolution Bicentennial Administration*] ... ARBAC
American Revolution Bicentennial Board [*American Revolution Bicentennial Administration*] ... ARBB
American Revolution Bicentennial Commission [*Later, ARBA*] ... ARBC
American Revolution II Committee (EA) ... AR II
American Revolution Round Table (EA) ... ARRT
American Reye's Syndrome Association [*Defunct*] (EA) ... ARSA
American Rheumatism Association [*Later, ACR*] (EA) ... ARA
American Rheumatism Association Medical Information System [*Information service or system*] (IID) ... ARAMIS
American Rhinologic Society (EA) ... ARS
American Rhododendron Society (EA) ... ARS
American Rice Growers Cooperative Association [*Defunct*] (EA) ... ARGCA
American Rice, Inc. [*Associated Press*] (SAG) ... AmRice
American Rice, Inc. [*NASDAQ symbol*] (SAG) ... RICE
American Riding Association of Berlin [*Post-World War II*] ... ARAB
American Right of Way Association [*Later, IRWA*] (EA) ... ARWA
American Right to Read [*Defunct*] (EA) ... ARR
American Risk and Insurance Association [*Orlando, FL*] (EA) ... ARIA
American River College, Sacramento, CA [*OCLC symbol*] (OCLC) ... ASR
American River College, Sacramento, CA [*Library symbol Library of Congress*] (LCLS) ... CSAR
American River Oil [*NASDAQ symbol*] (TTSB) ... AROC
American River Oil Co. [*Associated Press*] (SAG) ... AmRiverO
American River Oil Co. [*NASDAQ symbol*] (SAG) ... AROC
American River Touring Association ... ARTA
American Rivers (EA) ... AR
American Rivers Conservation Council [*Later, AR*] (EA) ... ARCC
American Road and Transportation Builders Association ... ARTB
American Road and Transportation Builders Association (EA) ... ARTBA
American Road Builders' Association [*Later, ARTBA*] ... ARBA
American Road Race of Champions ... ARRC
American Road Racing Association (EA) ... ARRA
American Robot Society (EA) ... ARS
American Rock Art Research Association (EA) ... ARARA
American Rock Garden Society (EA) ... ARGS
American Rocket Society [*Later, AIAA*] ... ARS
American Roentgen Ray Society (EA) ... ARRS
American Romagnola Association (EA) ... ARA
American Romanian Academy of Arts and Sciences (EA) ... ARA
American Romanian Committee for Assistance to Refugees (EA) ... ARCAR
American Romanian Orthodox Youth (EA) ... AROY
American Romney Breeders' Association (EA) ... ARBA
American Roque League (EA) ... ARL
American Rose Council [*Defunct*] (EA) ... ARC
American Rose Foundation (EA) ... ARF
American Rose Society (EA) ... ARS
American Rottweiler Club (EA) ... ARC
American Rowing Association (EA) ... ARA
American Royal Association (EA) ... ARA
American RSROA [*Roller Skating Rink Operators Association of America*] **Roller Hockey Association** (EA) ... ARRHA
American Rubberband Duckpin Bowling Congress (EA) ... ARDBC
American Running and Fitness Association (EA) ... AR & FA
American Rural Health Association (EA) ... ARHA
American Russian Aid Association (EA) ... ARAA
American Russian Institute, San Francisco, CA [*Library symbol Library of Congress*] (LCLS) ... CSfAR
American Sabbath Tract and Communications Council (EA) ... ASTCC
American Sabbath Tract Society [*Later, ASTCC*] (EA) ... ASTS
American Sable Rabbit Society (EA) ... ASRS
American Saddle Horse Breeders Association [*Later, ASHA*] (EA) ... ASHBA
American Saddle Horse Youth Club (EA) ... ASHYC
American Saddlebred Horse Association (EA) ... ASHA
American Saddlebred Pleasure Horse Association [*Later, ASHA*] (EA) ... ASPHA
[*The*] **American Safe Deposit Association** (EA) ... TASDA
American Safety Council (EA) ... ASC
American Safety Razor Co. [*Associated Press*] (SAG) ... AmSafRz
American Safety Razor Co. [*NASDAQ symbol*] (SAG) ... RAZR
American Sail Training Association (EA) ... ASTA
American Sailing Association (EA) ... ASA
American Sailing Council [*of the National Marine Manufacturers Association*] [*Chicago, IL*] ... ASC
American Sailing Foundation (EA) ... ASF
American Salers Association (EA) ... ASA
American Salers Junior Association (EA) ... ASJA
American Saluki Association (EA) ... ASA
American Salvage Pool Association (EA) ... ASPA
American Samoa ... AM SAM
American Samoa [*Postal code*] [*ANSI two-letter standard code*] (CNC) ... AS
American Samoa [*MARC country of publication code Library of Congress*] (LCCP) ... as
American Samoa [*ANSI three-letter standard code*] (CNC) ... ASM
American Samoa [*MARC geographic area code Library of Congress*] (LCCP) ... poas--
American Samoa Administrative Code [*A publication*] (DLA) ... ASAC
American Samoa Code [*A publication*] (DLA) ... Am Samoa
American Samoa Code [*A publication*] (DLA) ... AS Code
American Samoa Code. Annotated [*A publication*] (DLA) ... Am Samoa Code Ann
American Sanitary Engineering Intersociety Board [*Later, AAEE*] (EA) ... ASEIB
American Satellite (MCD) ... AMSAT
American Satellite Corp. (TSSD) ... ASC
American Satellite Television Alliance (EA) ... ASTA
American Satin Rabbit Breeders' Association (EA) ... ASRBA
American Saudi Roundtable (EA) ... ASR
American Savings and Loan Association (EA) ... ASLA
American Savings and Loan Institute [*Later, IFE*] (EA) ... ASLI
American Savings and Loan League [*Later, ALFI*] (EA) ... ASLL
American Scenic and Historic Preservation Society [*Defunct*] (EA) ... ASHPS
American Schizophrenia Association (EA) ... ASA
American Scholar [*A publication*] (BRI) ... AS
American School Achievement Test [*Education*] (AEBS) ... ASAT
American School and Community Safety Association [*Later, The Safety Society*] ... ASCSA
American School Band Directors' Association (EA) ... ASBDA
American School Counselor Association (EA) ... ASCA
American School Food Service Association (EA) ... ASFSA
American School Health Association (EA) ... ASHA
American School in London ... ASL
[*The*] **American School in Switzerland** ... TASIS
American School Intelligence Test [*Education*] (AEBS) ... ASIT
American Schools and Hospitals Abroad [*Program*] [*Agency for International Development*] ... ASHA
American Schools Association (EA) ... ASA
American Schools of Oriental Research (EA) ... ASOR
American Schooner Association (EA) ... ASA
American Science & Engineering, Inc. [*Associated Press*] (SAG) ... AsciE
American Science & Engineering, Inc. [*AMEX symbol*] (SPSG) ... ASE
American Science Fiction Association (EA) ... ASFA
American Science Film Association (EA) ... ASFA
American Science Information Institute ... ASII
American Scientific Affiliation (EA) ... ASA
American Scientific Engineering (KSC) ... ASE
American Scientific Glassblowers Society (EA) ... ASGS
American Scientific Institute ... ASI
American Scientific Laboratories (AEBS) ... ASL
American Scientist [*A publication*] (BRI) ... Am Sci
American Scotch Highland Breeders' Association (EA) ... ASHBA
American Scottish Foundation (EA) ... ASF
American Scouting Traders Association (EA) ... ASTA
American Scripture Gift Mission [*Later, SGM/USA*] (EA) ... ASGM
American Sea Songs and Chanteys [*A publication*] ... AmSS
American Seafood Distributors Association (EA) ... ASDA
American Seafood Harvesters Association ... ASHA
American Seafood Retailers Association (EA) ... ASRA
American Sealyham Terrier Club (EA) ... ASTC
American Seamen's Friend Society [*Defunct*] (EA) ... ASFS
American Seat Belt Council [*Later, AORC*] (EA) ... ASBC
American Section of the International Solar Energy Society (EA) ... AS of ISES
American Section of the Societe de Chimie Industrielle (EA) ... ASSCI
American Security Council (EA) ... ASC
American Security Council Foundation (EA) ... ASCF
American Seed Research Foundation (EA) ... ASRF
American Seed Trade Association (EA) ... ASTA
American Select Portfolio [*NYSE symbol*] (SPSG) ... SLA
American Select Portfolios, Inc. [*Associated Press*] (SAG) ... ASelPort
American Self-Protection Association ... ASP
American Self-Protection Association (EA) ... ASPA
American Selling Price ... ASP
American Selling Price System ... ASPS
American Senior Citizens Association (EA) ... ASCA
American Sensors, Inc. [*Associated Press*] (SAG) ... ASensrs
American Sensors, Inc. [*NASDAQ symbol*] (SAG) ... SNIF
American Sentic Association ... ASA
American Sephardi (BJA) ... ASe
American Sephardi Federation (EA) ... ASF
American Service Radio [*English-language broadcasting*] (VNW) ... ASR
American Servicemen's Union (EA) ... ASU
American Sewing Guild (EA) ... ASG
American Shared Hospital Services [*AMEX symbol*] (SPSG) ... AMS
American Shared Hospital Services [*Associated Press*] (SAG) ... AmShrd
American Shark Association (EA) ... ASA
American Sheep Industry Association (EA) ... ASIA
American Sheep Producers Council [*Later, ASIA*] (EA) ... ASPC
American Shellfisheries Association ... ASA
American Shetland Pony Club (EA) ... ASPC
American Shetland Sheepdog Association (EA) ... ASSA
American Shiatsu Association (EA) ... ASA
American Shih Tzu Club (EA) ... ASTC
American Shire Horse Association (EA) ... ASHA
American Shooting Sports Council ... ASSC
American Shore and Beach Preservation Association (NOAA) ... ASBA
American Shore and Beach Preservation Association (EA) ... ASBPA
American Short Line Railroad Association (EA) ... ASLRA
American Short Line Railroads ... ASLR
American Shorthorn Association (EA) ... ASA
American Shorthorn Breeders Association [*Later, ASA*] ... ASBA
American Shortwave Listeners Club (EA) ... ASWLC
American Shoulder and Elbow Surgeons (EA) ... ASES
American Shrimp Canners and Processors Association [*Later, ASPA*] (EA) ... ASCPA
American Shrimp Canners Association [*Later, ASPA*] ... ASCA
American Shrimp Processors Association (EA) ... ASPA
American Shrimpboat Association [*Defunct*] (EA) ... ASA
American Shropshire Registry Association (EA) ... ASRA
American Shuffleboard Co. (EA) ... ASC

American Shuffleboard Leagues (EA) ... ASL
American Sighthound Field Association (EA) ... ASFA
American Sightseeing Association [Later, ASI] ... ASA
American Sightseeing International (EA) ... ASI
American Sign Language [for the deaf] ... AMESLAN
American Sign Language [for the deaf] ... ASL
American Silk Council [Defunct] (EA) ... ASC
American Silkie Bantam Club (EA) ... ASBC
American Simmental Association (EA) ... ASA
American Simplified Keyboard [Typewriter] ... ASK
American Singers Club (EA) ... ASC
American Single Shot Rifle Association (EA) ... ASSRA
American Ski Association (EA) ... ASA
American Ski Federation (EA) ... ASF
American Ski Manufacturers' Association (EA) ... ASMA
American Ski Teachers Association of Natur Teknik (EA) ... ASTAN
American Skibob Association [Later, USSBF] (EA) ... ASBA
American Slovenian Catholic Union of the USA (EA) ... KSKJ
American Small and Rural Hospital Association (EA) ... ASRHA
American Small Businesses Association (EA) ... ASBA
American Smelting & Refining Co. (IIA) ... AR
American Smelting & Refining Co., Research Department Library, South Plainfield,NJ [Library symbol Library of Congress] (LCLS) ... NjSopA
American Smoking Pipe Manufacturers Association [Defunct] (EA) ... ASPMA
American SMR [Special Mobile Radio] Network Association (EA) ... ASNA
American Snowmobile Association [Defunct] ... ASA
American Snowplowing Association [Defunct] (EA) ... ASA
American Snowshoers Union (EA) ... ASU
American Soccer League ... ASL
American Social Communications Conference (EA) ... ASCC
American Social Health [formerly, Hygiene] Association (EA) ... ASHA
American Society for Abrasive Methods [Later, AES] (EA) ... ASAM
American Society for Abrasives [Superseded by AES] (EA) ... ASA
American Society for Adolescent Psychiatry (EA) ... ASAP
American Society for Adolescent Psychology (DAVI) ... ASAP
American Society for Advancement of Anesthesia in Dentistry (EA) ... ASAAD
American Society for Advancement of General Anesthesia in Dentistry [Later, ASAAD] (EA) ... ASAGAD
American Society for Aerospace Education (EA) ... ASAE
American Society for Aesthetic Plastic Surgery (EA) ... ASAPS
American Society for Aesthetics (EA) ... ASA
American Society for Amusement Park Security and Safety (EA) ... ASAPSS
American Society for Apheresis (EA) ... ASFA
American Society for Artificial Internal Organs (EA) ... ASAIO
American Society for Association Publishing (EA) ... ASAP
American Society for Automation in Pharmacy (EA) ... ASAP
American Society for Bariatric Obesity Surgery (HCT) ... ASBS
American Society for Biochemistry and Molecular Biology (EA) ... ASBMB
American Society for Blood and Marrow Transplantation ... ASBMT
American Society for Bone and Mineral Research (EA) ... ASBMR
American Society for Cell Biology (EA) ... ASCB
American Society for Church Architecture [Later, IFRAA] (EA) ... ASCA
American Society for Clinical Evoked Potentials (EA) ... ASCEP
American Society for Clinical Investigation (EA) ... ASCI
American Society for Clinical Nutrition (EA) ... ASCN
American Society for Colposcopy and Cervical Pathology (EA) ... ASCCP
American Society for Concrete Construction (EA) ... ASCC
American Society for Conservation Archaeology (EA) ... ASCA
American Society for Crippled Children in Israel (EA) ... ASCCI
American Society for Cybernetics (EA) ... ASC
American Society for Cytotechnology (EA) ... ASCT
American Society for Deaf Children [Defunct] (EA) ... ASDC
American Society for Dental Aesthetics (EA) ... ASDA
American Society for Dermatologic Surgery (EA) ... ASDS
American Society for Eastern Arts ... ASEA
American Society for Eighteenth-Century Studies (EA) ... ASECS
American Society for Engineering Education (EA) ... ASEE
American Society for Engineering Management (EA) ... ASEM
American Society for Enology and Viticulture (EA) ... ASEV
American Society for Environmental Education (EA) ... ASEE
American Society for Environmental History (EA) ... ASEH
American Society for Ethnohistory (EA) ... ASE
American Society for Experimental Pathology [Later, AAP] (EA) ... ASEP
American Society for Friendship with Switzerland [Later, ASA] (EA) ... ASFS
American Society for Gastrointestinal Endoscopy (EA) ... ASGE
American Society for Genetics (DAVI) ... ASG
American Society for Geriatric Dentistry (EA) ... ASGD
American Society for German Literature of the 16th and 17th Centuries (EA) ... ASGLSSC
American Society for Head and Neck Surgery (EA) ... ASHNS
American Society for Health Care Marketing and Public Relations (EA) ... ASHCMPR
American Society for Healthcare Central Service Personnel [American Hospital Association] (EA) ... ASHCSP
American Society for Healthcare Education and Training - of the American Hospital Association (EA) ... ASHET
American Society for Healthcare Environmental Services of the American Hospital Association (EA) ... ASHES
American Society for Healthcare Human Resources Administration (EA) ... ASHHRA
American Society for Healthcare Risk Management (EA) ... ASHRM
American Society for Histocompatibility and Immunogenetics (EA) ... ASHI
American Society for Horticultural Science (EA) ... ASHS
American Society for Hospital Engineering - of the American Hospital Association (EA) ... ASHE
American Society for Hospital Food Service Administrators (EA) ... ASHFSA
American Society for Hospital Marketing and Public Relations [Later, ASHCMPR] (EA) ... ASHMPR
American Society for Hospital Materials Management (EA) ... ASHMM
American Society for Hospital Personnel Administration [Later, ASHHRA] (EA) ... ASHPA
American Society for Hospital Planning ... ASHP
American Society for Hospital Planning (DMAA) ... ASHP
American Society for Hospital Purchasing and Materials Management [Later, ASHMM] (EA) ... ASHPMM
American Society for Industrial Security (EA) ... ASIS
American Society for Information Science [Formerly, ADI] (EA) ... ASIS
American Society for Information Science, Washington, DC [Library symbol] [Library of Congress] (LCLS) ... ASIS
American Society for Jewish Music (EA) ... ASJM
American Society for Laser Medicine and Surgery (EA) ... ASLMS
American Society for Legal History (EA) ... ASLH
American Society for Mass Spectrometry (EA) ... ASMS
American Society for Medical Technology (EA) ... ASMT
American Society for Metals [Later, ASMI] (EA) ... ASM
American Society for Metals Library, Metals Park, OH [Library symbol] [Library of Congress] (LCLS) ... OMpA
American Society for Microbiology (EA) ... ASM
American Society for Neo-Hellenic Studies (EA) ... ASNHS
American Society for Netherlands Philately (EA) ... ASNP
American Society for Neurochemistry (EA) ... ASN
American Society for Nondestructive Testing (EA) ... ASNT
American Society for Nursing Service Administrators [Later, AONE] (EA) ... ASNSA
American Society for Oceanography [Later, MTS] (EA) ... ASO
American Society for Parenteral and Enteral Nutrition (EA) ... ASPEN
American Society for Pediatric Neurosurgery (EA) ... ASPN
American Society for Performance Improvement [Defunct] (EA) ... ASPI
American Society for Personnel Administration [Later, SHRM] (EA) ... ASPA
American Society for Personnel Administration International (EA) ... ASPA/I
American Society for Pharmacology and Experimental Therapeutics (EA) ... ASPET
American Society for Pharmacy Law (EA) ... ASPL
American Society for Philatelic Pages and Panels (EA) ... ASPPP
American Society for Photobiology (EA) ... ASP
American Society for Photogrammetry and Remote Sensing (EA) ... ASPRS
American Society for Plasticulture (EA) ... ASP
American Society for Political and Legal Philosophy (EA) ... ASPLP
American Society for Portuguese Numismatics [Defunct] (EA) ... ASPN
American Society for Preventive Dentistry [Defunct] ... ASPD
American Society for Prophylaxis in Obstetrics (PAZ) ... ASPO/Lamaze
American Society for Psychical Research (EA) ... ASPR
American Society for Psychical Research, New York, NY [Library symbol Library of Congress] (LCLS) ... NNASP
American Society for Psychoprophylaxis in Obstetrics (EA) ... ASPO
American Society for Public Administration (EA) ... ASPA
American Society for Quality Control (EA) ... ASQC
American Society for Reformation Research ... ASRR
American Society for Reproductive Medicine (PAZ) ... ASRM
American Society for Russian Naval History (EA) ... ASRNH
American Society for Steel Treaters [Later, ASM] ... ASST
American Society for Stereotactic and Functional Neurosurgery (EA) ... ASSFN
American Society for Surface Mining and Reclamation (EA) ... ASSMR
American Society for Surgery of the Hand (EA) ... ASSH
American Society for Technion-Israel Institute of Technology (EA) ... ASTIIT
American Society for Testing and Development (AAGC) ... ASTD
American Society for Testing and Materials [Acronym is now organization's official name] (EAIO) ... ASTM
American Society for the Defense of Tradition, Family and Property (EA) ... TFP
American Society for the Preservation of Sacred, Patriotic, and Operatic Music (EA) ... ASPSPOM
American Society for the Prevention of Crime [Defunct] (EA) ... ASPC
American Society for the Prevention of Cruelty to Animals (EA) ... ASPCA
American Society for the Protection of Nature in Israel (EA) ... ASPNI
American Society for the Study of Arteriosclerosis [Later, CAAHA] ... ASSA
American Society for the Study of Ideological Belief Systems (EA) ... ASSIBS
American Society for the Study of Orthodontics (EA) ... ASSO
American Society for the Study of Religion (EA) ... ASSR
American Society for the Study of Sterility [Later, AFS] (EA) ... ASSS
American Society for Theatre Research (EA) ... ASTR
American Society for Therapeutic Radiology and Oncology (EA) ... ASTRO
American Society for Training and Development (EA) ... ASTD
American Society for Value Inquiry (EA) ... ASVI
American Society for Zero Defects [Later, American Society for Performance Improvement] ... ASZD
American Society of Abdominal Surgery (EA) ... ASAS
American Society of Access Professionals (EA) ... ASAP
American Society of Addiction Medicine (EA) ... ASAM
American Society of Adlerian Psychology (AEBS) ... ASAP
American Society of Adults with Pseudo-Obstruction ... ASAP
American Society of Advertising and Promotion, Inc. (NTCM) ... ASAP
American Society of Aeronautical Engineers [Later, SAE] (KSC) ... ASAE
American Society of Aerospace Pilots [Defunct] (EA) ... ASAP
American Society of African Culture [Defunct] (EA) ... AMSAC
American Society of Agricultural Consultants (EA) ... ASAC
American Society of Agricultural Engineers (EA) ... ASAE
American Society of Agronomy (EA) ... ASA
American Society of Allied Health Professions (EA) ... ASAHP
American Society of Ancient Instruments [Defunct] (EA) ... ASAI
American Society of Anesthesiologists (EA) ... ASA

American Society of Anesthesiologists, Park Ridge, IL [*Library symbol Library of Congress*] (LCLS) ... IParkA
American Society of Animal Production [*Later, ASAS*] ... ASAP
American Society of Animal Science (EA) ... ASAS
American Society of Anthropometric Medicine and Nutrition [*Defunct*] (EA) ... ASAMN
American Society of Appraisers [*Acronym also used as designation awarded to group's senior members*] [*Washington, DC*] (EA) ... ASA
American Society of Architectural Hardware Consultants [*Later, DHI*] (EA) ... ASAHC
American Society of Arms Collectors ... AS of AC
American Society of Arms Collectors (EA) ... ASAC
American Society of Artists (EA) ... ASA
American Society of Asset Managers (EA) ... ASAM
American Society of Association Executives (EA) ... ASAE
American Society of Auctioneers [*Defunct*] (EA) ... ASA
American Society of Aviation Artists [*An association*] ... ASAA
American Society of Aviation Writers [*Later, IATJ*] (EA) ... ASAW
American Society of Bacteriologists (BARN) ... ASB
American Society of Bacteriology (DAVI) ... ASB
American Society of Bakery Engineers (EA) ... ASBE
American Society of Bank Directors [*Arlington, VA*] (EA) ... ASBD
American Society of Bariatric Physicians (EA) ... ASBP
American Society of Bariatrics [*Later, ASBP*] ... ASB
American Society of Biological Chemists [*Later, ASBMB*] (EA) ... ASBC
American Society of Body Engineers (EA) ... ASBE
American Society of Bookplate Collectors and Designers (DGA) ... ABCD
American Society of Bookplate Collectors and Designers (EA) ... ASBC & D
American Society of Brewing Chemists (EA) ... ASBC
American Society of Business Press Editors (EA) ... ASBPE
American Society of Camera Collectors (EA) ... ASCC
American Society of Cartographers [*Defunct*] (EA) ... ASC
American Society of Cataract and Refractive Surgery (EA) ... ASCRS
American Society of Certified Engineering Technicians (EA) ... ASCET
American Society of Chartered Life Underwriters [*Later, ASCLU, ChFC*] (EA) ... ASCLU
American Society of Check Collectors (EA) ... ASCC
American Society of Chemical Engineers (BARN) ... ASChE
American Society of Childbirth Educators [*Inactive*] (EA) ... ASCE
American Society of Chinese Medicine [*Inactive*] ... ASCM
American Society of Chiropodical Roentgenology ... ASCR
American Society of Christian Ethics [*Later, SCE*] ... ASCE
American Society of Church History (EA) ... ASCH
American Society of Cinematographers (EA) ... ASC
American Society of Civil Engineers (WDAA) ... AM SOC CE
American Society of Civil Engineers (EA) ... ASCE
American Society of Civil Engineers and Architects (WDAA) ... ASCEA
American Society of Clinic Radiologists (EA) ... ASCR
American Society of Clinical Genetics and Dysmorphology [*Later, BDCGS*] (EA) ... ASCGD
American Society of Clinical Hypnosis (EA) ... ASCH
American Society of Clinical Hypnosis - Education and Research Foundation (EA) ... ASCH-ERF
American Society of Clinical Laboratory Technicians [*Later, ASMT*] ... ASCLT
American Society of Clinical Oncology (EA) ... ASCO
American Society of Clinical Pathologists (EA) ... ASCP
American Society of Clinical Pathologists (DMAA) ... ASCP
American Society of Clinical Pharmacology and Chemotherapy (DAVI) ... ASCPC
American Society of CLU [*Chartered Life Underwriters*] **and ChFC** [*Chartered Financial Consultants*] [*Bryn Mawr, PA*] (EA) ... ASCLU & ChFC
American Society of Colon and Rectal Surgeons (EA) ... ASCRS
American Society of Composers, Authors, and Publishers (EA) ... ASCAP
American Society of Computer Dealers (EA) ... ASCD
American Society of Construction Inspectors (EA) ... ASCI
American Society of Consultant Pharmacists (EA) ... ASCP
American Society of Consulting Arborists (EA) ... ASCA
American Society of Consulting Pharmacists (DMAA) ... ASCP
American Society of Consulting Planners (EA) ... ASCP
American Society of Contemporary Artists (EA) ... ASCA
American Society of Contemporary Medicine and Surgery (EA) ... ASCMS
American Society of Contemporary Ophthalmology (EA) ... ASCO
American Society of Corporate Secretaries [*New York, NY*] (EA) ... ASCS
American Society of Cosmetic Surgeons [*Later, AACS*] (EA) ... ASCS
American Society of Country Music (EA) ... ASCM
American Society of Crime Laboratory Directors (EA) ... ASCLD
American Society of Criminology (EA) ... ASC
American Society of Cytology (EA) ... ASC
American Society of Danish Engineers (EA) ... ASDE
American Society of Dental Radiographers ... ASDR
American Society of Dentistry for Children (EA) ... ASDC
American Society of Dermatological Retailers (EA) ... ASDR
American Society of Dermatopathology (EA) ... ASD
American Society of Design Engineers (EA) ... ASDE
American Society of Directors of Volunteer Services (EA) ... ASDVS
American Society of Disk Jockeys [*Defunct*] (EA) ... ASDJ
American Society of Dowsers (EA) ... ASD
American Society of Echocardiography (EA) ... ASE
American Society of Educators [*Later, AAMSL*] (EA) ... ASE
American Society of Electrical Engineers (NTCM) ... ASEE
American Society of Electroencephalographic Technologists (EA) ... ASET
American Society of Electro-Neurodiagnostic Technologists (EA) ... ASET
American Society of Electroplated Plastics (EA) ... ASEP
American Society of Employers (SRA) ... ASE
American Society of Engineers ... ASE
American Society of Engineers and Architects ... ASEA
American Society of Enologists (EA) ... ASE
American Society of Extra-Corporeal Technology (EA) ... AmSECT
American Society of Extra-Corporeal Technology [*Medicine*] (DAVI) ... ASECT
American Society of Farm Managers and Rural Appraisers (EA) ... ASFMRA
American Society of Forensic Odontology (EA) ... ASFO
American Society of Furniture Designers (EA) ... ASFD
American Society of Gas Engineers (EA) ... ASGE
American Society of Genealogists (EA) ... ASG
American Society of Geolinguistics (EA) ... ASG
American Society of Golf Course Architects (EA) ... ASGCA
American Society of Group Psychotherapy and Psychodrama (EA) ... ASGPP
American Society of Hand Therapists (EA) ... ASHT
American Society of Handicapped Physicians (EA) ... ASHP
American Society of Health-System Pharmacists [*Formerly, American Society of Hospital Pharmacists*] ... ASHP
American Society of Heating and Air-Conditioning Engineers [*Later, ASHRAE*] ... ASHACE
American Society of Heating and Air-Conditioning Engineers [*Later, ASHRAE*] ... ASHAE
American Society of Heating and Ventilating Engineers ... ASHVE
American Society of Heating, Refrigerating and Air-Conditioning Engineers (MHDB) ... ASHRACE
American Society of Heating, Refrigerating, and Air-Conditioning Engineers (EA) ... ASHRAE
American Society of Hematology (EA) ... ASH
American Society of Home Inspectors (EA) ... ASHI
American Society of Hospice Care [*Defunct*] (EA) ... ASHC
American Society of Hospital Attorneys (EA) ... ASHA
American Society of Hospital Pharmacists (EA) ... ASHP
American Society of Hospital Pharmacists Research and Education Foundation (EA) ... ASHPREF
American Society of Hospital-Based Emergency Air Medical Services (EA) ... ASHBEAMS
American Society of Human Genetics (EA) ... ASHG
American Society of Hypertension (EA) ... ASH
American Society of Ichthyologists and Herpetologists (EA) ... ASIH
American Society of Independent Business [*Defunct*] (EA) ... ASIB
American Society of Indexers (EA) ... ASI
American Society of Industrial Auctioneers (EA) ... ASIA
American Society of Industrial Designers [*Later, IDSA*] (EA) ... ASID
American Society of Insurance Management [*Later, RIMS*] (EA) ... ASIM
American Society of Interior Designers (EA) ... ASID
American Society of Internal Medicine (EA) ... ASIM
American Society of International Executives [*Blue Bell, PA*] (EA) ... ASIE
American Society of International Law (DLA) ... Am Soc Int L
American Society of International Law (EA) ... ASIL
American Society of International Law. Proceedings [*A publication*] (DLA) ... Am Soc'y Int'l Proc
American Society of Interpreters (EA) ... ASI
American Society of Inventors (EA) ... ASI
American Society of Irrigation Consultants (EA) ... ASIC
American Society of Journalism School Administrators (EA) ... ASJSA
American Society of Journalists and Authors (EA) ... ASJA
American Society of Knitting Technologists (EA) ... ASKT
American Society of Laboratory Animal Practitioners (EA) ... ASLAP
American Society of Landscape Architects (EA) ... ASLA
American Society of Law and Medicine (EA) ... ASLM
American Society of Law Enforcement Trainers (EA) ... ASLET
American Society of Learned Societies on the Protection of Cultural Treasures inWar Areas [*World War II*] ... ASLSPCTWA
American Society of Limnology and Oceanography (EA) ... ASLO
American Society of Local Officials [*Defunct*] (EA) ... ASLO
American Society of Lubrication Engineers (EA) ... ASLE
American Society of Magazine Editors (EA) ... ASME
American Society of Magazine Photographers (EA) ... ASMP
American Society of Mammalogists (EA) ... ASM
American Society of Marine Artists (EA) ... ASMA
American Society of Master Dental Technologists (EA) ... ASMDT
American Society of Mature Catholics [*Defunct Defunct*] (EA) ... ASMC
American Society of Maxillofacial Surgeons (EA) ... ASMS
American Society of Mechanical Engineers (WDAA) ... Am Soc ME
American Society of Mechanical Engineers (EA) ... ASME
American Society of Mechanical Engineers Auxiliary (EA) ... ASMEA
American Society of Medical Missionaries ... ASMM
American Society of Mental Hospital Business Administrators [*Later, AMHA*] (EA) ... ASMHBA
American Society of Military Comptrollers (EA) ... ASMC
American Society of Military Insignia Collectors (EA) ... ASMIC
American Society of Missiology (EA) ... ASM
American Society of Motion Picture and Television Engineers [*Formerly, ASMPE*] ... ASMPTE
American Society of Motion Picture Engineers [*Later, ASMPTE*] ... ASMPE
American Society of Music Arrangers (EA) ... ASMA
American Society of Music Copyists (EA) ... ASMC
American Society of Naturalists (EA) ... ASN
American Society of Naval Engineers (EA) ... ASNE
American Society of Nephrology (EA) ... ASN
American Society of Neuroimaging (EA) ... ASN
American Society of Neuroradiology (EA) ... ASNR
American Society of Newspaper Editors (EA) ... ASNE
American Society of Notaries (EA) ... ASN
American Society of Onomatologists [*Defunct*] (EA) ... ASO
American Society of Ophthalmic Administrators (EA) ... ASOA
American Society of Ophthalmic Registered Nurses (EA) ... ASORN

American Society of Ophthalmologic and Otolaryngologic Allergy [Later, AAOA] (EA) .... ASOOA
American Society of Oral Surgeons [Later, AAOMS] (EA) .... ASOS
American Society of Orthodontists [Later, AAO] .... ASO
American Society of Outpatient Surgeons (EA) .... ASOS
American Society of Papyrologists (EA) .... ASP
American Society of Paramedics (EA) .... ASPM
American Society of Parasitologists (EA) .... ASP
American Society of Pediatric Hematology/Oncology (EA) .... ASPHO
American Society of Pension Actuaries (EA) .... ASPA
American Society of Perfumers [Defunct] (EA) .... ASP
American Society of Periodontists [Later, AAP] .... ASP
American Society of Peru (EAIO) .... AmSoc
American Society of Petroleum Operations Engineers (EA) .... ASPOE
American Society of Pharmacognosy (EA) .... ASP
American Society of Photogrammetry [Later, ASPRS] (EA) .... ASP
American Society of Photographers (EA) .... ASP
American Society of Physician Analysts (EA) .... ASPA
American Society of Picture Professionals (EA) .... ASPP
American Society of Planning Officials [Later, American Planning Association] (EA) .... ASPO
American Society of Plant Physiologists (EA) .... ASPP
American Society of Plant Taxonomists (EA) .... ASPT
American Society of Plastic and Reconstructive Surgeons (EA) .... ASPRS
American Society of Plastic and Reconstructive Surgical Nurses (EA) .... ASPRSN
American Society of Plumbing Engineers (EA) .... ASPE
American Society of Podiatric Assistants [Later, ASPMA] (EA) .... ASPA
American Society of Podiatric Dermatology (EA) .... ASPD
American Society of Podiatric Medical Assistants (EA) .... ASPMA
American Society of Podiatric Medicine (EA) .... ASPM
American Society of Polar Philatelists (EA) .... ASPP
American Society of Post-Anesthesia Nurses (EA) .... ASPAN
American Society of Practicing Architects .... ASPA
American Society of Precision Nailmakers [Defunct] .... ASPN
American Society of Pre-Dental Students (EA) .... ASPS
American Society of Preventive Oncology (EA) .... ASPO
American Society of Primatologists (EA) .... ASP
American Society of Professional and Executive Women [Defunct] (EA) .... ASPEW
American Society of Professional Appraisers (EA) .... ASPA
American Society of Professional Automobile Racing .... ASPAR
American Society of Professional Biologists [Later, AIBS] (EA) .... ASPB
American Society of Professional Draftsmen and Artists (EA) .... ASPDA
American Society of Professional Ecologists (EA) .... ASPE
American Society of Professional Estimators (EA) .... ASPE
American Society of Professional Salesmen (EA) .... ASPS
American Society of Psychopathology of Expression (EA) .... ASPE
American Society of Psychosomatic Dentistry and Medicine [IPI] [Absorbed by] (EA) .... ASPDM
American Society of Questioned Document Examiners (EA) .... ASQDE
American Society of Radiologic Technologists (EA) .... ASRT
American Society of Range Management [Later, SRM] (EA) .... ASRM
American Society of Real Estate Counselors (EA) .... ASREC
American Society of Refrigerating Engineers [Later, ASHRAE] .... ASRE
American Society of Regional Anesthesia (EA) .... ASRA
American Society of Retired Dentists (EA) .... ASRD
American Society of Rocketry .... ASR
American Society of Roommate Services (EA) .... ASRS
American Society of Safety Engineers (EA) .... ASSE
American Society of Sanitary Engineering (EA) .... ASSE
American Society of Scientific and Engineering Translators .... ASSET
American Society of Senior Wire Rope Engineers (EA) .... AS²WRE
American Society of Sephardic Studies (EA) .... ASOSS
American Society of Sugar Beet Technologists (EA) .... ASSBT
American Society of Swedish Engineers (EA) .... ASSE
American Society of Tax Professionals (EA) .... ASTP
American Society of Teachers of Dancing (EA) .... ASTD
American Society of Test Engineers (EA) .... ASTE
American Society of the French Legion of Honor (EA) .... ASFLH
American Society of the Greek Order of Saint Dennis of Zante (EA) .... ASGOSDZ
American Society of Theater Consultants (EA) .... ASTC
American Society of Therapeutic Radiologists [Later, ASTRO] (EA) .... ASTR
American Society of Tool and Manufacturing Engineers [Later, SME] (EA) .... ASTME
American Society of Tool Engineers [Later, SME] (EA) .... ASTE
American Society of Traffic and Transportation (EA) .... ASTT
American Society of Transplant Surgeons (EA) .... ASTS
American Society of Transportation and Logistics [MTMC] (TAG) .... AST&L
American Society of Transportation and Logistics (EA) .... ASTL
American Society of Travel Agents (EA) .... ASTA
American Society of Trial Consultants (EA) .... ASTC
American Society of Tropical Medicine and Hygiene (EA) .... ASTMH
American Society of TV Cameramen (EA) .... ASTVC
American Society of Ultrasound Technical Specialists [Later, SDMS] (EA) .... ASUTS
American Society of University Composers (EA) .... ASUC
American Society of Utility Investors (EA) .... ASUI
American Society of Veterinary Ethology (EA) .... ASVE
American Society of Veterinary Ophthalmology (EA) .... ASVO
American Society of Veterinary Physiologists and Pharmacologists (EA) .... ASVPP
American Society of Wedding Professionals (EA) .... ASWP
American Society of Women Accountants (EA) .... ASWA
American Society of X-Ray Technicians [Later, ASRT] .... ASXT

American Society of Zoologists (EA) .... ASZ
American Society on Aging (EA) .... ASA
American Society to Save Biharis and Other Minorities .... ASSB & OM
American Sociological Association (EA) .... ASA
American Sociometric Association [Defunct] (EA) .... ASA
American Sod Producers' Association (EA) .... ASPA
American Software [NASDAQ symbol] (SAG) .... AMSW
American Software, Inc. [Associated Press] (SAG) .... ASoft
American Software Users Group (EA) .... ASUG
American Sokol Educational and Physical Culture Organization (EA) .... ASO
American Sokol Educational and Physical Culture Organization .... SOK
American Solar Energy Association (EA) .... ASEA
American Solar Energy Society (EA) .... ASES
American Soldier .... AMSOL
American Solidarity Movement [Defunct] (EA) .... ASM
American Songbag [A publication] .... AS
American Southdown Breeders' Association (EA) .... ASBA
American Sovereignty Task Force (EA) .... ASTF
American Soybean Association (EA) .... ASA
American Soybean Institute [Defunct] (EA) .... ASI
American Spa and Health Resort Association (EA) .... ASHRA
American Space and Development Agency (NUCP) .... ASADA
American Space Foundation [Defunct] (EA) .... ASF
American Space Frontier Committee [Defunct] (EA) .... ASFC
American Spaniel Club (EA) .... ASC
American Spanish Committee (EA) .... ASC
American Spanish Dance Theatre .... ASDT
American Spasmodic Torticollis Association (EA) .... ASTA
[The] American Specialty Surety Council [Later, ASA] (EA) .... TASSC
American Specification Institute [Defunct] .... ASI
American Spectator [A publication] (BRI) .... Am Spect
American Speech and Hearing Association (DAVI) .... ASHA
American Speech-Language-Hearing Association (EA) .... ASHA
American Speed Association .... ASA
American Spelean Historical Association (EA) .... ASHA
American Spice Trade Association (EA) .... ASTA
American Spinal Injury Association (EA) .... ASIA
American Spoon Collectors (EA) .... ASC
American Sport Horse Registry [Defunct] (EA) .... ASHR
American Sport Touring Rider's Association (EA) .... ASTRA
American Sportfishing Association .... ASA
American Sports Education Institute (EA) .... ASEI
American Sports Medicine Association Board of Certification .... ASMA
American Sportscasters Association (EA) .... ASA
American Sportsman's Club [Commercial firm] (EA) .... ASC
American Sprint Car Association [Auto racing] .... ASCA
American Sprocket Chain Manufacturers Association [Later, American Chain Association] .... ASCMA
American Squadron of Aviation Historians (EA) .... ASAH
American Squid Marketing Association [Defunct] (EA) .... ASMA
American Stamp Club of Great Britain (EA) .... ASCGB
American Stamp Dealers Association (EA) .... ASDA
American Standard (WDAA) .... AMER STD
American Standard .... AS
American Standard Building Code (IEEE) .... ASBC
American Standard Chinchilla Association [Later, ASCRA] .... ASCA
American Standard Chinchilla Rabbit Association (EA) .... ASCRA
American Standard Code (OA) .... ASC
American Standard Code for Information Interchange [Pronounced "ask-ee"] [American National Standards Institute] [Computer science] .... ASCII
American Standard Companies, Inc. [NYSE symbol] (SAG) .... ASD
American Standard Cos., Inc. [Associated Press] (SAG) .... AmStd
American Standard Elevator Code .... ASEC
American Standard of Testing Materials .... ASTM
American Standard Practice for Industrial Lighting (IAA) .... ASPIL
American Standard Version [of the Bible, 1901] .... ASV
American Standard Vocabulary for Information Processing (BUR) .... ASVIP
American Standardbred Breeders Association (EA) .... ASBA
American Standards Association [Later, USASI, ANSI] (EA) .... ASA
American Standards Institute (IAA) .... ASI
American Standards Test Manual .... ASTM
American State Papers [A publication] (DLA) .... Am St P
American State Papers [A publication] (DLA) .... Am St Papers
American State Papers [A publication] (DLA) .... Am State Papers
American State Reports [A publication] (DLA) .... Am SR
American State Reports [1886-1911] [A publication] (DLA) .... Am St R
American State Reports [A publication] (DLA) .... Am St Rep
American State Reports [A publication] (DLA) .... Am St Reports
American State Reports [A publication] (DLA) .... Am Sta Rep
American State Reports [A publication] (DLA) .... Am State Rep
American State Reports [A publication] (DLA) .... Amer St Rep
American State Reports [A publication] (DLA) .... Amer State Reps
American State Reports [A publication] (DLA) .... American State Rep
American State Reports [A publication] (DLA) .... ASR
American States Financial Corp. [Associated Press] (SAG) .... AmStFn
American States Financial Corp. [NYSE symbol] (SAG) .... ASX
American Statesmen [A publication] .... AS
American Statistical Association (EA) .... ASA
American Statistics Index [Congressional Information Service, Inc.] [Bibliographic database] [A publication] .... ASI
American Steamship Traffic Executives Committee .... ASTEC
American Steel and Wire Gauge .... AS & W
American Steel and Wire Gauge .... ASWG
American Steel Foundrymen's Association .... ASFA
American Steel Warehouse Association [Later, SSCI] .... ASWA

American Sterilizer Co. ... AMSCO
American Sternwheel Association (EA) ... ASA
American Stock Exchange [*New York, NY*] ... A
American Stock Exchange [*New York, NY*] (EA) ... AMEX
American Stock Exchange (EA) ... ASE
American Stock Exchange Clearing Corp. ... ASECC
American Stock Exchange Guide [*Commerce Clearing House*] [*A publication*] (DLA) ... Am Stock Ex Guide
American Stock Exchange Option Display Book ... AODB
American Stock Yards Association (EA) ... ASYA
American Stomatological Association (DAVI) ... ASA
American Stone Importers Association (EA) ... ASIA
American Stop Smoking Intervention Study [*National Institutes of Health*] (EGAO) ... ASSIST
American Stores Co. [*Associated Press*] (SAG) ... AmStores
American Stores Co. [*NYSE symbol*] (SPSG) ... ASC
American Strategic Income Portfolio [*Associated Press*] (SAG) ... AmSIP
American Strategic Income Portfolio [*NYSE symbol*] (SAG) ... ASP
American Strategic Income Portfolio [*NYSE symbol*] (SPSG) ... CSP
American Strategic Income Portfolio II [*Associated Press*] (SAG) ... AmSIP2
American Strategic Income Portfolio II [*NYSE symbol*] (SAG) ... BSP
American Strategic Income Portfolio III [*Associated Press*] (SAG) ... AmSIP3
American Strategic Income Portfolio III [*NYSE symbol*] (SAG) ... CSP
American Street Machines [*Defunct*] (EA) ... ASM
American Street Railway Decisions [*A publication*] (DLA) ... Am St RD
American Street Railway Decisions [*A publication*] (DLA) ... Am St Ry Dec
American Street Railway Reports [*A publication*] (DLA) ... Am St Ry Rep
American String Teachers Association (EA) ... ASTA
American Striped Bass Society (EA) ... ASBS
American Studebaker Club ... ASC
American Student Association (EA) ... ASA
American Student Committee of the Occupational Therapy Association [*American Occupational Therapy Association*] ... ASCOTA
American Student Dental Association (EA) ... ASDA
American Student Information Service ... ASIS
American Student Media Association (EA) ... ASMA
American Student Union ... ASU
American Studies Association (EA) ... ASA
American Studies Centre [*University of Sydney*] [*Australia*] ... ASC
American Studies in Papyrology [*New Haven, CT*] [*A publication*] (BJA) ... AMStPapyr
American Studies International [*A publication*] (BRI) ... ASInt
American Studios, Inc. [*NASDAQ symbol*] (SAG) ... AMST
American Studios, Inc. [*Associated Press*] (SAG) ... AStudio
American Study Program for Educational and Cultural Training (EA) ... ASPECT
American Subacute Care Association ... ASCA
American Subcontractors Association (EA) ... ASA
American Sudden Infant Death Syndrome Institute (EA) ... ASIDSI
American Suffolk Horse Association (EA) ... ASHA
American Suffolk Sheep Society (EA) ... ASSS
American Sugar Alliance (EA) ... ASA
American Sugar Beet Industry Policy Committee [*Defunct*] (EA) ... ASBIPC
American Sugar Cane League of the USA (EA) ... ASCL
American Sugar Refining Co., Philadelphia, PA [*Library symbol Library of Congress Obsolete*] (LCLS) ... PPAmSR
American Sugarbeet Growers Association (EA) ... ASGA
American Suicide Fund [*An association*] ... ASF
American Sunbathing Association (EA) ... ASA
American Sunday School Union [*Later, AMF*] ... ASSU
American Sunday School Union, Philadelphia, PA [*Library symbol Library of Congress Obsolete*] (LCLS) ... PPAmS
American Sunroof Corp., Inc. ... ASC
American Supercharger Club and Owner's Association (EA) ... ASCOA
American Superconductor Corp. [*NASDAQ symbol*] (SPSG) ... AMSC
American Superconductor Corp. [*Associated Press*] (SAG) ... AmSupr
American Supplier Institute (EA) ... ASI
American Supply and Machinery Manufacturers Association (EA) ... ASMMA
American Supply Association (EA) ... ASA
American Surety Association (EA) ... ASA
American Surfing Association (EA) ... ASA
American Surgical Association (EA) ... ASA
American Surgical Trade Association (EA) ... ASTA
American Survival Association [*Defunct*] (EA) ... ASA
American Swedish Historical Foundation and Museum (EA) ... ASHF
American Swedish Historical Foundation, Philadelphia, PA [*Library symbol Library of Congress*] (LCLS) ... PPAmSwM
American Swedish Institute (EA) ... ASI
American Swimming Coaches Association (EA) ... ASCA
American Swiss Foundation for Scientific Exchange (EA) ... ASFSE
American Symphony Orchestra ... ASO
American Symphony Orchestra League (EA) ... ASOL
American Synthetic Rubber Corp. ... ASRC
American Syringomyelia Alliance Project (EA) ... ASAP
American Tan Rabbit Specialty Club (EA) ... ATRSC
American Tang Soo Do Association [*Defunct*] (EA) ... ATSDA
American Tarantula Society [*Defunct*] (EA) ... ATS
American Tarentaise Association (EA) ... ATA
American Tariff League [*Later, TRC*] ... ATL
American Tarpan Studbook Association (EA) ... ATSA
American Tax Policy Institute (EA) ... ATPI
American Tax Reduction Movement (EA) ... ATRM
American Tax Reform Project (EA) ... ATRP
American Tax Token Society (EA) ... ATTS
American Taxation Association (EA) ... ATA
American Taxicab Association [*Later, ITA*] (EA) ... ATA
American Taxpayers Association (EA) ... ATA
American Taxpayers' Quarterly [*A publication*] (DLA) ... Am Tax Q
American Teachers Association [*Later, NEA*] (EA) ... ATA
American Teachers' Series [*A publication*] ... ATS
American Technical Ceramics [*AMEX symbol*] (SPSG) ... AMK
American Technical Ceramics [*Associated Press*] (SAG) ... ATechC
American Technical Education Association (EA) ... ATEA
American Technical Society ... ATS
American Technological University (MCD) ... ATU
American Technology & Information, Inc. [*Vancouver Stock Exchange symbol*] ... ATI
American Teilhard Association (EA) ... ATA
American Teilhard Association for the Future of Man [*Later, ATA*] (EA) ... ATAFM
American Teilhard de Chardin Association [*Later, ATAFM*] ... ATCA
American Telco, Inc. [*Telecommunications service*] (TSSD) ... ATI
American Telecasting, Inc. [*Associated Press*] (SAG) ... AmTele
American Telecasting, Inc. [*NASDAQ symbol*] (SAG) ... ATEL
American Telecommunications Corp. [*Vancouver Stock Exchange symbol*] ... AMT
American Telemarketing Association [*Deerfield, IL*] (EA) ... ATA
American Telephone & Telegraph Co. (ACRL) ... AT&T
American Telephone & Telegraph Co. [*New York, NY*] ... ATT
American Telephone & Telegraph Co. [*Wall Street slang name: "Telephone"*] [*NYSE symbol*] (SPSG) ... T
American Telephone & Telegraph Co. Commission. Leaflets [*A publication*] (DLA) ... AT & T Co Com L
American Telephone & Telegraph Co. Commission Telephone Cases [*A publication*] (DLA) ... AT & T Co TC
American Telephone & Telegraph Co., Corporate Research Library, New York, NY [*Library symbol Library of Congress*] (LCLS) ... NNAT
American Telephone & Telegraph Co. Information Systems (TEL) ... ATTIS
American Telephone & Telegraph Co. Interexchange Carrier (TEL) ... ATTIX
American Telephone & Telegraph Co. International (TEL) ... ATTI
American Telephone & Telegraph Co., Long Lines, Bedminister, NJ [*OCLC symbol*] (OCLC) ... ATT
American Telephone & Telegraph Co., Morristown Corporate Marketing Library, Morristown, NJ [*Library symbol Library of Congress*] (LCLS) ... NjMoAT
American Telephone & Telegraph Co. Resource Center, Piscataway, NJ [*Library symbol Library of Congress*] (LCLS) ... NjPwAT
American Telephone & Telegraph Co., Technical Process, Piscataway, NJ [*OCLC symbol*] (OCLC) ... ATP
American Telephone & Telegraph Co. Technologies (TEL) ... ATTT
American Telephone Fundraisers Association (NFD) ... ATFA
American Television & Communications Corp. [*Cable TV operator*] ... ATC
American Television Society (NTCM) ... ATS
American Temperance Society [*Later, AHTS*] (EA) ... ATS
American Tennis Association (EA) ... ATA
American Tennis Federation (EA) ... ATF
American Tennis Industry Federation (EA) ... ATIF
American Tentative Society ... ATS
American Terms [*Business term*] ... AT
American Textbook Council (EA) ... ATC
American Textbook Publishers Institute [*Later, AAP*] (EA) ... ATPI
American Textile Machinery Association (EA) ... ATMA
American Textile Machinery Exhibition - Yarn, Fiber, and Non-Woven ManufacturingProcesses (ITD) ... ATME
American Textile Manufacturers Institute (EA) ... ATMI
American Theater Productions, Inc. ... ATP
American Theatre [*A publication*] (BRI) ... Am Theat
American Theatre Annual [*A publication*] ... ATA
American Theatre Arts for Youth (EA) ... TAFY
American Theatre Association [*Defunct*] (EA) ... ATA
American Theatre Critics Association (EA) ... ATCA
American Theatre Organ Enthusiasts [*Later, ATOS*] ... ATOE
American Theatre Organ Society (EA) ... ATOS
American Theatre Society [*Commercial firm*] (EA) ... ATS
American Theatre Wing (EA) ... ATW
American Themis [*A publication*] (DLA) ... Am Them
American Themis [*A publication*] (DLA) ... Them
American Theological Library Association (EA) ... ATLA
American Theological Library Association. Indexes ... ATLAI
American Theological Library Association, Princeton, NJ [*OCLC symbol*] (OCLC) ... ATL
American Theological Library Association, Yale University Divinity School, New Haven, CT [*Library symbol Library of Congress*] (LCLS) ... ATLA
American Theological Society - Midwest Division (EA) ... ATS
American Therapeutic Recreation Association (EA) ... ATRA
American Therapeutic Society [*Later, American Society for Clinical Pharmacologyand Therapeutics*] (EA) ... ATS
American Thermographic Society [*Later, American Academy of Thermology*] (EA) ... ATS
American Thesaurus of Slang ... ATS
American Thoracic Society (EA) ... ATS
American Three-Quarter Midget Racing Association [*Auto racing*] ... ATQMRA
American Thyroid Association (EA) ... ATA
American Time Travel Society [*Defunct*] (EA) ... ATTS
American Tin Trade Association (EA) ... ATTA
American Tinnitus Association (EA) ... ATA
American Title Association [*Later, ALTA*] ... ATA
American Tobacco Co., Department of Research and Development, Hopewell, VA [*Library symbol Library of Congress*] (LCLS) ... ViHopAT
American Tolkien Society (EA) ... ATS
American Topical Association (EA) ... ATA
American Torah Shelemah Committee (EA) ... ATSC

American Tort Reform Association (EA) .... ATRA
American Tour Managers Association [*Defunct*] (EA) .... ATMA
American Toy Export Association (EA) .... ATEA
American Toy Goat Association (EA) .... ATGA
American Toy Retailers Association (EA) .... ATRA
American Toys, Inc. [*Associated Press*] (SAG) .... AmToys
American Toys, Inc. [*NASDAQ symbol*] (SAG) .... ATOY
American Toys, Inc. [*Associated Press*] (SAG) .... AToys
American Toys Non-Red Wrrt [*NASDAQ symbol*] (TTSB) .... ATOYZ
American Toys Wrrt [*NASDAQ symbol*] (TTSB) .... ATOYW
American Track [*National Railroad Passenger Corp.; formerly, Railpax*] .... AMTRAK
American Tract Society (EA) .... ATS
American Trade and Industrial Development .... ATID
American Trade Association Executives [*Later, ASAE*] .... ATAE
American Trade Association for British Woolens (EA) .... ATABW
American Trade Consortium .... ATC
American Trade Organization [*Commonwealth of Independent States*] .... AMTORG
American Trade Union Council for Histadrut (EA) .... ATUCH
American Trade-Mark Cases (Cox) [*A publication*] (DLA) .... Am T-M Cas
American Trade-Mark Cases (Cox) [*A publication*] (DLA) .... Am Trade Mark Cas
American Traders Group (EA) .... ATG
American Traffic Association .... ATA
American Traffic Safety Services Association (EA) .... ATSSA
American Traffic Services Association [*Later, ATSSA*] (EA) .... ATSA
American Trails Foundation [*Defunct*] (EA) .... ATF
American Train Dispatchers Association (EA) .... ATDA
American Train Dispatchers Association .... TDA
American Trainers Association (EA) .... ATA
American Trakehner Association (EA) .... ATA
American Tramp Shipowners Association (EA) .... ATSA
American Trans Air [*ICAO designator*] (AD) .... TZ
American Trans Air, Inc. [*ICAO designator*] (FAAC) .... AMT
American Transfer Printing Institute [*Later, ITPI*] (EA) .... ATPI
American Transit Association [*Later, APTA*] (EA) .... ATA
American Transit Collectors' Association (EA) .... ATCA
American Translation [*of the Bible*] .... AT
American Translators Association (EA) .... ATA
American Transplant Association (EA) .... ATA
American Transportation Advisory Council .... ATAC
American Transportation Bowling Association (EA) .... ATBA
American Trauma Society (EA) .... ATS
American Travel Association [*Later, ATI*] .... ATA
American Travel Inns (EA) .... ATI
American Travel Survey [*BTS*] (TAG) .... ATS
American Travellers Corp. [*Associated Press*] (SAG) .... ATravel
American Travellers Corp. [*NASDAQ symbol*] (NQ) .... ATVC
American Tree Association .... ATA
American Trial Lawyers Association. Journal [*A publication*] (DLA) .... ATLJ
American Truck Dealers (EA) .... ATD
American Truck Historical Society (EA) .... ATHS
American Truck Leasing Network, Inc. .... AMTRALEASE
American Truck Owners Association [*New York, NY*] (EA) .... ATOA
American Truck Stop Foundation (EA) .... ATSF
American Truck Stop Operators Association (EA) .... ATSOA
American Truckers Benevolent Association [*Defunct*] (EA) .... ATBA
American Trucking Associations (EA) .... ATA
American Trudeau Society [*Later, American Thoracic Society*] .... ATS
American Tube Association/FMA (EA) .... ATA
American Tunaboat Association (EA) .... ATA
American Tung Oil Association [*Defunct*] .... ATOA
American Turkey Hunters Association [*Defunct*] (EA) .... ATHA
American Turners (EA) .... AT
American Turners [*An association*] .... TUR
American Turpentine Farmers Association Cooperative (EA) .... ATFAC
American Type Culture Collection (EA) .... ATCC
American Type Founders (DGA) .... ATF
American Typecasting Fellowship (EA) .... ATF
American Underground-Space Association (EA) .... AUA
American Underground-Space Association (EA) .... AUSA
American Union of Men (EA) .... AUM
American Union of Students (EA) .... AUS
American Union of Swedish Singers (EA) .... AUSS
American Union Transport [*Steamship*] (MHDW) .... AUT
American Unitarian Association .... AUA
American Unitarian Christian Association (EA) .... AUCA
American United Global, Inc. [*NASDAQ symbol*] (SAG) .... AUGI
American United Global, Inc. [*Associated Press*] (SAG) .... AUtdG
American United Global, Inc. [*Associated Press*] (SAG) .... AUtdGlb
American United Global Wrrt [*NASDAQ symbol*] (TTSB) .... AUGIW
American United Telecom (NITA) .... AUT
American Universities Field Staff [*Later, UFSI-IWA*] (EA) .... AUFS
American Universities Field Staff - Institute of World Affairs [*Later, UFSI-IWA*] (EA) .... AUFS-IWA
American Universities Field Staff. Reports Series [*A publication*] .... AUFS
[*The*] **American University** (GAGS) .... Amer U
American University [*Washington, DC*] .... AU
American University Hospital [*Lebanon*] .... AUH
American University in Paris, Paris, France [*Library symbol*] [*Library of Congress*] (LCLS) .... FrPAUP
American University Institute for Risk Analysis [*American University*] [*Research center*] (RCD) .... AURA
American University Intramural Law Review [*A publication*] (DLA) .... Am U Int L Rev
American University Intramural Law Review [*A publication*] (DLA) .... Am U Intra L Rev
American University Law Review [*A publication*] (DLA) .... Am U L
American University of Beirut [*Lebanon*] .... AUB
American University of Beirut, Beirut, Lebanon [*Library symbol Library of Congress*] (LCLS) .... LeBAU
American University of Cairo .... AUC
American University of Paris .... AUP
American University of the Caribbean .... AUC
American University Press Services, Inc. [*Information service or system*] (IID) .... AUPS
American University Publishers Group Ltd. .... AUPG
American University, Washington College of Law, Washington, DC [*Library symbol Library of Congress*] (LCLS) .... DAU-L
American University, Washington, DC [*Library symbol Library of Congress*] (LCLS) .... DAU
American University, Washington, DC [*OCLC symbol*] (OCLC) .... EAU
American Urban and Regional Information Systems Association (EERA) .... URISA
American Urological Association (EA) .... AUA
American Urological Association Allied (EA) .... AUAA
American Vacuum Society (EA) .... AVS
American Values Center (EA) .... AVC
American Vanguard Corp. [*NASDAQ symbol*] (NQ) .... AMGD
American Vanguard Corp. [*Associated Press*] (SAG) .... AVang
American Vaulting Association (EA) .... AVA
American Vecturist Association (EA) .... AVA
American Vegan Society (EA) .... AVS
American Vegetarian (EA) .... AV
American Vegetarian Union [*Defunct*] (EA) .... AVU
American Veneer Package Association (EA) .... AVPA
American Venereal Disease Association (EA) .... AVDA
American Ventilation Association [*Defunct*] (EA) .... AVA
American Ventures [*Vancouver Stock Exchange symbol*] .... AVR
American Veterans Alliance (EA) .... AVA
American Veterans Association - National Headquarters .... AVA
American Veterans Committee (EA) .... AVC
American Veterans of Israel (EA) .... AVI
American Veterans of World War II, Korea, and Vietnam (GPO) .... AMVETS
American Veterinary Dental Society (EA) .... AVDS
American Veterinary Distributors Association (EA) .... AVDA
American Veterinary Exhibitors' Association (EA) .... AVEA
American Veterinary Holistic Medical Association [*Later, AHVMA*] (EA) .... AVHMA
American Veterinary Lyme Disease Society .... AVLDS
American Veterinary Medical Association (EA) .... AVMA
American Veterinary Medical Association, Chicago, IL [*Library symbol Library of Congress*] (LCLS) .... ICAV
American Veterinary Neurology Association [*Defunct*] (EA) .... AVNA
American Veterinary Radiology Society [*Defunct*] (EA) .... AVRS
American Veterinary Society for Computer Medicine (EA) .... AVSCM
American Veterinary Society of Animal Behavior (EA) .... AVSAB
American Victims of Abortion (EA) .... AVA
American Video Association (EA) .... AVA
American Video Channels, Inc. [*New York, NY*] [*Telecommunications*] (TSSD) .... AVC
American Video Institute [*Rochester Institute of Technology*] [*Research center*] (RCD) .... AVI
American Video Teleconferencing Corp. [*Farmingdale, NY*] [*Telecommunications*] (TSSD) .... AVTC
American Videotext Services, Inc. [*Peekskill, NY*] [*Telecommunications*] (TSSD) .... AVS
American Viennola [*Record label*] .... AmVien
American Viewcard Club (EA) .... AVC
American Viewpoint [*Later, ERC*] .... AV
American Vineyard Foundation (EA) .... AVF
American Viola Society (EA) .... AVS
American Viscose Co., Front Royal, VA [*Library symbol Library of Congress*] (LCLS) .... ViFroA
American Viscose Co., Roanoke, VA [*Library symbol Library of Congress*] (LCLS) .... ViRoA
American Visionary Art Museum .... AVAM
American Visions [*A publication*] (BRI) .... Am Vis
American Visions [*A publication*] .... Am Vis
American Viticultural Area Association (EA) .... AVAA
American Vocational Association (EA) .... AVA
American Vocational Education Personnel Development Association (EA) .... AVEPDA
American Vocational Education Research Association (EA) .... AVERA
American Voice Input/Output Society (EA) .... AVIOS
American Volkssport Association (EA) .... AVA
American Volleyball Coaches Association (EA) .... AVCA
American Volunteer Group [*Flying Tigers*] [*World War II*] .... AVG
American Vox [*Record label*] .... AmVox
American Voyager Association (EA) .... AVA
American Wagering, Inc. [*Associated Press*] (SAG) .... AmWagr
American Wagering, Inc. [*NASDAQ symbol*] (SAG) .... BETM
American Waldensian Aid Society [*Later, AWS*] (EA) .... AWAS
American Waldensian Society (EA) .... AWS
American Walking Horse Association (EA) .... AWHA
American Walking Pony Association (EA) .... AWPA
American Walnut Manufacturers Association [*Later, FHAWA*] (EA) .... AWMA
American War Dads (EA) .... AWD
American War Mothers (EA) .... AWM
American War Standards [*DoD*] .... AWS
American Warehousemen's Association (EA) .... AWA
American Warmblood and Sport Horse Guild (EA) .... AW & SHG

American Warmblood Registry (EA)	AWR
American Warmblood Society (EA)	AWS
American Wash and Wear Institute	AWWI
American Waste Services [*NYSE symbol*] (SPSG)	AW
American Waste Services [*Associated Press*] (SAG)	AWste
American Watch Association (EA)	AWA
American Watch Workers Union	AWWU
American Watchmakers Institute (EA)	AWI
American Water Color Society, New York [*1878, founded 1866 as American Society of Painters in Water Colors*] (NGC)	AWCS
American Water Resources Association (EA)	AWRA
American Water Ski Association (EA)	AWSA
American Water Ski Educational Foundation	AWSEF
American Water Works [*Associated Press*] (SAG)	AmWtr
American Water Works [*Associated Press*] (SAG)	AWat
American Water Works Association (EA)	AWWA
American Water Works Association, Denver, CO [*Library symbol Library of Congress*] (LCLS)	CoDAW
American Water Works Association Research Foundation (EPA)	AWWARF
American Water Works Co., Inc. [*NYSE symbol*] (SPSG)	AWK
American Watercolor Society (EA)	AWS
American Waterfowl Association	AWA
American Watershed Council (EA)	AWC
American Waterways Operators (EA)	AWO
American Waterways Shipyard Conference (EA)	AWSC
American Wax Importers and Refiners Association (EA)	AMERWAX
American Wax Importers and Refiners Association	AWIRA
American Weight Lifting Association (EA)	AWLA
American Welara Pony Society (EA)	AWPS
American Welders Association (EA)	AWA
American Welding Institute	AWI
American Welding Society (EA)	AWS
American West African Freight Conference (EA)	AWAFC
American West Capital [*Vancouver Stock Exchange symbol*]	ANW
American West Overseas Association	AWOA
American Westwater Technology Group Ltd. [*Vancouver Stock Exchange symbol*]	AWW
American Wheat Striate Mosaic Virus [*Plant pathology*]	AWSMV
American Wheelchair Bowling Association (EA)	AWBA
American Whippet Club (EA)	AWC
American White Cross [*Associated Press*] (SAG)	AmWhite
American White Cross [*Associated Press*] (SAG)	AmWhite
American White Cross [*NASDAQ symbol*] (SAG)	AWCI
American Whitewater Affiliation (EA)	AWA
American Wholesale Booksellers Association (EA)	AWBA
American Wholesale Horticultural Dealers Association [*Later, HDA*] (EA)	AWHDA
American Wholesalers and Distributors Directory [*Pronounced "awed"*] [*A publication*]	AWDD
American Wilderness Alliance [*Later, AW*] (EA)	AW
American Wildlands (EA)	AW
American Wildlands Alliance (GNE)	AWL
American Wind Energy Association (EA)	AWEA
American Window Covering Manufacturers Association (EA)	AWCMA
American Wine Association (EA)	AWA
American Wine Society (EA)	AWS
American Wire Cloth Institute (EA)	AWCI
American Wire Gauge [*Standard*]	AWG
American Wire Producers Association (EA)	AWPA
American Wire Weavers Protective Association	AWWPA
American Wit and Gags [*Book title*]	AWAG
American Woman above Ground [*Lifestyle classification*]	AWAG
American Woman's Association [*Defunct*] (EA)	AWA
American Woman's Economic Development Corp. (EA)	AWED
American Woman's Society of Certified Public Accountants [*Chicago, IL*] (EA)	AWSCPA
American Women Buyers Club (EA)	AWBC
American Women Composers (EA)	AWC
American Women in Radio and Television (EA)	AWRT
American Women Playwrights Association (EA)	AWPA
American Women's Association for Renewable Energy	AWARE
American Women's Association of Saigon (VNW)	AWAS
American Women's Clergy Association (EA)	AWCA
American Women's Himalayan Expeditions	AWHE
American Women's Hospital Reserve Corps [*British*] (DAS)	AWHRC
American Women's Hospitals [*Later, AWHS*]	AWH
American Women's Hospitals Service [*Formerly, AWH*] [*Later, AWHS/AWMA*] (EA)	AWHS
American Women's Hospitals Service Committee of AMWA [*American Medical Women's Association*] (EA)	AWHS/AMWA
American Women's Voluntary Services [*World War II*] (EA)	AWVS
American Wood Chip Export Association (EA)	AWCEA
American Wood Council (EA)	AWC
American Wood Fabric Institute	AWFI
American Wood Inspection Agency	AWIA
American Wood Preservers' Association (EA)	AWPA
American Wood Preservers Bureau [*Defunct*] (EA)	AWPB
American Wood Preservers Institute (EA)	AWPI
American Wood Window Institute (DAC)	AWWI
American Wooden Money Guild (EA)	AWMG
American Woodmark Corp. [*NASDAQ symbol*] (NQ)	AMWD
American Woodmark Corp. [*Associated Press*] (SAG)	AWood
American Wool Council (EA)	AWC
American Word Processing Association (EA)	AWPA
American Working Terrier Association (EA)	AWTA

American World's Boxing Association (BARN)	AWBA
American Wrestling Association (DAVI)	AWA
American Wrestling Coaches and Officials Association [*Later, NWCA*] (EA)	AWCOA
American Writers Theatre Foundation (EA)	AWTF
American Yachtsmen's Association [*Later, BOAT/US*] (EA)	AYA
American Yankee Association (EA)	AYA
American Yarn Spinners Association (EA)	AYSA
American Y-Flyer Yacht Racing Association (EA)	AYFYRA
American Yoga Association (EA)	AYA
American Yorkshire Club (EA)	AYC
American Youth Congress	AYC
American Youth for Democracy	AYD
American Youth Foundation (EA)	AYF
American Youth Hostels (EA)	AYH
American Youth Soccer Organization (EA)	AYSO
American Youth Work Center (EA)	AYWC
American Yugoslav Claims Committee (EA)	AYCC
American Zellter, Inc.	AZI
American Zinc Association (EA)	AZA
American Zinc Institute [*Later, ZI*] (EA)	AZI
American Zinc Institute, Inc. [*Later, ZI*] (MCD)	AZII
American Zionist (BJA)	AZi
American Zionist Council [*Later, AZF*] (EA)	AZC
American Zionist Federation	AZF
American Zionist Youth Council (EA)	AZYC
American Zionist Youth Foundation (EA)	AZYF
American Zombie Association [*Defunct*]	AZA
Americana Gold & Diamond Holdings [*NASDAQ symbol*] (SAG)	AGDM
Americana Gold & Diamond Holdings [*Associated Press*] (SAG)	AmGold
Americana Gold&Diamond Hldgs [*NASDAQ symbol*] (TTSB)	AGDM
Americana Hotels & Realty Corp. [*NYSE symbol*] (SPSG)	AHR
Americana Hotels & Realty Corp. [*Associated Press*] (SAG)	AmHotl
Americana Unit [*American Topical Association*] (EA)	AU
Americanae Antiquarianae Societatis Socius [*Fellow of the American Antiquarian Society*] [*Latin*]	AASS
Americanae Orientalis Societatis Socius [*Fellow of the American Oriental Society*]	AOSS
American-African Affairs Association (EA)	AAAA
American-Arab Affairs Council (EA)	AAAC
American-Arab Anti-Discrimination Committee (EA)	ADC
American-Arab Association for Commerce and Industry [*New York, NY*] (EA)	AAACI
American-Arab Relations Committee (EA)	AARC
American-ASEAN [*Association of South East Asian Nations*] **Trade Council** (EA)	AATC
American-Asian Educational Exchange [*Defunct*] (EA)	AAEE
American-Australian Studies Foundation	AASF
American-Austrian Society (EA)	A-AS
American-Born Chinese	ABC
American-British Conversation [*as ABC-1, a 1941 report that set forth Allied worldwide strategy*] [*World War II*]	ABC
American-British Forces [*World War II*]	ABFOR
American-British Intelligence [*NATO*] (NATG)	ABI
American-British Laboratory [*Harvard University*]	ABL
American-British-Canadian Air Standardization Agreement (NG)	ABCAIRSTD
American-British-Canadian Army Standardization Program	ABC-ASP
American-British-Canadian Standardization Program	ABCSP
American-British-Canadian Stores Catalogue (DEN)	ABCSC
American-British-Dutch-Australian Air Operational Command [*1942*]	ABDAIR
American-British-Dutch-Australian Army Operational Command [*1942*]	ABDARM
American-British-Dutch-Australian Naval Operational Command [*1942*]	ABDAFLOAT
American-British-Dutch-Australian Supreme Command [*1942*]	ABDACOM
American-Byelorussian Cultural Relief Association (EA)	ABCRA
American-Canadian Genealogical Society (EA)	ACGS
American-Canadian Tour [*Auto racing*]	ACT
American-European Express [*Railway*]	AEE
American-French Genealogical Society (EA)	AFGS
American-International Charolais Association (EA)	AICA
American-International Reiki Association (EA)	AIRA
Americanism Educational League [*Buena Park, CA*] (EA)	AEL
Americanism Foundation [*Norwalk, OH*] (EA)	AF
American-Israel Anti-Smoking Society (EA)	AIASS
American-Israel Numismatic Association (EA)	AINA
American-Italian Women of Achievement	AMITA
American-Italy Society, Inc.	AISI
American-Korean Foundation [*Later, IHAP*] (EA)	AKF
American-Mideast Business Association (EA)	AMBA
American-Nepal Education Foundation (EA)	ANEF
American-Netherlands Club of Rotterdam	ANCOR
American-Paraguayan Cultural Center [*Paraguay*] (EAIO)	APCC
American-Polish National Relief for Poland (EA)	APNRP
Americans Against Abortion	AAA
Americans Against Union Control of Government (EA)	AAUCG
Americans by Choice (EA)	ABC
Americans Combatting Terrorism [*Commercial firm*] (EA)	ACT
Americans Concerned about Corporate Power [*Defunct*] (EA)	ACACP
Americans Concerned about Southern Africa	ACSA
Americans for a Common Sense Budget [*Inactive Defunct*] (EA)	ACSB
Americans for a Music Library in Israel [*Defunct*] (EA)	AMLI
Americans for a Safe Israel (EA)	AFSI
Americans for a Sound AIDS [*Acquired Immune Deficiency Syndrome*] Policy (EA)	ASAP

Americans for Better Care (EA) .... ABC
Americans for Budget Equity [*Defunct*] (EA) .... ABE
Americans for Children's Relief [*Defunct*] (EA) .... ACR
Americans for Common Sense [*Defunct*] (EA) .... ACS
Americans for Community Cooperation in Other Nations (AEBS) .... ACCION
Americans for Constitutional Action (EA) .... ACA
Americans for Constitutional Freedom [*Later, MC/ACF*] (EA) .... ACF
Americans for Constitutional Training (EA) .... ACT
Americans for Customary Weight and Measure (EA) .... ACWM
Americans for Decency (EA) .... AFD
Americans for Democracy in Ukraine (EA) .... ADU
Americans for Democratic Action (EA) .... ADA
Americans for Due Process (EA) .... ADP
Americans for Economic Freedom (EA) .... AEF
Americans for Economic Reform (EA) .... AER
Americans for Educational Choice (EA) .... AEC
Americans for Effective Law Enforcement (EA) .... AELE
Americans for Energy Independence (EA) .... AFEI
Americans for Generational Equity (EA) .... AGE
Americans for God (EA) .... AFG
Americans for God (EA) .... AG
Americans for Historic Preservation (EA) .... AHP
Americans for Hope, Growth, & Opportunity .... AHGO
Americans for Human Rights and Social Justice (EA) .... AHRSJ
Americans for Human Rights in Ukraine (EA) .... AHRU
Americans for Immigration Control (EA) .... AIC
Americans for Indian Opportunity (EA) .... AIO
Americans for International Aid (EA) .... AIA
Americans for Justice in the Middle East [*Lebanon*] (EAIO) .... AJME
Americans for Justice on the Job [*Defunct*] (EA) .... AJJ
Americans for Life (EA) .... AFL
Americans for Medical Freedom [*Defunct*] (EA) .... AMF
Americans for Medical Progress Educational Foundation (EA) .... AMPEF
Americans for Middle East Understanding (EA) .... AMEU
Americans for More Power Sources [*Defunct*] (EA) .... AMPS
Americans for Nonsmokers' Rights (EA) .... ANR
Americans for Nuclear Energy (EA) .... AFNE
Americans for Nuclear Energy (EA) .... ANE
Americans for Peace [*Defunct*] (EA) .... AFP
Americans for Peace and Democracy in the Middle East (EA) .... APDME
Americans for Peace in the Americas (EA) .... APA
Americans for President Reagan's Foreign Policy [*Defunct*] (EA) .... APRFP
Americans for Progressive Israel (EA) .... API
Americans for Progressive Israel - Hashomer Hatzair (EA) .... API-HH
Americans for Religious Liberty (EA) .... ARL
Americans for Responsible Government [*Defunct*] (EA) .... ARG
Americans for Safe and Competitive Trucking (EA) .... ASCT
Americans for Safe Food (GNE) .... ASF
Americans for Substance Abuse Prevention and Treatment (EA) .... ASAPT
Americans for Tax Reform (EA) .... ATR
Americans for the Competitive Enterprise System [*Later, ACEE*] (EA) .... ACES
Americans for the Enforcement of Attorney Ethics .... AEAE
Americans for the Enforcement of Judicial Ethics .... AEJE
Americans for the Environment (EA) .... AFE
Americans for the National Interest [*Defunct*] (EA) .... ANI
Americans for the National Voter Initiative Amendment (EA) .... ANVIA
Americans for the Universality of UNESCO (EA) .... AUU
Americans for Undivided Israel USA (EA) .... AUIUSA
Americans in Israel Political Action Committee (EA) .... AMIPAC
Americans in New Caledonia [*Army's 23rd infantry; acronym used as name of division. Active in World War II, disbanded 1945; reactivated 1967-71*] .... AMERICAL
Americans Mutually Interested in Giving Others a Start [*Defunct*] (EA) .... AMIGOS
Americans of European Ancestry [*Psychometrics*] .... AEA
Americans of Italian Descent (EA) .... AID
Americans of Japanese Ancestry [*Psychometrics*] .... AJA
Americans (of Lebanese-Syrian Ancestry) for America (EA) .... ALSAA
Americans United for a Smoke Free Society [*Defunct*] (EA) .... AUSFS
Americans United for God and Country (EA) .... AUGC
Americans United for Life (EA) .... AUL
Americans United for Life Legal Defense Fund (EA) .... AULLDF
Americans United for Separation of Church and State (EA) .... AUSCS
Americans United Research Foundation (EA) .... AURF
Americans United to Combat Fluoridation [*Later, AUDF*] (EA) .... AUCF
Americans United to Outlaw Fluoridation (EA) .... AUOF
Americans Want to Know [*Defunct*] (EA) .... AWK
Americans with Disabilities Act [*of 1990*] (USGC) .... ADA
Americans with Disabilities Act [*An association*] (EA) .... ADA
American-Scandinavian Foundation (EA) .... ASF
American-Scandinavian Foundation, New York, NY [*Library symbol Library of Congress*] (LCLS) .... NNASF
American-Serbian Cultural Association (EA) .... ASCA
American-South African Study and Educational Trust .... ASSET
American-Southern Africa Chamber of Trade and Industry (EA) .... ASACOT
American-Southern Africa Council [*Defunct*] .... ASAC
American-Soviet Homestays (EA) .... ASH
American-Soviet Medical Society, New York, NY [*Library symbol Library of Congress Obsolete*] (LCLS) .... NNASovM
American-Soviet Textbook Study Project [*An association Defunct*] (EA) .... ASTSP
American-Swiss Association (EA) .... ASA
American-Turkish Friendship Council .... ATFC
American-Turkish Society (EA) .... ATS
Americares Foundation (EA) .... AF
Americas: A Quarterly Review of Inter-American Cultural History [*A publication*] (BRI) .... Ams
Americas Boychoir Federation (EA) .... ABF
America's Cup Organizing Committee .... ACOC
America's Ekiden Federation [*Defunct*] (EA) .... AEF
America's Foundation (EA) .... AF
America's Freedom Ride [*Defunct*] (EA) .... AFR
America's Funniest Home Videos [*Television program*] .... AFHV
America's Future [*New Rochelle, NY*] (EA) .... AF
Americas Growth Fund, Inc. [*NASDAQ symbol*] (SAG) .... AGRO
[*The*] **Americas Growth Fund, Inc.** [*Associated Press*] (SAG) .... AmersGF
Americas Income Trust [*Associated Press*] (SAG) .... AmsInco
Americas Income Trust [*NYSE symbol*] (SPSG) .... XUS
America's Manifest Destiny [*An association*] (EA) .... AMD
America's Most Wanted [*Television program*] .... AMW
America's New Foundations [*A publication*] .... ANF
Americas Review: A Review of Hispanic Literature and Art of the USA [*A publication*] (BRI) .... Amer R
America's Small Business Political Action Committee [*Defunct*] (EA) .... ASBPAC
Americas Society (EA) .... AS
America's Society of Separated and Divorced Men (EA) .... ASDM
America's Sound Transportation Review Organization [*AAR*] [*Defunct*] .... ASTRO
America's Top 40 [*Radio program*] AT40
Americas UNIVAC [*Universal Automatic Computer*] **Users Association** [*Formerly, USE, UUA*] (EA) .... AUUA
America's Victory Force [*An association*] (EA) .... AVF
Americas Watch (EA) .... AW
Americium [*Chemical element*] .... Am
Americredit Corp. [*NYSE symbol*] (SAG) .... ACF
AmeriCredit Corp. [*NYSE symbol*] (TTSB) .... ACF
Americredit Corp. [*Associated Press*] (SAG) .... Amercrd
Americus [*Georgia*] [*Seismograph station code, US Geological Survey*] (SEIS) .... AMG
Americus, GA [*Location identifier FAA*] (FAAL) .... ACJ
Americus, GA [*AM radio station call letters*] .... WDEC
Americus, GA [*FM radio station call letters*] .... WDEC-FM
Americus, GA [*AM radio station call letters*] .... WISK
Americus, GA [*FM radio station call letters*] .... WISK-FM
AmeriData Technol [*NYSE symbol*] (TTSB) .... ADA
Ameridata Technologies, Inc. [*Formerly, Sage Technologies*] [*NYSE symbol*] (SAG) .... ADA
Ameridata Technologies, Inc. [*Formerly, Sage Technologies*] [*Associated Press*] (SAG) .... Ameridta
Amerifax Cattle Association (EA) .... ACA
Ameriflight, Inc. [*ICAO designator*] (FAAC) .... AMF
Amerigas Partners LP [*Associated Press*] (SAG) .... Amerigas
Amerigas Partners LP [*Associated Press*] (SAG) .... Amrigs
Amerigas Partners LP [*NYSE symbol*] (SAG) .... APU
AmeriGas Partners L.P. [*NYSE symbol*] (TTSB) .... APU
Amerigon, Inc. [*Associated Press*] (SAG) .... Amerign
Amerigon, Inc. [*NASDAQ symbol*] (SAG) .... ARGN
Amerigon Inc.'A' [*NASDAQ symbol*] (TTSB) .... ARGNA
Amerihost Properties [*NASDAQ symbol*] (TTSB) .... HOST
Amerihost Properties, Inc. [*Associated Press*] (SAG) .... Amrhost
Amerihost Properties, Inc. [*NASDAQ symbol*] (NQ) .... HOST
Amerijet International [*ICAO designator*] (FAAC) .... AJT
Amerikanisch [*American*] [*German*] .... amerik
Amerikos Lietuviu Tautine Sajunga [*National Lithuanian Society of America*] (EA) .... ALTS
AmeriLink Corp. [*NASDAQ symbol*] (SAG) .... ALNK
AmeriLink Corp. [*Associated Press*] (SAG) .... AmrLink
Amerin Corp. [*Associated Press*] (SAG) .... Amerin
Amerin Corp. [*NASDAQ symbol*] (SAG) .... AMRN
Amerind Foundation (EA) .... AF
AmeriQuest Technol [*NYSE symbol*] (TTSB) .... AQS
Ameriquest Technology, Co. [*Formerly, CMS Enhancements*] [*Associated Press*] (SAG) .... AmeriqTc
Ameriquest Technology Co. [*Formerly, CMS Enhancements*] [*NYSE symbol*] (SAG) .... AQS
Amerisafe, Inc. [*Associated Press*] (SAG) .... Amrisfe
Amerisafe, Inc. [*NYSE symbol*] (SAG) .... ASF
AmeriSource Health Corp. [*NYSE symbol*] (SAG) .... AAS
AmeriSource Health Corp. [*Associated Press*] (SAG) .... AmeriSrc
AmeriSource Health Corp. [*Associated Press*] (SAG) .... AmriHlt
AmeriSource Health Corp. [*NASDAQ symbol*] (SAG) .... ASHC
AmeriSource Health'A' [*NYSE symbol*] (TTSB) .... AAS
Ameristar Casinos [*NASDAQ symbol*] (TTSB) .... ASCA
Ameristar Casinos, Inc. [*Associated Press*] (SAG) .... AmerCas
Ameristar Casinos, Inc. [*NASDAQ symbol*] (SAG) .... ASCA
Ameritech Corp. [*NYSE symbol*] (SPSG) .... AIT
Ameritech Corp. [*Associated Press*] (SAG) .... Ameritch
Ameritech Mobile Communications, Inc. [*Schaumburg, IL*] [*Telecommunications*] (TSSD) .... AMCI
Ameritech Network Management (ACRL) .... ANM
Ameritel Management, Inc. [*Vancouver Stock Exchange symbol*] .... AEL
Ameritex Resources Ltd. [*Vancouver Stock Exchange symbol*] .... ATX
AmeriVest Properties, Inc. [*Associated Press*] (SAG) .... AmriVst
AmeriVest Properties, Inc. [*Associated Press*] (SAG) .... AmrVst
AmeriVest Properties, Inc. [*NASDAQ symbol*] (SAG) .... AMVP
Ameriwood Indus Intl. [*NASDAQ symbol*] (TTSB) .... AWII
Ameriwood Industries International [*Associated Press*] (SAG) .... Ameriwd
Ameriwood Industries International Corp. [*NASDAQ symbol*] (SAG) .... AWII
Amerman's Reports [*111-115 Pennsylvania*] [*A publication*] (DLA) .... Amer
Ameroil Energy Corp. [*Vancouver Stock Exchange symbol*] .... ALN
Ameron, Inc. [*Associated Press*] (SAG) .... Ameron

Ameron, Inc. [*NYSE symbol*] (SPSG) .... AMN
Ameron, Inc. Corrosion Control Division, Brea, CA [*Library symbol Library of Congress*] (LCLS) .... CBreA
Ameron Intl. [*NYSE symbol*] (TTSB) .... AMN
Amersham [*England*] .... AMER
Amertool Services .... AS
AmerTranz Worldwide Holding Corp. [*Associated Press*] (SAG) .... AmTrnz
AmerTranz Worldwide Holding Corp. [*NASDAQ symbol*] (SAG) .... AMTZ
AmerTranz Worldwide Holding Corp. [*Associated Press*] (SAG) .... ATrnz
Amery, WI [*Location identifier FAA*] (FAAL) .... AHH
Amery, WI [*AM radio station call letters*] .... WXCE
Ames Aeronautical Laboratory [*Air Force*] .... AAL
Ames Aircrew/Aircraft Integration Program [*NASA*] (RDA) A3I
Ames' Cases on Bills and Notes [*A publication*] (DLA) .... Ames Cas B & N
Ames' Cases on Partnership [*A publication*] (DLA) .... Ames Cas Par
Ames' Cases on Pleading [*A publication*] (DLA) .... Ames Cas Pl
Ames' Cases on Suretyship [*A publication*] (DLA) .... Ames Cas Sur
Ames' Cases on Trusts [*A publication*] (DLA) .... Ames Cas Trusts
Ames Cubic Precision Ranging System [*NASA*] .... ACPRS
Ames Daily Tribune, Ames, IA [*Library symbol Library of Congress*] (LCLS) .... IaAT
Ames Department Stores [*NASDAQ symbol*] (TTSB) .... AMES
Ames Department Stores [*Associated Press*] (SAG) .... Ames
Ames Department Stores [*Associated Press*] (SAG) .... Ames DS
Ames Department Stores, Inc. [*NASDAQ symbol*] (SAG) .... AMES
Ames Dept Stores Wrrt 'C' [*NASDAQ symbol*] (TTSB) .... AMESW
Ames Dimensional Hypersonic Wind Tunnel (SAA) .... AHWT
Ames, IA [*Location identifier FAA*] (FAAL) .... AMW
Ames, IA [*AM radio station call letters*] .... KASI
Ames, IA [*FM radio station call letters*] .... KCCQ
Ames, IA [*FM radio station call letters*] .... KEZT
Ames, IA [*FM radio station call letters*] (RBYB) .... KURE-FM
Ames, IA [*FM radio station call letters*] .... KUSR
Ames, IA [*AM radio station call letters*] .... WOI
Ames, IA [*FM radio station call letters*] .... WOI-FM
Ames, IA [*Television station call letters*] .... WOI-TV
AMES Interactive Dynamic Display Editor (MCD) .... AIDDE
Ames', Knowles', and Bradley's Reports [*8 Rhode Island*] [*A publication*] (DLA) .... Ames K & B
Ames Laboratory Research Reactor .... ALRR
Ames Life Sciences Directorate (DNAB) .... ALSD
Ames Prototype Hypersonic Free Flight Facility (KSC) .... APHFFF
Ames, Public Library, Ames IA [*Library symbol Library of Congress*] (LCLS) .... IaA
Ames' Reports [*4-7 Rhode Island*] [*A publication*] (DLA) .... Ames
Ames' Reports [*1 Minnesota*] [*A publication*] (DLA) .... Ames
Ames Research Center [*Moffett Field, CA*] [*NASA*] .... ARC
Ames Unitary Plan (SAA) .... AUP
Ames Unitary Wind Tunnel (SAA) .... AUWT
Amesbury Historical Society, Amesbury, MA [*Library symbol Library of Congress*] (LCLS) .... MAmHi
Amesbury Public Library, Amesbury, MA [*Library symbol Library of Congress*] (LCLS) .... MAm
Ametek, Inc. [*NYSE symbol*] (SPSG) .... AME
Ametek, Inc. [*Associated Press*] (SAG) .... Ametek
Amethopterin [*Methotrexate*] [*Antineoplastic drug*] .... A
Amethopterin [*Methotrexate*] [*Also, A, M, MTX*] [*Antineoplastic drug*] (AAMN) .... AM
Amethopterin [*Methotrexate*] [*Antineoplastic drug*] (MAE) .... AMT
Ametropia [*Ophthalmology*] .... AM
AMEX [*American Stock Exchange*] **Commodities Exchange** .... ACE
AMEX [*American Stock Exchange*] **Communications** [*Network*] .... AMCOM
AMEX [*American Stock Exchange*] **Computerized Order Display and Execution System** .... AMCODE
AMEX [*American Stock Exchange*] **Options Switching System** .... AMOS
AMF Apollo Sailing Class Association (EA) .... ASCA
AMF Sunfish Racing Class Association (EA) .... SRC
AMF Windflite Sailboard Class Association (EA) .... AMFWSCA
Amfed Financial, Inc. [*Associated Press*] (SAG) .... Amfed
Amfed Financial, Inc. [*NASDAQ symbol*] (SAG) .... AMFF
Amfion [*Record label*] [*Mexico*] .... Amf
Amfonelic Acid [*Biochemistry*] .... AFA
Amgen, Inc. [*Associated Press*] (SAG) .... Amgen
Amgen, Inc. [*NASDAQ symbol*] (NQ) .... AMGN
Amharic [*MARC language code Library of Congress*] (LCCP) .... amh
Amhawk Resources Corp. [*Vancouver Stock Exchange symbol*] .... AHK
Amherst College, Amherst, MA [*OCLC symbol*] (OCLC) .... AMH
Amherst College, Amherst, MA [*Library symbol Library of Congress*] (LCLS) .... MA
Amherst County Public Library, Amherst, VA [*Library symbol*] [*Library of Congress*] (LCLS) .... ViAm
Amherst Historical Society, Amherst, MA [*Library symbol Library of Congress*] (LCLS) .... MAHi
Amherst, MA [*FM radio station call letters*] .... WAMH
Amherst, MA [*FM radio station call letters*] .... WFCR
Amherst, MA [*FM radio station call letters*] .... WMUA
Amherst, MA [*FM radio station call letters*] .... WRNX
Amherst, MA [*AM radio station call letters*] .... WTTT
Amherst, NS [*AM radio station call letters*] .... CKDH
Amherst, NY [*AM radio station call letters*] .... WUFO
Amherst Papyri [*A publication*] (OCD) .... PAmh
Amherst, VA [*AM radio station call letters*] .... WAMV
Amherst, VA [*FM radio station call letters*] .... WYYD
Amherstview Branch, Lennox and Addington County Public Library, Ontario [*Library symbol National Library of Canada*] (NLC) .... OALAC
AMI (Air Mercury International) [*Belgium ICAO designator*] (FAAC) .... MIA
Ami Frame Interface Development System [*Lotus Development Corp.*] (PCM) .... AFIDS
Amicable and Brotherly Society of Journeymen Millwrights [*A union*] [*British*] .... ABSJM
Amicable Society of Coachmakers [*A union*] [*British*] .... ASC
Amici Thomae Mori [*Angers, France*] [*An association*] (EA) .... ATM
Amicus Curiae [*Friend of the Court*] [*Latin Legal term*] (ADA) .... AM CUR
Amiens/Glisy [*France ICAO location identifier*] (ICLI) .... LFAY
Amiga [*Record label*] [*Germany*] .... Ami
AMIGOS [*Access Method for Indexed Data Generalized for Operating System*] **Bibliographic Council** (EA) .... ABC
AMIGOS [*Access Method for Indexed Data Generalized for Operating System*] **Bibliographic Council, Dallas, TX** [*OCLC symbol*] (OCLC) IIC
AMIGOS [*Access Method for Indexed Data Generalized for Operating System*] **Bibliographic Council, Dallas, TX** [*OCLC symbol*] (OCLC) .... TPQ
AMIGOS [*Access Method for Indexed Data Generalized for Operating System*] **Bibliographic Council, Dallas, TX** [*OCLC symbol*] (OCLC) .... TPR
AMIGOS [*Access Method for Indexed Data Generalized for Operating System*] **Bibliographic Council, Dallas, TX** [*Library symbol Library of Congress*] (LCLS) .... TxDaABC
Amilcar Cabral International/Sal Island [*Cape Verde*] [*ICAO location identifier*] (ICLI) .... GVAC
Amilcar Register (EA) .... AR
Amiloride Inhibitable Lithium Transport [*Biochemistry*] (DAVI) .... AILT
Amine Precursor Uptake and Decarboxylation [*Cytology*] .... APUD
Amine Precursor Uptake and Decarboxylation Tumor [*Endocrinology*] (DAVI) .... APUD-Oma
Amino [*As substituent on nucleoside*] [*Biochemistry*] .... n
Amino Acid [*Biochemistry*] .... AA
Amino Acid Adenylate [*Also called adenomonophosphate*] [*Biochemistry*] (DAVI) .... AA-AMP
Amino Acid Decarboxylase [*An enzyme*] .... AADC
Amino Acid Formula [*Biochemistry*] .... AAF
Amino Acid Formula with Glutamate [*Biochemistry*] .... AAFG
Amino Acid Nitrogen [*Analytical biochemistry*] .... AAN
Amino Acid Oxidase [*An enzyme*] .... AAO
Amino Acid Racemization [*Dating process*] .... AAR
Amino Acid Residue [*Biochemistry*] .... AA
Amino Acid, Unknown or Other [*Symbol*] [*Biochemistry*] X
Amino Acid-Activating Enzyme [*Biochemistry*] (MAE) .... AAAE
Amino Polycyclic Aromatic Hydrocarbon [*Environmental chemistry*] .... APAH
Aminoacetaldehyde Diethyl Acetal [*Organic chemistry*] .... AADEA
Aminoacetaldehyde Dimethyl Acetal [*Organic chemistry*] .... AADMA
Aminoacetone [*Organic chemistry*] .... AA
Aminoacetonitrile [*Organic chemistry*] .... AAN
Aminoacetylcatechol [*or Acetamidocatechol*] [*Biochemistry*] .... AAC
Aminoadenosine Triacid Ester [*Biochemistry*] .... AATE
Aminoadipic Acid [*Organic chemistry*] .... AAA
Aminoadipic Acid [*Biochemistry*] .... Aad
(Aminoadipyl)cysteinylvaline Synthetase [*An enzyme*] .... ACVS
Amino(aminophenyl)benzamide [*Organic chemistry*] .... AAPBA
AminoAzobenzene [*Organic chemistry*] .... AB
Aminobenzamide [*Organic chemistry*] .... AB
Aminobenzamidine [*Biochemistry*] .... ABD
Aminobenzoic Acid [*Organic chemistry*] .... ABOA
Aminobenzophenone [*Organic chemistry*] .... AB
Aminobenzyloxy Methyl Cellulose Paper (DOG) .... ABM Paper
Aminobiphenyl [*Biochemistry*] (OA) .... ABP
Amino(bromo)(phenyl)pyrimidinone [*Antiherpes compound*] .... ABPP
(Aminobutyl)ethylisoluminol [*Biochemistry*] .... ABEI
Aminobutyraldehyde [*Organic chemistry*] .... ABAL
Aminobutyric Acid [*Also, Abu*] [*Organic chemistry*] .... ABA
Aminobutyric Acid [*Also, ABA*] [*Biochemistry*] .... Abu
Aminocaproic Acid [*Organic chemistry*] .... ACA
Aminocaproic Acid [*Biochemistry*] .... Acp
Aminocaprolactam [*Organic chemistry*] .... ACL
Aminocephalosporanic Acid [*Pharmacology*] .... ACA
Aminochlorobenzophenone [*Organic chemistry*] .... ACB
Amino(chloro)pentenedioic Acid [*Organic chemistry*] .... ACPA
Amino(chloro)Pentenoic Acid [*Organic chemistry*] .... ACP
Aminocyclopentane Carboxylic [*Acid*] (DMAA) .... ACPC
Amino(cyclopentyl)dicarboxylate [*Organic chemistry*] .... ACPD
Aminocyclopropane-Carboxylic Acid [*Organic chemistry*] .... ACC
Aminocyclopropanecarboxylicacid Oxidase [*An enzyme*] .... ACCO
Aminodecephalosporanic Acid [*Biochemistry*] .... ADCA
Aminodeoxyclavulanic Acid [*Organic chemistry*] .... ADCA
Aminodihydroxytetrahydronaphthalene [*Organic chemistry*] .... ADTN
Amino(dimethyl)dihydrobenzofuran [*Organic chemistry*] .... ADD
Aminodiphenyl [*Organic chemistry*] .... ADP
Aminoethoxyvinylglycine [*Organic chemistry*] .... AVG
Aminoethyl [*Biochemistry*] .... Aet
Aminoethyl Benzene Sulfonyl Fluoride [*Organic chemistry*] .... AEBSF
Aminoethyl Cellulose [*Organic chemistry*] (OA) .... AEC
Aminoethyl Cysteine [*Biochemistry*] (OA) .... AEC
Aminoethylaminopropylsilane .... AEPS
Amino(ethyl)carbazole [*Organic chemistry*] .... AEC
Aminoethylethanolamine [*Organic chemistry*] .... AEEA
Aminoethylhomocysteine [*Biochemistry*] .... AEHC
Aminoethylhomocysteine [*Biochemistry*] (OA) .... AEOC
Aminoethylisothiuronium [*Radiology*] .... AET
Aminoethyl(methyl)sulfone [*Biochemistry*] .... AEMS
Aminoethylphosphonic Acid [*Organic chemistry*] .... AEP
Aminoethylphosphonic Acid [*Organic chemistry*] (PDAA) .... AEPA
Aminoethylpiperazine [*Organic chemistry*] .... AEP
Amino(ethyl)propanediol [*Organic chemistry*] .... AEPD
Aminoethyltricosadiynamide [*Organic chemistry*] .... AETDA
Aminofluorene [*Also, FA*] [*Carcinogen*] .... AF

Amino-Form Bind Medium [*Analytical biochemistry*] ... ABM
Aminoglutethimide [*Organic chemistry*] (MAE) ... AGL
Aminoglutethimide [*Antineoplastic drug*] (CDI) ... AGT
Aminoglycoside [*Endocrinology*] (DAVI) ... AG
Aminoguanosine [*Biochemistry*] ... AG
Aminohexanoic Acid [*Biochemistry*] ... Ahx
Aminohippurate (MAE) ... AH
Aminohydroxynaphthalenesulfonic Acid [*Organic chemistry*] ... ANSA
Aminohydroxypropane Diphosphonate ... APDP
Amino(hydroxy)propylidine [*Organic chemistry*] ... APD
Aminoimidazole Ribonucleotide [*Biochemistry*] ... AIR
Aminoimidazolecarboxamide [*Also, AICA*] [*Organic chemistry*] ... AIC
Aminoimidazolecarboxamide [*Also, AIC*] [*Organic chemistry*] ... AICA
Aminoimidazolecarboxamide Ribonucleotide [*Also, AICR*] [*Biochemistry*] ... AICAR
Aminoimidazolecarboxamide Ribonucleotide [*Also, AICAR*] [*Biochemistry*] ... AICR
Aminoimidazolecarboxylic Acid [*Organic chemistry*] ... AICA
Amino(iodoacetamido)valeric Acid [*Organic acid*] ... AIAVA
(Amino)(Iodo)ketanserin [*Biochemistry*] ... AMIK
Aminoisobutyrate (DMAA) ... AIB
Aminoisobutyric Acid [*Biochemistry*] ... AIB
Aminoisobutyric Acid [*Biochemistry*] (AAMN) ... AIBA
Aminolaevulinate [*or Aminolaevulinic*] **Acid** [*Biochemistry*] ... ALA
Aminolaevulinate Dehydratase [*Also, ALD*] [*An enzyme*] ... ALAD
Aminolaevulinate Dehydratase [*Also, ALAD*] [*An enzyme*] ... ALD
Aminolaevulinate Synthase [*An enzyme*] ... ALAS
Aminolaevulinic Acid [*Biochemistry*] ... AmLev
Aminomalonic Acid [*Organic chemistry*] ... AMA
Amino(mercapto)thiodiazole [*Organic chemistry*] ... AMTD
Amino(mercopto)thiadiazole [*Organic chemistry*] ... AMTD
Amino(methoxy)benzanilide [*Organic chemistry*] ... AMBA
Aminomethyl Anthracene [*Organic chemistry*] ... AMA
Aminomethyl Naphthalene [*Organic chemistry*] ... AMN
Aminomethyl Phosphonic Acid [*Organic chemistry*] ... AMPA
Aminomethylalizarindiacetic [*Organic chemistry*] ... AMADAC
Amino-Methyl-Coumarin ... AMC
Amino(methyl)coumarinacetate [*Organic chemistry*] ... AMCA
Aminomethylcyclohexanecarboxylic Acid [*Pharmacology*] (AAMN) ... AMCA
Aminomethylcyclohexanecarboxylic Acid [*Pharmacology*] ... AMCHA
Aminomethyl(methyl)benzothiadiazinedioxide [*Biochemistry*] ... AMBD
Amino(methyl)propanediol [*Organic chemistry*] ... AMPD
Amino(methyl)propanol [*Organic chemistry*] ... AMP
Aminomethyltrimethylpsoralen [*Cytology*] ... AMT
Aminomethyltrioxsalen [*Organic chemistry*] ... AMT
Aminomonophosphate [*Organic chemistry*] (DAVI) ... AMP
Amino-naphthalene-trisulfonic Acid [*Organic chemistry*] ... ANTS
Aminonaphtholsulfonic Acid [*Organic chemistry*] ... ANSA
Amino-(nitro)cyclopentanecarboxylic Acid [*Organic chemistry*] ... ANCPA
Aminonitrothiazole [*Biochemistry*] (DAVI) ... ANT
Aminonucleoside (DMAA) ... AMNS
Amino(octyl)guanidine [*Organic chemistry*] ... AOG
Amino-Oligopeptidase [*An enzyme*] ... AOP
Aminooxyacetic Acid [*Biochemistry*] ... AOAA
Aminopenicillanic Acid [*Biochemistry*] ... APA
Aminopentanoic Acid [*An amino acid*] ... APE
Aminopeptidase [*An enzyme*] (MAE) ... AP
Aminophenyl Disulfide [*Biochemistry*] ... APDS
Aminophenylacetylene [*Organic chemistry*] ... APA
Amino(phenyl)butanoic Acid [*Organic chemistry*] ... APBA
Aminophenylmercuric Acid [*Organic chemistry*] ... APMA
Aminophosphonobutyric Acid [*Organic chemistry*] ... APB
Amino(phosphono)heptanoic Acid [*Organic chemistry*] ... APH
Amino(phosphono)valerate [*Organic chemistry*] ... APV
Amino(phosphono)valeric Acid [*An amino acid*] ... APV
Aminophylline [*A drug*] ... AM
Aminophylline, Phenobarbital, Ephedrine [*Medicine*] (MAE) ... APE
Aminopimelic Acid [*An amino acid*] ... APM
(Aminopropylamino)ethylthiophosphate [*Biochemistry*] ... APAETP
Aminopropyldiethanolamine [*Organic chemistry*] ... APDEA
Aminopropylmorpholine [*Organic chemistry*] ... APM
(Aminopropyl)triethoxysilane [*Organic chemistry*] ... APTES
Aminopropyltrimethoxysilane [*Organic chemistry*] ... APTMS
Aminopropyltrimethoxysilane [*Organic chemistry*] ... APTS
Aminopterin [*Antineoplastic drug regimen*] (DAVI) ... AMPT
Aminopterin [*Antiviral compound*] ... AMT
Aminopteroylglutamic Acid [*Organic chemistry*] ... APGA
Aminopurine [*Biochemistry*] ... AP
Aminopyrazolopyrimidine [*Biochemistry*] ... APP
Aminopyrazolopyrimidine Ribonucleoside [*Biochemistry*] ... APPR
Aminopyrene-trisulfonate [*Organic chemistry*] ... APTS
Aminopyrine [*An antipyretic and anesthetic*] ... AP
Aminopyrine Breath Test [*Clinical chemistry*] ... APBT
Aminoquinoline [*Biochemistry*] (OA) ... AQ
Aminoquinoline Oxide [*Biochemistry*] (OA) ... AQO
Aminosalicyclic Acid [*Biochemistry*] ... ASA
(Amino)selenadiazole [*Antiviral compound*] ... ASD
Aminosultopride [*Biochemistry*] ... AST
Aminothiazolineacetic Acid [*Biochemistry*] ... ATAA
Aminotransferase [*An enzyme*] ... AT
Aminotriazole [*Herbicide*] (MAE) ... AT
Aminotriazole [*Herbicide*] ... ATA
Amiodarone [*Coronary vasodilator*] [*Cardiology*] ... AMIO
Amiodarone-Iodine-Induced Thyrotoxicosis [*Medicine*] (DMAA) ... AIIT
Amiprophos Methyl [*Organic chemistry*] ... APM
Amir Mines Ltd. [*Toronto Stock Exchange symbol*] ... AMM
Amiral Commandant le Groupe Anti-Sous-Marin [*Commander, Antisubmarine Force*] [*French*] (NATG) ... ALGASM
Amiral Commandant les Porte-Avions [*Admiral, Aircraft Carriers*] [*French*] (NATG) ... ALPA
Amiral Commandant l'Escadre [*Admiral, French Fleet*] (NATG) ... ALESC
Amiri Flight-Bahrain [*ICAO designator*] (FAAC) ... BAH
Amiridia, Genitourinary Abnormalities, and Mental Retardation [*Medicine*] (DMAA) ... AGR
Amis de la Terre [*Friends of the Earth*] [*Canada*] (EAIO) ... AT
Amisk Public Library, Alberta [*Library symbol National Library of Canada*] (NLC) ... AAMI
Amistad Recreation Area [*National Park Service designation*] ... AMIS
Amistad Research Center Library, New Orleans, LA [*Library symbol*] [*Library of Congress*] (LCLS) ... LNAC
Amistar Corp. [*Associated Press*] (SAG) ... Amistar
Amistar Corp. [*NASDAQ symbol*] (NQ) ... AMTA
AMISYS Managed Care Sys [*NASDAQ symbol*] (TTSB) ... AMCS
Amit Women (EA) ... AW
Amite, LA [*AM radio station call letters*] ... WABL
Amitie Franco-Afghane [*French Afghan Friendship Committee*] ... AFRANE
Amities Belgo-Congolaises [*Belgian-Congolese Friendship Association*] ... ABC
Amitriptyline [*Also, AT*] [*Antidepressant compound*] ... AMI
Amitriptyline [*Also, AMI*] [*Antidepressant compound*] ... AT
Amity International (EAIO) ... AI
Amity Public Library, Amity, OR [*Library symbol Library of Congress*] (LCLS) ... OrAm
Amityville Junior High School, Amityville, NY [*Library symbol*] [*Library of Congress*] (LCLS) ... NAmiJH
Amityville Memorial High School, Amityville, NY [*Library symbol*] [*Library of Congress*] (LCLS) ... NAmiHS
Amityville Public Library, Amityville, NY [*Library symbol Library of Congress*] (LCLS) ... NAmi
AML Communication, Inc. [*NASDAQ symbol*] (SAG) ... AMLJ
AML Communications [*NASDAQ symbol*] (TTSB) ... AMLJ
AML Communications, Inc. [*Associated Press*] (SAG) ... AML Com
Amli Residential Prop [*NYSE symbol*] (TTSB) ... AML
AMLI Residential Properties [*NYSE symbol*] (SAG) ... AML
AMLI Residential Properties [*Associated Press*] (SAG) ... AMLI Rs
Amlikon [*Switzerland ICAO location identifier*] (ICLI) ... LSPA
Amman [*Jordan*] [*Airport symbol*] (OAG) ... AMM
Amman [*Jordan*] [*ICAO location identifier*] (ICLI) ... OJAC
Amman [*Jordan*] [*ICAO location identifier*] (ICLI) ... OJAF
Amman [*Jordan*] [*ICAO location identifier*] (ICLI) ... OJZZ
Amman/Marka [*Jordan*] [*ICAO location identifier*] (ICLI) ... OJAM
Amman/Queen Alia [*Jordan*] [*ICAO location identifier*] (ICLI) ... OJAI
Amman World Trade Center [*Jordan*] (EAIO) ... AWTC
Ammanford [*District in Wales*] ... AMMAN
Ammeter (MDG) ... A
Ammeter ... AM
Ammeter ... AMM
Ammeter ... AMTR
Ammeter Switch (MSA) ... AS
Ammianus Marcellinus [*c. 330-395AD*] [*Classical studies*] (OCD) ... Amm Marc
Ammo War Reserve Level (CINC) ... AWRL
Ammonia (MAE) ... AMM
Ammonia ... AMMN
Ammonia ... ammon
Ammonia (MSA) ... AMNA
Ammonia (GNE) ... NH_3
Ammonia Double-Alkali [*Organic chemistry*] (DICI) ... ADA
Ammonia Freeze Explosion [*Chemical engineering*] ... AFEX
Ammonia Oxidation Plant (MCD) ... AOP
Ammonia Service [*Military*] (DNAB) ... AS
Ammonia System (DS) ... AMM SYS
Ammonia System Operations [*NASA*] (NASA) ... ASO
Ammoniacal Copper Arsenate [*Wood preservative*] ... ACA
Ammoniacal Copper Arsenite (OA) ... ACA
Ammoniacal Copper Zinc Arsenate [*Wood preservative*] ... ACZA
Ammonia-Fiber Explosion [*Agricultural engineering*] (PS) ... AFEX
Ammoniaque Synthetique et Derives [*Belgium*] ... ASED
Ammonium Biflouride [*Inorganic chemistry*] ... ABF
Ammonium Citrate [*Organic chemistry*] (OA) ... AC
Ammonium Diethyldithiocarbamate [*Organic chemistry*] ... ADDC
Ammonium Dihydrogen Arsenate [*Inorganic chemistry*] ... ADA
Ammonium Dihydrogen Phosphate [*Inorganic chemistry*] ... ADP
Ammonium Dihydrogen Phosphate (IDOE) ... adp
Ammonium Dimolybdate [*Inorganic chemistry*] ... ADM
Ammonium Dinitramide [*Potential rocket fuel component*] [*Inorganic chemistry*] ... ADN
Ammonium Diuranate [*Inorganic chemistry*] ... ADU
Ammonium Heptamolybdate [*Inorganic chemistry*] ... AHM
Ammonium Hydrogen Sulfate [*Inorganic chemistry*] ... AHS
Ammonium Lauryl Sulfate [*Organic chemistry*] ... ALS
Ammonium Metatungstate [*Inorganic chemistry*] ... AMT
Ammonium Metavanadate [*Inorganic chemistry*] ... AMV
Ammonium Molybdophosphate [*Inorganic chemistry*] ... AMP
Ammonium Nitrate [*Inorganic chemistry*] ... AN
Ammonium Nitrate and Fuel Oil [*Explosive*] ... ANFO
Ammonium Nitrate, Copper, Aluminum, and Plywood [*Proposed currency*] ... ANCAP
Ammonium Paratungstate [*Metallurgy*] ... APT
Ammonium Perchlorate [*Inorganic chemistry*] ... AP
Ammonium Perchlorate [*Inorganic chemistry*] ... APC
Ammonium Persulfate [*Inorganic chemistry*] ... APS

Ammonium Polyphosphate [*Fertilizer*] .... APP
Ammonium Polysulfide [*Fertilizer*] .... APS
Ammonium Pyrrolidinedithiocarbamate [*Also, APDTC*] [*Organic chemistry*] .... APDC
Ammonium Pyrrolidinedithiocarbamate [*Also, APDC*] [*Organic chemistry*] .... APDTC
Ammonium Sulfamate [*Inorganic chemistry*] .... AMS
Ammonium Sulfate-Nitrate [*Fertilizer*] .... ASN
Ammonium Thioglycolate .... ATG
Ammonium Thiosulfate [*Fertilizer*] .... ATS
Ammonium Uranyl Carbonate [*Inorganic chemistry*] .... AUC
Ammonium Uranyl Tricarbonate [*Inorganic chemistry*] .... AUT
Ammons Picture Vocabulary Test [*Speech and language therapy*] (DAVI) .... APVT
Ammunition (ADA) .... AM
Ammunition (KSC) .... AMM
Ammunition (AFM) .... AMMO
Ammunition .... AMMUN
Ammunition .... AMN
Ammunition and Hazardous Materials Handling Review Board (MCD) .... AMHAZ
Ammunition Base Load (MCD) .... ABL
Ammunition Bearer [*Military*] (INF) .... AB
Ammunition Bearer [*Military*] (AABC) .... AMMOBR
Ammunition, Casualties, and Equipment (INF) .... ACE
Ammunition Condition Report .... ACR
Ammunition Consolidated Stock Status Report .... ACSSR
Ammunition Control Point (AFM) .... ACP
Ammunition Disposition Request [*or Report*] .... ADR
Ammunition Distribution and Control [*Military*] (NG) .... AD & C
Ammunition Distribution System .... ADS
Ammunition Engineering Directorate [*Army*] (MCD) .... AED
Ammunition Examiner [*British and Canadian*] [*World War II*] .... AE
Ammunition Executive Office [*Military British*] .... AEO
Ammunition, Explosives, and Other Dangerous Articles .... AEDA
Ammunition Group - Picatinny Arsenal (MCD) .... AGPA
Ammunition Handling Equipment .... AHE
Ammunition Handling System (MCD) .... AHS
Ammunition Hoist .... AMOHST
Ammunition Hoist Drive .... AMOHSTDR
Ammunition Identification Code .... AIC
Ammunition Initiatives Task Force (MCD) .... AITF
Ammunition Lighter [*Navy symbol*] (DNAB) .... YEN
Ammunition Lighter [*Navy symbol*] (DNAB) .... YWN
Ammunition Loading (SAA) .... A/L
Ammunition Loading Production Engineering Center [*Army*] .... ALPEC
Ammunition Loading System (MCD) .... ALS
Ammunition Logistics [*Army*] (RDA) .... AMMOLOG
Ammunition Lot Number .... ALN
Ammunition Peculiar Equipment (AABC) .... APE
Ammunition Performance Report [*Military*] (NVT) .... APR
Ammunition Point .... AP
Ammunition Pontoon [*Navy symbol*] (DNAB) .... YWN
Ammunition Post Processor [*Computer science Military*] .... APP
Ammunition Procurement and Supply Agency [*Army*] .... APSA
Ammunition Rack .... AMMORK
Ammunition Railhead .... ARH
Ammunition Readiness Concept (MCD) .... ARC
Ammunition Refilling Point .... ARP
Ammunition Reliability Division [*Military*] .... ARD
Ammunition Reliability Evaluation Program (SAA) .... AREP
Ammunition Reliability Information Evolution System (MCD) .... ARIES
Ammunition Repair Workshop (NATG) .... ARW
Ammunition Reporting Management System [*Air Force*] (AFM) .... ARMS
Ammunition Resupply Projectile [*Military*] (RDA) .... ARP
Ammunition Ship [*Navy symbol*] .... AE
Ammunition Ship .... AFD
Ammunition Shipment Order [*Army*] .... AMSO
Ammunition Specialist [*Military*] (GFGA) .... AS
Ammunition Stock Recording System .... ASRS
Ammunition Stockpile Reliability Program (MCD) .... ASRP
Ammunition Storage Facility [*Military*] .... ASF
Ammunition Stores Issue Ship .... ASIS
Ammunition Stores Management and Remote Set Fuzing (MCD) .... SM/RSF
Ammunition Subdepot [*United Kingdom*] (NATG) .... ASD
Ammunition Sub-Park [*British military*] (DMA) .... ASP
Ammunition Supply Depot .... ASD
Ammunition Supply Dump [*British World War II*] .... ASD
Ammunition Supply Installation [*Army*] (INF) .... ASI
Ammunition Supply Officer (AFM) .... ASO
Ammunition Supply Plan [*Army*] .... ASP
Ammunition Supply Point .... ASP
Ammunition Supply Squadron [*Air Force*] .... AMMISSq
Ammunition Supply Squadron [*Air Force*] .... ASUPS
Ammunition Systems Reliability and Safety Division [*Picatinny Arsenal*] [*Army*] .... ASRSD
Ammunition Technical Officer [*Ireland*] .... ATO
Ammunition Technician [*British military*] (DMA) .... AT
Ammunition Technology Division [*Lake City Army Ammunition Plant*] [*Independence, MO*] .... ATD
Ammunition Torque (SAA) .... A/T
Ammunition Transfer Point [*or Pack*] (MCD) .... ATP
Ammunition Transport .... AKE
Ammunition War Reserve (CINC) .... AWR
Amnesic Shellfish Poisoning [*Medicine*] .... ASP
Amnesty International [*London, England*] (EAIO) .... AI
Amnesty International Canadian Section .... AICS
Amnesty International EC Representation [*Belgium*] (EAIO) .... AI-EC
Amnesty International Medical Group .... AIMG
Amnesty International of the USA (EA) .... AIUSA
Amnesty International Parliamentary Group .... AIPG
Amnesty Review Board [*Terminated, 1976*] .... ARB
Amnex, Inc. [*Associated Press*] (SAG) .... Amnex
AMNEX, Inc. [*Formerly, NYCOM Information Services*] [*NASDAQ symbol*] (SPSG) .... AMXI
Amniocentesis [*Obstetrics*] (DAVI) .... amnio
Amnion (DMAA) .... Am
Amnionic Fluid Volume [*Obstetrics*] (DAVI) .... AFV
Amniotic Alphafetoprotein [*Obstetrics*] .... AFP
Amniotic Deformity, Adhesion, Mutilation [*Syndrome*] [*Medicine*] (DMAA) .... ADAM
Amniotic Fluid [*Obstetrics*] .... AF
Amniotic Fluid Embolism [*Obstetrics*] .... AFE
Amniotic Fluid Glucose [*Obstetrics*] .... AFG
Amnistie Internationale Section Canadienne [*Amnesty International Canadian Section*] .... AISC
AMOCO Canada Petroleum Co. Ltd., Calgary, AB, Canada [*Library symbol Library of Congress*] (LCLS) .... CaACAC
AMOCO Canada Petroleum Co. Ltd., Calgary, Alberta [*Library symbol National Library of Canada*] (NLC) .... ACAC
AMOCO Chemicals Customer Service System .... ACCESS
AMOCO Corp. [*Associated Press*] (SAG) .... Amoco
Amoco Corp. [*NYSE symbol*] (SAG) .... AN
Amoco Corp. [*NYSE symbol*] (TTSB) .... AN
AMOCO Production Co., Library, Tulsa, OK [*OCLC symbol*] (OCLC) .... OUD
AMOCO Production Co., Research Center Geology Library, Tulsa, OK [*Library symbol Library of Congress*] (LCLS) .... OkTAm
Amoeba-Less Life Cycle (PDAA) .... ALC
Amoebocyte Lysate [*Biochemistry*] .... AL
Amol [*Iran*] [*ICAO location identifier*] (ICLI) .... OINA
Amold, CA [*FM radio station call letters*] .... KCFA
Amon Carter Museum of Western Art, Fort Worth, TX [*Library symbol Library of Congress*] (LCLS) .... TxFACM
Among .... AMG
Among Others .... AO
Amongst (ROG) .... AMGST
Amonium Zingiber [*Ginger*] [*Pharmacology*] (ROG) .... AMON ZINGIB
Amook [*Alaska*] [*Airport symbol*] (OAG) .... AOS
AMOON Distributing [*NASDAQ symbol*] (SAG) .... DIST
Amora (BJA) .... A
Amores [*of Ovid*] [*Classical studies*] (OCD) .... Am
Amorite Personal Names in the Mari Texts [*A publication*] (BJA) .... APNM
Amorphous (AAMN) .... AMOR
Amorphous [*Sediment*] [*Biochemistry*] (DAVI) .... AMORP
Amorphous .... amorph
Amorphous Hydrous Calcium Phosphate [*Inorganic chemistry*] .... ACP
Amorphous Inclusion [*Cytology*] .... AI
Amorphous Material [*Agronomy*] .... Am
Amorphous Material [*Clinical medicine*] .... A-MAT
Amorphous Polyalphaolefin [*Plastics technology*] .... APAO
Amorphous Polyamide [*Organic chemistry*] .... APA
Amorphous Polyolefin [*Organic chemistry*] .... APO
Amorphous Polypropylene [*Organic chemistry*] .... APP
Amorphous Semiconductor (PDAA) .... AS
Amorphous Sodium Aluminosilicate [*Inorganic chemistry*] .... ASAS
Amorphous Solid Water [*Materials science*] .... ASW
Amorphous Thin Film (PDAA) .... ATF
Amortization and Partial Prepayment [*Business term*] .... APP
Amory, MS [*FM radio station call letters*] .... WAFM
Amory, MS [*AM radio station call letters*] .... WAMY
Amos [*Old Testament book*] .... Am
Amos [*California*] [*Seismograph station code, US Geological Survey*] (SEIS) .... AMS
Amos and Ferard on Fixtures [*A publication*] (DLA) .... A & F Fix
Amos and Ferard on Fixtures [*A publication*] (DLA) .... Am & Fer
Amos and Ferard on Fixtures [*A publication*] (DLA) .... Amos & F
Amos and Ferard on Fixtures [*A publication*] (DLA) .... Amos & F Fixt
Amos and Ferard on Fixtures [*A publication*] (DLA) .... Ferard Fixt
Amos' Fifty Years of the English Constitution [*A publication*] (DLA) .... Amos Fifty Years
Amos on an English Code [*A publication*] (DLA) .... Amos Eng Code
Amos on International Law [*A publication*] (DLA) .... Amos Int Law
Amos on Laws for Regulation of Vice [*A publication*] (DLA) .... Amos Reg Vice
Amos, PQ [*AM radio station call letters*] .... CHAD
Amos' Primer of the English Constitution [*A publication*] (DLA) .... Amos Engl Const
Amos' Science of Jurisprudence [*A publication*] (DLA) .... Amos Jur
Amotopo [*Surinam*] [*ICAO location identifier*] (ICLI) .... SMAM
Amougies [*Belgium ICAO location identifier*] (ICLI) .... EBAM
Amount (ROG) .... A
Amount .... AMNT
Amount (AFM) .... AMT
Amount of Critical View .... ACV
Amount of Insulin Extractable from the Pancreas (MAE) .... AIEP
Amount of Substance [*Molecular quantity*] (MAE) .... ams
Amount of Substance [*Molecular quantity*] [*Symbol IUPAC*] .... n
Amount Tendered .... AT
Amount to Make the Property Operational [*Business term*] (EMRF) .... AMPO
Amoxicillin [*Medicine*] (DMAA) .... AMX
AMP Exploration & Mining Co. Ltd. [*Vancouver Stock Exchange symbol*] .... API
AMP, Inc. [*NYSE symbol*] (SPSG) .... AMP
AMP, Inc. [*FAA designator*] (FAAC) .... MMP
AMP, Inc., Harrisburg, PA [*Library symbol Library of Congress*] (LCLS) .... PHarA

Ampac Petroleum Resources, Inc. [*Vancouver Stock Exchange symbol*] .... AMP
Ampace Corp. [*Associated Press*] (SAG) .... Ampace
Ampace Corp. [*NASDAQ symbol*] (SAG) .... PACE
Ampal American Israel Corp. [*NASDAQ symbol*] (SAG) .... AMPL
Ampal-Amer Israel 6.50% Pfd [*NASDAQ symbol*] (TTSB) .... AMPLP
Ampal-Amer Israel Corp. [*AMEX symbol*] (SPSG) .... AIS
Ampal-American Israel Corp. [*Associated Press*] (SAG) .... Ampal
Ampanihy [*Madagascar*] [*Airport symbol*] (OAG) .... AMP
Ampanihy [*Madagascar*] [*ICAO location identifier*] (ICLI) .... FMSY
Amparafaravola [*Malagasy*] [*Airport symbol*] (AD) .... AMF
Amparafaravola [*Madagascar*] [*ICAO location identifier*] (ICLI) .... FMMP
Ampco-Pittsburgh [*NYSE symbol*] (TTSB) .... AP
Ampco-Pittsburgh Corp. [*Associated Press*] (SAG) .... Ampco
Ampco-Pittsburgh Corp. [*NYSE symbol*] (SPSG) .... AP
Ampenan [*Indonesia*] [*Airport symbol*] (AD) .... AMI
Ampere [*Unit of electric current*] [*SI symbol*] .... A
Ampere (DMAA) .... amp
Ampere (ODBW) .... amp
Ampere (IDOE) .... amp
Ampere [*or Amperage*] [*Unit of electric current*] (AFM) .... AMP
Ampere [*Unit of electric current*] (ROG) C
Ampere Demand Meter (MSA) .... AD
Ampere Direct Current (MCD) .... ADC
Ampere Hour .... A H
Ampere/Hour (MCD) .... A/HR
Ampere Hour (IDOE) .... Ah
Ampere Hour (IDOE) .... amp-hr
Ampere Minute (IAA) .... AM
Ampere per Meter [*Unit of magnetic field strength*] .... A/M
Ampere Second .... As
Ampere Turns per Motor (IAA) .... ATM
Ampere, Volt, Ohm (IAA) .... AVO
Ampere-Hour (MDG) .... AMP-HR
Ampere-Hour Capacity .... AHC
Ampere-Hour Meter .... AHM
Amperemeter (IAA) .... A
Amperemeter (MAE) .... AM
Amperes (KSC) .... AMPS
Amperes per Square Centimeter (IAA) .... ASC
Amperes per Square Foot .... ASF
Amperes per Square Inch .... APSI
Amperes per Square Inch [*Electrochemistry*] .... ASI
Amperes per Square Meter .... A/M^2
Amperes per Terminal .... A/T
Ampere-Seconds per Volt (IAA) .... ASV
Ampere-Turn [*Technical drawings*] .... A-T
Ampere-Turn per Meter (MCD) .... AT/M
Amperometric [*Electromagnetics*] .... Amp
Ampex Corp. [*Associated Press*] (SAG) .... Ampex
Ampex Corp. [*AMEX symbol*] (SAG) .... AXC
Ampex Corp.'A' [*AMEX symbol*] (TTSB) .... AXC
Ampex Corp., Redwood City, CA [*Library symbol Library of Congress*] (LCLS) .... CRcAm
Ampex Digital Optics [*Telecommunications*] (WDMC) .... ADO
Ampex Disk Controller [*Computer science*] (IAA) .... ADC
AMPEX [*Alexander M. Poniatoff, Excellence*] **Replacement Memory** (IAA) ...... ARM
Ampfing/Waldkraiburg [*Germany ICAO location identifier*] (ICLI) .... EDYA
Amphenol Corp'A' [*NYSE symbol*] (TTSB) .... APH
Amphenol Corp. (SAA) .... AMP
Amphenol Corp. [*Associated Press*] (SAG) .... Amphnl
Amphenol Corp. [*NYSE symbol*] (SAG) .... APH
Amphenol-Borg Electronics Corp. (MCD) .... ABEC
Amphetamine [*Also, AMT, amphet*] [*CNS stimulant*] .... A
Amphetamine [*Pharmacology*] (DAVI) .... AMP
Amphetamine [*Pharmacology*] (DAVI) .... AMPH
Amphetamine [*Also, A, AMT*] [*CNS stimulant*] .... amphet
Amphetamine [*Also, A, amphet*] [*CNS stimulant*] .... AMT
Amphetamine Sulfate [*Also callde Benzedrine*] [*Pharmacology*] (DAVI) .... A's
Amphiali [*Greece*] [*ICAO location identifier*] (ICLI) .... LGAM
Amphibian [*or Amphibious*] .... A
Amphibian [*Russian aircraft symbol*] .... E
Amphibian Boat Reconnaissance Aircraft .... ABR
Amphibian Imperial Forces .... AIF
Amphibian Papilla [*An auditory organ*] .... AP
Amphibian Reconnaissance [*Military*] .... AR
Amphibian Tank Escape Apparatus .... ATEA
Amphibian Technology Tested .... ATT
Amphibian [*or Amphibious*] **Tractor** [*or Truck*] .... AMTRAC
Amphibian [*or Amphibious*] **Tractor Battalion** [*or Truck*] .... AMTRACBN
Amphibians and Watercraft [*Army*] (RDA) .... AWC
Amphibians and Watercraft Product Manager [*Army*] (RDA) .... AWC-PM
Amphibious (AFM) .... AMPH
Amphibious .... AMPHBS
Amphibious .... AMPHIB
Amphibious [*JETDS*] .... K
Amphibious .... PHIB
Amphibious and Watercraft (MCD) .... AWC
Amphibious, Armored Infantry Combat Vehicle (MCD) .... AAICV
Amphibious Assault Bulk Fuel System [*Navy*] .... AABFS
Amphibious Assault Carrier [*or Ship*] **(Landing Helicopter Assault Ship)** [*Navy symbol*] .... LHA
Amphibious Assault Fire System (CAAL) .... AAFS
Amphibious Assault Fuel System [*Navy*] .... AAFS
Amphibious Assault Landing Craft [*Navy symbol*] .... AALC
Amphibious Assault Ship [*Military*] .... LAA
Amphibious Assault Ship (Landing Platform, Helicopter) [*Navy symbol*] ...... LPH
Amphibious Auto Club of America (EA) .... AACA
Amphibious Bases, United Kingdom .... PHIBSUKAY
Amphibious Beach Unit [*Military*] .... ABU
Amphibious Car [*British*] .... AC
Amphibious Cargo Ship [*Navy symbol*] .... LKA
Amphibious Coastal Reconnaissance Ship [*Navy symbol*] .... LSSR
Amphibious Command and Control System (MCD) .... ACCS
Amphibious Command Car (NATG) .... ACC
Amphibious Command Ship [*Formerly, AGC*] [*Navy symbol*] LCC
Amphibious Construction Battalion [*Also, PHIBCB*] .... ACB
Amphibious Construction Battalion [*Also, ACB*] (NVT) .... PHIBCB
Amphibious Corps [*Marine Corps*] .... AC
Amphibious Corps [*Marine Corps*] .... PHIBCORPS
Amphibious Corps, Atlantic Fleet [*Marine Corps*] .... ACAF
Amphibious Corps, Pacific Fleet [*Marine Corps*] .... ACPF
Amphibious Corps, Pacific Fleet [*Marine Corps*] .... PHIBCORPAC
Amphibious Detachment .... PHIBDET
Amphibious Detachment, India .... PHIBDETIND
Amphibious Exercise [*Navy, Marine Corps*] .... AMPHIBEX
Amphibious Exercise [*NATO*] .... PHIBEX
Amphibious Fire Support Ship [*Navy symbol*] .... LFS
Amphibious Flagship Data System [*Military*] (NVT) .... AFDS
Amphibious Follow-on-Echelon [*Navy*] (MCD) .... AFOE
Amphibious Force Flagship [*Later, LCC*] [*Navy symbol*] .... AGC
Amphibious Forces .... AMPHIBFOR
Amphibious Forces .... PHIBFOR
Amphibious Forces, Atlantic .... AMPHFORLANT
Amphibious Forces, Atlantic (MUGU) .... AMPHIBFORLANT
Amphibious Forces, Atlantic Fleet .... PHIBLANT
Amphibious Forces, Atlantic Fleet .... PHIBSLANT
Amphibious Forces, Central Pacific .... AMPHIBFORCENPAC
Amphibious Forces, Europe .... PHIBEU
Amphibious Forces, Europe .... PHIBSEU
Amphibious Forces, Mediterranean .... AMPHFORMED
Amphibious Forces, Mediterranean (MUGU) .... AMPHIBFORMED
Amphibious Forces, Northwest African Waters .... PHIBNAW
Amphibious Forces Ordnance Material Mobile Instruction Unit [*Obsolete Navy*] .... AF(F)MMIU
Amphibious Forces, Pacific .... AMPHFORPAC
Amphibious Forces, Pacific (MUGU) .... AMPHIBFORPAC
Amphibious Forces, Pacific Fleet .... PHIBPAC
Amphibious Forces, Pacific Fleet .... PHIBSFORPAC
Amphibious Forces, Pacific Fleet .... PHIBSPAC
Amphibious Group .... PHIBGROUP
Amphibious Group .... PHIBGRU
Amphibious Group Command [*NATO*] (NATG) .... AGC
Amphibious [*Warfare*] **Indoctrination** (DOMA) .... AMPHIBIND
Amphibious Infantry Combat Vehicle [*Army*] (ADDR) .... AICV
Amphibious Infantry Support Vehicle .... AISV
Amphibious Inhaul Device (PDAA) .... AID
Amphibious Intelligence (DOMA) .... AMPHIBINT
Amphibious Landing Exercise [*Navy*] (NVT) .... PHIBLEX
Amphibious Logistics Support Ashore [*Marine Corps*] (MCD) .... ALSA
Amphibious Logistics Systems [*Navy*] .... ALS
Amphibious Maintenance Support Unit (DNAB) .... AMSU
Amphibious Maintenance Support Unit, Atlantic (DNAB) .... AMSULANT
Amphibious Maintenance Support Unit, Pacific (DNAB) .... AMSUPAC
Amphibious Objective Area [*Navy*] .... AOA
Amphibious Objective Study [*Navy*] .... AOS
Amphibious Operating Area .... AOA
Amphibious Operational Training Element .... AOTE
Amphibious Operational Training Unit [*Military*] (DNAB) .... AOTU
Amphibious Operations [*Navy*] (NVT) .... PHIBOPS
Amphibious Operations Officer [*British military*] (DMA) .... AOO
Amphibious Pionier Erkundungsfahrzeug [*Amphibious Engineer Reconnaissance Vehicle*] [*German*] (MCD) .... APE
Amphibious Planning (DOMA) .... AMPHIBPLN
Amphibious Raid Exercise [*Navy*] (NVT) .... PHIBRAIDEX
Amphibious Ready Group .... ARG
Amphibious Ready Group-Special Landing Force (DNAB) .... ARG-SLF
Amphibious Reconnaissance Exercise [*Navy*] (NVT) .... PHIBRECONEX
Amphibious Refresher Training [*Navy*] (CAAL) .... PHIBREFTRA
Amphibious Refresher Training [*Navy*] (NVT) .... PHIBRFT
Amphibious Research Craft .... ARC
Amphibious River Crossing Equipment [*Military*] .... ARCE
Amphibious Schoolship [*Navy*] (NVT) .... PHIBSS
Amphibious Ship, Dock .... LSD
Amphibious Ship Shakedown Cruise [*Navy*] (NVT) .... PHIBSKDN
Amphibious Ship, Tank .... LST
Amphibious Squadron [*Army*] .... PHIBRON
Amphibious Supply Platform [*Army*] .... ASP
Amphibious Support Battalion [*Military*] .... ASB
Amphibious Support Information System (NVT) .... ASIS
Amphibious Tank [*Military*] .... AMTANK
Amphibious Tank [*Military*] .... AMTK
Amphibious Tanker Terminal Facility [*Navy*] .... ATTF
Amphibious Task Force [*Navy*] (NVT) .... ATF
Amphibious Task Force [*Navy*] (NVT) .... PHIBTF
Amphibious Task Group/Marine Amphibious Brigade (DNAB) .... ATG/MAB
Amphibious Task Unit [*Military*] (DNAB) .... ATU
Amphibious Tractor Exercise [*Navy*] (NVT) .... TRACEX
Amphibious Training Base [*Navy*] .... ATB
Amphibious Training Base [*Navy*] .... PHIBTRABASE
Amphibious Training Base [*Navy*] .... PHIBTRBASE

Amphibious Training Command Liaison Officer [*Navy*] ... ATCLO
Amphibious Training Demonstrator ... ADT
Amphibious Training Exercise [*Navy*] (NVT) ... AMTREX
Amphibious Training Exercise [*Navy*] (NVT) ... PHIBTRAEX
Amphibious Training Unit, Royal Marines [*British*] ... ATURM
Amphibious Transport [*Navy ship symbol*] ... LPA
Amphibious Transport [*Navy*] ... PHIBTRANS
Amphibious Transport Dock [*Landing Platform, Dock*] [*Navy ship symbol*] ... LPD
Amphibious Transport (Small) [*Navy ship symbol*] ... LPR
Amphibious Transport Submarine [*Landing Platform, Submarine*] [*Navy ship symbol*] ... LPSS
Amphibious Truck, 2 1/2-ton Cargo ... DUKW
Amphibious Warfare [*Navy*] (NVT) ... AMW
Amphibious Warfare [*British military*] (DMA) ... AW
Amphibious Warfare Branch [*Navy*] (DNAB) ... AWB
Amphibious Warfare Communications [*Navy*] (MCD) ... AWC
Amphibious Warfare Lift Capability [*Navy*] (MCD) ... AMWL
Amphibious Warfare School (DNAB) ... AWS
Amphibious Warfare Training Center [*Navy*] ... PHIBWARTRACEN
Amphibious Warfare Working Party (NATG) ... AWWP
Amphibious Warping Tug [*Navy symbol*] ... LWT
Amphibole [*A mineral*] ... Amph
Amphicar Owners Club (EA) ... AOC
Amphion [*Record label*] [*France*] ... Amph
Amphipathic Alpha Helix [*Genetics*] ... AAH
Amphipathic Helix-Loop-Helix [*Genetics*] ... A-HLH
Amphiphilic Flavin [*Chemistry*] ... AF
Amphiregulin [*Biochemistry*] ... AR
Amphitheater (VRA) ... ampth
Amphitheatre (ROG) ... AMPHI
Amphitruo [*of Plautus*] [*Classical studies*] (OCD) ... Amph
Amphoric [*Sound*] [*Medicine*] (DAVI) ... amph
Amphotericin B [*Antifungal agent*] ... AMB
Amphotericin B Lipid Complex [*Antifungal*] ... ABLC
Amphotericin B Methyl Ester [*A drug*] ... AME
Amphotrophic Murine Leukemia Virus [*Medicine*] (DMAA) ... AmuLV
Ampicillin [*Also, AM, AMP*] [*Antibacterial compound*] ... A
Ampicillin [*Also, A, AMP*] [*Antibacterial compound*] ... AM
Ampicillin [*Also, A, AM*] [*Antibacterial compound*] ... AMP
Amplicon, Inc. [*NASDAQ symbol*] (NQ) ... AMPI
Amplicon, Inc. [*Associated Press*] (SAG) ... Amplcn
Amplidyne [*Electricity*] (KSC) ... ADYN
Amplidyne [*Electricity*] (SAA) ... AMP
Amplidyne [*Electricity*] ... AMPLDN
Amplidyne Generator [*Electricity*] ... AMPLG
Amplidyne Motor Generator [*Electricity*] ... AMPLMG
Amplification [*Medicine*] (DAVI) ... amp
Amplification by Stimulated Emission of Radiation ... ASER
Amplification Controlling Element [*Genetics*] ... ACE
Amplification Factor ... AF
Amplification Ratio (MCD) ... AR
Amplification Refractory Mutation System [*Biochemistry*] ... ARMS
Amplified ... AMPLFD
Amplified Automatic Level Control [*Air Force*] ... AALC
Amplified Failure or Unsatisfactory Report ... AFUR
Amplified Failure or Unsatisfactory Report [*Obsolete*] ... AMFUR
Amplified Fragment Length Polymorphism [*Also, Ampli FLP*] [*Genetics*] ... AFLP
Amplified Fragment Length Polymorphism [*Genetics*] ... AmpliFLP
Amplified Immunoradiometric Assay ... AMIRA
Amplified Response Spectrum [*Nuclear energy*] (NRCH) ... ARS
Amplified Spontaneous Emission (MCD) ... ASE
Amplified Stimulated Emission (PDAA) ... ASE
Amplified Substrate/Alkaline Phosphatase ... AS/AP
Amplifier ... A
Amplifier [*JETDS nomenclature*] [*Military*] (CET) ... AM
Amplifier (KSC) ... AMP
Amplifier (ODBW) ... amp
Amplifier [*Electronic*] (WDMC) ... amp
Amplifier (AAG) ... AMPL
Amplifier (IAA) ... AR
Amplifier and Switch Assembly (MCD) ... ASA
Amplifier Buffer Attenuator (MCD) ... ABA
Amplifier Detector ... AD
Amplifier Detector Assembly ... ADA
Amplifier Discriminator [*Instrumentation*] ... AD
Amplifier Input ... AI
Amplifier Open Loop Response ... AOLR
Amplifier Oscillator, Radiofrequency ... AORF
Amplifier Output [*Computer science*] ... AO
Amplifier Output Stage ... AOS
Amplifier Power Supply ... APS
Amplifier Subsystem (NASA) ... AMS
Amplifier Unit (OA) ... AU
Amplifier-Control Intercommunications (MCD) ... ACI
Amplifier-Controlled Euphonic [*Electronics*] (IAA) ... ACE
Amplifying Failure, Unsatisfactory, or Removal Report (MCD) ... AMPFUR
Amplitude [*Physics*] ... A
Amplitude ... AMP
Amplitude ... AMPL
Amplitude (FAAC) ... AMPLTD
Amplitude (MSA) ... AMPTD
Amplitude Absorption Coefficient ... AAC
Amplitude and Latency Measuring Instrument with Digital Output (MCD) ... ALMIDO
Amplitude and Rise Time Compensation (IEEE) ... ARC
Amplitude Companded Single Sideband [*Electronics*] ... ACSB
Amplitude Comparison Monopulse [*Electronics*] (IAA) ... ACM
Amplitude Gain Control ... AGC
Amplitude Keyed ... AK
Amplitude Limiter [*Electronics*] (OA) ... AL
Amplitude Miss Distance Acoustical Scoring System (MCD) ... AMASS
Amplitude Modulation [*Electronics*] ... AM
Amplitude Modulation, Double Sideband [*Electronics*] (HGAA) ... AM-DBS
Amplitude Modulation, Double Sideband [*Electronics*] ... AMDSB
Amplitude Modulation, Double Sideband, Suppressed Carrier [*Electronics*] (CET) ... AMDSB/SC
Amplitude Modulation Equivalent [*Telecommunications*] (TEL) ... AME
Amplitude Modulation Generator ... AMG
Amplitude Modulation Link Program ... AMLP
Amplitude Modulation, Single Sideband [*Electronics*] ... AMSSB
Amplitude Modulation, Single Sideband, Suppressed Carrier [*Electronics*] (CET) ... AMSSB/SC
Amplitude Modulator (IDOE) ... AM
Amplitude Noise Limiting ... ANL
Amplitude of Accommodation [*Ophthalmology*] ... AA
Amplitude Phase Conversion [*Telecommunications*] (OA) ... APC
Amplitude Phase Keyed [*Telecommunications*] (NITA) ... APK
Amplitude Phase Shift Keying (MCD) ... APK
Amplitude Probability Distribution [*Telecommunications*] ... APD
Amplitude Ratio Characteristic (PDAA) ... ARC
Amplitude Shift Keying ... ASK
Amplitude Spectral Density [*Physics*] ... ASD
Amplitude Vibration Exciter Control (PDAA) ... AVEC
Amplitude-Companded Single Sideband (DA) ... ACSSB
Amplitude-Frequency Characteristic [*Telecommunications*] (OA) ... AFC
Amplitude-Frequency Distortion ... AFD
Amplitude-Frequency Response [*Telecommunications*] (OA) ... AFR
Amplitude-Modulated Link [*Electronics*] ... AML
Amplitude-Modulated Transmitter [*Electronics*] ... AMT
Amplitude-Modulation Noise Level (IDOE) ... AMNL
Amplitude-Weighted Mean Velocity (DMAA) ... AWMV
Amplus [*Large*] [*Pharmacy*] (ROG) ... AMP
Amplus [*Large*] [*Pharmacy*] ... AMPL
Ampoule ... AM
Ampthill [*England*] ... AMPT
Ampule [*Pharmacy*] ... AMP
Ampule (DMAA) ... amp
Ampulla [*Ampule*] [*Pharmacy*] ... AMPUL
Ampullary-Isthmic Junction [*Anatomy*] ... AIJ
Amputation [*Medicine*] ... AMP
Amputee [*Orthopedics and rehabilitation*] (DAVI) ... amp
Amputee Shoe and Glove Exchange (EA) ... ASGE
Amputee Sports Association [*Defunct*] (EA) ... ASA
Amputee Sports Association of Australia ... ASAA
Amputees' Association of Victoria [*Australia*] ... AAV
Amputees in Motion (EA) ... AIM
Amqui, PQ [*AM radio station call letters*] ... CFVM
AMR American Eagle, Inc. [*ICAO designator*] (FAAC) ... EGF
AMR Combs, Inc. [*AMR Services, Inc.*] [*ICAO designator*] (FAAC) ... XAM
AMR Corp. [*NYSE symbol*] (SPSG) ... AMR
AMRE, Inc. [*NYSE symbol*] (SPSG) ... AMM
AMRE, Inc. [*Associated Press*] (SAG) ... Amre
Amrep Corp. [*Associated Press*] (SAG) ... Amrep
AMREP Corp. [*NYSE symbol*] (SPSG) ... AXR
AMRESCO INC. [*NASDAQ symbol*] (TTSB) ... AMMB
Amresco, Inc. [*NASDAQ symbol*] (SAG) ... AMMB
Amresco, Inc. [*Associated Press*] (SAG) ... Amresco
Amrinone [*Cardiotonic*] ... AMR
Amrinone [*Cardiotonic*] ... AR
Amrion, Inc. [*NASDAQ symbol*] (SAG) ... AMRI
Amrion, Inc. [*Associated Press*] (SAG) ... Amrion
Amritsar [*India*] [*Airport symbol*] (OAG) ... ATQ
Amritsar [*India*] [*ICAO location identifier*] (ICLI) ... VIAR
Amron Information Services (IID) ... AIS
AMS Press, Inc., New York, NY [*Library symbol Library of Congress*] (LCLS) ... AmS
AMSA, [*Acridinylamine Methanesulphon-M-Aniside*] **Prednisone, and Chlorambucil** [*Antineoplastic drug regimen*] ... APC
AMSAA [*Army Materiel Systems Analysis Agency*] **Evade Sustained Operations Performance Simulation** (MCD) ... AESOPS
AMSAA [*Army Materiel Systems Analysis Agency*] **Missile End Game Simulation** (MCD) ... AMEGS
AMSAA [*Army Materiel Systems Analysis Agency*]/RARDE Combat Simulation [*Royal Armament Research and Development Establishment*] (MCD) ... ARCS
AMSAA [*Army Materiel Systems Analysis Agency*] **Simulation Wargame** (MCD) ... AMSWAG
Amsacrine [*Medicine*] (BABM) ... AMSA
Amsacrine [*Also, M-AMSA*] [*Antineoplastic drug*] (CDI) ... AMSA
Amsacrine [*Antineoplastic drug*] [*Also, AMSA*] (CDI) ... m-AMSA
Amscan Holdings, Inc. [*Associated Press*] (SAG) ... Amscan
Amscan Holdings, Inc. [*NASDAQ symbol*] (SAG) ... AMSN
AMSCO International [*Associated Press*] (SAG) ... Amsco
AMSCO International [*NYSE symbol*] (SPSG) ... ASZ
Amsele [*Sweden ICAO location identifier*] (ICLI) ... ESUA
Amserv Healthcare [*NASDAQ symbol*] (TTSB) ... AMSR
AMSERV Healthcare, Inc. [*Associated Press*] (SAG) ... Amserv
Amserv Healthcare, Inc. [*NASDAQ symbol*] (NQ) ... AMSR
AmSouth Bancorp [*Associated Press*] (SAG) ... AmSouth
AmSouth Bancorp. [*NYSE symbol*] (SPSG) ... ASO
Amstar American Petroleum [*Vancouver Stock Exchange symbol*] ... AAP

Amstar Venture Corp. [*Vancouver Stock Exchange symbol*] ... AMV
Amsterdam [*Netherlands*] [*Airport symbol*] (OAG) ... AMS
Amsterdam (BARN) ... Amst
Amsterdam [*Netherlands ICAO location identifier*] (ICLI) ... EHAA
Amsterdam Center for Mathematics and Computer Sciences ... ACM
Amsterdam Free Library, Amsterdam, NY [*Library symbol Library of Congress*] (LCLS) ... NAms
Amsterdam Institute of Finance ... AIF
Amsterdam, NY [*FM radio station call letters*] ... WBKK
Amsterdam, NY [*AM radio station call letters*] ... WBUG
Amsterdam, NY [*AM radio station call letters*] ... WCSS
Amsterdam, NY [*Television station call letters*] ... WOCD
Amsterdam, Rotterdam, Antwerp ... ARA
Amsterdam/Schiphol [*Netherlands ICAO location identifier*] (ICLI) ... EHAM
Amsterdam-Rotterdam Bank ... AMRO
Amsterdam-Rotterdam Bank [*Netherlands*] ... Amrobank
Amtech Corp. [*NASDAQ symbol*] (NQ) ... AMTC
Amtech Corp. [*Associated Press*] (SAG) ... AmtchCp
Amtech Sys Wrrt [*NASDAQ symbol*] (TTSB) ... ASYSW
Amtech Systems [*Associated Press*] (SAG) ... Amtch
Amtech Systems [*NASDAQ symbol*] (TTSB) ... ASYS
Amtech Systems, Inc. [*Associated Press*] (SAG) ... Amtech
Amtech Systems, Inc. [*NASDAQ symbol*] (NQ) ... ASYS
Am-Timan [*Chad*] [*Airport symbol*] (AD) ... AMC
Am-Timan [*Chad*] [*ICAO location identifier*] (ICLI) ... FTTN
AMTRAK Commuter Services Corp. [*Later, CSC*] ... ACSC
Amtrak Historical Society (EA) ... AHS
AMTRAK Library, Washington, DC [*OCLC symbol*] (OCLC) ... ATK
AMTRAK Library, Washington, DC [*Library symbol Library of Congress*] (LCLS) ... DAmL
Amtran, Inc. [*NASDAQ symbol*] (SAG) ... AMTR
Amtran, Inc. [*Associated Press*] (SAG) ... Amtran
Amtrol, Inc. [*NASDAQ symbol*] (SAG) ... AMTL
AMTROL, Inc. [*NASDAQ symbol*] (TTSB) ... AMTL
Amtrol, Inc. [*Associated Press*] (SAG) ... Amtrol
AmTrust Capital [*NASDAQ symbol*] (TTSB) ... ATSB
AmTrust Capital Corp. [*Associated Press*] (SAG) ... AmTrst
AmTrust Capital Corp. [*NASDAQ symbol*] (SAG) ... ATSB
Amtsblatt [*Official Gazette*] [*German*] (DLA) ... ABL
Amtsgericht [*Inferior Court*] [*German*] ... AG
Amubri [*Costa Rica*] [*ICAO location identifier*] (ICLI) ... MRAM
Amulet Resources Corp. [*Vancouver Stock Exchange symbol*] ... AUO
Amur River and Basin [*MARC geographic area code Library of Congress*] (LCCP) ... aa----
Amuraviatrans [*Former USSR*] [*FAA designator*] (FAAC) ... AAX
Amusement ... AMUSE
Amusement and Music Operators Association (EA) ... AMOA
Amusement and Vending Machine Distributors Association (EA) ... AVMDA
Amusement Caterers' Association [*British*] (BI) ... ACA
Amusement Game Manufacturers Association [*Later, AAMA*] (EA) ... AGMA
Amusement Machine Operators' Association [*Australia*] ... AMOA
Amusement Park Club International [*Defunct*] (EA) ... APCI
Amusement Parks and Arcades [*Public-performance tariff class*] [*British*] ... AP
Amusement Trades Association [*British*] (BI) ... ATA
Amusement Trades Exhibition International [*British*] (ITD) ... ATEI
Amusement with Prizes [*Pinball machines*] [*British*] ... AWP
AmVestors Financial [*Associated Press*] (SAG) ... Amvst
AmVestors Financial Co. [*NYSE symbol*] (SAG) ... AMV
AmVestors Financial Co. [*Associated Press*] (SAG) ... AmvestF
AmVestors Finl [*NYSE symbol*] (TTSB) ... AMV
AmVestors Fin'l Wrrt [*NASDAQ symbol*] (TTSB) ... AMVWW
AMVETS Auxiliary (EA) ... AA
Amway Asia Pacific [*NYSE symbol*] (SPSG) ... AAP
Amway Asia Pacific [*Associated Press*] (SAG) ... AmwyAs
Amway Japan Ltd. [*NYSE symbol*] (SAG) ... AJL
Amway Japan Ltd. [*Associated Press*] (SAG) ... AmwyJ
Amway Japan LtduADS [*NYSE symbol*] (TTSB) ... AJL
Amwest Insur Group [*AMEX symbol*] (TTSB) ... AMW
Amwest Insurance Group, Inc. [*AMEX symbol*] (SPSG) ... AMW
Amwest Insurance Group, Inc. [*Associated Press*] (SAG) ... AMwest
AMX Corp. [*Associated Press*] (SAG) ... AMXCo
AMX Corp. [*NASDAQ symbol*] (SAG) ... AMXX
Amygdala Pars Lateralis [*Neuroanatomy*] ... APL
Amygdala Pars Medialis [*Neuroanatomy*] ... APM
Amygdaloid Complex (PDAA) ... AC
Amygdalus [*Almond*] [*Pharmacology*] (ROG) ... AMYGD
Amyl [*Organic chemistry*] ... Am
Amyl Acetate [*Organic chemistry*] ... AMA
Amylas [*An enzyme*] (DAVI) ... AMY
Amylas Urine Spot [*Test*] [*Gastroenterology*] (DAVI) ... AMY-SP
Amylase [*An enzyme*] (MAE) ... AMS
Amylase [*An enzyme*] ... AMY
Amylase [*An enzyme*] (DAVI) ... AMYLAS
Amylase Clearance [*Biochemistry*] (DAVI) ... C_{am}
Amylase Inhibitor Activity [*Food technology*] ... AIA
Amylin Pharmaceuticals [*NASDAQ symbol*] (SPSG) ... AMLN
Amylin Pharmaceuticals, Inc. [*Associated Press*] (SAG) ... Amylin
Amyloglucosidase [*An enzyme*] ... AMG
Amyloid Beta Protein Precursor [*Biochemistry*] ... ABPP
Amyloid Enhancing Factor [*Biochemistry*] (DMAA) ... AEF
Amyloid of Immunoglobulin Origin [*Medicine*] ... AIO
Amyloid of Unknown Origin [*Medicine*] ... AUO
Amyloid Pack Core [*Pathology*] ... APC
Amyloid Precursor Protein Secretase [*Medicine*] (DMAA) ... APPS
Amyloid Precursor-Like Protein [*Medicine*] (DMAA) ... APLP
Amyloid Protein [*Biochemistry*] ... AP
Amyloid Protein Precursor [*Biochemistry*] ... APP
Amyloid Substance [*Medicine*] ... AS
Amyloid-A-Degrading Protease [*An enzyme*] ... AADP
Amyloid-Associated [*Protein*] [*Medicine*] ... AA
Amyloid-Associated Protein [*Biochemistry*] (DAVI) ... AA
Amyloplast Pressure Index [*Botany*] ... API
Amyltrichlorosilane [*Organic chemistry*] ... AMTCS
Amyotrophic Cerebellar Hypoplasia [*Medicine*] (DMAA) ... ACH
Amyotrophic Lateral Sclerosis [*Medicine*] ... ALS
Amyotrophic Lateral Sclerosis Association (EA) ... ALSA
Amyotrophic Lateral Sclerosis/Parkinsonism-Dementia [*Medicine*] ... ALS/P-D
Amyotrophic Lateral Sclerosis Society of America (EA) ... ALSSOA
Amyotrophic Lateral Sclerosis Society of Canada ... ALSSOC
AN [*Army-Navy*] **and MS Manual** [*Manufacturing Status*] (AAG) ... AAMM
An Chomhairle Ealaion [*Arts Council*] (EAIO) ... ACE
An Comhairle Oiliuna (ACII) ... AnCO
An Comunn Gaidhealach [*The Highland Association*] (EA) ... ACG
An Foras Forbartha [*National Institute for Physical Planning and ConstructionResearch*] [*Ireland*] [*Research center*] (IRC) ... AFF
An Foras Taluntais [*Agricultural Institute*] [*Ireland*] [*Research center*] (IRC) ... AFT
An Gluaiseacht Eireannach in Aghaidh Apartheid [*Irish Anti-Apartheid Movement*] (EAIO) ... AGEAA
An Oige [*The Irish Youth Hostels Association*] [*Founded in 1931*] ... O
An Old Bachelor [*Pseudonym used by William Lloyd Garrison Acronym also facetiously translated as "Ass, Oaf, and Blockhead"*] ... AOB
An Party Kenethlegek Kernow (EA) ... APKK
An Seni Respublica Gerenda Sit [*of Plutarch*] [*Classical studies*] (OCD) ... An Seni
Ana [*Of Each*] [*Pharmacy*] ... A
Ana [*Of Each*] [*Pharmacy*] ... AA
Ana G. Mendez Educational Foundation ... AGMEF
Ana Maria [*Ecuador*] [*ICAO location identifier*] (ICLI) ... SEAN
Ana Partes [*Equal Parts*] [*Latin*] ... aa
Anaa [*French Polynesia*] [*ICAO location identifier*] (ICLI) ... NTGA
ANAADIGICS Inc. [*NASDAQ symbol*] (TTSB) ... ANAD
Anabasis [*of Xenophon*] [*Classical studies*] (OCD) ... An
Anabasis [*of Arrian*] [*Classical studies*] (OCD) ... Anab
Anabolism-Promoting Factor (MAE) ... APF
Anacapa Island [*California*] [*Seismograph station code, US Geological Survey*] (SEIS) ... AIC
Anacharsis [*of Lucian*] [*Classical studies*] (OCD) ... Anach
Anachronism ... ANAC
Anaco [*Venezuela*] [*Airport symbol*] (OAG) ... AAO
Anaco, Anzoategui [*Venezuela ICAO location identifier*] (ICLI) ... SVAN
Anacomp, Inc. [*NYSE symbol*] (SPSG) ... AAC
Anacomp, Inc. [*Associated Press*] (SAG) ... Anacmp
Anacomp, Inc. [*Associated Press*] (SAG) ... Ancmp
Anacomp, Inc. [*NASDAQ symbol*] (SAG) ... ANCO
Anaconda American Brass Co., Waterbury, CT [*Library symbol Library of Congress*] (LCLS) ... CtWAB
Anaconda, MT [*FM radio station call letters*] ... KGLM
Anacortes Public Library, Anacortes, WA [*Library symbol Library of Congress*] (LCLS) ... WaAn
Anacortes, WA [*AM radio station call letters*] ... KLKI
Anacreon [*Greek poet, 527-488BC*] [*Classical studies*] (OCD) ... Anac
Anacreon [*Greek poet, 572-488BC*] [*Classical studies*] (ROG) ... ANACR
Anadarko, OK [*AM radio station call letters*] ... KRPT
Anadarko, OK [*FM radio station call letters*] ... KRPT-FM
Anadarko Petroleum [*Associated Press*] (SAG) ... Anadrk
Anadarko Petroleum [*NYSE symbol*] (SPSG) ... APC
Anadigics, Inc. [*NASDAQ symbol*] (SAG) ... ANAD
Anadigics, Inc. [*Associated Press*] (SAG) ... Anadigc
Anadromous Fish Conservation Act [*1965*] ... AFCA
Anaelectrodiabatic [*Nuclear wave*] ... AED
Anaerobe [*Biochemistry*] (DAVI) ... ANAERO
Anaerobic Attached-Film Expanded-Bed [*For treating wastewater*] ... AAFEB
Anaerobic Bacterial Flora [*Microbiology*] ... ABF
Anaerobic Broth Disk (PDAA) ... AnBD
Anaerobic Threshold ... AT
Anaerobic Upflow Fixed-Film Process [*For treating wastewater*] ... ANFLOW
Anaerobically Digested Municipal Sewage Solids [*Culture medium*] ... AD-MSS
Anaerobically Thioglycolate Broth Disk (PDAA) ... AnTBD
Anaesthesia [*or Anaesthetic*] (ADA) ... ANAES
Anaesthesia [*or Anaesthetic*] (ADA) ... ANAESTH
Anaesthesia Literature Abstracting Retrieval Method [*American Society of Anesthesiologists*] (NITA) ... ALARM
Anaesthetic ... An
Anaesthetic Research Society (EAIO) ... ARS
Anaesthetics [*Medical Officer designation*] [*British*] ... A
Anaesthetist (ADA) ... ANAES
Anaesthetist (ADA) ... ANAESTH
Anagram (ADA) ... ANAG
Anagrapha Falcifera Nuclear Polyhedrosis ... AfNPV
Anaheim, CA [*Location identifier FAA*] (FAAL) ... ANA
Anaheim, CA [*Television station call letters*] ... KDOC
Anaheim, CA [*FM radio station call letters*] ... KEZY
Anaheim, CA [*AM radio station call letters*] ... KORG
Anaheim Public Library, Anaheim, CA [*Library symbol Library of Congress*] (LCLS) ... CAna
Anahuac, TX [*Location identifier FAA*] (FAAL) ... CBC
Anair - Anich Airways [*Croatia*] [*ICAO designator*] (FAAC) ... ANH
Anaktuvuk Pass [*Alaska*] [*Airport symbol*] (OAG) ... AKP
Anal Fin Base [*Fish anatomy*] ... AFB
Anal Intraepithelial Neoplasia [*Oncology*] ... AIN
Anal Pore ... AP

Anal Sphincter [*Anatomy*]	AS
Analalava [*Madagascar*] [*ICAO location identifier*] (ICLI)	FMNL
Analalava [*Madagascar*] [*Airport symbol*] (OAG)	HVA
Analcime [*A zeolite*]	ANA
Analgesic [*Medicine*]	ANAL
Analgesic Abuse Nephropathy [*Medicine*] (DAVI)	AAN
Analgesic Dose	AD
Analgesic-Associated Nephropathy [*Medicine*]	AAN
Analog	A
Analog (NASA)	ANL
Analog (MSA)	ANLG
Analog	ANLG
Analog Alarm Section	AAS
Analog and Digital Monitoring System [*Computer science*] (MCD)	ADMS
Analog & Digital Peripherals, Inc. (PCM)	ADPI
Analog and Discrete Output (MCD)	A & DO
Analog Antenna Positioner	AAP
Analog Autopilot (KSC)	AAP
Analog Circuit Analysis and Partitioning System [*Computer science*]	ACAPS
Analog Command Module [*Computer science*] (NITA)	ACM
Analog Computer (AAG)	AC
Analog Computer	ANACOM
Analog Computer Facility	ACF
Analog Computer Subsystem	ACSS
Analog Computer System	ACS
Analog Computer Translator	ACTRAN
Analog Concept Learning System (PDAA)	ACLS
Analog Conditioning and Test System	ACTS
Analog Control Technology [*Computer science*]	ACT
Analog Data Acquisition Module	ADAM
Analog Data Aquisition System	ADAS
Analog Data Digitizer	ADD
Analog Data Distributor and Control [*Computer science*] (KSC)	ADDAC
Analog Data Handling Assembly (IAA)	ADHA
Analog Data Handling System (AAG)	ADHS
Analog Data Recorder Transcriber	ADRT
Analog Data Reduction System (CAAL)	ADAR
Analog Delay Unit	ADU
Analog Device [*Computer science*] (IAA)	AD
Analog Devices [*NYSE symbol*] (SAG)	ADI
Analog Devices, Inc. [*Associated Press*] (SAG)	Analog
Analog Digital/Digital Analog (RDA)	AD/DA
Analog Display Indicator (MCD)	ADI
Analog Display Services Interface [*Interactive television technology*] (PS)	ADSI
Analog Display Unit	ADU
Analog Divider [*Electronics*] (ECII)	AD
Analog Drive Assembly (MCD)	ADA
Analog Electronic Computer	AEC
Analog Event Distribution System [*Computer science*] (MCD)	AEDS
Analog Event Distributor [*Computer science*] (MCD)	AED
Analog Event System [*Computer science*] (MCD)	AES
Analog Facility Terminal [*Computer science*] (TEL)	AFT
Analog Factor Calibration Network	AFCAN
Analog Filter Assembly (MCD)	AFA
Analog Fly by Wire [*Aviation*]	AFBW
Analog Function Control [*Electronics*] (ECII)	AFC
Analog Function Generator	AFG
Analog Ground Bus	AGBUS
Analog Hybrid (OA)	AH
Analog Input	AI
Analog Input [*Electronics*] (ECII)	AIN
Analog Input Differential (MCD)	AID
Analog Input Module [*Computer science*]	AIM
Analog Input/Output Board [*Computer science*] (NITA)	AIB
Analog Input/Output Board [*Computer science*] (NITA)	AIO
Analog Input/Output Package [*Computer science*]	AIOP
Analog Input System	AIS
Analog Instrumentation Subsystem	AIS
Analog Interlock [*Electronics*] (ECII)	AINL
Analog Junction (TEL)	AJ
Analog Junction Module (TEL)	AJM
Analog Line Driver [*Computer science*] (BUR)	ALD
Analog Line Termination Subsystem [*Telecommunications*] (TEL)	ALTS
Analog Link [*Telecommunications*] (TEL)	AL
Analog Loop-Back [*Telecommunications*] (TEL)	AL
Analog Major Alarm (MCD)	AMA
Analog Matched Filter	AMF
Analog Mobile Phone System (PS)	AMPS
Analog Module [*Telecommunications*] (TEL)	AM
Analog Monitor Module [*Computer science*]	AMM
Analog Monolithic [*Electronics*] (OA)	AM
Analog Multiplexer Quantitizer [*Computer science*] (KSC)	AMQ
Analog Multiplier Unit (ECII)	AMU
Analog Number Identification [*Electronics*] (ECII)	ANI
Analog/Output	A/O
Analog Output [*Computer science*] (NASA)	AO
Analog Output Differential [*Computer science*] (MCD)	AOD
Analog Output Submodule (SAA)	AOS
Analog Panel Meter (IEEE)	APM
Analog Parameter Record (IAA)	APR
Analog Phased Processing Loop Equipment [*Computer science*] (MHDB)	APPLE
Analog Phased-Locked Loop (PDAA)	APLL
Analog Pressure Transducer	APT
Analog Private Line [*Telecommunications*] (ACRL)	APL
Analog Process Variable Measurement [*Process control*]	APVM
Analog Processing Unit [*Computer science*] (NITA)	APU
Analog Program Tape [*Computer science*]	APT
Analog Programming and Checking [*Computer science*]	APACHE
Analog Programming and Checking [*Computer science*]	APACHE
Analog RADAR Absorber	ARA
Analog RADAR Signal Processor (MCD)	ARSP
Analog Random Access Memory [*Computer science*] (HGAA)	ARAM
Analog Recording Dynamic Analyzer [*Computer science*]	ARDA
Analog Recording System	ARS
Analog Recurrent Neural Network [*Computer science*]	ARNN
Analog Recursive Computer (IAA)	ARC
Analog Remote Unit (MCD)	ARU
Analog Response Conditioner (MCD)	ARC
Analog Response Unit	ARU
Analog Rod Position Indicator [*Electronics*] (IAA)	ARPI
Analog Rotation Speed Control	ARSC
Analog Schematic Translator to Algebraic Language [*Computer science*] (MHDB)	ASTRAIL
Analog Schematic Translator to Algebraic Language [*Computer science*] (IEEE)	ASTRAL
Analog Science Fiction and Fact [*A publication*] (BRI)	Analog
Analog Select Keyboard [*Computer science*] (KSC)	ASK
Analog Self-Checking Automatic Tester	ASCAT
Analog Shift Register [*Computer science*]	ASR
Analog Signal Converter	ASC
Analog Signal Correlator	ASC
Analog Signal to Discrete Time Interval Converter [*NASA*]	ASDTIC
Analog Simulation System	ASS
Analog Simulator (MHDB)	ANSIM
Analog Stimulus Unit	ASU
Analog Strip Chart	ASC
Analog Strip Chart Recorder	ASCR
Analog Switching Subsystem [*Telecommunications*] (NITA)	ASS
Analog System Assembly Pack	ASAP
Analog Tape Recorder	ATR
Analog Technology Co.	ATC
Analog Threshold Logic	ATL
Analog to Frequency Converter	AFC
Analog to Pressure Converter	APC
Analog to Time (MCD)	A/T
Analog to Time to Digital [*Computer science*]	ATD
Analog Tone Signal (MCD)	ATS
Analog Translator [*Computer science*]	ANATRAN
Analog Tree-Organized Multiplexer	ATOM
Analog Tune in Progress (IAA)	ATIP
Analog Video Bandwidth	AVB
Analog Video Tape Recorder (MCD)	AVTR
Analog-Digital Automatic Program (DNAB)	ADAP
Analog-Digital Automatic Program Tester [*Computer science*]	ADAPT
Analog-Digital Converter (NITA)	ADCVR
Analog-Digital Input/Output System [*Computer science*]	ADIOS
Analog-Digital Integrating Translator [*Computer science*]	ADIT
Analog-Digital Recorder [*Computer science*]	ADR
Analog-Digital-Analog (IAA)	ADA
Analog-Digital-Designer [*Trademark*]	ADD
Analog-Discrete Data Converter [*Computer science*] (MCD)	ADDC
Analogic Corp. [*NASDAQ symbol*] (NQ)	ALOG
Analogic Corp. [*NASDAQ symbol*] (TTSB)	ALOG
Analogic Corp. [*Associated Press*] (SAG)	Anlogic
Analogical Circuit Technique (PDAA)	ACT
Analog-In Single-Ended (MCD)	AIS
Analogous (MSA)	ANLGS
Analogous Random Process (PDAA)	ARP
Analog-to-Digital (IDOE)	a/d
Analog-to-Digital (IDOE)	A/D
Analog-to-Digital [*Converter*] [*Computer science*] (AFM)	A-to-D
Analog-to-Digital [*Converter*] [*Computer science*]	A-to-D
Analog-to-Digital Computer [*Computer science*] (MCD)	ADC
Analog-to-Digital Conversion System [*Computer science*]	ADIC
Analog-to-Digital Converter [*Computer science*] (DOM)	A/D converter
Analog-to-Digital Converter (IDOE)	adc
Analog-to-Digital Converter [*Computer science*] (MUGU)	ADC
Analog-to-Digital Converter [*Computer science*]	ADCON
Analog-to-Digital Data Converter [*Computer science*] (MCD)	ADDC
Analog-to-Digital Data Recording System [*Computer science*] (IEEE)	ADRS
Analog-to-Digital Data Reduction System for Oceanographic Research	ADDRESOR
Analog-to-Digital-to-Analog Converter (IAA)	ADAC
Analog-to-Pulse Duration	APD
Analog-to-Pulse Width Converter	A/PW
Analog-to-Stochastic Converter (IAA)	ASC
Analogue/Digital/Analogue Process and Test System (PDAA)	ADAPTS
Analogue Large Scale Integration (NITA)	ALSI
Analogue Simulation of Competitive Operational Tactics [*Game*]	ASCOT
Analogy	ANAL
Analogy, Inc. [*Associated Press*] (SAG)	Analogy
Analogy, Inc. [*NASDAQ symbol*] (SAG)	ANLG
Analogy Inc. [*NASDAQ symbol*] (TTSB)	ANLG
Analysis (IAA)	A
Analysis (AABC)	ANAL
Analysis	ANALYS
Analysis	ANLY
Analysis	ANLYS
Analysis (FAAC)	ANLYS

Analysis Alarm [*Engineering*] ... AA
Analysis and Computation Division [*National Range Operations Directorate*] [*White Sands Missile Range, NM*] ... ACD
Analysis and Control Element [*Army*] ... ACE
Analysis and Digest of the Decisions of Sir George Jessel, by A. P Peter [*England*] [*A publication*] (DLA) ... Jes
Analysis and Digest of the Decisions of Sir George Jessel, by A. P. Peter [*England*] [*A publication*] (DLA) ... Peter
Analysis and Evaluation ... A & E
Analysis and Evaluation Division [*Environmental Protection Agency*] (GFGA) ... AED
Analysis and Evaluation Staff [*Environmental Protection Agency*] (GFGA) ... AES
Analysis and Forecasting, Inc. [*Database producer*] (IID) ... A & F
Analysis and Forecasting Mode ... AFM
Analysis and Information Branch [*Climate Analysis Center*] [*National Weather Service*] ... AIB
Analysis and Prediction [*Program*] [*Marine science*] (OSRA) ... A&P
Analysis and Prediction [*Program*] (USDC) ... A&P
Analysis and Production (MCD) ... AAP
Analysis and Program for Calculation of Optimum Propellant Performance for Liquid and Solid Rocket Fuels ... APCOPPLSRF
Analysis and Research of Methods for Management ... ARMM
Analysis and Simulation Tool for Resource Allocation (MCD) ... ASTRA
Analysis and Support Division [*Environmental Protection Agency*] (GFGA) ... ASD
Analysis & Technology [*NASDAQ symbol*] (TTSB) ... AATL
Analysis & Technology, Inc. [*NASDAQ symbol*] (NQ) ... AATI
Analysis & Technology, Inc. [*Associated Press*] (SAG) ... AnalyTc
Analysis/Architecture (SSD) ... A/A
Analysis Bar Charting (PDAA) ... ABC
Analysis by Synthesis (PDAA) ... AbS
Analysis Computer System ... ACS
Analysis Console (MCD) ... AC
Analysis Control Routine [*Computer science*] (OA) ... ACRT
Analysis Control Unit ... ACU
Analysis Coordination Element ... ACE
Analysis, Design, and Evaluation System (MCD) ... ADES
Analysis Division (ACII) ... AD
Analysis for Forces Objectives and Resources Determination (MCD) ... AFFORD
Analysis - Forcast Transport and Diffusion [*Marine science*] (OSRA) ... AFTAD
Analysis of Accounts ... A/A
Analysis of Automatic Line Insulation Test [*Bell System*] ... ANALIT
Analysis of Capabilities, Opportunities, and Prospects ... ACOP
Analysis of Coping Style [*Test*] ... ACS
Analysis of Covariance ... ANCOVA
Analysis of Critical Actions Program (SAA) ... ACAP
Analysis of Digitized Seismic Signals [*Computer science*] ... ADSS
Analysis of Dynamical Systems Online [*Computer science*] (MHDI) ... ADSOL
Analysis of Intelligence (MCD) ... ANALIT
Analysis of Interconnected Decision Areas [*Business term*] (PDAA) ... AIDA
Analysis of Internal Management Systems ... AIMS
Analysis of Large Data Sets [*Computer science*] (MHDB) ... ALDS
Analysis of Large Plastic Incremental Deformation (MCD) ... ALPID
Analysis of Linear Electronic Circuits (MHDI) ... ALEC
Analysis of Local Oriented Edges [*Cancer technology*] ... ALOE
Analysis of Longwall Pillar Stability [*Computer program*] [*US Bureau of Mines*] ... ALPS
Analysis of Means (PDAA) ... ANOM
Analysis of Military Organizational Effectiveness (MCD) ... AMORE
Analysis of Multiple Source Obscurants on Realistic Battlefield (MCD) ... AMSORB
Analysis of Pacific Area Communications for Hardening to Electromagnetic Pulse ... APACHE
Analysis of Packing Methods for Ammunition Storage and Transportation (MCD) ... APMAST
Analysis of Random Data [*System documentation*] [*Oregon State University*] ... ARAND
Analysis of Real-Time Systems / Data Base Oriented Systems (MHDI) ... ARTS/DB
Analysis of Spare Parts Change (MCD) ... ASPC
Analysis of Tactical Single Channel Net Radios (MCD) ... ATACNET
Analysis of Variance ... ANOV
Analysis of Variance ... ANOVA
Analysis of Variance (OA) ... AOV
Analysis Package (MHDI) ... ANAPAC
Analysis Production Persistency [*LIMRA*] ... APP
Analysis Program Linear Active Circuits (NASA) ... APLAC
Analysis, Refinement, and Extension of Nuclear Methodology [*Military*] ... ARENUM
Analysis, Requirements Determination, Design and Development, and Implementationand Evaluation (MHDB) ... ARDI
Analysis System for Static and Dynamic Problems (MCD) ... ANSYS
Analysis Time ... AT
Analysis-Forecast Transport and Diffusion (USDC) ... AFTAI
Analyst (DAVI) ... anal
Analyst ... ANLS
Analyst ... ANLYST
Analyst Capability ... ACAP
Analyst [*Information or Intelligence*] **Display and Exploitation System** ... AIDES
Analyst Intelligence Data System (MCD) ... AIDS
Analysts International Corp. [*Associated Press*] (SAG) ... Analysts
Analysts International Corp. [*NASDAQ symbol*] (NQ) ... ANLY
Analysts Intl. [*NASDAQ symbol*] (TTSB) ... ANLY
Analyst-to-Analyst Communications Service (MCD) ... ATACS
Analyst-to-Analyst Exchange Message Format (MCD) ... ANEX
Analytic ... ANLYTC
Analytic Approximation Theory [*Physics*] (OA) ... AAT
Analytic [*or Analytical*] **Chemist** ... AC
Analytic Decisions Corp. [*Information service or system*] (IID) ... ADC
Analytic Drag Control [*Aviation*] (NASA) ... ADC
Analytic Element Method ... AEM
Analytic Ephemeris Generator ... AEG
Analytic Hierarchy Process ... AHP
Analytic Intelligence Test [*Psychology*] ... AIT
Analytic Language Manipulation System ... ALMS
Analytic Learning Disability Assessment [*Child development test*] ... ALDA
Analytic Methodology for System Evaluation and Control [*Army*] ... AMSEC
Analytic Mission Reliability (MCD) ... AMR
Analytic Orbit Determination Program (MCD) ... ANODE
Analytic Plotter Coordinagraph [*Geoscience*] ... APC
Analytic Processing Unit ... APU
Analytic Reaction (AAMN) ... AR
[*The*] **Analytic Sciences Corp.** ... TASC
Analytic Services, Inc. ... ANSER
Analytic Solution to Queues (MHDI) ... ASQ
Analytic Trouble Shooting (MHDB) ... ATS
Analytica Chimica Acta [*A publication*] ... ACA
Analytica Posteriora [*of Aristotle*] [*Classical studies*] (OCD) ... An Post
Analytica Priora [*of Aristotle*] [*Classical studies*] (OCD) ... An Pr
Analytical ... ANLYTCL
Analytical Abstracts Online [*Royal Society of Chemistry*] [*Information service or system*] (CRD) ... AA
Analytical and Computer Laboratory ... ACL
Analytical Assessments Corp. (MCD) ... AAC
Analytical Calibration Curve ... ACC
Analytical Chemistry and Applied Spectroscopy (MUGU) ... ACAS
Analytical Chemistry by Open Learning [*A publication*] ... ACOL
Analytical Chemistry Laboratory [*Department of Energy*] ... ACL
Analytical Computer Program ... ACP
Analytical Condition Inspection [*Air Force*] (MCD) ... ACI
Analytical Condition Inspection Program [*Air Force*] (MCD) ... ACIP
Analytical Control and Data (MHDB) ... ANACONDA
Analytical Determination of the Values of Information to Combat Effectiveness (PDAA) ... ADVICE
Analytical Development Corp. ... ADC
Analytical Electron Microscope [*or Microscopy*] (DAVI) ... AEM
Analytical Electron Microscopy ... AEM
Analytical Grade [*Organic chemistry*] ... AG
[*An*] **Analytical Information Management System** (HGAA) ... AAIMS
Analytical Instrument Development, Inc. ... AID
Analytical Isoelectrofocusing Scanning Apparatus [*Analytical chemistry*] ... AISA
Analytical Laboratory (NRCH) ... AL
Analytical Laboratory Managers Association (EA) ... ALMA
Analytical Letters [*A publication*] ... AL
Analytical Limits (NRCH) ... AL
Analytical Liquid Chromatograph ... ALC
Analytical Maintenance Program [*Navy*] (NVT) ... AMP
Analytical Methodology Information Center [*Environmental Protection Agency*] ... AMIC
Analytical Methods, Inc. ... AMI
Analytical Mode for Performing Logistic Evaluation (DNAB) ... AMPLE
Analytical Nuclear Casualty Estimation Technique (PDAA) ... ANCET
Analytical Photogrammetric Positioning System (MCD) ... APPS
Analytical Photogrammetric Positioning System - II ... APPS II
Analytical Photogrammetric Processing System (MCD) ... APPS
Analytical Procedures Subsystem (MCD) ... APS
Analytical Processing for Improved Composite (MCD) ... APIC
Analytical Profile Index [*Microbiology*] ... API
Analytical Psychology ... AP
Analytical Psychology Club of New York (EA) ... APCNY
Analytical Quality Control Laboratory (IID) ... AQCL
Analytical Reagent [*Chemistry*] ... AR
Analytical Reports Gathering and Updating System [*Navy*] (NG) ... ARGUS
Analytical Research and Development Unit [*British*] ... ARDU
Analytical Results Database ... ARDB
Analytical Rework Program [*Navy*] (NG) ... ARP
Analytical Satellite Orbit Predictor (MCD) ... ASOP
Analytical Scanning Electron Microscope ... ASEM
Analytical Services Progam ... ASP
Analytical Solution of Groups [*Thermodynamics*] ... ASOG
Analytical Stereoplotter (DNAB) ... AS
Analytical Studies of Surface Effects of Submerged Submarines [*Navy*] (DNAB) ... ASSES
Analytical Studies of Surface Effects of Submerged Submarines [*Navy*] ... ASSESS
Analytical Surveys [*NASDAQ symbol*] (TTSB) ... ANLT
Analytical Surveys, Inc. [*NASDAQ symbol*] (NQ) ... ANLT
Analytical Surveys, Inc. [*Associated Press*] (SAG) ... AnlySur
Analytical Technology Applications Corp. ... ATAC
Analytical Transient One-, Two-, and Three-Dimensional Model ... AT123D
Analytical Transmission Electron Microscope ... ATEM
Analytical Tree [*Method used to analyze and design physical security for facilities*] [*Military*] (RDA) ... AT
Analytical Ultracentrifugation [*Separation science*] ... AU
Analyze (MSA) ... ANALY
Analyzer ... ANLYZ
Analyzer for FORTRAN [*Formula Translation*] **Incremental Reengineering Methodology** ... AFFIRM
Analyzer Unit (CAAL) ... AU
Analyzer-Recorder-Controller ... ARC
Anamilo Club of Detroit [*Michigan*] (EA) ... ACD

Anamosa Eureka, Anamosa, IA [Library symbol Library of Congress]
(LCLS) ..... IaAnaE
Anamosa, IA [AM radio station call letters] ..... KLEH
Anamosa Journal, Anamosa, IA [Library symbol Library of Congress]
(LCLS) ..... IaAnaJ
Anamosa Public Library, Anamosa, IA [Library symbol Library of Congress]
(LCLS) ..... IaAna
Ananda Marga (EA) ..... AM
Ananda Marga Universal Relief Team [India] ..... AMURT
Ananda Marga Women's Center [Australia] ..... AMWC
Ananeotiko Demokratiko Socialistiko Kinema [Democratic Socialist Reform
Movement] [Cyprus] [Political party] (EY) ..... ADISOK
Anangel American Shipholdings Ltd. [Associated Press] (SAG) ..... Anangel
Anangel American Shipholdings Ltd. [NASDAQ symbol] (SAG) ..... ASIP
Anangel-Amer Shiphldgs ADS [NASDAQ symbol] (TTSB) ..... ASIPY
Anaphase-Promoting Complex [Cytology] ..... APC
Anaphylactoid Purpura [Medicine] ..... AP
Anaphylactoid Reaction [Immunology] ..... AR
Anaphylatoxin [Immunology] ..... AT
Anaphylaxis [Medicine] ..... A
Anaplastic Lymphoma Kinase [An enzyme] ..... ALK
Anapolis [Brazil] [Airport symbol] (AD) ..... APS
Anapolis (Base Aerea) [Brazil ICAO location identifier] (ICLI) ..... SBAN
Anar [Iran] [ICAO location identifier] (ICLI) ..... OIKE
[The] Anarchiad [American satirical epic poem, 1786-1787] ..... Anarch
Anarchist Association of the Americas [Defunct] (EA) ..... AAA
Anarchist Federation [British] ..... AF
Anarchist Federation of Britain ..... AFB
Anarchist Red Cross ..... ARC
Anarchist-Communist Federation of North America [Canada] ..... ACFNA
Anaren Microwave [NASDAQ symbol] (TTSB) ..... ANEN
Anaren Microwave, Inc. [Associated Press] (SAG) ..... Anaren
Anaren Microwave, Inc. [NASDAQ symbol] (NQ) ..... ANEN
Anastomosis [Medicine] (MAE) ..... anast
Anastomosis Group [Plant pathology] ..... AG
Anatech International Corp. [La Jolla, CA] ..... ANA
Anatom [Vanuatu] [ICAO location identifier] (ICLI) ..... NVVA
Anatomic [Anatomy] (DAVI) ..... an
Anatomic Porous Replacement [Orthopedics] (DAVI) ..... APR
Anatomic Shunt Flow [Medicine] (DAVI) ..... Qsan
Anatomical Dead Space (DAVI) ..... ADS
Anatomical Society of Great Britain and Ireland (DAVI) ..... ASGB
Anatomical Society of Great Britain and Ireland ..... ASGBI
Anatomie [Anatomy] [German] ..... Anat
Anatomische Gesellschaft [Anatomical Society] [Germany] (EAIO) ..... AG
Anatomy [or Anatomical] ..... ANAT
Anatuberculin, Pertragnani's Integral [Pharmacology] (DAVI) ..... AIP
Anatuberculin, Petragnani's Integral [Medicine] (BABM) ..... AIP
Anatuberculina Diagnostica Petragnani [Petragnani Diagnostic Anatuberculin]
[Medicine] ..... ADP
Anavatan Partisi [Motherland Parties] (EAIO) ..... AP
Anax Aviation [France ICAO designator] (FAAC) ..... ANX
ANB Corp. [Associated Press] (SAG) ..... ANB
ANB Corp. [Associated Press] (SAG) ..... ANB Corp
ANB Corp. [NASDAQ symbol] (SAG) ..... ANBC
Ancaster High and Vocational School, Ontario [Library symbol National
Library of Canada] (NLC) ..... OAH
Ancenis [France ICAO location identifier] (ICLI) ..... LFFI
Ancestor ..... ANC
Ancestry Research Club (EA) ..... ARC
Anches [Reeds] [Music] ..... ANCH
Anchor (MSA) ..... AHR
Anchor ..... ANCHR
Anchor Bancorp (SPSG) ..... ABKR
Anchor Bancorp Wisc [NASDAQ symbol] (TTSB) ..... ABCW
Anchor Bancorp Wisconsin, Inc. [NASDAQ symbol] (SAG) ..... ABCW
Anchor Bancorp Wisconsin, Inc. [Associated Press] (SAG) ..... AncBWI
Anchor Bible Commentary [A publication] (BJA) ..... ABC
Anchor Bible Dictionary [A publication] ..... ABD
Anchor Block Foundation (EA) ..... ABF
Anchor Bolt [Technical drawings] ..... AB
Anchor Financial Corp. [NASDAQ symbol] (SAG) ..... AFSC
Anchor Financial Corp. [Associated Press] (SAG) ..... AnchFin
Anchor Gaming [Associated Press] (SAG) ..... AnchGm
Anchor Gaming [NASDAQ symbol] (SAG) ..... SLOT
Anchor Gold Corp. [Vancouver Stock Exchange symbol] ..... AHG
Anchor Handling Salvage Tug (DS) ..... AHST
Anchor Handling Tug (DS) ..... AHT
Anchor Handling Tug Supply Vessel (DS) ..... AHTS
Anchor Line [Steamship] (MHDW) ..... A
Anchor Line Ltd. [Steamship] (MHDB) ..... ALL
Anchor Machine & Manufacturing Ltd. [Toronto Stock Exchange symbol] ..... AKC
Anchor Order (MSA) ..... AOR
Anchor Placement Equipment ..... APE
Anchor Windlass ..... AWNDLS
Anchorage [Alaska Methodist University] [Alaska] [Seismograph station code,
US Geological Survey] [Closed] (SEIS) ..... AMU
Anchorage [Alaska] [Airport symbol] (OAG) ..... ANC
Anchorage [Maps and charts] ..... ANCH
Anchorage [Alaska] [ICAO location identifier] (ICLI) ..... PAZA
Anchorage, AK [Location identifier FAA] (FAAL) ..... CMQ
Anchorage, AK [Location identifier FAA] (FAAL) ..... EDF
Anchorage, AK [Television station call letters] ..... KAKM
Anchorage, AK [FM radio station call letters] ..... KASH
Anchorage, AK [FM radio station call letters] ..... KATB

Anchorage, AK [FM radio station call letters] ..... KBFX
Anchorage, AK [FM radio station call letters] ..... KBRJ
Anchorage, AK [AM radio station call letters] ..... KBYR
Anchorage, AK [Television station call letters] ..... KDMD
Anchorage, AK [FM radio station call letters] ..... KEAG
Anchorage, AK [AM radio station call letters] ..... KENI
Anchorage, AK [AM radio station call letters] ..... KFQD
Anchorage, AK [FM radio station call letters] ..... KGOT
Anchorage, AK [AM radio station call letters] ..... KHAR
Anchorage, AK [Television station call letters] ..... KIMO
Anchorage, AK [FM radio station call letters] ..... KKRO
Anchorage, AK [FM radio station call letters] ..... KLEF
Anchorage, AK [FM radio station call letters] (RBYB) ..... KMXS
Anchorage, AK [FM radio station call letters] (RBYB) ..... KNBA-FM
Anchorage, AK [FM radio station call letters] ..... KNIK
Anchorage, AK [FM radio station call letters] ..... KRUA
Anchorage, AK [FM radio station call letters] ..... KSKA
Anchorage, AK [Television station call letters] ..... KTBY
Anchorage, AK [Television station call letters] ..... KTUU-TV
Anchorage, AK [Television station call letters] ..... KTVA
Anchorage, AK [FM radio station call letters] ..... KWHL
Anchorage, AK [FM radio station call letters] (RBYB) ..... KWQJ-FM
Anchorage, AK [AM radio station call letters] ..... KYAK
Anchorage, AK [Television station call letters] ..... KYES
Anchorage, AK [FM radio station call letters] ..... KYMG
Anchorage, AK [Television station call letters] ..... KZXC
Anchorage, AK [Location identifier FAA] (FAAL) ..... LHD
Anchorage, AK [Location identifier FAA] (FAAL) ..... MRI
Anchorage, AK [Location identifier FAA] (FAAL) ..... TGN
Anchorage, AK [Location identifier FAA] (FAAL) ..... ZAN
Anchorage Community College, Anchorage, AK [Library symbol Library of
Congress] (LCLS) ..... AkAC
Anchorage Dependent Cell [Culture technology] ..... ADC
Anchorage/Elmendorf Air Force Base [Alaska] [ICAO location identifier]
(ICLI) ..... PAED
Anchorage/Ft. Richardson, AK [Location identifier FAA] (FAAL) ..... CSR
Anchorage Higher Education Consortium Library, Anchorage, AK [Library
symbol Library of Congress] (LCLS) ..... AkACon
Anchorage/International [Alaska] [ICAO location identifier] (ICLI) ..... PANC
Anchorage/Merrill Field [Alaska] [ICAO location identifier] (ICLI) ..... PAMR
Anchorage Prohibited [Nautical charts] ..... Anch Prohib
Anchorage School District, Library Resources, Anchorage, AK [Library
symbol Library of Congress] (LCLS) ..... AkAS
Anchored ..... ANCH
Anchored Catheter [Medicine] ..... A/C
Anchored Cell Analysis and Sorting [Cell culture] ..... ACAS
Anchored Filament ..... ANCFIL
Anchored Filament ..... ANF
Anchored Interplanetary Monitoring Platform ..... AIMP
Anchored Polymerase Chain Reaction [Genetics] ..... A-PCR
Anchored Radio Sonobuoy ..... ARSB
Anchored Radiosight ..... ARS
Anchoring Fibril [Anatomy] ..... AF
Anchorite ..... ANC
Anchors and Chains Proved [Shipping] ..... A & CP
Ancien Testament [Old Testament] [French] ..... AT
Anciens Moudjahidine et Victimes de la Guerre [War Veterans and Victims]
[Algeria] ..... AMVG
Ancient ..... ANC
Ancient (VRA) ..... anc
Ancient ..... ANCNT
Ancient ..... ANCT
Ancient and Accepted [Freemasonry] ..... A and A
Ancient and Accepted Rite [Freemasonry] ..... A and AR
Ancient and Accepted Scottish Rite [Freemasonry] (ROG) ..... A & ASR
Ancient and Accepted Scottish Rite [Freemasonry] ..... AASR
Ancient and Honorable Artillery Co. of Massachusetts (EA) ..... AHACM
Ancient and Honourable Guild of Town Criers (EAIO) ..... AHGTC
Ancient and Illustrious Order Knights of Malta [East Canton, OH]
(EA) ..... AIOK of M
Ancient and Modern [Hymns] ..... A and M
Ancient and Modern Palestine [A publication] (BJA) ..... AMP
Ancient Arts Fellowship [Australia] ..... AAF
Ancient Astronaut Society (EA) ..... AAS
Ancient Charters [1692] [A publication] (DLA) ..... Anc Charters
Ancient Classics for English Readers [A publication] ..... ACER
Ancient Conserved Region [Genetics] ..... ACR
Ancient Dialogue upon the Exchequer [A publication] (DLA) ..... Anc Dial Exch
Ancient Egypt Research Associates ..... AERA
Ancient Egyptian Arabic Order Nobles of the Mystic Shrine (EA) ..... AEAONMS
Ancient Egyptian Arabic Order Nobles of the Mystic Shrine (EA) ..... NMS
Ancient Egyptian Order of Sciots (EA) ..... AEOS
Ancient English Christmas Carols [A publication] ..... AnEC
Ancient Forest International [An association] ..... AFI
Ancient Free and Accepted Masons [Freemasonry] ..... AF & AM
Ancient Free and Accepted Masons [Freemasonry] ..... AFAM
Ancient Freemasons ..... AFM
Ancient Gneiss Complex [Geology] ..... AGC
Ancient History Documents Research Center [Macquarie University]
[Australia] ..... AHDRC
Ancient Israel: Its Life and Institutions [A publication] (BJA) ..... AncIsr
Ancient Mediterranean Research Association (EA) ..... AMRA
Ancient Monuments Act [Town planning] [British] ..... AM
Ancient Monuments Society (EAIO) ..... AMS

Ancient Mystic Order of Bagmen of Bagdad Imperial Guild [*Roanoke, VA*] (EA) ... AMOB
Ancient Mystic Order of Samaritans (EA) ... AMOS
Ancient Mystical Order Rosae Crucis [*Rosicrucian Order*] (EA) ... AMORC
Ancient Near East (BJA) ... ANE
[*The*] **Ancient Near East in Pictures** [*A publication*] (BJA) ... ANEP
Ancient Near Eastern Texts Relating to the Old Testament [*A publication*] (BJA) ... ANET
Ancient Order of Druids ... AOD
[*The*] **Ancient Order of Foresters** ... AOF
[*The*] **Ancient Order of Foresters** [*Freemasonry*] (ROG) ... FOREST
Ancient Order of Foresters of California [*Later, AOFPCJ*] (EA) ... AOFC
Ancient Order of Foresters of the Pacific Coast Jurisdiction [*Hilo, HI*] (EA) ... AOFPCJ
Ancient Order of Frothblowers [*British*] ... AOFB
Ancient Order of Hibernians in America (EA) ... AOH
Ancient Order of Maccabeans (BJA) ... AOM
Ancient Order of Shepherds ... AOS
Ancient Order United Workmen [*Seattle, WA*] (EA) ... AOUW
Ancient Parish ... AP
Ancient Petition ... AP
Ancient Philosophies for Modern Readers [*A publication*] ... APMR
Ancient Records of Assyria [*A publication*] (BJA) ... ARA
Ancient Records of Assyria and Babylonia [*A publication*] (BJA) ... ARAB
Ancient Records of Egypt [*A publication*] (BJA) ... ARE
Ancient York Mason [*Freemasonry*] ... AYM
Ancilla College [*Formerly, Ancilla Domini College*] [*Donaldson, IN*] ... AC
Ancillae Sacri Cordis Jesu [*Handmaids of the Sacred Heart of Jesus*] [*Roman Catholic religious order*] ... ACJ
Ancillary (MCD) ... ANC
Ancillary (MCD) ... ANCIL
Ancillary Armament Equipment (DNAB) ... AAE
Ancillary Communications Services [*Australia*] ... ACS
Ancillary Composing Equipment (DGA) ... ACE
Ancillary Control Processor ... ACP
Ancillary Education Establishment ... AEE
Ancillary Services Review Program [*Health insurance*] (GHCT) ... ASRP
Ancom ATM International, Inc. [*Toronto Stock Exchange symbol*] ... ANY
Ancon [*Peru*] [*ICAO location identifier*] (ICLI) ... SPNO
Ancona [*Italy*] [*Airport symbol*] (OAG) ... AOI
Ancona/Falconara [*Italy ICAO location identifier*] (ICLI) ... LIPY
Ancor Communications [*Associated Press*] (SAG) ... AncorCm
Ancor Communicatons [*NASDAQ symbol*] (SAG) ... ANCR
Ancud [*Chile*] [*Airport symbol*] (AD) ... ZUD
Ancud/Pupelde [*Chile*] [*ICAO location identifier*] (ICLI) ... SCAC
And (ROG) ... A
, and Chassigny [*Egypt*] [*Pronounced "snick" Classification for a group of meteorites recovered from these sites*] [*French*] ... SNC
And Elsewhere [*Mathematics*] ... ae
And Gate [*Logic element*] [*Computer science*] ... AG
AND JEF - Parti Africain pour la Democratie et le Socialisme [*Senegal*] [*Political party*] (EY) ... AJ-PADS
, and Nancy [*Dickerman*] [*Cook Democratic Party activists*] ... EMN
And/Or ... A/OR
And Others ... AO
And So Forth [*Et cetera*] [*Latin*] (WDMC) ... etc
And So To Bed [*Commercial firm British*] ... ASTB
and Subassembly Facility [*or Refurbishment*] [*NASA*] (NASA) ... SRSF
And The Following [*A notation*] (WDMC) ... et seq
Andahuaylas [*Peru*] [*Airport symbol Obsolete*] (OAG) ... ANS
Andahuaylas [*Peru*] [*ICAO location identifier*] (ICLI) ... SPHY
Andalgala [*Argentina*] [*Seismograph station code, US Geological Survey Closed*] (SEIS) ... ANL
Andalusia, AL [*Location identifier FAA*] (FAAL) ... JUY
Andalusia, AL [*Location identifier FAA*] (FAAL) ... RIU
Andalusia, AL [*FM radio station call letters*] ... WAAO
Andalusia, AL [*AM radio station call letters*] ... WKYD
Andalusia, AL [*FM radio station call letters*] (RBYB) ... WSTF
Andalusia, AL [*FM radio station call letters*] (RBYB) ... WWSF
Andalusian Horse Registry (EA) ... AHR
Andalusite [*Mineralogy*] ... AND
Andaman Islands ... AND
Andamooka [*Australia Airport symbol*] (OAG) ... ADO
Andante [*Slow*] [*Music*] ... AND
Andante [*Slow*] [*Music*] ... ANDTE
Andantino [*Slow*] [*Music*] ... ANDNO
Andantino [*Slow*] [*Music*] ... ANDO
Andapa [*Madagascar*] [*ICAO location identifier*] (ICLI) ... FMND
Andapa [*Madagascar*] [*Airport symbol*] (OAG) ... ZWA
Andaurex Resources, Inc. [*Vancouver Stock Exchange symbol*] ... AWX
Andco, Inc., Buffalo, NY [*Library symbol Library of Congress*] (LCLS) ... NBuAn
Andean Area [*MARC geographic area code Library of Congress*] (LCCP) ... sn----
Andean Commission of Jurists [*See also CAJ*] (EAIO) ... ACJ
Andean Common Market (EAIO) ... ANCOM
Andean Development Corp. [*NASDAQ symbol*] (SAG) ... ADCC
Andean Development Corp. [*Associated Press*] (SAG) ... Andean
Andean Development Corp. [*Associated Press*] (SAG) ... AndeanD
Andean Group ... AG
Andean Pact Organization [*Chile, Peru, Bolivia, Ecuador, Colombia*] ... APO
Andean Potato Latent Virus [*Plant pathology*] ... APLV
Andean Potato Mottle Virus [*Plant pathology*] ... APMV
Andean Trade Preference Act ... ATPA
Andelin Foundation for Education in Family Living (EA) ... AFEFL
Andenes [*Norway*] [*Airport symbol*] (OAG) ... ANX
Andere [*Other*] [*German*] ... and
Andernos-Les-Bains [*France ICAO location identifier*] (ICLI) ... LFCD
Anders Gaan Leven [*Live Differently*] [*Belgium Political party*] (PPW) ... AGALEV
Anders Gaan Leven-Geweldloos, Rechtvaardig, Open Ecologisch Netwerk [*Belgium*] [*Political party*] (ECED) ... A-G
Andersen Air Force Base, Guam Island [*Mariana Islands*] [*ICAO location identifier*] (ICLI) ... PGUA
Andersen Group [*NASDAQ symbol*] (TTSB) ... ANDR
Andersen Group, Inc. [*NASDAQ symbol*] (NQ) ... ANDR
Andersen Group, Inc. [*Associated Press*] (SAG) ... AndrGr
Andersen Laboratories, Inc. ... AL
Anderson [*South Carolina*] [*Airport symbol*] (OAG) ... AND
Anderson Air Force Base Flightline ... AAFBF
Anderson Associates Ltd., Willowdale, Ontario [*Library symbol National Library of Canada*] (NLC) ... OWAA
Anderson Aviation, Inc. [*FAA designator*] (FAAC) ... ADX
Anderson, CA [*FM radio station call letters*] ... KEWB
Anderson Carnegie Public Library, Anderson, IN [*Library symbol Library of Congress*] (LCLS) ... InAnd
Anderson, Clayton & Co., Foods Division Technical Library, Dallas, TX [*Library symbol Library of Congress*] (LCLS) ... TxDaAC
Anderson Clayton Foods [*of Anderson, Clayton & Co.*], Richardson, TX [*Library symbol Library of Congress*] (LCLS) ... TxRiA
Anderson College, Anderson, IN [*OCLC symbol*] (OCLC) ... INA
Anderson College, Anderson, IN [*Library symbol Library of Congress*] (LCLS) ... InAndC
Anderson College, Anderson, SC [*Library symbol*] [*Library of Congress*] (LCLS) ... ScAnC
Anderson College, Graduate School of Theology, Anderson, IN [*Library symbol Library of Congress*] (LCLS) ... InAcdC-T
Anderson College, Graduate School of Theology, Anderson, IN [*Library symbol*] [*Library of Congress*] (LCLS) ... InAndC-T
Anderson Co. ... ANCO
Anderson County Library, Anderson, SC [*OCLC symbol*] (OCLC) ... SAL
Anderson County Library, Anderson, SC [*Library symbol Library of Congress*] (LCLS) ... ScAn
Anderson Daily Bulletin, Anderson, IN [*Library symbol Library of Congress*] (LCLS) ... InAndB
Anderson - Darling Test [*Statistics*] ... AD
Anderson Exploration Ltd. [*Toronto Stock Exchange symbol*] ... AXL
Anderson Galleries ... AG
Anderson Herald, Anderson, IN [*Library symbol Library of Congress*] (LCLS) ... InAndH
Anderson, IN [*Location identifier FAA*] (FAAL) ... AID
Anderson, IN [*FM radio station call letters*] (RBYB) ... WBSB-FM
Anderson, IN [*AM radio station call letters*] ... WHBU
Anderson, IN [*AM radio station call letters*] ... WHUT
Anderson, IN [*FM radio station call letters*] ... WQME
Anderson, IN [*FM radio station call letters*] ... WXXP
Anderson [*H. H.*] **Line** [*Steamship*] (MHDB) ... HHA
Anderson Model [*Physics*] ... AM
Anderson on Church Wardens [*A publication*] (DLA) ... And Ch W
Anderson Public Library, Anderson, IN [*OCLC symbol*] (OCLC) ... IAM
Anderson Reservoir [*California*] [*Seismograph station code, US Geological Survey*] (SEIS) ... ADR
Anderson, SC [*Location identifier FAA*] (FAAL) ... ELW
Anderson, SC [*AM radio station call letters*] ... WAIM
Anderson, SC [*AM radio station call letters*] ... WANS
Anderson, SC [*Television station call letters*] (RBYB) ... WFBC-TV
Anderson, SC [*FM radio station call letters*] ... WJMZ
Anderson, SC [*FM radio station call letters*] ... WROQ
Anderson-Brinkman-Morel State [*Superconductivity*] ... ABM
Anderson's Agricultural Decisions [*Scotland*] [*A publication*] (DLA) ... And Agr Dec
Anderson's Agriculture Cases [*England*] [*A publication*] (DLA) ... And
Anderson's English Common Pleas Reports [*1534-1605*] [*A publication*] (DLA) ... And
Anderson's Examination Questions and Answers [*A publication*] (DLA) ... And Q & A
Anderson's History of Commerce [*A publication*] (DLA) ... And Com
Andersons Inc. [*NASDAQ symbol*] (TTSB) ... ANDE
Anderson's Law Dictionary [*A publication*] (DLA) ... And Law Dict
Anderson's Reports, English Court of Common Pleas [*A publication*] (DLA) ... Ander (Eng)
Anderson's Reports, English Court of Common Pleas [*A publication*] (DLA) ... Anders
Anderson's Reports, English Court of Common Pleas [*A publication*] (DLA) ... Anderson
Anderson's Uniform Commercial Code [*A publication*] (DLA) ... Anderson UCC
Anderstorp [*Sweden ICAO location identifier*] (ICLI) ... ESMP
Andhra Pradesh [*State in southeast India*] ... AP
Andimeshk [*Iran*] [*ICAO location identifier*] (ICLI) ... OIAN
Andizhan [*Former USSR Seismograph station code, US Geological Survey*] (SEIS) ... ANR
AND-JEF/Mouvement Revolutionnaire pour la Democratie Nouvelle [*AND-JEF/New Democratic Revolutionary Movement*] [*Senegal*] [*Political party*] ... AJ/MRDN
Andkhoi [*Afghanistan*] [*ICAO location identifier*] (ICLI) ... OAAK
Andocides [*Fifth century BC*] [*Classical studies*] (OCD) ... Andoc
Andong [*South Korea ICAO location identifier*] (ICLI) ... RKTA
And-Or Amplifier (HGAA) ... AO AMPL
And-Or Invert (IEEE) ... AOI
Andoraq Resources Corp. [*Vancouver Stock Exchange symbol*] ... ARQ
Andorra [*ANSI two-letter standard code*] (CNC) ... AD
Andorra [*MARC country of publication code Library of Congress*] (LCCP) ... an
Andorra [*ANSI three-letter standard code*] (CNC) ... AND

Andorra (VRA) .... And
Andorra [MARC geographic area code Library of Congress] (LCCP) .... e-an--
Andorran Philately Study Circle [Defunct] (EA) .... APSC
Andover Bancorp [NASDAQ symbol] (TTSB) .... ANDB
Andover Bancorp, Inc. [NASDAQ symbol] (NQ) ...... ANDB
Andover Bancorp, Inc. [Associated Press] (SAG) ...... AndvBc
Andover Distributors Association (EA) .... ADA
Andover Historical Society, Andover, MA [Library symbol Library of Congress] (LCLS) .... MAnHi
Andover, KS [FM radio station call letters] (RBYB) ... KDGS
Andover, MA [FM radio station call letters] .... WPAA
Andover Newton Theological School [Newton Center, MA] ..... ANTS
Andover Newton Theological School, Newton Center, MA [OCLC symbol] (OCLC) .... BAN
Andover Newton Theological School, Newton Center, MA [Library symbol Library of Congress] (LCLS) .... MNtcA
Andover Service Center [IRS] .... ANSC
Andover Togs, Inc. [Associated Press] (SAG) ...... AndvTog
Andover Togs, Inc. [NASDAQ symbol] (NQ) .... ATOG
Andoya [Norway ICAO location identifier] (ICLI) ...... ENAN
Andradina [Brazil] [Airport symbol] (AD) .... ARD
Andravida [Greece] [ICAO location identifier] (ICLI) ... LGAD
Andre and Coquelin [Often used as a pattern on clothes designed by Courreges, the initials represent the first names of the couturier and his wife] .... AC
Andre Marsan & Associes, Inc., Montreal, PQ, Canada [Library symbol Library of Congress] (LCLS) .... CaQMAMA
Andrea Airlines SA [Peru] [ICAO designator] (FAAC) ...... NDR
Andrea Electronics [AMEX symbol] (TTSB) .... AND
Andrea Electronics Corp. [AMEX symbol] (SPSG) ..... AND
Andrea Electronics Corp. [Associated Press] (SAG) ... Andrea
Andrea McArdle Fan Club (EA) .... AMFC
Andreafsky/St. Marys, AK [Location identifier FAA] (FAAL) ...... SMA
Andreas Acconzaioco de Ravello [Flourished, 1294-1300] [Authority cited in pre-1607 legal work] (DSA) ...... Andr Acza
Andreas Acconzaioco de Ravello [Flourished, 1294-1300] [Authority cited in pre-1607 legal work] (DSA) ...... Andr Azaio
Andreas Acconzaioco de Ravello [Flourished, 1294-1300] [Authority cited in pre-1607 legal work] (DSA) ...... Andr de Ra
Andreas Alciatus [Deceased, 1550] [Authority cited in pre-1607 legal work] (DSA) ...... A Alciat
Andreas Alciatus [Deceased, 1550] [Authority cited in pre-1607 legal work] (DSA) ...... Andr Alciat
Andreas Bonellus de Barulo [Flourished, 1260-71] [Authority cited in pre-1607 legal work] (DSA) ...... A de Ba
Andreas Bonellus de Barulo [Flourished, 1260-71] [Authority cited in pre-1607 legal work] (DSA) ...... An
Andreas Bonellus de Barulo [Flourished, 1260-71] [Authority cited in pre-1607 legal work] (DSA) ...... And
Andreas Bonellus de Barulo [Flourished, 1260-71] [Authority cited in pre-1607 legal work] (DSA) ...... And de Baro
Andreas Bonellus de Barulo [Flourished, 1260-71] [Authority cited in pre-1607 legal work] (DSA) ...... Andr
Andreas Bonellus de Barulo [Flourished, 1260-71] [Authority cited in pre-1607 legal work] (DSA) ...... Andr de Bar
Andreas Bonellus de Barulo [Flourished, 1260-71] [Authority cited in pre-1607 legal work] (DSA) ...... Andre
Andreas de Capua [Flourished, 1242-57] [Authority cited in pre-1607 legal work] (DSA) ...... An
Andreas de Capua [Flourished, 1242-57] [Authority cited in pre-1607 legal work] (DSA) ...... And de Ca
Andreas de Capua [Flourished, 1242-57] [Authority cited in pre-1607 legal work] (DSA) ...... Andr de Ca
Andreas de Capua [Flourished, 1242-57] [Authority cited in pre-1607 legal work] (DSA) ...... Andr de Cap
Andreas de Isernia [Deceased circa 1316] [Authority cited in pre-1607 legal work] (DSA) ...... An de Iser
Andreas de Isernia [Deceased circa 1316] [Authority cited in pre-1607 legal work] (DSA) ...... Andr
Andreas de Isernia [Deceased circa 1316] [Authority cited in pre-1607 legal work] (DSA) ...... Andr de Isern
Andreas de Isernia [Deceased circa 1316] [Authority cited in pre-1607 legal work] (DSA) ...... Andre
Andreas Fachineus [Deceased, 1622] [Authority cited in pre-1607 legal work] (DSA) ...... Andr Fachin
Andreas Pomates [Authority cited in pre-1607 legal work] (DSA) ...... Andr Pomat
Andreas Tiraquellus [Deceased, 1558] [Authority cited in pre-1607 legal work] (DSA) ...... And Tiraq
Andreas Tiraquellus [Deceased, 1558] [Authority cited in pre-1607 legal work] (DSA) ...... Andr Tiraq
Andrei Sakharov Institute [Later, FUWPH] (EA) ...... ASI
Andres Wines Ltd. [Toronto Stock Exchange symbol Vancouver Stock Exchange symbol] .... ADW
Andrew Bayne Memorial Library, Bellevue, PA [Library symbol Library of Congress] (LCLS) .... PBvu
Andrew College, Cuthbert, GA [Library symbol Library of Congress] (LCLS) .... GCuA
Andrew Corp. [Associated Press] (SAG) .... Andrew
Andrew Corp. [NASDAQ symbol] (NQ) .... ANDW
Andrew County Historical Society, Savannah, MO [Library symbol Library of Congress] (LCLS) .... MoSavHi
Andrew File System [Computer science] (TNIG) .... AFS
Andrew Jackson [US general and president, 1767-1845] .... AJ
Andrew Public Library, Alberta [Library symbol National Library of Canada] (NLC) .... AA

Andrew Public Library, Andrew, AB, Canada [Library symbol] [Library of Congress] (LCLS) .... CaAAn
Andrew R. Jennings Computing Center [Case Western Reserve University] [Research center] (RCD) .... ARJCC
Andrew W. Mellon Foundation, New York, NY [Library symbol Library of Congress] (LCLS) .... NNMel
Andrews Air Force Base [Washington, DC] .... AAFB
Andrews & McMeel [Publisher] .... A & M
Andrews and Stoney's Supreme Court of Judicature Acts [A publication] (DLA) .... And & Ston JA
Andrews Carnegie Library, Andrews, NC [Library symbol Library of Congress] (LCLS) .... NcAnd
Andrews' Digest of the Opinions of the Attorneys-General [A publication] (DLA) .... And Dig
Andrews' English King's Bench Reports [95 English Reprint] [A publication] (DLA) .... And
Andrews' English King's Bench Reports [95 English Reprint] [A publication] (DLA) .... Andr
Andrews' English King's Bench Reports [95 English Reprint] [A publication] (DLA) .... Andrews (Eng)
Andrews' Manual of the United States Constitution [A publication] (DLA) .... And Man Const
Andrews, McMeel & Parker [Later, A & M] [Publisher] ...... AM & P
Andrews/Nelson/Whitehead [Commercial firm] .... A/N/W
Andrews on Criminal Law [A publication] (DLA) ...... And Cr Law
Andrews on the Revenue Law [A publication] (DLA) ... And Rev Law
Andrews on United States Laws and Courts [A publication] (DLA) ..... And L & Cts
Andrews' Precedents of Leases [A publication] (DLA) ...... And Pr Lea
Andrews' Precedents of Mortgages [A publication] (DLA) ...... And Pr Mort
Andrews' Reports [63-73 Connecticut] [A publication] (DLA) ...... And
Andrews, SC [Location identifier FAA] (FAAL) .... PHH
Andrews, SC [FM radio station call letters] .... WGTN
Andrews Sisters Fan Club (EA) .... ASFC
Andrews, TX [Location identifier FAA] (FAAL) ...... ANR
Andrews, TX [AM radio station call letters] .... KACT
Andrews, TX [FM radio station call letters] .... KACT-FM
Andrews University (GAGS) .... Andrews U
Andrews University, Berrien Springs, MI [OCLC symbol] (OCLC) ...... EXN
Andrews University, Berrien Springs, MI [Library symbol Library of Congress] (LCLS) .... MiBsA
Andrews-Dallas Township Public Library, Andrews, IN [Library symbol Library of Congress] (LCLS) .... InAnw
Andrewsfield [British ICAO location identifier] (ICLI) ...... EGSL
Andria [of Terence] [Classical studies] (OCD) .... An
Andriamena [Madagascar] [Airport symbol] (OAG) ... WAD
Androecium [Botany] .... A
Androgen [Antineoplastic drug] (DAVI) .... And
Androgen Binding Protein [Endocrinology] .... ABP
Androgen Insensitivity Syndrome [Endocrinology] .... AIS
Androgen Receptors [Endocrinology] .... AR
Androgen-Deprivation Therapy [Medicine] .... ADT
Androgenic Anabolic Agent [Medicine] (DMAA) ..... AAA
Andromache [of Euripides] [Classical studies] (OCD) ...... Andr
Andromeda [Constellation] .... And
Andromeda [Constellation] .... Andr
Androne Resources Ltd. [Vancouver Stock Exchange symbol] ...... AND
Andronicus Publishing Co., Inc., New York, NY [Library symbol Library of Congress] (LCLS) .... ApC
Andros, Inc. [Associated Press] (SAG) .... Andros
Andros, Inc. [NASDAQ symbol] (NQ) .... ANDY
Andros Town [Bahamas] [Airport symbol] (OAG) ...... ASD
Andros Town, Andros Island [Bahamas] [ICAO location identifier] (ICLI) ...... MYAF
Androstanediene [Biochemistry] (DAVI) .... ADD
Androstanediene-Dione (BABM) .... ADD
Androstatrienedione [Organic chemistry] .... ATD
Androstenedione [Endocrinology] .... AD
Androsterone [Medicine] (DMAA) .... A
Androsterone [Pharmacology] (DAVI) .... ANDRO
Androsterone [Pharmacology] (DAVI) .... ANDROS
Androsterone Sulfate [Biochemistry] (AAMN) .... AS
Andrulis Research Corp. .... ARC
Andrulis Tracker [Military] (CAAL) .... ANTRAC
Andrus Gerontological Information Center [University of Southern California] (IID) .... AGIC
Andrx Corp. [NASDAQ symbol] (SAG) .... ADRX
Andrx Corp. [Associated Press] (SAG) .... AndrxCp
Anduki/Seria [Brunei] [ICAO location identifier] (ICLI) ...... WBAK
Andy Griffith Show Appreciation Society (EA) ...... AGSAS
[The] Andy Griffith Show Rerun Watchers Club (EA) ...... TAGSRWC
Andy Williams Fan Club (EA) .... AWFC
Andyne Computing [NASDAQ symbol] (TTSB) ...... ADYNF
Andyne Computing Ltd. [NASDAQ symbol] (SAG) ... ADYN
Andyne Computing Ltd. [Associated Press] (SAG) ... Andyne
Anechoic (MSA) .... ANCH
Anechoic Acoustic Test Facility (MCD) .... AATF
Anechoic Water Tank .... AWT
Anegada [Virgin Islands] [Seismograph station code, US Geological Survey] (SEIS) .... ABV
Aneityum [Vanuata] [Airport symbol] (OAG) .... AUY
Anekdote [Anecdote] [German] .... Anekd
Anemone [Botany] .... AN
Anergen, Inc. [Associated Press] (SAG) .... Anergen
Anergen, Inc. [NASDAQ symbol] (SPSG) .... ANRG
Aneroid (MSA) .... ANER
Anesta Corp. [Associated Press] (SAG) .... Anesta

Anesta Corp. [*NASDAQ symbol*] (SAG) .... NSTA
Anesthesia [*or Anesthetic*] [*Medicine*] (DAVI) .... AN
Anesthesia [*or Anesthetic*] [*Medicine*] .... ANESTH
Anesthesia .... ANSTHS
Anesthesia Standby [*Medicine*] .... ASB
Anesthesiologist's Assistant [*Medicine*] (DAVI) .... AA
Anesthesiology [*Medical specialty*] (DHSM) .... AN
Anesthesiology (AABC) .... ANES
Anesthesiology .... ANESTHLGY
Anesthesiology .... ANSTHSLGY
Anesthetic [*Medicine*] .... A
Anesthetic Gas Standards .... AGS
Anethole Dithiolthione [*Biochemistry*] .... ADT
Anethum [*Dill Seed*] [*Pharmacology*] (ROG) .... ANETH
Aneurysm .... AN
Aneurysm of Ascending Aorta [*Cardiology*] (DMAA) .... AAA
Aneurysm of Ascending Aorta [*Cardiology*] (DMAA) .... AAA
Anfang [*Beginning*] [*German*] .... Anf
Anfang Bedenk das Ende [*At the Beginning Consider the End*] [*Motto of Bruno II, Count of Mansfeld (1545-1615)*] [*German*] .... ABDE
Angavokely [*Madagascar*] [*Seismograph station code, US Geological Survey*] (SEIS) .... AVY
Angeborener Ausolsender Mechanismus [*Innate Release Mechanism*] [*Psychology*] .... AAM
Angeion Corp. [*Associated Press*] (SAG) .... Angeion
Angeion Corp. [*NASDAQ symbol*] (NQ) .... ANGN
Angel (ROG) .... A
Angel Collectors Club of America (EA) .... ACCA
Angel Fire, NM [*FM radio station call letters*] .... KAFR
Angel Flight (EA) .... AnF
Angel Island [*California*] [*Seismograph station code, US Geological Survey*] (SEIS) .... AGC
Angel, Jerald J., Los Angeles CA [*STAC*] .... AJJ
[*The*] **Angel Planes** [*An association*] (EA) .... AP
[*The*] **Angel Planes** (EA) .... TAP
Angel, Second Class [*Classification of angel Clarence Oddbody in 1947 film, "It's a Wonderful Life"*] AS2
Angelegenheit [*Affair*] [*German*] .... Angelegenh
Angeles Mortgage Partners [*Associated Press*] (SAG) .... AngMtg
Angeles Mortgage Partners [*AMEX symbol*] (SPSG) .... ANM
Angeles Mtge Inv Tr L.P. [*AMEX symbol*] (TTSB) .... ANM
Angeles Participating Mortgage Trust [*Associated Press*] (SAG) .... AngPar
Angeles Participating Mortgage Trust [*AMEX symbol*] (SPSG) .... APT
Angeles Ptc Mtge'A'SBI [*AMEX symbol*] (TTSB) .... APT
Angelholm [*Sweden ICAO location identifier*] (ICLI) .... ESDB
Angelholm/Helsingbord [*Sweden*] [*Airport symbol*] (OAG) .... AGH
Angelic Warfare Confraternity [*Defunct*] (EA) .... AWC
Angelica Corp. [*NYSE symbol*] (SPSG) .... AGL
Angelica Corp. [*Associated Press*] (SAG) .... Angelic
Angelica Free Library, Angelica, NY [*Library symbol Library of Congress*] (LCLS) .... NAng
Angelina & Neches River Railroad Co. [*AAR code*] .... ANR
Angelina College, Lufkin, TX [*Library symbol Library of Congress*] (LCLS) .... TxLufA
Angelina, Cotui [*Dominican Republic*] [*ICAO location identifier*] (ICLI) .... MDAN
Angelini Francesco [*Italy*] [*Research code symbol*] .... AF
Angell and Ames on Corporations [*A publication*] (DLA) .... A & A Corp
Angell and Ames on Corporations [*A publication*] (DLA) .... Ang & A Corp
Angell and Ames on Corporations [*A publication*] (DLA) .... Ang Corp
Angell and Durfee on Highways [*A publication*] (DLA) .... A & D High
Angell and Durfee on Highways [*A publication*] (DLA) .... Ang & D High
Angell and Durfee on Highways [*A publication*] (DLA) .... Ang High
Angell and Durfee on Highways [*A publication*] (DLA) .... Ang Highw
Angell and Durfee's Reports [*1 Rhode Island*] [*A publication*] (DLA) .... Ang
Angell and Durfee's Reports [*1 Rhode Island*] [*A publication*] (DLA) .... Ang & Dur
Angell on Adverse Enjoyment [*A publication*] (DLA) .... Ang Adv Enj
Angell on Assignment [*A publication*] (DLA) .... Ang Ass
Angell on Bank Tax [*A publication*] (DLA) .... Ang BT
Angell on Carriers [*A publication*] (DLA) .... Ang Car
Angell on Insurance [*A publication*] (DLA) .... Ang Ins
Angell on Limitation of Actions [*A publication*] (DLA) .... Ang Lim
Angell on Tide Waters [*A publication*] (DLA) .... Ang Tide Waters
Angell on Tide Waters [*A publication*] (DLA) .... Ang TW
Angell on Water Courses [*A publication*] (DLA) .... Ang Wat
Angell on Water Courses [*A publication*] (DLA) .... Ang Water Courses
Angell's Rhode Island Reports [*A publication*] (DLA) .... Ang
Angelman Syndrome [*Genetics*] .... AS
Angelo State University (GAGS) .... Angelo St U
Angelo State University, San Angelo, TX [*Library symbol Library of Congress*] (LCLS) .... TxSalA
Angel's Peak [*Nevada*] [*Seismograph station code, US Geological Survey*] (SEIS) .... APK
Angelus Carletus de Clavasio [*Deceased, 1492*] [*Authority cited in pre-1607 legal work*] (DSA) .... Angel de Clavas
Angelus de Gambilionibus de Aretio [*Flourished, 1422-51*] [*Authority cited in pre-1607 legal work*] (DSA) .... Ang
Angelus de Gambilionibus de Aretio [*Flourished, 1422-51*] [*Authority cited in pre-1607 legal work*] (DSA) .... Ang Are
Angelus de Gambilionibus de Aretio [*Flourished, 1422-51*] [*Authority cited in pre-1607 legal work*] (DSA) .... Ange
Angelus de Gambilionibus de Aretio [*Flourished, 1422-51*] [*Authority cited in pre-1607 legal work*] (DSA) .... Ange Aret
Angelus de Gambilionibus de Aretio [*Flourished, 1422-51*] [*Authority cited in pre-1607 legal work*] (DSA) .... Angel
Angelus de Periglis [*Deceased, 1446*] [*Authority cited in pre-1607 legal work*] (DSA) .... Ang de Perigl
Angelus de Ubaldis [*Deceased, 1407*] [*Authority cited in pre-1607 legal work*] (DSA) .... An
Angelus de Ubaldis [*Deceased, 1407*] [*Authority cited in pre-1607 legal work*] (DSA) .... Ang
Angelus de Ubaldis [*Deceased, 1407*] [*Authority cited in pre-1607 legal work*] (DSA) .... Ange
Angelus de Ubaldis de Perusio [*Deceased, 1407*] [*Authority cited in pre-1607 legal work*] (DSA) .... An de Peru
Angelus Domini [*Angel of the Lord*] [*Latin*] (BARN) .... AD
Angers/Avrille [*France ICAO location identifier*] (ICLI) .... LFRA
Angestellter [*Clerk, Employee*] [*German*] .... Angest
Angina Pectoris [*Medicine*] .... AP
Angina Threshold Heart Rate [*Cardiology*] (DAVI) .... ATHR
Angiocardiography [*Medicine*] .... ACG
Angiocatheter [*or Angiocatheterization*] [*Cardiology*] (DAVI) .... angio
Angiofollicular (Lymph Node) Hyperplasia [*Oncology*] .... AFH
Angiogenesis Factor [*Biochemistry*] .... AF
Angiogenesis Inhibitor [*Physiology*] .... AI
Angiogram [*Cardiology*] .... ANG
Angiogram [*Cardiology*] .... angio
Angiographically Occult Intracranial Vascular Malformation [*Neurosurgery*] (DAVI) .... AOIVM
Angiography [*Cardiology*] (DAVI) .... angio
Angioimmunoblastic Lymphadenopathy [*Medicine*] .... AIL
Angioimmunoblastic Lymphadenopathy with Dysproteinemia [*Medicine*] .... AILD
Angiotensin [*Biochemistry*] .... AII
Angiotensin [*Biochemistry*] .... ANG
Angiotensin [*Biochemistry*] .... AT
Angiotensin Converting Enzyme [*Biochemistry*] .... ACE
Angiotensin Converting Enzyme Inhibitor [*Biochemistry*] .... ATCEI
Angiotensin Generation Rate [*Biochemistry*] (MAE) .... Ang GR
Angiotensin I [*Biochemistry*] (MAE) .... AI
Angiotensin I Converting Enzyme (DMAA) .... AICE
Angiotensin Pressor Dose [*Medicine*] .... APD
Angiotensin Sensitivity Test [*Medicine*] .... AST
Angiotensin-Converting Enzyme [*Medicine*] (MEDA) .... ACE
Angiotensin-II-Ferritin [*Biochemistry*] .... ATF
Angiotensin-Like Substance [*Biochemistry*] (MAE) .... ALS
Angiotensinogen [*Biochemistry*] .... ATG
Angissoq [*Greenland*] [*ICAO location identifier*] (ICLI) .... BGAS
Angkatan Democratic Liberal Sabah [*Malaysis*] [*Political party*] (EY) .... Adil
Angkatan Keadilan Rakyat [*People's Justice Movement*] [*Malaysia*] [*Political party*] (EY) .... AKAR
Angkatan Perpaduan Ummah [*Muslim Unity Movement*] [*Malaysia*] [*Political party*] (EY) .... APU
Angle (MSA) .... ANG
Angle .... ANGL
Angle L
Angle at Leaf Base [*Botany*] .... BANG
Angle at Leaf Base [*Botany*] .... BANGLE
Angle at Tip of Leaf [*Botany*] .... TANGLE
Angle between Leaf Apex and Widest Point [*Botany*] .... AANG
Angle Bulkhead Jack .... ABHJ
Angle Bulkhead Jack .... ABJ
Angle Closure Glaucoma [*Ophthalmology*] .... ACG
Angle Data Assembly .... ADA
Angle Data Recorder .... ADR
Angle Data Subsystem .... ADS
Angle Deception Jamming .... ADJ
Angle Deception Jamming System .... ADJS
Angle Evaporated Vertical Channel Power MOSFET [*Metal-Oxide-Semiconductor Field-Effect Transistor*] (IAA) .... AEVMOST
Angle Frame (OA) .... AF
Angle Iron [*Freight*] .... AI
Angle Jamming System .... AJS
Angle Lock .... AL
Angle Measuring Equipment .... AME
Angle Measuring Equipment, Correlation Tracking and Ranging .... AME/COTAR
Angle, Meter (DAVI) .... AM
Angle Neovascularization [*Opthalmology*] .... ANV
Angle of Arrival .... AOA
Angle of Attack [*Military*] (NG) .... A/A
Angle of Attack [*Military*] (MCD) .... AOA
Angle of Attack Limiter (MCD) .... AAL
Angle of Attack Transmitter [*Military*] .... AOAT
Angle of Bank .... AOB
Angle of Beam .... AOB
Angle of Descent .... AOD
Angle of Elevation .... AE
Angle of Greatest Extension [*Orthopedics*] .... AGE
Angle of Greatest Flexion [*Orthopedics*] .... AGF
Angle of Incidence I
Angle of Incidence (IDOE) I
Angle of Inner Gimbal .... AIG
Angle of Middle Gimbal (KSC) .... AMG
Angle of Reflection .... AOR
Angle of Sight (IAA) .... AS
Angle of Site .... AOS
Angle of Train .... AT
Angle of Yaw Indicator .... AYI
Angle on Jam (MCD) .... AOJ
Angle on Target .... AOT
Angle on the Bow [*Navy*] (NVT) .... AOB

Angle Order (IEEE) ... ANLOR
Angle Panel Jack ... APJ
Angle Point ... AP
Angle Position Indicator ... API
Angle Rate Bombing Set (DWSG) ... ARBS
Angle Resolved [*Physics*] ... AR
Angle Resources Ltd. [*Vancouver Stock Exchange symbol*] ... AGU
Angle Shot [*Cinematography*] (NTCM) ... AS
Angle Side Angle [*Geometry*] (BARN) ... ASA
Angle Stop Valve [*Technical drawings*] ... ASV
Angle Template ... AT
Angle, Time, Range [*Computer science*] ... ATR
Angle Track on Target [*Military*] ... ATOT
Angle Tracker (MUGU) ... A/T
Angle Tracking Computer (MHDI) ... ATRAC
Angle Tracking System [*NASA*] ... ATS
Angle Versus Length [*Computer science*] ... AVL
Angled (NTCM) ... A
Angled End [*Outdoor advertising*] (NTCM) ... AE
Angled Single [*Outdoor advertising*] (NTCM) ... AS
Angle-Dispersed Electron Spectroscopy (MCD) ... ADES
Angle-Dispersed Photoelectron Spectroscopy ... ADPES
Angle-Integrated Ultraviolet Photoelectron Spectroscopy ... AIUPS
Angle-of-Approach Indicator [*Aviation*] (AFM) ... AAI
Angle-of-Attack Indicator [*Military*] ... AAI
Angle-of-Attack Indicator [*Military*] ... AOAI
Angle-of-Attack Sensor [*Military*] (MCD) ... AOAS
Angle-Only Track ... AOT
Angleplied Laminate ... APL
Angler ... ANGLR
Angle-Resolved Electron Energy Loss Spectroscopy ... AREELS
Angle-Resolved Inverse Photoelectron Spectroscopy ... ARIPES
Angle-Resolved Photoelectron Spectroscopy ... ARPES
Angle-Resolved Photoemission (MCD) ... ARP
Angle-Resolved Photoemission Extended Fine Structure [*Analytical technique*] ... ARPEFS
Angle-Resolved Ultraviolet Photoelectron Spectroscopy ... ARUPS
Anglers' Co-Operative Association [*British*] (EAIO) ... ACA
Angler's Library [*A publication*] ... AL
Anglesey [*Welsh island and county*] (ROG) ... AGL
Anglesey [*Welsh island and county*] ... ANG
Anglesey Antiquarian Society [*British*] (DBA) ... AAS
Anglia and Prefect Owners' Club [*British*] (BI) ... APOC
Anglian Water Authority [*British*] (DCTA) ... AWA
Anglian Water Services Ltd. [*Commercial firm British*] (ECON) ... AW
Anglican ... A
Anglican ... ANG
Anglican ... ANGL
Anglican ... ANGLCN
Anglican Accredited Layworkers' Federation [*British*] ... AALF
Anglican and Eastern Churches Association [*British*] (EAIO) ... A & ECA
Anglican Association of Musicians (EA) ... AAM
Anglican Church Handbooks [*A publication*] ... ACH
Anglican Church House, Toronto, ON, Canada [*Library symbol Library of Congress*] (LCLS) ... CaOTCH
Anglican Church House, Toronto, Ontario [*Library symbol National Library of Canada*] (NLC) ... OTCH
Anglican Church of Canada ... ACC
Anglican Church of Canada, Archives, Toronto, ON, Canada [*Library symbol Library of Congress*] (LCLS) ... CaOTCHAr
Anglican Church of Canada Archives, Toronto, Ontario [*Library symbol National Library of Canada*] (NLC) ... OTCHAR
Anglican Church of Canada, British Columbia Provincial Synod, Archives, Vancouver, BC, Canada [*Library symbol Library of Congress*] (LCLS) ... CaBVaABSA
Anglican Church of Canada, Diocese of Algoma, Synod Office, Sault Ste. Marie, ON, Canada [*Library symbol*] [*Library of Congress*] (LCLS) ... CaOStMAAS
Anglican Church of Canada, Diocese of Brandon, Synod Office, Brandon, MB, Canada [*Library symbol Library of Congress*] (LCLS) ... CaMBABS
Anglican Church of Canada, Diocese of Caledonia, Synod Office, Victoria, BC, Canada [*Library symbol Library of Congress*] (LCLS) ... CaBPRACS
Anglican Church of Canada, Diocese of Fredericton, Archives, Fredericton, NB, Canada [*Library symbol Library of Congress*] (LCLS) ... CaNBFAFA
Anglican Church of Canada, Diocese of Keewatin, Synod Office, Kenora, ON, Canada [*Library symbol Library of Congress*] (LCLS) ... CaOKeAKS
Anglican Church of Canada, Diocese of Montreal, Archives, Montreal, PQ, Canada [*Library symbol Library of Congress*] (LCLS) ... CaQMADMA
Anglican Church of Canada, Diocese of Moosonee, Synod Office, Schumacher, ON, Canada [*Library symbol Library of Congress*] (LCLS) ... CaOSAMS
Anglican Church of Canada, Diocese of Nova Scotia, Synod Office, Halifax, NS, Canada [*Library symbol Library of Congress*] (LCLS) ... CaNSHANSS
Anglican Church of Canada, Diocese of Ontario, Synod Office, Kingston, ON, Canada [*Library symbol Library of Congress*] (LCLS) ... CaOKAOS
Anglican Church of Canada, Diocese of Ottawa, Archives, Ottawa, ON, Canada [*Library symbol Library of Congress*] (LCLS) ... CaOOAOA
Anglican Church of Canada, Diocese of Quebec, Synod Office, Quebec, PQ, Canada [*Library symbol Library of Congress*] (LCLS) ... CaQQAQS
Anglican Church of Canada, Diocese of Saskatchewan, Synod Office, Prince Albert,SK, Canada [*Library symbol Library of Congress*] (LCLS) ... CaSPAASS
Anglican Church of Canada, Ecclesiastical Province of British Columbia, Vancouver, BC, Canada [*Library symbol*] [*Library of Congress*] (LCLS) ... CaBVaABS
Anglican Church of Canada, St. George's Cathedral, Kingston, ON, Canada [*Library symbol Library of Congress*] (LCLS) ... CaOKASG
Anglican Communion ... AC
Anglican Communion Office [*British*] (EAIO) ... ACO
Anglican Community Services Council [*Australia*] ... ACSC
Anglican Consultative Council [*British*] (EAIO) ... ACC
Anglican Council of North America and the Caribbean ... ACNAC
Anglican Evangelical Group Movement (BARN) ... AEGM
Anglican Fellowship of Prayer (EA) ... AFP
Anglican Men's Society in Australia ... AMSA
Anglican Pacifist Fellowship [*Oxford, England*] (EAIO) ... APF
Anglican Society (EA) ... AS
Anglican Young People's Association [*British*] ... AYPA
Anglican Youth Movement [*Canada*] ... AYM
Anglican-Roman Catholic International Commission ... ARCIC-II
Anglice [*In English*] [*Latin*] ... ANGL
Angling ... A
Angling Trade Association (EAIO) ... ATA
Anglistik [*Study of English language and literature*] [*German*] ... Angl
Anglo Am Gold Inv ADR [*NASDAQ symbol*] (TTSB) ... AAGIY
Anglo Amer So Afr ADR [*NASDAQ symbol*] (TTSB) ... ANGLY
Anglo American Corp. of South Africa Ltd. [*NASDAQ symbol*] (NQ) ... ANGL
Anglo American Corp. of South Africa Ltd. [*Associated Press*] (SAG) ... AngSA
Anglo American Gold [*Associated Press*] (SAG) ... AngAG
Anglo American Gold Investment Co. Ltd. [*NASDAQ symbol*] (NQ) ... AAGI
Anglo American Resources [*Vancouver Stock Exchange symbol*] ... AAM
Anglo Australian Resources ... AAR
Anglo Canadian Mining Corp. [*Toronto Stock Exchange symbol Vancouver Stock Exchange symbol*] ... ANP
Anglo Cargo Ltd. [*British ICAO designator*] (FAAC) ... ANC
Anglo Dominion Gold Exploration Ltd. [*Toronto Stock Exchange symbol*] ... ADE
Anglo-American ... AA
Anglo-American Air Force (DAS) ... AAAF
Anglo-American Associates (EA) ... AAA
Anglo-American Authority File of Authors ... AAAF
Anglo-American Cataloguing Rules [*American Library Association A publication*] ... AACR
Anglo-American Cataloguing Rules, Second Edition [*American Library Association A publication*] ... AACR2
Anglo-American Code [*Cataloging*] (DIT) ... AAC
Anglo-American Committee [*World War II*] ... AAC
Anglo-American Council on Productivity [*British*] (DI) ... AACP
Anglo-American Families Association [*British*] (BI) ... AAFA
Anglo-American Food Committee [*World War II*] ... AAFC
Anglo-American Joint Chiefs of Staff ... AAJCS
Anglo-American Judicial Exchange (ILCA) ... AAJE
Anglo-American Press Association of Paris [*See also APAAP*] [*France*] (EA) ... AAPAP
Anglo-American Racers ... AAR
Anglo-American Sporting Club ... AASC
Anglo-American-Hellenic Bureau of Education [*Defunct*] ... AAHBE
Anglo-Australian Observatory ... AAO
Anglo-Australian Telescope ... AAT
Anglo-Belgian Society (DBA) ... ABS
Anglo-Bomarc Mines [*Vancouver Stock Exchange symbol*] ... ANB
Anglo-Brazilian Information Service [*Information service or system*] (IID) ... ABIS
Anglo-Canadian Telephone Co. [*Toronto Stock Exchange symbol*] ... ACT
Anglo-Chilean Society (EAIO) ... ACS
Anglo-Continental Dental Society [*British*] ... ACDS
Anglo-Continental Society [*British*] ... ACS
Anglo-Dutch-United States ... ANDUS
Anglo-French [*Language, etc.*] ... AF
Anglo-French [*Language, etc.*] ... AFR
Anglo-French Supply and Purchases [*World War II*] ... AFSP
Anglo-French Variable-Geometry [*Combat aircraft*] ... AFVG
Anglo-Frisian [*Language, etc.*] ... AF
Anglo-German Variable Geometry [*Avaition*] (PDAA) ... AGVG
Anglo-Indian [*Language, etc.*] ... AI
Anglo-Indian (BARN) ... A-Ind
Anglo-Irish [*Language, etc.*] ... AI
Anglo-Irish Agreement [*1985*] ... AIA
Anglo-Irish Beef Processors Ltd. [*Northern Ireland*] ... AIBP
Anglo-Irish Free Trade Area [*British*] ... AIFTA
Anglo-Irish Free Trade Area Agreement (PDAA) ... AIFTAA
Anglo-Israel Association [*British*] (BI) ... AIA
Anglo-Israelism [*or Anglo-Israelite*] ... AI
Anglo-Italian Society [*British*] (DBA) ... AIS
Anglo-Ivorian Society [*British*] (DBA) ... AIS
Anglo-Japanese Economic Institute [*British*] (EAIO) ... AJEI
Anglo-Jewish Association [*British*] ... AJA
Anglo-Latin [*Language, etc.*] ... AL
Anglo-Malaysian Defence Agreement ... AMDA
Anglo-Mongolian Society (EAIO) ... AMS
Anglo-Norman [*Language, etc.*] ... AN
Anglo-Norman Text Society [*British*] ... ANTS
Anglo-Rhodesian Society (EA) ... ARS
Anglo-Saxon [*MARC language code Library of Congress*] (LCCP) ... ang
Anglo-Saxon ... Ang-Sax
Anglo-Saxon [*Language, etc.*] ... A-S
Anglo-Saxon Christian Patriot (EA) ... ASCP
Anglo-Saxon Chronicle ... ASC
Anglo-Saxon Protestant ... ASP
Anglo-Scandinavian Study of Early Thrombolysis ... ASSET
Anglo-Soviet Pact (DAS) ... ASP
Anglo-Soviet Recognition Signals ... ASRS

Anglo-Vernacular ... AV
Angmagssalik [*Greenland*] [*ICAO location identifier*] (ICLI) ... BGAM
Ango [*Zaire*] [*ICAO location identifier*] (ICLI) ... FZKO
Angoavia Angola [*FAA designator*] (FAAC) ... NGV
Angoche [*Mozambique*] [*ICAO location identifier*] (ICLI) ... FQAG
Angola [*ANSI three-letter standard code*] (CNC) ... AGO
Angola ... ANG
Angola [*MARC country of publication code Library of Congress*] (LCCP) ... ao
Angola [*ANSI two-letter standard code*] (CNC) ... AO
Angola [*Aircraft nationality and registration mark*] (FAAC) ... D2
Angola [*International civil aircraft marking*] (ODBW) ... D2
Angola [*MARC geographic area code Library of Congress*] (LCCP) ... f-ao--
Angola Air Charter Ltd. [*ICAO designator*] (FAAC) ... AAC
Angola Air Charter Ltd. [*ICAO designator*] (FAAC) ... AGO
Angola, IN [*Location identifier FAA*] (FAAL) ... ANQ
Angola, IN [*Location identifier FAA*] (FAAL) ... SJZ
Angola, IN [*FM radio station call letters*] ... WEAX
Angola, IN [*Television station call letters*] ... WINM
Angola, IN [*FM radio station call letters*] ... WLKI
Angola, LA [*FM radio station call letters*] ... KLSP
Angolan News Agency ... ANGOP
Angolia (VRA) ... Ang
Angoon [*Alaska*] [*Airport symbol*] (OAG) ... AGN
Angora [*Bolivia*] [*ICAO location identifier*] (ICLI) ... SLAN
Angora Goat Record and Registry (EA) ... AGRR
Angoram [*Papua New Guinea*] [*Airport symbol*] (OAG) ... AGG
Angouleme/Brie-Champniers [*France ICAO location identifier*] (ICLI) ... LFBU
Angra Do Heroismo [*Azores*] [*Seismograph station code, US Geological Survey*] (SEIS) ... ADH
Angry Revengeful Frequent Fliers [*Aeronautics*] ... ARFF
Angry Young Man (BARN) ... AYM
Angst, Revolution, Titillation [*Art films*] ... ART
Angstrom [*Also, AU*] ... A
Angstrom Pyrheliometric Scale ... APS
Angstrom Unit [*Also, A*] ... AU
Angstromeinheit [*Angstrom Unit*] [*German*] ... AE
Anguganak [*Papua New Guinea*] [*Airport symbol*] (OAG) ... AKG
Anguilla [*ANSI two-letter standard code*] (CNC) ... AI
Anguilla [*West Indies*] [*Airport symbol*] (OAG) ... AXA
Anguilla [*Leeward Islands*] [*Airport symbol*] (AD) ... AXA
Anguilla [*International civil aircraft marking*] (ODBW) ... VP-LA
Anguilla Democratic Party [*Political party*] (EY) ... ADP
Anguilla, MS [*Location identifier FAA*] (FAAL) ... RFK
Anguilla National Alliance (PPW) ... ANA
Anguilla People's Party [*Later, ADP*] [*Political party*] (PPW) ... APP
Anguilla Tourist Information and Reservation Office (EA) ... ATIRO
Anguilla Tourist Information Office [*Later, ATIRO*] (EA) ... ATIO
Angular ... ANLR
Angular Acceleration Susceptibility [*Orientation*] ... AAS
Angular Accelerometer [*NASA*] (MCD) ... AA
Angular Accelerometer Input Device (MCD) ... AAID
Angular Accelerometer Unit ... AAU
Angular Aperture (MCD) ... AA
Angular Blocky Soil [*Agronomy*] ... ABK
Angular Correlation of Annihilation Radiation [*Spectroscopy*] ... ACAR
Angular Dependent Photoelectron Diffraction (PDAA) ... ADPD
Angular Dialing Unit (IAA) ... ADU
Angular Differentiating-Integrating Accelerometer ... ADA
Angular Display Unit (IAA) ... ADU
Angular Distribution Auger Microscopy ... ADAM
Angular Distribution Data Tape ... ADDT
Angular Distribution Pattern [*Surface analysis*] ... ADP
Angular Intensity Light Scattering [*Physics*] ... AILS
Angular Magnetic-Hydrodynamic Integrating Accelerometer ... AMIA
Angular Mapping Transformation [*Computer science*] ... AMT
Angular Measurement Accuracy ... AMA
Angular Momentum ... AM
Angular Momentum [*Physics*] (BARN) ... J
Angular Momentum [*Symbol*] [*IUPAC*] ... L
Angular Momentum [*Symbol*] [*Physics*] ... M
Angular Momentum Wheel (KSC) ... AMW
Angular Motion Compensator ... AMC
Angular Motion Simulator (MCD) ... AMS
Angular Position Counter (SAA) ... APC
Angular Position Digitizer ... APD
Angular Position Sensor ... APS
Angular Rate Bombing System (MCD) ... ARBS
Angular Rate Sensor ... ARS
Angular Second Moment ... ASM
Angular Velocity (MCD) ... AV
Angular Velocity (BARN) ... W
Angular Yaw Velocity (AAG) ... r
Angurugu Community Government Council [*Australia*] ... ACGC
Angus [*County in Scotland*] (ROG) ... AGS
Angus & Robertson [*Publisher*] [*Australia*] ... A & R
Angus Aviation Ltd. [*Canada ICAO designator*] (FAAC) ... AAZ
Angus Resources Ltd. [*Vancouver Stock Exchange symbol*] ... AGS
Angus Society of Australia ... ASA
Angus Telemanagement Group, Inc. [*Pickering, ON*] [*Information service or system Telecommunications*] (TSSD) ... ATMG
Angwin, CA [*FM radio station call letters*] ... KCDS
Anhang [*Appendix*] [*German*] (EG) ... ANH
Anheuser Busch [*NYSE symbol*] (SAG) ... BUD
Anheuser-Busch Companies, Inc. [*Associated Press*] (SAG) ... Anheus
Anheuser-Busch Cos. [*NYSE symbol*] (TTSB) ... BUD
Anheuser-Busch, Inc. ... AB
Anheuser-Busch, Inc., Corporation Library, St. Louis, MO [*OCLC symbol*] (OCLC) ... ABS
Anheuser-Busch, Inc., St. Louis, MO [*Library symbol Library of Congress*] (LCLS) ... MoSAB
Anholt [*Denmark ICAO location identifier*] (ICLI) ... EKAT
Anhwei Province [*China, Mainland*] [*MARC geographic area code Library of Congress*] (LCCP) ... a-cc-an
Anhydride (MSA) ... ANHYD
Anhydrobis(beta-hydroxyethyl)biguanide [*Antiviral agent*] ... ABOB
Anhydroenneahepitol [*Organic chemistry*] ... AEH
Anhydroglucose [*Biochemistry*] ... AHG
Anhydroglucose Unit [*Biochemistry*] ... AGU
Anhydrotic Congenital Ectodermal Dysplasia [*Medicine*] (DMAA) ... ACED
Anhydrous ... AN
Anhydrous ... ANH
Anhydrous ... ANHY
Anhydrous ... ANHYD
Anhydrous Hydrazine [*Rocket propellant*] ... AH
Anhydrous Hydrogen Fluoride [*Inorganic chemistry*] ... AHF
Anhydrous Monocalcium Phosphate [*Inorganic chemistry*] ... AMCP
Anhydrous Sodium Metasilicate [*Inorganic chemistry*] ... ASM
Anhysteretic Remanent Magnetization ... ARM
Aniak [*Alaska*] [*Airport symbol*] (OAG) ... ANI
Anicom, Inc. [*NASDAQ symbol*] (SAG) ... ANIC
Anicom, Inc. [*Associated Press*] (SAG) ... Anicom
Anie/Kolokope [*Togo*] [*ICAO location identifier*] (ICLI) ... DXKP
Anika Research [*NASDAQ symbol*] (TTSB) ... ANIK
Anika Research, Inc. [*NASDAQ symbol*] (SAG) ... ANIK
Anika Research, Inc. [*Associated Press*] (SAG) ... AnikaRs
Aniline [*Philately*] ... anil
Aniline Association (EA) ... AA
Aniline Blue-Lactophenol Medium [*Botany*] ... ABLP
Aniline Gentian Violet ... AGV
Aniline Hydrogen Phthalate (OA) ... AHP
Aniline Point [*Measure of solvency*] ... AP
Aniline, Sulfur, and Formaldehyde [*Resin*] (AAMN) ... ASF
Aniline-Furfuryl Alcohol-Hydrazine (SAA) ... A-FA-H
Anilinonaphthalenesulfonic Acid [*Also, ANSA*] [*Organic chemistry*] ... ANS
(Anilino)naphthalenesulfonic Acid [*Also, ANS*] [*Organic chemistry*] ... ANSA
(Anilinonaphthyl)maleimide [*Organic chemistry*] ... ANM
Anima Dulcis [*Sweet Soul*] [*Latin*] ... AD
Anima Quiescat in Christo [*May His, or Her, Soul Repose in Christ*] [*Latin*] ... AQIC
Animal [*Psychology*] ... A
Animal ... AN
Animal ... ANI
Animal ... ANIM
Animal (WGA) ... ANL
Animal ... ANML
Animal Air Transportation Association (EA) ... AATA
Animal and Plant Health Inspection Service ... APHI
Animal and Plant Health Inspection Service [*Department of Agriculture*] [*Also, an information service or system*] (IID) ... APHIS
Animal Behavior Society (EA) ... ABS
Animal Breeding Research Organisation [*British*] ... ABRO
Animal Care Panel [*Later, AALAS*] ... ACP
Animal Damage Control [*Department of Agriculture*] ... ADC
Animal Defence League of Canada (AC) ... ADLC
Animal Defense/Anti-Vivisection Society of BC (AC) ... ADAV
Animal Detail [*Rorschach*] [*Psychology*] ... Ad
Animal Disease and Parasite Research Division [*of ARS, Department of Agriculture*] ... ADP
Animal Disease Eradication Division [*of ARS, Department of Agriculture*] ... ADE
Animal Disease Occurrence [*Database*] [*Commonwealth Agricultural Bureaux*] [*Information service or system*] (CRD) ... ADO
Animal Diseases Research Association [*Moredun Institute*] [*British*] (ARC) ... ADRA
Animal Diseases Research Institute [*Canada*] (IRC) ... ADRI
Animal Diseases Research Institute, Agriculture Canada [*Institut de Recherches Veterinaires, Agriculture Canada*] **Ottawa, Ontario** [*Library symbol National Library of Canada*] (NLC) ... OOAGA
Animal Diseases Research Institute (West), Agriculture Canada [*Institut de Recherches Veterinaires (Ouest), Agriculture Canada*] **Lethbridge, Alberta** [*Library symbol National Library of Canada*] (NLC) ... ALADR
Animal Drug Research Center [*Denver, CO*] [*Department of Health and Human Services*] (GRD) ... ADRC
Animal Educational League [*Defunct*] ... AEL
Animal Feed and Tissue Residue Research Center [*Department of Health and Human Services*] (GRD) ... AFTRRC
Animal Guild of America (EA) ... AGA
Animal Health Distributors Association [*British*] (DBA) ... AHDA
Animal Health Foundation (EA) ... AHF
Animal Health Institute (EA) ... AHI
Animal Health Technologists Association of BC (AC) ... AHTA of BC
Animal Health Trust [*British*] (BI) ... AHT
Animal Husbandry Research Division [*of ARS, Department of Agriculture*] ... AH
Animal Improvement Programs Laboratory [*Formerly, DHIA*] (EA) ... AIPL
Animal Industry Foundation (EA) ... AIF
Animal Inspection and Quarantine Division [*of ARS, Department of Agriculture*] ... AIQ
Animal Legal Defense Fund (EA) ... ALDF
Animal Liberation (EA) ... AL
Animal Liberation Front (EA) ... ALF
Animal Medical Center (EA) ... AMC

Animal Medicinal Drug Use Clarification Act of 1994 .... AMDUCA
Animal Models of Protecting Ischemic Myocardium [Cardiology
   project] .... AMPIM
Animal Nutrition Research Council (EA) .... ANRC
Animal Parasitic Systems .... APS
Animal Pathology Laboratory, Food Production and Inspection Branch,
  Agriculture Canada [Laboratoire de Pathologie Veterinaire, Direction
  Generale de la Production et de l'Inspection des Aliments, Agriculture
  Canada], Richmond, BritishColumbia [Library symbol National Library of
  Canada] (BIB) .... BRIAG
Animal Pathology Laboratory, Food Production and Inspection Branch,
  Agriculture Canada [Laboratoire de Pathologie Veterinaire, Direction
  Generale de la Production et de l'Inspection des Aliments, Agriculture
  Canada], Saskatoon, Saskatchewan [Library symbol National Library of
  Canada] (BIB) .... SSAGA
Animal Political Action Committee (EA) .... ANPAC
Animal Procurement Office [Military] .... APO
Animal Production and Health Commission for Asia [Australia] .... APHCA
Animal Protection Institute of America (EA) .... API
Animal Protective Association (EA) .... APA
Animal Protein Factor .... APF
Animal Psi [Parapsychology] .... ANPSI
Animal Research Centre [Canada] (ARC) .... ARC
Animal Research Committee .... ARC
Animal Research Facilities .... ARF
Animal Research Institute, Agriculture Canada [Institut de Recherches
  Zootechniques, Agriculture Canada] Ottawa, Ontario [Library symbol
  National Library of Canada] (NLC) .... OOAGAR
Animal Resources Center [University of Texas at Austin] [Research center]
  (RCD) .... ARC
Animal Resources Program [Bethesda, MD] [Department of Health and
  Human Services] (GRD) .... ARP
Animal Rights [An association Australia] .... AR
Animal Rights Coalition (EA) .... ARC
Animal Rights Information and Education Service (EA) .... ARIES
Animal Rights International (EA) .... ARI
Animal Rights Law Reporter [A publication] (DLA) .... Animal Rights L Rep
Animal Rights Mobilization (EA) .... ARM
Animal Rights Network (EA) .... ARN
Animal Transport [Navy ship symbol] [Obsolete] .... APA
Animal Transport [British and Canadian] [World War II] .... AT
Animal Tumor Research Facility [Rochester University] (PDAA) .... ATRE
Animal Virus Research Institute [British] (ARC) .... AVRI
Animal Welfare Information Center [Department of Agriculture Information
  service or system] (IID) .... AWIC
Animal Welfare Institute (EA) .... AWI
Animal Welfare League of South Australia .... AWLSA
Animal-Facilitated Therapy .... AFT
Animal-Tub-Sized [Paper] .... ATS
Animal-Unit Month .... AUM
Animal-Vues (EA) .... AV
Animate (WGA) .... AN
Animated .... ANMTD
Animated Backlighted Burtek Trainer .... ABBT
Animated Burtek Trainer .... ABT
Animated Computer Education .... ACE
Animated Dissection of Anatomy for Medicine [Interactive Multimedia
  Program] .... ADAM
Animated Film Language (BUR) .... AFL
Animated Graphics System (WDMC) .... AGS
Animated Movie Language (BUR) .... AML
Animated Reconstruction of Telemetry .... ART
Animation [Films, television, etc.] .... ANIM
Animation Photo Transfer [Animation technique developed by Disney
  Studio] .... APT
Animation Producers' Association [Defunct] (EA) .... APA
Animato [Lively, Animated] [Music] .... ANIMO
Anina Resources, Inc. [Vancouver Stock Exchange symbol] .... ANI
Anion .... A
Anion Exchanger 1 [Biochemistry] AE1
Anion Gap [Medicine] (DAVI) .... AG
Anion Vacancy (IAA) .... AV
Anion-Responsive Electrode .... ARE
Anisakan [Myanmar] [ICAO location identifier] (ICLI) .... VBAS
Anisean [Geology] .... A
Anisidine Value [Food science] .... AnV
Anisocytosis [Hematology] (DAVI) .... ANIS
Anisocytosis [Hematology] .... aniso
Anisometropia [Ophthalmology] .... AN
Anisometropia [Ophthalmology] .... Anisometr
Anisotropic Hypernetted Chain [Chemical physics] .... AHNC
Anisotropic Magnetoresistance .... AMR
Anisotropic Remanent Magnetism (PDAA) .... ARM
Anisotropic Saturation Recovery [NMR imaging] .... ASR
Anisotropic Source Flux Iteration Technique (PDAA) .... ASFIT
Anisotropic Spin-Orbit (PDAA) .... ASO
Anisotropic Stress Effect (PDAA) .... ASE
Anisotropically Conductive Silicone [Rubber] [Robotics] .... ACS
Anisotropy of Magnetic Susceptibility [Geophysics] .... AMS
Anisoyl [As substituent on nucleoside] [Biochemistry] .... an
Anisoylated-Plasminogen-Streptokinase Activator Complex
  [Thrombolytic] .... APSAC
Anistropy Telescope [Instrumentation] .... AT
Anisum [Anise Seed] [Pharmacology] (ROG) .... ANIS
Anisylacetone [Organic chemistry] .... AA

Anita Tribune, Anita, IA [Library symbol Library of Congress] (LCLS) .... IaAniT
Aniwa [Vanuatu] [ICAO location identifier] (ICLI) .... NVVB
Anixter International, Inc. [Associated Press] (SAG) .... Anixter
Anixter International, Inc. [NYSE symbol] (SAG) .... AXE
Anixter Intl. [NYSE symbol] (TTSB) .... AXE
Anjouan [Comoro Islands] [Airport symbol] (OAG) .... AJN
Anjouan/Ouani [Comoros] [ICAO location identifier] (ICLI) .... FMCV
Ankang [China] [Airport symbol] (OAG) .... AKA
Ankara [Turkey] [Seismograph station code, US Geological Survey] (SEIS) .... ANK
Ankara [Turkey] [Airport symbol] (OAG) .... ANK
Ankara [Turkey ICAO location identifier] (ICLI) .... LTAA
Ankara/Esenboga [Turkey ICAO location identifier] (ICLI) .... LTAC
Ankara/Etimesgut [Turkey ICAO location identifier] (ICLI) .... LTAD
Ankara/Murted [Turkey ICAO location identifier] (ICLI) .... LTAE
Ankara-Esenboga [Turkey] [Airport symbol] (OAG) .... ESB
Ankatan Udara Republik Indonesia .... AURI
Ankavandra [Madagascar] [ICAO location identifier] (ICLI) .... FMMK
Ankavandra [Madagascar] [Airport symbol] (OAG) .... JVA
Ankazoabo [Madagascar] [ICAO location identifier] (ICLI) .... FMSZ
Ankazoabo [Madagascar] [Airport symbol] (OAG) .... WAK
Ankeny, IA [FM radio station call letters] .... KJJY
Ankeny, IA [FM radio station call letters] .... KMXD
Ankeny Press-Citizen, Ankeny, IA [Library symbol Library of Congress]
  (LCLS) .... IaAnkP
Anker Data Systems (IAA) .... ADS
Ankina Breeders [Inactive] (EA) .... AB
Anklam [Germany ICAO location identifier] (ICLI) .... ETAM
Ankle (MAE) .... ank
Ankle Arm Index .... AAI
Ankle/Brachial Pressure Index .... A/B
Ankle/Brachial Pressure Index .... ABI
Ankle/Brachial Pressure Index .... ABPI
Ankle Jerk [Neurology] .... AJ
Ankle-Foot [Orthosis] [Orthopedics] (DAVI) .... A-F
Ankle-Foot Orthosis [Orthopedics] .... AFO
Ankole-Watusi International Registry (EA) .... AWIR
Ankylosing Spondylitis [Medicine] .... AS
Ankylosing Spondylitis [Medicine] (DMAA) .... ASP
Ankylosing Spondylitis Association (EA) .... ASA
Anmerkung [Note] [German] .... ANM
Ann [Myanmar] [ICAO location identifier] (ICLI) .... VBAN
Ann Arbor [Michigan] .... A²
Ann Arbor [Michigan] [Seismograph station code, US Geological Survey]
  (SEIS) .... AAM
Ann Arbor, MI [Location identifier FAA] (FAAL) .... ARB
Ann Arbor, MI [AM radio station call letters] .... WAAM
Ann Arbor, MI [Television station call letters] .... WBSX
Ann Arbor, MI [FM radio station call letters] .... WCBN
Ann Arbor, MI [FM radio station call letters] .... WIQB
Ann Arbor, MI [FM radio station call letters] .... WQKL
Ann Arbor, MI [AM radio station call letters] .... WTKA
Ann Arbor, MI [FM radio station call letters] .... WUOM
Ann Arbor Public Library, Ann Arbor, MI [Library symbol Library of
  Congress] (LCLS) .... MiAa
Ann Arbor Railroad Co. [AAR code] .... AA
Ann Taylor Stores [NYSE symbol] (SPSG) .... ANN
Ann Taylor Stores [Associated Press] (SAG) .... AnnTayl
Anna [Monetary unit] [India] .... A
Anna [Ohio] [Seismograph station code, US Geological Survey] (SEIS) AN1
Anna [Ohio] [Seismograph station code, US Geological Survey] (SEIS) AN3
Anna, IL [AM radio station call letters] .... WRAJ
Anna, IL [FM radio station call letters] .... WRAJ-FM
Anna Regina [Queen Anne] .... AR
Annaba [Algeria] [Airport symbol] (OAG) .... AAE
Annaba/El Mellah [Algeria] [ICAO location identifier] (ICLI) .... DABB
Annai [Guyana] [Airport symbol] (OAG) .... NAI
Annai [Guyana] [ICAO location identifier] (ICLI) .... SYAN
Annales [of Tacitus] [Classical studies] (OCD) .... Ann
Annales [Annals] [Latin] (GPO) .... ann
Annales Africaines [A publication] (ILCA) .... AA
Annales de Droit Commercial et Industriel Francais, Etranger, et
  International [A publication] (DLA) .... Ann Dr Com Ind Fr Etr
Annales de Droit Commercial Francais, Etranger, et International
  [A publication] (DLA) .... Ann Dr Com Fr Etr Int
Annales de Droit Economique [A publication] (DLA) .... Ann Econ
Annales de la Propriete Industrielle, Artistique, et Litteraire [A publication]
  (DLA) .... Ann de la Pro
Annales des Justices de Paix [France] [A publication] (ILCA) .... AJP
Annales des Justices de Paix [France] [A publication] (DLA) .... Ann JP
Annales Economiques [A publication] (DLA) .... Ann Econ
Annales. Faculte de Droit. Ecole Francaise de Droit de Beyrouth
  [A publication] (DLA) .... Ann Ec Fr Dr Beyrouth
Annales. Faculte de Droit et des Sciences Economiques [Beyrouth,
  Lebanon] [A publication] (DLA) ..... Ann de la Fac de Droit et des Sci Econ (Beyrouth)
Annales. Faculte de Droit et des Sciences Economiques de Beyrouth.
  Faculte de Droit [A publication] (DLA) .... Ann Fac Beyrouth
Annales. Faculte de Droit et des Sciences Economiques de Lille, France
  [A publication] (DLA) .... Ann de la Fac de Droit et des Sci Econ de Lille
Annales. Faculte de Droit et des Sciences Economiques de Lyon
  [A publication] (DLA) .... Ann Fac Lyon
Annales Malgaches [A publication] (DLA) .... Ann Malg
Annales Parlementaires [Belgium] [A publication] (DLA) .... Ann Parl
Annales. Universite de Madagascar [A publication] (DLA) .... Ann Malg
Annali di Diritto Internazionale [Milan] [A publication] (DLA) .... Ann Dir Int
Annali di Storia del Diritto [A publication] (ILCA) .... Ann St Dir

Annali. Facolta di Giurisprudenza. Universita di Bari [*A publication*] (DLA) ... Ann Fac Bari
Annali. Istituto di Corrispondenza Archeologica [*A publication*] (OCD) ... Ann Ist
Annali. Seminario Giuridico. Universita Catania [*A publication*] (ILCA) ... Ann Sem Giur Catania
Annali. Seminario Giuridico. Universita di Palermo [*A publication*] (ILCA) ... Ann Sem Giur
Annals ... ANN
Annals (DAVI) ... Annls
Annals Australia: Journal of Catholic Culture [*A publication*] (APTA) ... AA
Annals. Chinese Society of International Law [*Taipei, Taiwan*] [*A publication*] (DLA) ... Chinese Soc'y Int'l L Annals
Annals. Hitotsubashi Academy [*A publication*] (DLA) ... Ann Hitotsubashi Acad
Annals of Collective Economy [*Later, Annals of Public and Co-Operative Economy*] [*A publication*] ... ACE
Annals of Congress [*A publication*] (DLA) ... Ann C
Annals of Congress [*A publication*] (DLA) ... Ann Cong
Annals of Improbable Research [*A publication*] ... AIR
Annals of Philosophy [*A publication*] (BARN) ... AP
Annals of Science [*A publication*] (BARN) ... AS
Annals of the American Academy of Political and Social Science [*A publication*] (AAGC) ... Annals
Annals of the Kings of Assyria [*A publication*] (BJA) ... AKA
Annals. South Africa Museum [*A publication*] ... ASAM
Annaly's Lee Tempore Hardwicke [*7-10 George II, King's Bench*] [*1733-38*] [*A publication*] (DLA) ... Ann
Annamalainagar [*India*] [*Geomagnetic observatory code*] ... ANN
Annandale High School, Annandale, MN [*Library symbol*] [*Library of Congress*] (LCLS) ... MnAdH
Annandale Middle School, Annandale, MN [*Library symbol*] [*Library of Congress*] (LCLS) ... MnAdMS
Annandale Public Library, Annandale, MN [*Library symbol*] [*Library of Congress*] (LCLS) ... MnAd
Annapolis Bancshares [*NASDAQ symbol*] (TTSB) ... ANNB
Annapolis Bancshares, Inc. [*Associated Press*] (SAG) ... AnnapB
Annapolis Bancshares, Inc. [*NASDAQ symbol*] (SAG) ... ANNB
Annapolis Division [*Maryland*] [*Navy*] (DNAB) ... ANNADIV
Annapolis Lymphoblast Globulin [*Biochemistry*] (MAH) ... ALG
Annapolis, MD [*Location identifier FAA*] (FAAL) ... ANP
Annapolis, MD [*AM radio station call letters*] ... WANN
Annapolis, MD [*FM radio station call letters*] ... WFSI
Annapolis, MD [*FM radio station call letters*] ... WHFS
Annapolis, MD [*Television station call letters*] ... WMPT
Annapolis, MD [*AM radio station call letters*] ... WNAV
Annapolis, MD [*AM radio station call letters*] ... WYRE
Annapolis Region Community Arts Council (AC) ... ARCAC
Annapolis Science Center ... ASC
Annapolis Valley Regional Library, Annapolis Royal, NS [*Library symbol National Library of Canada*] (NLC) ... NSAR
Annapolis Valley Regional Library, Annapolis Royal, NS, Canada [*Library symbol Library of Congress*] (LCLS) ... CaNSAR
Annapurna Conservation Area Project [*Nepal*] ... ACAP
Anne Christy Fan Club (EA) ... ACFC
Anne Frank Fund [*Basel, Switzerland*] (EAIO) ... AFF
Anne Frank Institute of Philadelphia [*Formerly, NIH*] (EA) ... AFIP
Anne Frank Stichting [*Anne Frank Foundation*] [*Netherlands*] (EAIO) ... AFS
Anne Murray Fan Club (EA) ... AMFC
Anneal (KSC) ... ANL
Annealed ... ANN
Annealed Copper-Covered Steel ... ACS
Annealing (ABBR) ... A
Annealing Point (MCD) ... AP
Annecy [*France*] [*Airport symbol*] (OAG) ... NCY
Annecy/Meythet [*France ICAO location identifier*] (ICLI) ... LFLP
Annee Courante [*Of the Current Year*] [*French*] ... AC
Annee de Lumiere [*Light Year*] [*French*] ... AL
Annee Mondiale du Refugie ... AMR
Annemasse [*France ICAO location identifier*] (ICLI) ... LFLI
Annenberg Research Institute for Judaic and Middle Eastern Studies, Philadelphia, PA [*Library symbol*] [*Library of Congress*] (LCLS) ... PPAnR
Annesley on Insurance [*A publication*] (DLA) ... Ann Ins
Annette Funicello Fan Club (EA) ... AFFC
Annette Island [*Alaska*] [*Airport symbol Obsolete*] (OAG) ... ANN
Annette Island [*Alaska*] [*ICAO location identifier*] (ICLI) ... PANT
Annex ... AN
Annex [*Commonly used*] (OPSA) ... ANEX
Annex ... ANN
Annex [*Commonly used*] (OPSA) ... ANNX
Annex ... ANX
Annex (AABC) ... ANX
Annexure [*British and Canadian*] [*World War II*] ... annx
Anni [*Years*] [*Latin*] (GPO) ... ann
Anni Caesar [*Era of the Caesars*] [*Latin*] (ROG) ... A CAES
Anni Currentis [*Of the Current Year*] [*Latin*] (ROG) ... AC
Anni Praesentis [*In the Present Year*] [*Latin*] ... ap
Annie Penn Hospital, Medical Library, Reidsville, NC [*Library symbol Library of Congress*] (LCLS) ... NcReH
Annie People (EA) ... AP
Annihilation Radiation [*Physics*] ... ACAR
Anniston [*Alabama*] [*Airport symbol*] (OAG) ... ANB
Anniston, AL [*Location identifier FAA*] (FAAL) ... RLI
Anniston, AL [*AM radio station call letters*] ... WANA
Anniston, AL [*AM radio station call letters*] ... WDNG
Anniston, AL [*FM radio station call letters*] (RBYB) ... WGRW-FM
Anniston, AL [*AM radio station call letters*] ... WHMA
Anniston, AL [*FM radio station call letters*] ... WHMA-FM
Anniston, AL [*Television station call letters*] ... WJSU
Anniston Army Depot [*Alabama*] (AABC) ... ANAD
Anniston Museum of Natural History, Anniston, AL [*Library symbol Library of Congress*] (LCLS) ... AAnnM
Anniston Public Library, Anniston, AL [*Library symbol Library of Congress*] (LCLS) ... AAnn
Anniversary ... ANNIV
Anno [*or Annus*] [*Year*] [*Latin*] ... A
Anno [*or Annus*] [*Year*] [*Latin*] ... AN
Anno [*Year*] [*Latin*] ... ANN
Anno Ab Urbe Condita [*In the Year from the Building of the City (Rome)*] [*Latin*] (ROG) ... ANAUC
Anno ante Christum [*In the Year before Christ*] [*Latin*] ... AAC
Anno ante Christum [*In the Year before Christ*] (ROG) ... AN AC
Anno ante Christum Natum [*In the Year before the Birth of Christ*] [*Latin*] (DLA) ... AACN
Anno Christi [*In the Year of Christ*] [*Latin*] ... AC
Anno Christi [*In the Year of Christ*] [*Latin*] (ROG) ... AN C
Anno Christianis Aerae [*In the Year of the Christian Era*] [*Latin*] ... ACE
Anno Corrente [*In the Current Year*] [*Latin*] (ADA) ... AC
Anno Depositionis [*In the Year of the Deposit*] [*Freemasonry*] [*Latin*] ... A DEP
Anno Domini [*In the Year of Our Lord*] [*Latin*] (GPO) ... AD
Anno Domini [*In the Year of Our Lord*] [*Latin*] ... AN DO
Anno Futuro [*In the Next Year*] [*Latin*] (ADA) ... AF
Anno Hebraico [*In the Hebrew Year*] [*Since 3761 BC*] [*Latin*] ... AH
Anno Hegirae [*In the Year of the Hegira*] [*The flight of Mohammed from Mecca AD 622*] [*Latin*] ... AH
Anno Humanae Salutis [*In the Year of Human Salvation*] [*Latin*] ... AHS
Anno Inventionis [*In the Year of the Discovery*] [*Freemasonry*] [*Latin*] ... A INV
Anno Inventionis [*In the Year of the Discovery*] [*Latin*] ... AI
Anno Lucis [*In the Year of Light*] [*Latin*] ... AL
Anno Mundi [*In the Year of the World*] [*Since 4004 BC*] [*Latin*] (GPO) ... AM
Anno Orbis Conditi [*In the Year of the Creation*] [*Latin*] ... AOC
Anno Ordinis [*In the Year of the Order*] [*Used by the Knights Templar Freemasonry*] (ROG) ... AO
Anno post Christum Natum [*In the Year after Christ Was Born*] [*Latin*] (ROG) ... APC
Anno post Christum Natum [*In the Year after Christ Was Born*] [*Latin*] ... APCN
Anno post Roman Conditam [*In the Year after the Building of Rome*] [*753 BC*] [*Latin*] ... APRC
Anno Regni [*In the Year of the Reign*] [*Latin*] ... AR
Anno Regni Regis [*or Reginae*] [*In the Year of the King's, or Queen's, Reign*] [*Latin*] ... ARR
Anno Regni Victoriae Regina Vicesimo Secundo (DLA) ... ARVR 22
Anno Reparatae Salutis [*In the Year of Our Redemption*] [*Latin*] ... ARS
Anno Salvatoris [*or Salutis*] [*In the Year of Salvation*] [*Latin*] ... AS
Anno Urbis [*In the Year of the City of Rome*] [*Latin*] ... AU
Anno Urbis Conditae [*In the Year from the Building of the City (Rome)*] [*753 BC*] [*Latin*] ... AUC
Anno Vixit [*He Lived (a given number of) Years*] [*Latin*] ... AV
Annotate ... ANOT
Annotated (DLA) ... Ann
Annotated (DLA) ... Anno
Annotated ... ANNOT
Annotated Card Program ... AC
Annotated Code [*A publication*] (DLA) ... Ann Code
Annotated Code of Maryland [*A publication*] (DLA) ... MD Ann Code
Annotated Code of Maryland [*A publication*] (DLA) ... MD Code Ann
Annotated Law Reporter [*1932-35*] [*India*] [*A publication*] (DLA) ... Ann L Rep
Annotated Laws of Massachusetts [*A publication*] (DLA) ... Mass Ann Laws
Annotated Manual of Statutes and Regulations [*of the Federal Home Loan Bank Board*] ... AMSR
Annotated Predicate Calculus (MCD) ... APC
Annotated Statutes [*A publication*] (DLA) ... Ann St
Annotated Statutes of Indian Territory [*A publication*] (DLA) ... Ann St Ind T
Annotated Tax Cases [*England*] [*A publication*] (DLA) ... Ann Tax Cas
Annotated Tax Cases [*A publication*] ... ATC
Annotations to Official Florida Statutes [*A publication*] (DLA) ... Fla Stat Anno
Annotator [*MARC relator code*] [*Library of Congress*] (LCCP) ... ann
Announce (AABC) ... ANN
Announce (FAAC) ... ANNC
Announce Booth [*Soundproof room*] [*Television studio*] (NTCM) ... AB
Announced [*or Announcement of*] **Flight Opportunity** [*NASA*] (KSC) ... AFO
Announcement and Order Sheet (SAA) ... AOS
Announcement Day [*Military*] (DNAB) ... A (Day)
Announcement Number (DNAB) ... ANN NO
Announcement of Opportunity [*NASA*] (MCD) ... AO
Announcer (NTCM) ... ANN
Announcer ... ANNCR
Announcer (WDMC) ... anncr
Announcing (MSA) ... ANCG
Annoyance Call Bureau [*Telephone-pest control*] ... ACB
Annoyance Index [*Aviation*] (OA) ... AI
Annoyance Level [*Aircraft noise*] ... ANL
Annuaire (BJA) ... Ann
Annuaire. Academie Theologique (S. Clement D'Ochride) [*A publication*] (BJA) ... AnClemOchr
Annuaire de Legislation Francaise [*A publication*] (DLA) ... Ann Leg Fr
Annuaire de Legislation Francaise et Etrangere [*A publication*] (DLA) ... Ann de Leg
Annuaire. Faculte de Droit de Skopje [*A publication*] (DLA) ... Annu de la Fac de Droit de Skopje
Annuaire Francais de Droit International [*A publication*] ... ANFRIDI
Annuaire Judiciaire. [*A publication*] (DLA) ... Ann Jud

Annual ..... A
Annual (AABC) ..... ANL
Annual ..... ANN
Annual (ROG) ..... ANNL
Annual ..... ANNL
Annual Active Duty for Training [*Army*] ..... ANACDUTRA
Annual Advance Retainer Pay ..... AARP
Annual Aircraft Movements ..... AAM
Annual Allowance and Requirements Review [*Navy*] ..... AARR
Annual Authorizations Service [*of the Copyright Clearance Center*] ..... AAS
Annual Automated Controls Survey [*of a ship*] (DS) ..... AAS
Annual Average Daily Traffic [*on highways*] ..... AADT
Annual Average Score (AABC) ..... AAS
Annual Average Weekday Traffic [*TRB*] (TAG) ..... AAWDT
Annual Budget Authorization (AFM) ..... ABA
Annual Capital Charge ..... ACC
Annual Capital Grant [*Education*] (AIE) ..... ACG
Annual Change Traffic ..... ACT
Annual Conference (ADA) ..... AC
Annual Conference on Engineering in Medicine and Biology (HGAA) ..... ACEMB
Annual Conference Program Advisory Committee [*American Occupational Therapy Association*] ..... ACPAC
Annual Confidential Report ..... ACR
Annual Contracted Quantity (ADA) ..... ACQ
Annual Contributions Contract [*Public housing development*] ..... ACC
Annual Corrective Maintenance (CAAL) ..... ACM
Annual Cost of Ownership ..... ACO
Annual Course Contribution ..... ACC
Annual Curriculum Review [*Education*] (AIE) ..... ACR
Annual Customer Order [*Air Force*] (AFIT) ..... ANCO
Annual Cycle Energy System [*Energy Research and Development Administration*] ..... ACES
Annual Cycle of Readings from Torah and Prophets (BJA) ..... AC
Annual Cycle Thermal Energy Storage (PDAA) ..... ACTES
Annual Delegate Meeting [*British*] (DCTA) ..... ADM
Annual Demographic Survey [*Bureau of the Census*] (GFGA) ..... ADS
Annual Digest and Reports of Public International Law Cases [*A publication*] (DLA) ..... AD
Annual Digest and Reports of Public International Law Cases [*A publication*] (DLA) ..... ADILR
Annual Digest and Reports of Public International Law Cases [*A publication*] (DLA) ..... Ann Dig
Annual Digest and Reports of Public International Law Cases [*A publication*] (DLA) ..... Ann Dig ILC
Annual Digest of International Law [*A publication*] ..... ADIL
Annual Effective Yield [*Finance*] ..... AEY
Annual Efficiency Index [*Army*] ..... AEI
Annual Engineering Plan (AFIT) ..... AEP
Annual Estimated Usage ..... AEU
Annual Execution Plan (RDA) ..... AEP
Annual Field Training [*Army*] (AABC) ..... AFT
Annual Financial Plan ..... AFP
Annual Financial Target [*DoD*] ..... AFT
Annual Fuel Utilization Efficiency [*Furnaces*] ..... AFUE
Annual Funding Program [*Army*] ..... AFP
Annual General Inspection [*Army*] ..... AGI
Annual General Meeting ..... AGM
Annual Goal [*Education*] ..... AG
Annual Growth Rate ..... AGR
Annual High School Mathematics Examination [*Educational test*] ..... AHSME
Annual History Review (MCD) ..... AHR
Annual Hospital Report [*Program of the Department of Health and Human Services*] ..... AHR
Annual Housing Survey [*Department of Housing and Urban Development*] (GFGA) ..... AHS
Annual Hull Survey (DS) ..... AHS
Annual Implementation Plan [*Health Planning and Resource Development Act of 1974*] ..... AIP
Annual Improvement Factor (MCD) ..... AIF
Annual Improvement, Maintenance, and Support (MHDI) ..... AIMS
Annual Inert Gas System Survey (DS) ..... AIGSS
Annual Inspection and Overhaul [*Nuclear energy*] (NRCH) ..... AI & O
Annual Inspection Summary (MCD) ..... AIS
Annual Integrated Assessment of Security Assistance [*Military*] (DOMA) ..... AIASA
Annual Law Register of the United States [*A publication*] (DLA) ..... Ann L Reg US
Annual Law Review [*Australia A publication*] ..... Ann Law Review
Annual Lease [*Business term*] (MHDB) ..... AL
Annual Leave [*US Civil Service*] ..... AL
Annual Legal Bibliography [*Harvard Law School Library*] [*A publication*] (DLA) ..... Ann Leg Bibliog
Annual License Fee [*FCC*] (NTCM) ..... ALF
Annual Life Unit (MCD) ..... ALU
Annual Limit of Intake (MHDB) ..... ALI
Annual Logistic Estimate (NATG) ..... LOGEST
Annual Machinery Survey [*American Bureau of Shipping*] (DS) ..... AMS
Annual Maintenance Manhours [*Military*] (AABC) ..... AMMH
Annual Material Forecast [*Military*] (AFM) ..... AMF
Annual Military Inspection ..... AMI
Annual Military Personnel Inspection ..... AMPI
Annual National Information Retrieval Colloquium ..... ANIRC
Annual Northeast Regional Antipollution Conference ..... ANERAC
Annual Officer Billet Summary (DNAB) ..... AOBS
Annual Operating Budget [*Army*] ..... AOB
Annual Operating Hours (MCD) ..... AOH
Annual Operating Program [*Army*] ..... AOP
Annual Operating Requirements ..... AOR
Annual Ordinary Shareholders' Meeting [*Investment term*] ..... AOSM
Annual Percentage Rate ..... APR
Annual Percentage Yield ..... APY
Annual Permanent Improvement Program (AAGC) ..... APIP
Annual Plan ..... AP
Annual Planning Estimate [*Navy*] (NVT) ..... APE
Annual Planning Report ..... APR
Annual Practice [*A publication*] (DLA) ..... Ann Pr
Annual Practice [*A publication*] (DLA) ..... AP
Annual Print Awards (DGA) ..... APA
Annual Proceedings. National Association of Railway Commissions [*A publication*] (DLA) ..... Ann Proc Nat Asso R Coms
Annual Procurement Agreement (MCD) ..... APA
Annual Program Objectives [*Navy*] (NG) ..... APO
Annual Progress Report ..... APR
Annual Qualifications Questionnaire [*Navy*] (NVT) ..... AQQ
Annual Questionnaire ..... AQ
Annual Rate ..... AR
Annual Rate Plus Stock Dividend [*Investment term*] (DFIT) ..... B
Annual Reevaluation of Safe Areas (MCD) ..... ARSA
Annual Refrigerated Machinery Survey [*of a vessel*] (DS) ..... ARS
Annual Register [*London*] [*A publication*] (DLA) ..... Ann Reg
Annual Register [*A publication*] ..... AR
Annual Register, New Series [*A publication*] (DLA) ..... Ann Reg NS
Annual Renewable Term [*Insurance*] ..... ART
Annual Report [*A publication*] (DLA) ..... Ann Rep
Annual Report (DNAB) ..... ANNREPT
Annual Report ..... ANREP
Annual Report ..... AR
Annual Report and Official Opinions of the Attorney General of Indiana [*A publication*] (DLA) ..... Ann Rep & Op Ind Att'y Gen
Annual Report and Official Opinions of the Attorney General of Maryland [*A publication*] (DLA) ..... Ann Rep & Op MD Att'y Gen
Annual Report Council (EA) ..... ARC
Annual Report. Department of Mines. New South Wales [*Australia A publication*] ..... Ann Rept Dept Mines NSW
Annual Report of the Attorney General of Florida [*A publication*] (DLA) ..... Ann Rep Fla Att'y Gen
Annual Report of the Attorney General of South Carolina to the General Assembly [*A publication*] (DLA) ..... Ann Rep SC Att'y Gen
Annual Report on Transport Statistics ..... ARTS
Annual Report Producers Council ..... ARPC
Annual Report to Shareholders [*Securities and Exchange Commission*] (IID) ..... ARS
Annual Reports on Analytical Atomic Spectroscopy [*Later, JAAS*] [*A publication*] ..... ARAAS
Annual Research Conference [*Bureau of the Census*] (GFGA) ..... ARC
Annual Research Task Summary ..... ARTS
Annual Return ..... AR
Annual Return of Investment [*Business term*] ..... AROI
Annual Review (NATG) ..... AR
Annual Review and Information Symposium on the Technology of Training, Learning,and Education [*DoD*] ..... ARISTOTLE
Annual Review Committee [*NATO*] (NATG) ..... ARC
Annual Review of Information Science and Technology [*A publication*] ..... ARIST
Annual Review of International Affairs [*A publication*] (DLA) ..... Ann Rev Int'l Aff
Annual Review Questionnaire [*Military*] (AABC) ..... ARQ
Annual Review Traveling Team [*NATO*] (NATG) ..... ARTT
Annual Reviews (EA) ..... AR
Annual Schedule of Circuit Estimates [*Telecommunications*] (NITA) ..... ASCE
Annual Service Order ..... AnSO
Annual Service Practice [*Firings*] [*Military*] ..... ASP
Annual Summary Report ..... ASR
Annual Supply Inspection [*Military*] (NVT) ..... ASI
Annual Support Cost (MCD) ..... ASC
Annual Survey (DNAB) ..... AS
Annual Survey of African Law [*A publication*] (DLA) ..... Ann Surv Afr L
Annual Survey of American Law [*A publication*] (DLA) ..... Ann Surv Am
Annual Survey of Australian Law [*A publication*] ..... Ann Surv of Aust Law
Annual Survey of Australian Law [*A publication*] ..... ASAL
Annual Survey of Banking Law [*A publication*] (DLA) ..... Ann Surv Banking L
Annual Survey of Colleges [*The College Board*] [*Information service or system*] (CRD) ..... ASC
Annual Survey of Colorado Law [*A publication*] (DLA) ..... Ann Surv Colo L
Annual Survey of Indian Law [*A publication*] (DLA) ..... Ann Surv Ind L
Annual Survey of Manufactures [*Department of Commerce Information service or system*] ..... ASM
Annual Survey of Massachusetts Law [*A publication*] (DLA) ..... Ann Survey
Annual Survey of Massachusetts Law [*A publication*] (ILCA) ..... ASML
Annual Survey of South African Law [*A publication*] (DLA) ..... Ann Surv S Afr L
Annual System Operating Time (CAAL) ..... ASOT
Annual System Practice (MCD) ..... ASP
Annual Technical Conference [*Society of Plastics Engineers*] ..... ANTEC
Annual Technical Progress Report ..... ATPR
Annual Tour ..... AT
Annual Training [*Military*] (AFM) ..... AT
Annual Training Deployment (MCD) ..... ATD
Annual Training Duty [*Marine Corps*] ..... ATD
Annual Training Equipment Pools (AABC) ..... ATEP
Annual Value (ADA) ..... AV
Annual Wage Reporting [*Social Security Administration*] ..... AWR
Annual Wage Survey (OICC) ..... AWS
Annual Work Plan ..... AWP

Annual Work Schedule ... AWS
Annual Worldwide Industry Review (IMH) ... AWIR
Annual Yield [*Business term*] ... AY
Annualized Cost of Living Model ... ACOL
Annually (ROG) ... ANNLY
Annuario di Statistiche Guidiziarie [*A publication*] (ILCA) ... Ann Stat Guid
Annuitant (ROG) ... ANNUIT
Annuity (ROG) ... ANN
Annuity (DLA) ... ANNUI
Annuity ... ANNY
Annular ... A
Annular ... ANLR
Annular Base Drag ... ABD
Annular Bearing Engineers Committee (EA) ... ABEC
Annular Core Pulsed Reactor ... ACPR
Annular Core Research Reactor [*Nuclear energy*] (NRCH) ... ACRR
Annular Expansion Column [*Chromatography*] ... A/E
Annular Fire Missile ... AFM
Annular Linear Induction Pump [*Nuclear energy*] (NRCH) ... ALIP
Annular Momentum Control Device [*NASA*] ... AMCD
Annular Phased-Array System [*Cardiology*] (DAVI) ... APAS
Annular Pressure Loss [*Well drilling technology*] ... APL
Annular Primary Combustor ... APC
Annular Suspension and Pointing System (MCD) ... ASAP
Annular Suspension and Pointing System (SSD) ... ASPS
Annular Turbojet Combustor ... ATC
Annular Turbojet Combustor ... ATJC
Annular Vortex Combustor [*Coal technology*] (PS) ... AVC
Annulment (DLA) ... ANNUL
Annulment of Certification ... AC
Annuloaortic Ectasia [*Medicine*] (DMAA) ... AAE
Annulus Exhaust Gas Treatment System [*Nuclear energy*] (NRCH) ... AEGTS
Annulus Gas System [*Nuclear energy*] (NRCH) ... AGS
Annulus Vacuum Maintenance System [*Nuclear energy*] (NRCH) ... AVMS
Annunciation ... ANNUN
Annunciation [*or Annunciator*] (ROG) ... ANNUNC
Annunciator (NFPA) ... A
Annunciator [*Electronically controlled signal board*] (KSC) ... ANN
Annunciator ... ANNUN
Annunciator Control Assembly (MCD) ... ACA
Annunciator Control Unit [*Military*] (MCD) ... ACU
Annunciator Display Unit (MCD) ... ADU
Annunciator Response Procedure [*Nuclear energy*] (NRCH) ... ARP
Annus [*Year*] [*Latin*] ... ANN
Annus Erat Augusti [*It Was in the Year of Augustus*] [*Coin inscription*] [*Latin*] (ROG) ... AEA
Annus Mirabilis [*The Wonderful Year (1666)*] [*Latin*] (GPO) ... AM
Annville-Cleona, PA [*AM radio station call letters*] ... WWSM
Annydrous (BARN) ... anhydr
Anodal Closing Odor [*Physiology*] ... ACO
Anodal Closing Picture [*Physiology*] ... ACP
Anodal Closing Sound [*Physiology*] ... ACS
Anodal Closure [*Physiology*] ... AC
Anodal Closure Clonus [*Physiology*] (MAE) ... ACCI
Anodal Closure Contraction [*Also, AnCC*] [*Physiology*] ... ACC
Anodal Closure Contraction [*Also, ACC*] [*Physiology*] ... AnCC
Anodal Closure Tetanus [*Physiology*] ... ACTe
Anodal Contraction [*Physiology*] ... AC
Anodal Deviation [*Physiology*] ... AD
Anodal Duration [*Physiology*] (MAE) ... AD
Anodal Duration Contraction [*Physiology*] ... ADC
Anodal Duration Tetanus [*Physiology*] (DMAA) ... ADTe
Anodal Duration Tetanus [*Physiology*] ... AnDTe
Anodal Opening [*Physiology*] ... AO
Anodal Opening Clonus [*Medicine*] (DMAA) ... ANOCL
Anodal Opening Clonus [*Medicine*] (DMAA) ... AOCl
Anodal Opening Clonus [*Physiology*] ... AOCL
Anodal Opening Contraction [*Also, AOC*] [*Physiology*] ... AnOC
Anodal Opening Contraction [*Also, AnOC*] [*Physiology*] ... AOC
Anodal Opening Odor [*Physiology*] ... AOO
Anodal Opening Picture [*Physiology*] ... AOP
Anodal Opening Sound [*Physiology*] ... AOS
Anodal Opening Tetanus [*Medicine*] (MAE) ... AOTe
Anode [*Technical drawings*] ... A
Anode (IDOE) ... a
Anode (MSA) ... AD
Anode ... AN
Anode Circuit ... AC
Anode Current Efficiency [*Environmental science*] ... ACE
Anode Excitation (MAE) ... an ex
Anode Reaction ... AR
Anode Supply Voltage ... ASV
Anode Tapping Point (IAA) ... ATP
Anode Voltage Drop ... AVD
Anodic Iridium Oxide Film (PDAA) ... AIROF
Anodic Stripping Voltammetry [*Chemical analysis*] ... ASV
Anodically Electrodeposited Iridium Oxide Film [*Electrochemistry*] ... AEIROF
Anodize (MSA) ... ANDZ
Anodize (MSA) ... ANOD
Anodized Aluminum (VRA) ... anod alum
Anodizing ... ANDZNG
Anodyne [*Medicine*] (ROG) ... ANO
Anodynum [*A Soothing Medicament*] [*Pharmacy*] (ROG) ... ANODYN
Anoka Area Vocational Technical Institute, Anoka, MN [*Library symbol Library of Congress*] (LCLS) ... MnAnVT
Anoka County Genealogical Society, Anoka, MN [*Library symbol Library of Congress*] (LCLS) ... MnAnGS
Anoka County Historical Society, Anoka, MN [*Library symbol Library of Congress*] (LCLS) ... MnAnHi
Anoka County Library, Minneapolis, MN [*Library symbol Library of Congress*] (LCLS) ... MnMAC
Anoka, MN [*FM radio station call letters*] ... KQQL
Anoka-Ramsey Community College, Anoka, MN [*Library symbol Library of Congress*] (LCLS) ... MnAnA
Anomalistic Observational Phenomena [*In study of UFO's*] ... AOP
Anomalous Atrioventricular Conduction [*Cardiology*] ... AAVC
Anomalous Cirumflex [*Coronary Artery*] (DMAA) ... ACx
Anomalous Cosmic Ray ... ACR
Anomalous Dispersion Spherical Array Target [*for increasing radio reflectivity*] ... ADSAT
Anomalous Left Coronary Artery [*Cardiology*] (DMAA) ... ALCA
Anomalous Magnetic Moment ... AMM
Anomalous Photovoltaic Effect (MCD) ... APE
Anomalous Photovoltaic Effect (MCD) ... APV
Anomalous Propagation [*Telecommunications Electronics*] (NVT) ... ANAPROP
Anomalous Propagation [*Telecommunications Electronics*] (TEL) ... AP
Anomalous Pulmonary Venous Drainage [*Medicine*] (DAVI) ... APVD
Anomalous Retinal Correspondence [*Ophthalmology*] ... ARC
Anomalous Scattering [*Crystallography*] ... AS
Anomalous State of Knowledge [*Term used in artificial intelligence and concept experimentally used information systems*] (NITA) ... ASK
Anomalously Enriched Element [*Environmental chemistry*] ... AEE
Anomaly Dynamics Study [*NORPAX*] ... ADS
Anomaly Report (MCD) ... AR
Anomolous Skin Effect (PDAA) ... ASE
Anonim Sirketi [*Corporation, Joint-Stock Company*] ... AS
Anonima Lombarda Fabbrica Automobili ... ALFA
Anonymous ... A
Anonymous (WGA) ... AN
Anonymous ... ANON
Anonymous (VRA) ... anon
Anonymous ... ANON
Anonymous (WDMC) ... anon
Anonymous Arts Recovery Society (EA) ... AARS
Anonymous Donor's Sperm [*Obstetrics*] (DAVI) ... ADS
Anonymous Families History Project (EA) ... AFHP
Anonymous Peer Refereeing ... APR
Anonymous Reports at End of Benloe [*1661*] [*England*] [*A publication*] (DLA) ... AB
Anonymous Reports at End of Benloe [*1661*] [*England*] [*A publication*] (DLA) ... An
Anonymous Reports at End of Benloe [*1661*] [*England*] [*A publication*] (DLA) ... An B
Anonymous Society of Second Bananas (EA) ... ASSB
Anopheles (MAE) ... A
Anophthalmia (DMAA) ... ANOP
Anordnung [*Direction, Instruction*] [*German*] (ILCA) ... AnO
Anorectal Dressing (MAE) ... ARD
Anorexia and Bulimia Nervosa Foundation of Victoria [*Australia*] ... ABNFV
Anorexia Bulimia Nervosa Association (DBA) ... ABNA
Anorexia Nervosa [*Medicine*] ... AN
Anorexia Nervosa and Associated Disorders [*Later, ANAD-National Association of Anorexia Nervosa and Associated Disorders*] (EA) ... ANAD
Anorexia Nervosa and Related Eating Disorders (EA) ... ANRED
Anorexic Family Aid and National Information Centre [*British*] (CB) ... AFA
Anorthite [*CIPW classification*] [*Geology*] ... an
Anorthotiko Komma Ergazomenou Laou [*Progressive Party of the Working People*] [*Cyprus*] [*Political party*] (PPW) ... AKEL
Another ... ANO
Another (ROG) ... ANOR
Another (ROG) ... ANR
Another Boring Book Bi-Monthly Rag [*Subtitle for the periodical Slightly Soiled*] [*British A publication*] ... ABBBMR
Another Chicago Magazine [*A publication*] (BRI) ... ACM
Another Copy (ROG) ... AC
Another Debugger [*Computer science*] (BYTE) ... adb
Another Mother for Peace [*Defunct*] (EA) ... AMP
Another World Viewer Alliance (EA) ... AWVA
Anovular Menstruation ... AM
Anovulatory Persistent Proliferative Endometrium [*Medicine*] ... APPEM
Anovulatory Syndrome [*Medicine*] (DMAA) ... AS
Anoxic Encephalopathy [*Medicine*] ... AE
Anoxygenic Phototrophic Bacteria ... APB
Anpu [*Republic of China*] [*Seismograph station code, US Geological Survey*] (SEIS) ... ANP
ANQ: A Quarterly Journal of Short Articles, Notes, and Reviews [*A publication*] (BRI) ... ANQ:QJ
ANSA [*Agenzia Nazionale Stampa Associata*]'s Electronic Documentation Service [*ANSA Agency*] (IID) ... DEA
Ansaldo Signal [*Associated Press*] (SAG) ... Ansaldo
Ansaldo Signal [*NASDAQ symbol*] (SAG) ... ASIG
Ansan, Inc. [*Associated Press*] (SAG) ... Ansan
Ansan, Inc. [*NASDAQ symbol*] (SAG) ... ANSN
Ansan Inc. Unit [*NASDAQ symbol*] (TTSB) ... ANSNU
Ansan Inc. Wrrt'A' [*NASDAQ symbol*] (TTSB) ... ANSNW
Ansan Inc. Wrrt'B' [*NASDAQ symbol*] (TTSB) ... ANSNZ
Ansbach [*Germany ICAO location identifier*] (ICLI) ... EDEB
Ansbach/Petersdorf [*Germany ICAO location identifier*] (ICLI) ... EDQF
Anschliessend [*Following, Subsequent*] [*German*] ... anschl
Ansco Resources (BC) [*Vancouver Stock Exchange symbol*] ... ANS

Anselmus de Baggio de Lucca [*Deceased, 1086*] [*Authority cited in pre-1607 legal work*] (DSA) .... Ans
Ansett Airlines of Australia [*ICAO designator*] (FAAC) .... AAA
Ansett Airlines of Australia [*ICAO designator*] (AD) .... AN
Ansett Airlines of Australia .... ANSETT
Ansett Airlines of New South Wales [*Australia*] .... AANSW
Ansett Airlines of New South Wales [*Australia ICAO designator*] (FAAC) ...... NSW
Ansett Airlines of New South Wales [*ICAO designator*] (AD) .... WX
Ansett Airlines of South Australia .... AASA
Ansett Airlines of South Australia [*ICAO designator*] (AD) .... GJ
Ansett Express [*Airport symbol*] .... WX
Ansett New Zealand [*ICAO designator*] (AD) .... ZQ
Ansett New Zealand [*Airline flight code*] (ODBW) .... ZQ
Ansett Worldwide Aviation Services [*Australia*] .... AWAS
Ansoft Corp. [*Associated Press*] (SAG) .... Ansoft
Ansoft Corp. [*NASDAQ symbol*] (SAG) .... ANST
Ansoft Corp. [*NASDAQ symbol*] (TTSB) .... ANST
Anson County Library, Wadesboro, NC [*Library symbol Library of Congress*] (LCLS) .... NcWad
Anson County Senior High School, Medial Center, Wadesboro, NC [*Library symbol*] [*Library of Congress*] (LCLS) .... NcWadAS
Anson on Contracts [*A publication*] (DLA) .... Ans Con
Anson on Contracts [*A publication*] (DLA) .... Anson Cont
Anson Technical College, Learning Resources Center, Polk Campus, Polkton, NC [*Library symbol Library of Congress*] (LCLS) .... NcPolA
Anson Technical Institute, Ansonville, NC [*Library symbol Library of Congress*] (LCLS) .... NcAnA
Anson, TX [*FM radio station call letters*] .... KKHR
Anson Unit [*Of hydrolytic enzyme activity*] .... AU
Ansongo [*Mali*] [*ICAO location identifier*] (ICLI) .... GAAO
Ansonia, CT [*AM radio station call letters*] .... WADS
Anstey's Guide to the English Law and Constitution [*A publication*] (DLA) .... Anst Eng Law
Anstey's Pleader's Guide [*A publication*] (DLA) .... Anst Pl Gui
Anstruther's English Exchequer Reports [*145 English Reprint*] [*A publication*] (DLA) .... Anst
Anstruther's English Exchequer Reports [*145 English Reprint*] [*A publication*] (DLA) .... Anstr
Anstruther's English Exchequer Reports [*145 English Reprint*] [*A publication*] (DLA) .... Anstr (Eng)
Answer [*In transcripts*] .... A
Answer .... AN
Answer (AFM) .... ANS
Answer (WDMC) .... ans
Answer (ROG) .... ANSR
Answer Complete [*Telecommunications*] (TEL) .... AC
Answer Construct .... AC
Answer in Sentence [*Computer science*] (MHDB) .... AIS
Answer, No-Charge [*Telecommunications*] (TEL) .... ANN
Answer Only (TEL) .... AO
Answer Originate (IAA) .... AO
Answer Print (NTCM) .... AP
Answer Print, Optical (DOAD) .... APO
Answer Search Interface (MCD) .... ASI
Answer Send and Receive [*Telecommunications*] (DGA) .... ASR
Answer Unit (IAA) .... AU
Answerable (ROG) .... ANSABLE
Answer-Back Code [*Telecommunications*] (TEL) .... ABC
Answer-Back Tone [*Telecommunications*] (HGAA) .... ABT
Answered (ROG) .... ANSD
Answering (ROG) .... ANSG
Answering .... ANSWRNG
Answering Flag [*Navy British*] .... AN
Answering Machine Owner .... AMO
Answering, Recording, and Dialing .... ARD
Answering Service (LAIN) .... AS
Answering Time Recorder [*Telecommunications*] (TEL) .... ATR
[*The*] Answering Voice [*A publication*] .... AV
Answer-Return Query .... ARQ
Ansyl [*Organic radical*] .... Ans
Ansys, Inc. [*NASDAQ symbol*] (SAG) .... ANSS
Ansys, Inc. [*Associated Press*] (SAG) .... Ansys
Ant Guard Activity [*Ecology*] .... AA
Anta [*Peru*] [*Airport symbol*] (OAG) .... ATA
Anta/Comdte. FAP German Arias Grazziani [*Peru*] [*ICAO location identifier*] (ICLI) .... SPHZ
Antagonist (AAMN) .... ANTAG
Antagonist Cimetidine [*Ulcer medicine manufactured by SmithKline Beckman Corp.*] .... TAGAMET
Antagonistic (DAVI) .... antag
Antair, SA de CV [*Mexico*] [*FAA designator*] (FAAC) .... TIR
Antalaha [*Madagascar*] [*Airport symbol*] (OAG) .... ANM
Antalaha [*Madagascar*] [*ICAO location identifier*] (ICLI) .... FMNH
Antalya [*Turkey*] [*Airport symbol*] (OAG) .... AYT
Antalya [*Turkey ICAO location identifier*] (ICLI) .... LTAI
Antananarivo [*Madagascar*] [*ICAO location identifier*] (ICLI) .... FMMD
Antananarivo [*Madagascar*] [*ICAO location identifier*] (ICLI) .... FMMM
Antananarivo [*Madagascar*] [*Airport symbol*] (OAG) .... TNR
Antananarivo/Arivonimamo [*Madagascar*] [*ICAO location identifier*] (ICLI) .... FMMO
Antananarivo/Ivato [*Madagascar*] [*ICAO location identifier*] (ICLI) .... FMMI
Antarctic .... A
Antarctic [*Marguerite Bay*] [*Antarctica*] [*Seismograph station code, US Geological Survey*] [*Closed*] (SEIS) .... ANC
Antarctic .... ANT
Antarctic .... Antarc

Antarctic [*MARC geographic area code Library of Congress*] (LCCP) .... t------
Antarctic Bottom Water [*Oceanography*] .... AABW
Antarctic Bottom Water [*Marine science*] (OSRA) .... ABW
Antarctic Circle (ROG) .... AAC
Antarctic Circumpolar Current [*Oceanography*] .... ACC
Antarctic Cold Reversal [*Climatology*] .... ACR
Antarctic Current Experiment [*Global Atmospheric Research Program*] (USDC) .... ACE
Antarctic Current Experiment [*Marine science*] (OSRA) .... ACE
Antarctic Expedition .... AE
Antarctic Intermediate Water [*Marine science*] (OSRA) .... AAIW
Antarctic Marine Ecosystem Research at the Ice Edge Zone .... AMERIEZ
Antarctic Medal .... AntM
Antarctic Meteorite Bibliography [*Lunar and Planetary Institute*] [*Database*] .... AMB
Antarctic Muon and Neutrino Detector Array [*Astronomy*] (ECON) .... AMANDA
Antarctic Observation Team .... AOT
Antarctic Offshore Seismic Stratigraphy Project [*Australia*] .... ANTOSTRAT
Antarctic Operations [*Military*] (NVT) .... ANTOPS
Antarctic Polar Front [*Meteorology*] .... APF
Antarctic Research Advisory Council .... ARAC
Antarctic Search for Meteorites .... ANSMET
Antarctic Submillimeter Telescope and Remote Observatory Project [*AT & T Bell Labs, Boston University, University of Illinois*] .... ASTRO
Antarctic Support Activities .... ANTARCTICSUPPORT
Antarctic Task Force .... ATF
Antarctic Treaty Consultative Parties .... ATCP
Antarctic Treaty Meeting .... ATM
Antarctic Treaty Organization (ASF) .... ATO
Antarctic Treaty System .... ATS
Antarctica (VRA) .... Antar
Antarctica (BARN) .... Antarc
Antarctica [*ANSI two-letter standard code*] (CNC) .... AQ
Antarctica [*ANSI three-letter standard code*] (CNC) .... ATA
Antarctica [*MARC country of publication code Library of Congress*] (LCCP) .... ay
Antarctica [*MARC geographic area code Library of Congress*] (LCCP) .... t-ay--
Antarctica and Southern Oceans Coalition (EA) .... ASOC
Antarctica Project (EA) .... AP
[*The*] Antarctica Project [*An association*] (EAIO) .... TAP
Antarctica Service Medal [*Military decoration*] .... ASM
Antarctican Society (EA) .... AS
Antares Resources [*NASDAQ symbol*] (TTSB) .... ANTR
Antares Resources Corp. [*Associated Press*] (SAG) .... Antares
Antares Resources Corp. [*NASDAQ symbol*] (SAG) .... ANTR
Ante [*Before*] [*Latin*] .... A
Ante [*Before*] [*Latin*] .... an
Ante Christum [*Before Christ*] [*Latin*] .... A Ch
Ante Christum [*Before Christ*] [*Latin*] .... AC
Ante Christum [*Before Christ*] [*Latin*] .... AChr
Ante Christum Natum [*Before Christ's Birth*] [*Latin*] .... AChrn
Ante Christum Natum [*Before the Birth of Christ*] [*Latin*] .... ACN
Ante Cibum [*Before Meals*] [*Pharmacy*] .... AC
Ante Diem [*Before the Day*] [*Latin*] (GPO) .... ad
Ante Jentaculum [*Before Breakfast*] [*Pharmacy*] .... ANT JENTAC
Ante Lucem [*Before Daylight*] [*Latin*] .... Ant Luc
Ante Meridiem [*Before Noon*] [*Latin*] (GPO) .... AM
Ante Nativitatem Christi [*Before the Birth of Christ*] [*Latin*] (ROG) .... ANC
Ante Partum [*Obstetrics*] .... AP
Ante Prandium [*Before Dinner*] [*Pharmacy*] .... ANT PRAND
Ante Prandium [*Before Dinner*] [*Pharmacy*] .... AP
Antec Corp. [*NASDAQ symbol*] (SAG) .... ANTC
ANTEC Corp. [*NASDAQ symbol*] (TTSB) .... ANTC
Antec Corp. [*Associated Press*] (SAG) .... Antec
Antecedent Index (NOAA) .... AI
Antecedent Precipitation Index .... API
Ante-Communion .... AC
Antecubital [*Anatomy*] .... AC
Antediluvian Knight [*Old actor*] (IIA) .... AK
Antediluvian Order of Buffaloes [*British*] .... AOB
Antelope Island [*Utah*] [*Seismograph station code, US Geological Survey*] (SEIS) .... ANU
Antelope Resources [*Vancouver Stock Exchange symbol*] .... ATF
Antelope Valley Junior College [*Later, Antelope Valley College*] [*Lancaster, CA*] .... AVJC
Antelope Valley Junior College, Lancaster, CA [*Library symbol Library of Congress*] (LCLS) .... CLAV
Antenatal [*Medicine*] (DMAA) .... A/N
Antenatal [*Medicine*] .... AN
Antenatal Care .... ANC
Antenatal Clinic .... ANC
Antenatal Diagnosis .... AND
Antenna (IAA) .... A
Antenna (IDOE) .... ant
Antenna (AFM) .... ANT
Antenna Adjustable Current Distribution [*Telecommunications*] (OA) .... AACD
Antenna and Transmitter Improvement Study .... ATIS
Antenna Aspect Processor .... AAP
Antenna Assembly (IAA) .... AS
Antenna Base Spring .... ABS
Antenna Contour Measuring Equipment .... ACME
Antenna Control and Display Panel (MCD) .... ACDP
Antenna Control Console .... ACC
Antenna Control Display .... ACD
Antenna Control Unit .... ACU
Antenna Counterbalance Cylinder Assembly .... ACCA

Antenna Coupler Receiver (MCD) ... ACR
Antenna Coupling Regulator (IEEE) ... ACR
Antenna Cross Talk ... ACT
Antenna Current (IAA) ... AC
Antenna Directive Gain ... ADG
Antenna Dish Control ... ADC
Antenna Dummy Load ... ADL
Antenna Effective Height ... AEH
Antenna Effective Length for Electric-Field Antennas (IEEE) ... LE
Antenna Effective Length for Magnetic-Field Antennas (IEEE) ... LEM
Antenna Effective Resistance ... AER
Antenna Elevation Angle ... AEA
Antenna Feed Horn ... AFH
Antenna Feed System ... AFS
Antenna Field Charge Kit ... AFCK
Antenna Field Gain ... AFG
Antenna for Communications ... AFC
Antenna Homing System ... AHS
Antenna Impedance ... AI
Antenna Input Resistance ... AIR
Antenna Interface Subsystem (CAAL) ... AIS
Antenna Laboratory (MCD) ... AL
Antenna Lightning Arrester ... ALA
Antenna Loading Coil ... ALC
Antenna Lobe for Variable Ionospheric Nimbus (IEEE) ... ALVIN
Antenna Management (NASA) ... AM
Antenna Mast Group [*PATRIOT*] [*Army*] (RDA) ... AMG
Antenna Mast Set (MCD) ... AMS
Antenna Matching Unit ... AMU
Antenna Measurement Techniques Association (EA) ... AMTA
Antenna Noise Temperature ... ANT
Antenna Ohmic Resistance ... AOR
Antenna Pattern Analyzer ... APA
Antenna Pattern Correction [*for spacecraft data*] ... APC
Antenna Pattern Error Analysis ... APEA
Antenna Pattern Measurement Test [*Army*] (AABC) ... APMT
Antenna Pattern Test System [*Army*] (AABC) ... APATS
Antenna Pointing Angle Change ... APAC
Antenna Pointing Subsystem ... APS
Antenna Position Indicator ... API
Antenna Position Programmer [*Manned Space Flight Network*] ... APP
Antenna Position Recorder ... APR
Antenna Positioning Device ... ANPOD
Antenna Positioning Mechanism ... APM
Antenna Power Gain ... APG
Antenna Radiation Pattern ... ARP
Antenna Radiation Resistance ... ARR
Antenna RADOME [*RADAR Dome*] **Heater** ... ARH
Antenna Range Equipment ... ARE
Antenna Rotation Rate (NVT) ... ARR
Antenna Select Logic Unit [*NASA*] (NASA) ... ASLU
Antenna Slave Data Equipment (IAA) ... ASDE
Antenna Solar Panel Positioner ... ASPP
Antenna Steering Group ... ASG
Antenna Supports [*JETDS nomenclature*] [*Military*] (CET) ... AB
Antenna Switching Matrix ... ASM
Antenna System Readiness Monitor (MCD) ... ASRM
Antenna Systems Laboratory [*University of New Hampshire*] (PDAA) ... ASL
Antenna Test Facility ... ATF
Antenna Test Group [*Army*] (AABC) ... ATG
Antenna Test Model ... ATM
Antenna to Antenna Compatibility Analysis Program (MCD) ... ATACAP
Antenna Tracking Altitude, Azimuth, and Range by Electronic Scan (PDAA) ... ANTARES
Antenna Transmit Receive (IAA) ... ATR
Antenna Tuning Capacitor (IAA) ... ATC
Antenna Tuning Inductance (IAA) ... ATI
Antenna Tuning Unit (MSA) ... ATU
Antenna Turning Motor (IAA) ... ATM
Antenna with Reflector ... R
Antennapedia Complex [*Gene cluster in fruit fly*] ... ANT-C
Antenna-Receiver-Transmitter (IAA) ... ART
Antennas and Propagation (MCD) ... A/P
Antennas, Complex [*JETDS nomenclature*] [*Military*] (CET) ... AS
Antennas, Simple [*JETDS nomenclature*] [*Military*] (CET) ... AT
Antennule Length [*of Crustacea*] ... AL
Antennule Length to Total Body Length Ratio [*of Crustacea*] ... AL/TL
Antepartum Hemorrhage [*Medicine*] ... APH
Anterior ... A
Anterior ... ANT
Anterior and Posterior [*Medicine*] ... A & P
Anterior Aorta ... AA
Anterior Aortic Wall [*Medicine*] (DMAA) ... AAW
Anterior Auditory Field [*Physiology*] ... AAF
Anterior Axillary Line ... AAL
Anterior Axillary Line [*Anatomy*] (DAVI) ... Ant Ax
Anterior Basal Body ... ABB
Anterior Bulbar Cell [*Neurobiology*] ... ABC
Anterior Burster [*Neuron*] ... AB
Anterior Byssus Retractor Muscle [*Mollusk anatomy*] ... ABRM
Anterior Cerebral Artery [*Anatomy*] (AAMN) ... ACA
Anterior Cervical Diskectomy and Fusion [*Medicine*] (DAVI) ... ACDF
Anterior Chamber [*Ophthalmology*] ... AC
Anterior Chamber Diameter [*Ophthalmology*] (DAVI) ... ACD
Anterior Chamber Tube Shunt Encircling Band [*Ophthalmology*] (DAVI) ... ACTSEB
Anterior Chamber-Associated Immune Deviation [*For study of foreign tissue grafts*] ... ACAID
Anterior Chest Diameter ... ACD
Anterior Colporrhaphy [*Gynecology*] (CPH) ... AC
Anterior Commissure [*Neuroanatomy*] ... AC
Anterior Communicating Aneurysm (HGAA) ... ACA
Anterior Connective [*Anatomy*] ... AC
Anterior Convex Side ... ACS
Anterior Coronary Artery (HGAA) ... ACA
Anterior Cortical [*Anatomy*] ... AC
Anterior Cruciate [*Ligament*] [*Anatomy*] (DAVI) ... AC
Anterior Cruciate Ligament [*Anatomy*] ... ACL
Anterior Deltoid [*Myology*] ... AD
Anterior Dendritic Field [*Neurology*] ... ADF
Anterior Descending Artery [*Anatomy*] (MAE) ... ADA
Anterior Dorsolateral Scale Count ... ADLS
Anterior Ectosylvian Sulcus [*Neuroanatomy*] ... AES
Anterior Extreme Position [*Medicine*] ... AEP
Anterior Facial Height ... AFH
Anterior Faucial Pillar [*Anatomy*] (MAE) ... AFP
Anterior Fold from Typhlosole ... AFT
Anterior Fontanelle [*Neonatology and pediatrics*] (DAVI) ... AF
Anterior [*Part of*] **Foot** ... AF
Anterior Hyaloid Membrane [*Ophthalmology*] ... AHM
Anterior Hypothalamic Area ... AHA
Anterior Hypothalamic Nucleus [*Brain anatomy*] ... AH
Anterior Hypothalamic Preoptic (DMAA) ... AHPO
Anterior Hypothalamus, Preoptic Area [*Brain anatomy*] ... AHPOA
Anterior Inferior Cerebellar Artery [*Anatomy*] ... AICA
Anterior Inferior Communicating Artery [*Anatomy*] ... AICA
Anterior Informal Vertebral Vein [*Medicine*] (DMAA) ... AIVV
Anterior Internal Cerebral Artery [*Anatomy*] (DAVI) ... AICA
Anterior Interosseous Nerve Syndrome [*Medicine*] (DMAA) ... AIS
Anterior Interpositus Nucleus [*Anatomy*] ... AIN
Anterior Ischemic Optic Neuropathy [*Neurology and ophthalmology*] (DAVI) ... AION
Anterior [*Wall of*] **Kidney** ... AK
Anterior Lateral Dendrites [*Neurology*] ... ALD
Anterior Lateral Line Nerve [*Fish anatomy*] ... ALLN
Anterior Lateral Myocardial Infarct [*or Infarction*] [*Cardiology*] ... ALMI
Anterior Lateral Nerve ... ALN
Anterior Latissimus Dorsi [*Anatomy*] ... ALD
Anterior Leaflet of Mitral Valve [*Cardiology*] (AAMN) ... ALMV
Anterior Lobe Hormone [*Endocrinology*] (MAE) ... ALH
Anterior Lobe of Hypophysis [*Anatomy*] (AAMN) ... ALH
Anterior Lobe of Pituitary [*Gland*] ... ALP
Anterior Lymph Node [*Medicine*] (MAE) ... ALN
Anterior Middle Suprasylvian Association [*Area of cat cortex*] ... AMSA
Anterior Mitochondrion [*Cytology*] ... AM
Anterior Mitral Leaflet [*Cardiology*] ... AM
Anterior Mitral Leaflet [*Cardiology*] ... AML
Anterior Mitral Valve Leaflet [*Cardiology*] (AAMN) ... aMVL
Anterior Myocardial Infarction [*Medicine*] (DMAA) ... AMI
Anterior Nasal Discharge [*Medicine*] (DMAA) ... AND
Anterior Nasal Spine [*Medicine*] (DMAA) ... ANS
Anterior Oblique (MAE) ... AO
Anterior Octaval Nucleus [*Neuroanatomy*] ... AON
Anterior Papillary Muscle [*Cardiology*] (DAVI) ... APM
Anterior Pituitary [*Endocrinology*] ... ANT PIT
Anterior Pituitary [*Endocrinology*] ... AP
Anterior Pituitary Extract [*Endocrinology*] ... APE
Anterior Pituitary Hormone [*Endocrinology*] ... APH
Anterior Pituitary Lobe [*Anatomy*] ... AL
Anterior Pituitary Reaction [*Endocrinology*] (AAMN) ... APR
Anterior Pituitary Resection [*Medicine*] (MAE) ... APR
Anterior Pituitary-Like [*Endocrinology*] ... APL
Anterior Portion - Medial Collateral Ligament [*Anatomy*] ... A-MCL
Anterior Resection [*Medicine*] ... AR
Anterior Right Ventricular Wall [*Cardiology*] (DAVI) ... ARV
Anterior Sagittal Diameter [*Medicine*] (MEDA) ... ASD
Anterior Segmental Ocular Dysgenesis [*Medicine*] (DMAA) ... ASOD
Anterior Septal Artery [*Anatomy*] ... ASA
Anterior Sorting Area ... ASA
Anterior Subcapsular Cataract [*Ophthalmology*] (DAVI) ... ASC
Anterior Superior Iliac Spine [*Anatomy*] ... ASIS
Anterior Superior Spine [*Of ilium*] [*Anatomy*] (DAVI) ... Ant Sup Spine
Anterior Superior Spine [*Anatomy*] ... ASS
Anterior Tibial Compartment Syndrome [*Medicine*] (DMAA) ... ATCS
Anterior Tibial (Muscle) [*Anatomy*] ... AT
Anterior Tibialis [*Anatomy*] ... ATB
Anterior Trabeculae Carneae [*Heart anatomy*] ... ATC
Anterior Urethral Valve [*Medicine*] (DMAA) ... AUV
Anterior Ventral Microtubule [*Anatomy*] ... AVM
Anterior Ventral Neuron [*Neurophysiology*] ... AV
Anterior Wall [*Anatomy*] ... AW
Anterior Wall Infarction [*Cardiology*] (MAE) ... AWI
Anterior Wall Myocardial Infarction [*Cardiology*] (MAE) ... AWMI
Anterior Wall of Aortic Root [*Cardiology*] (DMAA) ... AWAR
Anterior Wall Thickness [*Anatomy*] ... AWT
Anterior-Median [*Ophthalmology*] ... AM
Anterior-Posterior and Lateral [*Chest x-ray*] (CPH) ... A-P & Lat
Anterior-Posterior Dual Energy Radiography [*Medicine*] (DMAA) ... APDER
Anterograde Amnesia [*Medicine*] ... AA

Anterolateral Pre-Olivary Nucleus [*Neuroanatomy*] ALPO
Anterolateral Rotatory [*or Rotational*] **Instability** [*Orthopedics*] ALRI
Anterolateral Sclerosis [*Neurology*] (DAVI) ALS
Anterolateral Wall Myocardial Infarction [*Cardiology*] ALWMI
Anteromeatal [*Anatomy*] (DAVI) AM
Anteromedial Puncture [*Medicine*] AMP
Anteromedial Rotatory Instability [*Medicine*] AMRI
Anteromedial-Anterolateral Rotatory Instability [*Medicine*] AM-ALRI
Anteroposterior [*Projection*] [*Radiology*] (DAVI) AP
Anteroposterior and Lateral [*X-ray views*] (AAMN) AP & L
Anteroposterior and Lateral [*X-ray views*] (AAMN) AP & Lat
Anteroposterior [*or Anterior-posterior*] **Diameter** [*Pelvic measurement*] [*Medicine*] A-PD
Anteroseptal Myocardial Infarct [*or Infarction*] [*Cardiology*] (MAE) ASMI
Anteroventral Cochlear Nucleus AVCN
Anteroventral Portion of the Third Ventricle [*Neuroanatomy*] AV 3V
Anteversion [*Medicine*] AV
Anteverted, Anteflexed [*Medicine*] (MAE) AV/AF
Antex Data Systems (HGAA) ADS
Anthelmintic [*Expelling Worms*] [*Medicine*] (ROG) ANTH
Anther [*Botany*] A
Anther [*Botany*] AN
Anther Primordium [*Botany*] AP
Anthes Industries, Inc. [*Toronto Stock Exchange symbol*] AII
Anthocyanin [*Fruit pigment*] ACN
Anthocyanin Pigmented Juices [*Food technology*] API
Anthologia Latina [*A publication*] (OCD) Anth Lat
Anthologia Lyrica Graeca [*A publication*] (OCD) Anth Lyr Graec
Anthologia Palatina [*Classical studies*] (OCD) Anth Pal
Anthologia Planudea [*Classical studies*] (OCD) Anth Plan
Anthologie [*Anthology*] [*German*] Anthol
Anthologie Sonore [*Record label*] [*France*] AS
Anthology ANTH
Anthology ANTHOL
Anthology Film Archives (EA) AFA
Anthology Film Archives, New York, NY [*Library symbol Library of Congress*] (LCLS) NNAn
Anthology Film Archives, New York, NY [*Library symbol*] [*Library of Congress*] (LCLS) NNAnF
Anthology for Famous English and American Poetry [*A publication*] AnFE
Anthology for the Enjoyment of Poetry [*A publication*] AnEnPo
Anthology of Catholic Poets [*A publication*] ACP
Anthology of Commonwealth Verse [*A publication*] ACV
Anthology of Contemporary Latin-American Poetry [*A publication*] AnCL
Anthology of English Verse [*A publication*] AEV
Anthology of French Poetry [*A publication*] AnFP
Anthology of German Poetry [*A publication*] AnGP
Anthology of German Poetry through the Nineteenth Century [*A publication*] AGP
Anthology of Irish Literature [*A publication*] AnIL
Anthology of Irish Verse [*A publication*] AnIV
Anthology of Light Verse [*A publication*] ALV
Anthology of Medieval Lyrics [*A publication*] AnML
Anthology of Mexican Poetry [*A publication*] AnMP
Anthology of Modern Poetry [*A publication*] AnMoPo
Anthology of New England Poets [*A publication*] AnNE
Anthology of New Zealand Verse [*A publication*] AnNZ
Anthology of Norwegian Lyrics [*A publication*] AnNoLy
Anthology of Old English Poetry [*A publication*] AnOE
Anthology of Spanish Poetry from Garsilaso to Garcia [*A publication*] AnSP
Anthology of Swedish Lyrics [*A publication*] AnSL
Anthology of World Poetry [*A publication*] AWP
Anthon Herald, Anthon, IA [*Library symbol Library of Congress*] (LCLS) IaAntH
Anthon Public Library, Anthon, IA [*Library symbol Library of Congress*] (LCLS) IaAnt
Anthon's Abridgment of Blackstone [*A publication*] (DLA) Anth Black
Anthon's Law Student [*A publication*] (DLA) Anth LS
Anthon's New Precedents of Declarations [*A publication*] (DLA) Anth Prec
Anthon's New York Nisi Prius Reports [*A publication*] (DLA) Anth
Anthon's New York Nisi Prius Reports [*A publication*] (DLA) Anth NP
Anthon's New York Nisi Prius Reports [*A publication*] (DLA) Anth NPR
Anthon's New York Nisi Prius Reports [*A publication*] (DLA) Anthon NP (NY)
Anthon's New York Nisi Prius Reports [*A publication*] (DLA) Anthon Rep
Anthon's New York Nisi Prius Reports [*A publication*] (DLA) Anthon's NP
Anthon's New York Nisi Prius Reports [*A publication*] (DLA) Anthon's Rep
Anthon's Nisi Prius Reports [*2nd ed.*] [*A publication*] (DLA) Anthon's NP (2d Ed)
Anthon's Study of Law [*A publication*] (DLA) Anth St
Anthony Colin Bruce Chapman [*British auto industrialist and engineer, founder of Lotus Cars*] ACBC
Anthony Indus [*NYSE symbol*] (TTSB) ANT
Anthony Industries, Inc. [*NYSE symbol*] (SPSG) ANT
Anthony Industries, Inc. [*Associated Press*] (SAG) Anthony
Anthony, KS [*Location identifier FAA*] (FAAL) ANY
Anthony on Consolidation of Railroad Companies [*A publication*] (DLA) Anth RR Cons
Anthony Pape Memorial Law Library, Hamilton Law Association, Ontario [*Library symbol National Library of Canada*] (BIB) OHLA
Anthony Sharp and Rachael Ellison Family Organization (EA) ASREFO
Anthony, Smallhorn & Associates [*British*] AS & A
Anthony's Edition of Shephard's Touchstone [*A publication*] (DLA) Anth Shep
Anthracene Scintillation Dosimeter ASD
Anthracenecarboxylic Acid [*Organic chemistry*] AC
Anthracenedicarboxaldehyde [*Biochemistry*] ADC
Anthracite (ABBR) A
Anthracite Industry Association (EA) AIA
Anthracite Information Bureau [*Defunct*] AIB
Anthracite Institute [*Absorbed by PCMA*] AI
Anthracite Railroads Historical Society (EA) ARHS
Anthrahydroquinone [*Organic chemistry*] AHQ
Anthrahydroquinone Disulfonate [*Organic chemistry*] AHDS
Anthranilamide [*Organic chemistry*] ATA
Anthranilate Synthase [*An enzyme*] AS
Anthranilate Synthase - Phosphoribosyl Transferase [*Enzyme complex*] AS-PRT
Anthranilic Acid [*Organic chemistry*] AA
Anthraquinone [*Organic chemistry*] AQ
Anthraquinone Disulfonate [*Organic chemistry*] AQDS
Anthraquinone Disulfonic Acid [*Organic chemistry*] ADA
Anthrax Antiserum [*Medicine*] AAS
Anthropogenic Climate Change [*Marine science*] (OSRA) ACC
Anthropogenic Hydrocarbons AHC
Anthropogenic Sulfate Aerosol [*Meteorology*] ASA
Anthropological [*or Anthropology*] ANTHR
Anthropological ANTHROPOL
Anthropological Institute (BARN) AI
Anthropological Research Center [*Memphis State University*] [*Research center*] (RCD) ARC
Anthropological Research Council [*British*] ARC
Anthropologie [*Anthropology*] [*German*] Anthropol
Anthropology ANTHRO
Anthropology (DD) Anthro
Anthropology (VRA) anthrop
Anthropology ANTHROP
Anthropology and Sociology Section [*Association of College and Research Libraries*] ANSS
Anthropology Case Materials Project [*National Science Foundation*] ACMP
Anthropology Film Center Foundation (EA) AFCF
Anthropology Film Institute [*Later, AFCF*] (EA) AFI
Anthropology of Development Programme [*McGill University*] [*Canada Research center*] (RCD) PAD
Anthropology Resource Center [*Defunct*] (EA) ARC
Anthropometric Survey [*Human figure simulation*] [*Army*] (RDA) ANSUR
Anthropometric Test Device [*Automotive safety*] ATD
Anthropomorphic Test Device [*MM*] (TAG) ATD
Anthropomorphic Test Dummy ATD
Anthroposophical Society in America (EA) ASA
Anthroposophical Society in Australia, Victorian Branch ASA(VB)
Anthroposophical Society in Great Britain (EAIO) ASGB
(Anthroyloxy)stearic Acid [*Organic chemistry*] AS
Anti Racist Teacher Education Network (AIE) ARTEN
Anti-Afterburn Valve [*Automotive engineering*] AAV
Antiair Artillery Order of Battle (MCD) AAAOB
Antiair Output AAO
Anti-Air Processing Program (SAA) AAP
Antiair Warfare AAW
Antiair Warfare Center AAWC
Antiair Warfare Commander [*or Coordinator*] (NVT) AAWC
Antiair Warfare Exercise [*Navy*] (NG) AAWEX
Antiair Warfare Exercise in Port [*Navy*] (NVT) AAWEXINPT
Antiair Warfare Readiness Assessment Training System (MCD) AAWRATS
Antiair Warfare Reporting [*Navy*] (NVT) AAW(R)
Antiair Warfare Support (NVT) AAWSUP
Antiair Warfare Systems [*Navy*] (MCD) AAWS
Antiair Warfare Training in Port [*Navy*] (NVT) AAWIPT
Antiair Weapon (SAA) AAW
Antiaircraft [*Officer's rating*] [*British Royal Navy*] A
Antiaircraft [*Army*] AA
Antiaircraft Armament AAA
Anti-Aircraft Armoured Truck [*Military*] (PDAA) AAAT
Antiaircraft Artillery (GPO) AAA
Antiaircraft Artillery and Guided Missile Center AAGMC
Antiaircraft Artillery Command AAAC
Antiaircraft Artillery Information [*or Intelligence*] **Service** AAAIS
Antiaircraft Artillery Information [*or Intelligence*] **Service** [*Army*] AAIS
Antiaircraft Artillery Operation Center AAAOC
Antiaircraft Artillery RADAR Crewman [*Military*] (IAA) AAARDRCRM
Antiaircraft Artillery Reception Center AAARC
Antiaircraft Assistant (SAA) AA-A
Antiaircraft Balloon [*Obsolete*] AA/B
Anti-Aircraft Battery (DOMA) AAB
Antiaircraft Cannon (KSC) AAC
Antiaircraft Command AAC
Antiaircraft Common [*Projectile*] AAC
Antiaircraft Control Station (MCD) AACS
Anti-Aircraft Co-Operation Unit [*British military*] (DMA) AACU
Anti-Aircraft Corps [*British military*] (DMA) AAC
Antiaircraft Defence Commander [*British*] AADC
Antiaircraft Defences [*British*] AAD
Antiaircraft Defended Point (MUGU) AADP
Antiaircraft Defense Area [*NATO*] AADA
Antiaircraft Defense System [*Army*] (AABC) AADS
Antiaircraft Director Center (MCD) AADC
Anti-Aircraft Experimental Section [*British military*] (DMA) AAES
Antiaircraft Fire Control AAFC
Antiaircraft Guided Missile (AAG) AAGM
Antiaircraft Guided Missile Center (SAA) AAGMC
Antiaircraft Guided Missile School (SAA) AAGMS
Antiaircraft Guided Missile System (NG) AAGMS
Antiaircraft Gun-Laying (DEN) AAGL
Antiaircraft Liaison Officer (SAA) AALO

Antiaircraft Light Cruiser [*Navy symbol*] ... CLAA
Antiaircraft Light Machine Gun ... AALMG
Antiaircraft Machine Gun [*Army*] ... AAMG
Antiaircraft Missile (KSC) ... AAM
Antiaircraft Missile Battalion [*Marine Corps*] ... AAMSBN
Antiaircraft Observation Post ... AAOP
Antiaircraft Officer (IIA) ... AAO
Antiaircraft Operations Center [*Air Force*] ... AAOC
Antiaircraft Operations Room (MCD) ... AAOR
Antiaircraft Searchlight ... AASL
Antiaircraft Self-Destroying ... AASD
Antiaircraft Station ... AASTA
Antiaircraft Talker (SAA) ... AAT
Antiaircraft Tank (IAA) ... AAT
Antiaircraft Technician (MCD) ... AAT
Antiaircraft Training and Test Center [*Navy*] ... AAT & TC
Antiaircraft Training Center [*Navy*] ... AATC
Antiaircraft Training Center [*Navy*] ... AATRACEN
Antiaircraft Volunteer ... AAV
Anti-alpha-staphylolysin [*Immunology*] ... ASTA
Anti-Antimissile Missile ... AAM
Anti-Antimissile Missile (IAA) ... AAMM
Anti-Apartheid Movement [*South Africa*] [*Political party*] (EA) ... AAM
Anti-Apartheids Beweging Nederland [*Anti-Apartheid Movement*] [*South Africa*] [*Political party*] (EAIO) ... AABN
Antiarmor Capabilities Study (MCD) ... AACS
Antiarmor Cluster Munition (MCD) ... ACM
Antiarmor Fuze ... AAF
Antiarmor Helicopter Troop (MCD) ... AAHT
Antiarmor Kill Zone [*Military*] (INF) ... AKZ
Antiarmor Missile System - Heavy [*Army*] (INF) ... AMS-H
Anti-Armour Helicopter [*Military*] (PDAA) ... AAH
Anti-Arteriosclerosis Polysaccharide Factor [*Medicine*] (DMAA) ... AAPF
Anti-Axial Compression/Liquid Chromatography ... AC/LC
Anti-Backfire Valve [*Automotive engineering*] ... ABFV
Antibacklash Gear ... ABG
Antibacklash Gear ... ABLG
Antibacterial Activity [*Medicine*] (MAE) ... ABA
Antiballistic Missile [*Air Force*] ... ABM
Antiballistic Missile Early Warning System [*Air Force*] ... ABMEWS
Antiballistic-Missile Missile [*Air Force*] (AFM) ... ABMM
Anti-Beevers-Ross [*Beta-alumina crystallography*] ... aBR
Antibiotic [*Pharmacology*] (DAVI) ... ATB
Antibiotic Concentrate [*Medicine*] (DMAA) ... AC
Antibiotic Removal Device [*Pharmacology*] (DAVI) ... ARD
Antibiotic-Acquired Pseudomembranous Colitis (DAVI) ... AAPC
Antibiotic-Associated Colitis [*Medicine*] ... AAC
Antibiotic-Associated Pseudomembranous Colitis [*Medicine*] (DMAA) ... AAC
Antibiotic-Associated Pseudomembranous Colitis [*Medicine*] ... AAPMC
Antibiotics [*Pharmacology*] (DAVI) ... ABx
Antibiotics in Animal Feeds (DICI) ... AAF
Antiblocking System (IAA) ... ABS
Antibodies [*Immunochemistry*] (DAVI) ... ABO
Antibodies to Cardiac Myosin [*Immunology*] (DAVI) ... AM
Antibodies to Murine Cardiac Myosin [*Immunology*] (DAVI) ... AMM
Antibodies to Nuclear Antigen [*Immunology*] ... ANA
Antibody [*Also, aby*] [*Immunology*] ... Ab
Antibody [*Medicine*] (DMAA) ... ab
Antibody [*Also, Ab*] [*Immunology*] ... aby
Antibody [*Biochemistry*] (DAVI) ... ANTI
Antibody Activity [*Immunology*] ... AA
Antibody Deficiency Syndrome [*Immunology*] (MAE) ... ADS
Antibody Hepatitis-Associated Antigen [*Immunology*] (MAE) ... anti-HAA
Antibody Mediated Cell Dependent Immune Lympholysis [*Immunology*] ... ABCIL
Antibody Nitrogen (DMAA) ... AbN
Antibody Positive ... ab+
Antibody Smooth Muscle-Ribonucleoprotein [*Genetics*] (DAVI) ... anti-SM/RNP
Antibody Thyroglobulin [*Immunology*] ... TGA
Antibody to Deoxyribonucleic Acid Test [*Rheumatology*] (DAVI) ... anti-DNA
Antibody to Extractable Nuclear Antigen Test [*Rheumatology*] (DAVI) ... anti-ENA
Antibody to Hepatitis A Virus [*Medicine*] (MEDA) ... anti-HAV
Antibody to Hepatitis B Core Antigen [*Medicine*] (MEDA) ... anti-HBc
Antibody to Hepatitis B Surface Antigen [*Immunology*] (DAVI) ... anti-HB$_s$Ag
Antibody to Hepatitis B Surface Antigen [*Medicine*] (MEDA) ... anti-HBs
Antibody Unit ... ABU
Antibody-Against-Panel [*Immunology*] (AAMN) ... AbAP
Antibody-Coated Bacteria [*Immunology*] ... ACB
Antibody-Coated Grid Technique [*Medicine*] (DMAA) ... ACGT
Antibody-Containing Cell [*Immunology*] ... ACC
Antibody-Dependent Cell-Mediated Cytotoxicity [*Immunology*] ... ADCC
Antibody-Dependent Cell-Mediated Cytotoxicity [*Immunology*] ... ADCMC
Antibody-Dependent Cellular Cytotoxicity (DOG) ... ADCC
Antibody-Dependent Enhancement [*of viral infection*] ... ADE
Antibody-Dependent Lymphocyte-Mediated Cytotoxicity [*Clinical chemistry*] ... ADLC
Antibody-Dependent Macrophage-Mediated Cytotoxicity [*Clinical chemistry*] ... ADMC
Antibody-Directed Enzyme Prodrug Therapy [*Oncology*] ... ADEPT
Antibody-Forming [*Immunology*] (MAE) ... AF
Antibody-Forming Cell [*Immunology*] ... AFC
Antibody-Induced Cell-Mediated Cytoxicity [*Medicine*] (PDAA) ... AICC
Antibody-Negative Mice with Latent Infection [*Immunology*] ... ANLI
Antibody-Producing Cell [*Medicine*] (DMAA) ... ABPC
Antibody-Secreting Cells [*Immunology*] ... ASC
Anti-Bureaucracy Special Interest Group [*Mensa*] (EA) ... ABSIG
Anti-Camout Ribbed Bit [*Screwdriving tool*] ... ACR
Anti-Cancer Foundation of the Universities of South Australia ... ACFUSA
Anticar Theft [*Campaign or Committee*] ... ACT
Anticardiolipin Antibody [*Immunochemistry*] ... ACA
Anticarrier Warfare (MCD) ... ACW
Anti-Catholic League (EA) ... ACL
Anticenter ... AC
Anticentromere Antibody [*Immunology*] ... ACA
Antichaff Circuit (IEEE) ... ANTC
Anti-Char Rapide Autopropulse [*French antitank weapon system*] ... ACRA
Antichymotrypsin [*Biochemistry*] ... ACT
Anticipate (FAAC) ... ANCPT
Anticipate (AABC) ... ANTCP
Anticipate Discharge Tomorrow [*Medicine*] (DAVI) ... ADS
Anticipated (WGA) ... ANT
Anticipated Engine Not Operationally Ready Supply [*Military*] (AFIT) ... AENORS
Anticipated Freight [*Commerce*] (BARN) ... ant frt
Anticipated Level of Business ... ALB
Anticipated Life Span [*Statistics*] (DAVI) ... ALS
Anticipated Not Mission Capable, Supply [*Military*] (NVT) ... ANMCS
Anticipated Not Operationally Ready, Maintenance (NVT) ... ANORM
Anticipated Not Operationally Ready, Supply (AFM) ... ANORS
Anticipated Operational Occurrence [*Nuclear energy*] (NRCH) ... AOO
Anticipated Transient Operating Guideline [*Nuclear energy*] (NRCH) ... ATOG
Anticipated Transient without Scram [*Physics*] ... ATWS
Anticipated Vacancy [*Civil Service*] ... AV
Anticipatory Avoidance [*Medicine*] ... AA
Anticipatory Goal Response [*Medicine*] ... AGR
Anticipatory Nausea and Vomiting [*Medicine*] ... ANV
Anticipatory Reactor Trips (NRCH) ... ART
Anticircling Run [*Navy*] (NG) ... ACR
Anticlockwise ... A
Anticlockwise ... ACW
Anticlonus Index [*Neurology*] [*Medicine*] (DAVI) ... ACI
Anticlutter (NATG) ... AC
Anticoagulant [*or Anticoagulation*] ... AC
Anticoagulant [*or Anticoagulation*] (AAMN) ... ANTICOAG
Anticoagulant Citrate Dextrose [*Hematology*] ... ACD
Anticoagulant Therapy [*Medicine*] ... ACT
Anticoagulants in the Secondary Prevention of Events in Coronary Thrombosis ... ASPECT
Anticoincidence Counter (OA) ... AC
Anticoincidence Detection System ... ADS
Anticollagen Antibody [*Immunology*] ... ACA
Anti-Collision Light System [*or Subsystem*] (MCD) ... ALS
Anticomet Tail (IAA) ... ACT
Anti-Comet Tail Gun [*Television*] (WDMC) ... ACT
Anti-Comintern Pact ... ACP
Anti-Common Market League [*British*] (BI) ... ACML
Anti-Communism International (EAIO) ... ACI
Anti-Communist (ADA) ... A-C
Anti-Communist Advisory Committee (EA) ... ACAC
Anti-Communist Committee (EA) ... ACC
Anti-Communist Confederation of Polish Freedom Fighters in USA (EA) ... ACCPFF
Anti-Communist International (EA) ... ACI
Anti-Communist League of America (EA) ... ACLA
Anti-Communist Society [*Belize*] (PD) ... ACS
Anticomplement Activity [*Medicine*] (DMAA) ... ACA
Anticomplement Immunofluorescence Test [*Immunochemistry*] ... ACIF
Anticomplementary [*Immunology*] ... AC
Anticompromise Emergency Destruction (MCD) ... ACED
Anticompromise Technique ... ACT
Anti-Concorde Project (EA) ... A-CP
Anticonstipation Regimen [*Medicine*] ... ACR
Anticorrosive ... AC
Anti-Corruption Agency ... ACA
Anti-Counterfeit Action Group [*Australia*] ... ACAG
Anticountermeasures Trainer ... ACTER
Anti-Crime (LAIN) ... AC
Anticrime Unit ... ACU
Anti-Cronyism Movement [*Philippines*] ... ACRONYM
Anticruise Missile (MCD) ... ACM
Anti-Curl System [*Intellifax*] [*Brother Industries USA, Inc.*] [*Telecommunications*] ... ACS
Anticyclonic [*Meteorology*] (BARN) ... ACYC
Anticytoplasmic Antibody [*Medicine*] (DMAA) ... ACA
Anti-Defamation League of B'nai B'rith (EA) ... ADL
Anti-Defamation League of B'nai B'rith, New York, NY [*Library symbol Library of Congress*] (LCLS) ... NNAD
Anti-Deficiency Act (AAGC) ... ADA
Antideoxyribonuclease [*Medicine*] (DMAA) ... ADN
Antidetonation Injection ... ADI
Antidiarrhea [*Medicine*] ... AD
Anti-Diesel Device [*Automotive engineering*] ... ADV
Anti-Digit Dialing League (EA) ... ADDL
Anti-Discrimination Act [*Australia*] ... ADA
Anti-Disturbance (MCD) ... AD
Antidiuretic Hormone [*Vasopressin*] [*Endocrinology*] ... ADH
Antidiuretic Substance ... ADS
Antidotum [*Antidote*] [*Latin*] ... Antid
Anti-Drainback Valve [*Automotive engineering*] ... ADV
Antidromic Potential [*Medicine*] (DMAA) ... AP
Anti-Drug Coalition [*Later, NADC*] (EA) ... ADC
Anti-Drug Network (DOMA) ... ADNET

Anti-Dumping [*International trade*] (GFGA) .... AD
Anti-Dumping Authority .... ADA
Anti-Dumping Tribunal [*Canada*] .... ADT
Anti-Embolic Stockings [*Medicine*] (DMAA) .... AES
Antient [*Archaic variation of "ancient"*] (ROG) .... ANT
Antiepileptic Drug .... AED
Anti-Estrogen Binding Site [*Biochemistry*] .... AEBS
Antietam National Battlefield Site .... ANTI
Antiexposure Flight Suit .... AEFS
Antifaschistischer Kampf Kaiserslautern [*Kaiserslautern Antifascist Struggle*] [*Germany*] (PD) .... AKK
Anti-Fascist Organization [*Later, AFPFL*] [*Burma*] [*World War II*] .... AFO
Anti-Fascist People's Freedom League [*Formerly, AFO*] [*Burma*] [*World War II*] .... AFPFL
Antifatty Liver [*Medicine*] .... AFL
Antiferromagnet [*Physics*] .... AFM
Antiferromagnetic .... AF
Antiferromagnetic Resonance .... AFMR
Antifibrinogen [*Hematology*] (DAVI) .... A-F
Anti-Flood Valve (MCD) .... AFV
Anti-Fluoridation Association of Victoria [*Australia*] .... AFAV
Anti-Fouling Paint (DNAB) .... AF
Anti-Fratricide Identification Device [*Military*] (DOMA) .... AFID
Antifreeze Glycoprotein [*Biochemistry*] .... AFGP
Antifreeze Polypeptide [*Biochemistry*] .... AFP
Antifreeze Protein .... AFP
Anti-Friction [*Lubricants*] .... AF
Antifriction Bearing .... AFB
Anti-Friction Bearing Distributors Association [*Later, BSA*] (EA) .... AFBDA
Anti-Friction Bearing Manufacturers Association (EA) .... AFBMA
Antifriction Metal .... AFM
Anti-G [*Gravity*] Straining Maneuver (DOMA) .... AGSM
Antigas [*Military*] .... AG
Antigas Gangrene Serum [*Medicine*] .... AGGS
Anti-Gas Instructor [*British military*] (DMA) .... A/GI
Antigen [*Also, a, Ag*] [*Immunology*] .... A
Antigen [*Also, A, a*] [*Immunology*] .... Ag
Antigen Detection Test [*Clinical chemistry*] .... ADT
Antigen E .... AgE
Antigen Receptor Response Element [*Immunology*] .... ARRE
Antigen Recognition Activation Motif [*Immunology*] .... ARAM
Antigen Recognition Site [*Genetics*] .... ARS
Antigen-Antibody [*Complex*] [*Immunology*] .... Ag-AB
Antigen-Antibody Crossed Electrophoresis [*Biochemistry*] (DAVI) .... AACE
Antigen-Antiglobulin Reaction [*Immunology*] (MAE) .... AAR
Antigen-Binding [*Immunology*] .... AB
Antigen-Binding Capacity [*Immunology*] .... ABC
Antigen-Binding Fragment [*Immunology*] .... Fab
Antigen-Binding Lymphocyte [*Immunology*] (AAMN) .... ABL
Antigen-Carrier Lipid [*Immunology*] .... ACL
Antigenic Determinant [*Medicine*] .... AD
Antigen-Inducing Unit [*Medicine*] (DMAA) .... AIU
Antigen-Presenting Cell [*Immunology*] .... APC
Antigen-Presenting Liposome [*Immunochemistry*] .... APL
Antigen-Reactive Cell [*Immunology*] .... ARC
Antigenreceptor Homology [*Immunochemistry*] .... ARH
Antigen-Transporting Cell [*Immunology*] .... ATC
Antiglare, Antireflective, Antistatic [*Cathode ray tube treatment*] (PCM) .... AGRAS
Antigliadin Antibodies [*Immunology*] .... AGA
Antiglobulin [*Clinical chemistry*] .... AG
Antiglobulin Test [*Hematology*] .... AGT
Antiglomerular Basement Antibody Test .... AGBM
Antiglomerular Basement Membrane [*Antibodies*] [*Cardiology*] (DAVI) .... anti-GMB
Antigo Public Library, Antigo, WI [*Library symbol Library of Congress*] (LCLS) .... WAn
Antigo, WI [*Location identifier FAA*] (FAAL) .... AIG
Antigo, WI [*AM radio station call letters*] .... WATK
Antigo, WI [*FM radio station call letters*] .... WRLO
Antigone [*of Sophocles*] [*Classical studies*] (OCD) .... Ant
Antigonish, NS [*Television station call letters*] CJCB-2
Antigonish, NS [*AM radio station call letters*] .... CJFX
Antigravity .... AG
Antigravity Suit [*NASA*] (MCD) .... AGS
Antigravity Suit [*Air Force clothing for supersonic flight*] .... G (Suit)
Antigua [*Antigua*] [*Seismograph station code, US Geological Survey*] (SEIS) .... ANG
Antigua (ROG) .... ANT
Antigua (ROG) .... ANTIG
Antigua [*IYRU nationality code*] [*Airport symbol*] .... ANU
Antigua [*MARC country of publication code Library of Congress*] (LCCP) .... aq
Antigua [*Antigua*] [*Seismograph station code, US Geological Survey Closed*] (SEIS) .... AWI
Antigua [*MARC geographic area code Library of Congress*] (LCCP) .... nwaq--
Antigua [*International civil aircraft marking*] (ODBW) V2
Antigua and Barbuda Airways International Ltd. [*ICAO designator*] (FAAC) .... ABI
Antigua and Barbuda Broadcasting Service (EY) .... ABBS
Antigua Caribbean Liberation Movement [*Political party*] (EAIO) .... ACLM
Antigua Labour Party [*Political party*] (PPW) .... ALP
Antigua-Barbuda [*ANSI two-letter standard code*] (CNC) .... AG
Antigua-Barbuda [*ANSI three-letter standard code*] (CNC) .... ATG
Antihalation .... AH
Antihalation Undercoat [*Photography*] (OA) .... AHU
Anti-Heart Antibody [*Medicine*] (DMAA) .... AHA
Anti-Helicopter Device .... AHD
Anti-Helicopter Mine [*Military*] .... AHM
Antihemophilic Factor [*Factor VIII*] [*Also, AHG, PTF, TPC Hematology*] .... AHF

Antihemophilic Globulin [*Factor VIII*] [*Hematology*] (DAVI) .... AGH
Antihemophilic Globulin [*Factor VIII*] [*Also, AHF, PTF, TPC Hematology*] .... AHG
Antihistone Antibody [*Medicine*] (DMAA) .... AHA
Antihuman Globulin [*Consumption test*] [*Medicine*] .... AHG
Antihuman Lymphocyte Globulin [*Medicine*] (DMAA) .... AHLG
Antihuman Lymphocyte Serum [*Immunochemistry*] (MAE) .... AHLS
Antihuman Thymocyte Gamma Globulin [*Immunochemistry*] .... AHTGG
Antihuman Thymocyte Globulin [*Medicine*] (DAVI) .... ATG
Antihuman Thymocytic Globulin [*Clinical chemistry*] (MAE) .... AHTG
Antihuman Thymocytic Plasma [*Clinical chemistry*] (MAE) .... AHTP
Antihuman Thymus Serum (DMAA) .... AHTS
Antihunt [*Circuit*] [*Electronics*] .... AH
Antihyaluronidase [*Clinical chemistry*] .... AH
Antihyaluronidase [*Bacteriology*] (DAVI) .... AHI
Antihyaluronidase Titer [*Clinical chemistry*] (MAE) .... AHT
Antihypertensive and Lipid-Lowering Heart Attack Trial [*Clinical trial*] .... ALLHAT
Antihypertensive Drug [*Medicine*] .... AHD
Antihypertensive Neural Renomedullary Liquid .... ANRL
Antihypertensive Neutral Renomedullary Lipids [*Cardiology*] (DAVI) .... ANRL
Anti-Ice/De-Ice System [*or Subsystem*] (MCD) .... ADS
Anti-Icing [*Technical drawings*] .... AI
Anti-Icing Additive (NATG) .... AIA
Anti-Icing Fluid [*Aviation*] (DA) .... AAF
Anti-Icing System [*Aircraft*] .... AIS
Anti_Immunoglobulin [*Medicine*] (DMAA) .... AIG
Anti-Immunoglobulin Antibodies (DOG) .... AIA
Anti-Inflammatory Corticoid [*Pharmacology*] (DAVI) .... AC
Anti-Inflammatory Drug [*Pharmacology*] (DAVI) .... AID
Anti-Inflammatory Nonsteroidal [*Agent or drug*] [*Pharmacology*] (DAVI) .... AINS
Anti-Inflammatory Protein (PDAA) .... AIP
Anti-Inflation Act [*Canada*] .... AIA
Anti-Inflation Appeal Tribunal [*Canada*] .... AIAT
Anti-Inflation Board .... AIB
Anti-Injunction Act of 1932 (WYGK) .... AIA
Anti-Insulin Antibody [*Endocrinology*] (DAVI) .... AI-Ab
Anti-Insulin Receptor Antibody [*Medicine*] (DMAA) .... AIRA
Anti-Insulin Serum [*Biochemistry*] (MAE) .... AIS
Anti-Intercontinental Ballistic Missile .... AICBM
Anti-Intermediate Range Ballistic Missile .... AIRBM
Anti-Intrusion Alarm .... AIA
Anti-Intrusion Alarm Set .... AIAS
Anti-Invasion Factor [*In bone resorption*] .... AIF
Anti-Jackknife System [*Automotive engineering*] .... AJS
Anti-Jam Control Modem [*Military*] (DOMA) .... AJCM
Antijam Display .... AJD
Antijam Equipment .... AJE
Antijam Frequency .... AJF
Antijam Frequency Hopper .... AJFH
Antijam Hopper .... AJH
Antijam Manpack Antenna (MCD) .... AJMA
Anti-Jam Modem Controller [*Computer science*] (LAIN) .... AJM/C
Antijam MODEM [*Modulate, Demodulate*], Very-Low Frequency (CAAL) .... VERDIN
Antijam Operator (CET) .... AJO
Antijam Synthesizer .... AJS
Antijam Technique .... AJT
Antijamming [*RADAR*] .... AJ
Antijamming/Anti-Interference (CET) .... AJ/AI
Antijamming Blackout .... AJBO
Antijamming Improvements (AABC) .... AJI
Anti-Knock Index [*Automotive industry*] .... AKI
AntiLASER Beam Coating .... ALBC
Antilla [*Cuba ICAO location identifier*] (ICLI) .... MUAT
Antillaanse Luchtvaart Maatschappij [*Airline*] [*Netherlands Antilles*] .... ALM
Antillana de Nevegacion Aerea SA [*Dominican Republic*] [*ICAO designator*] (FAAC) .... SUN
Antilles (VRA) .... L Anti
Antilles Air Boats (MHDB) .... AD
Antilles Command, United States Army Caribbean .... ANTCOMDUSARCARIB
Antilles Research Program [*Yale University*] .... ARP
Antilles Resources Ltd. [*Vancouver Stock Exchange symbol*] .... ARY
Antilliaanse Luchtvaart Maatschappij [*Netherlands ICAO designator*] (FAAC) .... ALM
Antilock Brake [*Automotive engineering*] .... ALB
Antilock Brake Control Module [*Automotive engineering*] .... ABCM
Antilock Braking System [*Automotive engineering*] .... ABS
Anti-Locust Research Centre [*Later, Centre for Overseas Pest Research*] [*British*] (MCD) .... ALRC
Antilog [*Mathematics*] (BARN) .... illog
Antilogarithm .... ANTILOG
Antilogarithmic Function .... ANLG
Antilymphocyte Antibody [*Medicine*] (DMAA) .... AL-Ab
Antilymphocyte [*or Antilymphocytic*] Globulin [*Immunology*] .... ALG
Antilymphocyte Plasma [*Immunology*] (MAE) .... ALP
Antilymphocyte [*or Antilympholytic*] Serum [*Immunology*] .... ALS
Antimacrophage Globulin (MAE) .... AMG
Antimacrophage Serum (MAE) .... AMS
Antimalaria Campaign .... AMC
Antimalarial Agent .... AMA
Antimassed Armor Strike Weapon System (MCD) .... AASWS
Antimateriel [*Munitions*] .... AM
Antimateriel Incendiary .... AMI
Antimateriel Warhead .... AMW
Antimateriel Warhead .... AMWH
Antimechanized [*Army*] (AABC) .... AMECZ
Anti-Metric Society of America [*An association*] .... AMSA

Antimicrobial Agent Associated Colitis [*Medicine*] ... AAAC
Antimicrobial Agent-Associated Colitis [*Medicine*] (DAVI) ... AAC
Antimicrobial Agents and Chemotherapy ... AAC
Antimicrobial Removal Device ... ARD
Antimicrosomal Antibody [*Clinical chemistry*] ... AMcA
Anti-Mine Countermeasure (MCD) ... AMCM
Antiminesweeping Explosive Float ... AMSEF
Antimissile Array RADAR ... AMAR
Antimissile Missile [*Air Force*] ... AMM
Antimissile Missile and Space Defense Office ... AMMSDO
Antimissile Missile Test Range [*Military*] ... AMMTR
Anti-Missile Research Advisory Council ... AMRAC
Antimissile Surface-to-Air Missile ... AMSAM
Antimissile Warfare ... AMW
Antimisting Kerosene [*Aviation*] ... AMK
Antimitochondral Antibody [*Immunology*] ... AMA
Antimonium [*Antimony*] [*Symbol is Sb*] [*Chemical element*] (ROG) ... ANT
Antimonium [*Antimony*] [*Symbol is Sb*] [*Chemical element*] (ROG) ... ANTIM
Antimony [*Chemical element*] (DOG) ... Sb
Antimony Sodium Dimercaptosuccinate [*Stibocaptate*] (BABM) ... TWSb/6
Antimony Tin Oxide (IAA) ... ATO
Antimony Trisisooctyl Mercaptoacetate (GNE) ... ATOM
Antimony Trisulfide Oxysulfide ... ASOS
Antimotor Torpedo Boat [*Navy*] ... AMTB
Antimotorboat ... AMB
Antimouse Lymphocyte Serum [*Immunology*] (MAE) ... AMLS
Anti-Muellerian Hormone [*Also, MIS*] [*Embryology*] [*Biochemistry*] ... AMH
Antimultipath Equipment ... AME
Antimuscle Factor [*Immunology*] ... AMF
Antimycin (DAVI) ... Ant
Antimycin A (DMAA) ... AntA
Antimyosin Antibody [*Medicine*] (DMAA) ... AMA
Antineoplastic Urinary Protein ... ANUP
Antineutrophil Cytoplasmic Antibody [*Immunology*] ... ANCA
Antineutrophilic Serum [*Hematology*] (DAVI) ... ANS
[*The*] **Antinoe Papyrus of Theocritus** [*Classical studies*] (OCD) ... PAntin
Antinoopolis Papyri [*A publication*] (OCD) ... PAntinoop
Antinuclear Antibody [*Medicine*] (DMAA) ... A
Antinuclear Antibody [*Immunology*] ... ANA
Antinuclear Antibody [*Medicine*] (DMAA) ... ANuA
Antinuclear Antibody Fluid [*Medicine*] (DAVI) ... ANA-FL
Anti-Nuclear Campaign [*British*] ... ANC
Antinuclear Factor [*Immunology*] ... ANF
Anti-Nuclear Force (DNAB) ... ANF
Anti-Nuclear Group Representing York (NRCH) ... ANGRY
Antinuclear Submarine Warfare [*Navy*] ... ANSW
Antinucleolar Antibodies [*Immunology*] (AAMN) ... ANoA
Antioch College, Yellow Springs, OH [*OCLC symbol*] (OCLC) ... ANC
Antioch College, Yellow Springs, OH [*Library symbol Library of Congress*] (LCLS) ... OYesA
Antioch Program for Interracial Education [*Antioch College*] (EA) ... APIE
Antioch Review [*A publication*] (BRI) ... Ant R
Anti-Ovotransferrin [*Biochemistry*] ... AOT
Antioxidant Activity [*Food technology*] ... AA
Antiparietal Antibody ... APA
Antiparkinsonian [*Medicine*] (MEDA) ... APK
Antiperiplanar [*Chemistry*] ... ap
Antipernicious Anemia Factor [*Also, APAF, EF, LLD*] [*Hematology*] (AAMN) ... APA
Antipernicious Anemia Factor [*Also, APA, EF, LLD*] [*Hematology*] ... APAF
Antipernicious Anemia Principle [*Hematology*] (IIA) ... AAP
Antipersonnel [*Projectile*] ... AP
Antipersonnel [*Projectile*] ... APER
Antipersonnel [*Projectile*] (AABC) ... APERS
Antipersonnel Antimaterial [*Weaponry*] (MCD) ... APAM
Antipersonnel Bomb ... APB
Antipersonnel Improved Conventional Munitions [*Army*] (ADDR) ... APICM
Antipersonnel Missile ... APM
Antipersonnel Obstacle Breaching System [*Marine Corps*] (INF) ... APOBS
Antipersonnel Projectile ... APP
Antiphase Boundaries [*Mineralogy*] ... APB
Anti-Phase Boundary Energy (PDAA) ... APBE
Antiphase Domains [*Mineralogy*] ... APD
Antiphlogistic-Corticoid [*Medicine*] (AAMN) ... AC
Antiphlogistic-Corticoid [*Medicine*] (MAE) ... APC
Antiphlogistic-Corticoid Conditioning Effect [*Medicine*] ... A-CC
Antiphon ... ANT
Antiphonale Sacrosanctae Romanae Ecclesiae ... AR
Antiphospholipid Antibody [*Medicine*] (DMAA) ... APAB
Antiphosphotyrosine [*Biochemistry*] ... APT
Antiplasmin [*Hematology*] ... AP
Antiplugging Relay ... APR
Anti-Poaching Unit (BARN) ... APU
Antipodal Propagation Phenomena ... APP
Antipolo [*Philippines*] [*Later, MUT*] [*Geomagnetic observatory code*] ... ANO
Antiprostaglandin Antiserum [*Immunology*] ... APS
Antiprotein Accumulator (DAVI) ... AA
Antiproton Accumulator [*Particle physics*] ... AA
Antiproton Collector [*Particle physics*] ... ACOL
Anti-Pseudomonas Human Plasma [*Immunology*] (MAE) ... APHP
Antipsychotic Drug ... APD
Antipyrine [*Analgesic*] (AAMN) ... AP
Antipyrylbenzoquinoneimine [*Organic chemistry*] ... ABQI
Antiquarian [*or Antiquities*] ... ANTIQ
Antiquarian Book and Collectibles Information Systems (IID) ... ABACIS
Antiquarian Booksellers Association [*International*] ... ABA
Antiquarian Booksellers Association of America (EA) ... ABAA
Antiquarian Booksellers Association of Canada ... ABAC
Antiquarian Booksellers' Center (EA) ... ABC
Antiquarian Horological Society (EA) ... AHS
Antiquarian House, Plymouth, MA [*Library symbol Library of Congress*] (LCLS) ... MPIA
Antiquarian Trade List Annual [*A publication*] ... ATLA
Antiquaries Journal [*A publication*] (OCD) ... Ant Journ
Antiquaries Journal [*A publication*] (BRI) ... Antiq J
Antiquariorum Regiae Societatis Socius [*Fellow of the Royal Society of Antiquaries*] [*Latin*] ... ARSS
Antique [*Bookbinding*] (ROG) ... ANTIQ
Antique (VRA) ... antq
Antique ... ANTQ
Antique Airplane Association (EA) ... AAA
Antique and Art Glass Salt Shaker Collectors Society (EA) ... AAGSSCS
Antique and Classic Boat Society (EA) ... ACBS
Antique and Historical Glass Foundation (EA) ... AHGF
Antique Appraisal Association of America (EA) ... AAAA
Antique Auto Racing Association (EA) ... AARA
Antique Automobile Club of America (EA) ... AACA
Antique Automobile Coalition [*Legislative lobbying group*] ... AAC
Antique Bicycle Club of America (EA) ... ABCA
Antique Boat and Yacht Club (EA) ... ABYC
Antique Boat Society (EA) ... ABS
Antique Bottle Collectors Association [*Defunct*] ... ABCA
Antique Bowie Knife Association (EA) ... ABKA
Antique Collectors' Club [*British*] (DBA) ... ACC
Antique Comb Collectors Club (EA) ... ACCC
Antique Doorknob Collectors of America (EA) ... ADCA
Antique Engine and Thresher Association (EA) ... AETA
Antique Laid [*Paper*] (ADA) ... ANTLD
Antique Latin (ADA) ... ANTLAT
Antique Motorcycle Club of America (EA) ... AMCA
Antique Old Style [*Paper*] (ADA) ... ANTOS
Antique Phonograph Collectors Club (EA) ... APCC
Antique Powercraft Historical Society [*Defunct*] (EA) ... APHS
Antique Radio Club of America (EA) ... ARCA
Antique Radio Guild of America ... ARGA
Antique Snowmobile Club of America (EA) ... ASCOA
[*The*] **Antique Stove Association** (EA) ... TASA
Antique Stove Information Clearinghouse (EA) ... ASIC
Antique Studebaker Club (EA) ... ASC
Antique Telephone Collectors Association [*Later, TCI*] (EA) ... ATCA
Antique Toy Collectors of America (EA) ... ATCA
Antique Trade Weekly, Dubuque, IA [*Library symbol Library of Congress*] (LCLS) ... IaDuAn
Antique Truck Club of America (EA) ... ATCA
Antique Wireless Association (EA) ... AWA
Antique Wove [*Paper*] (ADA) ... ANTWO
Antiques & Collecting Magazine [*A publication*] (BRI) ... Ant & CM
Antiques Dealers' Association of America (EA) ... ADA
Antiques Fairs Organisers Association [*British*] (DBA) ... AFOA
Antiquitates Judaicae [*Jewish Antiquities*] [*of Josephus*] [*Classical studies*] (OCD) ... AJ
Antiquitates Judaicae [*Jewish Antiquities*] [*of Josephus*] [*Classical studies*] (BJA) ... Ant
Antiquitates Romanae [*of Dionysius Halicarnassensis*] [*Classical studies*] (OCD) ... Ant Rom
Antiquite Classique [*A publication*] (OCD) ... Ant Class
Antiquities ... ANT
Antiquo [*I Oppose*] [*Used by Romans to signify a negative vote*] [*Latin*] ... A
Antirabies Serum [*Medicine*] ... ARS
Antiracketeering ... AR
AntiRADAR (NATG) ... AR
AntiRADAR Missile ... ARM
AntiRADAR Surveillance and Target Acquisition System ... ASTAS
Antiradiation Guidance Sensor ... ARGS
Antiradiation Homer ... ARH
Anti-Radiation Homing and Warning System [*Military*] (DNAB) ... ARHAWS
Anti-Radiation Homing / Infrared [*Military*] (PDAA) ... ARH/IR
Antiradiation Missile ... ARM
Antiradiation Projectile ... ARP
Antiradiation Projectile Simulation (MCD) ... ARPSIM
Antiradiation Weapon System (NVT) ... ARWS
Antirat Neutrophil Serum [*Medicine*] (DMAA) ... ANS
Antirat Thymocyte Serum [*Medicine*] (DMAA) ... ATS
Antirattler [*Automotive engineering*] ... A/RATLR
Antireceptor Antibody [*Immunology*] ... ARA
Antirecession Fiscal Assistance ... ARFA
Antireflection ... AR
Antireflection Coated Metal-Oxide Semiconductor (MCD) ... AMOS
Antireflective, Antiglare [*Cathode ray tube treatment*] (PCM) ... ARAG
Antireflective, Antistatic [*Cathode ray tube treatment*] (PCM) ... ARAS
Antirepeat Relay ... ARR
Anti-Repression Resource Team (EA) ... ARRT
Antireticular Cytotoxic Serum ... ACS
Antireticulo-Endothelial Serum [*Medicine*] (DMAA) ... ARES
Antireversionary [*Method of exhaust control*] [*Automotive engineering*] ... AR
Anti-Revolutionaire Partij - Evangelische Volkspartij [*Antirevolutionary Party*] [*Netherlands Political party*] (PPW) ... ARP
Antiribonucleoprotein [*Genetics*] (DAVI) ... anti-RNP
Antiriot Laws ... ARL
Anti-Saccade Oculomotor Delayed Response [*Neurobiology*] ... AS-OUR

Antisatellite	ASAT
Anti-Satellite Engagement Model [Military]	ASEM
Antisatellite Satellite	ASAT
Anti-Satellite Weapon (IAA)	ASW
Antisaturation Inverter	ASI
Antiself Homing [System] [Torpedo safety device] [Navy]	ASH
Antisense Orientation	AS
Antisense RNA [Ribonucleic Acid] [Genetics] (DOG)	asRNA
Antiseparation Tailored Contour (MCD)	ATC
Antiseptic (MSA)	ANTSPT
Antiseptic Biological Suppository [Medicine] (IIA)	ABS
Antiserum [Immunology]	AS
Antiserum/Horse [Medicine] (DMAA)	AS/Ho
Antiship Capable Missile (NVT)	ASCM
Antiship Cruise Missile	ASCM
Antiship Missile (NVT)	ASM
Antiship Missile Defense	ASMD
Anti-Ship Missile Defense / Electronic Warfare (PDAA)	ASMD/EW
Antiship Missile Defense Missile System (MCD)	ASMDMS
Antiship Missile Target (MCD)	ASMT
Antiship Phoenix	ASP
Antiship Surveillance and Targeting [Navy] (NVT)	ASST
Antiship Torpedo (IEEE)	ASTOR
Antiship Torpedo Defense [or Device] (MCD)	ASTD
Antiship Underwater Warfare (MCD)	ASUW
Anti-Shipping Campaign Model (MCD)	ASCAM
Antishock Body	ASB
Antisidetone [Telecommunications] (TEL)	AST
Antiskid Braking System [General Motors Corp.]	ABS
Antiskywave Antenna (NTCM)	ASWA
Antislack Device	ASD
Anti-Slavery International [England] (EAIO)	ASI
Anti-Slavery Society for the Protection of Human Rights (EA)	ASSPHR
Anti-Slip Differential [Automotive engineering]	ASD
Anti-Slip Regulation [Automotive engineering]	ASR
Anti-Smith [Antibody] [Hematology] (DAVI)	anti-Sm
Antismooth Muscle Antibody [Immunology]	ASMA
Antisnake Venom [Medicine]	ASV
Antisocial Personality [Psychology]	ASP
Antisocial Personality Disorder [Psychology] (WDAA)	APD
Anti-Socialist Party (ADA)	ANTI-SOC
Antisolar (KSC)	A-SOL
Antispasticity Index [Neurology] (DAVI)	ASTI
Antispleen Globulin [Medicine] (DMAA)	ASPG
Anti-Spoofing [Jamming resistance feature on global positioning satellites] (SSD)	A-S
Antisqueak [Automotive engineering]	A/SQK
Anti-Standoff Jammer [Defense system] (MCD)	ASOJ
Antistatic Additive	ASA
Antistatic Compound	ASC
Anti-Stoke Stimulated Raman Scattering [Spectrometry] (MCD)	ASRS
Antistreptococcal Hyaluronidase [Medicine] (DMAA)	ASH
Antistreptococcal Polysaccharide Test [Medicine] (DMAA)	ASPAT
Antistreptokinase [Immunology]	ASK
Antistreptolysin [Immunology] (MAE)	AS
Antistreptolysin [Immunology]	ASL
Antistreptolysin [Immunology] (DHSM)	ASTO
Antistreptolysin Factor (PDAA)	ASF
Anti-Streptolysin Reaction [Medicine] (DMAA)	ASR
Antistreptolysin Test [Medicine] (DMAA)	ASLT
Antistreptolysin-O [Also, ASO] [Clinical chemistry]	ASLO
Antistreptolysin-O [Also, ASLO] [Clinical chemistry]	ASO
Antistreptolysin-O Titer [Clinical chemistry] (AAMN)	ASOT
Antistreptozyme (DMAA)	ASTZ
Antistreptozyme Test [Clinical chemistry]	ASTZ
Antisubmarine	AS
Antisubmarine [Designation for all US military aircraft]	S
Antisubmarine Air Control [Navy] (MCD)	ASAC
Antisubmarine Attack Plotter [Navy]	ASAP
Antisubmarine Attack Teacher	ASAT
Antisubmarine Attack Teacher Training Unit	ASATTU
Antisubmarine Classification Analysis Test	ASCAT
Antisubmarine Classification and Analysis Center [Navy]	ASCAC
Antisubmarine Classification and Analysis Center/Tactical Support Center (DNAB)	ASCAC/TSC
Antisubmarine Combat Activity Center (DNAB)	ASCAC
Antisubmarine Composite Engineering Squadron	ACES
Antisubmarine Contact Evaluation System [Navy] (MCD)	ASCES
Antisubmarine Defense Forces, Atlantic [Obsolete Navy]	ASDEFORLANT
Antisubmarine Defense Forces, Pacific [Obsolete Navy]	ASDEFORPAC
Antisubmarine Defense Group	ASDG
Antisubmarine Detection Investigation Committee [A group in World War I that gave rise to the device that bore its name in World War II]	ASDIC
Antisubmarine Development Detachment [Atlantic Fleet] [Norfolk, VA]	ASDD
Antisubmarine Development Detachment [Navy] (DNAB)	ASDEVDET
Antisubmarine Development Detachment, Atlantic Fleet [Navy]	ASDEVLANT
Anti-Submarine Division [British military] (DMA)	ASD
Antisubmarine Establishment [Navy British]	ASE
Antisubmarine Experimental Establishment	A/SEE
Antisubmarine Fighter Squadron [Navy]	ANTISUBFITRON
Antisubmarine Fighter Squadron [Navy]	VSF
Antisubmarine Fixed Defenses Officer [Navy]	A/SFDO
Antisubmarine Helicopter (NATG)	HPS
Antisubmarine Launched Ballistic Missile	ASLBM
Antisubmarine Patrol	ASP

Antisubmarine Rocket [Navy]	ASROC
Antisubmarine Rocket Computer [Navy] (IAA)	ASROC
Antisubmarine Rocket (Extended Range) (DNAB)	ASROC(ERA)
Antisubmarine Submarine [Navy symbol]	SSK
Antisubmarine Systems Project Office [Navy]	ASPO
Antisubmarine Tactical Data System (DNAB)	ASTDS
Antisubmarine Technical Evaluation Center [Navy]	ASTEC
Antisubmarine Terrier Missile [Navy]	ASTER
Antisubmarine Test Requirement Outline	ASTRO
Antisubmarine Torpedo (MSA)	ASTOR
Antisubmarine Torpedo Ordnance Rocket (MCD)	ASTOR
Anti-Submarine Training Indicator [Military] (PDAA)	ASTI
Antisubmarine War Division [British]	A/SWD
Antisubmarine Warfare	ASW
Antisubmarine Warfare Advisory Committee	ASWAC
Antisubmarine Warfare Air Control Ship (NVT)	ASWACS
Antisubmarine Warfare Airborne Simulation Program [Navy] (CAAL)	ASWASP
Antisubmarine Warfare and Antiair Warfare	ASW/AAW
Antisubmarine Warfare Area System [Italy]	ASWAS
Antisubmarine Warfare Automated Detection Prediction System (MCD)	ADEPS
Antisubmarine Warfare Barrier Submarine Patrol Area [Navy] (NVT)	SUBPA
Antisubmarine Warfare Barrier Submarine Patrol Zone [Navy] (NVT)	SUBPZ
Antisubmarine Warfare Barrier Surface Patrol Area [Navy] (NVT)	SURFPA
Antisubmarine Warfare Barrier Surface Patrol Ship [Navy] (NVT)	SURF
Antisubmarine Warfare Barrier Surface Patrol Zone [Navy] (NVT)	SURFPZ
Antisubmarine Warfare Barriers [Military]	ASWB
Antisubmarine Warfare Center [NATO] (NATG)	ASWC
Antisubmarine Warfare Centers Command and Control System [Navy] (CAAL)	ASWCCCS
Antisubmarine Warfare Combat System Integration [Navy] (CAAL)	ASWCSI
Antisubmarine Warfare Command and Control Centers System (MCD)	ASWCCS
Antisubmarine Warfare Commander [Navy] (NVT)	ASWC
Antisubmarine Warfare Communications (DNAB)	ASCOMM
Antisubmarine Warfare Communications Detachment (DNAB)	ASCOMMDET
Antisubmarine Warfare Control System [Navy] (CAAL)	ASWCS
Antisubmarine Warfare Electronic Countermeasures System (MCD)	ASWEC
Antisubmarine Warfare Exercise (NVT)	ASWEX
Antisubmarine Warfare Fighter Squadron (DNAB)	ASWFITRON
Antisubmarine Warfare Fire Control Officer [Navy] (CAAL)	ASWFCO
Antisubmarine Warfare Force [Atlantic Fleet] [Norfolk, VA]	ASW
Antisubmarine Warfare Force, Sixth Fleet [Navy]	ASWFORSIXTHF
Antisubmarine Warfare Group	ASWGRU
Antisubmarine Warfare Improved Localization System (NVT)	ASWILS
Antisubmarine Warfare Information Exchange System [or Subsystem] [Navy] (NVT)	ASWIXS
Antisubmarine Warfare Installations [NATO] (NATG)	ASWI
Antisubmarine Warfare Integrated Combat System [Navy] (MCD)	ASWICS
Antisubmarine Warfare Laboratory [Military]	ASWL
Antisubmarine Warfare Missile [Navy] (CAAL)	ASWM
Antisubmarine Warfare Officer [Navy]	ASWO
Antisubmarine Warfare Operational Research Group [World War II]	ASWORG
Antisubmarine Warfare Operations Centers [Navy] (NVT)	ASWOC
Antisubmarine Warfare Operations Controller [Navy] (CAAL)	ASWOC
Antisubmarine Warfare Operations Patrol (NVT)	ASWPTL
Antisubmarine Warfare Program System [Navy] (GFGA)	ASWEPS
Antisubmarine Warfare Programs [Navy] (MCD)	AWP
Antisubmarine Warfare Project Office [Navy]	ASWPO
Antisubmarine Warfare RADAR (IIA)	ASWR
Antisubmarine Warfare Research Center [NATO] (NATG)	ASWRC
Antisubmarine Warfare Research Center [NATO]	ASWRECEN
Antisubmarine Warfare Schoolship [Navy] (NVT)	ASWSS
Antisubmarine Warfare Ship Command and Control System (NVT)	ASWSCCS
Antisubmarine Warfare Standoff Weapon	ASW/SOW
Antisubmarine Warfare Systems [Navy]	ASWS
Antisubmarine Warfare Systems Analysis Group [Navy]	ASWSAG
Antisubmarine Warfare Systems Project Office [Washington, DC Navy]	ASWR
Antisubmarine Warfare Systems Project Office [Navy]	ASWSPO
Antisubmarine Warfare Systems Project Office [Navy] (DNAB)	ASWSYSPROJOFC
Antisubmarine Warfare Tactical Data System [Navy] (NVT)	ASWTDS
Antisubmarine Warfare Tactical Navigation System [Navy] (NG)	ASWTNS
Antisubmarine Warfare Tactical School	ASWTACSCOL
Antisubmarine Warfare Target Vehicle (MCD)	ASWTV
Antisubmarine Warfare Test Requirement Outline (MCD)	ASWTRO
Antisubmarine Warfare Training Center [Navy]	ASWTC
Antisubmarine Warfare Training Center [Navy]	ASWTRACEN
Antisubmarine Warfare Training in Port [Navy] (NVT)	ASWIPT
Antisubmarine Warfare Training Unit	ASWTU
Antisubmarine Warfare/Underwater Warfare	ASW/UW
Antisubmarine Warfare Unit [Navy]	ASWU
Antisubmarine Warning - Long Range (NATG)	ASW-LR
Antisubmarine Warning - Short Range (NATG)	ASW-SR
Antisubmarine Weapon (NATG)	ASW
Antisubmarine Weapons Environmental Prediction Service [Navy]	ASWEPS
Anti-Submarine Wire-Guided Weapon [British military] (DMA)	ASWGW
Antisulfanilic Acid [Biochemistry] (DAVI)	anti-S
Antisurface [Military] (NVT)	A/S
Antisurface Boat	ASB
Anti-Surface Euromissile Consortium (PDAA)	ASEM
Antisurface Raiders Exercise [NATO] (NATG)	RAIDEX
Antisurface Ship Missile [NATO] (MCD)	ASSM
Antisurface Ship Surveillance and Targeting (MCD)	ASST
Antisurface Ship Warfare (MCD)	ASSW

Antisurface Ship Warfare [*Navy*] (CAAL) ... ASU
Antisurface Vessel [*Navy*] ... ASV
Antisurface Warfare [*Navy*] ... ASUW
Antisurface Warfare Commander [*Navy*] ... ASUWC
Antisurface Weapons Exchange and Reaction Simulation (MCD) ... ANSWERS
Antisymmetric [*Chemistry*] ... a
Antisymmetrized Geminal Power [*Chemical physics*] ... AGP
Antisyphilitic Treatment [*Medicine*] ... AST
Antitactical Ballistic Missile (MCD) ... ATB
Antitactical Ballistic Missile ... ATBM
Antitactical Missile ... ATM
Antitank [*Also, ATk*] ... AT
Antitank [*Also, AT*] (NATG) ... ATk
Antitank Air Defense System ... ATADS
Antitank Aircraft Rocket ... ATAR
Antitank/Antivehicle (MCD) ... AT/AV
Antitank Assault Air Defense (MCD) ... ATAAD
Antitank/Assault/Air Defense System (MCD) ... ATAADS
Antitank Assault Weapon [*Army*] ... ATAW
Antitank Battalion [*Marine Corps*] ... ATBN
Antitank Battery [*Military*] ... ATB
Antitank Grenade Launcher (AABC) ... ATGL
Antitank Guided Air Rocket ... ATGAR
Antitank Guided Missile ... ATGM
Antitank Guided Weapon (MCD) ... ATGW
Antitank Gun [*Military*] ... ATG
Antitank Helicopter (MCD) ... ATH
Antitank LASER-Assisted System [*British*] ... ATLAS
Antitank Mine Dispensing System (MCD) ... ATMDS
Antitank Missile [*Army*] ... ATM
Antitank Missile Test (MCD) ... ATMT
Antitank, Nonmetallic ... ATNM
Antitank Regiment [*Military*] ... ATR
Antitank Rocket Launcher Imagery Interpretation (AABC) ... ATRL
Antitank Target System [*Military*] (INF) ... ATTS
Antitank Weapon (NATG) ... ATW
Antitank Weapons Effect Signature Simulator [*Army*] (INF) ... ATWESS
Antitension Line (MAE) ... ATL
Antiterrain Avoidance RADAR System (MCD) ... ATARS
Antiterritorial Land Mine (MCD) ... ATLAM
Antiterrorism [*Measure*] [*DoD*] ... AT
Anti-Terrorism Assistance Program [*FAA*] (TAG) ... ATAP
Anti-Terrorism Coordinating Committee (DOMA) ... ATCC
Antiterrorism Operations and Intelligence Cell [*Army*] ... ATOIC
Anti-Terrorismo ETA [*Anti-ETA Terrorism*] [*Spanish*] (PPE) ... ATE
Anti-Terrorist Alert Center [*Navy*] (LAIN) ... ATAC
Anti-Terrorist Liberation Group [*Undercover anti-Basque terrorist interior-ministry network*] [*Acronym is based on foreign phrase Spain*] (ECON) ... GAL
Antitetanus Serum [*Medicine*] ... ATS
Anti-Tetany Substance 10 [*Same as DHT, Dihydrotachysterol*] [*Pharmacology*] ... AT-10
Antithrombin [*Hematology*] ... AT
Antithrombocyte Globulin [*Immunology*] (MAE) ... ATG
Antithrombotics in the Prevention of Reocclusion in Coronary Thrombolysis [*Cardiology study*] ... APRICOT
Antithymocyte Gamma-Globulin [*Immunology*] ... ATGAM
Antithymocyte Globulin [*Immunochemistry*] ... ATG
Antithymocyte Serum [*Immunochemistry*] ... ATS
Antithyroglobulin [*Immunochemistry*] (MAE) ... ATG
Antithyroglobulin Antibody [*Immunochemistry*] ... ATA
Antithyroid Drug (AAMN) ... ATD
Antithyroid Plasma Membrane Antibody [*Medicine*] (DMAA) ... ATMA
Antitorpedo [*Navy*] ... AT
Antitorpedo (MSA) ... ATORP
Anti-Torpedo Craft [*British military*] (DMA) ... ATC
Antitorque Pedal ... ATP
Anti-Torture Research [*Copenhagen, Denmark*] [*An association*] (EAIO) ... ATR
Antitoxin (MSA) ... ANTOX
Antitoxin Botulism Equine Trivalent [*Biochemistry*] (DAVI) ... ABE
Antitoxin Unit [*Immunology*] ... AU
Antitoxineinheit [*Antitoxin Unit*] [*German*] ... AE
Anti-Toxoplasma Antibody [*Immunology*] (MAE) ... ATA
Antitracking Control ... ATRC
Anti-Transmit-Receive ... ATR
Anti-Transmit-Receive Tube ... ATRT
Anti-Trust (LAIN) ... AT
Antitrust and Monopoly Subcommittee [*US Senate*] ... A & M
Antitrust Bulletin (AAGC) ... Antitrust Bull
Antitrust Law ... ATL
Antitrust Law and Trade Regulations Report [*Bureau of National Affairs*] [*A publication*] (ILCA) ... Antitrust L & Trade Reg Rep
Antitrust Procedural Improvements Act of 1980 ... APIA
Antitrypsin [*Biochemistry*] ... AT
Anti-U-Boat Warfare [*British World War II*] ... AU
Antiunderwater Warfare [*Navy*] (CINC) ... AUW
Antivaccinial Immunoglobulin [*Medicine*] (PDAA) ... AVIG
Antivehicle [*Munitions*] ... AV
Antivehicle Device [*Air Force*] (MCD) ... AVD
Antivehicle Land Mine ... AVLM
Antivehicle Mine ... AVM
Anti-Vermin [*Battle dress*] [*British and Canadian*] [*World War II*] ... A/V
Antivibration Joint ... AVJ
Antiviral Factor ... AVF
Antiviral Protein [*Immunology*] ... AVP
Antivirus [*Computer science*] ... AV
Anti-Virus Emergency Response Team [*Computer security system*] ... AVERT
Anti-Virus Emergency Response Team [*McAfee*] [*Computer science*] ... AVERT
Anti-Virus Toolkit for Windows [*Dr. Solomon's Software, Inc.*] ... AVTK
Anti-Vivisection Party [*British*] ... AV
Anti-Vivisection Society [*VIL*] [*Absorbed by*] (EA) ... AVS
Antivoice-Operated Transmission (CET) ... ANTIVOX
Antiwear ... AW
Anti-Whole Rabbit Serum [*Immunology*] ... AWRS
Antiyeast Factor [*Medicine*] ... AYF
Antler (VRA) ... atlr
Antlers, OK [*Location identifier FAA*] (FAAL) ... AEE
Antlia [*Constellation*] ... Ant
Antlia [*Constellation*] ... Antl
Antofagasta [*Chile*] [*Airport symbol*] (OAG) ... ANF
Antofagasta [*Chile*] [*Seismograph station code, US Geological Survey*] (SEIS) ... ANT
Antofagasta [*Chile*] [*ICAO location identifier*] (ICLI) ... SCFZ
Antofagasta & Bolivia Railroad Co. (MHDB) ... A & B
Antofagasta and Bolivia Railway Co. (MHDB) ... A & BRC
Antofagasta/Internacional Cerro Moreno [*Chile*] [*ICAO location identifier*] (ICLI) ... SCFA
Antoko Demokraty Kristiana Malagasy [*Malagasy Christian Democratic Party*] (AF) ... ADKM
Antokon'ny Kongresin'ny Fahaleovantenan'i Madagasikara [*Congress Party for Malagasy Independence*] [*Political party*] (AF) ... AKFM
Antoky ny Revolosiona Malagasy [*Vanguard of the Malagasy Revolution*] (PPW) ... AREMA
Anton Breini Center for Tropical Health and Medicine [*James Cook University*] [*Australia*] ... ABCTHM
Anton Chico, NM [*Location identifier FAA*] (FAAL) ... ACH
Antoniani Benedictini Armeni [*Mechitarists*] ... ABA
Antonine Sisters (TOCD) ... RA
Antonio Enes [*Mozambique*] [*Airport symbol*] (AD) ... ANO
Antonius [*of Plutarch*] [*Classical studies*] (OCD) ... Ant
Antonius Albergati [*Deceased, 1634*] [*Authority cited in pre-1607 legal work*] (DSA) ... An Albg
Antonius Augustinus [*Deceased, 1586*] [*Authority cited in pre-1607 legal work*] (DSA) ... A August
Antonius Augustinus [*Deceased, 1586*] [*Authority cited in pre-1607 legal work*] (DSA) ... AA
Antonius Augustinus [*Deceased, 1586*] [*Authority cited in pre-1607 legal work*] (DSA) ... Ant Aug
Antonius Augustinus [*Deceased, 1586*] [*Authority cited in pre-1607 legal work*] (DSA) ... Ant August
Antonius Boidus [*Flourished, 16th century*] [*Authority cited in pre-1607 legal work*] (DSA) ... Ant Boid
Antonius Burgos [*Deceased, 1525*] [*Authority cited in pre-1607 legal work*] (DSA) ... Anton Burg
Antonius Corsettus [*Flourished, 15th century*] [*Authority cited in pre-1607 legal work*] (DSA) ... Ant Corse
Antonius de Butrio [*Deceased, 1408*] [*Authority cited in pre-1607 legal work*] (DSA) ... An
Antonius de Butrio [*Deceased, 1408*] [*Authority cited in pre-1607 legal work*] (DSA) ... An de Bu
Antonius de Butrio [*Deceased, 1408*] [*Authority cited in pre-1607 legal work*] (DSA) ... Ant de But
Antonius de Butrio [*Deceased, 1408*] [*Authority cited in pre-1607 legal work*] (DSA) ... Anto
Antonius de Butrio [*Deceased, 1408*] [*Authority cited in pre-1607 legal work*] (DSA) ... Anto de But
Antonius de Rosellis [*Deceased, 1466*] [*Authority cited in pre-1607 legal work*] (DSA) ... Ant de Rosell
Antonius de Rosellis [*Deceased, 1466*] [*Authority cited in pre-1607 legal work*] (DSA) ... Ant Rosel
Antonius de Tremolis [*Flourished, 16th century*] [*Authority cited in pre-1607 legal work*] (DSA) ... Anto de Trem
Antonius Faber [*Deceased, 1624*] [*Authority cited in pre-1607 legal work*] (DSA) ... Ant Fab
Antonius Faber [*Deceased, 1624*] [*Authority cited in pre-1607 legal work*] (DSA) ... Anto Fab
Antonius Faber [*Deceased, 1624*] [*Authority cited in pre-1607 legal work*] (DSA) ... Anton Fab
Antonius Gabrielius (Romanus) [*Deceased, 1555*] [*Authority cited in pre-1607 legal work*] (DSA) ... Ant Gab Rom
Antonius Gabrielius (Romanus) [*Deceased, 1555*] [*Authority cited in pre-1607 legal work*] (DSA) ... Anton Gabr
Antonius Gabrielius (Romanus) [*Deceased, 1555*] [*Authority cited in pre-1607 legal work*] (DSA) ... Anton Gabr Roman
Antonius Gomez [*Flourished, l6th century*] [*Authority cited in pre-1607 legal work*] (DSA) ... An Go
Antonius Guibertus Costanus [*Flourished, 16th century*] [*Authority cited in pre-1607 legal work*] (DSA) ... Anton Costan
Antonius Nicellus [*Flourished, 15th century*] [*Authority cited in pre-1607 legal work*] (DSA) ... Anto Nice
Antonius Nicenus [*Authority cited in pre-1607 legal work*] (DSA) ... Anto Nice
Antonov [*Former USSR ICAO aircraft manufacturer identifier*] (ICAO) ... AN
Antonov Design Bureau [*Former USSR ICAO designator*] (FAAC) ... ADB
Antony and Cleopatra [*Shakespearean drama*] (BARN) ... A & C
Antony and Cleopatra [*Shakespearean work*] ... Ant
Antony and Cleopatra [*Shakespearean drama*] (BARN) ... Ant & Cl
Antony Resources [*Vancouver Stock Exchange symbol*] ... AYI
Antonym ... ANT
Antonym (ADA) ... ANTON
Antral Ethmoidal Sphenoidectomy [*Otorhinolaryngology*] (DAVI) ... AES
Antrim [*County in Ireland*] (ROG) ... ANT

Antrum [*Maxillary sinus*] [*Otorhinolaryngology*] (DAVI) ... A
Antrum-Corpus Boundary [*Anatomy*] ... ACB
Ants, Mice, and Gophers [*Electromagnetic antipest device*] ... AMIGO
Antsalova [*Madagascar*] [*ICAO location identifier*] (ICLI) ... FMMG
Antsalova [*Madagascar*] [*Airport symbol*] (OAG) ... WAQ
Antsirabe [*Madagascar*] [*ICAO location identifier*] (ICLI) ... FMME
Antsiranana/Arrachart [*Madagascar*] [*ICAO location identifier*] (ICLI) ... FMNA
Antsohihy [*Madagascar*] [*Airport symbol*] (OAG) ... WAI
Antsohihy/Ambalabe [*Madagascar*] [*ICAO location identifier*] (ICLI) ... FMNW
Antur Teifi [*Teifi Valley Business Centre*] [*British*] ... AT
Antwerp [*Belgium*] [*Airport symbol*] (OAG) ... ANR
Antwerp/Hamburg [*Range of ports between and including these two cities*] [*Shipping*] (DS) ... A/H
Antwerp-Anvers [*Belgium ICAO location identifier*] (ICLI) ... EBAW
Anuario Espanol e Hispano-Americano [*A publication*] ... AEHA
Anuhco, Inc. [*AMEX symbol*] (SPSG) ... ANU
Anuhco, Inc. [*Associated Press*] (SAG) ... Anuhco
Anuradhapura [*Ceylon*] [*Airport symbol*] (AD) ... ADP
Anuradhapura [*Sri Lanka*] [*ICAO location identifier*] (ICLI) ... VCCA
Anus ... A
Anuvrat Vishva Bharati [*Anuvrat Global Organization*] [*India*] (EAIO) ... ANUVIBHA
Anvik [*Alaska*] [*Airport symbol*] (OAG) ... ANV
Anvil Mountain [*Alaska*] [*Seismograph station code, US Geological Survey*] (SEIS) ... ANV
Anxiety [*Psychology*] (DAVI) ... anx
Anxiety Adjective Check List [*Psychology*] ... AACL
Anxiety Disorders Association of America (EA) ... ADAA
Anxiety Index [*Psychology*] ... AI
Anxiety Neurosis [*Psychology*] (DAVI) ... anx Neur
Anxiety Reaction [*Psychology*] (DAVI) ... anx reac
Anxiety Scale for the Blind [*Psychology*] ... ASB
Anxiety Scale Questionnaire [*Psychology*] ... ASQ
Anxiety Score [*Psychology*] ... AS
Anxiety Sign [*Psychology*] ... AxS
Anxiety State [*Psychology*] ... AS
Anxiety Status Inventory [*Medicine Medicine*] (DMAA) ... ASI
Anxiety Tension State [*Psychology*] ... ATS
Any Acceptable ... A/A
Any Boy Can [*Program*] [*Defunct*] (EA) ... ABC
Any Desired Thing [*Notation in a placebo prescription*] [*Medicine*] ... ADT
Any Good Brand ... AGB
Any Old Time [*Journalism*] (WDMC) ... AOT
Any One Accident [*Insurance*] (AIA) ... AOA
Any One Accident [*Insurance*] (AIA) ... AOAcc
Any One Aircraft [*Insurance*] (AIA) ... AOA
Any One Bottom [*Marine insurance*] (DS) ... AOB
Any One Location [*Marine insurance*] (DS) ... AOLOC
Any One Loss [*Insurance*] (AIA) ... AOL
Any One Occurrence [*Insurance*] (AIA) ... AOOcc
Any One Person [*Insurance*] (AIA) ... AOP
Any One Steamer [*Marine insurance*] (DS) ... AOS
Any One Vessel [*Marine insurance*] (DS) ... AOV
Any Other Business (ADA) ... AOB
Any Other Competent Business (ODBW) ... AOCB
Any Quantity ... AQ
Any Quantity ... AQAN
Any Reliable Brand [*Pharmacology*] ... ARB
Any Solid Color Other than Black [*Refers to cocker spaniels*] (IIA) ... ASCOB
Any Tape Search [*Computer program*] (KSC) ... ANTS
Anybody but Carter [*1976 presidential campaign*] ... ABC
Anybody but McGovern [*1972 presidential campaign*] ... ABM
Anybody but Wallace [*Political slogan referring to Alabama governor George Wallace*] ... ABW
Anyone (IAA) ... AY
Anything Invented Anywhere [*As opposed to NIH, Not Invented Here, an acronym indicating refusal to accept foreign technology*] ... AIA
Any-to-Come [*Type of wager where any cash forthcoming from earlier bets finances further bets*] [*British*] ... ATC
Anzac Community School, Fort McMurray, Alberta [*Library symbol National Library of Canada*] (BIB) ... AFMAS
ANZAC [*Australia-New Zealand Army Corps*] **Day Commemoration Committee, Queensland** ... ADCCQ
Anzar Road [*California*] [*Seismograph station code, US Geological Survey*] (SEIS) ... ANZ
Anzeiger [*or Anzeigen*] [*German*] (OCD) ... Anz
ANZHES [*Australian and New Zealand History of Education Society*] **Journal** [*A publication*] ... ANZHES Jl
AOL [*America Online*] **Instant Messenger** [*Computer science*] ... AIM
AOM-Minerve, SA [*France*] [*FAA designator*] (FAAC) ... AOM
Aomori [*Japan*] [*Airport symbol*] (OAG) ... AOJ
Aomori [*Japan*] [*Seismograph station code, US Geological Survey*] (SEIS) ... AOM
Aomori [*Japan ICAO location identifier*] (ICLI) ... RJSA
Aomori Outpost [*Japan*] [*Seismograph station code, US Geological Survey*] (SEIS) ... AOMJ
Aon Corp. [*NYSE symbol*] (SPSG) ... AOC
Aon Corp. [*Associated Press*] (SAG) ... Aon
Aon Corp. [*Associated Press*] (SAG) ... Aon Cp
Aon Cp 8% Perpetual Pfd [*NYSE symbol*] (TTSB) ... AOCPrA
Aon Cp 6.25% Cv Ex Pfd [*NYSE symbol*] (TTSB) ... AOCPrB
Aonde Vamos (BJA) ... AV
Aontas Fiontair Agus Spoirt [*Association for Adventure Sports*] [*British*] (EAIO) ... AFAS
Aontas Vaimheolochta na hEireann [*Speleological Union of Ireland*] (EAIO) ... AVE
Aorist [*Grammar*] (ROG) ... AOR
Aorta [*Cardiology*] (AAMN) ... Ao
Aortacoronary Bypass Graft [*Cardiology*] ... ACBG
Aorta-Iliac [*Cardiology*] (DAVI) ... ao-il
Aortic Aneurysm [*Cardiology*] (DAVI) ... AA
Aortic Arch Syndrome [*Medicine*] ... AAS
Aortic Artery [*Gradient*] [*Cardiology*] (DAVI) ... A-A
Aortic Blood Flow [*Medicine*] (DMAA) ... ABF
Aortic Closure [*Cardiology*] ... AC
Aortic Cross Clamping [*Cardiology*] ... ACC
Aortic First Heart Sound [*Cardiology*] ... A_1
Aortic Flow [*Cardiology*] ... AF
Aortic Incompetence [*or Insufficiency*] [*Medicine*] ... AI
Aortic Insufficiency [*Cardiology*] (DAVI) ... AInsuf
Aortic Plexus [*Anatomy*] ... AP
Aortic Posterior Wall [*Cardiology*] (DMAA) ... AOPW
Aortic Posterior Wall [*Cardiology*] (DMAA) ... AoPW
Aortic Pressure [*Medicine*] ... AoP
Aortic Pressure [*Medicine*] ... AP
Aortic Regurgitation [*Medicine*] (MEDA) ... AOR REGURG
Aortic Regurgitation [*Medicine*] (CPH) ... aort regurg
Aortic Regurgitation [*Medicine*] ... AR
Aortic Root [*Cardiology*] ... AR
Aortic Root Replacement [*Medicine*] (DMAA) ... ARR
Aortic Sac [*Cardiology*] (DAVI) ... AS
Aortic Second Heart Sound [*Cardiology*] ... A_2
Aortic Stenosis [*Medicine*] (BABM) ... A sten
Aortic Stenosis [*Cardiology*] (DAVI) ... A Sten
Aortic Stenosis [*Medicine*] (MEDA) ... AORT STEN
Aortic Stenosis [*Medicine*] ... AS
Aortic Stenosis and Aortic Insufficiency Murmurs [*Cardiology*] (MAE) ... ASAI
Aortic Valve [*Cardiology*] ... AV
Aortic Valve Closure [*Medicine*] ... AOC
Aortic Valve Cusp Separation [*On echocardiogram*] [*Cardiology*] (DAVI) ... AVSC
Aortic Valve Disease [*Cardiology*] ... AVD
Aortic Valve Echophonocardiogram [*Cardiology*] ... AVE
Aortic Valve Opening [*Cardiology*] ... AO
Aortic Valve Replacement [*Cardiology*] ... AVR
Aortic Valve Stenosis [*Cardiology*] (DMAA) ... AVS
Aortic Valve Stroke Volume [*Cardiology*] ... AVSV
Aorticopulmonary Septal Defect [*Medicine*] (DMAA) ... APSD
Aortobifemoral [*Medicine*] (DMAA) ... ABF
Aortocoronary Bypass [*Cardiology*] ... ACB
Aortocoronary Bypass Graft Surgery [*Cardiology*] (CPH) ... ACBGS
Aortocoronary Bypass Surgery [*Cardiology*] (CPH) ... ACBS
Aortocoronary Graft [*Cardiology*] (DMAA) ... ACG
Aortocoronary Saphenous Vein [*Cardiology*] (MAE) ... ACSV
Aortocoronary Saphenous Vein Bypass [*Cardiology*] (AAMN) ... ACB
Aortocoronary Venous Bypass [*Cardiology*] (DMAA) ... ACVB
Aorto-Femoral Bypass [*Medicine*] ... AFB
Aortofemoral Bypass Graft [*Cardiology*] (DMAA) ... AFBG
Aorto-Iliac Occlusive Disease [*Medicine*] ... AIOD
Aortopulmonary [*Cardiology*] ... AP
Aos-Oideachas Naisiunta Tri Aontu Saorlach [*National Association of Adult Education*] (EAIO) ... AONTAS
Aosta [*Italy ICAO location identifier*] (ICLI) ... LIMW
Aoulef [*Algeria*] [*ICAO location identifier*] (ICLI) ... DAAF
Aoulef [*Algeria*] [*Airport symbol*] (AD) ... WAE
AOUON [*All of Us or None*] **Archive** [*An association*] (EA) ... AA
APA Internacional [*Dominican Republic*] [*ICAO designator*] (FAAC) ... APY
APA Optics [*NASDAQ symbol*] (TTSB) ... APAT
APA Optics, Inc. [*Associated Press*] (SAG) ... APA
APA Optics, Inc. [*Blaine, MN*] [*NASDAQ symbol*] (NQ) ... APAT
APAC TeleServices [*NASDAQ symbol*] (TTSB) ... APAC
APAC TeleServices, Inc. [*NASDAQ symbol*] (SAG) ... APAC
APAC TeleServices, Inc. [*Associated Press*] (SAG) ... APACT
Apache [*MARC language code Library of Congress*] (LCCP) ... apa
APACHE [*Active Thermal Protection for Avionics Crew and Heat-Sensitve Equipment*] **Action Team** [*Army*] ... AAT
Apache Attack Helicopter [*Military*] (RDA) ... AAH
Apache, Black Hawk, and Chinook Self-Deployments [*Military*] ... ABCD
Apache Corp. [*NYSE symbol*] (SPSG) ... APA
Apache Corp. [*Associated Press*] (SAG) ... Apache
Apache Helicopter [*Anti-armor attack helicopter*] ... AH
Apache Junction, AZ [*FM radio station call letters*] ... KVVA-FM
Apache Medical Systems, Inc. [*NASDAQ symbol*] (SAG) ... AMSI
Apache Medical Systems, Inc. [*Associated Press*] (SAG) ... ApcheM
[*The*] **Apache Railway Co.** [*AAR code*] ... APA
APACHE [*Active Thermal Protection for Avionics Crew and Heat-Sensitive Equipment*] **Readiness Improvement Program** [*Army*] ... ARIP
Apachito [*Race of maize*] ... APA
Apalachee Community Mental Health Services, Inc., Tallahassee, FL [*Library symbol Library of Congress*] (LCLS) ... FTaA
Apalachicola, FL [*Location identifier FAA*] (FAAL) ... AAF
Apalachicola, FL [*Location identifier FAA*] (FAAL) ... AQQ
Apalachicola, FL [*FM radio station call letters*] ... WOYS
Apalachicola, FL [*FM radio station call letters*] (RBYB) ... WXGJ-FM
Apalachicola Northern Railroad Co. [*AAR code*] ... AN
Aparri, Cagayan [*Philippines*] [*ICAO location identifier*] (ICLI) ... RPUA
Apartamento ... APT
Apartment [*Classified advertising*] (ADA) ... APART
Apartment ... APT
Apartment ... APT
Apartment (VRA) ... apt
Apartment and Office Building Association [*of Metro Washington, DC*] (SRA) ... AOBA
Apartment Association of Indiana (SRA) ... AAI

Apartment Association of New Mexico (SRA) .... AANM
Apartment House Addressing Program [*US Postal Service*] .... AHAP
Apartment Investment & Management Co. [*NYSE symbol*] (SAG) .... AIV
Apartment Investment & Management Co. [*Associated Press*] (SAG) .... AptInv
Apartment Investment & Mgmt'A' [*NYSE symbol*] (TTSB) .... AIV
Apartment Owners and Managers Association of America (EA) .... AOMA
Apartments .... APTS
Apataki [*French Polynesia*] [*Airport symbol*] (OAG) .... APK
Apataki [*French Polynesia*] [*ICAO location identifier*] (ICLI) .... NTGD
Apatite [*CIPW classification*] [*Geology*] .... ap
Apatite Subgroup [*Apatite, fluorite, calcite, pyrite, iron*] [*CIPW classification Geology*] .... A
Apatity [*Former USSR Seismograph station code, US Geological Survey*] (SEIS) .... APA
APCE [*Automated Product Control Environment*] **Interface Set** (SSD) .... AIS
APCHE [*Automatic Program Checkout Equipment*] **Relay Box** .... ARB
Apco Argentina [*NASDAQ symbol*] (SAG) .... APAG
Apco Argentina [*NASDAQ symbol*] (TTSB) .... APAGF
Apco Argentina, Inc. [*Associated Press*] (SAG) .... Apco
APE [*Automatic Processing Equipment*] **Control Facility** .... ACF
APEA [*Australian Petroleum Exploration Association*] **Journal** [*A publication*] .... APEA Jl
Apeiranthos Of Naxos [*Greece*] [*Seismograph station code, US Geological Survey*] (SEIS) .... APE
Apel. Notation of Polyphonic Music [*A publication*] .... ApNPM
Apentina [*Surinam*] [*ICAO location identifier*] (ICLI) ...... SMPT
Aperient [*Pharmacy*] (ROG) .... APE
Aperient [*Pharmacy*] (ROG) .... APER
Aperiodic Stochastic Resonance [*Model of neurophysiological reactions*] .... ASR
Aperture .... AP
Aperture .... APER
Aperture (MSA) .... APERT
Aperture Card (MSA) .... APTC
Aperture Card Raster Image Scanner [*Versatec Co.*] (NITA) .... ACRIS
Aperture Current [*Medicine*] (DMAA) .... APC
Aperture Current Setting [*In Coulter counter*] [*Microbiology*] .... ACS
Aperture Direct Read-Out .... ADR
Aperture Distribution and Maintenance [*System*] .... ADAM
Aperture File Protocol [*Computer science*] .... AFP
Aperture Lip .... APL
Aperture Plate Character Generator .... APCG
Aperture Relay Experiment Definition (MCD) .... ARED
Aperture Value [*Photography*] .... AV
Apertus Technologies [*NASDAQ symbol*] (TTSB) .... APTS
Apertus Technologies, Inc. [*Associated Press*] (SAG) ..... Apertus
Apertus Technologies, Inc. [*NASDAQ symbol*] (SPSG) ...... APTS
Apex [*Medicine*] (DMAA) .... Ap
Apex Air Cargo [*ICAO designator*] (FAAC) .... APX
Apex Beat [*Medicine*] .... AB
Apex Cardiogram [*Medicine*] .... ACG
Apex Cardiogram [*Medicine*] .... APCG
Apex Clubs of Australia .... ACA
Apex Energy Corp. [*Vancouver Stock Exchange symbol*] ...... APG
Apex Global Information Services .... AGIS
Apex Global Information Services [*Computer science*] ...... AGIS
Apex Global Internet Service [*Computer science*] .... AGIS
Apex Global Internet Services .... AGIS
Apex Muni Fund [*NYSE symbol*] (TTSB) .... APX
Apex Municipal Fund, Inc. [*Associated Press*] (SAG) ...... Apex
Apex Municipal Fund, Inc. [*NYSE symbol*] (SPSG) .... APX
Aphanizomenon Flos-Aquae [*Blue green algae*] .... AFA
Aphasia [*Medicine*] (DMAA) .... Aph
Aphasia, Agnosia, Apraxia, Agraphia, Alexia [*Medicine*] (MEDA) .... AAAAA
Aphasia Language Performance Scale [*Speech and language therapy*] (DAVI) .... ALPS
Aphetic (BARN) .... aph
Aphorism .... APH
Aphoxide [*Also, TEPA*] [*Mutagen*] .... APO
Aphrodisiac [*Medicine*] (ROG) .... APHRO
Aphton Corp. [*NASDAQ symbol*] (SPSG) .... APHT
Aphton Corp. [*Associated Press*] (SAG) .... Aphton
API [*American Petroleum Institute*] **Literature** [*New York, NY*] [*Bibliographic database*] .... APILIT
Apia [*Samoa Islands*] [*Seismograph station code, US Geological Survey*] (SEIS) .... API
Apia [*Samoa Islands*] [*Airport symbol*] (OAG) .... APW
Apia [*Western Samoa*] [*ICAO location identifier*] (ICLI) .... NSAP
Apiary Inspectors of America (EA) .... AIA
Apical (DAVI) .... A
Apical Cell [*Botany*] .... AC
Apical Ectodermal Ridge [*Embryology, genetics*] .... AER
Apical Impulse [*Medicine*] (AAMN) .... AI
Apical Meristem [*Botany*] .... AP
Apical Pulse [*Medicine*] .... AP
Apical/Radial [*Pulse*] [*Medicine*] .... A/R
Apical Rate [*Medicine*] .... AR
Apiculture .... APIC
APL [*Applied Physics Laboratory*] **Management Planning and Engineering Resource Evaluation** [*Navy*] .... AMPERE
Aplasia Cutis Congenita [*Medicine*] (MEDA) .... ACC
Aplastic Anemia [*Medicine*] (DMAA) .... AA
Aplastic Anemia Foundation of America (EA) .... AAFA
Aplington Legion Memorial Library, Aplington, IA [*Library symbol Library of Congress*] (LCLS) .... IaAp
Apnea, Bradycardia, Cyanosis [*Medicine*] (MAE) .... ABC

Apnea of Infancy [*Also, AOP (Apnea of Prematurity)*] (PAZ) .... AOI
Apnea of Prematurity [*Also, AOI (Apnea of Infancy)*] (PAZ) .... AOP
Apnea-Bradycardia [*Spells*] [*Medicine*] (DAVI) .... AB
Apnea-Plus-Hypopnea Index [*Medicine*] (DMAA) .... AHI
Apneustic Center [*Brain anatomy*] .... APC
Apocalypse (BJA) .... Ap
Apocalypse (VRA) .... apcys
Apocalypse .... Apoc
Apocalypse of Abraham (BJA) .... ApocAbr
Apocalypse of Baruch [*Apocalyptic book*] .... APOC BAR
Apocalypse of Elijah (BJA) .... ApocElij
Apocalypse of Moses (BJA) .... ApocMos
Apocalypse of Peter (BJA) .... ApocPet
Apocalyptic (BJA) .... Apoc
Apochromatic [*Photography*] .... APO
Apocolocyntosis [*of Seneca the Younger*] [*Classical studies*] (OCD) .... Apocol
Apocrypha (BJA) .... Apcr
Apocrypha (BJA) .... Apoc
Apocrypha (ROG) .... APOCH
Apocrypha (VRA) .... apocph
Apocrypha .... APOCR
[*The*] **Apocrypha and Pseudepigrapha of the Old Testament** [*A publication*] (BJA) .... APOT
[*The*] **Apocryphal Literature: A Brief Introduction** [*1945*] [*A publication*] (BJA) .... TAL
[*The*] **Apocryphal New Testament** [*A publication*] (BJA) .... ANT
Apoenzyme [*Clinical chemistry*] (MAE) .... AE
Apoenzyme Reactivation Immunoassay System [*Clinical chemistry*] .... ARIS
Apogee .... APG
Apogee .... APO
Apogee .... APOG
Apogee Altitude (NASA) .... HA
Apogee and Maneuvering Stage [*Space flight*] .... AMS
Apogee Boost Motor [*Aerospace*] (MCD) .... ABM
Apogee Enterprises [*NASDAQ symbol*] (TTSB) .... APOG
Apogee Enterprises, Inc. [*NASDAQ symbol*] (NQ) .... APOG
Apogee Enterprises, Inc. [*Associated Press*] (SAG) ...... ApogEn
Apogee, Inc. [*NASDAQ symbol*] (SAG) .... APGG
Apogee, Inc. [*Associated Press*] (SAG) .... Apogee
Apogee Injection Module [*NASA*] .... AIM
Apogee Intercept Defense (MCD) .... AID
Apogee Kick [*NASA*] (KSC) .... AK
Apogee Kick Motor [*NASA*] (KSC) .... AKM
Apogee Motor Assembly with Paired Satellites [*NASA*] .... AMAPS
Apogee Motor Fire [*Aerospace*] .... AMF
Apogee Motor Igniter [*NASA*] .... AMI
Apogee Motor Timer [*NASA*] .... AMT
Apogee Structured Query Language [*Computer science*] .... ASQL
Apogee-Perigee Injection System (PDAA) .... APIS
Apolipoprotein [*Biochemistry*] .... Apo
Apolipoprotein A [*Biochemistry*] .... ApoA
Apolipoprotein C [*Biochemistry*] .... ApoC
Apolipoprotein E [*Biochemistry*] .... ApoE
Apolipoprotein-B [*Biochemistry*] (ECON) .... APOB
Apollo [*A publication*] (BRI) .... Apo
Apollo Abort System [*NASA*] (IAA) .... AAS
Apollo Access Arm [*NASA*] (KSC) .... AAA
Apollo Airlines [*Greece*] [*FAA designator*] (FAAC) ...... AOA
Apollo Airlines [*ICAO designator*] (AD) .... ID
Apollo Applications [*NASA*] .... AA
Apollo Applications Program [*NASA*] .... AAP
Apollo Applications Program Office [*NASA*] (MCD) .... AAPO
Apollo Applications Test Requirements [*NASA*] (MCD) ..... AATR
Apollo Bioenvironmental Information System (PDAA) .... ABIS
Apollo Command and Service Module [*NASA*] (IAA) .... ACSM
Apollo Command [*or Communications*] **System** [*NASA*] .... ACS
Apollo Computer Address Matrix [*NASA*] .... ACAM
Apollo Contractor Information Center [*NASA*] (KSC) ...... ACIC
Apollo Crew Systems Branch [*NASA*] (KSC) .... ACSB
Apollo Data Bank [*NASA*] (MCD) .... ADB
Apollo Data [*or Document*] **Descriptions Standards** [*NASA*] (MCD) .... ADDS
Apollo Data Manager [*NASA*] (KSC) .... ADM
Apollo Development [*NASA*] (KSC) .... AD
Apollo Display Console [*NASA*] .... ADC
Apollo Docking Test Device [*NASA*] .... ADTD
Apollo Document Distribution Requirements Index [*NASA*] (KSC) .... ADDRI
Apollo Document Index [*NASA*] (KSC) .... ADI
Apollo Document Preparation Standards [*Handbook*] [*NASA*] (KSC) .... ADPS
Apollo Documentation Administration Instruction [*NASA*] (KSC) .... ADAI
Apollo Documentation List [*NASA*] (MCD) .... ADL
Apollo Dynamic Programs [*NASA*] (KSC) .... ADP
Apollo Earth-Orbiting Station [*NASA*] .... AES
Apollo Engineering [*NASA*] (SAA) .... AE
Apollo Engineering and Technology Index [*NASA*] (KSC) .... AETI
Apollo Engineering Bulletin [*NASA*] (SAA) .... AEB
Apollo Engineering Documentation Board [*NASA*] (MCD) .... AEDB
Apollo Environmental Control System [*NASA*] (IAA) .... AECS
Apollo Experiment Pallet [*NASA*] .... AEP
Apollo Experiment Support [*NASA*] .... AES
Apollo Extension Program [*NASA*] .... AEP
Apollo Extension System [*NASA*] .... AES
Apollo Extension System / Apollo Logistics Support System / Lunar Exploration System for Apollo [*NASA*] (SAA) .... AES/ALSS/LESA
Apollo Flight Control [*NASA*] (MCD) .... AFC
Apollo Follow-On Missions [*NASA*] (SAA) .... AFM

Apollo/GOSS [*Ground Operations Support System*] **Navigation Qualifications** [*NASA*] .... AGNQ
Apollo Group, Inc. [*NASDAQ symbol*] (SAG) .... APOL
Apollo Group, Inc. [*Associated Press*] (SAG) .... ApolloG
Apollo Group 'A' [*NASDAQ symbol*] (TTSB) .... APOL
Apollo Guidance and Navigation Industrial Support [*NASA*] .... AGNIS
Apollo Guidance and Navigation Information [*NASA*] .... AGANI
Apollo Guidance Computer [*NASA*] .... AGC
Apollo Guidance Equipment [*NASA*] (KSC) .... AGE
Apollo Guidance Ground Display [*NASA*] (MCD) .... AGGD
Apollo Implementing Instructions [*NASA*] (KSC) .... AII
Apollo Initiator Resistance Measuring Equipment [*NASA*] (NASA) .... AIRME
Apollo Instrumentation Ships [*NASA*] (MCD) .... AIS
Apollo Intermediate Chart [*NASA*] (MCD) .... AIC
Apollo Launch Data System [*NASA*] .... ALDS
Apollo Launch Operation Panel [*NASA*] (KSC) .... ALOP
Apollo Launch Operations Committee [*NASA*] (KSC) .... ALOC
Apollo Launch Trajectory Data System [*NASA*] (KSC) .... ALTDS
Apollo Light-Flash Moving-Emulsion Detector [*NASA*] .... ALFMED
Apollo Logistic Support System [*NASA*] .... ALSS
Apollo Logistic Support System / Lunar Explorations System for Apollo [*NASA*] (SAA) .... ALSS/LESA
Apollo Lunar Excursion Module Sensors [*NASA*] .... ALEMS
Apollo Lunar Exploration Mission [*NASA*] .... ALEM
Apollo Lunar Hand Tool [*NASA*] .... ALHT
Apollo Lunar Hand Tool Carrier [*NASA*] .... ALHTC
Apollo Lunar Landing System [*NASA*] (SAA) .... ALLS
Apollo Lunar Logistic Support [*NASA*] .... ALLS
Apollo Lunar Module [*NASA*] .... ALM
Apollo Lunar Orbit [*NASA*] .... ALO
Apollo Lunar Orbital Science [*NASA*] (KSC) .... ALOS
Apollo Lunar Polar Orbiter [*NASA*] .... ALPO
Apollo Lunar Radioisotopic Heater [*NASA*] (MCD) .... ALRH
Apollo Lunar Sample Return Container [*NASA*] .... ALSRC
Apollo Lunar Sounder Experiment [*NASA*] .... ALSE
Apollo Lunar Surface Closeup Camera [*Apollo 11*] [*NASA*] .... ALSCC
Apollo Lunar Surface Drill [*NASA*] .... ALSD
Apollo Lunar Surface Experiments Package [*NASA*] .... ALSEP
Apollo Master Measurements Program [*NASA*] (KSC) .... AMMP
Apollo Mission Planning Task Force [*NASA*] (KSC) .... AMPTF
Apollo Mission Programs [*NASA*] (KSC) .... AMP
Apollo Mission Simulator [*NASA*] .... AMS
Apollo Navigation Working Group [*NASA*] (MCD) .... ANWG
Apollo Network [*NASA*] (KSC) .... ANW
Apollo Network Simulations [*NASA*] (KSC) .... ANS
Apollo Operations Director [*NASA*] (SAA) .... AOD
Apollo Operations Handbook [*NASA*] .... AOH
Apollo Orbital Research Laboratory [*NASA*] .... AORL
Apollo Orbiting Laboratory Module [*NASA*] .... AOLM
Apollo Owners Register (EA) .... AOR
Apollo, PA [*AM radio station call letters*] .... WAVL
Apollo Pad Test [*NASA*] (KSC) .... APT
Apollo Part Task Trainer [*NASA*] (KSC) .... APTT
Apollo Parts Information Center [*NASA*] (MCD) .... APIC
Apollo Payload Exploration [*NASA*] .... APPLE
Apollo Personnel Identification [*or Investigation*] **Program** [*NASA*] (KSC) .... APIP
Apollo Preflight Operations Procedures [*NASA*] (KSC) .... APOP
Apollo Problem Bulletin [*NASA*] .... APB
Apollo Program [*NASA*] .... AP
Apollo Program Control Center [*NASA*] (KSC) .... APCC
Apollo Program Control Room [*NASA*] (KSC) .... APCR
Apollo Program Definition Phase [*NASA*] (KSC) .... APDP
Apollo Program Directive [*NASA*] (KSC) .... APD
Apollo Program Logic Network [*NASA*] (KSC) .... APLN
Apollo Program Office [*NASA*] (KSC) .... APO
Apollo Program Requirements [*NASA*] (KSC) .... APR
Apollo Program Specifications [*NASA*] (KSC) .... APS
Apollo Propellant Gauging System [*NASA*] (KSC) .... APGS
Apollo Propulsion Analysis Program [*NASA*] .... APAP
Apollo Qualification [*NASA*] (KSC) .... AQ
Apollo Range Instrumentation Aircraft [*NASA*] .... ARIA
Apollo Reentry Communications Blackout Working Group [*NASA*] .... ACBWG
Apollo Reentry Ship [*NASA*] .... ARS
Apollo Reliability Engineering [*NASA*] (KSC) .... ARE
Apollo Reliability Engineering Electronics [*NASA*] .... AREE
Apollo Requirements Manual [*NASA*] (KSC) .... ARM
Apollo Service Module [*NASA*] (MCD) .... ASM
Apollo Ship's Operational Readiness Force [*NASA*] .... ASORF
Apollo Signal Definition Document [*NASA*] (KSC) .... ASDD
Apollo Simple Penetrometer [*NASA*] .... ASP
Apollo Simulated Remote Site [*NASA*] (KSC) .... ASRS
Apollo Simulation Checkout and Training System [*NASA*] .... ASCATS
Apollo Site Selection Board [*NASA*] (KSC) .... ASSB
Apollo Spacecraft Development Test Plan [*NASA*] (KSC) .... ASDTP
Apollo Spacecraft Hardware Utilization Request [*NASA*] .... ASHUR
Apollo Spacecraft Parts and Materials Information Services [*NASA*] (KSC) .... ASPMIS
Apollo Spacecraft Project [*NASA*] (IAA) .... ASP
Apollo Spacecraft Project Office [*NASA*] .... ASPO
Apollo Special Task Team [*NASA*] .... ASTT
Apollo Standard Detonator [*NASA*] .... ASD
Apollo Standard Initiator [*NASA*] .... ASI
Apollo Supplemental Procedural Information [*NASA*] (KSC) .... ASPI
Apollo Support Department [*NASA*] (KSC) .... ASD
Apollo Systems Manual [*A publication*] (MCD) .... ASM

Apollo Systems Test [*NASA*] (IAA) .... AST
Apollo Technical Documentation Distribution List [*NASA*] (KSC) .... ATDDL
Apollo Telemetry Aircraft Project [*NASA*] .... ATAP
Apollo Telescope Mount [*NASA*] .... ATM
Apollo Telescope Mount Console [*NASA*] .... ATMC(0)
Apollo Telescope Mount - Deployed [*NASA*] (MCD) .... ATM-D
Apollo Telescope Mount Deployment Assembly [*NASA*] .... ATMDA
Apollo Telescope Mount Digital Computer [*NASA*] .... ATMDC
Apollo Telescope Mount - Stowed [*NASA*] (MCD) .... ATM-S
Apollo Telescope Orientation Mount Program [*NASA*] (MCD) .... ATOM
Apollo Test Box [*NASA*] (SAA) .... ATB
Apollo Test Integration Working Groups [*NASA*] (KSC) .... ATIWG
Apollo Test Operations [*NASA*] (KSC) .... ATO
Apollo Test Requirements [*NASA*] (KSC) .... ATR
Apollo Test Unsatisfactory Report [*NASA*] (IAA) .... ATUR
Apollo Time Conditioner [*NASA*] .... ATC
Apollo Trajectory Decision Logic Prototype [*NASA*] .... ATDLP
Apollo Unified S-Band Circuit Margin [*Program*] [*NASA*] .... AUSBCM
Apollo Validation Test [*NASA*] (KSC) .... AVT
Apollo Vehicle Systems Section [*NASA*] (KSC) .... AVSS
Apollo Wind-Tunnel Testing Program [*NASA*] .... AWTTP
Apollo XI Collector Society [*Defunct*] (EA) .... AXICS
Apollodorus [*Second century BC*] [*Classical studies*] (OCD) .... Apollod
Apollonius Rhodius [*Third century BC*] [*Classical studies*] (OCD) .... Ap Rhod
Apollo-Saturn [*NASA*] (MCD) .... AS
Apollo-Soyuz Docking Module [*NASA*] .... ASDM
Apollo-Soyuz Test Project [*NASA/USSR*] .... ASTP
Apolo [*Bolivia*] [*ICAO location identifier*] (ICLI) .... SLAP
Apologeticus [*of Tertullian*] [*Classical studies*] (OCD) .... Apol
Apologia [*of Plato*] [*Classical studies*] (OCD) .... Ap
Apologia [*of Apuleius*] [*Classical studies*] (OCD) .... Apol
Apologia Socratis [*of Xenophon*] [*Classical studies*] (OCD) .... Ap
Apomict [*Biology*] (BARN) .... apm
Apomorphine [*Neurochemistry, pharmacology*] .... APO
Apophthegmata [*of Julian*] [*Classical studies*] (OCD) .... Apophth
Apopka, FL [*AM radio station call letters*] .... WTLN
Apopka, FL [*FM radio station call letters*] .... WTLN-FM
Apoprotein [*Biochemistry*] .... Apo
Apoptosis-Inducing Factor [*Biochemistry*] .... AIF
Apoptosis-Inducing Factor [*Cytology*] .... AIF
Apostilb [*Unit of luminance*] .... Asb
Apostle [*Church calendars*] .... A
Apostle (VRA) .... ap
Apostle .... AP
Apostle and Evangelist [*Church calendars*] .... AE
Apostle and Martyr [*Church calendars*] (ROG) .... A & M
Apostle, Evangelist, and Martyr [*Church calendars*] (ROG) .... AE & M
Apostles .... APP
Apostles of the Sacred Heart of Jesus [*Roman Catholic women's religious order*] .... ASCJ
Apostleship of Prayer (EA) .... AP
Apostleship of the Sea [*See also AM*] [*Vatican City, Vatican City State*] (EAIO) .... AOS
Apostleship of the Sea in the United States (EA) .... AOSUS
Apostleship of the Sea in the United States (EA) .... ASUS
Apostolate .... APSTLT
Apostolate for Family Consecration (EA) .... AFC
Apostolate of Christ the Worker .... ACW
Apostolate to Hungarians [*Diocesan abbreviation*] [*District of Columbia*] (TOCD) .... ATH
Apostolatus Maris [*Apostleship of the Sea - AOS*] (EA) .... AM
Apostolic .... A
Apostolic (BJA) .... Ap
Apostolic (BJA) .... apost
Apostolic .... APSTLC
Apostolic Anti-Communist Alliance [*Spain*] .... AAA
Apostolic Church .... AC
Apostolica Sedes [*Apostolic See*] [*Latin*] [*Reference to the papacy*] (BARN) .... Ap Sed
Apostolicam Actuositatem [*Decree on the Apostolate of the Laity*] [*Vatican II document*] .... AA
Apostrophe .... APOS
Apoteri [*Guyana*] [*ICAO location identifier*] (ICLI) .... SYAP
Apothecaries' Ounce (WDAA) .... OZ AP
Apothecaries Ounce (BARN) .... oz apoth
Apothecaries' Pound (BARN) .... lb ap
Apothecaries' Weight (BARN) .... ap wt
Apothecary (WGA) .... AP
Apothecary .... APOTH
Apovincaminic Acid [*Biochemistry*] .... AVA
Apoyeque [*Nicaragua*] [*Seismograph station code, US Geological Survey*] (SEIS) .... APY
Appal Pwr, 7.40% Pfd [*NYSE symbol*] (TTSB) .... AEWPrC
Appalachia Educational Laboratory [*Department of Education*] [*Charleston, WV*] .... AEL
Appalachia Science in the Public Interest [*An association*] .... ASPI
Appalachian (FAAC) .... APLCN
Appalachian Area [*MARC geographic area code Library of Congress*] (LCCP) .... n-usa-
Appalachian Bible Institute, Bradley, WV [*Library symbol Library of Congress*] (LCLS) .... WvBrA
Appalachian Community Service Network [*Cable-television system*] .... ACSN
Appalachian Consortium (EA) .... AC
Appalachian Educational Laboratory, Inc., Charleston, WV [*Library symbol Library of Congress*] (LCLS) .... WvCAE

Appalachian Environmental Laboratory [*University of Maryland Center for Environmental and Estuarine Studies*] [*Research center*] (RCD) .... AEL
Appalachian Finance Association [*Later, Eastern Finance Association*] (EA) .... APFA
Appalachian Flying Service, Inc. [*ICAO designator*] (FAAC) .... APL
Appalachian Forum [*An association*] (EA) .... AF
Appalachian Hall Medical Library, Asheville, NC [*Library symbol*] [*Library of Congress*] (LCLS) .... NcAAH
Appalachian Hardwood Manufacturers, Inc. (EA) .... AHMI
Appalachian Laboratory for Occupational Respiratory Diseases .... ALFORD
Appalachian Laboratory for Occupational Safety and Health [*Department of Health and Human Services*] (GFGA) .... ALOSH
Appalachian Land Stabilization and Conservation Program .... ALSCP
Appalachian Mountain Club (EA) .... AMC
Appalachian Mountains .... AM
Appalachian Power Co. [*NYSE symbol*] (SPSG) .... AEW
Appalachian Power Co. .... APC
Appalachian Power Co. [*NYSE symbol*] (SAG) .... APJ
Appalachian Power Co. [*Associated Press*] (SAG) .... ApPw
Appalachian Regional Commission [*Washington, DC*] .... ARC
Appalachian Regional Development Act of 1965 .... ARDA
Appalachian Regional Library, North Wilkesboro, NC [*Library symbol Library of Congress*] (LCLS) .... NcNwA
Appalachian Soil and Water Conservation Research Laboratory [*Beckley, WV*] [*Department of Agriculture*] (GRD) .... ASWCRL
Appalachian State Teachers College [*Later, ASU*] [*North Carolina*] .... ASTC
Appalachian State University (GAGS) .... Appal St U
Appalachian State University [*Boone, NC*] .... ASU
Appalachian State University, Boone, NC [*Library symbol Library of Congress*] (LCLS) .... NcBoA
Appalachian State University, Boone, NC [*OCLC symbol*] (OCLC) .... NJB
Appalachian Trail .... AT
Appalachian Trail Conference (EA) .... ATC
Appalachian Ultradeep Core Hole [*Project of seismic profiling*] .... ADCOH
Appalachian Volunteers, Inc. (EA) .... AVI
Appaloosa Color Breeders Association (EA) .... ACBA
Appaloosa Horse Club (EA) .... AHC
Appaloosa Horse Club (EA) .... ApHC
Appaloosa Horse Club of Canada (AC) .... ApHCC
Appaloosa Sport Horse Association (EA) .... ApSHA
Apparatus (MUGU) .... APAR
Apparatus (KSC) .... APP
Apparatus (AFM) .... APPAR
Apparatus .... APPRTS
Apparatus .... APTUS
Apparatus Carrier Telephone [*British military*] (DMA) .... ACT
Apparatus for Pore Examination [*Geophysics*] .... APEX
Apparatus Mounted in Plastic .... AMPLAS
Apparatus Repair - Strategy Evaiuation Guidelines [*Telecommunications*] (TEL) .... AREG
Apparatus Slide-In Unit [*Computer science*] (NITA) .... ASU
Apparel .... APPRL
Apparel Agents' Association of Queensland [*Australia*] .... AAAQ
Apparel Agents' Association of Victoria [*Australia*] .... AAAV
Apparel Agents' Association of Western Australia .... AAAWA
Apparel and Fashion Industry's Association [*British*] (BI) .... AFIA
Apparel Business Control [*System*] [*Computer science*] .... ABC
Apparel Guild (EA) .... AG
Apparel Importers' Association of Australia .... AIAA
Apparel Industries Inter-Association Committee [*Defunct*] (EA) .... AIIC
Apparel Industry Committee on Imports (EA) .... AICI
Apparel Manufacturers Association (EA) .... AMA
Apparel Manufacturing Executives Association (EA) .... AMEA
Apparel Manufacturing Technology Center [*Research center*] (RCD) .... AMTC
Apparel Performance Level Standards [*Pronounced "apples"*] .... APLS
Apparel Research Foundation [*Defunct*] .... ARF
Apparel-Computer Integrated Manufacturing Center [*Research center*] (RCD) .... A-CIM
Apparent (ADA) .... AP
Apparent .... APPAR
Apparent (MSA) .... APRNT
Apparent Activation Energy .... AAE
Apparent Body Orientation (PDAA) .... ABO
Apparent Bulk Density .... ABD
Apparent Candle Power .... ACP
Apparent Depth of Compensation [*Geology*] .... ADC
Apparent Digestible Energy [*Nutrition*] .... ADE
Apparent Elastic Thickness [*Geoscience*] .... AET
Apparent Free Testosterone Concentration [*Clinical chemistry*] .... AFTC
Apparent Half-Life (DMAA) .... AHL
Apparent Life-Threatening Episode [*Medicine*] .... ALTE
Apparent Metabolisable Energy .... AME
Apparent Mineralocorticoid Excess [*Medicine*] .... AME
Apparent Molar Quantity .... AMQ
Apparent Net Transfer Rate (MAE) .... ANTR
Apparent Norepinephrine Secretion Rate [*Medicine*] (DMAA) .... ANESR
Apparent Oxygen Utilization .... AOU
Apparent Polar Wander [*Paleomagnetism*] .... APW
Apparent Polar Wander Path [*Paleomagnetism*] .... APWP
Apparent Power [*Symbol*] (DEN) .... S
Apparent Sidereal Time (PDAA) .... AST
Apparent Solar Time (PDAA) .... AST
Apparent Time (ADA) .... AT
Apparent Time at Ship (DS) .... ATS
Apparent Total Nitroso Compound [*Organic chemistry*] .... ATNC

Apparent Volume of Distribution [*Clinical chemistry*] .... AVD
Apparent Watt [*Electricity*] (IAA) .... AW
Apparently .... APP
Appeal (ADA) .... APP
Appeal .... APPL
Appeal and Error [*Legal term*] (DLA) .... A & E
Appeal and Marathon Republic, Albert City, IA [*Library symbol Library of Congress*] (LCLS) .... IaAlcAM
Appeal Cases [*Canada*] [*A publication*] (DLA) .... AC
Appeal Cases [*A publication*] (DLA) .... App
Appeal Cases, District of Columbia [*A publication*] (DLA) .... ADC
Appeal Cases, District of Columbia [*1-74*] [*A publication*] (DLA) .... App Cas
Appeal Cases, District of Columbia [*1-74*] [*A publication*] (DLA) .... App Cas (DC)
Appeal Cases, District of Columbia [*A publication*] (DLA) .... App DC
Appeal Cases, English Law Reports [*1875-90*] [*A publication*] (DLA) .... App Cas
Appeal Cases, English Law Reports, Second Series [*A publication*] (DLA) .... App Cas 2d
Appeal Cases in the United States [*A publication*] (DLA) .... App Cas
Appeal Cases of the Different States [*A publication*] (DLA) .... App Cas
Appeal Court [*Legal*] [*British*] (ROG) .... AC
Appeal Court Reports [*Ceylon*] [*A publication*] (DLA) .... ACR
Appeal Court Reports, New Zealand [*A publication*] (DLA) .... App Ct Rep
Appeal Denied (DLA) .... app den
Appeal Dismissed (DLA) .... app dism
Appeal [*or Appeals*] Examiner (DLA) .... App Exam
Appeal of Conscience Foundation (EA) .... ACF
Appeal, Plain Facts, Personalities, Local Angle, Action, Uniqueness [*or Universality*], Significance, Energy .... APPLAUSE
Appeal Referee (DLA) .... App Ref
Appeal Reports, New Zealand [*A publication*] (DLA) .... App NZ
Appeal Reports, New Zealand [*A publication*] (DLA) .... App RNZ
Appeal Reports, New Zealand, Second Series [*A publication*] (DLA) ..... App NZ 2d
Appeal Reports, Upper Canada [*1846-66*] [*A publication*] (DLA) .... AR
Appeal Tribunal (DLA) .... App Trib
Appeal Tribunal (DLA) .... AT
Appeals (AAGC) .... App
Appeals Council [*Social Security Administration*] (OICC) .... AC
Appeals Examining Office [*CSC*] .... AEO
Appeals from Fisheries Commission [*1861-93*] [*Ireland*] [*A publication*] (DLA) .... App Fish Com
Appeals Notes [*A publication*] (DLA) .... AN
Appeals Relating to Tax on Servants [*1781*] [*England*] [*A publication*] (DLA) .... App Tax Serv
Appeals Review Board [*Formerly, BAR*] [*Civil Service Commission*] .... ARB
Appear (FAAC) .... APPR
Appearance [*In urinalysis*] [*Biochemistry*] (DAVI) .... APEAR
Appearance (MSA) .... APP
Appearance (ROG) .... APPCE
Appearance Energy [*Surface ionization*] .... AE
Appearance, Mood, Sensorium, Intelligence, and Thought Processes [*Mental status examination*] [*Medicine*] (DAVI) .... AMSIT
Appearance Potential [*Physics*] .... AP
Appearance Potential Spectroscopy [*Physics*] .... APS
Appearance Station (SAA) .... APS
Appeared (ROG) .... APPD
Appelbo [*Sweden*] [*Seismograph station code, US Geological Survey*] (SEIS) .... APP
Appellant [*Legal shorthand*] (LWAP) .... APPANT
Appellant (WDAA) .... APPL
Appellants (ROG) .... APPTS
Appellate [*Legal term*] (DLA) .... APP
Appellate (AAGC) .... App
Appellate Court (DLA) .... AC
Appellate Court (BARN) .... App Ct
Appellate Court Reports [*A publication*] (AAGC) .... III App Illinois
Appellate Department (DLA) .... App Dep't
Appellate Department of the Superior Court, California (ILCA) .... App Dept Super Ct
Appellate Division [*Legal term*] .... AD
Appellate Division (DLA) .... App Div
Appellate Division Reports [*Massachusetts*] [*A publication*] (DLA) .... ADR
Appellate Jurisdiction Act of 1876 [*39, 40 Victoria, c. 59*] (DLA) .... App Jur Act 1876
Appellation d'Origine Controle [*Official place name for wine*] .... AOC
Appellation d'Origine Vin de Qualite Superieure [*Trademark for Vintage Wine of Superior Quality*] .... AOVDQS
Appellee [*Legal shorthand*] (LWAP) .... APPLEE
Append [*or Appendix*] (AFM) .... APP
Appendage .... APPEN
Appendectomy [*Medicine*] .... AP
Appendectomy [*Medicine*] (AAMN) .... APPY
Appendectomy [*Medicine*] (DMAA) .... appy
Appendices of Proceedings of the Scottish Land Court [*A publication*] (DLA) .... SL Co
Appendices of Proceedings of the Scottish Land Court [*A publication*] (DLA) .... SL Co R
Appendices to the Report of the Scottish Land Court [*A publication*] (DLA) .... Sc La Rep Ap
Appendices to the Report of the Scottish Land Court [*A publication*] (DLA) .... Sc La Rep App
Appendicitis [*Medicine*] (DAVI) .... AP
Appendix [*Anatomy*] (DAVI) .... AP
Appendix (AAGC) .... App
Appendix (DLA) .... Append
Appendix (KSC) .... APPX

Appendix [*Medicine*] (DMAA) ... appx
Appendix (WGA) ... APX
Appendix to 11 Peters, United States Reports [*A publication*] (DLA) ... Bald App
Appendix to Breese's Reports [*Illinois*] [*A publication*] (DLA) ... Ap Bre
Appendix to Breese's Reports [*Illinois*] [*A publication*] (DLA) ... Appx Bre
Appendix to Tidd's Practice [*A publication*] (DLA) ... Tidd App
Appendix to Volume 10 of Hare's Vice-Chancellor's Reports [*England*] [*A publication*] (DLA) ... Ha App
Appendixes (DLA) ... apps
Appenweiler [*Germany ICAO location identifier*] (ICLI) ... EDZU
Appian [*Second century AD*] [*Classical studies*] (OCD) ... App
Appied Graphics Technologies, Inc. [*Associated Press*] (SAG) ... AppGrph
Applanation [*Ophthalmology*] ... APPLAN
Applanation Tonometry [*Ophthalmology*] ... AT
Applantus [*Flattened*] [*Latin*] (MAE) ... applan
Apple [*Philately*] ... ap
Apple and Pear Disease Workers (EA) ... APDW
Apple and Pear Growers' Association of South Australia ... APGASA
Apple AUI [*Attachment Unit Interface*] (CDE) ... AAUI
Apple Bulletin Board System [*Pronounced "abbies"*] ... ABBS
Apple Chlorotic Leafspot Virus [*Plant pathology*] ... ACLV
Apple Classroom of Tomorrow ... ACOT
Apple Computer [*NASDAQ symbol*] (TTSB) ... AAPL
Apple Computer, Inc. [*NASDAQ symbol*] (NQ) ... AAPL
Apple Computer, Inc. [*Associated Press*] (SAG) ... AppleC
Apple Desktop Bus [*Computer science*] ... ADB
Apple Desktop Bus Microcontroller [*Computer processor*] ... ADBM
Apple File Exchange [*Computer science*] ... AFE
Apple/IBM/Motorola (CDE) ... AIM
Apple [*Computer*] **Infected Disk Syndrome** (NHD) ... AIDS
Apple Management Association (EA) ... AMA
Apple Mosaic Virus ... ApMV
Apple Octopus Fan Club (EA) ... AOFC
Apple Open Collaboration Environment [*Computer science*] (PCM) ... AOCE
Apple Preferred Format [*Computer science*] ... APF
Apple Processors Association (EA) ... APA
Apple Programmers and Developers Association (DOM) ... APDA
Apple QuickTime [*Computer science*] ... mov
Apple Remote Access [*Apple Computer, Inc.*] (PCM) ... ARA
Apple Scar Skin Viroid [*Plant pathology*] ... ASSVd
Apple Shared Library Manager [*Computer science*] ... ASLM
Apple Sound Chip [*Apple Computer, Inc.*] (BYTE) ... ASC
Apple South [*NASDAQ symbol*] (SPSG) ... APSO
Apple South, Inc. [*Associated Press*] (SAG) ... ApplSou
Apple Stem Grooving Virus [*Plant pathology*] ... ASGV
Apple University Consortium ... AUC
Apple UNIX [*Computer science*] (ACRL) ... AUX
Apple Valley [*California*] [*Airport symbol Obsolete*] (OAG) ... APV
Apple Valley, CA [*AM radio station call letters*] (RBYB) ... KIXW
Apple Valley, CA [*AM radio station call letters*] (RBYB) ... KWRN
Apple Valley, CA [*FM radio station call letters*] ... KZXY-FM
Applebee's International, Inc. [*NASDAQ symbol*] (NQ) ... APPB
Applebee's International, Inc. [*Associated Press*] (SAG) ... Applebee
Applebee's Intl. [*NASDAQ symbol*] (TTSB) ... APPB
Appleby College, Oakville, ON, Canada [*Library symbol Library of Congress*] (LCLS) ... CaOOakA
Appleby College, Oakville, Ontario [*Library symbol National Library of Canada*] (NLC) ... OOAKA
Applejack ... AJ
Apples [*Phonetic alphabet*] [*Royal Navy World War I*] (DSUE) ... A
Apple's Kin [*An association Defunct*] (EA) ... AK
Applesauce, Bananas, Cereal [*Diet*] (MEDA) ... ABC
AppleTalk Data Stream Protocol [*Apple Computer, Inc.*] (PCM) ... ADSP
AppleTalk Echo Protocol [*Apple Computer, Inc.*] (PCM) ... AEP
AppleTalk Filing Protocol [*Apple Computer, Inc.*] (BYTE) ... AFP
AppleTalk Link Access Protocol [*Apple Computer, Inc.*] (BYTE) ... ALAP
AppleTalk Print Service [*Apple Computer, Inc.*] (PCM) ... ATPS
Appletalk Remote Access [*Apple Computer Inc.*] ... ARA
Appletalk Remote Access Protocol [*Apple Computer Inc.*] ... ARAP
AppleTalk Session Protocol [*Apple Computer, Inc.*] (BYTE) ... ASP
AppleTalk Transaction Protocol [*Apple Computer, Inc.*] ... ATP
Apple-Talk Update-Based Routing Protocol [*Computer science*] ... AURP
Appleton [*Wisconsin*] [*Airport symbol*] (OAG) ... ATW
Appleton Elementary School, Grand Junction, CO [*Library symbol Library of Congress*] (LCLS) ... CoGjAE
Appleton Memorial Hospital, Appleton, WI [*Library symbol Library of Congress*] (LCLS) ... WAM
Appleton, MN [*FM radio station call letters*] (RBYB) ... KNCM-FM
Appleton, MN [*FM radio station call letters*] ... KRSU
Appleton, MN [*Television station call letters*] ... KWCM
Appleton Municipal Hospital, Appleton, MN [*Library symbol*] [*Library of Congress*] (LCLS) ... MnApH
Appleton, OH [*Location identifier FAA*] (FAAL) ... APE
Appleton Post Crescent, Appleton, WI [*Library symbol*] [*Library of Congress*] (LCLS) ... WAPC
Appleton Public Library, Appleton, MN [*Library symbol*] [*Library of Congress*] (LCLS) ... MnAp
Appleton Public Library, Appleton, WI [*Library symbol Library of Congress*] (LCLS) ... WA
Appleton Public Library, Appleton, WI [*Library symbol*] [*Library of Congress*] (LCLS) ... WAPL
Appleton Public Library, Appleton, WI [*OCLC symbol*] (OCLC) ... WIQ
Appleton Public Schools, Appleton, MN [*Library symbol*] [*Library of Congress*] (LCLS) ... MnApPS
Appleton, WI [*Location identifier FAA*] (FAAL) ... FXV
Appleton, WI [*Television station call letters*] (RBYB) ... WACY
Appleton, WI [*FM radio station call letters*] ... WAPL
Appleton, WI [*FM radio station call letters*] (RBYB) ... WEMI
Appleton, WI [*FM radio station call letters*] ... WLFM
Appleton, WI [*AM radio station call letters*] ... WRJQ
Appleton-Century-Crofts [*Publisher*] ... ACC
Appleton's Reports [*19, 20 Maine*] ... App
Appleton's Reports [*19, 20 Maine*] [*A publication*] (DLA) ... Appleton
Appleton's Rules of Evidence [*A publication*] (DLA) ... App Ev
Appletree Companies [*Associated Press*] (SAG) ... Appltree
Appletree Companies [*NASDAQ symbol*] (SAG) ... ATRE
Applewoods, Inc. [*Associated Press*] (SAG) ... Aplewds
Applewoods, Inc. [*NASDAQ symbol*] (SAG) ... APWD
Applewoods Inc. [*NASDAQ symbol*] (TTSB) ... APWD
Appliance ... APPL
Appliance ... APPLNC
Appliance Leakage Current Interrupter (BARN) ... ALCI
Appliance Parts Distributors Association (EA) ... APDA
Appliance Parts Jobbers Association [*Later, APDA*] ... APJA
Appliance, Range, Adjust [*Computer science*] ... ARGA
Appliance Recycling Centers of America [*Associated Press*] (SAG) ... AplRecy
Appliance Recycling Centers of America (PS) ... ARCA
Appliance Recycling Centers of America [*NASDAQ symbol*] (SAG) ... ARCI
Appliance Recycling Ctrs Amer [*NASDAQ symbol*] (TTSB) ... ABCI
Appliance Wiring Material ... AWM
Applicability Code ... APCOD
Applicable (AFM) ... APPL
Applicable Approved Accounting Standard ... AAAS
Applicable Document Contractual Record [*Military*] ... ADCR
Applicable High-Yield Discount Obligation [*Finance*] ... AHYDO
Applicable or Relevant and Appropriate Requirement [*Environmental science*] ... ARAR
Applicandus [*To Be Applied*] [*Pharmacy*] ... APPLICAND
Applicant [*or Application*] (DNAB) ... APPL
Applicant Data System [*Department of Labor*] ... ADS
Applicant File Search [*US Employment Service*] [*Department of Labor*] ... AFS
Applicant Holding Office [*Employment*] ... AHO
Applicant Information Service [*Institute of International Education*] (AEBS) ... AIS
Applicant Master File [*State Employee Security Agency*] (OICC) ... AMF
Applicant Outreach Program [*Department of Labor*] ... AOP
Applicant Qualification Test [*Navy*] ... AQT
Applicant Tracking System [*Human resources*] (WYGK) ... ATS
Application [*Computer science*] ... app
Application ... APP
Application ... APPLCTN
Application ... APPLN
Application ... APPLON
Application and Resource Control (NASA) ... A & RC
Application Binary Interface [*Computer science*] (BYTE) ... ABI
Application Block (MSA) ... AB
Application Builder Class [*Computer science*] ... ABC
Application Builder Editor [*Computer science*] ... ABE
Application Channel Interface (TEL) ... ACHI
Application Code (CDE) ... app code
Application Control [*or Controller*] [*Computer science*] (NASA) ... AC
Application Control and Teleprocessing System (MHDI) ... ACTS
Application Control Architecture [*Computer science*] ... ACA
Application Control Architecture Service [*Computer science*] ... ACAS
Application Control Block [*Computer science*] (NITA) ... ACB
Application Control Block Generation [*Computer science*] (MHDI) ... ACBGEN
Application Control Language [*Computer science*] (BUR) ... ACL
Application Control Language [*Computer science*] (MHDI) ... ACOL
Application Control Management System (MCD) ... ACMS
Application Control Service Element (ACII) ... ACSE
Application Control Service Element (ACII) ... ASCE
Application Creation Made Easy [*Watcom International Corp.*] [*Computer science*] (PCM) ... ACME
Application Data Interchange [*Telecommunications*] (OSI) ... ADI
Application Data Management (IAA) ... ADM
Application Data Management Services (MCD) ... ADMS
Application Data Material Readiness List [*DoD*] ... ADMRL
Application Date [*Bell System*] (TEL) ... APP
Application Dedicated Terminal [*Computer science*] (IAA) ... ADT
Application Design Service [*IBM Corp.*] ... ADS
Application Development Environment [*Computer science*] (BTTJ) ... ADE
Application Development Facility [*IBM Corp.*] [*Computer science*] ... ADF
Application Development System/Online [*Computer science*] (HGAA) ... ADS/O
Application Development Systems [*Computer science*] ... ADS
Application Development Task Group [*Navy*] ... ADTG
Application Development Workbench [*Sterling Software, Atlanta, GA*] (CDE) ... ADW
Application Engineering ... AE
Application Executive [*Software interface for Integrated Modular Avionics*] [*Computer science*] ... APEX
Application Explorer Mission [*NASA*] ... AEM
Application Fit Analysis ... AFA
Application for Certiorari Denied [*Legal term*] (DLA) ... CD
Application for Federal Assistance (OICC) ... AFA
Application for Federal Assistance and Assurances (OICC) ... AFAA
Application for Federal Student Aid (GFGA) ... AFSA
Application for Mandamus Granted in Part [*Legal term*] (DLA) ... MGP
Application for New Stock Item ... ANSI
Application for Passport for Self and/or Dependents Accordance BUPERS Manual [*Navy*] ... PLYPASSPORT
Application for Review Decisions [*A publication*] (DLA) ... ARD

Application for Writ of Error Dismissed by Agreement of Parties [*Legal term*] (DLA) .... DAP
Application for Writ of Error Dismissed for Want of Jurisdiction [*Legal term*] (DLA) .... D
Application for Writ of Error Dismissed, Judgment Correct [*Legal term*] (DLA) .... DJC
Application for Writ of Error Granted [*Legal term*] (DLA) .... G
Application for Writ of Mandamus Dismissed for Want of Jurisdiction [*Legal term*] (DLA) .... MD
Application for Writ of Mandamus Refused [*Legal term*] (DLA) .... MR
Application for Writ of Mandamus Refused in Part [*Legal term*] (DLA) .... MRP
Application Foundation Classes [*Microsoft Corp.*] [*Computer science*] .... AFC
Application Frameworx [*Microsoft Corp.*] .... AFX
Application Functions Module [*Computer science*] .... AFM
Application Integration Module [*Telecommunications*] (TSSD) .... AIM
Application Interface Engine [*Computer science*] .... AIE
Application Language Liberator (MCD) .... ALL
Application Layer Structure [*Telecommunications*] (OSI) .... ALS
Application Library File [*Computer science*] .... ALF
Application Macro Language (PCM) .... AML
Application Module Library [*IBM Corp.*] .... AML
Application of Autonomous Passive Classification (MCD) .... AAPC
Application of Computers to Manufacturing Engineering .... ACME
Application of Filters to Demand Forecasting (MCD) .... APOFDF
Application of RADAR to Ballistic Acceptance Testing [*of ammunition*] (MCD) .... ARBAT
Application of Remote Manipulators in Space [*Robot*] [*NASA*] .... ARMS
Application of Science and Technology to Rural Areas [*An association*] .... ASTRA
Application of Space Techniques Relating to Aviation [*International Civil Aviation Organization*] .... ASTRA
Application of the 1973 Middle East War to CAA [*Concepts Analysis Agency*] War Games, Models, and Simulations .... AMWAR
Application Oriented Language [*Computer science*] (BUR) .... AOL
Application Package for Chemical Engineers .... APACHE
Application Process [*Telecommunications*] (OSI) .... AP
Application Process Invocation [*Telecommunications*] (OSI) .... API
Application Process [*or Program*] **(Structure)** [*Telecommunications*] (TEL) .... AP(S)
Application Process Subsystem [*Telecommunications*] (TEL) .... APS
Application Program [*Computer science*] (BUR) .... AP
Application Program Evaluator Tool [*Computer science*] (MHDB) .... APET
Application Program Generator [*Computer science*] .... APG
Application Program Interface [*Telecommunications*] (OSI) .... API
Application Program Interface .... API
Application Program Interface Association (BTTJ) .... APIA
Application Program Preparation Utility (MHDI) .... APPU
Application Programming Interface [*Telecommunications*] (ACRL) .... API
Application Protocol Data Unit [*Telecommunications*] (OSI) .... APDU
Application Quality Assurance [*Automotive engineering*] [*3M Co.*] .... AQA
Application Reference Manual (IAA) .... ARM
Application Replacement Factor .... ARF
Application Review (IAA) .... AR
Application Service Element [*Telecommunications*] (OSI) .... ASE
Application Software Module (MCD) .... ASM
Application Specific Coding Flag (NTCM) .... ASCF
Application Specific Standard Part (CDE) .... ASSP
Application Support System (IAA) .... APPS
Application Swapping Extensions [*Computer science*] (PCM) .... ASE
Application System (ADA) .... AS
Application System/400 [*IBM minicomputer series*] (CDE) AS/400
Application System Generator .... ASG
Application Systems Developer [*Army*] .... ASD
Application Terminal Unit [*Telecommunications*] (TEL) .... ATU
Application Transaction Program (ACRL) .... ATP
Application Transfer Study [*IBM problem solving process*] .... ATS
Application Transfer Teams [*IBM Corp.*] .... ATT
Application Visualization System [*Computer science*] (BTTJ) .... AVS
Application-by-Forms (HGAA) .... ABF
Application-Entity [*Telecommunications*] (OSI) .... AE
Application-Entity Invocation [*Telecommunications*] (OSI) .... AEI
Applications and Industry (MCD) .... AI
Applications Configuration Management Board [*NASA*] (NASA) .... ACMB
Applications Database [*Environmental Protection Agency*] (GFGA) .... ADB
Applications Development Environment [*Computer science*] .... ADE
Applications Environment System .... AES
Applications Experience .... AEXP
Applications Explorer [*NASA*] .... AE
Applications In Mathematics for High Schools .... AIM-HI
Applications Information Processing System (MCD) .... AIPS
Applications Interface Message Set .... AIMS
Applications Management [*Computer science*] .... AM
Applications Management System [*Computer application*] (PCM) .... AMS
Applications of Space Technology Panel to Requirements of Civil Aviation [*ICAO*] (DA) .... ASTRA
Applications Portability Profile [*Computer science*] (BARN) .... APP
Applications Processor (IEEE) .... AP
Applications Program Integration Board [*NASA*] .... APIB
Applications Research and Defense Fund (DNAB) .... ARDF
Applications Research Corp. .... ARC
Applications Server [*Computer science*] .... APPS
Applications Software [*Computer science*] .... ASW
Applications Systems Verification and Transfer (MCD) .... ASVT
Applications Systems Verification Test [*NASA*] .... ASVT
Applications Technology Satellite [*Communications satellite*] [*NASA*] .... ATS

Applications Technology Satellite Operations Control Center [*NASA*] .... ATSOCC
Applications Terminal Language [*Computer science*] (MHDB) .... ATL
Applications Vertical Test Program [*Communication Satellite program*] .... AVT
Application-Specific Integrated Circuit [*Electronics*] .... ASIC
Applicative Language Idealized Computing Engine [*Imperial College*] [*British*] .... ALICE
Applicator .... APPLCTR
Applicatur [*Let It Be Applied*] [*Pharmacy*] (ROG) .... APPLIC
Applicatur [*Let It Be Applied*] [*Pharmacy*] .... APPLICAT
Applied (MSA) .... APLD
Applied .... APP
Applied .... APPL
Applied (VRA) .... appl
Applied .... APPLD
Applied .... APPLD
Applied Agricultural Research, Inc. [*Research center*] (RCD) .... AAR
Applied Analytical Industries, Inc. [*NASDAQ symbol*] (SAG) .... AAII
Applied Analytical Industries, Inc. [*Associated Press*] (SAG) .... AppAnl
Applied Behavior Analysis [*Psychology*] .... ABA
Applied Biometrics [*NASDAQ symbol*] (TTSB) .... ABIO
Applied Biometrics, Inc. [*NASDAQ symbol*] (NQ) .... ABIO
Applied Biometrics, Inc. [*Associated Press*] (SAG) .... ApBiomet
Applied Bioscience [*NASDAQ symbol*] (TTSB) .... APBI
Applied Bioscience International [*Associated Press*] (SAG) .... ABiosci
Applied Bioscience International, Inc. [*NASDAQ symbol*] (NQ) .... APBI
Applied Biosystems, Inc. .... AB
Applied Business Technology Corp. .... ABT
Applied Business Telecommunications [*San Ramon, CA*] [*Information service or system Telecommunications*] (TSSD) .... ABC
Applied Carbon Technology [*NASDAQ symbol*] (TTSB) .... ACTYF
Applied Cellular Technology [*NASDAQ symbol*] (SAG) .... ACTC
Applied Cellular Technology [*Associated Press*] (SAG) .... AplCell
Applied Communication Research, Inc. [*Information service or system*] (IID) .... ACR
Applied Communications Systems Center [*AT & T*] .... ACSC
Applied Computer Research [*Information service or system*] (IID) .... ACR
Applied Computer Research Institute [*La Trobe University*] [*Australia*] .... ACRI
Applied Computer Science (IAA) .... ACS
Applied Computer Solution .... ACS
Applied Computer Tech [*NASDAQ symbol*] (TTSB) .... ACTI
Applied Computer Tech Wrrt [*NASDAQ symbol*] (TTSB) .... ACTIW
Applied Computer Techniques (TEL) .... ACT
Applied Computer Technology, Inc. [*NASDAQ symbol*] (SAG) .... ACTI
Applied Computer Technology, Inc. [*Associated Press*] (SAG) .... ApdCmp
Applied Computer Technology, Inc. [*Associated Press*] (SAG) .... ApdCptr
Applied Cost for Work Performed (SSD) .... ACWP
Applied Data Communication [*Computer science*] (IAA) .... ADC
Applied Data Research [*Commercial firm*] (NITA) .... ADR
Applied Data Research, Inc. [*Princeton, NJ*] (TSSD) .... ADR
Applied Decision Analysis .... ADA
Applied Decision Systems [*Information service or system*] (IID) .... ADS
Applied Demographic Research Group [*Database producer*] (IID) .... ADRG
Applied Digital Access [*NASDAQ symbol*] (SAG) .... ADAX
Applied Digital Access [*Associated Press*] (SAG) .... ApdDgtl
Applied Digital Data Systems [*Commercial firm*] (NITA) .... ADDS
Applied Dynamics (IAA) .... AD
Applied Dynamics International .... ADI
Applied Economic Research and Information Centre [*Conference Board of Canada*] [*Ottawa, ON*] .... AERIC
Applied Energy, Inc. [*Vancouver Stock Exchange symbol*] .... AEG
Applied Energy Services [*Commercial firm*] (ECON) .... AES
Applied Entomology .... AE
Applied Entomology Group [*Natick Labs, MA*] [*Army*] .... AE
Applied Extrasensory Projection [*Psychology*] (DAVI) .... AESP
Applied Extrusion Tech [*NASDAQ symbol*] (TTSB) .... AETC
Applied Extrusion Technologies [*NASDAQ symbol*] (SPSG) .... AETC
Applied Extrusion Technologies [*Associated Press*] (SAG) .... ApdExtr
Applied Forest Research Institute [*Syracuse University*] .... AFRI
Applied Graphics Technologies, Inc. [*NASDAQ symbol*] (SAG) .... AGTX
Applied Imagery Pattern Recognition .... AIPR
Applied Imaging Corp. [*NASDAQ symbol*] (SAG) .... AICX
Applied Imaging Corp. [*Associated Press*] (SAG) .... Applmg
Applied Immune Sciences, Inc. [*NASDAQ symbol*] (SAG) .... AISX
Applied Immune Sciences, Inc. [*Associated Press*] (SAG) .... Apdlmu
Applied Immunoenzymometric Assay [*Clinical chemistry*] .... AIMEA
Applied Industrial Technology [*Associated Press*] (SAG) .... ApldIndlT
Applied Industrial Technology [*NYSE symbol*] (SAG) .... APZ
Applied Information and Data Management Systems Section [*Battelle Memorial Institute*] [*Information service or system*] (IID) .... AIDMS
Applied Information and Documentation [*Database producer*] (IID) .... AID
Applied Information Management System [*Computer science*] (DIT) .... AIMS
Applied Information Resources [*Research center*] (RCD) .... AIR
Applied Information Technologies Research Center [*Information service or system*] (IID) .... AITRC
Applied Innovation [*NASDAQ symbol*] (TTSB) .... AINN
Applied Innovation, Inc. [*NASDAQ symbol*] (SAG) .... AINN
Applied Innovation, Inc. [*Associated Press*] (SAG) .... Apllnov
Applied Intelligence Group, Inc. [*Associated Press*] (SAG) .... AppGrp
Applied Intelligence Group, Inc. [*Associated Press*] (SAG) .... ApplGrp
Applied Intelligence Group, Inc. [*NASDAQ symbol*] (SAG) .... IQIQ
Applied Journalism .... AJ
Applied Knowledge Test [*Vocational guidance test*] .... AKT
Applied Laboratory Method (OA) .... ALM
Applied Language Technology .... ALTech
Applied LASER Projects Staff .... ALPS

Applied Magnetics [*NYSE symbol*] (SAG) ... APM
Applied Magnetics Corp. [*Associated Press*] (SAG) ... ApplMg
Applied Manufacturing Research and Process Development ... AMRPD
Applied Marine Research Laboratory [*Old Dominion University*] [*Research center*] (RCD) ... AMRL
Applied Materials [*NASDAQ symbol*] (TTSB) ... AMAT
Applied Materials [*Associated Press*] (SAG) ... ApldMat
Applied Materials, Inc. [*NASDAQ symbol*] (NQ) ... AMAT
Applied Materials, Inc. ... AMI
Applied Mathematics and Statistics Laboratory [*Stanford University*] (MCD) ... AMSL
Applied Mathematics Group [*Brown University*] (MCD) ... AMG
Applied Mathematics Institute [*University of Delaware*] [*Research center*] (RCD) ... AMI
Applied Mathematics Laboratory ... AML
Applied Mathematics Panel [*DoD*] ... AMP
Applied Mathematics Series ... AMS
Applied Mechanics Division [*American Society of Mechanical Engineers*] ... AMD
Applied Mechanics Engineer [*Academic degree*] ... App ME
Applied Mechanics Engineer (PGP) ... App ME
Applied Microbiology [*NASDAQ symbol*] (TTSB) ... AMBI
Applied Microbiology Group [*Natick Laboratories*] [*Army*] (RDA) ... AMG
Applied Microbiology, Inc. [*NASDAQ symbol*] (SAG) ... AMBI
Applied Microbiology, Inc. [*Associated Press*] (SAG) ... ApdM
Applied Microbiology, Inc. [*Associated Press*] (SAG) ... ApdMicr
Applied Microbiology Wrrt [*NASDAQ symbol*] (TTSB) ... AMBIW
Applied Microsystems [*NASDAQ symbol*] (TTSB) ... APMC
Applied Microsystems Corp. [*NASDAQ symbol*] (SAG) ... APMC
Applied Microsystems Corp. [*Associated Press*] (SAG) ... ApMicro
Applied Mineral Sciences (DD) ... AppMinSci
Applied Naturalist Guild [*Defunct*] ... ANG
Applied Parallel Programming Language Experiment [*Computer science*] (MCD) ... APPLE
Applied Peripheral System (IAA) ... APS
Applied Physics (IEEE) ... AP
Applied Physics and Materials Laboratory [*Princeton University*] ... APML
Applied Physics Branch [*Air Proving Ground Center*] ... APB
Applied Physics Laboratory [*Johns Hopkins University*] ... APL
Applied Physics Laboratory/Johns Hopkins University ... APL/JHU
Applied Physics Laboratory/University of Washington ... APL/UW
Applied Physics Research Section ... APRS
Applied Physics Staff (SAA) ... APS
Applied Potential Tomography [*Medicine*] ... APT
Applied Power A [*NYSE symbol*] (SAG) ... APW
Applied Power Cl'A' [*NYSE symbol*] (TTSB) ... APW
Applied Power, Inc. [*Associated Press*] (SAG) ... ApldPw
Applied Power, Inc. [*NYSE symbol*] (SPSG) ... APW
Applied Property Research [*British*] ... APR
Applied Psychological Services (KSC) ... APS
Applied Psychology Corp. (KSC) ... APC
Applied Psychology Panel [*of NDRC*] [*World War II*] ... APP
Applied Psychology Research Unit (SAA) ... APRU
Applied Psychology Unit ... APU
Applied Remote Sensing Program (MCD) ... ARSP
Applied Research ... APPRES
Applied Research [*of ASRA*] [*National Science Foundation*] ... AR
Applied Research and Design Center [*Research center*] (RCD) ... ARDC
Applied Research Corp. ... ARC
Applied Research Ethics National Association (EA) ... ARENA
Applied Research Laboratories [*Commercial firm*] ... ARL
Applied Research Laboratory [*Johns Hopkins University, University of Texas at Austin, Pennsylvania State University*] [*Research center*] ... ARL
Applied Research Management ... ARM
Applied Research Objective ... ARO
Applied Research of Cambridge [*British*] (NITA) ... ARC
Applied Research: Operation Weather Analysis [*Navy*] ... AROWA
Applied Research Program ... ARPO
Applied Science ... AS
Applied Science and Research Applications [*Program*] [*Supersedes RANN*] [*National Science Foundation*] ... ASRA
Applied Science & Tech [*NASDAQ symbol*] (TTSB) ... ASTX
Applied Science & Tech Wrrt [*NASDAQ symbol*] (TTSB) ... ASTXW
Applied Science & Technology, Inc. [*Associated Press*] (SAG) ... ApdSci
Applied Science & Technology, Inc. [*NASDAQ symbol*] (SAG) ... ASTX
Applied Science Associates ... ASA
Applied Science Corp. (MCD) ... ASC
Applied Science Corp. of Princeton (MCD) ... ASCOP
Applied Science Division [*GAO*] (AAGC) ... ASD
Applied Science Laboratory ... ASL
Applied Science Technologists & Technicians of British Columbia [*Formerly, Society of Engineering Technologists of BC*] (AC) ... ASTTBC
Applied Science through Research and Engineering ... ASTRE
Applied Scientist (PGP) ... App Sc
Applied Signal Technology [*NASDAQ symbol*] (TTSB) ... APSG
Applied Signal Technology, Inc. [*Associated Press*] (SAG) ... ApldSig
Applied Signal Technology, Inc. [*NASDAQ symbol*] (SAG) ... APSG
Applied Social Sciences Index and Abstracts [*Information service or system*] (IID) ... ASSIA
Applied Software Technology [*Computer science*] (HGAA) ... ASTEC
Applied Space Technology Regional Advancement (KSC) ... ASTRA
Applied Statistics Training Institute ... ASTI
Applied Superconductivity Conference, Inc. (MCD) ... ASC
Applied Superconductivity Research Center [*University of Wisconsin - Madison*] [*Research center*] (RCD) ... ASC
Applied Systems and Personnel (BUR) ... ASAP
Applied Systems Development and Evaluation Center ... ASDEC
Applied Systems Knowledge Ltd. [*British*] (NITA) ... ASK
Applied Technology Advanced Computer ... ATAC
Applied Technology Council (EA) ... ATC
Applied Technology Gasification [*Coal*] ... ATGAS
Applied Technology Laboratory [*Army*] (GRD) ... ATL
Applied to Previous Charge [*Business term*] ... APC
Applied Urbanetics, Inc. [*Information service or system*] (IID) ... AUI
Applied Videotex Systems, Inc. [*Telecommunications service*] (TSSD) ... AVS
Applied Voice Technology [*Telecommunications service*] (TSSD) ... AVT
Applied Voice Technology [*NASDAQ symbol*] (TTSB) ... AVTC
Applied Voice Technology, Inc. [*Associated Press*] (SAG) ... ApdVoice
Applied Voice Technology, Inc. [*NASDAQ symbol*] (SAG) ... AVTC
Applique ... A
Applique (VRA) ... apliq
Applique (MSA) ... APLQ
Applique ... APPLQ
Applix, Inc. [*NASDAQ symbol*] (SAG) ... APLX
Applix, Inc. [*Associated Press*] (SAG) ... Applix
Apply Fixture (AAG) ... APFX
Apply Force [*Industrial engineering*] ... AF
Apply Pressure [*Industrial engineering*] ... AP
Apply Template (MCD) ... AT
Appoint (FAAC) ... APNT
Appoint (AABC) ... APT
Appointed ... APP
Appointed ... APPNTD
Appointed ... APPTD
Appointed Factory Doctor (PDAA) ... AFD
Appointing Order ... AO
Appointment ... APPMT
Appointment (WGA) ... APPNT
Appointment (AFM) ... APPT
Appointment [*Medicine*] (DMAA) ... appt
Appointment (ROG) ... APPTNT
Appointment (ROG) ... APPTT
Appointment and Promotion Advisory Committee [*UN Food and Agriculture Organization*] ... APAC
Appointment of Agents - Excise [*Revenue Canada - Customs and Excise*] [*Information service or system*] (CRD) ... AAE
Appointment Recommended (NOAA) ... APRMD
Appointment Will Be Regarded as Having Terminated upon This Date ... POINTERM
Appointments Register ... AR
Appollo High School, St. Cloud, MN [*Library symbol*] [*Library of Congress*] (LCLS) ... MnStclA
Appomattox Court House National Historic Park ... APCO
Appomattox Regional Library, Hopewell, VA [*Library symbol Library of Congress*] (LCLS) ... ViHop
Appomattox, VA [*FM radio station call letters*] ... WLDJ
Appomattox, VA [*FM radio station call letters*] ... WTTX-FM
Appomattox, VA [*AM radio station call letters*] (RBYB) ... WWAR
Apportioned Effort (MCD) ... AE
Apportionment of Close Companies' Income [*Business term*] (NITA) ... ACCI
Appositive (WDAA) ... APPOS
Appraisal ... APPRSL
Appraisal & Valuation Consultants Ltd. [*British*] ... AVC
Appraisal Institute (EA) ... AI
Appraisal Institute of Canada ... AIC
Appraisal of Language Disturbance [*Test*] ... ALD
Appraisal of the Navy RDT & E [*Research, Development, Test, and Evaluation*] **Program** ... ANREP
Appraisal: Science Books for Young People [*A publication*] (BRI) ... ASBYP
Appraisals, Evaluation, and Sectoral Study ... AESS
Appraised (WGA) ... APP
Appraisement (ROG) ... APPRAIST
Appraiser ... APPRSER
Appraisers Association of America (EA) ... AAA
Appraisor ... APPRSOR
Appreciate [*Wire service abbreviation*] (WDMC) ... apc
Appreciate [*Wire service abbreviation*] (WDMC) ... APC
Appreciate ... Apc
Appreciation Index [*Television ratings*] [*British*] ... AI
Appreciation of Capital, Protection, Income [*Finance*] ... API
Apprehend (AABC) ... APP
Apprehend (AFM) ... APPR
Apprehended Violence Order [*A publication*] ... AVO
Apprentice ... APP
Apprentice (ROG) ... APPRCE
Apprentice ... APPRENT
Apprentice ... APPRNTC
Apprentice (AFM) ... APR
Apprentice Seaman ... AS
Apprentice Training Incentive ... ATI
Apprentices' Free Library, Philadelphia, PA [*Library symbol Library of Congress Obsolete*] (LCLS) ... PPAp
Apprentices National Insurance [*British*] ... ANI
Apprentices Union [*British*] ... AU
Apprenticeship (AABC) ... APPR
Apprenticeship and Training Conference [*Bureau of Apprenticeship and Training*] [*Department of Labor*] ... ATC
Apprenticeship and Training Representative [*Bureau of Apprenticeship and Training*] [*Department of Labor*] ... ATR
Apprenticeship Committee [*Department of Labor*] ... AC
Apprenticeship Information Center [*Department of Labor*] ... AIC

Apprenticeship News [*A publication*] ..... Apprent News
Apprenticeship Outreach Program [*Bureau of Apprenticeship and Training*] (OICC) ..... AOP
Apprenticeship Program (DD) ..... AP
Apprenticeship, Referral, and Outreach for Women [*An association Defunct*] (EA) ..... AROW
Approach [*Database terminology*] (NITA) ..... AP
Approach ..... APCH
Approach ..... APP
Approach (MSA) ..... APRCH
Approach Aid [*Aviation*] (IAA) ..... AA
Approach and Departure Control [*FAA*] (TAG) ..... AADC
Approach and Departure Control [*Aviation*] (FAAC) ..... AADC
Approach and Landing [*Aviation*] (NASA) ..... A & L
Approach & Landing [*MTMC*] (TAG) ..... AL
Approach and Landing Flight Test [*Aviation*] (MCD) ..... ALFT
Approach and Landing Procedures Simulator [*Aviation*] (MCD) ..... ALPS
Approach and Landing Simulator [*Aviation*] ..... ALS
Approach and Landing Test [*Aviation*] (MCD) ..... ALT
Approach and Landing Test Requirement [*NASA*] (NASA) ..... ALTR
Approach/Approach Mode (GAVI) ..... APPR
Approach Astrophysics Payload [*NASA*] ..... AAP
Approach Astrophysics Payload [*NASA*] (MCD) ..... APP
Approach by Concept [*Information retrieval*] ..... ABC
Approach Chart ..... AC
Approach Control [*Aviation*] ..... A/C
Approach Control [*Aviation*] ..... APC
Approach Control [*FAA*] ..... APCON
Approach Control [*Aviation*] (AFM) ..... APPCON
Approach Control Center (MCD) ..... ACC
Approach Control Function [*Aviation*] (AIA) ..... APF
Approach Control Office [*Aviation code*] ..... APP
Approach Control Office [*ICAO designator*] (ICDA) ..... ZA
Approach Control Office [*FAA designator*] (FAAC) ..... ZAZ
Approach Control RADAR [*Aviation*] ..... ACR
Approach Control RADAR (DA) ..... APP-R
Approach/Departure [*Aviation*] (DNAB) ..... APP/DEP
Approach Deterioration Parameter (MCD) ..... ADP
Approach End Barrier Engagement (MCD) ..... AEBE
Approach End Runway [*Aviation*] (FAAC) ..... AER
Approach, Horizon Indicator [*Aviation*] (PDAA) ..... AHI
Approach Indexer ..... APEXER
Approach/Landing ..... A/L
Approach Landing Autopilot System [*or Subsystem*] [*Aviation*] (MCD) ..... ALAS
Approach Landing System [*Aviation*] (MCD) ..... ALS
Approach Light Contact Height ..... ALCH
Approach Light Facility (PDAA) ..... ALF
Approach Light System [*Aviation*] ..... ALS
Approach Light System with Sequenced Flashing Lights in ILS CAT-I Configuration [*FAA*] (TAG) ..... ALSF-I
Approach Light System with Sequenced Flashing Lights in ILS CAT-II Modification [*FAA*] (TAG) ..... ALSF-II
Approach Lighting [*Aviation*] (DA) ..... A
Approach Lighting System Improvement Program [*FAA*] (TAG) ..... ALSIP
Approach Lighting System with Sequenced Flashers [*Aviation*] ..... ALSF
Approach Lighting System With Sequenced Flashing Lights [*FAA*] (TAG) ..... ALSF
Approach Lights [*Aviation*] (AIA) ..... AP
Approach, Naval Aviation Safety Review [*A publication*] ..... ANAR
Approach Path Alignment Panel [*Aviation*] (FAAC) ..... APAP
Approach Path Control System [*NASA*] (MCD) ..... APCS
Approach Positive Control ..... APC
Approach Power Compensator [*NASA*] ..... APC
Approach Power Compensator System [*NASA*] ..... APCS
Approach Power Control Set (NG) ..... APCS
Approach Resources, Inc. [*Vancouver Stock Exchange symbol*] ..... APH
Approach to Command and Control Implementation and Design (SAA) ..... ACCID
Approach to Distributed Processing Transaction [*Computer science*] (MHDB) ..... ADOPT
Approacher ..... APPRCHR
Approaches (NATG) ..... AP
Approaches [*Maps and charts*] ..... Apprs
Approaches to Behavior Change Inventory (EDAC) ..... ABC
Approaching ..... APCHG
Approaching Lactate Dehydrogenase [*LD*] **1:2 Flip** [*Cardiology*] (DAVI) ..... APPR
Approbation ..... APPRO
Appropriate (DMAA) ..... approp
Appropriate (AABC) ..... APROP
Appropriate Authority [*Office of Censorship*] [*World War II*] ..... AA
Appropriate Duty [*Air Force*] (AFM) ..... APDY
Appropriate for Gestational Age [*Medicine*] ..... AGA
Appropriate Health Resources and Technologies Action Group [*London, England*] ..... AHRTAG
Appropriate Home Energy Cooperative [*Canada*] ..... AHEC
Appropriate Labor Organization (OICC) ..... ALO
Appropriate National Authorities [*NATO*] (NATG) ..... ANA
Appropriate Superior Authority [*British military*] (DMA) ..... ASA
Appropriate Technology ..... AT
Appropriate Technology in the Third World [*G. V. Olsen Associates*] [*Information service or system*] (CRD) AT3
Appropriate Technology Information Service [*International Council of Scientific Unions*] ..... ATIS
Appropriate Technology International (EA) ..... ATI
Appropriate Technology Ltd. [*British*] (IRUK) ..... APTEC
Appropriate Technology Project [*Maintained by the Volunteers in Asia*] ..... ATP
Appropriate Technology Transfer for Rural Areas [*National Center for Appropriate Technology*] (GNE) ..... ATTRA
Appropriate Technology - United Kingdom Unit [*ITDG*] [*British*] ..... AT-UK
Appropriated (ROG) ..... APP
Appropriated Funds ..... AF
Appropriated Funds (AABC) ..... APF
Appropriateness Evaluation Protocol [*Medicine*] (MEDA) ..... AEP
Appropriating Property in Possession of Common Carrier [*FBI standardized term*] ..... APIPOCC
Appropriation ..... APPN
Appropriation ..... APPROP
Appropriation Account Data [*Business term*] ..... AAD
Appropriation Accounts and Data Processing Division [*Ministry of Agriculture, Fisheries, and Food*] [*British*] ..... AA & DPD
Appropriation and Budget Account Code ..... ABAC
Appropriation and Budget Activity [*Army*] (AABC) ..... ABA
Appropriation and Expense (AFM) ..... A & E
Appropriation and Expense (AFIT) ..... AAE
Appropriation Purchases Account ..... APA
Appropriation Transfer Account (AFM) ..... ATA
Appropriations and Allocations (OICC) ..... AA
Approval (ADA) ..... APP
Approval (AFM) ..... APPR
Approval ..... APPRO
Approval (ROG) ..... APPVAL
Approval (MSA) ..... APPVL
Approval (KSC) ..... APRVL
Approval ..... APVL
Approval for Full Production [*Navy*] (DOMA) ..... AFP
Approval for Service Use [*Military*] (NVT) ..... ASU
Approval in Principle (NRCH) ..... AIP
Approval MILSTRIP [*Military Standard Requisition and Issue Procedures*] **Change Letter** [*DoD*] ..... AMCL
Approval Request [*Military*] (DNAB) ..... APREQ
Approval Requests [*Military*] (AABC) ..... APREQS
Approval to Build Prototype [*Automotive project management*] ..... ABP
Approval to Start Production [*Automotive project management*] ..... ASP
Approve ..... APPRV
Approve (MSA) ..... APPV
Approve (KSC) ..... APRV
Approve ..... APV
Approved ..... A
Approved (KSC) ..... APPD
Approved (DAVI) ..... APPROV
Approved (ILCA) ..... apprvd
Approved (MSA) ..... APVD
Approved and Removed ..... A & R
Approved as Amended ..... AAA
Approved Auto Repair [*American Automobile Association*] ..... AAR
Approved Basic Stock Level of Ammunition (MCD) ..... ABSLA
Approved Capital Costs [*Canada*] ..... ACC
Approved Code of Practice (DS) ..... ACOP
Approved Conference Rate and Interconference Agreement [*of Steamship Lines in the Foreign Commerce of the United States*] ..... ACRA
Approved Consumer Information ..... ACI
Approved Cult ..... AC
Approved Data Element (AFM) ..... ADE
Approved Deferred Share Trust (ODBW) ..... ADST
Approved Departure Time (MCD) ..... ADT
Approved Deposit Fund (ADA) ..... ADF
Approved Driving Instructor [*British*] (DBQ) ..... ADI
Approved Drug Product [*Medicine*] (DMAA) ..... ADP
Approved Engineering Test Laboratory [*Military*] (CAAL) ..... AETL
Approved Equivalent Parts List ..... AEPL
Approved Fastener Substitution List (MCD) ..... AFSL
Approved Flight Manual [*FAA A publication*] (MCD) ..... AFM
Approved for Limited Production (MCD) ..... ALP
Approved for Release ..... AR
Approved Force Acquisition Objective [*Army*] (AABC) ..... AFAO
Approved Force Budget Objective [*Army*] (AABC) ..... AFBO
Approved Force Gross Requirement [*Army*] (AABC) ..... AFGR
Approved Force Inventory Objective [*Military*] ..... AFIC
Approved Force Inventory Objective [*Army*] (AABC) ..... AFIO
Approved Force Investment Level Requirement (AFIT) ..... AFILR
Approved Force Retention Stock [*Air Force*] (AFIT) ..... AFRS
Approved Force War Reserves (AFM) ..... AFWR
Approved Health Plan [*Medicine*] ..... AHP
Approved Item Name ..... AIN
Approved Item Name Reclassification Program [*DoD*] (AFIT) ..... AINRP
Approved MAPAD [*Military Assistance Program Address File*] **Change Letter** (AAGC) ..... AMCL
Approved Marine Devices Co. (MCD) ..... AMD
Approved Market [*Business term*] ..... AM
Approved Material Substitution List ..... AMSL
Approved Materials List [*NASA*] ..... AML
Approved Modernization Maintenance Program (AFM) ..... AMMP
Approved Operating Budget [*Army*] (AABC) ..... AOB
Approved Parts List ..... APL
Approved Prescription Services Ltd. [*British*] ..... APS
Approved Production Inspection System [*Manufacturing*] (MCD) ..... APIS
Approved Quality Assurance ..... AQA
Approved Research Institute ..... ARI
Approved Source List (SAA) ..... ASL
Approved Spare Parts List (MCD) ..... ASPL
Approved Species - Specfic Protocol [*Marine science*] (OSRA) ..... ASSP

Approved Species-Specific Protocol (USDC) ..... ASSP

Approved Study Structure ..... ASS

Approved Supplier Tab List ..... ASTL

Approved Suppliers' List (DNAB) ..... ASL

Approved System Requirement ..... ASR

Approved Tank Wagon ..... ATW

Approved Test Officer ..... ATO

Approved to British Standard [*British Standards Institution*] ..... ABS

Approved Training Organisation [*Manpower Services Commission*] (AIE) ..... ATO

Approved Type Certificate [*Governmental airworthiness certification for planes*] ..... ATC

Approved Vendors List ..... AVL

Approving Authority ..... AA

Approvisionnements et Services Canada [*Supply and Services Canada - SSC*] ..... ASC

Approximate [*Rate*] [*Value of the English pound*] ..... A

Approximate ..... APP

Approximate (ADA) ..... APPR

Approximate (EY) ..... APPROX

Approximate ..... APPRX

Approximate (VRA) ..... appx

Approximate (AFM) ..... APRX

Approximate Absolute [*Temperature*] ..... AA

Approximate Cubic Search [*Mathematics*] ..... ACS

Approximate Degrees of Freedom [*Statistics*] ..... ADF

Approximate Digestibility ..... AD

Approximate Exposure Time ..... AET

Approximate Lethal Concentration [*Medicine*] (DMAA) ..... ALC

Approximate Lethal Dose ..... ALD

Approximate Quadratic Search [*Mathematics*] ..... AQS

Approximate Ray Tracing [*Of seismic waves*] ..... ART

Approximate Theoretical Error Variance (MHDB) ..... ATEV

Approximately (DEN) ..... APRXLY

Approximately (WDMC) ..... apx

Approximation (DAVI) ..... APPROX

Approximation to English ..... ATE

Appurtenances (ROG) ..... APPURTS

AppWare Loadable Module [*Computer science*] (PCM) ..... ALM

Apraxia [*Neurology*] (DAVI) ..... aprax

Apres Jesus-Christ [*After Christ*] [*French*] ..... AP JC

Apres Livraison [*After Delivery of Goods*] [*French*] ..... AL

Apria Healthcare Group, Inc. [*NYSE symbol*] (SAG) ..... AHG

Apria Healthcare Group, Inc. [*NASDAQ symbol*] (SAG) ..... APRA

Apria Healthcare Group, Inc. [*Associated Press*] (SAG) ..... Apria

Apricot Producers of California (EA) ..... APC

April ..... A

April ..... AP

April ..... APL

April (AFM) ..... APR

April and October [*Denotes semiannual payments of interest or dividends in these months*] [*Business term*] ..... A & O

April Computing Executive [*Commercial firm British*] ..... ACE

April Fan Club (EA) ..... AFC

April Fools' Day ..... AFD

April, July, October, and January [*Denotes quarterly payments of interest or dividends in these months*] [*Business term*] ..... AJOJ

Aprobarbital [*Pharmacology*] (DAVI) ..... APRO

Aprogenex, Inc. [*AMEX symbol*] (SPSG) ..... APG

Aprogenex, Inc. [*Associated Press*] (SAG) ..... Aprognx

Apron [*Aviation*] ..... APN

Aprovecho Institute (EA) ..... AI

APS Holding 'A' [*NASDAQ symbol*] (TTSB) ..... APSI

APS Holding Corp. [*Associated Press*] (SAG) ..... APS Hld

APS Holding Corp. [*NASDAQ symbol*] (SAG) ..... APSI

APSDEP Information Network [*Islamabad, Pakistan*] [*Information service or system*] (IID) ..... APSDIN

Apt/Saint-Christol [*France ICAO location identifier*] (ICLI) ..... LFXI

APT Satellite Holdings Ltd. [*NYSE symbol*] (SAG) ..... ATS

Aptargroup, Inc. [*Associated Press*] (SAG) ..... Aptar

Aptargroup, Inc. [*NYSE symbol*] (SAG) ..... ATR

AptarGroup Inc. [*NYSE symbol*] (TTSB) ..... ATR

Aptitude (AABC) ..... APT

Aptitude Area ..... AA

Aptitude Area ..... APTA

Aptitude Assessment Battery Programming [*Computer science*] (IEEE) ..... AABP

Aptitude Index ..... AI

Aptitude Index Battery [*LIMRA*] ..... AIB

Aptitude Strategies (PDAA) ..... APSTRAT

Aptitude Test ..... AT

Aptitude Test Battery [*Educational test*] ..... ATB

Aptitude Test for Adults [*Psychoeducational test*] ..... AA

Aptitude Test for School Beginners [*Child development test*] ..... ASB

Aptitude-Treatment Interactions [*Education*] ..... ATI

Apud [*At, In the Works Of, According To*] [*Latin*] ..... AP

Apud Bonifacium [*Latin*] (DSA) ..... Ap Bon

Apud Bonifacium [*Latin*] (DSA) ..... Bon

Apud Gregorium [*Latin*] (DSA) ..... Ap Greg

Apud Justinianum [*Latin*] (DLA) ..... Ap Just

Apud Justinianum [*Latin*] (DLA) ..... Ap Justin

Apuleius [*Second century AD*] [*Classical studies*] (OCD) ..... Apul

Apus [*Constellation*] ..... Aps

Aputiteq [*Greenland*] [*ICAO location identifier*] (ICLI) ..... BGAT

Aqaba [*Jordan*] [*Airport symbol*] (OAG) ..... AQJ

Aqaba [*Jordan*] [*ICAO location identifier*] (ICLI) ..... OJAQ

Aqua [*Water*] [*Latin*] ..... A

Aqua [*Water*] [*Pharmacy*] ..... AQ

Aqua 1 Beverage [*Vancouver Stock Exchange symbol*] ..... AQB

Aqua Ammoniae [*Ammoniated Water*] [*Pharmacy*] (ROG) ..... AQ AMMON

Aqua Anethi [*Dill Water*] [*Pharmacy*] (ROG) ..... AQ ANETH

Aqua Anisi [*Anise Water*] [*Pharmacy*] (ROG) ..... AQ ANIS

Aqua Astricta [*Frozen Water*] [*Pharmacy*] (ROG) ..... AQ ASTR

Aqua Bulliens [*Boiling Water*] [*Pharmacy*] ..... AQ BULL

Aqua Bulliens [*Boiling Water*] [*Pharmacy*] (ROG) ..... AQ BULLIENS

Aqua Calida [*Hot Water*] [*Pharmacy*] ..... AQ CAL

Aqua Calida [*Hot Water*] [*Pharmacy*] (ROG) ..... AQ CALID

Aqua Care Sys Wrrt'A' [*NASDAQ symbol*] (TTSB) ..... AQCRW

Aqua Care Sys Wrrt'B' [*NASDAQ symbol*] (TTSB) ..... AOCRZ

Aqua Care Systems [*NASDAQ symbol*] (SAG) ..... AQCR

Aqua Care Systems [*Commercial firm Associated Press*] (SAG) ..... AquaC

Aqua Care Systems [*Commercial firm Associated Press*] (SAG) ..... AquaCre

Aqua Care Systems [*Commercial firm Associated Press*] (SAG) ..... AquC

Aqua Cinnamoni [*Cinnamon Water*] [*Pharmacy*] (ROG) ..... AQ CINNAM

Aqua Communis [*Tap Water*] [*Pharmacy*] ..... AQ COM

Aqua Communis [*Tap water*] [*Pharmacology*] (DAVI) ..... aq comm

Aqua Destillata [*Distilled Water*] [*Pharmacy*] ..... AQ DEST

Aqua Europa - European Federation for Water Treatment [*British*] (EAIO) ..... AEEFWT

Aqua Fervens [*Warm Water*] [*Pharmacy*] ..... AQ FERV

Aqua Fluviatilis [*River Water*] [*Pharmacy*] (ROG) ..... AQ FLUV

Aqua Fontis [*Spring Water*] [*Pharmacy*] (ROG) ..... AQ FONT

Aqua Fortis [*Sulphuric Acid*] [*Pharmacy*] (ROG) ..... AQ FORT

Aqua Frigida [*Cold Water*] [*Pharmacy*] ..... AQ FRIG

Aqua Frigida [*Cold Water*] [*Pharmacy*] (ROG) ..... AQ FRIGID

Aqua Gelida [*Cold Water*] [*Pharmacy*] ..... AQ GEL

Aqua Lung Dealers Association [*Defunct*] (EA) ..... ALDA

Aqua Marina [*Sea Water*] [*Pharmacy*] (ROG) ..... AQ MAR

Aqua Mentha [*Mint Water*] [*Pharmacy*] (ROG) ..... AQ MENTH

Aqua Mentha Piperitae [*Peppermint Water*] [*Pharmacy*] (ROG) ..... AQ MENTH PIP

Aqua Nivalis [*Snow Water*] [*Pharmacy*] (ROG) ..... AQ NIV

Aqua Pimentae [*Allspice Water*] [*Pharmacy*] (ROG) ..... AQ PIMENT

Aqua Pluvialis [*or Pluviatilis*] [*Rain Water*] [*Pharmacy*] (ROG) ..... AQ PLUV

Aqua Pura [*Pure Water*] [*Pharmacy*] (ROG) ..... AQ PUR

Aqua Rosa [*Rose Water*] [*Pharmacy*] (ROG) ..... AQ ROS

Aqua Ruta [*Rue Water*] [*Pharmacy*] (ROG) ..... AQ RUT

Aqua Soda [*Soda Water*] [*Pharmacy*] (ROG) ..... AQ SOD

Aqua Tepida [*Lukewarm Water*] [*Pharmacy*] ..... AQ TEP

Aqua Tepida [*Lukewarm Water*] [*Pharmacy*] (ROG) ..... AQ TEPID

Aqua-Cat Catamaran Sailing Association (EA) ..... ACSA

Aquaculture Information Center [*Department of Agriculture Information service or system*] (IID) ..... AIC

Aquaculture Research Center [*Texas A & M University*] [*Research center*] (RCD) ..... ARC

Aquada, PR [*Television station call letters*] ..... WQHA

Aquadag [*Graphite coating*] (NTCM) ..... DAG

Aquagenic Pruritus [*Medicine*] ..... AP

Aquagenix, Inc. [*Associated Press*] (SAG) ..... Aqgnx

Aquagenix, Inc. [*Associated Press*] (SAG) ..... Aquagnx

Aquagenix, Inc. [*NASDAQ symbol*] (SAG) ..... AQUX

Aquagenix Inc. Wrrt [*NASDAQ symbol*] (TTSB) ..... AQUXW

Aquair Luftfahrt GmbH [*Germany ICAO designator*] (FAAC) ..... AQU

Aquamarine [*Philately*] ..... Aqua

Aquanatural Co. [*NASDAQ symbol*] (TTSB) ..... AQQA

Aquaplaning Risk Indicator for Landings ..... APRIL

Aquarian Digest International [*A publication*] ..... ADI

Aquarian Research Foundation (EA) ..... ARF

Aquarion Co. [*Associated Press*] (SAG) ..... Aquarn

Aquarion Co. [*NYSE symbol*] (SPSG) ..... WTR

Aquarius [*Constellation*] ..... Aqar

Aquarius [*Constellation*] ..... Aqr

Aquarius [*Constellation*] ..... AQU

Aquarius Resources Ltd. [*Vancouver Stock Exchange symbol*] ..... AQR

Aquarius Seafarms [*Vancouver Stock Exchange symbol*] ..... AQS

Aquatic ..... AQUA

Aquatic Airlines [*ICAO designator*] (AD) ..... VZ

Aquatic Based Recreation Survey [*Environmental Protection Agency*] ..... ABRS

Aquatic Ecosystem Objectives Committee [*Great Lakes Science Advisory Board*] [*Canada*] ..... AEOC

Aquatic Environments Ltd., Calgary, AB, Canada [*Library symbol Library of Congress*] (LCLS) ..... CaACAqE

Aquatic Environments Ltd., Calgary, Alberta [*Library symbol National Library of Canada*] (NLC) ..... ACAQE

Aquatic Exercise Association (EA) ..... AEA

Aquatic Federation of Canada ..... AFC

Aquatic Information Retrieval (GNE) ..... ACQUIRE

Aquatic Information Retrieval Database [*Chemical Information Systems, Inc.*] [*Information service or system*] ..... AQUIRE

Aquatic Nuisance Species [*Oceanography*] ..... ANS

Aquatic Plant ..... AP

Aquatic Plant Control Research Program [*Army Corps of Engineers Waterways Experiment Station*] (MSC) ..... APCRP

Aquatic Plant Management Society (EA) ..... APMS

Aquatic Processes and Effects Group [*Army*] ..... APEG

Aquatic Research Institute (EA) ..... ARI

Aquatic Resource Division [*Environmental Protection Agency*] (GFGA) ..... ARD

Aquatic Sciences and Fisheries Abstracts [*Database producer*] (NITA) ..... ASFA

Aquatic Sciences and Fisheries Information System [*Food and Agriculture Organization*] [*United Nations*] (IID) ..... ASFIS

Aquatic Sciences Information Retrieval Center [*University of Rhode Island*] ..... ASIRC

Aquatic Toxicity ..... AQTX

Aquatic Toxicity [Environmental science] .... AT
Aquatint (VRA) .... aqut
Aqueduct (VRA) .... aqdt
Aqueous [Medicine] (DMAA) .... A
Aqueous .... AQ
Aqueous (AAMN) .... AQU
Aqueous Extraction Process .... AEP
Aqueous Film-Forming Foam [Firefighting chemical for ships] .... AFFF
Aqueous Flare Response [Physiology] .... AFR
Aqueous Homogeneous Reactor .... AHR
Aqueous Humor [Anatomy] (CPH) .... AH
Aqueous Makeup [Room] [Nuclear energy] (NRCH) .... AMU
Aqueous Powder Suspension [For coating plastics] .... APS
Aqueous Procaine Penicillin G [Antibiotic] .... APPG
Aqueous Solubility Database [Chemical Information Systems, Inc.]
  [Information service or system] (CRD) .... SOLUB
Aqueous Solution .... AS
Aqueous Suspension .... AS
Aqueous to Organic [Ratio] .... A/O
Aquidauana [Brazil] [Airport symbol] (AD) .... AQU
Aquifer Storage and Recovery [Water supply technology] .... ASR
Aquifer Test Solver .... AQTESOLV
Aquifer Test Toolbox [Computer science] .... ATT
Aquifer Test Toolbox .... ATT
Aquifer Thermal Energy Storage .... ATES
Aquila [Constellation] .... Aqil
Aquila [Constellation] .... Aql
Aquila [Italy] [Seismograph station code, US Geological Survey] (SEIS) .... AQU
Aquila Air, Inc. [FAA designator] (FAAC) .... CNH
Aquila Air, Inc. [ICAO designator] (FAAC) .... PCY
Aquila Air Ltd. [Canada ICAO designator] (FAAC) .... AQL
Aquila Airways Ltd. .... AQU
Aquila Biopharmaceuticals, Inc. [NASDAQ symbol] (SAG) .... AQLA
Aquila Biopharmaceuticals, Inc. [Associated Press] (SAG) .... AquilaB
Aquila Gas Pipeline [NYSE symbol] (SPSG) .... AQP
Aquila Gas Pipeline Corp. [Associated Press] (SAG) .... AquilaG
Aquila's Greek Translation of the Bible [A publication] (BJA) .... Aq
Aquinas College, Grand Rapids, MI [OCLC symbol] (OCLC) .... EXQ
Aquinas College, Grand Rapids, MI [Library symbol Library of Congress]
  (LCLS) .... MiGrA
Aquinas High School, Augusta, GA [Library symbol Library of Congress]
  (LCLS) .... GAuAH
Aquinas Institute, Dubuque, IA [Library symbol Library of Congress]
  (LCLS) .... IaDuA
Aquinas Institute Library, Rochester, NY [OCLC symbol] (OCLC) .... RVO
Aquinas Junior College, Nashville, TN [Library symbol] [Library of
  Congress] (LCLS) .... TNAC
Ara Appaloosa and Foundation Breeders International (EA) .... AAFBI
ARA Historical Foundation, ARA Industries, Philadelphia, PA [Closed]
  [Library symbol] [Library of Congress] (LCLS) .... PPARA
Arab [or Arabic] (BJA) .... A
Arab Agricultural Aviation [Egypt] [ICAO designator] (FAAC) .... AGC
Arab Air Cargo [Jordan] [ICAO designator] (FAAC) .... AWF
Arab Air Carriers Organization (EAIO) .... AACO
Arab Airways (Jerusalem) Ltd. .... AAJ
Arab, AL [FM radio station call letters] .... WCRQ
Arab, AL [AM radio station call letters] .... WRAB
Arab Amateur Athletic Federation [See also CAA] (EAIO) ...... AAAF
Arab American Democratic Federation (EA) .... AADF
Arab American Institute (EA) .... AAI
Arab American Medical Association (EA) .... AAMA
Arab American Republican Federation [Defunct] (EA) .... AARF
Arab Authority for Agricultural Investment and Development [Khartoum,
  Sudan] (EAIO) .... AAAID
Arab Bankers' Association .... ABA
Arab Canadian Association of the Atlantic Provinces (AC) .... ACAAP
Arab Center for the Study of Arid Zones and Dry Lands [of the League of
  Arab States] [Syria] [Research center] (IRC) .... ACSAD
Arab Common Market [United Arab Republic, Iraq, Jordan, Kuwait, and
  Syria] .... ACM
Arab Communist Party [Political party] .... ACP
Arab Co-Operation Council (ECON) .... ACC
Arab Deterrent Force [Palestine] (PD) .... ADF
Arab Federation for Food Industries (EA) .... AFFI
Arab Federation for Technical Education [Baghdad, Iraq] (EAIO) ..... AFTE
Arab Federation for the Organs of the Deaf [Damascus, Syria] (EAIO) .... AFOD
Arab Federation of Chemical Fertilizer Producers (EA) ..... AFCFP
Arab Fund for Technical Assistance to Arab and African Countries .... AFTA
Arab Gulf States Information Documentation Center [Information service or
  system] (IID) .... AGSIDC
Arab Gulf States Information Documentation Center [Information service or
  system] (IID) .... GSIDC
Arab Historians Association (EAIO) .... ARABHA
Arab Horse Society (EAIO) .... AHS
Arab Industrial Development Organization (EA) .... AIDO
Arab Information Bank [Information service or system] (IID) .... AIB
Arab Information Center, Arab League Office, Washington, DC [Library
  symbol] [Library of Congress] (LCLS) .... DArI
Arab Inter-Parliamentary Union [Syrian Arab Republic] (EAIO) ..... AIPU
Arab Latin American Bank .... ARLABANK
Arab Lawyers Union [See also UAA] [Cairo, Egypt] (EAIO) ..... ALU
Arab League .... AL
Arab League Educational, Cultural, and Scientific Organization
  [Tunisia] .... ALECSO
Arab Liberation Army .... ALA

Arab Liberation Front .... ALF
Arab Maghreb Union [Morocco, Algeria, Mauritania, Tunisia, and Libya] .... AMU
Arab Malaysian Development Bank .... AMDB
Arab Monetary Fund .... AMF
Arab Network of America (BARN) .... ANA
Arab News Agency .... ANA
Arab Oil and Economic Review [A publication] .... AOER
Arab Organization for Agricultural Development (EAIO) ..... AOAD
Arab Organization for Standardization and Metrology (EAIO) ... ASMO
Arab Organization of Administrative Sciences (EAIO) .... AOAS
Arab Organization of Petroleum Exporting Countries ...... AOPEC
Arab Petroleum Investments Corp. (ECON) .... APICORP
Arab Petroleum Training Institute [Defunct] (EA) .... APTI
Arab Political and Cultural Organization [Iran] (PD) .... APCO
Arab Postal Union .... APU
Arab Relief Agency .... ARA
Arab Report & Record [A publication] .... ARR
Arab Republic of Egypt .... ARE
Arab Republic of National Telephone Organization (ACRL) ..... ARENTO
Arab Research Centre [British] (CB) .... ARC
Arab Revolution News Agency .... ARNA
Arab Roads Association [Cairo, Egypt] (EAIO) .... ARA
Arab Satellite Communications Organization [Saudi Arabia]
  [Telecommunications] .... ARABSAT
Arab Satellite Communications Organization [League of Arab States]
  [Riyadh, Saudi Arabia] (EAIO) .... ASCO
Arab Socialist Party [Egypt] [Political party] (PPW) .... ASP
Arab Socialist Party [Syria] [Political party] (PPW) .... ASP
Arab Socialist Renaissance Party [Syria] .... ASRP
Arab Socialist Union [Syria] [Political party] (PPW) .... ASU
Arab Sports Confederation [Saudi Arabia] (EAIO) .... ASC
Arab States [MARC geographic area code Library of Congress] (LCCP) .... ma----
Arab States Broadcasting Union .... ASBU
Arab Sugar Federation [Khartoum, Sudan] (EAIO) .... ASF
Arab Telecommunications Union (EA) .... ATU
Arab Towns Organization [Safat, Kuwait] (EAIO) .... ATO
Arab Tunisian Bank .... ATB
Arab Union for Cement and Building Materials [See also UACMC]
  (EAIO) .... AUCBM
Arab Urban Development Institute (EA) .... AUDI
Arab Wings Co. [Jordan] [ICAO designator] (FAAC) .... AWS
Arab Women's Council (EA) .... AWC
Arab World and Islamic Resources and School Services (EA) ..... AWAIR
Arab-American Media Society (EA) .... AAMS
Arab-American Media Society (EA) .... AMS
Arab-American Press Guild (EA) .... AAPG
Arab-Burundi Bank SARL (EY) .... ABB
Arabesque [Embossed] [Bookbinding] (ROG) .... ARA
Arabesque (VRA) .... arbsq
Arabesque Resources Ltd. [Vancouver Stock Exchange symbol] ...... AAR
Arabia (VRA) .... Arab
Arabia [ICAO designator] (AD) .... RZ
Arabian .... ARBN
Arabian Bank Trade [Saudi Arabia] .... ABT
Arabian Bulk Trade [Saudi Arabia] [Commercial firm] .... ABT
Arabian Communication Satellite .... ARCOMSAT
Arabian Exhibition Management WLL [Manama, Bahrain] ..... AEM
Arabian Horse Club Registry of America [Later, AHR] ...... AHCRA
Arabian Horse Owners Foundation (EA) .... AHOF
Arabian Horse Registry of America (EA) .... AHR
Arabian Horse Trust (EA) .... AHT
Arabian Jockey Club (EA) .... AJC
Arabian Peninsula [MARC geographic area code Library of Congress]
  (LCCP) .... ar----
Arabian Sea and Area [MARC geographic area code Library of Congress]
  (LCCP) .... au----
Arabian Shield Dev [NASDAQ symbol] (TTSB) .... ARSD
Arabian Shield Development Co. [Associated Press] (SAG) ..... ArabSh
Arabian Shield Development Co. [NASDAQ symbol] (NQ) .... ARSD
Arabian Sport Horse Association (EA) .... ASHA
Arabian-American Oil Co. .... ARAMCO
Arabian-Nubian Shield [Geology] .... ANS
Arabic .... AR
Arabic [MARC language code Library of Congress] (LCCP) ...... ara
Arabic [Language, etc.] .... ARA
Arabidopsis Information Service .... AIS
Arabinofuranosyladenine [or Adenine Arabinoside] [Also, Vira-A Antiviral
  compound] .... ara-A
Arabinofuranosylfluorocytosine [Also, FCA] [Antineoplastic drug] ...... ara-FC
Arabinofuranosylthymine [Biochemistry] .... ara-T
Arabinogalactan Protein [Biochemistry] .... AGP
Arabinose [One-letter symbol; see Ara] [A sugar] .... a
Arabinose [Also, a] [A sugar] .... Ara
Arabinose (DMAA) .... ara
Arabinose Binding Protein [Biochemistry] .... ABP
Arabinoside .... Ar
Arabinosylazacytidine [Biochemistry] .... AAC
Arabinosylhypoxanthine [Biochemistry] .... ara-H
Arabinosylmercaptopurine [Antineoplastic drug] .... ara-MP
Arabis Mosaic Virus [Plant pathology] .... ARMV
Arab-Jewish Women's Dialogue for Peace [Defunct] (EA) .... AJWDFP
, ara-C , Prednisone [Vincristine] [Cytarabine] [Antineoplastic drug
  regimen] .... ROAP
, ara-C , Prednisone, Bleomycin [Vincristine] [Cytarabine] [Antineoplastic drug
  regimen] .... HOAP-BLEO

Aracaju [*Brazil*] [*Airport symbol*] (OAG) ... AJU
Aracaju/Santa Maria [*Brazil ICAO location identifier*] (ICLI) ... SBAR
Aracatuba [*Brazil*] [*Airport symbol*] (OAG) ... ARU
Aracatuba [*Brazil ICAO location identifier*] (ICLI) ... SBAU
Arachidonic Acid [*Biochemistry*] ... AA
Arachidonic Linoleic Acid Ratio [*Clinical chemistry*] ... ALR
Arachnoid Cyst of the Middle Fossa [*Medicine*] (DMAA) ... ACMF
Arachnology ... ARACH
Aracruz Celulose SA [*NYSE symbol*] (SPSG) ... ARA
Aracruz Celulose SA [*Associated Press*] (SAG) ... Aracruz
Aracruz Celulose SA [*Associated Press*] (SAG) ... Aracrz
Aracruz Celulose S.A. ADS [*NYSE symbol*] (TTSB) ... ARA
Aracytidine [*Cytarabine*] [*Also, CA, CAR*] [*Antineoplastic drug*] ... ara-C
Aracytidine, Hydroxyurea [*Antineoplastic drug regimen*] ... ara-C-HU
Arad [*Romania*] [*Airport symbol*] (OAG) ... ARW
Arad [*Romania*] [*ICAO location identifier*] (ICLI) ... LRAR
Aradigm Corp. [*Associated Press*] (SAG) ... Aradigm
Aradigm Corp. [*NASDAQ symbol*] (SAG) ... ARDM
Aragarcas [*Brazil*] [*Airport symbol*] (OAG) ... ARS
Aragip [*Papua New Guinea*] [*Airport symbol*] (OAG) ... ARP
Araguacema [*Brazil*] [*Airport symbol*] (AD) ... AGX
Araguaina [*Brazil*] [*Airport symbol*] (OAG) ... AUX
Arajuno [*Ecuador*] [*ICAO location identifier*] (ICLI) ... SEAR
Arak [*Iran*] [*ICAO location identifier*] (ICLI) ... OIHR
Arakan Independence Organization [*Myanmar*] [*Political party*] ... AIO
Arakan Liberation Army [*Myanmar*] [*Political party*] (EY) ... ALA
Arakan Liberation Party [*Myanmar*] [*Political party*] ... ALP
Arakhin [*or Arakin*] (BJA) ... Ar
Arakis Capital [*Vancouver Stock Exchange symbol*] ... AKS
Arakis Energy [*NASDAQ symbol*] (TTSB) ... AKSEF
Arakis Energy Corp. [*NASDAQ symbol*] (SAG) ... AKSE
Arakis Energy Corp. [*Associated Press*] (SAG) ... Arakis
Aral [*Kazakhstan*] [*FAA designator*] (FAAC) ... AZD
Aralsk [*Former USSR ICAO location identifier*] (ICLI) ... UATA
Aram Public Library, Delavan, WI [*Library symbol Library of Congress*] (LCLS) ... WDA
Aramac [*Australia Airport symbol*] (OAG) ... AXC
Aramaeische Papyri aus Elephantine [*A publication*] (BJA) ... APE
Aramaic [*Language, etc.*] ... A
Aramaic [*Language, etc.*] (ROG) ... AR
Aramaic [*Language, etc.*] ... ARAM
Aramaic [*MARC language code Library of Congress*] (LCCP) ... arc
[*The*] **Aramaic of the Old Testament** [*A publication*] (BJA) ... AOT
Aramaic Papyri Discovered at Assuan [*A publication*] (BJA) ... AP
Aramco Services Co., Corporate Information Center, Houston, TX [*Library symbol*] [*Library of Congress*] (LCLS) ... TxHAS
Aramed, Inc. Gensia Pharmaceuticals [*NASDAQ symbol*] (SAG) ... ARAM
Aramed Incorporated Gensia Pharmaceuticals [*Associated Press*] (SAG) ... Aramed
Aramex International Ltd. [*NASDAQ symbol*] (SAG) ... ARMX
Aramex International Ltd. [*Associated Press*] (SAG) ... ArmxIntl
Aramid Reinforced Aluminum Laminate (MCD) ... ARALL
Aramis en Rames Automatisees de Modules Independants dans les Stations [*Arrangement in Automated Trains of Independent Modules in Stations*] [*France*] ... ARAMMIS
Aran Energy Ltd. [*NASDAQ symbol*] (SAG) ... ARAN
Aran Energy Ltd. [*Associated Press*] (SAG) ... AranEgy
Arandis [*Namibia*] [*ICAO location identifier*] (ICLI) ... FAAR
Aranjuez [*Costa Rica*] [*ICAO location identifier*] (ICLI) ... MRAJ
Aranuka [*Kiribati*] [*Airport symbol*] (OAG) ... AAK
Aranuka [*Kiribati*] [*ICAO location identifier*] (ICLI) ... NGUK
Arapaho [*MARC language code Library of Congress*] (LCCP) ... arp
Arapahoe Community College, Littleton, CO [*Library symbol Library of Congress*] (LCLS) ... CoLiAJ
Arapahoe Community College, Littleton, CO [*OCLC symbol*] (OCLC) ... DVZ
Arapahoe County Evaluation Center, Englewood, CO [*Library symbol Library of Congress*] (LCLS) ... CoEnE
Arapahoe County School District 6, Littleton, CO [*Library symbol Library of Congress*] (LCLS) ... CoLiSD
Arapahoe Mining [*Vancouver Stock Exchange symbol*] ... ATH
Arapahoe Regional Library District, Littleton, CO [*Library symbol Library of Congress*] (LCLS) ... CoLiA
Arapicos [*Ecuador*] [*ICAO location identifier*] (ICLI) ... SEAP
Arapuni [*New Zealand*] [*Seismograph station code, US Geological Survey Closed*] (SEIS) ... ARA
Arar [*Saudi Arabia*] [*ICAO location identifier*] (ICLI) ... OERR
Arar [*Saudi Arabia*] [*Airport symbol*] (OAG) ... RAE
Araracuara [*Colombia*] [*Airport symbol*] (OAG) ... ACR
Araraquara [*Brazil*] [*Airport symbol Obsolete*] (OAG) ... AQA
Ararat [*Australia Airport symbol Obsolete*] (OAG) ... ARY
Aratea [*of Germanicus*] [*Classical studies*] (OCD) ... Arat
Aratica [*French Polynesia*] [*ICAO location identifier*] (ICLI) ... NTGR
Arator Society [*Defunct*] (EA) ... AS
Aratus [*of Plutarch*] [*Classical studies*] (OCD) ... Arat
Arauca [*Colombia*] [*Airport symbol*] (OAG) ... AUC
Arauca/Santiago Perez [*Colorado ICAO location identifier*] (ICLI) ... SKUC
Araucanian [*MARC language code Library of Congress*] (LCCP) ... arn
Aravco Ltd. [*British ICAO designator*] (FAAC) ... ARV
Arawa [*Papua New Guinea*] [*Airport symbol*] (OAG) ... RAW
Arawak [*MARC language code Library of Congress*] (LCCP) ... arw
Arawak Airlines (OAG) ... LK
Arax Airlines Ltd. [*Nigeria*] [*ICAO designator*] (FAAC) ... RXA
Araxa [*Brazil*] [*Airport symbol*] (OAG) ... AAX
Araxos [*Greece*] [*ICAO location identifier*] (ICLI) ... LGRX
Arba Minch [*Ethiopia*] [*ICAO location identifier*] (ICLI) ... HAAM
Arba Mintch [*Ethiopia*] [*Airport symbol*] (AD) ... AMH
Arba Sicula [*Sicilian Dawn*] (EA) ... AS
Arbeidernes Kommunistiske Parti [*Workers' Communist Party*] [*Norway Political party*] (PPE) ... AKP
Arbeidernes Kommunistparti (Marxist-Leninistene) [*Workers Communist Party (Marxist-Leninist)*] [*Norway Political party*] ... AKP (M-L)
Arbeit und Sitte in Palaestina [*A publication*] (BJA) ... AS
Arbeit und Sitte in Palaestina [*A publication*] (BJA) ... AuS
Arbeitgeber [*Employer*] [*German*] ... Arbeitg
Arbeits Gemeinschaft der Offentlichrechtlichen Rundfunk Anstalten der Bundesrepublik Deutschland [*Broadcasting organization*] ... ARD
Arbeitseinheit [*Work Unit*] [*German*] ... AE
Arbeitsgemeinschaft [*Study Group*] [*German*] ... Arbeitsgem
Arbeitsgemeinschaft Alpenlaender [*Working Group of Alpine Regions*] (EAIO) ... ARGE ALP
Arbeitsgemeinschaft der Bibliotheken und Dokumentationsstellen der Osteuropa-, Sudosteuropa und DDR-Forschung [*Association of Libraries and Documentation Centres for the Study of Eastern Europe, South-Eastern Europe and the German Democratic Republic*] (PDAA) ... ABDOSD
Arbeitsgemeinschaft der Grossfochungseinrichtungen [*The Association of National Research Centers of the Federal Republic of Germany*] [*Computer science*] (TNIG) ... AGFNET
Arbeitsgemeinschaft der Verbande der Europaischen Schloss- und Beschlagindustrie [*European Federation of Associations of Lock and Builders' Hardware Manufacturers*] (EAIO) ... ARGE
Arbeitsgemeinschaft Europaeischer Chorverbaende [*Federation of European Choirs*] [*Utrecht, Netherlands*] (EAIO) ... AGEC
Arbeitsgemeinschaft Europaeischer Chorverbaende [*European Choral Association - ECA*] (EA) ... EUROCHOR
Arbeitsgericht [*Labor Court*] [*German*] ... AG
Arbeitsgericht [*Labor Court*] [*German*] (DLA) ... Arb G
Arbeitsgerichtsgesetz [*Law on labor courts*] [*German*] (ILCA) ... Arb GG
Arbeitsgruppe fuer Menschenrechte [*Germany*] ... AFM
Arbeitskraft ... AK
Arbeitsschutz und Arbeitsmedizin [*Industrial Safety and Medicine*] [*German*] ... A & A
Arbeitsschutzinformationssystem [*Information System for Occupational Safety and Health*] [*West Germany*] (IID) ... ASIS
Arbeitsverwendungsfaehig [*Fit for labor duty only*] [*German military - World War II*] ... AV
Arbejdsloshedsstatistikkens Bruger-Bank [*Danmarks Statistik*] [*Denmark Information service or system*] (CRD) ... ABBA
Arberia Airlines [*Albania*] [*FAA designator*] (FAAC) ... ABE
Arberia Airways [*Albania*] [*FAA designator*] (FAAC) ... ABW
Arbet International Ltd. [*Hungary ICAO designator*] (FAAC) ... RBE
Arbetarnas och Smabrukarnas Socialdemokratiska Foerbund [*Social Democratic League of Workers and Smallholders*] [*Finland Political party*] (PPE) ... ASSF
Arbetarpartiet Kommunisterna [*Communist Workers' Party*] [*Sweden*] (PPE) ... APK
Arbetsmarknadsstyrelsen [*National Labor Market Board*] [*Sweden*] ... AMS
Arbiter (ADA) ... ARB
Arbitrage Pricing Theory [*Finance*] ... APT
Arbitrageur [*Stock exchange term*] ... Arb
Arbitrageur [*Stock exchange term*] (ODBW) ... ARB
Arbitrarily Primed Polymerase Chain Reaction [*Genetics*] ... APPCR
Arbitrary (MSA) ... ARB
Arbitrary ... ARBRY
Arbitrary Correction to Hit [*Gunnery term*] [*Navy*] ... ACTH
Arbitrary Degree of Freedom (MCD) ... ADOF
Arbitrary Evolution Index (DMAA) ... AEI
Arbitrary Function Generator (MUGU) ... AFG
Arbitrary Unit ... AU
Arbitrary Waveform Generator [*Electronics*] ... AWG
Arbitrated Access Timer [*Telecommunications*] (OSI) ... AAT
Arbitration (DLA) ... Arb
Arbitration (AAGC) ... ARB
Arbitration (DLA) ... Arbitr
Arbitration (ADA) ... ARBITRN
Arbitration (ROG) ... ARBRON
Arbitration (WGA) ... ARBTRN
Arbitration and Award [*Legal term*] (DLA) ... ARB & A
Arbitration & Mediation Institute of Canada Inc. [*Institut d'Arbitrage et de Mediation du Canada Inc.*] [*Formerly, Arbitrators' Institute of Canada*] (AC) ... AMIC
Arbitration & Mediation Institute of Saskatchewan Inc. (AC) ... AMIS
Arbitration as an Alternative (DICI) ... AAA
Arbitration Journal (AAGC) ... Arb J
Arbitration Law: A Digest of Court Decisions [*A publication*] (DLA) ... Arb L Dig
Arbitrator (DLA) ... Arb
Arbitrator (ROG) ... ARBR
Arbitrator (ROG) ... ARBROR
Arbitron Information on Demand [*Marketing service*] (DOAD) ... AID
Arbitron Radio Summary Data [*Arbitron Ratings Co.*] [*Information service or system*] ... ARB
Arbitron's Information on Demand [*Arbitron Co.*] [*Information service or system*] (NTCM) ... AID
Arboga [*Sweden ICAO location identifier*] (ICLI) ... ESQO
Arbois [*France ICAO location identifier*] (ICLI) ... LFGD
Arboletas [*Colombia*] [*Airport symbol*] (OAG) ... ARO
Arbor Drugs [*Associated Press*] (SAG) ... ArborD
Arbor Drugs [*NASDAQ symbol*] (TTSB) ... ARBR
Arbor Drugs, Inc. [*NASDAQ symbol*] (NQ) ... ARBR
Arbor Health Care Co. [*NASDAQ symbol*] (SAG) ... AHCC
Arbor Health Care Co. [*Associated Press*] (SAG) ... ArborHl

Arbor Property Tr [*NYSE symbol*] (TTSB) .... ABR
Arbor Property Trust Co. [*Formerly, EQK Green Acres Trust*] [*NYSE symbol*] (SAG) .... ABR
Arbor Property Trust Co. [*Formerly, EQK Green Acres Trust*] [*Associated Press*] (SAG) .... ArborPT
Arbor Resources, Inc. [*Vancouver Stock Exchange symbol*] .... AOR
Arbor Software [*NASDAQ symbol*] (TTSB) .... ARSW
Arbor Software Corp. [*Associated Press*] (SAG) .... ArborSft
Arbor Software Corp. [*NASDAQ symbol*] (SAG) .... ARSW
Arboricultural Association (EA) .... AA
Arboriculture .... ARBOR
Arbra [*Sweden ICAO location identifier*] (ICLI) .... ESUB
Arbuthnot's Select Criminal Cases [*Madras*] [*A publication*] (DLA) .... Arbuth
Arc (ABBR) .... A
Arc Brazing .... AB
ARC Cap Wrrt'A' [*NASDAQ symbol*] (TTSB) .... ARCCW
ARC Cap Wrrt'B' [*NASDAQ symbol*] (TTSB) .... ARCCZ
ARC Capital [*Associated Press*] (SAG) .... ARC
ARC Capital [*NASDAQ symbol*] (SAG) .... ARCC
ARC Capital [*Associated Press*] (SAG) .... ARCCap
ARC Capital [*NASDAQ symbol*] (SAG) .... ARCO
ARC Capital Cl'A' [*NASDAQ symbol*] (TTSB) .... ARCCA
Arc Current Time Simulator .... ACTS
Arc Cutting [*Welding*] .... AC
Arc Data Monitor [*Welding*] [*Automotive engineering*] .... ADM
Arc Detector Unit .... ADU
Arc Drop Voltage .... ADV
Arc Gas Heater .... AGH
Arc Heater Housing .... AHH
Arc Heating Device .... AHD
ARC International Corp. [*Associated Press*] (SAG) .... ARC
ARC International Corp. [*AMEX symbol*] (SPSG) .... ATV
ARC Intl. [*AMEX symbol*] (TTSB) .... ATV
Arc Jet .... AJ
Arc Lamp Assembly .... ALA
Arc Lamp Igniter .... ALI
Arc LASER Light .... ALL
Arc LASER Light Pump .... ALLP
Arc Melting Furnace .... AMF
Arc Resistance Tester .... ART
Arc Spraying [*Welding*] .... ASP
Arc Tangent Mechanism .... ATM
Arc Vacuum Cast .... AVC
ARC [*Agricultural Research Council*] Weed Research Organization [*Research center British*] (IRC) .... WRO
Arc Weld (KSC) .... ARC/W
Arc Welding .... AW
Arc Welding Machine .... AWM
Arc Xenon Lamp .... AXL
Arca Aerovias Colombians Ltda. [*Colombia*] [*ICAO designator*] (FAAC) .... AKC
Arcachon/La Teste De Buch [*France ICAO location identifier*] (ICLI) .... LFCH
Arcade (MCD) .... ARC
Arcade [*Commonly used*] (OPSA) .... ARC
Arcade .... ARC
Arcade [*Commonly used*] (OPSA) .... ARCADE
Arcade & Attica Railroad Corp. (IIA) .... A & A
Arcade & Attica Railroad Corp. [*AAR code*] .... ARA
Arcadia, CA [*FM radio station call letters*] (RBYB) .... KLYY-FM
Arcadia, CA [*FM radio station call letters*] .... KMAX
Arcadia, FL [*AM radio station call letters*] .... WKGF
Arcadia, FL [*FM radio station call letters*] .... WKGF-FM
Arcadia, FL [*FM radio station call letters*] (RBYB) .... WWRZ-FM
Arcadia Public Library, Arcadia, CA [*Library symbol Library of Congress*] (LCLS) .... CAr
Arcadian Corp. [*NYSE symbol*] (SAG) .... ACA
Arcadian Corp. Mand Cv Pfd [*NYSE symbol*] (TTSB) .... ACAPrA
Arcadian Partners Ltd. [*Associated Press*] (SAG) .... Arcadn
Arcana Workshops [*Teaches philosophy of Alice A. Bailey toward human relations*] (EA) .... AW
Arcane Order [*Defunct*] (EA) .... AO
ARCAS [*Atlantic Research Corporation Atmospheric Sounding Missile*] Piggyback Emulsion Experiment (MUGU) .... APEX
Arcata [*California*] [*Seismograph station code, US Geological Survey*] (SEIS) .... ARC
[*The*] Arcata & Mad River Rail Road Co. [*AAR code*] .... AMR
Arcata, CA [*Television station call letters*] .... KAEF
Arcata, CA [*AM radio station call letters*] .... KATA
Arcata, CA [*FM radio station call letters*] .... KHSU
Arcata, CA [*FM radio station call letters*] .... KXGO
Arcata Microfilm Corp., Winston-Salem, NC [*Library symbol Library of Congress*] (LCLS) .... AmC
Arcata Public Library, Arcata, CA [*Library symbol Library of Congress*] (LCLS) .... CArc
Arcata-Eureka [*California*] [*Airport symbol*] (AD) .... ACV
Arcato [*With the Bow*] [*Music*] .... ARC
Arcato [*With the Bow*] [*Music*] (ROG) .... ARCO
Arcavacata [*Italy*] [*Seismograph station code, US Geological Survey*] (SEIS) .... ACI
Arch (VRA) .... arh
Arch Communications Group [*NASDAQ symbol*] (SPSG) .... APGR
Arch Communications Group, Inc. [*Associated Press*] (SAG) .... ArchCm
Arch Development Corp. [*Vancouver Stock Exchange symbol*] .... ARV
Arch Petroleum [*Associated Press*] (SAG) .... ArchPet
Arch Petroleum, Inc. [*NASDAQ symbol*] (NQ) .... ARCH
Archaeologia Aeliana [*A publication*] (OCD) .... Arch Ael
Archaeologiae Christianae Doctor [*Doctor of Christian Archeology*] .... ACD

Archaeological Conservancy (EA) .... AC
Archaeological Institute of America (EA) .... AIA
Archaeological Journal [*A publication*] (OCD) .... Arch Journ
Archaeological Reports [*A publication*] (OCD) .... Arch Rep
Archaeological Research, Environment Canada [*Recherches Archeologiques, Environnement Canada*] Ottawa, Ontario [*Library symbol National Library of Canada*] (NLC) .... OOEAB
Archaeological Resources Management Service [*Ball State Univesity*] [*Research center*] (RCD) .... ARMS
Archaeological Resources Protection Act .... ARPA
Archaeological Sites Data Base [*Tucson*] [*Information service or system*] (IID) .... AZSITE
Archaeological Society of Alberta (AC) .... ASA
Archaeological Society of British Columbia (AC) .... ASBC
Archaeological Survey Association of Southern California, La Verne, CA [*Library symbol Library of Congress*] (LCLS) .... CLavA
Archäologischer Anzeiger in Jahrbuch des [*Kaiserlichen*] Deutschen Archäologischen Instituts [*A publication*] (OCD) .... Arch Anz
Archaeology [*or Archaeologist*] .... ARCHAE
Archaeology .... ARCHAEOL
Archaeology (VRA) .... archeo
Archaeology Abroad (EAIO) .... AA
Archaeology and the Religion of Israel [*A publication*] (BJA) .... ARI
[*The*] Archaeology of Palestine [*A publication*] (BJA) .... AP
[*The*] Archaeology of Palestine and the Bible [*A publication*] (BJA) .... APB
Archaeology Research Program [*Southern Methodist University*] [*Research center*] (RCD) .... ARP
Archaeology Subsection Office, Prairie Region Library, Parks Canada [*Recherches Archeologiques, Bibliotheque de la Region des Pres, Parcs Canada*] Winnipeg, Manitoba [*Library symbol National Library of Canada*] (NLC) .... MWPCPA
Archaeus Project (EA) .... AP
Archaic .... ARCH
Archaism .... ARCH
Archana Airways Ltd. [*India*] [*FAA designator*] (FAAC) .... ACY
Archangelos [*Greece*] [*Seismograph station code, US Geological Survey*] (SEIS) .... ARG
Archangelos [*Greece*] [*Seismograph station code, US Geological Survey*] (SEIS) .... RHD
Archangelsk Airlines [*Former USSR*] [*FAA designator*] (FAAC) .... AUL
Archbishop .... AABP
Archbishop (ROG) .... AB
Archbishop .... ABP
Archbishop .... ABSHP
Archbishop (ADA) .... Arch
Archbishop .... ARCHBP
Archbishop Carroll High School, Radnor, PA [*Library symbol*] [*Library of Congress*] (LCLS) .... PRaCHS
Archbishop of Canterbury's Certificate in Church Music [*British*] (DBQ) .... ACertCM
Archbishop of Canterbury's Diploma in Church Music [*British*] (DBQ) .... ADCM
Archbishop of Canterbury's Doctorate in Music [*British*] (DBQ) .... DMusCantuar
Archbishop Oscar Arnulfo Romero Relief Fund (EA) .... AOARRF
Archbold. Indictments, with Forms [*1916*] [*A publication*] (DLA) .... Arch Forms
Archbold. Justice of the Peace [*7th ed.*] [*1859*] [*A publication*] (DLA) ...... Arch JP
Archbold. Law of Landlord and Tenant [*3rd ed.*] [*1864*] [*A publication*] (DLA) .... Arch L & T
Archbold. Lunacy Laws [*5th ed.*] [*1915*] [*A publication*] (DLA) .... Arch Lun
Archbold. Municipal Corporations Act [*1836*] [*A publication*] (DLA) .... Arch Mun Corp
Archbold, OH [*FM radio station call letters*] .... WBCY
Archbold, OH [*FM radio station call letters*] .... WMTR
Archbold on Baines' Acts on Criminal Justice [*A publication*] (DLA) .... Arch Baines' Act
Archbold on Bankruptcy [*1825-56*] [*A publication*] (DLA) .... Arch Bank
Archbold. Practice of the Court of Common Pleas [*1829*] [*A publication*] (DLA) .... Arch PCP
Archbold's Abridgment of Poor Law Cases [*1842-58*] [*A publication*] (DLA) .... Arch PL Cas
Archbold's Bankrupt Law [*A publication*] (DLA) .... Arch BL
Archbold's Civil Pleading [*A publication*] (DLA) .... Archb Civil Pl
Archbold's Civil Pleading and Evidence [*A publication*] (DLA) ...... Arch Civ Pl
Archbold's Civil Pleading and Evidence [*A publication*] (ILCA) ...... Archb Civ Pl
Archbold's Criminal Law [*A publication*] (DLA) .... Arch Cr L
Archbold's Criminal Pleading [*A publication*] (DLA) .... Arch Cr Pl
Archbold's Criminal Pleading [*A publication*] (DLA) .... Archb Crim Pl
Archbold's Criminal Practice [*A publication*] (DLA) .... Arch Cr Prac
Archbold's Criminal Procedure [*A publication*] (DLA) .... Arch Cr Proc
Archbold's Edition of Blackstone's Commentaries [*A publication*] (DLA) .... Arch Black
Archbold's Forms in King's Bench and Common Pleas [*A publication*] (DLA) .... Arch KB Forms
Archbold's Forms of Indictment [*A publication*] (DLA) .... Arch Forms Ind
Archbold's King's Bench Practice [*A publication*] (DLA) .... Arch KB Pr
Archbold's Landlord and Tenant [*A publication*] (DLA) .... Archb Landl & Ten
Archbold's Law of Arbitration and Award [*A publication*] (DLA) .... Arch Arb
Archbold's Law of Nisi Prius [*A publication*] (DLA) .... Arch NP
Archbold's Law of Nisi Prius [*A publication*] (DLA) .... Archb NP
Archbold's Law of Partnership [*A publication*] (DLA) .... Arch Part
Archbold's New Common Law Practice [*A publication*] (DLA) .... Arch CL Pr
Archbold's New Practice [*A publication*] (DLA) .... Archb N Prac
Archbold's New Practice [*A publication*] (DLA) .... Archb New Pr
Archbold's New Practice in Poor Law Removals and Appeals [*A publication*] (DLA) .... Arch PL Pr

Archbold's Pleading and Evidence in Criminal Cases [*A publication*] (DLA) .... Arch Cr

Archbold's Pleading and Evidence in Criminal Cases [*A publication*] (DLA) .... Arch Cr Law

Archbold's Pleading and Evidence in Criminal Cases [*A publication*] (DLA) .... Archb Cr Prac & Pl

Archbold's Pleas of the Crown [*A publication*] (DLA) .... Arch PC
Archbold's Poor Law [*1840-1930*] [*A publication*] (DLA) .... Arch PL
Archbold's Poor Law Cases [*1842-58*] [*A publication*] (DLA) .... APL Cas
Archbold's Poor Law Cases [*1842-58*] [*A publication*] (DLA) .... Arch PLC
Archbold's Practice [*A publication*] (DLA) .... Archb Pr
Archbold's Practice, by Chitty [*A publication*] (DLA) .... Arch P Ch
Archbold's Practice, by Cholty [*A publication*] (DLA) .... Arch Pr Ch
Archbold's Practice in Judges Chambers [*A publication*] (DLA) .... Arch Pr JC
Archbold's Practice in Quarter Sessions [*A publication*] (DLA) .... Arch Pr QS
Archbold's Practice in the Common Pleas [*A publication*] (DLA) .... Arch Pr CP
Archbold's Practice in the Common Pleas [*A publication*] (DLA) .... Arch Pr CP
Archbold's Practice in the King's Bench [*A publication*] (DLA) .... Arch PKB
Archbold's Practice in the King's Bench [*A publication*] (DLA) .... Archb Pr KB
Archbold's Practice in the Queen's Bench [*A publication*] (DLA) .... Arch QB
Archbold's Summary of Laws of England [*A publication*] (DLA) .... Arch Sum
Arch-Chancellor .... AC
Archconfraternity of Christian Mothers (EA) .... ACM
Archconfraternity of Perpetual Adoration [*Defunct*] (EA) .... APA
Archconfraternity of Prayer for Israel (EA) .... API
Archconfraternity of the Holy Ghost (EA) .... AHG
Archdeacon .... ADCON
Archdeacon .... ADN
Archdeacon (ROG) .... ARCH
Archdeacon [*or Archdeaconry*] .... ARCHD
Archdeacon Nares [*Pseudonym used by Robert Nares*] .... AN
Archdeaconry .... AD
Archdeanery .... Achdny
Archdiocesan (ABBR) .... ADIOCN
Archdiocesan Development Fund [*Catholic*] .... ADF
Archdiocese (ABBR) .... ADIOC
Archdiocese (ADA) .... ARCHDIOC
Archduke .... AD
Archduke (WDAA) .... ARCH
Archduke .... ARCHD
Arc-Heated Materials Jet [*Langley Research Center*] .... AHMJ
Archelaus Smith Museum, Centreville (Shelburne Co.), Nova Scotia [*Library symbol National Library of Canada*] (NLC) .... NSCAS
Archelaus Smith Museum, Shelburne County, NS, Canada [*Library symbol*] [*Library of Congress*] (LCLS) .... CaNSCeAS
Archenemy (ABBR) .... AENM
Archeological .... ARCHEOL
Archeological Research Laboratory [*Texas A & M University*] [*Research center*] (RCD) .... ARL
Archeological Resources Protection Act [*1979*] .... ARPA
Archeology (BJA) .... Arch
Archeology and Ecology [*Coined by Paolo Soleri, Italian-born architect*] .... ARCHOLOGY
Archeology Section (EA) .... AS
Archer and Hogue. Reports [*2 Florida*] [*A publication*] (DLA) .... Archer & H
Archer Daniels Midland [*Commercial firm*] .... ADM
Archer Daniels Midland [*Associated Press*] (SAG) .... ArchDan
Archer Elementary School, Freeport, NY [*Library symbol Library of Congress*] (LCLS) .... NFreeAE
Archer International Developments Ltd. [*Vancouver Stock Exchange symbol*] .... ADV
Archer-Daniels-Midland Co. [*NYSE symbol*] (SPSG) .... ADM
Archer-Daniels-Midland Co. [*Associated Press*] (SAG) .... ArchDn
Archers Association of Nova Scotia (AC) .... AANS
Archer's Reports [*2 Florida*] [*A publication*] (DLA) .... Archer
Archery .... ARCH
Archery .... ARCHRY
Archery Association of Australia .... AAA
Archery Manufacturers and Dealers Association [*Later, AMO*] (EA) .... AMADA
Archery Manufacturers Association [*Later, AMO*] .... AMA
Archery Manufacturers Organization (EA) .... AMO
Archery Range and Retailers Organization (EA) .... ARRO
Archery Society of Tasmania [*Australia*] .... AST
Arches National Monument .... ARCH
Archeveche de Rimouski, Quebec [*Library symbol National Library of Canada*] (NLC) .... QRA
Archeveche de Sherbrooke, Sherbrooke, PQ, Canada [*Library symbol Library of Congress*] (LCLS) .... CaQSherA
Archibald. Country Solicitor's Practice in the Queen's Bench [*1881*] [*A publication*] (DLA) .... Arch CS Pr
Archibald Foundation, Regina, Saskatchewan [*Library symbol National Library of Canada*] (NLC) .... SRAF
Archibald Foundation, Regina, SK, Canada [*Library symbol Library of Congress*] (LCLS) .... CaSRAF
Archibald Library, Caronport, Saskatchewan [*Library symbol National Library of Canada*] (NLC) .... SCA
Archibald Library, Caronport, SK, Canada [*Library symbol Library of Congress*] (LCLS) .... CaSCA
Archibald on Practice of Judges' Chambers [*A publication*] (DLA) .... Arch JC Pr
Archidiaconal [*Ecclesiastical*] (ROG) .... ARCHIDIAC
Archidiaconus [*Authority cited in pre-1607 legal work*] (DSA) .... Ar
Archidiaconus [*Authority cited in pre-1607 legal work*] (DSA) .... Arch
Archidiaconus [*Authority cited in pre-1607 legal work*] (DSA) .... Archi
Archidiaconus [*Authority cited in pre-1607 legal work*] (DSA) .... Archid
Archidiaconus [*Authority cited in pre-1607 legal work*] (DSA) .... Archidi

Archidiaconus [*Authority cited in pre-1607 legal work*] (DSA) .... Ard
Archie Campbell Fan Club [*Defunct*] (EA) .... ACFC
Archie Frazer-Nash [*British auto industrialist and founder of AFN Cars*] .... AFN
Archignac [*France*] [*Seismograph station code, US Geological Survey*] (SEIS) .... ARH
Archilochus [*Seventh century BC*] [*Classical studies*] (OCD) .... Archil
Archipelago [*Maps and charts*] .... ARCH
Archipelago Mundi [*An international association*] (EA) .... AM
Architect .... A
Architect [*or Architecture*] .... ARCH
Architect .... ARCHT
Architect (VRA) .... archt
Architect .... ARCHT
Architect Member of the Incorporated Association of Architects and Surveyors [*British*] (DI) .... AIAA
Architect of the Capitol [*US*] .... AC
Architect of the Capitol [*US*] .... AOC
Architect-Engineer .... A-E
Architect-Engineer-Manager [*Plan*] .... AEM
Architect-Engineers Liaison Commission .... AELC
Architect-Engineers - Spanish Bases .... AESB
Architect-in-Training (OA) .... AIT
Architects and Designers [*Building*] [*New York City*] .... A & D
Architects and Engineers .... A & E
Architects and Planners in Support of Nicaragua (EA) .... APSN
Architects and Surveyors Institute (EAIO) .... ASI
Architect's Associate [*Army research program*] (RDA) .... AA
Architects Association of New Brunswick [*Association des Architectes du Nouveau-Brunswick*] (AC) .... AANB
Architects Association of Prince Edward Island (AC) .... AAPEI
Architects' Benevolent Society [*British*] (BI) .... ABS
Architects' Board of Western Australia .... ABWA
Architects' Central Constructional Engineering Surveying Service [*British*] (NITA) .... ACCESS
[*The*] Architects Collaborative [*Design firm*] .... TAC
Architects, Construction and Consulting Engineers, Specialist Service (MHDB) .... ACCESS
Architects Council of Europe (DAC) .... ACE
Architects/Designers/Planners for Social Responsibility (EA) .... ADPSR
Architects' Emergency Committee .... AEC
Architects for Social Responsibility (EA) .... ASR
Architects, Interior Designers, Landscape Designers [*British*] .... AIDLD
Architects Job Costing [*ICS*] [*Software package*] (NCC) .... ARCOS
Architects' Law Reports [*British A publication*] (DLA) .... Architects' LR
Architects' Law Reports [*British*] .... ARCHLR
Architects, Professional Engineers, Land Surveyors Council on Registration .... APELSCOR
Architects' Registration Council [*British*] .... ARC
Architects' Registration Council of the UK (DI) .... ARCUK
Architects Renewal Committee in Harlem [*Defunct*] .... ARCH
Architectural .... ARCHL
Architectural Acoustics Society (EA) .... AAS
Architectural Aluminum Association (DAC) .... AAA
Architectural Aluminum Manufacturers Association (MHDB) .... AAMA
Architectural and Engineering [*Also, A-E*] (AFM) .... A & E
Architectural and Engineering (AFIT) .... AAE
Architectural and Engineering [*Also, A & E*] (KSC) .... A-E
Architectural and Engineering Construction (BYTE) .... AEC
Architectural and Industrial Maintenance [*Coatings*] .... AIM
Architectural and Transportation Barriers Compliance [*Board*] (AAGC) .... ATBC
Architectural and Transportation Barriers Compliance Board [*Office of Human Development Services*] [*Washington, DC*] .... A & TBCB
Architectural and Transportation Barriers Compliance Board [*Office of Human Development Services*] [*Washington, DC*] .... ATBCB
Architectural Anodizers Council (EA) .... AAC
Architectural Association [*British*] (EA) .... AA
Architectural Association of Ireland (SLS) .... AAI
Architectural Barriers .... A/B
Architectural Barriers Act of 1968 (WYGK) .... ABA
Architectural Barriers Committee (EA) .... ABC
Architectural Block Diagram Language .... ABL
Architectural Cladding Association [*British*] (DBA) .... ACA
Architectural Control Document (SSD) .... ACD
Architectural Engineer .... Ar E
Architectural Engineer .... Arch E
Architectural Engineering (OICC) .... A/E
Architectural Engineering Firm (IAA) .... AEF
Architectural Fabric Structures Institute (EA) .... AFSI
Architectural Heritage Foundation (EA) .... AHF
Architectural Heritage Year [*1975*] [*British*] (DI) .... AHY
Architectural History Foundation (EA) .... AHF
Architectural Institute of British Columbia [*1914*] [*Canada*] (NGC) .... AIBC
Architectural Institute of British Columbia (AC) .... AIBC
Architectural Interaction Design System .... AIDS
Architectural Inventory Group [*Association of Canadian Archivists*] .... AIG
Architectural League of New York (EA) .... AL
Architectural League of New York [*Later, AL*] (EA) .... ALNY
Architectural Metal Craftsmen's Association [*British*] (BI) .... AMCA
Architectural Millwrights of Ontario (AC) .... AMO
Architectural Periodicals Index [*Royal Institute of British Architects*] [*Information service or system*] (IID) .... API
Architectural Photographers Association [*Defunct*] (EA) .... APA
Architectural Precast Association (EA) .... APA
Architectural Projected Window [*Technical drawings*] .... APW
Architectural Psychology Newsletter [*British*] .... AP

Architectural Secretaries Association [*Later, SAA*] (EA) ... ASA
Architectural Spray Coaters Association (EA) ... ASCA
Architectural Terra-Cotta [*Technical drawings*] (DAC) ... ATC
Architectural Woodwork Institute (EA) ... AWI
Architectural Woodwork Manufacturers Association of Canada (AC) ... AWMAC
Architecture ... AR
Architecture (VRA) ... arch
Architecture ... ARCH
Architecture ... ARCHIT
Architecture and Building Aids Computer Unit, Strathclyde University (PDAA) ... ABACUS
Architecture and Engineering (AAGC) ... A&E
Architecture and Engineering Performance Information Center [*University of Maryland*] [*College Park*] [*Information service or system*] (IID) ... AEPIC
Architecture and Fine Arts Library, University of Manitoba, Winnipeg, Manitoba [*Library symbol National Library of Canada*] (NLC) ... MWUAF
Architecture and Planning Research Laboratory [*University of Michigan*] [*Research center*] (RCD) ... APRL
Architecture Bulletin [*A publication*] ... AB
Architecture Description Language [*Computer science*] (CSR) ... ADL
Architecture Design and Assessment System [*Software package*] ... ADAS
Architecture Neutral Distributed Format (CDE) ... ANDF
Architecture New York [*A publication*] ... ANY
Architecture Technology Corp. [*Minneapolis, MN*] [*Information service or system Telecommunications*] (TSSD) ... ATC
Architectures for Heterogeneous European Distributed Databases ... ARCHEDDA
Architrave (VRA) ... archtr
Archiv des Kreises Asch, Fernleihe, Bayern, Federal Republic of Germany [*Library symbol Library of Congress*] (LCLS) ... GyBaA
Archiv des Oeffentlichen Rechts [*A publication*] (ILCA) ... Arch Off R
Archiv foer Retsvidenskaben og dens Anvendelse [*Denmark*] [*A publication*] (ILCA) ... AfR
Archiv fuer die Civilistische Praxis [*A publication*] (ILCA) ... ACP
Archiv fuer die Zivilistische Praxis [*A publication*] (ILCA) ... Arch Ziv Pr
Archiv fuer die Zivilistische Praxis [*A publication*] (ILCA) ... AZP
Archiv fuer Papyrusforschung [*A publication*] (OCD) ... Arch Pap
Archiv fuer Rechts und Sozialphilosophie [*A publication*] (ILCA) ... Arch R Soz Phil
Archival and Manuscripts Control [*USMARC format*] [*Computer science*] ... AMC
Archival Association of Atlantic Canada ... AAAC
Archival Micrographics, Midland Park, NJ [*Library symbol Library of Congress*] (LCLS) ... ArcM
Archival Research Catalog ... ARC
Archival Research Catalog [*A publication*] ... ARC
Archival Security Program [*An association Defunct*] (EA) ... ASP
Archivaria [*A publication*] (BRI) ... Archiv
Archive (MSA) ... ARCH
Archive (VRA) ... archv
Archive ... ARCHV
Archive and Records Centre [*Geneva, Switzerland*] [*United Nations*] (ECON) ... ARC
Archive Preservation Programme and Retrieval by Automated Techniques [*Computer science*] ... APPARAT
Archives Acadiennes, Universite de Moncton, New Brunswick [*Library symbol National Library of Canada*] (NLC) ... NBMOUA
Archives and General Library, College of Cape Breton, Sydney, Nova Scotia [*Library symbol National Library of Canada*] (NLC) ... NSSXA
Archives and Manuscripts [*A publication*] ... Arch Ms
Archives and Manuscripts [*A publication*] ... Archs Man
Archives and Record Cataloging and Indexing by Computer (MHDB) ... ARCAIC
Archives and Special Collections Department, University of New Brunswick, Fredericton, New Brunswick [*Library symbol National Library of Canada*] (NLC) ... NBFUA
Archives and Special Collections Division, McMaster University, Hamilton, Ontario [*Library symbol National Library of Canada*] (NLC) ... OHMA
Archives and Special Collections, Simon Fraser University, Burnaby, British Col umbia [*Library symbol National Library of Canada*] (NLC) ... BVASA
Archives, Archdiocese of Kingston, Catholic Church, Ontario [*Library symbol National Library of Canada*] (NLC) ... OKCAA
Archives, Archdiocese of Vancouver, Catholic Church, British Columbia [*Library symbol National Library of Canada*] (NLC) ... BVACAA
Archives Association of British Columbia (AC) ... AABC
Archives Association of Ontario [*L'Association des Archives de l'Ontario*] (AC) ... AAO
Archives, Brandon University, Manitoba [*Library symbol National Library of Canada*] (BIB) ... MBCA
Archives, British Columbia Conference, United Church, Vancouver, British Columbia [*Library symbol National Library of Canada*] (NLC) ... BVAUBCA
Archives, British Columbia Provincial Synod, Anglican Church of Canada, Vancouver, British Columbia [*Library symbol National Library of Canada*] (NLC) ... BVAABSA
Archives, City of Etobicoke, Ontario [*Library symbol National Library of Canada*] (BIB) ... OEA
Archives, Dalhousie University, Halifax, Nova Scotia [*Library symbol National Library of Canada*] (BIB) ... NSHDA
Archives de la Chancellerie, L'Archeveche de Montreal, Quebec [*Library symbol National Library of Canada*] (NLC) ... QMAA
Archives de la Chancellerie, Montreal, PQ, Canada [*Library symbol Library of Congress*] (LCLS) ... CaQMAA
Archives de la Compagnie de Jesus, Province du Canada - Francais, Saint-Jerome, Quebec, Quebec [*Library symbol National Library of Canada*] (NLC) ... QQACJ
Archives de la Congregation de Notre-Dame, Montreal, PQ, Canada [*Library symbol Library of Congress*] (LCLS) ... CaQMACN
Archives de la Congregation de Notre-Dame, Montreal, Quebec [*Library symbol National Library of Canada*] (NLC) ... QMACN
Archives de la Congregation de Sainte-Croix, Montreal, PQ, Canada [*Library symbol*] [*Library of Congress*] (LCLS) ... CaQMCSCA
Archives de la Congregation de Sainte-Croix, Montreal, Quebec [*Library symbol National Library of Canada*] (NLC) ... QMCSCA
Archives de l'Archeveche de Quebec, Quebec [*Library symbol National Library of Canada*] (NLC) ... QQAA
Archives de l'Archeveche de Quebec, Quebec, PQ, Canada [*Library symbol Library of Congress*] (LCLS) ... CaQQAA
Archives de Philosophie du Droit [*A publication*] (ILCA) ... APD
Archives des Augustines du Monastere de l'Hopital General de Quebec, Quebec [*Library symbol National Library of Canada*] (NLC) ... QQMAGA
Archives des Augustines du Monastere de l'Hopital General de Quebec, Quebec, PQ,Canada [*Library symbol*] [*Library of Congress*] (LCLS) ... CaQQMAGA
Archives des Clercs de Saint-Viateur, Province de Montreal, Outremont, PQ, Canada [*Library symbol*] [*Library of Congress*] (LCLS) ... CaQMCSVA
Archives des Clercs de Saint-Viateur, Province de Montreal, Outremont, Quebec [*Library symbol National Library of Canada*] (NLC) ... QMCSVA
Archives des Franciscains, Montreal, PQ, Canada [*Library symbol*] [*Library of Congress*] (LCLS) ... CaQMFRA
Archives des Franciscains, Montreal, Quebec [*Library symbol National Library of Canada*] (NLC) ... QMFRA
Archives des Freres de Saint-Gabriel, Montreal, PQ, Canada [*Library symbol*] [*Library of Congress*] (LCLS) ... CaQMFSGA
Archives des Freres de Saint-Gabriel, Montreal, Quebec [*Library symbol National Library of Canada*] (NLC) ... QMFSGA
Archives des Freres des Ecoles Chretiennes, Ville de Laval, Quebec [*Library symbol National Library of Canada*] (NLC) ... QLFECA
Archives des Freres Maristes, Iberville, PQ, Canada [*Library symbol*] [*Library of Congress*] (LCLS) ... CaQIFMA
Archives des Freres Maristes, Iberville, Quebec [*Library symbol National Library of Canada*] (NLC) ... QIFMA
Archives des Murasu [*A publication*] (BJA) ... AM
Archives des Peres Eudistes, Charlesbourg, PQ, Canada [*Library symbol*] [*Library of Congress*] (LCLS) ... CaQQPEA
Archives des Peres Eudistes, Charlesbourg, Quebec [*Library symbol National Library of Canada*] (NLC) ... QQPEA
Archives des Religieuses Hospitalieres de Saint-Joseph, Montreal, PQ, Canada [*Library symbol*] [*Library of Congress*] (LCLS) ... CaQMRSJA
Archives des Religieuses Hospitalieres de Saint-Joseph, Montreal, Quebec [*Library symbol National Library of Canada*] (NLC) ... QMRSJA
Archives des Soeurs de la Charite de Quebec, Quebec, Quebec [*Library symbol National Library of Canada*] (NLC) ... QQSCA
Archives des Soeurs de la Charite d'Ottawa, Ontario [*Library symbol National Library of Canada*] (NLC) ... OOSCA
Archives des Soeurs de la Charite d'Ottawa, Ottawa, ON, Canada [*Library symbol*] [*Library of Congress*] (LCLS) ... CaOOSCA
Archives des Soeurs de Sainte-Anne, Lachine, Quebec [*Library symbol National Library of Canada*] (NLC) ... QLSAA
Archives des Ursulines, Trois-Rivieres, PQ, Canada [*Library symbol Library of Congress*] (LCLS) ... CaQTUrA
Archives des Ursulines, Trois-Rivieres, Quebec [*Library symbol National Library of Canada*] (NLC) ... QTURA
Archives Deschatelets (Oblats de Marie-Immaculee), Ottawa, Ontario [*Library symbol National Library of Canada*] (NLC) ... OOADE
Archives Deschatelets [*Oblates de Marie-Immaculee*], Ottawa, ON, Canad a [*Library symbol*] [*Library of Congress*] (LCLS) ... CaOOAD
Archives, Diocese of Fredericton, Anglican Church of Canada, New Brunswick [*Library symbol National Library of Canada*] (NLC) ... NBFAFA
Archives, Diocese of Montreal, Anglican Church of Canada, Quebec [*Library symbol National Library of Canada*] (NLC) ... QMADMA
Archives, Diocese of Ottawa, Anglican Church of Canada, Ontario [*Library symbol National Library of Canada*] (NLC) ... OOAOA
Archives, Diocese of Yarmouth, Catholic Church, Nova Scotia [*Library symbol National Library of Canada*] (NLC) ... NSYCDA
Archives du Monastere des Augustines, Quebec, PQ, Canada [*Library symbol*] [*Library of Congress*] (LCLS) ... CaQQMAA
Archives du Monastere des Augustines, Quebec, Quebec [*Library symbol National Library of Canada*] (NLC) ... QQMAA
Archives du Monastere des Ursulines de Merici, Quebec, PQ, Canada [*Library symbol*] [*Library of Congress*] (LCLS) ... CaQQUA
Archives du Monastere des Ursulines de Merici, Quebec, Quebec [*Library symbol National Library of Canada*] (NLC) ... QQUA
Archives du Monastere Notre-Dame-Des-Anges, Quebec, PQ, Canada [*Library symbol Library of Congress*] (LCLS) ... CaQQAND
Archives du Monastere Notre-Dame-Des-Anges, Quebec, Quebec [*Library symbol National Library of Canada*] (NLC) ... QQAND
Archives du Seminaire de Quebec, Quebec, PQ, Canada [*Library symbol Library of Congress*] (LCLS) ... CaQQAS
Archives du Seminaire de Quebec, Quebec, Quebec [*Library symbol National Library of Canada*] (NLC) ... QQAS
Archives du Seminaire de Saint-Sulpice, Montreal, PQ, Canada [*Library symbol Library of Congress*] (LCLS) ... CaQMAS
Archives du Seminaire de Saint-Sulpice, Montreal, Quebec [*Library symbol National Library of Canada*] (NLC) ... QMAS
Archives Generales des Soeurs Grises, Montreal, Quebec [*Library symbol National Library of Canada*] (NLC) ... QMSGA
Archives Historiques, Universite du Quebec, Trois-Rivieres, Quebec [*Library symbol National Library of Canada*] (NLC) ... QTUAH
Archives Jean Piaget, Geneve, Switzerland [*Library symbol Library of Congress*] (LCLS) ... SzGPAr
Archives, Manuscripts, and Special Collections [*Research Libraries Group project*] (IT) ... AMSC

Archives, Maritime Conference, United Church of Canada Halifax, Nova Scotia [*Library symbol National Conference of Commissioners on Uniform State Laws*] (BIB) ... NSHMCA
Archives Nationales du Film, de la Television, et de l'Enregistrement Sonore [*National Film, Television, and Sound Archives*] [*NFTSA*] [*Canada*] ... ANFTES
Archives Nationales du Quebec, Quebec [*Library symbol National Library of Canada*] (NLC) ... QQA
Archives Nationales du Quebec, Rimouski, Quebec [*Library symbol National Library of Canada*] (BIB) ... QRAN
Archives Nationales du Quebec, Trois-Rivieres, PQ, Canada [*Library symbol Library of Congress*] (LCLS) ... CaQTA
Archives Nationales du Quebec, Trois-Rivieres, Quebec [*Library symbol National Library of Canada*] (NLC) ... QTA
Archives of American Art (EA) ... AAA
Archives of Ontario, Toronto, Ontario [*Library symbol National Library of Canada*] (NLC) ... OTAR
Archives of the Canadian Rockies, Banff, AB, Canada [*Library symbol Library of Congress*] (LCLS) ... CaABA
Archives of the Canadian Rockies, Banff, Alberta [*Library symbol National Library of Canada*] (NLC) ... ABA
Archives of the Ecclesiastical Province of British Columbia, Vancouver, BC, Canada [*Library symbol Library of Congress*] (LCLS) ... CaBVaRE
Archives of the Ecclesiastical Province of British Columbia, Vancouver, British Columbia [*Library symbol National Library of Canada*] (NLC) ... BVARE
Archives of the Miramichi Historical Society, Newcastle, New Brunswick [*Library symbol National Library of Canada*] (NLC) ... NBNAM
Archives of the Moravian Church, Bethlehem, PA [*Library symbol Library of Congress*] (LCLS) ... PBMCA
Archives of Yad Washem [*A publication*] (BJA) ... AYW
Archives Office (ADA) ... AO
Archives Providence, Montreal, PQ, Canada [*Library symbol*] [*Library of Congress*] (LCLS) ... CaQMPRA
Archives Providence, Montreal, Quebec [*Library symbol National Library of Canada*] (NLC) ... QMPRA
Archives Provinciales des Capucins, Montreal, PQ, Canada [*Library symbol Library of Congress*] (LCLS) ... CaQMArC
Archives Provinciales des Capucins, Montreal, Quebec [*Library symbol National Library of Canada*] (NLC) ... QMARC
Archives Provinciales des Clercs de Saint-Viateur, Joliette, Quebec [*Library symbol National Library of Canada*] (NLC) ... QJCSVA
Archives Publiques du Canada [*Public Archives of Canada - PAC*] ... APC
Archives, Queen's University, Kingston, Ontario [*Library symbol National Library of Canada*] (NLC) ... OKQAR
Archives, Region of Peel, Brampton, Ontario [*Library symbol National Library of Canada*] (BIB) ... OBRAPA
Archives, St. Paul University [*Archives, Universite St-Paul*] **Ottawa, Ontario** [*Library symbol National Library of Canada*] (NLC) ... OOSUA
Archives, Unitarian Church of Vancouver, British Columbia [*Library symbol National Library of Canada*] (NLC) ... BVAUCA
Archives, Universite d'Ottawa [*Archives, University of Ottawa*], Ontario [*Library symbol National Library of Canada*] (BIB) ... OOUA
Archiving Utility [*Computer science*] ... arc
Archiving Utility [*Computer science*] ... zip
Archivio Dati e Programmi per le Scienze Sociali [*Data and Program Archive for the Social Sciences*] [*University of Milan*] [*Italy*] [*Information service or system*] (IID) ... ADPSS
Archivio Dati Italiani di Geologia [*Italian Geological Data Archive*] [*National Research Council Database*] (IID) ... ADIGE
Archivio dei Libri Italiani, su Calcolatore Elettronica [*Editrice Bibliografica*] [*Italian Information service or system*] (CRD) ... ALICE
Archivo del Libertador, Caracas, Venezuela [*Library symbol Library of Congress*] (LCLS) ... VeCAL
Archivo General de Indias [*Archives of the Indies*], Seville, Spain [*Library symbol Library of Congress*] (LCLS) ... SpSAG
Archivolt (VRA) ... arvlt
Archivum Linguisticum [*A publication*] (BARN) ... ALing
Arch-Loop-Whorl [*Basis of Galton's System of Fingerprint Classifications*] ... ALW
Archonist Club (EA) ... AC
Archonist Club (EA) ... ARCLUB
Archons of Colophon (EA) ... AC
Arch-Treasurer ... AT
Archuleta County Public Library, Pagosa Springs, CO [*Library symbol Library of Congress*] (LCLS) ... CoPs
Archuleta County Public Library, Pagosa Springs, CO [*Library symbol*] [*Library of Congress*] (LCLS) ... CoPsC
Arcing (MSA) ... ARNG
Arc-Jet Wind Tunnel ... AWT
ARCNET Trade Association (EA) ... ATA
ARCO Chemical [*NYSE symbol*] (TTSB) ... RCM
ARCO Chemical Co. [*Associated Press*] (SAG) ... ARCOCh
ARCO Chemical Co. [*NYSE symbol*] (SPSG) ... RCM
ARCO Chemical Co., Channelview, TX [*Library symbol Library of Congress*] (LCLS) ... TxCvS
ARCO Exploration and Technology Co. ... AETC
ARCO-Alaska, Inc., Anchorage, AK [*Library symbol*] [*Library of Congress*] (LCLS) ... AkAArA
Arcola Community Unit School District, Arcola, IL [*Library symbol*] [*Library of Congress*] (LCLS) ... IArcSD
Arcola, IL [*FM radio station call letters*] (RBYB) ... WKJR
Arcola Public Library, Arcola, IL [*Library symbol Library of Congress*] (LCLS) ... IArc
Arcola, TX [*Location identifier FAA*] (FAAL) ... AXH
Arcola, TX [*Location identifier FAA*] (FAAL) ... SYG
Arc-Plasma Spraying [*Magnetic film*] ... APS
Arcseconds ... ARCSEC
ArcSys, Inc. [*NASDAQ symbol*] (SAG) ... ARCS
ArcSys, Inc. [*Associated Press*] (SAG) ... ArcSys
Arctco, Inc. [*NASDAQ symbol*] (SAG) ... ACAT
Arctco, Inc. [*Associated Press*] (SAG) ... Arctco
Arctec Canada Ltd., Calgary, Alberta [*Library symbol National Library of Canada*] (NLC) ... ACARC
Arctec Canada Ltd., Kanata, ON, Canada [*Library symbol Library of Congress*] (LCLS) ... CaOKanA
Arctec Canada Ltd., Kanata, Ontario [*Library symbol National Library of Canada*] (NLC) ... OKANA
Arctec, Inc., Columbia, MD [*Library symbol Library of Congress*] (LCLS) ... MdCoA
Arctec Ltd., Calgary, AB, Canada [*Library symbol Library of Congress*] (LCLS) ... CaACARC
Arctic [*Air mass*] [*Meteorological symbol*] ... A
Arctic [*Iceland*] [*ICAO designator*] (FAAC) ... AEB
Arctic (WDAA) ... ARC
Arctic ... Arct
Arctic Aeromedical Laboratory [*Later, AMRL*] [*Fort Wainwright, AK*] [*Air Force*] (KSC) ... AAL
Arctic Aeromedical Laboratory [*Later, AMRL*] [*Air Force*] ... AAML
Arctic and Antarctic Research Institute [*Russian Federation*] [*Marine science*] (OSRA) ... AARI
Arctic and Antarctic Research Institute [*Russia*] (USDC) ... AARI
Arctic and Antarctic Scientific Research Institute ... AASRI
Arctic and Marine Oil Spill Program [*Environment Canada*] ... AMOP
Arctic Approach Limitation (AFM) ... AAL
Arctic Bay, NT [*ICAO location identifier*] (ICLI) ... CYAB
Arctic Bibliography [*A publication*] ... AB
Arctic Biological Station, Fisheries and Oceans Canada [*Station Biologique del'Arctique, Peches et Oceans Canada*] **Ste-Anne-De-Bellevue, Quebec** [*Library symbol National Library of Canada*] (NLC) ... QMFR
Arctic Circle ... AC
Arctic Circle Service, Inc. [*ICAO designator*] (FAAC) ... CIR
Arctic Climate System Study (ECON) ... ACSYS
Arctic College, Iqualuit, Northwest Territories [*Library symbol National Library of Canada*] (BIB) ... NWIAC
Arctic Communication Satellite (IAA) ... ARCOM
Arctic Construction and Frost Effects Laboratory [*Army*] (PDAA) ... ACEFEL
Arctic Construction and Frost Effects Laboratory [*Boston, MA*] [*Army*] ... ACFEL
Arctic Control Area [*Aviation*] (FAAC) ... ACA
Arctic Drift Barge ... ADB
Arctic Drift Station ... ADS
Arctic Drilling System ... ADS
Arctic Environmental Buoy System (NOAA) ... AEB
Arctic Environmental Engineering Laboratory [*University of Alaska*] ... AEEL
Arctic Environmental Field Station [*Environmental Protection Agency*] (GFGA) ... AEFS
Arctic Environmental Information and Data Center [*University of Alaska, Fairbanks*] [*Research center*] (IID) ... AEIDC
Arctic Environmental Research Laboratory [*Environmental Protection Agency*] (NOAA) ... AERL
Arctic Forward Area Refueling Equipment (DWSG) ... AFARE
Arctic Fuel Dispensing Equipment (MCD) ... AFDE
Arctic Gas and Aerosol Sampling Program [*Marine science*] (OSRA) ... AGASP
Arctic Gas and Aerosol Sampling Program (USDC) ... AGASP
Arctic Goose Habitat Working Group ... AGHWG
Arctic Health Research Laboratory [*HEW*] ... AHRL
Arctic Health Services Research Center [*HEW*] ... AHSRC
Arctic Ice Dynamics Joint Experiment [*National Science Foundation - Canada*] ... AIDJEX
Arctic Institute ... AI
Arctic Institute of North America (EA) ... AINA
Arctic Institute of North America, Calgary, AB, Canada [*Library symbol Library of Congress*] (LCLS) ... CaACAI
Arctic Institute of North America, Montreal, PQ, Canada [*Library symbol Library of Congress Obsolete*] (LCLS) ... CaQMAI
Arctic Institute of North America, University of Calgary, Alberta [*Library symbol National Library of Canada*] (NLC) ... ACUAI
Arctic International Wildlife Range Society (EA) ... AIWRS
Arctic Islands Pipeline Program [*Canada*] ... AIPP
Arctic Marine Locomotive [*An icebreaker used in oil exploration in the Arctic*] ... AML
Arctic Marine Pipelaying System ... AMPS
Arctic Meteorology Photographic Probe ... AMPP
Arctic Missions [*Later, IM*] (EA) ... AM
Arctic Mobile Drilling Structure (PDAA) ... AMDS
Arctic National Wildlife Refuge [*Alaska*] ... ANWR
Arctic Ocean ... ARC
Arctic Ocean and Region [*MARC geographic area code Library of Congress*] (LCCP) ... r-----
Arctic Ocean Environment Simulator ... AOES
Arctic Ocean Radiative Fluxes [*Data set*] (OSRA) ... AORF
Arctic Ocean Science Board (OSRA) ... AOSB
Arctic Offshore Program [*National Science Foundation*] (GFGA) ... AOP
Arctic Operations [*Military*] (NVT) ... ARCOPS
Arctic Petroleum Operators' Association [*Canada*] ... APOA
Arctic Polynya Experiment [*Marine science*] (OSRA) ... APEX
Arctic Polynya Experiment (USDC) ... APEX
Arctic Red Resources [*Vancouver Stock Exchange symbol*] ... ARP
Arctic Research and Policy Act of 1984 ... ARPA
Arctic Research Consortium of the United States ... ARCUS
Arctic Research Directors Committee [*Canada*] ... ARDC
Arctic Research in Environmental Acoustics [*Navy*] (MSC) ... AREA
Arctic Research Laboratory [*Point Barrow, AK*] [*Army*] ... ARL

Arctic Research Laboratory Island [*A floating ice island in the Arctic Ocean*] [*Navy*] .... ARLIS
Arctic Research Vessel .... ARV
Arctic Science and Technology Information System [*Arctic Institute of North America*] [*University of Calgary*] [*Information service or system*] (IID) .... ASTIS
Arctic Slope Native Association .... ASNA
Arctic Small Tool Tradition [*Archeology*] .... ASTt
Arctic Submarine Laboratory [*Navy*] (MSC) .... ASL
Arctic Surface Effects Vehicle [*Navy*] .... ASEV
Arctic Survey Boat [*Coast Guard*] (DNAB) .... ASB
Arctic Survival Instructor [*British military*] (DMA) .... ASI
Arctic System Science [*Program*] [*Marine science*] (OSRA) .... ARCSS
Arctic System Science [*Program*] (USDC) .... ARCSS
Arctic Tent Stake Driver (MCD) .... ATSD
Arctic Test Branch [*Army*] (MCD) .... ATB
Arctic Test Center [*Army*] .... ATC
Arctic Vessel and Marine Research Institute [*National Research Council of Canada*] [*Later, Institute of Marine Dynamics*] [*Research center*] (RCD) .... AVMRI
Arctic Village [*Alaska*] [*Airport symbol*] (OAG) .... ARC
Arctic Warfare Training [*British military*] (DMA) .... AWT
Arctic Wings and Rotors Ltd. [*Canada*] [*FAA designator*] (FAAC) .... AWR
Arctic Winter Games International Committee [*Formerly, Arctic Winter Games Corporation*] (AC) .... AWGIC
Arctic Working Group [*University of Toronto*] [*Research center*] (RCD) .... AWG
Arctic-Desert-Tropic Information Center [*Air University*] [*Maxwell Air Force Base, AL*] .... ADTIC
Arcuate [*Brain anatomy*] .... AR
Arcuate Nucleus [*In the medulla oblongata*] .... AN
Arcuate Nucleus [*Neuroanatomy*] .... ARC
Arcuate-Median Eminence [*Anatomy*] .... A-ME
Arcus-Air-Logistic GmbH [*Germany ICAO designator*] (FAAC) .... AZE
Ardakan-E-Fars [*Iran*] [*ICAO location identifier*] (ICLI) .... OISC
Ardakan-E-Yazd [*Iran*] [*ICAO location identifier*] (ICLI) .... OIYA
Ardeer Double Cartridge Test [*Sensitivity to propagation test of an explosive*] .... ADC
Arden Branch, Frontenac County Library, Ontario [*Library symbol National Library of Canada*] (BIB) .... OAFC
Arden Group CI'A' [*NASDAQ symbol*] (TTSB) .... ARDNA
Arden Group, Inc. [*Associated Press*] (SAG) .... Arden
Arden Group, Inc. [*NASDAQ symbol*] (NQ) .... ARDN
Arden Hill Hospital Medical Library, Goshen, NY [*Library symbol Library of Congress*] (LCLS) .... NGosA
Arden Industrial Products [*NASDAQ symbol*] (SAG) .... AFAS
Arden Industrial Products [*Associated Press*] (SAG) .... ArdenPd
Arden Realty, Inc. [*Associated Press*] (SAG) .... ArdenRlt
Arden Realty, Inc. [*NYSE symbol*] (SAG) .... ARI
Ardent (DSUE) .... ARD
Ardestan [*Iran*] [*ICAO location identifier*] (ICLI) .... OIFD
Ardito [*Ardently*] [*Music*] (ROG) .... ARD
Ardito [*Ardently*] [*Music*] .... Ardo
Ardleigh [*England*] .... ARDL
Ardmore [*Oklahoma*] [*Airport symbol Obsolete*] (OAG) .... ADM
Ardmore [*Oklahoma*] [*Airport symbol Obsolete*] (OAG) .... AHD
Ardmore [*New Zealand*] [*Airport symbol*] (OAG) .... AMZ
Ardmore [*Oklahoma*] [*ICAO location identifier*] (ICLI) .... KADM
Ardmore [*New Zealand*] [*ICAO location identifier*] (ICLI) .... NZAR
Ardmore, OK [*Location identifier FAA*] (FAAL) .... AIW
Ardmore, OK [*Location identifier FAA*] (FAAL) .... AUV
Ardmore, OK [*FM radio station call letters*] (RBYB) .... KACO-FM
Ardmore, OK [*FM radio station call letters*] (RBYB) .... KKAJ-FM
Ardmore, OK [*FM radio station call letters*] (RBYB) .... KRXZ
Ardmore, OK [*AM radio station call letters*] (RBYB) .... KVSO
Ardmore, TN [*AM radio station call letters*] .... WSLV
Ardsley Public Library, Ardsley, NY [*Library symbol Library of Congress*] (LCLS) .... NArd
Arduously (ABBR) .... ADUY
Are [*Also, a*] [*A unit of area in the metric system*] .... A
Are You [*Communication*] .... RU
Are You OK? [*Internet language*] [*Computer science*] .... RUOK
Are You There? [*Computer science*] (DOM) .... ENQ?
Area .... A
Area (IDOE) .... a
Area .... AR
Area Advisory Group [*British Overseas Trade Board*] (DS) .... AAG
Area Agencies on Aging Association of Michigan (SRA) .... AAAAM
Area Agency on Aging (DHSM) .... AAA
Area Air Defense Commander [*Military*] .... AADC
Area Air Defense System (MCD) .... AADS
Area Airports Checked (FAAC) .... ARAC
Area Alarm Sum (ECII) .... AAS
Area Altitude Requirement (SAA) .... AR
Area Approach Control Center (DOMA) .... AACC
Area Approach Control Centre .... AACC
Area Bancshares [*NASDAQ symbol*] (TTSB) .... AREA
Area Bancshares Corp. [*NASDAQ symbol*] (SAG) .... AREA
Area Bancshares Corp. [*Associated Press*] (SAG) .... AreaBnc
Area Business Databank [*Information Access Co.*] [*Belmont, CA*] [*Information service or system*] (IID) .... ABD
Area Chart .... A
Area Chemist Contractors' Committee [*National Health Service*] [*British*] (DI) .... ACCC
Area Clearance Officer (MUGU) .... ACO
Area Club Management [*Military*] .... ACM
Area Code .... AC

Area Combined Headquarters [*World War II*] (DMA) .... ACH
Area Combined Headquarters [*World War II*] .... ACHQ
Area Combined Movements Center [*Army*] (AABC) .... ACMC
Area Command Information Exchange System (MCD) .... ARCIXS
Area Command Post (FAAC) .... ACP
Area Commander [*British military*] (DMA) .... AC
Area Commanders' Meeting [*NATO*] (NATG) .... ARCOMET
Area Commanders Operations Report .... AREAOPREP
Area Communications Control Function [*Defense Communications System*] (DNAB) .... ACCF
Area Communications Operations Center [*Telecommunications*] (TEL) ...... ACOC
Area Communications Terminal Subsystem [*Ground Communications Facility, NASA*] .... ACTS
Area Composition Machine (DGA) .... ACM
Area Composition Terminal (DGA) .... ACT
Area Computing Facilities (CET) .... ACF
Area Concept Papers [*Military*] .... ACP
Area Confinement Facility [*Military*] (AABC) .... ACF
Area Consultative Committee .... ACC
Area Control Center (DA) .... ACC
Area Control Center [*ICAO designator*] (ICDA) .... ZR
Area Control Centre [*FAA designator*] (FAAC) .... ZRZ
Area Control Computer Complex (AAGC) .... ACCC
Area Control Computer Complex [*FAA*] (TAG) .... ACCC
Area Control Error (OA) .... ACE
Area Control Facility [*FAA*] (TAG) .... ACF
Area Control Facility (GAVI) .... ACF
Area Control-RADAR (DA) .... ACC-R
Area Cooperative Educational Services [*Information service or system*] .... ACES
Area Coordinating Paper .... ACP
Area Coordination Center .... ACC
Area Coordination Group [*Air Force*] (AABC) .... ACG
Area Coordination Group [*Air Force*] (AFM) .... ACGp
Area Coordination Review .... ACR
Area Coordination Subgroup [*Air Force*] (AFM) .... ACSG
Area Coordination Subgroup [*Air Force*] (AFM) .... ACSGp
Area Coordination Subgroup [*Air Force*] .... ACSGRP
Area Coordination to Command Designated in Appropriate Instructions (MCD) .... AREACORD
Area Correlation Tracker [*Air Force*] .... ACT
Area Council for Economic Education (EA) .... ACEE
Area Coverage .... AC
Area Coverage File (MCD) .... ACF
Area Cutover Manager (DNAB) .... ACOM
Area Damage Control (MCD) .... ADC
Area Damage Control Center [*Army*] .... ADCC
Area Damage Control Center [*Army*] .... ADCOC
Area Damage Control Party [*Army*] .... ADCOP
Area Data Center .... ADC
Area Data Distribution System [*Army*] (ADDR) .... ADDS
Area Dean [*Church of England in Australia*] .... AD
Area Defense Counsel [*Military*] .... ADC
Area Defense Homing Interceptor .... ADHI
Area Defense Missile .... ADM
Area Denial Artillery Munition (AABC) .... ADAM
Area Denial Munition (MCD) .... ADM
Area Denial Visual Indication Security Equipment (MCD) .... ADVISE
Area Dental Laboratory [*Military*] .... ADL
Area Detection System [*Military*] (LAIN) .... ADS
Area Diastolic Pressure [*Cardiology*] (DAVI) .... ADP
Area Director .... AD
Area Discriminator [*SAGE*] .... AD
Area Distribution Officers [*Military British World War II*] .... ADOS
Area Distribution Panel .... ADP
Area Drain [*Technical drawings*] .... AD
Area Education Agency (OICC) .... AEA
Area Education Officer [*Military British*] .... AEO
Area Electronic Supervisor .... AES
Area Engineering Officer [*Army Corps of Engineers*] (AAG) .... AEO
Area Equipment Compounds [*Military*] (AABC) .... AEC
Area Fire Armor System .... AFAS
Area Forecast [*Aviation*] .... ARFOR
Area Forecast Center [*Meteorology*] (BARN) .... AFC
Area Forecast in Metric Unit [*Meteorology*] (BARN) .... ARMET
Area Frequency Coordinator (MUGU) .... AFC
Area Frequency Response Characteristic (PDAA) .... AFRC
Area Fuel Consumption Allocation [*Environmental Protection Agency*] (GFGA) .... AFCA
Area Full Value (ECII) .... AFV
Area Full Value Display (ECII) .... AFVD
Area Headquarters (NATG) .... AHQ
Area Health Authority .... AHA
Area Health Authority Full Time [*Chiropody*] [*British*] .... AHF
Area Health Authority (Teaching) [*British*] .... AHA(T)
Area Health Education Activity (DMAA) .... AHEA
Area Health Education Center [*Veterans Administration*] (DHSM) .... AHEC
Area Health Education Officer [*National Health Service*] [*British*] (DI) .... AHEO
Area II Library Services Authority [*Library network*] .... ALSA 2
Area Imaging Device (AID) .... AID
Area Inspector [*British railroad term*] .... AI
Area Interdiction Mine [*Air Force*] (MCD) .... AIM
Area Intrusion Detection System (MCD) .... AIDS
Area Junction [*Telecommunications*] (OA) .... AJ
Area L AHEC Library, Rocky Mount, NC [*Library symbol*] [*Library of Congress*] (LCLS) .... NcRmHE

Area Learning Resource Center .... ALRC
Area Letter of Acceptance [*Department of Housing and Urban Development*] (GFGA) .... ALA
Area Library Services Authority [*Indiana*] .... ALSA
Area Local Control Panel (NRCH) .... ALCP
Area Logistics Command .... ALC
Area Mail Processing [*US Postal Service*] .... AMP
Area Mail Processing Center [*US Postal Service*] .... AMPC
Area Maintenance Facility .... AMF
Area Maintenance Supply Facility [*Army*] (AABC) .... AMSF
Area Maintenance Support Activity (AABC) .... AMSA
Area Manpower Instructional Development Systems .... AMIDS
Area Manpower Review [*Department of Labor*] .... AMR
Area Medical Laboratory [*Military*] (AABC) .... AML
Area Microwave Assembly [*Ground Communications Facility, NASA*] .... AMWA
Area Minimum Altitude [*Aviation*] (FAAC) .... AMA
Area Monitoring Office [*Military*] (DNAB) .... AMO
Area Moving Target Indicator [*NASA*] (KSC) .... AMTI
Area Multiplexer (CAAL) .... AM
Area Naval Commander [*NATO*] (NATG) .... ANC
Area Navigation .... ANAV
Area Navigation .... RNAV
Area Notice (FAAC) .... ARNOT
Area of Cardiac Disease (MEDA) .... ACD
Area of Cardiac Dullness [*Cardiology*] (DAVI) .... ACD
Area of Concentration (RDA) .... AOC
Area of Concern (MCD) .... AOC
Area of Critical Environmental Concern [*Bureau of Land Management designation*] .... ACEC
Area of Dominant Influence [*Mapmaking*] [*Telecommunications*] .... ADI
Area of Intense Air Activity (DA) .... AIAA
Area of Interest (AABC) .... AOI
Area of Mutual Visibility [*Aviation*] (PDAA) .... AMV
Area of Operation [*Military*] (VNW) .... AO
Area of Operations [*Military*] (AABC) .... AO
Area of Outstanding Natural Beauty [*Great Britain*] .... AONB
Area of Positive Control [*FAA*] .... APC
Area of Possible Incompatibility [*Military*] (DNAB) .... API
Area of Probability (NVT) .... AOP
Area of Resolution .... AR
Area of Responsibility (MCD) .... AOR
Area of Responsibility Centre [*Aviation*] .... ARC
Area of Safe Operation .... ASO
Area of Strategic Value [*Military*] .... ASV
Area of Substantial Unemployment [*CETA*] [*Department of Labor*] .... ASU
Area of Uncertainty (CAAL) .... AOU
Area of Uncertainty Factor .... AOUF
Area Office .... AO
Area Office Director [*OFCCP*] (AAGC) .... AOD
Area Operations Office [*Employment and Training Administration*] (OICC) .... AOO
Area Passive Dosimeter (MCD) .... APD
Area Petroleum Office [*or Officer*] .... APO
Area Planning .... AP
Area Planning Council [*Department of Education*] (OICC) .... APC
Area Planning Report .... APR
Area Planning-Action Councils .... APAC
Area/Point Search System (CAAL) .... APSS
Area Postal Directory [*Army*] (AFIT) .... APD
Area Precipitation Measurement Equipment .... APME
Area Precipitation Measurement Indicator (IEEE) .... APMI
Area Production Urgency Committee .... APUC
Area RADAR Prediction Analysis (PDAA) .... ARPA
Area Radiation Monitor (NRCH) .... ARM
Area Radiological Monitoring System (NRCH) .... ARMS
Area Railway Transport Officer [*British military*] (DMA) .... ARTO
Area Real Estate Office .... AREO
Area Records Officer (MCD) .... ARO
Area Recruiting Concept Special Test Army Reserve .... ARCSTAR
Area Redesignation [*Environmental Protection Agency*] .... AR
Area Redevelopment Act .... ARA
Area Redevelopment Administration [*Terminated, 1965; functions transferred to Economic Development Administration*] [*Department of Commerce*] .... ARA
Area Redevelopment Program .... ARP
Area Reference Resource Center [*Library network*] .... ARRC
Area Requirements and Product Status [*Military*] (DNAB) .... ARAPS
Area Resident Officer-in-Charge of Construction (DNAB) .... AROICC
Area Resource Center [*Library network*] .... ARC
Area Resource File [*Public Health Service*] [*Information service or system*] (IID) .... ARF
Area Resource File System [*Department of Health and Human Services*] (GFGA) .... ARFS
Area Responsibilities Transfer (SAA) .... ART
Area Resupply .... ARS
Area Safety Officer .... ASO
Area Sales Manager (DS) .... ASM
Area Sampling Frames .... ASF
Area Scale Temperature Display .... ASTD
Area Scanning Alarm .... ASA
Area Search Program .... ASP
Area Security Coordination Center .... ASCC
Area Security Information Center .... ASIC
Area Security Surveillance System (SAA) .... ASSS
Area Service Unit .... ASU
Area Signal Center [*Army*] (AABC) .... ASIGCEN
Area Signal Conditioner (MCD) .... ASC

Area Source [*Environmental Protection Agency*] (GFGA) .... AS
Area Source Category [*Environmental Protection Agency*] (GFGA) .... ASC
Area Spatial Filtering (MCD) .... ASF
Area Specialist Program [*Air Force training program*] .... ASP
Area Specialist Team [*Army*] .... AST
Area Specialized Division [*Army*] (MCD) .... AS
Area Stores Module (NITA) .... ASM
Area Supervisor (FAAC) .... ARSUP
Area Supervisor [*Bureau of Apprenticeship and Training*] [*Department of Labor*] .... AS
Area Supply and Maintenance Facility (MCD) .... ASMF
Area Supply Officer [*Army*] .... ASO
Area Supply Support Activity [*Army*] (AFIT) .... ASSA
Area Supply Support Plan [*Military*] (DNAB) .... ASSP
Area Support and Coordination Committee [*Military*] (VNW) .... ASCC
Area Support Group [*Military*] (AABC) .... ASG
Area Surveillance .... AS
Area Surveillance Control System (IEEE) .... ASCS
Area Surveillance RADAR .... ASR
Area Systolic Pressure (MAE) .... ASP
Area Test Equipment .... ATE
Area Traffic Officer .... ATO
Area Training Center [*Environmental Protection Agency*] (GFGA) .... ATC
Area Training Director [*Red Cross*] .... TD
Area under Plasma Concentration Curve [*Hematology*] .... AUC
Area Under the Curve [*Medicine*] (DMAA) .... AUC
Area under the Disease Progress Curve [*Botany*] .... AUDPC
Area Utilization Office [*GSA*] .... AUO
Area Ventralis of Tsai [*Of the brain*] [*Neurology*] (DAVI) .... AVT
Area VI Area Library Services Authority [*Library network*] .... ALSA 6
Area Wage and Classification Office .... AWCO
Area Wage Survey (OICC) .... AWS
Area Weapon Forward (MCD) .... AF
Area Weapon Left (MCD) .... AL
Area Weapon Right (MCD) .... AR
Area Weapon Verify (MCD) .... AV
Area Weighted Average Resolution [*Photography*] .... AWAR
Area Weighted Average T-Number (IEEE) .... AWAT
Area Working Standards .... AWS
Area Youth Office [*British*] .... AYO
Area-by-Area-Allocation [*Marketing*] (DOAD) .... ABA
Area-Dominant Military Aircraft .... ADMA
Area-Inertial Navigation System (PDAA) .... AINS
Areal Hypolimnetic Oxygen Deficit [*Hydrobiology*] .... AHOD
Area-Oriented Depots [*Military*] (RDA) .... AOD
Area-Oriented Distribution [*DoD*] .... AOD
Areas of Change Questionnaire .... ACQ
Areas of Deeper Convection (PDAA) .... ADC
Areas of Development International Conference and Exhibition [*British*] (ITD) .... AD 2000
Areas Source Program [*Environmental Protection Agency*] .... ASP
Areawide Planning Organization [*Department of Housing and Urban Development*] (GFGA) .... APO
Arecaidine Propargyl Ester [*Biochemistry*] .... APE
Arecibo [*Puerto Rico*] [*Seismograph station code, US Geological Survey*] (SEIS) .... APR
Arecibo [*Diocesan abbreviation*] [*Puerto Rico*] (TOCD) .... ARE
Arecibo Ionospheric Observatory [*Later, National Astronomy and Ionospheric Observatory*] [*Puerto Rico*] .... AIO
Arecibo, PR [*Location identifier FAA*] (FAAL) .... ABO
Arecibo, PR [*Television station call letters*] .... WCCV
Arecibo, PR [*AM radio station call letters*] .... WCMN
Arecibo, PR [*FM radio station call letters*] .... WCMN-FM
Arecibo, PR [*Television station call letters*] .... WMEI
Arecibo, PR [*AM radio station call letters*] .... WMIA
Arecibo, PR [*AM radio station call letters*] .... WNIK
Arecibo, PR [*FM radio station call letters*] .... WNIK-FM
Arel Comm & Software [*NASDAQ symbol*] (TTSB) .... ARLCF
Arel Comm & Software Wrrt'A' [*NASDAQ symbol*] (TTSB) .... ARLWF
Arel Communications & Software Ltd. [*Associated Press*] (SAG) .... Arel C
Arel Communications & Software Ltd. [*Associated Press*] (SAG) .... ArelCom
Arel Communications & Software Ltd. [*NASDAQ symbol*] (SAG) .... ARLC
Arel Communications & Software Ltd. [*NASDAQ symbol*] (SAG) .... ARLW
Arena .... ARN
Arena Magazine [*A publication*] (BRI) .... Arena
Arena Managers Association [*Defunct*] (EA) .... AMA
Arena Managers Association, Inc. [*Defunct*] .... AMAI
Arena Meetings, Conventions and Exhibitions Proprietary Ltd. .... AMCE
Arequipa [*Peru*] [*Airport symbol*] (OAG) .... AQP
Arequipa [*Peru*] [*Seismograph station code, US Geological Survey*] (SEIS) .... ARE
Arequipa/Rodriguez Ballon [*Peru*] [*ICAO location identifier*] (ICLI) .... SPQU
Arethusa Off-Shore Ltd. [*Associated Press*] (SAG) .... Arethusa
Arethusa Off-Shore Ltd. [*NASDAQ symbol*] (SAG) .... ARTH
Arezzo [*Italy ICAO location identifier*] (ICLI) .... LIQB
Arfendazam [*Biochemistry*] .... ARF
Argcen Holdings [*Vancouver Stock Exchange symbol*] .... AGN
Argent [*Money*] [*French*] .... A
Argent [*Heraldry*] .... A
Argent [*Heraldry*] .... ARG
Argent Bank [*Associated Press*] (SAG) .... ArgentB
Argent Bank [*NASDAQ symbol*] (SAG) .... ARGT
Argenta Systems [*Vancouver Stock Exchange symbol*] .... AEA
Argentaffin [*Cytology*] .... AN
Argentan [*France ICAO location identifier*] (ICLI) .... LFAJ
ArgentBank [*NASDAQ symbol*] (TTSB) .... ARGT

Argentex Resource Exploration Corp. [*Vancouver Stock Exchange symbol*] .... AXR
Argentia, NF [*FM radio station call letters*] .... CFOZ
Argentia, NF [*Television station call letters*] (RBYB) .... CJOM
Argentina [*IYRU nationality code*] (IYR) .... A
Argentina [*MARC country of publication code Library of Congress*] (LCCP) .... ag
Argentina [*ANSI two-letter standard code*] (CNC) .... AR
Argentina [*ANSI three-letter standard code*] (CNC) .... ARG
Argentina (VRA) .... Arg
Argentina [*MARC geographic area code Library of Congress*] (LCCP) .... s-ag--
Argentina Association of Nuclear Technology (NUCP) .... AANT
Argentina, Brazil, Chile .... ABC
Argentina, Brazil, Chile, and Peru (IIA) .... ABCP
Argentina Fund [*NYSE symbol*] (SPSG) .... AF
Argentina Fund [*Associated Press*] (SAG) .... ArgentFd
Argentine Angel [*Record label*] .... ArgA
Argentine Anticommunist Alliance [*Political party*] (LAIN) .... AAA
Argentine Columbia [*Record label*] .... ArgC
Argentine Commission for Human Rights (EA) .... ACHR
Argentine Decca [*Record label*] .... ArgD
Argentine Information Service Center (EA) .... AISC
Argentine Interplanetary Association .... AIA
Argentine Island [*Antarctica*] [*Seismograph station code, US Geological Survey*] (SEIS) .... AIA
Argentine London [*Record label*] .... ArgLon
Argentine Odeon [*Record label*] .... ArgOd
Argentine Parlophone [*Record label*] .... ArgP
Argentine Pathe [*Record label*] .... ArgPat
Argentine Victor [*Record label*] .... ArgV
Argentinian Communist Party [*Political party*] .... AKP
Argentinian Hemorrhagic Fever [*Medicine*] (DMAA) .... AHF
Argentinien [*Argentina*] [*German*] .... Argent
Argenton-Sur-Creuse [*France ICAO location identifier*] (ICLI) .... LFEG
Argentum [*Silver*] [*Chemical element*] .... Ag
Argentum [*Silver*] [*Numismatics*] .... AR
Argentum [*Silver*] .... ARG
Arges [*Romania*] [*Seismograph station code, US Geological Survey*] (SEIS) .... ARR
Argillite (VRA) .... argil
Arginase [*An enzyme*] .... AS
Arginine [*Also, R*] [*An amino acid*] .... Arg
Arginine [*Also, R*] [*An amino acid*] (DOG) .... arg
Arginine [*One-letter symbol; see Arg*] .... R
Arginine Decarboxylase [*An enzyme*] .... ADC
Arginine, Glutamate, alpha-Ketoglutarate Oxalacetate .... AGKO
Arginine Insulin Tolerance Test [*Endocrinology*] (MAE) .... AITT
Arginine Maturity Index [*For prediction of peanut harvest date*] .... AMI
Arginine Rich Motif [*Biochemistry*] .... ARM
Arginine Tolerance Test [*Endocrinology*] .... ATT
Arginine Vasopressin [*Antidiuretic hormone*] .... AVP
Arginine Vasotocin [*Endocrinology*] .... AVT
Arginine-Vasopressin (DMAA) .... ARVP
Argininosuccinate [*Biochemistry*] (DAVI) .... ASA
Argininosuccinate Lyase [*Also, ASL*] [*An enzyme*] .... AL
Argininosuccinate Lyase [*Also, AL*] [*An enzyme*] .... ASL
Argininosuccinate Synthetase [*An enzyme*] .... AS
Argininosuccinate Synthetase [*An enzyme*] (AAMN) .... ASAS
Argininosuccinate Synthetase [*An enzyme*] .... ASS
Argininosuccinate Synthetase Pseudogene (DMAA) .... ASSP
Argininosuccinic Acid (MAE) .... ASA
Arginosuccinic Acid Lyase (DMAA) .... ASAL
Argles' French Law of Bills of Exchange [*A publication*] (DLA) .... Arg Bills Ex
Argo [*Constellation*] .... ARG
Argo Development Corp. [*Vancouver Stock Exchange symbol*] .... ARG
Argo, SA [*Dominican Republic*] [*ICAO designator*] (ICDA) .... DI
Argo SA [*Dominican Republic*] [*ICAO designator*] (FAAC) .... RGO
ARGO Systems, Inc., Sunnyvale, CA [*OCLC symbol*] (OCLC) .... ASI
Argon [*Chemical symbol is Ar*] [*Chemical element*] .... A
Argon [*Preferred form, but also see A*] [*Chemical element*] .... Ar
Argon Gas LASER .... AGL
Argon Glow Lamp .... AGL
Argon Ion LASER .... AIL
Argon Ionization Detector [*Medicine*] (DMAA) .... AID
Argon LASER Discharge Tube .... ALDT
Argon LASER Lining .... ALL
Argon LASER Trabeculoplasty [*Ophthalmology*] (DAVI) .... ALT
Argon Oxygen Decarburization .... AOD
Argon Oxygen Refining (DNAB) .... AOR
Argon Purge Cart [*Nuclear energy*] (NRCH) .... APC
Argonaut Group, Inc. [*NASDAQ symbol*] (NQ) .... AGII
Argonaut Group, Inc. [*Associated Press*] (SAG) .... ArgoGp
Argonaut Resources Ltd. [*Vancouver Stock Exchange symbol*] .... AGP
Argonautica [*of Apollonius Rhodius*] [*Classical studies*] (OCD) .... Argon
Argonex International Ltd. [*Vancouver Stock Exchange symbol*] .... AXI
Argonne Advanced Research Reactor (NRCH) .... A^{2}R^{2}
Argonne Advanced Research Reactor .... AARR
Argonne Boiling Water Reactor (NRCH) .... ARBOR
Argonne Cancer Research Hospital [*Illinois*] .... ACRH
Argonne Code Center [*Department of Energy*] (IID) .... ACC
Argonne Code Center Exchange and Storage System (MHDB) .... ACCESS
Argonne Computer-Aided Diffraction Equipment .... ARCADE
Argonne Dispersion Code (MCD) .... ARDISC
Argonne Fast Source Reactor .... AFSR
Argonne High-Flux Reactor (NRCH) .... AHFR
Argonne Institute of Nuclear Science and Engineering [*AEC*] .... AINSE
Argonne Interactive Display .... AID

Argonne Low-Power Reactor [*Obsolete*] .... ALPR
Argonne Microprocessor .... AMP
Argonne National Laboratory [*Argonne, IL*] [*Department of Energy*] (GRD) .... ANL
Argonne National Laboratory, Argonne, IL [*OCLC symbol*] (OCLC) .... ANL
Argonne National Laboratory, Argonne, IL [*Library symbol Library of Congress*] (LCLS) .... IArg
Argonne National Laboratory, Argonne-West Technical Library, Idaho Falls, ID [*Library symbol*] [*Library of Congress*] (LCLS) .... IdIfAL
Argonne National Laboratory Division of Environmental Impact Studies .... ANL/ES
Argonne National Laboratory Energy and Environmental Systems Division .... ANL/EES
Argonne National Laboratory Engineering and Technology Division [*Illinois*] .... ANL/ETD
Argonne National Laboratory, Idaho Division .... ANL ID
Argonne National Laboratory Illinois Site (AAGC) .... AIS
Argonne National Laboratory-East (DOGT) .... ANL-E
Argonne National Laboratory-East [*Argonne, IL*] (GAAI) .... ANL-E
Argonne National Laboratory-East .... ANL-E
Argonne National Laboratory-West .... ANL-W
Argonne National Laboratory-West .... ANL-W
Argonne National Laboratory-West [*Idaho Falls, ID*] (GAAI) .... ANL-W
Argonne National Laboratory-West (DOGT) .... ANL-W
Argonne Nuclear Assembly for University Training .... ARGONAUT
Argonne Reactor Computation (IEEE) .... ARC
Argonne Reactor Physics [*AEC*] (PDAA) .... ARP
Argonne Tandem/LINAC Accelerator System [*Department of Energy*] .... ATLAS
Argonne Thermal Source Reactor .... ATSR
Argonne Universities Association .... AUA
Argon-Oxygen Decarburization [*Steelmaking*] .... AOD
Argonz del Castillo Syndrome [*Medicine*] (DMAA) .... ADCS
Argos Public Library, Argos, IN [*Library symbol Library of Congress*] (LCLS) .... InAr
Argos Tribune, Argos, IN [*Library symbol Library of Congress*] (LCLS) .... InArT
Argostolion [*Greece*] [*Airport symbol*] (OAG) .... EFL
Argosy [*A publication*] (ROG) .... ARG
Argosy Airways [*Canada ICAO designator*] (FAAC) .... ARY
Argosy Gaming [*NASDAQ symbol*] (TTSB) .... ARGY
Argosy Gaming Co. [*NYSE symbol*] (SAG) .... AGY
Argosy Gaming Co. [*Associated Press*] (SAG) .... Argosy
Argosy Gaming Co. [*NASDAQ symbol*] (SAG) .... ARGY
Argosy Mining Corp. Ltd. [*Toronto Stock Exchange symbol*] .... AGY
Argrel Resources Ltd. [*Formerly, Sundance Gold Ltd.*] [*Vancouver Stock Exchange symbol*] .... AGL
Argument (OCD) .... ARG
Argument Programming (MSA) .... AP
Argumento [*By an argument drawn from such a law*] [*Latin*] .... ARG
Argus Corp. Ltd. [*Toronto Stock Exchange symbol*] .... AR
Argus Open Numerical Environments [*Computer science*] .... Argus ONE
Argus Press Group [*British*] .... APG
Argus Printing & Publishing Co., Butler, NJ [*Library symbol Library of Congress*] (LCLS) .... NjButA
Argyle Community Library, Port Loring, Ontario [*Library symbol National Library of Canada*] (NLC) .... OPLAC
Argyle School, Argyle, MN [*Library symbol*] [*Library of Congress*] (LCLS) .... MnArS
Argyle Television 'A' [*NASDAQ symbol*] (TTSB) .... ARGL
Argyle Television, Inc. [*NASDAQ symbol*] (SAG) .... ARGL
Argyle Television, Inc. [*Associated Press*] (SAG) .... ArgyleT
Argyle Ventures [*Vancouver Stock Exchange symbol*] .... AGV
Argyll [*County in Scotland*] .... ARG
Argyll and Sutherland Highlanders [*Military unit*] [*British*] .... A & SH
Argyll Energy Corp. [*Toronto Stock Exchange symbol*] .... AYE
Argyll Light Infantry [*Military unit*] [*British*] .... ALI
Argyll Robertson Pupil [*Ophthalmology*] (MAE) .... AR
Argyllshire [*County in Scotland*] .... ARGYL
Argyllshire [*County in Scotland*] (ROG) .... ARGYLLS
Argyre Planitia [*A filamentary mark on Mars*] .... AP
Argyrophil .... AL
Argyrophil, Fluorescent, Granulated [*Cells*] [*Anatomy*] .... AFG
Arhus/Kirstinesminde [*Denmark ICAO location identifier*] (ICLI) .... EKKM
ARI Network Services [*NASDAQ symbol*] (SPSG) .... ARIS
ARI Network Services, Inc. [*Associated Press*] (SAG) .... ARI Net
ARIA [*Apollo Range Instrumentation Aircraft*] Operations Control Center [*NASA*] .... AOCC
ARIA [*Advanced Range Instrumentation Aircraft*] Phased Array Telemetry System [*Air Force*] .... APATS
Ariad Pharmaceutical, Inc. [*NASDAQ symbol*] (SAG) .... ARIA
ARIAD Pharmaceuticals [*NASDAQ symbol*] (TTSB) .... ARIA
Ariad Pharmaceuticals, Inc. [*Associated Press*] (SAG) .... Ariad
Ariad Pharmaceuticals, Inc. [*Associated Press*] (SAG) .... AriadP
ARIAD Pharmaceuticals Wrrt [*NASDAQ symbol*] (TTSB) .... ARIAW
Ariana Afghan Airlines [*Afganistan*] [*ICAO designator*] (FAAC) .... AFG
Ariana Afghan Airlines [*ICAO designator*] (AD) .... FG
ARIANE [*Artificial Satellite*] Passenger Payload Experiment (PDAA) .... APPLE
Aribinda [*Burkina Faso*] [*ICAO location identifier*] (ICLI) .... DHOY
Arica [*Chile*] [*Airport symbol*] (OAG) .... ARI
Arica [*Chile*] [*Seismograph station code, US Geological Survey*] (SEIS) .... ARI
Arica Institute (EA) .... AI
Arica/Internacional Chacalluta [*Chile*] [*ICAO location identifier*] (ICLI) .... SCAR
Aricana Resources [*Vancouver Stock Exchange symbol*] .... ANO
Arid Land Ecology [*AEC project*] .... ALE
Arid Lands Agricultural Development [*Program*] [*Later, ICARDA Middle East*] .... ALAD
Arid Lands Ecology .... ARE
Arid Lands Ecology Reserve .... ALE

Arid Lands Environment Centre [*Australia*] ... ALEC
Arid Lands Information Center [*University of Arizona*] [*Tucson*] ... ALIC
Arid Lands Information System [*University of Arizona*] [*Tucson*] (IID) ... ALIS
Arida [*Japan*] [*Seismograph station code, US Geological Survey*] (SEIS) ... ARD
Ariel Corp. [*NASDAQ symbol*] (SAG) ... ADSP
Ariel Corp. [*Associated Press*] (SAG) ... Ariel
Ariel Corp. [*Associated Press*] (SAG) ... ArielCp
Ariel Corp. Unit 2000 [*NASDAQ symbol*] (TTSB) ... ADSPU
Ariel Corp. Wrrt [*NASDAQ symbol*] (TTSB) ... ADSPW
Ariel Owners' Motorcycle Club (EA) ... AOMC
Ariel Resources [*TS Symbol*] (TTSB) ... AU
Ariel Resources Ltd. [*Vancouver Stock Exchange symbol*] ... ALL
Ariely Advertising Ltd. [*Associated Press*] (SAG) ... Ariely
Ariely Advertising Ltd. [*NASDAQ symbol*] (SAG) ... RELE
Ariely Advertising Ltd [*NASDAQ symbol*] (TTSB) ... RELEF
Aries [*Constellation*] ... Ari
Aries [*Constellation*] ... Arie
Aries Air Cargo International [*Air carrier designation symbol*] ... AACX
Aries Resources [*Vancouver Stock Exchange symbol*] ... AIE
Aril Society International (EA) ... ASI
ARINC [*Aeronautical Radio, Inc.*] **Communications Addressing and Reporting System** ... ACARS
ARINC [*Aeronautical Radio, Inc.*] **Communications Addressing and Reporting System** (USDC) ... ACARS
ARINC [*Aeronautical Radio Inc.*] **Communications Addressing and Reporting Systems** [*Marine science*] (OSRA) ... ACARS
ARINC [*Aeronautical Radio Incorporated*] **Communications and Address Reporting System** [*Digital communications system used primarily for aircraft-to-airline messages*] (GAVI) ... ACARS
Arion Resources, Inc. [*Vancouver Stock Exchange symbol*] ... AIO
Arion Systems, Inc. ... ASI
Ariprandus [*Flourished, 12th century*] [*Authority cited in pre-1607 legal work*] (DSA) ... Ar
Ariprandus [*Flourished, 12th century*] [*Authority cited in pre-1607 legal work*] (DSA) ... Ari
Ariprandus [*Flourished, 12th century*] [*Authority cited in pre-1607 legal work*] (DSA) ... Arip
Ariprandus [*Flourished, 12th century*] [*Authority cited in pre-1607 legal work*] (DSA) ... Aripnd
Ariprandus [*Flourished, 12th century*] [*Authority cited in pre-1607 legal work*] (DSA) ... Arp
Ariprandus [*Flourished, 12th century*] [*Authority cited in pre-1607 legal work*] (DSA) ... Arpn
Arista Investors Corp. [*NASDAQ symbol*] (NQ) ... ARIN
Arista Investors Corp. [*Associated Press*] (SAG) ... AristIn
Arista Invs Corp. [*NASDAQ symbol*] (TTSB) ... ARINA
Aristo International [*NASDAQ symbol*] (TTSB) ... ATSP
Aristo International Corp. [*Associated Press*] (SAG) ... AristoIn
Aristo International Corp. [*NASDAQ symbol*] (SAG) ... ATSP
Aristocrat (DSUE) ... ARISTO
Aristocrat ... ARSTCRT
Aristophanes [*Greek playwright, c. 445-380BC*] [*Classical studies*] (OCD) ... Ar
Aristophanes [*Greek playwright, c. 445-380BC*] [*Classical studies*] (ROG) ... ARIST
Aristos Foundation (EA) ... AF
Aristos Guild (EA) ... AG
Aristotelian Society [*British*] (EAIO) ... AS
Aristotle [*Greek philosopher, 384-322BC*] [*Classical studies*] (ROG) ... ARIST
Aristotle Corp. [*Associated Press*] (SAG) ... Aristotle
Aristotle Corp. [*NASDAQ symbol*] (SPSG) ... ARTL
Aristotle's Nicomachean Ethics [*A publication*] (DLA) ... Eth Nic
Aristoxenus [*Fourth century BC*] [*Classical studies*] (OCD) ... Aristox
Arithemetic Mask Register (MHDI) ... AMR
Arithmetic (IAA) ... A
Arithmetic (DNAB) ... ARI
Arithmetic [*Flowchart*] ... ARITH
Arithmetic Age [*Education*] (BARN) ... Ar A
Arithmetic and Control Processor ... ACP
Arithmetic and Control Unit (BUR) ... ACU
Arithmetic and Controls (SAA) ... A & C
Arithmetic and Controls (IAA) ... AAC
Arithmetic and Logic Unit [*Computer science*] ... A & LU
Arithmetic Array Identification ... AAID
Arithmetic Assignment Statement ... AAS
Arithmetic Average ... AA
Arithmetic Building Element [*Computer science*] ... ABE
Arithmetic Bus [*Computer science*] (IAA) ... AB
Arithmetic, Coding, Information, and Digit Symbols [*Psychometrics*] ... ACID
Arithmetic Computation Test [*Military*] ... AC
Arithmetic Computer ... ACU
Arithmetic Device ... AD
Arithmetic Element (BUR) ... AE
Arithmetic Element Program ... ARELEM
Arithmetic Expression (IEEE) ... AE
Arithmetic Factor Register [*Computer science*] ... D
Arithmetic Flag Aspect Factor (MHDI) ... AF
Arithmetic Function Designator ... AFD
Arithmetic Function Identifier ... AFID
Arithmetic Input Left [*Computer science*] (MHDI) ... AIL
Arithmetic Input Right [*Computer science*] (MHDI) ... AIR
Arithmetic Logic and Control Unit [*Computer science*] ... ALCU
Arithmetic Logic Processor ... ALP
Arithmetic Logic Register Stack [*Computer science*] (MHDI) ... ALRS
Arithmetic Logic Section [*Computer science*] ... ALS
Arithemetic Logic Unit [*Computer science*] ... ALU
Arithmetic Mean [*Statistics*] (DCTA) ... AM
Arithmetic Mean [*Statistics*] ... X
Arithmetic Output Control Unit ... AOCU
Arithmetic Output Data [*Computer science*] ... AOD
Arithmetic Output Unit ... AOU
Arithmetic Processing Unit [*Computer science*] ... APU
Arithmetic Processor ... AP
Arithmetic Processor Queue (IAA) ... APQ
Arithmetic Proficiency Training Program [*Computer-assisted training program*] ... APTP
Arithmetic Progression ... AP
Arithmetic Project [*National Science Foundation*] ... AP
Arithmetic Quotient (BARN) ... Ar Q
Arithmetic Reading Test [*Military*] ... ART
Arithmetic Reasoning Test ... ART
Arithmetic Register ... AR
Arithmetic Series Weight Function (PDAA) ... ASWF
Arithmetic Shift Left [*Computer science*] ... ASL
Arithmetic Shift Right [*Computer science*] ... ASR
Arithmetic Simple Variable ... ASV
Arithmetic Statement Function ... ASF
Arithmetic Underachievers [*Education*] ... AUA
Arithmetic Unit [*Computer science*] ... ARITHU
Arithmetic Unit [*Computer science*] ... AU
Arithmetical Unit [*Computer science*] (NITA) ... ARU
Arivaca Silver Mines Ltd. [*Vancouver Stock Exchange symbol*] ... AVC
Arizako Mines Ltd. [*Vancouver Stock Exchange symbol*] ... AZK
Arizona ... ARI
Arizona (AFM) ... ARIZ
Arizona [*Postal code*] ... AZ
Arizona [*MARC country of publication code Library of Congress*] (LCCP) ... azu
Arizona [*MARC geographic area code Library of Congress*] (LCCP) ... n-us-az
Arizona Academy of Family Physicians (SRA) ... AzAFP
Arizona Administrative Code [*A publication*] (AAGC) ... Ariz Admin Code
Arizona Administrative Digest [*A publication*] (DLA) ... Ariz Admin Dig
Arizona Administrative Register [*A publication*] (AAGC) ... Ariz Admin Reg
Arizona Air [*Aviation Services West, Inc.*] [*ICAO designator*] (FAAC) ... AAE
Arizona Airways, Inc. [*ICAO designator*] (FAAC) ... AZY
Arizona Appeals Reports [*A publication*] (DLA) ... Ariz App
Arizona Articulation Proficiency Scale [*Speech and language therapy*] (DAVI) ... AAPS
Arizona Association for Economic Development (SRA) ... AAED
Arizona Association for Home Care (SRA) ... AAHC
Arizona Association of Chiropractic (SRA) ... AAC
Arizona Association of Counties (SRA) ... AACo
Arizona Association of Health Underwriters (SRA) ... AzAHU
Arizona Association of Homes and Housing for the Aging (SRA) ... AzAHA
Arizona Association of Industries (SRA) ... AAI
Arizona Association of Life Underwriters (SRA) ... AALU
Arizona Association of Medical Products Suppliers (SRA) ... AAMPS
Arizona Association of Mortgage Brokers (SRA) ... AAMB
Arizona Association of Realtors (SRA) ... AAR
Arizona Association of School Business Officials (SRA) ... AASBO
Arizona Association of School Psychologists (SRA) ... AASP
Arizona Automatic Fire Alarm Association (SRA) ... AAFAA
Arizona Automobile Dealers Association (SRA) ... AADA
Arizona Automotive Recyclers Association (SRA) ... AARA
Arizona Automotive Trade Organization (SRA) ... AzAUTO
Arizona Bankers Association (SRA) ... ABA
Arizona Basic Assessment and Curriculum Utilization System (EDAC) ... ABACUS
Arizona Beef Council (SRA) ... ABC
Arizona Broadcasters Association (SRA) ... ABA
Arizona Builders Alliance (SRA) ... ABA
Arizona Bureau of Geology and Mineral Technology [*University of Arizona*] [*Research center*] (RCD) ... ABGMT
Arizona Business Association (SRA) ... ABA
Arizona Cable Telecommunications Association (SRA) ... ACTA
Arizona Cactus and Succulent Research (EA) ... ACSR
Arizona Cattlemen's Association (SRA) ... ACA
Arizona City, AZ [*FM radio station call letters*] ... KONZ
Arizona Clearing House Association (SRA) ... ACHA
Arizona Concrete Contractors Association (SRA) ... ACCA
Arizona Constitution [*A publication*] (DLA) ... Ariz Const
Arizona Construction Industry Association (SRA) ... ACIA
Arizona Consulting Engineers Association (SRA) ... ACEA
Arizona Cotton Growers Association (SRA) ... ACGA
Arizona Court of Appeals Reports [*A publication*] (DLA) ... AZ A
Arizona Credit Union League (SRA) ... ACUL
Arizona Crop Improvement Association (SRA) ... ACIA
Arizona Crop Protection Association (SRA) ... ACPA
Arizona Dance Theatre ... ADT
Arizona Department of Library Archives, Tempe, AZ [*OCLC symbol*] (OCLC) ... AZP
Arizona Desert Bighorn Sheep Society (SRA) ... ADBSS
Arizona Dietetics Association (SRA) ... AZDA
Arizona Education Association (SRA) ... AEA
Arizona Employers Council (SRA) ... AEC
Arizona Energy Management Council (SRA) ... AEMC
Arizona Farm Bureau Federation (SRA) ... AFBF
Arizona Financial Services Association (SRA) ... AFSA
Arizona Funeral Directors Association (SRA) ... AFDA
Arizona Golden Pacific [*Vancouver Stock Exchange symbol*] ... AZA
Arizona Golf Association (SRA) ... AGA
Arizona Health Care Association (SRA) ... AHCA
Arizona Heat Pump Council (SRA) ... AHPC

Arizona Highway Users Conference (SRA) .... AzHUC
Arizona Historical Foundation, Arizona State University, Tempe, AZ [*Library symbol Library of Congress*] (LCLS) .... AzTeS-Hi
Arizona Historical Society, Tucson, AZ [*Library symbol Library of Congress*] (LCLS) .... AzTP
Arizona Hospital Association (SRA) .... ArHA
Arizona Hotel and Motel Association (SRA) .... AzHMA
Arizona Independent Auto Dealers Association (SRA) .... AIADA
Arizona Instrument [*NASDAQ symbol*] (TTSB) .... AZIC
Arizona Instrument Corp. [*Associated Press*] (SAG) .... ArizInst
Arizona Instrument Corp. [*NASDAQ symbol*] (SAG) .... AZIC
Arizona International Campus [*University of Arizona*] .... AIC
Arizona Jewelers Association (SRA) .... AJA
Arizona Job Colleges [*An association Defunct*] (EA) .... AJC
Arizona Jojoba Growers Association (EA) .... AJGA
Arizona Jojoba, Inc. [*Vancouver Stock Exchange symbol*] .... AJJ
Arizona Land Income Corp. [*Associated Press*] (SAG) .... ArizLd
Arizona Land Income Corp. [*AMEX symbol*] (SPSG) .... AZL
Arizona Land Income'A' [*AMEX symbol*] (TTSB) .... AZL
Arizona Landscape Contractors Association (SRA) .... ALCA
Arizona Library Association (SRA) .... AzLA
Arizona Licensed Beverage Association (SRA) .... ALBA
Arizona Long Term Care Gerontology Center [*University of Arizona*] [*Research center*] (RCD) .... ALTCGC
Arizona Macintosh Users Group .... AMUG
Arizona Masonry Guild (SRA) .... AMG
Arizona Medical Association (SRA) .... ArMA
Arizona Medical Center, University of Arizona, Tucson, AZ [*Library symbol Library of Congress*] (LCLS) .... AzTAM
Arizona Mining Association (SRA) .... AMA
Arizona Mobile Housing Association (SRA) .... AMHA
Arizona Mortgage Bankers Association (SRA) .... AMBA
Arizona Motor Tariff Bureau, Inc., Phoenix AZ [*STAC*] .... AZB
Arizona Motor Transport Association (SRA) .... AMTA
Arizona Multihousing Association (SRA) .... AMA
Arizona Newspapers Association (SRA) .... ANA
Arizona Nursery Association (SRA) .... ANA
Arizona Nurses Association (SRA) .... AzNA
Arizona Official Compilation of Administrative Rules and Regulations [*A publication*] (DLA) .... Ariz Admin Comp
Arizona Official Compilation of Administrative Rules and Regulations [*A publication*] (DLA) .... Ariz Admin Comp R
Arizona Optometric Association (SRA) .... AzOA
Arizona Osteopathic Medical Association (SRA) .... AOMA
Arizona Pacific Airways [*Arizona Flight School, Inc.*] [*ICAO designator*] (FAAC) .... AZP
Arizona Parks and Recreation Association (SRA) .... APRA
Arizona Pest Control Association (SRA) .... APCA
Arizona Pharmacy Association (SRA) .... APA
Arizona Photopolarimeter Telescope .... APT
Arizona Physical Therapy Association (SRA) .... AzPTA
Arizona Planning Association (SRA) .... APA
Arizona Pork Council (SRA) .... APC
Arizona Professional Photographers Association (SRA) .... APPA
Arizona Promotional Products Association (SRA) .... AZPPA
Arizona Psychiatric Society (SRA) .... APS
Arizona Pub SvAdj Rt Q Pfd [*NYSE symbol*] (TTSB) .... ARPPrQ
Arizona Pub Svc 10%'MIDS' [*NYSE symbol*] (TTSB) .... AZD
Arizona Pub Svc $1.8125 Pfd [*NYSE symbol*] (TTSB) .... ARPPrW
Arizona Public Service [*Associated Press*] (SAG) .... AriP
Arizona Public Services [*NYSE symbol*] (SPSG) .... ARP
Arizona Public Services Co. [*NYSE symbol*] (SAG) .... AZD
Arizona Regional Ecological Test Site [*Department of the Interior*] .... ARETS
Arizona Regional Library for the Blind and Physically Handicapped, Phoenix, AZ [*Library symbol Library of Congress*] (LCLS) .... Az-BPH
Arizona Research Information Center [*Information service or system*] (IID) .... ARIC
Arizona Restaurant Association (SRA) .... ARA
Arizona Retailers Association (SRA) .... ARA
Arizona Revised Statutes [*A publication*] (DLA) .... Ariz Rev Stat
Arizona Revised Statutes [*A publication*] (DLA) .... Ariz Rev State
Arizona Revised Statutes [*A publication*] (DLA) .... ARS
Arizona Revised Statutes, Annotated [*A publication*] (DLA) .... Ariz Rev Stat Ann
Arizona Road Dust [*Environmental chemistry*] .... AZRD
Arizona Rock Products Association (SRA) .... ARPA
Arizona Roofing Contractors Association (SRA) .... ARCA
Arizona School Administrators Association (SRA) .... ASA
Arizona School Boards Association (SRA) .... ASBA
Arizona Self-Insurers Association (SRA) .... ASIA
Arizona Session Laws [*A publication*] (DLA) .... Ariz Sess Laws
Arizona Sign Association (SRA) .... ASA
Arizona Silver Corp. [*Vancouver Stock Exchange symbol*] .... ARZ
Arizona Silver Corp. [*Vancouver Stock Exchange symbol*] .... ASC
Arizona Small Business Association (SRA) .... ASBA
Arizona Small Utilities Association (SRA) .... ASUA
Arizona Society of Association Executives (SRA) .... AzSAE
Arizona Society of Health System Pharmicists (SRA) .... AzSHP
Arizona Society of Practicing Accountants (SRA) .... ASPA
Arizona Society of Professional Engineers (SRA) .... ASPE
Arizona Software Association (SRA) .... ASA
Arizona Sports Network [*Cable TV programming service*] .... ASN
Arizona Star Resource Corp. [*Vancouver Stock Exchange symbol*] .... AZS
Arizona State College .... ASC
Arizona State Dental Association (SRA) .... ASDA
Arizona State Electronics Association (SRA) .... ASEA
Arizona State Law Journal [*A publication*] (DLA) .... Ariz State LJ
Arizona State Museum [*University of Arizona*] [*Research center*] (RCD) .... ASM
Arizona State Prison Library, Florence, AZ [*Library symbol Library of Congress*] (LCLS) .... AzFlP
Arizona State University (GAGS) .... Ariz St U
Arizona State University [*Arizona*] [*Seismograph station code, US Geological Survey*] (SEIS) .... ASU
Arizona State University, College of Educational Technology and Library Science,Tempe, AZ [*OCLC symbol*] (OCLC) .... ASE
Arizona State University, College of Law Library, Tempe, AZ [*OCLC symbol*] (OCLC) .... AZC
Arizona State University, College of Law, Tempe, AZ [*Library symbol Library of Congress*] (LCLS) .... AzTeS-L
Arizona State University, Tempe, AZ [*OCLC symbol*] (OCLC) .... AZS
Arizona State University, Tempe, AZ [*Library symbol Library of Congress*] (LCLS) .... AzTeS
Arizona Statistical Repetitive Analog Computer .... ASTRAC
Arizona Stock Exchange .... AZX
Arizona Territory [*Obsolete*] (ROG) .... AT
Arizona Thoroughbred Breeders Association (SRA) .... ATBA
Arizona Tire and Service Dealers Association (SRA) .... ATSDA
Arizona Trade-Off Model [*State of Arizona and Department of Commerce project to resolve conflicts between economic and environmental goals*] .... ATOM
Arizona Transportation Research Center [*Arizona State University*] [*Research center*] (RCD) .... ATRC
Arizona Travel Industry Association (SRA) .... ATIA
Arizona Travel Parks Association (SRA) .... ATPA
Arizona Trial Lawyers Association (SRA) .... AzTLA
Arizona Veterinary Medical Association (SRA) .... AzVMA
Arizona Vocational Association (SRA) .... AzVA
Arizona Water Quality Association (SRA) .... AWQA
Arizona Water Well Association (SRA) .... AzWWA
Arizona Western College, Yuma, AZ [*OCLC symbol*] (OCLC) .... AZY
Arizona Western College, Yuma, AZ [*Library symbol Library of Congress*] (LCLS) .... AzYAW
Arizona Wholesale Beer and Liquor Association (SRA) .... AWBLA
Arizona Wool Producers Association (SRA) .... AWPA
Arizona-Nogales [*Mexico*] [*Airport symbol*] (AD) .... NOG
Ark Energy Ltd. [*Vancouver Stock Exchange symbol*] .... ARK
Ark Restaurants [*NASDAQ symbol*] (SAG) .... ARKR
Ark Restaurants [*Associated Press*] (SAG) .... ArkRst
Arkadelphia, AR [*Location identifier FAA*] (FAAL) .... ADF
Arkadelphia, AR [*FM radio station call letters*] .... KDEL
Arkadelphia, AR [*Television station call letters*] .... KETG
Arkadelphia, AR [*FM radio station call letters*] .... KSWH
Arkadelphia, AR [*AM radio station call letters*] .... KVRC
Arkansas [*Postal code*] .... AR
Arkansas (AFM) .... ARK
Arkansas [*MARC country of publication code Library of Congress*] (LCCP) .... aru
Arkansas [*MARC geographic area code Library of Congress*] (LCCP) .... n-us-ar
Arkansas Aging Foundation (SRA) .... AAF
Arkansas Agricultural Aviation Association (SRA) .... AAAA
Arkansas & Louisiana Missouri Railway Co. [*AAR code*] .... ALM
Arkansas & Ozarks Railway [*AAR code*] .... AO
Arkansas Appellate Reports [*A publication*] (DLA) .... Ark App
Arkansas Appellate Reports [*A publication*] (DLA) .... Ark App Rep
Arkansas Arts Center, Little Rock, AR [*OCLC symbol*] (OCLC) .... AKA
Arkansas Arts Center, Little Rock, AR [*Library symbol Library of Congress*] (LCLS) .... ArLA
Arkansas Association of Bank Holding Companies (SRA) .... AABHC
Arkansas Association of Conservation Districts (SRA) .... AACD
Arkansas Association of Educational Administrators (SRA) .... AAEA
Arkansas Association of Oriental Medicine (SRA) .... AAOM
Arkansas Association of School Administrators (SRA) .... AASA
Arkansas Association of Secondary School Principals (SRA) .... AASSP
Arkansas Automobile Dealers Association (SRA) .... AADA
Arkansas Bar Association (SRA) .... ABA
Arkansas Bar Association. Proceedings [*A publication*] (DLA) .... Ark BA
Arkansas Best [*NASDAQ symbol*] (TTSB) .... ABFS
Arkansas Best $2.875 'A 'Pfd [*NASDAQ symbol*] (TTSB) .... ABFSP
Arkansas Best Corp. [*NASDAQ symbol*] (SAG) .... ABFS
Arkansas Best Corp. [*Associated Press*] (SAG) .... ArkBest
Arkansas Best Corp. [*Associated Press*] (SAG) .... ArkBst
Arkansas Broadcasters Association (SRA) .... ABA
Arkansas Cancer Research Center [*Little Rock*] .... ACRC
Arkansas Chiropractic Association (SRA) .... ACA
Arkansas City, KS [*AM radio station call letters*] .... KSOK
Arkansas City, KS [*FM radio station call letters*] .... KYQQ
Arkansas Code Annotated [*A publication*] (AAGC) .... Ark Code Ann
Arkansas College [*Batesville*] .... AC
Arkansas College, Batesville, AR [*Library symbol Library of Congress*] (LCLS) .... ArBaA
Arkansas Constitution [*A publication*] (DLA) .... Ark Const
Arkansas Corporation Commission Report [*A publication*] (DLA) .... Ark CC
Arkansas County Quality Deer Association .... ACQDA
Arkansas Credit Union League (SRA) .... ACUL
Arkansas Crop Protection Association (SRA) .... ACPA
Arkansas Democrat, Little Rock, AR [*Library symbol Library of Congress*] (LCLS) .... ArLAD
Arkansas Department of Public Utilities Report [*A publication*] (DLA) .... Ark PU
Arkansas Education Association (SRA) .... AEA
Arkansas Electric Cooperatives (SRA) .... AEC
Arkansas Environmental Federation (SRA) .... AEF
Arkansas Farm Bureau Federation (SRA) .... AFBF
Arkansas Farmers Union (SRA) .... AFU

Arkansas Forestry Association (SRA) ... AFA
Arkansas Health Care Association (SRA) ... AHCA
Arkansas History Commission, Department of Archives and History, Little Rock, AR [*Library symbol Library of Congress*] (LCLS) ... Ar-Hi
Arkansas Home Builders Association (SRA) ... AHBA
Arkansas Hospital Association (SRA) ... AHA
Arkansas Hospitality Association (SRA) ... AHA
Arkansas Independent Automobile Dealers Association (SRA) ... AIADA
Arkansas Law Journal [*A publication*] (DLA) ... Ark LJ
Arkansas League of Savings Institutions (SRA) ... ALSI
Arkansas Library Commission, Little Rock, AR [*OCLC symbol*] (OCLC) ... AKF
Arkansas Library Commission, Little Rock, AR [*Library symbol Library of Congress*] (LCLS) ... Ar
Arkansas Livestock Show Association (SRA) ... ALSA
Arkansas Louisiana Gas Co. (IIA) ... AKG
Arkansas Louisiana Gas Co. ... ARKLA
Arkansas Manufactured Housing Association (SRA) ... AMHA
Arkansas Medical Society (SRA) ... AMS
Arkansas Motor Carriers Association (SRA) ... AMCA
Arkansas Municipal League (SRA) ... AML
Arkansas Municipal Police Association (SRA) ... AMPA
Arkansas Music Operators Association (SRA) ... AMOA
Arkansas Nuclear One (NRCH) ... ANO
Arkansas Nurserymen's Association (SRA) ... ANA
Arkansas Nurses Association (SRA) ... ArNA
Arkansas Oil Marketers Association (SRA) ... AOMA
Arkansas Optometric Association (SRA) ... AOA
Arkansas Osteopathic Medical Association (SRA) ... AOMA
Arkansas Petroleum Council (SRA) ... APC
Arkansas Pharmacists Association (SRA) ... APA
Arkansas Polytechnic College [*Later, Arkansas Technical University*] ... APC
Arkansas Polytechnic College [*Later, Arkansas Technical University*], Russellville, AR [*Library symbol Library of Congress*] (LCLS) ... ArRuA
Arkansas Pork Producers Association (SRA) ... APPA
Arkansas Post National Monument ... ARPO
Arkansas Poultry Federation (SRA) ... APF
Arkansas Power & Light [*NYSE symbol*] (SAG) ... AKP
Arkansas Power and Light Co. (IIA) ... AKP
Arkansas Power & Light Co. [*Associated Press*] (SAG) ... ArkPL
Arkansas Press Association (SRA) ... APA
Arkansas Propane Gas Association (SRA) ... APGA
Arkansas Railroad Association (SRA) ... ARA
Arkansas Ready Mixed Concrete Association (SRA) ... ARMCA
Arkansas Realtors Association (SRA) ... ARA
Arkansas Register [*A publication*] (DLA) ... Ark Admin Reg
Arkansas Register [*A publication*] (AAGC) ... Ark Reg
Arkansas Reports [*A publication*] (DLA) ... Ak
Arkansas Reports [*A publication*] (DLA) ... Ark R
Arkansas Reports [*A publication*] (DLA) ... Ark Rep
Arkansas Reports [*A publication*] (DLA) ... Ark's
Arkansas Research Test Station ... ARTS
Arkansas River Valley Regional Library, Dardanelle, AR [*Library symbol Library of Congress*] (LCLS) ... ArDar
Arkansas River Valley Regional Library, Dardanelle, AR [*OCLC symbol*] (OCLC) ... AVR
Arkansas School Boards Association (SRA) ... ASBA
Arkansas Sheriffs' Association (SRA) ... ASA
Arkansas Society of Association Executives (SRA) ... ASAE
Arkansas Society of Professional Engineers (SRA) ... ASPE
Arkansas Soft Drink Association (SRA) ... ASDA
Arkansas State Association of Life Underwriters (SRA) ... ASALU
Arkansas State Chamber of Commerce (SRA) ... ASCC
Arkansas State College [*Later, ASU*] ... ASC
Arkansas State Dental Association (SRA) ... ASDA
Arkansas State Employees Association (SRA) ... ASEA
Arkansas State Library, Little Rock, AR [*OCLC symbol*] (OCLC) ... AST
Arkansas State Police Association (SRA) ... ASPA
Arkansas State Teachers College [*Later, University of Central Arkansas*] ... ASTC
Arkansas State University (GAGS) ... Ark St U
Arkansas State University [*Beebe*] ... ASU
Arkansas State University Library, State University, AR [*OCLC symbol*] (OCLC) ... ASU
Arkansas State University, State University, AR [*Library symbol Library of Congress*] (LCLS) ... ArStC
Arkansas Statutes [*A publication*] (DLA) ... Ark Stats
Arkansas Statutes, Annotated [*A publication*] (DLA) ... Ark Stat Ann
Arkansas Supreme Court Library, Little Rock, AR [*Library symbol Library of Congress*] (LCLS) ... Ar-SC
Arkansas Supreme Court Reports [*A publication*] (DLA) ... Ark
Arkansas Technical University, Russellville, AR [*OCLC symbol*] (OCLC) ... AKP
Arkansas Telephone Association (SRA) ... ATA
Arkansas Transit Association (SRA) ... ATA
Arkansas Trial Lawyers Association (SRA) ... ATLA
Arkansas Valley Regional Library Service System [*Library network*] ... AVRLSS
Arkansas Veterinary Medical Association (SRA) ... AVMA
Arkansas Vocational Association (SRA) ... ArVA
Arkansas Water Resources Research Center [*University of Arkansas*] [*Research center*] (RCD) ... AWRRC
[*The*] **Arkansas Western Railway Co.** [*AAR code*] ... ARW
[*The*] **Arkansas Western Railway Co.** (IIA) ... AW
Arkhangelsk [*Former USSR Geomagnetic observatory code*] ... ARK
Arkhangelsk 2 Aviation Division [*Former USSR*] [*FAA designator*] (FAAC) ... OAO
Arkia Israel Inland Airlines [*ICAO designator*] (FAAC) ... AIZ
Arkia-Israel Inland Airlines [*ICAO designator*] (AD) ... IZ
Arkib Negara [*National Archives of Malaysia*], Federal Government Building,Kuala Lumpur, Malaysia [*Library symbol Library of Congress*] (LCLS) ... MlyKA
Ark-La-Tex Genealogical Association (EA) ... ALTGA
Ark-La-Tex Industries [*Vancouver Stock Exchange symbol*] ... AKL
Arkley's Justiciary Reports [*Scotland*] [*A publication*] (DLA) ... Ark
Arkley's Justiciary Reports [*Scotland*] [*A publication*] (DLA) ... Ark Just
Arkley's Justiciary Reports [*Scotland*] [*A publication*] (DLA) ... Arkl
Arkley's Justiciary Reports [*Scotland*] [*A publication*] (DLA) ... Arkley
Arlen Communications, Inc. [*Bethesda, MD*] [*Information service or system Telecommunications*] (TSSD) ... ACI
Arli [*Burkina Faso*] [*ICAO location identifier*] (ICLI) ... DHER
Arlin J. Brown Information Center (EA) ... AJBIC
Arlin Test of Formal Reasoning [*Intelligence test*] ... ATFR
Arlington [*Diocesan abbreviation*] [*Virginia*] (TOCD) ... ARL
Arlington Annex [*Navy*] ... AA
Arlington Annex [*Navy*] (DNAB) ... ARLAN
Arlington Annex [*Navy*] (DNAB) ... ARLEX
Arlington Baptist Junior College, Arlington, TX [*Library symbol Library of Congress*] (LCLS) ... TxArB
Arlington College, Arlington, CA [*Library symbol Library of Congress*] (LCLS) ... CArlA
Arlington County Department of Libraries, Arlington, VA [*OCLC symbol*] (OCLC) ... VIA
Arlington County Department of Libraries, Arlington, VA [*Library symbol Library of Congress*] (LCLS) ... ViAr
Arlington County Department of Libraries, Aurora Hills Branch, Arlington, VA [*Library symbol Library of Congress*] (LCLS) ... ViAr-A
Arlington County Department of Libraries, Cherrydale Branch, Arlington, VA [*Library symbol Library of Congress*] (LCLS) ... ViAr-Ch
Arlington County Department of Libraries, Clarendon Branch, Arlington, VA [*Library symbol Library of Congress*] (LCLS) ... ViAr-Cl
Arlington County Department of Libraries, Fairlington Branch, Arlington, VA [*Library symbol Library of Congress*] (LCLS) ... ViAr-F
Arlington County Department of Libraries, Glencarlyn Branch, Arlington, VA [*Library symbol Library of Congress*] (LCLS) ... ViAr-G
Arlington County Department of Libraries, Westover Branch, Arlington, VA [*Library symbol Library of Congress*] (LCLS) ... ViAr-W
Arlington Development Center, Arlington, TN [*Library symbol Library of Congress*] (LCLS) ... TArDC
Arlington Hall Station [*Virginia*] [*Army*] (AABC) ... AHS
Arlington Heights, IL [*Location identifier FAA*] (FAAL) ... JLH
Arlington Heights, IL [*FM radio station call letters*] ... WCBR
Arlington Heights Public Library, Arlington Heights, IL [*Library symbol Library of Congress*] (LCLS) ... IArlh
Arlington Memorial Amphitheater Commission [*Abolished 1960, functions transferred to Department of Defense*] ... AMAC
Arlington National Cemetery ... ANC
Arlington Naval Annex (MCD) ... ANA
Arlington, NY [*FM radio station call letters*] ... WDSP
Arlington Public Library, Arlington, IA [*Library symbol Library of Congress*] (LCLS) ... IaArl
Arlington Public Library, Arlington, OR [*Library symbol Library of Congress*] (LCLS) ... OrAr
Arlington Public Library, Arlington, SD [*Library symbol Library of Congress*] (LCLS) ... SdAr
Arlington Public Library, Genealogy Department, Arlington, TX [*Library symbol Library of Congress*] (LCLS) ... TxAr-G
Arlington State College [*Texas*] ... ASC
Arlington, TN [*Location identifier FAA*] (FAAL) ... LHC
Arlington, TX [*FM radio station call letters*] (RBYB) ... KEWS-FM
Arlington, TX [*TV station call letters*] (RBYB) ... KINZ-TV
Arlington, TX [*FM radio station call letters*] ... KSNN
Arlington, TX [*Television station call letters*] ... KTXA
Arlington, VA [*AM radio station call letters*] ... WABS
Arlington, VA [*FM radio station call letters*] ... WAVA
Arlington, VA [*AM radio station call letters*] ... WMZQ
Arlington, VA [*Television station call letters*] ... WTMW
Arlington, VA [*AM radio station call letters*] (RBYB) ... WZHF-AM
Arlington, WA [*Location identifier FAA*] (FAAL) ... AWO
Arlit [*Niger*] [*ICAO location identifier*] (ICLI) ... DRZL
Arlit [*Niger*] [*Airport symbol*] (OAG) ... RLT
Arm (IAA) ... A
Arm and Hammer [*Brand of soda*] ... A & H
Arm Circumference ... AC
Arm/Destruct (KSC) ... A/D
ARM Financial Group [*AMEX symbol*] (SPSG) ... ARM
ARM Financial Group [*Associated Press*] (SAG) ... ARM F
ARM Fin'l 9.50% Pfd [*AMEX symbol*] (TTSB) ... ARMPr
Arm/Fire Device (MCD) ... AFD
Arm/Firing Mechanism (MCD) ... A/FM
Arm Girth, Chest Depth, and Hip Width [*Anatomical index*] ... ACH
Arm Length ... AL
Arm Length Index ... ALI
Arm Length Order ... ALO
Arm Lock Magnet ... ALM
Arm Muscle Circumference ... AMC
Arm Retracting Strut [*Nuclear energy*] (AAG) ... AR-RET-ST
Arm/Safe (SAA) ... A/S
Arm Width ... AW
Arm Width Index ... AWI
Armada Free Public Library, Armada, MI [*Library symbol Library of Congress*] (LCLS) ... MiArm
Armada Gold & Mining [*Vancouver Stock Exchange symbol*] ... ARM
Armadillo ... ARMDLL

Armadillo Breeders Association [*Defunct*] (EA) ... ABA

Armageddon Project [*Later, AAAP*] (EA) ... AP

Armagh [*County in Ireland*] (ROG) ... AR

Armagh [*County in Ireland*] (WGA) ... ARM

Armak Chemicals, Saskatoon, Saskatchewan [*Library symbol National Library of Canada*] (NLC) ... SSAC

Armak Chemicals, Saskatoon, SK, Canada [*Library symbol Library of Congress*] (LCLS) ... CaSSAC

Armak Co., McCook, IL [*Library symbol Library of Congress*] (LCLS) ... IMccA

Armament ... A

Armament (SAA) ... AR

Armament ... ARM

Armament (AFM) ... ARMT

Armament and Avionics Planning Guidance (MCD) ... AAPG

Armament and Chemical Acquisition and Logistics Agency [*Army*] (INF) ... ACALA

Armament and Combat Vehicle Center (MCD) ... ACVC

Armament and Disarmament Information Unit [*British*] ... ADIU

Armament and Electronic Maintenance Squadron [*Air Force*] ... A & EMSq

Armament and Electronics [*Air Force*] ... A & E

Armament and Electronics (AFIT) ... AAE

Armament and Electronics [*Air Force*] (IAA) ... ARMEL

Armament and Electronics Laboratory ... AEL

Armament and Electronics Test Laboratory [*NATO*] ... AETL

Armament and Fire Control (MCD) ... A & FC

Armament and Flight Control System (SAA) ... AFCS

Armament and Fuel Coordinator (MCD) ... AFC

Armament Artificer [*British and Canadian*] [*World War II*] ... AA

Armament Auxiliaries Test Set (MCD) ... AATS

Armament Boresight Line ... ABL

Armament Command [*Army*] (AABC) ... ARMCOM

Armament Concepts Office [*Army*] (RDA) ... ACO

Armament Control ... AC

Armament Control and Delivery System (MCD) ... ARCADS

Armament Control and Display Panel (PDAA) ... ACDP

Armament Control Computer (MCD) ... ACC

Armament Control Indicator Set (DWSG) ... ACIS

Armament Control Panel ... ACP

Armament Control Processor Set (CAAL) ... ACPS

Armament Control Relay Panel (MCD) ... ACRP

Armament Control System [*Air Force*] ... ACS

Armament Control System Checkout [*Air Force*] (SAA) ... ACSC

Armament Control Unit (DNAB) ... ACU

Armament Data Line [*Military*] (NVT) ... ADL

Armament Datum Line (MCD) ... ADL

Armament Delivery Analysis Programming System (PDAA) ... ADAPS

Armament Depot [*Military British*] ... AD

Armament Design Establishment [*British*] ... ADE

Armament Development and Test Center [*Eglin Air Force Base, FL*] (MCD) ... ADTC

Armament Development Center [*Army*] ... ADC

Armament Development, Enfield ... ADEN

Armament Development, Enfield/Direction Etude Fabrication [*Military*] (MCD) ... ADEN/DEFA

Armament Development Technical Report ... AD-TR

Armament Division [*Air Force Systems Command*] [*Eglin Air Force Base, FL*] ... AD

Armament Division, Deputy for Engineering [*Eglin Air Force Base, FL*] ... AD/EN

Armament Electronic Maintenance Squadron ... AEMS

Armament Engineering Directorate [*Dover, NJ*] [*Army*] (GRD) ... AED

Armament Enhancement Initiative [*DoD*] ... AEI

Armament Handling Equipment (MCD) ... AHE

Armament Logistics Command [*Army*] (PDAA) ... ALC

Armament Maintenance Management Information Center [*Navy*] (NG) ... AMMIC

Armament Material Bulletin (NG) ... AMB

Armament Material Change (NG) ... AMC

Armament Material Readiness Command ... AMRECOM

Armament Monitor and Control (CAAL) ... AMAC

Armament, Munitions, and Chemical Command Regulation [*Military*] ... AMCCOMR

Armament/Munitions Requirements, Acquisition and Development Committee [*Military Washington, DC*] ... AMRAD

Armament Practice Camp [*British military*] (DMA) ... APC

Armament Practice Station [*British military*] (DMA) ... APS

Armament Recording Program [*Military*] ... ARP

Armament Release Panel (DNAB) ... ARP

Armament Research and Development Center [*Army*] (RDA) ... ARDC

Armament Research and Development Command (MCD) ... ARDCOM

Armament Research and Development Establishment [*British*] (MCD) ... ARDE

Armament Research Development [*British*] (MCD) ... ARD

Armament Research, Development, and Engineering Center [*Picatinny Arsenal*] [*Dover, NJ*] [*Army*] (RDA) ... ARDEC

Armament Retooling and Manufacturing Support Initiative [*1993*] ... ARMS

Armament Sergeant Major [*British*] ... ASM

Armament Station Control Unit ... ASCU

Armament Stores Issuing Ship [*Navy*] ... ASIS

Armament Supply Department [*Navy British*] ... ASD

Armament Supply Officer [*British Navy slang*] [*World War II*] (DSUE) ... ARSO

Armament Supply Officer [*Navy British*] (DMA) ... ASO

Armament System Test Environment (MCD) ... ASTE

Armament System Test Set (MCD) ... ASTS

Armament Systems Control Unit (MCD) ... ASCU

Armament Systems Personnel Research Laboratory [*Lowry Air Force Base, CO*] ... ASPRL

Armament Systems Section [*Air Force*] ... ASS

Armament Technical Manual (SAA) ... ATM

Armament Technology Division [*Air Force*] (MCD) ... ATL

Armament Technology Laboratory [*Air Force*] ... ATL

Armament Test ... AT

Armament Test Center [*Military*] ... ATC

Armament Test Preparation Facility ... ATPF

Armament Training Camp [*Military*] (OA) ... ATC

Armament Training Station [*Military*] (OA) ... ATS

Armaments Command [*Formerly, Munitions Command*] [*Rock Island, IL*] [*Army*] ... AC

Armaments Control Agency [*Western European Union*] (NATG) ... ACA

Armaments Cooperation Steering Committee ... ACSC

Armaments Design Department [*Ministry of Supply*] [*British World War II*] ... ADD

Armaments Research Department [*Ministry of Supply*] [*British*] ... ARD

Armaments Standardization and Interoperability [*NATO*] (NATG) ... ASI

Armani Exchange (ECON) ... A/X

Armanino Foods Distinction [*NASDAQ symbol*] (TTSB) ... ARMF

Armanino Foods of Distinction, Inc. [*Associated Press*] (SAG) ... Arman

Armanino Foods of Distinction, Inc. [*NASDAQ symbol*] (SAG) ... ARMF

Arm-Ankle Indices [*Cardiology*] (DAVI) ... AAI

Armata Revoluzione Nucleare [*Armed Revolutionary Nucleus*] [*Italy*] ... ARN

Armatron International, Inc. [*Associated Press*] (SAG) ... Armtrn

Armatron International, Inc. [*AMEX symbol*] (SPSG) ... ART

Armature (IAA) ... A

Armature (KSC) ... ARM

Armature ... ARMA

Armature (VRA) ... armt

Armature ... armtr

Armature ... ARMTR

Armature Acceleration (IAA) ... ARMACCEL

Armature Accelerator ... AA

Armature Shunt [*Electromagnetism*] (IAA) ... ARMSH

Armature Shunt [*Electromagnetism*] ... ARMSHT

Armature Shunt [*Electromagnetism*] (IAA) ... AS

Armature Shunt [*Electromagnetism*] ... ASH

Armature Winding [*Wiring*] (DNAB) ... AW

Armbro Enterprises, Inc. [*Toronto Stock Exchange symbol*] ... ARE

Armchair Detective [*A publication*] (BRI) ... Arm Det

Armco $4.50 Cv B Pfd [*NYSE symbol*] (TTSB) ... ASPrA

Armco $3.625 Cv A Pfd [*NYSE symbol*] (TTSB) ... ASPrB

Armco Inc,$2.10 Cv Pfd [*NYSE symbol*] (TTSB) ... ASPr

Armco, Inc. [*Formerly, Armco Steel Corp.*] [*Associated Press*] (SAG) ... Armc

Armco, Inc. [*Formerly, Armco Steel Corp.*] [*Associated Press*] (SAG) ... Armco

Armco, Inc. [*Formerly, Armco Steel Corp.*] [*NYSE symbol*] (SPSG) ... AS

Armco, Inc., Advanced Materials Division, Research Library, Baltimore, MD [*Library symbol Library of Congress*] (LCLS) ... MdBAS

Armco, Inc., Research Center, Technical Library, Middletown, OH [*Library symbol Library of Congress*] (LCLS) ... OMidAR

Armed (CINC) ... ARMD

Armed ... ARMD

Armed Advanced Scout Helicopter (AABC) ... ARMEDASH

Armed Aircraft Qualification ... AAQ

Armed Boarding Vessel ... ABV

Armed Career Criminal Act of 1984 ... ACCA

Armed Combat Youth [*Government of South Vietnam training program*] (VNW) ... ACY

Armed Experimental [*British military*] (DMA) ... AE

Armed Forces ... AF

Armed Forces Acquisition Document (NASA) ... AFAD

Armed Forces Act ... AFA

Armed Forces Air Intelligence Training Center ... AFAITC

Armed Forces Americas ... AA

Armed Forces and Society [*A publication*] (BRI) ... Arm F & S

Armed Forces Assistance to Korea [*Military*] ... AFAK

Armed Forces Benefit and Aid Association (EA) ... AFBAA

Armed Forces Benefit Association ... AFBA

Armed Forces Broadcasters Association (EA) ... AFBA

Armed Forces Central Medical Registry [*School of Aerospace Medicine*] (PDAA) ... AFCMR

Armed Forces Chemical Association [*Later, ADPA*] (EA) ... AFCA

Armed Forces Chemical Association [*Later, ADPA*] (EA) ... AFCA

Armed Forces Christian Fellowship ... ACFC

Armed Forces Civilian Instructors Association (EA) ... AFCIA

Armed Forces Combat Bulletin ... AFCB

Armed Forces Communications and Electronics Association (EA) ... AFCEA

Armed Forces Communications Association [*Later, AFCEA*] (MCD) ... AFCA

Armed Forces Council ... AFC

Armed Forces Courier Service ... AFCOS

Armed Forces Courier Service ... ARFCOS

Armed Forces Courier Station (AFM) ... ARFCOSTA

Armed Forces Cycling Association ... AFCA

Armed Forces Day ... AFD

Armed Forces Dental Officers Association (EA) ... AFDOA

Armed Forces Development Board ... AFDB

Armed Forces Disciplinary Control Board ... AFDCB

Armed Forces Enlisted Personnel Benefit Association [*Later, MBA*] ... AFEPBA

Armed Forces Epidemiological Board [*Washington, DC*] ... AFEB

Armed Forces Europe ... AE

Armed Forces Examining and Entrance Stations (AFM) ... AFEES

Armed Forces Examining and Induction Stations ... AFEIS

Armed Forces Examining Station ... AFES

Armed Forces Exchange Service (DNAB) ... AFES

Armed Forces Expeditionary Medal [*Military decoration*] (AFM) ... AFEM

Armed Forces Financial Advisory Services [*British*] ... AFFAS

Armed Forces for the Liberation of Cabinda [*Angola*] (PD) ... FALC

Armed Forces Health Profession Scholarship Program .... AFHPSP
Armed Forces Hostess Association (EA) .... AFHA
Armed Forces Identification Review Board [*US Total Army Personnel Agency*] (EGAO) .... AFIRB
Armed Forces Induction Station .... AFIS
Armed Forces Information and Education (MCD) .... AFIE
Armed Forces Information and Education Center (SAA) .... AFIEC
Armed Forces Information and Education Division .... AFIED
Armed Forces Information Film (AFM) .... AFIF
Armed Forces Information Program .... AFIP
Armed Forces Information School .... AFIS
Armed Forces Information Service [*DoD*] .... AFIS
Armed Forces Institute .... AFI
Armed Forces Institute of Pathology [*DoD*] (DNAB) .... AFINSPATH
Armed Forces Institute of Pathology [*DoD*] (EA) .... AFIP
Armed Forces Institute of Technology .... AFIT
Armed Forces Insurance .... AFI
Armed Forces Intelligence Training Center .... AFITC
Armed Forces Language Program .... AFLP
Armed Forces Leave Act of 1946 .... AFLA
Armed Forces Liaison Representative [*Red Cross*] .... AFLR
Armed Forces Librarians Round Table [*American Library Association*] .... AFLRT
Armed Forces Librarians Section [*Public Library Association*] .... AFLS
Armed Forces Mail Call [*Defunct*] (EA) .... AFMC
Armed Forces Management (AABC) .... AFM
Armed Forces Management Association [*Later, ADPA*] (EA) .... AFMA
Armed Forces Marketing Council (EA) .... AFMC
Armed Forces Master Records [*Solicited phonograph records, and money to buy records, for the armed forces*] [*See also RFOFM*] [*World War II*] .... AFMR
Armed Forces Medical Intelligence Center [*Fort Detrick*] [*Frederick, MD*] .... AFMIC
Armed Forces Medical Library [*Later, National Library of Medicine, 1956*] .... AFML
Armed Forces Medical Procurement Agency .... AFMPA
Armed Forces Menu Service Committee (AABC) .... AFMSC
Armed Forces Military Report [*DoD*] .... AFMR
Armed Forces Movement [*Portugal*] .... AFM
Armed Forces National Research Council [*National Academy of Sciences*] .... AFNRC
Armed Forces Network [*Military*] .... AFN
Armed Forces Network [*TV-radio*] (DOMA) .... AFN
Armed Forces News Bureau [*Later, AFPS*] .... AFNB
Armed Forces of the Republic of Korea (CINC) .... AFK
Armed Forces of the United States .... AFUS
Armed Forces Optometric Society (EA) .... AFOS
Armed Forces Pacific .... AP
Armed Forces Pest Control Board [*Washington, DC*] .... AFPCB
Armed Forces Pest Management Board (RDA) .... AFPMB
Armed Forces Philippines Supply Center (CINC) .... AFPSC
Armed Forces Police .... AFP
Armed Forces Police Department [*or Detachment*] .... AFPD
Armed Forces Policy Council .... AFPC
Armed Forces Procurement Regulation .... AFPR
Armed Forces Product Evaluation Committee (AABC) .... AFPEC
Armed Forces Production Distribution Service (DNAB) .... AFPDS
Armed Forces Production Resources Agency (MUGU) .... APRA
Armed Forces Professional Entertainment Office .... AFPEO
Armed Forces Provisional Ruling Council [*Gambia*] [*Political party*] .... AFPRC
Armed Forces Qualification Test .... AFQT
Armed Forces Qualification Test, Verbal Arithmetic Subtest .... AFQTVA
Armed Forces Radio (ADA) .... AFR
Armed Forces Radio and Telegraph Service .... AFRTS
Armed Forces Radio and Television Service-Broadcast Center (GFGA) .... AFRTS-BC
Armed Forces Radio Service [*Military*] .... AFRS
Armed Forces Radio Service [*United States military*] [*Established during World War II*] [*Later, Armed Forces Radio and Television Service*] (WDMC) .... AFRS
Armed Forces Radiobiology Institute .... AFFRI
Armed Forces Radiobiology Research Institute .... AFRADBIORSCHINST
Armed Forces Radiobiology Research Institute [*Bethesda, MD*] [*DoD*] .... AFRRI
Armed Forces Radiobiology Research Institute, Bethesda, MD [*OCLC symbol*] (OCLC) .... AFR
Armed Forces Radio-Television [*Cable-television system*] .... AFRTS
Armed Forces Readiness Command (MCD) .... AFREDCOM
Armed Forces Recipe Service Committee (AABC) .... AFRSC
Armed Forces Recreation Center .... AFRC
Armed Forces Recruiting Stations [*DoD*] .... AFRS
Armed Forces Relief and Benefit Association (EA) .... AFRBA
Armed Forces Reporting Unit [*Red Cross*] .... AFRU
Armed Forces Research Institute of Medical Sciences [*Bangkok - collaboration of Thailand and United States*] .... AFRIMS
Armed Forces Reserve Act of 1952, as Amended .... AFRA
Armed Forces Reserve Center (AABC) .... AFRC
Armed Forces Reserve Medal [*Military decoration*] .... AFRESM
Armed Forces Reserve Medal [*Military decoration*] .... AFRM
Armed Forces Retirement Home .... AFRH
Armed Forces Revolutionary Council [*Ghana*] (PPW) .... AFRC
Armed Forces Screen Reports .... AFSR
Armed Forces Security Agency [*Obsolete*] .... AFSA
Armed Forces Security Agency [*Obsolete*] .... AFSAG
Armed Forces Security Agency Council [*Abolished, 1952*] .... AFSAC
Armed Forces Security Agency Council Intelligence Requirements Committee [*Obsolete*] .... AFSAC/IRC
Armed Forces Special Weapons Agency .... AFSWA
Armed Forces Special Weapons Project [*Later, DASA*] .... AFSWP
Armed Forces Sports Committee (EA) .... AFSC
Armed Forces Staff College .... AFSC
Armed Forces Stamp Exchange Club (EA) .... AFSEC
Armed Forces Supply Control Center [*DoD*] .... AFSCC
Armed Forces Supply Support Center [*Merged with Defense Logistics Services Center*] .... AFSSC
Armed Forces Surplus Property Bidders Registration and Sales Information Office [*Later, Defense Surplus Bidders Control Office*] .... AFSPBRSIO
Armed Forces Technical Information Agency (NATG) .... AFTIA
Armed Forces Television Service (NTCM) .... AFTS
Armed Forces Vocational Testing Group [*Randolph Air Force Base, TX*] (AFM) .... AFVTG
Armed Forces Women's Selection Test .... AFWST
Armed Forces Writers League [*Later, NAGC*] (EA) .... AFWL
Armed Guard .... AG
Armed Guard (MUGU) .... ARMGRD
Armed Guard Center .... AGC
Armed Guard Center Training School [*Obsolete*] .... AGCTS
Armed Guard Inspection Officer .... AGIO
Armed Guard Inspection Service .... AGIS
Armed Guard School .... AGS
Armed Islamic Group [*Anti-government faction*] [*Algeria*] [*Acronym is based on foreign phrase*] (ECON) .... GIA
Armed Merchant Cruiser [*Obsolete Navy British*] .... AMC
Armed Merchant Cruiser [*Navy symbol*] XCL
Armed Nuclear Bombardment Satellite .... ANBS
Armed Proletarian Nuclei [*Italy*] .... NAP
Armed Propaganda Team [*Military*] .... APT
Armed Public Security Force (CINC) .... APSF
Armed RECCE [*Reconnaissance*] [*Military*] (VNW) .... AR
Armed Reconnaissance (MUGU) .... A/R
Armed Resistance Movement (EA) .... ARM
Armed Resistance Unit (EA) .... ARU
Armed Revolutionary Movement [*Puerto Rico*] .... ARM
Armed Scout Mission [*Military*] (DOMA) .... ASM
Armed Services .... AS
Armed Services Biomedical Research and Evaluation Management Committee .... ASBREM
Armed Services Biomedical Research Evaluation and Management (RDA) .... ASBREM
Armed Services Blood Program Office (DOMA) .... ASBPO
Armed Services Board of Contract Appeals .... ASBCA
Armed Services Bulletin .... ASB
Armed Services - Civilian Interest Survey [*Test*] .... ASCVIS
Armed Services Commissary Store Regulations (DNAB) .... ASCSR
Armed Services Committee [*US Senate*] (AAG) .... ASC
Armed Services Court Lawyers Association [*Now BCALA*] (AAGC) .... ASCTLA
Armed Services Documents Intelligence Center [*DoD*] .... ASDIC
Armed Services Edition [*Publishing*] [*World War II*] .... ASE
Armed Services Electron Tube Committee .... ASETC
Armed Services Electro-Standards Agency [*Later, DESC*] .... ASESA
Armed Services Exchange Regulation [*DoD*] .... ASER
Armed Services Explosive Ordnance Disposal Coordinating Group .... ASEODCG
Armed Services Explosives Safety Board [*Army*] .... ASESB
Armed Services Explosives Safety Board [*Army*] (AABC) .... ASESBD
Armed Services Graves Registration Office [*Later, AFIRB*] .... ASGRO
Armed Services Industrial Readiness Council .... ASIRC
Armed Services Medical Material Coordination Committee (CINC) .... ASMMCC
Armed Services Medical Procurement Agency [*Later, Medical Material Directorate*] .... ASMPA
Armed Services Medical Regulating Office .... ASMRO
Armed Services Medical Regulating Office (DOMA) .... ASMRO
Armed Services Papers .... ASP
Armed Services Patent Advisory Board [*DoD*] .... ASPAB
Armed Services Personnel Interrogation Center (AFM) .... ASPIC
Armed Services Petroleum Agency .... ASPA
Armed Services Petroleum Board .... ASPB
Armed Services Petroleum Purchasing Agency .... ASPPA
Armed Services Pricing Manual [*A publication*] (AAGC) .... ASPM
Armed Services Procurement Act .... ASPA
Armed Services Procurement Manual (MCD) .... ASPM
Armed Services Procurement Medal .... ASPM
Armed Services Procurement Planning Officer .... ASPPO
Armed Services Procurement Regulation [*Later, DAR*] .... ASPR
Armed Services Procurement Regulation Manual (AABC) .... ASPRM
Armed Services Procurement Regulation Supplement (AABC) .... ASPRS
Armed Services Procurement Regulation Supplement .... ASPS
Armed Services Procurement Regulations .... ASPERS
Armed Services Production Planning Officer (MCD) .... ASPPO
Armed Services Renegotiation Board [*Later, RB*] .... ASRB
Armed Services Research Specialists Committee .... ASRSC
Armed Services Technical Information Agency [*Later, Defense Documentation Center*] .... ASTIA
Armed Services Technical Information Agency Bulletin [*A publication*] (DNAB) .... ASTIAB
Armed Services Textile and Apparel Procurement Agency (DNAB) .... ASTAPA
Armed Services Vocational Aptitude Battery [*Tests*] .... ASVAB
Armed Services Whole Blood Processing Laboratory (AABC) .... ASWBPL
Armed Services Young Men's Christian Association [*Military*] .... ASYMCA
Armed Strike Reconnaissance (AABC) .... ASR
Armed Surface Reconnaissance [*Navy*] (DOMA) .... ASR
Armed Tactical Fighter [*General Dynamics Corp.*] (ECON) .... ATF
Armed White Male (ECON) .... AWM
Armedia/El Elden [*Colorado ICAO location identifier*] (ICLI) .... SKAP

Armee de Liberation Nationale [*National Liberation Army*] [*Algeria*] [*Political party*] (AF) ..... ALN
Armee de Liberation Nationale [*National Liberation Army*] [*Guadeloupe*] [*Political party*] (PD) ..... ALN
Armee de Liberation Nationale de l'Angola [*Angolan Army of National Liberation*] ..... ALNA
Armee de Liberation Nationale Kamerounaise [*Cameroonese National Liberation Army*] ..... ALNK
Armee de Liberation Nationale Kamerunaise [*Cameroonian Army of National Liberation*] (AF) ..... ALNK
Armee Korps [*Army Corps*] [*German*] ..... AK
Armee Nationale Congolaise [*Congolese National Army*] ..... ANC
Armee Populaire Nationale [*National People's Army*] [*Congo*] (AF) ..... APN
Armee-Munitionslager [*Army ammunition depot*] [*German military - World War II*] ..... AML
Armenia ..... ARM
Armenia (VRA) ..... Arm
Armenia [*Colombia*] [*Airport symbol*] (OAG) ..... AXM
Armenian [*MARC language code Library of Congress*] (LCCP) ..... arm
Armenian (BJA) ..... Armen
Armenian Assembly Charitable Trust (EA) ..... AACT
Armenian Assembly of America, Student Affairs Division (EA) ..... AAASAD
Armenian Assembly Student Services [*Later, AAASAD*] (EA) ..... AASS
Armenian Catholic Exarchate [*Diocesan abbreviation*] [*Pennsylvania*] (TOCD) ..... ARM
Armenian Church Youth Organization of America (EA) ..... ACYOA
Armenian Educational Foundation (EA) ..... AEF
Armenian Express Canada [*Vancouver Stock Exchange symbol*] ..... APN
Armenian Film Foundation (EA) ..... AFF
Armenian General Benevolent Union (EA) ..... AGBU
Armenian General Benevolent Union of America [*Later, AGBU*] (EA) ..... AGBUA
Armenian International Airlines [*ICAO designator*] (FAAC) ..... RME
Armenian Literary Society (EA) ..... ALS
Armenian Missionary Association of America (EA) ..... AMAA
Armenian National Army [*Guerrilla force*] [*Former USSR*] (ECON) ..... ANA
Armenian National Committee (EA) ..... ANC
Armenian National Council of America (EA) ..... ANCA
Armenian National Education Committee (EA) ..... ANEC
Armenian National Federation (AC) ..... ANF
Armenian Numismatic Society (EA) ..... ANS
Armenian Pan-National Movement [*Political party*] (EY) ..... APM
Armenian Progressive League of America (EA) ..... APLA
Armenian Relief Society [*Later, ARSNA*] (EA) ..... ARS
Armenian Relief Society of North America (EA) ..... ARSNA
Armenian Revolutionary Federation [*Political party*] (EY) ..... ARF
Armenian Revolutionary Federation of America [*Later, ARF*] (EA) ..... ARFA
Armenian Rugs Society (EA) ..... ARS
Armenian Secret Army for the Liberation of Armenia [*Turkey*] (PD) ..... ASALA
Armenian Secret Liberation Army ..... ASLA
Armenian Soviet Socialist Republic [*MARC country of publication code Library of Congress*] (LCCP) ..... air
Armenian Soviet Socialist Republic ..... ArmSSR
Armenian Soviet Socialist Republic [*MARC geographic area code Library of Congress*] (LCCP) ..... e-ur-ai
Armenian Students Association of America (EA) ..... ASA
Armenian Students Association of America (EA) ..... ASAA
Armenian Women's Welfare Association (EA) ..... AWWA
Armenian Youth Federation of America - Youth Organization of the ARF [*Armenian Revolutionary Federation of America*] (EA) ..... AYF
Armeno Resources, Inc. [*Vancouver Stock Exchange symbol*] ..... ARO
Armidale [*Australia Airport symbol*] (OAG) ..... ARM
Armidale City and Dumarasq Shire War Memorial Library, Armidale, NSW, Australia [*Library symbol Library of Congress*] (LCLS) ..... AuAr
Armidale Historical Society. Journal [*A publication*] ..... Arm Hist Soc J
Armidale Newspaper Co. Ltd., Armidale, NSW, Australia [*Library symbol Library of Congress*] (LCLS) ..... AuArA
Armijo, NM [*FM radio station call letters*] (RBYB) ..... KNKT
Armillaria mellea [*A fungus*] ..... AM
Arming (MSA) ..... ARM
Arming and Fusing (AFM) ..... A & F
Arming and Fusing Device ..... AFD
Arming and Fusing System (MSA) ..... AFS
Arming Decision Device (MUGU) ..... ADD
Arming Device ..... ARMDEV
Arming Device Assemblies [*Army*] (MCD) ..... ADA
Arming, Safing, and Initiating (SAA) ..... AS & I
Arming System Tester (MCD) ..... AST
Arming Unit Distribution Box [*Army*] (MCD) ..... AUDB
Arming Wire [*Bombs*] ..... AW
Armingford [*England*] ..... ARMINGF
Armistice and Post-War Committee [*British World War II*] ..... APW
Armistice Terms and Civil Administration [*British World War II*] ..... ACA
Armitage Academy Library, Kenosha, WI [*Library symbol Library of Congress*] (LCLS) ..... WKenA
ARMMS [*Automated Reliability and Maintenance Management System*] **Control Executive System** [*NASA*] ..... ACES
Armor All Products [*NASDAQ symbol*] (TTSB) ..... ARMR
Armor All Products Corp. [*Associated Press*] (SAG) ..... Armor
Armor All Products Corp. [*NASDAQ symbol*] (NQ) ..... ARMR
Armor and Arms Club (EA) ..... AAC
Armor and Engineer Board [*Army*] (PDAA) ..... ARENBD
Armor, Armament, and Ammunition ..... AA & A
Armor, Artillery, and Engineers Aptitude Area [*Army*] ..... AE
Armor Board (MCD) ..... AB
Armor Combat Operations Model Support [*TCATA*] (RDA) ..... ARCOMS
Armor Development Corp. [*Vancouver Stock Exchange symbol*] ..... ADP
Armor Enhancement Initiative [*Army*] ..... AEI
Armor Full Crew Research Simulator Center - Laboratory ..... AFCIS-L
Armor Grating [*Technical drawings*] ..... AG
Armor Holdings, Inc. [*AMEX symbol*] (SAG) ..... ABE
Armor Holdings, Inc. [*Associated Press*] (SAG) ..... ArmorH
Armor Information Management System-Logistics ..... ARIMS-LOG
Armor Machine Gun (MCD) ..... AMG
Armor Management Information System - Logistics ..... ARMIS-LOG
Armor Plate (MUGU) ..... A/PL
Armor Plate (KSC) ..... ARM-PL
Armor Remoted Target System (RDA) ..... ARETS
Armor School [*Army*] (MCD) ..... AS
Armor Support Battalion (MCD) ..... ASB
Armor Systems Program Review (MCD) ..... ASPR
Armor Target Mechanism [*Army*] ..... ATM
Armor Training Devices (RDA) ..... ATD
Armoral Tutle Public Library, New Plymouth, ID [*Library symbol*] [*Library of Congress*] (LCLS) ..... IdNpm
Armored (ADA) ..... A
Armored (CINC) ..... ARM
Armored (AFM) ..... ARMD
Armored ..... ARMRD
Armored Ambulance ..... AA
Armored and Mechanized Unit Air Defense [*Army*] ..... ARMAD
Armored Antiaircraft System (MCD) ..... AAAS
Armored Artillery Resupply Vehicle (MCD) ..... AARV
Armored Box Launcher [*Shipboard launching system*] ..... ABL
Armored Cable ..... AC
Armored Cannon Vehicle (MCD) ..... ACV
Armored Cavalry Assault Vehicle ..... ACAV
Armored Cavalry Cannon Vehicle (MCD) ..... ACCV
Armored Cavalry Regiment ..... ACR
Armored Cavalry Trainer [*Army*] (AABC) ..... ACT
Armored Cavalry Vehicle ..... ACV
Armored Cavalry's Veterans of Vietnam and Cambodia ..... ACVVC
Armored Column Cover (MCD) ..... ACC
Armored Combat Earthmover [*Army*] ..... ACE
Armored Combat Equipment (DOMA) ..... ACE
Armored Combat Logistics Support Vehicle [*Army*] ..... ACLSV
Armored Combat Logistics Support Vehicle Family ..... ACLSVF
Armored Combat Vehicle ..... ACV
Armored Combat Vehicle Material Center (MCD) ..... ACVMC
Armored Combat Vehicle Technology (RDA) ..... ACVT
Armored Combat Vehicle Technology Program ..... ACVTP
Armored Command and Reconnaissance Vehicle [*Former USSR*] (AABC) ..... ACRV
Armored Command Post [*Army*] (RDA) ..... ACP
Armored Command Vehicle [*Army*] ..... ACV
Armored Crashworthy Crew Set (MCD) ..... ACCS
Armored Crew Seat ..... ACS
Armored Cruiser [*Navy symbol Obsolete*] ..... ACR
Armored Division [*Military*] (MCD) ..... AD
Armored Division [*Army*] ..... ARMD
Armored Division Equivalent [*Military*] ..... ADE
Armored Engineer Vehicle (MCD) ..... AEV
Armored Family of Vehicles [*Military*] (RDA) ..... AFV
Armored Fighting Vehicle [*Marine Corps*] ..... AFV
Armored Force Vehicle ..... AFV
Armored Forward Area Rearm Vehicle (MCD) ..... AFARV
Armored Forward Area Resupply Vehicle (MCD) ..... AFARV
Armored Gun System [*Army*] ..... AGS
Armored Gun System, Armament [*Army*] (RDA) ..... AGS ARMT
Armored Infantry Battalion ..... AIB
Armored Infantry Combat Vehicle ..... AICV
Armored Infantry Fighting Vehicle (NATG) ..... AIFV
Armored Infantry Vehicle (MSA) ..... AIV
Armored Maintenance Vehicle ..... AMV
Armored Personnel Carrier [*Military*] ..... APC
Armored Personnel Carrier/Qualification Course [*Army*] ..... APC/QC
Armored Personnel Vehicle [*Military*] (IAA) ..... APV
Armored Reconnaissance ..... AR
Armored Reconnaissance Airborne Assault Vehicle (AABC) ..... ARAAV
Armored Reconnaissance Carrier (MCD) ..... ARC
Armored Reconnaissance Scout Vehicle [*Army*] (AABC) ..... ARSV
Armored Reconnaissance Scout Vehicle [*Army*] (RDA) ..... RSV
Armored Reconnaissance Scout Vehicle - Task Force (MCD) ..... ARSV-TF
Armored Reconnaissance Vehicle (MCD) ..... ARV
Armored Recovery Vehicle ..... ARV
Armored Rifle Battalion ..... ARB
Armored Security Vehicle [*Army*] ..... ASV
Armored Support Patrol Boat [*Military*] ..... ASPB
Armored Support Vehicle (MCD) ..... ASV
Armored Systems Integration [*Army*] (RDA) ..... ASI
Armored Systems Modernization [*Formerly, Heavy Forces Modernization Program*] [*Army*] (RDA) ..... ASM
Armored Systems Modernization - Future [*Formerly, Heavy Forces Modernization Program*] [*Army*] (RDA) ..... ASM-F
Armored Tank Cannon [*Army*] ..... ATAC
Armored Training Devices [*Army*] (RDA) ..... ARD
Armored Transport Vehicle (NATG) ..... ATV
Armored Transportation Institute (EA) ..... ATI
Armored Troop Carrier [*Army*] ..... ATC
Armored Troop Carrier (Helicopter) [*Army*] (SAA) ..... ATC (H)
Armored, Universal Engineer Tractor ..... AUET

Armored Utility Vehicle ... AUV
Armored Vehicle (MCD) ... AV
Armored Vehicle General Purpose [*General Motors armored car*] [*Canada*] ... AVGP
Armored Vehicle Launched [*Military*] (MCD) ... AVL
Armored Vehicle Launched Bridge [*Military*] (INF) ... AVLB
Armored Vehicle Technology Associates [*Army*] (RDA) ... AVTA
Armored-Infantry-Mechanized (AABC) ... AIM
Armorer (AABC) ... ARMR
Armorial and Heraldry Society of Australasia ... AHSA
Armorican ... ARM
Armor-Piercing [*Ammunition*] ... AP
Armor-Piercing Capped [*Ammunition*] ... APC
Armor-Piercing, Carbide, Ballistic Cap [*Ammunition*] (NATG) ... APCBC
Armor-Piercing Discarding Sabot [*Ammunition*] (NATG) ... APDS
Armor-Piercing Discarding Sabot, Fin-Stabilized [*Ammunition*] (MCD) ... APDSFS
Armor-Piercing Discarding Sabot with Tracer [*Ammunition*] (AABC) ... APDS-T
Armor-Piercing Fin Stabilized Discarding Sabot [*Ammunition*] (MCD) ... APFSDS
Armor-Piercing Fin Stabilized Discarding Sabot with Tracer [*Ammunition*] (INF) ... APFSDS-T
Armor-Piercing High Explosive [*Ammunition*] ... APHE
Armor-Piercing High Explosive Weaponry [*Army*] (VNW) ... APHE
Armor-Piercing Incendiary [*Ammunition*] ... API
Armor-Piercing Incendiary Tracer [*Ammunition*] ... APIT
Armor-Piercing Infantry Light-Arm System [*Ammunition*] ... APILAS
Armor-Piercing Reduced (Caliber) [*Ammunition*] ... APCR
Armor-Piercing Sabot [*Ammunition*] (SAA) ... APS
Armor-Piercing with Tracer [*Ammunition*] ... APT
Armor-Piercing-Capped, Ballistic-Capped [*Ammunition*] (MSA) ... APCBC
Armor-Piercing-Capped Incendiary [*Ammunition*] ... APCI
Armor-Piercing-Capped Incendiary with Tracer [*Ammunition*] ... APCIT
Armor-Piercing-Capped with Tracer [*Ammunition*] ... APCT
Armory ... ARMRY
Armour & Co., Chicago, IL [*Library symbol Library of Congress Obsolete*] (LCLS) ... ICArmour
Armour Pharmaceutical Co. [*Research code symbol*] ... AB
Armour Pharmaceutical Co. [*Research code symbol*] ... P
Armour Piercing - Hard Core (PDAA) ... AP-HC
Armour Public Library, Armour, SD [*Library symbol Library of Congress*] (LCLS) ... SdArm
Armour. Queen's Bench and County Court Reports Tempore Wood [*Manitoba*] [*A publication*] (DLA) ... Manitoba
Armour Research Center Library, Scottsdale, AZ [*Library symbol Library of Congress*] (LCLS) ... AzSArm
Armour Research Center, Scottsdale, AZ [*OCLC symbol*] (OCLC) ... AZR
Armour Research Foundation [*Later, IITRI*] ... ARF
Armour Research Foundation Reactor ... ARR
Armoured Boarding Steamer [*British military*] (DMA) ... ABS
Armoured Car [*Military British*] ... AC
Armoured Car Section, Royal Naval Air Service [*British military*] (DMA) ... ACSRNAS
Armoured Combat Vehicle Weapon System [*Military*] (PDAA) ... ACVWS
Armoured Control Vehicle [*Military*] ... ACV
Armoured Mine Clearing Vehicle [*Military*] ... AMCV
Armoured Motor Battery [*British military*] (DMA) ... AMB
Armoured Observation Post [*British and Canadian*] [*World War II*] ... AOP
Armoured Replacement Group [*British and Canadian*] [*World War II*] ... ARG
Armoured Scout Reconnaissance Vehicle [*Military*] (PDAA) ... ASRV
Armoured Tank Destroyer [*Military*] (PDAA) ... ATD
Armoured Tractor [*British*] ... AT
Armoured Train [*British*] ... AT
Armoured Vehicle Bridge Launcher [*Military*] (PDAA) ... AVBL
Armoured Vehicle, Reconnaissance [*British military*] (DMA) ... AVR
Armoured Vehicle, Royal Engineers [*British and Canadian*] [*World War II*] ... AVRE
Armourer Quartermaster Sergeant [*British*] ... AQMS
Armour-Piercing Composite Rigid [*British military*] (DMA) ... APCR
Armour-Piercing Secondary Effects [*British military*] (DMA) ... APSE
Armpit [*Medicine*] (DHSM) ... AX
Arms and Ammunition Division [*Army*] ... AAD
Arms & Armor (VRA) ... ar/arm
Arms & Armour Press [*Publisher*] [*British*] ... A & AP
Arms and Armour Society (EA) ... AAS
Arms and Militaria Collectors' Association of New South Wales [*Australia*] ... AMCNSW
Arms and Services on Duty with Air Force ... ASWAF
Arms and Services with the Army Air Forces ... ASWAAF
Arms Control and Disarmament [*A publication*] ... ACD
Arms Control and Disarmament Act [*1961*] ... ACDA
Arms Control and Disarmament Agency [*Washington, DC*] ... ACDA
[*United States*] **Arms Control and Disarmament Agency** (USGC) ... ACDA
Arms Control and Disarmament Agency (AAGC) ... USACD
Arms Control and Disarmament Agency Military and Economic Affairs Bureau [*Washington, DC*] ... ACDA/MEA
Arms Control and Disarmament Agency Weapons Evaluation and Control Bureau [*Washington, DC*] ... ACDA/WEC
Arms Control and Disarmament Agency Weapons Evaluation and Control Bureau Field Operations Division [*Washington, DC*] ... ACDA/WEC/FO
Arms Control and Disarmament Research Unit [*British*] ... ACDRU
Arms Control and Foreign Policy Caucus (EA) ... ACFPC
Arms Control Association (EA) ... ACA
Arms Control Computer Network [*Defunct*] (EA) ... ACCN
Arms Control Education Project [*Defunct*] (EA) ... ACEP
Arms Control Impact Statement (MCD) ... ACIS
Arms Control Observation Satellite ... ACOS
Arms Control Simulation (SAA) ... ACSIM
Arms Control Technical Information and Analysis Center [*Department of State*] ... ACTIAC
Arms Control Verification Committee [*Pronounced "acey-veecee"*] ... ACVC
Arms Export Control Act ... AECA
Arms Export Control Board ... AECB
ARMS/FIRMS Users Association (EA) ... AFUA
Arms Material (AABC) ... AM
Arms Memorandum ... AM
ARMS [*Action Research into Multiple Sclerosis*] **of America** (EA) ... AA
Arms Transfer Management Group ... ATMG
Armstrong Air, Inc. [*Canada ICAO designator*] (FAAC) ... ARQ
Armstrong Aldren Collins [*Lunar mineral named after three astronauts*] ... ARMALCOLITE
Armstrong Association of Philadelphia, Philadelphia, PA [*Library symbol Library of Congress Obsolete*] (LCLS) ... PPArmA
Armstrong Browning Library [*Baylor University*] [*Research center*] (RCD) ... ABL
Armstrong Community Library, Ontario [*Library symbol National Library of Canada*] (NLC) ... OARMS
Armstrong. Contested Election Cases [*New York*] [*A publication*] (DLA) ... Arms Con El
Armstrong Journal, Armstrong, IA [*Library symbol Library of Congress*] (LCLS) ... IaArmJ
Armstrong, Macartney, and Ogle's Irish Nisi Prius Reports [*A publication*] (DLA) ... AM & O
Armstrong, Macartney, and Ogle's Irish Nisi Prius Reports [*A publication*] (DLA) ... Arm & O
Armstrong, Macartney, and Ogle's Irish Nisi Prius Reports [*A publication*] (DLA) ... Arm M & O
Armstrong, Macartney, and Ogle's Irish Nisi Prius Reports [*A publication*] (DLA) ... Arm Mac & Og
Armstrong, Macartney, and Ogle's Irish Nisi Prius Reports [*A publication*] (DLA) ... Arms M & O
Armstrong, Macartney, and Ogle's Irish Nisi Prius Reports [*A publication*] (DLA) ... Arms Mac & Og
Armstrong, Macartney, and Ogle's Irish Nisi Prius Reports [*A publication*] (DLA) ... Armstrong M & O (Ir)
Armstrong, ON [*ICAO location identifier*] (ICLI) ... CYYW
Armstrong Public Library, Armstrong, ON, Canada [*Library symbol*] [*Library of Congress*] (LCLS) ... CaOARMS
Armstrong Siddeley Car Club [*Australia*] ... ASCC
Armstrong Siddeley Owners Club (EA) ... ASOC
Armstrong State College (GAGS) ... Armstrong St C
Armstrong State College, Savannah, GA [*OCLC symbol*] (OCLC) ... GAC
Armstrong State College, Savannah, GA [*Library symbol Library of Congress*] (LCLS) ... GSA
Armstrong University (GAGS) ... Armstrong U
Armstrong World Indus [*NYSE symbol*] (TTSB) ... ACK
Armstrong World Industries, Inc. [*Formerly, Armstrong Cork Co.*] [*NYSE symbol*] (SPSG) ... ACK
Armstrong World Industries, Inc. [*Formerly, Armstrong Cork Co.*] [*Associated Press*] (SAG) ... ArmWI
Armstrong's Breach of Privilege Cases, New York [*A publication*] (DLA) ... Arms Br P Cas
Armstrong's Cases of Contested Elections, New York [*A publication*] (DLA) ... Arms Elect Cas
Armstrong's Limerick Trials [*Ireland*] [*A publication*] (DLA) ... Arms Tr
Armstrong's New York Contested Elections [*A publication*] (DLA) ... Arms Con Elec
Armstrong-Spallumcheen Museum and Archives Society, Armstrong, British Columbia [*Library symbol National Library of Canada*] (NLC) ... BARS
Armstrong-Whitworth Sperry Gyroscope (IAA) ... AWSG
Army ... A
Army ... AR
Army Achievement Medal (INF) ... AAM
Army Achievement Medal [*Military decoration*] ... ARAM
Army Acquisition Corps (RDA) ... AAC
Army Acquisition Corps Management Office (RDA) ... AACMO
Army Acquisition Corps Program (INF) ... AACP
Army Acquisition Executive ... AAE
Army Acquisition Executive Support Agency (RDA) ... AAESA
Army Acquisition Information System (AAGC) ... AAIS
Army Acquisition Objective ... AAO
Army Acquisition Pollution Prevention Support Office ... AAPSO
Army Acquisition Program Executive Review System [*Army*] ... AAPERS
Army Acquisition Workforce Management Information System (RDA) ... AAWMIS
Army Act (ILCA) ... AA
Army Adaptation Inventory ... AAI
Army Administration Center, Fort Benjamin Harrison (AABC) ... ADMINCEN
Army Advanced Marksmanship Unit ... AAMU
Army Advanced Materiel Concepts Agency (PDAA) ... AAMCA
Army Adviser Discharge Affairs [*British and Canadian*] [*World War II*] ... AADA
Army Advisory Group, China ... AGC
Army Advisory Group on Energy ... AAGE
Army Aerial Reconnaissance System ... AARS
Army Aeromedical Research Laboratory (RDA) ... AARL
Army Aeronautical Depot Maintenance Center [*AMC-ASMC*] ... ARADMAC
Army Aeronautical Research Center [*Ames Research Center*] ... AARL
Army Air Base (MCD) ... AAB
Army Air Corps [*British ICAO designator*] (FAAC) ... AAC
Army Air Corps Centre [*British military*] (DMA) ... AACC
Army Air Cushioned Vehicle (VNW) ... ACV
Army Air Defense ... AAD
Army Air Defense Area ... AADA

Army Air Defense Artillery Board ..... AADAB
Army Air Defense Board (KSC) ..... AADB
Army Air Defense Command [*or Commander*] [*Later, AADCOM*] ..... AADC
Army Air Defense Command [*or Commander*] [*Formerly, AADC, ARADCOM*] (AABC) ..... AADCOM
Army Air Defense Command [*or Commander*] [*Later, AADCOM*] ..... ARADCOM
Army Air Defense Command and Control (MCD) AADC2
Army Air Defense Command Post ..... AADCP
Army Air Defense Control and Coordination System (AABC) ..... AADCCS
Army Air Defense Information Service ..... AADIS
Army Air Defense Operations Office [*or Officer*] ..... AADOO
Army Air Defense School (KSC) ..... AADS
Army Air Defense School ..... ARADSCH
Army Air Defense Site ..... AADS
Army Air Defense Staff (MCD) ..... AADS
Army Air Defense System [*Formerly, FABMDS*] ..... AADS
Army Air Force Board ..... AAFB
Army Air Force Bulletin [*A publication*] (MCD) ..... AAFB
Army Air Force Central Flying Training Command ..... AAFCFTC
Army Air Force Central Technical Training Command ..... AAFCTTC
Army Air Force Classification Center ..... AAFCC
Army Air Force Clemency and Parole Board ..... AAFCPB
Army Air Force Eastern Flying Training Command ..... AAFEFTC
Army Air Force Eastern Technical Training Command ..... AAFETTC
Army Air Force Flying Training Detachment ..... AAFFTD
Army Air Force Headquarters, Mediterranean Theater of Operations ..... AAFMTO
Army Air Force Intelligence Report (MCD) ..... AAFIR
Army Air Force Manual [*A publication*] (MCD) ..... AAFM
Army/Air Force Motion Picture Service ..... AAFM
Army Air Force Nontechnical Intelligence Report (MCD) ..... AAFNTIR
Army Air Force Officer-in-Charge ..... AAFOIC
Army/Air Force Post Office (AAGC) ..... APO
Army Air Force Technical Intelligence Report (MCD) ..... AAFTIR
Army Air Force Technical Order (MCD) ..... AAFTO
Army Air Force Translation (MCD) ..... AAFT
Army Air Force Weather Service Bulletin (MCD) ..... AAFWSB
Army Air Force Weather Service Manual [*A publication*] (MCD) ..... AAFWSM
Army Air Forces ..... AAF
Army Air Forces Aid Society [*World War II*] ..... AAFAS
Army Air Forces Air Adjutant General [*World War II*] ..... AFMAG
Army Air Forces Antisubmarine Command ..... AFSUB
Army Air Forces Assistant Secretary of War for Air [*World War II*] ..... AFSWA
Army Air Forces Base Unit ..... AAFBU
Army Air Forces Basic Training Center ..... AAFBTC
Army Air Forces Bombardier School ..... AAFBS
Army Air Forces Center ..... AAFC
Army Air Forces Chief of the Air Staff [*World War II*] ..... AFCAS
Army Air Forces Commanding General [*World War II*] ..... AFACG
Army Air Forces Deputy Chiefs of Air Staff [*World War II*] ..... AFIAS
Army Air Forces Engineer Command ..... AAFEC
Army Air Forces Gunnery School ..... AAFGS
Army Air Forces Intelligence School ..... AAFIS
Army Air Forces Materiel Center ..... AAFMC
Army Air Forces Military Personnel [*World War II*] ..... AFPMP
Army Air Forces Navigation School ..... AAFNS
Army Air Forces, Pacific Ocean Areas ..... AAFPOA
Army Air Forces, Pacific Ocean Areas (Administrative) ..... AAFPOA (ADMIN)
Army Air Forces Pilot School ..... AAFPS
Army Air Forces Pre-Flight School (Pilot) ..... AAFPFS(P)
Army Air Forces Requirements Division [*World War II*] ..... AFREQ
Army Air Forces School of Applied Tactics [*World War II*] ..... AAFSAT
Army Air Forces Service Command ..... AAFSC
Army Air Forces Southeast Training Command [*World War II*] ..... AAFSETC
Army Air Forces Tactical Center [*World War II*] ..... AAFTAC
Army Air Forces Technical School [*World War II*] ..... AAFTS
Army Air Forces Technical Training Command [*World War II*] ..... AAFTTC
Army Air Forces Training Aids Division [*World War II*] ..... AAFTAD
Army Air Forces Training Command [*World War II*] ..... AAFTC
Army Air Forces Western Flying Training Command [*World War II*] ..... AAFWFTC
Army Air Forces Western Technical Training Command [*World War II*] ..... AAFWTTC
Army Air Mobility Research and Development Laboratories [*Army*] ..... AAMRDL
Army Air Movement Support Unit (MCD) ..... AAMSU
Army Air Operations (MCD) ..... AA
Army Air Reconnaissance for Damage Assessment in the Continental United States (AABC) ..... AARDAC
Army Air Service ..... AAS
Army Air Support Control [*British and Canadian*] [*World War II*] ..... A AIR SC
Army Air Traffic Control and Navigation System (MCD) ..... AATCAN
Army Air Traffic Coordinating Office (AABC) ..... AATCO
Army Air Traffic Regulation and Identification ..... AATRI
Army Air Traffic Regulation and Identification System (AFM) ..... AATRIS
Army Air Transport Organization ..... AATO
Army Air Transport Training and Development Centre [*England*] ..... AATDC
Army Airborne Electronics and Special Warfare Board ..... AAESWB
Army Aircraft (AABC) ..... AACFT
Army Aircraft Avionics Study (MCD) A3S
Army Aircraft Maintenance (AABC) ..... AAM
Army Aircraft Maintenance Shop (AABC) ..... AAMS
Army Aircraft Mobile Technical Assistance Program ..... AAMTAP
Army Aircraft Radio Laboratory (IAA) ..... AARL
Army Aircraft Repair Ship ..... AARS
Army Aircraft Requirements Review Committee ..... AARRC
Army Airfield ..... AAF
Army Air-Ground System ..... AAGS
Army Airspace Command and Control (DOMA) ..... A^2C^2
Army Airspace Command and Control ..... A^{2C2}
Army Airways Communications System ..... AACS
Army Alaska Communication System [*Air Force*] ..... AACS
Army Amateur Radio System ..... AARS
Army/American Council on Education (INF) ..... ACE
Army/American Council on Education Registry Transcript System (INF) ..... AARTS
Army Ammunition in Thailand (MCD) ..... AIT
Army Ammunition Plant (AABC) ..... AAP
[*The*] **Army Ammunition Reporting System** (AABC) ..... TAARS
Army Analysis of Intelligence ..... AAI
Army and Air Force Act [*British military*] (DMA) ..... A & AFA
Army and Air Force Air Intelligence School [*British*] ..... AAFAIS
Army and Air Force Base ..... AAFB
Army and Air Force Civilian Welfare Fund ..... AAFCWF
Army and Air Force Exchange and Motion Picture Service ..... AAFEMPS
Army and Air Force Exchange and Motion Picture Service Board of Directors [*DoD*] ..... AAFBD
Army and Air Force Exchange Service ..... A & AFES
Army and Air Force Exchange Service ..... AAFES
Army and Air Force Intelligence Staff [*British*] ..... AAFIS
Army and Air Force Motion Picture Service ..... AAFMPS
Army and Air Force Mutual Aid Association (EA) ..... AAFMAA
Army and Air Force Postal Service ..... AAFPS
Army and Air Force Wage Board ..... AAFWB
Army and Navy ..... A & N
Army and Navy ..... AN
Army and Navy Club, Washington, DC [*Library symbol Library of Congress*] (LCLS) ..... DAN
Army and Navy Life [*New York*] [*A publication*] (ROG) ..... A & NL
Army and Navy Munitions Board [*British*] (DAS) ..... A & NB
Army and Navy Staff College [*Redesignated National War College, 1946*] ..... ANSC
Army and Navy Staff College [*See ANSC*] ..... ANSCOL
Army and Navy Union, USA (EA) ..... ANU
Army Apprenticeship Program ..... AAP
Army Area Analysis Intelligence Agency (SAA) ..... AAIA
Army Area Calibration Facilities (MCD) ..... AACF
Army Area Communications [*System*] (IAA) ..... AACOM
Army Area Communications System (MCD) ..... AACOMS
Army Area Representative ..... AAR
Army Area Signal Center (AABC) ..... AASC
Army Area Signal System (IAA) ..... AASS
Army Armament Materiel Readiness Command ..... ARRCOM
Army Armament Research and Development Center [*or Command*] **Technical Support Directorate** [*Dover, NJ*] ..... ARTSD
Army Armament Research and Development Command [*Dover, NJ*] (MCD) ..... ARRADCOM
Army Armament Research and Development Command Chemical Systems Laboratory ..... ARCSL
Army Armament Research and Development Command Product Assurance Directorate ..... ARPAD
Army Armament Research Ballistic Research Laboratory [*Aberdeen Proving Ground, MD*] (MCD) ..... ARBRL
Army Armor Board (MCD) ..... A-ARM
Army Armor School (AAG) ..... AAMS
Army Artillery and Missile Center [*Fort Sill, OK*] (MCD) ..... AAMC
Army Artillery and Missile School ..... AAMS
Army Artillery Board (AAG) ..... AAB
Army Artillery Board (MCD) ..... A-ART
Army Artillery Group (AABC) ..... AAG
Army Aspirin (VNW) ..... APC
Army Assault Team ..... AAT
Army Atomic Weapons Systems Safety Committee [*Later, DNA*] (AABC) ..... AAWSSC
Army Attache ..... ARMA
Army Attache System ..... AAS
Army Attrition Rates Committee (NATG) ..... AARC
Army Audio-Visual Agency (PDAA) ..... AAVA
Army Audiovisual Center ..... AAC
Army Audit Agency ..... AAA
Army Authority for Major Commands to Disseminate Information and Take Appropriate Action ..... ACTCOM
Army Auto Plan and Progress Evaluation System ..... AAPPES
[*The*] **Army Automated Budget System** ..... TAABS
Army Automated Environmental Management Information System ..... AAEMIS
[*The*] **Army Automated Logistic Data System** ..... TAALODS
Army Automation and Communication Steering Committee ..... AACSC
Army Automation Command Operating Budget (AAGC) ..... AACOB
Army Automation Command Operating Budget Estimate ..... AACOBE
Army Automation Communications System (AAGC) ..... AACOMS
Army Automation Directorate [*Formerly, DMIS*] (MCD) ..... AAD
Army Automation Master Plan ..... AAMAP
Army Automation Memorandum Budget ..... AAMB
Army Automation Planning, Programming, and Evaluation System (MCD) ..... AAPES
Army Automation Planning, Programming, and Evaluation System ..... AAPPES
Army Automation Program ..... AAP
Army Automation Program Budget Guidance ..... AAPBG
Army Automation Security Program ..... AASP
Army Automation Steering Committee ..... AASC
Army Aviation (AABC) ..... AAVN
Army Aviation Association of America (EA) ..... AAAA
Army Aviation Board ..... AAB
Army Aviation Centre [*British*] (BI) ..... AAvnC

Army Aviation Control Center	AACC
Army Aviation Decontamination Station (DOMA)	AADS
Army Aviation Depot Maintenance Center (MCD)	AADMC
Army Aviation Development Plan (MCD)	AADP
Army Aviation Element (AABC)	AAE
Army Aviation Employment Conference	AVNEC
Army Aviation Engineering Flight Activity	AAEFA
Army Aviation Engineers	AAE
Army Aviation Maintenance Support Activity	AAMSA
Army Aviation Materiel Command	AAMC
Army Aviation Materiel Laboratory (MCD)	AAML
Army Aviation Medical Officer's Badge [Military decoration]	AR Av MO Bad
Army Aviation Mission Area Analysis	AAMAA
Army Aviation Modernization Plan (MCD)	AAMP
Army Aviation Operating Detachment	AAOD
Army Aviation Personnel Requirements of Sustained Operations Study (MCD)	AAPRSO
Army Aviation Planning Manual (AABC)	AAPM
Army Aviation Program Review (MCD)	AAPR
Army Aviation Research and Development Command [Fort Monmouth, NJ] (MCD)	AVRADCOM
Army Aviation Support Element (AABC)	AASE
Army Aviation Support Facility (MCD)	AASF
Army Aviation Systems Test Activity [Also, USAASTA]	AASTA
Army Aviation Test Board	AATB
Army Aviation Test Command [ATEC]	AATC
Army Aviation Unit Training Command (MCD)	AAUTC
Army Aviator (AABC)	ARAV
Army Aviator Badge [Military decoration]	AR Av Bad
Army Aviator Badge [Military decoration]	AVBAD
Army Avionics Program	AAP
Army Background Experiment	ABE
Army Ballistic Missile Agency [Redstone Arsenal, AL]	ABMA
Army Ballistic Research Laboratory (SAA)	ABRL
Army Base Information Transfer System (MCD)	ARBITS
Army Basic Training Unit [British military] (DMA)	ABTU
Army Battle Command System (RDA)	ABCS
Army Battle Command Systems [Army]	ABCS
Army Battle Damage Repair (GFGA)	ABDR
Army Battlefield Interface Concept (MCD)	ABIC
Army Benevolent Fund [British]	ABF
Army Biological Laboratory	ABL
Army Biological Warfare Research Center	ABWRC
Army Board for Correction of Military Records	ABCMR
Army Board of Contract Appeals (AAGC)	ABCA
Army Board of Review for Eliminations	ABRE
Army Book [British and Canadian] [World War II]	AB
Army Broadcasting Service (GFGA)	ABS
Army Budget Directive	ABD
Army Budget Office	ABO
Army Bureau of Current Affairs [To encourage British soldiers to think and talk about what they were fighting for] [World War II]	ABCA
Army Cadet Force [Military unit] [British]	ACF
Army Cadet Force Association [British military] (DMA)	ACFA
Army Calibration System	ACS
Army Capabilities Plan	ACP
Army Career and Alumni Program (INF)	ACAP
Army Career Education System	ACES
Army Career Group	ACGP
Army Catering Corps [British]	ACC
Army Cavalry Scout Experiment (MCD)	ARCAVEX
Army [Forces US] Central [Command] (DOMA)	ARCENT
Army Central Budget Office	ACBO
Army Central Logistics Data Bank (AABC)	ACLDB
Army Central Service Point	ACSP
Army Central Welfare Fund	ACWF
Army Chaplains Department [British military] (DMA)	ACD
Army Chemical Center	ACC
Army Chemical Center	ACMLC
Army Chemical Center Procurement Agency	ACCPA
Army Chemical Corps Medical Laboratories (KSC)	ACCML
Army Chemical Research and Development Labs (MCD)	ACRDL
Army Chemical Warfare Laboratory	ACWL
Army Chief of Research and Development (SAA)	ACRD
Army Chief of Staff (AAGC)	CSA
Army Chief of Support Services	ACSS
Army Child Advocacy Program (MCD)	ACAP
Army Circular [British military] (DMA)	AC
Army Civil Services' Union [Singapore]	ACSU
Army Civilian Career Evaluation System	ACCES
Army Civilian Personnel System	ACPERS
Army Civilian Training, Education, and Development System	ACTEDS
Army Class Manager Activity (AABC)	ACMA
Army Classification Battery [Military tests]	ACB
Army Classification Evaluation Board	ACEB
Army Clerical Speed Test	ACST
Army Clothing and Equipment Board (MCD)	ACEB
Army Clothing, Textile, and Materiel Center	ACTMC
Army Club Fund	ACF
Army Coastal Engineering Research Center	ACERC
Army Coating and Chemical Laboratory (MCD)	ACCL
Army Cohesion and Stability Program	ARCOST
Army Cohesion Study (MCD)	ARCOST
Army College Fund	ACF
Army Combat Artist Program	ACAP

Army Combat Development Committee [British]	ACDC
Army Combat Development Experimental Center (AAG)	ACDEC
Army Combat Developments Command	ACDC
Army Combat Engineers (CINC)	ACE
Army Combat Identification Systems	ACIS
Army Combat Operations Vietnam (AABC)	ARCOV
[The] Army Combined Arms Weapons System	TACAWS
Army Command and Administration Communication Agency (NATG)	ACACA
Army Command and Control Communications Network (MCD)	ARCCNET
Army Command and Control Communications Network (MCD)	ARCONET
Army Command and Control Management Information System	ACCMIS
Army Command and Control Master Plan	AC2MP
Army Command and Control Network (AABC)	ACCNET
Army Command and Control Network (MCD)	ARCNET
Army Command and Control Study (MCD)	ACCS
Army Command and Control System (MCD)	AC2S
Army Command and Control System (RDA)	ACCS
Army Command and Control System Engineering Implementation Plan	ASEIP
Army Command and General Staff College	ARCGSC
Army Command and General Staff School	ACGSC
Army Command Management System	ACMS
Army [Forces] Command Post	ARCP
Army Commanders' Conference	ACC
Army Commanders Initiatives Program (RDA)	ARCIP
Army Commanding Service	ACS
Army Commendation Medal [Military decoration]	ARCM
Army Commendation Medal [Military decoration]	ARCOM
Army Commercial Vehicle Code (AABC)	ACVC
Army Commissary Automation System (GFGA)	ACAS
Army Commissary Computer Entry Store System (AABC)	ACCESS
Army Common Operating Environment (RDA)	ACOE
Army Communication Operations Center Agency	ACOCA
Army Communications Administrative Network [Domestic and overseas integrated system of fixed radio, wire, cable, and associated communications facilities]	ACAN
Army Communications and Electronic Command	ACEC
Army Communications and Equipment Coordination	AC & EC
Army Communications Board	ACB
Army Communications Command [Fort Huachuca, AZ]	ACC
Army Communications Command Advanced Concepts Office [Fort Huachuca, AZ]	ACC-ACO
Army Communications Division	ACD
Army Communications Electronics School (MCD)	ACES
Army Communications Equipment Support (MCD)	ACES
Army Communications Objectives Measurement Survey [or System] (GFGA)	ACOMS
Army Communications - Service Division	ACSD
Army Communicative Systems [Provisional] (RDA)	ACS
Army Communicative Technology (RDA)	ACT
Army Communicative Technology Office	ACTO
Army Communities of Excellence	ACOE
Army Community Health Nursing [Army]	ACHN
Army Community Service	ACS
Army Competitive Category (RDA)	ACC
Army Component Command (CINC)	ACC
Army Computer Capabilities Online Repository and Disseminator (PDAA)	ACCORD
Army Computer Systems Command [Also, CSC]	ACSC
Army Computer-Aided Acquisition and Logistics Support	ACALS
Army COMSEC [Communications Security] Central Office of Record (AABC)	ACCOR
Army COMSEC [Communications Security] Commodity, Logistical, and Accounting Information Management System (AABC)	ACCLAIMS
Army Concept Team in Vietnam	ACTIV
Army Concepts Analysis Agency	ACAA
Army Consideration of Tactical Air Support	ACTAS
Army Container-Oriented Distribution Systems	ACODS
Army Continuing Education System	ACES
Army Continuing Evaluation Services	ACES
Army Contract Adjustment Board	ACAB
Army Contract Adjustment Region (MCD)	ACAR
Army Contract Appeals Panel	ACAP
Army Control Program Directive	ACPD
Army Controllership Program	ACP
Army Controlling Education Service	ACES
Army Co-Operation [British military] (DMA)	AC
Army Cooperation Command [British]	ACC
Army Co-Operation Squadron [British and Canadian] [World War II]	AC Sqn
Army Corporate Database (GFGA)	ACDB
Army Corps	AC
Army Corps of Engineers	ACE
Army Corps of Engineers (AAGC)	ACE
Army Corps of Engineers (AAGC)	COE
Army Corps of Engineers (AAGC)	ENG
Army Corps of Engineers Claims and Appeals Board (AAGC)	ENG C&A
Army Corps of Engineers/Naval Facilities Engineering Command	CE/NAVFAC
Army Corps of Engineers, Office of the Chief Engineer (AAGC)	ACE-OCE
Army Corps of Engineers Socioeconomic Information System [Information service or system] (IID)	ACESIS
Army Correspondence Course Program	ACCP
Army Cost Analysis Information and Data System (MCD)	ARCAIDS
Army Cost Analysis Paper	ACAP
Army Cost Position	ACP
Army Cost Reduction Program (AABC)	ACRP
Army Council (ADA)	AC

Army Council Instruction [*World War II*] ... ACI
Army Council of Review Boards ... ACRB
[*The*] **Army Counter-Air Weapons System** ... TACAWS
Army Countermine Mobility Equipment System (MCD) ... ACMES
Army Crisis Action System ... ACAS
Army Criteria Tracking System ... ACTS
Army Customer Order Control System ... ACOCS
Army Customer Order Program ... ACOP
Army Damage Assessment System (AABC) ... ARMDAS
Army Data Dictionary (RDA) ... ADD
Army Data Distribution System ... ADDS
Army Data Retrieval Engineering System (MCD) ... ADRES
Army Data Retrieval System (NITA) ... ADRES
Army Data Validation and Netting Capabilities Establishment ... ADVANCE
Army Decision Support System ... ADSS
Army Defense Acquisition Regulation [*Superseded by AFARS in 1984*] (AAGC) ... ADAR
Army Defense Acquisition Regulation Supplement (AABC) ... ADARS
Army DEIS [*Defense Energy Information System*] **Data Entry System** ... ADDS
Army Density Report ... ADR
Army Density Report, United States Army Reserve ... ADRUSAR
Army Dental Corps [*British*] ... AD
Army Dental Corps [*British*] ... ADC
Army Dental Service ... ADS
Army Department [*British*] (RDA) ... AD
Army Department Establishments [*British*] ... ADE
Army Dependents' Assurance Trust [*British*] (DI) ... ADAT
Army Deployment Reporting System (AABC) ... ADEPREP
Army Depot (AABC) ... AD
Army Depot Automatic Diagnostic System (RDA) ... ADADS
Army Depot Operations Management (MCD) ... ADOM
Army Depot Police [*British military*] (DMA) ... ADP
Army Development and Acquisition of Threat Simulators ... ADATS
Army Development and Employment Agency [*Fort Lewis, WA*] ... ADE
Army Development and Employment Agency [*Fort Lewis, WA*] (INF) ... ADEA
Army Digital Avionics System (MCD) ... ADAS
Army Digitalization Office ... ADO
Army Disability Rating Review Board (AABC) ... ADRRB
Army Disability Review Board ... ADRB
Army Discharge Review Board ... ADRB
Army Distaff Foundation (EA) ... ADF
Army Distribution Objective (MCD) ... ADO
Army Dollar Resource Allocation ... ADRA
Army Education ... AE
Army Education Center ... AEC
Army Education Information System (MCD) ... AREIS
Army Education Requirement System (DOMA) ... AERS
Army Education Review Board ... AERB
Army Educational Corps [*Later, RAEC*] [*British*] ... AEC
Army Educational Requirements Board ... AERB
Army Electronic Proving Ground ... AEPG
Army Electronic Proving Ground (IIA) ... AREPG
Army Electronic Warfare and Intelligence Board ... AEWIB
Army Electronic Warfare Board (MCD) ... AEWB
Army Electronic Warfare Information System ... AEWIS
Army Electronic Warfare Policy Committee (IAA) ... AEWPC
Army Electronics Command ... AEC
Army Electronics Command (MUGU) ... AECOM
Army Electronics Laboratories (KSC) ... AEL
Army Electronics Logistics Research Office (KSC) ... AELRO
Army Electronics Material Support Agency ... AEMSA
Army Electronics Research and Development Activity [*White Sands Missile Range, NM*] ... AERDA
Army Electronics Research and Development Laboratory (AABC) ... AERDL
Army Emergency Relief (EA) ... AER
Army Emergency Reserve [*British*] ... AER
Army Energy Office ... AEO
Army Engineer Center (SAA) ... AEC
Army Engineer District, Far East ... FED
Army Engineer Reactors Group [*Fort Belvoir, VA*] ... AERG
Army Engineer Research and Development Laboratories [*Fort Belvoir, VA*] ... AERDL
Army Engineer Topographic Laboratories (RDA) ... AETL
Army Engineer Waterways Experiment Station [*Vicksburg, MS*] ... AEWES
Army Enlisted Education Review Board (MCD) ... AEERB
Army Entertainment Scholarships and Awards Program (AABC) ... AESAP
Army Environmental Center [*Aberdeen Proving Ground, MD*] (RDA) ... AEC
Army Environmental Health Agency ... AEHA
Army Environmental Health Laboratory ... AEHL
Army Environmental Hygiene Agency ... AEHA
Army Equipment Authorizations Review Center (AABC) ... AEARC
Army Equipment Engineering Establishment ... AEEE
Army Equipment Policy [*British military*] (DMA) ... AEP
Army Equipment Policy Committee (AAG) ... AEPC
[*The*] **Army Equipment Record System** [*Later, TAMMS*] ... TAERS
Army Equipment Status Report ... AESR
Army Equipment Status Reporting System (AABC) ... AESRS
Army Excess Property (AABC) ... AES
Army Exchange Service [*Centralized the control of PX's in US*] [*World War II*] ... AES
Army Executives for Software Program [*Army Materiel Command*] (RDA) ... ARES
Army Exhibit Unit ... AEU
Army Experimental Flight Activity (MCD) ... AEFA
Army Extension Course Program (AABC) ... AECP
Army Extension Training (GFGA) ... AET
Army Extension Training Information System ... AETIS
Army Extension Training System ... AETS
Army Facilities Components System (AABC) ... AFCS
Army Facilities Energy Program (MCD) ... AFEP
Army Family Action Planning ... AFAP
Army Family Housing ... AFH
Army Family Term Building ... AFTB
Army Federal Acquisition Regulations Supplement ... AFARS
Army Field Artillery Combat Effectiveness Model (MCD) ... AFACE
Army Field Artillery School ... AFAS
Army Field Assistance and Technology ... AFAST
Army Field Commands ... AFC
Army Field Feeding System (INF) ... AFFS
Army Field Forces ... AFF
Army Field Forces Board ... AFFB
Army Field Headquarters ... AFHQ
Army Field Stock Control System (AABC) ... AFSCS
Army Field Workshop ... AFW
Army Film and Photographic Section [*British military*] (DMA) ... AFPS
Army Film and Photographic Unit [*British military*] (DMA) ... AFPU
Army Finance and Accounting Center (MCD) ... AFAC
Army Finance Association [*Defunct*] (EA) ... AFA
Army Finance Center ... AFC
Army Financial Stock Summary Analysis ... AFSSA
Army Fire Service ... AFS
Army Fixed Wing Aptitude Battery (AABC) ... AFWAB
Army Flight Activity ... AFA
Army Flying Corps [*British*] (AIA) ... AFC
Army Flying Time Report (MCD) ... AFTR
Army Food Management Information System (GFGA) ... AFMIS
Army Food Service Energy Management (AABC) ... AFSEM
Army Force ... AF
Army Force Development Plan ... AFDP
Army Force Guidance ... AFG
Army Force Integration Study ... AFIS
Army Force/Materiel Cost Methodology Improvement Project ... ACMIP
Army Force Modernization Coordination Office ... AFMCO
Army Force Planning Cost Handbook ... AFPCH
Army Force Planning Data and Assumptions (AABC) ... AFPDA
Army Force Program ... AFP
Army Force Status Reporting System (AABC) ... ARFORSTAT
Army Forces [*Element of a joint task force*] ... ARFOR
Army Forces [*Element of a joint task force*] ... ARFOR
Army Forces Atlantic (MCD) ... ARLANT
Army Forces Far East ... AFFE
Army Forces Readiness Command (MCD) ... ARRED
Army Foreign Science and Technology Center ... AFSTC
Army Form ... AF
Army Forwarding Officer [*British*] ... AFO
Army Fuels and Lubricants Laboratory ... AFLL
Army Fuels and Lubricants Research Laboratory ... AFLRL
Army Functional Component System ... AFCS
[*The*] **Army Functional Files System** ... TAFFS
[*The*] **Army Functional Files Test System** (MCD) ... TAFFTS
Army Fuze Program (MCD) ... AFP
Army Gas Dynamic LASER (MCD) ... A-GDL
Army Gas-Cooled Reactor System (SAA) ... AGCRS
Army Gas-Cooled Reactor Systems Program ... AGCRSP
Army General Classification Test [*Measurement of intelligence*] ... AGCT
Army General Council ... AGC
Army General Equipment Command ... AGEC
Army General Staff ... AGS
Army General Staff Civilian Personnel Office, Office of the Chief of Staff ... AGSCPO
Army General Supplies Commodity Center ... AGSCC
Army Global Command and Control System (RDA) ... AGCCS
Army Global Command and Control System [*Army*] ... AGCCS
Army Good Conduct Medal ... AGCM
Army Good Conduct Medal ... AGCMDL
Army Ground Forces ... AGF
Army Ground Pool [*for officers*] ... AGP
Army Ground Transportable Emitter Location Identification System ... AGTELIS
Army Group (NATG) ... AG
Army Group ... AGP
Army Group Effects Department ... AGED
Army Group Headquarters ... AGH
Army Group Royal Artillery [*British*] ... AGRA
Army Group, Royal Engineers [*British and Canadian*] [*World War II*] ... AGRE
Army Guidance ... AG
Army Gun Air Defense Systems (RDA) ... ARGADS
Army Gunner Training (MCD) ... AGT
Army Handicapped Employe of the Year (RDA) ... AHEY
Army Headquarters ... AHQ
Army Health Nurse (AABC) ... AHN
Army Helicopter [*British military*] (DMA) ... AH
Army Helicopter Improvement Program ... AHIP
Army Heliport (AABC) ... AHP
Army Help for Education and Development ... AHEAD
Army High Performance Computing Research Center [*University of Minnesota*] [*Research center*] (RCD) ... AHPCRC
Army High School Completion Program (MCD) ... AHSCP
Army High-Performance Computing Research (RDA) ... AHPCRC
Army Historical Foundation (EA) ... AHF
Army Hospital ... AH
Army Hospital Corps ... AHC

Army Housing Committee (AABC) .... ARHOC
Army Human Engineering Laboratory (MCD) .... AHEL
Army Human Factors Research Advisory Committee .... AHFRAC
Army Human Factors Research and Development Committee (AABC) .... AHFRDC
Army Imagery Intelligence Corps .... AIIC
Army in Burma Reserve of Officers [*British military*] (DMA) .... ABRO
Army in Europe .... AE
Army in the Field (MCD) .... AITF
Army in the Field Containers System Study (MCD) .... AFCSS
Army Industrial College .... AIC
Army Industrial Engineering Activity (AAGC) .... EA
Army Industrial Fund .... AIF
Army Industrial Preparedness Program .... AIPP
Army/Industry Materiel Information Liaison Office [*or Officer*] .... AIMILO
Army Infantry Board (RDA) .... AIB
Army Infantry Board (MCD) .... A-INF
Army Infantry School (KSC) .... AIS
Army In-Flight Data Transmission System (MCD) .... AIDATS
Army Information and Data Systems Command .... AIDSCOM
Army Information Architecture .... AIA
Army Information Digest .... AID
Army Information Engineering (GFGA) .... AIE
Army Information Management System .... AIMS
Army Information Processing Standards (MCD) .... AIPS
Army Information Program .... AIP
Army Information Radio Service (MCD) .... AIRS
Army Information Systems (RDA) .... AIS
Army Information Systems Command .... AISC
Army Information Systems / Information Systems Management Activity (RDA) .... AIS/ISMA
Army Insecticide Measuring System (RDA) .... AIMS
Army Inspector General (MCD) .... AIG
Army Installation Management .... AIM
Army Installation Management Course .... AIMC
Army Installations Planning Committee (AABC) .... AIPC
Army Institute for Professional Development (MCD) .... AIPD
Army Institute for Research in Management Information and Computer Science [*Atlanta, GA*] (IEEE) .... AIRMICS
Army Institute of Administration (MCD) .... AIA
Army Institute of Advanced Studies .... AIAS
Army Institute of Dental Research (RDA) .... AIDR
Army Institute of Surgical Research (RDA) .... AISR
Army Instructor Cadre Interceptor Transporter Loader Operations [*Course*] .... AICITLO
Army Instructor Cadre Interceptor Transporter / Loader Operations Maintenance Course .... AICITLOM
Army Integrated Decision Equipment .... AIMS
Army Integrated Meteorological Systems (NOAA) .... AIM
Army Integrated Meteorological Systems .... AIMS
Army Integrated Microfilm System .... AIMS
Army Intelligence .... AI
Army Intelligence Agency .... AIA
Army Intelligence and Security .... AIS
Army Intelligence Center .... AIC
Army Intelligence Center and School (MCD) .... AICS
Army Intelligence Department [*British*] .... AID
Army Intelligence/Electronic Warfare Reorganization Overwatch Committee (MCD) .... AIEWROC
Army Intelligence Interpreter .... AII
Army Intelligence Reserve .... AIR
Army Intelligence School .... AIS
Army Intelligence School, Fort Devens (MCD) .... AISD
Army Intelligence Survey [*ITAC*] (MCD) .... AIS
Army Intelligence Translator .... AIT
Army Internal Control Program (RDA) .... AICP
Army Interoperability Network (RDA) .... AIN
Army Inventory Control Point .... AICP
Army Inventory Data Systems .... AIDS
Army Inventory Objective (AABC) .... AIO
Army Investigational Drug Review Board (AABC) .... AIDRB
Army Job Activities Questionnaire .... AJAQ
Army Job Questionnaire .... AJQ
Army Key Management System .... AKMS
Army Kinematograph Corp. [*British military*] (DMA) .... AKC
Army Laboratory of the Year Award (RDA) .... ALYA
Army Land Forces .... ALANF
Army Language Aptitude Test [*Later, DLAT*] .... ALAT
[*The*] **Army Language School** .... TALS
Army LASER Target Designator System .... ALTDS
Army Launch Area .... ALA
Army Lawyer [*A publication*] (AAGC) .... Army Law
Army Legal Corps [*British military*] (DMA) .... ALC
Army Lessons Learned Management Information System (INF) .... ALLMIS
Army Liaison Element (MCD) .... ALE
Army Liaison Officer .... ALO
Army Liaison Officer (MCD) .... ARMLO
Army Library .... ALIB
Army Library Automated Systems (IID) .... ALAS
Army Life Cycle Cost Analysis Model (MCD) .... ALCCAM
Army Life Cycle Cost Model (MCD) .... ALCCM
Army Life-Support Power Source System (MCD) .... ALPSS
Army Limited War Laboratory .... ALWL
Army Linguist Personnel Study .... ALPS
Army List [*British military*] (DMA) .... AL
Army Logistic Development Committee [*British*] (RDA) .... ALDC
Army Logistics Assessment .... ALA
Army Logistics Center .... ALC
Army Logistics Command Japan (CINC) .... ALCJ
Army Logistics Data Base and Access System .... ALDBAS
Army Logistics Data Center .... ALDC
Army Logistics Evaluation Agency (MCD) .... ARLEA
Army Logistics Management College [*Fort Lee, VA*] .... ALMC
Army Logistics Management Integrated Data Systems (AABC) .... ALMIDS
Army Logistics Management Systems Activity .... ALMSA
Army Logistics Manpower Office [*Merged with Operations Personnel Office*] .... ALMO
Army Logistics Objectives Program .... ALOP
Army Logistics Policy Council (AABC) .... ALPC
Army Logistics Readiness Evaluation System .... ALRES
Army Logistics Research and Development .... ALRD
Army Logistics Specialty Committee (MCD) .... ALSC
Army Logistics Study Program .... ALSP
Army Long-Range Appraisal .... ALRA
Army Long-Range Capabilities Plan .... ALRCP
Army Long-Range Planning Guidance .... ALRPG
Army Long-Range Technological Forecast (AABC) .... ALRTF
Army Long-Range Training Plan (RDA) .... ALRTP
Army Low-Speed Air Research Tasks .... ALART
Army Maintenance and Supply Procedures [*or Publications*] (NATG) .... AMSP
Army Maintenance Board .... AMB
Army Maintenance Management (MCD) .... AMM
Army Maintenance Management Center .... AMMC
Army Maintenance Management System (MCD) .... AMMS
[*The*] **Army Maintenance Management System** [*Formerly, TAERS*] (AABC) .... TAMMS
Army Maintenance Training and Evaluation Simulation System (MCD) .... AMTESS
Army Management Engineering College (RDA) .... AMEC
Army Management Engineering Training Agency (RDA) .... AMETA
Army Management Fund .... AMF
Army Management Headquarters Activity (MCD) .... AMHA
Army Management Information Program (AABC) .... AMIP
Army Management Information System .... AMIS
Army Management Information Systems Course .... AMISC
Army Management Intern Program (RDA) .... AMIP
Army Management Milestone System .... AMMS
Army Management School (KSC) .... AMS
Army Management Staff College (RDA) .... AMSC
Army Management Structure .... AMS
Army Management Structure Code .... AMSCO
Army Management System .... AMS
Army Management System - Korea .... AMS-K
Army Manpower Cost System (RDA) .... AMCOS
Army Manual .... AM
Army Map Service [*Later, Defense Mapping Agency Topographic Center*] [*Washington, DC*] .... AMS
Army Marksmanship Training Unit [*CONARC*] (AABC) .... AMKTU
Army Marksmanship Training Unit [*CONARC*] (INF) .... AMTU
Army Marksmanship Unit .... AMU
Army Master Data File (AABC) .... AMDF
Army Master Data File Reader Microfilm System [*Later, ARMS*] (AABC) .... AMDFRMS
Army Master Data File Retrieval Microform System .... ARMS
Army Master Force Development Plan (MCD) .... AMFDP
Army Master Study Program (AABC) .... AMSP
Army Material Acquisition Reorganization Committee (MCD) .... AMARC
Army Material Command Circular (MCD) .... AMCC
Army Material Supply Command (KSC) .... AMSC
Army Materials and Mechanics Research Center [*Watertown, MA*] .... AMMRC
Army Materials Research Agency [*Later, AMMRC*] [*Watertown, MA*] .... AMRA
Army Materials Research Reactor .... AMRR
Army Materials Technology Laboratory [*Watertown, MA*] .... AMTL
Army Materiel Acquisition Guidance .... AMAG
Army Materiel Acquisition Review Committee [*Terminated, 1974*] .... AMARC
Army Materiel Command [*Formerly, DARCOM*] [*Alexandria, VA*] .... AMC
Army Materiel Command Administrative Data Center .... AMCADC
Army Materiel Command Announcement Distribution System (RDA) .... AMCADS
Army Materiel Command Automated Logistics Management Systems Agency (AABC) .... AMCALMSA
Army Materiel Command Board [*Aberdeen Proving Ground, MD*] (MCD) .... AMCB
Army Materiel Command Catalog Data Office (AABC) .... AMCCDO
Army Materiel Command Data Center .... AMCDC
Army Materiel Command Depot Data Center .... AMCDDC
Army Materiel Command Deputy Chief of Staff for Chemical and Nuclear Matters .... AMCCN
Army Materiel Command Deputy Chief of Staff for Developments Engineering and Acquisition .... AMCDE
Army Materiel Command Facilities and Services Center (AABC) .... AMCFASC
Army Materiel Command Field Assistance for Science and Technology Program (RDA) .... AMC-FAST
Army Materiel Command Field Office (RDA) .... AMCFO
Army Materiel Command Field Safety Agency (AABC) .... AMCFSA
Army Materiel Command General Order .... AMCGO
Army Materiel Command Information Center .... AMCIC
Army Materiel Command Inspector General, Western Inspection Activity .... AMCIGW
Army Materiel Command Installation Division .... AMCID
Army Materiel Command Installations and Service Agency (AABC) .... AMCI & SA
Army Materiel Command International Logistics Directorate (MCD) .... AMCIL

Army Materiel Command Logistic Data Center (AABC) ... AMCLDC
Army Materiel Command Logistics Systems Support Agency (AABC) ... AMCLSSA
Army Materiel Command Materiel Requirements Directorate (MCD) ... AMCMR
Army Materiel Command Memorandum ... AMCM
Army Materiel Command Mission Area Manager ... AMAM
Army Materiel Command Packaging, Storage, and Containerization Center [*Tobyhanna, PA*] ... AMCPSCC
Army Materiel Command Pamphlet (MCD) ... AMCP
Army Materiel Command Procurement and Production Directorate ... AMCPP
Army Materiel Command Procurement Instructions ... AMCPI
Army Materiel Command Regulations ... AMCR
Army Materiel Command Research and Development ... AMCRD
Army Materiel Command Support Activity ... AMCSA
Army Materiel Command Technical Committee ... AMCTC
Army Materiel Development and Readiness Command [*Now AMC*] (AAGC) ... DARCOM
Army Materiel Education and Training Activity [*School of Engineering at Red River Army Depot*] [*Texarkana, TX*] (RDA) ... AMETA
Army Materiel Plan (AABC) ... AMP
Army Materiel Plan Modernization ... AMPMOD
Army Materiel Status Committees (AABC) ... ARMATSC
Army Materiel Systems Analysis Activity [*or Agency*] [*Aberdeen Proving Ground, MD*] (MCD) ... AMSAA
Army Materiel Test and Evaluation Directorate [*White Sands Missile Range, NM*] ... ARMTE
Army Mathematics Research Center [*Madison, Wisconsin*] ... AMRC
Army Mathematics Steering Committee ... AMSC
Army Medical Bioengineering Research and Development Laboratory (RDA) ... AMBRDL
Army Medical Biomechanical Research Laboratory ... AMBRL
Army Medical Center ... AMC
Army Medical Corps ... AMC
Army Medical Corps/Dental Corps ... AMED/DC
Army Medical Department ... AMD
Army Medical Department (AABC) ... AMEDD
Army Medical Department ... ARMED
Army Medical Department Property Accounting System (AABC) ... AMEDDPAS
Army Medical Intelligence and Information Agency (MCD) ... AMIIA
Army Medical Library [*Became Armed Forces Medical Library, 1952; later, NLM*] ... AML
Army Medical Material Agency (MCD) ... AMMA
Army Medical Nutrition Laboratory (MCD) ... AMNL
Army Medical Research and Development Command ... AMRDC
Army Medical Research and Nutrition Laboratory (DAVI) ... AMRL
Army Medical Research and Nutrition Laboratory ... AMRNL
Army Medical Research Institute of Chemical Defense (RDA) ... AMRICD
Army Medical Research Institute of Infectious Diseases (RDA) ... AMRIID
Army Medical Research Laboratory ... AMRL
Army Medical Research Laboratory, Alaska (RDA) ... AMRLA
Army Medical Science ... AMEDS
Army Medical Service ... AMEDS
Army Medical Service [*British*] ... AMS
Army Medical Service Graduate School ... AMSGS
Army Medical Service Research and Development Command ... AMSRDC
Army Medical Service School [*Later, Medical Field Service School*] ... AMSS
Army Medical Specialist Corps ... AMSC
Army Medical Staff ... AMS
Army Medical Supply Control Officer ... AMSCO
Army Medical Supply Support Activity ... AMSSA
Army Medical Unit ... AMU
Army Member, Inter-American Defense Board (AABC) ... AMIADB
Army Methods of Instruction Centre [*British military*] (DMA) ... AMIC
Army Metrology and Calibration Center ... AMCC
Army Metrology and Calibration Center Metrology Development and Engineering Division ... AMCC-MM
Army Military Clothing Sales Store (DOMA) ... AMCSS
Army Military Intelligence Battalion (MCD) ... AMIB
Army Mine Planter ... AMP
Army Mine Planter Service ... AMPS
Army Missile and Rockets Directorate ... AMRD
Army Missile and Rockets Division - NATO Supply Center ... AMRD-NASC
Army Missile Command ... AMC
Army Missile Command ... AMICOM
Army Missile Command (MUGU) ... ARMSLC
Army Missile Defense Command (AABC) ... AMDC
Army Missile Development Center (MCD) ... AMDC
Army Missile Laboratory (RDA) ... AML
Army Missile Research and Development Command (MCD) ... AMRDC
Army Missile Test and Evaluation ... ARMTE
Army Missile Test Center [*White Sands Missile Range, NM*] ... AMTC
Army Missile Transport Systems (KSC) ... AMTRANS
Army Mobile Missile Operation ... AMMO
Army Mobility Command ... AMC
Army Mobility Command ... AMOCOM
Army Mobility Equipment Center (SAA) ... AMEC
Army Mobility Equipment Research and Development Center (MCD) ... AMERADC
Army Mobility Model (RDA) ... AMM
Army Mobility Research and Development Center ... AMRDC
Army Mobility Research Center ... AMRC
Army Mobility Support Center ... AMSC
Army Mobilization and Operations Planning System ... AMOPS
Army Mobilization Capabilities Study ... AMCS
Army Mobilization Planning and Programming Directive (AABC) ... AMPPD
Army Mobilization Planning and Programming Guidance Document (AABC) ... AMPPGD
Army Mobilization Program Directive ... AMPD
Army Model Improvement Program (RDA) ... AMIP
Army Model Improvement Program Management Office (RDA) ... AMMO
Army Modernization Information Memorandum (RDA) ... AMIM
Army Modernization Plan (RDA) ... AMP
Army Modernization Training ... AMT
Army Modernization Training Automation System ... AMTAS
Army Molecular Sieve Oxygen Generator (RDA) ... AMSOG
Army Morale Support Fund (AABC) ... AMSF
Army Mortar Program (RDA) ... ARMOP
Army Mortar Requirements Study ... AMOR
Army Motion Picture Service ... AMPS
Army Mounteering Association [*British military*] (DMA) ... AMA
Army Multibus Avionics Multi-Process (MCD) ... AMAMP
Army Munitions Command [*Later merged with Army Weapons Command*] ... AMC
Army Munitions Command [*Later merged with Army Weapons Command*] ... AMUCOM
Army Munitions Command [*Later merged with Army Weapons Command*] ... AMUNC
Army Mutual Aid Association [*Later, AAFMAA*] (EA) ... AMAA
Army Natick Laboratory ... ANL
Army National Guard ... ANG
Army National Guard ... ARNG
Army National Guard Management Information System (GFGA) ... ARNGMIS
Army National Guard of the United States ... ARNGUS
Army National Guard Troop Structure Program ... ARNG-TSP
Army Native Hospital Corps [*British military*] (DMA) ... ANHC
Army, Navy & Air Force Veterans in Canada [*Les Anciens Combattants de l'Armee, de la Marine et des Forces Aeriennes au Canada*] (AC) ... ANAVETS
Army, Navy Electronics Evaluation Group ... ANEEG
Army Navy/Fixed Communications Cabinet (MCD) ... AN/FCC
Army Navy/Fixed Satellite Communication (MCD) ... AN/FSC
Army Navy Integrated Presentation ... ANIP
Army, Navy, NASA, Air Force Geodetic Satellite ... ANNA
Army/Navy Number ... A/N
Army - Navy Retractor [*Surgery*] (DAVI) ... A/N
Army Net Assessment, Central Europe ... ANACE
Army Network Station ... ANS
Army News Features ... ANF
Army News Service ... ANS
Army News Service ... ARNEWS
Army Newspaper Service ... ANS
Army Nozzle Technology Program (MCD) ... ANTP
Army Nuclear Data System [*Study*] (AABC) ... ANUDS
Army Nuclear Defense Laboratory (MCD) ... ANDL
Army Nuclear Power Program ... ANPP
Army Nuclear Weapon Coordination Group ... ANWCG
Army Nuclear Weapons Stockpile Reliability Program ... ANWSRP
Army Nurse Corps ... ANC
Army Nursing Service [*British*] ... ANS
Army Observation Post [*British military*] (DMA) ... AOP
Army Occupational Survey Program [*Formerly, MODB*] ... AOSP
Army of Excellence [*Military program*] (INF) ... AOE
Army of Northern Virginia [*Civil War*] ... ANV
Army of Occupation Medal [*Military decoration*] ... AOM
Army of Occupation Medal [*Military decoration*] ... OCCMDL
Army of Occupation of Germany Medal [*Military decoration*] ... AOGM
Army of Occupation of Germany Medal [*Military decoration*] ... OCCGERMDL
Army of Tennessee, CSA [*An association*] (EA) ... AT
Army of the Republic of Vietnam [*Also, ARVN*] [*South Vietnam*] ... ARVIN
Army of the Republic of Vietnam [*Also, ARVIN*] [*South Vietnam*] [*Defunct*] ... ARVN
Army of the Republic of Vietnam Sea, Air, and Land Team (VNW) ... ARVN SEAL
Army of the United States ... AUS
Army of Tripura People's Liberation Organization [*India*] (PD) ... ATPLO
Army Officer Basic Course [*Army*] (RDA) ... AOBC
Army Officers' Emergency Reserve [*British*] ... AOER
Army Oil Analysis Program (MCD) ... AOAP
Army Operating Availability Data ... AOAD
Army Operational Research ... AOR
Army Operational Research Establishment [*British*] ... AORE
Army Operational Research Group [*British*] ... AORG
[*The*] **Army Operations Center** ... AOC
[*The*] **Army Operations Center** ... TAOC
[*The*] **Army Operations Center System** ... TARMOCS
Army Operations Research Symposia (RDA) ... AORS
Army Optical Station ... AOS
Army Order [*British*] ... AO
Army Ordnance Ammunition Command [*Merged with Munitions Command*] ... AOAC
Army Ordnance Ballistic Missile Office ... AOBMO
Army Ordnance Combat Equipment Office ... AOCEO
Army Ordnance Corps [*Later, RAOC*] [*British*] ... AOC
Army Ordnance Department [*British*] ... AOD
Army Ordnance Guided Missile School (MCD) ... AOGMS
Army Ordnance Missile Center (MCD) ... AOMC
Army Ordnance Missile Command [*Later, Missile Command*] [*Redstone Arsenal, AL*] ... AOMC
Army Ordnance Missile Support Agency ... AOMSA
Army Ordnance Missile Support Center (NATG) ... AOMSC
Army Ordnance Stores [*British*] ... AOS
Army Ordnance Submarine Mine Laboratory (KSC) ... AOSML
Army Ordnance Weapons Command ... AOWC

Army Ordnance Workshop [*British military*] (DMA) ... AOW
Army Orientation Training (MCD) ... AOT
Army Outward Bound School [*British military*] (DMA) ... AOBS
Army Pacific (CINC) ... ARPAC
Army Package Power Reactor ... APPR
Army Packaging Board (AABC) ... APB
Army Parachute Association [*British military*] (DMA) ... APA
Army Parachute Team ... APT
Army Part Number (MCD) ... APN
Army Pay Corps [*Later, RAPC*] [*British*] ... APC
Army Pay Department [*British*] ... APD
Army Pearl Harbor Board [*World War II*] ... APHB
Army Pensions ... AP
Army Performance-Oriented Review and Standards Program ... APORS
Army Performance-Oriented Reviews and Standards ... APORS
Army Personnel Attached to the Air Force for Duty ... ARWAF
Army Personnel Letter (AABC) ... APL
Army Personnel Research Committee (MCD) ... APRC
Army Personnel Research Establishment [*British*] ... APRE
Army Personnel Research Office [*Washington, DC*] ... APRO
Army Personnel Research Service ... APRS
Army Personnel System Committee ... APSC
Army Petroleum Center ... APC
Army Photo Interpretation Center ... APIC
Army Photo Interpretation Detachment ... APID
Army Photo Interpretation Unit (NATG) ... APIU
Army Photographic Interpretation Section [*British*] ... APIS
Army Physical Disability Activity (MCD) ... APDA
Army Physical Disability Appeal Board ... APDAB
Army Physical Evaluation Board ... APEB
Army Physical Fitness Program ... APFP
Army Physical Fitness Test (INF) ... APFT
Army Physical Fitness Training (ADDR) ... APFT
Army Physical Readiness Test (INF) ... APRT
Army Physical Review Council ... APRC
Army Physical Training Corps [*British*] ... APTC
Army Physical Training Staff [*British military*] (DMA) ... APTS
Army Physiological Research Establishment [*British*] ... ARPE
Army Pictorial Center ... APC
Army Pictorial Division ... APD
Army Pictorial Service ... APS
Army Pilot School ... APS
[*The*] **Army Plan** ... TAP
[*The*] **Army Plan for Equipment Records** ... TAPER
Army Planning and Programming Guidance Memorandum (MCD) ... APPGM
Army Planning Group ... APG
Army Plant Representative Office (AAGC) ... ARPRO
Army Plant Representative's Offices ... APRO
Army Point of Contact (AABC) ... APOC
Army Policy Council ... APC
Army Pollution Abatement Program (MCD) ... APAP
Army Port and Service Command ... AP & SC
[*The*] **Army Portion of Force Status and Identify Report** [*Force Status Report*] (AABC) ... TAPFOR
Army Post Office ... APO
Army Post Office Corps [*British military*] (DMA) ... APOC
Army Postal Clerk (AABC) ... APC
Army Postal Service ... APS
Army Postal Service Agency (AFM) ... ARPSA
Army Postal Unit ... APU
Army Power Procurement Office ... APPO
Army Power Procurement Officer Representative (MCD) ... APPOR
Army Precommission Extension Course (AABC) ... APCEC
Army Preliminary Evaluation ... APE
Army Primary Standards Laboratory ... APSL
Army Printing and Stationery Services [*British*] ... APSS
Army Procurement Appropriation ... APA
Army Procurement Appropriation Reporting System ... APARS
Army Procurement District ... APD
Army Procurement Procedure ... APP
Army Procurement Regulation [*or Requirement*] ... APR
Army Procurement Research Office ... APRO
Army Procurement - Sharpe General Depot ... APSGD
Army Program for Individual Training ... ARPRINT
Army Program Memorandum (AABC) ... APM
Army Projects Management Department (SAA) ... APM
Army Promotion List (AABC) ... APL
Army Propulsion Laboratory and Center (KSC) ... APLC
Army Prosthetics Research Laboratory ... APRL
Army Proving Grounds ... APG
Army Provisioning Process Course [*DoD*] (RDA) ... APPC
Army Pulse Radiation Directorate (PDAA) ... APRD
Army Pulse Radiation Facility [*Aberdeen Proving Ground, MD*] ... APRF
Army Pulse Radiation Facility Reactor [*Nuclear energy*] (OA) ... APRFR
Army Pulsed Experimental Research Assembly ... APRA
Army Qualification Battery [*of tests*] ... AQB
Army Quartermaster Corps [*Merged with Supply and Maintenance Command*] ... AQMC
Army Quartermaster Research and Engineering Command (MCD) ... AQREC
Army RADAR Approach Control Facility (FAAC) ... ARAC
Army Radiation Laboratory ... ARL
Army Radio Code ... ARC
Army Radio Code Aptitude Test (IAA) ... ARCAT
Army Radio Code Aptitude Test ... ARCT
Army Radio School [*British military*] (DMA) ... ARS
Army Radio Station (IAA) ... ARS
Army Ration Credit System (AABC) ... ARCS
Army Reactor Area (SAA) ... ARA
Army Reactor Experimental Area ... AREA
Army Reactor Systems Health and Safety Review Committee (AABC) ... ARCHS
Army Reactors Branch (SAA) ... ARB
Army Readiness and Mobilization Regions (MCD) ... ARMR
Army Readiness Evaluation System (MCD) ... ARES
Army Readiness Management [*or Measurement*] **System** (MCD) ... ARMS
Army Readiness Region (AABC) ... ARR
Army Readiness Region ... ARRED
Army Ready Materiel ... ARM
Army Rearming Base ... ARB
Army Receiving-Valve (IAA) ... AR
Army Records Society (EAIO) ... ARS
Army Recruiting and Accession Data System (GFGA) ... ARADS
Army Regional Threat ... ART
Army Registry of Physical Therapists ... ARPT
Army Registry of Special Educational Materials (AABC) ... ARSEM
Army Regulation ... AR
Army Regulations Supplement [*A publication*] (AAGC) ... ARS
Army Relief Society [*AER*] [*Absorbed by*] (EA) ... ARS
Army Renegotiation Division [*of ASRB*] ... ARD
Army Requirements and Management Board ... ARMB
Army Requirements Control Office (AABC) ... ARCO
Army Requirements Development Plan (AABC) ... ARDP
Army Requirements for Space Technologies (MCD) ... ARST
Army Requirements for Tactical Communications (AABC) ... ARTACOM
Army Research and Development [*Later, R, D & A*] [*A publication*] (SAA) ... ARD
Army Research and Development Bulletin [*A publication*] (RDA) ... ARAB
Army Research and Development Command ... ARDC
Army Research and Development Group (MCD) ... ARDG
Army Research and Development Group (Europe) ... ARDG(E)
Army Research and Development Group (Far East) ... ARDG(FE)
Army Research and Development Information Systems Office (RDA) ... ARDISO
Army Research and Development Test and Evaluation Information Systems ... ARDIS
Army Research Associates Program (DOMA) ... ARAP
Army Research Consortium (RDA) ... ARC
[*The*] **Army Research Council** ... TARC
Army Research, Development, and Acquisition ... ARDAA
Army Research, Development, and Acquisition ... ARDAC
Army Research Institute (RDA) ... ARI
Army Research Institute for Environmental Medicine ... ARIEM
Army Research Institute for the Behavioral and Social Sciences [*Alexandria, VA*] ... ARI
Army Research Laboratory (RDA) ... ARL
Army Research Office [*Research Triangle Park, NC*] ... ARO
Army Research Office - Durham ... ARO-D
Army Research Office - Europe ... ARO-E
Army Research Office - Far East (AABC) ... ARO-FE
Army Research Office - Japan ... ARO-J
Army Research Office/University Research Initiative (RDA) ... ARO/URI
Army Research Plan ... ARP
Army Research Task Summary ... ARTS
Army Reserve [*Formerly, ERC, ORC*] ... AR
Army Reserve and Reserve Officers Training Corps Affairs ... ARROTCA
Army Reserve Association ... ARA
Army Reserve Association ... AResA
Army Reserve Civilian Acquired Skills Program (MCD) ... ARCASP
Army Reserve Command ... ARCOM
Army Reserve Command (MCD) ... ARRCOM
Army Reserve Components (MCD) ... ARC
Army Reserve Components Achievement Medal [*Military decoration*] (AABC) ... ARCAM
Army Reserve Components Overseas Training Ribbon [*Military decoration*] (GFGA) ... ARCOTR
Army Reserve Forces Policy Council (MCD) ... ARFPC
Army Reserve Officers Training Corps (AEE) ... AROTC
Army Reserve Personnel Center [*St. Louis, MO*] (INF) ... ARPERCEN
Army Reserve Readiness Training Center [*Fort McCoy, WI*] (INF) ... ARRTC
Army Reserve Recruiting Unit ... ARRU
Army Reserve Review Committee ... ARRC
Army Reserve Technician ... ART
Army Resident Training (MCD) ... ART
Army Resource Management Advisory and Assessment Program ... ARMAAP
Army Retail Requirements ... ARR
Army Retiring Board ... ARB
Army Rifle Association [*British military*] (DMA) ... ARA
Army Rocket and Guided Missile Agency [*Redstone Arsenal, AL*] ... ARGMA
Army Rocket Transportation System (MCD) ... ARTP
Army Rotary Wing Aptitude Battery (AABC) ... ARWAB
Army Routine Order ... ARO
Army Safety Management Information System (MCD) ... ASMIS
Army Satellite Tracking Center ... AST
Army Satellite Tracking Center (IAA) ... ASTC
Army School of Education [*British*] ... ASE
Army School of Education and Depot [*British*] (BI) ... ASED
Army School of Physical Training [*British*] ... ASPT
Army School on Instructional Technology [*British*] ... ASI
Army School on Instructional Technology [*British*] ... ASIT
Army Schools Department [*British military*] (DMA) ... ASD
Army Science and Technology Master Plan (RDA) ... ASTMP
Army Science Board [*Formerly, ASAP*] (RDA) ... ASB
Army Scientific Advisory Panel [*Later, ASB*] ... ASAP

[*The*] **Army Scientific Advisory Panel** .... TASAP
Army Scientific and Technical Information Program (DIT) .... ASTIP
Army Scientific Assistance Program (RDA) .... ASAP
Army Scripture Reader [*British military*] (DMA) .... ASR
Army Seal of Approval .... ASA
Army Secure Operating System .... ASOS
Army Security .... AS
Army Security Agency [*Later, INSCOM*] [*Arlington, VA*] .... ASA
Army Security Agency, Pacific (CINC) .... ASAPAC
Army Security Agency School [*Merged with Defense Security Agency School*] .... ASAS
Army Security Assistance Coordinating Group .... ASACG
[*The*] **Army Security Assistance Program Study Group** .... TASAPS
Army Security Review Board .... ASRB
Army Selection Centre [*British*] .... ASC
Army Selective Aerial Rocket (MCD) .... ASAR
Army Serial Number .... ASN
Army Service [*British*] (ROG) .... AS
Army Service Command .... ASCOM
Army Service Corps [*Initialism also facetiously translated during World War I as "Ally Sloper's Cavalry," Ally Sloper being a comic-paper buffoon*] [*Later, RASC*] [*British*] .... ASC
Army Service Forces [*Formerly, SOS*] .... ASF
Army Service Forces Training Center .... ASFTC
Army Service Forces Training Center Unit .... ASFTCU
Army Service Number .... ASN
Army Service Reserve [*British*] (ROG) .... ASR
Army Service Ribbon [*Military decoration*] .... ASR
Army Service Squadron [*Corresponds to Navy's CASU*] .... ASSERON
Army Shipping Document .... ASD
Army Signal Corps [*Later, CEC*] .... ASC
Army Signal Corps, Communications Security Service (MUGU) .... ASCCSS
Army Signal Intelligence Agency .... ASIA
Army Signal Material [*or Missile*] **Support Agency** .... ASMSA
Army Signal Radio Propagation Agency .... ASRPA
Army Signal Research and Development Laboratory .... ASRDL
Army Signal School (MCD) .... ASIGSCH
Army Signal School [*British*] .... ASS
Army Signal Squadron (IAA) .... ASS
[*The*] **Army Signal Supply Agency** (MCD) .... ASSA
[*The*] **Army Signal Supply Agency** .... TASSA
Army Signal Support Agency .... ASSA
Army Ski Association [*British military*] (DMA) .... ASA
Army Small Arms Program .... ARSAP
Army Small Arms Requirements Simulation [*Battle model*] (MCD) .... ASARS
Army Small Arms Requirements Studies (MCD) .... ASARS
Army Small Computers Program .... ASCP
Army Snow, Ice, and Permafrost Research Establishment .... ASIPRE
Army Space [*Command*] .... ARSPAC
Army Space Exploitation Demonstration Program [*Army*] .... ASEDP
Army Space Initiatives Study .... ASIS
Army Space Operations Center .... ARSPOC
Army Space Program Office (MCD) .... ASPO
Army Space Technology and Research Office (RDA) .... ASTRO
Army Special Award for Accomplishment (RDA) .... ASAA
Army Special Operation Forces Command, Control, Communitions, Computers, Intelligences, Psychological Operations, and Civil Affairs System (RDA) .... ARSOF C4I PYSOP and CA
Army Special Operation Task Force .... ARSOTF
Army Special Operations Command (DOMA) .... ARSOC
Army Special Operations Force [*Army*] .... ASOF
Army Special Operations Forces (GFGA) .... ARSOF
Army Special Operations Forces Task Force (DOMA) .... ARSOFTF
Army Special Operations Pictorial Detachment .... ASOPD
Army Special Staff .... ASS
Army Special Warfare Center .... ASWC
Army Special Weapons Depot .... ASWD
Army Specialist Corps [*Functions transferred to Officer Procurement Service*] .... ASC
Army Specialized Training .... AST
Army Specialized Training Division .... ASTD
Army Specialized Training Program [*World War II*] .... ASTP
Army Specialized Training Reserve Program .... ASTRP
Army Specialized Training Unit .... ASTU
Army Spectrometric Oil Analysis Program (AABC) .... ASOAP
Army Spectrum Management Steering Committee (MCD) .... ASMSC
Army Sports Control Board [*British*] .... ASCB
[*The*] **Army Staff** (AABC) .... ARSTAF
Army Staff .... AS
[*The*] **Army Staff** .... TAS
Army Staff Automated Administrative Support System (MCD) .... ARSTADS
Army Staff College (DOMA) .... ASC
Army Staff Council .... ASC
Army Staff Counsel (AAGC) .... ASC
Army Standard Group Order of Battle System (MCD) .... ASGOBS
Army Standard Information Management System .... ASIMS
Army Standard Program Languages .... ASPL
Army Standardization Program .... ASP
Army Standards Laboratory .... ASL
Army Stationing and Installation Plan (AABC) .... ASIP
Army Status Report (AABC) .... ASR
Army Stock Fund .... ASF
Army Stock Fund/Non-Stock Fund .... ASF/NSF
Army Strategic and Tactical Reorganization Objective .... ASTRO
Army Strategic Appraisal .... ASA
Army Strategic Capabilities Plan .... ASCP
Army Strategic Command and Control Systems (MCD) .... ASTRACCS
Army Strategic Communications Command .... ASCC
Army Strategic Defense Command [*Huntsville, AL*] .... ASDC
Army Strategic Objectives Plan .... ASOP
Army Strategic Plan [*A document*] .... ASP
Army Streamlined Acquisition Process [*or Program*] (RDA) .... ASAP
Army Student Nurse Program (AABC) .... ASNP
Army Student Nurse Program Identification Badge (GFGA) .... ASNPIDBAD
Army Student Nurse Program Identification Badge (AABC) .... ASNPIdentBad
[*The*] **Army Studies Program** (AABC) .... TASP
Army Study Advisory Committee .... ASAC
Army Study Documentation and Information Retrieval System [*Later, ALAS*] .... ASDIRS
[*The*] **Army Study System** .... TASS
Army Subject Schedule (AABC) .... ASUBJSCD
Army Subordinate Command Management Information System [*Formerly, CARMOCS*] (AABC) .... ASMIS
Army Subsistence Center .... ASC
Army Subsistence Supply Center [*Merged with Defense Subsistence Supply Center*] .... ASSC
Army Summary Jurisdiction Regulations [*British military*] (DMA) .... ASJR
Army Supply and Maintenance Command .... ASMC
Army Supply and Maintenance Command (MUGU) .... ASMCOM
[*The*] **Army Supply and Maintenance System** (AABC) .... TASAMS
Army Supply Program .... ASP
Army Support Center (AABC) .... ASPTC
Army Surgeon General .... ASG
Army Survival Measures Plan (AABC) .... ASMP
Army Switched Data and Secure Voice Network .... ASD & SVN
Army Switched Data and Secure Voice Network .... ASDSVN
Army System Engineering Office (RDA) .... ASEO
Army System for Standardized Intelligence Support Terminals (MCD) .... ASSIST
Army System Management .... ASM
Army Systems Acquisition Review Council .... ASARC
Army Systems Acquisition Review Council (DOMA) .... ASARC
Army Systems Acquisition Review Council Independent Evaluation Team (MCD) .... ASARC IET
Army Systems Coordinating Documents .... ASCOD
Army Systems Development and Acquisition Priorities (MCD) .... ASDAP
Army Tactical Airspace Regulation System (MCD) .... ATARS
Army Tactical Area Communications System .... ATACS
Army Tactical Command (NVT) .... ATC
Army Tactical Command and Control/Information System (MCD) .... ATACCIS
Army Tactical Command and Control System .... ATCCS
Army Tactical Communication System Simulator (MCD) .... ATCSS
Army Tactical Data Link .... ATDL
Army Tactical Data Systems (AABC) .... ARTADS
Army Tactical Frequency Engineering System .... ATFES
Army Tactical Intelligence Agency Blueprint (MCD) .... ATIB
Army Tactical Intelligence Committee (MCD) .... ATIC
Army Tactical Intelligence Concept (MCD) .... ATIC
Army Tactical, Logistical, and Air Simulation (MCD) .... ATLAS
Army Tactical Missile System (MCD) .... ATACM
Army Tactical Missile System (RDA) .... ATACMS
Army Tactical Missile System Block II (RDA) .... ATACMS BLK II
Army Tactical Missile System-Brilliant Anti-Armor Submunition (RDA) .... ATACMS-BAT
Army Tactical Multichannel Communications System (MCD) .... ATMCS
Army Tactical Operations Central .... ARTOC
Army Tactical Requirements for Infrared Systems (MCD) .... ATAIRS
Army Tactical Requirements for National Reconnaissance (MCD) .... ATRN
Army Tank Office (RDA) .... ATO
Army Tank Plant .... ATP
Army Tank Program (MCD) .... ATP
Army Tank-Automotive Center [*or Command*] [*Warren, MI*] .... ATAC
Army Technical Architecture [*Military*] .... ATA
Army Technical Library Improvement Studies .... ATLIS
Army Technical School [*British military*] (DMA) .... ATS
Army Technical Service Corps .... ATSC
Army Technology Base Master Plan (RDA) .... ATBMP
Army Telecommunications Center Automatic Programming (MCD) .... ATCAP
Army Telecommunications Combat Theater and General Support [*5 Year Plan*] (MCD) .... ATCOGS
Army Telecommunications System (GFGA) .... ATS
Army Telegraph [*Stamp surcharge*] [*British*] (ROG) .... AT
Army Terminal Command .... ATC
Army Terrain Information [*or Intelligence*] **System** (MCD) .... ARTINS
Army Terrain Requirements Data Base .... ATRDB
Army Test and Evaluation Command [*AMC*] .... ATEC
Army Test and Evaluation Command [*AMC*] (MUGU) .... ATECOM
Army Test and Evaluation Seminar .... ATES
Army Test Technology Office .... ATTO
Army Theater Missile [*Air*] **Defense Element** [*Army*] .... ATMDE
Army Theatre Arts Association [*Defunct*] (EA) .... ATAA
Army TMDE Modernization (RDA) .... ATM
Army Topographic Command [*Formerly, Army Map Service*] .... ATC
Army Topographic Station (AABC) .... ATS
Army Training and Evaluation Program (AABC) .... ARTEP
Army Training Battle Simulation System (MCD) .... ARTBASS
Army Training Battle Simulation System .... ARTBSS
Army Training Board .... ATB
Army Training Center .... ATC
Army Training Device Agency [*Orlando, FL*] (AABC) .... ATDA
Army Training Effectiveness and Simulation System (MCD) .... AMTESS

Army Training Extension Course Program ... ATECP
Army Training Film ... ATF
Army Training Instruction ... ATI
Army Training Memorandum [*British*] ... ATM
Army Training Plan (MCD) ... ATP
Army Training Program ... ATP
[*The*] **Army Training Requirements and Resource System** ... ATARRS
Army Training Requirements and Resources System ... ATRRS
Army Training Study ... ARTS
Army Training Support Center [*Fort Eustis, VA*] ... ATSC
Army Training Target System (MCD) ... ATTS
Army Training Test ... ATT
Army Transport [*British military*] (DMA) ... AT
Army Transport Service [*Later, Military Sea Transportation Service, then Military Sealift Command*] [*Obsolete*] ... ATS
Army Transport Service Quartermaster Corps [*Obsolete*] ... ATSQMC
Army Transportation Association ... ATA
Army Transportation Board (MCD) ... ATB
Army Transportation Corps ... ATC
Army Transportation Plan in Support of the Army Strategic Capabilities Plan (AABC) ... ATP-ASCP
Army Transportation Research Command ... ATRC
Army Troops [*British and Canadian*] [*World War II*] ... A Tps
Army Tropic Test Center (MCD) ... ATTC
Army Type Classification Code ... ATCC
Army Uniform Data Inquiry Technique ... AUDIT
Army Unit ... AU
Army Unit Resiliancy Analysis [*Computer science*] (RDA) ... AURA
Army User Equipment (MCD) ... AUE
Army Validation Program ... AVP
Army Veterinary and Remount Services [*British*] ... AVR
Army Veterinary and Remount Services [*British military*] (DMA) ... AVRS
Army Veterinary Corps [*Facetious translation during World War I "All Very Cushy"*] [*Later, RAVC*] [*British*] ... AVC
Army Veterinary Department [*British*] ... AVD
Army Veterinary Service [*British*] (DAS) ... AVS
Army Victualling Department [*British*] ... AVD
Army Vietnam ... ARV
Army Volunteer Reserve [*British*] ... AVR
Army Volunteers Corps [*British*] ... AVC
Army War College (MCD) ... ARWARCOL
Army War College ... ARWC
Army War College ... AWC
Army War College Correspondence Studies (MCD) ... AWCCS
Army War College Corresponding Studies Course (INF) ... AWCCSC
Army War Room (AABC) ... AWR
Army War Room Information System ... AWRIS
Army Warranty Program ... AWP
Army Wartime Asset Distribution Study ... AWADS
Army Weapons and Mobility Command ... AWMC
Army Weapons Command [*AMC*] ... AWC
Army Weapons Command [*AMC*] (MCD) ... AWECOM
Army Weather Service (NATG) ... AWS
Army Welfare Officer [*British*] ... AWO
Army Welfare Services [*British*] ... AWS
Army Wholesale Logistic System (AABC) ... AWLOG
Army Wireless Officer [*Obsolete*] (IAA) ... AWO
Army with Navy [*Personnel*] ... ARNA
Army (Wives) Senior Assistance Program ... ASAP
Army Women's Services Officers School [*British military*] (DMA) ... AWSOS
Army Work Study Group ... AWSG
Army Worldwide Military Command and Control Information Systems (RDA) ... AWWMCCS
Army WWMCCS [*Worldwide Military Command and Control System*] **Information System** (GFGA) ... AWIS
Army Youth Team [*British*] ... AYT
Army-Air Force Center for Low-Intensity Conflict [*Langley Air Force Base, VA*] (INF) ... A-AF CLIC
Army-Navy Aeronautical (KSC) ... ANA
Army-Navy Anticorrosion Compound ... ANC
Army-Navy Communications Intelligence Board [*Later, STANCIB*] ... ANCIB
Army-Navy Communications Intelligence Coordinating Committee [*Later, ANCIB*] ... ANCICC
Army-Navy Communications Production Expediting Agency ... ANCPEA
Army-Navy Country Club ... ANCC
Army-Navy Design Standards ... AND
Army-Navy Electronics Production Agency ... ANEPA
Army-Navy Ground Radio Communications ... AN/GRC
Army-Navy Instrumentation Program ... ANIP
Army-Navy Joint Specifications Board ... ANJSB
Army-Navy Joint Type Ordnance ... AN
Army-Navy Liquidation Commission [*World War II*] ... ANLC
Army-Navy Medical Procurement Office (DNAB) ... ANMPO
Army-Navy Munitions Board [*Later, Munitions Board*] ... ANMB
Army-Navy Petroleum Board ... ANPB
Army-Navy Petroleum Pool, Pacific Coast ... ANPPPC
Army-Navy Shipping Information Agency ... ANSIA
Army-Navy Vehicular Radio Communications ... AN/VRC
Army-Navy-Air Force (MCD) ... ANA
Army-Navy-Air Force ... ANAF
Army-Navy-Air Force Times Alliance [*A publication*] ... ANAFTA
Army-Navy-British ... ANB
Army-Navy-British Standard (SAA) ... ANBS
Army-Navy-Civil (MSA) ... ANC
Army-Navy-Commerce ... ANC
Army-Navy-Industry (MCD) ... ANI
Army's Electronic Environmental Test Facility [*Military*] (IAA) ... AEETF
Army's Five-Year Defense Program ... AFYDP
Army's Incentive Awards Program (RDA) ... AIAP
Army's Mobility Opportunity Development Program ... AMOD
Army's Program for Individual Training (MCD) ... APRINT
Army's Requirement to Own and Operate Watercraft (MCD) ... ARROW
Army-Wide ... AW
Army-Wide Doctrinal and Training Literature Program ... ADTLP
Army-Wide Library Council (RDA) ... ALC
Army-Wide Signature Program (MCD) ... AWSP
Army-Wide Training and Doctrinal Literature Program ... ATDLP
Armywide Training Literature ... ATL
Army-Wide Training Literature Program (AABC) ... ATLP
Army-Wide Training Support (AABC) ... AWTS
Army-Wide Training Support System ... AWTSS
Arnada Resources [*Vancouver Stock Exchange symbol*] ... AAN
Arnbruck [*Germany ICAO location identifier*] (ICLI) ... EDYB
Arner Medical Alert [*NASDAQ symbol*] (TTSB) ... AMAC
Arnhem Resources, Inc. [*Vancouver Stock Exchange symbol*] ... AHR
Arnold Air Development Center [*Air Force*] ... AADC
Arnold Air Society (EA) ... AAS
Arnold and Hodges' English Bail Court Reports [*A publication*] (DLA) ... Arn & HBC
Arnold and Hodges' English Bail Court Reports [*A publication*] (DLA) ... Arn & Hod BC
Arnold and Hodges' English Practice Cases [*A publication*] (DLA) ... Arn & Hod PC
Arnold and Hodges' English Practice Cases [*A publication*] (DLA) ... Arn & Hod Pr Cas
Arnold and Hodges' English Queen's Bench Reports [*1840-41*] [*A publication*] (DLA) ... A & H
Arnold and Hodges' English Queen's Bench Reports [*1840-41*] [*A publication*] (DLA) ... Arn & H
Arnold and Hodges' English Queen's Bench Reports [*1840-41*] [*A publication*] (DLA) ... Arn & Hod
Arnold and Hodges' English Queen's Bench Reports [*1840-41*] [*A publication*] (DLA) ... Arnold & H
Arnold, CA [*FM radio station call letters*] ... KBYN
Arnold Cook Braille and Talking Book Library [*Australia*] ... ACBTBL
Arnold Engineering Development Center [*Arnold Air Force Base, TN*] ... AEDC
Arnold Engineering Development Center, Arnold Air Force Station, TN [*OCLC symbol*] (OCLC) ... TAF
Arnold Gregory Memorial Hospital, Albion, NY [*Library symbol Library of Congress*] (LCLS) ... NAlbiH
Arnold Indus [*NASDAQ symbol*] (TTSB) ... AIND
Arnold Industries, Inc. [*NASDAQ symbol*] (NQ) ... AIND
Arnold Industries, Inc. [*Associated Press*] (SAG) ... Arnold
Arnold, MO [*FM radio station call letters*] ... KCWA
Arnold Palmer Golf Co. (The) [*Associated Press*] (SAG) ... APalmer
Arnold Palmer Golf Co. (The) [*NASDAQ symbol*] (SAG) ... APGC
Arnold. Public Meetings and Political Societies [*1833*] [*A publication*] (DLA) ... Arn Pub M
Arnold. Public Meetings and Political Societies [*1833*] [*A publication*] (DLA) ... Arn Pub Meet
Arnold Ranch [*California*] [*Seismograph station code, US Geological Survey*] (SEIS) ... ARN
Arnold Schoenberg Institute [*University of Southern California*] [*Research center*] (RCD) ... ASI
Arnold Schoenberg Institute, Los Angeles, CA [*Library symbol Library of Congress*] (LCLS) ... CLAS
Arnold Transit Co. [*Later, ATCO*] [*AAR code*] ... ATC
Arnold Transit Co. [*Formerly, ATC*] [*AAR code*] ... ATCO
Arnold, White & Durkee, Houston, TX [*Library symbol Library of Congress*] (LCLS) ... TxHAWD
Arnold-Chiari Malformation [*Medicine*] ... ACM
Arnolds Cove Public Library, Arnolds Cove, NF, Canada [*Library symbol Library of Congress*] (LCLS) ... CaNfAC
Arnolds Cove Public Library, Newfoundland [*Library symbol National Library of Canada*] (NLC) ... NFAC
Arnold's Election Cases [*England*] [*A publication*] (DLA) ... Arn El Cas
Arnold's English Common Pleas Reports [*1838-39*] [*A publication*] (DLA) ... Arn
Arnold's English Common Pleas Reports [*1838-39*] [*A publication*] (DLA) ... Arnold
Arnold's Geological Series ... AGS
Arnold's Municipal Corporations [*A publication*] (DLA) ... Arn Mun Cor
Arnolt-Bristol Owners Club [*Later, ABR*] (EA) ... ABOC
Arnolt-Bristol Registry (EA) ... ABR
Arnot's Criminal Cases [*1536-1784*] [*Scotland*] [*A publication*] (DLA) ... Arnot Cr C
Arnot's Criminal Trials [*1536-1784*] [*Scotland*] [*A publication*] (DLA) ... Arn
Arnould on Marine Insurance [*A publication*] (DLA) ... Arn
Arnould on Marine Insurance [*A publication*] (DLA) ... Arn Ins
Arnprior, ON [*AM radio station call letters*] ... CHVR-2
Arnprior Public Library, Arnprior, ON, Canada [*Library symbol*] [*Library of Congress*] (LCLS) ... CaOARB
Arnprior Public Library, Ontario [*Library symbol National Library of Canada*] (NLC) ... OAR
Arnsberg [*Germany ICAO location identifier*] (ICLI) ... EDLA
ARO, Inc., AEDC Library, Arnold Air Force Station, TN [*Library symbol Library of Congress*] (LCLS) ... TArnA
Aromatic [*Chemistry*] ... ar
Aromatic (MSA) ... AROM
Aromatic Amine Terminated Butadiene/Acrylonitrile [*Organic chemistry*] ... AATBN
Aromatic Amino Acid Decarboxylase [*Also, AADC*] [*An enzyme*] ... AAAD

Aromatic Amino Acid Decarboxylase [Also, AAAD] [An enzyme] .... AADC
Aromatic Amino Acids [Biochemistry] .... AAA
Aromatic Hydrocarbon Hydroxylase [An enzyme] .... AHH
Aromatic Red Cedar Closet Lining Manufacturers Association (EA) .... ARCCLMA
Aromatic Solvent-Induced Shift [Physical chemistry] .... ASIS
Aromatic Weathering Ratio [Ecology] (DAVI) .... AWR
Aromatica [Essence] [Chemistry] (ROG) .... AROMAT
Aromatics [Organic chemistry] .... Aro
Aromatics Hydrogenation [Fuel technology] .... AHYD
Arona [New Guinea] [Airport symbol] (AD) .... AON
Aronex Pharmaceuticals [NASDAQ symbol] (TTSB) .... ARNX
Aronex Pharmaceuticals, Inc. [NASDAQ symbol] (SAG) .... ARNX
Aronex Pharmaceuticals, Inc. [Associated Press] (SAG) .... AronexPh
Aronex Pharmaceuticals, Inc. [Associated Press] (SAG) .... AronxPh
Aroostook Aviation, Inc. [FAA designator] (FAAC) .... PXX
Aroostook State Teachers College [Merged with University of Maine] .... ASTC
Aroostook Valley Railroad Co. [AAR code] .... AVL
Arorae [Kiribati] [Airport symbol] (OAG) .... AIS
Arorae [Kiribati] [ICAO location identifier] (ICLI) .... NGTR
Around (FAAC) .... ARND
Around the Clock [Medicine] .... ATC
Arousal .... A
Arousal Mechanism [Medicine] .... AM
ARPA Calibration Satellite (MCD) .... ACS
ARPA [Advanced Research Projects Agency] Environmental Test
    Satellite .... ARENTS
ARPA [Advanced Research Projects Agency]/Lincoln C-Band Observable
    RADAR [Army] (AABC) .... ALCOR
ARPA [Advanced Research Projects Agency] Long-Range Tracking and
    Instrument RADAR .... ALTAIR
ARPA [Advanced Research Projects Agency] Maui Optical Station
    (MUGU) .... AMOS
ARPA [Advanced Research Projects Agency] Measurements RADAR
    [Raytheon] .... AMRAD
ARPA [Advanced Research Projects Agency] Network Terminal System ...... ANTS
Arpad Academy of Hungarian Scientists, Writers, and Artists Abroad
    (EA) .... AAHSWAA
Arpad Federation (EA) .... AF
Arpeggio [Music] .... ARP
Arpeggio [Record label] [Italy] .... Arp
Arpeggio [Music] .... ARPO
ArQule, Inc. [NASDAQ symbol] (SAG) .... ARQL
ArQule, Inc. [Associated Press] (SAG) .... ArQule
Arracacha Virus A [Plant pathology] .... AVA
Arracacha Virus B [Plant pathology] .... AVB
Ar-Rajhi Banking & Investment Co. [Saudi Arabia] (EY) .... ARABIC
Arrange (AABC) .... ARNG
Arrange (ROG) .... ARRE
Arranged .... ARR
Arranged .... ARRD
Arranged Total Loss [Insurance] .... ARRTL
Arranged Total Loss [Insurance] (AIA) .... ATL
Arrangement [Music] .... ARR
Arrangement (DLA) .... Arrang
Arrangement .... ARRANGT
Arrangement (ROG) .... ARRGT
Arranger [MARC relator code] [Library of Congress] (LCCP) .... arr
Arras/Roclincourt [France ICAO location identifier] (ICLI) .... LFQD
Array (NASA) .... ARR
Array Bending (SSD) .... AB
Array Element Study .... AES
Array Interconnection Logic [Computer science] .... AIL
Array Interface Unit [Computer science] (CAAL) .... AIU
Array Machine Language [Computer science] .... AML
Array Motion Sensor .... AMS
Array of Building Blocks (MHDI) .... ABB
Array Processing Instruction Set [Computer science] (MSA) .... APIS
[An] Array Processing Language [Programming language] .... AAPL
Array Processor [Computer science] (BUR) .... AP
Array Processor Access Method [Computer science] (BUR) .... APAM
Array Processor Assembly Language [Computer science] .... APAL
Array Processor Software [Computer science] (IEEE) .... APS
Array Processor Subroutine Package [Computer science] (BUR) .... APSP
Array Reduction Analysis Circuit (MHDB) .... ARAC
Array Signal Processing (MCD) .... ASP
Array Structure Experiment Package [Computer science] (IAA) .... ASEP
Array Transform Processor .... ATP
Arrears in Pay [Military] .... ARSIP
Arrecife [Canary Islands] [Airport symbol] (OAG) .... ACE
Arrecife/Lanzarote [Canary Islands] [ICAO location identifier] (ICLI) .... GCRR
Arrendamiento de Aviones Jets, SA [Mexico] [FAA designator] (FAAC) .... JTS
Arrest (FAAC) .... ARST
Arrest after Arrival [Medicine] (DMAA) .... AAA
Arrested Relaxation [Molecular dynamics] .... AR
Arrester [Electricity] (IAA) .... AR
Arrester [Electricity] (KSC) .... ARR
Arrester [Electricity] .... ARSR
Arresting .... ARG
Arresting Gear [Aviation] .... A-G
Arresting Gear Officer [Military] (MCD) .... AGO
Arresting Gear Tester .... AGT
Arret de la Chambre Civile de la Cour de Cassation [Decision of the Court of
    Appeal, Civil Division] [French] (ILCA) .... Cass Civ
Arret de la Chambre Civile de la Cour de Cassation [Decision of the Court of
    Appeal, Civil Division] [French] (ILCA) Civ

Arret de la Chambre Criminelle de la Cour de Cassation [Decision of the
    Court of Appeal, Criminal Division] [French] (ILCA) .... Cass Crim
Arret de la Chambre Criminelle de la Cour de Cassation [Decision of the
    Court of Appeal, Criminal Division] [French] (ILCA) .... Crim
Arret de la Chambre des Requetes de la Cour de Cassation [Decision of the
    Court of Appeal, Chamber of Requests] [French] (ILCA) .... Cass Req
Arret de la Cour de Cassation [Decision of the Court of Appeal] [Belgium]
    (ILCA) .... Cass
Arret de la Cour de Cassation Toutes Chambres Reunies [Decision of the
    Full Court of the Court of Appeal] [French] (ILCA) .... Ch Reun
Arret de la Section Commerciale de la Cour de Cassation [Decision of the
    Commercial Section of the Court of Appeal] [French] (ILCA) .... Cas Com
Arret de la Section Sociale de la Cour de Cassation [Decision of the Social
    Security and Labor Division of the Court of Appeal] [French] (ILCA) ..... Cass Soc
Arrete [Decision, Ordinance, By-law] [French] .... AR
Arrete [Decision, Order] [French] (ILCA) .... Arr
Arrhenatherum Blue Dwarf Virus [Plant pathology] .... ABDV
Arrhythmia [Cardiology] (DAVI) .... Arry
Arrhythmia Research Tech [AMEX symbol] (TTSB) .... HRT
Arrhythmia Research Technology [AMEX symbol] (SPSG) .... HRT
Arrhythmia Research Technology, Inc. [Associated Press] (SAG) .... Arhyth
Arrhythmogenic Dose of Epinephrine [Medicine] .... ADE
Arrhythmogenic Right Ventricular Dysplasia [Cardiology] (DMAA) .... ARVI
Arrian [Second century AD] [Classical studies] (OCD) .... Arr
Arricaccato (VRA) .... arric
Arrick, Douglas B., Denver CO [STAC] .... ARK
Arriflex [Camera] [Named for manufacturers Arnold and Richter] .... ARRI
Arrington [England] .... ARR
Arris Pharmaceutical [NASDAQ symbol] (TTSB) .... ARRS
Arris Pharmaceutical Corp. [Associated Press] (SAG) .... ArrisPh
Arris Pharmaceutical Corp. [NASDAQ symbol] (SAG) .... ARRS
Arrival .... AR
Arrival [or Arrive] .... ARR
Arrival Aircraft Interval [FAA] (TAG) .... AAI
Arrival Aircraft Interval [Aviation] (FAAC) .... AAITVL
Arrival Airfield Control Group [Military] (AABC) .... AACG
Arrival and Assembly Area [Marine Corps] (DOMA) .... AAA
Arrival and Assembly Operations Element [Navy] (ANA) .... AAOE
Arrival and Assembly Operations Group [Navy] (ANA) .... AAOG
Arrival and Assembly Support Party [Navy] (ANA) .... AASP
Arrival and Return [Shipping] .... AR
Arrival Angle [Army] .... AA
Arrival Date (DOMA) .... ARRDATE
Arrival Delay [Air Traffic Control] (FAAC) .... ADLY
Arrival/Departure Airfield Control Group (DOMA) .... A/DACG
Arrival Further Proceed Immediately and Report [Navy] .... ARPROIMREP
Arrival Further Proceed Port in which Activity Designated May Be
    [Navy] .... ARPROPORICH
Arrival Locator .... AL
Arrival Message [Aviation code] .... ARR
Arrival Notice [Shipping] .... AN
Arrival of Goods (WDMC) .... AOG
Arrival Report [Navy] .... ARREP
Arrival Report [Navy] (NVT) .... ARRIVEDREP
Arrival Report Commanding Officer that Vessel Duty [Navy] .... ARREPCOVES
Arrival Report Immediate Superior in Command [Navy] .... ARREPISIC
Arrival Report Will be Filed With [Aviation] (FAAC) .... FIRIV
Arrival Sequencing Program [FAA] (TAG) .... ASP
Arrival Time (AABC) .... AT
Arrival Time [Aviation] .... PX In
Arrival Time Distribution [Chemical physics] .... ATD
Arrival Unknown [Aviation] .... ARUNK
Arrive (ADA) .... A
Arrive (WGA) .... ARV
Arrived .... ARRD
Arrived Notification Form [British] (DCTA) .... ANF
Arrived Within Continental Limits of US [Navy] .... ARRUS
ARRL [American Radio Relay League] Foundation (EA) .... ARRLF
Arrocillo Amarillo [Race of maize] [Mexico] .... A-A
Arrow .... ARW
Arrow Airways, Inc. [ICAO designator] (FAAC) .... APW
Arrow Automotive Industries, Inc. [AMEX symbol] (SPSG) .... AI
Arrow Automotive Industries, Inc. [Associated Press] (SAG) .... ArrowA
Arrow Aviation Ltd. [Canada ICAO designator] (FAAC) .... ARO
Arrow Bank Corp. [NASDAQ symbol] (NQ) .... AROW
Arrow Bank Corp. [Associated Press] (SAG) .... ArowFn
Arrow Diagramming Method (MCD) .... ADM
Arrow Electronics [NYSE symbol] (TTSB) .... ARW
Arrow Electronics, Inc. [Associated Press] (SAG) .... ArowE
Arrow Electronics, Inc. [NYSE symbol] (SPSG) .... ARW
Arrow Financial [NASDAQ symbol] (TTSB) .... AROW
Arrow International [NASDAQ symbol] (TTSB) .... ARRO
Arrow International, Inc. [Associated Press] (SAG) .... ArowInt
Arrow International, Inc. [NASDAQ symbol] (SAG) .... ARRO
Arrow Transportation [NASDAQ symbol] (TTSB) .... ARRW
Arrow Transportation Co. [Associated Press] (SAG) .... ArrowTrn
Arrow Transportation Co. [NASDAQ symbol] (SAG) .... ARRW
Arrowfield Resources [Vancouver Stock Exchange symbol] .... ARW
Arrowhead [Military decoration] (AABC) .... Ahd
Arrowhead Airways [ICAO designator] (FAAC) .... ARH
Arrowhead Library System [Library network] .... ALS
Arrowhead Library System, Janesville Public Library, Janesville, WI [OCLC
    symbol] (OCLC) .... WIJ
Arrowhead Library System, Virginia, MN [Library symbol Library of
    Congress] (LCLS) .... MnVA

Arrowhead Professional Libraries Association [*Library network*] .... APLA
Arrowhead Resources Ltd. [*Vancouver Stock Exchange symbol*] .... AWR
Arrow-Magnolia International, Inc. [*Associated Press*] (SAG) .... ArrowM
Arrow-Magnolia International, Inc. [*NASDAQ symbol*] (SAG) .... ARWM
Arrow-Magnolia Intl. [*NASDAQ symbol*] (TTSB) .... ARWM
Arrows Ltd. [*British ICAO designator*] (FAAC) .... ARW
Arrowwood Municipal Library, Alberta [*Library symbol National Library of
    Canada*] (NLC) .... AARM
Arroyo Grande, CA [*AM radio station call letters*] .... KKAL
Ars Aequi; Juridisch Studentenblad [*Netherlands*] (ILCA) .... AAe
Ars Amatoria [*of Ovid*] [*Classical studies*] (OCD) .... Ars Am
Ars Poetica [*of Horace*] [*Classical studies*] (OCD) .... Ars P
Ars Rhetorica [*of Dionysius Halicarnassensis*] [*Classical studies*] (OCD) .... Rhet
ARS [*American Rocket Society*] Structures and Materials Committee .... ASTMC
Arsanilic Acid [*Organic chemistry*] .... ARS
'Arse over Kettle [*Head over heels*] [*Slang British*] (DSUE) .... AK
'Arse over Top [*Head over Heels*] [*Bowdlerized version*] (ADA) ...... AOT
Arsenal (AABC) .... ARS
Arsenal (MCD) .... ARSL
Arsenal .... ARSNL
Arsenal Exchange Model (MCD) .... AEM
Arsenal Family and Children's Center [*Research center*] (RCD) ..... AFCC
Arsenal Management Information System .... ARMIS
Arsenal Operations Directorate [*Rock Island Arsenal*] [*Army*] ...... AOD
Arsendinus de Forlivio [*Authority cited in pre-1607 legal work*] (DSA) ...... Ar
Arsendinus de Forlivio [*Authority cited in pre-1607 legal work*] (DSA) ...... Ar de For
Arsenic [*Chemical element*] (DAVI) .... ARSEN
Arsenic [*Chemical element*] .... As
Arsenic Atmosphere Czochralski [*System for growing crystals*] .... AAC
Arshan [*Former USSR Seismograph station code, US Geological Survey*]
    (SEIS) .... ARS
Arsine [*Inorganic chemistry*] .... ARS
Arsine [*Medicine*] (ADDR) .... SA
Arso [*Indonesia*] [*ICAO location identifier*] (ICLI) .... WAJA
Arson [*Criminology*] (LAIN) .... ARS
Arson Information Management System [*Developed by National Fire
    Administration*] [*Emmitsburg, MD*] .... AIMS
Arson Task Force Assistance Program .... ATFAP
Arsphenamine [*Antisyphilitic compound*] (MAE) .... AR
Arsphenamine [*Antisyphilitic compound*] .... ARS
Art (ADA) .... A
Art Advisory Committee .... AAC
Art and Antique Dealers League of America (EA) .... AADLA
Art and Architecture Thesaurus Program, Bennington College,
    Bennington, VT [*Library symbol*] [*Library of Congress*] (LCLS) ...... AatP
Art and Australia [*A publication*] .... Art Aust
Art and Craft Materials Institute (EA) .... ACMI
Art and Mechanical [*Graphics*] (NTCM) .... A & M
Art and Mechanical [*Graphic arts*] (WDMC) .... AM
Art and Requirements of Command (MCD) .... ARC
Art and Text [*A publication*] .... Art & T
Art and the Law [*A publication*] (DLA) .... Art & Law
Art Bulletin [*A publication*] (BRI) .... Art Bull
Art Center College of Design, Los Angeles, CA [*Library symbol Library of
    Congress*] (LCLS) .... CLArt
Art Center School .... ACS
Art Circle Public Library, Crossville, TN [*Library symbol Library of
    Congress*] (LCLS) .... TCrA
Art Class Teacher's Certificate [*British*] .... ACTC
Art Collectors Club of America (EA) .... ACCA
Art Complete (MCD) .... AC
Art Dealers Association of America (EA) .... ADAA
Art Deco Societies of America (EA) .... ADSA
Art Direction [*A publication*] (BRI) .... Art Dir
Art Director [*Films, television, etc.*] .... AD
Art Directors Annual [*A publication*] .... ADA
Art Directors Club (EA) .... ADC
Art Directors Club of Montreal [*1950*] [*Canada*] (NGC) .... ADCM
Art Directors Club of Toronto [*1947*] [*Canada*] (NGC) .... ADCT
Art Dreco Institute (EA) .... ADI
Art Education Society of New South Wales [*Australia*] .... AESNW
Art Exhibitions Australia .... AEA
Art Exhibitions Bureau .... AEB
Art For All .... AFA
Art for World Friendship (AEBS) .... AWF
Art Galleries Association [*British*] (DBA) .... AGA
Art Gallery .... AG
Art Gallery, Mount Saint Vincent University, Halifax, Nova Scotia [*Library
    symbol National Library of Canada*] (NLC) .... NSHVA
Art Gallery of Cobourg, Cobourg, ON, Canada [*Library symbol Library of
    Congress*] (LCLS) .... CaOCoA
Art Gallery of Cobourg, Ontario [*Library symbol National Library of Canada*]
    (NLC) .... OCOA
Art Gallery of Greater Victoria, Victoria, BC, Canada [*Library symbol Library
    of Congress*] (LCLS) .... CaBViA
Art Gallery of Greater Victoria, Victoria, British Columbia [*Library symbol
    National Library of Canada*] (NLC) .... BVIA
Art Gallery of Hamilton, Hamilton, ON, Canada [*Library symbol Library of
    Congress*] (LCLS) .... CaOHAG
Art Gallery of Hamilton, Ontario [*Library symbol National Library of Canada*]
    (NLC) .... OHAG
Art Gallery of Nova Scotia, Halifax, Nova Scotia [*Library symbol National
    Library of Canada*] (NLC) .... NSHAG
Art Gallery of Nova Scotia, Halifax, NS, Canada [*Library symbol Library of
    Congress*] (LCLS) .... CaNSHAG

Art Gallery of Ontario [*UTLAS symbol*] .... AGO
Art Gallery of Ontario, Audiovisual Library, Toronto, ON, Canada [*Library
    symbol Library of Congress*] (LCLS) .... CaOTAGAV
Art Gallery of Ontario, Toronto, ON, Canada [*Library symbol Library of
    Congress*] (LCLS) .... CaOTAG
Art Gallery of Ontario, Toronto, Ontario [*Library symbol National Library of
    Canada*] (NLC) .... OTAG
Art Gallery of South Australia .... AGSA
Art Gallery of Windsor, Ontario [*Library symbol National Library of Canada*]
    (NLC) .... OWAG
Art Gallery of Windsor, Windsor, ON, Canada [*Library symbol Library of
    Congress*] (LCLS) .... CaOWAG
Art Glass Suppliers Association (EA) .... AGSA
Art Hazards Information Center (EA) .... AHIC
Art in America [*A publication*] (BRI) .... Art Am
Art Information Center (EA) .... AIC
Art Institute of Chicago .... AIC
Art Institute of Chicago, Chicago, IL [*Library symbol Library of Congress*]
    (LCLS) .... ICA
Art Institute of Fort Lauderdale, Fort Lauderdale, FL [*Library symbol*]
    [*Library of Congress*] (LCLS) .... FFIAI
Art Institute of Light (EA) .... AIL
Art Journal [*A publication*] (BRI) .... Art J
Art Leather [*Abbreviation of artificial*] [*Visual material*] (WDMC) ...... art
Art Libraries Society [*British*] (BI) .... ARLIS
Art Libraries Society/North America (EA) .... ARLIS/NA
Art Master's Certificate .... AMC
Art Master's Teaching Certificate [*British*] .... AMTC
Art Material Club [*Later, AMMA*] (EA) .... AMC
Art Material Manufacturers Association [*Defunct*] (EA) .... AMMA
Art Metalware Manufacturers' Association [*British*] (DBA) .... AMMA
Art Museum Association of America (EA) .... AMAA
Art Museum Development Association (NFD) .... AMDA
Art Museum of Princeton University, Princeton, NJ [*Library symbol*] [*Library
    of Congress*] (LCLS) .... NjP-A
Art Museum of South Texas, Corpus Christi, TX [*Library symbol Library of
    Congress*] (LCLS) .... TxCcMST
Art Patrons Association of America (EA) .... APAA
Art Research Libraries of Ohio [*Library network*] .... ARLO
Art Resources in Collaboration (EA) .... ARC
Art Self-Concept Inventory (EDAC) .... ASCI
Art Services Grants [*British*] .... ASG
Art Students' League of New York (EA) .... ASLNY
Art Teacher's Certificate [*British*] .... ATC
Art Teacher's Diploma [*British*] .... ATD
Art Teacher's Diploma [*British*] .... ATDip
Art Therapist, Registered .... ATR
Art Velum [*Abbreviation of artificial*] [*Visual material*] (WDMC) ...... art
Art Workers Guild (EAIO) .... AWG
Arta [*Djibouti*] [*Seismograph station code, US Geological Survey Closed*]
    (SEIS) .... ART
Arta Group [*NYSE symbol*] (TTSB) .... ATA
Arta Observatory [*Djibouti*] (SEIS) .... ARO
Artac [*Spain*] [*FAA designator*] (FAAC) .... AVS
ARTADS Requirements Coordinating Committee .... ARCC
Artagraph Reproduction Technology [*NASDAQ symbol*] (SAG) ...... XARO
Artbibliographies Modern [*Database*] [*Clio Press Ltd.*] [*Information service or
    system*] (CRD) .... ABM
ARTCC Maintenance Control Center [*FAA*] (TAG) .... AMCC
Artem-Avia [*Ukraine*] [*FAA designator*] (FAAC) .... ABA
ARTEP [*Army Training and Evaluation Program*] Mission Training Plan
    (INF) .... AMTP
Arteria [*Artery*] [*Latin*] .... A
Arterial Blood [*Medicine*] (MAE) .... a
Arterial Blood Gas [*Medicine*] .... ABG
Arterial Blood Pressure [*Medicine*] .... ABP
Arterial Cannulation Support [*Cardiology*] (DAVI) .... ACS
Arterial Carbon Dioxide Pressure, Tension [*Medicine*] (MAE) ...... $Paco_2$
Arterial Flow Rate .... AFR
Arterial Gas Embolism .... AGE
Arterial Hypertension [*Medicine*] .... AH
Arterial in the Blood Phase [*Medicine*] (DAVI) .... A
Arterial Insufficiency of the Lower Extremities [*Medicine*] ...... AILE
Arterial Occlusive Disease [*Medicine*] .... AOD
Arterial Oxygen Pressure (MAE) .... PAO_2
Arterial Oxygen Pressure (WDAA) .... PAO_2
Arterial Oxygen Saturation [*Medicine*] (DAVI) .... SO_2
Arterial Partial Pressure of Oxygen [*Medicine*] (DAVI) .... PaO_2
Arterial pH [*Hydrogen ion concentration*] [*Medicine*] (DAVI) ...... PHA
Arterial Premature Beat [*Cardiology*] .... APB
Arterial Premature Contraction [*Cardiology*] .... APC
Arterial Presssure [*Medicine*] (DHSM) .... AP
Arterial Pulse Wave Transducer .... APWT
Arterial Vascular Engineering [*NASDAQ symbol*] (TTSB) .... AVEI
Arterial Vascular Engineering, Inc. [*Associated Press*] (SAG) ...... ArtVasc
Arterial Vascular Engineering, Inc. [*NASDAQ symbol*] (SAG) ...... AVEI
Arterial/Venous [*Ratio in fundi*] [*Ophthalmology*] (DAVI) .... A:V
Arterialized Capillary Blood [*Medicine*] (AAMN) .... ACB
Arteries [*Medicine*] (DMAA) .... AA
Arterio/Deep Venous [*Medicine*] .... A/DV
Arterio/Superficial Venous [*Medicine*] (MAE) .... A/SV
Arteriofemoral Bypass Graft [*Medicine*] .... AFBG
Arteriolar [*Medicine*] (DAVI) .... A
Arteriolonephrosclerosis [*Urology*] .... ANS
Arteriosclerosis [*Medicine*] .... AS

Arteriosclerosis [*or Arteriosclerotic*] [*Medicine*] .... ASC
Arteriosclerosis [*Cardiology*] (DAVI) .... ASCL
Arteriosclerosis [*Medicine*] (MAE) .... ATS
Arteriosclerosis Obliterans [*Medicine*] .... ASO
Arteriosclerosis Obliterans [*Cardiology*] (DAVI) .... ASOblit
Arteriosclerotic Brain Syndrome [*Cardiology and neurology*] (DAVI) .... ASBS
Arteriosclerotic Cardiovascular Disease [*Cardiology*] .... ASCVD
Arteriosclerotic Cardiovascular Renal Disease [*Medicine*] (DAVI) .... ACVRD
Arteriosclerotic Cardiovascular Renal Disease [*Medicine*] (DAVI) .... ASCVRD
Arteriosclerotic Coronary Artery Disease [*Cardiology*] (MAE) .... ASCAD
Arteriosclerotic Heart Disease [*Cardiology*] .... AHD
Arteriosclerotic Heart Disease [*Cardiology*] .... ASHD
Arteriosclerotic Nephritis [*Medicine*] (DMAA) .... ASN
Arteriosclerotic Peripheral Vascular Disease [*Medicine*] (MEDA) .... ASPVD
Arteriosclerotic Renal Vascular Disease [*Medicine*] .... ARVD
Arteriosclerotic Vascular [*or Vessel*] **Disease** [*Cardiology*] (DAVI) .... ASVD
Arteriovenous [*Medicine*] .... AV
Arteriovenous Anastomosis [*Medicine*] .... AVA
Arteriovenous Fistula [*Medicine*] .... AVF
Arteriovenous Internal Mammary [*Fistula*] [*Cardiology*] (DAVI) .... A-V IMA
Arteriovenous Malformation [*Medicine*] (CPH) .... ARM
Arteriovenous Malformation [*Medicine*] .... AVM
Arteriovenous Oxygen Content Difference [*Medicine*] (DAVI) .... $C(a\text{-}v)O_2$
Arteriovenous Oxygen Difference [*Medicine*] (MAE) .... $A\text{-}VO_2$
Arteriovenous Oxygen Differnce [*Biochemistry*] (DAVI) .... $AV\ DO_2$
Arteriovenous Oxygen Saturation Difference [*Medicine*] (DMAA) .... AVDO
Arteriovenous Shunt [*Cardiology*] .... AVS
Artery [*or Arterial*] .... ART
Artery .... ARTRY
Artery and Nerve [*Cardiology*] (DAVI) .... A/N
Artesia, MS [*FM radio station call letters*] .... WQNN
Artesia, MS [*FM radio station call letters*] (RBYB) .... WSMS-FM
Artesia, NM [*Location identifier FAA*] (FAAL) .... ATS
Artesia, NM [*AM radio station call letters*] .... KSVP
Artesia, NM [*FM radio station call letters*] .... KTZA
Artesia Public Library, Artesia, NM [*OCLC symbol*] (OCLC) .... ANM
Artesia Public Library, Artesia, NM [*Library symbol Library of Congress*] (LCLS) .... NmAr
Artesia Public Library, Artesia, NM [*Library symbol*] [*Library of Congress*] (LCLS) .... NmArP
Artesian Resources Corp. [*Associated Press*] (SAG) .... ArtesRes
Artesian Resources Corp. [*NASDAQ symbol*] (SAG) .... ARTN
Artesian Resources'A' [*NASDAQ symbol*] (TTSB) .... ARTNA
Arthmetic Ratio (BARN) .... Ar R
Arthritic Dose [*Medicine*] (BABM) .... AD
Arthritis (DMAA) .... arth
Arthritis and Musculoskeletal and Skin Diseases Database [*National Arthritis and Musculoskeletal and Skin Diseases Information Clearinghouse*] [*Information service or system*] (CRD) .... AMS
Arthritis and Rheumatic Disease [*Medicine*] (DAVI) .... ARD
Arthritis and Rheumatic Diseases Abstracts [*A publication*] .... ARD
Arthritis and Rheumatism Council for Research [*British*] (IRUK) .... ARC
Arthritis and Rheumatism Foundation [*Later, Arthritis Foundation*] .... ARF
Arthritis Care [*An association*] (EAIO) .... AC
Arthritis Care Association [*British*] .... ACA
Arthritis Foundation (EA) .... AF
Arthritis Foundation of Australia (Australian Capital Territory) .... AFA(ACT)
Arthritis Foundation of Australia, Queensland .... AFAQ
Arthritis Foundation of New South Wales [*Australia*] .... AFNSW
Arthritis Foundation of South Australia .... AFSA
Arthritis Foundation of Tasmania [*Australia*] .... AFT
Arthritis Foundation of Victoria [*Australia*] .... AFV
Arthritis Foundation of Western Australia .... AFWA
Arthritis Health Professions Association (EA) .... AHPA
Arthritis Impact Measurement Scales [*Medicine*] .... AIMS
Arthritis Information Clearinghouse [*Public Health Service*] (EA) .... AIC
Arthritis Rehabilitation Center (EA) .... ARC
Arthritis Society, Winnipeg, Manitoba [*Library symbol National Library of Canada*] (NLC) .... MWAS
Arthritis Society, Winnipeg, MB, Canada [*Library symbol Library of Congress*] (LCLS) .... CaMWAS
ArthroCare Corp. [*NASDAQ symbol*] (SAG) .... ARTC
ArthroCare Corp. [*NASDAQ symbol*] (TTSB) .... ARTC
ArthroCare Corp. [*Associated Press*] (SAG) .... ArthroC
Arthrodentosteodysplasia [*Medicine*] (DMAA) .... ADOD
Arthrogryposis Association (EA) .... AA
Arthrogryposis Multiplex Congenita [*Medicine*] (MEDA) .... AMC
Arthropod-Borne [*Also, ARBOR*] [*Virology*] .... ARBO
Arthropod-Borne [*Also, ARBO*] [*Virology*] .... ARBOR
Arthropod-Borne Animal Diseases Research Laboratory [*Department of Agriculture*] (GRD) .... ABADRL
Arthropod-Borne Virus [*Medicine*] (DMAA) .... ABV
Arthropods of La Selva [*Costa Rica*] .... ALAS
Arthroscopy [*Orthopedics*] (DAVI) .... arthro
Arthroscopy Association of North America (EA) .... AANA
Arthur Adaptation of the Leiter International Performance Scale [*Psychology*] .... AALIPS
Arthur Andersen & Co., Carolinas Central Library, Charlotte, NC [*Library symbol*] [*Library of Congress*] (LCLS) .... NcCA
Arthur Anderson & Co., Portland, OR [*Library symbol Library of Congress*] (LCLS) .... OrPAA
Arthur Brown's Compendious View of the Civil Law [*A publication*] (DLA) .... Bro (A) CL
Arthur Community School District, Arthur, IL [*Library symbol*] [*Library of Congress*] (LCLS) .... IArtSD
Arthur D. Little [*Commercial firm*] (NITA) .... ADL
Arthur D. Little, Inc. [*Cambridge, MA*] [*Research code symbol*] .... ADL
Arthur D. Little, Inc. .... ALI
Arthur D. Little, Inc. [*Research code symbol*] .... NSC
Arthur D. Little, Inc., Cambridge, MA [*OCLC symbol*] (OCLC) .... ADL
Arthur D. Little, Inc., Cambridge, MA [*Library symbol Library of Congress*] (LCLS) .... MCA
Arthur D. Little, Inc., Cambridge, MA [*Library symbol*] [*Library of Congress*] (LCLS) .... MCAL
Arthur District High School, Arthur, ON, Canada [*Library symbol*] [*Library of Congress*] (LCLS) .... CaOAtD
Arthur District High School, Arthur, Ontario [*Library symbol National Library of Canada*] (NLC) .... OARD
Arthur G. McKee & Co., Cleveland, OH [*Library symbol Library of Congress*] (LCLS) .... OCIAM
Arthur Johnson Memorial Library, Raton, NM [*OCLC symbol*] (OCLC) .... AJM
Arthur Johnson Memorial Library, Raton, NM [*Library symbol Library of Congress*] (LCLS) .... NmRa
Arthur Machen Society [*Defunct*] (EA) .... AMS
Arthur, ND [*FM radio station call letters*] .... KCQV
Arthur Public Library, Arthur, IL [*Library symbol Library of Congress*] (LCLS) .... IArt
[*The*] **Arthur Ransome Society** [*British*] (EAIO) .... TARS
Arthur Vining Davis Corp. .... ARVIDA
Arthurian Resources Ltd. [*Vancouver Stock Exchange symbol*] .... ATU
Arthur's Town [*Bahamas*] [*Airport symbol*] (OAG) .... ATC
Arthur's Town, Eleuthera Island [*Bahamas*] [*ICAO location identifier*] (ICLI) .... MYCA
Arti [*Former USSR Seismograph station code, US Geological Survey*] (SEIS) .... ARU
Artibus Asiae [*A publication*] .... Art Asiae
Artic Aerospace Laboratory [*Air Force*] .... AAL
Artic Military Environmental Cooperation [*U.S., Russia, and Norway study of radioactive waves*] .... AMEC
Artichoke Advisory Board (EA) .... AAB
Artichoke Italian Latent Virus [*Plant pathology*] .... AILV
Artichoke Mottled Crinkle Virus [*Plant pathology*] .... AMCV
Artichoke Vein Banding Virus [*Plant pathology*] .... AVBV
Artichoke Yellow Ringspot Virus [*Plant pathology*] .... AYRV
Article .... A
Article (AFM) .... ART
Article 19 - International Centre Against Censorship [*British*] (EAIO) A19
Article 19 - International Centre on Censorship (EAIO) ICC
Article Number Association (EAIO) .... ANA
Article Numbering Association [*Retailing*] [*British*] (NITA) .... ANA
Article Numbering Association of Ireland (EAIO) .... ANAI
Article Procurement with Online Local Ordering [*Document delivery system*] [*Telecommunications*] .... APOLLO
Article Type [*Database terminology*] (NITA) .... AT
Articled Clerk [*1867-68*] [*A publication*] (DLA) .... Artic Cl
Articled Clerk and Debater [*1866*] [*A publication*] (DLA) .... Artic Cl Deb
Articled Clerks' Journal and Examiner [*1879-81*] [*A publication*] (DLA) .... Artic Cl J Exam
Articles for the Government of the Navy [*Obsolete*] .... AGN
Articles of War .... AOW
Articles of War .... AW
Articulare [*Craniometric point*] .... AR
Articulated (DCTA) .... A
Articulated [*or Articulation*] (ADA) .... ART
Articulated .... ARTCLD
Articulated Computing Hierarchy [*British*] .... ARCH
Articulated Dump Truck [*Caterpillar Tractor Co.*] .... ADT
Articulated Instructional Media (SAA) .... AIM
Articulated Leg Platform [*Drilling technology*] .... ALP
Articulated Linear Thrust Engine [*Submarine technology*] .... ALTEN
Articulated Mirror System [*Astronomy*] .... AMS
Articulated Requirements Transaction System [*NASA*] .... ARTS
Articulated Subject Index (NITA) .... ASI
Articulated Total Body (MCD) .... ATB
Articulated Total Body .... ATB
Articulated Vehicle Dynamic Simulator (PDAA) .... AVDS
Articulated-Frame Mechanical-Drive Vehicle [*Automotive engineering*] .... AMV
Articulating Dolly [*Trailer engineering*] .... A (Dolly)
Articulation .... ARTIC
Articulation Control Subsystem [*NASA*] .... ARTC
Articulation Index .... AI
Articulation Loss of Consonants [*Audiology*] .... ALcons
Articulation Score [*Percentage of words correctly understood over a radio channel perturbed by interference*] [*Telecommunications*] .... AS
Articulation Screening Assessment [*Speech development test*] .... ASA
Articuli Cleri [*Articles of the Clergy*] [*Latin*] (DLA) .... Artic Cleri
Articuli Super Chartas [*Articles upon the Charters*] [*Latin*] (DLA) .... Artic Sup Chart
Articulotrochanteric Distance (PDAA) .... ATD
Artificer .... ART
Artificer (ADA) .... ARTIF
Artificer Diver [*British military*] (DMA) .... AD
Artificer Quartermaster Sergeant [*British*] .... AQMS
Artificer Sergeant Major [*British*] .... ASM
Artificial .... ARFL
Artificial (TEL) .... ART
Artificial (MSA) .... ARTF
Artificial .... ARTIF
Artificial (VRA) .... artif
Artificial .... ARTIFCL
Artificial Aerial (DEN) .... AA

Artificial Beta Cells [*Biochemistry*] (DAVI) .... ABC
Artificial Breeding Box .... ABB
Artificial Breeding Center, Victoria [*Australia*] .... ABCV
Artificial Cerebrospinal Fluid [*Medicine*] .... ACSF
Artificial Circus Movement Tachycardia [*Medicine*] (DMAA) .... ACMT
Artificial Cloud Nucleation [*Rainmaking*] .... ACN
Artificial Compression Method .... ACM
Artificial Delay Line (IAA) .... ADL
Artificial Earth Research and Orbiting Satellite (NATG) .... AEROS
Artificial Earth Satellite [*NASA*] .... AES
Artificial Earth Satellite Observation Program [*Navy*] .... AESOP
Artificial Endocrine Pancreas [*Medicine*] .... AEP
Artificial Erythrocyte [*Hematology*] .... AE
Artificial Flower Manufacturers' Association of Great Britain (BI) .... AFMA
Artificial Flower Manufacturers Board of Trade [*Defunct*] (EA) .... AFMBT
Artificial Gravity (NASA) .... AG
Artificial Gravity Structure .... AGS
Artificial Heart [*Medicine*] .... AH
Artificial Heart Energy System .... AHES
Artificial Hip Joint (DMAA) .... AHJ
Artificial Horizon (MCD) .... AH
Artificial Horizon Indicator [*Aerospace*] (MCD) .... AHI
Artificial Insemination [*Medicine*] .... AI
Artificial Insemination [*Medicine*] (HGAA) .... art insem
Artificial Insemination [*From George Orwell's novel, "1984"*] .... ARTSEM
Artificial Insemination by Donor [*Medicine*] .... AID
Artificial Insemination by Husband [*Medicine*] .... AIH
Artificial Insemination Centre [*Australia*] .... AIC
Artificial Insemination, Homologous [*Medicine*] (MAE) .... AIH
Artificial Intelligence [*Computer science*] .... AI
Artificial Intelligence and Expert System .... AL/ES
Artificial Intelligence Applications Institute [*British*] .... AIAI
Artificial Intelligence Expert System .... AIES
Artificial Intelligence for Engineering Design, Analysis, and Manufacturing [*A publication*] .... AI EDAM
Artificial Intelligence Group [*MIT*] .... AIG
Artificial Intelligence in Medicine .... AIM
Artificial Intelligence Job Performance Aid [*Army*] .... AIJPA
Artificial Intelligence Knowledge Representation [*Computer science*] (NITA) .... AIKR
Artificial Intelligence Laboratory [*Massachusetts Institute of Technology*] [*Research center*] (RCD) .... AIL
Artificial Intelligence Project Office (SSD) .... AIPO
Artificial Intelligence Research [*Computer science*] (DAVI) .... AIR
Artificial Intelligence Research Support [*Program*] [*Computer science*] .... AIRS
Artificial Intelligence-Transaction Security Ltd. [*British*] (NITA) .... AI-TSL
Artificial Interference to Transmission or Reception [*Broadcasting*] .... QRM
Artificial Life [*Computer science*] .... AL
Artificial Limb (HGAA) .... AFL
Artificial Limb and Appliance Centre [*British*] .... ALAC
Artificial Line [*Electricity*] (OA) .... AL
Artificial Luminance [*Theory proposed by James Clerk Maxwell in 1864*] .... AL
Artificial Luminous Cloud .... ALC
Artificial Lung-Expanding Compound [*Medicine*] (DMAA) .... ALEC
Artificial Methods Analyst (MCD) .... ARMAN
Artificial Neural Network .... ANN
Artificial Neural Network .... ANN
Artificial Neuron .... ARTRON
Artificial Nutrition and Hydration [*Medicine*] .... ANH
Artificial Pacemaker-Induced Ventricular Rhythm [*Medicine*] (DMAA) .... APIVR
Artificial Personality .... AP
Artificial Pneumothorax [*Medicine*] .... AP
Artificial Pneumothorax [*Medicine*] .... APN
Artificial Pupil (SAA) .... AP
Artificial Respiration [*Medicine*] .... AR
Artificial Resynthesis Technology [*Mechanical mouth used in dental research*] .... ART
Artificial Rupture of Membrane [*Medicine*] (CPH) .... AROM
Artificial Rupture of Membranes [*Medicine*] .... ARM
Artificial Satellite .... AS
Artificial Satellite Time and Radio Orbit (MCD) .... ASTRO
Artificial Seawater .... ASW
Artificial Site Tuff [*Geology*] .... AST
Artificial Sweetener .... AS
Artificial Time History [*Nuclear energy*] (NRCH) .... ATH
Artificial Top Component [*Virology*] .... ATC
Artificial Traffic Equipment [*Telecommunications*] (NITA) .... ATE
Artificial Transmission Line .... ATL
Artificial Vagina [*Veterinary science*] (OA) .... AV
Artificial White Light .... AWL
Artificially Fed .... AF
Artificially Induced Aurora .... AIA
Artificially Intelligent Computer Performer .... AICP
Artificially Intelligent Devices and Techniques (NITA) .... ADAT
Artificially Random Self-Motivated (MHDI) .... ARASEM
Artificially Sweetened (HGAA) .... asw
Artigas [*Uruguay*] [*Airport symbol*] (OAG) .... ATI
Artigas/Aeropuerto Deptal [*Uruguay*] [*ICAO location identifier*] (ICLI) .... SUAG
Artikelen [*Articles*] [*Dutch*] (ILCA) .... artt
Artikkel-Indeks Database [*Norwegian Center for Informatics*] [*Information service or system*] .... AID
Artikkel-Indeks Tidsskrifter [*Norwegian Center for Informatics*] [*Database*] .... AITI
Artillerie [*Artillery*] [*German*] .... ArtI
Artilleriefuehrer [*Division artillery commander*] [*German military - World War II*] .... AF

Artillery .... A
Artillery .... ART
Artillery .... ARTIL
Artillery .... ARTILL
Artillery .... ARTLY
Artillery (AFM) .... ARTY
Artillery (CINC) .... AT
Artillery Air Observer (DNAB) .... AAO
Artillery Ammunition and Rocket Development Laboratory [*Army*] (MCD) .... AARDL
Artillery and Missile School [*Army*] (MCD) .... AMS
Artillery Ballistic Meteorological System (MCD) .... ABMS
Artillery Barge [*Navy symbol Obsolete*] .... APB
Artillery Command Reconnaissance Vehicle [*Former USSR*] .... ACRV
Artillery Computer System .... ACS
Artillery Control Console [*British*] .... ACC
Artillery Controller (NATG) .... AC
Artillery Counterfire Information [*Army*] (ADDR) .... ACIF
Artillery Delivered Antipersonnel Munitions (MCD) .... ADAM
Artillery Destruction Program .... ADP
Artillery Direct Fire Trainer (AABC) .... ADFT
Artillery Division [*Military*] (MCD) .... AD
Artillery Engagement Simulation System (MCD) .... ARES
Artillery Equipment School [*British*] (DAS) .... AES
Artillery Fire Data Computer (PDAA) .... AFDC
Artillery Flash Ranging [*Army*] (AABC) .... AFR
Artillery Forces Simulation Model (MCD) .... AFSM
Artillery Forward Observer .... AFO
Artillery Ground Burst Simulator (MCD) .... AGBS
Artillery Liaison Officer [*Army*] .... AIO
Artillery Liaison Office [*or Officer*] (DNAB) .... ARTYLO
Artillery Location Acoustic System (MCD) .... ALAS
Artillery Meteorological System (NATG) .... AMETS
Artillery Meteorological Team [*Army*] (ADDR) .... ARTYMET
Artillery Observation Post [*British military*] (DMA) .... AOP
Artillery/Ordnance (MCD) .... AO
Artillery Reconnaissance [*British and Canadian*] [*World War II*] .... arty R
Artillery Registration/Adjustment System [*ARRADCOM*] (MCD) .... ARADS
Artillery Registration/Adjustment System [*ARRADCOM*] (MCD) .... ARAS
Artillery Repair Truck [*British*] .... ART
Artillery Resources Ltd. [*Vancouver Stock Exchange symbol*] .... ARY
Artillery Saturation Rocket System [*Army*] .... ASTROS
Artillery Siege Train Traction Engine [*British*] .... ASTTE
Artillery Spotting Division [*Air Force*] .... ASD
Artillery Supply Truck [*British*] .... AST
Artillery Tactical Terminal .... ATT
Artillery Target Intelligence (MCD) .... ATI
Artillery Test Board [*Army*] .... ATB
Artillery Towing Light Auxiliary System [*Army*] (MCD) .... ATLAS
Artillery Tractor [*British*] .... AT
Artillery Volunteer Corps [*British*] .... AVC
Artillery Volunteers .... AV
Artillery Weapons Data Transmission System (MCD) .... AWDATS
Artillery-Delivered Antipersonnel Mine (RDA) .... ADAM
Artillery-Delivered Antitank Mine (MCD) .... ADATM
Artillery-Delivered Expendable Jammer [*Army*] .... ADEXJAM
Artillery-Delivered Multipurpose Submunition (AABC) .... ARDEMS
Artillery-Fired Atomic Projectile .... AFAP
Artillery-Launched Television System (PDAA) .... ALTEL
Artillery-Locating RADAR .... ALR
Artina Resources Ltd. [*Vancouver Stock Exchange symbol*] .... ARS
ARTINS [*Army Terrain Information System*] Requirements Coordination Committee (RDA) .... ARCC
Artisan .... ARTSN
Artisan Quartermaster Sergeant [*British*] .... AQMS
Artisan Works Co. [*British and Canadian*] [*World War II*] .... art wks coy
Artisans Order of Mutual Protection [*Philadelphia, PA*] (EA) .... AOMP
Artisoft, Inc. [*Associated Press*] (SAG) .... Artsft
Artisoft, Inc. [*NASDAQ symbol*] (SPSG) .... ASFT
Artisoft LAN [*Linked Access Network*] Interface Chip for Ethernet [*Artisoft, Inc.*] [*Computer science*] (PCM) .... ALICE
Artist [*MARC relator code*] [*Library of Congress*] (LCCP) .... art
Artist .... ART
Artist .... ART
Artist [*Record label*] .... Atst
Artist and Repertoire (WDMC) .... A & R
Artist Blacksmith Association of North America (EA) .... ABANA
Artist Direct [*Record label*] .... AD
Artist in Residence (BARN) .... AIR
Artistic .... ARTSTC
Artistic Crafts Series of Technical Handbooks [*A publication*] .... ACSTH
Artistic Greetings [*NASDAQ symbol*] (TTSB) .... ARTG
Artistic Greetings, Inc. [*NASDAQ symbol*] (NQ) .... ARTG
Artistic Greetings, Inc. [*Associated Press*] (SAG) .... ArtistG
Artistic License (EA) .... AL
Artistic Roller Skating Federation (EA) .... ARSF
Artist-Owned Label [*Music*] .... AOL
Artistry .... ARTSTRY
Artistry [*Record label*] .... Asty
Artists and Athletes Against Apartheid (EA) .... AAAA
Artists and Repertory .... A & R
Artists Civil Rights Assistance Fund [*Defunct*] .... ACRAF
Artist's Collection (VRA) .... artist coll
Artists Confronting AIDS [*An association*] (EA) .... ACA
Artist's Diploma (PGP) .... AD

Artist's Diploma (PGP) .... ADP
Artists Equity Association [*Later, NAEA*] (EA) .... AEA
Artists Equity Fund [*of the National Artists Equity Association*] (EA) .... AEF
Artists' Fellowship (EA) .... AF
Artists for Nuclear Disarmament [*Defunct*] (EA) .... AND
Artists' General Benevolent Institution [*British*] .... AGBI
Artists Guild .... AG
Artists' Guild of Australia .... AGA
Artists Guild of Chicago [*Defunct*] (EA) .... AGC
Artists Guild of New York (EA) .... AGNY
Artists in Bark Association of Australia .... AIBAA
Artists in Christian Testimony (EA) .... ACT
Artists in Stained Glass [*Canada*] .... AISG
Artists in the Schools Program (EDAC) .... AIS
Artists' Legal Advice Services (AC) .... ALAS
Artist's Proof .... AP
Artist's Proof (ADA) .... ART PF
Artists' Representatives Association [*Defunct*] (EA) .... ARA
Artists Rights Association [*Defunct*] .... ARA
Artists' Service Bureau (NTCM) .... ASB
Artists Space (EA) .... AS
Artists Technical Research Institute (EA) .... ATRI
Artists United Against Apartheid (EA) .... AUAA
Artium Baccalaureus [*Bachelor of Arts*] .... AB
Artium Elegantium Doctor [*Doctor of Fine Arts*] .... AED
Artium Liberalium Magister [*Master of the Liberal Arts*] .... ALM
Artium Magister [*Master of Arts*] .... AM
Artium Magister [*Master of Arts*] in Social Work (IIA) .... AMSW
Artlantic Offshore Fish and Lobster Association (USDC) .... AOFLA
ARTnews [*A publication*] (BRI) .... Art N
Artra Group, Inc. [*Associated Press*] (SAG) .... Artra
Artra Group, Inc. [*NYSE symbol*] (SPSG) .... ATA
Arts Action Australia [*An association*] .... AAA
Arts and Business Council (EA) .... ABC
Arts and Crafts Movement [*c. 1860-1920*] .... A & C
Arts and Crafts Society of New South Wales [*Australia*] .... ACSNSW
Arts and Crafts Society of Victoria [*Australia*] .... ACSV
Arts & Entertainment Network [*Cable-television system*] .... A & E
Arts and Humanities .... AH
Arts and Letters Club, Toronto [*1908*] [*Canada*] (NGC) .... ALCT
Arts and Letters Club, Toronto, ON, Canada [*Library symbol Library of Congress*] (LCLS) .... CaOTAL
Arts and Letters Club, Toronto, Ontario [*Library symbol National Library of Canada*] (NLC) .... OTAL
Arts and Sciences .... A & S
Arts Anonymous (EA) .... AA
Arts Centre Group (EAIO) .... ACG
Arts Council (EAIO) .... AC
Arts Council of Australia .... ACA
Arts Council of Great Britain (EAIO) .... AC
Arts Council of Great Britain .... ACGB
Arts Councils of America [*Later, American Council for the Arts*] .... ACA
Arts Development Association [*British*] (DBA) .... ADA
Arts Documentation Service [*Australian Council Library*] [*Information service or system*] .... ARTS
[*The*] Arts, Education, and Americans (EA) .... AEA
Arts Education for a Multicultural Society (AIE) .... AEMS
Arts et Metiers [*Arts and Crafts*] [*French*] .... A et M
Arts for a New Nicaragua (EA) .... ANN
Arts in Danger [*An association British*] (DI) .... AID
Arts International (EA) .... AI
Arts Law Australia [*A publication*] .... ALA
Arts Management Training Initiative, Scotland (AIE) .... AMTIS
Arts of the Church [*A publication*] .... AC
Arts Recognition and Talent Search [*National Foundation for Advancement in the Arts*] .... ARTS
Arts Training New South Wales [*An association Australia*] .... ATN
Art's Way Manufacturing Co. [*Associated Press*] (SAG) .... ArtWay
Art's Way Manufacturing Co., Inc. [*NASDAQ symbol*] (NQ) .... ARTW
Art's Way Mfg [*NASDAQ symbol*] (TTSB) .... ARTW
Arturo Rodriguez Martinez [*Mexico*] [*FAA designator*] (FAAC) .... MTI
Arturo Toscanini Society (EA) .... ATS
Artwork (WDMC) .... A/W
Artwork (WDMC) .... art
Artwork-Interactive Design System (MCD) .... AIDS
Arua [*Uganda*] [*Airport symbol*] (AD) .... AAU
Arua [*Uganda*] [*ICAO location identifier*] (ICLI) .... HUAR
Arua [*Uganda*] [*Airport symbol*] (OAG) .... RUA
Aruada, CO [*AM radio station call letters*] .... KQXI
Aruba [*ANSI three-letter standard code*] (CNC) .... ABW
Aruba [*Netherlands Antilles*] [*Airport symbol*] .... AUA
Aruba [*ANSI two-letter standard code*] (CNC) .... AW
Aruba [*Aircraft nationality and registration mark*] (FAAC) P4
Aruba, Bonaire, and Curacao [*Islands*] .... ABC
Arubaanse Volks Partij [*Aruban People's Party*] [*Netherlands Antilles*] [*Political party*] (PPW) .... AVP
Arubair [*Aruba*] [*ICAO designator*] (FAAC) .... ARB
Aruban Florin [*Monetary unit*] (ODBW) .... Af
Arunachal People's Conference [*India*] [*Political party*] (PPW) .... APC
Arundell on the Law of Mines [*A publication*] (DLA) .... Arun Mines
Arusha [*Tanzania*] [*Airport symbol*] (AD) .... ARY
Arusha [*Tanzania*] [*ICAO location identifier*] (ICLI) .... HTAR
Arussi Liberation Army [*Ethiopia*] (AF) .... ALA
Arutua [*French Polynesia*] [*ICAO location identifier*] (ICLI) .... NTGU
ARV Assisted Living [*NASDAQ symbol*] (TTSB) .... ARVI

ARV Assisted Living, Inc. [*NASDAQ symbol*] (SAG) .... ARVI
ARV Assisted Living, Inc. [*Associated Press*] (SAG) .... ARVLiv
Arvada Public Library, Arvada, CO [*Library symbol Library of Congress*] (LCLS) .... CoAr
Arvika [*Sweden ICAO location identifier*] (ICLI) .... ESKV
Arvin Indus [*NYSE symbol*] (TTSB) .... ARV
Arvin Industries [*NYSE symbol*] (SAG) .... ARV
Arvin Industries, Inc. [*Associated Press*] (SAG) .... Arvin
Arwick International Resources Ltd. [*Vancouver Stock Exchange symbol*] .... AWK
Aryepiglottic [*Medicine*] (DAVI) .... AE
Aryl [*Chemistry*] .... Ar
Aryl Hydrocarbon Hydroxylase [*An enzyme*] .... AHH
Aryl Hydrocarbon Receptor [*Biochemistry*] .... AHR
Arylated Poly(phenylene Sulfide) [*Organic chemistry*] .... APPS
Arylene Isopropylidene Polymers [*Organic chemistry*] .... AIP
Arylhydrocarbon-Receptor Nuclear Translocator [*Genetics*] .... ARNT
Arylhydroxamic(acyltransferase) [*An enzyme*] .... AHAT
Arylsulfatase A (DMAA) .... ARSA
Arylsulfatase C (DMAA) .... ARSC
Arylsulfatase-A (MAE) .... ASA
Aryt Inds Ltd [*NASDAQ symbol*] (TTSB) .... ARYTF
Aryt Industries Ltd. [*Associated Press*] (SAG) .... ArytInd
Aryt Optronics Industries Ltd. [*NASDAQ symbol*] .... ARYT
Arzaero [*Azerbaijan*] [*FAA designator*] (FAAC) .... AZO
Arzan International Ltd. [*Associated Press*] (SAG) .... ArzanInt
Arzan International Ltd. [*NASDAQ symbol*] (SAG) .... ARZN
Arzan International Ltd. [*NASDAQ symbol*] (SAG) .... ARZW
Arzan Intl(1991) Ltd [*NASDAQ symbol*] (TTSB) .... ARZNF
Arzan Intl(1991) Wrrt [*NASDAQ symbol*] (TTSB) .... ARZWF
Arzana [*United Arab Emirates*] [*ICAO location identifier*] (ICLI) .... OMAR
As Amended By [*Army*] .... AABY
As Before .... AB
As Design Changes Occur (MCD) .... ADCO
As Drawn (MSA) .... AD
As Far As I Know [*Internet language*] [*Computer science*] .... AFAIK
As Found (ODBW) .... A/F
As Generated (MCD) .... ASGEN
As Good As .... AGA
As Interest May Appear [*Insurance*] .... AIMA
As Late as Possible (PCM) .... ALAP
As Low as Possible [*or Practical*] (NRCH) .... ALAP
As Low as Reasonably Achievable [*Radiation exposure*] [*Nuclear Regulatory Commission*] .... ALARA
As Low as Reasonably Practicable [*Radiation exposure*] [*Nuclear Regulatory Commission*] .... ALARP
As Low as Technically Achievable (NUCP) .... ALATA
AS Lufttransport [*Norway ICAO designator*] (FAAC) .... LTR
AS Morefly [*Norway ICAO designator*] (FAAC) .... MOR
As Much As Possible [*Medicine*] .... AMAP
As Needed (NRCH) .... A/N
AS Norving [*Norway ICAO designator*] (FAAC) .... NOR
As Often As Possible (DAVI) .... AOAP
As per List .... APL
As Planned Parts List (MCD) .... APPL
As Prescribed (AFM) .... AP
As Purchased .... AP
As Quoted [*Business term*] .... AQ
As Required (AFM) .... AR
As Required (MCD) .... ASR
As Rolled [*Technical drawings*] (DAC) .... AR
As Soon as Possible .... ASAP
As Soon As Possible [*Internet language*] [*Computer science*] .... ASAP
As Soon As Possible (ODBW) .... asap
As Soon As Possible [*Pronounced a-sap*] (WDMC) .... asap
As Soon as Possible .... ASP
As Stated .... AS
As The Subject Says [*Internet language*] [*Computer science*] .... ATSS
As the World Turns [*A television program*] .... ATWT
As the World Turns Fan Club (EA) .... ATWTFC
As Their Respective Interests May Appear [*Legal term*] (ADA) .... ATRIMA
As Tolerated [*Medicine*] (CPH) .... as tol
As Trustee For [*Banking*] .... ATF
As You Like It [*Shakespearean work*] .... AYL
As You Like It [*Shakespearean drama*] (BARN) .... AYLI
ASA [*Former USSR ICAO designator*] (FAAC) .... SPB
ASA, Air Starline, AG [*Switzerland ICAO designator*] (FAAC) .... ACR
ASA Holdings, Inc. [*Associated Press*] (SAG) .... ASA Hold
ASA Holdings, Inc. [*NASDAQ symbol*] (SAG) .... ASAI
ASA International Ltd. [*Associated Press*] (SAG) .... ASA Int
ASA International Ltd. [*NASDAQ symbol*] (NQ) .... ASAA
ASA Intl Ltd [*NASDAQ symbol*] (TTSB) .... ASAA
Asa Lafitte Stark Family Association [*Defunct*] (EA) .... ALSFA
ASA Ltd. [*Formerly, American-South African Investment Co. Ltd.*] [*NYSE symbol*] (SPSG) .... ASA
ASA Ltd. [*Formerly, American-South African Investment Co. Ltd.*] [*Associated Press*] (SAG) .... ASA Ltd
Asab [*United Arab Emirates*] [*ICAO location identifier*] (ICLI) .... OMAC
Asad Abad [*Iran*] [*ICAO location identifier*] (ICLI) .... OIHB
ASAHI/AMERICA [*NASDAQ symbol*] (TTSB) .... ASAM
Asahi/America, inc. [*NASDAQ symbol*] (SAG) .... ASAM
Asahi/America, Inc. [*Associated Press*] (SAG) .... AsahiAm
Asahi Chemical Exchange Process [*Nuclear energy*] (NUCP) .... ACEP
Asahi New Cast [*Metal fabrication*] .... ANC
Asahikawa [*Japan*] [*Airport symbol*] (OAG) .... AKJ

Asahikawa [*Japan*] [*Seismograph station code, US Geological Survey*] (SEIS) .... ASA
Asahikawa [*Japan ICAO location identifier*] (ICLI) .... RJCA
Asahikawa [*Japan ICAO location identifier*] (ICLI) .... RJEC
Asama [*Japan*] [*Seismograph station code, US Geological Survey*] (SEIS) .... ASM
Asamblea Majorera [*Spain Political party*] (EY) .... AM
Asamblea Nicaraguense de Unidad Democratica [*Nicaraguan Assembly Democratic Unity*] (PD) .... Anude
Asamera Minerals Ltd. [*Toronto Stock Exchange symbol*] .... AUA
Asante Technologies, Inc. [*Associated Press*] (SAG) .... Asante
Asante Technologies, Inc. [*NASDAQ symbol*] (SAG) .... ASNT
Asanteman Association (EA) .... AA
Asantle Technologies [*NASDAQ symbol*] (TTSB) .... ASNT
ASAP and Computer Interface Unit .... ACIU
ASAP Interface Unit .... AIU
ASARCO, Inc. [*Formerly, American Smelting & Refining Co.*] [*NYSE symbol*] (SPSG) .... AR
ASARCO, Inc. [*Formerly, American Smelting & Refining Co.*] [*Associated Press*] (SAG) .... Asarco
Asarhaddon (BJA) .... Asarh
Asatru Alliance (EA) .... AA
Asatru Free Assembly [*Later, AA*] (EA) .... AFA
Asau [*Western Samoa*] [*ICAO location identifier*] (ICLI) .... NSAU
ASB Financial [*NASDAQ symbol*] (TTSB) .... ASBR
ASB Financial Corp. [*Associated Press*] (SAG) .... ASB Fn
ASB Financial Corp. [*NASDAQ symbol*] (SAG) .... ASBP
Asbestos (MSA) .... A
Asbestos (KSC) .... ASB
Asbestos (VRA) .... asb
Asbestos .... ASB
Asbestos .... ASBSTS
Asbestos Action Program [*Environmental Protection Agency*] (GFGA) .... AAP
Asbestos & Danville [*AAR code*] .... ASDA
Asbestos and Danville [*Railroad*] (MHDB) .... ASDE
Asbestos and Small Business Ombudsman [*Environmental Protection Agency*] .... ASBO
Asbestos Bodies .... AB's
Asbestos Body (DAVI) .... AB
Asbestos Cement [*Technical drawings*] .... AC
Asbestos Cement Manufacturers Association [*British*] (BI) .... ACMA
Asbestos Cement Sheet (ADA) .... ACS
Asbestos Claims Council (EA) .... ACC
Asbestos Cloth Neck (OA) .... ACN
Asbestos Compensation Coalition (EA) .... ACC
Asbestos Contractor Tracking System [*Environmental Protection Agency*] (ERG) .... ACTS
Asbestos Corp. Ltd. [*Toronto Stock Exchange symbol*] .... AB
Asbestos Hazard Emergency Response Act of 1986 .... AHERA
Asbestos Hill [*Canada*] [*Airport symbol Obsolete*] (OAG) .... YAF
Asbestos Information Association/North America (EA) .... AIA/NA
Asbestos Information Centre Ltd. [*British*] (CB) .... AIC
Asbestos Inspection and Management Plan Assistance Program [*Environmental Protection Agency*] .... AIMPAP
Asbestos Institute (EA) .... AI
Asbestos Insulated Wire .... AIW
Asbestos International Association [*British*] (EAIO) .... AIA
Asbestos Litigation Group (EA) .... ALG
Asbestos Lung Disease .... ALD
Asbestos Medical Surveillance Program [*Military*] (DNAB) .... AMSP
Asbestos Mill Board [*Technical drawings*] .... AMB
Asbestos, PQ [*AM radio station call letters*] .... CJAN
Asbestos Related Illness .... ARI
Asbestos Removal and Treatment Contractors' Association [*Australia*] .... ARTCA
Asbestos Removal Contractors Association (EAIO) .... ARCA
Asbestos Roof Shingles [*Technical drawings*] .... ARS
Asbestos School Hazard Abatement Act (GFGA) .... ASHAA
Asbestos Textile Institute .... ATI
Asbestos Victims of America (EA) .... AVA
Asbestos-Cement Board [*Technical drawings*] .... ACB
Asbestos-Cement Pressure [*Construction*] (DICI) .... ACP
Asbestos-Cement Products Association [*Defunct*] (EA) .... A-CPA
Asbestos-Containing Building Material (ERG) .... ACBM
Asbestos-Containing Material .... ACM
Asbestos-Covered Metal [*Technical drawings*] .... ACM
Asbestosis Research Council [*British*] .... ARC
As-Built Configuration File (MCD) .... ABCF
As-Built Configuration Lists .... ABCL
As-Built Configuration Record (NASA) .... ABCR
Asbury College, Wilmore, KY [*OCLC symbol*] (OCLC) .... KWW
Asbury College, Wilmore, KY [*Library symbol Library of Congress*] (LCLS) .... KyWA
Asbury, IA [*FM radio station call letters*] .... KIKR
Asbury, MO [*FM radio station call letters*] .... KWXD
Asbury Park Free Public Library, Asbury Park, NJ [*Library symbol Library of Congress*] (LCLS) .... NjAs
Asbury Park/Monmouth County [*New Jersey*] [*Airport symbol*] (OAG) .... ARX
Asbury Park, NJ [*AM radio station call letters*] .... WJLK
Asbury Park, NJ [*FM radio station call letters*] .... WJLK-FM
Asbury Park Press, Asbury Park, NJ [*Library symbol Library of Congress*] (LCLS) .... NjAsP
Asbury Theological Seminary, Wilmore, KY [*OCLC symbol*] (OCLC) .... KAT
Asbury Theological Seminary, Wilmore, KY [*Library symbol Library of Congress*] (LCLS) .... KyWAT
Ascazubi [*Ecuador*] [*ICAO location identifier*] (ICLI) .... SEAS
Ascencion De Guarayos [*Bolivia*] [*ICAO location identifier*] (ICLI) .... SLAS

Ascend Communications [*NASDAQ symbol*] (TTSB) .... ASND
Ascend Communications, Inc. [*Associated Press*] (SAG) .... Ascend
Ascend Communications, Inc. [*NASDAQ symbol*] (SAG) .... ASND
Ascendance-Submission [*Psychology*] .... AS
Ascending .... ASC
Ascending and Descending (MAE) .... A & D
Ascending Aorta [*Anatomy*] .... AA
Ascending Horizon Crossing Time (OA) .... AHCT
Ascending Neuron [*Neurology*] .... AN
Ascending Order Arrangement (MHDB) .... AOA
Ascending Pharyngeal System [*Anatomy*] .... APS
Ascending Reticular Activating [*or Activation*] **System** .... ARAS
Ascensio Recta [*Right Ascension*] [*Latin*] .... ar
Ascension [*Bolivia*] [*Airport symbol Obsolete*] (OAG) .... ASC
Ascension Island [*MARC geographic area code Library of Congress*] (LCCP) .... Isai--
Ascension Island Station [*NASA*] (SAA) .... AIS
Ascension Island Tracking Station [*NASA*] (NASA) .... ACN
Ascension of Isaiah (BJA) .... AscIs
Ascension Parish Library, Donaldsonville, LA [*Library symbol Library of Congress*] (LCLS) .... LDA
Ascension Poetry Reading Series (EA) .... APRS
Ascent .... AS
Ascent (MCD) .... ASC
Ascent/Abort (MCD) .... ASC/ABT
Ascent Air Data System (NASA) .... AADS
Ascent Closed Loop (MCD) .... ACL
Ascent Descent Director (PDAA) .... ADD
Ascent Engine Arming Assembly [*NASA*] (KSC) .... AEAA
Ascent Engine Latching Device [*NASA*] (KSC) .... AELD
Ascent Entertainment Group, Inc. [*Associated Press*] (SAG) .... AscentEnt
Ascent Entertainment Group, Inc. [*NASDAQ symbol*] (SAG) .... GOAL
Ascent Entertainment Grp [*NASDAQ symbol*] (TTSB) .... GOAL
Ascent Flight Systems Integration Group [*NASA*] (NASA) .... AFSIG
Ascent Guidance and Control System [*NASA*] (KSC) .... AGS
Ascent Phase .... AP
Ascent Propulsion System [*NASA*] .... APS
Ascent Stage .... A/S
Ascent Stage [*NASA*] (MCD) .... AS
Ascent Thrust Vector Control [*or Controller*] [*NASA*] (MCD) .... ATVC
Ascent Thrust Vector Control Driver [*NASA*] (MCD) .... ATVCD
Aschaffenburg [*Germany ICAO location identifier*] (ICLI) .... EDEC
Aschaffenburg-Grossostheim [*Germany ICAO location identifier*] (ICLI) .... EDFC
Ascheim-Zondek Test [*Medicine*] .... AZT
Aschheim-Zondek [*Pregnancy*] **Test** [*Medicine*] (AAMN) .... AZ
ASCII COBOL [*Computer science*] .... ACOB
ASCII COBOL Data Manipulation Language-Preprocessor [*Computer science*] .... ADMLP
ASCII [*American Standard Code for Information Interchange*] **Message De finition Table** (NITA) .... AMDT
Ascites Hepatoma [*Medicine*] .... AH
Ascites-Plasma Ratio [*Medicine*] (MAE) .... A/P
Ascitic Fluid (MAE) .... Ascit Fl
ASCLA [*Association of Specialized and Cooperative Library Agencies*] **Libraries Serving Special Populations Section** .... ASCLA LSSPS
ASCLA LSSPS [*Association of Specialized and Cooperative Library Agencies - Libraries Serving Special Populations Section*] **Academic Librarians Assisting the Disabled Discussion Group** .... ASCLA LSSPS ALAD
ASCLA LSSPS [*Association of Specialized and Cooperative Library Agencies - Libraries Serving Special Populations Section*] **Bibliotherapy Forum** .... ASCLA LSSPS BF
ASCLA LSSPS [*Association of Specialized and Cooperative Library Agencies - Libraries Serving Special Populations Section*] **Health Care Libraries Forum** .... ASCLA LSSPS HCLF
ASCLA LSSPS [*Association of Specialized and Cooperative Library Agencies - Libraries Serving Special Populations Section*] **Library Service to Developmentally Disabled Persons Membership Activity Group** .... ASCLA LSSPS LSDDP MAG
ASCLA LSSPS [*Association of Specialized and Cooperative Library Agencies - Libraries Serving Special Populations Section*] **Library Service to Prisoners Forum** .... ASCLA LSSPS LSPF
ASCLA LSSPS [*Association of Specialized and Cooperative Library Agencies - Libraries Serving Special Populations Section*] **Library Service to the Blind andPhysically Handicapped Forum** .... ASCLA LSSPS LSBPHF
ASCLA LSSPS [*Association of Specialized and Cooperative Library Agencies - Libraries Serving Special Populations Section*] **Library Service to the Deaf Forum** .... ASCLA LSSPS LSDF
ASCLA LSSPS [*Association of Specialized and Cooperative Library Agencies - Libraries Serving Special Populations Section*] **Library Service to the Impaired Elderly Forum** .... ASCLA LSSPS LSIEF
ASCLA [*Association of Specialized and Cooperative Library Agencies*] **Multitype Library Networks and Cooperatives Section** .... ASCLA Multi-LINCS
ASCLA [*Association of Specialized and Cooperative Library Agencies*] **State Library Agency Section** .... ASCLA SLAS
Asclepius [*of Apuleius*] [*Classical studies*] (OCD) .... Asclep
Ascochinga [*Argentina ICAO location identifier*] (ICLI) .... SACN
Ascom City [*South Korea ICAO location identifier*] (ICLI) .... RKSA
Ascona [*Switzerland ICAO location identifier*] (ICLI) .... LSZD
Ascor Flyservice AS [*Norway ICAO designator*] (FAAC) .... NOC
Ascorbic Acid [*Vitamin C*] [*Biochemistry*] .... AA
Ascorbic Acid [*Also called vitamin C*] (DAVI) .... ASC
Ascorbic Acid [*Vitamin C*] (DAVI) C
Ascorbic Acid Factor [*Biochemistry*] .... AAF
Ascorbic Free Radical [*Biochemistry*] .... AFR
Ascorbyl Dipalmitate [*Organic chemistry*] .... ADP

Ascot Investment Corp. [*Toronto Stock Exchange symbol Vancouver Stock Exchange symbol*] .... AIP

Ascot Resources Ltd. [*Vancouver Stock Exchange symbol*] .... AOT

Ascriptum [*Ascribed To*] [*Latin*] (MAE) .... ascr

ASD (Production and Logistics) (DOMA) .... ASD(P & L)

ASE Test Ltd. [*Associated Press*] (SAG) .... ASE Tst

ASE Test Ltd. [*NASDAQ symbol*] (SAG) .... ASTS

ASE [*National Institute for Automotive Service Excellence*] **Test Registration Booklet** [*A publication*] (EAAP) .... R/B

ASEA AB [*NASDAQ symbol*] (NQ) .... ASEA

Asea Brown Boveri [*Swedish-Swiss manufacturing company*] (ECON) .... ABB

ASEA [*Allmaenna Svenska Elektriska Aktiebolaget*] **Brown Boveri, Inc., Montreal, Quebec** [*Library symbol National Library of Canada*] (BIB) .... QMASBB

ASEAN [*Association of South East Asian Nations*] **Association for Planning and Housing** (EAIO) .... AAPH

ASEAN [*Association of South East Asian Nations*] **Association of Museums** (EAIO) .... ASEANAM

ASEAN [*Association of South East Asian Nations*] **- Australia Business Council** .... ASEAN-ABC

ASEAN [*Association of Southeast Asian Nations*] **- Australia Consultative Meeting** .... AACM

ASEAN [*Association of South East Asian Nations*] **Bankers Association** [*Singapore, Singapore*] (EAIO) .... ABA

ASEAN [*Association of South East Asian Nations*] **Council on Petroleum** [*Indonesia*] .... ASCOPE

ASEAN [*Association of South East Asian Nations*] **Federation of Cement Manu facturers** [*Indonesia*] (EAIO) .... AFCM

ASEAN [*Association of South East Asian Nations*] **Federation of Engineering Organizations** (EAIO) .... AFEO

ASEAN [*Association of South East Asian Nations*] **Free Trade Area** (ECON) .... AFTA

ASEAN [*Association of South East Asian Nations*] **Inter-Parliamentary Organisation** .... AIPO

ASEAN [*Association of South East Asian Nations*] **Japan Development Fund** .... AJDF

ASEAN [*Association of South East Asian Nations*] **Port Authorities Association** (DS) .... APAA

ASEAN [*Association of Southeast Asian Nations*] **Regional Forum** (ECON) .... ARF

ASEAN [*Association of South-East Asian Nations*] **Specialized Meteorological Centre** [*Marine science*] (OSRA) .... ASMC

ASEAN [*Association of South East Asian Nations*] **- United States Business Council** [*Bangkok, Thailand*] (EAIO) .... AUSBC

ASEAN [*Association of South East Asian Nations*] **Valuers Association** [*Kuala Lumpur, Malaysia*] (EAIO) .... AVA

Aseco Corp. [*NASDAQ symbol*] (SAG) .... ASEC

Aseco Corp. [*Associated Press*] (SAG) .... Aseco

Aseki [*Papua New Guinea*] [*Airport symbol Obsolete*] (OAG) .... AEK

Asele [*Sweden ICAO location identifier*] (ICLI) .... ESUS

Aseptic Bone Necrosis [*Medicine*] .... ABN

Aseptic Epiphyseal Necrosis [*Medicine*] (DMAA) .... AEN

Aseptic Fluid Transfer System [*NASA*] .... AFTS

Aseptic Food Processing System .... AFPS

Aseptic Maintenance by Pressurization [*NASA*] .... AMP

Aseptic Meningitis [*Medicine*] .... AM

Aseptic Necrosis [*Medicine*] .... AN

Aseptic Packaging Council (EA) .... APC

Aserradero [*Nicaragua*] [*Seismograph station code, US Geological Survey*] (SEIS) .... ASE

ASFE [*Association of Soil and Foundation Engineers*]/Association of Engineering Firms Practicing in the Geosciences (EA) .... ASFEAEFPG

ASG Industries, Inc. [*Formerly, American St. Gobain*] .... ASG

Ash Grove, MO [*FM radio station call letters*] (RBYB) .... KQMO-FM

Ash Grove, MO [*FM radio station call letters*] .... KZPD

Ash Lighter [*Navy symbol*] .... YA

Ashanti Goldfields Co. Ltd. [*Associated Press*] (SAG) .... Ashanti

Ashanti Goldfields Co. Ltd. [*NYSE symbol*] (SAG) .... ASL

Ashanti Goldfields Ltd GDS [*NYSE symbol*] (TTSB) .... ASL

Ashbrooke-Pembleton-Ffrench [*Mythical British family appearing in "Announcements" column of Times of London*] .... A-P-F

Ashburn, GA [*FM radio station call letters*] .... WFFM

Ashburner. Principles of Equity [*2nd ed.*] [*1933*] [*A publication*] (DLA) .... Ashb

Ashburton Oil Ltd. [*Vancouver Stock Exchange symbol*] .... ASB

Ashbury College, Ottawa, ON, Canada [*Library symbol*] [*Library of Congress*] (LCLS) .... CaOOASH

Ashbury College, Ottawa, Ontario [*Library symbol National Library of Canada*] (NLC) .... OOASH

Ashby Public School, Ashby, MN [*Library symbol*] [*Library of Congress*] (LCLS) .... MnAshS

Ashcroft, BC [*ICAO location identifier*] (ICLI) .... CYZA

Ashcroft Museum, British Columbia [*Library symbol National Library of Canada*] (NLC) .... BASM

Ashdown, AR [*FM radio station call letters*] .... KARQ

Ashdown, AR [*FM radio station call letters*] .... KHSP

Ashe County Public Library, West Jefferson, NC [*Library symbol Library of Congress*] (LCLS) .... NcWj

Asheboro, NC [*Location identifier FAA*] (FAAL) .... CQJ

Asheboro, NC [*FM radio station call letters*] .... WKRR

Asheboro, NC [*AM radio station call letters*] .... WKXR

Asheboro, NC [*FM radio station call letters*] (RBYB) .... WPER

Asheboro, NC [*AM radio station call letters*] .... WZOO

Ashendon [*England*] .... ASH

Ashe's Tables to the Year Books, Coke's Reports, or Dyer's Reports [*A publication*] (DLA) .... Ashe

Asheville [*North Carolina*] [*Airport symbol*] (OAG) .... AVL

Asheville, NC [*Location identifier FAA*] (FAAL) .... BRA

Asheville, NC [*Location identifier FAA*] (FAAL) .... IMO

Asheville, NC [*Location identifier FAA*] (FAAL) .... SUG

Asheville, NC [*Television station call letters*] .... WASV

Asheville, NC [*FM radio station call letters*] .... WCQS

Asheville, NC [*Television station call letters*] .... WHNS

Asheville, NC [*AM radio station call letters*] .... WISE

Asheville, NC [*AM radio station call letters*] .... WKJV

Asheville, NC [*FM radio station call letters*] .... WKSF

Asheville, NC [*FM radio station call letters*] .... WLFA

Asheville, NC [*Television station call letters*] .... WLOS

Asheville, NC [*AM radio station call letters*] .... WSKY

Asheville, NC [*Television station call letters*] .... WUNF

Asheville, NC [*AM radio station call letters*] .... WWNC

Asheville-Buncombe Technical Institute, Asheville, NC [*Library symbol Library of Congress*] (LCLS) .... NcAAB

Asheville-Henderson [*North Carolina*] [*Airport symbol*] (AD) .... AVL

Ashford Press Publishing [*British*] .... APP

Ash-Free Dry Mass [*Analytical chemistry*] .... AFDM

Ash-Free Dry Weight (DMAA) .... AFDW

Ashiya [*Japan ICAO location identifier*] (ICLI) .... RJFA

Ashizuri [*Japan*] [*Seismograph station code, US Geological Survey*] (SEIS) .... ASZ

Ashkenazic [*Jews from Central or Eastern Europe*] (BJA) .... Ashken

Ashkezar [*Iran*] [*ICAO location identifier*] (ICLI) .... OIYZ

Ashkhabad [*Former USSR Airport symbol*] (OAG) .... ASB

Ashkhabad [*Former USSR Seismograph station code, US Geological Survey*] (SEIS) .... ASH

Ashland [*Wisconsin*] [*Airport symbol Obsolete*] (OAG) .... ASX

Ashland Chemical Co., Research Library, Columbus, OH [*OCLC symbol*] (OCLC) .... ASO

Ashland City, TN [*AM radio station call letters*] .... WQSV

Ashland Coal [*NYSE symbol*] (SPSG) .... ACI

Ashland Coal, Inc. [*Associated Press*] (SAG) .... AsCoal

Ashland College, Ashland, OH [*OCLC symbol*] (OCLC) .... ASC

Ashland College, Ashland, OH [*Library symbol Library of Congress*] (LCLS) .... OAsC

Ashland Community College [*Ashland, KY*] .... ACC

Ashland, Inc. [*NYSE symbol*] (SAG) .... ASH

Ashland Inc. [*NYSE symbol*] (TTSB) .... ASH

Ashland, Inc. [*Formerly, Ashland Oil*] [*Associated Press*] (SAG) .... Ashland

Ashland, Inc. [*Associated Press*] (SAG) .... AshInd

Ashland Inc. $3.125 Cv Pfd [*NYSE symbol*] (TTSB) .... ASHPr

Ashland, KY [*Location identifier FAA*] (FAAL) .... AJY

Ashland, KY [*AM radio station call letters*] .... WCMI

Ashland, KY [*FM radio station call letters*] (RBYB) .... WDGG

Ashland, KY [*Television station call letters*] .... WKAS

Ashland, KY [*Television station call letters*] .... WTSF

Ashland, MO [*FM radio station call letters*] .... KBXR

Ashland, OH [*Location identifier FAA*] (FAAL) .... AAU

Ashland, OH [*AM radio station call letters*] .... WNCO

Ashland, OH [*FM radio station call letters*] .... WNCO-FM

Ashland, OH [*FM radio station call letters*] .... WRDL

Ashland Oil Canada Ltd., Calgary, AB, Canada [*Library symbol Library of Congress*] (LCLS) .... CaACAO

Ashland, OR [*AM radio station call letters*] .... KCMX

Ashland, OR [*FM radio station call letters*] .... KCMX-FM

Ashland, OR [*FM radio station call letters*] (RBYB) .... KKJJ-FM

Ashland, OR [*FM radio station call letters*] .... KSMF

Ashland, OR [*Location identifier FAA*] (FAAL) .... KSOR

Ashland, OR [*FM radio station call letters*] (RBYB) .... KSRG

Ashland Public Library, Ashland, KY [*Library symbol Library of Congress*] (LCLS) .... KyA

Ashland Public Library, Ashland, MA [*Library symbol Library of Congress*] (LCLS) .... MAsl

Ashland State General Hospital, Ashland, PA [*OCLC symbol*] (OCLC) .... PHZ

Ashland Theological Seminary, Ashland, OH [*Library symbol Library of Congress*] (LCLS) .... OAsT

Ashland, VA [*Location identifier FAA*] (FAAL) .... LJK

Ashland, VA [*Location identifier FAA*] (FAAL) .... OFP

Ashland, VA [*Television station call letters*] .... WAWB

Ashland, VA [*AM radio station call letters*] .... WPES

Ashland, VA [*FM radio station call letters*] .... WYFJ

Ashland, WI [*Location identifier FAA*] (FAAL) .... ENY

Ashland, WI [*AM radio station call letters*] .... WATW

Ashland, WI [*FM radio station call letters*] .... WBSZ

Ashland, WI [*FM radio station call letters*] .... WJJH

Ashland-Lineville, AL [*FM radio station call letters*] .... WASZ

Ashley Community Consolidated District 15, Ashley, IL [*Library symbol Library of Congress*] (LCLS) .... IAsyCD

Ashley, Drew & Northern Railway Co. [*AAR code*] .... ADN

Ashley, MI [*FM radio station call letters*] .... WJSZ

Ashley, ND [*Location identifier FAA*] (FAAL) .... ASY

Ashley Public Library, Ashley, IL [*Library symbol Library of Congress*] (LCLS) .... IAsy

Ashmead's Pennsylvania Reports [*1808-41*] [*A publication*] (DLA) .... Ash

Ashmead's Pennsylvania Reports [*1808-41*] [*A publication*] (DLA) .... Ashm

Ashmead's Pennsylvania Reports [*1808-41*] [*A publication*] (DLA) .... Ashm (PA)

Ashmead's Pennsylvania Reports [*1808-41*] [*A publication*] (DLA) .... Ashmead

Ashmead's Pennsylvania Reports [*1808-41*] [*A publication*] (DLA) .... Ashmead (PA)

Ashmead's Pennsylvania Reports [*1808-41*] [*A publication*] (DLA) .... Ashmead's Penn Rep

Ashmont, AB [*Television station call letters*] CFRN-4

Ashmont Public Library, Alberta [*Library symbol National Library of Canada*] (NLC) .... AAS

Ashmont Public Library, Ashmont, AB, Canada [*Library symbol*] [*Library of Congress*] (LCLS) ... CaAAs
Ashmore and Cartier Islands [*at (Australia) used in records cataloged after January 1978*] [*MARC country of publication code Library of Congress*] (LCCP) ... ac
Ashmore and Cartier Islands [*MARC geographic area code Library of Congress*] (LCCP) ... u-ac--
Ashoka Society [*Later, Ashoka: Innovators for the Public*] (EA) ... AS
Ashore Coordinated ASW [*Antisubmarine Warfare*] **Training** [*Navy*] (DOMA) ... ACAT
Ashpit [*British*] (ROG) ... AP
Ashridge Centre for Transport Management [*Ashridge Management College*] [*British*] (CB) ... ACTM
Ashtabula County District Library, Ashtabula, OH [*Library symbol Library of Congress*] (LCLS) ... OAsht
Ashtabula, OH [*AM radio station call letters*] ... WFUN
Ashtabula, OH [*FM radio station call letters*] ... WREO
Ashton Public Library, Ashton, ID [*Library symbol*] [*Library of Congress*] (LCLS) ... IdAs
Ashton Tech Group [*NASDAQ symbol*] (TTSB) ... ASTN
Ashton Tech Group Wrrt [*NASDAQ symbol*] (TTSB) ... ASTNW
Ashton Technology Group, Inc. (The) [*Associated Press*] (SAG) ... AshtnT
Ashton Technology Group, Inc. (The) [*NASDAQ symbol*] (SAG) ... ASTN
Ashton-Potter America [*Printer of U.S. postage stamps*] (BARN) ... APA
Ashton's Reports [*9-12 Opinions of the United States Attorneys General*] [*A publication*] (DLA) ... Ashton
Ashton-Under-Lyne Public Library, Ashton-Under-Lyne, United Kingdom [*Library symbol Library of Congress*] (LCLS) ... UkAul
Ashurst's Manuscript Reports, Printed in Volume 2, Chitty [*A publication*] (DLA) ... Ashurst
Ashurst's Manuscript Reports, Printed in Volume 2, Chitty [*A publication*] (DLA) ... Ashurst MS
Ashurst's Paper Books, Lincoln's Inn Library [*A publication*] (DLA) ... APB
Ashurst's Paper Books, Lincoln's Inn Library [*A publication*] (DLA) ... Ashurst
Ashurst's Paper Books, Lincoln's Inn Library [*A publication*] (DLA) ... Ashurst MS
Ashworth, Inc. [*NASDAQ symbol*] (SAG) ... ASHW
Ashworth, Inc. [*Associated Press*] (SAG) ... Ashwrth
Asia [*MARC geographic area code Library of Congress*] (LCCP) ... a-----
Asia ... AS
Asia (VRA) ... As
Asia Aero Survey & Consulting Engineers, Inc. [*Korea*] [*ICAO designator*] (FAAC) ... KAA
Asia and Pacific Plant Protection Commission [*Formerly, Plant Protection Committeefor the Southeast Asia and Pacific Region*] (EA) ... APPPC
Asia and Pacific Special Interest Group [*Australian Library and Information Association*] ... APSIG
Asia and the Pacific Commission on Agricultural Statistics [*Formerly, Asia and theFar East Commission on Agricultural Statistics*] (EA) ... APCAS
Asia, Central [*MARC geographic area code Library of Congress*] (LCCP) ... ac----
Asia Crime Prevention Foundation (EAIO) ... ACPF
Asia Data Research, Inc. [*Database producer*] (IID) ... ADR
Asia, East [*MARC geographic area code Library of Congress*] (LCCP) ... ae----
Asia Education Foundation ... AEF
[*The*] **Asia Foundation** (EA) ... TAF
Asia House [*An association*] (EA) ... AH
Asia Library Services, Auburn, NY [*Library symbol Library of Congress*] (LCLS) ... AIS
Asia Minor (VRA) ... As Min
Asia Pac Resources Intl'A' [*NYSE symbol*] (TTSB) ... ARH
Asia Pacific Air Cargo PTE Ltd. [*Singapore*] [*ICAO designator*] (FAAC) ... APK
Asia Pacific Association of Japan ... APAJ
Asia Pacific Broadcasting Union (EAIO) ... ABU
Asia Pacific Business Association ... APBA
Asia Pacific Capital Corp. [*Vancouver Stock Exchange symbol*] ... APP
Asia Pacific Christian Mission ... APCM
Asia Pacific Distribution [*Australia ICAO designator*] (FAAC) ... APD
Asia Pacific Economic Cooperation [*Forum*] ... APEC
Asia Pacific Economic Cooperation Council ... APECC
Asia Pacific Economic Group ... APEG
Asia Pacific Foundation of Canada [*Fondation Asie Pacifique du Canada*] (AC) ... APFC
Asia Pacific Foundation of Canada, Information Services, Vancouver, BC, Canada [*Library symbol*] [*Library of Congress*] (LCLS) ... CaBVaAP
Asia Pacific Fund [*NYSE symbol*] (SPSG) ... APB
Asia Pacific Fund [*Associated Press*] (SAG) ... AsiaPc
Asia/Pacific Market Analysis [*MMS International*] [*Information service or system*] (CRD) ... APMA
Asia Pacific Network Information Center ... APNIC
Asia Pacific Resources International Holdings Ltd. [*NYSE symbol*] (SAG) ... ARH
Asia Pacific Resources International Holdings Ltd. [*Associated Press*] (SAG) ... AsiaPR
Asia Pacific Resources Ltd. [*NASDAQ symbol*] (SAG) ... APQC
Asia Pacific Resources Ltd. [*Associated Press*] (SAG) ... AsiaPac
Asia Pacific Resources Ltd [*NASDAQ symbol*] (TTSB) ... APQCF
Asia Pacific Wire & Cable Corp. Ltd. [*Associated Press*] (SAG) ... AsiaPWi
Asia Pacific Wire & Cable Corp. Ltd. [*NYSE symbol*] (SAG) ... AWC
ASIA Project, Los Angeles, CA [*Library symbol Library of Congress*] (LCLS) ... CLASIA
Asia Pulp & Paper ADS [*NYSE symbol*] (TTSB) ... PAP
Asia Pulp and Paper Co. Ltd. [*Associated Press*] (SAG) ... AsiaPlp
Asia Pulp and Paper Co. Ltd. [*NYSE symbol*] (SAG) ... PAP
Asia Resource Center (EA) ... ARC
Asia Satellite Telecommunications Holdings Ltd. [*Associated Press*] (SAG) ... AsiaSat
Asia Satellite Telecommunications Holdings Ltd. [*NYSE symbol*] (SAG) ... SAT
Asia Service Airlines [*Kazakhstan*] [*FAA designator*] (FAAC) ... ASQ
Asia Society (EA) ... AS
Asia, Southeastern [*MARC geographic area code Library of Congress*] (LCCP) ... as----
Asia, Southwestern [*MARC geographic area code Library of Congress*] (LCCP) ... aw----
Asia Tigers Fund [*Associated Press*] (SAG) ... AsiaTigr
Asia Tigers Fund [*NYSE symbol*] (SPSG) ... GRR
Asia Watch Committee (EA) ... AsW
Asiaamerica Holdings [*Vancouver Stock Exchange symbol*] ... AAK
Asialoglycoprotein [*Biochemistry*] ... ASG
Asialoglycoprotein Receptor [*Biochemistry*] ... ASGPR
Asialo-Orosomucoid [*Liver metabolism*] ... ASOr
Asiamerica Equities Ltd. [*Vancouver Stock Exchange symbol*] ... AEQ
Asian Agricultural Journalists and Writers Association [*Jakarta, Indonesia*] (EAIO) ... AAJWA
Asian Agriculture, Agrotechnology, and Agribusiness Exhibition and Conference ... AGASIA
Asian Alliance of Appropriate Technology Practitioners (EA) ... AAATP
Asian Amateur Swimming Federation [*Dhaka, Bangladesh*] (EAIO) ... AASF
Asian American Arts Alliance (EA) ... AAAA
Asian American Caucus for Disarmament (EA) ... AACD
Asian American Certified Public Accountants (EA) ... AACPA
Asian American Free Labor Institute (EA) ... AAFLI
Asian American Journalists Association (EA) ... AAJA
Asian American Legal Defense and Education Fund (EA) ... AALDEF
Asian American Librarians Association [*Defunct*] (EA) ... AALA
Asian American Librarians Caucus (EA) ... AALC
[*The*] **Asian American Magazine** [*A publication*] ... ASIAM
Asian American Manufacturers Association (EA) ... AAMA
Asian American Psychological Association (EA) ... AAPA
Asian American Voters Coalition (EA) ... AAVC
Asian Americans Information Directory [*A publication*] ... AAID
Asian and African American Materials [*Association for Library Collections and Technical Services*] ... AAM
Asian and African Section [*Association of College and Research Libraries*] ... AAS
Asian and Pacific Americans for Nuclear Awareness (EA) ... APANA
Asian and Pacific Centre for Transfer of Technology [*India*] (EAIO) ... APCTT
Asian and Pacific Coconut Community [*Jakarta, Indonesia*] (EAIO) ... APCC
Asian and Pacific Council ... ASPAC
Asian and Pacific Development Centre (EAIO) ... APDC
Asian and Pacific Energy Planning Network [*of the Asian and Pacific Development Centre*] (EAIO) ... APENPLAN
Asian and Pacific Information Network on Medicinal and Aromatic Plants [*UNESCO*] [*United Nations*] (DUND) ... APINMAP
Asian and Pacific Professional Language and Education Services [*Defunct*] (EA) ... APPLES
Asian and Pacific Regional Agricultural Credit Association (EA) ... APRACA
Asian and Pacific Skill Development Information Network [*ILO*] [*United Nations*] (DUND) ... APSDIN
Asian Association of Agricultural Colleges and Universities [*Philippines*] ... AAACU
Asian Association of Convention and Visitor Bureaus (EA) ... AACVB
Asian Association of Insurance Commissioners (EAIO) ... AAIC
Asian Association of Management Organisations [*Kuala Lumpur, Malaysia*] ... AAMO
Asian Association of Occupational Health (EA) ... AAOH
Asian Automotive and Accessories Exhibition ... AAAE
Asian Basketball Confederation (EA) ... ABC
Asian Benevolent Corps (EA) ... ABC
Asian Broadcasting Conference (NTCM) ... ABC
Asian Bureau Australia Newsletter [*A publication*] ... ABAN
Asian Business League [*Later, ABL-SF*] (EA) ... ABL
Asian Business League of San Francisco [*California*] (EA) ... ABL-SF
Asian Canadian Resources Ltd. [*Vancouver Stock Exchange symbol*] ... ANC
Asian Center for the Progress of Peoples [*Hong Kong*] (EAIO) ... ACPP
Asian Christian Association [*Taiwan*] (EAIO) ... ACA
Asian CineVision [*Later, ACV*] [*An association*] (EA) ... AC
Asian CineVision (EA) ... ACV
Asian Clearing Union ... ACU
Asian Club Federation (EAIO) ... ACF
Asian Coconut Community [*Later, APCC*] ... ACC
Asian Committee for Standardization of Physical Fitness Tests [*Obu-Shi, Japan*] (EAIO) ... ACSPFT
Asian Communist [*Later, B Group*] [*Division of National Security Agency*] ... ACOM
Asian Comparative Law Review [*A publication*] (DLA) ... Asian Comp L Rev
Asian Confederation of Credit Unions [*of the World Council of Credit Unions*] [*Bangkok, Thailand*] (EAIO) ... ACCU
Asian Confederation of Physical Therapy (EAIO) ... ACPT
Asian Conference on Religion and Peace [*Singapore, Singapore*] (EAIO) ... ACRP
Asian Cultural Centre for UNESCO ... ACCU
Asian Cultural Council (EA) ... ACC
Asian Cultural Exchange Foundation (EA) ... ACEF
Asian Cultural Forum on Development - USA [*Defunct*] (EA) ... ACFOD-USA
Asian Currency Unit ... ACU
Asian Development Bank ... ADB
Asian Development Bank (GNE) ... ADB
Asian Development Bank (EY) ... AsDB
Asian Development Center ... ADC
Asian Development Fund [*Asian Development Bank*] ... ADF
Asian Dust Input to the Oceanic System [*Research project*] ... ADIOS
Asian Federation for the Mentally Retarded [*Singapore*] (EAIO) ... AFMR
Asian Federation of Library Associations [*Japan*] ... AFLA
Asian Federation of Obstetrics and Gynaecology (PDAA) ... AFOG
Asian Finance/Investment Corp. [*Proposed*] (ECON) ... AFIC

Asian Fisheries Society [*Marine science*] (OSRA) .... AFS
Asian Folklore Studies Group [*Later, ISA*] (EA) .... AFSG
Asian Football Confederation (EAIO) .... AFC
Asian Geotechnical Engineering Information Center [*Information service or system*] (IID) .... AGE
Asian Geotechnology Engineering Database [*Asian Institute of Technology*] [*Information service or system*] (CRD) .... AGE
Asian Indian Chamber of Commerce (EA) .... AICC
Asian Infrastructure Consortia Program [*Australia*] .... AICP
Asian Institute for Economic Development and Planning .... AIEDP
Asian Institute of Management [*Philippines*] .... AIM
Asian Institute of Technology [*Bangkok, Thailand*] (MCD) .... AIT
Asian Institute of Technology Alumni Association [*Thailand*] (EAIO) .... AITAA
Asian International Chemical and Process Engineering and Contracting Show and Conference .... CHEMASIA
Asian International Hardware Exposition .... AIHEX
Asian Law Centre [*University of Melbourne*] [*Australia*] .... ALC
Asian Literature Division - of MLA [*Modern Language Association of America*] (EA) .... ALD
Asian Manpower Skill Development Program [*United Nations*] .... AMSDEP
Asian Mass Communication Research and Information Centre [*Singapore*] (EAIO) .... AMIC
Asian Media Coalition [*Inactive*] (EA) .... AMC
Asian Monetary Unit .... AMU
Asian NonGovernmental Organizations Coalition for Agrarian Reform and Rural Development [*Philippines*] (EAIO) .... ANGOC
Asian Oceanic Postal Union [*Later, APPU*] [*China, Korea, Philippines, Thailand*] .... AOPU
Asian Pacific Alliance for Creative Equality .... APACE
Asian/Pacific American .... APA
Asian Pacific American Heritage Council (EA) .... APAHC
Asian/Pacific American Librarians Association (EA) .... APALA
Asian Pacific Center for Theoretical Physics [*Institute, based in Seoul, Korea*] .... APCTP
Asian Pacific Confederation of Chemical Engineering (EAIO) .... APCChE
Asian Pacific Dental Federation/Asian Pacific Regional Organisation (EAIO) .... APDF/APRO
Asian Pacific Dental Students' Association [*Singapore, Singapore*] (EAIO) .... APDSA
Asian Pacific Law and Tax Review [*A publication*] .... APLTR
Asian Pacific Materials and Corrosion Association .... APMCA
Asian Pacific Weed Science Society (EA) .... APWSS
Asian Pacific Youth Forum (EA) .... APYF
Asian Pacific Youth Freedom League [*Tokyo, Japan*] (EAIO) .... APYFL
Asian Parasite Control Organization [*Japan*] (EAIO) .... APCO
Asian Parliamentarians' Union .... APU
Asian Patent Attorneys Association (EA) .... APAA
Asian Peoples' Anti-Communist League .... APACL
Asian Political Scientists Group in USA (EA) .... APSGUSA
Asian Productivity Organization [*Japan*] (EAIO) .... APO
Asian Profiles [*Database*] [*SRG International Ltd.*] [*Information service or system*] (CRD) .... APR
Asian Program for Education Innovation for Development .... APEID
Asian Racing Conference .... ARC
Asian Recycling Association (EAIO) .... ARA
Asian Regional Organization .... ARO
Asian Regional Organization - International Confederation of Free Trade Unions .... ARO-ICFTU
Asian Regional Training and Development Organization .... ARTDO
Asian Religio-Cultural Forum on Development .... ARCFOD
Asian Science Communicators' Organization [*International Council of Scientific Unions*] .... ASCO
Asian Scientific and Technological Information Network (EAIO) .... ASTINFO
Asian Securities Analysts Council [*See also CAAF*] [*Japan*] (EAIO) .... ASAC
Asian Socialist Conference .... ASC
Asian Statistical Institute .... ASI
Asian Students' Association [*Kowloon, Hong Kong*] (EAIO) .... ASA
Asian Studies Association of Australia .... ASAA
Asian Studies Association of Australia. Review [*A publication*] .... ASAA Rev
Asian Studies Centre [*St. Antony's College*] [*British*] (CB) .... ASC
Asian Studies Council [*Australia*] .... ASC
Asian Surgical Association (EAIO) .... ASA
Asian Track and Field Coaches Association [*India*] (EAIO) .... ATFCA
Asian University [*EDUCATSS*] [*UTLAS symbol*] .... AUT
Asian Vegetable Research and Development Center (EA) .... AVRDC
Asiana Airlines [*South Korea ICAO designator*] (FAAC) .... AAR
Asian-American Almanac [*A publication*] .... AAA
Asian-American Women's Political Caucus (EA) .... AAWPC
Asian-Australasian Society of Neurological Surgeons [*Kowloon, Hong Kong*] (EAIO) .... AASNS
Asian-Indian Women in America (EA) .... AIWA
Asia-North America Eastbound Rate Agreement [*Shipping*] .... Anera
Asian-Pacific Association for the Study of the Liver .... AsPASL
Asian-Pacific Association of LASER Medical Surgery .... AsPALMS
Asian-Pacific Parliamentary Union .... APPU
Asian-Pacific Postal Union [*Manila, Philippines*] (EAIO) .... APPU
Asian-Pacific Section [*International Union of Local Authorities*] [*Australia*] .... ASPAC
Asian-Pacific Section - IPRS [*International Confederation for Plastic and Reconstructive Surgery*] [*Singapore*] (EAIO) .... APS-IPRS
Asian-Pacific Society for Digestive Endoscopy .... AsPCDE
Asian-Pacific Society of Cardiology (EA) .... APSC
Asian-Pacific Society of Cardiology .... AsPSC
Asian-Pacific Society of Nephrology .... AsPSN
Asian-Pacific Society of Paediatric Gastroenterology and Nutrition .... AsPSPGN
Asian-Pacific Tax and Investment Research Centre [*Singapore*] (EA) .... APTIRC
Asia-Oceania Clinical Oncology Association .... AsOCOA
Asia-Oceania Federation of Nuclear Medicine .... AsOFNM
Asia-Oceania Workshop [*Computer science*] (TNIG) .... AOW
Asia-Pacific Academy of Ophthalmology [*Tokyo, Japan*] (EAIO) .... APAO
Asia-Pacific Association for Agricultural Education .... APAAE
Asia-Pacific Aviation Medicine Association .... AsPAvMA
[*Annual*] **Asia-Pacific Conference** .... ASPAC
Asia-Pacific Council of American Chambers of Commerce (EA) .... APCAC
Asia-Pacific Fellowship .... APF
Asia-Pacific Forestry Commission [*UN Food and Agriculture Organization*] .... APFC
Asia-Pacific Information Network in Social Sciences .... APINESS
Asia-Pacific Institute for Broadcasting Development (EAIO) .... AIBD
Asia-Pacific News Network .... ANN
Asia-Pacific People's Environment Network [*Penang, Malaysia*] (EAIO) .... APPEN
Asia-Pacific Petroleum Conference .... APPEC
Asia-Pacific Railway Cooperation Group (MHDB) .... APRCG
Asia-Pacific Resources [*Vancouver Stock Exchange symbol*] .... APQ
Asia-Pacific Socialist Organization [*Political party Tokyo, Japan*] (EAIO) .... APSO
Asia-Pacific Society for Impotence Research .... AsPSIR
Asia-Pacific Technology Information System [*ESCAP*] [*United Nations*] (DUND) .... APTIS
Asia-Pacific Telecommunity [*Thailand*] [*Telecommunications*] .... APT
Asiatic Fleet [*Obsolete Navy*] .... AF
Asiatic-Pacific Campaign Medal [*Military decoration*] .... APCM
Asiatic-Pacific Theater of War .... APTW
Asinaria [*of Plautus*] [*Classical studies*] (OCD) .... Asin
Asistencia Reciproca Petrolera Estatal Latinoamericana [*Mutual Assistance of the Latin American Government Oil Companies*] (EAIO) .... ARPEL
Asitka Resources Corp. [*Vancouver Stock Exchange symbol*] .... ATK
Ask a Friend to Explain Reconstruction [*An association*] (EA) .... AFTER
ASK Information Search, Anchorage, AK [*Library symbol*] [*Library of Congress*] (LCLS) .... AkAAS
Askania Cine-Theodolite Optical-Tracking Range .... ACTOR
Askania Optical Tracker .... AOT
Askania Theodolite Camera (MUGU) .... ASK
Asked .... A
Asking [*Automotive advertising*] .... ASKNG
Asking Price .... AP
Aslib Economics and Business Information Group (NITA) .... AEBIG
ASM [*American Society for Metals*] **Foundation for Education and Research** [*ASM International*] .... ASMFER
ASM [*American Society for Metals*] **International** (EA) .... ASMI
ASM International NV [*Associated Press*] (SAG) .... ASM Intl
ASM Lithography Holding NV [*Associated Press*] (SAG) .... ASM Lit
ASM Lithography Holding NV [*Associated Press*] (SAG) .... ASM Litho
ASM Lithography Holding NV [*NASDAQ symbol*] (SAG) .... ASML
ASM Litography Hldg NV [*NASDAQ symbol*] (TTSB) .... ASMILF
Asmar [*Afghanistan*] [*ICAO location identifier*] (ICLI) .... OAAS
Asmara [*Ethiopia*] [*Airport symbol*] (OAG) .... ASM
Asmara [*Ethiopia*] [*Airport symbol*] (AD) .... ASM
Asmara App [*Ethiopia*] [*ICAO location identifier*] (ICLI) .... HAAS
Asmara/Yohannes IV [*Ethiopia*] [*ICAO location identifier*] (ICLI) .... HAAY
ASME [*American Society of Mechanical Engineers*] **International Gas Turbine Institute** (EA) .... ASMEIGTI
Asmonean (BJA) .... AS
Asnuntuck Community College, Learning Resources Center, Enfield, CT [*Library symbol Library of Congress*] (LCLS) .... CtEnA
Aso [*Japan*] [*Seismograph station code, US Geological Survey Closed*] (SEIS) .... ASO
Asociacion [*Association*] [*Spanish*] .... ASOC
Asociacion Argentina de Tecnologia Nuclear (NUCP) .... AATN
Asociacion Argentino-Norteamericana para el Avance de la Ciencia, Technologia, yCultura [*Argentine-North American Association for the Advancement of Science, Technology, and Culture*] (EA) .... ANACITEC
Asociacion Bancaria de Panama (EY) .... ABP
Asociacion Centroamericana de Armadores [*Central American Association of Shipowners*] [*Guatemala, Guatemala*] (EAIO) .... ACAMAR
Asociacion Chilena de Empresas de Turismo [*Chile*] (EY) .... ACHET
Asociacion Cristiana de Jovenes [*Young Men's Christian Association*] (EAIO) .... ACJ
Asociacion de Bancos e Instituciones Financieras de Bolivia (EY) .... ASOBAN
Asociacion de Empresas Estatales de Telecomunicaciones del Acuerdo Subregional Andino [*Association of State Telecommunication Undertakings of the Andean Sub regional Agreement*] [*Ecuador*] (EAIO) .... ASETA
Asociacion de Familiares de Uruguayos Desaparecidos [*France*] .... AFUDE
Asociacion de Ferias Internacionales de America [*Association of International Trade Fairs of America*] (EAIO) .... AFIDA
Asociacion de Industriales Latinoamericanos [*Latin American Industrialists Association - LAIA*] [*Uruguay*] .... AILA
Asociacion de Linguistica y Filologia de America Latina .... ALFAL
Asociacion de Universidades del Caribe [*Association of Caribbean Universities and Research Institutes*] (EAIO) .... AUC
Asociacion de Universidades del Caribe [*Association of Caribbean Universities and Research Institutes*] (EA) .... UNICA
Asociacion del Congreso Panamericano de Ferrocarriles [*Pan American Railway Congress Association*] (EAIO) .... ACPF
Asociacion Filatelica de Filipinas [*Philatelic Association of the Philippines*] (EA) .... AFF
Asociacion Guatemalteca de Agentes de Viajes [*Guatemalan Association of Travel Agents*] (EY) .... AGAV
Asociacion Guatemalteca Pro Naciones Unidas [*Guatemala*] (EAIO) .... AGNU
Asociacion Hispanoamericana de Centros de Investigacion y Estudios de Telecomunicaciones (EA) .... AHCIET

Asociacion Iberoamericana de Camaras de Comercio [*Ibero-American Association of Chambers of Commerce - IACC*] [*Bogota, Colombia*] (EAIO) ... AICO
Asociacion Interamericana de Bibliotecarios y Documentalistas Agricolas [*Inter-American Association of Agricultural Librarians and Documentalists*] (EAIO) ... AIBDA
Asociacion Interamericana de Contabilidad [*Interamerican Accounting Association - IAA*] [*Mexico City, Mexico*] (EAIO) ... AIC
Asociacion Interamericana de Gastroenterologia [*Interamerican Association of Gastroenterology*] [*Guatemala*] ... AIGE
Asociacion Interamericana de Hombres de Empresa [*Inter-American Businessmen's Association*] ... AIHE
Asociacion Interamericana de Ingeniera Sanitaria [*Inter-American Assocation of Sanitary and Environmental Engineering*] (EA) ... AIDIS
Asociacion Interamericana de la Propiedad Industrial [*Inter-American Association of Industrial Property - IAAIP*] (EAIO) ... ASIPI
Asociacion Interamericana de Radiodifusion [*Inter-American Association of Broadcasters - IAAB*] [*Montevideo, Uruguay*] (EA) ... AIR
Asociacion Interamericana pro Democracia y Libertad [*Interamerican Association for Democracy and Freedom*] ... AIDL
Asociacion Internacional de Beisbol Amateur [*International Association of Amateur Baseball*] (EA) ... AINBA
Asociacion Internacional de Derecho de Aguas [*International Association for Water Law - IAWL*] [*Spain*] (EAIO) ... AIDA
Asociacion Internacional de Escritores Policiacos [*International Association of Crime Writers*] (EAIO) ... AIEP
Asociacion Internacional de Estructuras Laminares y Espaciales [*International Association for Shell and Spatial Structures*] ... AIEL
Asociacion Internacional de Estudio Integral del Deporte [*International Association of Sport Research*] ... AIEID
Asociacion Internacional de Fomento [*International Development Association*] ... AIF
Asociacion Internacional de Hispanistas [*International Association of Hispanists*] [*Aalst, Belgium*] (EA) ... AIH
Asociacion Internacional de Investigacion para la Paz [*International Peace Research Association*] (EAIO) ... AIIP
Asociacion Internacional de Mercadotecnia Social [*Social Marketing International Association - SMIA*] [*Defunct Mexico*] (EAIO) ... AIMS
Asociacion Internacional de Planificacion Familiar [*Social Marketing International Association - SMIA*] (EAIO) ... AIPF
Asociacion Internacional de Radiodifusion [*International Association of Broadcasting - IAB*] (EAIO) ... AIR
Asociacion Internacional para el Progreso de la Ensenanza y de la Investigacion de la Propiedad Intelectual [*International Association for the Advancement of Teaching and Research in Intellectual Property*] (EAIO) ... ATRIP
Asociacion Latinoamericana de Administracion Publica ... ALAP
Asociacion Latinoamericana de Agentes de Carga Aerea y Transporte [*Latin American Association of Freight and Transport Agents - LAFTA*] (EA) ... ALACAT
Asociacion Latinoamericana de Analisis y Modificacion del Comportamiento [*Latin American Association of Behavior Analysis and Modification*] (EAIO) ... ALAMOC
Asociacion Latinoamericana de Archivos [*Latin American Association of Archives - LAAA*] (EAIO) ... ALA
Asociacion Latinoamericana de Armadores [*Latin American Shipowners' Association*] (EAIO) ... ALAMAR
Asociacion Latinoamericana de Ciencias Fisiologicas [*Latin American Association of Physiological Sciences*] [*ICSU*] (EAIO) ... ALACF
Asociacion Latinoamericana de Derecho Aeronautico y Espacial ... ALADA
Asociacion Latinoamericana de Derecho Constitucional [*Latin American Constitutional Law Association - LACLA*] (EAIO) ... ALDC
Asociacion Latinoamericana de Editores en Geociencias ... ALEGEO
Asociacion Latinoamericana de Educacion Agricola Superior ... ALEAS
Asociacion Latinoamericana de Escuelas de Bibliotecologia y Ciencias de la Informacion ... ALEBCI
Asociacion Latinoamericana de Estudios Afroasiaticos [*Latin American Association for Afro-Asian Studies - LAAAAS*] (EAIO) ... ALADAA
Asociacion Latinoamericana de Facultades y Escuelas de Medicina de America Latina [*Latin American Association of Medical Schools and Faculties - LAAMSF*] [*Quito, Ecuador*] (EAIO) ... ALAFEM
Asociacion Latinoamericana de Ferrocarriles [*Latin American Railways Association - LARA*] [*Argentina*] ... ALAF
Asociacion Latinoamericana de Industrias Farmaceuticas [*Latin American Association of Pharmaceutical Industries - LAAPI*] (EAIO) ... ALIFAR
Asociacion Latinoamericana de Instituciones Financieras de Desarrollo [*Latin American Association of Development Financing Institutions*] [*Lima, Peru*] (EAIO) ... ALIDE
Asociacion Latinoamericana de Libre Comercio [*Also, LAFTA*] [*Latin American Free Trade Association*] ... ALALC
Asociacion Latinoamericana de Politica Cientifica y Tecnologica [*Latin American Association for Science and Technology*] [*Mexico*] (EAIO) ... ALPCyT
Asociacion Latinoamericana de Produccion Animal ... ALPA
Asociacion Latinoamericana de Psicologia Social [*Latin American Association for Social Psychology - LAASP*] (EAIO) ... ALPS
Asociacion Latinoamericana de Sociologia Rural [*Latin American Rural Sociological Association - LARSA*] (EAIO) ... ALASRU
Asociacion Latinoamericana para el Desarrollo y la Integracion de la Mujer [*Latin American Association for the Development and Integration of Women - LAADIW*] [*Santiago, Chile*] (EAIO) ... ALADIM
Asociacion Latinoamericana y del Caribe de Mundazas Internacionales [*Latin American and Caribbean International Moving*] [*Panama*] (EAIO) ... ALCMI
Asociacion Mexicana de Bibliotecarios, Asociacion Civil [*Spanish*] ... AMBAC
Asociacion Mexicana para las Naciones Unidas [*United Nations Association of Mexico*] (EAIO) ... AMNU
Asociacion Mundial de Veterinarios Higienistas de los Alimentos [*World Association of Veterinary Food-Hygienists - WAVFH*] [*Berlin, Federal Republic of Germany*] (EAIO) ... AMVHA
Asociacion Mundial Veterinaria de Avicola [*World Veterinary Poultry Association - WVPA*] [*Huntingdon, Cambridgeshire, England*] (EAIO) ... AMVA
Asociacion Mundial Veterinaria de Pequenos Animales [*World Small Animal Veterinary Association - WSAVA*] [*Hatfield, Hertfordshire, England*] (EAIO) ... AMVPA
Asociacion Nacional Campesina Pro-Tierra [*National Peasant Association for Land*] [*Guatemala*] [*Political party*] ... ANC
Asociacion Nacional de Universidades e Institutos de Ensenanza Superior [*The Mexican Association of Universities and Public Institutes of Higher Education*] (CROSS) ... ANUIES
Asociacion Nacional pro Personas Mayores [*National Association for Hispanic Elderly*] (EA) ... ANPPM
Asociacion Nicaraguense de Agencias de Viajes (EY) ... ANAVIT
Asociacion Panamena de Agencias de Viajes y Turismo (EY) ... APAVIT
Asociacion Panamericana de Instituciones de Credito Educativo [*Pan American Association of Educational Credit Institutions - PAAECI*] (EAIO) ... APICE
Asociacion Panamericana de Oftalmologia [*Panamerican Association of Ophthalmology*] [*Washington, DC*] ... APO
Asociacion para el Progreso de Honduras [*Association for the Progress of Honduras*] [*Political party*] ... APROH
Asociacion Petroquimica Latinoamericana [*Argentina*] (EAIO) ... APLA
Asociacion pro Derechos Humanos de Espana [*Spanish Human Rights Association*] ... APDH
Asociacion pro Derechos Humanos de Espana [*Spanish Human Rights Association*] (EAIO) ... APDHE
Asociacion pro Zarzuela en America (EA) ... APZA
Asociacion Universal de Federalistas Mundiales [*World Association of World Federalists*] ... AUFM
Asociacion Universitaria Interamericana [*Interamerican University Association*] [*Spanish*] ... AUI
Asocial Personality ... ASP
Asociatiunea Reuniunilor Femeilor Ortodoxe Romane-Americane [*Association of Romanian-American Orthodox Ladies Auxiliaries*] ... ARFORA
As-Of Date (AFM) ... AOD
Asom Gana Parishad [*Assam People's Council*] [*India*] [*Political party*] (FEA) ... AGP
Asosa [*Ethiopia*] [*Airport symbol*] (OAG) ... ASO
Asosan [*Japan*] [*Seismograph station code, US Geological Survey*] (SEIS) ... ASJ
Asotin County Library, Clarkston, WA [*Library symbol Library of Congress*] (LCLS) ... WaCl
Asotin, WA [*AM radio station call letters*] ... KCLK
Asparaginase [*An enzyme*] (AAMN) ... ASP
Asparaginase [*Antineoplastic drug*] (CDI) ... ASP
Asparaginase, Vincreistine, Doxorubicin, Prednisone [*Antineoplastic drug*] (CDI) ... AVDP
Asparagine [*One-letter symbol; see Asn*] ... A
Asparagine [*Also, Asp(NH*$_2$*), N*] [*An amino acid*] ... Asn
Asparagine [*Also, N*] [*An amino acid*] (DOG) ... asn
Asparagine (BARN) ... Asp N
Asparagine [*Also, Asn, N*] [*An amino acid*] ... $Asp(NH_2)$
Asparagine [*Biochemistry*] (DAVI) ... N
Asparagus Club (EA) ... AC
Asparagus Stunt Virus [*Plant pathology*] ... ASV
Asparagus Virus ... AV
Asparagus Virus II [*Plant pathology*] ... AVII
Aspartame [*Sweetening agent*] ... APM
Aspartame Committee of the International Food Information Council (EA) ... ACIFIC
aspartate (DOG) ... asp
Aspartate Aminotransferase [*Also, ASAT, AST, GOT*] [*An enzyme*] ... AAT
Aspartate Aminotransferase [*Also, AAT, AST, GOT*] [*An enzyme*] ... ASAT
Aspartate Aminotransferase [*Also, AAT, ASAT, GOT*] [*An enzyme*] ... AST
Aspartate Aminotransferase [*An enzyme*] (DAVI) ... GOT
Aspartate Transcarbamylase [*Also, ATCase*] [*An enzyme*] ... ATC
Aspartate Transcarbamylase [*Also, ATC*] [*An enzyme*] ... ATCase
Aspartic Acid [*Also, D*] [*An amino acid*] ... Asp
Aspartic Acid [*Also, D*] [*An amino acid*] (DOG) ... asp
Aspartic Acid [*or Asparagine*] [*Also, B An amino acid*] ... Asx
Aspartic Acid [*or Asparagine*] [*Also, Asx An amino acid Symbol*] ... B
Aspartic Acid [*One-letter symbol; see Asp*] ... D
Aspartocin [*Endocrinology*] ... AT
Aspartyl Naphthylamide (MAE) ... ANA
Aspartyl-Hydroxamic Acid (MAE) ... AHA
Aspect (ROG) ... ASP
Aspect Angle Radiation Code (MCD) ... AARAD
Aspect Development [*NASDAQ symbol*] (SAG) ... ASDV
Aspect Development [*NASDAQ symbol*] (TTSB) ... ASDV
Aspect Development [*Associated Press*] (SAG) ... AspctDv
Aspect Factor (PDAA) ... AF
Aspect Ratio ... AR
Aspect Ratio Dependent Etching [*Microlithography*] ... ARDE
Aspect Ratio Enhancement (MCD) ... ARE
Aspect Telecommunications [*Associated Press*] (SAG) ... AspectTel
Aspect Telecommunications [*NASDAQ symbol*] (TTSB) ... ASPT
Aspect Telecommunications Corp. [*Associated Press*] (SAG) ... AspctTl
Aspect Telecommunications Corp. [*NASDAQ symbol*] (SAG) ... ASPT
Aspects of Gymnastics and Independent Learning Experience (AIE) ... AGILE
Aspen [*Colorado*] [*Airport symbol*] (OAG) ... ASE
Aspen Airways [*ICAO designator*] (AD) ... AP
Aspen Airways [*Air carrier designation symbol*] ... APN
Aspen Bancshares [*NASDAQ symbol*] (TTSB) ... ASBK

Aspen Bankshares, Inc. [*NASDAQ symbol*] (SAG) ... ASBK
Aspen Bankshares, Inc. [*Associated Press*] (SAG) ... AspenB
Aspen, CO [*Location identifier FAA*] (FAAL) ... BUK
Aspen, CO [*FM radio station call letters*] ... KAJX
Aspen, CO [*AM radio station call letters*] ... KRKE
Aspen, CO [*FM radio station call letters*] ... KSPN
Aspen, CO [*Location identifier FAA*] (FAAL) ... PKN
Aspen, CO [*Location identifier FAA*] (FAAL) ... RDY
Aspen, CO [*Location identifier FAA*] (FAAL) ... RNE
Aspen Exploration Corp. [*Vancouver Stock Exchange symbol*] ... ASP
Aspen Imaging International [*NASDAQ symbol*] (NQ) ... ARIB
Aspen Imaging International, Inc. [*Associated Press*] (SAG) ... Aspnlm
Aspen Imaging Intl. [*NASDAQ symbol*] (TTSB) ... ARIB
Aspen Institute for Humanistic Studies (EA) ... AIHS
Aspen Institute Program on Communications and Society (NTCM) ... AIPCS
Aspen Law Center, Aspen, CO [*Library symbol Library of Congress*] (LCLS) ... CoAsL
Aspen Technology [*NASDAQ symbol*] (TTSB) ... AZPN
Aspen Technology, Inc. [*Associated Press*] (SAG) ... AspenTc
Aspen Technology, Inc. [*NASDAQ symbol*] (SAG) ... AZPN
Aspencade Motorcyclists Convention (EA) ... ASP/MC
Aspergillosis [*A fungal disease*] (DAVI) ... ASPER
Aspergillus Asthma ... AA
Aspergillus fumigatus [*A fungus*] ... Af
Aspergillus niger [*Factor*] ... AN
Asphalt ... ASP
Asphalt (KSC) ... ASPH
Asphalt ... ASPHLT
Asphalt and Vinyl Asbestos Tile Institute [*Later, RFCI*] (EA) ... AVATI
Asphalt Coking Technology ... ASCOT
Asphalt Composition (KSC) ... AC
Asphalt Concrete [*FHWA*] (TAG) ... AC
Asphalt Contractors Association of Florida (SRA) ... ACAF
Asphalt Employees Protection Society [*A union*] [*British*] ... AEPS
Asphalt Emulsion Manufacturers Association (EA) ... AEMA
Asphalt Institute (EA) ... AI
Asphalt Pavement Association of Indiana (SRA) ... APAI
Asphalt Paving Association of Iowa (SRA) ... APAI
Asphalt Paving Association of Washington (SRA) ... APAW
Asphalt Recycling and Reclaiming Association (EA) ... ARRA
Asphalt Residual Treatment [*Petroleum refining*] ... ART
Asphalt Roads Association [*British*] (BI) ... ARA
Asphalt Roof Shingles [*Technical drawings*] ... ASPHRS
Asphalt Roofing Industry Bureau [*Later, ARMA*] (EA) ... ARIB
Asphalt Roofing Manufacturers Association (EA) ... ARMA
Asphalt Rubber Producers Group (EA) ... ARPG
Asphalt Surface Course (DAC) ... ASC
Asphalt Tile [*Technical drawings*] ... AT
Asphalt Treated Base [*FHWA*] (TAG) ... ATB
Asphaltenic Bottom Cracking [*Hydrocarbon processing*] ... ABC
Asphaltic Concrete ... AC
Asphaltic Concrete Pavement ... ACP
Asphalt-Plank Floor (MSA) ... ASPHPF
Asphalt-Plastic-Asphalt-Chip (PDAA) ... APAC
Asphalt-Tile Base [*Technical drawings*] ... ATB
Asphalt-Tile Floor [*Technical drawings*] ... ATF
Asphodel Township Public Library, Westwood, Ontario [*Library symbol National Library of Canada*] (BIB) ... OWEST
Asphyxiating Thoracic Dystrophy [*Medicine*] ... ATD
Aspinall's Maritime Law Cases [*1871-1940*] [*England*] [*A publication*] (DLA) ... Asp
Aspinall's Maritime Law Cases [*1871-1940*] [*England*] [*A publication*] (DLA) ... Asp Cas
Aspinall's Maritime Law Cases [*1871-1940*] [*England*] [*A publication*] (DLA) ... Asp Mar L Cas (Eng)
Aspinall's Maritime Law Cases [*1871-1940*] [*England*] [*A publication*] (DLA) ... Asp Mar Law Cas
Aspinall's Maritime Law Cases [*1871-1940*] [*England*] [*A publication*] (DLA) ... Asp MC
Aspinall's Maritime Law Cases [*1871-1940*] [*A publication*] (DLA) ... Asp MCL
Aspinall's Maritime Law Cases [*1871-1940*] [*England*] [*A publication*] (DLA) ... Asp MLC
Aspinall's Maritime Law Cases [*1871-1940*] [*A publication*] (DLA) ... Asp Rep
Aspinall's Maritime Law Cases [*1871-1940*] [*England*] [*A publication*] (DLA) ... Aspin
Aspira of America (EA) ... AOA
Aspiration Biopsy Cytology [*Medicine*] ... ABC
Aspiration Percutaneus Lumber Dickectomy [*Medicine*] ... APLD
Aspirator (NASA) ... ASP
Aspirator (MSA) ... ASPRTR
Aspirator Air System [*Automotive engineering*] ... AAS
Aspirator-Assisted Vacuum System [*Automotive engineering*] ... AAVS
Aspirin, Caffeine, Phenacetin [*Medicine*] (AAMN) ... ACP
Aspirin Compound [*Pharmacology*] (DAVI) ... APC
Aspirin Foundation of America (EA) ... AFA
Aspirin Myocardial Infarction Study [*Medicine*] ... AMIS
Aspirin, Phenacetin, Caffeine [*Medicine*] (DHSM) ... APC
Aspirin, Phenacetin, Caffeine with Codeine [*Medicine*] (MAE) ... APC-C
Aspirin Tolerance Time [*Medicine*] (DMAA) ... ATT
Aspirin-Induced Asthma [*Medicine*] ... AIA
Aspiryl Chloride [*Organic chemistry*] (MAH) ... ACI
ASPP [*Atmospheric and Space Plasma Physics*] **Sortie Laboratory** [*NASA*] (NASA) ... ASPSL
Aspres-Sur-Buech [*France ICAO location identifier*] (ICLI) ... LFNJ
ASR Investments [*AMEX symbol*] (TTSB) ... ASR
ASR Investments Corp. [*Formerly, American Southwest Mortgage Investment Co.*] [*Associated Press*] (SAG) ... ASR
ASR Investments Corp. [*Associated Press*] (SAG) ... ASR Inv
ASROC [*Antisubmarine Rocket*] **Missile Assembly** ... AMA
ASROC [*Antisubmarine Rocket*] **Splashpoint Telemetry System** [*Navy*] ... ASTS
As-Run Procedure [*Military*] (MCD) ... ARP
Assab [*Ethiopia*] [*Airport symbol*] (OAG) ... ASA
Assab [*Ethiopia*] [*ICAO location identifier*] (ICLI) ... HASB
Assafoetida [*Pharmacy*] (ROG) ... ASSAFOET
Assam, India (ILCA) ... Ass Ind
Assam Valley Light Horse [*British military*] (DMA) ... AVLH
Assamese [*MARC language code Library of Congress*] (LCCP) ... asm
Assassination (ROG) ... ASS
Assassination (ROG) ... ASSAS
Assassination Archives and Research Center (EA) ... AARC
Assassination Information Bureau [*An association*] (EA) ... AIB
Assateague Island National Seashore [*National Park Service designation*] ... ASIS
Assault [*FBI standardized term*] ... A
Assault (AFM) ... ASLT
Assault Airlift Control Officer ... AACO
Assault Amphibian Vehicle [*Military*] ... AAV
Assault Amphibious Battalion (DNAB) ... ASLTPHIBBN
Assault and Battery ... A & B
Assault and Battery [*Legal term*] (DLA) ... ASSLT & B
Assault and Battery with Intent to Kill ... ABWIK
Assault Battalion Task Force (MCD) ... ABTF
Assault Breaker (MCD) ... AB
Assault Craft Division (DNAB) ... ACDIV
Assault Craft Unit (NVT) ... ACU
Assault Crisis Center ... ACC
Assault Data System (DNAB) ... ADS
Assault Echelon (NVT) ... AE
Assault Engineer [*British military*] (DMA) ... AE
Assault Fire Command Console [*Army*] ... AFCC
Assault Fire Unit [*Army*] ... AFU
Assault Follow-On Echelon [*Marine Corps*] (MCD) ... AFOE
Assault Gun (MCD) ... AG
Assault Gun (AABC) ... ASLTG
Assault Gun Battalion (INF) ... AGB
Assault Helicopter Aircraft Carrier [*Navy symbol Obsolete*] ... CVHA
Assault Helicopter Battalion [*Military*] ... AHB
Assault Helicopter Company [*Army*] (AABC) ... AHC
Assault Helicopter Company [*Air Force*] (AFM) ... AHCo
Assault Helicopter Support Company [*Air Force*] (AFM) ... AHSCo
Assault Hospital Ship [*Navy symbol*] (VNW) ... LPH
Assault Landing Zone (AFM) ... ALZ
Assault Occasioning Actual Bodily Harm [*Criminology*] ... AOABH
Assault Occasioning Grievous Bodily Harm [*Criminology*] ... AOGBH
Assault on Illiteracy Program (EA) ... AIP
Assault on Illiteracy Program (EA) ... AOIP
Assault Regiment Royal Engineers [*British military*] (DMA) ... ARRE
Assault Squadron [*British military*] (DMA) ... AS
Assault Support Helicopter [*Military*] ... ASH
Assault Support Helicopter Company [*Army*] (VNW) ... ASHC
Assault Support Patrol Boat (DNAB) ... ASP
Assault Support Patrol Boat [*Navy symbol*] ... ASPB
Assault to Kill [*FBI standardized term*] ... A to K
Assault Vehicle, Royal Engineers [*British*] ... AVRE
Assault with Deadly Weapon ... ADW
Assaulting Federal Officer [*FBI standardized term*] ... AFO
Assay Ton ... AT
Asselin, Benoit, Boucher, Ducharme & Lapointe, Inc., Montreal, PQ, Canada [*Library symbol Library of Congress*] (LCLS) ... CaQMABB
Assemblage (VRA) ... asmblg
Assemble (AABC) ... ASBL
Assemble (IAA) ... ASMBL
Assemble (MSA) ... ASSEM
Assemble ... ASSMBL
Assemble and Checkout (MCD) ... A/C
Assemble and Recycle (SAA) ... A & R
Assemble and Test ... A & T
Assemble/Load [*Computer science*] ... A/L
Assembled ... ASMBD
Assembled Air-Launched Weapon ... AALW
Assembled Electronic Component ... AEC
Assemblee de l'Atlantique Nord [*North Atlantic Assembly*] [*Brussels, Belgium*] (EAIO) ... AAN
Assemblee des Franco-Americains/Association of Franco-Americans (EA) ... AFA
Assemblee des Gestionnaires de Reseaux Electriques Municipalises et Cooperatives [*Assembly of Managers of Municipal and Cooperative Electrical Systems*] [*Canada*] ... AGREMC
Assemblee des Nations Captives d'Europe [*Assembly of Captive European Nations*] ... ANCE
Assemblee des Premieres Nations (AC) ... APN
Assemblee des Regions d'Europe [*Later, AER*] (EAIO) ... ARE
Assemblee Generale des Federations Internationales Sportives [*General Assembly of International Sports Federations*] ... AGFIS
Assemblee Generale du Contentieux, Conseil d'Etat [*France*] (ILCA) ... Ass
Assemblee Generale Permanente des Comites Nationaux Olympiques [*Permanent General Assembly of National Olympic Committees*] ... AGP-CNO
Assemblee Internationale des Parlementaires de Langue Francaise (AC) ... AIPLF
Assemblee Mondiale de la Jeunesse [*World Assembly of Youth*] ... AMJ

Assemblee Mondiale des Petites et Moyennes Entreprises [*World Assembly of Small and Medium Enterprises - WASME*] [*See also AMEPM New Delhi,India*] (EAIO) .... AMPME
Assemblee Parlementaire Europeenne .... APE
Assemblee Populaire Communale [*People's Communal Assembly*] [*Algeria*] (AF) .... APC
Assemblee Populaire Nationale [*Haiti*] [*Political party*] (EY) .... APN
Assembler [*Computer science*] (IAA) .... AS
Assembler [*Computer science*] .... ASM
Assembler (NITA) .... ASM
Assembler (MHDB) .... asmblr
Assembler (NITA) .... ASS
Assembler [*Computer science*] .... ASSM
Assembler .... ASSMBLR
Assembler Language [*Computer science*] (CMD) .... ASS
Assembler Language for MULTICS .... ALM
Assembler Unit [*Computer science*] (IAA) .... AU
Assemblies, Components, Spare Parts, and Materials [*NATO*] (NATG) .... ACSM
Assemblies of God (ADA) .... AOG
Assemblies of God Graduate School, Springfield, MO [*OCLC symbol*] (OCLC) .... MOG
Assemblies of God Graduate School, Springfield, MO [*Library symbol Library of Congress*] (LCLS) .... MoSpA
Assembling [*FBI standardized term*] .... ASMB
Assembly (IAA) .... A
Assembly (AFM) .... ASBLY
Assembly (WGA) .... ASM
Assembly .... ASMBLY
Assembly .... ASS
Assembly (AAMN) .... ASSBY
Assembly (DLA) .... Assem
Assembly .... ASSY
Assembly (DNAB) .... AY
Assembly Aid [*Tool*] (AAG) .... ASAD
Assembly and Checkout [*Minuteman*] [*Military*] (AFIT) .... A & CO
Assembly and Checkout [*Minuteman*] [*Military*] (AFIT) .... AAC
Assembly and Disassembly (IAA) .... AAD
Assembly and Equipment (SAA) .... A & E
Assembly and Equipment (IAA) .... AAE
Assembly and Erection (SAA) .... A & E
Assembly and Fabrication .... AF
Assembly and Maintenance (KSC) .... A & M
Assembly and Maintenance (IAA) .... AAM
Assembly and Operations Plan .... AOP
Assembly and Repair .... A & R
Assembly and Repair (IAA) .... AAR
Assembly and Rework Operation .... ARO
Assembly and Structure Test .... AST
Assembly and Test [*Aerospace*] (AAG) .... A/T
Assembly and Test (IAA) .... AAT
Assembly and Test Area [*NASA*] (KSC) .... ATA
Assembly and Test Pit [*Nuclear energy*] (NRCH) .... A & TP
Assembly and Test Pit [*Nuclear energy*] (IAA) .... AATP
Assembly and Verification Review (SSD) .... AVR
Assembly Area .... AA
Assembly Area (IAA) .... ASSA
Assembly Area Command .... AAC
Assembly Bill [*in state legislatures*] .... AB
Assembly Breakdown List .... ABL
Assembly Concept for Construction of Erectable Space Structures [*Space shuttle experiment*] [*NASA*] .... ACCESS
Assembly Control System [*IBM Corp.*] (BUR) .... ACS
Assembly Coordination Advice (MCD) .... ACA
Assembly Decay Indicator .... ADI
Assembly Department Shortage List .... ADSL
Assembly Detail Purchased Parts (AAG) .... ADPP
Assembly/Disassembly Facility .... A/D
Assembly District .... AD
Assembly Drawing .... AD
Assembly Facility Tool (MCD) .... AFT
Assembly Fixture (MCD) .... AF
Assembly Fixture [*Tool*] (AAG) .... ASFX
Assembly Fixture Accessory (MCD) .... AFA
Assembly for Behavioral and Social Sciences [*National Research Council*] .... ABASS
Assembly, Handling, and Shipping Equipment .... AHSE
Assembly History Tag .... AHT
Assembly Identification Number (NG) .... AIN
Assembly Inspection Record (SAA) .... AIR
Assembly Instruction Device (DNAB) .... AID
Assembly Instruction Mnemonics [*Computer science*] .... AIM
Assembly Integration and Test .... AI & T
Assembly Jig .... AJ
Assembly Joint Resolution [*Congress*] .... AJR
Assembly Language [*Computer science*] .... AL
Assembly Language Coding [*Computer science*] .... ALC
Assembly Language Preprocessor [*Computer science*] (IEEE) .... ALP
Assembly Language Program [*Computer science*] .... ALP
Assembly Language Translator [*Xerox Corp.*] .... ALTRAN
Assembly Layout [*Computer science*] (MHDB) .... ASLO
Assembly Line Communications Link [*General Motors computerized automotive production*] .... ALCL
Assembly Line Diagnostic Link [*Automotive engineering*] .... ALDL
Assembly Line Effectiveness Center .... ALEC
Assembly Line Planning System (MHDB) .... ALPS

Assembly Line Shortages Log .... ALSL
Assembly List Shortage Log (AAG) .... ALSL
Assembly Machine Fixture (MCD) .... AMF
Assembly, Maintenance, and Servicing (SSD) .... AMS
Assembly Management Operating System (MCD) .... AMOS
Assembly Manufacturing Payroll System (MHDB) .... AMPS
Assembly of Captive European Nations (EA) .... ACEN
Assembly of Episcopal Hospitals and Chaplains (EA) .... AEHC
Assembly of European Regions [*Later, AER*] (EAIO) .... ARE
Assembly of First Nations [*Canadian Indian organization*] .... AFN
Assembly of First Nations, Ottawa, Ontario [*Library symbol National Library of Canada*] (NLC) .... OOAFN
Assembly of Free Spirit Baptist Churches (EA) .... AFSBC
Assembly of God in Australia .... AOGA
Assembly of Governmental Employees [*Defunct*] (EA) .... AGE
Assembly of Hospital Schools of Nursing (EA) .... AHSN
Assembly of Librarians of the Americas [*Defunct*] (EA) .... ALA
Assembly of Librarians of the Americas [*Defunct*] .... ALOA
Assembly of Mathematical and Physical Sciences [*National Research Council*] .... AMPS
Assembly of National Postsecondary Educational Organizations (EDAC) .... ANPEO
Assembly of National Tourist Office Representatives in New York [*Defunct*] (EA) .... ANTOR
Assembly of Parties [*INTELSAT*] .... AP
Assembly of State Conferences [*American Association of University Professors*] (EDAC) .... ASC
Assembly of Turkish American Associations (EA) .... ATAA
Assembly Operation and Inspection Report .... AOIR
Assembly Operations Record .... AOR
Assembly Order .... AO
Assembly Order Control Number .... AOCN
Assembly Outline .... AO
Assembly Outline Tooling .... AOT
Assembly Over-Ships Records .... AO-SR
Assembly Page Change Notice (SAA) .... APCN
Assembly Page Listing (SAA) .... APL
Assembly Page Maintenance (SAA) .... APM
Assembly Part List .... APL
Assembly Process Flow Chart (IAA) .... APFC
Assembly Production Order [*Manufacturing*] (AAG) .... APO
Assembly Programming Language [*Computer science*] .... APL
Assembly Programming System [*Computer science*] (IEEE) .... APS
Assembly Quality Record .... AQR
Assembly Sequence Record Sheet .... ASRS
Assembly Sequence Record Sheet - Work Sheet .... ASRSWS
Assembly Shortage Control (MCD) .... ASC
Assembly System .... AS
Assembly System for Central Processor [*Computer science*] .... ASCENT
Assembly System for Peripheral Processors [*Computer science*] .... ASPER
Assembly Telling (SAA) .... AT
Assembly, Test, and System Support .... AT & SS
Assembly Test Program (IAA) .... ATP
Assembly Test Record (IAA) .... ATR
Assembly Test Recording System .... ATRS
Assembly Text Chip [*Computer science*] .... ATC
Assembly Time Standard Estimating Sheet (MCD) .... ATSES
Assembly Tool (AAG) .... ASTO
Assembly Tracking and Management System (MCD) .... ATMS
Assembly Truss and Structure (SSD) .... ATS
Assembly Type Supply Directive [*Military*] (AFIT) .... ATSD
Assembly Week (MCD) .... AW
Assembly Work Schedule Order .... AWSO
Assembly Workstand [*NASA*] (NASA) .... AW
Assembly-Line Preventive Maintenance [*Automotive engineering*] .... ALPM
Assented [*Investment term*] .... A
Assented [*Investment term*] .... ASD
Assented [*Securities*] .... ASST
Assented (WGA) .... ASSTD
Assented [*Economics*] .... AST
Assented [*Investment term*] .... ASTD
Assented Security [*Investment term*] .... AS
Assertive Behavior Inventory Tool [*Psychology*] (DMAA) .... ABIT
Assertive Sentence Title [*Report writing*] .... AST
Assertiveness Training (WGA) .... AT
Assessable Stock [*Investment term*] .... AS
Assessed (WGA) .... ASSD
Assessed Annual Value [*Accounting*] (ADA) .... AAV
Assessed Tax Case (DLA) .... ATC
Assessed Taxes (Decisions of Judges) [*A publication*] (DLA) .... Ass Tax
Assessing Severity: Age of Patient, Systems Involved, State of Disease, Complications, Response to Therapy [*Medicine*] (MEDA) .... AS-SCORE
Assessing the Cognitivie Consequences of Computer Environments for Learning Project (EDAC) .... ACCCEL
Assessment [*Medicine*] .... A
Assessment .... ASMNT
Assessment .... ASMT
Assessment (KSC) .... ASSESMT
Assessment [*Business term*] .... ASSMT
Assessment .... ASST
Assessment .... AST
Assessment Adjustment Pass [*Psychiatry*] (DAVI) .... AAP
Assessment and Career Development Centre [*Australia*] .... ACDC

Assessment and Coordination Branch, Environmental Protection Service, Environment Canada [*Direction de l'Evaluation et de la Coordination, Service de la Protection de l'Environnement, Environnement Canada*] Yellowknife, Northwest Territories [*Library symbol National Library of Canada*] (NLC) .... NWYEEP
Assessment and Evaluation [*Educational Resources Information Center (ERIC) Clearinghouse*] [*The Catholic University of America*] (PAZ) .... TM
Assessment and Information Services Center [*National Oceanic and Atmospheric Administration Information service or system*] (IID) .... AISC
Assessment and Plans [*Medicine*] .... AP
Assessment and Remediation of Contaminated Sediments [*Environmental science*] .... ARCS
Assessment and Training for Employment (AIE) .... ATE
[*Kaufman*] Assessment Battery for Children [*Diagnostic assessment test*] (PAZ) .... ABC
Assessment Biological and Chemical [*Warfare*] (NATG) .... ABC
Assessment Center [*Business term*] .... AC
Assessment for Community Care Services [*Health Care Financing Administration*] .... ACCESS
Assessment Guidance Centre [*British*] .... AGC
Assessment, Improvement, and Monitoring System [*School milk programs*] .... AIMS
Assessment Models in Support of Hazard Assessment Handbook (MCD) .... AMSHAH
Assessment of Basic Competencies [*Child development test*] .... ABC
Assessment of Career Decision Making [*Vocational guidance test*] .... ACDM
Assessment of Children's Language Comprehension [*Education*] .... ACLC
Assessment of Cognitive Skills .... ACS
Assessment of Combat Effectiveness [*Army*] (AABC) .... ACE
Assessment of Fluency in School-Age Children [*Speech evaluation test*] ..... AFSC
Assessment of Instructional Terms (EDAC) .... AIT
Assessment of Intelligibility of Dysarthric Speech [*Speech and language therapy*] (DAVI) .... AIDS
Assessment of Language and Reading Maturity Test (EDAC) .... ALARM
Assessment of Language Proficiency of Bilingual Persons Project (EDAC) .... ALPBP
Assessment of Motor and Process Skills [*Occupational therapy*] .... AMPS
Assessment of Performance Unit [*Education*] [*British*] .... APU
Assessment of Prior Learning .... APL
Assessment of Safety Significant Events Team [*IAEA*] (NUCP) .... ASSET
Assessment of Skills in Computation [*Mathematics test*] .... ASC
Assessment of Survivability Against LASER Threat (MCD) .... ASALT
Assessment of the Provision of Part Time Training [*Education*] (AIE) .... APPT
Assessment of Theater Warfare [*Model*] (MCD) .... ATWAR
Assessment Paid [*Billing*] .... AP
Assessment Paid .... Apd
Assessment, Plan, Implementation, and Evaluation [*Medicine*] (DMAA) .... APIE
Assessment Policy Committee [*National Assessment of Educational Progress*] (EDAC) .... APC
Assessment Quality Report (MCD) .... AQR
Assessment Statute Expiration Date [*IRS*] .... ASED
Assessment Subgroup [*NATO*] (NATG) .... ASG
Assessments for Integration into Mainstream Settings .... AIMS
Assessor [*Assistant, Assessor*] [*German*] .... Ass
Assessor of Archdeaconry [*Ecclesiastical*] (ROG) .... ASSER
Assessors Association of Pennsylvania (SRA) .... AAP
Assessor's Data Exchange [*A publication*] (EAAP) .... ADE
Asset .... ASST
Asset [*or Availability*] Balance File [*Military*] (AABC) .... ABF
Asset Capitalization Program [*Air Force*] (DOMA) .... ACP
Asset Control System [*or Subsystem*] [*Army*] (AABC) .... ACS
Asset Control Techniques [*TRW, Inc.*] .... ACT
Asset Depreciation Range [*IRS*] .... ADR
Asset Depreciation Range System [*Accounting*] .... ADRS
Asset Investors Corp. [*NYSE symbol*] (SPSG) .... AIC
Asset Investors Corp. [*Associated Press*] (SAG) .... AsetInv
Asset/Liability Management [*Banking*] .... ALM
Asset/Locating (LAIN) .... AL
Asset Management Account .... AMA
Asset Management Performance (HGAA) .... AMP
Asset Master Balance File [*Military*] (AABC) .... AMBF
Asset Position .... AP
Asset Protection Trust .... APT
Asset Report Request .... ARR
Asset Requirements Depot Maintenance Data (MCD) .... ARDMA
Asset Share Value [*Insurance*] .... ASV
Asset Source for Software Engineering Technology .... ASSET
Asset Status Cards .... ASC
Asset Support Request .... ASR
Asset Type [*Database terminology*] (NITA) .... AT
Asset Value (WDAA) .... AV
Asset-Backed Security [*Finance*] .... ABS
Asset-Liability Committee [*Banking*] .... ALCO
Assets Accounting [*Business term*] .... AA
Assets and Depreciation [*Accounting*] .... A/D
Assets Availability Code (MCD) .... AAC
Assets Less Than (NITA) .... AL
Assets Management System .... AMS
Assets Repriced Before Liabilities [*Business term*] (MHDB) .... ARBL
Assia Regis David [*A publication*] (DLA) .... Ass Reg Da
Assicurazioni Generali [*General Assurance*] [*Commercial firm Italy*] .... AG
Assiginack Public Library, Manitowaning, Ontario [*Library symbol National Library of Canada*] (NLC) .... OMAS
Assign (AABC) .... ASG
Assign (AFM) .... ASGN

Assign .... ASSN
Assign Missile RADAR (CAAL) .... AMR
Assign Symbolic Device (IAA) .... ASD
Assign Volume (IAA) .... ASVOL
Assignable Square Feet .... ASF
Assignation (DSUE) .... ASSIG
Assigned (AABC) .... ASGD
Assigned .... ASGED
Assigned (DLA) .... Assd
Assigned (BARN) .... assnd
Assigned Activity Standardization Office [*Air Force*] (AFIT) .... AASO
Assigned Altitude Deviation [*Aviation*] (DA) .... AAD
Assigned Contractor (SAA) .... AC
Assigned Night Answer [*Telecommunications*] (TEL) .... ANA
Assigned Procurement Responsibility (AAG) .... APR
Assigned Rating [*Sailing*] .... AR
Assigned Responsible Agency [*DoD*] .... ARA
Assigned Service Contractor .... ASC
Assigned Slot Release (MHDI) .... ASR
Assignee [*MARC relator code*] [*Library of Congress*] (LCCP) .... asg
Assignee [*Legal shorthand*] (LWAP) .... ASGEE
Assignee .... ASSGN
Assignee Name [*Database terminology*] (NITA) .... AN
Assignment [*FCC*] (NTCM) .... A
Assignment .... ASGMT
Assignment (WDMC) .... asgmt
Assignment (IAA) .... ASSG
Assignment (ROG) .... ASSGT
Assignment .... ASSIGT
Assignment (ROG) .... ASSMT
Assignment (ROG) .... ASST
Assignment Action Number (AFM) .... AAN
Assignment and Status Chart .... A & S
Assignment Control and Tracking System [*Computer science*] .... ACTS
Assignment Control Authority [*Military*] (NVT) .... ACA
Assignment Control Number [*Army*] .... ACN
Assignment Control Trainee (MCD) .... ACT
Assignment Date [*Telecommunications*] (TEL) .... AD
Assignment Eligibility and Availability [*Military*] (AABC) .... AEA
Assignment Instructions .... AI
Assignment Instructions Remain Firm [*Army*] .... AIRF
Assignment Instructions Were Furnished Your Command [*Military*] .... AIFURC
Assignment Instructions Will Include MOS [*Military Occupational Specialty*]within Army Career Group (AABC) .... AIMOSACGP
Assignment Memorandum [*Army*] (AABC) .... AM
Assignment of Claims Act [*1940*] (OICC) .... ACA
Assignment of (Construction) Permit [*FCC*] (NTCM) .... AP
Assignment of (Construction) Permit and License [*FCC*] (NTCM) .... APL
Assignment of License [*FCC*] (NTCM) .... AL
Assignment of Mortgage [*Business term*] (EMRF) .... A/M
Assignment Oriented Training .... AOT
Assignment Selection Date [*Military*] (AFM) .... ASD
Assignments for Benefits of Creditors [*A publication*] (DLA) .... Assign for Crs
Assignor [*Legal shorthand*] (LWAP) .... ASGOR
Assigns (ROG) .... ASS
Assigns (ROG) .... ASSNS
Assigns (ROG) .... ASSS
Assimilable Organic Carbon [*Environmental chemistry*] .... AOC
Assimilated .... ASSIM
Assimilation and Fractional Crystallization [*Geology*] .... AFC
Assimilation Efficiency .... AE
Assimilation Regulatory Protein [*Medicine*] (DMAA) .... ARP
Assimilations per Second .... APS
Assimulatory Quotient .... AQ
Assinado [*Signed*] [*Portuguese Business term*] .... a
Assiniboine Community College, Brandon, Manitoba [*Library symbol National Library of Canada*] (NLC) .... MBAC
Assiniboine Community College, Brandon, MB, Canada [*Library symbol Library of Congress*] (LCLS) .... CaMBAC
Assiniboine South School Division No. 3, Winnipeg, Manitoba [*Library symbol National Library of Canada*] (NLC) .... MWASD
Assist [*Health care*] .... A
Assist [*Sports*] .... A
Assist Card International (EA) .... ACI
Assist Control (DAVI) .... AC
Assist for Telecommunications Program and Control (IAA) .... ATPC
Assist Order .... AO
Assist Ship's Force Funds [*Navy*] (NVT) .... ASF
Assist Work Authorization .... AWA
Assistance [*or Assist*] (DAVI) .... ASST
Assistance (MSA) .... ASSTN
Assistance .... ASSTNCE
Assistance Aeroportuaire de l'Aeroport de Paris [*France ICAO designator*] (ICDA) .... XJ
Assistance Aeroportuaire de l'Aeroport de Paris [*France*] [*FAA designator*] (FAAC) .... XJA
Assistance and Independence for the Disabled [*British*] .... AID
Assistance and Instructions (MCD) .... AI
Assistance aux Createurs d'Entreprises du Nord-Ouest Europeen [*Multinational organization*] (EAIO) .... ACENOE
Assistance Dogs International (EA) .... ADI
Assistance Dogs of America [*An association*] (EA) .... ADAI
Assistance for Disabled Students in Post-Secondary Education [*Australia*] .... ADSPSE
Assistance for the Blind .... AB

Assistance in Divorce [*British*] (DI) .... AID
Assistance in Ministries (EA) .... AIM
Assistance Information and Data Acquisition Center [*Navy*] .... AIDAC
Assistance Medicale a l'Afrique Centrale [*Medical Assistance to Central Africa*] [*Belgium*] (AF) .... AMAC
Assistance Medicale Internationale [*International Medical Assistance*] [*Canada*] .... AMI
Assistance Militaire Technique [*Military Technical Assistance*] [*Niger*] (AF) .... AMT
Assistance Payments [*Social Security Administration*] .... AP
Assistance Payments Administration [*Later, Office of Family Assistance*] [*Social Security Administration*] .... APA
Assistance Technique de l'Organisation des Nations Unies .... ATONU
Assistance-in-Kind [*Funds*] .... AIK
Assistant [*Military*] .... A
Assistant .... ASS
Assistant .... ASSIST
Assistant .... ASSIST
Assistant (WDMC) .... asst
Assistant (EY) .... ASST
Assistant (DD) .... asst
Assistant [*Navy*] .... AST
Assistant Adjutant .... AA
Assistant Adjutant and Quartermaster-General [*British*] .... AA & QMG
Assistant Adjutant-General [*Military*] .... AAG
Assistant Administrator (GFGA) .... AA
Assistant Air Attache [*British*] .... AAA
Assistant Air Force Postal Clerk (AFM) .... AAFPC
Assistant Airport Traffic Controller (IAA) .... AAPTC
Assistant Airway Traffic Controller (IAA) .... AAWTC
Assistant and Deputy Director of Naval Recruiting [*British*] .... ADDNR
Assistant [*US*] **Army Military Attache** (CINC) .... AARMA
Assistant Auditor Freight Accounts [*Business term*] .... AAFA
Assistant Barrister [*British*] (ROG) .... AB
Assistant Base Operations Manager [*NASA*] (KSC) .... ABOM
Assistant Battalion Officer-of-the-Watch (DNAB) .... ABOOW
Assistant Beach Master [*British*] .... ABM
Assistant Cameraman .... AC
Assistant Camp Commandant [*British*] .... ACC
Assistant Captain [*Worn on assistant captains' uniforms*] [*Hockey*] .... A
Assistant Casework Supervisor [*Red Cross*] .... ACWS
Assistant Cashier [*Banking*] .... AC
Assistant Cashier (MHDB) .... Asst Cash
Assistant Catering Accountant [*British military*] (DMA) .... ACA
Assistant Chaplain-General [*British*] .... ACG
Assistant Chief, Chemical Warfare Service .... ACCWS
Assistant Chief Fire Officer [*British*] .... ACFO
Assistant Chief for Research .... ACR
Assistant Chief Medical Director .... ACMD
Assistant Chief Observer [*Navy*] (NVT) .... ACHOBS
Assistant Chief of Air Staff [*Army British*] .... AC of AS
Assistant Chief of Air Staff [*Army British*] .... ACAS
Assistant Chief of Air Staff (Intelligence) [*Army British*] .... ACAS(I)
Assistant Chief of Air Staff (Operations) [*Army British*] .... ACAS(O)
Assistant Chief of Air Staff (Policy) [*Army British*] .... ACAS(P)
Assistant Chief of Air Staff (Technical) [*Army British*] .... ACAS(T)
Assistant Chief of Air Staff (Technical Requirements) [*Army British*] .... ACAS(TR)
Assistant Chief of Defence Staff [*British Australia*] (NATG) .... ACDS
Assistant Chief of Engineers [*Military*] .... ACE
Assistant Chief of Fleet Support [*Navy British*] .... ACFS
Assistant Chief of Mission [*Foreign Service*] .... ACM
Assistant Chief of Mission Operations [*NASA*] .... ACMO
Assistant Chief of Naval Operations .... ACNO
Assistant Chief of Naval Operations (Communications)/Director, Naval Communications (DNAB) .... ACNO(COMM)/DNC
Assistant Chief of Naval Operations for Communications and Cryptology (IAA) .... ACNOCOMM
Assistant Chief of Naval Operations (Transportation) .... ACNOT
Assistant Chief of Staff .... AC of S
Assistant Chief of Staff (MCD) .... ACOFS
Assistant Chief of Staff .... ACOS
Assistant Chief of Staff .... ACS
Assistant Chief of Staff, Air Force .... AC/SAF
Assistant Chief of Staff for Automation and Communications [*Military*] (AABC) .... ACSAC
Assistant Chief of Staff for Command and Control Information Management .... ACSCCIM
Assistant Chief of Staff for Communications - Electronics [*Army*] (AABC) .... ACSC-E
Assistant Chief of Staff for Force Development [*Army*] .... ACSFOR
Assistant Chief of Staff for Information Management [*Army*] .... ACSIM
Assistant Chief of Staff for Information Management-Command, Control, Communications, and Computers [*Military*] (GFGA) ACSIM-C4
Assistant Chief of Staff for Intelligence [*Washington, DC*] [*Army*] .... ACSI
Assistant Chief of Staff for Reserve Components [*Army*] .... ACSRC
Assistant Chief of Staff for Studies and Analysis [*Air Force*] .... CSA
Assistant Chief of Staff, Intelligence (NATG) .... ACINTEL
Assistant Chief of Staff, Intelligence [*Air Force*] (MCD) .... AFIN
Assistant Chief of Staff, Logistics (NATG) .... ACLOG
Assistant Chief of Staff, Organization and Training Division (NATG) .... ACOT
Assistant Chief of Staff, Plans and Policy Division (NATG) .... ACPANDP
Assistant Chief of Staff, Programs Division (NATG) .... ACPROG
Assistant Chief of Staff, Studies and Analysis [*Air Force*] (MCD) .... ACS/S & A
Assistant Chief of Supplies [*British military*] (DMA) .... ACS
Assistant Chief of the General Staff [*Military British*] .... ACGS
Assistant Chief of the General Staff (Operational Requirements) [*British*] (RDA) .... ACGS(OR)
Assistant Chief of the Imperial General Staff [*British*] .... ACIGS
Assistant Chief of the Naval Staff [*British*] .... ACNS
Assistant Chief of the Naval Staff (Air) [*British*] .... ACNS(A)
Assistant Chief of Transportation [*Army*] .... AC of T
Assistant Chief Patrol Inspector [*Immigration and Naturalization Service*] .... ACPI
Assistant Chief Statistician .... ACS
Assistant Civil Engineer Adviser [*Military British*] .... ACEA
Assistant Clerk [*Navy British*] (ROG) .... AC
Assistant Clerks Association [*A union*] [*British*] .... ACA
Assistant Combat Cargo Officer, Well Deck (CAAL) .... ACCOW
Assistant Combat Information Center Officer (MUGU) .... ACICO
Assistant Command Director [*Military*] (MCD) .... ACD
Assistant Command Duty Officer [*Military*] (MCD) .... ACDO
Assistant Commandant [*Army/Marine Corps*] .... AC
Assistant Commandant [*Coast Guard*] .... CA
Assistant Commandant of the [*US*] **Marine Corp** (DOMA) .... ACMC
Assistant Commissary General .... ACG
Assistant Commissioner .... AC
Assistant Commissioner of the Metropolitan Police [*British*] (DAS) .... ACMP
Assistant Comptroller of the Army for Finance and Accounting .... ACOA(F & A)
Assistant Controller (DCTA) .... AC
Assistant Controller of the Navy [*British*] .... AC of N
Assistant Controller, Personnel and Logistics [*Navy British*] .... ACPL
Assistant Controller, Research and Development [*Admiralty*] [*British*] .... AC(R & D)
Assistant Cook [*British military*] (DMA) .... ACK
Assistant County Architect [*British*] .... ACA
Assistant Cub Master [*Scouting*] .... ACM
Assistant Customs Officer .... ACO
Assistant Data Recording System Analyst (MUGU) .... ADRSA
Assistant Defence Advisor [*British military*] (DMA) .... ADA
Assistant Defense Counsel .... ADC
Assistant Deputy Chief of Naval Material (MCD) .... ADCNM
Assistant Deputy Chief of Naval Operations (DNAB) .... ADCNO
Assistant Deputy Chief of Naval Operations (Civilian Personnel/Equal Employment Opportunity) (DNAB) .... ADCNO(CP/EEO)
Assistant Deputy Chief of Staff for Combat Developments [*Army*] .... ADCSCD
Assistant Deputy Chief of Staff for Logistics [*Army*] .... ADCSLOG
Assistant Deputy Chief of Staff for Logistics for Security Assistance [*Military*] .... ADCSLOG-SA
Assistant Deputy Chief of Staff for Operations and Plans [*Military*] .... ADCSOPS
Assistant Deputy Chief of Staff for Operations and Plans (Joint Affairs) [*Military*] .... ADCSOPS (JA)
Assistant Deputy Chief of Staff for Research, Development, and Acquisition [*Military*] .... ADCSRDA
Assistant Deputy Chief of Staff, in Test and Evaluation [*Army*] .... ADCSTE
Assistant Deputy Judge Advocate General [*Military British*] .... ADJAG
Assistant Deputy Military Governor [*US Military Government, Germany*] .... ADMG
Assistant Deputy Minister [*Canada*] .... ADM
Assistant Deputy Postmaster-General [*Canada*] .... ADPMG
Assistant Deputy Registrar General [*Canada*] .... ADRG
Assistant Director .... AD
Assistant Director, Army Postal Services [*British military*] (DMA) .... ADPS
Assistant Director, Auxiliary Territorial Service [*British military*] (DMA) .... ADATS
Assistant Director, Curatorial .... ADC
Assistant Director, Flight Operations [*NASA*] (KSC) .... ADFO
Assistant Director for Education [*Vietnam*] .... ADEDU
Assistant Director for Legal and Legislative Affairs [*National Security Agency*] [*Obsolete*] .... ADLA
Assistant Director for Plans and Resources [*National Security Agency*] [*Obsolete*] .... ADPR
Assistant Director for Policy and Liaison [*National Security Agency*] [*Obsolete*] .... ADPL
Assistant Director for Training [*National Security Agency*] .... ADT
Assistant Director of Administrative Planning [*Military British*] .... ADAP
Assistant Director of Army Health [*British*] .... ADAH
Assistant Director of Army Psychiatry [*British*] .... ADAP
Assistant Director of Army Welfare Services [*British*] .... ADAWS
Assistant Director of Artillery [*British*] .... ADA
Assistant Director of Ceremonies [*Freemasonry*] .... ADC
Assistant Director of Contracts [*Military British*] .... ADC
Assistant Director of Dental Services .... ADDS
Assistant Director of Expense Accounts [*Navy British*] .... ADEA
Assistant Director of Fortifications and Works [*Military British*] .... ADFW
Assistant Director of Hygiene [*Military British*] .... ADH
Assistant Director of Intelligence [*British military*] (DMA) .... ADI
Assistant Director of Intelligence, Department K [*Air Ministry*] [*British*] .... ADI(K)
Assistant Director of Light Railways [*British military*] (DMA) .... ADLR
Assistant Director of Mechanical Engineering [*British military*] (DMA) .... ADME
Assistant Director of Medical Services .... ADMS
Assistant Director of Naval Accounts [*British*] .... ADNA
Assistant Director of Naval Construction [*British*] .... ADNC
Assistant Director of Naval Intelligence [*British*] .... ADNI
Assistant Director of Nursing (BARN) .... ADN
Assistant Director of Operations Division [*British military*] (DMA) .... ADOD
Assistant Director of Ordnance Factories [*Ministry of Supply*] [*British World War II*] .... ADOF
Assistant Director of Ordnance Services [*British*] .... ADOS
Assistant Director of Pathology [*Military British*] .... ADP
Assistant Director of Psychiatry [*British*] (DAVI) .... ADAP
Assistant Director of Public Relations [*Military British*] .... ADPR
Assistant Director of Railway Transport [*British military*] (DMA) .... ADRT
Assistant Director of Signals (IAA) .... ADSIGS

Assistant Director of Supplies and Transport [*Military British*] ADS & T
Assistant Director of the Army Budget ADAB
Assistant Director of the Army Budget (Financial Systems Management) ADAB (FSM)
Assistant Director of Torpedoes [*Navy British*] ADT
Assistant Director of Transportation [*British military*] (DMA) ADTn
Assistant Director of Veterinary and Remount Services [*British military*] (DMA) ADVRS
Assistant Director of Veterinary Services [*Military British*] ADVS
Assistant Director of Works, Electrical and Mechanical [*Military British*] ADWE & M
Assistant Director-General [*British*] ADG
Assistant Director-General of Medical Services [*Military British*] ADGMS
Assistant Director-General of Transportation [*British military*] (DMA) ADGT
Assistant District Attorney ADA
Assistant District Commission (MCD) ADC
Assistant District Manager (DCTA) ADM
Assistant District Postmaster [*British*] (DCTA) ADP
Assistant Division Commander [*Military*] ADC
Assistant Division Commander for Maneuver [*Military*] (INF) ADC(M)
Assistant Division Communications Electronics Officer [*Military*] (AABC) ADCEO
Assistant Division Engineer [*Army*] (AABC) ADE
Assistant Division Supply Officer [*Army*] ADSO
Assistant Editor [*Publishing*] AE
Assistant Engineer AE
Assistant Executive Engineer [*British*] (DCTA) AEE
Assistant Experimental Officer [*Ministry of Agriculture, Fisheries, and Food*] [*Also, AExO, AXO*] [*British*] AEO
Assistant Experimental Officer [*Ministry of Agriculture, Fisheries, and Food*] [*Also, AEO, AXO*] [*British*] AExO
Assistant Experimental Officer [*Ministry of Agriculture, Fisheries, and Food*] [*Also, AEO, AExO*] [*British*] AXO
Assistant Field Director [*Red Cross*] AFD
Assistant Fighter Director Office [*Navy*] AFDO
Assistant Fire Support Coordinator [*Military*] (AABC) AFSCOORD
Assistant Firemaster [*British*] AFMR
Assistant Flight Director [*NASA*] (KSC) AFD
Assistant Flight Dynamics Officer [*NASA*] AFDO
Assistant Flying Instructor (DA) AFI
Assistant for Development Planning [*Air Force*] AFDAP
Assistant for Materiel Program Control [*Air Force*] AFMPC
Assistant Freight Agent AFA
Assistant Freight Claim Agent AFCA
Assistant Freight Traffic Manager AFTM
Assistant General Freight Agent AGFA
Assistant General Manager [*AEC*] AGM
Assistant General Manager for Administration [*AEC*] AGMA
Assistant General Manager for International Activities [*AEC*] AGMIA
Assistant General Manager for Operations [*AEC*] AGMO
Assistant General Manager for Plans and Production [*AEC*] AGMPP
Assistant General Manager for Research and Development [*AEC*] AGMRD
Assistant General Secretary (DCTA) AGS
Assistant Grand Director of Ceremonies [*Freemasonry*] AGDC
Assistant Grand Sojourner [*Freemasonry*] AGS
Assistant Gunner/Driver [*Military*] (INF) AG/DR
Assistant Head Nurse (AAMN) AHN
Assistant Head of Section (DCTA) AHS
Assistant Head Postmaster (DCTA) AHP
Assistant House Physician AHP
Assistant House Surgeon AHS
Assistant in Nursing AIN
Assistant in Private Practice [*Chiropody*] [*British*] P
Assistant Industrial Manager [*of Naval District*] (MUGU) AIM
Assistant Industrial Manager [*of Naval District*] (MUGU) ASTINDMAN
Assistant Information Officer (DCTA) AIO
Assistant Inspector (DCTA) AI
Assistant Inspector Armourer [*British and Canadian*] [*World War II*] AIA
Assistant Inspector General [*Military*] AIG
Assistant Inspector General for Auditing (DNAB) AIG(A)
Assistant Inspector of Naval Materiel AINM
Assistant Inspector of Naval Materiel AINSMAT
Assistant Inspector of Naval Ordnance AINO
Assistant Inspector of Physical Training [*Military British*] AIPT
Assistant Inspector-General, Royal Irish Constabulary (ROG) AIGRIC
Assistant Instructor AI
Assistant Instructor in Gunnery [*British military*] (DMA) AIG
Assistant Instrumentation Operations Coordination (KSC) AIOC
Assistant Judge Advocate General [*Army*] AJAG
[*The*] **Assistant Judge Advocate General** [*Army*] (AABC) TAJAG
Assistant Judge Advocate General for Civil Law [*Army*] (AABC) AJAG/CIV
Assistant Judge Advocate General for Military Law [*Army*] (AABC) AJAG/MIL
Assistant Laboratory Director ALD
Assistant Language Teacher ALT
Assistant Local Director (DCTA) ALD
Assistant Major-General [*Military British*] (ROG) AM-G
Assistant Manager AM
Assistant Marshal of the Diplomatic Corps [*British*] AMDC
Assistant Master-General of Ordnance [*British*] AMGO
Assistant Masters and Mistresses Association (EAIO) AMMA
Assistant Masters' Association [*British*] AMA
Assistant Medical Officer AMO
Assistant Military Landing Officer [*British and Canadian*] [*World War II*] AMLO
Assistant Military Secretary [*British*] AMS
Assistant Missile Flight Safety Officer (MUGU) AMFSO
Assistant Naval Attache [*British*] ANA
Assistant Naval Science Instructor (DNAB) ANSI
Assistant Naval Stores Officer ANSO
Assistant Navy Mail Clerk ANMC
Assistant Network Controller [*NASA*] (KSC) ANC
Assistant Network Operations Manager [*NASA*] (KSC) ANOM
Assistant Officer in Charge [*DoD*] AOIC
Assistant Operations Director [*Air Force/Army*] (MCD) AOD
Assistant Ordnance Mechanical Engineer [*British military*] (DMA) AOME
Assistant Parachute Jump Instructor [*British military*] (DMA) APJI
Assistant Patrol Leader (DI) APL
Assistant Paymaster AP
Assistant Paymaster [*Marine Corps*] APM
Assistant Polaris Systems Officer [*British military*] (DMA) APSO
Assistant Poor Law Commissioner [*British*] (ROG) APLC
Assistant Postmaster-General [*British*] APMG
Assistant Principal Chaplain [*British*] (ADA) APC
Assistant Private Secretary to the First Sea Lord [*Navy British*] APSFSL
Assistant Professor of Military S cience (INF) APMS
Assistant Project Engineer APE
Assistant Project Manager [*NASA*] (NASA) APM
Assistant Project Manager for Business Administration APMBA
Assistant Project Manager for Logistics APML
Assistant Project Officer APO
Assistant Provost Marshal [*Facetious translation: "A Permanent Malingerer"*] APM
Assistant Public Works Officer APWO
Assistant Quartermaster AQM
Assistant Quartermaster-General [*Military*] AQMG
Assistant Regional Administrator [*Environmental Protection Agency*] (GFGA) ARA
Assistant Regional Commissioner [*IRS*] ARC
Assistant Regional Commissioner Disability Insurance [*Social Security Administration*] (OICC) ARCDI
Assistant Regional Manager ARM
Assistant Registrar (ROG) AR
Assistant Research Officer [*Ministry of Agriculture, Fisheries, and Food*] [*British*] ARO
Assistant Secretary AS
Assistant Secretary, Controller [*Admiralty*] [*British*] AS(C)
Assistant Secretary for Administration and Management [*Department of Labor*] ASAM
Assistant Secretary for Conservation and Renewable Energy ASCRE
Assistant Secretary for Defense Programs ASDP
Assistant Secretary for Employment and Training [*Department of Labor*] ASET
Assistant Secretary for Employment Standards [*Department of Labor*] ASES
Assistant Secretary for Environment, Safety, and Health ASESH
Assistant Secretary for Fossil Energy ASFE
Assistant Secretary for Health [*HEW*] ASH
Assistant Secretary for International Affairs and Energy Emergencies ASIAEE
Assistant Secretary for Labor-Management Relations [*Department of Labor*] ASLMR
Assistant Secretary for Nuclear Energy ASNE
Assistant Secretary for Occupational Safety and Health [*Department of Labor*] ASOSH
Assistant Secretary for Planning and Evaluation [*Department of Health and Human Services*] ASPE
Assistant Secretary for Policy Evaluation and Research [*Department of Labor*] ASPER
Assistant Secretary General (NATG) ASG
Assistant Secretary General (NATG) ASYG
Assistant Secretary General for Air Navigation [*ICAO*] ASGAN
Assistant Secretary General for Infrastructure, Logistics, and Council Operations [*NATO*] ASG ILCO
Assistant Secretary of Defense ASD
Assistant Secretary of Defense (DNAB) ASSTSECDEF
Assistant Secretary of Defense (Administration) (AABC) ASD (A)
Assistant Secretary of Defense (Civil Defense) ASD (CD)
Assistant Secretary of Defense (Communications, Command-Control, and Intelligence) (AABC) ASD(C3I)
Assistant Secretary of Defense (Comptroller) ASD (C)
Assistant Secretary of Defense (Comptroller) (DNAB) ASSTSECDEF(COMPT)
Assistant Secretary of Defense for Acquisition and Logistics ASD(A & L)
Assistant Secretary of Defense for Economic Security (RDA) ASD(ES)
Assistant Secretary of Defense (Force Management and Personnel) (DOMA) ASD(FM & P)
Assistant Secretary of Defense (Health Affairs) (AABC) ASD(HA)
Assistant Secretary of Defense (Health Affairs) (DNAB) ASSTSECDEF(HELAFF)
Assistant Secretary of Defense (Health and Environment) ASD (H & E)
Assistant Secretary of Defense (Health and Medical) ASD/H & M
Assistant Secretary of Defense (Installations and Logistics) ASD (I & L)
Assistant Secretary of Defense (Intelligence) ASD (I)
Assistant Secretary of Defense (Intelligence) (DNAB) ASSTSECDEF(INTEL)
Assistant Secretary of Defense (International Security Affairs) ASD/ISA
Assistant Secretary of Defense (International Security Affairs) (DNAB) ASSTSECDEF(INTSECAFF)
Assistant Secretary of Defense (Legislative Affairs) (DOMA) ASD(LA)
Assistant Secretary of Defense (Manpower) ASD (M)
Assistant Secretary of Defense (Manpower and Reserve Affairs) [*Later, ASD (MRA & L)*] (AABC) ASD (M & RA)
Assistant Secretary of Defense (Manpower, Personnel, and Reserves) ASD/MP & R
Assistant Secretary of Defense (Manpower, Reserve Affairs, and Logistics) [*Formerly, ASD (M & RA)*] ASD (MRA & L)

Assistant Secretary of Defense (Manpower, Reserve Affairs, and Logistics) (DNAB) ... ASSTSECDEF(MPRRESAFFLOG)
Assistant Secretary of Defense (Program Analysis and Evaluation) (AABC) ... ASD (PA & E)
Assistant Secretary of Defense (Properties and Installations) ... ASD/P & I
Assistant Secretary of Defense (Public Affairs) ... ASD (PA)
Assistant Secretary of Defense (Public Affairs) (DNAB) ... ASSTSECDEF(PUBAFF)
Assistant Secretary of Defense (Research and Development) ... ASD/R & D
Assistant Secretary of Defense (Research and Engineering) ... ASD/R & E
Assistant Secretary of Defense (Reserve Affairs) [*DoD*] (GFGA) ... ASD(RA)
Assistant Secretary of Defense (Supply and Logistics) ... ASD/S & L
Assistant Secretary of Defense (Systems Analysis) (AABC) ... ASD (SA)
Assistant Secretary of Defense (Telecommunications) ... ASD (T)
Assistant Secretary of State (DAS) ... ASS
Assistant Secretary of the Air Force ... AS of AF
Assistant Secretary of the Air Force (MCD) ... ASAF
Assistant Secretary of the Air Force ... ASOFAF
Assistant Secretary of the Air Force ... ASTSECAF
Assistant Secretary of the Air Force (Acquisition) (DOMA) ... ASAF(A)
Assistant Secretary of the Air Force (Financial Management) ... ASAF(FM)
Assistant Secretary of the Air Force for Acquisition (AAGC) ... SAF/AQ
Assistant Secretary of the Air Force (Manpower and Personnel) ... SAFMP
Assistant Secretary of the Air Force (Manpower, Reserve Affairs and Installations Logistics) ... ASAF (MRA & 1L)
Assistant Secretary of the Air Force (Materiel) ... ASAFMA
Assistant Secretary of the Air Force (Research and Development) ... SAFRD
Assistant Secretary of the Air Force (Research, Development, and Acquisition) (MCD) ... ASAF(RD & A)
Assistant Secretary of the Air Force (Research, Development, and Logistics) (MCD) ... ASAF(RDL)
Assistant Secretary of the Air Force (Research, Development, and Logistics) ... SAF/AL
Assistant Secretary of the Army ... AS of A
Assistant Secretary of the Army ... ASA
[*The*] **Assistant Secretary of the Army** ... TASA
Assistant Secretary of the Army (Acquisition) ... ASA(A)
Assistant Secretary of the Army (Civil Works) ... ASA(CW)
Assistant Secretary of the Army (Financial Management) ... ASA (FM)
Assistant Secretary of the Army for Installations, Logistics, and Financial Management (MCD) ... IL & FM
Assistant Secretary of the Army (Installations and Logistics) ... ASA (I & L)
Assistant Secretary of the Army (Installations, Logistics, and Financial Management) (AABC) ... ASA(IL & FM)
Assistant Secretary of the Army (Manpower and Reserve Affairs) (AABC) ... ASA (M & RA)
Assistant Secretary of the Army, Materiel (SAA) ... ASAMAT
Assistant Secretary of the Army (Research and Development) ... ASA (R & D)
Assistant Secretary of the Army (Research, Development, and Acquisition) ... ASA(RDA)
Assistant Secretary of the General Staff ... ASGS
Assistant Secretary of the Navy ... ASN
Assistant Secretary of the Navy ... ASTSECNAV
Assistant Secretary of the Navy (Financial Management) ... ASN (FM)
Assistant Secretary of the Navy (Financial Management) (DNAB) ... ASSTSECNAVFINMGMT
Assistant Secretary of the Navy (Financial Management) ... ASTSECNAVFIN
Assistant Secretary of the Navy for Air ... ASTSECNAVAIR
Assistant Secretary of the Navy (Installation and Logistics) ... ASN(I & L)
Assistant Secretary of the Navy (Installation and Logistics) (DNAB) ... ASSTSECNAVINSTLOG
Assistant Secretary of the Navy (Installation and Logistics) ... ASTSECNAVINSLOG
Assistant Secretary of the Navy (Manpower and Reserve Affairs) (MCD) ... ASN(M & RA)
Assistant Secretary of the Navy (Manpower and Reserve Affairs) (DNAB) ... ASSTSECNAVMPRESAFF
Assistant Secretary of the Navy (Research and Development) ... ASN(R & D)
Assistant Secretary of the Navy (Research and Development) (DNAB) ... ASN(RES)
Assistant Secretary of the Navy (Research and Development) (DNAB) ... ASSTSECNAVRES
Assistant Secretary of the Navy (Research and Development) ... ASTSECNAVRESDEV
Assistant Secretary of the Navy (Research, Development, and Acquisition) (DOMA) ... ASN(RD & A)
Assistant Secretary of the Navy (Research, Engineering, and Systems) (DNAB) ... ASN(RE & S)
Assistant Secretary of the Navy (Research, Engineering, and Systems) (DNAB) ... ASSTSECNAVRESENGSYS
Assistant Secretary of the Navy (Shipbuilding and Logistics) (MCD) ... ASN(S & L)
Assistant Secretary of the Navy (Shipbuilding and Logistics) (DNAB) ... ASSTSECNAVSHIPLOG
Assistant Secretary of War ... ASW
Assistant Secretary of War for Air [*World War II*] ... ASWA
Assistant Secretary's Office [*Navy*] ... ASO
Assistant Section Officer [*Air Force British*] ... ASO
Assistant Sector Controller [*Aviation*] (DA) ... ASC
Assistant Sector Programming Leader (SAA) ... ASPL
Assistant Sector System Training Leader (SAA) ... ASSTL
Assistant Senior Naval Officer Landing [*British and Canadian*] [*World War II*] ... ASNOL
Assistant Service Manager [*Automobile sales*] ... ASM
Assistant Solicitor-General (DAS) ... ASG
Assistant Special Agent in Charge ... ASAIC
Assistant Staff Duty Officer (CINC) ... ASDO
Assistant Staff Judge Advocate [*Air Force*] ... ASJA
Assistant Staff Meteorologist [*NASA*] (KSC) ... ASM
Assistant Stage Manager ... ASM
Assistant State Director ... ASD
Assistant Station Master [*British*] (ADA) ... ASM
Assistant Steward [*British military*] (DMA) ... ASTD
Assistant Stores Accountant [*British military*] (DMA) ... ASA
Assistant Superintendent (DCTA) ... A/SUPT
Assistant Superintendent, Range Operations [*NASA*] (KSC) ... ASRO
Assistant Supervisor of Shipbuilding [*Navy*] ... ASOS
Assistant Surgeon (DAS) ... AS
Assistant Surgeon [*Department of Health and Human Services*] (GFGA) ... Asst Surg
Assistant Surgeon General (DAS) ... ASG
Assistant Tactical Officer [*Navy*] (CAAL) ... ATACO
Assistant Test Chief ... ATC
Assistant Test Conductor ... ATC
Assistant Test Director ... ATD
Assistant to the Secretary of Defense (DOMA) ... ATSD
Assistant to the Secretary of Defense (Atomic Energy) ... ATSD (AE)
Assistant to the Secretary of Defense (Intelligence Oversight) (DOMA) ... ATSD(IO)
Assistant to the Secretary of Defense (Intelligence Policy) (DOMA) ... ATSD(IP)
Assistant to the Secretary of Defense (Review and Oversight) ... ATSD(R & O)
Assistant Town Clerk [*British*] ... ATC
Assistant Traffic Manager ... ATM
Assistant Traffic Supervisor (DCTA) ... ATS
Assistant Transmission Controller ... ATC
Assistant Trial Counsel ... ATC
Assistant Under-Secretary (ADA) ... AUS
Assistant Under-Secretary, General [*Air Ministry*] [*British*] ... AUS(G)
Assistant Under-Secretary of State (DAS) ... AUSS
Assistant United States Attorney (EPA) ... AUSA
Assistant Veterans Employment Representative [*Department of Labor*] ... AVER
Assistant Vice Chancellor (DLA) ... AVCH
Assistant Vice Chief of Staff ... AVCS
Assistant Vice Chief of Staff, Army [*Later, AVCSA*] (AABC) ... AVC of SA
Assistant Vice Chief of Staff, Army [*Formerly, AVC of SA*] (AABC) ... AVCSA
Assistant Vice Director for Estimates (MCD) ... DE
Assistant Vice President ... AVP
Assistant Weapons Control Officer ... AWCO
Assistant Writer [*British military*] (DMA) ... AWTR
Assistant Yard Master [*Railroads*] [*British*] ... AYM
Assistant-Commissary-General [*British*] ... Ass Com Gen
Assist-Control Mechanical Ventilation [*Medicine*] ... ACMV
Assisted Control (MEDA) ... AC
Assisted Health Insurance Plan ... AHIP
Assisted Home-Ownership Program [*Canada*] ... AHOP
Assisted Hydrothermal Oxidation [*Of hazardous wastes*] ... AHO
Assisted Living Concepts [*AMEX symbol*] (TTSB) ... ALF
Assisted Living Concepts, Inc. [*AMEX symbol*] (SAG) ... ALF
Assisted Living Concepts, Inc. [*Associated Press*] (SAG) ... AstLiving
Assisted Living Facilities Association of America ... ALFAA
Assisted Maintenance Period [*British military*] (DMA) ... AMP
Assisted Mechanical Ventilation [*Medicine*] (DAVI) ... AMV
Assisted Places Committee [*Education*] [*British*] ... APC
Assisted Places Scheme (AIE) ... APS
Assisted Rental Program [*Canada*] ... ARP
Assisted Resonance (NTCM) ... AR
Assisted Takeoff [*British aviation and rocket term*] ... ATO
Assisted Takeoff System ... ATOS
Assisted-Draught Crossflow Tower (PDAA) ... ADCT
Assisted-Living Facility [*Health care*] ... ALF
Assistent [*Assistant*] [*German*] ... Assist
Assisting ... ASSTG
Assisting Women to Advance through Resources and Encouragement Project (EDAC) ... AWARE
Assisting Work Center ... AWC
Assistive Device Center [*Research center*] (RCD) ... ADC
Assistive Listening Device (WYGK) ... ALD
Assistive Listening Devices (PAZ) ... ALDs
Assiut [*Egypt*] [*Airport symbol*] (AD) ... ATZ
Assize Rolls [*British*] ... ASS
Assizes of Jerusalem [*A publication*] (DLA) ... Ass Jerus
Asso and Manuel's Institutes of Spanish Civil Law [*A publication*] (DLA) ... Asso & Man
Assoc Estates Rlty 9.75% Dep Pfd [*NYSE symbol*] (TTSB) ... AECPrA
Associacao Brasileira de Imprensa [*Brazilian Press Association*] ... ABI
Associacao Brasileiro dos Colectionadores de Discos [*Record label*] [*Brazil*] ... ABCD
Associacao Catolica Interamericana de Filosofia (EAIO) ... ACIF
Associacao Civica Angolana [*Political party*] (EY) ... ACA
Associacao Internacional de Missoes dos Israelitas [*International Board of Jewish Missions*] (EAIO) ... AIMI
Associacao Latino-Americana de Direito Agrario ... ALADA
Associacao Social Democrata Independente [*Independent Social Democrat Association*] [*Portugal Political party*] (PPE) ... ASDI
Associacao Universitaria Interamericana [*Interamerican University Association*] [*Portuguese*] ... AUI
Associacion Latino Americana para la Promocion de l'Habitat la Arquitectura y elUrbanismo [*Latin American Association for the Promotion of the Habitat, Architecture and Town Planning*] [*Ecuador*] (PDAA) ... ALAHUA
Associate [*In an academic degree*] ... A
Associate ... ASSO

Associate [*or Association*] (AFM) .... ASSOC
Associate .... ASSOC
Associate (AAGC) .... Assoc
Associate Administrator [*NASA*] .... AA
Associate Administrator for Information Systems [*Social and Rehabilitation Service, HEW*] .... AAIS
Associate Administrator for Management [*Social and Rehabilitation Service, HEW*] .... AA/M
Associate Administrator for Manned Space Flight [*NASA*] (KSC) .... AA/MSF
Associate Administrator for Minority Small Business and Capital Ownership Development (AAGC) .... AA/MSB&COD
Associate Administrator for NAS Development [*FAA*] (TAG) .... AND
Associate Administrator for Space Flight [*NASA*] (MCD) .... AASF
Associate Chief Medical Director (DMAA) .... ACMD
Associate Citizens for Responsible Education [*Group opposing sex education in schools*] .... ACRE
Associate Client Program [*Business International Corp.*] [*Information service or system*] (IID) .... ACP
Associate, College of Violinists .... ACV
Associate Collegiate Players .... ACP
Associate Committee of Geodesy and Geophysics [*Canada*] .... ACGG
Associate Committee on Aerodynamics [*National Research Council*] [*Canada*] .... ACOA
Associate Committee on Air Cushion Technology [*Canada*] (HGAA) .... ACACT
Associate Committee on Aviation Medical Research [*Canada*] .... ACAMR
Associate Committee on Geo-Technical Research [*Canada*] (HGAA) .... ACGR
Associate Committee on the National Building Code [*National Research Council Canada*] .... ACNBC
Associate Computer Professional .... ACP
Associate Contractor .... AC
Associate Contractor (SAA) .... ACR
Associate Contractor Agreement (MCD) .... ACA
Associate Contractor Program Manager [*NASA*] (NASA) .... ACPM
Associate Contractor Projects Office [*NASA*] (NASA) .... ACPO
Associate Creative Director [*Advertising*] (WDMC) .... ACD
Associate Credit Executive [*Society of Certified Consumer Credit Executives*] [*Designation awarded by*] .... ACE
Associate Degree .... AD
Associate Degree Completion Program [*Navy*] (NG) .... ADCOP
Associate Degree in Nursing .... ADN
Associate Deputy Director for Operations/Military Affairs .... ADDO/MA
Associate Diploma .... AssocDip
Associate Diploma Built Environment Technician .... AssocDipBltEnvir
Associate Diploma in Aboriginal Community Management and Development .... AssocDipAbComMgt & Dev
Associate Diploma in Aboriginal Health .... AssocDipAbHlth
Associate Diploma in Aboriginal Health and Community Development .... AssocDipAHCD
Associate Diploma in Aboriginal Studies .... ADipAborStud
Associate Diploma in Aboriginal Studies .... AssocDipAbStudies
Associate Diploma in Accounting .... AssocDipAcctg
Associate Diploma in Administration .... AssocDipAdmin
Associate Diploma in Advertising .... AssocDipAdvrt
Associate Diploma in Agricultural Production .... AssocDipAgProd
Associate Diploma in Agricultural Services .... AssocDipAgServs
Associate Diploma in Agriculture .... AssocDipAg
Associate Diploma in Agriculture .... AssocDipAgr
Associate Diploma in Applied Biology .... AssocDipAppBiol
Associate Diploma in Applied Science .... AssocDipAppSc
Associate Diploma in Applied Science (Agriculture) .... AssocDipAppSci(Ag)
Associate Diploma in Applied Science (Animal Science) .... AssocDipAppSci(AnimalSc)
Associate Diploma in Applied Science (Animal Technology) .... AssocDipAppSci(AnimalTech)
Associate Diploma in Applied Science (Grain Management) .... AssocDipAppSci(GrainMgmt)
Associate Diploma in Architectural Drafting .... AssocDipArchDraft
Associate Diploma in Architectural Technology .... AssocDipArchTech
Associate Diploma in Arts (ADA) .... ADipA
Associate Diploma in Arts .... AssocDipArts
Associate Diploma in Arts (Applied Photography) .... AssocDipArts(AppPhotog)
Associate Diploma in Arts (Commercial Art) .... AssocDipArts(ComArt)
Associate Diploma in Asian Studies .... AssocDipAsianSt
Associate Diploma in Biological Science (Animal Technology) .... AssocDipBiolSc(AnimalTech)
Associate Diploma in Building Construction .... AssocDipBuildCons
Associate Diploma in Business .... AssocDipBus
Associate Diploma in Cartography (ADA) .... AssocDipCart
Associate Diploma in Civil Engineering .... AssocDipCivEng
Associate Diploma in Clinical Laboratory Techniques .... AssocDipClinLabTech
Associate Diploma in Clinical Nursing Studies (Gerontology) .... AssocDipClinNursStud(Gerontol)
Associate Diploma in Community Health Nursing .... AssocDipCHN
Associate Diploma in Computer Applications .... AssocDipCompAppl
Associate Diploma in Computing .... ADC
Associate Diploma in Diversional Therapy .... AssocDipDT
Associate Diploma in Education .... AssocDipEd
Associate Diploma in Electrical Engineering .... AssocDipElecEng
Associate Diploma in Fine Arts .... ADipFA
Associate Diploma in Forestry .... AssDipFor
Associate Diploma in Forestry .... AssocDipFor
Associate Diploma in Furniture Technology .... AssocDipFurnTechnology
Associate Diploma in Geology .... ADipGeol
Associate Diploma in Horse Management .... AssocDipHorseMgmt
Associate Diploma in Horticulture .... AssocDipHort

Associate Diploma in Human Studies .... AssocDipHumanSt
Associate Diploma in International Trade .... AssocDipIntTrade
Associate Diploma in Legal Practice .... AssocDipLegPrac
Associate Diploma in Library Studies .... ADipLibStud
Associate Diploma in Local and Applied History .... AssocDipLoc&AppHist
Associate Diploma in Marketing .... AssocDipMktg
Associate Diploma in Marketing and Japanese .... AssocDipMktgJap
Associate Diploma in Mechanical Engineering .... ADipME
Associate Diploma in Mechanical Engineering .... AssocDipMechEng
Associate Diploma in Medical Laboratory Technology .... AssocDipMedLabTech
Associate Diploma in Music .... AssocDipMus
Associate Diploma in Nurse Education .... AssocDipNursEd
Associate Diploma in Nursing Studies .... AssocDipNursStudies
Associate Diploma in Occupational Health and Safety .... AssocDipOccHlth&Saft
Associate Diploma in Office Administration .... AssocDipOffAdmin
Associate Diploma in Photography .... ADipPhot
Associate Diploma in Physiotherapy .... ADipPhysio
Associate Diploma in Political Studies .... AssocDipPolSt
Associate Diploma in Professional Writing .... ADipProWri
Associate Diploma in Recreation .... ADipRec
Associate Diploma in Recreation .... AssocDipRec
Associate Diploma in Rehabilitation Counselling .... AssocDipRc
Associate Diploma in Science .... AssocDipSc
Associate Diploma in Science (Animal Science) .... AssocDipSc(AnimalScience)
Associate Diploma in Science (Systems Agriculture) .... AssocDipSc(SystemsAg)
Associate Diploma in Security Management .... AssocDipSecMgt
Associate Diploma in Small Business Management .... AssocDipSmallBusMgt
Associate Diploma in Social Welfare .... ADipSocWel
Associate Diploma in Social Work .... ADipSW
Associate Diploma in Sports Science .... AssocDipSptSc
Associate Diploma in Surveying and Mapping .... AssocDipSurvMap
Associate Diploma in Training and Development .... AssocDipTrainDev
Associate Diploma in Valuation .... ADipVal
Associate Diploma of Mining and Mineral Technology .... AssocDipMMT
Associate Diploma of Modern Languages .... AssocDipModLang
Associate Diploma of Social Science .... AssocDipSocSc
Associate Diploma of Surveying .... AssocDipSurv
Associate Director .... AD
Associate Directorate for Design [*Kennedy Space Center*] [*NASA*] (NASA) .... DD
Associate Directorate for Facilities and Systems Management [*Kennedy Space Center*] [*NASA*] (NASA) .... DF
Associate Directorate for LPS [*Launch Processing System*] Development [*Kennedy Space Center*] [*NASA*] (NASA) .... DL
Associate Editor [*Publishing*] .... AE
Associate Enforcement Counsel [*Environmental Protection Agency*] (GFGA) .... AEC
Associate Engraver [*British*] (ROG) .... AE
Associate Engraver, Royal Academy [*British*] .... AERA
Associate Fellow (ADA) .... AF
Associate Fellow of American College of Allergists (DHSM) .... AFACAL
Associate Fellow of the American Institute of Aeronautics and Astronautics [*Formerly, AFIAS*] .... AFAIAA
Associate Fellow of the British Interplanetary Society (DI) .... AFBIS
Associate Fellow of the Canadian Aeronautic and Space Institute (DD) .... AFCASI
Associate Fellow of the Canadian Aeronautical Institute .... AFCAI
Associate Fellow of the Catering Institute of Australia .... AFCIA
Associate Fellow of the Institute of Aeronautical Sciences [*Later, AFAIAA*] .... AFIAS
Associate Fellow of the Institute of Civil Defence [*British*] .... AFICD
Associate Fellow of the Institute of Industrial Managers [*British*] .... AFIIM
Associate Fellow of the Institute of Mathematics and Its Applications [*British*] (DBQ) .... AFIMA
Associate Fellow of the Institute of Petroleum [*British*] .... AF Inst Pet
Associate Fellow of the Royal Aeronautical Society [*British*] .... AFR Ae S
Associate Fellow of the Royal Aeronautical Society [*British*] .... AFRAS
Associate Fellow of the Society of Electronic and Radio Technicians [*British*] (DBQ) .... AFSERT
Associate Fellow of the Society of Licensed Aircraft Engineers and Technologists [*British*] (DBQ) .... AFSLAET
Associate Fellowship of Youth Development [*British*] (DBQ) .... FYDA
Associate for Radiation Research [*British*] .... ARR
Associate for Reform of Latin Teaching [*British*] .... ARLT
Associate for Religious Education for Teachers and Lecturers [*British*] .... ARETL
Associate for Research in Ophthalmology (DMAA) .... ARO
Associate in Accounting .... AA
Associate in Administration .... A Adm
Associate in Aeronautical Engineering .... A Ae E
Associate in Agriculture .... A Agri
Associate in Agriculture (NADA) .... AAgric
Associate in Air-Conditioning and Refrigeration Technology .... AA-C & Ref Tech
Associate in Applied Arts .... AAA
Associate in Applied Science .... AAS
Associate in Architecture .... A Arch
Associate in Arts .... AA
Associate in Arts (ROG) .... AIA
Associate in Arts in Agriculture .... AA Ag
Associate in Arts in Arts and Science .... AAA & S
Associate in Arts in Business .... AA Bus
Associate in Arts in Business .... AAB
Associate in Arts in Fine Arts .... AAFA
Associate in Arts in Home Economics .... AAHE
Associate in Arts in Judaic Studies (BJA) .... AAJS
Associate in Arts in Law Enforcement .... AALE
Associate in Arts in Liberal Arts .... AALA

Associate in Arts in Music	AAMus
Associate in Arts in Nursing	AAN
Associate in Arts in Terminal Education	AA Ter Ed
Associate in Automotive Technology	AA Tech
Associate in Aviation Technology	A Av Tech
Associate in Business	AB
Associate in Business Administration	ABA
Associate in Business Administration	ABus
Associate in Business Management	ABM
Associate in Business Management	ASBM
Associate in Business Science	ABS
Associate in Business Technology	ABT
Associate in Chemistry	A Chem
Associate in Commerce	A Com
Associate in Commerce	AC
Associate in Commercial Arts	ACA
Associate in Commercial Education	AC Ed
Associate in Commercial Science	ACS
Associate in Criminal Justice	ACJ
Associate in Customer Service [Canada] (DD)	ACS
Associate in Diesel Technology	A Dies Tech
Associate in Drafting and Design	A Dr & Dgn
Associate in Education	A Ed
Associate in Education	AE
Associate in Electrical Technology (IAA)	AELECTECH
Associate in Electrical Technology	AET
Associate in Electronics Technology (IAA)	AELECTRTECHN
Associate in Elementary Education	A El Ed
Associate in Engineering	A Eng
Associate in Engineering	A Engr
Associate in Engineering	AE
Associate in Engineering	AEE
Associate in Engineering	ASE
Associate in Engineering Administration	AEA
Associate in Engineering Electronics	A Eng Elect
Associate in Engineering Technology	AET
Associate in Engineering Technology (WGA)	ASET
Associate in English	A En
Associate in Fine Arts	AFA
Associate in Fine Arts in Art	AFA Art
Associate in Fine Arts in Dance	AFA Dance
Associate in Fine Arts in Drama	AFA Drama
Associate in Fine Arts in Music	AFA Mus
Associate in General Education	A in G Ed
Associate in General Education	AGE
Associate in General Education	AGEd
Associate in General Studies	AGS
Associate in Home Economics	AH Ec
Associate in Home Economics	AHE
Associate in Industrial Education	AI Ed
Associate in Industrial Management	AIM
Associate in Industrial Management	ASIM
Associate in Journalism	AJ
Associate in Letters	A Litt
Associate in Letters, Arts, and Sciences	ALAS
Associate in Liberal Arts	ALA
Associate in Literature	A Lit
Associate in Local Government Administration (ADA)	ALGA
Associate in Mechanical Technology	AMT
Associate in Medical Technology	AMT
Associate in Metallurgy [British]	A Met
Associate in Music	AMus
Associate in Music of the London College of Music (ROG)	A MUS LCM
Associate in Music of Trinity College of Music, London [British] (DBQ)	AMusTCL
Associate in Nursing	AN
Associate in Nursing	ASN
Associate in Nursing Science (DAVI)	ANS
Associate in Nursing Science	ASN
Associate in Philosophy	A Ph
Associate in Physical Education	AP Ed
Associate in Practical Arts	APA
Associate in Public Administration	APA
Associate in Public Service Technology	APST
Associate in Recreation Leadership	ARL
Associate in Religion	A Rel
Associate in Religious Arts	ARA
Associate in Religious Education	ARE
Associate in Retailing	AR
Associate in Risk Management [Canada] (DD)	ARM
Associate in Science	AS
Associate in Science	ASc
Associate in Science	Assoc Sc
Associate in Science Education	ASEd
Associate in Science in Basic Engineering	ASBE
Associate in Science in Business	ASB
Associate in Science in Commerce	ASC
Associate in Science in Electronic Engineering (IAA)	ASEE
Associate in Science in Electronic Engineering Technology	ASEET
Associate in Science in Engineering	ASE
Associate in Science in Medical Secretarial	ASMS
Associate in Science in Recreation Leadership	ASRL
Associate in Science in Secretarial Studies	ASSS
Associate in Science in Teacher Training	ASTT
Associate in Secretarial Administration	ASA

Associate in Secretarial Science	A Se S
Associate in Secretarial Science	A Se Sc
Associate in Secretarial Science	ASS
Associate in Secretarial Science	SSA
Associate in Secretarial Studies	ASS
Associate in Specialized Business	ASB
Associate in Technical Arts	ATA
Associate in Technical Education	ATE
Associate in Technology	AT
Associate in Technology (NADA)	ATECH
Associate in the Technology of Surface Coatings [British] (DBQ)	ATSC
Associate in Theology	A Th
Associate in Theology (ADA)	ThA
Associate in Therapy	ATh
Associate in Wildlife Technology	AWT
Associate Infantry Officer Career Course [Army]	AIOCC
Associate, Institute of Hospital Administrators [or Administration] (DAVI)	AHA
Associate Insurance Broker (DD)	AIB
Associate Jewelers [Defunct] (EA)	AJ
Associate Justice [US Supreme Court]	AJ
Associate Logistics Executive Development Course	ALEDC
Associate Managing Editor (WDMC)	AME
Associate Member	AM
Associate Member of Engineering Institute of Canada	AMEIC
Associate Member of Institute of Accredited Public Accountants	APA
Associate Member of Institution of Aeronautical Engineers [British]	AMI Ae E
Associate Member of the American Society of Civil Engineers	AM Am Soc CE
Associate Member of the American Society of Mechanical Engineers	AMASME
Associate Member of the Association of Business Executives [British] (DCTA)	AMABE
Associate Member of the Association of Medical Secretaries, Practice Administrators, and Receptionists [British] (DBQ)	AAMS
Associate Member of the Association of Supervisory and Executive Engineers [British] (DBQ)	AMASEE
Associate Member of the Australian Association of Neurologists	AMAAN
Associate Member of the British Arts Association (DBQ)	AMBA
Associate Member of the British Computer Society (DBQ)	AMBCS
Associate Member of the British Institute of Management	AMBIM
Associate Member of the British Institution of Radio Engineers [Later, AMIERE]	AM Brit IRE
Associate Member of the Chartered Institute of Transport [British] (DI)	AMCIT
Associate Member of the Commonwealth Institute of Accountants [British] (ODBW)	AICA
Associate Member of the Construction Surveyor's Institute [British] (DBQ)	AMCSI
Associate Member of the Corporation of Insurance Brokers [British] (DI)	AMCIB
Associate Member of the Fundraising Institute-Australia, Inc. (NFD)	AMFIA
Associate Member of the Guild of Cleaners and Launderers [British] (DBQ)	AGCL
Associate Member of the Highway and Traffic Technicians' Association [British] (DBQ)	AMHTTA
Associate Member of the Incorporated Advertising Managers' Association (DGA)	AMIAMA
Associate Member of the Institute of Aeronautical Engineers [British] (DI)	AMIAE
Associate Member of the Institute of Asphalt Technology [British] (DBQ)	AMIAT
Associate Member of the Institute of Automobile Engineers [British] (ROG)	AMIAE
Associate Member of the Institute of Automotive Engineer Assessors [British] (DBQ)	AMInstAEA
Associate Member of the Institute of Biology [British] (DI)	AIBiol
Associate Member of the Institute of Business and Technical Management [British] (DBQ)	AMInstBTM
Associate Member of the Institute of Clerks of Works [British] (DI)	AMICW
Associate Member of the Institute of Commercial Management [British] (DCTA)	AM Inst CM
Associate Member of the Institute of Credit Management [British] (DBQ)	MICM
Associate Member of the Institute of Electronics [British]	AM Inst E
Associate Member of the Institute of Employment Consultants [British] (DBQ)	AECI
Associate Member of the Institute of Export [British]	AMIEx
Associate Member of the Institute of Fuel [British]	AM Inst F
Associate Member of the Institute of Fuel [British]	AMIF
Associate Member of the Institute of Gas Engineers [British] (ROG)	AM INST GE
Associate Member of the Institute of Heating and Ventilating Engineers [British] (DI)	AMIHVE
Associate Member of the Institute of Management Specialists [British] (DBQ)	AMIMS
Associate Member of the Institute of Manufacturing [British] (DBQ)	AMIManf
Associate Member of the Institute of Marine Engineers [British]	AMI Mar E
Associate Member of the Institute of Marine Engineers [British] (DS)	AMIME
Associate Member of the Institute of Materials Handling [British] (DBQ)	AMIMH
Associate Member of the Institute of Medical and Biological Illustration [British] (DBQ)	AIMBI
Associate Member of the Institute of Metallurgists [British] (DBQ)	AMIM
Associate Member of the Institute of Plant Engineers [British]	AMI Plant E
Associate Member of the Institute of Practitioners in Advertising [British] (DI)	AMIPA

Associate Member of the Institute of Printing (DGA) .... AMIOP
Associate Member of the Institute of Printing Management (DGA) ..... AMI PTG M
Associate Member of the Institute of Production Control [*British*] (DBQ) .... AMIPC
Associate Member of the Institute of Public Cleansing [*British*] (DI) ..... AMInstPC
Associate Member of the Institute of Quality Assurance (ODBW) .... AMIQM
Associate Member of the Institute of Quarrying [*British*] (DBQ) .... AMIQ
Associate Member of the Institute of Radio and Electronic Engineers (Australia) .... AMIREE (Aust)
Associate Member of the Institute of Refrigeration [*British*] .... AMInstR
Associate Member of the Institute of Road Transport Engineers [*British*] (DBQ) .... AMIRTE
Associate Member of the Institute of Structural Engineers [*British*].... AMIStruct E
Associate Member of the Institute of Supervisory Management [*British*] (DBQ) .... AMISM
Associate Member of the Institute of the Motor Industry [*British*] .... AMIMI
Associate Member of the Institute of Training and Development [*British*] (DBQ) .... AMITD
Associate Member of the Institute of Transport [*British*] (EY) .... AMInstT
Associate Member of the Institute of Transport Administration [*British*] (DCTA) .... AM Inst TA
Associate Member of the Institute of Water Engineers [*British*] .... AMI Water E
Associate Member of the Institute of Water Pollution Control [*British*] (DBQ) .... AMIWPC
Associate Member of the Institute of Welding [*British*] .... AM Inst W
Associate Member of the Institute of Welding [*British*] .... AMIW
Associate Member of the Institute of Wood Science [*British*] (DBQ) .... AIWSc
Associate Member of the Institute of Work Study Practitioners [*British*] .... AIWSP
Associate Member of the Institution of Aeronautical Engineers [*British*] .... AssocMIAeE
Associate Member of the Institution of Agricultural Engineers [*British*] .... AMIAgrE
Associate Member of the Institution of Body Engineers [*British*] (DBQ) .... AMBEI
Associate Member of the Institution of British Engineers .... AMInstBE
Associate Member of the Institution of Chemical Engineers [*British*] .... AMI Chem E
Associate Member of the Institution of Civil Engineers [*Later, MICE*] [*British*] .... AMICE
Associate Member of the Institution of Civil Engineers [*British*] (EY)..... AMInstCE
Associate (Member) of the Institution of Civil Engineers [*British*] .... Assoc (M) Inst CE
Associate Member of the Institution of Corrosion Science and Technology [*British*] (DBQ) .... AMICorrST
Associate Member of the Institution of Electrical and Electronics Incorporated Engineers [*British*] (DBQ) .... AMIElecIE
Associate Member of the Institution of Electrical Engineers [*Later, MIEE*] [*British*] (EY) .... AMIEE
Associate Member of the Institution of Electronic and Radio Engineers [*Formerly, AM Brit IRE*] [*British*] .... AMIERE
Associate Member of the Institution of Engineering Designers [*British*] .... AMIED
Associate Member of the Institution of Fire Engineers [*British*] .... AMIFireE
Associate Member of the Institution of Gas Engineers [*British*] .... AMIGasE
Associate Member of the Institution of Highway Engineers [*British*] (DBQ) .... AMIHT
Associate Member of the Institution of Highway Engineers [*British*] ..... AMInstHE
Associate Member of the Institution of Locomotive Engineers [*British*] .... AMILocoE
Associate Member of the Institution of Mechanical and General Technician Engineers [*British*] (DBQ) .... AMIMGTechE
Associate Member of the Institution of Mechanical Engineers [*Later, MIMechE*] [*British*] (EY) .... AMIMechE
Associate Member of the Institution of Mining and Metallurgy [*British*].... AMIMM
Associate Member of the Institution of Mining Engineers [*British*] .... AMIME
Associate Member of the Institution of Mining Engineers [*British*] (EY) .... AMIMinE
Associate Member of the Institution of Municipal Engineers [*British*] .... AMI Mun E
Associate Member of the Institution of Naval Architects [*British*] .... AMINA
Associate Member of the Institution of Occupational Safety and Health [*British*] (DCTA) .... AMIOSH
Associate Member of the Institution of Production Engineers [*British*] ..... AMIPE
Associate Member of the Institution of Production Engineers [*British*] (DBQ) .... AMI-ProdE
Associate Member of the Institution of Sales Management [*British*] (DI) .... AMInstSM
Associate Member of the Institution of Water Engineers and Scientists [*British*] (DI) .... AMIWES
Associate Member of the Institution of Works and Highways Technician Engineers [*British*] (DBQ) .... AMIWHTE
Associate Member of the Institution of Works Managers [*British*] .... AMIWM
Associate Member of the International Institute of Arts and Letters .... AIAL
Associate Member of the International Institute of Social Economics [*British*] (DBQ) .... AMIISE
Associate Member of the Master Photographers Association [*British*] (DBQ) .... AMPA
Associate Member of the Nautical Institute [*British*] .... AMNI
Associate Member of the Pensions Management Institute [*British*] (DBQ) .... APMI
Associate Member of the Royal Institution of Naval Architects [*British*] .... AMRINA
Associate Member of the Royal School of Church Music [*British*] .... ARSCM
Associate Member of the Royal Society of Health [*Formerly, ARSH*] [*British*] .... AMRSH
Associate Member of the Society of Cardiological Technicians [*British*] (DBQ) .... ASCT
Associate Member of the Society of Certified Professionals [*British*] (DBQ) .... AMSCP
Associate Member of the Society of Commercial Teachers [*British*] (DBQ) .... ASCT
Associate Member of the Society of Electronic and Radio Technicians [*British*] (DBQ) .... AMSERT
Associate Member of the Society of Engineers, Inc. [*British*] (DBQ) .... AMSE
Associate Member of the Society of Hearing Aid Audiologists [*British*] (DI) .... AMSHAA
Associate Member of the Society of Licensed Aircraft Engineers and Technologists [*British*] (DBQ) .... AMSLAET
Associate Member of the Town Planning Institute [*British*] (EY) .... AMTPI
Associate Member of the Women's Engineering Society [*British*] (DBQ) .... AMWES
Associate Mercantile Market (DICI) .... AMM
Associate Missionaries of the Assumption (EA) .... AMA
Associate, National Academician .... ANA
Associate of Accountants' and Executives' Corp. of Canada .... AAE
Associate of American Guild of Organists .... AAGO
Associate of Association of Certified and Corporate Accountants [*British*] .... AACCA
Associate of British Theatre Technicians .... ABTT
Associate of Canadian Institute of Chemistry .... ACIC
Associate of Heriot-Watt College, Edinburgh .... AH-WC
Associate of Incorporated Secretaries Association .... AISA
Associate of King's College [*London*] .... AKC
Associate of King's College London .... AKCL
Associate of Manchester College of Technology [*British*] .... AMCT
Associate of New Era Academy of Dance [*British*] .... ANEA
Associate of Public Health Association .... APHA
Associate of Queen's College [*London*] .... AQC
Associate of Speech and Drama, Australia .... ASDA
Associate of the Ambulance Service Institute [*British*] (DBQ) .... AASI
Associate of the American Institute of Electrical Engineers .... AAIEE
Associate of the American Institute of Mining and Metallurgical Engineers .... AAIMME
Associate of the American Institute of Physics .... AAIP
Associate of the American Society of Mechanical Engineers .... AASME
Associate of the Association of Computer Professionals [*British*] (DBQ) .... AACP
Associate of the Association of Cost Accountants (ADA) .... AACA
Associate of the Association of Health Care Information and Medical Record Officers [*British*] (DBQ) .... AMR
Associate of the Association of International Accountants [*British*] .... AAIA
Associate of the Australian College of Health .... AHA
Associate of the Australian Institute of Food Science and Technology .... AAIFScT
Associate of the Australian Psychological Society .... AAPS
Associate of the Benesh Institute of Choreology [*British*] (DBQ) .... AIChor
Associate of the Birmingham and Midland Institute School of Music [*British*] .... ABSM
Associate of the British Association of Accountants and Auditors (BARN) .... ABAA
Associate of the British Ballet Organisation .... ABBO
Associate of the British Display Society (DBQ) .... ABDS
Associate of the British Hypnotherapy Association (DBQ) .... ABHA
Associate of the British Institute of Certified Carpenters .... ABICC
Associate of the British Institute of Interior Design (DBQ) .... ABID
Associate of the British Institute of Professional Photography (DBQ) .... ABIPP
Associate of the British Institution of Radio Engineers .... Assoc Brit IRE
Associate of the British Interplanetary Society (IAA) .... ABIS
Associate of the British Psychological Society .... AB Ps S
Associate of the British Society of Commerce .... ABSC
Associate of the Building Societies [*Institute*] [*British*] [*German*] (BARN) .... ABS
Associate of the Camborne School of Mines [*British*] .... ACSM
Associate of the Canadian Bankers Association (DD) .... ACBA
Associate of the Canadian College of Organists .... ACCO
Associate of the Casualty Actuarial Society [*Designation awarded by Casualty Actuarial Society*] .... ACAS
Associate of the Chartered Auctioneers' and Estate Agents' Institute [*British*] .... AAI
Associate of the Chartered Building Societies Institute [*British*] (DBQ) ...... ACBSI
Associate of the Chartered Institute of Arbitrators [*British*] (DBQ) .... ACIArb
Associate of the Chartered Institute of Loss Adjustors [*Insurance*] .... ACILA
Associate of the Chartered Institute of Secretaries [*Later, Institute of Chartered Secretaries and Administrators*] [*British*] (EY) .... ACIS
Associate of the Chartered Insurance Institute [*British*] (EY) .... ACII
Associate of the Chartered Land Agents' Society [*British*] .... ALAS
Associate of the City and Guilds of London Institute [*British*] .... ACGI
Associate of the College of Craft Education [*British*] (DI) .... ACCEd
Associate of the College of Engineering [*British*] (ROG) .... ACE
Associate of the College of Preceptors [*British*] .... ACP
Associate of the College of Technology [*British*] .... ACT
Associate of the Confederation of Professional Management [*British*] (DBQ) .... ACPM
Associate of the Corporation of Insurance Agents (ODBW) .... ACIA
Associate of the Corporation of Insurance Brokers [*Canada*] (DD) .... ACIB
Associate of the Corporation of Insurance Brokers [*British*] .... ACIB
Associate of the Corporation of Secretaries [*Associate of the Corp. of Certified Secretaries*] [*Acronym is based on former name, British*] (DI) ...... ACCS
Associate of the Drama Board (Education) [*British*] (DI) .... ADB(Ed)
Associate of the Drama Board (Special) [*British*] (DI) .... ADB(S)
Associate of the Educational Institute of Scotland .... AEIS
Associate of the Faculty of Actuaries [*British*] .... AFA

Associate of the Faculty of Architects and Surveyors [British] ..... AFAS
Associate of the Faculty of Architects and Surveyors [British] (DBQ) ..... AFS
Associate of the Faculty of Astrological Studies [British] ..... AFAS
Associate of the Faculty of Commerce and Industry [British] (DBQ) ..... AFCI
Associate of the Faculty of Physiatrics [British] ..... AFPhys
Associate of the Faculty of Teachers in Commerce [British] (DBQ) ..... AFTCom
Associate of the Farriers Co. of London [British] (DI) ..... AFCL
Associate of the Federal Institute of Accountants [Australia] (ODBW) ..... AFIA
Associate of the Geological Society [British] (DBQ) ..... AMIGeol
Associate of the Greek Institute [British] (DI) ..... AGI
Associate of the Guildhall School of Music [British] ..... AGSM
Associate of the Hotel, Catering, and Institutional Management Association [British] (DBQ) ..... AHCIMA
Associate of the Imperial College of Tropical Agriculture [British] ..... AICTA
Associate of the Imperial Society of Teachers of Dancing [British] (DBQ) ..... AISTD
Associate of the Incorporated British Institute of Certified Carpenters (DI) ..... AIBICC
Associate of the Incorporated Guild of Church Musicians [British] ..... AIGCM
Associate of the Incorporated Society of Auctioneers and Landed Property Agents [British] ..... AALPA
Associate of the Incorporated Society of Organ Builders [British] (DBQ) ..... AISOB
Associate of the Incorporated Society of Valuers and Auctioneers [British] (DBQ) ..... ASVA
Associate of the Institute of Actuaries [British] ..... AIA
Associate of the Institute of Administrative Accounting and Data Processing [British] (DCTA) ..... AAAI
Associate of the Institute of Administrative Management [British] (DCTA) ..... A Inst AM
Associate of the Institute of Animal Technicians [British] (DI) ..... AIAT
Associate of the Institute of Arbitrators [British] ..... AI Arb
Associate of the Institute of Arbitrators Australia ..... AIArbA
Associate of the Institute of Automobile Engineers [British] (MCD) ..... AIAE
Associate of the Institute of Automotive Engineer Assessors [British] (DBQ) ..... AssocInstAEA
Associate of the Institute of Automotive Engineer Assessors (Body Division) [British] (DBQ) ..... AssocInstAEA (Body Dvn)
Associate of the Institute of Bankers [British] (EY) ..... AIB
Associate of the Institute of Bankers in Scotland (DBQ) ..... AIB(Scot)
Associate of the Institute of British Bakers (DBQ) ..... AInstBB
Associate of the Institute of British Decorators ..... AIBD
Associate of the Institute of British Photographers ..... AIBP
Associate of the Institute of Builders [British] ..... AIOB
Associate of the Institute of Burial and Cremation Administration [British] (DBQ) ..... AInstBCA
Associate of the Institute of Canadian Bankers (DD) ..... AICB
Associate of the Institute of Carpenters [British] (DBQ) ..... AIOC
Associate of the Institute of Ceramics [British] ..... AI Ceram
Associate of the Institute of Certificated Grocers [British] ..... AGI
Associate of the Institute of Chartered Accountants [British] (EY) ..... ACA
Associate of the Institute of Chartered Shipbrokers [British] ..... AICS
Associate of the Institute of Chemistry [Later, ARIC] [British] ..... AIC
Associate of the Institute of Chiropodists [British] (DBQ) ..... ACh
Associate of the Institute of Civil Engineers [British] ..... AICE
Associate of the Institute of Clerks of Works [British] (DI) ..... AICW
Associate of the Institute of Commerce [British] (DCTA) ..... ACI
Associate of the Institute of Company Accountants [British] ..... AIAC
Associate of the Institute of Cost and Management Accountants [British] ..... ACMA
Associate of the Institute of Cost and Works Accountants [British] ..... ACWA
Associate of the Institute of Data Processing Management [British] (DCTA) ..... AIDPM
Associate of the Institute of Electrical Engineers [British] ..... AIEE
Associate of the Institute of Electrical Engineers of Canada (DD) ..... AIEE
Associate of the Institute of Executives and Managers [British] (DBQ) ..... AIEM
Associate of the Institute of Explosives Engineers [British] (DBQ) ..... AIExpE
Associate of the Institute of Factory Managers [British] (DI) ..... AIFM
Associate of the Institute of Food Science and Technology [British] (DBQ) ..... AIFST
Associate of the Institute of Freight Forwarders [British] (DBQ) ..... AInstFF
Associate of the Institute of Freight Trades Association (DS) ..... AIFTA
Associate of the Institute of Health Service Administrators [British] (DCTA) ..... AHA
Associate of the Institute of Hospital Almoners [British] ..... AIHA
Associate of the Institute of Incorporated Photographers [British] (DI) ..... AIIP
Associate of the Institute of Incorporated Practitioners in Advertising (DGA) ..... AIPA
Associate of the Institute of Incorporated Technologists [British] (DI) ..... AIITech
Associate of the Institute of Information Scientists [British] ..... AI Inf Sc
Associate of the Institute of Land Agents [British] (DI) ..... AILA
Associate of the Institute of Landscape Architects [British] ..... AILA
Associate of the Institute of Leisure and Amenity Management [British] (DBQ) ..... AILAM
Associate of the Institute of Linguists [British] ..... AIL
Associate of the Institute of Local Government Administrators [British] (DI) ..... AILGA
Associate of the Institute of Management Services [British] (DBQ) ..... AMS
Associate of the Institute of Marine Engineers [British Australia] ..... AI Mar E
Associate of the Institute of Marine Engineers [British] ..... AIME
Associate of the Institute of Market Officers [British] (DI) ..... AInstMO
Associate of the Institute of Marketing [British] (DCTA) ..... A Inst M
Associate of the Institute of Marketing and Sales Management [British] ..... A Inst MSM
Associate of the Institute of Mechanical Engineers ..... AIME
Associate of the Institute of Medical Laboratory Sciences [British] (DBQ) ..... AIMLS
Associate of the Institute of Mining and Metallurgy [British] ..... Assoc Inst MM
Associate of the Institute of Mining Engineers ..... AIME
Associate of the Institute of Municipal Building Management [British] (DBQ) ..... AIMBM
Associate of the Institute of Municipal Treasurers and Accountants [British] ..... AIMTA
Associate of the Institute of Musical Instrument Technology [British] (DBQ) ..... AIMIT
Associate of the Institute of Naval Architects ..... AINA
Associate of the Institute of Patentees and Inventors [British] (EY) ..... AInstPI
Associate of the Institute of Personnel Management (ADA) ..... AIPM
Associate of the Institute of Personnel Management of Australia ..... AIMPA
Associate of the Institute of Petroleum [British] (DI) ..... AInstPet
Associate of the Institute of Physicians [British] ..... AIP
Associate of the Institute of Physics (ADA) ..... AIP
Associate of the Institute of Physics and the Physical Society [British] (EY) ..... AInstP
Associate of the Institute of Plumbing [British] (DBQ) ..... AIP
Associate of the Institute of Printing (DGA) ..... ASSOC IOP
Associate of the Institute of Purchasing and Supply [British] (DCTA) ..... A Inst PS
Associate of the Institute of Qualified Private Secretaries [British] (DI) ..... AIQPS
Associate of the Institute of Quantity Surveyors [British] ..... AIQS
Associate of the Institute of Road Transport Engineers (DBQ) ..... AIRTE
Associate of the Institute of Sales and Marketing Management [British] (DBQ) ..... AInstSMM
Associate of the Institute of Sales Technology and Management [British] (DBQ) ..... AISTM
Associate of the Institute of Shipping and Forwarding Agents (ODBW) ..... ASF
Associate of the Institute of Statisticians [Later, MIS] [British] ..... AIS
Associate of the Institute of Structural Engineers [British] ..... AI Struct E
Associate of the Institute of Taxation [British] (DBQ) ..... ATII
Associate of the Institute of the Rubber Industry [British] ..... AIRI
Associate of the Institute of Trading Standards Administration [British] (DBQ) ..... AITSA
Associate of the Institute of Transport Administration [British] (DBQ) ..... AInstTA
Associate of the Institution of Agricultural Engineers [British] (DBQ) ..... AIAgrE
Associate of the Institution of Analysts and Programmers [British] (DBQ) ..... AMIAP
Associate of the Institution of Business Agents [British] (DBQ) ..... AIBA
Associate of the Institution of Certified Public Accountants [British] ..... ACPA
Associate of the Institution of Electrical and Electronics Incorporated Engineers [British] (DBQ) ..... AssociateIElecIE
Associate of the Institution of Electrical Engineers [British] ..... Assoc IEE
Associate of the Institution of Electronic and Radio Engineers [British] ..... AIERE
Associate of the Institution of Fire Engineers [British] ..... AIFireE
Associate of the Institution of Industrial Managers [British] (DCTA) ..... AIIM
Associate of the Institution of Locomotive Engineers [British] ..... AI Loco E
Associate of the Institution of Mechanical Engineers [British] ..... AI Mech E
Associate of the Institution of Mechanical Engineers [British] ..... AIMEE
Associate of the Institution of Mechanical Engineers [British] ..... Assoc I Min E
Associate of the Institution of Metallurgists [British] ..... AIM
Associate of the Institution of Mining and Metallurgy [British] ..... AIMM
Associate of the Institution of Naval Architects [British] ..... Assoc INA
Associate of the Institution of Production Engineers [British] ..... AIPE
Associate of the Institution of Public Health Engineers [British] (DBQ) ..... AssocIPHE
Associate of the Institution of Works and Highways Technician Engineers [British] (DBQ) ..... AIWHTE
Associate of the Insurance Institute of America ..... AIIA
Associate of the Insurance Institute of Canada ..... AIIC
Associate of the International Association of Book-Keepers (DCTA) ..... AIAB
Associate of the International Council of Psychologists ..... AICP
Associate of the International Dance Teachers' Association [British] (DBQ) ..... AIDTA
Associate of the International Institute of Arts and Letters [British] (DI) ..... AIIAL
Associate of the International Institute of Sports Therapy [British] (DBQ) ..... AISTC
Associate of the Iron and Steel Institute ..... AISI
Associate of the Iron and Steel Institute [British] ..... AssocISI
Associate of the Landscape Institute [British] (DBQ) ..... ALI
Associate of the Library Association [British] (EY) ..... ALA
Associate of the Linnaean Society [British] ..... ALS
Associate of the London and Counties Society of Physiologists [British] (DBQ) ..... LSCP(Assoc)
Associate of the London Association of Certified and Corporate Accountants [British] (EY) ..... ALAA
Associate of the London College of Divinity [British] ..... ALCD
Associate of the London College of Music [British] ..... ALCM
Associate of the Museums Association [British] (EY) ..... AMA
Associate of the National Academy of Design ..... ANA
Associate of the National Academy of Design, New York (NGC) ..... ANA
Associate of the National Association of Estate Agents [British] (DBQ) ..... ANAEA
Associate of the National College of Rubber Technology [British] (DI) ..... ANCRT
Associate of the National Institute of Hardware [British] (DBQ) ..... ANIH
Associate of the New Zealand Institute of Chemistry ..... ANZIC
Associate of the Non-Destructive Testing Society [British] ..... ANDTS
Associate of the Normal School of Science ..... ANSS
Associate of the Northeast Coast Institution of Engineers and Shipbuilders [British] ..... ANECInst
Associate of the Pharmaceutical Society [British] ..... APS
Associate of the Plastics and Rubber Institute (ODBW) ..... APRI
Associate of the Plastics Institute [British] ..... API
Associate of the Psychological Society of Ireland ..... APsSI

Associate of the Rating and Valuation Association [*British*] (DBQ) .... ARVA
Associate of the Retail Management Institute of Australia .... ARMIA
Associate of the Royal Academy [*British*] .... ARA
Associate of the Royal Academy of Dancing [*British*] .... ARAD
Associate of the Royal Academy of Music [*British*] .... ARAM
Associate of the Royal Aeronautical Society [*British*] .... ARAeS
Associate of the Royal Agricultural College [*British*] (BARN) .... ARAC
Associate of the Royal Astronomical Society [*British*] .... ARAS
Associate of the Royal Birmingham Society of Artists [*British*] (DI) .... ARBSA
Associate of the Royal British Colonial Society of Artists .... ARBC
Associate of the Royal Cambrian Academy [*British*] .... ARCA
Associate of the Royal Cambrian Academy [*British*] .... ARCamA
Associate of the Royal Canadian Academy .... ARCA
Associate of the Royal Canadian Academy of Arts (NGC) .... ARCA
Associate of the Royal Canadian College of Organists .... ARCCO
Associate of the Royal College of Advanced Technology [*British*] .... Assoc RCATS
Associate of the Royal College of Art [*British*] (EY) .... ARCA
Associate of the Royal College of Dancing [*British*] .... ARCD
Associate of the Royal College of Music [*British*] (EY) .... ARCM
Associate of the Royal College of Organists [*British*] (EY) .... ARCO
Associate of the Royal College of Organists (Choir-Training Diploma) [*British*] .... ARCO(CHM)
Associate of the Royal College of Psychiatrists [*British*] (DI) .... ARCPsych
Associate of the Royal College of Science [*British*] (EY) .... ARCS
Associate of the Royal College of Science [*British*] .... ARCSc
Associate of the Royal College of Science and Technology, Glasgow [*Later, ARTC*] [*Scotland*] .... ARCST
Associate of the Royal College of Surgeons [*British*] (ROG) .... ARCS
Associate of the Royal College of Veterinary Surgeons [*British*] .... ARCVS
Associate of the Royal Colonial Institute [*British*] .... ARCI
Associate of the Royal Conservatory of Music of Toronto .... ARCT
Associate of the Royal Drawing Society [*British*] .... ARDS
Associate of the Royal Hibernian Academy [*British*] .... ARHA
Associate of the Royal Incorporation of Architects in Scotland .... ARIAS
Associate of the Royal Institute of British Architects .... ARIBA
Associate of the Royal Institute of Chemistry [*Formerly, AIC*] [*British*] .... ARIC
Associate of the Royal Institute of Public Health and Hygiene [*British*] .... ARIPHH
Associate of the Royal Institution of Chartered Surveyors [*Formerly, PASI*] [*British*] .... ARICS
Associate of the Royal Institution of Naval Architects [*British*] (DI) .... ARINA
Associate of the Royal Institution of Naval Architects [*British*] .... AssocRINA
Associate of the Royal Photographic Society [*British*] .... ARPS
Associate of the Royal Red Cross [*British*] .... ARRC
Associate of the Royal Sanitary Institute [*British*] (ROG) .... ARSANI
Associate of the Royal Sanitary Institute [*British*] .... ARSI
Associate of the Royal School of Mines [*British*] (EY) .... ARSM
Associate of the Royal Scottish Academy .... ARSA
Associate of the Royal Scottish Society of [*Painting*] **in Water Colours** (BARN) .... ARSW
Associate of the Royal Society for the Promotion of Health [*British*] (DAVI) .... ARSPH
Associate of the Royal Society of Antiquaries [*British*] .... ARSA
Associate of the Royal Society of Arts [*British*] (EY) .... ARSA
Associate of the Royal Society of British Artists .... ARBA
Associate of the Royal Society of British Sculptors .... ARBS
Associate of the Royal Society of Chemistry [*British*] (DAVI) .... ARSC
Associate of the Royal Society of Health [*Later, AMRSH*] [*British*] .... ARSH
Associate of the Royal Society of Literature [*British*] .... ARSL
Associate of the Royal Society of Miniature Painters [*British*] .... ARMS
Associate of the Royal Society of Musicians [*British*] .... ARSM
Associate of the Royal Society of Painter-Etchers and Engravers [*British*] .... ARE
Associate of the Royal Society of Painters in Water Colours [*British*] .... ARWS
Associate of the Royal Society of Sciences [*British*] (ROG) .... ARSSC
Associate of the Royal Technical College, Glasgow [*Formerly, ARCST*] .... ARTC
Associate of the Royal Technical College (Salford) [*British*] .... ARTC(S)
Associate of the Royal Victoria Institute of Architects [*British*] .... ARVIA
Associate of the Royal Water-Colour Society [*British*] (ROG) .... ARWS
Associate of the Royal West of England Academy .... ARWA
Associate of the Society of Actuaries [*Society of Actuaries*] [*Designation awarded by*] .... ASA
Associate of the Society of Art Masters [*British*] .... ASAM
Associate of the Society of Chiropodists [*British*] .... AChS
Associate of the Society of Commercial Accountants [*British*] .... A Comm A
Associate of the Society of Company and Commercial Accountants [*British*] (DCTA) .... ASCA
Associate of the Society of Dyers and Colourists [*British*] (DBQ) .... ASDC
Associate of the Society of Health and Beauty Therapists [*British*] (DBQ) .... ASBTh
Associate of the Society of Incorporated Accountants and Auditors [*British*] .... ASAA
Associate of the Society of Industrial Artists (Education) [*British*] .... ASIA(Ed)
Associate of the Society of Investment Analysts [*British*] (DBQ) .... ASIA
Associate of the Society of Licensed Aircraft Engineers and Technologists [*British*] (DBQ) .... AssocSLAET
Associate of the Society of Surveying Technicians [*British*] (DBQ) .... AMSST
Associate of the Society of Typographic Designers (DGA) .... ASTD
Associate of the South African Institute of Mechanical Engineers .... ASAI Mech E
Associate of the Swimming Teachers' Association [*British*] (DBQ) .... ASTA
Associate of the Textile Institute [*British*] .... ATI
Associate of the Toronto Conservatory of Music .... ATCM
Associate of the Welding Institute [*British*] (DBQ) .... AWeldI
Associate of Theological Study [*British*] .... ATS
Associate of Trinity College of Music, London [*British*] .... ATCL
Associate of Youth Development [*British*] (DBQ) .... AYD
Associate Presbyterian (IIA) .... AP
Associate Producer .... AP
Associate Professor (ADA) .... Aspro
Associate Pulmonary Technologist [*Academic degree*] .... A-Put
Associate Regional Administrator .... ARA
Associate, Royal Manchester College of Music [*British*] (ROG) .... ARMCM
Associate Safety Professional [*Board of Certified Safety Professionals*] [*Designation awarded by*] .... ASP
Associate Scottish Hospital Bureau of Management (DAVI) .... ASHBM
Associate Surveyor Member of the Incorporated Association of Architects and Surveyors [*British*] .... AIAS
Associate Technical Aide .... ATA
Associate Technical Director for Engineering and Test [*Army*] (RDA) .... ATDE/T
Associate Technical Project Officer .... ATPO
Associate, Trinity College of Music [*Canadian*] .... ATCM
Associated .... ASSD
Associated (EY) .... ASSOCD
Associated .... ASSOCD
Associated .... ASSTD
Associated Accounting Firms International [*Washington, DC*] (EA) .... AAFI
Associated Actors and Artistes of America .... AAA
Associated Actors and Artistes of America (EA) .... AAAA
Associated Aero Science Laboratories (SAA) .... AASL
Associated African States and Madagascar (MHDB) .... AAASM
Associated African States, Madagascar and Mauritius [*Later, Association of African, Caribean and Pacific States*] (PDAA) .... AASMM
Associated Agents of America (EA) .... AAA
Associated Air Balance Council (EA) .... AABC
Associated Airlines [*ICAO designator*] (AD) CV
Associated Antique Dealers of America (EA) .... AADA
Associated Australasian Banks in London .... AABL
Associated Aviation Underwriters .... AAU
Associated Baby Carriage Dealers (EA) .... ABCD
Associated Banc-Corp [*NASDAQ symbol*] (NQ) .... ASBC
Associated Banc-Corp. [*Associated Press*] (SAG) .... AsdBnc
[*The*] **Associated Banks of Europe Corp.** (IID) .... ABECOR
Associated Banks of Europe Corp. (ODBW) .... ABERCOR
Associated Beer Distributors of Illinois (SRA) .... ABDI
Associated Biomedic Systems, Inc. .... ABS
Associated Birdkeepers and Traders [*Australia*] .... ABKT
Associated Blacksmiths, Forge, and Smithy Workers Society [*A union*] [*British*] .... ABFSWS
Associated Blacksmiths of Scotland [*A union*] .... ABS
Associated Board of the Royal Schools of Music [*British*] (BI) .... ABRSM
Associated Body of Church Schoolmasters [*A union*] [*British*] .... ABCS
Associated Bodywork and Massage Professionals (EA) .... ABMP
Associated Book Publishers [*Subsidiary of International Thomson Organisation*] .... ABP
Associated Booksellers of Great Britain and Ireland (DGA) .... ABGBI
Associated Borrowers Endorsement [*British*] .... ABE
Associated Bread Manufacturers of Australia and New Zealand .... ABMANZ
Associated British Cinemas .... ABC
Associated British Foods [*Commercial firm*] .... ABF
Associated British Ports (DS) .... ABP
Associated Broadcast News [*Cable-television system*] .... ABN
Associated Builders and Contractors (EA) .... ABC
Associated Builders and Owners of Greater New York (SRA) .... ABOGNY
Associated Building Material Distributors of America (EA) .... ABM
Associated Building Material Distributors of America (EA) .... ABMDA
Associated Business Papers (NTCM) .... ABP
Associated Business Writers of America (EA) .... ABWA
Associated California Loggers (SRA) .... ACL
Associated Carpenters and Joiners Society of Scotland [*A union*] .... ACJSS
Associated Carters Society of Scotland [*A union*] .... ACSS
Associated Chain Drug Stores (EA) .... ACDS
Associated Chiropodists of America .... ACA
[*The*] **Associated Christian Colleges of Oregon** [*Library network*] .... ACCO
Associated Church Press (EA) .... ACP
[*The*] **Associated Clubs** (EA) .... AC
Associated Collection Agencies [*Colorado*] (SRA) .... ACA
Associated Collectors of El Salvador (EA) .... ACES
Associated College Libraries of Central Pennsylvania [*Library network*] .... ACLCP
Associated Colleges of the Chicago Area .... ACCA
Associated Colleges of the Midwest (EA) .... ACM
Associated Colleges of the Midwest, Periodical Bank, Chicago, IL [*Library symbol Library of Congress*] (LCLS) .... ICACM
Associated Colleges of Upper New York .... ACUNY
Associated Collegiate Press (EA) .... ACP
Associated Committee of Friends on Indian Affairs (EA) .... ACFIA
Associated Communications Corp. .... ACC
Associated Computer System (MHDI) .... ACS
Associated Concrete Contractors of Michigan (SRA) .... ACCM
Associated Construction Distributors International (EA) .... ACD
Associated Construction Distributors, International .... ACDI
Associated Construction Publications (EA) .... ACP
Associated Container Transportation .... ACT
Associated Contractor Originated Change (AAG) .... ACOC
Associated Cooperage Industries of America (EA) .... ACIA
Associated Corpuscular Emission .... ACE
Associated Correspondents News Service .... ACNS
Associated Corset and Brassiere Manufacturers (EA) .... ACBM
Associated Councils of the Arts [*Later, American Council for the Arts*] .... ACA

Associated Country Women of the World [*British*] .... ACWW
Associated Court and Commercial Newspapers (DGA) .... ACCN
Associated Credit Bureaus [*Houston, TX*] (EA) .... ACB
[*The*] Associated Daimler Co. [*British*] (DCTA) .... ADC
Associated Dairies [*Commercial firm British*] .... ASDA
Associated Day Care Centers .... ADCC
Associated Deliveries Limited [*British*] .... ADL
Associated Designers of Canada (AC) .... ADC
Associated Disbursing Officer [*Military*] (DNAB) .... ADO
Associated Driving Schools of Australia .... ADSA
Associated Drug and Chemical Industries of Missouri .... ADACIOM
Associated Electrical Industries [*British*] .... AEI
Associated Employers of Montana (SRA) .... AEM
Associated Engineering Services [*Canada*] .... AESL
Associated Engineering Services Ltd., Vancouver, BC, Canada [*Library
    symbol Library of Congress*] (LCLS) .... CaBVaAE
Associated Engineering Services Ltd., Vancouver, British Columbia [*Library
    symbol National Library of Canada*] (NLC) .... BVAAE
Associated Enterprises, Inc. (TSSD) .... AEI
Associated Equipment Distributors (EA) .... AED
Associated Equipment Distributors of Arizona (SRA) .... AEDA
Associated Equipment Distributors' Research and Services
    Operation .... AED/R & S
Associated Estates Realty [*NYSE symbol*] (SPSG) .... AEC
Associated Estates Realty [*NYSE symbol*] (SPSG) .... AEC
Associated Estates Realty [*Associated Press*] (SAG) .... AsdEst
Associated Estates Realty [*Associated Press*] (SAG) .... AsdEstat
Associated Examining Board [*British*] .... AEB
Associated Factory Mutual Fire Insurance Companies [*Later, FMS*]
    (EA) .... AFMFIC
Associated Fantasy Publishers .... AFP
Associated Film Distribution (BARN) .... AFD
Associated Foam Manufacturers (EA) .... AFM
Associated Food Dealers of Michigan (SRA) .... AFD
Associated Fraternities of America .... AFA
Associated Fraternity of Iron Forgers [*A union*] [*British*] .... AFIF
Associated Fresh Foods [*British*] .... AFF
Associated Funeral Directors Service (EA) .... AFDS
Associated Funeral Directors Service International (EA) .... AFDSI
Associated Fur Manufacturers (EA) .... AFM
Associated Gas Distributors .... AGD
Associated General Contractors of America (EA) .... AGC
Associated General Contractors of America .... AGCA
Associated General Contractors of California (AAGC) .... AGCC
Associated Geographers of America .... AGA
Associated Glass and Pottery Manufacturers (EA) .... AGPM
Associated Gospel Churches of Canada (AC) .... AGO
Associated Granite Craftsmen's Guild (EA) .... AGCG
Associated Grantmakers of Massachusetts (SRA) .... AGM
Associated Ground Equipment (CINC) .... AGE
[*The*] Associated Group, Inc. [*NASDAQ symbol*] (SAG) .... AGRP
Associated Group, Inc. (The) [*Associated Press*] (SAG) .... AscdGp
Associated Health Foundation (EA) .... AHF
Associated Heat Services [*Energy management contractor*] [*British*] .... AHS
Associated Humane Societies (EA) .... AHS
Associated Humber Lines [*Steamship*] (MHDB) .... AHL
Associated Independent Dairies of America (EA) .... AIDA
Associated Independent Distributors [*Later, IDA*] .... AID
Associated Independent Electrical Contractors of America [*Later, IEC*]
    (EA) .... AIECA
Associated Industrial Photographic Dealers [*Defunct*] .... AIPD
Associated Industries of Florida (SRA) .... AIF
Associated Industries of Kentucky (SRA) .... AIK
Associated Industries of Massachusetts .... AIM
Associated Industries of Missouri (SRA) .... AIM
Associated Industries of the Inland Northwest (SRA) .... AIIN
Associated Industries of Vermont (SRA) .... AIV
Associated Information Managers (EA) .... AIM
Associated In-Group Donors .... AID
Associated Iron Moulders of Scotland [*A union*] .... AIMS
Associated Japan-America Societies of the United States (EA) .... AJAS
Associated Japanese Bank (International) Ltd. .... AJB
Associated Knowledge Systems [*Imperial Chemical Industries Ltd.*]
    [*Information service or system*] (IID) .... AKS
Associated Koi Clubs of America (EA) .... AKCA
Associated Laboratories (EA) .... AL
Associated Landscape Contractors of America (EA) .... ALCA
Associated Landscape Contractors of Colorado (SRA) .... ALCC
Associated Landscape Contractors of Massachusetts (SRA) .... ALCM
Associated Legislative Rabbinate of America (EA) .... ALRA
Associated Licensed Detectives of New York State (SRA) .... ALDONYS
Associated Locksmiths of America .... ALA
Associated Locksmiths of America (EA) .... ALOA
Associated Logic Parallel System (BUR) .... ALPS
Associated Long-Distance Interstate Message [*Telecommunications*]
    (TEL) .... ALDI
Associated Lutheran Charities [*Later, Lutheran Social Welfare Conference of
    America*] (EA) .... ALC
Associated Mail and Parcel Centers (EA) .... AMPC
Associated Maintenance Module [*Telecommunications*] (TEL) .... AMM
Associated Male Choruses of America (EA) .... AMC of A
Associated Manitoba Arts Festivals, Inc. (AC) .... AMAF
Associated Marine Officers Association of the Philippines .... AMOAP
Associated Mariners' Society [*A union*] [*British*] .... AMS

Associated Master Barbers and Beauticians of America [*Later, HI/AMBBA*]
    (EA) .... AMBBA
Associated Memory Equipment .... AME
Associated Merchandising Corp. .... AMC
Associated Metal Workers Society [*A union*] [*British*] .... AMWS
Associated Metal Workers Union [*British*] .... AMWU
Associated Metalworkers' Union [*British*] (DCTA) .... AMU
Associated Microfilming Service, Inc., Mountain Lakes, NJ [*Library symbol
    Library of Congress*] (LCLS) .... AssM
Associated Midwestern Universities, Inc. .... AMU
Associated Migrant Opportunity Services .... AMOS
Associated Milk Producers, Inc. .... AMPI
Associated Milk Producers/Southern Region [*Texas*] (SRA) .... AMP/S
Associated Millinery Men (EA) .... AMM
Associated Minicomputer Dealers of America (EA) .... AMDA
Associated Minority Contractors of America (EA) .... AMC
Associated Missile Products Corp. .... AMPCO
[*The*] Associated Missions (EA) .... TAM
Associated Motion Picture Advertisers (EA) .... AMPA
Associated Motor Carriers Tariff Bureau (EA) .... AMCTB
Associated Motor Carriers Tariff Bureau, Saint Paul MN [*STAC*] .... AMC
Associated Multiplier Agency Liaison Group [*Australia*] .... AMALG
Associated Music Publishers (NTCM) .... AMP
Associated Music Publishers [*Musical slang*] .... AMPS
Associated Name [*MARC relator code*] [*Library of Congress*] (LCCP) .... asn
Associated Negro Press (IIA) .... ANP
Associated Networks for European Research [*EC*] (ECED) .... RARE
Associated New York State Food Processors (SRA) .... ANYSFP
Associated Newspaper Holdings [*British*] .... ANH
Associated Newspapers Ltd., London, United Kingdom [*Library symbol
    Library of Congress*] (LCLS) .... UkLA
Associated Nuclear Services [*British*] (IRUK) .... ANS
Associated Nursery Guides Emphatically Lacking in Leisure .... ANGELL
Associated of Correctors of the Press [*Later, NGA*] (DGA) .... ACP
Associated Oklahoma Trucking Association (SRA) .... AMCO
Associated Oregon Industries (SRA) .... AOI
Associated Oregon Loggers (SRA) .... AOL
Associated Organizations for Professionals in Education [*Defunct*] (EA) .... AOPE
Associated Organizations for Teacher Education [*Later, AOPE*] .... AOTE
Associated Overseas Countries and Territories (DS) .... AOCT
Associated Overseas Countries of the European Economic Community .... AOC
Associated Paper Industries [*British*] .... API
Associated Parishes (EA) .... AP
Associated Patternmakers of Scotland [*A union*] .... APS
Associated Pennsylvania Constructors (SRA) .... APC
Associated Period [*Medicine*] (DAVI) .... AP
Associated Person [*Stock exchange term*] .... AP
Associated Petroleum Industries of Michigan (SRA) .... APIM
Associated Petroleum Industries of Pennsylvania (SRA) .... API-PA
Associated Pharmacologists and Toxicologists (EPA) .... APT
Associated Photographers International (EA) .... API
Associated Pimiento Canners [*Defunct*] (EA) .... APC
Associated Pipe Organ Builders of America (EA) .... APOBA
Associated Porcupine Mines Ltd. [*Toronto Stock Exchange symbol*] .... APC
Associated Portland Cement Manufacturers of Great Britain .... APCM
Associated Pot and Kettle Clubs of America [*Later, IPKC*] (EA) .... APKCA
Associated Poultry and Egg Industries [*Defunct*] (EA) .... APEI
Associated Presbyterian [*British*] (ROG) .... AP
Associated Press [*News agency and wire service*] (EA) .... AP
Associated Press Broadcasters .... APB
Associated Press Broadcasters Association [*Later, APB*] (EA) .... APBA
Associated Press Managing Editors (EA) .... APME
Associated Press Managing Editors Association (DGA) .... APMEA
Associated Press of Pakistan .... APP
Associated Press Radio .... APR
Associated Press Radio Network (NTCM) .... APRN
Associated Press Radio-Television Association [*Later, APB*] .... APRTA
Associated Press Service .... APS
Associated Press Sports Editors [*Defunct*] (EA) .... APSE
Associated Press Television .... APTV
Associated Professional Massage Therapists and Bodyworkers [*Later,
    ABMP*] (EA) .... APMT
Associated Public School Systems .... APSS
Associated Public-Safety Communications Officers (EA) .... APCO
Associated Publishers (EA) .... AP
Associated Pulp and Paper Mills (DGA) .... APPM
Associated Purchasing Publications .... APP
Associated Rare Breeds of New England [*Defunct*] (EA) .... ARBNE
[*The*] Associated Readers of Tarot International (EA) .... TAROT
Associated Rediffusion [*Television*] .... AR
Associated Reformed Presbyterian .... ARP
Associated Regional Accounting Firms [*Atlanta, GA*] (EA) .... ARAF
Associated Reinforcing Bar Producers (EA) .... ARBP
Associated Retail Bakers of America [*Later, Retail Bakers of America*]
    (EA) .... ARBA
Associated Retail Confectioners of North America [*Later, RCI*] (EA) .... ARC
Associated Retail Confectioners of the United States [*Later, RCI*] .... ARCUS
Associated Risk Managers International [*Austin, TX*] (EA) .... ARMI
Associated Risk Managers of New York State (SRA) .... ARMNY
Associated Risk Managers of Ohio (SRA) .... ARM/OH
Associated Rocky Mountain Universities [*AEC*] .... ARMU
Associated Roller Rink Operators of Wisconsin (SRA) .... ARROW
Associated Roofing Contractors of Maryland (SRA) .... ARCOM
Associated Sandblasting Contractors (EA) .... ASC
Associated School Boards of South Dakota (SRA) .... ASBSD

Associated Schools of Construction (EA) .... ASC
Associated Schools Project in Education for International Cooperation and Peace [UNESCO] [Paris, France] (EAIO) .... ASPEICP
Associated Scottish Life Offices (EAIO) .... ASLO
Associated Services for the Blind (EA) .... ASB
Associated Sheet Metal/Roofing Contractors, Connecticut Chapter (SRA) .... ASMRCC
Associated Society of Locomotive Engineers and Firemen [British] (ODBW) .... Aslef
Associated Society of Locomotive Engineers and Firemen [A union] [British] (DCTA) .... ASLEF
Associated Society of Moulders [A union] [British] .... ASM
Associated Society of Range Stove and Ornamental Workers [A union] [British] .... ASRSOW
Associated Specialty Contractors (EA) .... ASC
Associated Spring Corp. .... ASCO
Associated States of Indochina (NATG) .... ASIC
Associated Stenotypists of America [Later, NSRA] (EA) .... ASA
Associated Students of the University of California .... ASUC
Associated Students Promoting Individual Rights for Everyone .... ASPIRE
Associated Subcontractors of Massachusetts (SRA) .... ASM
Associated Support Items of Equipment (MCD) .... ASIOE
Associated Surplus Dealers (EA) .... ASD
Associated Surplus Dealers and Associated Merchandise Dealers Trade Show (ITD) .... ASD/AMD
Associated Talmud Torahs [A publication] (BJA) .... ATT
Associated Technical Services, Inc. [Glen Ridge, NJ] [Information service or system] .... ATS
Associated Technical Services, Inc., Glen Ridge, NJ [Library symbol Library of Congress] (LCLS) .... NjGlrIA
Associated Technology Co. [Information service or system] (IID) .... ATC
Associated Telemanagement, Inc. [Newburyport, MA] [Telecommunications] (TSSD) .... ATI
Associated Telephone Answering Exchanges [Formerly, ATE] (EA) .... ATAE
Associated Telephone Exchanges [Later, ATAE] .... ATE
Associated Television Ltd. [British independent, commercial television company] .... ATV
Associated Third Class Mail Users [Later, TCMA] (EA) .... ATCMU
Associated Tie Manufacturers of Australia .... ATMA
Associated Tobacco Manufacturers [Defunct] (EA) .... ATM
Associated Traffic Clubs of America [Later, TCI] (EA) .... ATC
Associated Training Specialist (SAA) .... ATS
[The] Associated Turtles [Defunct] (EA) .... TAT
Associated Two-Year Schools in Construction [Defunct] (EA) A2YSC
Associated Underground Contractors (SRA) .... AUC
Associated Unions of America [Later, OPEIU] (EA) .... AUA
Associated Universities for Toxicology Research and Education [Research center] (RCD) .... AUTRE
Associated Universities, Inc. (EA) .... AUI
Associated University Bureaus of Business and Economic Research [Later, AUBER] .... AUBBER
Associated Utility Contractors of Maryland (SRA) .... AUCM
Associated Veterinary Laboratories [Defunct] (EA) .... AVL
Associated Video Dealers of America [Defunct] (EA) .... AVDA
Associated Water Colour Painters, Toronto [1912] [Canada] (NGC) .... AWCP
Associated Western Universities [Salt Lake City, UT] [Department of Energy] .... AWU
Associated Wire Rope Fabricators (EA) .... AWRF
Associated with Brokers [London Stock Exchange] .... AB
Associated with Dual Capacity Firms [London Stock Exchange] .... AD
Associated with Jobbers [London Stock Exchange] .... AJ
Associated Workers' Union [Philippines] .... AWU
Associated Writing Programs (EA) .... AWP
Associates (VRA) .... assoc
Associates and Advisory Committee to the Special Committee on Electronic Data Retrieval (MCD) .... AACSCEDR
Associates Catalog Librarians, Richmond, VA [Library symbol] [Library of Congress] (LCLS) .... ViRACL
Associates First Capital Corp. [NYSE symbol] (SAG) .... AFS
Associates First Capital Corp. [Associated Press] (SAG) .... AscFCap
Associates First Captial'A' [NYSE symbol] (TTSB) .... AFS
Associates for Radio Astronomy .... ARA
Associates for Religion and Intellectual Life (EA) .... ARIL
Associates of Clinical Pharmacology (EA) .... ACP
Associates of Elvis Presley Fan Clubs (EA) .... AEPFC
Associates of the Graymoor Ecumenical Institute [Defunct] (EA) .... AGEI
Associateship of Loughborough University of Technology [British] (DBQ) .... ALUT
Associateship of the London School of Polymer Technology [British] (DBQ) .... ALSPT
Associateship of the Manchester College of Technology [British] .... AssocMCT
Associateship of the University of Manchester Institute of Science and Technology [British] (DI) .... AUMIST
Associatin of British Brush Machinery Manufacturers (MHDB) .... ABBMM
Association .... A
Association .... ASS
Association (EY) .... ASSCN
Association .... ASSN
Association (DD) .... Assn
Association .... ASSN
Association (ODBW) .... assn
Association (AAGC) .... Assn
Association (AAGC) .... Assoc
Association (ODBW) .... Assoc
Association .... ASSOCN

Association Actuarielle Internationale [International Actuarial Association - IAA] [Brussels, Belgium] .... AAI
Association Adjustment Inventory [Psychology] .... AAI
Association Africaine de Cartographie [African Association of Cartography] (EAIO) .... AAC
Association Algerienne des Transports Automobiles [Algerian Automobile Transport Association] [Algeria] .... ATA
Association Belge pour le Developpement Pacifique de l'Energie Atomique [Belgium Association for the Peaceful Development of Atomic Energy] (NUCP) .... ADEA
Association Belgo-Americaine [Later, American-Belgian Association] (EA) .... ABA
Association Belgo-Congolaise du Textile [Belgo-Congolese Textile Association] [Zaire] .... ABCT
Association Beton Quebec (AC) .... ABQ
Association Botanique du Canada (AC) .... ABC
Association Canadienne Contre la Tuberculose et les Maladies Respiratoires [Canadian Association Against Tuberculosis and Respiratory Diseases] .... ACTMR
Association Canadienne d'Administrateurs de Recherche Universitaire [Canadian Association of University Research Administrators - CAURA] .... ACARU
Association Canadienne d'Archaeologie [Canadian Archaeological Association - CAA] .... ACA
Association Canadienne d'Assistance Juridique, d'Information et de Recherche desHandicapes [Canadian Legal Advocacy Information and Research Association of the Disabled] .... CAJIR
Association Canadienne d'Athletisme [Canadian Athletics Association] .... ACA
Association Canadienne de Badminton [Canadian Badminton Association] .... ACB
Association Canadienne de Cinema-Television [Canada] .... ACC-T
Association Canadienne de Cross (AC) .... ACC
Association Canadienne de Direction D'Artists (AC) .... ACDA
Association Canadienne de Documentation Professionnelle (AC) .... ACADOP
Association Canadienne de Fabricants d'Armoires de Cuisine (AC) .... ACAC
Association Canadienne de Financement et de Location (AC) .... ACFL
Association Canadienne de Football Amateur [Canadian Association of Amateur Football] .... ACFA
Association Canadienne de Gestion des Achats [Purchasing Management Association of Canada - PMAC] .... ACGA
Association Canadienne de Hockey Amateur [Canadian Amateur Hockey Association - CAHA] .... ACHA
Association Canadienne de la Construction [Canadian Construction Association] .... ACC
Association Canadienne de la Courtepointe (AC) .... ACC
Association Canadienne de la Gestion du Personnel des Services Publics [Canadian Association of Public Service Personnel Management] .... ACGPSP
Association Canadienne de la Presse Syndicale [Canadian Syndicated Press Association] .... ACPS
Association Canadienne de la Recherche Operationnelle [Canadian Association of Operational Research] .... ACRO
Association Canadienne de l'Acoustique [Canadian Acoustics Association] .... ACA
Association Canadienne de l'Ataxie de Friedreich [Canadian Association of Friedreich's Ataxia] .... ACAF
Association Canadienne de l'Electricite (AC) .... ACE
Association Canadienne de l'Enseignement a Distance [Canadian Association for Distance Education - CADE] .... ACED
Association Canadienne de l'Habitation et du Developpement Urbain [Canadian Association of Housing and Urban Development] .... ACHDU
Association Canadienne de l'Immeuble [Canadian Real Estate Association - CREA] .... ACI
Association Canadienne de l'Imprimerie (EAIO) .... ACI
Association Canadienne de l'Industrie du Bois (AC) .... ACIB
Association Canadienne de l'Informatique [Canadian Information Processing Society - CIPS] .... ACI
Association Canadienne de Linguistique Appliquee [Canadian Association of Applied Linguistics - CAAL] .... ACLA
Association Canadienne de Litterature Comparee [Canadian Comparative Literature Association - CCLA] .... ACLC
Association Canadienne de Maisons Mobiles [Canadian Association of Mobile Homes] .... ACMM
Association Canadienne de Nage Synchronisee Amateur [Canadian Association of Amateur Synchronized Swimmers] .... ACNSA
Association Canadienne de Normalisation [Canadian Association of Standardization] .... ACNOR
Association Canadienne de Patinage Artistique [Canada] .... ACPA
Association Canadienne de Philosophie [Canadian Philosophical Association - CPA] .... ACP
Association Canadienne de Recherche en Evaluation Nondestructifs (AC) .... ACREND
Association Canadienne de Recherche et d'Education pour la Paix [Canadian Peace Research and Education Association - CPREA] .... ACREP
Association Canadienne de Recherches Sociales Appliquees [Canadian Association of Applied Social Research - CAASR] .... ACRSA
Association Canadienne de Sante Publique (AC) .... ACSP
Association Canadienne de Science Politique [Canadian Political Science Association - CPSA] .... ACSP
Association Canadienne de Semiotique [Canadian Semiotic Association - CSA] .... ACS
Association Canadienne de Sociologie et d'Anthropologie [Canadian Sociology and Anthropology Association - CSAA] .... ACSA
Association Canadienne de Softball Amateur [Canadian Association of Amateur Softball] .... ACSA
Association Canadienne de Technologie Avancee [Canadian Association of Advanced Technology] .... ACTA

Association Canadienne de Therapie Animale [*Canadian Animal Therapy Association*] .... ACTA

Association Canadienne de Traitement d'Images et Reconnaissance des Formes [*Canada*] .... ACTIRF

Association Canadienne de Vexillologie (AC) .... CFA

Association Canadienne de Vol a Voile [*Canada*] .... ACVV

Association Canadienne d'Economique [*Canadian Economics Association - CEA*] .... ACE

Association Canadienne d'Education [*Canadian Education Association - CEA*] .... ACE

Association Canadienne d'Education de Langue Francaise (AC) .... ACELF

Association Canadienne d'Entraineurs de Badminton [*Canadian Association of Badminton Coaches*] .... ACEB

Association Canadienne des Adjoints Juridiques (AC) .... ACAJ

Association Canadienne des Administrateurs et des Administratrices Scolaires (AC) .... ACAS

Association Canadienne des Administrateurs Scolaires [*Canadian Association of Academic Administrators*] .... ACAS

Association Canadienne des Arbitres de Badminton [*Canadian Association of Badminton Referees*] .... ACAB

Association Canadienne des Bibliothecaires de Langue Francaise [*Later, ASTED*] .... ACBLF

Association Canadienne des Bibliotheques [*Canadian Library Association - CLA*] .... ACB

Association Canadienne des Bibliotheques de Droit [*Canadian Association of Law Libraries - CALL*] .... ACBD

Association Canadienne des Bibliotheques Musicales [*Canadian Association of Music Libraries*] .... ACBM

Association Canadienne des Boursiers Rhodes [*Canadian Association of Rhodes Scholars - CARS*] .... ACBR

Association Canadienne des Cadres en Informatique [*Canadian Association of Information Officials*] .... ACFOR

Association Canadienne des Centres de Vie Autonome (AC) .... ACCVA

Association Canadienne des Chefs de Pompiers [*Canadian Association of Fire Chiefs*] .... ACCP

Association Canadienne des Chercheurs en Education [*Canadian Educational Researchers Association - CERA*] .... ACCE

Association Canadienne des Chirurgiens Generaux [*Canadian Association of General Surgeons - CAGS*] .... ACCG

Association Canadienne des Cinq Quilles [*Formerly, Canadian Bowling Congress*] (AC) .... L'ACSQ

Association Canadienne des Communications [*Canadian Communication Association - CCA*] .... ACC

Association Canadienne des Communications entre l'Homme et l'Ordinateur [*Canadian Association of Communications between Man and Computers*] .... ACCHO

Association Canadienne des Courtiers en Valeurs Mobilieres [*Investment Dealers' Association of Canada - IDA*] .... ACCOVAM

Association Canadienne des Dessinateurs Editoriaux (AC) .... ACDE

Association Canadienne des Detaillants en Quincaillerie (AC) .... ACDQ

Association Canadienne des Dietetistes [*Canadian Association of Dietitians*] .... ACD

Association Canadienne des Eaux Potables et Usees (AC) .... ACEPU

Association Canadienne des Ecoles de Bibliothecaires [*Canadian Association of Library Schools*] .... ACEB

Association Canadienne des Ecoles de Traduction (AC) .... ACET

Association Canadienne des Ecoles du Service Social [*Canadian Association of Schools of Social Work - CASSW*] .... ACESS

Association Canadienne des Ecoles Universitaires de Musique [*Canadian Association of University Schools of Music - CAUSM*] .... ACEUM

Association Canadienne des Ecoles Universitaires de Nursing [*Canadian Association of University Schools of Nursing - CAUSN*] .... ACEUN

Association Canadienne des Editeurs de Musique [*Canadian Music Publishers Association - CMPA*] .... ACEM

Association Canadienne des Editeurs de Quotidiens [*Canadian Association of Newspaper Editors*] .... ACEQ

Association Canadienne des Educateurs de Musique [*Canadian Music Educators' Association*] .... CAEM

Association Canadienne des Employes de Telephone [*Canadian Telephone Employees' Association - CTEA*] .... ACET

Association Canadienne des Employes du Transport Aerien [*Canadian Air Line Employees' Association - CALEA*] .... ACETA

Association Canadienne des Enseignants Noirs [*Canadian Association of Black Teachers*] .... ACEN

Association Canadienne des Entraineurs [*Canadian Association of Coaches*] .... ACE

Association Canadienne des Entrepreneurs en Couverture [*Canadian Association of Bedding Entrepreneurs*] .... ACEC

Association Canadienne des Entreprises de Telecommunications [*Canadian Association of Telecommunication Businesses*] .... ACET

Association Canadienne des Etudes Africaines [*Canadian Association of African Studies*] (EAIO) .... ACEA

Association Canadienne des Etudes Asiatiques [*Canadian Asian Studies Association - CASA*] .... ACEA

Association Canadienne des Etudes Avancees (AC) .... ACDEA

Association Canadienne des Etudes Cinematographiques [*Canadian Association of Film Studies*] .... ACEC

Association Canadienne des Etudes Ecossaises [*Canadian Association for Scottish Studies - CASS*] .... ACEE

Association Canadienne des Etudes Finno-Ougriennes [*Finno-Ugrian Studies Association - FUSAC*] .... ACEFO

Association Canadienne des Etudes Hongroises [*Canadian Association of Hungarian Studies - CAHS*] .... ACEH

Association Canadienne des Etudes Latino-Americaines [*Canadian Association of Latin American Studies - CALAS*] .... ACELA

Association Canadienne des Etudes Latino-Americaines et Caraibes [*Canadian Association of Latin American and Caribbean Studies*] .... ACELAC

Association Canadienne des Etudes Patristiques [*Canadian Society of Patristic Studies - CSPS*] .... ACEP

Association Canadienne des Etudes Prospectives [*Canadian Association for Future Studies - CAFS*] .... ACEP

Association Canadienne des Fabricants de Panneaux de Particules (AC) .... ACFPP

Association Canadienne des Fabricants de Tuyaux de Beton (AC) .... ACTB

Association Canadienne des Femmes Arabes (AC) .... ACFA

Association Canadienne des Femmes en Radio et Television (AC) .... ACFR

Association Canadienne des Fondements de l'Education (AC) .... ACFE

Association Canadienne des Geographes [*Canadian Association of Geographers*] .... ACG

Association Canadienne des Gerants de la Redaction [*Canadian Association of Editorial Directors*] .... ACGR

Association Canadienne des Hispanistes [*Canadian Association of Hispanists - CAH*] .... ACH

Association Canadienne des Humanites [*Humanities Association of Canada - HAC*] .... ACH

Association Canadienne des Implantes Intraoculaires [*Canadian Implant Association*] (EAIO) .... ACII

Association Canadienne des Infirmieres et Infirmiers en Sante du Travail [*Formerly, National Association of Occupation Health Nurses*] (AC) .... ACIIST

Association Canadienne des Infirmieres et Infirmiers Pediatriques (AC) .... ACIIP

Association Canadienne des Laboratoires d'Analyse Environmenmentale (AC) .... ACLAE

Association Canadienne des Laboratoires d'Essais [*Canadian Testing Association*] (AC) .... ACLE

Association Canadienne des Maitres de Poste et Adjoints [*Canadian Postmasters and Assistants Association - CPAA*] .... ACMPA

Association Canadienne des Manufacturiers de Fenetres et Portes [*Canadian Association of Window and Door Manufacturers*] .... ACMFP

Association Canadienne des Manufacturiers de Maconnerie en Beton (AC) .... ACMMB

Association Canadienne des Manufacturiers de Palettes et Contenants [*Canadian Wood Pallet and Container Association*] (EAIO) .... ACMPC

Association Canadienne des Optometristes [*Canadian Association of Optometrists*] .... ACO

Association Canadienne des Orchestres de Jeunes [*Canadian Association of Youth Orchestras - CAYO*] .... ACOJ

Association Canadienne des Paiements (AC) .... ACP

Association Canadienne des Patineurs Professionnels [*Canadian Association of Professional Skaters*] .... ACPP

Association Canadienne des Periodiques Catholiques [*Canadian Association of Catholic Periodicals*] .... ACPC

Association Canadienne des Physiciens et Physiciennes (AC) .... ACP

Association Canadienne des Pigistes de l'Edition [*Canada*] .... ACPE

Association Canadienne des Presidents de Departements d'Anglais [*Canadian Association of Chairmen of English Departments - CACE*] .... ACPDA

Association Canadienne des Producteurs de Films d'Animation [*Canada*] .... ACPFA

Association Canadienne des Professeures et Professeurs d'Universite (AC) .... ACPPU

Association Canadienne des Professeurs de Comptabilite [*Canadian Association of Professors of Accounting*] .... ACPC

Association Canadienne des Professeurs de Droit [*Canadian Association of Law Teachers - CALT*] .... ACPD

Association Canadienne des Professeurs de Langue Seconde (AC) .... ACPLS

Association Canadienne des Professeurs de Redaction Technique et Scientifique [*Canadian Association of Teachers of Technical Writing - CATTW*] .... ACPRTS

Association Canadienne des Professeurs d'Immersion (AC) .... ACPI

Association Canadienne des Professeurs d'Universite [*Canadian Association of University Professors*] .... ACPU

Association Canadienne des Quotidiens (AC) .... ACQ

Association Canadienne des Radiodiffuseurs (AC) .... ACR

Association Canadienne des Redacteurs Agricoles de Langue Francaise (AC) .... ACRA

Association Canadienne des Regulateurs des Vols [*Canadian Air Line Dispatchers' Association - CALDA*] .... ACRV

Association Canadienne des Relations Industrielles [*Canadian Industrial Relations Association - CIRA*] .... ACRI

Association Canadienne des Resources Hydriques [*Canadian Water Resources Association*] (EAIO) .... ACRH

Association Canadienne des Responsables de l'Habitation et de l'Urbainisme [*Canada*] .... ACRHU

Association Canadienne des Restaurateurs Professionnels [*Canadian Association of Professional Conservators - CAPC*] .... ACRP

Association Canadienne des Sciences de l'Information [*Canadian Association for Information Science*] .... ACSI

Association Canadienne des Sciences Geodesiques et Cartographiques [*Canadian Institute of Surveying and Mapping*] (EAIO) .... ACSGC

Association Canadienne des Sciences Regionales [*Canadian Regional Science Association - CRSA*] .... ACSR

Association Canadienne des Sciences Sportives [*Canadian Association of Sports Sciences*] .... ACSS

Association Canadienne des Slavistes [*Canadian Association of Slavists - CAS*] .... ACS

Association Canadienne des Societes d'Investissement en Capital de Risque .... ACSICR

Association Canadienne des Sociologues et Anthropologues de Langue Francaise [*Canadian Association of French-Language Sociologists and Anthropologists*] .... ACSALF

Association Canadienne des Soins Palliatifs (AC) .... ACSP

Association Canadienne des Techniciens en Radiation Medicale [*Canadian Association of Medical Radiation Technologists*] (EAIO) ... ACTRM
Association Canadienne des Techniciens et Technologistes en Sante Animale (AC) ... ACTTSA
Association Canadienne des Techniques de l'Asphalte [*Canadian Technical AsphaltAssociation*] (EAIO) ... ACTA
Association Canadienne des Travailleurs Sociaux [*Canadian Association of Social Workers - CASW*] ... ACTS
Association Canadienne des Utilisateurs SAS (AC) ... ACUS
Association Canadienne des Veterans du Hockey [*Canadian Association of Hockey Veterans*] ... ACVH
Association Canadienne des Veterinaires [*Canadian Veterinary Medical Association*] (EAIO) ... ACV
Association Canadienne d'Etudes Fiscales (AC) ... ACEF
Association Canadienne d'Exportation [*Canadian Export Association*] ... ACE
Association Canadienne d'Habitation et de Renovation Urbaine (AC) ... ACHRU
Association Canadienne d'Hygiene Publique [*Canadian Association of Public Health*] ... ACHP
Association Canadienne d'Orthopedie (AC) ... ACO
Association Canadienne Droit et Societe [*Canadian Law and Society Association - CLSA*] ... ACDS
Association Canadienne du Canotage Recreatif [*Canadian Association of Recreational Boating*] ... ACCR
Association Canadienne du Commerce des Semences (AC) ... ACCS
Association Canadienne du Contreplaque de Bois Dur (AC) ... ACCBD
Association Canadienne du Controle du Trafic Aerien [*Canadian Air Traffic Control Association - CATCA*] ... ACCTA
Association Canadienne du Droit de l'Environnement [*Canadian Association of Environmental Law*] ... ACDE
Association Canadienne du Genie Eolien [*Canada*] ... ACGE
Association Canadienne du Marketing Direct (AC) ... ACMD
Association Canadienne du Personnel Administratif Universitaire [*Canadian Association of University Administration Personnel*] ... ACPAU
Association Canadienne d'Urbanisme [*Canadian City Planning Association*] ... ACU
Association Canadienne Fournisseurs Bibliotheque [*Canadian Association of Library Suppliers*] ... ACFB
Association Canadienne Linguistique [*Canadian Linguistic Association - CLA*] ... ACL
Association Canadienne pour la Formation des Enseignants (AC) ... ACFE
Association Canadienne pour la Gestion de la Production et let Stocks [*Also, APICS Region VIII*] (AC) ... ACGPS
Association Canadienne pour la Recherche en Economie de Sante [*Canadian Health Economics Research Association - CHERA*] ... ACRES
Association Canadienne pour la Recherche en Economie Familiale [*Canadian Association for Research in Home Economics - CARHE*] ... ACREF
Association Canadienne pour la Technologie des Animaux de Laboratoire [*Canadian Association for Laboratory Animals Technology*] ... ACTA
Association Canadienne pour l'Avancement de la Litterature de Jeunesse [*Canadian Association for the Advancement of Children's Literature*] ... ACALJ
Association Canadienne pour l'Avancement des Etudes Neerlandaises [*Canadian Association for the Advancement of Netherlandic Studies - CAANS*] ... ACAEN
Association Canadienne pour le Droit a l'Avortement [*Canadian Abortion Rights Action League - CARAL*] ... ACDA
Association Canadienne pour le Soustitrage (AC) ... ACST
Association Canadienne pour les Deficients Mentaux [*Canadian Association for the Mentally Retarded*] ... ACDM
Association Canadienne pour les Etudes du Folklore [*Canadian Folklore Studies Association*] ... ACEF
Association Canadienne pour les Etudes en Cooperation [*Canadian Association for Studies in Cooperation - CASC*] ... ACEC
Association Canadienne pour les Etudes Rurales [*Canadian Association of Rural Studies - CARS*] ... ACER
Association Canadienne pour les Etudes sur les Femmes [*Canadian Women's Studies Association - CWSA*] ... ACEF
Association Canadienne pour les Nations-Unies [*United Nations Association in Canada*] (EAIO) ... ACNU
Association Canadienne pour les Structures et Materiaux Composites (AC) ... ACSMAC
Association Canadienne pour l'Etude de la Litterature et des Langues du Commonwealth [*Canadian Association for Commonwealth Literature and Language Studies - CACLALS*] ... ACELLC
Association Canadienne pour l'Etude de l'Administration Scolaire [*Canadian Association for the Study of Academic Administration*] ... ACEAS
Association Canadienne pour l'Etude de l'Education des Adultes [*Canadian Association for the Study of Adult Education - CASAE*] ... ACEEA
Association Canadienne pour l'Integration Communautarie [*Canadian Association for Community Living*] (EAIO) ... ACIC
Association Canadienne-Francaise de l'Alberta (AC) ... ACFA
Association Canadienne-Francaise de l'Ontario (AC) ... ACFO
Association Canadienne-Francaise pour l'Avancement des Sciences ... ACFAS
Association Canado-Americaine (EA) ... ACA
Association Candienne de la Formation Professionelle (AC) ... ACFP
Association Candienne de Television par Cable [*Formerly, National Community Antenna Television Association of Canada*] (AC) ... ACTC
Association Candienne sur la Qualite de l'Eau [*Also, Canadian National Committee of the Internation Association on Water Quality*] [*Formerly, Canadian Association on Water Pollution Research & Control*] (AC) ... ACQE
Association Catholique Canadienne de la Sante [*Canadian-Catholic Health Association*] ... ACCS
Association Catholique de la Jeunesse Canadienne-Francaise [*Catholic Association of Francophone Youth*] [*Canada*] ... ACJC
Association Catholique des Etudes Bibliques au Canada [*Catholic Association of Bible Studies in Canada*] ... ACEBAC
Association Catholique Internationale des Oeuvres de Protection de la Jeune Fille [*Later, ACISJF*] ... ACIOPJF
Association Catholique Internationale des Services de la Jeunesse Feminine [*International Catholic Society for Girls*] [*Geneva, Switzerland*] (EAIO) ... ACISJF
Association Cerification Comite European de Normalisation (OSI) ... CENCER
Association Chiropratique Canadienne [*Canadian Chiropractic Association*] ... ACC
Association Cinematographique Professionnelle de Conciliation et d'Arbitrage (EAIO) ... ACPCA
Association Congolaise pour les Nations Unies [*United Nations Association of the Congo*] (EAIO) ... ACNU
Association Control Service Element [*Telecommunications*] (OSI) ... ACSE
Association Cooperative de Productions Audio-Visuelles (AC) ... ACPAV
Association Cooperative d'Economie Familiale - Montreal (Nord) (AC) ... ACEF du Nord
Association Cooperative Feminine du Quebec (AC) ... ACFQ
Association County Commissioners of Georgia (SRA) ... ACCG
Association Culturelle et Touristique des Cantons [*Cultural and Tourist Association of Cantons*] [*Canada*] ... ACTC
Association Culturelle Franco-Manitobaine (AC) ... ACFM
Association Culturelle Internationale: Reliance [*Leucate, France*] (EAIO) ... ACIR
Association d'Amitie et de Solidarite Franco-Algerienne [*Franco-Algerian Friendship and Solidarity Association*] ... AASFA
Association Danse au Canada [*Dance Association of Canada*] ... ADAC
Association de Climatologie du Quebec (AC) ... ACLIQ
Association de Comites Nationaux Olympiques d'Afrique [*Association of National Olympic Committees of Africa - ANOCA*] (EA) ... ACNOA
Association de Consultants Internationaux en Droits de l'Homme [*Association of International Consultants on Human Rights*] [*Geneva, Switzerland*] (EAIO) ... CID
Association de Coureurs Internationaux en Multicoques Oceaniques [*Association of International Competitors on Oceanic Multihulls*] (EAIO) ... ACIMO
Association de Gestion Internationale Collective des Oeuvres Audiovisuelles [*Association for the International Collective Management of Audiovisual Works*] [*Geneva, Switzerland*] (EAIO) ... AGICOA
Association de Gestion Portuaire de l'Afrique de l'Est et de l'Afrique Australe [*Port Management Association of Eastern and Southern Africa - PMAESA*] (EAIO) ... AGPAEA
Association de Golf du Quebec (AC) ... AGQ
Association de la Construction de l'Outaouais [*Outaouais Construction Association*] (AC) ... ACO
Association de la Construction du Quebec [*Construction Association of Quebec*] (AC) ... ACQ
Association de la Jeunesse Rurale du Quebec (AC) ... AJRQ
Association de la Librairie Ancienne du Canada [*Association of Antique Bookstores of Canada*] ... ALAC
Association de la Paralysie Cerebrale du Quebec [*Quebec Cerebral Palsy Association*] (AC) ... APCQI
Association de la Presse Anglo-Americaine de Paris [*Anglo-American Press Association of Paris*] (EAIO) ... APAAP
Association de la Presse Eurafricaine [*Eurafrican Press Association*] [*Belgium*] ... APEA
Association de la Presse Sportive du Quebec (AC) ... APSQ
Association de la Recherche en Communication du Quebec (AC) ... ARCQ
Association de la Securite Industrielle du Canada [*Industrial Security Association of Canada*] ... ASIC
Association de l'Evangelisation des Enfants (AC) ... AEF
Association de l'Huile a Chauffage du Quebec (AC) ... AHCQ
Association de l'Industrie de la Fonte de Fromage de la CEE [*Association of the Processed Cheese Industry of the European Economic Community*] ... ASSIFONTE
Association de l'Industrie de l'Aluminium du Quebec (AC) ... AIAQ
Association de l'Industrie des Fruits et Legumes au Vinaigre, en Saumure, a l'Huile et des Produits Similaires des CE [*Association of the Industry of Fruit and Vegetables in Vinegar, Brine, Oil and Similar Products of the EC*] (ECED) ... AIFLV
Association de l'Industrie des Just et Nectars de Fruits et de Legumes de la CEE [*Association of the Industry of Juices and Nectars from Fruits and Vegetables of the EEC*] (ECED) ... AIJN
Association de l'Industrie Laitiere de la CE [*European Community Dairy Trade Association*] [*Belgium*] (EAIO) ... ASSILEC
Association de l'Industrie Touristique du Canada [*Travel (later, Tourism) Industry Association of Canada - TIAC*] ... AITC
Association de Manutention du Quebec (AC) ... AMQ
Association de Placement Universitaire et Collegial [*University and College Placement Association*] [*Canada*] ... APUC
Association de Planification Fiscale et Financiere (AC) ... APFF
Association de Prevention des Accidents dans l'Industrie Forestiere [*Forest Products Accident Prevention Association*] [*Canada*] ... APAIF
Association de Psychologie du Travail de Langue Francaise [*French-Language Association of Work Psychology*] (EAIO) ... APTLF
Association de Psychologie Scientifique de Langue Francaise [*French-Language Association of Scientific Psychology*] (EAIO) ... APSLF
Association de Recherche et d'Exploitation de Diamant et de l'Or [*Guinea*] [*ICAO designator*] (FAAC) ... GIN
Association de Recherches Theatrales au Canada (AC) ... ARTC
Association de Recyclage du Polystyrene du Canada (AC) ... ARPC
Association de Reseaux Informatique en Systeme Totalement et Tres Elabore [*Association of Information Networks in a Completely Open and Very Elaborate System*] [*France*] [*Computer science*] (TNIG) ... ARISTOTE
Association de Sante et Securite des Industries de la Foret du Quebec [*Quebec Logging Health & Safety Association Inc.*] (AC) ... ASSIFQ
Association de Sante et Securite des Pates et Papiers du Quebec Inc. [*Quebec Pulp & Paper Health & Safety Association Inc.*] (AC) ... ASSPPQ

Association de Ski Nautique du Canada [*Canadian Water Ski Association*] .... ASNC
Association de Textiles des Cantons de l'Est (AC) .... ATCE
Association d'Economie Familiale du Quebec (AC) .... AEFQ
Association d'Economie Politique [*Political Economic Association*] [*Canada*] .... AEP
Association d'Education Prescolaire du Quebec (AC) ...... AEPQ
Association Democratique des Francais de l'Etranger [*Democratic Association of French Citizens Abroad*] (PPW) .... ADFE
Association d'Entraide pour les Agoraphobes (AC) .... ADEPA
Association des Administrateurs de Recherches Universitaires du Quebec (AC) .... ADARUQ
Association des Administrateurs du Personnel de la Fonction Publique [*Association of Personnel Administrators of Public Functions*] [*Canada*] ...... AAP
Association des Agences de Publicite du Quebec [*Association of Quebec Advertising Agencies*] (AC) .... AAPQ
Association des Agents de Voyages du Quebec (AC) .... ACTA-Quebec
Association des Amenagistes Regionaux du Quebec (AC) .... AARQ
Association des Amidonneries de Cereales de la CEE [*EC*] (ECED) ....:........ AAC
Association des Amidonneries de Mais de la CEE [*Association of the Maize Starch Industries of the European Economic Community*] .... AAM
Association des Amis de Maurice Zundel [*Paris, France*] (EAIO) .... AAMZ
Association des Amis du Musee International des Hussards [*Association of Friends of the International Museum of the Hussars*] [*France*] (EAIO) ...... AAMIH
Association des Anciens Fonctionnaires Internationaux [*Association of Former International Civil Servants - AFICS*] [*Geneva, Switzerland*] (EA) .... AAFI
Association des Animateurs et Animatrices de Pastorale de la Sante du Quebec (AC) .... AAAPSQ
Association des Architectes en Pratique Privee du Quebec (AC) .... AAPPQ
Association des Architectes Paysagistes du Quebec (AC) .... AAPQ
Association des Archivistes du Quebec (AC) .... AAQ
Association des Armateurs Canadiens [*Formerly, Dominion Marine Association*] (AC) .... AAC
Association des Artisans du Film Canadien (AC) .... AAFC
Association des Artisans Glaciers et des Fabricants de Mix pour Glace des Pays de la CEE [*Association of Home-Made Ice-Cream and Ice-Mix Manufacturers in the European Economic Community*] .... ASSOGLACE
Association des Artistes Non Figuratifs de Montreal [*1956-61*] [*Canada*] (NGC) .... AANFM
Association des Arts Graphiques du Quebec, Inc. (AC) .... AAGQ
Association des Arts Plastiques, Montreal [*1955*] [*Canada*] (NGC) .... AAP
Association des Assureurs Cooperatifs Europeens [*Association of European Cooperative Insurers - AECI*] [*Brussels, Belgium*] (EAIO) ...... AACE
Association des Assureurs-Vie du Canada [*Association of Life Insurers of Canada*] .... AAVC
Association des Auditeurs et Anciens Auditeurs de l'Academie [*Association of Attenders and Alumni of the Hague Academy of International Law*] (EAIO) .... AAA
Association des Auteurs des Cantons de l'Est [*Association of Writers of Cantons of the East*] [*Canada*] .... AACE
Association des Auxiliaires Familiales et Sociales du Quebec (AC) .... AAFSQ
Association des Banques Centrales Africaines [*Association of African Central Banks*] (EAIO) .... ABCA
Association des Banquiers Canadiens [*Canadian Bankers Association*] .... ABC
Association des Bibliothecaires du Quebec (AC) .... ABQ
Association des Bibliothecaires Parlementaires au Canada [*Association of Parliamentary Librarians of Canada*] .... ABPAC
Association des Bibliothecaires Professionel du Nouveau-Brunswick (AC) .... ABPNB
Association des Bibliotheques de la Sante Affiliee a l'Universite de Montreal (AC) .... ABSAUM
Association des Bibliotheques de la Sante du Canada [*Canadian Association of Health Libraries*] .... ABSC
Association des Bibliotheques de Recherche du Canada [*Canadian Association of Research Libraries*] (EAIO) .... ABRC
Association des Bibliotheques des Provinces de l'Atlantique [*Atlantic Provinces Association of Libraries*] [*Canada*] .... ABPA
Association des Bibliotheques Publiques de l'Estrie (AC) .... ABIPE
Association des Bureaux de Congres du Quebec (AC) .... ABCQ
Association des Bureaux de l'Information des Universites [*Association of University Information Bureaus*] [*Canada*] .... ABUIC
Association des Cablodistributeurs du Quebec Inc. (AC) .... ACQ
Association des Cadres des Colleges du Quebec (AC) .... ACCQ
Association des Cadres d'Institutions Culturelles (AC) .... ACIC
Association des Cadres Intermediaires de la Sante et des Services Sociaux du Quebec (AC) .... ACISSSQ
Association des Cadres Intermediaires des Affaires Sociales (AC) .... ACIAS
Association des Camps du Canada (AC) .... ACC
Association des Cartotheques et des Archives Cartographiques du Canada [*Association of Canadian Map Libraries and Archives*] (EAIO) .... ACACC
Association des Centres de Ski de Fond du Quebec (AC) .... ACSFQ
Association des Centres Hospitaliers et Centres d'Accueil Prives du Quebec (AC) .... ACHAB
Association des Chantiers Maritimes Canadiens [*Association of Canadian Maritime Shipyards*] .... ACMC
Association des Chefs de Service d'Incendie du Quebec [*Quebec Fire Chief Association*] (AC) .... ACSIQ
Association des Chimistes de l'Industrie Textile [*Association of Chemists of the Textile Industry*] (EAIO) .... ACIT
Association des Citoyens de Culture Francaise d'Amerique [*American Association of Citizens of French Culture*] [*Canada*] .... ACCFA
Association des Classes Moyennes Africaines [*African Middle Classes Association*] .... ACMAF
Association des Collaboratrices et Partenaires en Affaires (AC) .... ACPA

Association des Comites Nationaux Olympiques [*Association of National Olympic Committees - ANOC*] [*Paris, France*] (EAIO) .... ACNO
Association des Comites Nationaux Olympiques d'Europe [*Association of the European National Olympic Committees - ENOC*] [*Brussels, Belgium*] (EAIO) .... ACNOE
Association des Commissaires Industriels du Quebec (AC) .... ACIQ
Association des Communicateurs Municipaux du Quebec (AC) .... ACMQ
Association des Communicateurs Scientifiques du Quebec (AC) .... ACSQ
Association des Conseillers en Environnement du Quebec (AC) .... ACEQ
Association des Conseillers et Conseilleres Scolaires Francophones du Nouveau-Brunswick (AC) .... ACCSFNB
Association des Conseils Sub-Aquatiques Canadiens [*Association of Canadian Underwater Councils*] .... ASCS
Association des Consommateurs du Canada [*Consumers' Association of Canada - CAC*] .... ACC
Association des Consommateurs du Quebec (AC) .... ACQ
Association des Constructeurs de Machines a Coudre de la CEE [*Association of Sewing Machine Manufacturers of the EEC*] .... ASCOMACE
Association des Constructeurs de Routes et Grands Travaux du Quebec [*Quebec Road Builders & Heavy Construction Association*] (AC) .... ACRGTQ
Association des Constructeurs Europeens d'Automobiles [*Association of European Car Manufacturers*] [*EC*] (ECED) .... ACEA
Association des Constructeurs Europeens de Systemes d'Alarme Incendie et Vol [*Association of European Manufacturers of Fire and Intruder Alarm Systems*] (EAIO) .... EURALARM
Association des Cooperatives d'Epargne et de Credit d'Afrique [*African Confederation of Cooperative Savings and Credit Associations - ACCOSCA*] [*Nairobi, Kenya*] (EAIO) .... ACECA
Association des Coordonnateurs de Congres des Universites et des Colleges du Canada (AC) .... ACCUCC
Association des Courtiers d'Assurances de la Province de Quebec [*Insurance Brokers Association of Quebec*] (AC) .... ACAPQ
Association des Createurs et Intervenants de la Bande Dessinee (AC) .... ACIBD
Association des Denturologistes du Quebec (AC) .... ADQ
Association des Dermatologistes du Quebec [*Association of Dermatologists of Quebec*] (AC) .... ADQ
Association des Designers Industriels du Quebec (AC) .... ADIQ
Association des Detaillants de Materiaux de Construction du Quebec [*Quebec Building Materials Dealers Association*] (AC) .... ADMACQ
Association des Detaillants en Alimentation du Quebec [*Quebec Food Retailers Association*] (AC) .... ADA
Association des Directeurs d'Agence-Vie de Montreal (AC) .... ADAM
Association des Directeurs de Departements de Sante Communautaire [*Association of Public Health Department Directors*] [*Canada*] .... ADDSC
Association des Directeurs de Departements d'Etudes Francaises des Universites et Colleges du Canada [*Association of Directors of Departments of French Studies of Canadian Universities and Colleges*] .... ADEFUCC
Association des Directeurs de Recherche Industrielle du Quebec (AC) .... ADRIQ
Association des Directeurs d'Ecole de Montreal (AC) .... ADEM
Association des Directeurs des Centres Europeens des Plastiques [*Association of Directors of European Centres for Plastics*] (EAIO) .... ADICEP
Association des Directeurs Generaux des Commissions Scolaires du Quebec (AC) .... ADIGECS
Association des Distributeurs Aux Services Alimentaires du Quebec (AC) .... ADSAQ
Association des Distributeurs Exclusifs de Livres en Langue Francaise [*Association of Exclusive Distributors of French-Language Books*] [*Canada*] .... ADELF
Association des Distributeurs Independants de Produits Petroliers (AC) .... ADIP
Association des Ecoles Internationales .... AEI
Association des Economistes, Sociologues, et Statisticiens [*Economists', Sociologists', and Statisticians' Association ESSA*] [*Canada*] .... AESS
Association des Ecrivains de Langue Francaise [*Association of French-Language Writers*] (EAIO) .... ADELF
Association des Editeurs Canadiens [*Association of Canadian Editors*] .... AEC
Association des Eglises Evangelique (AC) .... AEE
Association des Electrolystes du Quebec (AC) .... AEQ
Association des Employes du Conseil de Recherches [*Research Council Employees' Association - RCEA*] [*Canada*] .... AECR
Association des Employes du Trafic [*Association of Traffic Employees*] [*Canada*] .... AET
Association des Employes d'Universites et de Colleges [*Association of University and College Employees - AUCE*] [*Canada*] .... AEUC
Association des Enducteurs, Calandreurs et Fabricants de Revetements de Sols Plastiques de la CEE [*Association of Coated Fabrics, Plastic Films and Plastic and Synthetic Floor Coverings of the European Economic Community*] (PDAA) .... AEC
Association des Enseignantes et des Enseignants Franco-Ontariens [*Franco-Ontarien Teachers' Association*] (AC) .... AEFO
Association des Enseignants de la Construction et du Meuble du Quebec (AC) .... AECMQ
Association des Enseignants des Metiers du Vetement du Quebec (AC) .... AEMVQ
Association des Enseignants en Imprimerie du Quebec (AC) .... AEIQ
Association des Enseignants en Refrigeration et Climatisation du Quebec (AC) .... AERCQ
Association des Entomologistes Amateurs du Quebec (AC) .... AEAQ
Association des Entrepreneurs de Services en Environnement du Quebec (AC) .... AESEQ
Association des Entrepreneurs en Construction du Quebec (AC) .... AECQ
Association des Entrepreneurs en Couture du Quebec (AC) .... AECQ
Association des Entrepreneurs en Isolation de la Province du Quebec (AC) .... AIQ

Association des Etablissements Multiplicateurs de Semences Fourrageres des Communautes Europeennes [*Association of Forage Seed Breeders of the European Community*] [*Brussels, Belgium*] .... AMUFOC

Association des Etudes Canadiennes [*Association for Canadian Studies - ACS*] .... AEC

Association des Etudes de l'Europe Centrale et de l'Europe de l'Est du Canada [*Central and East European Studies Association of Canada - CEESAC*] .... AEECEEC

Association des Etudiants et Etudiantes en Medecine de l'Universite de Montreal (AC) .... AEMUM

Association des Etudiants Musulmans Nord-Africains [*North African Muslim Students Association*] (AF) .... AEMNA

Association des Etudiants Tchadiens en France [*Association of Chadian Students in France*] [*Chad*] (AF) .... AETF

Association des Evangeliques d'Afrique et Madagascar [*Association of Evangelicals of Africa and Madagascar*] (EAIO) .... AEAM

Association des Fabricants de Cafe Soluble des Pays de la CEE [*Association of Soluble Coffee Manufacturers of the Countries of the European Economic Community*] .... AFCASOLE

Association des Fabricants de Glucose de la CEE [*Association of the Glucose Producers in the European Economic Community*] .... AFG

Association des Fabricants de Laits de Conserve des Pays de la CEE [*Association of Powdered Milk Manufacturers of the EEC*] .... ASFALEC

Association des Fabricants de Material Agricole du Quebec (AC) .... AFMAQ

Association des Fabricants d'Engrais du Quebec (AC) .... AFEQ

Association des Fabricants et Distributeurs de l'Industrie de la Cuisine du Quebec (AC) .... AFDICQ

Association des Fabricants Europeens d'Appareils de Controle [*European Control Manufacturers Association*] (EAIO) .... AFECOGAZ

Association des Fabricants Europeens d'Appareils de Controle et de Regulation [*European Control Device Manufacturers' Association*] [*EC*] (ECED) .... AFECOR

Association des Fabricants Europeens de Chauffe-Bains et Chauffe-Eau Instantaneset de Chaudieres Murales au Gaz [*Association of European Manufacturers of Instantaneous Gas Water Heaters and Wall-Hung Boilers*] (EA) .... AFECI

Association des Fabricants Europeens de Rubans Auto-Adhesifs [*Association of European Manufacturers of Self-Adhesive Tapes - AEMSAT*] (EAIO) .... AFERA

Association des Fabricants Europeens d'Emulsifants Alimentaires [*Association of European Manufacturers of Food Emulsifiers*] (EAIO) .... EFEMA

Association des Fabricants Europeens d'Equipements Ferroviaires [*Association of European Railway Equipment Manufacturers*] (EAIO) .... AFEDEF

Association des Facultes de Medecine du Canada [*Association of Medical Faculties of Canada*] .... AFMC

Association des Facultes de Pharmacie du Canada [*Association of Faculties of Pharmacy of Canada*] .... AFPC

Association des Facultes Dentaires du Canada [*Association of Dentistry Faculties in Canada*] .... AFDC

Association des Familles Paguin [*Association of the Paguin Family*] [*Canada*] .... AFP

Association des Federations Africaines de Basketball Amateur [*African Association of Basketball Federations*] [*Egypt*] .... AFABA

Association des Femmes Africaines pour la Recherche sur le Developpement [*Association of African Women for Research and Development - AAWORD*] (EAIO) .... AFARD

Association des Femmes Collaboratrices [*Association of Feminine Collectives*] [*Canada*] .... ADFC

Association des Femmes d'Affaires du Quebec (AC) .... AFAQ

Association des Fermieres de l'Ontario (AC) .... AFO

Association des Firmes-Conseils en Technologie de l'Information de Quebec (AC) .... AFTIQ

Association des Fournisseurs d'Hotels et Restaurants Inc. (AC) .... AFHR

Association des Gens d'Affaires Haitiens de Montreal [*Haitian Businessmen's Association of Montreal*] (AC) .... AGAHM

Association des Grandes Entreprises de Distribution de Belgique [*Trade organization*] [*Belgium*] (EY) .... AGED

Association des Graveurs du Quebec [*1971, CGQ from 1978, CQE from 1984*] [*Canada*] (NGC) .... AGQ

Association des Groupements de Negoce Interieur du Bois et des Produits Derives dans les Pays de la CEE [*Association of National Trade Groups for Wood and Derived Products in Countries of the European Economic Community*] .... AGNIB

Association des Groupes d'Astronomes Amateurs [*Association of Amateur Astronomy Groups*] [*Canada*] .... AGAA

Association des Hommes d'Affaires et Professionnels du Quebec (AC) .... AHAPQ

Association des Hopitaux Catholiques du Canada [*Association of Catholic Hospitals of Canada*] .... AHCC

Association des Hopitaux du Canada [*Association of Hospitals of Canada*] .... AHC

Association des Hopitaux du Quebec [*Quebec Hospital Association*] (AC) .... AHQ

Association des Industries de Cidre et Vins de Fruits de la CE [*Belgium*] (EAIO) .... AICVF-CE

Association des Industries de Glaces Alimentaires de la CEE [*Association of the Ice Cream Industries of the European Economic Community*] .... EUROGLACES

Association des Industries de la Chocolaterie, Biscuiterie-Biscotterie et Confiserie de la CEE [*Association of the Chocolate, Biscuit and Confectionery Industries of the EEC*] (ECED) .... CAOBISCO

Association des Industries des Aliments Dietetiques de la CEE [*Association of Dietetic Foods Industries of the European Economic Community*] .... IDACE

Association des Industries des Carrieres [*Federations of Quarrying Industries*] [*Belgium*] (EY) .... AIC

Association des Industries des Cidres et Vins de Fruits de la CEE [*Association of the Cider and Fruit Wine Industries of the EEC*] (ECED) .... AICV

Association des Industries des Fruits et Legumes Deshydrates de la CEE [*European Organization of the Dehydrated Fruit and Vegetable Industries*] [*EC*] (ECED) .... AIFLD

Association des Industries des Fruits et Legumes Deshydrates de la CEE [*European Organization of the Dehydrated Fruit and Vegetable Industries*] (EAIO) .... AJFLD

Association des Industries du Jute Europeennes [*Association of European Jute Industries*] .... AIJE

Association des Industries Margarinieres des Pays de la CEE [*Association of Margarine Industries of the EEC Countries*] [*Belgium*] .... IMACE

Association des Infirmieres Canadiennes [*Canadian Nurses' Association - CNA*] .... AIC

Association des Infirmieres et Infirmiers du Canada (EAIO) .... AIIC

Association des Infirmieres et Infirmiers en Sante du Travail du Quebec (AC) .... AIISTQ

Association des Ingenieurs Municipaux du Quebec [*Association of Quebec Municipal Engineers*] (AC) .... AIMQ

Association des Ingenieurs-Conseils du Canada [*Association of Canadian Engineer-Councils*] .... AICC

Association des Ingenieurs-Conseils du Quebec [*Consulting Engineers of Quebec*] (AC) .... AICQ

Association des Institutions de Niveaux Prescolaire et Elementaire du Quebec (AC) .... AIPEQ

Association des Institutions d'Enseignement Secondaire (AC) .... AIES

Association des Instituts de Theologie du Moyen-Orient [*Association of Theological Institutes in the Middle East - ATIME*] (EAIO) .... AITME

Association des Instituts d'Etudes Europeennes [*Association of Institutes for European Studies*] .... AIEE

Association des Intermediaires en Assurance de Personnes du Quebec (AC) .... AIAPQ

Association des Intervenants en Toxicomanie du Quebec (AC) .... AITQ

Association des Jeunes Juristes Africains [*France*] .... AJJAF

Association des Journalistes Independants du Quebec [*Quebec Association of Independent Journalists*] (AC) .... AJIQ

Association des Journaux Regionaux du Quebec (AC) .... AJRQ

Association des Juifs Anciens Resistants [*Association of Jews in the Resistance*] [*Acronym is pseudonym of writer Romain Gary*] .... AJAR

Association des Juristes d'Expression Francaise de l'Ontario (AC) .... AJEFO

Association des Libraires du Quebec (AC) .... ALQ

Association des Litteratures Canadiennes et Quebecoises [*Association for Canadian and Quebec Literatures - ACQL*] .... ALCQ

Association des Maitres Couvreurs du Quebec [*Quebec Master Roofers Association*] (AC) .... AMCQ

Association des Malentendants Canadiens (AC) .... AMEC

Association des Manoeuvres Interprovinciaux [*Interprovincial Labourers Association*] (AC) .... AMI

Association des Manufacturiers de Bois de Sciage du Quebec [*Quebec Lumber Manufacturers Association*] (AC) .... AMBSQ

Association des Manufacturiers de Maconnerie de Beton (AC) .... AMMB

Association des Manufacturiers de Produits Alimentaires du Quebec [*Quebec Food Processors Association*] (AC) .... AMPAQ

Association des Marchands de Bois en Gros du Quebec [*Quebec Wholesale Lumber Association*] (AC) .... AMBQ

Association des MBA du Quebec (AC) .... AMBAQ

Association des Medecins Biochimistes du Canada (AC) .... AMBC

Association des Medecins de Langue Francaise [*Canada*] (EAIO) .... AMLF

Association des Medecins Haitiens a l'Etranger [*Association of Haitian Physicains Abroad*] (EA) .... AMHE

Association des Medecins Psychiatres du Quebec [*Quebec Psychiatrists' Association*] (AC) .... AMPQ

Association des Media et de la Technologie en Education au Canada [*Association for Media and Technology in Education in Canada - AMTEC*] .... AMTE

Association des Medias Ecrits Communautaires du Quebec (AC) .... AMECQ

Association des Microbiologistes du Quebec (AC) .... AMQ

Association des Mines d'Aminante du Quebec (AC) .... AMAQ

Association des Municipalities du Nouveau-Brunswick (AC) .... AMNB

Association des Numismates Francophones du Canada (AC) .... ANFC

Association des Obtenteurs de Pommes de Terre du Marche Commun [*Association of Certified Seed Potato Suppliers of the Common Market*] .... ASSOPOMAC

Association des Optometristes du Quebec (AC) .... AOQ

Association des Orchestres de Jeunes du Canada [*Canadian Association of Youth Orchestras*] .... AOJC

Association des Organisations Nationales de la Boulangerie et de la Patisserie de la CE [*Association of National Organizations in the Bakery and Confectionery Trade in the European Community*] [*Belgium*] (EAIO) .... AONBP-CE

Association des Organisations Nationales d'Entreprises de Peche de la CEE [*Association of National Organizations of Fishing Enterprises in the European Economic Community*] .... EUROPECHE

Association des Organisations Professionnelles du Commerce des Sucres pour les Pays de la Communaute Economique Europeenne [*Association of Sugar Trade Organizations for the European Economic Community Countries*] [*Belgium*] .... ASSUC

Association des Parents Catholiques du Quebec (AC) .... APCQ

Association des Parents Francophones de la Colombie-Britannique (AC) .... APFCB

Association des Parlementaires du Commonwealth [*Commonwealth Parliamentary Association*] [*Canada*] .... APC

Association des Pays Exportateurs de Mineral de Fer [*Association of Iron Ore Exporting Countries*] [*Switzerland*] (EAIO) .... APEF.

Association des Peres Gais de Montreal Inc. [*Gay Fathers of Montreal Inc.*] (AC) .... APGM

Association des Pharmaciens des Etablissements de Sante du Quebec (AC) ... APES
Association des Physiciens et Ingenieurs Biomedicaux du Quebec (AC) ... APIBQ
Association des Policiers Provinciaux du Quebec [*Quebec Provincial Police Association*] (AC) ... APPQ
Association des Presses Universitaires Canadiennes [*Association of Canadian University Presses - ACUP*] ... APUC
Association des Producteurs de Films et Television du Quebec (AC) ... APFTQ
Association des Producteurs de Theatre Professionnel (AC) ... APTP
Association des Producteurs d'Isoglucose de la CE [*Association of the Producers of Isoglucose of the European Community*] [*Common Market*] ... API
Association des Producteurs Europeens d'Azote [*European Association of Nitrogen Manufacturers*] (EAIO) ... APEA
Association des Professeurs d'Allemand des Universites Canadiennes [*Canadian Association of University Teachers of German - CAUTG*] ... APAUC
Association des Professeurs d'Anglais des Universites Canadiennes [*Association of Canadian University Teachers of English - ACUTE*] ... APAUC
Association des Professeurs de Francais des Universites Canadiennes [*Association of Canadian University Teachers of French*] ... APFUC
Association des Professeurs de Francais des Universites et Colleges Canadiens [*Association of Canadian University and College Teachers of French - ACUCTF*] ... APFUCC
Association des Professeurs de Francais en Afrique [*Association of French Teachers in Africa - AFTA*] [*Khartoum, Sudan*] (EAIO) ... APFA
Association des Professeurs de Sciences du Quebec (AC) ... APSQ
Association des Professeurs Franco-Americains [*Defunct*] (EA) ... APFA
Association des Professionnels du Chauffage (AC) ... APC
Association des Professionnels en Exposition du Quebec (AC) ... APEQ
Association des Proprietaires d'Autobus du Quebec (AC) ... APAQ
Association des Proprietaires de Camions-Remorques Independants du Quebec Inc. (AC) ... APCRIQ
Association des Proprietaires de Machinerie Lourde du Quebec Inc. (AC) ... APMLQ
Association des Proprietaires du Quebec Inc. (AC) ... APQ
Association des Prospecteurs du Quebec [*Quebec Prospectors Association*] (AC) ... APQ
Association des Psychiatres du Canada [*Canadian Psychiatric Association*] (EAIO) ... APC
Association des Psychologues de l'Ocean Indien (EAIO) ... APsyOI
Association des Psychologues du Quebec [*Quebec Psychological Association*] (AC) ... APQ
Association des Radiodiffuseurs Communautaires du Quebec (AC) ... ARCQ
Association des Redacteurs de Devis du Canada [*Specification Writers Association of Canada*] ... ARDC
Association des Registraires d'Universites et de Colleges du Canada [*Association of Registrars of the Universities and Colleges of Canada*] ... ARUCC
Association des Religieuses Enseignantes du Quebec (AC) ... AREQ
Association des Residences d'Accueil du Quebec (AC) ... ARAQ
Association des Responsables des Bibliotheques [*Centres de Documentation Universitaires et Recherche d'Expression Francaise au Canada*] (AC) ... ABCDEF-Canada
Association des Ressortissants du Haut et du Moyen Congo [*Association of Natives of the Upper and Middle Congo*] ... ASSORECO
Association des Restaurateurs du Quebec [*Quebec Restaurant Association*] (AC) ... ARQ
Association des Restauratrices-Cuisinieres (EA) ... ARC
Association des Routes et Transports du Canada [*Roads and Transportation Association of Canada*] ... ARTC
Association des Scientifiques, Ingenieurs, et Techniciens du Canada [*Association of the Scientific, Engineering, and Technological Community of Canada*] ... ASITC
Association des Sculpteurs du Quebec [*1961, CSQ from 1978*] [*Canada*] (NGC) ... ASQ
Association des Secretaires et Tresoriers Municipaux de l'Ontario (AC) ... ASTMO
Association des Services aux Etudiants des Colleges et Universites du Canada [*Canadian Association of College and University Student Services*] ... ASECUC
Association des Services d'Aide aux Jeunes Entrepreneurs du Quebec (AC) ... ASAJEQ
Association des Services de Rehabilitation Sociale du Quebec Inc. [*Association of Social Rehabilitation Agencies of Quebec Inc.*] (AC) ... ASRSQ
Association des Services Geologiques Africains [*Association of African Geological Surveys - AAGS*] [*ICSU*] (EAIO) ... ASGA
Association des Sexologues du Quebec (AC) ... ASQ
Association des Societes Nationales, Europeennes, et Mediterraneennes de Gastroenterologie [*Association of National, European, and Mediterranean Societies of Gastroenterology*] (EAIO) ... ASNEMGE
Association des Specialistes de la Mesure en Education [*Association of Specialists in Educational Measures*] [*Canada*] ... ASME
Association des Statisticiens de l'Athletisme [*Association of Track and Field Statisticians*] (EAIO) ... ASA
Association des Syndicats de Cheminots Canadiens [*Canadian Railway Labour Association - CRLA*] ... ASCC
Association des Techniciens Congolais des Telecommunications [*Association of Congolese Telecommunications Technicians*] [*Zaire*] ... ATCT
Association des Techniciens en Sante Animal du Quebec (AC) ... ATSAQ
Association des Technologistes Agricoles [*Association of Agricultural Technologists*] [*Canada*] ... ATA
Association des Technologistes Agro-Alimentaires [*Association of Subsistence Agriculture Technologists*] [*Canada*] ... ATA
Association des Traducteurs Anglophones du Quebec [*Association of Anglophone Translators of Quebec*] ... ATAQ
Association des Traducteurs et Traductrices Litteraires du Canada [*Literary Translators Association of Canada*] (EAIO) ... ATTLC
Association des Traducteurs Litteraires [*Literary Translators' Association*] [*Canada*] ... ATL
Association des Transitaires Internationaux Canadiens, inc. (AC) ... ATIC
Association des Transporteurs Aeriens de la Zone Franc [*Association of Air Transporters of the Franc Zone*] (AF) ... ATAF
Association des Transports du Canada [*Transportation Association of Canada*] (EAIO) ... ATC
Association des Tremblay d'Amerique [*Tremblay (Family) Association of America*] [*Canada*] ... ATA
Association des Universitaires d'Europe ... AUE
Association des Universites Africaines [*Association of African Universities - AAU*] (EAIO) ... AUA
Association des Universites Partiellement ou Entierement de Langue Francaise [*Association of Wholly or Partially French Language Universities*] [*Montreal, PQ*] (EA) ... AUPELF
Association d'Etudes Baha'ies [*Association for Baha'i Studies*] (EAIO) ... AEB
Association d'Etudes Linguistiques Interculturelles Africaines [*Canada*] ... AELIA
Association d'Etudes Politiques Transeuropeennes [*Trans European Policy Studies Association - TEPSA*] (EA) ... ADEPT
Association d'Histoire du Theatre du Canada [*Association for Canadian Theatre History - ACTH*] ... AHTC
Association d'Ileostomie & Colostomie de Montreal [*Colostomy Association of Montreal*] (AC) ... AICM
Association d'Instituts Europeens de Conjoncture Economique [*Association of European Conjuncture Institutes*] (EAIO) ... AIECE
Association du Camionnage du Quebec, Inc. [*Quebec Trucking Association Inc.*] (AC) ... ACQ
Association du Commerce et de l'Industrie du Cafe dans la CEE [*Association for the Coffee Trade and Industry in the EEC*] ... ACICAFE
Association du Disque et de l'Industrie du Spectacle Quebecoise [*Quebec Association of the Record and Entertainment Industry*] [*Canada*] ... ADISQ
Association du Droit de Retransmission Canadien (AC) ... ADRC
Association du Negoce des Grains Oleagineuses, Huiles, et Graisses Animales et Vegetales et Leurs Derives de la CEE [*Trade Association for Oilseeds, Oil, Vegetable and Animal Fats, and Their Derivatives of the European Economic Community*] ... ANGO
Association du Patrimoine d'Aylmer (AC) ... APA
Association du Personnel de Geneve OMS [*Geneva Staff Association World Health Organization*] [*Switzerland*] (EAIO) ... APGOMS
Association du Personnel Navigant des Lignes Aeriennes Canadiennes [*Canadian Air Line Flight Attendants' Association - CALFA*] ... APENAC
Association du Peuple pour l'Unite et l'Action [*Algeria*] [*Political party*] (EY) ... APUA
Association du Quebec pour Enfants avec Problemes Auditifs (AC) ... AQEPA
Association du Quebec pour l'Integration Sociale [*Quebec Association for Community Living*] (AC) ... AQIS
Association du Traite Atlantique [*Atlantic Treaty Association*] (EAIO) ... ATA
Association Educative et Culturelle Canada Egypte (AC) ... AECCE
Association Europea de Profesores de Espanol (AIE) ... AEPE
Association Europeene de Saint Vladimir (EAIO) ... AESV
Association Europeene des Decafeineurs [*European Association of Decaffeinators*] [*France*] (EAIO) ... AED
Association Europeene des Enseignants Dentaires [*European Association of Teachers of Dentistry*] (PDAA) ... AEED
Association Europeenne d'Athletisme [*European Athletic Association - EAA*] (EA) ... AEA
Association Europeenne de Ceramique [*European Ceramic Association*] [*France*] ... AEC
Association Europeenne de la Boyauderie [*European Natural Sausage Casings Association - ENSCA*] (EA) ... AEB
Association Europeenne de Laboratoires de Teledetection [*European Association of Remote Sensing Laboratories - EARSEL*] (EA) ... AELT
Association Europeenne de l'Asphalte [*European Mastic Asphalt Association - EMAA*] (EAIO) ... AEA
Association Europeenne de Libre-Echange [*European Free Trade Association - EFTA*] [*Geneva, Switzerland*] ... AELE
Association Europeenne de Radiologie [*European Association of Radiology - EAR*] (EA) ... AER
Association Europeenne de Vente par Correspondance [*European Mail Order Traders' Association*] [*Belgium*] (ECED) ... AEVPC
Association Europeenne des Assures de l'Industrie [*European Association of Industrial Insurers*] [*Brussels, Belgium*] (EAIO) ... AEAI
Association Europeenne des Audioprothesistes [*European Association of Hearing Aid Dispensers*] (EAIO) ... AEA
Association Europeenne des Centres d'Audiophonologie [*European Association of Audiophonological Centres - EAAC*] (EAIO) ... AECA
Association Europeenne des Centres Nationaux de Productivite [*European Association for National Productivity Centers - EANPC*] (EAIO) ... AECNP
Association Europeenne des Conservatoires [*European Association of Conservatories - EAC*] (EAIO) ... AEC
Association Europeenne des Conservatoires, Academies de Musique, et Musikhochschulen [*European Association of Music Conservatories, Academies, and High Schools*] (EAIO) ... AECAH
Association Europeenne des Constructeurs de Materiel Aerospatial [*European Association of Aerospace Manufacturers*] (EAIO) ... AECMA
Association Europeenne des Contribuables [*European Taxpayers Association - ETA*] (EA) ... AEC
Association Europeenne des Directeurs de Bureaux de Concerts et Spectacles [*European Association of Directors of the Bureau of Concerts and Events*] [*France*] (EAIO) ... AEDBCS
Association Europeenne des Directeurs d'Hopitaux [*Later, EAHM*] (EA) ... AEDH

Association Europeenne des Ecoles et Colleges d'Optometre [*European Association of Schools and Colleges of Optometry - EASCO*] (EA) .... AESCO
Association Europeenne des Editeurs d'Annuaires [*European Association of Directory Publishers - EADP*] (EA) .... AEEA
Association Europeenne des Exploitations Frigorifiques [*European Association of Refrigeration Enterprises*] [*Common Market*] [*Belgium*] .... AEEF
Association Europeenne des Fabricants de Blocs de Mousse Souple de Polyurethane [*European Association of Flexible Foam Block Manufacturers*] (EAIO) .... EUROPUR
Association Europeenne des Festivals [*European Association of Festivals*] [*Switzerland*] (EAIO) .... AEF
Association Europeenne des Festivals de Musique [*European Association of Music Festivals - EAMF*] (EAIO) .... AEFM
Association Europeenne des Gaz de Petrole Liquefies [*European Liquefied Petroleum Gas Association - ELPGA*] (EAIO) .... AEGPL
Association Europeenne des Graveurs et des Flexographes [*European Association of Engravers and Flexographers*] (EAIO) .... AEGRAFLEX
Association Europeenne des Industries de l'Habillement [*European Association of Clothing Industries*] (EA) .... AEIH
Association Europeenne des Industries de Produits de Marque [*European Association of Industries of Branded Products*] (EAIO) .... AIM
Association Europeenne des Institutions d'Amenagement Rural [*European Association of Country Planning Institutions*] (EAIO) .... AEIAR
Association Europeenne des Marches aux Bestiaux [*European Association of Livestock Markets - EALM*] [*Brussels, Belgium*] (EAIO) .... AEMB
Association Europeenne des Metaux [*European Association of Metals*] [*Belgium*] (EAIO) .... AEM
Association Europeenne des Musees de l'Histoire des Sciences Medicales [*European Association of Museums of the History of Medical Sciences - EAMHMS*] (EAIO) .... AEMHSM
Association Europeenne des Officiers Professionnels de Sapeurs-Pompiers [*European Association of Professional Fire Brigade Officers - EAPFBO*] (EAIO) .... AE
Association Europeenne des Organisations Nationales des Commercants Detaillants en Textiles [*European Association of National Organizations of Textile Manufacturers*] .... AEDT
Association Europeenne des Photographes Professionnels [*European Association of Professional Photographers*] .... EUROPHOT
Association Europeenne des Producteurs d'Acides Gras [*European Association of Fatty Acid Producing Companies*] (EAIO) .... APAG
Association Europeenne des Reserves Naturelles Libres [*European Association for Free Nature Reserves*] [*Inactive*] (EAIO) .... EUREL
Association Europeenne des Specialites Pharmaceutiques Grand Public [*European Proprietary Association*] (EA) .... AESGP
Association Europeenne des Vehicules Electriques Routiers [*European Electric Road Vehicle Association*] (EAIO) .... AVERE
Association Europeenne d'Etudes Chinoises [*European Association of Chinese Studies - EACS*] (EAIO) .... AEDEC
Association Europeenne du Commerce en Gros des Viandes [*European Association Wholesale Trade in Meat*] [*EC*] (ECED) .... AECGV
Association Europeenne du Laser [*European Laser Association - ELA*] (EA) .... AEL
Association Europeenne du Moulinage [*European Throwsters Association - ETA*] (EA) .... AEM
Association Europeenne l'Anodisation [*European Anodisers' Association*] (EA) .... EURAS
Association Europeenne pour la Cooperation [*European Association for Cooperation*] .... AEC
Association Europeenne pour l'Echange de la Litterature Technique dans le Domaine de la Siderurgie [*European Association for the Exchange of Technical Literature in the Field of Ferrous Metallurgy - EAETLFFM*] (EAIO) .... ASELT
Association Europeenne pour l'Etude de la Population [*European Association for Population Studies - EAPS*] (EAIO) .... AEEP
Association Europeenne pour l'Etude de l'Alimentation et Developpement de l'Enfant [*European Association of Nutrition and Child Development*] (EAIO) .... ADE
Association Europeenne pour l'Etude du Diabete [*European Association for the Study of Diabetes - EASD*] (EAIO) .... AEED
Association Europeenne Rubans, Tresses, Tissus Elastiques [*European Ribbon, Braid, and Elastic Material Association*] .... AERTEL
Association Europeenne Thyroide [*European Thyroid Association - ETA*] (EAIO) .... AET
Association Executives Human Rights Caucus (EA) .... AEHRC
Association Executives of North Carolina (SRA) .... AENC
Association Feeling Truth and Living It .... AFTLI
Association Feminine d'Education et d'Action Sociale [*Women's Association of Education and Social Action*] [*Canada*] .... AFEAS
Association Football Club [*British*] (DI) .... AFC
Association for a National Recycling Policy (EA) .... ANRP
Association for a World Language (EA) .... AWL
Association for Academic Surgery (EA) .... AAS
Association for Academic Travel Abroad (EA) .... ATA
Association for Administration of Volunteer Services [*Later, AVA*] (EA) .... AAVS
Association for Adult Continuing Education [*British*] .... AACE
Association for Adult Development and Aging (EA) .... AADA
Association for Adult Education (AIE) .... AAE
Association for Advanced Life Underwriting [*Washington, DC*] (EA) .... AALU
Association for Advancement of Behavior Therapy (EA) .... AABT
Association for Advancement of Blind and Retarded (EA) .... AABR
Association for Advancement of Blind Children [*Later, AABR*] (EA) .... AABC
Association for Advancement of Maternity Care [*British*] (DBA) .... AAMC
Association for Advancement of Modelling and Simulation Techniques in Enterprises [*France*] (EAIO) .... AMSE
Association for Advancement of Psychoanalysis (of the Karen Horney Psychoanalytic Institute and Center) (EA) .... AAP
Association for Advancement of Psychology (EA) .... AAP
Association for Affiliated College and University Offices [*Later, ACUO*] (EA) .... AACUO
Association for Agricultural Education Staffs [*British*] (DBA) .... AAES
Association for All Speech Impaired Children (EAIO) .... AFASIC
Association for Ambulatory Pediatric Services [*Later, APA*] (EA) .... AAPS
Association for Anesthesiologists' Assistants Training Program (DAVI) .... AAATP
Association for Applied Hypnosis (EAIO) .... AAH
Association for Applied Poetry (EA) .... AAP
Association for Applied Psychoanalysis (EA) .... AAP
Association for Applied Psychophysiology and Biofeedback (EA) .... AAPB
Association for Applied Solar Energy [*Later, International Solar Energy Society*] .... AASE
Association for Applied Solar Energy [*Later, International Solar Energy Society*] .... AFASE
Association for Archery in Schools (EAIO) .... AAS
Association for Arid Lands Studies (EA) .... AALS
Association for Armenian Information Professionals (EA) .... AAIP
Association for Asian Studies (EA) .... AAS
Association for Asian Studies, Committee on American Library Resources on the Far East, Center for Research Libraries, Chicago, IL [*Library symbol Library of Congress*] (LCLS) .... CALRFE
Association for Astrological Networking (EA) .... AFAN
Association for Astrological Psychology (EA) .... AAP
Association for Astronomy Education [*British*] (DBA) .... AAE
Association for Australian Rural Nurses .... AARN
Association for Automated Reasoning (EA) .... AAR
Association for Baha'i Studies (EAIO) .... ABS
Association for Balance of Political Power (EA) .... BOP
Association for Behavior Analysis (EA) .... ABA
Association for Behaviorial Sciences and Medical Education (EA) .... ABSAME
Association for Biology Laboratory Education (EA) .... ABLE
Association for Biomedical Research (EA) .... ABR
Association for Birth Psychology (EA) .... ABP
Association for Brain Tumor Research (EA) .... ABTR
Association for Brain Tumor Research (EA) .... AFBTR
Association for Bridge Construction and Design (EA) .... ABCD
Association for Bright Children [*Societe pour Enfants Doues et Surdoues*] [*Ontario*] (AC) .... ABC
Association for Bright Children [*Canada*] .... CBA
Association for British Music (EAIO) .... ABM
Association for Broadcast Engineering Standards [*Defunct*] (EA) .... ABES
Association for Business Communication [*Urbana, IL*] (EA) .... ABC
Association for Business Simulation and Experiential Learning [*Tulsa, OK*] (EA) .... ABSEL
Association for Business Sponsorship of the Arts [*British*] (EAIO) .... ABSA
Association for Canada Educational Resources (AC) .... ACER
Association for Canadian and Quebec Literatures .... ACQL
Association for Canadian Registered Safety Professionals [*Association des Professionnels en Securite Agrees du Canada*] (AC) .... ACRSP
Association for Canadian Studies [*See also AEC*] .... ACS
Association for Canadian Studies in the United States (EA) .... ACSUS
Association for Canadian Theatre History .... ACTH
Association for Canadian Theatre Research (AC) .... ACTR
Association for Central Asian Studies (EA) .... ACAS
Association for Chemoreception Sciences (EA) .... AChemS
Association for Child Psychiatrists (DAVI) .... ACP
Association for Child Psychoanalysis (EA) .... ACP
Association for Child Psychology and Psychiatry [*British*] .... ACPP
Association for Childbirth at Home, International (EA) .... ACHI
Association for Childhood Education International .... ACE
Association for Childhood Education International (EA) .... ACEI
Association for Children and Adults with Learning Disabilities [*Later, LDA*] (EA) .... ACALD
Association for Children for Enforcement of Support (EA) .... ACES
Association for Children with Down Syndrome (EA) .... ACDS
Association for Children with Learning Disabilities [*Later, LDA*] (EA) .... ACLD
Association for Children with Retarded Mental Development (EA) .... A/CRMD
Association for Children with Russell-Silver Syndrome (EA) .... ACRSS
Association for Christian Ethics [*Vatican*] (EA) .... ACE
Association for Christian Schools [*Defunct*] (EA) .... ACS
Association for Christian Training and Service (EA) .... ACTS
Association for Citizens with Special Needs [*Australia*] .... ACSN
Association for Classical Music [*Later, MA*] (EA) .... ACM
Association for Classical Music [*Later, MA*] (EA) .... AFCM
Association for Clinical Pastoral Education (EA) .... ACPE
Association for Clinical Theological Training and Care [*British*] (EAIO) .... ACTTCL
Association for Colleges (AIE) .... AFC
Association for Commonwealth Literature and Language Studies (EAIO) .... ACLALS
Association for Commonwealth Literature and Languages Studies .... ACLLS
Association for Communication Administration (EA) .... ACA
Association for Communist Unity [*Australia*] .... ACU
Association for Community Based Education (EA) .... ACBE
Association for Community Based Educational Institutions [*Later, ACBE*] (EA) .... ACBEI
Association for Community Living (SRA) .... ACL
Association for Community Organizations for Refaring Now .... ACORN
Association for Commuter Transportation (EA) .... ACT
Association for Comparative Economic Studies [*Notre Dame, IN*] (EA) .... ACES
Association for Comparative Economics [*Later, ACES*] .... ACE
Association for Composite Tanks (EA) .... ACT

Association for Computational Linguistics (EA) .... ACL
Association for Computer Art and Design Education [Defunct] (EA) .... ACADE
Association for Computer Assisted Learning (AIE) .... ACAL
Association for Computer Operations Management (EA) .... ACOM
Association for Computer-Based Systems for Career Information
　(OICC) .... ACSCI
Association for Computers and Information Technology in Teaching
　(AIE) .... ACITT
Association for Computers and the Humanities (EA) .... ACH
Association for Computing Machinery (EA) .... ACM
Association for Conflict Resolution [Defunct] (EA) .... ACR
Association for Conservation Information (EA) .... ACI
Association for Constitutional Democracy in Liberia (EA) .... ACDL
Association for Consumer Research (EA) .... ACR
Association for Continuing Education (EA) .... ACE
Association for Continuing Higher Education (EA) .... ACHE
Association for Continuing Professional Education [Formerly, AFSTE]
　(EA) .... ACPE
Association for Convention Operations Management (EA) .... ACOM
Association for Cooperation in Banana Research in the Caribbean and
　Tropical America [Guadeloupe, French West Indies] (EAIO) .... ACORBAT
Association for Cooperation in Engineering [Defunct] .... ACE
Association for Co-Ordinated Rural Development [Government body]
　[British] .... ACCORD
Association for Corporate Growth [Deerfield, IL] (EA) .... ACG
Association for Corporate Growth and Diversification [Later, ACG]
　(EA) .... ACGD
Association for Correctional Research and Information Management
　(EA) .... ACRIM
Association for Correctional Research and Statistics (OICC) .... ACRS
Association for Counselor Education and Supervision (EA) .... ACES
Association for Couples in Marriage Enrichment (EA) .... ACME
Association for Creative Change within Religious and Other Social
　Systems (EA) .... ACC
Association for Cultural Exchange .... ACE
Association for Cultural Exchange (EA) .... CULTUREX
Association for Cultural Interchange (EA) .... ACI
Association for Dance Movement Therapy (EAIO) .... ADMT
Association for Data Processing and Computer Management (NITA) ...... ADPCM
Association for Death Education and Counseling (EA) .... ADEC
Association for Denture Prosthesis (EAIO) .... ADP
Association for Development of Computer-Based Instructional Systems
　(EA) .... ADCIS
Association for Development of Instructional Systems [Later, ADCIS]
　[Western Washington University Bellingham, WA] (BUR) .... ADIS
Association for Direct Instruction (EA) .... ADI
Association for Documentary Editing (EA) .... ADE
Association for Dressings and Sauces (EA) .... ADS
Association for Education and Cultural Advancement [South Africa] .... ASECA
Association for Education and Rehabilitation of the Blind and Visually
　Impaired (EA) .... AER
Association for Education by Radio-Television [Defunct] (AEBS) .... AERT
Association for Education in International Business [Later, AIB] (EA) .... AEIB
Association for Education in Journalism [Later, AEJMC] (EA) .... AEJ
Association for Education in Journalism and Mass Communication
　(EA) .... AEJMC
Association for Education of the Visually Handicapped [Later, AER]
　(EA) .... AEVH
Association for Educational and Training Technology (EAIO) .... AETT
Association for Educational Communications and Technology (NTCM) ...... ACET
Association for Educational Communications and Technology [Washington,
　DC] .... AECT
Association for Educational Data Processing .... AEDP
Association for Educational Data Systems (EA) .... AEDS
Association for Educational Development (EA) .... AED
Association for Electronic Data Systems [Database producer] (ECII) .... AEDS
Association for Electronics Manufacturing of the Society of Manufacturing
　Engineers (EA) .... AEM/SME
Association for Employee Health and Fitness (EA) .... AEHF
Association for Environmental and Outdoor Education (EA) .... AEOE
Association for Environmental Education (New South Wales)
　[Australia] .... AEE(NSW)
Association for Equine Sports Medicine (EA) .... AESM
Association for Evolutionary Economics [Lincoln, NE] (EA) .... AFEE
Association for Experiential Education (EA) .... AEE
Association for Faculty in the Medical Humanities (EA) .... AFMH
Association for Fair Play for Children in Scotland (EAIO) .... AFPCS
Association for Family Living [Defunct] (EA) .... AFL
Association for Federal Information Resources Management (EA) .... AFFIRM
Association for Field Archaeology [Defunct] (EA) .... AFFA
Association for Field Services in Teacher Education [Later, ACPE] .... AFSTE
Association for Finishing Processes of SME [Society of Manufacturing
　Engineers] (EA) .... AFP
Association for Finishing Processes of the Society of Manufacturing
　Engineers (EAIO) .... AFP/SME
Association for Food Self-Sufficiency (EAIO) .... AFS
Association for Food Service Management [Later, SFM] (EA) .... AFSM
Association for Gay and Lesbian Issues in Counseling [Later, AGLBIC]
　(EA) .... AGLIC
Association for Gay, Lesbian, and Bisexual Issues in Counseling
　(EA) .... AGLBIC
Association for General and Liberal Studies (EA) .... AGLS
Association for Gerontology in Higher Education (EA) .... AGHE
Association for Gifted and Talented Students (EA) .... AGTS
Association for Glycogen Storage Disease (EA) .... AGSD

Association for Gnotobiotics (EA) .... AG
Association for Government Assisted Housing [Defunct] (EA) .... AGAH
Association for Governmental Leasing and Finance [Washington, DC]
　(EA) .... AGLF
[The] Association for Graduate Education and Research .... TAGER
Association for Gravestone Studies (EA) .... AGS
Association for Group Psychoanalysis and Process (EA) .... AGPP
Association for Health Records [Later, AHQ] (EA) .... AHR
Association for Health Services Research (EA) .... AHSR
Association for Healthcare Philanthropy .... AHP
Association for Healthcare Philanthropy (NFD) .... AHP
Association for Healthcare Philanthropy Foundation (NFD) .... AHP Foundation
Association for Healthcare Quality [Defunct] (EA) .... AHQ
Association for High Speed Photography [British] (BI) .... AHSP
Association for Higher Education [of the NEA] [Later, AAHE] (EA) .... AHE
Association for Higher Education, Dallas, TX [OCLC symbol] (OCLC) .... IUC
Association for Hispanic Handicapped of New Jersey (EA) .... AHH
Association for Holistic Health [Defunct] (EA) .... AHH
Association for Holistic Living (EA) .... AHL
Association for Hospital Medical Education (EA) .... AHME
Association for Human Emergence [Defunct] (EA) .... AHE
Association for Human Rights (EA) .... AHR
Association for Humanist Sociology (EA) .... AHS
Association for Humanistic Education (EA) .... AHE
Association for Humanistic Education and Development (EA) .... AHEAD
Association for Humanistic Psychology (EA) .... AHP
Association for Humanistic Psychology in Britain (EAIO) .... AHPB
Association for Improvements in the Maternity Services (EAIO) .... AIMS
Association for Improving Moral Standards [British] (BI) .... AIMS
Association for Independent Disabled Self-Sufficiency [British] .... AIDS
Association for Indiana Media Educators (SRA) .... AIME
Association for Individually Guided Education (EA) .... AIGE
Association for Infant Massage (EA) .... AIM
Association for Informal Logic and Critical Thinking (EA) .... AILACT
Association for Information and Image Management (EA) .... AIIM
Association for Information Management [Aslib] (NITA) .... AIM
Association for Informational Media and Equipment (EA) .... AIME
Association for Innovation in Higher Education [Defunct] (EA) .... AIHE
Association for Innovative Marketing (EA) .... AIM
Association for Institutional Research (EA) .... AIR
Association for Integrated Manufacturing Technology [Later,
　NCS/AIMTECH] (EAAP) .... AIM Tech
Association for Integrated Manufacturing Technology [Later,
　NCS/AIMTECH] (EA) .... AIMT
Association for Integrative Studies (EA) .... AIS
Association for Intelligent Systems Technology (EA) .... AIST
Association for Intercollegiate Athletics for Women (EA) .... AIAW
Association for International Agricultural and Extension Education
　(EA) .... AIAEE
Association for International Agriculture and Rural Development (EA) .... AIARD
Association for International Cancer Research (EAIO) .... AICR
Association for International Children and Youth (EA) .... AICY
Association for International Cotton Emblem [Brussels, Belgium] (EAIO)..... AFICE
Association for International Development [Defunct] (EA) .... AID
Association for International Medical Study [Defunct] (EA) .... AIMS
Association for International Practical Training (EA) .... AIPT
Association for International Technical Promotion .... AITEP
Association for Investment Management and Research (EA) .... AIMR
Association for Jewish Studies (EA) .... AJS
Association for Jewish Youth [British] .... AJY
Association for Korean Studies (EA) .... AKS
Association for Laboratory Automation (EA) .... ALA
Association for Latin American Studies [Defunct] .... ALAS
Association for Latin Liturgy (EA) .... ALL
Association for Legal Justice [Northern Ireland] .... ALJ
Association for Liberal Education [British] .... ALE
Association for Library and Information Science Education (EA) .... ALISE
Association for Library Automation Research Communications (EA) .... LARC
Association for Library Collections and Technical Services .... ALCTS
Association for Library Information [Duquesne University Library]
　[Information service or system] (IID) .... AFLI
Association for Library Information, Pittsburgh, PA [OCLC symbol]
　(OCLC) .... AFL
Association for Library Service to Children (EA) .... ALSC
Association for Literary and Linguistic Computing [University College of
　North Wales] [Gwynedd] (EA) .... ALLC
Association for Living Historical Farms and Agricultural Museums
　(EA) .... ALHFAM
Association for Loss Prevention and Security (EA) .... ALPS
Association for Machine Translation and Computational Linguistics [Later,
　Association for Computational Linguistics] (EA) .... AMTCL
Association for Macular Diseases (EA) .... AMD
Association for Maintained Girls' Schools (AIE) .... AMGS
Association for Management Excellence [Later, AAIM] (EA) .... AME
Association for Manufacturing Excellence (EA) .... AME
Association for Manufacturing Technology (EA) .... AMT
Association for Maternal and Child Health and Crippled Children's
　Programs (EA) .... AMCHCCP
Association for Measurement and Evaluation in Counseling and
　Development (EA) .... AMECD
Association for Measurement and Evaluation in Guidance [Later, AMECD]
　(EA) .... AMEG
Association for Mechanical Translation and Computation Linguistics
　(NITA) .... AMTC

Association for Media and Technology in Education in Canada [*See also AMTE*] ... AMTEC
Association for Media Psychology (EA) ... AMP
Association for Media-Based Continuing Education for Engineers (EA) ... AMCEE
Association for Medical Education in Europe [*Scotland*] ... AMEE
Association for Medical Education in the Eastern Mediterranean Region [*United Arab Emirates*] (EAIO) ... AMEEMR
Association for Medical Physics Technology [*British*] ... AMPT
Association for Men in Psychology ... AMP
Association for Mental Health Affiliation with Israel (EA) ... AMHAI
Association for Mexican Cave Studies (EA) ... AMCS
Association for Middle-Income Housing [*Later, MMHA*] (EA) ... AMIH
Association for Moral and Social Hygiene [*British*] (BI) ... AMSH
Association for Multicultural Counseling and Development (EA) ... AMCD
Association for Multi-Image (EA) ... AMI
Association for Native Development in the Performing and Visual Arts [*Canada*] ... ANDPVA
Association for Non-White Concerns in Personnel and Guidance (EA) ... ANWC
Association for Nordic Transplant and Dialysis Personnel (EAIO) ... NORDIATRANS
Association for Nuclear Development and Research in Electrical Engineering (MCD) ... ANDREE
Association for Parents of Addicts [*British*] (BI) ... APA
Association for Past-Life Research and Therapy (EA) ... APRT
Association for Pediatric Education in Europe (PDAA) ... APEE
Association for People with Arthritis [*Defunct*] (EA) ... APA
Association for Petroleum and Explosives Administration [*British*] ... APEA
Association for Philosophy of the Unconscious (EA) ... APU
Association for Physical and Mental Rehabilitation [*Later, ACTA*] (EA) ... APMR
Association for Physical and System Mathematics (EA) ... APSM
Association for Poetry Therapy [*Later, NAPT*] (EA) ... APT
Association for Politics and the Life Sciences (EA) ... APLS
Association for Population/Family Planning Libraries and Information Centers - International [*Also, an information service or system*] (IID) ... APLIC
Association for Population/Family Planning Libraries and Information Centers, International (EA) ... APLIC-Intl
Association for Practical and Professional Ethics (EA) ... APPE
Association for Practical Theology (EA) ... APT
Association for Practitioners in Infection Control (EA) ... APIC
Association for Precision Graphics [*Defunct*] (EA) ... APG
Association for Pre-School Education of Deaf Children ... APSEDC
Association for Preservation Technology [*Later, APTI*] (EA) ... APT
Association for Prevention of Disabilities (EAIO) ... APD
Association for Productive Teaching (AEBS) ... APT
Association for Professional Broadcasting Education [*Later, Broadcast EducationAssociation*] (EA) ... APBE
Association for Professional Education for Ministry [*Later, APT*] (EA) ... APEM
Association for Professional Environmental Auditing in Nova Scotia [*Formerly, Association for Professional Environmental Auditors*] (AC) ... APEA
Association for Programmed Learning and Educational Technology ... APLET
Association for Progressive Communications ... APC
Association for Progressive Education (EA) ... AFPE
Association for Promoting Christian Knowledge [*Church of Ireland*] ... APCK
Association for Promoting Retreats [*British*] (BI) ... APR
Association for Promoting the Reform of Convocation [*British*] ... APRC
Association for Promoting Unity of Christendom ... APUC
Association for Protection of Fur-Bearing Animals [*Canada*] ... APFA
Association for Psychoanalytic Medicine (EA) ... APM
Association for Psychological Type (EA) ... APT
Association for Psychotheatrics [*Defunct*] (EA) ... AP
Association for Public Broadcasting (EA) ... APB
Association for Public Justice (EA) ... APJ
Association for Public Justice Education Fund [*Later, CPJ*] (EA) ... APJEF
Association for Public Policy Analysis and Management (EA) ... APPAM
Association for Puerto Rican-Hispanic Culture (EA) ... APRHC
Association for Quality and Participation (EA) ... AQP
Association for Radiation Research [*British*] (NRCH) ... ARR
Association for Rational Environmental Alternatives [*Defunct*] (EA) ... AREA
Association for Realistic Philosophy [*Defunct*] (EA) ... ARP
Association for Recognizing the Life of Stillborns (EA) ... ARLS
Association for Recorded Sound Collections (EA) ... ARSC
Association for Recreation and Cultural Activities with People in Detention [*Canada*] ... ARCAD
Association for Recurrent Education [*British*] ... ARE
Association for Regulatory Reform (EA) ... ARR
Association for Relatives of the Mentally, Emotionally, and Nervously Disturbed [*British*] (BI) ... AMEND
Association for Religious and Value Issues in Counseling (EA) ... ARVIC
Association for Religious Education ... ARE
Association for Research, Administration, Professional Councils, and Societies (EA) ... ARAPCS
Association for Research and Enlightenment (EA) ... ARE
Association for Research and Enlightenment, Virginia Beach, VA [*Library symbol Library of Congress*] (LCLS) ... ViVbRE
Association for Research in Cosmecology (EA) ... ARC
Association for Research in Growth Relationships [*Defunct*] (EA) ... ARGR
Association for Research in Nervous and Mental Disease (EA) ... ARNMD
Association for Research in Ophthalmology [*Later, ARVO*] (EA) ... ARO
Association for Research in Vision and Ophthalmology (EA) ... ARVO
Association for Research into Restricted Growth [*British*] ... ARRG
Association for Research into the Folklore of Imagination [*French*] (ECON) ... ARFI
Association for Research of Childhood Cancer (EA) ... AROCC
Association for Research on Nonprofit Organizations and Voluntary Action (EA) ... ARNOVA
Association for Residential Care [*British*] (EAIO) ... ARC
Association for Responsible Dissent (EA) ... ARD
Association for Restriction of Radio and Television Commercials [*Defunct*] (EA) ... ARRTVC
Association for Restriction of TV Commercials [*Later, ARRTVC*] (EA) ... ARTVC
Association for Retarded Children (DAVI) ... ARC
Association for Retarded Citizens (EA) ... ARC
Association for Rural Mental Health [*Later, NARMH*] (EA) ... ARMH
Association for Sane Psychiatric Practices (EA) ... ASPP
Association for School, College, and University Staffing (EA) ... ASCUS
Association for Science Education [*British*] (DEN) ... ASE
Association for Science, Technology, and Innovation (EA) ... ASTI
Association for Scientific Journals (EA) ... ASJ
Association for Scottish Literary Studies [*Aberdeen, Scotland*] (EAIO) ... ASLS
Association for Service Management ... AFSM
Association for Services Management International (EA) ... ASMI
Association for Short Term Psychotherapy (EA) ... ASTP
Association for Sickle Cell Anemia [*Defunct*] ... ASCA
Association for Singles (EA) ... AS
Association for Small Business Advancement [*Defunct*] (EA) ... ASBA
Association for Social Anthropology in Oceania (EA) ... ASAO
Association for Social Design [*Later, BRI*] (EA) ... ASD
Association for Social Economics (EA) ... ASE
Association for Social Work Education in Africa [*See also AESA*] (EAIO) ... ASWEA
Association for Software Protection (EA) ... ASP
Association for Software Testing and Evaluation [*Defunct*] (EA) ... ASTE
Association for Special Education [*British*] (BI) ... ASE
Association for Special Education [*British*] ... ASPE
Association for Special Education Technology ... ASET
Association for Specialists in Group Work (EA) ... ASGW
Association for Spina Bifida and Hydrocephalus [*Australia British*] (IRUK) ... ASBAH
Association for Spiritual Awareness (EA) ... AFSA
Association for Stammerers (EAIO) ... AFS
Association for Stamp Exhibitions [*Defunct*] ... ASE
Association for Strengthening Agricultural Research in Eastern and Central Africa (ECON) ... ASERCA
Association for Student Counsellors (AIE) ... ASC
Association for Student Teaching [*Later, ATE*] (EA) ... AST
Association for Studies in the Conservation of Historic Buildings [*British*] ... ASCHB
Association for Study of Internal Fixation (DMAA) ... ASIF
Association for Study of Karma (EA) ... ASK
Association for Supervision and Curriculum Development (EA) ... ASCD
Association for Surgical Education (EA) ... ASE
Association for Symbolic Logic (EA) ... ASL
Association for Systematics Collections [*Taxonomy*] ... ASC
Association for Systems Management (EA) ... ASM
Association for Teacher Education in Europe [*Belgium*] (EAIO) ... ATEE
Association for Teaching of Psychology [*British*] (DBA) ... ATPsych
Association for Technical Education in Schools [*British*] (BI) ... ATES
Association for Technology in Music Instruction (EA) ... ATMI
Association for Tele-Education in Canada (AC) ... ATEC
Association for the Advancement of Aeronautical Research [*France*] ... AAAR
Association for the Advancement of Aging Research [*Defunct*] (EA) ... AAAR
Association for the Advancement of Agricultural Sciences in Africa (EAIO) ... AAASA
Association for the Advancement of Automotive Medicine (EA) ... AAAM
Association for the Advancement of Baltic Studies (EA) ... AABS
Association for the Advancement of British Biotechnology (EAIO) ... AABB
Association for the Advancement of Central Asian Research (EA) ... AACAR
Association for the Advancement of Civil Rights [*Gibraltar*] [*Political party*] (PPE) ... AACR
Association for the Advancement of Creative Musicians (EA) ... AACM
Association for the Advancement of Dutch-American Studies (EA) ... AADAS
Association for the Advancement of Family Stability [*Later, AFCO*] ... AAFS
Association for the Advancement of Health Care Managers [*Defunct*] (EA) ... AAHCM
Association for the Advancement of Health Education (EA) ... AAHE
Association for the Advancement of Instruction about Alcohol and Narcotics [*Defunct*] ... AAIAN
Association for the Advancement of International Education (EA) ... AAIE
Association for the Advancement of Invention and Innovation [*Patent lobby*] [*Defunct*] ... AAII
Association for the Advancement of Medical Education [*Defunct*] (EA) ... AAME
Association for the Advancement of Medical Instrumentation (EA) ... AAMI
Association for the Advancement of Ophthalmology [*Defunct*] (EA) ... AAO
Association for the Advancement of Policy, Research, and Development in the Third World (EA) ... AAPRDTW
Association for the Advancement of Psychotherapy (EA) ... AAP
Association for the Advancement of Scandinavian Studies in Canada GG2 [*See also AAESC*] ... AASSC
Association for the Advancement of Science in Canada ... AASC
Association for the Advancement of Sports Potential (EA) ... AASP
Association for the Advancement of Teacher Education in Music (AIE) ... AATEM
Association for the Aid of Crippled Children [*Later, Foundation for Child Development*] (EA) ... AACC
Association for the Alleviation of Asinine Abbreviations and Absurd Acronyms [*Satirical nonassociation*] ... AAAAAA
Association for the American Dance Festival (EA) ... AADF
[*The*] **Association for the Anthropological Study of Play** (EA) ... TAASP

Association for the Behavioral Treatment of Sexual Abusers (EA) .... ABTSA
Association for the Bibliography of History (EA) .... ABH
Association for the Blind [*Australia*] .... AFTB
Association for the Blind of Western Australia .... AFTBWA
Association for the Blind, Queensland [*Australia*] .... AFTBQ
Association for the Care of Asthma (EA) .... ACA
Association for the Care of Children's Health (EA) .... ACCH
Association for the Conservation of Energy [*British*] (IRUK) .... ACE
Association for the Coordination of University Religious Affairs (EA) .... ACURA
Association for the Development of Human Potential (EA) .... ADHP
Association for the Development of Religious Information Systems (EA) .... ADRIS
Association for the Development of Social Therapy [*Defunct*] (EA) .... ADST
[*The*] **Association for the Education and Welfare of the Visually Handicapped** [*British*] .... AEWVH
Association for the Education of Teachers in Science (EA) .... AETS
Association for the Encouragement of Correct Punctuation, Spelling, and Usage inPublic Communications (EA) .... AECPSUPC
Association for the Evaluation of the Elementary School (AEBS) .... AEES
Association for the Export of Canadian Books [*Association pour l'Exportation du Livre Canadien*] (AC) .... AECB
Association for the Free Distribution of the Scriptures [*British*] .... AFDS
[*The*] **Association for the Gifted** (EA) .... TAG
Association for the History of Chiropractic (EA) .... AHC
Association for the Improvement of Community College Teaching [*Defunct*] (EA) .... AICCT
Association for the Improvement of the Mississippi River (EA) .... AIMR
Association for the Integration of Management [*New York, NY*] (EA) .... AIM
Association for the Introduction of New Biological Nomenclature [*Belgium*] (EAIO) .... AINBN
Association for the Legal Right to Abortion (Western Australia) .... ALRA(WA)
Association for the Liberation of Ukraine [*Defunct*] (EA) .... ALU
Association for the Monetary Union of Europe .... AMUE
Association for the Neurologically Disabled of Canada (AC) .... AND
Association for the Preservation and Presentation of the Arts .... APPA
Association for the Preservation of Anti-Psychiatric Artifacts [*Defunct*] (EA) .... APAPA
Association for the Preservation of Political Americana (EA) .... APPA
Association for the Preservation of Rural Life [*British*] (BI) .... APRL
Association for the Preservation of Rural Scotland (BI) .... APRS
Association for the Preservation of the Auction Market [*Defunct*] (EA) .... APAM
Association for the Preservation of Virginia Antiquities (EA) .... APVA
Association for the Prevention of Thefts in Shops [*British*] .... APTS
Association for the Professional Treatment of Offenders [*Defunct*] (EA) .... APTO
Association for the Promotion & Advancement of Science Education (AC) .... APASE
Association for the Promotion of African Community Initiatives (EAIO) .... APACI
Association for the Promotion of Humor in International Affairs (EA) .... APHIA
Association for the Promotion of the International Circulation of the Press [*Distipress*] .... APICP
Association for the Protection of Evolution [*British*] .... APE
Association for the Protection of Fur-Bearing Animals (EAIO) .... APFBA
Association for the Protection of Rural Australia .... APRA
Association for the Protection of Rural Scotland [*British*] .... APRS
Association for the Protection of the Adirondacks (EA) .... APA
Association for the Psychiatric Study of Adolescents [*British*] .... APSA
Association for the Psychophysiological Study of Sleep [*Later, Sleep Research Society - SRS*] .... APSS
Association for the Reduction of Aircraft Noise (EA) .... ARAN
Association for the Rehabilitation of the Brain Injured (AC) .... ARBI
Association for the Rights of Catholics in the Church (EA) .... ARCC
Association for the Scientific Study of Anomalous Phenomena .... ASSAP
Association for the Sexually Harassed (EA) .... ASH
Association for the Sociological Study of Jewry (EA) .... ASSJ
Association for the Sociology of Religion (EA) .... ASR
Association for the Study and Advancement of Supportive Values (EA) .... ASASV
Association for the Study of Abortion [*Later, NAF*] .... ASA
Association for the Study of Abortion. Newsletter [*A publication*] (DLA) .... ASA Newsl
Association for the Study of Afro-American Life and History (EA) .... ASALH
Association for the Study of Animal Behavior .... ASAB
Association for the Study of Canadian Radio and Television [*Pronounced "Askrat"*] [*See also AERTC*] .... ASCRT
Association for the Study of Canadian Radio & Television [*Association pour les Etudes sur la Radio-Television Canadienne*] (AC) .... ASCRT
Association for the Study of Classical African Civilizations (EA) .... ASCAC
Association for the Study of Dada and Surrealism (EA) .... ASDS
Association for the Study of Dreams (EA) .... ASD
Association for the Study of Food and Society (EA) .... ASFS
Association for the Study of Higher Education (EA) .... ASHE
Association for the Study of Human Infertility (DAVI) .... ASHI
Association for the Study of International Development [*See also AEDI*] [*Canada*] .... ASID
Association for the Study of Jewish Languages [*Haifa, Israel*] (EAIO) .... ASJL
Association for the Study of Literature and Alchemy (EA) .... ASLA
Association for the Study of Man-Environment Relations (EA) .... ASMER
Association for the Study of Medical Education .... ASME
Association for the Study of Negro Life and History [*Later, Association for theStudy of Afro-American Life and History*] (EA) .... ASNLH
Association for the Study of Obesity (EAIO) .... ASO
Association for the Study of Primary Education (AIE) .... ASPE
Association for the Study of Soviet-Type Economies [*Later, ACES*] (EA) .... ASTE
Association for the Study of the Grants Economy (EA) .... ASGE
Association for the Study of the Nationalities (USSR and East Europe) (EA) .... ASN
Association for the Study of the World Refugee Problem [*Vaduz, Liechtenstein*] (EAIO) .... AWR
Association for the Support and Diffusion of Art (EA) .... ASDA
Association for the Teaching of Psychology [*British*] .... ATP
Association for the Therapeutic Education [*British*] .... ATE
Association for the Understanding of Man (EA) .... AUM
Association for the United Nations in Russia (EAIO) .... UNAR
Association for the World University (EA) .... AWU
Association for Theatre and Disability (EA) .... ATD
Association for Theatre in Higher Education (EA) .... ATHE
Association for Theological Education in South East Asia (EAIO) .... ATESEA
Association for Theological Education in the Near East [*Later, ATIME*] .... ATENE
Association for Totally Dependent Persons of South Australia .... TDPSA
Association for Transarmament Studies [*Later, CBDA*] (EA) .... ATS
Association for Transpersonal Psychology (EA) .... ATP
Association for Tropical Biology (EA) .... ATB
Association for Union Democracy (EA) .... AUD
Association for University Business and Economic Research [*University, AL*] (EA) .... AUBER
Association for Unmanned Vehicle Systems (EA) .... AUVS
Association for Vertical Market Computing [*Defunct*] (EA) .... AVMC
Association for Vital Records and Health Statistics (EA) .... AVRHS
Association for Voluntary Action in Europe [*See also AVE*] (EAIO) .... AVAE
Association for Voluntary Sterilization, Inc. [*New York, NY Research center*] .... AVS
Association for Voluntary Sterilization, Inc., International Project, New York, NY [*Library symbol Library of Congress*] (LCLS) .... NNAVS
Association for Voluntary Surgical Contraception (EA) .... AVSC
Association for Volunteer Administration (EA) .... AVA
Association for Women Geoscientists (EA) .... AWG
Association for Women in Computing (EA) .... AWC
Association for Women in Development (EA) .... AWD
Association for Women in Development (EA) .... AWID
Association for Women in Mathematics (EA) .... AWM
Association for Women in Psychology (EA) .... AWP
Association for Women in Science (EA) .... AWIS
Association for Women in Sports Media (EA) .... AWSM
Association for Women Veterinarians (EA) .... AWV
Association for Women's Active Return to Education [*Defunct*] .... AWARE
Association for Women's AIDS [*Acquired Immune Deficiency Syndrome*] **Research and Education** .... AWARE
Association for Workplace Democracy [*Defunct*] (EA) .... AWD
Association for World Education (EA) .... AWE
Association for World Evangelism (EA) .... AWE
Association for World Peace [*Founded in 1951*] [*Defunct British*] .... AWP
Association for World Travel Exchange (EA) .... AWTE
Association Forestiere Canadienne [*Canadian Forestry Association*] (EAIO) .... AFC
Association Forestiere de la Vallee du St-Maurice Inc. (AC) .... AFVSM
Association Forestiere de l'Abitibi-Temiscamingue, Inc. (AC) .... AFAT
Association Forestiere Quebecoise Inc. [*Quebec Forestry Association Inc.*] (AC) .... AFQ
Association Forestiere Saguenay-Lac St-Jean Inc. (AC) .... AFSL
Association Francaise De Lutte Contre La Mucoviscidose [*French Cystic Fibrosis Association*] .... AFLM
Association Francaise de Normalisation [*French Association for Standardization*] [*Database producer*] (IID) .... AFNOR
Association Francaise de Terminologie [*French Association of Terminology*] [*Canada*] .... AFTERM
Association Francaise des Documentalistes et des Bibliothecaires Specialises (NITA) .... AFDBS
Association Francaise des Entreprises pour l'Environnement [*French Environmentalist Association*] .... AFEE
Association Francaise des Etudes Canadiennes [*French Association of Canadian Studies*] .... AFEC
Association Francaise d'Experts de la Cooperation Technique Internationale [*French Association of Experts Assigned to International Technical Cooperation*] (AF) .... AFECTI
Association Francaise pour la Cybernetique Economique et Technique [*French Association for Economic and Technical Cybernetics*] .... AFCET
Association Francaise pour l'Accueil des Travailleurs Africains et Malgaches [*French Association for the Reception of African and Malagasy Workers*] (AF) .... AFTAM
Association Francaise pour l'Etude des Eaux [*French Water Study Association*] [*Paris*] [*Information service or system*] (IID) .... AFEE
Association France-Etats-Unis [*France-United States Association*] (EA) .... AFEU
Association Francophone d'Amitie et de Liaison (EA) .... AFAL
Association Francophone de Spectrometrie de Masse de Solides [*French-Speaking Association of Solids Mass Spectrometry*] (EAIO) .... AFSMAS
Association Francophone d'Education Comparee [*French-Speaking Comparative Education Association - FSCEA*] (EAIO) .... AFEC
Association Francophone Internationale des Directeurs d'Etablissements Scolaires [*International Association of French-Speaking Directors of Educational Institutions*] [*Anjou, PQ*] .... AFIDES
Association Francophone Internationale des Groupes d'Animation de la Paraplegie [*International French-Speaking Association of Paraplegic Therapy Groups*] [*Brie-Comte-Robert, France*] (EAIO) .... AFIGAP
Association Franco-Yukonnaise (AC) .... AFY
Association Generale des Eleves et Etudiants du Dahomey en France [*General Association of Dahomean Pupils and Students in France*] [*Dahomey*] .... AGEED
Association Generale des Etudiants Reunionnais en Metropole [*General Association of Reunionese Students in France*] (AF) .... AGERM

Association Generale des Federations Internationales de Sports [*General Association of International Sports Federations - GAISF*] (EA) .... AGFIS

Association Generale des Hygienistes et Techniciens Municipaux [*General Association of Municipal Health and Technical Experts*] (EAIO) .... AGHTM

Association Geologique Carpatho-Balkanique [*Carpathian Balkan Geological Association - CBGA*] (EA) .... AGCB

Association Guineenne des Editeurs de la Presse Independente [*Press association*] [*Guinea*] (EY) .... AGEPI

Association Henri Capitant (EA) .... AHC

Association in Occupational Studies [*Associate degree*] (PAZ) .... AOS

Association in Scotland to Research into Astronautics (EAIO) .... ASTRA

Association in Solidarity with Guatemala (EA) .... ASOGUA

Association Institute (EA) .... AI

Association Intercontinentale du Mais Hybride .... INTERHYBRID

Association Internationale Contre la Torture [*International Association Against Torture*] [*Milan, Italy*] (EAIO) .... AICT

Association Internationale Contre la Violence dans le Sport [*International Association for Non-Violent Sport - IANVS*] [*Monte Carlo, Monaco*] (EAIO) .... AICVS

Association Internationale Contre le Bruit [*International Association Against Noise*] [*ICSU*] (EAIO) .... AICB

Association Internationale d'Allergologie [*International Association of Allergology*] .... AIA

Association Internationale de Bibliophile [*International Association of Bibliophiles - IAB*] [*Paris, France*] (EAIO) .... AIB

Association Internationale de Boxe Amateur [*International Amateur Boxing Association*] (EA) .... AIBA

Association Internationale de Bryozoologie [*International Bryozoology Association - IBA*] [*Paris, France*] (EAIO) .... AIB

Association Internationale de Chimie Cerealiere [*International Association for Cereal Chemistry*] [*Also, ICC*] .... AICC

Association Internationale de Chimie Cerealiere [*International Association for Cereal Chemistry*] [*Also, AICC*] ICC

Association Internationale de Cybernetique [*International Association for Cybernetics - IAC*] (EAIO) .... AIC

Association Internationale de Defense des Artistes [*International Association for the Defence of Artists*] (EAIO) .... AIDA

Association Internationale de Defense des Artistes [*International Associationfor the Defense of Artists*] - USA (EA) .... AIDA-USA

Association Internationale de Developpement et d'Action Communautaires [*International Association for Community Development*] [*Marcinelle, Belgium*] (EAIO) .... AIDAC

Association Internationale de Droit Constitutionnel [*International Association of Constitutional Law - IACL*] (EAIO) .... AIDC

Association Internationale de Droit des Assurances [*International Association for Insurance Law*] [*Belgium*] (EAIO) .... AIDA

Association Internationale de Droit Penal [*International Association of Penal Law*] .... AIDP

Association Internationale de Geodesie [*International Association of Geodesy*] .... AIG

Association Internationale de Geologie de l'Ingenieur [*International Association of Engineering Geology*] .... AIGI

Association Internationale de Geomagnetisme et d'Aeronomie [*International Association of Geomagnetism and Aeronomy*] .... AIGA

Association Internationale de Grands Magasins [*International Association of Department Stores - IADS*] (EAIO) .... AIGM

Association Internationale de la Boulangerie Industrielle [*International Association of the Bread Industry*] (EAIO) .... AIBI

Association Internationale de la Couleur [*International Color Association*] [*Soesterberg, Netherlands*] (EA) .... AIC

Association Internationale de la Distribution [*International Association of Distribution*] [*Belgium*] (EAIO) .... AIDA

Association Internationale de la Distribution des Produits Alimentaires et des Produits de Grande Consommation [*International Association for the Distribution of Food Products and General Consumer Goods*] (EAIO) .... AIDA

Association Internationale de la Fonction Publique [*Avignon, France*] (EAIO) .... AIFP

Association Internationale de la Gestion du Personnel [*International Association of Personnel Administration*] [*Canada*] .... AIGP

Association Internationale de la Meunerie [*International Milling Association - IMA*] (EAIO) .... AIM

Association Internationale de la Mutualite [*International Association for Mutual Assistance*] [*Switzerland*] .... AIM

Association Internationale de la Presse Echiqueenne [*International Association of Chess Press*] [*Kerteminde, Denmark*] (EAIO) .... AIPE

Association Internationale de la Presse Sportive [*International Sport Press Association*] (EAIO) .... AIPS

Association Internationale de la Psychologie Adlerienne [*International Association of Adlerian Psychology*] .... AIPA

Association Internationale de la Savonnerie et de la Detergence [*International Association of the Soap and Detergent Industry*] (EAIO) .... AIS

Association Internationale de la Science du Sol [*International Society of Soil Science - ISSS*] (EAIO) .... AISS

Association Internationale de la Securite Sociale [*International Social Security Association*] .... AISS

Association Internationale de la Soie [*International Silk Association - ISA*] (EAIO) .... AIS

Association Internationale de la Teinture et de l'Impression Textiles [*International Association of Textile Dyers and Printers*] (EAIO) .... AITIT

Association Internationale de l'Etancheite [*International Waterproofing Association - IWA*] (EAIO) .... AIE

Association Internationale de l'Industrie des Bouillons et Potages [*International Association of the Manufacture of Soups and Broths*] (EAIO) .... AIIBP

Association Internationale de l'Industrie des Engrais [*International Fertilizer Industry Association - IFA*] (EAIO) .... IFA

Association Internationale de Linguistique Appliquee [*International Association of Applied Linguistics*] (EA) .... AILA

Association Internationale de Litterature Comparee [*International Comparative Literature Association*] .... AILC

Association Internationale de Medecine et de Biologie de l'Environnement [*International Association of Medicine and Biology of Environment - IAMBE*] [*France*] (EAIO) .... AIMBE

Association Internationale de Medecine Traditionnelle Chinoise [*International Association of Traditional Chinese Medicine*] [*Canada*] .... AIMTC

Association Internationale de Musees de Transports [*International Association of Transport Museums - IATM*] (EAIO) .... AIMT

Association Internationale de Mycologie [*International Mycological Association*] (EAIO) .... AIM

Association Internationale de Numerotation des Articles [*International Article Numbering Association*] (EAIO) .... EAN

Association Internationale de Paleontologie Humaine (EAIO) .... AIPH

Association Internationale de Papyrologues [*International Association of Papyrologists*] (EAIO) .... AIP

Association Internationale de Pedagogie Experimentale de Langue Francaise [*International Association of Experimental French Language Education*] [*Canada*] .... AIPELF

Association Internationale de Pediatrie [*International Pediatric Association - IPA*] [*Paris, France*] (EAIO) .... AIP

Association Internationale de Philosophie du Droit et de Philosophie Sociale [*See also IAPLSP*] .... AIPDPS

Association Internationale de Photobiologie [*International Photobiology Association*] [*Epalinges, Switzerland*] (EA) .... AIP

Association Internationale de Presse pour l'Etude des Problemes d'Outre-Mer [*International Press Association for Studying Overseas Problems*].... AIPEPO

Association Internationale de Prophylaxie de la Cecite [*International Association for the Prevention of Blindness*] .... AIPC

Association Internationale de Psychologie Appliquee [*International Association of Applied Psychology*] .... AIPA

Association Internationale de Relations Professionnelles [*International Industrial Relations Association - IIRA*] (EAIO) .... AIRP

Association Internationale de Science Politique [*International Political Science Association - IPSA*] [*Canada*] .... AISP

Association Internationale de Sociologie [*International Sociological Association - ISA*] (EAIO) .... AIS

Association Internationale de Standardisation Biologique [*International Association of Biological Standardization - IABS*] (EAIO) .... AISB

Association Internationale de Terminologie [*International Association of Terminology*] [*Quebec, PQ*] (EAIO) .... TERMIA

Association Internationale de Volcanologie [*International Association of Volcanology*] .... AIV

Association Internationale d'Epigraphie Grecque et Latine [*International Association for Greek and Latin Epigraphy*] (EAIO) .... AIEGL

Association Internationale d'Epigraphie Latine [*International Association for Latin Epigraphy*] .... AIEL

Association Internationale des Aeroports Civils [*International Civil Airports Association - ICAA*] (EAIO) .... AIAC

Association Internationale des Approvisionneurs de Navires [*British*] (EAIO) .... AIAN

Association Internationale des Arbitres de Water Polo [*International Association of Water Polo Referees - IAWPR*] (EAIO) .... AIA

Association Internationale des Arts Plastiques [*International Association of Art - IAA*] (EAIO) .... AIAP

Association Internationale des Assureurs Contre la Grele [*International Association of Hail Insurers*] .... AIAG

Association Internationale des Automobile Clubs Reconnus [*International Automobile Federation*] .... AIACR

Association Internationale des Bibliotheques, Archives, et Centres de Documentation Musicaux [*International Association of Music Libraries, Archives, and Documentation Centres - IAML*] (EAIO) .... AIBM

Association Internationale des Charites [*International Association of Charities - IAC*] (EAIO) .... AIC

Association Internationale des Charites de St. Vincent De Paul [*International Association of Charities of St. Vincent De Paul*] (EAIO) .... AIC

Association Internationale des Circuits Permanents [*Circuits International*] [*Germany*] (EAIO) .... AICP

Association Internationale des Constructeurs de Materiel Aerospatial [*International Association of Aerospace Equipment Manufacturers*] .... AICMA

Association Internationale des Constructeurs de Materiel Roulant [*International Association of Rolling Stock Builders - IARSB*] (EAIO) .... AICMR

Association Internationale des Cordeliers [*International Songwriters' Association - ISA*] (EAIO) .... AIC

Association Internationale des Critiques d'Art [*International Association of Art Critics*] (EAIO) .... AICA

Association Internationale des Critiques de Theatre [*International Association of Theatre Critics*] .... AICT

Association Internationale des Critiques Litteraires [*International Association of Literary Critics*] (EAIO) .... AICL

Association Internationale des Debardeurs [*International Longshoremen's Association - ILA*] [*Canada*] .... AID

Association Internationale des Demographes de Langue Francaise (EAIO) .... AIDELF

Association Internationale des Diffuseurs d'Oeuvres d'Art Originales [*International Association of Original Art Diffusors - IAOAD*] (EAIO) .... AIDOAO

Association Internationale des Distributions d'Eau .... AIDE

Association Internationale des Docteurs (Lettres et Sciences Humaines) de l'Universite de Paris et des Autres Universites de France [*International Association of Doctors (Letters and Liberal Studies) of the University of Paris and Other Universities of France*] [*Canada*] .... AIDLUPA

Association Internationale des Documentalistes et Techniciens de l'Information [*International Association of Documentalists and Information Officers*] ... AID
Association Internationale des Documentaristes [*International Association of Documentary Filmmakers*] ... AID
Association Internationale des Ecoles de Service Social [*International Association of Schools of Social Work - IASSW*] (EA) ... AIESS
Association Internationale des Ecoles de Voile [*International Sailing Schools Association*] [*France*] (EAIO) ... ISSA
Association Internationale des Ecoles des Sciences de l'Information [*International Association of Information Sciences Schools*] [*Canada*] (EAIO) ... AIESI
Association Internationale des Ecoles Privees Europeennes ... AIEPE
Association Internationale des Ecoles Superieures d'Education Physique [*International Association for Physical Education in Higher Education*] (EAIO) ... AIESEP
Association Internationale des Editeurs de Catalogues de Timbres-Poste [*International Association of Publishers of Postage Stamp Catalogues*] (EA) ... ASCAT
Association Internationale des Educateurs de Jeunes Inadaptes [*International Association of Workers for Troubled Children and Youth*] (EAIO) ... AIEJI
Association Internationale des Entreprises d'Equipement Electrique [*International Association of Electrical Contractors - IAEC*] (EAIO) ... AIE
Association Internationale des Etudes Byzantines [*International Association for Byzantine Studies - IABS*] (EAIO) ... AIEB
Association Internationale des Etudes de l'Asie du Sud-Est [*Paris, France*] (EAIO) ... AIEAS
Association Internationale des Etudes et Recherches sur l'Information [*International Association of Mass Communications Research*] ... AIERI
Association Internationale des Etudes Francaises [*Paris, France*] (EAIO) ... AIEF
Association Internationale des Etudiants Dentaires [*International Association of Dental Students - IADS*] [*British*] (EA) ... AIED
Association Internationale des Etudiants en Agriculture [*International Association of Agriculture Students - IAAS*] (EAIO) ... AIEA
Association Internationale des Etudiants en Sciences Economiques et Commerciales [*International Association of Students in Economics and Commerce*] [*Brussels, Belgium*] (EAIO) ... AIESEC
Association Internationale des Etudiants en Sciences Economiques et Commerciales (AIE) ... AIESEC
Association Internationale des Femmes d'Affaires Noires [*Black Business Women - International - BBWI*] [*France*] (EAIO) ... AIFAN
Association Internationale des Femmes Medecins [*Medical Women's International Association - MWIA*] [*Germany*] (EAIO) ... AIFM
Association Internationale des Hautes Juridictions Administratives [*International Association of Supreme Administrative Jurisdictions*] (EAIO) ... AIHJA
Association Internationale des Hydrogeologues [*International Association of Hydrogeologists - IAH*] ... AIH
Association Internationale des Interets Radio-Maritimes ... AIIRM
Association Internationale des Interpretes de Conference [*International Association of Conference Interpreters*] (EAIO) ... AIIC
Association Internationale des Jeunes Avocats [*Young Lawyers' International Association*] (EAIO) ... AIJA
Association Internationale des Journalistes de la Presse Feminine et Familiale [*International Association of Women and Home Page Journalists - IAWHPJ*] (EAIO) ... AIJPF
Association Internationale des Journalistes Philateliques [*International Association of Philatelic Journalists*] [*Germany*] ... AIJP
Association Internationale des Juges des Enfants ... AIJE
Association Internationale des Juristes Democrates [*International Association of Democratic Lawyers*] ... AIJD
Association Internationale des Lotteries d'Etat [*International Association of State Lotteries*] [*Canada*] (EAIO) ... AILE
Association Internationale des Magistrats de la Jeunesse [*International Association of Youth Magistrates*] ... AIJE
Association Internationale des Maires et Responsables des Capitales et Metropoles Partiellement ou Entierement Francophones [*International Association of Mayors Responsible for Capital Cities or Metropolises Partially or Entirely French-Speaking*] (EA) ... AIMF
Association Internationale des Maires Francophones - Bureau a Quebec (AC) ... AIMF
Association Internationale des Metiers et Enseignements d'Art [*International Association for Crafts and the Teaching of Art*] ... AIMEA
Association Internationale des Musees d'Agriculture [*International Association of Agricultural Museums*] (EAIO) ... AIMA
Association Internationale des Navigants de Langue Francaise (EAIO) ... AINLF
Association Internationale des Numismates Professionnels [*International Association of Professional Numismatists - IAPN*] [*Switzerland*] (EAIO) ... AINP
Association Internationale des Organisateurs de Courses Cyclistes [*International Association of Organizers of Cycle Competitions*] [*France*] (EAIO) ... AIOCC
Association Internationale des Palais des Congres [*International Association of Congress Centers*] [*Zagreb, Yugoslavia*] (EA) ... AIPC
Association Internationale des Parlementaires de Langue Francaise [*International Association of French-Speaking Parliamentarians*] (EAIO) ... AIPLF
Association Internationale des Ponts et Charpentes [*International Association of Bridges and Construction*] [*Switzerland*] ... AIPC
Association Internationale des Ports [*International Association of Ports and Harbors - IAPH*] [*Tokyo, Japan*] (EAIO) ... AIP
Association Internationale des Presses Universitaires de Langue Francaise [*International Association of French Language University Presses*] [*Canada Defunct*] ... AIPULF
Association Internationale des Producteurs de l'Horticulture [*International Association of Horticultural Producers*] [*Netherlands*] ... AIPH
Association Internationale des Professeurs de Philosophie [*International Association of Teachers of Philosophy*] (EAIO) ... AIPPh
Association Internationale des Sciences de l'Education [*International Association for the Advancement of Educational Research*] ... AISE
Association Internationale des Sciences Economiques [*International Economic Association - IEA*] [*Paris, France*] (EAIO) ... AISE
Association Internationale des Sciences Juridiques [*International Association of Legal Science - IALS*] (EAIO) ... AISJ
Association Internationale des Secretaires Professionnelles [*International Association of Professional Secretaries*] [*Canada*] ... AISP
Association Internationale des Selectionneurs pour la Protection des Obtentions Vegetales [*International Association of Plant Breeders for the Protection of Plant Varieties - IAPBPPV*] (EAIO) ... ASSINSEL
Association Internationale des Skal Clubs [*International Association of Skal Clubs*] (EAIO) ... AISC
Association Internationale des Societes d'Assurance Mutuelle [*International Association of Mutual Insurance Companies*] [*Paris, France*] (EAIO) ... AISAM
Association Internationale des Sociologues de Langue Francaise [*International Association of French Language Sociologists*] (EAIO) ... AISLF
Association Internationale des Statisticiens d'Enquetes [*International Association of Survey Statisticians*] (EAIO) ... AISE
Association Internationale des Traducteurs de Conference [*International Association of Conference Translators*] (EAIO) ... AITC
Association Internationale des Travailleurs [*International Association of Workers*] [*France*] ... AIT
Association Internationale des Travaux en Souterrain - International Tunneling Association [*Bron, France*] (EA) ... AITES-ITA
Association Internationale des Universites [*International Association of Universities - IAU*] (EAIO) ... AIU
Association Internationale des Universites du Troisieme Age [*International Association of Universities of the Third Age*] (EAIO) ... AIUTA
Association Internationale des Urbanistes [*International Society of City and Regional Planners - ISOCARP*] (EAIO) ... AIU
Association Internationale des Usagers d'Embranchements Particuliers [*International Association of Users of Private Sidings*] ... AIEP
Association Internationale des Utilisateurs de Files de Fibres Artificielles et Synthetiques [*International Association of Users of Yarn of Man-Made Fibers*] ... AIUFFAS
Association Internationale des Villes d'Avenir [*International Association of Cities of the Future*] (EA) ... AIVA
Association Internationale des Villes Francophones des Congres [*International Association of French-Speaking Congress Towns - IAFCT*] (EAIO) ... AIVFC
Association Internationale d'Etude des Civilisations Mediterraneennes [*International Association of Studies on Mediterranean Civilizations*] (EAIO) ... AIECM
Association Internationale d'Etudes du Sud-Est Europeen [*International Association of South-East European Studies - IASEES*] (EAIO) ... AIESEE
Association Internationale d'Etudes Patristiques [*International Association for Patristic Studies*] (EAIO) ... AIEP
Association Internationale d'Etudes pour la Protection des Investissements ... ADPI
Association Internationale d'Eutonie Gerda Alexander [*International Association for Gerda Alexander Eutony*] [*Switzerland*] (EAIO) ... AIEGA
Association Internationale d'Experts Scientifiques du Tourisme [*International Association of Scientific Experts in Tourism*] (EAIO) ... AIEST
Association Internationale d'Histoire Contemporaine de l'Europe [*International Association for Contemporary History of Europe*] [*Defunct*] (EAIO) ... AIHCE
Association Internationale d'Hotellerie [*International Hotel Association - IHA*] (EAIO) ... AIH
Association Internationale d'Hydrologie Scientifique ... AIH
Association Internationale d'Information et de Documentation en Administration Publique [*International Association for Information and Documentation in Public Administration*] (EAIO) ... AIIDAP
Association Internationale d'Information Scolaire, Universitaire, et Professionelle [*International Association for Educational and Vocational Information - IAEVI*] (EAIO) ... AIISUP
Association Internationale d'Irradiation Industrielle [*Association of International Industrial Irradiation*] (EAIO) ... AIII
Association Internationale: Donnees pour le Developpement [*Data for Development International Association - DFD*] (EA) ... DD
Association Internationale d'Orientation Professionnelle ... AIOP
Association Internationale d'Orientation Scolaire et Professionnelle [*International Association for Educational and Vocational Guidance - IAEVG*] (EAIO) ... AIOSP
Association Internationale du Cinema Scientifique [*International Scientific Film Association*] ... AICS
Association Internationale du Congres des Chemins de Fer [*International Railway Congress Association - IRCA*] (EAIO) ... AICCF
Association Internationale du Droit Nucleaire [*International Nuclear Law Association - INLA*] (EA) ... AIDN
Association Internationale du Film d'Animation [*International Animated Film Association*] (EAIO) ... ASIFA
Association Internationale du Mohair [*International Mohair Association*] (EAIO) ... AIM
Association Internationale du Nouvel Objet Visuel [*International Association for New Visual Objects*] [*Paris, France*] (EAIO) ... INOV
Association Internationale du Registre des Bateaux du Rhin [*International Association of the Rhine Ships Register*] ... AIRBR
Association Internationale du Theatre Amateur [*International Amateur Theatre Association - IATA*] (EAIO) ... AITA
Association Internationale du Theatre pour l'Enfance et de la Jeunesse [*International Association of Theatre for Children and Youth*] (EAIO) ... ASSITEJ
Association Internationale Francophone des Aines [*Canada*] (EAIO) ... AIFA

Association Internationale Futuribles [*Futuribles International*] (EAIO) .... AIF
Association Internationale Permanente des Congres de la Route [*Permanent International Association of Road Congresses - PIARC*] (EAIO) .... AIPCR
Association Internationale pour la Defense des Langues et Cultures Menacees [*International Association for the Defence of Threatened Languages and Cultures*] (EAIO) .... AIDLCM
Association Internationale pour la Lecture (EAIO) .... AIL
Association Internationale pour la Mobilisation de la Creativite [*International Association for the Mobilization of Creativity*] [*Canada*] .... AIMC
Association Internationale pour la Prevention du Suicide [*International Association for Suicide Prevention*] .... AIPS
Association Internationale pour la Protection de la Propriete Industrielle [*International Association for the Protection of Industrial Property*] [*Zurich, Switzerland*] (EA) .... AIPPI
Association Internationale pour la Recherche et la Diffusion des Methodes Audio-Visuelles et Structuro-Globales [*International Association for Research and Diffusion of Audio-Visual and Structural-Global Methods*] (EA) .... AIMAV
Association Internationale pour la Recherche Medicale et les Echanges Culturels [*International Association for Medical Research and Cultural Exchange*] [*Paris, France*] (EAIO) .... AIRMEC
Association Internationale pour la Securite Aerienne [*International Air Safety Association*] .... AISA
Association Internationale pour le Calcul Analogique [*International Association for Analogue Computation*] [*Later, IMACS*] .... AICA
Association Internationale pour le Calcul Analogique [*International Association for Analogue Computation*] [*Later, IMACS*] .... ASICA
Association Internationale pour le Developpement des Bibliotheques en Afrique [*International Association for the Development of Libraries in Africa*] .... AIDBA
Association Internationale pour le Developpement des Universites Internationaleset Mondiales [*International Association for the Development of International and World Universities - IADIWU*] [*Aulnay-Sous-Bois, France*] (EAIO) .... AIDUIM
Association Internationale pour le Developpement des Universites Internationaleset Mondiales [*International Association for the Development of International and World Universities - IADIWU*] .... AIDUM
Association Internationale pour le Developpement en Afrique des Sciences Humaines Appliquees [*International Association for the Development of Applied Human Sciences in Africa*] (AF) .... AIDASA
Association Internationale pour le Progres Social .... AIPS
Association Internationale pour le Sport des Aveugles [*International Blind Sports Association - IBSA*] [*Farsta, Sweden*] (EAIO) .... AISA
Association Internationale pour l'Education Integrative [*International Association for Integrative Education - IAIE*] (EAIO) .... AIEI
Association Internationale pour les Etudes Sanskrites [*France*] (EAIO) .... AIES
Association Internationale pour les Recherches au Bas Fourneau d'Ougree .... AIRBO
Association Internationale pour les Residus Solides et le Nettoiement des Vil les [*International Solid Wastes and Public Cleansing Association*] [*INTAPUC and IRGRD*] [*Formed by a merger of*] [*Denmark*] (EAIO) .... ISWA
Association Internationale pour les Voiles Minces [*en Beton*] [*International Association for Shell Structures*] .... AIVM
Association Internationale pour l'Etude de la Mosaique Antique [*International Association for the Study of Ancient Mosaics*] .... AIEMA
Association Internationale pour l'Etude de l'Economie de l'Assurance [*Switzerland*] (EAIO) .... AIEEA
Association Internationale pour l'Etude des Argiles [*International Association for the Study of Clays*] (EAIO) .... AIPEA
Association Internationale pour l'Etude du Foie [*International Association for the Study of the Liver*] (EAIO) .... AIEF
Association Internationale pour l'Etude du Quaternaire [*International Association for the Study of the Quaternary*] [*Canada*] .... AIEQ
Association Internationale pour l'Evaluation du Rendement Scolaire [*International Association for the Valuation of Educational Achievement*] (EAIO) .... AIERS
Association Internationale pour l'Histoire du Verre [*International Association for the History of Glass*] (EAIO) .... AIHV
Association Internationale pour l'Oceanographie Biologique [*International Association of Biological Oceanography - IABO*] (EAIO) .... AIOB
Association Internationale Urbanisme et Commerce [*International Association for Town Planning and Distribution*] (EAIO) .... URBANICOM
Association Internationale Veterinaire de Production Animale [*International Veterinary Association for Animal Production - IVAAP*] [*Brussels, Belgium*] (EAIO) .... AIVPA
Association Jeunesse Fransaskoise [*Canada*] .... AJF
Association Litteraire et Artistique Internationale [*International Literary and Artistic Association*] .... ALAI
Association Lyrique Internationale [*Toulouse, France*] (EAIO) .... ALI
Association Management Centre (AC) .... AMC
Association Marketing Roundtable (EA) .... AMR
Association Mathematique du Quebec (AC) .... AMQ
Association Media Independents Ltd. [*British*] (DBA) .... AMI
Association Medicale Canadienne [*Canadian Medical Association - CMA*] ..... AMC
Association Medicale du Quebec (AC) .... AMQ
Association Medicale Franco-Americaine (EA) .... AMFA
Association Medicale Internationale pour l'Etudes des Conditions de Vie et de Sante [*International Medical Association for the Study of Living Conditions and Health*] [*Sofia, Bulgaria*] (EAIO) .... AMIEV
Association Medicale Mondiale [*World Medical Association - WMA*] [*Ferney-Voltaire, France*] .... AMM
Association Member of the Plastics and Rubber Institute [*British*] (DBQ) .... AMPRI
Association Miniere du Quebec (AC) .... AMQ
Association Mondiale de Hockey [*World Hockey Association - WHA*] [*Canada*] .... AMH
Association Mondiale de Lutte Contre la Faim [*World Association for the Struggle Against Hunger*] .... ASCOFAM
Association Mondiale de Prospective Sociale [*World Social Prospects Study Association*] [*Geneva, Switzerland*] (EAIO) .... AMPS
Association Mondiale de Zootechnie [*World Association for Animal Production*] .... AMZ
Association Mondiale des Amis de l'Enfance [*World Association of Children's Friends*] [*Monaco*] (EAIO) .... AMADE
Association Mondiale des Arts Divinatoires [*Divinatory Arts World Association - DAWA*] [*Rillieux-La-Pape, France*] (EAIO) .... AMAD
Association Mondiale des Federalistes Mondiaux [*World Association of World Federalists - WAWF*] (EA) .... AMFM
Association Mondiale des Guides et des Eclaireuses [*World Association of Girl Guides and Girl Scouts - WAGGGS*] [*London, England*] (EAIO) .... AMGE
Association Mondiale des Inventeurs [*World Association of Inventors and Researchers*] (EAIO) .... AMINA
Association Mondiale des Medecins Francophones [*Ottawa, ON*] (EAIO) .... AMMF
Association Mondiale des Sciences de l'Education [*World Association for Educational Research - WAER*] (EAIO) .... AMSE
Association Mondiale des Travailleurs Scientifiques [*Scientific Workers World Association*] (NATG) .... AMTS
Association Mondiale des Veterinaires Microbiologistes, Immunologistes, et Specialistes des Maladies Infectieuses [*World Association of Veterinary Microbiologists, Immunologists, and Specialists in Infectious Diseases - WAVMI*] [*Maisons-Alfort, France*] (EAIO) .... AMVMI
Association Mondiale pour l'Ecole Instrument de Paix [*World Association for the School as an Instrument of Peace*] [*Geneva, Switzerland*] (EAIO) .... EIP
Association Mondiale pour l'Energie Non-Polluante [*Planetary Association for Clean Energy - PACE*] .... AMEN
Association Mondiale Veterinaire [*World Veterinary Association - WVA*] [*Madrid, Spain*] (EAIO) .... AMV
Association Montessori International - USA (EA) .... AMI-USA
Association Montessori Internationale [*International Montessori Association*] [*Amsterdam, Netherlands*] (EAIO) .... AMI
Association Multinationale des Producteurs et Revendeurs d'Electricite-Documentation [*Multinational Association of Producers and Retailers of Electricity-Documentation*] [*Electricity Supply Board*] [*Information service or system*] (IID) .... AMPEREDOC
Association Museums New Brunswick [*Association des Musees du Nouveau-Brunswick*] (AC) .... AMNB
Association Nationale d'Aide aux Handicapes [*National Association of Aids to Handicapped Persons*] [*Canada*] .... ANAH
Association Nationale de la Recherche Technique [*National Association of Technical Research - NATR*] [*France Information service or system*] (IID) .... ANRT
Association Nationale des Anciens Detenus et Internes Resistants [*National Association of Former Resistance Prisoners and Internees*] [*Algeria*] (AF) .... ANADIR
Association Nationale des Anciens Moudjahidine et Mutiles de Guerre [*National Association of War Veterans and War Wounded*] [*Algeria*] .... ANAMMG
Association Nationale des Camionneurs Artisans (AC) .... ANCAI
Association Nationale des Distributeurs de Tabac et de Confiserie (AC) .... ANDTC
Association Nationale des Editeurs de Livres (AC) .... ANEL
Association Nationale des Forblantiers et Couvreurs, Section Locale 2020 [*National Association of Tinsmiths & Tilers, Local 2020*] (AC) .... ANFC
Association Nationale des Telespectateurs [*National Association of Telespectators*] [*Canada*] .... ANT
Association Nationale d'Etudes pour la Documentation Automatique [*National Association for Studies in Automatic Documentation*] [*French*] (NITA) .... ANEDA
Association Nationale pour l'Infographie [*National Computer Graphics Association of Canada*] .... ANI
Association Nordique des Etudes Canadiennes [*Nordic Association for Canadian Studies*] .... ANEC
Association Nucleaire Canadienne [*Canadian Nuclear Association - CNA*] ..... ANC
Association of Abrasive Blastcleaners and Protective Coaters, Queensland [*Australia*] .... AABPC(Qld)
Association of Academic Health Centers (EA) .... AAHC
Association of Academic Health Sciences Library Directors (EA) .... AAHSLD
Association of Academic Physiatrists (EA) .... AAP
Association of Academies of Science [*Later, NAAS*] .... AAS
Association of Accommodation and Welfare Officers [*British*] (DBA) .... AAWO
Association of Accounting Administrators [*Commercial firm Washington, DC*] (EA) .... AAA
Association of Accounting Technicians (EAIO) .... AAT
Association of Accredited Medical Laboratory Schools [*Later, NAHCS*] (EA) .... AAMLS
Association of Accredited Practitioners in Advertising (DGA) .... AAPA
Association of Administrative Assistants [*Association des Adjoints Administratifs*] (AC) .... AAA
Association of Administrative Assistants and Secretaries to United States Senators (EA) .... AAASUSS
Association of Administrators of the Interstate Compact on the Placement of Children (EA) .... AAICPC
Association of Advanced Rabbinical and Talmudic Schools (EA) .... AARTS
Association of Adventist Forums (EA) .... AAF
Association of Advertisers in Ireland (EAIO) .... AAI
Association of Advertising Film Companies .... AAFC
Association of Advertising Lawyers [*Defunct*] (EA) .... AAL
Association of Advertising Men and Women [*Later, Advertising and Marketing Association*] (EA) .... AAMW

Association of Advisers, Craft, Design, and Technology [*British*] (DBA) .... AACDT
Association of Advisors in Design and Technical Studies [*British*] .... AADTS
Association of Aerial Surveyors Australia .... AASA
Association of African Airlines .... AAFRA
Association of African American People's Legal Council (EA) .... AAPLC
Association of African Central Banks [*Dakar, Senegal*] .... AACB
Association of African Development Finance Institutions (MHDB) .... AADFI
Association of African Geological Surveys [*See also ASGA*] (EAIO) .... AAGS
Association of African Industrial Technology Organizations .... AAITO
Association of African Physicians in North America (EA) .... AAPNA
Association of African Sports Confederations [*See also UCSA*] [*Yaounde, Cameroon*] (EAIO) .... AASC
Association of African Studies Programs (EA) .... AASP
Association of African Trade Promotion Organizations [*Tangier, Morocco*] (EAIO) .... AATPO
Association of African Universities (EAIO) .... AAU
Association of African Women for Research and Development (EAIO) .... AAWORD
Association of Agricultrual Computer Companies (EA) .... AACC
Association of Agricultural Education Staffs [*British*] .... AAES
Association of Air Transport Unions [*Defunct*] (EA) .... AATU
Association of Airborne Ranger Companies of the Korean War (EA)..... AARCKW
Association of Alaska School Boards (SRA) .... AASB
Association of Alcohol/Addictions Programs in Washington State (SRA)..... AAP
Association of Allergists for Mycological Investigations [*Defunct*] (EA) ..... AAMI
Association of Allied Health Professionals Ontario [*Association des Professionnels Unis de la Sante, Ontario*] (AC) .... AAHP-O
Association of Alternate Postal Systems (EA) .... AAPS
Association of Alternative Newsweeklies .... AAN
Association of Amateur Magicians [*Defunct*] (EA) .... AAM
Association of American Air Travel Clubs [*Defunct*] (EA) .... AAATC
Association of American and Canadian Importers of Green Olives [*Later, Green Olive Trade Association*] (EA) .... AACIGO
Association of American Battery Manufacturers [*Later, BCI*] (EA) .... AABM
Association of American Boards of Examiners in Veterinary Medicine [*Later, AAVSB*] (EA) .... AABEVM
Association of American Cancer Institutes (EA) .... AACI
Association of American Chambers of Commerce in Latin America (EA) .... AACCLA
Association of American Choruses [*Later, Drinker Library of Choral Music*] (EA) .... AAC
Association of American CIRP [*College Internationale pour l'Etude Scientifique des Techniques de Production Mechanique*] **Industrial Sponsors** (EA) .... AACIS
Association of American Colleges (EA) .... AAC
Association of American Collegiate Literary Societies (EA) .... AACLS
Association of American Correspondents in London [*England*] (EA) .... AACL
[*The*] **Association of American Cultures** (EA) .... TAAC
Association of American Dance Companies [*Defunct*] (EA) .... AADC
Association of American Dentists .... AAD
Association of American Editorial Cartoonists (EA) .... AAEC
Association of American Feed Control Officials (EA) .... AAFCO
Association of American Fertilizer Control Officials [*Later, AAPFCO*] (EA) .... AAFCO
Association of American Foreign Service Women (EA) .... AAFSW
Association of American Geographers (EA) .... AAG
Association of American Geographers Annals [*A publication*] (BRI) .... AAAGA
Association of American Historic Inns (EA) .... AAHI
Association of American Indian and Alaska Native Social Workers [*Later, NISWA*] (EA) .... AAIANSW
Association of American Indian Physicians (EA) .... AAIP
Association of American Indian Social Workers [*Later, NISWA*] (EA) .... AAISW
Association of American Jurists (EA) .... AAJ
Association of American Law Schools (EA) .... AALS
Association of American Library Schools (BARN) .... AAIS
Association of American Medical Book Publishers [*Later, AMPA*] (EA).... AAMBP
Association of American Medical Colleges (EA) .... AAMC
Association of American Military Uniform Collectors (EA) .... AAMUC
Association of American Motorcycle Road Racers [*Defunct*] (EA) .... AAMRR
Association of American Pesticide Control Officials (EA) .... AAPCO
Association of American Physicians (EA) .... AAP
Association of American Physicians and Surgeons (EA) .... AAPS
Association of American Plant Food Control Officials (EA) .... AAPFCO
Association of American Playing Card Manufacturers [*Defunct*] (EA) ...... AAPCM
Association of American Publishers (EA) .... AAP
Association of American Railroad Dining Car Officers (EA) .... AARDCO
Association of American Railroads (EA) .... AAR
Association of American Railroads, Economics and Finance Department Library, Washington, DC [*Library symbol Library of Congress*] (LCLS) .... DBRE
Association of American Rhodes Scholars .... AAR
Association of American Rhodes Scholars (EA) .... AARS
Association of American Rod and Gun Clubs, Europe (EA) .... AARGCE
Association of American Schools in South America (EA) .... AASSA
Association of American Seed Control Officials (EA) .... AASCO
Association of American Ship Owners (EA) .... AASO
Association of American State Boards of Examiners in Veterinary Medicine [*Later, AAVSB*] (EA) .... AASBEVM
Association of American State Geologists [*Defunct*] (EA) .... AASG
Association of American Steel Manufacturers .... AASM
[*The*] **Association of American Sword Collectors** (EA) .... TAASC
Association of American Universities (EA) .... AAU
Association of American University Presses (EA) .... AAUP
Association of American Veterinary Medical Colleges (EA) .... AAVMC
Association of American Vintners (EA) .... AAV
Association of American Volunteer Physicians (EA) .... AAVP
Association of American Weather Observers (EA) .... AAWO
Association of American Wives of Europeans (EA) .... AAWE
Association of American Wood Pulp Importers (EA) .... AAWPI
Association of American Youth of Ukrainian Descent (EA) .... ODUM
Association of American-Chinese Professionals (EA) .... AACP
Association of Americans and Canadians for Aliyah [*Later, North American AliyahMovement*] .... AACA
Association of Americans and Canadians in Israel (EA) .... AACI
Association of Americans Resident Overseas (EA) .... AARO
Association of Anaesthetists (DAVI) .... AA
Association of Analytical Chemists, Inc. .... AAC
Association of Analytical Chemists, Inc. (EA) .... ANACHEM
Association of Ancient Historians (EA) .... AAH
Association of Anglican Musicians (EA) .... AAM
Association of Apex Clubs of Australia .... AACA
Association of Apollo-Soyuz Test Project Philatelists (EA) .... A-ASTP-P
Association of Appliance and Home Entertainment Distributors [*Defunct*] (EA) .... AAHED
Association of Applied Biologists [*Midlothian, Scotland*] (EA) .... AAB
Association of Applied Insect Ecologists (EA) .... AAIE
Association of Arab Universities [*Amman, Jordan*] (EAIO) .... AARU
Association of Arab-American University Graduates (EA) .... AAUG
Association of Architectural Hardware Manufacturers (EA) .... AAHM
Association of Architectural Librarians (EA) .... AAL
Association of Architectural Technologists of Ontario (AC) .... AATO
Association of Area Business Publications (EA) .... AABP
Association of Area Medical Officers [*British*] .... AAMO
Association of Arizona Food Banks (SRA) .... AAFB
Association of Arkansas Counties (SRA) .... AAC
Association of Art Historians [*British*] (EAIO) .... AAH
Association of Art Institutions [*British*] .... AAI
Association of Art Museum Directors (EA) .... AAMD
Association of Artist-Run Galleries (EA) .... AARG
Association of Arts Administration Educators (EA) .... AAAE
Association of Arts Centres in Scotland [*British*] .... AACS
Association of Asbestos Cement Pipe Producers (EA) .... AACPP
Association of Asian Indians in America (EA) .... AAIA
Association of Asian/Pacific American Artists (EA) .... AAPAA
Association of Asian/Pacific Community Health Organizations (EA) ...... AAPCHO
Association of Asian Social Science Research Councils [*New Delhi, India*] .... AASSREC
Association of Asian-American Chambers of Commerce [*Washington, DC*] (EA) .... AAACC
Association of Asphalt Paving Technologists (EA) .... AAPT
Association of Assistant Librarians .... AAL
Association of Assistant Mistresses in Secondary Schools [*British*] (BI) .... AAM
Association of Assistant Mistresses, Inc. [*British*] .... AAMI
Association of Astronomy Educators .... AAE
Association of Atlantic Universities [*Association des Universites de l'Atlantique*] (AC) .... AAU
Association of Atlantic Universities/Blackwell North America [*Project*] [*Information service or system*] (IID) .... AAU/BNA
Association of Attenders and Alumni of The Hague Academy of International Law (EA) .... AAAHAIL
Association of Audio-Visual Technicians (EA) .... AAVT
Association of Australian Investigators .... AAI
Association of Australian University Presses .... AAUP
Association of Authorized Public Accountants (EAIO) .... AAPA
Association of Authorized Public Accountants [*British*] (DBA) .... AAPA
Association of Authors' Agents (EAIO) .... AAA
Association of Auto and Truck Recyclers [*Later, ADRA*] (EA) .... AATR
Association of Autoelectrical Technicians Ltd. [*British*] (BI) .... AET
Association of Automotive Aftermarket Distributors (EA) .... AAAD
Association of Average Adjusters of the United States [*New York, NY*] (EA) .... AAA
Association of Average Adjusters of the United States .... AAAUS
Association of Avian Veterinarians (EA) .... AAV
Association of Aviation and Space Museums [*Defunct*] (EA) .... AASM
Association of Aviation Maintenance Organizations (EAIO) .... AMOSA
Association of Aviation Psychologists (EA) .... AAP
Association of Balloon and Airship Constructors (EA) .... ABAC
Association of Ballrooms [*British*] (EAIO) .... ABL
Association of Bank Holding Companies [*Washington, DC*] (EA) .... ABHC
Association of Bank Travel Bureaus [*Defunct*] (EA) .... ABTB
Association of Banking Teachers [*British*] (DBA) .... ABT
Association of Bankrupts (EAIO) .... AB
Association of Baptist Chaplains (EA) .... ABC
Association of Baptist Churches of the Australian Capital Territory .... ABCACT
Association of Baptist Homes and Hospitals [*Later, ABHHA*] (EA) .... ABHH
Association of Baptist Professors of Religion .... ABPR
Association of Baptists for World Evangelism (EA) .... ABWE
Association of Battlefords Realtors (AC) .... BREB
Association of Beauty Teachers [*British*] .... ABT
Association of Bedding and Furniture Law Officials (EA) .... ABFLO
Association of Bendectin Children [*Later, ABDC*] (EA) .... ABC
Association of Better Business Bureaus [*Later, CBBB*] .... ABBB
Association of Better Computer Dealers [*Later, ABCD: The Microcomputer IndustryAssociation*] (EA) .... ABCD
Association of Beverage Container Recyclers (EA) .... ABCR
Association of Bibliographic Agencies of Britain, Australia, Canada, and the United States (ADA) .... ABACUS
Association of Biological Collections Appraisers (EA) .... ABCA
Association of Biomedical Communication Directors (EA) .... ABCD
Association of Biotechnology Companies (EA) .... ABC
Association of Birth Defect Children (EA) .... ABDC

Association of Bituminous Contractors (EA) .... ABC
Association of Black Admissions and Financial Aid Officers of the Ivy League andSister Schools (EA) .... ABAFAOILSS
Association of Black Anthropologists (EA) .... ABA
Association of Black Cardiologists (EA) .... ABC
Association of Black Catholics Against Abortion (EA) .... ABC
Association of Black CPA [*Certified Public Accountant*] **Firms** [*Defunct*] (EA) .... ABCPAF
Association of Black Foundation Executives (EA) .... ABFE
Association of Black Motion Picture and Television Producers (EA) .... ABMPTP
Association of Black Nursing Faculty in Higher Education (EA) .... ABNF
Association of Black Psychologists (EA) .... ABP
Association of Black Psychologists (EA) .... ABPsi
Association of Black Sociologists (EA) .... ABS
Association of Black Storytellers (EA) .... ABS
Association of Black Women Historians (EA) .... ABWH
Association of Black Women in Higher Education (EA) .... ABWHE
Association of Blauvelt Descendants (EA) .... ABD
Association of Blind and Partially Sighted Teachers and Students [*British*] .... ABPSTS
Association of Blind and Partially-Sighted Teachers and Students [*British*] .... ABAPSTAS
Association of Blind Chartered Physiotherapists .... ABCP
Association of Blind Citizens of New South Wales [*Australia*] .... ABCNSW
Association of Blind Piano Tuners [*British*] (BI) .... ABPT
Association of Blood Donor Recruiters [*Defunct*] (EA) .... ABDR
Association of Board Makers [*British*] (DBA) .... ABM
Association of Boards of Certification (EA) .... ABC
Association of Boiler Setters, Chimney and Furnace Constructors [*British*] (BI) .... ABSC
Association of Bone and Joint Surgeons (EA) .... ABJS
Association of Book Publishers of British Columbia (AC) .... ABPBC
Association of Book Travelers (EA) .... ABT
Association of Bottled Beer Collectors (EAIO) .... ABBC
Association of Boys and Girls Clubs Professionals (EA) .... ABGCP
Association of Boys and Students Clothing Manufacturers (EA) .... ABSCM
Association of Brass and Bronze Ingot Manufacturers (EA) .... ABBIM
Association of Breastfeeding Mothers (EAIO) .... ABM
Association of Brewers [*Later, AOB*] (EA) .... AB
Association of Brewers (EA) .... AOB
Association of Bridal Consultants (EA) .... ABC
Association of British Adoption and Fostering Agencies (DI) .... ABAFA
Association of British Aero Clubs (BI) .... ABAC
Association of British and International Hairdressers and Hairdressing Schools (DBA) .... ABIH
Association of British Aviation Consultants (DA) .... ABAC
Association of British Chambers of Commerce .... ABCC
Association of British Chemical Manufacturers (BARN) .... ABCM
Association of British Climatologists (EAIO) .... ABC
Association of British Columbia Grape Growers (AC) .... ABCGG
Association of British Columbia Professional Foresters (AC) .... ABCPF
Association of British Conference Organisers (BI) .... ABCO
Association of British Correspondence Colleges (EAIO) .... ABCC
Association of British Counties (DBA) .... ABC
Association of British Dental Surgery Assistants .... ABDSA
Association of British Detectives (DI) .... ABD
Association of British Directory Publishers (EAIO) .... ABDP
Association of British Dispensing Opticians (DBA) .... ABDO
Association of British Editors (EAIO) .... ABE
Association of British Factors .... ABF
Association of British Factors and Discounters (EAIO) .... ABFD
Association of British Foam Laminators (BI) .... ABFL
Association of British Generating Set Manufacturers (MHDB) .... ABGSM
Association of British Geodesists .... ABG
Association of British Hairdressers and Hairdressing Schools .... ABH
Association of British Hispanists .... ABH
Association of British Independent Oil Exploration Companies .... BRINDEX
Association of British Insecticide Manufacturers (DI) .... ABIM
Association of British Insurers (EAIO) .... ABI
Association of British Introduction Agencies (EAIO) .... ABIA
Association of British Investigators (EAIO) .... ABI
Association of British Launderers and Cleaners (DI) .... ABLC
Association of British Library and Information Science Schools .... ABLISS
Association of British Library and Information Studies Schools (DBA) .... ABLISS
Association of British Library Schools .... ABLS
Association of British Manufacturers of Agricultural Chemicals (BI) .... ABMAC
Association of British Manufacturers of Printers' Machinery (DI) .... ABMPM
Association of British Marketing Research Companies (DBA) .... ABMRC
Association of British Meat Processors (DBA) .... ABMP
Association of British Mining Equipment Companies (EAIO) .... ABMEC
Association of British Mining Equipment Exporters (MHDB) .... ABMEX
Association of British Neurologists .... ABN
Association of British Oceanic Industries (DS) .... ABOI
Association of British Offshore Industries (DBA) .... ABOI
Association of British Orchestras (DBA) .... ABO
Association of British Organic and Compound Fertilisers Ltd. (BI) .... ABOCF
Association of British Orientalists .... ABO
Association of British Packing Contractors (BI) .... ABPC
Association of British Paediatric Nurses .... ABPN
Association of British Pewter Craftsmen .... ABPC
Association of British Picture Restorers .... ABPR
Association of British Plywood and Veneer Manufacturers (BI) .... ABPVM
Association of British Reclaimed Rubber Manufacturers (BI) .... ABRRM
Association of British Riding Schools (BI) .... ABRS
Association of British Roofing Felt Manufacturers Ltd. (BI) .... ABRFM
Association of British Sailmakers (DBA) .... ABS
Association of British Science Writers .... ABSW
Association of British Secretaries in America .... ABSA
Association of British Solid Fuel Appliance Manufacturers (DBA) .... ABSAM
Association of British Spectroscopists (DBA) .... ABS
Association of British Steriliser Manufacturers (EAIO) .... ABSM
Association of British Theological and Philosophical Libraries .... ABTAPL
Association of British Transport Museums .... ABTM
Association of British Travel Agents .... ABTA
Association of British Tree Surgeons and Arborists (DI) .... ABTSA
Association of British Veterinary Acupuncture (DBA) .... ABVA
Association of British Wild Animal Keepers (DBA) .... ABWAK
Association of British Yacht Agents (BI) .... ABYA
Association of British Zoologists (BI) .... ABZ
Association of Broadcasting Staff [*A union*] [*British*] (DCTA) .... ABS
Association of Brokers and Yacht Agents [*British*] (DBA) .... ABYA
Association of Bronze and Brass Founders [*British*] (BI) .... ABBF
Association of Builders' Hardware Manufacturers (EAIO) .... ABHM
Association of Building Centres [*British*] (BI) .... ABC
Association of Building Component Manufacturers (EAIO) .... ABCM
Association of Building Contractors of Quebec (AC) .... ABCQ
Association of Building Technicians [*A union*] [*British*] .... ABT
Association of Burglary Insurance Surveyors [*British*] (DI) .... ABIS
Association of Business Administration Studies [*British*] (EAIO) .... ABAS
Association of Business Advertising Agencies [*British*] (DBA) .... ABAA
Association of Business and Administrative Computing (MHDB) .... ABAC
Association of Business and Industry [*Iowa*] (SRA) .... ABI
Association of Business and Professional Women in Construction (EA) .... ABPWC
Association of Business Centres [*British*] (DBA) .... ABC
Association of Business Executives [*British*] (DBA) .... ABE
Association of Business Forms Manufacturers [*Defunct*] (EA) .... ABFM
Association of Business Officers of Preparatory Schools (EA) .... ABOPS
Association of Business Product Manufacturers (EA) .... ABPM
Association of Business Publishers (EA) .... ABP
Association of Button Merchants (EAIO) .... ABM
Association of Buying Offices [*Defunct*] (EA) .... ABO
Association of Cable Television Suppliers (EA) .... ACTS
Association of California Enhanced Telemessaging Services (SRA) .... ACETS
Association of California Hospital Districts (SRA) .... ACHD
Association of California Insurance Companies (SRA) .... ACIC
Association of California Life Insurance Companies (SRA) .... ACLIC
Association of California School Administrators (SRA) .... ACSA
Association of California State Attorneys (SRA) .... ACSA
Association of California Surety Companies (SRA) .... ACSC
Association of California Water Agencies (SRA) .... ACWA
Association of Cambodian Survivors of America (EA) .... ACSA
Association of Camps Farthest Out (EA) .... CFO
Association of Canadaian Teaching Hospitals (AC) .... ACTH
Association of Canadian Advertisers, Inc. (WDMC) .... ACA
Association of Canadian Alumni Administrators (NFD) .... ACAA
Association of Canadian Alumni Administrators .... ACAA
Association of Canadian Archivists .... ACA
Association of Canadian Bible Colleges (AC) .... ACBC
Association of Canadian Biscuit Manufacturers [*Association Canadienne des Manufacturiers de Biscuits*] (AC) .... ACBM
Association of Canadian Choral Conductors [*Association des Chefs des Choeurs Canadiens*] .... ACCC
Association of Canadian College and University Teachers of French .... ACCUTF
Association of Canadian Commercial Testing Laboratories and Consultants .... ACCTLC
Association of Canadian Community Colleges [*Association des Colleges Communautaires du Canada*] .... ACCC
Association of Canadian Courts Administrators (AC) .... ACCA
Association of Canadian Distillers [*Association des Distallateurs Canadiens*] (AC) .... ACD
Association of Canadian Editorial Cartoonists (AC) .... ACEC
Association of Canadian Faculties of Dentistry .... ACFD
Association of Canadian Film Craftspeople (AC) .... ACFC
Association of Canadian Financial Corporations (AC) .... ACFC
Association of Canadian Fire Marshals & Fire Commissioners [*L'Association Canadienne des Directeurs et Commissaires des Incendies*] (AC) .... ACFM-FC
Association of Canadian Industrial Designers .... ACID
Association of Canadian Interpreters .... ACI
Association of Canadian Law Teachers .... ACLT
Association of Canadian Manufacturers (BARN) .... ACM
Association of Canadian Map Libraries and Archives (EAIO) .... ACMLA
Association of Canadian Medical Colleges (AC) .... ACMC
Association of Canadian Mountain Guides [*Association des Guides de Montagne Canadiens*] (AC) .... ACMG
Association of Canadian Orchestras .... ACO
Association of Canadian Pension Management .... ACPM
Association of Canadian Publishers .... ACP
Association of Canadian Television and Radio Artists .... ACTRA
Association of Canadian Underwater Councils .... ACUC
Association of Canadian Universities for Northern Studies .... ACUNS
Association of Canadian University and College Teachers of French .... ACUCTF
Association of Canadian University Information Bureaus [*See also ABUIC*] .... ACUIB
Association of Canadian University Presses .... ACUP
Association of Canadian University Teachers of English .... ACUTE
Association of Canadian University Teachers of French .... ACUTF
Association of Canadian Venture Capital Companies .... ACVCC
Association of Canadian Women Composers .... ACWC

Association of Car Fleet Operators [*British*] (DBA) ... ACFO
Association of Career Teachers [*British*] ... ACT
Association of Career Training Schools [*Defunct*] (EA) ... ACTS
Association of Caribbean Historians [*Nassau, Bahamas*] (EAIO) ... ACH
Association of Caribbean Studies (EA) ... ACS
Association of Caribbean University and Research Institute Libraries ... ACURIL
Association of Cartonboard Makers [*British*] (DBA) ... ACBM
Association of Casing Importers Ltd. [*British*] (BI) ... ASCIM
Association of Casualty Accountants and Statisticians [*Later, SIA*] ... ACAS
Association of Casualty and Surety Companies [*Later, AIA*] (EA) ... ACSC
Association of Casualty Care Personnel [*Canada*] ... ACCP
Association of Catholic Colleges and Universities (EA) ... ACCU
Association of Catholic Diocesan Archivists (EA) ... ACDA
Association of Catholic School Principals [*Australia*] ... ACSP
Association of Catholic Teachers [*Defunct*] ... ACT
Association of Catholic Trade Unionists (EA) ... ACTU
Association of Catholic TV and Radio Syndicators (EA) ... ACTRS
Association of CCTV [*Closed Circuit Television*] **Surveyors** (EAIO) ... ACCTVS
Association of Centers of Medieval and Renaissance Studies [*Later, CARA*] (EA) ... ACOMARS
Association of Cereal Food Manufacturers (EAIO) ... ACFM
Association of Certification Bodies [*British*] (DBA) ... ACB
Association of Certified Accountants (EAIO) ... ACA
Association of Certified and Corporate Accountants [*British*] ... ACCA
Association of Certified Liquidators (EA) ... ACL
Association of Certified Public Accountant Examiners [*Later, NASBA*] (EA) ... ACPAE
Association of Certified Servers (EA) ... ACS
Association of Chairmen of Departments of Mechanics (EA) ... ACDM
Association of Chambers of Commerce of Ireland (DI) ... ACCI
Association of Charity Officers (EAIO) ... ACO
Association of Chart and Technical Analysts [*British*] ... ACTA
Association of Charter Trustees [*British*] ... ACT
Association of Charter Trustees and Urban Parish Councils [*British*] (DBA) ... ACT & UPC
Association of Chartered Accountants in the United States (EA) ... ACAUS
Association of Chartered Industrial Designers of Ontario (AC) ... ACIDO
Association of Chartered Physiotherapists in Sports Medicine (EAIO) ... ACPSM
Association of Chemical Industry of Texas (SRA) ... ACIT
Association of Chief Administrators of Health Authorities [*British*] ... ACAHA
Association of Chief Ambulance Officers [*British*] (DBA) ... ACAO
Association of Chief Architects of Scottish Local Authorities (EAIO) ... ACASLA
Association of Chief Education Officers [*British*] (BI) ... ACEO
Association of Chief Education Social Workers [*British*] (DBA) ... ACESW
Association of Chief Officers of Police [*British*] (DI) ... ACOP
Association of Chief Officers of Probation [*British*] (DBA) ... ACOP
Association of Chief Police Officers [*British*] ... ACPO
Association of Chief State School Audio-Visual Officers [*Defunct*] (EA) ... ACSSAVO
Association of Chief Technical Officers (EAIO) ... ACTO
Association of Child Advocates (EA) ... ACA
Association of Child and Adolescent Psychiatric Nurses ... ACAPN
Association of Child Care Centers in New South Wales [*Australia*] ... ACCCNSW
Association of Child Care Officers [*British*] (DI) ... ACCO
Association of Child Psychotherapists (EAIO) ... ACP
Association of Children's Officers [*British*] (DI) ... ACO
Association of Children's Prosthetic-Orthotic Clinics (EA) ... ACPOC
Association of Chinese and American Engineers ... ACAE
Association of Chinese from Indochina [*Later, SEAC*] (EA) ... ACI
Association of Chiropodists (NADA) ... NAC
Association of Chiropractic Colleges (EA) ... ACC
Association of Choral Conductors (EA) ... ACC
Association of Christian Church Educators (EA) ... ACCE
Association of Christian Librarians (EA) ... ACL
Association of Christian Schools International (EA) ... ACSI
Association of Christian Teachers [*British*] (EAIO) ... ACT
Association of Christian Universities and Colleges in Asia (EA) ... ACUCA
Association of Christians in Local Broadcasting [*British*] ... ACLB
Association of Church Missions Committees (EA) ... ACMC
Association of Cinema and Video Laboratories (EA) ... ACVL
Association of Cinema Laboratories [*Later, ACVL*] (EA) ... ACL
Association of Cinematograph, Television, and Allied Technicians [*Canada*] ... ACTT
Association of Circus Proprietors of Great Britain (BI) ... ACP
Association of Civil Defence and Emergency Planning Officers [*British*] (DBA) ... ACDEPO
Association of Civil Service Temporary Clerks and Writers [*A union*] [*British*] ... ACSTCW
Association of Civilian Technicians (EA) ... ACT
Association of Civilian Technicians ... CTA
Association of Civilian Widows of Australia ... ACWA
Association of Clandestine Radio Enthusiasts (EA) ... ACE
Association of Classroom Teachers [*Defunct*] ... ACT
Association of Clerical, Technical, and Supervisory Staffs [*British*] (DCTA) ... ACTS
Association of Clerks and Stewards in Mental Hospitals [*A union*] [*British*] ... ACSMH
Association of Clinical Biochemists [*British*] ... ACB
Association of Clinical Pathologists ... ACP
Association of Clinical Research [*British*] (DBA) ... ACR
Association of Clinical Research Pharmaceutical Industries [*British*] (DBA) ... ACRPI
Association of Clinical Scientists (EA) ... ACS
Association of College Admissions Counselors [*Later, NACAC*] (EA) ... ACAC
Association of College and Research Libraries [*American Library Association*] (EA) ... ACRL
Association of College and University Auditors [*Madison, WI*] (EA) ... ACUA
Association of College and University Broadcasting Stations (NTCM) ... ACUBS
Association of College and University Business Officers (NFD) ... ACUBO
Association of College and University Concert Managers [*Later, ACUCAA*] ... ACUCM
Association of College and University Housing Officers [*Later, ACUHO-I*] (EA) ... ACUHO
Association of College and University Housing Officers - International (EA) ... ACUHO-I
Association of College and University Museums and Galleries (EA) ... ACUMG
Association of College and University Offices (EA) ... ACUO
Association of College and University Printers (EA) ... ACUP
Association of College and University Telecommunications Administrators (EA) ... ACUTA
Association of College Auxiliary Services [*Later, NACAS*] (EA) ... ACAS
Association of College Honor Societies (EA) ... ACHS
Association of College Management [*British*] (DBA) ... ACM
Association of College Professors of Textiles and Clothing (EA) ... ACPTC
Association of College Registrars [*British*] ... ACR
Association of College Registrars and Administrators [*British*] ... ACRA
Association of College Unions [*Later, ACU-I*] (EA) ... ACU
Association of College Unions - International (EA) ... ACU-I
Association of College, University, and Community Arts Administrators [*Later, APAP*] (EA) ... ACUCAA
Association of Colleges and Secondary Schools [*Later, SACS*] (EA) ... ACSS
Association of Colleges and Secondary Schools for Negroes [*Later, ACSS*] ... ACSSN
Association of Colleges and Universities for International-Intercultural Studies [*Defunct*] (EA) ... ACUIIS
Association of Colleges for Further and Higher Education [*British*] (EAIO) ... ACFHE
Association of Colleges Implementing the Diploma of Higher Education [*British*] ... ACID
Association of Colleges of Applied Arts & Technology of Ontario [*Association des Colleges d'Arts Appliquees et de Technologie de l'Ontario*] (AC) ... ACAATO
Association of Collegiate Business Schools and Programs (PGP) ... ACBSP
Association of Collegiate Entrepreneurs (EA) ... ACE
Association of Collegiate Schools of Architecture (EA) ... ACSA
Association of Collegiate Schools of Nursing [*Later, NLN*] ... ACSN
Association of Collegiate Schools of Planning (EA) ... ACSP
Association of Combined Youth Clubs [*British*] (DBA) ... ACYC
[*The*] **Association of Comedy Artists** (EA) ... TACA
Association of Comics Enthusiasts (EAIO) ... ACE
Association of Commerce and Industry (EA) ... ACI
Association of Commerce and Industry of New Mexico (SRA) ... ACI-NM
Association of Commercial Diving Educators (EA) ... ACDE
Association of Commercial Finance Attorneys (EA) ... ACFA
Association of Commercial Finance Companies of New York [*Later, NCFA*] (EA) ... ACFC
Association of Commercial Mail Receiving Agencies [*Defunct*] (EA) ... ACMRA
Association of Commercial Records Centers (EA) ... ACRC
Association of Commissioned Officers (USDC) ... ACO
Association of Commodity Exchange Firms [*Later, Futures Industry Association*] (EA) ... ACEF
Association of Commonwealth Archivists and Records Managers (EAIO) ... ACARM
Association of Commonwealth Students [*British*] (BI) ... ACS
Association of Commonwealth Universities [*British*] (EAIO) ... ACU
Association of Communication Engineers [*Charlotte, NC*] (TSSD) ... ACE
Association of Communications Technicians (EA) ... ACT
Association of Community Arts Agencies of Kansas (SRA) ... ACAAK
Association of Community Cancer Centers (EA) ... ACCC
Association of Community College Trustees (EA) ... ACCT
Association of Community Colleges for Excellence in Systems and Services [*Consortium*] ... ACCESS
Association of Community Home Schools [*British*] ... ACHS
Association of Community Information Centres in Ontario (AC) ... ACICO
Association of Community Mental Health Centers of Kansas (SRA) ... ACMHCK
Association of Community Organizations for Reform Now (EA) ... ACORN
Association of Community Technical Aid Centres (EAIO) ... ACTAC
Association of Community Travel Clubs (EA) ... ACTC
Association of Community Tribal Schools (EA) ... ACTS
Association of Community Workers [*British*] ... ACW
Association of Commuter Airlines [*Later, NATA*] ... ACA
Association of Compact Disk Publishers (EA) ... ACDP
Association of Company Registration Agents [*British*] (DBA) ... ACRA
Association of Comparative Haematology [*British*] (DBA) ... ACH
Association of Competitive Telecommunications Suppliers (AC) ... ACTS
Association of Computer Consultants (EA) ... ACC
Association of Computer Professionals (EA) ... ACP
Association of Computer Programmers and Analysts (EA) ... ACPA
Association of Computer Retailers (EA) ... ACR
Association of Computer Time-Sharing Users ... ACTSU
Association of Computer Users (EA) ... ACU
Association of Concentrated and Powdered Milk Manufacturers of the EEC (EAIO) ... ACPMME
Association of Concern for Ultimate Reality and Meaning (EA) ... ACURM
Association of Concern for Ultimate Reality & Meaning (AC) ... URAM
Association of Concerned African Scholars (EA) ... ACAS
Association of Concert Bands (EA) ... ACB
Association of Concert Bands of America [*Later, ACB*] (EA) ... ACBA
Association of Condominium Managers of Ontario (AC) ... ACMO

Association of Conference and Events Directors-International (EA) .... ACED-I
Association of Connecticut Career Schools (SRA) .... ACCS
Association of Connecticut Fairs (SRA) .... ACF
Association of Conservation Engineers (EA) .... ACE
Association of Conservation Officers (EAIO) .... ACO
Association of Conservative Clubs [*British*] (DBA) .... ACC
Association of Consultant Architects (EAIO) .... ACA
Association of Consultant Quantity Surveyors (MHDI) .... ACQS
Association of Consulting Actuaries (EAIO) .... ACA
Association of Consulting Architects Australia .... ACAA
Association of Consulting Chemists and Chemical Engineers (EA) ..... ACC & CE
Association of Consulting Engineers [*British*] (DI) .... ACE
Association of Consulting Engineers of Alberta (AC) .... CEA
Association of Consulting Engineers of Canada .... ACEC
Association of Consulting Engineers of Great Britain .... ACE
Association of Consulting Engineers of Great Britain .... ACEGB
Association of Consulting Engineers of Ireland (EAIO) .... ACEI
Association of Consulting Engineers of Manitoba (AC) .... ACEM
Association of Consulting Engineers of Ontario (AC) .... CEO
Association of Consulting Engineers of Saskatchewan (AC) .... ACES
Association of Consulting Engineers of the Yukon (AC) .... CEY
Association of Consulting Foresters (EA) .... ACF
Association of Consulting Foresters of Australia .... ACFA
Association of Consulting Management Engineers (EA) .... ACME
Association of Consulting Structural Engineers of New South Wales [*Australia*] .... ACSENSW
Association of Consumers and Taxpayers [*Political Group*] [*New Zealand*].... ACT
Association of Contact Lens Manufacturers [*British*] (DBA) .... ACLM
Association of Contact Lens Practitioners [*British*] (BI) .... ACLP
Association of Contemplative Sisters (EA) .... ACS
Association of Contemporary Historians (EA) .... ACH
Association of Continuing Legal Education Administrators (EA) .... ACLEA
Association of Cooperative Banks of the EC [*Economy Community*] [*Belgium*] (EAIO) .... ACB-EC
Association of Cooperative Educators (EA) .... ACE
Association of Cooperative Library Organizations [*Later, ASCLA*] .... ACLO
Association of Cooperative Retailers-Owned Wholesalers of Europe (EAIO) .... ACROWE
Association of Corporate Travel Executives (EA) .... ACTE
Association of Corporate Treasurers (EAIO) .... ACT
[*The*] **Association of Corporate Trustees** [*British*] (EAIO) .... TACT
Association of Correctional Administrators .... ACA
Association of Correctional Psychologists .... ACP
Association of Correctors of the Press (BARN) .... ACP
Association of Correspondence School Teachers (AEBS) .... ACST
Association of Corrugated Papermakers [*British*] (BI) .... ACPM
Association of Cosmetologists [*Later, ACH*] (EA) .... AC
Association of Cosmetologists and Hairdressers (EA) .... ACH
Association of Cost and Executive Accountants [*British*] (EAIO) .... ACEA
Association of Cost Engineers [*British*] (DBA) .... ACE
Association of Cotton Textile Merchants of New York [*Later, ATMI*] (EA) .... ACTM
Association of Cotton Yarn Distributors [*Later, AYD*] .... ACYD
Association of Council Secretaries [*Later, NAES*] (EA) .... ACS
Association of Country Entertainers (EA) .... ACE
Association of Country Greyhound Clubs [*Australia*] .... ACGC
Association of County Archivists [*British*] (DBA) .... ACA
Association of County Chief Executives [*British*] (EAIO) .... ACCE
Association of County Commissioners of Oklahoma (SRA) .... ACCO
Association of County Commissions of Alabama (SRA) .... ACCA
Association of County Councils [*British*] .... ACC
Association of County Public Health Officers [*British*] .... AssCPHO's
Association of County Supplies Officers [*British*] (DBA) .... ACSO
Association of Coupon Processors (EA) .... ACP
Association of Crafts and Creative Industries (EA) .... ACCI
Association of Crane Makers [*British*] (BI) .... ACM
Association of Credit Union League Executives (EA) .... ACULE
Association of Cricket Statisticians (EAIO) .... ACS
Association of Cricket Umpires (EAIO) .... ACU
Association of Crossroads Care Attendant Schemes (EAIO) .... ACCAS
Association of Cuban Architects in Exile (EA) .... ACAE
Association of Cultural Advancement through Visual Art [*British*] (DBA) .... ACAVA
Association of Cultural Executives [*Canada*] .... ACE
Association of Customers' Brokers [*Later, AIB*] (EA) .... ACB
Association of Cycle Exhibitors [*Later, NABEA*] (EA) .... ACE
Association of Cycle Traders (EAIO) .... ACT
Association of Cytogenetic Technologists (EA) .... ACT
Association of Dairymen's Assistants [*A union*] [*British*] .... ADA
Association of Dandyroll and Mould Makers (DGA) .... ADMM
Association of Dark Leaf Tobacco Dealers and Exporters (EA) .... ADLTDE
Association of Data Communications Users [*Defunct*] (EA) .... ADCU
Association of Data Processing Service Organizations [*Later, CSSIA*] [*US and Canada*] (EA) .... ADAPSO
Association of Data Processing Service Organizations [*Includes American and Canadian companies*] [*Later, ADAPSO - The Computer Software and Services Industry Association*] (EA) .... ADPSO
Association of Data Processing Service Organizations Panels .... ADAPSP
Association of Data Terminal Distributors .... ADTD
Association of Database Producers (IID) .... ADP
Association of Day Care Operators of Ontario (AC) .... ADCO
Association of Deans of American Colleges of Veterinary Medicine [*Later, Association of American Veterinary Medical Colleges*] (AEBS) .... ADACVM
Association of Defense Counselors (EA) .... ADC
Association of Defense Trial Attorneys (EA) .... ADTA
Association of Delaware Hospitals (SRA) .... ADH
Association of Dental Hospitals of Great Britain and Northern Ireland (BI) .... ADH
Association of Department Heads of Catering [*British*] (DBA) .... ADHOC
Association of Departments of English (EA) .... ADE
Association of Departments of Foreign Languages (EA) .... ADFL
Association of Desk and Derrick Clubs (EA) .... ADDC
Association of Development Financing Institutions in Asia and the Pacific [*Manila, Philippines*] (EA) .... ADFIAP
Association of Development Institutes for the Pacific and Asia .... ADIPA
Association of Diesel Specialists (EA) .... ADS
Association of Direct Labour Organisations [*British*] .... ADLO
Association of Direct Marketing Agencies [*Defunct*] (EA) .... ADMA
Association of Directors and Producers [*British*] .... ADP
Association of Directors of Education (AIE) .... ADE
Association of Directors of Education, Scotland (DI) .... ADES
Association of Directors of Recreation, Leisure, and Tourism [*British*] (DBA) .... ADRLT
Association of Directors of Social Services (EAIO) .... ADSS
Association of Directors of Social Work (EAIO) .... ADSW
Association of Disabled Professionals (EAIO) .... ADP
Association of Disciples for Theological Discussion (EA) .... ADTD
Association of Dispensing Opticians [*British*] (DBQ) .... ADO
Association of Distributors of Advertising Material (EAIO) .... ADAM
Association of District Council Treasurers [*British*] .... ADCT
Association of District Councils [*British*] .... ADC
Association of District Secretaries [*British*] .... ADS
Association of Diving Contractors (EA) .... ADC
Association of Drainage Authorities [*British*] (DCTA) .... ADA
Association [*or Associate*] **of Drama Boards** [*British*] .... ADB
Association of Drilled Shaft Contractors (EA) .... ADSC
Association of Drinkwatchers International [*Defunct*] (EA) .... DW
Association of Driver Educators for the Disabled (EA) .... ADED
Association of Drug Referral Centers [*Australia*] .... ADRC
Association of Drum Manufacturers [*British*] (DBA) .... ADM
Association of DX [*Distance*] **Reporters** (EA) .... ADXR
Association of Early Childhood Educators, Ontario (AC) .... AECEO
Association of Earth Science Editors (EA) .... AESE
Association of Ecosystem Research Centers (EA) .... AERC
Association of Edison Illuminating Companies (EA) .... AEIC
Association of Editorial Businesses (EA) .... AEB
Association of Education Committees [*British*] .... AEC
Association of Education Officers [*British*] .... AEO
Association of Educational Advisers Scotland (DBA) .... AEAS
Association of Educational Negotiators [*Later, NAEN*] (EA) .... AEN
Association of Educational Psychologists [*British*] .... AEP
Association of Educational Research Officers of Ontario [*Association Ontarienne des Agents de Recherche en Education*] (AC) .... AERO
Association of Educators of Homebound and Hospitalized Children [*Later, DPH*] (EA) .... AEHHC
Association of Electric Companies of Texas (SRA) .... AECT
Association of Electrical Contractors Ireland (EAIO) .... AECI
Association of Electrical Machinery Trades (EAIO) .... AEMT
Association of Electrical Wiremen [*A union*] [*British*] .... AEW
Association of Electronic Cottagers [*Defunct*] (EA) .... AEC
Association of Electronic Distributors (EA) .... AED
Association of Electronic Guard Manufacturers [*British*] .... AEGM
Association of Electronic Manufacturers [*Later, EIA*] (EA) .... AEM
Association of Electronic Manufacturers, Eastern Division (EA) .... AEM-ED
Association of Electronic Parts and Equipment Manufacturers [*Later, EIA*] .... AEPEM
Association of Embroiderers and Pleaters [*British*] (BI) .... AEP
Association of Emergency Medical Technicians [*British*] (DBA) .... AEMT
Association of Employees Supporting Education Services [*Canada*] .... AESES
Association of Energy Engineers (EA) .... AEE
Association of Engineering Distributors [*British*] (BI) .... AED
Association of Engineering Employees of Oregon (SRA) .... AEE
Association of Engineering Geologists (EA) .... AEG
Association of Engineering Technicians & Technologists of Newfoundland (AC) .... AETTN
Association of Engineers and Scientists (Independent) .... AES(I)
Association of Engineers and Scientists of the Bureau of Naval Weapons [*Later, ASE*] .... AESBNW
Association of English Singers and Speakers [*British*] (DBA) .... AES & S
Association of Enrolled Agents [*Later, NAEA*] (EA) .... AEA
Association of Entertainers (EA) .... AE
Association of Entertainment Industry Computer Professionals (EA) .... AEICP
Association of Environmental and Resource Economists (EA) .... AERE
Association of Environmental Authorities (SRA) .... AEA
Association of Environmental Conscious Builders [*British*] (DBA) .... AECB
Association of Environmental Engineering Professors (EA) .... AEEP
Association of Environmental Scientists and Administrators [*Defunct*] (EA) .... AESA
Association of Episcopal Colleges (EA) .... AEC
Association of Episcopal Conferences of Anglophone West Africa (EAIO) .... AECAWA
Association of Equipment Distributors (MHDB) .... AED
Association of Equipment Lessors [*Later, AAEL*] .... AEL
Association of Escort/Interpreters (EA) .... AEI
Association of Ethnic Broadcasters and Coordinators of New South Wales [*Australia*] .... AEBCNSW
Association of European Aeronautical and Astronautical Students (PDAA) .... EUROAVIA
Association of European Airlines (EAIO) .... AEA
Association of European Battery Manufacturers (EA) .... EUROBAT

Association of European Candle Manufacturers (EA) .... AECM
Association of European Conjuncture Institutes (EA) .... AECI
Association of European Cooperative Insurers [Brussels, Belgium]
    (EAIO) .... AECI
Association of European Correspondence Schools (EA) .... AECS
Association of European Express Carriers (DA) .... AEEC
Association of European Federations of Agro-Engineers [EC] (ECED) .... AEFA
Association of European Jute Industries .... AEJI
Association of European Machine Tool Merchants [Berkhamsted,
    Hertfordshire, England] (EAIO) .... AEMTM
Association of European Manufacturers of Self-Adhesive Tapes
    (EA) .... AEMSAT
Association of European Metal Sink Manufacturers (EAIO) ..... AEMSM
Association of European Steel Producers (PDAA) .... EUROFER
Association of Evangelical Lutheran Churches .... AELC
Association of Evangelical Professors of Missions (EA) .... AEPM
Association of Evangelical Relief and Development Organizations
    (DICI) .... AERDO
Association of Evangelicals for Italian Missions (EA) .... AEIM
Association of Executive Recruiting Consultants [Later, AESC] (EA) ..... AERC
Association of Executive Search Consultants (EA) .... AESC
Association of Exhibition Organisers [British] (DBA) .... AEO
Association of Existential Psychology and Psychiatry [Defunct] (EA) ..... AEPP
Association of Exploration Geochemists [ICSU] (EAIO) .... AEG
Association of Export Subscription Newsagents (DGA) .... AESN
Association of Fair Housing Committees [Defunct] .... AFHC
Association of Family and Conciliation Courts (EA) .... AFCC
Association of Family Case-Workers [British] (BI) .... AFCW
Association of Family Farmers (EA) .... AFF
Association of Family Practice Residency Directors (EA) .... AFPRD
Association of Family Therapy [British] (DBA) .... AFT
Association of Fancy Box Makers [A union] [British] .... AFBM
Association of Farmworker Opportunity Programs (EA) .... AFOP
Association of Fashion Advertising and Editorial Photographers
    (EAIO) .... AFAEP
Association of Fashion and Image Consultants (EA) .... AFIC
Association of Fatty Acid Distillers [British] (BI) .... AFAD
Association of Federal Appraisers [Later, Association of Governmental
    Appraisers] .... AFA
Association of Federal Architects .... AFA
Association of Federal Communications Consulting Engineers (NITA) .... AFCC
Association of Federal Communications Consulting Engineers (EA) .... AFCCE
Association of Federal Computer Users [Defunct] (EA) .... AFCU
Association of Federal Fiscal Technicians (EA) .... AFFT
Association of Federal Investigators (EA) .... AFI
Association of Federal Photographers [Defunct] (EA) .... AFP
Association of Federal Safety and Health Professionals [Defunct] (EA)..... AFSHP
Association of Federal Woman's Award Recipients [Defunct] (EA) ..... AFWAR
Association of Feminine Collectives [Canada] .... AFC
Association of Field Ornithologists (EA) .... AFO
Association of Field Service Managers [Later, ASMI] (EA) ..... AFSM
Association of Field Service Managers, International [Later, ASMI]
    (EA) .... AFSMI
Association of Film Commissioners (EA) .... AFC
Association of Finnish Electric Industries .... AFEI
Association of Firearm and Tool Mark Examiners (EA) .... AFTE
Association of First Class Mailers .... AFCM
Association of First Division Civil Servants [British] .... AFDCS
Association of Fish Canners [British] (DBA) .... AFC
Association of Fish Meal Manufacturers [British] (DBA) .... AFMM
Association of Flight Attendants (EA) .... AFA
Association of Flight Training Organizations [British] (DBA) .... AFTO
Association of Flock Processors [Defunct] (EA) .... AFP
Association of Flooring Contractors [British] (BI) .... AFC
Association of Florida Community Developers (SRA) .... AFCD
Association of Fluorocarbon Consumers and Manufacturers
    [Australia] .... AFCAM
Association of Folding Furniture Manufacturers [British] (BI) .... AFFM
Association of Food and Drug Officials (EA) .... AFDO
Association of Food and Drug Officials of the United States [Later, AFDO]
    (EA) .... AFDOUS
Association of Food Distributors [Later, AFI] (EA) .... AFD
Association of Food Industries (EA) .... AFI
Association of Food Marketing Agencies in Asia and the Pacific (EA) ...... AFMA
Association of Football Statisticians [British] (DBA) .... AFS
Association of Footwear Distributors [Defunct] (EA) .... AFD
Association of Foreign Investors in US Real Estate (EA) .... AFIRE
Association of Foreign Trade Representatives (EA) .... AFTR
Association of Foremen and Supervisors [Australia] .... AFS
Association of Foremen Iron Founders [A union] [British] ..... AFIF
Association of Forensic Document Examiners (EA) .... AFDE
Association of Forest Service Employees for Environmental Ethics
    (EA) .... AFSEEE
Association of Former Agents of the US Secret Service (EA) ..... AFAUSSS
Association of Former Intelligence Officers (EA) .... AFIO
Association of Former Intelligence Officers (DOMA) .... AFIO
Association of Former Members of Congress [Formerly, FMC] (EA) ..... AFMC
Association of Former Senate Aides (EA) .... AFSA
Association of Former Students of the College of Europe (EAIO) ..... AFSCE
Association of Franchised Distributors of Electronic Components
    [British] .... AFDEC
Association of Fraternity Advisors (EA) .... AFA
Association of Free French in the US (EA) .... AFFUS
Association of Free Lutheran Congregation and Seminary Headquarters,
    Minneapolis, MN [Library symbol Library of Congress] (LCLS) ..... MnMFL

Association of Free Lutheran Congregations .... AFLC
Association of Free Magazines (DGA) .... AFM
Association of Free Magazines and Periodicals [British] (EAIO) ..... AFMP
Association of Free Methodist Educational Institutions (EA) .... AFMEI
Association of Free Newspapers [British] (EAIO) .... AFN
Association of Free Trade Unions [Former USSR] .... AFTU
Association of Freestanding Radiation Oncology Centers (EA) .... AFROC
Association of French Host Centers [Paris] [Information service or system]
    (IID) .... ACSF
Association of French Language Epidemiologists (EAIO) .... AFLE
Association of French Mechanical Industries (EA) .... AFMI
Association of French Teachers in Africa [See also AFPA] [Khartoum,
    Sudan] (EAIO) .... AFTA
Association of French-Language Leprologists [Paris, France] (EAIO) ..... AFLL
Association of Fund Raisers and Direct Sellers (EA) .... AFRDS
Association of Fund Raising Professionals of British Columbia
    [Canada] .... AFRP BC
Association of Fundamental Institutions of Religious Education ..... AFIRE
Association of Futures Brokers and Dealers (EAIO) .... AFBD
Association of Futures Investment [British] (DBA) .... AFI
Association of Gardening and Hardware Wholesalers [British] (DBA) ..... AGHW
Association of Gaugers and Appraisers Ltd. [British] (BI) ...... AGA
Association of Gay and Lesbian Psychiatrists (EA) .... AGLP
Association of Gay Psychologists [Later, ALGP] (EA) .... AGP
Association of Genealogists and Record Agents [British] (EAIO) ..... AGRA
Association of General Heating and Domestic Engineer Assistants [A
    union] [British] .... AGHDEA
Association of General Merchandise Chains [NMRI] [Absorbed by]
    (EA) .... AGMC
Association of General Practitioner Community Hospitals [British]
    (EAIO) .... AGPCH
Association of Geography Teachers of Ireland (AIE) .... AGTI
Association of Geoscientists for International Development [Bangkok,
    Thailand] (EAIO) .... AGID
Association of German Broadcasters (EA) .... AGB
Association of German Chambers of Industry and Commerce (EA) .... AGCIC
Association of German Language Authors in America [Defunct] (EA) ..... AGLAA
Association of Gifted-Creative Children (EA) .... AGCC
Association of Girl Scout Executive Staff (EA) .... AGSES
Association of Girl Scout Professional Workers [Later, AGSES] (EA) ..... AGSPW
Association of Golf Club Secretaries (EAIO) .... AGCS
Association of Golf Writers (EAIO) .... AGW
Association of Good Motorists [British] (BI) .... AGM
Association of Governing Boards (NFD) .... AGB
Association of Governing Boards of Universities and Colleges (EA) ..... AGB
Association of Government Accountants [Arlington, VA] (EA) ..... AGA
Association of Government Auditors (AAGC) .... AGA
Association of Government Marketing Assistance Specialists (EA) ..... AGMAS
Association of Government Supervisors and Radio Officers [British] ..... AGSRO
Association of Governmental Appraisers [American Society of Appraiser]
    [Absorbed by] (EA) .... AGA
Association of Graduate Careers Advisory Services [British] (DBA) ..... AGCAS
Association of Graduate Liberal Studies Programs (EA) .... AGLSP
Association of Graduate Recruiters [British] (DBA) .... AGR
Association of Graduate Schools in Association of American Universities
    (EA) .... AGS
Association of Graduates of the United States Air Force Academy (EA) ..... AOG
Association of Graphic Arts Consultants (EA) .... AGAC
Association of Graphic Communications (SRA) .... AGC
Association of Graphic Designers (DGA) .... AGD
Association of Great Lakes Outdoor Writers (SRA) .... AGLOW
Association of Green Crop Driers [British] (BI) .... AGCD
Association of Grey Board Makers [British] (DBA) .... AGBM
Association of Ground Investigation Specialists [British] (DBA) ..... AGIS
Association of Ground Water Scientists and Engineers (EA) .... AGWSE
Association of Group Travel Executives (EA) .... AGTE
Association of Gut Processors [British] (BI) .... AGP
Association of Gypsy Organizations [British] (DBA) .... AGO
Association of Halfway House Alcoholism Programs of North America
    (EA) .... AHHAP
Association of Handicapped Artists (EA) .... AHA
Association of Head and Neck Oncologists of Great Britain ..... AHNO
Association of Head Mistresses, Inc. [British] .... AHMI
Association of Headmistresses [British] (DI) .... AH
Association of Headmistresses [British] (BI) .... AHM
Association of Headmistresses of Preparatory Schools [British] ..... AHMPS
Association of Headmistresses of Preparatory Schools [British] (BI) ..... AHPS
Association of Heads of Girls Boarding Schools [British] .... AHGBS
Association of Heads of Independent and Direct Grant Girls Schools
    [British] .... AHIDGS
Association of Heads of Independent Schools [British] .... AHIS
Association of Heads of Outdoor Education Centres [British] (DBA) ..... AHOEC
Association of Heads of Polytechnic Student Services [British] (AIE) ..... AHOPSS
Association of Health Care Information and Medical Records Officers
    (EAIO) .... AMRO
Association of Health Facility Licensure and Certification Directors
    (EA) .... AHFLCD
Association of Health Management Organizations in Michigan (SRA) ..... AHMOM
Association of Health Occupations Teacher Educators (EA) .... AHOTE
Association of Health Professionals [Australia] .... AHP
Association of Health Service Treasurers [British] .... AHST
Association of Hebrew Catholics (EA) .... AHC
Association of Heritage Approved Specialists [An association] (EAIO) ..... AHAS
Association of High Medicare Hospitals (EA) .... AHMH
Association of High Tech Distributors (EA) .... AHTD

Association of Higher Education and Disabilities ... AHEAD
Association of Higher Educational Institutions Concerned with Home Economics [*British*] (DBA) ... AHEIHE
Association of Highway Steel Transporters (EA) ... AHST
Association of Hillel/Jewish Campus Professionals (EA) ... AHJCP
Association of Hispanic Arts (EA) ... AHA
Association of Hispanists [*British*] ... AH
Association of Hispanists of Great Britain and Ireland (AIE) ... ABH
Association of Holocaust Organizations (EA) ... AHO
Association of Home Appliance Manufacturers (EA) ... AHAM
Association of Home Study Schools [*Later, ACTS*] (EA) ... AHSS
Association of Hospital and Institution Libraries [*of ALA*] [*Later, ASCLA*] ... AHIL
Association of Hospital and Welfare Administrators [*British*] (BI) ... AHWA
Association of Hospital Directors of Medical Education [*Later, AHME*] (EA) ... AHDME
Association of Hospital Management Committees ... AHMC
Association of Hospital Pharmacists of Victoria [*Australia*] ... AHPV
Association of Hospital Security Administrators ... AHSA
Association of Hospital Television Networks (EA) ... AHTN
Association of Hotel Booking Agents [*British*] (BI) ... AHBA
Association of House Democratic Press Assistants (EA) ... AHDPA
Association of Household Distributors [*British*] (EAIO) ... AHD
Association of Housing Aid [*British*] (DBA) ... AHA
Association of Human Resource Systems Professionals (EA) ... HRSP
Association of Human Resources Management and Organizational Behavior [*Later, AM*] (EA) ... HRMOB
Association of Human Services in Alberta (AC) ... AHSA
Association of Humanistic Psychology Practitioners (EAIO) ... AHPP
Association of Humanistic Rabbis (EA) ... AHR
Association of Hungarian Students in North America [*Defunct*] (EA) ... AHS
Association of Hydraulic Equipment Manufacturers ... AHEM
Association of Idaho Cities (SRA) ... AIC
Association of Illinois Electric Cooperatives (SRA) ... AIEC
Association of Illinois Middle-Level Schools (SRA) ... AIMS
Association of Illustrators [*British*] (DBA) ... AOL
Association of Image Consultants (EA) ... AIC
Association of Immigration and Nationality Lawyers [*Later, AILA*] (EA) ... AINL
Association of Immigration Attorneys (EA) ... AIA
Association of Importers and Producers of Admixtures [*Belgium*] (EAIO) ... AIPA
Association of Importers-Manufacturers for Muzzleloading (EA) ... AIMM
Association of Incorporated Managers and Administrators [*British*] (EAIO) ... AIMA
Association of Indepedent Liberal Arts Colleges for Teacher Education (EDAC) ... AILACTE
Association of Independent Businesses (EAIO) ... AIB
Association of Independent California Colleges and Universities (SRA) ... AICCU
Association of Independent Camps (EA) ... AIC
Association of Independent Church Schools (AC) ... AICS
Association of Independent Cinemas [*British*] ... AIC
Association of Independent Clinical Research Contractors [*British*] (DBA) ... AICRC
Association of Independent Colleges and Schools (EA) ... AICS
Association of Independent Colleges of Music (EA) ... AICM
Association of Independent Commercial Editors (NTCM) ... AICE
Association of Independent Commercial Producers [*New York, NY*] (EA) ... AICP
Association of Independent Composers and Performers (EA) ... AICP
Association of Independent Computer Specialists (EAIO) ... AICS
Association of Independent Consultants (AC) ... AIC
Association of Independent Contract Research Organisations [*British*] ... AICRO
Association of Independent Copy Machine Dealers and Manufacturers (EA) ... AICMDM
Association of Independent Corrugated Converters (EA) ... AICC
Association of Independent Crop Consultants [*British*] (DBA) ... AICC
Association of Independent Electricity Producers [*British*] (DBA) ... AIEP
Association of Independent Hospitals and Kindred Organisations [*British*] (BI) ... AIH
Association of Independent Information Professionals (EA) ... AIIP
Association of Independent Investment Managers [*Formerly, National Micrographics Association*] (EAIO) ... AIIM
Association of Independent Kentucky Colleges and Universities (SRA) ... AIKCU
Association of Independent Living Centers in New York (SRA) ... AILCNY
Association of Independent Mailing Equipment Dealers (EA) ... AIMED
Association of Independent Maryland Schools (EDAC) ... AIMS
Association of Independent Medical Equipment Suppliers (EA) ... AIMES
Association of Independent Merchant Stockists (DGA) ... AIMS
Association of Independent Metropolitan Stations (NTCM) ... AIMS
Association of Independent Microdealers [*Later, CMC*] (EA) ... AIM
Association of Independent Motor Stores [*British*] (DBA) ... AIMS
Association of Independent Museums [*British*] (EAIO) ... AIM
Association of Independent Music Publishers (EA) ... AIMP
Association of Independent Optical Wholesalers [*Later, OLA*] ... AIOW
Association of Independent Producers [*British*] ... AIP
Association of Independent Radio Contractors [*British*] ... AIRC
Association of Independent Railways [*British*] (DBA) ... AIR
Association of Independent Research and Technology Organizations [*British*] (DBA) ... AIRTO
Association of Independent Research Institutes (EA) ... AIRI
Association of Independent Schools & Colleges in Alberta (AC) ... AISCA
Association of Independent Schools of New South Wales [*Australia*] ... AISNSW
Association of Independent Schools of Queensland [*Australia*] ... AISQ
Association of Independent Schools of the Australian Capital Territory ... AISACT
Association of Independent Schools of Western Australia ... AISWA
Association of Independent Software Companies [*Later, ADAPSO*] (EA) ... AISC
Association of Independent Television Stations (EA) ... INTV
Association of Independent Television Stations, Inc. (NTCM) ... AITS
Association of Independent Tour Operators [*British*] (DBA) ... AITO
Association of Independent Video and Filmmakers (EA) ... AIVF
Association of Indian Muslims (EA) ... AIM
Association of Indians in America (EA) ... AIA
Association of Industrial Advertisers [*Later, B/PAA*] (EA) ... AIA
Association of Industrial Archaeology (EAIO) ... AIA
Association of Industrial Colleges and Schools (OICC) ... AICS
Association of Industrial Filter and Separator Manufacturers [*British*] (DBA) ... AIFSM
Association of Industrial Medical Officers [*British*] (BI) ... AIMO
Association of Industrial Metallizers, Coaters, and Laminators (EA) ... AIMCAL
Association of Industrial Road Safety Officers [*British*] (DBA) ... AIRSO
Association of Industrial Scientists [*affiliated with*] **Marine Engineers Beneficial Association** [*A union*] ... AIS-MEBA
Association of Industrial Truck Trainers [*British*] (DBA) ... AITT
Association of Industrialized Building Component Manufacturers Ltd. [*British*] (BI) ... AIBCM
Association of Industry Manufacturers Representatives (EA) ... AIM/R
Association of Information and Dissemination Centers (MHDB) ... ASDIC
Association of Information and Dissemination Centers (EA) ... ASIDIC
Association of Information Managers (NITA) ... AIM
Association of Information Managers for Financial Institutions [*Defunct*] (EA) ... AIM
Association of Information Officers in the Pharmaceutical Industry [*British*] ... AIOPI
Association of Information Systems Professionals [*Defunct*] (EA) ... AISP
Association of Information Technology Professionals ... AITP
Association of Information Technology Professionals ... AITP
Association of Informed Senior Citizens [*Defunct*] (EA) ... AISC
Association of Inplant Managers (DGA) ... AIM
Association of Insolvency Accountants [*Chicago, IL*] (EA) ... AIA
Association of Inspectors, Advisers, and Consultants for Religious Education (AIE) ... AREIAC
Association of Inspectors of Taxes [*British*] ... AIT
Association of Institute and School of Education In-Service Tutors [*British*] ... AISEIT
Association of Institutional Distributors [*Later, FOOD*] (EA) ... AID
Association of Insulin-Dependent Diabetics [*Defunct*] (EA) ... AIDD
Association of Insurance Advertisers [*Defunct*] (EA) ... AIA
Association of Insurance and Risk Managers in Industry and Commerce (EAIO) ... AIRMIC
Association of Insurance Attorneys [*Later, ADTA*] (EA) ... AIA
Association of Insurance Brokers Ltd. [*British*] (BI) ... AIB
Association of Insurance Managers in Industry and Commerce [*British*] (BI) ... AIMC
Association of Insurance Teachers [*British*] (DBA) ... AIT
Association of Interior Decor Specialists [*Later, ASCR*] ... AIDS
Association of Internal Management Consultants [*East Bloomfield, NY*] (EA) ... AIMC
Association of International Accountants [*British*] (EAIO) ... AIA
Association of International Advertising Agencies (EA) ... AIAA
Association of International Automobile Manufacturers (EA) ... AIAM
Association of International Automobile Manufacturers of Canada [*Association des Fabricants Internationaux d'Automobiles du Canada*] (AC) ... AIAMC
Association of International Bond Dealers [*Zurich, Switzerland*] (EAIO) ... AIBD
Association of International Bond Dealers Quotation [*Stock exchange term*] ... AIBDQ
Association of International Border Agencies (EA) ... AIBA
Association of International Colleges and Universities (EA) ... AICU
Association of International Courier and Express Services (EAIO) ... AICES
Association of International Education Administrators (EA) ... AIEA
Association of International Health Researchers (EA) ... AIHR
Association of International Institute of Arts and Letters ... AIAL
Association of International Insurance Agents [*Later, Intersure*] (EA) ... AIIA
Association of International Libraries/North America ... AIL/NA
Association of International Marathons and Road Races [*New Zealand*] (EAIO) ... AIMS
Association of International Marketing (EAIO) ... AEME
Association of International Marketing [*British*] (EAIO) ... AIM
Association of International Meeting Planners (EA) ... AIMP
Association of International Photography Art Dealers (EA) ... AIPAD
Association of International Relations Clubs (EA) ... AIRC
Association of International Schools in Africa (EA) ... AISA
Association of Interpreters and Translators of South Australia ... AITSA
Association of Interpretive Naturalists [*Later, NAI*] (EA) ... AIN
Association of Interracial Marriages ... AIM
Association of Interstate Commerce Commission Practitioners (EA) ... AICCP
Association of Interstate Motor Carriers [*Defunct*] ... AIMC
Association of Interstate Motor Carriers, Newark NJ [*STAC*] ... AIC
Association of Investment Brokers [*New York, NY*] (EA) ... AIB
Association of Investment Trust Companies (ODBW) ... AITC
Association of Investment Trusts [*British*] (BI) ... AIT
Association of Invoice Factors [*British*] (DBA) ... AIF
Association of Iowa Fairs (SRA) ... AIF
Association of Iowa Merchants (SRA) ... AIM
Association of Irish Musical Societies (EAIO) ... AIMS
Association of Iron and Steel Engineers (EA) ... AISE
Association of Iron Ore Exporting Countries ... AIOEC
Association of Island Marine Laboratories of the Caribbean (EA) ... AIMLC
Association of Italian Families and Friends of Handicapped Children [*Australia*] ... HANDITAL
Association of Jamaican Trusts (United Kingdom) [*British*] ... AJT(UK)
Association of Jensen Owners (EA) ... AJO

Association of Jesuit Colleges and Universities (EA) .... AJCU
Association of Jewish Anti-Poverty Workers [*Superseded by ECJF*] .... AJAPW
Association of Jewish Book Publishers (EA) .... AJBP
Association of Jewish Center Workers (EA) .... AJCW
Association of Jewish Chaplains of the Armed Forces (EA) .... AJCAF
Association of Jewish Community Relations Workers (EA) .... AJCRW
Association of Jewish Day Schools [*Association des Ecoles Juives*] (AC) .... AJDS
Association of Jewish Ex-Servicemen [*British*] (DI) .... AJEX
Association of Jewish Family and Children's Agencies (EA) .... AJFCA
Association of Jewish Family, Children's Agency Professionals (EA) .... NACHES
Association of Jewish Genealogical Societies (EA) .... AJGS
Association of Jewish Libraries (EA) .... AJL
Association of Jewish Refugees in Great Britain .... AJR
Association of Jewish Sponsored Camps (EA) .... AJSC
Association of Jewish Women's Organisations [*British*] (DI) .... AJWO
Association of Journalists Against Extremism [*British*] (DI) .... AJAX
Association of Junior Leagues (EA) .... AJL
Association of Jute Spinners and Manufacturers [*British*] (DBA) .... AJSM
Association of Kew Gardeners in America [*Defunct*] (EA) .... AKGA
Association of Kinsmen Clubs (EA) .... KIN
Association of Knitted Fabrics Manufacturers (EA) .... AKFM
Association of Korean University Presses .... AKUP
Association of Labor Mediation Agencies [*Later, ALRA*] (EA) .... ALMA
Association of Labor Relations Agencies (EA) .... ALRA
Association of Labor-Management Administrators and Consultants on Alcoholism (EA) .... ALMACA
Association of Ladies of Charity of the United States (EA) .... ALCUS
Association of Land and Property Owners .... ALPO
Association of Land Grant Colleges and Universities [*Later, NASULGC*] .... ALGCU
Association of Language Learning [*British*] (DBA) .... ALL
Association of Late-Deafened Adults (EA) .... ALDA
Association of Latvian Academic Societies [*Defunct*] (EA) .... ALAS
Association of Law Costs Draftsmen [*British*] (DBA) .... ALCD
[*The*] **Association of Law Teachers** [*British*] .... ALT
Association of Lawyers for the Defence of the Unborn (EAIO) .... ALDU
Association of Leadership Educators (EA) .... ALE
Association of Learned and Professional Society Publishers [*British*] .... ALPSP
Association of Learned Societies in Social Sciences [*British*] (DBA) .... ALSISS
Association of Learning Disabled Adults [*Defunct*] (EA) .... ALDA
Association of Lecturers in Accountancy [*British*] .... ALIA
Association of Lecturers in Colleges of Education in Scotland .... ALCES
Association of Lecturers in Scottish Central Institutions (AIE) .... ALSCI
Association of Legal Administrators (EA) .... ALA
Association of Legal Aid Attorneys of the City of New York (EA) .... ALAA
Association of Legal Secretaries [*British*] (DBA) .... ALS
Association of Lesbian and Gay Psychologists (EA) .... ALGP
Association of Liberal Trade Unionists [*British*] (DI) .... ALTU
Association of Libertarian Feminists (EA) .... ALF
Association of Librarians in the History of the Health Sciences (EA) .... ALHHS
Association of Libraries of Judaica and Hebraica in Europe .... ALJH
Association of Library Magazines of America (DGA) .... ALMA
Association of Licensed Aircraft Engineers [*A union*] [*British*] .... ALAE
Association of Licensed Automobile Manufacturers .... ALAM
Association of Licensed Clubs of Western Australia .... ALCWA
Association of Licensed Trade Relief Agencies [*British*] (DBA) .... ALTRA
Association of Life Agency Officers [*Later, LIMRA*] .... ALAO
Association of Life Insurance Counsel (EA) .... ALIC
Association of Life Insurance Medical Directors of America (EA) .... ALIMDA
Association of Life Underwriters of South Dakota (SRA) .... ALU
Association of Light Alloy Refiners and Smelters Ltd. [*British*] (BI) .... ALAR
Association of Lightweight Agggregate Manufacturers (MHDB) .... ALAM
Association of Liquidpaperboard Carton Manufacturers .... ALCM
Association of Literary Magazines of America [*Later, CCLM*] (EA) .... ALMA
Association of Lithuanian Foresters in Exile [*Defunct*] (EA) .... LMSI
Association of Lithuanian Workers (EA) .... ALW
Association of Litigation Support Managers [*Australia*] .... ALSM
Association of Little Presses (DGA) .... ALP
Association of Little Theatre Groups [*Australia*] .... ALTG
Association of Lloyd's Members [*British insurers' organization*] (ECON) .... ALM
Association of Loading and Elevating Equipment Manufacturers [*British*] (EAIO) .... ALEM
Association of Local Air Pollution Control Officers [*Environmental Protection Agency*] (ERG) .... ALAPO
Association of Local Air Pollution Control Officials (EA) .... ALAPCO
Association of Local Authority Chief Executives [*British*] (DBA) .... ALACE
Association of Local Government Engineers and Surveyors [*British*] (DI) .... ALGES
Association of Local Government Financial Officers [*British*] (DI) .... ALGFO
Association of Local Housing Finance Agencies (EA) .... ALHFA
Association of Local Official Health Agencies (AC) .... ALOHA
Association of Local Transport Airlines [*Defunct*] (EA) .... ALTA
Association of London Borough Engineers and Surveyors [*British*] (BI) .... ALBES
Association of London Chief Librarians .... ALCL
Association of London Computer Clubs (NITA) .... ALCC
Association of London Housing Estates [*British*] (DI) .... ALHE
Association of Long Distance Telephone Companies (EA) .... ALTEL
Association of Louisiana Electric Cooperatives (SRA) .... ALEC
Association of Lunar and Planetary Observers (EA) .... ALPO
Association of Lutheran College Faculties (EA) .... ALCF
Association of Lutheran Men (EA) .... ALM
Association of Lutheran Secondary Schools (EA) .... ALSS
Association of Machinery and Equipment Appraisers (EA) .... AMEA
Association of Magisterial Officers [*British*] (DBA) .... AMO
Association of Mail Order Publishers (DGA) .... AMOP
Association of Major Charitable Associations .... AMCO
Association of Major City Building Officials (EA) .... AMCBO
Association of Major Power Consumers in Ontario (AC) .... AMPCO
Association of Major Symphony Orchestra Volunteers (EA) .... AMSO
Association of Makers of Packaging Papers [*British*] (DBA) .... AMPP
Association of Makers of Printing and Writing Papers (DGA) .... AMPW
Association of Makers of Printings and Writings [*British*] (DBA) .... AMPW
Association of Makers of Soft Tissue Papers [*British*] (DBA) .... AMSTP
Association of Malt Products Manufacturers [*British*] (BI) .... AMPM
Association of Management (EA) .... AM
Association of Management Analysts in State and Local Government (EA) .... AMASLG
Association of Management Analysts in State and Local Government (EA) .... MASLIG
Association of Management and Business Education (AIE) .... AMBE
Association of Management and Professional Staffs [*British*] (DBA) .... AMPS
Association of Management Consultants (EA) .... AMC
Association of Management Education and Development [*British*] (DBA) .... AMED
Association of Management Education Centres [*British*] .... AMEC
Association of Management in Public Health [*Later, AAHA*] (EA) .... AMPH
Association of Managerial Electrical Executives [*British*] (BI) .... AMEE
Association of Manipulative Medicine [*British*] (BI) .... AMM
Association of Manitoba Museums (AC) .... AMM
Association of Manpower Franchise Owners (EA) .... AMFO
Association of Manufacturers and Exporters of Concentrated and Unconcentrated Soft Drinks [*British*] (BI) .... AMECUSD
Association of Manufacturers and Suppliers for the Graphic Arts (DGA) .... AMSGA
Association of Manufacturers of Animal-Derived Food Enzymes [*EC*] (ECED) .... AMAFE
Association of Manufacturers of Confectionery and Chocolate (EA) .... AMCC
Association of Manufacturers of Domestic Electric Appliances [*British*] (DI) .... AMDEA
Association of Map Memorabilia Collectors (EA) .... AMMC
Association of Marian Helpers (EA) .... AMH
Association of Marine and General Engineers [*A union*] [*British*] .... AMGE
Association of Marine Catering and Supply [*British*] (DBA) .... AMCS
Association of Marine Engine Manufacturers (EA) .... AMEM
Association of Marine Engineering Schools [*Liverpool, Merseyside, England*] (EAIO) .... AMES
Association of Marine Laboratories of the Caribbean (EAIO) .... AMLC
Association of Marine Traders [*British*] (BI) .... AMT
Association of Marine Underwriters of British Columbia (AC) .... AMUBC
Association of Marine Underwriters of the United States (EA) .... AMUUS
Association of Maritime Transport Users in the Central American Isthmus [*Guatemala*] (EAIO) .... USARIOS
Association of Maritime Transport Users in the Central American Isthmus [*Guatemala, Guatemala*] (EAIO) .... USUARIOI
Association of Market Survey Organisations [*British*] .... AMSO
Association of Marriage Enrichment [*British*] (DBA) .... AME
Association of Married Women (EA) .... AMW
Association of Marshall Scholars (EA) .... AMS
Association of Mary Immaculate (EA) .... AIM
Association of Maryland Pilots (SRA) .... AMP
Association of Massachusetts Homes and Services for the Aging (SRA) .... AMHSA
Association of Massage Therapists [*Australia*] .... AMT
Association of Master Lightermen and Barge Owners [*British*] (BI) .... AML
Association of Master of Business Administration Executives [*New York, NY*] (EA) .... AMBAE
Association of Master Upholsterers [*British*] (BI) .... AMU
Association of Mature Canadians (AC) .... AMC
Association of Maximum Service Telecasters .... AMST
Association of Maximum Service Telecasters (EA) .... MST
Association of Meat Inspectors [*British*] .... AMI
Association of Media Producers [*ICIA*] [*Absorbed by*] (EA) .... AMP
Association of Media Sales Executives [*British*] (BI) .... AMSE
Association of Medical Advertising Agencies (EA) .... AMAA
Association of Medical Deans in Europe (EAIO) .... AMDE
Association of Medical Education and Research in Substance Abuse (EA) .... AMERSA
Association of Medical Group Psychoanalysts (EA) .... AMGP
Association of Medical Illustrators (EA) .... AMI
Association of Medical Record Consultants [*Defunct*] (EA) .... AMRC
Association of Medical Record Officers [*British*] (BI) .... AMRO
Association of Medical Rehabilitation Administrators (EA) .... AMRA
Association of Medical Rehabilitation Directors and Coordinators [*Later, AMRA*] (EA) .... AMRDC
Association of Medical Research Charities [*British*] .... AMRC
Association of Medical School Pediatric Department Chairmen (EA) .... AMSPDC
Association of Medical Secretaries [*British*] (BI) .... AMS
Association of Medical Secretaries, Practice Administrators, and Receptionists [*British*] (DBA) .... AMSPAR
Association of Medical Superintendents of Mental Hospitals [*Later, AAPA*] (EA) .... AMSMH
Association of Medical Technologists [*British*] (DBA) .... AMT
Association of Medical Women in Western Australia .... AMWWA
Association of Members and Friends of the Historic Southern Tenant Farmers Union [*Defunct*] (EA) .... AMFHSTFU
Association of Members of Boards of Visitors [*British*] (DI) .... AMBOV
Association of Membership Executives (EA) .... AME
Association of Memoirists and Family Historians (EA) .... AMFH
Association of Men's Belt Manufacturers [*BA*] [*Absorbed by*] (EA) .... AMBM

Association of Mental Health Administrators (EA) .... AMHA
Association of Mental Health Clergy (EA) .... AMHC
Association of Mental Health Librarians (EA) .... AMHL
Association of Mental Health Practitioners with Disabilities [*Defunct*] (EA) .... AMHPD
Association of Mental Health Specialties (EA) .... AMHS
Association of Mercy Colleges (EA) .... AMC
Association of Messenger Services .... AMS
Association of Metal Sprayers [*British*] (EAIO) .... AMS
Association of Methodist Historical Societies [*Later, General Commission on Archives and History of the United Methodist Church*] (EA) .... AMHS
Association of Metropolitan Authorities [*British*] .... AMA
Association of Metropolitan Chief Librarians [*London*] .... AMCL
Association of Metropolitan District Chief Librarians [*British*] .... AMDCL
Association of Metropolitan District Education and Children's Librarians [*British*] (DBA) .... AMDECL
Association of Metropolitan Sewerage Agencies (EA) .... AMSA
Association of Metropolitan Water Agencies (EA) .... AMWA
Association of Mexican-American Educators (OICC) .... AMAE
Association of Microbial Food Enzyme Producers (EA) .... AMFEP
Association of Microbiological Diagnostic Manufacturers (EA) .... AMDM
Association of Midwest Fish and Game Commissioners [*Later, AMFWA*] .... AMFGC
Association of Midwest Fish and Wildlife Agencies (EA) .... AMFWA
Association of Midwest Fish and Wildlife Commissioners [*Later, AMFWA*] (EA) .... AMFWC
Association of Migrants from Turkey [*Australia*] .... AMFT
Association of Military Banks of America [*Bethesda, MD*] (EA) .... AMBA
Association of Military Colleges and Schools of the US (EA) .... AMCS
Association of Military Dental Surgeons .... AMDS
Association of Military Surgeons of the United States (RDA) .... AMS
Association of Military Surgeons of the United States (EA) .... AMSUS
Association of Mill and Elevator Mutual Insurance Companies (EA) .... AMEMIC
Association of Miniature Engine Manufacturers [*British*] (DBA) .... AMEM
Association of Minicomputer Users (EA) .... AMU
Association of Mining, Electrical, and Mechanical Engineers [*British*] (DI) .... AMEME
Association of Minnesota Counties (SRA) .... AMC
Association of Minority Health Professions Schools (EA) .... AMHPS
Association of Missile and Rocket Industries .... AMRI
Association of Missouri Electric Cooperatives (SRA) .... AMEC
Association of Model Agents [*British*] (DBA) .... AMA
Association of Motion Picture Producers [*Later, AMPTP*] (EA) .... AMPP
Association of Motor Racing Circuit Owners [*British*] (DBA) .... AMRCO
Association of Motor Vehicle Training Agents [*British*] (DBA) .... AMVTA
Association of Multiracial Playgroups .... AMP
Association of Municipal Administrators, Nova Scotia (AC) .... AMANS
Association of Municipal Authorities [*British*] (DCTA) .... AMA
Association of Municipal Clerks & Treasurers of Ontario (AC) .... AMCTO
Association of Municipal Corporationss [*British*] .... AMC
Association of Municipal Recycling Coordinators (AC) .... AMRC
Association of Municipalities of Ontario (AC) .... AMO
Association of Museum Stores (EA) .... AMS
Association of Music Video Broadcasters [*Defunct*] (EA) .... AMVB
Association of Musical Instrument Industries [*British*] (BI) .... AMII
Association of Muslim Scientists and Engineers (EA) .... AMSE
Association of Muslim Social Scientists (EA) .... AMSS
Association of Mutual Fire Insurance Engineers [*Later, ILCA*] .... AMFIE
Association of Mutual Fund Plan Sponsors [*Later, ICI*] (EA) .... AMFPS
Association of Mutual Insurance Engineers [*Later, ILCA*] (EA) .... AMIE
Association of National Advertisers (EA) .... ANA
Association of National Grasslands (EA) .... ANG
Association of National Health Service Corps Scholarship Recipients [*Defunct*] (EA) .... ANHSCSR
Association of National Health Service Officers [*British*] .... ANHSO
Association of National Health Service Supplies Officers [*British*] (DBA) .... ANHSSO
Association of National Non-Profit Artists' Centres [*Canada*] .... ANNPAC
Association of National Olympic Committees [*See also ACNO*] [*Paris, France*] (EAIO) .... ANOC
Association of National Olympic Committees of Africa (EA) .... ANOCA
Association of National Organizations in the Bakery and Confectionery Trade in the EC [*European Community*] [*Belgium*] (EAIO) .... ANOBCT-EC
Association of National Park Officers [*British*] .... ANPO
Association of National Trade Groups of Wood and Derived Products in the EEC [*European Economic Community*] **Countries** [*Denmark*] (EAIO) .... ANTGWDPEC
Association of Natural Resource Enforcement Trainers (EA) .... ANRET
Association of Natural Rubber Producing Countries [*Kuala Lumpur, Malaysia*] (EAIO) .... ANRPC
Association of Naturopathic Physicians of British Columbia (AC) .... ANPBC
Association of Naval Aviation (EA) .... ANA
Association of Naval Weapons, Engineers, and Scientists [*Later, ASE*] .... ANWES
Association of Navy Safety Professionals [*Defunct*] (EA) .... ANSP
Association of Nebraska Community Action Agencies (SRA) .... ANCAA
Association of Negro Press Photographers .... ANPP
Association of Neighbourhood Councils [*British*] .... ANC
Association of Neighbourhood Houses of Greater Vancouver (AC) .... ANH
Association of Neuro-Metabolic Disorders (EA) .... ANMD
Association of New Brunswick Land Surveyors [*Association des Arpenteurs-Geometres du Nouveau-Brunswick*] (AC) .... ANBLS
Association of New Jersey Environmental Commissions (SRA) .... ANJEC
Association of Newfoundland & Labrador Archivists [*L'Association des Archivistes de Terre-Neuve et de Labrador*] (AC) .... ANLA
Association of Newspaper Classified Advertising Managers (EA) .... ANCAM
Association of Noise Consultants [*British*] .... ANC
Association of Nonsmokers' Rights [*British*] (DBA) .... ANSR
Association of Nordic Aeroclubs (EA) .... ANA
Association of Nordic Paper Historians [*See also FNPH*] [*Sweden*] (EAIO) .... NPH
Association of North American Directory Publishers (EA) .... ANADP
Association of North American Missions (EA) .... ANAM
Association of North American Radio Clubs (EA) .... ANARC
Association of Northwest Steelheaders (EA) .... ANWS
Association of Norwalk School Administration .... ANSA
Association of Nova Scotia Hairdressers (AC) .... ANSH
Association of Nuclear Instrument Manufacturers [*Later, SAMA*] .... ANIM
Association of Nurse Administrators [*British*] (DBA) .... ANA
Association of Nursery Training Colleges [*British*] .... ANTC
Association of Nurses Endorsing Transplantation (EA) .... ANET
Association of Nurses in AIDS [*Acquired Immune Deficiency Syndrome*] **Care** (EA) .... ANAC
Association of Nurses of Prince Edward Island (AC) .... ANPEI
Association of Nursing Directors & Supervisors of Ontario Official Health Agencies (AC) .... ANDSOOHA
Association of Nursing Religious [*British*] (DBA) .... ANR
Association of Obedience Clubs and Judges (EA) .... AOCJ
Association of Occupational Therapists [*British*] (BI) .... AOT
Association of Occupational Therapists of Manitoba [*Association des Ergotherapeutes du Manitoba*] (AC) .... AOTM
Association of Official Agricultural Chemists (DAVI) .... AOAC
Association of Official Analytical Chemists (EA) .... AOAC
Association of Official Analytical Chemists - Europe [*Bennekom, Netherlands*] (EAIO) .... AOAC Europe
Association of Official Architects [*British*] .... AOA
Association of Official Racing Chemists (EA) .... AORC
Association of Official Seed Analysts (EA) .... AOSA
Association of Official Seed Certifying Agencies (EA) .... AOSCA
Association of Offshore Diving Contractors [*British*] (DBA) .... AODC
Association of Ohio Children's Hospitals (SRA) .... AOCH
Association of Ohio Life Insurance Companies (SRA) .... AOLIC
Association of Ohio Longrifle Collectors (EA) .... AOLRC
Association of Ohio Philanthropic Homes and Housing for the Aging (SRA) .... AOPHA
Association of Oil Pipe Lines (EA) .... AOPL
Association of Oilwell Servicing Contractors (EA) .... AOSC
Association of Oklahoma General Contractors (SRA) .... AOGC
Association of Old Crows (EAIO) .... AOC
Association of Oldetime Barbell and Strongmen (EA) .... AOBS
Association of Online Professionals .... AOP
Association of Ontario Health Centres [*Association des Centres de Sante de l'Ontario*] (AC) .... AOHC
Association of Ontario Midwives [*Association des Sages-Femmes de l'Ontario*] [*Formerly, Ontario Association of Midwives*] (AC) .... AOM
Association of Ontario Road Superintendents (AC) .... AORS
Association of Operating Room Nurses (EA) .... AORN
Association of Operating Room Nurses, Denver, CO [*Library symbol*] [*Library of Congress*] (LCLS) .... CoDORN
Association of Operating Room Technicians [*Later, AST*] (EA) .... AORT
Association of Operative Millers (EA) .... AOM
Association of Optical Practitioners [*British*] (BI) .... AOP
Association of Optical Workers and Spectacle Frame Makers [*A union*] [*British*] .... AOWSFM
Association of Optometric Educators (EA) .... AOE
Association of Optometrists [*British*] (DBA) .... AOP
Association of Oregon Community Development Organizations (SRA) .... AOCDO
Association of Oregon Counties (SRA) .... AOC
Association of Organisers of Music, Scotland .... AOMS
Association of Organisers of Physical Education, Scotland .... AOPES
Association of Orthodox Jewish Scientists (EA) .... AOJS
Association of Orthodox Jewish Teachers (EA) .... AOJT
Association of Orthodox Jews in Communications (EA) .... AOJC
Association of Orthopaedic Chairmen (EA) .... AOC
Association of Osteopathic Publications [*Defunct*] .... AOP
Association of Osteopathic State Executive Directors (EA) .... AOSED
Association of Otolaryngology Administrators (EA) .... AOA
Association of Our Lady of Salvation [*Defunct*] .... AOLS
Association of Outplacement Consulting Firms (EA) .... AOCF
Association of Overseas Educators [*Defunct*] (EA) .... AOE
Association of Pacific Fisheries [*Later, PSPA*] (EA) .... APF
Association of Package Tour Travellers [*British*] (DBA) .... APTT
Association of Paediatric Anaesthetists of Great Britain and Ireland [*Birmingham, England*] (EAIO) .... APA
Association of Paid Circulation Publications (EA) .... APCP
Association of Painting Craft Teachers [*British*] .... APCT
Association of Pakistani Physicians (EA) .... APP
Association of Palm Oil Importers [*British*] (DBA) .... APOI
Association of Paper Distributors (DGA) .... APD
Association of Parents of Vaccine Damaged Children [*British*] .... APVDC
Association of Parents Paying Child Support (EA) .... APPCS
Association of Parliamentary Librarians in Canada .... APLIC
Association of Parliamentary Librarians of Australasia .... APLA
Association of Paroling Authorities International (EA) .... APA
Association of Part-Time Professionals (EA) .... AP-TP
Association of Passenger Transport Executives and Managers [*British*] (DCTA) .... APTEM
Association of Pastoral Care of the Mentally Ill [*British*] (DBA) .... APCMI
Association of Pathology Chairmen (EA) .... APC

Association of Patternmakers and Allied Craftsmen [*A union*] [*British*] (DCTA) ... APAC
Association of Payment Clearing Services [*British*] (DBA) ... APACS
Association of Pediatric Oncology Nurses (EA) ... APON
Association of Pediatric Oncology Social Workers (EA) ... APOSW
Association of Pediatric Societies of the Southeast Asian Region (EA) ... APSSEAR
Association of Pennsylvania State College and University Faculties (SRA) ... APSCUF
Association of Pension Lawyers [*British*] (DBA) ... APL
Association of Pensioneer Trustees [*British*] (DBA) ... APT
Association of Pensioners & Injured Workmen of Ontario (AC) ... APIO
Association of Performing Arts Presenters (EA) ... APAP
Association of Personal Assistants and Secretaries [*Leamington Spa, Warwickshire, England*] [*Defunct*] (EAIO) ... APAS
Association of Personal Computer User Groups (PCM) ... APCUG
Association of Personnel Agencies of New York ... APANY
Association of Petrochemical Producers in Europe (ECON) ... APPE
Association of Petroleum Geologists (IID) ... AAPG
Association of Petroleum Re-Refiners (EA) ... APR
Association of Petroleum Writers (EA) ... APW
Association of Pharmaceutical Importers [*British*] (DBA) ... API
Association of Philippine Coconut Desiccators ... APCD
Association of Philippine Physicians in America (EA) ... APPA
Association of Philippine Practicing Physicians in America [*Later, APPA*] (EA) ... APPPA
Association of Philippine-American Women (EA) ... APAW
Association of Philosophy Journal Editors (EA) ... APJE
Association of Photo Sensitizers (EA) ... APS
Association of Photographic Importers and Distributors (EA) ... APID
Association of Photographic Laboratories [*British*] (DBA) ... APL
Association of Physical Fitness Centers (EA) ... APFC
Association of Physical Plant Administrators of Universities and Colleges (EA) ... APPA
Association of Physical Plant Administrators of Universities and Colleges (EA) ... APPAUC
Association of Physician Assistant Programs (EA) ... APAP
Association of Physician's Assistants in Cardio-Vascular Surgery (EA) ... APACVS
Association of Piano Class Teachers [*British*] (BI) ... APCT
Association of Planned Parenthood Professionals [*Later, ARHP*] (EA) ... APPP
Association of Plastic Cable Makers [*British*] (BI) ... APCM
Association of Plastic Raw Material Distributors [*Defunct*] (EA) ... APRMD
Association of Plastics Manufacturers in Europe (EA) ... APME
Association of Playing Fields' Officers [*British*] (BI) ... APFO
Association of Playing Fields Officers and Landscape Managers [*British*] (DBA) ... APFO & LM
Association of Pleasure Craft Operators [*British*] (BI) ... APCO
Association of Podiatrists in Federal Service [*Later, FSPMA*] (EA) ... APFS
Association of Point-of-Sale-Advertising [*British*] ... APSA
Association of Police Surgeons of Great Britain ... APSGB
Association of Polish Women in the United States (EA) ... APWUS
Association of Political Risk Analysts [*Later, CIBRM*] (EA) ... APRA
Association of Polysomnographic Technologists (EA) ... APT
Association of Polytechnic Teachers [*British*] ... APT
Association of Port Authorities ... APA
Association of Post Production Companies [*British*] (DBA) ... APPCo
Association of Postal Officials of Canada ... APOC
Association of Poultry Processors and Poultry Import- and Export-Trade in the EEC Countries (EAIO) ... AVEC
Association of Poultry Slaughterhouse Operators (EA) ... APSO
Association of Practicing Accountants ... APA
Association of Practicing Certified Public Accountants (SRA) ... APCPA
Association of Practising Accountants [*British*] (DBA) ... APA
Association of Presbyterian Colleges and Universities (EA) ... APCU
Association of Preserved Milk Manufacturers of the EEC [*European Economic Community*] [*France*] (EAIO) ... APMM-EEC
Association of Principals of Colleges [*British*] ... APC
Association of Principals of Colleges for Adult Education [*British*] ... APCAE
Association of Principals of Technical Institutions [*British*] ... APTI
Association of Principals, Wardens, and Advisers of University Women Students [*British*] (AIE) ... APWA
Association of Printing Machinery Importers (DGA) ... APMI
Association of Printing Technologists [*Later, IOP*] (DGA) ... APT
Association of Private Camps [*Later, AIC*] (EA) ... APC
Association of Private Client Investment Managers and Stockbrokers (ODBW) ... APCIMS
Association of Private Colleges and Universities in Georgia (SRA) ... APCUG
Association of Private Enterprise Education (EA) ... APEE
Association of Private Hospitals (EA) ... APH
Association of Private Investors [*British*] (DBA) ... API
Association of Private Libraries (EA) ... APL
Association of Private Office Personnel Agencies ... APOPA
Association of Private Pension and Welfare Plans (EA) ... APPWP
Association of Private Postal Systems [*Later, AAPS*] (EA) ... APPS
Association of Private Traders [*British*] (BI) ... APT
Association of Private Weather Related Companies (EA) ... APWRC
Association of Privately Owned Seventh-Day Adventist Services and Industries (EA) ... ASI
Association of Producing Artists ... APA
Association of Productivity Specialists (EA) ... APS
Association of Professional and Executive Staff [*British*] ... APEX
Association of Professional Ball Players of America (EA) ... APBPA
Association of Professional Baseball Physicians (EA) ... APBP
Association of Professional Boardsailing Centres [*British*] (DBA) ... APBC
Association of Professional Bridge Players (EA) ... APBP
Association of Professional Collectors ... APC
Association of Professional Color Laboratories (EA) ... APCL
Association of Professional Composers [*British*] (DBA) ... APC
Association of Professional Computer Consultants [*Canada*] (EAIO) ... APCC
Association of Professional Conservatories of Music (EA) ... APCM
Association of Professional Design Firms (EA) ... APDF
Association of Professional Energy Managers (EA) ... APEM
Association of Professional Engineers & Geoscientists of British Columbia (AC) ... APEG BC
Association of Professional Engineers & Geoscientists of Newfoundland [*Formerly, Association of Professional Engineers of Newfoundland*] (AC) ... APEGN
Association of Professional Engineers, Geologists & Geophysicists of Alberta (AC) ... APEGGA
Association of Professional Engineers, Geologists, and Geophysicists of Alberta [*Canada*] (DD) ... APEGGA
Association of Professional Engineers, Geologists & Geophysicists of the Northwest Territories (AC) ... NAPEGG
Association of Professional Engineers of Manitoba (AC) ... APEM
Association of Professional Engineers of New Brunswick (AC) ... APENB
Association of Professional Engineers of Nova Scotia (AC) ... APENS
Association of Professional Engineers of Prince Edward Island (AC) ... APEPEI
Association of Professional Engineers of Saskatchewan (AC) ... APES
Association of Professional Engineers, Scientists, and Managers, Australia ... APESMA
Association of Professional, Executive, Clerical, and Computer Staff (AIE) ... APEX
Association of Professional Foresters (EAIO) ... APF
Association of Professional Genealogists (EA) ... APG
Association of Professional Geological Scientists [*Later, AIPG*] (EA) ... APGS
Association of Professional Insurance Women [*Acronym is now organization's official name*] (EA) ... APIW
Association of Professional Landscape Designers (EA) ... APLD
Association of Professional Librarians of New Brunswick (AC) ... APLNB
Association of Professional Material Handling Consultants (EA) ... APMHC
Association of Professional Music Therapists [*British*] (DBA) ... APMT
Association of Professional Photogrammetrists (EA) ... APP
Association of Professional Placement Agencies & Consultants [*Association de Placement en Personnel Agences et Conseillers*] (AC) ... APPAC
Association of Professional Police Investigators (EA) ... APPI
Association of Professional Recording Studios Ltd. [*British*] (BI) ... APRS
Association of Professional Schools of International Affairs (EA) ... APSIA
Association of Professional Sleep Societies (EA) ... APSS
Association of Professional Student Services Personnel [*Association du Personnel Professionnel des Services aux Etudiants*] (AC) ... APSSP
Association of Professional Video Distributors [*British*] (DBA) ... APVD
Association of Professional Vocal Ensembles [*Later, Chorus America*] (EA) ... APVE
Association of Professional Writing Consultants (EA) ... APWC
Association of Professions for the Mentally Handicapped [*British*] ... APMH
Association of Professors and Researchers in Religious Education (EA) ... APRRE
Association of Professors of Cardiology (EA) ... APC
Association of Professors of Gynecology and Obstetrics (EA) ... APGO
Association of Professors of Medicine (EA) ... APM
Association of Professors of Mission (EA) ... APM
Association of Professors of Modern Languages in Technological Universities (AIE) ... APMLTU
Association of Profiles Consultants (EA) ... APC
Association of Program Directors in Internal Medicine (EA) ... APDIM
Association of Programmed Learning [*London, England*] (MCD) ... APL
Association of Progressive Rental Organizations (EA) ... APRO
Association of Proposal Management Professionals ... APMP
Association of Psychiatric Outpatient Centers of America [*Psychiatric Out patient Centers of America*] [*Acronym is based on former name,*] (EA) ... POCA
Association of Psychiatric Social Workers [*British*] (BI) ... APSW
Association of Psychological Counselling and Training [*British*] (DBA) ... APCT
Association of Psychology Internship Centers (EA) ... APIC
Association of Public Address Engineers [*British*] (BI) ... APAE
Association of Public Analysts [*British*] ... APA
Association of Public and Private Labor Employees ... APPLE
Association of Public Authority Surveyors [*Australia*] ... APAS
Association of Public Broadcasting Stations of New York (SRA) ... APBSNY
Association of Public Corporations [*Miami, FL*] (EA) ... APC
Association of Public Data Users (EA) ... APDU
Association of Public Health Inspectors ... APHI
Association of Public Lighting Engineers [*British*] (BI) ... APLE
Association of Public Radio Stations [*Later, NPR*] (EA) ... APRS
Association of Public Service Administrative Staff [*British*] (DBA) ... APSAS
Association of Public Service Financial Administrators [*Association des Gestionnaires Financiers de la Fonction Publique*] (AC) ... APSFA
Association of Publication Production Managers (EA) ... APPM
Association of Publicly Traded Companies (EA) ... APTC
Association of Publicly Traded Investment Funds [*Defunct*] (EA) ... APTIF
Association of Publishers ... AAP
Association of Publishers' Educational Representatives [*British*] ... APER
Association of Publishers Representatives [*Later, NAPR*] (EA) ... APR
Association of Pulp Consumers, Inc. [*Later, American Paper Institute*] (EA) ... APC
Association of Pulp Consumers, Inc. ... APCI
Association of Qualified Curative Hypnotherapists [*British*] (DBA) ... AQCH
Association of Quality Management Consultants [*British*] (DBA) ... AQMC
Association of Racing Commissioners International (EA) ... ARCI

Association of Racquetsports Manufacturers and Suppliers [*Inactive*] (EA) ... ARMS
Association of Radical Midwives [*British*] (DBA) ... ARM
Association of Radio and Electrical Engineers [*A union*] [*British*] ... AREE
Association of Radio and Television Employees of Canada ... ARTEC
Association of Radio Broadcasters (BARN) ... ARB
Association of Radio News Analysts [*Later, ARTNA*] ... ARNA
Association of Radio Reading Services (EA) ... ARRS
Association of Radio-Television News Analysts [*Defunct*] (EA) ... ARTNA
Association of Railroad Advertising and Marketing (EA) ... ARAM
Association of Railroad Editors [*Formerly, ARMEA*] (EA) ... ARE
Association of Railway Communicators (EA) ... ARC
Association of Railway Museums (EA) ... ARM
Association of Railway Preservation Societies Ltd. [*British*] ... ARPS
Association of Railway Trainmen and Locomotive Firemen (EA) ... ARTLF
Association of Railway Trainmen and Locomotive Firemen ... RTLF
Association of Rain Apparel Contractors (EA) ... ARAC
Association of Real Estate Syndicators (EA) ... ARES
Association of Reclaimed Textile Processors [*British*] (DBA) ... ARTP
Association of Recognised English Language Schools [*British*] ... ARELS
Association of Recognition Business Schools [*British*] (DBA) ... ARBS
Association of Records Executives and Administrators [*Later, ARMA*] (EA) ... AREA
Association of Records Managers and Administrators (EA) ... ARMA
Association of Recovering Motorcyclists (EA) ... ARM
Association of Reform Zionists of America (EA) ... ARZA
Association of Refrigerant and Desuperheating Manufacturing (EA) ... ARDM
Association of Regional Religious Communicators (EA) ... ARRC
Association of Registered Bank Holding Companies [*Later, ABHC*] (EA) ... ARBHC
Association of Registered Child Care Centers of Western Australia ... ARCCCWA
Association of Registered Driving Instructors [*British*] (BI) ... ARDI
Association of Registered Interior Designers of New Brunswick [*Association des Designers d'Interieur Immatricules du Nouveau-Brunswick*] (AC) ... IDNB
Association of Registered Interior Designers of Ontario [*Formerly, Interior Designers of Ontario*] (AC) ... ARIDO
Association of Registered Nurses of Newfoundland (AC) ... ARNN
Association of Registered Professional Foresters of New Brunswick [*Association des Forestiers Agrees du Nouveau-Brunswick*] (AC) ... ARPFNB
Association of Registrars of the Universities and Colleges of Canada ... ARUCC
Association of Regular Army Sergeants (EA) ... ARAS
Association of Regulatory and Clinical Scientists ... ARCS
Association of Rehabilitation Centers [*Later, NARF*] (EA) ... ARC
Association of Rehabilitation Ltd. ... AOR
Association of Rehabilitation Nurses (EA) ... ARN
Association of Rehabilitation Programs in Data Processing (EA) ... ARPDP
Association of Religion and Applied Behavioral Science [*Later, ACC*] (EA) ... ARABS
Association of Relocation Agents [*British*] (DBA) ... ARA
Association of Representatives of Old Pupils' Societies [*British*] ... AROPS
Association of Representatives of Old Pupils' Societies (AIE) ... AROPS
Association of Representatives of Professional Athletes (EA) ... ARPA
Association of Reproduction Materials Manufacturers (EA) ... ARMM
Association of Reproductive Health Professionals (EA) ... ARHP
Association of Research Directors (EA) ... ARD
Association of Research Libraries (EA) ... ARL
Association of Research Libraries Collection Analysis Project ... ARLCAP
Association of Researchers in Medical Sciences [*British*] ... ARMS
Association of Researchers in Voluntary Action and Community Involvement [*British*] ... ARVAC
Association of Reserve City Bankers (EA) ... ARCB
Association of Reserve Officers of the US Public Health Service [*Defunct*] (EA) ... AROUSPHS
Association of Reserves for Improving Social Economics (AC) ... ARISE
Association of Residential Care Homes of New Jersey (SRA) ... ARCH
Association of Residential Communities [*British*] (DBA) ... ARC
Association of Residential Letting Agents [*British*] (DBA) ... ARLA
Association of Residential Resources in Minnesota (SRA) ... ARRM
Association of Resort Publicity Officers [*British*] (BI) ... ARPO
Association of Retail Candy Shops ... ARCS
Association of Retail Travel Agents ... ARTA
Association of Retailer-Owned Wholesalers in Foodstuffs [*Later, ACROWE*] (EAIO) ... AROWF
Association of Retired Americans (EA) ... ARA
Association of Retired Naval Officers [*British military*] (DMA) ... ARNO
Association of Retired Persons International [*Later, IARP*] ... ARP
Association of Rhode Island Health Sciences Librarians [*Library network*] ... ARIHSL
Association of Rhodesian and Nyasaland Industries ... ARNI
Association of River Authorities [*British*] (BI) ... ARA
Association of Road Racing Athletes (EA) ... ARRA
Association of Road Racing Clubs [*British*] (DBA) ... ARRC
Association of Road Surface Dressing Contractors [*British*] (BI) ... ARSD
Association of Road Traffic Sign Makers [*British*] (EAIO) ... ARTSM
Association of Romanian Catholics of America (EA) ... ARCA
Association of Romanian-American Orthodox Ladies Auxiliaries (EA) ... ARAOLA
Association of Rooflight Manufacturers [*British*] (DBA) ... ARM
Association of Rotational Molders (EA) ... ARM
Association of Round Tables in Central Africa ... ARTCA
Association of Rover Clubs (EAIO) ... ARC
Association of Rural District Council Surveyors [*British*] (BI) ... ARDCS
Association of Russian Imperial Medical Officers [*Defunct*] (EA) ... ARIMO
Association of Russian Imperial Naval Officers in America (EA) ... ARINOA
Association of Russian War Invalids of World War II (EA) ... ARWI
Association of Russian-American Scholars in the United States of America (EA) ... ARASUSA
Association of Sacred Heart Schools [*Australia*] ... ASHS
Association of Safety Council Executives (EA) ... ASCE
Association of Sales Administration Managers (EA) ... ASAM
Association of Sanitary Protection Manufacturers [*British*] (DBA) ... ASPM
Association of School Business Officials International (EA) ... ASBO
Association of School Natural History Societies [*British*] ... ASNHS
Association of Schools and Colleges of Optometry (EA) ... ASCO
Association of Schools of Journalism and Mass Communication (EA) ... ASJMC
Association of Schools of Public Health (EA) ... ASPH
Association of Schools of Public Health (EA) ... ASPH
Association of Schools of Public Health in the European Region (EAIO) ... ASPHER
Association of Science Museum Directors (EA) ... ASMD
Association of Science-Technology Centers (EA) ... ASTC
Association of Science-Technology Centers ... ASTEC
Association of Scientific Information Dissemination Centers (NITA) ... ASIDIC
Association of Scientific, Technical, and Managerial Staffs [*British*] ... ASTMS
Association of Scientific Workers [*British*] ... AScW
Association of Scientists and Engineers of the Naval Sea Systems Command (EA) ... ASE
Association of Scientists and Professional Engineering Personnel ... ASPEP
Association of Scottish Climbing Clubs (BI) ... ASCC
Association of Scottish Games and Festivals (EA) ... ASGF
Association of Scottish Local Health Councils [*British*] ... ASLHC
Association of Screen Magazine Publishers [*Defunct*] ... ASMP
Association of Sea and Air Ports Health Authority [*British*] ... ASAPHA
Association of Sea Fisheries Committees of England and Wales (DCTA) ... ASFC
Association of Sea Grant Program Institutes [*Marine science*] (OSRA) ... ASGPI
Association of Sea Grant Program Institutes (USDC) ... ASGPI
Association of Sea Training Organisations [*British*] (DBA) ... ASTO
Association of Seafood Importers (EA) ... ASI
Association of Sealant Applicators [*British*] (DBA) ... ASA
Association of Search and Selection Consultants [*British*] (DBA) ... ASSC
Association of Second Class Mail Publishers (EA) ... ASCMP
Association of Secondary Teachers, Ireland (BI) ... ASTI
Association of Secretaries General of Parliaments (EA) ... ASGP
Association of Secretaries Young Men's Christian Associations [*Later, YMCA*] ... ASYMCA
Association of Securities and Exchange Commission Alumni (EA) ... ASECA
Association of Self Employment Developers of Ontario (AC) ... ASEDO
Association of Seminary Professors in the Practical Fields [*Later, APT*] (EA) ... ASPPF
Association of Semi-Rotary Wing Pump Manufacturers (MHDB) ... ASRWPM
Association of Senior Engineers [*NAVSHIPS*] ... ASE
Association of Senior Engineers of the Bureau of Ships [*Later, ASE*] (EA) ... ASEBS
Association of Seventh Day Pentecostal Assemblies (EA) ... ASDPA
Association of Seventh-Day Adventist Educators (EA) ... ASDAE
Association of Seventh-Day Adventist Engineers and Architects (EA) ... AEA
Association of Seventh-Day Adventist Librarians (EA) ... ASDAL
Association of Sexual and Marital Therapists [*British*] (DBA) ... ASMT
Association of Shareware Professionals [*Canada*] ... ASP
Association of Shareware Professionals ... ASP
Association of Shell Boilermakers [*British*] (DBA) ... ASB
Association of Ship Brokers and Agents - USA (EA) ... ASBA
Association of Ships' Compositions Manufacturers [*British*] (BI) ... ASCM
Association of Shopfront Section Manufacturers [*British*] (BI) ... ASSM
Association of Short-Circuit Testing Authorities, Inc. [*British*] (BI) ... ASTA
Association of Show and Agricultural Organisations [*British*] ... ASAO
Association of SIDS [*Sudden Infant Death Syndrome*] Program Professionals (EA) ... ASPP
Association of Ski Schools in Great Britain ... ASSGB
Association of Sleep Disorders Centers (EA) ... ASDC
Association of Small Business Development Centers [*Washington, DC*] (EA) ... ASBDC
Association of Small Computer Users [*Later, ACU*] (EA) ... ASCU
Association of Small Computer Users [*Later, ACU*] (CSR) ... ASCUE
Association of Small Computer Users in Education (NITA) ... ASCUE
Association of Small Public Libraries of Ontario (AC) ... ASPLO
Association of Smoked Fish Processors (EA) ... ASFP
Association of Social and Behavioral Scientists (EA) ... ASBS
Association of Social Anthropologists of the Commonwealth [*British*] (EAIO) ... ASA
Association of Social Research Organisations [*British*] ... ASRO
Association of Social Science Teachers [*Later, ASBS*] (EA) ... ASST
Association of Social Workers [*British*] (BI) ... ASW
Association of Societies for Growing Australian Plants ... ASGAP
Association of Software Brokers (EA) ... ASB
Association of Soil and Foundation Engineers [*Later, ASFE/The Association of Engineering Firms Practicing in the Geosciences*] (EA) ... ASFE
Association of Soil Conservation Officer Trainees ... ASCOT
Association of Solid Woven Belting Manufacturers [*British*] (BI) ... ASWB
Association of Sorbitol Producers in the European Community (EAIO) ... ASPEC
Association of South Asian Archaeologists in Western Europe (EAIO) ... ASAAWE
Association of South Carolina Life Insurance Companies (SRA) ... ASCLIC
Association of South East Asian Nations: Indonesia-Singapore [*Submarine cable*] [*Telecommunications*] ... ASEANIS
Association of South East Asian Nations: Philippines-Singapore [*Submarine cable*] [*Telecommunications*] (TEL) ... ASEANPS
Association of South East Field Naturalists Societies ... ASEFNS

Association of South Pacific Airlines ASPA
Association of South Pacific Environmental Institutions ASPEI
Association of Southeast Asian Institutions of Higher Learning [*Bangkok, Thailand*] ASAIHL
Association of South-East Asian Marine Scientists [*Marine science*] (OSRA) ASEAMS
Association of Southeast Asian Nations (ECON) ASEAN
Association of Southeast Asian Nations (DOMA) ASEAN
Association of South-East Asian States ASAS
Association of Southeast Asian Studies in the (United Kingdom) ASEAS(UK)
Association of Southeast Asian University Students ASEAUS
Association of Southeastern Research Libraries [*Library network*] ASERL
Association of Southern Agricultural Workers [*Later, SAAS*] ASAW
Association of Southern Baptist Campus Ministers (EA) ASBCM
Association of Southern Baptist Colleges and Schools (EA) ASBCS
Association of Space Explorers [*Later, ASE-USA*] (EA) ASE
Association of Space Explorers - USA (EAIO) ASE-USA
Association of Speakers Clubs [*British*] (DBA) ASC
Association of Special Education Administrators in Queensland [*Australia*] ASEAQ
Association of Special Events Professionals (SRA) ASEP
Association of Special Libraries and Information Bureaux [*Acronym is now organization's official name*] Aslib
Association of Special Libraries and Information Bureaux [*Association for Information Management*] [*British*] (AIE) ASLIB
Association of Special Libraries of the Philippines ASLP
Association of Specialised Film Producers [*British*] (BI) ASFP
Association of Specialists in Cleaning and Restoration (EA) ASCR
Association of Specialized and Cooperative Library Agencies (EA) ASCLA
Association of Specialized Film Exhibitors [*Defunct*] (EA) ASFE
Association of Spectacle Makers [*Australia*] ASM
Association of Sports Information Directors (EA) ASID
Association of Sports Museums and Halls of Fame [*Later, IASMHF*] (EA) ASMHF
Association of Sprocket Chain Manufacturers [*Defunct*] ASCM
Association of Sri-Lankans in America (EA) ASIA
Association of Standards Laboratories ASL
Association of State and Interstate Water Pollution Control Administrators (EA) ASIWPCA
Association of State and Provincial Safety Coordinators [*Later, ASPSO*] (EA) ASPSC
Association of State and Provincial Safety Officials [*Formerly, ASPSC*] (EA) ASPSO
Association of State and Territorial Chronic Disease Program Directors (EA) ASTCDPD
Association of State and Territorial Dental Directors (EA) ASTDD
Association of State and Territorial Directors of Local Health Services [*Defunct*] (EA) ASTDLHS
Association of State and Territorial Directors of Nursing (EA) ASTDN
Association of State and Territorial Directors of Public Health Nursing [*Later,ASTDN*] (EA) ASTDPHN
Association of State and Territorial Health Officials (EA) ASTHO
Association of State and Territorial Nutrition Directors ASTND
Association of State and Territorial Public Health Laboratory Directors (EA) ASTPHLD
Association of State and Territorial Public Health Nutrition Directors [*Defunct*] (EA) ASTPHND
Association of State and Territorial Solid Waste Management Officials (EA) ASTSWMO
Association of State Colleges and Universities [*Later, AASCU*] ASCU
Association of State Colleges and Universities Forestry Research Organizations ASCUFRO
Association of State Correctional Administrators (EA) ASCA
Association of State Dam Safety Officials (EA) ASDSO
Association of State Democratic Chairs (EA) ASDC
Association of State Drinking Water Administrators (EA) ASDWA
Association of State Employees in Management (SRA) ASEM
Association of State Floodplain Managers ASFM
Association of State Floodplain Managers (EA) ASFPM
Association of State Foresters [*Later, NASF*] ASF
Association of State Juvenile Justice Administrators [*NAJCA*] [*Absorbed by*] (EA) ASJJA
Association of State Labor Relations Agencies (EA) ASLRA
Association of State Library Agencies [*Formerly, Association of State Libraries*] [*Later, ASCLA*] ASLA
Association of State Maternal and Child Health and Crippled Children's Directors[*Later, AMCHCCP*] (EA) ASMCHCCD
Association of State Mediation Agencies [*Later, ALRA*] ASMA
Association of State Medical Officers [*Western Australia*] ASMO
Association of State Planning and Development Agencies [*Later, NASDA*] (EA) ASPDA
Association of State Public Health Veterinarians [*Later, NASPHV*] (EA) ASPHV
Association of State Supervisors of Mathematics (EA) ASSM
Association of State Universities and Land-Grant Colleges (EA) ASULGC
Association of State Wetland Managers (EA) ASWM
Association of Statisticians of American Religious Bodies (EA) ASARB
Association of Steel Distributors (EA) ASD
Association of Steel Drum Manufacturers [*British*] (BI) ASDM
Association of Sterilizer and Disinfector Equipment Manufacturers [*British*] (EAIO) ASDEM
Association of Stock Exchange Firms [*Later, SIA*] (EA) ASEF
Association of Strategic Planning Consultants (EA) ASPC
Association of Street Lighting Contractors [*British*] (DBA) ASLC
Association of Street Lighting Erection Contractors [*British*] (BI) ASLEC
Association of String Class Teachers [*British*] (BI) ASCT
Association of Structural Draftsmen of America (EA) ASDA
Association of Structural Fire Protection Contractors and Manufacturers Ltd. [*British*] (DBA) ASFPCM
Association of Stud Sheep Breeders of Australia ASSBA
Association of Student and Professional Italian-Americans (EA) ASPI
Association of Student Chapters, American Institute of Architects ASC/AIA
Association of Student Councils [*Canada*] AOSC
Association of Student Counselling [*British*] (DBA) ASC
Association of Student Governments ASG
Association of Student International Law Societies (EA) ASILS
Association of Study Curriculum [*British*] (DBA) ASC
Association of Subscription Agents [*British*] (DBA) ASA
Association of Sugar Producers of Puerto Rico [*Defunct*] (EA) ASPPR
Association of Summer Session Deans and Directors [*Later, AUSS*] (EA) ASSDD
Association of Summer Villages of Alberta (AC) ASVA
Association of Sun Tanning Organisations [*British*] (DBA) ASTO
Association of Supervisors in Purchasing and Supply [*British*] (DBQ) ASPS
Association of Supervisory and Executive Engineers [*A union*] [*British*] ASEE
Association of Supervisory Public Health Inspectors (Ontario) (AC) ASPHIO
Association of Supervisory Staffs, Executives, and Technicians (KSC) ASSET
Association of Suppliers to Airlines, Airports, and Shipping [*British*] (DBA) ASAAS
Association of Suppliers to the Furniture Industries Show [*Wood Work Industrial Exhibition*] (TSPED) AFSI
Association of Suppliers to the Furniture Industry [*British*] (EAIO) ASFI
Association of Supportive Care Homes ASCH
Association of Surf Angling Clubs (EA) ASAC
Association of Surfing Professionals (EA) ASP
Association of Surgeons in Training [*British*] (DBA) ASIT
Association of Surgeons of Great Britain and Ireland (BI) AS
Association of Surgeons of South East Asia (EAIO) ASSEA
Association of Surgical Technologists (EA) AST
Association of Swimming Pool Contractors [*British*] (BI) ASPC
Association of Swimming Therapy [*British*] AST
Association of Synthetic Yarn Manufacturers (EA) ASYM
Association of System 2000 Users for Technical Exchange ASTUTE
Association of Talent Agents (EA) ATA
Association of Tasmanian Forum Clubs [*Australia*] ATFC
Association of Tax Consultants (EA) ATC
Association of Teacher Educators (EA) ATE
Association of Teacher Training Colleges and Departments of Education [*British*] (DI) ATTCDE
Association of Teachers and Lecturers (AIE) ATL
Association of Teachers in Colleges and Departments of Education [*British*] ATCDE
Association of Teachers in Colleges and Departments of Education (AIE) ATCODE
Association of Teachers in Independent Schools in New York City and Vicinity (EA) ATIS
Association of Teachers in Independent Schools in New York City and Vicinity (EA) ATISNYCV
Association of Teachers in Penal Establishments [*British*] ATPE
Association of Teachers in Sixth Form and Tertiary Colleges [*British*] (AIE) ATVIC
Association of Teachers in Technical Institutions [*British*] ATTI
Association of Teachers of Domestic Science [*British*] (BI) ATDS
Association of Teachers of Dramatic Science [*British*] ATDS
Association of Teachers of Electrical Engineering [*British*] ATEE
Association of Teachers of English as a Second Language (EA) ATESL
Association of Teachers of English in Quebec (AC) ATEQ
Association of Teachers of French (AIE) ATF
Association of Teachers of Geology [*British*] ATG
Association of Teachers of German [*British*] ATG
Association of Teachers of German [*British*] ATGER
Association of Teachers of Italian [*British*] ATI
Association of Teachers of Japanese (EA) ATJ
Association of Teachers of Latin American Studies (EA) ATLAS
Association of Teachers of Lipreading to Adults [*British*] (DBA) ATLA
Association of Teachers of Management [*British*] ATM
Association of Teachers of Maternal and Child Health (EA) ATMCH
Association of Teachers of Mathematics [*Derby, England*] (EAIO) ATM
Association of Teachers of Preventive Medicine (EA) ATPM
Association of Teachers of Printing and Allied Subjects [*British*] ATPAS
Association of Teachers of Russian [*British*] ATR
Association of Teachers of Social Studies [*British*] ATSS
Association of Teachers of Spanish and Portuguese [*British*] ATSP
Association of Teachers of Technical Writing (EA) ATTW
Association of Technical and Supervisory Professionals (EA) ATSP
Association of Technical Artists [*Later, IG*] ATA
Association of Technical Institutions (EY) ATI
Association of Technical Professionals [*Defunct*] (EA) ATP
Association of Technical Studies Advisers [*British*] ATSA
Association of Telemessaging Services International (EA) ATSI
Association of Telephone Answering Services (EA) ATAS
Association of Telephone Information and Entertainment Providers [*British*] ATIEP
Association of Telephone Messaging Suppliers [*Defunct*] (EA) ATMS
Association of Temporary Office Services ATOS
Association of Temporary Personnel Contractors ATPC
Association of Tennis Professionals [*Defunct*] (EA) ATP
Association of Tequila Producers (EA) ATP
Association of Texas Colleges and Universities (SRA) ATCU
Association of Texas Graduate Schools (SRA) ATGS
Association of Texas Professional Educators (SRA) ATPE

Association of Texas Soil and Water Conservation Districts (SRA) .... ATSWCD
Association of Thalidomide-Damaged Children .... ATDC
Association of the Bar of the City of New York. Committee on Amendment of the Law. Bulletin [*A publication*] (DLA) .... CAL Bull
Association of the Bar of the City of New York, New York, NY [*Library symbol Library of Congress*] (LCLS) .... NNB
Association of the British Pharmaceutical Industry .... ABPI
Association of the Chemical Profession of Ontario (AC) .... ACPO
Association of the Cider and Fruit Wine Industry of the EC [*Economic Community*] [*Belgium*] (EAIO) .... ACFWI-EC
Association of the Customs Bar [*Later, CITBA*] (EA) .... ACB
Association of the European Independent Informatics Industry (PDAA) .... EIII
Association of the European National Olympic Committees [*See also ACNOE*] [*Brussels, Belgium*] (EAIO) .... ENOC
Association of the German Nobility in North America (EA) .... DAGNA
Association of the Graphic Arts (EA) .... AGA
Association of the Institute for Certification of Computer Professionals (EA) .... AICCP
Association of the Institute of Asphalt Technology [*British*] (DBQ) .... AIAT
Association of the International Christian Youth Exchange in Europe (EAIO) .... AICYEE
Association of the International Winter Sports Federations [*Switzerland*] (EAIO) .... AIWF
Association of the International Winter Sports Federations [*Berne, Switzerland*] (EAIO) .... AIWSF
Association of the IOC Recognized International Sports Federations [*Seoul, Republic of Korea*] (EAIO) .... ARISF
Association of the Junior Leagues of America [*Later, AJL*] (EA) .... AJLA
[*The*] **Association of the Scientific, Engineering, and Technological Community of Canada** .... SCITEC
Association of the Sons of Poland (EA) .... SSP
Association of the United States Army (EA) .... AUSA
Association of the Wall and Ceiling Industries - International (EA) .... AWCI
Association of the Wholesale Licensed Trade of Northern Ireland (BI) .... AWLTNI
Association of Theaters of Emilia and Romagna [*Ballet company*] .... ATER
Association of Theatre Benefit Agents [*Defunct*] (EA) .... ATBA
Association of Theatre Screen Advertising Companies [*Defunct*] .... ATSAC
Association of Theatrical Press Agents and Managers (EA) .... ATPAM
Association of Theological Institutes in the Middle East (EAIO) .... ATIME
Association of Theological Schools (EA) .... ATS
Association of Theological Schools in the United States and Canada (PGP) .... ATS
Association of Third World Affairs (EA) .... ATWA
Association of Third World Studies (EA) .... ATWS
Association of Thrift Holding Companies [*Washington, DC*] (EA) .... ATHC
Association of Tile, Terrazzo, Marble Contractors and Affiliates [*Later, NTCA*] (EA) .... ATTMCA
Association of Time-Sharing Users [*Later, ACU*] (EA) .... ATSU
Association of Tin Producing Countries [*Australia*] .... ATPC
Association of Toilet Paper Manufacturers [*British*] (BI) .... ATPM
Association of Tongue Depressors (EA) .... ATD
Association of Touring and Production Managers [*British*] (BI) .... ATPM
Association of Toy and Fancy Goods Factors [*British*] (BI) .... ATFGF
Association of Track and Field Statisticians [*British*] (EAIO) .... ATFS
Association of Track and Structure Suppliers [*Later, REMSA*] (EA) .... ATSS
Association of Trading Standards Officers [*British*] (DBA) .... ATSO
Association of Trailer Manufacturers [*British*] (DBA) .... ATM
Association of Training and Employment Professionals (EA) .... ATEP
Association of Translation Companies [*British*] (DBA) .... ATC
Association of Translators & Interpreters of Ontario [*Association des Traducteurs et Interpretes de l'Ontario*] (AC) .... ATIO
Association of Translators & Interpreters of Saskatchewan [*Association des Traducteurs et Interpretes de la Saskatchewan*] (AC) .... ATIS
Association of Transport Coordinating Officers (DCTA) .... ATCC
Association of Transport Co-ordinating Officers [*British*] (DBA) .... ATCO
Association of Transportation Practitioners (EA) .... ATP
Association of Travel Marketing Executives (EA) .... ATME
Association of Trial Behavior Consultants [*Later, ASTC*] (EA) .... ATBC
Association of Trial Lawyers of America (EA) .... ATLA
Association of Trial Lawyers of America. Newsletter [*A publication*] (DLA) .... Ass'n Trial Law Am Newsl
Association of Tutors [*British*] .... AOT
Association of Tutors in Adult Education [*British*] .... ATAE
Association of Ukrainian Sports Clubs in North America (EA) .... AUSC-NA
Association of Ukrainians in Great Britain Ltd. (BI) .... AUGB
Association of Ukrainians in Tasmania [*Australia*] .... AUT
Association of Umbrella Manufacturers and Suppliers [*Defunct*] (EA) .... AUM
Association of Unclaimed Property Administrators [*Later, NAUPA*] .... AUPA
Association of Unit Trust Managers [*British*] (BI) .... AUTM
Association of United Contractors of America [*Defunct*] (EA) .... AUCOA
Association of United Kingdom Media Librarians (DBA) .... AUKML
Association of United Kingdom Oil Independents .... AUKOI
Association of United States Night Vision Manufacturers (EA) .... ANVM
Association of United States Night Vision Manufacturers (EA) .... AUSNVM
Association of United Ukrainian Canadians (AC) .... AUUC
Association of Unity Churches (EA) .... AUC
Association of Universities and Colleges of Canada [*Association des Universites et Colleges du Canada*] .... AUCC
Association of Universities and Colleges of Canada, Ottawa, ON, Canada [*Library symbol Library of Congress*] (LCLS) .... CaOOCU
Association of Universities and Colleges of Canada [*Association des Universites et Colleges du Canada*], Ottawa, Ontario [*Library symbol National Library of Canada*] (NLC) .... OOCU
Association of Universities for Research in Astronomy (EA) .... AURA
Association of Universities of the British Commonwealth .... AUBC
Association of University Affiliated Facilities [*Later, AAUAP*] (EA) .... AUAF
Association of University and College Counseling Center Directors (EA) .... AUCCCD
Association of University and College Employees [*See also AEUC*] [*Canada*] .... AUCE
Association of University Anesthetists (EA) .... AUA
Association of University Architects (EA) .... AUA
Association of University Clinical Academic Staff [*British*] .... AUCAS
Association of University Environmental Health/Sciences Centers (EA) .... AUEHSC
Association of University Evening Colleges [*Later, ACHE*] (EA) .... AUEC
Association of University Fisheries and Wildlife Program Administrators (EA) .... AUFWPA
Association of University Forestry Schools of Canada [*Association des Ecoles Forestieres Universitaires du Canada*] (AC) .... AUFSC
Association of University Interior Designers (EA) .... AUID
Association of University Professors (French) [*British*] .... AUP(Fr)
Association of University Professors of Ophthalmology (EA) .... AUPO
Association of University Programs in Health Administration (EA) .... AUPHA
Association of University Programs in Occupational Health and Safety (EA) .... AUPOHS
Association of University Radiation Protection Officers [*British*] .... AURPO
Association of University Radiologists (EA) .... AUR
Association of University Related Research Parks (EA) .... AURRP
Association of University Summer Sessions (EA) .... AUSS
Association of University Teachers [*A union*] [*British*] .... AUT
Association of University Teachers in Accounting [*British*] .... AUTA
Association of University Technology Managers (AAGC) .... AUTM
Association of Uptown Converters (EA) .... AUC
Association of Urban Universities [*Defunct*] (EA) .... AUU
Association of US Chess Journalists [*Later, CJA*] (EA) .... AUSCJ
Association of US Members of the International Institute of Space Law (EA) .... AUSMIISL
Association of US University Directors of International Agricultural Programs [*Later, AIARD*] (EA) .... AUSUDIAP
Association of Used Tyre Merchants [*British*] (BI) .... AUTM
Association of Users of Research Agencies [*British*] (DBA) .... AURA
Association of Vacuum Equipment Manufacturers (EA) .... AVEM
Association of Valuers of Licensed Property [*British*] (DBA) .... AVLP
Association of Vegetarian Dietitians and Nutrition Educators (EA) .... VEGEDINE
Association of Vehicle Recovery Operators [*British*] (DBA) .... AVRO
Association of Venture Capital Clubs [*Defunct*] (EA) .... AVCC
Association of Venture Founders [*Defunct*] (EA) .... AVF
Association of Vermiculite Exfoliators Ltd. [*British*] (BI) .... AVE
Association of Vermont Independent Colleges (SRA) .... AVIC
Association of Veterinary Anaesthetists [*British*] .... AVA
Association of Veterinary Inspectors .... AVI
Association of Veterinary Students of Great Britain and Ireland (BI) .... AVS
Association of Veterinary Teachers and Research Workers [*British*] .... AVTRW
Association of Vice-Principals in Colleges [*British*] .... AVPC
Association of Victorian Greyhound Clubs [*Australia*] .... AVGC
Association of Viewdata Information Providers (EA) .... AVIP
Association of Visual Communicators (EA) .... AVC
Association of Visual Merchandise Representatives (EA) .... AVMR
Association of Visual Science Librarians (EA) .... AVSL
Association of Vitamin Chemists (EA) .... AVC
Association of Volleyball Professionals (EA) .... AVP
Association of Voluntary Action Scholars [*Later, ARNOVA*] (EA) .... AVAS
Association of Voluntary Agencies on Narcotics Treatment .... AVANT
Association of Voluntary Aided Secondary Schools [*British*] .... AVASS
Association of Voluntary Groups [*Republic of Ireland*] (BI) .... AVG
Association of Voluntary/Independent Schools [*British*] (DBA) .... AVIS
Association of Volunteer Bureaus [*Later, NVC*] (EA) .... AVB
Association of Volunteer Emergency Radio Teams .... AVERT
Association of Waldorf Schools of North America (EA) .... AWSNA
Association of Wall and Ceiling Contractors of Queensland [*Australia*] .... AWCCQ
Association of Wall and Ceiling Contractors of Victoria [*Australia*] .... AWCCV
Association of Wall and Ceiling Contractors of Western Australia .... AWCCWA
Association of Washington Business (SRA) .... AWB
Association of Washington Cities (SRA) .... AWC
Association of Washington School Principals (SRA) .... AWSP
Association of Waste Hazardous Materials Transporters .... AWHMT
Association of Water Officers [*British*] (DBA) .... AWO
Association of Water Transportation Accounting Officers [*New York, NY*] (EA) .... AWTAO
Association of Waterloo Groups [*British*] (DI) .... AWG
Association of Waterworks Officers [*British*] (BI) .... AWO
Association of Webbing Load Restraint Equipment Manufacturers [*British*] (DBA) .... AWLREM
Association of Welding Distributors [*British*] (DBA) .... AWD
Association of West European Shipbuilders [*London, England*] (EAIO) .... AWES
Association of Western Hospitals [*Later, HCF*] .... AWH
Association of Western Pulp and Paper Workers (EA) .... AWPPW
Association of Western Pulp and Paper Workers .... WPPW
Association of Western Railways [*Later, WRA*] .... AWR
Association of Wholesale Electrical Bulk Buyers [*British*] (DBA) .... AWEBB
Association of Wholesale Woollen Merchants Ltd. [*British*] (BI) .... AWWM
Association of Wind Teachers [*British*] .... AWT
Association of Winery Suppliers (EA) .... AWS
Association of Wisconsin Cleaning Contractors (SRA) .... AWCC
Association of Wisconsin School Administrators (SRA) .... AWSA
Association of Women Broadcasters .... AWB
Association of Women Executives [*Canada*] .... AWE

Association of Women Gemologists [*Defunct*] (EA) .... AWG
Association of Women Highway Safety Leaders .... AWHSL
Association of Women in Architecture [*Defunct*] (EA) .... AWA
Association of Women in Natural Foods (EA) .... AWIN
Association of Women in Public Relations [*British*] (DBA) .... AWPR
Association of Women Launderers [*British*] (BI) .... AWL
Association of Women Soil Scientists (EA) .... AWSS
Association of Women Surgeons (EA) .... AWS
Association of Women Tax Clerks [*A union*] [*British*] .... AWTC
Association of Women Welders [*A union*] [*British*] .... AWW
Association of Women Workers in the Bedstead Trade [*A union*] [*British*] .... AWWBT
Association of Women's Forum Clubs of Australia .... AWFCA
Association of Workers for Maladjusted Children [*British*] .... AWMC
Association of Workshop Way Consultants (EA) .... AWWC
Association of World Citizens (EA) .... AWC
Association of World Colleges and Universities [*Later, AWE*] .... AWCU
Association of World Trade Chamber Executives (EA) .... AWTCE
Association of Wyoming Insurance Agents (SRA) .... AWIA
Association of X-Ray Equipment Manufacturers [*British*] (DBA) .... AXrEM
Association of Yarn Distributors (EA) .... AYD
Association of Young Computer Enthusiasts (AIE) .... AYCF
Association of Yugoslav Jews in the USA (EA) .... AYJUSA
Association of Yukon Communities [*Formerly, Association of Yukon Municipalities*] (AC) .... AYC
Association Olympique Canadienne [*Canadian Olympic Association - COA*] .... AOC
Association on American Indian Affairs (EA) .... AAIA
Association on Broadcasting Standards [*Later, Association for Broadcast Engineering Standards*] .... ABS
Association on Handicapped Student Service Programs in Postsecondary Education (EA) .... AHSSPPE
Association on Japanese Textile Imports [*Defunct*] (EA) .... AJTI
Association on Programs for Female Offenders (EA) .... APFO
Association Package Sequence Number (MCD) .... APSN
Association Paritaire pour la Sante et la Securite du Travail - Affaires Municipales (AC) .... APSAM
Association Paritaire pour le Sante et le Securite du Travail - Mines (AC) .... APSM
Association Parlementaire Europe-Afrique [*Eur-African Parliamentary Association*] .... APEA
Association Period (MAE) .... AP
Association Petroliere pour la Conservation de l'Environnement Canadien [*Petroleum Association for Conservation of the Canadian Environment*] .... APCE
Association Pharmaceutique Canadienne [*Canadian Pharmaceutical Association*] (EAIO) .... APhC
Association Phonetique Internationale [*International Phonetic Association*] .... API
Association pour la Conservation et la Reproduction Photographique de la Presse,Paris, France [*Library symbol Library of Congress*] (LCLS) .... ACRPP
Association pour la Cooperation Islamique [*Senegal*] (EY) .... ACIS
Association pour la Prevention de la Contamination Atmospherique (AC) .... APCA
Association pour la Promotion des Initiatives Communautaires Africaines [*Association for the Promotion of African Community Initiatives - APACI*] (EAIO) .... APICA
Association pour la Promotion Industrie - Agriculture [*Association for the Promotion of Industry - Agriculture*] (EAIO) .... APIA
Association pour la Promotion Sociale de la Masse [*Association for the Social Betterment of the Masses*] [*Burundi and Rwanda*] (AF) .... APROSOMA
Association pour la Protection des Automobilistes [*Canada*] .... APA
Association pour la Protection des Interets des Consommateurs [*Association for the Protection of Consumer Interests*] [*Canada*] .... APIC
Association pour la Recherche dans l'Industrie Siderurgique Canadienne (AC) .... ARISC
Association pour la Recherche en Tourisme [*Travel Research Association*] [*Canada*] .... ART
Association pour la Recherche et le Developpement en Informatique Chimique [*Association for Research and Development of Chemical Informatics*] [*Information service or system*] (IID) .... ARDIC
Association pour la Reduction des Depenses Publiques [*Association for the Reduction of Public Spending*] (AC) .... ARDP
Association pour la Sante et la Securite du Travail, Secteur Affaires Sociales [*Association for the Health and Safety of Labour, Social Affairs Sector*] [*Canada*] .... ASSTSAS
Association pour la Sante et la Securite du Travail, Secteur Affaires Sociales, Centre de Documentation, Montreal, PQ, Canada [*Library symbol Library of Congress*] (LCLS) .... CaQMASSAS
Association pour la Sante Publique du Quebec [*Quebec Public Health Association*] (AC) .... ASPQ
Association pour la Solidarite Franco-Algerienne [*Association for Franco-Algerian Solidarity*] [*French*] (AF) .... ASFA
Association pour l'Anthropologie Physique au Canada [*Association for Physical Anthropology in Canada*] .... AAPC
Association pour l'Avancement de la Micro-Informatique [*Association for the Advancement of Micro-Information*] [*Canada*] .... AMIQ
Association pour l'Avancement des Etudes Scandinaves au Canada [*Association for the Advancement of Scandinavian Studies in Canada - AASSC*] .... AAESC
Association pour l'Avancement des Sciences et des Techniques de la Documentation [*Acronym is now organization's official name*] .... ASTED
Association pour l'Avancement en Afrique des Sciences de l'Agriculture [*Association for the Advancement of Agricultural Sciences in Africa*] [*Addis Ababa, Ethiopia*] .... AAASA
Association pour le Developpement de la Riziculture en Afrique de l'Ouest [*West Africa Rice Development Association - WARDA*] (EAIO) .... ADRAO
Association pour le Developpement de l'Administration de l'Education [*Association for the Development of Educational Administration*] [*Canada*] .... ADAE
Association pour le Developpement de l'Audiovisuel et de la Technologie en Education [*Canada*] .... ADATE
Association pour le Developpement de l'Enseignement Technique d'Outre-Mer [*Association for the Development of Overseas Technical Education*] [*French*] (AF) .... ADETOM
Association pour le Developpement des Oeuvres Sociales d'Outre-Mer [*Association for the Development of Social Welfare Projects Overseas*] [*French*] (AF) .... ADOSOM
Association pour le Developpement du Tourisme International [*Louveciennes, France*] (EAIO) .... ADTI
Association pour le Rayonnement de l'Opera de Paris [*France*] .... AROP
Association pour le Retablissement des Institutions et Oeuvres Israelites en France (EA) .... ARIF
Association pour le Socialisme au Gabon [*Political party*] (EY) .... APSG
Association pour le Volontariat a l'Acte Gratuit en Europe [*Association for Voluntary Action in Europe - AVAE*] (EAIO) .... AVE
Association pour l'Education Interculturelle du Quebec [*Quebec Association for Intercultural Education*] (AC) .... APEIQ
Association pour l'Education Permanente dan les Universites du Canada (AC) .... AEPUC
Association pour l'Enseignement Medical en Europe [*Association for Medical Education in Europe - AMEE*] (EA) .... AEME
Association pour l'Enseignement Social en Afrique [*Association for Social Work Education in Africa - ASWEA*] (EAIO) .... AESA
Association pour les Etudes sur la Radio-Television Canadienne [*Association for the Study of Canadian Radio and Television - ASCRT*] .... AERTC
Association pour les Recherches sur les Parodontopathies [*International Association for Research in Paradentosis*] .... ARPA
Association pour l'Etude des Etats Proches de la Mort [*International Association for Near-Death Studies*] (EAIO) .... AEEPM
Association pour l'Etude des Langues Juives [*Association for the Study of Jewish Languages*] (EAIO) .... AELJ
Association pour l'Etude des Problemes d'Outre-Mer [*Association for the Study of Overseas Problems*] [*French*] (AF) .... AEPOM
Association pour l'Etude du Developpement International [*Association for the Study of International Development ASID*] [*Canada*] .... AEDI
Association pour l'Etude Taxonomique de la Flore d'Afrique Tropicale [*Association for the Taxonomic Study of Tropical African Flora*] [*French*] (AF) .... AETFAT
Association pour l'Histoire de la Science et de la Technologies au Canada (AC) .... AHSTC
Association pour l'Union Monetaire de l'Europe [*Association for the Monetary Union of Europe*] [*France*] (EAIO) .... AUME
Association Professionnelle Catholique des Voyageurs de Commerce du Canada [*Catholic Professional Association of Commercial Representatives of Canada*] .... APCV
Association Professionnelle de Mesure en Education [*Professional Association of Educational Measures*] [*Canada*] .... APME
Association Professionnelle des Aides Pedagogiques Individuels [*Professional Association of Individual Educational Assistants*] [*Canada*] .... APAPI
Association Professionnelle des Criminologues du Quebec (AC) .... APCQ
Association Professionnelle des Enseignants de Technologie du Quebec (AC) .... APETQ
Association Professionnelle des Enseignants et Enseignantes en Commerce (AC) .... APEC
Association Professionnelle des Geographes du Quebec (AC) .... APGQ
Association Professionnelle des Infirmieres et Infirmiers Cadres du Quebec (AC) .... APIICQ
Association Professionnelle des Ingenieurs du Gouvernement du Quebec [*Association of Professional Engineers of the Government of Quebec*] (AC) .... APIGQ
Association Professionnelle des Meuniers du Quebec [*Quebec Feed Manufacturer's Association*] (AC) .... APMQ
Association Professionnelle des Nettoyeurs et Buandiers du Quebec (AC) .... APNB
Association Professionnelle des Pharmaciens Salaries du Quebec (AC) .... APPSQ
Association Professionnelle des Techniciens en Documentation du Quebec (AC) .... APTDQ
Association Professionnelle des Technologues Diplomes en Electrophysiologie Medicale (AC) .... APTDEPM
Association Professionnelle Internationale des Medicins [*International Professional Association of Physicians*] .... APIM
Association Provinciale des Constructeurs d'Habitations du Quebec Inc. [*Provincial Home Builders Association of Quebec Inc.*] (AC) .... APCHQ
Association Provinciale des Parents Fransaskois [*Fransaskois Parents Association*] (AC) .... APPF
Association Quebec Solaire (AC) .... AQS
Association Quebec-France (AC) .... AQF
Association Quebecoise de Canoe-Kayak de Vitesse (AC) .... AQCKV
Association Quebecoise de la Fibrose Kystique [*Quebec Cystic Fibrosis Association*] (AC) .... AGFK
Association Quebecoise de la Qualite (AC) .... AQQ
Association Quebecoise de l'Industrie de la Peche [*Quebec Fish Processor Association*] (AC) .... AQIP
Association Quebecoise de l'Industrie de la Peinture (AC) .... AQIP
Association Quebecoise de l'Industrie du Nautisme [*Quebec Marine Trades Association*] (AC) .... AQIN
Association Quebecoise de Loisir pour Personnes Handicapees [*Quebec Leisure Association for Handicapped Persons*] (AC) .... AQLPH

Association Quebecoise de Lutte Contre la Pollution Atmospherique (AC) .... AQLPA

Association Quebecoise de Pedagogie Collegiale (AC) .... AQPC

Association Quebecoise des Archivistes Medicales (AC) .... AQAM

Association Quebecoise des Auteurs Dramatiques (AC) .... AQAD

Association Quebecoise des Consommateurs Industriels d'Electricite (AC) .... AQCIE

Association Quebecoise des Critiques de Cinema (AC) .... AQCC

Association Quebecoise des Critiques de Theatre (AC) .... AQCT

Association Quebecoise des Directeurs et Directrices du Loisir Municipal (AC) .... AQDLM

Association Quebecoise des Ecoles de Francais (AC) .... AQEFT

Association Quebecoise des Editeurs de Magazines (AC) .... AQEM

Association Quebecoise des Educateurs du Primaire (AC) .... AQEP

Association Quebecoise des Enseignants de Francais Langue Seconde [Quebec Association of Teachers of French as a Second Language] (AC) .... AQUEFLS

Association Quebecoise des Enterprises Adaptees (AC) .... AQEA

Association Quebecoise des Fabricants de l'Industrie Medicale (AC) .... AQFIM

Association Quebecoise des Marionnettistes (AC) .... AQM

Association Quebecoise des Organismes de Co-operation Internationale [Canada] (CROSS) .... AQOCI

Association Quebecoise des Personnes de Petite Taille (AC) .... AQPPT

Association Quebecoise des Presses Universitaires (AC) .... AQPU

Association Quebecoise des Professeurs de Francais (AC) .... AQPF

Association Quebecoise des Professionnels de la Philatelie (AC) .... AQPP

Association Quebecoise des Realisateurs et Realisatrices de Cinema et de Television (AC) .... AQRRCT

Association Quebecoise des Soins Palliatifs (AC) .... AQSP

Association Quebecoise des Sports en Fauteuil Roulants (AC) .... AQSFR

Association Quebecoise des Techniques de l'Eau [Canada] (ASF) .... AQTE

Association Quebecoise des Transporteurs Aeriens (AC) .... AQTA

Association Quebecoise des Utilisateurs de l'Ordinateur au Primaire et au Secondaire (AC) .... AQUOPS

Association Quebecoise d'Etudes Americaines (AC) .... AQEA

Association Quebecoise d'Information Scolaire et Professionnelle (AC) .... AQISEP

Association Quebecoise d'Interpretation du Patrimoine (AC) .... AQIP

Association Quebecoise du Personnel de Direction des Ecoles (AC) .... AQPDE

Association Quebecoise du Personnes de Direction des Ecoles (AC) .... AQPPT

Association Quebecoise du Propane (AC) .... AQP

Association Quebecoise du Theatre Amateur Inc. (AC) .... AQTA

Association Quebecoise du Transport et des Routes Inc. (AC) .... AQTR

Association Quebecoise Plaidoyer-Victimes (AC) .... PV

Association Quebecoise pour la Defense des Droits des Retraites et des Pre-Retraites (AC) .... AQDR

Association Quebecoise pour la Maitrise de l'Energie (AC) .... AQME

Association Quebecoise pour le Patrimoine Industriel (AC) .... AQPI

Association Quebecoise pour les Troubles d'Apprentissage (AC) .... AQETA

Association Quebecoise pour les Troubles d'Apprentissage (AC) .... LDAQ

Association Referral Information Service .... ARIS

Association Regionale Caraibeenne des Infirmieres [Martinique] (EAIO) .... ARCI

Association Resource Institute [Commercial firm] (EA) .... ARI

Association Reunion Departement Francais [Association for Reunion as a French Department] [Political party] (PPW) .... ARDF

Association Scientifique de l'Industrie Europeenne du Talc [Scientific Association of European Talc Industry] (EAIO) .... EUROTALC

Association Scientifique et Technique pour la Recherche en Informatique Documentaire [Scientific and Technical Association for Research in Documentary Information] [Belgium] [Information service or system] .... ASTRID

Association Scientifique Europeenne pour la Prevision Economique a Moyen et LongTerme [European Scientific Association for Medium and Long-Term Economic Forecasts] .... ASEPELT

Association Scientifique Internationale du Cafe [International Scientific Association of Coffee] (EAIO) .... ASIC

Association Sectorielle de Fabrication d'Equipement de Transport et de Machines,St.-Leonard, Quebec [Library symbol National Library of Canada] (NLC) .... OSLEAS

Association Sectorielle, Fabrication d'Equipement de Transport et de Machines (AC) .... ASFETM

Association Social-Democrate du Cameroun [Political party] (EY) .... ASDC

Association Stomatologique Internationale [International Stomatological Association] .... ASI

Association Suisse d'Usagers de Telecommunications [Swiss Association of Telecommunications Users] [Zurich] (TSSD) .... ASUT

Association Technique de l'Importation Charbonniere (EA) .... ATIC

Association Technique de l'Industrie des Liants Hydrauliques [Technical Association for the Hydraulic Binders Industry] (IID) .... ATILH

Association Technique du Tourisme [Tourism Technique Association] [Canada] .... ATT

Association Technique Internationale des Bois Tropicaux [International Technical Tropical Timber Association] (EAIO) .... ATIBT

Association to Advance Ethical Hypnosis .... AAEH

Association to Combat Huntington's Chorea [British] (EAIO) .... ACHC

Association to Remind Husbands to Remember Birthdays and Anniversaries [Probably mythical] .... ATRHTRBAA

Association to Repeal Abortion Laws (EA) .... ARAL

Association to Resource Co-Operative Housing [Australia] .... ATRCH

Association to Unite the Democracies (EA) .... AUD

Association Touristique Regionale de la Monteregie (AC) .... ATRM

Association Typographique Internationale [International Typographic Association] .... ATYPI

Association Universelle d'Aviculture Scientifique [World's Poultry Science Association - WPSA] (EAIO) .... AVI

Association Universitaire Canadienne d'Etudes Nordiques [Association of Canadian Universities for Northern Studies] .... AUCEN

Association Universitaire Interamericaine [Interamerican University Association] [France] .... AUI

Association Universitaire pour le Developpement de l'Enseignement et de la Culture en Afrique et a Madagascar [University Association for the Development of Teaching and Culture in Africa and Madagascar] [Paris, France] (AF) .... AUDECAM

Association Value [Psychometrics] .... AV

Association Vocanologique Europeenne [European Volcanological Association] [Paris, France] (EAIO) .... LAVE

Association Zen Internationale [International Zen Association - IZA] (EAIO) .... AZI

Associational Fluency [Personality research] [Psychology] .... AF

Associations Canadienne pour l'Education Pastorale (AC) .... ACEP

Associations Council of the National Association of Manufacturers (EA) .... ACNAM

Associations des Industries du Poisson de la CEE [Association of the Fish Industries of the European Economic Community] .... AIPCEE

Associations' Publications in Print [Database] [R. R. Bowker Co.] [Information service or system] (CRD) .... APIP

Associations Touristiques Regionales Associees du Quebec [Quebec Regional Tourist Associations Inc.] .... ATRAQ

Association-Sensation [Psychology] (BARN) .... AS

Association-Storing Processor [Computer science] .... ASP

Associative Array Processor (MCD) .... AAP

Associative Communication Multiplexer .... ACM

Associative Computer Device .... ACD

Associative Content Retrieval Network [A. D. Little, Inc.] [Information service or system] .... ACORN

Associative Crosspoint Processor (MHDI) .... AXP

Associative File Processors (NITA) .... AFP

Associative Index Method .... AIM

Associative Information Processing Unit (PDAA) .... AIPU

Associative Interactive Dictionary [for databases] [National Library of Medicine] .... AID

Associative Learning from Relative Environmental Data .... ALFRED

Associative Light Searcher (SAA) .... ALS

Associative Linear Array Processor [Computer science] .... ALAP

Associative List Selection .... ALS

Associative Memory [Computer science] .... AM

Associative Memory Address [Computer science] .... AMA

Associative Memory Array [Computer science] .... AMA

Associative Memory Computer [Computer science] .... AMC

Associative Memory Device [Computer science] (DIT) .... AMD

Associative Memory Organizing System .... AMOS

Associative Memory Processor [Computer science] (BUR) .... AMP

Associative Memory System [Computer science] (DIT) .... AMS

Associative Output Control Unit [Computer science] .... AOCU

Associative Output Unit [Computer science] .... AOU

Associative Parallel Processor [Computer science] .... APP

Associative Principle for Addition [Mathematics] .... APA

Associative Principle for Multiplication [Mathematics] .... APM

Associative Processing Element (MCD) .... APE

Associative Processor [Computer science] (BUR) .... AP

Associative Processor [Computer science] (MCD) .... ASPRO

Associative Processor Computer System .... APCS

Associative Processor Control [Computer science] .... APC

Associative Processor Microelectronic Element .... APME

Associative Processor Programming Language Evaluation .... APPLE

Associative Programming Language [Computer science] (BUR) .... APL

Associative Push Down Memory [Computer science] (MHDB) .... APDM

Associative Read-Only Memory [Computer science] (IAA) .... AROM

Associative Register [Computer science] .... AR

Associative Registers for Generalized User Switching [Computer typesetting system] .... ARGUS

Associative String Processor (MCD) .... ASP

Associative Structure Computer (BUR) .... ASC

Associative Structures Package (BUR) .... ASP

Associative Surface Ionization [Organic chemistry] .... ASI

Associative Visual Cortex [Anatomy] .... AVC

Associaton for Responsible Communication (AC) .... ARC

Associaton of Commissioned Officers [Marine science] (OSRA) .... ACO

Associazione degli Industriali delle Conserve Animali [Meat Products Manufacturers Association] [Italy] (EY) .... AICA

Associazione Generale Italiana dello Spettacolo [General Italian Entertainments Association] [Italy] (EY) .... AGIS

Associazione Internazionale dei Professori d'Italiano [International Association of Teachers of Italian] (EAIO) .... AIPI

Associazione Internazionale di Archeologia Classica [International Association for Classical Archaeology - IACA] (EAIO) .... AIAC

Associazione Internazionale Mosaicisti Contemporanei [International Association of Contemporary Mosaicists] (EAIO) .... AIMC

Associazione Internazionale per gli Studi di Lingua e Letteratura Italiane [International Association for the Study of the Italian Language and Literature - IASILL] (EAIO) .... AISLLI

Associazione Italiana dei Fornitori e Distributori di Informazione Telematica [Italian Association for the Production and Distribution of Online Information] [Rome] [Information service or system] (IID) .... AFDIT

Associazione Italiana di Studi Canadesi [Italian Association of Canadian Studies] .... AISC

Associazione Italiana Industriali Prodotti Alimentari [Food manufacturers association] [Italy] (EY) .... AIIPA

Associazione Italiana Manufatture Ombrelli [Umbrella manufacturers association] [Italy] (EY) .... AIMO

Associazione Italiana Manufatturieri Pelli-Cuoio e Succedanei [*Leather and Imitation Skins Association*] [*Italy*] (EY) .... AIMPES
Associazione Italiana Pellicceria [*Furriers association*] [*Italy*] (EY) .... AIP
Associazione Italiana per il Calcolo Automatico [*Italian Association for Automatic Data Processing*] .... AICA
Associazione Italiana per la Documentazione Avanzata [*Italian Association forAdvanced Documentation*] [*Information service or system*] (IID) .... AIDA
Associazione Italiana per la Documentazione e l'Informazione [*Italian Association for Documentation and Information*] (NITA) .... AIDI
Associazione la Nostra Famiglia [*Ponte Lambro, Italy*] (EAIO) .... ANF
Associazione Nazionale Ex-Deportati Politici nei Campi Nazisti [*National Association of Political Ex-Deportees of the Nazi Camps*] [*Italy Political party*] (EAIO) .... ANED
Associazione Nazionalista Italiana [*Italian Nationalist Association*] [*Political party*] (PPE) .... ANI
Associes Benevoles Qualifies au Service des Jeunes (AC) .... ABQSJ
Associometrics Data Management System (IEEE) .... ADAM
Associometrics Remote Terminal Inquiry Control System (IEEE) .... ARTIC
Associu di Patrioti Corsi [*Association of Corsican Patriots*] [*France Political party*] (PPE) .... APC
Assort (MSA) .... ASRT
Assort .... ASST
Assorted (ROG) .... ASSD
Assorted .... ASSTD
Assortment .... ASMT
Assortment [*Business term*] .... ASSMT
Assortment .... AT
Assosa [*Ethiopia*] [*ICAO location identifier*] (ICLI) .... HASO
Assumed .... ASD
Assumed (FAAC) .... ASMD
Assumed Investment Return [*Business term*] (DICI) .... AIR
Assumed Latitude [*Navigation*] .... AL
Assumed Mean .... AM
Assumed Position [*Navigation*] .... AP
Assumpsit [*Legal shorthand*] (LWAP) .... ASSPT
Assumption .... ASSMPTN
Assumption College (GAGS) .... Assump C
Assumption College, Worcester, MA [*OCLC symbol*] (OCLC) .... AZM
Assumption College, Worcester, MA [*Library symbol Library of Congress*] (LCLS) .... MWAC
Assumption Guild (EA) .... AG
Assumption High School, East St. Louis, IL [*Library symbol Library of Congress*] (LCLS) .... IEsAHS
Assumption of Control Message [*Aviation*] .... AOC
Assumption of Moses [*Apocalyptic book*] .... ASMP M
Assumption of Moses (Pseudepigrapha) (BJA) .... AssMos
Assumption Parish Library, Napoleonville, LA [*Library symbol Library of Congress*] (LCLS) .... LNapA
Assumption-Based Truth Maintenance System [*Philosophy*] .... ATMS
Assumptionists (TOCD) .... AA
Assumptionists (TOCD) .... aaa
Assurance [*Insurance*] [*French*] (ILCA) .... Ass
Assurance [*Insurance*] [*French*] .... Assce
Assurance .... ASSNCE
Assurance .... Assur
Assurance .... ASSURNC
Assurance and Stabilization Trends for Reliability by Analysis of Lots (MHDI) .... ASTRAIL
Assurance Control Economics System (MUGU) .... ACES
Assurance Engineering [*or Effectiveness*] Division [*Military*] (DNAB) .... AED
Assurance Engineering Field Facility (DNAB) .... AEFF
Assurance Medical Society [*British*] .... AMS
Assurance Problem .... AP
Assurance sur la Vie [*Life Insurance*] [*French*] .... ASLV
Assurances Generales de France .... AGF
Assurbanipal [*King of ancient Assyria*] (BJA) .... Assurb
Assure .... ASSUR
Assure Competitive Transportation [*Truckers' lobby*] .... ACT
Assure Contre l'Incendie [*Insured Against Fire*] [*French*] .... ACI
Assured (ROG) .... ASSD
Assured Crew Return Vehicle [*Aerospace*] .... ACRV
Assured Depot Task .... ADT
Assured Destruction [*Capability*] [*of missiles*] .... AD
Assured Destruction Force [*Military*] .... ADF
Assured Field Shop Task .... AFST
Assured Intermediate Task (MCD) .... AIT
Assurex International (EA) .... AI
Assyria .... ASS
Assyria .... ASSYR
Assyrian and Babylonian Letters Belonging to the Kouyunjik Collection(s) of the British Museum [*A publication*] (BJA) .... ABL
Assyrian and Babylonian Religious Texts [*A publication*] (BJA) .... ABRT
Assyrian Australian Association .... AAA
Assyrian Medical Texts [*A publication*] (BJA) .... AMT
Assyrian Personal Names [*A publication*] (BJA) .... APN
Assyrische Rechtsurkunden [*A publication*] (BJA) .... ARu
AST/Quadram/Ashton-Tate Enhanced Memory Specification [*Quadram*] [*Norcross, GA*] [*Computer science*] .... AQA EMS
AST Research [*NASDAQ symbol*] (TTSB) .... ASTA
AST Research, Inc. [*Associated Press*] (SAG) .... AST
AST Research, Inc. [*NASDAQ symbol*] (NQ) .... ASTA
Asta Funding, Inc. [*NASDAQ symbol*] (SAG) .... ASFI
Asta Funding, Inc. [*Associated Press*] (SAG) .... AstaFd
Asta Werke AG [*Germany*] [*Research code symbol*] .... A
Asta Werke AG [*Germany*] [*Research code symbol*] .... P

Astable (MSA) .... ASTB
Astable Blocking Oscillator .... ABO
Astable Multivibrator .... AMV
Astara [*Iran*] [*ICAO location identifier*] (ICLI) .... OIGA
Astatine [*Chemical element*] .... At
Astea International, Inc. [*Associated Press*] (SAG) .... Astea
Astea International, Inc. [*NASDAQ symbol*] (SAG) .... ATEA
Astea Intl. [*NASDAQ symbol*] (TTSB) .... ATEA
Astec Industries [*NASDAQ symbol*] (TTSB) .... ASTE
Astec Industries, Inc. [*NASDAQ symbol*] (NQ) .... ASTE
Astec Industries, Inc. [*Associated Press*] (SAG) .... Astec
Astemizole [*Pharmacology*] .... AST
Aster Growth with Aster [*Ecology*] .... AA
Aster Growth with Brown Sedge [*Ecology*] .... AB
Aster Yellows [*A plant disease*] .... AY
Asterism (DGA) .... ASTM
Astern .... ASTN
Astern Flag [*Navy British*] .... AT
Asteroid Belt Probe .... ABP
Asteroid Meteoroid Detector .... AMD
Asterriquinone [*Antineoplastic drug*] .... ARQ
Asthenopia [*Ophthalmology*] [*Medicine*] .... ASTH
Asthma and Allergic Disease Center [*Department of Health and Human Services*] (GRD) .... AADC
Asthma and Allergy Foundation of America (EA) .... A & AFA
Asthma and Allergy Foundation of America (PAZ) .... AAFA
Asthma Care Association of America [*Defunct*] (EA) .... ACAA
Asthma Care Training (MEDA) .... ACT
Asthma Research Council [*British*] .... ARC
Asthma Rhinitis [*Immunology*] .... AR
Asthma Society of Canada [*Societe Canadienne de l'Asthme*] (AC) .... ASC
Asthmatic Bronchitis [*Medicine*] (ADA) .... AB
Asthmatic Children's Foundation of New York (EA) .... ACFNY
ASTIA [*Armed Services Technical Information Agency*] **Document** .... AD
ASTIA [*Armed Services Technical Information Agency*] **Report Bibliography** (MCD) .... ARB
Astigmatic Spectral Line .... ASL
Astigmatism [*Also, Ast*] [*Ophthalmology*] .... As
Astigmatism [*Also, As*] [*Ophthalmology*] .... Ast
Astigmatism [*Electronics*] .... ASTIG
Astigmatism [*Ophthalmology*] (DAVI) .... Astigm
Astigmatism, Hypermetropic [*Also, AsH*] [*Ophthalmology*] .... AH
Astigmatism, Hypermetropic [*Also, AH*] [*Ophthalmology*] .... AsH
Astigmatism, Myopic [*Also, AsM*] [*Ophthalmology*] .... AM
Astigmatism, Myopic [*Also, AM*] [*Ophthalmology*] .... AsM
Aston Dark Space [*Physics*] .... ADS
Aston Martin Owners Club (EA) .... AMOC
Aston Martin Racing [*British*] .... AMR
Aston Resources Ltd. [*Vancouver Stock Exchange symbol*] .... ASU
Aston Whole Number [*Chemistry*] .... AWN
Aston's Entries [*1673*] [*A publication*] (DLA) .... Ast Ent
Astor Home for Children, Rhinebeck, NY [*Library symbol Library of Congress*] (LCLS) .... NRhbA
Astor Library, Astoria, OR [*Library symbol Library of Congress*] (LCLS) .... OrAst
Astoria [*Oregon*] [*Airport symbol Obsolete*] (OAG) .... AST
Astoria Financial [*NASDAQ symbol*] (SAG) .... ASFC
Astoria Financial [*Associated Press*] (SAG) .... AstoriaF
Astoria, OR [*AM radio station call letters*] .... KAST
Astoria, OR [*FM radio station call letters*] .... KAST-FM
Astoria, OR [*FM radio station call letters*] .... KMUN
Astoria, OR [*AM radio station call letters*] .... KVAS
Astoria, OR [*Location identifier FAA*] (FAAL) .... NMW
Astoria, OR [*Location identifier FAA*] (FAAL) .... PEN
Astorville Branch, East Ferris Township Public Library, Ontario [*Library symbol National Library of Canada*] (NLC) .... OAEFT
Astqa Funding [*NASDAQ symbol*] (TTSB) .... ASFI
Astra AB [*NYSE symbol*] (SAG) .... A
Astra AB [*NYSE symbol*] (SAG) .... AAB
Astra AB [*Associated Press*] (SAG) .... AstraA
Astra AB [*Associated Press*] (SAG) .... AstraB
Astra AB'A'ADS [*NYSE symbol*] (TTSB) .... A
Astra AB'B' ADS [*NYSE symbol*] (TTSB) .... AAB
ASTRA Compania Argentina [*BA Symbol*] (TTSB) .... AST.BA
Astra Pharmaceuticals Canada Ltd., Mississauga, Ontario [*Library symbol National Library of Canada*] (NLC) .... OMAPC
Astragal (MSA) .... A
A-Strain Spontaneous Leukemia [*Type of cell line*] .... ASL
Astrakhan [*Former USSR*] [*FAA designator*] (FAAC) .... ASZ
Astral Aviation, Inc. d/b/a Skyway Airlines [*FAA designator*] (FAAC) .... SYX
Astral Bellevue Pathe, Inc. [*Toronto Stock Exchange symbol*] .... ACM
Astrida [*Rwanda*] [*Seismograph station code, US Geological Survey Closed*] (SEIS) .... AST
Astro Air International, Inc. [*Philippines*] [*ICAO designator*] (FAAC) .... AAP
Astro Communications System [*NASA*] (KSC) .... ACS
Astro Guidance Digital Computer (IEEE) .... AGDIC
Astro Launch Circuit [*NASA*] (KSC) .... ALC
Astro Musical Research (EA) .... AMR
Astro Research Corp. (KSC) .... ARC
ASTRO Satellite Operations Center (MCD) .... ASOC
Astro Sciences Corp. [*NASDAQ symbol*] (SAG) .... AOSC
Astro Sciences Corp. [*Associated Press*] (SAG) .... AstroSci
Astro Systems Research Laboratory (SAA) .... ASRL
Astrocyte-Conditioned Medium [*Analytical biochemistry*] .... ACM
Astrodigital Doppler Speedometer [*Electronics*] .... ADDS
Astrodynamical Report (SAA) .... AR

Astro-Electronics Division [*RCA*] .... AED
Astro-Geodetic Geoid Data Station Spacing and Distribution (SAA) .... AGGDSSD
Astrogeodetic World Datum .... AWD
Astrogeophysical Transmission Network [*Air Force's Air Weather Service Teletypewriter circuit*] .... ATN
Astrograph Mean Time [*Navigation*] .... AMT
Astroinertial Guidance Equipment .... AIGE
Astrologers' Guild of America (EA) .... AGA
Astrologers International [*Defunct*] (EA) .... AI
Astrological Association (EAIO) .... AA
Astrology .... AST
Astrology [*or Astrologer*] .... ASTROL
Astrology Encyclopedia [*A publication*] .... AE
Astrology Information Centre (AC) .... AIC
Astromechanics Research Division (SAA) .... ARD
Astro-Med [*NASDAQ symbol*] (TTSB) .... ALOT
Astro-Med, Inc. [*NASDAQ symbol*] (NQ) .... ALOT
Astro-Med, Inc. [*Associated Press*] (SAG) .... AstroM
Astrometric Interferometry Mission [*to determine locations of stars*] (ECON) .... AIM
Astrometric Telescope Facility (SSD) .... ATF
Astronaut Activities Office [*NASA*] (KSC) .... AAO
Astronaut Communications (MCD) .... ASTROCOM
Astronaut Control Console [*NASA*] .... ACC
Astronaut Control Panel [*NASA*] (NASA) .... ACP
Astronaut Life Support Assembly [*NASA*] .... ALSA
Astronaut Life Support Equipment [*NASA*] (MCD) .... ALSE
Astronaut Maneuvering Equipment [*NASA*] (MCD) .... AME
Astronaut Maneuvering Research Vehicle [*NASA*] .... AMRV
Astronaut Maneuvering Unit [*Gemini*] [*NASA*] .... AMU
Astronaut Operations Requirement Document [*NASA*] (KSC) .... AORD
Astronaut Preference Kit [*NASA*] .... APK
Astronaut Preference Test [*NASA*] (NASA) .... APT
Astronaut Rescue Air Pack [*NASA*] (KSC) .... ARAP
Astronaut Survival Kit [*NASA*] .... ASK
Astronaut Work Station [*NASA*] .... AWS
Astronaut-Actuated Abort [*NASA*] (MCD) .... AAA
Astronautic .... ASTRNTC
Astronautical (MSA) .... ASNAUT
Astronautical .... ASTRO
Astronautical Defensive-Offensive System .... ADOS
Astronautical Research and Development Agency (SAA) .... ARDA
Astronautical Research Laboratory (SAA) .... ARL
Astronautical Society of Canada .... ASC
Astronautics (DD) .... Astro
Astronautics and Space (KSC) .... ASTROSPACE
Astronautics Notice (AAG) .... AN
Astronautics Standard Practice (AAG) .... ASP
Astronautics Support Center .... ASC
Astronautics Test Procedures (AAG) .... ATP
Astronauts' Wives Club .... AWC
Astronavigation (NATG) .... AN
Astronics Corp. [*Associated Press*] (SAG) .... Astron
Astronics Corp. [*NASDAQ symbol*] (NQ) .... ATRO
Astronomer [*or Astronomy*] .... ASTRON
Astronomiae Professor Greshamii [*Professor of Astronomy at Gresham College, London*] .... APG
Astronomic (AABC) .... ASTN
Astronomical .... Astro
Astronomical and Space Techniques for Research on the Atmosphere [*National Science Foundation project*] .... ASTRA
Astronomical, Atmospheric, Earth, and Ocean Sciences [*National Science Foundation*] (GRD) .... AAEO
Astronomical Constant .... AC
Astronomical Explorer Satellite .... AES
Astronomical Great Circle Course .... ACC
Astronomical Guidance System for Air Navigation (OA) .... AGSAN
Astronomical Image Processing System .... AIPS
Astronomical Information Processing System [*Computer program*] .... AIPS
Astronomical League (EA) .... AL
Astronomical Netherlands Satellite .... ANS
Astronomical Observatory .... AO
Astronomical Observatory Satellite (KSC) .... AOS
Astronomical Radio Interferometric Earth Survey [*or Surveying*] [*NASA*] .... ARIES
Astronomical Society of the Pacific (EA) .... ASP
Astronomical Space Telescope Research Assembly (MCD) .... ASTRA
Astronomical Studies of Extrasolar Planetary Systems [*NASA*] .... ASEPS
Astronomical Telescope Orientation Mount [*NASA*] .... ATOM
Astronomical Time .... AT
Astronomical Time Switch .... ATS
Astronomical Unit [*Equal to average distance from earth to sun*] .... AU
Astronomische Einheit [*Astronomical Unit*] [*German*] .... AE
Astronomy (ROG) .... AS
Astronomy (NASA) .... AST
Astronomy .... ASTR
Astronomy [*A publication*] (BRI) .... Astron
Astronomy Information Service [*Space Telescope Science Institute*] [*Information service or system*] (IID) .... ASTIS
Astronomy Institute Potsdam .... AIP
Astronomy Missions Board [*NASA*] .... AMB
Astronomy Space and Radio Board [*Science and Engineering Research Council*] (PDAA) .... ASR
Astronomy Spacelab Payloads [*NASA*] (MCD) .... ASP
Astronomy Study Unit [*American Topical Association*] (EA) .... ASU
Astronomy Unit [*Later, ASU*] [*American Topical Association*] (EA) .... AU
Astronuclear Laboratory [*Westinghouse Electric Corp.*] (MCD) .... AL
Astrophysical Observatory [*Smithsonian Museum*] .... APO
Astrophysical Research Consortium .... ARC
Astrophysics Data System .... ADS
Astrophysics Payload [*NASA*] (MCD) .... APP
Astrophysics Transient Explorer .... ATREX
Astropower Laboratory [*Douglas Aircraft Corp.*] (MCD) .... AL
Astro-Psychology Institute (EA) .... API
Astro-Space Lab, Inc. (MCD) .... ASL
Astrosurveillance Science Laboratory .... ASL
Astrosystems, Inc. [*NASDAQ symbol*] (NQ) .... ASTR
Astrosystems, Inc. [*Associated Press*] (SAG) .... Astrosy
Astrotech International Corp. [*AMEX symbol*] (SPSG) .... AIX
Astrotech International Corp. [*Associated Press*] (SAG) .... Astrotc
Astrotech Intl. [*AMEX symbol*] (TTSB) .... AIX
Astruxius [*Authority cited in pre-1607 legal work*] (DSA) .... Astrux
Asuncion [*Paraguay*] [*Airport symbol*] (OAG) .... ASU
Asuncion [*Paraguay*] [*ICAO location identifier*] (ICLI) .... SGFA
Asuncion/Presidente General Stroessner [*Paraguay*] [*ICAO location identifier*] (ICLI) .... SGAS
ASV, Inc. [*Associated Press*] (SAG) .... ASV Inc
ASV, Inc. [*NASDAQ symbol*] (SAG) .... ASVI
ASW [*Antisubmarine Warfare*] **Acoustic Deception Device** (MCD) .... ADDS
ASW [*Antisubmarine Warfare*] **Coordinator** (MCD) .... ASWC
ASW [*Antisubmarine Warfare*] **Formatted Message Reporting System** .... AFMRS
ASW [*Antisubmarine Warfare*], Gun, and Missile Escort Ship [*Navy symbol*] .... DX/DXG
ASW [*Antisubmarine Warfare*] **Module** [*Navy*] .... ASWM
ASW [*Antisubmarine Warfare*] **Submarine System Evaluation Technique**.... ASSET
ASW [*Antisubmarine Warfare*] **Support Aircraft Carrier** [*Navy symbol*] .... CVS
ASW [*Antisubmarine Warfare*] **Tactical Center Systems** [*Data or Support*] (MCD) .... ASTACS
ASW [*Antisubmarine Warfare*] **Torpedo-Carrying Helicopter** (MCD) .... ATCH
Aswan [*Egypt*] [*Airport symbol*] (OAG) .... ASW
Aswan [*Egypt*] [*ICAO location identifier*] (ICLI) .... HESN
ASWEPS [*Antisubmarine Warfare Environmental Prediction Service*] **Submarine Oceanographic Digital Data System** .... ASODDS
Asylum .... ASY
Asylum .... ASYL
Asymmetric .... A
Asymmetric [*Chemistry*] .... as
Asymmetric (MSA) .... ASYM
Asymmetric Aminohydroxylation [*Organic chemistry*] .... AA
Asymmetric Balance (USDC) .... AB
Asymmetric Balance [*Marine science*] (OSRA) .... AB
Asymmetric Data Exchange .... ADX
Asymmetric Digital Subscriber Line [*Telecommunications*] .... ADSL
Asymmetric Dihydroxylation [*Organic chemistry*] .... AD
Asymmetric Epoxidation [*Organic chemistry*] .... AE
Asymmetric Illumination Contrast [*Microscopy*] .... AIC
Asymmetric Multiprocessing [*Computer science*] (PCM) .... AMP
Asymmetric Multiprocessing (CDE) .... ASMP
Asymmetric Multiprocessing System [*IBM Corp.*] .... AMS
Asymmetric Multiprocessing System [*Electronics*] (ECII) .... ASP
Asymmetric Resonant Cavity [*Physics*] .... ARC
Asymmetric [*or Asymmetrical*] **Septal Hypertrophy** [*Medicine*] .... ASH
Asymmetric Silicon Controlled Rectifier [*Electronics*] (TEL) .... ASCR
Asymmetric Stress Analysis of Axisymmetric Solids [*Computer program*] .... ASAAS
Asymmetrical [*Chemistry*] (BARN) .... U
Asymmetrical Digital Single Line (DMAA) .... ADSL
Asymmetrical Sideband .... ASB
Asymmetrical Tonic Neck Reflex .... ATNR
Asymmetry, Border, Color, and Diameter [*Rule*] [*Dermatology*] .... ABCD
Asymmetry Factor [*Mathematics*] .... AF
Asymptomatic [*Medicine*] (MEDA) .... Asx
Asymptomatic Bacteriuria [*Medicine*] (DMAA) .... ABU
Asymptomatic Bacteriuria [*Medicine*] (PDAA) .... ASB
Asymptomatic Carotid Bruit [*Medicine*] (DMAA) .... ACB
Asymptomatic Variance .... AVAR
Asymptote [*Mathematics*] .... ASYMP
Asymptotic Conical Dipole (PDAA) .... ACD
Asymptotic Giant Branch [*Astronomy*] .... AGB
Asymptotic Relative Efficiency [*Statistics*] .... ARE
Asymptotic Standard Error [*Statistics*] .... ASE
Asymptotic Temporary Threshold Shift (PDAA) .... ATTS
Asymptotic Threshold Shift [*Hearing*] .... ATS
Asymptotically Admissible Linear Unbiased Estimator [*Statistics*] .... AALUE
Asymptotically Best Linear Estimate (PDAA) .... ABLE
Asymptotically Best Linear Unbiased Estimator [*Statistics*] .... ABLUE
Asymptotically Most Powerful Rank Test [*Statistics*] .... AMPRT
Asymptotically Pointwise Optimal (DNAB) .... APO
Asynchronous .... A
Asynchronous (MSA) .... ASYN
Asynchronous .... ASYNC
Asynchronous .... ASYNCH
Asynchronous Address Communications Systems .... AACS
Asynchronous Balanced Mode [*Computer science*] .... ABM
Asynchronous Balanced Mode Extended [*Telecommunications*] (OSI) .... ABME
Asynchronous Bipolar Pulse Length Modulation [*Electronics*] (IAA) .... ABPLM
Asynchronous Circuit Design Language [*Computer science*] (PDAA) .... ACDL
Asynchronous Communication Adapter [*Computer science*] (IAA) .... ACA
Asynchronous Communication Control Module (MHDI) .... ACM
Asynchronous Communication Element (MHDB) .... ACE
Asynchronous Communication Procedure (BUR) .... ASC

Asynchronous Communications Control	ACC
Asynchronous Communications Control Attachment	ACCA
Asynchronous Communications Interface [*Computer science*] (HGAA)	ACI
Asynchronous Communications Interface Adapter [*Computer science*] (MDG)	ACIA
Asynchronous Communications Server [*Computer science*] (IT)	ACS
Asynchronous Computer Conferencing	ACC
Asynchronous Data Channel (MCD)	ADC
Asynchronous Data Communications Channel	ADCC
Asynchronous Data Multiplexer Synchronizer	ADMS
Asynchronous Data Transceiver	ADT
Asynchronous Data Transfer [*Transmission technique*] (CDE)	ADT
Asynchronous DataLink Control [*IBM Corp.*]	ADLC
Asynchronous Digital Combiner (MCD)	ADC
Asynchronous Digital Subscriber Loop [*Computer science*]	ADSL
Asynchronous Disconnected Mode	ADM
Asynchronous Framing Technique [*Computer science*]	AFT
Asynchronous Line Control Unit [*Telecommunications*]	ALCU
Asynchronous Line Driver [*Prentice Corp.*]	ALD
Asynchronous Line Interface [*Telecommunications*]	ALI
Asynchronous Line Module	ALM
Asynchronous Line Multiplexer [*Telecommunications*]	ALM
Asynchronous Line Unit [*Telecommunications*]	ALU
Asynchronous Look-Ahead Simulator (IEEE)	ALAS
Asynchronous MODEM	AM
Asynchronous Multiline Communications Coupler [*Telecommunications*] (NITA)	AMLCC
Asynchronous Multiline Controller [*Telecommunications*]	AMLC
Asynchronous Processing Unit [*Computer science*] (NITA)	APU
Asynchronous Pulse Length Modulation [*Electronics*] (IAA)	APLM
Asynchronous Response Mode [*Computer science*]	ARM
Asynchronous Serial Interface [*Telecommunications*] (NITA)	ASI
Asynchronous Single Sideband [*Electronics*] (IAA)	ASSB
Asynchronous State Machine (IEEE)	ASM
Asynchronous Synchronous Programmable Interface [*Computer science*]	ASPI
Asynchronous Synchronous Transmitter Receiver [*Electronics*] (IAA)	ASTR
Asynchronous Task Storage [*NASA*] (NASA)	ATS
Asynchronous Terminal Adapter [*Telecommunications*]	ATA
Asynchronous Terminal Concentrator [*Telecommunications*] (TSSD)	ATC
Asynchronous Time Diversity Device (MCD)	ATDD
Asynchronous Time Division	ATD
Asynchronous Time Division Multiplexing [*Telecommunications*]	ATDM
Asynchronous Time Multiplexing (IAA)	ATM
Asynchronous Time-Division Multiplexing [*Computer science*] (IAA)	ARDM
Asynchronous Traction Motor (PDAA)	ATM
Asynchronous Transfer Mode [*Computer science*]	ATM
Asynchronous Unit Delay [*Computer science*] (IAA)	AUD
Asyst Technologies [*Commercial firm Associated Press*] (SAG)	AsystTch
Asyst Technologies [*NASDAQ symbol*] (SAG)	ASYT
Asyut [*Egypt*] [*ICAO location identifier*] (ICLI)	HEAT
At	A
At [*An altitude*] (GAVI)	AT
At a Discount	AAD
At a Later Date	ALD
At and Maintain [*Aviation*] (FAAC)	ATAM
AT & T Aviation Group [*ICAO designator*] (FAAC)	XAT
AT & T Capital Corp. [*Associated Press*] (SAG)	ATT Cap
AT & T Capital Corp. (SPSG)	TCC
AT & T College and University System [*Bedminster, NJ*] [*Telecommunications service*] (TSSD)	ACUS
AT & T Communications [*Telecommunications*] (TSSD)	ATTCOM
AT & T Information Systems [*Telecommunications*]	ATTIS
AT & T Information Systems [*Telecommunications*] (TSSD)	ATTIS
AT & T Philips Telecommunications	APT
AT & T Stock Fund [*Equity Income Fund*] [*AMEX symbol*] (SPSG)	ATF
AT & T Stock Fund (Equity Income Fund) [*Associated Press*] (SAG)	ATT Fd
AT & T Technologies, Inc., Winston-Salem, NC [*Library symbol*] [*Library of Congress*] (LCLS)	NcWsAT-R
AT & T Transfer System [*Telecommunications*]	ATS
AT & Technologies, Inc., Winston-Salem, NC [*Library symbol*] [*Library of Congress*] (LCLS)	NcWsAT
AT [*Advanced Technology*] Attachment Packet Interface (CDE)	ATAPI
At Bat [*Baseball*]	AB
At Bed Side [*Medicine*]	ABS
At Earliest Convenience [*Medicine*] (AAMN)	AEC
At Fault (DI)	af
At Gage Marks (SAA)	AGM
At Gestational Age [*Medicine*] (DAVI)	AGA
At Home	AH
At Home Series [*Baseball*]	AHS
At No Expense to the Government	ANEXGOVT
At Occupation [*An underwriting designation for an occupational accident*] [*Insurance*]	AO
At or Above [*Aviation*]	AOA
At or After (FAAC)	AOAF
At or Before (FAAC)	AOBF
At or Below [*Aviation*]	AOB
At or Below [*Constrained Altitude*] (GAVI)	B
At Own Risk [*Medicine*] (BARN)	AOR
AT Plastics [*AMEX symbol*] (TTSB)	ATJ
AT Plastics, Inc. [*Associated Press*] (SAG)	AT Plas
AT Plastics, Inc. [*AMEX symbol*] (SAG)	ATJ
At Reactor Storage [*Nuclear energy*] (NUCP)	ARS
At Risk (MAE)	AR
At Risk Period (MAE)	ARP
At Risk Provision (DICI)	ARP
At Same Time	AST
At Sight	AS
At the Center of Things [*Slang*]	ACT
At the Market [*Market order*] [*Stock exchange term*]	ATM
At the Opening [*Investment term*]	ATO
At the Rate Of (MUGU)	A/R
At the Suit Of	ATS
At the Time of Bombing [*Radiation Effects Research Foundation, Japan*]	ATB
At the Umbilicus [*Obstetrics*] (DAVI)	U/
At This Time	ATTM
At Your Service	AYS
Ata-Aerocondor Transportes Aereos Ltda. [*Portugal ICAO designator*] (FAAC)	ARD
Atacames [*Ecuador*] [*ICAO location identifier*] (ICLI)	SEAT
Atactic Polypropylene [*Organic chemistry*]	APP
Atakpame/Akpaka [*Togo*] [*ICAO location identifier*] (ICLI)	DXAK
Atalanta Sosnoff Capital Corp. [*Associated Press*] (SAG)	AtalSos
Atalanta Sosnoff Capital Corp. [*NYSE symbol*] (SPSG)	ATL
Atambua/Haliwen [*Indonesia*] [*ICAO location identifier*] (ICLI)	WRKA
Atanasoff-Berry Computer [*Early computer*]	ABC
AT&T Capital [*NYSE symbol*] (TTSB)	TCC
AT&T Capital Corp. [*NYSE symbol*] (SAG)	TOC
AT&T Corp. [*NYSE symbol*] (TTSB)	T
AT&T Global Information Solutions [*Computer science*]	AT&T GIS
AT&T Global Information Solutions [*Dayton, OH*] [*Formerly, NCR Corp.*] (CDE)	AT&T GIS
AT&T Technologies Inc., Legal Library, Greensboro, NC [*Library symbol*] [*Library of Congress*] (LCLS)	NcGAT
AT&T Technologies Inc., Technical Library, Burlington, NC [*Library symbol*] [*Library of Congress*] (LCLS)	NcBurAT
Ataq [*People's Democratic Republic of Yemen*] [*ICAO location identifier*] (ICLI)	ODAT
Atar [*Djibouti*] [*Seismograph station code, US Geological Survey*] (SEIS)	ATA
Atar [*Mauritania*] [*Airport symbol*] (OAG)	ATR
Atar [*Mauritania*] [*ICAO location identifier*] (ICLI)	GQPA
Atari Corp. [*Associated Press*] (SAG)	Atari
Atari Corp. [*AMEX symbol*] (SPSG)	ATC
Atari Users Association (EA)	AUA
Atari-Version American Standard Code for Information Interchange [*Character code*]	ATASCII
Atascadero, CA [*FM radio station call letters*]	KIQO
Atascadero State Hospital, Atascadero, CA [*Library symbol Library of Congress*] (LCLS)	CAtaH
Atauro [*East Timor*] [*ICAO location identifier*] (ICLI)	WPAT
Ataxia Telangiectasia [*Genetic disease*]	AT
Ataxia Telangiectasia Mutated [*Medicine*]	ATM
Ataxia Telangiectasia Mutated	ATM
Atbara [*Sudan*] [*Airport symbol*] (OAG)	ATB
Atbara [*Sudan*] [*ICAO location identifier*] (ICLI)	HSAT
ATC Communications [*NASDAQ symbol*] (TTSB)	ATCT
ATC Communications, Inc. [*Associated Press*] (SAG)	ATC Com
ATC Communications, Inc. [*NASDAQ symbol*] (SAG)	ATCT
ATC Environmental [*NASDAQ symbol*] (TTSB)	ATCE
ATC Environmental, Inc. [*Associated Press*] (SAG)	ATC EnC
ATC Environmental, Inc. [*Associated Press*] (SAG)	ATC Env
ATC Environmental, Inc. [*NASDAQ symbol*] (NQ)	ATCE
ATC Environmental Wrrt 'C' [*NASDAQ symbol*] (TTSB)	ATCEL
ATC Group Services, Inc. [*Associated Press*] (SAG)	ATC Grp
ATC Group Services, Inc. [*NASDAQ symbol*] (SAG)	ATCS
ATC Group Srvices, Inc. [*Associated Press*] (SAG)	ATC GrpC
ATC [*Air Training Command*] Operations Center	ATC OPSCEN
ATC [*Air Traffic Control*] Systems Command Center [*Marine science*] (OSRA)	ATCSCC
ATC [*Air Traffic Control*] Systems Command Center (USDC)	ATCSCO
ATCCS [*Army Tactical Command and Control System*] Test Bed	ATB
Atcheson's Election Cases [*England*] [*A publication*] (DLA)	Atch EC
Atchison Casting [*NASDAQ symbol*] (TTSB)	ACCX
Atchison Casting Corp. [*NASDAQ symbol*] (SAG)	ACCX
Atchison Casting Corp. [*Associated Press*] (SAG)	AtchCst
Atchison Casting Corp. [*NYSE symbol*] (SAG)	FDY
Atchison. English Navigation and Trade Reports [*A publication*] (DLA)	Atch
Atchison, KS [*Location identifier FAA*] (FAAL)	JNL
Atchison, KS [*AM radio station call letters*] (RBYB)	KAIR-AM
Atchison, KS [*AM radio station call letters*]	KERE
[*The*] Atchison, Topeka & Santa Fe Railway Co. [*Also known as Santa Fe*]	AT & SF
[*The*] Atchison, Topeka & Santa Fe Railway Co. [*Also known as Sante Fe*]	AT & SFR
[*The*] Atchison, Topeka & Santa Fe Railway Co. [*Also known as Santa Fe*] [*AAR code*]	ATSF
[*The*] Atchison, Topeka & Santa Fe Railway Co. - DF Loaders [*AAR code*]	SFRB
[*The*] Atchison, Topeka & Santa Fe Railway Co. - Refrigerator Cars [*AAR code*]	SFRD
Atco Ltd. [*Toronto Stock Exchange symbol*]	ACO
ATE Computer (MCD)	ATC
ATE Management Service Co., Inc., Cincinnati, OH [*OCLC symbol*] (OCLC)	ATE
Ateba Mines, Inc. [*Toronto Stock Exchange symbol*]	ABA
ATEC Group [*NASDAQ symbol*] (TTSB)	ATEC
ATEC Group, Inc. [*Associated Press*] (SAG)	ATEC
ATEC Group, Inc. [*NASDAQ symbol*] (SAG)	ATEC
ATEC Group, Inc. [*Associated Press*] (SAG)	ATEC Gp

ATEC Group Wrrt [*NASDAQ symbol*] (TTSB) .... ATECW
Ateitis Association of Lithuanian Catholic Intellectuals (EA) ..... AALCI
Atelier de Modelisation de l'Architecture des Plantes [*Software manufacturer*] [*Paris, France*] .... AMAP
Atelier de Production et Creation [*French fashion label*] .... APC
Atelier Parisien d'Urbanisme [*Paris Office of Urbanization*] [*France*] [*Information service or system*] (IID) .... APUR
Ateliers de Constructions Electriques de Charleroi [*SA, Belgium*] (NUCP) .... ACEC
Ateliers de Constructions Electriques de Charleroi [*Telecommunications equipment manufacturers*] [*Belgium*] (NITA) .... ACEC
Ateliers de Gestion Integree des Ressources Limitees [*Canada*] .... AGIR
Ateliers d'Ingenierie Dominion, Lachine, Quebec [*Library symbol National Library of Canada*] (NLC) .... QLAID
Ateliers et Chantiers de Bretagne [*France*] (NUCP) .... ACB
Ateliers et Chantiers de l'Afrique Equatoriale [*Equatorial Africa Shipyards*] [*Gabon*] .... ACAE
Ateneo de Manila University, Manila, Philippines [*Library symbol Library of Congress*] (LCLS) .... PiMA
Ateneo Law Journal [*A publication*] (DLA) .... Ateneo LJ
Atex Commercial Users Group (EA) .... ACUG
Atex Newspaper Users Group (EA) .... ANUG
Athabasca, AB [*AM radio station call letters*] .... CKBA
Athabasca Public Library, Alberta [*Library symbol National Library of Canada*] (NLC) .... AATH
Athabasca Public Library, Athabasca, AB, Canada [*Library symbol*] [*Library of Congress*] (LCLS) .... CaAAth
Athabasca University, Alberta [*Library symbol National Library of Canada*] (NLC) .... AEAU
Athabasca University, Edmonton, AB, Canada [*Library symbol Library of Congress*] (LCLS) .... CaAEAU
Athabasca University Library [*UTLAS symbol*] .... AUL
Athabasca University Students' Association (AC) .... AUSA
Athabaska Airways Ltd. [*Canada ICAO designator*] (FAAC) .... ABS
Athabaska Delta Community School, Fort Chipewyan, Alberta [*Library symbol National Library of Canada*] (BIB) .... AFCAS
Athabaska Gold [*Vancouver Stock Exchange symbol*] .... AHB
Athapascan [*MARC language code Library of Congress*] (LCCP) .... ath
Atharan Hazari [*Pakistan*] [*Airport symbol*] (AD) .... ARH
Atheist Association (EA) .... AA
Atheist Foundation of Australia .... AFA
Atheists United (EA) .... AU
Athena Gold Corp. [*Vancouver Stock Exchange symbol*] .... AGC
Athena Neurosciences [*NASDAQ symbol*] (SPSG) .... ATHN
Athena Neurosciences, Inc. [*Associated Press*] (SAG) .... Athena
Athenaeum of Ohio, Eugene H. Maly Library, Cincinnati, OH [*Library symbol*] [*Library of Congress*] (LCLS) .... OCAO
Athenaeum of Ohio, Norwood, OH [*OCLC symbol*] (OCLC) .... ATO
Athenaeum of Ohio, Norwood, OH [*Library symbol Library of Congress*] (LCLS) .... ONowdM
Athenaeum of Philadelphia (EA) .... PAT
Athenaeum of Philadelphia, Philadelphia, PA [*OCLC symbol*] (OCLC) .... PAT
Athenaeum of Philadelphia, Philadelphia, PA [*Library symbol Library of Congress*] (LCLS) .... PPA
Athenaeus [*First century AD*] [*Classical studies*] (OCD) .... Ath
Athenagence [*News agency*] [*Greece*] (EY) .... ANA
[*The*] Athenian Tribute Lists [*A publication*] (OCD) .... ATL
Athens [*Georgia*] [*Airport symbol*] (OAG) .... AHN
Athens [*Greece*] [*Airport symbol*] (OAG) .... ATH
Athens Air [*Greece*] [*ICAO designator*] (FAAC) .... THN
Athens, AL [*AM radio station call letters*] .... WKAC
Athens, AL [*AM radio station call letters*] .... WVNN
Athens, AL [*FM radio station call letters*] .... WZYP
Athens/Albany, OH [*Location identifier FAA*] (FAAL) .... UNI
Athens Are Technical Institute, Athens, GA [*Library symbol*] [*Library of Congress*] (LCLS) .... GAtT
Athens College, Athens, GA [*Library symbol Library of Congress*] (LCLS) .... AAthC
Athens Community Hospital, Athens, TN [*Library symbol Library of Congress*] (LCLS) .... TACH
Athens Environmental Research Laboratory [*Athens, GA*] [*Environmental Protection Agency*] (GRD) .... ERL/ATH
Athens, GA [*FM radio station call letters*] .... WALR
Athens, GA [*AM radio station call letters*] .... WGAU
Athens, GA [*Television station call letters*] .... WGTV
Athens, GA [*FM radio station call letters*] .... WMSL
Athens, GA [*FM radio station call letters*] .... WNGC
Athens, GA [*Television station call letters*] .... WNGM
Athens, GA [*AM radio station call letters*] .... WRFC
Athens, GA [*FM radio station call letters*] .... WUGA
Athens, GA [*FM radio station call letters*] .... WUOG
Athens, GA [*AM radio station call letters*] (RBYB) .... WXAG
Athens News Agency [*Greece*] .... ANA
Athens Observatory [*Greece*] [*Seismograph station code, US Geological Survey*] (SEIS) .... ATH
Athens, OH [*AM radio station call letters*] .... WATH
Athens, OH [*AM radio station call letters*] .... WOUB
Athens, OH [*FM radio station call letters*] .... WOUB-FM
Athens, OH [*Television station call letters*] .... WOUB-TV
Athens, OH [*FM radio station call letters*] .... WXTQ
Athens Regional Library, Athens, GA [*Library symbol Library of Congress*] (LCLS) .... GAt
Athens Regional Library, Athens, GA [*Library symbol*] [*Library of Congress*] (LCLS) .... GAtL
Athens, TN [*Location identifier FAA*] (FAAL) .... MMI
Athens, TN [*FM radio station call letters*] .... WJSQ

Athens, TN [*AM radio station call letters*] .... WLAR
Athens, TN [*AM radio station call letters*] .... WYXI
Athens Township Library, Athens, MI [*Library symbol Library of Congress*] (LCLS) .... MiAth
Athens, TX [*Location identifier FAA*] (FAAL) .... AHX
Athens, TX [*Location identifier FAA*] (FAAL) .... CSZ
Athens, TX [*AM radio station call letters*] .... KLVQ
Athens, TX [*Location identifier FAA*] (FAAL) .... LIQ
Athens University [*Greece*] [*Seismograph station code, US Geological Survey*] (SEIS) .... ATU
Atherectomy Imaging Device [*Medicine*] .... AID
Atherley on Marriage Settlements [*A publication*] (DLA) .... Ath Mar Set
Atherogenic Index [*By ultracentrifugation*] [*Cardiology*] (DAVI) .... AI
Atherosclerosis [*Medicine*] (MAE) .... AS
Atherosclerosis [*Medicine*] .... ATHSC
Atherosclerosis [*Cardiology*] (DAVI) .... ATS
Atherosclerosis Risk in Communities Study [*Department of Health and Human Services*] (GFGA) .... ARIC
Atherosclerotic Brain Infarction [*Medicine*] (CPH) .... ABI
Atherosclerotic Cardiovascular Disease [*Medicine*] (MAE) .... ASCVD
Atherosclerotic Heart Disease [*Cardiology*] (DAVI) .... AHD
Atherothrombotic Brain Infarction [*Medicine*] (DAVI) .... ABI
Atherton, CA [*FM radio station call letters*] .... KCEA
Athey Products [*NASDAQ symbol*] (TTSB) .... ATPC
Athey Products Corp. [*Associated Press*] (SAG) .... Athey
Athey Products Corp. [*NASDAQ symbol*] (NQ) .... ATPC
Athinai [*Greece*] [*ICAO location identifier*] (ICLI) .... LGAC
Athinai [*Greece*] [*ICAO location identifier*] (ICLI) .... LGAT
Athinai [*Greece*] [*ICAO location identifier*] (ICLI) .... LGGG
Athinaikon Praktoreion Eidiseon [*Athens News Agency*] [*Greece*] .... APE
Athlete Assistance Program [*See also PAA*] [*Canada*] .... AAP
Athlete Information Bureau [*Canada*] .... AIB
Athletes' Advisory Council [*See also CCA*] [*Canada*] .... AAC
Athletes for a Better Education .... AthBE
Athletes in Action (EA) .... AIA
Athletes United for Peace (EA) .... AUP
Athletic (ADA) .... A
Athletic (MUGU) .... ATH
Athletic .... ATHL
Athletic .... ATHL
Athletic and Recreation Federation of College Women (EA) .... ARFCW
Athletic Association .... AA
Athletic Association of Western Universities (BARN) .... AAWU
Athletic Clothing Manufacturers' Association [*British*] (BI) .... ACMA
Athletic Club [*Usually in combination with proper noun, as, DAC, Detroit Athletic Club*] .... AC
Athletic Conference of American College Women [*Later, ARFCW*] .... ACACW
Athletic Director .... AD
Athletic Equipment Managers Association (EA) .... AEMA
Athletic Footwear Association (EA) .... AFA
Athletic Footwear Council [*Later, AFA*] (EA) .... AFC
Athletic Goods Manufacturers Association [*Later, SGMA*] (EA) .... AGMA
Athletic Goods Team Distributors (EA) .... AGTD
Athletic Institute (EA) .... AI
[*The*] Athletics Congress [*Track*] [*An association*] .... TAC
[*The*] Athletics Congress/USA (EA) .... TAC/USA
[*The*] Athletics Congress/USA Trust Fund .... TACTRUST
Athletics New Brunswick [*Athletisme du Nouveau-Brunswick*] (AC) .... ANB
Athlone Resources Ltd. [*Vancouver Stock Exchange symbol*] .... AT
Athol, MA [*FM radio station call letters*] .... WCAT
Athrotomy [*Orthopedics*] (DAVI) .... arthr
Athwartships .... ATH
Athwartships Reference Axis .... ASRA
Ati [*Chad*] [*Airport symbol*] (AD) .... ATV
Ati [*Chad*] [*ICAO location identifier*] (ICLI) .... FTTI
ATI Multimedia Channel [*Computer science*] .... AMC
Atico [*Peru*] [*Seismograph station code, US Geological Survey*] (SEIS) .... ATI
Atico [*Peru*] [*ICAO location identifier*] (ICLI) .... SPOY
Atico Financial Corp. (IIA) .... ATF
Atigaru Point, AK [*Location identifier FAA*] (FAAL) .... AUJ
Atikameg-Sovereign School, Alberta [*Library symbol National Library of Canada*] (BIB) .... AATS
Atikokan [*Canada*] [*Airport symbol*] (OAG) .... YIB
Atikokan Centennial Museum, Ontario [*Library symbol National Library of Canada*] (BIB) .... OATM
Atikokan High School, Atikokan, ON, Canada [*Library symbol Library of Congress*] (LCLS) .... CaOAtH
Atikokan High School, Ontario [*Library symbol National Library of Canada*] (NLC) .... OATH
Atikokan, ON [*AM radio station call letters*] CKDR-6
Atikokan, ON [*ICAO location identifier*] (ICLI) .... CYIB
Atikokan Public Library, Ontario [*Library symbol National Library of Canada*] (NLC) .... OAT
Atirro [*Costa Rica*] [*ICAO location identifier*] (ICLI) .... MRAR
Atiu [*Cook Islands*] [*Airport symbol*] (OAG) .... AIU
Atiu [*Cook Islands*] [*ICAO location identifier*] (ICLI) .... NCAT
Atkasuk Village, AK [*Location identifier FAA*] (FAAL) .... ATK
Atkins Research & Development [*W.S. Atkins Group Ltd.*] [*Research center British*] .... AR & D
Atkins Stress Analysis System [*Atkins Research & Development*] [*Software package*] (NCC) .... ASAS
Atkins Structural Analysis System (MCD) .... ASAS
Atkinson [*Guy F.*] Co. of California [*Associated Press*] (SAG) .... Atkinsn
Atkinson [*Guy F.*] Co. of California [*NASDAQ symbol*] (NQ) .... ATKN

Atkinson Elementary School, Houston, TX [Library symbol] [Library of Congress] (LCLS) .... TxHAE
Atkinson (Guy F.)Calif [NASDAQ symbol] (TTSB) .... ATKN
Atkinson on Conveyancing [A publication] (DLA) .... Atk Con
Atkinson on Marketable Titles [A publication] (DLA) .... Atk Titles
Atkinson on Sheriffs [A publication] (DLA) .... Atk Sher
Atkinson's Chancery Practice [A publication] (DLA) .... Atk Ch Pr
Atkinson's Law of Solicitors' Liens [1905] [A publication] (DLA) .... Atkinson
Atkinson's Quarter Sessions Records [Yorkshire, England] [A publication] (DLA) .... Atk
Atkyn's English Chancery Reports [1736-55] [A publication] (DLA) .... Atk
Atkyn's Parliamentary Tracts [A publication] (DLA) .... Atk PT
Atlanta [Iceland] [ICAO designator] (FAAC) .... ABD
Atlanta [Georgia] [Seismograph station code, US Geological Survey] (SEIS) .... ATL
Atlanta [Branch in the Federal Reserve regional banking system] (BARN) .... F
Atlanta [Georgia] [ICAO location identifier] (ICLI) .... KRTL
Atlanta Aerospace Rescue and Recovery Center [Air Force] .... AARRC
Atlanta & Saint Andrews Bay Railway Co. [AAR code] .... ASAB
Atlanta & West Point Rail Road Co. .... A & WP
Atlanta & West Point Rail Road Co. [AAR code] .... AWP
Atlanta Army Depot [Georgia] (AABC) .... ATAD
Atlanta Art Institute, Atlanta, GA [Library symbol] [Library of Congress] (LCLS) .... GAAI
Atlanta, Birmingham & Coast Railroad Co. .... AB & C
Atlanta Cancer Surveillance Center [Emory University] [Research center] (RCD) .... ACSC
Atlanta Centennial Olympic Games .... ACOG
Atlanta Chamber of Commerce, Atlanta, GA [Library symbol Library of Congress] (LCLS) .... GACC
Atlanta College of Art Library, Atlanta, GA [OCLC symbol] (OCLC) .... GAA
Atlanta Committee for the Olympic Games .... ACOG
Atlanta [Georgia] De Kalb/Peachtree Airport [Airport symbol Obsolete] (OAG) .... PDK
Atlanta Flames Fan Club (EA) .... AFFC
Atlanta, GA [Location identifier FAA] (FAAL) .... AFA
Atlanta, GA [Location identifier FAA] (FAAL) .... BRU
Atlanta, GA [Location identifier FAA] (FAAL) .... FSQ
Atlanta, GA [Location identifier FAA] (FAAL) .... FTY
Atlanta, GA [Location identifier FAA] (FAAL) .... FUN
Atlanta, GA [Location identifier FAA] (FAAL) .... HZK
Atlanta, GA [Location identifier FAA] (FAAL) .... LYN
Atlanta, GA [Location identifier FAA] (FAAL) .... RHX
Atlanta, GA [Location identifier FAA] (FAAL) .... SZJ
Atlanta, GA [FM radio station call letters] .... WABE
Atlanta, GA [AM radio station call letters] .... WAEC
Atlanta, GA [AM radio station call letters] .... WAFS
Atlanta, GA [Television station call letters] .... WAGA
Atlanta, GA [AM radio station call letters] (RBYB) .... WALR
Atlanta, GA [AM radio station call letters] .... WAOK
Atlanta, GA [Television station call letters] .... WATC
Atlanta, GA [Television station call letters] .... WATL
Atlanta, GA [FM radio station call letters] .... WCLK
Atlanta, GA [AM radio station call letters] .... WGKA
Atlanta, GA [Television station call letters] .... WGNX
Atlanta, GA [AM radio station call letters] .... WGST
Atlanta, GA [AM radio station call letters] .... WGUN
Atlanta, GA [FM radio station call letters] .... WKHX
Atlanta, GA [FM radio station call letters] .... WKLS
Atlanta, GA [AM radio station call letters] .... WNIV
Atlanta, GA [FM radio station call letters] .... WNNX
Atlanta, GA [Television station call letters] .... WPBA
Atlanta, GA [FM radio station call letters] .... WPCH
Atlanta, GA [AM radio station call letters] .... WQXI
Atlanta, GA [AM radio station call letters] .... WRAS
Atlanta, GA [FM radio station call letters] .... WREK
Atlanta, GA [FM radio station call letters] .... WRFG
Atlanta, GA [AM radio station call letters] .... WSB
Atlanta, GA [FM radio station call letters] .... WSB-FM
Atlanta, GA [Television station call letters] .... WSB-TV
Atlanta, GA [Television station call letters] .... WTBS
Atlanta, GA [TV station call letters] (RBYB) .... WUPA-TV
Atlanta, GA [FM radio station call letters] .... WVEE
Atlanta, GA [Television station call letters] .... WVEU
Atlanta, GA [Television station call letters] .... WXIA
Atlanta, GA [AM radio station call letters] .... WYZE
Atlanta, GA [FM radio station call letters] .... WZGC
Atlanta, GA [Location identifier FAA] (FAAL) .... ZTL
Atlanta Gas & Light Co. [NYSE symbol] (SPSG) .... ATG
Atlanta Gas & Light Co. [Associated Press] (SAG) .... AtlGas
Atlanta Gas & Light Co. [Associated Press] (SAG) .... AtlGs
Atlanta Gas Lt 7.70% Dep Pfd [NYSE symbol] (TTSB) .... ATGPr
Atlanta Gold Corp. [Vancouver Stock Exchange symbol Toronto Stock Exchange symbol] .... AAG
Atlanta, Hampton [Georgia] [ICAO location identifier] (ICLI) .... KZTL
Atlanta Historical Society, Atlanta, GA [Library symbol Library of Congress] (LCLS) .... GAHi
Atlanta Information Services, Decatur, GA [Library symbol Library of Congress] (LCLS) .... GDAIS
Atlanta Journal-Constitution .... AJC
Atlanta Junior College, Atlanta, GA [Library symbol Library of Congress] (LCLS) .... GAJ
Atlanta, MI [FM radio station call letters] .... WAIR
Atlanta Motor Speedway .... AMS
Atlanta Public Library, Atlanta, GA [Library symbol Library of Congress] (LCLS) .... GA

Atlanta Public Library, Atlanta, GA [OCLC symbol] (OCLC) .... GAP
Atlanta Public Schools, Professional Library, Atlanta, GA [Library symbol Library of Congress] (LCLS) .... GAP
Atlanta School of Art, Atlanta, GA [Library symbol Library of Congress] (LCLS) .... GAA
Atlanta Service Center [IRS] .... ATSC
Atlanta/Sosnoff [NYSE symbol] (TTSB) .... ATL
[The] Atlanta, Stone Mountain & Lithonia Railway Co. [AAR code] .... ASML
Atlanta Street Railroad .... A ST
AtLANta Technologies, Inc. [Atlanta, GA] [Telecommunications service] (TSSD) .... ATI
Atlanta/The William B. Hartsfield Atlanta International [Georgia] [ICAO location identifier] (ICLI) .... KATL
Atlanta, TX [Location identifier FAA] (FAAL) .... ATA
Atlanta, TX [AM radio station call letters] .... KALT
Atlanta, TX [FM radio station call letters] .... KPYN
Atlanta University, Atlanta, GA [Library symbol Library of Congress] (LCLS) .... GAU
Atlanta University Center, Atlanta, GA [OCLC symbol] (OCLC) .... AUU
Atlantair Ltd. [Canada ICAO designator] (FAAC) .... ATB
Atlantic [Ocean] (ABBR) .... A
Atlantic [Record label] .... Atl
Atlantic (AFM) .... ATL
Atlantic .... ATL
Atlantic .... LANT
Atlantic Aero, Inc. [ICAO designator] (FAAC) .... MDC
Atlantic Air BVI Ltd. [British ICAO designator] (FAAC) .... BLB
Atlantic Airborne Early Warning [Military] .... AAEW
Atlantic Airline Ltd. [Gambia] [FAA designator] (FAAC) .... AWA
Atlantic Airways, PF (Faroe Islands) [Denmark ICAO designator] (FAAC) .... FLI
Atlantic Alliance for Maritime Heritage Conservation (EA) .... AAMHC
Atlantic American [NASDAQ symbol] (TTSB) .... AAME
Atlantic American Corp. [NASDAQ symbol] (NQ) .... AAME
Atlantic American Corp. [Associated Press] (SAG) .... AtlAm
Atlantic Amphibious Force [Navy] .... AAF
Atlantic Amphibious Ready Group (MCD) .... AARG
Atlantic & East Carolina Railway Co. [AAR code] .... AEC
Atlantic & Great Western Railroad .... A & GW
Atlantic and Gulf American Flag Berth Operators .... AGAFBO
Atlantic & St. Lawrence Railroad .... A & StL
Atlantic and West Indies .... A & WI
Atlantic & Western [Railroad] (MHDB) .... A & W
Atlantic & Western Railway Co. (IIA) .... A & W
Atlantic & Western Railway Co. [AAR code] .... ATW
Atlantic & Yadkin Railroad (IIA) .... A & Y
Atlantic Antisubmarine Warfare Communication Net (NVT) .... AMANET
Atlantic Area [Services to the Armed Forces] [Red Cross] .... AA
Atlantic Art Institute .... AAI
Atlantic Association of Broadcasters (AC) .... AAB
Atlantic Association of Teacher Educators [Canada] .... AATE
Atlantic Association of Young Political Leaders (EA) .... AAYPL
Atlantic Avenue School, Lynbrook, NY [Library symbol] [Library of Congress] (LCLS) .... NLynAE
Atlantic Aviation Services (SAA) .... AAS
Atlantic Ballistic Missile Range .... ABMR
Atlantic Bank & Trust [NASDAQ symbol] (TTSB) .... ATLB
Atlantic Bank and Trust Co. [NASDAQ symbol] (SAG) .... ATLB
Atlantic Bank and Trust Co. [Associated Press] (SAG) .... AtlBkTC
Atlantic Barrier Patrol [Eastern seaward extension of the DEW Line] [Obsolete] .... BARLANT
Atlantic Base Section .... ABS
Atlantic Beach, FL [FM radio station call letters] .... WFYV
Atlantic Beach, FL [AM radio station call letters] .... WNCM
Atlantic Beach, SC [AM radio station call letters] .... WMIW
Atlantic Beverage [NASDAQ symbol] (TTSB) .... ABEV
Atlantic Beverage Corp. [NASDAQ symbol] (SAG) .... ABEV
Atlantic Beverage Corp. [Associated Press] (SAG) .... AtlBev
Atlantic Books Today [A publication] (BRI) .... Atl BT
Atlantic Booster Test (KSC) .... ABT
Atlantic Building Supply Dealers Association (AC) .... ABSDA
Atlantic Canada Opportunities Agency .... ACOA
Atlantic Canada Society for Human Resource Development .... ACSHRD
Atlantic Capital I [NYSE symbol] (SAG) .... ATE
Atlantic Capital I [Associated Press] (SAG) .... AtlCap
Atlantic Centennial Olympic Properties .... ACOP
Atlantic Center for the Environment (EA) .... ACE
Atlantic Charter .... AC
Atlantic Christian College [Wilson, NC] .... ACC
Atlantic Christian College, Wilson, NC [Library symbol Library of Congress] (LCLS) .... NcWilA
Atlantic Circulation and Climate Experiment [Marine science] (OSRA) .... ACCE
Atlantic City [New Jersey] [Airport symbol] (OAG) .... ACY
Atlantic City [New Jersey] [Airport symbol] (OAG) .... AIY
Atlantic City & Shore Railroad .... AC & S
Atlantic City/Atlantic City [New Jersey] [ICAO location identifier] (ICLI) .... KACY
Atlantic City Free Public Library, Atlantic City, NJ [OCLC symbol] (OCLC) .... ACP
Atlantic City Free Public Library, Atlantic City, NJ [Library symbol Library of Congress] (LCLS) .... NjAc
Atlantic City, NJ [Location identifier FAA] (FAAL) .... PVO
Atlantic City, NJ [Television station call letters] .... WACI
Atlantic City, NJ [FM radio station call letters] .... WAYV
Atlantic City, NJ [AM radio station call letters] .... WFPG
Atlantic City, NJ [FM radio station call letters] .... WFPG-FM
Atlantic City, NJ [FM radio station call letters] .... WMGM

Atlantic City, NJ [*AM radio station call letters*] ... WMID
Atlantic City, NJ [*FM radio station call letters*] ... WNJN
Atlantic City, NJ [*AM radio station call letters*] ... WUSS
Atlantic City, NJ [*Television station call letters*] ... WWAC
Atlantic City Remodelers Exposition [*Remodeling Contractors Association*] (TSPED) ... ACRE
Atlantic City Reporter, Atlantic City, NJ [*Library symbol Library of Congress*] (LCLS) ... NjAcR
Atlantic Climate Change Program (USDC) ... ACCP
Atlantic Climate Change Program [*Marine science*] (OSRA) ... ACCP
Atlantic Coast Air Service ... ACAS
Atlantic Coast Airlines [*NASDAQ symbol*] (TTSB) ... ACAI
Atlantic Coast Airlines [*Westair Airlines, Inc.*] [*ICAO designator*] (FAAC) ... BLR
Atlantic Coast Airlines, Inc. [*NASDAQ symbol*] (SAG) ... ACAI
Atlantic Coast Airlines, Inc. [*Associated Press*] (SAG) ... AtlCstAir
Atlantic Coast Conference (EA) ... ACC
Atlantic Coast Copper Corp. Ltd. [*Toronto Stock Exchange symbol*] ... ATC
Atlantic Coast Football League ... ACFL
Atlantic Coast Line R. R. [*AAR code*] ... ACL
Atlantic Coast Line R. R. ... ACLRR
Atlantic Command [*Navy*] ... LANTCOM
Atlantic Command Inspector General (DNAB) ... LANTCOMINSGEN
Atlantic Command Intelligence Operating Procedures (MCD) ... ACIOP
Atlantic Command Military Blood Program Office (DNAB) ... LANTCOMMBPO
Atlantic Command Operations Support Facility (DNAB) ... LANTCOMOPSUPPFAC
Atlantic [*Fleet*] **Commander Operational Control Center** [*Navy*] ... ACOCC
Atlantic [*Fleet*] **Commander Operational Control Center** [*Navy*] ... LANTCOMOPCONCEN
Atlantic [*Fleet*] **Commander Operational Control Center** [*Navy*] ... LCOCC
Atlantic Communication and Technical Workers Union ... AC & TWU
Atlantic Community College, Mays Landing, NJ [*OCLC symbol*] (OCLC) ... ANJ
Atlantic Community College, Mays Landing, NJ [*Library symbol Library of Congress*] (LCLS) ... NjMlAC
Atlantic Community Development Group for Latin America [*Joint US-European private investment company*] ... ADELA
Atlantic Community Newspapers Association (AC) ... ACNA
Atlantic Community Quarterly [*A publication*] (DLA) ... Atl Comm Q
Atlantic Congress ... AC
Atlantic Container Line [*British*] ... ACL
Atlantic Contract Management District (SAA) ... ATCMD
Atlantic Co-Operator, Antigonish, Nova Scotia [*Library symbol National Library of Canada*] (NLC) ... NSAAC
Atlantic Co-Operator, Antigonish, NS, Canada [*Library symbol*] [*Library of Congress*] (LCLS) ... CaNSAAC
Atlantic Council [*Later, ACUS*] [*NATO*] (NATG) ... AC
Atlantic Council of Canada (EAIO) ... ACC
Atlantic Council of the United States (EA) ... ACUS
Atlantic County Advertiser, Northfield, NJ [*Library symbol Library of Congress*] (LCLS) ... NjNoA
Atlantic County Clerk, Atlantic City, NJ [*Library symbol Library of Congress*] (LCLS) ... NjAcCoC
Atlantic County Clerk, Mays Landing, NJ [*Library symbol Library of Congress*] (LCLS) ... NjMlCoC
Atlantic County Historical Society, Somers Point, NJ [*Library symbol Library of Congress*] (LCLS) ... NjSomHi
Atlantic County Library, Mays Landing, NJ [*Library symbol Library of Congress*] (LCLS) ... NjMlA
Atlantic County Record, Mays Landing, NJ [*Library symbol Library of Congress*] (LCLS) ... NjMlR
Atlantic Dairy Council (AC) ... ADC
Atlantic Daylight Time ... ADT
Atlantic Deeper Waterways Association (EA) ... ADWA
Atlantic Development Council Canada ... ADCC
Atlantic Division Naval Facilities Engineering Command ... LANTNAVFACENGCOM
Atlantic Division Transport Control Center [*Military*] ... ATCC
Atlantic Economic Society (EA) ... AES
Atlantic Education Association [*Canada*] ... AEA
Atlantic Educational Research Council [*Canada*] ... AERC
Atlantic Energy [*Vancouver Stock Exchange symbol*] ... ACG
Atlantic Energy [*NYSE symbol*] (SPSG) ... ATE
Atlantic Energy, Inc. [*Associated Press*] (SAG) ... AtlEnrg
Atlantic Environmental Group [*National Marine Fisheries Service*] ... AEG
Atlantic Episcopal Assembly (AC) ... AEA
Atlantic Estuarine Fisheries Center [*National Oceanic and Atmospheric Administration*] (MSC) ... AEFC
Atlantic Estuarine Research Society (EA) ... AERS
Atlantic Estuarine Society ... AES
Atlantic Ferry Organization [*Based in Canada under Ministry of Aircraft Production*] [*British World War II*] ... ATFERO
Atlantic Ferry Service [*World War II*] ... AFS
[*The*] **Atlantic Fertilizer Institute** (AC) ... AFI
Atlantic Filmmakers' Co-Operative (AC) ... AFCOOP
Atlantic Fleet ... LANTFLT
Atlantic Fleet Amphibious Force [*Navy*] ... AFAF
Atlantic Fleet Amphibious Ready Group (MCD) ... ARG
Atlantic Fleet Antisubmarine Warfare Tactical School [*Navy*] ... LANTFLEASWTACSCOL
Atlantic Fleet Audio-Visual Center [*Navy*] (DNAB) ... AFAVC
Atlantic Fleet Chief of Naval Reserve Representative (DNAB) ... LANTREPCNAVRES
Atlantic Fleet Combat Camera Group [*Obsolete*] ... AFCCG
Atlantic Fleet Headquarters Support Activity [*Navy*] (DNAB) ... LANTFLTHEDSUPPACT
Atlantic Fleet Material Control Office [*Navy*] (DNAB) ... LANTFLTMATCONOFF
Atlantic Fleet Naval Forces Intelligence Collection Manual (MCD) ... AFNFICM
Atlantic Fleet Naval Forces Intelligence Collection Manual ... ANFICM
Atlantic Fleet Organization ... AFO
Atlantic Fleet Propulsion Examining Board [*Navy*] (DNAB) ... LANTFLTPEB
Atlantic Fleet Range Support Facility [*Navy*] (DNAB) ... AFRSF
Atlantic Fleet Signals Security Operations Center [*Navy*] (DNAB) ... LANTSOC
Atlantic Fleet Training Support Facilities ... LANTFLTRANSUPPFAC
Atlantic Fleet Weapons Range [*Later, AFRSF*] [*Navy*] ... AFWR
Atlantic Fleet Weapons Range [*Later, AFRSF*] [*Navy*] ... LANTFLTWPNRAN
Atlantic Fleet Weapons Training Facility [*Navy*] ... AFWTF
Atlantic Fleet Weapons Training Facility [*Navy*] (DNAB) ... LANTFLTWPNTRAFAC
Atlantic Fleet Worldwide Military Command Control System [*Navy*] (DNAB) ... LANTWWMCCS
Atlantic Forward Area Support Team [*Military*] (DNAB) ... LANTFAST
Atlantic Free Trade Area ... AFTA
Atlantic Gas Research Exchange (MHDB) ... AGRE
Atlantic Generating Station [*Nuclear energy*] (NRCH) ... AGS
Atlantic Geoscience Association ... AGS
Atlantic Gulf Airlines, Inc. [*ICAO designator*] (FAAC) ... AGF
Atlantic Gulf Communities Corp. [*NASDAQ symbol*] (SAG) ... AGLF
Atlantic Gulf Communities Corp. [*Associated Press*] (SAG) ... AtlGulf
Atlantic, Gulf, West Indies [*Marine insurance*] (ODBW) ... AGWI
Atlantic Highlands Public Library Association, Atlantic Highlands, NJ [*Library symbol Library of Congress*] (LCLS) ... NjAt
Atlantic, IA [*Location identifier FAA*] (FAAL) ... AIO
Atlantic, IA [*AM radio station call letters*] ... KJAN
Atlantic, IA [*FM radio station call letters*] ... KXKT
Atlantic Independent Film & Video Association (AC) ... AIFVA
Atlantic Independent Union ... AIU
Atlantic Information Centre for Teachers [*Defunct*] (EA) ... AICT
Atlantic Institute for International Affairs [*France*] (EA) ... AIIA
Atlantic Institute of Education, Halifax, NS, Canada [*Library symbol Library of Congress*] (LCLS) ... CaNSHAI
Atlantic Institution, Correctional Service Canada [*Etablissement Atlantique, Service Correctionnel Canada*], Renous, New Brunswick [*Library symbol National Library of Canada*] (BIB) ... NBRCA
Atlantic Intelligence Center [*Navy*] ... AIC
Atlantic Intelligence Center [*Navy*] ... LANTINTCEN
Atlantic International Air and Surface Search and Rescue Seminar (PDAA) ... LANTSAR
Atlantic International Marketing Committee [*Maryland, Virginia, North Carolina, and South Carolina*] ... AIM
Atlantic Island Air [*Iceland*] [*ICAO designator*] (FAAC) ... TRG
Atlantic Lottery Corp. [*Societe des Loteries de l'Atlantique*], Moncton, New Brunswick [*Library symbol National Library of Canada*] (NLC) ... NBMOAL
Atlantic Margin Coring Project ... AMCOR
Atlantic Marine Center [*National Oceanic and Atmospheric Administration*] ... AMC
Atlantic Merchant Shipping Instructions ... AMSI
Atlantic Missile Range [*Later, Eastern Test Range*] ... AMR
Atlantic Missile Range [*later, Eastern Test Range*] **Operations** ... AMRO
Atlantic Missile Range [*later, Eastern Test Range*] **Operations Office** ... AMROO
Atlantic Missile Range [*Later, Eastern Test Range*] **Telemetry Submodule** (SAA) ... AMRTS
Atlantic Missile Test Range (KSC) ... AMTR
Atlantic Monthly [*A publication*] (BRI) ... Atl
Atlantic Monthly Press ... AMP
Atlantic Motorcycle Competition Riders' Association (AC) ... AMCRA
Atlantic Naval Intelligence Summary (MCD) ... LNIS
Atlantic, NC [*FM radio station call letters*] ... WTKF
Atlantic News-Telegraph, Atlantic, IA [*Library symbol Library of Congress*] (LCLS) ... IaAtNT
Atlantic Nuclear Force [*NATO*] ... ANF
Atlantic Nutritional Association (EA) ... ANA
Atlantic Ocean ... AT
Atlantic Ocean ... AtlO
Atlantic Ocean (SAA) ... ATO
Atlantic Ocean [*MARC geographic area code Library of Congress*] (LCCP) ... l-----
Atlantic Ocean Air Traffic Control [*NATO*] (NATG) ... AOATC
Atlantic Ocean Area ... AOA
Atlantic Ocean Recovery Area [*NASA*] ... AORA
Atlantic Ocean Region [*INTELSAT*] ... AOR
Atlantic Ocean Ship [*INTELSAT*] ... AOS
Atlantic Oceanographic and Meteorological Laboratory [*Miami, FL*] [*National Oceanic and Atmospheric Administration*] ... AOML
Atlantic Oceanographic Laboratories [*of Environmental Science Services Administration*] ... AOL
Atlantic Offshore Fish and Lobster Association (OSRA) ... AOFLA
Atlantic Offshore Fishermen's Association (EA) ... AOFA
Atlantic Offshore Lobstermen's Association (SRA) ... AOLA
Atlantic Operating Area [*Military*] (DNAB) ... AOA
Atlantic Operations Supply Facilities (MCD) ... LANTOPS
Atlantic Operations Supply Facilities ... LANTOPSSUPFAC
Atlantic Outer Continental Shelf ... AOCS
Atlantic Pharmaceuticals [*NASDAQ symbol*] (TTSB) ... ATLC
Atlantic Pharmaceuticals, Inc. [*Associated Press*] (SAG) ... AtlPharm
Atlantic Pharmaceuticals, Inc. [*Associated Press*] (SAG) ... AtlPhr
Atlantic Pharmaceuticals,Inc. [*NASDAQ symbol*] (SAG) ... ATLC
Atlantic Pharma'l Units 2000 [*NASDAQ symbol*] (TTSB) ... ATLCU
Atlantic Pharm'l Wrrt 2000 [*NASDAQ symbol*] (TTSB) ... ATLCW
Atlantic Pilotage Authority ... APA
Atlantic Political Advisory Group [*NATO*] ... APAG
Atlantic Professional Boatman's Association [*Defunct*] (EA) ... APBA
Atlantic Province Reports [*Information service or system A publication*] (DLA) ... Atl PR
Atlantic Province Reports [*Information service or system A publication*] (DLA) ... Atl Prov

Atlantic Provinces Art Gallery Association [*Canada*] ...... APAGA
Atlantic Provinces Association of Landscape Architects (AC) ...... APALA
Atlantic Provinces Association of Learning Materials and Education
  Representatives [*Canada*] ...... APALMER
Atlantic Provinces Council on the Sciences (AC) ...... APCS
Atlantic Provinces Economic Council ...... APEC
Atlantic Provinces Library Association (AC) ...... APLA
Atlantic Provinces Linguistic Association [*Canada*] ...... APLA
Atlantic Provinces Numismatic Association [*Canada*] ...... APNA
Atlantic Provinces Power Development Act [*Canada*] ...... APPDA
[*The*] Atlantic Provinces Resource Centre for the Visually-Impaired, Hal
  ifax, NS, anada [*Library symbol*] [*Library of Congress*] (LCLS) ...... CaNSHAVI
[*The*] Atlantic Provinces Resource Centre for the Visually-Impaired,
  Halifax, Nova Scotia [*Library symbol National Library of Canada*]
  (NLC) ...... NSHAVI
Atlantic Provinces Trucking Association [*Canada*] ...... APTA
Atlantic Public Library, Atlantic, IA [*Library symbol Library of Congress*]
  (LCLS) ...... IaAt
Atlantic Public Library, Atlantic, IA [*Library symbol*] [*Library of Congress*]
  (LCLS) ...... IaAtL
Atlantic Publishers Association (AC) ...... APA
Atlantic Range Instrumentation Ship ...... ARIS
Atlantic Readiness Exercise (MCD) ...... LANTREADEX
Atlantic Realty Trust [*NASDAQ symbol*] (TTSB) ...... ATLRS
Atlantic Realty Trust SBI [*NASDAQ symbol*] (SAG) ...... ATLR
Atlantic Realty Trust SBI [*Associated Press*] (SAG) ...... AtlReal
Atlantic Refining Co., Philadelphia, PA [*Library symbol Library of Congress*]
  (LCLS) ...... PPAtR
Atlantic Region, Atmospheric Environment Service, Environment Canada
  [*Bureau Regional de l'Atlantique, Service de l'Environnement
  Atmospherique, Environnement Canada*] Halifax, Nova Scotia [*Library
  symbol National Library of Canada*] (NLC) ...... NSHW
Atlantic Regional Laboratory, National Research Council [*Laboratoire
  Regionale de l'Atlantique, Conseil National de Recherches du Canada*]
  Halifax, Nova Sco tia [*Library symbol National Library of Canada*]
  (NLC) ...... NSHM
Atlantic Regional Library, Parks Canada [*Bibliotheque Regionale de
  l'Atlantique, Parcs Canada*] Halifax, Nova Scotia [*Library symbol National
  Library of Canada*] (NLC) ...... NSHIAP
Atlantic Regional Library, Public Works Canada [*Bibliotheque Regionale de
  l'Atlantique, Travaux Publics Canada*] Halifax, Nova Scotia [*Library symbol
  National Library of Canada*] (NLC) ...... NSHPW
Atlantic Regional Library, Transport Canada [*Bibliotheque Regionale de
  l'Atlantique, Transports Canada*], Moncton, New Brunswick [*Library symbol
  National Library of Canada*] (NLC) ...... NBMOTAR
Atlantic Remote Sensing Land Ocean Experiment (MCD) ...... ARSLOE
Atlantic Reporter [*A publication*] (DLA) ...... A
Atlantic Reporter [*A publication*] (DLA) ...... A Rep
Atlantic Reporter [*A publication*] (DLA) ...... AR
Atlantic Reporter [*A publication*] (DLA) ...... At
Atlantic Reporter [*A publication*] (DLA) ...... At Rep
Atlantic Reporter [*A publication*] (BARN) ...... Atl
Atlantic Reporter [*A publication*] (DLA) ...... Atl R
Atlantic Reporter [*A publication*] (DLA) ...... Atl Rep
Atlantic Reporter [*A publication*] (DLA) ...... Atl Repr
Atlantic Reporter, Second Series [*West*] [*A publication*] (AAGC) A2d
Atlantic Reporter, Second Series [*A publication*] (DLA) A2d
Atlantic Reporter, Second Series (West) [*A publication*] (DLA) ...... Atl 2d
Atlantic Representative for Commander Naval Surface Reserve Force
  (DNAB) ...... LANTREPCOMNAVSURFRES
Atlantic Research Center (KSC) ...... ARC
Atlantic Research Centre for Mental Retardation [*Dalhousie University*]
  [*Canada Research center*] (RCD) ...... ARCMR
Atlantic Research Corp. (MCD) ...... ARC
Atlantic Research Corporation Atmospheric Sounding [*Missile*]
  (MUGU) ...... ARCAS
Atlantic Research Laboratories [*National Research Council of Canada*]
  (MCD) ...... ARL
Atlantic Reserve Fleet ...... LANTRESFLT
Atlantic Rich $3 Cv Pref [*NYSE symbol*] (TTSB) ...... ARCPrA
Atlantic Rich 9% Exch Nts'97 [*NYSE symbol*] (TTSB) ...... LYX
Atlantic Rich$2.80 Cv Pref [*NYSE symbol*] (TTSB) ...... ARCPrC
Atlantic Richfield [*NYSE symbol*] (TTSB) ...... ABC
Atlantic Richfield Canada Ltd. ...... ARCAN
Atlantic Richfield Co. [*NYSE symbol*] (SPSG) ...... ARC
Atlantic Richfield Co. ...... ARCO
Atlantic Richfield Co. [*Associated Press*] (SAG) ...... AtlRc
Atlantic Richfield Co. [*Associated Press*] (SAG) ...... AtlRich
Atlantic Richfield Co. [*Associated Press*] (SAG) AtlRich97
Atlantic Richfield Co. [*NYSE symbol*] (SAG) ...... LYX
Atlantic Richfield Co. [*ICAO designator*] (FAAC) ...... NRS
Atlantic Richfield Co., Geoscience Library, Dallas, TX [*OCLC symbol*]
  (OCLC) ...... ATR
Atlantic Richfield Co., Geoscience Library, Dallas, TX [*Library symbol Library
  of Congress*] (LCLS) ...... TxDaAR-G
Atlantic Richfield Co., R and D Library, Dallas, TX [*OCLC symbol*]
  (OCLC) ...... ATC
Atlantic Richfield Co., R and D Library, Dallas, TX [*Library symbol Library of
  Congress*] (LCLS) ...... TxDaAR-R
Atlantic Richfield Co., Technical Library, Dallas, TX [*Library symbol Library
  of Congress*] (LCLS) ...... TxDaAR-T
Atlantic Richfield Hanford Co. (MCD) ...... ARH
Atlantic Richfield Hanford Co. ...... ARHCO
Atlantic Richfield Hanford Co., Richland, WA [*Library symbol Library of
  Congress*] (LCLS) ...... WaRiAR

Atlantic Route [*Aviation*] (FAAC) ...... AR
Atlantic Salmon Association (EA) ...... ASA
Atlantic Salmon Convention Act of 1982 ...... ASCA
Atlantic Salmon Federation (EA) ...... ASF
Atlantic Satellite Network [*Cable-television system*] ...... ASN
Atlantic School of Theology [*Canada*] ...... AST
Atlantic School of Theology, Halifax, Nova Scotia [*Library symbol National
  Library of Canada*] (NLC) ...... NSHPH
Atlantic School of Theology, Halifax, NS, Canada [*Library symbol Library of
  Congress*] (LCLS) ...... CaNSHPH
Atlantic Sea Run Salmon Commission (EA) ...... ASRSC
Atlantic Seaboard Circuit [*Horse racing*] ...... ASC
Atlantic Semiconductor (IAA) ...... AS
Atlantic Shopping Centres Ltd. [*Toronto Stock Exchange symbol*] ...... ATS
Atlantic Site 1 (GAAI) ...... ATL 1
Atlantic Site 2 (GAAI) ...... ATL 2
Atlantic, SL [*Spain*] [*FAA designator*] (FAAC) ...... RCU
Atlantic So'east Air [*NASDAQ symbol*] (TTSB) ...... ASAI
Atlantic Southeast [*ICAO designator*] (AD) ...... EV
Atlantic Southeast Airlines [*Associated Press*] (SAG) ...... AtlSeAir
Atlantic Southeast Airlines, Inc. ...... ASA
Atlantic Southeast Airlines, Inc. [*NASDAQ symbol*] (NQ) ...... ASAI
Atlantic Southeast Airlines, Inc. [*ICAO designator*] (FAAC) ...... ASE
Atlantic Southeast Airlines, Inc. [*Air carrier designation symbol*] ...... ASEX
Atlantic Squadron ...... ATRON
Atlantic Standard Time ...... AST
Atlantic Standard Time ...... AT
Atlantic Standard Time ...... ATST
Atlantic States Marine Fisheries Commission (EA) ...... ASMFC
Atlantic Steam Navigation (MHDW) ...... ASN
Atlantic Stratocumulus Transition Experiment [*Meteorology*] ...... ASTEX
Atlantic Systems Conference [*Navy/NATO*] (MCD) ...... ASC
Atlantic Tele-Network [*NASDAQ symbol*] (SPSG) ...... ATNI
Atlantic Tele-Network, Inc. [*Associated Press*] (SAG) ...... AtlTele
Atlantic Test Site (SAA) ...... ATS
Atlantic to the Urals [*Conventional forces in Europe treaty zone*] ...... ATTU
Atlantic Tracking Range [*NASA*] ...... ATR
Atlantic Tracking Ship [*NASA*] (KSC) ...... ATS
Atlantic Trade Study ...... ATS
Atlantic Tradewind [*or Tropical*] Experiment [*National Science
  Foundation*] ...... ATEX
Atlantic Transportation Terminal Command [*Army*] ...... ATTC
Atlantic Treaty Association (EA) ...... ATA
Atlantic Treaty Education Committee [*NATO*] (NATG) ...... ATEC
Atlantic Tropical Oceanic Lower Layer [*National Oceanic and Atmospheric
  Administration*] ...... ATOLL
Atlantic Tuna Convention Act of 1975 ...... ATCA
Atlantic Undersea Test and Evaluation Center [*Acronym also used to refer to
  device for detection, amplification, and transmission of undersea noise*]
  [*Navy*] ...... AUTEC
Atlantic Union (DAS) ...... AU
Atlantic Union College [*South Lancaster, MA*] ...... AUC
Atlantic Union College, South Lancaster, MA [*Library symbol Library of
  Congress*] (LCLS) ...... MSIA
Atlantic Union College, South Lancaster, MA [*Library symbol*] [*Library of
  Congress*] (LCLS) ...... MSIA
Atlantic Universities Athletic Association [*Association Sportive
  Interuniversitaire de l'Atlantique*] (AC) ...... AUAA
Atlantic Varnish & Paint Co., Richmond, VA [*Library symbol Library of
  Congress*] (LCLS) ...... ViRAV
Atlantic Waterfowl Council (EA) ...... AWC
Atlantic Wind Test Site, Tignish, Prince Edward Island [*Library symbol
  National Library of Canada*] (NLC) ...... PTAWT
Atlantic World Airways, Inc. [*ICAO designator*] (FAAC) ...... BJK
Atlantic-Gulf Coastwise Steamship Freight Bureau ...... AGCSB
Atlantic-Gulf Coastwise Steamship Freight Bureau, Elizabeth NJ [*STAC*] ...... AGC
Atlantic-Intercoastal Waterway (WDAA) ...... AIW
Atlantis [*ICAO designator*] (AD) ...... SG
Atlantis Airlines [*ICAO designator*] (FAAC) ...... AAO
Atlantis Airlines [*ICAO designator*] (AD) ...... MP
Atlantis Commodities Purchasing Service ...... ATCOPS
Atlantis Enterprise [*Vancouver Stock Exchange symbol*] ...... ATE
Atlantis Group, Inc. [*AMEX symbol*] (SPSG) ...... AGH
Atlantis Group, Inc. [*NASDAQ symbol*] (SAG) ...... ATLA
Atlantis Group, Inc. [*Associated Press*] (SAG) ...... AtlantisG
Atlantis Plastics, Inc. [*Formerly, Atlantis Group*] [*AMEX symbol*] (SAG) ...... AGH
Atlantis Plastics, Inc. [*Associated Press*] (SAG) ...... Atlantis
Atlantis Research Centre (EA) ...... ARC
Atlantis Research Group (EA) ...... ARG
Atlantis Resources Ltd. [*Toronto Stock Exchange symbol*] ...... AIN
Atlantis Tank Landing Craft ...... ATL
Atlantis Transportation Services Ltd. [*Canada ICAO designator*] (FAAC) ...... ATE
Atlantische Passatwind Experiment [*Atlantic Tradewind Experiment*] [*US,
  England, Germany*] (MSC) ...... APEX
Atlantoaxial Subluxation (PDAA) ...... AAS
Atlantodens Interval [*Neurosurgery and orthopedics*] (DAVI) ...... ADI
Atlant-Soyuz [*Former USSR*] [*FAA designator*] (FAAC) ...... AYZ
Atlant-SV [*Ukraine*] [*FAA designator*] (FAAC) ...... ATG
Atlas (ROG) ...... ATL
Atlas ...... ATLS
Atlas Agena [*NASA*] ...... AA
Atlas Air [*NASDAQ symbol*] (TTSB) ...... ATLS
Atlas Air, Inc. [*Associated Press*] (SAG) ...... AtlasAir
Atlas Air, Inc. [*NASDAQ symbol*] (SAG) ...... ATLS
Atlas Air, Inc. [*Associated Press*] (SAG) ...... AtlsAir

Atlas Air, Inc. [*ICAO designator*] (FAAC) ... GTI
Atlas Airlines [*ICAO designator*] (FAAC) ... ATR
Atlas Aviation Simera (Pty) Ltd. [*South Africa*] [*FAA designator*] (FAAC) ... SMA
Atlas [*Abbreviated Test Language for Avionics Systems*] **Basic Language** [*Computer science*] ... ABL
Atlas Basic Language [*Computer science*] (ECII) ... ATL
Atlas Biomedical Literature System ... ABLS
ATLAS Block Structure (MCD) ... ABS
Atlas Chemical Industries, Inc. [*Research code symbol*] ... AT
Atlas Chemical Industries, Inc., Wilmington, DE [*Library symbol Library of Congress*] (LCLS) ... DeWAt
Atlas Commercial Language [*Computer science*] (BUR) ... ACL
Atlas Configuration Control Board [*Aerospace*] (AAG) ... ACCB
Atlas Corp. [*Associated Press*] (SAG) ... Atlas
Atlas Corp. [*NYSE symbol*] (SPSG) ... AZ
Atlas Corp. [*NYSE symbol*] (TTSB) ... AZ
Atlas Corp. Wrrt [*AMEX symbol*] (TTSB) ... AZ.WS
ATLAS Crew Procedures Laboratory [*NASA*] (MCD) ... ACPL
Atlas Economic Research Foundation (EA) ... AERF
Atlas Educational Center (EA) ... AEC
Atlas Explorer [*Computer geography tutorial*] (PCM) ... AE
Atlas Gemini [*NASA*] (KSC) ... AG
Atlas General Survey Program (IEEE) ... AGSP
Atlas Historique du Canada [*Historical Atlas of Canada*] [*Project*] ... AHC
Atlas LISP [*Library and Information Software Packaging*] **Algebraic Manipulator** (PDAA) ... ALAM
Atlas Microfilming Service, Pennsauken, NJ [*Library symbol*] [*Library of Congress*] (LCLS) ... AtMcS
Atlas Mountain Region [*MARC geographic area code Library of Congress*] (LCCP) ... fa----
Atlas of Australian Resources [*A publication*] ... AAR
Atlas [*Missile*] **Operational Data Summary** ... AODS
Atlas Pacific Ltd. [*NASDAQ symbol*] (SAG) ... APCF
Atlas Pacific Ltd. [*Associated Press*] (SAG) ... AtlasPac
Atlas Pacific Limited [*All Symbol*] (TTSB) ... ATP
Atlas Reliability Group ... ARG
Atlas Yellowknife Resources Ltd. [*Toronto Stock Exchange symbol*] ... AY
Atlas-Centaur [*Missile*] ... A-C
Atlin Historical Museum, British Columbia [*Library symbol National Library of Canada*] (NLC) ... BATM
ATM [*Apollo Telescope Mount*] **Electrical Power System** [*NASA*] ... AEPS
ATM [*Apollo Telescope Mount*] **Experiments Officer** [*NASA*] ... AEO
ATM [*Apollo Telescope Mount*] **Navigation and Timing Summary** [*NASA*] ... ANTS
Atmautluak [*Alaska*] [*Airport symbol*] (OAG) ... ATT
ATMDC [*Apollo Telescope Mount Digital Computer*] **Software Control Officer** [*NASA*] ... ASCO
Atmel Corp. [*Associated Press*] (SAG) ... Atmel
Atmel Corp. [*NASDAQ symbol*] (SPSG) ... ATML
Atmore, AL [*AM radio station call letters*] ... WASG
Atmore, AL [*FM radio station call letters*] ... WDWG
Atmore, AL [*AM radio station call letters*] ... WGYJ
Atmore, AL [*FM radio station call letters*] ... WYDH
Atmos Energy Corp. [*Associated Press*] (SAG) ... ATMOS
Atmos Energy Corp. [*NYSE symbol*] (SPSG) ... ATO
Atmosphere (ABBR) ... A
Atmosphere ... ATM
Atmosphere (KSC) ... ATMOS
Atmosphere (VRA) ... atmos
Atmosphere, Absolute ... ATA
Atmosphere and Land Surface Processes (OSRA) ... ALSP
Atmosphere and Land Surface Processes (USDC) ... ALSP
Atmosphere and Space ... AS
Atmosphere Boundary Layer Facility (MCD) ... ABLF
Atmosphere Climate Study [*National Science Foundation*] (MSC) ... ACS
Atmosphere Control System [*NASA*] (KSC) ... ACS
Atmosphere Defense Initiative (LAIN) ... ADF
Atmosphere Explorer B [*Satellite*] [*NASA*] ... AE-B
Atmosphere Explorer E [*Satellite*] [*NASA*] ... AE-E
Atmosphere General Circulation Experiment (MCD) ... AGCE
Atmosphere, Magnetosphere, and Plasmas in Space [*Space shuttle payload*] [*NASA*] ... AMPS
Atmosphere, Normal (MAE) ... An
Atmosphere Normale Internationale [*International Normal Atmosphere*] ... ANI
Atmosphere/Ocean Chemistry Experiment (USDC) ... AEROCE
Atmosphere/Ocean Chemistry Experiment [*Marine science*] (OSRA) ... AEROCE
Atmosphere Particulate Radioactivity Detector (IEEE) ... APRD
Atmosphere Radiation Monitor (IEEE) ... ARM
Atmosphere Reactants Supply Subsystem ... ARSS
Atmosphere Reactants Supply Subsystem Group (MCD) ... ARSSG
Atmosphere Revitalization Section [*or System*] [*NASA*] ... ARS
Atmosphere Sensing and Maintenance System [*NASA*] (KSC) ... ASMS
Atmosphere Sounding Projectile ... ASP
Atmosphere, Standard [*Unit of pressure*] ... atm
Atmosphere/Surface Turbulent Exchange Research ... ASTER
Atmosphere, Technical [*Unit of pressure*] ... at
Atmosphere Transport Model Evaluation Study (OSRA) ... ATMES
Atmospheric ... ATMO
Atmospheric Aerosols and Optics Data Library (RDA) ... AAODL
Atmospheric Analysis and Prediction [*National Center for Atmospheric Research*] ... AAP
Atmospheric and Ocean Sciences Program (OSRA) ... AOSP
Atmospheric and Ocean Sciences Program (USDC) ... AOSP
Atmospheric and Oceanographic Information Processing System [*Satellite image enhancing system*] (MCD) ... AOIPS
Atmospheric and [*Space*] **Physics** ... AP
Atmospheric and Space Plasma Physics [*NASA*] (NASA) ... ASPP
Atmospheric Angular Momentum [*Geophysics*] ... AAM
Atmospheric Applications (MCD) ... AA
Atmospheric Attenuation of Sound (MCD) ... ATMAT
Atmospheric Boundary Layer [*Marine science*] (OSRA) ... ABL
Atmospheric Boundary Layer Experiment [*National Oceanic and Atmospheric Administration*] ... ABLE
Atmospheric Burst Locator (MCD) ... ABL
Atmospheric Change (IAA) ... ATMCHG
Atmospheric Cloud Physics Laboratory [*Spacelab*] [*NASA*] ... ACPL
Atmospheric Collection Equipment [*Marine science*] (OSRA) ... ACE
Atmospheric Collection Equipment (USDC) ... ACE
Atmospheric Composition Payload Group [*NASA*] (SSD) ... ACG
Atmospheric Composition Satellite [*NASA*] ... ATCOS
Atmospheric Containment Atmosphere Dilution (PDAA) ... ACAD
Atmospheric Contamination Potential ... ACP
Atmospheric Control Experimentation ... ACE
Atmospheric Deposition Monitoring Program [*Environmental Protection Agency*] ... ADMN
Atmospheric Devices Laboratory [*Cambridge, MA*] (AAG) ... ADL
Atmospheric Diffusion Measuring System ... ADMS
Atmospheric Diffusion of Beryllium Program [*NASA*] (KSC) ... ADOBE
Atmospheric Diving Suit [*Deep sea diving*] ... ADS
Atmospheric Diving System ... ADS
Atmospheric Dump Valves [*Nuclear energy*] (NRCH) ... ADV
Atmospheric Dynamic Payload Group [*NASA*] (SSD) ... ADG
Atmospheric Dynamics Program [*National Oceanic and Atmospheric Administration*] ... ADP
Atmospheric Electric Detection System (KSC) ... AEDS
Atmospheric Electricity Hazards Protection ... AEHP
Atmospheric Electromagnetic Pulse ... AEMP
Atmospheric Emissions Photometric Imaging [*Plasma physics*] ... AEPI
Atmospheric Entry ... AE
Atmospheric Environment Service [*Canada*] ... AES
Atmospheric Environment Service, Environment Canada [*Service de l'Environnement Atmospherique, Environnement Canada*] **Dorval, Quebec** [*Library symbol National Library of Canada*] (NLC) ... QMEA
Atmospheric Environment Service, Environment Canada [*Service de l'Environnement Atmospherique, Environnement Canada*] **Downsview, Ontario** [*Library symbol National Library of Canada*] (NLC) ... OTM
Atmospheric Environment Service, Environment Canada [*Service de l'Environnement Atmospherique, Environnement Canada*] **Edmonton, Alberta** [*Library symbol National Library of Canada*] (NLC) ... AEEAE
Atmospheric Environment Service, Environment Canada [*Service de l'Environnement Atmospherique, Environnement Canada*] **Vancouver, British Columbia** [*Library symbol National Library of Canada*] (NLC) ... BVAEAE
Atmospheric Environment Service, Environment Canada [*Service de l'Environnement Atmospherique, Environnement Canada*] **Ville St-Laurent, Quebec** [*Library symbol National Library of Canada*] (NLC) ... QVSLEA
Atmospheric Environment Service (ODIT Ontario Weather Centre), Environment Canada [*Service de l'Environnement Atmospherique (Centre Meteorologique de l'Ontario), Environnement Canada*] **Toronto, Ontario** [*Library symbol National Library of Canada*] (NLC) ... OTEAOW
Atmospheric Explorer [*Satellite*] [*NASA*] ... AE
Atmospheric Flight ... AF
Atmospheric Flight Test (NASA) ... AFT
Atmospheric Fluidized Bed [*Chemical engineering*] ... AFB
Atmospheric Fluidized Bed Coal [*Energy technology*] ... AFBC
Atmospheric Fluidized-Bed Combustion [*Fuel technology*] ... AFBC
Atmospheric Forcings for the Mid-Atlantic Bight [*Oceanography*] (MSC) ... AFMAB
Atmospheric Gas Oil [*Petroleum technology*] ... AGO
Atmospheric General Circulation Model [*Meteorology*] ... AGCM
Atmospheric Head (AAG) ... H
Atmospheric Infrared Attenuation Coefficient ... AIRAC
Atmospheric Infrared Sounder (SSD) ... AIRS
Atmospheric Integrated Research Monitoring Network (OSRA) ... AIRMoN
Atmospheric Integrated Research Monitoring Network (USDC) ... AIRMoN
Atmospheric Laboratory for Applications and Science [*Satellite mission*] ... ALAS
Atmospheric Laboratory for Applications and Science [*NASA*] (OSRA) ... ATLAS
Atmospheric Layer and Density Distribution of Ions and Neutrals [*Rocket*] [*NASA*] ... ALADDIN
Atmospheric LIDAR [*LASER Infrared RADAR*] (SSD) ... ATLID
Atmospheric Lifetime Experiment [*Environmental science*] ... ALE
Atmospheric Lifetime Experiment Station [*Adrigole, Ireland*] ... ALE
Atmospheric Light Detection and Ranging Facility [*Los Alamos, NM*] [*Los Alamos National Laboratory*] [*Department of Energy*] (GRD) ... LIDAR
Atmospheric Magnetospheric Plasma System (NASA) ... AMPS
Atmospheric Maneuvering Reentry Vehicle (IEEE) ... AMRV
Atmospheric Mass Balance of Industrially Emitted and Natural Sulfur [*Environmental Protection Agency*] (GFGA) ... AMBIENS
Atmospheric Model Intercomparison Project (OSRA) ... AMIP
Atmospheric Model Intercomparison Project (USDC) ... AMIP
Atmospheric Monitor Oxygen Analyzer (IEEE) ... AMOA
Atmospheric Monitor System (IEEE) ... AMS
Atmospheric Nutrient Input to Coastal Areas [*Project*] (USDC) ... ANICA
Atmospheric Nutrient Input to Coastal Areas [*Project*] (OSRA) ... ANICA
Atmospheric Observation Bell (PDAA) ... AOB
Atmospheric or Remote Manipulator System [*Deep-sea diving*] ... ARMS
Atmospheric Physical and Chemical Monitor ... APACM
Atmospheric Physics Programme [*International Council of Scientific Unions*] ... APP
Atmospheric Pollution Sensor ... APS
Atmospheric Pressure ... AP
Atmospheric Pressure (IAA) ... ATMPR

Atmospheric Pressure and Ambient Temperature .... APAT
Atmospheric Pressure and Composition Control (NASA) .... APCC
Atmospheric Pressure Chemical Ionization .... APCI
Atmospheric Pressure Chemical Vapor Deposition [*Photovoltaic energy systems*] .... APCVD
Atmospheric Pressure Converted to Mean Sea Level E levation [*Aviation code*] (AIA) .... QFF
Atmospheric Pressure Ion Evaporation .... APIE
Atmospheric Pressure Ionization [*Physics*] .... API
Atmospheric Pressure Plasma Sprayed [*Thermal barrier coating*] .... APPS
Atmospheric Pressure Sensor .... APS
Atmospheric Pressure Supply System [*or Subsystem*] [*NASA*] (NASA) .... APSS
Atmospheric Quality and Modification [*National Center for Atmospheric Research*] .... AQM
Atmospheric Radiation Measurement [*Program*] .... ARM
Atmospheric Radiation Measurement Program [*Department of Energy*] (ECON) .... ARM
Atmospheric Radio Noise .... ARN
Atmospheric Radio Wave .... ARW
Atmospheric Reentry Materials and Structural Evaluation Facility (MCD) .... ARMSEF
Atmospheric Release Advisory Capability [*Energy Research and Development Administration*] .... ARAC
Atmospheric Rendezvous Space Logistics [*NASA*] (MCD) .... ARSL
Atmospheric Research and Environment Program [*Marine science*] (OSRA) .... AREP
Atmospheric Research and Exposure Assessment Laboratory [*Environmental Protection Agency*] .... AREAL
Atmospheric Research and Remote Sensing Plane [*Marine science*] (OSRA) .... ARAT
Atmospheric Research Equipment .... ARE
Atmospheric Research Program Staff [*Environmental Protection Agency*] (GFGA) .... ARPS
Atmospheric Resid Desulfurization [*Petroleum technology*] .... ARDS
Atmospheric Residue Hydrosulfurization [*Petroleum technology*] .... ARHDS
Atmospheric Revitalization (MCD) .... AR
Atmospheric Revitalization Pressure Control System (MCD) .... ARPCS
Atmospheric Roving Manipulator System (PDAA) .... ARMS
Atmospheric Science Facility [*NASA*] (NASA) .... ASF
Atmospheric Sciences Laboratory [*Army Laboratory Command*] [*White Sands Missile Range, NM*] .... ASL
Atmospheric Sciences Modeling Division [*Marine science*] (OSRA) .... ASMD
Atmospheric Sciences Modeling Division [*Air Resources Laboratory*] (USDC) .... ASMD
Atmospheric Sciences Research Center [*State University of New York*] [*Research center*] .... ASRC
Atmospheric Sciences Research Laboratory [*Research Triangle Park, NC*] [*Environmental Protection Agency*] (GRD) .... ASRL
Atmospheric Simulation Facility (MCD) .... ASF
Atmospheric Sound Refraction .... ASR
Atmospheric Sound-Focusing Gain .... ASFG
Atmospheric Storage and Control Section [*Spacelab*] [*NASA*] .... ASCS
Atmospheric Structure Satellite (SAA) .... ASS
Atmospheric Studies in Complex Terrain (PDAA) .... ASCOT
Atmospheric Surface Layer [*Marine science*] (OSRA) .... ASL
Atmospheric Surface Layer (USDC) .... ASL
Atmospheric Surveillance Technology (MCD) .... AST
Atmospheric Tactical Warning (MCD) .... ATW
Atmospheric Thermonuclear Weapons Testing .... ATWT
Atmospheric Trace Molecules Observed by Spectroscopy .... ATMOS
Atmospheric Transmission Measurement Equipment .... ATME
Atmospheric Transport and Dispersion [*Model*] [*Marine science*] (OSRA)..... ATAD
Atmospheric Transport and Dispersion [*Model*] (USDC) .... ATAD
Atmospheric Turbulence and Diffusion Division [*Air Resources Laboratory*] (USDC) .... ATDD
Atmospheric Turbulence and Diffusion Division [*Marine science*] (OSRA) .... ATDD
Atmospheric Turbulence and Diffusion Laboratory [*Oak Ridge, Tennessee*] .... ATDL
Atmospheric Turbulence Measuring Set (MCD) .... ATMS
Atmospheric Variability Experiment [*NASA*] .... AVE
Atmospheric Vehicle Detection .... AVD
Atmospheric Wind Velocity .... AWV
Atmospheric Winds Aloft .... AWA
Atmospheric X-Ray Imaging Spectrometer (MCD) .... AXIS
Atmospherics [*NWS*] (FAAC) .... SFERICS
Atna Resources Ltd. [*Vancouver Stock Exchange symbol*] .... ATN
Atoka, OK [*AM radio station call letters*] .... KEOR
Atoka, OK [*FM radio station call letters*] .... KHKC
Atoll Commander [*In Pacific operations*] [*World War II*] .... ATCOM
Atom [*or Atomic*] .... A
Atom Bomb .... A (Bomb)
Atom Flourescence for Chemical Analysis (PDAA) .... AFCA
Atom Parts per Million (MCD) .... APPM
Atom Transfer Radical Polymerization [*Chemistry*] .... ATRP
Atomedic Research Center (EA) .... ARC
Atomic .... AT
Atomic .... ATMC
Atomic Absorption [*Environmental Protection Agency*] .... AA
Atomic Absorption [*Chemical analysis*] .... AA
Atomic Absorption Coefficient .... AAC
Atomic Absorption Flame Spectrometer .... AAFS
Atomic Absorption Spectrometer [*or Spectrophotometer or Spectroscopy*] ..... AAS
Atomic Age (IAA) .... AA
Atomic Air Raid Precaution (IAA) .... AARP

Atomic and Molecular Physical Data Program [*American Society for Testing and Materials*] (IID) .... AMD
Atomic and Molecular Processes Information Center [*ORNL*] .... AMPIC
Atomic Bargain Analysis Report (CINC) .... ATBAN
Atomic Beam Method .... ABM
Atomic, Biological, and Chemical [*as, ABC Officer, ABC Warfare*] [*Obsolete*] .... ABC
Atomic, Biological, Chemical, and Damage Control .... ABCD
Atomic, Biological, Chemical, and Radiological [*Warfare*] (NATG) .... ABCR
Atomic, Biological, Chemical Warfare .... ABCW
Atomic Bomb (ODBW) .... A-bomb
Atomic Bomb Casualty Commission [*Later, RERF*] .... ABCC
Atomic Bomb Casualty Commission, Seattle, WA [*Library symbol Library of Congress*] (LCLS) .... WaSAB
Atomic Cesium Beam MASER .... ACBM
Atomic Collision Cross Sections Information Center [*ORNL*] .... ACCSIC
Atomic Coordinating Office (Washington, DC) [*British Defense Staff*] ...... ACO(W)
Atomic Coordination Office [*British*] .... ACO
Atomic Damage Template [*Military drafting*] .... ADT
Atomic Defense .... ATOMDEF
Atomic Defense and Space Group [*Westinghouse Electric Corp.*] (MCD) ..... ADSG
Atomic Defense Engineering (MUGU) .... ADE
Atomic Defense Support Agency .... ADSA
Atomic Demolition Munition .... ADM
Atomic Development Authority [*Proposed by Bernard Baruch to exercise control over those aspects of atomic energy inimical to global security; never organized*] .... ADA
Atomic Device [*Military*] .... ATOMDEV
Atomic Drive (AAG) .... AD
Atomic Drive .... A-DRV
Atomic Emission .... AE
Atomic Emission Detector [*Instrumentation*] .... AED
Atomic Emission Spectroscopy .... AES
Atomic Energy (ADA) .... AE
Atomic Energy Act [*1954*] .... AEA
Atomic Energy Authority [*British*] .... AEA
Atomic Energy Bureau [*Korea*] (NUCP) .... AEB
Atomic Energy Bureau [*Japan*] (NUCP) .... AEB
Atomic Energy Bureau of Science and Technics Agency [*Japan*] .... AEBSTA
Atomic Energy Centre - Lahore .... AECL
Atomic Energy Commission [*Functions divided, 1975, between Nuclear Regulatory Commission and Energy Research and Development Administration*] .... AEC
Atomic Energy Commission - Armed Forces Special Weapons Project Technical Publication (MCD) .... AEC-AFSWP-TP
Atomic Energy Commission Board of Contract Appeals [*Replaced by the Energy Research and Development Administration Board of Contract Appeals in 1975*] (AAGC) .... AECBCA
Atomic Energy Commission Declassified Report (NUCP) .... AECD
Atomic Energy Commission - Defense Atomic Support Agency Technical Publication (MCD) .... AEC-DASA-TP
Atomic Energy Commission - Defense Atomic Support Agency Technical Publication (MCD) .... AEC-DASA-TP
Atomic Energy Commission - Defense Nuclear Agency Technical Publication (MCD) .... AEC-DNA-TP
Atomic Energy Commission Manual .... AECM
Atomic Energy Commission Procurement Regulations [*Obsolete*] .... AECPR
Atomic Energy Commission. Reports [*A publication*] (DLA) .... AEC
Atomic Energy Commission/Technical Information Center (MCD) .... AEC/TIC
Atomic Energy Commission Unclassified Report (NUCP) .... AECU
Atomic Energy Control Board [*Canada*] .... AECB
Atomic Energy Control Board, Ottawa, ON, Canada [*Library symbol Library of Congress*] (LCLS) .... CaOOAECB
Atomic Energy Control Board [*Commission de Controle de l'Energie Atomique*]Ottawa, Ontario [*Library symbol National Library of Canada*] (NLC) .... OOAECB
Atomic Energy Corporation [*South Africa*] [*Research center*] .... AEC
Atomic Energy Detection System [*Nuclear energy*] .... AEDS
Atomic Energy Establishment [*Libya*] (NUCP) .... AEE
Atomic Energy Establishment [*British*] .... AEE
Atomic Energy Establishment, [*Trombay, India*] (NUCP) .... AEET
Atomic Energy Establishment, Winfrith [*England*] .... AEEW
Atomic Energy Labor Management Relations Panel .... AELMRP
Atomic Energy Law Journal [*A publication*] (DLA) .... AELJ
Atomic Energy Law Journal [*A publication*] (DLA) .... Atom Energy LJ
Atomic Energy Law Journal [*A publication*] (AAGC) .... Atom Energy LJ
Atomic Energy Law Reporter (Commerce Clearing House) [*A publication*] (DLA) .... Atom En L Rep CCH
Atomic Energy Law Reporter (Commerce Clearing House) [*A publication*] (DLA) .... CCH Atom En L Rep
Atomic Energy Level .... AEL
Atomic Energy Levels Data Center .... AELDC
Atomic Energy of Canada, Chalk River, ON, Canada [*Library symbol Library of Congress*] (LCLS) .... CaOCkA
Atomic Energy of Canada [*L'Energie Atomique du Canada*] Chalk River, Ontario [*Library symbol National Library of Canada*] (NLC) .... OCKA
Atomic Energy of Canada Chemical Co., Ottawa, ON, Canada [*Library symbol Library of Congress*] (LCLS) .... CaOOAEC
Atomic Energy of Canada Ltd. .... AECL
Atomic Energy of Canada Ltd. Library [*UTLAS symbol*] .... ATM
Atomic Energy of Canada Ltd., Research Co., Ottawa, ON, Canada [*Library symbol Library of Congress*] (LCLS) .... CaOOAER
Atomic Energy of Canada, Montreal, PQ, Canada [*Library symbol Library of Congress*] (LCLS) .... CaQMAEC

Atomic Energy of Canada [*L'Energie Atomique du Canada*] **Montreal, Quebec** [*Library symbol National Library of Canada*] (NLC) .... QMAEC
Atomic Energy of Canada, Ottawa, ON, Canada [*Library symbol Library of Congress*] (LCLS) .... CaOOAE
Atomic Energy of Canada, Toronto, ON, Canada [*Library symbol Library of Congress*] (LCLS) .... CaOTAE
Atomic Energy of Canada [*L'Energie Atomique du Canada*] **Toronto, Ontario** [*Library symbol National Library of Canada*] (NLC) .... OTAE
Atomic Energy of Canada, Whiteshell Nuclear Research Establishment, **Pinawa, MB, Canada** [*Library symbol Library of Congress*] (LCLS) .... CaMPW
Atomic Energy Organisation [*Iran*] (NUCP) .... AEO
Atomic Energy Project .... AEP
Atomic Energy Regulatory Board [*India*] .... AERB
Atomic Energy Research Department [*NASA*] (KSC) .... AERD
Atomic Energy Research Establishment [*of United Kingdom Atomic Energy Authority*] .... AERE
Atomic Energy Research Establishment, Didcot, Oxfordshire, United Kingdom [*Library symbol Library of Congress*] (LCLS) .... UkHA
Atomic Energy Society of Japan (NUCP) .... AESJ
Atomic Explosion .... ATXPL
Atomic Fluid Cell (OA) .... AFC
Atomic Fluorescence .... AF
Atomic Fluorescence Spectroscopy .... AFS
Atomic Force Microscope .... AFM
Atomic Forum (IEEE) .... AF
Atomic Frequency Standard .... AFS
Atomic Fuel Corp. [*Japan*] .... AFC
Atomic Ground Intercept (MCD) .... ATGIN
Atomic Hydrogen Weld .... AT/W
Atomic Hydrogen Welding .... AHW
Atomic Incident Control Plan .... AICP
Atomic Industrial Forum [*Later, USCEA*] (EA) .... AIF
Atomic International - Combustion Engineering .... AI-CE
Atomic Layer Epitaxy [*Physical chemistry*] .... ALE
Atomic Layer-by-Layer Molecular Beam Epitaxy .... ALL-MBE
Atomic Line Molecular Spectroscopy .... ALMS
Atomic Magneto-Optic Resonance Spectrometry .... AMORS
Atomic Mass (IIA) .... ATM
Atomic Mass Number .... AMN
Atomic Mass Unit .... AMU
Atomic Mass Unit (IDOE) .... amu
Atomic Migration .... AM
Atomic, Molecular, and Optical Physics .... AMO
Atomic/Nuclear Energy Study Group (EA) .... ANESG
Atomic Number .... AN
Atomic Number .... ATNO
Atomic Number [*Symbol*] .... Z
Atomic Orbital .... AO
Atomic Orbital with Angular Momentum Quantum Number 3 [*Symbol*] (DAVI) .... f
Atomic Ordnance Cataloging Office .... AOCO
Atomic Ordnance Platoon (NG) .... AOP
Atomic Packing Factor (IEEE) .... APF
Atomic Photoelectric Effect .... APE
Atomic Physics Consortium at Oak Ridge .... APCOR
Atomic Post-Strike Analysis Report .... ATPOS
Atomic Power Construction Ltd. .... APC
Atomic Power Construction Ltd. .... APCL
Atomic Power Development Associates, Inc. .... APDA
Atomic Power Equipment Department (SAA) .... APED
Atomic Power Group [*Nuclear energy*] (NUCP) .... APG
Atomic Power Station (NRCH) .... APS
Atomic Powered .... AP
Atomic Reactor in Space (MUGU) .... ARIS
Atomic Research and Development Authority [*Nuclear Regulatory Commission*] (GFGA) .... ARDA
Atomic Resolution Microscope .... ARM
Atomic Resonance Absorption Spectroscopy [*Physics*] .... ARAS
Atomic Resonance Filter Optical Receiver Module (MCD) .... ARFORM
Atomic Resonance Optical Filter (MCD) .... AROF
Atomic Safety and Licensing Appeal Board (NRCH) .... ASLAB
Atomic Safety and Licensing Appeal Panel [*Nuclear Regulatory Commission*] .... ASLAP
Atomic Safety and Licensing Board [*Nuclear Regulatory Commission*] .... ASLB
Atomic Safety and Licensing Board Panel [*Nuclear Regulatory Commission*] .... ASLBP
Atomic Safety Line (IAA) .... ASL
Atomic Scattering Factor .... ASF
Atomic Scientists' Association [*Great Britain*] .... ASA
Atomic Security Agency [*Army*] .... ASA
Atomic Shell of 98 Electrons per Shell (BARN) .... Q
Atomic Solution Diffusion .... ASD
Atomic Solvation Parameter [*Physical chemistry*] .... ASP
Atomic Space and Development Authority [*Nuclear energy*] (NRCH) .... ASADA
Atomic Space and Development Authority [*Nuclear energy*] .... ASDA
Atomic Spin Orbital (IAA) .... ASO
Atomic Standing Operating Procedures (NATG) .... ASOP
Atomic Status Report (NATG) .... ATOMSTATSREP
Atomic Strike Evaluation Center .... ASTREC
Atomic Strike Net (AABC) .... ASN
Atomic Strike Plan (AFM) .... ASP
Atomic Strike Plan Control Group Alternate (AABC) .... ASPCGA
Atomic Strike Recording [*Air Force*] .... ASR
Atomic Strike Recording System [*Air Force*] .... ASTREC
Atomic Time .... AT

Atomic Time Unit .... ATU
Atomic Torpedo [*Military*] .... ATORP
Atomic Transition Probabilities Data Center .... ATPDC
Atomic Units (MCD) .... AU
Atomic Value (ADA) .... AV
Atomic Vapor LASER Isotope Separation (NUCP) .... ALVIS
Atomic Vapor LASER Isotope Separation .... AVLIS
Atomic Volume (DNAB) .... AT VOL
Atomic Warfare .... AW
Atomic Weapon Detection, Recognition and Yield (PDAA) .... AWDREY
Atomic Weapon Retrofit Order .... AWRO
Atomic Weapons Research Establishment [*British Ministry of Defense*] [*Research center*] .... AWRE
Atomic Weapons Special Transport (DNAB) .... AWST
Atomic Weapons Training Group [*DASA*] .... AWTG
Atomic Weight .... A
Atomic Weight .... ATWT
Atomic Weight .... AW
Atomic Weight (IAA) .... AWT
Atomic Weight Unit .... AWU
Atomicity, Consistency, Isolation, and Durability .... ACID
Atomicity, Consistency, Isolation, and Durability Test (DOM) .... ACID test
Atomicity Controller .... AC
Atomics International (NRCH) .... AI
Atomics International, Canoga Park, CA [*Library symbol Library of Congress*] (LCLS) .... CCpA
Atomics International Division .... AID
Atomics International Evaluated Nuclear Data Files (KSC) .... AIENDF
Atomic-Type Field Army (SAA) .... ATFA
Atomized Suspension Technique .... AST
Atomizing .... ATMG
Atom-Probe Field-Ion Microscopy .... APFIM
Atonement .... Aton
Atonement Seminary of the Holy Ghost, Washington, DC [*Library symbol Library of Congress*] (LCLS) .... DAtS
Atopic Dermatitis [*Medicine*] .... AT
ATP [*Adenosine Triphosphate*]-Binding Cassette [*Biochemistry*] .... ABC
Atqasuk [*Alaska*] [*Airport symbol*] (OAG) .... ATK
A-Track Initiator (SAA) .... ATI
Atraumatic [*Medicine*] (DAVI) .... AT
Atraumatic Normocephalic [*Medicine*] .... ATNC
Atresia [*Medicine*] .... ATR
Atria/Carotid/Ventricular [*Anatomy*] .... ACV
Atria Communities, Inc. [*NASDAQ symbol*] (SAG) .... ATRC
Atria Communities, Inc. [*Associated Press*] (SAG) .... AtriaCo
Atria Software [*NASDAQ symbol*] (TTSB) .... ATSW
Atria Software, Inc. [*Associated Press*] (SAG) .... AtriaSft
Atria Software, Inc. [*NASDAQ symbol*] (SAG) .... ATSW
Atrial [*Cardiology*] (DAVI) .... AT
Atrial [*Cardiology*] (DAVI) .... atr
Atrial Bolus Dynamic Computer Tomography [*Cardiology*] (DAVI) .... ABDCT
Atrial Diastolic Gallop [*Cardiology*] (MAE) .... ADG
Atrial Ectopic Tachycardia [*Medicine*] .... AET
Atrial Ectopy [*Cardiology*] .... AT-ECT
Atrial Emptying Index [*Medicine*] (DMAA) .... AEI
Atrial Fibrillation [*Cardiology*] .... AF
Atrial Fibrillation [*Cardiology*] .... AFIB
Atrial Fibrillation [*Cardiology*] .... AT FIB
Atrial Fibrillation [*Cardiology*] (MAE) .... atr fib
Atrial Fibrillation and/or Flutter [*Cardiology*] (DAVI) .... AF/F
Atrial Filling Fraction [*Cardiology*] .... AFF
Atrial Filling Pressure [*Cardiology*] (DAVI) .... AFP
Atrial Filling Rate [*Cardiology*] .... AFR
Atrial Flutter [*Cardiology*] .... Af
Atrial Flutter [*Cardiology*] (MAE) .... AFL
Atrial Gallop [*Cardiology*] .... AG
Atrial His-Bundle [*Cardiology*] .... AH
Atrial Inhibited Pacemaker [*Cardiology*] (DMAA) .... AAI
Atrial Insufficiency [*Cardiology*] (AAMN) .... AI
Atrial Myxoma [*Medicine*] (DAVI) .... AM
Atrial Natriuretic Factor [*Biochemistry*] .... ANF
Atrial Natriuretic Peptide [*Biochemistry*] .... ANP
Atrial Overdrive Stimulation Rate [*Cardiology*] (DMAA) .... AST
Atrial Pore Field [*Botany*] .... APF
Atrial [*or Auricular*] Premature Beat [*Cardiology*] (DAVI) .... APB
Atrial Premature Beats [*Cardiology*] .... APB
Atrial Premature Contraction [*Cardiology*] .... APC
Atrial Premature Depolarization [*Cardiology*] .... APD
Atrial Rate [*Cardiology*] .... AR
Atrial Septal Defect [*Cardiology*] .... ASD
Atrial Stenosis [*Cardiology*] (AAMN) .... AS
Atrial Synchronous Ventricular Inhibited Pacemaker [*Cardiology*] .... ASVIP
Atrial Tachycardia with Block [*Cardiology*] (AAMN) .... ATB
Atrial Vascular Relaxant Substance [*Biochemistry*] .... AVRS
Atrialelectrogram [*Cardiology*] .... AEG
Atriocarotid [*Medicine*] .... AC
Atrion Corp. [*NASDAQ symbol*] (SAG) .... ATRI
Atrion Corp. [*NASDAQ symbol*] (TTSB) .... ATRI
Atrion Corp. [*Associated Press*] (SAG) .... Atrion
Atriopeptin [*Biochemistry*] .... AP
Atrioseptal Heart Disease [*Cardiology*] (DMAA) .... ASHD
Atrioventricular [*Cardiology*] .... AV
Atrioventricular Block [*Cardiology*] (DMAA) .... AVB
Atrioventricular Canal [*Cardiology*] .... AVC

Atrioventricular Canal Defect [*Also called endocardial cushion defect*] [*Cardiology*] (DAVI) .... AVCD
Atrioventricular Conduction System [*Cardiology*] .... AVCS
Atrioventricular Heart Block [*Cardiology*] (DAVI) .... AVHB
Atrioventricular Junction [*Medicine*] (DMAA) .... AVJ
Atrioventricular Nodal Reentry [*Cardiology*] .... AVNR
Atrioventricular Node [*Cardiology*] .... AVN
Atrioventricular Node Dysfunction [*Medicine*] (DMAA) .... AVND
Atrioventricular Reentrant Tachycardia [*Cardiology*] (DMAA) .... AVRT
Atrioventricular Refractory Period [*Cardiology*] (MAE) .... AVRP
Atrioventricular Septal Defect [*Cardiology*] (DMAA) .... AVSD
Atrioventricular Valve Opening (DAVI) .... AO
Atrium [*Medicine*] (DMAA) .... A
Atrium Pace [*Cardiology*] .... AP
Atrix International [*NASDAQ symbol*] (TTSB) .... ATXI
Atrix International, Inc. [*Associated Press*] (SAG) .... AtrixInt
Atrix International, Inc. [*NASDAQ symbol*] (SAG) .... ATXI
Atrix Laboratories [*NASDAQ symbol*] (TTSB) .... ATRX
Atrix Laboratories, Inc. [*Associated Press*] (SAG) .... AtrixL
Atrix Laboratories, Inc. [*NASDAQ symbol*] (SAG) .... ATRX
Atrophic Rhinitis [*Medicine*] (DMAA) .... AR
Atrophy (MAE) .... atr
Atropine (MAE) .... A
Atropine-Like Psycho-Chemical Substance (PDAA) .... APS
Atroxin-Defibrinated Plasma [*Clinical chemistry*] .... ADFP
Atruvera [*Former USSR*] [*FAA designator*] (FAAC) .... AUV
ATS Aircharter Ltd. [*British ICAO designator*] (FAAC) .... AVT
ATS Med Inc. Wrrt [*NASDAQ symbol*] (TTSB) .... ATSIW
ATS Medical [*NASDAQ symbol*] (TTSB) .... ATSI
ATS Medical, Inc. [*Associated Press*] (SAG) .... ATS M
ATS Medical, Inc. [*Associated Press*] (SAG) .... ATS Med
ATS Medical, Inc. [*NASDAQ symbol*] (SAG) .... ATSI
At-Sea Calibration Procedure .... ASCAP
ATS-Servicii de Transport Aerian [*Italy ICAO designator*] (FAAC) .... ROS
Atsugi [*Japan ICAO location identifier*] (ICLI) .... RJTA
Attach [*or Attachment*] (AFM) .... ATCH
Attach (KSC) .... ATT
Attach on Morning Report the Following Named EM [*Enlisted Man*] Who Has Been Authorized to Report to Your Station upon Expiration of Leave. Retain Him/Her Pending Further Instructions (AABC) .... ATCHEMPI
Attach Points Only (MCD) .... APO
Attach-Detach Kit .... ADK
Attache .... ATT
Attache .... ATT
Attache Support Message (MCD) .... ASM
Attached .... ATCHD
Attached (WDMC) .... att
Attached Applications Processor .... AAP
Attached FORTRAN Processor [*Burroughs Corp.*] [*Computer science*] (BUR) .... AFP
Attached Gingiva [*Medicine*] (DMAA) .... AG
Attached Inflatable Decelerator [*Aerodynamics*] .... AID
Attached Inflatable Detector .... AID
Attached Payload Accommodations Equipment (SSD) .... APAE
Attached Payload and Associated Equipment (SSD) .... AP & AE
Attached Pressurized Module [*European Space Agency*] .... APM
Attached Processor [*Computer science*] (BUR) .... AP
Attached Processor for Speech [*IBM Corp.*] (NITA) .... APS
Attached Processor System [*Telecommunications*] (TEL) .... APS
Attached Resource Computer (MHDB) .... ARC
Attached Resource Computer Network .... ARCnet
Attached Resources Computer Network [*Microcomputer LAN*] [*Datapoint Corp.*] (NITA) .... ARCNET
Attached Support Processor [*Computer science*] .... ASP
Attached to Other Correspondence [*Business term*] .... A to OC
Attached to Other Correspondence [*Business term*] .... AOC
Attached Trailer Towed Vehicle Weight [*Automotive engineering*] .... ATVW
Attached Training Vessel [*Navy*] .... ATV
Attached Virtual Processor [*Computer science*] (NITA) .... AVP
Attachie [*British Columbia*] [*Seismograph station code, US Geological Survey Closed*] (SEIS) .... ATC
Attachment (MUGU) .... ATCHMT
Attachment [*Telecommunications*] (TEL) .... ATT
Attachment .... ATTACHT
Attachment Plaque .... AP
Attachment Point [*Genetics*] (DOG) .... ap
Attachment Unit (MCD) .... AU
Attachment Unit Interface [*Computer science*] (PCM) .... AUI
Attack [*Designation for all US military aircraft*] .... A
Attack [*Men's lacrosse position*] .... A
Attack (DNAB) .... ATAK
Attack (MSA) .... ATCK
Attack (AABC) .... ATK
Attack .... ATTK
Attack Air Mobility System [*Army*] .... AAMS
Attack Aircraft Carrier (MCD) .... AAC
Attack Aircraft Carrier [*Navy symbol*] .... CVA
Attack Aircraft Carrier (Nuclear Propulsion) [*Navy symbol*] .... CVAN
Attack Assessment [*Military*] .... AA
Attack Assessment System (MCD) .... AAS
Attack Cargo Ship [*Navy symbol*] .... AKA
Attack Cargo Ship [*Navy symbol*] .... LKA
Attack Carrier Air Wing [*Navy*] .... ATKCARAIRWING
Attack Carrier Air Wing [*Navy symbol*] .... CVW
Attack Carrier Striking Force .... ACSF

Attack Center .... AC
Attack Center Display .... ACD
Attack Center Indicator Panel .... ACIP
Attack Center Panel .... ACP
Attack Center Switchboard .... ACS
Attack Characterization (MCD) .... AC
Attack Class Patrol Boat [*Navy*] .... ACPB
Attack Console .... AC
Attack Control Concept .... ACC
Attack Control Console .... ACC
Attack Cut Out [*Military*] (NG) .... ACO
Attack/Decay/Sustain/Release [*Audio programming parameters*] .... ADSR
Attack Director [*Military*] (MCD) .... AD
Attack Display Group (MCD) .... ADG
Attack Evaluation Model (MCD) .... AEM
Attack Experimental [*Air Force*] (MCD) .... AX
Attack Geometry Display (DNAB) .... AGD
Attack Guidance Matrix [*Military*] (INF) .... AGM
Attack Heading Slot (SAA) .... AHS
Attack Heavy (DNAB) .... AH
Attack Helicopter (CINC) .... AH
Attack Helicopter [*MTMC*] (TAG) .... ATK HEL
Attack Helicopter Battalion .... AHB
Attack Helicopter Battalion [*Army*] (ADDR) .... ATKHB
Attack Helicopter Company [*Military*] .... AHC
Attack Helicopter Company [*Military*] (AABC) .... ATKHC
Attack Helicopter Instrument Test (MCD) .... AHIT
Attack Helicopter Interface Unit (MCD) .... AIU
Attack Helicopter Operations (CAAL) .... AHO
Attack Helicopter Operations and Analysis Group .... AHOAG
Attack Helicopter Organization [*Military*] .... ATHELO
Attack Helicopter Self Test (MCD) .... AHST
Attack Helicopter Support (MCD) .... AHS
Attack Helicopter Team .... AHT
Attack Information Center (AFM) .... AIC
Attack Jet .... AJ
Attack Plan (MCD) .... AP
Attack Plotter (NVT) .... AP
Attack Reference Point .... ARP
Attack Response Evaluation (MCD) .... ARE
Attack Response Exercise (MCD) .... ARE
Attack Squadron [*Navy*] (MUGU) .... ATKRON
Attack Squadron [*Symbol*] (MCD) .... VA
Attack Squadron Detachment [*Navy*] (DNAB) .... ATKRONDET
Attack Surveillance Committee [*Army*] (AABC) .... ATKSC
Attack Surveillance Coverage [*Army*] (AABC) .... ATKSC
Attack, Sustain, Release [*Electronic musical instruments*] .... ASR
Attack Teacher .... A/T
Attack Transport [*Later, LPA*] [*Navy symbol*] .... APA
Attack Warning Processing and Display System (MCD) .... AWPDS
Attack Warning System [*Civil Defense*] .... AWS
Attack Working Group [*Military*] .... AWG
Attacking Hardened Air Bases [*Air Force*] (PDAA) .... AHAB
Attain (ROG) .... ATTN
Attained Competency Level .... ACL
Attainment Quotient .... AQ
Attainment Target (AIE) .... AT
Attala, AL [*FM radio station call letters*] .... WKXX
Attawapiskat [*Canada*] [*Airport symbol*] (OAG) .... YAT
Attawapiskat Band Library, Attawapiskat, ON, Canada [*Library symbol*] [*Library of Congress*] (LCLS) .... CaOAttB
Attawapiskat Band Library, Ontario [*Library symbol National Library of Canada*] (BIB) .... OAB
Attempt (FAAC) .... ATMT
Attempt Break and Enter [*Criminology*] .... AB & E
Attempt to Contact (FAAC) .... ATMTC
Attempt to Locate (FAAC) .... ALCT
Attempt to Locate .... ATL
Attempt to Steal from Motor Vehicle [*Criminology*] .... ASFMV
Attempted [*FBI standardized term*] .... ATT
Attempted Corporate Integration of Dividends [*Economics*] .... ACID
Attempts .... ATT
Attempts per Circuit per Hour [*Telecommunications*] (TEL) .... ACH
Attend (ROG) .... ATTD
Attendance [*Sports*] .... A
Attendance (ROG) .... ATTCE
Attendance and Labor System (MCD) .... ATLAS
Attendant [*Telecommunications*] (TEL) .... AD
Attendant (MUGU) .... ATDNT
Attendant .... ATDT
Attendant (MSA) .... ATT
Attendant (AABC) .... ATTND
Attendant .... ATTNDNT
Attendant Care Evaluation .... ACE
Attendant Care Scheme .... ACS
Attendant Control of Facilities [*Western Electric Co.*] .... ACOF
Attended Pay Station [*Attended Public Telephone*] (TEL) .... APS
Attended Public Telephone [*Telecommunications*] (TEL) .... ATT
Attended Resource Computer [*Datapoint Corp.*] (NITA) .... ARC
Attending .... ATT
Attending .... ATTG
Attending .... ATTNG
Attending Physician (DMAA) .... AtP
Attending Physician Work Station (DMAA) .... APWS
Attending Physician's Statement .... APS

Attending's Admission Notes [*Medicine*] (DMAA) .... AAN
Attente [*Leave on*] [*Knitting term*] [*French*] (BARN) .... ATSDR
Attention [*Electronics*] .... AT
Attention .... ATN
Attention .... ATT
Attention (WDMC) .... att
Attention .... ATTEN
Attention (AFM) .... ATTN
Attention .... ATTN
Attention (ODBW) .... attn
Attention Control Training .... ACT
Attention Deficit and Distractability Disorder with Hyperactivity [*Medicine*]
    (DAVI) .... ADDD/H
Attention Deficit Disorder [*Psychology*] .... ADD
Attention Deficit Disorder with Hyperactivity [*Psychology*] (DAVI) .... ADD W H
Attention Deficit Disorder with Hyperactivity [*Medicine*] .... ADD-H
Attention Deficit Disorder with Hyperactivity [*Medicine*] .... ADD-HA
Attention Deficit Disorder-Residual Type .... ADD-RT
Attention Deficit Hyperactivity Disorder [*Medicine*] .... ADHD
Attention Dial Tone [*Computer science*] (DOM) .... ATDT
Attention Director (MCD) .... ATTNDIR
Attention Display [*Communications device*] .... AD
Attention Getting [*by the hearing-impaired*] .... AG
Attention, Interest, Desire, Conviction, Action, and Satisfaction [*Sales*]
    (WDMC) .... AIDCAS
Attention Invited (MCD) .... ATTNINV
Attention Operating Characteristic [*Psychometrics*] .... AOC
Attention-Deficit Disorder Association (EA) .... ADDA
Attention-Interest-Desire-Action [*Formula*] [*Marketing*] .... AIDA
Attenuated RADAR Monitor .... ARM
Attenuated Total Reflectance [*Instrumentation*] .... ATR
Attenuation (IAA) .... A
Attenuation (DEN) .... AT
Attenuation [*Instrumentation*] .... ATT
Attenuation Efficiency Score (PDAA) .... AES
Attenuation Equalizer (IAA) .... AE
Attenuation Index .... AI
Attenuation Reaction .... AR
Attenuator (KSC) .... ATTEN
Attenuator .... ATTN
Attenuator-Thermoelement Voltmeter .... ATVM
Attestation .... ATTESTN
Attesting (ROG) .... ATTESTG
At-the-Knee Amputation (VNW) .... AK Amp
Atti della Settimana Biblica [*A publication*] (BJA) .... AtSetBib
Atti Parlamentari [*Parliamentary Acts*] [*Italian*] (ILCA) .... Atti Parl
Attic [*Greek dialect*] (ROG) .... ATT
Attic .... ATTC
Attica [*New York*] [*Seismograph station code, US Geological Survey Closed*]
    (SEIS) .... ATT
Attica Daily Ledger Tribune, Attica, IN [*Library symbol Library of Congress*]
    (LCLS) .... InAttLT
Attica Friendly Oracle, Attica, IN [*Library symbol Library of Congress*]
    (LCLS) .... InAttFO
Attica, IN [*FM radio station call letters*] .... WGBD
Attica, NY [*FM radio station call letters*] .... WBTF
Attica Public Library, Attica, IN [*Library symbol Library of Congress*]
    (LCLS) .... InAtt
Atticus [*of Nepos*] [*Classical studies*] (OCD) .... Att
Attitude .... ATT
Attitude (KSC) .... ATTD
Attitude .... ATTTD
Attitude Acquisition Technique .... AAT
Attitude and Antenna Control System [*NASA*] (MCD) .... AACS
Attitude and Articulation Control Subsystem [*NASA*] .... AACS
Attitude and Orbit Control Electronics [*Aerospace*] (NASA) .... AOCE
Attitude and Orbit Control System [*or Subsystem*] (MCD) .... AOCS
Attitude and Pointing (MCD) .... AP
Attitude and Pointing Control System [*NASA*] (MHDW) .... APC
Attitude and Pointing Control System [*NASA*] (KSC) .... APCS
Attitude and Pointing Control System [*NASA*] .... APS
Attitude and Rate Indicating System .... ARIS
Attitude and Spin Control Subsystem [*NASA*] .... ASCS
Attitude and Translation Control Assembly [*Aviation*] (MCD) .... ATCA
Attitude and Translation Control Electronics .... ATCE
Attitude and Translation Control System (MCD) .... ATCS
Attitude and Translation Control Unit .... ATCU
Attitude Angle Transducer .... AAT
Attitude Axis Emergency Control [*Aerospace*] (MCD) .... AAEC
Attitude Command System (IEEE) .... ACS
Attitude Configuration System (SSD) .... ACS
Attitude Control [*System*] [*Aerospace*] .... AC
Attitude Control (IDOE) .... ac
Attitude Control and Determination Subsystem (MCD) .... ACDS
Attitude Control and Maneuver Rate [*Aerospace*] .... ACMR
Attitude Control and Maneuvering Electronics [*Aerospace*] (MCD) .... ACME
Attitude Control and Maneuvering Electronics System [*Aerospace*]
    (MCD) .... ACMES
Attitude Control and Stabilization [*NASA*] (KSC) .... ACS
Attitude Control and Translation System [*Aerospace*] (MCD) .... ACTS
Attitude Control and Translation System/Propulsion [*Aerospace*] ...... ACTS/PROP
Attitude Control and Translation System/Stabilization and Control
    Electronics [*Aerospace*] .... ACTS/SCE
Attitude Control Development [*Aerospace*] (SSD) .... ACD
Attitude Control Document (SSD) .... ACD

Attitude Control Electronics [*Aerospace*] .... ACE
Attitude Control Indicator [*Aerospace*] (IAA) .... ACI
Attitude Control Jet [*Aerospace*] .... ACJ
Attitude Control Propulsion Motor [*Aerospace*] .... ACPM
Attitude Control Propulsion System [*or Subsystem*] [*NASA*] .... ACPS
Attitude Control System [*or Subsystem*] [*Aerospace*] .... ACS
Attitude Control Torquing Device [*Aerospace*] .... ACTD
Attitude Controller Assembly [*NASA*] (KSC) .... ACA
Attitude Coordinate Converter System (AAG) .... ACCS
Attitude Determination and Control Software [*Orbital satellites*] .... ADACS
Attitude Determination and Control System (MCD) .... ADACS
Attitude Direction Indicator [*Aerospace*] .... ADI
Attitude Director Indicator System (PDAA) .... ADIS
Attitude Display Indicator [*Aerospace*] (MCD) .... ADI
Attitude Display System (MCD) .... ADS
Attitude Ground Support System (MCD) .... AGSS
Attitude Gyro (MCD) .... AG
Attitude Gyro Accelerometer Assembly (MCD) .... AGAA
Attitude Gyro Accelerometer Package (KSC) .... AGAP
Attitude Gyro Assembly (MCD) .... AGA
Attitude Gyro Coupling Unit (KSC) .... AGCU
Attitude Heading Gyroscope System .... AHGS
Attitude Heading Reference System (NG) .... AHRS
Attitude Heading Reference Unit .... AHRU
Attitude Hold (MCD) .... AH
Attitude Hold Pitch [*Axis*] .... AHP
Attitude Hold Roll [*Axis*] (NASA) .... AHR
Attitude Horizon Sensor (IIA) .... AHS
Attitude Indicating System (MCD) .... AIS
Attitude Indicator [*NASA*] (KSC) .... AI
Attitude Maneuvering System (SAA) .... AMS
Attitude Monitor Switching Unit (MCD) .... AMSU
Attitude Nutation Control Electronics (NASA) .... ANCE
Attitude Processor (NASA) .... AP
Attitude Propulsion Subsystem .... APS
Attitude Reaction Wheel .... ARW
Attitude Reference Assembly (MCD) .... ARA
Attitude Reference Bombing Computer (MCD) .... ARBC
Attitude Reference Bombing Computer Set [*or System*] (MCD) .... ARBCS
Attitude Reference Program [*NASA*] .... ATTREF
Attitude Reference System (KSC) .... ARS
Attitude Reference Unit .... ARU
Attitude Sensor Parachute Staging Unit (MCD) .... ASPSU
Attitude Set [*Aerospace*] .... AS
Attitude Set and Gimbal Position Display [*NASA*] (KSC) .... AS/GPD
Attitude Set and Gimbal Position Indicator [*NASA*] .... AS/GPI
Attitude Set Control Panel [*Aerospace*] (NASA) .... ASCP
Attitude Stabilization and Control System (MCD) .... ASCS
Attitude Thrustor System .... ATS
Attitude toward Caring for the Dying Scale .... ACD
Attitude toward School Questionnaire [*Test*] .... ASQ
Attitude Transfer System (MCD) .... ATS
Attitude Vapor Crystal Growth (SSD) .... AVCG
Attitude-Interest Analysis Test [*Psychology*] .... AIAT
Attitude-Referenced Radiometer Study [*NASA*] .... ARRS
Attitudes, Interests, and Opinions of Individuals [*Psychographics*]
    (WDMC) .... AIO Inventory
Attitudes Toward Blindness Questionnaire [*Psychology*] (EDAC) .... ATBQ
Attitudes toward Disabled Persons [*Psychology*] .... ATDP
Attitudes Toward Educational Research Scale [*Psychology*] (EDAC) .... ATERS
Attitudes Toward Feminist Issues Scales [*Psychology*] (EDAC) .... ATFI
Attitudes Toward Handicapped Individuals Scale [*Psychology*] (EDAC) .... ATHI
Attitudes toward Industrialization [*Psychology*] .... ATI
Attitudes Toward Mainstreaming Scale [*Psychology*] (EDAC) .... ATMS
Attitudes toward Parental Control of Children [*Psychology*] .... ATPCC
Attitudes Toward Sex Roles Instrument [*Psychology*] (EDAC) .... ATSR
Attitudinal Information Data System (NVT) .... AIDS
Attiyeh Foundation (EA) .... AF
Attleboro, MA [*AM radio station call letters*] .... WARA
Attleboro Public Library, Attleboro, MA [*Library symbol Library of
    Congress*] (LCLS) .... MAtt
Atto [*Act*] [*Italian*] .... A
Atto [*A prefix meaning divided by 10 to the 18th power*] [*SI symbol*] .... a
Attofarad (IDOE) .... aF
Attohenry (IDOE) .... aH
Attopeu [*Laos*] [*ICAO location identifier*] (ICLI) .... VLAP
Attorney (WGA) .... AT
Attorney .... ATT
Attorney (AFM) .... ATTY
Attorney .... ATTY
Attorney General (AAGC) .... Ag
Attorney General .... AG
Attorney General (ADA) .... ATTGEN
Attorney General (WGA) .... Atty Gen
Attorney General of England (ROG) .... AGE
Attorney General of Ontario, Crown Law Office, Toronto, ON, Canada
    [*Library symbol Library of Congress*] (LCLS) .... CaOTAGC
Attorney General of the Duchy of Lancaster (ILCA) .... AGDL
Attorney General of the Queen's Troop [*Military British*] (ROG) .... AGQT
Attorney General's Annual Report [*A publication*] (DLA) .... Att'y Gen Ann Rep
Attorney General's Decisions [*A publication*] (DLA) .... AG Dec
Attorney General's Department (ADA) .... AGD
Attorney General's Law Journal [*A publication*] (DLA) .... Att'y Gen LJ
Attorney General's Ministry [*Canada*] .... AGM
Attorney General's Opinions [*A publication*] (DLA) .... AG

Attorney General's Opinions ..... AGO
Attorney General's Opinions [*A publication*] (DLA) ..... Atty Gen Op
Attorney General's Opinions [*A publication*] (DLA) ..... Atty Gen Op NY
Attorneys, Certified Public Accountants, and Enrolled Agents [*In "Operation ACE," IRS investigation of these occupations as sources of income tax evasion*] ..... ACE
Attorneys for Animal Rights (EA) ..... AFAR
[*The*] **Attorneys Group** (EA) ..... TAG
Attraktiv und Preiswert [*Attractive and Priced Right*] [*West German grocery products brand*] ..... A & P
Attribute ..... A
Attribute ..... ATR
Attribute ..... ATTRIB
Attribute Distributed Tree (MHDI) ..... ADT
Attribute Requirement Inventory ..... ARI
Attribute Value (MHDI) ..... ATRVAL
Attributed (VRA) ..... attr
Attributed ..... ATTRIB
Attrition and Modification Work Order ..... AMWO
Attrition and Pregnancy [*Reasons for high turnover rate among women employees*] ..... A and P
Attrition Reserve ..... AR
Attrition, Utilization, and Loss Rate (AFM) ..... AULR
Attu, AK [*Location identifier FAA*] (FAAL) ..... ATU
Atuona [*Marquesas Islands*] [*Airport symbol*] (OAG) ..... AUQ
ATV [*All-Terrian Vehicle*] **Safety Institute** (EA) ..... ASI
Atwater, CA [*FM radio station call letters*] ..... KVRQ
Atwater Kent Museum, Philadelphia, PA [*Library symbol Library of Congress*] (LCLS) ..... PPAK
Atwater Library, Montreal, PQ, Canada [*Library symbol Library of Congress*] (LCLS) ..... CaQMMI
Atwater Library [*Formerly, Mechanics Institute Library*] **Montreal, Quebec** [*Library symbol National Library of Canada*] (NLC) ..... QMMI
Atwater Library of the Mechanics' Institute of Montreal [*UTLAS symbol*] ..... ATW
Atwater, NM [*FM radio station call letters*] ..... KYRS
Atwater Public Library, Atwater, MN [*Library symbol*] [*Library of Congress*] (LCLS) ..... MnAt
Atwater-Grove City Junior High School, Grove City, MN [*Library symbol*] [*Library of Congress*] (LCLS) ..... MnGcJH
Atwater-Grove City Public Schools, Atwater, MN [*Library symbol*] [*Library of Congress*] (LCLS) ..... MnAtPS
Atwater's Reports [*1 Minnesota*] [*A publication*] (DLA) ..... Atw
Atwater's Reports [*1 Minnesota*] [*A publication*] (DLA) ..... Atwater
Atwood, KS [*Location identifier FAA*] (FAAL) ..... ADT
Atwood Oceanics [*NASDAQ symbol*] (TTSB) ..... ATWD
Atwood Oceanics, Inc. [*NASDAQ symbol*] (NQ) ..... ATWD
Atwood Oceanics, Inc. [*Associated Press*] (SAG) ..... AtwdOc
ATWS [*Anticipated Transient without Scram*] **Mitigating System Actuation Circuitry** [*Nuclear energy*] (NRCH) ..... AMSAC
ATWS [*Anticipated Transient without Scram*] **Rod Injection System** [*Nuclear energy*] (NRCH) ..... ARI
Atypical Acid-Fast Bacilli [*Microbiology*] ..... AAFB
Atypical Chest Pain [*Medicine*] ..... ACP
Atypical Chronic Myeloid Leukemia [*Medicine*] (DMAA) ..... ACMI
Atypical Glandular Cells of Undetermined Significance [*Gynecology*] ..... AGUS
Atypical Legionella-Like Organism ..... ALLO
Atypical Lymphocyte [*Hematology*] (DAVI) ..... A-LYM
Atypical Lymphocytes (DAVI) ..... ATL
Atypical Lymphoepitheloid Cell Proliferation [*Medicine*] ..... ALEP
Atypical Lymphoid Hyperplasia [*Medicine*] ..... ALH
Atypical Measles Syndrome [*Medicine*] ..... AMS
Atypical Mole Syndrome ..... AMS
Atypical Odontalgia [*Dental pain that has no apparent organic cause*] ..... AO
Atypical Squamous Cells of Undetermined Significance [*Medicine*] ..... ASCUS
Atypical Transformation Zone [*Gynecology*] (DAVI) ..... ATZ
Atypical Ventricular Tachycardia [*Cardiology*] (DAVI) ..... AVT
Au Bon Pain [*NASDAQ symbol*] (SPSG) ..... ABPC
Au Bon Pain, Inc. [*Associated Press*] (SAG) ..... AuBon
Au Bon Pain'A' [*NASDAQ symbol*] (TTSB) ..... ABPCA
Au Resources Ltd. [*Vancouver Stock Exchange symbol*] ..... AUE
Au Tau [*Hong Kong*] [*Later, HKO*] [*Geomagnetic observatory code*] ..... AUT
Aua [*Papua New Guinea*] [*Airport symbol*] (OAG) ..... AUI
Aubenas [*France*] [*Airport symbol*] (OAG) ..... OBS
Aubenas-Vals-Lanas [*France ICAO location identifier*] (ICLI) ..... LFHO
Auberger [*Blood group*] ..... Au
Auberry, CA [*FM radio station call letters*] (RBYB) ..... KLBN
Aubeville [*Congo*] [*ICAO location identifier*] (ICLI) ..... FCBU
Aubigny-Sur-Nere [*France ICAO location identifier*] (ICLI) ..... LFEH
Auburn [*Nebraska*] [*Seismograph station code, US Geological Survey*] (SEIS) ..... ABN
Auburn [*New York*] [*Airport symbol*] (AD) ..... SSN
Auburn, AL [*AM radio station call letters*] ..... WAUD
Auburn, AL [*FM radio station call letters*] ..... WEGL
Auburn, AL [*FM radio station call letters*] ..... WKKR
Auburn, CA [*Location identifier FAA*] (FAAL) ..... AUN
Auburn, CA [*AM radio station call letters*] ..... KAHI
Auburn, CA [*FM radio station call letters*] ..... KHYL
Auburn Community College [*New York*] ..... ACC
Auburn Dam [*California*] [*Seismograph station code, US Geological Survey*] (SEIS) ..... ADC
Auburn Enterprise, Auburn, IA [*Library symbol Library of Congress*] (LCLS) ..... IaAubE
Auburn Evening Star, Auburn, IN [*Library symbol Library of Congress*] (LCLS) ..... InAubS
Auburn High School, Rockford, IL [*Library symbol*] [*Library of Congress*] (LCLS) ..... IRoAH
Auburn Hills, MI [*FM radio station call letters*] ..... WAHS
Auburn, IN [*FM radio station call letters*] (RBYB) ..... WGLL
Auburn, IN [*AM radio station call letters*] ..... WIFF
Auburn/Lewiston, ME [*Location identifier FAA*] (FAAL) ..... LEW
Auburn/Lewiston, ME [*Location identifier FAA*] (FAAL) ..... PDS
Auburn, ME [*FM radio station call letters*] ..... WKZS
Auburn Memorial Hospital, Learning Resources Center, Auburn, NY [*Library symbol Library of Congress*] (LCLS) ..... NAuMH
Auburn National [*NASDAQ symbol*] (SAG) ..... AUBN
Auburn National [*Associated Press*] (SAG) ..... AubNB
Auburn Natl Bancorp [*NASDAQ symbol*] (TTSB) ..... AUBN
Auburn, NE [*FM radio station call letters*] (RBYB) ..... KNCY-FM
Auburn, NY [*AM radio station call letters*] ..... WAUB
Auburn, NY [*FM radio station call letters*] ..... WDWN
Auburn, NY [*AM radio station call letters*] ..... WMBO
Auburn, NY [*FM radio station call letters*] ..... WPCX
Auburn/Opelika [*Alabama*] [*Airport symbol*] (OAG) ..... AUO
Auburn Public Library, Auburn, IA [*Library symbol Library of Congress*] (LCLS) ..... IaAub
Auburn Public Library, Auburn, IL [*Library symbol Library of Congress*] (LCLS) ..... IAub
Auburn Public Library, Auburn, ME [*Library symbol Library of Congress*] (LCLS) ..... MeAu
Auburn Public Library, Auburn, ME [*Library symbol*] [*Library of Congress*] (LCLS) ..... MeAub
Auburn Public Library, Auburn, WA [*Library symbol Library of Congress*] (LCLS) ..... WaAu
Auburn Research Foundation (KSC) ..... ARF
Auburn Theological Seminary, Auburn, NY [*Library symbol Library of Congress Obsolete*] (LCLS) ..... NAuT
Auburn University [*Alabama*] ..... AU
Auburn University (GAGS) ..... Auburn U
Auburn University, Archives, Auburn, AL [*Library symbol*] [*Library of Congress*] (LCLS) ..... AAP-A
Auburn University at Montgomery (GAGS) ..... Auburn U (Montgomery)
Auburn University at Montgomery, Montgomery, AL [*OCLC symbol*] (OCLC) ..... AAM
Auburn University at Montgomery, Montgomery, AL [*Library symbol Library of Congress*] (LCLS) ..... AMU
Auburn University, Auburn, AL [*OCLC symbol*] (OCLC) ..... AAA
Auburn University, Auburn, AL [*Library symbol Library of Congress*] (LCLS) ..... AAP
Auburn, WA [*AM radio station call letters*] ..... KBSG
Auburn, WA [*FM radio station call letters*] ..... KGRG
Auburn-Cord-Duesenberg Club (EA) ..... ACDC
Auburndale, FL [*AM radio station call letters*] ..... WTWB
Auburndale, WI [*AM radio station call letters*] ..... WLBL
Auburn-Lewiston [*Maine*] [*Airport symbol*] (AD) ..... LEW
Auburn-Placer County Library, Auburn, CA [*OCLC symbol*] (OCLC) ..... APR
Auburn-Placer County Library, Auburn, CA [*Library symbol Library of Congress*] (LCLS) ..... CAuP
Auch/Lamothe [*France ICAO location identifier*] (ICLI) ..... LFDH
Auchinleck's Manuscript Cases, Scotch Court of Session [*A publication*] (DLA) ..... Auch
Auchinoon [*Scotland*] [*Seismograph station code, US Geological Survey*] (SEIS) ..... EAU
Auckland [*New Zealand*] [*Airport symbol*] (OAG) ..... AKL
Auckland [*New Zealand*] [*Seismograph station code, US Geological Survey*] (SEIS) ..... AUC
Auckland [*New Zealand*] [*ICAO location identifier*] (ICLI) ..... NZAK
Auckland [*New Zealand*] [*ICAO location identifier*] (ICLI) ..... NZAQ
Auckland [*New Zealand*] [*ICAO location identifier*] (ICLI) ..... NZZA
Auckland [*New Zealand*] [*ICAO location identifier*] (ICLI) ..... NZZO
Auckland Explorations Ltd. [*Vancouver Stock Exchange symbol*] ..... AUK
Auckland/International [*New Zealand*] [*ICAO location identifier*] (ICLI) ..... NZAA
Auckland Regional Rescue Helicopter Trust [*New Zealand*] [*FAA designator*] (FAAC) ..... WPR
Auckland University, Auckland, New Zealand [*Library symbol Library of Congress*] (LCLS) ..... NzAU
Auction (ROG) ..... AUCN
Auction ..... AUCT
Auction Preferred Stock [*Investment term*] (DFIT) ..... APS
Auction Register and Law Chronicle [*A publication*] (DLA) ..... Auct Reg & L Chron
Auction Transfer Authority ..... ATA
Auctioneer ..... AUCTNR
Auctioneer ..... AUCTNR
Auctioneering ..... ACTNRG
Auctioneering ..... AUCTNRG
Auctioneers and Valuers' Association of Western Australia ..... AVAWA
Auctioneers and Valuers of Western Australia [*An association*] ..... AVWA
Auctioneers Association of Canada ..... AA of C
Auction-Market Preferred Stock ..... AMPS
Auctores Antiquissimi [*Classical studies*] ..... AA
Auctoris [*One that Gives Increase; an Originator*] [*Latin*] ..... auct
Auctorum [*Of Authors*] [*Biology, taxonomy*] ..... auct
Audeli Air Express [*Spain ICAO designator*] (FAAC) ..... ADI
Audemars Piguet [*Trademark for line of watches*] (ECON) ..... AP
Audi Air, Inc. [*ICAO designator*] (FAAC) ..... AUD
Audi International Motor Car Club (EA) ..... AIMCC
Audi Space Frame [*Concept car*] [*Automotive engineering*] ..... ASF
Audible (WGA) ..... AUD
Audible Alarm (IAA) ..... AA
Audible Current Meter [*Electronics*] (DICI) ..... ACM

Audible Doppler Enhancer [*Telecommunications*] (TEL) ... ADE
Audible Rumble Loudness Level [*Stereo*] ... ARLL
Audible Signal Devices [*JETDS nomenclature*] [*Military*] (CET) ... BZ
Audibly Instructed Manufacturing Operations [*Military*] ... AIMO
Audience Development Committee (EA) ... AUDELCO
Audience Interest Factor ... AIF
Audience Measurement by Market for Outdoor (NTCM) ... AMMO
Audience Reaction Assessment [*Television ratings*] [*British*] ... AURA
Audience Reaction Indicator (IIA) ... ARI
Audience Research (NTCM) ... AR
Audience Research Bureau (IIA) ... ARB
Audience Research Institute [*Also, AIPO*] (NTCM) ... ARI
Audience Studies, Inc. [*Television program testing system*] ... ASI
Audiences (WDMC) ... auds
Audimeter/Diary System [*A. C. Nielson Co.*] (NTCM) ... A/D
Audio (WDMC) ... a
Audio (WDMC) ... A
Audio [*or Audible or Audiology*] (MSA) ... AUD
Audio ... AUD
Audio Alarm Module [*Automotive engineering*] ... AAM
Audio and Electroacoustics [*IEEE*] ... AU
Audio and Power Connectors [*JETDS nomenclature*] [*Military*] (CET) ... U
Audio Archives [*Record label*] ... AudA
Audio Bandpass Filter ... ABF
Audio Bandpass Filter ... ABPF
Audio Bandwidth ... AB
Audio Capture and Playback Adapter (PCM) ... ACPA
Audio Cartridge (WDMC) ... ACR
Audio Cassette Recorder (RDA) ... ACR
Audio Cassette Recorder (IDOE) ... acr
Audio Cassette Recording (IDOE) ... acr
Audio Center [*Command and Service Module*] [*NASA*] ... AC
Audio Center Equipment (SAA) ... ACP
Audio Center Module [*NASA*] (IAA) ... ACM
Audio Center - Receiver (KSC) ... ACRC
Audio Center - Receiver (KSC) ... ACRV
Audio Center - Transmitter (KSC) ... ACTM
Audio Central Control Unit (NASA) ... ACCU
Audio Collectors [*Record label*] ... AudC
Audio Commercial Message Repeating Unit [*Device delivering a recorded commercial from cigarette vending machines*] ... ACMRU
Audio Communications System ... ACS
Audio Conducted Susceptibility (IAA) ... ACS
Audio Control Center ... ACC
Audio Control Panel (NASA) ... ACP
Audio Data Communication [*Computer science*] (IAA) ... ADC
Audio Data Sequence [*Telecommunications*] (NTCM) ... ADSQ
Audio Decode Oscillator ... ADO
Audio/Digital Systems [*Telecommunications service*] (TSSD) ... A/DS
Audio Distribution Amplifier ... ADA
Audio Distribution System (NASA) ... ADS
Audio End Instrument (MCD) ... AEI
Audio Engineering Society (EA) ... AES
Audio Engineering Society/European Broadcast Union (DOM) ... AES/EBU
Audio Enhanced Computer Aided Learning (AIE) ... AECAL
Audio Equipment (IAA) ... AUDEQUIP
Audio Fidelity (NTCM) ... AF
Audio Flat Panel [*Speaker system*] ... AFP
Audio Follow Video [*Tape editing*] (NTCM) ... AFV
Audio Frequency [*Data transmission*] ... AF
Audio Frequency Amplifier ... AFA
Audio Frequency Apparatus ... AFA
Audio Frequency Change ... AFC
Audio Frequency Choke ... AFC
Audio Frequency Coder ... AFC
Audio Frequency Interference ... AFI
Audio Frequency Magnetotelluric ... AMT
Audio Frequency Modulation ... AFM
Audio Frequency Shift (IEEE) ... AFS
Audio Frequency Shift Key ... AFSK
Audio Frequency Shift Keying (NITA) ... AFSK
Audio Frequency Transformer ... AFT
Audio Function Generator (MCD) ... AFG
Audio High Density ... AHD
Audio Input Frequency Tolerance ... AIFT
Audio Input Level ... AIL
Audio Institutional Membership [*Telecommunications*] ... AIM
Audio Integrating System (DA) ... AIS
Audio Interchange File Format [*Computer science*] (BTTJ) ... AIFF
Audio Junction Box (MCD) ... AJB
Audio King [*NASDAQ symbol*] (TTSB) ... AUDK
Audio King, Inc. [*NASDAQ symbol*] (SAG) ... AUDK
Audio King, Inc. [*Associated Press*] (SAG) ... AudKng
Audio Level Meter ... ALM
Audio Library Services of Northwestern Ontario, Lakehead University, Thunder Bay, Ontario [*Library symbol National Library of Canada*] (NLC) ... OTBLA
Audio Lingual Education Press (KSC) ... ALEP
Audio Load Compensator (MCD) ... ALC
Audio Media Integration Standard [*Telecommunications*] (BARN) ... AMIS
Audio News Release (WDMC) ... ANR
Audio Operator (NTCM) ... AO
Audio Oscillator ... AO
Audio Peak Clipping Amplifier ... APCA
Audio Playback Unit ... APU
Audio Precision Series One Analyzer [*CD-sound quality test*] (PCM) ... APSO
Audio Publishers Association [*Defunct*] (EA) ... APA
Audio Rarities [*Record label*] ... AudR
Audio Receive Only (NTCM) ... ARO
Audio Recording Rights Coalition [*Defunct*] (EA) ... ARRC
Audio Renaissance Tapes [*Los Angeles, CA*] ... ART
Audio Reply (IEEE) ... AUDREY
Audio Response ... AR
Audio Response Control (BUR) ... ARC
Audio Response Interface System (PDAA) ... ARIS
Audio Response System ... ARS
Audio Response Time-Shared System [*Computer science*] (MHDB) ... ARTS
Audio Response Unit ... ARU
Audio Sensitivity ... AS
Audio Signal (IAA) ... AUDSNL
Audio Stream Handler (PCM) ... ADSH
Audio Support Equipment ... ASE
Audio Switch Assembly [*Ground Communications Facility, NASA*] ... ASWA
Audio Tape Cassette Player Set ... ATCPS
Audio Tape Recording ... ATR
Audio Techniques and Evaluation Laboratory [*NASA*] ... ATEL
Audio Teleconference Network [*Acadia University*] [*Wolfville, NS*] (TSSD) ... ATN
Audio Terminal Unit (NASA) ... ATU
Audio Test Set (NITA) ... ATS
Audio Thermal Unit (MCD) ... ATU
Audio Tone Decoder ... ATD
Audio/Video (WDMC) ... A/V
Audio Video (WDMC) ... AV
Audio Video Interleave [*Computer science*] ... AVI
Audio Video Market Place [*A publication*] ... AVMP
Audio Video Review Digest [*A publication*] ... AVRD
Audio/Visual (WDMC) ... A/V
Audio Visual Association [*British*] (DBA) ... AVA
Audio Visual Authoring [*Computer programming language*] (PCM) ... AVA
Audio Visual Drive (CDE) ... AV drive
Audio Visual Innovations [*Computer science*] ... AVI
Audio/Visual Interleave [*Windows*] [*Computer science*] ... avi
Audio Visual Interleaved [*Computer science*] (PCM) ... AVI
Audio, Visual, Kinesthetic, and Oral [*Teaching techniques*] (EA) ... AVKO
Audio Visual Library, University of Toronto [*UTLAS symbol*] ... AVL
Audio Voice Exchange ... AVX
Audio Warning Amplifier (AAG) ... AWA
Audio Wave Analyzer ... AWA
Audiobook Service to the Handicapped, British Columbia Library Services Branch, Burnaby [*Library symbol National Library of Canada*] (NLC) ... BBLA
Audiofrequency Control [*Electronics*] (ECII) ... AFC
Audiofrequency Magnetic Fields [*Prospecting technique*] ... AFMAG
Audiogenic Seizure [*Neurophysiology*] ... AS
Audiographic Teleconference ... AGT
Audiolingual Language Programming [*Computer science*] ... ALLP
Audiological Society of Australia ... ASA
Audiologist ... AUDLGST
Audiology ... AUDLGY
Audiology and Speech Pathology (DAVI) ... AUSPE
Audiometer Telephone Interface [*for the hearing-impaired*] ... ATI
Audiometry Sweep Test ... AST
Audio-Monitored Talk Amplifier (DNAB) ... AMTA
Audio-Only ... AO
Audiophile [*Record label*] ... Aphe
Audioprothesis ... AUDIOPR
Audiosonometry (IAA) ... ASM
Audio-Tactile Display (PDAA) ... ATD
Audiotape Recorder (WDMC) ... ATR
[*The*] **Audiotex Group** [*Princeton, NJ*] [*Telecommunications service*] (TSSD) ... TAG
Audio-Video Interactive ... AVI
Audio-Video Interleaved [*Computer science*] ... AVI
Audio-Video Recording System [*Air Force*] ... AVRS
Audio-Visual (IDOE) ... a/v
Audiovisual ... AV
Audio-Visual Aids Committee [*British*] ... AVAC
Audiovisual Annunciator ... AVA
Audiovisual, Computer, and Communication Office Automation ... AVCCOA
Audio-Visual Connection (PCM) ... AVC
Audio-Visual Credit Interchange [*Defunct*] (EA) ... AVCI
Audiovisual Display Unit ... AVDU
Audiovisual Distribution System (MCD) ... AVDS
Audio-Visual Division [*Environmental Protection Agency*] (GFGA) ... AVD
Audiovisual Education in Neurosurgery ... AVENS
Audiovisual Information System ... AVIS
Audiovisual Instructional Technology [*Military*] (AABC) ... AVIT
Audio-Visual Integrated Trainer (PDAA) ... AVIT
Audiovisual Kit [*Army*] ... AVK
Audio-Visual Language Association [*British*] ... AVLA
Audiovisual Liaison Officer [*Army*] ... AVLO
Audiovisual Library, Art Gallery of Ontario, Toronto, Ontario [*Library symbol National Library of Canada*] (NLC) ... OTAGAV
Audio-Visual Library, University of Toronto, Ontario [*Library symbol National Library of Canada*] (NLC) ... OTUAV
Audiovisual Machine Readable Catalogue [*A database*] [*British Library Automated Dissemination of Information*] (NITA) ... AVMARC
Audio-Visual Management Association (EA) ... AVMA
Audiovisual Modulator ... AVM
Audio-Visual Squadron [*Air Force*] ... AVS
Audiovisual Squadron [*Air Force*] ... AVSq
Audiovisual Superimposed Electrocardiogram Presentation ... AVSEP

Audiovisual Support Center [*Army*] (AABC) .... AVSC
Audiovisuals On-Line [*National Library of Medicine*] [*Rockville Pike, MD Database*] .... AVLINE
Audiovisual-Tutorial [*Instruction*] [*Media System Corp.*] .... AVT
Audiovox CI'A' [*AMEX symbol*] (TTSB) .... VOX
Audiovox Corp. [*Associated Press*] (SAG) .... Audvox
Audiovox Corp. [*AMEX symbol*] (SAG) .... VOX
Audit [*or Audited*] .... A
Audit .... AU
Audit [*or Auditor*] (AFM) .... AUD
Audit (ODBW) .... aud
Audit .... AUDT
Audit Agency .... AA
Audit and Management Consulting Division [*United Nations*] (ECON) ..... AMCD
Audit Base Inventory System [*IRS*] .... ABIS
Audit Basic Learning Examination (MCD) .... ABLE
Audit Bureau of Circulations (EA) .... ABC
Audit Bureau of Marketing Services (DOAD) .... ABMS
Audit Central Control Network (MCD) .... ACCN
Audit Command Language .... ACL
Audit Compliance (MCD) .... AC
Audit, Control, and Evaluation (PDAA) .... ACE
Audit Control Point .... ACP
Audit Discrepancy Report (NRCH) .... ADR
Audit Entry [*Accounting, finance*] (BUR) .... AE
Audit Entry Language [*Burroughs Corp.*] .... AEL
Audit Error List .... AEL
Audit Information Management System [*Department of the Treasury*] ...... AIMS
Audit Information Management-Systems File [*IRS*] .... AIMF
Audit Integrated Reporting System [*IRS*] .... AIRS
Audit Item Disposition (MCD) .... AID
Audit Liaison Division (AAGC) .... OAL
Audit Operations Staff [*Environmental Protection Agency*] (GFGA) .... AOS
Audit Organization (DNAB) .... AO
Audit Programs Division (AAGC) .... OPD
Audit Reports Handbook [*IRS*] .... ARH
Audit Technical Time Report [*IRS*] .... ATTR
Audit Trail .... AT
Audit Trail Report [*Military*] .... AUDITRPT
Audita Querela [*A publication*] (DLA) .... Aud Q
Auditing .... ADTNG
Auditing Order Error .... AOE
Auditing Practices Board [*British*] (ECON) .... APB
Auditing Practices Committee [*British*] .... APC
Auditing Standards Board .... ASB
Auditor (MSA) .... AUDTR
Auditor .... AUDTR
Auditor Camerae [*Auditor of the Papal Treasury*] .... AC
Auditor Freight Accounts .... AFA
Auditor Freight Claims .... AFC
Auditor Freight Overcharge Claim .... AFOC
Auditor Freight Receipts .... AFR
Auditor Freight Traffic .... AFT
Auditor General [*Military*] .... AG
Auditor General of the Navy .... AUDGENAV
Auditor General of the Navy (DNAB) .... AUDGENNAV
Auditor General's Department [*Air Force*] .... AGD
Auditor General's Office .... AGO
Auditor General's Report [*Canada Information service or system*] (IID) .. AGR
Auditor of Receipts .... AR
Auditor of Revenue .... AR
Auditor of Traffic Accounts .... ATA
Auditor Overcharge Claims .... AOC
Auditorium .... ADTRM
Auditorium (DAC) .... AUD
Auditorium (VRA) .... audit
Auditorium and Training Facility [*NASA*] (NASA) .... ATF
Auditoriums (WDMC) .... auds
Auditory (ABBR) .... A
Auditory (DAVI) .... aud
Auditory Apperception Test [*Psychology*] .... AAT
Auditory Brain Response [*Neurology*] (DAVI) .... ABR
Auditory Brainstem Evoked Response [*Medicine*] (DMAA) .... ABER
Auditory Brainstem Implant [*Hearing technology*] .... ABI
Auditory Brainstem Response [*Neurophysiology*] .... ABR
Auditory Brain-Stem-Evoked Potential [*Neurology*] (DAVI) .... ABEP
Auditory Cortex [*Neurology*] .... AC
Auditory Discrimination in Depth [*Program*] [*Education*] .... ADD
Auditory Discrimination Test [*"Wepman"*] [*Education*] .... ADT
Auditory Gross Error .... AGE
Auditory Induction .... AI
Auditory Information Display .... AID
Auditory Input Task [*Computer science*] .... AUDIT
Auditory Integrative Abilities Test .... AIAT
Auditory Interneuron [*Neurology*] .... AIN
Auditory, Kinesthetic, Tactile Approach [*Teaching method*] .... AKT
Auditory Memory Span [*Psychometrics*] .... AMS
Auditory Nerve Activating Substance [*Physiology*] .... ANAS
Auditory Sensation Area .... ASA
Auditory Vocal Sequencing [*Medicine*] (DMAA) .... AVS
Auditory-Evoked Magnetic Field [*Neurophysiology*] .... AEF
Auditory-Evoked Potential [*Neurophysiology*] .... AEP
Auditory-Evoked Response [*Neurophysiology*] .... AER
Auditory-Flutter Fusion (PDAA) .... AFF
Auditory-Flutter Fusion Threshold (PDAA) .... AFFT

Auditory-Visual (DAVI) .... AV
Audits & Surveys Worldwide [*AMEX symbol*] (TTSB) .... ASW
Audits & Surveys Worldwide, Inc. [*AMEX symbol*] (SAG) .... ASW
Audits & Surveys Worldwide, Inc. [*Associated Press*] (SAG) .... AudSurv
Audits of Great Britain .... AGB
Audit Polycystic Kidney Disease [*Medicine*] (CPH) .... ADPKD
Audre Recognition Systems, Inc. [*Vancouver Stock Exchange symbol*] .... ADY
Audrey Resources, Inc. [*Toronto Stock Exchange symbol*] .... AUY
Audubon [*A publication*] (BRI) .... Aud
Audubon Artists (EA) .... AA
Audubon County Courthouse, Audubon, IA [*Library symbol Library of Congress*] (LCLS) .... IaAuCoC
Audubon County Journal, Exira, IA [*Library symbol Library of Congress*] (LCLS) .... IaExJ
Audubon, IA [*Location identifier FAA*] (FAAL) .... ADU
Audubon, IA [*FM radio station call letters*] (RBYB) .... KSOM
Audubon News-Advocate, Audubon, IA [*Library symbol Library of Congress*] (LCLS) .... IaAuNA
Audubon Public Library, Audubon, IA [*Library symbol Library of Congress*] (LCLS) .... IaAu
Audubon Public School, Audubon, MN [*Library symbol*] [*Library of Congress*] (LCLS) .... MnAudS
Audubon Regional Library, Clinton, LA [*Library symbol Library of Congress*] (LCLS) LCli
Audubon Society of Rhode Island, Providence, RI [*Library symbol Library of Congress*] (LCLS) .... RPAS
Auer Bodies [*Medicine*] .... AB
Auerbach Power Index (NITA) .... API
Auf Bestellung [*On Order*] [*German*] (ILCA) .... aB
Auffuehrung [*Performance*] [*German*] .... Auff
Aufgabe [*Task*] [*German*] .... Aufg
Aufklaerungsgruppe [*Air Forces Reconnaissance Unit*] [*German military - World War II*] .... AG
Auflage [*Edition*] [*German*] .... AUFL
Aufsatz [*Essay*] [*German*] .... Aufs
Aufschlagzuender ohne Verzoegerung [*Nondelay fuze*] [*German military - World War II*] .... AZOV
Aufsichtsrat [*Supervisory Board*] [*German*] .... AR
Auftrag [*Order*] [*German*] .... Auftr
Aufzeichnung [*Note*] [*German*] .... Aufz
Augat, Inc. [*NYSE symbol*] (SPSG) .... AUG
Augat, Inc. [*Associated Press*] (SAG) .... Augat
Augdome Corp. [*Vancouver Stock Exchange symbol*] .... AUG
Auger and Elevator Manufacturers Council (EA) .... AEMC
Auger Electron Analysis .... AEA
Auger Electron Appearance Potential Spectroscopy .... AEAPS
Auger Electron Spectrometry [*or Spectroscopy*] .... AES
Augere [*Increase*] [*Pharmacy*] .... AUG
Aughey Spark Chamber .... ASC
Augment (MSA) .... AGMT
Augment (AABC) .... AUG
Augmentation [*Music*] .... A
Augmentation .... AGN
Augmentation [*Music*] .... Aug
Augmentation [*Music*] .... Augm
Augmentation Concentration [*Biochemistry*] .... AC
Augmentation Reliability (MCD) .... AR
Augmentation Research Center [*Stanford Research Institute*] .... ARC
Augmentation Stabilization Equipment .... ASE
Augmentation System .... AS
Augmentative .... AUGM
Augmentative and Alternative Communication [*A publication*] .... AAC
Augmented Air Jet .... AAJ
Augmented Assault Fire Units [*Army*] (AABC) .... AAFU
Augmented Bibliographic Citation (ADA) .... ABC
Augmented Built-In Test .... AMBIT
Augmented Catalytic Thruster (MCD) .... ACT
Augmented Contact Support Set [*TOW*] .... ACSS
Augmented Content-Addressed Memory .... ACAM
Augmented Deflector Exhaust Nozzle [*Aviation*] .... ADEN
Augmented Energy Management (MCD) .... AEM
Augmented Final Fade (SAA) .... AF
Augmented Finite State Machine [*Computer science*] .... AFSM
Augmented Histamine Test [*Medicine*] (MAE) .... AHT
Augmented Human Intellect (KSC) .... AHI
Augmented Ignition Delay Sensor (CAAL) .... AIDS
Augmented Index and Digest [*Information Retrieval Ltd.*] [*British*] (NITA) ... AID
Augmented Logistics Support (MCD) .... ALS
Augmented Lunar Module (MCD) .... ALM
Augmented Lunar Payload Module .... ALPM
Augmented Off-Gas System [*Nuclear energy*] (NRCH) .... AOG
Augmented Phase Wave [*Thermodynamics*] .... APW
Augmented Plane Wave .... APW
Augmented Predictive Analyzer [*Computer science*] (DIT) .... APA
Augmented Programming Training [*Computer science*] (IEEE) .... APT
Augmented Reentry Test (IAA) .... ART
Augmented Roman (ADA) .... AR
Augmented Roman Alphabet (DGA) .... ARA
Augmented Satellite Launch Vehicle [*India*] .... ASLV
Augmented Spark Igniter [*NASA*] .... ASI
Augmented Support Period [*or Plan*] .... ASP
Augmented Surveyor [*NASA*] (MCD) .... AS
Augmented Synoptic Oceanographic Data Acquisition System [*Navy*] (MSC) .... ASODAS
Augmented System Ignition [*NASA*] (KSC) .... ASI

Augmented Target Docking Adapter [*Gemini*] [*NASA*] ATDA
Augmented Target Screening Subsystem (MCD) ATSS
Augmented Telemetry ATM
Augmented Thermally Electric Propulsion ATEP
Augmented Thrust Propulsion ATP
Augmented Transition Network [*Language analysis*] ATN
Augmented Transition Tree (MCD) ATT
Augmented V Lead, Left Arm [*Electrocardiogram*] [*Medicine*] AVL
Augmented V Lead, Left Leg [*Electrocardiogram*] [*Medicine*] AVF
Augmented V Lead, Right Arm [*Electrocardiogram*] [*Medicine*] AVR
Augmented Visual Carrier Aircraft Recovery System (MCD) AVCARS
Augmenter Wing Jet STOL [*Short Takeoff and Landing*] **Research Aircraft** AWJSRA
Augmenting Unit [*Navy*] AUGU
Augmentor Fuel Flow Test Unit (MCD) AFFTU
Augmentor of Liver Regeneration [*Biochemistry*] ALR
Augmentor Wing Research Aircraft [*Aviation*] (MCD) AWRA
Augmentor-Wing [*Aviation*] AW
Augmitto Explorations Ltd. [*Toronto Stock Exchange symbol*] AU
Augsburg College and Seminary, Minneapolis, MN [*Library symbol Library of Congress*] (LCLS) MnMA
Augsburg College, Minneapolis, MN [*OCLC symbol*] (OCLC) MNA
Augsburg/Gablingen [*Germany ICAO location identifier*] (ICLI) EDOX
Augsburg Hospital [*Germany ICAO location identifier*] (ICLI) EDII
Augsburg/Muehlhausen [*Germany ICAO location identifier*] (ICLI) EDMA
Augsburg Transmission Upgrade (MCD) ATU
August (CDAI) A
August AG
August AU
August (EY) AUG
August (ROG) AUGT
August 15 and February 15 [*Denotes interest payable on these dates*] [*Business term*] A & F 15
August and February [*Denotes semiannual payments of interest or dividends in these months*] [*Business term*] A & F
August Derleth Society (EA) ADS
August, November, February, and May [*Denotes quarterly payments of interest or dividends in these months*] [*Business term*] ANFM
Augusta [*Georgia*] [*Airport symbol*] AGS
Augusta [*Maine*] [*Airport symbol*] (OAG) AUG
Augusta [*Maine*] [*ICAO location identifier*] (ICLI) KAUG
Augusta Airways [*ICAO designator*] (AD) BH
Augusta & Summerville Railroad Co. [*AAR code*] AUS
Augusta, AR [*FM radio station call letters*] KABK
Augusta Area Committee for Health Information Resources [*Library network*] AACHIR
Augusta Chronicle-Herald, Augusta, GA [*Library symbol Library of Congress*] (LCLS) GAuACH
Augusta College (GAGS) Augusta C
Augusta College, Augusta, GA [*Library symbol Library of Congress*] (LCLS) GAuA
Augusta College, Augusta, GA [*OCLC symbol*] (OCLC) GJG
Augusta, GA [*Location identifier FAA*] (FAAL) DNL
Augusta, GA [*Location identifier FAA*] (FAAL) EMR
Augusta, GA [*Location identifier FAA*] (FAAL) MZX
Augusta, GA [*FM radio station call letters*] WACG
Augusta, GA [*Television station call letters*] WAGT
Augusta, GA [*AM radio station call letters*] WBBQ
Augusta, GA [*FM radio station call letters*] WBBQ-FM
Augusta, GA [*FM radio station call letters*] WEKL
Augusta, GA [*AM radio station call letters*] WFAM
Augusta, GA [*FM radio station call letters*] WFXA
Augusta, GA [*Television station call letters*] WFXG
Augusta, GA [*AM radio station call letters*] WGAC
Augusta, GA [*Television station call letters*] WJBF
Augusta, GA [*AM radio station call letters*] WKIM
Augusta, GA [*FM radio station call letters*] WLPE
Augusta, GA [*AM radio station call letters*] WRDW
Augusta, GA [*Television station call letters*] WRDW-TV
Augusta, GA [*AM radio station call letters*] WTHB
Augusta, GA [*FM radio station call letters*] WZNY
Augusta Huiell Seaman Society [*Defunct*] (EA) AHSS
Augusta, IL [*FM radio station call letters*] (RBYB) WAHI-FM
Augusta, KS [*FM radio station call letters*] KLLS
Augusta, ME [*Location identifier FAA*] (FAAL) CCM
Augusta, ME [*Television station call letters*] WCBB
Augusta, ME [*AM radio station call letters*] (RBYB) WEZW
Augusta, ME [*FM radio station call letters*] WKCG
Augusta, ME [*AM radio station call letters*] WMDR
Augusta, ME [*FM radio station call letters*] WMME-FM
Augusta Mental Health Institute, Augusta, ME [*Library symbol Library of Congress*] (LCLS) MeAM
Augusta Mental Health Institute, Augusta, ME [*OCLC symbol*] (OCLC) MEZ
Augusta Railroad Co. [*AAR code*] AUG
Augusta Technical Institute, Augusta, GA [*Library symbol*] [*Library of Congress*] (LCLS) GAuT
Augusta Township Public Library, Brockville, Ontario [*Library symbol National Library of Canada*] (NLC) OBAT
Augusta Warshaw Advertising Library, New York, NY [*Library symbol Library of Congress*] (LCLS) NNAA
Augustan Prose Sample [*Machine readable selection of English prose*] (NITA) APS
Augustan Reprint Society (EA) ARS
Augustan Society (EA) AS
Augustana College (GAGS) Augustana C
Augustana College, Rock Island, IL [*OCLC symbol*] (OCLC) ICY
Augustana College, Rock Island, IL [*Library symbol Library of Congress*] (LCLS) IRA
Augustana College, Sioux Falls, SD [*OCLC symbol*] (OCLC) SDA
Augustana College, Sioux Falls, SD [*Library symbol Library of Congress*] (LCLS) SdSifA
Augustana Historical Society (EA) AHS
Augustana Hochschule Bibliothek, Neuendettelsau, Federal Republic of Germany [*Library symbol Library of Congress*] (LCLS) GyNeA
Augustana Luther League [*Later, ILLL*] ALL
Augustana Swedish Institute [*Later, AHS*] ASI
Augusta-Richmond County Library, Augusta, GA [*Library symbol Library of Congress*] (LCLS) GAu
Augusta-Richmond County Library, Augusta, GA [*Library symbol*] [*Library of Congress*] (LCLS) GAuCL
Augusta-Ross Township District Library (McKay Library), Augusta, MI [*Library symbol Library of Congress*] (LCLS) MiAu
Augustine [*Deceased, 430*] [*Authority cited in pre-1607 legal work*] (DSA) Ag
Augustine [*354-430AD*] [*Classical studies*] (OCD) August
Augustine Island [*Alaska*] [*Seismograph station code, US Geological Survey*] (SEIS) AGI
Augustine Island [*Alaska*] [*Seismograph station code, US Geological Survey*] (SEIS) AUF
Augustine Island [*Alaska*] [*Seismograph station code, US Geological Survey*] (SEIS) AUI
Augustine Island [*Alaska*] [*Seismograph station code, US Geological Survey*] (SEIS) AUM
Augustines de la Misericorde de Jesus [*Religious order*] [*Canada*] AMJ
Augustinian Educational Association [*Defunct*] (EA) AEA
Augustinian Historical Institute, Villanova University, Villanova, PA [*Library symbol Library of Congress*] (LCLS) PVAHI
Augustinian Nuns of Contemplative Life (TOCD) OSA
Augustinian Recollect Sisters [*An association Australia*] AR
Augustinian Recollect Sisters (TOCD) OAR
Augustinian Secondary Educational Association (EA) ASEA
Augustinian Sisters of Our Lady of Consolation (TOCD) OSA
Augustiniani Assumptionis [*Assumptionists*] [*Roman Catholic men's religious order*] AA
[*The*] **Augustinians** (TOCD) osa
[*The*] **Augustinians** (TOCD) OSA
Augustinus Berous [*Deceased, 1554*] [*Authority cited in pre-1607 legal work*] (DSA) Aug Bero
Augustinus Berous [*Deceased, 1554*] [*Authority cited in pre-1607 legal work*] (DSA) Augu
Augustus Downs [*Australia Airport symbol Obsolete*] (OAG) AUD
Augustus Downs [*Queensland*] [*Airport symbol*] (AD) AUD
Augustus Resources Ltd. [*Vancouver Stock Exchange symbol*] AST
AUI Peace Language International (EA) APLI
Aujourd'hui [*Today*] [*French*] AUJ
Auke Bay Coastal Fisheries Research Center [*National Oceanic and Atmospheric Administration*] (PDAA) ABCFRC
Auki [*Solomon Islands*] [*Airport symbol*] (OAG) AKS
Auki [*Solomon Islands*] [*Seismograph station code, US Geological Survey*] (SEIS) AUK
Ault & Wiborg (DGA) A & W
Ault, Inc. [*NASDAQ symbol*] (NQ) AULT
Ault Public Library, Ault, CO [*Library symbol Library of Congress*] (LCLS) CoAul
Aulus Caius Decimus [*Coin inscription*] (ROG) ACD
Aumentado [*Enlarged*] [*Spanish*] (BARN) aum
Aunes [*French Ells*] AU
Aupracondylar Knee-Ankle[*Orthosis*] [*Orthopedics*] (DAVI) SKA
Aupraorbita Artery [*Anatomy*] (DAVI) SOA
Aur [*Marshall Islands*] [*Airport symbol*] (OAG) AUL
AUR Resources, Inc. [*Toronto Stock Exchange symbol*] AUR
Aura Systems, Inc. [*NASDAQ symbol*] (NQ) AURA
Aura Systems, Inc. [*Associated Press*] (SAG) AuraSy
Aurakhmat [*Former USSR Seismograph station code, US Geological Survey Closed*] (SEIS) AUR
Aural AUR
Aural Bearing Generator ABG
Aural Comprehension Course (DNAB) ACC
Aural Perception Heterodyne Exciter [*Inter-Technology Exchange Ltd.*] [*Psychoacoustics*] APHEX
Aural Warning Logic Unit (MCD) AWLU
Aurally Coded English [*in The ACE Spelling Dictionary*] [*British*] ACE
Auramine-O [*A biological stain*] AO
Aurangabad [*India*] [*Airport symbol*] (OAG) IXU
Aurangabad [*India*] [*ICAO location identifier*] (ICLI) VAAU
Auranofin [*An organogold*] AF
Auranteum [*Orange (Rind)*] [*Pharmacy*] (ROG) AURANT
Aurelia Public Library, Aurelia, IA [*Library symbol Library of Congress*] (LCLS) IaAur
Aurelia Sentinel, Aurelia, IA [*Library symbol Library of Congress*] (LCLS) IaAurS
Aurelian [*of Scriptores Historiae Augustae*] [*Classical studies*] (OCD) Aurel
Aurelio y Gustavo Pompa Estrella [*Mexico*] [*FAA designator*] (FAAC) POM
Aurelius Corbulus [*Flourished, 16th century*] [*Authority cited in pre-1607 legal work*] (DSA) Aurel Corbul
Aures Unitas [*Both Ears*] [*Latin*] AU
Aurex Resources, Inc. [*Vancouver Stock Exchange symbol*] ARX
Aurich [*Germany ICAO location identifier*] (ICLI) EDZR
Auricular [*or Auricle*] [*Also, AUR*] [*Medicine*] A
Auricular [*or Auricle*] [*Also, A*] [*Medicine*] AUR
Auricular [*Cardiology*] (DAVI) auric
Auricular Fibrillation [*Medicine*] AF
Auricular Fibrillation [*Medicine*] (MAE) aur fib

Auricular Premature Beat [*Medicine*] (MAE) .... APB
Auriculocarotid [*Medicine*] (MAE) .... AC
Auriculo-Osteodysplasia [*Medicine*] .... AOD
Auriculoventricular [*Medicine*] .... AV
Auriga [*Constellation*] .... Aur
Auriga [*Constellation*] .... Auri
Aurignacian (VRA) .... Aurig
Aurigny Air Services [*ICAO designator*] (AD) .... GR
Aurigny Air Services Ltd. [*British ICAO designator*] (FAAC) .... AUR
Aurillac [*France*] [*Airport symbol Obsolete*] (OAG) .... AUR
Aurillac [*France ICAO location identifier*] (ICLI) .... LFLW
Aurinarium [*Ear Cone*] [*Medicine*] .... AURIN
Aurintricarboxylic Acid (MAE) .... ATA
Auris [*Ear*] [*Latin*] .... A
Auris [*Ear*] [*Latin*] .... AUR
Auris Dextra [*Right Ear*] [*Latin*] .... AD
Auris Dextra [*Right Ear*] [*Otorhinolaryngology*] (DAVI) .... Aurd
Auris Laeva [*Left Ear*] [*Medicine*] .... AL
Auris Sinistra [*Left Ear*] [*Latin*] .... AS
Auris Sinistra [*Left Ear*] [*Otorhinolaryngology*] (DAVI) .... Aurs
Auris Uterque [*Each Ear*] [*Latin*] .... AU
Auristillae [*Ear Drops*] [*Pharmacy*] .... AURIST
Auristillae [*Ear Drops*] [*Pharmacy*] .... AURISTILL
Aurizon Mines Ltd. [*Toronto Stock Exchange symbol Vancouver Stock Exchange symbol*] .... ARZ
Aurogin Resources [*Vancouver Stock Exchange symbol*] .... AUQ
Auropalpebral Reflex [*Response to sound*] .... APR
Aurora Borealis .... AURBO
Aurora, Canadian Forces Base, Greenwood, Nova Scotia [*Library symbol National Library of Canada*] (NLC) .... NSGCFA
Aurora, CO [*AM radio station call letters*] .... KEZW
Aurora, CO [*AM radio station call letters*] (RBYB) .... KMXA-AM
Aurora, CO [*AM radio station call letters*] .... KYBG
Aurora College, Aurora, IL [*Library symbol Library of Congress*] (LCLS) .... IAurC
Aurora College, Aurora, IL [*Library symbol*] [*Library of Congress*] (LCLS) .... IAurC
Aurora College, Aurora, IL [*OCLC symbol*] (OCLC) .... ICA
Aurora Electronics [*AMEX symbol*] (TTSB) .... AUR
Aurora Electronics Co., Inc. [*Formerly, BSN Corp.*] [*AMEX symbol*] (SPSG) .... AUR
Aurora Electronics Co., Inc. [*Formerly, BSN Corp.*] [*Associated Press*] (SAG) .... AurorEl
Aurora, Elgin & Fox River Electric R. R. [*AAR code*] .... AEFR
Aurora Environmental, Inc. [*NASDAQ symbol*] (NQ) .... AURE
Aurora Foundation (EA) .... AF
Aurora High School PRECIS Project [*UTLAS symbol*] .... AUE
Aurora High School PRECIS Project [*UTLAS symbol*] .... AUR
Aurora High School, PRECIS Project, Aurora, ON, Canada [*Library symbol*] [*Library of Congress*] (LCLS) .... CaOAuHS
Aurora Historical Society, Aurora, ON, Canada [*Library symbol*] [*Library of Congress*] (LCLS) .... CaOAuH
Aurora Historical Society, Ontario [*Library symbol National Library of Canada*] (NLC) .... OAUH
Aurora, IL [*Location identifier FAA*] (FAAL) .... ARR
Aurora, IL [*AM radio station call letters*] .... WBIG
Aurora, IL [*Television station call letters*] .... WEHS
Aurora, IL [*AM radio station call letters*] .... WKKD
Aurora, IL [*FM radio station call letters*] .... WKKD-FM
Aurora, IL [*FM radio station call letters*] .... WYSY
Aurora, IN [*FM radio station call letters*] .... WSCH
Aurora, MO [*FM radio station call letters*] .... KGMY
Aurora, MO [*AM radio station call letters*] .... KSWM
Aurora Museum, Aurora, ON, Canada [*Library symbol*] [*Library of Congress*] (LCLS) .... CaOAUM
Aurora Museum, Ontario [*Library symbol National Library of Canada*] (BIB) .... OAUM
Aurora, NC [*Location identifier FAA*] (FAAL) .... AUR
Aurora, NE [*Location identifier FAA*] (FAAL) .... AUH
Aurora, NE [*FM radio station call letters*] .... KLRB
Aurora, OR [*Location identifier FAA*] (FAAL) .... HBU
Aurora Public Library, Aurora, CO [*Library symbol Library of Congress*] (LCLS) .... CoAur
Aurora Public Library, Aurora, CO [*OCLC symbol*] (OCLC) .... COB
Aurora Public Library, Aurora, IL [*Library symbol Library of Congress*] (LCLS) .... IAur
Aurora Public Library, Aurora, IL [*Library symbol*] [*Library of Congress*] (LCLS) .... IAur
Aurora Public Library, Aurora, IN [*Library symbol Library of Congress*] (LCLS) .... InAur
Aurora Public Library, Aurora, MN [*Library symbol*] [*Library of Congress*] (LCLS) .... MnAur
Aurora Public Library, Aurora, ON, Canada [*Library symbol Library of Congress*] (LCLS) .... CaOAu
Aurora Public Library, Ontario [*Library symbol National Library of Canada*] (NLC) .... OAU
Auroral Absorption Index (CET) .... Ka
Auroral Electrojet [*Index*] .... AE
Auroral Hydrogen Line .... AHL
Auroral Hydrogen Line Emission .... AHLE
Auroral Infrasonic Wave [*Substorm*] .... AIW
Auroral Intrasonic Wave [*Substorm*] (PDAA) .... AIW
Auroral Kilometric Radiation [*Planetary science*] .... AKR
Auroral Large Imaging System .... ALIS
Auroral Time [*Geophysics*] .... AT
Aurtex, Inc. [*NASDAQ symbol*] (SAG) .... AURT
Aurtex, Inc. [*Associated Press*] (SAG) .... Aurtex
Aurukun Mission [*Australia Airport symbol*] (OAG) .... AUU
Aurum [*Gold*] [*Chemical element*] .... Au
Aurum [*Gold*] [*Latin*] .... AUR
Aurum [*Gold*] [*Numismatics*] .... AV
Aurum Software, Inc. [*NASDAQ symbol*] (SAG) .... AURM
Aurum Software, Inc. [*Associated Press*] (SAG) .... AurmSft
Aus Alter und Neuer Zeit [*Illustrated Addition to Israelitisches Familienblatt, Hamburg*] [*A publication*] (BJA) .... AAUNZ
Aus-Air [*Australia ICAO designator*] (FAAC) .... AUZ
Ausbildung [*Education*] [*German*] .... Ausb
Auscultation [*Medicine*] (AAMN) .... AUS
Auscultation [*Medicine*] (AAMN) .... AUSC
Auscultation [*Medicine*] (AAMN) .... AUSCUL
Auscultation and Palpation [*Medicine*] (AAMN) .... A & P
Auscultation and Percussion [*Medicine*] .... A & P
Ausfrech-Melcher-Grossapach [*Mercedes-Benz cars*] [*High-performance parts supplier*] .... AMG
Ausfuehrungsanweisung [*Regulatory Instructions*] [*German*] (DLA) .... AA
Ausfuehrungsgesetz zur Burgerlichen Gesetzbuch [*Implementing law to the civil code*] [*German*] (ILCA) .... AGBGB
Ausgabe [*Edition*] [*German*] .... AUSG
Ausgabestelle [*Distribution Point*] [*German military - World War II*] .... A
AUSLANG [*Australian Supply Language*] **Dictionary of Item Names** [*A publication*] .... ADIN
Ausonius [*Fourth century AD*] [*Classical studies*] (OCD) .... Auson
Auspex Gold Ltd. [*Vancouver Stock Exchange symbol*] .... APJ
Auspex Systems [*NASDAQ symbol*] (TTSB) .... ASPX
Auspex Systems, Inc. [*NASDAQ symbol*] (SAG) .... ASPX
Auspex Systems, Inc. [*Associated Press*] (SAG) .... Auspex
Auspuff-Turbolaeder [*Exhaust turbocharger*] [*German Automotive engineering*] .... ATL
Ausserdem [*Furthermore*] [*German*] .... ausserd
Ausstellung [*Exhibition*] [*German*] .... Ausst
Ausstellungs-Tegung fuer Chemisches Apparatewesen [*Triennial international chemical engineering exhibition*] .... ACHEMA
Aust&N.ZealandBk9.125%Pfd [*NYSE symbol*] (TTSB) .... ANZPr
Austast-Synchron-Signal (MCD) .... AS-SIGNAL
Austell, GA [*AM radio station call letters*] .... WAOS
Austempered Ductile Iron [*Metallurgy*] .... ADI
Austen Riggs Center, Inc., Stockbridge, MA [*Library symbol Library of Congress*] (LCLS) .... MStocA
Austenite (IAA) .... A
Austenite and Ferrite [*Manufacturing materials*] (IAA) .... AAF
Austere Airborne Ranging and Sighting System (MCD) .... AARSS
Austere Heads-Up Display [*Aviation*] (MCD) .... AHUD
Austere Surface-to-Air Missile System .... ASAMS
Austere Version (MCD) .... AV
Austin [*Nevada*] [*Airport symbol Obsolete*] (OAG) .... ASQ
Austin [*Minnesota*] [*Airport symbol*] (AD) .... AUM
Austin [*Texas*] [*Seismograph station code, US Geological Survey Closed*] (SEIS) .... AUS
Austin Airways [*ICAO designator*] (AD) .... UH
Austin Area Vocational-Technology Institute, Austin, MN [*OCLC symbol*] (OCLC) .... AVT
Austin/Bergstrom Air Force Base [*Texas*] [*ICAO location identifier*] (ICLI) .... KBSM
Austin College, Sherman, TX [*OCLC symbol*] (OCLC) .... IAU
Austin College, Sherman, TX [*Library symbol Library of Congress*] (LCLS) .... TxShA
Austin Community College, Austin, MN [*OCLC symbol*] (OCLC) .... ACO
Austin Community College, Austin, TX [*OCLC symbol*] (OCLC) .... TAC
Austin Community College, Austin, TX [*Library symbol Library of Congress*] (LCLS) .... TxAuCC
Austin Concept Vehicle .... ACV
Austin Data Recorder [*Military*] (SAA) .... ADR
Austin, IN [*FM radio station call letters*] .... WJAA
Austin, IN [*FM radio station call letters*] (RBYB) .... WJCP-FM
Austin, IN [*FM radio station call letters*] .... WJLR
Austin Junior College [*Later, Austin Community College*] [*Minnesota*] .... AJC
Austin, MN [*Location identifier FAA*] (FAAL) .... AUM
Austin, MN [*Television station call letters*] .... KAAL
Austin, MN [*AM radio station call letters*] .... KAUS
Austin, MN [*FM radio station call letters*] .... KAUS-FM
Austin, MN [*FM radio station call letters*] .... KMSK
Austin, MN [*AM radio station call letters*] .... KNFX
Austin, MN [*Television station call letters*] .... KSMQ
Austin Moore Prosthesis [*Medicine*] (DAVI) .... AM Pros
Austin Peay State College [*Later, Austin Peay State University*] [*Tennessee*] .... APSC
Austin Peay State University [*Tennessee*] .... APSU
Austin Peay State University (GAGS) .... Aus Peay St U
Austin Peay State University, Clarksville, TN [*Library symbol Library of Congress*] (LCLS) .... TClA
Austin Peay State University, Clarksville, TN [*OCLC symbol*] (OCLC) .... TPA
Austin Presbyterian Theological Seminary, Austin, TX [*Library symbol Library of Congress*] (LCLS) .... TxAuP
Austin Public Library, Austin, MN [*Library symbol Library of Congress*] (LCLS) .... MnAu
Austin Public Library, Austin, TX [*Library symbol Library of Congress*] (LCLS) .... TxAu
Austin Public Library, Austin, TX [*OCLC symbol*] (OCLC) .... TXG
Austin Public Library, Austin-Travis County Collection, Austin, TX [*Library symbol Library of Congress*] (LCLS) .... TxAu-AT
Austin Public Schools Media, Austin, MN [*OCLC symbol*] (OCLC) .... APS
Austin Public Schools Media, Austin, MN [*Library symbol Library of Congress*] (LCLS) .... MnAuPS

Austin Resources, Inc. [*Vancouver Stock Exchange symbol*] .... AUS
Austin/Robert Mueller Municipal [*Texas*] [*ICAO location identifier*] (ICLI) ...... KAUS
Austin Rover [*British-built automobile*] .... AR
Austin Rover Cars of North America, Inc. .... ARCONA
Austin Rover Group Ltd. .... ARG
Austin Rover Japan .... ARJ
Austin Service Center [*IRS*] .... AUSC
Austin Seven Clubs Association (EAIO) A7CA
Austin State Hospital, Austin, TX [*Library symbol Library of Congress*] (LCLS) .... TxAuSHos
Austin State Junior College, Austin, MN [*Library symbol Library of Congress*] (LCLS) .... MnAuS
Austin Ten Drivers Club [*High Wycombe, Buckinghamshire, England*] (EAIO) .... ATDC
Austin Trumbull Radio [*Air transport radio prior to April 15, 1967*] (MCD) .... ATR
Austin, TX [*Location identifier FAA*] (FAAL) .... BSM
Austin, TX [*Location identifier FAA*] (FAAL) .... EBL
Austin, TX [*Location identifier FAA*] (FAAL) .... GFQ
Austin, TX [*FM radio station call letters*] .... KASE
Austin, TX [*FM radio station call letters*] .... KAZI
Austin, TX [*Television station call letters*] (RBYB) .... KEYE-TV
Austin, TX [*AM radio station call letters*] .... KFON
Austin, TX [*FM radio station call letters*] .... KKMJ
Austin, TX [*AM radio station call letters*] .... KLBJ
Austin, TX [*FM radio station call letters*] .... KLBJ-FM
Austin, TX [*Television station call letters*] .... KLRU
Austin, TX [*FM radio station call letters*] .... KMFA
Austin, TX [*Television station call letters*] .... KNVA
Austin, TX [*FM radio station call letters*] .... KPEZ
Austin, TX [*Television station call letters*] .... KTBC
Austin, TX [*FM radio station call letters*] .... KUT
Austin, TX [*AM radio station call letters*] .... KVET
Austin, TX [*FM radio station call letters*] .... KVET-FM
Austin, TX [*FM radio station call letters*] .... KVRX
Austin, TX [*Television station call letters*] .... KVUE
Austin, TX [*Television station call letters*] .... KXAN
Austin, TX [*Location identifier FAA*] (FAAL) .... MMR
Austin Vocational Technical Institute, Austin, MN [*Library symbol Library of Congress*] (LCLS) .... MnAuV
Austin-Crothersville News, Austin, IN [*Library symbol Library of Congress*] (LCLS) .... InAusN
Austin-Healey Club of America (EA) .... AHCA
Austin-Healey Sports and Touring Club (EA) .... AHSTC
Austin-Moore [*Prosthesis*] [*Medicine*] .... A-M
Austin-Moore Prosthesis [*Medicine*] (DMAA) .... A-M Pr
Austin-Moore Prosthesis [*Medicine*] .... A-MP
Austin's Appeal Reports [*Ceylon*] [*A publication*] (ILCA) .... Aus Rep
Austin's Ceylon Reports [*A publication*] (DLA) .... Austin (Ceylon)
Austin's English County Court Cases [*1867-69*] [*A publication*] (DLA) .... Aust
Austin's English County Court Reports [*A publication*] (DLA) .... Austin CC
Austins International [*NASDAQ symbol*] (SAG) .... AUST
Austin's International [*NASDAQ symbol*] (TTSB) .... AUST
Austin's International, Inc. [*Associated Press*] (SAG) .... AustInt
Austin's Kandran Appeals [*Ceylon*] [*A publication*] (DLA) .... Aust KA
Austin's Lectures on Jurisprudence [*A publication*] (DLA) .... Aust Jr
Austin's Lectures on Jurisprudence [*A publication*] (ILCA) .... Aust Jur
Austin's Lectures on Jurisprudence, Abridged [*A publication*] (DLA) .... Aust Jur Abr
Austin's Reports [*Ceylon*] [*A publication*] (DLA) .... Austin
Austins Steak & Saloon, Inc. [*Associated Press*] (SAG) .... Austins
Austins Steak & Saloon, Inc. [*NASDAQ symbol*] (SAG) .... STAK
Austins Steaks & Saloon [*NASDAQ symbol*] (TTSB) .... STAK
Austra Resources Corp. [*Vancouver Stock Exchange symbol*] .... ARC
Austrain Institute Library, New York, NY [*Library symbol*] [*Library of Congress*] (LCLS) .... NNAIL
Austral Lineas Aereas [*Airline*] [*Argentina*] (EY) .... ALA
Austral Lineas Aereas [*ICAO designator*] (AD) .... AU
Austral Lineas Aereas [*Argentina ICAO designator*] (FAAC) .... AUT
Australasia (ADA) .... A'ASIA
Australasia (BARN) .... AUSTL
Australasia (ADA) .... AUSTSIA
Australasia [*MARC geographic area code Library of Congress*] (LCCP) .... u-----
Australasia and South East Asia Network [*Computer science*] (TNIG) .... AUSEAnet
Australasian (ADA) .... A'ASIAN
Australasian (ROG) .... AUSTRAL
Australasian (ADA) .... AUSTSN
Australasian Academy of Broadcast Arts and Sciences .... AABAS
Australasian Association for Logic .... AAL
Australasian Association of Secretaries and Managers .... AASM
Australasian Business Conditions Bulletin [*A publication*] .... Aust Bus Cond Bull
Australasian Catholic Record [*A publication*] .... Australas Cath Rec
Australasian College of Physical Scientists and Engineers in Medicine .... ACPSEM
Australasian Conference of Assessment and Certification Agencies .... ACACA
Australasian Corrosion Association (EAIO) .... ACA
Australasian Drama Studies .... Aus Drama St
Australasian Drug Information Services .... ADIS
Australasian Electrical Times [*A publication*] .... Aust Elec Times
Australasian Engineer [*A publication*] .... Aust Eng
Australasian Genetic Support Group Association .... AGSA
Australasian Institute of Chartered Accountants .... AICA
Australasian Institute of Fundraising .... AIF
[*The*] **Australasian Institute of Fundraising** .... TAIF
Australasian Insurance and Banking Record [*A publication*] .... Australas Insur Banking Rec
Australasian Insurance Journal [*A publication*] .... Australas Insur J
Australasian Journal of Philosophy [*A publication*] (APTA) .... AJP
Australasian Journal of Philosophy [*A publication*] .... Aus J Phil
Australasian Law Students Association .... ALSA
Australasian Medical Index [*A publication*] .... AMI
Australasian Performing Right Association (EAIO) .... APRA
Australasian Photo Review [*A publication*] .... Aust Photo Rev
Australasian Porcelain Art Teachers [*An association*] .... APAT
Australasian Presentation and Multi-Media Association .... APMMA
Australasian Public Libraries and Information Services [*A publication*] ...... APLIS
Australasian Regional Association of Zoological Parks and Aquaria .... ARAZP
Australasian Register of Agricultural Consultants .... ARAC
Australasian Religion Index [*A publication*] (APTA) .... ARI
Australasian Schoolmaster and Literary Review [*A publication*] .... Australas Schoolmaster
Australasian Seabird Group (EA) .... ASG
Australasian Sketcher [*A publication*] .... AS
Australasian Smaller Companies Trust .... ASCT
Australasian Society for HIV [*Human Immunodeficiency Virus*] **Medicine** .... ASHM
Australasian Society for the Study of Animal Behaviour .... ASSAB
Australasian Society of Engineers .... ASE
Australasian Species Management Plan .... ASMP
Australasian Study of Parliament Group .... ASPG
Australasian Typographical Journal [*A publication*] .... ATJ
Australasian Universities Language and Literature Association (EAIO)..... AULLA
Australasians in Property in London .... AIPIL
Australia .... AS
Australia [*MARC country of publication code Library of Congress*] (LCCP) .... at
Australia [*ANSI two-letter standard code*] (CNC) .... AU
Australia [*ANSI three-letter standard code*] (CNC) .... AUS
Australia .... AUSTL
Australia .... AUSTR
Australia (VRA) .... Austr
Australia .... AUSTRAL
Australia [*IYRU nationality code*] (IYR) .... KA
Australia [*MARC geographic area code Library of Congress*] (LCCP) .... u-at--
Australia 1938 Bulletin [*A publication*] .... A 1938 B
Australia Air Publications [*A publication*] .... AAP
Australia & New Zealand Bank [*NYSE symbol*] (SPSG) .... ANZ
Australia & New Zealand Banking Group [*Associated Press*] (SAG) .... AusNZ
Australia & New Zealand Banking Group [*Associated Press*] (SAG) .... AustNZ
Australia and New Zealand Funds Management [*Banking*] .... ANZFM
Australia and New Zealand Trade Advisory Committee [*British Overseas Trade Board*] (DS) .... ANZTAC
Australia & N.Z. Bk ADS [*NYSE symbol*] (TTSB) .... ANZ
Australia Antigen [*Immunology*] (DAVI) .... AA
Australia Antigen [*Immunology*] .... Au
Australia Antigen [*Immunology*] (MAE) .... Au Ag
Australia Antigen [*Medicine*] (MAH) .... Au(I)
Australia Antigen Radioimmunoassay [*Immunology*] (AAMN) .... AAR
Australia Asia Airlines [*Air carrier designation symbol*] .... AAA
Australia Asia Airlines Ltd. [*ICAO designator*] (FAAC) .... AAU
Australia Braford Society .... ABS
Australia Canada Association (ADA) .... ACA
Australia, Canada, United Kingdom, United States (ADA) .... AUCANUKUS
Australia, Canada, United Kingdom, United States (MCD) .... AUSCANUKUS
Australia Council Press Clips [*Database*] .... ACP
Australia. Department of Foreign Affairs. Treaty Series [*A publication*] .... Aust DFA Treaty Series
Australia Fan Club (EA) .... AFC
Australia First [*Political party*] .... AF
Australia Hepatitis-Associated Antigen [*Immunology*] (MAE) .... AUHAA
Australia in Print [*Book distributor*] .... AIP
Australia. Institute of Science and Industry. Bulletin [*A publication*] .... Inst Sci & Indust Bull
Australia International Defence Equipment Exhibition .... AIDEX
Australia Kangaroo Club [*Defunct*] (EA) .... AKC
Australia, New Zealand, and Malaysia [*Defense pact*] (BARN) .... ANZAM
Australia, New Zealand, and the United States [*Signatories to the Tripartite Security Treaty of 1951*] .... ANZUS
Australia, New Zealand, and United Kingdom .... ANZUK
Australia - Papua New Guinea [*Submarine cable*] [*Telecommunications*] ...... APNG
Australia. Radio Propagation Committee. Ionospheric Bulletin [*A publication*] .... ARPC Ionospheric Bull
Australia Serum Hepatitis [*Medicine*] (DMAA) .... AuS
Australia Serum Hepatitis [*Antigen*] [*Immunology*] (MAE) .... AuSH
Australia Standard White [*Variety of wheat*] .... ASW
Australia Telescope Compact Array .... ATCA
Australia Telescope National Facility .... ATNF
Australia Television International .... ATVI
Australia-Brazil Chamber of Commerce .... ABCC
Australia-Britain Society .... ABS
Australia-British Trade Association .... ABTA
Australia-China Business Co-Operation Committee .... ACBCC
Australia-China Business Council .... ACBC
Australia-China Chamber of Commerce .... ACCC
Australia-China Friendship Society .... ACFS
Australia-France Technological Exchange Scheme .... AFTEX
Australia-India Chamber of Commerce .... AICC
Australia-Indonesia Business Council .... AIBC
Australia-Indonesia Youth Exchange Program .... AIYEP
Australia-Israel Chamber of Commerce and Industry .... AICCI
Australia-Japan Research Centre [*Australian National University*] .... AJRC
Australia-Korea Chamber of Commerce and Industry .... AKCCI
Australia-Korea Foundation .... AKF

Australia-Malaysia Chamber of Commerce ... AMCC
Australian ... A
Australian ... AUST
Australian Abalone Producers' Association ... AAPA
Australian Aboriginal Studies [*A publication*] ... Aus Ab St
Australian Academic and Research Libraries [*A publication*] ... Aust Acad Res Libs
Australian Academic and Research Network [*Computer science*] (TNIG) ... AARNet
Australian Academy of Anatomy ... AAA
Australian Academy of Art ... AAA
Australian Academy of Cricket ... AAC
Australian Academy of Optometry ... AAO
Australian Academy of Paediatrics ... AAP
Australian Accountancy Student [*A publication*] ... Aust Account Student
Australian Accountant [*A publication*] ... Aust Acctnt
Australian Administrative Law Bulletin [*A publication*] ... AAL Bull
Australian Administrative Law Bulletin [*A publication*] ... AALB
Australian Administrative Law Bulletin [*A publication*] ... ADL Bull
Australian Advanced Air Traffic Services (GAVI) ... AAATS
Australian Aerobatic Club ... AAC
Australian Aeronautical Academy ... AAA
Australian Affiliation of Herpetological Societies ... AAHS
Australian Agricultural Machinery Manufacturers' Association ... AAMMA
Australian Air International ... AAI
Australian Air League New South Wales Boys Group ... AALNSWBG
Australian Air League Victorian Group ... AALVG
Australian Air Pilots Mutual Benefit Fund ... AAPMBF
Australian Aircraft Consortium (LAIN) ... AAC
Australian Airlines ... AA
Australian Airlines [*ICAO designator*] (FAAC) ... AUS
Australian Airlines [*Airline flight code*] (ODBW) ... TN
Australian Amateur Football Council ... AAFC
Australian Amateur Ice Racing Council ... AAIRC
Australian Amateur Water Polo Association ... AAWPA
Australian and New Zealand Association for Canadian Studies ... ANZACS
Australian and New Zealand Commentary on Halsbury's Laws of England [*A publication*] ... ANZC Hals
Australian and New Zealand Conveyancing Report [*A publication*] ... ACR
Australian and New Zealand Environment and Conservation Council ... ANZECC
Australian and New Zealand Equal Opportunity Law and Practice [*A publication*] ... AEOP
Australian and New Zealand Federation of Animal Societies ... ANZFAS
Australian and New Zealand Income Tax Reports [*A publication*] (DLA) ... ANZITR
Australian and New Zealand Insurance Reporter [*A publication*] ... AIN
Australian and New Zealand Journal of Criminology [*A publication*] ... ANZJ of Crim
Australian and New Zealand Journal of Criminology [*A publication*] ... Aust & NZJ Crim
Australian and New Zealand Journal of Criminology [*A publication*] ... Aust NZ Jl Criminol
Australian and New Zealand Journal of Sociology [*A publication*] ... Aust NZ Jl Sociol
Australian and New Zealand Journal of Surgery [*A publication*] ... Aust NZ Jl Surgery
Australian and New Zealand Merchants' and Shippers' Association (DS) ... ANZMSA
Australian and New Zealand Physicist [*A publication*] ... Aust & NZ Phys
Australian Animal Protection Society ... AAPS
Australian Annual Digest [*A publication*] (DLA) ... Austl AD
Australian Antarctic Expedition [*1911-14*] ... AAE
Australian Antarctic Territory ... AAT
Australian Anti-Apartheid Movement [*An association*] ... AAM
Australian Apple and Pear Growers' Association ... AAPGA
Australian Apple and Pear Shippers' Association ... AAPSA
Australian Appliance Association ... AAA
Australian Architectural Periodicals Index (ADA) ... AAPI
Australian Archives Electronic Research Project ... AAERP
Australian Armed Forces Radio ... AAFR
Australian Army ... AA
Australian Army Training Team, Vietnam (VNW) ... AATTV
Australian Army Training Team, Vietnam (VNW) ... AATTVV
Australian Aromatherapists' Association ... AAA
Australian Art Index [*Database*] ... AART
Australian Art Index [*Australian National Gallery Library*] [*Database*] (ADA) ... AARTI
Australian Asian Association ... AAA
Australian Associated Press Party Ltd. ... AAP
Australian Associated Stock Exchanges (ADA) ... AASE
Australian Association Against Painful Experiments on Animals ... AAAPEA
Australian Association for Armed Neutrality ... AAAN
Australian Association for Deserted Children ... AADC
Australian Association for Engineering Education ... AAEE
Australian Association for Environmental Education ... AAEE
Australian Association for Quality and Participation ... AAQP
Australian Association of Bush Regenerators ... AABR
Australian Association of Cattle Veterinarians ... AACV
Australian Association of Ceramic Tile Merchants ... AACTM
Australian Association of Chief Information Officers ... AACIO
Australian Association of Community Language Services ... AACLS
Australian Association of Consulting Planners ... AACP
Australian Association of Farm Management Consultants ... AAFMC
Australian Association of Film and Video Libraries ... AAFVL
Australian Association of Independent Businesses Ltd. ... AAIB
Australian Association of Mental Health ... AAMH
Australian Association of Musical Instrument Makers ... AAMIM
Australian Association of Nematologists ... AAN
Australian Association of Pathology Practices ... AAPP
Australian Association of Philanthropy ... AAP
Australian Association of Police Citizens' Youth Clubs ... AAPCYC
Australian Association of Prisoner Support Organizations ... AAPSO
Australian Association of Rural Fire Authorities ... AARFA
Australian Association of Taxation and Management Accountants ... AATMA
Australian Association of University Teachers of Accounting ... AAUTA
Australian Association of Veterans' Athletic Clubs ... AAVAC
Australian Atomic Energy Commission (NUCP) ... AAEC
Australian Audio-Visual Reference Book [*A publication*] (APTA) ... AAVRB
Australian Automotive Manufacturers' Association ... AAMA
Australian Aviation Underwriters' Pool ... AAUP
Australian Avocado Growers' Association ... AAGF
Australian Ayrshire Breeders' Association ... AABA
Australian Babji Joga Sangam [*An association*] ... ABJS
Australian Ballet ... AB
Australian Ballet School ... ABS
Australian Banana Growers' Council ... ABGC
Australian Bank Ltd. ... ABL
Australian Bank of Commerce ... ABC
Australian Baptist [*A publication*] (APTA) ... AB
Australian Bar Review [*A publication*] ... Aust Bar Rev
Australian Barefoot Association ... ABA
Australian Barley Marketing Federation ... ABMF
Australian Bartenders' Guild ... ABG
Australian Baseball League ... ABL
Australian Baton Twirling Association ... ABTA
Australian Beef Promotion Committee ... ABPC
Australian Biathlon Association Victoria ... ABAV
Australian Bibliographic Network [*National Library of Australia*] [*Information service or system*] (IID) ... ABN
Australian Bicentennial Authority ... ABA
Australian Bicycle Motocross Association ... ABMXA
Australian Billiards and Snooker Council ... ABSC
Australian Biographical and Genealogical Record [*A publication*] (ADA) ... ABGR
Australian Biological Resources Advisory Committee ... ABRAC
Australian Bird Count ... ABC
Australian Birthright Movement [*An association*] ... ABM
Australian Blind Sports Federation ... ABSF
Australian Bloodhorse Breeders Association ... ABBA
Australian Board of Translators ... ABT
Australian Boating [*A publication*] ... AB
Australian Bone Marrow Transplant Foundation ... ABMTF
Australian Book Heritage Resources Project ... ABHR
Australian Book Review [*A publication*] (BRI) ... Aust Bk R
Australian Book Trade Directory [*A publication*] (APTA) ... ABTD
Australian Boot Trade Employees' Federation ... ABTEF
Australian Borrowers' Association ... ABA
Australian Bowling Federation ... ABF
Australian Bowls Board ... ABB
Australian Boys' Choir ... ABC
Australian Brangus Cattle Association ... ABCA
Australian Breeding Center ... ABC
Australian Bridge [*A publication*] ... AB
Australian Bridge Federation ... ABF
Australian British Chamber of Commerce (DBA) ... ABCC
Australian Broadcasting Co. ... ABC
Australian Broadcasting Corporation Senior Executives' Association ... ABCSOA
Australian Brown Swiss and Braunvieh Association ... ABSBA
Australian Brushmakers' Union ... ABU
Australian Builder [*A publication*] ... Aust Build
Australian Builder and Land Advertiser [*A publication*] ... AB & LA
Australian Builders' Laborers Federated Union of Workers ... ABLFUW
Australian Building Cost Database ... ABCD
Australian Bulletin of Labour [*A publication*] ... Aust BL
Australian +Bureau of Agricultural and Resource Economics (IID) ... ABARE
Australian Bureau of Animal Health ... ABAH
Australian Bureau of Criminal Intelligence ... ABCI
Australian Bureau of Meteorology [*Marine science*] (OSRA) ... ABOM
Australian Bureau of Statistics Database ... ABSDATA
Australian Business and Estate Planning Reporter [*A publication*] ... AEB
Australian Business Brief [*A publication*] ... Aust Bus Brief
Australian Business Brief and Hansard Service [*Australian Chamber of Commerce*] [*Information service or system Defunct*] (IID) ... BBHS
Australian Business Communications Directory [*A publication*] ... ABCD
Australian Business Directory [*A publication*] ... ABD
Australian Business Forms Association ... ABFA
Australian Business Law Review [*A publication*] ... ABLR
Australian Business Law Review [*A publication*] ... Aust Bus Law Rev
Australian Business Law Review [*A publication*] ... Aust Bus Rev
Australian Business Lawyer [*A publication*] ... Aust Bus Lawyer
Australian Business Monthly [*A publication*] ... ABM
Australian Cable and Subscription Communications Association ... ACSCA
Australian Calisthenics Federation ... ACF
Australian Camellia Research Society ... ACRS
Australian Cane Farmers' Association ... ACFA
Australian Canvas and Synthetic Products Association ... ACSPA
Australian Capital Territory (PPW) ... ACT
Australian Capital Territory Amateur Weightlifting Association ... ACTAWA
Australian Capital Territory Association for the Teaching of English ... ACTATE
Australian Capital Territory Athletics [*An association*] ... ACTA
Australian Capital Territory Basketball ... ACTB
Australian Capital Territory Bridge Association ... ACTBA
Australian Capital Territory Continence Promotion Group ... ACTCPG

Australian Capital Territory Council of Cultural Societies ACTCCS
Australian Capital Territory Credit Union Association Cooperative ACTCUAC
Australian Capital Territory Education Information Network ACTEIN
Australian Capital Territory Geographical Society ACTGS
Australian Capital Territory Geography Teachers' Association ACTGTA
Australian Capital Territory Hockey Association ACTHA
Australian Capital Territory Injury Surveillance and Prevention Project ACTISPP
Australian Capital Territory Institute of Technical and Further Education ACTITFE
Australian Capital Territory Lieder Society ACTLS
Australian Capital Territory Marching Association ACTMA
Australian Capital Territory Master Joiners' Association ACTMJA
Australian Capital Territory Nurses' Board ACTNB
Australian Capital Territory Pistol Association ACTPA
Australian Capital Territory Racing Club ACTRC
Australian Capital Territory Recycling Campaign ARC
Australian Capital Territory Smallbore Rifle Club ACTSRC
Australian Capital Territory Soccer Federation ACTSF
Australian Capital Territory Softball Association ACTSA
Australian Capital Territory Sport and Recreational Fishing Council ACTSRFC
Australian Capital Territory Touch Association ACTTA
Australian Capitol [*Record label*] ACap
Australian Cardiacs' Association ACA
Australian Carpet Wool Council ACWC
Australian Carpetmaster Sheepbreeders' Association ACSA
Australian Casemix Bulletin [*A publication*] ACB
Australian Cashmere Growers' Association ACGA
Australian Catholic Bishops' Conference ACBC
Australian Catholic Health Care Association ACHCA
Australian Catholic Theological Association ACTA
Australian Catholic University Aquinas Campus ACU Aq
Australian Catholic University Castle Hill Campus ACU CH
Australian Catholic University Christ Campus ACU Christ
Australian Catholic University Mackillop Campus ACU MacK
Australian Catholic University McAuley Campus ACU McA
Australian Catholic University Mercy Campus ACU Mercy
Australian Catholic University Mount St. Mary Campus ACU MSM
Australian Catholic University Signadou Campus ACU Sign
Australian Cattle Dog Club of America (EA) ACDCA
Australian Cattle Dog Society of New South Wales ACDSNSW
Australian Center for Leadership Research and Development ACLRD
Australian Centre for Advanced Risk and Reliability Engineering ACARRE
Australian Centre for Egyptology ACE
Australian Centre for Remote Sensing ACRES
Australian Cerebral Palsy Sports Federation ACPSF
Australian Chamber Music Society ACMS
Australian Chamber of Fruit and Vegetable Industries ACFVI
Australian Chemical Industry Council ACIA
Australian Cherry Growers' Federation ACGF
Australian Chicken Growers' Council ACGC
Australian Chicken Meat Federation ACMF
Australian Child and Family Welfare [*A publication*] Aust Child Family Welf
Australian Children's Foundation ACF
Australian Children's Television Committee. Newsletter [*A publication*] Aust Children TV Com Newsl
Australian Childrens Television Foundation ACTVF
Australian Chinese Community Association of New South Wales ACCANSW
Australian Choreographic Ensemble ACE
Australian Christian [*A publication*] (APTA) AC
Australian Christian Party [*Political party*] ACP
Australian Cinema Advertising Council ACAC
Australian Citrus Exporters' Association ACEA
Australian Citrus Industry Council ACIC
Australian Citrus Processors' Association ACPA
Australian Civil Affairs Unit (VNW) ACAU
Australian Civil Aviation Authority, Flying Unit [*ICAO designator*] (FAAC) ADA
Australian Civil Engineering and Construction [*A publication*] Aust Civil Engng Constr
Australian Civil Police AUSTCIVPOL
Australian Clay Pipe Manufacturers' Association ACPMA
Australian Clay Target Association ACTA
Australian Coal Marketing and Technology Council ACMTC
Australian Coal Trade and Technology Committee ACTTC
Australian Coalition of Young People ACYP
Australian Coffee Growers Association ACGA
Australian College of Education. Queensland Chapter. Newsletter [*A publication*] Newsl Aust Coll Ed Qd
Australian College of Metaphysical Studies ACMS
Australian College of Midwives ACM
Australian College of Travel and Hospitality ACTH
Australian Colleges and Universities Staff Association ACUSA
Australian Commercial Law Association ACLA
Australian Commission for the Future ACF
Australian Committee on Africa ACA
Australian Commodities [*Database*] AUSTCOM
Australian Community Languages and Cultural Program ACLCP
Australian Community Theatre ACT
Australian Companies Legislation [*A publication*] ACL
Australian Company Law and Practice [*A publication*] ACP
Australian Co. Secretary's Business Law Manual [*A publication*] LABL
Australian Co. Secretary's Letter [*A publication*] ACSL
Australian Company Secretary's Practice Manual [*A publication*] LSEC
Australian Computer Equipment Manufacturers' Association ACEMA
Australian Computer-Aided Design Systems ACADS
Australian Construction Industry Law Letter [*A publication*] ACILL
Australian Construction Law Newsletter [*A publication*] ACLN
Australian Construction Law Reporter [*A publication*] Aust Con LR
Australian Consulate-General, Australian Reference Library, New York, NY [*Library symbol*] [*Library of Congress*] (LCLS) NNAUR
Australian Consumer Sales and Credit Law Cases [*A publication*] ACSCC
Australian Consumers' Association (ODBW) ACA
Australian Conveyancer and Solicitors' Journal [*A publication*] (DLA) Austl Convey & Sol J
Australian Conveyor Manufacturers Association ACMA
Australian Corporate Law [*Database*] ACLID
Australian Corporation Law Bulletin [*A publication*] ACLB
Australian Corporations and Securities Reports [*A publication*] ACSR
Australian Cotton Foundation ACF
Australian Cotton Growers' Research Association ACGRA
Australian Council for Aeronautics ACA
Australian Council for Aeronautics. Report [*A publication*] Aust Council Aeronautics Rept
Australian Council for Children's Films and Television ACCFTV
Australian Council for Educational Research, Hawthorn, V, Australia [*Library symbol Library of Congress*] (LCLS) AuHaA
Australian Council for Private Education and Training ACPET
Australian Council for Teaching Foreign Languages ACTFL
Australian Council for the Care of Animals in Research and Teaching ACCART
Australian Council of Alcohol and Other Drug Associations ACAODA
Australian Council of Churches ACOC
Australian Council of Egg Producers ACEP
Australian Council of Employers' Federations ACEF
Australian Council of Independent Business Schools ACIBS
Australian Council of Manufacturing Associates ACMA
Australian Council of Marriage Counselling ACMC
Australian Council of Recyclers ACR
Australian Council of Rural Youth ACRY
Australian Council of Social Service ACSS
Australian Country Music Awards ACMA
Australian Country Party [*Political party*] (BARN) ACP
Australian Country Party [*Political party*] AustCP
Australian Courier and Taxi Truck Operators' Association ACTTOA
Australian Cranio-Facial Foundation ACFF
Australian Credit Unions Magazine [*A publication*] Aust Credit Unions Mag
Australian Cricket Association ACA
Australian Crime Prevention Council. Quarterly Journal [*A publication*] ACPCQJ
Australian Criminal Lawyers' Association ACLA
Australian Croatian Association ACA
Australian Croquet Association ACA
Australian Cruiser (DMA) AC
Australian Cultural Center Association ACCA
Australian Curling Association ACA
Australian Current Case Annotator [*A publication*] ACCA
Australian Current Law Articles [*A publication*] ACL AT
Australian Current Law Review [*A publication*] (DLA) Austl Current L Rev
Australian Customer Service Association ACSA
Australian Customs Notice [*A publication*] ACN
Australian Cystic Fibrosis Associations Federation ACFAF
Australian Czech Association of New South Wales ACANSW
Australian Dairy Foods Advisory Bureau ADFAB
Australian Dairy Products Federation ADPF
Australian Dairy Products Standards Organization ADPSO
Australian Dairy Traders' Federation ADTF
Australian Dance Foundation ADF
Australian Dance Theatre [*Adelaide*] ADT
Australian Database Development Association Database ADDABASE
Australian De Facto Relationships Law [*A publication*] ADR
Australian Deaf Sports Federation ADSF
Australian Deer Farmers' Federation ADFF
Australian Deerstalkers' Federation ADF
Australian Defence Force (ADA) ADF
Australian Defense Force Warfare Center [*Military*] ADFWC
Australian Defense Formatted Message System [*Military*] ADFORMS
Australian Democratic Labor Party [*Political party*] (PPW) ADLP
Australian Democratic Party [*Political party*] (PPW) ADP
Australian Democrats [*Political party*] (EAIO) AD
Australian Dental Research Fund ADRF
Australian Design Council ADC
Australian Design Rule [*Automotive technology*] ADR
Australian Diabetes Foundation ADF
Australian Dictionary of Acronyms and Abbreviations [*A publication*] ADAA
Australian Die Casting Association ADCA
Australian Digest [*A publication*] ADA
Australian Digest [*A publication*] (DLA) Austl D
Australian Digest, Second Edition [*A publication*] (DLA) Aust D 2d
Australian Directory of Vocational Education and Training [*A publication*] ADVET
Australian Disabilities Review [*A publication*] ADR
Australian Disabled Skiers' Federation ADSF
Australian Dispute Resolution Journal [*A publication*] ADRJ
Australian Diving Association ADA
Australian Dollar [*Monetary unit*] AUD
Australian Down Syndrome Association ADSA
Australian Drama Studies Association ADSA
Australian Driver Trainers' Association ADTA
Australian Driving Society ADS
Australian Drug and Alcohol Foundation ADAF

Australian Drug Database ... ADDB
Australian Drug Database (Law Enforcement Component) ... ADDBLEC
Australian Duty Free Operators' Association ... ADFOA
Australian Early Childhood Education Association ... AECEA
Australian Early Holden Association ... AEHA
Australian Earth Sciences Information System [*Database on AUSINET*] (NITA) ... AESI
Australian Eastern Daylight Saving Time (ADA) ... AEDST
Australian Economic Indicators [*A publication*] ... AEI
Australian Economic Papers [*A publication*] ... Aust Econ P
Australian Economic Review [*A publication*] ... Aust Econ R
Australian Education directory [*A publication*] ... AED
Australian Education Researcher [*A publication*] ... Aus Ed Res
Australian Education Researcher [*A publication*] ... Aust Ed Res
Australian Education Review [*A publication*] ... Aust Ed Rev
Australian Educational Allowance Fund ... AEAF
Australian Egg Marketing Council ... AEMC
Australian Electric Transport Association (South Australia) ... AETM(SA)
Australian Embassy, Washington, DC [*Library symbol Library of Congress*] (LCLS) ... DAusE
Australian Employee Survey Group ... AESG
Australian Employers' Federation ... AEF
Australian Employment Law Guide [*A publication*] ... AEM
Australian Employment Legislation [*A publication*] ... AEL
Australian Energy Management News [*A publication*] ... AEMN
Australian Energy Research Laboratory ... AERL
Australian Environmental Law News [*A publication*] ... AELN
Australian Equestrian Trade Association ... AETA
Australian Equine Research Foundation ... AERF
Australian Equine Veterinary Association ... AEVA
Australian Ethnic Democrats [*Political party*] ... AED
Australian Ethnic Democrats [*An association*] ... AUSED
Australian Export Commodity Classification ... AECC
Australian Export Statistics [*Database*] ... AEEC
Australian Fabian Society ... AFS
Australian Factors' Guild ... AFG
Australian Faculty Directory [*A publication*] ... AFD
Australian Family Association ... AFA
Australian Family Law Bulletin [*A publication*] ... AFLB
Australian Family Law Guide [*A publication*] ... AFAM
Australian Family Lawyer [*A publication*] ... AFL
Australian Family Research Bulletin [*A publication*] (ADA) ... AFRB
Australian Family Studies Database ... AFAM
Australian Federal Police [*A publication*] ... Aust Fed Police
Australian Federal Tax Reporter [*A publication*] ... FTR
Australian Federation of Air Freight Forwarders ... AFAFF
Australian Federation of Credit Unions ... AFCU
Australian Federation of Homeopaths ... AFH
Australian Federation of Pipe Band Associations ... AFPBA
Australian Federation of Right to Life Associations ... AFRTLA
Australian Federation of the Women's International Zionist Organization ... AFWIZO
Australian Federation of Timber Merchants' Associations ... AFTMA
Australian Federation of Travel Agents (BARN) ... AFTA
Australian Feeds Information Centre [*Database*] ... AFIC
Australian Fencing Federation ... AFF
Australian Fertilizer Manufacturers' Committee ... AFMC
Australian Festival [*Record label*] ... AFest
Australian Festival of Life ... AFL
Australian Film Corp. ... AFC
Australian Film Finance Corp. ... AFFC
Australian Film Institute Distribution ... AFID
Australian Film Making Association ... AFMA
Australian Finance Availability Guide [*A publication*] ... AFIN
Australian Financial Futures Market ... AFFM
Australian Financial Review [*A publication*] ... Fin Rev
Australian Financial Review Property Review [*A publication*] (ADA) ... FRPR
Australian Firms Information System ... AFIS
Australian Fish Health Reference Laboratory ... AFHRL
Australian Fisheries [*A publication*] ... Aust Fisheries
Australian Fisheries Service [*Marine science*] (OSRA) ... AFS
Australian Fishing Zone Authority ... AFZA
Australian Flour Export Promotion Committee ... AFEPC
Australian Flute Association ... AFA
Australian Folk Music Associates ... AFMA
Australian Folklore Association ... AFA
Australian Folkloric Dance Company [*An association*] ... AFDC
Australian Foodservice Manufacturers' Association ... AFMA
Australian Football Coaches Association ... AFCA
Australian Foreign Affairs Record [*A publication*] ... Aust For Aff Rec
Australian Foreign Trade Office ... AFTO
Australian Forest Grower [*A publication*] ... Aust Forest Grower
Australian Foundation for the Disabled ... AFD
Australian Foundation for the Peoples of the South Pacific ... AFPSP
Australian Freedom from Hunger Campaign ... AFHC
Australian Fresh Juice and Cordial Manufacturers' Association ... AFJCMA
Australian Fresh Juice Association ... AFJA
Australian Friendly Societies' Association ... AFSA
Australian Friesian Sahiwal [*Cattle terminology*] ... AFS
Australian Fringe Benefits Tax Guide for Employers [*A publication*] ... AFB
Australian Fruit Growers [*An association*] ... AFG
Australian Futsal Federation ... AFF
Australian Garden History Society ... AGHS
Australian Garlic Association ... AGA
Australian Genome Research Facility ... AGAP
Australian Geographer [*A publication*] ... Aus Geo
Australian Geographical Studies [*A publication*] ... AGS
Australian Geographical Studies [*A publication*] ... Aus G Stud
Australian Geological Survey Organisation ... AGSO
Australian Geological Survey Organisation [*Formerly, BMR - Bureau of Mineral Resources*] ... AGSO
Australian Geriatrics' Society ... AGS
Australian Glass Workers' Union ... AGWU
Australian Gold [*Vancouver Stock Exchange symbol*] ... AZG
Australian Golf Course Superintendents' Association ... AGCSA
Australian Government Solicitors' Office ... AGSO
Australian Graduate of the School of Management (ODBW) ... AGSM
Australian Grain Exporters' Association ... AGEA
Australian Grape Exporters' Committee ... AGEC
Australian Greeting Card Association ... AGCA
Australian Gruen Party [*Political party*] ... AGP
Australian Guild of Music and Speech ... AGMS
Australian Guild of Screen Composers ... AGSC
Australian Guitar Journal [*A publication*] (APTA) ... AGJ
Australian Hairdressers, Wigmakers, and Hairworkers Employees Federation ... AHWHEF
Australian Handball Council ... AHC
Australian Handball Federation ... AHF
Australian Hard Wheat [*Agriculture*] ... AHW
Australian Hardwood Quality Council ... AHQC
Australian Harness Racing Council ... AHRC
Australian Hayward Kiwifruit Growers Association ... AHKGA
Australian Health Ethics Committee ... AHEC
Australian Health Professionals Association ... AHPA
Australian Health Services ... AHS
Australian Health Services Commission ... AHSC
Australian Hepatitis Antigen [*Biochemistry*] (DAVI) ... AHA
Australian Heraldic Archival Record ... AHAR
Australian Heritage Award ... AHA
Australian Hides, Skins, and Leather Exports Association ... AHSLEA
Australian Historic Records Register [*Database*] ... AHRR
Australian Historical Bibliography [*A publication*] ... Aust Hist Bibl
Australian Historical Geography [*A publication*] ... AHG
Australian Historical Statistics [*A publication*] ... AHS
Australian Historical Studies [*A publication*] (APTA) ... AHS
Australian Historical Studies [*A publication*] ... Aust Hist Stud
Australian Home Owners' Club ... AHOC
Australian Horticultural Correspondence School ... AHCS
Australian Horticultural Export Council ... AHEC
Australian Horticultural Exporters Association ... AHEA
Australian Horticultural Trades Exhibition ... AHTE
Australian Housing Industry Development Council ... AHIDC
Australian Hungarian Association of Western Australia ... AHAWA
Australian Immigration Research Center ... AIRC
Australian Income Tax Guide [*A publication*] ... AITG
Australian Income Tax Guide [*A publication*] ... ITG
Australian Income Tax Legislation [*A publication*] ... ATL
Australian Income Tax Reports [*A publication*] (DLA) ... ITR
Australian Income Tax Rulings [*A publication*] ... ATRU
Australian Indonesian Association of Victoria [*Australia*] ... AIAV
Australian Indoor Bias Bowls Council ... AIBBC
Australian Indoor Cricket Federation ... AICF
Australian Indoor Soccer Federation ... AISF
Australian Industrial and Intellectual Property [*A publication*] ... ALEC
Australian Industrial Safety, Health, and Welfare [*A publication*] ... ASH
Australian Industrial Safety, Health, and Welfare Cases [*A publication*] ... AISHWC
Australian Industrial Union of Academic Staff ... AIUAS
Australian Industries Development Association. Bulletin [*A publication*] ... Bull Aust Ind Devt Ass
Australian Information Network (NITA) ... AUSINET
Australian Infrastructure Fund ... AIF
Australian Insolvency Bulletin [*A publication*] ... AIB
Australian Insolvency Management Practice [*A publication*] ... AISP
Australian Institute for International Understanding ... AIIU
Australian Institute for Rational Emotive Therapy ... AIRET
Australian Institute of Archaeology ... AIA
Australian Institute of Bankers ... AIB
Australian Institute of Cartographers (Queensland) ... AIC(Q)
Australian Institute of Consultant Valuers ... AICV
Australian Institute of Higher Energy Physics ... AUSHEP
Australian Institute of Homeopathy ... AIH
Australian Institute of Jewish Affairs ... AIJA
Australian Institute of Loss Adjusters ... AILA
Australian Institute of Materials Management ... AIMM
Australian Institute of Medical Scientists ... AIMS
Australian Institute of Mining and Metallurgy (NUCP) ... AIMM
Australian Institute of Parapsychological Research ... AIPR
Australian Institute of Purchasing and Supply Management ... AIPSM
Australian Institute of Radio and Television ... AIRT
Australian Institute of Radiography (EAIO) ... AIR
Australian Institute of Sales and Marketing Executives ... AISME
Australian Institute of Surgical and Dental Technicians ... AISDT
Australian Institute of Tourism Officers ... AITO
Australian Institute of Travel and Tourism ... AITT
Australian Intellectual Disabilities Research Foundation ... AIDRF
Australian Intellectual Property Cases [*A publication*] ... AIP
Australian Intellectual Property Cases [*A publication*] ... AIPC
Australian Intellectual Property Law Bulletin [*A publication*] ... AIPLB
Australian Interactive Multimedia Industry Association ... AIMIA

Australian International Development Assistance Bureau .... AIDAB
Australian International Hotel School .... AIHS
Australian International Law News [A publication] .... AILN
Australian International Law Review [A publication] .... AILR
Australian International Pilots' Industrial Organisation .... AIPIO
Australian International Tax Agreements [A publication] .... AIX
Australian International Technology Exhibition .... AITE
Australian International UFO [Unidentified Flying Object] Research .... AIUFOR
Australian Internationals (EA) .... AI
Australian Inventory of Chemical Substances .... AICS
Australian Investment Planning Guide [A publication] .... AVST
Australian Investor [A publication] (ADA) .... AI
Australian Irish Dancing Association .... AIDA
Australian Irish Welfare Bureau .... AIWB
Australian Jaycees .... AJ
Australian Jersey Breeders' Association .... AJBA
Australian Joint Citrus Exporters [An association] .... AJCE
Australian Joint Lamb and Sheepmeat Promotion Committee .... AJLSPC
Australian Journal for Health, Physical Education, and Recreation
   [A publication] .... AJHPER
Australian Journal. Institute of Transport [A publication] .... Aust J Inst Transp
Australian Journal of Advanced Education [A publication] .... Aust J Adv Ed
Australian Journal of Advanced Nursing [A publication] (APTA) ...... AJAN
[The] Australian Journal of Anthropology [A publication] .... TAJA
Australian Journal of Ecology [A publication] .... AJ Ecol
Australian Journal of Education [A publication] .... AJ Ed
Australian Journal of Educational Technology [A publication] ...... AJET
Australian Journal of Experimental Agriculture [A publication] ..... AJEA
Australian Journal of Experimental Biology and Medical Science
   [A publication] .... Aust J Exper Biol & Med Sci
Australian Journal of Family Law [A publication] .... AJFL
Australian Journal of Forensic Sciences [A publication] .... Aust J Foren Sci
Australian Journal of Health, Physical Education, and Recreation
   [A publication] .... Aust J Hlth Phys Ed Rec
Australian Journal of Holistic Nursing [A publication] .... AJOHN
Australian Journal of Labour Law [A publication] .... AJLL
Australian Journal of Law and Society [A publication] .... Aust JLS
Australian Journal of Law and Society [A publication] (DLA) ...... Austl JL Soc'y
Australian Journal of Linguistics [A publication] .... AJL
Australian Journal of Linguistics [A publication] .... Aus J Lin
Australian Journal of Liturgy [A publication] (APTA) .... AJL
Australian Journal of Management [A publication] .... Aust J Mgmt
Australian Journal of Management [A publication] .... Aust JM
Australian Journal of Mining [A publication] .... AJM
Australian Journal of Pharmacy [A publication] .... AJP
Australian Journal of Psychology and Philosophy
   [A publication] .... Aust J Psych & Phil
Australian Journal of Public Administration [A publication] .... Aust J Publ Admin
Australian Journal of Sex, Marriage, and Family [A publication] (APTA) ..... AJSMF
Australian Journal of Social Issues [A publication] .... AJ Soc Is
Australian Journal of Social Issues [A publication] .... Aust J Soc Is
Australian Journal of Social Issues [A publication] .... Aust Jnl of Social Issues
Australian Journal of Special Education [A publication] .... Aust J Spec Ed
Australian Journal of Teacher Education [A publication] .... Aust J Teach Ed
Australian Journalism Review [A publication] (APTA) .... AJR
Australian Journalist [A publication] .... AJ
Australian Journalist [A publication] .... J
Australian Ju Jitsu Association .... AJJA
Australian Junior Chamber of Commerce .... AJCC
Australian Junior Rugby Football Union .... AJRFU
Australian Jurist [A publication] (DLA) .... Austl Jr
Australian Jurist Reports [A publication] (ILCA) .... Aust Jur R
Australian Karate Federation .... AKF
Australian Kelpie Club of New South Wales .... AKCNSW
Australian Kendo Federation .... AKF
Australian Key Center in Land Information Studies .... AKCLIS
Australian Kite Association .... AKA
Australian Kiwifruit Growers' Association .... AKGA
Australian Korea Business Council .... AKBC
Australian Korfball Association .... AKA
Australian Labour Party [Political party] (PPW) .... ALP
Australian Lace Guild .... ALG
Australian Land Transport Development Program .... ALTD
Australian LANDSAT [Land Satellite] Station .... ALS
Australian Law Reports [A publication] (DLA) .... Austl LR
Australian Law Times [A publication] (DLA) .... Austl L Times
Australian Lawyer [A publication] (DLA) .... Austl Law
Australian Lead/Zinc Development Association .... ALZDA
Australian League of Ex-Servicemen and Women .... ALESW
Australian Leather and Suede Clothing Association .... ALSCA
Australian Leave and Holidays Practice Manual [A publication] ...... ALVE
Australian Lecture Foundation .... ALF
Australian Left Review [A publication] .... Aus L Rev
Australian Left Review [A publication] .... Aust Left R
Australian Left Review [A publication] .... Aust Left Rev
Australian Legal Monthly Digest [A publication] (DLA) .... Austl LMD
Australian Leisure Index [Information service or system A publication] ...... ALI
Australian Liberation Front [Political party] .... ALF
Australian Libraries: the Essential Directory [A publication] ..... ALED
Australian Library and Information Professionals [A publication] .... ALIP
Australian Library Fair .... ALF
Australian Library News [A publication] .... Aust Libr News
Australian Library-Based Information System [National Library of Australia]
   (NITA) .... ALBIS
Australian Lighthouse Association .... ALA

Australian Limousin Breeders' Society .... ALBS
Australian Literary Awards and Fellowships [A publication] ..... ALAF
Australian Literature [A database] (NITA) .... ALIT
Australian Literature Index [A publication] .... ALI
Australian Lithuanian Catholic Federation .... ALCF
Australian Lithuanian Community .... ALC
Australian Livestock Exporters' Association .... ALEA
Australian Loan Council .... ALC
Australian Logic Teachers' Association .... ALTA
Australian Lutheran World Service .... ALWS
Australian Lychee Growers' Association .... ALGA
Australian Macadamia Growers' Society .... AMGS
Australian Macadamia Manufacturers' Association .... AMMA
Australian Macadamia Society .... AMS
Australian Machine Readable Cataloguing Record Service [National Library
   of Australia] (NITA) .... AMRS
Australian Major Energy Statistics [Database] .... AMES
Australian Malaysian Singaporean Association .... AMSA
Australian Malaysian Society .... AMS
Australian Management College Mount Eliza Association .... AMCMEA
Australian Management Industrial Association .... AMIA
Australian Manager [A publication] .... Aust Mger
Australian Manufacturing Production Commodity Classification ...... AMPCC
Australian Marathon Swimming Federation .... AMSF
Australian MARC [Machine readable catalogue] (NITA) .... AUSMARC
Australian MARC [Machine Readable Catalogue] Distribution Service
   (NITA) .... AMDS
Australian Marching Association .... AMA
Australian Marine Data Information Service .... AMDIS
Australian Marine Sciences Association .... AMSA
Australian Maritime Safety Authority .... AMSA
Australian Market Basket Survey .... AMB
Australian Master Tax Guide Updater [A publication] .... MTGU
Australian Mathematics Olympiad Committee .... AMOC
Australian Meatworks Federal Council .... AMFC
Australian Media Contacts [A publication] (ADA) .... AMC
Australian Merchant Vessel [Shipping] (ADA) .... AMV
Australian Meteorological and Oceanographic Society .... AMOS
Australian Meteorological Magazine [A publication] .... AMM
Australian Migration Consultants' Association .... AMCA
Australian Milk Vendors' Council .... AMVC
Australian Milking Zebu Breed [Agriculture] .... AMZB
Australian Minesweeper [A publication] .... AMS
Australian Mining Standard [A publication] .... Aust Mining Stand
Australian Ministry [A publication] (APTA) .... AM
Australian Modern Pentathlon Union .... AMPU
Australian Mohair Breeders' Association .... AMBA
Australian Molasses Pool [An association] .... AMP
Australian Monopoly Association .... AMA
Australian Monthly Magazine [A publication] .... Aust Mon Mag
Australian Monthly Newspapers and Periodicals Association ...... AMNPA
Australian Motorcycle Trailriders' Association .... AMTRA
Australian Mountain Bike Association .... AMBA
Australian Museum Society .... AMS
Australian Musicians' Guild .... AMG
Australian Nashi Growers' Association .... ANGA
Australian National Airways .... ANA
Australian National Antarctic Research Satellite .... ANARESAT
Australian National Association for Mental Health. Newsletter
   [A publication] .... Newsl Aust Natn Ass Ment Hlth
Australian National Capital Dancers [An association] .... ANCD
Australian National Committee of the International Dairy Federation ...... ANCIDF
Australian National Committee, World Energy Council .... ANCWEC
Australian National Dictionary [A publication] .... AND
Australian National Eisteddfod Society .... ANES
Australian National Field Days .... ANFD
Australian National Field Days Committee .... ANFDC
Australian National Flower Show Organising Committee .... ANFSOC
Australian National Formulary .... ANF
Australian National Four Wheel Drive Council .... ANFWDC
Australian National Kennel Council .... ANKC
Australian National Kung Fu Federation .... ANKFF
Australian National Party [Political party] .... ANP
Australian National Review [A publication] .... Aust National Rev
Australian National Review [A publication] .... Aust Natn Rev
Australian National Sportfishing Association (EAIO) .... ANSA
Australian National University .... ANU
Australian National University, Canberra, ACT, Australia [Library symbol
   Library of Congress] (LCLS) .... AuCU
Australian National University, Canberra, ACT, Australia [Library symbol
   Library of Congress] (LCLS) .... AuU
Australian National University Library and Information Service ...... ANULIS
Australian National University Staff Association .... ANUSA
Australian National Word Festival .... ANWF
Australian Native Dog Training Society of New South Wales
   [Australia] .... ANDTSNSW
Australian Naval Reserve .... ANR
Australian Netherlands Chamber of Commerce .... ANCC
Australian Neurological Research Institute .... ANRI
Australian Neutron Beam Users' Group .... ANBUG
Australian, New Zealand, African [Radio network] .... ANZA
Australian Nixa [Record label] .... ANix
Australian Noise Exposure Index .... ANEI
Australian Nuclear Science and Technology Organisation .... ANSTO
Australian Nuffied Farming Scholars' Association .... ANFSA

Australian Nurses' Journal [*A publication*] (APTA)	ANJ
Australian Nursing Homes and Extended Care Association	ANHECA
Australian Nutgrowers' Council	ANC
Australian Oceanographic Data Centre	AODC
Australian Oilseed Crushers' Association	AOCA
Australian Oilseeds Federation	AOF
Australian Onion Association	AOA
Australian Ordnance Council	AOC
Australian Organizations Industrial Policy	AOIP
Australian Osteopathic Association	AOA
Australian Outlook [*A publication*]	Aus Outl
Australian Outward Bound Foundation	AOBF
Australian Overseas Construction Council	AOCC
Australian Owned Companies Association	AOCA
Australian Packet Switching Service [*Telecommunications*] (NITA)	AUSTPAC
Australian PaintBall Players' Association	APBPA
Australian Parliamentary Paper [*A publication*]	Aust Parl Paper
Australian Particleboard Research Institute	APRI
Australian Payments Clearing Association	APCA
Australian Payroll Tax Manual [*A publication*]	APY
Australian Peak Shippers' Association	APSA
Australian Perendale Association	APA
Australian Periodicals in Print [*A publication*] (APTA)	APIP
Australian Pesticides Analytical Committee	APAC
Australian Pet Industry Joint Advisory Council	APIJAC
Australian Petanque Federation	APF
Australian Petroleum Industry Research Association	APIRA
Australian Petroleum Institute	API
Australian Picture Framers' Association	APFA
Australian Pig Artificial Breeding Association	APABA
Australian Pig Breeders' Association	APBA
Australian Pig Breeders' Society	APBS
Australian Pioneers' Club	APC
Australian Pistacio Growers' Association	APGA
Australian Plaiters and Whipmakers' Association	APWA
Australian Plastic Modellers' Association	APMA
Australian Podiatry Association	APA
Australian Podiatry Council	APC
Australian Police Journal [*A publication*]	A Pol J
Australian Police Journal [*A publication*]	Aust Pol J
Australian Police Ministers' Council, Senior Officers' Group	APMCSOG
Australian Political Register [*Australian Consolidated Press*] [*Database*]	APOL
Australian Poll Dorset Association	APDA
Australian Poll Hereford Association	APHA
Australian Polo Council	APC
Australian Pony Club Council	APCC
Australian Population Association	APA
Australian Population Research Institute	APRU
Australian Porcelain Decorators' Association	APDA
Australian Potato Industry Council	APIC
Australian Powerlifting Federation	APF
Australian Presbyterian Life [*A publication*]	Aust Presb Life
Australian Pre-School Quarterly [*A publication*]	Aust Presch Q
Australian Preservation and Conservation Abroad Group	APACA
Australian Product Liability Association	APLA
Australian Product Liability Reporter [*A publication*]	APLR
Australian Product Number Association	APNA
Australian Productivity Action [*A publication*]	Aust Prod Action
Australian Products First [*An association*]	APF
Australian Professional Rodeo Association	APRA
Australian Professional Triathletes Association	APTA
Australian Property Law Bulletin [*A publication*]	APLB
Australian Property News [*A publication*] (ADA)	APN
Australian Prosthodontic Society	APS
Australian Protea Growers' Association	APGA
Australian Psychoanalytical Society	APS
Australian Psychologist [*A publication*]	Aus Psych
Australian Psychologists Press [*A publication*]	APP
Australian Psychology and Hypnotherapy Association	APHA
Australian Public Library Issues [*A publication*]	Aust Publ Libr Issues
Australian Public Risk Insurance Management Association	APRIMA
Australian Public Sector and Broadcasting Union	APSBU
Australian Public Service Benevolent Society Inc.	APSBSI
Australian Publishers' Bureau	APB
Australian Pulp and Paper Institute [*Monash University*] [*Australia*]	APPI
Australian Queen Bee Breeders' Association	AQBBA
Australian Queensland Fever (DAVI)	QuF
Australian Quilters' Association	AQA
Australian Railways Industry Commission	ARIC
Australian Rainfall and Runoff [*Meteorology*]	ARR
Australian Records Management Association	ARMA
Australian Red Poll Cattle Breeders' Association	ARPCBA
Australian Red Poll Society	ARPS
Australian Region of the International Plant Propagators' Society	ARIPPS
Australian Register of Therapeutic Goods	ARTG
Australian Registrars Committee	ARC
Australian Religion Studies Review [*A publication*] (APTA)	ARSR
Australian Renderers' Association	ARA
Australian Research Council	ARC
Australian Resources Quarterly [*A publication*]	ARQ
Australian Retinitis Pigmentosa Association	ARPA
Australian Review [*A publication*]	Aust R
Australian Review Council	ARC
Australian Rights Movement	ARM
Australian Road Index [*Australian Road Research Board*] (NITA)	ARi

Australian Romney Association	ARA
Australian Rope and Cordage Workers' Union	ARCWU
Australian Rotary Health Research Fund	ARHRF
Australian Rowing Council	ARC
Australian Rules Football League of Sydney	ARFLS
Australian Rural Publishers' Association	ARPA
Australian Rural Research in Progress [*Database*]	ARRIP
Australian Rural Youth	ARY
Australian Safety News [*A publication*]	Aust Saf N
Australian Sahiwal Society	ASS
Australian Sales Tax Cases [*Australia*]	ASTC
Australian Salvadorian Association	ASA
Australian Satellite [*Telecommunications*] (NITA)	AUSSAT
Australian Scholarly Newsletter [*A publication*]	ASN
Australian School Catalogue Information Service (ADA)	ASCIS
Australian School Librarian [*A publication*]	Aust School Libn
Australian School of Health and Beauty	ASHB
Australian School of Hypnotherapy	ASH
Australian Schools' Cricket Council	ASCC
Australian Schools' Rugby Football Union	ASRFU
Australian Schools Sports Council	ASSC
Australian Science Advisory Committee	ASAC
Australian Science and Technology Counsellor Network	ASTCON
Australian Scientific Research Liaison [*British*]	ASRL
Australian Scrabble Players' Association	ASPA
Australian Screen Directors' Association	ASDA
Australian Secret Intelligence Organization (LAIN)	ASIO
Australian Security Industry Association	ASIA
Australian Seed Industry Advisory Council	ASIAC
Australian Seismological Center	ASC
Australian Sentencing Digest [*A publication*]	ASD
Australian Sentencing Judgements Bulletin [*A publication*]	ASJB
Australian Serials in Print [*A publication*]	ASIP
Australian Sheep and Wool Information Service [*Database*]	ASWIS
Australian Sheep Breeders' Association	ASBA
Australian Shiatsu College	ASC
Australian Shipbuilders' Association	ASA
Australian Shooters Party [*Political party*]	ASP
Australian Silky Terrier Club	ASTC
Australian Skeptics, Inc. [*An association*]	ASI
Australian Ski Areas Association	ASAA
Australian Small Business Awards	ASBA
Australian Small-Bore and Air Rifle Association	ASARA
Australian Social Security Cases [*A publication*]	ASSC
Australian Social Security Guide [*A publication*]	ASS
Australian Social Welfare [*A publication*]	Aust Soc Welf
Australian Social Welfare Impact [*A publication*]	Aust Soc Welf Impact
Australian Social Work [*A publication*]	Aus Soc W
Australian Social Work [*A publication*]	Aust Soc Work
Australian Society [*A publication*] (ADA)	AS
Australian Society [*A publication*]	Aus Soc
Australian Society [*A publication*] (APTA)	Aust Soc
Australian Society for Classical Studies	ASCS
Australian Society for Intercountry Aid (Children)	ASIAC
Australian Society for Sports History	ASSH
Australian Society of Accountants (ODBW)	ASA
Australian Society of Association Executives	ASAE
Australian Society of Calligraphers	ASC
Australian Society of Engineers	ASOE
Australian Society of Horticultural Science	ASHS
Australian Society of Infectious Diseases	ASID
Australian Society of New York [*Later, Australia-New Zealand Society of New York*] (EA)	AS of NY
Australian Society of Real Estate Agents and Valuers	ASREAV
Australian Society of Rheology	ASR
Australian Society of Sport Administrators	ASSA
Australian Society of Travel Writers	ASTW
Australian Sociological Association	ASA
Australian Softwood Producers' Council	ASPC
Australian Sogetsu Teachers' Association	ASTA
Australian Soil and Plant Analysis Council	ASPAC
Australian Songwriters' Association	ASA
Australian Special Air Services (VNW)	ASAS
Australian Special Libraries [*A publication*]	ASL
Australian Speedway Media Association	ASMA
Australian Sport Aviation Confederation	ASAC
Australian Sport Climbing Federation	ASCF
Australian Sport Index [*Database*]	AUSPORT
Australian Sporting Goods Association	ASGA
Australian Sports Acrobatic Federation	ASAF
Australian Sports and Economics Institute	ASEI
Australian Sports Science Council	ASSC
Australian Stamp Duties [*A publication*]	ASTM
Australian Standard Research Classification	ASRC
Australian Standard White [*Wheat*] (ADA)	ASW
Australian State Family Law Legislation [*A publication*]	ASFL
Australian Statistics [*Database*]	AUSSTATS
Australian Steel Association	ASA
Australian Stevedoring Supervisors' Association	ASSA
Australian Stock Exchange	ASX
Australian Stock Exchange Indices [*Database*] [*Sydney Stock Exchange*] [*Information service or system*] (CRD)	ASE
Australian Stock Exchange Indices [*Database*] [*Sydney Stock Exchange*] [*Information service or system*]	ASEINDEX
Australian Stock Exchanges Share Prices [*Database*]	AUSTOCK

Australian Stock Horse Society	ASHS
Australian Street Machine Federation	ASMF
Australian String Teachers' Association	ASTA
Australian Studies Association	ASA
Australian Studies Resources [Database]	AUST STUDY
Australian Studies Schools Project	ASSP
Australian Sunflower Association	ASA
Australian Superfine Wool Growers' Association	ASWGA
Australian Surfers' Union	ASA
Australian Surfriders' Association	ASA
Australian Swimming [An association]	AS
Australian Synchronised Swimming	ASS
Australian Synchrotron Beam Users' Group	ASBUG
Australian Table Grape Growers' Association	ATGGA
Australian Table Tennis Association	ATTA
Australian Tax Decisions [A publication] (DLA)	Austr Tax
Australian Tax Monitor [A publication]	ATM
Australian Taxation Office Practice [A publication]	ATOP
Australian Teacher [A publication]	Aust Teacher
Australian Teachers of Media [An association]	ATM
Australian Technology Export Committee	ATEC
Australian Telecommunication Standardization Committee (ACRL)	ATSC
Australian Television Network	ATN
Australian Terrier Club of America (EA)	ATCA
Australian Territory (EERA)	TER
Australian Textile, Clothing, and Footwear Industry Training Council	ATCFITC
Australian Tibet Council	ATC
Australian Timber Importers' Federation	ATIF
Australian Timber Industry Stabilization Conference	AUSTIS
Australian Timber Research Institute	ATRI
Australian Tin Producers' Association	ATPA
Australian Tin Producers' Council	ATPC
Australian Tire Manufacturers' Association	ATMA
Australian Tomato Processors' Association	ATPA
Australian Torts Reporter [A publication]	ATOR
Australian Torts Reports [A publication]	Aust Torts Reports
Australian Touch Association	ATA
Australian Tourism Commission	ATCO
Australian Tourism Exchange	ATE
Australian Tourism Industry Association	ATIA
Australian Tourism Research Institute	ATRI
Australian Toy Association	ATA
Australian Toy Library Association	ATLA
Australian Trade Commission (EA)	ATC
Australian Trade Commission	AUSTRADE
Australian Trade Practices Reporter. Cases and Decisions Digest [A publication]	ATPR (Digest)
Australian Trade Practices Reporter. Commission Decisions [A publication]	ATPR (Com)
Australian Transcontinental Airways	ATA
Australian Transplant Sports Association	ATSA
Australian Transport Literature Informatin System [Database on AUSINET] (NITA)	ATLS
Australian Tropical Research Foundation	AUSTROP
Australian Trust for Conservation Volunteers	ATFCV
Australian Tug-of-War Association	ATOWA
Australian Tuna Boat Owners' Association	ATBOA
Australian Turkey Federation	ATF
Australian Turkish Islamic Federation	ATIF
Australian Tyre Dealers' Association	ATDA
Australian Underground Construction and Tunnelling Association	AUCTA
Australian Underwater Hockey Association	AUHA
Australian United Fresh Fruit and Vegetable Association	AUFFVA
Australian United Press	AUP
Australian Universities Sports Federation	AUSF
Australian Unlisted Securities Quotation System	AUSQS
Australian Vegetable Growers' Federation	AVGF
Australian Vegetarian Society	AVS
Australian Veterans and Defence Services Council [Also, AVADSC]	AVDSC
Australian Veterans and Defense Services Council [Also, AVADSC]	AVADSC
Australian Veterinary Emergency Plan	AUSVETPLAN
Australian/Victorian Biathlon Association	AVBA
Australian Vietnam War Veterans' Trust	AVWVT
Australian Visual Copyright Society	AVCS
Australian Vocational Training System	AVTS
Australian Volleyball Association	AVA
Australian Waste Management Association	AWMA
Australian Water Ski Association	AWSKA
Australian Waterbird Association	AWA
Australian Weightlifting Federation	AWF
Australian Wheat Starch Producers' Association	AWSPA
Australian Wheelchair Athletes [An association]	AWA
Australian Wheelchair Sports Federation	AWSF
Australian White [Cattle]	AW
Australian Wide Array of Geomagnetic Stations	AWA
Australian Wide Array of Geomagnetic Stations	AWAGS
Australian Wildlife Protection Council	AWPC
Australian Window Roller Shutter Association	AWRSA
Australian Windscreen Association	AWA
Australian Wine and Brandy Producers' Association	AWBPA
Australian Wine Foundation	AWF
Australian Winemakers' Forum	AWF
Australian Women's Book Review [A publication]	AWBR
Australian Women's Bowling Council	AWBC
Australian Women's Tennis Association	AWTA

Australian Women's Vigoro Association	AWVA
Australian Wood Panels Association	AWPA
Australian Wool Processors' Council	AWPC
Australian Wool Selling Brokers Employers' Federation	AWSBEF
Australian Worker [A publication]	AW
Australian Worker's Compensation Case Digests [A publication]	AWCCD
Australian Workers' Compensation Guide [A publication]	AWK
Australian Workman [A publication]	AW
Australian Wrestling Union	AWU
Australian Writers and Editors' Guide [A publication]	AWEG
Australian Yearbook of International Law [A publication] (DLA)	Aust Y Int L
Australian Youth Initiatives Grant	AYIG
Australian Yugoslav Welfare Society	AYWS
Australian Zebu Association	AZA
Australiana Society	AS
Australian-Antarctic Discordance [Geology]	AAD
Australian-Arab Association	AAA
Australian-Arab Chamber of Commerce and Industry	AACCI
Australian-Asian Society of Queensland	AASQ
Australian-British Chamber of Commerce	ABCC
Australian-British Trade Association. Bulletin [A publication]	ABTA Bull
Australia-New Zealand Association [Also, The ANZA Club] (AC)	ANZA
Australia-New Zealand Business Council	ANZBC
Australia-New Zealand Closer Economic Relations Trade Agreement (BARN)	ANZCERTA
Australia-New Zealand Direct Line	ANZDL
Australia-New Zealand Studies Centre [Pennsylvania State University]	ANZSC
Australian-German Welfare Society	AGWS
Australian-Greek Welfare Society	AGWS
Australian-Indian Society	AIS
Australian-New Zealand Army Corps (VNW)	ANZAC
Australian-New Zealand Society of New York (EA)	A-NZSNY
Australian-New Zealand-Canada [Cable]	ANZCAN
Australians Against Further Immigration [An association]	AAFI
Australians against Further Immigration [Political party]	AFI
Australians Against Further Immigration Party [An association]	AAFIP
Australians for Reconciliation [An association]	AFR
Australian-United States Ministerial Talks [Conference]	AUSMIN
Australia-Papua New Guinea Friendship Association	APNGFA
Australia's Heritage [A publication]	Aust Her
Australia's Independent Optometrists [An association]	AIO
Australia's Indigenous Peoples Party [Political party]	AIP
Australia's International Engineering Exhibition	AIEE
Australia's Library, Information and Archives Services: an Encyclopaedia of Practice and Practitioners [A publication]	ALIAS
Australia's Strategic Planning in the Nineties [An association]	ASP90
Australia-Taiwan Business Council	ATBC
Australia-Thailand Association	ATA
Australia-Thailand Business Council	ATBC
Australia-Wide Funeral Information [Database]	AFIN
Austria	A
Austria [ANSI two-letter standard code] (CNC)	AT
Austria	AU
Austria [MARC country of publication code Library of Congress] (LCCP)	au
Austria	AUS
Austria	AUST
Austria (VRA)	Aust
Austria [ANSI three-letter standard code] (CNC)	AUT
Austria [MARC geographic area code Library of Congress] (LCCP)	e-au--
Austria [International civil aircraft marking] (ODBW)	OE
Austria Erit In Orbe Ultima [Austria Will Be The Last in the World] [Variation of 15th-century inscription]	AEIOU
Austria Fund [Associated Press] (SAG)	Austr
Austria Fund [NYSE symbol] (SPSG)	OST
Austria Microsystems International (NITA)	AMI
Austria Philatelic Society of New York (EA)	APSNY
Austria Presse Agentur [Press agency] [Austria]	APA
Austria (Republic) SIGNs [NYSE symbol] (TTSB)	SPJ
Austria [Republic of] Stock Index Growth Notes [Associated Press] (SAG)	AustStk
Austria [Republic of] Stock Index Growth Notes [NYSE symbol] (SPSG)	SPJ
Austriae Est Imperare Orbi Universo [It Is Given to Austria to Rule the Whole World] [Variation of 15th-century inscription]	AEIOU
Austrian Air [ICAO designator] (AD)	SO
Austrian Air Ambulance [ICAO designator] (FAAC)	OAF
Austrian Air Services [ICAO designator] (FAAC)	AAS
Austrian Air Services [Austria ICAO designator] (ICDA)	SO
Austrian Airlines [ICAO designator] (FAAC)	AUA
Austrian Airlines [ICAO designator] (AD)	OS
Austrian Airtransport [ICAO designator] (FAAC)	AAT
Austrian Airways [Oesterreichische Luftverkehrs AG]	AUA
Austrian Communist Party [Political party]	AKP
Austrian Cultural Institute (EA)	ACI
Austrian Documentation Centre for Media and Communication Research [Information service or system] (IID)	ADMAC
Austrian Forum [Defunct] (EA)	AF
Austrian Institute [Later, ACI] (EA)	AI
Austrian National Tourist Office (EA)	ANTO
Austrian Press and Information Service (EA)	APIS
Austrian RADAR Site Analysis	ARSA
Austrian Schilling [Monetary unit]	AS
Austrian Society of Acupuncture and Auricular Therapy [Multinational organization] (EAIO)	ASAAT
Austrian Telefunken [Record label]	AusT
Austrian Trade Commission (EA)	ATC

Austrian Trade Union Federation ... ATUF
Austria's Empire Is Obviously Upset [*Variation of 15th-century inscription*] ... AEIOU
Austria's Empire Is Overall Universal [*Variation of 15th-century inscription*] ... AEIOU
Austro-Daimler Motoren AG [*Automobile manufacturer*] ... ADM
Austroton [*Austria, Germany, etc.*] [*Record label*] ... Attn
Auswaertiges [*Nonresident*] [*German*] ... Ausw
Auswaertiges Amt [*Foreign Ministry*] [*German*] ... AA
Auswaschung [*Erosion*] [*German*] ... Auswasch
Authentic ... A
Authentic ... AUTH
Authentic (WDMC) ... auth
Authentic (AABC) ... AUTHEN
Authentic (VRA) ... authn
Authentic Fitness [*NYSE symbol*] (TTSB) ... ASM
Authentic Fitness Corp. [*NYSE symbol*] (SPSG) ... ASM
Authentic Fitness Corp. [*Associated Press*] (SAG) ... AuthFit
Authentic Reproduction of an Independent Earth Satellite ... ARIES
Authentication (AFM) ... AUTHN
Authentication Center ... AUC
Authentication Header [*Computer science*] ... AH
Authentication Maneuver [*Aviation*] (FAAC) ... ATM
Authenticator Organization (MCD) ... AO
Authenticis Pandectis [*Latin*] (DSA) ... Aut Pand
Authenticum [*A publication*] (DSA) ... A
Authenticum [*A publication*] (DSA) ... Aut
Authenticum [*A publication*] (DSA) ... Authen
Author ... A
Author [*Online database field identifier*] [*Computer science*] ... AU
Author [*Editing notation*] (WDMC) ... au
Author [*Editing notation*] (WDMC) ... Au
Author [*Online database field identifier*] [*Computer science*] ... AUT
Author ... AUTH
Author (VRA) ... auth
Author (WDMC) ... auth
Author and Keyword in Context ... AKWIC
Author and Keywords in Alphabetical Sequence (ADA) ... AKWAS
Author Catalogue (ROG) ... AC
Author Comfort Index [*Publishing*] ... ACI
Author Earn-Out [*Publishing*] ... AEO
Author Index ... AUTDEX
Author of "Southern Harmony" [*Initials singer Billy Walker put after his name*] ... ASH
Author Organization Source [*Database terminology*] (NITA) ... AOS
Authoring of Instructional Materials ... AIM
Authorised Computer Distributors (NITA) ... ACD
Authorised Unregistered Vehicle Inspection Station [*Australia*] ... AUVIS
Authority ... ATHRTY
Authority ... AUT
Authority (AFM) ... AUTH
Authority ... AUTHY
Authority and Format Identifier [*Telecommunications*] (OSI) ... AFI
Authority Coordinating the Transport of Inland Continental Europe [*NATO*] ... ACTICE
Authority Directing Arrest or Confinement [*Military*] ... ADA
Authority for Expenditure ... AFE
Authority for Intellectually Handicapped Persons [*Western Australia*] ... AIHP
Authority for Issue Indicator (AFIT) ... AI
Authority for Material Substitution (MCD) ... AMS
Authority for Purchase ... AFP
Authority for Removal of Accepted Spacecraft Installations (MCD) ... AFROASI
Authority for the Coordination of Inland Transport in Southern Europe [*NATO*] ... ACTISUD
Authority for Tooling Expenditures ... AFTE
Authority for Uniform Specification of Meat and Livestock [*Australia*] ... AUSMEAT
Authority Granted (NOAA) ... AUGRA
Authority Granted [*Army*] ... AUTHGR
Authority Granted [*Military*] (NVT) ... AUTHGRA
Authority Granted to Execute Acceptance and Oath of Office for ___ ... AUTHEXANDO
Authority Is Requested (NOAA) ... AUREQ
Authority Is Requested to Inter [*the remains of*] [*Army*] (AABC) ... ARI
Authority Record [*Database terminology*] (NITA) ... AR
Authority Sequence Number [*Online bibliographies*] ... ASN
Authority Supervising the Aerodome [*FAA designator*] (FAAC) ... YDY
Authority Supervising the Aerodrome [*ICAO designator*] (ICDA) ... YD
Authority to Participate Card ... ATP
Authority to Pay [*or Purchase*] ... A/P
Authority to Proceed (MCD) ... ATP
Authority to Prospect (ADA) ... A to P
Authority, Worldliness, and Power ... AW & P
Authorization [*or Authorized*] (EY) ... AUTH
Authorization and Consent (OICC) ... AC
Authorization Control Facility [*Computer access security software*] (NITA) ... ACF
Authorization for Disposal of Overhead Supplies (MCD) ... ADOS
Authorization for Interceptor Operations (MCD) ... AFIO
Authorization for Local Purchase ... ALP
Authorization for Program Development [*NASA*] (NASA) ... AFPD
Authorization for Sale of Salvage Material ... ASSM
Authorization for Temporary Admission [*Customs*] ... ATA
Authorization of Special Types General Order [*British*] (DCTA) ... ASTGO
Authorization Response ... AUTHR
Authorization Source Code (SAA) ... ASC
Authorization to Copy [*Computer science*] (ODBW) ... ATC
Authorization to Purchase [*Food stamp card*] [*Department of Agriculture*] ... ATP
Authorization to Transfer Material ... ATTM
Authorization under Consideration (DCTA) ... AC
Authorizations Subsystem [*Military*] ... AS
Authorized (WDMC) ... auth
Authorized (ROG) ... AUTHD
Authorized Abbreviation (MCD) ... AUTHAB
Authorized About ... AUTHAB
Authorized Absence (DAVI) ... AA
Authorized Accounting Activity [*DoD*] ... AAA
Authorized Acquisition Objective [*Army*] (AABC) ... AAO
Authorized Active Inventory (MCD) ... AAI
Authorized Allowance ... AA
Authorized Allowance List (MCD) ... AAL
Authorized Bond Allotment (MCD) ... ABA
Authorized Code Number (AFM) ... ACN
Authorized Commanders Atomic Air Defense (CINC) ... ACAAD
Authorized Consumption List [*Military*] (AABC) ... ACL
Authorized Contracting Officer (SAA) ... ACO
Authorized Control Material Order (AAGC) ... ACM
Authorized Controlled Material Order [*Military*] (AFIT) ... ACMO
Authorized Controller Material ... ACM
Authorized Data Chain (AFM) ... ADC
Authorized Data Distributor (HGAA) ... ADD
Authorized Data Element ... ADE
Authorized Data Item Description Manual [*A publication*] (MCD) ... ADM
Authorized Data List [*DoD*] ... ADL
Authorized Dental Allowance List [*Military*] (DNAB) ... ADAL
Authorized Depot Stockage List [*Army*] ... ADSL
Authorized Direct Expenditure Plan (SAA) ... ADEP
Authorized Equipment Listing (AABC) ... AEL
Authorized in Accordance with Bureau of Naval Personnel Manual ... ABPM
Authorized in Bureau of Naval Personnel Manual ... AUTHBUPERSMAN
Authorized "In Excess" ... AIE
Authorized Inspector ... AI
Authorized Item Identification Data Collaborator Code ... AIIDC
Authorized Item Identification Data Receiver Code ... AIIDR
Authorized Item Identification Data Submitter Code ... AIIDS
Authorized Landing Area (ADA) ... ALA
Authorized Level of Organization (AABC) ... ALO
Authorized Medical Allowance List (CAAL) ... AMAL
Authorized Medical Examiner (DA) ... AME
Authorized Military Occupational Specialty Code (AABC) ... AMOSC
Authorized Notice of Change ... ANOC
Authorized Nuclear Inspector (NRCH) ... ANI
Authorized Order ... AO
Authorized Ordering Agency (MCD) ... AOA
Authorized Organizational Storage List [*Army*] ... AOSL
Authorized Part Number ... APN
Authorized Parts Substitution List ... APSL
Authorized Pick-Up [*Trucking terminology*] ... APU
Authorized Possession Limits [*Nuclear energy*] (NRCH) ... APL
Authorized Price List ... APL
Authorized Procurement Information Requirements Description [*NASA*] (NASA) ... APIRD
Authorized Procurement Information Requirements List [*NASA*] (NASA) ... APIRL
Authorized Program Analysis Report [*Computer science*] (IBMDP) ... APAR
Authorized Program Facility [*Computer science*] (BUR) ... APF
Authorized Program File [*Computer science*] (PCM) ... APF
Authorized Protective Connecting Module (MHDB) ... APCM
Authorized Repair Unaccomplished at Base [*Military*] (AFIT) ... ARUB
Authorized Retention Level [*Military*] (AABC) ... ARL
Authorized Review Officer ... ARO
Authorized Revisit Above-Mentioned Places and Vary Itinerary as Necessary ... REVAR
Authorized Rotational Retention [*Navy*] ... RORET
Authorized Selling Representative [*Marketing*] (WDMC) ... ASR
Authorized Shortages and Discrepancies (KSC) ... ASAD
Authorized Signature Card (MCD) ... ASC
Authorized Standard Version [*of the Bible*] [*A publication*] ... ASV
Authorized Stock Level (CINC) ... ASL
Authorized Stockage List [*Army*] ... ASL
Authorized Terminal Strength ... ATS
Authorized to Delay [*Number of Days*], Any Portion of Which May Be Taken inCONUS [*Navy*] ... DELINUS
Authorized to Delay [*Number of Days*], Any Portion of Which May Be Taken Prior to or after Arrival in United States [*Navy*] ... DELREPARUS
Authorized to Delay [*Number of Days*], Any Portion of Which May Be Taken Prior to or after Departure [*Navy*] ... DELPARTURE
Authorized to Delay [*Number of Days*], in Reporting [*Navy*] ... DELREP
Authorized to Delay [*Number of Days*], in Reporting, Any Portion of Which May Be Taken Prior to or after Reporting at Temporary Duty Station [*Navy*] ... DELREPANY
Authorized to Delay [*Number of Days*], in Reporting, Keep New Station Advised Address [*Navy*] ... DELREPVAN
Authorized to Delay [*Number of Days*], in Reporting, to Count as GraduationLeave [*Navy*] ... DELREPGRAD
Authorized to Proceed On or About [*Date*] [*Military*] ... AUTHPROBOUT
Authorized to Travel [*Military*] (DNAB) ... AUTHTRAV
Authorized Training Associate Program [*Novell, Inc.*] ... ATA
Authorized User (DCTA) ... AU
Authorized Validating Agency (AIE) ... AVA
Authorized Version [*or King James Version of the Bible, 1611*] (ROG) ... AUTH

Authorized Version [*or King James Version of the Bible, 1611*] ..... AV
Authorized Walk-In [*Patient*] [*Medicine*] (DAVI) ..... AWI
Author's Alteration [*Publishing*] ..... AA
Authors and Artists for Young Adults [*A publication*] ..... AAYA
Authors' and Printers' Dictionary [*A publication*] (DGA) ..... APD
Authors' and Publishers' Lending Right Association Committee ..... APLA
Authors at Auction [*A publication*] ..... AAA
Author's Correction [*Publishing*] ..... AC
Authors Guild (EA) ..... AG
Authors Guild of the Authors League of America (EA) ..... AGALA
Authors Institute of America (EA) ..... AIA
Authors League of America (EA) ..... ALA
Authors' Lending and Copyright Society [*British*] ..... ALCS
Authors' Lending Royalty ..... ALR
Authors' Licensing and Collecting Society [*British*] (DBA) ..... ALCS
Author's Licensing and Correcting Society [*British*] ..... ALCS
Author's Proof [*Publishing*] ..... AP
Author's Proof [*Publishing*] (WDMC) ..... ap
Author's Resource Kit [*Asymetrix Co.*] [*Computer software*] (PCM) ..... ARK
Author's Standard Pre-Press Interface Code [*Mark-up code for word processing/typesetter interface*] (NITA) ..... ASPIC
Authors' Symbolic Pre-Press Interfacing Codes (DGA) ..... ASPIC
Author's Time [*Publishing*] ..... AT
Autism Association [*Australia*] ..... AA
Autism Network International (EA) ..... ANI
Autism Screening Instrument for Educational Planning ..... ASIEP
Autism Services Center (EA) ..... ASC
Autism Society Canada ..... ASC
Autism Society Nova Scotia [*Formerly, Nova Scotia Society for Autistic Children*] (AC) ..... ASNS
Autism Society of America (EA) ..... ASA
Autistic Children's Association of Queensland [*Australia*] ..... ACAQ
Autistic Children's Association of South Australia ..... ACASA
Autistic Citizens' Residential and Resources Society of Victoria [*Australia*] ..... ACRRSV
Autistics and Cousins ..... AC
Auto Acquisition [*RADAR*] ..... AA
Auto Alliance International [*Joint manufacturing venture of Ford Motor Co. and Mazda*] ..... AAI
Auto and Truck Recyclers Association of New Hampshire (SRA) ..... ATRANH
Auto and Truck Recyclers of Illinois (SRA) ..... ATRI
Auto Answer (CDE) ..... AA
Auto/Axial Compression [*Chromatography*] ..... AC
Auto/Axial Compression/Liquid Chromatography ..... AC/LC
Auto Backlight Control [*Photography*] ..... ABC
Auto Beacon (KSC) ..... AB
Auto Body Computer [*Software*] [*Automotive Computer Group*] [*Automotive engineering*] ..... ABC
Auto Body Representatives Council (EA) ..... ABRC
Auto Bracketing Control [*Photography*] ..... ABC
Auto Camping Club Ltd. [*British*] (BI) ..... ACC
Auto Car Guard ..... ACG
Auto Chek Centres [*Vancouver Stock Exchange symbol*] ..... ACN
Auto Collision Repair Association ..... ACRA
Auto Dealers Traffic Safety Council [*HUF*] [*Absorbed by*] (EA) ..... ADTSC
Auto Defense Ordinance (CINC) ..... ADO
Auto Directional Antenna ..... ADA
Auto Enthusiasts International [*Defunct*] (EA) ..... AEI
Auto Exhaust Testing ..... AET
Auto Exposure Bracketing [*Photography*] ..... AEB
Auto Exposure Lock [*Photography*] ..... AEL
Auto Force Generator [*Military*] (DOMA) ..... AFG
Auto Glass Industry Committee for Highway Safety [*Later, AGIC*] (EA) ..... AGICHS
Auto Glass Industry Council (EA) ..... AGIC
Auto Headway Control [*Mitsubishi*] [*Automotive engineering*] ..... AHC
Auto Hold Fire (KSC) ..... AHF
Auto Industries Highway Safety Committee [*Later, DSMC*] (EA) ..... AIHSC
Auto Insurance Plans Services Office [*A rule and rate-making association*] ..... AIPSO
Auto Internacional Association (EA) ..... AIA
Auto Marine Electric Ltd. [*Vancouver Stock Exchange symbol*] ..... AUM
Auto Part (NRCH) ..... AP
Auto Parts Advisory Committee [*US Committee designed to combat the trade deficit with Japan*] (ECON) ..... APAC
Auto Read Reallocation [*Computer science*] ..... ARRE
Auto Sequential (NRCH) ..... AS
Auto Steel Partnership Program [*Industry manufacturing standards*] ..... ASPP
Auto Theft Prevention Authority ..... ATPA
Auto Tracking Scan System [*for television video quality*] [*Sony Corp.*] ..... ATSS
Auto Transport de l'Ouest [*Western Auto Transport*] [*Madagascar*] ..... ATO
Auto Trol Technology Corp. [*Associated Press*] (SAG) ..... AutTrT
Auto Workers Action Caucus (EA) ..... AWAC
Autoanalyzer ..... AA
Autoantibodies to Human Thyroglobulin [*Endocrinology*] (DAVI) ..... AHT
Autoantibodies to Nuclear Antigens (MCD) ..... ANA
Autoantibody [*Panel*] [*Biochemistry*] (DAVI) ..... AUTOAB
AutoBaud Rate [*Detect*] (CDE) ..... ABR
Autobody and Paint Association of Hawaii (SRA) ..... ABPAH
Autobody Craftsman Association (SRA) ..... ACA
Autobody Filler Manufacturers Association [*ASEMC*] [*Absorbed by*] (EA) ..... AFMA
Autobody Supply and Equipment Manufacturers Council [*Defunct*] (EA) ..... ASEMC
AutoBond Acceptance Corp. [*NASDAQ symbol*] (SAG) ..... ABND
AutoBond Acceptance Corp. [*Associated Press*] (SAG) ..... AtoBond
Autobond Welder ..... ABW
AutoCAD [*Computer-Aided Design*] **Development System** (PCM) ..... ADS
AutoCAD [*Computer-Aided Design*] **Sequel Extension** [*Computer science*] ..... ASE
AutoCAD [*Computer-Aided Design*] **SQL Extension** [*Structured Query Language*] (PCM) ..... ASE
Autocam Corp. [*NASDAQ symbol*] (SAG) ..... ACAM
Autocam Corp. [*Associated Press*] (SAG) ..... Autocam
Autocarrier [*Predecessor of British auto maker, AC Cars*] ..... AC
Autochrome (VRA) ..... ATCH
Auto-Cite [*VERALEX, Inc.*] [*Information service or system*] (CRD) ..... AC
Autoclave Engineers, Inc. ..... AE
Autoclaved Aerated Concrete Products Association [*British*] (DBA) ..... AACPA
Autocoder-to-COBOL Conversion Aid Program [*IBM Corp.*] [*Computer science*] ..... ACCAP
Autocoder-to-COBOL Translating Service [*Computer science*] (IEEE) ..... ACTRAN
Autocollimator ..... AC
Autocontex [*Freight-forwarding company*] [*British*] ..... AC
Autocorrelation Function [*Statistics*] ..... ACF
Autocorrelation Histogram [*Statistics*] ..... ACH
Autocorrelator Photon Spectroscopy ..... APS
Autocostruzioni Societa per Azione [*Automobile manufacturing company*] [*Italy*] ..... ASA
Autocovariance Generating Function [*Statistics*] ..... ACGF
Autocrine Differentiation-Inhibiting Factor [*Biochemistry*] ..... ADIF
Autocrine Mobility Factor [*Oncology*] ..... AMF
Autocycle Union [*British*] ..... ACU
Autodecoder (IAA) ..... AC
Autodesk Development System [*Computer science*] (PCM) ..... ADS
Autodesk, Inc. [*Sausalito, CA*] [*NASDAQ symbol*] (NQ) ..... ACAD
Autodesk, Inc. [*NASDAQ symbol*] (SAG) ..... ADSK
Autodesk, Inc. [*NASDAQ symbol*] (TTSB) ..... ADSK
Autodesk, Inc. [*Associated Press*] (SAG) ..... Autodesk
Auto-Dialed Remote Message Players [*Telecommunications*] ..... ADRMPS
Auto-Diesel Technician Program [*Association of Independent Colleges and Schools specialization code*] ..... AD
AUTODIN/AUTOVON Interface (CET) ..... AAI
AUTODIN Coordination Station (CET) ..... ADCS
AUTODIN CRT for Secure Reserve Force (MCD) ..... RESFOR
AUTODIN Digital Subscriber Terminal (AABC) ..... ADST
AUTODIN Enhancement Program [*Computer science*] (MCD) ..... AEP
AUTODIN Facility (MCD) ..... AUTOFAC
AUTODIN Interface Control Unit (MCD) ..... AICU
AUTODIN Memory/Memory Control Replacement Program (MCD) ..... M/MCRP
AUTODIN Multimedia Terminal (NVT) ..... AMT
AUTODIN Station Maintenance Console (AABC) ..... ASMC
AUTODIN Switch Upgrade Project (MCD) ..... ASUP
AUTODIN Switching Center ..... ASC
AUTODIN Upgrade Program (MCD) ..... AUP
Autodyne Detection and Ranging ..... AUDAR
Autoerotic Asphyxiation [*Medicine*] ..... AEA
Auto-Fiche (MCD) ..... AF
Autofocus [*Cameras*] ..... AF
Autofocus RADAR Projector ..... ARP
Auto-Free Ottawa (AC) ..... AFO
Auto-Free Zone [*TRB*] (TAG) ..... AFZ
Autogenetically-Controlled Cesium Electro-Nuclear Thrust System (MCD) ..... ACCENT
Autogenic Feedback Training (MCD) ..... AFT
Autogenic Training [*Influencing the body through autosuggestion*] ..... AT
Autogenous Ignition Temperature (DNAB) ..... AIT
Autogenous Saphenous Vein (Graft) [*Surgery*] ..... ASV
Autograph ..... AUT
Autograph ..... AUTOG
Autograph Card Signed [*Manuscript descriptions*] ..... ACS
Autograph Chapter of the American First Day Cover Society [*Defunct*] (EA) ..... ACAFDCS
Autograph Document [*Manuscript descriptions*] ..... AD
Autograph Document Signed [*Manuscript descriptions*] ..... ADS
Autograph Letter [*Manuscript descriptions*] ..... AL
Autograph Letter Signed [*Manuscript descriptions*] ..... ALS
Autograph Letter Signed [*Manuscript description*] (ODBW) ..... als
Autograph Manuscript Signed [*Manuscript descriptions*] ..... AMSS
Autograph Note (BARN) ..... AN
Autograph Note Signed [*Manuscript descriptions*] ..... ANS
Autograph Poem Signed [*Manuscript descriptions*] (ADA) ..... APS
Autograph Postcard Signed [*Manuscript descriptions*] ..... APS
Autographa Californica Multipnucleocapsid Nuclear Polyhedrosis Virus [*Entomology*] ..... ACMNPV
Autographa Californica Nuclear Polyhedrosis Virus ..... AcNPV
Autographed Manuscript [*Manuscript description*] (WGA) ..... AMS
Autographed Presentation Copy ..... APC
Autographic Theme Extraction [*System*] ..... ATE
Auto-Graphics Interactive Library Exchange [*Auto-Graphics, Inc.*] [*Information service or system*] (IID) ..... AGILE
Autographics International (EA) ..... AI
Auto-Igniting Propellant (SAA) ..... AIP
Autoignition Temperature ..... AIT
Autoimmune Chronic Active Hepatitis [*Medicine*] ..... ACAH
Autoimmune Collagen Vascular Disease [*Medicine*] (CPH) ..... A-CVD
Autoimmune Complement Fixation [*Immunochemistry*] ..... AICF
Autoimmune Deficiency [*or Disease*] [*Immunology*] ..... AID
Autoimmune Encephalomyelitis [*Hematology*] ..... AE
Autoimmune Hemolytic Anemia [*Hematology*] ..... AHA
Autoimmune Hemolytic Anemia [*Hematology*] ..... AIHA

Autoimmune Hemolytic Disease [*Medicine*] ... AHD
Autoimmune, Inc. [*NASDAQ symbol*] (SAG) ... AIMM
Autoimmune, Inc. [*Associated Press*] (SAG) ... Autoimu
Autoimmune Oophoritis [*Medicine*] ... AO
Autoimmune Progesterone Dermatitis [*Medicine*] (DMAA) ... APD
Autoimmune Thyroid Disease [*Endocrinology*] ... AITD
Autoimmune Thyroid Disease (DAVI) ... ATD
AutoInfo, Inc. [*NASDAQ symbol*] (SPSG) ... AUTO
AutoInfo, Inc. [*Associated Press*] (SAG) ... AutoInf
Auto-Initiate Manual-Confirm (CAAL) ... AIMC
Auto-Instructional Device (AEBS) ... AID
Auto-Instructional Media for Library Orientation [*Colorado University Library*] (NITA) ... AIMLO
Auto-Interactive Design [*Combines operator-executed and automatic features*] [*Computer science*] ... AID
AUTOLAND [*Automatic Landing*] (NASA) ... A/L
AUTOLAND [*Automatic Landing*] **Flight Tests** [*NASA*] (MCD) ... AFL
AUTOLAND [*Automatic Landing*] **Rollout** [*NASA*] (MCD) ... A/R
Autoleather Guild (EA) ... AG
AutoLend Group, Inc. [*Associated Press*] (SAG) ... AutoL
AutoLend Group, Inc. [*Associated Press*] (SAG) ... AutoLend
Autolend Group, Inc. [*NASDAQ symbol*] (SAG) ... CARS
Auto-Lock Channel Tuning [*Television technology*] ... ACT
Autologic Information International, Inc. [*NASDAQ symbol*] (SAG) ... AIII
Autologic Information International, Inc. [*Associated Press*] (SAG) ... Autolog
Autologic Paginating and Photoimaging System [*Typography*] (DGA) ... APPS
Autologous Blood Transfusion [*Medicine*] (DMAA) ... ABT
Autologous Bone Marrow Transpantation [*Medicine*] (DMAA) ... ABMI
Autologous Bone Marrow Transplant [*Medicine*] ... ABMT
Autologous Bone-Marrow Transplantation [*Medicine*] (PDAA) ... ABMS
Autologous Mixed Lymphocyte Reaction [*Immunochemistry*] ... AMLR
Autologous Peripheral Blood Stem Cell Transplantation [*Medicine*] ... ABSCT
Autologous Rosette-Forming Cell [*s*] [*Immunology*] ... ARFC
Autolymphocyte Therapy [*Oncology*] ... ALT
Autolysed Yeast Protein [*Biochemistry*] (DAVI) ... AYP
Auto-Magnetic Plasma-Filled Ion Diode (MCD) ... AMPFION
Auto-Manual Bridge Control [*Telecommunications*] (TEL) ... AMB
Auto-Manual Center [*Telecommunications*] (TEL) ... AMC
Auto-Manual Switching Unit [*Telecommunications*] (DCTA) ... AMSU
Automatech Graphics Corp. [*Information service or system*] (IID) ... AGC
Automated ... AUTOM
Automated Accounting System (BUR) ... AAS
Automated Acoustic Detection System (MCD) ... AADS
Automated Adaptive Flight Training System (MCD) ... AAFTS
Automated Agency Accounting ... AAA
Automated Air Facilities Intelligence File [*Naval Oceanographic Office*] ... AAFIF
Automated Air Facility Information File [*Defense Mapping Agency*] (MCD) ... AAFIF
Automated Air Information Production System (MCD) ... AAIPS
Automated Air Load Planning System [*Developed for the Army by SRI International*] ... AALPS
Automated Aircrew Escape System (MCD) ... AAES
Automated Airlift Analysis [*MTMC*] (TAG) ... AAA
Automated Airload Planning System ... AALP
Automated Ambulatory Medical Record System [*Medicine*] (DMAA) ... AAMRS
Automated Amino Acid Analysis [*Food technology*] ... AAA
Automated Analytical Electrophoresis Facility [*NASA*] (MCD) ... AAEF
Automated Armed Forces Examining and Entrance Station ... AFEES
Automated Armed Forces Examining and Entrance Station System (MCD) ... AAFEESS
Automated Assessment Signal Processor ... AASP
Automated Assessment Tool (MCD) ... AAT
Automated Astronomic Positioning Device [*Defense Mapping Agency*] (MCD) ... AAPD
Automated Astronomic Positioning System [*Defense Mapping Agency*] ... AAPS
Automated Attendance Accounting System [*Jet Propulsion Laboratory, NASA*] ... AAAS
Automated Attendance Reporting System (MCD) ... AARS
Automated Attitude Hold [*Manned maneuvering unit*] [*Aerospace*] (NASA) ... AAH
Automated Auger Microprobe ... A^2M
Automated Azimuth Measuring System (MCD) ... AAMS
Automated Banking ... AB
Automated Batch Manufacturing System [*Computer science*] (MHDI) ... ABMS
Automated [*or Automatic*] **Batch Mixing** [*Computer science*] ... ABM
Automated Batch Weighing ... ABW
Automated Battlefield Interface Concept [*Army*] ... ABIC
Automated Behavioral Intelligence (MCD) ... ABI
Automated Bibliography ... AB
Automated Bioassay System (MCD) ... ABS
Automated Biological and Chemical Data [*System*] ... ABCD
Automated Biological Laboratory [*NASA*] ... ABL
Automated Blood Inventory Information System (PDAA) ... ABIIS
Automated Bond System [*Investment term*] (DFIT) ... ABS
Automated Book Request System [*Computer science*] ... ABRS
Automated Breathing Metabolic Simulator [*Medicine*] (PDAA) ... ABMS
Automated Broker Interface [*Customs Service*] (GFGA) ... ABI
Automated Budget System ... AUTOBUS
Automated Bulk Items List System (MCD) ... ABILS
Automated Business Mail Processing System [*Computer science*] (MHDI) ... ABMPS
Automated Calibration Procedure ... ACP
Automated Calibration Temperature Activated [*Electronic balance*] ... ACTA
Automated Camera Effects System ... ACES
Automated Car Identification [*Railroads*] ... ACI
Automated Career Management Information System ... ACMIS
Automated Career Management System ... ACMS
Automated Cargo Clearance and Enforcement Processing Technique [*US Customs Service*] ... ACCEPT
Automated Cargo Document System ... ACDS
Automated Carrier Landing System [*Military*] ... ACLS
Automated Carrier Landing Systems Project [*Military*] ... ACLSP
Automated Cartographic Drafting and Photogrammetric System (HGAA) ... ACDPS
Automated Catalog of Computer Equipment and Software Systems [*Army*] (NITA) ... ACCESS
Automated Cell-Injection System ... AIS
Automated Chemical Analysis for Process Solutions System [*Hughes Aircraft Co.*] (ECON) ... ACAPS
Automated Chemistry Program [*Computer science*] ... ACP
Automated Circuit Card Etching Layout [*Computer science*] ... ACCEL
Automated Circuit Card Lay-Out and Implementation [*Computer science*] (PDAA) ... ACCLAIM
Automated Circulation and Enquiry System [*University of Aberdeen*] [*British*] (NITA) ... ACES
Automated Circulation Control System [*Library management*] ... ACCS
Automated Circulation System [*Computer science*] ... ACS
Automated Claims Information System [*Air Force*] (DNAB) ... ACIS
Automated Classification of Medical Entities [*National Center for Health Statistics*] (GFGA) ... ACME
Automated Classified Document Control System ... ACDCS
Automated Classified Material Accountability System ... ACMAS
Automated Clearinghouse [*Banking*] ... ACH
Automated Cloud Observation System (MCD) ... ACOS
Automated Coagulation Laboratory ... ACL
Automated Code Evaluation System ... ACES
Automated Coder of Report Narrative [*Computer science*] (DIT) ... ACORN
Automated Collection Management System ... ACOMS
Automated Color Separation System (PDAA) ... ACSS
Automated Combat Mission Folder System (MCD) ... ACMFS
Automated Combustor [*Computer code*] ... AUTOCOM
Automated Command and Control System (MCD) ... ACCS
Automated Command Control Executive Support System [*Air Force*] (DOMA) ... ACCESS
Automated Command Response Verification (MCD) ... ACRV
Automated Commercial System [*US Customs Service computerized system*] ... ACS
Automated Commitment Tracking System [*Nuclear energy*] (NRCH) ... ACTS
Automated Communications and Control System [*Navy*] (MCD) ... ACCS
Automated Communications and Electronics Management Information System [*Army*] ... ACEMIS
Automated Communications and Message Processing System [*Army*] (RDA) ... ACAMPS
Automated Communications and Message Processing System [*Army*] (MCD) ... ACMPS
Automated Communications Publications (AFIT) ... ACP
Automated Communications Set (BUR) ... ACS
Automated Communications System (PCM) ... ACS
Automated Component Trading System ... ACTS
Automated Computer Controlled Editing Sound System ... ACCESS
Automated Computer Program ... ACP
Automated Computer Science Education ... ACSED
Automated Computer Science Education System ... ACSES
Automated Computer Time Service ... ACTS
Automated Computerized Axial Tomography [*Radiology*] (DAVI) ... ACAT
Automated Computerized Tomography [*Radiology*] (DAVI) ... ACT
Automated Computerized Transverse [*Axial scanner*] [*Radiology*] (DAVI) ... ACTH
Automated Computing Engine (PDAA) ... ACE
Automated CONARC Command Echelon Standard Systems (MCD) ... ACCESS
Automated Configuration Management System [*NASA*] (NASA) ... ACMS
Automated Configuration Status Accounting System [*Navy*] ... ACSAS
Automated Configuration Tracking System (MCD) ... ACTS
Automated Contingency Support Capability (AFM) ... ACSC
Automated Contingency Support System ... ACSS
Automated Contingency Translator [*Computer science*] ... ACT
Automated Continuous Acceptance of Propellants (MCD) ... AUTOCAP
Automated Contract Specification System ... ACSS
Automated Control and Checking of Electrical Systems Support (MCD) ... ACCESS
Automated Control and Distribution of Trainees [*Army*] (MCD) ... ACT
Automated Control and Landing System [*Aerospace*] ... ACLS
Automated Control of a Document Management System [*Computer science*] (DIT) ... ACDMS
Automated Cost Estimates ... ACE
Automated Cost Model ... ACM
Automated Costing and Planning System (DNAB) ... ACAPS
Automated Credit Enquiry [*British Information service or system*] (IID) ... ACE
Automated Cross-Section Analysis Program [*Computer science*] ... ACSAP
Automated Culture System ... ACUSYST
Automated Custom Terminal System ... ACTS
Automated Data Acquisition and Control System (MCD) ... ADACS
Automated Data Acquisition System [*GCA Corp.*] ... ADAS
Automated Data Analysis and Presentation Techniques (MCD) ... ADAPT
Automated Data and Telecommunications Service [*Later, Office of Information andResources Management*] ... ADTS
Automated Data Collection [*Computer science*] (BTTJ) ... ADC
Automated Data Entry Measurement System [*Computer science*] (IAA) ... ADEMS
Automated Data Entry System [*Computer science*] (IAA) ... ADES
Automated Data Interchange Systems Panel [*Computer science*] (MHDB) ... ADIP
Automated Data Management (IAA) ... ADM
Automated Data Management Information System ... ADMIS

Automated Data Network System [*Army*] ..... ADNS
Automated Data on Instructional Technology ..... ADIT
Automated Data Preparation by Electronic Photocomposition (MCD) ..... ADPEP
Automated Data Preparation Evaluation Program (MCD) ..... ADPEP
Automated Data Processing [*FAA*] (TAG) ..... ADP
Automated Data Processing and Communications Service (MHDI) ..... ADPACS
Automated Data Processing System Security Enhancement Program (GFGA) ..... ADPSSEP
Automated Data Processing Telecommunications (MCD) ..... ADP-T
Automated Data Reports Submission System ..... ADRSS
Automated Data Retrieval System (NRCH) ..... ADRS
Automated Data Subsystem (AABC) ..... ADSS
Automated Data System Development Plan [*Military*] (MCD) ..... ADSDP
Automated Data Systems Manual [*Military*] (GFGA) ..... ADSM
Automated Data Unit Movement (AABC) ..... ADUM
Automated Data Wiring ..... ADW
Automated Debugging Environment [*Applied Data Research, Inc.*] ..... ADE
Automated Declassification System (MCD) ..... ADS
Automated Deferred Discrepancy File ..... ADDF
Automated Demand Resolution [*FAA*] (TAG) ..... ADR
Automated Deposition of Advanced Materials [*Materials technology*] ..... ADAM
Automated Depot Maintenance ..... ADM
Automated Design and Documentation (SAA) ..... ADD
Automated Design and Manufacturing (SAA) ..... ADAM
Automated Design Engineering [*Telecommunications*] (TEL) ..... ADE
Automated Design Facility (MCD) ..... ADF
Automated Design of Damage Resistant Structures (MCD) ..... ADDRESS
Automated Design System (MCD) ..... ADS
Automated Diagram Drafting (SAA) ..... ADD
Automated Dictionary Support System [*Army*] (RDA) ..... ADSS
Automated Differential Agglutination (PDAA) ..... ADA
Automated Digital Data System ..... ADDS
Automated Digital Design System [*Raytheon Co.*] ..... ADDS
Automated Digital Interior Communications (MCD) ..... ADIC
Automated Digital Weather Communications Program [*Air Force*] (AFM) ..... ADWCP
Automated Digitized Document Storage, Retrieval and Transmission System [*Computer science*] (MHDB) ..... ADDSRTS
Automated Direct Entry Packaging Technique ..... ADEPT
Automated Direct Labor Reporting (MCD) ..... ADLR
Automated Directional Solidification Furnace [*Materials processing*] ..... ADSF
Automated Dispatch System [*Telecommunications*] ..... ADS
Automated Dispensing Analyzer (PDAA) ..... ADA
Automated Dithionate Test (AAMN) ..... ADT
Automated Document Control and Retrieval System [*Computer science*] (GFGA) ..... ADCAR
Automated Document Control System [*Computer science*] (MCD) ..... ADCS
Automated Document Delivery Over Networked Information Service (NITA) ..... ADONIS
Automated Document Management Information Network (NITA) ..... ADMIN
Automated Document Management Systems (DGA) ..... ADMS
Automated Documentation (IAA) ..... AUTODOC
Automated Documentation Development and Maintenance [*FAA*] (TAG) ..... ADDM
Automated Documentation Systems [*Computer science*] ..... ADS
Automated Drafting and Digitizing Machine [*Computer science*] (RDA) ..... ADDM
Automated Drafting Machine ..... ADM
Automated Drafting System ..... ADS
Automated Drawing Parts List (MCD) ..... ADPL
Automated Drawing Parts List System (MCD) ..... ADPLS
Automated Dredging and Disposal System [*U.S. Army Corps of Engineers*] ..... ADDAMS
Automated Drug Identification ..... AUDRI
Automated Durability Road ..... ADR
Automated Dynamic Analysis of Mechanical Systems [*Mechanical Dynamics, Inc.*] [*Automotive engineering*] ..... ADAMS
Automated EAM Processing and Dissemination System (MCD) ..... AEPDS
Automated Edge Match System (MCD) ..... AEMS
Automated Educational Services On-Line Processing (MCD) ..... AESOP
Automated Electrocardiograph Interpretive System [*Veterans Administration*] ..... AECGIS
Automated Electronic Maintenance Training (MCD) ..... AEMT
Automated Electrophoresis Microscope System (MCD) ..... AEMS
Automated Eligibility Verification System (MEDA) ..... AEVS
Automated Endoscopic System for Optimal Positioning [*Medicine*] ..... AESOP
Automated Engineering and Scientific Optimization Program [*NASA*] ..... AESOP
Automated Engineering Design [*Programming language*] [*1960*] [*Computer science*] ..... AED
Automated Engineering Design Circuit Analysis Program (MHDB) ..... AEDCAP
Automated Engineering Design of Networks [*Computer science*] (IAA) ..... AEDNET
Automated Engineering Document Preparation System (MCD) ..... AEDPS
Automated En-Route Air Traffic Control [*Proposed*] [*FAA*] ..... AERA
Automated Environmental Control System (MCD) ..... AECS
Automated Environmental Prediction (CAAL) ..... AEP
Automated Environmental Prediction System (MCD) ..... AEPS
Automated Equipment Identification (BTTJ) ..... AEI
Automated Execution [*FAA*] (TAG) ..... AEX
Automated External Defibrillator-Pacemaker [*Cardiology*] ..... AEDP
Automated Fare Collection ..... AFC
Automated Fault Tree Analyzer (MCD) ..... AFTA
Automated Fiber Winner System ..... AFWS
Automated Field Evaluation and Test System (MCD) ..... AUTO-FETS
Automated Field Fire ..... AFF
Automated Field Interview System ..... AFIS
Automated Financial Improvement Program [*Navy*] (GFGA) ..... AFIP
Automated Financial Information System [*Computer science*] (MHDI) ..... AFIS
Automated Fingerprint Identification System [*NEC Corp.*] ..... AFIS
Automated Fire Support Artillery (MCD) ..... AFSA
Automated Flaw Detector ..... AFD
Automated Flight Information Service [*ICAO designator*] (FAAC) ..... FISA
Automated Flight Service Station [*FAA*] (TAG) ..... AFSS
Automated Flight Service Station (FAAC) ..... AFSS
Automated Flight Test Data System (MCD) ..... AFTDS
Automated Flow Technology ..... AFT
Automated Forces [*Air Force*] (RDA) ..... AFOR
Automated Forward Area Alerting RADAR [*Army*] ..... AFAAR
Automated Frequency Assignment System [*Telecommunications*] ..... AFAS
Automated Frequency Deconfliction [*Telecommunications*] (LAIN) ..... AFD
Automated General Experimental Device [*Animal performance testing*] ..... AGED
Automated Generic Case Analysis Program (MCD) ..... AGCAP
Automated Genetic Analyzer [*Instrumentation*] ..... AGA
Automated Geomagnetic Airborne Survey System [*Aviation*] (PDAA) ..... AGASS
Automated Graphics Application Program (MCD) ..... AGAP
Automated Ground Engine Test System (MCD) ..... AGETS
Automated Ground Network System ..... AGNS
Automated Ground Operations Scheduling System [*Also, AUTO-GOSS*] (MCD) ..... AGOSS
Automated Ground Operations Scheduling System [*Also, AGOSS*] (MCD) ..... AUTO-GOSS
Automated Group Learning (PDAA) ..... AGL
Automated Guideway Transit [*TRB*] (TAG) ..... AGT
Automated Gun Laying (Turret) Training [*British military*] (DMA) ..... AGL(T)TRG
Automated Gyro Test Set ..... AGTS
Automated Highway System ..... AHS
Automated Highway System ..... AHS
Automated Highway Systems [*FHWA*] (TAG) ..... AHS
Automated Historical Data Base ..... AHDB
Automated Hospital Data Management System [*Medicine*] (DMAA) ..... AHDMS
Automated Hospital Information System [*Veterans Administration*] (IID) ..... AHIS
Automated Identification Division System [*FBI*] ..... AIDS
Automated Identification System [*FBI*] ..... AIS
Automated Image Analysis [*Instrumentation*] ..... AIA
Automated Image Data Extraction System (MCD) ..... AIDES
Automated Image Device Evaluator [*Electronics*] ..... AIDE
Automated Imagery Processing (PDAA) ..... AIP
Automated Imaging Association (EA) ..... AIA
Automated Imaging System (DGA) ..... AIS
Automated Immunochemistry System ..... AutoICS
Automated Immunonephelometric Assay [*Medicine*] (DMAA) ..... AINA
Automated Immunoprecipitin [*System*] [*Clinical chemistry*] ..... AIP
Automated Implementation Plan ..... AIP
Automated Import Inspection System [*Department of Agriculture*] (GFGA) ..... AIIS
Automated Incendiary Submunition (MCD) ..... AMIS
Automated Indicator System (MCD) ..... AIS
Automated Industrial Control System [*Computer science*] (MHDB) ..... AICS
Automated Industrial Drilling (MHDI) ..... AID
Automated Industrial Management System ..... AIMS
Automated Information and Management System (BUR) ..... AIMS
Automated Information and Management Systems (MCD) ..... AIMES
Automated Information and Reservation Computer Operated Network ..... AIRCON
Automated Information Data System ..... AIDS
Automated Information Directory Update System (PDAA) ..... AIDUS
Automated Information Dissemination System (NITA) ..... AIDS
Automated Information Management (NASA) ..... AIM
Automated Information Processing [*Computer science*] (MCD) ..... AIP
Automated Information Processing Request (MCD) ..... AIPR
Automated Information Reference Systems, Inc. [*Information service or system*] (IID) ..... AIRS
Automated Information System ..... AIS
Automated Information Transfer [*FAA*] (TAG) ..... AIT
Automated Information Transfer System [*Department of Commerce*] [*Database*] ..... AITS
Automated Input and Document Update Service [*International Data Corp.*] ..... AIDUS
Automated Inspection of Data ..... AIDA
Automated Installation File (MCD) ..... AIF
Automated Installation Intelligence File ..... AIIF
Automated Instruction (DNAB) ..... AI
Automated Instruction Fetch Unit [*Computer science*] (MHDI) ..... AIFU
Automated Instructional Management System [*Army*] ..... AIMS
Automated Instructional Materials Services [*Developed by the System Development Corp.*] (IID) ..... AIMS
Automated Instrumentation System ..... AIS
Automated Insurance Service ..... AIS
Automated Integrated Debugging System (MCD) ..... AIDS
Automated Integrated Design Engineering (IEEE) ..... AIDE
Automated Integrated Manufacturing (MCD) ..... AIM
Automated Integrative Design Engineering (NITA) ..... AIDE
Automated Intelligence Data System [*Air Force*] ..... AIDS
Automated Intelligence File [*Military*] (AABC) ..... AIF
Automated Intelligence Processing System (MCD) ..... AIPS
Automated Intelligent Cruise Control [*FHWA*] (TAG) ..... AICC
Automated Intelligent Microscope ..... AIM
Automated Interactive Microscope ..... AIM
Automated International Flight Service Station [*FAA*] (TAG) ..... AIFSS
Automated Inventory Distribution System ..... AIDS
Automated Inventory Management Evaluation System (IEEE) ..... AIMES
Automated Jail Information System ..... AJIS

Automated Joint Application Development [*Computer science*] (BTTJ) .... AJAD
Automated Juvenile Law Archive [*National Center for Juvenile Justice*] [*Information service or system*] (CRD) .... AJLA
Automated Keyed Continuous Wave (DNAB) .... ACW
Automated Labor and Attendance Subsystem (SAA) .... ALAS
Automated Laboratory Diagnostic Instrument .... ALADIN
Automated Lamellar Kerotaplasty [*Medicine*] .... ALK
Automated Land and Minerals Records System [*Department of the Interior*] (GFGA) .... ALMRS
Automated Land Titles System (ADA) .... ALTS
Automated Language Processing (NITA) .... ALP
Automated Language Processing Systems [*Electronic translation of foreign languages*] [*Commercial firm*] (NITA) .... ALPS
Automated Language Processing Systems, Inc. (MHDW) .... AILP
Automated Large Experiment [*NASA*] .... ALE
Automated LASER Seeker Performance Evaluation System (MHDI) .. ALSPEC
Automated LASER Seeker Performance Evaluation System (MCD) .... ALSPES
Automated Law Enforcement Response Team (DICI) .... ALERT
Automated Layout Design Program [*IBM Corp.*] .... ALDEP
Automated Learning Process .... ALP
Automated Leave and Pay System [*Military*] (DNAB) .... ALPS
Automated Library Acquisitions System [*Suggested name for the Library of Congress computer system*] .... ALAS
Automated Library Expandable Program, Hebrew University of Jerusalem [*Israel*] [*Information service or system*] (IID) .... ALEPH
Automated Library Information System [*National Technological Library of Denmark*] [*Lyngby*] (IID) .... ALIS
Automated Library Information System [*Dataphase Systems, Inc.*] (IID) .... ALIS
Automated Library Issue Document (NVT) .... ALID
Automated Library Processing Services [*System Development Corp.*] (IID) .... ALPS
Automated Library Program [*Computer science*] (DIT) .... ALP
Automated Library System [*Foundation for Library Research, Inc.*] [*Information service or system*] (IID) .... ALS
Automated Library Technical Services [*Program*] [*Los Angeles Public Library*] .... ALTS
Automated Light Survey .... ALS
Automated Line Record Update [*Telecommunications*] (TEL) .... ALRU
Automated Lines of Communications and Target System (MCD) .... ALCATS
Automated Linguistic Extraction and Retrieval Technique .... ALERT
Automated Linguistic Fieldworker [*Computer science*] (DIT) .... AUTOLING
Automated Liquid Sampler [*Instrumentation*] .... ALS
Automated Literature Alerting System [*Computer science*] (DIT) .... ALAS
Automated Litigation Support [*Department of Justice*] (GFGA) .... ALS
Automated Living User Intervention Anarchy [*Computer science*] .... ALUIA
Automated Loans System [*Library science*] .... ALS
Automated Local Evaluations in Real Time [*National Oceanic and Atmospheric Administration*] .... ALERT
Automated Location of Isolation and Continuity Error [*Module*] [*Raytheon Co.*] .... ALICE
Automated Logic Diagram [*Computer science*] (IBMDP) .... ALD
Automated Logic Implementation [*Computer science*] (IEEE) .... ALI
Automated Logic Mapping System (PDAA) .... ALMS
Automated Logistics Data Processing System .... ALDPS
Automated Logistics Management and Inventory Control System (MCD) .... ALMICS
Automated Logistics Management System (SSD) .... ALMS
Automated Logistics Management Systems Agency [*DoD*] .... ALMSA
Automated Logistics Planning System (MCD) .... ALPS
Automated Logistics System for Tracking, Analysis, and Reporting .... ALSTAR
Automated Logistics Systems Review (MCD) .... ALSR
Automated Low-Cost Weather Observation System (MCD) .... ALWOS
Automated Maintenance Control and Records System (MCD) .... AMCARS
Automated Maintenance Data Exchange (MCD) .... AMDEX
Automated Maintenance Depot .... AMD
Automated Maintenance Information System (MCD) .... AMIS
Automated Management and Reporting System [*Department of Housing and Urban Development*] (GFGA) .... AMRS
Automated Management Information Center (SSD) .... AMIC
Automated Management Information Civil Users System [*Department of Justice*] (GFGA) .... AMICUS
Automated Management Information System (DIT) .... AMIS
Automated Management Reports (BUR) .... AMR
Automated Manifest System (DA) .... AMS
Automated Manpower Data Department of the Navy Reports (MCD) .... AMDAR
Automated Manpower Management Information System .... AMMIS
Automated Manufacturing Research Facility [*Gaithersburg, MD*] [*Department of Commerce*] (GRD) .... AMRF
Automated Map Information File [*DoD*] (PDAA) .... AMIF
Automated Mapping [*Cartography*] .... AM
Automated Mapping/Facility Management [*Computer science*] .... AMFM
Automated Mask Inspection System (PDAA) .... AMIS
Automated Material Parts Request System (MCD) .... AMPRS
Automated Material Processing System [*Computer science*] .... AMPS
Automated Material System (SAA) .... AMS
Automated Material System (MCD) .... AUTOMAT
Automated Materials Handling System [*Computer science*] .... AMHS
Automated Materials Handling Systems Association [*British*] (DBA) .... AMHSA
Automated Measurement Evaluator and Director System (MHDB) .... AMEDS
Automated Measurement of Lineups [*A. C. Nielsen Co.*] (WDMC) .... AMOL
Automated Mechanical Transmission [*Automotive engineering*] .... AMT
Automated Medical Examination System (PDAA) .... AMES
Automated Medical History .... AMH
Automated Medical Record System (AAMN) .... AMRS
Automated MEDICARE Log (MEDA) .... AML

Automated Merchandise Processing System [*US Customs Service*] .... AMPS
Automated [*formerly, Atlantic*] Merchant Vessel Report [*Coast Guard*] .... AMVER
Automated [*formerly, Atlantic*] Merchant Vessel Report System [*Coast Guard*] .... AMVERS
Automated Message Handling System .... AMHS
Automated Message Management System (MCD) .... AMMS
Automated Message Processing Dissemination System (MCD) .... AMPDS
Automated Message Processing Exchange System [*Military*] (GFGA) ... AMPES
Automated Meteorogical Observing System (USDC) .... AMOS
Automated Meteorological and Terminal Information Service .... AMATIS
Automated Microbial Metabolism Laboratory [*NASA*] .... AMML
Automated Microbial Systems (MCD) .... AMS
Automated Microfiche Terminal (PDAA) .... AMT
Automated Microfilm Aperture Card Updating System [*Army*] .... AMACUS
Automated Microfilm Storage and Retrieval [*Army*] (IID) .... AMSR
Automated Microform Storage and Retrieval [*Computer science*] (MHDI) .... AMSO
Automated Microhemagglutination Assay for Antibodies to Treponema pallidum [*Serology*] .... AMHA-TP
Automated Military Construction Progress Reporting System (GFGA) .... AMPRS
Automated Military Justice Analysis and Management System .... AMJAMS
Automated Military Outpatient System (RDA) .... AMOS
Automated Military Outpatient System Specialist (MCD) .... AMOSIST
Automated Minefield System (MCD) .... AMS
Automated Minerals Information System [*Bureau of Mines*] [*Database*] .... AMIS
Automated Mixed Traffic Transit (PDAA) .... AMTT
Automated Modification Analyzer [*Computer science*] .... AMA
Automated Modular Preplanner Programming System (MCD) .... AMPPS
Automated Molding Plant [*Manufacturing*] .... AMP
Automated Mooney Decay [*Chemical engineering*] .... AMD
Automated Mortgage Management Information Network [*Computer science*] (MHDI) .... AMMINET
Automated Multimedia Exchange [*Communications*] [*Army*] (MCD) ...... AMME
Automated Multi-Media Switch (PDAA) .... AMMS
Automated Multiparameter Analyzer for Cells .... AMAC
Automated Multiphasic Health Testing .... AMHT
Automated Multiphasic Health Testing and Services (KSC) .... AMHTS
Automated Multiphasic Screening [*Medicine*] (MAH) .... AMS
Automated Multiple Development [*Chromatography*] .... AMD
Automated Multistage Substructuring (MCD) .... AMSS
Automated Multitest Laboratory .... AML
Automated Mutual-Assistance Vessel Rescue System (DS) .... AMVER
Automated Nautical Chart Index File [*System*] [*DoD*] .... ANCIF
Automated Nautical Charting System (USDC) .... ANCS-II
Automated Nautical Charting System (OSRA) .... ANCS-II
Automated Naval Architecture (PDAA) .... ANA
Automated Near-Term Improvement (MCD) .... ANTI
Automated Nephelometric Immunoassay [*Medicine*] (DMAA) .... ANIA
Automated Network Control Center [*Military*] (DOMA) .... ANCC
Automated Network Schedule with Evaluation of Resources (MCD) ...... ANSWER
Automated Newspaper Delivery System (PDAA) .... ANDS
Automated Non-Destructive Inspector [*Robotics*] (PS) .... ANDI
Automated Notices to Mariners System .... ANMS
Automated Nuclear, Biological, and Chemical Information System [*Military*] (DOMA) .... ANBACIS
Automated Office Battery [*Selection and career development test*] .... AOB
Automated Office Support System [*Department of Energy*] .... AOSS
Automated Office System (HGAA) .... AOS
Automated Offset Unit [*Air Force*] .... AOU
Automated Onboard Gravimeter .... AOG
Automated Optical Inspection .... AOI
Automated Optical Navigation (MCD) .... AON
Automated Orbit Control System (MCD) .... AOCS
Automated Order Writing Process (MCD) .... AOWP
Automated Order Writing System (MCD) .... AOWS
Automated Overseas Employment Referral Program .... AOERP
Automated Packaging Code [*Army*] (MCD) .... APC
Automated Packaging Planning System (MCD) .... APPS
Automated Parking Lot Control (MCD) .... APLC
Automated Parking Support System [*Vehicle storage*] .... AUTOPASS
Automated Parking System .... APS
Automated Patent Searching [*Computer science*] .... APS
Automated Payload Processing Facility [*NASA*] (NASA) .... APPF
Automated Payment and Deposit [*Banking*] .... APD
Automated Payroll, Cost, and Personnel System [*Defense Supply Agency*] .... APCAPS
Automated PEMA [*Procurement of Equipment and Munition Appropriations*] Bud get System [*Military*] (AABC) .... APBS
Automated People Mover [*MOCD*] [*TXDOT*] (TAG) .... APM
Automated Percutaneous Discectomy [*Spinal surgery*] .... APD
Automated Performance Measurement (MCD) .... APM
Automated Performance Measurement System [*FAA*] (TAG) .... APMS
Automated Performance Measurement System (GAVI) .... APMS
Automated Peritoneal Dialysis [*Medicine*] .... APD
Automated Personnel Accounting, Cost, Historical Estimating System [*Army*] .... APACHES
Automated Personnel Information Exchange (DNAB) .... APIX
Automated Photogrammetric Positioning System (DNAB) .... APPS
Automated Pilot Aptitude Measurement System (MCD) .... APAMS
Automated Pit Trading [*Developed by London International Financial Futures Exchange*] [*Stock exchange term*] .... APT
Automated Planning Fabrication Outline (MCD) .... APFO
Automated Plate Measuring [*for Spectrography*] .... APM
Automated Powder Diffractometer .... APD
Automated Procedures for Engineering Consultants, Inc. .... APEC
Automated Process Information File [*Library of Congress*] .... APIF

Automated Process Planning System (PDAA) .... AUTOPROS
Automated Procurement and Production Scheduling and Management System [*Army*] .... APPSMS
Automated Procurement Documentation System [*Environmental Protection Agency*] (GFGA) .... APDS
Automated Procurement Planning, Execution, and Control .... APEX
[*The*] Automated Procurement Planning System .... TAPPS
Automated Product Control Environment (SSD) .... APCE
Automated Production and Control [*Industrial engineering*] .... APC
Automated Productivity Services (MCD) .... APS
Automated Program Debugging System (MCD) .... APD
Automated Program for Aerospace-Vehicle Synthesis .... APAS
Automated Program Search [*Tape recorder feature*] .... AMPS
Automated Program Support System [*Computer science*] .... APSS
Automated Program Testing Facility (MHDI) .... APTF
Automated Program to Project AIT [*Advanced Individual Training*] **Training Spaces** [*DoD*] .... APPATS
Automated Programmable Assembly System [*Computer science*] .... APAS
Automated Programming, Budgeting, and Operational Evaluation [*Army*] .... AUTOPROBE
Automated Project Management Information System [*Computer science*] .... APMIS
Automated Projective Drawing [*GMW Computers Ltd.*] [*Software package*] (NCC) .... AUTOPROD
Automated Pronunciation Instructor .... API
Automated Propeller Optical Measurement System .... APOMS
Automated Publication Preparation System [*Army*] (MCD) .... APPS
Automated Publications Maintenance System (DNAB) .... APMS
Automated Purchase and Payment System [*United Nations*] (DUND) .... APPS
Automated Quality of Care Evaluation Support System [*Military*] .... AQCESS
Automated Quotation System (IAA) .... AQS
Automated RADAR Measurement System (MCD) .... ARMS
Automated RADAR Monitor System .... ARM
Automated Radar Terminal System (GAVI) .... ARTS
Automated Radar Terminal System [*FAA*] (TAG) .... ARTS
Automated RADAR Tracking System (MCD) .... ARTS
Automated Radioimmunoassay .... AR
Automated Radioimmunoassay [*Immunology*] (DAVI) .... ARIA
Automated Radiotheodolite [*Marine science*] (OSRA) .... ARC
Automated Radiotheodolite (USDC) .... ARC
Automated Range Management System (MCD) .... ARMS
Automated Reactor Inspection System [*Nuclear energy*] (NRCH) .... ARIS
Automated Readability Index (MCD) .... ARI
Automated Reading Aid for the Physically Handicapped .... ARAPH
Automated Ready-Supply Stores System (DNAB) .... ARSSS
Automated Reagin [*Serology*] .... AR
Automated Reagin Test [*Serology*] .... ART
Automated Real-Time Imaging System .... ARIS
Automated Real-Time Investments Exchange [*NASDAQ trading computer*] .... ARIEL
Automated Real-time Mapping System [*Navigation systems*] .... ARMS
Automated Real-Time Radiography Inspection System .... ARTRIS
Automated Reasoning Assistant (IAA) .... AURA
Automated Reasoning Tool (MCD) .... ART
Automated Records Control System .... ARCS
Automated Records Management System [*Computer science*] (HGAA) .... ARMS
Automated Reference Service [*Ohio State University Libraries*] (OLDSS) .... ARS
Automated Registration, Indexing, and Enquiries System [*Computer science*] .... ARIES
Automated Reiter Protein Complement - Fixation Test (PDAA) .... ARPCFT
Automated Reliability and Maintenance Management [*or Measurement*] System [*Navy*] (NG) .... ARMMS
Automated Reliability Assessment Program [*FAA*] .... ARAP
Automated Reliability Estimation Program [*Computer science*] .... ARIES
Automated Remote Recognition and Tracking System .... ARRTS
Automated Remote Tracking Station (MCD) .... ARTS
Automated Rent Collections .... ARC
Automated Repair Service Bureau (TEL) .... ARSB
Automated Reporting and Management Information System [*Federal Communications Commission*] (GFGA) .... ARMIS
Automated Reporting, Tracking, and Evaluation Management Information System (SSD) .... ARTEMIS
Automated Reports Control Handling (MCD) .... ARCH
Automated Reproduction and Collating System (MCD) .... ARCS
Automated Request Transmission (MHDB) .... ART
Automated Request Transmission by Telephone (PDAA) .... ARTTel
Automated Requirement Computation System Initial Provisioning [*Army*] .... ARCSIP
Automated Requirements Allocation Data (MCD) .... ARAD
Automated Requirements Development System (MCD) .... ARDS
Automated Requirements Traceability System (SSD) .... ARTS
Automated Research Facility [*National Bureau of Standards*] (NITA) .... AMRF
Automated Resource Management System (MCD) .... ARMS
Automated Resource Planning and Analysis System (MCD) .... ARPAS
Automated Response to Query .... ARQ
Automated Responsive Environment (BUR) .... ARE
Automated Retail Outlet System (MCD) .... AUTOROS
Automated Revenue Collection System [*Business term*] (MHDW) .... ARCS
Automated Ring Code Search (DIT) .... ARCS
Automated Roadside Safety Inspection [*FHWA*] (TAG) .... ARSI
Automated Route Management (DEN) .... ARM
Automated Runbook/Library System .... ARLS
Automated Safety Officer .... ASO
Automated Scanning Low-Energy Electron Probe (IEEE) .... ASLEEP
Automated Schedule Information System .... ASIS

Automated Schedule Procedures .... ASP
Automated Screen Trading [*Business term*] .... AST
Automated Seat Reservation System [*Aviation*] .... ASRS
Automated Seavan Shipment Planning System [*MTMC*] (TAG) .... ASSP
Automated Security Enhancement Tool .... ASET
Automated Security Holdings ADS [*NYSE symbol*] (SPSG) .... ASI
Automated Security Holdings Ltd. [*Associated Press*] (SAG) .... AutSec
Automated Seismic Processor [*Earthquake analyzer*] .... ASP
Automated Seismological Observation System [*Marine science*] (OSRA) .... ASOS
Automated Sequential Trace Enrichment of Dialysate .... ASTED
Automated Service Center .... ASC
Automated Service Center .... AUTOSERVCEN
Automated Shareholder Records System (MCD) .... ASRS
Automated Shell Theory for Rotating Structures [*NASA*] .... ASTROS
Automated Ship Classification System (MCD) .... ASCS
Automated Ship Data Library (IEEE) .... ASDL
Automated Ship Location and Attitude Measuring System .... ASLAMS
Automated Shipboard Forecasting System .... ASFS
Automated Signal Excess Prediction (MCD) .... ASEP
Automated Single Area Field Scanner [*Department of Agricultural Meteorology, University of Nebraska*] .... ASAFS
Automated Small Purchase System [*DoD*] .... ASPS
Automated Soft Lander [*Aerospace*] (MCD) .... ASL
Automated Software Evaluation System .... ASES
Automated Software System Used for Reliability Evaluation .... ASSURE
Automated Software Trouble Report .... ASTR
Automated Space Production Experimenters Network [*Robotics*] .... ASPEN
Automated Spares Simulation Estimating Technique [*The Boeing Co.*] .... ASSET
Automated Specifications [*Computer science*] (DIT) .... AUTOSPEC
Automated Speech Technology (MCD) .... AST
Automated Speed Enforcement .... ASE
Automated Speed Enforcement Device .... ASED
Automated Spooling Priority [*Computer science*] .... ASP
Automated Staff Message Processing System .... ASMPS
Automated Statistical Analysis Program .... ASAP
Automated Statistical Analysis Technique (DNAB) .... ASAT
Automated Status Board .... ASB
Automated Status Board (DNAB) .... ASTAB
Automated Stock Transfer System (MCD) .... ASTS
Automated Storage Control System (MCD) .... ASCS
Automated Storage, Kitting, and Retrieval Systems [*Tandem Computers*] [*Navy*] .... ASKARS
Automated Storage/Retrieval [*Computer science*] .... AS/R
Automated Storage/Retrieval Systems (EA) .... AS/RS
Automated Structural Design [*NASA*] .... ASD
Automated Structural Optimization Program [*Air Force*] .... ASOP
Automated Submarine Frame [*Navy*] .... ASF
Automated Support System for Army Unit Logistics Training .... ASSAULT
Automated Surface Observing System [*Meteorology*] (FAAC) .... ASOS
Automated Surface Perspective (MHDI) .... ASPEX
Automated Switched Communications Network (MCD) .... ASCON
Automated System (ACRL) .... AS
Automated System Analysis Technique .... AUTOSATE
Automated System Charter (IAA) .... ASC
Automated System for Composing, Revising, Illustrating, and Phototypesetting .... AUTOSCRIPT
Automated System for Production Management (IAA) .... ASPM
Automated System for Sequential Extraction and Tabulation (NVT) .... ASSET
Automated System for Storing and Subsequently Selecting Information [*Developed by ICI, Inc.*] .... ASSASSIN
Automated System for the Control of Atmospheric Sampling [*Marine science*] (MSC) .... ASCAS
Automated System for Transportation Data [*Military*] .... AUTOSTRAD
Automated System for Transportation Intelligence [*Army*] (RDA) .... ASTI
Automated Systems and Services Branch [*NTIS*] .... AS & SB
Automated Systems and Software Engineering Technology (MCD) .... ASSET
Automated Systems Army Commissaries (AABC) .... ASAC
Automated Systems Management System (MCD) .... ASMS
Automated Tactical Environmental System .... ATES
Automated Tactical Environmental System (MCD) .... ATESS
Automated Tactical Fusion Division .... ATFD
Automated Tactical Target Graphic .... ATTG
Automated Tape Label Assignment System (MCD) .... ATLAS
Automated Tape Library .... ATL
Automated Target Recognition [*Military*] .... ATR
Automated Tariff Filing and Information System [*Washington, DC*] (EGAO) .... ATFI
Automated Technical Control [*System*] [*Honeywell, Inc.*] [*Army*] (RDA) .... ATC
Automated Technical Control [*System*] [*Honeywell, Inc.*] [*Army*] .... ATEC
Automated Technical Information (MCD) .... ATI
Automated Technical Information Support .... ATIS
Automated Technical Order Maintenance Sequences [*or Systems*] [*The Boeing Co.*] (MCD) .... ATOMS
Automated Technical Order System [*Air Force*] (MCD) .... ATOS
Automated Technique for Spacecraft Monitoring [*NASA*] .... ATSM
Automated Telecommunications Center (MCD) .... ATC
Automated Telecommunications Center .... ATCC
Automated Telecommunications System [*Army*] (ADDR) .... ATS
Automated [*or Automatic*] Teller Machine (ADA) .... AT
Automated [*or Automatic*] Teller Machine [*Banking*] .... ATM
Automated Terminal Weather Dissemination Display System (MCD) .... ATWDDS
Automated Terrain Information .... ARTINS
Automated Test Data Base Management System [*Army*] .... ATDBMS
Automated Test Data Generator [*Computer science*] .... ATDG
Automated Test Equipment .... ATE

Automated Test Plan (BUR) .... ATP
Automated Test Validation .... ATV
Automated Test-Case Guidance [*Computer science*] .... ATG
Automated Testing Analyzer [*Computer science*] .... ATA
Automated Ticket and Boarding Pass [*Travel industry*] .... ATB
Automated Ticket Dispenser .... ATD
Automated Time and Attendance Procedures (MHDB) .... ATAP
Automated Time Standards (MCD) .... ATS
Automated Tracking and Monitoring System .... ATAMS
Automated Trading System [*NYSE computer*] .... ATS
Automated Traffic Advisory and Resolution Service [*Collision-avoidance system*] [*Aviation*] .... ATARS
Automated Traffic Overload Protection (DNAB) .... ATOP
Automated Traffic Surveillance and Control [*Automotive engineering*] .... ATSAC
Automated Train Operation by Minicomputer [*Computer science*] (PDAA) .... ATOMIC
Automated Transfer Vehicle [*Space technology*] .... ATV
Automated Transponder Navigation System (PDAA) .... AUTRANAV
Automated Travel Agents Reservation .... ATAR
Automated Travel Agents Reservation Systems (PDAA) .... ATARS
Automated Ultrasonic Scanner (MCD) .... AUS
Automated Unit Equipment List .... AUEL
Automated Unit Placement Model .... AUPM
Automated Unit Reference Sheets (MCD) .... AURS
Automated Universal Array (MCD) .... AUA
Automated Urease-Chromous Method [*Analytical chemistry*] .... AUCM
Automated Vacuum .... AVAC
Automated Vacuum-Assisted Collection System [*Disney World trash disposal system*] .... AVAC
Automated Vendor Selection System (NRCH) .... AVSS
Automated Verification System [*Computer science*] (MCD) .... AVS
Automated Vibration Diagnostic System (MCD) .... AVID
Automated Video Maintenance Information (MCD) .... AVMI
Automated Video Target Scoring System .... AVTSS
Automated Viscoelastic Grain Structural Analysis Program (MCD) .... AVGSAP
Automated Vision Association [*Later, AIA*] (EA) .... AVA
Automated Visual Sensitivity Tester .... AVST
Automated Vocabulary Control [*Subsystem of PLIS*] [*Computer science*] .... AVOCON
Automated Voice Annunciator Systems [*FTA*] (TAG) .... AVAS
Automated Voice Response System [*DoD*] .... AVRS
Automated Volt Left [*Medicine*] (DMAA) .... aVL
Automated Voltammetric Electrode [*Electrochemistry*] .... AVE
Automated Want and Warrant System [*Data processing system used in police work*] .... AWWS
Automated Weapons Test Analysis System .... AWTAS
Automated Weather Acquisition and Retrieval Data System [*Marine science*] (OSRA) .... AWARDS
Automated Weather Acquisition and Retrieval Data System (USDC) .... AWARDS
Automated Weather Advisory Station (GAVI) .... AWAS
Automated Weather Data Network [*National Climate Program Office*] .... AWDN
Automated Weather Distribution System (MCD) .... AWDS
Automated Weather Information Processing System .... AWIPS
Automated Weather Network [*Air Force*] .... AWN
Automated Weather Network Coordinating Station [*Air Force*] .... AWNCS
Automated Weather Network Management Center [*Military*] .... AWNMC
Automated Weather Observing Station [*FAA*] (TAG) .... AWOS
Automated Wire Data System .... AWDS
Automated Wire List [*NASA*] (NASA) .... AWL
Automated Wiring System (MCD) .... AWS
Automated Work Authorization System (MCD) .... AWAS
Automated Work Request (NVT) .... AWR
Automated Worthless Document Index .... AWDI
Automated Wreck and Obstruction Information System [*National Oceanic and Atmospheric Administration Information service or system*] (IID) .... AWOIS
Automated X-Ray Orientation System (MCD) .... AXROS
Automatic (IAA) .... A
Automatic (IAA) .... AU
Automatic .... AUT
Automatic .... AUTM
Automatic (AFM) .... AUTO
Automatic .... AUTOMTC
Automatic 4-Speed Heavy Duty Transmission [*Automotive engineering*] A4HD
Automatic 4-Speed Light Duty Transmission [*Automotive engineering*] A4LD
Automatic Abort-Sensing System [*NASA*] .... AASS
Automatic Adaptation Data (DNAB) .... AUTOMAD
Automatic Adaptive Equalization [*Telecommunications*] .... AAE
Automatic Address Recognition System [*or Subsystem*] [*Computer science*] .... AARS
Automatic Addressing System [*Computer science*] .... AAS
Automatic Aimpoint Selection and Maintenance (MCD) .... AUASAM
Automatic Aimpoint Selection and Maintenance (DNAB) .... AUASM
Automatic Air Data Calibration System [*Aerospace*] .... AADCS
Automatic Air Traffic Control [*System*] (IEEE) .... AATC
Automatic Aircraft Diagnostic System .... AADS
Automatic Aircraft Intercept Control System .... AAICS
Automatic Aircraft Vectoring Control System [*Air Force*] .... AAVCS
Automatic Aircraft Vectoring System [*Air Force*] (MUGU) .... AAVS
Automatic Air-Valving Surface Effects Device [*Army*] (MCD) .... AAVSED
Automatic Alternate Voice/Data [*Computer science*] .... AAVD
Automatic Alternative Routing [*Telecommunications*] (TEL) .... AAR
Automatic Altitude Trim System [*for helicopters*] (NG) .... AATS
Automatic Amplitude Control (CET) .... AAC
Automatic and Dynamic Monitor with Immediate Relocation, Allocation, and Loading (IEEE) .... ADMIRAL
Automatic Anechoic Chamber Test System [*Navy*] (MCD) .... AACTS
Automatic Announcement Subsystem [*Telecommunications*] (TEL) .... AAS
Automatic Answer [*Telecommunications*] (TEL) .... AA
Automatic Answer Trunk [*Computer science*] (IAA) .... AAT
Automatic Answering Equipment [*Telecommunications*] (IAA) .... AAE
Automatic Answering Unit [*Telecommunications*] (TEL) .... AAU
Automatic Antenna Timer .... AAT
Automatic Antijam Circuit (CET) .... AAJAC
Automatic Antitheft System [*Electronic lock*] .... AATS
Automatic Aperture Control .... AAC
Automatic Approach/AUTOLAND (NASA) .... AA/AL
Automatic Approach Control [*Aviation*] (AAG) .... AAC
Automatic Approach Control Coupler [*or Complex*] [*Aviation*] (MCD) .... AACC
Automatic Armor Cluster Munition .... AACM
Automatic Assemble Editing (NTCM) .... AAE
Automatic Attack Warning System (AFM) .... AAWS
Automatic Autocollimator .... AAC
Automatic Azimuth Laying Theodolite (KSC) .... AALT
Automatic Back Bias [*RADAR*] .... ABB
Automatic Backlight Compensation [*Photography*] .... ABLC
Automatic Backup and Recovery [*Computer science*] (IAA) .... ABR
Automatic Band Rate (IEEE) .... ABR
Automatic Bandwidth Control .... ABC
Automatic Bandwidth Control (MSA) .... ABWC
Automatic Bar Checker .... ABC
Automatic Base Communication Systems (PDAA) .... ABCS
Automatic Baseband Monitor (PDAA) .... ABBM
Automatic Bass Compensation [*Radio*] .... ABC
Automatic Bass Compensation (IDOE) .... abc
Automatic Bass Compensation [*Radio*] (MSA) .... ABSC
Automatic Bass Control .... ABC
Automatic Battery Test .... ABT
Automatic Beam Control (IAA) .... ABC
Automatic Beam Current Stabilizing (IAA) .... ABS
Automatic Bias Compensation .... ABC
Automatic Bias Compensation (MSA) .... ABCP
Automatic Bias Control .... ABC
Automatic Bias Control (IDOE) .... abc
Automatic Bill Calling [*Later, MCCS*] [*Telecommunications*] .... ABC
Automatic Binary Computer (ADA) .... ABC
Automatic Binary Data Link [*Computer science*] (CET) .... ABDL
Automatic BIT [*Binary Digit*] **Error Rate Test** [*Computer science*] (MCD) .... ABERT
Automatic Black Signal [*TRB*] (TAG) .... ABS
Automatic Blip Counter .... ABC
Automatic Blip Counter System .... ABCS
Automatic Blip-Scan Counter .... ABSC
Automatic Blip-Scan Counter System .... ABSCS
Automatic Block Controller (MCD) .... ABC
Automatic, Block-Schematic Advanced Control User-Oriented System (PDAA) .... ABACUS
Automatic Blow Down (IEEE) .... AB
Automatic Boiling-Column Reactor .... ABC
Automatic Bootstrap Loader [*Computer science*] .... ABL
Automatic Braking System (MCD) .... ABS
Automatic Braking Technology [*Rollerblade, Inc.*] (PS) .... ABT
Automatic Branch Control (IAA) .... ABC
Automatic Bridge Control [*Navy*] (MCD) .... ABC
Automatic Brightness Compensation (IDOE) .... abc
Automatic Brightness Control (IDOE) .... abc
Automatic Brightness Control [*Telecommunications*] (TEL) .... ABC
Automatic Broadcast (BARN) .... ABCST
Automatic Broadcasting Control System [*Japan*] .... ABCS
Automatic Bulk Tape Degausser .... ABTD
Automatic Bus Terminal [*Computer science*] (MCD) .... ABT
Automatic Bus Transfer (NVT) .... ABT
Automatic Cable Pair Identification [*Computer science*] (IAA) .... ACPI
Automatic Cable Tester .... ACT
Automatic Call Director [*Telecommunications*] .... ACD
Automatic Call Distribution [*Switching system*] [*Telecommunications*] .... ACD
Automatic Call Distributor [*Datapoint Corp.*] (NITA) .... ACD
Automatic Call Distributor - Electronic Switching System [*Telecommunications*] (TEL) .... ACD-ESS
Automatic Call Number Identification [*Telecommunications*] (IAA) .... ACNI
Automatic Call Origination [*Telecommunications*] .... ACO
Automatic Call Recording [*Telecommunications*] (CMD) .... ACR
Automatic Call Recording Equipment [*Telecommunications*] .... ACRE
Automatic Call [*or Calling*] **Unit** [*Telecommunications*] (TEL) .... ACU
Automatic Calling and Answering Unit [*Telecommunications*] (OA) .... ACAU
Automatic Calling Card Service [*Telecommunications*] (TEL) .... ACCS
Automatic Calling Equipment [*Telecommunications*] (BUR) .... ACE
Automatic Calling Unit Interface [*Telecommunications*] (IEEE) .... ACUI
Automatic Cancellation (CAAL) .... ACNX
Automatic Cancellation of Extended Targets (AABC) .... ACET
Automatic Cannon Technology (MCD) .... ACT
Automatic Capacitor Tester .... ACT
Automatic Car Wash Association International [*Later, ICA*] .... ACWA
Automatic Card Control Entrance Security System [*Computer science*] .... ACCESS
Automatic Card Identification .... ACI
Automatic Card Reader .... ACR
Automatic Carriage Return .... ACR
Automatic Carrier Control [*Telecommunications*] (TEL) .... ACC
Automatic Carrier Landing System [*Military*] .... ACL
Automatic Carrier Landing System [*FAA*] (TAG) .... ACLS
Automatic Cartographic System .... ACS

Automatic Cartridge, Pistol [Military] (VNW) .... ACP
Automatic Case Control System .... ACCS
Automatic Celestial Navigation [Air Force] .... ACN
Automatic Central Communications Electronic Switching System .... ACCESS
Automatic Centrifugal Tinning Apparatus .... ACTA
Automatic Channel and Time [Toshiba Corp.] [Programmable television set] .... ACT
Automatic Check Personalization (DGA) .... ACP
Automatic Check Valve (MSA) .... AUTO CV
Automatic Checkout (BUR) .... AC
Automatic Checkout and Control System .... ACCS
Automatic Checkout and Evaluation System [Air Force] .... ACES
Automatic Checkout and Readiness Equipment .... ACRE
Automatic Checkout and Recording Equipment .... ACORN
Automatic Checkout Equipment .... ACE
Automatic Checkout Equipment .... ACOE
Automatic Checkout Equipment Sequencer (NASA) .... ACES
Automatic Checkout Set (AAG) .... ACOS
Automatic Checkout System [NASA] (AAG) .... ACHS
Automatic Checkout System [NASA] .... ACS
Automatic Checkout Technician [or Technique] (MCD) .... ACT
Automatic Checkout Test Equipment (AAG) .... ACTE
Automatic Chemical Agent Alarm [Military] (RDA) .... ACAA
Automatic Chemical Agent Alarm [Military] (RDA) .... ACADA
Automatic Chemical Agent Alarm System (MCD) .... ACAAS
Automatic Chemical Biological Warning System .... ACBWS
Automatic Chemical Reaction System .... ACRS
Automatic Chrominance Control (DEN) .... ACC
Automatic Chrominance Control (IDOE) .... acc
Automatic Circuit Analysis Program .... ACAP
Automatic Circuit Analyzer .... ACA
Automatic Circuit Assurance Feature (CET) .... ACAF
Automatic Circuit Board Card Tester .... ACBCT
Automatic Circuit Board Tester .... ACBT
Automatic Circuit Exchange .... ACE
Automatic Circuit Exchange (MSA) .... ACKTX
Automatic Circuit Quality Monitoring (PDAA) .... ACOM
Automatic Circuit Quality Monitoring (MHDI) .... ACQM
Automatic Circuit Tester .... ACT
Automatic Classification and Interpretation of Data (BUR) .... ACID
Automatic Climate Control [Automotive engineering] .... ACC
Automatic Climatological Recording Equipment [Meteorology] (PDAA) .... ACRE
Automatic Clinical Analyzer [Medicine] (MAE) .... ACA
Automatic Closed Transition Transfer Switch .... ACTTS
Automatic Closing Device (DAC) .... ACD
Automatic Closure and Interlock [Nuclear energy] (NRCH) .... ACI
Automatic Clutch and Throttle System [Automotive powertrain] .... ACTS
Automatic Clutch System [Powertrain] [Automotive engineering] .... ACS
Automatic Clutter Eliminator [FAA] .... ACE
Automatic Clutter Eliminator (MSA) .... ACLE
Automatic Clutter Mapping .... ACM
Automatic Coating Machine .... ACM
Automatic Code Generator .... ACG
Automatic Code Translation [Computer science] .... ACT
Automatic Code Translator (NITA) .... ACT
Automatic Coding Machine [Computer science] (CET) .... ACOM
Automatic Coding System [Computer science] (IAA) .... ACS
Automatic Coin Telephone Service .... ACTS
Automatic Color Compensation (IDOE) .... acc
Automatic Color Control .... ACC
Automatic Color Killer [Video recording] .... ACK
Automatic Color-Scanned Device (MCD) .... ACSD
Automatic Colt Pistol (DICI) .... ACP
Automatic Combat Intelligence Center (MCD) .... ACIC
Automatic Combustion Control .... ACC
Automatic Combustion Control and Feedwater Control (DNAB) .... ACC/FWC
Automatic Combustion Control Unmanned (PDAA) .... ACCU
Automatic Command to Line of Sight [Military British] .... ACLOS
Automatic Communication Relay (NVT) .... AUTOCAT
Automatic Communications Addressing and Reporting System [FAA] (TAG) .... ACARS
Automatic Communications Program (DWSG) .... ACP
Automatic Component Tester .... ACT
Automatic Comprehensive Display System [Computer science] .... ACDS
Automatic Compression Regulator (IEEE) .... ACR
Automatic Compression - Release .... ACR
Automatic Compression - Release Device .... ACRD
Automatic Computer .... AC
Automatic Computer (IDOE) .... ac
Automatic Computer Calculation of Optical Systems (MCD) .... ACCOS
Automatic Computer Evaluation (BUR) .... ACE
Automatic Computer, Ministry of Supply [British] (DEN) .... AMOS
Automatic Computer Telex Services .... ACTS
Automatic Computer Voltage Stabilizer (MHDI) .... ACVS
Automatic Computer-Controlled Electronic Scanning System [National Institute of Standards and Technology] .... ACCESS
Automatic Computerized Transverse Axial [Computer X-ray system] .... ACTA
Automatic Computing Engine [Early computer] [National Physical Laboratory] .... ACE
Automatic Computing Equipment (IAA) .... ACE
Automatic Computing Transfer Oscillator (IEEE) .... ACTO
Automatic Conference Arranger (CET) .... ACA
Automatic Configuration Management Tool .... ACMT
Automatic Continuity Equipment .... ACE
Automatic Continuous Air Monitoring System (MCD) .... ACAMS

Automatic Continuous Evaporation .... ACE
Automatic Continuous Function Generation [Computer science] .... ACFG
Automatic Contour Digitizer .... ACD
Automatic Contrast Control .... ACC
Automatic Control .... AC
Automatic Control Center [Purdue University] .... ACC
Automatic Control Certified (DCTA) .... ACC
Automatic Control Certified for Unattended Engine Room (DS) .... ACCU
Automatic Control Certified for Unattended Engine Room - Open Seas (DS) .... ACCU-OS
Automatic Control Console (NASA) .... ACC
Automatic Control Distribution (IAA) .... ACD
Automatic Control Equipment .... ACE
Automatic Control Evaluation Simulator [Spaceflight training machine] .... ACES
Automatic Control Features (NRCH) .... ACF
Automatic Control Instrumentation .... ACI
Automatic Control Module .... ACM
Automatic Control of Air Transmissions (NATG) .... AUTOCAT
Automatic Control of Training Unit (IAA) .... ACTU
Automatic Control Operations Center (DNAB) .... ACOC
Automatic Control System .... ACS
Automatic Control Unit (IAA) .... ACU
Automatic Controlled Exposure .... ACE
Automatic Controlled Instrument Landing (NASA) .... ACIL
Automatic Cop Feeder (PDAA) .... ACF
Automatic Corps [Communications System] [General Electric Co.] .... AutoKo
Automatic Correlation Guidance .... ACG
Automatic Coulometric Titration (PDAA) .... ACT
Automatic Counter System .... ACS
Automatic Countermeasures Dispensing System (PDAA) .... ACDS
Automatic Coupling [Music] .... Auto
Automatic Course Control [Air Force] .... ACC
Automatic Course Keeping (IAA) .... ACK
Automatic Crane Control Storage System .... ACCESS
Automatic Credit Transfer (CDAI) .... ACT
Automatic Cross-Connection Equipment [Computer science] .... ACE
Automatic Cutout [Valve] [Aviation] (AIA) .... ACO
Automatic Daily System Operability Test .... ADSOT
Automatic Damper Arm (KSC) .... ADA
Automatic Damper Manufacturers Association [Defunct] (EA) .... ADMA
Automatic Damping Control [Automotive suspensions] .... ADC
Automatic Data Accumulation and Transfer .... ADAT
Automatic Data Acquisition [Programming language named for Augusta Ada Byron] .... ADA
Automatic Data Acquisition and Computer Complex [Air Force] .... ADACC
Automatic Data Acquisition and Computer Complex [Computer science] (MHDB) .... ADAEX
Automatic Data Acquisition and Processing Techniques [Army] (RDA) .... ADAPT
Automatic Data Aids (MCD) .... ADA
Automatic Data and Select Program (KSC) .... ADASP
Automatic Data Center (ECII) .... ADC
Automatic Data Collection and Analysis System [Fort Huachuca, AZ] [United States Army Electronic Proving Ground] (GRD) .... ADCAS
Automatic Data Collection System (RDA) .... ADCS
Automatic Data Collector [National Weather Service] .... ADC
Automatic Data Computing [Computer science] (IAA) .... ADC
Automatic Data Correlation System (MCD) .... ADCS
Automatic Data Descriptor .... ADD
Automatic Data Digitizing System [Air Force] .... ADDS
Automatic Data Distribution System [Army] (AABC) .... ADDS
Automatic Data Entry [Air Force] .... ADE
Automatic Data Entry Unit .... ADEU
Automatic Data Evaluation .... ADE
Automatic Data Exchange .... ADX
Automatic Data Extraction Routine (CAAL) .... ADER
Automatic Data Extractor and Plotting Table .... ADEPT
Automatic Data Field Systems Command [Fort Belvoir, VA] [Army] .... ADFSC
Automatic Data Handling [Computer science] .... ADH
Automatic Data Interchange System [International Civil Aviation Organization] .... ADIS
Automatic Data Link [Computer science] .... ADL
Automatic Data Link Plotting System .... ADLIPS
Automatic Data Logger (PDAA) .... ADL
Automatic Data Material Requirements List .... ADMRL
Automatic Data Network .... ADN
Automatic Data Plotter .... ADP
Automatic Data Proc [NYSE symbol] (TTSB) .... AUD
Automatic Data Processing (IDOE) .... adp
Automatic Data Processing .... ADP
Automatic Data Processing [Associated Press] (SAG) .... AutoDt
Automatic Data Processing Budget (DNAB) .... ADPBUD
Automatic Data Processing Budget Control Totals .... ADPBCT
Automatic Data Processing by Equipment Systems .... ADPES
Automatic Data Processing Center .... ADPC
Automatic Data Processing Engineering .... ADPE
Automatic Data Processing Equipment .... ADPE
Automatic Data Processing Equipment/Data System (AAGC) .... ADPE/DS
Automatic Data Processing Equipment Selection Office [Navy] .... ADPESO
Automatic Data Processing Field Branch [BUPERS] .... ADPFB
Automatic Data Processing, Inc. [Trademark for data processing services] .... ADP
Automatic Data Processing, Inc. [NYSE symbol] (SPSG) .... AUD
Automatic Data Processing, Inc. [Associated Press] (SAG) .... AutoDta
Automatic Data Processing Liaison Officer [Military] (MCD) .... ADPLO
Automatic Data Processing Machine .... ADPM
Automatic Data Processing Management Information System (AABC) .... ADPMIS

Automatic Data Processing Modification Order .... ADPMO
Automatic Data Processing Planning and Development Branch [*BUPERS*] .... ADPP & DB
Automatic Data Processing Production Branch [*BUPERS*] .... ADPPB
Automatic Data Processing Program Reporting System [*Military*] (MCD) .... ADPPRS
Automatic Data Processing Programming and Processing Branch [*BUPERS*] .... ADPP & PB
Automatic Data Processing Requirements Office [*Jet Propulsion Laboratory, NASA*] .... ADPRO
Automatic Data Processing Resource Estimating Procedures .... ADPREP
Automatic Data Processing Resource Estimating Procedures .... ADREP
Automatic Data Processing Security [*Military*] (MCD) .... ADPS
Automatic Data Processing Selection Office [*Military*] (MCD) .... ADPSO
Automatic Data Processing Service Center [*Service of the US military*] (AABC) .... ADPSC
Automatic Data Processing Services .... ADPS
Automatic Data Processing System [*or Subsystem*] .... ADPS
Automatic Data Processing System Security Officer (MCD) .... ADPSSO
Automatic Data Processing Systems and Equipment (GFGA) .... ADPSE
Automatic Data Processing Tactical Operation System (DNAB) .... ADPTOS
Automatic Data Processing Training Center [*Military*] (MCD) .... ADPTC
Automatic Data Processing Unit (IAA) .... ADPU
Automatic Data Rate Changer .... ADRC
Automatic Data Relay .... ADR
Automatic Data Reporting System (NATG) .... ADRS
Automatic Data Routing Group (AAG) .... ADRG
Automatic Data Service Center .... ADSC
Automatic Data Set Editing Program [*NASA*] (KSC) .... ADSEP
Automatic Data Switching System [*Deep Space Network*] .... ADSS
Automatic Data System [*Computer science*] .... ADS
Automatic Data System Uniform Practices [*A programming language*] .... ADSUP
Automatic Data System within the Army in the Field .... ADSAF
Automatic Data Test System [*Bell System*] .... ADTS
Automatic Data Transfer System (MCD) .... ADTS
Automatic Data Translator [*or Transmitter*] .... ADT
Automatic Data Unit .... ADU
Automatic Dead Reckoning Instrument Systems [*Navigation*] [*Canada*] .... ADRIS
Automatic Dead-Reckoning Instrument [*Aviation*] (PDAA) .... ADRI
Automatic Debit Transfer [*Banking*] .... ADT
Automatic Debiting and Electronic Payment for Transport [*Automotive engineering*] (ECON) .... ADEPT
Automatic Decisions Optimizing Predicted Estimates .... ADOPE
Automatic Defense Operation Center .... ADOC
Automatic Defense System (MCD) .... ADS
Automatic Degaussing (IAA) .... ADG
Automatic Degaussing System (DWSG) .... ADS
Automatic Degreasing Machine .... ADM
Automatic Deletion Procedure (DNAB) .... ADP
Automatic Dependence Surveillance System [*International Civil Aviation Organisation*] .... ADS
Automatic Dependent Surveillance [*FAA*] (TAG) .... ADS
Automatic Dependent Surveillance Unit [*ICAO designator*] (FAAC) .... ADSU
Automatic Depositor [*Banking*] (BUR) .... AD
Automatic Depressurization System [*Nuclear energy*] (NRCH) .... ADS
Automatic Depth Control (MCD) .... ADC
Automatic Depth/Deployed Moored Sweep (MCD) .... ADDMS
Automatic Depth Keeping (IAA) .... ADK
Automatic Derivation of Invariants (MCD) .... ADI
Automatic Design Optimization Techniques (MCD) .... ADOPT
Automatic Destruct Program (MUGU) .... ADP
Automatic Detection [*Air Force*] .... AD
Automatic Detection and Integrated Tracking (MCD) .... ADIT
Automatic Detection and Tracking (MCD) .... ADT
Automatic Detection/Automatic Classification [*Antisubmarine warfare*] (MCD) .... AD/AC
Automatic Detection Mark (NVT) .... ADM
Automatic Development System (MCD) .... ADS
Automatic Deviation Control (MCD) .... ADC
Automatic Device for Mechanical Order Selection .... ADMOS
Automatic Diagnostic Input/Output System [*Computer science*] .... ADIOS
Automatic Diagnostic Maintenance Information Retrieval [*Computer science*] (IAA) .... ADMIR
Automatic Diagnostic Maintenance Information Retrieval System [*Computer science*] (MCD) .... ADMIRE
Automatic Dial Order Wire [*Military*] (NVT) .... ADOW
Automatic Dialer with Recorded Message Player [*Telecommunications*] .... ADRMP
Automatic Dialing Alarm System (PDAA) .... ADAS
Automatic Dialing and Indicating Equipment [*Telecommunications*] (IAA) .... ADIE
Automatic Dialing Unit [*Telecommunications*] .... ADU
Automatic Dialing Unit (IDOE) .... adu
Automatic Dialogue Replacement .... ADR
Automatic Dial-Out (NITA) .... ADO
Automatic Die Positioner [*Electronics*] (EECA) .... ADP
Automatic Diffemic Identification of Speakers [*University of Bonn*] .... ADIS
Automatic Digit Recognition .... AUDREY
Automatic Digital Assembly Test Equipment (MCD) .... ADATE
Automatic Digital Calculator [*Computer science*] (ADA) .... ADC
Automatic Digital Data Acquisition and Recording [*Computer science*] .... ADDAR
Automatic Digital Data Assembly System [*Computer science*] .... ADDAS
Automatic Digital Depth (IAA) .... ADD
Automatic Digital Encoding System [*Computer science*] .... ADES
Automatic Digital Exchange [*Telecommunications*] (ODBW) .... ADX
Automatic Digital Input/Output System [*Computer science*] .... ADIOS
Automatic Digital Message Switch Equipment (MCD) .... ADMSE
Automatic Digital Message Switching .... ADMS
Automatic Digital Message Switching Center [*AUTODIN*] .... ADMSC
Automatic Digital Network [*DoD*] .... AUTODIN
Automatic Digital Network - Evolutionary Modernization [*Military*] (DNAB) .... AUTODIN EMOD
Automatic Digital Network - Integrated Circuits Communications Data Processor [*Military*] (DNAB) .... AUTODIN ICCDP
Automatic Digital On-Line Instrumentation System .... ADONIS
Automatic Digital Optical Tracker [*Army*] (AABC) .... ADOT
Automatic Digital Processor (MCD) .... ADP
Automatic Digital Recording and Control .... ADRAC
Automatic Digital Switch .... ADS
Automatic Digital Switching Center (IEEE) .... ADSC
Automatic Digital Test Unit .... ADTU
Automatic Digital Weather Switch [*Air Force*] (AFM) .... ADWS
Automatic Digital-Data-Error Recorder [*Computer science*] .... ADDER
Automatic Direct Access to Information with the On-Line UDC [*Universal Decimal Classification*] **System** [*American Institute of Physics*] [*Information retrieval*] .... AUDACIOUS
Automatic Direct Analog Computer (BUR) .... ADAC
Automatic Direct-Distance Dialing System [*Telecommunications*] (IEEE) .... ADDDS
Automatic Direction Finder [*Military*] .... ADF
Automatic Direction Finder, Remote Control (AAG) .... ADFR
Automatic Direction Finding Approach (SAA) .... ADFA
Automatic Direction Finding Approach .... ADFAP
Automatic Direction Finding System .... ADFS
Automatic Direction Indicator (AFM) .... ADI
Automatic Dish Detergent .... ADD
Automatic Dispatch System [*Nuclear energy*] (NRCH) .... ADS
Automatic Dispatching Stick Repeater .... ADSP
Automatic Display [*Computer science*] .... AD
Automatic Display and Plotting System (BUR) .... ADAPS
Automatic Display Finder [*Computer science*] (NASA) .... ADF
Automatic Display Mode [*Computer science*] (BUR) .... ADM
Automatic Display Plotting System (MCD) .... ADPS
Automatic Display Switching Oscilloscope .... ADSO
Automatic Distance and Angle Measurement .... ADAM
Automatic Distortion Reduction (IAA) .... ADR
Automatic Distribution of Documents [*DoD*] .... ADD
Automatic Distribution of Microfiche .... ADM
Automatic Dividend Reinvestment [*Investment term*] .... ADR
Automatic Document Abstracting Method (NITA) .... ADAM
Automatic Document Analysis (DIT) .... ADA
Automatic Document Distribution (MCD) .... ADD
Automatic Document Feeder [*For copying machines*] .... ADF
Automatic Document Online Information System [*Document delivery system*] [*Association of European Publishers*] (NITA) .... ADONIS
Automatic Document Request (AIE) .... ADRS
Automatic Document Request Service [*or System*] .... ADRS
Automatic Document Storage and Retrieval [*Computer science*] .... ADSTAR
Automatic Door Isolating Cock [*British railroad term*] .... DIC
Automatic Door Seal [*Technical drawings*] .... ADS
Automatic Drafting Equipment (IEEE) .... ADE
Automatic Drafting Machine (DIT) .... ADMA
Automatic Drawing Device (DIT) .... ADD
Automatic Drift Control (AFM) .... ADC
Automatic Drip Coffee [*Brand name*] .... ADC
Automatic Drive Control (IAA) .... ADC
Automatic Drivetrain Management [*Automotive engineering*] .... ADM
Automatic Dynamic Digital Test System (MHDB) .... AUDDIT
Automatic Dynamic Evaluation by Programmed Organizations .... ADEPO
Automatic Dynamic Evaluation by Programmed Test .... ADEPT
Automatic Dynamic Incremental Nonlinear Analysis (MCD) .... ADINA
Automatic Dynamic Response Analyzer (PDAA) .... ADRA
Automatic Earnings Recomputation Operation [*Social Security*] .... AERO
Automatic Electric (MCD) .... AE
Automatic Electric Energy Management System [*Aviation*] (OA) .... AEEMS
Automatic Electronic Production (IAA) .... AEP
Automatic Electronic Range Instrumentation System (MCD) .... AERIS
Automatic Electronic Switching Center .... AESC
Automatic Electronic Switching System .... AESRS
Automatic Electronic Switching System (MCD) .... AESS
Automatic Electronic Voice Switch (RDA) .... AEVS
Automatic Emergency Broadcast Alert [*Telecommunications*] (IAA) .... AEBA
Automatic Emission Spectroscopy (MCD) .... AES
Automatic End Point .... AEP
Automatic Engine Control [*Heavy-duty diesel engines*] .... AEC
Automatic Environment Monitoring (BUR) .... AEM
Automatic Equalization/Analyzation System .... AEAS
Automatic Error Analysis .... AEA
Automatic Error Interrogation [*Telecommunications*] (OA) .... AEI
Automatic Error Request Equipment [*Aviation*] .... ARQ
Automatic Exciter Control .... AEC
Automatic Execute Batch (CDE) .... AUTOEXEC BAT
Automatic Exposure Camera .... AE
Automatic Exposure Control [*In reprographic systems*] .... AEC
Automatic Exposure Control Technique .... AECT
Automatic External Defibrillator (PDAA) .... AED
Automatic External Standard [*or Standardization*] [*Radioactivity measurement*] .... AES
Automatic Extracting Program .... AEP
Automatic Extraction System [*Computer science*] (MHDI) .... AES
Automatic False Alarm Rate .... AFAR

Automatic Fare Collection [*TRB*] (TAG) .... AFC
Automatic Fare Collection System .... AFCS
Automatic Fast Demagnetization .... AFD
Automatic Fast Feed (NITA) .... AFF
Automatic Fault Isolation .... AFI
Automatic Fault Isolation Test .... AFIT
Automatic Fault Location .... AFL
Automatic Fault Simulator .... AFS
Automatic Fault-Finding and Maintenance (SAA) .... AFM
Automatic Feature Extraction System (MCD) .... AFES
Automatic Feature Negotiation [*Computer science*] .... AFN
Automatic Fidelity Control .... AFC
Automatic Field Analog Computer .... AFAC
Automatic Field Assistant (MCD) .... AFA
Automatic Field Control (MHDB) .... AFC
Automatic Field/Format Recognition [*Computer science*] (NITA) .... AFR
Automatic File Distribution [*Computer science*] [*Telecommunications*] .... AFD
Automatic Film Data Collection System (MCD) .... AFDCS
Automatic Filter (ADA) .... AF
Automatic Fine Cull Machine (MHDB) .... AFCM
Automatic Fine Tuning .... AFT
Automatic Fingerprint Verification Computer System .... AFVCS
Automatic Fire Alarm Association (EA) .... AFAA
Automatic Fire Control .... AFC
Automatic Fire Control System (AAG) .... AFCS
Automatic Fire Detection (NITA) .... AFD
Automatic Fire Extinguisher (MCD) .... AFE
Automatic Firearms Identification System [*Jet Propulsion Laboratory, NASA*] .... AFIDS
Automatic Firing Sequencer .... AFS
Automatic Five Speed [*DOE*] (TAG) A5
Automatic Flexible Test Station .... AFTS
Automatic Flight Control .... AFC
Automatic Flight Control and Augmentation System (DA) .... AFCAS
Automatic Flight Control Equipment .... AFCE
Automatic Flight Control Panel (MCD) .... AFCP
Automatic Flight Control System [*Aerospace*] .... AFCS
Automatic Flight Control System Control Panel (MCD) .... AFCSCP
Automatic Flight Director System (MCD) .... AFDS
Automatic Flight Inspection (DA) .... AFIS
Automatic Flight Management .... AFM
Automatic Flight Operation Center [*Army*] (RDA) .... AFOC
Automatic Flight Path Control System [*Aviation*] (PDAA) .... AFPCS
Automatic Flight Planning and Monitoring .... AFPAM
Automatic Flight Reference System (DNAB) .... AFRS
Automatic Flight Stabilization and Control System (SAA) .... AFSC
Automatic Flight System [*Aviation*] (AIA) .... AFS
Automatic Flight System (GAVI) .... AFS
Automatic Flight Termination .... AFT
Automatic Flow Control .... AFC
Automatic Flow Process Analysis (IEEE) .... AFPA
Automatic Flowcharting .... AUTOFLOW
Automatic Fluorescent Penetrant Processing Facility (MCD) .... AFPPF
Automatic Focusing [*Photography*] .... AF
Automatic Focusing Random Scene Tracker (MCD) .... AFRST
Automatic Following [*RADAR*] .... AF
Automatic Format Recognition [*Computer science*] (ADA) .... AFR
Automatic Formation Drone Control (MCD) .... AFDC
Automatic Four Speed [*DOE*] (TAG) A4
Automatic Frame Scan Control (PDAA) .... AFSC
Automatic Frequency Assignment Model [*Telecommunications*] .... AFAM
Automatic Frequency Control [*Electronics*] .... AFC
Automatic Frequency Control (IDOE) .... AFC
Automatic Frequency Follower .... AFF
Automatic Frequency/Phase-Controlled [*Loop*] (IEEE) .... AF/PC
Automatic Frequency Ratio Controller (MHDB) .... AFRC
Automatic Frequency Stabilization .... AFS
Automatic Frequency Tone Shift (NVT) .... AFTS
Automatic Frequency Tuner .... AFT
Automatic Front Feed (ECII) .... AFF
Automatic Fuel Cutoff [*NASA*] (KSC) .... AFCO
Automatic Function Generator (HGAA) .... AFG
Automatic Functional Test and Evaluation Routine [*Raytheon Co.*] .... AFTER
Automatic Funds Transfer .... AFT
Automatic Fuze Radiograph Inspection Device (PDAA) .... AFRID
Automatic Gain Adjusting Amplifier [*Telecommunications*] .... AGAA
Automatic Gain Adjusting Amplifier [*Telecommunications*] (TEL) .... AGAMP
Automatic Gain Calibration Program .... AGCP
Automatic Gain Control [*Electronics*] .... AGC
Automatic Gain Control/Constant False Alarm Rate .... AGC/CFAR
Automatic Gain Ranging Amplifier (MCD) .... AGRA
Automatic Gain Stabilization .... AGS
Automatic Gas Analyzer [*Nuclear energy*] (NRCH) .... AGA
Automatic Gauge .... AG
Automatic Gauge Control [*or Controller*] .... AGC
Automatic Generation and Retrieval of Information on Chemical Components (PDAA) .... AGRICC
Automatic Generation Control (ACII) .... AGC
Automatic Generation of Requests [*Computer science*] (DIT) .... AUTOQEST
Automatic Gimbaled-Antenna Vectoring Equipment [*Air Force*] .... AGAVE
Automatic Governing Valve Control [*Nuclear energy*] (NRCH) .... AGVC
Automatic Government Source Inspection .... AGSI
Automatic Gravity Gradient .... AGGD
Automatic Ground Checkout System (KSC) .... AGCS
Automatic Ground Computer System (KSC) .... AGCS
Automatic Ground Control Station (KSC) .... AGCS
Automatic Ground Control System Computer (KSC) .... AGCSC
Automatic Ground Effect Augmentation System (MCD) .... AGEAS
Automatic Ground Equipment .... AGE
Automatic Ground Position Indicator [*Military*] .... AGPI
Automatic Ground Spoiler - Rejected Takeoff (MCD) .... AGS-RTO
Automatic Ground Transportable Emitter Location and Identification System [*Army*] .... AGTELIS
Automatic Ground Unit .... AGU
Automatic Ground-Controlled Approach [*RADAR*] .... AGCA
Automatic Ground-Controlled Intercept (MCD) .... AGCI
Automatic Ground-Controlled Landing .... AGCL
Automatic Ground-to-Air Communications System .... AGACS
Automatic Grouping System [*Hospital records*] (DHSM) .... AUTOGRP
Automatic Guard Receiver Terminals [*Navy*] (MCD) .... AGRT
Automatic Guidance and Control System .... AGCS
Automatic Guidance Electronics .... AGE
Automatic Guidance Programming (NATG) .... AGP
Automatic Guided Flight (MUGU) .... AGF
Automatic Guided Vehicle [*Robotic manufacturing equipment*] .... AGV
Automatic Guided Vehicle System [*Robotics*] .... AGVS
Automatic Guided Vehicle Systems (EA) .... AGVS
Automatic Gun Positioning System .... AGPS
Automatic Gunfire Control System (DNAB) .... AGFCS
Automatic Gun-Laying (DEN) .... AGL
Automatic Gun-Laying Turrets [*World War II British*] .... AGLT
Automatic Half Barrier .... AHB
Automatic Heading Reference System .... AHRS
Automatic Headway Control .... AHC
Automatic Helicopter Approach System [*Army*] .... AHAS
Automatic Hydrologic Observing System [*National Weather Service*] .... AHOS
Automatic Hydrologic Radio Reporting Network (DNAB) .... AHRRN
Automatic Identification [*Computer science*] .... Auto ID
Automatic Identification Manufacturers (EA) .... AIM
Automatic Identification Technology [*Army*] (RDA) .... AIT
Automatic Identified Outward Dialing [*Telecommunications*] .... AIOD
Automatic Idle Speed [*Automotive engineering*] .... AIS
Automatic Illustrated Documentation System [*Information International, Inc.*] .... AIDS
Automatic Image Density Control [*Photocopying toning technique*] (NITA) .... AIDC
Automatic Image Retrieval System (MCD) .... AIRS
Automatic Image Screening .... AIS
Automatic Imagery Interpretation .... AII
Automatic Implantable Cardiovascular Defibrillator [*Unit*] [*Cardiology*] (DAVI) .... AICD
Automatic Implantable Cardioverter-Defibrillator [*Cardiology*] .... AICD
Automatic Implantable Defibrillator [*Cardiology*] .... AID
Automatic Incident Detector (DI) .... AID
Automatic Indexing and Proofreading System .... AIPS
Automatic Industries Holdings [*Associated Press*] (SAG) .... AutoInd
Automatic Inflation Module .... AIM
Automatic In-Flight Insertion (NG) .... AIFI
Automatic Information Distribution [*Computer science*] (MHDI) .... AID
Automatic Information Retrieval System [*Information service or system*] (BUR) .... AIRS
Automatic Information Station [*or System*] (BUR) .... AIST
Automatic Information Test [*Military*] .... AIT
Automatic Initial Distribution (DNAB) .... AID
Automatic Initiation Circuit (IEEE) .... AIC
Automatic Inlet Control System (NG) .... AICS
Automatic In-Process Microcircuit Evaluation (MCD) .... AIME
Automatic Input [*Computer science*] (BUR) .... AI
Automatic Input Processing [*Computer science*] (MCD) .... AIP
Automatic Inspection Device for Explosive Charge Shell (AABC) .... AIDECS
Automatic Inspection, Diagnostic, and Prognostic [*System*] [*Army*] .... AIDAP
Automatic Inspection, Diagnostic, and Prognostic System [*Army*] .... AIDAPS
Automatic Instrument Landing Approach System [*Aviation*] .... AILAS
Automatic Instrument Landing System (FAAC) .... AILS
Automatic Instrumented Diving Assembly .... AIDA
Automatic Integrated Circuit Tester .... AICT
Automatic Integrated Container Handling (PDAA) .... AICH
Automatic Integrated Debugging System [*Computer science*] (BUR) .... AIDS
Automatic Integrated Director Equipment .... AIDE
Automatic Integrated Dynamic Avionics Tester .... AIDAT
Automatic Integrated Telephone System [*Telecommunications*] (OA) .... AITS
Automatic Integrating Fluctuation Meter .... AIFM
Automatic Interaction Detection [*or Detector*] [*Computer science*] .... AID
Automatic Interactive Computer Control (MCD) .... AICC
Automatic Intercept Bureau [*Telecommunications*] (TEL) .... AIB
Automatic Intercept Center [*Bell System*] .... AIC
Automatic Intercept System [*Bell System*] .... AIS
Automatic Intercity Station [*Telecommunications*] (OA) .... AIS
Automatic Intercity Telephone Exchange [*Telecommunications*] (OA) .... AITE
Automatic Intercom Switching System .... AISS
Automatic Interference Limiter [*Automotive sound systems*] .... AIL
Automatic Interference Measurement System (MCD) .... AIMS
Automatic Intermediate Station (MCD) .... AIS
Automatic Interrogation Distortion [*Telecommunications*] (OA) .... AID
Automatic Intersection Control System .... AICS
Automatic Intruder Detector Alarm [*Military British*] .... AIDA
Automatic Iris Control (PDAA) .... AIC
Automatic "J" Relay (MCD) .... AJR
Automatic Jamming Avoidance Circuitry (AABC) .... AJAC
Automatic Key Distribution .... AKD
Automatic Kinetic Enzyme System (PDAA) .... AKES

Automatic Label Exchange ..... ALEX
Automatic Landing [*NASA*] (NASA) ..... AUTOLAND
Automatic Landing Autopilot Subsystem (NASA) ..... ALAS
Automatic Landing Control (SAA) ..... ALC
Automatic Landing Flight Experiment [*Japan*] ..... ALFLEX
Automatic Landing Positioning System ..... ALPS
Automatic Landing System ..... ALS
Automatic Language Data Processing ..... ALDP
Automatic Language Identification (MCD) ..... ALI
Automatic Language Processing Advisory Committee [*National Research Council*] ..... ALPAC
Automatic LASER Encoder ..... ALE
Automatic LASER Instrumentation Measuring System (MCD) ..... ALIMS
Automatic LASER Test Set [*Hughes Aircraft Co.*] ..... ALTS
Automatic Launch Control System (DNAB) ..... ALCS
Automatic Layshaft Transmission [*Automotive engineering*] ..... ALT
Automatic Lead Former ..... ALF
Automatic Letter Facer ..... ALF
Automatic Level Control [*Camera*] [*Aviation*] ..... ALC
Automatic Level Control (IDOE) ..... alc
Automatic Level Control Assembly (MCD) ..... ALCA
Automatic Level Recorder ..... ALR
Automatic Level Setting ..... ALS
Automatic Leveling Seat [*Automotive engineering*] ..... ALS
Automatic License Plate Scanning ..... ALPS
Automatic License Revocation ..... ALR
Automatic Life Testing and Recording of Electronic Components [*Canada*] ..... ALTREC
Automatic Light Aircraft Readiness Monitor ..... ALARM
Automatic Light Control (KSC) ..... ALC
Automatic Lightning Detection System [*To aid in the prevention of forest fires*] ..... ALDS
Automatic Line Buildout [*Bell Laboratories*] ..... ALBO
Automatic Line Fault Analysis (MHDB) ..... ALFA
Automatic Line Feed [*Telecommunications*] ..... ALF
Automatic Line Insulation Test [*or Tester*] [*Bell System*] ..... ALIT
Automatic Line Integration (NVT) ..... ALI
Automatic Line Test and Administrative System [*Taiwan International Standard Electronics Ltd., a subsidiary of ITT*] (NITA) ..... ALTA
Automatic Line Test Set [*Telecommunications*] (TEL) ..... ALTS
Automatic Line Testing [*Telecommunications*] (TEL) ..... ALT
Automatic Line Tracer and Programming Equipment ..... ALTAPE
Automatic Linear Positioning System ..... ALPS
Automatic Linear Temperature Programmer ..... ALTP
Automatic Link Establishment (DOMA) ..... ALE
Automatic Liquid Agent Detector (AABC) ..... ALAD
Automatic Liquid Nitrogen Transfer System ..... ALNTS
Automatic List Classification and Profile Production ..... ALCAPP
Automatic Literature Processing, Handling, and Analysis ..... ALPHA
Automatic Load Alleviation System (MCD) ..... ALAS
Automatic Load Control ..... ALC
Automatic Load Regulator ..... ALR
Automatic Local Frequency Control ..... ALFC
Automatic Location Identification [*Street crime locator*] ..... ALI
Automatic Loc-Bottom [*Packaging*] ..... ALB
Automatic Locking Differential ..... ALD
Automatic Lock-On (MCD) ..... ALO
Automatic Lockup Four Speed [*DOE*] (TAG) L4
Automatic Logging Electronic Reporting and Telemetering System [*Maintains surveillance over petroleum wells and pipelines*] ..... ALERT
Automatic Logic Testing and Recording Equipment ..... ALTARE
Automatic Logical Equipment Readiness Tester ..... ALERT
Automatic Logical Translation and Information Retrieval [*Computer science*] (DIT) ..... ALTAIR
Automatic Louver Damper (OA) ..... ALD
Automatic Low Date Rate Input ..... ALDRI
Automatic Low-Altitude Bombing System (MCD) ..... AUTOLABS
Automatic Low-Frequency Gain-Limiting Circuit (RDA) ..... ALFGL
Automatic Lubrication System ..... ALS
Automatic Machine Loading ..... AML
Automatic Machining Program ..... AUTOMAP
Automatic Magazine Loading ..... AML
Automatic Magnetic Data Acquisition System (MCD) ..... AMDAS
Automatic Magnetic Guidance ..... AMG
Automatic Magnetic Tape Dissemination [*Defense Documentation Center*] ..... AMTD
Automatic Magnetic Tape Distribution [*Program*] ..... AMTD
Automatic Maintenance Monitor ..... AMM
Automatic Malfunction Analysis (KSC) ..... AMA
Automatic Management Switch [*Communication Devices, Inc.*] ..... AMS
Automatic Maneuvering Attack System [*Air Force*] ..... AMAS
Automatic Maneuvering Control (DNAB) ..... AMC
Automatic Manifold Pressure Regulator [*Aviation*] ..... AMPR
Automatic/Manual (MDG) ..... A/M
Automatic Map Display (MCD) ..... AMD
Automatic Mapping and Planning System [*Environmental Protection Agency*] (ERG) ..... AMPS
Automatic Master Sequence Selector ..... AMSS
Automatic Mathematical Analysis and Symbolic Translation [*Computer science*] ..... AUTOMAST
Automatic Mathematical Translator [*Programming language*] [*1970*] ..... AMTRAN
Automatic Measuring, Computing, and Sorting ..... AMECOS
Automatic Memory Allocation [*Computer science*] (BUR) ..... AMA
Automatic Merchandising Association of Florida (SRA) ..... AMAF
Automatic Message Accounting [*Bell Laboratories*] [*Telecommunications*] ..... AMA
Automatic Message Accounting Collecting System [*Telecommunications*] (TEL) ..... AMACS
Automatic Message Accounting / Magnetic Tape Recording [*Computer science*] (MHDB) ..... AMA/MTR
Automatic Message Accounting Recording Center [*Telecommunications*] (TEL) ..... AMARC
Automatic Message Accounting Recording System [*Bell System*] ..... AMARS
Automatic Message Accounting System (MCD) ..... AMAS
Automatic Message Address Routing System (AABC) ..... AMARS
Automatic Message Counting ..... AMC
Automatic Message Distribution System (CET) ..... AMDS
Automatic Message Entry System [*Computer science*] (MCD) ..... AMES
Automatic Message Exchange ..... AMX
Automatic Message Exchange Service ..... AUTOMEX
Automatic Message Processing Center ..... AMPC
Automatic Message Processing System [*USAERDL*] ..... AMPS
Automatic Message Processor (MCD) ..... AMP
Automatic Message Recording ..... AMR
Automatic Message Registering ..... AMR
Automatic Message Routing (BUR) ..... AMR
Automatic Message Routing Device ..... AMRD
Automatic Message Switching Center (NOAA) ..... AMSC
Automatic Meteorological Correction [*A missile guidance technique*] ..... AUTOMET
Automatic Meteorological Data Acquisition and Processing System (MCD) ..... AMDAPS
Automatic Meteorological Observation [*or Observing*] **Station** [*or System*] ..... AMOS
Automatic Meteorological, Oceanographic, (and Radiation) Station ..... AMO(R)S
Automatic Meteorological Oceanographic Buoy [*Marine science*] (MSC) ..... AMOB
Automatic Meteorological System (RDA) ..... AMS
Automatic Meteorological System - Artillery (MCD) ..... AMS-A
Automatic Meter Reading ..... AMR
Automatic Meter Reading Association (EA) ..... AMRA
Automatic Microfiche Editor ..... AME
Automatic Microfilm Information System ..... AMFIS
Automatic Microscope Electronic Data Accumulator (MHDB) ..... AMEDA
Automatic Miss Distance Indicator ..... AMDI
Automatic Mission Control ..... AMC
Automatic Mixture Control ..... AMC
Automatic Modal Tuning and Analysis System (NASA) ..... AMTAS
Automatic Mode Status (CAAL) ..... AMS
Automatic Modulation Control (DEN) ..... AMC
Automatic Module for Industrial Control Analysis ..... AMICA
Automatic Monitoring (CET) ..... AM
Automatic Monitoring Circuit [*Telecommunications*] (OA) ..... AMC
Automatic Monitoring Equipment ..... AME
Automatic Monitoring System [*Aviation*] ..... AMS
Automatic Moon Tracking ..... AMT
Automatic Motion Control System (MCD) ..... AMCS
Automatic Motion Inhibit [*Nuclear energy*] (NRCH) ..... AMI
Automatic Motor Tester ..... AMT
Automatic Moving Target Indicator (MSA) ..... AMTI
Automatic Multiaddress Segregation System (MCD) ..... AMASS
Automatic Multiaddress Segregation System ..... AMSS
Automatic Multiloop Optimal Approach Controller [*Navy*] ..... AMOAC
Automatic Multimode Mass Spectrometry ..... AMMS
Automatic Multiparameter Semiconductor Test Set ..... AMSTS
Automatic Multipattern Metering [*Photography*] ..... AMP
Automatic Multiple Blade Damper (OA) ..... AMBD
Automatic Multiple-Parameter Collection Processing System [*Air Force*] (MCD) ..... AMCAPS
Automatic Multi-Program Selection [*Photography*] [*Minolta Corp.*] ..... AMPS
Automatic Musical Instrument Collectors Association (EA) ..... AMICA
Automatic Navigation and Data Acquisition System ..... ANDAS
Automatic Navigation Computer for Land and Amphibious Vehicles ..... ANCLAV
Automatic Navigation Kit (MCD) ..... ANK
Automatic Navigation System ..... ANS
Automatic Nesting Program [*Kongsberg Vaapenfabrikk*] [*Software package*] (NCC) ..... AUTONEST
Automatic Network Analyzer ..... ANA
Automatic Network Dialing [*Telecommunications*] (TEL) ..... AND
Automatic Network Display ..... AUTONET
Automatic Network Routing [*Telecommunications*] (ACRL) ..... ANR
Automatic Nitrogen Transfer System ..... ANTS
Automatic Noise Figure Indicator (MCD) ..... ANFI
Automatic Noise Limiter [*Electronics*] ..... ANL
Automatic Noise Reduction Circuit [*Electronics*] ..... ANRC
Automatic Noise-Landing (DNAB) ..... ANL
Automatic Null Steering/Surveillance Array System (MCD) ..... ANSAS
Automatic Number Analysis (NITA) ..... ANA
Automatic Number Announcer [*Telecommunications*] (TEL) ..... ANA
Automatic Number Identification [*Telecommunications*] ..... ANI
Automatic Number Identification Failure [*Telecommunications*] (TEL) ..... ANF
Automatic Observer ..... AO
Automatic Operating and Scheduling Program [*Computer science*] ..... AOSP
Automatic Operating System [*IBM Corp.*] ..... AUTOPSY
Automatic Operation Control ..... AOC
Automatic Operations Panel ..... AOP
Automatic Optical Bench [*Hughes Aircraft Co.*] ..... AOB
Automatic Outgoing Message Processor System (NVT) ..... AOMPS
Automatic Outgoing Trunk Test [*Bell System*] ..... AOTT
Automatic Output Control ..... AOC
Automatic Overdrive ..... AOD
Automatic Overdrive Transaxle [*Automotive engineering*] ..... AXOD
Automatic Overload (IAA) ..... AUTOOVLD

Automatic Overload Circuit .... AOC	Automatic Programming [*Computer science*] .... AP
Automatic Overload Circuit (MSA) .... AOVC	Automatic Programming [*Computer science*] .... AUTO PROG
Automatic Overload Control (IEEE) .... AOC	Automatic Programming and Recording [*Computer science*] .... APAR
Automatic Page Composition (DGA) .... APC	Automatic Programming and Recording [*Computer science*] (MCD) .... APR
Automatic Page Search [*Imtec Co.*] [*Information retrieval*] (NITA) .... APS	Automatic Programming for Positioning System (DNAB) .... AUTOPROPS
Automatic Paralleling Relay (MCD) .... APR	Automatic Programming Information Centre [*British*] .... APIC
Automatic Particle Size Analyzer (OA) .... APSA	Automatic Programming Instruction [*Computer science*] .... API
Automatic Parts Handler .... APH	Automatic Programming Language [*Computer science*] (CMD) .... APL
Automatic Parts Testing (IAA) .... APT	Automatic Programming Machine [*Computer science*] .... APM
Automatic Passbook Reader (BUR) .... APR	Automatic Programming National Information Center .... APNIC
Automatic Passenger Counter [*FTA*] (TAG) .... APC	Automatic Programming of Lathes (PDAA) .... AUTOPOL
Automatic Passenger Counting .... APC	Automatic Programming of Machine Tools [*IBM Corp.*] .... AUTOPROMT
Automatic Patching System (IEEE) .... APS	Automatic Programming System Extended [*Computer science*] (IAA) .... APX
Automatic Pattern Recognition .... APR	Automatic Programming Tool [*Computer science*] (NITA) .... APT
Automatic Payroll Deposit Plan (DNAB) .... APDP	Automatic Progression Testing (TEL) .... APT
Automatic Performance Analysis System .... APAS	Automatic Proof of Delivery .... AUTOPOD
Automatic Performance Control .... APC	Automatic Propulsion Control System (DNAB) .... APS
Automatic Performance Reserve .... APR	Automatic Protection Switching [*Telecommunications*] (ACRL) .... APS
Automatic Performance Review [*Aerospace*] .... APR	Automatic Provisioning System [*Military*] (CAAL) .... APS
Automatic Permanent Magnetic-Field Compensator (PDAA) .... APMC	Automatic Pulse-Analyzer (DNAB) .... APA
Automatic Personal Accident [*Insurance*] (AIA) .... Auto PA	Automatic Quench Calibration [*or Correction*] .... AQC
Automatic Personal Identification Code [*IBM Corp.*] .... AUTOPIC	Automatic Quench Compensation [*Beckman Instruments, Inc.*]
Automatic Personnel Locator .... APL	[*Instrumentation*] .... AQC
Automatic Phase and Amplitude Data System (MCD) .... APADAS	Automatic RADAR Beacon .... ARB
Automatic Phase Control [*Telecommunications*] (TEL) .... APC	Automatic RADAR Beacon Sequencer .... ARBS
Automatic Phase Lock .... APL	Automatic RADAR Chain Acquisition System [*Air Force*] .... ARCAS
Automatic Phase Shifter .... APS	Automatic RADAR Control and Data Equipment .... ARCADE
Automatic Phase Synchronization .... APS	Automatic RADAR Data Measuring Equipment .... ARDME
Automatic Phased-Locked Loop (PDAA) .... APLL	Automatic RADAR Distance Measuring Equipment (MSA) .... ARDME
Automatic Phase-Locked Loop [*Electronics*] (IAA) .... APLL	Automatic RADAR Pattern Recognition (MCD) .... ARPR
Automatic Phono-Cardiac Analyzer (SAA) .... APCA	Automatic RADAR Plotting Aids .... ARPA
Automatic Phonograph Manufacturers Association .... APMA	Automatic Radar Plotting Disc [*Navy*] .... ARPD
Automatic Photographic Analysis .... APA	Automatic RADAR Plotting System [*Collision avoidance aid*] .... ARPS
Automatic Picture Control (IDOE) .... APC	Automatic RADAR Reconnaissance Exploitation System .... ARRES
Automatic Picture Taking (IEEE) .... APT	Automatic Radiating Tester .... ART
Automatic Picture Transmission [*NASA*] .... APT	Automatic Radiation Monitoring System (MCD) .... ARMS
Automatic Picture Transmission Ground System (NOAA) .... APTGS	Automatic Radio Control .... ARC
Automatic Picture Transmission System [*or Subsystem*] [*NASA*] .... APTS	Automatic Radio Control (ECII) .... ARC
Automatic Pilot (MCD) .... A/P	Automatic Radio Information [*System which relays traffic information through
Automatic Pilot System .... APS	car radios*] .... ARI
Automatic Pistol .... AUTOP	Automatic Radio Location Beacon (PDAA) .... ARLB
Automatic Pitch Control .... APC	Automatic Radio Manufacturing Co., Inc. .... AR
Automatic Planetary Station [*Astronomy*] .... APS	Automatic Radio Meteorological Measurements and Survey (IAA) .... ARMS
Automatic Plate Processor .... APP	Automatic Radiotheodolite [*Meteorology*] .... ART
Automatic Plotting Routine (ADA) .... AUTOPLOT	Automatic Ram Control (CAAL) .... ARC
Automatic Plugging Meter (PDAA) .... APM	Automatic Random Access Transport .... ARAT
Automatic Point Marking, Measuring, and Recording Instrument .... APMMRI	Automatic Range Compensating [*Firearms*] .... ARC
Automatic Point of Sale System (IAA) .... APOSS	Automatic Range Control .... ARC
Automatic Point Positioning System (MCD) .... APPS	Automatic Range Detection and Measuring Equipment .... ARDME
Automatic Point Transfer Instrument (MCD) .... APTI	Automatic Range Only .... ARO
Automatic Polarity Indication (IAA) .... AUTPOL	Automatic Range Tracker [*or Tracking*] .... ART
Automatic Polling [*Computer science*] (EECA) .... AUTOPOLL	Automatic Range Tracking Unit [*Military*] .... ARTU
Automatic Position Planning .... APP	Automatic Range Unit .... ARU
Automatic Position Reference Monitor (IEEE) .... APRM	Automatic Ranging Telescope [*Weaponry*] (INF) .... ART
Automatic Position Reference System .... APRS	Automatic Rate Changer .... ARC
Automatic Position Telemetering .... APT	Automatic Rate Control .... ARC
Automatic Positioning Equipment .... APE	Automatic Reasoning Tool (MCD) .... ART
Automatic Positioning Telemetering Antenna .... APOTA	Automatic Receiving and Measuring System (MCD) .... ARMS
Automatic Potential Control (MHDI) .... APC	Automatic Recirculation Valve [*Engineering*] .... ARC
Automatic Power Control (NTCM) .... APC	Automatic Reclosing (IAA) .... AUTORECL
Automatic Power Input Controller .... APIC	Automatic Recogniton of Continuous Speech (PDAA) .... ARCS
Automatic Power Plant Checker .... APPC	Automatic Record Analysis Language [*Computer science*] .... ARAL
Automatic Power Reserve [*Aeronautics*] .... APR	Automatic Record Evaluation .... ARE
Automatic Power-Factor-Control Systems (IEEE) .... APFCS	Automatic Record Evaluation System .... ARES
Automatic Precipitation Gauge (NOAA) .... APG	Automatic Record Level (IAA) .... ARL
Automatic Predictive Maintenance (MHDI) .... APM	Automatic Recording and Reduction Facility .... ARRF
Automatic Premium Loan [*Insurance*] .... APL	Automatic Recording Infrared Spectrometer .... ARIS
Automatic Press Feed .... APF	Automatic Recording Spectrometer .... ARS
Automatic Pressure Conveyor .... APC	Automatic Recovery Option [*NCR Corp.*] (NITA) .... ARO
Automatic Pressure Relief [*Nuclear energy*] (NRCH) .... APR	Automatic Recovery Process (MCD) .... ARP
Automatic Pressure Relief System [*Military*] (CAAL) .... APRS	Automatic Recovery System .... ARS
Automatic Printed Circuit Board Routing with Intermediate Control of the	Automatic Reel Mounting .... ARM
Tracking (MHDB) .... APRICOT	Automatic Reentry Flight Dynamics Simulator [*NASA*] (NASA) .... ARFDS
Automatic Priority Group [*Fujitsu Ltd.*] [*Japan*] (MCD) .... APG	Automatic Reference System .... ARS
Automatic Priority Interrupt [*Computer science*] .... API	Automatic Reference System/Sequential Launch Adapter .... ARS/SLA
Automatic Processing and Recording (NITA) .... APAR	Automatic Regulation and Electronic Protection .... AREP
Automatic Processing of Jezebel [*Sonobuoy System*] Information .... APOJI	Automatic Relative Plotter (IAA) .... ARP
Automatic Processing System (MCD) .... APS	Automatic Relay Calculator [*Early computer*] [*Birkbeck College*] [*British*]
Automatic Procurement Capability System .... AUTOPROC	(MCD) .... ARC
Automatic Production Line .... APL	Automatic Relay Computer (IAA) .... ARC
Automatic Production Record System .... APRS	Automatic Release Data (AAGC) .... ARD
Automatic Production Recording .... APR	Automatic Release Date [*Military*] (AABC) .... ARD
Automatic Production Test Equipment (DNAB) .... APTE	Automatic Reliability Mathematical Model (DNAB) .... ARMM
Automatic Program Analysis Report [*Computer science*] (BUR) .... APAR	Automatic Remote Cassette Handler (NTCM) .... ARCH
Automatic Program Finding [*Electronics*] .... APF	Automatic Remote Control (DEN) .... ARC
Automatic Program Loading Unit [*Computer science*] .... APLU	Automatic Remote Data Terminal (IAA) .... ARDT
Automatic Program Selection [*Automobile accessory*] .... APS	Automatic Remote Manned System (MCD) .... ARMS
Automatic Program System [*Computer science*] .... APS	Automatic Remote Terminal Information System .... ARTIS
Automatic Program Unit, High-Speed [*Component of ADIS*] .... APUHS	Automatic Repeat Request [*Computer science*] (MCD) .... ARQ
Automatic Program Unit, Low-Speed [*Component of ADIS*] .... APULS	Automatic Repeat Request Mode Counter [*Computer science*] (IAA) .... ARMC
Automatic Programmed Checkout Equipment .... APCHE	Automatic Reporting Feature (MCD) .... ARF
Automatic Programmed Test Input (NASA) .... APTI	Automatic Reporting Maintenance System (MCD) .... ARMS
Automatic Programmer and Data System [*Air Force*] .... APADS	Automatic Reporting Post [*Air defense*] [*NATO*] (NATG) .... ARP
Automatic Programmer and Test System [*Army*] .... APATS	Automatic Reporting Telephone [*Telecommunications*] (TEL) .... ART
Automatic Programmer and Test System [*Army*] (MCD) .... APTS	Automatic Request (IAA) .... ARQ

Automatic Request [*Computer science*] (DOM) .... ARQ
Automatic Request for Correction (NITA) .... ARQ
Automatic Requirements Engineering Systems (MCD) .... ARES
Automatic Rerouting [*Telecommunications*] (TEL) .... ARR
Automatic Reseau Measuring Equipment (MCD) .... ARME
Automatic Reservation and Communication (IAA) .... ARCO
Automatic Reserve Ripcord Release [*for a parachute*] (RDA) AR3
Automatic Reset Counter .... ARC
Automatic Resistance Test Set .... ARTS
Automatic Resolution Selection Control (NITA) .... ARSC
Automatic Responsivity Control (MCD) .... ARC
Automatic Resupply (NVT) .... AR
Automatic Resupply and Buildup Time [*Air Force*] (AFIT) .... AIRBUT
Automatic Resupply Logistics System (AFM) .... ARLS
Automatic Retailers of America (MCD) .... ARA
Automatic Retransmission Exchange [*ITT World Communications, Inc.*]
  [*Secaucus, NJ*] (TSSD) .... ARX
Automatic Retransmission Queue [*Computer science*] (HGAA) .... ARQ
Automatic Retransmission Request for Correction [*Computer science*]
  (NTCM) .... ARQ
Automatic Retrieval of Text from Europe's Multinational Information
  Service .... ARTEMIS
Automatic Retrieval of Text through European Multipurpose Information
  (NITA) .... ARTEMIS
Automatic Return Fire [*ARPA*] .... ARF
Automatic Return Item List (MCD) .... ARIL
Automatic Return Items (AABC) .... ARI
Automatic Ride Control Suspension [*Automotive engineering*] .... ARC
Automatic Rifle [*or Rifleman*] [*DoD*] .... AR
Automatic Road Analyzer [*FHWA*] (TAG) .... ARAN
Automatic Rocket Impact Predictor .... ARIP
Automatic Route Advancement (MCD) .... ARA
Automatic Route Control System [*Truck-delivery computer system*] .... ARCS
Automatic Route Selection [*Also, MERS*] [*Bell System*]
  [*Telecommunications*] .... ARS
Automatic Routine Generating and Updating System [*Compiler*] [*Computer
  science*] .... ARGUS
Automatic Rubber Tensile Tester (PDAA) .... ARTT
Automatic Rudder Control (MUGU) .... ARCON
Automatic Safety Monitor [*PUR*] (PS) .... ASM
Automatic Sample Preparation Extraction Column [*Chromatography*] .... ASPEC
Automatic Sample Processor (KSC) .... ASP
Automatic Sample Processor and Injector .... ASPI
Automatic Sampling Injector .... ASI
Automatic Satellite / Computer Aid to Navigation [*Computer science*]
  (PDAA) .... AUTOSCAN
Automatic Scan Counter .... ASC
Automatic Scan Counter System .... ASCS
Automatic Scan Tracking [*Videotape head*] (NTCM) .... AST
Automatic Scanning Control Unit .... ASCU
Automatic Scanning Correlator .... AUSCOR
Automatic Scanning Unit Out of Service (FAAC) .... SCANO
Automatic Scanning Unit Returned to Service (FAAC) .... SCAOK
Automatic Schedule Procedure .... ASP
Automatic Scheduling and Operating Program (BUR) .... ASOP
Automatic Scheduling Message (GFGA) .... ASM
Automatic Scheduling with Time-Integrated Resource Allocation .... ASTRA
Automatic Science Citation Alerting (IEEE) .... ASCA
Automatic SDI [*Selective Dissemination of Information*] [*British Library
  Automated Information Service*] (NITA) .... AUTOSD
Automatic Secure Voice Communications (CAAL) .... ASVC
Automatic Secure Voice Communications .... AUTOSEVCOM
Automatic Secure Voice Communications (NVT) .... AUTOSEVOCOM
Automatic Secure Voice Communications Network .... AUTOSEVOCON
Automatic Selection of Any Channel (IAA) .... ASAC
Automatic Selection of Digital Electronic Computers .... ASDEC
Automatic Selective Dissemination of Information .... ASDI
Automatic Selectivity Control (DEN) .... ASC
Automatic Self-Powered Cannon (MCD) .... ASP
Automatic Self-Verification .... ASV
Automatic Send/Receive Teletypewriter [*or Terminal*] [*Communications
  equipment*] .... AS/R
Automatic Sensitivity Control [*Aviation*] .... ASC
Automatic Sequence Control [*Computer science*] (EECA) .... ASC
Automatic Sequence Controlled Calculator [*First all-automatic calculating
  machine*] .... ASCC
Automatic Sequence Enable .... ASE
Automatic Sequence Execution and Processor (MCD) .... ASEP
Automatic Sequence Register (NTCM) .... ASR
Automatic Services and Products .... ASP
Automatic Servo Plotter .... ASP
Automatic Shaft-Position Data Encoder .... ASPDE
Automatic Sheet Feeder .... ASF
Automatic Shift Keying (HGAA) .... ASK
Automatic Shipboard Checkout and Readiness Equipment (MCD) .... ASCORE
Automatic Shipboard Launch Aircraft Data System .... ASLADS
Automatic Ship's Heading Measurement System (DNAB) .... ASHMS
Automatic Shop Tester (OA) .... AST
Automatic Shorebased Acceptance Checkout Equipment (PDAA) .... AutoSACE
Automatic Shot Dispensing Pump .... ASDP
Automatic Shutdown [*Automotive engineering*] .... ASD
Automatic Shuttle Valve .... ASV
Automatic Signal Excess Prediction System [*Military*] (CAAL) .... ASEPS
Automatic Signal Filtration [*Electronics*] (IAA) .... ASF
Automatic Signal Processing Unit (MCD) .... ASPU

Automatic Signal Recognition Unit (IAA) .... ASRU
Automatic Signature Verification System .... ASVS
Automatic Skin [*NASA*] (KSC) .... AS
Automatic Sky Quality Assessment (MCD) .... ASQA
Automatic Slack Adjuster [*Truck brakes*] .... ASA
Automatic Solution Crystal Growth [*Materials processing*] .... ASCG
Automatic SONAR Readout .... ASR
Automatic Sorting, Testing, Recording Analysis .... ASTRA
Automatic Space Management .... ASM
Automatic Space Plasma Experiment with a Rotating Analyser
  [*Instrumentation*] .... ASPERA
Automatic Spares Analysis Technique .... ASAT
Automatic Sparrow Operational Test Systems (MCD) .... ASOTS
Automatic Specimen Positioning .... ASP
Automatic Specimen Positioning System .... ASPS
Automatic Speckle Cancellation Techniques (PDAA) .... ASPECT
Automatic Spectrum Analyzer (MHDB) .... ASA
Automatic Spectrum Display and Signal Recognition System (IEEE) .... ASDSRS
Automatic Speech Exchange System [*Voice messaging*] .... ASPEN
Automatic Speech Recognition .... ASR
Automatic Speed Control Device .... ASCD
Automatic Spooling with Asynchronous Processing [*Computer science*]
  (PDAA) .... ASAP
Automatic Spray Gun .... ASG
Automatic Sprinkler [*Technical drawings*] .... AS
Automatic Sprinkler Riser [*Technical drawings*] .... ASR
Automatic Stability Control System [*Bavarian Motor Works*] [*Automotive
  engineering*] .... ASC
Automatic Stability Regulation [*Automotive engineering*] .... ASR
Automatic Stabilization and Control System .... ASCS
Automatic Stabilization Equipment .... ASE
Automatic Stabilization System .... ASS
Automatic Standard Magnetic Observatory .... ASMO
Automatic Standard Magnetic Observatory - Remote .... ASMOR
Automatic Starter .... ASt
Automatic Starter .... AUTOSTRT
Automatic Starting .... AUTOSTRTG
Automatic Start-Up System [*Reactor*] .... ASS
Automatic Station Identification Device .... ASID
Automatic Station Keeping System .... ASKS
Automatic Status Board Subsystem (MCD) .... ASTABS
Automatic Steam-Temperature Control .... ASTC
Automatic Steerable Null Antenna Processor .... ASNAP
Automatic Steering Antenna .... ASA
Automatic Stellar Tracking, Recognition, and Orientation Computer .... ASTROC
Automatic Step Regulator .... ASR
Automatic Stereo Broadcast Scanner (IAA) .... AUTOSCAN
Automatic Stereo Recording Amplifier .... ASRA
Automatic Stiffening (MSA) .... AUTOSTIF
Automatic Stop and Check Valve (AAG) .... AUTO S & CV
Automatic Stop Announcement .... ASA
Automatic Store and Forward .... ASF
Automatic Storm Observation Service [*AFCRL*] .... ASOS
Automatic Strength Regulation (IAA) .... ASR
Automatic Strobe Tracking (CET) .... ASTRA
Automatic Structure Analysis of Mass Spectra .... ASAMS
Automatic Submarine Control [*Navy*] (MCD) .... ASC
Automatic Submerged Arc Welding Process (NUCP) .... ASAW
Automatic Support Equipment [*Military*] .... ASE
Automatic Surveillance Receiver (MCD) .... ASR
Automatic Sustainer Cutoff (MUGU) .... ASCO
Automatic Switching [*Telecommunications*] (OA) .... AS
Automatic Switching and Processing [*Command Communications, Inc.*]
  [*Telecommunications*] (PCM) .... ASAP
Automatic Switching Center .... ASC
Automatic Switching Panel .... ASP
Automatic Switching Unit [*Telecommunications*] .... ASU
Automatic Synchronized Control (DEN) .... ASC
Automatic Synchronized Discriminator (DEN) .... ASD
Automatic Synchronizer .... AS
Automatic Synthesis Program .... ASP
Automatic System Checkout Program .... ASCP
Automatic System Control .... ASC
Automatic System for Positioning Tools .... AUTOSPOT
Automatic System for Selection of Receiver and Transmitter [*Computer
  science*] (MHDB) .... ASSORT
Automatic System Self-Test [*Aviation*] (MCD) .... ASST
Automatic System Trouble Analysis [*Computer science*] (MHDB) .... ASTA
Automatic Systems Analysis (KSC) .... ASA
Automatic Systems for Kinematic Analysis [*NASA*] (NASA) .... ASKA
Automatic Systems Management and Control [*Aviation*] (OA) .... ASMC
Automatic Systems Pressure Alarm (PDAA) .... ASPA
Automatic Systems Test Unit .... ASTU
Automatic Tabulating, Listing, and Sorting System [*Software*] .... ATLAS
Automatic Tactical Air Control Center (MCD) .... ATACC
Automatic TAEM [*Terminal Area Energy Management*] [*NASA*] (NASA) .... AT
Automatic Takeoff Thrust Control System (IEEE) .... ATTCS
Automatic Tally and Sort (PDAA) .... ATS
Automatic Tank Target System [*Military*] (INF) .... ATTS
Automatic Tap Changing .... ATC
Automatic Tape Degausser .... ATD
Automatic Tape Handler (IAA) .... ATH
Automatic Tape Load Audit System .... ATLAS
Automatic Tape Reader (DNAB) .... ATR
Automatic Tape Winder (IAA) .... ATW

Automatic Target Acquisition (MCD) ... ATA
Automatic Target Acquisition, Detection (MCD) ... ATAD
Automatic Target and Battery Evaluation [*Military*] ... ATABE
Automatic Target Counting ... ATC
Automatic Target Designation ... ATAD
Automatic Target Designation ... ATD
Automatic Target Detection (MCD) ... ATD
Automatic Target Evaluator and Weapon Assignor ... ATEWA
Automatic Target Finder (IAA) ... ATF
Automatic Target Follow ... ATF
Automatic Target Handoff Computer (MCD) ... ATHOC
Automatic Target Handoff System (DOMA) ... ATAH
Automatic Target Handover System [*Army*] ... ATHS
Automatic Target Handover System/Avionics Integration ... ATHS/AI
Automatic Target Identification ... ATI
Automatic Target Recognition ... ATR
Automatic Target Recognition Analysis ... AUTRAN
Automatic Target Recognition Device ... ATRD
Automatic Target Recognition, Identification, and Detection ... ATRID
Automatic Target Scoring Systems (MCD) ... ATSS
Automatic Target Selection File (CINC) ... ATSF
Automatic Target Tracking (MCD) ... ATT
Automatic Teaching Device ... ATD
Automatic Technical Reliability Assessment of PATRIOT [*Phased Array Tracking to Intercept of Target*] ... ATRAP
Automatic Techniques for Selection and Identification of Targets [*Army/Air Force*] (MCD) ... ATSIT
Automatic Telecommunications Switching System ... ATSS
Automatic Telecommunications Switching System - Data Services [*Computer science*] (MHDI) ... ATSS-D
Automatic Telecommunications System Security Manager [*Military*] (GFGA) ... ATSSM
Automatic Telegram Transmission with Computers [*Telecommunications*] (TEL) ... ATECO
Automatic Telegraph Message Switching System (PDAA) ... ATMSS
Automatic Telegraph Subsystem [*Navy British*] (MCD) ... ATSS
Automatic Telemetry Decommutation System ... ATDS
Automatic Telemetry System ... ATS
Automatic Telemetry Tracking Antenna System (MCD) ... ATTRAS
Automatic Telemetry Tracking Receiving Antenna ... ATTRA
Automatic Telemetry Tracking System [*NASA*] ... ATTS
Automatic Telephone (IAA) ... AT
Automatic Telephone Call (IAA) ... ATC
Automatic Telephone Call Distribution (PDAA) ... ACTD
Automatic Telephone Exchange (NITA) ... ATE
Automatic Telephone Set ... ATS
Automatic Telephone Switching System (NITA) ... ATSS
Automatic Telephone Using Radio [*Telecommunications service*] (TEL) ... ATUR
Automatic Teleprinter Exchange Service [*of Western Union Corp.*] ... TEX
Automatic Teletypewriter Exchange Service [*of Western Union*] ... TELEX
Automatic TELEX Exchange [*Telecommunications*] (TEL) ... ATX
Automatic Telling [*Banking*] (IAA) ... ATL
Automatic Temperature Compensation ... ATC
Automatic Temperature Control ... ATC
Automatic Temporary Roof Support [*Mining industry*] ... ATRS
Automatic Terminal Approach System (MCD) ... ATAS
Automatic Terminal Information Service [*Aviation*] (AFM) ... ATIS
Automatic Terminal System [*NASA*] (NASA) ... ATS
Automatic Terrain Avoidance [*Air Force*] ... ATA
Automatic Terrain Avoidance System [*Military*] ... ATAS
Automatic Terrain Following [*Military*] (MCD) ... ATF
Automatic Terrain Following/Automatic Terrain Avoidance [*Military*] ... ATF/ATA
Automatic Terrain Recognition and Identification Device (PDAA) ... ATRID
Automatic Terrain Recognition and Navigation Guidance System ... ATRAN
Automatic Terrain-Following RADAR [*Military*] ... ATFR
Automatic Test ... AT
Automatic Test Analysis System ... ATAS
Automatic Test and Checkout Equipment (AFM) ... ATCE
Automatic Test and Evaluation ... ATE
Automatic Test Break and Access [*Telecommunications*] (TEL) ... ATBA
[*An*] **Automatic Test Control System** (MCD) ... AATCS
Automatic Test Control System [*Air Force*] ... ATCS
Automatic [*or Automated*] **Test Equipment** [*or Testing*] (NASA) ... ATE
Automatic Test Equipment (AAGC) ... ATE
Automatic Test Equipment Complex (MCD) ... ATEC
Automatic Test Equipment Compute [*or Computer*] ... ATC
Automatic Test Equipment for Internal Combustion Engines (MCD) ... ATE/ICE
Automatic Test Equipment Language Standardization (MCD) ... ATLAS
Automatic Test Equipment Materiel Manager ... ATEMM
Automatic Test Equipment, Missile (MCD) ... ATEM
Automatic Test Equipment Software Support Environment [*Computer science*] ... ATESSE
Automatic Test Equipment Support Center [*Army*] ... ATESC
Automatic Test Formatter (NITA) ... ATF
Automatic Test Generation Facility (MHDI) ... ATGF
Automatic Test Generator ... ATG
Automatic Test Grading ... ATG
Automatic Test Guide ... ATG
Automatic Test Language for All Systems [*DoD*] ... ATLAS
Automatic Test Line ... ATL
Automatic Test Message Handling (MCD) ... ATMH
Automatic Test Pattern [*or Program*] **Generation** (MCD) ... ATPG
Automatic Test Scoring ... ATS
Automatic Test Set [*Support*] [*Military*] (DOMA) ... ATSE
Automatic Test Support Systems (RDA) ... ATSS
Automatic Test System ... ATS
Automatic Test System Jet Engine Accessories ... ATSJEA
Automatic Testing Committee (AAGC) ... ATC
Automatic Testing, Evaluation, and Reporting ... ATER
Automatic Testing Multiple Operating System (MCD) ... ATMOS
Automatic Text Formatter ... ATF
Automatic Thin-Layer Analytical System ... ATLAS
Automatic Threat Detection System [*Aviation*] (DA) ... ATD
Automatic Three Speed [*DOE*] (TAG) ... A3
Automatic Three-Axis Stabilization ... ATAS
Automatic Three-Dimensional Electronics Scanning Array (IAA) ... ATDESA
Automatic Three-Dimensional Electronics Scanning Array (MUGU) ... ATHESA
Automatic Threshold Circuit (MCD) ... ATC
Automatic Threshold Variation ... ATV
Automatic Throttle Control (SAA) ... ATC
Automatic Throttle/Speed Control System (MCD) ... ATS
Automatic through Center [*Telecommunications*] (OA) ... ATC
Automatic through Junction [*Telecommunications*] (OA) ... ATJ
Automatic Thrust Vector Control [*NASA*] ... ATVC
Automatic Ticket Vendors (ADA) ... ATV
Automatic Ticketing ... AT
Automatic Time Element Compensator (SAA) ... AMTEC
Automatic Time Interval Measurement System [*Air Force*] ... ATIMS
Automatic Timing Corrector ... ATC
Automatic Timing Device [*Diesel engines*] ... ATD
Automatic Tint Control [*Electronics*] (IAA) ... ATC
Automatic Toll Ticketing (TEL) ... ATT
Automatic Tone Control ... ATC
Automatic Tone Correction ... ATC
Automatic Toning Machine [*Color printing technology*] ... ATM
Automatic Tool Changer ... ATC
Automatic Topographic Mapper ... ATOM
Automatic Torque Biasing Differential [*Automotive engineering*] ... ATBD
Automatic Track Acquisition ... ATA
Automatic Track Finding [*System*] [*Video technology*] ... ATF
Automatic Track Initiation ... ATI
Automatic Tracking (IAA) ... AT
Automatic Tracking Antenna ... ATA
Automatic Tracking Antenna System ... ATAS
Automatic Tracking Control (MSA) ... ATC
Automatic Tracking Feature (NVT) ... ATF
Automatic Tracking LASER Illumination System (MCD) ... ATLIS
Automatic Tracking Razor Action [*The Gillette Co.*] ... ATRA
Automatic Tracking Telemetry Receiving System (DNAB) ... ATTRS
Automatic Tracking Unit ... ATU
Automatic Track-while-Scan [*Radar*] ... ATWS
Automatic Traction Control [*Automotive engineering*] ... ATC
Automatic Traffic Control ... ATC
Automatic Traffic Engineering and Management Information System (MHDI) ... ATEMIS
Automatic Traffic Recorder [*Telecommunications*] (NITA) ... ATR
Automatic Traffic Recording and Analysis Complex (IAA) ... AUTRAX
Automatic Traffic Usage Recording System (TEL) ... ATURS
Automatic Traffic-Flow Control (MHDB) ... ATFC
Automatic Traffic-Flow Control (MHDB) ... ATFC
Automatic Train Control ... ATC
Automatic Train Operation (BARN) ... ATO
Automatic Train Protection [*TRB*] (TAG) ... ATP
Automatic Train Stop (SAA) ... ATS
Automatic Train Supervision (BARN) ... ATS
Automatic Transaxle ... ATX
Automatic Transfer of Savings [*Banking*] ... ATS
Automatic Transfer Service [*Banking*] ... ATS
Automatic Transfer Switch ... ATS
Automatic Transfer Switches [*Standby electrical power systems*] ... ATS
Automatic Transformer (IEEE) ... AXFMR
Automatic Transient Detection System (MCD) ... ATDS
Automatic Transistor Test Equipment ... ATTE
Automatic Translation ... AT
Automatic Translation ... AUTOTRAN
Automatic Transmission [*Automotive engineering*] ... A/T
Automatic Transmission [*Automotive engineering*] ... A/TRANS
Automatic Transmission Control Unit [*Automotive engineering*] ... ATCU
Automatic Transmission Fluid ... ATF
Automatic Transmission Measuring Equipment [*Telecommunications*] (TEL) ... ATME
Automatic Transmission Measuring System [*Terminated*] ... ATMS
Automatic Transmission of Mail [*Early electronic mail system*] ... ATOM
Automatic Transmission Rebuilders Association (EA) ... ATRA
Automatic Transmission System [*Telecommunications*] (NTCM) ... ATS
Automatic Transmission Test and Control [*Telecommunications*] (TEL) ... ATTC
Automatic Transmitter ... AT
Automatic Transmitter Identification System [*Citizens band radio*] ... ATIS
Automatic Transportation Research Investigation Program (PDAA) ... AUTO-TRIP
Automatic Trim System (PDAA) ... ATS
Automatic Trouble Analysis (TEL) ... ATA
Automatic Trunk Measuring System [*Bell System*] ... ATMS
Automatic Trunk Office [*Telecommunications*] (OA) ... ATO
Automatic Trunk Routiner (MCD) ... ATR
Automatic Trunk Synchronizer [*Telecommunications*] (TEL) ... ATS
Automatic Tuned Circuit Adjustment [*Telecommunications*] (OA) ... ATCA
Automatic Tuned Circuit Adjustment Amplitude [*Telecommunications*] (OA) ... ATCAA
Automatic Tuning (IAA) ... ATTUN
Automatic Tuning (IAA) ... AUTTUN

Automatic Tuning Control ATC
Automatic Tuning Device ATD
Automatic Tuning System ATS
Automatic Turbidity Compensation Hemoglobin Test ATC
Automatic Turbine Tester (NRCH) ATT
Automatic Turret Lathe ATL
Automatic Type Placement System ATPS
Automatic Typewriter (IAA) AT
Automatic Unattended Detection Inspection Transmitter [*Raytheon Co.*] AUDIT
Automatic Unit for National Taxation and Insurance (MHDB) AUNTIE
Automatic Universal Translator AUNT
Automatic Unmanned Weather Station AUWS
Automatic Update Transaction System [*DoD*] AUTS
Automatic Utility Translator (IEEE) AUTRAN
Automatic Vacuum Deposition System (IAA) AVDS
Automatic Valve Control (IEEE) AVC
Automatic Vapor Crystal Growth [*Materials processing*] AVCG
Automatic Variable Character Compensation (DGA) AVCC
Automatic Variable Orifice [*Steam trap of Agontz Corp.*] AVO
Automatic Variable Perforating AVP
Automatic Vehicle Classification [*Automotive engineering*] AVC
Automatic Vehicle Identification [*Automotive engineering*] AVI
Automatic Vehicle Location (IEEE) AVL
Automatic Vehicle Location System (DA) AVLS
Automatic Vehicle Monitoring [*Antihijack device*] AVM
Automatic Vehicle Monitoring System [*Army*] (MCD) AVMS
Automatic Vending Association of Britain (EAIO) AVAB
Automatic Vending Machine Association [*British*] (BI) AVMA
Automatic Vent Control (IEEE) AVC
Automatic Verification, Evaluation, and Readiness Tester AVERT
Automatic Vertical Electrophoresis System [*Instrumentation*] AVES
Automatic VFR [*Visual Flight Rules*] **Advisory Service** [*Aviation*] (OA) AVAS
Automatic Vibration Control AVC
Automatic Vibration Exciter Control AVEC
Automatic Video Noise Leveling [*or Limiting*] AVNL
Automatic Video Scoring System [*Army*] (INF) AVSS
Automatic Video Tracker AVT
Automatic Vision Testing (NITA) AVT
Automatic Visual Inspection System [*NASA*] AVIS
Automatic Vocal Transaction Analysis (IAA) AVTA
Automatic Voice Alerting Device (DA) AVAD
Automatic Voice Answering [*Computer-generated recording unit for telephone directory assistance*] AVA
Automatic Voice Data (MCD) AVD
Automatic Voice Link Observation AVOLO
Automatic Voice Network [*DoD*] AUTOVON
Automatic Voice Recognition (NITA) AVR
Automatic Voice Relay AVR
Automatic Voice Response [*Telephone*] (WDMC) AVR
Automatic Voice Switching Network (AFIT) AVSN
Automatic Voltage Control (NATG) AVC
Automatic Voltage Digitizer AVD
Automatic Voltage Regulator AVR
Automatic Volume [*Electronics*] (ECII) AV
Automatic Volume Control [*Telecommunications*] AVC
Automatic Volume Expansion AVE
Automatic Volume Recognition (MCD) AVR
Automatic Voting Machine AVM
Automatic Wage Payments (MCD) AWP
Automatic Warning and Control System AWCS
Automatic Water Check [*Freight*] AUTM WTR CK
Automatic Waveform Digitizing System (MCD) AWDS
Automatic Weapon (DNAB) AUTOWEAP
Automatic Weapons AW
Automatic Weapons Control System AWCS
Automatic Weapons Effect Signature Simulator (MCD) AWESS
Automatic Weapons Release System (DNAB) AWRS
Automatic Weapons (Self-Propelled) [*Military*] AWSP
Automatic Weather Broadcast (DA) AB
Automatic Weather Broadcast Equipment (FAAC) AWBE
Automatic Weather Observing/Reporting System (FAAC) AWOS
Automatic Weather Station AWS
Automatic Welding AW
Automatic Welding Machinery Association [*Defunct*] (EA) AWMA
Automatic Welding System AWS
Automatic Winder (IAA) AUW
Automatic Wire Data System (MCD) AWDS
Automatic Wire Wrap Machine AWWM
Automatic Withdrawal Prohibit [*Nuclear energy*] (NRCH) AWP
Automatic Word (SAA) AW
Automatic Work Control System [*Military*] (MCD) AWCS
Automatic Writing Machine AWM
Automatic X-Ray Inspection (MCD) AXIS
Automatic X-Ray Radiograph AXR
Automatic Yaw Control AYC
Automatic Zero Set [*Military*] AZS
Automatical Digital Relay (PDAA) ADR
Automatically Controlled Electrical System [*NASA*] (MCD) ACES
Automatically Controlled Transportation [*Airport passenger shuttle*] [*Ford Motor Co.*] ACT
Automatically Controlled Turbine Run-Up System [*Navigation*] ACTRUS
Automatically Cued Target Detecting System (MCD) ACTDS
Automatically Data Equalized MODEM [*Computer science*] (IAA) ADEM
Automatically Deployable Emergency Locator Transmitter [*Aviation*] (DA) ADELT
Automatically Directed Outgoing Intertoll Trunk [*Bell System*] ADOIT
Automatically Directed Outgoing Trunk [*Bell System*] ADOT
Automatically Erectable Modular Torus AEMT
Automatically Generated Test Analysis and Programs (MCD) AGTP
Automatically Operated Inlet Valve AOIV
Automatically Processed WIR [*Weapons Inspection Report*] **List** (CET) APWL
Automatically Programmed Remote Indication Logged APRIL
Automatically Programmed Tool [*Computer software*] [*Computer science*] APT
Automatically Programmed Tool - Advanced Contouring [*IBM Corp.*] APT-AC
Automatically Programmed Tool - Intermediate Contouring [*IBM Corp.*] APT-IC
Automatically Reconfigurable Modular Multiprocessor [*or Multiprocessing*] **System** [*Computer science*] ARMMS
Automatically Stabilized Maneuvering Unit [*NASA*] ASMU
Automatically Synchronous [*Remote-indicating system*] [*Trade name Western Electric Co.*] AUTOSYN
Automatically-Adjustable Shock-Absorber [*System*] [*Automotive engineering*] AAS
Automatically-Generated Integrated Circuit (DNAB) AGIC
Automatiches Schaltgetriebe ASG
Automatic-Landing Flight Experiment [*Space program*] [*Japan*] AFLEX
Automatic-Landing Flight Experiment [*Space program*] [*Japan*] ALFLEX
Automation (DS) A
Automation (MSA) AUTOMN
Automation AUTOMTN
Automation (AFM) AUTON
Automation and Control A & C
Automation and Robotics (SSD) A & R
Automation and Robotics Panel ARP
Automation and Robotics Research Institute [*University of Texas at Arlington*] [*Research center*] (RCD) ARRI
Automation Communication Resource Management Plan [*Army*] ACRMP
Automation Co. of Kentucky [*McDonnell Douglas Corp.*] AUT/KY
Automation Co. of Texas [*McDonnell Douglas Corp.*] AUT/TEX
Automation Composition System (MCD) ACS
Automation Device (IAA) AE
Automation Economic Analysis AEA
Automation Engineering Laboratory AEL
Automation for Storage and Retrieval of Information AFSARI
Automation Foundation AF
Automation GMBH [*McDonnell Douglas Corp.*] [*Germany*] AUT/GMBH
Automation Industries Research Laboratory (KSC) AIRL
Automation Institute (MCD) AI
Automation Instrument Data Service [*Computer-based industrial information system*] [*Indata Ltd.*] [*British*] AIDS
Automation Management Office [*Military*] (AABC) AMO
Automation of Bibliography through Computerization [*ABC-Clio Press*] ABC
Automation of Data Processing/Computerization of Information Systems [*Food Stamp Program*] [*Department of Agriculture*] (GFGA) ADP/CIS
Automation of Field Observations and Services AFOS
Automation of Field Operations and Services [*National Weather Service*] (MSC) AFOS
Automation of Interlending by Microcomputer [*British*] (NITA) AIM
Automation of Procurement and Accounting Data Entry [*Navy*] (GFGA) APADE
Automation of Wartime Functional Supply Requirements (MCD) AWFSR
Automation on Air Traffic Flow Management (DA) AUT-ATFM
Automation Planning and Technology APT
Automation Resource Group [*Wellesley, MA*] ARG
Automation Robotics and Machine Intelligence System (PDAA) ARAMIS
Automation Security Committee [*Military*] (GFGA) ASC
Automation Services - System Improvement - Solution and Tracking (MCD) ASSIST
Automation Society (EA) AS
Automation System for Scientific Experiments ASSE
Automation Techniques, Inc. ATI
Automation Technology Center [*Vicksburg, MS*] [*Army*] ATC
Automation Training Center (MCD) ATC
Automatische Korpsstamunetz [*Tactical Communications System*] [*Germany*] Autoko
Automatisering Landbouwkundige Dokumentatie-En Informatievespreiding in Nederland [*Automation of Agricultural Documentation and Information in the Netherlands*] [*Centre for Agricultural Publishing and Documentation*] (NITA) ALADIN
Automative Student Service Educational Training ASSET
Automator Control Language [*Computer science*] ACL
Automedica Corp. [*An association Defunct*] (EA) AM
Automic Fire Control System [*Army*] AFSC
Automicrobic System AMS
Automix Keyboards, Inc. AKI
Automized Medical Anamnesis Dialog Assistant [*Computer*] AMANDA
Automobil Versuchs- und Untersuchungs Strecke [*Automobile Test Track*] [*Department of Energy*] AVUS
Automobile A
Automobile AU
Automobile AUTO
Automobile AUTO
Automobile Accident (CPH) AA
Automobile Association [*British*] AA
Automobile Builders' Combination Designed Especially for Getting Hitler including Japan [*Suggested name for Automotive Council for War Production*] [*World War II*] ABCDEFGHIJ
Automobile Cases [*Commerce Clearing House*] [*A publication*] (DLA) Auto C

Automobile Cases [*Commerce Clearing House*] [*A publication*] (DLA) .... Auto Cas
Automobile Cases, Second Series [*Commerce Clearing House*] [*A publication*] (DLA) .... Auto Cas 2d
Automobile Club .... AC
Automobile Club of Great Britain and Ireland [*Later, Royal Automobile Club*] .... ACGBI
Automobile Club of Italy (BARN) .... ACI
Automobile Club of Philadelphia, Philadelphia, PA [*Library symbol Library of Congress Obsolete*] (LCLS) .... PPAuC
Automobile Competition Committee for the United States FIA [*Federation Internationale de l'Automobile*] (EA) .... ACCUS
Automobile Dealers Association .... ADA
Automobile Dealers Association of Indiana (SRA) .... ADAI
Automobile Dealers Association of North Dakota (SRA) .... ADAND
Automobile Dealers Parts Association .... ADPA
Automobile Defog/Defrost System Model (PDAA) .... ADSYM
Automobile Drivers Radio Information [*System for turning on car radio automatically, e.g. important messages*] (NITA) .... ARi
Automobile Engineering and Manufacturing [*Commercial firm British*] .... AEM
Automobile Fuel Efficiency Act [*1980*] .... AFEA
Automobile Importers Compliance Association [*Defunct*] (EA) .... AICA
Automobile Importers of America [*Later, AIAM*] (EA) .... AIA
Automobile Information Disclosure Act [*1958*] .... AIDA
Automobile Insurance Cases [*Commerce Clearing House*] [*A publication*] (DLA) .... Auto Ins Cas
Automobile Labor Board .... ALB
Automobile Law Reporter [*Commerce Clearing House*] [*A publication*] (DLA) .... Auto L Rep
Automobile Legal Association [*Defunct*] (EA) .... ALA
Automobile Liability [*Insurance*] .... AL
Automobile License Plate Collectors Association (EA) .... ALPCA
Automobile Manufacturers' Association [*Later, MVMA*] (EA) .... AMA
Automobile Manufacturers' Association, Inc., Detroit, MI [*Library symbol Library of Congress*] (LCLS) .... MiDAMA
Automobile Mechanic Training Evaluation Project [*Southern Association of Colleges and Schools*] (EDAC) .... AMTEP
Automobile Mutual Insurance Co. of America .... AMICA
Automobile Objets d'Art Club (EA) .... AODC
Automobile Owners Action Council [*Defunct*] (EA) .... AOAC
Automobile Parts [*Freight*] .... AUTO PTS
Automobile Physical Damage [*Insurance*] .... APD
Automobile Protection Association [*Canada*] .... APA
Automobile Protection Corp. [*NASDAQ symbol*] (NQ) .... APCO
Automobile Protection Corp. [*Associated Press*] (SAG) .... AutProt
Automobile Protection-APCO [*NASDAQ symbol*] (TTSB) .... APCO
Automobile Racing Club of America .... ARCA
Automobile Road Information [*Traffic management*] .... ARI
Automobile Seat Cover Association of America (EA) .... ASCAA
Automobile Shredder Residue .... ASR
Automobile Transporters Tariff Bureau, Inc., Southfield MI [*STAC*] .... ATB
Automobile Utility Trailer Rental Association (EA) .... AUTRA
Automobili Turismo Sport [*Auto manufacturing company*] [*Italy*] .... ATS
Automobilvertriebs Aktiengesellschaft [*Austria ICAO designator*] (FAAC) .... MBA
Automobil-Werke Eisenach [*Automobile manufacturer*] [*Germany*] .... AWE
Automotive (MUGU) .... AUTMV
Automotive (MSA) .... AUTOM
Automotive .... AUTOMTV
Automotive (AABC) .... AUTOMV
Automotive Accessories Manufacturers of America (MHDB) .... AAMA
Automotive Advertisers Council [*Chicago, IL*] (EA) .... AAC
Automotive Affiliated Representatives (EA) .... AAR
Automotive Aftermarket News [*A publication*] .... AAN
Automotive Aftermarket Professional [*AWDA University*] .... AAP
Automotive Air Conditioning Association [*Later, IMACA*] (EA) .... AACA
Automotive and Construction Equipment Overhaul and Repair Plant [*Navy*] .... ACEORP
Automotive and Construction Equipment Parts Depot [*Navy*] .... ACEPD
Automotive Battery Charger Manufacturers Council [*Defunct*] (EA) .... ABCMC
Automotive Billing Module [*GSA*] (TAG) .... AUTOBILL
Automotive Booster Clubs International (EA) .... ABC
Automotive Booster Clubs International (EA) .... ABCI
Automotive Chemical Manufacturers Council (EA) .... ACMC
Automotive Climate Control .... ACC
Automotive Committee for Air Defense [*World War II*] .... ACAD
Automotive Competitive Assessment Data Bank [*Ward's Research*] [*Database*] .... COMPASS
Automotive Component Group [*Automotive engineering*] .... ACG
Automotive Composites Consortium .... ACC
Automotive Composities Consortium [*General Motors Corp., Ford Motor Co., and Chrysler Corp.*] .... ACC
Automotive Consortium on Recycling and Disposal [*Industry research group*] .... ACORD
Automotive Consumer Action Program (EA) .... AUTOCAP
Automotive Cooling Systems Institute (EA) .... ACSI
Automotive Crash Injury Research .... ACIR
Automotive Development Group [*LTV Steel Corp.*] .... ADG
Automotive Diesel Fuel .... ADF
Automotive Diesel Oil (ADA) .... ADO
Automotive Dismantlers and Recyclers Association (EA) .... ADRA
Automotive Dismantlers and Recyclers Association (EA) .... ADRA
Automotive Distillate Oil (ADA) .... ADO
Automotive Electric Association [*ASIA*] [*Absorbed by*] (EA) .... AEA
Automotive Emissions and Fuel Economy Office [*Division of automaker certifying compliance with government exhaust emission and fuel economy standards*] .... AEFEO
Automotive Energy Efficiency Program [*Department of Transportation*] .... AEEP
Automotive Engine Rebuilders Association (EA) .... AERA
Automotive Engine Rebuilders Association. Service Bulletin [*A publication*] (EAAP) .... SB
Automotive Engine Rebuilders Association. Technical Bulletin [*A publication*] (EAAP) .... TB
Automotive Exhaust Research Institute [*Defunct*] (EA) .... AERI
Automotive Exhaust Systems Manufacturers Council (EA) .... AESMC
Automotive Exhibitors' Association of South Australia .... AEASA
Automotive Filter Manufacturers Council [*Later, FMC*] (EA) .... AFMC
Automotive Fine Arts Society .... AFAS
Automotive Fleet and Leasing Association (EA) .... AFLA
Automotive Hall of Fame .... AHOF
Automotive Industrial Motor .... AIM
Automotive Industries [*A publication*] .... AI
Automotive Industries Association of Canada .... AIA
Automotive Industries Association of Canada .... AIAC
Automotive Industry Action Group (EA) .... AIAG
Automotive Industry Data [*British*] .... AID
Automotive Industry Matters [*A publication*] (ADA) .... AIM
Automotive Information Council (EA) .... AIC
Automotive Information Management System [*Computer software*] [*Automotive engineering*] .... AIMS
Automotive Information Network Service .... AINS
Automotive Information Test (AABC) .... AIT
Automotive Layshaft Transmission .... ALT
Automotive Legislative Council of America (EA) .... ALCA
Automotive Lift Institute (EA) .... ALI
Automotive Machine & Parts Association .... AMPA
Automotive Maintenance and Repair Association .... AMRA
Automotive Manufacturers EDP [*Electronic Data Processing*] **Council** (EA) .... AMEDPC
Automotive Market Research Council (EA) .... AMRC
Automotive Mechanical and Electrical [*Test*] .... AME
Automotive, Metal, and Engineering Union .... AMEU
Automotive Occupant Protection Association (EA) .... AOPA
Automotive Occupant Restraints Council (EA) .... AORC
Automotive Organization Team (EA) .... AOT
Automotive Original Equipment Manufacturers .... AOEM
Automotive Parts and Accessories Association (EA) .... APAA
Automotive Parts Association of the Carolinas (SRA) .... APAC
Automotive Parts Manufacturers' Association [*Association des Fabricants de Pieces d'Automobile*] (AC) .... APMA
Automotive Parts Rebuilders Association (EA) .... APRA
Automotive Payment Module [*GSA*] (TAG) .... AUTOPAY
Automotive Performance Execution and Layout .... APEAL
Automotive Pigeon Loft .... APL
Automotive Planner's Handbook .... APH
Automotive Presidents Council (EA) .... APC
Automotive Press Association .... APA
Automotive Products [*Commercial firm British*] .... AP
Automotive Products Emissions Committee (EA) .... APEC
Automotive Products Export Council [*Defunct*] (EA) .... APEC
Automotive Products Trade Act of 1965 .... APTA
Automotive Public Relations Council (EA) .... APRC
Automotive Recyclers Association [*Salvage yards*] .... ARA
Automotive Recyclers of Indiana (SRA) .... ARI
Automotive Recycling Industry of Nebraska (SRA) .... ARIN
Automotive Refrigeration Products Institute (EA) .... ARPI
Automotive Repair Management Systems [*3M Co.*] .... ARMS
Automotive Research and Marketing Services .... ARMS
Automotive Restoration Market Organization .... ARMO
Automotive Restoration Market Organization .... ARMO
Automotive Retailers Association [*Canada*] .... ARA
Automotive Safety Foundation (EA) .... ASF
Automotive Sales Council (EA) .... ASC
Automotive Satellite Television Network [*Automotive engineering*] .... ASTN
Automotive Sensor Instrumentation System Van [*Automotive engineering*] .... ASIS
Automotive Service Association (EA) .... ASA
Automotive Service Association of Georgia (SRA) .... ASAG
Automotive Service Councils [*Later, ASA*] (EA) .... ASC
Automotive Service Education Program [*General Motors*] (EDAC) .... ASEP
Automotive Service Excellence .... ASE
Automotive Service Industry Association (EA) .... ASIA
Automotive Service Reports [*A publication*] (EAAP) .... ASR
Automotive Services Marketing Association [*Canada*] .... ASMA
Automotive Specialty Warehouse .... ASW
Automotive Study Unit [*American Topical Association*] (EA) .... ASU
Automotive Technicians Association International (EA) .... ATA
Automotive Test Rig [*Military*] (RDA) .... ATR
Automotive Trade Association Executives (EA) .... ATAE
Automotive Trade Association Managers [*Later, ATAE*] .... ATAM
Automotive Trades Association Inc. (AC) .... ATA
Automotive Training Managers Council (EA) .... ATMC
Automotive Transportation Center [*Purdue University*] [*Research center*] (RCD) .... ATC
Automotive Warehouse Distributors Association (EA) .... AWDA
Automotive Wholesalers Association Executives (EA) .... AWAE
Automotive Wholesalers Association of Alabama and Georgia (SRA) .... AWAAG
Automotive Wholesalers Association of Tennessee (SRA) .... AWAT
Automotive Wholesalers of Arizona (SRA) .... AWOA
Automotive Wholesalers of Illinois (SRA) .... AWOI
Automotive Wholesalers of New England (SRA) .... AWANE
Automotive Wholesalers of Oklahoma (SRA) .... AWO

Automotive Wholesalers of Texas (SRA) .... AWOT
Automotors Salta SACYF [*Argentina ICAO designator*] (FAAC) .... LES
Automovile Journalists Association of Canada [*Association des Journalistes Automobile du Canada*] (AC) .... AJAC
Autonetics (KSC) .... AN
Autonetics Base-Line Equipment .... ABLE
Autonetics Business & Control United Systems, Inc. .... ABACUS
Autonetics General Information Learning Equipment .... AGILE
Autonetics Generalized Reset .... AGR
Autonetics Kalman Utilization of Reference for Optimal Navigation (MCD) .... AKURON
Autonetics Modular Airborne RADAR System .... AMARS
Autonome Transfer Unit [*Computer science*] (DIT) .... ATU
Autonomic Dysreflexia [*Neurology*] (DAVI) .... AD
Autonomic Hyperreflexia [*Medicine*] .... AH
Autonomic Hyperreflexia [*Medicine*] (MEDA) .... AHR
Autonomic Lability Score [*In ion detection*] .... ALS
Autonomic Nervous System [*Medicine*] .... ANS
Autonomic Perception Questionnaire [*Psychology*] (EDAC) .... APQ
Autonomous .... AUT
Autonomous Air Vehicle [*Drone-formerly RPV*] [*Military*] (DOMA) .... AAV
Autonomous Anarchist Groups [*Spanish*] (PD) .... GAS
Autonomous Area .... AA
Autonomous Benthic Explorer [*Oceanography*] .... ABE
Autonomous Data Transfer .... ADT
Autonomous Fire and Forget [*Military*] .... AFAF
Autonomous Free-Flight Dispenser System [*Air Force*] .... AFDS
Autonomous Guidance for Conventional Weapons [*Air Force*] .... AGCW
Autonomous Guided Weapon (DOMA) .... AGW
Autonomous Helicopter System [*Military*] (LAIN) .... AHS
Autonomous Infantry Mortar [*Military*] (INF) .... AIM
Autonomous Intelligent Cruise Control [*Automotive engineering*] .... AICC
Autonomous Lagrangian Circulation Explorer [*Oceanography*] .... ALACE
Autonomous Lagrangian Circulation Explorer (OSRA) .... ALACE
Autonomous Land Vehicle [*Military*] (RDA) .... ALV
Autonomous Land Vehicle in a Neural Network [*Military*] .... ALVINN
Autonomous Learner Index .... ALI
Autonomous Line Scanning Unit (MCD) .... ALSU
Autonomous Listening Stations [*Instrumentation*] .... ALS
Autonomous Lock-On After Launch (MCD) .... ALOAL
Autonomous Marine Power Source [*Navy*] .... AMPS
Autonomous Missile Site RADAR (AABC) .... AMSR
Autonomous Multiplexer Channel .... AMC
Autonomous Navigation System .... ANS
Autonomous Navigation System Concept (MCD) .... ANSC
Autonomous Navigation Technology (MCD) .... ANT
Autonomous Oblast [*Former USSR*] .... AO
Autonomous Precision Approach and Landing System [*Lockheed-Martin's radical landing-guidance system*] .... APALS
Autonomous Precision-Guided Munition [*NATO*] .... APGM
Autonomous Remotely Controlled Submersible [*Autonomous underwater vehicle*] .... ARCS
Autonomous Replication Core-Consensus Sequence [*Genetics*] .... ACS
Autonomous Replication Sequence [*Genetics*] .... ARS
Autonomous Republic .... AR
Autonomous Soviet Socialist Republic .... ASSR
Autonomous Spacecraft Maintenance (MCD) .... ASM
Autonomous Switch Unit [*Telecommunications*] (NITA) .... ASU
Autonomous Tactical All-Weather Strike (MCD) .... ATAWS
Autonomous Tech [*NASDAQ symbol*] (TTSB) .... ATCI
Autonomous Technologies Corp. [*NASDAQ symbol*] (SAG) .... ATCI
Autonomous Technologies Corp. [*Associated Press*] (SAG) .... AutonoT
Autonomous Temperature Line Acquisition System [*Moorings*] [*Marine science*] (OSRA) .... ATLAS
Autonomous Temperature Line Acquisition System [*Moorings*] (USDC) .... ATLAS
Autonomous Terminal Homing [*Air Force*] .... ATH
Autonomous Terminal Homing Program (MCD) .... ATHP
Autonomous Underwater Vehicle [*Navy*] .... AUV
Autonomously Functioning Thyroid Nodule [*Endocrinology*] .... AFTN
Autonomously Functioning Thyroid Nodule [*Endocrinology*] .... ATN
Autonomously Replicating Sequence [*Genetics*] .... ARS
Auto-Oxidation Inhibitor (BARN) .... AI
Autophagic Vacuole [*Botany*] .... AV
Autopilot (GAVI) .... A/P
Autopilot Capsule .... A/PC
Autopilot Control (AAG) .... A/P CTL
Autopilot Disengage Switch (MCD) .... ADS
Autopilot Flight Director .... APFD
Autopilot Flight Director System (GAVI) .... AFDS
Autopilot Ground Control Unit (AAG) .... AGCU
Autopilot Ground Control Unit .... APGCU
Autopilot Mode Selector .... AMS
Autopilot Monitor (AAG) .... A/P MON
Autopilot Monitor and Control Unit .... A/P MCU
Autopilot Positioning Indicator .... A/P POI
Autopilot Rate Control .... ARC
Autopilot Surface Servo .... ASS
Autopilot Test Monitor (AAG) .... A/P TSTMN
Autopilot Test Programmer (AAG) .... A/P TSTPG
Autopilot Zero .... APO
Autopiloted Vehicle .... APV
Autoplot Controller (IEEE) .... APC
AutoPrep 5000 Users Group (EA) .... APUG
Autopsy [*Also, AUT*] [*Medicine*] .... AU
Autopsy [*Also, AU*] [*Medicine*] .... AUT
Autoquote [*Computer science*] (TEL) .... AQ
Autoradiographic .... AR
Autoradiographic Immunoassay (MCD) .... ARIA
Autoradiography [*Medicine*] (DAVI) .... AR
Autoradiography .... ARG
Auto-Refresh Direct Memory Access [*Computer science*] (PDAA) .... ARDMA
Autoregressive [*Mathematical bioscience*] .... AR
Autoregressive Conditional Heteroscedastic [*Electronics*] (PCM) .... ARCH
Autoregressive Moving Average [*Statistics*] .... ARMA
Auto-Regressive Random Field (PDAA) .... ARF
Autoregressive-Integrated-Moving-Average [*Statistics*] .... ARIMA
Auto-Regulated Inspiratory Support [*Medicine*] (DMAA) .... ARIS
Auto-Resonant Accelerator [*For atomic particles*] .... ARA
Auto-Restricted Zone [*Environmental Protection Agency*] (GFGA) .... ARZ
Autoroute (DD) .... aut
Autosampler .... AS
Autosomal Dominant [*Genetics*] .... AD
Autosomal Dominant Polycystic Kidney Disease [*Medicine*] .... ADPKD
Autosomal Dominant Retinitis Pigmentosa [*Ophthalmology*] .... ADRP
Autosomal Dominant Vitreo-Retinochoroidopathy [*Medicine*] (DMAA) .... ADVIRC
Autosomal Recessive [*Genetics*] .... AR
Autosomal Recessive Distal Muscular Dystrophy [*Medicine*] .... ARDMD
Autosomal Recessive Polycystic Disease [*Medicine*] (DMAA) .... ARPD
Autosomal Recessive Polycystic Kidney Disease [*Medicine*] .... ARPKD
Autosomal-Dominant Compelling Helioophthalmic Outburst .... ACHOO
Autosome [*Genetics*] .... A
Autothrottle [*Aerospace*] .... A/T
Auto-Throttle Actuator (MCD) .... ATA
Auto-Throttle Actuator Assembly (MCD) .... ATAA
Autothrust System (GAVI) .... ATHR
Autotote Corp. [*Associated Press*] (SAG) .... Autotote
Autotote Corp. [*NASDAQ symbol*] (NQ) .... TOTE
Autotote Corp. Cl'A' [*AMEX symbol*] (TTSB) .... TTE
Auto-Trace Steam Analysis Program [*Computer software*] .... ASAP
Autotrack Vulcan Air Defense System .... AVADS
Autotransformer .... AUTOTR
Auto-trol Technology [*NASDAQ symbol*] (TTSB) .... ATTC
Auto-Trol Technology Corp. [*NASDAQ symbol*] (NQ) .... ATTC
Autotumorolytic Factor [*Oncology*] .... ATF
Autotuned [*NAVAID, Navigational Aid*] (GAVI) .... A
Autovend Technology Corp. [*Vancouver Stock Exchange symbol*] .... AVT
AUTOVON (MCD) .... AV
AUTOVON [*Automatic Voice Network*] **Assistance Operator** (DNAB) .... AAO
AUTOVON Centralized Alarm System .... ACAS
Autozone, Inc. [*Associated Press*] (SAG) .... AutoZone
AutoZone, Inc. [*NYSE symbol*] (SPSG) .... AZO
AutoZone Inc. [*NYSE symbol*] (TTSB) .... AZO
Autrex, Inc. [*Toronto Stock Exchange symbol*] .... AUT
Autry Family Association .... AFA
Autumn .... Au
Autumn .... AUT
Autumn Circulation Experiment [*Denmark, Great Britain, Norway, West Germany*] [*1987-88 Oceanography*] .... ACE
Autumnal Equinox .... AE
Autumn-Burned [*Ecology*] .... A
Autun/Bellevue [*France ICAO location identifier*] (ICLI) .... LFQF
Aux Bons Soins De [*Care Of, c/o*] [*Correspondence*] [*French*] .... ABS
Aux Soins De [*Care Of, c/o*] [*French*] .... A/S
Aux Soins De [*Care Of, c/o*] [*French*] .... A/S DE
Auxaire-Bretagne [*ICAO designator*] (AD) .... BS
Auxerre/Moneteau [*France ICAO location identifier*] (ICLI) .... LFLA
Auxiliaries of Our Lady of the Cenacle (EA) .... AOLC
Auxiliaries of the Blessed Sacrament (TOCD) .... ABS
Auxiliary (DNAB) .... A
Auxiliary (AFM) .... AUX
Auxiliary .... AUX
Auxiliary (WDMC) .... aux
Auxiliary .... AUXIL
Auxiliary Acceleration Pump [*Automotive engineering*] .... AAP
Auxiliary Active Digital Display [*Sonar*] (DNAB) A2D2
Auxiliary Active Digital Display [*Sonar*] (DNAB) .... AADD
Auxiliary Aiming Mark [*Target*] (IAA) .... AAM
Auxiliary Air Control [*Automotive engineering*] .... AAC
Auxiliary Air Force [*Later, R Aux AF*] [*British*] .... AAF
Auxiliary Air Force Base .... AAFB
Auxiliary Air Force General List [*British military*] (DMA) .... AAFGL
Auxiliary Air Force Reserve [*British*] .... AAFR
Auxiliary Air Units [*Naval Reserve*] .... AAU
Auxiliary Airborne Command Post (MCD) .... AUXCP
Auxiliary Airborne Power Plant .... AAPP
Auxiliary Aircraft Carrier [*Navy symbol*] .... ACV
Auxiliary Aircraft Training Ship .... AVT
Auxiliary Aircraft Transport [*Navy symbol Obsolete*] .... AVT
Auxiliary Aircraft Warning Service .... AAWS
Auxiliary Ambulance Service (DAS) .... AAS
Auxiliary Amplifier (AAG) .... XA
Auxiliary and Fuel Handling Building [*Nuclear energy*] (NUCP) .... AFHB
Auxiliary and RADWASTE Area Ventilation System [*Nuclear energy*] (NRCH) .... ARAVS
Auxiliary Area Emergency Gas Treatment System [*Nuclear energy*] (NRCH) .... AAEGTS
Auxiliary Area Environmental Control System [*Nuclear energy*] (NRCH) .... AAECS
Auxiliary Array Antenna [*Army*] .... AAA
Auxiliary Array Guard Band [*Military*] .... AAGB
Auxiliary Array Signal Band [*Military*] .... AASB

Auxiliary Artillery Corps [*British military*] (DMA) .... AAC
Auxiliary Assembly [*JETDS nomenclature*] .... AA
Auxiliary Attitude Control System [*Aviation*] (MCD) ...... AACS
Auxiliary Balance Line Evaluation [*Nuclear energy*] (NUCP) .... ABLE
Auxiliary Ballast Tank .... ABT
Auxiliary Barracks Ship (Self-Propelled) (DNAB) .... APB
Auxiliary Battery Acquisition RADAR (MCD) .... ABAR
Auxiliary Boiler [*of a ship*] (DS) .... AXB
Auxiliary Boiler Survey [*of a ship*] (DS) .... AXBS
Auxiliary Building Filter System [*Nuclear energy*] (NRCH) ..... ABFS
Auxiliary Building Gas Treatment System [*Nuclear energy*] (NRCH) ...... ABGTS
Auxiliary Building Isolation [*Nuclear energy*] (NRCH) ..... ABI
Auxiliary Building Special Ventilation System [*Nuclear energy*] (NRCH) .... ABSVS
Auxiliary Building Sump [*Nuclear energy*] (IEEE) .... ABS
Auxiliary Building Sump Tank [*Nuclear energy*] (NRCH) ..... ABST
Auxiliary Building Ventilation [*Nuclear energy*] (NRCH) ... ABV
Auxiliary Checkpoint .... ACP
Auxiliary Coastal Minesweepers [*Navy symbol*] .... AMC
Auxiliary Coastguard [*British*] .... ACG
Auxiliary Code Storage [*Computer memory*] (NITA) .... ACS
Auxiliary Combat Information Center .... ACIC
Auxiliary Command .... AC
Auxiliary Command Post (SAA) .... ACP
Auxiliary Communications .... AUX COMMO
Auxiliary Component Cooling Water System [*Nuclear energy*] (NRCH) ..... ACCWS
Auxiliary Computer Input Multiplexer .... ACIM
Auxiliary Computer Power Unit .... ACPU
Auxiliary Computer Room [*Apollo*] [*NASA*] .... ACR
Auxiliary Conditioning Unit .... ACU
Auxiliary Console (SAA) .... AC
Auxiliary Contractor Logistic Support [*Military*] .... ACLS
Auxiliary Control Panel [*Aerospace*] (AAG) .... ACP
Auxiliary Conversion Equipment .... ACE
Auxiliary Cooling System [*Nuclear energy*] (NRCH) .... ACS
Auxiliary Core Memory [*Computer science*] (MCD) .... ACM
Auxiliary Core Storage [*Computer science*] (BUR) .... ACS
Auxiliary Crane Ship [*Navy symbol*] .... TACS
Auxiliary Crew Compartment (MCD) .... ACC
Auxiliary Current Transformer .... AuCT
Auxiliary Data Acquisition Unit [*Computer science*] (MHDI) ...... ADAU
Auxiliary Data Annotation Set [*or System*] .... ADAS
Auxiliary Data Processing Equipment .... ADPE
Auxiliary Data Translator Unit .... ADTU
Auxiliary Deception Generator (MCD) .... ADG
Auxiliary Deep Submergence Support Ship [*Navy symbol*] (NVT) ..... AGDS
Auxiliary Detonation Fuze (NG) .... ADF
Auxiliary Display Equipment Group (KSC) .... ADEG
Auxiliary Display Request Keyboard .... ADRK
Auxiliary Display Unit .... ADU
Auxiliary Drum (CET) .... AXD
Auxiliary Emission Control Device [*Automotive engineering*] ...... AECD
Auxiliary Encoder System .... AES
Auxiliary Engineering Signal Processor .... AESP
Auxiliary Equation [*Mathematics*] (OA) .... AE
Auxiliary Equipment (KSC) .... AE
Auxiliary Equipment Building [*Nuclear energy*] (NRCH) .... AEB
Auxiliary Essential Raw Cooling Water [*Nuclear energy*] (NRCH) ..... AERCW
Auxiliary Feed [*Nuclear energy*] (NRCH) .... AF
Auxiliary Feed Pump Turbine (IEEE) .... AFPT
Auxiliary Feedwater [*Nuclear energy*] (NRCH) .... AF
Auxiliary Feedwater [*Nuclear energy*] (NRCH) .... AFW
Auxiliary Feedwater Actuating System [*Nuclear energy*] (NRCH) ..... AFAS
Auxiliary Feedwater Actuating System [*Nuclear energy*] (NRCH) ..... AFWAS
Auxiliary Feedwater Control [*Nuclear energy*] (NRCH) .... AFWC
Auxiliary Feedwater Storage Tank [*Nuclear energy*] (IEEE) ..... AFST
Auxiliary Feedwater System [*Nuclear energy*] (NRCH) ..... AFS
Auxiliary Feedwater System [*Nuclear energy*] (NRCH) ..... AFWS
Auxiliary Ferry Service Unit .... AFSU
Auxiliary Field (MUGU) .... AF
Auxiliary Fighter Director Ship [*Navy*] .... AFDS
Auxiliary Fire Service [*British*] .... AFS
Auxiliary Fire Tube Boiler [*of a ship*] (DS) .... AXFTB
Auxiliary Fire Tube Boiler Survey [*of a ship*] (DS) ..... AXFBS
Auxiliary Fire Tube Boiler Survey [*of a ship*] (DS) ..... AXFTBS
Auxiliary Flight Reference System .... AFRS
Auxiliary Flight Service Station [*Aviation*] (FAAC) ..... XFSS
Auxiliary Floating Dry Dock [*Navy symbol*] .... AFD
Auxiliary Floating Dry Dock (Big) [*Non-self-propelled*] [*Navy symbol*] ..... AFDB
Auxiliary Floating Dry Dock (Concrete) [*Non-self-propelled*] [*Navy symbol*] ..... AFDC
Auxiliary Floating Dry Dock (Little) [*Non-self-propelled*] [*Navy symbol*] ..... AFDL
Auxiliary Floating Dry Dock (Little, Concrete) [*Non-self-propelled*] [*Navy symbol*] ..... AFDL(C)
Auxiliary Floating Dry Dock (Medium) [*Non-self-propelled*] [*Navy symbol*] ..... AFDM
Auxiliary Force, India [*British military*] (DMA) .... AFI
Auxiliary Force Medical Corps [*British military*] (DMA) .. AFMC
Auxiliary Force Veterinary Corps [*British military*] (DMA) ..... AFVC
Auxiliary Fresh Water (DNAB) .... AFW
Auxiliary Fuel Oil (System) [*Nuclear energy*] (NRCH) .... AFO(S)
Auxiliary Functional Unit [*Data link*] (NG) .... AFU
Auxiliary General Electronics Research Ship [*Navy*] ..... AGERS
Auxiliary General for Environmental Research [*Ship*] [*Military*] (LAIN) ..... AGER
Auxiliary General Missile .... AGM
Auxiliary General Oceanographic Research Ship [*Navy*] (MSC) ..... AGOR
Auxiliary General Survey [*Navy*] (MSC) .... AGS

Auxiliary Generating Plant [*Aviation*] (AIA) .... AGP
Auxiliary Ground Control Station [*NASA*] (KSC) .... AUXGCS
Auxiliary Ground Equipment .... AGE
Auxiliary Handling Machine [*Nuclear energy*] (NRCH) ..... AHM
Auxiliary Hydraulic Power Supply .... AHPS
Auxiliary Inerting Gas Subsystem [*Nuclear energy*] (NRCH) ..... AIGS
Auxiliary Inshore Minesweeper [*NATO*] .... AMI
Auxiliary Intelligence Collection Ship [*Navy*] (CAAL) ... AGI
Auxiliary Interface Unit [*NASA*] .... AIU
Auxiliary Intermediate Heat Exchanger [*Nuclear energy*] (NRCH) ..... AIHX
Auxiliary Killing Ground [*British and Canadian*] [*World War II*] ..... AKG
Auxiliary Landing Field .... ALF
Auxiliary Library Service Collections .... ALSC
Auxiliary Library Service Organization .... ALSO
Auxiliary Light [*Navigation signal*] .... Aux
Auxiliary Lighter Ship (DNAB) .... ALS
Auxiliary Liquid Metal System [*Nuclear energy*] (NRCH) .. ALMS
Auxiliary Loans to Assist Students .... ALAS
Auxiliary Machinery Room (CAAL) .... AMR
Auxiliary Machinery Space (DNAB) .... AMS
Auxiliary Marine Power Source [*For submarines*] (DOMA) .. AMPS
Auxiliary Marker [*Telecommunications*] (TEL) .... AM
Auxiliary Memory .... AM
Auxiliary Memory Drum .... AMD
Auxiliary Memory Set (MCD) .... AMS
Auxiliary Memory Unit .... AMU
Auxiliary Mexican Border Veterans (EA) .... AMBV
Auxiliary Military Pioneer Corps [*British*] .... AMPC
Auxiliary Minelayer [*Navy symbol*] .... ACM
Auxiliary Minelayer .... AML
Auxiliary Minesweeper [*NATO*] .... AM
Auxiliary Minesweeper [*NATO*] .... AMS
Auxiliary Motor Launches (NATG) .... MLA
Auxiliary Motor Minesweeper [*Navy symbol*] .... YMS
Auxiliary Ocean Tug [*Navy symbol*] .... ATA
Auxiliary of the Decalogue Society of Lawyers (EA) .... ADSL
Auxiliary Oil Replenisher [*or Replenishment*] [*Navy British*] ..... AOR
Auxiliary Oiler (MCD) .... AO
Auxiliary Oiler [*Military Sea Transportation Service*] .. TAO
Auxiliary Operational Members [*Coast Guard*] .... AUXOPS
Auxiliary Oscillator .... AO
Auxiliary Oscillator .... AUXOSC
Auxiliary Output Tester .... AOT
Auxiliary Pastoral Ministry [*Church of England*] .... APM
Auxiliary Patrol [*British military*] (DMA) .... AP
Auxiliary Payload Power System (MCD) .... APPS
Auxiliary Personnel, Attack [*Navy designation for combat landing craft*] [*World War II*] ..... APA
Auxiliary Personnel, Destroyer [*British military*] (DMA) ..... APD
Auxiliary Pneumatic (AAG) .... APNEU
Auxiliary Pneumatics Panel .... APP
Auxiliary Police (LAIN) .... AP
Auxiliary Potential Transformer .... AuPT
Auxiliary Power (CAAL) .... AP
Auxiliary Power Distribution (KSC) .... APD
Auxiliary Power Package (MCD) .... APP
Auxiliary Power Plant .... APP
Auxiliary Power Subsystem (MCD) .... APS
Auxiliary Power Supply .... APS
Auxiliary Power Supply Unit (MCD) .... APSU
Auxiliary Power System (NRCH) .... APS
Auxiliary Power [*or Propulsion*] Unit [*Military*] ...... APU
Auxiliary Power Unit Subsystem (MCD) .... APUS
Auxiliary Power Unit System Module (MCD) .... APUSM
Auxiliary Power Unit Test (MCD) .... APUT
Auxiliary Printer (ECII) .... AP
Auxiliary Processing Unit .... APU
Auxiliary Program Storage [*Computer science*] (BUR) ..... APS
Auxiliary Propelled Anti-Tank [*Military*] (PDAA) .... APAT
Auxiliary Propulsion System [*or Subsystem*] [*Apollo*] [*NASA*] ..... APS
Auxiliary Propulsion System Aft POP (MCD) .... APSAP
Auxiliary Pump-Drive Assembly .... APDA
Auxiliary Reactor Area .... ARA
Auxiliary Readout (CAAL) .... ARO
Auxiliary Read-Out Unit [*Computer science*] (MHDB) ...... ARU
Auxiliary Recording Control [*Circuit*] [*Bell System*] .. AUXRC
Auxiliary Recovery Antenna [*NASA*] (KSC) .... ARA
Auxiliary Register .... AUXR
Auxiliary Regulation Excitation Principle [*Industrial engines*] ..... AREP
Auxiliary Removable Memory Media/Tape-Transport Cartridge (MCD) ..... ARMM/TTC
Auxiliary Repair Battle Damage [*British military*] (DMA) ..... ARB
Auxiliary Repair Dry Dock [*Non-self-propelled*] [*Navy ship symbol*] ..... ARD
Auxiliary Repair Dry Dock, Concrete [*Later, AFDL*] [*Navy symbol Obsolete*] ..... ARDC
Auxiliary Rescue Team Chief [*Air Force*] .... ARTC
Auxiliary Resources Control Office .... ARCO
Auxiliary Rocket Engine .... ARE
Auxiliary Roll Control .... ARC
Auxiliary Routine (IAA) .... AR
Auxiliary Seaplane Tender [*Ship symbol*] .... XAV
Auxiliary Segment Table [*Electronics*] (OA) .... AST
Auxiliary Sensor Unit (MCD) .... ASU
Auxiliary Service Force, Transition Training Squadron, Pacific ..... ASFTRNTRARONPAC

Auxiliary Ship Information System [*Navy*] (CAAL) .... ASIS
Auxiliary Spacecraft Power [*NASA*] (MCD) .... ASP
Auxiliary Stabilizing Support - "A" Frame .... ASF
Auxiliary Stage [*NASA*] (NASA) .... A/S
Auxiliary Steam [*Nuclear energy*] (NRCH) .... AS
Auxiliary Steam Generator [*Nuclear energy*] (NRCH) .... ASG
Auxiliary Steam (System) [*Nuclear energy*] (NRCH) .... AS(S)
Auxiliary Storage [*Computer science*] .... AS
Auxiliary Storage and Playback [*Assembly*] [*Apollo Telescope Mount*] [*NASA*] .... ASAP
Auxiliary Storage and Playback Assembly [*Apollo Telescope Mount*] [*NASA*] (KSC) .... ASPA
Auxiliary Storage Manager [*Computer science*] .... ASM
Auxiliary Storage Unit [*Computer science*] (IAA) .... ASU
Auxiliary Submarine [*Navy symbol*] .... AGSS
Auxiliary Submarine [*Navy symbol*] .... SSAC
Auxiliary Submarine Rescue Ship [*Navy symbol*] .... ASR
Auxiliary Support Reaction System .... ASRS
Auxiliary Supporting Feature (IEEE) .... ASF
Auxiliary Surface Simulator Platform [*Navy*] (CAAL) .... ASSP
Auxiliary Survey Vessel [*Oceanography*] (MSC) .... ASV
Auxiliary Switch [*Electricity*] .... ASW
Auxiliary Switch [*Electricity*] .... AuS
Auxiliary Switch [*Breaker*] **Normally Closed** [*Electricity*] .... ASC
Auxiliary Switch [*Breaker*] **Normally Open** [*Electricity*] .... ASO
Auxiliary System for Interactive Statistics [*Sweden Information service or system*] (IID) .... AXIS
Auxiliary Systems Function Test Stand [*NASA*] (KSC) .... ASFTS
Auxiliary Tape Memory [*Spacecraft guidance*] .... ATM
Auxiliary Territorial Service [*Later, WRAC*] [*British women's service*] [*World War II*] .... ATS
Auxiliary Test Unit .... ATU
Auxiliary Timer .... AT
Auxiliary Timer Assembly .... ATA
Auxiliary to Sons of Union Veterans of the Civil War (EA) .... ASUVCW
Auxiliary to the American Dental Association (EA) .... AADA
Auxiliary to the American Optometric Association [*Later, AFVA*] (EA) .... AAOA
Auxiliary to the American Osteopathic Association (EA) .... AAOA
Auxiliary to the National Dental Association (EA) .... ANDA
Auxiliary to the National Medical Association (EA) .... ANMA
Auxiliary Tool Production (MCD) .... ATP
Auxiliary Track (MUGU) .... AUXTRAC
Auxiliary Training Submarine [*Navy symbol*] .... ATSS
Auxiliary Tug Service (PDAA) .... ATS
Auxiliary Turbopump Assembly .... ATPA
Auxiliary Unit .... AU
Auxiliary Utility Equipment Area (NRCH) .... AUEA
Auxiliary Vessel (NOAA) .... AV
Auxiliary Vessels [*Navy symbol*] (MUGU) .... AA
Auxiliary Video Switching Matrix .... AVSM
Auxiliary Waste Heat Boiler [*of a ship*] (DS) .... AXWHB
Auxiliary Waste Heater Boiler Survey [*of a ship*] (DS) .... AXWHBS
Auxiliary Waste Tube Boiler Survey [*of a ship*] (DS) .... AXWTBS
Auxiliary Water Tube Boiler [*of a ship*] (DS) .... AXWTB
Auxiliary Winding .... AW
Auxilium Meum a Deo [*My Help Cometh from the Lord*] [*(Ps., CXXI. 2) Motto of Christian, Margrave of Brandenburg-Baireuth (1581-1655)*] .... AMAD
Auxin Response Factor [*Biochemistry*] .... ARF
Auyuittuq National Park, Parks Canada [*Parc National Auyuittuq, Parcs Canada*] **Pangnirtung, Northwest Territories** [*Library symbol National Library of Canada*] (NLC) .... NWPPCA
AV [*Audiovisual*] **Pansophic Users Group** [*Defunct*] (EA) .... AVPUG
Ava, IL [*FM radio station call letters*] .... WXAN
Ava, MO [*Location identifier FAA*] (FAAL) .... AOV
Ava, MO [*AM radio station call letters*] .... KKOZ
Ava, MO [*FM radio station call letters*] .... KKOZ-FM
'Avadim (BJA) .... 'Avad
Availability (NITA) .... AV
Availability .... AVBLTY
Availability .... AVLBLTY
Availability Balance File [*Military*] (AABC) .... ABF
Availability Centered Inventory Model (MCD) .... ACIM
Availability Code .... AC
Availability Computation - Element Transient and Asymptotic Repair Process (PDAA) .... AVACOM-ETARP
Availability Control Unit (IAA) .... ACU
Availability Date [*Banking*] .... AD
Availability Factor [*Generating time ratio*] (IEEE) .... AF
Availability Factor .... AVF
Availability Guarantee [*Military*] .... AG
Availability of Logistics Support Elements (MCD) .... ALSE
Availability Rate .... AR
Availability, Reliability, and Maintainability [*Computer performance*] .... ARM
Availability, Steady .... AS
Available [*or Availability*] (MCD) .... A
Available [*or Availability*] [*Online database field identifier*] [*Computer science*] .... AV
Available [*or Availability*] (KSC) .... AVAIL
Available [*or Availability*] (AFM) .... AVAL
Available [*or Availability*] .... AVBL
Available (ECII) .... AVBLE
Available [*or Availability*] (MSA) .... AVLBL
Available but Not Installed .... ABNI
Available Database Management System .... ADBMS
Available for Local Use (MCD) .... AFLU
Available for Reassignment .... AVFR
Available for Release (MCD) .... AFR
Available Hours [*Electronics*] (IEEE) .... AH
Available Labor Pool Model (MCD) .... AVPOOL
Available Machine Time .... AMT
Available Manhours (AFM) .... AVMH
Available Pay Survey Reports [*Information service or system*] (IID) .... APSR
Available Phosphoric Acid .... APA
Available Potential Energy [*Geophysics*] .... APE
Available Power Efficiency .... APE
Available Power Response .... APR
Available Seat Miles [*Airlines term*] .... ASM
Available Seat-Kilometres [*Air travel*] .... ASK
Available Space List [*Computer science*] .... ASL
Available Space List [*Computer science*] (IAA) .... AVSL
Available Supply Rate .... ASR
Available Time .... AT
Available Time (AFM) .... AVT
Available Tonne-Kilometer (ADA) .... ATK
Available Vehicle Occupancy [*VDOT*] (TAG) .... AVO
Available Water-Holding Capacity [*Soil science*] .... AWC
Available Water-Holding Capacity [*Soil science*] (OA) .... AWHC
Available-to-Load Date (AABC) .... ALD
Avair, Inc. [*ICAO designator*] (FAAC) .... FVA
Avaj [*Iran*] [*ICAO location identifier*] (ICLI) .... OIHJ
Avalanche Controlled Rectifier (PDAA) .... ACR
Avalanche Diode (KSC) .... AD
Avalanche Diode Oscillator .... ADO
Avalanche Injection Diode .... AID
Avalanche Injection Metal-Oxide Semiconductor .... AMOS
Avalanche Mode Photodiode .... AMP
Avalanche Photodiode [*Solid state physics*] .... APD
Avalanche Photodiode Detector .... APD
Avalanche Punch-Through Erase (MCD) .... APTE
Avalanche Transit Time .... ATT
Avalanche Transit Time Diode .... ATTD
Avalanche Transit Time Oscillator (IAA) .... ATTO
Avalanche-Induced Migration (MCD) .... AIM
Avalanching Junction Light Output .... AJLO
Avallon [*France ICAO location identifier*] (ICLI) .... LFGE
Avalon [*Australia ICAO location identifier*] (ICLI) .... AMAV
Avalon Bay [*Santa Catalina, California*] [*Airport symbol*] (AD) .... AVX
Avalon, CA [*Location identifier FAA*] (FAAL) .... AVX
Avalon, CA [*AM radio station call letters*] .... KBRT
Avalon, CA [*FM radio station call letters*] .... KISL
Avalon, CA [*FM radio station call letters*] .... KRCI
Avalon Capital [*NASDAQ symbol*] (TTSB) .... MIST
Avalon Capital, Inc. [*Associated Press*] (SAG) .... AvalonC
Avalon Capital, Inc. [*NASDAQ symbol*] (SAG) .... MIST
Avalon Community Services, Inc. [*Associated Press*] (SAG) .... Avalon
Avalon Community Services, Inc. [*NASDAQ symbol*] (SAG) .... CITY
Avalon Community Svcs [*NASDAQ symbol*] (TTSB) .... CITY
Avalon, NJ [*FM radio station call letters*] .... WCZT
Avalon Prop 9% Sr'A'Pfd [*NYSE symbol*] (TTSB) .... AVNPrA
Avalon Properties [*Associated Press*] (SAG) .... Avaln
Avalon Properties [*Associated Press*] (SAG) .... AvalonPr
Avalon Properties [*NYSE symbol*] (SPSG) .... AVN
Avalon Resources, Inc. [*Vancouver Stock Exchange symbol*] .... AGM
Avanavero [*Surinam*] [*ICAO location identifier*] (ICLI) .... SMVO
Avance International, Inc. [*Vancouver Stock Exchange symbol*] .... AVA
Avancer [*Fast, as clocks*] [*French*] .... A
Avanguardia Operaia [*Worker's Vanguard*] [*Italy Political party*] (PPE) .... AO
Avant Corp. [*Associated Press*] (SAG) .... Avanti
Avant Corp. [*NASDAQ symbol*] (SAG) .... AVNT
Avant Corp. [*NASDAQ symbol*] (TTSB) .... AVNT
Avant Jesus-Christ [*Before Christ*] [*French*] .... AV J-C
Avant-Garde (VRA) .... av-gd
Avantgarde de la Revolution Malgache [*Vanguard of the Malagasy Revolution*] [*Political party*] (PPW) .... AREMA
Avant-Garde Francaise d'Amerique [*French Avant-Garde of America*] [*Canada*] .... AGFA
Avanti Air [*Austria ICAO designator*] (FAAC) .... ATV
Avanti Owners Association International (EA) .... AOAI
Avanti Productions, Inc. [*Vancouver Stock Exchange symbol*] .... AVN
Avaric [*MARC language code Library of Congress*] (LCCP) .... ava
Avarua/Rarotonga International [*Cook Islands*] [*ICAO location identifier*] (ICLI) .... NCRG
Avascular Necrosis [*Medicine*] (AAMN) .... AN
Avascular Necrosis of Bone [*Medicine*] (DMAA) .... ANB
Avascular Necrosis of Bone [*Medicine*] .... AVNB
Avascular Necrosis of the Femoral Head [*Medicine*] (DMAA) .... AVNFH
Avascular Zone [*Medicine*] (DMAA) .... AVZ
Avatar Hldgs [*NASDAQ symbol*] (TTSB) .... AVTR
Avatar Holdings, Inc. [*Associated Press*] (SAG) .... Avatar
Avatar Holdings, Inc. [*NASDAQ symbol*] (NQ) .... AVTR
Avatar Resources Corp. [*Vancouver Stock Exchange symbol*] .... AAV
AVCAL Change Request (MCD) .... ACR
Avco Airway Express, Inc. [*FAA designator*] (FAAC) .... AEX
Avco Data Analysis and Prediction Technique [*for sunspot prediction*] .... ADAPT
Avco Systems Development (MCD) .... AVSD
Avco-Everett Research Laboratory (MCD) .... AERL
Avco-Everett Research Laboratory, Everett, MA [*OCLC symbol*] (OCLC) .... AVC
Avco-Everett Research Laboratory, Everett, MA [*Library symbol Library of Congress*] (LCLS) .... MEvA
Avcon AG [*Switzerland ICAO designator*] (FAAC) .... AVX
Avcon, Aviation Consulting Ltd. [*Switzerland*] [*FAA designator*] (FAAC) .... VCN

Avcorp Industries, Inc. [*Toronto Stock Exchange symbol*] ... AVP
Ave Maria ... AM
Ave Maria ... AVM
Avecor Cardiovascular [*NASDAQ symbol*] (TTSB) ... AVEC
Avecor, Inc. [*NASDAQ symbol*] (SAG) ... AVEC
Avecor, Inc. [*Associated Press*] (SAG) ... Avecor
Aveiro [*Portugal ICAO location identifier*] (ICLI) ... LPAV
AVEMCO Corp. [*NYSE symbol*] (SPSG) ... AVE
AVEMCO Corp. [*Associated Press*] (SAG) ... AVEMCO
Avenal, CA [*Tactical Air Navigation Station*] [*Air Force*] ... AVE
Avenal, CA [*FM radio station call letters*] ... KAAX
Avenger Control Electronics [*Navy*] ... ACE
Avenida [*Avenue*] (EY) ... AVDA
Avenor Inc. [*TS Symbol*] (TTSB) ... AVR
Avensa Aerovias Venezolanas SA [*Venezuela*] [*ICAO designator*] (FAAC) ... AVE
Aventi Cristo [*Before Christ*] [*Italian*] ... AvC
Avenue [*Correspondence*] (EY) ... AV
Avenue (DD) ... av
Avenue (DD) ... Ave
Avenue (VRA) ... ave
Avenue [*Correspondence*] (AFM) ... AVE
Avenue [*Postal Service standard*] (OPSA) ... AVE
Avenue ... AVE
Avenue [*Commonly used*] (OPSA) ... AVEN
Avenue [*Commonly used*] (OPSA) ... AVENU
Avenue [*Commonly used*] (OPSA) ... AVENUE
Avenue [*Commonly used*] (OPSA) ... AVN
Avenue [*Commonly used*] (OPSA) ... AVNUE
Avenue of Approach [*Army*] (AABC) ... AA
Avenue Resources, Inc. [*Vancouver Stock Exchange symbol*] ... AVE
Average (DAVI) ... A
Average ... AV
Average ... AVE
Average ... AVER
Average (AFM) ... AVG
Average (ADA) ... AVGE
Average Absolute Control Movement (MCD) ... AACM
Average Absolute Deviation [*Statistics*] ... AAD
Average Absolute Error (MCD) ... AAE
Average Absolute Percentage Error [*Statistics*] ... AAPE
Average Acceleration ... AA
Average Adjuster [*Insurance*] (DS) ... AA
Average Adjustment Factor (MCD) ... AAF
Average Alarm ... AVA
Average and Excess Demand (IAA) ... AED
Average Annual Cost [*Business term*] (MHDB) ... AAC
Average Annual Daily Traffic [*FHWA*] (TAG) ... AADT
Average Annual Growth Rate (MHDI) ... AAGR
Average Annual Performance Rate ... AAPR
Average Annual Precipitation (PDAA) ... AAP
Average Annual Rainfall (PDAA) ... AAR
Average Annual Temperature (PDAA) ... AAT
Average Aptitude Requirement per Unit Time ... AARPUT
Average Audience [*Television ratings*] ... AA
Average Blank Data [*Computer science*] ... AVEBD
Average Body Dose [*Radiation technology*] (WDAA) ... ABD
Average Body Weight (DMAA) ... ABW
Average Branching Factor (IAA) ... ABF
Average Business Day [*Bell System*] ... ABD
Average Busy Hour [*Telecommunications*] (TEL) ... ABH
Average Busy Season [*Telecommunications*] (TEL) ... ABS
Average Busy Season Busy Hour [*Telecommunications*] (TEL) ... ABSBH
Average Busy Stream [*Computer science*] (ACRL) ... ABS
Average Carbonaceous Chondrite [*Meteorology*] ... AVCC
Average Consumer ... AC
Average Consumer Extraodinaire . ... ACE
Average Correlation Coefficient (PDAA) ... ACC
Average Cost ... AC
Average Cost [*Accounting term*] ... AVCO
Average Cost per Patient Day [*Medicine*] ... ACPPD
Average Crop Yield [*Agriculture*] (WDAA) ... ACY
Average Cumulative Error (PDAA) ... ACE
Average Current-Mantle Adiabat [*Geochemistry*] ... ACMA
Average Customer Wait Time ... ACWT
Average Daily Allowance (ADA) ... ADA
Average Daily Attendance ... ADA
Average Daily Balance ... ADB
Average Daily Census ... ADC
Average Daily Dose [*Pharmacy*] (DAVI) ... ADD
Average Daily Gain [*of weight*] [*Cattle*] ... ADG
Average Daily Member Load ... ADML
Average Daily Membership ... ADM
Average Daily Patient Load [*Medicine*] ... ADPL
Average Daily Rate [*Hotels*] ... ADR
Average Daily Service Charge [*Hospitals*] ... ADSC
Average Daily Traffic ... ADT
Average Decreasing Line ... ADL
Average Deferral Percentage ... ADP
Average Depth (IAA) ... AD
Average Depth (NOAA) ... AVDTH
Average Deviation [*Statistics*] ... AD
Average Diameter ... AD
Average Effectiveness Level (IAA) ... AEL
Average Efficiency (IAA) ... AVEFF
Average Efficiency Index ... AEI
Average Electrode Current ... AEC
Average Error (MCD) ... AE
Average Evoked Potential [*Neurophysiology*] ... AEP
Average Evoked Response [*Neurophysiology*] ... AER
Average Excitation Energy [*Physics*] ... AEE
Average Extent of Burning ... AEB
Average Failure Number ... AFN
Average Female Mass [*Ecology*] ... FMA
Average Female Weekly Earnings ... AFWE
Average Fixed Cost [*Economics*] ... AFC
Average Flying Hours per Sortie [*Air Force*] (AFIT) ... AFHS
Average for Gestational Age [*Medicine*] (DAVI) ... AGA
Average Freight Rate Assessment [*Shipping*] ... AFRA
Average Global Automobile [*Emissions to atmosphere*] ... AGA
Average Goals Against per Period [*Hockey*] ... AGP
Average Grid Heading (SAA) ... AVGH
Average Heading ... AVH
Average Hearing Level ... AHL
Average Holding Time [*Telecommunications*] (TEL) ... AHT
Average Index Sequential Access Method [*Computer science*] (MHDI) ... AVISAM
Average Indexed Monthly Earnings [*Social Security Administration*] ... AIME
Average Indexed Yearly Earnings (GFGA) ... AIYE
Average Instruction Execution Time [*Computer parameter*] ... AIET
Average Instructions per Second [*Computer science*] ... AIP
Average Integral Square Error (PDAA) ... AISE
Average Intravascular Pressure [*Medicine*] (MAE) ... AIP
Average Inventory Level ... AIL
Average Length of Stay [*of patients in a health care institution*] ... ALOS
Average Linear Planar Heat Generation Rate [*Nuclear energy*] (NRCH) ... ALPHGR
Average Load Factor ... ALF
Average Magnitude for Velocity [*Military*] ... AMV
Average Male Mass ... MMA
Average Male Weekly Earnings ... AMWE
Average Man-Hours per Day (DNAB) ... AMHD
Average Mean Pressure ... AMP
Average Miles Driven Per Day [*DOE*] (TAG) ... AMPD
Average Month Program [*Air Force*] (AFIT) ... AMP
Average Monthly Consumption (MCD) ... AMC
Average Monthly Demand ... AMD
Average Monthly Earnings ... AME
Average Monthly Sales (MCD) ... AMS
Average Monthly Usage (KSC) ... AMU
Average Monthly Wage ... AMW
Average Mutual Information (PDAA) ... AMI
Average Net Cost [*Insurance*] ... ANC
Average Octane Number ... AON
Average of Normals ... AON
Average Operating Cost (KSC) ... AOC
Average Operation Time ... AOT
Average Out [*Business term*] ... AO
Average Outgoing Quality [*Quality control*] ... AOQ
Average Outgoing Quality Laboratory ... AOQL
Average Outgoing Quality Level [*or Limit*] [*Quality control*] ... AOQL
Average Oxidation State [*Physical chemistry*] ... AOS
Average Page Exposure [*Advertising*] (WDMC) ... apx
Average Particle Diameter ... APD
Average Peak Noise (MAE) ... APN
Average per Pupil Expenditure [*Education*] (GFGA) ... APPE
Average Percentage Damage [*Meteorology*] ... APD
Average Percentage Difference [*Mathematics*] ... APD
Average Picture Level ... APL
Average Picture Level (MSA) ... AVPL
Average Planar Heat Generation Rate [*Nuclear energy*] (NRCH) ... APLHGR
Average Pore Diameter [*Filtration*] ... APD
Average Power Control [*Telecommunications*] (TEL) ... APC
Average Power Dissipation ... APD
Average Power Range Monitor [*Nuclear energy*] (NRCH) ... APRM
Average Price ... AP
Average Product [*Economics*] ... AP
Average Product of Labor ... AP_L
Average Propensity to Consume [*Economics*] ... APC
Average Propensity to Save [*Economics*] ... APS
Average Quality Limit ... AQL
Average Quality of the Lot (IAA) ... AQL
Average Quantity Repaired Monthly ... AQRM
Average Quarter Hour (WDMC) ... AQH
Average Quarter Hour Rating [*Television*] [*Radio*] (WDMC) ... AQH
Average Quarter-Hour Rating [*Of radio and television programming*] (WDMC) ... AQR
Average Quarterly Demand ... AQD
Average Rating ... AR
Average Rectified Forward Current [*Electronics*] (IAA) ... ARFC
Average Rectified Slope [*FHWA*] (TAG) ... ARS
Average Recurrent Interval ... ARI
Average Relationship Index ... ARI
Average Relative Representation Error (IAA) ... ARRE
Average Remaining Lifetime (MAE) ... ARL
Average Response Amplitude ... ARA
Average Response Amplitude Data ... ARAD
Average Response Computer ... ARC
Average Response Data ... ARD
Average Response Latency [*Biochemistry*] ... ARL
Average Response Time ... ART
Average Retrieval Time (OA) ... ART
Average Revenue ... AR

Average Revenue/Average Physical Product [*Economics*] ... ARAP
Average Revenue/Marginal Physical Product [*Economics*] ... ARMP
Average Revenue per Message ... ARPM
Average Run Length [*Statistics*] ... ARL
Average Sample Number [*Quality control*] ... ASN
Average Sample Run Length [*Statistics*] (PDAA) ... ASRL
Average Sampling Time [*Statistics*] ... AST
Average Season Busy Hour Call Attempts [*Telecommunications*] (TEL) ... ASBHCA
Average Season Busy Hour Call Completions [*Telecommunications*] (TEL) ... ASBHCC
Average Service Life ... ASL
Average Sorties per Aircraft Actually Possessed [*Air Force*] (AFIT) ... ASAXP
Average Sorties per Day [*Air Force*] (AFIT) ... ASD
Average Specific Polymerization Rate (OA) ... ASPR
Average Speech Power ... ASP
Average Staffing Level ... ASL
Average Standing Crop ... ASC
Average Straight Time Hourly Earnings [*Accounting*] ... ASTHE
Average Student Hours [*Education*] (AIE) ... ASH
Average Task Time ... ATT
Average Temperature (NOAA) ... AVTMP
Average Temperature (NRCH) ... TAVE
Average Time between Maintenance ... ATBM
Average Time of Burning ... ATB
Average Time to Repair (MCD) ... ATTR
Average T-Matrix Approximation (MCD) ... ATA
Average Total Cost ... ATC
Average Total Diametrical Displacement (IAA) ... ATDD
Average Total Episode Cost [*Medicine*] ... ATEC
Average Total Inspection [*QCR*] ... ATI
Average Total Operating Cost (KSC) ... ATOC
Average Total Unit Cost ... ATUC
Average Transfer Rate of Information BITS [*Binary Digits*] [*Computer science*] (IEEE) ... ATRIB
Average Turnaround [*Computer science*] ... ATA
Average Unit Cost ... AUC
Average Unit of Council Funding [*Higher Education Funding Council*] (AIE) ... AUCF
Average Unit Procurement Cost [*Military*] (DOMA) ... AUPC
Average Useful Life ... AUL
Average Utilization Factor ... AUF
Average Value (NASA) ... AV
Average Variability ... AV
Average Variable Cost [*Of production*] ... AVC
Average Variable Costs ... AVC
Average Visual Evoked Potential [*Neurophysiology*] ... AVEP
Average Wage ... AW
Average Weekday Daily Traffic [*TXDOT*] (TAG) ... AWDT
Average Weekly Earnings ... AWE
Average White Back [*Football*] ... AWB
[*The*] **Average White Band** [*Rock music group*] ... AWB
Average Wholesale Price ... AWP
Average Width ... AVW
Average Work Load ... AWL
Average Work Time ... AWT
Average Working Depth ... AWD
Average Yarding Distance [*Forestry*] ... AYD
Average Yearly Demands ... AYD
Averaged [*Motor Octane Number*] [*Antiknock index Fuel technology*] ... R & M/2
Averaged Magnitude Squared Coherence (MCD) ... AMSC
Averaged Probability Ratio Sequential Test (MHDI) ... APRST
Averaged-Coupled Pair Functional [*Quantum chemistry*] ... ACPF
Averbach on Handling Accident Cases [*A publication*] (DLA) ... Averbach Acci Cas
Averette College, Danville, VA [*Library symbol Library of Congress*] (LCLS) ... ViDA
Averroes [*Morocco*] [*Seismograph station code, US Geological Survey*] (SEIS) ... AVE
Avert Disruption of Operation ... AVERDISROP
Avert, Inc. [*Associated Press*] (SAG) ... Avert
Avert, Inc. [*NASDAQ symbol*] (SAG) ... AVRT
Avert Inc. Wrrt [*NASDAQ symbol*] (TTSB) ... AVRTW
Avery [*Printer of U.S. postage stamps*] (BARN) ... AVR
Avery and Hobb's Bankrupt Law [*A publication*] (DLA) ... Av & HBL
Avery and Hobbs' Bankrupt Law of United States [*A publication*] (DLA) ... A & H Bank
Avery Dennison Corp. [*Associated Press*] (SAG) ... AveryD
Avery Dennison Corp. [*NYSE symbol*] (SPSG) ... AVY
Avery Point [*Connecticut*] [*Seismograph station code, US Geological Survey Closed*] (SEIS) ... APT
Avery-Mitchell-Yancey Regional Library, Spruce Pine, NC [*Library symbol Library of Congress*] (LCLS) ... NcSppA
Avery-Morrison Public Library, Newland, NC [*Library symbol Library of Congress*] (LCLS) ... NcNew
Aves [*Birds*] [*of Aristophanes*] [*Classical studies*] (OCD) ... Av
Avesen SA de CV [*Mexico ICAO designator*] (FAAC) ... ESE
Avesta [*Language, etc.*] ... Av
Avesta [*MARC language code Library of Congress*] (LCCP) ... ave
Avesta [*Sweden ICAO location identifier*] (ICLI) ... ESVA
Avestan (BARN) ... Av
Avia [*Francis Lombardi eC*] [*Italy ICAO aircraft manufacturer identifier*] (ICAO) ... AD
Avia Airlines [*South Africa*] [*FAA designator*] (FAAC) ... AGW
Avia Airlines [*Ghana*] [*FAA designator*] (FAAC) ... VIL
Avia Express Ltd. [*Hungary*] [*ICAO designator*] (FAAC) ... AEH
Avia Filipines International, Inc. [*Philippines*] [*ICAO designator*] (FAAC) ... FIL
Avia Kargo Sisitem, AS [*Turkey*] [*FAA designator*] (FAAC) ... AVK
Avia Sud [*France ICAO designator*] (FAAC) ... AVU
Aviacion Colombiana Ltd. [*Colombia*] [*ICAO designator*] (FAAC) ... VCO
Aviacion Comercial de America, SA de DV [*Mexico*] [*FAA designator*] (FAAC) ... VME
Aviacion de Chiapas [*Mexico ICAO designator*] (FAAC) ... CHP
Aviacion del Noroeste SA de CV [*Mexico ICAO designator*] (FAAC) ... ANW
Aviacion Ejecutiva del Noroeste SA de CV [*Mexico ICAO designator*] (FAAC) ... NST
Aviacion Ejecutiva Mexicana SA [*Mexico ICAO designator*] (FAAC) ... AVM
Aviacion y Comercio SA [*Aviation and Trade Corporation*] [*Airline*] [*Spain*] ... AVIACO
Aviacion y Comercio SA [*Spain ICAO designator*] (FAAC) ... AYC
Aviacor [*Former USSR*] [*FAA designator*] (FAAC) ... VCR
Aviaeskadra [*Russian term for an air squadron*] ... AS
Aviair Aviation Ltd. [*Canada ICAO designator*] (FAAC) ... AVF
Avial (Russian Co. Ltd.) [*Former USSR ICAO designator*] (FAAC) ... RLC
Avialgarve, Taxis Aereos do Algarve Ltd. [*Portugal ICAO designator*] (FAAC) ... AVG
Aviall, Inc. [*Associated Press*] (SAG) ... Aviall
Aviall, Inc. [*NYSE symbol*] (SPSG) ... AVL
Aviamilano [*Construzioni Aeronautiche SpA*] [*Italy ICAO aircraft manufacturer identifier*] (ICAO) ... AM
Avian Aircraft Ltd. [*Canada ICAO aircraft manufacturer identifier*] (ICAO) ... VA
Avian Basal Medium [*Culture media*] ... ABM
Avian Embryo Nutrient Cartridge ... AENC
Avian Erythroblastosis [*Medicine*] (DMAA) ... AEB
Avian Erythroblastosis Virus ... AEV
Avian Herpes Virus (DMAA) ... AHV
Avian Infectious Bronchitis [*Medicine*] (DMAA) ... AIB
Avian Influenza ... AI
Avian Leukosis Complex (MAE) ... ALC
Avian Leukosis Virus ... ALV
Avian Lymphoblastosis [*Medicine*] (DMAA) ... ALB
Avian Myeloblastic Virus Reverse Transcription [*Genetics*] ... AMVRT
Avian Myeloblastosis [*Medicine*] (DMAA) ... AMB
Avian Myeloblastosis Virus ... AMV
Avian Nephritis Virus [*Medicine*] (DMAA) ... ANV
Avian Pancreatic Polypeptide ... APP
Avian Philately Unit [*Defunct*] (EA) ... APU
Avian Retrovirus ... ARV
Avian Retrovirus ... AVRV
Avian Sarcoma Virus [*Same as RSV*] ... ASV
Avian Sarcoma-Leukosis Virus ... ASLV
Avian Tumor Virus [*Medicine*] (DMAA) ... ATV
Avianca [*ICAO designator*] (AD) ... AV
Avianca (GAVI) ... AV
AVIANCA [*Aerovias Nacionales de Colombia SA*] [*Colombian airline*] ... AVN
Avianca, Aerovias Nacionales de Colombia SA [*ICAO designator*] (FAAC) ... AVA
Aviano [*Italy ICAO location identifier*] (ICLI) ... LIPA
Aviano [*Italy ICAO location identifier*] (ICLI) ... LIYW
Avianova SpA [*Italy ICAO designator*] (FAAC) ... NOV
Aviaobshemash [*Former USSR*] [*FAA designator*] (FAAC) ... OBM
Aviapaslauga [*Lithuania*] [*FAA designator*] (FAAC) ... AVX
Aviapolk [*Russian term for an air regiment*] ... AP
Aviaprima [*Russian Federation*] [*ICAO designator*] (FAAC) ... PRL
Aviaross [*Russian Federation*] [*ICAO designator*] (FAAC) ... RAR
Aviata [*Former USSR*] [*FAA designator*] (FAAC) ... TVL
Aviateca [*ICAO designator*] (AD) ... GU
Aviation [*FCC*] (NTCM) ... A
Aviation [*Special duties officer*] [*British*] ... AV
Aviation (DLA) ... AVI
Aviation (AFM) ... AVN
Aviation ... AVN
Aviation Administrative Communication (DA) ... AAC
Aviation Amos [*M et J*], Inc. [*Canada ICAO designator*] (FAAC) ... AMJ
Aviation and Air Defense Division [*US Army Human Engineering Laboratory, Aberdeen Proving Ground, MD*] (RDA) ... AADD
Aviation and Computer Enthusiasts [*Defunct*] (EA) ... ACE
Aviation and Fire Management Centre, Ontario Ministry of Natural Resources, Sault Ste. Marie [*Library symbol National Library of Canada*] (BIB) ... OSTMNA
Aviation and Surface Effects Department [*David W. Taylor Naval Ship Research and Development Center*] ... ASED
Aviation and Surface Material Command [*Air Force*] ... AVSCOM
Aviation and Troop Command [*Army*] ... ATCOM
Aviation and Troop Support Command [*Army*] (RDA) ... ATCOM
Aviation Annex [*Air Force*] ... AA
Aviation Antisubmarine Warfare Basic Operational Trainer ... AAWBOT
Aviation Applied Technology Directorate [*Fort Eustis, VA*] [*Army*] (RDA) ... AATD
Aviation Armament Bulletin (MCD) ... AAB
Aviation Armament Change (MCD) ... AAC
Aviation Armament Laboratory [*Later, Naval Air Development Center*] [*Navy*] ... AAL
Aviation Associates, Inc. [*St. Croix*] [*ICAO designator*] (FAAC) ... SUA
Aviation Association of Indiana (SRA) ... AAI
Aviation ASW [*Antisubmarine Warfare*] **Operator** [*Navy rating*] ... AW
Aviation ASW [*Antisubmarine Warfare*] **Operator, First Class** [*Navy rating*] ... AW1
Aviation ASW [*Antisubmarine Warfare*] **Operator, Master Chief** [*Navy rating*] ... AWCM
Aviation ASW [*Antisubmarine Warfare*] **Operator, Second Class** [*Navy rating*] ... AW2
Aviation ASW [*Antisubmarine Warfare*] **Operator, Senior Chief** [*Navy rating*] ... AWCS

Aviation ASW [*Antisubmarine Warfare*] **Operator, Third Class** [*Navy rating*] ... AW3
Aviation ASW [*Antisubmarine Warfare*] **Technician** [*Navy rating*] ... AX
Aviation ASW [*Antisubmarine Warfare*] **Technician, Chief** [*Navy rating*] ... AXC
Aviation ASW [*Antisubmarine Warfare*] **Technician, First Class** [*Navy rating*] ... AX1
Aviation ASW [*Antisubmarine Warfare*] **Technician, Master Chief** [*Navy rating*] ... AXCM
Aviation ASW [*Antisubmarine Warfare*] **Technician, Second Class** [*Navy rating*] ... AX2
Aviation ASW [*Antisubmarine Warfare*] **Technician, Senior Chief** [*Navy rating*] ... AXCS
Aviation ASW [*Antisubmarine Warfare*] **Technician, Third Class** [*Navy rating*] ... AX3
Aviation Automated Weather Observation System (NOAA) ... AV-AWOS
Aviation Base Responsibility List (AFIT) ... ABRL
Aviation Baseship ... AVB
Aviation Battalion [*Army*] ... AB
Aviation Battalion [*Army*] ... AVBAT
Aviation Beauport Ltd. [*British ICAO designator*] (FAAC) ... AVB
Aviation Billet Indicator (DNAB) ... ABI
Aviation Boatswain [*Navy rating*] ... AB
Aviation Boatswain's Mate [*Navy rating*] ... ABM
Aviation Boatswain's Mate, Arresting Gear and Barriers [*Navy rating*] ... ABMAG
Aviation Boatswain's Mate, Catapult [*Navy rating*] ... ABMCP
Aviation Boatswain's Mate, Chief [*Navy rating*] ... ABC
Aviation Boatswain's Mate, First Class [*Navy rating*] ... AB1
Aviation Boatswain's Mate, Fuel [*Navy rating*] ... ABF
Aviation Boatswain's Mate, Fuel, Airman [*Navy rating*] ... ABFAN
Aviation Boatswain's Mate, Fuel, Airman Apprentice [*Navy rating*] ... ABFAA
Aviation Boatswain's Mate, Fuel, Second Class [*Navy rating*] (DNAB) ... ABF2
Aviation Boatswain's Mate, Fuel, Third Class [*Navy rating*] (DNAB) ... ABF3
Aviation Boatswain's Mate, Gasoline System [*Navy rating*] ... ABMGA
Aviation Boatswain's Mate, Handler [*Navy rating*] ... ABH
Aviation Boatswain's Mate, Handler, Airman [*Navy rating*] ... ABHAN
Aviation Boatswain's Mate, Handler, Airman Apprentice [*Navy rating*] ... ABHAA
Aviation Boatswain's Mate, Handler, First Class [*Navy rating*] (DNAB) ... ABH1
Aviation Boatswain's Mate, Handler, Second Class [*Navy rating*] (DNAB) ... ABH2
Aviation Boatswain's Mate, Handler, Third Class [*Navy rating*] (DNAB) ... ABH3
Aviation Boatswain's Mate, Launch and Recovery Equipment [*Navy rating*] ... ABE
Aviation Boatswain's Mate, Launch and Recovery Equipment, Airman [*Navy rating*] ... ABEAN
Aviation Boatswain's Mate, Launch and Recovery Equipment, Airman Apprentice [*Navy rating*] ... ABEAA
Aviation Boatswain's Mate, Plane Handler [*Navy rating*] ... ABMPH
Aviation Boatswain's Mate, Second Class [*Navy rating*] ... AB2
Aviation Boatswain's Mate, Senior Chief [*Navy rating*] ... ABCS
Aviation Boatswain's Mate, Third Class [*Navy rating*] ... AB3
Aviation Cadet [*Air Force*] ... AC
Aviation Cadet ... AvC
Aviation Cadet [*Navy*] ... AVCAD
Aviation Cadet Alumni Association (EA) ... ACAA
Aviation Cadet Qualifying Test [*Military*] ... ACQT
Aviation Calibration Equipment (MCD) ... AVCAL
Aviation Career Incentive Act [*1974*] (AABC) ... ACIA
Aviation Career Incentive Pay [*Air Force*] (AFM) ... ACIP
Aviation Carrier Turbine Fuel ... AVCAT
Aviation Cases [*Commerce Clearing House*] [*A publication*] (DLA) ... Av Cas
Aviation Center [*Army*] ... AVNC
Aviation Charter & Management [*British ICAO designator*] (FAAC) ... FTN
Aviation Chief Boatswain's Mate, Arresting Gear and Barriers [*Navy rating*] ... ACBMAG
Aviation Chief Boatswain's Mate, Catapult [*Navy rating*] ... ACBMCP
Aviation Chief Boatswain's Mate, Gasoline System [*Navy rating*] ... ACBMGA
Aviation Chief Boatswain's Mate, Plane Handler [*Navy rating*] ... ACBMPH
Aviation Chief Electrician's Mate [*Navy*] ... ACEM
Aviation Chief Fire Controlman [*Navy*] ... ACFC
Aviation Chief Machinist's Mate [*Navy*] ... ACMM
Aviation Chief Machinist's Mate, Carburetor Mechanic [*Navy*] ... ACMMC
Aviation Chief Machinist's Mate, Flight Engineer [*Navy*] ... ACMMF
Aviation Chief Machinist's Mate, Gas Turbine Mechanic [*Navy*] ... ACMMT
Aviation Chief Machinist's Mate, Hydraulic Mechanic [*Navy*] ... ACMMH
Aviation Chief Machinist's Mate, Instrument Mechanic [*Navy*] ... ACMMI
Aviation Chief Machinist's Mate, Propeller Mechanic [*Navy*] ... ACMMP
Aviation Chief Metalsmith [*Navy*] ... ACM
Aviation Chief Ordnanceman [*Navy*] ... ACOM
Aviation Chief Ordnanceman, Turret Mechanic [*Navy*] ... ACOMT
Aviation Chief Radio Technician [*Navy*] ... ACRT
Aviation Chief Radioman [*Navy*] ... ACRM
Aviation Circular Letter ... ACL
Aviation Classification Repair Activity Depot [*Army*] (RDA) ... AVCRAD
Aviation Classification Test ... ACT
Aviation Clothing and Survival Equipment Bulletin (MCD) ... ACSEB
Aviation Combat Development Agency [*CDC*] ... ACDA
Aviation Combat Element [*Marine Corps*] (DOMA) ... ACE
Aviation Combat Training System [*Military*] ... ACTS
Aviation Combined Arms Tactical Trainer [*Army*] ... AVCATT
Aviation Combined Arms Team Trainer ... ACATT
Aviation Command Screening Board (DNAB) ... ACSB
Aviation Commission Date (DNAB) ... ACD
Aviation Company [*Military*] (VNW) ... AVN
Aviation Co. Meridian [*Former USSR*] [*FAA designator*] (FAAC) ... MMM
Aviation Co. Mostransgas [*Former USSR*] [*FAA designator*] (FAAC) ... MTG
Aviation Consolidated Allowance List [*Military*] (NVT) ... AVCAL
Aviation Construction Engineers [*Military*] ... ACE
Aviation Consumer Action Project (EA) ... ACAP
Aviation Continuation Pay [*Navy*] (DOMA) ... ACP
Aviation Control Center ... ACC
Aviation Crash Injury Research (MUGU) ... ACIR
Aviation Credit Corps ... ACC
Aviation Crime Prevention Institute (EA) ... ACPI
Aviation Cruiser (MCD) ... CH
Aviation Daily ... AD
Aviation Data Analysis Center (MCD) ... AVDAC
Aviation Data and Analysis System [*BTS*] (TAG) ... ADA
Aviation Data Service, Inc. [*Information service or system*] (IID) ... ADS
Aviation Depot Group (AAG) ... ADG
Aviation Depot Level Repairables (MCD) ... AVDLRS
Aviation Depot Squadron [*Air Force*] ... ADS
Aviation Depot Squadron [*Air Force*] ... AVDS
Aviation Design Research [*Navy*] ... ADR
Aviation Detachment [*Military*] (VNW) ... AD
Aviation Development Co. Nigeria Ltd. [*ICAO designator*] (FAAC) ... ADK
Aviation Development Council (EA) ... ADC
Aviation Development Test Activity [*Test and Evaluation Command*] [*Army*] (RDA) ... ADTA
Aviation Development Test Activity [*Test and Evaluation Command*] [*Army*] (RDA) ... AVNDTA
Aviation Development Test Facility (MCD) ... ADTF
Aviation Distributors and Manufacturers Association (EA) ... ADMA
Aviation Distributors, Inc. [*NASDAQ symbol*] (SAG) ... ADIN
Aviation Distributors, Inc. [*Associated Press*] (SAG) ... AviDist
Aviation Division [*Marine science*] (OSRA) ... AD
Aviation Division [*Forecast Systems Laboratory*] (USDC) ... AD
Aviation Electric Ltd., Montreal, PQ, Canada [*Library symbol Library of Congress*] (LCLS) ... CaQMAE
Aviation Electric Ltd., Montreal, Quebec [*Library symbol National Library of Canada*] (NLC) ... QMAE
Aviation Electrician's Mate [*Navy rating*] ... AE
Aviation Electrician's Mate [*Navy rating*] ... AEM
Aviation Electrician's Mate, Chief [*Navy rating*] ... AEC
Aviation Electrician's Mate, First Class [*Navy rating*] ... AE1
Aviation Electrician's Mate, Master Chief [*Navy rating*] ... AECM
Aviation Electrician's Mate, Second Class [*Navy rating*] ... AE2
Aviation Electrician's Mate, Senior Chief [*Navy rating*] ... AECS
Aviation Electrician's Mate, Third Class [*Navy rating*] ... AE3
Aviation Electronic Combat [*Army*] (RDA) ... AEC
Aviation Electronic Equipment Information Exchange System (MCD) ... AVEXS
Aviation Electronic Technician's Mate [*Navy*] ... AETM
Aviation Electronic Technician's Mate, Combat Aircrewman [*Navy*] ... AETAC
Aviation Electronics ... AVIONICS
Aviation Electronics Technician [*Navy rating*] ... AT
Aviation Electronics Technician Airborne CIC [*Combat Information Center*] **Equipment** ... ATW
Aviation Electronics Technician, Chief [*Navy rating*] ... ATC
Aviation Electronics Technician, First Class [*Navy rating*] ... AT1
Aviation Electronics Technician, Master Chief [*Navy rating*] ... ATCM
Aviation Electronics Technician, Second Class [*Navy rating*] ... AT2
Aviation Electronics Technician, Senior Chief [*Navy rating*] ... ATCS
Aviation Electronics Technician, Third Class [*Navy rating*] ... AT3
Aviation Electronicsman [*Military*] ... AL
Aviation Engineer (IAA) ... AE
Aviation Engineer Battalion [*Marine Corps*] ... AVNENGRBN
Aviation Engineer Force ... AEF
Aviation Engineering Corp. (MCD) ... AVIEN
Aviation Engineering Flight Activity [*Formerly, ASTA*] [*Edwards Air Force Base, CA*] [*Army*] ... AEFA
Aviation Enterprises [*Denmark ICAO designator*] (FAAC) ... AVP
Aviation Facilities Energy Association [*Defunct*] (EA) ... AFEA
Aviation Facilities Service [*of FAA*] ... AFS
Aviation Financial Services, Inc. ... AFSI
Aviation Fire Control Technician [*Navy rating*] ... AQ
Aviation Fire Control Technician, Bomb Direction [*Navy rating*] ... AQB
Aviation Fire Control Technician, Chief [*Navy rating*] ... AQC
Aviation Fire Control Technician, Fire Control [*Navy rating*] ... AQF
Aviation Fire Control Technician, First Class [*Navy rating*] ... AQ1
Aviation Fire Control Technician, Master Chief [*Navy rating*] ... AQCM
Aviation Fire Control Technician, Second Class [*Navy rating*] ... AQ2
Aviation Fire Control Technician, Senior Chief [*Navy rating*] ... AQCS
Aviation Fire Control Technician, Third Class [*Navy rating*] ... AQ3
Aviation Fire Controlman [*Navy*] ... AFC
Aviation Fleet Maintenance (NVT) ... AFM
Aviation Foot Lockers [*Army*] (RDA) ... AFL
Aviation Force Structure for the Army (MCD) ... AFSA
Aviation Forecast Verification Program [*Marine science*] (OSRA) ... AFVP
Aviation Forecast Verification Program (USDC) ... AFVP
Aviation Forum [*British*] ... AF
Aviation Fuel (MSA) ... AVFUEL
Aviation Fuel [*Gasoline/Kerosene*] [*NATO*] ... AVTAG
Aviation Fuel, High-Flash Point [*NATO*] ... AVCAT
Aviation Fuels Logistical Area Summary [*Air Force*] (AFIT) ... AFLAS
Aviation Fuels, Lubricants, and Associated Products [*NATO*] (NATG) ... F & L
Aviation Gas Turbine (KSC) ... AGT
Aviation Gasoline [*Navy*] ... AGAS
Aviation Gasoline ... AVGAS
Aviation Gridded Forecast System [*Marine science*] (OSRA) ... AGFS
Aviation Gridded Forecast System (USDC) ... AGFS
Aviation Ground Equipment (AAGC) ... AGE
Aviation Ground Power Unit (MCD) ... AGPU

Aviation Ground Unit [*Naval Reserve*] ... AGU
Aviation Guided Flight (MUGU) ... AGF
Aviation Gunnery Officers School ... AGOS
Aviation Historical Society (EA) ... AHS
Aviation Human Research Unit [*Army*] ... AHRU
Aviation Impact Variable (OSRA) ... AIV
Aviation Impact Variable (USDC) ... AIV
Aviation Indoctrination Program [*Military*] (DNAB) ... AIP
Aviation Industries of China (ECON) ... AVIC
Aviation Industry Advisory Council (ADA) ... AVIAC
Aviation Information Services Ltd. (IID) ... AISL
Aviation Instrument Laboratory [*Navy*] ... AIL
Aviation Insurance Officers Association (DA) ... AIOA
Aviation Insurance Rating Bureau [*Defunct*] (EA) ... AIRB
Aviation Intensive Management Items (AABC) ... AIMI
Aviation Intermediate Maintenance [*Army*] (MCD) ... AVIM
Aviation Investigator (LAIN) ... AI
Aviation Item Reports ... AIR
Aviation Kamchatka-California Organization for Reconstruction and Development (ECON) ... AKCORD
Aviation Laboratories [*Army*] ... AVLABS
Aviation LASER Device ... AVLD
Aviation Law Reporter [*Commerce Clearing House*] [*A publication*] (DLA) ... Av L Rep
Aviation Legere de l'Armee de Terre [*France ICAO designator*] (FAAC) ... LAT
Aviation Life Support Equipment (AABC) ... ALSE
Aviation Life Support Systems (MCD) ... ALSS
Aviation Logistics and Operations Center [*Military*] (DOMA) ... ALOC
Aviation Logistics Officer Course [*Army*] (INF) ... AVLOC
Aviation Lubricant (MUGU) ... AVLUB
Aviation Machinist Mate Jet, Chief [*Navy rating*] ... ADJC
Aviation Machinist Mate Jet, Master Chief [*Navy rating*] ... ADJM
Aviation Machinist Mate Jet, Senior Chief [*Navy rating*] ... ADJS
Aviation Machinist's Mate [*Navy rating*] ... AD
Aviation Machinist's Mate [*Navy rating*] ... AMM
Aviation Machinist's Mate, Carburetor Mechanic [*Navy rating*] ... AMMC
Aviation Machinist's Mate, Combat Aircrewman [*Navy rating*] ... AMMAC
Aviation Machinist's Mate, Flight Engineer [*Navy rating*] ... AMMF
Aviation Machinist's Mate, Hydraulic Mechanic [*Navy rating*] ... AMMH
Aviation Machinist's Mate, Instrument Mechanic [*Navy rating*] ... AMMI
Aviation Machinist's Mate, Jet Engine Mechanic [*Navy rating*] ... ADJ
Aviation Machinist's Mate, Jet Engine Mechanic, First Class [*Navy rating*] (DNAB) ... ADJ1
Aviation Machinist's Mate, Jet Engine Mechanic, Second Class [*Navy rating*] (DNAB) ... ADJ2
Aviation Machinist's Mate, Jet Engine Mechanic, Third Class [*Navy rating*] (DNAB) ... ADJ3
Aviation Machinist's Mate, Propeller Mechanic [*Navy rating*] ... AMMP
Aviation Machinist's Mate, Reciprocating Engine Mechanic [*Navy rating*] ... ADR
Aviation Machinist's Mate, Reciprocating Engine Mechanic, Chief [*Navy rating*] ... ADRC
Aviation Machinist's Mate, Reciprocating Engine Mechanic, First Class [*Navy rating*] ... ADR1
Aviation Machinist's Mate, Reciprocating Engine Mechanic, Master Chief [*Navy rating*] ... ADRCM
Aviation Machinist's Mate, Reciprocating Engine Mechanic, Second Class [*Navy rating*] ... ADR2
Aviation Machinist's Mate, Reciprocating Engine Mechanic, Senior Chief [*Navy rating*] ... ADRCS
Aviation Machinist's Mate, Reciprocating Engine Mechanic, Third Class [*Navy rating*] ... ADR3
Aviation Machinist's Mate, Turret Mechanic [*Navy rating*] ... AMMT
Aviation Maintenance Administrationman [*Navy rating*] ... AZ
Aviation Maintenance Administrationman, Chief [*Navy rating*] ... AZC
Aviation Maintenance Administrationman, First Class [*Navy rating*] ... AZ1
Aviation Maintenance Administrationman, Master Chief [*Navy rating*] ... AZCM
Aviation Maintenance Administrationman, Second Class [*Navy rating*] ... AZ2
Aviation Maintenance Administrationman, Senior Chief [*Navy rating*] ... AZCS
Aviation Maintenance Administrationman, Third Class [*Navy rating*] ... AZ3
Aviation Maintenance and Logistics Evaluation (MCD) ... AMLE
Aviation Maintenance Costs ... AMC
Aviation Maintenance Foundation, Inc. (EA) ... AMFI
Aviation Maintenance Officer [*Military*] (NVT) ... AMO
Aviation Maintenance Technician [*Military*] (DNAB) ... AVMAINTECH
Aviation Management Corp. [*ICAO designator*] (FAAC) ... AAM
Aviation Marine-Outillage ... AMO
Aviation Material Change (SAA) ... AMC
Aviation Material Combat Ready In-Country (MCD) ... AMCRIC
Aviation Material Office [*Military*] (AFIT) ... AMO
Aviation Material Office, Atlantic [*Military*] (DNAB) ... AVNMATOLANT
Aviation Material Office, Reserve [*Military*] (DNAB) ... AVNMATORES
Aviation Materiel Command [*St. Louis, MO*] [*Army*] ... AVCOM
Aviation Materiel Laboratories [*Army*] ... AML
Aviation Materiel Management Center (AABC) ... AMMC
Aviation Materiel Management Improvement Program [*Military*] (NG) ... AMMIP
Aviation Medical ... AVM
Aviation Medical Acceleration Laboratory (MCD) ... AMAL
Aviation Medical Examiner ... AME
Aviation Medical Officer [*Military*] (AABC) ... AMO
Aviation Medical Reports ... AMR
Aviation Medicine [*Medical officer designation*] [*British*] ... A/M
Aviation Medicine ... AM
Aviation Medicine [*Military*] (AABC) ... AVNMED
Aviation Medicine Technician [*Navy*] ... AVT
Aviation Metalsmith ... AM
Aviation Meteorological Facsimile [*National Weather Service*] ... AMFAX
Aviation Network (IAA) ... AVNET
Aviation News Features ... ANF
Aviation Observation (NOAA) ... AVIOB
Aviation Officer [*MTMC*] (TAG) ... AO
Aviation Officer Candidate [*Navy*] ... AOC
Aviation Officer Candidate Airman [*Navy*] (DNAB) ... AOCAN
Aviation Officer Candidate School [*Navy*] ... AOCS
Aviation Officer Continuation Pay [*Navy*] ... AOCP
Aviation Officer of the Day [*MTMC*] (TAG) ... AOD
Aviation Officers' Quarters ... AOQ
Aviation Officers Training Corps ... AOTC
Aviation Oil [*Military*] ... A OIL
Aviation Oil [*Military*] ... AVOIL
Aviation Operating Detachment (CINC) ... AOD
Aviation Operations Technician (DNAB) ... AVOPTECH
Aviation Ordnance Officer ... AOO
Aviation Ordnance Technician (DNAB) ... AVORDTECH
Aviation Ordnanceman [*Navy rating*] ... AO
Aviation Ordnanceman [*Navy rating Obsolete*] ... AOM
Aviation Ordnanceman, Airman Apprentice, Striker [*Navy rating*] ... AOAA
Aviation Ordnanceman, Airman, Striker [*Navy rating*] ... AOAN
Aviation Ordnanceman, Bombsight Mechanic [*Navy rating Obsolete*] ... AOMB
Aviation Ordnanceman, Chief [*Navy rating*] ... AOC
Aviation Ordnanceman, Combat Aircrewman [*Navy rating Obsolete*] ... AOMAC
Aviation Ordnanceman, Combat Aircrewman, Air Bomber [*Navy rating Obsolete*] ... AOACB
Aviation Ordnanceman, First Class [*Navy rating*] ... AO1
Aviation Ordnanceman, Master Chief [*Navy rating*] ... AOCM
Aviation Ordnanceman, Second Class [*Navy rating*] ... AO2
Aviation Ordnanceman, Senior Chief [*Navy rating*] ... AOCS
Aviation Ordnanceman, Third Class [*Navy rating*] ... AO3
Aviation Ordnanceman, Turret Mechanic [*Navy rating*] ... AOMT
Aviation Pay [*Navy*] ... AVIA
Aviation Pay (Crewmember) [*Navy*] ... AVN(CM)
Aviation Pay (Non-Crewmember) [*Navy*] ... AVN(NCM)
Aviation Performance Assessment in a Chemical Environment (PDAA) ... APACHE
Aviation Personnel and Survival Equipment Team [*Navy*] (NG) ... APSET
Aviation Personnel Planning Data [*Navy*] (NG) ... APPD
Aviation Petroleum Coordinating Committee, Latin American ... APCCLA
Aviation Petroleum Products Allocation Committee ... APPAC
Aviation Petroleum Products Allocation Committee, London ... APPAC-L
Aviation Pilot [*Navy*] ... AP
Aviation Pilot, Airship [*Navy*] ... APLA
Aviation POL [*Petroleum, Oil, and Lubrication*] **Handling Equipment** (NATG) ... PHE
Aviation Procurement Authorization [*Army*] ... APA
Aviation Procurement, Navy (MCD) ... APN
Aviation Professionals International [*New Orleans*] ... API
Aviation Psychology Laboratory [*Ohio State University*] [*Research center*] (RCD) ... APL
Aviation Publication (MCD) ... AVP
Aviation Qualification Test ... AQT
Aviation Quebec Labrador Ltd. [*Canada ICAO designator*] (FAAC) ... QLA
Aviation Radio and RADAR Countermeasures Technician [*Navy*] ... RCM
Aviation Radio Technician ... ART
Aviation Radioman [*Navy*] ... ARM
Aviation Radioman, Combat Aircrewman [*Navy*] ... ARMAC
Aviation Radionavigation, Land [*FCC*] (IEEE) ... AR
Aviation Readiness Evaluation (NVT) ... ARE
Aviation Regulatory Advisory Committee [*FAA*] (TAG) ... ARAC
Aviation Repair and Overhaul Unit ... AROU
Aviation Repair Supply Depot ... ARSD
Aviation Requirements for the Combat Structure of the Army (AABC) ... ARCSA
Aviation Research and Development Service [*FAA*] ... ARDS
Aviation Research and Technology Activity [*Moffett Field, CA*] [*Army*] (RDA) ... ARTA
Aviation Research Development and Engineering Center [*Army*] (RDA) ... AVRDEC
Aviation Research Laboratory [*University of Illinois*] (MCD) ... ARL
Aviation Reserve Officers Candidate Program ... AVROC
Aviation Resources Management and Control System ... ARMACS
Aviation Route Forecast (MCD) ... ARF
Aviation Routine Weather Report [*ICAO*] (FAAC) ... METAR
Aviation Rulemaking Advisory Committee (GAVI) ... ARAC
Aviation Safety Analysis System [*FAA*] (GFGA) ... ASAS
Aviation Safety and Health Association (EA) ... ASHA
Aviation Safety District Office ... ASDO
Aviation Safety Engineering and Research (KSC) ... AVSER
Aviation Safety Institute (EA) ... ASI
Aviation Safety Office [*or Officer*] [*Military*] (MCD) ... ASO
Aviation Safety Program [*FAA*] (TAG) ... ASP
Aviation Safety Programs, Transport Canada [*Programme de la Securite Aerienne, Transports Canada*], Vancouver, British Columbia [*Library symbol National Library of Canada*] (NLC) ... BVATAS
Aviation Safety Regulation ... ASR
Aviation Safety Reporting System (MCD) ... ASRS
Aviation Sales Co. [*Associated Press*] (SAG) ... Aviation
Aviation Sales Co. [*NYSE symbol*] (SAG) ... AVS
Aviation Satellite (DNAB) ... AVSAT
Aviation School [*Army*] ... AVNS
Aviation School of Medicine ... ASM
Aviation Section Signal Reserve Corps ... ASSRC

Aviation Security Association of America - International [*Defunct*] (EA) ... ASAA-I
Aviation Security Command [*Philippines*] ... AVSECOM
Aviation Security Improvement Act [*FAA*] (TAG) ... ASIA
Aviation Security Panel [*ICAO*] (DA) ... AVSEC
Aviation Selected Reserve Programs Branch [*BUPERS*] ... ASRPB
Aviation Service Code (AFM) ... ASC
Aviation Service Date (AFM) ... ASD
Aviation Service Entry Data (AABC) ... ASED
Aviation Services [*ICAO designator*] (AD) ... ML
Aviation Services, Inc. ... ASI
Aviation Services, Inc. [*ICAO designator*] (FAAC) ... AVQ
Aviation Services Ltd. [*Guam*] [*ICAO designator*] (FAAC) ... FRE
Aviation Seychelles Ltd. [*ICAO designator*] (FAAC) ... AVS
Aviation Ships Planning Document (MCD) ... ASPD
Aviation Signal Light Gun [*Military*] (PDAA) ... ASLG
Aviation/Space Writers Association ... A/SWA
Aviation/Space Writers Association (EA) ... AWA
Aviation Standards [*FAA*] (TAG) ... AVS
Aviation Standards National Field Office [*ICAO designator*] (FAAC) ... FLC
Aviation Status Indicator (DNAB) ... ASI
Aviation Storekeeper [*Navy rating*] ... AK
Aviation Storekeeper, Chief [*Navy rating*] ... AKC
Aviation Storekeeper, First Class [*Navy rating*] ... AK1
Aviation Storekeeper, Master Chief [*Navy rating*] ... AKCM
Aviation Storekeeper, Second Class [*Navy rating*] ... AK2
Aviation Storekeeper, Senior Chief [*Navy rating*] ... AKCS
Aviation Storekeeper, Third Class [*Navy rating*] ... AK3
Aviation Structural Mechanic [*Navy rating*] ... AM
Aviation Structural Mechanic, Chief [*Navy rating*] ... AMC
Aviation Structural Mechanic, First Class [*Navy rating*] ... AM1
Aviation Structural Mechanic, Hydraulic Mechanic [*Navy rating*] ... AMH
Aviation Structural Mechanic, Hydraulics, Airman [*Navy rating*] ... AMHAN
Aviation Structural Mechanic, Hydraulics, Airman Apprentice [*Navy rating*] ... AMHAA
Aviation Structural Mechanic, Hydraulics, Chief [*Navy rating*] (DNAB) ... AMHC
Aviation Structural Mechanic, Hydraulics, First Class [*Navy rating*] (DNAB) ... AMH1
Aviation Structural Mechanic, Hydraulics, Second Class [*Navy rating*] (DNAB) ... AMH2
Aviation Structural Mechanic, Hydraulics, Third Class [*Navy rating*] (DNAB) ... AMH3
Aviation Structural Mechanic, Master Chief [*Navy rating*] ... AMCM
Aviation Structural Mechanic, Safety Equipment [*Navy rating*] ... AME
Aviation Structural Mechanic, Safety Equipment, Airman [*Navy rating*] ... AMEAN
Aviation Structural Mechanic, Safety Equipment, Airman Apprentice [*Navy rating*] ... AMEAA
Aviation Structural Mechanic, Safety Equipment, First Class [*Navy rating*] (DNAB) ... AME1
Aviation Structural Mechanic, Safety Equipment, Second Class [*Navy rating*] (DNAB) ... AME2
Aviation Structural Mechanic, Safety Equipment, Third Class [*Navy rating*] (DNAB) ... AME3
Aviation Structural Mechanic, Second Class [*Navy rating*] ... AM2
Aviation Structural Mechanic, Senior Chief [*Navy rating*] ... AMCS
Aviation Structural Mechanic, Structures [*Navy rating*] ... AMS
Aviation Structural Mechanic, Structures, Airman [*Navy rating*] ... AMSAN
Aviation Structural Mechanic, Structures, Airman Apprentice [*Navy rating*] ... AMSAA
Aviation Structural Mechanic, Structures, First Class [*Navy rating*] (DNAB) ... AMS1
Aviation Structural Mechanic, Structures, Second Class [*Navy rating*] (DNAB) ... AMS2
Aviation Structural Mechanic, Structures, Third Class [*Navy rating*] (DNAB) ... AMS3
Aviation Structural Mechanic, Third Class [*Navy rating*] ... AM3
Aviation Supply Annex ... ASA
Aviation Supply Control Center (NVT) ... ASCC
Aviation Supply Depot ... ASD
Aviation Supply Depot - Naval Supply Center (MCD) ... ASD-NSC
Aviation Supply Office [*Philadelphia, PA*] [*Navy*] ... ASO
Aviation Supply Office/Inventory Control Point ... ASO/ICP
Aviation Supply Office Philadelphia [*Navy*] ... ASOP
Aviation Supply Officer (DOMA) ... ASO
Aviation Supply Ship [*Navy symbol*] ... AVS
Aviation Support Command [*Military*] (DOMA) ... AVSCOM
Aviation Support, Electrical [*Navy rating*] ... ASE
Aviation Support Equipment (CAAL) ... ASE
Aviation Support Equipment Technician [*Navy rating*] ... AS
Aviation Support Equipment Technician, Chief [*Navy rating*] ... ASC
Aviation Support Equipment Technician, Electrical, Airman Apprentice [*Navy rating*] (DNAB) ... ASEAA
Aviation Support Equipment Technician, Electrical, Second Class [*Navy rating*] (DNAB) ... ASE2
Aviation Support Equipment Technician, Electrical, Third Class [*Navy rating*] (DNAB) ... ASE3
Aviation Support Equipment Technician, First Class [*Navy rating*] ... AS1
Aviation Support Equipment Technician, Hydraulics and Structures, Airman [*Navy rating*] (DNAB) ... ASHAN
Aviation Support Equipment Technician, Hydraulics and Structures, Airman Apprentice [*Navy rating*] (DNAB) ... ASHAA
Aviation Support Equipment Technician, Hydraulics and Structures, Second Class [*Navy rating*] (DNAB) ... ASH2
Aviation Support Equipment Technician, Hydraulics and Structures, Third Class [*Navy rating*] (DNAB) ... ASH3
Aviation Support Equipment Technician, Master Chief [*Navy rating*] ... ASCM
Aviation Support Equipment Technician, Mechanical, Airman [*Navy rating*] (DNAB) ... ASMAN
Aviation Support Equipment Technician, Mechanical, Airman Apprentice [*Navy rating*] (DNAB) ... ASMAA
Aviation Support Equipment Technician, Mechanical, Second Class [*Navy rating*] (DNAB) ... ASM2
Aviation Support Equipment Technician, Mechanical, Third Class [*Navy rating*] (DNAB) ... ASM3
Aviation Support Equipment Technician, Second Class [*Navy rating*] ... AS2
Aviation Support Equipment Technician, Senior Chief [*Navy rating*] ... ASCS
Aviation Support Equipment Technician, Third Class [*Navy rating*] ... AS3
Aviation Support, Hydraulic [*Navy rating*] ... ASH
Aviation Support Material and Equipment (MCD) ... ASME
Aviation Support, Mechanical [*Navy rating*] ... ASM
Aviation Surface Material Command (MCD) ... ASMC
Aviation System Capacity Plan [*FAA*] (TAG) ... ASCP
Aviation Systems Command [*Army*] (RDA) ... ASC
Aviation Systems Command [*St. Louis, MO*] [*Army*] ... AVSCOM
Aviation Systems Command [*Army*] (MCD) ... AVSYCOM
Aviation Systems Laboratory (MCD) ... ASL
Aviation Systems Program Review (MCD) ... ASPR
Aviation Systems Test Activity [*Later, AEFA*] (MCD) ... ASTA
Aviation Tactical Coordinator [*Navy*] (NVT) ... ATACCO
Aviation Tactical Data System ... ATDS
Aviation Technical Test Center [*Army*] (RDA) ... ATTC
Aviation Technical Training Center ... ATTC
Aviation Technical Training Division [*Military*] (DNAB) ... ATTD
Aviation Technician Education Council (EA) ... ATEC
Aviation Technician, Navigation ... ATN
Aviation Technician, RADAR ... ATR
Aviation Test Office [*Edwards Air Force Base, CA*] [*Army*] ... ATO
Aviation Traders Engineering Ltd. [*British*] ... ATEL
Aviation Training Aids ... ATA
Aviation Training Aids Branch [*Military*] (DNAB) ... ATAB
Aviation Training Center ... ATC
Aviation Training Devices (Provisional) [*Army*] (RDA) ... AVD
Aviation Training Jacket (DNAB) ... ATJ
Aviation Training Record ... ATR
Aviation Training Support System [*Navy*] (GFGA) ... ATSS
Aviation Transport Services [*Italy ICAO designator*] (FAAC) ... ATS
Aviation Turbine Fuel ... ATF
Aviation Turbine Fuel (ADA) ... AVTUR
Aviation Turbine Kerosine (IAA) ... ATK
Aviation Unit [*Marine Corps*] ... AVNU
Aviation Unit Maintenance [*Army*] (MCD) ... AVUM
Aviation VHF [*Very High Frequency*] **Packet Communications** [*Computer science*] (TNIG) ... AVPAC
Aviation Warfare Specialist (DNAB) ... AWS
Aviation Warrant Officer Career Course [*Army*] ... WOCAR
Aviation Weapons Movement Control System (MCD) ... AWMCS
Aviation Weather and Notice to Airmen System (MCD) ... AWANS
Aviation Weather Development Laboratory [*FAA*] (TAG) ... AWDL
Aviation Weather Facility ... AWF
Aviation Weather Processor [*ICAO designator*] (FAAC) ... AWP
Aviation Weather Products Generator [*FAA*] (TAG) ... AWPG
Aviation Weather Reporting Station ... AWRS
Aviation Weather Service [*of National Weather Service*] ... AWS
Aviation Wide-Angle Visual System (MCD) ... AWAVS
Aviation-Automatic/Weather Observing System Developmental Model (T) (MCD) ... AV-AWOS-T
Aviation-Electromagnetic Efects Policy Board [*Military*] ... A-EMEPB
Aviaton [*Ukraine*] [*FAA designator*] (FAAC) ... UAN
Aviator (AABC) ... AVR
Aviator Readiness Level (MCD) ... ARL
Aviator SA [*Greece*] [*ICAO designator*] (FAAC) ... AVW
Aviator's Breathing Oxygen [*Air Force*] ... ABO
Aviator's Night Vision Imaging System (RDA) ... ANVIS
Aviator's Oxygen Helmet (NG) ... AOH
Aviator's Protective Helmet (NG) ... APH
Aviatrans [*Former USSR ICAO designator*] (FAAC) ... VAS
Aviatsiia Dalnego Deistviia [*Long-Range Aviation*] [*Strategic bombing force of USSR*] ... ADD
Aviatsionnaya Diviziya [*Air Division*] [*Former USSR*] ... AD
Aviatsiya Voenno Morskogo Flota [*Aviation - Naval Fleet*] [*Former USSR*] ... AVMF
AVIC Group International, Inc. [*AMEX symbol*] (SAG) ... AV
AVIC Group International, Inc. [*Associated Press*] (SAG) ... AVIC Gp
Avicaya [*Bolivia*] [*ICAO location identifier*] (ICLI) ... SLAV
Avicultural Advancement Council of Canada (AC) ... AACC
Avicultural Federation of Australia ... AFA
[*The*] **Avicultural Society** [*British*] ... AS
Avicultural Society of America (EA) ... ASA
Avicultural Society of America (EA) ... ASOA
Avid Technology [*NASDAQ symbol*] (TTSB) ... AVID
Avid Technology, Inc. [*NASDAQ symbol*] (SAG) ... AVID
Avid Technology, Inc. [*Associated Press*] (SAG) ... AvidTch
Avidin-Biotin Complex [*Immunochemistry*] ... ABC
Avies [*Estonia*] [*FAA designator*] (FAAC) ... AIA
Avigen Inc. [*NASDAQ symbol*] (TTSB) ... AVGN
Avigen, Inc. [*NASDAQ symbol*] (SAG) ... AVGN
Avigen, Inc. [*Associated Press*] (SAG) ... Avigen
Avignon [*France*] [*Airport symbol*] (OAG) ... AVN
Avignon/Caumont [*France ICAO location identifier*] (ICLI) ... LFMV
Avignon-Pujaut [*France ICAO location identifier*] (ICLI) ... LFNT

Avijet SA de CV [*Mexico ICAO designator*] (FAAC) ... IJE
Avila College, Kansas City, MO [*OCLC symbol*] (OCLC) ... HOO
Avila College, Kansas City, MO [*Library symbol Library of Congress*] (LCLS) ... MoKAv
Aviles/Asturias [*Spain ICAO location identifier*] (ICLI) ... LEAS
Avilond, TAC [*Ukraine*] [*FAA designator*] (FAAC) ... LON
Avinda Video, Inc. [*Toronto Stock Exchange symbol*] ... AVV
Avino Mines & Resources Ltd. [*Vancouver Stock Exchange symbol*] ... AVO
Aviogenex [*Yugoslavia*] [*ICAO designator*] (FAAC) ... AGX
Avioimpex [*Yugoslavia*] [*ICAO designator*] (FAAC) ... AXX
Avion a Grande Vitesse [*French high-speed train*] ... AGV
Avion Taxi Canada, Inc. [*ICAO designator*] (FAAC) ... ADQ
Aviona [*ICAO designator*] (AD) ... RD
Avionair, Inc. [*Canada ICAO designator*] (FAAC) ... ANU
Aviones Are, SA de CV [*Mexico*] [*FAA designator*] (FAAC) ... NRE
Aviones de Renta de Quintana Roo, SA de CV [*Mexico*] [*FAA designator*] (FAAC) ... AQT
Aviones de Sonora SA [*Mexico ICAO designator*] (FAAC) ... ADS
Aviones Ejecutivos, JFA [*Mexico*] [*FAA designator*] (FAAC) ... JFA
Aviones Unidos SA de CV [*Mexico ICAO designator*] (FAAC) ... AUN
Aviones y Servicios del Golfo SA de CV [*Mexico ICAO designator*] (FAAC) ... ADG
Avionic ... AVNC
Avionic Flight Control System ... AFCS
Avionic Instrument (MCD) ... AI
Avionic Integration Support Facility (MCD) ... AISF
Avionic Ltd. [*Greece*] [*FAA designator*] (FAAC) ... VIO
Avionic Observation of Intruder Danger Systems [*Army*] ... AVOIDS
Avionic Subsystem Requirement Document (MCD) ... ASRD
Avionic System Integration Plan (MCD) ... ASIP
Avionic System Simulation (MCD) ... AVSIM
Avionic Systems Demonstrator Rig (PDAA) ... ASDR
Avionic Test Set (MCD) ... ATS
Avionics (NASA) ... AV
Avionics Automatic Transmission Line ... AATE
Avionics Bay (MCD) ... AB
Avionics Bay (MCD) ... AVBAY
Avionics Bay Cooling System ... ABCS
Avionics Bulletin (MCD) ... AVB
Avionics Change (MCD) ... AVC
Avionics, Control, and Information Systems (MCD) ... ACIS
Avionics Cooling Loop (MCD) ... ACL
Avionics Cooling Unit [*Aerospace*] (NASA) ... ACU
Avionics Cooling Unit Operator (MCD) ... ACUO
Avionics Decision Notice (MCD) ... ADN
Avionics Depot Test Station (MCD) ... ADTS
Avionics Development and Integration Facility (MCD) ... ADIF
Avionics Development Laboratory [*Rockwell International-Space Division*] [*NASA*] (NASA) ... ADL
Avionics Electrical Distribution (MCD) ... AED
Avionics Engineering Division [*Air Force*] ... AVED
Avionics Equipment Design Review ... AEDR
Avionics Expert System (MCD) ... AES
Avionics Fault Tree Analyzer (MCD) ... AFTA
Avionics Integrated Maintenance Expert System (MCD) ... AIMES
Avionics Integrated Support Networks (PDAA) ... AVISNET
Avionics Integration ... AI
Avionics Integration Bench (MCD) ... AIB
Avionics Integration Laboratories [*NASA*] (NASA) ... AIL
Avionics Integration Plan [*NASA*] (NASA) ... AIP
Avionics Integration Research (SSD) ... AIR
Avionics Interface Unit (MCD) ... AIU
Avionics Intermediate Shop (MCD) ... AIS
Avionics Intermediate Shop Mobile Facility Support (DWSG) ... AISMF
Avionics Laboratory [*Air Force*] ... AL
Avionics Laboratory Predictive Operations and Support (MCD) ... ALPOS
Avionics Laboratory Technical Information Handling Profile ... ALTIHP
Avionics Maintenance Conference (EA) ... AMC
Avionics Maintenance Shop ... AMS
Avionics Maintenance Squadron [*Air Force/Navy*] (MCD) ... AMS
Avionics Maintenance Squadron [*Air Force*] (AFM) ... AMSq
Avionics Modernization Program [*Air Force*] (DOMA) ... AMP
Avionics Module Repair Improvement Program [*Navy*] ... AMRIP
Avionics Module Unit ... AMU
Avionics Multiplex ... AMUX
Avionics Operating Instruction (MCD) ... AOI
Avionics Operating Time (MCD) ... AOT
Avionics Overall Test (NASA) ... AOT
Avionics Processing System ... APS
Avionics Repairable Assemblies (AFIT) ... ARA
Avionics Requirements (MCD) ... AR
Avionics Research Aircraft (MCD) ... ARA
Avionics Research and Development Activity [*Fort Monmouth, NJ*] [*Army*] (GRD) ... AVRADA
Avionics Shop Maintenance ... ASM
Avionics Software Support Cost Model (MCD) ... ASSCM
Avionics Standard Communications Bus (DA) ... ASCB
Avionics Status Panel (MCD) ... ASP
Avionics Subsystem for Strategic Bombers ... ASSB
Avionics Subsystem Group [*NASA*] (NASA) ... ASG
Avionics Subsystem Interface Unit (MCD) ... ASSIU
Avionics Subsystems Interface Contractor [*Air Force*] ... ASIC
Avionics System Integration and Acquisition (MCD) ... ASIA
Avionics System Project Officer ... ASPO
Avionics System Review (NASA) ... ASR
Avionics System Test Equipment Comparator (MCD) ... ASTEC
Avionics System Test Specification (MCD) ... ASTS
Avionics Systems Engineering Division [*Johnson Space Center*] [*NASA*] (NASA) ... ASED
Avionics Technical Note ... ATN
Avionics Test Article (NASA) ... ATA
Avionics Test Station (MCD) ... ATS
Avionics Unit Maintenance (MCD) ... AVUM
Avionics Verification Laboratory (MCD) ... AVL
Avionics Verification Status Room [*NASA*] (NASA) ... AVSR
Avions Mudry & Cie. [*France ICAO aircraft manufacturer identifier*] (ICAO) ... CE
Avions Mudry & Cie. [*France*], Lockheed Aircraft Corp. [*ICAO aircraft manufacturer identifier*] (ICAO) ... CP
Avior [*ICAO designator*] (AD) ... XP
Avior Pty Ltd. [*Australia ICAO designator*] (FAAC) ... AVR
Aviorrenta SA [*Mexico ICAO designator*] (FAAC) ... AVI
Aviron [*NASDAQ symbol*] (SAG) ... AVIR
Aviron [*Associated Press*] (SAG) ... Aviron
Avirulence ... AVR
Avis de Reception [*Return Receipt*] [*French*] ... AR
Avis Licensee Association (EA) ... ALA
Avis, PA [*FM radio station call letters*] ... WQBR
Avis Rent a Car ... ARAC
Avisco [*ICAO designator*] (AD) ... AO
Aviser SA [*Spain ICAO designator*] (FAAC) ... AVH
Avistar (Cyprus) Ltd. [*ICAO designator*] (FAAC) ... KJA
Avitar, Inc. [*NASDAQ symbol*] (SAG) ... AVIT
Avitar, Inc. [*Associated Press*] (SAG) ... Avitar
Avitar Inc. Wrrt [*NASDAQ symbol*] (TTSB) ... AVITW
Avitat [*British ICAO designator*] (FAAC) ... ESO
Aviva Petroleum Dep [*AMEX symbol*] (TTSB) ... AVV
Aviva Petroleum, Inc. [*Associated Press*] (SAG) ... AvivaPet
Aviva Petroleum, Inc. [*AMEX symbol*] (SAG) ... AVV
Aviva Resources, Inc. [*Vancouver Stock Exchange symbol*] ... AVS
AVKO Educational Research Foundation (EA) ... AVKOERF
Avnet, Inc. [*Associated Press*] (SAG) ... Avnet
Avnet, Inc. [*NYSE symbol*] (SPSG) ... AVT
Avno [*Denmark ICAO location identifier*] (ICLI) ... EKAV
Avoca Journal-Herald, Avoca, IA [*Library symbol Library of Congress*] (LCLS) ... IaAvJH
Avoca Public Library, Avoca, IA [*Library symbol Library of Congress*] (LCLS) ... IaAv
Avocado Growers' Association of Western Australia ... AGAWA
Avocado Growers Bargaining Council [*Defunct*] (EA) ... AGBC
Avocado Growers Council [*Later, AGBC*] (EA) ... AGC
Avocado-Sunblotch Viroid ... ASBV
Avocado-Sunblotch Viroid [*Plant pathology*] ... ASBVd
Avocat General [*District Attorney*] [*French*] (ILCA) ... Av Gen
Avocet Ventures, Inc. [*Vancouver Stock Exchange symbol*] ... AVZ
'Avodah Zarah (BJA) ... 'AvZar
Avogadro Constant [*Symbol*] [*IUPAC*] ... L
Avogadro Number [*Number of molecules in one gram-molecular weight of a substance*] ... N
Avogadro's Number [*Chemistry*] (DAVI) ... Na
Avoid Verbal Instructions [*DoD*] (MCD) ... AVI
Avoid Verbal Orders [*Military*] ... AVO
Avoidable Delay ... AD
Avoidable Mortality from Cancer in Black Populations Survey [*Department of Health and Human Services*] (GFGA) ... AMCBPS
Avoir [*Credit*] [*French*] ... AV
Avoirdupois ... AV
Avoirdupois [*Unit of measurement*] (KSC) ... AVDP
Avoirdupois [*Unit of measurement*] ... AVDPS
Avoirdupois ... AVOIR
Avoirdupois (ADA) ... AVP
Avoirdupois Ounce ... advp oz
Avon [*Australia Seismograph station code, US Geological Survey*] (SEIS) ... AVO
Avon, CO [*FM radio station call letters*] ... KZYR
Avon, CO [*Location identifier FAA*] (FAAL) ... VON
Avon Elementary School, Avon, MN [*Library symbol*] [*Library of Congress*] (LCLS) ... MnAvoE
Avon Junior/Senior High School Library, Avon, NY [*OCLC symbol*] (OCLC) ... RVP
Avon, NY [*FM radio station call letters*] (RBYB) ... WHRR
Avon, NY [*FM radio station call letters*] (RBYB) ... WRQV-FM
Avon, NY [*AM radio station call letters*] ... WYSL
Avon Park, FL [*Location identifier FAA*] (FAAL) ... AGR
Avon Park, FL [*Location identifier FAA*] (FAAL) ... AVO
Avon Park, FL [*AM radio station call letters*] ... WAVP
Avon Park, FL [*FM radio station call letters*] ... WWOJ
Avon Products [*NYSE symbol*] (TTSB) ... AVP
Avon Products, Inc. [*Associated Press*] (SAG) ... Avon
Avon Products, Inc. [*NYSE symbol*] (SPSG) ... AVP
Avon Products, Inc., Suffern, NY [*Library symbol Library of Congress*] (LCLS) ... NSufA
Avondale Financial [*NASDAQ symbol*] (TTSB) ... AVND
Avondale Financial Corp. [*NASDAQ symbol*] (SAG) ... AVND
Avondale Financial Corp. [*Associated Press*] (SAG) ... AvondF
Avondale Industries [*NASDAQ symbol*] (TTSB) ... AVDL
Avondale Industries, Inc. [*NASDAQ symbol*] (NQ) ... AVDL
Avondale Industries, Inc. [*Associated Press*] (SAG) ... Avndle
Avondale Public Library, Avondale, AZ [*Library symbol*] [*Library of Congress*] (LCLS) ... AzAv
Avondale Resources, Inc. [*Vancouver Stock Exchange symbol*] ... AVD
Avonics Management System ... AMS

Avonmore Branch, Stormont, Dundas, and Glengarry County Public Library, Ontario [*Library symbol National Library of Canada*] (BIB) ...... OAVSDG
Avord [*France ICAO location identifier*] (ICLI) ...... LFOA
Avoyelles Parish Library, Marksville, LA [*Library symbol Library of Congress*] (LCLS) ...... LMarA
Avranches/Le Val Saint-Pere [*France ICAO location identifier*] (ICLI) ...... LFRW
Avril Sur Loire [*France*] [*Seismograph station code, US Geological Survey*] (SEIS) ...... AVF
Avro International Aerospace [*British*] [*FAA designator*] (FAAC) ...... WFD
AVSCOM [*Aviation Systems Command*] **Integrated Microfilm Systems** [*Army*] ...... AIMS
AVTEAM, Inc. [*NASDAQ symbol*] (SAG) ...... AVTM
Avtomat Kalashnikov [*Submachine Gun*] [*Commonwealth of Independent States*] ...... AK
Avtomobilei Zavod Lenin Komsomol [*Lenin Collective Automobile Works*] [*Former USSR*] ...... AZLK
Avu Avu [*Solomon Islands*] [*Airport symbol*] (OAG) ...... AVU
AVVI [*Altimeter Vertical Velocity Indicator*] **RADAR Altitude** (GFGA) ...... ARA
Avvocato [*Solicitor*] [*Italian*] (EY) ...... AVV
AVX Corp. [*NYSE symbol*] (SAG) ...... AVX
AVX Corp. [*Associated Press*] (SAG) ...... AVX Cp
AW Computer Systems [*Associated Press*] (SAG) ...... AW
AW Computer Systems, Inc. [*NASDAQ symbol*] (NQ) ...... AWCS
AW Computer Systems'A' [*NASDAQ symbol*] (TTSB) ...... AWCSA
Awadhi [*MARC language code Library of Congress*] (LCCP) ...... awa
Await ...... AWT
Awaiting Action Deck Court-Martial ...... AADCM
Awaiting Action General Court-Martial ...... AAGCM
Awaiting Action [*of*] **Higher Authority** [*Army*] ...... AAHA
Awaiting Action Summary Court-Martial ...... AASCM
Awaiting Additional Funds (AAGC) ...... AAF
Awaiting Aircraft Availability ...... AAA
Awaiting Bad Conduct Discharge [*Military*] ...... ABCD
Awaiting Berth [*Military*] (DNAB) ...... AWBER
Awaiting Combat Assignment (MUGU) ...... ACA
Awaiting Connection [*Telecommunications*] (TEL) ...... AC
Awaiting Contract Record Disposition Notice (AAGC) ...... ACRDN
Awaiting Delivery (MCD) ...... A/D
Awaiting Delivery of Data (AAGC) ...... ADD
Awaiting Discharge [*Military*] (DNAB) ...... AWDISCH
Awaiting Disciplinary Action This Command [*Army*] ...... AWDISCOM
Awaiting Disconnection [*Telecommunications*] (TEL) ...... AD
Awaiting Final Invoice (AAGC) ...... AFI
Awaiting Forward Release [*Telecommunications*] (TEL) ...... AFR
Awaiting Incoming Continuity [*Telecommunications*] (TEL) ...... AIC
Awaiting Incoming Message [*Telecommunications*] (TEL) ...... AIM
Awaiting Instruction [*Military*] (DNAB) ...... AI
Awaiting Laboratory Input ...... ALI
Awaiting Maintenance ...... AM
Awaiting Maintenance (AFM) ...... AWM
Awaiting Number Received [*Telecommunications*] (TEL) ...... ANR
Awaiting Office Hours ...... AOH
Awaiting Orders [*Military*] (DNAB) ...... AWORD
Awaiting Outgoing Continuity [*Telecommunications*] (TEL) ...... AOC
Awaiting Overhaul (NG) ...... AOH
Awaiting Parts ...... AP
Awaiting Parts (AFM) ...... AWP
Awaiting Patent and Royalty Clearance (AAGC) ...... APRC
Awaiting Plant Clearance (AAGC) ...... APC
Awaiting Price Redetermination (AAGC) ...... APR
Awaiting Removal of Excess Funds (AAGC) ...... AREF
Awaiting Reply [*Telecommunications*] (TEL) ...... AR
Awaiting Report of Survey (AAGC) ...... ARS
Awaiting Results of Trial [*Military*] ...... ARTL
Awaiting Sentence [*of court-martial*] ...... AWS
Awaiting Transportation (AFM) ...... AT
Awaiting Trial ...... ATL
Awaiting Trial [*by court-martial*] ...... AWT
Awaiting Weather [*Military*] (DNAB) ...... AWEA
Awake, Alert, and Oriented (HGAA) ...... AAO
Awake and Aware [*Neurology*] (DAVI) ...... A & A
Awake and Oriented Times Four [*Neurology and psychiatry*] (DAVI) ...... A & OX4
Awake and Oriented Times Three [*Neurology and psychiatry*] (DAVI) ...... A & OX3
Awake and Oriented to Person, Place, and Time [*Neurology and psychiatry*] (DAVI) ...... A & OX3
Awake and Oriented to Person, Place, Time, and Date [*Neurology and psychiatry*] (DAVI) ...... A & OX4
Awake and Oriented to Time, Place, and Person [*Neurology*] (DAVI) AAOX3
Awami Action Committee [*India*] [*Political party*] (PPW) ...... AAC
Awami League [*Bangladesh*] [*Political party*] (FEA) ...... AL
Awami National Party [*Pakistan*] [*Political party*] (FEA) ...... ANP
Awana Clubs International (EAIO) ...... ACI
Awana Youth Association (EA) ...... AYA
Award (AABC) ...... AWD
Award ...... AWRD
Award Central Control Unit [*NASA*] (NASA) ...... ACCU
Award Fee ...... AF
Award Fee Determination Plan (AAGC) ...... AFDP
Award Fee Determining Official (AAGC) ...... AFDO
Award Fee Evaluation Board [*NASA*] (NASA) ...... AFEB
Award Fee Evaluation Committee [*NASA*] (NASA) ...... AFEC
Award Fee Review Board ...... AFRB
Award of Contract ...... AOC
Award of Merit [*Royal Horticultural Society*] [*British*] ...... AM
Award of Merit for Group Achievement [*Military*] (DNAB) ...... AMGA
Award Processing [*Social Security Administration*] (OICC) ...... AP
Award Resources [*Vancouver Stock Exchange symbol*] ...... ADR
Award Scheme for Science, Industry and School-Teaching [*Science Research Council*] (PDAA) ...... ASSIST
Award Software International, Inc. [*NASDAQ symbol*] (SAG) ...... AWRD
Award Software International, Inc. [*Associated Press*] (SAG) ...... AwrdSft
Award to Honor Excellent Newspaper Advertising (DGA) ...... ATHENA
Awardee [*Database terminology*] (NITA) ...... AW
Awards Almanac [*A publication*] ...... AA
Awards and Obligations (GFGA) ...... AO
Awards for Cablecasting Excellence ...... ACE
Awards for Publication Excellence ...... APEX
Awards, Honors, and Prizes [*A publication*] ...... AHP
Aware, Inc. [*Associated Press*] (SAG) ...... Aware
Aware, Inc. [*NASDAQ symbol*] (SAG) ...... AWRE
Awareness (KSC) ...... AWRN
Awareness Center [*Defunct*] (EA) ...... AC
Awareness Research Foundation (EA) ...... ARF
Awareness Vision Imagination Responsibility Action ...... AVIRA
Awaruwaunawa [*Guyana*] [*ICAO location identifier*] (ICLI) ...... SYAW
Awash [*Ethiopia*] [*ICAO location identifier*] (ICLI) ...... HAAW
Awash [*Ethiopia*] [*ICAO location identifier*] (ICLI) ...... HALA
Away from Home ...... AFH
Away from Keyboard [*Computer hacker terminology*] (NHD) ...... AFK
Away from Reactor [*Storage facilities*] ...... AFR
Away from Reactor Storage [*Nuclear energy*] (NUCP) ...... AFRS
Away without Authorization ...... AWA
Aweil [*Sudan*] [*ICAO location identifier*] (ICLI) ...... HSAW
Awesome Resources Ltd. [*Vancouver Stock Exchange symbol*] ...... AWE
AWIPS [*Advanced Weather Interactive Processing System*] **Forecast Preparation System** [*Marine science*] (OSRA) ...... AFPS
AWIPS [*Advanced Weather Interactive Processing System*] **Forecast Preparation System** (USDC) ...... AFPS
AWIPS [*Advanced Weather Interactive Processing System*] **Program Office** (USDC) ...... APO
AWIPS [*Advanced Weather Interactive Processing System*] **Program Office** [*Marine science*] (OSRA) ...... APO
Awkward Expression or Construction [*Used in correcting manuscripts, etc.*] ...... AWK
Awning (MSA) ...... AWN
Awning ...... AWN
Awning Deck [*of a ship*] (DS) ...... Adk
Awning Deck [*of a ship*] (DS) ...... AWD
Awood Air Ltd. [*Canada ICAO designator*] (FAAC) ...... AWO
AWOS Data Acquisition System [*FAA*] (TAG) ...... ADAS
AWS Ammunition Magazine (MCD) ...... AAM
AXA ADS [*NYSE symbol*] (SAG) ...... AXA
Axa Midi Assurances [*Commercial firm France*] ...... AMA
Axactic Polypropylene ...... APP
Axel Heiberg Island [*Canada*] ...... AHI
Axel Rent SA [*Mexico ICAO designator*] (FAAC) ...... AXR
AXENT Technologies [*NASDAQ symbol*] (TTSB) ...... AXNT
Axent Technologies, Inc. [*Associated Press*] (SAG) ...... AxentT
Axent Technologies, Inc. [*NASDAQ symbol*] (SAG) ...... AXNT
Axial ...... A
Axial (DAVI) ...... ax
Axial Centrifugal (AAG) ...... AC
Axial Flow (AAG) ...... AF
Axial Flow ...... AXFL
Axial Flow Compressor ...... AFC
Axial Flow Reactor [*Chemical engineering*] ...... AFR
Axial Flow Wheel ...... AFW
Axial Flux Density (IEEE) ...... AFD
Axial Flux Difference [*Nuclear energy*] (NRCH) ...... AFD
Axial Flux Difference Alarm (IEEE) ...... AFDA
Axial Flux Offset (IEEE) ...... AFO
Axial Gear Differential (OA) ...... AGD
Axial Gear Differential/Constant-Speed Drive (DNAB) ...... AGD/CSD
Axial Gradient (MAE) ...... ax grad
Axial Magma Chamber [*Geology*] ...... AMC
Axial Next-Nearest-Neighbor Interactions [*Crystallography*] ...... ANNNI
Axial Pitch (IEEE) ...... AXP
Axial Power Distribution Monitoring Systems [*Nuclear energy*] (NRCH) ...... APDMS
Axial Power Imbalance Limit (IEEE) ...... APIL
Axial Power Shaping Rods [*Nuclear energy*] (NRCH) ...... APSR
Axial Power Shaping Rods Assembly [*Nuclear energy*] (NRCH) ...... APSRA
Axial Pressure Angle [*Gears*] ...... APA
Axial Rotating Filtration ...... ARF
Axial Seamount Hydrothermal Emissions Study [*Marine science*] (OSRA) ...... ASHES
Axial Seamount Hydrothermal Emissions Study (USDC) ...... ASHES
Axial Shape Index (NRCH) ...... ASI
Axial Summit Caldera [*Volcanology*] ...... ASC
Axial Thrust Misalignment ...... ATM
Axial Turbo Machine ...... ATM
Axial Vapor Deposition [*Coating technology*] ...... AVD
Axial Vapor-Phase Oxidation Process [*Optical fibre technology*] (EECA) ...... AVPO
Axial Vector Dominance Model ...... AVDM
Axial Velocity Ratio ...... AVR
Axial Width ...... AW
Axially Magnetized Plasma ...... AMP
Axially Scattering Spectrometer Probe (MCD) ...... ASSP
Axially Symmetric Nozzle ...... ASN
Axilla (DAVI) ...... ax
Axilla, Shoulder, Elbow [*Bandage*] ...... ASE

Axillary [*Medicine*] ... AX
Axillary Dissection [*Medicine*] (DMAA) ... AXD
Axim [*Ghana*] [*ICAO location identifier*] (ICLI) ... DGTX
Axiobuccal [*Dentistry*] (MAE) ... AB
Axiobuccocervical [*Dentistry*] ... ABC
Axiobuccogingival [*Dentistry*] ... ABG
Axiobuccolingual [*Dentistry*] ... ABL
Axiocervical [*Dentistry*] ... AC
Axiodistal [*Dentistry*] ... AD
Axiodistocervical [*Dentistry*] ... ADC
Axiodistogingival [*Dentistry*] ... ADG
Axiodistoincisal [*Dentistry*] ... ADI
Axiodisto-Occlusal [*Dentistry*] ... ADO
Axiogingival [*Dentistry*] ... AG
Axioincisal [*Dentistry*] ... AI
Axiolabial [*Dentistry*] ... ALa
Axiolabiogingival [*Dentistry*] ... ALaG
Axiolabiolingual [*Dentistry*] ... ALaL
Axiolingual [*Dentistry*] ... AL
Axiolinguocervical [*Dentistry*] ... ALC
Axiolinguogingival [*Dentistry*] ... ALG
Axiolinguo-Occlusal [*Dentistry*] ... ALO
Axiom ... AX
Axiom Information Resources ... AIR
Axiom International Development Corp. [*Formerly, Axiom Explorations, Inc.*] [*Vancouver Stock Exchange symbol*] ... AXX
Axiom of Choice [*Logic*] ... AC
Axiomatic Requirements Engineering (MCD) ... ARE
Axiomesial [*Dentistry*] ... AM
Axiomesiocervical [*Dentistry*] ... AMC
Axiomesiodistal [*Dentistry*] ... AMD
Axiomesiogingival [*Dentistry*] ... AMG
Axiomesioincisal [*Dentistry*] ... AMI
Axiomesio-Occlusal [*Dentistry*] ... AMO
Axio-Occlusal [*Dentistry*] ... AO
Axiopulpal [*Dentistry*] ... AP
Axis (ABBR) ... A
Axis (AAG) ... AX
Axis [*of a cylindrical lens*] [*Ophthalmology*] (DAVI) ... x
Axis Crossing Interval Meter [*SONAR*] ... ACIM
Axis Deviation (MAE) ... AD
Axis of Orientation [*Imaginary vertical line at the left of a block of text*] [*Also, mental margin*] (WDMC) ... A/O
Axis of Orientation (WDMC) ... AO
Axis [*or Axes*] **of Signal Communication** [*Army*] ... AXSIGCOMM
Axis Select (IAA) ... AS
Axisymmetric Blunt Body ... ABB
Axisymmetric Duct Aeroacoustic Modeling (MCD) ... ADAM
Axisymmetric Jet Stretcher ... AJS
Axisymmetric Spiral [*Astronomy*] ... ASS
Axisymmetrical and Planar Structural Analysis (MCD) ... APSA
Axisymmetrical Conical Flow ... ACF
Axisymmetrical Flow Field ... AFF
Axle Detector ... AD
Axle Flange Gasket [*Automotive engineering*] ... AF
Axle Housing Cover Gasket [*Automotive engineering*] ... AX
Axle Nut (DICI) ... AN
Axminster [*England*] ... AXMIN
Axogen Ltd. [*AMEX symbol*] (SAG) ... AXG
Axogen Ltd. [*Associated Press*] (SAG) ... Axogen
Axon Cylinder Membrane ... ACM
Axonal Arborization [*Medicine*] (DMAA) ... AA
Axonometric (VRA) ... axon
Axsys Technologies, Inc. [*Associated Press*] (SAG) ... AxsysTch
Axsys Technologies, Inc. [*NASDAQ symbol*] (SAG) ... AXYS
Axum [*Ethiopia*] [*Airport symbol*] (OAG) ... AXU
Axum [*Ethiopia*] [*ICAO location identifier*] (ICLI) ... HAAX
Ayacucho [*Peru*] [*Airport symbol*] (OAG) ... AYP
Ayacucho/Coronel FAP Alfredo Mendivil Duarte [*Peru*] [*ICAO location identifier*] (ICLI) ... SPHO
Ayagualo [*El Salvador*] [*Seismograph station code, US Geological Survey Closed*] (SEIS) ... AYA
Ayckbourn's Chancery Forms [*A publication*] (DLA) ... Ayck Ch F
Ayckbourn's Chancery Practice [*A publication*] (DLA) ... Ayck Ch Pr
Ayckbourn's Jurisdiction of the Supreme Court of Judicature [*A publication*] (DLA) ... Ayck Jur
Aydin [*Turkey*] [*Airport symbol*] (AD) ... ADN
Aydin [*Turkey ICAO location identifier*] (ICLI) ... LTBD
Aydin Corp. [*NYSE symbol*] (SPSG) ... AYD
Aydin Corp. [*Associated Press*] (SAG) ... Aydin
Ayeet Aviation & Tourism [*Israel*] [*FAA designator*] (FAAC) ... AYT
Ayenquera [*Peru*] [*Seismograph station code, US Geological Survey*] (SEIS) ... AYE
Ayer, Ft. Devens, MA [*Location identifier FAA*] (FAAL) ... DKO
Ayer Information Center [*Information service or system*] (IID) ... AIC
Ayer Public Library, Delavan, IL [*Library symbol Library of Congress*] (LCLS) ... IDelav
Ayer Public Library, Delavan, IL [*OCLC symbol*] (OCLC) ... ISG
Ayerok Petroleum [*Vancouver Stock Exchange symbol*] ... AYK
Ayers Rock [*Australia Airport symbol*] (OAG) ... AYQ
Ayerst Laboratories [*Research code symbol*] ... AY
Ayerst, McKenna & Harrison, Inc. Montreal, Quebec [*Library symbol National Library of Canada*] (NLC) ... QMAY
Ayerst, McKenna & Harrison Ltd., Montreal, PQ, Canada [*Library symbol Library of Congress*] (LCLS) ... CaQMAy
Ayerst Science Laboratory, Rouses Point, NY [*Library symbol Library of Congress*] (LCLS) ... NRpA
Ayian Leukosis [*Medicine*] (DMAA) ... AL
Aylesbeare [*England*] ... AYLB
Aylesbury [*England*] ... AYLB
Aylesbury/Thame [*British ICAO location identifier*] (ICLI) ... EGTA
Ayliffe's Calendar of Ancient Charters [*1774*] [*A publication*] (DLA) ... Ayl Char
Ayliffe's Introduction to the Calendar of Ancient Charters [*A publication*] (DLA) ... Ayl Int
Ayliffe's Pandect of the Roman Civil Law [*A publication*] (DLA) ... Ayl Pan
Ayliffe's Pandect of the Roman Civil Law [*A publication*] (DLA) ... Ayl Pand
Ayliffe's Pandects [*A publication*] (DLA) ... Ayliffe
Ayliffe's Parergon Juris Canonici Anglicani [*A publication*] (DLA) ... Ayl Par
Ayliffe's Parergon Juris Canonici Anglicani [*A publication*] (DLA) ... Ayliffe
Aylmer District Museum, Aylmer, ON, Canada [*Library symbol*] [*Library of Congress*] (LCLS) ... CaOAYM
Aylmer District Museum, Ontario [*Library symbol National Library of Canada*] (BIB) ... OAYM
Aylmer Heritage Association (AC) ... AHA
Ay-Luri [*Bolivia*] [*ICAO location identifier*] (ICLI) ... SLAX
Aymara [*MARC language code Library of Congress*] (LCCP) ... aym
Aymo Cravetta [*Deceased, 1569*] [*Authority cited in pre-1607 legal work*] (DSA) ... Aym
Ayn Rand Institute (EA) ... ARI
Ayn Rand Memorial Library Association [*Defunct*] (EA) ... ARMLA
Ayolas [*Paraguay*] [*ICAO location identifier*] (ICLI) ... SGAY
Ayr and Wigton's Registration Cases [*Scotland*] [*A publication*] (DLA) ... Ayr & Wig
Ayr Research Station [*Queensland, Australia*] ... ARS
Ayres Space Test [*Psychology*] ... AST
Ayr's Registration Cases [*Scotland*] [*A publication*] (DLA) ... Ayr
Ayrshire [*County in Scotland*] (WGA) ... AYR
Ayrshire [*County in Scotland*] ... AYRS
Ayrshire Artillery Volunteers [*British military*] (DMA) ... AAV
Ayrshire Breeders' Association (EA) ... ABA
Ayrshire Breeders Association of Canada (AC) ... ABAC
Ayrshire Cattle Society of Australia ... ACSA
Ayrshire Imperial Yeomanry [*British military*] (DMA) ... AIY
Ayrshire Yeomanry [*British military*] (DMA) ... AY
Ayrton's Land Transfer Act [*A publication*] (DLA) ... Ayr Land Tr
Aza [*As substituent on nucleoside*] [*Biochemistry*] ... z
Azacitidine [*Pharmacology*] (DAVI) ... 5-AC
Azacycloheptane Diphosphonate [*Organic chemistry*] ... AHDP
Azacytidine [*or Azacitidine*] [*Also, AZA, Aza-C*] [*Antineoplastic drug*] ... AC
Azacytidine [*or Azacitidine*] [*Also, AC, Aza-C*] [*Antineoplastic drug*] ... AZA
Azacytidine [*or Azacitidine*] [*Also, AC, AZA*] [*Antineoplastic drug*] ... Aza-C
Azad Hind Fauj [*Indian National Army*] ... AHF
Azad Kashmir Muslim Conference [*Pakistan*] [*Political party*] (FEA) ... AKMC
Azad Shahr [*Iran*] [*ICAO location identifier*] (ICLI) ... OINP
Azaguanine (MAE) ... azg
Azahypoxanthine [*Biochemistry*] ... AHX
Azalavia-Azerbaijan Hava Yollari [*ICAO designator*] (FAAC) ... AHY
Azalea Society of America (EA) ... ASA
Azamat [*Kazakhstan*] [*ICAO designator*] (FAAC) ... AZB
Aza(methyl)pregnanedione [*Biochemistry*] ... AMPD
Azania Liberation Front [*South Africa*] ... ALF
Azanian Co-Ordinating Committee [*South Africa Political party*] (EY) ... AZACCO
Azanian People's Organization [*South Africa*] (PPW) ... AZAPO
Azar Shahr [*Iran*] [*ICAO location identifier*] (ICLI) ... OITW
Azathioprine [*Also, AZA, AZT*] [*Immunosuppressive drug*] ... AZ
Azathioprine [*Also, AZ, AZT*] [*Immunosuppressive drug*] ... AZA
Azathioprine [*Also, AZ, AZA*] [*Immunosuppressive drug*] ... AZT
Azauracil [*Antineoplastic drug*] (DAVI) ... AZU
Azauridine (MAE) ... AU
Azauridine [*Antineoplastic drug*] (DAVI) ... AZUR
Azco Mining [*AMEX symbol*] (TTSB) ... AZC
Azco Mining, Inc. [*AMEX symbol*] (SAG) ... AZC
Azco Mining, Inc. [*Associated Press*] (SAG) ... Azco
Azerbaijan Democratic Party [*Iran*] [*Political party*] ... ADP
Azerbaijan Soviet Socialist Republic [*MARC country of publication code Library of Congress*] (LCCP) ... ajr
Azerbaijan Soviet Socialist Republic [*MARC geographic area code Library of Congress*] (LCCP) ... e-ur-aj
Azerbaijani [*MARC language code Library of Congress*] (LCCP) ... aze
Azerbaijani (BARN) ... Azerb
Azerbaydzhani Soviet Socialist Republic ... AzerSSR
Azia Keizai Kenkyujo [*Institute for Developing Economies*], Tokyo, Japan [*Library symbol Library of Congress*] (LCLS) ... JTA
Azidodeoxythymidine [*Biochemistry*] ... AZT
Azidodideoxyadenosine [*Antiviral*] ... AZA
Azidodideoxyguanosine [*Antiviral*] ... AZG
Azidodideoxyuridine [*Antiviral*] ... AZDDU
Azidodideoxyuridine [*Antiviral*] ... AZDU
Azido(ethyl)dideoxyuridine [*Antiviral*] ... AZEU
Azidonitrophenyl Phosphate [*Also, ACN*] [*Organic chemistry*] ... ANPP
Azidophenyl Norisocarbacyclin [*Organic chemistry*] ... APNIC
Azidophenylglyoxal [*Organic chemistry*] ... APG
(Azidophenylthio)phthalimide [*Organic chemistry*] ... APTP
Azidothymidine [*Later, ZDV*] [*Antiviral*] ... AZI
Azidothymidine [*Later, ZDV*] [*Antiviral*] ... AZT
Azidothymidine-Triphosphate [*Biochemistry*] ... AZT-TP
Azilda Branch, Rayside-Balfour Public Library, Ontario [*Library symbol National Library of Canada*] (NLC) ... OARB
Azimut SA [*Spain ICAO designator*] (FAAC) ... AZT
Azimuth (IAA) ... A

Azimuth (AFM) .... AZ
Azimuth .... AZM
Azimuth Alignment System [*Aerospace*] (AAG) .... AAS
Azimuth and Elevation .... A & E
Azimuth and Elevation (IAA) .... AAE
Azimuth and Elevation (MSA) .... AZEL
Azimuth and Range .... AZRAN
Azimuth and Range (MSA) .... AZRNG
Azimuth Angle .... Z
Azimuth Angle Increment .... AAI
Azimuth Change Pulse .... ACP
Azimuth Comparator .... AC
Azimuth Control Amplifier .... ACA
Azimuth Control System .... ACS
Azimuth Control Torquer .... ACT
Azimuth Determining System [*Army Space Technology and Research*
   Office] (RDA) .... ADS
Azimuth Drive (GFGA) .... AD
Azimuth Drive Assembly (MCD) .... ADA
Azimuth Drive Local Control .... ADLC
Azimuth, Elevation, and Range Overtake (SAA) .... AERO
Azimuth Elevation Range (KSC) .... AER
Azimuth Error Indicator .... AEI
Azimuth Error Test Feature .... AETF
Azimuth Error Test Fixture (MCD) .... AETF
Azimuth Follow-Up Amplifier .... AFA
Azimuth Follow-Up System (MCD) .... AFS
Azimuth Gimbal Assembly (MCD) .... AGA
Azimuth Guidance Nose in Stands (MCD) .... AGNIS
Azimuth Indicator .... AI
Azimuth Laying Set (AABC) .... ALS
Azimuth Mark Pulse Amplifier .... AMPA
Azimuth Only .... AZON
Azimuth Orientation System [*Military*] .... AOS
Azimuth Orientation Unit [*Military*] (AABC) .... AOU
Azimuth Pulse Generator .... APG
Azimuth Quantized Gated Video [*Air Force*] .... AQGV
Azimuth/Range (RDA) .... A/R
Azimuth Range and Timing Group (KSC) .... ARTG
Azimuth Reference System (MCD) .... ARS
Azimuth Reset Pulse .... ARP
Azimuth Servo Assembly .... ASA
Azimuth, Speed, Altitude .... AZUSA
Azimuth Speed Indicator .... ASI
Azimuth Steering Line (MCD) .... ASL
Azimuth Torquer Amplifier .... ATA
Azimuth Versus Amplitude .... AVA
Azimuthal Quantum Number .... AQN
Azimuthal Quantum Number [*or Orbital Angular Momentum Quantum*
   Number] [*Symbol*] I
Azimuthal Quantum Number [*or Orbital Angular Momentum Quantum*
   Number] - **Total** [*Symbol*] L

Azimuthally Varying Field .... AVF
Azimuth-Elevation (IDOE) .... AZ-EL
Azimuth-Stabilized Plan Position Indicator (DEN) ...... ASPPI
Azione Dynamico-Specifico [*Dynamic-Specific Action*] [*Italian Medicine*] .... ADS
Aziridinyl Benzoquinone [*Organic chemistry*] .... AZQ
Azna [*Iran*] [*ICAO location identifier*] (ICLI) .... OICA
Azo Group [*Chemical group with two nitrogen atoms*] (MEDA) .... N:N
Azobenzene Derivative [*Organic chemistry*] .... ABD
Azobenzenearsonate [*Also, ARS*] [*Organic chemistry*] ... ABA
Azobenzenearsonate [*Also, ABA*] [*Organic chemistry*] .. ARS
Azobisformamide [*Organic chemistry*] .... ABFA
Azobisisobutyronitrile [*Organic chemistry*] .... AIBN
Azodicarbonamide (OA) .... ADA
Azoospermia Factor [*Genetics*] .... AZF
Azora Minerals [*Vancouver Stock Exchange symbol*] .. AZM
Azores (VRA) .... Azo
Azores Fixed Acoustic Range [*NATO*] .... AFAR
Azores Hot Spot [*Geology*] .... AHS
Azores Islands .... AZ
Azores Islands [*MARC geographic area code Library of Congress*] (LCCP)..... lnaz--
Azote [*Nitrogen*] [*French*] .... AZ
Azoxymethane [*A carcinogen*] .... AZM
Aztar Corp. [*NYSE symbol*] (SPSG) .... AZR
Aztar Corp. [*Associated Press*] (SAG) .... Aztar
Aztec Manufacturing Co. [*NASDAQ symbol*] (NQ) ..... AZTC
Aztec Manufacturing Co. [*Associated Press*] (SAG) ... AztcM
Aztec Mfg Co. [*NASDAQ symbol*] (TTSB) .... AZTC
Aztec, NM [*AM radio station call letters*] .... KCQL
Aztec, NM [*FM radio station call letters*] .... KWYK
Aztec Ruins National Monument .... AZRU
Azul [*Race of maize*] .... AZU
Azul [*Argentina ICAO location identifier*] (ICLI) .... SAZA
Azuni's Maritime Law [*A publication*] (DLA) .... Az Mar Law
Azuni's Maritime Law [*A publication*] (DLA) .... Azuni Mar Law
Azure (ABBR) .... A
Azure [*Heraldry*] [*Philately*] .... AZ
Azure Laid [*Paper*] (DGA) .... AL
Azure Laid (ADA) .... AZLD
Azure Resources [*Vancouver Stock Exchange symbol*] .. AZR
Azure Wove [*Paper*] (DGA) .... AW
Azure Wove (ADA) .... AZWO
Azurin .... AZU
Azurophil-Derived Bactericidal Factor .... ADBF
Azusa Ground Station .... AZGS
Azusa Pacific College, Azusa, CA [*OCLC symbol*] (OCLC) .... CAP
Azusa Pacific College, Azusa, CA [*Library symbol Library of Congress*]
   (LCLS) .... CAzPC
Azusa Pacific University (GAGS) .... Azusa Pac U
Azusa Public Library, Azusa, CA [*Library symbol Library of Congress*]
   (LCLS) .... CAz
Azusa Transponder .... AZT
Azusa Transponder Coherent .... AZTC
Azza Transport Co. Ltd. [*Sudan*] [*FAA designator*] (FAAC) .... AZZ

B & B Productions [*New Jersey*] [*Record label*] .... B & B
B and Better [*Lumber*] .... BB
B & H Maritime Carriers Ltd. [*Associated Press*] (SAG) .... B & H Mr
B & H Maritime Carriers Ltd. [*AMEX symbol*] (CTT) .... BHM
B & H Ocean Carriers Ltd. [*Associated Press*] (SAG) .... B & HO
B & H Ocean Carriers Ltd. [*AMEX symbol*] (CTT) .... BHO
"B" Corp. [*Toronto Stock Exchange symbol*] .... XBC
B. F. Goodrich Chemical Co. [*of B. F. Goodrich Co.*], Development Center
　Library, Avon Lake, OH [*Library symbol Library of Congress*] (LCLS) .... OAvG
B. F. Goodrich Co. .... BFG
B. F. Goodrich Co., Akron, OH [*Library symbol Library of Congress*]
　(LCLS) .... OAkGr
B. F. Goodrich Co., Information Center, Brecksville, OH [*OCLC symbol*]
　(OCLC) .... OGR
B. F. Goodrich Co., Technical Library, Brecksville, OH [*Library symbol
　Library of Congress*] (LCLS) .... OBrG
B. F. Goodrich Institute for Personnel Development .... GIPD
B. F. Jones Memorial Library, Aliquippa, PA [*OCLC symbol*] (OCLC) .... BFJ
B. F. Jones Memorial Library, Aliquippa, PA [*Library symbol Library of
　Congress*] (LCLS) .... PA
B. J. Thomas Fan Club (EA) .... BJTFC
B M J Financial [*NASDAQ symbol*] (TTSB) .... BMJF
B negative [*Blood type*] (DAVI) .... BNEG
B. W. Flinn Middle School, Rockford, IL [*Library symbol*] [*Library of
　Congress*] (LCLS) .... IRoFM
Ba [*Fiji*] [*Airport symbol*] (OAG) .... BFJ
Ba [*Fiji*] [*ICAO location identifier*] (ICLI) .... NFFA
BA Merchant Services, Inc. [*Associated Press*] (SAG) .... BA Mrch
BA Merchant Services, Inc. [*NYSE symbol*] (SAG) .... BPI
BA Resources [*Vancouver Stock Exchange symbol*] .... BAP
Baader-Meinhof Group [*Revolutionary group*] [*Germany*] .... BMG
Baan Co. NV [*NASDAQ symbol*] (SAG) .... BAAN
Baan Co.NV [*NASDAQ symbol*] (TTSB) .... BAANF
BAB Holdings [*NASDAQ symbol*] (TTSB) .... BAGL
BAB Holdings, Inc. [*Associated Press*] (SAG) .... BABHld
BAB Holdings, Inc. [*NASDAQ symbol*] (SAG) .... BAGL
Baba Bathra [*or Bava Batra*] (BJA) .... BB
Baba Kama [*or Bava Kamma*] (BJA) .... BK
Baba Mezi'a [*or Bava Mezi'a*] (BJA) .... BM
Baba Qama [*or Bava Qamma*] (BJA) .... BQ
Babahoyo [*Ecuador*] [*ICAO location identifier*] (ICLI) .... SEBA
[*The*] Babbage Society (EA) .... BABS
Babbing [*Fishing for eels*] .... BAB
Babbitt [*Metallurgy*] .... BAB
Babbitt [*Metallurgy*] .... Bb
Babbitt Metal [*Freight*] .... BAB MTL
Babbitt, MN [*FM radio station call letters*] (RBYB) .... KAOD
Babbitt Public Library, Babbitt, MN [*Library symbol*] [*Library of Congress*]
　(LCLS) .... MnBab
Babcock & Wilcox Co. .... B & W
Babcock & Wilcox Co., Alliance, OH [*Library symbol Library of Congress*]
　(LCLS) .... OAIB
Babcock & Wilcox Co., Lynchburg, VA [*Library symbol Library of Congress*]
　(LCLS) .... ViLBW
Babcock and Wilcox Nuclear Environmental Services (GAAI) .... B&W-NES
Babcock & Wilcox Standard Safety Analysis Report [*Nuclear energy*]
　(NRCH) .... BSSAR
Babcock & Wilcox Test Reactor .... BAWTR
Babcock & Wilcox Test Reactor .... BWTR
Babcock Easy Terminal Access System (MCD) .... BETA
Babcock Test of Mental Efficiency [*Psychology*] .... BTME
Babcock Woodall-Duckham Ltd. [*British*] (IRUK) .... BWD
Babe Ruth Baseball (EA) .... BRB
Babe Ruth Birthplace Foundation (EA) .... BRBF
Babe Ruth League (EA) .... BRL
Babel Language Editing and Checking (PDAA) .... BLEACH
Babenhausen [*Germany ICAO location identifier*] (ICLI) .... EDEF
Babilonia [*Costa Rica*] [*ICAO location identifier*] (ICLI) .... MRBB
Babinet Absorption Rule .... BAR
Babinet Jamin Compensator .... BJC
Babington's Law of Auctions [*A publication*] (DLA) .... Bab Auc
Babington's Law of Set-Off [*A publication*] (DLA) .... Bab Set-Off
Babinski [*Reflex*] [*Medicine*] .... BAB
Babo [*Indonesia*] [*Airport symbol*] (OAG) .... BXB
Babo [*Indonesia*] [*ICAO location identifier*] (ICLI) .... WASO
Babolsar [*Iran*] [*ICAO location identifier*] (ICLI) .... OINB

Baboon Endogenous Virus .... BaEV
Baboon Endogenous Virus .... BEV
Baboon Kidney (DMAA) .... BabK
Babson College (GAGS) .... Babson C
Babson College, Babson Park, MA [*OCLC symbol*] (OCLC) .... BAB
Babson College, Babson Park, MA [*Library symbol Library of Congress*]
　(LCLS) .... MBBI
Babson Institute of Business Administration [*Massachusetts*] .... BIBA
Babson's Reports, Inc. (IIA) .... BRI
Baby Bond [*Investment term*] .... BB
Baby Boomers in Debt [*Lifestyle Classification*] .... Biddies
Baby Born Dead [*Medicine*] .... BBD
Baby Brother Tender Love [*Doll manufactured by Mattel, Inc.*] .... BBTL
Baby Hamster Kidney .... BHK
Baby Incendiary Bomb .... B/B
Baby Incendiary Bomb .... BIB
Baby Life Support System (DI) .... BLISS
Baby Mouse Kidney Cells .... BMK
Baby "N" Connector (IEEE) .... BNC
Baby or Doll [*Freight*] .... BB DL
Baby Rat Kidney [*Immunology*] .... BRK
Baby Superstore [*NASDAQ symbol*] (TTSB) .... BSST
Baby Superstore, Inc. [*Associated Press*] (SAG) .... BabySst
Baby Superstore, Inc. [*NASDAQ symbol*] (SAG) .... BSST
Babylon, NY [*Location identifier FAA*] (FAAL) .... BBN
Babylon, NY [*FM radio station call letters*] .... WBAB
Babylon, NY [*AM radio station call letters*] .... WGLI
Babylon, NY [*AM radio station call letters*] .... WNYG
Babylon, NY [*AM radio station call letters*] (RBYB) .... WZZU-AM
Babylon Public Library, Babylon, NY [*Library symbol Library of Congress*]
　(LCLS) .... NBab
Babylonia (BJA) .... Bab
Babylonia [*or Babylonian*] .... BABYL
[*The*] Babylonian Genesis [*A publication*] (BJA) .... BG
Babylonian Historical Texts Relating to the Capture and Downfall of
　Babylon [*A publication*] (BJA) .... BHT
Babylonian Inscriptions in the Collection of James B. Nies (BJA) .... BIN
Babylonian Legal and Business Documents [*A publication*] (BJA) .... BLBD
Babylonian Records in the Library of J. Pierpont Morgan (BJA) .... BRM
Babylonian Seleucid Era (BJA) .... SelBab
Babylonian Talmud (BJA) .... Bab
Babylonian Talmud (BJA) .... BT
Babylonian Vocalization (BJA) .... BV
Babylonien und Assyrien [*A publication*] (BJA) .... BuA
Babylonische Briefe aus der Zeit der Hammurapi Dynastie [*A publication*]
　(BJA) .... BB
Babylonische Busspsalmen [*A publication*] (BJA) .... BB
Babylonische Rechtsurkunden aus der Regierungszeit Artaxerxes I und
　Darius II [*A publication*] (BJA) .... BRU
Babylonische Texte [*A publication*] (BJA) .... BT
Babysitting Association of South Australia .... BASA
Babystar, Inc. [*Associated Press*] (SAG) .... Babyst
Babystar, Inc. [*Associated Press*] (SAG) .... Babystr
Babystar, Inc. [*NASDAQ symbol*] (SAG) .... DATA
BAC Aircraft Ltd. [*British ICAO designator*] (FAAC) .... RPX
BAC Leasing Ltd. [*British*] [*FAA designator*] (FAAC) .... BAC
Baca County Public Library, Springfield, CO [*Library symbol Library of
　Congress*] (LCLS) .... CoSp
Bacau [*Romania*] [*Seismograph station code, US Geological Survey*] (SEIS) .... BAC
Bacau [*Romania*] [*Airport symbol*] (OAG) .... BCM
Bacau [*Romania*] [*ICAO location identifier*] (ICLI) .... LRBC
Baccalaureat en Administration des Affaires [*Canada*] (DD) .... BAA
Baccalaureat en Ingenerie [*Canada*] (DD) .... Bing
Baccalaureat en Loisirs [*Canada*] (DD) .... BL
Baccalaureat en Sciences Administratives [*Canada*] (DD) .... BAS
Baccalaureat en Sciences Administratives [*Canada*] (DD) .... BSA
Baccalaureate .... B
Baccalaureate .... BACC
Baccalaureate Exam [*France*] .... BAC
Baccalaureus .... BAC
Baccalaureus Artium [*Bachelor of Arts*] [*Latin*] .... BA
Baccalaureus Chirurgiae [*Bachelor of Surgery*] .... B Ch
Baccalaureus Chirurgiae [*Bachelor of Surgery*] .... B Chir
Baccalaureus Chirurgiae [*Bachelor of Surgery*] .... BC
Baccalaureus Chirurgiae Dentium [*Bachelor of Dental Surgery*] .... B Ch D
Baccalaureus in Arte Ingeniaria [*Bachelor of Engineering*] (EY) .... BAI

Baccalaureus Juris [*Bachelor of Law*] (DLA) ... B Jur
Baccalaureus Legum [*Bachelor of Laws*] ... BLL
Baccalaureus Literarum [*Bachelor of Literature*] [*Latin*] ... LB
Baccalaureus Medicinae, Chirurgiae Magister [*Bachelor of Medicine, Master of Surgery*] ... MBCM
Baccalaureus Procurationis (DLA) ... B Proc
Baccalaureus Scientiae [*Bachelor of Science*] [*Latin*] ... B Sc
Baccalaureus Scientiae Didacticae [*Bachelor of Didactic Science*] ... BSD
Baccalaureus Utriusque Juris [*Bachelor of Both Laws; i.e., Canon and Civil Laws*] ... BUJ
Bacchae [*of Euripides*] [*Classical studies*] (OCD) ... Bacch
Bacchides [*of Plautus*] [*Classical studies*] (OCD) ... Bacch
Bacchylides [*Fifth century BC*] [*Classical studies*] (OCD) ... Bacchyl
Bac-Giang [*Vietnam*] [*Seismograph station code, US Geological Survey*] (SEIS) ... BGV
Bach Choir [*Record label*] ... BC
Bach Jahrbuch [*A publication*] ... B-J
Bach Society of Queensland [*Australia*] ... BSQ
Bach Werke-Verzeichnis [*Music*] ... BWV
Bachad Organization of North America (EA) ... BONA
Bachelier des Arts [*Bachelor of Arts*] [*French*] ... B des A
Bachelier des Lettres [*Bachelor of Letters*] [*French*] ... B des L
Bachelier des Sciences [*Bachelor of Science*] [*French*] ... B des S
Bachelier en Arts Visuels [*Bachelor of Visual Arts*] [*French*] ... BAV
Bachelier en Droit [*Bachelor of Laws*] [*French*] ... B en Dr
Bachelier en Droit Canonique [*Bachelor of Canon Law*] [*French*] ... BDC
Bachelier en Sciences Administratives [*Bachelor in Administrative Sciences*] [*French*] ... BSA
Bachelier en Service Social [*Bachelor of Social Work*] [*French*] ... BSerSoc
Bachelier es Sciences [*Bachelor of Science*] [*French*] (ROG) ... B es SC
Bachelier es Sciences Appliquees [*Bachelor of Applied Science*] [*French*] ... BScA
Bachelor ... B
Bachelor ... BACH
Bachelor ... BACHR
Bachelor ... BCHLR
Bachelor Airmen's Quarters [*Air Force*] ... BAQ
Bachelor Degrees for Soldiers [*Program*] ... BDFS
Bachelor Enlisted Quarters ... BEQ
Bachelor in Dental Science [*British*] ... BDentSc
Bachelor in Interior Architecture ... BIntArch
Bachelor in Interior Design ... BIntDesign
Bachelor in Landscape Architecture ... BLandArch
Bachelor in Law (DD) ... BL
Bachelor in Library Science (ADA) ... BLibSc
Bachelor in Surgery (DD) ... BCh
Bachelor in Surgery (DD) ... BChir
Bachelor Lake Gold Mines, Inc. [*Toronto Stock Exchange symbol*] ... BLG
Bachelor Noncommissioned Officers' Quarters [*Air Force*] (AFM) ... BNCOQ
Bachelor of Accountancy ... B Acc
Bachelor of Accounts ... B Ac
Bachelor of Accounts ... B Acc's
Bachelor of Actuarial Sciences (DD) ... BActSci
Bachelor of Acupuncture [*British*] (DBQ) ... BAc
Bachelor of Administration ... B Adm
Bachelor of Administration ... BAdmin
Bachelor of Administrative Engineering ... B Adm Eng
Bachelor of Advertising Arts and Design ... B of Adv Art & Des
Bachelor of Aeronautical Administration ... B of AA
Bachelor of Aeronautical and Astronautical Engineering (WGA) ... BAAE
Bachelor of Aeronautical Engineering ... B Ae E
Bachelor of Aeronautical Engineering ... B Ae Eng
Bachelor of Aeronautical Engineering ... B Aero E
Bachelor of Aeronautical Engineering ... B of AE
Bachelor of Aeronautical Engineering ... BAE
Bachelor of Aeronautical Science ... B Ae S
Bachelor of Aeronautical Science ... B Ae Sc
Bachelor of Aeronautics ... B Ae
Bachelor of Agricultural Economics (WDAA) ... B AG ECO
Bachelor of Agricultural Economics (IIA) ... BAE
Bachelor of Agricultural Economics (ADA) ... BAgEc
Bachelor of Agricultural Economics (NADA) ... BAgoEco
Bachelor of Agricultural Economics ... BAgrEcon
Bachelor of Agricultural Engineering ... B Ag E
Bachelor of Agricultural Engineering ... B Agr E
Bachelor of Agricultural Engineering ... B Eng A
Bachelor of Agricultural Engineering ... BAE
Bachelor of Agricultural Research and Economics ... BAgResEcon
Bachelor of Agricultural Science ... B Agr S
Bachelor of Agricultural Science ... B Agr Sc
Bachelor of Agricultural Science ... BA Sc
Bachelor of Agricultural Science (ADA) ... BAgSc
Bachelor of Agricultural Science (BARN) ... BAgSci
Bachelor of Agricultural Science ... BAS
Bachelor of Agricultural Science (NADA) ... BSA
Bachelor of Agriculture ... B Ag
Bachelor of Agriculture ... B Agr
Bachelor of Agriculture ... BA
Bachelor of Agriculture ... BAgri
Bachelor of Agriculture [*British*] ... BAgric
Bachelor of Air Conditioning Engineering ... BAC Eng
Bachelor of Air Conditioning Engineering ... BACE
Bachelor of Animal Science ... BAnimSc
Bachelor of Applied Arts ... B/A
Bachelor of Applied Arts ... BAA
Bachelor of Applied Arts (NADA) ... BAppArts
Bachelor of Applied Chemistry ... BA Chem
Bachelor of Applied Economics (ADA) ... BAppEc
Bachelor of Applied Mathematics ... BAM
Bachelor of Applied Music ... BMusA
Bachelor of Applied Science (WDAA) ... B APP SCI
Bachelor of Applied Science ... B Applied Sc
Bachelor of Applied Science ... BA Sc
Bachelor of Applied Science (ADA) ... BAppSc
Bachelor of Applied Science ... BAS
Bachelor of Applied Science (ADA) ... BScApp
Bachelor of Applied Science - Built Environment ... BAppSc-BltEnvir
Bachelor of Applied Science - Computing ... BAppSc-Comptg
Bachelor of Applied Science - Construction Management ... BAppSc-ConstMgmt
Bachelor of Applied Science - Electronic Systems and Computing ... BAppSc-ElectSysComptg
Bachelor of Applied Science - Information ... BAppScInfo
Bachelor of Applied Science (Nursing) (ADA) ... BAppSci(Nsg)
Bachelor of Applied Science (Optometry) ... BAppSci(Optom)
Bachelor of Applied Science - Optometry ... BAppSc-Optom
Bachelor of Applied Science - Quantity Surveying ... BAppSc-QuantSurv
Bachelor of Applied Science (Social Ecology) ... BAppSci(SocEcol)
Bachelor of Applied Science - Surveying ... BAppSc-Surv
Bachelor of Architectural Design ... B Arch Des
Bachelor of Architectural Engineering ... B Ar E
Bachelor of Architectural Engineering ... B Arc E
Bachelor of Architectural Engineering ... B Arch Eng
Bachelor of Architectural Engineering ... BAE
Bachelor of Architectural Engineering (NADA) ... BArchE
Bachelor of Architectural History ... BArchHist
Bachelor of Architectural Science ... BAS
Bachelor of Architectural Studies ... BArchSt
Bachelor of Architectural Studies ... BArchStudies
Bachelor of Architectural Technology ... BArchTech
Bachelor of Architecture ... B Ar
Bachelor of Architecture ... B Arch
Bachelor of Architecture (NADA) ... BArch
Bachelor of Architecture and Town Planning (ADA) ... BArch & TP
Bachelor of Architecture in Architectural Engineering ... B Arch (ArchE)
Bachelor of Architecture in Architecture ... B Arch (Arch)
Bachelor of Architecture in City Planning ... B Arch in City Pl
Bachelor of Art and Architecture (ADA) ... BAA
Bachelor of Art Education ... BA Ed
Bachelor of Art Education ... BAE
Bachelor of Art Education ... BArtEd
Bachelor of Art of Oratory ... BAO
Bachelor of Art Theory ... BArtTh
Bachelor of Arts (AEE) ... AB
Bachelor of Arts ... BA
Bachelor of Arts and Sciences ... B Ar Sc
Bachelor of Arts and Sciences ... BAS
Bachelor of Arts (Asian Studies) ... BA(AsianStudies)
Bachelor of Arts/Bachelor of Laws (ADA) ... BA/LLB
Bachelor of Arts/Bachelor of Management Combines (DD) ... BA/BMgmt
Bachelor of Arts/Bachelor of Science Combined (DD) ... BA/BS
Bachelor of Arts - Classical ... BA Class
Bachelor of Arts (Economics) ... BA (Econ)
Bachelor of Arts (Education) ... BA(Educ)
Bachelor of Arts in Arts and Sciences ... BA in A & Sci
Bachelor of Arts in Bible ... AB (Bible)
Bachelor of Arts in Business Administration ... BA in BA
Bachelor of Arts in Business and Economics ... BA in B & E
Bachelor of Arts in Ceramic Art ... BA in Cer A
Bachelor of Arts in Chemical Engineering ... AB in Ch E
Bachelor of Arts in Chemistry (WDAA) ... BA CHEM
Bachelor of Arts in Civil Engineering ... AB in CE
Bachelor of Arts in Economics and Business ... BA in E & B
Bachelor of Arts in Education ... AB Ed
Bachelor of Arts in Education ... BA Ed
Bachelor of Arts in Education ... BAE
Bachelor of Arts in Electrical Engineering ... AB in EE
Bachelor of Arts in Elementary Education ... BA in E Ed
Bachelor of Arts in Elementary Education (WGA) ... BAEE
Bachelor of Arts in General Studies [*British*] (DBQ) ... BA(GenStud)
Bachelor of Arts in General Studies ... BAGS
Bachelor of Arts in Home Economics ... AB in H Ec
Bachelor of Arts in Human Relations ... BAH Re
Bachelor of Arts in Information Systems ... BAIS
Bachelor of Arts in Journalism ... AB in J
Bachelor of Arts in Journalism (BARN) ... B A Jour
Bachelor of Arts in Journalism ... BA in J
Bachelor of Arts in Journalism ... BAJ
Bachelor of Arts in Law ... BA(Law)
Bachelor of Arts in Library Science ... ABLS
Bachelor of Arts in Library Science (WDAA) ... BALS
Bachelor of Arts in Mechanical Engineering ... AB in ME
Bachelor of Arts in Mechanical Engineering ... ABME
Bachelor of Arts in Music ... BAM
Bachelor of Arts in Music Education ... BA in M Ed
Bachelor of Arts in Music Education (BARN) ... BAMusEd
Bachelor of Arts in Nursing (WDAA) ... BA NURS
Bachelor of Arts in Pedagogy (DD) ... BAPed
Bachelor of Arts in Physical Education (NADA) ... BAPE
Bachelor of Arts in Practical Christian Training ... BAPCT
Bachelor of Arts in Religious Education ... BA in Rel Ed
Bachelor of Arts in Sacred Music (BJA) ... BASM

Bachelor of Arts in Secondary Education	AB in Sec Ed
Bachelor of Arts in Secretarial Studies (ADA)	BASecStud
Bachelor of Arts in Social Science (WDAA)	BASS
Bachelor of Arts in Speech	BA in Sp
Bachelor of Arts in Speech	BAS
Bachelor of Arts in Teaching	BAT
Bachelor of Arts in Theology	AB in TH
Bachelor of Arts in Theology (BARN)	B A Theol
Bachelor of Arts in Theology	BA Theo
Bachelor of Arts in Visual Communication	BAVisCom
Bachelor of Arts (Information Management)	BA(InfoMan)
Bachelor of Arts (Leisure Studies)	BA(LeisureStud)
Bachelor of Arts (Library Science)	BA(LibSc)
Bachelor of Arts, Master of Science	BASM
Bachelor of Arts (Music)	BA (Mus)
Bachelor of Arts - Non-Classical	BA Non-Class
Bachelor of Arts (Open University) [British] (DI)	BA(OU)
Bachelor of Arts (Visual Arts)	BA(VA)
Bachelor of Arts with Religious Major	AB (Rel)
Bachelor of Asian Studies	BAsianStudies
Bachelor of Association Science	B As S
Bachelor of Association Science	B As Sc
Bachelor of Automobile Engineering	B Au E
Bachelor of Automobile Engineering	B Au Eng
Bachelor of Ayurvedic Medicine	BAM
Bachelor of Bacteriology	B Bac
Bachelor of Bacteriology	BB
Bachelor of Beauty Culture	BBC
Bachelor of Behavioral Sciences	BBehavSci
Bachelor of Behavioural Science	BBSc
Bachelor of Biblical Arts	B Bib Arts
Bachelor of Biological Chemistry	B Bi Ch
Bachelor of Biological Chemistry	B Bi Chem
Bachelor of Biological Engineering	B Bi E
Bachelor of Biological Engineering	B Bi Eng
Bachelor of Biological Physics	B Bi Phy
Bachelor of Biological Sciences	B Bi S
Bachelor of Biological Sciences	B Bi Sc
Bachelor of Biomedical Sciences	BBiomed
Bachelor of Building (ADA)	BBldg
Bachelor of Building (ADA)	BBuild
Bachelor of Building	BBuilding
Bachelor of Building Construction	B of BC
Bachelor of Building Construction	BBC
Bachelor of Building Science	BBldgSc
Bachelor of Building Science (ADA)	BBldSc
Bachelor of Business	BB
Bachelor of Business (ADA)	BBus
Bachelor of Business - Accountancy	BBus-Accy
Bachelor of Business Administration	BB Ad
Bachelor of Business Administration	BB Adm
Bachelor of Business Administration	BBA
Bachelor of Business Administration (ADA)	BBusAd
Bachelor of Business Administration	BBusAdmin
Bachelor of Business - Communication	BBus-Comn
Bachelor of Business - Computing	BBus-Comptg
Bachelor of Business Education	BB Ed
Bachelor of Business - Health Administration	BBusHA
Bachelor of Business - Health Administration	BBus-HealthAdmin
Bachelor of Business Management	BBM
Bachelor of Business Management	BBusMgmt
Bachelor of Business - Management	BBus-Mgt
Bachelor of Business - Public Administration	BBus-PubAdmin
Bachelor of Business Science	BB Sc
Bachelor of Business Science	BBS
Bachelor of Business Studies	BBS
Bachelor of Canon Law	B Can L
Bachelor of Canon Law	BCL
Bachelor of Cement Engineering	B Ce Eng
Bachelor of Ceramic Engineering	B Cer E
Bachelor of Ceramic Engineering	B Cer Eng
Bachelor of Chemical Engineering	B Ch E
Bachelor of Chemical Engineering	B Ch Eng
Bachelor of Chemical Engineering	B Chem E
Bachelor of Chemical Engineering	BCE
Bachelor of Chemical Engineering (DD)	BChemEng
Bachelor of Chemical Engineering (ADA)	BEChem
Bachelor of Chemical Science	BCS
Bachelor of Chemistry	B Ch
Bachelor of Chemistry	B Chem
Bachelor of Chemistry	BC
Bachelor of Chemistry	Ch B
Bachelor of Christian Education	B Chr Ed
Bachelor of Christian Education	BCE
Bachelor of Christian Science	BSC
Bachelor of Christian Science	CSB
Bachelor of Christian Training	BCT
Bachelor of Chromatics	BChrom
Bachelor of Church Music	BCM
Bachelor of City Forestry	BCF
Bachelor of City Planning	BCP
Bachelor of Civil Engineering	BCE
Bachelor of Civil Law	BCL
Bachelor of Civil Law	CLB
Bachelor of Classics	BA. BC

Bachelor of College Studies	BCS
Bachelor of Combined Studies [British] (DBQ)	BCombStuds
Bachelor of Combined Studies [British] (DI)	BComStuds
Bachelor of Commerce	B Com
Bachelor of Commerce	B Comm
Bachelor of Commerce	BC
Bachelor of Commerce (Accounting)	BCom(Acc)
Bachelor of Commerce and Administration (BARN)	BCA
Bachelor of Commerce-Bachelor of Laws	BCom-LLB
Bachelor of Commercial Administration	B Com Adm
Bachelor of Commercial Arts	BCA
Bachelor of Commercial Education	BC Ed
Bachelor of Commercial Law	BCL
Bachelor of Commercial Science	BC Sc
Bachelor of Commercial Science	BCommSc
Bachelor of Commercial Science	BComSc
Bachelor of Commercial Science	BCS
Bachelor of Commercial Science	BScCom
Bachelor of Commercial Science (DD)	BScComm
Bachelor of Commercial Service	BC Se
Bachelor of Community Welfare	BCW
Bachelor of Community Work	BCW
Bachelor of Computer and Mathematical Sciences	BCM
Bachelor of Computer Management (DD)	BCM
Bachelor of Computer Science	BCompSc
Bachelor of Computer Science	BCS
Bachelor of Computer Science and Engineering	BCompScEng
Bachelor of Computer Systems Engineering	BComSysEng
Bachelor of Computing	BComp
Bachelor of Construction Economics	BConstrucEc
Bachelor of Creative Arts	BA(Creative)
Bachelor of Creative Arts	BCA
Bachelor of Creative Arts	BCreativeArts
Bachelor of Criminal Science (NADA)	BCS
Bachelor of Criminology	B Cr
Bachelor of Dental Science	BD Sc
Bachelor of Dental Science [British] (BABM)	BDentSci
Bachelor of Dental Surgery	BDS
Bachelor of Dental Surgery (NADA)	BDS
Bachelor of Dentistry	BDentistry
Bachelor of Design	B Des
Bachelor of Design	BDesign
Bachelor of Design in Art Education	B Des A Ed
Bachelor of Didactics	B Did
Bachelor of Didactics	BDi
Bachelor of Diesel Engineering	B Di E
Bachelor of Diesel Engineering	B Di Eng
Bachelor of Diplomacy	B Dipl
Bachelor of Divine Literature	BDL
Bachelor of Divinity	BD
Bachelor of Divinity	DB
Bachelor of Divinity and Master of Hebrew Literature (BJA)	BDMHL
Bachelor of Divinity in Education	BD in E
Bachelor of Domestic Arts	ADB
Bachelor of Domestic Arts	BDA
Bachelor of Dramatic Art	B Dr Art
Bachelor of Dramatic Art	BDA
Bachelor of Economics	B Ec
Bachelor of Economics	BEcon
Bachelor of Economics/Bachelor of Laws (ADA)	BEc/LLB
Bachelor of Economics (Social Sciences)	BEc(SocSc)
Bachelor of Education	B Ed
Bachelor of Education	BE
Bachelor of Education	Ed B
Bachelor of Education (Industrial Arts)	BEd(IndArts)
Bachelor of Education (Preliminary Studies)	BEd(Prelim)
Bachelor of Education (Technical and Further Education)	BEd(TAFE)
Bachelor of Education (Technological and Applied Studies)	BEd(TAS)
Bachelor of Educational Science (ADA)	BEdSc
Bachelor of Educational Studies (ADA)	BEdSt
Bachelor of Educational Studies	BEdStud
Bachelor of Electrical Engineering	BEE
Bachelor of Electrical Engineering	BEngE
Bachelor of Electrical Engineering, Communication Option	B of EE (Com Opt)
Bachelor of Electrical Engineering, Power Option	B of EE (Power Opt)
Bachelor of Electro-Chemical Engineering	BECE
Bachelor of Electronics and Telecomunications Engineering (NADA)	BElec&TelEng
Bachelor of Elements	B Ele
Bachelor of Elocution	B El
Bachelor of Elocution	BE
Bachelor of Engineering	B Eng
Bachelor of Engineering (WGA)	B Engr
Bachelor of Engineering	BE
Bachelor of Engineering	BEn
Bachelor of Engineering (Agriculture)	BE(Ag)
Bachelor of Engineering/Bachelor of Business	BEng/BBus
Bachelor of Engineering - Civil	BEng-Civil
Bachelor of Engineering Construction	BEC
Bachelor of Engineering - Electrical	BEng-Elec
Bachelor of Engineering - Electrical	BEng-Elect
Bachelor of Engineering in Mechanical Engineering	BE-ME
Bachelor of Engineering - Mechanical	BEng-Mech
Bachelor of Engineering of Mines	BEM
Bachelor of Engineering Physics	B of EP

Bachelor of Engineering Physics	BE Phy
Bachelor of Engineering Physics	BEP
Bachelor of Engineering Science (WGA)	B Eng S
Bachelor of Engineering Science (DD)	BE
Bachelor of Engineering Science (ADA)	BEngSc
Bachelor of Engineering Science (NADA)	BEngSci
Bachelor of Engineering Science	BESc
Bachelor of Engineering Sciences	BES
Bachelor of Engineering (Technology)	B Eng (Tech)
Bachelor of Engineering Technology	BET
Bachelor of English	B En
Bachelor of English	BE
Bachelor of English Divinity	BED
Bachelor of English Literature	BEL
Bachelor of English Literature	ELB
Bachelor of Entomology	B Ent
Bachelor of Environmental Science	BEnvSc
Bachelor of Environmental Science	BEnvSci
Bachelor of Environmental Studies	BES
Bachelor of Expression	B Ex
Bachelor of Expression	BE
Bachelor of Family Life	BFL
Bachelor of Film and Television	BFTV
Bachelor of Finance	BF
Bachelor of Finance	BFin
Bachelor of Financial Administration	BFA
Bachelor of Financial Administration (ADA)	BFinAdmin
Bachelor of Fine Arts	BFA
Bachelor of Fine Arts in Dramatic Art	BFA in DA
Bachelor of Fine Arts in Education	BFA in Ed
Bachelor of Fine Arts in Landscape Architecture	BFALA
Bachelor of Fine Arts in Music	BFA in Mus
Bachelor of Fine Arts in Painting and Sculpture	BFA in PS
Bachelor of Fine Arts in Speech	BFA in Sp
Bachelor of Fisheries Science	BFSc
Bachelor of Foreign Service	BFS
Bachelor of Foreign Trade	BFT
Bachelor of Forest Engineering	BF Eng
Bachelor of Forest Engineering	BFE
Bachelor of Forestry (ADA)	B For
Bachelor of Forestry	BF
Bachelor of Forestry Science (ADA)	BForSc
Bachelor of Forestry Science (NADA)	BForSci
Bachelor of General Education	B Gen Ed
Bachelor of General Laws (DLA)	BGL
Bachelor of General Studies	BGS
Bachelor of Geological Engineering	B Ge E
Bachelor of Geological Engineering	B Ge Eng
Bachelor of Geological Engineering	BGE
Bachelor of Graphic Design	BGD
Bachelor of Hamburgerology [McDonald's Corp. Hamburger University]	BH
Bachelor of Health Science	BHlthSc
Bachelor of Health Science	BHS
Bachelor of Health Science	BHSc
Bachelor of Health Science	BHthSc
Bachelor of Hebrew	BH
Bachelor of Hebrew Letters	BHL
Bachelor of Hebrew Literature	BHL
Bachelor of Home Economics	BH Ec
Bachelor of Home Economics (NADA)	BHE
Bachelor of Home Science	BHS
Bachelor of Horticultural Science	BHortSc
Bachelor of Horticultural Science	BHortSci
Bachelor of Horticultural Science (NADA)	BHortSci
Bachelor of Horticulture	B Hor
Bachelor of Horticulture	BHort
Bachelor of Hospital Administration	BH Adm
Bachelor of Hospital Administration	BHA
Bachelor of Hospitality	BHospitality
Bachelor of Household Economics	BHE
Bachelor of Household Economy	B Ho Ec
Bachelor of Household Science	B Ho Sc
Bachelor of Household Science	BHSc
Bachelor of Household Science (NADA)	BHSci
Bachelor of Human Biology	BHB
Bachelor of Human Movement	BHUMMVT
Bachelor of Human Movement Studies	BHMS
Bachelor of Humane Letters	BHL
Bachelor of Humane Letters [or Bachelor of Literature or Bachelor of the More Humane Letters]	LHB
Bachelor of Humanics	BH
Bachelor of Humanities	B Hu
Bachelor of Hygiene	B Hy
Bachelor of Hygiene	B HYG
Bachelor of Indian Medicine (NADA)	BIM
Bachelor of Industrial Administration (WGA)	BIA
Bachelor of Industrial Arts	BIA
Bachelor of Industrial Design	BID
Bachelor of Industrial Design	BIndDes
Bachelor of Industrial Education	B Ind Ed
Bachelor of Industrial Engineering	B Ind E
Bachelor of Industrial Engineering	BI Eng
Bachelor of Industrial Engineering	BIE
Bachelor of Industrial Management	B Ind Mgt
Bachelor of Industrial Management	B of IM

Bachelor of Industrial Management	BIM
Bachelor of Industrial Relations (DD)	BIR
Bachelor of Industrial Technology	BIndTech
Bachelor of Industrial Technology	BIT
Bachelor of Industry	B Ind
Bachelor of Informatics	BIn
Bachelor of Information Science	BInfoSc
Bachelor of Information Systems	BInfoSys
Bachelor of Information Technology and Communication	BInfoTech
Bachelor of Interdisciplinary Studies	BIS
Bachelor of Interior Architectural Engineering	BI Arch E
Bachelor of Interior Architectural Engineering	BI Arch Eng
Bachelor of Interior Architecture	BI Arch
Bachelor of Interior Design	B of ID
Bachelor of International Law	B Int L
Bachelor of Irrigation Engineering	B Ir E
Bachelor of Irrigation Engineering	B Ir Eng
Bachelor of Jewish Education	BJ Ed
Bachelor of Jewish Education (BJA)	BJE
Bachelor of Jewish Literature (BJA)	BJL
Bachelor of Jewish Pedagogy	BJP
Bachelor of Journalism	BJ
Bachelor of Judicial Science	JSB
Bachelor of Juridical and Social Sciences (DLA)	B Jur & Soc S
Bachelor of Jurisprudence	BJ
Bachelor of Jurisprudence	BJuris
Bachelor of Land Information	BLandInfo
Bachelor of Land Management (NADA)	BLM
Bachelor of Land Resource Science	BLandResSc
Bachelor of Landscape Architecture	BL Arch
Bachelor of Landscape Architecture	BLA
Bachelor of Landscape Design	BL Des
Bachelor of Landscape Design [British] (DBQ)	BLD
Bachelor of Landscape Engineering	BL Eng
Bachelor of Landscape Management	BLM
Bachelor of Languages [British] (DBQ)	BA(Lan)
Bachelor of Latin Letters	B La L
Bachelor of Latin Letters	BLL
Bachelor of Law Administration	BLAdmin
Bachelor of Law and Administration	BLA
Bachelor of Laws	BL
Bachelor of Laws (PGP)	LL B
Bachelor of Laws (DD)	LLB
Bachelor of Legal Studies (ADA)	BLegS
Bachelor of Legal Studies	BLegSt
Bachelor of Leisure Studies	BLeisureStud
Bachelor of Letters	B Lit
Bachelor of Letters	B Litt
Bachelor of Letters	BL
Bachelor of Letters (ODBW)	BLitt
Bachelor of Letters in Journalism	BLJ
Bachelor of Liberal Arts	BLA
Bachelor of Liberal Studies	BLibSt
Bachelor of Liberal Studies	BLibStudies
Bachelor of Liberal Studies	BLS
Bachelor of Library and Information Studies	BLS
Bachelor of Library Economics	BL Ec
Bachelor of Library Economics	BLE
Bachelor of Library Science	BL Sc
Bachelor of Library Science (ADA)	BLib
Bachelor of Library Science (NADA)	BLibS
Bachelor of Library Science (NADA)	BLibSci
Bachelor of Library Science	BLS
Bachelor of Library Service (NADA)	BLS
Bachelor of Life Science	LSB
Bachelor of Linguistics, University of Manchester [British] (DBQ)	BLing
Bachelor of Literary Interpretation	BLI
Bachelor of Literature	B Lit
Bachelor of Literature	B Litt
Bachelor of Literature	B Lt
Bachelor of Literature	BL
Bachelor of Literature	Lt B
Bachelor of Literature and Communication	BLittComm
Bachelor of Management (DD)	BMgmt
Bachelor of Management Arts (DD)	BMA
Bachelor of Management Engineering	B Mgt E
Bachelor of Management Engineering (NADA)	BMgtEng
Bachelor of Manufacturing Management	BMfgMgt
Bachelor of Manufacturing Technology	BManufTech
Bachelor of Marine Engineering	B Ma E
Bachelor of Marine Engineering	B Ma Eng
Bachelor of Marine Engineering	B Mar E
Bachelor of Marine Engineering (NADA)	BMarEng
Bachelor of Marine Science	BMS
Bachelor of Mathematics	BM
Bachelor of Mathematics	BMath
Bachelor of Mathematics	BMaths
Bachelor of Mechanic Arts	AMB
Bachelor of Mechanical Engineering	B Mech E
Bachelor of Mechanical Engineering	BM Eng
Bachelor of Mechanical Engineering	BME
Bachelor of Mechanical Engineering (Aeronautical Option)	BME (Aero Option)
Bachelor of Mechanical Engineering, Manufacture, and Management [British] (DBQ)	BEng and Man
Bachelor of Mechanical Science	BM Sc

Bachelor of Mechanical Science	BMS
Bachelor of Mechanical Sciences	B Ms Sc
Bachelor of Mechanics	B Mech
Bachelor of Medical Biology	B Med Biol
Bachelor of Medical Laboratory Science	BMedLabSc
Bachelor of Medical Science	BMS
Bachelor of Medical Science, University of Dundee [British] (DBQ)	BMSc
Bachelor of Medical Sciences	B Med Sc
Bachelor of Medical Sciences	B Med Sci
Bachelor of Medical Technology	BMT
Bachelor of Medicine	B Med
Bachelor of Medicine	BM
Bachelor of Medicine [Other than from Oxford]	MB
Bachelor of Medicine and Bachelor of Science [British] (ROG)	MBBSC
Bachelor of Medicine and Bachelor of Surgery	BMBS
Bachelor of Medicine, Bachelor of Surgery	BMBCh
Bachelor of Medicine, Master of Surgery	MBMS
Bachelor of Metallurgical Engineering	B Met E
Bachelor of Metallurgical Engineering	B Met Eng
Bachelor of Metallurgical Engineering	B Metal E
Bachelor of Metallurgy	B Met
Bachelor of Metaphysics	Me B
Bachelor of Microbiology	B Mic
Bachelor of Mining and Metallurgy	BMM
Bachelor of Mining Engineering	B Mi E
Bachelor of Mining Engineering	B Mi Eng
Bachelor of Mining Engineering	BEM
Bachelor of Mining Engineering	BME
Bachelor of Mining Engineering	BMinE
Bachelor of Mining Engineering	BMiningE
Bachelor of Ministry	BMin
Bachelor of Modern Languages	BML
Bachelor of Municipal Administration	BMA
Bachelor of Music	B Mu
Bachelor of Music	B Mus
Bachelor of Music (ODBW)	B Mus
Bachelor of Music (BARN)	BAC MUS
Bachelor of Music	BM
Bachelor of Music (WDAA)	MB
Bachelor of Music Education	B Mus E
Bachelor of Music Education	BM Ed
Bachelor of Music Education	BME
Bachelor of Music Education	BMusEd
Bachelor of Music Education	Mus Ed B
Bachelor of Music in Public School Music	B Mus (PSM)
Bachelor of Music (Performance)	BMusPerf
Bachelor of Music Teaching	BMusT
Bachelor of Natural Resources (ADA)	BNatRes
Bachelor of Natural Science (BARN)	BNS
Bachelor of Naval Architecture	BN Arch
Bachelor of Naval Engineering	BN Eng
Bachelor of Naval Engineering	BNE
Bachelor of Naval Science	BNS
Bachelor of Navigation	B Na
Bachelor of Navigation (NADA)	BNav
Bachelor of Nursing	BN
Bachelor of Nursing	BNursing
Bachelor of Nursing Education	BN Ed
Bachelor of Nursing, Nursing Studies, University of Southampton [British] (DBQ)	BN Nursing Studies
Bachelor of Nursing Science	BN Sc
Bachelor of Nursing Science	BNS
Bachelor of Nursing, University of Manchester [British] (DBQ)	BNurs
Bachelor of Nutrition and Dietetics	BND
Bachelor of Occupational Therapy (ADA)	BOccThy
Bachelor of Occupational Therapy	BOT
Bachelor of Optometry	B Opt
Bachelor of Optometry (ADA)	BOptom
Bachelor of Optometry	BOptometry
Bachelor of Oral English	BOE
Bachelor of Oratory	B Or
Bachelor of Oratory	BO
Bachelor of Oriental Language	BOL
Bachelor of Oriental Studies	B Orient
Bachelor of Osteopathy	BO
Bachelor of Paediatrics (ADA)	BPaed
Bachelor of Painting	B Pa
Bachelor of Painting	BP
Bachelor of Patent Law	BPL
Bachelor of Pedagogy [or Pedagogics]	B Pd
Bachelor of Pedagogy	B Pe
Bachelor of Pedagogy [or Pedagogics]	B Ped
Bachelor of Pedagogy	B Py
Bachelor of Pedagogy	BP
Bachelor of Pedagogy	BPaed
Bachelor of Pedagogy	Pd B
Bachelor of Pedagogy (ROG)	PE B
Bachelor of Pedagogy	Ped B
Bachelor of Pedagogy	Pg B
Bachelor of Pedagogy	Py B
Bachelor of Pediatrics	Pe B
Bachelor of Pediatrics (WDAA)	PED B
Bachelor of Performing Arts	BPerfArts
Bachelor of Petroleum Engineering	B Pe E
Bachelor of Petroleum Engineering	B Pe Eng

Bachelor of Petroleum Engineering	B Pet E
Bachelor of Petroleum Engineering (WGA)	BPE
Bachelor of Pharmaceutical Chemistry	B Ph C
Bachelor of Pharmacy	B Pharm
Bachelor of Pharmacy	BP
Bachelor of Pharmacy (DD)	BPh
Bachelor of Pharmacy	Ph B
Bachelor of Pharmacy	Phm B
Bachelor of Philosophy	B Ph
Bachelor of Philosophy	B Phil
Bachelor of Philosophy	BP
Bachelor of Philosophy (WDAA)	PB
Bachelor of Philosophy (DAVI)	PhB
Bachelor of Philosophy (Education), University of Birmingham [British] (DBQ)	BPhil(Ed)
Bachelor of Philosophy in Architecture	Ph B in Arch
Bachelor of Philosophy in Commerce	Ph B in Com
Bachelor of Philosophy in Education	Ph B in Ed
Bachelor of Philosophy in Journalism (NADA)	PhBJ
Bachelor of Philosophy in Speech (NADA)	PhBSp
Bachelor of Photography	B Pho
Bachelor of Physic	BM
Bachelor of Physical and Health Education	BPHE
Bachelor of Physical Biology	BPB
Bachelor of Physical Culture	Ph B
Bachelor of Physical Education	BP Ed
Bachelor of Physical Education	BPE
Bachelor of Physical Education	BPhysEd
Bachelor of Physical Health Education	BPhysHlthEd
Bachelor of Physical Science	B Ph S
Bachelor of Physical Therapy (WDAA)	B PHYS THY
Bachelor of Physical Therapy	BPT
Bachelor of Physics	B Phy
Bachelor of Physics (NADA)	BPhys
Bachelor of Physiotherapy (ADA)	BPhty
Bachelor of Physiotherapy	BPhysio
Bachelor of Physiotherapy (NADA)	BPT
Bachelor of Planning and Design	BPD
Bachelor of Planning, University of Manchester [British]	BPI
Bachelor of Political Science	B Pol Sc
Bachelor of Practical Theology	P Th B
Bachelor of Professional Arts	BPA
Bachelor of Professional Studies	BPS
Bachelor of Psychic Sciences	B Ps Sc
Bachelor of Psychology	B Ps
Bachelor of Psychology	BPsy
Bachelor of Psychology	BPsych
Bachelor of Psychotherapy	B Ps Th
Bachelor of Public Administration	BP Adm
Bachelor of Public Administration	BPA
Bachelor of Public Administration	BPubAdmin
Bachelor of Public Health	BPH
Bachelor of Public Health Education	BPH Ed
Bachelor of Public Health Engineering	BPH Eng
Bachelor of Public Health Engineering	BPHE
Bachelor of Public Health Nursing	BPHN
Bachelor of Public Policy	BPubPol
Bachelor of Public School Art	BPSA
Bachelor of Public School Music	BPSM
Bachelor of Radio and Television Engineering	BRT Eng
Bachelor of Radio and Television Engineering	BRTE
Bachelor of Radio Engineering	B Ra E
Bachelor of Radio Engineering	B Ra Eng
Bachelor of Recreation Education (DD)	BRE
Bachelor of Refrigeration Engineering	B Re E
Bachelor of Refrigeration Engineering	B Re Eng
Bachelor of Regional and Town Planning (ADA)	BRTP
Bachelor of Religion	B Re
Bachelor of Religious Education	BR Ed
Bachelor of Religious Education	BRE
Bachelor of Religious Sciences	BRSc
Bachelor of Religious Studies	BRS
Bachelor of Rural Engineering	B Ru E
Bachelor of Rural Engineering	B Ru Eng
Bachelor of Rural Science (ADA)	BRurSc
Bachelor of Rural Science (NADA)	BRuSci
Bachelor of Rural Science Education	BRurScEd
Bachelor of Sacred Literature	BSL
Bachelor of Sacred Music	BS Mu
Bachelor of Sacred Music	BS Mus
Bachelor of Sacred Music	BSM
Bachelor of Sacred Music	SMB
Bachelor of Sacred Sciences	B Sa Sc
Bachelor of Sacred Theology	BST
Bachelor of Sacred Theology (NADA)	STB
Bachelor of Sanitary Engineering	BS Eng
Bachelor of Sanitary Engineering	BSE
Bachelor of Sanitary Science	BS Sc
Bachelor of Sanitary Science	BSS
Bachelor of School Music	B Sch Mus
Bachelor of School Music	BS Mus
Bachelor of School Music	BSM
Bachelor of School Music	Sch Mus B
Bachelor of Science	B Sc
Bachelor of Science	BS

Bachelor of Science [*Academic degree*] (AIE)	BSc
Bachelor of Science	SB
Bachelor of Science	Sc B
Bachelor of Science and English Literature	BSEL
Bachelor of Science (Animal Husbandry) (ADA)	BSc(AH)
Bachelor of Science (Architecture)	BSc(Arch)
Bachelor of Science (Chemical Engineering) (ADA)	BSc(ChemEng)
Bachelor of Science (Civil Engineering)	BSCE
Bachelor of Science (Dentistry)	BSc (Dent)
Bachelor of Science (Design Studies)	BSc(DesStud)
Bachelor of Science (Domestic Science)	B Sc (Dom Sc)
Bachelor of Science (Education)	BSc(Educ)
Bachelor of Science Education (NADA)	BSE
Bachelor of Science, Engineering (DD)	BScE
Bachelor of Science (Engineering) (EY)	BSc(Eng)
Bachelor of Science (Engineering)	BSc(Engg)
Bachelor of Science (Engineering)	BSc(Engin)
Bachelor of Science (Estate Management)	B Sc (Est Man)
Bachelor of Science (Forestry)	BSc(Forestry)
Bachelor of Science (General Science) (ADA)	BSc(GenSc)
Bachelor of Science (Home Science)	BSc(HomeSc)
Bachelor of Science (Home Science)	BSc(HomeSci)
Bachelor of Science in Accounting (WDAA)	B SC ACC
Bachelor of Science in Accounting	BS (Acc)
Bachelor of Science in Accounting	BS in Acc
Bachelor of Science in Administrative Engineering	BS in AE
Bachelor of Science in Advertising	BS Adv
Bachelor of Science in Aeronautical Administration	BS in Aero Adm
Bachelor of Science in Aeronautical Engineering	BS Ae E
Bachelor of Science in Aeronautical Engineering	BS (Aero E)
Bachelor of Science in Aeronautical Engineering	BS in AE
Bachelor of Science in Aeronautical Engineering	BS in Ae E
Bachelor of Science in Aeronautical Engineering	BS in Aero E
Bachelor of Science in Aeronautical Engineering	BSAE
Bachelor of Science in Aeronautical Engineering - Electronics Major	BSAE-E
Bachelor of Science in Agricultural Administration	BS in AM
Bachelor of Science in Agricultural Administration	BSA Adm
Bachelor of Science in Agricultural Biology (NADA)	BScAgrBio
Bachelor of Science in Agricultural Economics (NADA)	BScAgrEco
Bachelor of Science in Agricultural Education	BS in AD
Bachelor of Science in Agricultural Education	BS in Agr Ed
Bachelor of Science in Agricultural Engineering	B Sc in Agr Engr
Bachelor of Science in Agricultural Engineering	BS Ag E
Bachelor of Science in Agricultural Engineering	BS in Ag E
Bachelor of Science in Agricultural Engineering	BS in Agr E
Bachelor of Science in Agricultural Engineering	BS in Agr Eng
Bachelor of Science in Agricultural Engineering	BS in AN
Bachelor of Science in Agricultural Engineering (WGA)	BSAE
Bachelor of Science in Agricultural Engineering (NADA)	BScAgrEng
Bachelor of Science in Agricultural Engineering	BSc(AgricEng)
Bachelor of Science in Agriculture	B Sc Agr
Bachelor of Science in Agriculture (DD)	BAS
Bachelor of Science in Agriculture	BS Ag
Bachelor of Science in Agriculture	BS Agr
Bachelor of Science in Agriculture	BS in Ag
Bachelor of Science in Agriculture	BSA
Bachelor of Science in Agriculture	BScA
Bachelor of Science in Agriculture	BScAg
Bachelor of Science in Agriculture	BScAgri
Bachelor of Science in Agriculture	BScAgric
Bachelor of Science in Agriculture and Animal Husbandry (NADA)	BScAg&AH
Bachelor of Science in Agriculture and Chemistry	BS in Agr & Chem
Bachelor of Science in Agriculture and Education	BS in Ag & Ed
Bachelor of Science in Agriculture in Dairy Manufacturing	BS in Ag (DM)
Bachelor of Science in Air Transportation	BSAT
Bachelor of Science in Aircraft Maintenance Engineering	BSAME
Bachelor of Science in Applied Arts (WGA)	BSAA
Bachelor of Science in Applied Mathematics	BS (A Math)
Bachelor of Science in Applied Mathematics	BS in Math
Bachelor of Science in Applied Mathematics	Sc BAM
Bachelor of Science in Architectural Engineering	BS Arch E
Bachelor of Science in Architectural Engineering	BS in AE
Bachelor of Science in Architectural Engineering	BSAE
Bachelor of Science in Architectural Engineering (NADA)	BSArchEng
Bachelor of Science in Architecture	BS in Arch
Bachelor of Science in Architecture (NADA)	BSArch
Bachelor of Science in Architecture (NADA)	BScArch
Bachelor of Science in Architecture in Architectural Engineering	BS Arch (Arch E)
Bachelor of Science in Architecture in Architecture	BS Arch (Arch)
Bachelor of Science in Art Education	BS Art Ed
Bachelor of Science in Bacteriology	B Sc in Bact
Bachelor of Science in Basic Medical Science	BS in Med S
Bachelor of Science in Basic Medical Sciences	BS in BMS
Bachelor of Science in Biology	BS Biol
Bachelor of Science in Biomedical Engineering	BS in Biomed Eng
Bachelor of Science in Business	BS Bus
Bachelor of Science in Business	BS in Bus
Bachelor of Science in Business	BSB
Bachelor of Science in Business Administration	BS Bus Ad
Bachelor of Science in Business Administration	BS in B Ad
Bachelor of Science in Business Administration	BS in BA
Bachelor of Science in Business Administration	BS in Bus Ad
Bachelor of Science in Business Administration	BSB Ad
Bachelor of Science in Business Administration	BSBA
Bachelor of Science in Business Administration (NADA)	BScBA
Bachelor of Science in Business Education	BS in B Ed
Bachelor of Science in Business Education	BS in Bus Ed
Bachelor of Science in Business Education	BSB Ed
Bachelor of Science in Business Education	BSBusEd
Bachelor of Science in Business - Medical Records	BS (Bus-MR)
Bachelor of Science in Cartography	BS in Cart
Bachelor of Science in Ceramic Engineering	BS (Cer E)
Bachelor of Science in Ceramic Engineering	BS Cr E
Bachelor of Science in Ceramic Engineering	BS in Cer E
Bachelor of Science in Ceramic Technology	BS in Cer Tech
Bachelor of Science in Ceramics	BS in Cer
Bachelor of Science in Chemical Engineering	BS in Ch E
Bachelor of Science in Chemical Engineering	BS Ch Eng
Bachelor of Science in Chemical Engineering	BS Chem E
Bachelor of Science in Chemical Engineering	BS in CE
Bachelor of Science in Chemical Engineering	BS in Ch E
Bachelor of Science in Chemical Engineering	BS in Ch Eng
Bachelor of Science in Chemical Engineering	BS in Chem E
Bachelor of Science in Chemical Engineering	BS in CN
Bachelor of Science in Chemical Engineering (NADA)	BScChemE
Bachelor of Science in Chemical Technology	BS in Chem Tech
Bachelor of Science in Chemistry	BS in C
Bachelor of Science in Chemistry	BS in Ch
Bachelor of Science in Chemistry	BS in Chm
Bachelor of Science in Chemistry	BSCh
Bachelor of Science in Chemistry (NADA)	BSChm
Bachelor of Science in Chemistry	Sc BC
Bachelor of Science in Christian Education - Music	BS in CE - Music
Bachelor of Science in Civil Engineering	B Sc in CE
Bachelor of Science in Civil Engineering	BS in CE
Bachelor of Science in Civil Engineering (NADA)	BScCE
Bachelor of Science in Civil Engineering	SBCE
Bachelor of Science in Commerce	BS in C
Bachelor of Science in Commerce	BS in Com
Bachelor of Science in Commerce	BS in Comm
Bachelor of Science in Commerce	BSC
Bachelor of Science in Commerce and Business	BS in Com & Bus
Bachelor of Science in Commerce and Economics	BS in C & Ec
Bachelor of Science in Commercial and Business Administration	BS in C & BA
Bachelor of Science in Commercial Education	BS in Com Ed
Bachelor of Science in Communications	BS Com
Bachelor of Science in Community Recreation	BS in Comm Rec
Bachelor of Science in Computer Science	BSCompSci
Bachelor of Science in Criminal Justice	BSCJ
Bachelor of Science in Dental Hygiene	BS in DH
Bachelor of Science in Dental Hygiene	BSD Hyg
Bachelor of Science in Dental Hygiene (NADA)	BSDH
Bachelor of Science in Dentistry	BS in Dent
Bachelor of Science in Dentistry (ADA)	BSD
Bachelor of Science in Dentistry (NADA)	BSDent
Bachelor of Science in Design	BS Des
Bachelor of Science in Design	BSD
Bachelor of Science in Design in Decorative Design	BS Des (Dec Des)
Bachelor of Science in Dianoetics	B Sc (Dn)
Bachelor of Science in Economics	B Sc Econ
Bachelor of Science in Economics	BS Ec
Bachelor of Science in Economics (WGA)	BS Econ
Bachelor of Science in Economics	BS in Ec
Bachelor of Science in Education	BS Ed
Bachelor of Science in Education	BS in E
Bachelor of Science in Education	BS in Ed
Bachelor of Science in Education	BScEd
Bachelor of Science in Education	BSE
Bachelor of Science in Electrical and Mechanical Engineering	BSEE-ME
Bachelor of Science in Electrical Engineering	B Sc in EE
Bachelor of Science in Electrical Engineering	BS in EE
Bachelor of Science in Electrical Engineering	BSEE
Bachelor of Science in Electrical Engineering	SBEE
Bachelor of Science in Electronic Engineering	BS El E
Bachelor of Science in Electronic Engineering	BS in Elect Eng
Bachelor of Science in Elementary Education	BS El Ed
Bachelor of Science in Elementary Education	BS Elem
Bachelor of Science in Elementary Education	BS in Elem Ed
Bachelor of Science in Elementary Education (ADA)	BScElEd
Bachelor of Science in Elementary Education	BSEE
Bachelor of Science in Engineering (DD)	BE
Bachelor of Science in Engineering	BES
Bachelor of Science in Engineering	BS in E
Bachelor of Science in Engineering	BS in Eng
Bachelor of Science in Engineering (DD)	BSc(Eng)
Bachelor of Science in Engineering	BSE
Bachelor of Science in Engineering (NADA)	BSEng
Bachelor of Science in Engineering	Sc BE
Bachelor of Science in Engineering Administration	BS Engr Ad
Bachelor of Science in Engineering and Civil Engineering	BSE (CE)
Bachelor of Science in Engineering and Economics	BSE & E
Bachelor of Science in Engineering in Aeronautical Engineering	BSE (Ae E)
Bachelor of Science in Engineering in Chemical Engineering	BSE (Ch E)
Bachelor of Science in Engineering in Electrical Engineering	BSE (EE)
Bachelor of Science in Engineering in Engineering Mechanics	BSE (EM)
Bachelor of Science in Engineering in Geodesy and Surveying	BSE (Geod & Surv)

Bachelor of Science in Engineering in Industrial Engineering ... BSE (Ind E)
Bachelor of Science in Engineering in Materials Engineering ... BSE (Mat E)
Bachelor of Science in Engineering in Mechanical and Industrial Engineering ... BSE (M & Ind E)
Bachelor of Science in Engineering in Mechanical Engineering ... BSE (ME)
Bachelor of Science in Engineering in Metallurgical Engineering ... BSE (Met E)
Bachelor of Science in Engineering in Naval Architecture and Marine Engineering ... BSE (Nav Arch & Mar E)
Bachelor of Science in Engineering Mathematics ... BS in E Math
Bachelor of Science in Engineering Mechanics ... BS in Mech
Bachelor of Science in Engineering of Mines ... BS in EM
Bachelor of Science in Engineering of Mines ... BSEM
Bachelor of Science in Engineering Physics ... BS Engr Phys
Bachelor of Science in Engineering Physics ... BS in E Phys
Bachelor of Science in Engineering Physics ... BS in EP
Bachelor of Science in Engineering Physics ... BSE Phys
Bachelor of Science in Engineering Physics ... BSEP
Bachelor of Science in Engineering Science ... BS Engr Sci
Bachelor of Science in Engineering Sciences ... BS Eng Sci
Bachelor of Science in Engineering Sciences ... BS in ES
Bachelor of Science in Engineering Sciences ... BSE Sc
Bachelor of Science in Engineering Sciences ... BSES
Bachelor of Science in Engineering Technology (IEEE) ... BSET
Bachelor of Science in Finance ... BS (Fin)
Bachelor of Science in Finance ... BS in Fin
Bachelor of Science in Fisheries Management ... BSF Mgt
Bachelor of Science in Foreign Service ... BS in FS
Bachelor of Science in Foreign Service ... BSFS
Bachelor of Science in Forest Management ... BSFM
Bachelor of Science in Forestry ... B Sc F
Bachelor of Science in Forestry ... B Sc For
Bachelor of Science in Forestry ... BS For
Bachelor of Science in Forestry ... BS Fsty
Bachelor of Science in Forestry ... BS in For
Bachelor of Science in Forestry ... BS in Fy
Bachelor of Science in Forestry ... BSF
Bachelor of Science in Fuel Technology ... BSFT
Bachelor of Science in Game Management ... BSG Mgt
Bachelor of Science in General Business ... BS in Gen Bus
Bachelor of Science in General Education ... BS Gen Ed
Bachelor of Science in General Engineering ... BS in GE
Bachelor of Science in General Engineering ... BS in Gen Eng
Bachelor of Science in General Engineering ... BSGE
Bachelor of Science in General Nursing ... BS in Gen Nurs
Bachelor of Science in General Nursing (NADA) ... BSGenNur
Bachelor of Science in General Science ... BS in Gen Sci
Bachelor of Science in General Science and Mathematics ... BS in GSM
Bachelor of Science in General Studies ... BS in Gen Std
Bachelor of Science in General Studies ... BS in GS
Bachelor of Science in Geodesy and Surveying ... BS in Geod & Surv
Bachelor of Science in Geography ... BS (Geog)
Bachelor of Science in Geography ... BS Ggr
Bachelor of Science in Geological Engineering (NADA) ... BCGeolEng
Bachelor of Science in Geological Engineering ... BS Geol E
Bachelor of Science in Geological Engineering ... BS Gl E
Bachelor of Science in Geological Engineering ... BS in Ge E
Bachelor of Science in Geological Engineering ... BS in Geol E
Bachelor of Science in Geology ... BS (Geol)
Bachelor of Science in Geology ... BS Gl
Bachelor of Science in Geology and Physics ... BSGP
Bachelor of Science in Geophysical Engineering ... BS in Gph E
Bachelor of Science in Geophysics ... BS Gph
Bachelor of Science in Group Work Education ... BS in GWE
Bachelor of Science in Health and Physical Education ... BS in H & PE
Bachelor of Science in Health and Physical Education ... BS in HPE
Bachelor of Science in Health Education ... BS in H Ed
Bachelor of Science in Health Education ... BSHE
Bachelor of Science in Health Education (NADA) ... BSHEd
Bachelor of Science in Hebrew Education (BJA) ... BSHE
Bachelor of Science in Home Economics ... B Sc in HE
Bachelor of Science in Home Economics ... BS H Ec
Bachelor of Science in Home Economics ... BS in H Ec
Bachelor of Science in Home Economics ... BS in H Econ
Bachelor of Science in Home Economics ... BS in HE
Bachelor of Science in Home Economics ... BSc(HEc)
Bachelor of Science in Home Economics ... BSHE
Bachelor of Science in Home Economics (NADA) ... BSHEco
Bachelor of Science in Home Economics Education ... BS in HD
Bachelor of Science in Home Science ... BSc(HomeScience)
Bachelor of Science in Horticulture ... BSc(Hort)
Bachelor of Science in Hospital Administration ... BSHA
Bachelor of Science in Hotel and Restaurant Administration ... BS in H & RA
Bachelor of Science in Industrial Art ... BS in Ind Art
Bachelor of Science in Industrial Art (NADA) ... BSIndArt
Bachelor of Science in Industrial Arts ... BS in IA
Bachelor of Science in Industrial Chemistry ... BS in Ind Ch
Bachelor of Science in Industrial Chemistry (NADA) ... BSIndChem
Bachelor of Science in Industrial Education ... BS in Ind Ed
Bachelor of Science in Industrial Education ... BSIE
Bachelor of Science in Industrial Education ... BSIndEd
Bachelor of Science in Industrial Engineering ... BS in IE
Bachelor of Science in Industrial Engineering ... BS in Ind E
Bachelor of Science in Industrial Engineering ... BS Ind Eng
Bachelor of Science in Industrial Engineering ... BSIE
Bachelor of Science in Industrial Engineering and Management ... BS in IE & M
Bachelor of Science in Industrial Management ... BS in IM
Bachelor of Science in Industrial Management ... BS Ind Mgt
Bachelor of Science in Industrial Management ... BSIM
Bachelor of Science in Industrial Relations ... BSIR
Bachelor of Science in Industrial Technology ... BSIndTech
Bachelor of Science in Industrial Technology ... BSIT
Bachelor of Science in Jewish Education (BJA) ... BSJE
Bachelor of Science in Journalism ... BS in J
Bachelor of Science in Journalism ... BS Jr
Bachelor of Science in Journalism ... BSJ
Bachelor of Science in Judaic Studies (BJA) ... BSJS
Bachelor of Science in Labor Relations ... BS Lab Rel
Bachelor of Science in Laboratory Technology ... BS in LT
Bachelor of Science in Land Planning ... BS in LP
Bachelor of Science in Land Surveying (ADA) ... BScSur
Bachelor of Science in Landscape Architecture ... BSL Arch
Bachelor of Science in Landscape Architecture ... BSLA
Bachelor of Science in Landscape Management ... BSLM
Bachelor of Science in Languages ... BSL
Bachelor of Science in Latin ... BS in Lat
Bachelor of Science in Law ... BSL
Bachelor of Science in Letters and Science ... BS in L & S
Bachelor of Science in Library Science ... BSLS
Bachelor of Science in Library Service ... BS in LS
Bachelor of Science in Linguistics ... BSL
Bachelor of Science in Management Engineering ... BS in Mgt Engr
Bachelor of Science in Management Science ... BS in Mgt Sc
Bachelor of Science in Management Science (NADA) ... BSMgtSci
Bachelor of Science in Marine Engineering (NADA) ... BSMarEng
Bachelor of Science in Mathematical Statistics ... BS in Math Stat
Bachelor of Science in Mathematics and Chemistry ... BSMC
Bachelor of Science in Mechanical Arts ... BS in MA
Bachelor of Science in Mechanical Engineering ... B Sc in ME
Bachelor of Science in Mechanical Engineering ... BS in M Engr
Bachelor of Science in Mechanical Engineering ... BS in ME
Bachelor of Science in Mechanical Engineering ... BS in Mech Eng
Bachelor of Science in Mechanical Engineering ... BSME
Bachelor of Science in Mechanical Industries ... BS in Mech Ind
Bachelor of Science in Mechanics ... BS in Mech
Bachelor of Science in Medical Laboratory Science (ADA) ... BSc(MLS)
Bachelor of Science in Medical Record Library Science ... BS in MRL
Bachelor of Science in Medical Records ... BS in Med Rec
Bachelor of Science in Medical Records (NADA) ... BSMedRec
Bachelor of Science in Medical Records Libarianship (NADA) ... BSMedRecLib
Bachelor of Science in Medical Records Librarianship ... BS in Med Rec Lib
Bachelor of Science in Medical Secretarial Science ... BS in Med Sc
Bachelor of Science in Medical Technology ... B Sc in Med Tech
Bachelor of Science in Medical Technology ... BS in Md
Bachelor of Science in Medical Technology ... BS in Med Tech
Bachelor of Science in Medical Technology ... BS in MT
Bachelor of Science in Medical Technology ... BS Med T
Bachelor of Science in Medical Technology ... BS Med Tech
Bachelor of Science in Medical Technology ... BSMT
Bachelor of Science in Medicine ... B Sc in Med
Bachelor of Science in Medicine ... BS in Med
Bachelor of Science in Medicine ... BSM
Bachelor of Science in Medicine (NADA) ... BSMed
Bachelor of Science in Metallurgical Engineering ... BS in Met E
Bachelor of Science in Metallurgical Engineering ... BS in Met Engin
Bachelor of Science in Metallurgical Engineering ... BS Met E
Bachelor of Science in Metallurgical Engineering ... BS Met Eng
Bachelor of Science in Metallurgical Engineering ... BS Mt E
Bachelor of Science in Metallurgy ... B Sc Met
Bachelor of Science in Metallurgy ... BS in Met
Bachelor of Science in Metallurgy (NADA) ... BSMet
Bachelor of Science in Meteorology ... BS in Met
Bachelor of Science in Meteorology ... BS Met
Bachelor of Science in Military Science ... BS in MS
Bachelor of Science in Mineralogy ... BS Min
Bachelor of Science in Mining ... BS in Min
Bachelor of Science in Mining (ADA) ... BScMin
Bachelor of Science in Mining (NADA) ... BSMIN
Bachelor of Science in Mining Engineering ... BS in Min E
Bachelor of Science in Mining Engineering ... BS in Min Eng
Bachelor of Science in Mining Engineering ... BS Mg E
Bachelor of Science in Mining Engineering ... BS Min E
Bachelor of Science in Mining Engineering ... BS Mng E
Bachelor of Science in Mining Engineering (DAS) ... BScME
Bachelor of Science in Mining Engineering ... BSME
Bachelor of Science in Mining Engineering (NADA) ... BSMinEng
Bachelor of Science in Music ... BS Mus
Bachelor of Science in Music ... BSM
Bachelor of Science in Music Education ... BS in M Educ
Bachelor of Science in Music Education ... BS in Mu Ed
Bachelor of Science in Music Education ... BS Mus Ed
Bachelor of Science in Music Education ... BSM Ed
Bachelor of Science in Music Education ... BSME
Bachelor of Science in Musical Education ... BS in Mus Ed
Bachelor of Science in Natural History ... BS in Nat Hist
Bachelor of Science in Natural History (NADA) ... BSNatHist
Bachelor of Science in Natural Science ... BS in N Sc
Bachelor of Science in Natural Science ... BS in NS
Bachelor of Science in Natural-Gas Engineering ... BS in Nat G Engin
Bachelor of Science in Nautical Industrial Technology (NADA) ... BSNIT
Bachelor of Science in Nursing ... B Sc in Nurs

Bachelor of Science in Nursing ... BS in N
Bachelor of Science in Nursing ... BS in Nr
Bachelor of Science in Nursing ... BS in Nurs
Bachelor of Science in Nursing ... BS Nurs
Bachelor of Science in Nursing ... BScN
Bachelor of Science in Nursing (NADA) ... BScNurs
Bachelor of Science in Nursing ... BSN
Bachelor of Science in Nursing Administration ... BSNA
Bachelor of Science in Nursing Education ... BS in N Ed
Bachelor of Science in Nursing Education ... BS in NE
Bachelor of Science in Nursing Education ... BS in Nurs Ed
Bachelor of Science in Nursing Education ... BS Nurs Ed
Bachelor of Science in Nursing Education ... BSN Ed
Bachelor of Science in Nursing Education ... BSNE
Bachelor of Science in Occupational Therapy ... B Sc in Occ Ther
Bachelor of Science in Occupational Therapy ... BS in Occ Ther
Bachelor of Science in Occupational Therapy ... BS in OT
Bachelor of Science in Occupational Therapy (NADA) ... BSOccTher
Bachelor of Science in Occupational Therapy ... BSOT
Bachelor of Science in Oceanography ... BS in Ocean
Bachelor of Science in Optics ... BS in Opt
Bachelor of Science in Optometry ... B Sc in Opt
Bachelor of Science in Optometry ... BS in Opt
Bachelor of Science in Optometry ... BS (Opt)
Bachelor of Science in Ornamental Horticulture ... BS in OH
Bachelor of Science in Ornamental Horticulture ... BS Orn Hort
Bachelor of Science in Orthoptics ... BS in Ortho
Bachelor of Science in Personnel and Industrial Relations ... BS (Per & Ind Rel)
Bachelor of Science in Personnel and Public Relations (NADA) ... BSPer&PubRel
Bachelor of Science in Petroleum ... BS in Pet
Bachelor of Science in Petroleum (NADA) ... BSPet
Bachelor of Science in Petroleum Engineering ... BS in PE
Bachelor of Science in Petroleum Engineering ... BS in Pet Engin
Bachelor of Science in Petroleum Engineering ... BS in Petr E
Bachelor of Science in Petroleum Engineering (NADA) ... BSPetEng
Bachelor of Science in Pharmacy ... B Sc in Phar
Bachelor of Science in Pharmacy ... BS in Ph
Bachelor of Science in Pharmacy ... BS in Phar
Bachelor of Science in Pharmacy ... BS Ph
Bachelor of Science in Pharmacy ... BS Phar
Bachelor of Science in Pharmacy (DAS) ... BScP
Bachelor of Science in Pharmacy ... BSc(Pharm)
Bachelor of Science in Pharmacy ... BSP
Bachelor of Science in Pharmacy ... BSPharm
Bachelor of Science in Physical and Occupational Therapy ... BS in Th
Bachelor of Science in Physical and Occupational Therapy ... BSc (P & OT)
Bachelor of Science in Physical Education ... BS in P Ed
Bachelor of Science in Physical Education ... BS in PE
Bachelor of Science in Physical Education ... BS in Phy Ed
Bachelor of Science in Physical Education ... BS in Phys Ed
Bachelor of Science in Physical Education ... BSc(PE)
Bachelor of Science in Physical Education (ADA) ... BSc(PEd)
Bachelor of Science in Physical Education ... BSPE
Bachelor of Science in Physical Education (NADA) ... BSPhysEd
Bachelor of Science in Physical Education (NADA) ... BSPhysEdu
Bachelor of Science in Physical Therapy ... B Sc in Phys Ther
Bachelor of Science in Physical Therapy ... BS in Phys Th
Bachelor of Science in Physical Therapy ... BS in Phys Ther
Bachelor of Science in Physical Therapy ... BS in PT
Bachelor of Science in Physical Therapy ... BS Ph Th
Bachelor of Science in Physical Therapy (NADA) ... BSPhysTher
Bachelor of Science in Physical Therapy ... BSPT
Bachelor of Science in Physics ... B Sc in Phys
Bachelor of Science in Physics ... BS Phys
Bachelor of Science in Physics ... Sc BP
Bachelor of Science in Practical Arts ... BS in PA
Bachelor of Science in Practical Arts ... BS in Prac Arts
Bachelor of Science in Practical Arts and Letters ... BS in PAL
Bachelor of Science in Professional Geology ... BS in Pr Ge
Bachelor of Science in Professional Meteorology ... BS in Pr Met
Bachelor of Science in Public Administration ... BS in PA
Bachelor of Science in Public Administration ... BSPA
Bachelor of Science in Public Health ... BSPH
Bachelor of Science in Public Health and Preventative Medicine ... BS in PHPM
Bachelor of Science in Public Health Nursing ... BS in PHN
Bachelor of Science in Public Health Nursing ... BSPHN
Bachelor of Science in Public School Music ... BS in PSM
Bachelor of Science in Pure Science ... BS
Bachelor of Science in Quantity Surveying (ADA) ... BSc(QS)
Bachelor of Science in Radiologic Technology (ADA) ... BScRT
Bachelor of Science in Radiological Technology ... BS in RT
Bachelor of Science in Radiological Technology ... BSRT
Bachelor of Science in Railway and Mechanical Engineering ... BS in Ry ME
Bachelor of Science in Range Animal Husbandry ... BS in RAH
Bachelor of Science in Recreation ... BS in Rec
Bachelor of Science in Recreation ... BS Rec
Bachelor of Science in Recreation ... BSR
Bachelor of Science in Recreation Leadership ... BS in Rec Lead
Bachelor of Science in Rehabilitation (NADA) ... BSR
Bachelor of Science in Religious Education (BJA) ... BSinRE
Bachelor of Science in Restaurant Management ... B Sc in Rest Mgt
Bachelor of Science in Retailing ... BS Ret
Bachelor of Science in Sanitary Engineering ... BS in San E
Bachelor of Science in Sanitary Engineering ... BSSanE
Bachelor of Science in Sanitary Engineering ... SBSanE
Bachelor of Science in Sanitary Science ... BS in San Sci
Bachelor of Science in Science ... BSS
Bachelor of Science in Science Engineering ... BS Sc E
Bachelor of Science in Science Engineering (NADA) ... BSScEng
Bachelor of Science in Secondary Education ... BS in Sec Ed
Bachelor of Science in Secondary Education ... BS Sec
Bachelor of Science in Secondary Education ... BS Sec Ed
Bachelor of Science in Secondary Education ... BSSE
Bachelor of Science in Secretarial Administration ... BS (Sec Adm)
Bachelor of Science in Secretarial Administration ... BSSA
Bachelor of Science in Secretarial Science ... BS in Sec Sc
Bachelor of Science in Secretarial Science ... BS in Sec Sci
Bachelor of Science in Secretarial Science ... BSS Sci
Bachelor of Science in Secretarial Science (NADA) ... BSSecSci
Bachelor of Science in Secretarial Studies (ADA) ... BScSS
Bachelor of Science in Secretarial Studies ... BSSS
Bachelor of Science in Social Administration ... B Sc in Soc Adm
Bachelor of Science in Social Science ... BS in S Sc
Bachelor of Science in Social Science ... BS in SS
Bachelor of Science in Social Science ... BSSS
Bachelor of Science in Social Science (NADA) ... BSSSc
Bachelor of Science in Social Service ... BS in Soc Serv
Bachelor of Science in Social Service (NADA) ... BSSocServ
Bachelor of Science in Social Studies ... BS in Soc St
Bachelor of Science in Social Studies (NADA) ... BSSocSt
Bachelor of Science in Social Work ... BS (Soc Wk)
Bachelor of Science in Special Fields ... BS in Spec Flds
Bachelor of Science in Speech ... BS Sp
Bachelor of Science in Statistics ... BS in Stat
Bachelor of Science in Structural Engineering ... BS in Struc E
Bachelor of Science in Structural Engineering (NADA) ... BSStrucEng
Bachelor of Science in Teaching (ADA) ... B Sc Tchg
Bachelor of Science in Teaching ... BST
Bachelor of Science in Technology ... BSTech
Bachelor of Science in Textile Engineering ... BS in TE
Bachelor of Science in Textile Engineering (ADA) ... BSc(TE)
Bachelor of Science in Textiles ... BA in Text
Bachelor of Science in Textiles (ADA) ... BSc(Text)
Bachelor of Science in Textiles (NADA) ... BSText
Bachelor of Science in the Social Sciences, University of Southampton [*British*] ... BSc(Social Sciences)
Bachelor of Science in Trade and Industrial Engineering ... BST & IE
Bachelor of Science in Transportation ... BS Trans
Bachelor of Science in Veterinary Science (NADA) ... BScVetSc
Bachelor of Science in Vocational Agriculture ... BS in Voc Ag
Bachelor of Science in Vocational Education ... BS in Voc Ed
Bachelor of Science in Vocational Education (NADA) ... BSVocEd
Bachelor of Science in Zoological Sciences ... BS in ZS
Bachelor of Science (Industrial Arts) ... BSc(IndArts)
Bachelor of Science (Mechanical Engineering) ... BSc(MechEng)
Bachelor of Science (Medical) ... BSc(Med)
Bachelor of Science (Medical Science) ... B Sc (Med Sci)
Bachelor of Science (Nursing) ... BSc(Nursing)
Bachelor of Science (Nutrition) ... BSc(Nutr)
Bachelor of Science (Occupational Therapy) ... BSc(OT)
Bachelor of Science (Oenology) ... BSc(Oen)
Bachelor of Science (Physical Therapy) ... BSc(PT)
Bachelor of Science (Rural Science) (ADA) ... BSc(RS)
Bachelor of Science (Social Science), University of Edinburgh [*British*] ... BSc(Social Science)
Bachelor of Science (Social Sciences) ... BSc(SocSc)
Bachelor of Science (Sociology) ... B Sc (Soc)
Bachelor of Science (Surgery) ... BSc(Surg)
Bachelor of Science (Technology) ... B Sc (Tech)
Bachelor of Science (Town and Regional Planning), University of Dundee [*British*] (DBQ) ... BSc(Town & Regional Planning)
Bachelor of Science (Veterinary) ... BSc(Vet)
Bachelor of Science with Aeronautical Engineering Electives ... BS (Ae Elec)
Bachelor of Science with Chemical Engineering Electives ... BS (Ch E Elect)
Bachelor of Science with Mechanical Engineering Electives ... BS (ME Elect)
Bachelor of Scientific Agriculture ... BSA
Bachelor of Scientific Didactics ... BS Di
Bachelor of Scientology ... B Scn
Bachelor of Secretarial Arts ... B Se A
Bachelor of Secretarial Science ... B Sec Sc
Bachelor of Secretarial Science ... BSS
Bachelor of Secretarial Studies ... B Se St
Bachelor of Social Administration ... BSocAdmin
Bachelor of Social Science ... B So Sc
Bachelor of Social Science ... BS Sc
Bachelor of Social Science ... BScSoc
Bachelor of Social Science (NADA) ... BSocSci
Bachelor of Social Science ... BSS
Bachelor of Social Sciences ... BSocSc
Bachelor of Social Service ... B So Se
Bachelor of Social Studies (ADA) ... BSocSt
Bachelor of Social Studies (ADA) ... BSocStud
Bachelor of Social Work ... B So W
Bachelor of Social Work ... BSocW
Bachelor of Social Work ... BSocWk
Bachelor of Social Work ... BSW
Bachelor of Sociology ... B So
Bachelor of Special Education ... BSpecEd
Bachelor of Special Education ... BSpEd
Bachelor of Special Studies ... BSS

Bachelor of Speech	B Sp
Bachelor of Speech Therapy	BSpeechTherapy
Bachelor of Speech Therapy (ADA)	BSpThy
Bachelor of Statistics	B St
Bachelor of Structural Engineering	B St E
Bachelor of Structural Engineering	B St Eng
Bachelor of Surgery	B Sur
Bachelor of Surgery	BS
Bachelor of Surgery (DD)	ChB
Bachelor of Surveying	BSurv
Bachelor of Surveying Science	BSurvSc
Bachelor of Systematic Theology	B Sy Th
Bachelor of Teaching	BT
Bachelor of Teaching	BTeach
Bachelor of Technical Science	B Sc Tech
Bachelor of Technical Science	BTechSc
Bachelor of Technological Science	BTS
Bachelor of Technology	B Tech
Bachelor of Technology	BT
Bachelor of Technology Education	BTechEd
Bachelor of Technology in Information Systems	BTechInfSys
Bachelor of Telecommunications Engineering (ADA)	BTelE
Bachelor of Textile Chemistry	B of TC
Bachelor of Textile Chemistry	BT Ch
Bachelor of Textile Chemistry	BTC
Bachelor of Textile Design	BT Des
Bachelor of Textile Dyeing	BTD
Bachelor of Textile Engineering	B of TE
Bachelor of Textile Engineering	BT Eng
Bachelor of Textile Engineering	BTE
Bachelor of Textile Management	B of TM
Bachelor of Textile Technology	BTT
Bachelor of Textiles	BText
Bachelor of the Art of Obstetrics	BAO
Bachelor of the Elements	BE
Bachelor of the Science of Law	B Sc L
Bachelor of the Science of Oratory	B Or Sc
Bachelor of the Science of Oratory	B Sc O
Bachelor of the Science of Oratory	BSO
Bachelor of the Science of Theology	STB
Bachelor of Theatre	BT
Bachelor of Theology	B Th
Bachelor of Theology	BT
Bachelor of Theology	BTheol
Bachelor of Town and Regional Planning (ADA)	BT & RP
Bachelor of Town and Regional Planning (ADA)	BTRP
Bachelor of Town Planning	BTP
Bachelor of Unani Medicine and Surgery	BUMS
Bachelor of Urban and Regional Planning	BUrbRegPlan
Bachelor of Urban and Regional Planning	BURP
Bachelor of Urban Planning	B Urb Pl
Bachelor of Urban Studies	BUS
Bachelor of Veterinary Medicine	B Vet Med
Bachelor of Veterinary Medicine	BVM
Bachelor of Veterinary Medicine	Vet MB
Bachelor of Veterinary Medicine and Science [Academic degree] (DMAA)	BVMS
Bachelor of Veterinary Medicine and Surgery	BVM & S
Bachelor of Veterinary Medicine and Surgery	BVMS
Bachelor of Veterinary Science	BV Sc
Bachelor of Veterinary Science (ADA)	BVetSc
Bachelor of Veterinary Science (NADA)	BVetSci
Bachelor of Veterinary Science	BVS
Bachelor of Veterinary Science and Animal Husbandry	BVSc & AH
Bachelor of Veterinary Surgery (NADA)	BVetSur
Bachelor of Veterinary Surgery	BVS
Bachelor of Visual Arts	BVA
Bachelor of Vocational Agriculture	BVA
Bachelor of Vocational Arts	BVocArts
Bachelor of Vocational Education	BVE
Bachelor of Vocational Education	BVocEd
Bachelor of Welding Engineering	BWE
Bachelor of Zoological Science	BZ Sc
Bachelor Officers' Quarters [Army]	BOQ
Bachelor Sergeant Quarters [Air Force]	BSQ
Bachelor Staff Quarters [Military] (DNAB)	BSQ
Bachelors' and Spinsters' Dance (ADA)	B & S
Bachelor's Degree (Honours) [British]	Bh
Bachelor's Degree (Pass) [British]	Bp
Bache's Pennsylvania Justice's Manual [A publication] (DLA)	Bache Pa Just
Bachman Information Sys [NASDAQ symbol] (TTSB)	BACH
Bachman Information Systems [NASDAQ symbol] (SPSG)	BACH
Bachman Information Systems, Inc. [Associated Press] (SAG)	BachInf
Bachman-Turner Overdrive [Rock music group]	BTO
Bach's Reports [19-21 Montana] [A publication] (DLA)	Bach
Bacillary Angiomatosis [Medicine]	BA
Bacillary Angiomatosis-Bacillary Peliosis	BAP
Bacillary Emulsion [Tuberculin] [Medicine] (MAE)	BE
Bacillary White Diarrhea [Veterinary medicine]	BWD
Bacille Acido-Resistant [Acid-Fast Bacillus] [Medicine]	BAR
Bacillen Emulsion [Clinical chemistry] (AAMN)	BE
Bacillus [Bacteriology]	B
Bacillus [or Bacilli] [Bacteriology] (WDAA)	BAC
Bacillus Calmette-Guerin [TB vaccine] (GPO)	BCG
Bacillus Emulsion [Medicine] (DAVI)	TBN
Bacillus globigii [Biological warfare with bacteria]	BG
Bacillus Pumilis [Bacteriology]	BP
Bacillus thuringiensis [Also, Bt] [Bacteriology]	BT
Bacillus Thuringiensis Israelensis [Bacteriology]	BTI
Bacitracin Methylene Disalicylate [Animal antibiotic]	BMD
Bacitracin, Polymyxin B, Neomycin Sulfate [Medicine] (DMAA)	BPN
Bacitracin V [Antibacterial compound]	BV
Bacitracin V and X [Antibacterial compound]	BVX
Bacitracin X [Antibacterial compound]	BX
Back	B
Back	BCK
Back [Dance terminology]	BK
Back Again to Hoover [Slogan during 1974 economic downturn]	BATH
Back, Arm, Neck, Scalp [Medicine]	BANS
Back Association of Canada	BAC
Back Bay Restaurant Group, Inc. [Associated Press] (SAG)	BackBay
Back Bay Restaurant Group, Inc. [NASDAQ symbol] (SAG)	PAPA
Back Bay Restaurant Grp [NASDAQ symbol] (TTSB)	PAPA
Back Course (FAAC)	BC
Back Course Marker (FAAC)	BCM
Back Cover [Publishing] (WDMC)	BC
Back Dividends	BD
Back Door Trot [i.e., a call of nature] [Obsolete slang]	BDT
Back Electromotive Force (DEN)	BEMF
Back Emergency Speed (DNAB)	BEM
Back End (MSA)	BE
Back Face (SAA)	BF
Back Fat [Animal husbandry]	BF
Back Focal	BF
Back Focal Distance (MSA)	BFD
Back Focal Length [Optics]	BFL
Back Folded [Freight]	BF
Back Full Speed (DNAB)	BF
Back Gear [Technical drawings]	BG
Back Judge [Football]	BJ
Back Lay Welding (NUCP)	BLW
Back Loading Point [Military British]	BLP
Back Marker [Aviation]	BM
Back of Board (MSA)	B of B
Back of Book	BOB
Back of Cab [TII] (TAG)	BOC
Back Office Crunch [Business term]	BOC
Back Order	BO
Back Order and Selection	BOS
Back Order Release (DNAB)	BO REL
Back Pain Association [British Research center] (EAIO)	BPA
Back Pain Classification Scale [Medicine] (DMAA)	BPCS
Back Plane (MCD)	BP
Back Plaster [Technical drawings]	BP
Back Porch Effect	BPE
Back Pressure	BP
Back Pressure Regulator	BPR
Back Pressure Transducer [Automotive engineering]	BPT
Back Projection (DEN)	BP
Back Reflection (DNAB)	BR
Back Scatter Factor [Medicine] (MAE)	BSF
Back Shelf	BKSLF
Back Shunt Keying	BSK
Back Spread [Investment term]	BS
Back Stage Left [A stage direction]	BSL
Back Stage Right [A stage direction]	BSR
Back Surface Field [Photovoltaic energy systems]	BSF
Back Surface Reflectance [Photovoltaic energy systems]	BSR
Back Tape Reader	BTR
Back Taxiing [Aviation] (FAAC)	BT
Back Telling (SAA)	B-TELL
Back to Back [Technical drawings]	B to B
Back to School (WDAA)	BTS
Back to the Bible Broadcast (NTCM)	BBB
Back to the City [An association Defunct] (EA)	BC
Back to the Future Fan Club	BTTFFC
Back, Training [Parachute]	BT
Back Up [Automotive engineering]	B/UP
Back Up Register	BUR
Back View (MSA)	BV
Back Widow Spider Toxin [Medicine] (DMAA)	BWST
Back Yard Burgers [NASDAQ symbol] (TTSB)	BYBI
Back Yard Burgers, Inc. [Associated Press] (SAG)	BackYrd
Back Yard Burgers, Inc. [NASDAQ symbol] (SAG)	BYBI
Backache [Medicine]	BA
Back-Action Evasion [Physics]	BAE
Backamo [Sweden ICAO location identifier] (ICLI)	ESGA
Back-Arc-Basin Basalt [Geology]	BABB
Backboard [Telecommunications] (TEL)	BB
Backbone Concentrator Node [Routing device] [Telecommunications] (PCM)	BCN
Backbord [Portside] [German military]	BB
Back-Connected [Technical drawings]	BC
Backdoor Financing [Public debt transactions] [Investment term]	BF
Backed With [Used by record companies and trade papers to indicate music on the alternative side of a disk]	b/w
Back-End Processor [Computer] (TSSD)	BEP
Back-end Storage Network [Computer science] (EECA)	BSN
Backer Petroleum Corp. [Vancouver Stock Exchange symbol]	BCM
Backer Resources [Vancouver Stock Exchange symbol]	BAK

Backer Spielvogel Bates Worldwide [*Commercial firm British*] (ECON) .... BSBW
Backface (MSA) .... BF
Back-Feed .... BF
Backfile Conversion Project [*European Patent Office*] .... BACON
Backfire Suppressor Valve [*Automotive engineering*] .... BSV
Back-Gate Metal-Oxide Semiconductor (IAA) .... BMOS
Back-Gate Metal-Oxide Semiconductor Field-Effect Transistor (IAA)..... BMOSFET
Background .... BCGD
Background [*Low-priority processing*] [*Computer science*] .... BG
Background (WDMC) .... bg
Background (NTCM) .... BKG
Background .... BKGD
Background (VRA) .... bkgr
Background [*Low-priority processing*] [*Computer science*] .... BKGRD
Background Air Pollution Monitoring Network (GNE) .... BAPMoN
Background Compiler COBOL [*Common Business-Oriented Language*] (IAA) .... BGCOB
Background Diabetic Retinopathy [*Endocrinology and ophthalmology*] (DAVI) .... BDR
Background Elimination Technique (MCD) .... BET
Background Emission Index [*Automotive engineering*] .... BGEI
Background Equivalent Activity .... BEA
Background Equivalent Concentration [*Computer science*] .... BEC
Background Heat Flux .... BHF
Background Illumination Intensity .... BII
Background Information (MCD) .... BI
Background Information Document [*Environmental Protection Agency*] .... BID
Background Investigation .... BI
Background Listening [*Music*] .... BL
Background Luminance Monitor [*Aviation*] (DA) .... BLM
Background Mapping Sensor .... BMS
Background Measurement Satellite (NASA) .... BMS
Background Measurements Program (MCD) .... BMP
Background Music (WDAA) .... BGM
Background Natural Organic Matter [*Environmental chemistry*] .... BNOM
Background Natural Sound .... BGNS
Background Noise Level (CAAL) .... BNL
Background Noise Level (CAAL) .... LN
Background Noise Power .... BNP
Background Noise Suppression Amplifier (DICI) .... BNSA
Background Operating System (IEEE) .... BOS
Background Paper .... BP
Background Perfume .... BGP
Background Radiation (SAA) .... BR
Background Storage and Control Unit .... BSCU
Background-Limited Infrared Photoconductor (IAA) .... BIP
Background-Limited Infrared Photography .... BLIP
Backhoe .... BCKHOE
Backhoe Trench [*Archaeology*] .... BHT
Backhoe Trench [*Archaeology*] .... T
Backing [*Publishing*] (WDMC) .... back
Backing (FAAC) .... BCKG
Backlash (MSA) .... BL
Backlash Allowance (MSA) .... BA
Backlight Burtek Trainer .... BBT
Backlight Compensation [*Photography*] .... BLC
Backlog of Essential Maintenance and Repair (AFM) .... BEMAR
Backlog of Maintenance and Repair (MCD) .... BMAR
Backmixing [*Chemical engineering*] .... BM
Back-Off System .... BOS
Backorder Problem Working Group [*DoD*] .... BOPWG
Backpack .... BP
Backpack Survival Kit (MCD) .... BSK
Backpackers Club [*Reading, Berkshire, England*] (EAIO) .... BC
Back-Pressure Control .... BPC
Backscatler / Absorption Chamber (PDAA) .... BACH
Backscatter/Absorption Gas Imaging (MCD) .... BAGI
Backscatter Electron .... BSE
Backscatter Imaging Tomography [*Factory automation*] (BTTJ) .... BIT
Backscatter Ultraviolet [*Spectrometry*] (MCD) .... BUV
Backscatter Ultraviolet Spectrometer .... BUS
Backscatter Ultraviolet Spectrometer .... BUVS
Backscattered Electron (MCD) .... BE
Back-Scattered Electron [*Microscopic imaging*] .... BSE
Backscattered Electron Microscopy .... BSEM
Backscattered LASER Energy Digitizing Equipment (MCD) .... BLEDE
Backscattering Spectroscopy [*Surface analysis*] .... BS
Backsight (DNAB) .... BS
Backspace [*ASCII format effector*] [*Computer science*] (NITA) .... BS
Backspace Character [*Keyboard*] [*Computer science*] (BUR) .... BKSP
Backspace Character [*Keyboard*] [*Computer science*] .... BS
Backspace Contact .... BSC
Backspace File (BUR) .... BSF
Backspace Recorder .... BSR
Backstage [*Theater*] (WDMC) .... back
Backstage (ADA) .... BS
Backstairs [*Gossip*] .... BS
Backstamp .... BKST
Backstrip [*Book-binding*] (WDMC) .... back
Backstrip (WGA) .... BKS
Backtell (IAA) .... BTL
Backtell Lateraltell Output (SAA) .... BLO
Backup (KSC) .... BKUP
Backup (KSC) .... BU
Backup Acquisition System .... BACS
Backup Aerospace Vehicle [*or Aircraft*] .... BA
Backup Aerospace Vehicle [*or Aircraft*] **Authorization** .... BAA
Backup Aerospace Vehicle [*or Aircraft*] **Inventory** .... BAI
Backup Air Data Sensor Assembly (MCD) .... BADSA
Backup Alert Force .... BAF
Backup Attitude Reference System .... BARS
Backup Auxiliary Transformer [*Nuclear energy*] (GFGA) .... BAT
Backup Avionics Subsystem Software (MCD) .... BASS
Backup Block (MCD) .... BUB
Backup Bus Controller [*Computer science*] .... BBC
Backup Computer (CET) .... BUC
Backup Control Electronics (MCD) .... BCE
Backup Control System .... BCS
Backup Control System (MCD) .... BUCS
Backup Controller (MCD) .... BUC
Backup Digital Computer .... BDC
Backup Digital Computer .... BUDC
Backup Digital System .... BUDS
Backup Drive Amplifier (MCD) .... BDA
Backup Emergency Communications .... BUEC
Backup Facility [*Nuclear war games*] .... BUF
Backup File [*Computer science*] .... BAK
Backup File (CDE) .... BAK file
Backup Flight Control (MCD) .... BFC
Backup Flight Control System [*NASA*] (NASA) .... BFCS
Backup Flight Control System (MCD) .... BUFCS
Backup Flight System (MCD) .... BFS
Backup Force .... BF
Backup Gimbal Servo .... BGS
Backup Guidance System [*NASA*] .... BGS
Backup Guidance System [*NASA*] .... BUGS
Backup Interceptor Control [*System*] [*Air Force*] .... BUIC
Backup Interceptor Control System [*Air Force*] .... BUICS
Backup Maintenance Activity (MCD) .... BMA
Backup Operating System (NASA) .... BOS
Backup Optical Storage System [*Aquidneck Data Corp.*] (NITA) .... BOSS
Backup Optical Unit (NASA) .... BUOU
Backup Plate .... BUP
Backup Plate, Perforated .... BUPP
Back-Up Quantity .... BQ
Backup Rate [*Ventilator*] [*Medicine*] (DAVI) .... BUR
Backup Rate of Pitch .... BURP
Backup Rate of Roll .... BURR
Backup Rate of Yaw .... BURY
Backup Scram System [*Nuclear energy*] (NRCH) .... BUSS
Backup Study Sheets [*Military*] .... BUSS
Backup System Services [*NASA*] (NASA) .... BSS
Backup System Services .... BSS
Backup System Test Console .... BUSTC
Backus Naur [*or Normal*] **Form** [*ALGOL*] [*Computer science*] (BUR) .... BNF
Backus Normal [*or Naur*] **Form** [*ALGOL*] [*Computer science*] .... BNO
Backus on Sheriffs [*A publication*] (DLA) .... Back Sher
Backus School, Backus, MN [*Library symbol*] [*Library of Congress*] (LCLS) .... MnBacS
Backward (WDAA) .... BKD
Backward (KSC) .... BKWD
Backward [*Telecommunications*] (TEL) .... BWD
Backward Chaining [*Psychology*] .... BC
Backward Diode .... BD
Backward Edge [*Skating*] .... B
Backward Indicator [*Telecommunications*] (TEL) .... BI
Backward Indicator BIT [*Binary Digit*] [*Telecommunications*] (TEL) .... BIB
Backward Internal Rotation [*Orthopedics*] (DAVI) .... BIR
Backward Interworking Telephony Event [*Telecommunications*] (TEL) .... BITE
Backward Limit Photocell .... BLPC
Backward Sequence Number [*Telecommunications*] (TEL) .... BSN
Backward Signaling [*Telecommunications*] (TEL) .... BS
Backward Traveling Wave .... BTW
Backward Volume Wave [*Telecommunications*] (TEL) .... BVW
Backward Wave [*Telecommunications*] (IAA) .... BW
Backward Wave Amplifier .... BWA
Backward Wave Converter (CET) .... BWC
Backward Wave Magnetron (MSA) .... BWM
Backward Wave Oscillator .... BWO
Backward Wave Oscillator Synchronizer .... BWOS
Backward Wave Oscillator Tube .... BWOT
Backward Wave Power Amplifier .... BWPA
Backward Wave Sweep Oscillator .... BWSO
Backward Wave Tube [*Physics*] .... BWT
Backwardation [*Commodity futures trading*] (ROG) .... BACK
Backwardation [*Commodity futures trading*] .... BK
Backward-Explicit Congestion Notification [*Computer science*] .... BECN
Backwards Differentiation Formula (MHDI) .... BDF
Back-Water Valve .... BWV
Backyard Boat Builders [*USCG*] (TAG) .... BYBB
BACM Industries Ltd. [*Formerly, British-American Construction & Materials Ltd.*] .... BACM
Baco [*Ethiopia*] [*ICAO location identifier*] (ICLI) .... HABC
Bacolod [*Philippines*] [*Airport symbol*] (OAG) .... BCD
Bacolod, Negros Occidental [*Philippines*] [*ICAO location identifier*] (ICLI) .... RPVB
Bacon and Meat Manufacturers' Association [*British*] .... BMMA
Bacon. Arguments in Law [*A publication*] (DLA) .... Bacon
Bacon Families Association [*Defunct*] (EA) .... BFA
Bacon, Lettuce, and Tomato Sandwich .... BLT

Bacon Memorial Public Library, Wyandotte, MI [*Library symbol Library of Congress*] (LCLS) ..... MiWy
Bacon on Benefit Societies and Life Insurance [*A publication*] (DLA) ..... Bac Ben Soc
Bacon on Benefit Societies and Life Insurance [*A publication*] (DLA) ..... Bac Ins
Bacon on Government [*A publication*] (DLA) ..... Bac Gov
Bacon on Government [*A publication*] (DLA) ..... Bacon
Bacon on Leases and Terms of Years [*A publication*] (DLA) ..... Bac Lease
Bacon on Leases and Terms of Years [*A publication*] (DLA) ..... Bacon
Bacon's Abridgment [*1736-1832*] [*A publication*] (DLA) ..... Bac Ab
Bacon's Abridgment [*1736-1832*] [*A publication*] (DLA) ..... Bac Abr
Bacon's Abridgment [*1736-1832*] [*A publication*] (DLA) ..... Bacon
Bacon's Case of Treason [*1641*] [*A publication*] (DLA) ..... Bac Ca
Bacon's Chancery Cases [*England*] [*A publication*] (DLA) ..... Bac Chanc
Bacon's Complete Arbitrator [*A publication*] (DLA) ..... Bac Comp Arb
Bacon's Complete Arbitrator [*A publication*] (DLA) ..... Bacon
Bacon's Decisions (Ritchie) [*England*] [*A publication*] (DLA) ..... Bac Dec
Bacon's Decisions (Ritchie) [*England*] [*A publication*] (DLA) ..... Bac Rep
Bacon's Elements of the Common Law [*A publication*] (DLA) ..... Bac El
Bacon's Elements of the Common Law [*A publication*] (DLA) ..... Bacon
Bacon's Essay on Uses [*A publication*] (DLA) ..... Bac Uses
Bacon's Essay on Uses [*A publication*] (DLA) ..... Bacon
Bacon's Georgia Digest [*A publication*] (DLA) ..... Bac Dig
Bacon's Liber Regis [*A publication*] (DLA) ..... Bacon
Bacon's Liber Regis, vel Thesaurus Rerum Ecclesiasticarum [*A publication*] (DLA) ..... Bac Lib Reg
Bacon's Liber Regis, vel Thesaurus Rerum Ecclesiasticarum [*A publication*] (DLA) ..... Bac TE
Bacou USA [*NASDAQ symbol*] (TTSB) ..... BACU
Bacteria (DAVI) ..... BAC
Bacterial Adherent Colonies ..... BAC
Bacterial Adhesion to Hydrocarbons ..... BATH
Bacterial Agglutination (MAE) ..... BA
Bacterial Alkaline Phosphatase [*or Bacterial Alkaline Phosphomonoesterase*] [*An enzyme*] ..... BAP
Bacterial Antigen Complex [*Immunochemistry*] ..... BAC
Bacterial Artificial Chromosome [*Genetics*] ..... BAC
Bacterial Artificial Chromosome [*Genetics*] ..... BAC
Bacterial Artificial Chromosome [*Genetics*] ..... BAC
Bacterial Automated Identification Technique ..... BAIT
Bacterial Carbon Demand [*Marine biology*] ..... BCD
Bacterial Endocarditis [*Medicine*] ..... BE
Bacterial Endocarditis ..... BEC
Bacterial Ice Nucleation Diagnosis [*DNA Plant Technology Corp. test*] ..... BIND
Bacterial Identification ..... BID
Bacterial Intravenous Protein (MAE) ..... BIP
Bacterial Kidney Disease [*Ichthyology*] ..... BKD
Bacterial Organic Carbon [*Water chemistry*] ..... BOC
Bacterial Phosphatidylethanolamine [*Physiological chemistry*] ..... BPE
Bacterial Releasing Agent [*Microbiology*] ..... BRA
Bacterial Secondary Production [*Water chemistry*] ..... BSP
Bacterial Sulfate Reduction ..... BSR
Bacterial Vaginosis [*Medicine*] ..... BV
Bactericidal Concentration (MAE) ..... BC
Bactericidal/Permeability Increasing [*Protein*] [*Immunology*] ..... BPI
Bacteriochlorophyll [*Biochemistry*] ..... BChl
Bacteriochlorophyll-B [*Biochemistry*] ..... BC-B
Bacteriologic Index [*Clinical microbiology*] ..... BI
Bacteriological ..... BAC
Bacteriological Analytical Manual [*A publication*] ..... BAM
Bacteriological Oxygen Demand [*Water pollution*] ..... BOD
Bacteriological Warfare ..... BW
Bacteriological Warfare, Defence [*British World War II*] ..... BW(D)
Bacteriological Warfare, Operational Panel [*British World War II*] ..... BW(O)
Bacteriological Warfare, Policy Panel [*British World War II*] ..... BW(P)
Bacteriological Warhead ..... BW
Bacteriology [*Biochemistry*] (DAVI) ..... bact
Bacteriology ..... BACTER
Bacteriology ..... BACTLGY
Bacteriology Laboratory (DAVI) ..... Bacti Lab
Bacteriopheophytin [*Biochemistry*] ..... Bphe
Bacteriopheophytin [*Biochemistry*] ..... BPheo
Bacteriopheophytin-B [*Biochemistry*] ..... BP-B
Bacteriorhodopsin [*Biochemistry*] ..... bR
Bacteriostatic Water for Injection [*Medicine*] ..... BWFI
Bacterium [*Bacteria*] [*Latin*] ..... BACT
Bacteroids Bile Esculin [*Agar*] [*Microbiology*] ..... BBE
Bactometer Data Management System ..... BDMS
Bactrian (VRA) ..... Bactr
Baculovirus Expression Vector [*Biochemistry*] ..... BEV
Bacus/B'Gosh Families [*An association Defunct*] (EA) ..... BBF
Bad and Doubtful Debt (DCTA) ..... B & D
Bad Axe, MI [*Location identifier FAA*] (FAAL) ..... BAX
Bad Axe, MI [*AM radio station call letters*] ..... WLEW
Bad Axe, MI [*FM radio station call letters*] ..... WLEW-FM
Bad Axe, MI [*Television station call letters*] ..... WUCX-TV
Bad Axe Public Library, Bad Axe, MI [*Library symbol Library of Congress*] (LCLS) ..... MiBa
Bad Black Brother ..... BBB
Bad Bramstedt [*Germany ICAO location identifier*] (ICLI) ..... EDHX
Bad Breath ..... BB
Bad Cannstatt Hospital [*Germany ICAO location identifier*] (ICLI) ..... EDOG
Bad Character ..... BC
Bad Check [*Banking*] ..... BC
Bad Conduct [*British military*] (DMA) ..... BC
Bad Conduct Discharge [*Military*] ..... BCD
Bad Conduct Discharge, General Court-Martial, after Confinement in Prison [*Navy*] ..... BDGC
Bad Conduct Discharge, General Court-Martial, after Violation of Probation [*Navy*] ..... BDGP
Bad Conduct Discharge, General Court-Martial, Immediate [*Navy*] ..... BDGI
Bad Conduct Discharge, Sentence of Summary Court-Martial, Immediate [*Navy*] ..... BDSI
Bad Conduct Discharge, Summary Court-Martial, after Violation of Probation [*Navy*] ..... BDSP
Bad Data Lister ..... BDL
Bad Delivery [*Investment term*] ..... BD
Bad Demographic Risk [*Television*] ..... BDR
Bad Duerkheim [*Germany ICAO location identifier*] (ICLI) ..... EDRF
Bad Gandersheim [*Germany ICAO location identifier*] (ICLI) ..... EDVA
Bad Hersfeld [*Germany ICAO location identifier*] (ICLI) ..... EDOZ
Bad Kissingen [*Germany ICAO location identifier*] (ICLI) ..... EDEG
Bad Kissingen [*Germany ICAO location identifier*] (ICLI) ..... EDFK
Bad Kreuznach [*Germany ICAO location identifier*] (ICLI) ..... EDEH
Bad Order [*i.e., requiring repair*] ..... BO
Bad Ragaz [*Switzerland ICAO location identifier*] (ICLI) ..... LSZC
Bad Ragaz [*Switzerland ICAO location identifier*] (ICLI) ..... LSZE
Bad Reichenhall [*Federal Republic of Germany*] [*Seismograph station code, US Geological Survey*] (SEIS) ..... BHG
Bad Tolz [*Germany ICAO location identifier*] (ICLI) ..... EDOV
Bada [*Indonesia*] [*ICAO location identifier*] (ICLI) ..... WAMQ
Badajoz [*Spain*] [*Airport symbol*] (OAG) ..... BJZ
Badajoz/Talavera La Real [*Spain ICAO location identifier*] (ICLI) ..... LEBZ
Badana [*Saudi Arabia*] [*Airport symbol Obsolete*] (OAG) ..... BDN
Badbury [*England*] ..... BADB
Bade [*Indonesia*] [*Airport symbol*] (OAG) ..... BXD
Bade [*Indonesia*] [*ICAO location identifier*] (ICLI) ..... WAKE
Baden Explorations [*Vancouver Stock Exchange symbol*] ..... BEX
Baden-Baden [*Germany ICAO location identifier*] (ICLI) ..... EDTB
Badfinger Fan Club (EA) ..... BFC
Badge Card Reader (MHDI) ..... BCR
Badge Collectors Circle [*British*] [*An association*] (DBA) ..... BCC
Badger Army Ammunition Plant (AABC) ..... BAAP
Badger Meter [*AMEX symbol*] (TTSB) ..... BMI
Badger Meter, Inc. [*Associated Press*] (SAG) ..... BadgrM
Badger Meter, Inc. [*AMEX symbol*] (SPSG) ..... BMI
Badger Mountain [*Washington*] [*Seismograph station code, US Geological Survey*] (SEIS) ..... BDG
Badger Paper Mills [*NASDAQ symbol*] (TTSB) ..... BPMI
Badger Paper Mills, Inc. [*Associated Press*] (SAG) ..... BadgrP
Badger Paper Mills, Inc. [*NASDAQ symbol*] (NQ) ..... BPMI
Badger School, Badger, MN [*Library symbol*] [*Library of Congress*] (LCLS) ..... MnBadS
Badger State Car Wash Association [*Wisconsin*] (SRA) ..... BSCWA
Badger Union High School District, Lake Geneva, WI [*Library symbol Library of Congress*] (LCLS) ..... WLagB
Badgery's Creek Airport [*Australia*] ..... BCA
Badische Anilin und Soda-Fabrik [*Automotive industry supplier*] ..... BASF
Badlands National Monument [*South Dakota*] ..... BADL
Badminton Association of England (DBA) ..... BA of E
Badminton Association of England (EAIO) ..... BAE
Badminton Association of Western Australia ..... BAWA
Badminton Library [*A publication*] ..... BL
Badminton Union of Ireland (EAIO) ..... BUI
Bado Lite [*Zaire*] [*Airport symbol*] (OAG) ..... BDT
Baende [*Volumes*] [*German*] ..... BDE
Bafata [*Guinea-Bissau*] [*ICAO location identifier*] (ICLI) ..... GGBF
Baffle [*Regulating device*] (KSC) ..... BAF
Baffle/Liner Interface Seal [*Nuclear energy*] (NRCH) ..... BLIS
Bafgh [*Iran*] [*ICAO location identifier*] (ICLI) ..... OIYB
Bafia [*Cameroon*] [*ICAO location identifier*] (ICLI) ..... FKAF
Bafoulabe [*Mali*] [*ICAO location identifier*] (ICLI) ..... GABF
Bafour, Blanchard, and Raymond [*Computer typesetting*] (DGA) ..... BBR
Bafoussam [*Cameroon*] [*Airport symbol*] (OAG) ..... BFX
Bafoussam [*Cameroon*] [*ICAO location identifier*] (ICLI) ..... FKKU
Baft [*Iran*] [*ICAO location identifier*] (ICLI) ..... OIKF
Bag [*Shipping*] ..... B
Bag ..... BG
Bag All Garbage ..... BAG
Bag Cell Peptide [*Biochemistry*] ..... BCP
Bag in Box [*Packaging*] ..... BIB
Bag of Waters [*Medicine*] ..... BOW
Bagabag, Neuva Viscaya [*Philippines*] [*ICAO location identifier*] (ICLI) ..... RPUZ
Bagala [*Ship's rigging*] (ROG) ..... BLA
Bagarottus dei Corradi da Bologna [*Flourished, 1200-42*] [*Authority cited in pre-1607 legal work*] (DSA) ..... B
Bagarottus dei Corradi da Bologna [*Flourished, 1200-42*] [*Authority cited in pre-1607 legal work*] (DSA) ..... Ba
Bagarottus dei Corradi da Bologna [*Flourished, 1200-42*] [*Authority cited in pre-1607 legal work*] (DSA) ..... Bag
Bagatelle ..... BGTTL
Bagdad, AZ [*FM radio station call letters*] (RBYB) ..... KAKP
Bagdogra [*India*] [*Airport symbol*] (OAG) ..... IXB
Bage [*Brazil*] [*Airport symbol*] (OAG) ..... BGX
Bagehot. English Constitution [*8th ed.*] [*1904*] [*A publication*] (DLA) ..... Bag Eng Const
Bagehot. English Constitution [*8th ed.*] [*1904*] [*A publication*] (DLA) ..... Bag Engl Const
Baggage (AFM) ..... BAG
Baggage for Air Cargo ..... CARBAGAIR

Baggage Improvement Program [*IATA*] (DS) ..... BIP
Bagged White Cell Study [*Cytology*] (DAVI) ..... BWCS
Baghdad [*Iraq*] [*Airport symbol*] (OAG) ..... BGW
Baghdad/Muthenna [*Iraq*] [*ICAO location identifier*] (ICLI) ..... ORBW
Baghdad Pact (CINC) ..... BP
Baghdad/Rasheed [*Iraq*] [*ICAO location identifier*] (ICLI) ..... ORBR
Baghdad/Saddam International [*Iraq*] [*ICAO location identifier*] (ICLI) ..... ORBS
Baghdad/Soica Headquarters [*Iraq*] [*ICAO location identifier*] (ICLI) ..... ORBC
Baghdad-Saddam [*Iraq*] [*Airport symbol*] (OAG) ..... SDA
Baghdogra [*India*] [*ICAO location identifier*] (ICLI) ..... VEBD
Baghlan [*Afghanistan*] [*ICAO location identifier*] (ICLI) ..... OABG
Bagley and Harman's Reports [*17-19 California*] [*A publication*] (DLA) ..... Bagl & H
Bagley and Harman's Reports [*17-19 California*] [*A publication*] (DLA) ..... Bagl & Har
Bagley and Harman's Reports [*17-19 California*] [*A publication*] (DLA) ..... Bagl & Har (Cal)
Bagley Elementary School, Bagley, MN [*Library symbol*] [*Library of Congress*] (LCLS) ..... MnBagE
Bagley Gazette, Bagley, IA [*Library symbol Library of Congress*] (LCLS) ..... IaBagG
Bagley Public Library, Bagley, IA [*Library symbol Library of Congress*] (LCLS) ..... IaBag
Bagley Public Library, Bagley, MN [*Library symbol*] [*Library of Congress*] (LCLS) ..... MnBag
Bagley's Practice at Chambers [*1834*] [*A publication*] (DLA) ..... Bag Ch Pr
Bagley's Reports [*16 California*] [*A publication*] (DLA) ..... Bagl
Bagley's Reports [*16-19 California*] [*A publication*] (DLA) ..... Bagl (Cal)
Baglung [*Nepal*] [*Airport symbol*] (OAG) ..... BGL
Baglung [*Nepal*] [*ICAO location identifier*] (ICLI) ..... VNBL
Bagneres De Bigorre [*France*] [*Seismograph station code, US Geological Survey*] (SEIS) ..... BDB
Bagneres De Luchon [*France ICAO location identifier*] (ICLI) ..... LFCB
Bagnole-De-L'Orne [*France ICAO location identifier*] (ICLI) ..... LFAO
Bagong Alyansang Makabayan [*Philippines*] [*Political party*] (EY) ..... Bayan
Bagotville Canadian Forces Base, PQ [*ICAO location identifier*] (ICLI) ..... CYBG
Bagra [*Pakistan*] [*Seismograph station code, US Geological Survey*] (SEIS) ..... BGP
Bags ..... BGS
Bags, Barrels, or Boxes [*Freight*] ..... BBB
Bagua [*Peru*] [*ICAO location identifier*] (ICLI) ..... SPGU
Baguio [*Philippines*] [*Seismograph station code, US Geological Survey*] (SEIS) ..... BAG
Baguio, Benguet [*Philippines*] [*ICAO location identifier*] (ICLI) ..... RPUB
Baha Resources Ltd. [*Vancouver Stock Exchange symbol*] ..... BAH
Bahaa Esperanto-Ligo (EA) ..... BEL
Baha'i Community [*Australia*] ..... BC
Baha'i Faith ..... BF
Baha'i International Community ..... BIC
Baha'i National Spiritual Assembly [*Australia*] ..... BNSA
Bahama Islands (WDAA) ..... BA I
Bahama Islands (BARN) ..... Ba Is
Bahama Resources Ltd. [*Vancouver Stock Exchange symbol*] ..... BHA
Bahama Route [*Aviation*] (FAAC) ..... BR
Bahamas [*IYRU nationality code*] (IYR) ..... BA
Bahamas (ROG) ..... BAH
Bahamas (VRA) ..... Baha
Bahamas [*MARC country of publication code Library of Congress*] (LCCP) ..... bf
Bahamas [*ANSI three-letter standard code*] (CNC) ..... BHS
Bahamas [*ANSI two-letter standard code*] (CNC) ..... BS
Bahamas [*Aircraft nationality and registration mark*] (FAAC) C6
Bahamas [*MARC geographic area code Library of Congress*] (LCCP) ..... nwbf--
Bahamas Air [*ICAO designator*] (AD) ..... UP
Bahamas Law Reports [*A publication*] (DLA) ..... Bah LR
Bahamas Law Reports [*A publication*] (DLA) ..... BLR
Bahamas Red Cross Society (EAIO) ..... BRCS
Bahamas Telecommunications Corp. [*Telecommunications service*] (TSSD) ..... BATELCO
Bahamasair Holdings Ltd. [*Bahamas*] [*ICAO designator*] (FAAC) ..... BHS
Bahamian Democratic Party [*Political party*] (PPW) ..... BDP
Bahar Dar [*Ethiopia*] [*Airport symbol*] (OAG) ..... BJR
Bahar Dar [*Ethiopia*] [*ICAO location identifier*] (ICLI) ..... HABD
Bahau [*Malaysia*] [*ICAO location identifier*] (ICLI) ..... WMAA
Bahawalnagar [*Pakistan*] [*ICAO location identifier*] (ICLI) ..... OPBR
Bahawalpur [*Pakistan*] [*Airport symbol*] (AD) ..... BWP
Bahawalpur [*Pakistan*] [*ICAO location identifier*] (ICLI) ..... OPBW
Bahia Blanca [*Argentina*] [*Airport symbol*] (OAG) ..... BHI
Bahia Blanca/Comdte. Espora [*Argentina ICAO location identifier*] (ICLI) ..... SAZB
Bahia De Caraquez [*Ecuador*] [*ICAO location identifier*] (ICLI) ..... SEBC
Bahia De Los Angeles [*Mexico*] [*Seismograph station code, US Geological Survey*] (SEIS) ..... LAX
Bahia Oral Language Test (EDAC) ..... BOLT
Bahia Solano [*Colombia*] [*Airport symbol*] (OAG) ..... BSC
Bahia Solano/Jose Celestino Mutis [*Colorado ICAO location identifier*] (ICLI) ..... SKBS
Bahn Post Amt [*Railway Post Office*] [*German*] ..... BPA
Bahrain [*Aircraft nationality and registration mark*] (FAAC) A9C
Bahrain [*MARC geographic area code Library of Congress*] ..... a-ba--
Bahrain [*MARC country of publication code Library of Congress*] (LCCP) ..... ba
Bahrain ..... BAHR
Bahrain (VRA) ..... Bahr
Bahrain [*IYRU nationality code*] [*ANSI two-letter standard code*] (CNC) ..... BH
Bahrain [*ANSI three-letter standard code*] (CNC) ..... BHR
Bahrain [*Bahrain*] [*ICAO location identifier*] (ICLI) ..... OBBB
Bahrain Development Bank (EY) ..... BDB
Bahrain Dinar [*Monetary unit*] (BJA) ..... BD
Bahrain/International [*Bahrain*] [*ICAO location identifier*] (ICLI) ..... OBBI
Bahrain Islands [*Airport symbol*] (OAG) ..... BAH
Bahrain Middle East Bank ..... BMB
Bahrain Monetary Agency (IMH) ..... BMA
Bahrain Telecommunications Co. ..... BATELCO
Bahrain Tourism Co. (EY) ..... BTC
Bahraini Saudi Bank (EY) ..... BSB
Baht [*Monetary unit*] [*Thailand*] ..... B
Baht [*Monetary unit*] [*Thailand*] ..... BHT
Bahujan Samaj Party [*Political party Italy*] (ECON) ..... BSP
Bahujan Samaj Party [*India*] ..... BSP
Baia Mare [*Romania*] [*Airport symbol*] (OAG) ..... BAY
Baia Mare/Tauti Magherusi [*Romania*] [*ICAO location identifier*] (ICLI) ..... LRBM
Baibara [*Papua New Guinea*] [*Airport symbol*] (OAG) ..... BAP
Baidoa [*Somalia*] [*ICAO location identifier*] (ICLI) ..... HCMB
Baie Comeau [*Canada*] [*Airport symbol*] (OAG) ..... YBC
Baie Comeau, PQ [*FM radio station call letters*] ..... CBMI
Baie Comeau, PQ [*AM radio station call letters*] ..... CHLC
Baie Comeau, PQ [*FM radio station call letters*] (RBYB) ..... CHLC-FM
Baie Comeau, PQ [*ICAO location identifier*] (ICLI) ..... CYBC
Baie Johan Beetz [*Canada*] [*Airport symbol*] (OAG) ..... YBJ
Baie Verte, NF [*Television station call letters*] CBNAT-1
Baie Verte, NF [*AM radio station call letters*] ..... CKIM
Baie Verte Public Library, Baie Verte, NF, Canada [*Library symbol Library of Congress*] (LCLS) ..... CaNfBV
Baie Verte Public Library, Newfoundland [*Library symbol National Library of Canada*] (NLC) ..... NFBV
Baie-Trinite, PQ [*Television station call letters*] ..... CIVF
Baika Women's College [*EDUCATSS*] [*UTLAS symbol*] ..... BAI
Baikal [*Russian Federation*] [*ICAO designator*] (FAAC) ..... BKL
Baikal Commodity Exchange [*Russian Federation*] (EY) ..... BCE
Baikal-Amur Mainline [*USSR railroad in Siberia*] ..... BAM
Baikonur [*Satellite launch complex*] [*Former USSR*] ..... BAI
Bail Bond (DLA) ..... BB
Bail Court [*Legal term*] (DLA) ..... BC
Bail Court Cases [*A publication*] ..... Bail CC
Bail Court Cases [*Legal*] [*British*] ..... BCC
Bail Court Cases (Lowndes and Maxwell) [*England*] [*A publication*] (DLA) ..... BC Rep
Bail Court Cases (Lowndes and Maxwell) [*England*] [*A publication*] (DLA) ..... BCR
Bail Court Reports [*Legal*] [*British*] ..... BCR
Bail Court Reports (Saunders and Cole) [*England*] [*A publication*] (DLA) ..... Bail Ct R
Bail Court Reports (Saunders and Cole) [*England*] [*A publication*] (DLA) ..... BC Rep
Bail Court Reports (Saunders and Cole) [*England*] [*A publication*] (DLA) ..... BCC
Bail Court Reports (Saunders and Cole) [*England*] [*A publication*] (DLA) ..... BCR
Bail Out ..... BO
Bailadores [*Venezuela*] [*Seismograph station code, US Geological Survey*] (SEIS) ..... BLV
Baildon's Select Cases in Chancery [*Selden Society Publication, Vol. 10*] [*A publication*] (DLA) ..... Baild
Bailed Aircraft Repairables (MCD) ..... BAR
Bailett Weighting Function ..... BWF
Bailey Corp. [*NASDAQ symbol*] (CTT) ..... BAIB
Bailey Corp. [*Associated Press*] (SAG) ..... Bailey
Bailey Elementary School, Pasadena, TX [*Library symbol*] [*Library of Congress*] (LCLS) ..... TxPBE
Bailey, G. R., Escanaba MI [*STAC*] ..... BGR
Bailey Oil Content Monitor [*Ship ballast discharge*] ..... BOCM
Bailey's Chancery Reports [*South Carolina*] [*A publication*] (DLA) ..... Bailey Ch
Bailey's Equity Reports [*South Carolina*] [*A publication*] (DLA) ..... Bai Eq
Bailey's Equity Reports [*South Carolina*] [*A publication*] (DLA) ..... Bail Eq
Bailey's Equity Reports [*South Carolina*] [*A publication*] (DLA) ..... Bail Eq (SC)
Bailey's Equity Reports [*South Carolina*] [*A publication*] (DLA) ..... Bailey
Bailey's Equity Reports, South Carolina Court of Appeals [*A publication*] (DLA) ..... Bailey Eq
Bailey's Law of Master's Liability for Injuries to Servant [*A publication*] (DLA) ..... Bailey Mast Liab
Bailey's Law Reports [*South Carolina*] [*A publication*] (DLA) ..... Bai
Bailey's Law Reports [*South Carolina*] [*A publication*] (DLA) ..... Bail
Bailey's Law Reports [*South Carolina*] [*A publication*] (DLA) ..... Bail L
Bailey's Law Reports [*South Carolina*] [*A publication*] (DLA) ..... Bail L (SC)
Bailey's Law Reports [*South Carolina*] [*A publication*] (DLA) ..... Bailey
Bailey's North Carolina Digest [*A publication*] (DLA) ..... Bail Dig
Bailie [*British*] (ROG) ..... B
Bailiff Grand Cross ..... BGC
Bailiff Grand Cross of [*the Order of*] **Saint John of Jerusalem** [*British*] (ADA) ..... GCStJ
Bailing ..... BLG
Bailleau-Armenonville [*France ICAO location identifier*] (ICLI) ..... LFFL
Bailliere's Medical Transparencies [*A publication*] (DAVI) ..... BMT
Baillie's Digest of Mohammedan Law [*A publication*] (DLA) ..... Baill Dig
Baillie's Mohammedan Law of Inheritance [*A publication*] (DLA) ..... Baill Inher
Bailly Generating Station [*Nuclear energy*] (NRCH) ..... BGS
Bailment [*Legal term*] (DLA) ..... Bailm
Bailment (AAGC) ..... BLMT
Bailment Flight Test Program ..... BFTP
Baimuru [*Papua New Guinea*] [*Airport symbol*] (OAG) ..... VMU
Bainbridge, GA [*Location identifier FAA*] (FAAL) ..... BGE
Bainbridge, GA [*AM radio station call letters*] ..... WMGR
Bainbridge, GA [*FM radio station call letters*] ..... WMGR-FM
Bainbridge, GA [*Television station call letters*] ..... WTLH
Bainbridge Junior College, Bainbridge, GA [*Library symbol Library of Congress*] (LCLS) ..... GBaB
Bainbridge, OH [*FM radio station call letters*] ..... WKHR
Bainbridge on Mines and Minerals [*A publication*] (DLA) ..... Bainb M & M

Bainbridge on Mines and Minerals [*A publication*] (DLA) ... Bainb Mines
Baird-Associates, Inc. (MCD) ... BAI
Bairnco Corp. [*Associated Press*] (SAG) ... Bairnco
Bairnco Corp. [*NYSE symbol*] (SPSG) ... BZ
Bairnsdale [*Australia Airport symbol Obsolete*] (OAG) ... BSJ
Baitadi [*Nepal*] [*Airport symbol*] (OAG) ... BIT
Baitadi [*Nepal*] [*ICAO location identifier*] (ICLI) ... VNBT
Baiting Hollow Free Library, Calverton, NY [*Library symbol Library of Congress*] (LCLS) ... NCalv
Baiyer River [*New Guinea*] [*Airport symbol*] (AD) ... BYV
Baja California [*Mexico*] ... BC
Baja California - Territorio Norte ... BCTN
Baja California - Territorio Sur ... BCTS
Bajawa [*Indonesia*] [*Airport symbol*] (OAG) ... BJW
Bajawa/Padhameleda [*Indonesia*] [*ICAO location identifier*] (ICLI) ... WRKB
Baje/Cmt. Gustavo Kraemer [*Brazil ICAO location identifier*] (ICLI) ... SBBG
Bajhang [*Nepal*] [*Airport symbol*] (OAG) ... BJH
Bajhang [*Nepal*] [*ICAO location identifier*] (ICLI) ... VNBG
Bajocian [*Geology*] ... B
Bajura [*Nepal*] [*ICAO location identifier*] (ICLI) ... VNBR
Bakalalan [*Malaysia*] [*Airport symbol*] (OAG) ... BKM
Baked ... BKD
Bakel [*Senegal*] [*Seismograph station code, US Geological Survey*] (SEIS) ... BKL
Bakel [*Senegal*] [*Airport symbol*] (OAG) ... BXE
Bakel [*Senegal*] [*ICAO location identifier*] (ICLI) ... GOTB
Bakelalan [*Malaysia*] [*ICAO location identifier*] (ICLI) ... WBGQ
Baker [*Phonetic alphabet*] [*World War II*] (DSUE) ... B
Baker [*Diocesan abbreviation*] [*Oregon*] (TOCD) ... BAK
Baker ... BKR
Baker Analyzed Reagent [*Chemistry*] ... BAR
Baker and Taylor Automated Buying [*A teleordering system*] (NITA) ... BATAB
Baker & Taylor Co. ... B & T
Baker & Taylor Co. [*ACCORD*] [*UTLAS symbol*] ... BTE
Baker & Taylor Electronic Book Ordering Service [*Baker & Taylor Companies*] [*Trademark*] ... BaTaSYSTEMS
Baker and Taylor's Automated Buying System [*Teleordering system*] [*Baker & Taylor Companies*] [*Information service or system*] (IID) ... BATAB
Baker Aviation, Inc. [*ICAO designator*] (FAAC) ... BAJ
Baker, Botts, Shepherd & Coates, Houston, TX [*Library symbol Library of Congress*] (LCLS) ... TxHBB
Baker, CA [*FM radio station call letters*] ... KBXY
Baker, CA [*FM radio station call letters*] ... KIXF
Baker City, OR [*AM radio station call letters*] ... KBKR
Baker City, OR [*FM radio station call letters*] ... KCMB
Baker City, OR [*FM radio station call letters*] ... KKBC
Baker [*Michael*] **Corp.** [*Associated Press*] (SAG) ... Baker
Baker [*Michael*] **Corp.** [*AMEX symbol*] (SPSG) ... BKR
Baker County Public Library, Baker, OR [*Library symbol Library of Congress*] (LCLS) ... OrBak
Baker Elementary School, Great Neck, NY [*Library symbol Library of Congress*] (LCLS) ... NGrnBE
Baker, Fentress & Co. [*Associated Press*] (SAG) ... BakrF
Baker, Fentress & Co. [*NYSE symbol*] (CTT) ... BKF
Baker, FL [*FM radio station call letters*] ... WTJT
Baker Gold Ltd. [*Vancouver Stock Exchange symbol*] ... BKG
Baker High School, Baker, MT [*Library symbol*] [*Library of Congress*] (LCLS) ... MtBaHS
Baker Hughes, Inc. [*Associated Press*] (SAG) ... BakrHu
Baker Hughes, Inc. [*NYSE symbol*] (SPSG) ... BHI
Baker [*J.*], Inc. [*Associated Press*] (SAG) ... BakerJ
Baker [*J.*], Inc. [*NASDAQ symbol*] (NQ) ... JBAK
Baker Island Army Air Field [*Baker Island*] [*ICAO location identifier*] (ICLI) ... PBAR
Baker, LA [*FM radio station call letters*] ... WBBU
Baker Lake [*Northwest Territories*] [*Seismograph station code, US Geological Survey*] (SEIS) ... BLC
Baker Lake [*Canada*] [*Airport symbol*] (OAG) ... YBK
Baker Lake, NT [*FM radio station call letters*] ... CKQN
Baker Lake, NT [*ICAO location identifier*] (ICLI) ... CYBK
Baker, MT [*Location identifier FAA*] (FAAL) ... BKU
Baker, MT [*AM radio station call letters*] ... KFLN
Baker on the Law Relating to Burials [*A publication*] (DLA) ... Bak Bur
Baker, OR [*Location identifier FAA*] (FAAL) ... BKE
Baker River Audiovisual Center [*Library network*] ... BRAVC
Baker Street Irregulars (EA) ... BSI
Baker University, Baldwin City, KS [*Library symbol Library of Congress*] (LCLS) ... KBB
Baker University, Baldwin City, KS [*OCLC symbol*] (OCLC) ... KKB
Bakers' and Allied Traders' Golfing Society [*British*] (BI) ... BATS
Bakers and Pastrycooks' Association of Tasmania [*Australia*] ... BPAT
Baker's Antifol, Cyclophosphamide, Adriamycin, and Cisplatin [*Antineoplastic drug regimen*] (DAVI) ... T-CAP
Bakers' Food and Allied Workers' Union [*British*] (DCTA) ... BFAWU
Baker's Health Laws [*A publication*] (DLA) ... Bak Health L
Baker's Law of Highways [*A publication*] (DLA) ... Bak Highw
Baker's Law of Quarantine [*A publication*] (DLA) ... Baker Quar
Baker's New York Corporation Laws [*A publication*] (DLA) ... Bak Corp
Bakers' Union [*British*] (DI) ... BU
Baker-Schmidt Telescope (PDAA) ... BST
Baker-Schulberg Community Mental Health Ideology Scale [*Psychology*] ... CMHI
Bakersfield [*California*] [*Airport symbol*] (OAG) ... BFL
Bakersfield, CA [*TACAN station*] (NASA) ... BFL
Bakersfield, CA [*AM radio station call letters*] ... KAFY
Bakersfield, CA [*Television station call letters*] ... KBAK
Bakersfield, CA [*AM radio station call letters*] ... KBID
Bakersfield, CA [*AM radio station call letters*] ... KCWR
Bakersfield, CA [*AM radio station call letters*] ... KERN
Bakersfield, CA [*FM radio station call letters*] ... KERN-FM
Bakersfield, CA [*Television station call letters*] ... KERO
Bakersfield, CA [*FM radio station call letters*] (RBYB) ... KFRB-FM
Bakersfield, CA [*AM radio station call letters*] ... KGEO
Bakersfield, CA [*Television station call letters*] ... KGET
Bakersfield, CA [*FM radio station call letters*] ... KGFM
Bakersfield, CA [*AM radio station call letters*] ... KHIS
Bakersfield, CA [*FM radio station call letters*] ... KHIS-FM
Bakersfield, CA [*FM radio station call letters*] ... KIWI
Bakersfield, CA [*FM radio station call letters*] ... KKBB
Bakersfield, CA [*AM radio station call letters*] ... KNZR
Bakersfield, CA [*FM radio station call letters*] ... KPRX
Bakersfield, CA [*FM radio station call letters*] ... KTIE
Bakersfield, CA [*FM radio station call letters*] ... KTQX
Bakersfield, CA [*FM radio station call letters*] ... KUZZ
Bakersfield, CA [*Television station call letters*] ... KUZZ-TV
Bakersfield, CA [*AM radio station call letters*] ... KWAC
Bakersfield, CA [*AM radio station call letters*] (RBYB) ... KXEM
Bakersfield, CA [*AM radio station call letters*] ... KZPM
Bakersfield Individualized Process (EDAC) ... BIP
Bakersfield/Meadows Field [*California*] [*ICAO location identifier*] (ICLI) ... KBFL
Bakertalc, Inc. [*Toronto Stock Exchange symbol*] ... BKT
Bakery ... BAK
Bakery (AABC) ... BKRY
Bakery ... BKRY
Bakery and Allied Trades Association Ltd. [*British*] (BI) ... BATA
Bakery and Confectionery Workers' International Union of America [*Later, BCTWIU*] ... BCW
Bakery and Confectionery Workers' International Union of America [*Later, BCTWIU*] (EA) ... BCWIU of A
Bakery, Confectionery, and Tobacco Workers' International Union (EA) ... BCTWIU
Bakery Employees and Salesmen's Federation of Australia ... BESFA
Bakery Equipment Manufacturers Association (EA) ... BEMA
Bakery Equipment Manufacturers Society (PDAA) ... BEMS
Bakery Industry Employees' Association of New South Wales [*Australia*] ... BIEANSW
Bakery Students Association of Scotland (BI) ... BSAS
Bakhon Phanom/Mukdahan [*Thailand*] [*ICAO location identifier*] (ICLI) ... VTUB
Bakhtar Afghan Airlines [*ICAO designator*] (AD) ... BJ
Bakhtaran [*Iran*] [*ICAO location identifier*] (ICLI) ... OICC
Bakhtaran [*Iran*] [*ICAO location identifier*] (ICLI) ... OICT
Bakhuys [*Surinam*] [*ICAO location identifier*] (ICLI) ... SMBG
Baking ... BKG
Baking Industry and Teamster Labor Conference (EA) ... BITLC
Baking Industry Association of New South Wales [*Australia*] ... BIANSW
Baking Industry Sanitation Standards Committee (EA) ... BISSC
Baking Powder (WDAA) ... B/P
Baking Sands Tactical Underwater Range [*Oahu, HI*] ... BASTUR
Baking Trade Union of South Australia ... BTUSA
Baking Trades Employees' Union of New South Wales [*Australia*] ... BTEUNSW
Bakkafjordur [*Iceland*] [*Airport symbol*] (OAG) ... BJD
Bakken Library of Electricity in Life, Minneapolis, MN [*Library symbol Library of Congress*] (LCLS) ... MnMBL
Bakra Resources Ltd. [*Vancouver Stock Exchange symbol*] ... BKQ
Bakshi Ka Talab [*India*] [*ICAO location identifier*] (ICLI) ... VIBL
Baku [*Former USSR Seismograph station code, US Geological Survey*] (SEIS) ... BAK
Bakuai [*China*] [*ICAO location identifier*] (ICLI) ... RCUK
Bakuriani [*Former USSR Seismograph station code, US Geological Survey*] (SEIS) ... BKR
Balair AG [*Switzerland ICAO designator*] (FAAC) ... BBB
Balalae [*Solomon Islands*] [*Airport symbol*] (OAG) ... BAS
Balalae, Shortland Islands [*Solomon Islands*] [*ICAO location identifier*] (ICLI) ... AGGE
Balalaika and Domra Association of America (EA) ... BDAA
Balance [*Medicine*] (DAVI) ... bal
Balance [*Accounting*] (AFM) ... BAL
Balance ... BAL
Balance [*Bookkeeping*] (ODBW) ... bal
Balance [*Accounting*] (ROG) ... BALCE
Balance (WGA) ... BLC
Balance (ADA) ... BLCE
Balance Calibration Machine ... BCM
Balance Fixture (MCD) ... BAF
Balance Forward Master ... BFM
Balance General Mobilization Reserve Acquisition Objective [*DoD*] ... BGMRAO
Balance Location ... BALOC
Balance Magnetometric Zero (NOAA) ... BMZ
Balance Mobilization Reserve Materiel Objective [*Army*] (AABC) ... BMRMO
Balance of Commitments ... BCOM
Balance of Material (MCD) ... BM
Balance of Need Campaign [*Red Cross fund-raising*] ... BON
Balance of Payments [*Accounting*] ... BALPA
Balance of Payments [*International trade*] ... B-of-P
Balance of Payments [*International trade*] ... BOP
Balance of Payments [*International trade*] ... BP
Balance of Payments Act [*International trade*] (AABC) ... BOPA
Balance of Payments Program (AAGC) ... BALPRO
Balance of Payments Programmed [*International trade*] (AABC) ... BOPP
Balance of Payments Report [*A publication*] (DLA) ... Bal Pay't Rep
Balance of Plant [*Nuclear energy*] (NRCH) ... BOP

Balance of Plant Standard Safety Analysis Report [*Nuclear energy*] (NRCH) ... BOPSSAR
Balance of Power (IEEE) ... BOP
Balance of Space to Space Control Agencies ... BALSPACON
Balance of State [*Department of Labor*] ... BOS
Balance of Trade [*International trade*] ... B-of-T
Balance of Trade [*International trade*] ... BOT
Balance Resources Ltd. [*Vancouver Stock Exchange symbol*] ... BLD
Balance Return Loss [*Telecommunications*] (TEL) ... BRL
Balance Sheet [*Accounting*] ... BS
Balance to Follow (WDAA) ... BTF
Balance/Transferred [*Banking*] (WDAA) ... B/TF
Balanced ... B
Balanced Asynchronous (ACRL) ... BA
Balanced Budget ... BB
Balanced Budget Amendment ... BBA
Balanced Budget and Emergency Deficit Control Reaffirmation Act [*1987*] ... BBEDCRA
Balanced Colorimeter Chamber (MCD) ... BCC
Balanced Crystal Mixer (IAA) ... BCM
Balanced Current [*Electronics*] (IAA) ... BC
Balanced Diet Certificates [*Economics simulation game*] ... BALDICER
Balanced Digital Transmission Device [*Army*] ... BDTD
Balanced Electrolyte Solution [*Physiology*] ... BES
Balanced Expansion Technique (MCD) ... BET
Balanced Extravehicular Training Aircraft [*NASA*] ... BETA
Balanced File Organization Scheme (MHDI) ... BFS
Balanced Force Requirements Analysis (MCD) ... BALFRAN
Balanced Forearm Orthosis [*Medicine*] ... BFO
Balanced Fund [*Investment term*] ... B
Balanced Half-Sample Replication [*Statistics*] ... BHSR
Balanced in Plane (IEEE) ... BIP
Balanced Income & Growth Fund Trust Units [*Toronto Stock Exchange symbol*] ... BIF
Balanced Incomplete Block [*Statistical design*] ... BIB
Balanced Incomplete Block Design [*Mathematics*] ... BIBD
Balanced Indigenous Population ... BIP
Balanced Inductor Logical Element ... BILE
Balanced Line Driver (MSA) ... BLD
Balanced Line Logical Element ... BLLE
Balanced Line System ... BLS
Balanced Magnetic Amplifier ... BMA
Balanced Nuclear Economy Code (IAA) ... BANEC
Balanced Nutrient Solution ... BNS
Balanced Parametric Amplifier ... BPA
Balanced Pressure Joint ... BPJ
Balanced Pressure Plane Swivel Joint ... BPPSJ
Balanced Pressure Swivel Joint ... BPSJ
Balanced Processing Monitor [*Mitsubishi*] (NITA) ... BPM
Balanced Property Management (ADA) ... BPM
Balanced Property Trust (ADA) ... BPT
Balanced Repeated Replication [*Statistics*] ... BRR
Balanced Resource Allocation Information for Logical Lucid Evaluation (PDAA) ... BRAILLE
Balanced Salt Solution [*Cell incubation medium*] ... BSS
Balanced Swivel Joint ... BSJ
Balanced Tape Drive ... BTD
Balanced Technology Initiative [*DoD*] (RDA) ... BTI
Balanced Technology Institute (AAGC) ... BTI
Balanced, Total [*Business term*] ... BT
Balanced Transformer (IAA) ... BTL
Balanced Valve Regulator ... BVR
Balanced Voltage ... BV
Balanced-Deficit Diet ... BDD
Balanced-Emitter Technology (IAA) ... BET
Balanced-to-Unbalanced Line Transformer [*Telecommunications*] (TEL) ... BALUN
Balanced-Tree [*Technique for organizing indexes*] (CDE) ... B-tree
Balance-of-System [*Power plant efficiency*] ... BOS
Balance-to-Unbalance Network [*Telecommunications*] ... BALUN
Balancing ... BALNCNG
Balancing Network (IAA) ... BALNET
Balancing Network ... BN
Balancing Rheostat ... BALRHEO
Balancing Set (IEEE) ... BALS
Balancing the Budget on the Backs of the Elderly [*Political charge*] ... B^3E
Balancing the Budget on the Backs of the Poor [*Political charge*] ... B^3P
Balancing Transformer (IAA) ... BALTR
Balancing Unit [*Radio*] ... BALUN
Balanitis Xerotica Obliterans (DMAA) ... BXO
Balantidium [*Biochemistry*] (DAVI) ... B
Balao Chico [*Ecuador*] [*ICAO location identifier*] (ICLI) ... SEBH
Balasingham's Notes of Cases [*Ceylon*] [*A publication*] (ILCA) ... Bal Notes
Balasingham's Notes of Cases [*Ceylon*] [*A publication*] (DLA) ... Balas NC
Balasingham's Reports [*Ceylon*] [*A publication*] (DLA) ... Bal
Balasingham's Reports of Cases [*Ceylon*] [*A publication*] (ILCA) ... Bal Rep
Balasingham's Reports of Cases [*1904-09*] [*Ceylon*] [*A publication*] (DLA) ... Balas RC
Balasingham's Reports of Cases [*Ceylon*] [*A publication*] (ILCA) ... Balasingham Rep
Balasingham's Supreme Court Reports [*Ceylon*] [*A publication*] (DLA) ... Balas
Balaton Public Library, Balaton, MN [*Library symbol*] [*Library of Congress*] (LCLS) ... MnBa
Balaton Public Schools, Balaton, MN [*Library symbol*] [*Library of Congress*] (LCLS) ... MnBaPS
Balboa [*Monetary unit*] [*Panama*] ... B
Balboa/Albrook [*Panama*] [*ICAO location identifier*] (ICLI) ... MPLB
Balboa, Canal Zone [*Location identifier FAA*] (FAAL) ... ZLB
Balboa Heights [*Canal Zone*] [*Seismograph station code, US Geological Survey*] (SEIS) ... BHP
Balch Institute [*Philadelphia, PA*] ... BI
Balch Institute Library, Philadelphia, PA [*OCLC symbol*] (OCLC) ... BAI
Balch Institute, Philadelphia, PA [*Library symbol Library of Congress*] (LCLS) ... PPBI
Balch Springs, TX [*AM radio station call letters*] ... KSKY
Balchem Corp. [*Associated Press*] (SAG) ... Balchem
Balchem Corp. [*AMEX symbol*] (SAG) ... BCP
Balco Industries [*Toronto Stock Exchange symbol Vancouver Stock Exchange symbol*] ... BFP
Balcony (WDAA) ... BAL
Balcony [*Classified advertising*] (ADA) ... BALC
Balcor Resources Corp. [*Vancouver Stock Exchange symbol*] ... BAL
Bald Eagle [*District of Columbia*] [*Seismograph station code, US Geological Survey Closed*] (SEIS) ... BED
Bald Eagle Protection Act [*1940*] ... BEPA
Bald Eagle Total Value ... BETV
Bald Knob, AR [*AM radio station call letters*] ... KAPZ
Bald Knob, AR [*FM radio station call letters*] ... KKSY
Bald with Bridgework, Bifocals, Baywindow, and Bunions [*A humorous unofficial Selective Service Class*] ... 5B
Baldachino (VRA) ... baldc
Baldasseroni on Maritime Law [*A publication*] (DLA) ... Bald
Baldasseroni on Maritime Law [*A publication*] (DLA) ... Bald CC
Baldeva Ram Dave. Privy Council Judgment [*India*] [*A publication*] (DLA) ... Bal RD
Baldeva Ram Dave. Privy Council Judgment [*India*] [*A publication*] (DLA) ... Baldev PC
Bald-Headed Men of America (EA) ... BHMA
Baldor Electric [*NYSE symbol*] (SAG) ... BEZ
Baldor Electric [*NYSE symbol*] (TTSB) ... BEZ
Baldor Electric Co. [*Associated Press*] (SAG) ... Baldor
Baldus Bartolinus Novellus [*Deceased, 1490*] [*Authority cited in pre-1607 legal work*] (DSA) ... Bal Novel
Baldus Bartolinus Novellus [*Deceased, 1490*] [*Authority cited in pre-1607 legal work*] (DSA) ... Bald Novell
Baldus (Commentator on the Code) [*A publication*] (DLA) ... Bald
Baldus (Commentator on the Code) [*A publication*] (DLA) ... Bald CC
Baldus de Ubaldis [*Deceased, 1400*] [*Authority cited in pre-1607 legal work*] (DSA) ... B
Baldus de Ubaldis [*Deceased, 1400*] [*Authority cited in pre-1607 legal work*] (DSA) ... Bal
Baldwin & Lyons Cl'A' [*NASDAQ symbol*] (TTSB) ... BWINA
Baldwin & Lyons Cl'B' [*NASDAQ symbol*] (TTSB) ... BWINB
Baldwin & Lyons, Inc. [*Associated Press*] (SAG) ... BaldLy
Baldwin & Lyons, Inc. [*Associated Press*] (SAG) ... BaldLyB
Baldwin & Lyons, Inc. [*Associated Press*] (SAG) ... BaldwLy
Baldwin & Lyons, Inc. [*NASDAQ symbol*] (NQ) ... BWIN
Baldwin. Appendix to 11 Peters [*A publication*] (DLA) ... Bald App 11 Pet
Baldwin City, KS [*FM radio station call letters*] ... KNBU
Baldwin, FL [*FM radio station call letters*] ... WXQL
Baldwin. Law of Bankruptcy [*11th ed.*] [*1915*] [*A publication*] (DLA) ... Bald Bank
Baldwin Locomotive Works, Eddystone, PA [*Library symbol Library of Congress Obsolete*] (LCLS) ... PEddyB
Baldwin on Bankruptcy [*A publication*] (DLA) ... Baldwin
Baldwin Piano [*NASDAQ symbol*] (SAG) ... BPAO
Baldwin Piano & Organ [*NASDAQ symbol*] (TTSB) ... BPAO
Baldwin Piano & Organ Co. [*Associated Press*] (SAG) ... BaldPia
Baldwin Public Library, Baldwin, NY [*Library symbol Library of Congress*] (LCLS) ... NBald
Baldwin Public Library, Birmingham, MI [*Library symbol Library of Congress*] (LCLS) ... MiBir
Baldwin Senior High School, Baldwin, NY [*Library symbol Library of Congress*] (LCLS) ... NBaldSH
Baldwin Technology Corp. [*Associated Press*] (SAG) ... Baldw
Baldwin Technology Corp. [*AMEX symbol*] (SPSG) ... BLD
Baldwin Technology'A' [*AMEX symbol*] (TTSB) ... BLD
Baldwin's Connecticut Digest [*A publication*] (DLA) ... Bald Conn Dig
Baldwin's Connecticut Digest [*A publication*] (DLA) ... Baldw Dig
Baldwin's Kentucky Revised Statutes, Annotated [*A publication*] (DLA) ... KY Rev Stat Ann
Baldwin's Patent, Copyright, Trade-Mark Cases [*A publication*] (DLA) ... Bald Pat Cas
Baldwin's Patent, Copyright, Trade-Mark Cases [*A publication*] (DLA) ... Bald Pat Etc Cas
Baldwin's United States Circuit Court Reports [*A publication*] (DLA) ... Bald
Baldwin's United States Circuit Court Reports [*A publication*] (DLA) ... Bald CC
Baldwin's United States Circuit Court Reports [*A publication*] (DLA) ... Bald Cir C
Baldwin's United States Circuit Court Reports [*A publication*] (DLA) ... Bald Rep
Baldwin's United States Circuit Court Reports [*A publication*] (DLA) ... Baldw
Baldwin's United States Circuit Court Reports [*A publication*] (DLA) ... Baldwin's CC US Rep
Baldwin's United States Circuit Court Reports [*A publication*] (DLA) ... Baldwin's Rep
Baldwin's View of the United States Constitution with Opinions [*A publication*] (DLA) ... Bald Const
Baldwin's View of the United States Constitution with Opinions [*A publication*] (DLA) ... Bald Op
Baldwinsville, NY [*FM radio station call letters*] ... WBXL
Baldwinsville, NY [*AM radio station call letters*] ... WFBL
Baldwinsville, NY [*FM radio station call letters*] ... WSEN
Baldwin-Wallace College [*Berea, OH*] ... BWC

Baldwin-Wallace College, Berea, OH [Library symbol Library of Congress]
(LCLS) .... OBerB
Baldwin-Wallace College, Berea, OH [OCLC symbol] (OCLC) .... OXB
Baldwyn, MS [FM radio station call letters] .... WESE
Baldy Mountain, MB [Television station call letters] .... CBWST
Bale [Shipping] .... B
Bale .... BE
Bale .... BL
Bale [Switzerland ICAO location identifier] (ICLI) .... LSZM
Bale/Mulhouse [France/Switzerland] [ICAO location identifier] (ICLI) .... LFSB
Balearic Islands .... BAL IS
Balearic Islands .... Bal Isls
Balearic Islands .... BI
Balen/Keiheuvel [Belgium ICAO location identifier] (ICLI) .... EBKH
Baler, Aurora Sub-Province [Philippines] [ICAO location identifier] (ICLI) .... RPUR
Bales of Cotton [Shipping] .... B/C
Bales or Rolls [Freight] .... B or R
Balfour Declaration [1917] [For protection of the Jewish settlement of Palestine] (BJA) .... BD
Balfour's Practice Laws of Scotland [A publication] .... Balf
Balfour's Practice Laws of Scotland [A publication] (DLA) .... Balf Pr
Bali [Papua New Guinea] [Airport symbol] (OAG) .... BAJ
Bali [Cameroon] [Airport symbol] (OAG) .... BLC
Bali [Cameroon] [ICAO location identifier] (ICLI) .... FKKG
Bali [Indonesia] [ICAO location identifier] (ICLI) .... WRRZ
Bali International Air Service [Indonesia] [ICAO designator] (FAAC) .... BLN
Bali International/Ngurah Rai [Indonesia] [ICAO location identifier] (ICLI) .... WRRR
Balikesir [Turkey] [Airport symbol] (AD) .... BZI
Balikesir [Turkey ICAO location identifier] (ICLI) .... LTBF
Balikpapan [Indonesia] [Airport symbol] (OAG) .... BPN
Balikpapan/Sepinggan [Indonesia] [ICAO location identifier] (ICLI) .... WRLL
Balimo [Papua New Guinea] [Airport symbol] (OAG) .... OPU
Balkan [ICAO designator] (AD) .... LZ
Balkan Intelligence Centre [British World War II] .... BIC
Balkan Supply Center [Navy] .... BSC
Balkan Turks of America [Later, BTAA] (EA) .... BTA
Balkan Turks of America Association (EA) .... BTAA
Balkan-Bulgarian Airlines [ICAO designator] (FAAC) .... LAZ
Balkan-ji-Bari International [Children's Own Garden International - COGI] (EAIO) .... BjBI
Balks [Baseball] .... BK
Ball .... B
Ball .... BA
Ball and Beatty's Irish Chancery Reports [1807-14] [A publication] (DLA) .... B & B
Ball and Beatty's Irish Chancery Reports [1807-14] [A publication] (ILCA) .... Ba & B
Ball and Beatty's Irish Chancery Reports [1807-14] [A publication] (DLA) .... Ba & Be
Ball and Beatty's Irish Chancery Reports [1807-14] [A publication] (DLA) .... Ball & B
Ball and Beatty's Irish Chancery Reports [1807-14] [A publication] (DLA) .... Ball & B (Ir)
Ball and Beatty's Irish Chancery Reports [1807-14] [A publication] (DLA) .... Ball & Beatty
Ball and Chain [Slang for a wife] .... B & C
Ball and Socket Joint .... BSJ
Ball and Socket Upper Bearing .... BSUB
Ball and Tube [Photography] .... B & T
Ball Bearing [Technical drawings] .... BB
Ball Bearing .... BBRG
Ball Bearing Joint .... BBJ
Ball Bearing Swivel Joint .... BBSJ
Ball Bearing Torque .... BBT
Ball Brothers Research Corp. .... BBRC
Ball Brothers Research Corp., Boulder, CO [Library symbol Library of Congress] (LCLS) .... CoBBRC
Ball Change [Dance terminology] .... BC
Ball Check Valve .... BCV
Ball Corp. [Associated Press] (SAG) .... Ball
Ball Corp. [NYSE symbol] (SPSG) .... BLL
Ball Joint [Automotive engineering] .... B/JNT
Ball Joint Actuator .... BJA
Ball Joint Fitting .... BJF
Ball, LA [AM radio station call letters] .... KWDF
Ball Lightning .... BL
Ball Lock Pin .... BLP
Ball Manufacturers Engineers Committee (EA) .... BMEC
Ball on Back (DAVI) .... BOB
Ball On Cylinder Lubricity Evaluator [Fuels and lubricants testing] .... BOCLE
Ball on National Banks [A publication] (DLA) .... Ball Banks
Ball on National Banks [A publication] (DLA) .... BB
Ball On Three Disk .... BOTD
Ball Reduction Drive .... BRD
Ball Spin Frequency [Machinery] .... BSF
Ball Spinning Friction .... BSF
Ball State Teachers College [Later, Ball State University] [Indiana] .... BSTC
Ball State University (GAGS) .... Ball St U
Ball State University, Muncie, IN [OCLC symbol] (OCLC) .... IBS
Ball State University, Muncie, IN [Library symbol Library of Congress] (LCLS) .... InMuB
Ball Tooth Gear .... BTG
Ball Tooth Gear Joint .... BTGJ
Ball Tooth Joint .... BTJ
[The] Ballad Book [A publication] .... BaBo

Ballantine/Del Rey/Fawcett/Ivy [Publishing group] .... B/DR/F/I
Ballantine. Statute of Limitations [1810] [A publication] (DLA) .... Ball Lim
Ballantyne of Omaha [AMEX symbol] (TTSB) .... BTN
Ballantyne of Omaha, Inc. [Associated Press] (SAG) .... Ballntyn
Ballantyne of Omaha, Inc. [AMEX symbol] (SAG) .... BTN
Ballarat Music Lovers' Club [Australia] .... BMLC
Ballarat Tramway Preservation Society [Australia] .... BTPS
Ballard Community Hospital Library, Seattle, WA [Library symbol] [Library of Congress] .... WaSBH
Ballard Medical Prod [NYSE symbol] (TTSB) .... BMP
Ballard Medical Products [Associated Press] (SAG) .... Ballard
Ballard Medical Products [NYSE symbol] (SPSG) .... BMP
Ballard Power Systems [NASDAQ symbol] (TTSB) .... BLDPF
Ballard Power Systems, Inc. [Associated Press] (SAG) .... Ballard
Ballard Power Systems, Inc. [NASDAQ symbol] (SAG) .... BLDP
Ballard Research, Inc., North Vancouver, BC, Canada [Library symbol Library of Congress] (LCLS) .... CaBNvBR
Ballard Research, Inc., North Vancouver, British Columbia [Library symbol National Library of Canada] (NLC) .... BNVBR
Ballard's Somerton Court Rolls [Oxford Archaeological Society, No. 50] [England] [A publication] (DLA) .... Ball
Ballast (IAA) .... B
Ballast (KSC) .... BALL
Ballast (MSA) .... BLST
Ballast Aerating Retrieval Boom (MCD) .... BARB
Ballast Control Panel .... BCP
Ballast Flood Valve .... BFV
Ballast Lumen Factor (PDAA) .... BLF
Ballast Rack (MCD) .... BR
Ballast Tank Meter .... BTM
Ballast Tube (IAA) .... BALLT
Ballast Tube Resistor .... BTR
Ballastable Earthmoving Sectionalized Tractor [Formerly, UET] [Army] .... BEST
Ballastable Tractor .... BALTRAC
Ballatar Explorations [Vancouver Stock Exchange symbol] .... BLE
Ball-Burton-Hill-Hatch Plan [Senate resolution calling for international cooperation during wartime, named after four senators who introduced plan] B2H2
Balled [Freight] .... BLD
Balled and Burlapped [Plant industry] .... B & B
Ballen Booksellers International, Inc. [UTLAS symbol] .... BII
Ballentine's Law Dictionary [A publication] (DLA) .... Ballentine
Ballentine's Self Pronouncing Law Dictionary [A publication] (DLA) .... Ballentine's Law Dict
Baller .... BLLR
Ballet America Concert Dancers .... BACD
Ballet Contemporani de Barcelona .... BCB
Ballet Intensive from Moscow .... BIM
Ballet Theatre Foundation (EA) .... BTF
Ballet Theatre of Queensland [Australia] .... BTQ
Ballets de San Juan [Puerto Rico] .... BST
Ballett der Deutschen Opera [Berlin] .... BDO
Balletto di Toscana [Florence, Italy] .... BDT
Ballina [Australia Airport symbol] .... BNK
Ballinger Publishing Co. .... B
Ballinger, TX [FM radio station call letters] (RBYB) .... KCSE-FM
Ballinger, TX [AM radio station call letters] .... KRUN
Ballinger, TX [FM radio station call letters] .... KRUN-FM
Ballinger's Annotated Codes and Statutes [Washington] [A publication] (DLA) .... Bal Ann Codes
Ballinger's Annotated Codes and Statutes [Washington] [A publication] (DLA) .... Ballinger's Ann Codes & St
Balliol College [Oxford, England] (BARN) .... Ball
Ballistic .... B
Ballistic [or Ballistics] (MSA) .... BAL
Ballistic (AFM) .... BALL
Ballistic Advanced Missile (MCD) .... BAM
Ballistic Aerial Target System .... BATS
Ballistic Aimpoint [Military] (CAAL) .... BAP
Ballistic Analysis Research System .... BARS
Ballistic and LASER Eye Protection Spectacles [Army] (INF) .... BLEPS
Ballistic and LASER Protective Spectacles [Military] (RDA) .... BLPS
Ballistic Armor Subsystem [Military] (DOMA) .... BASS
Ballistic Attack Game .... BAG
Ballistic Camera .... BC
Ballistic Camera Control (KSC) .... BCC
Ballistic Coefficient .... BC
Ballistic Compressor Computer Code .... BCCC
Ballistic Computer Systems (AAGC) .... BCS
Ballistic Correction of the Moment .... BCM
Ballistic Correction to Normal .... BCN
Ballistic Damage Tolerance (MCD) .... BDT
Ballistic Data Acquisition System (MCD) .... BALDAS
Ballistic Defense Missile .... BDM
Ballistic Density .... BALDNY
Ballistic Environmental Characteristics and Measurement Program [Army] (AABC) .... BECAMP
Ballistic Evaluation Motor (MCD) .... BEM
Ballistic Evaluation Static Test (MCD) .... BEST
Ballistic Flight Test Missile (MCD) .... BFTM
Ballistic Height Correction .... BHC
Ballistic Hull and Turret Vehicle (MCD) .... BH & T
Ballistic LASER Holographic System (MCD) .... BLHS
Ballistic LASER Protection System [Army] (INF) .... BLEPS
Ballistic LORAN Assist Device .... BALLAD

Ballistic Missile (MUGU) .... BALMI

Ballistic Missile (AFM) .... BM

Ballistic Missile Acquisition RADAR .... BMAR

Ballistic Missile Analyst Technician-Specialist .... BMAT/S

Ballistic Missile Bombardment [*or Boost*] **Interceptor** [*Military*] .... BAMBI

Ballistic Missile Branch .... BMB

Ballistic Missile Center [*Air Materiel Command*] [*Obsolete*] .... BMC

Ballistic Missile Center, Air Materiel Command [*Obsolete*] .... BMC/AMC

Ballistic Missile Checkout Equipment Technician-Specialist .... BMCET/S

Ballistic Missile Construction Office .... BMCO

Ballistic Missile Defense .... BMD

Ballistic Missile Defense Advanced Technology Center (AABC) .... BMDATC

Ballistic Missile Defense Center (MCD) .... BMDC

Ballistic Missile Defense Command .... BMDC

Ballistic Missile Defense Command Post (AABC) .... BMDCP

Ballistic Missile Defense Committee .... BMDC

Ballistic Missile Defense Emergency Action Report (AABC) .... BMDEAR

Ballistic Missile Defense Engagement Simulator .... BMDES

Ballistic Missile Defense Integrated Training Plan (AABC) .... BMDITP

Ballistic Missile Defense Master Plan (AABC) .... BMDMP

Ballistic Missile Defense Materials Program Office (MCD) .... BMDMPO

Ballistic Missile Defense Missile Battalion (AABC) .... BMDMB

Ballistic Missile Defense - Nuclear Effects and Threat Committee (AABC) .... BMD-NEAT

Ballistic Missile Defense Operations [*or Organization*] [*or Office*] (AABC) .... BMDO

Ballistic Missile Defense Operations Activity (AABC) .... BMDOA

Ballistic Missile Defense Organization .... BMDO

Ballistic Missile Defense Organization (AAGC) .... BUDO

Ballistic Missile Defense Program Manager (AABC) .... BMDPM

Ballistic Missile Defense Program Office (AABC) .... BMDPO

Ballistic Missile Defense Surveillance Battalion (AABC) .... BMDSB

Ballistic Missile Defense System .... BMDS

Ballistic Missile Defense Systems Command [*Huntsville, AL*] .... BMD

Ballistic Missile Defense Systems Command (AABC) .... BMDSCOM

Ballistic Missile Division [*Ballistic Research Laboratory*] .... BMD

Ballistic Missile Division - Field Office [*Ballistic Research Laboratory*] (SAA) .... BMD-FO

Ballistic Missile Early Warning [*System*] .... BMEW

Ballistic Missile Early Warning System .... BMEWS

Ballistic Missile Inertial Guidance Technician (IAA) .... BMIGT

Ballistic Missile Inertial Guidance Technician-Mechanic .... BMIGT/M

Ballistic Missile Interceptor .... BMI

Ballistic Missile Launch Equipment Technician-Repairman .... BMLET/R

Ballistic Missile Logistics Office .... BMLO

Ballistic Missile Manager .... BMM

Ballistic Missile Office [*Norton Air Force Base, CA*] [*United States Air Force Systems Command*] (GRD) .... BMO

Ballistic Missile Operational Training Readiness .... BMOTR

Ballistic Missile Orientation Course .... BMOC

Ballistic Missile Radiation Analysis Center .... BAMIRAC

Ballistic Missile Reentry System .... BMRS

Ballistic Missile Reentry System (AABC) .... BMRSYS

Ballistic Missile Ship [*Navy*] .... BMS

Ballistic Missile Specification (IAA) .... BMS

Ballistic Missile Submarine [*Navy symbol*] .... SSB

Ballistic Missile Surface Force .... BMSF

Ballistic Missile Systems Command [*Army*] (RDA) .... BMSC

Ballistic Missile Target System (MCD) .... BMTS

Ballistic Missile Terminal Defense .... BMTD

Ballistic Missile Test System (IEEE) .... BMTS

Ballistic Missile Test Vessel .... BMTV

Ballistic Missiles European Task Organization [*Military*] .... BMETO

Ballistic Missiles Weapon System .... BMWS

Ballistic Number (MCD) .... BN

Ballistic Offense Suppressive System [*Military*] .... BOSS

Ballistic Particle Manufacturing [*Desktop manufacturing*] .... BPM

Ballistic Processor [*Military*] (CAAL) .... BP

Ballistic Protected Shelter (MCD) .... BPS

Ballistic Range for Aircraft Survivability Studies (DNAB) .... BRASS

Ballistic Recording System .... BRS

Ballistic Recoverable Booster (MCD) .... BRB

Ballistic Recovery of Orbiting Man (KSC) .... BROOM

Ballistic Reentry Body .... BRB

Ballistic Reentry Vehicle .... BRV

Ballistic Research Laboratories Electronic Scientific Computer .... BRLESC

Ballistic Research Laboratory [*Aberdeen Proving Ground, MD*] [*Army*] .... BRL

Ballistic Rocket Air Suppression .... BRAS

Ballistic Shell .... BS

Ballistic Sight Technology Improving Night/(Day) Gunnery [*Project*] [*Military*] .... BSTING

Ballistic Simulated Round (MCD) .... BSR

Ballistic Systems Division [*Norton Air Force Base, CA*] .... BSD

Ballistic Systems Education Division [*Air University*] [*Air Force*] .... BSED

Ballistic Systems Zeus [*Aerospace*] .... BSZ

Ballistic Test and Evaluation Systems (KSC) .... BATES

Ballistic Test Facility [*Air Research and Development Command*] (AAG) .... BTF

Ballistic Test Site Terminal (MCD) .... BTST

Ballistic Test Submodule (RDA) .... BTSM

Ballistic Track Assignor (AAG) .... BTA

Ballistic Trajectory (DNAB) .... BT

Ballistic Wind .... BALLWIN

Ballistic Wind .... BALWND

Ballistic Wind Plotter .... BWP

Ballistically Launched Aerodynamic Missile .... BLAM

Ballistics Computer Unit .... BCU

Ballistics Dispensing System (MCD) .... BDS

Ballistics Force Integrator and Analyzer System (MCD) .... BFIAS

Ballistocardiogram [*Medicine*] .... BCG

Ball-Jointed [*Body*] [*Doll collecting*] .... bj

Ball-Lock Separation Bolt .... BLSB

Ballon De Servance [*France*] [*Seismograph station code, US Geological Survey*] (SEIS) .... BSF

Ball-on-Cylinder Lubricity Evaluator .... BOCLE

Balloon (AFM) .... BLN

Balloon .... BLN

Balloon Altitude Mosaic Measurements (MCD) .... BAMM

Balloon and Nike Scaled High Explosive Experiment (KSC) .... BANSHEE

Balloon Aortic Valvuloplasty [*Cardiology*] (DAVI) .... BAVP

Balloon Astronomy .... BALAST

Balloon Atmospheric Propagation Experiment [*NASA*] .... BAPE

Balloon Atrial Septostomy [*Cardiology*] (DMAA) .... BAS

Balloon Barrage .... BB

Balloon Barrage Training Center [*Army*] .... BBTC

Balloon Catheter Angioplasty .... BCA

Balloon Command (DAS) .... BC

Balloon Destroyer [*British*] .... BD

Balloon Dilation Angioplasty [*Cardiology*] (DMAA) .... BDA

Balloon Federation of America (EA) .... BFA

Balloon Infrared Astronomy Platform .... BIRAP

Balloon Interrogation Package .... BIP

Balloon Launching Station .... BLS

Balloon Parachute .... BALLUTE

Balloon Platoon of America [*Later, HBC*] (EA) .... BPA

Balloon Post Collectors Club (EA) .... BPCC

Balloon Radio System .... BRS

Balloon Supported Rocket .... BSR

Balloon Temperature and Humidity [*Sonde*] [*Meteorology*] .... BALTHUM

Balloon Transport System .... BTS

Balloon-Assisted Takeoff [*Air Force*] .... BATO

Balloon-Borne Astronomical Studies (MCD) .... BBAS

Balloon-Borne Filter .... BBF

Balloon-Borne Filter Radiometer .... BBFR

Balloon-Borne LASER In-Situ Sensor [*Spectrometer*] .... BLISS

Balloon-Borne Microwave Limb Sounder [*Atmospheric research*] .... BMLS

Balloon-Borne Nephelometer .... BBN

Balloon-Borne Polar Nephelometer .... BBPN

Balloon-Borne Polar Nephelometer .... BPN

Balloon-Borne Radio .... BBR

Balloon-Borne Radio System .... BBRS

Balloon-Borne Solar Pointer .... BBSP

Balloon-Borne Ultraviolet Stellar Spectrometer .... BUSS

Balloon-Launched Decelerator Test [*Air Force*] .... BLDT

Ball-Pass Frequency, Inner Race [*Machinery*] .... BPF(I)

Ball-Pass Frequency, Outer Race [*Machinery*] .... BPF(O)

Ballroom .... BLLRM

Ballroom Dancers Federation [*British*] (DBA) .... BDF

Ball's Digest of the Common Law [*A publication*] (DLA) .... Ball Dig

Ball's Index to Irish Statutes [*A publication*] (DLA) .... Ball Ind

Ball's Popular Conveyancer [*A publication*] (DLA) .... Ball Conv

Ball's Student Guide to the Bar [*A publication*] (DLA) .... Ball St Guide

Ballston Spa, NY [*FM radio station call letters*] (RBYB) .... WXCR-FM

Ballston Spa, NY [*FM radio station call letters*] .... WZRQ

Ballstop (MSA) .... BSP

Ballwin, MO [*FM radio station call letters*] .... KYMC

Bally Entertainment [*NYSE symbol*] (TTSB) .... BLY

Bally Entertainment Corp. [*Formerly, Bally Manufacturing*] [*Associated Press*] (SAG) .... BallyEnt

Bally Entertainment Corp. [*Formerly, Bally Manufacturing*] [*NYSE symbol*] (SAG) .... BLY

Bally Entertain't8.00%'PRIDES' [*NYSE symbol*] (TTSB) .... BLYPrP

Bally Gaming International [*NASDAQ symbol*] (SPSG) .... BGII

Bally Gaming International Corp. [*Associated Press*] (SAG) .... BalyGm

Bally Gaming Intl. [*NASDAQ symbol*] (TTSB) .... BGII

Bally Total Fitness Holding [*NASDAQ symbol*] (TTSB) .... BFIT

Bally Total Fitness Holding Corp. [*Associated Press*] (SAG) .... BallyTot

Bally Total Fitness Holding Corp. [*NASDAQ symbol*] (SAG) .... BFIT

Ballykelly [*British ICAO location identifier*] (ICLI) .... EGQB

Bally's Grand [*NASDAQ symbol*] (TTSB) .... BGLV

Ballys Grand, Inc. [*Associated Press*] (SAG) .... Ballys

Ballys Grand, Inc. [*Associated Press*] (SAG) .... BallysGr

Ballys Grand, Inc. [*NASDAQ symbol*] (SAG) .... BGLV

Ballys Grand Wrrt [*NASDAQ symbol*] (TTSB) .... BGLVW

Balmaceda [*Chile*] [*Airport symbol*] (OAG) .... BBA

Balmaceda/Balmaceda [*Chile*] [*ICAO location identifier*] (ICLI) .... SCBA

Balmertown Public Library, Ontario [*Library symbol National Library of Canada*] (NLC) .... OBAL

Balmoral Shoe [*Orthosis*] .... Bal

Balneum [*Bath*] [*Medicine*] .... B

Balneum [*Bath*] [*Medicine*] (ROG) .... BALN

Balneum Arenae [*Sand Bath*] [*Medicine*] .... BA

Balneum Arenae [*Sand Bath*] [*Medicine*] .... BAL ARENAE

Balneum Calidum [*Warm Bath*] [*Medicine*] (ROG) .... BALN CAL

Balneum Mariae [*Salt-Water Bath*] [*Medicine*] .... BAL MAR

Balneum Marinum [*Sea-Water Bath*] [*Medicine*] .... BM

Balneum Vaporis [*Vapor Bath*] [*Medicine*] .... BAL VAP

Balneum Vaporis [*Vapor Bath*] [*Medicine*] .... BV

Balopticon (IEEE) .... BALOP

Balopticon [*An opaque projector*] (WDMC) .... balop

Balsa Wood (VRA) .... bal wd

Balsam Lake, WI [*FM radio station call letters*] (RBYB) .... WWLC-FM

Balsam Resources, Inc. [*Vancouver Stock Exchange symbol*] ... BSM
Balsam School, Bovey, MN [*Library symbol*] [*Library of Congress*] (LCLS) ... MnBovS
Balsamic [*Mild, Healing*] [*Medicine*] (ROG) ... BAL
Balsamum [*Balsam*] [*Pharmacy*] ... BALS
Balsas [*Brazil*] [*Airport symbol*] (AD) ... BSS
Baltek Corp. [*Associated Press*] (SAG) ... Baltek
Baltek Corp. [*NASDAQ symbol*] (NQ) ... BTEK
Balthazar Scales of Adaptive Behavior [*Psychology*] ... BSAB
Baltia Air Lines, Inc. [*ICAO designator*] (FAAC) ... BTL
Baltic [*MARC language code Library of Congress*] (LCCP) ... bat
Baltic Airlines Ltd. [*ICAO designator*] (FAAC) ... HOT
Baltic American Freedom League (EA) ... BAFL
Baltic and Bothnian Echoes from the Lithosphere [*Collaborative seismic project*] [*Britain, Denmark, Finland, Germany, and Sweden*] ... BABEL
[*The*] **Baltic and International Maritime Conference** ... BIMC
Baltic and International Maritime Conference [*or Council*] [*Copenhagen, Denmark*] (EAIO) ... BIMCO
Baltic Aviation, Inc. [*ICAO designator*] (FAAC) ... BLT
Baltic Bankers Ltd. [*Finland*] ... BBL
Baltic Council of Victoria [*Australia*] ... BCV
Baltic Freight Index [*of spot market rates*] [*Shipping*] (DS) ... BFI
Baltic International Airlines [*Latvia*] [*ICAO designator*] (FAAC) ... BIA
Baltic International Freight Futures Exchange [*London, England*] ... BIFFEX
Baltic International USA, Inc. [*Associated Press*] (SAG) ... Baltic
Baltic International USA, Inc. [*Associated Press*] (SAG) ... BalticInt
Baltic International USA, Inc. [*NASDAQ symbol*] (SAG) ... BISA
Baltic Intl. USA [*NASDAQ symbol*] (TTSB) ... BISA
Baltic Intl USA Wrrt [*NASDAQ symbol*] (TTSB) ... BISAW
Baltic Marine Environment Protection Commission - Helsinki Commission (EAIO) ... HELCOM
Baltic Open Sea Experiment (GNE) ... BOSEX
Baltic Research Foundation [*Australia*] (EAIO) ... BRF
Baltic States [*MARC geographic area code Library of Congress*] (LCCP) ... eb----
Baltic Steamship Co. (MHDB) ... BSC
Baltic Student Federation ... BSF
Baltic Women's Council (EA) ... BWC
Baltic World Council [*Defunct*] (EA) ... BWC
Baltimore [*Diocesan abbreviation*] [*Maryland*] (TOCD) ... BAL
Baltimore [*Maryland*] ... BALT
Baltimore [*Maryland*] ... BALTO
Baltimore [*Maryland*] [*Name derived from Baltimore-Washington International Airport*] [*Airport symbol*] ... BWI
Baltimore & Annapolis Railroad Co. (IIA) ... B & A
[*The*] **Baltimore & Annapolis Railroad Co.** [*AAR code*] ... BLA
Baltimore & Eastern Railroad Co. [*Absorbed into Consolidated Rail Corp.*] [*AAR code*] ... BE
[*The*] **Baltimore & Ohio Chicago Terminal Railroad Co.** ... B & OCT
[*The*] **Baltimore & Ohio Chicago Terminal Railroad Co.** [*AAR code*] ... BOCT
[*The*] **Baltimore & Ohio Railroad Co.** [*Chessie System, Inc.*] ... B & O
[*The*] **Baltimore & Ohio Railroad Co.** [*Chessie System, Inc.*] ... B & O RR
[*The*] **Baltimore & Ohio Railroad Co., Employees' Library, Baltimore, MD** [*Library symbol Library of Congress Obsolete*] (LCLS) ... MdBBO
Baltimore & Ohio Railroad Historical Society (EA) ... B & ORHS
Baltimore/Baltimore-Washington International [*Maryland*] [*ICAO location identifier*] (ICLI) ... KBWI
Baltimore Bar Library, Baltimore, MD [*Library symbol Library of Congress*] (LCLS) ... MdBB
Baltimore Biological Laboratory ... BBL
Baltimore City Court House, Baltimore, MD [*Library symbol Library of Congress*] (LCLS) ... MdBCH
Baltimore City Hospitals, Doctors' Library, Baltimore, MD [*Library symbol Library of Congress*] (LCLS) ... MdBH
Baltimore City Reports [*A publication*] (DLA) ... Balt C Rep
Baltimore City Reports [*A publication*] (DLA) ... BR
Baltimore College of Commerce [*Maryland*] ... BCC
Baltimore Conference, Inc., United Methodist Historical Society, Baltimore, MD [*Library symbol Library of Congress*] (LCLS) ... MdBBC
Baltimore County Public Library, Towson, MD [*Library symbol Library of Congress*] (LCLS) ... MdBCP
Baltimore Gas & El [*NYSE symbol*] (TTSB) ... BGE
Baltimore Gas & Electric Co. [*Associated Press*] (SAG) ... BaltGE
Baltimore Gas & Electric Co. [*NYSE symbol*] (SPSG) ... BGE
Baltimore Gas & Electric Co. [*Associated Press*] (SAG) ... BltGE
Baltimore Hebrew College (BJA) ... BHC
Baltimore Hebrew College, Baltimore, MD [*Library symbol Library of Congress*] (LCLS) ... MdBHC
Baltimore Huntington's Disease Project [*Johns Hopkins University*] [*Research center*] (RCD) ... BHDP
Baltimore Junior College [*Maryland*] ... BJC
Baltimore Law Transcript [*A publication*] (DLA) ... Balt L Tr
Baltimore Law Transcript [*A publication*] (DLA) ... Balt LT
Baltimore Law Transcript [*A publication*] (DLA) ... BLT
Baltimore Longitudinal Study of Aging [*Department of Health and Human Services*] (GFGA) ... BLSA
Baltimore, Maryland, and Ohio ... BM & O
Baltimore, MD [*Location identifier FAA*] (FAAL) ... FND
Baltimore, MD [*Location identifier FAA*] (FAAL) ... IUB
Baltimore, MD [*Location identifier FAA*] (FAAL) ... MDV
Baltimore, MD [*Location identifier FAA*] (FAAL) ... MTN
Baltimore, MD [*Location identifier FAA*] (FAAL) ... OEH
Baltimore, MD [*Location identifier FAA*] (FAAL) ... RUX
Baltimore, MD [*AM radio station call letters*] ... WBAL
Baltimore, MD [*Television station call letters*] ... WBAL-TV
Baltimore, MD [*Television station call letters*] ... WBFF
Baltimore, MD [*AM radio station call letters*] ... WBGR
Baltimore, MD [*FM radio station call letters*] ... WBJC
Baltimore, MD [*AM radio station call letters*] ... WBMD
Baltimore, MD [*FM radio station call letters*] ... WBYQ
Baltimore, MD [*AM radio station call letters*] ... WCAO
Baltimore, MD [*AM radio station call letters*] ... WCBM
Baltimore, MD [*FM radio station call letters*] ... WEAA
Baltimore, MD [*FM radio station call letters*] ... WERQ
Baltimore, MD [*Television station call letters*] ... WHSW
Baltimore, MD [*AM radio station call letters*] ... WITH
Baltimore, MD [*FM radio station call letters*] ... WIYY
Baltimore, MD [*AM radio station call letters*] ... WJFK
Baltimore, MD [*FM radio station call letters*] ... WJHU
Baltimore, MD [*Television station call letters*] ... WJZ
Baltimore, MD [*FM radio station call letters*] ... WLIF
Baltimore, MD [*Television station call letters*] ... WMAR
Baltimore, MD [*Television station call letters*] ... WMPB
Baltimore, MD [*Television station call letters*] ... WNUV
Baltimore, MD [*FM radio station call letters*] ... WOCT
Baltimore, MD [*AM radio station call letters*] ... WOLB
Baltimore, MD [*FM radio station call letters*] ... WPOC
Baltimore, MD [*FM radio station call letters*] ... WRBS
Baltimore, MD [*AM radio station call letters*] ... WWIN
Baltimore, MD [*AM radio station call letters*] ... WWLG
Baltimore, MD [*FM radio station call letters*] ... WWMX
Baltimore, MD [*FM radio station call letters*] ... WXYV
Baltimore Museum of Art, Baltimore, MD [*Library symbol Library of Congress*] (LCLS) ... MdBMA
Baltimore, Ohio & Southwestern Railway ... BO & SW
Baltimore Photo & Blue Print Co., Baltimore, MD [*Library symbol Library of Congress*] (LCLS) ... BPB
Baltimore Publishers Association (EA) ... BPA
Baltimore Regional Planning Commission [*Library network*] ... RPC
Baltimore Steam Packet Co. [*AAR code*] ... BSP
Baltimore Vegetarians [*Later, VRG*] (EA) ... BV
Baltischer Weltrat [*Baltic World Council*] (EAIO) ... BW
Baluchi [*MARC language code Library of Congress*] (LCCP) ... bal
Baluchi Students' Organization [*Pakistan*] (PD) ... BSO
Baluchistan Liberation Front [*Pakistan*] [*Political party*] (PD) ... BLF
Baluchistan, Pakistan (ILCA) ... Bal Pak
Balurghat [*India*] [*ICAO location identifier*] (ICLI) ... VEBG
Balustrade (VRA) ... balstr
Balzac Deflection Door ... BDD
Balzers/FL [*Switzerland ICAO location identifier*] (ICLI) ... LSXB
Bam [*Iran*] [*ICAO location identifier*] (ICLI) ... OIKM
Bama Band Fan Club (EA) ... BBFC
Bamaga [*Australia Airport symbol*] (OAG) ... ABM
Bamako [*Mali*] [*Airport symbol*] (OAG) ... BKO
Bamako [*Mali*] [*ICAO location identifier*] (ICLI) ... GABV
Bamako/Senou [*Mali*] [*ICAO location identifier*] (ICLI) ... GABS
Bamar [*Afghanistan*] [*ICAO location identifier*] (ICLI) ... OABR
Bambadinca [*Guinea-Bissau*] [*ICAO location identifier*] (ICLI) ... GGBB
Bambara [*MARC language code Library of Congress*] (LCCP) ... bam
Bambari [*Central African Republic*] [*ICAO location identifier*] (ICLI) ... FEFM
Bamberg [*Germany ICAO location identifier*] (ICLI) ... EDEJ
Bamberg, SC [*FM radio station call letters*] ... WWBD
Bamberg-Denmark, SC [*AM radio station call letters*] ... WRIT
Bambili-Dingila [*Zaire*] [*ICAO location identifier*] (ICLI) ... FZKB
Bamboo Mosaic Virus [*Plant pathology*] ... BAMV
Bamburi [*Kenya*] [*Airport symbol Obsolete*] (OAG) ... BMQ
Bamenda [*Cameroon*] [*ICAO location identifier*] (ICLI) ... FKKV
Bamfield Marine Station, Bamfield, British Columbia [*Library symbol National Library of Canada*] (BIB) ... BBAM
Bamian [*Afghanistan*] [*Airport symbol Obsolete*] (OAG) ... BIN
Bampoor [*Iran*] [*ICAO location identifier*] (ICLI) ... OIZP
Bampton [*England*] ... BAMP
Bamu [*Papua New Guinea*] [*Airport symbol*] (OAG) ... BMZ
Bamyan [*Afghanistan*] [*ICAO location identifier*] (ICLI) ... OABN
Ban (WGA) ... B
Ban Houei Sai [*Laos*] [*Airport symbol*] (AD) ... OUI
Ban the Soviets Coalition (EA) ... BTSC
Ban Unsafe Schoolbuses Which Regularly Endanger Children [*Student legal action organization*] ... BUSWREC
Banak [*Norway ICAO location identifier*] (ICLI) ... ENNA
Banana Growers' Federation Cooperative [*Australia*] ... BGFC
Banana Industry Committee [*New South Wales, Australia*] ... BIC
Banana Industry Protection Board [*Australia*] ... BIPB
Banana Plug Resistor ... BPR
Banana, Rice Cereal, Apple Sauce, and Tea [*Diet*] (DAVI) ... BRAT
Banana River Repeater Station [*NASA*] (KSC) ... BRRS
Bananas, Rice, Apple Sauce, Tea, and Toast [*Diet*] (DAVI) ... BRATT
Bananas, Rice Cereal, Applesauce, and Toast [*Bland diet*] [*Medicine*] ... BRAT
Bananera [*Guatemala*] [*ICAO location identifier*] (ICLI) ... MGBN
Banankoro/Gbenko [*Guinea*] [*ICAO location identifier*] (ICLI) ... GUGO
Banaras Law Journal [*India*] [*A publication*] (DLA) ... Ban LJ
Banaras Law Journal [*India*] [*A publication*] (DLA) ... Banaras LJ
Banat Air Service Ltd. [*Romania*] [*FAA designator*] (FAAC) ... BAT
Banbury [*British depot code*] ... BAN
Banbury. English Exchequer Reports [*145 English Reprint*] [*A publication*] (DLA) ... Banbury (Eng)
Banbury Gold Mines [*Vancouver Stock Exchange symbol*] ... BBG
Banc Cymru [*Bank of Wales*] ... BC
Banc One $3.50 Cv Pfd [*NASDAQ symbol*] (TTSB) ... BONEO
Banc One Corp. [*Associated Press*] (SAG) ... BancOne
Banc One Corp. [*Associated Press*] (SAG) ... BcOne

Banc One Corp. [*NASDAQ symbol*] (SAG) ... BONE
Banc One Corp. [*NYSE symbol*] (SPSG) ... ONE
Banc Texas Group [*Associated Press*] (SAG) ... BanTex
Banca, Borsa, e Titoli di Credito [*A publication*] (ILCA) ... Banca Borsa Tit Cred
Banca Brignone [*Italy*] ... BB
Banca Commerciale Italiana [*Italy*] ... BCI
Banca del Gottardo [*Gotthard Bank*] [*Switzerland*] ... BG
Banca della Svizzera Italiana [*Swiss-Italian Bank*] [*Switzerland*] ... BSI
Banca Europea degli Investimenti [*European Investment Bank - EIB*] [*Italian*] ... BEI
Banca Internationala de Investitii [*International Investment Bank*] ... BII
Banca Mondiale [*World Bank*] [*Italian*] ... BM
Banca Nazionale del Lavoro [*National Bank of Labor*] [*Italy*] (ECON) ... BNL
Banca Nazionale dell'Agricoltura [*National Bank of Agriculture*] [*Italy*] (ECON) ... BNA
Banca QuadruADS [*NASDAQ symbol*] (TTSB) ... QDRMY
Banca Quadrum SA [*Associated Press*] (SAG) ... BncQuad
Banca Quadrum SA [*NASDAQ symbol*] (SAG) ... QDRM
BancFirst Corp. [*NASDAQ symbol*] (TTSB) ... BANF
BancFirst Corp. Oklahoma [*NASDAQ symbol*] (SAG) ... BANF
BancFirst Corp. Oklahoma [*Associated Press*] (SAG) ... BncFstOK
Bancfirst Ohio Corp. [*NASDAQ symbol*] (SAG) ... BFOH
Bancfirst Ohio Corp. [*Associated Press*] (SAG) ... BncfstOH
Bancinsurance Corp. [*Associated Press*] (SAG) ... Bancins
Bancinsurance Corp. [*NASDAQ symbol*] (SAG) ... BCIS
Banco Amazonas [*Amazon Bank*] [*Ecuador*] ... BA
Banco BHIF [*NYSE symbol*] (SAG) ... BB
Banco BHIF [*Associated Press*] (SAG) ... BcoBHIF
Banco Bilbao Vizcaya (ECON) ... BBV
Banco Bilbao Vizcaya [*NYSE symbol*] (SPSG) ... BVG
Banco Bilbao Vizcaya 9% ADS [*NYSE symbol*] (TTSB) ... BVGPrB
Banco Bilbao Vizcaya ADS [*NYSE symbol*] (TTSB) ... BBV
Banco Bilbao Vizcaya International [*Associated Press*] (SAG) ... BncBil
Banco Bilbao Vizcaya International [*Associated Press*] (SAG) ... BncBl
Banco Bilbao Vizcaya SA [*NYSE symbol*] (CTT) ... BBV
Banco Bilbao Vizcaya SA [*Associated Press*] (SAG) ... BcBilV
Banco Cent Hispanoamer ADS [*NYSE symbol*] (TTSB) ... BCH
Banco Central [*Toronto Stock Exchange symbol*] ... BCY
Banco Central Hispanoamericano [*NYSE symbol*] (SAG) ... BCH
Banco Central Hispanoamericano SA [*Associated Press*] ... BncCtrl
Banco Centroamericano de Integracion Economica [*Central American Bank for Economic Integration*] [*Spanish*] (BARN) ... BCIE
Banco Comercial de Mocambique ... BCM
Banco Comercial Portugues [*Portuguese Commercial Bank*] (ECON) ... BCP
Banco Comercial Portugues [*NYSE symbol*] (SPSG) ... BPC
Banco Comercial Portugues SA [*Associated Press*] (SAG) ... BnCPort
Banco Coml Portugues ADS [*NYSE symbol*] (TTSB) ... BPC
Banco de A. Edwards [*Associated Press*] (SAG) ... BcoAEdw
Banco de A Edwards ADS [*NYSE symbol*] (TTSB) ... AED
Banco de Bilbao [*Italian*] ... BB
Banco de Bilbao [*Spain*] ... BB
Banco de Cabo Verde [*Bank of Cape Verde*] (EY) ... BCV
Banco de Credito Nacional SA [*Private bank*] [*Brazil*] (EY) ... BCN
Banco de Desenvolvimento de Minas Gerais SA [*Brazil*] (EY) ... BDMG
Banco de Desenvolvimento do Estado de Sao Paulo SA [*Brazil*] (EY) ... BADESP
Banco de Galicia y Buenos Aires [*NASDAQ symbol*] (SAG) ... BGAL
Banco de Galicia y Buenos Aires [*Commercial firm Associated Press*] (SAG) ... BncGalic
Banco de Galicia-Buenos Aires [*NASDAQ symbol*] (TTSB) ... BGALY
Banco de la Nacion [*National Bank*] [*Peru*] ... BN
Banco de la Nacion Argentina [*National Bank of Argentina*] ... BNA
Banco de Latinoamerica, SA [*Panama*] (EY) ... BANCOLAT
Banco de Mexico [*ICAO designator*] (FAAC) ... BMX
Banco de Santander SA [*NYSE symbol*] (SPSG) ... STD
Banco de Santander Sociedad Anonima de Credito [*Associated Press*] ... BnSant
Banco De Santiago [*Associated Press*] (SAG) ... BcoSanti
Banco De Santiago [*NYSE symbol*] (SAG) ... SAN
Banco di Napoli [*Italy*] ... BDN
Banco di Sicilia [*Italy*] ... BdS
Banco do Estado do Rio de Janiero SA [*Brazil*] (EY) ... BANERJ
Banco Espanol de Credito [*Spain*] (ECON) ... BANESTO
Banco Europeo de Inversion [*European Investment Bank - EIB*] [*Spanish*] ... BEI
Banco Europeu para a America Latina [*Bank*] [*Portuguese*] (EY) ... BEAL
Banco Fonsecas & Burnay [*Fonsecas & Burnay Bank*] [*Portugal*] ... BFB
Banco Frances del Rio ADS [*NYSE symbol*] (TTSB) ... BFR
Banco Frances del Rio La Plata [*NYSE symbol*] (SAG) ... BFR
Banco Frances del Rio La Plata [*Associated Press*] (SAG) ... BncoFrn
Banco Ganadero [*NYSE symbol*] (SAG) ... BGA
Banco Ganadero [*Associated Press*] (SAG) ... BGanadro
Banco Ganadero [*Associated Press*] (SAG) ... BGandro
Banco Ganadero [*Associated Press*] (SAG) ... BGndo
Banco Ganadero ADS [*NYSE symbol*] (TTSB) ... BGA
Banco Ganadero 'C'Pref ADS [*NYSE symbol*] (TTSB) ... BGAPr
Banco Hipotecario de la Construccion SA [*The Dominican Republic*] (EY) ... BANHICO
Banco Holandes Unido [*Dutch Union Bank*] [*Ecuador*] ... BHU
Banco Indl Colombiano Pref ADS [*NYSE symbol*] (TTSB) ... CIB
Banco Industrial Columbiano SA [*Associated Press*] (SAG) ... BcoIndl
Banco Industrial Columbiano SA [*NYSE symbol*] (SAG) ... CIB
Banco Industrial del Mediterraneo [*Industrial Bank of the Mediterranean*] [*Spain*] ... BIM
Banco Inmobilario [*Nicaragua*] (EY) ... BIN
Banco Interamericano de Desarrollo [*Inter-American Development Bank*] [*Spanish*] ... BID
Banco Internacional [*International Bank*] [*Ecuador*] ... BI
Banco Internacional de Reconstruccion y Fomento [*International Bank for Reconstruction and Development; also known as World Bank*] [*Spanish*] ... BIRF
Banco Latinamericano de Exportaciones [*Associated Press*] (SAG) ... BcLatn
Banco Latinoamer de Export'E' [*NYSE symbol*] (TTSB) ... BLX
Banco Latinoamericano de Export 'E' [*NYSE symbol*] (SPSG) ... BLX
Banco Mundial [*World Bank*] [*Spanish*] ... BM
Banco Nacional de Angola [*National Bank of Angola*] ... BNA
Banco Nacional de Desarrollo [*National Development Bank*] [*Argentina*] ... BND
Banco Nacional de Mexico [*National Bank of Mexico*] ... Banamex
Banco Nacional de Trabajadores [*Paraguay*] (EY) ... BNT
Banco Nacional do Desenvolvimento Economico [*National Economic Development Bank*] [*Brazil*] ... BNDE
Banco OHiggins [*Associated Press*] (SAG) ... BcOHig
Banco OHiggins [*NYSE symbol*] (SAG) ... OHG
Banco O'Higgins ADS [*NYSE symbol*] (TTSB) ... OHG
Banco Osorno y La Union [*Associated Press*] (SAG) ... BcOsorno
Banco Osorno y La UnionADS [*NYSE symbol*] (TTSB) ... BOU
Banco Panamericano [*Panama*] (EY) ... PANABANK
Banco Popular de Desenvolvimento ... BPD
Banco Portugues do Atlantico [*Portuguese Bank of the Atlantic*] (ECON) ... BPA
Banco Portugues do Investimento [*Portuguese Investment Bank*] ... BPI
Banco Regis [*or Reginae*] [*The King's (or Queen's) Bench*] [*Latin*] ... BR
Banco Resources Ltd. [*Vancouver Stock Exchange symbol*] ... BAR
Banco Santander ADS [*NYSE symbol*] (TTSB) ... STD
Banco Santander Chile [*Associated Press*] (SAG) ... BcSantCh
Banco Santander Chile [*NYSE symbol*] (SAG) ... BSB
Banco Wiese ADS [*NYSE symbol*] (TTSB) ... BWP
Banco Wiese Limitado [*Associated Press*] (SAG) ... BcoWiese
Banco Wiese Limitado [*NYSE symbol*] (SAG) ... BWP
BancoBilbaoVizcaya8.00%ADS [*NYSE symbol*] (TTSB) ... BVGPrC
BancoBilbaoVizcaya9.75% ADS [*NYSE symbol*] (TTSB) ... BVGPr
Bancode A Edwards [*NYSE symbol*] (SAG) ... AED
Bancode A Edwards [*Associated Press*] (SAG) ... BcoAEd
Bancorp Connecticut [*NASDAQ symbol*] (TTSB) ... BKCT
Bancorp Connecticut, Inc. [*NASDAQ symbol*] (SAG) ... BKCT
Bancorp Connecticut, Inc. [*Associated Press*] (SAG) ... Bncp CT
Bancorp Hawaii [*NYSE symbol*] (TTSB) ... BOH
Bancorp Hawaii, Inc. [*Associated Press*] (SAG) ... BcpHaw
Bancorp Hawaii, Inc. [*Associated Press*] (SAG) ... BcpHw
Bancorp Hawaii, Inc. [*NYSE symbol*] (SPSG) ... BOH
Bancorp South, Inc. [*Associated Press*] (SAG) ... BcpSou
Bancorp South, Inc. [*NASDAQ symbol*] (SAG) ... BOMS
BancorpSouth [*NASDAQ symbol*] (TTSB) ... BOMS
Bancroft, Avery & McAlister, San Francisco, CA [*Library symbol*] [*Library of Congress*] (LCLS) ... CSFBA
Bancroft Convertible Fd [*AMEX symbol*] (TTSB) ... BCV
Bancroft Convertible Fund, Inc. [*Associated Press*] (SAG) ... BanFd
Bancroft Convertible Fund, Inc. [*AMEX symbol*] (SPSG) ... BCV
Bancroft, ON [*Television station call letters*] ... CIII-2
Bancroft, ON [*AM radio station call letters*] ... CJNH
Bancroft Public Library, Bancroft, ON, Canada [*Library symbol Library of Congress*] (LCLS) ... CaOBan
Bancroft Public Library, Ontario [*Library symbol National Library of Canada*] (NLC) ... OBAN
Bancroft Public Library, Salem, NY [*Library symbol Library of Congress*] (LCLS) ... NSa
Bancroft Register, Bancroft, IA [*Library symbol Library of Congress*] (LCLS) ... IaBanR
Bancshare Portfolio Corp. [*Toronto Stock Exchange symbol*] ... XBP
Banctec, Inc. [*Associated Press*] (SAG) ... Banctec
Banctec, Inc. [*NYSE symbol*] (SAG) ... BTC
BancTec, Inc. [*NASDAQ symbol*] (NQ) ... BTEC
BancTec,Inc. [*NYSE symbol*] (TTSB) ... BTC
Banctexas Group, Inc. [*NYSE symbol*] (SPSG) ... BTX
Bancus [*Common Bench*] [*Legal*] [*British*] (ROG) ... B
Bancus Superior [*King's Bench*] [*British Legal term*] (ROG) ... BANC SUP
Bancus Superior [*King's Bench*] [*British Legal term*] (DLA) ... BS
Band ... B
Band [*Volume*] [*German*] ... BD
Band (KSC) ... BD
Band (KSC) ... BND
Band Amplitude Product ... BAP
Band and Orchestra [*Musical slang*] ... B & O
[*The*] **Band Appreciation Society** (EAIO) ... TBAS
Band Approximation Method (MCD) ... BAM
Band Archive Management Service (IAA) ... BAMS
Band Colour Sergeant [*British military*] (DMA) ... Bd/CSgt
Band Corporal ... BC
Band Corporal [*British military*] (DMA) ... Bd/Cpl
Band Display ... BNDDIS
Band Edge Energy ... BEE
Band Elimination ... BE
Band Elimination Filter ... BEF
Band Filter Cutoff (MSA) ... BFCO
Band Filter Set ... BFS
Band Ignitor Tube ... BIT
Band Limiting Filter [*Electronics*] (OA) ... BLF
Band of Hope [*British*] ... B of H
Band of Hope [*British*] (DAS) ... BOH
Band Pressure Level ... BPL
Band Reject (IAA) ... BR
Band Sergeant [*British military*] (DMA) ... Bd/Sgt
Band Setting (IAA) ... BS
Band System (IAA) ... BS

Band Training and Advisory Services Branch [*Canada, Indian and Inuit Affairs Program*] [*Canada*] .... BTAS
Banda [*Indonesia*] [*ICAO location identifier*] (ICLI) .... WAPC
Banda Aceh [*Indonesia*] [*Airport symbol*] (OAG) .... BTJ
Banda Aceh/Blangbintang [*Indonesia*] [*ICAO location identifier*] (ICLI) .... WITT
Banda Aceh/Maimun Saleh [*Indonesia*] [*ICAO location identifier*] (ICLI) .... WIAB
Banda Atjeh [*Indonesia*] [*Airport symbol*] (AD) .... BTJ
Bandag, Inc. [*Associated Press Associated Press*] (SAG) .... Bandag
Bandag, Inc. [*Associated Press*] (SAG) .... Bandg
Bandag, Inc. [*NYSE symbol*] (SPSG) .... BDG
Bandag Inc.'A' [*NYSE symbol*] (TTSB) .... BDG A
Bandanaira [*Indonesia*] [*Airport symbol*] (OAG) .... NDA
Bandar Abbas [*Iran*] [*Airport symbol*] (OAG) .... BND
Bandar Abbas [*Iran*] [*ICAO location identifier*] (ICLI) .... OIKB
Bandar Anzali [*Iran*] [*ICAO location identifier*] (ICLI) .... OIGP
Bandar Deylam [*Iran*] [*ICAO location identifier*] (ICLI) .... OIBD
Bandar Khamir [*Iran*] [*ICAO location identifier*] (ICLI) .... OIKI
Bandar Lampung [*Indonesia*] [*Airport symbol*] (OAG) .... TKG
Bandar Lengeh [*Iran*] [*Airport symbol*] (OAG) .... BDH
Bandar Lengeh [*Iran*] [*ICAO location identifier*] (ICLI) .... OIBL
Bandar Mahshahr [*Iran*] [*ICAO location identifier*] (ICLI) .... OIAM
Bandar Seri Begawan [*Brunei*] [*Airport symbol*] (OAG) .... BWN
Bandar Torkaman [*Iran*] [*ICAO location identifier*] (ICLI) .... OINY
Bandblock (IAA) .... BB
Bande Dessinee [*Comic strip*] [*French*] .... BD
Banded Iron Formation [*Geology*] .... BIF
Banded Two Sides and One End [*Lumber*] (DAC) B2S1E
Bandeirante [*Airplane code*] .... Emb
Bandelier National Monument .... BAND
Bandera, TX [*FM radio station call letters*] .... KEEP
B&H Maritime Carriers [*AMEX symbol*] (TTSB) .... BHM
B&H Ocean Carriers [*AMEX symbol*] (TTSB) .... BHO
Bandiagara [*Mali*] [*ICAO location identifier*] (ICLI) .... GABD
Bandinus Familiatus de Pisa [*Deceased, 1218*] [*Authority cited in pre-1607 legal work*] (DSA) .... Ba
Bandinus Familiatus de Pisa [*Deceased, 1218*] [*Authority cited in pre-1607 legal work*] (DSA) .... Ban
Bandinus Familiatus de Pisa [*Deceased, 1218*] [*Authority cited in pre-1607 legal work*] (DSA) .... Band
Bandirma [*Turkey ICAO location identifier*] (ICLI) .... LTBG
Bandkamalkhan [*Afghanistan*] [*ICAO location identifier*] (ICLI) .... OABK
Band-Limited Hiss [*NASA*] .... BLH
Band-Limited Signal .... BLS
Bandmaster [*Military British*] (ROG) .... BANDMR
Bandmaster [*Military British*] (ROG) .... BANDR
Bandmaster [*Military British*] (ROG) .... BDR
Bandmaster (ROG) .... BM
Bandmaster .... BMSTR
Bandmaster [*Military British*] (DMA) .... Bndr
Bando McGlocklin Adj Rt'A'Pfd [*NASDAQ symbol*] (TTSB) .... BMCCP
Bando McGlocklin Capital [*NASDAQ symbol*] (TTSB) .... BMCC
Bando McGlocklin Capital Corp. [*Associated Press*] (SAG) .... Bando
Bando McGlocklin Capital Corp. [*Associated Press*] (SAG) .... BandoM
Bando McGlocklin Capital Corp. [*NASDAQ symbol*] (NQ) .... BMCC
Bandolier .... BAND
Bandolier (MSA) .... BDLR
Bandon, OR [*FM radio station call letters*] (RBYB) .... KBDN
Bandon Public Library, Bandon, OR [*Library symbol Library of Congress*] (LCLS) .... OrBan
Bandpass .... BP
Bandpass (IDOE) .... bp
Bandpass Crystal .... BPC
Bandpass Crystal Filter .... BCF
Bandpass Crystal Filter .... BPCF
Bandpass Filter .... BF
Bandpass Filter .... BPF
Bandpass Limiter (IAA) .... BPL
Bandpass Network .... BPN
Bandpass Transformer .... BPT
Bandrejection Filter (IAA) .... BRF
Bands (Civilian and Military) [*Public-performance tariff class*] [*British*] .... B
Bands of America (EA) .... BA
Bandsman [*Military British*] .... BDSM
Bandsman [*Military British*] .... BDSMN
Bands-of-Performance (MCD) .... BOP
Bandstop [*Electronics*] (IAA) .... BS
Bandstop Filter (PDAA) .... BSF
Bandstop Filter (MSA) .... BSFL
Bandundu [*Zaire*] [*Airport symbol*] (OAG) .... FDU
Bandundu [*Zaire*] [*ICAO location identifier*] (ICLI) .... FZBO
Bandung [*Indonesia*] [*Airport symbol*] (OAG) .... BDO
Bandung [*Indonesia*] [*Seismograph station code, US Geological Survey Closed*] (SEIS) .... BND
Bandung/Husein Sastranegara [*Indonesia*] [*ICAO location identifier*] (ICLI) .... WIIB
Bandwidth [*Frequency range*] .... B
Bandwidth [*Frequency range*] .... BW
Bandwidth (IDOE) .... bw
Bandwidth Allocation Control Protocol [*Telecommunications*] (ACRL) .... BACP
Bandwidth Allocation Control Protocol [*Computer science*] (PCM) .... BACP
Bandwidth Allocation Control Protocol (PCM) .... BACP
Bandwidth Allocation Protocol [*Telecommunications*] (ACRL) .... BAP
Bandwidth Compression Technique .... BCT
Bandwidth on Demand (PCM) .... BOND
Bandwidth on Demand Interoperability Working Group [*Telecommunications*] (ACRL) .... BONDING
Bandwidth Radio (MCD) .... BWR
Bandwidth Ratio .... BWR
Bandwidth Ratio [*Telecommunications*] (NITA) .... BWT
Bandwidth Reduction and Intelligence Target Tracking (MCD) .... BRITT
Bandwidth Shape Factor .... BSF
Bane Houei Say [*Laos*] [*ICAO location identifier*] (ICLI) .... VLHS
Baneh [*Iran*] [*ICAO location identifier*] (ICLI) .... OICB
Banff [*Alberta*] [*Seismograph station code, US Geological Survey Closed*] (SEIS) .... BAN
Banff, AB [*ICAO location identifier*] (ICLI) .... CYBA
Banff Centre Library, Alberta [*Library symbol National Library of Canada*] (NLC) .... ABSFA
Banff Library, Alberta [*Library symbol National Library of Canada*] (NLC) .... AB
Banff Library, Banff, AB, Canada [*Library symbol Library of Congress*] (LCLS) .... CaAB
Banff Municipal Library, Improvement District No. 9, Banff, AB, Canada [*Library symbol Library of Congress*] (LCLS) .... CaABIDM
Banff School of Fine Arts, Banff, AB, Canada [*Library symbol Library of Congress*] (LCLS) .... CaABSFA
Banfora [*Burkina Faso*] [*ICAO location identifier*] (ICLI) .... DHOB
Bang for the Buck .... BFB
Bang on a Can Festival .... BOAC
Banga [*Zaire*] [*ICAO location identifier*] (ICLI) .... FZCI
Bangala Law Reporter [*India*] [*A publication*] (DLA) .... Bang LR
Bangalore [*India*] [*Airport symbol*] (OAG) .... BLR
Bangalore [*India*] [*ICAO location identifier*] (ICLI) .... VOBG
Bangalore Volunteer Rifles [*British military*] (DMA) .... BVR
Bangamba [*Congo*] [*ICAO location identifier*] (ICLI) .... FCPB
Bangassou [*Central African Republic*] [*ICAO location identifier*] (ICLI) .... FEFG
Bang-Bang Erection System [*Electronics*] (IAA) .... BBES
Bang-Bang-Bang Surfaces (PDAA) .... BBBS
Bangkok [*Thailand*] (WDAA) .... BGK
Bangkok [*Thailand*] [*Airport symbol*] (OAG) .... BKK
Bangkok [*Thailand*] [*ICAO location identifier*] (ICLI) .... VTBA
Bangkok [*Thailand*] [*ICAO location identifier*] (ICLI) .... VTBB
Bangkok Airways [*Thailand*] [*ICAO designator*] (FAAC) .... BKP
Bangkok Bank [*Thailand*] .... BB
Bangkok/International [*Thailand*] [*ICAO location identifier*] (ICLI) .... VTBD
Bangladash .... BANGLA
Bangladesh [*MARC geographic area code Library of Congress*] .... a-bg--
Bangladesh (ILCA) .... Bang
Bangladesh [*ANSI two-letter standard code*] (CNC) .... BD
Bangladesh [*MARC country of publication code Library of Congress*] (LCCP) .... bg
Bangladesh [*ANSI three-letter standard code*] (CNC) .... BGD
Bangladesh (WDAA) .... BNGL
Bangladesh [*Aircraft nationality and registration mark*] (FAAC) S2
Bangladesh Biman [*ICAO designator*] (FAAC) .... BBC
Bangladesh Biman [*ICAO designator*] (AD) .... BG
Bangladesh Cultural Association (EA) .... BCA
Bangladesh House Building Finance Corp. (EY) .... BHBFC
Bangladesh Krishi Bank (EY) .... BKB
Bangladesh Medical Association of North America (EA) .... BMA
Bangladesh National Awami Party [*Political party*] (PPW) .... NAP
Bangladesh National Party [*Bangladesh Jatiyabadi Dal*] (PPW) .... BNP
Bangladesh National Scientific and Technical Documentation Centre [*Information service or system*] (IID) .... BANSDOC
Bangladesh Nationalist Party [*Political party*] .... BNP
Bangladesh News Agency .... BNA
Bangladesh Population and Health Consortium/NGO Project .... BPHC
Bangladesh Press International .... BPI
Bangladesh Rural Advancement Committee [*Development program*] .... BRAC
Bangladesh Samabaya Bank Ltd. (EY) .... BSBL
Bangladesh Samajtantrik Dal [*Bangladesh Socialist Party*] (PPW) .... BSD
Bangladesh Sanwad Sanstha [*News agency*] .... BSS
Bangladesh Shilpa Bank [*Industrial Development Bank*] (EY) .... BSB
Bangladesh-Australia Society of South Australia .... BASSA
Bangledesh [*E. Pakistan*] (VRA) .... Bangl
Bangles Fan Club [*Later, Bangles n' Mash International*] [*Defunct*] (EA) .... BFC
Bangles n' Mash International [*Defunct*] (EA) .... BMI
Bango Whiplash [*Military*] .... BW
Bangong-Nujiang Suture [*Paleogeography*] .... BNS
Bangor [*City in Wales*] (ROG) .... BAN
Bangor [*Maine*] [*Airport symbol*] (OAG) .... BGR
Bangor Air Defense Sector (SAA) .... BAADS
Bangor & Aroostook Railroad Co. (IIA) .... B & A
Bangor & Aroostook Railroad Co. .... B & AR
Bangor & Aroostook Railroad Co. [*AAR code*] .... BAR
Bangor Historical Society, Bangor, ME [*Library symbol Library of Congress*] (LCLS) .... MeBaHi
Bangor Hydro Electric [*NYSE symbol*] (TTSB) .... BGR
Bangor Hydro Electric Co. [*NYSE symbol*] (SPSG) .... BGR
Bangor Hydro-Electric Co. [*Associated Press*] (SAG) .... BangH
Bangor/International [*Maine*] [*ICAO location identifier*] (ICLI) .... KBGR
Bangor International Airport .... BIA
Bangor, ME [*Location identifier FAA*] (FAAL) .... JVH
Bangor, ME [*AM radio station call letters*] .... WABI
Bangor, ME [*Television station call letters*] .... WABI-TV
Bangor, ME [*FM radio station call letters*] .... WEZQ
Bangor, ME [*FM radio station call letters*] .... WHCF
Bangor, ME [*FM radio station call letters*] .... WHSN
Bangor, ME [*Television station call letters*] .... WLBZ
Bangor, ME [*FM radio station call letters*] .... WMEH
Bangor, ME [*Television station call letters*] .... WVII
Bangor, ME [*FM radio station call letters*] (RBYB) .... WWBX
Bangor, ME [*AM radio station call letters*] .... WZON

Bangor Mental Health Institute, Bangor, ME [*OCLC symbol*] (OCLC) ... MEB
Bangor [*Wales*] **Orange Position Estimating Equipment for Pastures** [*Electronic beeper to be attached to sheep*] ... BO PEEP
Bangor Public Library, Bangor, ME [*OCLC symbol*] (OCLC) ... BYN
Bangor Public Library, Bangor, ME [*Library symbol Library of Congress*] (LCLS) ... MeBa
Bangor Theological Seminary, Bangor, ME [*Library symbol Library of Congress*] (LCLS) ... MeBaT
Bangor, Wicklow, McClure, and Monteagle Union Public Library, Maynooth, Ontario [*Library symbol National Library of Canada*] (BIB) ... OMBW
Bangsa Moro National Liberation Front [*Philippines*] [*Political party*] (FEA) ... BMNLF
Bangui [*Central African Republic*] [*Airport symbol*] (OAG) ... BGF
Bangui [*Central African Republic*] [*Seismograph station code, US Geological Survey*] (SEIS) ... BNG
Bangui [*Central African Republic*] [*ICAO location identifier*] (ICLI) ... FEFV
Bangui/M'Poko [*Central African Republic*] [*ICAO location identifier*] (ICLI) ... FEFF
Bangula [*Malawi*] [*ICAO location identifier*] (ICLI) ... FWBG
Bani [*Monetary unit*] [*Romania*] ... B
Banihal [*India*] [*ICAO location identifier*] (ICLI) ... VIBH
Banished (ROG) ... BAN
Banister Continental Ltd. [*Toronto Stock Exchange symbol*] ... BAC
Banister Foundation [*Formerly, Banister, Inc.*] [*AMEX symbol*] (SPSG) ... BAN
Banister, Foundation [*Associated Press*] (SAG) ... Banstr
Banja Luka [*Yugoslavia*] [*Seismograph station code, US Geological Survey*] (SEIS) ... BLY
Banja Luka [*Former Yugoslavia*] [*ICAO location identifier*] (ICLI) ... LYBK
Banjarmasin [*Indonesia*] [*Airport symbol*] (OAG) ... BDJ
Banjarmasin Sector [*Indonesia*] [*ICAO location identifier*] (ICLI) ... WRBZ
Banjarmasin/Syamsuddin Noor [*Indonesia*] [*ICAO location identifier*] (ICLI) ... WRBB
Banjo ... BJO
Banjul [*Gambia*] [*Airport symbol*] (OAG) ... BJL
Banjul [*Gambia*] [*ICAO location identifier*] (ICLI) ... GBYD
Bank ... B
Bank ... BK
Bank ... BK
Bank (ROG) ... BNK
Bank Acceptance ... BA
Bank Account Debits Tax (ADA) ... BAD
Bank Account Debits Tax (ADA) ... BADT
Bank Administration [*Bank Administration Institute*] [*A publication*] ... BA
Bank Administration Institute (EA) ... BAI
Bank Analysis System [*Robinson-Humphrey Co.*] [*Defunct Information service or system*] (CRD) ... BANKANAL
Bank and Trust ... B & T
Bank and Turn Indicator [*Aviation*] ... BTI
Bank Angle ... BA
Bank Atlantic Bancorp, Inc. [*NASDAQ symbol*] (SAG) ... BANCA
Bank Atlantic Bancorp, Inc. [*Associated Press*] (SAG) ... BkAtlB
Bank Automated Service Information System (BUR) ... BASIS
Bank Book ... BB
Bank Book ... BK
Bank Bumiputra Malaysia Berhad (FEA) ... BBMB
Bank Burglary ... BB
Bank Cable (IAA) ... BKCA
Bank Capital Markets Association [*Washington, DC*] (EA) ... BCMA
Bank Cash Ratio (ADA) ... BCR
Bank Cash Reserve (ADA) ... BCR
Bank Clearing [*Business term*] (ADA) ... BC
Bank [*Joseph A.*] **Clothiers, Inc.** [*NASDAQ symbol*] (SAG) ... JOSB
Bank [*Joseph A.*] **Clothiers, Inc.** [*Associated Press*] (SAG) ... JosBank
Bank Corp. (GA) [*NASDAQ symbol*] (TTSB) ... BCGA
Bank Corp. of Georgia [*NASDAQ symbol*] (SAG) ... BCGA
Bank Corp. of Georgia [*Associated Press*] (SAG) ... BkCpGa
Bank Credit Transfer (DI) ... BCT
Bank Descriptor Index [*Computer science*] ... BDI
Bank Descriptor Registers [*Computer science*] ... BDR
Bank Descriptor Word [*Computer science*] ... BDW
Bank Dividend (IIA) ... BD
Bank Draft (DS) ... B/DFT
Bank Draft ... BD
Bank Draft Number (TEL) ... BDN
Bank Economic and Social Database [*World Bank*] [*United Nations*] (DUND) ... BESD
Bank Education Service [*British*] (BI) ... BES
Bank Error ... BE
Bank Export Services Act [*1982*] ... BESA
Bank for Cooperatives ... BC
Bank for Foreign Trade of the USSR ... BFT
Bank for International Settlements [*Basel, Switzerland*] (AF) ... BIS
Bank for International Settlements, Quarterly [*Database*] [*I. P. Sharp Associates*] [*Information service or system*] (CRD) ... BISQ
Bank for International Settlements, Semi-Annual [*Database*] [*I. P. Sharp Associates*] [*Information service or system*] (CRD) ... BISS
Bank fuer Gemeinwirtschaft [*Germany*] ... BfG
Bank fuer Internationalen Zahlungsausgleich [*Bank for International Settlements*] [*German*] ... BIZ
Bank fuer Kredit und Aussenhandel AG [*Bank for Credit and Export Trade*] [*German*] ... BKA
Bank/Fund Conferences Office [*World Bank, IMF*] ... BFCO
Bank Giro Credit [*British*] (DCTA) ... BGC
Bank Holding Company ... BHC
Bank Holding Company Act [*of 1956*] (TDOB) ... BHCA
Bank Holiday ... BH
Bank Identification Number ... BIN
Bank in Liechtenstein ... BIL
Bank Information System Network ... BISNET
Bank Insurance Fund ... BIF
Bank Investment Contract ... BIC
Bank Larceny ... BL
Bank Management Information System ... BMIS
Bank Markazi Iran. Bulletin [*A publication*] ... BMIB
Bank Marketing Association [*Chicago, IL*] (EA) ... BMA
Bank Marketing Association, Chicago, IL [*Library symbol Library of Congress*] (LCLS) ... ICBM
Bank Marketing Association, Chicago, IL [*OCLC symbol*] (OCLC) ... IDZ
Bank Mees & Hope NV ... BMH
Bank Melli Iran ... BMI
Bank of Africa [*Mali*] (EY) ... BOA
Bank of Alberta [*Toronto Stock Exchange symbol*] ... BNT
Bank of America ... B of A
Bank of America ... BA
Bank of America Australia ... BAA
Bank of American National Trust and Savings Association (MHDW) ... BANTSA
Bank of Boston [*NYS*] (TTSB) ... BKB
Bank of Boston 8.60% Dep Pfd [*NYSE symbol*] (TTSB) ... BKBPrE
Bank of Boston 7.875%DepPfd [*NYSE symbol*] (TTSB) ... BKBPrF
Bank of Boston Adj Rt A Pfd [*NYSE symbol*] (TTSB) ... BKBPrA
Bank of Boston Adj Rt B Ptd [*NYSE symbol*] (TTSB) ... BKBPrB
Bank of Boston Adj Rt C Pfd [*NYSE symbol*] (TTSB) ... BKBPrC
Bank of Boston Corp. [*NYSE symbol*] (SPSG) ... BKB
Bank of Boston Corp. [*Associated Press*] (SAG) ... BkBost
Bank of British Columbia [*Toronto Stock Exchange symbol Vancouver Stock Exchange symbol*] ... BBC
Bank of California, San Francisco, CA [*Library symbol Library of Congress*] (LCLS) ... CSfB
Bank of Canada [*Banque du Canada*] ... BC
Bank of Canada, Ottawa, ON, Canada [*Library symbol Library of Congress*] (LCLS) ... CaOOB
Bank of Canada [*Banque du Canada*] **Ottawa, Ontario** [*Library symbol National Library of Canada*] (NLC) ... OOB
Bank of Canada Weekly Financial Statistics [*I. P. Sharp Associates*] [*Information service or system*] (CRD) ... WBANK
Bank of China Trust and Consultancy Co. ... BOCTC
Bank of Commerce (California) [*Associated Press*] (SAG) ... BCmCA
Bank of Commerce (California) [*NASDAQ symbol*] (SAG) ... BCOM
Bank of Commerce, Technical Information Facility, Toronto, ON, Canada [*Library symbol*] [*Library of Congress*] (LCLS) ... CaOTBCO
Bank of Communications [*China*] ... BOC
Bank of Communications [*China*] ... BoCom
Bank of Credit and Commerce Australia ... BCCA
Bank of Credit & Commerce International [*Facetious Translation: Bank of Crooks and Criminals International*] (ECON) ... BCCI
Bank of Credit and Commerce Niger (EY) ... BCCN
Bank of England ... B of E
Bank of England Staff Organisation ... BESO
Bank of Ghana ... B of G
Bank of Ghana ... BofG
Bank of Granite [*Associated Press*] (SAG) ... BkGranit
Bank of Granite [*NASDAQ symbol*] (SAG) ... GRAN
Bank of Granite [*NASDAQ symbol*] (TTSB) ... GRAN
Bank of Ireland Asset Management ... BIAM
Bank of Japan ... BOJ
Bank of Japan (ODBW) ... BoJ
Bank of Kuwait & the Middle East (ECON) ... BKME
Bank of London and South America ... BOLSA
Bank of Los Angeles [*Associated Press*] (SAG) ... BankLA
Bank of Los Angeles [*NASDAQ symbol*] (SAG) ... BKLA
Bank of Los Angeles [*Associated Press*] (SAG) ... BnkLA
Bank of Maldives Ltd. (FEA) ... BML
Bank of Melbourne [*Australia*] ... BOM
Bank of Mitsubishi Ltd. [*Associated Press*] (SAG) ... BkTokyo
Bank of Mitsubishi Ltd. [*NYSE symbol*] (SAG) ... MBK
Bank of Montreal [*Associated Press*] (SAG) ... BkMont
Bank of Montreal [*Toronto Stock Exchange symbol Vancouver Stock Exchange symbol*] ... BMO
Bank of Montreal, Canadian Imperial Bank of Commerce, Bank of Nova Scotia, and Toronto-Dominion Bank ... MINT
Bank of Montreal, Montreal, PQ, Canada [*Library symbol Library of Congress*] (LCLS) ... CaQMBMo
Bank of Montreal [*Banque de Montreal*], Quebec [*Library symbol National Library of Canada*] (NLC) ... QMBMO
Bank of Montreal, Technical Information Centre, Willowdale, ON, Canada [*Library symbol Library of Congress*] (LCLS) ... CaOTBM
Bank of Nashville [*Associated Press*] (SAG) ... BkNash
Bank of Nashville [*Associated Press*] (SAG) ... BkNsh
[*The*] **Bank of Nashville** [*NASDAQ symbol*] (NQ) ... TBON
Bank of Nauru ... BON
Bank of New Hampshire Corp. [*NASDAQ symbol*] (NQ) ... BNHC
Bank of New Hampshire Corp. [*Associated Press*] (SAG) ... BnkNH
Bank of New South Wales. Circular [*A publication*] ... Bank NSW Circular
Bank of New York [*Associated Press*] (SAG) ... Bank NY
Bank of New York [*NYSE symbol*] (TTSB) ... BK
Bank of New York Co., Inc. [*NYSE symbol*] (SPSG) ... BK
Bank of New York Co., Inc. [*Associated Press*] (SAG) ... BkNY
Bank of Nova Scotia [*Toronto Stock Exchange symbol Vancouver Stock Exchange symbol*] ... BNS
Bank of Nova Scotia, Toronto, ON, Canada [*Library symbol Library of Congress*] (LCLS) ... CaOTNS

Bank of Nova Scotia [*Banque de Nouvelle-Ecosse*], Toronto, Ontario [*Library symbol National Library of Canada*] (NLC) .... OTNS
Bank of Queensland Ltd. .... BOQ
Bank of Queensland Ltd. [*Australia*] .... BQL
Bank of Santa Clara [*Associated Press*] (SAG) .... BkSClara
Bank of Santa Clara [*NASDAQ symbol*] (SAG) .... BNSC
Bank of Singapore .... BOS
Bank of Small Industries and Commerce [*Bangladesh*] (EY) .... BASIC
[*The*] Bank of South Carolina [*NASDAQ symbol*] (NQ) .... BKSC
Bank of South Carolina (The) Charleston [*Associated Press*] (SAG) .... BankSC
Bank of Southington [*Associated Press*] (SAG) .... BkSthg
[*The*] Bank of Southington [*AMEX symbol*] (SPSG) .... BSO
Bank of Southington [*AMEX symbol*] (TTSB) .... BSO
Bank of Thailand (IMH) .... BOT
Bank of the United States .... BUS
Bank of Tokyo .... BOT
Bank of Tokyo Australia Ltd. .... BOTA
Bank of Tokyo-MitsubishiADS [*NYSE symbol*] (TTSB) .... MBK
Bank of Tonga .... BT
Bank of Uganda .... BoU
Bank of Valletta [*Malta*] .... BV
Bank of Western Samoa .... BWS
Bank of Yorba Linda [*NASDAQ symbol*] (SAG) .... BOYL
Bank of Yorba Linda [*Associated Press*] (SAG) .... BYrbLin
Bank Official Loan Act [*1933*] .... BOLA
Bank Pass Book (ROG) .... BPB
Bank Personnel Selection Inventory [*Test*] .... BPSI
Bank Plus Corp. [*Associated Press*] (SAG) .... BnkPlus
Bank Plus Corp. [*NASDAQ symbol*] (SAG) .... BPLS
Bank Plus Corp. [*NASDAQ symbol*] (TTSB) .... BPLS
Bank Post Bill [*Business term*] .... BPB
Bank Public Relations and Marketing Association [*Later, BMA*] .... BPRMA
Bank Rate [*Banking*] .... BR
Bank Robbery .... BR
Bank Secrecy Act (TDOB) .... BSA
Bank Settlement Plan (ADA) .... BSP
Bank South Corp. [*NASDAQ symbol*] (NQ) .... BKSO
Bank South Corp. [*Associated Press*] (SAG) .... BkSouth
Bank Standing Order (DI) .... BSO
Bank Stationers Association [*Later, FSA*] (EA) .... BSA
Bank Street College of Education (GAGS) .... Bank St C
Bank Street College of Education, New York, NY [*Library symbol Library of Congress*] (LCLS) .... NNBSC
Bank Street Writer [*A computer program manufactured by Bank Street and Intentional Educations, Inc.*] .... BSW
Bank to Turn [*Aviation*] (MCD) .... BTT
Bank United Corp. [*NASDAQ symbol*] (SAG) .... BNKU
Bank United Corp. [*Associated Press*] (SAG) .... BnkUntd
Bank United of Texas FSB [*NYSE symbol*] (SPSG) .... BKU
Bank United of Texas FSB [*Associated Press*] (SAG) .... BkUtd
Bank Utd Texas 9.60% 'B' Pfd [*NYSE symbol*] (TTSB) .... BKUPrB
Bank Utd Texas FSB Pfd [*NYSE symbol*] (TTSB) .... BKUPrA
Bank West Financial [*NASDAQ symbol*] (TTSB) .... BWFC
Bank West Financial Corp. [*Associated Press*] (SAG) .... Bk West
Bank West Financial Corp. [*NASDAQ symbol*] (SAG) .... BWFC
Bank Wire Transfer of Funds .... BWTF
Bankair [*ICAO designator*] (AD) .... JA
Bankair, Inc. [*ICAO designator*] (FAAC) .... BKA
BankAmer 9% cm Ser'H'Pfd [*NYSE symbol*] (TTSB) .... BACPrH
BankAmer 8.16% cm Ser'L'Pfd [*NYSE symbol*] (TTSB) .... BACPrL
BankAmer 8.50% cm Ser'N'Pfd [*NYSE symbol*] (TTSB) .... BACPrN
BankAmer 7.875% cm Ser'M'Pfd [*NYSE symbol*] (TTSB) .... BACPrM
BankAmer 8.375% cm Ser'K'Pfd [*NYSE symbol*] (TTSB) .... BACPrK
BankAmer Adj cm A Pfd [*NYSE symbol*] (TTSB) .... BACPrA
BankAmer Adj cm B Pfd [*NYSE symbol*] (TTSB) .... BACPrB
BankAmerica Corp. [*Formerly, Security Pacific Corp.*] [*NYSE symbol*] (SPSG) .... BAC
BankAmerica Corp. [*Associated Press*] (SAG) .... BankAm
BankAmerica Corp. [*Associated Press*] (SAG) .... BkA
BankAmerica Corp. [*Associated Press*] (SAG) .... BkAm
BankAmericard [*Later, Visa*] [*Credit card*] .... BA
BankAmericard [*Later, Visa*] [*Credit card*] .... BAC
BankAmericard Service Exchange .... BASE
BankAtlantic, a Federal Savings Bank [*Associated Press*] (SAG) .... BankAtl
BankAtlantic Bancorp, Inc. [*NASDAQ symbol*] (SAG) .... BANC
BankAtlantic Bancorp, Inc. [*Associated Press*] (SAG) .... BnkAtla
BankAtlantic Bancorp'A' [*NASDAQ symbol*] (TTSB) .... BANCA
BankAtlantic Bancorp'B' [*NASDAQ symbol*] (TTSB) .... BANC
Bankcard .... BC
Bankcard Holders of America (EA) .... BHA
BankcAtlantic Bancorp, Inc. [*NASDAQ symbol*] (SAG) .... BANC
Banked Breast Milk [*Neonatology*] (DAVI) .... BBM
Banked Position Withdrawal Sequence (IEEE) .... BPWS
Bankeno Resources Ltd. [*Toronto Stock Exchange symbol*] .... BKE
Banker .... BNKR
Bankers' [*Rate*] [*Value of the English pound*] .... BK
Bankers Association for Foreign Trade [*Washington, DC*] (EA) .... BAFT
Bankers' Automated Clearing Services [*British*] (DCTA) .... BACS
Bankers' Blanket Bond [*Investment term*] .... BBB
Bankers Clearing House [*California*] (SRA) .... BCH
Bankers Committee (EA) .... BC
Bankers Committee for Tax Equality [*of the National Tax Equality Association*] (EA) .... BCTE
Bankers Committee to Eliminate Favoritism to Credit Unions (EA) .... BCEFCU
Bankers Corp. [*Associated Press*] (SAG) .... Bankrs Cp

Bankers Corp. [*NASDAQ symbol*] (SAG) .... BKCO
Bankers First Corp. [*NASDAQ symbol*] (NQ) .... BNKF
Bankers First Corp. [*Associated Press*] (SAG) .... BnkFst
Banker's Law Journal [*A publication*] (DLA) .... Banker's LJ
Bankers Life Holding Corp. [*Associated Press*] (SAG) .... BkrsLH
Bankers Life Holding Corp. [*NYSE symbol*] (SPSG) .... BLH
Bankers Life Holdings [*NYSE symbol*] (TTSB) .... BLH
Banker's Note [*Associated Press*] (SAG) .... BnkrN
Banker's Note [*AMEX symbol*] (SAG) .... TBN
Banker's Note [*ECM Symbol*] (TTSB) .... TBN.EC
Banker's Order .... BO
Bankers Tr N.Y. 7.625%Dep Pfd [*AMEX symbol*] (TTSB) .... BPR
Bankers Tr N.Y. Adj Dep'Q'Pfd [*NYSE symbol*] (TTSB) .... BTPrQ
Bankers Tr N.Y. Adj Dep'R'Pfd [*NYSE symbol*] (TTSB) .... BTPrR
Bankers Tr N.Y.7.50% Dep Pfd [*AMEX symbol*] (TTSB) .... BPB
Bankers Tr N.Y.7.75% Dep'S'Pfd [*NYSE symbol*] (TTSB) .... BTPrS
Bankers Tr N.Y.8.55% Sr'I'Pfd [*NYSE symbol*] (TTSB) .... BTPrI
Bankers Tr6% Cap Sec [*AMEX symbol*] (TTSB) .... BTB
Bankers Tr6.125%CapSec [*AMEX symbol*] (TTSB) .... BND
Bankers Trust Co. (MHDW) .... BTC
Bankers Trust Information Service [*Database producer*] .... BTIS
Bankers Trust New York Corp. [*Associated Press*] (SAG) .... BankTr
Bankers Trust New York Corp. [*AMEX symbol*] (SPSG) .... BND
Bankers Trust New York Corp. [*Associated Press*] (SAG) .... BnkT
Bankers Trust New York Corp. [*AMEX symbol*] (SAG) .... BPB
Bankers Trust New York Corp. [*AMEX symbol*] (SAG) .... BPR
Bankers Trust New York Corp. [*NYSE symbol*] (SPSG) .... BT
Bankers Trust New York Corp. [*AMEX symbol*] (SPSG) .... BTB
Bankers Trust New York Corp. [*NYSE symbol*] (TTSB) .... BTU
Bankers Trust NY [*NYSE symbol*] (TTSB) .... BT
Bankgesellschaft Berlin [*Germany*] (ECON) .... BGB
Bankim Barotra [*Commerce Bank*] [*Malagasy*] (AF) .... BB
Banking .... BKG
Banking (ODBW) .... bkg
Banking (ADA) .... BNKG
Banking .... BNKNG
Banking and Currency Committee [*US Senate*] .... B & C
Banking and Securities Industry Committee [*Inactive*] .... BASIC
Banking Cases [*A publication*] (DLA) .... Bank Cas
Banking Code [*A publication*] (DLA) .... Bank C
Banking Communication System (IAA) .... BCS
Banking Federation of the European Economic Community [*Belgium*] (EAIO) .... BFEC
Banking Federation of the European Economic Community [*Belgium*] (EAIO) .... BFEEC
Banking, Finance, and Urban Affairs (DLA) .... BFUA
Banking, Housing, and Urban Affairs (DLA) .... BHUA
Banking Information Processing System [*Computer science*] (BUR) .... BIPS
Banking Information Service [*British*] .... BIS
Banking, Insurance, and Finance Union [*British*] (DBA) .... BIFU
Banking Law Bulletin [*Australia A publication*] .... BLB
Banking Law Institute (EA) .... BLI
Banking Literature Index [*A publication*] .... BLI
Banking On-Line Package System (BUR) .... BOPS
Banking Profession Political Action Committee [*Acronym now used as official name of organization*] (EA) .... BANKPAC
Banking Research and Economic Analysis [*Unit*] [*Department of the Treasury*] (GRD) .... BR & EA
Banking Systems Information Exchange .... BSIE
Banking Users' Group [*British*] .... BAKUP
Bankit Resource Corp. [*Vancouver Stock Exchange symbol*] .... BKR
Banknorth Group [*NASDAQ symbol*] (TTSB) .... BKNG
Banknorth Group, Inc. [*NASDAQ symbol*] (NQ) .... BKNG
Banknorth Group, Inc. [*Associated Press*] (SAG) .... Bknth
Banknote .... BN
Banknote Corp of America [*Printer of U.S. postage stamps*] (BARN) .... BCA
Bankroll [*Slang*] .... BR
Bankrupt (ROG) .... BKPT
Bankrupt .... BKRPT
Bankrupt (ROG) .... BKRUPT
Bankrupt [*or Bankruptcy*] (DCTA) .... BRUPT
Bankrupt Court Reporter [*New York*] [*A publication*] (DLA) .... Bank Ct Rep
Bankrupt Register [*A publication*] (DLA) .... B Reg
Bankruptcy [*Legal term*] (DLA) .... Bank
Bankruptcy .... BANKCY
Bankruptcy [*Legal term*] (DLA) .... Bankr
Bankruptcy [*Legal term*] (DLA) .... Bcy
Bankruptcy .... BKCY
Bankruptcy (ODBW) .... bkcy
Bankruptcy [*Legal shorthand*] (LWAP) .... BKPTCY
Bankruptcy (ADA) .... BKRPCY
Bankruptcy .... BKRPTCY
Bankruptcy .... BKTCY
Bankruptcy .... BKY
Bankruptcy Act [*Legal term*] (DLA) .... Bankr Act
Bankruptcy and Insolvency Cases [*Legal*] [*British*] .... B & I
Bankruptcy and Insolvency Reports [*1853-55*] [*England*] [*A publication*] (DLA) .... B & I
Bankruptcy and Insolvency Reports [*1853-55*] [*England*] [*A publication*] (DLA) .... Bank & Ins
Bankruptcy and Insolvency Reports [*1853-55*] [*England*] [*A publication*] (DLA) .... Bank & Ins R
Bankruptcy and Insolvency Reports [*1853-55*] [*England*] [*A publication*] (DLA) .... Bank & Insol Rep

Bankruptcy and Insolvency Reports [*1853-55*] [*England*] [*A publication*] (DLA) ... Bank Insol Rep
Bankruptcy and Insolvency Reports [*1853-55*] [*England*] [*A publication*] (DLA) ... Bankr Ins R
Bankruptcy Annulment Order [*Legal term*] (DLA) ... BAO
Bankruptcy Bar Bulletin [*A publication*] (DLA) ... Bankr B Bull
Bankruptcy Cases [*A publication*] (DLA) ... BC
Bankruptcy Court [*Legal term*] (DLA) ... Bank
Bankruptcy Court [*Legal term*] (DAS) ... BC
Bankruptcy Court Decisions [*A publication*] (DLA) ... Bankr Ct Dec
Bankruptcy Fee (ADA) ... BF
Bankruptcy File [*Canada Systems Group*] [*Ottawa, ON*] [*Information service or system*] (IID) ... BKRP
Bankruptcy Forms [*A publication*] (DLA) ... Bankr Form
Bankruptcy Gazette [*A publication*] (DLA) ... Bank Gaz
Bankruptcy Law Reports [*CCH*] [*A publication*] (AAGC) ... Bankr L Rep
Bankruptcy Official Receivers' Information System ... BORIS
Bankruptcy Reform Act [*1978*] ... BRA
Bankruptcy Register [*A publication*] (DLA) ... Bank Reg
Bankruptcy Register [*A publication*] (DLA) ... BR
Bankruptcy Reporter [*West*] [*A publication*] (AAGC) ... BR
Bankruptcy Reports [*A publication*] (DLA) ... BR
Banks & Barns [*Commercial firm British*] ... B & B
Banks Automated Clearing System [*British*] (NITA) ... BACS
Banks Community Library, Banks, OR [*Library symbol Library of Congress*] (LCLS) ... OrBa
Banks, OR [*FM radio station call letters*] ... KDBX
Banks' Reports [*1-5 Kansas*] [*A publication*] (DLA) ... Banks
Bank-Share Owners Advisory League [*Inactive*] ... BSOAL
Bankson Language Screening Test [*Child development test*] ... BLST
Bank-Switching [*Computer technology*] ... BS
Bankter's Institutes of Scottish Law [*A publication*] (DLA) ... Bank I
Bankter's Institutes of Scottish Law [*A publication*] (DLA) ... Bank Inst
Bankter's Institutes of Scottish Law [*A publication*] (DLA) ... Bankt I
BankUnited Financial Corp. [*NASDAQ symbol*] (NQ) ... BKUN
BankUnited Financial Corp. [*Associated Press*] (SAG) ... BkUtF
BankUnited Financial Corp. [*Associated Press*] (SAG) ... BnkUt
BankUnited Financial Corp. [*Associated Press*] (SAG) ... BnkUtd
BankUnited Financial'A' [*NASDAQ symbol*] (TTSB) ... BKUNA
BankUnited Finl 8% Cv Pfd [*NASDAQ symbol*] (TTSB) ... BKUNP
BankUnited Finl 9% Perp Pfd [*NASDAQ symbol*] (TTSB) ... BKUNO
Banner [*Record label*] ... Ban
Banner Aerospace [*Associated Press*] (SAG) ... BanrAer
Banner Aerospace [*NYSE symbol*] (SPSG) ... BAR
Banner Blade Length [*Botany*] ... BBLL
Banner Claw Length [*Botany*] ... BCLL
Banner Elk, NC [*Location identifier FAA*] (FAAL) ... BAR
Banner Elk, NC [*FM radio station call letters*] ... WZJS
Banner Entertainment [*Vancouver Stock Exchange symbol*] ... BNN
Banner Reflex [*Botany*] ... BREX
Banning and Arden's Patent Cases [*United States*] [*A publication*] (DLA) ... Ban & A
Banning and Arden's Patent Cases [*United States*] [*A publication*] (DLA) ... Bann & A
Banning and Arden's Patent Cases [*United States*] [*A publication*] (DLA) ... Bann & A Pat Cas
Banning and Arden's Patent Cases [*United States*] [*A publication*] (DLA) ... Bann & Ard
Banning and Arden's Patent Reports [*United States*] [*A publication*] (DLA) ... B & A
Banning, CA [*Location identifier FAA*] (FAAL) ... BNG
Banning, CA [*AM radio station call letters*] ... KMET
Banning. Limitations of Actions [*3rd ed.*] [*1906*] [*A publication*] (DLA) ... Bann Lim
Banning Union Public Library, Banning, CA [*Library symbol Library of Congress*] (LCLS) ... CBan
Bannister Research & Consulting ... BRC
Bannister's Edition of Orlando Bridgman's English Common Pleas Reports [*A publication*] (DLA) ... Bann Br
Bannister's Reports, English Common Pleas [*A publication*] (DLA) ... Bann
Bannock Regional Medical Center, Medical Library [*Library symbol*] [*Library of Congress*] (LCLS) ... IdPBH
Bannon, E. J., Buffalo NY [*STAC*] ... BEJ
Bannu [*Pakistan*] [*Airport symbol*] (OAG) ... BNP
Bannu [*Pakistan*] [*ICAO location identifier*] (ICLI) ... OPBN
BanPonce 8.35%.Mthly Inc. Pfd [*NASDAQ symbol*] (TTSB) ... BPOPP
BanPonce Corp. [*Associated Press*] (SAG) ... BanPn
BanPonce Corp. [*Associated Press*] (SAG) ... BanPonc
BanPonce Corp. [*NASDAQ symbol*] (NQ) ... BPOP
Banque Africaine de Developpement [*African Development Bank*] [*Use ADB*] (AF) ... BAD
Banque al-Baraka Mauritanienne Islamique (EY) ... BAMIS
Banque Arabe et Internationale d'Investissement [*France*] ... BAII
Banque Arabe-Libyenne-Burkinabe pour le Commerce et le Developpement (EY) ... BALIB
Banque Bruxelles Lambert [*Belgium*] (ECON) ... BBL
Banque Canadienne Nationale ... BCN
Banque Centrale de la Republique de Guinee [*Central Bank of the Republic of Guinea*] (AF) ... BCRG
Banque Centrale de Syrie [*Central Bank of Syria*] (BJA) ... BCS
Banque Centrale de Tunisie [*Central Bank of Tunisia*] (AF) ... BCT
Banque Centrale des Etats de l'Afrique de l'Ouest [*Central Bank of the West African States*] [*Dakar, Senegal*] (AF) ... BCEAO
Banque Centrale des Etats de l'Afrique Equatoriale et de Cameroun [*Central Bank of the States of Equatorial Africa and Cameroon*] (AF) ... BCEAEC
Banque Centrale du Congo Belge et du Ruanda-Urundi [*Central Bank of the Belgian Congo and Rwanda-Urandi*] ... BCCBRU
Banque Commerciale du Burundi (EY) ... BANCOBU
Banque Commerciale du Rwanda [*Commercial Bank of Rwanda*] (AF) ... BCR
Banque Commerciale du Senegal (EY) ... BCS
Banque d'Afrique Occidentale [*Bank of French West Africa*] ... BAO
Banque Dahomeenne de Developpement [*Dahomean Development Bank*] ... BDD
Banque de Credit Agricole et de Developpement [*Central African Republic*] (EY) ... BCAD
Banque de Developpement de la Republique du Niger [*Development Bank of the Republic of Niger*] (AF) ... BDRN
Banque de Developpement de l'Afrique de l'Est [*East African Development Bank - EADB*] (EAIO) ... BDAE
Banque de Developpement des Etats du Grand Lac [*Development Bank of the Great Lakes States*] (EAIO) ... BDEGL
Banque de Developpement du Tchad [*Development Bank of Chad*] (AF) ... BDT
Banque de Developpement Local [*Algeria*] (EY) ... BDL
Banque de Donnees a acces direct de l'Universite du Quebec [*Database of the holdings of the University of Quebec*] [*Canada*] (NITA) ... BADADUQ
Banque de Donnees Internationales de Biometrie Humaine et d'Ergonomie [*International Database of Human Biometrics and Ergonomics*] [*Universite Rene Descartes*] [*France*] [*Information service or system*] (CRD) ... ERGODATA
Banque de Donnees Locales [*Local Area Data Bank*] [*National Institute of Statistics and Economic Studies*] [*Information service or system*] (IID) ... BDL
Banque de Donnees Macroeconomiques [*Macroeconomic Data Bank*] [*National Institute of Statistics and Economic Studies*] [*Information service or system*] ... BDM
Banque de Donnees Socio-Economiques des Pays Mediterraneens [*Socioeconomic Data Bank on the Mediterranean Countries*] [*International Center for Advanced Mediterranean Agronomic Studies*] [*Information service or system*] (IID) ... MEDISTAT
Banque de Donnees Urbaines de Paris et de la Region d'Ile-De-France [*Urban Data Bank of Paris and the Paris Region*] [*Paris Office of Urbanization France*] [*Information service or system*] (IID) ... BDU
Banque de France [*Bank of France*] ... BF
Banque de l'Union Europeenne [*European Union Bank*] [*France*] ... BUE
Banque de Madagascar et des Comores [*Bank of Madagascar and of the Comoro Islands*] (AF) ... BMC
Banque de Nouvelle - Caledonie (EY) ... BNC
Banque de Terminologie de Quebec [*Terminology Bank of Quebec*] [*French Language Board*] [*Information service or system*] ... TERMINOQ
Banque de Terminologie du Quebec [*Terminology Bank of Quebec*] [*French Language Board*] [*Information service or system*] (IID) ... BTQ
Banque des Connaissances et des Techniques [*Knowledge and Technique Bank*] [*National Agency for the Promotion of Research*] [*Information service or system*] (IID) ... BCT
Banque des Etats de l'Afrique Centrale [*Bank of Central African States*] (AF) ... BEAC
Banque des Reglements Internationaux [*Bank for International Settlements*] ... BRI
Banque d'Expansion Industrielle [*Industrial Development Bank*] [*Canada*] ... BEI
Banque d'Information Automatisee sur les Medicaments Principes Actifs [*Databank on active ingredients of drugs*] [*French*] (NITA) ... BIAM PA
Banque d'Information Industrielle [*Industrial Information Data Base*] [*Industrial Research Center of Quebec*] [*Information service or system*] (IID) ... BII
Banque d'Information Industrielle de Pont-A-Mousson et du CTIF [*Centre Technique des Industries de la Fonderie*] [*French Information service or system*] (CRD) ... BIIPAM-CTIF
Banque d'Information Robert Debre [*Centre International de l'Enfance*] [*Database*] ... BIRD
Banque d'Information sur les Recherches [*INSERM Research Information Bank*] [*National Institute for Health and Medical Research*] [*Information service or system*] (IID) ... BIR
Banque d'Informations Automatisees sur les Medicaments [*Data Bank for Medicaments*] [*Information service or system*] (IID) ... BIAM
Banque d'Informations Politiques et d'Actualite [*Political and Current Events Information Bank*] [*Database Telesystems - Questel*] [*Information service or system*] (IID) ... BIPA
Banque du Congo Belge [*Bank of the Belgian Congo*] ... BCB
Banque Europeenne de Credit [*Belgium*] ... BEC
Banque Europeenne d'Investissement [*European Investment Bank - EIB*] [*French*] ... BEI
Banque Europeenne pour l'Amerique Latine [*Bank*] [*French*] (EY) ... BEAL
Banque Exterieure d'Algerie [*Algerian Foreign Bank*] (AF) ... BEA
Banque Federale de Developpement [*Federal Business Development Bank - FBDB*] [*Canada*] ... BFD
Banque Francaise Commerciale Ocean Indian [*Reunion*] (EY) ... BFCOI
Banque Francaise du Commerce Exterieur [*French state-owned bank*] ... BFCE
Banque Francaise pour le Commerce [*French Commercial Bank*] (AF) ... BFC
Banque Franco-Arabe d'Investissements Internationaux ... FRAB
Banque Gabonaise de Developpement [*Gabonese Development Bank*] (AF) ... BGD
Banque Guineenne du Commerce Exterieur [*Guinean Bank of Foreign Commerce*] (AF) ... BGCE
Banque Interamericaine de Developpement [*Inter-American Development Bank*] [*French*] ... BID
Banque International de Placement ... BIP
Banque Internationale a Luxembourg SA (ECON) ... BIL
Banque Internationale des Comores (EY) ... BIC
Banque Internationale du Burkina [*Burkina Faso*] (EY) ... BIB
Banque Internationale pour la Reconstruction et le Developpement [*International Bank for Reconstruction and Development; also known as the World Bank*] [*French*] ... BIRD
Banque Internationale pour l'Afrique en Guinee (EY) ... BIAG

Banque Internationale pour l'Afrique Occidentale [*International Bank for West Africa*] [*France*] (AF) ... BIAO
Banque Internationale pour l'Afrique Occidentale - Cote d'Ivoire (EY) ... BIAO-CI
Banque Ivoirienne de Developpement Industriel [*Ivorian Bank for Industrial Development*] (AF) ... BIDI
Banque Malgache de l'Ocean Indien [*Indian Ocean Malagasy Bank*] [*Madagascar*] (EY) ... BMOI
Banque Malgache d'Escompte et de Credit [*Malagasy Discount and Credit Bank*] (AF) ... BAMES
Banque Malienne de Credits et de Depots [*Malian Credit and Deposits Bank*] (AF) ... BMCD
Banque Marocaine pour le Commerce Exterieur [*Moroccan Foreign Trade Bank*] (AF) ... BMCE
Banque Mauritanienne de Developpement [*Mauritanian Development Bank*] (AF) ... BMD
Banque Nationale Agricole [*National Agricultural Bank*] [*Tunisia*] (AF) ... BNA
Banque Nationale de Belgique [*National Bank of Belgium*] ... BNB
Banque Nationale de Credit Rural [*Gabon*] (EY) ... BNCR
Banque Nationale de Devellopement du Burkina (EY) ... BNDB
Banque Nationale de Developpement de la Haute-Volta [*National Development Bank of Upper Volta*] (AF) ... BNDHV
Banque Nationale de Developpement du Congo [*National Development Bank of the Congo*] (AF) ... BNDC
Banque Nationale de Developpement Economique [*National Economic Development Bank*] [*France*] (AF) ... BNDE
Banque Nationale de Mauritanie (EY) ... BNM
Banque Nationale de Paris [*National Bank of Paris*] [*France*] ... BNP
Banque Nationale du Canada, Centre de Documentation, Montreal, PQ, Canada [*Library symbol*] [*Library of Congress*] (LCLS) ... CaQMBAN
Banque Nationale du Congo [*National Bank of the Congo*] ... BNC
Banque Nationale Malgache de Developpement [*Malagasy National Development Bank*] (AF) ... BNM
Banque Nationale pour le Commerce et l'Industrie [*National Bank for Commerce and Industry*] [*Togo*] [*French*] ... BNCI
Banque Nationale pour le Developpement Agricole [*National Agricultural Development Bank*] [*Ivory Coast*] (AF) ... BNDA
Banque Nationale pour le Developpement Economique [*National Bank for Economic Development*] [*Morocco*] (IMH) ... BNDE
Banque Ouest Africaine de Developpement [*West African Development Bank - WADB*] (EAIO) ... BOAD
Banque pour le Financement du Commerce et des Investissements du Burkina (EY) ... BFCIB
Banque pour l'Expansion Industrielle [*Industrial Development Bank*] [*France*] (EY) ... BANEXI
Banque Senegalo-Koweitienne [*Senegal-Kuwait Bank*] ... BSK
Banque Senegalo-Tunisienne (EY) ... BST
Banque Tchadienne de Credit et de Depots [*Chad*] (EY) ... BTCD
Banquet Event Order [*Food service industry*] ... BEO
Banqueting/Catered Functions [*Public-performance tariff class*] [*British*] ... BF
Banta Corp. [*Associated Press*] (SAG) ... Banta
Banta Corp. [*NASDAQ symbol*] (NQ) ... BNTA
Bantam (ABBR) ... BTM
Bantam, Doubleday, Dell Publishing Group ... BDD
Bantam Reconnaissance-Command [*Jeep prototype*] ... BRC
Bantamweight (ABBR) ... BTMWT
Banting Research Centre Library, Department of National Health and Welfare [*Bibliotheque du Centre de Recherches Banting, Ministere de la Sante Nationale et du Bien-Etre Social*] **Ottawa, Ontario** [*Library symbol National Library of Canada*] (NLC) ... OONHBR
Banting-Best Physiology Library, University of Toronto, Ontario [*Library symbol National Library of Canada*] (NLC) ... OTUBP
Bantock Society (EA) ... BS
Banyan Hotel Inv Fund [*AMEX symbol*] (TTSB) ... VHT
Banyan Hotel Investment Fund (SAG) ... BanyHI
Banyan Hotel Investment Fund [*Formerly, VMS Hotel Investment Fund*] [*AMEX symbol*] (SPSG) ... VHT
Banyan Mortgage Inv Fund [*NYSE symbol*] (TTSB) ... VMG
Banyan Mortgage Investment Fund [*Associated Press*] (SAG) ... BanyMF
Banyan Mortgage Investment Fund [*Formerly, VMS Mortgate Investment Fund*] [*NYSE symbol*] (SPSG) ... VMG
Banyan Short Term Income Trust [*Associated Press*] (SAG) ... BanynSh
Banyan Short Term Income Trust [*Formerly, VMS Short Term Income Trust*] [*AMEX symbol*] (SPSG) ... VST
Banyan Strategic Land Fd II [*NASDAQ symbol*] (TTSB) ... VSLF
Banyan Strategic Land Fund [*Associated Press*] (SAG) ... BanySL
Banyan Strategic Land Fund [*NASDAQ symbol*] (SAG) ... VSLF
Banyan Strategic Land Fund II [*Associated Press*] (SAG) ... BanySL2
Banyan Strategic Land Fund II [*NASDAQ symbol*] (SAG) ... VSLF
Banyan Strategic Realty Tr [*NASDAQ symbol*] (TTSB) ... VLANS
Banyan Strategic Realty Trust [*Associated Press*] (SAG) ... BanyRT
Banyan Strategic Realty Trust [*NASDAQ symbol*] (SAG) ... VLAN
Banyan Systems [*NASDAQ symbol*] (TTSB) ... BNYN
Banyan Systems, Inc. [*Associated Press*] (SAG) ... BanynSy
Banyan Systems, Inc. [*NASDAQ symbol*] (SAG) ... BNYN
Banyo [*Cameroon*] [*ICAO location identifier*] (ICLI) ... FKAB
Banyumas/Wirasaba [*Indonesia*] [*ICAO location identifier*] (ICLI) ... WIAP
BANZ [*British-Australian-New Zealand*] [*Papua New Guinea*] [*Airport symbol*] [*Obsolete*] (OAG) ... BNZ
Banza-Lute [*Zaire*] [*ICAO location identifier*] (ICLI) ... FZCL
Baoshan [*China*] [*Airport symbol*] (OAG) ... BSD
Baotou [*China*] [*Airport symbol*] (OAG) ... BAV
Baotou [*China*] [*ICAO location identifier*] (ICLI) ... ZBOW
BAPTA [*Bearing and Power Transfer Assembly*] **Accelerometer and Conditioner** [*Aerospace*] ... BAC
Baptist ... B
Baptist ... BAP
Baptist ... BAPT
Baptist (VRA) ... bapt
Baptist ... BAPT
Baptist Association of Hospital Chaplains (EA) ... BAHC
Baptist Bible College, Denver, CO [*Library symbol Library of Congress*] (LCLS) ... CoDBB
Baptist Bible College of Pennsylvania, Clarks Summit, PA [*Library symbol Library of Congress*] (LCLS) ... PCsB
Baptist Bible College, Springfield, MO [*Library symbol Library of Congress*] (LCLS) ... MoSpBB
Baptist Bible Fellowship International (EA) ... BBFI
Baptist College at Charleston, Charleston, SC [*OCLC symbol*] (OCLC) ... SBC
Baptist College at Charleston, Charleston, SC [*Library symbol Library of Congress*] (LCLS) ... ScCB
Baptist Community Service [*Australia*] ... BCS
Baptist Convention of Ontario & Quebec (AC) ... BCOQ
Baptist Counselling Service [*Australia*] ... BCS
Baptist General Conference of Canada (AC) ... BGC
[*The*] **Baptist Historical Society** [*British*] ... BHS
Baptist Historical Society of New South Wales [*Australia*] ... BHSNSW
Baptist Hospital Association (EA) ... BHA
Baptist Hospital, Medical Library, Nashville, TN [*Library symbol Library of Congress*] (LCLS) ... TNBH
Baptist Hospital of Miami, Health Sciences Library, Miami, FL [*Library symbol Library of Congress*] (LCLS) ... FMBH
Baptist Independent Church [*Also, BIC*] ... BI
Baptist Independent Church [*Also, BI*] ... BIC
Baptist Information Retrieval System [*Southern Baptist Convention*] [*Nashville, TN*] [*Library network*] [*Defunct*] ... BIRS
Baptist Joint Committee on Public Affairs (EA) ... BJCPA
Baptist Life Association [*Buffalo, NY*] (EA) ... BLA
Baptist Medical Center (Montclair), Medical Library, Birmingham, AL [*Library symbol Library of Congress*] (LCLS) ... ABBM-M
Baptist Medical Center (Princeton), Medical Library, Birmingham, AL [*Library symbol Library of Congress*] (LCLS) ... ABBM-P
Baptist Medical Center, School of Nursing, Birmingham, AL [*Library symbol Library of Congress*] (LCLS) ... ABBM
Baptist Memorial Hospital, Kansas City, MO [*Library symbol Library of Congress*] (LCLS) ... MoKBH
Baptist Memorial Hospital, Memphis, TN [*Library symbol Library of Congress*] (LCLS) ... TMBH
Baptist Memorial Hospital, School of Nursing, Memphis, TN [*Library symbol Library of Congress*] (LCLS) ... TMBH-N
Baptist Mid-Missions (EA) ... BMM
Baptist Mission of North America [*Defunct*] (EA) ... BMNA
Baptist Mission Society ... BMS
Baptist Missionary Association Theological Seminary, Jacksonville, TX [*Library symbol Library of Congress*] (LCLS) ... TxJaB
Baptist Peace Fellowship ... BPF
Baptist Peace Fellowship of North America (EAIO) ... BPFNA
Baptist Public Relations Association (EA) ... BPRA
Baptist Revival Fellowship [*British*] ... BRF
Baptist Student Union (IIA) ... BSU
Baptist Students Concerned [*Defunct*] (EA) ... BSC
Baptist Telecommunications Network [*Nashville, TN*] [*Cable-television system*] ... BTN
Baptist Union ... BU
Baptist Union of Australia ... BUA
Baptist Women's Missionary Auxilliary [*British*] (BI) ... BWMA
Baptist Women's Union of the South West Pacific [*Australia*] ... BWUSWP
Baptist World Aid (EA) ... BWA
Baptist World Aid (EA) ... BWAid
Baptist World Alliance (EA) ... BWA
Baptist World Relief [*Later, Baptist World Aid*] (EA) ... BWARF
Baptist Young People's Union ... BYPU
Baptists for Life (EA) ... BFL
Baptized ... BA
Baptized ... BAP
Baptized ... BAPT
Baptized ... BP
Bar ... B
Bar [*Freight*] ... BA
Bar ... BR
Bar Address Register [*Computer science*] (NITA) ... BAR
Bar and Legal World [*England*] [*A publication*] (DLA) ... Bar & Leg W
Bar Association Bulletin, Los Angeles [*A publication*] (DLA) ... BA Bull LA
Bar Association for Commerce, Finance, and Industry [*British*] (DBA) ... BACA
Bar Association for Human Rights of Greater New York (EA) ... BAHRGNY
Bar Association of Metropolitan St. Louis. Bankruptcy Reporter [*A publication*] (DLA) ... BAMSL
Bar Association of Queensland [*Australia*] ... BAQ
Bar Association of the District of Columbia (SRA) ... BADC
Bar Association of the District of Columbia, Washington, DC [*Library symbol Library of Congress*] (LCLS) ... DBA
Bar Bulletin [*A publication*] (DLA) ... B Bull
Bar Bulletin, New York County Lawyers' [*A publication*] (DLA) ... Bar Bull (NY County La)
Bar Chart Report (MCD) ... BCR
Bar Coded Label (NITA) ... BCL
Bar. Das Internationale Privat-und-Strafrecht [*A publication*] (DLA) ... Bar Int Pr R
Bar Draft [*Depth of water over a bar*] ... BD
Bar Examination Annual [*1893-94*] [*A publication*] (DLA) ... Bar Ex Ann
Bar Examination Guide [*1895-99*] [*A publication*] (DLA) ... Bar Ex Guide
Bar Examination Journal [*A publication*] (DLA) ... B Exam J

Bar Examination Journal [*A publication*] (DLA) .... Bar Ex J
Bar Examination Journal [*A publication*] (DLA) .... Bar Ex Jour
Bar (Handle) Control [*Early automobiles*] (ROG) .... BC
Bar Harbor [*Maine*] [*Airport symbol*] (OAG) .... BHB
Bar Harbor Airlines [*ICAO designator*] (FAAC) .... AJC
Bar Harbor Airlines [*ICAO designator*] (AD) .... QO
Bar Harbor, ME [*FM radio station call letters*] .... WLKE
Bar Harbor, ME [*FM radio station call letters*] .... WMDI
Bar Joist [*Building construction*] (OA) .... BJ
Bar Journal [*A publication*] .... BJ
Bar Keel [*Shipping*] (DS) .... BK
Bar Leader [*A publication*] (DLA) .... B Leader
Bar Library Association of Kansas City, Kansas City, MO [*Library symbol Library of Congress*] (LCLS) .... MoKB
Bar Mitzvah (BJA) .... BM
Bar Reports [*1865-71*] [*A publication*] (DLA) .... Bar Rep
Bar Reports in All Courts [*England*] [*A publication*] (DLA) .... Bar
Bar Reports in All Courts [*England*] [*A publication*] (DLA) .... Bar Re
Bar Resources Ltd. [*Vancouver Stock Exchange symbol*] .... BSL
Baraboo, WI [*FM radio station call letters*] .... WOLX
Baraboo, WI [*AM radio station call letters*] .... WRPQ
Baracoa [*Cuba*] [*Airport symbol*] (OAG) .... BCA
Baracoa/Oriente [*Cuba ICAO location identifier*] (ICLI) .... MUBA
Baracoa Playa/Habana [*Cuba ICAO location identifier*] (ICLI) .... MUPB
Barahona [*Dominican Republic*] [*Airport symbol*] (OAG) .... BRX
Barahona [*Dominican Republic*] [*ICAO location identifier*] (ICLI) .... MDBH
Barair SA [*Spain ICAO designator*] (FAAC) .... BAI
Barakoma [*Solomon Islands*] [*Airport symbol*] (OAG) .... VEV
Baramita [*Guyana*] [*Airport symbol*] (OAG) .... BMJ
Baramita [*Guyana*] [*ICAO location identifier*] (ICLI) .... SYBR
Barandium Resources [*Vancouver Stock Exchange symbol*] .... BRM
Baranof, AK [*Location identifier FAA*] (FAAL) .... BNF
Barat [*Yemen*] [*ICAO location identifier*] (ICLI) .... OYBT
Barat College of the Sacred Heart [*Later, Barat College*] [*Lake Forest, IL*] .... BCSH
Barat College of the Sacred Heart, Lake Forest, IL [*OCLC symbol*] (OCLC) .... ICB
Barat College of the Sacred Heart, Lake Forest, IL [*Library symbol Library of Congress*] (LCLS) .... ILfB
Barbacena [*Brazil ICAO location identifier*] (ICLI) .... SBBQ
Barbadensis [*Pharmacy*] (ROG) .... BB
Barbadensis [*Pharmacy*] (ROG) .... Bbds
Barbados [*Aircraft nationality and registration mark*] (FAAC) 8P
Barbados (ROG) .... BARB
Barbados (VRA) .... Barb
Barbados [*MARC country of publication code Library of Congress*] (LCCP) .... bb
Barbados [*ANSI two-letter standard code*] (CNC) .... BB
Barbados [*Seismograph station code, US Geological Survey*] (SEIS) .... BDS
Barbados [*Airport symbol*] (OAG) .... BGI
Barbados [*Seismograph station code, US Geological Survey Closed*] (SEIS) .... BRB
Barbados [*ANSI three-letter standard code*] (CNC) .... BRB
Barbados [*IYRU nationality code*] (IYR) .... KBA
Barbados [*MARC geographic area code Library of Congress*] (LCCP) .... nwbb--
Barbados Board of Tourism (EA) .... BBT
Barbados Environmental Association (EAIO) .... BEA
Barbados Labor Party .... BLP
Barbados Law Reports [*A publication*] (DLA) .... Barb LR
Barbados Law Reports [*A publication*] (DLA) .... BLR
Barbados Oceanographic and Meteorological Analysis Project .... BOMAP
Barbados Oceanographic and Meteorological Experiment [*National Oceanic and Atmospheric Administration*] .... BOMEX
Barbara Bain International .... BBI
Barbara Bush Foundation for Family Literacy (EA) .... BBFFL
Barbara Eden International Fan Club (EA) .... BEIFC
Barbecon, Inc. [*Toronto Stock Exchange symbol*] .... BEC
Barbecue (ADA) .... BBQ
Barbecue Briquet Institute [*Later, BIA*] .... BBI
Barbecue Industry Association (EA) .... BIA
Barber [*Charles E.*] [*Designer's mark, when appearing on US coins*] .... B
Barber .... BARB
Barber, Albert P., Kenosha WI [*STAC*] .... BAA
Barber Coin Collector Society (EA) .... BCCS
Barber Colman Co., Technical Library, Loves Park, IL [*Library symbol*] [*Library of Congress*] (LCLS) .... ILpB
Barber Hairstyling for Men and Women [*Associated Press*] (SAG) .... BarHair
Barber Hairstyling for Men and Women [*NASDAQ symbol*] (SAG) .... BBHF
Barber on Insurance [*A publication*] (DLA) .... Barb Ins
Barber Pole (KSC) .... BP
Barber Steamship Lines (MHDW) .... BSL
Barber Suggestibility Scale [*Psychology*] .... BBS
Barber's Digest [*New York*] [*A publication*] (DLA) .... Barb App Dig
Barber's Digest of Kentucky [*A publication*] (DLA) .... Barb Dig
Barber's Gold Law [*South Africa*] [*A publication*] (DLA) .... B
Barber's Gold Law [*South Africa*] [*A publication*] (DLA) .... Barb
Barber's Gold Law [*South Africa*] [*A publication*] (DLA) .... Barber
Barbers Point Naval Air Station, Oahu Island [*Hawaii*] [*ICAO location identifier*] (ICLI) .... PHNA
Barber's Reports [*14-42 Arkansas*] [*A publication*] (DLA) .... Bar
Barber's Reports [*14-42 Arkansas*] [*A publication*] (DLA) .... Barb
Barber's Reports [*14-42 Arkansas*] [*A publication*] (DLA) .... Barb Ark
Barber's Reports [*14-42 Arkansas*] [*A publication*] (DLA) .... Barbe
Barber's Reports [*14-42 Arkansas*] [*A publication*] (DLA) .... Barber
Barber-Scotia College [*Concord, NC*] .... BSC
Barber-Scotia College, Concord, NC [*OCLC symbol*] (OCLC) .... NCB
Barber-Scotia College, Concord, NC [*Library symbol Library of Congress*] (LCLS) .... NcCoB
Barbers,Hairstyling Men&Women [*NASDAQ symbol*] (TTSB) .... BBHF
Barberton [*South Africa*] [*ICAO location identifier*] (ICLI) .... FABN
Barberton Public Library, Barberton, OH [*Library symbol Library of Congress*] (LCLS) .... OBarb
Barbette [*Military*] .... BARB
Barbeyrac's Edition of Grotius on War and Peace [*A publication*] (DLA) .... Barb Gro
Barbeyrac's Edition of Puffendorf's Law of Nature and Nations [*A publication*] (DLA) .... Barb Puf
Barbil [*India*] [*ICAO location identifier*] (ICLI) .... VEBL
Barbital-Dependent [*Medicine*] (DMAA) .... BD
Barbiturate [*Pharmacology*] .... barb
Barbiturate Dependence [*Medicine*] (DMAA) .... BD
Barbiturate Screen [*Biochemistry*] (DAVI) .... BARB
Barbour and Carroll's Kentucky Statutes [*A publication*] (DLA) ...... Barb & C KY St
Barbour Elementary School, Rockford, IL [*Library symbol*] [*Library of Congress*] (LCLS) .... IRoBaE
Barbour on Parties in Law and Equity [*A publication*] (DLA) .... Barb Par
Barbour on the Law of Set-Off [*A publication*] (DLA) .... Barb Set-Off
Barbour's Abstracts of Chancellor's Decisions [*New York*] [*A publication*] (DLA) .... Barb Abs
Barbour's Chancery Practice [*New York*] [*A publication*] (DLA) .... Barb Ch Pr
Barbour's Chancery Reports [*New York*] [*A publication*] (DLA) .... B Ch
Barbour's Chancery Reports [*New York*] [*A publication*] (DLA) .... Barb Ch
Barbour's Chancery Reports [*New York*] [*A publication*] (DLA) .... Barb Ch (NY)
Barbour's Chancery Reports [*New York*] [*A publication*] (DLA) .... Barb Ch Rep
Barbour's Chancery Reports [*New York*] [*A publication*] (DLA) .... Barb Chancery Rep
Barbour's Chancery Reports [*New York*] [*A publication*] (DLA) .... Barbour's Ch R
Barbour's Criminal Law [*A publication*] (DLA) .... Barb Cr L
Barbour's Criminal Law [*A publication*] (DLA) .... Barb Cr Law
Barbour's Criminal Pleadings [*A publication*] (DLA) .... Barb Cr P
Barbour's Criminal Practice [*A publication*] (DLA) .... Barb Cr P
Barbour's New York Reports [*A publication*] (DLA) .... B
Barbour's Supreme Court Reports [*New York*] [*A publication*] (DLA) .... Bar SC Rep
Barbour's Supreme Court Reports [*New York*] [*A publication*] (DLA) .... Barb
Barbour's Supreme Court Reports [*New York*] [*A publication*] (DLA) .... Barb (NY) SCR
Barbour's Supreme Court Reports [*New York*] [*A publication*] (DLA) .... Barb R
Barbour's Supreme Court Reports [*New York*] [*A publication*] (DLA) .... Barb SC
Barbour's Supreme Court Reports [*New York*] [*A publication*] (DLA) ...... Barb SCR
Barbour's Supreme Court Reports [*New York*] [*A publication*] (DLA) .... Barb Sup Ct
Barbour's Supreme Court Reports [*New York*] [*A publication*] (DLA) .... Barb Sup Ct Reports
Barbour's Supreme Court Reports [*New York*] [*A publication*] (DLA) .... Barbour
Barbour's Supreme Court Reports [*New York*] [*A publication*] (DLA) .... Barbour (NY)
Barbour's Supreme Court Reports [*New York*] [*A publication*] (DLA) .... Barbour's Sup Court Rep
Barbourville, KY [*AM radio station call letters*] .... WYWY
Barbourville, KY [*FM radio station call letters*] .... WYWY-FM
Barbuda [*West Indies*] [*Airport symbol*] (OAG) .... BBQ
Barbuda [*MARC geographic area code Library of Congress*] (LCCP) .... nwbc--
Barbuda People's Movement [*Antigua*] [*Political party*] (PD) .... BPM
Barca [*Ship's rigging*] (ROG) .... BCA
Barcaldine [*Australia Airport symbol*] (OAG) .... BCI
Barcan Communications, Inc. [*Vancouver Stock Exchange symbol*] .... BNC
Barcelona [*Spain*] [*Airport symbol*] (OAG) .... BCN
Barcelona [*Venezuela*] [*Airport symbol*] (OAG) .... BLA
Barcelona [*Spain ICAO location identifier*] (ICLI) .... LEBL
Barcelona [*Spain ICAO location identifier*] (ICLI) .... LECB
Barcelona/Gral. Jose Antonio Anzoategui Internacional Anzoategui [*Venezuela ICAO location identifier*] (ICLI) .... SVBC
Barcelona Olympic Organizing Committee [*Spain*] (EAIO) .... BOOC
Barcelona, Spain - Pisa, Italy [*Submarine cable*] [*Telecommunications*] .... BAPI
Barceloneta, PR [*AM radio station call letters*] .... WBQN
Barcelonnette/Saint-Pons [*France ICAO location identifier*] (ICLI) .... LFMR
Barch, John R., New York NY [*STAC*] .... BJR
Barcklay Flying Service [*ICAO designator*] (FAAC) .... ACH
Barclay Classroom Assessment System [*Student personality test*] .... BCAS
Barclay Early Childhood Skill Assessment Center (EDAC) .... BECSAS
Barclays Australia Investment Services Consensus Earnings Profile .... BARCEP
Barclays Bank [*Associated Press*] (SAG) .... BarB
Barclays Bank [*NYSE symbol*] (SPSG) .... BCB
Barclays Bank Australia .... BBA
Barclays Bk C1/C2Unit ADS [*NYSE symbol*] (TTSB) .... BCBPrC
Barclays Bk D1/D2Unit ADS [*NYSE symbol*] (TTSB) .... BCBPrD
Barclays Bk E1/E2 UnitADS [*NYSE symbol*] (TTSB) .... BCBPr
Barclays de Zoete Wedd [*Investment firm*] [*British*] .... BZW
Barclays Development Fund [*Barclay's Bank*] [*British*] .... BDF
Barclay's Digest of the Law of Scotland [*A publication*] (DLA) .... Bar Dig
Barclay's Digest of the Law of Scotland [*A publication*] (DLA) ...... Barc Dig Law Sc
Barclays Home Mortgage Rate [*British*] (DCTA) .... BHMR
Barclay's Law of Highways [*A publication*] (DLA) .... Barc High
Barclays Ltd. [*Associated Press*] (SAG) .... Barclay
Barclays Ltd. [*NYSE symbol*] (SPSG) .... BCS
Barclays Merchant Bank [*British*] .... BMB
Barclay's Missouri Digest [*A publication*] (DLA) .... Barc Dig
Barclay's Missouri Digest [*A publication*] (DLA) .... Barc Mo Dig
Barclays PLC [*Associated Press*] (SAG) .... Barclay
Barclays PLC [*NYSE symbol*] (SAG) .... BCS
Barclays plc ADS [*NYSE symbol*] (TTSB) .... BCS
Barco Rotary Joint .... BRJ
Bar-Code Reader/Sorter [*Marketing*] (PDAA) .... BCRS

Bard College, Annandale-On-Hudson, NY [*Library symbol Library of Congress*] (LCLS) .... NAnB
Bard College, Annandale-On-Hudson, NY [*OCLC symbol*] (OCLC) .... VVP
Bard (C.R.) [*NYSE symbol*] (TTSB) .... BCR
Bard [*C.R.*], Inc. [*Associated Press*] (SAG) .... Bard
Bard [*C. R.*], Inc. [*NYSE symbol*] (SPSG) .... BCR
Bard Silver & Gold [*Vancouver Stock Exchange symbol*] .... BDS
Bardai-Zougra [*Chad*] [*ICAO location identifier*] (ICLI) .... FTTZ
Bardeen-Cooper-Schrieffer Theory [*Theoretical physics*] .... BCS
Bardenas Reales [*Spain ICAO location identifier*] (ICLI) .... LEBR
Bardera [*Somalia*] [*ICAO location identifier*] (ICLI) .... HCMD
Bardet-Beidl Syndrome [*Medicine*] .... BBS
Bardine Oils Ltd. [*Vancouver Stock Exchange symbol*] .... BAO
Bardsey Bird and Field Observatory [*British*] (BI) .... BBFO
Bardstown, KY [*Location identifier FAA*] (FAAL) .... BRY
Bardstown, KY [*AM radio station call letters*] .... WBRT
Bardstown, KY [*FM radio station call letters*] .... WOKH
Bardufoss [*Norway*] [*Airport symbol*] (OAG) .... BDU
Bardufoss [*Norway ICAO location identifier*] (ICLI) .... ENDU
Bare Aluminum Wire .... BAW
Bare and Painted (BARN) .... b & p
Bare Base [*Air Force*] (AFM) .... BB
Bare Base Set [*Air Force*] .... BBS
Bare Base Support Package (MCD) .... BBSP
Bare Beryllium Copper Wire .... BBCW
Bare Brass Wire .... BBW
Bare Copper .... BC
Bare Copper Wire .... BCW
Bare Copper-Clad Wire .... BCCW
Bare Equipment Modernization Officer [*Military*] (DNAB) .... BEMO
Bare Essentials of Surface Transfer .... BEST
Bare Gold-Plated Wire .... BGPW
Bare Lymphocytes Syndrome [*Medicine*] .... BLS
Bare Metal Arc Welding .... BMAW
Bare Molybdenum Wire .... BMW
Bare Nickel Chrome Wire .... BNCW
Bare Phosphor Bronze Wire .... BPBW
Bare Platinum Wire .... BPW
Bare Reactor Experiment at Nevada .... BREN
Bare Refractory, Double Containment [*Boiler*] [*NASA*] .... BRDC
Bare Silver-Plated Wire .... BSPW
Bare Stainless-Steel Wire .... BSSW
Bare Steel Wire .... BSW
Bare Tungsten Wire .... BTW
Bare Zirconium Wire .... BZW
Bareboat Charter (DNAB) .... BBC
Bareboat Charter (DNAB) .... BC
Barefoot, Inc. [*NASDAQ symbol*] (SPSG) .... BARE
Barefoot, Inc. [*Associated Press*] (SAG) .... Barefoot
Bareilly [*India*] [*ICAO location identifier*] (ICLI) .... VIBY
Barexor Minerals, Inc. [*Vancouver Stock Exchange symbol*] .... BXR
Bargain (ADA) .... BARG
Bargain (ROG) .... BARGN
Bargain .... BRGN
Bargaining Unit (GFGA) .... BU
Bargaining Unit Member [*of a faculty union*] .... BUM
Barge .... B
Barge .... BG
Barge (ROG) .... BGE
Barge Aboard Catamaran .... BACAT
Barge, Amphibious, Resupply, Cargo .... BARC
Barge, Amphibious, Resupply Craft [*Navy*] (VNW) .... BARC
Barge and Canal Development Association [*British*] .... BCDA
Barge Builders Trade Union [*British*] .... BBTU
Barge Cargo (AAG) .... BC
Barge Cargo Ship .... TALS
Barge Carrying Vessel .... BCV
Barge, Knockdown (MSA) .... BK
Barge Off Loading Facility .... BOLF
Barge, Training (MSA) .... BT
Barge Transportation Appraisal Program [*Military*] (MCD) .... BARTAP
Barge-Mounted Methanol Plant [*Chemical industry*] .... BMMP
Barge-Mounted Production and Storage System (DS) .... BPSS
Barges on Board [*Shipping*] .... BOB
Bargmann Bowen and Kemp, Inc. [*Telecommunications service*] (TSSD) .... BBK
Barham's Student's Guide to the Preliminary Examinations [*A publication*] (DLA) .... Barh Pre Ex
Bari [*Italy*] [*Seismograph station code, US Geological Survey Closed*] (SEIS) .... BAI
Bari [*Italy*] [*Airport symbol*] (OAG) .... BRI
Bari/Palese Macchie [*Italy ICAO location identifier*] (ICLI) .... LIBD
Bar-Ilan University (BJA) .... BIU
Barile-Yaguchi-Eveland [*Growth medium*] [*Microbiology*] .... BYE
Barinas [*Venezuela*] [*Airport symbol*] (OAG) .... BNS
Barinas, Barinas [*Venezuela ICAO location identifier*] (ICLI) .... SVBI
Baring Unit Trust Management Service [*Finance British*] .... BUTM
Bario [*Malaysia*] [*Airport symbol*] (OAG) .... BBN
Bario [*Malaysia*] [*ICAO location identifier*] (ICLI) .... WBGZ
Barisal [*Bangladesh*] [*Airport symbol*] (AD) .... BZL
Barisan Nasional [*Malaysia*] [*Political party*] (EY) .... BN
Barisan Nasional Penbebasan Pattani [*Thailand*] [*Political party*] .... BNPP
Barisan Revolusi Nasional [*Thailand*] [*Political party*] .... BRN
Baritone [*Music*] .... B
Baritone [*Music*] .... BAR
Baritone [*Music*] (ADA) .... barit
Barium [*Chemical element*] .... Ba

Barium Boron Oxide [*Inorganic chemistry*] .... BBO
Barium Chloranilate [*Organic chemistry*] .... BCA
Barium Cloud Experiment [*NASA*] .... BCE
Barium Contrast Enema [*Medicine*] (CPH) .... BCE
Barium Crown .... BC
Barium Enema [*Medicine*] (DMAA) .... Ba
Barium Enema [*Medicine*] (BABM) .... Ba enem
Barium Enema [*Medicine*] (DAVI) .... Ba Enem
Barium Enema [*Medicine*] .... BaE
Barium Enema [*Medicine*] (MEDA) .... BaEn
Barium Enema [*Medicine*] .... BE
Barium Ferrite Magnet .... BFM
Barium Ion Cloud [*NASA*] .... BIC
Barium Meal [*Medicine*] .... BaM
Barium Oxide Ferrite .... BOF
Barium Sodium Niobate [*Crystal*] .... BSN
Barium-Magnesia-Alumina-Silicate [*Inorganic chemistry*] .... BMAS
Bark (WGA) .... BAR
Bark [*or Barque*] (ROG) .... BK
Bark (VRA) .... brk
Bark Dieback [*Plant pathology*] .... BD
Bark Forager [*Ornithology*] .... BF
Bark Thickness [*Botany*] .... BARKTH
Barkcloth (VRA) .... brkcth
Barken International, Inc. [*ICAO designator*] (FAAC) .... BKJ
Barker & Dobson [*British*] .... B & D
Barker Code Processing .... BCP
Barker Free Library, Barker, NY [*Library symbol Library of Congress*] (LCLS) .... NBar
Barker-Henderson [*Theory*] [*Chemical physics*] .... BH
Barkerville Historic Park, British Columbia [*Library symbol National Library of Canada*] (NLC) .... BBHP
Barkhausen-Kurz Oscillator .... BKO
Barkhausen-Kurz Oscillator .... BO
Barkhor Resources, Inc. [*Vancouver Stock Exchange symbol*] .... BHO
Barking [*Borough in England*] .... BARK
Barking Sands, Kauai Island [*Hawaii*] [*ICAO location identifier*] (ICLI) .... PHBK
Barking Sands Tactical Underwater Range [*Naval Oceanographic Office*] .... BARSTUR
Barking Sands Underwater Range Expansion [*Naval Oceanographic Office*] (MCD) .... BSURE
Barkley Dam [*TVA*] .... BD
Barksdale, LA [*Location identifier FAA*] (FAAL) .... BYU
Barkston Ashe and Skyrac Volunteers [*British military*] (DMA) .... B & SV
Barkston Heath [*British ICAO location identifier*] (ICLI) .... EGYE
Barkston-Heath FTU [*British*] [*Military*] [*FAA designator*] (FAAC) .... BHH
Bar-Le-Duc [*France ICAO location identifier*] (ICLI) .... LFEU
Barley Alkaline Protease Inhibitor [*Medicine*] (DMAA) .... BAPI
Barley and Malt Institute [*Defunct*] (EA) .... BMI
Barley Canyon [*New Mexico*] [*Seismograph station code, US Geological Survey*] (SEIS) .... BRC
Barley Leaf Piece Agar [*Microbiology*] .... BLPA
Barley Marketing Board of New South Wales [*Australia*] .... BMBNSW
Barley Research Committee for Queensland [*Australia*] .... BRCQ
Barley Research Committee for South Australia .... BRCSA
Barley Research Committee for Western Australia .... BRCWA
Barley Research Committee, New South Wales [*Australia*] .... BRCNSW
Barley Research Council [*Australia*] .... BRC
Barley Stripe Mosaic Virus .... BSMV
Barley Yellow Dwarf [*Plant pathology*] .... BYD
Barley Yellow Dwarf Virus .... BYDV
Barley Yellow Mosaic Virus [*Plant pathology*] .... BAYMV
Barley Yellow Striate Mosaic Virus [*Plant pathology*] .... BYSMV
Barleycorn [*Unit of weight*] [*Obsolete British*] (ROG) .... BAR
Barleycorn [*Unit of weight*] [*Obsolete British*] (ROG) .... BC
Barling, AR [*FM radio station call letters*] .... KOLX
Barlow. Justice of Peace [*1745*] [*A publication*] (DLA) .... Barl Just
Barlow Sanatorium, Elks Tuberculosis Library, Los Angeles, CA [*Library symbol Library of Congress*] (LCLS) .... CLE
Barn [*Area of nuclear cross-section*] .... b
Barn .... BN
Barn Cleaner, Cattle Feeder, and Silo Unloader Association [*Later, FEA*] (EA) .... BCCFSUA
Barn Equipment Association [*Later, FEA*] (EA) .... BEA
Barnabites [*Also, CRSP*] [*Roman Catholic men's religious order*] .... Barn
Barnard [*Star second closest to the sun*] (BARN) .... Barn
Barnard College, Columbia University, New York, NY [*Library symbol Library of Congress*] (LCLS) .... NNBa
Barnardiston's English Chancery Cases [*1740-41*] [*A publication*] (DLA) .... Barnardiston CC
Barnardiston's English Chancery Reports [*A publication*] (DLA) .... Bar Ch
Barnardiston's English Chancery Reports [*A publication*] (DLA) .... Bar Chy
Barnardiston's English Chancery Reports [*1740-41*] [*A publication*] (DLA) .... Barn C
Barnardiston's English Chancery Reports [*1740-41*] [*A publication*] (DLA) .... Barn Ch
Barnardiston's English Chancery Reports [*1740-41*] [*A publication*] (DLA) .... Barnard Ch
Barnardiston's English Chancery Reports [*1740-41*] [*A publication*] (DLA) .... Barnard Ch (Eng)
Barnardiston's English Chancery Reports [*1740-41*] [*A publication*] (DLA) .... Barnard Ch Rep
Barnardiston's English King's Bench Reports [*A publication*] (DLA) .... Bar
Barnardiston's English King's Bench Reports [*A publication*] (DLA) .... Barn
Barnardiston's English King's Bench Reports [*A publication*] (DLA) .... Barn KB

Barnardiston's English King's Bench Reports [*A publication*] (DLA) .... Barnard
Barnardiston's English King's Bench Reports [*A publication*] (DLA)..... Barnard KB
Barnardiston's Tempore Hardwicke Reports, Chancery [*1740-41*] [*England*] [*A publication*] (DLA) .... Barnard
Barnaul [*Former USSR ICAO location identifier*] (ICLI) .... UNBB
Barnes & Noble [*NYSE symbol*] (TTSB) .... BKS
Barnes & Noble, Inc. [*Associated Press*] (SAG) .... BarNbl
Barnes & Noble, Inc. [*NYSE symbol*] (SPSG) .... BKS
Barnes Engineering Co. (KSC) .... BEC
Barnes' English Common Pleas Reports [*A publication*] (DLA) .... Barn
Barnes' Equity Practice [*A publication*] (DLA) .... Barn Eq Pr
Barnes' Exposition of the Law Respecting Sheriff [*1816*] [*A publication*] (DLA) .... Barn Sh
Barnes Group [*NYSE symbol*] (TTSB) .... B
Barnes Group, Inc. [*NYSE symbol*] (SPSG) .... B
Barnes Group, Inc. [*Associated Press*] (SAG) .... BarnGp
Barnes, Hickam, Pantzer & Boyd, Indianapolis, IN [*OCLC symbol*] (OCLC)..... IHB
Barnes, Hickam, Pantzer & Boyd, Law Library, Indianapolis, IN [*Library symbol Library of Congress*] (LCLS) .... InIBHP
Barnes' Notes of Cases of Practice in Common Pleas [*94 English Reprint*] [*A publication*] (DLA) .... Bar N
Barnes' Notes of Cases of Practice in Common Pleas [*94 English Reprint*] [*A publication*] (DLA) .... Barn No
Barnes' Notes of Cases of Practice in Common Pleas [*94 English Reprint*] [*A publication*] (DLA) .... Barnes
Barnes' Notes of Cases of Practice in Common Pleas [*94 English Reprint*] [*A publication*] (DLA) .... Barnes NC
Barnes' Notes of Cases of Practice in Common Pleas [*94 English Reprint*] [*A publication*] (DLA) .... Barnes Notes
Barnes' Notes of Cases of Practice in Common Pleas [*94 English Reprint*] [*A publication*] (DLA) .... Barnes Notes (Eng)
Barnes' Notes on the New Testament [*A publication*] .... BNNT
Barnesboro, PA [*AM radio station call letters*] .... WNCC
Barnes-Hind/Hydrocurve [*Commercial firm*] (DAVI) .... BH
Barnes-Hind Pharmaceutical (DAVI) .... B-H
Barnes's Federal Code [*A publication*] (DLA) .... Barnes's Fed Code
Barnesville, GA [*AM radio station call letters*] .... WBAF
Barnesville High School, Barnesville, MN [*Library symbol*] [*Library of Congress*] (LCLS) .... MnBarH
Barnesville, OH [*FM radio station call letters*] .... WBNV
Barnesville Public Library, Barnesville, MN [*Library symbol*] [*Library of Congress*] (LCLS) .... MnBar
Barnesville Public Library, Barnesville, OH [*Library symbol Library of Congress*] (LCLS) .... OBarn
Barnet's English Central Criminal Courts Reports [*27-92*] [*A publication*] (DLA) .... Barnet
Barnett Banks, Inc. [*Associated Press*] (SAG) .... Barnett
Barnett Banks, Inc. [*Associated Press*] (SAG) .... Barnt
Barnett Banks, Inc. [*NYSE symbol*] (SPSG) .... BBI
Barnett, Inc. [*Associated Press*] (SAG) .... Barnett
Barnett, Inc. [*NASDAQ symbol*] (SAG) .... BNTT
Barnett Inc. [*NASDAQ symbol*] (TTSB) .... BNTT
Barnewall and Adolphus' English King's Bench Reports [*109-110 English Reprint*] [*1830-34*] [*A publication*] (DLA) .... B & A
Barnewall and Adolphus' English King's Bench Reports [*109-110 English Reprint*] [*1830-34*] [*A publication*] (DLA) .... B & Ad
Barnewall and Adolphus' English King's Bench Reports [*109-110 English Reprint*] [*1830-34*] [*A publication*] (DLA) .... Bar & Ad
Barnewall and Adolphus' English King's Bench Reports [*109-110 English Reprint*] [*1830-34*] [*A publication*] (DLA) .... Barn & A
Barnewall and Adolphus' English King's Bench Reports [*109-110 English Reprint*] [*A publication*] (DLA) .... Barn & Ad
Barnewall and Adolphus' English King's Bench Reports [*109-110 English Reprint*] [*A publication*] (DLA) .... Barn & Ad (Eng)
Barnewall and Adolphus' English King's Bench Reports [*109-110 English Reprint*] [*1830-34*] [*A publication*] (DLA) .... Barn & Adol
Barnewall and Alderson's English King's Bench Reports [*1817-22*] [*A publication*] (DLA) .... B & A
Barnewall and Alderson's English King's Bench Reports [*A publication*] (DLA) .... B & Ald
Barnewall and Alderson's English King's Bench Reports [*A publication*] (DLA) .... Bar & Al
Barnewall and Alderson's English King's Bench Reports [*A publication*] (DLA) .... Barn & A
Barnewall and Alderson's English King's Bench Reports [*A publication*] (DLA) .... Barn & Ald
Barnewall and Alderson's English King's Bench Reports [*A publication*] (DLA) .... Barn & Ald (Eng)
Barnewall and Alderson's English King's Bench Reports [*1st part*] [*A publication*] (DLA) .... Selw & Barn
Barnewall and Cresswell's English King's Bench Reports [*107-109 English Reprint*] [*A publication*] (DLA) .... B & C
Barnewall and Cresswell's English King's Bench Reports [*A publication*] (DLA) .... Bar & Cr
Barnewall and Cresswell's English King's Bench Reports [*107-109 English Reprint*] [*A publication*] (DLA) .... Barn & C
Barnewall and Cresswell's English King's Bench Reports [*107-109 English Reprint*] [*A publication*] (DLA) .... Barn & C (Eng)
Barnewall and Cresswell's English King's Bench Reports [*107-109 English Reprint*] [*A publication*] (DLA) .... Barn & Cr
Barnewall and Cresswell's English King's Bench Reports [*107-109 English Reprint*] [*A publication*] (DLA) .... Barn & Cress
Barney Children's Medical Center, Dayton, OH [*Library symbol Library of Congress*] (LCLS) .... ODaMC
Barnfield and Stiness' Reports [*20 Rhode Island*] [*A publication*] (DLA) .... Barnf & S
Barnfield's Reports [*19-20 Rhode Island*] [*A publication*] (DLA) .... Barn
Barnhart Dictionary of Etymology [*A publication*] .... BDE
Barns Olson Aeroleasing Ltd. [*British ICAO designator*] (FAAC) .... CLN
Barnstable Law Library, Barnstable, MA [*Library symbol*] [*Library of Congress*] (LCLS) .... MBarL
Barnstable, MA [*FM radio station call letters*] .... WQRC
Barnstaple [*Municipal borough in England*] .... BARNST
Barnstaple's Printed Minutes and Proceedings [*A publication*] (DLA) .... Barn Pr M
Barnum Elementary School, Barnum, MN [*Library symbol*] [*Library of Congress*] (LCLS) .... MnBmE
Barnum High School, Barnum, MN [*Library symbol*] [*Library of Congress*] (LCLS) .... MnBmH
Barnum Woods Elementary School, East Meadow, NY [*Library symbol Library of Congress*] (LCLS) .... NEmBWE
Barnwall's Digest of the Year Books [*A publication*] (DLA) .... Barnw Dig
Barnwell Indus [*AMEX symbol*] (TTSB) .... BRN
Barnwell Industries, Inc. [*Associated Press*] (SAG) .... Barnwl
Barnwell Industries, Inc. [*Toronto Stock Exchange symbol*] .... BNW
Barnwell Industries, Inc. [*AMEX symbol*] (SPSG) .... BRN
Barnwell Municipal Library, Alberta [*Library symbol National Library of Canada*] (NLC) .... ABARM
Barnwell Nuclear Fuel Plant (NRCH) .... BNFP
Barnwell, SC [*Commercial waste site*] (GAAI) .... BARN
Barnwell, SC [*Location identifier FAA*] (FAAL) .... BNL
Barnwell, SC [*AM radio station call letters*] .... WBAW
Barnwell, SC [*FM radio station call letters*] .... WBAW-FM
Baroclinic Prognosis [*NWS*] (FAAC) .... BACLIN
Baroclinic Waves [*Astronomy*] .... BW
Baroda Law Reports [*India*] [*A publication*] (DLA) .... Baroda LR
Baroda/Vadodara [*India*] [*ICAO location identifier*] (ICLI) .... VABO
Barograph Display Unit .... BDU
Baromedical Nurses Association (EA) .... BNA
Barometer [*or Barometric*] .... BAR
Barometer (AABC) .... BARO
Barometer (FAAC) .... BRM
Barometric [*Medicine*] (DAVI) .... B
Barometric (WGA) .... BRMC
Barometric Absolute Pressure [*Automotive engineering*] .... BAP
Barometric Altimeter (MCD) .... BA
Barometric Altitude (MCD) .... BALT
Barometric Altitude (GAVI) .... HBARO
Barometric Altitude Control .... BAC
Barometric Altitude Indicator (NASA) .... BAI
Barometric Altitude Reference Unit .... BARU
Barometric and Manifold Absolute Pressure [*Automotive engineering*] .... BMAP
Barometric Pressure .... BP
Barometric Pressure Correction [*Symbol*] .... B
Barometric Read Solenoid [*Automotive engineering*] .... BRS
Baron .... B
Baron (ROG) .... BA
Baron .... BN
Baron (ROG) .... BON
Baron (ROG) .... BR
Baron Aviation Services, Inc. [*ICAO designator*] (FAAC) .... BVN
Baron of Exchequer [*British*] (ROG) .... BE
Baron on Chattel Mortgages [*A publication*] (DLA) .... Baron Ch Mort
Baroness (ROG) .... BNSS
Baroness (ROG) .... BSS
Baroness Publications Ltd., Inc. [*Publisher*] .... B
Baronet [*British*] .... BART
Baronet (EY) .... BT
Baronet of British Kingdom [*Initials used by Arthur Orton in his diary*] (ROG) .... B of BK
Baronial Order of Magna Charta (EA) .... BOMC
Baronne [*Baroness*] [*French*] (BARN) .... Bonnet
Barons Oil Ltd. [*Toronto Stock Exchange symbol*] .... BN
Barony of Urie Court Records [*1604-1747*] [*Scotland*] [*A publication*] (DLA) .... Baron
Baroque (VRA) .... Barq
Baroque All Style High [*Acronym is title of silk screen by sculptor Eduardo Paolozzi*] .... BASH
Baroque Resources Ltd. [*Vancouver Stock Exchange symbol*] .... BRQ
Barora [*Solomon Islands*] [*Airport symbol*] (OAG) .... RRI
Barossa Valley Vintage Festival Association [*Australia*] .... BVVFA
Barossa Winemakers' Association [*Australia*] .... BWA
Barostat (KSC) .... BARO
Baroswitch .... BS
Barotropic Electromagnetic and Pressure Experiment [*North Pacific, 1986-87*] [*Marine science*] (OSRA) .... BEMPEX
Barotropic Prognosis (FAAC) .... BATROP
Bar-Pattern Response [*Computer science*] (IAA) .... BPR
Barque [*Bark, Boat*] [*French*] (ROG) .... BAR
Barque .... BK
Barque [*Bark, Boat*] [*French*] .... BQ
Barque [*Bark, Boat*] [*French*] .... BQUE
Barquentine [*Ship*] .... BKN
Barquisimeto [*Venezuela*] [*Airport symbol*] (OAG) .... BRM
Barquisimeto/Internacional, Lara [*Venezuela ICAO location identifier*] (ICLI) .... SVBM
Barr Laboratories [*AMEX symbol*] (TTSB) .... BRL
Barr Laboratories, Inc. [*Associated Press*] (SAG) .... BarrLb
Barr Laboratories, Inc. [*AMEX symbol*] (SPSG) .... BRL
Barra [*Brazil*] [*Airport symbol*] (OAG) .... BQQ

Barra [*Hebrides Islands*] [*Airport symbol*] (OAG) .... BRR
Barra [*British ICAO location identifier*] (ICLI) .... EGPR
Barra Colorado [*Costa Rica*] [*Airport symbol*] (OAG) .... BCL
Barra De Parismina [*Costa Rica*] [*ICAO location identifier*] (ICLI) .... MRBP
Barra De Tortuguero [*Costa Rica*] [*ICAO location identifier*] (ICLI) ..... MRBT
Barra Del Colorado [*Costa Rica*] [*ICAO location identifier*] (ICLI) ..... MRBC
Barra Do Garcas [*Brazil ICAO location identifier*] (ICLI) .... SBBW
Barra Do Garcas/Xingu [*Brazil ICAO location identifier*] (ICLI) ... SBXG
Barra, Inc. [*Associated Press*] (SAG) .... Barra
BARRA, Inc. [*NASDAQ symbol*] (SPSG) .... BARZ
Barraca [*Peru*] [*ICAO location identifier*] (ICLI) .... SPCA
Barrack Department [*British military*] (DMA) .... BD
Barrack Warden [*British military*] (DMA) .... BW
Barracks .... BAKS
Barracks (AABC) .... BKS
Barracks and Quarters [*Army*] .... B & Q
Barracks Craft [*Non-self-propelled*] [*Navy symbol*] .... APL
Barracks Master-at-Arms .... BMAA
Barracks Petty Officer (DNAB) .... BPO
Barrackville, WV [*FM radio station call letters*] .... WMMN
Barrackville, WV [*FM radio station call letters*] (RBYB) .... WVUC
Barracuda Resources Ltd. [*Vancouver Stock Exchange symbol*] ... BCZ
Barradall. Manuscript Reports [*Virginia*] [*A publication*] (DLA) ... Barr M
Barradall. Manuscript Reports [*Virginia*] [*A publication*] (DLA) ... Barr MSS
Barrage Balloon .... BRGBLN
Barrage Balloon [*Navy symbol*] .... ZK
Barrage Jammers [*RADAR*] .... BJ
Barrage Mansour Eddahbi [*Morocco*] [*Seismograph station code, US Geological Survey*] (SEIS) .... BME
Barrage Rocket (NATG) .... BR
Barrancabermeja [*Colombia*] [*Airport symbol*] (OAG) .... EJA
Barrancabermeja/Yariguis [*Colorado ICAO location identifier*] (ICLI) ... SKEJ
Barranquilla [*Colombia*] [*Airport symbol*] (OAG) .... BAQ
Barranquilla [*Colorado ICAO location identifier*] (ICLI) .... SKEC
Barranquilla/Ernesto Cortissoz [*Colorado ICAO location identifier*] (ICLI) ... SKBQ
Barranquitas, PR [*AM radio station call letters*] .... WOLA
Barratry [*FBI standardized term*] .... BARR
Barre & Chelsea Railroad (IIA) .... B & C
Barre Granite Association (EA) .... BGA
Barre, VT [*FM radio station call letters*] (RBYB) .... WCMD-FM
Barre, VT [*FM radio station call letters*] .... WORK
Barre, VT [*AM radio station call letters*] .... WSNO
Barreau de Montreal, Bibliotheque des Avocats, Montreal, PQ, Canada [*Library symbol Library of Congress*] (LCLS) .... CaQMAv
Barred .... BRRD
Barred Trunk [*Telecommunications*] (NITA) .... BT
Barreiras [*Brazil*] [*Airport symbol*] (OAG) .... BRA
Barrel [*Shipping*] .... B
Barrel [*Shipping*] .... BAR
Barrel (AFM) .... BBL
Barrel (MCD) .... BL
Barrel .... BRL
Barrel .... BRL
Barrel Bulk [*Shipping*] (ROG) .... BB
Barrel Cactus Virus [*Plant pathology*] .... BACV
Barrel Cactus Virus .... BCV
Barrel Coating .... BC
Barrel Futurities of America (EA) .... BFA
Barrel Roll (CINC) .... BR
Barrel Switch (IAA) .... BSW
Barrel Vault (VRA) .... bar vlt
Barrel-Launched Adaptive Munitions .... BLAM
Barrels [*or Boxes*] [*Freight*] .... BB
Barrels [*Shipping*] .... BBLS
Barrels (ROG) .... BLL
Barrels [*Shipping*] .... BLS
Barrels, Boxes, or Crates [*Freight*] .... BBC
Barrels of New Oil (MHDB) .... BNO
Barrels of Oil Equivalent .... BOE
Barrels of Oil Equivalent per Day .... BOED
Barrels of Oil per Day (WGA) .... BOPD
Barrels or Bags [*Freight*] .... B BGS
Barrels per Calendar Day (IAA) .... BCD
Barrels per Calendar Day .... BPCD
Barrels per Day (IMH) .... bbl/d
Barrels per Day .... BD
Barrels per Day .... BPD
Barrels per Day Oil Equivalent .... B/DOE
Barrels per Hour .... BPH
Barrels per Minute .... BPM
Barrels per Month (IAA) .... BM
Barrels per Month (IAA) .... BPM
Barrels per Stream Day [*Also, BSD*] .... BPSD
Barrels per Stream Day [*Also, BPSD*] .... BSD
Barrel-Tile Roof [*Technical drawings*] .... BTR
Barremian-Aptian [*Paleontology*] .... BA
Barre-Montpelier, VT [*Location identifier FAA*] (FAAL) .... VKN
Barren Foundation [*Defunct*] (EA) .... BF
Barretos [*Brazil ICAO location identifier*] (ICLI) .... SBBT
Barrett [*California*] [*Seismograph station code, US Geological Survey*] (SEIS) .... BAR
Barrett Business Services [*Associated Press*] (SAG) .... BarrettB
Barrett Business Services [*Associated Press*] (SAG) .... BarrettB
Barrett Business Services, Inc. [*NASDAQ symbol*] (SAG) .... BBSI
Barrett Business Svcs [*NASDAQ symbol*] (TTSB) .... BBST

Barrett Memorial Library, Petersburg, IN [*Library symbol Library of Congress*] (LCLS) .... InPet
Barrett Memorial Library, Williams Bay, WI [*Library symbol Library of Congress*] (LCLS) .... WWil
Barrett Resources [*Associated Press*] (SAG) .... BaretRs
Barrett Resources [*NYSE symbol*] (SAG) .... BRR
Barrett Resources [*NYSE symbol*] (TTSB) .... BRR
Barrette [*Hawaii*] [*Seismograph station code, US Geological Survey Closed*] (SEIS) .... BAH
Barrett-Lennard Relationship Inventory (EDAC) .... BLRI
Barrett's Esophagus [*Medicine*] .... BE
[*The*] Barretts of Wimpole Street [*A play by Rudolf Besier*] .... BOWS
Barrhead Public Library, Alberta [*Library symbol National Library of Canada*] (NLC) .... ABARR
Barriada .... BDA
Barrick Gold [*NYSE symbol*] (TTSB) .... ABX
Barrick Gold Corp. [*NYSE symbol*] (SAG) .... ABX
Barrick Gold Corp. [*Associated Press*] (SAG) .... BarrickG
Barrick Resources Corp. [*Toronto Stock Exchange symbol*] .... BRC
Barrick-Cullaton Gold Trust Units [*Toronto Stock Exchange symbol*] .... BC
Barrie & Jenkins [*Publisher's imprint*] .... B & J
Barrie, ON [*FM radio station call letters*] .... CFJB
Barrie, ON [*FM radio station call letters*] .... CHAY
Barrie, ON [*FM radio station call letters*] (RBYB) .... CIQB
Barrie, ON [*Television station call letters*] .... CKVR
Barrie Public Library, Barrie, ON, Canada [*Library symbol Library of Congress*] (LCLS) .... CaOBa
Barrie Public Library, Ontario [*Library symbol National Library of Canada*] (NLC) .... OBA
Barriefield Branch, Frontenac County Library, Ontario [*Library symbol National Library of Canada*] (BIB) .... OBFC
Barrier (NVT) .... BAR
Barrier (MSA) .... BARR
Barrier and Countersurveillance Division [*Army*] (RDA) .... B & CD
Barrier Arresting Kit (PDAA) .... BAK
Barrier Coat (MSA) .... BC
Barrier Combat Air Patrol [*Navy*] .... BARCAP
Barrier Doctrine [*Military*] (NVT) .... BARDOC
Barrier Film Rectifier .... BFR
Barrier Filter [*Medicine*] .... BF
Barrier, Grease Proof (MSA) .... BGP
Barrier Injection Transit Time [*Physics*] .... BARITT
Barrier Layer Cell .... BLC
Barrier Layer Rectifier .... BLR
Barrier, Moisture Vapor Proof (MSA) .... BMVP
Barrier Operations [*Military*] (NVT) .... BAROPS
Barrier Paper Manufacturers Association [*Defunct*] (EA) .... BPMA
Barrier Preparation (MCD) .... BP
Barrier Pressure [*Medicine*] .... BRP
Barrier Ready Light System (MSA) .... BRLS
Barrier Ready Light System (IAA) .... BRLSYS
Barrier Reef Resources [*Vancouver Stock Exchange symbol*] ..... BAF
Barrier Tech [*Vancouver Stock Exchange symbol*] .... BAE
Barrier Terminal Strip .... BTS
Barrier Up Indicator System (MSA) .... BUIS
Barrier Up Indicator System .... BUISYS
Barrier, Waterproof (MSA) .... BWP
Barrier-Equivalent Velocity [*Automotive safety*] .... BEV
Barrigada, GU [*FM radio station call letters*] (RBYB) .... KHMG
Barrincorp Industries, Inc. [*Toronto Stock Exchange symbol*] ... BCP
Barring .... BRRG
Barringer Research Ltd., Rexdale, ON, Canada [*Library symbol Library of Congress*] (LCLS) .... CaOTBR
Barringer Research Ltd., Rexdale, Ontario [*Library symbol National Library of Canada*] (NLC) .... OTBR
Barringer Resources [*Associated Press*] (SAG) .... BarrngTch
Barringer Resources, Inc. [*NASDAQ symbol*] (NQ) .... BARR
Barringer Resources, Inc. [*Associated Press*] (SAG) .... BarTc
Barringer Resources, Inc. [*Associated Press*] (SAG) .... BarTch
Barringer Technologies Inc. [*NASDAQ symbol*] (TTSB) .... BARR
Barrington Area Library District, Barrington, IL [*Library symbol*] [*Library of Congress*] (LCLS) .... IBa
Barrington Bancorp [*NASDAQ symbol*] (TTSB) .... BABC
Barrington Bancorp, Inc. [*NASDAQ symbol*] (SAG) .... BABC
Barrington Bancorp, Inc. [*Associated Press*] (SAG) .... Barrngtn
Barrington College, Barrington, RI [*Library symbol Library of Congress*] (LCLS) .... RBaB
Barrington Historical Society, Barrington, NJ [*Library symbol Library of Congress*] (LCLS) .... NjBarHi
Barrington Petroleum Ltd. [*Formerly, Barrington Properties Ltd.*] [*Toronto Stock Exchange symbol*] .... BPL
Barrington Properties Ltd. [*Toronto Stock Exchange symbol Vancouver Stock Exchange symbol*] .... BGP
Barrington Public Library, Barrington, RI [*Library symbol Library of Congress*] (LCLS) .... RBa
Barrington's Magna Charta [*A publication*] (DLA) .... Bar Mag
Barrington's Observations upon the Statutes from Magna Charta to 21 James [*A publication*] (DLA) .... Bar Ob Stat
Barrington's Observations upon the Statutes from Magna Charta to 21 James [*A publication*] (DLA) .... Barr Ob
Barrington's Observations upon the Statutes from Magna Charta to 21 James I [*A publication*] (DLA) .... Bar Anc Stat
Barrington's Observations upon the Statutes from Magna Charta to 21 James I [*A publication*] (DLA) .... Bar Obs St

Barrington's Observations upon the Statutes from Magna Charta to 21 James I [*A publication*] (DLA) .... Barr Obs St
Barrington's Observations upon the Statutes from Magna Charta to 21 James I [*A publication*] (DLA) .... Barr St
Barrington's Observations upon the Statutes from Magna Charta to 21 James I [*A publication*] (DLA) .... Barring Obs St
Barrington's Observations upon the Statutes from Magna Charta to 21 James I [*A publication*] (DLA) .... Barring St
Barrio Florida [*Puerto Rico*] [*Seismograph station code, US Geological Survey*] (SEIS) .... PWP
Barrister (ADA) .... bar
Barrister .... BARR
Barrister .... BRRSTR
Barrister (ABBR) .... BRSTR
Barrister Info Sys [*AMEX symbol*] (TTSB) .... BIS
Barrister Information Systems Corp. [*Associated Press*] (SAG) .... Baristr
Barrister Information Systems Corp. [*AMEX symbol*] (SPSG) .... BIS
Barrister-at-Law .... BL
Barristers and Solicitors Admission Board of New South Wales [*Australia*] .... BSABNSW
Barristers and Solicitors' Admission Board of the Australian Capital Territory .... BSABACT
Barro Colorado Island [*Canal Zone*] [*Site of Smithsonian Tropical Research Institute*] .... BCI
Barroll. Chancery Practice [*Maryland*] [*A publication*] (DLA) .... Barr Ch Pr
Barron and Arnold's English Election Cases [*1843-46*] [*A publication*] (DLA) .... B & A
Barron and Arnold's English Election Cases [*1843-46*] [*A publication*] (DLA) .... B & Arn
Barron and Arnold's English Election Cases [*1843-46*] [*A publication*] (DLA) .... Bar & Arn
Barron and Arnold's English Election Cases [*1843-46*] [*A publication*] (DLA) .... Barr & Arn
Barron and Austin's English Election Cases [*1842*] [*A publication*] (DLA) .... B & A
Barron and Austin's English Election Cases [*1842*] [*A publication*] (DLA) .... B & Aust
Barron and Austin's English Election Cases [*1842*] [*A publication*] (DLA) .... B & Aust Cases (Eng)
Barron and Austin's English Election Cases [*1842*] [*A publication*] (DLA) .... Bar & Au
Barron and Austin's English Election Cases [*1842*] [*A publication*] (DLA) .... Bar & Aust
Barron and Austin's English Election Cases [*1842*] [*A publication*] (DLA) .... Barr & Aus
Barron and Holtzoff's Federal Practice and Procedure [*A publication*] (DLA) .... Barron & H Fed Pr & Proc
Barron's Mirror of Parliament [*A publication*] (DLA) .... Barron Mir
Barron-Welsh Art Scale [*Psychology*] .... BWAS
Barros & Associates Ltd. [*Information service or system*] (IID) .... B & A
Barrow [*Alaska*] [*Seismograph station code, US Geological Survey Closed*] (SEIS) .... BRW
Barrow [*Alaska*] [*Airport symbol*] (OAG) .... BRW
Barrow [*Alaska*] [*ICAO location identifier*] (ICLI) .... PABR
Barrow, AK [*Location identifier FAA*] (FAAL) .... IEY
Barrow, AK [*AM radio station call letters*] .... KBRW
Barrow, AK [*FM radio station call letters*] (RBYB) .... KBRW-FM
Barrow, AK [*Location identifier FAA*] (FAAL) .... NMT
Barrow High School, Barrow, AK [*Library symbol*] [*Library of Congress*] (LCLS) .... AkBarH
Barrow/Walney Island [*British ICAO location identifier*] (ICLI) .... EGNL
Barrows' Reports [*18 Rhode Island*] [*A publication*] (DLA) .... Bar
Barrows' Reports [*18 Rhode Island*] [*A publication*] (DLA) .... Barr
Barrows' Reports [*18 Rhode Island*] [*A publication*] (DLA) .... Barrows
Barrows' Reports [*18 Rhode Island*] [*A publication*] (DLA) .... Barrows (RI)
Barr's Reports [*1-10 Pennsylvania*] [*A publication*] (DLA) .... Barr
Barr's Reports [*1-10 Pennsylvania*] [*A publication*] (DLA) .... Barr (PA)
Barry [*Cardiff*] [*Welsh depot code*] .... BRY
Barry All the Time (EA) .... BATT
Barry Bostwick Fan Club (EA) .... BBFC
Barry College, Miami Shores, FL [*Library symbol Library of Congress*] (LCLS) .... FMsB
Barry College, North Miami, FL [*OCLC symbol*] (OCLC) .... FBC
Barry College, North Miami, FL [*Library symbol Library of Congress*] (LCLS) .... FNmB
Barry [*R.G.*] **Corp.** [*Associated Press*] (SAG) .... BarryR
Barry Gibb Record (EA) .... BGR
Barry Melton Band [*Pop music group*] .... BMB
Barry Morse Fan Club (EA) .... BMFC
Barry on Building Societies [*A publication*] (DLA) .... Barry Build Soc
Barry on Forms and Precedents in Conveyancing [*A publication*] (DLA) .... Barry Forms Conv
Barry on Tenures [*A publication*] (DLA) .... Barr Ten
Barry on Tenures [*A publication*] (DLA) .... Barry Ten
Barry. Practice of Conveyancing [*1865*] [*A publication*] (DLA) .... Barry Conv
Barry Railway [*Wales*] .... BR
Barry (R.G.) [*NYSE symbol*] (TTSB) .... RGB
Barry RG Corp. [*NYSE symbol*] (SAG) .... RGB
Barry (R.G.) Corp. [*NYSE symbol*] (SAG) .... RGB
Barry. Statutory Jurisdiction of Chancery [*1861*] [*A publication*] (DLA) .... Barry Ch Jur
Barry. Statutory Jurisdiction of Chancery [*1861*] [*A publication*] (DLA) .... Barry Ch Pr
Barry University (GAGS) .... Barry U
Barry's Babes [*Later, BGR*] (EA) .... BB
Barry's Bay Public Library, Ontario [*Library symbol National Library of Canada*] (NLC) .... OBB
Barrys Jewelers [*Associated Press*] (SAG) .... BarryJwl
Barry's Jewelers [*NASDAQ symbol*] (TTSB) .... BARY
Barry's Jewelers, Inc. [*NASDAQ symbol*] (NQ) .... BARY
Barry's Jewelers, Inc. [*Associated Press*] (SAG) .... BaryJ
Barry's Jewelers, Inc. [*Associated Press*] (SAG) .... BaryJw
Barry's Jewelers Wrrt [*NASDAQ symbol*] (TTSB) .... BARYW
Barryton Public Library, Barryton, MI [*Library symbol Library of Congress*] (LCLS) .... MiBar
Barsalogho [*Burkina Faso*] [*ICAO location identifier*] (ICLI) .... DHCB
Barsand Resources, Inc. [*Vancouver Stock Exchange symbol*] .... BSD
Barstow, CA [*Location identifier FAA*] (FAAL) .... BYS
Barstow, CA [*FM radio station call letters*] .... KDUC
Barstow, CA [*Television station call letters*] .... KHIZ
Barstow, CA [*AM radio station call letters*] .... KIQQ
Barstow, CA [*AM radio station call letters*] .... KSZL
Barstow, CA [*FM radio station call letters*] .... KXXZ
Barstow School, Kansas City, MO [*Library symbol Library of Congress*] (LCLS) .... MoKBa
Bar-Sur-Seine [*France ICAO location identifier*] (ICLI) .... LFFR
Bart Resources Ltd. [*Vancouver Stock Exchange symbol*] .... BK
Bartender (ABBR) .... BRTNDR
Barter (ABBR) .... BRTR
Barter Clubs (EA) .... BC
Barter Island [*Alaska*] [*Seismograph station code, US Geological Survey*] (SEIS) BI1
Barter Island [*Alaska*] [*Seismograph station code, US Geological Survey*] (SEIS) BI2
Barter Island [*Alaska*] [*Seismograph station code, US Geological Survey*] (SEIS) BI3
Barter Island [*Alaska*] [*Seismograph station code, US Geological Survey*] (SEIS) BI4
Barter Island [*Alaska*] [*Airport symbol*] (OAG) .... BTI
Barter Island [*Alaska*] [*ICAO location identifier*] (ICLI) .... PABA
Barter Worldwide, Inc. [*Information service or system*] (IID) .... BWW
Barth [*Germany ICAO location identifier*] (ICLI) .... ETBH
Bartholin and Skene [*Glands*] [*Medicine*] .... B & S
Bartholin's Skene's, and Urethral [*Glands*] [*Gynecology*] (DAVI) .... BSU
Bartholin's, Urethral, and Skene's Glands and External Genitalia [*Gynecology*] (DAVI) .... BUSEG
Bartholin's, Urethral, Skene's [*Glands*] [*Medicine*] .... BUS
Bartholomaeus [*Authority cited in pre-1607 legal work*] (DSA) .... Barto
Bartholomaeus Archamonus [*Authority cited in pre-1607 legal work*] (DSA) .... Bar Ar
Bartholomaeus Archamonus [*Authority cited in pre-1607 legal work*] (DSA) .... Bar Archa
Bartholomaeus Belenzinus de Modena [*Deceased, 1478*] [*Authority cited in pre-1607 legal work*] (DSA) .... Barth Belenz
Bartholomaeus Belenzinus de Modena [*Deceased, 1478*] [*Authority cited in pre-1607 legal work*] (DSA) .... Bartho Belenz
Bartholomaeus Belenzinus (Mutinensis) [*Deceased, 1478*] [*Authority cited in pre-1607 legal work*] (DSA) .... Bartho Mutinen
Bartholomaeus Brixiensis [*Deceased circa 1258*] [*Authority cited in pre-1607 legal work*] (DSA) .... B
Bartholomaeus Brixiensis [*Deceased circa 1258*] [*Authority cited in pre-1607 legal work*] (DSA) .... B Bri
Bartholomaeus Brixiensis [*Deceased circa 1258*] [*Authority cited in pre-1607 legal work*] (DSA) .... B Brix
Bartholomaeus Brixiensis [*Deceased circa 1258*] [*Authority cited in pre-1607 legal work*] (DSA) .... B Bx
Bartholomaeus Brixiensis [*Deceased circa 1258*] [*Authority cited in pre-1607 legal work*] (DSA) .... Bar
Bartholomaeus Brixiensis [*Deceased circa 1258*] [*Authority cited in pre-1607 legal work*] (DSA) .... Bar Brix
Bartholomaeus Brixiensis [*Deceased circa 1258*] [*Authority cited in pre-1607 legal work*] (DSA) .... Bar Brixi
Bartholomaeus Brixiensis [*Deceased circa 1258*] [*Authority cited in pre-1607 legal work*] (DSA) .... Bar Brixien
Bartholomaeus Brixiensis [*Deceased circa 1258*] [*Authority cited in pre-1607 legal work*] (DSA) .... Bart Bri
Bartholomaeus Brixiensis [*Deceased circa 1258*] [*Authority cited in pre-1607 legal work*] (DSA) .... Barth
Bartholomaeus Brixiensis [*Deceased circa 1258*] [*Authority cited in pre-1607 legal work*] (DSA) .... Barth Brix
Bartholomaeus Brixiensis [*Deceased circa 1258*] [*Authority cited in pre-1607 legal work*] (DSA) .... Bthol
Bartholomaeus Camerarius [*Deceased, 1564*] [*Authority cited in pre-1607 legal work*] (DSA) .... Bartol Camer
Bartholomaeus Cepolla [*Deceased, 1477*] [*Authority cited in pre-1607 legal work*] (DSA) .... Bart Cepol
Bartholomaeus de Capua [*Deceased, 1328*] [*Authority cited in pre-1607 legal work*] (DSA) .... B
Bartholomaeus de Capua [*Deceased, 1328*] [*Authority cited in pre-1607 legal work*] (DSA) .... B de C
Bartholomaeus de Capua [*Deceased, 1328*] [*Authority cited in pre-1607 legal work*] (DSA) .... B de Ca
Bartholomaeus de Capua [*Deceased, 1328*] [*Authority cited in pre-1607 legal work*] (DSA) .... Ba de Ca
Bartholomaeus de Capua [*Deceased, 1328*] [*Authority cited in pre-1607 legal work*] (DSA) .... Bar de C
Bartholomaeus de Capua [*Deceased, 1328*] [*Authority cited in pre-1607 legal work*] (DSA) .... Bar de Ca
Bartholomaeus de Capua [*Deceased, 1328*] [*Authority cited in pre-1607 legal work*] (DSA) .... Bar de Cap

Bartholomaeus de Capua [*Deceased, 1328*] [*Authority cited in pre-1607 legal work*] (DSA) .... Bart de Cap
Bartholomaeus de Exeter [*Flourished, 12th century*] [*Authority cited in pre-1607 legal work*] (DSA) .... Barthol
Bartholomaeus de Saliceto [*Deceased, 1411*] [*Authority cited in pre-1607 legal work*] (DSA) .... B de Sa
Bartholomaeus de Saliceto [*Deceased, 1411*] [*Authority cited in pre-1607 legal work*] (DSA) .... Bar
Bartholomaeus de Saliceto [*Deceased, 1411*] [*Authority cited in pre-1607 legal work*] (DSA) .... Bar de Sa
Bartholomaeus de Saliceto [*Deceased, 1411*] [*Authority cited in pre-1607 legal work*] (DSA) .... Bar de Sal
Bartholomaeus de Saliceto [*Deceased, 1411*] [*Authority cited in pre-1607 legal work*] (DSA) .... Bar de Sali
Bartholomaeus de Saliceto [*Deceased, 1411*] [*Authority cited in pre-1607 legal work*] (DSA) .... Bartho de Sali
Bartholomaeus Socinus [*Deceased, 1507*] [*Authority cited in pre-1607 legal work*] (DSA) .... Bart Socin
Bartholoman's Reports, Yorkshire Lent Assize [*March 9, 1911*] [*England*] [*A publication*] (DLA) .... Bartholoman
Bartholomew County Historical Society, Columbus, IN [*Library symbol Library of Congress*] (LCLS) .... InColuHi
Bartholomew County Library, Columbus, IN [*OCLC symbol*] (OCLC) .... INB
Bartholomew County Library, Columbus, IN [*Library symbol Library of Congress*] (LCLS) .... InColo
Bartholomew County Library, Columbus, IN [*Library symbol Library of Congress*] (LCLS) .... InColu
Bartholomew Sales & Distribution Services [*British*] .... BSDS
Barth's Aviation [*France ICAO designator*] (FAAC) .... BTH
Bartica [*Guyana*] [*Airport symbol*] (OAG) .... GFO
Bartica [*Guyana*] [*ICAO location identifier*] (ICLI) .... SYBT
Bartle Bogle Hegarty [*Commercial firm British*] .... BBH
Bartlesville [*Oklahoma*] [*Airport symbol*] (AD) .... BVO
Bartlesville Energy Research Center [*Department of Energy*] .... BERC
Bartlesville Energy Technology Center [*Later, NIPER*] [*Department of Energy Bartlesville, OK*] [*Information service or system*] (GRD) .... BETC
Bartlesville, OK [*Location identifier FAA*] (FAAL) .... BVO
Bartlesville, OK [*Television station call letters*] .... KDOR
Bartlesville, OK [*AM radio station call letters*] .... KWON
Bartlesville, OK [*FM radio station call letters*] .... KYFM
Bartlesville Project Office [*Bartlesville, OK*] [*Department of Energy*] (GRD) .... BPO
Bartlesville Public Library, Bartlesville, OK [*Library symbol Library of Congress*] (LCLS) .... OkB
Bartlet & Richards, Windsor, Ontario [*Library symbol National Library of Canada*] (BIB) .... OWBR
Bartlett Cove, AK [*Location identifier FAA*] (FAAL) .... BQV
Bartlett, TN [*AM radio station call letters*] (RBYB) .... WGSF
Bartlett, TN [*FM radio station call letters*] (RBYB) .... WMFS
Bartlett's Congressional Election Cases [*A publication*] (DLA) .... Bart Cong Election Cases
Bartlett's Congressional Election Cases [*A publication*] (DLA) .... Bart El Cas
Bartlett's Congressional Election Cases [*A publication*] (DLA) .... Bart Elec Cas
Bartlett's Index of the Laws of Rhode Island [*A publication*] (DLA) .... Bart Ind
Bartlett's Law of Mining [*1850*] [*A publication*] (DLA) .... Bart Mines
Bartley Herbarium, Ohio University [*Athens, OH*] .... BHO
Bartok Archives Z-Symbol Rhythm Extraction [*Computer science*] .... BARZREX
Bartok Recording Studio [*Record label*] .... BRS
Bartolus de Sassoferrato [*Deceased, 1357*] [*Authority cited in pre-1607 legal work*] (DSA) .... B
Bartolus de Sassoferrato [*Deceased, 1357*] [*Authority cited in pre-1607 legal work*] (DSA) .... Bar
Bartolus de Sassoferrato [*Deceased, 1357*] [*Authority cited in pre-1607 legal work*] (DSA) .... Bart
Bartolus de Sassoferrato [*Deceased, 1357*] [*Authority cited in pre-1607 legal work*] (DSA) .... Barto
Bartolus de Sassoferrato [*Deceased, 1357*] [*Authority cited in pre-1607 legal work*] (DSA) .... Bto
Barton & Guestier [*Wine*] .... B & G
Barton County Community College, Great Bend, KS [*Library symbol Library of Congress*] (LCLS) .... KGbB
Barton Regis [*England*] .... BART REG
Bartone [*Record label*] .... Bne
Bartonian Metaphysical Society, Ottawa, ON, Canada [*Library symbol Library of Congress*] (LCLS) .... CaOOBM
Bartonian Metaphysical Society, Ottawa, Ontario [*Library symbol National Library of Canada*] (NLC) .... OOBM
Barton's Law Practice [*A publication*] (DLA) .... Bart L Pr
Barton's Maxims in Conveyancing [*A publication*] (DLA) .... Bart Max
Barton's Modern Precedents in Conveyancing [*A publication*] (DLA) .... Bar Prec Conv
Barton's Modern Precedents in Conveyancing [*3rd ed.*] [*1826*] [*A publication*] (DLA) .... Bart Prec Conv
Barton's Science of Conveyancing [*2nd ed.*] [*1810-22*] [*A publication*] (DLA) .... Bart Conv
Barton's Suit in Equity [*A publication*] (DLA) .... Bar Eq
Barton's Suit in Equity [*A publication*] (DLA) .... Bart Eq
Bartonville, IL [*FM radio statio call letters*] (RBYB) .... WIXO-FM
Bartow, FL [*Location identifier FAA*] (FAAL) .... BOW
Bartow, FL [*AM radio station call letters*] .... WBAR
Bartow, FL [*AM radio station call letters*] .... WWBF
Bartow Public Library, Bartow, FL [*Library symbol Library of Congress*] (LCLS) .... FB
Bartram Trail Regional Library, Washington, GA [*Library symbol Library of Congress*] (LCLS) .... GWasB
Baruch [*Book of the Bible*] (BJA) .... Ba

Baruch [*Book of the Bible*] .... Bar
Baruch College, New York, NY [*OCLC symbol*] (OCLC) .... VVB
Baruch Retrieval of Automated Information for Negotiations [*City University of New York*] [*Information service or system*] (IID) .... BRAIN
Barwick Community Library, Barwick, ON, Canada [*Library symbol*] [*Library of Congress*] (LCLS) .... CaOBC
Barwick Community Library, Ontario [*Library symbol National Library of Canada*] (BIB) .... OBC
Barymin Explorations Ltd. [*Toronto Stock Exchange symbol*] .... BYX
Baryon Scale (WDAA) .... B
Baryon Symmetric Big Band (PDAA) .... BSBB
Baryonic Dark Matter [*Galactic science*] .... BDM
Baryon-Isobar Rest System .... BARS
Baryta Light Fling (MSA) .... BLF
Barytex Resources Corp. [*Vancouver Stock Exchange symbol*] .... BTX
Barzona Breeders Association of America (EA) .... BBAA
BAS Airlines [*ICAO designator*] (AD) .... GS
Bas Relief (VRA) .... barlf
BASA [*British Australian Studies Association*] **Magazine** [*A publication*] .... BASA Mag
Basaba Enterprises, Inc. [*Vancouver Stock Exchange symbol*] .... BSE
Basair AB [*Sweden ICAO designator*] (FAAC) .... BSR
Basal Acid Output [*Medicine*] .... BAO
Basal Acid Output to Maximal Acid Output [*Ratio*] [*Medicine*] (AAMN) .... BAO-MAO
Basal Area Increment [*Forestry*] .... BAI
Basal Body Temperature [*Medicine*] .... BBT
Basal Cell Atypia [*Medicine*] (DAVI) .... BCA
Basal Cell Carcinoma [*Medicine*] .... BCC
Basal Cell Carcinoma [*Medicine*] (DAVI) .... BCCA
Basal Cell Dysplasia [*Medicine*] (DAVI) .... BCD
Basal Cell Epithelioma [*Obsolete Medicine*] .... BCE
Basal Cell Hyperplasia [*Medicine*] .... BCH
Basal Cell Nevus Syndrome [*Medicine*] (DMAA) .... BCNS
Basal Cell Vigilance (DAVI) .... BCV
Basal Cerebral Vigilance [*Sleep*] .... BCV
Basal Energy Expenditure [*Nutrition*] (DMAA) .... BEE
Basal Energy Requirement [*Nutrition*] .... BER
Basal Fold .... BF
Basal Ganglion [*Medicine*] (DMAA) .... BG
Basal Granule .... BGR
Basal Groove .... BG
Basal Heart Rate [*Medicine*] .... BHR
Basal Insulin Level [*Medicine*] (DMAA) .... BIL
Basal Lamina [*Neuroanatomy*] .... BL
Basal Leaf Area [*Botany*] .... BAREA
Basal Level Element [*Genetics*] .... BLE
Basal Level Enhancer [*Genetics*] .... BLE
Basal Medium [*Microbiology*] .... BM
Basal Medium, Eagle's [*Diploid cell cultures*] (MAE) .... BME
Basal Metabolic Rate (CPH) .... BMET
Basal Metabolic Rate [*Medicine*] .... BMR
Basal Metabolism [*Medicine*] .... BM
Basal Pepsin Output [*Medicine*] (DMAA) .... BPO
Basal Period .... BP
Basal Retinal Neuron [*Neurology*] .... BRN
Basal [*or Baseline*] Skin Resistance [*Medicine*] .... BSR
Basal Starch Cycloheximide Antibiotic Agar [*Microbiology*] .... BSCAA
Basal Web .... BW
Basal-Ganglion Calcification [*Neurology*] (DAVI) .... BGC
Basalt (VRA) .... bst
Basalt, CO [*FM radio station call letters*] (RBYB) .... KNFO
Basalt Public Library, Basalt, CO [*Library symbol Library of Congress*] (LCLS) .... CoBa
Basalt Waste Isolation Project [*Department of Energy*] .... BWIP
Basaltic Achondrite Best Initial (DICI) .... BABI
Basaltic Achondrite Parent [*Planetary body*] .... BAP
Basaltic Volcanism Study Project [*Planetary science*] .... BVSP
Basankusu [*Zaire*] [*Airport symbol*] (OAG) .... BSU
Basankusu [*Zaire*] [*ICAO location identifier*] (ICLI) .... FZEN
Basco [*Philippines*] [*Airport symbol*] (OAG) .... BSO
Basco, Batanes Island [*Philippines*] [*ICAO location identifier*] (ICLI) .... RPUO
Base .... B
Base (DCTA) .... BAS
Base (IAA) .... BS
Base Accountable Supply Officer [*Air Force*] .... BASO
Base Accounting and Finance Office [*Air Force*] (AFM) .... BAFO
Base Activation .... BA
Base Activation Central Control Committee .... BACCC
Base Activation Change Order .... BACO
Base Activation Instruction .... BAI
Base Activation Notice .... BAN
Base Activation Statistical Control .... BASC
Base Activation Test Equipment .... BATE
Base Address and Transfer [*Military*] .... BAT
Base Address Register [*Computer science*] (BUR) .... BUR
Base Air Defense Ground Environment [*Air Force*] .... BADGE
Base Air Depot Area [*Air Force*] .... BADA
Base Aircraft Maintenance and Engineering Organization [*Canadian Navy*] .... BAMEO
Base Allowance List (MUGU) .... BAL
Base Ammunition Depot (NATG) .... BAD
Base and Increment [*Technical drawings*] .... B & I
Base and Installation Security System [*Military*] .... BISS
Base Area Commandant .... BAC
Base Area Refueling Equipment .... BARE

Base Assembly ... BA
Base Assembly and Test Equipment (SAA) ... BATE
Base Assembly Parts List (IAA) ... BAPL
Base Augmentation Support Set (MCD) ... BASS
Base Authorization List ... BAL
Base Automated Mobility System (MCD) ... BAMS
Base Automotive Maintenance ... BAM
Base Auxiliary Power (KSC) ... BAP
Base Burning (MCD) ... BB
Base Burning/Lateral Injection Propulsion (MCD) ... BBLIP
Base Capacitance (IDOE) ... C_B
Base Case Coordinating Instructions (DOMA) ... BCCI
Base Circle Diameter (IAA) ... BCD
Base Civil Engineer [*Military*] (AFM) ... BCE
Base Civil Engineer Real Property Office (SAA) ... BCERPO
Base Civil Engineering Course [*Air Force*] ... BCECRS
Base Civil Engineering School [*Air Force*] ... BCESCH
Base Closing Economic Injury [*Loan*] ... BCEI
Base Closure Action (MCD) ... BCA
Base Closure and Realignment Act [*Military*] ... BCRA
Base Closure and Realignment Commission [*DoD*] ... BCARS
Base Coat/Clear Coat [*Automotive body and refinishing*] ... BC/CC
Base Collector ... BC
Base Command ... BC
Base Communications Plan [*United States Army Communications Command*] (MCD) ... BASCOP
Base Composite Price Index (MCD) ... BI
Base Condemnation Percent (NASA) ... BCP
Base Connection [*Engineering*] (IAA) ... BC
Base Consolidation Control Office (AFM) ... BCCO
Base Construction Depot Detachment [*Navy*] ... BCDD
Base Construction Liaison Unit (SAA) ... BCLU
Base Contracting Automated System [*Computer science*] ... BCAS
Base Contracting Officer [*Military*] ... BCO
Base Correlation Matrix [*Air Force*] (DOMA) ... BCM
Base Count (IAA) ... BC
Base Course Wear Rate [*Tire testing*] ... BCWR
Base Data Processing Installation ... BDPI
Base Data System (AFM) ... BDS
Base de Datos Geomagneticos [*Instituto Geografico Nacional*] [*Database*] ... BASEMAG
Base de Documentos en Politica Criminal [*Criminal Law Documents Data Base*] [*United Nations Latin American Institute for Crime Prevention and Treatment of Offenders*] (IID) ... DPOC
Base de Donnees des Obligations Francaises [*DAFSA*] [*Database*] ... BDO
Base Defense Force [*Military*] (NVT) ... BDF
Base Deficit ... BD
Base des Forces Canadiennes [*Canadian Forces Base - CFB*] ... BFC
Base Design Section [*Military*] (IAA) ... BDS
Base Design Section - Operational Facility Installation [*Military*] (IAA) ... BDSOFI
Base Design Section - Support Facility Installation [*Military*] (IAA) ... BDSSFI
Base Detonating ... BD
Base Detonating Fuse ... BDF
Base Detonating Fuze (MCD) ... BDEF
Base Detonating, Self-Destroying ... BDSD
Base Development Board [*Military*] (AABC) ... BDB
Base Development Feasibility Study [*Navy*] ... BDFS
Base Development Plan (AABC) ... BDP
Base Development Report ... BASEDEV
Base Development Survey (MCD) ... BDS
Base Diameter ... BD
Base Diameter ... BDIA
Base Diameter [*Manufacturing term*] ... Db
Base Diffusion Isolation ... BDI
Base d'Information Robert Debre [*Robert Debre Information Base*] [*International Children's Center*] [*Information service or system*] (IID) ... BIRD
Base Distribution System [*Air Force*] (AFM) ... BDS
Base Divider Strip (AAG) ... BDS
Base Ejection ... BE
Base Electronics System Engineering Plan (NG) ... BESEP
Base Engineer Emergency Force [*Air Force*] (AFM) ... BEEF
Base Engineering Automated Management System (AFM) ... BEAMS
Base Equipment Container ... BEC
Base Equipment Management Office [*Air Force*] (AFM) ... BEMO
Base Excess [*Medicine*] ... BE
Base Excess [*Biochemistry*] (DAVI) ... Bex
Base Excess [*Medicine*] ... BXS
Base Exchange ... BX
Base Extension Course ... BEC
Base Facilities for SACLANT [*NATO*] (NATG) ... BFS
Base Field Effect Register [*Electronics*] (OA) ... BFER
Base File ... BF
Base Flight Management Data System (AFM) ... BFMDS
Base for Uniform Language Definition [*Computer science*] (IEEE) ... BUILD
Base Force ... BASEFOR
Base Frequency (ADA) ... BF
Base Fuels Management Officer [*Air Force*] (AFM) ... BFMO
Base Fuels Supply Officer [*Air Force*] (AFM) ... BFSO
Base Funded (AFM) ... BF
Base Fuze ... BF
Base Fuze Hole Plug ... BFHP
Base Heat Shield ... BHS
Base Helix Angle [*NASA*] ... BHA
Base Hospital [*Military*] ... BH
Base Ignition ... BI
Base Industrial Relations Office [*or Officer*] [*Military*] ... BIRO
Base Information Transfer Center [*Military*] ... BITC
Base Information Transfer System [*Navy*] (GFGA) ... BITS
Base Injection (IAA) ... BI
Base Inspection Questionnaire [*Air Force*] ... BIQ
Base Installation Action Requirements ... BIAR
Base Installation Department (SAA) ... BID
Base Installation - Minuteman [*Military*] (IAA) ... BIMM
Base Installation Officer ... BIO
Base Installation Test Equipment [*Military*] (IAA) ... BITE
Base Interface Surveillance Unit (IAA) ... BISU
Base Interrupt Address Register (IAA) ... BIAR
Base Intrusion Detection System (MCD) ... BIDS
Base Intrusion Surveillance System (MCD) ... BISS
Base Isolation Level (IAA) ... BIL
Base Level Commercial Equipment [*DoD*] ... BCE
Base Level Inquiry System ... BLIS
Base Level Maintenance Cost System (AFIT) ... BLMCS
Base Level Military Personnel System ... BLMPS
Base Level of Treatment (DICI) ... BLT
Base Level Operations ... BLO
Base Level Personnel System [*Air Force*] (GFGA) ... BLPS
Base Level Self-Sufficiency [*Air Force*] ... BLSS
Base Line Configuration Identification (SAA) ... BCI
Base Loaded Antenna ... BLA
Base Loading System (DNAB) ... BLS
Base Locator Linkage (MHDI) ... BLL
Base Logistical Command ... BALOG
Base Mail Distribution Scheme [*Air Force*] (AFM) ... BMDS
Base Maintenance [*Air Force*] (AFM) ... BM
Base Maintenance and Operations Model ... BMOM
Base Maintenance and Repair ... BMAR
Base Maintenance Building (MCD) ... BMB
Base Maintenance Division [*Navy*] ... BMD
Base Maintenance Operation (MCD) ... BMO
Base Maintenance Removal Interval [*Air Force*] (AFIT) ... BMRI
Base Management Engineering Data System ... BMEDS
Base Manager Data System ... BMDS
Base Manager's Notice ... BMN
Base Manpower Data System [*Air Force*] (OAG) ... BMDS
Base Marambio [*Argentina ICAO location identifier*] (ICLI) ... SAWB
Base Medical Supply Office [*or Officer*] [*Air Force*] (AFM) ... BMSO
Base Metal Catalyst [*Automotive engineering*] ... BMC
Base Mount Valve ... BMV
Base Neutralizing Capacity [*Chemistry*] ... BNC
Base of Air Operations ... BAO
Base of Dorsal Lip ... BDL
Base of Lateral Lip ... BLL
Base of Natural Logarithms [*Mathematics*] (DAVI) ... e
Base of Overcast [*Meteorology*] ... BOVC
Base of Preference Program [*for reenlisting airmen*] ... BOP
Base of Prism Down [*Medicine*] (DMAA) ... BD
Base of Terminal Service [*for airmen*] ... BTS
Base of Tongue [*Anatomy and otorhinolaryngology*] (DAVI) ... BOT
Base Only Density (DGA) ... BOD
Base Operacional de Tropas Paraquedistas [*Paratroopers Operational Base*] [*Air Force Portugal*] ... BOTP
Base Operating Information System [*Formerly, COCOAS*] ... BASOPS
Base Operating Information System (Supply Management System) ... BASOPS (SMS)
Base Operating Service [*Contract*] [*DoD*] ... BOS
Base Operating Supplies ... BOS
Base Operating Supply System ... BOSS
Base Operating Support (AFM) ... BOS
Base Operation Manager ... BOM
Base Operations ... BAOPS
Base Operations ... BASEOPS
Base Operations Contract (SSD) ... BOC
Base Operations Division [*NASA*] (KSC) ... BOD
Base Operations Maintenance Simulator (MHDI) ... BOMS
Base Operations Office ... BASOPS
Base Order ... BO
Base Ordnance Depot ... BOD
Base Ordnance Workshop [*British and Canadian*] ... BOW
Base Organization and Maintenance Processor (IEEE) ... BOMP
Base Pairs [*Genetics*] (DOG) ... bp
Base Pairs in DNA [*Genetics*] ... BP
Base Pay [*Military*] ... BP
Base Percussion ... BP
Base Perimeter Security System ... BPSS
Base Period Density ... BPD
Base Personnel Staff Officer [*Air Force British*] ... BPSO
Base Pioneer [*Cell neuron*] ... BP
Base Pitch (MSA) ... BP
Base Planning Board [*Military*] (DNAB) ... BPB
Base Point ... BP
Base Point ... BPT
Base Point Configuration (AAG) ... BPC
Base Point Defense Launching System (DNAB) ... BPDLS
Base Pointer [*Computer science*] ... BP
Base Position [*Phylogenetic analysis*] ... BP
Base Post Office ... BPO
Base Postal Section [*Air Force*] (AFM) ... BPS
Base Precision Measurement Equipment Laboratories (AFM) ... BPMEL
Base Procured (AFM) ... BP

Base Procured/Central Procured (AFM) .... BP/CP
Base Procurement Office [Air Force] (AFM) .... BPO
Base Procurement Service Stores [Air Force] (AFM) .... BPSS
Base Production Unit [Army] (AABC) .... BPU
Base Productivity Factor (MCD) .... BPF
Base Program Preparation Facility [Computer science] (MHDI) ...... BPPF
Base Protein .... BP
Base Quartermaster [Marine Corps] .... BQM
Base Quota .... BQ
Base Rate Area [Telecommunications] (TEL) .... BRA
Base Rate Boundary [Telecommunications] (TEL) .... BRB
Base Realignment Aid Closure [Military] .... BRAC
Base Realignment and Closure [DoD] (RDA) .... BRAC
Base Realignment and Closure (AAGC) .... BRAC
Base Recirculation Insulation (IAA) .... BRI
Base Reclamation [of critical materials] (AAG) .... BR
Base Records Unit (SAA) .... BRU
Base Recovery After Attack (MCD) .... BRAAT
Base Recovery Course [Military] (NVT) .... BRC
Base Register [Computer science] (IAA) .... BAR
Base Register (CMD) .... BR
Base Register [Computer science] .... BX
Base Remount Depot [British military] (DMA) .... BRD
Base Repair Cycle (MCD) .... BRC
Base Requirements Overseas (CINC) .... BRO
Base Residence Course .... BRC
Base Resistance (IDOE) .... R_B
Base Resistance Transistor .... BRT
Base [or Basic] Retirement Date [Air Force] .... BRD
Base Salvage (AAG) .... BS
Base Salvage Officer (MCD) .... BSO
Base Section [Military] .... BASEC
Base Section [Military] .... BS
Base Security Council [Air Force] (AFM) .... BSC
Base Service Battalion [Marine Corps] .... BSERBN
Base Service Store [Air Force] (AFIT) .... BSS
Base Service Unit [Navy] .... BASESERVUNIT
Base Service Unit [Navy] .... BSU
Base Shell .... BS
Base Shield (IAA) .... BS
Base Shop Test Facility [Military] .... BSTF
Base Shop Test Station [Military] .... BSTS
Base Shop Tester .... BST
Base Signal Officer [Military] (IAA) .... BSO
Base Skirt .... BS
Base Spares Allowance List (MCD) .... BSAL
Base Spares Group .... BSG
Base Station [ITU designation] (CET) .... FB
Base Statistical Control (AAG) .... BSC
Base Supply (KSC) .... BS
Base Supply Airfield [British and Canadian] .... B Sup Airfld
Base Supply Depot .... BSD
Base Supply Management Office [Air Force] (AFM) .... BSMO
Base Supply Officer [Navy] .... BSO
Base Support Area [Military] .... BSA
Base Support Equipment [Military] .... BSE
Base Support Group [Air Force] .... BSGP
Base Support Group System [Air Force] .... BSGS
Base Target (MCD) .... BT
Base Ten Sys CI'A' [NASDAQ symbol] (TTSB) .... BASEA
Base Ten Sys CI'B' [NASDAQ symbol] (TTSB) .... BASEB
Base Ten Systems [Associated Press] (SAG) .... BsTn
Base Ten Systems, Inc. [NASDAQ symbol] (NQ) .... BASE
Base Transceiver Station .... BTS
Base Unit .... BU
Base Value (IDOE) V
Base Vehicle Reporting Officer .... BVRO
Base Voltage (IDOE) .... V_B
Base Weather Station (MCD) .... BWS
Base Wire and Telephone System [Air Force] (MCD) .... BWTS
Base Wire and Telephone System Development Schedule [Air Force].... BWTSDS
Base Wire Communications Program [Air Force] .... BWCP
Base Wire Communications System [Air Force] (CET) .... BWCS
Base Work Order (AAG) .... BWO
Base Workshop [British and Canadian] [Military] .... B Wksp
Base Year (DOMA) .... BY
Base Year Dollars (MCD) .... BYS
Baseball (ABBR) .... BSBL
Baseball .... BSBLL
Baseball Canada [Also, Canadian Federation of Amateur Baseball] (AC) .... CFAB
Baseball Club .... BBC
Baseball Hall of Fame Committee on Baseball Veterans (EA) .... BHFCBV
Baseball Hall of Shame [Defunct] (EA) .... BHS
Baseball Umpires Council of Australia .... BUCA
Baseball Writers Association of America (EA) .... BBWAA
Baseball Writers Association of America (EA) .... BWAA
Baseband (AAG) .... BB
Baseband (MUGU) .... BSB
Baseband Assembly Unit .... BAU
Baseband Breadboard .... BBB
Baseband Distribution Unit .... BDU
Baseband Level Control (MCD) .... BLC
Baseband Modulator-Demodulator (IAA) .... BMD
Baseband RADAR Bag Initiator (PDAA) .... BARBI
Baseband RADAR Sensor Technology (PDAA) .... BARS

Baseband Separation Unit (MCD) .... BSU
Baseboard (ABBR) .... BSBD
Baseboard Hot Water [Heating system] [Classified advertising] .... BBHW
Base-Catalysed Dechlorination .... BCD
Base-Catalyzed Decomposition Process .... BCDP
Base-Catalyzed Destination [Environmental science] .... BCD
Base-Coupled Logic [Computer science] (PDAA) .... BCL
Based (ABBR) .... BSD
Base-Down (Prism) [Ophthalmology] .... BD
Base-Emitter (DNAB) .... BE
Base-Excision Repair [Genetics] .... BER
Basegram [Navy] .... BGM
Base-Height Ratio .... B/H
Base-In (Prism) [Ophthalmology] .... BI
Basel [Bale] [Switzerland] [Seismograph station code, US Geological Survey] .... BAS
Basel Club (EAIO) .... BC
Basel/Mulhouse [Switzerland] [Airport symbol] (OAG) .... BSL
Baseless (ABBR) .... BSLS
Base-Level Self-Sufficiency Spare [Air Force] (DOMA) .... BLSSS
Baseline .... BL
Baseline Accounting and Reporting System (NASA) .... BARS
Baseline Armor Reliability Test [Army] (MCD) .... BART
Baseline Calibration Equipment .... BLCE
Baseline Comparison System [Army] .... BCS
Baseline Configuration .... BLC
Baseline Configuration Document (SSD) .... BCD
Baseline Correlation Matrix [Air Force] (AAGC) .... BCM
Baseline Cost Estimate (AABC) .... BCE
Baseline Data Collection Facility (MCD) .... BDCF
Baseline Definition Document (NASA) .... BDD
Baseline Demonstration LASER (MCD) .... BDL
Baseline Design Data Book (MCD) .... BDDB
Baseline Document Change Request (MCD) .... BDCR
Baseline Documentation (MCD) .... BLD
Baseline Electronic Warfare System (MCD) .... BLEWS
Baseline Flight Vehicle Mission Time Line .... BFVMTL
Baseline Intelligence Summary Supplement (MCD) .... BIS
Baseline Monitoring Report [Environmental Protection Agency] (GFGA) .... BMR
Baseline Operations Plan (MCD) .... BOP
Baseline Program Document (NASA) .... BPD
Baseline Reference Flight Plan (KSC) .... BRFP
Baseline Reference Mission (MCD) .... BRM
Baseline Restorer (IEEE) .... BLR
Baseline Schedule Plan (MCD) .... BSP
Baseline Surface Radiation Network [Marine science] (OSRA) .... BSRN
Baseline Surface Radiation Network [World Meteorlogical Organization] (USDC) .... BSRN
Baseline Waste Management Strategy (NUCP) .... BWMS
Baselined Software Library (MCD) .... BSL
Basement .... BSMNT
Basement .... BSMT
Basement (MSA) .... BSMT
Basement Membrane [Medicine] .... BM
Basement Membrane Matrix [Biochemistry] .... BMM
Basement Membrane Zones [Anatomy] .... BMZ
Basenji Club of America (EA) .... BCA
Basenji Club of America (EA) .... BCOA
Baseops International, Inc. [ICAO designator] (FAAC) .... XBO
Base-Out (Prism) [Ophthalmology] .... BO
Baseplate [Technical drawings] .... BAPE
Baseplate [Technical drawings] .... BP
Baseplate [Technical drawings] .... BPL
Base-Region Width (IDOE) .... W_B
Bases and Stations Information System [Navy] (GFGA) .... BASIS
Bases on Balls [Baseball] .... BB
Base-Stored Image Sensor .... BASIS
Base-Up (Prism) [Ophthalmology] .... BU
Base-Voltage Supply (IDOE) .... V_{BB}
Bashaw Public Library, Alberta [Library symbol National Library of Canada] (NLC) .... ABASH
Bashful (ABBR) .... BSHFL
Bashfully (ABBR) .... BSHFLY
Bashfulness (ABBR) .... BSHFLNS
Bashkir [MARC language code Library of Congress] (LCCP) .... bak
Bashkir Soviet Socialist Republic .... BashSSR
Bashkirian Airlines [Former USSR] [International] (FAAC) .... BTC
Basic [Rate] [Value of the English pound] (BAS) .... BAS
Basic (MUGU) .... BSC
Basic .... BSC
Basic Access Method [Computer science] .... BAM
Basic Achievement Skills Individual Screener [Educational test] .... BASIS
Basic Acoustic Warfare System (MCD) .... BAWS
Basic Acrylic Monomer Manufacturers Association (EA) .... BAMM
Basic Active Service Date (AABC) .... BASD
Basic Activity Subset [Telecommunications] (OSI) .... BAS
Basic Adaptive Hardware .... BAH
Basic Additional Teleprocessing Support [Computer science] (BUR) .... BATS
Basic Administration and Management .... BAAM
Basic Advance Training .... Bas Adv Tra
Basic Advanced Integrated Navigation System .... BAINS
Basic Agreement .... BA
Basic Air Navigation School [Military] (OA) .... BANS
Basic Air Temperature .... BAT
Basic Aircraft Check-Out Equipment (PDAA) .... BACE

Basic Airman [*Air Force*] ... E1
Basic Airspeed [*Aviation*] ... BAS
Basic Algebraic Symbolic Interpretive Compiler (IEEE) ... BASIC
Basic Allowance for Quarters [*Military*] ... BAQ
Basic Allowance for Quarters for Adopted Child [*Military*] ... BAQ(AC)
Basic Allowance for Quarters for Father [*Military*] ... BAQ(F)
Basic Allowance for Quarters for Husband [*Military*] ... BAQ(H)
Basic Allowance for Quarters for Legitimate Children [*Military*] ... BAQ(LC)
Basic Allowance for Quarters for Mother [*Military*] ... BAQ(M)
Basic Allowance for Quarters for Stepchildren [*Military*] ... BAQ(SC)
Basic Allowance for Quarters for Wife [*Military*] ... BAQ(W)
Basic Allowance for Quarters Pending Disability Retirement [*Military*] ... BAQ(DIS RET)
Basic Allowance for Subsistence [*Military*] ... BAS
Basic Allowance for Subsistence (DOMA) ... BAS
Basic Alteration Class Drawing [*Navy*] (CAAL) ... BACD
Basic Analog Simulation System (PDAA) ... BASS
Basic Analysis and Mapping Program (DNAB) ... BAMP
Basic and Applied Myology [*A publication*] ... BAM
Basic and Logically Applied Norms - Civil Engineering (AFM) ... BALANCE
Basic and Long-term Research ... BLR
Basic and Traditional Food Association [*Inactive*] (EA) ... BTFA
Basic Angle System ... BAS
Basic Appraisal System for Incoming Components ... BASIC
Basic Approved Jury Instructions (HGAA) ... BAJI
Basic Area of Interest [*Army*] (ADDR) ... BAI
Basic Armed Forces Communication Plan ... BAFCOM
Basic Armor Reliability Test (MCD) ... BART
Basic Armor Training (MCD) ... BAT
Basic Army Administrative Course ... BAAC
Basic Army Strategic Estimate [*A document*] ... BASE
Basic Artillery Force Simulation Model (MCD) ... BAFSM
Basic Assembler [*Computer science*] (IAA) ... BA
Basic Assembler Program [*Computer science*] ... BAP
Basic Assembly Language [*Programming language*] [*Sperry UNIVAC*] [*Computer science*] ... BAL
Basic Assembly Unit (WDAA) ... BAU
Basic Assessment System for Children ... BASC
Basic Attack Helicopter Team [*Army*] (RDA) ... BAHT
Basic Attack Option (MCD) ... BAO
Basic Authorization ... BA
Basic Automatic Checkout Equipment ... BACE
Basic Automatic Stored Instruction Computer (BUR) ... BASIC
Basic Automation Systems Elements ... BASE
Basic Aviation Sub-System Integration Concept (PDAA) ... BASIC
Basic Avionics Procedure Trainer [*British military*] (DMA) ... BAPT
Basic Boxed Base ... BBB
Basic Brazeau Medium [*Culture media*] ... BBM
Basic Building Code ... BBC
Basic Business Language [*Computer science*] (IEEE) ... BBL
Basic Calcium Phosphate [*Biochemistry*] (DAVI) ... BCP
Basic Call Processing System [*Telecommunications*] (NITA) ... BCPS
Basic Carbonate White Lead [*Paint technology*] ... BCWL
Basic Cardiac Life Support [*System*] [*Medicine*] ... BCLS
Basic Carriage Service [*Telecommunications*] ... BCS
Basic Combat Maneuver (MCD) ... BCM
Basic Combat Training [*Later, BT*] [*Army*] ... BCT
Basic Combined Programming Language ... BCPL
Basic Combined Subset [*Telecommunications*] (OSI) ... BCS
Basic Communication Access Method [*Computer science*] (IAA) ... BCAM
Basic Comparison Element (MHDI) ... BCE
Basic Computer Unit ... BCU
Basic Concepts Inventory [*Psychology*] ... BCI
Basic Configuration ... BSC
Basic Consolidated Requirements Document (NASA) ... BCRD
Basic Contour Line ... BCL
Basic Contract Specification ... BCS
Basic Control [*Mode*] [*Computer science*] ... BC
Basic Control Frequency ... BCF
Basic Control Monitor (BUR) ... BCM
Basic Control Program (DNAB) ... BCP
Basic Control System [*For satellites*] (MDG) ... BCS
Basic Copy [*Genetics*] ... BC
Basic Cost Information (AFIT) ... BCI
Basic Court System (PDAA) ... BCS
Basic Cryptanalysis Course ... BCC
Basic Cycle Length [*Medicine*] (DAVI) ... BCL
Basic Daily Food Allowance (AABC) ... BDFA
Basic Data Access Method [*Computer science*] (EECA) ... BDAM
Basic Data Base Environment [*Computer science*] (MHDI) ... BDBE
Basic Data Set Project [*National Science Foundation*] ... BDSP
Basic Data Transmission Routine (IAA) ... BDTR
Basic Dead Load [*Construction*] (DICI) ... BDL
Basic Decision Height [*Aviation*] (DA) ... BCH
Basic Democrats [*Pakistan*] ... BD
Basic Design Engineering (MCD) ... BDE
Basic Device Unit [*Computer science*] (IBMDP) ... BDU
Basic Direct Access Method [*IBM Corp.*] [*Computer science*] (BUR) ... BDAM
Basic Direct Shipping Instructions ... BDSI
Basic Disk Access Method (MCD) ... BDAM
Basic Disk Operating System ... BDOS
Basic Display Unit [*Computer science*] ... BDU
Basic Economics Test [*Educational test*] ... BET
Basic Editor Monitor [*Computer science*] (MHDI) ... BEM
Basic Education Assistance Material Service [*National Multimedia Center for Adult Basic Education*] (IID) ... BEAMS
Basic Education Development System (OICC) ... BEDS
Basic Education Program (EDAC) ... BEP
Basic Educational Opportunity Grants [*Office of Education*] ... BEOG
Basic Educational Skills Test ... BEST
Basic Educational Skills through Technology Project [*U.S. Department of Education*] (EDAC) ... BEST
Basic Electric Arc (PDAA) ... BEA
Basic Electrical Rhythm [*Neurophysiology*] ... BER
Basic Electricity and Electronics ... BE & E
Basic Electricity and Electronics Individualized Learning System [*Military*] (DNAB) ... BE/E INLS
Basic Electricity and Electronics School [*Military*] (DNAB) ... BEES
Basic Electronics Maintenance Trainer ... BEMT
Basic Element of Performance [*Medicine*] (DMAA) ... BEP
Basic Encoding Rule [*Telecommunications*] (OSI) ... BER
Basic Encoding Unit ... BEU
Basic Encyclopedia [*Army*] (AABC) ... BE
Basic Encyclopedic Redundancy Media (IEEE) ... BERM
Basic Energy Reduction Technology (IEEE) ... BERT
Basic Energy Sciences Committee [*Department of Energy Washington, DC*] (EGAO) ... BESAC
Basic Energy Sciences Program [*Department of Energy*] [*Washington, DC*] ... BES
Basic Energy Sciences Program [*Department of Energy*] [*Washington, DC*] ... BESP
Basic Engineering (DNAB) ... BENG
Basic Engineering Casualty Control Exercise [*Military*] (NVT) ... BECCE
Basic Engineering Damage Control Exercise [*Military*] (NVT) ... BEDCE
Basic Engineering Development ... BED
Basic Engineering Product Assumption ... BEPA
Basic English ... BE
Basic English for Testing Applications (PDAA) ... BETA
Basic Enlisted Service Date (AABC) ... BESD
Basic Enlisted Submarine School [*Navy*] (DOMA) ... BESS
Basic Entry Pay Date ... BEPD
Basic Equipment List (MCD) ... BEL
Basic Error Control System ... BECS
Basic Essential Skills Testing ... BEST
Basic Exchange Rate Planning Model [*Telecommunications*] (TEL) ... BERPM
Basic Exchange Telephone Radio [*Telecommunications*] (TNIG) ... BETR
Basic Executive Scheduler and Timekeeper (PDAA) ... BEST
Basic Executive System [*Honeywell, Inc.*] ... BES
Basic Exercises ... BX
Basic Experimental Automatic Syntactic Translator [*Bunker Ramo Corp.*] (NITA) ... BEAST
Basic Experimental Language [*Computer science*] (IAA) ... BASEX
Basic Extension to Alpha [*Alaska long period array*] ... BETA
Basic Extraction Sludge Treatment ... BEST
Basic Facility Requirements List [*Navy*] ... BFRL
Basic Fibroblast Growth Factor [*Biochemistry*] ... BFGF
Basic Field Manual [*Military*] ... BFM
Basic Fighter Maneuver [*Air Force*] (MCD) ... BFM
Basic Fighter Transition [*Air Force*] (DOMA) ... BFT
Basic File Access System ... BFAS
BASIC [*Bank Automated Service Information System*] **File Directory** (HGAA) ... BFD
BASIC [*Bank Automated Service Information System*] **File System** [*Computer science*] (HGAA) ... BFS
Basic Filter Power Handling Capacity (IAA) ... BFPHC
Basic Fitness Test [*British military*] (DMA) ... BFT
Basic Flight Maneuvering [*Navy*] (DOMA) ... BFM
Basic Floppy Disk ... BFD
Basic Fluid Power Research Program (IAA) ... BFPR
Basic Gastrin [*Medicine*] (DMAA) ... BG
Basic Graphic Access Method (IAA) ... BGAM
Basic Health Profile ... BHP
Basic Health Unit (DMAA) ... BHU
Basic Helix-Loop-Helix [*Genetics*] ... BHLH
Basic Heterostructure (IAA) ... BH
Basic Hole System ... BHS
Basic Human Factor Technology (SSD) ... BHFT
Basic Human Needs ... BHN
Basic Hytran Simulation Language [*Computer science*] (PDAA) ... BHSL
Basic Identification Number (EECA) ... BIN
Basic Imagery File (MCD) ... BIF
Basic Imagery Interpretation Brief (MCD) ... BIIB
Basic Imagery Interpretation Report (MCD) ... BIIR
Basic Impulse Insulation Level [*Electronics*] ... BIL
Basic in Flow (NRCH) ... BIF
Basic Incidence Rate [*Medicine*] ... BIR
Basic Income Unit (WDAA) ... BIU
Basic Index (NITA) ... BI
Basic Indexed Sequential Access Method [*IBM Corp.*] [*Computer science*] ... BISAM
Basic Indexing and Retrieval System [*Computer science*] (DIT) ... BIRS
Basic Industrial Control Engineering Programming System (IAA) ... BICEPS
Basic Industrial Materials [*Program*] [*Navy*] ... BIM
Basic Industry Research Laboratory ... BIRL
Basic Infantry ... BI
Basic Information Package ... BIP
Basic Information Retrieval System (NITA) ... BIRS
Basic Information Unit (BUR) ... BIU
Basic Initial Entry Test (MCD) ... BIET
Basic Initial Entry Training (MCD) ... BIET
Basic Input/Output System [*Computer science*] (WDMC) ... bio

Basic Input-Output Support Program Package (IAA) ... BIO
Basic Input-Output System [*IBM Corp.*] ... BIOS
Basic Institutional Development Program [*Under Title III of the Higher Education Act*] ... BIDP
Basic Instruments and Selected Documents of the GATT (AAGC) ... BISD
Basic Integrated Aircraft Command and Control [*Navy*] ... BIACC
Basic Interpersonal Communicative Skills (EDAC) ... BICS
BASIC Interpreter Package [*Computer science*] ... BIP
Basic Intrinsic Noise Ratio (CET) ... BINR
Basic Inventory of Natural Language [*Test*] ... BINL
Basic Iron Aluminum Silicate [*Du Pont trademark*] ... BIASILL
Basic Issue Items [*Army*] (AABC) ... BII
Basic Issue Items List [*Army*] (AABC) ... BIIL
Basic Issue List Items [*Army*] ... BILI
Basic Jet Navigation (DNAB) ... BJN
Basic Journal Abstracts [*A publication*] ... BJA
Basic Knowledge and Skills [*Training*] [*Military*] ... BK & S
Basic Language Concepts Test [*Child development test*] ... BLCT
Basic Language for the Implementation of System Software [*Computer science*] ... BLISS
Basic Language Machine [*Computer*] (BUR) ... BLM
BASIC [*Beginner's All-Purpose Symbolic Instruction Code*] **Language Translator** [*Computer science*] (MCD) ... BLT
Basic Launch Plan [*NASA*] (KSC) ... BLP
Basic Learning Institute ... BLI
Basic Level Automation of Data through Electronics ... BLADE
Basic Liberation of Smokers and Sympathizers of Marijuana ... BLOSSOM
Basic Library Inquiry Subsystem [*Computer science*] ... BLISS
Basic Life Support [*System*] ... BLS
Basic Linear Algebra Subroutines (MCD) ... BLAS
Basic Link Unit [*Computer science*] (BUR) ... BLU
Basic Literal Automatic Coding ... BALITAC
Basic Load [*Ammunition*] (AABC) ... BL
Basic Load Storage Area [*Military*] ... BLSA
Basic Logic Unit (IEEE) ... BLU
Basic Machine Cycle (IAA) ... BMC
Basic Magnesium, Inc., Las Vegas, NV [*Library symbol Library of Congress Obsolete*] (LCLS) ... NvLBM
Basic Main Frame (NATG) ... BMF
Basic Maintenance Allowance ... BMA
Basic Manufacturing Division ... BMD
Basic Mapping Support [*Computer science*] ... BMS
Basic Medical Insurance Plan [*UN Food and Agriculture Organization*] ... BMIP
Basic Memory Access Controller [*Memory management unit*] [*Computer science*] ... BMAC
Basic Message Switching Center [*Computer science*] ... BSC
Basic Metabolic Rate [*Biochemistry*] (DAVI) ... BMR
Basic Metabolic Unit [*Medicine*] (DMAA) ... BMU
Basic Metabolism Rate and Electrocardiogram [*Medicine*] ... BMR & ECG
Basic Metals and Minerals Processing Industry Council [*Australia*] ... BMMPIC
Basic Metals Industry Council [*Australia*] ... BMIC
Basic Meteorological Services (FAAC) ... BMS
Basic Military Compensation (MCD) ... BMC
Basic Military Journalist [*Department of Defense Information School course*] (DNAB) ... BMJ
Basic Military Requirement ... BMR
Basic Military Training ... BMT
Basic Military Training School ... BMTS
Basic Military Training School, United States Air Force ... BMTS USAF
Basic Military Training Squadron [*Air Force*] ... BMTS
Basic Minimum Descent Height [*Aviation*] (DA) ... BMDH
Basic Minute Value (PDAA) ... BMV
Basic Missile Checker (NATG) ... BMC
Basic Mission, Design Number, and Series [*Aircraft*] (AFM) ... BMDNS
Basic Mission Qualified [*NASA*] ... BMQ
Basic Mobile Facility (MCD) ... BMF
Basic Monthly Maintenance Charge (NITA) ... BMMC
Basic Morse Mission Trainer [*Military*] ... BMMT
Basic Motion-Time Study ... BMT
Basic Motor Ability Test [*Education*] ... BMAT
Basic Multicellular Unit [*Medicine*] (DMAA) ... BMU
Basic Multiline Controller [*Computer science*] (MHDI) ... BMLC
Basic Multi-Minutes (PDAA) ... BMM
Basic Multi-Role Avionics (PDAA) ... BMRA
Basic National Security Police (MCD) ... BNSP
Basic Naval Aviation Officers School (DNAB) ... BANAVAVNOFFSCOL
Basic Naval Aviation Officers School (DNAB) ... BNAO
Basic Naval Establishment Plan ... BNEP
Basic Net Radio Interface Device (MCD) ... BNRID
Basic Network (IAA) ... BASNET
Basic Networking Utilities ... BNU
Basic Noncommissioned Officer Course [*Army*] (INF) ... BNCOC
Basic Noncommissioned Officer Course [*Army*] ... BNOC
Basic Notch Unit ... BNU
Basic Oblate Spheroid ... BOS
Basic Occupational Language Training ... BOLT
Basic Occupational Literacy Test ... BOLT
Basic Occupational Preparation ... BOP
Basic Officers Training Battalion [*Army*] (INF) ... BOTB
Basic Operating Consumer-Oriented Language [*Computer science*] ... BOCOL
Basic Operating Monitor ... BOM
Basic Operating Program [*Computer science*] (NITA) ... BOP
Basic Operating System [*IBM Corp.*] [*Computer science*] ... BOS
Basic Operating System [*Computer science*] (NITA) ... BOSS
Basic Operating System Software [*Toshiba Corp.*] [*Japan*] ... BOSS
Basic Operation Memory [*Computer science*] (IAA) ... BOM
Basic Operation Plan [*Army*] ... BOP
Basic Operational Capability (SSD) ... BOC
Basic Operational Data ... BOD
Basic Operational Requirements and Planning Criteria Group [*ICAO*] (DA) ... BORG
Basic Operational Training Unit (Fixed Wing) ... BOTU(FW)
Basic Operational Training Unit (Rotary Wing) ... BOTU(RW)
Basic Ordering Agreement ... BOA
Basic Ordering Unit ... BOU
Basic Organizing/Optimizing Training Schedules (MCD) ... BOOTS
Basic Overall Polarity (IAA) ... BOP
Basic Oxygen Furnace [*Steelmaking*] ... BOF
Basic Oxygen Process [*Steelmaking*] ... BOP
Basic Oxygen Process Furnace [*Steelmaking*] (EG) ... BOPF
Basic Oxygen Steel [*Steelmaking*] ... BOS
Basic Parameter Input Tape [*Computer science*] (IAA) ... BPIT
Basic Partitioned Access Method [*IBM Corp.*] [*Computer science*] ... BPAM
Basic Parts List ... BPL
Basic Pay ... BP
Basic Pay Entry Date ... BPED
Basic Peripheral Channel ... BPC
Basic Petroleum International Ltd. [*Associated Press*] (SAG) ... BasPetr
Basic Petroleum International Ltd. [*NASDAQ symbol*] (NQ) ... BPIL
Basic Petroleum Intl. [*NASDAQ symbol*] (TTSB) ... BPILF
Basic Physical Fitness Test (MCD) ... BPFT
Basic Planning Document [*Military*] (AABC) ... BPD
Basic Planning Memorandum (NATG) ... BASPM
Basic Point Defense [*Military*] (NVT) ... BPD
Basic Point Defense Missile System (MCD) ... BPDMS
Basic Point Defense Surface Missile System (NVT) ... BPDSMS
Basic Point Defense System (MCD) ... BPDS
Basic Pole Unit ... BPU
Basic Postflight (MCD) ... BPO
Basic Pressure Altitude ... BPA
Basic Process (ECII) ... BP
Basic Processing Unit (CET) ... BPU
BASIC [*Beginner's All-Purpose Symbolic Instruction Code*] **Processor and Computer** ... BASICPAC
Basic Production Scheduling System (IAA) ... BPSS
BASIC [*Beginner's All-Purpose Symbolic Instruction Code*] **Program File** [*Computer science*] ... BAS
Basic Programming Knowledge Test (MCD) ... BPKT
Basic Programming Support [*IBM Corp.*] (BUR) ... BPS
Basic Programming System ... BPS
Basic Proline-Rich Protein (DMAA) ... PRB
Basic Protein [*Immunology*] ... BP
Basic Psychological Study (MCD) ... BPS
Basic Purchase Agreement (MCD) ... BPA
Basic Qualification Course (DNAB) ... BQC
Basic Query Language [*Computer science*] (BUR) ... BQL
Basic Radiation Effects Reactor ... BRER
Basic Rate Interface [*Telecommunications*] (PCM) ... BRI
Basic Rate Interface Transmission Equipment [*Telecommunications*] (ACRL) ... BRITE
Basic Reading Inventory (EDAC) ... BRI
Basic Recommended Reading (ADA) ... BRR
Basic Reference Coordinate System (MCD) ... BRCS
Basic Reference Lottery Ticket (PDAA) ... BRLT
Basic Research ... BAS-R
Basic Research ... BR
Basic Research in Adaptive Intelligence [*EEC*] ... BRAIN
Basic Research in Industrial Technology for Europe ... BRITE
Basic Research, Inc. (EA) ... BRINC
Basic Research Vehicle [*Automotive engineering*] ... BRV
Basic Resolution Unit [*Computer science*] ... BRU
Basic Rest-Activity Cycle [*Medicine*] (DMAA) ... BRAC
Basic Rifle Maintenance ... BRM
Basic Rifle Marksmanship [*Program of instruction*] [*Army*] (INF) ... BRM
Basic Schedule of Quantified Items (MHDI) ... BSQI
Basic School Skills Inventory [*Education*] ... BSSI
Basic School Skills Inventory - Diagnostic ... BSSI-D
Basic School Skills Inventory - Screen ... BSSI-S
Basic Sediment [*Petroleum*] ... BS
Basic Sediment and Water [*in crude oil*] ... BS & W
Basic Selection Unit [*Computer science*] (IAA) ... BSU
Basic Semantic Element [*Computer science*] (DIT) ... BASE
Basic Sequential Access Method [*IBM Corp.*] [*Computer science*] ... BSAM
Basic Sequential Access Method [*Electronics*] [*Computer science*] (ECII) ... BSAM
Basic Service Arrangement (ACRL) ... BSA
Basic Service Element [*Computer science*] (TNIG) ... BSE
Basic Shaft System ... BSS
Basic Shipping Instructions (NASA) ... BSI
Basic Size [*Printing*] (WDMC) ... BS
Basic Skills Assessment Program [*Academic achievement and aptitude test*] ... BSAP
Basic Skills Education Program [*Army*] ... BSEP
Basic Skills Learning System (EDAC) ... BSLS
Basic Skills Trainer [*Army*] (INF) ... BST
Basic Sounding Unit [*Telecommunications*] (TEL) ... BSU
Basic Spline (DOM) ... B-spline
Basic Standardization Agreement [*Military*] ... BSA
Basic Stock Allowance [*Military*] ... BSA
Basic Stock Allowance List [*Military*] (NVT) ... BSAL
Basic Storage Module (MCD) ... BSM

Basic Storage Unit [Computer science] (IAA) .... BST
Basic Stripping Method [DICI] .... BSM
Basic Structural Design Gross Weight (MCD) .... BSDG
Basic Structural Unit .... BSU
Basic Subsystem Module .... BSM
Basic Sustainment Materiel [Army] .... BSM
Basic Switching Impulse Insulation Level (IAA) .... BSIL
Basic Switching-Surge Level (IAA) .... BSL
Basic Synchronized Subset [Telecommunications] (OSI) .... BSS
Basic Synchronous Communication [Computer science] (IAA) .... BSC
Basic System (IEEE) .... BASYS
Basic System Memory [Computer science] (BUR) .... BSM
Basic System Reference Frequency (ACRL) .... BSRF
Basic System Release (MCD) .... BSR
Basic Systems, Inc., Huntington, WV [Library symbol Library of Congress] (LCLS) .... WvHuB
Basic Tables of Commissioning Allowances [Navy] .... BTCA
Basic Takeoff Gross Weight [Aviation] (MCD) .... BTOGW
Basic Tape Access Method [Computer science] .... BTAM
Basic Technical Course [Military] .... BTC
Basic Technique [Parapsychology] .... BT
Basic Telecommunication (MCD) .... BTMA
Basic Telecommunications Access Method [IBM Corp.] [Computer science] .... BTAM
Basic Teleprocessing Access Method .... BTAM
Basic Terminal Access Method [Computer science] .... BTAM
Basic Test Battery [Navy] .... BTB
Basic Timesharing, Inc. [Later,] (NITA) .... BTI
Basic Time-Sharing System (BUR) .... BTSS
Basic Trading Area (ACRL) .... BTA
[Rand McNally] Basic Trading Areas .... BTA
Basic Traffic Control Center (IAA) .... BTCC
Basic Trainer [Air Force] .... BT
Basic Training [Military] (NVT) .... BASICTNG
Basic Training [Military] .... BT
Basic Training Center [Military] .... BTC
Basic Training School .... BTS
Basic Transcription Factor [Genetics] .... BTF
Basic Transient Diode Logic [Computer science] (BUR) .... BTDL
Basic Transmission Header [Computer science] (IBMDP) .... BTH
Basic Transmission Unit [Computer science] .... BTU
Basic Transmission Unit per Square Foot per Minute (IAA) .... BTUSQFTMIN
Basic Transportation Vehicle .... BTV
Basic Trauma Life Support [Medicine] (DMAA) .... BTLS
Basic Travel Allowance .... BTA
Basic Underwater Demolition/SEAL [Sea, Air, and Land Capability] Training Department [Navy] .... BUD/S
Basic Underwater Demolition Team [Marine Corps] .... BUD
Basic Unit Training .... BUT
Basic Update Generator (MHDB) .... BUG
Basic Update Matrix Program .... BUMP
Basic User Unit (MCD) .... BUU
Basic War Plan [Navy] .... BWP
Basic Weight Controller .... BWC
Basic Work Data (MHDB) .... BWD
BASIC-52 Computer/Controller BCC-52
Basically (ABBR) .... BSCY
Basic-Extension (IAA) .... BASEX
Basics of Adult Teaching (OICC) .... BOAT
Basics of Language [Method] .... BOL
Basics of Supervisory Skills .... BOSS
Basilar Artery [Anatomy] .... BA
Basilar Membrane [Ear anatomy] .... BM
Basilar Papilla [Anatomy] .... BP
Basile, LA [FM radio station call letters] .... KSIG
Basilian Fathers (TOCD) .... CSB
Basilian Fathers (TOCD) .... csb
Basilian Salvatorian Fathers [Roman Catholic religious order] .... BS
Basilian Salvatorian Fathers (TOCD) .... BSO
Basilic Vein [Anatomy] (AAMN) .... BV
Basilica (VRA) .... basl
Basin [of a river] [Geology] .... B
Basin [Board on Geographic Names] .... BSN
Basin Exploration [NASDAQ symbol] (SAG) .... BSNX
Basin Exploration, Inc. [Associated Press] (SAG) .... BasExpl
Basin Petroleum Resources Ltd. [Vancouver Stock Exchange symbol] .... BSN
Basing (ABBR) .... BSG
Basioccipital [Anatomy] .... BO
Basion [Craniometric point] .... BA
Basis Computer Center (IAA) .... BCC
Basis of Allocation .... BOA
Basis of Estimate (AAGC) .... BOE
Basis of Issue [Army] .... BOI
Basis of Issue Monitoring and Recording System [Army] (AABC) .... BOIMARS
Basis of Issue Plan [Army] .... BOIP
Basis of Issue Plan - Complete [Army] .... BOIP-C
Basis of Issue Plan II [Army] (AABC) .... BOIP II
Basis of Issue Plan - Tentative [Army] .... BOIP-T
Basis of Issue System [Army] .... BOIS
Basis of Standard System (IAA) .... BOSS
Basis Point [Finance] (ODBW) .... BP
Basis Quote [Investment term] .... BQ
Basis Set Extension [Physical chemistry] .... BSE
Basis Set Superposition Error [Physical chemistry] .... BSSE
Basisian Salvatorian Fathers (TOCD) .... bso

Basisphenoid [Anatomy] .... BS
Bask [Iran] [ICAO location identifier] (ICLI) .... OIZR
Basked (ABBR) .... BSKD
Basket .... BKT
Basket .... BSK
Basket .... BSK
Basket (KSC) .... BSKT
Basket (VRA) .... bskt
Basket Loading Pool [Nuclear energy] (NRCH) .... BLP
Basket, Skip, and Hamper Makers Association [A union] [British] .... BSHMA
Basketball (ADA) .... BB
Basketball (ABBR) .... BSKBL
Basketball .... BSKTBLL
Basketball Australia [An association] .... BA
Basketball Federation of the United States of America [Defunct] .... BFUSA
Basketball Northern Territory [Australia An association] .... BNT
Basketball Saskatchewan Inc. [Formerly, Saskatchewan Basketball] (AC) .... BSI
Basketry (ABBR) .... BSKTY
Baskets or Hampers [Freight] .... BH
Basking (ABBR) .... BSKG
Basle Nomina Anatomica [Basel Anatomical Nomenclature] [Medicine] .... BNA
Basler Airlines, Inc. [Air carrier designation symbol] .... BASX
Basler Flight Service, Inc. [ICAO designator] (FAAC) .... BFC
Basolateral [Anatomy] .... BL
Basongo [Zaire] [ICAO location identifier] (ICLI) .... FZVR
Basophil [Hematology] .... B
Basophil [Hematology] .... Bas
Basophil [Hematology] (DHSM) .... BASO
Basophil Chemotactic Factor [Hematology] .... BCF
Basophilic Degeneration [Hematology] .... BD
Basophilic Stippling [Biochemistry] (DAVI) .... STIP
Basotho Congress Party [Lesotho] [Political party] (PPW) .... BCP
Basotho Democratic Alliance [Lesotho] [Political party] (EY) .... BDA
Basotho National Party [Lesotho] [Political party] (PPW) .... BNP
Basotho Unity Party [South Africa] [Political party] (PPW) .... BUP
Basque [MARC language code Library of Congress] (LCCP) .... bag
Basque (ABBR) .... BSQ
Basque Educational Organization (EA) .... BEO
Basque Left - Left for Socialism (PPW) .... EE-IS
Basra [Iraq] [Airport symbol] (AD) .... BSR
Basrah/Magal [Iraq] [ICAO location identifier] (ICLI) .... ORMM
Basrah/Shaibah [Iraq] [ICAO location identifier] (ICLI) .... ORMS
Bass [or Basso] [Music] .... B
Bass (IDOE) .... b
Bass [or Basso] [Music] .... Bs
Bass ADS [NYSE symbol] (SPSG) .... BAS
Bass Anglers Sportsman Society (EA) .... BASS
Bass Baritone [Music] .... BBAR
Bass Clarinet .... BC
Bass Clarinet [Music] .... BCLAR
Bass Klarinette [Bass Clarinet] [Music] .... B KI
Bass PLC [NYSE symbol] (SAG) .... BAS
Bass Public Ltd. [Associated Press] (SAG) .... Bass
Bass Research Foundation (EA) .... BRF
Bass Transistor (IDOE) .... b
Bassano Del Grappa [Italy ICAO location identifier] (ICLI) .... LIPJ
Bassano Public Library, Alberta [Library symbol National Library of Canada] (NLC) .... ABAS
Bassari [Togo] [ICAO location identifier] (ICLI) .... DXBS
Basse Pression [Low Pressure] [French] .... BP
Basse Tension [Low Tension] [French] .... BT
Bassein [Myanmar] [Airport symbol] (OAG) .... BSX
Bassein [Myanmar] [ICAO location identifier] (ICLI) .... VBBS
Bassel, Sullivan & Leake, Toronto, Ontario [Library symbol National Library of Canada] (NLC) .... OTBSL
Basses-Alpes [Lower Alps] [French] (BARN) .... B Alp
Basset Hound Club of America (EA) .... BHCA
Basse-Terre [Guadeloupe] [Airport symbol] (OAG) .... BBR
Basse-Terre/Baillif [French Antilles] [ICAO location identifier] (ICLI) .... TFFB
Basseterre/Golden Rock [St. Kitts Island] [ICAO location identifier] (ICLI) .... TKPK
Bassett Furniture [Associated Press] (SAG) .... BassettF
Bassett Furniture [NASDAQ symbol] (TTSB) .... BSET
Bassett Furniture Industries, Inc. [NASDAQ symbol] (NQ) .... BSET
Bassett, NE [FM radio station call letters] .... KMNE
Bassett, NE [Television station call letters] .... KMNE-TV
Bassett, NE [Location identifier FAA] (FAAL) .... RBE
Bassett, VA [AM radio station call letters] .... WCBX
Bassett's Illinois Criminal Pleading and Practice [A publication] (DLA) .... Bass Crim Pl
Basso [Music] .... BAS
Basso Continuo [Continued Bass] [Music] (ROG) .... BAS CON
Basso Continuo [Continued Bass] [Music] .... BASS CON
Basso Continuo [Continued Bass] [Music] .... BASS CONT
Basso Continuo [Continued Bass] [Music] .... BC
Basso Continuo [Continued Bass] [Music] (ROG) C
Bassoon [Music] (ROG) .... BN
Bassoon [Music] .... BN
Bassoon [Music] .... Bsn
Bassposaune [Bass Trombone] [Music] .... BP
Basswood (VRA) .... baswd
Bastak [Iran] [ICAO location identifier] (ICLI) .... OIBH
Bastard [Slang] (DSUE) .... B
Bastard [Slang] (DSUE) .... BAS
Bastard (DLA) .... BAST
Bastard [Size or material] .... BSTD

Bastard (ABBR) .... BSTRD
Bastard Amber [*Stage-lighting filter*] (WDMC) .... BA
Bastardize (ABBR) .... BSTRDZ
Bastardized (ABBR) .... BSTRDZD
Bastardizing (ABBR) .... BSTRDZG
Bastardly (ABBR) .... BSTRDY
Bastardy [*FBI standardized term*] .... BAST
Baste (ABBR) .... BST
Basted (ABBR) .... BSTD
Bastia [*Corsica*] [*Airport symbol*] (OAG) .... BIA
Bastia/Poretta, Corse [*France ICAO location identifier*] (ICLI) .... LFKB
Basting (ABBR) .... BSTG
Bastrop, LA [*Location identifier FAA*] (FAAL) .... BQP
Bastrop, LA [*FM radio station call letters*] (RBYB) .... KLMB-FM
Bastrop, LA [*FM radio station call letters*] .... KRVV
Bastrop, LA [*AM radio station call letters*] .... KTRY
Bastrop, LA [*FM radio station call letters*] .... KTRY-FM
Bastrop, TX [*FM radio station call letters*] .... KGSR
Basutoland (BARN) .... Bas
Basutoland .... BL
Bat .... B
Bat Conservation International (EA) .... BCI
Bat Conservation Society of Canada (AC) .... BCSC
Bat Conservation Trust [*British*] (EAIO) .... BCT
Bat Groups of Britain (EAIO) .... BGB
BAT Industries Ltd. [*Associated Press*] (SAG) .... BAT
BAT Industries Ltd. [*AMEX symbol*] (SPSG) .... BTI
Bata [*Spanish Guinea*] [*Airport symbol*] (AD) .... BSG
Bata [*Equatorial Guinea*] [*ICAO location identifier*] (ICLI) .... FGBT
Bata Shoe Museum Foundation (AC) .... BSMF
Bataan [*Costa Rica*] [*ICAO location identifier*] (ICLI) .... MRBN
Bataan Ocean Petroleum Depot (CINC) .... BOPD
Batabano [*Cuba ICAO location identifier*] (ICLI) .... MUBO
Bataillon de Commandement et d'Appui [*Headquarters and Support Battalion*] [*Algeria*] (AF) .... BCA
Batallon Vasco Espanol [*Spanish Basque Battalion*] (PD) .... BVE
Batam/Hang Nadim [*Indonesia*] [*ICAO location identifier*] (ICLI) .... WIKB
Batavia [*Indonesia*] [*Later, TNG*] [*Geomagnetic observatory code*] .... BTV
Batavia Area Office [*Energy Research and Development Administration*] .... BAO
Batavia Beacon, Batavia, IA [*Library symbol Library of Congress*] (LCLS) .... IaBatB
Batavia, NY [*Location identifier FAA*] (FAAL) .... GVQ
Batavia, NY [*TV station call letters*] (RBYB) .... WAQF-TV
Batavia, NY [*AM radio station call letters*] .... WBTA
Batavia, NY [*FM radio station call letters*] .... WGCC-FM
Batavia, OH [*FM radio station call letters*] .... WOBO
Batch [*Computer science*] .... B
Batch [*Computer science*] (CDE) .... BAT
Batch Automated Balancing System [*Computer science*] (MHDI) .... BABS
Batch Data Class [*Telecommunications*] .... BDC
Batch Data Transmission System .... BDTS
Batch Disk Operating System .... BDOS
Batch Execution System [*Computer science*] [*Engineering*] .... BES
Batch Executive (IAA) .... BATEX
Batch Fabrication .... BF
Batch Fabrication Technique .... BFT
Batch File [*Computer science*] .... BAT
Batch Freeform Input [*Computer science*] (MHDI) .... BFI
Batch Input (NITA) .... BI
Batch Job Foreground [*Computer science*] .... BJF
Batch Mixer .... BMXR
Batch Operating Software System .... BOSS
Batch Operating System [*Computer science*] .... BOS
Batch Processing .... BP
Batch Processing Monitor [*Xerox Corp.*] [*Computer science*] (MCD) .... BPM
Batch Processing Multilanguage Operating System [*Computer science*] (IAA) .... BAMOS
Batch Processing Operating System (IAA) .... BPOS
Batch Processing System .... BPS
Batch Query Language [*Programming language*] .... BQL
Batch Reactor [*Chemical engineering*] .... BR
Batch, Stirred-Tank Reactor (PDAA) .... BSTR
Batch Terminal Controller [*Computer science*] (IAA) .... BTC
Batch Terminal Simulator [*Computer science*] .... BTS
Batch Time-Sharing Monitor [*Xerox Corp.*] [*Computer science*] (MCD) .... BTM
Batch Transfer Program .... BTP
Batch Weighing Kit .... BWK
Batch Weighing System .... BWS
Batched (ABBR) .... BTCHD
Batchelder's Law of Massachusetts Manufacturing Corporations [*A publication*] (DLA) .... Batch Mfg Cor
Batchewana Indian Band, Sault Ste. Marie, Ontario [*Library symbol National Library of Canada*] (NLC) .... OSTMB
Batching (ABBR) .... BTCHG
Batean [*Ship's rigging*] (ROG) .... BAT
Bateau Torpilleur [*Torpedo Boat*] [*French*] .... BT
Bateaux Resources, Inc. [*Vancouver Stock Exchange symbol*] .... BTU
Bateman. General Laws of Excise [*2nd ed.*] [*1840*] [*A publication*] (DLA) .... Bate Exc
Bateman. Law of Auctions [*11th ed.*] [*1953*] [*A publication*] (DLA) .... Bate Auct
Bateman on Agency [*A publication*] (DLA) .... Bate Ag
Bateman's Commercial Law [*A publication*] (DLA) .... Bate Com L
Bateman's United States Constitutional Law [*A publication*] (DLA) .... Bate Const
Bateria Artifical Chromosome [*Genetics*] .... BAC
Bateria de Examenes de Aptitud General [*General Aptitude Test Battery*] [*Spanish*] .... BEAG
Bateria General de Preubas de Aptitud [*General Aptitude Test Battery*] [*Spanish*] .... BGPA
Bates' Annotated Revised Statutes [*Ohio*] [*A publication*] (DLA) .... Bates' Ann St
Bates College, Lewiston, ME [*OCLC symbol*] (OCLC) .... BTS
Bates College, Lewiston, ME [*Library symbol Library of Congress*] (LCLS)..... MeLB
Bates' Delaware Chancery Reports [*A publication*] (DLA) .... Bates
Bates' Delaware Chancery Reports [*A publication*] (DLA) .... Bates Ch
Bates' Digest [*Ohio*] [*A publication*] (DLA) .... Bates' Dig
Bates' Law of Partnership [*A publication*] (DLA) .... Bates Part
Batesburg, SC [*AM radio station call letters*] .... WBLR
Batesburg, SC [*FM radio station call letters*] .... WKWQ
Batesville [*Arkansas*] [*Airport symbol*] (OAG) .... BVX
Batesville, AR [*Location identifier FAA*] (FAAL) .... BVX
Batesville, AR [*Location identifier FAA*] (FAAL) .... INY
Batesville, AR [*AM radio station call letters*] .... KAAB
Batesville, AR [*AM radio station call letters*] .... KBTA
Batesville, AR [*FM radio station call letters*] .... KZLE
Batesville, AR [*Location identifier FAA*] (FAAL) .... LYY
Batesville Herald Tribune, Batesville, IN [*Library symbol Library of Congress*] (LCLS) .... InBaHT
Batesville, IN [*Location identifier FAA*] (FAAL) .... HLB
Batesville, IN [*FM radio station call letters*] .... WRBI
Batesville, MS [*FM radio station call letters*] .... WBLE
Batesville, MS [*AM radio station call letters*] .... WJBI
Bath .... B
Bath (WGA) .... BA
Bath (ADA) .... BTH
Bath and Basin [*Classified advertising*] (ADA) .... B & B
Bath & Body Works .... BBW
Bath & Hammondsport Railroad Co. [*AAR code*] .... BH
Bath Blanket [*Medicine*] (MEDA) .... BB
Bath Branch, Lennox and Addington County Public Library, Ontario [*Library symbol National Library of Canada*] (NLC) .... OBLAC
Bath Information and Data Services [*Computer science*] [*British*] (TNIG) ...... BIDS
Bath Institute of Medical Engineering [*University of Bath*] [*British*] (IRUK) .... BIME
Bath Iron Works [*Maine*] (DOMA) .... BIW
Bath, Laxative, Enema, Shampoo, and Shower [*Medicine*] (AAMN) .... BLESS
Bath, ME [*FM radio station call letters*] (RBYB) .... WBC
Bath, ME [*FM radio station call letters*] (RBYB) .... WBCI-FM
Bath, ME [*AM radio station call letters*] .... WJTO
Bath, NY [*AM radio station call letters*] .... WABH
Bath, NY [*FM radio station call letters*] .... WCIK
Bath, NY [*FM radio station call letters*] .... WVIN
Bath Road [*Bristol*] [*British depot code*] .... BL
Bath Unit [*British and Canadian*] [*Military*] .... BU
Bath University Computing Services [*British*] (AIE) .... BUCS
Bathophenanthroline [*Organic chemistry*] .... BP
Bathophenanthroline [*Analytical chemistry*] .... BPT
Bathophenanthroline Disulphonate [*Organic chemistry*] .... BPDS
Bathroom [*Classified advertising*] .... BA
Bathroom [*Classified advertising*] (ADA) .... BATHRM
Bathroom (VRA) .... bathrm
Bathroom .... BR
Bathroom (ADA) .... BTH
Bathroom [*Classified advertising*] (ADA) .... BTHRM
Bathroom Privileges [*Medicine*] .... BP
Bathroom Privileges [*Medicine*] .... BRP
Bathtub (ABBR) .... BT
Bathurst [*Australia Airport symbol*] (OAG) .... BHS
Bathurst [*Gambia*] [*Airport symbol*] (AD) .... BTH
Bathurst College, Bathurst, NB, Canada [*Library symbol Library of Congress*] (LCLS) .... CaNBBB
Bathurst Island [*Australia Airport symbol*] (OAG) .... BRT
Bathurst, NB [*AM radio station call letters*] .... CKBC
Bathurst, NB [*FM radio station call letters*] .... CKLE
Bathurst Paper Ltd. [*Toronto Stock Exchange symbol*] .... BAT
Bathyconductograph .... BC
Bathymetric Navigation Equipment .... BNE
Bathymetric Swath [*Survey System*] [*National Ocean Survey*] (PDAA) .... BS
Bathymetric Swath Survey System [*National Ocean Survey*] (MSC) .... BSSS
Bathyscaphe Oceanographic Program .... BOP
Bathythermal Data (MCD) .... BTD
Bathythermal Traces .... BT
Bathythermograph [*Oceanography*] (MSC) .... BATHY
Bathythermograph [*Oceanography*] .... BT
Bathythermographic Data Collection and Processing Facility [*Oceanography*] .... BTDCPF
Bathythermographic Data Processing and Analysis Facility [*Oceanography*] .... BTDPAF
B.A.T.Idus Ord ADR [*AMEX symbol*] (TTSB) .... BTI
Batie [*Burkina Faso*] [*ICAO location identifier*] (ICLI) .... DHCE
Batik (ABBR) .... BTK
Batik (VRA) .... btk
Batman [*Turkey ICAO location identifier*] (ICLI) .... LTCJ
Batna [*Algeria*] [*ICAO location identifier*] (ICLI) .... DABT
Baton (WDAA) .... BTN
Baton Broadcasting, Inc. [*Toronto Stock Exchange symbol*] .... BNB
Baton Rouge [*Diocesan abbreviation*] [*Louisiana*] (TOCD) .... BR
Baton Rouge [*Louisiana*] [*Airport symbol*] (OAG) .... BTR
Baton Rouge, LA [*Location identifier FAA*] (FAAL) .... CLZ
Baton Rouge, LA [*AM radio station call letters*] .... KBRH
Baton Rouge, LA [*FM radio station call letters*] .... KLSU
Baton Rouge, LA [*Television station call letters*] .... WAFB
Baton Rouge, LA [*FM radio station call letters*] .... WBRH
Baton Rouge, LA [*Television station call letters*] .... WBRZ

Baton Rouge, LA [*FM radio station call letters*] .... WFMF
Baton Rouge, LA [*FM radio station call letters*] .... WGGZ
Baton Rouge, LA [*Television station call letters*] .... WGMB
Baton Rouge, LA [*AM radio station call letters*] .... WIBR
Baton Rouge, LA [*AM radio station call letters*] .... WJBO
Baton Rouge, LA [*FM radio station call letters*] .... WJFM
Baton Rouge, LA [*Television station call letters*] .... WLPB
Baton Rouge, LA [*FM radio station call letters*] (RBYB) .... WLSS-FM
Baton Rouge, LA [*AM radio station call letters*] .... WNDC
Baton Rouge, LA [*FM radio station call letters*] .... WRKF
Baton Rouge, LA [*FM radio station call letters*] .... WTGE
Baton Rouge, LA [*Television station call letters*] .... WVLA
Baton Rouge, LA [*AM radio station call letters*] .... WXOK
Baton Rouge, LA [*AM radio station call letters*] .... WYNK
Baton Rouge, LA [*FM radio station call letters*] .... WYNK-FM
Baton Rouge/Ryan Field [*Louisiana*] [*ICAO location identifier*] (ICLI) .... KBTR
Batouri [*Cameroon*] [*ICAO location identifier*] (ICLI) .... FKKI
Batouri [*Cameroon*] [*Airport symbol*] (OAG) .... OUR
Batrachotoxin [*Biochemistry*] .... BTX
Bats Both Right-Handed and Left-Handed [*Baseball*] .... BB
Bats Left-Handed [*Baseball*] .... BL
Bats Right-Handed [*Baseball*] .... BR
Batse Coordinates Distribution Network .... BACODINE
Batsfjord [*Norway*] [*Airport symbol*] (OAG) .... BJF
Batsfjord [*Norway ICAO location identifier*] (ICLI) .... ENBS
Batsman (ADA) .... B
Battaillon des Jeunes Ruraux [*Rural Youth Battalion*] [*Zaire*] .... BJR
Battalion .... BAT
Battalion (ROG) .... BATN
Battalion .... BATT
Battalion (ADA) .... BATTN
Battalion (AFM) .... BN
Battalion (ABBR) .... BTLN
Battalion .... BTN
Battalion Administration Officer (MCD) .... BAO
Battalion Aid Station [*Army*] .... BAS
Battalion Analyzer and Tactical Trainer for Local Engagements (MCD) .... BATTLE
Battalion and Below Command and Control [*Army*] B2C2
Battalion Antitank Recoilless Rifle .... BAT
Battalion Artillery Group (MCD) .... BAG
Battalion Automated Personnel System .... BAPERS
Battalion Battle Simulation [*Army*] .... BBS
Battalion Beachhead [*Army*] .... BBH
Battalion/Brigade Signal Officer Course [*Military*] (INF) .... BBSOC
Battalion Close Support Weapon System (MCD) .... BCSWS
Battalion Combat Team .... BCT
Battalion Command and Coordination [*Military*] .... BCAC
Battalion Command Inspection [*Army*] (INF) .... BCI
Battalion Command Post (DNAB) .... BN-CP
Battalion Commander (MCD) .... BC
Battalion Control Group [*Army*] .... BCG
Battalion Equipment Evaluation Program [*DoD*] .... BEEP
Battalion Etranger de Parachutistes [*Foreign Battalion of Parachutists*] [*French Foreign Legion*] .... BEP
Battalion Expeditionary Force (CINC) .... BEF
Battalion Field Exercise [*Military*] (NVT) .... BNFEX
Battalion Field Training Days (MCD) .... BFTD
Battalion Fire Distribution Center (AABC) .... BFDC
Battalion Ground Surveillance Section [*Army*] (AABC) .... BGSS
Battalion Headquarters [*British military*] (DMA) .... BHQ
Battalion Headquarters [*Marine Corps*] .... BNHQ
Battalion Infantry (CINC) .... BI
Battalion Input/Output Device (MCD) .... BIOD
Battalion Landing Exercise [*Military*] (NVT) .... BLTLEX
Battalion Landing Team [*Military*] .... BLT
Battalion Landing Team [*Marine Corps*] (DOMA) .... BLT
Battalion Landing Team Landing Exercise [*Military*] (NVT) .... BTLEX
Battalion Level Training Model [*DoD*] .... BLTM
Battalion Logistical Operations Center [*Military*] (INF) .... BLOC
Battalion Maintenance Equipment [*Military*] .... BME
Battalion Maintenance Officer [*Army*] (INF) .... BMO
Battalion Maintenance Sergeant [*Military*] (INF) .... BMS
Battalion Maintenance Technician [*Military*] (INF) .... BMT
Battalion Mortar and Davy Crockett Platoon [*Army*] (AABC) .... BMDCP
Battalion Mortar System [*Army*] .... BMS
Battalion Motor Officer [*Military*] (INF) .... BMO
Battalion Officer-of-the-Watch (DNAB) .... BOOW
Battalion Operated Surveillance System [*Army*] (INF) .... BOSS
Battalion Operations Center (AABC) .... BOC
Battalion Orderly Corporal [*British and Canadian*] .... BOC
Battalion Orderly Room [*British*] .... BOR
Battalion Orderly Sergeant [*British and Canadian*] .... BOS
Battalion Orders [*British military*] (DMA) .... BO
Battalion Shore Fire Control Party .... BNSFCP
Battalion Signal Officer (INF) .... BSO
Battalion Supply and Maintenance Equipment [*Military*] .... BSME
Battalion Supply Point [*Army*] (INF) .... BSP
Battalion Tactical Initialization [*Military*] .... BATI
Battalion Tactical Operations Center [*Military*] .... BTOC
Battalion Targeting System (DOMA) .... BTS
Battalion Task Force (MCD) .... BNTF
Battalion Training Management System [*Army*] (INF) .... BTMS
Battalion Training Model [*Military*] .... BTM
Battalion Transport Officer [*British military*] (DMA) .... BTO
Battambang [*Cambodia*] [*ICAO location identifier*] (ICLI) .... VDBG
Batted In [*Short form for RBI, Runs Batted In*] [*Baseball*] .... BI
Battelle Automated Search Information System [*Database management system*] [*Battelle Memorial Institute*] [*Information service or system*] .... BASIS
Battelle Columbus Laboratories Decommissioning Project [*Department of Energy*] (GAAI) .... BCLDP
Battelle Columbus Laboratories Decommissioning Project .... BCLDP
Battelle Columbus Laboratories Decommissioning Project (DOGT) .... BCLDP
Battelle Defense Document Center [*Battelle Memorial Institute*] (SAA) .... BDDC
Battelle - Defense Information Analysis Center [*Battelle Memorial Institute*] .... BDIAC
Battelle - Defense Information Center [*Battelle Memorial Institute*] (MCD) .... BDIC
Battelle Human Affairs Research Center [*Seattle, WA*] .... BHARC
Battelle Human Affairs Research Center, Seattle, WA [*Library symbol Library of Congress*] (LCLS) .... WaSBa
Battelle Institute Learning Automation [*Battelle Memorial Institute*] (IEEE) .... BILA
Battelle Memorial Institute (EA) .... BMI
Battelle Memorial Institute, Columbus, OH [*OCLC symbol*] (OCLC) .... BKM
Battelle Memorial Institute, Pacific Northwest Laboratory, Richland, WA [*Library symbol Library of Congress*] (LCLS) .... WaRiB
Battelle Monte Carlo [*Computer science*] .... BMC
Battelle New England Marine Research Laboratory [*Battelle Memorial Institute*] [*Research center*] (RCD) .... BNEMRL
Battelle Northwest Laboratories .... BNL
Battelle Northwest Laboratories (KSC) .... BNWL
Battelle Pacific Northwest Laboratories [*Nuclear energy*] (NRCH) .... BPNL
Battelle Research Reactor .... BRR
Battelle-Columbus Laboratories .... BCL
Battelle-Columbus Laboratories, Columbus, OH [*Library symbol Library of Congress*] (LCLS) .... OCoB
Battelle-Northwest Hospital, Life Science Library, Richland, WA [*Library symbol Library of Congress*] (LCLS) .... WaRiBN
Battelle's Educational Computer User's Network [*Battelle Memorial Institute*] [*Information service or system*] (IID) .... BECUN
Batten (KSC) .... BATT
Batten, Barton, Durstine & Osborn [*Advertising agency*] .... BBD & O
Batten, Barton, Durstine, and Osborn [*An advertising agency*] [*New York, NY*] (WDMC) .... BBDO
Batten on the Stannaries Act [*A publication*] (DLA) .... Bat Stan
Batten. Specific Performance on Contracts [*1849*] [*A publication*] (DLA) .... Bat Sp Perf
Batten's Disease [*Medicine*] .... BD
Batten's Disease Support and Research Association (EA) .... BDSRA
Batten-Spielmyer-Vogt [*Syndrome*] [*Medicine*] (AAMN) .... BSV
Batten-Turner Muscular Dystrophy [*Syndrome*] [*Medicine*] .... BTMD
Batter .... BAT
Battered Child (CPH) .... BC
Battered Child Syndrome .... BCS
Battered Woman [*or Wife*] **Syndrome** [*Medicine Defunct*] .... BWS
Batterers Anonymous (EA) .... BA
Batteries Batteries [*NASDAQ symbol*] (TTSB) .... BATS
Batteries Batteries, Inc. [*NASDAQ symbol*] (SAG) .... BATS
Batteries Batteries, Inc. [*Associated Press*] (SAG) .... Batter
Batteries Batteries, Inc. [*Associated Press*] (SAG) .... Batteries
Batteries Batteries Wrrt [*NASDAQ symbol*] (TTSB) .... BATSW
Batters Faced by Pitcher [*Baseball*] .... BFP
Battery .... B
Battery (IAA) .... BA
Battery (AAG) .... BAT
Battery .... BATRY
Battery [*FBI standardized term*] .... BATT
Battery .... BATT
Battery .... BATTY
Battery (AFM) .... BTRY
Battery .... BTY
Battery Acquisition RADAR .... BAR
Battery Adjust (AABC) .... BA
Battery Booster Cable .... BBC
Battery Capability .... BC
Battery Charge Regulator .... BCR
Battery Charger [*Military*] (MSA) .... BAT CHG
Battery Charger [*Military*] .... BC
Battery Command Post [*Army*] .... BCP
Battery Command Post [*Army*] .... BTRY CP
Battery Commander [*Army*] .... BC
Battery Computer System (MCD) .... BCS
Battery Condition Indicator (MCD) .... BCI
Battery Control and Monitor [*Army*] .... BCM
Battery Control Area [*Army*] .... BCA
Battery Control Building [*Army*] .... BCB
Battery Control Central [*Army*] .... BCC
Battery Control Data Processor [*Army*] .... BCDP
Battery Control Officer [*Army*] (AABC) .... BCO
Battery Control RADAR [*Army*] .... BCR
Battery Control Trailer (NATG) .... BCT
Battery Control Van (NATG) .... BCV
Battery/Coolant Unit (RDA) .... BCU
Battery Council International (EA) .... BCI
Battery Cutoff [*Telecommunications*] (IAA) .... BATCO
Battery Cutoff [*Telecommunications*] (TEL) .... BCO
Battery Data Link [*Air Force*] .... BDL
Battery Data Link System [*Air Force*] .... BDLS
Battery Display Unit [*Army*] .... BDU
Battery Echelon Operating Control (AFM) .... BEOC
Battery Energy Storage System (DWSG) .... BESS

Battery Energy Storage Test .... BEST
Battery Exhaust Emergency Recirculation (DNAB) .... BEER
Battery Firing Device (MCD) .... BFD
Battery Fuse (IAA) .... BATFU
Battery Fuse Panel (IAA) .... BFP
Battery Guidance Command Group .... BGCG
Battery Information Index [Battelle Memorial Institute] (IID) .... BII
Battery Integration and RADAR Display Equipment [Air defense system] .... BIRDIE
Battery Integration Routing Display Equipment (MCD) .... BIRDIE
Battery Interconnecting Cables (NATG) .... BIC
Battery Interface Unit (MCD) .... BIU
Battery Inverter (AAG) .... BI
Battery Inverter Accessory Power Supply .... BIAPS
Battery Inverter Instrument Power Supply (IAA) .... BIIPS
Battery Level Computer (MCD) .... BLC
Battery Maintenance Group [Military] .... BMG
Battery of Leukocyte Tests [Clinical medicine] .... BLT
Battery Operated (IAA) .... BATTOPER
Battery Operated Device .... BOD
Battery Operations Center [Air Force] .... BOC
Battery, Overvoltage Protection, Ringing, Supervision, Coding, Hybrids, Testing [Seven basic functions performed by line circuits] [Telecommunications] .... BORSCHT
Battery Package .... BP
Battery Park City [New York City] .... BPC
Battery Plotting Room .... BPR
Battery Protection and Reconditioning Circuit (MCD) .... BPRC
Battery Quartermaster-Sergeant [British] .... BQMS
Battery Random Access Memory [External storage system] [Computer science] .... BATRAM
Battery Replacement Unit (MCD) .... BRU
Battery Sergeant-Major .... BSM
Battery Shop Maintenance [NASA] (KSC) .... BSM
Battery Simulator .... BS
Battery Status Indicator (NATG) .... BSI
Battery Supply (IAA) .... BATSUP
Battery Target [British and Canadian] [Military] .... BT
Battery Tech, Inc. [Associated Press] (SAG) .... BatTech
Battery Tech, Inc. [NASDAQ symbol] (SAG) .... BTIO
Battery Technologies [NASDAQ symbol] (TTSB) .... BTIOF
Battery Terminal Equipment .... BTE
Battery Test Set .... BTS
Battery Timing Equipment (AAG) .... BTE
Battery Timing Group .... BTG
Battery Training Corps [British] .... BTC
Battery Vehicle Society [British] .... BVS
Battery Voltage [Automotive engineering] .... VBAT
Battery-Powered (ADA) .... BP
Battery-Powered Electrically Heated Catalyst [Automotive exhaust emissions] .... BPEHC
Battery-Powered Recorder .... BPR
Battery-Voltage Limit System .... BVLS
Batticaloa [Ceylon] [Airport symbol] (AD) .... BTC
Batticaloa [Sri Lanka] [ICAO location identifier] (ICLI) .... VCCB
Batting Average [Baseball] .... BA
Batting Practice [Baseball] .... BP
Battle .... B
Battle (AABC) .... BAT
Battle (WGA) .... BATT
Battle (ABBR) .... BTL
Battle Area Control Unit [Military] .... BACU
Battle Area Surveillance and Integrated Communications System [Marine Corps] .... BASIC
Battle Area Surveillance and Integrated Communications System [Marine Corps] (IEEE) .... BASICS
Battle Area Surveillance and Integrated Communications System Processor and Computer [Marine Corps] .... BASICPAC
Battle Bridge Tier [Shipping] (ROG) .... BBTR
Battle Casualty (MAE) .... BC
Battle Casualty Vietnam .... BCV
Battle Command Battle Laboratory [Army] .... BCBL
Battle Command Training Program [Army] .... BCTP
Battle Coordination Element [Army] (MCD) .... BCE
Battle Correlator Display .... BCD
Battle Creek [Michigan] [Airport symbol] (OAG) .... BTL
Battle Creek College, Battle Creek, MI [Library symbol Library of Congress Obsolete] (LCLS) .... MiBatC
Battle Creek, MI [AM radio station call letters] .... WBCK
Battle Creek, MI [FM radio station call letters] .... WBXX
Battle Creek, MI [AM radio station call letters] .... WELL
Battle Creek, MI [Television station call letters] .... WJUE
Battle Creek, MI [FM radio station call letters] .... WKFR
Battle Creek, MI [AM radio station call letters] .... WOLY
Battle Creek, MI [Television station call letters] .... WOTV
Battle Creek, MI [AM radio station call letters] (RBYB) .... WWKN-AM
Battle Creek Public School, Battle Creek, MI [Library symbol Library of Congress] (LCLS) .... MiBat
Battle Creek Times, Battle Creek, IA [Library symbol Library of Congress] (LCLS) .... IaBcT
Battle Cruiser [Navy] .... BC
Battle Cruiser [Navy symbol] .... CB
Battle Cruiser [Navy] CC
Battle Cruiser Flag [Navy British] .... BC
Battle Cruiser Force [British military] (DMA) .... BCF

Battle Cruiser Squadron [Navy] .... BCS
Battle Damage and Assessment Review [Military] .... BDAR
Battle Damage Assessment .... BDA
Battle Damage Assessment and Reporting Team .... BDART
Battle Damage Assessment Team [Navy] (DOMA) .... BDAT
Battle Damage Information Script (SAA) .... BDIS
Battle Damage Repair [Army] (RDA) .... BDR
Battle Damage Repair Ship [Navy symbol] .... ARB
Battle Damage Umpire (SAA) .... BDU
Battle Dress [Military] .... BD
Battle Dress Overgarment [Military] (INF) .... BDO
Battle Dress Uniform [Military] .... BDU
Battle Dressing Station [Military] (NVT) .... BDS
Battle Energy Corp. [Vancouver Stock Exchange symbol] .... BTE
Battle Fatigue (INF) .... BF
Battle Field Tactical Trainer .... BFTT
Battle Force .... BATFOR
Battle Force Combatant [Navy] .... BFC
Battle Force Inport Training [Navy] (DOMA) .... BFIT
Battle Ground, IN [FM radio station call letters] (RBYB) .... WASK-FM
Battle Group .... BG
Battle Group Anti-Air Warfare Coordinator [No longer used] [Navy] (DOMA) .... BGAAWC
Battle Group Commander (MCD) .... BG/CDR
Battle Group Commanders Team Training (DOMA) .... BGCTT
Battle Group Exercise [Navy] (DOMA) .... BGE
Battle Group Landing Team .... BGLT
Battle Group Operational Readiness System (DOMA) .... BGORS
Battle Group Passive Horizon Extension System [Reconnaissance] .... BGPHES
Battle Group Passive Horizon Extension System - Surface Terminal [Reconnaissance] (DWSG) .... BGPHES-ST
Battle Group Tactical Training [Navy] (DOMA) .... BGTT
Battle Harbour, NF [ICAO location identifier] (ICLI) .... CWBF
Battle Injury or Wound .... BIW
Battle Lake Public School, Battle Lake, MN [Library symbol] [Library of Congress] (LCLS) .... MnBatS
Battle Management [Military] (SDI) .... BM
Battle Management/Command, Control, Communications (MCD) BM/C3
Battle Management/Command, Control, Communications, and Intelligence [Military] .... BM/C^{3}I
Battle Management Node .... BMN
Battle Manning (DNAB) .... BM
Battle Mountain [Nevada] [Airport symbol Obsolete] (OAG) .... BAM
Battle Mountain [Nevada] [Seismograph station code, US Geological Survey] (SEIS) .... BMN
Battle Mountain Gold Co. [Associated Press] (SAG) .... BatlMt
Battle Mountain Gold Co. [Toronto Stock Exchange symbol NYSE symbol] .... BMG
Battle Mtn Gold [NYSE symbol] (TTSB) .... BMG
Battle Mtn Gold $3.25 Cv Pfd [NYSE symbol] (TTSB) .... BMGPr
Battle of Atlantic [World War II] .... BA
Battle Position (AABC) .... BP
Battle Practice Target [Obsolete Navy British] .... BPT
Battle Readiness and Competition Instructions (NVT) .... BATREADCOM
Battle Readiness and Competition Instructions (NVT) .... BATREADCOMP
Battle Reconnaissance (MCD) .... BATRECON
Battle Short Relay .... BSR
Battle Simulation Center (MCD) .... BSC
Battle Simulation Officer (SAA) .... BSO
Battle Staff Noncommissioned Officer Course [Army] (INF) .... BSNCOC
Battle Staff Support Center [Air Force] .... BSSC
Battle Staff Team .... BST
Battle Star .... BS
Battle Watch Captain (MCD) .... BWC
Battle Wound Injury (CINC) .... BWI
Battled (ABBR) .... BTLD
Battlefield (ABBR) .... BTLFLD
Battlefield Air Interdiction (MCD) .... BAI
Battlefield Airborne Illumination System (CINC) .... BAIS
Battlefield Area Reconnaissance System [RADAR] [Army] .... BARCS
Battlefield Area Surveillance System (MCD) .... BASS
Battlefield Artillery Target Engagement System (MCD) .... BATES
Battlefield Automated System Engineering Support [Army] .... BASES
Battlefield Automated Systems [Computer science Military] (RDA) .... BAS
Battlefield Automated Tactical Support System (MCD) .... BATSS
Battlefield Automation Appraisal (MCD) .... BAA
Battlefield Automation Interoperability System Engineering Management Plan [Army] .... BAISEMP
Battlefield Automation Management (MCD) .... BAM
Battlefield Automation Management Plan [or Program] (MCD) .... BAMP
Battlefield Combat Identification [Army] (RDA) .... BCID
Battlefield Combat Identification System [Army] (RDA) .... BCIS
Battlefield Commanders' Aid [Army] .... BCA
Battlefield Communications Review .... BCR
Battlefield Computer System .... BCS
Battlefield Damage Assessment and Repair [Technical manual] [Army] (RDA) .... BDAR
Battlefield Data System .... BDS
Battlefield Day (RDA) .... BFD
Battlefield Development Plan (RDA) .... BDP
Battlefield Distributed Simulation - Developmental Program [Army] (RDA) .... BDS-D
Battlefield Distributed Simulation-Developmental [Army] (RDA) .... BDS-D
Battlefield Electromagnetic Environment Office [Fort Huachuca, AZ] [United States Electronic Proving Ground] (GRD) .... BEEO
Battlefield Electronic Communications System (DWSG) .... BECS

Battlefield Environment (MCD) ..... BE
Battlefield Environment LASER Designator [*MIRADCOM*] (MCD) ..... BELD
Battlefield Environment LASER Designator/Weapon System Simulation
　[*MIRADCOM*] (RDA) ..... BELDWSS
Battlefield Environmental Effects Software [*Army*] ..... BEES
Battlefield Estimate ..... BFE
Battlefield Exercise (DNAB) ..... BFE
Battlefield Exploitation and Target Acquisition (MCD) ..... BETA
Battlefield Functional Area [*Army*] ..... BFA
Battlefield Functional System (MCD) ..... BFS
Battlefield Functional System Concept (MCD) ..... BFSC
Battlefield Guided Weapon (MCD) ..... BGW
Battlefield Identification Friend or Foe (MCD) ..... BIFF
Battlefield Identification System Study [*NATO*] (NATG) ..... BISS
Battlefield Illumination (AABC) ..... BI
Battlefield Illumination Airborne System (AFM) ..... BIAS
Battlefield Illumination Integrated Night Vision Devices (MCD) ..... BIINVD
Battlefield Illumination L System (MCD) ..... BTL ILUM-L
Battlefield Illumination System ..... BIS
Battlefield Information Center [*Army*] (AABC) ..... BIC
Battlefield Information Collection and Exploitation System ..... BICES
Battlefield Information Communications Center (MCD) ..... BICC
Battlefield Information Control Center [*Army*] (AABC) ..... BICC
Battlefield Information Distribution System (MCD) ..... BIDS
Battlefield Information System [*Army*] (RDA) ..... BIS
Battlefield Information Transmission System [*Army*] ..... BITS
Battlefield Integrated Information Center (MCD) ..... BIIC
Battlefield Integration Coordination Center ..... BICC
Battlefield Integration Management System [*Army*] ..... BIMS
Battlefield Intelligence Coordinator [*Army*] (DOMA) ..... BIC
Battlefield Interdiction (MCD) ..... BFI
Battlefield Interdiction (MCD) ..... BI
Battlefield Location and Information System [*Army*] (RDA) ..... BLAIS
Battlefield Management System [*Military*] (INF) ..... BMS
Battlefield Mobility / Target Acquistion [*Military*] ..... BM/TA
Battlefield Nuclear Warfare [*Army*] ..... BNW
Battlefield Operating System [*Military*] (RDA) ..... BOS
Battlefield Period (MCD) ..... BFP
Battlefield Plan Development (MCD) ..... BPD
Battlefield Related Electronic Warfare Simulator (MCD) ..... BREWS
Battlefield Related Evaluation of Countermeasure Hardware [*Model*]
　(MCD) ..... BREACH
Battlefield Situation Display [*DoD*] ..... BSD
Battlefield Surveillance (MCD) ..... BS
Battlefield Surveillance Airship System (PDAA) ..... BSAS
Battlefield Surveillance and Target Acquisition RADAR (MCD) ..... BSTAR
Battlefield Surveillance Devices (MCD) ..... BSD
Battlefield Surveillance [*RADAR*] Electronics (MCD) ..... BASE
Battlefield Surveillance/Moving Target Acquisition Plan (MCD) ..... BS/MTAR
Battlefield Surveillance RADAR (MCD) ..... BSR
Battlefield System Architecture (MCD) ..... BSA
Battlefield System Integration Center (MCD) ..... BSICEN
Battlefield Systems Integration (MCD) ..... BSI
Battlefield Systems Project Management ..... BSPM
Battlefield Visualization Graphics (AABC) ..... BVG
Battlefield Weapons System ..... BWS
Battlefield Weapons System Laboratory ..... BWSL
Battleford Union Hospital Memorial Library, North Battleford,
　Saskatchewan [*Library symbol National Library of Canada*] (BIB) ..... SNBH
Battlefords Early Childhood Intervention Home-Based Program Inc.
　(AC) ..... BECIP
Battlement (ABBR) ..... BTLMT
Battle's Digest [*North Carolina*] [*A publication*] (DLA) ..... Bat Dig
Battle's Revised Statutes of North Carolina [*1873*] [*A publication*]
　(DLA) ..... Bat Rev St
Battle's Revised Statutes of North Carolina [*1873*] [*A publication*]
　(DLA) ..... Bat Stat
Battle's Revised Statutes of North Carolina [*1873*] [*A publication*]
　(DLA) ..... Battle's Revisal
Battleship (MUGU) ..... BAT
Battleship ..... BATSHIP
Battleship [*Navy symbol*] ..... BB
Battleship ..... BS
Battleship (ABBR) ..... BTLSP
Battleship Battle Group [*Usually BBG*] [*Navy*] (DOMA) ..... BBBG
Battleship Battle Group [*Sometimes the more awkward BBBG*] [*Navy*]
　(DOMA) ..... BBG
Battleship Division ..... BATDIV
Battleship Firing (SAA) ..... BF
Battleship Flag [*Navy British*] ..... BS
Battleship Observation Squadron [*Navy symbol*] ..... VO
Battleship Squadron ..... BATRON
Battleship Squadron ..... BS
Battleships and Cruisers, Atlantic Fleet ..... BATCRULANT
Battleships and Cruisers, Pacific Fleet ..... BATCRUPAC
Battleships, Atlantic Fleet ..... BATLANT
Battleships, Atlantic Fleet ..... BATSHIPSLANT
Battleships, Battle Force, Pacific Fleet ..... BATSHIPSBATFORPAC
Battleships, Pacific Fleet ..... BATPAC
Battleships, Pacific Fleet ..... BATSHIPSPAC
Battlesight Zero (MCD) ..... BSZ
Battle-Unit Short-Range Antitank Weapon System (NATG) ..... BUSRAT
Battling (ABBR) ..... BTLG
Batts' Annotated Revised Civil Statutes [*Texas*] [*A publication*]
　(DLA) ..... Batts' Ann St

Batts' Annotated Revised Civil Statutes [*Texas*] [*A publication*]
　(DLA) ..... Batts' Rev St
Batty's Irish King's Bench Reports [*A publication*] (DLA) ..... Batt
Batty's Irish King's Bench Reports [*A publication*] (DLA) ..... Batty (Ir)
Batu Besar [*Indonesia*] [*Airport symbol*] (OAG) ..... BTH
Batu Licin [*Indonesia*] [*ICAO location identifier*] (ICLI) ..... WRBC
Batu Pahat [*Malaysia*] [*ICAO location identifier*] (ICLI) ..... WMAB
Batu Putih/Talisayam [*Indonesia*] [*ICAO location identifier*] (ICLI) ..... WRLD
Batumi [*Former USSR Airport symbol*] (OAG) ..... BUS
Bau [*Zaire*] [*ICAO location identifier*] (ICLI) ..... FZFF
Bau Bau [*Indonesia*] [*Airport symbol*] (OAG) ..... BUW
Bau Bau/Betoambari [*Indonesia*] [*ICAO location identifier*] (ICLI) ..... WAAB
Baucau [*East Timor*] [*ICAO location identifier*] (ICLI) ..... WPEC
Baud [*Unit of data transmission speed*] (MCD) ..... B
Baud [*Unit of data transmission speed*] (CET) ..... Bd
Baud Programming System [*Computer science*] (IAA) ..... BPS
Baud Rate [*Data transmission speed*] [*Computer science*] ..... BDRT
Baud Rate Generator [*Computer science*] ..... BRG
Baudeloeque's Diameter [*External conjugate diameter of pelvis*] [*Obstetrics*]
　(DAVI) ..... DB
Baudette [*Minnesota*] [*ICAO location identifier*] (ICLI) ..... KBDE
Baudette, MN [*Location identifier FAA*] (FAAL) ..... BDE
Baudette Public Library, Baudette, MN [*Library symbol*] [*Library of
Congress*] (LCLS) ..... MnBau
Baudot (IAA) ..... BAUD
Baudot Code ..... BAUD
Baudot Code (IAA) ..... BD
Baudot-Verdan Differential Analyzer [*Electronics*] (IAA) ..... BV
Bauer Hospital-Saint Mary Medical Center, Long Beach, CA [*Library symbol
Library of Congress*] (LCLS) ..... CLobB
Bauer Publishing & Printing Ltd., Rahway, NJ [*Library symbol Library of
Congress*] (LCLS) ..... NjRahB
Bauforschungsprojekte [*Building Research Projects*] [*Fraunhofer Society*]
　[*Information service or system*] (IID) ..... BAUFO
Baughan, E. F., Baltimore MD [*STAC*] ..... BEF
Baume [*Scale*] [*Measurement*] (GPO) ..... B
Baume ..... BA
Baume [*Hydrometer scale or specific gravity*] [*Organic chemistry*] (DAVI) ..... Be
Baumholder [*Germany ICAO location identifier*] (ICLI) ..... EDEK
Bauobjektdokumentation [*Buildings Documentation*] [*Fraunhofer Society*]
　[*Germany*] [*Information service or system*] (IID) ..... BODO
Baures [*Bolivia*] [*ICAO location identifier*] (ICLI) ..... SLBU
Bauru [*Brazil*] [*Airport symbol*] (OAG) ..... BAU
Bauru [*Brazil ICAO location identifier*] (ICLI) ..... SBBU
Bausch & Lomb [*NYSE symbol*] (TTSB) ..... BOL
Bausch & Lomb, Inc. [*Associated Press*] (SAG) ..... BauschL
Bausch & Lomb, Inc. [*NYSE symbol*] (SAG) ..... BOL
Bausch & Lomb, Inc., Library, Rochester, NY [*OCLC symbol*] (OCLC) ..... VQB
Bausch & Lomb, Inc., Rochester, NY [*Library symbol Library of Congress*]
　(LCLS) ..... NRBL
Bausch & Lomb, Inc., SOFLENS Division, Technical Information Center,
Rochester, NY [*Library symbol Library of Congress*] (LCLS) ..... NRBL-S
Bauxite & Northern Railway Co. [*Later, BXN*] [*AAR code*] ..... BN
Bauxite & Northern Railway Co. [*AAR code*] ..... BXN
Bavanat [*Iran*] [*ICAO location identifier*] (ICLI) ..... OISB
Bavaria [*State in West Germany*] (ROG) ..... BAV
Bavarian Border Police [*Germany*] ..... BBP
Bavarian Dance Group of North America (EA) ..... BDGNA
Bavarian Lion Industries Ltd. [*Vancouver Stock Exchange symbol*] ..... BAV
Bavli [*or Babylonian Talmud*] (BJA) ..... b
Baw Faw Mountain [*Washington*] [*Seismograph station code, US Geological
Survey*] (SEIS) ..... BFW
Bawdsey [*British ICAO location identifier*] (ICLI) ..... EGVB
Bawlf Municipal Library, Alberta [*Library symbol National Library of Canada*]
　(NLC) ..... ABAM
Baxley, GA [*FM radio station call letters*] ..... WBYZ
Baxley, GA [*Television station call letters*] ..... WUBI
Baxley, GA [*AM radio station call letters*] ..... WUFE
Baxter Elementary School, Baxter, MN [*Library symbol*] [*Library of
Congress*] (LCLS) ..... MnBaxE
Baxter International [*NYSE symbol*] (SPSG) ..... BAX
Baxter International, Inc. [*Associated Press*] (SAG) ..... Baxter
Baxter Laboratories, Inc. [*of Baxter Travenol Laboratories, Inc.*] [*Research
code symbol*] ..... BAX
Baxter, MN [*AM radio station call letters*] ..... WWWI
Baxter New Era, Baxter, IA [*Library symbol Library of Congress*] (LCLS) ..... IaBaxNE
Baxter on Judicature Acts and Rules [*A publication*] (DLA) ..... Bax Jud Acts
Baxter Springs, KS [*FM radio station call letters*] ..... KMOQ
Baxter Technologies Corp. [*Toronto Stock Exchange symbol*] ..... BTC
Baxter, TN [*FM radio station call letters*] ..... WBXE
Baxter Women's Club, Baxter, IA [*Library symbol Library of Congress*]
　(LCLS) ..... IaBaxWC
Baxter's Reports [*60-68 Tennessee*] [*A publication*] (DLA) ..... Bax
Baxter's Reports [*60-68 Tennessee*] [*A publication*] (DLA) ..... Baxt
Baxter's Reports [*60-68 Tennessee*] [*A publication*] (DLA) ..... Baxt (Tenn)
Baxter's Reports [*60-68 Tennessee*] [*A publication*] (DLA) ..... Baxter
Bay [*Maps and charts*] ..... B
Bay [*Thoroughbred racing*] ..... B
Bay (ADA) ..... BY
Bay Air Aviation [*New Zealand*] [*ICAO designator*] (FAAC) ..... BAY
Bay Air Cargo, SA [*Brazil*] [*FAA designator*] (FAAC) ..... BAO
Bay Ann Resources, Inc. [*Vancouver Stock Exchange symbol*] ..... BYA
Bay Apartment Communities [*Associated Press*] (SAG) ..... BayApt
Bay Apartment Communities [*NYSE symbol*] (SAG) ..... BYA
Bay Area Army Terminal Center ..... BAATC

Bay Area Cryonics Society [*Later, American Cryonics Society*] (EA) .... BACS
Bay Area Functional Performance Evaluation [*Personality research*] [*Psychology*] .... BAFPE
Bay Area Gigabit Network [*Computer science*] (TNIG) .... BAGNet
Bay Area Library and Information System [*Library network*] .... BALIS
Bay Area Library and Information System [*Library network*] .... EBC
Bay Area Library and Information System, Hayward, CA [*OCLC symbol*] (OCLC) .... BAS
Bay Area Library and Information System, Hayward, CA [*Library symbol Library of Congress*] (LCLS) .... CHB
Bay Area Physicians for Human Rights (EA) .... BAPHR
Bay Area Rapid Transit [*San Francisco area, California*] .... BART
Bay Area Reference Center [*San Francisco Public Library*] [*San Francisco, CA*] [*Library network*] .... BARC
Bay Area Regional Research Network [*Acquired from Stanford University by Bolt Beranek and Newman*] [*Internet service*] [*Also, an information service or system*] .... BARRnet
Bay Area Religious Channel [*Cable TV programming service*] .... BARC
Bay Area Seismic Imaging Experiment [*Geology*] .... BASIX
Bay Area Spatial Information System [*Geogroup Corp.*] [*Information service or system*] (IID) .... BASIS
Bay Cabinet Unit .... BCU
Bay City Junior College [*Michigan*] .... BCJC
Bay City, MI [*FM radio station call letters*] .... WCHW
Bay City, MI [*FM radio station call letters*] .... WHNN
Bay City, MI [*FM radio station call letters*] .... WIOG
Bay City, MI [*AM radio station call letters*] .... WMAX
Bay City, MI [*Television station call letters*] .... WNEM
Bay City, MI [*FM radio station call letters*] .... WTRK
Bay City, MI [*FM radio station call letters*] .... WUCX
Bay City, MI [*AM radio station call letters*] .... WXOX
Bay City Public Library, Bay City, MI [*Library symbol Library of Congress*] (LCLS) .... MiBay
Bay City, TX [*Location identifier FAA*] (FAAL) .... BYY
Bay City, TX [*AM radio station call letters*] (RBYB) .... KFCC
Bay City, TX [*FM radio station call letters*] .... KMKS
Bay City, TX [*FM radio station call letters*] .... KXGJ
Bay City-Midland-Saginaw [*Michigan*] [*Airport symbol*] (AD) .... MBS
Bay County Library System, Auburn Branch Library, Auburn, MI [*Library symbol Library of Congress*] (LCLS) .... MiBayS-A
Bay County Library System, Bay City, MI [*Library symbol Library of Congress*] (LCLS) .... MiBayS
Bay County Library System, Broadway Branch Library, Bay City, MI [*Library symbol Library of Congress*] (LCLS) .... MiBayS-B
Bay County Library System, Linwood Branch Library, Linwood, MI [*Library symbol Library of Congress*] (LCLS) .... MiBayS-L
Bay County Library System, Pinconning Branch Library, Pinconning, MI [*Library symbol Library of Congress*] (LCLS) .... MiBayS-P
Bay County Library System, Sage Branch Library, Bay City, MI [*Library symbol Library of Congress*] (LCLS) .... MiBayS-S
Bay County Public Library, Panama City, FL [*Library symbol Library of Congress*] (LCLS) .... FPc
Bay De Noc Community College, Escanaba, MI [*Library symbol Library of Congress*] (LCLS) .... MiEscB
Bay Gelding [*Horse*] .... BG
Bay Horse (BARN) .... b h
Bay Meadows Operating Co. [*Associated Press*] (SAG) .... BayMea
Bay Meadows Operating Co. [*AMEX symbol*] (SPSG) .... CJ
Bay Meadows Oper(Unit) [*AMEX symbol*] (TTSB) .... CJ
Bay Medical Center, Bay City, MI [*Library symbol Library of Congress*] (LCLS) .... MiBayM
Bay Microfilm, Incorporated, Palo Alto, CA [*Library symbol Library of Congress*] (LCLS) .... BMI
Bay Mills Ltd. [*Toronto Stock Exchange symbol*] .... BAY
Bay Minette, AL [*FM radio station call letters*] .... WAVH
Bay Minette, AL [*AM radio station call letters*] .... WBCA
Bay Minette, AL [*FM radio station call letters*] .... WNSP
Bay Networks [*NYSE symbol*] (TTSB) .... BAY
Bay Networks, Inc. [*NYSE symbol*] (SAG) .... BAY
Bay Networks, Inc. [*Associated Press*] (SAG) .... BayNtwk
Bay Networks, Inc. [*NASDAQ symbol*] (SAG) .... BNET
Bay of Biscay Subarea [*NATO*] .... BISCLANT
Bay of Islands Complex [*Newfoundland*] [*Geology*] .... BOI
Bay of Pigs Veterans Association (EA) .... BPVA
Bay Path Junior College [*Longmeadow, MA*] .... BPJC
Bay Resources [*Vancouver Stock Exchange symbol*] .... BAU
Bay Ridge Bancorp [*Associated Press*] (SAG) .... BayRidge
Bay Ridge Bancorp [*NASDAQ symbol*] (SAG) .... BRBC
Bay Roberts Public Library, Bay Roberts, NF, Canada [*Library symbol Library of Congress*] (LCLS) .... CaNfBR
Bay Roberts Public Library, Newfoundland [*Library symbol National Library of Canada*] (NLC) .... NFBR
Bay St. George Community College [*UTLAS symbol*] .... BSG
Bay St. George Community College, Stephenville, Newfoundland [*Library symbol National Library of Canada*] (NLC) .... NFSBS
Bay St. Louis, MS [*AM radio station call letters*] .... WBSL
Bay Shore, NY [*FM radio station call letters*] .... WBZO
Bay Shore Senior High School, Bay Shore, NY [*Library symbol Library of Congress*] (LCLS) .... NBysSH
Bay Shore-Brightwaters Public Library, Brightwaters, NY [*Library symbol Library of Congress*] (LCLS) .... NBri
Bay Springs, MS [*AM radio station call letters*] .... WIZK
Bay Springs, MS [*FM radio station call letters*] .... WIZK-FM
Bay State Gas [*NYSE symbol*] (TTSB) .... BGC
Bay State Gas [*NYSE symbol*] (SAG) .... BGC
Bay State Gas Co. [*Associated Press*] (SAG) .... BaySGs
Bay View Capital [*NASDAQ symbol*] (TTSB) .... BVFS
Bay View Capital Corp. [*Associated Press*] (SAG) .... BayVw
Bay View Capital Corp. [*NASDAQ symbol*] (NQ) .... BVFS
Bay View Elementary School, Duluth, MN [*Library symbol*] [*Library of Congress*] (LCLS) .... MnDuBVE
Bayamo [*Cuba*] [*Airport symbol*] (OAG) .... BYM
Bayamo [*Cuba ICAO location identifier*] (ICLI) .... MUBY
Bayamon Central University, Bayamon, PR [*OCLC symbol*] (OCLC) .... BCU
Bayamon Central University (Universidad Central de Bayamon), Bayamon, Puerto Rico [*Library symbol Library of Congress*] (LCLS) .... PrBayC
Bayamon, PR [*FM radio station call letters*] (RBYB) .... WCOM
Bayamon, PR [*Television station call letters*] .... WDWL
Bayamon, PR [*AM radio station call letters*] .... WLUZ
Bayamon, PR [*AM radio station call letters*] .... WRSJ
Bayamon, PR [*FM radio station call letters*] .... WXYX
Bayandai [*Former USSR Seismograph station code, US Geological Survey Closed*] (SEIS) .... BAY
Bayard News, Bayard, IA [*Library symbol Library of Congress*] (LCLS) .... IaBayN
Bayard, NM [*AM radio station call letters*] .... KNFT
Bayard, NM [*FM radio station call letters*] .... KNFT-FM
Bayard on Evidence [*A publication*] (DLA) .... Bay Ev
Bayard on the Constitution of the United States [*A publication*] (DLA) .... Bay Cons
Bayard Public Library, Bayard, IA [*Library symbol Library of Congress*] (LCLS) .... IaBay
Bayard Taylor Memorial Library, Kennett Square, PA [*Library symbol Library of Congress*] (LCLS) .... PKs
Bay-Area Random Access Information Network [*Defunct*] (TSSD) .... BRAIN
Baybanks, Inc. [*Associated Press*] (SAG) .... BayBks
BayBanks, Inc. [*NASDAQ symbol*] (NQ) .... BBNK
Bayboro, NC [*FM radio station call letters*] .... WKZF
Bayerische Flugzeug Werke [*Bavarian Airplane Works*] [*German*] .... BFW
Bayerische Koenigpartei [*Bavarian Royalist Party*] [*Pre-World War II*] .... BKP
Bayerische Motoren Werke [*Bavarian Motor Works*] [*German automobile manufacturer; initialism used as name of its cars and motorcycles*] .... BMW
Bayerische Motoren Werke [*Bavarian Motor Works*] **North America** .... BMWNA
Bayerische Rundfunk [*Radio network*] [*West Germany*] .... BR
Bayerische Staatspartei [*Bavarian State Party*] [*Germany*] (PPW) .... BSP
Bayerische Vereinsbank [*Union Bank of Bavaria*] [*Munich, West Germany*] .... BV
Bayerische Volkspartei [*Bavarian People's Party*] [*Germany Political party*] (PPE) .... BVP
Bayerisches Landwirtschaftliches Informationssystem [*Bavarian Agricultural Information System*] [*Databank*] [*Germany*] (IID) .... BALIS
Bayernpartei [*Bavarian Party*] [*Germany Political party*] (PPE) .... BP
Bayes Fixed Sample-Size Procedure [*Statistics*] .... BFP
Bayes Information Criterion .... BIC
Bayes Operating Characteristic .... BOC
Bayes Sequential Procedure [*Statistics*] .... BSP
Bayesian Analysis Modified by Inspection [*Computer science*] .... BAMBI
Bayesian Reliability Demonstration Test [*Computer science*] .... BRDT
Bayesian Zero-Failure [*Computer science*] (MCD) .... BAZE
Bayfield Laboratory, Ocean Science and Surveys, Fisheries and Oceans Canada [*Laboratoire Bayfield, Science et Leves Oceaniques, Peches et Oceans Canada*] **Burlington, Ontario** [*Library symbol National Library of Canada*] (NLC) .... OBUFBL
Bayfield Public Library, Bayfield, CO [*Library symbol Library of Congress*] (LCLS) .... CoBay
Baykit [*Former USSR ICAO location identifier*] (ICLI) .... UNKW
Bayley on Bills [*A publication*] (DLA) .... Bayl B
Bayley on Bills [*A publication*] (DLA) .... BB
Bayley on Bills and Notes [*A publication*] (DLA) .... Bay Bills
Bayley on Fines and Recoveries [*A publication*] (DLA) .... Bayl F & R
Bayley Scales of Infant Development .... BSID
Bayley's Commentaries on the Laws of England [*A publication*] (DLA) .... Bayl Ch Pr
Bayley's Questions and Answers for Students [*A publication*] (DLA).... Bayl Q & A
Baylies' Digested Index of English and American Reports [*A publication*] (DLA) .... Bay Dig Ind
Baylies on Domestic Servants [*A publication*] (DLA) .... Bay Dom Serv
Baylis Elementary School, Syosset, NY [*Library symbol Library of Congress*] (LCLS) .... NSyoBaE
Baylis Public Library, Sault Ste. Marie, MI [*Library symbol Library of Congress*] (LCLS) .... MiSsB
Baylles on Sureties and Guarantors [*A publication*] (DLA) .... Baylles Sur
Baylor College of Dentistry, Dallas, TX [*OCLC symbol*] (OCLC) .... IBD
Baylor Computing Center [*Baylor College of Medicine*] [*Research center*] (RCD) .... BCC
Baylor Rapid Autologous Transfusion [*System*] [*Medicine*] (DMAA) .... BRAT
Baylor University (GAGS) .... Baylor U
Baylor University, Armstrong Browning Library, Waco, TX [*Library symbol Library of Congress*] (LCLS) .... TxWB-B
Baylor University in Dallas, Dallas, TX [*Library symbol Library of Congress*] (LCLS) .... TxDaBU
Baylor University, Law School Library, Waco, TX [*Library symbol Library of Congress*] (LCLS) .... TxWB-L
Baylor University, Museum Collection, Waco, TX [*Library symbol Library of Congress*] (LCLS) .... TxWB-Mus
Baylor University School of Nursing, Dallas, TX [*Library symbol*] [*Library of Congress*] (LCLS) .... TxWB-N
Baylor University, Waco, TX [*OCLC symbol*] (OCLC) .... IYU
Baylor University, Waco, TX [*Library symbol Library of Congress*] (LCLS) .... TxWB
Bayly Moore. English Common Pleas Reports [*A publication*] (DLA) .... B Moore
Bayonet (MSA) .... BAY
Bayonet Base [*Lens mount*] (NTCM) .... BB

Bayonet Candelabra ... BAYC
Bayonet Candelabra Double Contact ... BAYCANDDC
Bayonet Candelabra Single Contact ... BAYCANDSC
Bayonet Cap ... BC
Bayonet Coaxial Connector [*Telecommunications*] (ECII) ... BNC
Bayonet Fighting ... BF
Bayonet Naval Connector [*Electronics*] (NTCM) ... BNC
Bayonet Neil Councilman [*Telecommunications*] (ACRL) ... BNC
Bayonet Nut Coupling [*Telecommunications*] (EECA) ... BNC
Bayonet Skirted ... BAYSK
Bayonet Workers' Trade Society [*A union*] [*British*] ... BWTS
Bayonette Connector, for Coaxial Cable [*Electronics*] (NITA) ... BNC
Bayonne Free Public Library, Bayonne, NJ [*Library symbol Library of Congress*] (LCLS) ... NjBa
Bayoo [*Commonly used*] (OPSA) ... BAYOO
Bayou [*Maps and charts*] ... B
Bayou ... BYU
Bayou ... BYU
Bayou Steel Corp. of La Place [*Associated Press*] (SAG) ... Bayou
Bayou Steel Corp. of La Place [*AMEX symbol*] (SPSG) ... BYX
Bayou Steel'A' [*AMEX symbol*] (TTSB) ... BYX
Bayou Vista, LA [*AM radio station call letters*] ... KDLP
Bayou Vista, LA [*FM radio station call letters*] ... KQKI
Bayport Restaurant Group [*NASDAQ symbol*] (TTSB) ... PORT
Bayport Restaurant Group, Inc. [*Associated Press*] (SAG) ... Bayport
Bayport Restaurant Group, Inc. [*NASDAQ symbol*] (SAG) ... PORT
Bayport-Blue Point Public Library, Blue Point, NY [*Library symbol Library of Congress*] (LCLS) ... NBp
Bayport-Blue Point Public Library, Blue Point, NY [*Library symbol*] [*Library of Congress*] (LCLS) ... NBpP
Bayrak Radio & TV Corp. [*Turkish Cyprus*] (EY) ... BRTK
Bayrak Radyo-Televisyon [*Bayrak Radio-Television*] ... BRT
Bayram-Ali [*Former USSR Seismograph station code, US Geological Survey Closed*] (SEIS) ... BAT
Bayreuth [*Germany Airport symbol*] (OAG) ... BYU
Bayreuth [*Germany ICAO location identifier*] (ICLI) ... EDEL
Bayreuth [*Germany ICAO location identifier*] (ICLI) ... EDQD
Bayridge Development [*Vancouver Stock Exchange symbol*] ... BYD
Bay's Reports [*1-3, 5-8 Missouri*] [*A publication*] (DLA) ... Bay
Bay's South Carolina Reports [*1783-1804*] [*A publication*] (DLA) ... Bay
Bayshore Independent, Matawan, NJ [*Library symbol Library of Congress*] (LCLS) ... NjMatB
Bayside, CA [*FM radio station call letters*] ... KZPN
Baytoun, TX [*Television station call letters*] ... KVVV
Baytown, TX [*Location identifier FAA*] (FAAL) ... HPY
Baytown, TX [*AM radio station call letters*] ... KWWJ
Bayu Indonesia Air PT [*ICAO designator*] (FAAC) ... BYU
Bayview Avenue Elementary School, Freeport, NY [*Library symbol*] [*Library of Congress*] (LCLS) ... NFreeBE
Bayview Community Hospital, Mastic Beach, NY [*Library symbol Library of Congress*] (LCLS) ... NMbCH
Bayville Elementary School, Bayville, NY [*Library symbol*] [*Library of Congress*] (LCLS) ... NBayvE
Bayville Free Library, Bayville, NY [*Library symbol Library of Congress*] (LCLS) ... NBayv
Bayville Intermediate School, Bayville, NY [*Library symbol*] [*Library of Congress*] (LCLS) ... NBayvI
Bayville Intermediate School, Locust Valley, NY [*Library symbol Library of Congress*] (LCLS) ... NLvBI
Bayville Primary School, Bayville, NY [*Library symbol*] [*Library of Congress*] (LCLS) ... NBayvP
Baywest Capital [*Vancouver Stock Exchange symbol*] ... BAW
Baz Resources Ltd. [*Vancouver Stock Exchange symbol*] ... BZR
Bazaar ... BZR
Bazianus [*Deceased, 1197*] [*Authority cited in pre-1607 legal work*] (DSA) ... B
Bazianus [*Deceased, 1197*] [*Authority cited in pre-1607 legal work*] (DSA) ... Bas
Bazianus [*Deceased, 1197*] [*Authority cited in pre-1607 legal work*] (DSA) ... Baz
Bazianus [*Deceased, 1197*] [*Authority cited in pre-1607 legal work*] (DSA) ... Baza
Bazianus [*Deceased, 1197*] [*Authority cited in pre-1607 legal work*] (DSA) ... Bazan
Bazianus de Baldone de Vaude [*Flourished, 13th century*] [*Authority cited in pre-1607 legal work*] (DSA) ... Baz
Bazil [*Red sheep*] [*Bookbinding*] (ROG) ... BAZ
Bazillenemulsion [*Bacillary emulsion*] [*Immunology*] ... BE
Bazman [*Iran*] [*ICAO location identifier*] (ICLI) ... OIZN
BBC Realty Investors [*Toronto Stock Exchange symbol Vancouver Stock Exchange symbol*] ... BBT
BBN Corp. [*NYSE symbol*] (SAG) ... BBN
BBN Corp. [*NYSE symbol*] (TTSB) ... BBN
BC (VRA) ... BC
BC [*British Columbia*] **Bancorp** [*Toronto Stock Exchange symbol Vancouver Stock Exchange symbol*] ... BBC
BC Biotechnology Alliance (AC) ... BCBA
BC Central Credit Union, Vancouver, BC, Canada [*Library symbol Library of Congress*] (LCLS) ... CaBVaCCU
BC Council for the Family (AC) ... BCCF
BC [*British Columbia*] **Court House Library Society, Vancouver, British Columbia,** [*Library symbol National Library of Canada*] (NLC) ... BVAL
BC Deaf Sports Federation (AC) ... BCDSF
BC Environmental Network (AC) ... BCEN
BC Gas [*TS Symbol*] (TTSB) ... BCG
BC Gymnastics Association (AC) ... BCGA
BC Lung Association (AC) ... BCLA
BC Multicultural Education Society (AC) ... BCMES
B.C. Native Women's Society, Kamloops, BC, Canada [*Library symbol*] [*Library of Congress*] (LCLS) ... CaBKNW
BC Parents in Crisis Society (AC) ... BCPIC
BC [*British Columbia*] **Rail Ltd.** [*Toronto Stock Exchange symbol Vancouver Stock Exchange symbol*] ... BCL
BC Salmon Farmers Association (AC) ... BCSFA
BC Shellfish Growers Association (AC) ... BCSGA
BC Snowmobile Federation (AC) ... BCSF
BC [*British Columbia*] **Sugar Refinery Ltd.** [*Toronto Stock Exchange symbol*] ... BCS
BC Therapeutic Riding Association (AC) ... BCTRA
BCA Charter [*British ICAO designator*] (FAAC) ... BRC
BCA Credit Information [*Later, Broadcast Credit Association*] (EA) ... BCA
BCAM International, Inc. [*Associated Press*] (SAG) ... BCAM
BCAM International, Inc. [*Associated Press*] (SAG) ... BCAM Int
BCAM Intl Wrrt'B' [*NASDAQ symbol*] (TTSB) ... BCAML
BCAM Intl Wrrt'E' [*NASDAQ symbol*] (TTSB) ... BCAMZ
BCB Financial Services Corp. [*Associated Press*] (SAG) ... BCB Fin
BCB Financial Services Corp. [*NASDAQ symbol*] (SAG) ... BCBF
BCB Financial Svcs [*NASDAQ symbol*] (TTSB) ... BCBF
BCC Library, CANMET, Energy, Mines, and Resources Canada [*Bibliotheque du CBC, CANMET, Energie, Mines, et Ressources Canada*], Nepean, Ontario [*Library symbol National Library of Canada*] (NLC) ... ONEMRCM
BCE, Inc. [*Formerly, Bell Canada Enterprises*] [*Toronto Stock Exchange symbol*] ... B
BCE, Inc. [*Formerly, Bell Canada Enterprises*] [*Vancouver Stock Exchange symbol*] ... B
BCE, Inc. [*Formerly, Bell Canada Enterprises*] [*NYSE symbol*] (SPSG) ... BCE
BCE Mobile Communications, Inc. [*Associated Press*] (SAG) ... BCE MC
BCE Mobile Communications, Inc. [*Toronto Stock Exchange symbol*] ... BCX
BCE Place Finance Corp. [*Toronto Stock Exchange symbol Vancouver Stock Exchange symbol*] ... BDF
BCED Capital Investment Corp. [*Toronto Stock Exchange symbol Vancouver Stock Exchange symbol*] ... BDP
B-Cell Activating Factor [*Immunology*] ... BAF
B-Cell Acute Lymphoblastic Leukemia [*Medicine*] ... B-ALL
B-Cell Antigen Receptor [*Immunology*] ... BCR
B-Cell Chronic Lymphocytic Leukemia [*Medicine*] ... B-CLL
B-Cell Differentiation Factor [*Immunology*] ... BCDF
B-Cell Growth Factor [*Biochemistry*] ... BCGF
B-Cell Line [*Cytology*] ... BCL
B-Cell Maturation Factor [*Immunology*] ... BMF
B-Cell Precursor [*Biochemistry*] ... BCP
B-Cell Prolymphocytic Leukemia ... B-PLL
B-Cell Stimulatory Factor [*Biochemistry*] ... BSF
B-Cell-Lymphadenopathy Associated Virus ... B-LAV
BCNU [*Carmustine*] **and Triazinate** [*Antineoplastic drug*] (DAVI) ... BT
BCNU [*Carmustine*], ara-C, Cyclophosphamide, Thioguanine [*Antineoplastic drug regimen*] ... BACT
BCNU [*Carmustine*], Cyclophosphamide, Oncovin , Prednisone [*Vincristine*] [*Antineoplastic drug regimen*] ... BCOP
BCNU [*Carmustine*], Cyclophosphamide, Prednisone [*Antineoplastic drug regimen*] ... BCP
BCNU [*Carmustine*], Cyclophosphamide, Vinblastine, Procarbazine, Prednisone [*Antineoplastic drug regimen*] ... BCVPP
BCNU [*Carmustine*], Cyclophosphamide, Vincristine, Prednisone [*Antineoplastic drug regimen*] ... BCVP
BCNU [*Carmustine*], Hydroxyurea, Dacarbazine [*Antineoplastic drug regimen*] ... BHD
BCNU [*Carmustine*], Hydroxyurea, Dacarbazine, Vincristine [*Antineoplastic drug regimen*] ... BHDV
BCNU [*Carmustine*], Methotrexate, Procarbazine [*Antineoplastic drug regimen*] ... BMP
BCNU [*Carmustine*], Prednisone [*Antineoplastic drug regimen*] ... BP
BCNU [*Carmustine*], Vinblastine, Cyclophosphamide, Procarbazine, Prednisone [*Antineoplastic drug regimen*] ... BVCPP
BCNU [*Carmustine*], Vinblastine, Procarbazine, and Prednisone [*Antineoplastic drug regimen*] (DAVI) ... BCUPP
BCNU [*Carmustine*], Vincristine, Adriamycin, Prednisone [*Antineoplastic drug regimen*] ... BVAP
BCNU [*Carmustine*], Vincristine, and arbazine [*DTIC*] [*Antineoplastic drug regimen*] (DAVI) ... BVD
BCNU [*Carmustine*], Vincristine, Procarbazine, Prednisone [*Antineoplastic drug regimen*] ... BVPP
B-Colony Forming Cells ... B-CFC
BCP International Bank Ltd. [*Associated Press*] (SAG) ... BCP Bk
BCP International Bank Ltd. [*NYSE symbol*] (SAG) ... BPC
BCR [*Bituminous Coal Research*] **National Laboratory** [*Defunct*] (EA) ... BCRNL
BCS [*Boeing Computer Services*] **Interactive Graphics** ... BIG
BCT International [*NASDAQ symbol*] (SAG) ... BCTI
BCT International, Inc. [*Associated Press*] (SAG) ... BCT Int
BCU Industries, Inc. [*Toronto Stock Exchange symbol*] ... BCU
BDM Corp., Albuquerque, NM [*Library symbol*] [*Library of Congress*] (LCLS) ... NmABD
BDM Federal, Inc. (GAAI) ... BDM
BDM International, Inc. [*NASDAQ symbol*] (SAG) ... BDMI
BDM International, Inc. [*Associated Press*] (SAG) ... BDMInt
BDM International, Information Service Center, Kettering, OH [*Library symbol*] [*Library of Congress*] (LCLS) ... OKetBD
BDM Intl. [*NASDAQ symbol*] (TTSB) ... BDM
BDM Service Co. (MCD) ... BDMSC
BE Aerospace [*NASDAQ symbol*] (TTSB) ... BEAV
BE Aerospace, Inc. [*Associated Press*] (SAG) ... BE Aero
BE Aerospace, Inc. [*NASDAQ symbol*] (SPSG) ... BEAV
Be Back Later [*Computer hacker terminology*] (NHD) ... BBL
Be Back Later [*Internet language*] [*Computer science*] ... bbl

Be Ever Alert, Vigilant/Error Removal [*United States Air Force Security System's acronym for the Zero Defects Program*] ... BEAVER
Be On the Lookout [*Police term*] ... BOL
Be On the Lookout [*Police term*] ... BOLO
Be Right Back [*Computer hacker terminology*] (NHD) ... BRB
Be Right Back [*Internet language*] [*Computer science*] ... brb
Be Seein' You [*Computer science*] (DOM) ... BCNU
BE Semiconductor Indus [*NASDAQ symbol*] (TTSB) ... BESIF
Be Specific ... BS
Be Undressed, Ready, My Angel [*Correspondence*] (DSUE) ... BURMA
BEA Income Fd [*NYSE symbol*] (TTSB) ... FBF
BEA Income Fund [*Associated Press*] (SAG) ... BEA Inco
BEA Income Fund [*NYSE symbol*] (SAG) ... FBF
BEA Strategic Income Fd [*NYSE symbol*] (TTSB) ... FBI
BEA Strategic Income Fund [*Associated Press*] (SAG) ... BEA Strat
BEA Strategic Income Fund [*NYSE symbol*] (SAG) ... FBI
Beach ... BCH
Beach (MCD) ... BCH
Beach [*Commonly used*] (OPSA) ... BEACH
Beach (ADA) ... BH
Beach Abort ... BA
Beach Armored Recovery Vehicle ... BARV
Beach Boys Freaks United (EA) ... BBFU
Beach Boys Stomp Fan Club (EAIO) ... BBSFC
Beach, Dewey W., Denver CO [*STAC*] ... BDW
Beach Discharge Lighter ... BDL
Beach Discharge Point (MCD) ... BDP
Beach Erosion Board [*Army*] ... BEB
Beach Front USA [*An association*] (EA) ... BFUSA
Beach Group ... BG
Beach Grove, IN [*AM radio station call letters*] ... WNTS
Beach Jumper Unit ... BJU
Beach Landing Site [*Military*] (DOMA) ... BLS
Beach Maintenance Area [*British and Canadian*] [*World War II*] ... BMA
Beach Master Unit [*Navy*] ... BMU
Beach Modulator Oscillator ... BMO
Beach on Contributory Negligence [*A publication*] (DLA) ... Beach Contrib Neg
Beach on Injunctions [*A publication*] (DLA) ... Beach Inj
Beach on Private Corporations [*A publication*] (DLA) ... Beach Priv Corp
Beach on Public Corporations [*A publication*] (DLA) ... Beach Pub Corp
Beach on the Law of Receivers [*A publication*] (DLA) ... Beach Rec
Beach Party ... BP
Beach Party Division [*Navy*] (NVT) ... BPD
Beach Party Group [*Navy*] (NVT) ... BPG
Beach Party Guard [*Navy*] (NVT) ... BPG
Beach Party Team [*Navy*] (NVT) ... BPT
Beach Patrol Craft [*British military*] (DMA) ... BPC
Beach Protection Program [*Australia*] ... BPP
Beach Signal Office [*Military*] (IAA) ... BSO
Beach Support Area (CINC) ... BSA
Beach Support Unit [*Military*] (DNAB) ... BSU
Beach Support Vehicle [*Navy*] (CAAL) ... BSV
Beachcomber, Ship Bottom, NJ [*Library symbol Library of Congress*] (LCLS) ... NjSbB
[*The*] **Beaches Environmental Assessment, Closure, and Health Act 1993** ... BEACH
Beachhead (AFM) ... BHD
Beachhead Air Defense (MCD) ... BHAD
Beachmaster ... BM
Beachmaster ... BMR
Beach's Commentaries on Modern Equity Jurisprudence [*A publication*] (DLA) ... Beach Mod Eq Jur
Beach's Modern Practice in Equity [*A publication*] (DLA) ... Beach Eq Prac
Beachville Ye Olde Museum, Beachville, ON, Canada [*Library symbol*] [*Library of Congress*] (LCLS) ... CaOBEM
Beachville Ye Olde Museum, Ontario [*Library symbol National Library of Canada*] (BIB) ... OBEM
Beacon [*Aviation*] ... B
Beacon [*Aviation*] (AFM) ... BCN
Beacon ... BN
Beacon Airborne S-Band (IAA) ... BAS
Beacon Airborne X-Band (IAA) ... BAX
Beacon Aircraft Position (MUGU) ... BAP
Beacon and Wayland News, Winfield, IA [*Library symbol Library of Congress*] (LCLS) ... IaWinfB
Beacon Antenna Equipment ... BAE
Beacon Buoy (IAA) ... BB
Beacon College [*Defunct*] (EA) ... BC
Beacon Collision Avoidance System [*Aviation*] (DA) ... BACS
Beacon Collision Avoidance System [*Aviation*] ... BCAS
Beacon Control Console (IAA) ... BCC
Beacon Data [*Aviation*] (FAAC) ... BDAT
Beacon Data Generation (SAA) ... BDG
Beacon Experiment and Auroral Research ... BEAR
Beacon Explorer [*Satellite*] [*NASA*] ... BE
Beacon Explorer A [*Satellite*] [*NASA*] ... BE-A
Beacon Explorer B [*Satellite*] [*NASA*] ... BE-B
Beacon Identification Method (DNAB) ... BIM
Beacon Instrumented Guided Ordnance (MCD) ... BINGO
Beacon, NY [*AM radio station call letters*] ... WBNR
Beacon Only Bombing System ... BOBS
Beacon, Pequannock, NJ [*Library symbol Library of Congress*] (LCLS) ... NjPeqB
Beacon Point ... BP
Beacon Portable Packset ... BPP
Beacon Press [*Publisher*] ... BP
Beacon Processing System ... BPS
Beacon Properties [*NYSE symbol*] (TTSB) ... BCN
Beacon Properties Corp. [*NYSE symbol*] (SAG) ... BCN
Beacon Properties Corp. [*Associated Press*] (SAG) ... BeacnP
Beacon Properties Corp. [*Associated Press*] (SAG) ... BeacnPr
Beacon Ranging Pulse ... BRP
Beacon Reply Group [*Aviation*] (OA) ... BRG
Beacon Tracking Level (KSC) ... BTL
Beacon Tracking System ... BTS
Beacon Trigger Generator ... BTG
Beacon, Ultra Portable "S" Band [*Navy*] ... BUPS
Beacon, Ultra Portable X Band [*Navy*] (IAA) ... BUPX
Beacon Video Digitizer ... BVD
Beacon Video Processing System ... BVPS
Beacon Video Processor ... BVP
Beacon-Radio Set ... BRS
Beacons and Blind Landing (IAA) ... BBL
Beaconsfield [*Urban district in England*] ... BEAC
Beaconsfield Public Library, Beaconsfield, PQ, Canada [*Library symbol Library of Congress*] (LCLS) ... CaQBE
Beaconsfield Public Library, Quebec [*Library symbol National Library of Canada*] (NLC) ... QBE
Bead (IAA) ... BD
Bead and Stone Importers Association (EA) ... BSIA
Bead Society (EA) ... BS
Beaded [*or Banded*] **One Side** [*Lumber*] ... B1S
Beaded [*or Banded*] **Two Sides** [*Lumber*] ... B2S
Beading Device [*Tool*] (AAG) ... BDDV
Beading Die ... BDDI
Beads (VRA) ... bea
Beadwork (VRA) ... beawk
Beagle Pup Club [*British*] ... BPC
Beak ... B
Beak Consultants, Mississauga, ON, Canada [*Library symbol Library of Congress*] (LCLS) ... CaOMBC
Beak Consultants, Mississauga, Ontario [*Library symbol National Library of Canada*] (NLC) ... OMBC
Beak Line ... BL
Bealanana [*Madagascar*] [*Airport symbol*] (OAG) ... WBE
Beale Cypher Association (EA) ... BCA
Beam [*of a ship*] ... B
Beam (KSC) ... BM
Beam Accessed Metal Oxide Semiconductor [*Memory technology*] (NITA) ... BEAMOS
Beam Addressed Metal Oxide Semiconductor [*Memory technology*] ... BEAMOS
Beam and Plate System (PDAA) ... BAPS
Beam Approach (DEN) ... B/A
Beam Approach Beacon System [*Aviation*] (KSC) ... BABS
Beam Approach Seeker Evaluation System [*Air Force*] (MCD) ... BASES
Beam Approach Training [*Military*] ... BAT
Beam Approach Training Flight [*British military*] (DMA) ... BATF
Beam Calibrator (PDAA) ... BECA
Beam Candle Watt Power (MCD) ... BCWP
Beam Candle Watt Seconds (MCD) ... BCWS
Beam Candlepower ... BCP
Beam Candlepower Seconds ... BCPS
Beam Collimation Error (MUGU) ... BCE
Beam Collimator ... BC
Beam Communications Set ... BCS
Beam Control Subsystem (MCD) ... BCS
Beam Correction Factor ... BCF
Beam Coupling Coefficient ... BCC
Beam Coupling Tube (NATG) ... BEACOTRON
Beam Deflection Tube ... BDT
Beam Degrader ... BD
Beam Experiment Aboard Rocket (MCD) ... BEAR
Beam Forming ... BF
Beam Lead Sealed Junction [*Electronics*] (IAA) ... BLSJ
Beam Lead Sealed Junction Integrated Circuit Package (AABC) ... BLSJICP
Beam Monitor ... BM
Beam of Light Transistor (MSA) ... BOLT
Beam of Light Transmitter ... BOLT
Beam Packing Loss (IAA) ... BPL
Beam Plasma Amplification (MCD) ... BPA
Beam Position Monitor ... BPM
Beam Positioning Drive (OA) ... BPD
Beam Positioning Magnet ... BPM
Beam Ride (AAG) ... BR
Beam Ride Actuator ... BRA
Beam Ride Error ... BRE
Beam Rider Tail Control Fragmentation [*Missile*] (MCD) ... BTF
Beam Shape Loss (IAA) ... BSL
Beam Spacer (DAC) ... BS
Beam Splitter [*Instrumentation*] ... BS
Beam Steering ... BS
Beam Steering Computer ... BSC
Beam Steering Device ... BSD
Beam Steering Group ... BSG
Beam Steering Processor [*Military*] ... BSP
Beam Steering Programmer Microprocessor [*Military*] ... BSPUP
Beam Steering Shift Register [*Military*] ... BSSR
Beam Steering System ... BSS
Beam Steering Transducer ... BST
Beam Steering Ultrasonic Transducer ... BSUT
Beam Steering Unit (DA) ... BSU

Beam Stop ... BS
Beam Tape Packaging [*Computer science*] ... BTP
Beam to Waterline Length ... B/LWL
Beam Tracking Nuclear [*Military*] (CAAL) ... BTN
Beam Transfer Area [*LASER technology*] ... BTA
Beam Transport System ... BTS
Beam Width (CET) ... BW
Beam Zero Indication (MCD) ... BZI
Beam-Driven Thermonuclear (MCD) ... BDTN
Beames' Commitments in Bankruptcy [*A publication*] (DLA) ... Bea Bank
Beames' Costs in Equity [*A publication*] (DLA) ... Bea CE
Beames' Costs in Equity [*A publication*] (DLA) ... Bea Costs
Beames' Costs in Equity [*A publication*] (DLA) ... CE
Beames' Equity Pleading [*A publication*] (DLA) ... Bea Eq Pl
Beames' Glanville [*A publication*] (DLA) ... Beames Glanv
Beames on the Writ of Ne Exeat Regno [*A publication*] (DLA) ... Bea Ne Ex
Beames' Orders in Chancery [*England*] [*A publication*] (DLA) ... Bea Ord
Beames' Pleas in Equity [*A publication*] (DLA) ... Bea Pl Eq
Beam-Foil (PDAA) ... BF
Beam-Foil Spectroscopy ... BFS
Beam-Forming Electrode ... BFE
Beam-Forming Interfact (PDAA) ... BFI
Beam-Forming Network ... BFN
Beam-Heated Cathode ... BHC
Beaminster [*England*] ... BEAM
Beam-Lead Device (IEEE) ... BLD
Beam-Lead Individual Carrier (PDAA) ... BLIC
Beam-Rider Tail Control ... BT
Beam-Rider Terrier [*Missile*] (MCD) ... BT
Beam-Riding Tail-Controlled Nuclear Missile ... BTN
Beams and Stringers [*Technical drawings*] ... B & S
Beamsteering (MSA) ... BMSTRG
Beamsville District Secondary School, Beamsville, ON, Canada [*Library symbol Library of Congress*] (LCLS) ... CaOBeD
Beamsville District Secondary School, Ontario [*Library symbol National Library of Canada*] (NLC) ... OBED
Beam-Switching Tube ... BST
Beam-to-Beam Correlation (NVT) ... BBC
Beamwidth (MSA) ... BMW
Bean Common Mosaic Virus ... BCMV
Bean Curly Dwarf Mosaic Virus [*Plant pathology*] ... BCDMV
Bean Golden Mosaic Virus ... BGMV
Bean Growers Cooperative Association [*Australia*] ... BGCA
Bean Mild Mosaic Virus [*Plant pathology*] ... BMMV
Bean Pod Mottle Virus [*Plant pathology*] ... BPMV
Bean Rugose Mosaic Virus [*Plant pathology*] ... BRMV
Bean Summer Death Virus [*Plant pathology*] ... BSDV
Bean Yellow Mosaic Virus ... BYMV
Bean Yellow Vein Banding Virus [*Plant pathology*] ... BYVBV
Beance Tubaire Volontaire [*Voluntary opening of eustachian tubes*] [*Deep-sea diving*] [*French*] ... BTV
Bear Canyon [*Utah*] [*Seismograph station code, US Geological Survey Closed*] (SEIS) ... BCU
Bear Canyon School, Alberta [*Library symbol National Library of Canada*] (BIB) ... ABCS
Bear Creek, AK [*Location identifier FAA*] (FAAL) ... BCC
Bear Gulch [*California*] [*Seismograph station code, US Geological Survey*] (SEIS) ... BGH
Bear Island [*Formerly, Bjornoya*] [*Norway*] [*Geomagnetic observatory code*] ... BJN
Bear Lake County District Library, Montpelier, ID [*Library symbol*] [*Library of Congress*] (LCLS) ... IdMonB
Bear Lake County District Paris Branch, Paris, ID [*Library symbol*] [*Library of Congress*] (LCLS) ... IdMonB-P
Bear Lake, MI [*FM radio station call letters*] ... WZTU
Bear Lake Resources Ltd. [*Vancouver Stock Exchange symbol*] ... BLA
Bear Market [*Investment term*] ... BM
Bear Mountain Trailside Museum, Bear Mountain, NY [*Library symbol*] [*Library of Congress*] (LCLS) ... NBmtT
Bear Point Community Library, Bear Canyon, AB, Canada [*Library symbol*] [*Library of Congress*] (LCLS) ... CaABcBC
Bear Point Community Library, Bear Canyon, Alberta [*Library symbol National Library of Canada*] (NLC) ... ABCBC
Bear River Historical Society, Bear River, NS, Canada [*Library symbol*] [*Library of Congress*] (LCLS) ... CaNSBrH
Bear River Historical Society, Nova Scotia [*Library symbol National Library of Canada*] (NLC) ... NSBRH
Bear River Range [*Idaho*] [*Seismograph station code, US Geological Survey*] (SEIS) ... BEI
Bear Stearns [*Associated Press*] (SAG) ... BS VPt
Bear Stearns 7.60%'C'Dep Pfd [*NYSE symbol*] (TTSB) ... BSCPrC
Bear Stearns 7.88%'B'Dep Pfd [*NYSE symbol*] (TTSB) ... BSCPrB
Bear Stearns Adj Rt Pfd [*NYSE symbol*] (TTSB) ... BSCPrA
Bear Stearns Companies, Inc. [*Associated Press*] (SAG) ... BearS
Bear Stearns Companies, Inc. [*Associated Press*] (SAG) ... BearSt
Bear Stearns Companies, Inc. [*AMEX symbol*] (SAG) ... BJC
Bear Stearns Companies, Inc. [*AMEX symbol*] (SAG) ... BJP
Bear Stearns Companies, Inc. [*Associated Press*] (SAG) ... BS MRK
Bear Stearns Companies, Inc. [*NYSE symbol*] (SPSG) ... BSC
Bear Stearns Companies, Inc. [*Associated Press*] (SAG) ... BSCUB
Bear Stearns Companies, Inc. [*Associated Press*] (SAG) ... BSHK
Bear Stearns Companies, Inc. [*Associated Press*] (SAG) ... BSJpn
Bear Stearns Companies, Inc. [*Associated Press*] (SAG) ... BSNk
Bear Stearns Companies, Inc. [*Associated Press*] (SAG) ... BSYn
Bear Stearns Companies, Inc. [*AMEX symbol*] (SAG) ... BYE
Bear Stearns Companies, Inc. [*AMEX symbol*] (SAG) ... BYN
Bear Stearns Companies, Inc. [*AMEX symbol*] (SAG) ... HXC
Bear Stearns Companies, Inc. [*AMEX symbol*] (SAG) ... HXP
Bear Stearns Companies, Inc. [*AMEX symbol*] (SAG) ... KBB
Bear Stearns Companies, Inc. [*AMEX symbol*] (SAG) ... MCP
Bear Stearns Companies, Inc. [*AMEX symbol*] (SAG) ... NKB
Bear Stearns Cos. [*NYSE symbol*] (TTSB) ... BSC
Bear Stearns Cos.'CUBS''98 [*AMEX symbol*] (TTSB) ... KBB
Bear Stearns Fin LLC'EPICS' [*NYSE symbol*] (TTSB) ... BSCPrZ
Bear Sterns 5.50%MRK'CHIPS' [*AMEX symbol*] (TTSB) ... MCP
Bear Valley [*California*] [*Seismograph station code, US Geological Survey*] (SEIS) ... BVL
Bear Valley Observatory [*California*] [*Seismograph station code, US Geological Survey Closed*] (SEIS) ... BVC
Bearbeiter [*Editor*] [*German*] (BARN) ... Bearb
Bearbeitet [*Revised*] [*German*] (BARN) ... bearb
Bearblock. Treatise upon Tithes [*6th ed.*] [*1832*] [*A publication*] (DLA) ... Bear Tithes
Beard Co. [*Associated Press*] (SAG) ... BeardCo
Beard Co. [*AMEX symbol*] (SPSG) ... BOC
Bearded Collie Club of America (EA) ... BCCA
Bearded Iris Mosaic Virus [*Plant pathology*] ... BIMV
Beardlsey-Brown Valley Public Schools, Beardlsey, MN [*Library symbol*] [*Library of Congress*] (LCLS) ... MnBeaPS
Beardmore Public Library, Ontario [*Library symbol National Library of Canada*] (NLC) ... OBEAR
Beardmore Resources [*Vancouver Stock Exchange symbol*] ... BDR
Beardsley-Browns Valley Public Schools, Browns Valley, MN [*Library symbol*] [*Library of Congress*] (LCLS) ... MnBrvPS
Beardstown, IL [*AM radio station call letters*] ... WRMS
Beardstown, IL [*FM radio station call letters*] ... WRMS-FM
Beardstown Public Library, Beardstown, IL [*Library symbol Library of Congress*] (LCLS) ... IBea
Bearer ... BRR
Bearer Bond [*Investment term*] (ADA) ... BB
Bearer Channel [*A component of ISDN interfaces*] (PCM) ... B-channel
Bearer Company [*British military*] (DMA) ... Br Coy
Bearer Depositary Receipt [*Investment term*] ... BDR
Bearing [*Angle*] ... B
Bearing ... BG
Bearing (WDAA) ... BR
Bearing (AFM) ... BRG
Bearing ... BRNG
Bearing Altitude Indicator [*Aerospace*] ... BAI
Bearing and Power Transfer Assembly [*Aerospace*] ... BAPTA
Bearing and Range Indicator ... BRI
Bearing Bronze [*Metallurgy*] ... BBz
Bearing Capacity Ratio [*Materials technology*] ... BCR
Bearing/Confidence ... B/CONF
Bearing Deviation Indicator [*Aerospace*] ... BDI
Bearing, Distance, and Heading ... BDH
Bearing, Distance, and Heading Indicator ... BDHI
Bearing Error [*Military*] (CAAL) ... BE
Bearing Factor [*Mechanical engineering*] ... BF
Bearing Frequency Indicator (NVT) ... BFI
Bearing Indicator (MCD) ... BI
Bearing Indicator and Navigator to Grounded Operator (MCD) ... BINGO
Bearing Magnetic [*Navigation*] (IAA) ... BM
Bearing Mounted Clutch ... BMC
Bearing Pennant [*Navy British*] ... BG
Bearing per Gyro Compass [*Navigation*] ... BPGC
Bearing per Standard Compass [*Navigation*] ... BPSC
Bearing per Steering Gyro Compass [*Navigation*] ... BPSTGC
Bearing Pile [*Technical drawings*] (DAC) ... BP
Bearing Plate [*Technical drawings*] ... BPL
Bearing Procurement Specification (MSA) ... BPS
Bearing Repeater Unit (IAA) ... BRU
Bearing Specialists Association (EA) ... BSA
Bearing Supplies Ltd. [*British ICAO designator*] (FAAC) ... PVO
Bearing Technology ... BT
Bearing Time Recorder ... BTR
Bearingless Main Rotor (RDA) ... BMR
Bearing-Only Launch [*Navy*] (CAAL) ... BOL
Bearings, Inc. [*Associated Press*] (SAG) ... Bearng
Bearings, Inc. [*NYSE symbol*] (SPSG) ... BER
Bearn-Fabre, PQ [*Television station call letters*] ... CKRN-3
Bears, Lions, Eagles, Steelers, Vikings, Colts, Dolphins, and Bills [*Computerized scouting combine for professional football teams; name comprises membership teams*] ... BLESTO-VIII
Bearskin Lake [*ICAO designator*] (AD) ... JV
Bearskin Lake Air Service Ltd. [*Canada ICAO designator*] (FAAC) ... BLS
Beasley's New Jersey Chancery Reports [*A publication*] (DLA) ... Beas
Beasley's New Jersey Equity Reports [*12-13*] [*A publication*] (DLA) ... Beas
Beasley's New Jersey Equity Reports [*A publication*] (DLA) ... Beasl
Beat ... BT
Beat Matsushita Whatsoever [*Facetious translation of BMW - Bavarian Motor Works, Originated by Sony Corp.*] (ECON) ... BMW
Beat Oscillator ... BO
Beata Maria [*The Blessed Virgin*] [*Latin*] ... BM
Beata Maria Virgo [*Blessed Mary the Virgin*] [*Latin*] ... BMV
Beata Virgo [*Blessed Virgin*] [*Latin*] ... BV
Beata Virgo Maria [*Blessed Virgin Mary*] [*Latin*] ... BVM
Beatae Memoriae [*Of Blessed Memory*] [*Latin*] ... BM
Beaten Favourite [*Horse racing*] [*British*] ... BF
Beat-Frequency ... BF
Beat-Frequency Detection (IAA) ... BFD

Beat-Frequency Interferometer (PDAA)	BFI
Beat-Frequency Oscillator	BFO
Beating [FBI standardized term]	BTG
Beating the Gun [Investment term]	BTG
Beatissime Pater [Most Holy Father] [Latin]	BP
Beatitudo Vestra [Your Holiness] [Latin]	BV
Beatles Connection [An association] (EA)	BC
Beatles Information Center [Sweden] (EAIO)	BIC
Beatles Unlimited (EA)	BU
Beatrice Foods Co., Chicago, IL [Library symbol Library of Congress] (LCLS)	ICBF
Beatrice M. Murphy Foundation (EA)	BMMF
Beatrice, NE [Location identifier FAA] (FAAL)	BIE
Beatrice, NE [Location identifier FAA] (FAAL)	BJU
Beatrice, NE [FM radio station call letters]	KTGL
Beatrice, NE [AM radio station call letters]	KWBE
Beatrice Public Library, Beatrice, NE [Library symbol Library of Congress] (LCLS)	NbB
Beatrice Public Library, Beatrice, NE [Library symbol] [Library of Congress] (LCLS)	NbBea
Beatrix Mine [South Africa] [ICAO location identifier] (ICLI)	FABX
Beats per Minute [Cardiology]	BPM
Beats per Minute [Medicine] (DMAA)	bpm
Beats per Second [Cardiology]	BPS
Beatty [Nevada] [Seismograph station code, US Geological Survey Closed] (SEIS)	BEA
Beatty [Nevada] [Seismograph station code, US Geological Survey Closed] (SEIS)	BTY
BEATTY, NV [Commercial waste site] (GAAI)	BETY
Beatty, NV [Location identifier FAA] (FAAL)	BTY
Beatty's Irish Chancery Reports [1814-36] [A publication] (DLA)	Beat
Beatty's Irish Chancery Reports [1814-36] [A publication] (DLA)	Beatt
Beatty's Irish Chancery Reports [1814-36] [A publication] (DLA)	Beatty
Beatty's Irish Chancery Reports [1814-36] [A publication] (DLA)	Beatty Ir Ch
Beattyville, KY [FM radio station call letters]	WLJC
Beattyville, KY [Television station call letters]	WLJC-TV
Beau Canada Exploration Ltd. [Toronto Stock Exchange symbol]	BAU
Beau Val Mines [Vancouver Stock Exchange symbol]	BVM
Beauchamp Exploration, Inc. [Vancouver Stock Exchange symbol]	BPE
Beauchemin, Beaton, LaPointe, Inc., Montreal, PQ, Canada [Library symbol Library of Congress] (LCLS)	CaQMBBL
Beauchemin, Beaton, Lapointe, Inc., Montreal, Quebec [Library symbol National Library of Canada] (NLC)	QMBBL
Beaufield Resources, Inc. [Toronto Stock Exchange symbol]	BFD
Beauford Resources Ltd. [Vancouver Stock Exchange symbol]	BFR
Beaufort [South Carolina] [Airport symbol] (OAG)	BFT
Beaufort & Morehead Railroad Co. [AAR code]	BMH
Beaufort/Beaufort Marine Corps Air Station [South Carolina] [ICAO location identifier] (ICLI)	KNBC
Beaufort County Library, Beaufort, SC [Library symbol Library of Congress] (LCLS)	ScB
Beaufort County Technical Institute, Washington, NC [Library symbol Library of Congress] (LCLS)	NcWaB
Beaufort, Hyde, Martin Regional Library, Washington, NC [Library symbol Library of Congress] (LCLS)	NcWaBHM
Beaufort Leasing Ltd. [Canada] [FAA designator] (FAAC)	QTX
Beaufort, NC [Location identifier FAA] (FAAL)	MRH
Beaufort, NC [AM radio station call letters]	WBTB
Beaufort, SC [Location identifier FAA] (FAAL)	NBC
Beaufort, SC [Location identifier FAA] (FAAL)	NGJ
Beaufort, SC [FM radio station call letters]	WAGP
Beaufort, SC [AM radio station call letters]	WBEU
Beaufort, SC [FM radio station call letters]	WJWJ
Beaufort, SC [Television station call letters]	WJWJ-TV
Beaufort, SC [AM radio station call letters]	WVGB
Beaufort, SC [FM radio station call letters]	WYKZ
Beaufort Technical College, Beaufort, SC [Library symbol] [Library of Congress] (LCLS)	ScBTC
Beaufort West [South Africa] [ICAO location identifier] (ICLI)	FABW
Beaufort West/Wes Town [South Africa] [ICAO location identifier] (ICLI)	FABY
Beaufort Wind Scale	BWS
Beaumont [Diocesan abbreviation] [Texas] (TOCD)	BEA
[Francis] Beaumont and [John]Fletcher [17th century English dramatists] (BARN)	Beau & Fl
Beaumont Art Museum, Beaumont, TX [Library symbol Library of Congress] (LCLS)	TxBeaAM
Beaumont. Bills of Sale [1855] [A publication] (DLA)	Beau Bills
Beaumont, CA [Location identifier FAA] (FAAL)	BUO
Beaumont, CA [FM radio station call letters]	KAEH
Beaumont Enterprise & Journal, Beaumont, TX [Library symbol Library of Congress] (LCLS)	TxBeaE
Beaumont Library District Library, Beaumont, CA [Library symbol Library of Congress] (LCLS)	CBea
Beaumont. Life and Fire Insurance [2nd ed.] [1846] [A publication] (DLA)	Beau Ins
Beaumont Municipal Library, Alberta [Library symbol National Library of Canada] (NLC)	ABEAM
Beaumont/Port Arthur [Texas] [Airport symbol] (OAG)	BPT
Beaumont Port-Arthur/Jefferson County [Texas] [ICAO location identifier] (ICLI)	KBPT
Beaumont, Sour Lake & Western Railway Co.	BSL & W
Beaumont, TX [Location identifier FAA] (FAAL)	BMT
Beaumont, TX [Location identifier FAA] (FAAL)	GDE
Beaumont, TX [AM radio station call letters] (RBYB)	KAYD
Beaumont, TX [FM radio station call letters]	KAYD-FM

Beaumont, TX [Television station call letters]	KBMT
Beaumont, TX [Television station call letters]	KFDM
Beaumont, TX [Television station call letters]	KITU
Beaumont, TX [AM radio station call letters] (RBYB)	KJUS
Beaumont, TX [AM radio station call letters]	KLVI
Beaumont, TX [FM radio station call letters]	KQXY
Beaumont, TX [FM radio station call letters] (RBYB)	KTCX-FM
Beaumont, TX [FM radio station call letters]	KTXB
Beaumont, TX [FM radio station call letters]	KVLU
Beaumont, TX [FM radio station call letters]	KXTJ
Beaumont, TX [FM radio station call letters]	KYKR
Beaumont, TX [FM radio station call letters]	KZZB
Beaune/Challanges [France ICAO location identifier] (ICLI)	LFGF
Beaupre Explorations [Vancouver Stock Exchange symbol]	BPD
Beauregard. Organisation de la Famille [A publication] (DLA)	Beaur Org
Beauregard Parish Library, DeRidder, LA [Library symbol Library of Congress] (LCLS)	LDeB
Beausoleil Indian Band Library, Christian Island, Ontario [Library symbol National Library of Canada] (BIB)	OCIB
Beauti Control Cosmetics, Inc. [Associated Press] (SAG)	BeauCtl
Beautician	BTCN
Beautician (ABBR)	BTCN
BeautiControl Cosmetics [NASDAQ symbol] (TTSB)	BUTI
BeautiControl Cosmetics, Inc. [NASDAQ symbol] (NQ)	BUTI
Beautification (ABBR)	BTFCN
Beautiful (ABBR)	BTFL
Beautiful Books [A publication]	BB
Beautiful Music (NTCM)	BM
Beautiful Music/Easy Listening [Radio station format] (WDMC)	B/EZ
Beautiful Music Friends (EA)	BMF
Beautiful Old House	BOH
Beautiful People [Slang for the wealthy, world-traveling, partying set]	BP
Beautiful Poems on Jesus [A publication]	BePJ
Beautiful Wife (IIA)	BW
Beautifully (ABBR)	BTFLY
Beautifulness (ABBR)	BTFLNS
Beautify (ABBR)	BTFY
Beautifying (ABBR)	BTFYG
Beauty	BTY
Beauty and Barber Supply Institute (EA)	BBSI
Beauty and the Beast International [An association Defunct] (EA)	BBI
Beauty Counselors International, Inc. [Toronto Stock Exchange symbol]	BCN
Beauty, Divinity, Wisdom, Power, Honor, Glory, Strength [Freemasonry] (ROG)	BDWPHGS
Beauty [or Bottom] (Quark) [Atomic physics]	b
Beauty Without Cruelty Society [Australia]	BWCS
Beauty without Cruelty USA (EA)	BWC
Beauvais [France] [Airport symbol] (AD)	BVA
Beauvais/Tille [France ICAO location identifier] (ICLI)	LFOB
Beauval Public Library, Beauval, SK, Canada [Library symbol] [Library of Congress] (LCLS)	CaSBe
Beauval Public Library, Saskatchewan [Library symbol National Library of Canada] (NLC)	SB
Beauvechain [Belgium ICAO location identifier] (ICLI)	EBBE
Beauvoir, the Jefferson Davis Shrine, Biloxi, MS [Library symbol Library of Congress] (LCLS)	MsBB
Beavan and Walford's Railway and Canal Cases [England] [A publication] (DLA)	Beav & W
Beavan and Walford's Railway and Canal Cases [England] [A publication] (DLA)	Beav & W Ry Cas
Beavan and Walford's Railway and Canal Cases [England] [A publication] (DLA)	Beav & Wal
Beavan and Walford's Railway and Canal Cases [England] [A publication] (DLA)	Beav & Wal Ry Cas
Beavan. Railway and Canal Cases [England] [A publication] (DLA)	Beav R & C
Beavan's English Rolls Court Reports [A publication] (DLA)	B
Beavan's English Rolls Court Reports [A publication] (DLA)	Beav
Beavan's English Rolls Court Reports [A publication] (DLA)	Beav (Eng)
Beavan's English Rolls Court Reports [A publication] (DLA)	Beavan Ch
Beavan's Ordines Cancellariae [A publication] (DLA)	Beav OC
Beaver [On lead tokens used as payment in the Canadian fur trade during the 1700's]	B
Beaver [Record label] [Canada]	Bea
Beaver [A publication] (BRI)	Beav
Beaver	BVR
Beaver [Alaska] [Airport symbol] (OAG)	WBQ
Beaver, AK [Location identifier FAA] (FAAL)	WBQ
Beaver Army Terminal [Oregon]	BEART
Beaver College, Glenside, PA [OCLC symbol] (OCLC)	BEA
Beaver College, Glenside, PA [Library symbol Library of Congress] (LCLS)	PGIB
Beaver County Court House, Beaver, PA [Library symbol Library of Congress] (LCLS)	PBeC
Beaver Dam, WI [AM radio station call letters]	WBEV
Beaver Dam, WI [FM radio station call letters]	WXRO
Beaver Defenders (EA)	BD
Beaver Falls [Pennsylvania] [Airport symbol] (OAG)	BFP
Beaver Falls, PA [Location identifier FAA] (FAAL)	BVI
Beaver Falls, PA [AM radio station call letters]	WBVP
Beaver Falls, PA [FM radio station call letters]	WGEV
Beaver Falls, PA [FM radio station call letters]	WITX
Beaver Falls, PA [FM radio station call letters] (RBYB)	WXDX
Beaver Island Mormon Colony Library, St. James, Beaver Island, MI [Library symbol Library of Congress Obsolete] (LCLS)	MiBeiM
Beaver Lake Branch, Walden Public Library, Ontario [Library symbol National Library of Canada] (NLC)	OWBL

Beaver, Meade & Englewood [*AAR code*] ... BME
Beaver Memorial Library, Beaver, PA [*Library symbol Library of Congress*] (LCLS) ... PBe
Beaver Resources, Inc. [*Toronto Stock Exchange symbol Vancouver Stock Exchange symbol*] ... BGI
Beaver Springs, PA [*FM radio station call letters*] (RBYB) ... WLZS-FM
Beaver Springs, PA [*FM radio station call letters*] ... WWBV
Beaver Valley Power Station (NRCH) ... BVPS
Beaver Valley Public Library, Fruitvale, British Columbia [*Library symbol National Library of Canada*] (NLC) ... BFBV
Beaverbrook Branch, Kanata Public Library, Ontario [*Library symbol National Library of Canada*] (NLC) ... OKAB
Beaverbrook Collection, New Brunswick Archives, Fredericton, New Brunswick [*Library symbol National Library of Canada*] (NLC) ... NBFB
Beaverbrook Newspapers Ltd., London, United Kingdom [*Library symbol Library of Congress*] (LCLS) ... UkLB
Beavercreek, OH [*FM radio station call letters*] (RBYB) ... WXEG
Beaverhead Resources [*Vancouver Stock Exchange symbol*] ... BVH
Beaverlodge Elementary School, Alberta [*Library symbol National Library of Canada*] (BIB) ... ABES
Beaverlodge High School, Alberta [*Library symbol National Library of Canada*] (BIB) ... ABBS
Beaverton Branch, Brock Township Public Library, Ontario [*Library symbol National Library of Canada*] (BIB) ... OBEAB
Beaverton City Library, Beaverton, OR [*Library symbol Library of Congress*] (LCLS) ... OrB
Beaverton, MI [*FM radio station call letters*] ... WMRX
Beaverton, OR [*FM radio station call letters*] ... KKCW
Beaverton-Thorah Eldon Historical Society, Inc., Ontario [*Library symbol National Library of Canada*] (NLC) ... OBEATE
Beavertown Historical Society, Lincoln Park, NJ [*Library symbol Library of Congress*] (LCLS) ... NjLpBHi
Beawes' Lex Mercatoria [*England*] [*A publication*] (DLA) ... Beaw
Beawes' Lex Mercatoria [*England*] [*A publication*] (DLA) ... Beaw Lex Mer
Beawes' Lex Mercatoria [*England*] [*A publication*] (DLA) ... Beawes' Lex Merc
Beazer Homes USA [*Associated Press*] (SAG) ... BeazHm
Beazer Homes USA [*Associated Press*] (SAG) ... Beazr
Beazer Homes USA [*Associated Press*] (SAG) ... BeazrHm
Beazer Homes USA [*NYSE symbol*] (SAG) ... BZH
Beazer HomesUSA$2.00CvExPfd [*NYSE symbol*] (TTSB) ... BZHPrA
BEC Group [*NYSE symbol*] (TTSB) ... EYE
BEC Group, Inc. [*Associated Press*] (SAG) ... BEC Gp
BEC Group, Inc. [*NYSE symbol*] (SAG) ... EYE
Because (ADA) ... BEC
Because It's There Network [*Electronic mail system*] (TNIG) ... BITNET
Because It's Time Network [*Interuniversity communications network*] ... BITNET
Beccaria on Crimes and Punishments [*A publication*] (DLA) ... Bec Cr
Beccles [*British ICAO location identifier*] (ICLI) ... EGSM
Bechar [*Algeria*] [*Airport symbol*] (OAG) ... CBH
Bechar/Ouakda [*Algeria*] [*ICAO location identifier*] (ICLI) ... DAOC
Bechar/Ouakda [*Algeria*] [*ICAO location identifier*] (ICLI) ... DAOR
Bechard. Histoire du Droit Municipal [*A publication*] (DLA) ... Bech Hist
Bechtel Client Letter (IEEE) ... BCL
Bechtel Group, Inc., San Francisco, CA [*Library symbol Library of Congress*] (LCLS) ... CSfBe
Bechtel Group, Inc., Technical Library, Houston, TX [*Library symbol Library of Congress*] (LCLS) ... TxHBec
Bechtel Information Services (IID) ... BIS
Bechtel National, Inc. (GAAI) ... BNI
Beck Depression Inventory [*Psychology*] ... BDI
Becker [*Blood group*] ... Be
Becker & Hayes, Inc. [*Information service or system*] (IID) ... B & H
Becker County Historical Society, Detroit Lakes, MN [*Library symbol*] [*Library of Congress*] (LCLS) ... MnDlHi
Becker Elementary School, Becker, MN [*Library symbol*] [*Library of Congress*] (LCLS) ... MnBE
Becker High School, Becker, MN [*Library symbol*] [*Library of Congress*] (LCLS) ... MnBH
Becker Junior College, Worcester, MA [*Inactive*] [*OCLC symbol*] (OCLC) ... BQM
Becker Junior College, Worcester, MA [*Library symbol Library of Congress*] (LCLS) ... MWBe
Becker Milk Co. Ltd. [*Toronto Stock Exchange symbol*] ... BEK
Becker Muscular Dystrophy [*Medicine*] ... BMD
Becker Public Library, Becker Elementary School, Becker, MN [*Library symbol*] [*Library of Congress*] (LCLS) ... MnB
Becker's Muscular Dystrophy [*Medicine*] (DMAA) ... BDM
Becket [*Bracket*] ... BCKT
Beckley [*West Virginia*] [*Airport symbol*] (OAG) ... BKW
Beckley College, Beckley, WV [*Library symbol Library of Congress*] (LCLS) ... WvBC
Beckley, WV [*Location identifier FAA*] (FAAL) ... MQU
Beckley, WV [*FM radio station call letters*] ... WCIR
Beckley, WV [*AM radio station call letters*] ... WIWS
Beckley, WV [*AM radio station call letters*] ... WJLS
Beckley, WV [*FM radio station call letters*] ... WJLS-FM
Beckley, WV [*FM radio station call letters*] ... WVPB
Beckley, WV [*AM radio station call letters*] ... WWNR
Beckley-Raleigh County Library, Beckley, WV [*Library symbol Library of Congress*] (LCLS) ... WvB
Becklin-Neugebauer [*Astronomy*] ... BN
Beckman Instruments [*NYSE symbol*] (TTSB) ... BEC
Beckman Instruments, Inc. [*Associated Press*] (SAG) ... BckIns
Beckman Instruments, Inc. [*NYSE symbol*] (CTT) ... BEC
Beckman Instruments Inc. (IAA) ... BII
Beckman Instruments, Inc., Fullerton, CA [*Library symbol Library of Congress*] (LCLS) ... CFIB
Beckman Instruments, Inc., Technical Library, Palo Alto, CA [*Library symbol Library of Congress*] (LCLS) ... CPaB
Beckman Translation [*Programming language*] [*Beckman Instruments, Inc.*] ... BECKTRAN
Beck's Colorado Reports [*12-16 Colorado and 1 Colorado Court of Appeals*] [*A publication*] (DLA) ... Beck
Beck's Colorado Reports [*12-16 Colorado and 1 Colorado Court of Appeals*] [*A publication*] (DLA) ... Beck (Colo)
Beck's Depression Index-Short Form [*Psychiatry*] (DAVI) ... BDI SF
Beck's Medical Jurisprudence [*A publication*] (DLA) ... Beck Med Jur
Beckwith-Wiedemann Support Network (EA) ... BWSN
Beckwith-Wiedemann Syndrome [*Medicine*] ... BWS
Beclobrinic Acid [*Biochemistry*] ... BBA
Beclomethasone Dipropionate [*Pharmacology*] ... BDP
Become (DA) ... BC
Become (FAAC) ... BCM
Becoming [*ICAO*] (FAAC) ... BECMG
Becoming One's Own Man [*Psychology*] ... BOOM
Becoming the Gift [*Religious education test*] ... BTG
Becquerel [*Symbol*] [*SI unit of activity of ionizing radiation source*] ... Bq
Becton, Dickinson [*NYSE symbol*] (TTSB) ... BDX
Becton, Dickinson & Co. [*Initialism used in titles of a series of technical publications*] ... B-D
Becton, Dickinson & Co. [*NYSE symbol*] (SPSG) ... BDX
Becton, Dickinson & Co. [*Associated Press*] (SAG) ... BectDk
Becton, Dickinson & Co., Paramus, NJ [*OCLC symbol*] (OCLC) ... JBD
Becton, Dickinson & Co. Research Center ... BDRC
Becton, Dickinson & Co., Research Center Library, Research Triangle Park, Durham, NC [*Library symbol Library of Congress*] (LCLS) ... NcDurBD
Becton, Dickinson & Co., Rutherford, NJ [*Library symbol Library of Congress*] (LCLS) ... NjRuB
Becton Dickinson Diagnostics [*Commercial firm*] (DAVI) ... BDI
Becton-Dickinson [*Spinal needle*] [*Medicine*] (DAVI) ... BD
Bed [*Medicine*] ... b
Bed and Board (WDAA) ... B & B
Bed and Breakfast [*Tourist accommodations*] ... B & B
Bed and Breakfast League (EA) ... BBL
Bed & Breakfast Reservation Services World-Wide [*An association*] ... B&BRSWW
Bed and Chair [*Rest*] [*Medicine*] ... B & C
Bed and Light Breakfast [*Hotel accomodations*] ... BLB
Bed Bath [*Medicine*] ... BB
Bed Bath & Beyond [*NASDAQ symbol*] (TTSB) ... BBBY
Bed Bath & Beyond, Inc. [*NASDAQ symbol*] (SAG) ... BBBY
Bed Bath & Beyond, Inc. [*Associated Press*] (SAG) ... BedBath
Bed, Breakfast, and Bath [*Tourist accommodations*] ... BBB
Bed, Breakfast, and Evening Meal [*Tourist accommodations*] ... BB & EM
Bed Depth Service Time [*Wastewater treatment*] ... BDST
Bed Joint [*Technical drawings*] ... BJT
Bed Nucleus of the Stria Terminalis [*Brain anatomy*] ... BNST
Bed Rest [*Medicine*] ... BR
Beda [*Deceased, 735*] [*Authority cited in pre-1607 legal work*] (DSA) ... B
Beda [*Deceased, 735*] [*Authority cited in pre-1607 legal work*] (DSA) ... Be
Bedanda [*Guinea-Bissau*] [*ICAO location identifier*] (ICLI) ... GGBE
Bedarfsflugunternehmen Dr. L. Polsterer [*Austria ICAO designator*] (FAAC) ... OPV
Bedarieux-La-Tour-Sur-Orb [*France ICAO location identifier*] (ICLI) ... LFNX
Bedarride. Droit Commercial [*A publication*] (DLA) ... Bed Dr Comm
Bedding (MSA) ... BDNG
Bedding ... BEDG
Beddingfield High School Library, Wilson, NC [*Library symbol*] [*Library of Congress*] (LCLS) ... NcWilB
Bedell Advertising Selling Improvement Corp. ... BASIC
Bedell's Reports [*163-191 New York*] [*A publication*] (DLA) ... Bedell
Bederation of British Tape Recordists (DBA) ... FBTR
Bedford [*Massachusetts*] [*Airport symbol*] (OAG) ... BED
Bedford [*Borough and county in England*] ... BEDFD
Bedford [*British ICAO location identifier*] (ICLI) ... EGVW
Bedford Bancshares [*NASDAQ symbol*] (TTSB) ... BFSB
Bedford Bancshares, Inc. [*Associated Press*] (SAG) ... BedfrdBc
Bedford Bancshares, Inc. [*NASDAQ symbol*] (SAG) ... BFSB
Bedford/Castle Mill [*British ICAO location identifier*] (ICLI) ... EGSB
Bedford Free Library, Bedford, NY [*Library symbol Library of Congress*] (LCLS) ... NBed
Bedford Free Public Library, Bedford, MA [*Library symbol Library of Congress*] (LCLS) ... MBd
Bedford Hills Free Library, Bedford Hills, NY [*Library symbol Library of Congress*] (LCLS) ... NBedh
Bedford, IN [*Location identifier FAA*] (FAAL) ... BFR
Bedford, IN [*AM radio station call letters*] ... WBIW
Bedford, IN [*FM radio station call letters*] ... WQRK
Bedford Institute of Oceanography [*Canada*] (MSC) ... BIO
Bedford Institute of Oceanography [*Institut Oceanographique de Bedford*] **Dartmouth, Nova Scotia** [*Library symbol National Library of Canada*] (NLC) ... NSDB
Bedford/Laurence G. Hanscom Field [*Massachusetts*] [*ICAO location identifier*] (ICLI) ... KBED
Bedford, MA [*Location identifier FAA*] (FAAL) ... BED
Bedford, MA [*Location identifier FAA*] (FAAL) ... SKR
Bedford, MA [*Location identifier FAA*] (FAAL) ... ULJ
Bedford, NH [*FM radio station call letters*] ... WAEF
Bedford, NH [*FM radio station call letters*] (RBYB) ... WOXF-FM
Bedford, NS [*ICAO location identifier*] (ICLI) ... CWHX
Bedford, PA [*AM radio station call letters*] ... WAYC

Bedford, PA [*AM radio station call letters*] .... WBFD
Bedford, PA [*FM radio station call letters*] .... WOOX
Bedford, PA [*FM radio station call letters*] .... WWCW
Bedford Park Public Library District, Bedford Park, IL [*Library symbol Library of Congress*] (LCLS) .... IBpB
Bedford Prop Investors(New) [*NYSE symbol*] (TTSB) .... BED
Bedford Property Investors [*Associated Press*] (SAG) .... BedfrdP
Bedford Property Investors, Inc. [*NYSE symbol*] (SPSG) .... BED
Bedford Property Investors, Inc. [*Associated Press*] (SAG) .... BedfrdPr
Bedford Public Library, Bedford, IN [*Library symbol Library of Congress*] (LCLS) .... InB
Bedford Public Library, Bedford, OH [*Library symbol Library of Congress*] (LCLS) .... OBed
Bedford Rae [*British ICAO designator*] (FAAC) .... RRS
Bedford Software Ltd. [*Toronto Stock Exchange symbol*] .... BFS
Bedford Systems Users Group (EA) .... BSUG
Bedford Times-Mail, Bedford, IN [*Library symbol Library of Congress*] (LCLS) .... InBTM
Bedford Times-Press, Bedford, IA [*Library symbol Library of Congress*] (LCLS) .... IaBedTP
Bedford, VA [*AM radio station call letters*] .... WBLT
Bedford, VA [*FM radio station call letters*] (RBYB) .... WLQE-FM
Bedfordshire [*England*] (BARN) .... Bedford
Bedfordshire [*County in England*] .... BEDS
Bedfordshire [*County in England*] (ODBW) .... Beds
Bedfordshire Imperial Yeomanry [*British military*] (DMA) .... BIY
Bedfordshire Yeomanry [*British military*] (DMA) .... BY
Bedlington Terrier Club of America (EA) .... BTCA
Bedourie [*Australia Airport symbol Obsolete*] (OAG) .... BEU
Bedpan (MSA) .... BDPN
Bedpan .... BP
Bedrock Resources Ltd. [*Vancouver Stock Exchange symbol*] .... BDK
Bedroom (ROG) .... B
Bedroom .... BDRM
Bedroom [*Classified advertising*] (ADA) .... BEDRM
Bedroom (VRA) .... bedrm
Bedroom .... BR
Bedroom [*Classified advertising*] (ADA) .... B'RM
Bedroom Steward [*In the first class aboard an ocean liner*] .... BR
Beds and Patients Report .... BAPREPT
Beds Occupied .... BEDOC
Bedside [*Medicine*] .... BS
Bedside Commode (CPH) .... BSC
Bedside Drainage [*Medicine*] .... BSD
Bedside Drainage [*Medicine*] (DMAA) .... BSD
Bedside Glucose Monitoring [*Medicine*] (DMAA) .... BGM
Bedside Network of the Veterans Hospital Radio and TV Guild [*Later, VBN*] (EA) .... BNVHRTVG
Bedspread Blanket .... BB
Bedstead Alliance [*A union*] [*British*] .... BA
Bedstead Workmens Association [*A union*] [*British*] .... BWA
Bedtime .... BT
Bedtime Insulin, Daytime Sulfonylurea [*Therapy*] [*Pharmacology*] (DAVI) .... BIDS
Bee Biology and Systematics Laboratory [*Department of Agriculture*] [*Research center*] (RCD) .... BBSL
Bee County College, Beeville, TX [*Library symbol Library of Congress*] (LCLS) .... TxBeeC
Bee County Public Library, Beeville, TX [*Library symbol Library of Congress*] (LCLS) .... TxBee
Bee Industries Association [*Defunct*] (EA) .... BIA
Bee Keepers Association .... BKA
Bee Research Association [*Later, IBRA*] .... BRA
Bee Venom [*Entomology*] .... BV
Beebas [*NASDAQ symbol*] (SAG) .... BEBA
Beeba's Creations, Inc. [*Associated Press*] (SAG) .... Beebas
Beebe, AR [*FM radio station call letters*] .... KPIK
Beebe Ranch [*California*] [*Seismograph station code, US Geological Survey*] (SEIS) .... BBR
Beebee's Analysis of Common Law Practice [*A publication*] (DLA) .... Bee Anal
Beebe's Ohio Citations [*A publication*] (DLA) .... Beebe Cit
Beech (VRA) .... becwd
Beech Aircraft Corp. (KSC) .... BAC
Beech Aircraft Corp. [*ICAO aircraft manufacturer identifier*] (ICAO) .... BE
Beech Aircraft Corp. [*ICAO designator*] (FAAC) .... BEC
Beech Mountain, NC [*FM radio station call letters*] .... WECR
Beech Mountain Railroad (MHDB) .... BMRR
Beech Mountain Railroad Co. [*AAR code*] .... BEEM
Beecham Bovril Brands [*Commercial firm British*] .... BBB
Beecham Laboratories, White Hall, IL [*Library symbol Library of Congress*] (LCLS) .... IWhhB
Beecham Products-Western Hemisphere Research, Parsippany, NJ [*OCLC symbol*] (OCLC) .... BEE
Beecham Research Laboratories Ltd. [*Great Britain*] [*Research code symbol*] .... BRL
Beechcraft [*Airplane code*] .... Bec
Beechcraft Kingair [*Airplane code*] .... Bek
Beef (ROG) .... BF
Beef Cattle Price Index .... BCPI
Beef Cattle Research Center [*Michigan State University*] [*Research center*] (RCD) .... BCRC
Beef Friesian Society (EA) .... BFS
Beef Heart Infusion Broth [*Microbiology*] .... BHIB
Beef Heart Infusion Supplement [*Broth or agar*] [*Growth medium*] (DAVI) .... BHIS
Beef Improvement Association of Australia .... BIAA
Beef Improvement Federation (EA) .... BIF
Beef Industry Council (EA) .... BIC
Beef Island [*British Virgin Islands*] [*Airport symbol*] (AD) .... EIS
Beef Liver Catalase [*An enzyme*] (OA) .... BLC
Beef Promotion and Research Board (EA) .... BPRB
Beef Recording Association [*British*] (BI) .... BRA
BEEF [*Base Engineer Emergency Forces*] **Reporting, Analysis, and Status System** [*Air Force*] (AFM) .... BRASS
Beef Research and Information Act [*1976*] .... BRIA
Beef Serum Albumin [*Medicine*] (MEDA) .... BSA
Beef Shorthorn [*Cattle*] .... BS
Beef Shorthorn Society of Australia .... BSSA
Beef Thyroid-Stimulating Hormone [*Endocrinology*] (MAE) .... BTSH
Beefmaster Breeders Universal (EA) .... BBU
Beekeeper .... BK
Beekeeper Serum [*Medicine*] (DMAA) .... BKS
Beekman Community Library Reading Center, Poughquag, NY [*Library symbol Library of Congress*] (LCLS) .... NPoq
Beeler, J. L., Los Angeles CA [*STAC*] .... BJL
Beeler's Reports [*Tennessee*] [*A publication*] (DLA) .... Beeler
Been .... BN
Been Here Since Day One [*Group of Reagan administration staffers*] .... BHSDO
Been to America [*Slang British*] .... BTA
Beer [*Phonetic alphabet*] [*Pre-World War II*] (DSUE) .... B
Beer Barrel (WDAA) .... BB
Beer, Bum, and Bacca [*Nautical*] [*Slang British*] (DSUE) .... 3B's
Beer Can Collectors of America (EA) .... BCCA
Beer Drinkers of America (EA) .... BDA
Beer Firkin .... BF
Beer House (ROG) .... BH
Beer Industry League of Louisiana (SRA) .... BILL
Beer Industry of Florida (SRA) .... BIF
Beer Institute (EA) .... BI
Beer Wholesalers Association of New Jersey (SRA) .... BWANJ
Be-'eravon Mugbal (BJA) .... BM
Beersheba [*Israel*] [*Airport symbol Obsolete*] (OAG) .... BEV
Beersheba/Teyman [*Israel*] [*ICAO location identifier*] (ICLI) .... LLBS
Beery Development Test of Visual-Motor Integration [*Psychiatry*] (DAVI) .... BDTVMI
Bee's Admiralty. An Appendix to Bee's District Court Reports [*A publication*] (DLA) .... Bee Adm
Bee's English Crown Cases Reserved [*A publication*] (DLA) .... Bee CCR
Bee's United States District Court Reports [*A publication*] (DLA) .... Bee
Beeswax (ABBR) .... BSWX
Beet Armyworm Larvae [*Entomology*] .... BAW
Beet Cryptic Virus [*Plant pathology*] .... BCV
Beet Curly Top Virus [*Plant pathology*] .... BCTV
Beet Invert Syrup [*Food sweetener*] .... BIS
Beet Leaf Curl Virus [*Plant pathology*] .... BLCV
Beet Medium Invert Syrup [*Food sweetener*] .... BMIS
Beet Mild Yellowing Virus [*Plant pathology*] .... BMYV
Beet Mosaic Virus [*Plant pathology*] .... BTMV
Beet Necrotic Yellow Vein Virus .... BNYVV
Beet Sugar Development Foundation (EA) .... BSDF
Beet Temperate Virus [*Plant pathology*] .... BTEV
Beet Western Yellows Virus .... BWYV
Beet Yellow Stunt Virus [*Plant pathology*] .... BYSV
Beet Yellows Virus .... BYV
Beeton Public Library, Ontario [*Library symbol National Library of Canada*] (BIB) .... OBEE
Beevers-Ross [*Beta-alumina crystallography*] .... BR
Beeville/Chase Field Naval Air Station [*Texas*] [*ICAO location identifier*] (ICLI) .... KNIR
Beeville, TX [*Location identifier FAA*] (FAAL) .... BEA
Beeville, TX [*AM radio station call letters*] .... KIBL
Beeville, TX [*FM radio station call letters*] .... KTKO
Beeville, TX [*FM radio station call letters*] .... KYTX
Beeville, TX [*Location identifier FAA*] (FAAL) .... NIR
Beeville, TX [*Location identifier FAA*] (FAAL) .... NNL
Befandriana [*Madagascar*] [*Airport symbol*] (OAG) .... WBD
Befandriana Nord [*Madagascar*] [*ICAO location identifier*] (ICLI) .... FMNF
Before .... B
Before [*Slang*] (DAVI) B4
Before [*Internet language*] [*Computer science*] b4
Before (VRA) .... bef
Before .... BEF
Before .... BEFE
Before (MSA) .... BFR
Before Bottom Center [*Valve position*] .... BBC
Before Bottom Dead Center [*Valve position*] .... BBDC
Before Business Clearance (NASA) .... BBC
Before Calculators .... BC
Before Casinos .... BC
Before Christ .... BC
Before Christian Era .... BCE
Before Cloning [*Cytology*] .... BC
Before Columbus Foundation (EA) .... BCF
Before Commercialism .... BC
Before Competition [*Term associated with the divestiture of AT & T*] .... BC
Before Computer .... BC
Before Cook [*Era preceding discovery of Australia by British explorer, James Cook*] (ECON) .... BC
Before Credit Cards [*Slang*] .... BC
Before Croonery [*Musical slang*] .... BC
Before Dark (FAAC) .... BFDK
Before Dead Center [*Valve position*] .... BDC

Before Divestiture [*AT & T*] (IT) .... BD
Before Flight (MCD) .... BF
Before Flight Abort [*NASA*] (MCD) .... BFA
Before Flight Reliability (MCD) .... BFR
Before Full Moon [*Freemasonry*] (ROG) .... BFM
Before Girls [*i.e., before women became part of armed forces*] [*Military*] .... BG
Before Goetz [*A reference to "vigilante" Bernhard Goetz, who shot four youths on a New York subway in 1984 after allegedly being threatened by them*] [*See also AG*] .... BG
Before Infantry Light and Lethal [*Antitank*] (MCD) .... BILL
Before Initial Release [*Information system*] (MCD) .... BIR
Before Marriage .... BM
Before Meals and At Bedtime [*Pharmacy*] (DAVI) .... AC & HS
Before Mentioned [*Legal*] [*British*] (ROG) .... BEFEMENTD
Before Midnight (ROG) .... BM
Before Morning Twilight (SAA) .... BMT
Before New Moon [*Freemasonry*] (ROG) .... BNM
Before Proceeding on Course [*Aviation*] .... BPOC
Before Queues [*Referring to pre-World War II period*] [*Slang British*] .... BQ
Before Rotary Cutting [*Quilting*] .... BRC
Before Sleep [*Pharmacy*] (DAVI) .... BS
Before Stephen Sondheim [*A reference to simpler, less sophisticated, and more sentimental musicals*] .... BSS
Before the Common Era [*Jewish equivalent of BC*] .... BCE
Before the Crash [*i.e., before the 1929 stock market collapse*] [*Slang*] .... BC
Before the Present .... BP
Before the Romantics [*A publication*] .... BeR
Before Top Center [*Valve position*] .... BTC
Before Top Dead Center [*Valve position*] .... BTDC
Before Touching [*Parapsychology*] .... BT
Before Video .... BV
Before Your Very Eyes (DGA) .... BVE
Befrienders International [*Later, BISW*] (EAIO) .... BI
Befrienders International Samaritans Worldwide (EA) .... BISW
Begg. Conveyancing Code [*Scotland*] [*A publication*] (DLA) .... Begg Code
Begg. Law Agents [*Scotland*] [*A publication*] (DLA) .... Begg L Ag
Begign Paroxysmal Positional Vertigo [*Medicine*] .... BPPV
Begin Bracket [*Indicator*] [*Computer science*] (IBMDP) .... BB
Begin Standard Refuel Orbit [*Aviation*] (FAAC) .... BSRO
Begin Telemetry Cycle .... BTC
Begin Transmission, Break .... BT
Beginners Algebraic Symbolic Interpretive Compiler [*Computer science*] (NITA) .... BASIC
Beginner's All-Purpose Symbolic Instruction Code [*Programming language invented by T. E. Kurtz and J. G. Kemeny at Dartmouth College in 1963-64*] .... BASIC
Beginning .... BEG
Beginning (VRA) .... beg
Beginning .... BGNG
Beginning and Ending (ADA) .... B & E
Beginning Assessment Test of Reading (EDAC) .... BATR
Beginning Climb [*Aviation*] (FAAC) .... BC
Beginning Descent [*Aviation*] (FAAC) .... BGND
Beginning Education Assessment [*Educational development test*] .... BEA
Beginning Entrepreneurial Support Team .... BEST
Beginning Evening Nautical Twilight .... BENT
Beginning Event (DNAB) .... BE
Beginning Morning Astronomical Twilight [*Navigation*] (MCD) .... BMAT
Beginning Morning Civil Twilight [*Navigation*] .... BMCT
Beginning Morning Nautical Twilight [*Navigation*] .... BMNT
Beginning Morning Nautical Twilight [*Navigation*] (CINC) .... BMT
Beginning, Negative, Positive, Finish [*ASCII subset*] .... BNPF
Beginning of Business .... BOB
Beginning of Cycle (NRCH) .... BOC
Beginning of Equilibrium Cycle [*Nuclear energy*] (NRCH) .... BEC
Beginning of Equilibrium Cycle [*Nuclear energy*] (NRCH) .... BOEC
Beginning of Equilibrium Life (NUCP) .... BOEL
Beginning of File (NASA) .... BOF
Beginning of Information [*Computer science*] (NITA) .... BOI
Beginning of Information Marker [*Computer science*] .... BIM
Beginning of Life .... BOL
Beginning of Magnetic Tape [*Computer science*] (MDG) .... BMT
Beginning of Message (IAA) .... BOM
Beginning of Month [*Accounting*] (NASA) .... BOM
Beginning of Period .... BOP
Beginning of Quarter [*Accounting*] .... BOQ
Beginning of Record [*Computer science*] (IAA) .... BOR
Beginning of Tape [*Computer science*] .... BOT
Beginning of Tape [*Computer science*] (IAA) .... BT
Beginning of Tape Level (NITA) .... BTL
Beginning of Year [*Accounting*] .... BOY
Beginning of Year Significant Non-Complier [*Environmental Protection Agency*] (ERG) .... BOYSNC
Beginning of Year Significant NonCompliers [*Environment*] (GNE) .... BOYSNC
Beginning Period (AABC) .... BP
Beginning Procedure Turn (FAAC) .... BPT
Beginning Professional Salary .... BPS
Beginning Standard Holding Procedure [*Aviation*] (FAAC) .... BSHP
Beginning Standard Instrument Approach [*Aviation*] (IAA) .... BGSIA
Beginning Standard Range Approach [*Aviation*] (FAAC) .... BSRAP
Beginning Straight-In Approach [*Aviation*] (IAA) .... BGSTA
Beginning Straight-In Approach [*Aviation*] (FAAC) .... BSIAP
Beginning Tape Label [*Computer science*] (BUR) .... BTL
Beginning Teacher Evaluation Study (EDAC) .... BTES
Beginning to Tape Test .... BTT
Begleitung [*Accompaniment*] [*Music*] .... BEGL
Behalf (ROG) .... BEHF
Behavior (WGA) .... B
Behavior (AAMN) .... BEH
Behavior Analysis in Ireland (EAIO) .... BAI
Behavior and Systems Research Laboratory [*Army*] .... BESERL
Behavior and Systems Research Laboratory [*Arlington, VA*] [*Army*] (IEEE) .... BESRL
Behavior Cards [*Psychological testing*] .... BC
Behavior Classification Checklist [*Psychology*] .... BCC
Behavior Disorder .... BD
Behavior Engineering Model (EDAC) .... BEM
Behavior Evaluation Scale [*Educational testing*] .... BES
Behavior Genetics Association (EA) .... BGA
Behavior Modification [*Psychology*] (DAVI) .... AMOD
Behavior Modification [*Psychology*] .... B-MOD
Behavior Monitor System .... BMS
Behavior of Offshore Structures [*Conference*] .... BOSS
Behavior Pattern (ADA) .... BP
Behavior Problem Checklist (EDAC) .... BPC
Behavior Rating Instrument for Autistic and Other Atypical Children [*Child development test*] [*Psychology*] .... BRIAAC
Behavior Rating Profile [*Educational testing*] .... BRP
Behavior Replication by Analog Instruction of the Nervous System [*Electrical stimulation of the brain*] .... BRAINS
Behavior Research Institute (EA) .... BRI
Behavior Sciences and the Law [*A publication*] (DLA) .... Behav Sci & L
Behavior Status Inventory [*Personality development test*] [*Psychology*] .... BSI
Behavior Style Questionnaire [*Medicine*] (DMAA) .... BSQ
Behavior Therapy [*Psychology*] .... BT
Behavior Therapy and Research Society (EA) .... BTRS
Behavioral .... BEHAV
Behavioral (AFM) .... BEHVL
Behavioral .... BHVRL
Behavioral Academic Self-Esteem [*Student personality test*] [*Psychology*] .... BASE
Behavioral Alcohol Research Laboratory (DICI) .... BARLAB
Behavioral and Social Sciences .... BASS
Behavioral and Social Sciences .... BSS
Behavioral and Social Sciences Survey Committee (EA) .... BSSSC
Behavioral Approach Scale [*Psychology*] .... BAS
Behavioral Assertiveness Test for Children .... BAT-C
Behavioral Assessment Grid .... BAG
Behavioral Assessment of Speech Anxiety (EDAC) .... BASA
Behavioral Avoidance Test [*Psychometrics*] .... BAT
Behavioral Books Institute [*Book club*] .... BBI
Behavioral Characteristics Progression [*Scale*] .... BCP
Behavioral Checklist [*Psychology*] .... BCL
Behavioral Differential .... BD
Behavioral Effects of Infectious Diseases [*Army*] .... BEID
Behavioral Emergency Committee [*Medicine*] (HCT) .... BEC
Behavioral Inventory .... BI
Behavioral Kinesiology [*Book title*] .... BK
Behavioral Neuropsychology Special Interest Group (EA) .... BNSIG
Behavioral Objective .... BO
Behavioral Pharmacology Society (EA) .... BPS
Behavioral Research Aspects of Safety and Health Working Group [*University of Kentucky*] [*Research center*] (RCD) .... BRASH
Behavioral Research Council (EA) .... BRC
Behavioral Research Laboratories .... BRL
Behavioral Risk Factor Surveillance System .... BRESS
Behavioral Risk Factor Surveillance System [*Health survey*] .... BRFSS
Behavioral Role-Playing Test (EDAC) .... BRPT
Behavioral Science Programming Language [*Computer science*] .... BSPL
Behavioral Sciences Laboratory [*University of Cincinnati*] [*Information service or system*] (IID) .... BSL
Behavioral Skills Training [*Navy*] .... BEST
Behavioral Skills Training Unit [*Navy*] (DNAB) .... BEHSTU
Behavioral Task Analysis (MCD) .... BTA
Behaviorally Anchored Rating Scale .... BARS
Behavior-Based Incentive Compensation [*Human resources*] (WYGK) .... BBIC
Behavior-Based Personnel Systems .... BBPS
Behaviorism [*Psychology*] (DAVI) .... beh
Behaviorists for Social Action (EA) .... BFSA
Behaviour Modification Information Test (AIE) .... BMIT
Behaviroal Assertiveness Test [*Psychometrics*] (EDAC) .... BAT
Behcet Syndrome [*Medicine*] (DMAA) .... BS
Behcet's Disease [*Medicine*] .... BD
Beheaded (ROG) .... BEH
Behind (ROG) .... BEHD
Behind (FAAC) .... BHND
Behind Armor Debris [*Army*] (RDA) .... BAD
Behind Completion Date .... BCD
Behind Schedule .... B/S
Behind Tape Reader (MCD) .... BTR
Behind the Ear [*Hearing aid*] [*Audiology*] .... BTE
Behind the Lens (NTCM) .... BTL
Behind the Line [*Air Force*] .... BTL
Behind The Scenes [*Film*] [*Television*] (WDMC) .... BTS
Behnken's Unit [*Of Roentgen-Ray Exposure*] [*Radiology*] (DAVI) .... R
Behshahr [*Iran*] [*ICAO location identifier*] (ICLI) .... OINH
Behsood [*Afghanistan*] [*ICAO location identifier*] (ICLI) .... OABD
Bei [*At, With*] [*German*] .... B
BEI Electronics [*NASDAQ symbol*] (TTSB) .... BEII
BEI Electronics, Inc. [*Associated Press*] (SAG) .... BEI El
BEI Electronics, Inc. [*NASDAQ symbol*] (NQ) .... BEII

Beica [*Ethiopia*] [*Airport symbol*] (OAG) .... BEI
Beica [*Ethiopia*] [*ICAO location identifier*] (ICLI) .... HABE
Beida [*Libya*] [*Airport symbol*] (OAG) .... LAQ
Beifolgend [*Herewith*] [*German*] .... BEIF
Beige (WGA) .... BG
Beigebunden [*Bound With*] [*German*] (BARN) .... beigeb
Beigetretene Teile Deutschlands [*Newly Adhered Parts of Germany*] [*Name given to former East German territory after unification*] .... BGTD
Beihan [*People's Democratic Republic of Yemen*] [*ICAO location identifier*] (ICLI) .... ODAB
Beijer Institute Centre for Resource Assessment and Management [*British*] (IRUK) .... BICRAM
Beijing [*China*] [*Airport symbol*] (OAG) .... PEK
Beijing [*China*] [*ICAO location identifier*] (ICLI) .... ZBPE
Beijing/Capital [*China*] [*ICAO location identifier*] (ICLI) .... ZBAA
Beijing City [*China*] [*ICAO location identifier*] (ICLI) .... ZBBB
Beijing Dance Institute [*China*] .... BDI
Beijing Electron-Positron Collider [*High-energy physics*] [*China*] .... BEPC
Beijing Institute of Modern Physics [*China*] .... BIMP
Beijing Institute of Technology [*China*] .... BIT
Beijing Polytechnic University [*China*] .... BPU
Beijing Proton Synchrotron [*China*] .... BPS
Beijing Publications Import & Export Corp. .... BPIEC
Beijing Royal Jelly [*Biochemistry*] .... BRJ
Beijing University of Chemical Technology .... BUCT
Beilingries [*Germany ICAO location identifier*] (ICLI) .... EDYG
Beilstein Registry Connection Tables [*Chemistry*] .... BRET
Beilstein Unique Sequence [*Chemistry*] .... BUS
Beilstein Unique Sequence Number [*Chemistry*] .... BUSEN
Beilstein-Institut, Frankfurt/Main, Germany [*Library symbol Library of Congress*] (LCLS) .... GyFmB
Being (ROG) .... BEG
Being .... BG
Being for Carter before the Convention [*One of the Carter Administration's criteria for appointment of federal judges*] .... BCBC
Beira [*Mozambique*] [*Airport symbol*] (OAG) .... BEW
Beira [*Mozambique*] [*ICAO location identifier*] (ICLI) .... FQBE
Beira [*Mozambique*] [*ICAO location identifier*] (ICLI) .... FQBR
Beirut [*Lebanon*] [*Airport symbol*] (OAG) .... BEY
Beirut [*Lebanon*] [*ICAO location identifier*] (ICLI) .... OLBV
Beirut [*Lebanon*] [*ICAO location identifier*] (ICLI) .... OLDD
Beirut [*Lebanon*] [*ICAO location identifier*] (ICLI) .... OLLL
Beirut/International [*Lebanon*] [*ICAO location identifier*] (ICLI) .... OLBA
Beiseker Municipal Library, Alberta [*Library symbol National Library of Canada*] (NLC) .... ABEM
Beiseker Municipal Library, Beiseker, AB, Canada [*Library symbol Library of Congress*] (LCLS) .... CaABeM
Beispiel [*Example*] [*Music*] [*German*] .... BEISP
Beit Bridge [*Zimbabwe*] [*ICAO location identifier*] (ICLI) .... FVBB
Beit Mikra (BJA) .... BM
Beit Zeiroth Mizrachi (BJA) .... BZM
Beitraeg [*or Beitraege*] [*Contribution, Share*] [*German*] (OCD) .... Beitr
Beitraege zum Altbabylonischen Privatrecht [*A publication*] (BJA) .... BAbPr
Beitraege zum Assyrischen Woerterbuch [*A publication*] (BJA) .... BaWb
Beitraege zur Danziger Statistik [*Danzig*] .... BDS
Beitraege zur Semitischen Sprachwissenschaft [*A publication*] (BJA) .... BSS
Beitraege zur Statistik der Republik Oesterreich [*Austria*] .... BSRO
Beja [*MARC language code Library of Congress*] (LCCP) .... bej
Beja [*Portugal ICAO location identifier*] (ICLI) .... LPBE
Beja [*Portugal ICAO location identifier*] (ICLI) .... LPBJ
Bejaia [*Algeria*] [*Airport symbol*] (OAG) .... BJA
Bejaia/Soummam [*Algeria*] [*ICAO location identifier*] (ICLI) .... DAAE
Bekesy Ascending Descending Gap Evaluation .... BADGE
Bekily [*Madagascar*] [*ICAO location identifier*] (ICLI) .... FMSL
Bekily [*Madagascar*] [*Airport symbol*] (OAG) .... OVA
Bekol/Thomas [*Congo*] [*ICAO location identifier*] (ICLI) .... FCMT
Bel [*Ten decibels*] .... B
Bel Air, MD [*FM radio station call letters*] .... WHFC
Bel Air, MD [*AM radio station call letters*] .... WHRF
Bel and the Dragon [*Old Testament book*] [*Apocrypha*] .... Bel and Dr
Bel Exemplaire [*Typography*] (DGA) .... BEL EX
Bel Fuse, Inc. [*NASDAQ symbol*] (NQ) .... BELF
Bel Fuse, Inc. [*Associated Press*] (SAG) .... BelFuse
Bela [*Pakistan*] [*ICAO location identifier*] (ICLI) .... OPBL
Bela Lugosi Society [*Defunct*] (EA) .... BLS
Bela Lyons Pratt [*Designer's mark, when appearing on US coins*] .... BLP
Bela Vista [*Brazil*] [*Airport symbol*] (AD) .... BVS
Belacker [*France*] [*Seismograph station code, US Geological Survey*] (SEIS) .... BAF
Belady Optimum Replacement [*Algorithm*] [*Computer science*] .... BOR
Belaga [*Malaysia*] [*Airport symbol*] (OAG) .... BLG
Belaga [*Malaysia*] [*ICAO location identifier*] (ICLI) .... WBGC
Belair [*Belarus*] [*ICAO designator*] (FAAC) .... BLI
Bel-Air Ltd. [*Slovakia*] [*FAA designator*] (FAAC) .... BLJ
Bel-Air Resources [*Vancouver Stock Exchange symbol*] .... BLS
Belarusky Narodny Front [*Belarussian Popular Front*] [*Political party*] (EY) .... BNF
Belarussian Literary Association [*Canada*] (EAIO) .... BLA
Belavia [*Belarus*] [*ICAO designator*] (FAAC) .... BRU
Belbek-5P [*Ukraine*] [*FAA designator*] (FAAC) .... BEK
Belchamp [*England*] .... BELCH
Belco Oil & Gas [*NYSE symbol*] (TTSB) .... BOG
Belco Oil & Gas Corp. [*Associated Press*] (SAG) .... Belco
Belco Oil & Gas Corp. [*NYSE symbol*] (SAG) .... BOG
Belcourt, ND [*FM radio station call letters*] .... KEYA
Belden & Blake Corp. [*NASDAQ symbol*] (TTSB) .... BELD
Belden & Blake Energy Co. [*NASDAQ symbol*] (SAG) .... BELD

Belden & Blake Energy Co. [*Associated Press*] (SAG) .... BeldBlk
Belden, Inc. [*Associated Press*] (SAG) .... Belden
Belden, Inc. [*NYSE symbol*] (SPSG) .... BWC
Belding Heminway [*NYSE symbol*] (TTSB) .... BHY
Belding Heminway Co., Inc. [*Associated Press*] (SAG) .... BeldHem
Belding Heminway Co., Inc. [*NYSE symbol*] (SPSG) .... BHY
Beleaguered (AABC) .... BEL
Belem [*Brazil*] [*Airport symbol*] (OAG) .... BEL
Belem [*Brazil ICAO location identifier*] (ICLI) .... SBBL
Belem/Julio Cesar [*Brazil ICAO location identifier*] (ICLI) .... SBJC
Belem/Val-De-Caes [*Brazil ICAO location identifier*] (ICLI) .... SBBE
Belen, NM [*AM radio station call letters*] .... KARS
Belen, NM [*FM radio station call letters*] (RBYB) .... KLVO
Belep [*New Caledonia*] [*Airport symbol*] (OAG) .... BMY
Belet Uen [*Somalia*] [*ICAO location identifier*] (ICLI) .... HCMN
Belfast [*City in Northern Ireland*] (ROG) .... BELF
Belfast [*Northern Ireland*] [*Airport symbol*] (OAG) .... BFS
Belfast [*City in Northern Ireland*] .... BLFST
Belfast/Aldergrove [*British ICAO location identifier*] (ICLI) .... EGAA
Belfast & Moosehead Lake Railroad Co. [*AAR code*] .... BML
Belfast and North Counties Railway [*British*] (ROG) .... B & NCR
Belfast Association of Engineers [*Northern Ireland*] (BARN) .... BAE
Belfast Banking Co. [*Ireland*] .... BBC
Belfast [*Northern Ireland*] Harbour [*Airport symbol*] (OAG) .... BHD
Belfast Harbour [*British ICAO location identifier*] (ICLI) .... EGAC
Belfast, ME [*Location identifier FAA*] (FAAL) .... BST
Belfast, ME [*FM radio station call letters*] .... WWFX
Belfast, Mersey and Manchester [*Steamship*] (MHDB) .... BMM
Belfast Public Library, Belfast, NY [*Library symbol Library of Congress*] (LCLS) .... NBelf
Belfort [*France*] [*Airport symbol*] (OAG) .... BOR
Belfort/Chaux [*France ICAO location identifier*] (ICLI) .... LFGG
Belfort/Fontaine [*France ICAO location identifier*] (ICLI) .... LFSQ
Belga [*Monetary unit*] [*Belgium*] .... B
Belgaum [*India*] [*Airport symbol*] (OAG) .... IXG
Belgaum [*India*] [*ICAO location identifier*] (ICLI) .... VABM
Belgavia (Societe de Handling) [*Belgium ICAO designator*] (FAAC) .... BLG
Belgian (ODBW) .... Bel
Belgian Air Force .... BAF
Belgian Air Staff [*NATO*] (NATG) .... BELAIR
Belgian American Educational Foundation (EA) .... BAEF
Belgian and Luxembourg Association of Penal Law (EAIO) .... BLAPL
Belgian Antarctic Expedition [*1897-99, 1957-58*] .... BelgAE
Belgian Archives for the Social Sciences [*Information service or system*] (IID) .... BASS
Belgian Begonia Growers Association [*Defunct*] (EA) .... BBGA
Belgian Centre for Information Processing .... BCIP
Belgian Chamber of Commerce for Australia .... BCCA
Belgian Chamber of Commerce in the United States [*Later, Belgian American Chamber of Commerce in the United States*] .... BCCUS
Belgian Circle in Victoria [*An association Australia*] .... BCV
Belgian Congo .... CB
Belgian Draft Horse Corp. of America (EA) .... BDHCA
Belgian Educational Student Travel Service .... BESTS
Belgian Engineers in North America [*Defunct*] (EA) .... BENA
Belgian Flight Centre [*ICAO designator*] (FAAC) .... ABF
Belgian Fourragere [*Military decoration*] .... BEFOURRA
Belgian Fourragere [*Military decoration*] .... BEFourragere
Belgian Fourragere [*Military decoration*] .... BF
Belgian Franc [*Monetary unit*] .... BFc
Belgian Futures and Options Exchange [*Stock exchange*] [*Belgium*] (EY) .... BELFOX
Belgian Information and Dissemination Service [*European host database system*] [*Ministry of Economic Affairs*] (IID) .... BELINDIS
Belgian International Air Carriers [*ICAO designator*] (FAAC) .... BIC
Belgian Linen Association [*Later, ILPC*] (EA) .... BLA
Belgian Naval Staff [*NATO*] (NATG) .... BELNAV
Belgian Reactor .... BR
Belgian Review of International Law [*A publication*] (DLA) .... Belg Rev Int'l L
Belgian Sheepdog Club of America (EA) .... BSCA
Belgian Socialist Party .... BSP
Belgian Telecommunications User Group (ACRL) .... BELTUG
Belgian Tourist Office (EA) .... BTO
Belgian-American Association (EAIO) .... ABA
Belgian-Luxembourg American Studies Association [*Belgium*] (EAIO) .... BLASA
Belgic [*Language*] (BARN) .... Bel
Belgique Judiciaire [*A publication*] (ILCA) .... Belg Jud
Belgique Judiciaire [*A publication*] (ILCA) .... ILCA
Belgische Radio en Televisie [*Belgian Radio and Television - Dutch Service*] .... BRT
Belgische Socialistische Partij [*Belgian Socialist Party*] (PPW) .... BSP
Belgische Werkliedenpartij [*Belgian Workers' Party*] [*Later, Belgian Socialist Party*] [*Political party*] (PPE) .... BWP
Belgisch-Luxembourg Wissel Instituut [*Benelux*] .... BLWI
Belgium [*IYRU nationality code*] .... B
Belgium [*ANSI two-letter standard code*] (CNC) .... BE
Belgium [*MARC country of publication code Library of Congress*] (LCCP) .... be
Belgium [*ANSI three-letter standard code*] (CNC) .... BEL
Belgium (ODBW) .... Bel
Belgium (VRA) .... Belg
Belgium [*MARC geographic area code Library of Congress*] (LCCP) .... e-be-
Belgium [*International civil aircraft marking*] (ODBW) .... OO
Belgium, Netherlands, Luxembourg [*Economic union*] .... BENELUX
Belgium Pharmacopoeia [*A publication*] .... Belg P

Belgium Philatelic Society (EA) .... BPS
Belgium-Luxembourg Chamber of Commerce [*Australia*] .... B-LCC
Belgium-Luxembourg Economic Union [*Political party*] (PPE) .... BLEU
Belgrade [*Former Yugoslavia*] [*Airport symbol*] (OAG) .... BEG
Belgrade Elementary School, Belgrade, MN [*Library symbol*] [*Library of Congress*] (LCLS) .... MnBgE
Belgrade High School, Media Center, Belgrade, MN [*Library symbol*] [*Library of Congress*] (LCLS) .... MnBgH
Belgrade, MT [*AM radio station call letters*] .... KGVW
Belgrade, MT [*FM radio station call letters*] .... KSCY
Belhaven College, Jackson, MS [*Library symbol Library of Congress*] (LCLS) .... MsJB
Belhaven, NC [*FM radio station call letters*] .... WKJA
Beli, AK [*Location identifier FAA*] (FAAL) .... BEK
Beliefs about Science and Science Education Scale (EDAC) .... BSSE
Believe It or Not .... BION
Believe the Children [*An association*] (EA) .... BTC
Belinfante-Swihart [*Theory*] .... BS
Beling and Vanderstraaten's Ceylon Reports [*A publication*] (DLA) .... B & V
Beling and Vanderstraaten's Ceylon Reports [*A publication*] (DLA) .... Beling & Van
Beling's Ceylon Reports [*A publication*] (DLA) .... Bel
Beling's Ceylon Reports [*A publication*] (DLA) .... Beling
Belize (BARN) .... Bel
Belize [*ANSI three-letter standard code*] (CNC) .... BLZ
Belize [*ANSI two-letter standard code*] (CNC) .... BZ
Belize [*International civil aircraft marking*] (ODBW) V3
Belize Action Movement (PD) .... BAM
Belize Airways [*ICAO designator*] (AD) .... ST
Belize Broadcasting Network (EY) .... BBN
Belize City [*Belize*] [*Airport symbol*] (OAG) .... BZE
Belize Defense Forces [*Military*] .... BDF
Belize Institute of Social Research and Action .... BISRA
Belize/International [*Belize*] [*ICAO location identifier*] (ICLI) .... MZBZ
Belize Popular Party [*Political party*] (EY) .... BPP
Belize Trans Air [*ICAO designator*] (FAAC) .... JGR
Belize Transair [*ICAO designator*] (FAAC) .... BTR
Belkin, Inc. [*Toronto Stock Exchange symbol*] .... BKN
Belknap's Probate Law of California [*A publication*] (DLA) .... Bel Prob
Bell (NFPA) .... B
Bell [*Computer science*] (DOM) .... BEL
Bell (IEEE) .... BL
Bell Adjustment Inventory (EDAC) .... BAI
Bell Administrative Network Communication System [*Telecommunications*] (TEL) .... BANCS
Bell Administrative Network Communications System [*Telecommunications*] (ACRL) .... BANCS
Bell Advanced Tilt Rotor (MCD) .... BAT
Bell Aerospace Co. .... BAC
Bell Aerospace Co., New Orleans, LA [*Library symbol Library of Congress*] (LCLS) .... LNBA
Bell Aerospace Textron .... BAT
Bell Aerospace Textron, Technical Library, Niagara Falls, NY [*Library symbol Library of Congress*] (LCLS) .... NNiaB
Bell Aerosystems Co. (KSC) .... BA
Bell Aerosystems Co., Buffalo, NY [*Library symbol Library of Congress*] (LCLS) .... NBuBA
Bell Aircraft Corp. (MCD) .... BAC
Bell Alarm (IAA) .... BA
Bell Alarm Switch (AAG) .... BASW
Bell and Bell [*Technical drawings*] .... B & B
Bell and Flange [*Technical drawings*] .... B & F
Bell & Howell [*NYSE symbol*] (TTSB) .... BHW
Bell & Howell Co. .... BH
Bell & Howell Co., Research Laboratories, Pasadena, CA [*Library symbol Library of Congress*] (LCLS) .... CPBH
Bell & Howell Holdings Co. [*Associated Press*] (SAG) .... BellHwl
Bell & Howell Holdings Co. [*NYSE symbol*] (SAG) .... BHW
Bell & Howell/Mamiya Co. .... BHMC
Bell and Spigot [*Technical drawings*] .... B & S
Bell Atlantic .... BA
Bell Atlantic Corp. [*NYSE symbol*] (SPSG) .... BEL
Bell Atlantic Corp. [*Associated Press*] (SAG) .... BellAtl
Bell Atlantic Mobile Systems [*Telecommunications*] .... BAMS
Bell Audit Relate System [*Bell Laboratories*] .... BARS
Bell Audit System [*Bell Laboratories*] .... BAS
Bell Bancorp [*NASDAQ symbol*] (TTSB) .... BELL
Bell Bancorp, Inc. [*NASDAQ symbol*] (SAG) .... BELL
Bell Bancorp, Inc. [*Associated Press*] (SAG) .... BellBcp
Bell Cablemedia [*NASDAQ symbol*] (TTSB) .... BCMPY
Bell Cablemedia Ltd. [*NASDAQ symbol*] (SAG) .... BCMP
Bell Cablemedia Ltd. [*Associated Press*] (SAG) .... BellCabl
Bell. Calcutta Reports [*A publication*] (DLA) .... Bell
Bell Canada [*Toronto Stock Exchange symbol*] .... BC
Bell Canada Data Resource Center, Ottawa, ON, Canada [*Library symbol Library of Congress*] (LCLS) .... CaOOBDR
Bell Canada Documentation Resource Center, Hull, PQ, Canada [*Library symbol*] [*Library of Congress*] (LCLS) .... CaQHB
Bell Canada Enterprises, Inc. [*Toronto Stock Exchange symbol Vancouver Stock Exchange symbol*] .... B
Bell Canada, Headquarters Economics Library, Hull, PQ, Canada [*Library symbol*] [*Library of Congress*] (LCLS) .... CaQHBE
Bell Canada, Headquarters Engineering Economics Reference Centre, Hull, PQ, Canada [*Library symbol*] [*Library of Congress*] (LCLS) .... CaQHBEER
Bell Canada Headquarters Regulatory Matters-Regulatory Information Bank, Hull, PQ, Canada [*Library symbol*] [*Library of Congress*] (LCLS) .... CaQHBRM
Bell Canada Headquarters, Regulatory Matters-Regulatory Information Bank, Hull, Quebec [*Library symbol National Library of Canada*] (NLC) .... QHBRM
Bell Canada Information Resource Centre, Toronto, ON, Canada [*Library symbol Library of Congress*] (LCLS) .... CaOTBCIR
Bell Canada Information Resource Centre, Toronto, Ontario [*Library symbol National Library of Canada*] (NLC) .... OTBCIR
Bell Canada International, Inc. [*Ottawa, ON*] [*Telecommunications*] (TSSD) .... BCI
Bell Canada Market Information Centre, Ottawa, ON, Canada [*Library symbol*] [*Library of Congress*] (LCLS) .... CaOOBMI
Bell Canada Market Information Centre, Ottawa, Ontario [*Library symbol National Library of Canada*] (NLC) .... OOBMI
Bell Character [*Keyboard*] .... BEL
Bell College Technical Information Service, Hamilton [*British*] (NITA) .... BECTIS
Bell Communications Research, Inc. (TSSD) .... Bellcore
Bell. Competing Titles [*Scotland*] [*A publication*] (DLA) .... BCT
Bell. Competing Titles [*Scotland*] [*A publication*] (DLA) .... Bell CT
Bell Cord [*Technical drawings*] .... BC
Bell Crank [*Automotive engineering*] .... B/CRK
Bell Crank [*Automotive engineering*] .... BELCRK
Bell Data Network [*Telecommunications*] .... BDN
Bell Doesn't Ring [*Telecommunications*] (TEL) .... BDR
Bell. Election Law of Scotland [*A publication*] (DLA) .... Bell Elec
Bell End .... BE
Bell FLICKS [*Programming language*] [*1973*] (CSR) .... BEFLIX
Bell Helicopter Co. (MCD) .... BHC
Bell Helicopter Co., Brantly Helicopter Corp., Brditschka [*Heinrich Brditschka Flugzeugbau*] [*ICAO aircraft manufacturer identifier*] (ICAO) .... HB
Bell Helicopter Co., Fort Worth, TX [*Library symbol Library of Congress*] (LCLS) .... TxFBH
Bell Helicopter, Textron Canada [*FAA designator*] (FAAC) .... TXB
Bell Helicopter Textron, Inc. .... BHT
Bell Industries [*NYSE symbol*] (TTSB) .... BI
Bell Industries, Inc. [*Associated Press*] (SAG) .... BellInd
Bell Industries, Inc. [*NYSE symbol*] (SPSG) .... BI
Bell Information Network .... BIN
Bell Integrated Optical Device [*Electronics*] (EECA) .... BIOD
Bell Island, AK [*Location identifier FAA*] (FAAL) .... KBE
Bell Island Public Library, Bell Island, NF, Canada [*Library symbol Library of Congress*] (LCLS) .... CaNfBI
Bell Island Public Library, Newfoundland [*Library symbol National Library of Canada*] (NLC) .... NFBI
Bell Jar System .... BJS
Bell Laboratories Automatic Design System [*Computer program*] .... BLADES
Bell Laboratories Automatic Design System [*Computer program*] .... BLADS
Bell Laboratories Automatic Device .... BLADE
Bell Laboratories Formula Translation Assembly Program (IAA) .... BETAP
Bell Laboratories FORTRAN Assembly Program [*Computer science*] (IEEE) .... BEFAP
Bell Laboratories Interpretive System [*Computer program*] .... BLIS
Bell Laboratories Library Real-Time Loan System .... BELLREL
Bell Laboratories Machine-Aided Technical Information Center (DIT) .... BELLMATIC
Bell. Lecture on Conveyancing [*Scotland*] [*A publication*] (DLA) .... Bell Convey
Bell Little Electrodata Symbolic System for the Electrodata [*Symbolic assembly program*] .... BLESSED
Bell Log System .... BLS
Bell Memorial Public Library, Mentone, IN [*Library symbol Library of Congress*] (LCLS) .... InMe
Bell Microproducts [*NASDAQ symbol*] (TTSB) .... BELM
Bell Microproducts, Inc. [*Associated Press*] (SAG) .... BellMic
Bell Microproducts, Inc. [*NASDAQ symbol*] (SAG) .... BELM
Bell Molybdenum Mines [*Vancouver Stock Exchange symbol*] .... BLY
Bell Northern Research [*Telecommunications*] (TEL) .... BNR
Bell Northern Research, Bramalea, ON, Canada [*Library symbol Library of Congress*] (LCLS) .... CaOBramB
Bell Northern Research, Bramalea, Ontario [*Library symbol National Library of Canada*] (NLC) .... OBRAMB
Bell Northern Research, Inc., Learning Resources Center, Morrisville, NC [*Library symbol*] [*Library of Congress*] (LCLS) .... NcMorB
Bell Northern Research, Montreal, PQ, Canada [*Library symbol Library of Congress*] (LCLS) .... CaQMBNR
Bell Northern Research, Montreal, Quebec [*Library symbol National Library of Canada*] (NLC) .... QMBNR
Bell Northern Research, Ottawa, ON, Canada [*Library symbol Library of Congress*] (LCLS) .... CaOONorE
Bell Northern Research, Ottawa, ON, Canada [*Library symbol*] [*Library of Congress*] (LCLS) .... CaOONorE
Bell Northern Research, Ottawa, Ontario [*Library symbol National Library of Canada*] (NLC) .... OONORE
Bell Northern Software Research, Toronto, ON, Canada [*Library symbol Library of Congress*] (LCLS) .... CaOTBNS
Bell Northern Software Research, Toronto, Ontario [*Library symbol National Library of Canada*] (NLC) .... OTBNS
Bell Number Screening [*Telecommunications*] (TEL) .... BNS
Bell on Excise [*A publication*] (DLA) .... Bel Ex
Bell on Expert Testimony [*A publication*] (DLA) .... Bell Exp Test
Bell on Landlord and Tenant [*Bengal*] [*A publication*] (DLA) .... Bell L & T
Bell on Leases [*Scotland*] [*A publication*] (DLA) .... Bell Leas
Bell on Leases [*A publication*] (DLA) .... BL
Bell Operating Co. [*Also, BSOC*] [*Post-divestiture division of American Telephone & Telegraph Co.*] .... BOC

Bell Operating System [*Telecommunications*] (TEL) .... BOS
Bell Owned and Maintained [*Telecommunications*] (TEL) .... BOAM
Bell. Property as Arising from the Relation of Husband and Wife [*1849*] [*A publication*] (DLA) .... Bell HW
Bell Propulsion Laboratory (IAA) .... BPL
Bell Rings Faintly [*Telecommunications*] (TEL) .... BRF
Bell. Sale of Food and Drugs [*14th ed.*] [*1968*] [*A publication*] (DLA) .... Bell S
Bell. Sale of Food and Drugs [*14th ed.*] [*1968*] [*A publication*] (DLA) .... Bell Sale
Bell Sports [*NASDAQ symbol*] (TTSB) .... BSPT
Bell Sports Corp. [*Associated Press*] (SAG) .... BellSpt
Bell Sports Corp. [*NASDAQ symbol*] (SAG) .... BSPT
Bell System Center for Technical Education .... BSCTE
Bell System Common Language [*Telecommunications*] (TEL) .... BSCL
Bell. System of the Forms of Deeds [*Scotland*] [*A publication*] (DLA) .... Bell Deeds
Bell. System of the Forms of Deeds (Styles) [*Scotland*] [*A publication*] (DLA) .... Bell Sty
Bell System Operating Co. [*Also, BOC*] [*Post-divestiture division of American T elephone & Telegraph Co.*] .... BSOC
Bell System Practices .... BSP
Bell System Reference Frequency Standard [*Telecommunications*] (TEL) .... BSRFS
Bell System Repair Specification [*Telecommunications*] (TEL) .... BSRS
Bell Tech Group Ltd [*NASDAQ symbol*] (TTSB) .... BELT
Bell Technology Group Ltd. [*Associated Press*] (SAG) .... BellTch
Bell Technology Group Ltd. [*Associated Press*] (SAG) .... BellTech
Bell Technology Group Ltd. [*NASDAQ symbol*] (SAG) .... BELT
Bell Technology Wrrt [*NASDAQ symbol*] (TTSB) .... BELTW
Bell Telephone .... BELLTEL
Bell Telephone Co. of Canada (IIA) .... BTC
Bell Telephone Co. of Canada, Law Department Library, Montreal, PQ, Canada [*Library symbol Library of Congress*] (LCLS) .... CaQMBL
Bell Telephone Co. of Canada, Montreal, PQ, Canada [*Library symbol Library of Congress*] (LCLS) .... CaQMB
Bell Telephone Laboratories, Inc. [*Murray Hill, NJ*] .... BTL
Bell Telephone Laboratories, Inc., Holmdel, NJ [*OCLC symbol*] (OCLC) .... BTL
Bell Telephone Laboratories, Inc., Murray Hill, NJ [*Library symbol Library of Congress*] (LCLS) .... NjMuB
Bell Telephone Laboratories, Inc., Technical Information Library, Holmdel, NJ [*Library symbol Library of Congress*] (LCLS) .... NjHolB
Bell Telephone Laboratories, Inc., Technical Information Library, Whippany, NJ [*Library symbol Library of Congress*] (LCLS) .... NjWhiB
Bell Telephone Manufacturing Co. [*Telecommunications*] .... BTM
Bell. Testing of Deeds [*Scotland*] [*A publication*] (DLA) .... Bell TD
Bell. Testing of Deeds [*Scotland*] [*A publication*] (DLA) .... BTD
Bell Wire .... BW
Bella Bella [*Canada*] [*Airport symbol*] (OAG) .... ZEL
Bella Coola [*Canada*] [*Airport symbol*] (OAG) .... QBC
Bella Coola Museum, Bella Coola, BC, Canada [*Library symbol*] [*Library of Congress*] (LCLS) .... CaBBCM
Bella Coola Museum, British Columbia [*Library symbol National Library of Canada*] (NLC) .... BBCM
Bella Union [*Bolivia*] [*ICAO location identifier*] (ICLI) .... SLBN
Bella Vista [*Paraguay*] [*ICAO location identifier*] (ICLI) .... SGBV
Bella Vista, AR [*FM radio station call letters*] .... KBVA
Bellabon Resources [*Vancouver Stock Exchange symbol*] .... BLJ
Belladonna [*Deadly Nightshade (or its medicinal extract)*] .... BD
Belladonna [*Deadly Nightshade (or its medicinal extract)*] (ROG) .... BELLAD
Belladonna [*Deadly Nightshade (or its medicinal extract)*] (ROG) .... BELLADON
Belladonna and Opium [*Toxicology*] .... B & O
Belladonna Mottle Virus [*Plant pathology*] .... BEMV
Bell-Air [*ICAO designator*] (AD) LL
Bell-Air Executive Air Travel Ltd. [*New Zealand*] [*ICAO designator*] (FAAC) .... BEL
Bellaire City Library, Bellaire, TX [*Library symbol Library of Congress*] (LCLS) .... TxBl
Bellaire, MI [*Location identifier FAA*] (FAAL) .... ACB
Bellaire, MI [*Location identifier FAA*] (FAAL) .... CXK
Bellaire, OH [*Location identifier FAA*] (FAAL) .... AIR
Bellaire, OH [*AM radio station call letters*] .... WOMP
Bellaire, OH [*FM radio station call letters*] .... WOMP-FM
Bellaire Public Library, Bellaire, MI [*Library symbol Library of Congress*] (LCLS) .... MiBela
Bellaire, Zanesville & Cincinnati Railroad [*Nickname: Bent, Zigzagged, and Crooked*] .... BZ & C
Bellairs Research Institute [*Canada*] (MSC) .... BRI
Bellamy Brothers Fan Club (EA) .... BBFC
Bellanca Aircraft Corp. [*ICAO aircraft manufacturer identifier*] (ICAO) .... BL
Bellanca Aircraft Corp., Champion Aircraft Corp. [*ICAO aircraft manufacturer identifier*] (ICAO) .... CH
Bellanca Contact (EA) .... BC
Bellar & Lichtenberg [*Device*] .... B & L
Bellarmine College, Louisville, KY [*OCLC symbol*] (OCLC) .... KBC
Bellarmine College, Louisville, KY [*Library symbol Library of Congress*] (LCLS) .... KyLoB
Bellarmine College, Plattsburgh, NY [*Library symbol Library of Congress*] (LCLS) .... NPlaB
Bellarmine College, Thomas Merton Studies Center, Louisville, KY [*Library symbol Library of Congress*] (LCLS) .... KyLoB-M
Bellary [*India*] [*ICAO location identifier*] (ICLI) .... VOBI
Bellasis. Bombay Reports [*A publication*] (DLA) .... Bel
Bellasis. Bombay Reports [*A publication*] (DLA) .... Bell
Bellasis. Civil Cases [*Bombay*] [*A publication*] (DLA) .... Bell CC
Bellasis. Civil Cases [*Bombay*] [*A publication*] (DLA) .... Bellas
Bellasis. Criminal Cases [*Bombay*] [*A publication*] (DLA) .... Bell CC
Bellasis. Criminal Cases [*Bombay*] [*A publication*] (DLA) .... Bellas
Bellavista/Huallaga [*Peru*] [*ICAO location identifier*] (ICLI) .... SPBL
Bellco Energy Corp. [*Vancouver Stock Exchange symbol*] .... BLO
Belle Chasse, LA [*FM radio station call letters*] .... KMEZ
Belle Chasse State School, Belle Chasse, LA [*Library symbol Library of Congress*] (LCLS) .... LBcS
Belle Fourche Public Library, Belle Fourche, SD [*Library symbol Library of Congress*] (LCLS) .... SdBf
Belle Fourche, SD [*AM radio station call letters*] .... KBFS
Belle Fourche, SD [*FM radio station call letters*] (RBYB) .... KZZI
Belle Glade, FL [*FM radio station call letters*] .... WBGF
Belle Glade, FL [*AM radio station call letters*] .... WSWN
Belle Plaine, IA [*FM radio station call letters*] .... KXPW
Belle Plaine, KS [*FM radio station call letters*] .... KANR
Belle Plaine Union, Belle Plaine, IA [*Library symbol Library of Congress*] (LCLS) .... IaBepU
Belle River Public Library, Ontario [*Library symbol National Library of Canada*] (NLC) .... OBRI
Belle Valley School, Belleville, IL [*Library symbol Library of Congress*] (LCLS) .... IBelVS
Bellechasse [*Switzerland ICAO location identifier*] (ICLI) .... LSTB
Belleek Collector's Society [*Commercial firm*] (EA) .... BCS
Bellefontaine, OH [*Location identifier FAA*] (FAAL) .... RUV
Bellefontaine, OH [*AM radio station call letters*] .... WBLL
Bellefontaine, OH [*FM radio station call letters*] .... WPKO
Bellefonte, AR [*AM radio station call letters*] .... KNWA
Bellefonte Central Railroad Co. [*AAR code*] .... BFC
Bellefonte District Library Center [*Library network*] .... CPDLC
Bellefonte Nuclear Plant (NRCH) .... BNP
Bellefonte, PA [*AM radio station call letters*] .... WBLF
Bellefonte, PA [*FM radio station call letters*] .... WZWW
Bellefonte-Clearfield-Philipsburg [*Pennsylvania*] [*Airport symbol*] (AD) .... PSB
Bellegarde, SK [*Television station call letters*] CBKFT-9
Bellegarde/Vouvray [*France ICAO location identifier*] (ICLI) .... LFHN
Bellerive Foundation (EAIO) .... BF
Bellerophon [*of Euripides*] [*Classical studies*] (OCD) .... Beller
Beller's Criminal Cases [*Bombay*] [*A publication*] (DLA) .... Bell Cr C
Beller's Criminal Cases [*Bombay*] [*A publication*] (DLA) .... Bell Cr Ca
Beller's Criminal Cases [*Bombay*] [*A publication*] (DLA) .... Bell Cr Cas
Beller's Delineation of Universal Law [*A publication*] (DLA) .... Bell UL
Beller's Delineations of Universal Law [*A publication*] (DLA) .... Bell Del
Bellerville/Scott Air Force Base [*Illinois*] [*ICAO location identifier*] (ICLI) .... KBLV
Belles Lettres [*A publication*] (BRI) .... Belles Let
Belleville [*Diocesan abbreviation*] [*Illinois*] (TOCD) .... BEL
Belleville & District Chamber of Commerce (AC) .... BCC
Belleville Area College, Belleville, IL [*Library symbol Library of Congress*] (LCLS) .... IBelC
Belleville Area College, Belleville, IL [*OCLC symbol*] (OCLC) .... IDF
Belleville Free Public Library, Belleville, NJ [*Library symbol Library of Congress*] (LCLS) .... NjBe
Belleville, IL [*Location identifier FAA*] (FAAL) .... BLV
Belleville, IL [*Location identifier FAA*] (FAAL) .... OXK
Belleville, IL [*Location identifier FAA*] (FAAL) .... RCC
Belleville, IL [*Location identifier FAA*] (FAAL) .... SKE
Belleville, IL [*AM radio station call letters*] .... WIBV
Belleville, KS [*FM radio station call letters*] .... KREP
Belleville, KS [*Location identifier FAA*] (FAAL) .... RPB
Belleville, ON [*FM radio station call letters*] .... CIGL
Belleville, ON [*AM radio station call letters*] .... CJBQ
Belleville, ON [*FM radio station call letters*] .... CJLX
Belleville, ON [*FM radio station call letters*] .... CJOJ
Belleville Public Library, Belleville, IL [*Library symbol Library of Congress*] (LCLS) .... IBel
Belleville Public Library, Belleville, ON, Canada [*Library symbol Library of Congress*] (LCLS) .... CaOBE
Belleville Public Library, Ontario [*Library symbol National Library of Canada*] (NLC) .... OBE
Belleville Public Schools District 118, Belleville, IL [*Library symbol Library of Congress*] (LCLS) .... IBelSD
Belleville Telegram, Belleville, NJ [*Library symbol Library of Congress*] (LCLS) .... NjBeT
Belleville Township High School District 201, Belleville, IL [*Library symbol Library of Congress*] (LCLS) .... IBelTSD
Belleville-Villie-Morgon [*France ICAO location identifier*] (ICLI) .... LFHW
Bellevue Community College, Bellevue, WA [*Library symbol Library of Congress*] (LCLS) .... WaBB
Bellevue Herald-Leader, Bellevue, IA [*Library symbol Library of Congress*] (LCLS) .... IaBevHL
Bellevue Index of Depression .... BID
Bellevue Municipal Library, Alberta [*Library symbol National Library of Canada*] (NLC) .... ABELM
Bellevue, NE [*AM radio station call letters*] .... KOIL
Bellevue, OH [*FM radio station call letters*] .... WNRR
Bellevue Oil & Minerals [*Vancouver Stock Exchange symbol*] .... BEU
Bellevue Public Library, Bellevue, IA [*Library symbol Library of Congress*] (LCLS) .... IaBev
Bellevue Public Library, Bellevue, ID [*Library symbol*] [*Library of Congress*] (LCLS) .... IdBe
Bellevue Public Library, Bellevue, NE [*OCLC symbol*] (OCLC) .... BLL
Bellevue Public Library, Bellevue, NE [*Library symbol Library of Congress*] (LCLS) .... NbBe
Bellevue Public Library, Bellevue, NE [*Library symbol*] [*Library of Congress*] (LCLS) .... NbBeL
Bellevue Public Library, Bellevue, OH [*Library symbol Library of Congress*] (LCLS) .... OBv
Bellevue School District, Instructional Materials Center, Bellevue, WA [*Library symbol Library of Congress*] (LCLS) .... WaBS

Bellevue Township Library, Bellevue, MI [*Library symbol Library of Congress*] (LCLS) .... MiBel
Bellevue Ventures Ltd. [*Vancouver Stock Exchange symbol*] .... BVL
Bellevue, WA [*Location identifier FAA*] (FAAL) .... BVU
Bellevue, WA [*FM radio station call letters*] .... KASB
Bellevue, WA [*FM radio station call letters*] .... KBCS
Bellevue, WA [*Television station call letters*] .... KBEH
Bellevue, WA [*Television station call letters*] (RBYB) .... KBGE
Bellevue, WA [*AM radio station call letters*] .... KBLV
Bellevue, WA [*FM radio station call letters*] .... KLSY
Bellewe's Cases Tempore Henry VIII [*Brooke's New Cases*] [*England*] [*A publication*] (DLA) .... Pet Br
Bellewe's Cases Tempore Richard II [*1378-1400*] [*A publication*] (ILCA) .... Bel Cas T R II
Bellewe's Cases Tempore Richard II [*1378-1400*] [*A publication*] (DLA) .... Bellewe's Ca Temp R II
Bellewe's English King's Bench Reports [*A publication*] (DLA) .... Bell
Bellewe's English King's Bench Reports [*A publication*] (DLA) .... Bellewe
Bellewe's English King's Bench Reports [*A publication*] (DLA) .... Bellewe (Eng)
Bellewe's English King's Bench Reports Tempore Richard II [*1378-1400*] [*A publication*] (DLA) .... Bel
Bellewe's English King's Bench Reports Tempore Richard II [*1378-1400*] [*A publication*] (DLA) .... Bell Cas T R II
Bellewe's English King's Bench Reports Tempore Richard II [*1378-1400*] [*A publication*] (DLA) .... Bell Cas T Rich II
Bellewe's Les Ans du Roy Richard le Second [*1378-1400*] [*A publication*] (DLA) .... YB Rich II
Belley-Peyrieu [*France ICAO location identifier*] (ICLI) .... LFKY
Bellfield [*Australia Seismograph station code, US Geological Survey*] (SEIS) .... BFD
Bellin Memorial Hospital, Green Bay, WI [*Library symbol Library of Congress*] (LCLS) .... WGrB
Bell-Independent Relations [*Telecommunications*] (TEL) .... B-IR
Belling .... BLNG
Bellinger and Cotton's Annotated Codes and Statutes [*Oregon*] [*A publication*] (DLA) .... Ann Codes & St
Bellinger and Cotton's Annotated Codes and Statutes [*Oregon*] [*A publication*] (DLA) .... B & C Comp
Bellinger's Reports [*4-8 Oregon*] [*A publication*] (DLA) .... Bel
Bellinger's Reports [*4-8 Oregon*] [*A publication*] (DLA) .... Bell
Bellinger's Reports [*4-8 Oregon*] [*A publication*] (DLA) .... Bell (Or)
Bellinger's Reports [*4-8 Oregon*] [*A publication*] (DLA) .... Bellinger
Bellingham [*Washington*] [*Airport symbol*] (OAG) .... BLI
Bellingham [*Washington*] [*Seismograph station code, US Geological Survey Closed*] (SEIS) .... BLL
Bellingham/International [*Washington*] [*ICAO location identifier*] (ICLI) .... KBLI
Bellingham Public Library, Bellingham, WA [*Library symbol Library of Congress*] (LCLS) .... WaBe
Bellingham Public Schools, Bellingham, MN [*Library symbol*] [*Library of Congress*] (LCLS) .... MnBelPS
Bellingham, WA [*FM radio station call letters*] .... KAFE
Bellingham, WA [*Television station call letters*] .... KBCB
Bellingham, WA [*AM radio station call letters*] .... KGMI
Bellingham, WA [*FM radio station call letters*] (RBYB) .... KISM-FM
Bellingham, WA [*AM radio station call letters*] .... KPUG
Bellingham, WA [*FM radio station call letters*] .... KUGS
Bellingham, WA [*Television station call letters*] .... KVOS-TV
Bellingham, WA [*FM radio station call letters*] .... KZAZ
Bellingham, WA [*Location identifier FAA*] (FAAL) .... LUM
Bellingham-Ferndale, WA [*AM radio station call letters*] .... KBFW
Bellini-Tose System .... BT
Bellini-Tose System .... BTS
Belli's Modern Trials [*A publication*] (DLA) .... Belli's Mod Trials
Bellmore Memorial Library, Bellmore, NY [*Library symbol Library of Congress*] (LCLS) .... NBellm
Bellmouth [*Design engineering*] .... BLMTH
Bellofram Rolling Diaphragm .... BRD
Bellona Island [*Solomon Islands*] [*Airport symbol*] (OAG) .... BNY
Bellows (MSA) .... BLWS
Bellows Falls, VT [*FM radio station call letters*] .... WBFL
Bellows Tankage Module .... BTM
Bellows Valve .... BV
Bellport Memorial Library, Bellport, NY [*Library symbol Library of Congress*] (LCLS) .... NBel
Bellport Senior High School, Brookhaven, NY [*Library symbol Library of Congress*] (LCLS) .... NBrooHS
Bell's Appeals to House of Lords from Scotland [*A publication*] (DLA) .... Bell Sc App
Bell's Cases in Parliament: Scotch Appeals [*A publication*] (DLA) .... Bell PC
Bell's Cases in the Scotch Court of Session [*A publication*] (DLA) .... Bell
Bell's Cases in the Scotch Court of Session [*A publication*] (DLA) .... Bell Cas
Bell's Cases in the Scotch Court of Session [*A publication*] (DLA) .... Bell Sc Cas
Bell's Cases in the Scotch Court of Session [*A publication*] (DLA) .... Bell Ses Cas
Bell's Commentaries on the Laws of Scotland [*A publication*] (DLA) .... BC
Bell's Commentaries on the Laws of Scotland [*A publication*] (DLA) .... Bell Comm
Bell's Decisions, Scotch Court of Session [*A publication*] (DLA) .... Bell Ct of Sess Fol R
Bell's Dictionary and Digest of the Laws of Scotland [*A publication*] (DLA) .... Bell Dict
Bell's Dictionary of Decisions, Scotch Court of Session [*A publication*] (DLA) .... Bell Dict Dec
Bell's Dictionary of Decisions, Scotch Court of Session [*A publication*] (DLA) .... Bell's Dict
Bell's English Crown Cases [*A publication*] (DLA) .... Bell Cr C
Bell's English Crown Cases [*A publication*] (DLA) .... Bell Cr Ca
Bell's English Crown Cases [*A publication*] (DLA) .... Bell Cr Cas
Bell's English Crown Cases Reserved [*169 English Reprint*] [*A publication*] (DLA) .... Bell
Bell's English Crown Cases Reserved [*169 English Reprint*] [*A publication*] (DLA) .... Bell CC
Bell's English Crown Cases Reserved [*169 English Reprint*] [*A publication*] (DLA) .... Bell CC (Eng)
Bell's Folio Reports, Scotch Court of Session [*1794-95*] [*A publication*] (DLA) .... Bell Fol
Bell's House of Lords Scotch Appeal Cases [*1842-50*] [*A publication*] (DLA) .... Bell App
Bell's House of Lords Scotch Appeal Cases [*1842-50*] [*A publication*] (DLA) .... Bell App Bell (SC)
Bell's House of Lords Scotch Appeal Cases [*1842-50*] [*A publication*] (DLA) .... Bell App Cas
Bell's House of Lords Scotch Appeal Cases [*1842-50*] [*A publication*] (DLA) .... Bell HL
Bell's House of Lords Scotch Appeal Cases [*1842-50*] [*A publication*] (DLA) .... Bell HL Sc
Bell's House of Lords Scotch Appeal Cases [*1842-50*] [*A publication*] (DLA) .... Bell's App
Bell's House of Lords Scotch Appeal Cases [*1842-50*] [*A publication*] (DLA) .... S Bell
Bell's Illustrations of Principles [*A publication*] (DLA) .... Bell Illus
Bell's Law of Arbitration in Scotland [*A publication*] (DLA) .... Bell Arb
Bell's Law of Awards [*A publication*] (DLA) .... Bell Aw
Bell's Medico-Legal Journal [*A publication*] (DLA) .... Bell Med LJ
Bell's Octavo Reports, Scotch Court of Sessions [*1790-92*] [*A publication*] (DLA) .... Bell 8vo
Bell's Octavo Reports, Scotch Court of Sessions [*1790-92*] [*A publication*] (DLA) .... Bell Oct
Bell's Palsy [*Medicine*] (DMAA) .... BP
Bell's Principles of the Law of Scotland [*10 eds.*] [*1829-99*] [*A publication*] (DLA) .... Bell Prin
Bell's Putative Marriage Case [*Scotland*] [*A publication*] (DLA) .... Bell Put Mar
Bell's Reports, Court of Session [*1790-92*] [*Scotland*] [*A publication*] (DLA) .... Bell C
Bell's Reports, High Court of Calcutta [*India*] [*A publication*] (DLA) .... Bell CHC
Bell's Reports, High Court of Calcutta [*India*] [*A publication*] (DLA) .... Bell HC
Bell's Reports, High Court of Calcutta [*India*] [*A publication*] (DLA) .... Bell (In)
Bell's Science Series [*A publication*] .... BSS
Bell's Scotch Appeal Cases [*A publication*] (DLA) .... Bell
Bell's Scotch Appeal Cases [*A publication*] (DLA) .... Bell Ap Ca
Bell's Scotch Appeal Cases [*A publication*] (DLA) .... Bell Sc App Cas
Bell's Scottish Digest [*A publication*] (DLA) .... Bell Sc Dig
Bell's Scottish Digest [*A publication*] (DLA) .... Bell Scot Dig
Bell's Supplemented Notes to Hume on Crimes [*A publication*] (DLA) .... Bell No
BellSouth Corp. [*Associated Press*] (SAG) .... BellSo
BellSouth Corp. [*NYSE symbol*] (SPSG) .... BLS
Bellsouth Services, Birmingham, AL [*Library symbol*] [*Library of Congress*] (LCLS) .... ABBsS
Bellum Actiacum [*of Ausonius*] [*Classical studies*] (OCD) .... B Act
Bellum Africum [*of Ausonius*] [*Classical studies*] (OCD) .... B Afr
Bellum Alexandrinum [*of Ausonius*] [*Classical studies*] (OCD) .... B Alex
Bellum Catilinae [*or De Catilinae Coniuratione*] [*of Sallust*] [*Classical studies*] (OCD) .... Cat
Bellum Civile [*of Caesar*] [*Classical studies*] (OCD) .... BCiv
Bellum Gallicum [*of Caesar*] [*Classical studies*] (OCD) .... BGall
Bellum Iugurthinum [*of Sallust*] [*Classical studies*] (OCD) .... Iug
Bellum Judaicum [*Josephus*] [*Classical studies*] (BJA) .... BelJud
Bellum Judaicum [*Josephus*] [*Classical studies*] (OCD) .... BJ
Bellum Judaicum [*Josephus*] [*Classical studies*] (BJA) .... JBJ
Bell-View Airlines Ltd. [*Nigeria*] [*ICAO designator*] (FAAC) .... BLV
Bellville, TX [*AM radio station call letters*] .... KFRD
Bellwether Expl Co. [*Associated Press*] (SAG) .... Bellweth
Bellwether Exploration [*NASDAQ symbol*] (TTSB) .... BELW
Bellwether Exploration Co. [*Associated Press*] (SAG) .... Bellweth
Bellwether Exploration Co. [*NASDAQ symbol*] (NQ) .... BELW
Bellwether Resources [*Vancouver Stock Exchange symbol*] .... BLW
Bellwether Stock [*Investment term*] .... BS
Bellwood, PA [*FM radio station call letters*] .... WALY
Bellwood Public Library, Bellwood, IL [*Library symbol Library of Congress*] (LCLS) .... IBelw
Belly Button to Medial Malleolus [*Measurement*] [*Anatomy*] (DAVI) .... BB to MM
Belmac Corp. [*Associated Press*] (SAG) .... Belmac
Belmac Corp. [*AMEX symbol*] (SPSG) .... BLM
Belmar/Farmingdale, NJ [*Location identifier FAA*] (FAAL) .... BLM
Belmar Public Library, Belmar, NJ [*Library symbol Library of Congress*] (LCLS) .... NjBel
Belmond Independent, Belmond, IA [*Library symbol Library of Congress*] (LCLS) .... IaBelmI
Belmond Public Library, Belmond, IA [*Library symbol Library of Congress*] (LCLS) .... IaBelm
Belmont [*Australia Airport symbol*] .... BEO
Belmont Abbey College [*North Carolina*] .... BAC
Belmont Abbey College, Belmont, NC [*Library symbol Library of Congress*] (LCLS) .... NcBe
Belmont and Methuen Township Public Library, Nephton, Ontario [*Library symbol National Library of Canada*] (BIB) .... ONBM
Belmont Bancorp [*Associated Press*] (SAG) .... BelBcp
Belmont Bancorp [*NASDAQ symbol*] (SAG) .... BLMT
Belmont College, Nashville, TN [*OCLC symbol*] (OCLC) .... TBC
Belmont College, Nashville, TN [*Library symbol Library of Congress*] (LCLS) .... TNBe
Belmont Elementary School, North Babylon, NY [*Library symbol*] [*Library of Congress*] (LCLS) .... NNbBE

Belmont Homes [*Associated Press*] (SAG) ... BelmH
Belmont Homes [*NASDAQ symbol*] (SAG) ... BHIX
Belmont Memorial Library, Belmont, MA [*Library symbol Library of Congress*] (LCLS) ... MBelm
Belmont, NC [*AM radio station call letters*] ... WCGC
Belmont, NC [*Television station call letters*] ... WJZY
Belmont, NH [*FM radio station call letters*] ... WNHI
Belmont Resources [*Vancouver Stock Exchange symbol*] ... BEO
Belmont Technical Institute, St. Clairsville, OH [*Library symbol Library of Congress*] (LCLS) ... OStcB
Belmonte [*Brazil*] [*Airport symbol*] (OAG) ... BVM
Belmoral Mines Ltd. [*Toronto Stock Exchange symbol*] ... BME
Belo [*Madagascar*] [*Airport symbol*] (OAG) ... BMD
Belo (A.H.)Cl'A' [*NYSE symbol*] (TTSB) ... BLC
Belo [*A.H.*] **Corp.** [*Associated Press*] (SAG) ... BeloAH
Belo [*A. H.*] **Corp.** [*NYSE symbol*] (SPSG) ... BLC
Belo Horizonte [*Brazil*] [*Airport symbol*] (OAG) ... BHZ
Belo Horizonte/Confins [*Brazil ICAO location identifier*] (ICLI) ... SBCF
Belo Horizonte/Pampulha [*Brazil ICAO location identifier*] (ICLI) ... SBBH
Belo Information Systems Online Network [*A. H. Belo Corp.*] [*Discontinued service*] [*Information service or system*] (IID) ... BISON
Beloit College, Beloit, WI [*Library symbol Library of Congress*] (LCLS) ... WBB
Beloit College Library, Beloit, WI [*OCLC symbol*] (OCLC) ... WII
Beloit/Janesville [*Wisconsin*] [*Airport symbol*] (OAG) ... JVL
Beloit, KS [*AM radio station call letters*] ... KVSV
Beloit, KS [*FM radio station call letters*] ... KVSV-FM
Beloit Memorial Hospital, Beloit, WI [*Library symbol Library of Congress*] (LCLS) ... WBM
Beloit, WI [*FM radio station call letters*] ... WBCR
Beloit, WI [*AM radio station call letters*] ... WGEZ
Belo-Luxembourg Chamber of Commerce (DS) ... BLCC
Belorussian [*MARC language code Library of Congress*] (LCCP) ... bel
Belorussian Soviet Socialist Republic [*MARC country of publication code Library of Congress*] (LCCP) ... bwr
Belorussian Soviet Socialist Republic [*MARC geographic area code Library of Congress*] (LCCP) ... e-ur-bw
Belorussian Yiddish (BJA) ... BrY
Belo-Sur-Tsiribihina [*Madagascar*] [*ICAO location identifier*] (ICLI) ... FMML
Belousov-Zhabotinskii [*Physical chemistry*] ... BZ
Below [*Technical drawings*] ... BEL
Below ... BLO
Below (MSA) ... BLW
Below All Clouds [*Aviation*] ... BAC
Below Bridges [*Navigation*] ... BB
Below Bridges [*Transportation*] ... BBS
Below Center of Mass [*Command report*] [*Army*] (INF) ... BCM
Below Clouds [*Aviation code*] ... BLO
Below Deck [*of a ship*] (DS) ... BD
Below Deck Communications System [*Navy*] (LAIN) ... BDCS
Below Diaphragm [*Medicine*] (DAVI) ... BD
Below Elbow [*Medicine*] ... BE
Below Elbow [*Orthopedics*] (DAVI) ... BELB
Below Ground Level (WDAA) ... BGL
Below Ground Surface ... BGS
Below/Hook Lifters Section of the Material Handling Institute (EA) ... BHLS
Below Knee [*Medicine*] ... BK
Below Knee Amputation [*Medicine*] ... BKA
Below Knee to Toe [*Medicine*] (MAE) ... BKTT
Below Knee Walking Cast (MEDA) ... BKWC
Below Knee Walking Plaster [*Medicine*] (MAE) ... BKWP
Below Layer Range (NVT) ... BLR
Below Limit of Detection ... BLD
Below Lower Limit (IEEE) ... BLL
Below Market Interest Rate (GFGA) ... BMIR
Below Minimum Standards [*TV ratings*] ... BMS
Below Proof ... BP
Below Regulatory Concern [*Nuclear Regulatory Commission classification*] ... BRC
Below Right Costal Margin [*Anatomy*] (DAVI) ... BRCM
Below Slab (OA) ... BS
Below the Detectable Limit ... BDL
Below the Line [*Budget*] ... BTL
Below the Treatment Zone (GNE) ... BTZ
Below Threshold Change [*Air Force*] ... BTC
Below Waist [*Medicine*] ... BW
Below Watch ... BW
Below Water (NG) ... BW
Below-Knee Orthosis [*Orthopedics*] (DAVI) ... BKO
Belozyorsk [*Former USSR ICAO location identifier*] (ICLI) ... ULWB
Belpre, OH [*FM radio station call letters*] ... WCVV
Belpre, OH [*FM radio station call letters*] ... WMBP
Belpre, OH [*FM radio station call letters*] ... WNUS
Belsk [*Poland*] [*Seismograph station code, US Geological Survey Closed*] (SEIS) ... BEL
Belt Association (EA) ... BA
Belt Driven Retrofit [*Cosworth racing engines*] [*Automotive engineering*] ... BDR
Belt Driven Turbocharged [*Cosworth racing engines*] [*Automotive engineering*] ... BDT
Belt Driven Type A [*Cosworth racing engines*] [*Automotive engineering*] ... BDA
[*The*] **Belt Railway Co. of Chicago** ... BR of C
[*The*] **Belt Railway Co. of Chicago** [*AAR code*] ... BRC
Belt Weather Kit (MCD) ... BWK
Belt Work Line ... BWL
Belt Work Line ... BWL
Beltec Enterprises Ltd. [*Vancouver Stock Exchange symbol*] ... BET
Belted Galloway Society (EA) ... BGS
Belting [*Freight*] ... BLTG
Belton Railroad Co. [*AAR code*] ... BRR
Belton, SC [*FM radio station call letters*] ... WEPC
Belton, SC [*AM radio station call letters*] ... WHPB
Belton, TX [*Television station call letters*] ... KNCT
Belton, TX [*FM radio station call letters*] ... KOOC
Belton, TX [*AM radio station call letters*] ... KTON
Belt's Edition of Brown's Chancery Reports [*1778-94*] [*A publication*] (DLA) ... Belt Bro
Belt's Edition of Vesey, Senior's, English Chancery Reports [*A publication*] (DLA) ... Belt Ves Sen
Belt's Supplement to Vesey, Senior's, English Chancery Reports [*1746-56*] [*A publication*] (DLA) ... Belt Sup
Belt's Supplement to Vesey, Senior's, English Chancery Reports [*1746-56*] [*A publication*] (DLA) ... Belt Sup Ves
Belt's Supplement to Vesey, Senior's, English Chancery Reports [*1746-56*] [*A publication*] (DLA) ... Belt Supp
Belt's Supplement to Vesey, Senior's, English Chancery Reports [*1746-56*] [*A publication*] (DLA) ... Belt's Supp (Eng)
Beltsville Agricultural Research Center [*Maryland*] [*Department of Agriculture*] ... BARC
Beltsville Human Nutrition Research Center [*Department of Agriculture*] ... BHNRC
Beltsville Space Center [*Later, Goddard Space Flight Center*] [*NASA*] ... BSC
Beluga, AK [*Location identifier FAA*] (FAAL) ... BLG
Belvedere, SC [*FM radio station call letters*] ... WAFJ
Belves-Saint-Pardoux [*France ICAO location identifier*] (ICLI) ... LFIB
Belvidere, IL [*FM radio station call letters*] ... WXRX
Belvidere, NJ [*FM radio station call letters*] ... WRNJ
Belview Public School, Bleview, MN [*Library symbol*] [*Library of Congress*] (LCLS) ... MnBevPS
Belvoir Fuels and Lubricants Research Facility [*Southwest Research Institute*] [*San Antonio, TX*] ... BFLRF
Belvoir Research, Development, and Engineering Center [*Fort Belvoir, VA*] [*Army*] (RDA) ... BRDEC
Belzoni, MS [*AM radio station call letters*] ... WELZ
Belzoni, MS [*FM radio station call letters*] ... WVRD
Bem Sex-Role Inventory [*Research test*] [*Psychology*] ... BSRI
Bema Gold [*AMEX symbol*] (TTSB) ... BGO
Bema Gold Corp. [*Associated Press*] (SAG) ... BemaGold
Bema Gold Corp. [*AMEX symbol*] (SAG) ... BGO
Bema Gold Ltd. [*Toronto Stock Exchange symbol Vancouver Stock Exchange symbol*] ... BGO
Bemba [*MARC language code Library of Congress*] (LCCP) ... bem
Bembridge [*British ICAO location identifier*] (ICLI) ... EGHJ
Bement Community Unit School District, Bement, IL [*Library symbol*] [*Library of Congress*] (LCLS) ... IBemSD
Bement Public Library, St. Johns, MI [*Library symbol Library of Congress*] (LCLS) ... MiStjo
Bement Township Library, Bement, IL [*Library symbol Library of Congress*] (LCLS) ... IBem
Bemichi [*Guyana*] [*Airport symbol*] (OAG) ... BCG
Bemidji [*Minnesota*] [*Airport symbol*] (OAG) ... BJI
Bemidji Aviation Services, Inc. [*ICAO designator*] (FAAC) ... BMJ
Bemidji High School, Bemidji, MN [*Library symbol*] [*Library of Congress*] (LCLS) ... MnBemH
Bemidji, MN [*Television station call letters*] ... KAWE
Bemidji, MN [*FM radio station call letters*] ... KBHP
Bemidji, MN [*FM radio station call letters*] ... KBSB
Bemidji, MN [*AM radio station call letters*] ... KBUN
Bemidji, MN [*FM radio station call letters*] ... KCRB
Bemidji, MN [*AM radio station call letters*] ... KKBJ
Bemidji, MN [*FM radio station call letters*] ... KKBJ-FM
Bemidji, MN [*FM radio station call letters*] ... KNBJ
Bemidji, MN [*Location identifier FAA*] (FAAL) ... MDI
Bemidji Public Library, Bemidji, MN [*Library symbol*] [*Library of Congress*] (LCLS) ... MnBem
Bemidji State College [*Later, Bemidji State University*] [*Minnesota*] ... BSC
Bemidji State College [*Later, Bemidji State University*], Bemidji, MN [*Library symbol Library of Congress*] (LCLS) ... MnBemS
Bemidji State University (GAGS) ... Bemidji St U
Bemidji State University, Bemidji, MN [*OCLC symbol*] (OCLC) ... MNB
Bemis Co. [*NYSE symbol*] (TTSB) ... BMS
Bemis Co., Inc. [*Associated Press*] (SAG) ... Bemis
Bemis Co., Inc. [*NYSE symbol*] (SPSG) ... BMS
Bemis Memorial Library, Robbinsville, NC [*Library symbol Library of Congress*] (LCLS) ... NcRob
Bemoair [*Czechoslovakia*] [*FAA designator*] (FAAC) ... BMI
Ben (BJA) ... b
Ben & Jerry's Cl'A' [*NASDAQ symbol*] (TTSB) ... BJICA
Ben & Jerry's Homemade, Inc. [*Associated Press*] (SAG) ... BenJerry
Ben & Jerry's Homemade, Inc. [*NASDAQ symbol*] (NQ) ... BJIC
Ben Chajim (BJA) ... BCh
Ben Franklin Retail Stores, Inc. [*Associated Press*] (SAG) ... BFrankR
Ben Franklin Retail Stores, Inc. [*NASDAQ symbol*] (SAG) ... BFRS
Ben Franklin Society [*Defunct*] (EA) ... BFS
Ben Franklin Technology Center [*Research center*] (RCD) ... BFTC
Ben Gurion [*Israel*] [*ICAO location identifier*] (ICLI) ... LLAD
Ben Hur Life Association [*Crawfordsville, IN*] (EA) ... BHLA
Ben Line Steamers (MHDB) ... BLS
Ben Marcato [*Well Marked*] [*Music*] (ROG) ... BM
Ben May Laboratory for Cancer Research [*University of Chicago*] [*Research center*] (RCD) ... BML
Ben Monroe's Kentucky Reports [*A publication*] (DLA) ... B Mon (KY)
Ben Monroe's Kentucky Reports [*A publication*] (DLA) ... B Monr
Ben Monroe's Kentucky Reports [*A publication*] (DLA) ... Ben Monroe

Ben Monroe's Kentucky Reports [*A publication*] (DLA) .... BM
Ben Monroe's Kentucky Supreme Court Reports [*A publication*] (DLA) ...... B Mon
Ben Naphtali (BJA) .... BN
Ben Slimane [*Morocco*] [*ICAO location identifier*] (ICLI) .... GMMB
Bena-Dibele [*Zaire*] [*ICAO location identifier*] (ICLI) .... FZVO
Benair [*Italy ICAO designator*] (FAAC) .... BEI
Benard Convection Cell .... BCC
Benbecula [*Hebrides Islands*] [*Airport symbol*] (OAG) .... BEB
Benbecula [*British ICAO location identifier*] (ICLI) .... EGPL
Bence Jones [*As in Bence Jones protein, Bence Jones reaction, etc.*] [*Named for Henry Bence Jones, 19th century London physician*] .... BJ
Bence Jones Protein [*Named for Henry Bence Jones, 19th century London physician*] (DAVI) .... B J PR
Bence Jones Protein [*Named for Henry Bence Jones, 19th century London physician*] (MAE) .... BJP
Bench (MSA) .... BNCH
Bench Check (NASA) .... B/C
Bench Checkout Equipment .... BCE
Bench Checkout Equipment .... BCOE
Bench Detergency Dispersancy Test (PDAA) .... BDDT
Bench Maintenance [*NASA*] (KSC) .... BM
Bench Maintenance Equipment [*NASA*] (KSC) .... BME
Bench Maintenance Test Set (SAA) .... BMTS
Bench Mark Control Point (NASA) .... BCP
Bench Mark Control Point [*Nautical charts*] .... BM
Bench Mark Test Files (MCD) .... BMTF
Bench Model Solar Receiver (MCD) .... BMSR
Bench Order .... BO
Bench Replaceable Assembly (MCD) .... BRA
Bench Scale Calorimeter .... BSC
Bench Stock [*Air Force*] (AFIT) .... B/S
Bench Stock Support Unit [*Military*] .... BSSU
Bench Test Console .... BTC
Bench Test Fixture .... BTF
Bench Test Specification .... BTS
Bench Welder Control Panel .... BWCP
Benchboard (KSC) .... BNCHBD
Benchmark [*Computer system evaluation*] .... BM
Benchmark Electronics [*AMEX symbol*] (TTSB) .... BHE
Benchmark Electronics, Inc. [*Associated Press*] (SAG) .... BenchE
Benchmark Electronics, Inc. [*AMEX symbol*] (SAG) .... BHE
Benchmark Interface Format [*Computer science*] (BTTJ) .... BIF
Benchmark Monitor Display System [*Sperry UNIVAC*] .... BMD
Benchmark Portability System (PDAA) .... BPS
Benchmark Soils Project [*University of Hawaii, University of Puerto Rico*] .... BSP
BENCHMARQ Microelectronics [*NASDAQ symbol*] (TTSB) .... BMRQ
Bend [*Commonly used*] (OPSA) .... BEND
Bend .... BND
Bend Down .... BD
Bend Down .... BDN
Bend Line (MSA) .... BL
Bend, OR [*AM radio station call letters*] .... KBND
Bend, OR [*FM radio station call letters*] .... KICE
Bend, OR [*FM radio station call letters*] .... KNLR
Bend, OR [*FM radio station call letters*] .... KOAB
Bend, OR [*Television station call letters*] .... KOAB-TV
Bend, OR [*FM radio station call letters*] .... KQAK
Bend, OR [*Television station call letters*] .... KTVZ
Bend, OR [*FM radio station call letters*] .... KTWS
Bend, OR [*FM radio station call letters*] .... KXIX
Bend, OR [*AM radio station call letters*] .... KXUX
Bend Over, Here It Comes Again [*Business term*] .... BOHICA
Bend Radius (MCD) .... BR
Bend Radius Template (MCD) .... BRT
Bend Research, Inc., Bend, OR [*Library symbol*] [*Library of Congress*] (LCLS) .... OrBeBR
Bend Senior High School, Bend, OR [*Library symbol*] [*Library of Congress*] (LCLS) .... OrBeHS
Bend Tangency Line (MCD) .... BTL
Bend Up .... BU
Bend Up [*Technical drawings*] .... BUP
Benday [*Type of dye*] (WDMC) .... BD
Benday [*Engraving*] (NTCM) .... DAY
Bend-Down Virginia [*A picked-up stub of a cigarette*] .... BDV
Bender Visual-Motor Gestalt [*Test*] [*Psychology*] (DAVI) .... BVMG
Bender Visual-Motor Gestalt Test [*Education*] .... BVMGT
Bender-Gestalt Test [*Psychology*] .... B-G
Bender-Gestalt Test [*Psychology*] .... BGT
Bendigo Agricultural Show Society [*Australia*] .... BASS
Bending (MSA) .... BNG
Bending Allowance [*Engineering*] (IAA) .... BA
Bending Feedback Control .... BFC
Bending Form [*Tool*] (AAG) .... BEFM
Bending Magnet .... BM
Bending Mode Filters .... BMF
Bending Moment [*Aerospace*] .... BM
Bending Moment [*Aerospace*] (AAG) .... M
Bendix Antiskid System [*Automotive engineering*] .... BAS
Bendix Atlantic Inflator Co. [*Automotive industry supplier*] .... BAICO
Bendix Aviation Corp. [*Later, Bendix Corp.*] .... BAC
Bendix Aviation Corp. [*Later, Bendix Corp.*] (MCD) .... BDX
Bendix Aviation Corp. [*Later, Bendix Corp.*], Pacific Division, North Hollywood, CA [*Library symbol Library of Congress*] (LCLS) .... CNhB
Bendix Corp., Baltimore, MD [*Library symbol Library of Congress*] (LCLS) .... MdBBR

Bendix Corp., Electrical Components Division, Engineering Library, Sidney, NY [*Library symbol Library of Congress*] (LCLS) .... NSidS
Bendix Corp., Engineering Development Center, Bendix Center, Southfield, MI [*Library symbol Library of Congress*] (LCLS) .... MiSfB
Bendix Corp., Technical Information Center, Kansas City, MO [*Library symbol Library of Congress*] .... MoKBen
Bendix Elementary School Annandale, MN [*Library symbol*] [*Library of Congress*] (LCLS) .... MnAdBE
Bendix Engineering Development Center, Southfield, MI [*OCLC symbol*] (OCLC) .... EEB
Bendix Field Engineering Corp. [*of Bendix Corp.*] .... BFEC
Bendix Integrated Data System .... BIDS
Bendix Missile Systems Division (MCD) .... BMSD
Bendix Optimum Configuration Satellite (IEEE) .... BOCS
Bendix-Westinghouse Automotive Air Brake Co. .... BW
Bendloe's [*or Benloe's*] English Common Pleas [*1531-1628*] [*A publication*] (DLA) .... Bendl
Bendloe's [*or Benloe's*] Reports, English Common Pleas [*Edition of 1661*] [*A publication*] (DLA) .... Bendloe
Bend-Over Point (PDAA) .... BOP
Bendroflumethiazide [*Organic chemistry*] (MEDA) .... BFM
Bene [*Well*] [*Pharmacy*] .... BEN
Bene Merenti [*To the Well-Deserving*] [*Latin*] .... BM
Bene Merenti [*To the Well-Deserving*] [*Latin*] .... BMT
Bene Merenti Fecit [*He Erected This to the Well-Deserving*] [*Latin*] .... BMF
Bene Quiescat [*May He, or She, Rest Well*] [*Latin*] .... BQ
Bene Vale [*Farewell*] [*Latin*] .... BV
Bene Vixit [*He Lived a Good Life*] [*Latin*] .... BV
Beneath (FAAC) .... BNTH
Benecke on Marine Insurance [*A publication*] (DLA) .... Ben Ins
Benedicite [*Bless You*] [*Latin*] .... Bte
Benedict College, Columbia, SC [*OCLC symbol*] (OCLC) .... BDC
Benedict College, Columbia, SC [*Library symbol Library of Congress*] (LCLS) .... ScCoB
Benedictine .... BENED
Benedictine and Brandy .... B & B
Benedictine College, Atchison, KS [*OCLC symbol*] (OCLC) .... KKA
Benedictine College, North Campus, Atchison, KS [*Library symbol Library of Congress*] (LCLS) .... KAS
Benedictine College, South Campus, Atchison, KS [*Library symbol Library of Congress*] (LCLS) .... KAM
Benedictine Congregation of Our Lady of Monte (TOCD) .... OSB
Benedictine Heights College [*Oklahoma*] .... BHC
Benedictine High School, Cleveland, OH [*Library symbol Library of Congress*] (LCLS) .... OCIBHS
Benedictine Hospital, Medical Library, Kingston, NY [*Library symbol Library of Congress*] (LCLS) .... NKiB
Benedictine Monks (TOCD) .... OSB
Benedictine Monks, Olivetan Benedictines, Sylvestrine Benedictines (TOCD) .... osb
Benedictine Nuns (TOCD) .... OSB
Benedictine Nuns of the Congregation of Solesmes (TOCD) .... OSB
Benedictine Nuns of the Primitive Observance (TOCD) .... OSB
Benedictine Sisters (TOCD) .... OSB
Benedictine Sisters of Liberty (TOCD) .... OSB
Benedictine Sisters of Pontifical Jurisdiction (TOCD) .... OSB
Benedictine Sisters of Sacred Heart (TOCD) .... OSB
Benedictines for Peace (EA) .... BP
Benedictio [*Blessing*] [*Latin*] (ADA) .... BEN
Benediction .... B
Benedict's American Admiralty Practice [*A publication*] (DLA) .... Ben Adm
Benedict's American Admiralty Practice [*A publication*] (DLA) .... Ben Adm Prac
Benedict's New York Civil and Criminal Justice [*A publication*] (DLA) .... Ben Just
Benedict's United States District Court Reports [*A publication*] (DLA) .... Ben
Benedict's United States District Court Reports [*A publication*] (DLA) .... Bene
Benedict's United States District Court Reports [*A publication*] (DLA) .... Bened
Benedict's United States District Court Reports [*A publication*] (DLA) .... Benedict
Benedict's United States District Court Reports [*A publication*] (DLA) .... Bt
Benedictus [*Blessed*] [*Latin*] .... Bs
Benedictus de Isernia [*Flourished, 1221-52*] [*Authority cited in pre-1607 legal work*] (DSA) .... B
Benedictus de Isernia [*Flourished, 1221-52*] [*Authority cited in pre-1607 legal work*] (DSA) .... Be
Benedictus de Isernia [*Flourished, 1221-52*] [*Authority cited in pre-1607 legal work*] (DSA) .... Bene
Benedictus de Isernia [*Flourished, 1221-52*] [*Authority cited in pre-1607 legal work*] (DSA) .... Bn
Benedict-Webb-Rubin [*Equation of state*] .... BWR
Benediktinische Monatsschrift [*A publication*] (BJA) .... BenM
Benedum Civic Center Public Library, Bridgeport, WV [*Library symbol Library of Congress*] (LCLS) .... WvBri
Benefice .... BNFC
Beneficial (ROG) .... BENEFL
Beneficial .... BNFCL
Beneficial Communications [*Computer system*] [*Beneficial Management Corp.*] .... BENCOM
Beneficial Corp. [*Associated Press*] (SAG) .... Benef
Beneficial Corp. [*Wall Street slang name: "Big Nose Louie"*] [*Associated Press*] (SAG) .... BenefCp
Beneficial Corp. [*NYSE symbol*] (SAG) .... BNL
Beneficial Corp.,5% Pfd [*NYSE symbol*] (TTSB) .... BNLPrVF
Beneficial Corp.,$4.30 Pfd [*NYSE symbol*] (TTSB) .... BNLPrB
Beneficial Corp.,$4.50 Pfd [*NYSE symbol*] (TTSB) .... BNLPrA
Beneficial Corp.,$5.50 Cv Pfd [*NYSE symbol*] (TTSB) .... BNLPrC

Beneficial Insects Research Laboratory [Department of Agriculture] [Newark, DE] (GRD) .... BIRL
Beneficial Occupancy .... BO
Beneficial Occupancy Date .... BOD
Beneficial Rays of the Sun [In reference to suntanning, supposedly occuring between 10am and 2pm] [See also SROTS] .... BROTS
Beneficial Suggestion (MCD) .... BS
Beneficial Suggestions [Program] (DNAB) .... BEN SUG
Beneficial Suggestions [Program] .... BENNY SUGG
Beneficial Suggestions [Program] (DNAB) .... BENNY SUGGS
Beneficial Use Date .... BUD
Beneficiary [Legal shorthand] (LWAP) .... BEN
Beneficiary .... BENE
Beneficiary (AFM) .... BENEF
Beneficiary (ROG) .... BENEFY
Beneficiary .... BFCY
Beneficiary Data Exchange System [between state welfare agencies and the Social Security Administration] .... BENDEX
Beneficiary Developing Country [Trade status] .... BDC
Beneficiary Evaluation Survey Service [LIMRA] .... BESS
Beneficiary Government Production Program .... BGPP
Beneficiary Identification Records Location Subsystem (MCD) .... BIRLS
Benefit .... BNFT
Benefit (ADA) .... BT
Benefit and Donation Claims, Selected Decisions of Umpire [England] [A publication] (DLA) .... OUUISD
Benefit Assessment for System Change (MHDB) .... BASYC
Benefit Cost Analysis [Accounting] .... BCA
Benefit Decisions of the British Umpire [A publication] (DLA) .... OUUIBD
Benefit Eligibility Interview [Unemployment insurance] (OICC) .... BEI
Benefit Performance [Theater] [Slang] (WDMC) .... ben
Benefit Principles (DLA) .... BP
Benefit Rights Interview [Unemployment insurance] .... BRI
Benefit Service Series, Unemployment Insurance [Department of Labor] [A publication A publication] (DLA) .... BSSUI
Benefit Service Series, Unemployment Insurance [Department of Labor] [A publication] .... BSUI
Benefit Systems Testing Section [Social Security Administration] .... BSTS
Benefit Week Number [Unemployment insurance] (OICC) .... BWN
Benefit Year Ending [Unemployment insurance] .... BYE
Benefit-Cost [Ratio] .... B-C
Benefit-Cost Analysis of Federal Programs: Guidelines and Discounts [OMB Circular] (AAGC) A-94
Benefit-Cost Ratio [Finance] .... BCR
Benefits (BARN) .... bnfts
Benefits Analysis Program [Environmental Protection Agency] (GFGA) .... BAP
Benefits and Use Division [Environmental Protection Agency] (GFGA) .... BUD
Benefits Control System [Insurance] .... BCS
Benefits Review Board [Department of Labor] (OICC) .... BRB
Benefits Review Board Service (Matthew Bender) [A publication] (DLA) .... BRBS
Benelli Owner's Club of America (EA) .... BOCA
Benelux Countries [MARC geographic area code Library of Congress] (LCCP) .... el----
BENELUX Economische Union [Belgium, Netherlands, and Luxembourg Economic Union] (EAIO) .... BEU
Benelux Falcon Service [Belgium ICAO designator] (FAAC) .... BFS
BENELUX Group on Mortality (EAIO) .... BGM
Benelux Phlebology Society (EA) .... BPS
BENELUX [Belgium, Netherlands, Luxembourg] Subarea Channel [NATO] (NATG) .... BENECHAN
Benet on Military Law and Courts-Martial [A publication] (DLA) .... Benet Ct-M
Benetton Group ADS [NYSE symbol] (TTSB) .... BNG
Benetton Group SpA [Associated Press] (SAG) .... Beneton
Benetton Group SpA [NYSE symbol] (SPSG) .... BNG
Benetton Group S.p.A [ML, exchange symbol] (TTSB) .... BTON
Benevento [Italy] [Seismograph station code, US Geological Survey Closed] (SEIS) .... BNV
Benevolent (ROG) .... BENEV
Benevolent .... BNVLNT
Benevolent and Loyal Order of Pessimists (EA) .... BLOOP
Benevolent and Protective Order of Elks (EA) .... BPOE
Benevolent Association for Naming All Nonentities After Schools .... BANANAS
Benevolent Orders (DLA) .... Ben Ord
Benevolent Society of Coachmakers [British] .... BSC
Benevolent Society of New South Wales [Australia] .... BSNSW
Benevolent Society of St. Patrick .... BSSP
Benevolenti Lectori Salutem [Greeting to the Well-Wishing Reader] [Latin] .... BLS
Benewah County Library District, St. Maries, ID [Library symbol] [Library of Congress] (LCLS) .... IdSmB
Bengal .... BENG
Bengal [or Bengalese] (WDAA) .... BG
Bengal & North-Western Railway Battalion [British military] (DMA) .... B & NW RY BN
Bengal Army Native Hospital Corps [British military] (DMA) .... BANHC
Bengal, Bay of [MARC geographic area code Library of Congress] (LCCP) .... ab----
Bengal Cavalry [British military] (DMA) .... BC
Bengal Civil Service [British] .... BCS
Bengal Civil Service [British] (ROG) .... BEN CS
Bengal Full Bench Rulings [North-Western Provinces, India] [A publication] (DLA) .... Full BR
Bengal Fusiliers [British military] (DMA) .... BF
Bengal Horse Artillery [British military] (DMA) .... BHA
Bengal Lancers [British military] (DMA) .... BL
Bengal Law Reports [India] [A publication] (DLA) .... Ben
Bengal Law Reports [India] [A publication] (DLA) .... Beng

Bengal Law Reports [India] [A publication] (DLA) .... Beng LR
Bengal Law Reports, Appeal Cases [India] [A publication] (DLA) .... Beng LR App Cas
Bengal Law Reports, Appeal Cases [India] [A publication] (DLA) .... BLRAC
Bengal Law Reports, High Courts [India] [A publication] (DLA) .... BLR
Bengal Law Reports, Privy Council [India] [A publication] (DLA) .... Beng LRPC
Bengal Law Reports, Privy Council [India] [A publication] (DLA) .... BLRPC
Bengal Law Reports, Supplement [India] [A publication] (DLA) .... Beng LR Supp
Bengal Law Reports, Supplemental Volume, Full Bench Rulings [India] [A publication] (ILCA) .... BLR Sup Vol
Bengal Law Reports, Supplemental Volume, Full Bench Rulings [India] [A publication] (DLA) .... BLR Suppl Vol
Bengal Light Cavalry [British military] (DMA) .... BLC
Bengal Medical Department [British military] (DMA) .... BMD
Bengal Native Infantry [Military British] (ROG) .... BEN NI
Bengal Native Infantry [Military British] .... BNI
Bengal Sadr Diwani Adalat Cases [India] [A publication] (DLA) .... Beng SDA
Bengal Sadr Diwani Adalat Decisions [A publication] (DLA) .... Dec SDA
Bengal Staff Corps [Military British] (ROG) .... BEN SC
Bengal Staff Corps [British Military] .... BSC
Bengal Yeomanry Cavalry [British military] (DMA) .... BYC
Bengali [MARC language code Library of Congress] (LCCP) .... ben
Bengali [Language, etc.] (ROG) .... BENG
Bengal-Nagpore Railway Volunteer Rifles [British military] (DMA) .... BNRVR
Benghazi [Libya] [Airport symbol] (OAG) .... BEN
Benghazi/Benina [Libya] [ICAO location identifier] (ICLI) .... HLLB
Bengis Aviation (Pty) Ltd. [South Africa] [FAA designator] (FAAC) .... SPT
Bengkalis/Sungai Pakning [Indonesia] [ICAO location identifier] (ICLI) .... WIBS
Bengkayang [Indonesia] [ICAO location identifier] (ICLI) .... WIOB
Bengkulu [Indonesia] [Airport symbol] (OAG) .... BKS
Bengkulu/Padang Kemiling [Indonesia] [ICAO location identifier] (ICLI) .... WIPL
Benguela [Angola] [Airport symbol] (OAG) .... BUG
Benguela [Angola] [ICAO location identifier] (ICLI) .... FNBG
Benguet Corp. [NYSE symbol] (SPSG) .... BE
Benguet Corp. [Associated Press] (SAG) .... BengtB
Ben-Gurion University (BJA) .... BGU
Beni [Zaire] [ICAO location identifier] (ICLI) .... FZNP
Beni Abbes [Algeria] [Airport symbol] (AD) .... KBA
Beni Hasan [Egyptology] (ROG) .... BH
Beni-Abbes [Algeria] [Seismograph station code, US Geological Survey] (SEIS) .... BAB
Benicia Free Public Library, Benicia, CA [Library symbol Library of Congress] (LCLS) .... CBen
Benidji Middle School, Bemidji, MN [Library symbol] [Library of Congress] (LCLS) .... MnBemMS
Benign Breast Disease [Medicine] (DMAA) .... BBD
Benign Epileptiform Transients of Sleep [Neurology] (DAVI) .... BETS
Benign Essential Blepharospasm [Medicine] (EA) .... BEB
Benign Essential Blepharospasm Research Foundation (EA) .... BEBRF
Benign Exertional Headache [Medicine] (DMAA) .... BEH
Benign Familial Hematuria [Medicine] (DMAA) .... BFH
Benign Familial Neonatal Convulsions [Medicine] .... BFNC
Benign Febrile Convulsion [Medicine] (MAE) .... BFC
Benign Focal Epilepsy of Childhood [Medicine] (DMAA) .... BFEC
Benign Intracranial Hypertension [Medicine] .... BIH
Benign Intradermal Nevus [Dermatology] (DAVI) .... BIN
Benign Lichenoid Keratosis [Medicine] .... BLK
Benign Lymphocytic Angiitis and Granulomatosis [Medicine] .... BLAG
Benign Monoclonal B-Cell Lymphocytosis [Medicine] (DMAA) .... BMBL
Benign Monoclonal Gammopathy [Immunochemistry] .... BMG
Benign Monoclonal Hypergammaglobulinemia [Medicine] .... BMH
Benign Mucous Membrane Pemphigus [Medicine] (MAE) .... BMMP
Benign Mucous Membrane Pemphigus [Dermatology] (DAVI) .... BMPP
Benign Nephrosclerosis [Medicine] (MAE) .... BNS
Benign Occipital Epilepsy [Medicine] (DMAA) .... BOE
Benign Paroxysmal Positioning Nystagmus [Medicine] (DMAA) .... BPPN
Benign Paroxysmal Positioning Vertigo [Medicine] .... BPPV
Benign Paroxysmal Torticollis [Medicine] (DMAA) .... BPT
Benign Paroxysmal Vertigo [Medicine] (DMAA) .... BPV
Benign Positional Vertigo [Neurology] (DAVI) .... BPV
Benign Proliferative Lesion [Medicine] (DMAA) .... BPL
Benign Prostatic Hyperplasia [Medicine] .... BPH
Benign Prostatic Hyperplasia [Medicine] (CDI) .... BPH
Benign Prostatic Hypertrophy [Medicine] .... BPH
Benign Recurrent Intrahepatic Cholestasis [Medicine] (DMAA) .... BRIC
Benign Senescent Forgetfulness [Medicine] .... BSF
Benign Sexual Headache [Medicine] (DMAA) .... BSH
Benign Symmetric Lipomatosis [Medicine] .... BSL
Benign Tertian Malaria [Medicine] (DMAA) .... BTM
Benihana Inc. [NASDAQ symbol] (TTSB) .... BNHN
Benihana Inc.'A' [NASDAQ symbol] (TTSB) .... BNHNA
Benihana National Corp. [Associated Press] (SAG) .... Benhn
Benihana National Corp. [Associated Press] (SAG) .... Benihan
Benihana National Corp. [NASDAQ symbol] (NQ) .... BNHN
Beni-Mellal [Morocco] [ICAO location identifier] (ICLI) .... GMMD
Benin [ANSI three-letter standard code] (CNC) .... BEN
Benin [ANSI two-letter standard code] (CNC) .... BJ
Benin [Nigeria] [ICAO location identifier] (ICLI) .... DNBE
Benin [Aircraft nationality and registration mark] (FAAC) .... TY
Benin Air Express [ICAO designator] (FAAC) .... BEX
Benin City [Nigeria] [Airport symbol] (OAG) .... BNI
Benito Juarez [Argentina ICAO location identifier] (ICLI) .... SAZJ
Benjamin and Slidell's Louisiana Digest [A publication] (DLA) .... Ben & S Dig
Benjamin Franklin High School Library, Rochester, NY [OCLC symbol] (OCLC) .... RVQ

Benjamin Franklin Junior Stamp Club [*Later, BFSC*] (EA) .... BFJSC
Benjamin Franklin Literary and Medical Society (EA) .... BFLMS
Benjamin Franklin Stamp Club (EA) .... BFSC
Benjamin Franklin University [*Washington, DC*] .... BFU
Benjamin Harrison [*US president, 1833-1901*] .... BH
Benjamin on Sales of Personal Property [*1868-1955*] [*A publication*] (DLA) .... Benj
Benjamin on Sales of Personal Property [*1868-1955*] [*A publication*] (DLA) .... Benj Sa
Benjamin on Sales of Personal Property [*1868-1955*] [*A publication*] (DLA) .... Benj Sales
Benjamin's Chalmer's Bills and Notes [*A publication*] (DLA) .... Benj Chalm Bills & N
Benjamin's New York Annotated Cases [*A publication*] (DLA) .... Benj
Benloe and Dalison's English Common Pleas Reports [*A publication*] (DLA) .... B & D
Benloe and Dalison's English Common Pleas Reports [*A publication*] (DLA) .... Ben & D
Benloe and Dalison's English Common Pleas Reports [*A publication*] (DLA) .... Ben & Dal
Benloe and Dalison's English Common Pleas Reports [*A publication*] (DLA) .... Benl
Benloe and Dalison's English Common Pleas Reports [*A publication*] (DLA) .... Benl & D
Benloe and Dalison's English Common Pleas Reports [*A publication*] (DLA) .... Benl & D (Eng)
Benloe and Dalison's English Common Pleas Reports [*A publication*] (DLA) .... Benl & Dal
Benloe and Dalison's English Common Pleas Reports [*A publication*] (DLA) .... Benl Old
Benloe and Dalison's English Common Pleas Reports [*A publication*] (DLA) .... Dal
Benloe at the End of Ashe's Tables [*A publication*] (DLA) .... Benl in Ashe
Benloe in Benloe and Dalison's English Common Pleas Reports [*A publication*] (DLA) .... Old Ben
Benloe in Benloe and Dalison's English Common Pleas Reports [*A publication*] (DLA) .... Old Benloe
Benloe in Keilway's Reports [*A publication*] (DLA) .... Benl in Keil
Benloe's English King's Bench and Common Pleas Reports [*A publication*] (DLA) .... Ben
Benloe's English King's Bench and Common Pleas Reports [*A publication*] (DLA) .... Benl New
Benloe's English King's Bench Reports [*73 English Reprint*] [*1531-1628*] [*A publication*] (DLA) .... Ben in Keil
Benloe's English King's Bench Reports [*73 English Reprint*] [*1531-1628*] [*A publication*] (DLA) .... Benl
Benloe's English King's Bench Reports [*73 English Reprint*] [*1531-1628*] [*A publication*] (DLA) .... Benl (Eng)
Benloe's English King's Bench Reports [*73 English Reprint*] [*1531-1628*] [*A publication*] (DLA) .... Benl KB
Benloe's English King's Bench Reports [*73 English Reprint*] [*1531-1628*] [*A publication*] (DLA) .... Benloe
Bennett and Heard's Leading Criminal Cases [*England*] [*A publication*] (DLA) .... B & H Cr Cas
Bennett and Heard's Leading Criminal Cases [*England*] [*A publication*] (DLA) .... B & H Crim Cas
Bennett and Heard's Leading Criminal Cases [*England*] [*A publication*] (DLA) .... B & H Lead Ca
Bennett and Heard's Leading Criminal Cases [*England*] [*A publication*] (DLA) .... B & H Lead Cas
Bennett and Heard's Leading Criminal Cases [*England*] [*A publication*] (DLA) .... Ben & HLC
Bennett and Heard's Leading Criminal Cases [*England*] [*A publication*] (DLA) .... Benn & H Cr Cas
Bennett and Heard's Leading Criminal Cases [*England*] [*A publication*] (DLA) .... Benn & H Lead Crim Cas
Bennett and Heard's Massachusetts Digest [*A publication*] (DLA) .... B & H Dig
Bennett and Heard's Massachusetts Digest [*A publication*] (DLA) .... Benn & H Dig
Bennett College, Greensboro, NC [*OCLC symbol*] (OCLC) .... BEN
Bennett College, Greensboro, NC [*Library symbol Library of Congress*] (LCLS) .... NcGB
Bennett College, Millbrook, NY [*Library symbol Library of Congress*] (LCLS) .... NMbrB
Bennett County Library, Martin, SD [*Library symbol Library of Congress*] (LCLS) .... SdMa
Bennett, D. L., Wheeling WV [*STAC*] .... BDL
Bennett Junior College [*New York*] .... BJC
Bennett Mechanical Comprehension Test [*Mechanical ability test*] .... BMCT
Bennett on Receivers [*A publication*] (DLA) .... Benn Rec
Bennett, Richard A., Stockton CA [*STAC*] .... BRA
Bennett's Dakota Cases [*A publication*] (DLA) .... Benn (Dak)
Bennett's Dissertation on Practice of Masters in Chancery [*A publication*] (DLA) .... Benn Pr MC
Bennett's Fire Insurance Cases [*A publication*] (DLA) .... Ben Fl Cas
Bennett's Fire Insurance Cases [*A publication*] (DLA) .... Benn Fl Cas
Bennett's Insurance Cases [*A publication*] (DLA) .... Ben Ins Cas
Bennett's Missouri Cases [*A publication*] (DLA) .... Benn (MO)
Bennett's Reports [*1 Dakota*] [*A publication*] (DLA) .... Benn
Bennett's Reports [*1 California*] [*A publication*] (DLA) .... Benn
Bennett's Reports [*16-21 Missouri*] [*A publication*] (DLA) .... Benn
Bennett's Reports [*1 California*] [*A publication*] (DLA) .... Benn Cal
Bennett's Rights and Liabilities of Farmers [*A publication*] (DLA) .... Benn Farm
Bennett's Transport [*Commercial firm British*] .... BET
Bennettsville & Cheraw Railroad (IIA) .... B & C
Bennettsville, SC [*Location identifier FAA*] (FAAL) .... BBP
Bennettsville, SC [*Location identifier FAA*] (FAAL) .... BES
Bennettsville, SC [*AM radio station call letters*] .... WBSC
Bennington Aviation, Inc. [*ICAO designator*] (FAAC) .... BEN
Bennington Bunch [*An association*] (EA) .... BB
Bennington College (GAGS) .... Bennington C
Bennington College, Bennington, VT [*OCLC symbol*] (OCLC) .... BNT
Bennington College, Bennington, VT [*Library symbol Library of Congress*] (LCLS) .... VtBennC
Bennington Free Library, Bennington, VT [*Library symbol Library of Congress*] (LCLS) .... VtBenn
Bennington Museum, Inc., Bennington, VT [*Library symbol Library of Congress*] (LCLS) .... VtBennM
Bennington, NE [*FM radio station call letters*] .... KRRK
Bennington, NE [*FM radio station call letters*] (RBYB) .... KTNP-FM
Bennington, VT [*AM radio station call letters*] .... WBTN
Bennington, VT [*FM radio station call letters*] .... WHGC
Benny Goodman [*Clarinetist*] .... BG
Benny Wilson Fan Club (EA) .... BWFC
Beno [*Zaire*] [*ICAO location identifier*] (ICLI) .... FZBE
Benoctol [*French illicit drug available in Vietnam*] (VNW) .... BT's
Benoist Scale (MAE) .... B
Bensbach [*Papua New Guinea*] [*Airport symbol*] (OAG) .... BSP
Bensberg [*Federal Republic of Germany*] [*Seismograph station code, US Geological Survey*] (SEIS) .... BNS
Benson [*British ICAO location identifier*] (ICLI) .... EGUB
Benson & Hedges (ADA) .... B & H
Benson, AZ [*FM radio station call letters*] .... KAVV
Benson Eyecare Corp. [*Associated Press*] (SAG) .... BenEye
Benson Eyecare Corp. [*NYSE symbol*] (SAG) .... EYE
Benson Financial [*NASDAQ symbol*] (TTSB) .... BFCX
Benson Financial Corp. [*Associated Press*] (SAG) .... BensonF
Benson Financial Corp. [*NASDAQ symbol*] (SAG) .... BFCX
Benson, MN [*Location identifier FAA*] (FAAL) .... BBB
Benson, MN [*AM radio station call letters*] .... KSCR
Benson, MN [*FM radio station call letters*] .... KSCR-FM
Benson, NC [*AM radio station call letters*] .... WPYB
Benson Needham Univas [*International advertising network*] .... BNU
Benson Public Library, Benson, AZ [*Library symbol Library of Congress*] (LCLS) .... AzBe
Benson Public Schools, Benson, MN [*Library symbol*] [*Library of Congress*] (LCLS) .... MnBenPS
Benson's Remarkable Trials and Notorious Characters [*A publication*] (DLA) .... Rem Tr No Ch
Bensselaerville, NY [*FM radio station call letters*] (RBYB) .... WGKP-FM
Bent .... BNT
Bent (MSA) .... BT
Bent Knees [*Doll collecting*] .... BK
Bent Logarithmically Periodic Zig-Zags .... BLPZZ
Bent Wire Antenna .... BWA
Benta [*Malaysia*] [*ICAO location identifier*] (ICLI) .... WMAC
Bentall Capital Corp. [*Toronto Stock Exchange symbol*] .... BCC
Bentayan [*Indonesia*] [*ICAO location identifier*] (ICLI) .... WIPY
Bentham on Rationale of Judicial Evidence [*A publication*] (DLA) .... Benth Ev
Bentham on Rationale of Judicial Evidence [*A publication*] (DLA) .... Benth Jud Ev
Bentham's Act of Packing as Applied to Special Juries [*1821*] [*A publication*] (DLA) .... Bent Pack Jur
Bentham's Codification [*A publication*] (DLA) .... Bent Cod
Bentham's Constitutional Code for All Nations [*A publication*] (DLA) .... Bent Const Code
Bentham's Judicial Evidence [*A publication*] (DLA) .... Bent Ev
Bentham's Judicial Evidence [*A publication*] (DLA) .... Bent Jud Ev
Bentham's Judicial Evidence [*A publication*] (DLA) .... Benth Jud Ev
Bentham's Principles of Morals and Legislation [*A publication*] (DLA) .... Bent Mor Leg
Bentham's Rationale of Punishment [*A publication*] (DLA) .... Bent Pun
Bentham's Theory of Legislation [*A publication*] (DLA) .... Bent The Leg
Benthic Acoustic Stress Sensor [*Oceanographic instrument*] .... BASS
Benthic Boundary Layer [*Oceanography*] .... BBL
Benthic Inflatable Toolstore Enclosure (PDAA) .... BITE
Benthic Layer Interactive Profiling System [*Marine science*] (OSRA) .... BLIPS
Benthic Layer Interactive Profiling System (USDC) .... BLIPS
Benthic Metabolism Measurement .... BMM
Benthic Mixed Layer [*Nuclear energy*] (NUCP) .... BML
Benthic Nepheloid Layer [*Oceanography*] .... BNL
Bentley College, Waltham, MA [*OCLC symbol*] (OCLC) .... BET
Bentley College, Waltham, MA [*Library symbol Library of Congress*] (LCLS) .... MWalBe
Bentley Drivers Club (EA) .... BDC
Bentley Pharmaceutical [*Associated Press*] (SAG) .... BentPh
Bentley Pharmaceutical [*AMEX symbol*] (SAG) .... BNT
Bentley Pharmaceuticals [*AMEX symbol*] (TTSB) .... BNT
Bentley Public Library, Alberta [*Library symbol National Library of Canada*] (NLC) .... ABEN
Bentley Resources Ltd. [*Vancouver Stock Exchange symbol*] .... BYT
Bentley School, New York, NY [*Library symbol Library of Congress*] (LCLS) .... NNBeS
Bentley's Irish Chancery Reports [*A publication*] (DLA) .... Bent
Bentley's Reports [*13-19 Attorneys-General's Opinions*] [*A publication*] (DLA) .... Bentl Atty-Gen
Bent-Mescalero School Library, Mescalero, NM [*Library symbol Library of Congress*] (LCLS) .... NmMeB
Benton & Bowles [*Advertising agency*] .... B & B
Benton, AR [*AM radio station call letters*] .... KEWI
Benton, AR [*FM radio station call letters*] .... KMVK
Benton County Historical Museum, Sauk Rapids, MN [*Library symbol*] [*Library of Congress*] (LCLS) .... MnSrB

Benton County Public Library, Fowler, IN [*Library symbol Library of Congress*] (LCLS) .... InFo
Benton County Recorder's Office, Fowler, IN [*Library symbol Library of Congress*] (LCLS) .... InFoCR
Benton Harbor [*Michigan*] [*Airport symbol*] (OAG) .... BEH
Benton Harbor, MI [*AM radio station call letters*] .... WHFB
Benton Harbor, MI [*FM radio station call letters*] .... WHFB-FM
Benton Harbor Public Library, Benton Harbor, MI [*Library symbol*] [*Library of Congress*] (LCLS) .... MiBh
Benton, IL [*Location identifier FAA*] (FAAL) .... BEE
Benton, IL [*FM radio station call letters*] .... WQRL
Benton, KY [*FM radio station call letters*] (RBYB) .... WAAJ-FM
Benton, KY [*AM radio station call letters*] .... WCBL
Benton, KY [*FM radio station call letters*] .... WCBL-FM
Benton, KY [*FM radio station call letters*] .... WVHM
Benton, LA [*FM radio station call letters*] .... KLKL
Benton Oil & Gas [*NASDAQ symbol*] (TTSB) .... BNTN
Benton Oil & Gas Co. [*Associated Press*] (SAG) .... BentOG
Benton Oil & Gas Co. [*NASDAQ symbol*] (SAG) .... BNTN
Benton Oil & Gas Co. [*Associated Press*] (SAG) .... BntOG
Benton Oil & Gas Wrrt [*NASDAQ symbol*] (TTSB) .... BNTNW
Benton, PA [*FM radio station call letters*] .... WKXP
Benton Resources Ltd. [*Vancouver Stock Exchange symbol*] .... BRX
Benton/Stearns Special Education Professional Library, St. Cloud, MN [*Library symbol*] [*Library of Congress*] (LCLS) .... MnStclBS
Benton, TN [*AM radio station call letters*] .... WBIN
Benton, TN [*FM radio station call letters*] .... WBIN-FM
Benton Township - Potterville District Library, Potterville, MI [*Library symbol Library of Congress*] (LCLS) .... MiPot
Benton Visual Retention Test [*Psychology*] (DAVI) .... BVRT
Benton Visual Retention Test, Revised [*Psychology*] (DAVI) .... BVRTR
Benton Visual Retention Time [*Psychiatry*] .... BVRT
Bentong [*Malaysia*] [*ICAO location identifier*] (ICLI) .... WMAD
Bentonite Agglutination (OA) .... BA
Bentonite Agglutination Inhibition (OA) .... BAI
Bentonite Flocculation [*Test*] .... BF
Bentonite Flocculation Test (AAMN) .... BFT
Benton's Abridgement of the Debates of Congress [*A publication*] (DLA) .... Bent Abr
Bentonville, AR [*FM radio station call letters*] (RBYB) .... KFAY
Bentonville-Bella Vista, AR [*AM radio station call letters*] (RBYB) .... KESE
Bent's Old Fort National Historic Site .... BEOL
Bentu [*Sudan*] [*ICAO location identifier*] (ICLI) .... HSBT
Bentwaters [*British ICAO location identifier*] (ICLI) .... EGVJ
Bentwood (VRA) .... bntwd
Benyzlimidazole [*Organic chemistry*] .... BZI
Benzaldehyde [*Organic chemistry*] .... BAL
Benzalkonium and Heparin (MAE) .... BH
Benzalkonium Chloride [*Organic chemistry*] .... BAC
Benzamide (DMAA) .... Bam
Benzanthracene [*Also, BzAnth*] [*Organic chemistry*] .... BA
Benzanthracene [*Also, BA*] [*Organic chemistry*] .... BzAnth
Benzathine Penicillin G [*Antibacterial*] .... BPG
Benzedrine .... B
Benzene [*Organic chemistry*] (ADA) .... BZ
Benzene Hexachloride [*Also, GBH, HCH*] [*Insecticide*] .... BHC
Benzene, Toluene, and Xylene .... BTX
Benzenecarboxylic Acid [*Organic chemistry*] .... BCA
Benzenediazonium Chloride [*Organic chemistry*] .... BDC
Benzene-Soluble Organics [*Pollutant*] .... BSO
Benzenesulfonic Acid [*Organic chemistry*] .... BSA
Benzenesulfonohydrazide [*Organic chemistry*] .... BSH
Benzenetricarboxylate [*Organic chemistry*] .... BTC
Benzhydryl [*As substituent on nucleoside*] [*Biochemistry*] .... bh
Benzhydryl [*Biochemistry*] .... Bzh
Benzidine [*Carcinogen*] .... BENZ
Benzidine [*Carcinogen*] .... BZD
Benziger, Bruce & Glencoe, Inc. .... BBG
Benzilic Acid Tropine Ester [*Also, BETE, BTE*] [*Pharmacology*] .... BAT
Benzilic Acid Tropine Ester [*Also, BAT, BTE*] [*Pharmacology*] .... BETE
Benzilic Acid Tropine Ester [*Also, BAT, BETE*] [*Pharmacology*] .... BTE
Benzimidazole [*Biochemistry*] .... Bza
Benzimidazolyl [*Biochemistry*] .... Bza
Benzimidazolylphenylmaleimide [*Organic chemistry*] .... BIPM
Benzing Retrograde (DAVI) .... BR
Benzo(a)pyrene .... BaP
Benzoate (MAE) .... B
Benzo(c)phenanthrene [*Organic chemistry*] .... BcPh
Benzocyclobutene [*Organic chemistry*] .... BCB
Benzodiazepine [*Also, BZD*] [*Organic chemistry*] .... BZ
Benzodiazepine [*Also, BZ*] [*Organic chemistry*] .... BZD
Benzodiazepine [*Pharmacology*] (DAVI) .... BZDZ
Benzo(e)pyridoindole [*Organic chemistry*] .... BePI
Benzoic Acid [*Organic chemistry*] .... BOA
Benzon [*Denmark*] [*Research stone symbol*] .... U
Benzonia Public Library, Benzonia, MI [*Library symbol Library of Congress*] (LCLS) .... MiBen
Benzonitrile [*Organic chemistry*] .... BN
Benzophenone Tetracarboxylic Acid Dianhydride (PDAA) .... BTAD
Benzophenonetetracarboxylic Dianhydride [*Organic chemistry*] .... BTDA
Benzophenonetetracarboxylic Diethylester [*Organic chemistry*] .... BTDE
Benzopyrene [*or Benzpyrene*] [*Also, BZ Carcinogen*] .... BP
Benzopyrene [*or Benzpyrene*] [*Also, BP Carcinogen*] .... BZ
Benzopyrenedihydrodiolepoxide [*Organic chemistry*] .... BPDE
Benzothiophene [*Organic chemistry*] .... BT

Benzothiopyranoindazole [*Organic chemistry*] .... BTPI
Benzotriazole [*Organic chemistry*] .... BTA
Benzotriazole [*Lubricants*] .... BTA
Benzotrifuroxan [*Organic chemistry*] .... BTF
Benzoyl [*Organic chemistry*] .... Bz
Benzoyl Leuco Methylene Blue [*Organic chemistry*] .... BLMB
Benzoyl Peroxide [*Also, BPO*] [*Organic chemistry*] .... BP
Benzoyl Peroxide [*Also, BP*] [*Organic chemistry*] .... BPO
Benzoylacetone [*Organic chemistry*] .... BZAC
Benzoylarginine Amide [*Biochemistry*] .... BAA
Benzoylarginine Ethyl Ester [*Biochemistry*] .... BAEE
Benzoylarginine Methyl Ester [*Biochemistry*] .... BAME
Benzoylarginine p-Nitroanilide [*Also, BAPA*] [*Biochemistry*] .... BAPA
Benzoylarginine p-Nitroanilide [*Also, BAPA*] [*Biochemistry*] .... BAPNA
Benzoylargininenaphthylamide .... BANA
Benzoylargininenitroanilide [*Organic chemistry*] .... BANI
Benzoylated DEAE [*Diethylaminoethyl*] [*Organic chemistry*] .... BD
Benzoylated-Naphthoylated DEAE [*Diethylaminoethyl*] .... BND
Benzoylated-Naphthoylated (DEAE)[*Diethylaminoethyl*]-Cellulose [*Analytical biochemistry*] .... BNC
Benzoylbenzoic Acid [*Organic chemistry*] .... BBA
Benzoylecgonine [*Cocaine metabolite*] .... BE
Benzoylecgonine [*Biochemistry*] .... BZE
Benzoyloxime [*Organic chemistry*] .... BO
Benzoyl-para-aminosalicylate [*Pharmacology*] .... BPAS
Benzoyl(Phenylalanyl)Proline [*Biochemistry*] .... BPAP
Benzoylphenylhydroxylamine (NRCH) .... BPHA
Benzoyl(sulfamoyl)(thenyloxy)benzoic Acid [*Biochemistry*] .... BSTBA
Benzoyltrifluoroacetone [*Organic chemistry*] .... BTA
Benzoyltrifluoroacetone [*Organic chemistry*] (NRCH) .... BTFA
Benzoyltyrosine [*Biochemistry*] .... BT
Benzoyltyrosine Ethyl Ester [*Biochemistry*] .... BTEE
Benzoyl-Tyrosyl Para-Aminobenzoic Acid [*Organic chemistry*] .... BT PABA
Benzoyl-Tyrosyl-Para-Aminobenzoic Acid [*Test*] (MEDA) .... Bz-Ty-PABA
Benzquinamide [*Pharmacology*] .... BZQ
Benzyl [*Organic chemistry*] .... Bn
Benzyl [*Organic chemistry*] .... Bzl
Benzyl Analogue of Serotonin [*Medicine*] (DAVI) .... BAS
Benzyl Butyl Phthalate [*Organic chemistry*] .... BBP
Benzyladenine [*Biochemistry*] .... BA
Benzyl-Aminophenol [*Organic chemistry*] .... BAP
Benzylaminopurine [*Biochemistry*] .... BAP
Benzylantiserotonin [*Pharmacology*] .... BAS
(Benzyl)benzylidenecyclopentanone [*Organic chemistry*] .... BBCP
Benzylcinchonidinium Chloride [*Organic chemistry*] .... BCDC
Benzylcinchoninium Chloride [*Organic chemistry*] .... BCNC
Benzylcyclopropylamine [*Organic chemistry*] .... BCA
Benzyldimethylamine [*Organic chemistry*] .... BDMA
Benzylfurancarboxylic Acid [*Organic chemistry*] .... BFCA
Benzylfurylmethyl Alcohol [*Organic chemistry*] .... BFA
Benzylideneglucose [*Biochemistry*] .... BG
Benzylidenemalononitrile [*Organic chemistry*] .... BMN
Benzyl-Iso-Thiourea [*Organic chemistry*] .... BITU
Benzyloxymethyl [*Organic chemistry*] .... BOM
Benzylpenicilloyl [*Organic chemistry*] .... BPO
Benzylpenicilloyl Polylysine [*Organic chemistry*] .... BPL
Benzylselenocyanate [*Antineoplastic drug*] .... BSC
Benzylthiomethyl [*Biochemistry*] .... Btm
Benzyltrichlorosilane [*Organic chemistry*] .... BTCS
Benzyltrimethylammonium Chloride [*Also, TMBAC*] [*Organic chemistry*] .... BTM
Benzyl(vinyl)pyridinium Bromide [*Organic chemistry*] .... BVP
Beobachtung [*Observation*] [*German*] .... BB
Beobachtungsstelle [*Observation post*] [*German military - World War II*] .... BST
Beograd [*Belgrade*] [*Yugoslavia*] [*Seismograph station code, US Geological Survey*] (SEIS) .... BEO
Beograd [*Former Yugoslavia*] [*ICAO location identifier*] (ICLI) .... LYBA
Beograd [*Former Yugoslavia*] [*ICAO location identifier*] (ICLI) .... LYBB
Beograd [*Former Yugoslavia*] [*ICAO location identifier*] (ICLI) .... LYBE
Beograd [*Former Yugoslavia*] [*ICAO location identifier*] (ICLI) .... LYYY
Beongo [*Zaire*] [*ICAO location identifier*] (ICLI) .... FZEO
Bepaling [*Provision in statute or contract*] [*Netherlands*] (ILCA) .... Bep
Bephenium Hydroxynaphthoate (MAE) .... BHN
Beppu [*Japan*] [*Seismograph station code, US Geological Survey Closed*] (SEIS) .... BEP
Bequeath [*Legal term*] (WDAA) .... BEQ
Bequeath [*Legal term*] (ROG) .... BEQTH
Bequeathed [*Legal term*] .... BEQD
Bequeathed [*Legal term*] .... BEQTHD
Bequest .... BEQT
Berachampa [*India*] [*ICAO location identifier*] (ICLI) .... VEBC
Berakhot [*or Berakot*] (BJA) .... Ber
Berar Law Journal [*India*] [*A publication*] (DLA) .... Berar
Berau [*Indonesia*] [*Airport symbol*] (OAG) .... BEJ
Berber [*MARC language code Library of Congress*] (LCCP) .... ber
Berbera [*Somalia*] [*Airport symbol*] (OAG) .... BBO
Berbera [*Somalia*] [*ICAO location identifier*] (ICLI) .... HCMI
Berberati [*Central African Republic*] [*ICAO location identifier*] (ICLI) .... FEFT
Berck-Sur-Mer [*France ICAO location identifier*] (ICLI) .... LFAM
Berclair, TX [*Location identifier FAA*] (FAAL) .... NGT
Berea College, Berea, KY [*OCLC symbol*] (OCLC) .... KBE
Berea College, Berea, KY [*Library symbol Library of Congress*] (LCLS) .... KyBB
Berea, KY [*AM radio station call letters*] .... WKXO
Berea, KY [*FM radio station call letters*] .... WKXO-FM
Berea, OH [*FM radio station call letters*] .... WBWC

Berean Bible College, Calgary, AB, Canada [*Library symbol Library of Congress*] (LCLS) .... CaACBB
Berean Bible Society (EA) .... BBS
Bereave (ABBR) .... BRVE
Bereaved (ABBR) .... BRVED
Bereaved Children's Program [*Later, BC*] (EA) .... BCP
Bereavement Center (EA) .... BC
Bereavement Services & Community Education (AC) .... LIFT
Bereina [*Papua New Guinea*] [*Airport symbol*] (OAG) .... BEA
Bereitschaftsstellung [*Line of support*] [*German military - World War II*] .... BST
Berens River [*Canada*] [*Airport symbol*] (OAG) .... YBV
Beresford Public Library, Beresford, SD [*Library symbol Library of Congress*] (LCLS) .... SdBer
Bereshit Rabba (BJA) .... BerRabb
Bereshit Rabba (BJA) .... BR
Berg Electronics [*NYSE symbol*] (TTSB) .... BEI
Berg Electronics Corp. [*NYSE symbol*] (SAG) .... BEI
Berg Electronics Corp. [*Associated Press*] (SAG) .... BergElc
Berga [*Sweden ICAO location identifier*] (ICLI) .... ESQP
Bergamo [*Italy*] [*Airport symbol*] (OAG) .... BGY
Bergamo/Orio Al Serio [*Italy ICAO location identifier*] (ICLI) .... LIME
Bergen [*Norway*] [*Seismograph station code, US Geological Survey*] (SEIS) .... BER
Bergen [*Norway*] [*Airport symbol*] (OAG) .... BGO
Bergen [*Norway ICAO location identifier*] (ICLI) .... ENVV
Bergen Brunswig [*Associated Press*] (SAG) .... BergBr
Bergen Brunswig 'A' [*NYSE symbol*] (TTSB) .... BBC
Bergen Brunswig Corp. [*NYSE symbol*] (SPSG) .... BBC
Bergen Citizen, Edgewater, NJ [*Library symbol Library of Congress*] (LCLS) .... NjEwB
Bergen Community College, Paramus, NJ [*OCLC symbol*] (OCLC) .... BER
Bergen Community College, Paramus, NJ [*Library symbol Library of Congress*] (LCLS) .... NjParB
Bergen County Historical Society, North Hackensack, NJ [*Library symbol Library of Congress*] (LCLS) .... NjNhBHi
Bergen/Flesland [*Norway ICAO location identifier*] (ICLI) .... ENBR
Bergen Gazette, Inc., Garfield, NJ [*Library symbol Library of Congress*] (LCLS) .... NjGaB
Bergen News, Palisades Park, NJ [*Library symbol Library of Congress*] (LCLS) .... NjPalN
Bergen Reading Center, Bergen, NY [*Library symbol Library of Congress*] (LCLS) .... NBerR
Bergen Record, Hackensack, NJ [*Library symbol Library of Congress*] (LCLS) .... NjHackR
Bergenfield Free Public Library, Bergenfield, NJ [*Library symbol Library of Congress*] (LCLS) .... NjBer
Bergen-Hohne [*Germany ICAO location identifier*] (ICLI) .... EDZB
Berger Hldgs Ltd [*NASDAQ symbol*] (TTSB) .... BGRH
Berger Holdings, Inc. [*Associated Press*] (SAG) .... BergHld
Berger Holdings, Inc. [*NASDAQ symbol*] (SAG) .... BGRH
Bergerac [*France*] [*Airport symbol Obsolete*] (OAG) .... EGC
Bergerac/Roumaniere [*France ICAO location identifier*] (ICLI) .... LFBE
Berger's Disease [*Medicine*] .... BD
Berggiesshubel [*German Democratic Republic*] [*Seismograph station code, US Geological Survey*] (SEIS) .... BRG
Berglynn Resources [*Vancouver Stock Exchange symbol*] .... BGN
Bergneustadt/Auf Dem Dumpel [*Germany ICAO location identifier*] (ICLI) .... EDKF
Bergstrom Capital [*AMEX symbol*] (SPSG) .... BEM
Bergstrom Capital Corp. [*Associated Press*] (SAG) .... BergCa
Berhad [*Public Limited Company*] [*Malaysia*] (FEA) .... BHD
Beriault Branch, Gloucester Public Library, Ontario [*Library symbol National Library of Canada*] (NLC) .... OGB
Berichte. Verhandlungen der Saechsischen Gesellschaft der Wissenschaften zu Leipzig [*A publication*] (OCD) .... Ber Sachs Ges Wiss
Beriev [*Russian aircraft designation*] (DOMA) Be2
Bering [*Komandorsky Islands*] [*Former USSR Seismograph station code, US Geological Survey*] (SEIS) .... BKI
Bering Air, Inc. [*ICAO designator*] (FAAC) .... BRG
Bering Sea, AK [*Location identifier FAA*] (FAAL) .... OCV
Bering Sea Expedition [*or Experiment*] .... BESEX
Bering Sea Fisheries-Oceanography Cooperation Investigations [*Marine science*] (OSRA) .... BS FOCI
Bering Sea FOCI [*Fisheries-Oceanography Cooperative Investigations*] (USDC) .... BS FOCI
Bering Sea Marine Mammal Experiment [*National Oceanic and Atmospheric Administration*] (MSC) .... BESMEX
Bering Sea Patrol [*Navy*] .... BERSEAPAT
Bering Standard Time (HGAA) .... BST
Beringovsky [*Former USSR ICAO location identifier*] (ICLI) .... UHMR
Berkeley [*England*] .... BERK
Berkeley [*California*] (BARN) .... Berk
Berkeley Association (EA) .... BA
Berkeley, CA [*Location identifier FAA*] (FAAL) .... JBK
Berkeley, CA [*FM radio station call letters*] .... KALX
Berkeley, CA [*FM radio station call letters*] (RBYB) .... KBLX
Berkeley, CA [*FM radio station call letters*] .... KPFA
Berkeley, CA [*FM radio station call letters*] .... KPFB
Berkeley, CA [*AM radio station call letters*] .... KVTO
Berkeley County Library, Moncks Corner, SC [*Library symbol*] [*Library of Congress*] (LCLS) .... ScMoc
Berkeley Elites Automated Retrieval [*University of California at Berkeley*] [*Information service or system*] (NITA) .... BEAR
Berkeley Enthusiasts Club [*Woking, Surrey, England*] (EAIO) .... BEC
Berkeley Exchange (EA) .... BE
Berkeley Geochronology Center .... BGC

Berkeley Historical Society, Berkeley, CA [*Library symbol*] [*Library of Congress*] (LCLS) .... CBHi
Berkeley Macintosh Users' Group (IID) .... BMUG
Berkeley Nuclear Laboratories [*England*] .... BNL
Berkeley Particle Data Center .... BPDC
Berkeley Particle Data Group [*Lawrence Radiation Laboratory*] .... BPDG
Berkeley Public Library, Berkeley, CA [*Library symbol Library of Congress*] (LCLS) .... CB
Berkeley Public Library, Berkeley, IL [*Library symbol Library of Congress*] (LCLS) .... IBerk
Berkeley Roundtable on the International Economy [*University of California*] .... BRIE
Berkeley Software Design, Inc. .... BSDI
Berkeley Software Design, Inc. .... BSDI
Berkeley Software Distribution [*University of California*] [*Computer science*] (TNIG) .... BSD
Berkeley Software Distribution UNIX (CDE) .... BSD UNIX
Berkeley Springs, WV [*AM radio station call letters*] .... WCST
Berkeley Springs, WV [*FM radio station call letters*] .... WCST-FM
Berkeley Springs, WV [*FM radio station call letters*] (RBYB) .... WDHC-FM
Berkeley Standard Distribution [*Computer science*] (BYTE) .... BSD
Berkeley Version (BJA) .... BV
Berkeley-Byerly [*California*] [*Seismograph station code, US Geological Survey*] (SEIS) .... BKS
Berkeley-Haviland [*California*] [*Seismograph station code, US Geological Survey*] (SEIS) .... BRK
Berkeley-Illinois-Maryland Association [*Consortium for astronomical study*] .... BIMA
Berkeley-Oakland Service System [*Library network*] .... BOSS
Berkelium [*Chemical element*] .... Bk
Berkely [*W.R.*] Corp. [*Associated Press*] (SAG) .... Berkly
Berkley [*W.R.*] Corp. [*Associated Press*] (SAG) .... Berkley
Berkley [*W. R.*] Corp. [*NASDAQ symbol*] (NQ) .... BKLY
Berkley Heights Public Library, Berkley Heights, NJ [*Library symbol Library of Congress*] (LCLS) .... NjBh
Berkley Resources, Inc. [*Vancouver Stock Exchange symbol*] .... BKS
Berkley(W.R.)7.375% Dep'A'Pfd [*NASDAQ symbol*] (TTSB) .... BKLYZ
Berks Community Television [*Reading, PA*] [*Telecommunications*] (TSSD) .... BCTV
Berkshire [*County in England*] .... BERKS
Berkshire [*County in England*] (ODBW) .... Berks
Berkshire (FAAC) .... BRKSHR
Berkshire and Westminster Dragoons [*British military*] (DMA) .... B & W Dgns
Berkshire Athenaeum, Pittsfield, MA [*Library symbol Library of Congress*] (LCLS) .... MPB
Berkshire Christian College, Lenox, MA [*Library symbol Library of Congress*] (LCLS) .... MLenB
Berkshire Community College [*Pittsfield, MA*] .... BCC
Berkshire Community College, Pittsfield, MA [*Library symbol Library of Congress*] (LCLS) .... MPBC
Berkshire Gas [*NASDAQ symbol*] (TTSB) .... BGAS
Berkshire Gas Co. [*Associated Press*] (SAG) .... BerkGs
Berkshire Gas Co. [*NASDAQ symbol*] (NQ) .... BGAS
Berkshire Hathaway [*Associated Press*] (SAG) .... BerkH
Berkshire Hathaway, Inc. [*Associated Press*] (SAG) .... BerkHa
Berkshire Hathaway, Inc. [*NYSE symbol*] (CTT) .... BRK
Berkshire Law Library Association, Pittsfield, MA [*Library symbol Library of Congress*] (LCLS) .... MPBL
Berkshire Realty [*NYSE symbol*] (TTSB) .... BRI
Berkshire Realty Co., Inc. [*Associated Press*] (SAG) .... BerkR
Berkshire Realty Company, Inc. [*Associated Press*] (SAG) .... BerkRty
Berkshire Realty, Inc. [*NYSE symbol*] (SPSG) .... BRI
Berkshire Yeomanry Cavalry [*British military*] (DMA) .... BYC
Berle Resources Ltd. [*Vancouver Stock Exchange symbol*] .... BRL
Berlevag [*Norway*] [*Airport symbol*] (OAG) .... BVG
Berlevag [*Norway ICAO location identifier*] (ICLI) .... ENBV
Berlin [*Germany*] [*Airport symbol*] (OAG) .... BER
Berlin (ROG) .... BERL
Berlin [*New Hampshire*] [*Seismograph station code, US Geological Survey*] (SEIS) .... BNH
Berlin [*West Germany*] [*Seismograph station code, US Geological Survey*] (SEIS) .... BRN
Berlin [*Germany ICAO location identifier*] (ICLI) .... EDBA
Berlin [*Germany Airport symbol*] (OAG) .... SXF
Berlin [*Germany Airport symbol*] (OAG) .... TXL
Berlin Air Safety Center .... BASC
Berlin Airlift Device [*Military decoration*] .... BAD
Berlin Airlift Device [*Military decoration*] (AABC) .... BerADev
Berlin Airlift Device [*Military decoration*] .... BERDEV
Berlin Border Guard [*East Germany*] .... BBG
Berlin Brigade .... BB
Berlin Brigade .... BBDE
Berlin Command [*Allied German Occupation Forces*] .... BC
Berlin Commission British [*Post-World War II*] .... BERCOMB
Berlin Contingency [*NATO*] (NATG) .... BERCON
Berlin Control Zone [*Allied German Occupation Forces*] .... BCZ
Berlin, CT [*FM radio station call letters*] .... WERB
Berlin District [*Allied German Occupation Forces*] .... BD
Berlin Document Center [*Allied German Occupation Forces*] .... BDC
Berlin Electron Storage Ring for Synchrotron Radiation .... BESSY
Berlin European [*ICAO designator*] (FAAC) .... ECJ
Berlin European [*ICAO designator*] (AD) .... WZ
Berlin Fan Club [*Defunct*] (EA) .... BFC
Berlin - Free University [*West Germany*] [*Seismograph station code, US Geological Survey*] (SEIS) .... BRL

Berlin/Gatow [*Germany ICAO location identifier*] (ICLI) .... EDBG
Berlin Kommandatura .... BK
Berlin, MD [*FM radio station call letters*] .... WOCQ
Berlin Mills [*AAR code*] .... BMS
Berlin, NH [*Location identifier FAA*] (FAAL) .... BML
Berlin, NH [*Location identifier FAA*] (FAAL) .... HXK
Berlin, NH [*AM radio station call letters*] .... WMOU
Berlin, NH [*FM radio station call letters*] (RBYB) .... WPKQ-FM
Berlin, NH [*FM radio station call letters*] .... WZPK
Berlin, NJ [*FM radio station call letters*] .... WNJS
Berlin Papyri [*A publication*] (OCD) .... PBerol
Berlin Philharmonic Orchestra .... BPO
Berlin Public Library, Berlin, WI [*Library symbol Library of Congress*] (LCLS) .... WBer
Berlin/Schonefeld [*Germany ICAO location identifier*] (ICLI) .... ETBN
Berlin/Schonefeld [*Germany ICAO location identifier*] (ICLI) .... ETBS
Berlin Sector [*Allied German Occupation Forces*] .... BS
Berlin State Opera Orchestra .... BSOO
Berlin/Tegel [*Germany ICAO location identifier*] (ICLI) .... EDBT
Berlin/Tempelhof [*Germany ICAO location identifier*] (ICLI) .... EDBB
Berlin U.S.A. [*ICAO designator*] (AD) .... ZF
Berlin, WI [*AM radio station call letters*] .... WISS
Berlin, WI [*FM radio station call letters*] .... WISS-FM
[*The*] **Berline, Berlin-Brandenburgisches Luftfahrtunternehmen GmbH** [*Germany ICAO designator*] (FAAC) .... TBL
Berliner Beitraege zur Keilschriftforschung [*A publication*] (BJA) .... BBK
Berliner, Cohen & Biogini, Law Library, San Jose, CA [*Library symbol Library of Congress*] (LCLS) .... CSjB
Berliner, Coher & Biogini, Law Library, San Jose, CA [*Library symbol*] [*Library of Congress*] (LCLS) .... CSjBC
Berliner Griechische Urkunden [*A publication*] (OCD) .... BGU
Berliner Handels- & Frankfurter Bank [*Berlin & Frankfurt Bank*] .... BHF
Berliner Klassikertexte [*A publication*] (OCD) .... BKT
Berliner Konferenz Europaischer Katholiken [*Berlin Conference of European Catholics*] [*Germany*] (EAIO) .... BK
Berliner Philologische Wochenschrift [*A publication*] (OCD) .... B Phil Woch
Berliner Verkehrs-Gesellschaft [*Later, Berliner Verkehrs-Betriebe*] [*Berlin Transport West Berlin*] .... BVG
Berliner Zionistische Vereinigung [*A publication*] (BJA) .... BZV
Berlinetta Boxer [*Ferrari sports car*] .... BB
Berlitz International [*Associated Press*] (SAG) .... Berlitz
Berlitz International [*NYSE symbol*] (SPSG) .... BTZ
Bermejo [*Bolivia*] [*ICAO location identifier*] (ICLI) .... SLBJ
Bermuda [*Airport symbol*] (OAG) .... BDA
Bermuda (DLA) .... BERM
Bermuda [*MARC country of publication code Library of Congress*] (LCCP) .... bm
Bermuda [*ANSI two-letter standard code*] (CNC) .... BM
Bermuda [*ANSI three-letter standard code*] (CNC) .... BMU
Bermuda [*IYRU nationality code*] (IYR) .... KB
Bermuda [*MARC geographic area code Library of Congress*] (LCCP) .... lnbm--
Bermuda Atlantic Time Series [*Oceanographic Station*] .... BATS
Bermuda Base Command [*World War II*] .... BBC
Bermuda Benevolent Association .... BBA
Bermuda Dunes, CA [*Location identifier FAA*] (FAAL) .... UDD
Bermuda Island (NASA) .... BDA
Bermuda Islands (BARN) .... Ber Is
Bermuda Islands .... BI
Bermuda Law Reports [*A publication*] (DLA) .... BLR
Bermuda Library, Hamilton, Bermudas [*Library symbol Library of Congress*] (LCLS) .... BmuHB
Bermuda Naval Air Station [*Bermuda*] [*ICAO location identifier*] (ICLI) .... TXKF
Bermuda - Navy [*Bermuda*] [*Seismograph station code, US Geological Survey Closed*] (SEIS) .... BEN
Bermuda Plan [*Travel accomodations*] .... BP
Bermuda Range Safety Officer [*NASA*] (KSC) .... BRSO
Bermuda Resources Ltd. [*Vancouver Stock Exchange symbol*] .... BDA
Bermuda Star Lines, Inc. (MHDW) .... BSL
Bermuda Tracking Station [*NASA*] (KSC) .... BDA
Bermuda-Columbia [*Bermuda*] [*Seismograph station code, US Geological Survey*] (SEIS) .... BEC
Bermuda-Schwortz Industries, Inc. [*Vancouver Stock Exchange symbol*] .... BWT
Bern/Belp [*Switzerland ICAO location identifier*] (ICLI) .... LSZB
Bern. Office Federal de l'Air [*Switzerland ICAO location identifier*] (ICLI) .... LSSO
Bern Radio [*Switzerland ICAO location identifier*] (ICLI) .... LSSB
Bern Resources Ltd. [*Vancouver Stock Exchange symbol*] .... BER
Bernadia [*Italy*] [*Seismograph station code, US Geological Survey*] (SEIS) .... BERI
Bernard Berenson [*American art critic, 1865-1959*] .... BB
Bernard Geis Associates [*Publisher*] [*Obsolete*] .... BGA
Bernard Haldane [*Commercial firm Associated Press*] (SAG) .... BerHald
Bernard Haldane [*NASDAQ symbol*] (SAG) .... BHAL
Bernard Haldane Assoc Inc. [*NASDAQ symbol*] (TTSB) .... BHAL
Bernard Herrmann Society (EA) .... BHS
Bernard Johnson, Inc., Houston, TX [*Library symbol*] [*Library of Congress*] (LCLS) .... TxHBJ
Bernard M. Baruch College of the City University of New York (GAGS) .... Baruch C (CUNY)
Bernard M. Baruch College of the City University of New York, New York, NY [*Library symbol Library of Congress*] (LCLS) .... NNBBC
Bernard Shaw Society (EA) .... BSS
Bernard van Risenburgh [*Label stamped on works by the master ebeniste*] .... BVRB
Bernard-Henri Levy [*French writer and philosopher*] .... BHL
Bernardine Sisters of the Third Order of St. Francis (TOCD) .... OSF
Bernardo De Irigoyen [*Argentina ICAO location identifier*] (ICLI) .... SATI
Bernard's Church Cases [*Ireland*] [*A publication*] (DLA) .... Bern
Bernard's Church Cases [*Ireland*] [*A publication*] (DLA) .... Bern Ch Cas
Bernards Township Library, Inc., Basking Ridge, NJ [*Library symbol Library of Congress*] (LCLS) .... NjBas
Bernard-Soulier Syndrome [*Hematology*] .... BSS
Bernardsville Library Association, Bernardsville, NJ [*Library symbol Library of Congress*] (LCLS) .... NjBern
Bernardsville News, Bernardsville, NJ [*Library symbol Library of Congress*] (LCLS) .... NBernN
Bernardsville News, Bernardsville, NJ [*Library symbol Library of Congress*] (LCLS) .... NjBernN
Bernardus Compostellanus [*Authority cited in pre-1607 legal work*] (DSA) .... B Compos
Bernardus Compostellanus [*Authority cited in pre-1607 legal work*] (DSA) .... Ber Compos
Bernardus Compostellanus, Junior [*Deceased, 1267*] [*Authority cited in pre-1607 legal work*] (DSA) .... B
Bernardus Compostellanus, Senior [*Flourished, 1198-1216*] [*Authority cited in pre-1607 legal work*] (DSA) .... B
Bernardus Compostellanus, Senior [*Flourished, 1198-1216*] [*Authority cited in pre-1607 legal work*] (DSA) .... Ber
Bernardus de Bottone de Parma [*Deceased, 1266*] [*Authority cited in pre-1607 legal work*] (DSA) .... B
Bernardus de Bottone de Parma [*Deceased, 1266*] [*Authority cited in pre-1607 legal work*] (DSA) .... Ber
Bernardus de Bottone de Parma [*Deceased, 1266*] [*Authority cited in pre-1607 legal work*] (DSA) .... Bern
Bernardus de Bottone de Parma [*Deceased, 1266*] [*Authority cited in pre-1607 legal work*] (DSA) .... Bernar
Bernardus de Pavia [*Deceased, 1213*] [*Authority cited in pre-1607 legal work*] (DSA) .... B
Bernardus Maynardi [*Authority cited in pre-1607 legal work*] (DSA) .... B May
Bernardus Maynardi [*Authority cited in pre-1607 legal work*] (DSA) .... Ber May
Bernardus Papiensis [*Deceased, 1213*] [*Authority cited in pre-1607 legal work*] (DSA) .... B Pa
Bernardus Saporis [*Flourished, 1327-36*] [*Authority cited in pre-1607 legal work*] (DSA) .... B Sapo
Bernardus Saporis [*Flourished, 1327-36*] [*Authority cited in pre-1607 legal work*] (DSA) .... B Sapor
Bernay/Saint-Martin [*France ICAO location identifier*] (ICLI) .... LFPD
Berne [*Switzerland*] [*Airport symbol*] (OAG) .... BRN
Berne, IN [*FM radio station call letters*] .... WZBD
Berne Public Library, Berne, IN [*Library symbol Library of Congress*] (LCLS) .... InBer
Berne Public Library, Berne, IN [*OCLC symbol*] (OCLC) .... XBB
Berne/Radio Suisse SA [*Switzerland ICAO location identifier*] (ICLI) .... LSSR
Berner High School, Massapequa, NY [*Library symbol Library of Congress*] (LCLS) .... NMassBH
Berner Oberland-Bahnen [*Bernese Overland Railways*] .... BOB
Bernese Mountain Dog Club of America (EA) .... BMDCA
Bernice Pauahi Bishop Museum, Honolulu, HI [*Library symbol Library of Congress*] (LCLS) .... HHB
Bernie [*Missouri*] [*Seismograph station code, US Geological Survey Closed*] (SEIS) .... BRM
Bernoulli Disk .... BD
Bernoulli Number [*Mathematics*] .... B
Bernoulli Society for Mathematical Statistics and Probability [*Voorburg, Netherlands*] (EA) .... BSMSP
Bernstein & Associates [*Computer science*] .... B&A
Bernstein, Lee, Yang, Primakoff [*Physicists*] .... BLYP
Beroroha [*Madagascar*] [*Airport symbol*] (OAG) .... WBO
Beroroha/Antsoa [*Madagascar*] [*ICAO location identifier*] (ICLI) .... FMSB
Berre-La-Fare [*France ICAO location identifier*] (ICLI) .... LFNR
Berridale [*Airport symbol*] .... BRE
Berrien Springs, MI [*FM radio station call letters*] .... WAUS
Berry (ABBR) .... BRY
Berry .... BRY
Berry Aviation, Inc. [*ICAO designator*] (FAAC) .... AHS
Berry College (GAGS) .... Berry C
Berry College, Mount Berry, GA [*OCLC symbol*] (OCLC) .... GBC
Berry College, Mount Berry, GA [*Library symbol Library of Congress*] (LCLS) .... GMtbC
Berry, Fruit, or Vegetable [*Freight*] .... BERRY F V
Berry Hill Elementary School, Syosset, NY [*Library symbol Library of Congress*] (LCLS) .... NSyoBE
Berry Hill, TN [*AM radio station call letters*] .... WVOL
Berry Petroleum Co. [*Associated Press*] (SAG) .... BerryP
Berry Petroleum Co. Class A [*NYSE symbol*] (SPSG) .... BRY
Berry Petroleum'A' [*NYSE symbol*] (TTSB) .... BRY
Berry Pseudorotation .... BPR
Berry, R. H., San Leandro CA [*STAC*] .... BRH
Berrying (ABBR) .... BRYG
Berryman [*Missouri*] [*Seismograph station code, US Geological Survey Closed*] (SEIS) .... BRR
Berry's Reports [*1-28 Missouri Appeals*] [*A publication*] (DLA) .... Berry
Berryville, AR [*AM radio station call letters*] .... KTHS
Berryville, AR [*FM radio station call letters*] .... KTHS-FM
Berryville, VA [*FM radio station call letters*] .... WAPP
Bersatu Rakyat Jelata Sabah [*Sabah People's Union*] [*Malaysia*] [*Political party*] (PPW) .... BERJAYA
Berserk (ABBR) .... BSRK
Bert Leston Taylor [*American columnist, 1866-1921*] [*Initials used as pseudonym*] .... BLT
Bertelsmann Music Group [*Record company*] (ECON) .... BMG
Bertelsmann Printing & Manufacturing Corp. .... BPMC
Berth (MSA) .... BTH

Berth Terms [Shipping] .... BT

Bertha Hill [Idaho] [Seismograph station code, US Geological Survey Closed] (SEIS) .... BHI

Bertha-Hweitt School, Bertha, MN [Library symbol] [Library of Congress] (LCLS) .... MnBeB

Berthing .... BERTH

Berthing Latch Interface Mechanism (SSD) .... BLIM

Berthoud Public Library, Berthoud, CO [Library symbol Library of Congress] (LCLS) .... CoBer

Berton's New Brunswick Reports [A publication] (DLA) .... Ber

Berton's New Brunswick Reports [A publication] (DLA) .... Bert

Berton's New Brunswick Reports [A publication] (DLA) .... NBR Ber

Bertoua [Cameroon] [Airport symbol] (OAG) .... BTA

Bertoua [Cameroon] [ICAO location identifier] (ICLI) .... FKKO

Bertrand Chaffee Hospital, Springville, NY [Library symbol Library of Congress] (LCLS) .... NSprvCH

Bertrand Russell Peace Foundation (EA) .... BRPF

Bertrand Russell Society (EA) .... BRS

Bertrandus [Authority cited in pre-1607 legal work] (DSA) .... Bert

Bertrandus [Authority cited in pre-1607 legal work] (DSA) .... Bertran

Bertrandus [Authority cited in pre-1607 legal work] (DSA) .... Btran

Bertrandus de Montefaventino [Deceased, 1342] [Authority cited in pre-1607 legal work] (DSA) .... B

Bertrandus de Montefaventino [Deceased, 1342] [Authority cited in pre-1607 legal work] (DSA) .... B de Monfa

Bertrandus de Montefaventino [Deceased, 1342] [Authority cited in pre-1607 legal work] (DSA) .... Bertr

Bertrix [Belgium ICAO location identifier] (ICLI) .... EBBX

Bertucci's, Inc. [NASDAQ symbol] (SPSG) .... BERT

Bertuccis, Inc. [Associated Press] (SAG) .... Bertuci

Beru [Kiribati] [Airport symbol] (OAG) .... BEZ

Beru [Kiribati] [ICAO location identifier] (ICLI) .... NGBR

Berufungsgericht [Court of Appeal] [German] (ILCA) .... BG

Berul Associates Ltd. [Information service or system] (IID) .... BAL

Berwick [Former county in Scotland] (WGA) .... BERW

Berwick, LA [FM radio station call letters] .... KBZE

Berwick, PA [FM radio station call letters] .... WKAB

Berwick, PA [AM radio station call letters] .... WSQV

Berwickshire [County in England] .... Berwicks

Berwyn Public Library, Berwyn, IL [Library symbol Library of Congress] (LCLS) .... IBer

Berwyn School, Alberta [Library symbol National Library of Canada] (BIB) .... ABWS

Berwyn WI Municipal Library, Alberta [Library symbol National Library of Canada] (NLC) .... ABWM

Berwyn W.I. Municipal Library, Berwyn, AB, Canada [Library symbol] [Library of Congress] (LCLS) .... CaABerWM

Beryl [Jewelry] (ROG) .... BERL

Beryllium [Chemical element] .... Be

Beryllium Oxide (IDOE) .... beO

Beryllium Oxide Reactor Experiment [Formerly, EBOR] [Nuclear energy] .... BORE

Beryllium Oxide Washer .... BOW

Beryllium Physics Reactor (NRCH) .... BPR

Beryllium Thrust Chamber .... BTC

Besah (BJA) .... Bes

Besalampy [Madagascar] [Airport symbol] (OAG) .... BPY

Besalampy [Madagascar] [ICAO location identifier] (ICLI) .... FMNQ

Besancon [France] [Seismograph station code, US Geological Survey] (SEIS) .... BES

Besancon/Thise [France ICAO location identifier] (ICLI) .... LFSA

Besancon-La-Veze [France ICAO location identifier] (ICLI) .... LFQM

Beseech (ABBR) .... BSCH

Beseech (ABBR) .... BSECH

Beseeched (ABBR) .... BSCHD

Beseeched (ABBR) .... BSECHD

Beseeching (ABBR) .... BSCHG

Besicorp Group [Associated Press] (SAG) .... Besicp

Besicorp Group [AMEX symbol] (SAG) .... BGI

Besicorp Group [ECM Symbol] (TTSB) .... BGIEC

Beside (ABBR) .... BSD

Beside (ABBR) .... BSID

Besiege (ABBR) .... BSEG

Besiege (ABBR) .... BSG

Besieged (ABBR) .... BSEGD

Besieged (ABBR) .... BSGD

Besieging (ABBR) .... BSEGG

Besieging (ABBR) .... BSGG

Besloten Vennootschap [Private or Closed Limited Company] [Dutch] .... BV

Besmear (ABBR) .... BSMER

Besmear (ABBR) .... BSMR

Besmeared (ABBR) .... BSMRD

Besmearing (ABBR) .... BSMRG

Besmirch (ABBR) .... BSMRCH

Besonders [Particularly] [German] .... BSD

Bess Kaiser Foundation Hospital, Medical Library, Portland, OR [Library symbol Library of Congress] (LCLS) .... OrPBK

Bess Kaiser Foundation Hospital, Medical Library, Portland, OR [Library symbol Library of Congress] (LCLS) .... OrPK

Bess Tilson Sprinkle Memorial Library, Weaverville, NC [Library symbol Library of Congress] (LCLS) .... NcWea

Bessel Function [Mathematics] (IAA) .... BES

Bessel Function Model (MCD) .... BFM

Besseler. Musik des Mittelalters und der Renaissance [A publication] .... BeMMR

Bessemer [Metallurgy] .... BESS

Bessemer, AL [Location identifier FAA] (FAAL) .... BEQ

Bessemer, AL [AM radio station call letters] .... WSMQ

Bessemer & Lake Erie Railroad Co. .... B & LE

Bessemer & Lake Erie Railroad Co. [AAR code] .... BLE

Bessemer Public Library, Bessemer, MI [Library symbol Library of Congress] (LCLS) .... MiBes

Bessey-Lowry Unit [Medicine] (MAE) .... BL

Bessey-Lowry Unit (MAE) .... BLU

Bessey-Lowry-Brock Unit [Medicine] (MAE) .... BLB

Bessie Smith Society (EA) .... BSS

Besson [Frank S.] Memorial Award [American Defense Preparedness Association] (RDA) .... BMA

Besson's New Jersey Precedents [A publication] (DLA) .... Bess Prec

Best [Moody's bond rating] [Investment term] .... Aaa

Best (IAA) .... B

Best (ROG) .... BST

Best Adaptive Path [NASA] .... BAP

Best Alternative Equally Effective Data System .... BAEDS

Best and Final Offer .... B/F

Best and Final Offer [DoD] (MCD) .... BAFO

Best and Revised Final Offer [DoD] .... BARFO

Best and Smith's English Queen's Bench Reports [A publication] (DLA) .... B & S

Best and Smith's English Queen's Bench Reports [A publication] (DLA) .... Best & S

Best and Smith's English Queen's Bench Reports [A publication] (DLA) .... Best & S (Eng)

Best and Smith's English Queen's Bench Reports [A publication] (DLA) .... Best & Sm

Best Asymptotically Normal [Estimates] [Econometrics] .... BAN

Best Available (WDMC) .... BA

Best Available (WDMC) .... ba

Best Available and Safest Technology .... BAST

Best Available Control Technology [Environmental Protection Agency] .... BACT

Best Available Demonstrated Control Technology [Environmental Protection Agency] .... BADCT

Best Available Demonstrated Technology [Environmental Protection Agency] (FFDE) .... BADT

Best Available Retrofit Facility [Environmental Protection Agency] (GFGA) .... BARF

Best Available Retrofit Technology [Environmental Protection Agency] .... BART

Best Available Shelter Survey [of fallout shelters] [Civil Defense] .... BASS

Best Available Technology .... BAT

Best Available Technology Economically Achievable [Wastewater treatment] .... BATEA

Best Available Technology Not Entailing Excessive Costs [British] .... BATNEEC

Best Available Treatment (MCD) .... BAT

Best Available True Heading (MCD) .... BATH

Best Average Definition Over the Picture Area (SAA) .... BADOPA

Best Berlin Broadcast [Radio program broadcast from Berlin by Robert H. Best, former South Carolina journalist] [World War II] .... BBB

Best Black [Pencil leads] (ROG) .... BB

Best Building Economic Solutions Together [Committee redesigning the defunct Charleston Navy Base and Shipyard] (ECON) .... BEST

Best Buy Cap 6.50%'MIPS' [NYSE symbol] (TTSB) .... BBYPrM

Best Buy Capital Ltd. [Associated Press] (SAG) .... BestB

Best Buy Capital LP [NYSE symbol] (SAG) .... BBY

Best Buy Co. [Bloomington, MN] [NYSE symbol] (SPSG) .... BBY

Best Buy Co. [Associated Press] (SAG) .... BestBuy

Best Candidate Committee (EA) .... BCC

Best Commercial Flight Line Test Set (MCD) .... BCFLS

Best Control Technology [Environmental Protection Agency] (ERG) .... BCT

Best Controlled Similar Source Emission [Environmental Protection Agency] .... BCSSE

Best Conventional Pollutant Control Technology (GNE) .... BCT

Best Conventional Technology [Environmental Protection Agency] .... BCT

Best Copy Available .... BCA

Best Corrected Visual Acuity [Ophthalmology] .... BVA

Best Critical Region (IAA) .... BCR

Best Cruise Altitude .... BCA

Best Cruise Mach Number [Aviation] .... BCM

Best Dark Virginia [Tobacco] [British] (ROG) .... BDV

Best Delay [Audiometry] .... BD

Best Demonstrated Available Technology .... BDAT

Best Demonstrated Technology (GFGA) .... BDT

Best Depth Range [Military] (NVT) .... BDR

Best Developed Alternate [Environmental Protection Agency] .... BDAT

Best Dressed List .... BDL

Best Educational Systems for Teaching .... BEST

Best Efficiency Point (KSC) .... BEP

BEST [Beneficial Employees Security Trust] Employers Association (EA) .... BEA

Best Engineering Judgement [Environmental Protection Agency] (FFDE) .... BEJ

Best Estimate Constrained .... BEC

Best Estimate Model (NRCH) .... BE

Best Estimate of Orbital Parameters .... BEOP

Best Estimate of Trajectory [Apollo] [NASA] .... BET

Best Estimate Unconstrained .... BEU

Best Estimated Quantity (AAGC) .... BEQ

Best Ever Bottled [Wines and spirits] .... BEB

Best Evidence Rule [Legal shorthand] (LWAP) .... BER

Best Excitatory Frequency [Neurophysiology] .... BEF

Best Execution Analysis Tabulation [Computer science] .... BEAT

Best Expert Judgment [Environmental Protection Agency] (ERG) .... BEJ

Best Fit Algorithm [Mathematics] (IAA) .... BF

Best Fit Sphere (MCD) .... BFS

Best Fixed-Sample Procedure [Statistics] .... BFSP

Best Friend [Initialism used by author E. B. White to describe his wife] .... BF

Best Game [Billiards] (BARN) .... BG

Best Holiday Trav-L-Park Association (EA) ..... BHTPA
Best in Group ..... BIG
Best in Match ..... BIM
Best in Show [*Dog show term*] ..... BIS
Best Inhibitory Frequency [*Neurophysiology*] ..... BIF
Best Linear Unbiased Estimator [*Statistics*] ..... BLUE
Best Linear Unbiased Prediction [*Genetics*] ..... BLUP
Best Loiter Mach Number [*Aviation*] ..... BLM
[*The*] **Best Love Story Poems** [*A publication*] ..... BeLS
Best Loved Poems of the American People [*A publication*] ..... BLPA
Best Loved Religious Poems [*A publication*] ..... BLRP
Best Management Practice [*Environmental Protection Agency*] ..... BMP
Best Noise Figure (IAA) ..... BNF
Best of a Bad Situation ..... BBS
Best of a Kind (BARN) ..... A
Best of Both Worlds [*Apple Computer's Macintosh Due System's nickname*] [*Pronounced as a proper name: Bob W.*] ..... Bob W
Best of Breed ..... BB
Best of Breed ..... BOB
Best of Variety (WDAA) ..... BOV
Best of Winners [*Dog show term*] ..... BW
Best Offer [*Classified advertising*] ..... BO
Best on Best (MCD) ..... BOB
Best on Evidence [*A publication*] (DLA) ..... Best Ev
Best on Presumptions of Law and Fact [*A publication*] (DLA) ..... Best Pres
Best on Presumptions of Law and Fact [*A publication*] (DLA) ..... Best Presumptions
Best on the Right to Begin and Reply [*A publication*] (DLA) ..... Best Beg & Rep
Best on Trial by Jury [*A publication*] (DLA) ..... Best Jur Tr
Best Operational Capability ..... BOC
Best Opposite Sex (to Best of Breed) [*Dog show term*] ..... BOS
Best Output and Color [*Computer science*] (IAA) ..... BOC
Best Practicable Control Technology [*Wastewater treatment*] ..... BPCT
Best Practicable Control Technology Currently Available (MCD) ..... BPCTCA
Best Practicable Control Technology Currently Available [*Clean Water Act*] (ERG) ..... BPTCA
Best Practicable Environmental Option (ECON) ..... BPEO
Best Practicable Means ..... BPM
Best Practicable Technology [*Environmental Protection Agency*] ..... BPT
Best Practicable Treatment (GNE) ..... BPT
Best Practicable Waste Treatment Technology (EG) ..... BPWTT
Best Practical Control Method [*Wastewater treatment*] (DICI) ..... BPCM
Best Practical Means [*Business term*] (DCTA) ..... BPM
Best Preliminary Estimate (AFM) ..... BPE
Best Products [*NASDAQ symbol*] (TTSB) ..... BEST
Best Products Co., Inc. [*NASDAQ symbol*] (SAG) ..... BEST
Best Products Company, Inc. [*Associated Press*] (SAG) ..... BestPd
Best Professional Judgment [*Environmental Protection Agency*] ..... BPJ
Best Range of Aging Verified Oscillator (MUGU) ..... BRAVO
Best Replacement Factor (CAAL) ..... BRF
Best Resources, Inc. [*Vancouver Stock Exchange symbol*] ..... BST
Best Speed Rating [*of a horse*] ..... BSR
Best Straight Line [*Mathematics*] ..... BSL
Best Support Concept Approach ..... BSCA
Best Technical Approach [*Military*] (AABC) ..... BTA
Best Technology Generally Available [*Environmental Protection Agency*] ..... BTGA
Best Time of the Day [*Automotive racing*] ..... BTD
Best Times Available [*Television*] ..... BTA
Best Value Selection (AAGC) ..... BVS
Best Western Motels [*Motel chain*] ..... BWM
Bestand Juedischer Gemeinden in Staatsarchiv Hamburg [*A publication*] (BJA) ..... BJG
Best-Estimated Evaluation Trajectory [*NASA*] (KSC) ..... BEET
Best-Fit Central Y-Plane ..... BFCY-P
Best-Fit Optic Z-Plane ..... BFOZ-P
Bestial (ABBR) ..... BSTL
Bestiality (ABBR) ..... BSTLT
Bestially (ABBR) ..... BSTLY
Bestow (ABBR) ..... BSTO
Bestow (ABBR) ..... BSTW
Bestowable (ABBR) ..... BSTWB
Bestowal (ABBR) ..... BSTWL
Bestowed (ABBR) ..... BSTWD
Bestowing (ABBR) ..... BSTWG
Bestowment (ABBR) ..... BSTWT
Best's Law Dictionary [*A publication*] (DLA) ..... Best Law Dic
Bestway Inc. [*NASDAQ symbol*] (TTSB) ..... BSTW
Bet 'Eked Sefarim (BJA) ..... BES
BET Holdings [*NYSE symbol*] (SPSG) ..... BTV
Bet Holdings, Inc. [*Associated Press*] (SAG) ..... BetHld
BET Holdings'A' [*NYSE symbol*] (TTSB) ..... BTV
Bet Ltd. ADS [*NYSE symbol Toronto Stock Exchange symbol*] (SPSG) ..... BEP
Bet Midrash le Torah (BJA) ..... BMT
Bet Nahrain (EA) ..... BN
BET PLC [*Associated Press*] (SAG) ..... BET Plc
BET Public Ltd ADS [*NYSE symbol*] (TTSB) ..... BEP
Bet Ya'akov Lekhu ve-Nelkhah (BJA) ..... BILU
Beta ..... B
Beta Absorption Gauge ..... BAG
Beta Activity [*Measure of radioactivity*] ..... BA
Beta Alpha Psi (EA) ..... BAP
Beta Alternating Transmission System (MCD) ..... BATS
Beta Anneal (PDAA) ..... BA
Beta, Atla, and Themis [*Regions on planet Venus*] ..... BAT
Beta, Beta-Dicyano-O-Chlorostyrene [*Organic chemistry*] (DAVI) ..... CS
Beta Disintegration Energy ..... BDE
Beta Environmental Fine Structure [*Physics*] ..... BEFS
Beta Gamma Sigma ..... BGS
Beta Human Chorionic Gonadotropin [*Endocrinology*] (DAVI) ..... B-HCG
Beta Solar Array Drive (SSD) ..... BSAD
Beta Spectrometer ..... BS
Beta Thickness Gauge (DEN) ..... BTG
Beta-1-C [*Also called complement C_3*] [*Biochemistry*] (DAVI) B-1-C
Beta-Alumina Solid Electrolyte ..... BASE
Beta-Aminoisobutyric Acid (MAE) ..... BAIB
Beta-Aminopropionitrile [*Organic chemistry*] ..... BAPN
Beta-Amyloid Precursor Protein ..... BAPP
Beta-Androgenic Receptor Kinase [*An enzyme*] ..... B-ARK
Beta-Anyloid Protein Bi-Anyloid Protein ..... BAP
Beta-Blocker [*Pharmacology*] (DAVI) ..... BB
Beta-Blocker Heart Attack Trial [*Cardiology*] ..... BHAT
Beta-Carotene [*Biochemistry*] ..... BC
Beta-Cedrene ..... BCDR
Beta-Cyclodextrin [*Organic chemistry*] ..... BCD
Beta-Endorphin [*Biochemistry*] ..... B-END
Betagalactoside ..... BGal
Beta-Gamma ..... BG
Beta-Glucuronidase [*Organic chemistry*] (DAVI) ..... GRS
Beta-Glycerophosphatase (MAE) ..... BGP
Beta-Hemolytic Streptococcus [*Medicine*] ..... BHS
Beta-Hydroxybutyric Acid (MAE) ..... BHBA
Beta-Hydroxyethylhydrazine [*Plant growth compound*] ..... BOH
(Beta-Hydroxyethyl)theophylline [*Biochemistry*] ..... BHET
(Beta-Hydroxypropyl)theophylline [*Biochemistry*] ..... BHPT
Beta-Hydroxysteroid Dehydrogenase [*An enzyme*] ..... BHD
Beta-Hydroxytheophylline [*Medicine*] (DMAA) ..... BHT
Beta-Ionone [*Biochemistry*] ..... BI
Beta-Lactamase Inhibitory Protein [*Biochemistry*] ..... BLIP
Beta-Lactoglobulin [*Biochemistry*] ..... BLG
Beta-Lipoprotein [*Medicine*] (DMAA) ..... BLP
Betamax [*First home VCR (Video Cassette Recorder) format*] (CDE) ..... Beta
Beta-Mercaptoethanol [*Organic chemistry*] ..... BME
Betamethasone Acetate [*Medicine*] (DMAA) ..... BA
Betamethasone Valerate [*Glucocorticoid*] ..... BV
Beta-Methylamino-alanine [*An amino acid*] ..... BMAA
Beta-Methylheptadecanoic Acid [*Organic chemistry*] ..... BMHDA
Beta-Naphthoflavone [*Organic chemistry*] ..... BNF
Beta-Naphthol [*Organic chemistry*] ..... BN
Beta-Naphthoxyacetic Acid [*Plant growth compound*] ..... BNOA
Beta-Naphthylamine [*Organic chemistry*] ..... BNA
Beta-Nitropropionic Acid [*Organic chemistry*] ..... BNPA
Beta-Oxalylamino-alanine [*An amino acid*] ..... BOAA
Beta-Oxybutyric Acid [*Organic chemistry*] (MAE) ..... BOBA
Beta-Oxynaphthoic Acid [*Also, BONA*] [*Organic chemistry*] ..... BON
Beta-Oxynaphthoic Acid [*Also, BON*] [*Organic chemistry*] ..... BONA
Beta-Propriolactone [*Organic chemistry*] ..... BPL
Betar Brith Trumpeldor (EA) ..... BBT
Betare-Oya [*Cameroon*] [*ICAO location identifier*] (ICLI) ..... FKAO
Beta-Resorcylic Acid [*Organic chemistry*] ..... BRA
Beta-Streptococcus Group A [*Bacteriology*] (DAVI) ..... BSGA
Beta-Thromboglobulin [*Hematology*] ..... BTG
Betera [*Spain ICAO location identifier*] (ICLI) ..... LEBT
Beth Din of America (EA) ..... BDA
Beth Israel (BJA) ..... BI
Beth Israel Ambulatory Center (DAVI) ..... BIAC
Beth Israel Hospital, Medical Library, Denver, CO [*Library symbol Library of Congress*] (LCLS) ..... CoDBI-M
Beth Israel Medical Center, New York, NY [*Library symbol Library of Congress*] (LCLS) ..... NNBI
Beth Israel Medical Center, New York, NY [*OCLC symbol*] (OCLC) VVI
Beth Simchat Torah (BJA) ..... BST
Bethalto Community Unit 8, Bethalto, IL [*Library symbol Library of Congress*] (LCLS) ..... IBethCU
Bethalto, IL [*FM radio station call letters*] ..... WFUN
Bethalto Public Library, Bethalto, IL [*Library symbol Library of Congress*] (LCLS) ..... IBeth
Bethania Mennonite Personal Care Home, Winnipeg, Manitoba [*Library symbol National Library of Canada*] (NLC) ..... MWBM
Bethania Mennonite Personal Care Home, Winnipeg, MB, Canada [*Library symbol Library of Congress*] (LCLS) ..... CaMWBM
Bethany and Northern Baptist Theological Seminaries Library, Oak Brook, IL [*OCLC symbol*] (OCLC) ..... IDI
Bethany and Northern Baptist Theological Seminaries Library, Oak Brook, IL [*Library symbol Library of Congress*] (LCLS) ..... IObT
Bethany Beach, DE [*FM radio station call letters*] ..... WOSC
Bethany Beach, DE [*FM radio station call letters*] (RBYB) ..... WZSK
Bethany College, Bethany, WV [*OCLC symbol*] (OCLC) ..... WVB
Bethany College, Bethany, WV [*Library symbol Library of Congress*] (LCLS) ..... WvBeC
Bethany College, Lindsborg, KS [*OCLC symbol*] (OCLC) ..... KFB
Bethany College, Lindsborg, KS [*Library symbol Library of Congress*] (LCLS) ..... KLindB
Bethany Fellowship Missions (EA) ..... BFM
Bethany Lutheran College, Mankato, MN [*OCLC symbol*] (OCLC) ..... MBE
Bethany Lutheran College, Mankato, MN [*Library symbol Library of Congress*] (LCLS) ..... MnManBC
Bethany Lutheran Theological Seminary, Mankato, MN [*OCLC symbol*] (OCLC) ..... MBS
Bethany Lutheran Theological Seminary, Mankato, MN [*Library symbol Library of Congress*] (LCLS) ..... MnManBS

Bethany Medical Center, Kansas City, KS [*Library symbol Library of Congress*] (LCLS) ..... KKcBM
Bethany, MO [*AM radio station call letters*] ..... KAAN
Bethany, MO [*FM radio station call letters*] ..... KAAN-FM
Bethany Nazarene College [*Oklahoma*] ..... BNC
Bethany Nazarene College, Bethany, OK [*OCLC symbol*] (OCLC) ..... OKA
Bethany Nazarene College, Bethany, OK [*Library symbol Library of Congress*] (LCLS) ..... OkBetC
Bethany, OK [*FM radio station call letters*] ..... KNTL
Bethany, WV [*FM radio station call letters*] ..... WVBC
Bethel [*Alaska*] [*Seismograph station code, US Geological Survey Closed*] (SEIS) ..... BET
Bethel [*Alaska*] [*ICAO location identifier*] (ICLI) ..... PABE
Bethel, AK [*Location identifier FAA*] (FAAL) ..... JBT
Bethel, AK [*FM radio station call letters*] ..... KYKD
Bethel, AK [*AM radio station call letters*] ..... KYUK
Bethel, AK [*Television station call letters*] ..... KYUK-TV
Bethel, AK [*Location identifier FAA*] (FAAL) ..... OSE
Bethel Bancorp [*Associated Press*] (SAG) ..... BethlBc
Bethel Bancorp [*NASDAQ symbol*] (NQ) ..... BTHL
Bethel College, Learning Resources Center, St. Paul, MN [*OCLC symbol*] (OCLC) ..... MNK
Bethel College, McKenzie, TN [*Library symbol Library of Congress*] (LCLS) ..... TMckB
Bethel College, Mishawaka, IN [*Library symbol Library of Congress*] (LCLS) ..... InMisB
Bethel College, North Newton, KS [*Library symbol Library of Congress*] (LCLS) ..... KNnB
Bethel College, St. Paul, MN [*Library symbol Library of Congress*] (LCLS) .... MnSB
Bethel Hospital, Winkler, Manitoba [*Library symbol National Library of Canada*] (NLC) ..... MWBH
Bethel Hospital, Winkler, MB, Canada [*Library symbol Library of Congress*] (LCLS) ..... CaMWinBH
Bethe-Salpeter Equation [*Physics*] (OA) ..... BS
Bethe-Salpeter Equation [*Physics*] ..... BSE
Bethesda Base Hospital, Information Resource Center, Cincinnati, OH [*Library symbol Library of Congress*] (LCLS) ..... OCBH
Bethesda Hospital, Medical Library, Denver, CO [*Library symbol Library of Congress*] (LCLS) ..... CoDBH-M
Bethesda Lutheran Hospital, St. Paul, MN [*Library symbol Library of Congress*] (LCLS) ..... MnSBH
Bethesda, MD [*FM radio station call letters*] ..... WARW
Bethesda, MD [*FM radio station call letters*] ..... WMMJ
Bethesda, MD [*AM radio station call letters*] ..... WTEM
Bethesda Military Librarians Group [*Library network*] ..... NMCLA
Bethesda National Christian Resource Center (EA) ..... BNCRC
Bethesda Research Laboratories [*Life Technologies, Inc.*] [*Gaithersburg, MD*] ..... BRL
Bethlehem [*South Africa*] [*ICAO location identifier*] (ICLI) ..... FABM
Bethlehem Corp. [*AMEX symbol*] (SPSG) ..... BET
Bethlehem Corp. [*Associated Press*] (SAG) ..... BethCp
Bethlehem, PA [*Television station call letters*] ..... WBPH
Bethlehem, PA [*AM radio station call letters*] ..... WGPA
Bethlehem, PA [*FM radio station call letters*] ..... WLVR
Bethlehem, PA [*FM radio station call letters*] ..... WZZO
Bethlehem Public Library, Bethlehem, PA [*Library symbol Library of Congress*] (LCLS) ..... PB
Bethlehem Public Library, Bethlehem, PA [*OCLC symbol*] (OCLC) ..... PBL
Bethlehem Resources Corp. [*Toronto Stock Exchange symbol Vancouver Stock Exchange symbol*] ..... BTH
Bethlehem Steel [*NYSE symbol*] (TTSB) ..... BS
Bethlehem Steel $5 cm Cv Pfd [*NYSE symbol*] (TTSB) ..... BSPr
Bethlehem Steel Corp. [*Associated Press*] (SAG) ..... BethStl
Bethlehem Steel Corp. [*Wall Street slang name: "Bessie"*] [*NYSE symbol*] (SPSG) ..... BS
Bethlehem Steel Corp. [*Wall Street slang name: "Bessie"*] [*Associated Press*] (SAG) ..... BthS
Bethlehem Steel Corp. [*Wall Street slang name: "Bessie"*] [*Associated Press*] (SAG) ..... BthSt
Bethlehem Steel Corp., Charles H. Herty, Jr., Memorial Library, Bethlehem, PA [*Library symbol Library of Congress*] (LCLS) ..... PBS
Bethlehem Steel Corp., Charles M. Schwab Memorial Library, Bethlehem, PA [*Library symbol Library of Congress*] (LCLS) ..... PBSteel
Bethlehem Steel$2.50cmCv Pfd [*NYSE symbol*] (TTSB) ..... BSPrB
Bethlehem Transportation Corp. [*Steamship*] (MHDW) ..... BTC
Bethlehem, WV [*FM radio station call letters*] ..... WHLX
Bethlehem, WV [*FM radio station call letters*] (RBYB) ..... WRIR-FM
Bethlemita, Daughters of the Sacred Heart of Jesus (TOCD) ..... Bethl
Bethpage, NY [*Location identifier FAA*] (FAAL) ..... BPA
Bethpage Public Library, Bethpage, NY [*Library symbol Library of Congress*] (LCLS) ..... NBet
Bethpage Senior High School, Bethpage, NY [*Library symbol Library of Congress*] (LCLS) ..... NBethSH
Bethpage Senior High School, Bethpage, NY [*Library symbol*] [*Library of Congress*] (LCLS) ..... NBetSH
Bethune-Cookman College [*Daytona Beach, FL*] ..... BCC
Bethune-Cookman College, Daytona Beach, FL [*OCLC symbol*] (OCLC) ..... DBB
Bethune-Cookman College, Daytona Beach, FL [*Library symbol Library of Congress*] (LCLS) ..... FDbBC
Betioky [*Madagascar*] [*Airport symbol*] (OAG) ..... BKU
Betioky [*Madagascar*] [*ICAO location identifier*] (ICLI) ..... FMSV
Bet-Nahrain Democratic Party [*Political party*] (BJA) ..... BNDP
Betoken (ABBR) ..... BTKN
Betonvereniging van Suidelike Africa [*Concrete Society of South Africa*] (EAIO) ..... BSA
Betoota [*Queensland*] [*Airport symbol*] (AD) ..... BTX
Betou [*Congo*] [*ICAO location identifier*] (ICLI) ..... FCOT
Betreffend [*Referring To*] [*German*] ..... BETR
Betriebsberufsschule [*Factory Training School*] [*Germany*] ..... BBS
Betriebsforschungsinstitut [*Institute for Industrial Research*] [*German Iron and Steel Engineers Association Dusseldorf*] [*Information service or system*] (IID) ..... BFI
Betriebsgewerkschaftsleitung [*Factory Union Headquarters*] [*Germany*] ..... BGL
Betriebsrategesetz [*Law on Works Councils*] [*German*] (ILCA) ..... BetrRG
Betriebsverfassungsgesetz [*Law on the Representation of Workers and Works Councils*] [*German*] (ILCA) ..... BetrVG
Betriebswirtschaftliches Literatursuchsystem [*Business Literature Search System*] [*Society for Business Information*] [*Information service or system*] (IID) ..... BLISS
Betroka [*Madagascar*] [*ICAO location identifier*] (ICLI) ..... FMSE
Betrust Investments [*Vancouver Stock Exchange symbol*] ..... BTR
Betsie Valley District Library, Thompsonville, MI [*Library symbol Library of Congress*] (LCLS) ..... MiTho
Betsy-Tacy Society (EA) ..... BTS
Bettendorf, IA [*FM radio station call letters*] (RBYB) ..... KORB
Bettendorf News, Bettendorf, IA [*Library symbol Library of Congress*] (LCLS) ..... IaBetN
Better ..... BETR
Better (BARN) ..... BTR
Better Boys Foundation (EA) ..... BBF
Better Business Bureau ..... BBB
[*A*] **Better Chance** (EA) ..... ABC
Better Education thru Simplified Spelling (EA) ..... BEtSS
Better Electronic Service Technicians ..... BEST
Better Fabrics Test Bureau ..... BFTB
Better Government Association (EA) ..... BGA
Better Hearing and Speech Month ..... BH & SM
Better Hearing Australia [*An association*] (EAIO) ..... BHA
Better Hearing Institute (EA) ..... BHI
Better Heating-Cooling Council [*Later, HI*] (EA) ..... BHC
Better Highways Information Foundation [*Later, ARTBA*] ..... BHIF
Better Home Heat Council of New Hampshire (SRA) ..... BHHCNH
Better Homes and Gardens [*Information service or system A publication*] (IID) ..... BH & G
Better Humanity League [*Commercial firm*] (EA) ..... BHL
Better Kitchens Institute (EA) ..... BKI
Better Lawn and Turf Institute (EA) ..... BLTI
Better Light Better Sight Bureau [*Defunct*] (EA) ..... BLBSB
Better on Lips than on Paper [*Put at the end of a letter with kisses*] [*British*] ..... BOLTOP
Better Opportunities for Single Soldiers [*Army*] ..... BOSS
Better Packaging Advisory Council (EA) ..... BPAC
Better Postcard Collectors' Club [*Later, D of A*] (EA) ..... BPCC
Better Resources Ltd. [*Vancouver Stock Exchange symbol*] ..... BRZ
Better Roads and Transportation Council (EA) ..... BR & TC
Better Sleep Council [*National Association of Bedding Manufacturers*] (EA) .... BSC
Better Sound Reproduction (IAA) ..... BSR
Better than Average ..... BTA
Better than Expected [*Politics*] ..... BTE
Better Vision Institute (EA) ..... BVI
Better World Society [*Defunct*] (EA) ..... BWS
Bettering Oregon's Opportunity for Saving Talent [*Educational project*] (EA) ..... BOOST
Betting Office Licensees Association [*British*] (DBA) ..... BOLA
Bettis Atomic Power Laboratory [*AEC*] (MCD) ..... BAPL
Bettis Corp. [*NASDAQ symbol*] (SAG) ..... BETT
Bettis Corp. [*Associated Press*] (SAG) ..... Bettis
Bettles [*Alaska*] [*Airport symbol*] (OAG) ..... BTT
Bettles [*Alaska*] [*ICAO location identifier*] (ICLI) ..... PABT
Bettles, AK [*Location identifier FAA*] (FAAL) ..... EAV
[*The*] **Bettmann Archive** [*A publication*] ..... TBA
Betts' Admiralty Practice [*A publication*] (DLA) ..... Betts' Adm Pr
Betty Lake, AK [*Location identifier FAA*] (FAAL) ..... BDY
Betty White Fan Club (EA) ..... BWFC
Between (KSC) ..... BET
Between (VRA) ..... bet
Between (ROG) ..... BETN
Between (ROG) ..... BETW
Between ..... BTN
Between ..... BTW
Between (AABC) ..... BTWN
Between Centers [*Technical drawings*] ..... BC
Between Comfort and Discomfort ..... BCD
Between Commands Testing [*Computer science*] ..... BCT
Between Great Trochanters [*Orthopedics*] (DAVI) ..... BiT
Between Ischial Spines [*Pelvic measurement*] [*Gynecology*] ..... BISp
Between Ischial Tuberosities [*Gynecology*] (BABM) ..... Bi Isch
Between Ischial Turberosities [*Medicine*] (MEDA) ..... Bi Isch
Between Job Monitor [*Computer science*] ..... BJM
Between Layers [*ICAO*] (FAAC) ..... BTL
Between Perpendiculars [*Technical drawings*] ..... BP
Between Two Outfielders [*Baseball*] [*Also, a lifestyle classification*] ..... Tweener
Betz Laboratories [*NYSE symbol*] (SPSG) ..... BTL
Betz Laboratories, Inc. [*Associated Press*] (SAG) ..... BetzLb
Betz Laboratories, Inc., Trevose, PA [*Library symbol Library of Congress*] (LCLS) ..... PTrB
BetzDearborn, Inc. [*Associated Press*] (SAG) ..... BetzDearb
BetzDearborn, Inc. [*NYSE symbol*] (SAG) ..... BTL
Betzdorf/Kirchen [*Germany ICAO location identifier*] (ICLI) ..... EDKI
Beulah, MI [*FM radio station call letters*] (RBYB) ..... WBVE-FM

Beulah, ND [*AM radio station call letters*] ... KHOL
Beulah Public Library, Beulah, MI [*Library symbol Library of Congress*] (LCLS) ... MiBeu
Beurre, Oeufs, Fromages [*Butter, Eggs, Cheese*] [*French*] ... BOF
Bev Tyme 10% Cv'C' Pfd [*NASDAQ symbol*] (TTSB) ... BEVTP
Beva [*A prefix meaning multiplied by one billion; same as "giga"*] ... B
Bevatron ... BEV
Bevatron/Super-HILAC [*Combination of accelerators*] ... BEVALAC
Bevel ... BEV
Bevel (VRA) ... bev
Bevel Gear ... BG
Beveled [*Technical drawings*] ... BVL
Beveled on Four Edges [*Lumber*] (DAC) ... B4E
Beveled on Three Edges [*Lumber*] (DAC) ... B3E
Beveled Plate Glass (DAC) ... BPG
Beveled Wood Siding [*Technical drawings*] ... BWS
Bevelled Deckle Edges [*Cards*] (DGA) ... BDE
Bevelled Edges [*Printing*] (DGA) ... BE
Beven and Siebel's Reports [*Ceylon*] [*A publication*] (DLA) ... B & S
Beven and Siebel's Reports [*Ceylon*] [*A publication*] (DLA) ... Bev & Sieb
Beven on Negligence in Law [*1889-1928*] [*A publication*] (DLA) ... Beven
Beven's Ceylon Reports [*A publication*] (DLA) ... Be (Ceylon)
Beven's Ceylon Reports [*A publication*] (ILCA) ... Bev Ceylon
Beven's Ceylon Reports [*A publication*] (DLA) ... Beven
Beverage ... BEV
Beverage (DMAA) ... bev
Beverage ... BEV
Beverage (KSC) ... BV
Beverage (MSA) ... BVGE
Beverage Canners International Corp. ... BCI
Beverage Container Control Coalition [*Later, WCFR*] (EA) ... B3C
Beverage Machinery Manufacturers Association (EA) ... BMMA
Beverage Manufacturers' Agents Association (EA) ... BMAA
Beverage Network [*An association*] (EA) ... BN
Beveren Rabbit Club [*Defunct*] (EA) ... BRC
Beverley [*Jamaica*] [*Seismograph station code, US Geological Survey Closed*] (SEIS) ... BEV
Beverly Bancorporation, Inc. [*NASDAQ symbol*] (SAG) ... BEVB
Beverly Bancorporation, Inc. [*Associated Press*] (SAG) ... BevBanc
Beverly Development, Inc. [*Toronto Stock Exchange symbol*] ... BVD
Beverly Enterprises [*NYSE symbol*] (SPSG) ... BEV
Beverly Enterprises [*Associated Press*] (SAG) ... Bevrly
Beverly Farms Public Library, Beverly, MA [*Library symbol Library of Congress*] (LCLS) ... MBev-F
Beverly Foundation (EA) ... BF
Beverly Hills (IIA) ... BH
Beverly Hills Bar Association. Journal [*A publication*] (DLA) ... Bev Hills BAJ
Beverly Hills, CA [*AM radio station call letters*] (RBYB) ... KNNS
Beverly Hills, FL [*FM radio station call letters*] ... WXOF
Beverly Hills Intermediate School, Houston, TX [*Library symbol*] [*Library of Congress*] (LCLS) ... TxHBhI
Beverly Hills Public Library, Beverly Hills, CA [*OCLC symbol*] (OCLC) ... BHP
Beverly Hills Public Library, Beverly Hills, CA [*Library symbol Library of Congress*] (LCLS) ... CBev
Beverly Hills Racquets Club [*Book title*] ... BHRC
Beverly Historical Society, Beverly, MA [*Library symbol Library of Congress*] (LCLS) ... MBevHi
Beverly, MA [*Location identifier FAA*] (FAAL) ... BVY
Beverly, MA [*Location identifier FAA*] (FAAL) ... TOF
Beverly, MA [*AM radio station call letters*] ... WNSH
Beverly Public Library, Beverly, MA [*Library symbol Library of Congress*] (LCLS) ... MBev
Beverly Springs [*Australia Airport symbol Obsolete*] (OAG) ... BVZ
Beverly Times, Beverly, MA [*Library symbol Library of Congress*] (LCLS) ... MBevT
Bevier and Southern [*Railroad*] (MHDB) ... B & S
Bevier & Southern Railroad Co. [*AAR code*] ... BVS
Bevil on Homicide [*A publication*] (DLA) ... Bev Hom
Bevill's Patent Cases [*England*] [*A publication*] (DLA) ... Bev Pat
Bevin and Mill's Reports [*Ceylon*] [*A publication*] (DLA) ... Bev & M
Bevin on Employer's Liability for Negligence of Servants [*A publication*] (DLA) ... Bev Emp L
Bevitron Orbit Code ... BOC
Bev-Tyme, Inc. [*Associated Press*] (SAG) ... BevT
Bev-Tyme, Inc. [*NASDAQ symbol*] (SAG) ... BEVT
Bev-Tyme Inc. [*NASDAQ symbol*] (TTSB) ... BEVTC
Bev-Tyme, Inc. [*Associated Press*] (SAG) ... BevTym
Bev-Tyme Inc.Wrrt'C' [*NASDAQ symbol*] (TTSB) ... BEVTZ
Bewani [*Papua New Guinea*] [*Airport symbol*] (OAG) ... BWP
Bewley and Naish on Common Law Procedure [*A publication*] (DLA) ... Bew & N Pr
Bewusstein [*Consciousness*] [*Psychology*] ... BW
Bex [*Switzerland ICAO location identifier*] (ICLI) ... LSTX
Bexar County Medical Library Association, San Antonio, TX [*Library symbol Library of Congress*] (LCLS) ... TxSaBM
Bexhill Museum [*British*] ... BEX
Bexley Public Library, Columbus, OH [*Library symbol Library of Congress*] (LCLS) ... OCoBex
Bexley-Maudsley Automated Psychological Screening [*Test*] ... BMAPS
Beyer Elementary School, Rockford, IL [*Library symbol*] [*Library of Congress*] (LCLS) ... IRoBeE
Beyla [*Guinea*] [*ICAO location identifier*] (ICLI) ... GUBL
Beynes/Thiverval [*France ICAO location identifier*] (ICLI) ... LFPF
Beynhurst [*England*] ... BEYN
Beyond (FAAC) ... BYD
Beyond Baroque Foundation (EA) ... BBF
Beyond Capacity of Intermediate Maintenance [*Army*] (MCD) ... BCIM
Beyond Capacity of Maintenance (MCD) ... BCM
Beyond Economical Repair (MCD) ... BER
Beyond Line of Sight (MCD) ... BLOS
Beyond Local Repair [*Weaponry*] [*British*] ... BLR
Beyond the Horizon (MCD) ... BTH
Beyond Visual Range (MCD) ... BVR
Beyond Visual Range Air-to-Air Missile (MCD) ... BVRAAM
Beyond Visual Range Missile (MCD) ... BVRM
Beyond War Foundation (EA) ... BWF
Bezafibrate Coronary Atherosclerosis Intervention Trial ... BECAIT
Bezah (BJA) ... Bez
Bezanson School, Alberta [*Library symbol National Library of Canada*] (BIB) ... ABEZS
Bezene, Toluene, Ethylbenzene, and Xylene [*Organic mixture*] ... BTEX
Beziehungsweise [*Respectively*] [*German*] ... BEZW
Beziehungsweise [*Respectively*] [*German*] ... BZW
Beziers [*France*] [*Airport symbol*] (OAG) ... BZR
Beziers/Vias [*France ICAO location identifier*] (ICLI) ... LFMU
Bezirksgericht [*District Court*] [*German*] (DLA) ... Bez G
Bezirksgericht [*District Court*] [*German*] (DLA) ... Bez Ger
Bezold-Type Reflex [*Medicine*] (MAE) ... BTR
Bezpartyjny Blok Wspolpracy z Rzadem [*Non-Party Bloc of Cooperation with the Government*] [*Poland Political party*] (PPE) ... BBWR
Bezueglich [*Concerning*] [*German*] ... BEZ
Bezueglich [*In Regard To, With Reference To*] [*German*] ... BZGL
BF Enterprises [*NASDAQ symbol*] (TTSB) ... BFEN
BF Enterprises, Inc. [*Associated Press*] (SAG) ... BF Ent
BF Enterprises, Inc. [*NASDAQ symbol*] (NQ) ... BFEN
BF Realty Holdings Ltd. [*Toronto Stock Exchange symbol*] (SPSG) ... BFR
BFS Bancorp, Inc. [*Associated Press*] (SAG) ... BFS NY
BFS Bankorp [*NASDAQ symbol*] (TTSB) ... BFSI
BFS Bankorp, Inc. [*NASDAQ symbol*] (NQ) ... BFSI
BFS [*Berliner Spezial Flug*], Luftahrtunternehmen GmbH [*Germany ICAO designator*] (FAAC) ... SBY
BGM Diversified Energy, Inc. [*Vancouver Stock Exchange symbol*] ... BGD
BGR Precious Metals, Inc. [*Toronto Stock Exchange symbol*] ... BPT
BGS Systems [*NASDAQ symbol*] (TTSB) ... BGSS
BGS Systems, Inc. [*Associated Press*] (SAG) ... BGS
BGS Systems, Inc. [*NASDAQ symbol*] (NQ) ... BGSS
BHA Group, Inc. [*Associated Press*] (SAG) ... BHA
BHA Group, Inc. [*NASDAQ symbol*] (NQ) ... BHAG
BHA Group'A' [*NASDAQ symbol*] (TTSB) ... BHAG
Bhabba Atomic Research Centre [*India*] ... BARC
Bhadrapur [*Nepal*] [*Airport symbol*] (OAG) ... BDP
Bhagtanwala [*Pakistan*] [*ICAO location identifier*] (ICLI) ... OPBG
Bhairawa [*Nepal*] [*Airport symbol*] (OAG) ... BWA
Bhairawa [*Nepal*] [*ICAO location identifier*] (ICLI) ... VNBW
Bhakra [*India*] [*Seismograph station code, US Geological Survey*] (SEIS) ... BHK
Bhamo [*Myanmar*] [*Airport symbol*] (OAG) ... BMO
Bhamo [*Myanmar*] [*ICAO location identifier*] (ICLI) ... VBBM
Bharat Heavy Electricals Ltd. [*India*] ... BHEL
Bharatiya Janata Party [*Indian People's Party*] [*Political party*] ... BJ
Bharatiya Janata Party [*Indian People's Party*] [*Political party*] (PPW) ... BJP
Bharatiya Lok Dal [*India*] [*Political party*] (PPW) ... BLD
Bharatpur [*Nepal*] [*Airport symbol Obsolete*] (OAG) ... BHR
Bharatpur [*Nepal*] [*ICAO location identifier*] (ICLI) ... VNBP
Bhatinda [*India*] [*ICAO location identifier*] (ICLI) ... VIBT
Bhatnagar-Gross-Krook [*Equation*] ... BGK
Bhaunagar [*India*] [*ICAO location identifier*] (ICLI) ... VABV
Bhavnagar [*India*] [*Airport symbol*] (OAG) ... BHU
BHC Communications [*Associated Press*] (SAG) ... BHC
BHC Communications, Inc. [*AMEX symbol*] (SPSG) ... BHC
BHC Communications'A' [*AMEX symbol*] (TTSB) ... BHC
BHC Financial [*NASDAQ symbol*] (TTSB) ... BHCF
BHC Financial, Inc. [*Associated Press*] (SAG) ... BHC Fncl
BHC Financial, Inc. [*NASDAQ symbol*] (SAG) ... BHCF
BHI Corp. [*Associated Press*] (SAG) ... BHI Cp
BHI Corp. [*NASDAQ symbol*] (SAG) ... BHIK
BHI Corp. [*NASDAQ symbol*] (TTSB) ... BHIKF
Bhiwani [*India*] [*ICAO location identifier*] (ICLI) ... VIBW
Bhoja Airlines [*Pakistan*] [*ICAO designator*] (FAAC) ... BHO
Bhojpur [*Nepal*] [*Airport symbol*] (OAG) ... BHP
Bhojpur [*Nepal*] [*ICAO location identifier*] (ICLI) ... VNBJ
Bhojpuri [*MARC language code Library of Congress*] (LCCP) ... bho
Bhopal [*India*] [*Airport symbol*] (OAG) ... BHO
Bhopal [*India*] [*ICAO location identifier*] (ICLI) ... VABP
BHP [*Broken Hill Proprietary Ltd.*] **Journal** [*A publication*] ... BHP Jl
Bhubaneswar [*India*] [*Airport symbol*] (OAG) ... BBI
Bhubaneswar [*India*] [*ICAO location identifier*] (ICLI) ... VEBS
Bhuj [*India*] [*Airport symbol*] (OAG) ... BHJ
Bhuj [*India*] [*ICAO location identifier*] (ICLI) ... VABJ
Bhumibol Dam [*Thailand*] [*Seismograph station code, US Geological Survey*] (SEIS) ... BDT
Bhutan [*Aircraft nationality and registration mark*] (FAAC) ... A5
Bhutan [*MARC geographic area code Library of Congress*] ... a-bt--
Bhutan ... Bhu
Bhutan ... BHUT
Bhutan [*ANSI two-letter standard code*] (CNC) ... BT
Bhutan [*MARC country of publication code Library of Congress*] (LCCP) ... bt
Bhutan [*ANSI three-letter standard code*] (CNC) ... BTN
Bhutan Broadcasting Service (EY) ... BBS
Bhutan People's Party [*Political party*] ... BPP
Bhutan Philatelic Society (EA) ... BPS
Bhutan Tourism Corp. (EY) ... BTC

BI, Inc. [*Associated Press*] (SAG) .... BI Inc
BI, Inc. [*NASDAQ symbol*] (NQ) .... BIAC
Biacore International AB [*NASDAQ symbol*] (SAG) ..... BCOR
Biacore International AB [*Associated Press*] (SAG) .... Biacore
Biafra [*MARC geographic area code Library of Congress*] (LCCP) .... f-by--
Biafra Relief Services Foundation (EA) .... BRSF
Biak [*Indonesia*] [*Airport symbol*] (OAG) .... BIK
Biak [*Indonesia*] [*ICAO location identifier*] (ICLI) ..... WABZ
Biak/Frans Kaisiepo [*Indonesia*] [*ICAO location identifier*] (ICLI) ... WABB
Biak/Manuhua [*Indonesia*] [*ICAO location identifier*] (ICLI) ... WABU
Bialla [*Papua New Guinea*] [*Airport symbol*] (OAG) .... BAA
Biamperometric [*Electromagnetics*] .... Biamp
Biarritz [*France*] [*Airport symbol*] (OAG) .... BIQ
Biarritz-Bayonne/Anglet [*France ICAO location identifier*] (ICLI) ... LFBZ
Biaru [*Papua New Guinea*] [*Airport symbol*] (OAG) ... BRP
Bias [*Telecommunications*] .... B
Bias Oscillator Frequency .... BOF
Bias Power and Temperature Step Stress (PDAA) .... BPATSS
Bias Telegraph Distortion .... BTD
Bias Temperature .... BT
Biased Antiworld Paw Entry [*Testing of left and right laterality in mice*] .... BAWPE
Biased Optimal Steering Selector (PDAA) .... BOSS
Biased Predictive Proportional Guidance .... BPPG
Biased Proportional Guidance .... BPG
Biased Random Walk [*Mathematics*] .... BRW
Biased World Paw Entry [*Testing of left and right laterality in mice*] .... BWPE
Biaxial (IAA) .... BIAX
Biaxial Shock Test Machine [*CERL*] [*Army*] (RDA) .... BSTM
Biaxially-Oriented Polypropylene [*Plastics technology*] .... BOPP
Bibanga [*Zaire*] [*ICAO location identifier*] (ICLI) .... FZWB
Bibas in Christo [*May You Live in Christ*] [*Latin*] .... BIC
Bibbia e Oriente [*A publication*] (BJA) .... BO
Bibbia e Oriente [*A publication*] (BJA) .... BOr
Bibbia e Oriente Fossano, Cuneo (BJA) .... BibO
Bibbia e Oriente Fossano, Cuneo (BJA) .... BieOr
Bibb's Kentucky Reports [*4-7 Kentucky*] [*1808-17*] [*A publication*] (DLA) .... Bibb
Bibb's Kentucky Reports [*4-7 Kentucky*] [*1808-17*] [*A publication*]
   (DLA) .... Bibb (KY)
Bibe [*Drink*] [*Pharmacy*] .... BIB
Bibel und Liturgie [*A publication*] (BJA) .... BL
Bibelforskaren (BJA) .... BF
Bibel-Lexikon [*A publication*] (BJA) .... BL
Biberach Aerodrome Riss [*Germany ICAO location identifier*] (ICLI) .... EDMB
Bibi Besch Fan Club (EA) .... BBFC
Bible .... B
Bible (WDMC) .... b
Bible .... BB
Bible .... BIB
[*The*] Bible - An American Translation (1935) [*A publication*] (BJA) .... AT
Bible and Medical Missionary Fellowship [*Later, BMMFI/USA*] (EA) .... BMMF
Bible Atlas [*Hurblut*] [*A publication*] (BJA) ...... HBA
Bible Christian Union (EA) .... BCU
Bible Churchmen's Missionary Society [*Church of England*] ..... BCMS
Bible Club Movement (EA) .... BCM
Bible de Jerusalem [*A publication*] (BJA) .... BJer
Bible Dictionary [*A publication*] (BJA) .... BD
Bible du Centenaire [*A publication*] (BJA) .... BCent
Bible et Terre Sainte [*A publication*] (BJA) .... BTS
Bible Grove, IL [*Location identifier FAA*] (FAAL) ... BIB
Bible Holiness Movement (EA) .... BHM
[*The*] Bible in Current Catholic Thought [*A publication*] .... BCCT
Bible Institute of Los Angeles .... BILA
Bible Key Words [*London, 1949-1965*] [*A publication*] (BJA) .... BKW
Bible Lands' Missions Aid Society [*British*] (BI) ... BLMAS
Bible League (EA) .... BL
Bible Literature International (EA) .... BLI
Bible Meditation League [*Later, BLI*] (EA) .... BML
Bible Memory Association, International (EA) .... BMA
Bible Protestant Missions (EA) .... BPM
Bible Reading Fellowship [*British*] .... BRF
Bible Research Systems [*Information service or system*] (IID) .... BRS
Bible Sabbath Association (EA) .... BSA
Bible Seminary in New York .... BSNY
Bible Study League of America [*Defunct*] (EA) ...... BSLA
Bible Version [*As opposed to the Prayer Book version of the Psalms*] .... BV
Bibles for the World (EA) .... BFW
Bibles for the World (EA) .... BW
Bible-Science Association (EA) .... BSA
Bibletone [*Record label*] .... Bib
Biblia Hebraica (BJA) .... BH
Biblia Hebraica (R. Kittel) [*A publication*] (BJA) ... BHK
Biblia Hebraica Stuttgartensia [*A publication*] (BJA) ... BHS
Biblia Rabbinica [*A publication*] (BJA) .... BR
Biblia Revuo [*A publication*] (BJA) .... BRe
Biblial Research Institute, Inc., Buffalo, NY [*Library symbol*] [*Library of Congress*] (LCLS) .... NBuBR
Biblica [*A publication*] (BJA) .... Bb
Biblica et Orientalia. Sacra Scriptura Antiquitatibus Orientalibus Illustrata
   [*Rome*] [*A publication*] (BJA) .... BietOr
Biblical (ROG) .... B
Biblical (ROG) .... BIB
Biblical .... BIBL
Biblical Aramaic (BJA) .... BA
Biblical Archaeologist Reader [*A publication*] (BJA) ... BAR
Biblical Colloquium [*Defunct*] (EA) .... BC

Biblical Creation Society [*British*] .... BCS
Biblical Essays [*A publication*] (BJA) .... BE
Biblical Evangelism (EA) .... BE
Biblical Fine Arts Association (EA) .... BFAA
Biblical Hebrew (BJA) .... BH
Biblical History and Literature (BJA) .... BHL
Biblical Institute for Social Change (EA) .... BISC
Biblical Numismatic Society [*Defunct*] (EA) ...... BNS
Biblical Research [*A publication*] (BJA) .... BRe
Biblical School of Theology, Hatfield, PA [*Library symbol Library of Congress*] (LCLS) .... PHatfB
Biblical Seminary in New York, New York, NY [*Library symbol Library of Congress*] (LCLS) .... NNBS
Biblical Theologians (EA) .... BT
Biblical Theology Bulletin [*A publication*] (BRI) ... BTB
Biblical Topics Study Unit [*American Topical Association*] (EA) .... BTSU
Biblical Witness Fellowship (EA) .... BWF
Bibliografia di Informatica e Diritto [*Bibliography of Legal/Rights Information*] [*CSC-Corte Suprema di Cassazione*] [*Italy*] (NITA) .... BID
Bibliografia Espanola [*Ministerio de Cultura*] [*Spain Information service or system*] (CRD) .... BIBL
Bibliografia Espanola de Ciencias de la Informacion [*Database*] [*Universidad Complutense de Madrid*] [*Spanish*] [*Information service or system*] (CRD) .... BECI
Bibliografia Extranjera Depositada en la Biblioteca Nacional [*Ministerio de Cultura*] [*Spain Information service or system*] (CRD) .... BNBE
Bibliografia General Espanola e Hispanoamericana [*A bibliographic publication*] [*Spain*] .... BEH
Bibliografia (Nazionale Italiano) (NITA) .... BIBLIO
Bibliographia Huntiana [*Computer-based bibliography*] ... BH
Bibliographic Access and Control System [*Washington University*] [*Information service or system*] (IID) .... BACS
Bibliographic Access System (EDAC) .... BAS
Bibliographic and Grouping System [*A software program for iconography*] (NITA) .... BAG
Bibliographic and Library Information Search Service [*Louisiana State University*] .... BLISS
Bibliographic and Library Instruction for Secondary Schools .... BLISS
Bibliographic Automation of Large Library Operations Using a Time-Sharing System [*Later, RLIN*] [*Stanford University*] .... BALLOTS
Bibliographic Center for Research, Denver, CO [*OCLC symbol*] (OCLC) .... TPS
Bibliographic Center for Research, Denver, CO [*OCLC symbol*] (OCLC) .... TPT
Bibliographic Centre, Ontario Ministry of Government Services, Toronto, Ontario [*Library symbol National Library of Canada*] (NLC) .... OTGSB
Bibliographic Classification [*System of library classification devised by Henry Evelyn Bliss*] .... BC
Bibliographic Control System (ADA) .... BCS
Bibliographic Cooperative Program [*American Library Association*] .... BIBCO
Bibliographic Data (ADA) .... BIBDATA
Bibliographic Data Entry System [*Computer science*] (PDAA) .... BIBDES
Bibliographic Data Processing Program [*For keyword indexing*] [*Information retrieval software*] .... BIDAP
Bibliographic Database .... BDB
Bibliographic Database Search Service [*University of Wyoming Libraries*] (OLDSS) .... BDS
Bibliographic Index of Library Documents [*Helsinki School of Economics*] [*Database*] .... BILD
Bibliographic Information on Southeast Asia [*University of Sydney Library*] [*Database*] [*Information service or system*] (IID) .... BISA
Bibliographic Information Service for Vocational Training [*ILO*] [*United Nations*] (DUND) .... BISVOT
Bibliographic Instruction [*Library science*] ...... BI
Bibliographic Instruction Section [*Association of College and Research Libraries*] .... BIS
Bibliographic Network [*OCLC retrieval system*] [*Computer science*] ... BIBNET
Bibliographic On-Line Display [*Document storage and retrieval system*] [*Computer science*] .... BOLD
Bibliographic Online Library Display [*Scientific Documentation Centre*] [*British*] (NITA) .... BOLD
Bibliographic On-Line Organized Knowledge [*Computer science*] (KSC) .... BOOK
Bibliographic Pattern Discovery Algorithm (PDAA) ... BPDA
Bibliographic Retrieval Services, Inc. [*Database host system*] [*Scotia, NY*] .... BRS
Bibliographic Search Services [*University of Minnesota*] (OLDSS) .... BSS
Bibliographic Service Development Program [*Council on Library Resources*] (NITA) .... BSDP
Bibliographic Services Division [*The British Library*] (NITA) .... BSD
Bibliographic Systems Center [*Case Western Reserve University*] (IID) .... BSC
Bibliographical Center for Research, Denver, CO [*OCLC symbol*] (OCLC) .... BCR
Bibliographical Center for Research, Rocky Mountain Region [*Library network*] .... BCR
Bibliographical Center for Research, Rocky Mountain Region, Denver, CO [*Library symbol Library of Congress*] (LCLS) .... CoDB
Bibliographical Footnotes .... bibl-f
Bibliographical Note (DSUE) .... BIBLIO
Bibliographical Services Section [*of a library*] ... BSS
Bibliographical Society [*British*] (DIT) .... BS
Bibliographical Society of America (EA) .... BSA
Bibliographical Society of America Papers [*A publication*] (BRI) .... BSA-P
Bibliographical Society of Canada (DGA) .... BSC
Bibliographical Society of the University of Virginia (EA) .... BSUV
Bibliographie Linguistischer Literatur [*Bibliography of Linguistic Literature*] [*Stadt- und Universitatbibliothek Frankfurt*] [*Information service or system*] [*Information service or system*] (CRD) .... BLL

Bibliographie Topographique des Principales Cites Grecques de l'Italie Meridionale et de la Sicile dans l'Antiquite [*A publication*] (OCD) .... Bibl Topogr

Bibliographie zur Offentlichen Unternehmung und Verwaltung [*Bibliography of Public Management and Administration*] [*NOMOS Datapool*] [*Information service or system*] .... BOWI

Bibliography (ROG) .... BIB

Bibliography .... BIBL

Bibliography .... BIBLIOG

Bibliography Master Index [*A database*] [*Gale Research*] (NITA) .... BMI

Bibliography of Agriculture [*Oryx Press*] [*Phoenix, AZ*] [*A publication*] .... B of A

Bibliography of American Literature [*A publication*] .... BAL

Bibliography of Australian Medicine and Health Services [*A publication*] .... BIBAM

Bibliography of Bioethics [*A publication*] .... BOB

Bibliography of Jewish Communities in Europe [*Catalog at General Archives for the History of the Jewish People, Jerusalem*] [*A publication*] (BJA) ...... BJCE

Bibliography of Medical Translations [*A publication*] .... BMT

Bibliography of Newfoundland, Memorial University [*UTLAS symbol*] .... BON

Bibliography of Old Norse-Icelandic Studies [*A publication*] .... BONIS

Bibliography of Research Studies in Education, 1926-1940 [*A publication*] .... BRSE

Bibliography of Soil Science [*A publication*] .... BSS

Bibliography of the Computer in Environmental Design [*A publication*] ...... BCED

Bibliography on Cable Television [*A publication*] (TSSD) .... BCTV

Bibliography on Cold Regions Science and Technology [*A publication*] .... BCRST

Bibliography on Incineration of Refuse and Waste [*Air Pollution Control Association*] [*A publication*] .... BIR

Bibliography Section, Alberta Public Affairs Bureau, Edmonton, Alberta [*Library symbol National Library of Canada*] (NLC) .... AEPA

Biblioteca Apostolica Vaticana, Vatican City, Vatican City [*Library symbol Library of Congress*] (LCLS) .... VatBA

Biblioteca Benjamin Franklin, Guadalajara, Mexico [*Library symbol Library of Congress*] (LCLS) .... MxGuBF

Biblioteca Benjamin Franklin, Mexico City, Mexico [*Library symbol Library of Congress*] (LCLS) .... MxMBF

Biblioteca Berenson, Florence, Italy [*Library symbol Library of Congress*] (LCLS) .... ItFB

Biblioteca Centrala de Stat a R.S. Romania [*Central State Library of Romania*], Bucharest, Romania [*Library symbol Library of Congress*] (LCLS) .... RoBBC

Biblioteca Comunale "Angelillo", Servizio Prestito, Bari, Italy [*Library symbol Library of Congress*] (LCLS) .... ItBa

Biblioteca Comunale di Barletta, Barletta, Italy [*Library symbol Library of Congress*] (LCLS) .... ItBar

Biblioteca Marucelliana di Firenze, Servizio Prestito, Florence, Italy [*Library symbol Library of Congress*] (LCLS) .... ItFBM

Biblioteca Nacional, Buenos Aires, Argentina [*Library symbol Library of Congress*] (LCLS) .... Aa

Biblioteca Nacional, Caracas, Venezuela [*Library symbol Library of Congress*] (LCLS) .... Ve

Biblioteca Nacional de Agricultura [*National Library of Agriculture*] [*Brazil*] [*Information service or system*] (IID) .... BINAGRI

Biblioteca Nacional de Chile, Santiago, Chile [*Library symbol Library of Congress*] (LCLS) .... Chl

Biblioteca Nacional de Mexico, Mexico City, Mexico [*Library symbol Library of Congress*] (LCLS) .... MxMBN

Biblioteca Nacional, Madrid, Spain [*Library symbol Library of Congress*] (LCLS) .... Sp

Biblioteca Nacional, Rio De Janeiro, Brazil [*Library symbol Library of Congress*] (LCLS) .... Br

Biblioteca Nazional Universitaria di Torino, Servizio Prestito, Turin, Italy [*Library symbol Library of Congress*] (LCLS) .... ItTU

Biblioteca Nazionale Centrale, Florence [*Italy*] .... BNCF

Biblioteca Nazionale Centrale, Rome, Italy [*Library symbol Library of Congress*] (LCLS) .... It

Biblioteca Publica, Palma De Mallorca, Spain [*Library symbol Library of Congress*] (LCLS) .... SpPm

Biblioteca Statale di Cremona, Cremona, Italy [*Library symbol Library of Congress*] (LCLS) .... ItCr

Biblio-Tech Ltd., Three Fathom Harbor, Nova Scotia [*Library symbol National Library of Canada*] (NLC) .... NSTB

Biblio-Techniques Library and Information System [*Washington Library Network*] (NITA) .... BLIS

Bibliotechno-Bibliograficheskaya Klassifikatsiya [*Library Bibliographical Classification*] [*Russian Federation*] (NITA) .... BBK

Biblioteka Golowna Politechniki Warszawsjiej (Warsaw Technical University Central Library), Warsaw, Poland [*Library symbol Library of Congress*] (LCLS) .... PoWP

Biblioteka Narodowa [*National Library*], Warsaw, Poland [*Library symbol Library of Congress*] (LCLS) .... PoWBN

Bibliotekernes Oplysningskontor, Centre de Pret International, Kobenhavn, Denmark [*Library symbol Library of Congress*] (LCLS) .... DnKBO

Bibliotekstjanst AB [*Library Service Ltd.*] [*Sweden Information service or system*] (IID) .... BTJ

Bibliotheca [*Library*] [*Latin*] .... BIBL

Bibliotheca [*of Photius*] [*Classical studies*] (OCD) .... Bibl

Bibliotheca [*of Apollodorus*] [*Classical studies*] (OCD) .... Bibl

Bibliotheca Judaica [*A publication*] (BJA) .... BJ

Bibliotheca Orientalis [*A publication*] (BJA) .... BiblOr

Bibliotheca Parsoniana, New Orleans, LA [*Library symbol Library of Congress Obsolete*] (LCLS) .... LNP

Bibliotekarisch-Analytiches Siches System zur Informations Speicherung-Erschleissung [*Library analytical system for information storage/retrieval*] [*Federal Republic of Germany*] (NITA) .... BASIS-E

Bibliotheks Ausleihverwaltungssystem [*Library circulation system*] [*Federal Republic of Germany*] (NITA) .... BIAS

Bibliotheks Automatisierung-System [*Online Cataloguing System*] [*Federal Republic of Germany*] (NITA) .... BAS

Bibliotheks- und Informationssystem [*Library and Information System*] [*German*] .... BIS

Bibliothek-Verbund-System [*Library Network System*] [*Siemens AG*] [*Information service or system*] (IID) .... BVS

Bibliotheque (VRA) .... bibl

Bibliotheque Adelard-Berger, St.-Jean-Sur-Richelieu, Quebec [*Library symbol National Library of Canada*] (BIB) .... QSTJA

Bibliotheque Administrative du Quebec [*UTLAS symbol*] .... BAQ

Bibliotheque Administrative, (Edifice H), Ministere des Communications du Quebec, Quebec [*Library symbol National Library of Canada*] (NLC) ..... QQMCH

Bibliotheque Administrative, Ministere des Affaires Inter-Gouvernementales du Quebec, Quebec, Quebec [*Library symbol Obsolete National Library of Canada*] (NLC) .... QQAI

Bibliotheque Americaine de Nantes, Universite de Nantes Chemin du Tertre, Nantes, France [*Library symbol*] [*Library of Congress*] (LCLS) .... FrNALP

Bibliotheque Americaine, Universite de Grenoble III, Domaine Universitaire, Grenoble, France [*Library symbol*] [*Library of Congress*] (LCLS) .... FrGrALP

Bibliotheque Americaine, Universite de Nancy II, Nancy, France [*Library symbol*] [*Library of Congress*] (LCLS) .... FrNanALP

Bibliotheque Americaine, Universite de Toulouse-Le Mirail, Toulouse, France [*Library symbol*] [*Library of Congress*] (LCLS) .... FrTlALP

Bibliotheque Americaine, Universite Paul-Valery, Montpellier, France [*Library symbol*] [*Library of Congress*] (LCLS) .... FrMpALP

Bibliotheque Battelle, Centre de Recherche, Geneve, Switzerland [*Library symbol Library of Congress*] (LCLS) .... SzGB

Bibliotheque Calvet, Avignon, France [*Library symbol Library of Congress*] (LCLS) .... FrAv

Bibliotheque Cantonal et Universitaire de Lausanne, Lausanne, Switzerland [*Library symbol Library of Congress*] (LCLS) .... SzLaCU

Bibliotheque Centrale de Pret d'Abitibi-Temiscamingue, Rouyn-Noranda, Quebec [*Library symbol National Library of Canada*] (NLC) .... QRBC

Bibliotheque Centrale de Pret de la Cote-Nord, Sept-Iles, Quebec [*Library symbol National Library of Canada*] (NLC) .... QSIBCP

Bibliotheque Centrale de Pret de la Mauricie, Trois-Rivieres, PQ, Canada [*Library symbol Library of Congress*] (LCLS) .... CaQTBC

Bibliotheque Centrale de Pret de la Mauricie, Trois-Rivieres, Quebec [*Library symbol National Library of Canada*] (NLC) .... QTBC

Bibliotheque Centrale de Pret de l'Estrie, Sherbrooke, Quebec [*Library symbol National Library of Canada*] (BIB) .... QSHERB

Bibliotheque Centrale de Pret d'Outaouais, Hull, Quebec [*Library symbol National Library of Canada*] (BIB) .... QHBC

Bibliotheque de Documentation des Archives, Ville de Montreal, Quebec [*Library symbol National Library of Canada*] (NLC) .... QMCIH

Bibliotheque de Droit, Universite de Moncton, New Brunswick [*Library symbol National Library of Canada*] (NLC) .... NBMOUD

Bibliotheque de Droit, Universite de Sherbrooke, Quebec [*Library symbol National Library of Canada*] (NLC) .... QSHERUD

Bibliotheque de la Faune, Ministere du Loisir, de la Chasse et de la Peche, Montreal, Quebec [*Library symbol National Library of Canada*] (NLC) .... QMLCPF

Bibliotheque de la Faune, Ministere du Loisir, de la Chasse, et de la Peche, Orsainville, Quebec [*Library symbol National Library of Canada*] (NLC) .... QOLCPF

Bibliotheque de la Legislature de la Province de Quebec, Quebec, PQ, Canada [*Library symbol Library of Congress*] (LCLS) .... CaQQL

Bibliotheque de la Sante, Centre Hospitalier Restigouche, Campbellton, New Brunswick [*Library symbol National Library of Canada*] (BIB) .... NBCHR

Bibliotheque de la Ville de Montreal, Montreal, PQ, Canada [*Library symbol Library of Congress*] (LCLS) .... CaQMBM

Bibliotheque de la Ville de Montreal, Quebec [*Library symbol National Library of Canada*] (NLC) .... QMBM

Bibliotheque de l'Ambassade de France, Ottawa, ON, Canada [*Library symbol*] [*Library of Congress*] (LCLS) .... CaOOAF

Bibliotheque de l'Ambassade de France, Ottawa, Ontario [*Library symbol National Library of Canada*] (BIB) .... OOAF

Bibliotheque de l'Arsenal, Paris, France [*Library symbol Library of Congress*] (LCLS) .... FrPBA

Bibliotheque de l'Assemblee Nationale, Quebec, Quebec [*Library symbol National Library of Canada*] (NLC) .... QQL

Bibliotheque de l'Institut d'Etudes Medievales, Universite de Montreal, Quebec [*Library symbol National Library of Canada*] (NLC) .... QMUE

Bibliotheque de Quebec, Quebec [*Library symbol National Library of Canada*] (NLC) .... QQ

Bibliotheque de Theologie, les Facultes de la Compagnie de Jesus, Montreal, Quebec [*Library symbol National Library of Canada*] (NLC) .... QMFCJ

Bibliotheque Dentinger [*Dentinger Library*] Falher, Alberta [*Library symbol National Library of Canada*] (NLC) .... AFD

Bibliotheque des Archives de la Province de Quebec, Quebec, PQ, Canada [*Library symbol Library of Congress*] (LCLS) .... CaQQA

Bibliotheque des Avocats, Barreau de Montreal, Quebec [*Library symbol National Library of Canada*] (NLC) .... QMAV

Bibliotheque des Ecoles Francaises d'Athenes et de Rome [*A publication*] (OCD) .... Bibl Ec Franc

Bibliotheque des Freres des Ecoles Chretiennes, Quebec [*Library symbol National Library of Canada*] (NLC) .... QQBL

Bibliotheque des Instituteurs, Montreal, PQ, Canada [*Library symbol Library of Congress*] (LCLS) .... CaQMBI

Bibliotheque des Nations Unies, Geneve, Switzerland [*Library symbol Library of Congress*] (LCLS) .... SzGBNU

Bibliotheque des Sciences de la Sante, Universite de Sherbrooke, Quebec [*Library symbol National Library of Canada*] (NLC) .... QSHERC

Bibliotheque des Sciences, Universite de Sherbrooke, Quebec [*Library symbol National Library of Canada*] (NLC) .... QSHERUS

Bibliotheque des Sciences, Universite du Quebec, Montreal [*Library symbol National Library of Canada*] (BIB) .... QMUQS

Bibliotheque des Services Diocesains, Archeveche de Quebec, Quebec [*Library symbol National Library of Canada*] (BIB) .... QQAQ

Bibliotheque des Services Infirmiers, Hopital Notre-Dame, Montreal, Quebec [*Library symbol National Library of Canada*] (NLC) .... QMHNDI

Bibliotheque Deschatelets, Peres Oblats, Ottawa, ON, Canada [*Library symbol Library of Congress*] (LCLS) .... CaOOSJ

Bibliotheque d'Ingenierie, BG Checo International Ltee., Montreal, Quebec [*Library symbol National Library of Canada*] (NLC) .... QMBGC

Bibliotheque du Grand Seminaire, Sherbrooke, Quebec [*Library symbol National Library of Canada*] (NLC) .... QSHERG

Bibliotheque du Monastere des Augustines, Quebec, PQ, Canada [*Library symbol*] [*Library of Congress*] (LCLS) .... CaQQMAB

Bibliotheque du Monastere des Augustines, Quebec, Quebec [*Library symbol National Library of Canada*] (NLC) .... QQMAB

Bibliotheque du Parlement [*Library of Parliament*] [*Canada*] .... BP

Bibliotheque Felix-Leclerc, Val-Belair, Quebec [*Library symbol National Library of Canada*] (NLC) .... QVBFL

Bibliotheque Franciscaine, Quebec, PQ, Canada [*Library symbol Library of Congress*] (LCLS) .... CaQQF

Bibliotheque Franciscaine, Quebec, Quebec [*Library symbol National Library of Canada*] (NLC) .... QQF

Bibliotheque Gabrielle-Roy, Quebec, PQ, Canada [*Library symbol*] [*Library of Congress*] (LCLS) .... CaQQGR

Bibliotheque Gabrielle-Roy, Quebec, Quebec [*Library symbol National Library of Canada*] (BIB) .... QQGR

Bibliotheque Gaspesienne, Cap-Chat, PQ, Canada [*Library symbol Library of Congress*] (LCLS) .... CaQCC

Bibliotheque Gaspesienne, Cap-Chat, Quebec [*Library symbol National Library of Canada*] (NLC) .... QCC

Bibliotheque Generale et Archives, Rabat, Morocco [*Library symbol Library of Congress*] (LCLS) .... MorR

Bibliotheque Generale, Universite de Sherbrooke, Quebec [*Library symbol National Library of Canada*] (NLC) .... QSHERU

Bibliotheque Intermunicipale de Pierrefonds et Dollard-des-Ormeaux, Pierrefonds,PQ, Canada [*Library symbol*] [*Library of Congress*] (LCLS) .... CaQPfD

Bibliotheque Intermunicipale de Pierrefonds et Dollard-Des-Ormeaux, Pierrefonds,Quebec [*Library symbol National Library of Canada*] (NLC) .... QPD

Bibliotheque Lasallienne, Quebec, PQ, Canada [*Library symbol*] [*Library of Congress*] (LCLS) .... CaQQBL

Bibliotheque Medicale, Hopital Charles Lemoyne, Greenfield Park, Quebec [*Library symbol National Library of Canada*] (NLC) .... QMHCL

Bibliotheque Medicale, Hopital du Haut-Richelieu, St.-Jean-Sur-Richelieu, Quebec [*Library symbol National Library of Canada*] (BIB) .... QSTJH

Bibliotheque Medicale, Hopital General La Salle, Quebec [*Library symbol National Library of Canada*] (NLC) .... QLSHG

Bibliotheque Medicale, Hopital Regional Chaleur [*Medical Library, Chaleur Regional Hospital*] Bathurst, New Brunswick [*Library symbol National Library of Canada*] (NLC) .... NBBC

Bibliotheque Medicale, Hotel-Dieu de Roberval, Quebec [*Library symbol National Library of Canada*] (NLC) .... QRHD

Bibliotheque Medicale, Hotel-Dieu Saint-Joseph-De-Tracadie, New Brunswick [*Library symbol National Library of Canada*] (BIB) .... NBTH

Bibliotheque Municipale, Alma, Quebec [*Library symbol National Library of Canada*] (NLC) .... QA

Bibliotheque Municipale, Arthabaska, PQ, Canada [*Library symbol Library of Congress*] (LCLS) .... CaQArM

Bibliotheque Municipale, Arthabaska, Quebec [*Library symbol National Library of Canada*] (NLC) .... QARM

Bibliotheque Municipale, Asbestos, PQ, Canada [*Library symbol Library of Congress*] (LCLS) .... CaQAsB

Bibliotheque Municipale, Asbestos, Quebec [*Library symbol National Library of Canada*] (NLC) .... QASB

Bibliotheque Municipale, Aylmer, Quebec [*Library symbol National Library of Canada*] (NLC) .... QAY

Bibliotheque Municipale, Beauport, Quebec [*Library symbol National Library of Canada*] (BIB) .... QBEAU

Bibliotheque Municipale, Becancour, PQ, Canada [*Library symbol Library of Congress*] (LCLS) .... CaQBEC

Bibliotheque Municipale, Becancour, Quebec [*Library symbol National Library of Canada*] (NLC) .... QBEC

Bibliotheque Municipale, Boucherville, PQ, Canada [*Library symbol Library of Congress*] (LCLS) .... CaQBO

Bibliotheque Municipale, Boucherville, Quebec [*Library symbol National Library of Canada*] (NLC) .... QBO

Bibliotheque Municipale, Brossard, Quebec [*Library symbol National Library of Canada*] (BIB) .... QB

Bibliotheque Municipale, Buckingham, Quebec [*Library symbol National Library of Canada*] (NLC) .... QBU

Bibliotheque Municipale, Candiac, Quebec [*Library symbol National Library of Canada*] (BIB) .... QCA

Bibliotheque Municipale, Cap-De-La Madeleine, PQ, Canada [*Library symbol Library of Congress*] (LCLS) .... CaQCmM

Bibliotheque Municipale, Cap-De-La-Madeleine, Quebec [*Library symbol National Library of Canada*] (NLC) .... QCMM

Bibliotheque Municipale, Cap-Rouge, Quebec [*Library symbol National Library of Canada*] (BIB) .... QCRM

Bibliotheque Municipale, Charlesbourg, Quebec [*Library symbol National Library of Canada*] (BIB) .... QQBMC

Bibliotheque Municipale, Chateauguay, Quebec [*Library symbol National Library of Canada*] (BIB) .... QCM

Bibliotheque Municipale, Coaticook, PQ, Canada [*Library symbol Library of Congress*] (LCLS) .... CaQCB

Bibliotheque Municipale, Coaticook, Quebec [*Library symbol National Library of Canada*] (NLC) .... QCB

Bibliotheque Municipale, Cowansville, Quebec [*Library symbol National Library of Canada*] (BIB) .... QC

Bibliotheque Municipale de la Ville de Montreal-Est, Quebec [*Library symbol National Library of Canada*] (BIB) .... QMEM

Bibliotheque Municipale de Lachine, Quebec [*Library symbol National Library of Canada*] (NLC) .... QLM

Bibliotheque Municipale de Lyon, Lyon, France [*Library symbol Library of Congress*] (LCLS) .... FrLy

Bibliotheque Municipale de Saint Raphael de l'Ile Bizard, Saint Raphael de l'IleBizard, PQ, Canada [*Library symbol*] [*Library of Congress*] (LCLS) .... CaQStR

Bibliotheque Municipale de Saint-Laurent [*UTLAS symbol*] .... STL

Bibliotheque Municipale de Saint-Raphael-De-L'Ile-Bizard, Quebec [*Library symbol National Library of Canada*] (NLC) .... QSTR

Bibliotheque Municipale de Sherbrooke, Sherbrooke, PQ, Canada [*Library symbol Library of Congress*] (LCLS) .... CaQSherN

Bibliotheque Municipale, Dorval, Quebec [*Library symbol National Library of Canada*] (BIB) .... QD

Bibliotheque Municipale, Drummondville, PQ, Canada [*Library symbol Library of Congress*] (LCLS) .... CaQDM

Bibliotheque Municipale, Gatineau, Quebec [*Library symbol National Library of Canada*] (NLC) .... QG

Bibliotheque Municipale, Granby, PQ, Canada [*Library symbol Library of Congress*] (LCLS) .... CaQGM

Bibliotheque Municipale, Granby, Quebec [*Library symbol National Library of Canada*] (NLC) .... QGM

Bibliotheque Municipale, Grand'Mere, PQ, Canada [*Library symbol Library of Congress*] (LCLS) .... CaQGmM

Bibliotheque Municipale, Grand'Mere, Quebec [*Library symbol National Library of Canada*] (NLC) .... QGMM

Bibliotheque Municipale, Hull, PQ, Canada [*Library symbol Library of Congress*] (LCLS) .... CaQH

Bibliotheque Municipale, Hull, Quebec [*Library symbol National Library of Canada*] (NLC) .... QH

Bibliotheque Municipale, Jonquiere, Quebec [*Library symbol National Library of Canada*] (BIB) .... QJ

Bibliotheque Municipale, La Salle, PQ, Canada [*Library symbol Library of Congress*] (LCLS) .... CaQLs

Bibliotheque Municipale, La Salle, Quebec [*Library symbol National Library of Canada*] (NLC) .... QLS

Bibliotheque Municipale, La Tuque, PQ, Canada [*Library symbol Library of Congress*] (LCLS) .... CaQLt

Bibliotheque Municipale, La Tuque, Quebec [*Library symbol National Library of Canada*] (NLC) .... QLT

Bibliotheque Municipale, Lachine, PQ, Canada [*Library symbol*] [*Library of Congress*] (LCLS) .... CaQLaM

Bibliotheque Municipale, Laval, PQ, Canada [*Library symbol Library of Congress*] (LCLS) .... CaQLA

Bibliotheque Municipale, Laval, Quebec [*Library symbol National Library of Canada*] (NLC) .... QLA

Bibliotheque Municipale, Levis, PQ, Canada [*Library symbol Library of Congress*] (LCLS) .... CaQLe

Bibliotheque Municipale, Levis, Quebec [*Library symbol National Library of Canada*] (NLC) .... QLE

Bibliotheque Municipale, Longueuil, PQ, Canada [*Library symbol Library of Congress*] (LCLS) .... CaQLo

Bibliotheque Municipale, Longueuil, Quebec [*Library symbol National Library of Canada*] (NLC) .... QLO

Bibliotheque Municipale, Magog, PQ, Canada [*Library symbol Library of Congress*] (LCLS) .... CaQMgB

Bibliotheque Municipale, Magog, Quebec [*Library symbol National Library of Canada*] (NLC) .... QMAGB

Bibliotheque Municipale, Mascouche, Quebec [*Library symbol National Library of Canada*] (BIB) .... QMASC

Bibliotheque Municipale, Mont-Laurier, Quebec [*Library symbol National Library of Canada*] (BIB) .... QMLM

Bibliotheque Municipale, Montreal-Nord, PQ, Canada [*Library symbol Library of Congress*] (LCLS) .... CaQMn

Bibliotheque Municipale, Nantes, France [*Library symbol Library of Congress*] (LCLS) .... FrN

Bibliotheque Municipale, Plessisville, PQ, Canada [*Library symbol Library of Congress*] (LCLS) .... CaQPIM

Bibliotheque Municipale, Plessisville, Quebec [*Library symbol National Library of Canada*] (NLC) .... QPLM

Bibliotheque Municipale, Port-Alfred, PQ, Canada [*Library symbol Library of Congress*] (LCLS) .... CaQPA

Bibliotheque Municipale, Port-Alfred, Quebec [*Library symbol National Library of Canada*] (NLC) .... QPA

Bibliotheque Municipale, Port-Cartier, Quebec [*Library symbol National Library of Canada*] (BIB) .... QPCM

Bibliotheque Municipale, Princeville, PQ, Canada [*Library symbol Library of Congress*] (LCLS) .... CaQPrM

Bibliotheque Municipale, Princeville, Quebec [*Library symbol National Library of Canada*] (NLC) .... QPRM

Bibliotheque Municipale, Quebec, PQ, Canada [*Library symbol Library of Congress*] (LCLS) .... CaQQ

Bibliotheque Municipale, Repentigny, PQ, Canada [*Library symbol*] [*Library of Congress*] (LCLS) .... CaQRe

Bibliotheque Municipale, Repentigny, Quebec [*Library symbol National Library of Canada*] (NLC) .... QRE

Bibliotheque Municipale, Rimouski, Quebec [*Library symbol National Library of Canada*] (NLC) .... QRM

Bibliotheque Municipale, Riviere-Du-Loup, Quebec [*Library symbol National Library of Canada*] (BIB) .... QRL

Bibliotheque Municipale, Rock Island, PQ, Canada [*Library symbol Library of Congress*] (LCLS) .... CaQRIB

Bibliotheque Municipale, St.-Eustache, Quebec [*Library symbol National Library of Canada*] (BIB) .... QE

Bibliotheque Municipale, Ste.-Foy, PQ, Canada [*Library symbol Library of Congress*] (LCLS) .... CaQSF

Bibliotheque Municipale, Ste.-Foy, Quebec [*Library symbol National Library of Canada*] (NLC) .... QSF

Bibliotheque Municipale, Saint-Bruno-De-Montarville, Quebec [*Library symbol National Library of Canada*] (BIB) .... QSTB

Bibliotheque Municipale, Saint-Jean, PQ, Canada [*Library symbol Library of Congress*] (LCLS) .... CaQStJB

Bibliotheque Municipale, Saint-Jean, Quebec [*Library symbol National Library of Canada*] (NLC) .... QSTJB

Bibliotheque Municipale, Saint-Jerome, PQ, Canada [*Library symbol Library of Congress*] (LCLS) .... CaQStJe

Bibliotheque Municipale, Saint-Jerome, Quebec [*Library symbol National Library of Canada*] (NLC) .... QSTJE

Bibliotheque Municipale, Saint-Laurent, PQ, Canada [*Library symbol Library of Congress*] (LCLS) .... CaQStL

Bibliotheque Municipale, Saint-Laurent, Quebec [*Library symbol National Library of Canada*] (NLC) .... QSTL

Bibliotheque Municipale, Saint-Leonard, PQ, Canada [*Library symbol Library of Congress*] (LCLS) .... CaQStLe

Bibliotheque Municipale, Saint-Leonard, Quebec [*Library symbol National Library of Canada*] (NLC) .... QSLE

Bibliotheque Municipale, Sept-Iles, PQ, Canada [*Library symbol Library of Congress*] (LCLS) .... CaQSi

Bibliotheque Municipale, Sept-Iles, Quebec [*Library symbol National Library of Canada*] (NLC) .... QSI

Bibliotheque Municipale, Sherbrooke, Quebec [*Library symbol National Library of Canada*] (NLC) .... QSHERN

Bibliotheque Municipale, Sorel, PQ, Canada [*Library symbol Library of Congress*] (LCLS) .... CaQSo

Bibliotheque Municipale, Sorel, Quebec [*Library symbol National Library of Canada*] (NLC) .... QSO

Bibliotheque Municipale, Terrebonne, Quebec [*Library symbol National Library of Canada*] (NLC) .... QTER

Bibliotheque Municipale, Trois-Rivieres, PQ, Canada [*Library symbol Library of Congress*] (LCLS) .... CaQT

Bibliotheque Municipale, Trois-Rivieres, Quebec [*Library symbol National Library of Canada*] (NLC) .... QT

Bibliotheque Municipale, Verdun, Quebec [*Library symbol National Library of Canada*] (BIB) .... QVE

Bibliotheque Municipale, Victoriaville, PQ, Canada [*Library symbol Library of Congress*] (LCLS) .... CaQV

Bibliotheque Municipale, Victoriaville, Quebec [*Library symbol National Library of Canada*] (NLC) .... QV

Bibliotheque Nationale de Luxembourg, Service du Pret, Luxembourg, Luxembourg [*Library symbol Library of Congress*] (LCLS) .... LuxLBN

Bibliotheque Nationale du Canada [*National Library of Canada - NLC*] .... BNC

Bibliotheque Nationale du Quebec [*UTLAS symbol*] .... BNQ

Bibliotheque Nationale du Quebec, Montreal, PQ, Canada [*Library symbol Library of Congress*] (LCLS) .... CaQMBN

Bibliotheque Nationale du Quebec, Montreal, Quebec [*Library symbol National Library of Canada*] (NLC) .... QMBN

Bibliotheque Nationale et Universitaire, Affaires Generales, Strasbourg, France [*Library symbol*] [*Library of Congress*] (LCLS) .... FrSU

Bibliotheque Nationale, Paris, France [*Library symbol Library of Congress*] (LCLS) .... FrPBN

Bibliotheque Pere Champagne [*Pere Champagne Library*], Notre-Dame-De-Lourdes, Manitoba [*Library symbol National Library of Canada*] (BIB) .... MNDP

Bibliotheque Publique Cambridge-St.-Albert, St.-Albert, Ontario [*Library symbol National Library of Canada*] (NLC) .... OSTAC

Bibliotheque Publique Cambridge-St-Albert, St.-Albert, ON, Canada [*Library symbol*] [*Library of Congress*] (LCLS) .... CaOSTAC

Bibliotheque Publique de Dubreuilville, Ontario [*Library symbol National Library of Canada*] (NLC) .... ODUB

Bibliotheque Publique de St.-Isidore, Ontario [*Library symbol National Library of Canada*] (NLC) .... OSTI

Bibliotheque Publique du Canton d'Alfred [*Alfred Township Public Library*],Lefaivre, Ontario [*Library symbol National Library of Canada*] (BIB) .... OLAL

Bibliotheque Publique Mgr. Paquet, Caraquet, New Brunswick [*Library symbol National Library of Canada*] (NLC) .... NBCBP

Bibliotheque Regionale du Haut Saint-Jean, Edmundston, NB, Canada [*Library symbol Library of Congress*] (LCLS) .... CaNBEBR

Bibliotheque Regionale du Haut Saint-Jean, Edmundston, New Brunswick [*Library symbol National Library of Canada*] (NLC) .... NBEBR

Bibliotheque Royale d'Albert 1er, American Studies Center, Bruxelles, Belgium [*Library symbol Library of Congress*] (LCLS) .... Be-Am

Bibliotheque Royale d'Albert 1er, Bruxelles, Belgium [*Library symbol Library of Congress*] (LCLS) .... Be

Bibliotheque Scientifique Nationale [*National Science Library*] [*Canada*] .... BSN

Bibliotheque Scientifique, Universite Laval, Quebec, Quebec [*Library symbol National Library of Canada*] (NLC) .... QQLAS

Bibliotheques Vertes pour le Monde [*Green Library - GL*] [*Saint Egreve, France*] (EAIO) .... BVM

Bibliotherapy Forum [*Association of Specialized and Cooperative Library Agencies*] .... BF

Biblische Untersuchungen [*A publication*] (BJA) .... BU

Biblische Zeit-und Streitfragen (BJA) .... BZStF

Biblischer Kommentar zum Alten Testament [*A publication*] (BJA) .... BK

Biblisches Reallexikon [*A publication*] (BJA) .... BR

Biblisch-Historisches Handwoerterbuch [*A publication*] (BJA) .... BHH

Biblisch-Historisches Handwoerterbuch [*A publication*] (BJA) .... BHHW

Biblisch-Theologisches Handwoerterbuch [*A publication*] (BJA) .... BTHW

Bibliotheque et Audiovisuel, Alma, Quebec [*Library symbol National Library of Canada*] (NLC) .... QABA

Bic Corp. [*NYSE symbol*] (SAG) .... BIC

Bic Corp. [*Associated Press*] (SAG) .... BicCp

Bicarbonate .... BICARB

Bicarbonate [*Pharmacology*] (DAVI) HCO3

Bicarbonate (GNE) HCO3

Bicaz [*Romania*] [*Seismograph station code, US Geological Survey*] (SEIS) .... BIZ

Bicentenary [*or Bicentennial*] .... BICENT

Bicentennial Council of the Thirteen Original States [*Later, CTOS*] (EA) .... BCTOS

Bicentennial Information Network [*American Revolution Bicentennial Administration*] .... BINET

Bicentennial Junior Committees of Correspondence [*American Revolution Bicentennial Administration, US Postal Service, and National Association of Elementary School Principals*] .... BJCC

Bicentennial Park Trust [*Australia*] .... BPT

Bicentennial Youth Debates [*National Endowment for the Humanities program*] .... BYD

Biceps Brachii [*A muscle*] .... BB

Biceps Femoris [*A muscle*] [*Anatomy*] .... BF

Biceps Jerk [*Neurology*] .... BJ

Biceps Tendon [*Anatomy*] .... BT

Biceps Tendon Reflex [*Medicine*] (DMAA) .... BTR

Bicer Medical Systems [*Vancouver Stock Exchange symbol*] .... BCJ

Bichon Frise Club of America (EA) .... BFCA

Bichromate (VRA) .... BICH

Biciklista Esperantista Movado Internacia [*International Movement of Esperantist Bicyclists - IMEB*] (EAIO) .... BEMI

Bicinchoninic Acid [*Organic chemistry*] .... BCA

Bicknell and Hawley's Reports [*10-20 Nevada*] [*A publication*] (DLA) .... Bick

Bicknell and Hawley's Reports [*10-20 Nevada*] [*A publication*] (DLA) .... Bick & H

Bicknell and Hawley's Reports [*10-20 Nevada*] [*A publication*] (DLA) .... Bick & Hawl

Bicknell, IN [*FM radio station call letters*] .... WUZR

Bicknell's Indiana Civil Practice [*A publication*] (DLA) .... Bick Civ Pr

Bicknell's Indiana Criminal Practice [*A publication*] (DLA) .... Bick Cr Pr

Bicknell's Reports [*India*] [*A publication*] (DLA) .... Bick (In)

Bicolor .... Bi

Bicolor Guaiac [*Test*] [*Medicine*] .... BCG

Bicolor Guaiac [*Test*] [*Medicine*] .... BG

Bicomponent [*Laboratory tubing*] .... BC

Biconditional .... BICOND

Biconvex .... BCVX

Bi-County Community Hospital, Warren, MI [*Library symbol Library of Congress*] (LCLS) .... MiWarBH

Bicuculline [*Organic chemistry*] .... BIC

Biculturalism and Bilingualism [*Canada*] .... B & B

Biculturalism and Bilingualism [*Canada*] .... BI & BI

Bicuspid [*Dentistry*] .... B

Bicuspid Aortic Valve [*Cardiology*] (DMAA) .... BAV

Bicycle (MSA) .... BCL

Bicycle (ROG) .... BIKE

Bicycle .... BIKE

Bicycle Association of Great Britain (EAIO) .... BAGB

Bicycle Australia [*An association*] .... BA

Bicycle Club [*Generic term*] (WGA) .... BC

Bicycle Club of America .... BCA

Bicycle Federation of America (EA) .... BF of A

Bicycle Helmet Safety Institute (EA) .... BHSI

Bicycle Institute of America [*Defunct*] .... BIA

Bicycle Manufacturers Association of America (EA) .... BMA

Bicycle Motocross .... BMX

Bicycle Network (EA) .... BN

Bicycle Ride Directors Association of America (EA) .... BRDAA

Bicycle Stamps Club (EA) .... BSC

Bicycle Study Unit [*American Topical Association*] (EA) .... BSU

Bicycle Touring Club [*British*] .... BTC

Bicycle Traders' Association of South Australia .... BTASA

Bicycle Transportation Action (EA) .... BTA

Bicycle Wholesale Distributors Association (EA) .... BWDA

Bicycle-Motocross Industrial Guild (EA) .... BIG

Bicycles on Stamps [*Study unit*] [*American Topical Association*] (EA) .... BOS

Bicycling Parking Foundation (EA) .... BPF

Bicycling Promotion Organization [*Later, BIA*] (EA) .... BPO

Bicyclists Educational and Legal Foundation (EA) .... BELF

Bid [*Stock exchange term*] (SPSG) .... B

Bid Analysis and Reporting System (AAGC) .... BARS

Bid and Asked [*Investment term*] .... B & A

Bid and Proposal .... B & P

Bid Bond Service Undertaking .... BBSU

Bid in Die [*Twice a Day*] [*Symbol*] [*Pharmacology*] (DAVI) ii

Bid Opening Date .... BOD

Bid Wanted [*Business term*] .... BW

Bida [*Nigeria*] [*ICAO location identifier*] (ICLI) .... DNBI

Bidar [*India*] [*ICAO location identifier*] (ICLI) .... VOBR

Biddeford, ME [*FM radio station call letters*] .... WCYY

Biddeford, ME [*AM radio station call letters*] .... WIDE

Biddeford, ME [*Television station call letters*] .... WMEA

Bidder's Court of Referees Reports [*England*] [*A publication*] (DLA) ... Bid
Bidders Early Alert Message (PDAA) ... BEAM
Bidder's List Control (SAA) ... BILCO
Bidder's Locus Standi Reports [*England*] [*A publication*] (DLA) ... Bid
Bidder's Locus Standi Reports, I [*1820-36*] [*A publication*] (DLA) ... Bidd
Bidders Mailing List (AAGC) ... BML
Bidders Master File Listing [*DoD*] ... BMFL
Biddle on Insurance [*A publication*] (DLA) ... Bid Ins
Biddle on Retrospective Legislation [*A publication*] (DLA) ... Bid Retr Leg
Biddle on Warranties in Sale of Chattels [*A publication*] (DLA) ... Bid War Sale Chat
Biddle's Table of Statutes [*A publication*] (DLA) ... Bid Tab Stat
Biddy [*Slang*] (DSUE) ... BID
Bide-a-Wee Home Association (EA) ... BAWHA
Bideford [*Municipal borough in England*] ... BIDEF
Bidens Mottle Virus [*Plant pathology*] ... BIMV
Bidirectional Associative Memory [*Computer science*] ... BAM
Bidirectional Categorical Grammar ... BCG
Bidirectional Category System ... BCS
Bidirectional Computer Interface Program ... BCI
Bi-Directional Converter (NASA) ... BDC
Bidirectional Line Switched Ring [*Telecommunications*] (ACRL) ... BLSR
Bi-Directional Line-Switched Rings ... BLSR
Bidirectional Output Switch Field Effect Transistor [*Electronics*] (NITA) ... BOSFET
Bidirectional Reference Array, Internally Derived [*Computer science*] (DIT) ... BRAID
Bidirectional Reflectance-Distribution Function ... BRDF
Bidirectional Test Fixture (MCD) ... BTF
Bidirectional Transceiver Element [*Telecommunications*] ... BTE
Bi-Doppler Scoring System (MCD) ... BIDOPS
Bidor [*Malaysia*] [*ICAO location identifier*] (ICLI) ... WMAE
Bi-Drive Recreational All-Terrain Transporter [*Subaru automobile*] ... BRAT
Bids Accepted for the Following Vacancies (FAAC) ... BAFVC
Bids per Circuit per Hour [*Telecommunications*] ... BCH
Bids Solicited (FAAC) ... BDSLD
Bids Solicited as Follows ... BSAF
Bidston [*England*] [*Seismograph station code, US Geological Survey Closed*] (SEIS) ... BID
Bi-Duplexed Redundancy [*Telecommunications*] ... BDR
Bidwell Mansion State Historic Park, Chico, CA [*Library symbol*] [*Library of Congress*] (LCLS) ... CChiBP
Bie [*Angola*] [*Airport symbol*] (OAG) ... SVP
Biel/Kappelen [*Switzerland ICAO location identifier*] (ICLI) ... LSZP
Bielefeld/Windelsbleiche [*Germany ICAO location identifier*] (ICLI) ... EDLI
Biel's Microfilm Co., West Seneca, NY [*Library symbol Library of Congress*] (LCLS) ... BMC
Bielschowsky-Jansky Syndrome [*Medicine*] (DMAA) ... BJ
Biennial ... B
Biennial ... BE
Biennial [*Botany*] ... bien
Biennial ... BIENN
Biennial Flight Review [*Aviation*] (DA) ... BFR
Biennial General Meeting ... BGM
Biennial National Atomic Spectroscopy Symposium ... BNASS
Biennial Report and Official Opinions of the Attorney General of the State of West Virginia [*A publication*] (DLA) ... Biennial Rep & Op W Va Atty's Gen
Biennial Report of the Attorney General of the State of Iowa [*A publication*] (DLA) ... Biennial Rep Iowa Att'y Gen
Biennial Report of the Attorney General of the State of Michigan [*A publication*] (DLA) ... Mich Att'y Gen Biennial Rep
Biennial Report of the Attorney General of the State of South Dakota [*A publication*] (DLA) ... Biennial Rep SD Att'y Gen
Biennial Report of the Attorney General of the State of Vermont [*A publication*] (DLA) ... Biennial Rep VT Att'y Gen
Bienville Parish Library, Arcadia, LA [*Library symbol Library of Congress*] (LCLS) ... LArB
Biet-Dong-Quan [*South Vietnamese Rangers*] (VNW) ... BDQ
Bifascicular Block [*Electrocardiogram*] (CPH) ... BFB
Bifidus Acidophilus Live [*Health-food product*] ... BA
Bifurcation Analysis and Catastrophy Theory Methodology (MCD) ... BACTM
Big ... BG
Big Apple Triathlon Club (EA) ... BATC
Big B, Inc. [*Associated Press*] (SAG) ... Big B
Big B, Inc. [*NASDAQ symbol*] (NQ) ... BIGB
Big Band [*Music*] (WDMC) ... BB
Big Band [*Radio station format*] (WDMC) ... BBnd
Big Band Academy of America (EA) ... BBAA
Big Bands Collectors' Club (EA) ... BBCC
Big Bar Gold Corp. [*Vancouver Stock Exchange symbol*] ... BBK
Big Bear [*California*] [*Seismograph station code, US Geological Survey Closed*] (SEIS) ... BBC
Big Bear City, CA [*FM radio station call letters*] ... KBHR
Big Bear Lake, CA [*AM radio station call letters*] ... KBBV
Big Bear Lake, CA [*FM radio station call letters*] (RBYB) ... KXSB
Big Bear Solar Observatory [*California Institute of Technology*] [*Research center*] (RCD) ... BBSO
Big Bear Stores Co. (IIA) ... BB
Big Ben Report [*World War II*] ... BENREP
Big Ben Resources, Inc. [*Vancouver Stock Exchange symbol*] ... BGB
Big Bend [*Idaho*] [*Seismograph station code, US Geological Survey*] (SEIS) ... BBI
Big Bend [*Montana*] [*Seismograph station code, US Geological Survey Closed*] (SEIS) ... BBM
Big Bend Community College, Moses Lake, WA [*Library symbol Library of Congress*] (LCLS) ... WaMIB
Big Bend National Park ... BIBE
Big Bend Natural History Association (EA) ... BBNHA
Big Big Gastrin [*Endocrinology*] ... BBG
Big Block [*Series of Chevrolet V-8 engines*] ... BB
Big Board [*The New York Stock Exchange, Inc.*] [*Slang*] ... BB
Big Brand Names [*i.e., well-established writers*] [*Publishing slang*] ... BBN
Big Brother [*From George Orwell's novel, "1984"*] ... BB
Big Brothers/Big Sisters of America (EA) ... BB/BSA
Big Brothers of America [*Later, BB/BSA*] (EA) ... BBA
Big City Bagels [*NASDAQ symbol*] (TTSB) ... BIGC
Big City Bagels, Inc. [*Associated Press*] (SAG) ... BgCtyB
Big City Bagels, Inc. [*NASDAQ symbol*] (SAG) ... BIGC
Big City Bagels, Inc. [*Associated Press*] (SAG) ... BigCityB
Big City Bagels Wrrt [*NASDAQ symbol*] (TTSB) ... BIGCW
Big Close-Up [*A photograph or motion picture sequence taken from a short distance*] ... BCU
Big Creek [*Nevada*] [*Seismograph station code, US Geological Survey Closed*] (SEIS) ... BGN
Big Creek Baldy [*Montana*] [*Seismograph station code, US Geological Survey Closed*] (SEIS) ... BCB
Big Creek News, Polk City, IA [*Library symbol Library of Congress*] (LCLS) ... IaPolcN
Big Deal [*An association*] (EA) ... BD
Big Delta [*Alaska*] [*ICAO location identifier*] (ICLI) ... PABG
Big Dumb Booster Rocket ... BDB
Big Dutch Hollow [*Utah*] [*Seismograph station code, US Geological Survey*] (SEIS) ... BDU
Big East Conference (EA) ... BEC
Big Eight Conference (EA) ... BEC
Big Eight Council on Black Student Government (EA) ... BECBSG
Big Electronic Human-Energized Machine, Only Too Heavy [*High technology*] ... BEHEMOTH
Big Emerging Markets (ACII) ... BEM
Big Entertainment, Inc. [*NASDAQ symbol*] (SAG) ... BIGE
Big Entertainment, Inc. [*Associated Press*] (SAG) ... BigEnt
Big Entertainment'A' [*NASDAQ symbol*] (TTSB) ... BIGE
Big European Bubble Chamber [*Nuclear particle detector*] ... BEBC
Big Falls Elementary School, Big Falls, MN [*Library symbol*] [*Library of Congress*] (LCLS) ... MnBfaE
Big Fat Wide Shot [*Photography*] (WDMC) ... BFWS
Big Fatal Disease [*Slang*] (DNAB) ... BFD
Big Fine Deal ... BFD
Big Flats, NY [*FM radio station call letters*] ... WGMM
Big Flower Holdings, Inc. [*NYSE symbol*] (SAG) ... BGF
Big Flower Holdings, Inc. [*Associated Press*] (SAG) ... BigFlower
Big Flower Holdings, Inc. [*Associated Press*] (SAG) ... BigFlwr
Big Flower Press Hldgs [*NYSE symbol*] (TTSB) ... BGF
Big Foot Financial Corp. [*NASDAQ symbol*] (SAG) ... BFFC
Big Foot Financial Corp. [*Associated Press*] (SAG) ... BigFoot
Big Friendly Giant [*In the children's bestseller "The BFG" by Roald Dahl*] ... BFG
Big Hole National Battlefield ... BIHO
Big Horn County Public Library, Hardin, MT [*Library symbol Library of Congress*] (LCLS) ... MtHar
Big I Development Ltd. [*Vancouver Stock Exchange symbol*] ... BID
Big, Intrusive Government ... BIG
Big Island Air, Inc. [*ICAO designator*] (FAAC) ... BIG
Big Island Rainforest Action Group (EA) ... BIRAG
Big Lake, AK [*Location identifier FAA*] (FAAL) ... BGQ
Big Lake Elementary School, Big Lake, MN [*Library symbol*] [*Library of Congress*] (LCLS) ... MnBIE
Big Lake High School, Big Lake, MN [*Library symbol*] [*Library of Congress*] (LCLS) ... MnBIH
Big Lake Public Library, Big Lake, MN [*Library symbol*] [*Library of Congress*] (LCLS) ... MnBI
Big Lake, TX [*Location identifier FAA*] (FAAL) ... LUJ
Big Little Book [*of comic strips*] ... BLB
Big Little Book Collector's Club of America (EA) ... BLBCCA
Big Liver and Spleen Disease [*Poultry*] ... BLS
Big Lost River [*Idaho*] [*Seismograph station code, US Geological Survey Closed*] (SEIS) ... LRI
Big M Petroleum, Inc. [*Vancouver Stock Exchange symbol*] ... BIM
Big Machine on Campus [*Computer*] ... BMOC
Big Mahogany Desk ... BMD
Big Man on Campus [*Slang*] ... BMOC
Big Man's Fan Club (EA) ... BMFC
Big Maria Mountains [*California*] [*Seismograph station code, US Geological Survey*] (SEIS) ... BMM
Big Mountain [*Alaska*] [*Seismograph station code, US Geological Survey*] (SEIS) ... BIG
Big Mountain Air Force Station [*Alaska*] [*ICAO location identifier*] (ICLI) ... PABM
Big Name Fan [*of science fiction or fantastic literature*] [*See also LNF*] ... BNF
Big O Tires, Inc. [*NASDAQ symbol*] (NQ) ... BIGO
Big O Tires, Inc. [*Associated Press*] (SAG) ... BigOTir
Big Office Head Office [*Business term*] (PCM) ... BOHO
Big Oil Bail Out [*Reference by Rep. James H. Scheuer (NY) to a particular toxic waste clean-up bill*] ... BOBO
Big Optical Array [*Proposed, 1992*] ... BOA
Big Pine, CA [*FM radio station call letters*] (RBYB) ... KRHV
Big Pine Key, FL [*FM radio station call letters*] ... WWUS
Big Piney, WY [*Location identifier FAA*] (FAAL) ... BPI
Big Plasma Glucagon [*Endocrinology*] ... BPG
Big Rapids Community Library, Big Rapids, MI [*Library symbol Library of Congress*] (LCLS) ... MiBr
Big Rapids, MI [*AM radio station call letters*] ... WBRN
Big Rapids, MI [*FM radio station call letters*] ... WBRN-FM
Big Rapids, MI [*FM radio station call letters*] ... WYBR

Big Red Bike Ride [*Fundraising event*] [*British*] ..... BRBR
Big Red Switch [*Computer science*] (NHD) ..... BRS
Big Rock Brewery [*NASDAQ symbol*] (SAG) ..... BEER
Big Rock Brewery [*NASDAQ symbol*] (TTSB) ..... BEERF
Big Rock Brewery [*Associated Press*] (SAG) ..... BigRck
Big Rock Point Nuclear Plant (NRCH) ..... BRPNP
Big Sandy, TX [*Location identifier FAA*] (FAAL) ..... ABG
Big Sandy, TX [*FM radio station call letters*] (RBYB) ..... KBAU
Big Sisters Association of Ontario (AC) ..... BSAO
Big Sky Airline [*ICAO designator*] (FAAC) ..... BSY
Big Sky Airlines [*ICAO designator*] (AD) ..... GQ
Big Sky Hospice, Billings, MT [*Library symbol*] [*Library of Congress*] (LCLS) ..... MtBilBH
Big Smith Brands [*NASDAQ symbol*] (TTSB) ..... BSBI
Big Smith Brands, Inc. [*NASDAQ symbol*] (SAG) ..... BSBI
Big Smith Brands, Inc. [*Associated Press*] (SAG) ..... BSmith
Big Smith Brands Wrrt [*NASDAQ symbol*] (TTSB) ..... BSBIW
Big Spring [*Texas*] [*Airport symbol*] (AD) ..... HCA
Big Spring, TX [*Location identifier FAA*] (FAAL) ..... BGS
Big Spring, TX [*AM radio station call letters*] ..... KBST
Big Spring, TX [*FM radio station call letters*] ..... KBST-FM
Big Spring, TX [*FM radio station call letters*] ..... KBTS
Big Spring, TX [*AM radio station call letters*] ..... KBYG
Big Spring, TX [*Television station call letters*] ..... KWAB
Big Spring/Webb Air Force Base [*Texas*] [*ICAO location identifier*] (ICLI) ..... KBGS
Big Stone Gap, VA [*FM radio station call letters*] ..... WAXM
Big Stone Gap, VA [*AM radio station call letters*] ..... WLSD
Big Stone Hutterite Colony School, Graceville, MN [*Library symbol*] [*Library of Congress*] (LCLS) ..... MnGraBS
Big Strike Resources [*Vancouver Stock Exchange symbol*] ..... BTK
Big Sur, CA [*Location identifier FAA*] (FAAL) ..... BSR
Big Thicket Association (EA) ..... BTA
Big Thicket Conservation Association (EA) ..... BTCA
Big Thicket Coordinating Committee [*Defunct*] (EA) ..... BTCC
Big Trout Lake [*Canada*] [*Airport symbol*] (OAG) ..... YTL
Big Trout Lake, ON [*ICAO location identifier*] (ICLI) ..... CYTL
Big Ugly Dish [*Traditional satellite dish antenna*] ..... BUD
Big Ugly Fat Fellow [*Nickname for B-52 bomber*] ..... BUFF
Big Ugly Fellow [*Slang for B-52 bomber or other large aircraft*] [*Bowdlerized version*] (DOMA) ..... BUF
Big West Conference (EA) ..... BWC
Big Whale Cay, Berry Island [*Bahamas*] [*ICAO location identifier*] (ICLI) ..... MYBW
Big White Set [*Type of lush movie set used in 1930's musical-comedy films*] ..... BWS
Big White Ski Village, BC [*FM radio station call letters*] (RBYB) ..... CKFR-FM
Big White Ski Village, BC [*FM radio station call letters*] ..... CKIQ
Big Woman on Campus [*Slang*] ..... BWOC
Bigamy [*or Bigamist*] (WDAA) ..... BIG
Bigelow on Equity [*A publication*] (DLA) ..... Big Eq
Bigelow on Estoppel [*A publication*] (DLA) ..... Big Est
Bigelow on Estoppel [*A publication*] (DLA) ..... Bigelow Estop
Bigelow on Frauds [*A publication*] (DLA) ..... Big Fr
Bigelow on Torts [*A publication*] (DLA) ..... Big Torts
Bigelow's Bench and Bar of New York [*A publication*] (DLA) ..... Big B & B
Bigelow's Cases on Bills and Notes [*A publication*] (DLA) ..... Big B & N
Bigelow's Cases on Bills and Notes [*A publication*] (DLA) ..... Big Cas B & N
Bigelow's Cases, William I to Richard I [*A publication*] (DLA) ..... Big Cas
Bigelow's Cases, William I to Richard I [*A publication*] (DLA) ..... Cas Wm I
Bigelow's Edition of Jarman on Wills [*A publication*] (DLA) ..... Big Jarm Wills
Bigelow's English Procedure [*A publication*] (DLA) ..... Big Eng Proc
Bigelow's English Procedure [*A publication*] (DLA) ..... Big Proc
Bigelow's Leading Cases on Bills and Notes, Torts, or Wills [*A publication*] (DLA) ..... Big Lead Cas
Bigelow's Leading Cases on Bills and Notes, Torts, or Wills [*A publication*] (DLA) ..... Bigelow Lead Cas
Bigelow's Leading Cases on Torts [*A publication*] (DLA) ..... Big Cas Torts
Bigelow's Life and Accident Insurance Cases [*A publication*] (DLA) ..... Big L & A Ins Cas
Bigelow's Life and Accident Insurance Cases [*A publication*] (DLA) ..... Big LI Cas
Bigelow's Life and Accident Insurance Reports [*A publication*] (DLA) ..... Big L & A Ins Rep
Bigelow's Life and Accident Insurance Reports [*A publication*] (DLA) ..... Life and Acc Ins R
Bigelow's Overruled Cases [*United States, England, Ireland*] [*A publication*] (DLA) ..... Big Ov Cas
Bigelow's Placita Anglo-Normanica [*A publication*] (DLA) ..... Big Plac
Bigelow's Placita Anglo-Normanica [*A publication*] (DLA) ..... Plac Ang Nor
Bigfork School, Bigford, MN [*Library symbol*] [*Library of Congress*] (LCLS) ..... MnBfoS
Biggers, Whitten, and Whittingham [*Growth medium*] [*Gynecology*] ..... BWW
Biggin Executive Aviation Ltd. [*British ICAO designator*] (FAAC) ..... BHE
Biggin Hill [*British ICAO location identifier*] (ICLI) ..... EGKB
Biggleswade [*Urban district in England*] ..... BIGGL
Bigg's Criminal Law [*A publication*] (DLA) ..... Bigg Cr L
Biggs Free Public Library, Biggs, CA [*Library symbol Library of Congress*] (LCLS) ..... CBi
Biggs Free Public Library, Biggs, CA [*Library symbol*] [*Library of Congress*] (LCLS) ..... CBiP
Biggs on Acts Relating to Railways [*A publication*] (DLA) ..... Bigg RR Acts
Bighorn Airways, Inc. [*ICAO designator*] (FAAC) ..... BHR
Bighorn Canyon National Recreation Area ..... BICA
Bighorn Development Corp. [*Vancouver Stock Exchange symbol*] ..... BHD
Bight ..... B
Bight (ROG) ..... BGT
Bignell's Reports [*India*] [*A publication*] (DLA) ..... Big
Bignell's Reports [*India*] [*A publication*] (DLA) ..... Bign
Bigstone Minerals [*Vancouver Stock Exchange symbol*] ..... BIG
Big-Time Operator [*Slang*] ..... BTO
Bihar Law Journal Reports [*India*] [*A publication*] (DLA) ..... Bih LJ Rep
Bihar Law Journal Reports [*India*] [*A publication*] (DLA) ..... BLJ
Bihar Light Horse [*British military*] (DMA) ..... BLH
Bihar Mounted Rifles [*British military*] (DMA) ..... BMR
Bihar Reports [*India*] [*A publication*] (DLA) ..... Bih Rep
Biharmonic Equation ..... BHE
Bihorium [*During Two Hours*] [*Pharmacy*] ..... BIHOR
BII Enterprises, Inc. [*Toronto Stock Exchange symbol*] ..... BII
Bijar [*Iran*] [*ICAO location identifier*] (ICLI) ..... OICE
Bijbels Woordenboek [*A publication*] (BJA) ..... BW
Bijou ..... BIJ
Bijouterie ..... BIJTR
Bikaner [*India*] [*ICAO location identifier*] (ICLI) ..... VIBK
Bikers Against Manslaughter (EA) ..... BAM
Bikes for Africa (EA) ..... BA
Bikes Not Bombs (EA) ..... BNB
Bikini Atoll Rehabilitation Committee [*Federal government*] ..... BARC
Bikitaite [*A zeolite*] ..... BIK
Bikoro [*Zaire*] [*ICAO location identifier*] (ICLI) ..... FZBC
Bilaspur [*India*] [*ICAO location identifier*] (ICLI) ..... VABI
Bilateral [*Anatomy*] (DAVI) ..... B
Bilateral ..... BIL
Bilateral ..... BILAT
bilateral (DMAA) ..... bilat
Bilateral Acoustic Neurofibromatosis [*Medicine*] ..... BANF
Bilateral Agreements ..... BLA
Bilateral Asymmetrical [*Medicine*] (DMAA) ..... BA
Bilateral Breath Sounds [*Medicine*] (DAVI) ..... BBS
Bilateral Bundle Branch Block [*Cardiology*] ..... BBBB
Bilateral Cartoid Body Resection [*Medicine*] (DMAA) ..... BCBR
Bilateral Cleft of Lip and Palate [*Medicine*] (DMAA) ..... BCLP
Bilateral Cortical Necrosis [*Medicine*] ..... BCN
Bilateral Cystogram [*Radiography*] (DAVI) ..... BCG
Bilateral Firm (Hand) Grips (MEDA) ..... BLFG
Bilateral Hilar Lymphadenopathy [*Medicine*] (DMAA) ..... BHL
Bilateral Impedance Rheograph [*Instrumentation*] ..... BR
Bilateral, Independent, Periodic, Lateralized Epileptiform Discharge [*Medicine*] (DMAA) ..... BIPLED
Bilateral Inguinal Herniae [*Gastroenterology*] (DAVI) ..... BIH
Bilateral Internal Mammary Arteries [*Anatomy*] (DAVI) ..... BIMA
Bilateral Iterative Network ..... BITN
Bilateral Myringotomy Tubes [*Otorhinolaryngology*] (DAVI) ..... BMT
Bilateral/Non-Governmental Organization (ADA) ..... BI/NGO
Bilateral Otitis Externa [*Otorhinolaryngology*] (DAVI) ..... BOE
Bilateral Otitis Media [*Medicine*] (MAE) ..... BOM
Bilateral Pelvic Lymph Node [*Medicine*] (DAVI) ..... BPLN
Bilateral Pelvic Lymph Node Dissection [*Medicine*] (DAVI) ..... BPLND
Bilateral Quarantine Agreement ..... BQA
Bilateral Renal Agenesis [*Medicine*] (DMAA) ..... BRA
Bilateral Sagittal Osteotomy [*Medicine*] (MAE) ..... BSO
Bilateral Salpingo-Oophorectomy [*Gynecology*] (DAVI) ..... BILAT SXO
Bilateral Salpingo-Oophorectomy [*Gynecology*] ..... BSO
Bilateral Salpingo-Oophorectomy with Hysterectomy [*Medicine*] ..... BSOTH
Bilateral School [*British*] ..... B
Bilateral Serous Otitis [*Otorhinolaryngology*] (DAVI) ..... BSO
Bilateral Serous Otitis Media [*Otorhinolaryngology*] (DAVI) ..... BSOM
Bilateral Short-Leg Casts [*Orthopedics*] (DAVI) ..... BILAT SLC
Bilateral Sphenoethmoidectomy [*Medicine*] ..... BSE
Bilateral, Symmetrical, and Equal (MAE) ..... BSE
Bilateral Tubal Interruption [*Gynecology*] ..... BTI
Bilateral Tubal Ligation [*Gynecology*] (DAVI) ..... BLT
Bilateral Tubal Ligation [*Gynecology*] ..... BTL
Bilateral Upper Dorsal Sympathectomy [*Medicine*] (DMAA) ..... BUDS
Bilateral Upper Extremity [*Occupational therapy*] ..... BUE
Bilateral Vas Ligation [*Medicine*] ..... BVL
Bilateration Ranging Transponder (MCD) ..... BRT
Bilateration Ranging Transponder System (MCD) ..... BRTS
Bilayer Lipid Membrane [*Physical chemistry*] ..... BLM
Bilbao [*Spain*] [*Airport symbol*] (OAG) ..... BIO
Bilbao [*Spain ICAO location identifier*] (ICLI) ..... LEBB
Bilbilographic Records Conversion (EDAC) ..... BIBCON
Bild Zeitung [*Picture newspaper*] [*German*] ..... BZ
Bilderberg Continuum Atmosphere ..... BCA
Bildschirmtext [*Viewdata system*] [*Federal Ministry of Posts and Telecommunications*] [*Germany*] ..... BTX
Bildudalur [*Iceland*] [*Airport symbol*] (OAG) ..... BIU
Bile [*Blood group*] ..... Bi
Bile Acid [*Gastroenterology*] (AAMN) ..... BA
Bile Acid Concentration [*Gastroenterology*] ..... BAC
Bile Acid-Dependent Fraction [*Medicine*] ..... BADF
Bile Acid-Independent Canalicular Fraction [*Medicine*] ..... BAICF
Bile Acid-Independent Fraction [*Medicine*] ..... BAIF
Bile Canalicular Membrane ..... BCM
Bile Canaliculi [*Anatomy*] ..... BC
Bile Driver (DWSG) ..... BD
Bile Duct [*Medicine*] ..... BD
Bile Duct Examination [*Medicine*] ..... BDE
Bile Duct Exploration [*Gastroenterology*] (DAVI) ..... BDE
Bile Duct Growth Factor [*Biochemistry*] ..... BDGF
Bile Duct Obstruction [*Medicine*] ..... BDO
Bile Esculin [*Medicine*] ..... BE
Bile Flow [*Physiology*] ..... BF

Bile Flow Rate [*Physiology*] ..... BFR
Bile Salt Independent Fraction [*Medicine*] (DMAA) ..... BSIF
Bile Salts [*Biochemistry*] ..... BS
Bile Salts/Phospholipid [*Ratio*] ..... BS/PL
Bilene [*Mozambique*] [*ICAO location identifier*] (ICLI) ..... FQBI
Bile-Salt Limited Lipase [*An enzyme*] ..... BSL
Bilevel (MCD) ..... BL
Bilevel Positive Airway Pressure [*Medicine*] (DMAA) ..... BIPAP
Bilevel Pulse (MCD) ..... BLP
Bilevel Quality Assurance Program [*NASA*] (KSC) ..... BQAP
Bilevel Response Unit ..... BRU
Bilevel Stimulus Unit ..... BSU
Biliary Atresia [*Medicine*] (DMAA) ..... BA
Biliary Colic [*Medicine*] (DMAA) ..... BC
Biliary Protein Fraction ..... BPF
Biliary Tract Disease [*Medicine*] (DMAA) ..... BTD
Bilin-Binding Protein [*Biochemistry*] ..... BBP
Bilinear Target Factor Analysis [*Mathematics*] ..... BTFA
Bilingual [*Texts*] (BJA) ..... bil
Bilingual Community Educator ..... BCE
Bilingual Counsellor ..... BC
Bilingual Education (EDAC) ..... BE
Bilingual Education Bibliographic Abstracts [*National Clearinghouse for Bilingual Education*] [*Rosslyn, VA Database*] ..... BEBA
Bilingual Education Telecommunications Network [*National Clearinghouse for Bilingual Education*] [*Wheaton, MD*] (TSSD) ..... BETNET
Bilingual Evaluation Technical Assistance Project (EDAC) ..... BETA
Bilingual Foundation of the Arts (EA) ..... BFA
Bilingual Information Instructor ..... BII
Bilingual Information Officer ..... BIO
Bilingual Obstetric Liaison Officer ..... BOLO
Bilingual Syntax Measure [*English and Spanish test*] ..... BSM
Bilinugal Education Act of 1968 (EDAC) ..... BEA
Bilirubin [*Biochemistry*] (AAMN) ..... BIL
Bilirubin [*Medicine*] (DMAA) ..... BIL
Bilirubin [*Clinical chemistry*] ..... bili
Bilirubin [*Gastroenterology and neonatology*] (DAVI) ..... BILIR
Bilirubin [*Gastroenterology and neonatology*] (DAVI) ..... bilirub
Bilirubin [*Biochemistry*] ..... BR
Bilirubin Clearance [*Gastroenterology*] (DAVI) ..... C_{BR}
Bilirubin Diglucuronide [*Biochemistry*] ..... BDG
Bilirubin, Direct and Indirect [*Clinical chemistry*] (CPH) ..... Bili D/I
Bilirubin Monoglucuronide [*Biochemistry*] ..... BMG
Bilirubin of Unknown Origin [*Gastroenterology*] (DAVI) ..... BUO
Bilirubin Oxidase [*An enzyme*] ..... BOX
Bilirubin Production [*Biochemistry*] (MAE) ..... BRP
Bilirubin, Total [*Clinical chemistry*] (CPH) ..... Bili T
Bill Blass [*Couturier*] ..... BB
Bill Book [*Shipping*] ..... BB
Bill Farrar Fan Club (EA) ..... BFFC
Bill for Collection ..... B/C
Bill Glass Evangelistic Association (EA) ..... BGEA
Bill in Care Of [*Telecommunications*] (TEL) ..... BCO
Bill Lodged [*British*] (ADA) ..... BL
Bill of Entry [*Shipping*] ..... B/E
Bill of Exchange [*Accounting*] ..... BE
Bill of Health ..... BH
Bill of Lading [*MARAD*] (TAG) ..... B/L
Bill of Lading ..... BIL
Bill of Lading [*Shipping*] (NOAA) ..... BILDG
Bill of Lading [*Shipping*] ..... BL
Bill of Lading [*Shipping*] ..... BLADING
Bill of Lading [*Shipping*] ..... BoL
Bill of Material Processor (IAA) ..... BIMAP
Bill of Material Processor ..... BOMP
Bill of Material Status (MCD) ..... BOMS
Bill of Material System (MCD) ..... BMS
Bill of Materials [*Manufacturing*] (MUGU) ..... BM
Bill of Materials (DNAB) ..... BMAT
Bill of Materials [*Digital Dynamics Ltd.*] [*Software package*] ..... BOM
Bill of Materials [*Manufacturing*] (ODBW) ..... bom
Bill of Parcels ..... BP
Bill of Rights ..... BR
Bill of Rights Foundation (EA) ..... BORF
Bill of Rights Journal [*A publication*] (DLA) ..... Bill of Rights J
Bill of Rights Journal [*A publication*] (DLA) ..... Bill Rts J
Bill of Rights Journal [*A publication*] (DLA) ..... BRJ
Bill of Rights of Virginia [*A publication*] (DLA) ..... BRV
Bill of Rights Review [*A publication*] (DLA) ..... Bill Rights Rev
Bill of Sale ..... BS
Bill of Sight [*Customs*] ..... B/ST
Bill of Sight (ODBW) ..... B/St
Bill of Sight [*Customs*] ..... BS
Bill of Store ..... BS
Bill of Work (NASA) ..... BOW
Bill Tomorrow [*Business term*] ..... BT
Billboard (VRA) ..... bilbd
Billboard Information Network [*Billboard Publications, Inc.*] [*Information service or system*] (IID) ..... BIN
Billboard Publications, Inc. ..... BPI
Billed At [*Commerce*] ..... B/A
Billed but Not Received (AFIT) ..... BNR
Billed Office Account Code [*Army*] (AFIT) ..... BOAC
Billerica Historical Society, Billerica, MA [*Library symbol Library of Congress*] (LCLS) ..... MBilHi

Billericay [*England*] ..... BILL
Billet [*Bill*] [*French Business term*] (ROG) ..... BET
Billet (AABC) ..... BIL
Billet (MSA) ..... BL
Billet a Payer [*Bill Payable*] [*French Business term*] ..... BAP
Billet a Recevoir [*Bill Receivable*] [*French Business term*] ..... BAR
Billet Master [*Military British*] (ROG) ..... BM
Billet Occupational Code [*Military*] (CAAL) ..... BOC
Billet Selection Program [*Military*] (DNAB) ..... BSP
Billet Sequence Code ..... BSC
Billet Split Lens ..... BSL
Billet Steel (MSA) ..... BLSTL
Billeting ..... BLLTNG
Billeting and Accommodations Advisory [*Military communications*] ..... BAA
Billeting and Inventory [*Military*] ..... B & I
Billiard [*Freight*] ..... BILLD
Billiard ..... BILLD
Billiard and Bowling Institute of America (EA) ..... BBIA
Billiard Congress of America (EA) ..... BCA
Billiard Players Association of America ..... BPA
Billiards ..... BILL
Billiards and Snooker Association of Western Australia ..... BSAWA
Billiards and Snooker Control Council [*An association*] (EAIO) ..... BSCC
Billiards Association [*British*] (BI) ..... BA
Billiards Trade Association [*British*] (BI) ..... BTA
Billie Jo Spears Fan Club (EA) ..... BJSFC
Billikin Resources, Inc. [*Vancouver Stock Exchange symbol*] ..... BIL
Billing ..... BLLKNG
Billing, Accounts Receivable, Sales Analysis (IBMDP) ..... BARSA
Billing Advice Code ..... BAC
Billing and Instruction Book ..... B & IB
Billing and Ordering Forum [*Exchange Carriers Standards Association*] [*Telecommunications*] ..... BOF
Billing and Prince's Law and Practice of Patents [*A publication*] (DLA) ..... Bill & Pr Pat
Billing Cease Date (TEL) ..... BC
Billing Day (DCTA) ..... BD
Billing Group [*Telecommunications*] (TEL) ..... BG
Billing Information Concepts [*NASDAQ symbol*] (SAG) ..... BILL
Billing Information Concepts [*Associated Press*] (SAG) ..... Bill Info
Billing Instructions [*Telecommunications*] (TEL) ..... BI
Billing, Inventory Control, Accounts Receivable, Sales Analysis (IBMDP) ..... BICARSA
Billing. Law of Awards and Arbitration [*1845*] [*A publication*] (DLA) ..... Bil Aw
Billing. Law Relating to Pews [*1845*] [*A publication*] (DLA) ..... Bil Pews
Billing Memo Charge [*Business term*] ..... BMC
Billing Name and Address ..... BNA
Billing Telephone Number [*Telecommunications*] (TEL) ..... BTN
Billing Validation Application ..... BVA
Billing-Collecting-Remitting [*Accounting*] (TEL) ..... BCR
Billings [*Montana*] [*Airport symbol*] (OAG) ..... BIL
Billings Clinic, Billings, MT [*Library symbol*] [*Library of Congress*] (LCLS) ..... MtBilC
Billings Family Life Center [*Australia*] ..... BFLC
Billings Mental Health Center, Billings, MT [*Library symbol*] [*Library of Congress*] (LCLS) ..... MtBilMH
Billings, MT [*FM radio station call letters*] (RBYB) ..... KBBB-FM
Billings, MT [*FM radio station call letters*] ..... KBKO
Billings, MT [*AM radio station call letters*] ..... KBLG
Billings, MT [*FM radio station call letters*] ..... KCTR-FM
Billings, MT [*AM radio station call letters*] (RBYB) ..... KDWG
Billings, MT [*FM radio station call letters*] ..... KEMC
Billings, MT [*AM radio station call letters*] ..... KGHL
Billings, MT [*FM radio station call letters*] ..... KIDX
Billings, MT [*FM radio station call letters*] ..... KKBR
Billings, MT [*AM radio station call letters*] ..... KMAY
Billings, MT [*FM radio station call letters*] ..... KRKX
Billings, MT [*Television station call letters*] ..... KSVI
Billings, MT [*Television station call letters*] ..... KTVQ
Billings, MT [*Television station call letters*] ..... KULR
Billings, MT [*AM radio station call letters*] ..... KURL
Billings, MT [*FM radio station call letters*] ..... KYYA
Billings, MT [*Location identifier FAA*] (FAAL) ..... LKO
Billings Ovulation Method Association of the United States (EA) ..... BOM
Billings Public Library, Billings, MT [*Library symbol Library of Congress*] (LCLS) ..... MtBil
Billings Public Schools, Billings, MT [*Library symbol*] [*Library of Congress*] (LCLS) ..... MtBils
Billings Township Public Library, Kagawong, Ontario [*Library symbol National Library of Canada*] (NLC) ..... OKBT
Billion (MCD) ..... B
Billion ..... BIL
Billion (EECA) ..... BILLI
Billion ..... BN
Billion Barrels [*Shipping*] ..... BB
Billion Barrels of Oil ..... BBO
Billion Channel Extraterrestrial Assay [*Search for intelligent life*] ..... BETA
Billion Conductor Feet [*Telecommunications*] (TEL) ..... BCF
Billion Cubic Feet ..... BCF
Billion Cubic Meters ..... BCM
Billion Electron Volts ..... BeV
Billion Floating-Point Operations per Second [*Computer science*] ..... BFLOPS
Billion Gallons (EPA) ..... BG
Billion Gallons per Day ..... BGD
Billion Instructions [*Power measurement*] [*Computer science*] (IAA) ..... BIN

Billion Instructions per Second [*Computing power measurement*] [*Computer science*]	BIPS
Billion Liters per Day	BLD
Billion Years	BY
Billion Years	BYR
Billionaire Boys Club (EA)	BBC
Billions of Barrels of Oil Equivalent (MCD)	BBOE
Billions of Cubic Feet per Day [*of gas*]	BCFD
Billions of Operations per Second (DOMA)	BOPS
Billionth (IDOE)	nano-
Billot. Traite de l'Extradition [*A publication*] (DLA)	Billot Extrad
Bills (ROG)	B
Bills and Notes [*Legal term*] (DLA)	B & N
Bills and Notes	BN
Bills Discounted	BD
Bills of Exchange Act [*1882*] [*British*]	BEA
Bills of Lading (ODBW)	Bs/L
Bills of Lading Act	BLA
Bills Payable [*Business term*]	BP
Bills Payable [*Business term*]	BSP
Bills Receivable [*Business term*] (ODBW)	b rec
Bills Receivable [*Business term*]	BR
Bills Recoverable [*Business term*] (ADA)	BREC
Billund [*Denmark*] [*Airport symbol*] (OAG)	BLL
Billund [*Denmark ICAO location identifier*] (ICLI)	EKBI
Billy Barty Foundation for Little People (EA)	BBFLP
Billy Blanton Fan Club (EA)	BBFC
Billy Cate Fan Club (EA)	BCFC
Billy "Crash" Craddock Fan Club (EA)	BCCFC
Billy Graham Evangelistic Association (EA)	BGEA
Billy Troy Fan Club [*Defunct*] (EA)	BTFC
Bilma [*Niger*] [*ICAO location identifier*] (ICLI)	DRRI
Biloela [*Australia Airport symbol*]	THG
Biloxi [*Diocesan abbreviation*] [*Mississippi*] (TOCD)	BLX
Biloxi/Keesler Air Force Base [*Mississippi*] [*ICAO location identifier*] (ICLI)	KBIX
Biloxi, MS [*Location identifier FAA*] (FAAL)	BIX
Biloxi, MS [*Location identifier FAA*] (FAAL)	EKE
Biloxi, MS [*Location identifier FAA*] (FAAL)	OLQ
Biloxi, MS [*Television station call letters*]	WLOX
Biloxi, MS [*FM radio station call letters*]	WMAH
Biloxi, MS [*Television station call letters*]	WMAH-TV
Biloxi, MS [*FM radio station call letters*]	WMJY
Biloxi, MS [*AM radio station call letters*]	WVMI
Biloxi, MS [*AM radio station call letters*]	WXBD
Biloxi Public Library, Biloxi, MS [*Library symbol Library of Congress*] (LCLS)	MsB
Biltine [*Chad*] [*ICAO location identifier*] (ICLI)	FTTE
Biltmore Forest, NC [*FM radio station call letters*]	WZLS
Biltrite Nightingale, Inc. [*Toronto Stock Exchange symbol*]	BLT
Bima [*Indonesia*] [*Airport symbol*] (OAG)	BMU
Bima/Palibelo [*Indonesia*] [*ICAO location identifier*] (ICLI)	WRRB
Bimbereke [*Benin*] [*ICAO location identifier*] (ICLI)	DBBR
Bimetal Heat Sensor [*Automotive engineering*]	BHS
Bimetal Steel-Aluminum (OA)	BSA
Bimetal Turbine Wheel	BTW
Bimetal Vacuum Switching Valve [*Automotive engineering*]	BVSV
Bimetallic	BMTLC
Bimini [*Bahamas*] [*Airport symbol*] (OAG)	BIM
Bimini-North [*Bahamas*] [*Airport symbol*] (OAG)	NSB
Bimodal Filter (PDAA)	BMF
Bimodular [*Journalism*] (WDMC)	bimo
Bimolecular Lipid Membrane	BLM
Bimolecular Liquid Membrane [*Biochemistry*] (DAVI)	BLM
Bi-Monthly	b
Bimonthly	BI-M
Bimonthly	BM
Bi-Monthly Law Review. University of Detroit [*A publication*] (DLA)	Bi-Mo L Rev
Bimonthly Progress Report	BMPR
Bimonthly Progress Report	BPR
Binary (BUR)	B
Binary (AFM)	BIN
Binary Adaptation Kit [*Computer science*] (PCM)	BAK
Binary Add [*Computer science*]	BA
Binary Angular Measurement [*Military*] (CAAL)	BAM
Binary Asymmetric Channel	BAC
Binary Asymmetric Dependent Channel	BADC
Binary Asymmetric Independent Channel	BAIC
Binary Automatic Computer [*Eckert-Maudely Computer Corp.*]	BINAC
Binary Automatic Data Annotation System	BADAS
Binary BIT [*Binary Digit*] Mapped [*Computer science*]	BBM
Binary Chemical Warhead System (DWSG)	BCW
Binary Code	BC
Binary Code Box	BCB
Binary Code Frequency Shift Keying [*SAGE*]	BCFSK
Binary Code Procedural Language [*Computer science*]	BCPL
Binary Coded Decimal (NITA)	BCD
Binary Coded Decimal Digit (IAA)	BCDD
Binary Coded Matrix [*Telecommunications*] (TEL)	BCM
Binary Communications: Synchronous [*Computer science*] (NITA)	BCS
Binary Compatibility Layer [*Computer science*] (PCM)	BCL
Binary Compatibility Specification [*Computer science*] (PCM)	BCS
Binary Compatibility Standard (CDE)	BCS
Binary Constitution Information Service (MCD)	BCIS
Binary Convolutional Code (IAA)	BCC
Binary Convolutional Self-Orthogonal Code [*Computer science*] (PDAA)	BCSOC

Binary Counter	BC
Binary Counting Unit (IEEE)	BCU
Binary Cycle High-Temperature Gas-Cooled Reactor [*Nuclear energy*] (NUCP)	BI-HTGR
Binary Decimal Counter [*Computer science*]	BDC
Binary Deck-to-Tape [*Computer science*]	BDT
Binary Decode Scaler [*Computer science*]	BDS
Binary Decoder [*Computer science*]	BD
Binary Delta Modulation	BDM
Binary Differential Phase-Shift Keying [*Telecommunications*] (TEL)	BDPSK
Binary Digit [*Computer science*] (MCD)	BD
Binary Digit (IAA)	BIGIT
Binary Digit (IDOE)	BIT
Binary Digit (IDOE)	bit
Binary Digital Data [*Computer science*]	BDD
Binary Digital Multiplier [*Computer science*]	BDM
Binary Digits per Second [*Computer science*] (HGAA)	BIT/SEC
Binary Discrete (MCD)	BD-
Binary Discriminant Analysis [*Statistics*]	BDA
Binary Divide	BD
Binary Divide (MSA)	BDV
Binary Dump Routine	BDR
Binary Electromagnetic Signal Signature	BESS
Binary Electronics Sequence Computer (BARN)	BESC
Binary Encoded Quaternary (MCD)	BEQ
Binary Encoded Ternary (MCD)	BET
Binary Encounter Approximation [*Nuclear physics*]	BEA
Binary Entity-Relationship Model [*Computer science*] (HGAA)	BERM
Binary Envelope Locked Loop (MCD)	BELL
Binary Error Erasure Channel (IEEE)	BEEC
Binary Exponential Backoff [*Telecommunications*] (OSI)	BEB
Binary Fault Analysis Program [*Computer science*] (MHDB)	BFAP
Binary Fault Isolation Chart [*Computer science*] (MHDB)	BFIC
Binary File Transfer (CDE)	BFT
Binary Floating Point Resistor [*Computer science*] (MHDB)	BFPR
Binary Floating-Point Digital Differential Analyzer (IEEE)	BFPDDA
Binary Fourier Representation (PDAA)	BIFORE
Binary Frequency Generator (IEEE)	BFG
Binary Homing Device	BHD
Binary Image Processor [*Computer science*]	BIP
Binary Information Exchange	BIX
Binary Information Transfer System (IAA)	BITS
Binary Input - Binary Output Machine (IAA)	BIBOM
Binary Input - Binary Output Moore Machine (IAA)	BIBOMM
Binary Interchange File Format (CDE)	BIFF
Binary Intersystem Transmission Standard	BITS
Binary Large Object [*Computer science*]	BLOB
Binary Light Beam Deflector	BLBD
Binary Load Dump [*Computer science*] (MHDI)	BLD
Binary Logic Element [*Computer science*] (BUR)	BLE
Binary Logical Association	BLA
Binary Magnetic Core	BMC
Binary Metal and Metalloid Constitution Data Center [*Illinois Institute of Technology*]	BMMCDC
Binary Mobile Phase [*Chromatography*]	BMP
Binary Multiply	BM
Binary Munitions	BIN MUN
Binary Northrop Automatic Computer [*Computer science*] (HGAA)	BINAC
Binary Number [*Computer science*]	BN
Binary Number System [*Computer science*]	BNS
Binary Order of Magnitude [*Computer science*]	BOM
Binary Output Program	BOP
Binary Oxide Film [*Memory*]	BOF
Binary Pattern Detector	BIPAD
Binary Phase Shifting Key [*Computer science*] (ACRL)	BPSK
Binary Phase-Only Filter [*Optics*]	BPOF
Binary Phase-Shift Keying [*Computer science*] (IEEE)	BPSK
Binary Program Loader	BPL
Binary Program Space [*Computer science*]	BPS
Binary Rate Divider	BRD
Binary Rate Multiplier (IAA)	BRM
Binary Read [*Computer science*] (HGAA)	BRD
Binary Relationship Model [*Computer science*] (NITA)	BRM
Binary Ring Sequence	BRS
Binary Run Tape [*Computer science*] (BUR)	BRT
Binary Scale (AAG)	BS
Binary Search Tree (IAA)	BST
Binary Space Partition [*Computer science*] (PCM)	BSP
Binary Subtract	BS
Binary Symmetric Channel [*Computer science*]	BSC
Binary Symmetric Dependent Channel [*Computer science*]	BSDC
Binary Symmetric Independent Channel [*Computer science*]	BSIC
Binary Synchronous [*Telecommunications*] (NITA)	BSC
Binary Synchronous Communication [*IBM Corp.*] [*Computer science*]	BSC
Binary Synchronous Communication System (MHDB)	BSCS
Binary Synchronous Communications [*Protocol*] [*IBM Co.*] (ACRL)	BSC
Binary Synchronous Communications Adapter [*Computer science*]	BSCA
Binary Synchronous Communications Controller [*Computer science*] (MHDI)	BSCC
Binary Synchronous Communications Macro	BSCM
Binary Synchronous Communications protocol [*IBM Co.*] (ACRL)	BISYNC
Binary Synchronous Communications/Start-Stop	BSC/SS
Binary Synchronous Control	BSC
Binary Synchronous Transmission [*or Communication*] [*Computer science*]	BISYNC

Binary Term [*Computer science*] ... byte
Binary Time Code (MCD) ... BTC
Binary to Decimal [*Computer science*] ... B/D
Binary to Decimal [*Computer science*] (BUR) ... BTD
Binary to Hexadecimal (BUR) ... BH
Binary to Octal [*Computer science*] (BUR) ... BO
Binary to Seven Segment [*Computer science*] ... BINSS
Binary to Text Encoding [*Computer science*] ... UUEncode
Binary Transversal Filter (IAA) ... BTF
Binary Universal for Representation [*Computer science*] ... BUFR
Binary Voltage Weigher ... BVW
Binary Workstation [*Computer science*] ... BW
Binary-Analog Conversion [*Computer science*] (DIT) ... BAC
Binary-Coded Data [*or Decimal*] [*Computer science*] ... BCD
Binary-Coded Decimal/Binary (DEN) ... BCD/B
Binary-Coded Decimal Counter ... BCDC
Binary-Coded Decimal Interchange Code (IEEE) ... BCDIC
Binary-Coded Decimal Interchange Code ... BDIC
Binary-Coded Decimal Nonadjacent Form [*Computer science*] (MHDI) ... BCDNAF
Binary-Coded Decimal/Quaternary (DEN) ... BCD/Q
Binary-Coded Hexadecimal (MCD) ... BCH
Binary-Coded Hollerith ... BCH
Binary-Coded Information ... BCI
Binary-Coded Octal [*Computer science*] ... BCO
Binary-Coded Range Time (MUGU) ... BCRT
Binary-Coded Range Time Signal (MUGU) ... BCRTS
Binary-Element Error Ratio (IAA) ... BEER
Binary-Erasure Channel (IAA) ... BEC
Binary-File Transfer - Non-Standard Facilities Frame [*Microsoft Corp.*] (PCM) ... BFT-NSF
Binary-Floating-Decimal [*Computer science*] ... BFD
Binary-to-Decimal Converter [*Computer science*] ... BIDEC
Binary-to-Decimal Decoder [*Computer science*] ... BDD
Binary-to-Decimal Transmitter [*Computer science*] (NOAA) ... BDT
Binasal Pharyngeal Airway [*Anatomy*] (MAE) ... BNPA
Binational Agricultural Research and Development Fund [*US-Israeli*] [*Research center*] (IRC) ... BARD
Binational Science Foundation [*U.S.-Israel*] [*Research center*] ... BSF
Binaural Alternate Loudness Balance Test (MAE) ... BALB
Binaural Analysis System [*Noise testing*] [*Automotive engineering*] ... BAS
Binaural Hearing Impairment ... BHI
Binaural Intensity Effect ... BIE
Binaural Masking Level Difference (PDAA) ... BMLD
Binaural Phase Effect ... BPE
Binbrook [*British ICAO location identifier*] (ICLI) ... EGXB
Binder (MSA) ... BDR
Binder ... BDR
Binder [*MARC relator code*] [*Library of Congress*] (LCCP) ... bnd
Binder ... BNDR
Binder (VRA) ... bndr
Binder ... BR
Binder Aviatik, Scheibe-Bruns, Schleicher-Bruns [*Germany ICAO aircraft manufacturer identifier*] (ICAO) ... BS
Binder Control Subsystem ... BINCOS
Binders' Guild (EA) ... BG
Bindery ... BDRY
Binding (MSA) ... BDG
Binding ... BDNG
Binding (ROG) ... BIND
Binding Capacity ... BC
Binding Chain [*Toxin*] ... B
Binding Designer [*MARC relator code*] [*Library of Congress*] (LCCP) ... bdd
Binding Edge (ADA) ... BE
Binding Energy ... BE
Binding Energy per Atom (IAA) ... BEPA
Binding Energy per Particle (IAA) ... BEPP
Binding Head ... BDGH
Binding Head (IAA) ... BDH
Binding Head Steel (IAA) ... BHS
Binding Industries of America (EA) ... BIA
Binding Margin [*Bookbinding*] (ADA) ... BM
Binding/No Date [*Publishing*] (DGA) ... B/ND
Binding Post (KSC) ... BP
Binding Post Chamber [*Telecommunications*] (TEL) ... BPC
Binding Protein [*Biochemistry*] ... BP
Binding Unit (IEEE) ... BU
Bindings [*Publishing*] ... BDS
Bindja [*Zaire*] [*ICAO location identifier*] (ICLI) ... FZBQ
Bindley Western Indus [*NYSE symbol*] (TTSB) ... BDY
Bindley Western Industries [*NYSE symbol*] (SAG) ... BDY
Bindley Western Industries [*Associated Press*] (SAG) ... Bindly
Bindura [*Zimbabwe*] [*ICAO location identifier*] (ICLI) ... FVBD
Binet-Simon [*Test*] [*Psychology*] (DAVI) ... BS
Bing Crosby Historical Society (EA) ... BCHS
Bing Crosby Productions ... BCP
Bingham and Colvin on Rents [*A publication*] (DLA) ... Bing & Colv Rents
Bingham. Infancy and Coveture [*1826*] [*A publication*] (DLA) ... Bing Inf
Bingham. Judgments and Executions [*1815*] [*A publication*] (DLA) ... Bing Ex
Bingham. Judgments and Executions [*1815*] [*A publication*] (DLA) ... Bing Judg
Bingham. Landlord and Tenant [*1820*] [*A publication*] (DLA) ... Bing L & T
Bingham Memorial Hospital, Medical Library, Blackfoot, ID [*Library symbol*] [*Library of Congress*] (LCLS) ... IdBfBH
Bingham. New Cases, English Common Pleas [*131-133 English Reprint*] [*A publication*] (DLA) ... Bing N Cas
Bingham. New Cases, English Common Pleas [*131-133 English Reprint*] [*A publication*] (DLA) ... Bing NC
Bingham. New Cases, English Common Pleas [*131-133 English Reprint*] [*A publication*] (DLA) ... Bing NC (Eng)
Bingham. New Cases, English Common Pleas [*A publication*] (DLA) ... BNC
Bingham Oceanographic Collection ... BOC
Bingham Oceanographic Laboratory (NOAA) ... BOL
Bingham on the Law of Real Property [*A publication*] (DLA) ... Bing RP
Bingham on the Laws of Descent [*A publication*] (DLA) ... Bing Des
Bingham Township Library, Suttons Bay, MI [*Library symbol Library of Congress*] (LCLS) ... MiSb
Bingham's Actions and Defences in Real Property [*A publication*] (DLA) ... Bing Act & Def
Bingham's English Common Pleas Reports [*130-131 English Reprint*] [*A publication*] (DLA) ... Bing
Bingham's English Common Pleas Reports [*130-131 English Reprint*] [*A publication*] (DLA) ... Bing (Eng)
Bingham's Executory Contracts, Etc. [*A publication*] (DLA) ... Bing Ex Cont
Binghamton [*New York*] [*Airport symbol*] (OAG) ... BGM
Binghamton [*New York*] [*Seismograph station code, US Geological Survey*] (SEIS) ... BNY
Binghamton, NY [*Location identifier FAA*] (FAAL) ... AAJ
Binghamton, NY [*Location identifier FAA*] (FAAL) ... IMZ
Binghamton, NY [*FM radio station call letters*] ... WAAL
Binghamton, NY [*Television station call letters*] ... WBNG
Binghamton, NY [*FM radio station call letters*] ... WHRW
Binghamton, NY [*FM radio station call letters*] ... WHWK
Binghamton, NY [*Television station call letters*] ... WICZ
Binghamton, NY [*AM radio station call letters*] ... WINR
Binghamton, NY [*FM radio station call letters*] ... WJIK
Binghamton, NY [*AM radio station call letters*] ... WKOP
Binghamton, NY [*Television station call letters*] ... WMGC
Binghamton, NY [*AM radio station call letters*] ... WNBF
Binghamton, NY [*FM radio station call letters*] ... WSKG
Binghamton, NY [*Television station call letters*] ... WSKG-TV
Binghamton, NY [*FM radio station call letters*] ... WSQX
Binghamton Public Library, Binghamton, NY [*Library symbol Library of Congress*] (LCLS) ... NBi
Bingo ... BNG
Bingo Clubs and Halls [*Public-performance tariff class*] [*British*] ... BO
Bing's Friends and Collectors Society (EA) ... BFCS
Biniguni [*Papua New Guinea*] [*Airport symbol*] (OAG) ... XBN
Binks Manufacturing Co. [*AMEX symbol*] (SPSG) ... BIN
Binks Manufacturing Co. [*Associated Press*] (SAG) ... BinkMf
Binks Mfg. [*AMEX symbol*] (TTSB) ... BIN
Binmore's Index-Digest of Michigan Reports [*A publication*] (DLA) ... Bin Dig
Binmore's Index-Digest of Michigan Reports [*A publication*] (DLA) ... Binm Ind
Binnacle (MSA) ... BNCL
Binney's Pennsylvania Reports [*1799-1814*] [*A publication*] (DLA) ... Bin
Binney's Pennsylvania Reports [*1799-1814*] [*A publication*] (DLA) ... Binn (PA)
Binney's Pennsylvania Supreme Court Reports [*1799-1814*] [*A publication*] (DLA) ... Binn
Binns' Pennsylvania Justice [*A publication*] (DLA) ... Binn Jus
Binns' Pennsylvania Justice [*A publication*] (DLA) ... Binns' Just
Binocular (MSA) ... BNCLR
Binocular Deprivation [*Optics*] ... BD
Binocular Earth Sensor (MCD) ... BES
Binocular Single Vision [*Ophthalmology*] ... BSV
Binocular Visual Efficiency ... BVE
Binoculars [*Slang British*] (DSUE) ... BINOCS
Binoculars (VNW) ... BINO(S)
Binomial Expansion [*Mathematics*] ... BINOMEXP
Binomial Probability Distributions (MCD) ... BINDIS
Binomial Proportion Test (MCD) ... BITEST
Bin-Tainer [*Shipping*] (DCTA) ... B
Binter Canarais [*Spain ICAO designator*] (FAAC) ... IBB
Binter-Mediterraneo [*Spain ICAO designator*] (FAAC) ... BIM
Bintulu [*Malaysia*] [*Airport symbol*] (OAG) ... BTU
Bintulu [*Malaysia*] [*ICAO location identifier*] (ICLI) ... WBGB
Bintuni [*Indonesia*] [*Airport symbol*] (OAG) ... NTI
Binza [*Leopoldville*] [*Zaire*] [*Seismograph station code, US Geological Survey*] (SEIS) ... BIN
Bio Imaging Technol Wrrt'G' [*NASDAQ symbol*] (TTSB) ... BITIW
Bio Imaging Technologies Inc. [*NASDAQ symbol*] (TTSB) ... BITI
Bio Technica Intl. [*NASDAQ symbol*] (TTSB) ... BIOT
Bio Technology Gen Wrrt'A' [*NASDAQ symbol*] (TTSB) ... BTGCL
Bio Transplant Inc. [*NASDAQ symbol*] (TTSB) ... BTRN
Bioaccumulation Factor [*Nuclear energy*] (NRCH) ... BAF
Bioactive ... B
Bioactive Aortic Substance [*Biochemistry*] ... BAS
Bioanalytical Systems ... BAS
Bioartificial Liver ... BAL
Bioassay Program ... BP
Bioassay Reagent ... BR
Bioassay Tank [*Spacecraft*] [*NASA*] ... BAT
Bioastronautic Orbiting Space Station [*or System*] (MUGU) ... BOSS
Bioastronautics Laboratory Research Tool (IEEE) ... BIOALRT
Bioastronautics Operational Support Unit (MCD) ... BOSU
Bioastronautics Orbital Space Program [*Air Force*] ... BOSP
Bio-Automated Roving Target [*Gun-like toy*] ... BART
Biobreeding/Worcester [*Rat variety*] ... BB/W
BioChem Pharma [*NASDAQ symbol*] (TTSB) ... BCHXF
Biochem Pharma, Inc. [*NASDAQ symbol*] (SAG) ... BCHX
Biochem Pharma, Inc. [*Associated Press*] (SAG) ... BioPhar
Biochemical [*or Biochemistry*] ... BIOCHEM

Biochemical Modeling [*Computer science*] ... BIOMOD
Biochemical Oxygen Demand ... BOD
Biochemical Oxygen Demand Over Five Days [*Biological*] (GNE) ... BOD5
Biochemical Process Industry ... BPI
Biochemical Profile (DAVI) ... BCP
Biochemical Research Foundation, Franklin Institute, Newark, DE [*Closed*] [*Library symbol*] [*Library of Congress*] (LCLS) ... PPF-B
Biochemical Society [*London, England*] (EAIO) ... BS
Biochemical Systems Theory ... BST
Biochemical Test Monitor ... BTM
Biochemistry (DD) ... Biochem
Biochemistry ... BIOCHEM
Biocide Injection System (MCD) ... BIS
Biocircuits Corp. [*NASDAQ symbol*] (SAG) ... BIOC
Biocircuits Corp. [*Associated Press*] (SAG) ... Biocirc
Biocompatible Orthopedic Polymer [*Medicine*] ... BOP
Bioconcentration Factor [*of chemicals by living organisms*] ... BCF
Biocontrol Science and Technology [*A publication*] ... BST
Biocontrol Technology [*NASDAQ symbol*] (TTSB) ... BICO
Biocontrol Technology, Inc. [*NASDAQ symbol*] (NQ) ... BICO
Biocontrol Technology, Inc. [*Associated Press*] (SAG) ... Bioctrl
Biocraft Laboratories, Inc. [*NYSE symbol*] (SPSG) ... BCL
Biocraft Laboratories, Inc. [*Associated Press*] (SAG) ... Biocft
Biocraft Labs [*NYSE symbol*] (TTSB) ... BCL
Biocryst Pharmaceuticals, Inc. [*NASDAQ symbol*] (SAG) ... BCRX
Biocryst Pharmaceuticals, Inc. [*Associated Press*] (SAG) ... Biocryst
BioCryst Pharm'l [*NASDAQ symbol*] (TTSB) ... BCRX
Biocular Display Driver's Viewer ... BDDV
Bio-Degradable Plastics, Inc. ... BPI
Biodegradable Volatile Solids [*Analytical chemistry*] ... BVS
Biodegrade [*or Biodegradable*] (WDAA) ... BIODEG
Bio-Dental Technologies [*NASDAQ symbol*] (TTSB) ... BDTC
BioDental Technologies Corp. [*NASDAQ symbol*] (SAG) ... BDTC
BioDental Technologies Corp. [*Associated Press*] (SAG) ... BioDent
Biodeterioration Information Centre [*British*] ... BIC
Biodiversity Institute [*Center established to inventory wildlife*] (PS) ... INBio
Bio-Dynamic Agricultural Association [*British*] ... BDAA
Bio-Dynamic Farming and Gardening Association (EA) ... BDFGA
Biodynamic Farming and Gardening Association [*Australia*] ... BFGA
Bio-Dynamics, Inc., BMC Library, Indianapolis, IN [*Library symbol Library of Congress*] (LCLS) ... InIBio
Biodynamics International [*NASDAQ symbol*] (SAG) ... BDYN
Biodynamics International [*Associated Press*] (SAG) ... BiodyInt
Biodynamics Intl. [*NASDAQ symbol*] (TTSB) ... BDYN
Bio-Dyne Corp. [*Associated Press*] (SAG) ... Bio-Dyn
Bio-Dyne Corp. [*NASDAQ symbol*] (SPSG) ... BODY
Bioelectrical Repair and Growth Society (EA) ... BRAGS
Bioelectrochemical Society (EA) ... BES
Bioelectrochemistry ... BEC
Bio-Electro-Magnetics Institute (EA) ... BEMI
Bioelectromagnetics Society (EA) ... BEMS
Bioelectromagnetics Special Interest Group (EA) ... BEM SIG
Bio-Energy Council [*Defunct*] (EA) ... BEC
Bioengineering ... BIOENG
Bioengineering and Research to Aid the Handicapped Program [*Washington, DC National Science Foundation*] (GRD) ... BRAH
Bioenvironmental ... BIOENVMT
Bioethic Citation Maintenance System (DMAA) ... BCMS
Bioethics Online [*Database*] ... BIOETHICSLINE
Bio-Feed Industries Ltd. [*Vancouver Stock Exchange symbol*] ... BOF
Biofeedback ... BFB
Bio-Feedback Research Society [*Later, BSA*] (EA) ... BFRS
Biofeedback Research Society [*Later, BSA*] (EA) ... BRS
Biofeedback Society of America [*Later, AAPB*] (EA) ... BSA
Biofeedback Training [*Physiology*] ... BFT
Bioferm Corp., Research Library, Wasco, CA [*Library symbol Library of Congress*] (LCLS) ... CWasB
Biofield Corp. [*Associated Press*] (SAG) ... Biofield
Biofield Corp. [*NASDAQ symbol*] (SAG) ... BZET
Biofield Corp. [*NASDAQ symbol*] (TTSB) ... BZET
Biofilm Electrode ... BFE
Biogen, Inc. [*NASDAQ symbol*] (NQ) ... BGEN
Biogen, Inc. [*Associated Press*] (SAG) ... Biogen
Biogenic Carbon [*Chemistry*] ... BC
Biogenic Institutes of America [*Later, AHMI*] (EA) ... BIA
Biogenic Silica [*In water sediments*] ... BSI
Biogeochemical Ocean Flux Study [*Oceanography*] ... BOFS
Biogeography (ADA) ... BIOGEOG
Biografias [*Database*] [*Ministerio de Cultura*] [*Spanish*] [*Information service or system*] (CRD) ... BIOG
Biographer (ROG) ... BIOG
Biographical Dictionaries and Related Works [*A publication*] ... BD
Biographical Dictionaries and Related Works. Supplement [*A publication*] ... BDS
Biographical Dictionaries Master Index [*A publication*] ... BDMI
Biographical Dictionary of Australian Librarians [*A publication*] ... BDAL
Biographical Dictionary of Federal Judiciary [*A publication*] ... BDFJ
Biographical Index of South Australians [*A publication*] (APTA) ... BISA
Biographical Information Blank ... BIB
Biographical Inventory Creativity ... BIC
Biographical Inventory for Medicine ... BIM
Biographical Inventory for Students [*Psychology*] ... BIS
Biographics (AABC) ... BIO
Biography (DSUE) ... BIO
Biography (WDMC) ... bio
Biography ... BIOG
Biography Almanac [*Later, Almanac of Famous People*] [*A publication*] ... BA
Biography: An Interdisciplinary Quarterly [*A publication*] (BRI) ... Biography
Biography and Genealogy Master Index [*A publication*] ... BGMI
Biography Master Index [*Gale Research, Inc.*] [*Information service or system A publication*] (IID) ... BMI
Bio-Imaging Technologies [*NASDAQ symbol*] (SAG) ... BITI
Bio-Imaging Technologies, Inc. [*Associated Press*] (SAG) ... BioIm
Bio-Imaging Technologies, Inc. [*Associated Press*] (SAG) ... BioImag
Bioimpedance Venous Analysis [*Biochemistry*] (DAVI) ... BVA
Bioindustry Association [*Great Britain*] ... BIA
Bioinstrumentation Advisory Council [*Defunct*] ... BIAC
Bioinstrumentation Harness Assembly ... BHA
Bio-Integral Resource Center (EA) ... BIRC
Bioisolator Suit System [*NASA*] (MCD) ... BISS
Bioject Medical Systems Ltd. [*Vancouver Stock Exchange symbol*] ... BJM
Bioject Medical Technologies [*NASDAQ symbol*] (NQ) ... BJCT
Bioject Medical Technologies, Inc. [*Associated Press*] (SAG) ... Bioject
Bioject Medl Technologies [*NASDAQ symbol*] (TTSB) ... BJCT
Biola College, La Mirada, CA [*OCLC symbol*] (OCLC) ... CBC
Biola Library, La Mirada, CA [*Library symbol Library of Congress*] (LCLS) ... CLamB
BIOLASE Technology [*NASDAQ symbol*] (TTSB) ... BLTI
BioLase Technology, Inc. [*Associated Press*] (SAG) ... BioLase
BioLase Technology, Inc. [*NASDAQ symbol*] (SAG) ... BLTI
Biologic False-Positive Reactor (MAE) ... BFR
Biologic Safety Level ... BSL
Bio-Logic Systems [*NASDAQ symbol*] (TTSB) ... BLSC
Bio-Logic Systems Corp. [*Associated Press*] (SAG) ... BioLogic
Bio-Logic Systems Corp. [*NASDAQ symbol*] (NQ) ... BLSC
Biological (ROG) ... BIOL
Biological ... BIOL
Biological Abstracts on Tape [*Biosciences Information Service*] [*Information service or system*] ... BAT
Biological Abstracts' Subjects in Context [*A publication*] ... BASIC
Biological Activated Carbon [*Water treatment*] ... BAC
Biological Activity ... BA
Biological Aerosol Detection [*Army*] (MCD) ... BAD
Biological Aerosol Test Facility [*Army*] ... BATF
Biological Agent Casualty Assessment System (MCD) ... BACAS
Biological Agent Decontamination Simulant (MCD) ... BADS
Biological Agent Simulant (MCD) ... BAS
Biological Agricultural Reactor of the Netherlands ... BARN
Biological Analysis Detection Instrumentation and Control ... BADIC
Biological and Agricultural Sciences Information Service [*University of Minnesota, St. Paul*] [*Information service or system*] (IID) ... BASIS
Biological and Chemical ... BC
Biological and Chemical Warfare (NATG) ... BC
Biological and Chemical Warfare ... BCW
Biological and Chemical Warfare Division [*DoD*] ... BCWD
Biological and Climatic Effects Research ... BACER
Biological and Electronic (NITA) ... BIONIC
Biological and Environmental Reference Materials ... BERM
Biological and Environmental Research Program [*Department of Energy*] ... BER
Biological Anthropological Section (EA) ... BAS
Biological Antiseptic Tampon (IIA) ... BAT
Biological Assessment Laboratory ... BAL
Biological, Behavioral, and Social Sciences [*Directorate*] ... BBS
Biological/Chemical Attack Report ... BIOREP/CHEMREP
Biological/Chemical Detector (DOMA) ... BCD
Biological Control Agent [*Agriculture*] ... BCA
Biological Control of Insects Research Laboratory [*Department of Agriculture*] (GRD) ... BCIRL
Biological Cosmic Ray Experiment (MCD) ... BIOCORE
Biological Damage Indicator ... BDI
Biological Defense [*Military*] ... BIODEF
Biological Defense [*Military*] (AABC) ... BIOLDEF
Biological Defense Research Laboratory ... BDRL
Biological Defense Research Program [*DoD*] ... BDRP
Biological Defense Research Program [*Military*] (DOMA) ... BDRP
Biological Defense System ... BDS
Biological Detection and Alarm Training Simulant (MCD) ... BDATS
Biological Detection System ... BDS
Biological Diversity Advisory Committee [*Australia*] ... BDAC
Biological Effect Monitoring [*Toxicology*] ... BEM
Biological Effects [*of Nonionizing*] **Electromagnetic Radiation** (MCD) ... BEER
Biological Effects of Atomic Radiation ... BEAR
Biological Effects of Ionizing Radiation ... BEIR
Biological Effects Program [*IDOE project*] [*Terminated, 1978*] (MSC) ... BEP
Biological Electronics (IEEE) ... BIONICS
Biological Energy Research [*Department of Energy*] ... BER
Biological Engineering Society [*British*] ... BES
Biological Exposure Index ... BEI
Biological False Positive [*Clinical chemistry*] ... BFP
Biological Farmers of Australia ... BFA
Biological Half-Life ... BHL
Biological Hazard Potential [*Atomic energy*] ... BHP
Biological Indicator [*Microbiology*] ... BI
Biological Indicator Unit [*Food testing*] ... BIU
Biological Information-Processing Organization [*Later, SIGBIO*] ... BIO
Biological Institute of Tropical America (EA) ... BIOTA
Biological Integrated Detection System [*Army*] ... BIDS
Biological Integrated Detection System [*US Army*] ... BIDS
Biological Inventory ... BI
Biological Investigation of Marine Antarctic Systems and Stocks Program [*Texas A & M University*] [*Research center*] (RCD) ... BIOMASS

Biological Investigation of Space [*NASA*] .... BIOS
Biological Isolation Garment [*NASA*] .... BIG
Biological Isolator Suit System (MCD) .... BISS
Biological Laboratory [*Army*] (MCD) .... BL
Biological Laboratory, Brunswick, Georgia [*US Bureau of Commercial Fisheries; later, National Marine Fisheries Service*] .... BLBG
Biological Medicine .... BIOMED
Biological Nitrogen Fixation [*Agriculture*] .... BNF
Biological Nuclear Solvent [*Physiology*] .... BNS
Biological Operations [*Military*] (GFGA) .... BIOLOPS
Biological Orbiting Satellite (MCD) .... BIOS
Biological Orbiting Space Station (IAA) .... BOSS
Biological Origin .... BO
Biological Oxygen Demand .... BOD
Biological Packs (DNAB) .... BIOPAC
Biological Packs (NG) .... BIOPACK
Biological Photographic Association (EA) .... BPA
Biological Processing (SSD) .... BP
Biological Production Module (SSD) .... BPM
Biological Radio Communications .... BRC
Biological Reagent [*Peptide grade*] .... bR
Biological Receptors - Atrial Natriuretic Factor .... B-ANF
Biological Records Centre [*Institute of Terrestrial Ecology*] [*Information service or system*] (IID) .... BRC
Biological Reference Materials .... BRM
Biological Report (AABC) .... BIOLREPT
Biological Report .... BIOREP
Biological Research (AABC) .... BIOLRSCH
Biological Research (NVT) .... BR
Biological Research Center [*Philippines*] .... BRC
Biological Research Laboratories [*Syracuse University*] [*Research center*] (RCD) .... BRL
Biological Research Module [*NASA*] (NASA) .... BIO
Biological Research Module [*NASA*] (NASA) .... BRM
Biological Research Resources .... BRR
Biological Response Modifier Technology [*Biotechnology*] .... BRM
Biological Response Modifiers Program [*National Cancer Institute*] .... BRMP
Biological Safety Cabinet [*Pharmaceutical processing*] .... BSC
Biological Safety Officer [*National Institutes of Health*] .... BSO
Biological Satellite .... BIOS
Biological Satellite (KSC) .... BIOSAT
Biological Sciences Communication Project [*American Institute of Biological Sciences*] .... BSCP
Biological Sciences Curriculum Study [*Colorado College*] [*Research center National Science Foundation*] .... BSCS
Biological Sciences Division [*Office of Naval Research*] (DNAB) .... BSD
Biological Sciences Research Center [*University of North Carolina at Chapel Hill*] [*Research center*] (RCD) .... BSRC
Biological, Social, Machine [*Combination*] .... BIOSOMA
Biological Space Experiments (MCD) .... BIOSPEX
Biological Species Concept [*Theory of E. Mayr-1942*] .... BSC
Biological Stain Commission (EA) .... BSC
Biological Standards Control Laboratory [*Medical Research Council*] (PDAA) .... BSCL
Biological Station, Fisheries and Oceans Canada [*Station de Biologie, Peches et Oceans Canada*] **St. Andrews, New Brunswick** [*Library symbol National Library of Canada*] (NLC) .... NBAB
Biological Threshold Limit Value (PDAA) .... BTLV
Biological Value .... BV
Biological Variation .... BV
Biological Warfare .... BIOWAR
Biological Warfare .... BW
Biological Warfare/Chemical Warfare (NG) .... BW/CW
Biological Warfare Defense .... BWD
Biological Warfare Laboratory .... BWL
Biological Warfare Rapid Warning System [*Army*] .... BWRWS
Biological Weapons [*Military*] (AABC) .... BIOLWPN
Biological Weapons [*Military*] .... BW
Biological Weapons Command (DOMA) .... BWC
Biological Weapons Convention .... BWC
Biological Weapons System [*Military*] (AABC) .... BIOLWPNSYS
Biological Weapons System [*Military*] .... BWS
Biological-Chemical .... BIO-CHEM
Biologically Induced Mineralization [*Microbial metabolism*] .... BIM
Biologist .... BIOGST
Biologist's Toolbox .... BT
Biologix (BC) Ltd. [*Vancouver Stock Exchange symbol*] .... BGX
Biology [*Secondary school course*] [*British*] .... B
Biology (DSUE) .... BI
Biology [*or Biological*] (KSC) .... BIO
Biology (DD) .... Bio
Biology .... BIO
Biology (DMAA) .... biol
Biology (EY) .... BIOL
Biology, Chemistry, Physics (DD) .... BCP
Biology Classroom Activity Checklist (EDAC) .... BCAC
Biology, Electronics, Aesthetics, Mechanics [*Robotics competition*] .... BEAM
Biology Information Retrieval System [*Marine science*] (MSC) .... BIRS
Biology Unit [*American Topical Association*] (EA) .... BU
Bioluminescence .... BL
Biomagnetic Tech [*NASDAQ symbol*] (TTSB) .... BTIX
Biomagnetic Technology [*Commercial firm Associated Press*] (SAG) .... Biomag
Biomagnetic Technology [*NASDAQ symbol*] (SAG) .... BTIX
Biomass [*Biology*] .... B
Biomass Energy and Alcohol Fuels Act of 1980 .... BEAFA
Biomass Energy Coordinating Committee [*Department of Energy*] .... BECC
Biomass Energy Research Association (EA) .... BERA
Biomass Energy Systems Program [*Department of Energy*] .... BES
Biomass Protein .... BMP
Biomass Research Center [*University of Arkansas*] .... BRC
Biomaterials Profiling Center [*University of Utah*] [*Research center*] (RCD) .... BPC
Biomatrix .... BM
Biomatrix, Inc. [*Associated Press*] (SAG) .... Biomatr
Biomechanical Combined Oxidation [*Water treatment*] .... BMCO
Biomechanically Faithful Side Impact Dummy [*Automotive engineering*] .... BIOSID
Biomechanics Corp. of America [*NASDAQ symbol*] (SAG) .... BCAM
Biomedical .... BIOMDCL
Biomedical .... BMD
Biomedical Analog Signal Processor (IAA) .... BASP
Biomedical Application Teams [*NASA*] .... BAT
Biomedical Belt [*NASA*] .... BMB
Biomedical Chromatography [*A publication*] .... BMC
Biomedical Communications Inventory [*National Library of Medicine*] .... BCI
Biomedical Communications Network [*Proposed*] [*National Library of Medicine*] .... BCN
Biomedical Computer .... BMC
Biomedical Computing Society [*Later, SIGBIO*] (BUR) .... BCS
Biomedical Computing Technology Information Center [*Oak Ridge National Laboratory*] [*Department of Energy*] (IID) .... BCTIC
Biomedical Data Analysis and Display System [*NASA*] .... BMDADS
Biomedical Display Unit (KSC) .... BDU
Biomedical Electronics (MCD) .... BME
Biomedical Engineering (DD) .... BiomedEng
Biomedical Engineering and Instrumentation Branch [*National Institutes of Health*] .... BEIB
Biomedical Engineering Current Awareness Notification [*Database, publication*] [*Brunel University*] [*Information service or system*] (CRD) .... BECAN
Biomedical Engineering Program [*Carnegie-Mellon University*] [*Research center*] (RCD) .... BME
Biomedical Engineering Research Corp. [*Illinois*] .... BERC
Biomedical Engineering Society (EA) .... BMES
Biomedical Engineering Unit [*McGill University*] [*Canada Research center*] (RCD) .... BMEU
Biomedical Equipment Technology .... BMET
Biomedical Experiment Scientific [*or Support*] **Satellite** [*NASA*] (NASA) .... BESS
Biomedical Informatics Today (ACII) .... BMIT
Biomedical Information Service [*University of Minnesota, Minneapolis*] [*Information service or system*] (IID) .... BIS
Biomedical Instrumentation Advisory Service [*Clinical Research Centre*] [*British*] (NITA) .... BIAS
Biomedical Instrumentation Consultant .... BIC
Biomedical Interdisciplinary Curriculum Project [*National Science Foundation*] .... BICP
Biomedical Laboratory, Aberdeen Proving Grounds, MD [*OCLC symbol*] (OCLC) .... ADF
Biomedical Marketing Association (EA) .... BMA
Biomedical Measurement and Control Panel (ACII) .... BCMP
Biomedical Monitoring System .... BMS
Biomedical Primate Research Centre [*The Netherlands*] .... BPRC
Biomedical Recovery Capsule (MUGU) .... BRC
Biomedical Research and Development Laboratory [*Army*] (RDA) .... BRDL
Biomedical Research Defense Fund [*Defunct*] (EA) .... BRDF
Biomedical Research Development Grants .... BRDG
Biomedical Research in Progress (ECII) .... BRIP
Biomedical Research Institute [*American Foundation for Biological Research*] [*Research center*] (RCD) .... BRI
Biomedical Research Support Advisory Committee [*National Institutes of Health*] (EGAO) .... BRSAC
Biomedical Research Support Grants .... BRSG
Biomedical Research Support Program [*Bethesda, MD*] [*National Institutes of Health*] (GRD) .... BRS
Biomedical Research Technology Program [*Bethesda, MD*] [*National Institutes of Health*] (GRD) .... BRTP
Biomedical Sciences Corps [*Air Force*] (AFM) .... BSC
Biomedical Sciences Program (DMAA) .... BMSP
Biomedical Signal Conditioner .... BSC
Biomedical Studies Section [*Oak Ridge National Laboratory*] (IID) .... BMS
Biomedical Technology Transfer Team .... BATEAM
Biomedical Urine Sampling System (KSC) .... BUSS
Biomedical Waste .... BMW
Biomedical Waste Incinerator [*or Incineration*] .... BMWI
Biomedicine and Health Program .... BMHP
Bio-Mega, Inc., Montreal, Quebec [*Library symbol National Library of Canada*] (NLC) .... QMBIM
Biomerica, Inc. [*Associated Press*] (SAG) .... Biomer
Biomerica, Inc. [*Associated Press*] (SAG) .... Biomerica
Biomerica, Inc. [*NASDAQ symbol*] (NQ) .... BMRA
Biomet, Inc. [*Associated Press*] (SAG) .... Biomet
Biomet, Inc. [*NASDAQ symbol*] (NQ) .... BMET
Biomet Tech, Inc. [*Vancouver Stock Exchange symbol*] .... BTS
Biometric Computer Service, Inc. .... BCSI
Biometric Society .... BS
Biometric Society, Western North American Region (EA) .... WNAR
Biometrics Research Laboratory (DAVI) .... BRL
Biometry .... BIOMET
Biometry and Epidemiology Program [*Department of Health and Human Services*] (GFGA) .... BEPP
Biometry and Risk Assessment Program (GNE) .... BRAP
Biomimetic Affinity Chromatography .... BMC
Biomira, Inc. [*NASDAQ symbol*] (SAG) .... BIOM

Biomira Inc. [*NASDAQ symbol*] (TTSB) .... BIOMF
Biomira, Inc. [*Associated Press*] (SAG) .... Biomira
Biomira, Inc. [*Toronto Stock Exchange symbol*] .... BRA
Biomolecular Engineering Program [*EC*] (ECED) .... BEP
Biomolecular Engineering Research Institute [*Formerly, PERI*] [*Japan*] .... BERI
Biomune Systems [*NASDAQ symbol*] (TTSB) .... BIME
Biomune Systems, Inc. [*NASDAQ symbol*] (SAG) .... BIME
Biomune Systems, Inc. [*Associated Press*] (SAG) .... Biomne
Bionaire, Inc. [*Toronto Stock Exchange symbol*] .... ION
Bionetics Research Institute [*Rockville, MD*] .... BRI
Bionics Adaptive Network .... BAN
Bionomic .... BIONMC
Bionomics, Environment, Plasmodium, Treatment, Immunity [*Malaria epidemiology*] (AAMN) .... BEPTI
Bionucleonics .... BIONUCL
Biopack [*NASA*] (KSC) .... BP
Biopack Subsystem [*NASA*] (KSC) .... BPSS
Biopharmaceutics Research Branch [*Washington, DC Department of Health and Human Services*] (GRD) .... BRB
Biophysical Society .... BP
Biophysical Society (EA) .... BPS
Biophysical Society (MCD) .... BS
Biophysical Society of Canada [*La Societe de Biophysique du Canada*] (AC) .... BSC
Biophysics (ADA) .... BIO
Biophysics (DAVI) .... Biophys
Bio-Plexus, Inc. [*Associated Press*] (SAG) .... BioPlex
Bio-Plexus, Inc. [*NASDAQ symbol*] (SAG) .... BPLX
Biopool International, Inc. [*Associated Press*] (SAG) .... Biopool
Biopool International, Inc. [*NASDAQ symbol*] (NQ) .... BIPL
Biopool Intl. [*NASDAQ symbol*] (TTSB) .... BIPL
BioProcess Engineering Society International (EA) .... BESI
Bioprocessing Aid .... BPA
Bioprocessing Research Facility [*Oak Ridge, TN*] [*Oak Ridge National Laboratory*] [*Department of Energy*] (GRD) .... BRF
Bioprocessing Technology [*Technical Insights, Inc.*] [*Information service or system*] (CRD) .... BT
Bio-Products Laboratory [*Central Blood Laboratories Authority*] [*British*] (IRC) .... BPL
Biopsy [*Medicine*] .... B
Biopsy [*Medicine*] .... BX
Biopsy and Curettage [*Gynecology*] .... B & C
Bioquant .... BQ
Bio-Rad Laboratories, Inc. [*AMEX symbol*] (SPSG) .... BIO
Bio-Rad Laboratories, Inc. [*Associated Press*] (SAG) .... BioR
Bio-Rad Labs Cl'A' [*AMEX symbol*] (TTSB) .... BIO.A
Bio-Rad Labs Cl'B' [*AMEX symbol*] (TTSB) .... BIO.B
Bioradioimmunoassay .... BRIA
Bioradiotelemetric System .... BRTS
Bio-Reference Laboratories, Inc. [*Associated Press*] (SAG) .... BioRef
Bio-Reference Laboratories, Inc. [*Associated Press*] (SAG) .... BioRf
Bio-Reference Laboratories, Inc. [*NASDAQ symbol*] (NQ) .... BRLI
Bio-Reference Labs [*NASDAQ symbol*] (TTSB) .... BRLI
Bio-Reference Labs Wrrt'A' [*NASDAQ symbol*] (TTSB) .... BRLIW
Bio-Reference Labs Wrrt'B' [*NASDAQ symbol*] (TTSB) .... BRLIZ
Bioregional Project (EA) .... BP
Bioren and Duane's United States Laws [*A publication*] (DLA) .... Bior & D Laws
BioResearch, Inc., Farmingdale, NY [*Library symbol Library of Congress*] (LCLS) .... NFarB
Bio-Research Laboratories Ltd., Pointe-Claire, PQ, Canada [*Library symbol Library of Congress*] (LCLS) .... CaQMBR
Bio-Research Laboratories Ltd., Pointe-Claire, Quebec [*Library symbol National Library of Canada*] (NLC) .... QMBR
Bio-Research Laboratory, Senneville, Quebec [*Library symbol National Library of Canada*] (NLC) .... QSBR
Bio-Research Module (MCD) .... BIO
BioResearch Titles (DIT) .... BRT
Bioresmethrin [*Biochemistry*] .... BR
Bioresources Research Facility [*University of Arizona*] [*Research center*] (RCD) .... BRF
Biorex, Ste.-Foy, Quebec [*Library symbol National Library of Canada*] (BIB) .... QSFB
Biorka [*Alaska*] [*Seismograph station code, US Geological Survey Closed*] (SEIS) .... BIO
BIOS [*Basic Input-Output System*] Parameter Block [*Computer science*] (PCM) .... BPB
BioSafe International, Inc. [*Associated Press*] (SAG) .... BioSafe
BioSafe International, Inc. [*Associated Press*] (SAG) .... BioSf
BioSafe International, Inc. [*NASDAQ symbol*] (SAG) .... BSFE
BioSafe Intl. [*NASDAQ symbol*] (TTSB) .... BSFE
BioSafe Intl. Wrrt'C' [*NASDAQ symbol*] (TTSB) .... BSFEW
BioSafe Intl. Wrtt'E' [*NASDAQ symbol*] (TTSB) .... BSFEL
Biosafety Level - Large Scale [*For laboratories utilizing biological agents*] .... BL-LS
Biosafety Systems [*NASDAQ symbol*] (SAG) .... BSSI
Biosafety Systems, Inc. [*Associated Press*] (SAG) .... BioSafety
BioScience [*A publication*] (BRI) .... BioSci
Bioscience Program [*NASA*] .... BP
Bio-Sciences Information Exchange [*Smithsonian Institution*] .... BSIE
BioSciences Information Service [*Database producer*] [*Philadelphia, PA*] .... BIOSIS
Bioscope [*The cinema*] [*Obsolete British*] (DSUE) .... BIO
Biosedra [*France*] [*Research code symbol*] .... Biosedra
Biosepra, Inc. [*Associated Press*] (SAG) .... Biosepra
Biosepra, Inc. [*NASDAQ symbol*] (SAG) .... BSEP
BioSepra Inc. [*NASDAQ symbol*] (TTSB) .... BSEP

Bioshield Power Assembly [*NASA*] .... BPA
Bioshield Pyrotechnic Control Assembly [*for Mariner Venus-Mercury Project spacecraft*] [*NASA*] .... BPCA
BIOSIS/CAS [*BioSciences Information Service/Chemical Abstracts Service*] Registry Number Concordance [*American Chemical Society*] [*Information service or system*] (CRD) .... BIOCAS
BIOSIS [*BioSciences Information Service*] Information Transfer Service .... BITS
Biosophical Institute, Inc. [*Defunct*] .... BII
BioSource International [*NASDAQ symbol*] (SAG) .... BIOI
BioSource International [*Associated Press*] (SAG) .... BioSrce
BioSource Intl. [*NASDAQ symbol*] (TTSB) .... BIOI
Biospecific Affinity Chromatography .... BAC
BioSpecifics Technologies [*NASDAQ symbol*] (TTSB) .... BSTC
BioSpecifics Technologies, Inc. [*Associated Press*] (SAG) .... BioSpecif
BioSpecifics Technologies, Inc. [*NASDAQ symbol*] (SAG) .... BSTC
Biosphere [*Self-contained scientific experimental community*] B2
Biosphere Reserve (GNE) .... BR
Biosphere-Atmosphere Transfer Scheme [*Meteorology*] .... BATS
Biospheric Aspects of the Hydrological Cycle [*Marine science*] (OSRA) ..... BAHC
Biospherics [*NASDAQ symbol*] (TTSB) .... BINC
Biospherics, Inc. [*NASDAQ symbol*] (NQ) .... BINC
Biospherics, Inc. [*Associated Press*] (SAG) .... Biosph
Biossay of Luteinizing Hormone (DMAA) .... bioLH
Biostatistics .... BIOSTAT
Biostructures Participating Research Team [*Biostructures Institute*] (RCD) .... BPRT
Biosynthetic Antibody Binding Site [*Biochemistry*] .... BABS
Biosynthetic Human Insulin [*Medicine*] .... BHI
Biosys [*Associated Press*] (SAG) .... Biosys
Biosys, Inc. [*NASDAQ symbol*] (NQ) .... BIOS
biosys Inc. [*NASDAQ symbol*] (TTSB) .... BIOS
Biosys Medical [*NASDAQ symbol*] (TTSB) .... BIOP
Biosystematic Code [*Databank terminology*] (NITA) .... BC
Biosystematic Code [*Online database field identifier*] .... BS
Biosystematics Research Institute [*Canada*] (ARC) .... BRI
Biot [*Also, aA*] [*Unit of electric current*] .... Bi
Biotech Electronics Ltd. [*Toronto Stock Exchange symbol*] .... ION
Biotechnica Canada, Calgary, AB, Canada [*Library symbol*] [*Library of Congress*] (LCLS) .... CaACBC
Biotechnica Canada, Calgary, Alberta [*Library symbol National Library of Canada*] (BIB) .... ACBC
Biotechnica International, Inc. .... BII
Biotechnica International, Inc. .... BIT
Biotechnica International, Inc. .... BTI
Biotechnical Research Project [*EC*] (ECED) .... BIOREP
Biotechnical Research Technology [*NIH*] .... BRT
Biotechnics International, Inc. [*NASDAQ symbol*] (NQ) .... BIOT
Biotechnics International, Inc. [*Associated Press*] (SAG) .... BioTInt
Biotechnology .... BIOTEC
Biotechnology .... BIOTECH
Biotechnology .... BIOTECH
Biotechnology .... BT
Biotechnology Advisory Committee [*Environmental Protection Agency*] (GFGA) .... BAC
Biotechnology and Biological Sciences Research Council [*British*] .... bbscrc
Biotechnology and Biological Sciences Research Council [*British*] .... BBSRC
Biotechnology and Human Research .... BHR
Biotechnology Branch, CISTI , Montreal, Quebec [*Canada Institute for Scienctific and Technical Information*] [*Annexe de Biotechnologie, ICIST*] [*Library symbol*] [*National Library of Canada*] (BIB) .... QMNB
Biotechnology Equipment Suppliers [*Deutsche Gesellschaft fuer Chemisches Apparatewesen, Chemische Technik, und Biotechnologie eV*] [*Germany*] (IID) .... BIOQUIP
Bio-Technology Exhibition (TSPED) .... BIOTEX
Biotechnology Facility (SSD) .... BTF
Biotechnology Gen Corp. [*Associated Press*] (SAG) .... BioTcG
Biotechnology Gen Corp. [*Associated Press*] (SAG) .... BioTG
Bio-Technology General Corp. [*NASDAQ symbol*] (SP86) .... BTGG
Bio-Technology Genl [*NASDAQ symbol*] (TTSB) .... BTGC
Biotechnology Industry Organization .... BIO
Biotechnology Investment Opportunities [*Database*] [*High Tech Publishing Co.*] [*Information service or system*] (CRD) .... BIO
Biotechnology Orbital Laboratory (KSC) .... BOL
Bio-Technology Purchasing Management Association [*Defunct*] (EA) .... BPMA
Biotechnology Research for Innovation, Development, and Growth in Europe [*EC*] (ECED) .... BRIDGE
Biotechnology Research Institute [*Montreal, PQ*] [*Canada*] .... BRI
Biotechnology Science Coordinating Committee [*An interagency governmental group*] [*Washington, DC*] .... BSCC
Biotechnology Thrust .... BT
Biotelemetry System .... BTS
Biotic Potential .... BP
BioTime, Inc. [*Associated Press*] (SAG) .... Biotime
Biotime, Inc. [*NASDAQ symbol*] (SAG) .... BTIM
Biotin B7
Biotin [*Pharmacology*] (DAVI) B7
Biotin Carboxyl Carrier Protein [*Biochemistry*] .... BCCP
Biotin-Avidin-Linked Immunoassay [*Immunochemistry*] .... BALIA
Biotinoyl (Iodoacetyl) Ethylenediamine [*An enzyme*] .... BIE
Biotin-X Cadaverine [*Biochemical labelling compound*] .... BXC
Biotinyl-para-aminobenzoate [*Biochemistry*] .... BPAB
Biotite Granite Schist [*Geology*] .... BIOT GR SCH
BioTransplant, Inc. [*Associated Press*] (SAG) .... BioTrans
BioTransplant, Inc. [*NASDAQ symbol*] (SAG) .... BTRN
Biot-Savart Law [*Physics*] .... BSL

Biovail Corp. International [*Associated Press*] (SAG) .... Biovail
Biovail Corp. International [*AMEX symbol*] (SAG) .... BVF
Biovail Corp. Intl. [*AMEX symbol*] (TTSB) .... BVF
Bio-Vascular, Inc. [*Associated Press*] (SAG) .... BioVasc
Bio-Vascular, Inc. [*NASDAQ symbol*] (NQ) .... BVAS
Biowaste Monitoring System (MCD) .... BMS
BioWhittaker, Inc. [*Associated Press*] (SAG) .... Biowht
BioWhittaker, Inc. [*NYSE symbol*] (SPSG) .... BWI
Bipara [*Having borne two children*] [*Gynecology and Obstetrics*] (DAVI) .... Para II
Biparietal Diameter [*Gynecology*] (MAE) .... BIP
Biparietal Diameter [*Obstetrics*] (DAVI) .... BiPD
Biparietal Diameter [*Gynecology*] .... BP
Biparietal Diameter [*Gynecology*] .... BPD
Biparting Door .... BIPD
Bipartisan [*Politics*] (WDMC) .... bipart
Bipartite Board [*Post-World War II, Germany*] .... BIB
Bipartite Civil Aviation Panel [*Post-World War II, Germany*] .... BCAP
Bipartite Civil Service Advisors [*Post-World War II, Germany*] .... BICIV
Bipartite Communications Panel [*Post-World War II, Germany*] .... BICOM
Bipartite Control Office [*Post-World War II, Germany*] .... BICO
Bipartite Decartelization Commission [*Berlin*] [*Post-World War II, Germany*] .... BIDEC
Bipartite Decartelization Sub-Commission [*Minden*] [*Post-World War II, Germany*] .... BIDESC
Bipartite Economic Panel [*Post-World War II, Germany*] .... BIECO
Bipartite Economic Panel Railway Supplies Committee [*Post-World War II, Germany*] .... BIECO/RAIL
Bipartite Economics Control Group [*Post-World War II, Germany*] .... BECG
Bipartite Finance Panel [*Post-World War II, Germany*] .... BIFIN
Bipartite Food and Agriculture Panel [*Post-World War II, Germany*] .... BIF & A
Bipartite News Office [*Post-World War II, Germany*] .... BNO
Bipartite Secretariat [*Post-World War II, Germany*] .... BISEC
Bipartite Transport Control Group [*Post-World War II, Germany*] .... BTCG
Bi-Petro Resources [*Vancouver Stock Exchange symbol*] .... BIP
Bi-Phase Mark (MHDI) .... BIO-M
Bi-Phase Modulation (IAA) .... BPM
Biphenyl Dianhydride [*Organic chemistry*] .... BPDA
Biphenyl Work Group (EA) .... BWG
Biphenylamine [*Organic chemistry*] .... BPA
(Biphenylyl)phenyloxazole [*Organic chemistry*] .... BPO
Bipiperidyl Mustard [*Pharmacology*] .... BPM
Biplabi Bangla Congress [*India*] [*Political party*] (PPW) .... BBC
Biplane .... B
Biplane Experimental [*Aircraft*] [*World War I*] .... BE
Biplane Ultra-Light Research Device (PDAA) .... BURD
Bipod Heavy Barrel [*Weaponry*] [*Military*] (INF) .... BHB
Bipolar Active-Plastic Cell .... BAC
Bipolar Affective Disorder [*Psychology*] (DAVI) .... BAD
Bipolar Affective Disorder [*Genetics*] .... BPAD
Bipolar Cell [*Biochemistry*] .... BC
Bipolar Cell [*In the retina*] .... Bi
Bipolar Complementary Metal Oxide Semiconductor [*Electronics*] (BARN) .... BICMOS
Bipolar Complementary Metal-Oxide Semiconductor (IAA) .... BCMOS
Bipolar Field Effect Transistor (IAA) .... BIFET
Bipolar Illness [*Psychiatry*] (CPH) .... BPI
Bipolar Insulated Gate Field-Effect Transistor [*Bell Laboratories*] .... BIGFET
Bipolar Integrated Circuit [*Electronics*] (EECA) .... BIC
Bipolar Inversion Channel Field Effect Transistor (MCD) .... BICFET
Bipolar Junction Transistor [*Electronics*] .... BJT
Bipolar Line Unit [*Electronics*] (IAA) .... BLU
Bipolar Magnetic Region (OA) .... BMR
Bipolar Metal-Oxide Semiconductor (IEEE) .... BiMOS
Bipolar Operational Amplifier .... BOA
Bipolar Operational Power .... BOP
Bipolar Power Supply (DWSG) .... BPS
Bipolar Psychological Inventory [*Personality development test*] [*Psychology*] .... BPI
Bipolar Read Only Memory [*Computer science*] (MHDI) .... BROM
Bipolar Return to Zero [*Electronics*] (ACRL) .... BPRZ
Bipolar with Eight-Zero Substitution [*Coding*] [*Telecommunications*] B8ZS
Bipolar with N Zeros Substitution [*Electronics*] (NITA) .... BNZS
Bipolar-CMOS-DMOS (MCD) .... BCDMOS
Bipolar-Mode Static Induction Transistor (MCD) .... BSIT
Bipost [*Lamp base*] (NTCM) .... Bp
Bipost .... BPT
Bipropellant (KSC) .... BIP
Bipropellant Valve (MCD) .... BPV
Bipyridine [*Also, BPY*] [*Organic chemistry*] .... BIPY
Bipyridine [*Also, BIPY*] [*Organic chemistry*] .... BPY
Bipyridinium Chlorochromate [*Organic chemistry*] .... BPCC
Bir Moghrein [*Mauritania*] [*ICAO location identifier*] (ICLI) .... GQPT
Birao [*Central African Republic*] [*ICAO location identifier*] (ICLI) .... FEFI
Birao [*Central African Republic*] [*Airport symbol*] (AD) .... IRO
Biratnagar [*Nepal*] [*Airport symbol*] (OAG) .... BIR
Biratnagar [*Nepal*] [*ICAO location identifier*] (ICLI) .... VNVT
Birch (VRA) .... bir
Birch Creek [*Alaska*] [*Airport symbol*] (OAG) .... KBC
Birch Elementary School, Massapequa, NY [*Library symbol Library of Congress*] (LCLS) .... NMassBE
Birch Elementary School, Merrick, NY [*Library symbol*] [*Library of Congress*] (LCLS) .... NMerkBE
Birch Hill [*Alaska*] [*Seismograph station code, US Geological Survey Closed*] (SEIS) .... BRH
Birch, Raymond Sr., Southampton PA [*STAC*] .... BRS
Birch Tree, MO [*AM radio station call letters*] .... KBMV
Birch Tree, MO [*FM radio station call letters*] .... KBMV-FM
Birchwood Elementary School, Duluth, MN [*Library symbol*] [*Library of Congress*] (LCLS) .... MnDuBE
Birchwood Elementary School, Huntington Station, NY [*Library symbol*] [*Library of Congress*] (LCLS) .... NHsBE
Bird Aircraft Strike Hazard .... BASH
Bird Airplane Club (EA) .... BAC
Bird Association of California (EA) .... BAC
Bird Corp. [*NASDAQ symbol*] (NQ) .... BIRD
Bird Corp. [*Associated Press*] (SAG) .... BirdC
Bird Corp. [*Associated Press*] (SAG) .... BirdCp
Bird Corp. $1.85 Cv Pref [*NASDAQ symbol*] (TTSB) .... BIRDP
Bird Dog Association, International (EA) .... BDAI
Bird Friends Society [*Defunct*] (EA) .... BFS
Bird Impact Resistant Transparency (PDAA) .... BIRT
Bird Investigation, Review, and Deterrent [*NASA*] .... BIRD
Bird Island [*Seychelles Islands*] [*Airport symbol*] (OAG) .... BDI
Bird Island Public Library, Bird Island, MN [*Library symbol*] [*Library of Congress*] (LCLS) .... MnBi
Bird Island-Danube-Renville-Sacred Heart (BDRSH) Public Schools, Renville, MN [*Library symbol*] [*Library of Congress*] (LCLS) .... MnRenBPS
Bird. Laws Respecting Landlords, Tenants, and Lodgers [*11th ed.*] [*1833*] [*A publication*] (DLA) .... Bird L & T
Bird Leasing, Inc. [*ICAO designator*] (FAAC) .... BIR
Bird Lovers Anthology [*A publication*] .... BLA
Bird. New Pocket Conveyancer [*5th ed.*] [*1830*] [*A publication*] (DLA) .... Bird Conv
Bird Protection League of South Australia .... BPLSA
Bird Resistant [*Sorghum variety*] .... BR
Bird. Solution of Precedents of Settlements [*1800*] [*A publication*] (DLA) .... Bird Sol Pr
Bird Strike Committee Europe [*Denmark*] (EAIO) .... BSCE
Bird Sweep Completed [*Aviation*] (FAAC) .... BSC
Bird-Fanciers Lung [*Medicine*] .... BFL
Birds of Prey Rehabilitation Foundation (EA) .... BPRF
[*The*] **Birds of Western Palearctic** [*Book series*] [*British A publication*] .... BWP
Bird's Supplement to Barton's Conveyancing [*A publication*] (DLA) .... Bird Supp
Birdseye's Statutes [*New York*] [*A publication*] (DLA) .... Birds St
Bird's-Eye-View .... BEV
Birdsville [*Australia Airport symbol*] (OAG) .... BVI
Birdwood's Printed Judgments [*India*] [*A publication*] (DLA) .... Birdw
Birgenair [*Turkey*] [*ICAO designator*] (FAAC) .... BHY
Birjand [*Iran*] [*ICAO location identifier*] (ICLI) .... OIMB
Birkbeck College Computation Laboratory [*British*] .... BCCL
Birkenhead [*British depot code*] .... BHD
Birkenhead's Judgments, House of Lords [*1919-22*] [*England*] [*A publication*] (DLA) .... Birk J
Birlesmis Milletler Turk Dernegi [*United Nations Association of Turkey*] (EAIO) .... BMTD
Birmingham [*City, county borough, and university in England*] .... BHAM
Birmingham [*Alabama*] [*Airport symbol*] .... BHM
Birmingham [*England*] [*Airport symbol*] (OAG) .... BHX
Birmingham [*Diocesan abbreviation*] [*Alabama*] (TOCD) .... BIR
Birmingham [*City, county borough, and university in England*] .... BIRM
Birmingham [*British ICAO location identifier*] (ICLI) .... EGBB
Birmingham [*Alabama*] [*ICAO location identifier*] (ICLI) .... KBHM
Birmingham Aerocentre, Ltd. [*British*] [*FAA designator*] (FAAC) .... HOT
Birmingham, AL [*Location identifier FAA*] (FAAL) .... ROE
Birmingham, AL [*Location identifier FAA*] (FAAL) .... VUZ
Birmingham, AL [*Television station call letters*] .... WABM
Birmingham, AL [*AM radio station call letters*] .... WAGG
Birmingham, AL [*AM radio station call letters*] .... WAPI
Birmingham, AL [*AM radio station call letters*] .... WATV
Birmingham, AL [*AM radio station call letters*] .... WAYE
Birmingham, AL [*FM radio station call letters*] .... WBFR
Birmingham, AL [*FM radio station call letters*] .... WBHM
Birmingham, AL [*Television station call letters*] .... WBIQ
Birmingham, AL [*Television station call letters*] .... WBMG
Birmingham, AL [*Television station call letters*] .... WBRC
Birmingham, AL [*AM radio station call letters*] (RBYB) .... WDJC-AM
Birmingham, AL [*FM radio station*] (RBYB) .... WDJC-FM
Birmingham, AL [*FM radio station call letters*] .... WENN
Birmingham, AL [*AM radio station call letters*] .... WERC
Birmingham, AL [*FM radio station call letters*] .... WGIB
Birmingham, AL [*AM radio station call letters*] .... WJOX
Birmingham, AL [*FM radio station call letters*] .... WJSR
Birmingham, AL [*FM radio station call letters*] .... WLJR
Birmingham, AL [*FM radio station call letters*] .... WMJJ
Birmingham, AL [*FM radio station call letters*] .... WMXQ
Birmingham, AL [*FM radio station call letters*] .... WODL
Birmingham, AL [*Television station call letters*] .... WTTO
Birmingham, AL [*FM radio station call letters*] .... WVSU
Birmingham, AL [*Television station call letters*] .... WVTM
Birmingham, AL [*AM radio station call letters*] .... WYDE
Birmingham, AL [*FM radio station call letters*] .... WZRR
Birmingham, AL [*AM radio station call letters*] .... WZZK
Birmingham, AL [*FM radio station call letters*] .... WZZK-FM
Birmingham & Midland Motor Omnibus Co. Ltd. [*British*] (DCTA) .... BMMD
Birmingham & Southeastern R. R. [*AAR code*] .... BSE
Birmingham Aviation Ltd. [*British ICAO designator*] (FAAC) .... ATX
Birmingham Belt R. R. [*AAR code*] .... BB
Birmingham Contemporary Music Group [*British*] .... BCMG
Birmingham European Airways [*ICAO designator*] (AD) .... VB
Birmingham European Airways [*Airline flight code*] (ODBW) .... VB
Birmingham Gauge .... BG

Birmingham Libraries Cooperative Mechanisation Project [Later, Library Services Ltd.] (NITA) .... BLCMP
Birmingham Library and Information Network [British] (NITA) .... B-LINK
Birmingham Loughborough Electronic Network Development [British] (NITA) .... BLEND
Birmingham, MI [FM radio station call letters] .... WCSX
Birmingham Post & Mail Ltd., Birmingham, United Kingdom [Library symbol Library of Congress] (LCLS) .... UkBP
Birmingham Public and Jefferson County Free Library, Birmingham, AL [Library symbol Library of Congress] (LCLS) .... AB
Birmingham Public Libraries, Birmingham, United Kingdom [Library symbol Library of Congress] (LCLS) .... UkB
Birmingham Public Library [Alabama] .... BPL
Birmingham Repair [British military] (DMA) .... BR
Birmingham Revision [of BNA] [Medicine British] .... BR
Birmingham Small Arms, Inc. (MCD) .... BSA
Birmingham Solar Oscillations Network .... BISON
Birmingham Southern College [Alabama] .... BSC
Birmingham Southern College, Birmingham, AL [Library symbol Library of Congress] (LCLS) .... ABS
Birmingham Southern Railroad Co. [AAR code] .... BS
Birmingham Standard [Wire gauge] .... BS
Birmingham Steel [NYSE symbol] (TTSB) .... BIR
Birmingham Steel Corp. [NYSE symbol] (SPSG) .... BIR
Birmingham Steel Corp. [Associated Press] (SAG) .... BirStl
Birmingham Technology Ltd. at Aston Science Park [Research center British] (IRUK) .... BTL
Birmingham University, Birmingham, United Kingdom [Library symbol Library of Congress] (LCLS) .... UkBU
Birmingham University Industrial Liaison for Technology [Research center British] .... BUILT
Birmingham Utilities, Inc. [NASDAQ symbol] (SAG) .... BIRM
Birmingham Utilities, Inc. [Associated Press] (SAG) .... BirmUtl
Birmingham Utils [NASDAQ symbol] (TTSB) .... BIRM
Birmingham Wire Gauge (IDOE) .... BG
Birmingham Wire Gauge .... BWG
Birmingham-Jefferson Library, Birmingham, AL [OCLC symbol] (OCLC) .... ABJ
Birnamwood, WI [FM radio station call letters] .... WHET
Birrfeld [Switzerland ICAO location identifier] (ICLI) .... LSZF
Birth .... B
Birth (ADA) .... BTH
Birth Certificate .... BC
Birth Control .... BC
Birth Control Advisory Bureau [British] (BI) .... BCAB
Birth Control Clinic .... BCC
Birth Control Investigation Committee (BABM) .... BCIC
Birth Control Medication .... BCM
Birth Control Pill [Medicine] .... BCP
Birth Defect [Neonatology] (DAVI) .... BD
Birth Defect and Clinical Genetic Society [Defunct] (EA) .... BDCGS
Birth Defects Information System [Center for Birth Defects Information Services, Inc.] [Information service or system] (IID) .... BDIS
Birth Education, Training, and Acceptance .... BETA
Birth Support Providers, International [Affiliated with National Association of Childbirth Assistants (NACA)] (PAZ) .... BSPI
Birth Visit (ROG) .... BV
Birth Weight [Medicine] .... BW
Birth Weight [Medicine] .... BWT
Birthdate (DD) .... b
Birthday (ABBR) .... BRTDY
Birthday (ABBR) .... BRTHDY
Birthday Honours [Titles conferred on the sovereign's birthday] [British] .... BH
Birthmark [Dermatology] (DAVI) .... BMK
Birthmark (ABBR) .... BRTHMK
Birthmark (ABBR) .... BRTMK
Birthparent & Relative Group Society (AC) .... BRGS
Birthplace .... BP
Birthplace .... BPL
Birthplace (ABBR) .... BRTHPL
Birthplace (ABBR) .... BRTPLC
Birthrate .... BR
Birthright (ABBR) .... BRTHRGT
Birthright (ABBR) .... BRTRT
Births, Deaths, and Marriages .... BDM
Births, Marriage and Deaths (WDAA) .... BMD
Birthstone (ABBR) .... BRTHSTN
Birthstone (ABBR) .... BRTST
Bis [Twice] [Pharmacy] .... B
Bis Horis [Every Two Hours] [Pharmacy] (ROG) .... BIS HOR
Bis in Die [Twice a Day] [Pharmacy] .... BD
Bis in Die [Twice a Day] [Pharmacy] .... BID
Bis in Die [Twice a Day] [Pharmacy] (ROG) .... BIS in D
Bis in Die Sumendus [To Be Taken Twice a Day] [Pharmacy] .... BDS
Bis in Noctus [Twice a Night] [Pharmacy] .... BIN
Bis in Septem Diebus [Twice a Week] [Pharmacy] bi7d
Bis in Septem Dies [Twice in Seven Days] [Pharmacy] (ROG) .... BIS in 7 D
Bis Terve in Die [Two or Three Times a Day] [Pharmacy] .... BTID
Bis Tris Propane [Biological buffer] .... BTP
Bis(acetatomercurimethyl)dioxane [Organic chemistry] .... BAMD
Bis(acryloyl)cystamine [Organic chemistry] .... BAC
Bis(amidino-benzimidazolyl)methane [Biochemistry] .... BABIM
Bis(aminomethyl)cyclohexane [Organic chemistry] .... BAC
Bis(aminophenoxy)ethanetetraacetic Acid [Organic chemistry] .... BAPTA
Bisaminophenyloxadiazole [Organic chemistry] .... BAO
Bis(aminopropyl)piperazine [Organic chemistry] .... BAPP

Bisbee [Arizona] [Airport symbol] (OAG) .... BSQ
Bisbee, AZ [FM radio station call letters] (RBYB) .... KRMB-FM
Bisbee, AZ [FM radio station call letters] .... KWCD
Bisbee, AZ [FM radio station call letters] (RBYB) .... KWRB
Bis(benzimidazole) [Organic chemistry] .... BBI
Bis(benzylidene)thiocarbohydrazone [Organic chemistry] .... BTH
Bis(biphenyl)oxadiazole [Organic chemistry] .... BBOD
Bis(biphenylyl)oxazole [Organic chemistry] .... BBO
Bis(bromomethyl)oxetane [Organic chemistry] .... BBMO
Bisbutoxybenzylidenebitoluidine [Organic chemistry] .... BBBT
Bis(carboxyethyl)carboxyfluorescein [Organic chemistry] .... BCECF
Biscarosse/Parentis [France ICAO location identifier] (ICLI) .... LFBS
Biscayan .... BISC
Biscayne Apparel [AMEX symbol] (TTSB) .... BHA
Biscayne Apparel, Inc. [Formerly, Biscayne Holdings, Inc.] [AMEX symbol] (SPSG) .... BHA
Biscayne Apparel, Inc. [Associated Press] (SAG) .... BiscApp
Biscayne Bay, FL [Location identifier FAA] (FAAL) .... BSY
Biscayne Chemical Laboratories, Inc., Miami, FL [Library symbol Library of Congress] (LCLS) .... FMB
Biscayne College, Miami, FL [OCLC symbol] (OCLC) .... FBM
Biscayne College, Miami, FL [Library symbol Library of Congress] (LCLS) .... FMBC
Biscayne College, St. Thomas University Law School, Miami, FL [Library symbol] [Library of Congress] (LCLS) .... FMBC-L
Bis(chloroethyl)nitrosourea [Carmustine] [Also, BiCNU] [Antineoplastic drug regimen] .... BCNU
Bis(chloroethyl)nitrosourea [Carmustine] [Also, BCNU] [Antineoplastic drug regimen] .... BiCNU
Bis(chloroethyl)sulfide [Biochemistry] .... BCES
Bis(chloromethyl) Ether [Organic chemistry] .... BCME
Bis(chloromethyl)oxetane [Organic chemistry] .... BCMO
Bis(chlorosulfophenyl)phenanthrolinedicarboxylic Acid [Organic chemistry] .... BCPDA
Biscuit .... BSCT
Biscuit (ABBR) .... BSCUT
Biscuit and Cracker Distributors Association (EA) .... BCDA
Biscuit and Cracker Manufacturers' Association (EA) .... B & CMA
Biscuit Bakers Institute [B & CMA] [Absorbed by] (EA) .... BBI
Biscuit, Cake, Chocolate, and Confectionery Alliance (EAIO) .... BCCCA
Bis-diazotized Benzidine [Hematology] .... BDB
Bis((dimethylaminoethyl)indole)sulfide [Biochemistry] .... BDIS
Bis(dimethylsilyl)acetamide [Organic chemistry] .... BDSA
Bisegmental Neuron [Neurology] .... BSN
Bis(ethylenedithiolo)tetrathiafulvalene [Organic chemistry] .... BEDT-TTF
Bis(ethylhexyl) Phthalate [Organic chemistry] .... BEHP
Bisexual [Psychiatry and infectious disease] (DAVI) .... AC-DC
Bisexual (DSUE) .... BI
Bisexual Center [Defunct] (EA) .... BC
Bisexual White Male .... BiWM
Bisha [Saudi Arabia] [Airport symbol] (OAG) .... BHH
Bisha [Saudi Arabia] [ICAO location identifier] (ICLI) .... OEBH
Bis(hexamethylene)triamine [Organic chemistry] .... BHMT
Bishop [Chess] .... B
Bishop [Ecclesiastical] .... B
Bishop .... BHP
Bishop [California] [Airport symbol] (OAG) .... BIH
Bishop (DSUE) .... BISH
Bishop .... BP
Bishop .... BP
Bishop .... BSHP
Bishop and Martyr [Church calendars] .... BM
Bishop Baraga Association (EA) .... BBA
Bishop, CA [Location identifier FAA] (FAAL) .... CDT
Bishop, CA [AM radio station call letters] .... KBOV
Bishop, CA [FM radio station call letters] .... KIBS
Bishop College, Dallas, TX [Inactive] [OCLC symbol] (OCLC) .... BIS
Bishop College, Dallas, TX [Library symbol Library of Congress] (LCLS) .... TxDaBC
Bishop. First Book of the Law [A publication] (DLA) .... Bish First Bk
Bishop Kearney High School Library, Rochester, NY [OCLC symbol] (OCLC) .... RVR
Bishop Method of Clothing Construction Council (EA) .... BMCCC
Bishop of Carlisle [British] .... CARIOL
Bishop of Chichester [British] .... CICESTR
Bishop of Durham [British] .... DUNELM
Bishop of Salisbury [British] .... SARUM
Bishop on Contracts [A publication] (DLA) .... Bish Con
Bishop on Contracts [A publication] (DLA) .... Bish Cont
Bishop on Criminal Law [A publication] (DLA) .... Bish Cr Law
Bishop on Criminal Procedure [A publication] (DLA) .... Bich Crim Proc
Bishop on Criminal Procedure [A publication] (DLA) .... Bish Cr Proc
Bishop on Insolvent Debtors [A publication] (DLA) .... Bish Ins
Bishop on Marriage and Divorce [A publication] (DLA) .... Bish Mar & Div
Bishop on Marriage, Divorce, and Separation [A publication] (DLA) .... Bish Mar Div & Sep
Bishop on Married Women [A publication] (DLA) .... Bish Mar Wom
Bishop on Non-Contract Law, Rights, and Torts [A publication] (DLA) .... Bish Non-Cont Law
Bishop on Statutory Crimes [A publication] (DLA) .... Bish St Crimes
Bishop on Statutory Crimes [A publication] (DLA) .... Bish Stat Cr
Bishop on Written Law [A publication] (DLA) .... Bish Wr L
Bishop Resources Development Ltd. [Vancouver Stock Exchange symbol] .... BIS
Bishop Routhier School, High Prairie, Alberta [Library symbol National Library of Canada] (BIB) .... AHPBS
Bishop State Junior College, Mobile, AL [Library symbol Library of Congress] (LCLS) .... AMobB

Bishop Suffragan .... BS
Bishop Suffrogan [*or Suffrogan Bishop*] (BARN) .... Bp Suff
Bishop, TX [*FM radio station call letters*] .... KFLZ
Bishopric .... BHPRIC
Bishops (ADA) .... BB
Bishops' Committee for Ecumenical and Interreligious Affairs (EA) .... BCEIA
Bishops' Committee for Education [*Australia*] .... BCE
Bishops' Committee for Industrial Affairs [*Australia*] .... BCIA
Bishops' Committee for the Spanish Speaking [*Later, SHA*] .... BCSS
Bishops' Committee on Priestly Formation (EA) .... BCPF
Bishops' Committee on the Liturgy (EA) .... BCL
Bishop's Committee on Vocations (EA) .... BCV
Bishops Court [*British ICAO location identifier*] (ICLI) .... EGOC
Bishop's Digest [*Montana*] [*A publication*] (DLA) .... Bishop Dig
Bishop's Edition of Burrill on Assignments [*A publication*] (DLA) .... Bish Burr
Bishops Falls Public Library, Bishops Falls, NF, Canada [*Library symbol*] [*Library of Congress*] (LCLS) .... CaNfBF
Bishops Falls Public Library, Newfoundland [*Library symbol National Library of Canada*] (NLC) .... NFBF
Bishop's Law of Nolle Prosequi [*A publication*] (DLA) .... Bish Noll Pros
Bishop's New Criminal Law [*A publication*] (DLA) .... Bish New Cr Law
Bishop's New Criminal Procedure [*A publication*] (DLA) .... Bish New Cr Proc
Bishop's Transcript [*British*] (ROG) .... BT
Bishop's Trial [*A publication*] (DLA) .... B Tr
Bishop's University, Department of Geography, Lennoxville, PQ, Canada [*Library symbol Library of Congress*] (LCLS) .... CaQLBG
Bishop's University, Lennoxville, PQ, Canada [*Library symbol Library of Congress*] (LCLS) .... CaQLB
Bishop's University, Lennoxville, Quebec [*Library symbol National Library of Canada*] (NLC) .... QLB
Bishop's University Library [*UTLAS symbol*] .... BHP
Bishopville, SC [*AM radio station call letters*] .... WAGS
Bishopville, SC [*FM radio station call letters*] .... WKHT
Bis(hydroxybenzyl)ethylenediaminediacetic Acid [*Organic chemistry*] .... HBED
Bis(hydroxycyclohexyl)nitrosourea [*Antineoplastic drug*] .... BHCNU
Bis(hydroxyethyl)aminoethanesulfonic Acid [*A buffer*] [*Organic chemistry*] .... BES
Bis(hydroxyethyl)dimerate [*Organic chemistry*] .... BHED
Bis(hydroxyethyl)glycine [*A buffer*] [*Organic chemistry*] .... BICINE
Bis(hydroxyethyl)piperazine [*Organic chemistry*] .... BHEP
Bis(hydroxyethyl)terephthalate [*Organic chemistry*] .... BHET
Bis(hydroxymethyl)ferrocene [*Organic chemistry*] .... BHMF
Bis(hydroxymethyl)furan [*Organic chemistry*] .... BHMF
Bis(hydroxymethyl)peroxide [*Organic chemistry*] .... BHMP
Bis(hydroxyphenyl)trichloroethane [*Organic chemistry*] .... HPTE
Biskra [*Algeria*] [*Airport symbol*] (OAG) .... BSK
Biskra [*Algeria*] [*ICAO location identifier*] (ICLI) .... DAUB
Bislig [*Philippines*] [*Airport symbol*] (OAG) .... BPH
Bislig, Surigao Del Sur [*Philippines*] [*ICAO location identifier*] (ICLI) .... RPWZ
Bismaleimide [*Organic chemistry*] .... BMI
Bismaleimide [*Plastics*] .... BMI
Bis(maleimido)hexane [*Organic chemistry*] .... BMH
Bismarck [*North Dakota*] [*Airport symbol*] (OAG) .... BIS
Bismarck Hospital, School of Nursing Library, Bismarck, ND [*Library symbol Library of Congress*] (LCLS) .... NdBH
Bismarck Junior College [*North Dakota*] .... BJC
Bismarck Junior College, Bismarck, ND [*Library symbol Library of Congress*] (LCLS) .... NdBC
Bismarck, ND [*Location identifier FAA*] (FAAL) .... BZX
Bismarck, ND [*FM radio station call letters*] (RBYB) .... KACL-FM
Bismarck, ND [*Television station call letters*] .... KBME
Bismarck, ND [*AM radio station call letters*] .... KBMR
Bismarck, ND [*Television station call letters*] .... KBMY
Bismarck, ND [*FM radio station call letters*] .... KBYZ
Bismarck, ND [*FM radio station call letters*] .... KCND
Bismarck, ND [*AM radio station call letters*] .... KFYR
Bismarck, ND [*Television station call letters*] .... KFYR-TV
Bismarck, ND [*FM radio station call letters*] .... KKCT
Bismarck, ND [*FM radio station call letters*] .... KQDY
Bismarck, ND [*FM radio station call letters*] .... KSSS
Bismarck, ND [*Television station call letters*] .... KXMB
Bismarck, ND [*AM radio station call letters*] (RBYB) .... KXMR
Bismarck, ND [*FM radio station call letters*] .... KYYY
Bismarck [*Veterans Memorial*] **Public Library, Bismarck, ND** [*Library symbol Library of Congress*] (LCLS) .... NdBV
Bismarck-Henning Community Unit School District, Bismarck, IL [*Library symbol*] [*Library of Congress*] (LCLS) .... IBisSD
Bismarck-Mandan, ND [*AM radio station call letters*] .... KLXX
Bis(methyloxybenzylidene)bitoluidine [*Organic chemistry*] .... BMBT
Bis(methylstyryl)benzene [*Organic chemistry*] .... BMSB
Bismorpholinecarbamylsulfenamide [*Organic chemistry*] .... BCMS
Bismuth [*Chemical element*] .... Bi
Bismuth [*Chemical element*] (ROG) .... BIS
Bismuth Germanate [*Inorganic chemistry*] .... BGO
Bismuth, Germanium, and Oxygen [*Inorganic chemistry*] .... BGO
Bismuth Glycine Glucose Yeast [*Medicine*] (DMAA) .... BIGGY
Bismuth Institute [*Brussels, Belgium*] (EAIO) .... BI
Bismuth Iodoform and Paraffin Paste [*Medicine*] .... BIPP
Bismuth Iodoform Paraffin [*Medicine*] .... BIP
Bismuth Iodoform Petrolatum Paste [*Biochemistry*] (DAVI) .... BIPP
Bismuth Silicon Oxide [*LASER Crystal*] (NITA) .... BSO
Bismuth, Strontium, Calcium, Copper, Oxide [*Inorganic chemistry*] .... BSCCO
Bismuth Subsalicylate [*Antidiarrhea agent*] .... BS
Bismuth Sulfite [*Agar*] [*Bacteriology*] .... BS
Bismuth-Sulfite Agar [*Medicine*] (MAE) .... BSA
Bis(nitrophenyl)ethyl [*Organic radical*] .... BNPE
Bis(nitrophenyl)ethyloxycarbonyl [*Organic radical*] .... BNPEOC
Bison (ABBR) .... BSN
Bison Petroleum & Minerals [*Vancouver Stock Exchange symbol*] .... BSP
Bispham's Principles of Equity [*A publication*] (DLA) .... Bisp Eq
Bispham's Principles of Equity [*A publication*] (DLA) .... Bisph Eq
Bisphenol A-Glycidyl Methacrylate [*Organic chemistry*] .... BIS-GMA
Bisphosphoglycerate [*Biochemistry*] .... BPG
Bispinous [*or Interspinous*] [*Gynecology*] .... bisp
Bispinous [*or Interspinous*] **Diameter** [*Orthopedics*] (DAVI) .... Bisp
Bispinous Diameter [*Pelvic measurement*] (CPH) .... Bisp Diam
Bis(pyridiniumtrimethylene) [*Dichloride*] [*Biochemistry*] .... BPT
Bissau [*Portuguese Guinea*] [*Airport symbol*] (OAG) .... BXO
Bissau/Oswaldo Vieira International [*Guinea-Bissau*] [*ICAO location identifier*] (ICLI) .... GGOV
Bissell's Minnesota Statutes [*A publication*] (DLA) .... Biss Stat
Bissell's United States Circuit Court Reports [*A publication*] (DLA) .... Bis
Bissell's United States Circuit Court Reports [*A publication*] (DLA) .... Biss
Bissell's United States Circuit Court Reports, Seventh Circuit [*A publication*] (DLA) .... Biss (US)
Bissell's United States Circuit Court Reports, Seventh Circuit [*A publication*] (DLA) .... Bissell
Bisset's Partnership and Joint Stock Companies [*1847*] [*A publication*] (DLA) .... Biss Part
Bissett and Smith's Digest [*South Africa*] [*A publication*] (DLA) .... Biss & Sm
Bissett on Estates for Life [*A publication*] (DLA) .... Biss Est
Bissett on Estates for Life [*A publication*] (DLA) .... Bissett Est
Bissextile Year [*Leap Year*] (ROG) .... BIS
Bissora [*Guinea-Bissau*] [*ICAO location identifier*] (ICLI) .... GGBI
Bissync Data Link Control (LAIN) .... BDLC
Bista Bancorp [*Associated Press*] (SAG) .... VistaBcP
Bistable (NRCH) .... B/S
Bistable Magnetic Core [*Computer science*] .... BIMAC
Bistable Magnetic Core [*Computer science*] .... BIMAG
Bistable Multivibrator [*Electronics*] (IAA) .... BM
Bistable Multivibrator .... BMV
Bistable Multivibrator .... BSM
Bistable Multivibrator (MUGU) .... BSMV
Bistable Optical Device .... BOD
Bistable Optical Differential Amplifier (MCD) .... BODA
Bistable Optically Controlled Semiconductor Switch (IAA) .... BOSS
Bistaple .... BSTL
Bi-State Academic Libraries [*Library network*] .... BI-SAL
Bistatic Coherent RADAR Display (MCD) .... BICORD
Bistatic Identification, Friend or Foe (MCD) .... BIFF
Bistatic RADAR (LAIN) .... B/R
Bistatic RADAR Identification of Hostile Target .... BRIHT
Bistatic RADAR Intelligence Generation and Analysis System (NVT) .... BRIGAND
Bistatic RADAR System (MCD) .... BRASS
Bistatic Reflected Energy Target (MCD) .... BRET
Bistatic SONAR (CAAL) .... BSS
Bistatic Synthetic Aperture Harmonic RADAR (MCD) .... BISAHR
Bistatic Thinned Array RADAR (MCD) .... BISTAR
Bis(tert-butylbenzoxazolyl)thiophene [*Organic chemistry*] .... BBOT
Bistre [*Yellowish Brown*] (ROG) .... BIS
Bistre (VRA) .... bist
Bis(tribromophenoxy)ethane [*Flame retardant*] [*Organic chemistry*] .... BTBPE
bis(Trichlorophenyl) Oxalate [*Organic chemistry*] .... TCPO
Bistrifluoroacetamide [*Organic chemistry*] .... BTFA
Bis(trimethylsilyl)acetamide [*Organic chemistry*] .... BSA
Bis(trimethylsilyl)acetylene [*Organic chemistry*] .... BTMSA
Bis(trimethylsilyl)carbamate [*Organic chemistry*] .... BSC
Bis(trimethylsilyl)formamide [*Organic chemistry*] .... BSF
Bis(trimethylsilyl)trifluoroacetamide [*Organic chemistry*] .... BSTFA
Bis(trimethylsilyl)urea [*Organic chemistry*] .... BSU
Bis(trinitroethyl)carbonate [*An explosive*] .... BTNEC
Bis(trinitroethyl)nitramine [*An explosive*] .... BTNEN
Bistro .... BSTR
Bisymmetric Spiral [*Astronomy*] .... BSS
Bisync [*Protocol*] (PCM) .... BSC
BISYNC Packet Assembler/Disassembler [*Telecommunications*] (ACRL) ...... BPAD
Bisynchronous (NITA) .... BISYNC
Bisynchronous Communications Macro (NITA) .... BSCM
Bisynchronous Communications Processor (NITA) .... BCP
Bisynchronous Frame Level [*Telecommunications*] (NITA) .... BSCFL
BISYS Group [*NASDAQ symbol*] (TTSB) .... BSYS
BISYS Group, Inc. [*Associated Press*] (SAG) .... BISYS
BISYS Group, Inc. [*NASDAQ symbol*] (SAG) .... BSYS
BIT [*Binary Digit*] [*Data transmission speed*] [*Computer science*] (DIT) .... B
BIT [*Binary Digit*] (IAA) .... BT
BIT [*Binary Digit*] **Attention Deficit Disorder** [*Computer science*] .... BADD
BIT [*Binary Digit*]-Block Transfer .... BITBLT
BIT [*Binary Digit*] **Buffer Unit** [*Computer science*] (CET) .... BBU
BIT [*Binary Digit*]/Byte Conversion [*Telecommunications*] (TEL) .... BB
BIT [*Binary Digit*] **Control** .... BC
BIT [*Binary Digit*] **Control Block** [*Computer science*] (IBMDP) .... BCB
BIT [*Binary Digit*] **Control Panel** [*Computer science*] (MCD) .... BCP
BIT [*Binary Digit*] **Count Appendage** [*Computer science*] (MHDI) .... BCA
BIT [*Binary Digit*] **Count Integrity** [*Telecommunications*] (TEL) .... BCI
BIT [*Binary Digit*] **Density** [*Computer science*] .... BD
BIT [*Binary Digit*] **Effectiveness Report** (CAAL) .... BER
BIT [*Binary Digit*] **Error Probability** [*Computer science*] (KSC) .... BEP
BIT [*Binary Digit*] **Error Rate** [*Computer science*] .... BER
BIT [*Binary Digit*] **Error Rate Monitor** .... BERM
BIT [*Binary Digit*] **Error Rate Test** [*Computer science*] .... BERT
BIT [*Binary Digit*] **Image Memory** [*Computer science*] .... BIM

Bit Interleaved Parity [*Electronics*] (ACRL) ... BIP
BIT [*Binary Digit*] **Light Inspection** (DNAB) ... BLIN
BIT [*Binary Digit*] **Manipulate Load** ... BML
BIT [*Binary Digit*] **Manipulate Store** ... BMS
BIT [*Binary Digit*] **Map** [*Computer science*] (PCM) ... BMP
BIT [*Binary Digit*] **Map Font** [*Computer science*] (PCM) ... BMF
BIT [*Binary Digit*] **Mark Sequencing** [*Computer science*] (IAA) ... BMS
BIT [*Binary Digit*] **Matched Filter** ... BMF
[*A*] **Bit of Money and a Cat** [*Lifestyle classification*] ... Abomac
BIT [*Binary Digit*]-Oriented Message (RDA) ... BOM
BIT [*Binary Digit*]-Oriented Protocol ... BOP
BIT [*Binary Digit*] **per Circuit per Hour** [*Computer science*] (IAA) ... BCH
BIT [*Binary Digit*]-Plane Encoding [*Computer science*] ... BPE
Bit Processor (NITA) ... BP
BIT [*Binary Digit*] **Rate** [*Data transmission speed*] [*Computer science*] (MCD) ... BR
BIT [*Binary Digit*] **Rate Low** [*Computer science*] (IAA) ... BRL
BIT [*Binary Digit*] **Reversion Circuit** [*Computer science*] (MHDI) ... BRC
BIT [*Binary Digit*] **Scan** [*Computer science*] (BUR) ... BSCN
BIT [*Binary Digit*] **Scan Command** [*Computer science*] ... BSC
BIT [*Binary Digit*] **Serial Link** ... BSL
BIT [*Binary Digit*] **Slippage Rate** [*Computer science*] ... BSR
BIT [*Binary Digit*] **Space** [*Computer science*] (IAA) ... BS
BIT [*Binary Digit*] **Storage and Sense** [*Computer science*] (IAA) ... BSS
BIT [*Binary Digit*] **Storage Density** [*Computer science*] ... BSD
BIT [*Binary Digit*] **Sync** [*Computer science*] ... BS
BIT [*Binary Digit*] **Sync Acquisition** [*Computer science*] ... BSA
BIT [*Binary Digit*] **Sync Generator** [*Computer science*] ... BSG
BIT [*Binary Digit*] **Sync Matched Filter** [*Computer science*] ... BSMF
BIT [*Binary Digit*] **Synchronizer / Signal Conditioner** (PDAA) ... BSSC
BIT [*Binary Digit*] **Test** [*Computer science*] ... BTST
BIT [*Binary Digit*] **Time Counter** [*Computer science*] ... BTC
Bitam [*Gabon*] [*Airport symbol*] (OAG) ... BMM
Bitam [*Gabon*] [*ICAO location identifier*] (ICLI) ... FOOB
Bit-Block Transfers [*Computer science*] ... blts
BITBLT [*Binary Digit-Block Transfer*] **Processing Unit** ... BPU
Bitburg [*Germany ICAO location identifier*] (ICLI) ... EDAB
Bitch ... B
Bite Detector ... BD
BITE [*Built-In Test Equipment*] **Status Register** (MCD) ... BSR
Bitec Development Corp. [*Vancouver Stock Exchange symbol*] ... BTD
Bitemporal (ROG) ... BT
Bithionol [*A Bacteriostatic*] [*Pharmacology*] (DAVI) ... TBP
Bithionol Sulfoxide [*Pharmacology*] ... BTS
Bithorax Complex [*Gene cluster in fruit fly*] ... BX-C
Biting (ABBR) ... BTG
BitMap Image [*Computer science*] ... bmp
BITmap Images ... BMAP
Bit-Mapped Graphics [*Computer science*] ... BMP
BITNET [*Because It's Time Network*] **Development and Operations Center** ... BITDOC
BITNET [*Because It's Time Network*] **Network Support Center** ... BITNSC
Bitolterol [*Pharmacology*] ... BTL
BITs [*Binary Digits*] **per Inch** [*Data density measurement*] [*Computer science*] ... BPI
Bits per Inch (IDOE) ... bpi
BITs [*Binary Digits*] **per Millimeter** [*Data density measurement*] [*Computer science*] ... BPMM
BITs [*Binary Digits*] **per Minute** [*Data transmission speed*] [*Computer science*] ... BPM
BITs [*Binary Digits*] **per Sample** (NASA) ... B/SMPL
BITs [*Binary Digits*] **per Sample** (MCD) ... BISMPL
BITs [*Binary Digits*] **per Second** [*Data transmission speed*] [*Computer science*] (CET) ... B/S
BITs [*Binary Digits*] **per Second** [*Data transmission speed*] [*Computer science*] (NASA) ... B/sec
BITS [*Binary Digits*] **per second** (NITA) ... BIT/s
BITs [*Binary Digits*] **per Second** [*Data transmission speed*] [*Computer science*] ... BPS
Bits Per Second [*Computer science*] (WDMC) ... bps
BITS [*Binary Digit*] **per Second per Hertz** [*Telecommunications*] (NITA) ... B/S/Hz
BITs [*Binary Digits*] **per Square Inch** [*Data density measurement*] [*Computer science*] ... BPSI
Bitstream font [*Bitstream Inc.*] (CDE) ... BT font
Bitstream, Inc. [*NASDAQ symbol*] (SAG) ... BITS
Bitstream, Inc. [*Associated Press*] (SAG) ... Bitstrm
Bitter and Burton [*British*] (DSUE) ... BB
Bitter National Magnet Laboratory ... BNML
Bitter Root Public Library, Hamilton, MT [*Library symbol*] [*Library of Congress*] (LCLS) ... MtHam
Bitterroot Resources Ltd. [*Vancouver Stock Exchange symbol*] ... BTT
Bitterwater Creek [*California*] [*Seismograph station code, US Geological Survey*] (SEIS) ... BTW
Bittleston and Wise. New Magistrates' Cases [*England*] [*A publication*] (DLA) ... Bit & Wise
Bittleston, Wise, and Parnell's Magistrates' Cases [*England*] [*A publication*] (DLA) ... Mag Cas
Bittleston, Wise, and Parnell's Reports [*2, 3 New Practice Cases*] [*England*] [*A publication*] (DLA) ... Bitt W & P
Bittleston's Chamber Cases [*1883-84*] [*A publication*] (DLA) ... Bitt Cha Cas
Bittleston's Chamber Cases [*1883-84*] [*A publication*] (DLA) ... Rep in Cha
Bittleston's Practice Cases [*A publication*] (ILCA) ... Bitt Prac Cas
Bittleston's Practice Cases under Judicature Acts [*England*] [*A publication*] (DLA) ... Bit Prac Cas
Bittleston's Practice Cases under Judicature Acts [*England*] [*A publication*] (DLA) ... Bitt PC
Bittleston's Practice Cases under Judicature Acts [*England*] [*A publication*] (DLA) ... Bitt Pr Cas
Bittleston's Practice Cases under Judicature Acts [*England*] [*A publication*] (DLA) ... Bitt Pr Case
Bittleston's Reports in Chambers, Queen's Bench Division [*England*] [*A publication*] (DLA) ... Bitt
Bittleston's Reports in Chambers, Queen's Bench Division [*England*] [*A publication*] (DLA) ... Bitt Ch
Bittleston's Reports in Chambers, Queen's Bench Division [*England*] [*A publication*] (DLA) ... Bitt Ch Cas
Bittleston's Reports in Chambers, Queen's Bench Division [*England*] [*A publication*] (DLA) ... Bitt Chamb Rep
Bittleston's Reports in Chambers, Queen's Bench Division [*England*] [*A publication*] (DLA) ... Bitt Rep in Ch
Bituberous [*Anatomy*] (DAVI) ... BT
Bitumen ... BITN
Bituminized [*Freight*] ... BITUMD
Bituminous [*Technical drawings*] ... BIT
Bituminous (MSA) ... BITUM
Bituminous Aggregate Mixture (OA) ... BAM
Bituminous and Aggregate Equipment Bureau (EA) ... BAEB
Bituminous Coal Institute [*Absorbed by NCA*] ... BCI
Bituminous Coal Operators' Association (EA) ... BCOA
Bituminous Coal Research (EA) ... BCR
Bituminous Equipment Manufacturers Bureau [*Later, BAEB*] (EA) ... BEMB
Bituminous Pipe Institute [*Defunct*] (EA) ... BPI
Bituminous Treated Base (DAC) ... BTB
Bitwise Designs [*Associated Press*] (SAG) ... Bitwse
Bitwise Designs [*NASDAQ symbol*] (SAG) ... BTWS
Bi-University Institutional Liaison for Development (SAA) ... BUILD
Biuret-Reactive Material [*Biochemistry*] (MAE) ... BRM
Bivariant Function Generator (DEN) ... BIVAR
Bivariate Exponential [*Distribution*] [*Statistics*] ... BVE
Bivariate Normal Mixture [*Statistics*] ... BVN
Bivariate Thematic Mapping ... BVTM
Biventricular Assist Device [*Medicine*] (DMAA) ... BVAD
Biventricular Assistance [*Cardiology*] ... BVA
Biventricular Hypertrophy [*Cardiology*] ... BVH
Bivouac (AABC) ... BIV
Biweekly ... BI-W
Biweekly ... BW
Biweekly Report (MCD) ... BWR
Bixby Memorial Free Library, Vergennes, VT [*Library symbol Library of Congress*] (LCLS) ... VtVe
Bixby, OK [*FM radio station call letters*] ... KJMM
Bizant [*Australia Airport symbol Obsolete*] (OAG) ... BZP
Bizarre (DAVI) ... BIZ
Bizarre People [*Extension of BP - Beautiful People*] [*Slang*] ... BP
Bizerte/Sidi Ahmed [*Tunisia*] [*ICAO location identifier*] (ICLI) ... DTTB
BJ Services [*NYSE symbol*] (TTSB) ... BJS
BJ Services Co. [*NYSE symbol*] (SPSG) ... BJS
BJ Services Wrrt [*NYSE symbol*] (TTSB) ... BJS.WS
Bjerrum Double Band [*Physics*] ... BDB
Bjorkvik [*Sweden ICAO location identifier*] (ICLI) ... ESKX
Bjornoya [*Norway ICAO location identifier*] (ICLI) ... ENBJ
Bk of N.Y.8.60% Dep Pfd [*NYSE symbol*] (TTSB) ... BKPrB
BKC Semiconductors [*NASDAQ symbol*] (TTSB) ... BKCS
BKC Semiconductors, Inc. [*Associated Press*] (SAG) ... BKC Sem
BKC Semiconductors, Inc. [*NASDAQ symbol*] (SAG) ... BKCS
Black [*Philately*] ... B
Black [*Pencils*] ... B
Black [*Buoy*] ... B
Black (VRA) ... b
Black (WDMC) ... b
Black ... BK
Black ... BL
Black (WDMC) ... bl
Black ... BLCK
Black (KSC) ... BLK
Black [*Thoroughbred racing*] ... BLK
Black (WDMC) ... K
Black Academy of Arts and Letters [*Defunct*] (EA) ... BAAL
Black Action Movement ... BAM
Black Affairs Center [*Later, BACTOD*] (EA) ... BAC
Black Affairs Center for Training and Organizational Development (EA) ... BACTOD
[*The*] **Black Agenda** [*An association*] ... TBA
Black American Baptist Churchmen [*An association*] (EA) ... BABC
Black American Cinema Society (EA) ... BACS
Black American Colleges and Universities [*A publication*] ... BACU
Black American Law Students Association (EA) ... BALSA
Black American Response to the African Crisis (EA) ... BARAC
Black American Travel Association [*Defunct*] ... BATA
Black Americans for Bush [*Defunct*] (EA) ... BAB
Black Americans Information Directory [*A publication*] ... BAID
Black and Coloured Sheep Breeders' Association of New South Wales [*Australia*] ... BCSBANSW
Black & Decker Corp. [*NYSE symbol*] (SPSG) ... BDK
Black & Decker Corp. [*Associated Press*] (SAG) ... BlackD
Black & Decker Manufacturing Co. ... B & D
Black and Multiethnic Christian Education Resources Center (EA) ... BMCERC
Black and Non-White YMCA Staffs [*An association Defunct*] (EA) ... BANWYS
Black & Veatch Consulting Engineers, Central Library, Kansas City, MO [*Library symbol Library of Congress*] (LCLS) ... MoKBV
Black and White [*Photography, television, etc.*] ... B

Black and White [*Photography, television, etc.*] ... B & W
Black and White [*Milk of magnesia and aromatic cascara fluid extract*] [*Pharmacy*] ... B & W
Black and White [*Photography*] [*Art*] (WDMC) ... b/w
Black and White [*Photography*] [*Art*] (WDMC) ... B/W
Black and White (IDOE) ... b/w
Black and White (IDOE) ... b&w
Black and White (IDOE) ... B&W
Black & White (VRA) ... b&w
Black and White [*Photography, television, etc.*] (KSC) ... BW
Black and White Horizontal Bands [*Navigation markers*] ... BWHB
Black and White Vertical Blinds [*Navigation markers*] (DNAB) ... BWVB
Black and White Vertical Stripes [*Navigation markers*] ... BWVS
Black Audio Network, Inc. (NTCM) ... BAN
Black Awareness in Television (EA) ... BAIT
Black Ball Transport, Inc. [*AAR code*] ... BBT
Black Beetle Virus ... BBV
Black Body Cavity (PDAA) ... BBC
Black Body Radiator ... BBR
Black Bolt and Nut Association [*British*] (DBA) ... BBNA
Black Box Corp. [*NASDAQ symbol*] (SAG) ... BBOX
Black Box Corp. [*Associated Press*] (SAG) ... BlackBx
Black Box Under Glass Variable Angle Controlled Temperature [*Automotive paint durability testing*] ... BBUGVACT
Black Business Alliance (EA) ... BBA
Black Business & Professional Association (AC) ... BBPA
Black Business Women - International [*French*] (EAIO) ... BBWI
Black Butte [*New Mexico*] [*Seismograph station code, US Geological Survey Closed*] (SEIS) ... BBN
Black Butte [*Montana*] [*Seismograph station code, US Geological Survey Closed*] (SEIS) ... BLK
Black Canyon, AZ [*AM radio station call letters*] (RBYB) ... KUET
Black Canyon of the Gunnison National Monument ... BLCA
Black Caucus of Health Workers (EA) ... BCHW
Black Caucus of the American Library Association (EA) ... BCALA
Black Child Development Institute [*Later, NBCDI*] (EA) ... BCDI
Black Christian Nationalist Church ... BCNC
Black Citizens for a Fair Media (EA) ... BCFM
Black Cliff Mines Ltd. [*Toronto Stock Exchange symbol*] ... BKC
Black Coaches Association (EA) ... BCA
Black Code [*Law passed after the Civil War limiting the rights of Negroes in the South*] ... BC
Black College Educational Network (TSSD) ... BCEN
Black Colt (ROG) ... BC
Black Community Crusade for Children [*Children's Defense Fund (CDF)*] (PAZ) ... BCCC
Black Country Development Corp. [*Department of Environment*] [*British*] ... BCDC
Black Country Society [*British*] ... BCS
Black Crossover Vote [*Political science*] ... BCROS
Black Cultural Centre for Nova Scotia, Westphal [*Library symbol National Library of Canada*] (BIB) ... NSWBC
Black Data Processing Associates (EA) ... BDPA
Black Data Processing Associates (EA) ... DPA
Black Death [*1348-49*] ... BD
Black Development Foundation ... BDF
Black Diamond Municipal Library, Alberta [*Library symbol National Library of Canada*] (NLC) ... ABDM
Black Diamond Municipal Library, Black Diamond, AB, Canada [*Library symbol Library of Congress*] (LCLS) ... CaABdM
Black Diamond Resources [*Vancouver Stock Exchange symbol*] ... BLK
Black Diamond Steamship Corp. (MHDW) ... BDSC
Black Economic Research Center (EA) ... BERC
Black Educational Resources Center [*Later, BMCERC*] (EA) ... BERC
Black Educational Services, Inc. ... BESI
Black Efforts for Soul in Television ... BEST
Black Elderly Twin Study [*National Institute on Aging*] ... BETS
Black Elected Official ... BEO
Black Employees of the Library of Congress (EA) ... BELC
Black Employment Program (EPA) ... BEP
Black Enamel Slate (MSA) ... BES
Black Enamelled ... BE
Black English [*Dialect*] ... BE
Black English Vernacular [*Dialect*] ... BEV
Black Enterprise [*A publication*] (BRI) ... B Ent
Black Enterprise [*A publication*] ... BE
Black Entertainment and Sports Lawyers Association (EA) ... BESLA
Black Entertainment Lawyers Association [*Later, BESLA*] (EA) ... BELA
Black Entertainment Television [*Cable-television system*] ... BET
Black Executive Exchange Program [*of The National Urban League*] (EA) ... BEEP
Black Family Research Organization (EA) ... BFRO
Black Female ... BF
Black, Female Republican ... BFR
Black Filly [*Horse racing*] (ROG) ... BF
Black Film & Video Network (AC) ... BFVN
Black Filmmaker Foundation (EA) ... BFF
Black Filmmakers Hall of Fame, Inc. (EA) ... BFHFI
Black Firsts [*A publication*] ... BF
Black Fox Nuclear Station (NRCH) ... BFNS
Black Fox Station [*Nuclear energy*] (NRCH) ... BFS
Black Gelding [*Horse racing*] (ROG) ... BG
Black Giant Mines Ltd. [*Vancouver Stock Exchange symbol*] ... BG
Black Gold Cooperative Library System, Ventura, CA [*OCLC symbol*] (OCLC) ... BGC
Black Gold Cooperative Library System, Ventura, CA [*Library symbol Library of Congress*] (LCLS) ... CVtB
Black Granite Gauge ... BGG
Black Hawk [*Military*] (MCD) ... BH
Black Hawk College, East Campus, Gustav E. Lundberg Learning Center, Kewanee, I L [*OCLC symbol*] (OCLC) ... ISY
Black Hawk College, East Campus, Kewanee, IL [*Library symbol Library of Congress*] (LCLS) ... IKeB
Black Hawk College, Moline, IL [*Library symbol Library of Congress*] (LCLS) ... IMolB
Black Hawk County Sun, Evansdale, IA [*Library symbol Library of Congress*] (LCLS) ... IaEvS
Black Hawk Gaming & Development [*Associated Press*] (SAG) ... BlkHG
Black Hawk Gaming & Development Co. [*Associated Press*] (SAG) ... BlkHwkG
Black Hawk Gaming & Development Co., Inc. [*NASDAQ symbol*] (SAG) ... BHWK
Black Hawk Gaming & Dvlp [*NASDAQ symbol*] (TTSB) ... BHWK
Black Hawk Gaming Wrrt 'A' [*NASDAQ symbol*] (TTSB) ... BHWKW
Black Hawk Gaming Wrrt 'B' [*NASDAQ symbol*] (TTSB) ... BHWKZ
Black Hawk Mining, Inc. [*Toronto Stock Exchange symbol*] ... BHK
Black Hill [*Scotland*] [*Seismograph station code, US Geological Survey*] (SEIS) ... EBH
Black Hill Resources Ltd. [*Vancouver Stock Exchange symbol*] ... BHR
Black Hills (FAAC) ... BLKHLS
Black Hills Army Depot ... BHAD
Black Hills Corp. [*NYSE symbol*] (SPSG) ... BKH
Black Hills Corp. [*Associated Press*] (SAG) ... BlkHICp
Black Hills State College (GAGS) ... Black Hills St C
Black Hills State College, Spearfish, SD [*OCLC symbol*] (OCLC) ... BHS
Black Hills State College, Spearfish, SD [*Library symbol Library of Congress*] (LCLS) ... SdSpeT
Black Hills Teachers College [*Later, Black Hills State College*] [*South Dakota*] ... BHTC
Black History Month Resource Book [*A publication*] ... BHMRB
Black Hole Ocarina (MCD) ... BHO
Black Human Resources Network [*An association*] (EA) ... BHRN
Black Incumbent ... BINC
Black, Indian, Hispanic, and Asian Women in Action [*An association*] (EA) ... BIHA
Black Information [*Banking*] [*British*] ... BI
Black Intelligence Test of Cultural Homogeneity [*Sometimes facetiously translated "Black Intelligence Test to Counter Honkeyism"*] ... BITCH
Black Iron ... BI
Black, James F., Baltimore MD [*STAC*] ... BJF
Black Jumbo [*Diplomatic codes*] [*World War II*] ... BJ
Black Knight [*Missile*] ... BK
Black Label Resources, Inc. [*Vancouver Stock Exchange symbol*] ... BLB
Black Law Student Association (EA) ... BLSA
Black Legal Action for Soul in Television [*Student legal action organization*] ... BLAST
Black Leghorn [*Poultry*] ... BL
Black Letter [*Printing*] ... BKLR
Black Letter [*Printing*] ... BL
Black Liberation Army (EA) ... BLA
Black Librarians Caucus (EA) ... BCALA
Black Light ... BL
Black Light Blue [*Source for near ultraviolet radiation*] ... BLB
Black Liquor [*Pulp and paper technology*] ... BL
Black Liquor Oxidation [*For pollution control in paper mills*] ... BLO
Black Liquor Solids [*Pulp and paper technology*] ... BLS
Black Literature Criticism [*A publication*] ... BLC
Black Lung [*Social Security Administration*] (OICC) ... BL
Black Lung Association (EA) ... BLA
Black Lung Benefits Act [*1972*] ... BLBA
Black Magic Project Ltd. [*British ICAO designator*] (FAAC) ... BLM
Black Male ... BM
Black Marlin Energy [*Vancouver Stock Exchange symbol*] ... BMY
Black Mental Health Alliance (EA) ... BMHA
Black Mesa & Lake Powell [*AAR code*] ... BLKM
Black Mesa Defense Fund (EA) ... BMDF
Black Methodists for Church Renewal (EA) ... BMCR
Black Military History Institute of America (EA) ... BMHIA
Black Mountain [*California*] ... BM
Black Mountain College [*1933-1956*] ... BMC
Black Mountain, NC [*AM radio station call letters*] ... WFGW
Black Mountain, NC [*FM radio station call letters*] ... WMIT
Black Mountain, NC [*AM radio station call letters*] ... WZQR
Black Mountain Public Library, Black Mountain, NC [*Library symbol Library of Congress*] (LCLS) ... NcBlm
Black Music Association [*Defunct*] (EA) ... BMA
Black Music Association of Canada (AC) ... BMAC
Black Muslim ... BM
Black Oil Finish Slate (MSA) ... BOFS
Black on Constitutional Law [*A publication*] (DLA) ... Black Const Law
Black on Construction and Interpretation of Laws [*A publication*] (DLA) ... Black Interp Laws
Black on Construction and Interpretation of Laws [*A publication*] (DLA) ... Black St Const
Black on Employer's Liability [*A publication*] (DLA) ... Bl Emp L
Black on Employer's Liability [*A publication*] (DLA) ... Black Emp Li
Black on Judgments [*A publication*] (DLA) ... Bl Judgm
Black on Judgments [*A publication*] (DLA) ... Black Judg
Black on Judgments [*A publication*] (DLA) ... Black Judgm
Black on the Laws Regulating the Manufacture and Sale of Intoxicating Liquors [*A publication*] (DLA) ... Black Intox Liq
Black on Tone [*Printing*] (DGA) ... BOT
Black Ordinary Working People ... BOWP
Black Panel Temperature [*Automotive paint durability testing*] ... BPT

Black Panther Party [*Defunct Political party*] .... BPP
Black Peak [*Arizona*] [*Seismograph station code, US Geological Survey Closed*] (SEIS) .... BPK
Black Pearl Resources Ltd. [*Vancouver Stock Exchange symbol*] .... BKP
Black People's Convention [*South Africa*] (PD) .... BPC
Black People's Party [*South Africa*] [*Political party*] (PPW) .... BPP
Black Photo Corp. Ltd. [*Toronto Stock Exchange symbol*] .... BPK
Black Pigmented Bacteria [*Microbiology*] .... BPB
Black Political Women's Caucus .... BPWC
Black Powder .... BP
Black Psychiatrists of America (EA) .... BPA
Black Radical Action Group .... BRAG
Black Rapids [*Alaska*] [*Seismograph station code, US Geological Survey*] (SEIS) .... BLR
Black Raspberry Latent Virus [*Plant pathology*] .... BRLV
Black Resources and Information Centre [*Canada*] .... BRIC
Black Resources Information Coordinating Services [*Information service or system*] (IID) .... BRICS
Black Revolutionary War Patriots Foundation (EA) .... BRWPF
Black River [*Jamaica*] [*Seismograph station code, US Geological Survey Closed*] (SEIS) .... BRJ
Black River & Western Corp. [*AAR code*] .... BRW
Black River Falls, WI [*Location identifier FAA*] (FAAL) .... BCK
Black River Falls, WI [*AM radio station call letters*] .... WWIS
Black River Falls, WI [*FM radio station call letters*] .... WWIS-FM
Black Rock Coalition (EA) .... BRC
Black Scale (MSA) .... BS
Black Scholar [*A publication*] (BRI) .... Bl S
Black Sea and Area [*MARC geographic area code Library of Congress*] (LCCP) .... mb----
Black Sea Expedition [*1969*] [*Turkey, US*] (MSC) .... BSE
Black September Organization [*Israel*] .... BSO
Black Sheep Ventures, Inc. [*Vancouver Stock Exchange symbol*] .... BSV
Black Silent Majority Committee of the USA (EA) .... BSMC
Black Silk Suture [*Medicine*] .... BSS
Black Star Line [*Steamship*] (MHDB) .... BSL
Black Students Psychological Association .... BSPA
Black Students Union .... BSU
Black Stuntmen's Association (EA) .... BSA
Black Swan Gold Mines Ltd. [*Vancouver Stock Exchange symbol*] .... BSW
Black, Syvalls & Bryson, Inc., HOMCO Division, Houston, TX [*Library symbol Library of Congress*] (LCLS) .... TxHH
Black Tennis and Sports Foundation (EA) .... BTSF
Black Theater Alliance (EA) .... BTA
Black Thunder Petroleum [*Vancouver Stock Exchange symbol*] .... BTP
Black Top and National Delaine Merino Sheep Association (EA) .... BLNDMSA
Black Turnout [*Political science*] .... BTURN
Black Turtle Soup .... BTS
Black United Front [*South Africa*] (PD) .... BUF
Black Urban Professional [*Lifestyle classification*] .... Buppie
Black Varnish Cambric [*Insulation*] (MSA) .... BVC
Black Veterans, Inc. (EA) .... BV
Black Void Reactor .... BVR
Black Watch [*Military unit*] [*British*] .... BW
Black Widow Spider Toxin .... BWSTx
Black Widow Spider Venom .... BWSV
Black Women in Church and Society (EA) .... BWCS
Black Women in Publishing (EA) .... BWIP
Black Women Organized for Educational Development (EA) .... BWOED
Black Women's Association (EA) .... BWA
Black Women's Educational Alliance (EA) .... BWEA
Black Women's Educational Policy and Research Network (EA) .... BWEPRN
Black Women's Health Project [*Later, NBWHP*] (EA) .... BWHP
Black Women's Network [*An association*] (EA) .... BWN
Black Women's Roundtable on Voter Participation (EA) .... BWRVP
Black World Foundation (EA) .... BWF
Black Writers [*A publication*] .... BW
Blackader/Lauterman Library of Architecture and Art, McGill University, Montreal, Quebec [*Library symbol National Library of Canada*] (NLC) .... QMMB
Blackall [*Australia Airport symbol*] (OAG) .... BKQ
Black-and-White (IDOE) .... bw
Blackberry Gold Resources, Inc. [*Vancouver Stock Exchange symbol*] .... BLC
Blackboard .... BBD
Blackboard (MSA) .... BKD
Blackbody Limited Line (PDAA) .... BBLL
Black-Bordered [*Stationery*] .... BB
Blackburn College, Carlinville, IL [*OCLC symbol*] (OCLC) .... IBN
Blackburn College, Carlinville, IL [*Library symbol Library of Congress*] (LCLS) .... ICarlB
Blackburn Family Association (EA) .... BFA
Blackburn Hamlet Branch, Gloucester Public Library, Ontario [*Library symbol National Library of Canada*] (NLC) .... OGBH
Blackburn on Sales [*A publication*] (DLA) .... Black Sal
Blackburn on Sales [*A publication*] (DLA) .... Blackb
Blackburn on Sales [*A publication*] (DLA) .... Blackb Sales
Blackbushe [*British ICAO location identifier*] (ICLI) .... EGLK
Black-Capped Chickadee [*Ornithology*] .... BC
Blackdome Mining Corp. [*Toronto Stock Exchange symbol Vancouver Stock Exchange symbol*] .... BDM
Blackduck Elementary School, Blackduck, MN [*Library symbol*] [*Library of Congress*] (LCLS) .... MnBlaE
Blackduck High School, Blackduck, MN [*Library symbol*] [*Library of Congress*] (LCLS) .... MnBlaH
Blackduck, MN [*FM radio station call letters*] .... WBJI
Blackduck Public Library, Blackduck, MN [*Library symbol*] [*Library of Congress*] (LCLS) .... MnBla
Blacken .... BLKN
Blackening .... BLKNG
Blackerby's Justices' Cases [*England*] [*A publication*] (DLA) .... Black Jus
Blackerby's Justices' Cases [*England*] [*A publication*] (DLA) .... Black Just
Blackerby's Magistrates' Reports [*1327-1716*] [*England*] [*A publication*] (DLA) .... Black
Blacker-Wood Library of Zoology and Ornithology, McGill University, Montreal, Quebec [*Library symbol National Library of Canada*] (NLC) .... QMMBZ
Blackeye Cowpea Mosaic Virus [*Plant pathology*] .... BICMV
Blackfalds Public Library, Alberta [*Library symbol National Library of Canada*] (NLC) .... ABLA
Blackfeet Community College Library, Browning, MT [*Library symbol*] [*Library of Congress*] (LCLS) .... MtBwB
Blackfoot [*MARC language code Library of Congress*] (LCCP) .... bla
Blackfoot, ID [*FM radio station call letters*] .... KCVI
Blackfoot, ID [*AM radio station call letters*] (RBYB) .... KECN-AM
Blackfoot, ID [*FM radio station call letters*] .... KLCE
Blackfoot Public Library, Blackfoot, ID [*Library symbol*] [*Library of Congress*] (LCLS) .... IdBf
Blackford County Historical Society, Hartford City, IN [*Library symbol Library of Congress*] (LCLS) .... InHarBHi
Blackford, VA [*Location identifier FAA*] (FAAL) .... GZG
Blackford's Indiana Reports [*1817-47*] [*A publication*] (DLA) .... Bl
Blackford's Indiana Reports [*1817-47*] [*A publication*] (DLA) .... Black
Blackford's Indiana Reports [*1817-47*] [*A publication*] (DLA) .... Black R
Blackford's Indiana Reports [*1817-47*] [*A publication*] (DLA) .... Blackf
Blackford's Indiana Reports [*1817-47*] [*A publication*] (DLA) .... Blackf (Ind)
Blackford's Indiana Reports [*1817-47*] [*A publication*] (DLA) .... Blackford's Ia R
Blackgram Mottle Virus [*Plant pathology*] .... BMOV
Blackham, Dundas, and Osborne's Irish Nisi Prius Reports [*1846-48*] [*A publication*] (DLA) .... BD & O
Blackham, Dundas, and Osborne's Irish Nisi Prius Reports [*1846-48*] [*A publication*] (DLA) .... Bl D & O
Blackham, Dundas, and Osborne's Irish Nisi Prius Reports [*1846-48*] [*A publication*] (DLA) .... Bl D & Osb
Blackham, Dundas, and Osborne's Irish Nisi Prius Reports [*1846-48*] [*A publication*] (DLA) .... Black D & O
Blackhawk Airways, Inc. [*ICAO designator*] (FAAC) .... BAK
Blackhawk Technical Institute, Janesville, WI [*Library symbol Library of Congress*] (LCLS) .... WJaB
Blackhealth Kindergarten School, Long Beach, NY [*Library symbol*] [*Library of Congress*] (LCLS) .... NLobBK
Blackie's Science Text Books [*A publication*] .... BSTB
Black-Jewish Information Center [*Defunct*] (EA) .... BJIC
Blackman's Volunteer Army of Liberation [*An association*] (EA) .... BVAL
Blackmist Resources, Inc. [*Vancouver Stock Exchange symbol*] .... BKA
Blackmore [*England*] .... BLACKM
Blackout .... BO
Blackout Door [*Military*] .... BOD
Blackout Exit Time .... BOE
Blackout Initiation Time .... BOI
Blackout Preparedness .... BP
Blackout Restrictions [*British World War II*] .... BR
Blackout Restrictions in Industrial Establishments [*British World War II*] .... BIE
Blackout Window [*Military*] .... BOW
Blackpool [*England*] [*Airport symbol*] (OAG) .... BLK
Blackpool [*British ICAO location identifier*] (ICLI) .... EGNH
Blackpool Central Library, Blackpool, United Kingdom [*Library symbol Library of Congress*] (LCLS) .... UkBl
Blackpool Gazette & Herald Ltd., Blackpool, United Kingdom [*Library symbol Library of Congress*] (LCLS) .... UkBlG
Blackrock 1998 Term Tr [*NYSE symbol*] (TTSB) .... BBT
Blackrock 1998 Term Trust [*NYSE symbol*] (SPSG) .... BBT
Blackrock 1998 Term Trust, Inc. [*Associated Press*] (SAG) Blk1998
Blackrock 1999 Term Tr [*NYSE symbol*] (TTSB) .... BNN
Blackrock 1999 Term Trust [*Associated Press*] (SAG) Blk1999
Blackrock 1999 Term Trust [*NYSE symbol*] (SAG) .... BNN
Blackrock 2001 Term Trust [*NYSE symbol*] (TTSB) .... BLK
Blackrock 2001 Term Trust [*Associated Press*] (SAG) Blk2001
Blackrock 2001 Term Trust Inc. [*NYSE symbol*] (SPSG) .... BLK
Blackrock Advantage Term [*NYSE symbol*] (TTSB) .... BAT
Blackrock Advantage Term Trust [*NYSE symbol*] (SPSG) .... BAT
Blackrock Advantage Term Trust [*Associated Press*] (SAG) .... BlkAdv
Blackrock Broad Inv Gr 2009 [*AMEX symbol*] (TTSB) .... BCT
Blackrock Broad Investment Grade 2009 Term Trust [*AMEX symbol*] (SPSG) .... BCT
Blackrock Broad Investment Grade 2009Term Trust [*Associated Press*] (SAG) BlkBI09
Blackrock CA Ins Muni 2008 Tr [*NYSE symbol*] (TTSB) .... BFC
Blackrock CA Inv Qual Muni [*AMEX symbol*] (TTSB) .... RAA
Blackrock California Insurance Municipal 2008 Trade [*NYSE symbol*] (SPSG) .... BFC
Blackrock California Insured Municipal 2008 Term Trust [*Associated Press*] (SAG) BlkCA08
Blackrock California Investment Quality Municipal [*AMEX symbol*] (SPSG) .... RAA
Blackrock California Investment Quality Municipal Trust [*Associated Press*] (SAG) .... BCAIQ
Blackrock Fl Ins Muni 2008 Tr [*NYSE symbol*] (TTSB) .... BRF
Blackrock FL Inv Qual Muni [*AMEX symbol*] (TTSB) .... RFA
Blackrock Florida Insurance Municipal 2008 Trade [*NYSE symbol*] (SPSG) .... BRF

Blackrock Florida Insured Municipal 2008 Term Trust [*Associated Press*] (SAG) ... BlkFL08
Blackrock Florida Investment Quality Municipal [*AMEX symbol*] (SPSG) ... RFA
Blackrock Florida Investment Quality Municipal Trust [*Associated Press*] (SAG) ... BFLIQ
Blackrock Income Trust [*NYSE symbol*] (SPSG) ... BKT
Blackrock Income Trust [*Associated Press*] (SAG) ... BlkIT
Blackrock Ins Muni 2008 Tr [*NYSE symbol*] (TTSB) ... BRM
Blackrock Ins Muni Term [*NYSE symbol*] (TTSB) ... BMT
Blackrock Insurance Municipal 2008 Trade [*NYSE symbol*] (SPSG) ... BRM
Blackrock Insurance Municipal Term Trust [*NYSE symbol*] (SPSG) ... BMT
Blackrock Insured Municipal 2008 Term Trust [*Associated Press*] (SAG) ... Blk2008
Blackrock Inv Qual Muni Tr [*NYSE symbol*] (TTSB) ... BKN
Blackrock Inv Qual Term Tr [*NYSE symbol*] (TTSB) ... BQT
Blackrock Investment Quality Municipal Trust [*NYSE symbol*] (SPSG) ... BKN
Blackrock Investment Quality Municipal Trust [*Associated Press*] (SAG) ... BlkIQM
Blackrock Investment Quality Term Trust [*Associated Press*] (SAG) ... BlkIQT
Blackrock Investment Quality Term Trust [*NYSE symbol*] (SPSG) ... BQT
Blackrock Muni Target Term [*NYSE symbol*] (TTSB) ... BMN
Blackrock Municipal Target Term Trust [*Associated Press*] (SAG) ... BlkMTar
Blackrock Municipal Target Term Trust [*NYSE symbol*] (SPSG) ... BMN
Blackrock New Jersey Investment Quality Municipal [*AMEX symbol*] (SPSG) ... RNJ
Blackrock New Jersey Investment Quality Municipal Trust [*Associated Press*] (SAG) ... BNJIQ
Blackrock New York Insurance Municipal 2008 Trade [*NYSE symbol*] (SPSG) ... BLN
Blackrock New York Insured Municipal 2008 Term Trust [*Associated Press*] (SAG) ... BlkNY08
Blackrock New York Investment Quality Municipal [*AMEX symbol*] (SPSG) ... RNY
Blackrock New York Investment Quality Municipal Trust [*Associated Press*] (SAG) ... BNYIQ
Blackrock NJ Inv Qual Muni [*AMEX symbol*] (TTSB) ... RNJ
Blackrock No Amer Gvt Inc. [*NYSE symbol*] (TTSB) ... BNA
Blackrock North American Government Income Trust [*Associated Press*] (SAG) ... BlkNA
Blackrock North American Government, Inc. [*NYSE symbol*] (SPSG) ... BNA
Blackrock NY Ins Muni 2008 Tr [*NYSE symbol*] (TTSB) ... BLN
Blackrock NY Inv Qual Muni [*AMEX symbol*] (TTSB) ... RNY
Blackrock Strategic Term [*NYSE symbol*] (TTSB) ... BGT
Blackrock Strategic Term Trust [*NYSE symbol*] (SPSG) ... BGT
Blackrock Strategic Term Trust [*Associated Press*] (SAG) ... BlkStr
Blackrock Target Term [*NYSE symbol*] (TTSB) ... BTT
Blackrock Target Term Trust [*Associated Press*] (SAG) ... BlkTT
Blackrock Target Term Trust [*NYSE symbol*] (SAG) ... BTT
Blacks Against Nukes (EA) ... BAN
Black's Constitutional Prohibitions [*A publication*] (DLA) ... Black Const Prohib
Black's Decisions in Shipping Cases [*A publication*] (DLA) ... Black Ship Ca
Blacks in Government (EA) ... BIG
Blacks in Law Enforcement [*An association*] (EA) ... BLE
Blacks in Media Broadcasting Organization ... BIMBO
Black's Law Dictionary [*A publication*] (DLA) ... Bl Dict
Black's Law Dictionary [*A publication*] (DLA) ... Bl LD
Black's Law Dictionary [*A publication*] (DLA) ... Black Dict
Black's Law Dictionary [*A publication*] (DLA) ... Black Law Dict
Black's Law Dictionary [*A publication*] (DLA) ... Black LD
Black's Law Dictionary [*A publication*] (DLA) ... Black's Law Dict
Black's Reports [*30-53 Indiana*] [*A publication*] (DLA) ... Black
Black's United States Supreme Court Reports [*66-67 United States Reports*] [*A publication*] (DLA) ... Bk
Black's United States Supreme Court Reports [*66-67 United States Reports*] [*A publication*] (DLA) ... Bl
Black's United States Supreme Court Reports [*66-67 United States Reports*] [*A publication*] (DLA) ... Black
Black's United States Supreme Court Reports [*66-67 United States Reports*] [*A publication*] (DLA) ... Black R
Black's United States Supreme Court Reports [*66-67 United States Reports*] [*A publication*] (DLA) ... Black Rep
Blacksburg [*Virginia*] [*Seismograph station code, US Geological Survey*] (SEIS) ... BAV
Blacksburg [*Virginia*] [*Seismograph station code, US Geological Survey*] (SEIS) ... BLA
Blacksburg, VA [*Location identifier FAA*] (FAAL) ... BCB
Blacksburg, VA [*Location identifier FAA*] (FAAL) ... TEC
Blacksburg, VA [*AM radio station call letters*] ... WFNR
Blacksburg, VA [*AM radio station call letters*] ... WKEX
Blacksburg, VA [*FM radio station call letters*] ... WUVT
Blacksburg, VA [*FM radio station call letters*] (RBYB) ... WVMJ
Blackshear, GA [*AM radio station call letters*] ... WGIA
Blackshear, GA [*FM radio station call letters*] ... WKUB
Blacksmith ... BSMITH
Blacksmith ... BSMITH
Blackstone on Magna Charta [*A publication*] (DLA) ... Black Mag Ch
Blackstone, VA [*Location identifier FAA*] (FAAL) ... BKT
Blackstone, VA [*FM radio station call letters*] ... WBBC
Blackstone, VA [*AM radio station call letters*] ... WKLV
Blackstone's Analysis of the Laws of England [*A publication*] (DLA) ... Black Anal
Blackstone's Commentaries on the Laws of England [*A publication*] (DLA) ... Bl
Blackstone's Commentaries on the Laws of England [*A publication*] (DLA) ... Bl Com
Blackstone's Commentaries on the Laws of England [*A publication*] (DLA) ... Bl Comm
Blackstone's Commentaries on the Laws of England [*A publication*] (DLA) ... Bla Com
Blackstone's Commentaries on the Laws of England [*A publication*] (ILCA) ... Bla Comm
Blackstone's Commentaries on the Laws of England [*A publication*] (DLA) ... Black Com
Blackstone's Commentaries on the Laws of England [*A publication*] (DLA) ... Blackstone's Commen
Blackstone's Commentaries on the Laws of England [*A publication*] (DLA) ... Com
Blackstone's Commentaries on the Laws of England [*A publication*] (DLA) ... Comm
Blackstone's Commentaries on the Laws of England, Abridged [*A publication*] (DLA) ... Black Abr
Blackstone's Law Tracts [*A publication*] (DLA) ... Bl Law Tracts
Blackstone's Law Tracts [*A publication*] (DLA) ... Bl LT
Blackstone's Law Tracts [*A publication*] (DLA) ... Black L Tr
Blackstrap [*Freight*] ... BLKSTP
Black-Top Delaine Merino Sheep Breeders' Association (EA) ... BTDMSBA
Blacktown Agoraphobia Support Group [*Australia*] ... BASG
Blackville, SC [*FM radio station call letters*] (RBYB) ... WIIZ
Blackware (VRA) ... bwr
Blackwater [*Australia Airport symbol*] (OAG) ... BLT
Blackwell North America, Inc. [*Information service or system*] (IID) ... B/NA
Blackwell North America, Inc. [*New Jersey*] [*ACCORD*] [*UTLAS symbol*] ... BNA
Blackwell North America, Inc. [*Oregon*] [*ACCORD*] [*UTLAS symbol*] ... BNW
Blackwell, OK [*Location identifier FAA*] (FAAL) ... BWL
Blackwell, OK [*AM radio station call letters*] ... KOKB
Blackwell Retail Group [*British*] ... BRG
Blackwell's Condensed Illinois Reports [*A publication*] (DLA) ... Black Cond
Blackwell's Condensed Illinois Reports [*A publication*] (DLA) ... Black Cond Rep
Blackwell's Condensed Illinois Reports [*A publication*] (DLA) ... Blackw Cond
Blackwell's Scotch Acts [*A publication*] (DLA) ... Blackw Sc Act
Blackwell's Tax Titles [*A publication*] (DLA) ... Bl TT
Blackwell's Tax Titles [*A publication*] (ILCA) ... Black Tax Tit
Blackwell's Tax Titles [*A publication*] (DLA) ... Blackw Tax Titles
Blackwell's Tax Titles [*A publication*] (DLA) ... Blackw TT
Black-White Infrared [*Film*] ... BWIR
Blackwood Hodge (Canada) Ltd. [*Toronto Stock Exchange symbol*] ... BHG
Blackwood, NJ [*FM radio station call letters*] ... WDBK
Blacky Pictures [*Psychological testing*] ... BP
Blacky Test [*Psychology*] (DAVI) ... BT
Blacrock Insured Municipal Term Trust [*Associated Press*] (SAG) ... BlkIMT
Bladder Neck Contracture [*Medicine*] (MAE) ... BNC
Bladder Neck Obstruction [*Medicine*] ... BNO
Bladder Neck Resection [*Medicine*] ... BNR
Bladder Neck Retraction [*Urology*] (DAVI) ... BNR
Bladder Observation [*Medicine*] (CPH) ... bl obs
Bladder Obstruction [*Medicine*] ... BLOBS
Bladder Outlet Obstruction [*Urology*] (DAVI) ... BOO
Bladder Tremor [*Urology*] (DAVI) ... BT
Bladder Tumor [*Oncology and urology*] (DAVI) ... BLT
Bladder Tumor [*Medicine*] ... BT
Bladder Tumor Recheck [*Urology*] (DAVI) ... BTR
Bladder Urine [*Urology*] (DAVI) ... BLAC
Bladder Washout [*Urology*] ... BW
Blade (MSA) ... BL
Blade Area Ratio ... BAR
Blade Inspection Method ... BIM
Blade Inspection Method System (MCD) ... BIMS
Blade Integrity Monitor [*Aviation*] (DA) ... BIM
Blade Loading Harmonics [*Helicopter*] ... BLH
Blade Passage Tone [*Aviation*] ... BPT
Blade Rate (NVT) ... BR
Blade Slap Factor [*Helicopter*] ... BSF
Blade-Brake Clutch [*on lawn mowers*] ... BBC
Bladed Disc [*Turbine component*] ... BLISK
Bladed Ring [*Turbine component*] ... BLING
Bladen County Public Library, Elizabethtown, NC [*Library symbol Library of Congress*] (LCLS) ... NcE
Bladen Technical College, Dublin, NC [*Library symbol Library of Congress*] (LCLS) ... NcDubB
Bladen Technical Institute, Elizabethtown, NC [*Library symbol Library of Congress*] (LCLS) ... NcEB
Blade-Passing Frequency (PDAA) ... BPF
Bladzijde [*Page*] [*Netherlands*] (ILCA) ... blz
Blaettchenpulver [*Flake powder*] [*German military - World War II*] ... BLP
Blagden Management Training Programme [*British*] (AIE) ... BMTP
Blaine County library, Chinook, MT [*Library symbol*] [*Library of Congress*] (LCLS) ... MtCh
Blaine County Medical Center, Medical Library, Hailey, ID [*Library symbol*] [*Library of Congress*] (LCLS) ... IdHIH
Blaine, WA [*AM radio station call letters*] ... KARI
Blair Bell Research Society [*British*] ... BBRS
Blair Corp. [*AMEX symbol*] (SPSG) ... BL
Blair Corp. [*Associated Press*] (SAG) ... BlairCp
Blair County Law Reports [*Pennsylvania*] [*A publication*] (DLA) ... Blair Co
Blair County Law Reports [*Pennsylvania*] [*A publication*] (DLA) ... Blair Co LR
Blair County Law Reports [*Pennsylvania*] [*A publication*] (DLA) ... Blair Co LR (PA)
Blair House Library Foundation [*Defunct*] (EA) ... BHLF
Blair. Manual for Scotch Justices of the Peace [*A publication*] (DLA) ... Blair
Blair, NE [*FM radio station call letters*] ... KDCV
Blair, NE [*FM radio station call letters*] ... KISP
Blair, NE [*FM radio station call letters*] (RBYB) ... KMRV-FM

Blair Public Library, Blair, NE [*Library symbol Library of Congress*] (LCLS) .... NbBla
Blairmore, AB [*AM radio station call letters*] .... CJPR
Blairmore Public Library, Alberta [*Library symbol National Library of Canada*] (NLC) .... ABL
Blairstown, NJ [*FM radio station call letters*] .... WHCY
Blairstown Press, Blairstown, NJ [*Library symbol Library of Congress*] (LCLS) .... NjBlaiP
Blairsville, PA [*Location identifier FAA*] (FAAL) .... BSI
Blairsville, PA [*FM radio station call letters*] .... WLCY
Blairsville Public Library, Blairsville, PA [*Library symbol Library of Congress*] (LCLS) .... PBI
Blairsville Public Library, Blairsville, PA [*Library symbol*] [*Library of Congress*] (LCLS) .... PBIP
BLAISE [*British Library Automated Information Service*] **number** [*Database terminology*] (NITA) .... BL
Blake and Hedges' Reports [*2-3 Montana*] [*A publication*] (DLA) .... Bl & H
Blake and Hedges' Reports [*2-3 Montana*] [*A publication*] (DLA) .... Blake & H
Blake, Cassels & Graydon, Law Library, Toronto, ON, Canada [*Library symbol Library of Congress*] (LCLS) .... CaOTBCG
Blake, Cassels & Graydon, Toronto, Ontario [*Library symbol National Library of Canada*] (NLC) .... OTBCG
Blake. Chancery Practice [*A publication*] (DLA) .... Bl Chy Pr
Blake Resources Ltd. [*Toronto Stock Exchange symbol*] .... BLE
Blakely, GA [*AM radio station call letters*] .... WBBK
Blakely, GA [*FM radio station call letters*] .... WBBK-FM
Blakely Island [*Washington*] [*Airport symbol*] (OAG) .... BYW
Blake's Reports [*1-3 Montana*] [*A publication*] (DLA) .... Blake
Blakesburg Public Library, Blakesburg, IA [*Library symbol Library of Congress*] (LCLS) .... IaBlak
Blalock-Taussig [*Cardiology*] .... BT
Blanc Sablon [*Canada*] [*Airport symbol*] (OAG) .... YBX
Blanca Flor [*Bolivia*] [*ICAO location identifier*] (ICLI) .... SLBF
Blanch [*E.W.*] **Holdings, Inc.** [*Associated Press*] (SAG) .... Blanch
Blanch [*E.W.*] **Holdings, Inc.** [*NYSE symbol*] (SPSG) .... EWB
Blanchard and Weeks' Leading Cases on Mines [*A publication*] (DLA) .... Bl & W Mines
Blanchard and Weeks' Leading Cases on Mines [*A publication*] (DLA) .... Blan & W Lead Cas
Blanchard and Weeks' Leading Cases on Mines [*A publication*] (DLA) .... Blanc & WLC
Blanchard Community Library, Santa Paula, CA [*Library symbol Library of Congress*] (LCLS) .... CStp
Blanchester Public Library, Blanchester, OH [*Library symbol Library of Congress*] (LCLS) .... OBla
Blanchi-Backlund Transformation [*Engineering*] .... BT
Blandford [*England*] .... BLANDF
Blanding [*Utah*] [*Airport symbol*] (OAG) .... BDG
Blanding Free Public Library, Rehoboth, MA [*Library symbol Library of Congress*] (LCLS) .... MReh
Blanding, UT [*Location identifier FAA*] (FAAL) .... BDG
Blanding, UT [*AM radio station call letters*] .... KUTA
Bland's Chancery Reports [*A publication*] (DLA) .... Bl Chr R
Bland's Maryland Chancery Reports [*A publication*] (DLA) .... Bla Ch
Bland's Maryland Chancery Reports [*A publication*] (DLA) .... Bland
Bland's Maryland Chancery Reports [*A publication*] (DLA) .... Bland Ch (MD)
Bland's Maryland Chancery Reports [*A publication*] (DLA) .... Bland Ch R
Bland's Maryland Chancery Reports [*A publication*] (DLA) .... Bland's Ch
Bland's Maryland Chancery Reports [*A publication*] (DLA) .... Bland's Ch R
Bland's Maryland Chancery Reports [*A publication*] (DLA) .... Bland's Chy Rep
Blaney, Pasternak, Smela, Eagleson & Watson, Toronto, ON, Canada [*Library symbol Library of Congress*] (LCLS) .... CaOTBP
Blaney, Pasternak, Smela, Eagleson & Watson, Toronto, Ontario [*Library symbol National Library of Canada*] (NLC) .... OTBP
Blank (BUR) .... B
Blank [*Microtiter plate*] .... BL
Blank (MSA) .... BLK
Blank (HGAA) .... Blnk
Blank Carbon Copy .... BCC
Blank Corrected Sample Data [*Computer science*] .... BCSD
Blank Die .... BLDI
Blank Display (MHDI) .... BD
Blank Film Door .... BFD
Blank Firing Adaptor [*Army*] (MCD) .... BFA
Blank Firing Attachment (MCD) .... BFA
Blank Flange .... BF
Blank Line [*Computer science*] .... BL
Blank Recording Disc .... BRD
Blank Spike .... BS
Blank Spike Duplicate .... BSD
Blank when Zero .... BZ
Blanke Bevrydingsbeweging [*White Protection Movement*] [*South Africa Political party*] (EY) .... BBB
Blanked Picture Signal .... BPS
Blanked Ventricular Sense [*Medicine*] (DMAA) .... BVS
Blanket (MSA) .... BLKT
Blanket (AAG) .... BLNKT
Blanket Agreement .... BA
Blanket Bath [*Medicine*] .... BB
Blanket Crime Policy [*Insurance*] .... BCP
Blanket Delivery Date [*Military*] (AABC) .... BDD
Blanket Delivery Order (MCD) .... BDO
Blanket Gas (SAA) .... BG
Blanket Open End [*Contract*] [*Business term*] (MCD) .... BOE
Blanket Position Bond [*Insurance*] .... BPB
Blanket Purchase Agreement (KSC) .... BPA
Blanket Purchase Authority .... BPA
Blanket Tool Expenditure Control (MCD) .... BTEC
Blanket Tool Order .... BTO
Blanket Travel Order (MCD) .... BTO
Blanket Tritium Recovery [*Subsystem*] (MCD) .... BTR
Blanking (DEN) .... BL
Blanking (MSA) .... BLKG
Blanking Amplifier (IAA) .... BA
Blanking Die .... BLKGD
Blanking Input (IEEE) .... BI
Blanking Oscillator (MCD) .... BO
Blanking Pulse .... BLKP
Blanshard. Statutes of Limitations [*A publication*] (DLA) .... Blan Lim
Blanshard. Statutes of Limitations [*A publication*] (DLA) .... Blansh Lim
Blantyre [*Malawi*] [*Airport symbol*] (OAG) .... BLZ
Blantyre/Chileka [*Malawi*] [*ICAO location identifier*] (ICLI) .... FWCL
Blare Lake, AK [*Location identifier FAA*] (FAAL) .... TEH
Blaser [*Blower*] [*Wind instrument player*] .... BL
Blashfield. Instructions to Juries [*A publication*] (DLA) .... Blash Juries
Blasinstrumente [*Wind Instruments*] [*Music*] .... BI
Blasius de Morcono [*Flourished, 14th century*] [*Authority cited in pre-1607 legal work*] (DSA) .... BM
Blasphemy (DLA) .... BLAS
Blast .... BL
Blast Danger Area (NASA) .... BDA
Blast Furnace [*Ironmaking*] .... BF
Blast Furnace Research, Inc. [*Defunct*] (EA) .... BFR
Blast Furnace Slag .... BFS
Blast Gauge (MUGU) .... BG
Blast Propagation (AAG) .... BP
Blast Resistant Artillery Camouflage Screen (MCD) .... BRACS
Blast Response and Collapse of Buildings (MCD) .... BRACOB
Blast Saturation Temperature (PDAA) .... BST
Blast Suppression Device .... BSD
Blast Test .... BT
Blast Test Missile (NG) .... BTM
Blast Test Motor (MCD) .... BTM
Blast Test Vehicle (NG) .... BTV
Blast Wave Yield .... BWY
Blast-Furnace Portland Cement (PDAA) .... BPC
Blasthole .... BH
Blast-Induced Distortion (MCD) .... BID
Blasting Agent (MCD) .... BA
Blasting Gelatine (IAA) .... BG
Blastodermal Cell [*Insect embryology*] .... BC
Blastogenic Factor [*Immunochemistry*] .... BF
Blastomere Analysis before Implantation .... BABI
Blastomyces [*A fungus*] [*Biochemistry*] (DAVI) .... BLASTO
Blatant Self-Promotion .... BS
Blatchford and Howland's Reports [*United States*] [*A publication*] (DLA) .... Blatchford & H
Blatchford and Howland's United States District Court Reports [*A publication*] (DLA) .... B & H
Blatchford and Howland's United States District Court Reports [*A publication*] (DLA) .... Betts' Dec
Blatchford and Howland's United States District Court Reports [*A publication*] (DLA) .... Bl & H
Blatchford and Howland's United States District Court Reports [*A publication*] (DLA) .... Bl & How
Blatchford and Howland's United States District Court Reports [*A publication*] (DLA) .... Blatch & H
Blatchford and Howland's United States District Court Reports [*A publication*] (DLA) .... Blatchf & H
Blatchford's Prize Cases [*United States*] [*A publication*] (DLA) .... Bl Pr Cas
Blatchford's Prize Cases [*United States*] [*A publication*] (DLA) .... Bl Prize
Blatchford's Prize Cases [*United States*] [*A publication*] (DLA) .... Blatchf Pr Cas
Blatchford's Prize Cases [*United States*] [*A publication*] (DLA) .... Blatchf Prize Cas
Blatchford's United States Circuit Court Reports [*A publication*] (DLA) .... Bl
Blatchford's United States Circuit Court Reports [*A publication*] (DLA) .... Bl CC
Blatchford's United States Circuit Court Reports [*A publication*] (DLA) .... Bl CCR
Blatchford's United States Circuit Court Reports [*A publication*] (DLA) .... Blat CCR
Blatchford's United States Circuit Court Reports [*A publication*] (DLA) .... Blatch
Blatchford's United States Circuit Court Reports [*A publication*] (DLA) .... Blatch (US Cir Ct)
Blatchford's United States Circuit Court Reports [*A publication*] (DLA) .... Blatchf
Blatchford's United States Circuit Court Reports [*A publication*] (DLA) .... Blatchf CC
Blatchford's United States Circuit Court Reports [*A publication*] (DLA) .... Blatchf CC Rep
Blatchford's United States Circuit Court Reports [*A publication*] (DLA) .... Blatchf (US Circ Ct)
Blatchley Junior High School, Sitka, AK [*Library symbol Library of Congress*] (LCLS) .... AkSB
Blatt [*Newspaper, Sheet*] [*German*] (BJA) .... Bl
Blauvelt Free Library, Blauvelt, NY [*Library symbol Library of Congress*] (LCLS) .... NBla
Blaxland's Codex Legum Anglicanum [*A publication*] (DLA) .... Blax Eng Co
Blayney. Life Annuities [*1817*] [*A publication*] (DLA) .... Blay Ann
Blayney. Life Assurance [*1837*] [*A publication*] (DLA) .... Bla Life Ass
Blayney. Life Assurance [*1837*] [*A publication*] (DLA) .... Blay Life Ins
Blazer Horse Association (EA) .... BHA
Blazon .... BLZN

BLCMP [*Birmingham Libraries Cooperative Mechanisation Project*] **Online Support Services** (NITA) .... BOSS
Bleach Filtrate Recycle [*Pulp and paper technology*] .... BFR
Bleachable Absorber LASER Amplifier and Detector .... BALAD
Bleach-Accelerator-Releasing Couplers [*Photography*] .... BAR
Bleached [*Freight*] .... BLCHD
Bleached Chemimechanical Pulping Process [*Pulp and paper technology*] .... BCMP
Bleached Chemi-Thermomechanical Pulp .... BCTMP
Bleached Eucalypt Kraft .... BEK
Bleached Eucalypt Kraft Mill .... BEKM
Bleached Kraft Mill Effluent [*Pulp and paper processing*] .... BKME
Bleached Semichemical Pulping Process [*Pulp and paper technolgy*] .... BSCP
Bleach-Fix [*Photography*] .... BLIX
Bleaching [*Freight*] .... BLCHG
Bleaching Treatment [*Dentistry*] .... BT
Bleckley's Reports [*34, 35 Georgia*] [*A publication*] (DLA) .... Bleck
Bleckley's Reports [*34, 35 Georgia*] [*A publication*] (DLA) .... Bleckley
Bledisloe [*England*] .... BLED
Bleed (MSA) .... BL
Bleed Air Precooler .... BAP
Bleed Air System .... BAS
Bleed Door Actuator .... BDA
Bleed Hose Assembly .... BHA
Bleed Storage Tank [*Nuclear energy*] (NRCH) .... BST
Bleed Valve (MCD) .... BLV
Bleed Valve (MCD) .... BV
Bleeder (MSA) .... BLDR
Bleeding Frequency [*Medicine*] .... BF
Bleeding [*or Bruising*] **of Undetermined Origin** [*Medicine*] .... BUO
Bleeding Time [*Clinical chemistry*] .... bl x
Bleeding Time [*Hematology*] (DAVI) .... BLEED
Bleeding Time [*Clinical chemistry*] .... BT
Blend .... B
Blend .... BLEN
Blend (MSA) .... BLN
Blended Credit Program [*Federal government*] .... BCP
Blended Old Scotch [*Whiskey*] (ROG) .... BOS
Blended Wing Body [*Megaplane*] .... BWB
Blender Control Unit (ECII) .... BCU
Blending Octane Number [*Petroleum technology*] .... BON
Blending Octane Value .... BOV
Blending Value Octane Number [*Petroleum technology*] .... BVON
Blendkoerper [*Frangible-glass smoke grenade*] [*German military - World War II*] .... BK
Blenheim [*New Zealand*] [*Airport symbol*] (OAG) .... BHE
Bleomycin [*Also, Bl, Bleo, BLM*] [*Antineoplastic drug*] .... B
Bleomycin [*Also, B, Bleo, BLM*] [*Antineoplastic drug*] .... Bl
Bleomycin [*Also, B, Bl, BLM*] [*Antineoplastic drug*] .... Bleo
Bleomycin [*Sulfate*] [*Also, B, Bl, Bleo*] [*Antineoplastic drug*] .... BLM
Bleomycin, Adriamycin, CCNU [*Lomustine*], Oncovin [*Vincristine*] [*Antineoplastic drug regimen*] (DAVI) .... BACO
Bleomycin, Adriamycin, Cyclophosphamide, Oncovin [*Vincristine*], Dexamethasone [*Antineoplastic drug regimen*] .... BACOD
Bleomycin, Adriamycin, Cyclophosphamide, Oncovin [*Vincristine*], Prednisone [*Antineoplastic drug regimen*] .... BACOP
Bleomycin, Adriamycin, Cytoxan, Oncovin, Methotrexate with Leucovorin Rescue [*Antineoplastic drug*] (CDI) .... M-BACOS
Bleomycin, Adriamycin, Cytoxan, Tamoxifen [*Antineoplastic drug regimen*] (DAVI) .... BACT
Bleomycin, Adriamycin, Methotrexate, Oncovin [*Vincristine*], Nitrogen mustard [*Antineoplastic drug regimen*] .... BAMON
Bleomycin, Adriamycin, Prednisone [*Antineoplastic drug regimen*] (DAVI) .... BAP
Bleomycin, Adriamycin, Vinblastine, Imidazole carboxamide [*Dacarbazine*], Prednisone [*Antineoplastic drug regimen*] .... BAVIP
Bleomycin, CCNU [*Lomustine*], Adriamycin, and Velban [*Antineoplastic drug regimen*] (DAVI) .... B-CAVe
Bleomycin, CCNU [*Lomustine*], Adriamycin, Vinblastine [*Antineoplastic drug regimen*] .... BCAVE
Bleomycin, Cyclophosphamide, Dactinomycin [*Antineoplastic drug regimen*] .... BCD
Bleomycin, Cyclophosphamide, Hydroxydaunomycin [*Adriamycin*], Oncovin , Prednisone [*Vincristine*] [*Antineoplastic drug regimen*] .... B-CHOP
Bleomycin, Cyclophosphamide, Methotrexate, Fluorouracil [*Antineoplastic drug regimen*] .... BCMF
Bleomycin, Cyclophosphamide, Oncovin [*Vincristine*], Methotrexate, Fluorouracil [*Antineoplastic drug regimen*] .... BLEO-COMF
Bleomycin, Dacarbazine, Oncovin [*Vincristine*], Prednisone, Adriamycin [*Antineoplastic drug regimen*] .... B-DOPA
Bleomycin, Dacarbazine [*DTIC*], Vincristine, Adriamycin, Prednisone [*Antineoplastic drug regimen*] (DAVI) .... BAVIP
Bleomycin, Etoposide, Platinol [*Cisplatin*] [*Antineoplastic drug regimen*] .... BEP
Bleomycin Hydrolase [*An enzyme*] .... BH
Bleomycin, Mustargen, Oncovin [*Vincristine*], Procarbazine, Prednisone [*Antineoplastic drug regimen*] .... B-MOPP
Bleomycin, Nitrogen Mustard, Oncovin [*Vincristine*], Procarbazine, and Prednisone [*Antineoplastic drug regimen*] (DAVI) .... BLEO-MOPP
Bleomycin, Oncovin [*Vincristine*], Adriamycin, Prednisone [*Antineoplastic drug regimen*] .... BOAP
Bleomycin, Oncovin [*Vincristine*], Lomustine, Dacarbazine [*Antineoplastic drug regimen*] .... BOLD
Bleomycin, Oncovin [*Vincristine*], Natulan , Prednisolone [*Procarbazine hydrochloride*] [*Antineoplastic drug regimen*] .... BONP
Bleomycin, Oncovin [*Vincristine*], Prednisone [*Antineoplastic drug regimen*] (DAVI) .... BOP
Bleomycin, Oncovin [*Vincristine*], Prednisone, Adriamycin, Mustargen , Methotrexate [*Nitrogen mustard*] [*Antineoplastic drug regimen*] .... BOPAM
Bleomycin Sulfate [*Antineoplastic drug*] (DAVI) .... BLEO
Bleomycin Sulphate [*Antineoplastic drug*] (DAVI) .... BMS
Bleomycin, Vinblastine, Doxorubicin, Streptozocin [*Antineoplastic drug regimen*] .... BVDS
Blepharophimosis, Ptosis, Epicanthus Inversus [*Medicine*] (DMAA) .... BPEI
Blepharophimosis-Ptosis-Epicanthus Inversus Syndrome [*Medicine*] (DMAA) .... BPES
Blepharoplasty [*Ophthalmology and plastic surgery*] (DAVI) .... bleph
Bleriot Experimental [*British military*] (DMA) .... BE
Blessed .... B
Blessed .... BL
Blessed .... BLSSD
Blessed Kateri Tekakwitha League (EA) .... BKTL
Blessed Kateri Tekakwitha School, Gloucester, Ontario [*Library symbol National Library of Canada*] (NLC) .... OGBKT
Blessed Mary [*or Mother*] (BARN) .... BM
Blessed Mary the Virgin (DAS) .... BMV
Blessed Memory (BARN) .... BM
Blessed Sacrament .... BS
Blessed Sacrament Seminary, Cleveland, OH [*Library symbol Library of Congress*] (LCLS) .... OCIBS
Blessed Trinity Society [*Defunct*] .... BTS
Blessed Virgin .... BV
Blessed Virgin Mary .... BVM
Blessed Virgin Missionaries of Carmel (TOCD) .... BVMC
Blessings Co. [*Associated Press*] (SAG) .... Blessings
Blessings Corp. [*AMEX symbol*] (SPSG) .... BCO
Bletchley [*British ICAO location identifier*] (ICLI) .... EGGE
Bletsoe [*England*] .... BLET
Blickenaderfer. Law Student's Review [*A publication*] (DLA) .... Blick Rev
Blida [*Algeria*] [*ICAO location identifier*] (ICLI) .... DAAB
Bligh's English House of Lords Reports [*A publication*] (DLA) .... Bli
Bligh's English House of Lords Reports, New Series [*A publication*] (DLA) .... Bl NS
Bligh's English House of Lords Reports, New Series [*1827-37*] [*A publication*] (DLA) .... Bli NS
Bligh's English House of Lords Reports, New Series [*1827-37*] [*A publication*] (DLA) .... Bligh NS (Eng)
Bligh's English House of Lords Reports, Old Series [*1819-21*] [*A publication*] (DLA) .... Bli (OS)
Bligh's English House of Lords Reports, Old Series [*1819-21*] [*A publication*] (DLA) .... Bligh
Blimp Squadron [*Navy*] .... BLIMPRON
Blimp Squadron [*Later separated into BLIMPRON and Blimp-HEDRON*] [*Navy*] .... ZEDRON
Blimped Noiseless Reflex Camera (NTCM) .... BNC
Blimpie International, Inc. [*Associated Press*] (SAG) .... Blimpie
Blimpie International, Inc. [*NASDAQ symbol*] (SAG) .... BMPE
Blimpie Int'l [*NASDAQ symbol*] (TTSB) .... BMPE
Blind .... BLND
Blind Approach [*Aviation*] .... BA
Blind Approach Beacon System [*Aviation*] .... BABS
Blind Approach Landing System [*Aviation*] .... BALS
Blind Approach System [*Aviation*] (MCD) .... BAS
Blind Approach Training [*Air Force*] .... BAT
Blind Blocking [*Bookbinding*] (DGA) .... BLD BKG
Blind Book Auxiliary (DGA) .... BBA
Blind Bronchial Sampling [*Clinical chemistry*] .... BBS
Blind Carbon Copy .... BCC
Blind Carbon Copy (ODBW) .... bcc
Blind Carbon Copy (WDMC) .... bcc
Blind Child [*Social Security Administration*] (OICC) .... BC
Blind Copy (DNAB) .... BC
Blind Fire Director (NATG) .... BFD
Blind Individual [*Social Security Administration*] (OICC) .... BI
Blind Landing Experimental Unit [*Aviation*] .... BLEU
Blind Learning Aptitude Test [*Education*] .... BLAT
Blind Loaded and Blind Plugged [*Projectile*] (MCD) .... BLBP
Blind Loaded and Plugged [*Projectile*] .... BL & P
Blind Loaded and Traced [*Projectile*] .... BL & T
Blind Loop Syndrome [*Medicine*] (DMAA) .... BLS
Blind Manufacturers' Association of Tasmania [*Australia*] .... BMAT
Blind Matching [*Parapsychology*] .... BM
Blind Mating Connector (MCD) .... BMC
Blind Mobility Research Unit [*University of Nottingham*] [*British*] (IRC) .... BMRU
Blind Navigation .... BN
Blind Outdoor Leisure Development (EA) .... BOLD
Blind Persons Resettlement Officer [*Department of Employment*] [*British*] .... BPRO
Blind Persons Technical Officer [*British*] (AIE) .... BPTO
Blind Purchase .... BP
Blind River, ON [*AM radio station call letters*] .... CJNR
Blind River Public Library, Blind River, ON, Canada [*Library symbol*] [*Library of Congress*] (LCLS) .... CaOBLR
Blind River Public Library, Ontario [*Library symbol National Library of Canada*] (NLC) .... OBLR
Blind River Refinery, Eldorado Resources Ltd., Ontario [*Library symbol National Library of Canada*] (NLC) .... OBRER
Blind Riveted Joint .... BRJ
Blind Service Association (EA) .... BSA
Blind Soldiers Association of Victoria [*Australia*] .... BSAV
Blind Sporting Association of New South Wales [*Australia*] .... BSANSW
Blind Sports [*Later, LBSF*] (EA) .... BS
Blind Spouse [*Title XVI*] [*Social Security Administration*] (OICC) .... BS

Blind Tooling [*Bookbinding*] (DGA) .... BLD TLG
Blind Toss .... BT
Blind Transmission Broadcast [*Army*] (ADDR) .... BTB
Blind Welfare Society of South Australia .... BWASA
Blind Workers' Union of South Australia .... BWUSA
Blind Workers' Union of Victoria [*Australia*] .... BWUV
Blinded American Veterans Foundation (EA) .... BAVF
Blinded Veterans Association (EA) .... BVA
Blinder (MSA) .... BLD
Blind-Made Products .... BMP
Blindmakers' Association of Australia .... BAA
Blindmakers' Association of New South Wales [*Australia*] .... BANSW
Blinds [*Classified advertising*] (ADA) .... BLDS
Blinker Tube .... BKT
Blinkers [*Horse racing*] .... B
Blinking Light Monitor .... BLM
Blinn College, Brenham, TX [*Library symbol Library of Congress*] (LCLS) .... TxBreB
Blip Counter System .... BCS
Blip/Frame (CET) .... B/F
Blip/Scan (MUGU) .... B/S
Blip-Frame Ratio (MSA) .... BFR
Blip-Scan Counter .... BSC
Blip-Scan Counter System .... BSCS
Blip-Scan RADAR (IAA) .... BSP
Blip-Scan Ratio .... BSR
Bliss & Laughlin Industries, Inc. [*NASDAQ symbol*] (CTT) .... BLIS
Bliss & Laughlin Industries, Inc. [*Associated Press*] (SAG) .... BlisLau
Bliss Classification .... BC
Bliss Classification Association [*London, England*] .... BCA
Bliss Memorial Public Library, Bloomville, OH [*Library symbol Library of Congress*] (LCLS) .... OBlv
Bliss' New York Code [*A publication*] (DLA) .... Bliss NY Co
Bliss' New York Code, Annotated [*A publication*] (DLA) .... Bliss NY Code
Bliss on Code Pleading [*A publication*] (DLA) .... Bliss Co Pl
Bliss on Life Insurance [*A publication*] (DLA) .... Bliss Ins
Blissymbolics Communication Resource Centre [*British*] (CB) .... BCRC
Blister Gas [*US Chemical Corps symbol*] CX
Blister Pack .... BP
Blit [*Computer science*] (NHD) .... BLT
Blitter Objects [*Amiga computer hardware*] .... BOB's
Blizzard [*NWS*] (FAAC) .... BLZD
Blizzard Resources, Inc. [*Vancouver Stock Exchange symbol*] .... BZD
Bloated Clay Aggregate [*Engineering*] .... BCA
Bloc Africain de Guinee [*African Bloc of Guinea*] .... BAG
Bloc Democratique Gabonais [*Gabonese Democratic Bloc*] [*Later, PDG*] .... BDG
Bloc Democratique Senegalais [*Senegal*] [*Political party*] (PPW) .... BDS
Bloc des Masses Senegalaises [*Bloc of the Senegalese Masses*] (AF) .... BMS
Bloc d'Esquerra d'Alliberament Nacional [*Left Bloc for National Liberation*] [*Spain*] (PPW) .... BEAN
Bloc Populaire Senegalais [*Senegal*] (PPW) .... BPS
Bloc pour la Social-Democratie [*Benin*] [*Political party*] (EY) .... BSD
Bloc Quebecois [*Canada Political party*] (ECON) .... BQ
Bloch & Co., Cleveland, OH [*Library symbol Library of Congress*] (LCLS) .... BL
Block (WGA) .... BK
Block (WDMC) .... bk
Block .... BL
Block (BUR) .... BLCK
Block [*Unit of data*] .... BLK
Block (VRA) .... blk
Block .... BLK
Block (FAAC) .... BLX
Block Access Method [*Computer science*] .... BAM
Block Adaptive Rate Controlled [*Computer science*] .... BARC
Block Address Translation [*Computer science*] (PCM) .... BAT
Block Allocating Map (IAA) .... BAM
Block and List Manipulator [*Computer science*] (CSR) .... BALM
Block Automation System [*NYSE trading computer*] .... BAS
Block Availability Map (IAA) .... BAM
Block Brazing .... BB
Block Calls Cleared [*Telecommunications*] (ACRL) .... BCC
Block Check [*or Control*] Character [*Computer science*] .... BCC
Block Check Character [*Computer science*] (TNIG) .... BCC
Block Check Code [*Telecommunications*] (OSI) .... BCC
Block Check Error [*Electronics*] (ECII) .... BCER
Block Check Sequence [*Computer science*] (IAA) .... BCS
Block Control Header [*Computer science*] (IBMDP) .... BCH
Block Control Sheet [*Computer science*] .... BCS
Block Control Signal [*Telecommunications*] (TEL) .... BCS
Block Control Unit [*Computer science*] (IBMDP) .... BCU
Block Copolymer [*Organic chemistry*] .... BCP
Block (Copolymerized) [*Organic chemistry*] .... b
Block Count [*Computer science*] .... BC
Block Data Transfer (MCD) .... BDT
Block Decoder Assembly [*Space Flight Operations Facility, NASA*] .... BDA
Block Delete (IAA) .... BD
Block Demultiplexer [*Ground Communications Facility, NASA*] .... BDXR
Block Design [*Psychometrics*] .... BD
Block Diagram (IAA) .... BD
Block Diagram Compiler .... BLODI
Block Diagram Compiler [*Engineering program*] (IAA) .... BLODIC
Block Diagram Compiler B (IEEE) .... BLODIB
Block Diagram - Graphics (PDAA) .... BLODI-G
Block Downconverter [*Satellite communications*] .... BD
Block Downconverter [*Satellite communications*] .... BDC
Block Drug Co. [*Associated Press*] (SAG) .... BlckD

Block Drug Co., Inc. [*NASDAQ symbol*] (NQ) .... BLOC
Block Drug'A'non-vtg [*NASDAQ symbol*] (TTSB) .... BLOCA
Block Error Detector (MCD) .... BED
Block Error Rate [*Computer science*] (MHDI) .... BKER
Block Error Rate Test [*Telecommunications*] .... BLERT
Block Error Status (IAA) .... BES
Block Floating Point Quantizer (MCD) .... BFPQ
Block Format Recording .... BFR
Block Grant Authority .... BGA
Block Group [*Bureau of the Census*] (GFGA) .... BG
Block Handler [*Computer science*] .... BH
Block Handler Routine [*Computer science*] (BUR) .... BHR
Block (H&R) [*NYSE symbol*] (TTSB) .... HRB
Block Header Record [*Computer science*] .... BHR
Block Improved Abrams [*Battle tank*] [*Army*] .... BIA
Block Improvement Program [*for M1A1 tank*] [*Army*] .... BIP
Block in Posteroinferior Division of Left Branch [*Medicine*] (DMAA) .... BIDLB
Block in the Anterosuperior Division of the Left Branch [*Cardiology*] (DAVI) .... BSDLB
Block [*H. & R.*], Inc. [*Associated Press*] (SAG) .... BlckHR
Block [*H. & R.*], Inc. [*NYSE symbol*] (SPSG) .... HRB
Block Input Length [*Computer science*] (BUR) .... BIL
Block Input-Output Output [*Computer science*] (MHDI) .... BIOO
Block Island [*Rhode Island*] [*Airport symbol*] (OAG) .... BID
Block Island - Fisher Island Range [*Navy*] (GFGA) .... BIFI
Block Island, RI [*Location identifier FAA*] (FAAL) .... SEY
Block Island, RI [*FM radio station call letters*] .... WBLQ
Block Island, RI [*Television station call letters*] .... WOST
Block Island, RI [*FM radio station call letters*] .... WVBI
Block Label [*Computer science*] (IAA) .... BL
Block Length .... BL
Block Length Error [*Computer science*] (IAA) .... BLE
Block Load Request [*Military*] .... BLR
Block Mode Terminal Interface [*Computer science*] .... BMTI
Block Multiplexer [*Ground Communications Facility, NASA*] .... BMXR
Block Multiplexer Channel (MHDI) .... BLMPX
Block Multiplexer Channel (IAA) .... BLMUX
Block Multiplexer Channel .... BMC
Block Numbering Area [*Bureau of the Census*] (GFGA) .... BNA
Block of Four [*Philately*] B4
Block on Tithes [*A publication*] (DLA) .... BI Ti
Block Order Exposure System [*Business term*] .... BLOX
Block out of Balance [*Computer science*] .... BOOB
Block Parity [*Error checking method*] [*Telecommunications*] (TEL) .... BP
Block Point Plan Scheduling Procedure (SAA) .... BPPSP
Block Print (VRA) .... blkpr
Block Proof List [*Computer science*] .... BPL
Block Proof Record [*Computer science*] .... BPR
Block Received Signal [*Telecommunications*] (TEL) .... BRS
Block Replacement .... BR
Block Sale [*Investment term*] .... BS
Block Specification (MCD) .... BS
Block Store Zero [*Computer science*] (IAA) .... BSZ
Block Structured Assembly Language .... BSAL
Block Structured Assembly Language [*Computer science*] (NITA) .... BSAL
Block Tape Recorder .... BTR
Block Template .... BT
Block Terminal [*Telecommunications*] (NITA) .... BT
Block Terminating Character [*Computer science*] (IAA) .... BTC
Block Transfer [*Computer science*] .... BLT
Block Transfer Controller [*Computer science*] .... BTC
Block Transfer Unit [*Computer science*] (IAA) .... BTU
Block Translation Lookaside Buffer [*Computer science*] (PCM) .... BTLB
Block Type Manipulation Facility .... BTMF
Block Unit Numbers (MCD) .... BUNS
Blockade (AABC) .... BLOC
Blockade Intelligence Department [*Ministry of Economic Warfare*] [*British World War II*] .... BID
Blockade Operations [*Military*] (NVT) .... BLOKOPS
Blockage .... BLOC
Block-a-Matic, Block-a-Gram, and Block-a-Text (SAA) .... BAMAGAT
Block-Connected Graph [*Mathematics*] [*Used in GPRS*] .... BCG
Block-Cutpoint-Tree [*Mathematics*] [*Used in ASAMS*] .... BCT
Blocked .... BLKD
Blocked Asynchronous Transmission [*Message protocol*] [*Computer science*] (PCM) .... BLAST
Blocked Calls Cleared [*Telecommunications*] .... BCC
Blocked Calls Delayed [*Telecommunications*] .... BCD
Blocked Calls Held [*Telecommunications*] .... BCH
Blocked Calls Released [*Telecommunications*] .... BCR
Blocked Data Format (MCD) .... BDF
Blocked Precedence Announcement (DNAB) .... BPA
Blocked Random Access Method (MCD) .... BRAM
Blocker Deflector [*Aviation*] (OA) .... BD
Blockhouse [*NASA*] (KSC) .... BH
Blockhouse [*NASA*] (AAG) .... BKHS
Blockhouse Battery Charger [*NASA*] .... BBC
Blockhouse Computer [*NASA*] (KSC) .... BHC
Blockhouse Equipment Switching Test (SAA) .... BEST
Blockhouse Operation [*NASA*] .... BO
Block-In (MCD) .... BI
Blocking (MSA) .... BLKG
Blocking [*Telecommunications*] (TEL) .... BLO
Blocking Acknowledgement Signal [*Telecommunications*] (NITA) .... BLA
Blocking Acknowledgment [*Telecommunications*] (TEL) .... BLA

Blocking Antibody [*Immunology*] (MAE) ... BA
Blocking Back [*Football*] ... BB
Blocking, Bracing, and Tie-Down [*Military*] (DOMA) ... BB & T
Blocking, Bracing, Packing, Crating, and Tiedown Materials [*Military*] (INF) ... BBPCT
Blocking Device [*Nuclear energy*] (OA) ... BD
Blocking Factor ... BF
Blocking Factor (CMD) ... BKF
Blocking Factor [*Computer science*] (IAA) ... BLF
Blocking Oscillator ... BO
Blocking Signal [*Telecommunications*] (NITA) ... BLO
Blocking-Tube Oscillator ... BTO
Block-Oriented Compiler ... BLOC
Block-Oriented Computer ... BOC
Block-Oriented Network Simulator [*Computer science*] ... BONES
Block-Oriented Random-Access Memory [*Computer science*] ... BORAM
Block-Oriented Systems Simulator [*Computer software*] ... BOSS
Blockout ... BO
Blocks [*Freight*] ... BLKS
Block-Switching Digital Network ... BSDN
Block-Write Mode [*Computer graphics*] (BYTE) ... BWM
Blodgett Memorial Library, Fishkill, NY [*Library symbol Library of Congress*] (LCLS) ... NFisk
Bloedel-Donovan Railroad (IIA) ... BD
Bloemfontein [*South Africa*] [*Airport symbol*] (OAG) ... BFN
Bloemfontein [*South Africa*] [*Seismograph station code, US Geological Survey*] (SEIS) ... BLF
Bloemfontein [*South Africa*] (ROG) ... BLOEMF
Bloemfontein/J. B. M. Hertzog [*South Africa*] [*ICAO location identifier*] (ICLI) ... FABL
Bloemfontein/New Tempe [*South Africa*] [*ICAO location identifier*] (ICLI) ... FATP
Blois/Le Breuil [*France ICAO location identifier*] (ICLI) ... LFOQ
Blomatrix, Inc. [*NASDAQ symbol*] (SPSG) ... BIOX
Blomkest Elementary School, Blomkest, MN [*Library symbol*] [*Library of Congress*] (LCLS) ... MnBkES
Blond (WGA) ... BLD
Blonde d'Aquitaine Breeders Society [*British*] (DBA) ... BDABS
Blonde D'Aquitaine Society of Australia and New Zealand ... BDSANZ
Blonder Tongue Laboratories, Inc. [*AMEX symbol*] (SAG) ... BDR
Blonder Tongue Laboratories, Inc. [*Associated Press*] (SAG) ... BlondT
Blonder Tongue Labs [*AMEX symbol*] (TTSB) ... BDR
Blonduos [*Iceland*] [*ICAO location identifier*] (ICLI) ... BIBL
Blonduos [*Iceland*] [*Airport symbol*] (OAG) ... BLO
Blood (AAMN) ... B
Blood ... BL
Blood [*Philately*] ... bld
Blood Agar [*Growth medium*] ... BA
Blood Agar Base [*Growth medium*] ... BAB
Blood Agar Plate [*Microbiology*] ... BAP
Blood Alcohol (WGA) ... BA
Blood Alcohol Concentration [*or Content*] [*Sobriety test*] ... BAC
Blood Alcohol Level [*Medicine*] ... BAL
Blood and Bone (ADA) ... b & b
Blood and Guts [*Code name used to refer to Oliver North, National Security Council aide during Reagan administration*] ... BG
Blood and Lymphatic System [*Medicine*] ... BLS
Blood Bank ... BB
Blood Bank (DAVI) ... Bld Bk
Blood Bank Technologist (DAVI) ... BBT
Blood Banking [*Medical specialty*] (DHSM) ... BLB
Blood Brain Barrier [*Neurology*] ... BBB
Blood Buffer Base [*Biochemistry*] (DAVI) ... BB
Blood Cadmium Level ... BCd
Blood Cancer Foundation [*Defunct*] (EA) ... BCF
Blood Cell Separator [*Medicine*] ... BCS
Blood Chemistry (DAVI) ... Bld Chem
Blood Color Analyzer [*Medicine*] ... BCA
Blood Culture [*Medicine*] ... BC
Blood Culture [*Medicine*] ... Bl C
Blood Culture [*Medicine*] (AAMN) ... BL CULT
Blood Culture [*Medicine*] (DMAA) ... BIC
Blood Derived Serum ... BDS
Blood Erythrocytes Particle Counter [*Medicine*] ... BEpc
Blood Ethanol Concentration [*Medicine*] ... BEC
Blood Ethanol Level [*Medicine*] (DMAA) ... BEL
Blood Extracellular Fluid [*Medicine*] (DMAA) ... BECF
Blood Fasting Sugar [*Medicine*] (DMAA) ... BFS
Blood Flow [*Medicine*] ... BF
Blood Flow Energy [*Medicine*] (DMAA) ... BFE
Blood Flow Rate [*Medicine*] ... BFR
Blood Gas [*US Chemical Corps symbol*] ... AC
Blood/Gas [*Clinical chemistry*] ... B/G
Blood Gas Analyzer [*Physiology*] ... BGA
Blood Glucose [*Medicine*] ... BG
Blood Glucose [*Medicine*] (MAE) ... BGlu
Blood Glucose Reagent Strip [*Endocrinology*] (DAVI) ... BGRS
Blood Granulocyte-Specific Activity [*Hematology*] (MAE) ... BGSA
Blood Group (ADA) ... BG
Blood Group Class ... BGC
Blood Group Substances [*Hematology*] ... BGS
Blood Group-Degrading [*Medicine*] (MAE) ... BGD
Blood Information Service (NITA) ... BIS
Blood Information Service [*Information service or system*] (IID) ... BLDIS
Blood Isotope Clearance [*Medicine*] (DMAA) ... BIC
Blood Lead Level [*Medicine*] ... BLL
Blood Loss [*Medicine*] (AAMN) ... BL
Blood Lymphocytes Particle Counter [*Instrumentation*] [*Medicine*] ... Blpc
Blood Oxygen Capacity [*Medicine*] (DMAA) ... BOC
Blood Oxygen Saturation [*On blood gas determinations*] [*Medicine*] (DAVI) ... $B-O_2S$
Blood Oxygenation Level-Dependent [*Physiology*] ... BOLD
Blood Partial Pressure of Carbon Dioxide [*On blood gas determinations*] (DAVI) ... $B-PCO_2$
Blood Partial Pressure of Oxygen [*On blood gas determinations*] (DAVI) ... $B-PO_2$
Blood Plasma Measuring System [*Medicine*] ... BPMS
Blood Precautions [*Isolation*] [*Medicine*] ... B/P
Blood Pressure [*Medicine*] (DMAA) ... B/P
Blood Pressure [*Medicine*] (MAE) ... bl pr
Blood Pressure [*Medicine*] ... BLP
Blood Pressure [*Medicine*] (DMAA) ... BIP
Blood Pressure [*Medicine*] ... BP
Blood Pressure Assembly (KSC) ... BPA
Blood Pressure Cuff [*Cardiology*] (DAVI) ... BCP
Blood Pressure Decreased [*Medicine*] (MAE) ... BPD
Blood Pressure Gauge [*Medicine*] ... BPG
Blood Pressure Increased [*Medicine*] (MAE) ... BPI
Blood Pressure, Pulse, Respiration, and Temperature [*On examination*] [*Medicine*] (DAVI) ... BPPRT
Blood Pressure Recorder [*Medicine*] ... BPR
Blood Pressure, Systolic ... BPsys
Blood Program [*Red Cross*] ... BP
Blood Program Directives [*Red Cross*] ... BPD
Blood Program Office (DNAB) ... BPO
Blood Research Foundation (EA) ... BRF
Blood Sedimentation Rate [*Medicine*] ... BSR
Blood Serological Test [*Medicine*] ... BST
Blood Sugar [*Medicine*] ... Bl S
Blood Sugar [*Medicine*] (DMAA) ... BIS
Blood Sugar [*Medicine*] ... BS
Blood Sugar Level [*Clinical chemistry*] ... BSL
Blood Supply Unit [*Military British*] ... BSU
Blood, Sweat, and Tears [*Rock music group*] ... BS & T
Blood Transfusion [*Hematology*] (DAVI) ... BT
Blood Transfusion Association (EA) ... BTA
Blood Transfusion Centre [*British*] ... BTC
Blood Transfusion Service [*Medicine*] ... BTS
Blood Triacylglycerol [*Hematology*] ... BTG
Blood Type [*Medicine*] ... Bl T
Blood Urea Nitrogen [*Medicine*] ... BUN
Blood Uric Acid [*Clinical chemistry*] (CPH) ... BUA
Blood Vessel [*Medicine*] ... BV
Blood Vessel Invasion [*Medicine*] (MAE) ... BVI
Blood Vessel of Branchial Filament ... BVBRF
Blood Vessel of Palp ... BVPP
Blood Vessel of Pinnule ... BVP
Blood Vessel Prosthesis [*Medicine*] ... BVP
Blood Viscosity [*Medicine*] (DMAA) ... BIV
Blood Volume [*Medicine*] ... BV
Blood Volume (DAVI) ... Q
Blood Volume Quantity per Unit of Time [*Cardiology*] (DAVI) ... QT
Blood Wassermann [*Medicine*] ... BW
Blood-Activated Recalcification [*Medicine*] (DMAA) ... BART
Blood-Clot Lysis Time [*Medicine*] ... BLT
Blood-Fasting [*Glucose tolerance test*] [*Endocrinology*] (DAVI) ... BL-FST
Blood-Products Laboratory [*British*] ... BPL
Blood-Retinal Barrier [*Ophthalmology*] (DAVI) ... BRB
Blood-Stage Variant Antigen Type [*Immunology*] ... BVAT
Bloodstone (VRA) ... bldst
Bloody [*Slang British*] (DSUE) ... B
Bloody Bastard [*British slang*] ... BB
Bloody Fool [*British slang*] ... BF
Bloody Hell [*British slang*] ... BH
Bloody Nuisance [*British slang*] ... BN
Bloody Public Nuisance [*British slang*] ... BPN
Bloody Young Fool [*Officer under the age of 30*] [*British*] (DSUE) ... BYF
Bloom [*or Blossom*] (ROG) ... BL
Bloom Analogies Test [*Intelligence test*] ... BAT
Bloom Elementary School, Rockford, IL [*Library symbol*] [*Library of Congress*] (LCLS) ... IRoBIE
Bloom Syndrome [*Medicine*] (DMAA) ... BLS
Bloom Syndrome [*Medicine*] ... BS
Bloomer Learning Test [*Intelligence test*] ... BLT
Bloomer, WI [*FM radio station call letters*] ... WQRB
Bloomfield College, Bloomfield, NJ [*OCLC symbol*] (OCLC) ... BLO
Bloomfield College, Bloomfield, NJ [*Library symbol Library of Congress*] (LCLS) ... NjBIC
Bloomfield, CT [*AM radio station call letters*] ... WRDM
Bloomfield Democrat, Bloomfield, IA [*Library symbol Library of Congress*] (LCLS) ... IaBID
Bloomfield Evening World and News, Bloomfield, IN [*Library symbol Library of Congress*] (LCLS) ... InBIWN
Bloomfield Hills, MI [*FM radio station call letters*] ... WBFH
Bloomfield, IA [*Location identifier FAA*] (FAAL) ... BEX
Bloomfield, IA [*FM radio station call letters*] ... KXOF
Bloomfield, IN [*FM radio station call letters*] ... WBHQ
Bloomfield, NM [*FM radio station call letters*] ... KKFG
Bloomfield Public Library, Bloomfield, IA [*Library symbol Library of Congress*] (LCLS) ... IaBI
Bloomfield Public Library, Bloomfield, IN [*Library symbol Library of Congress*] (LCLS) ... InBI

Bloomfield Public Library, Bloomfield, NJ [*Library symbol Library of Congress*] (LCLS) ... NjBl
Bloomfield-Hallowell Union Library, Bloomfield, Ontario [*Library symbol National Library of Canada*] (BIB) ... OBLH
Bloomfield's Manumission (or Negro) Cases [*New Jersey*] [*A publication*] (DLA) ... Blm Neg
Bloomfield's Manumission (or Negro) Cases [*New Jersey*] [*A publication*] (DLA) ... Bloom Man
Bloomfield's Manumission (or Negro) Cases [*New Jersey*] [*A publication*] (DLA) ... Bloom Man Neg Cas
Bloomfield's Manumission (or Negro) Cases [*New Jersey*] [*A publication*] (DLA) ... Manum Cas
Bloomfield's Manumission (or Negro) Cases [*New Jersey*] [*A publication*] (DLA) ... Manum Cases
Bloomfield's Manumission (or Negro) Cases [*New Jersey*] [*A publication*] (DLA) ... Neg Cas
Bloomfield's Manumission (or Negro) Cases [*New Jersey*] [*A publication*] (DLA) ... Negro Cas
Blooming Gate (IAA) ... BLG
Blooming Prairie, MN [*FM radio station call letters*] (RBYB) ... KOWZ-FM
Bloomington [*Indiana*] [*Seismograph station code, US Geological Survey*] (SEIS) ... BLO
Bloomington [*Indiana*] [*Airport symbol*] (OAG) ... BMG
Bloomington [*Illinois*] [*Airport symbol*] (OAG) ... BMI
Bloomington Academic Computer Services [*Indiana University*] [*Research center*] (RCD) ... BACS
Bloomington Herald-Telephone, Bloomington, IN [*Library symbol Library of Congress*] (LCLS) ... InBloHT
Bloomington, IL [*FM radio station call letters*] ... WBNQ
Bloomington, IL [*FM radio station call letters*] ... WESN
Bloomington, IL [*AM radio station call letters*] ... WJBC
Bloomington, IL [*Television station call letters*] ... WYZZ
Bloomington, IN [*FM radio station call letters*] ... WBWB
Bloomington, IN [*Television station call letters*] ... WCLJ
Bloomington, IN [*FM radio station call letters*] ... WFHB
Bloomington, IN [*FM radio station call letters*] ... WFIU
Bloomington, IN [*AM radio station call letters*] ... WGCL
Bloomington, IN [*Television station call letters*] ... WIIB
Bloomington, IN [*Television station call letters*] ... WTIU
Bloomington, IN [*FM radio station call letters*] ... WTTS
Bloomington, IN [*Television station call letters*] ... WTTV
Bloomington Public Schools, Bloomington, MN [*Library symbol*] [*Library of Congress*] (LCLS) ... MnBloPS
Bloomington, TX [*FM radio station call letters*] ... KLUB
Bloomsburg, PA [*FM radio station call letters*] ... WBUQ
Bloomsburg, PA [*AM radio station call letters*] ... WCNR
Bloomsburg, PA [*FM radio station call letters*] ... WHLM
Bloomsburg, PA [*AM radio station call letters*] ... WJMW
Bloomsburg State College, Bloomsburg, PA [*OCLC symbol*] (OCLC) ... PBB
Bloomsburg State College, Bloomsburg, PA [*Library symbol Library of Congress*] (LCLS) ... PBbS
Bloomsburg University of Pennsylvania (GAGS) ... Bloomsburg U
Bloomsbury Review [*A publication*] (BRI) ... Bloom Rev
Bloomsday Club (EA) ... BC
Bloorview Children's Hospital, Health Sciences Library, Willowdale, ON, Canada [*Library symbol*] [*Library of Congress*] (LCLS) ... CaOWBC
Bloque ... BL
Bloque Antiguerrillero del Oriente [*Eastern Anti-Guerrilla Bloc*] [*El Salvador*] (PD) ... BAGO
Bloque de la Vanguardia Revolucionaria [*Bolivia*] [*Political party*] (PPW) ... BVR
Bloque Nacional Popular de Galicia - Partido Socialista Gallego [*Popular National Bloc of Galicia - Galician Socialist Party*] [*Political party*] (PPW) ... BNPG-PSG
Bloque Nacionalista Galego [*Galician Nationalist Block*] [*Spain Political party*] (EY) ... BNG
Bloque Popular Revolucionario [*Popular Revolutionary Bloc*] [*El Salvador*] (PD) ... BPR
Blotting Paper Manufacturers' Association (DGA) ... BPMA
Blount. Fragmenta Antiquitatis [*A publication*] (DLA) ... Blount Frag Ant
Blount, Inc., Montgomery, AL [*Library symbol Library of Congress*] (LCLS) ... AMB
Blount International [*Associated Press*] (SAG) ... Blount
Blount International [*NYSE symbol*] (SAG) ... BLT
Blount Intl Cl'A' [*NYSE symbol*] (TTSB) ... BLT.A
Blount Intl Cv'B' [*NYSE symbol*] (TTSB) ... BLT.B
Blount Memorial Hospital, Medical Library, Maryville, TN [*Library symbol Library of Congress*] (LCLS) ... TMaryB
Blount on Tenures [*A publication*] (DLA) ... Blount Ten
Blount's Impeachment Trial [*A publication*] (DLA) ... Blount Tr
Blount's Law Dictionary [*A publication*] (DLA) ... Bl
Blount's Law Dictionary [*A publication*] (DLA) ... Bl D
Blount's Law Dictionary [*A publication*] (DLA) ... Bl LD
Blount's Law Dictionary [*A publication*] (DLA) ... Blount
Blount's Law Dictionary [*A publication*] (DLA) ... Blount LD
Blountstown, FL [*FM radio station call letters*] ... WPHK
Blountstown, FL [*AM radio station call letters*] ... WYBT
Blountville, TN [*AM radio station call letters*] ... WGOC
Blow Bottle [*Medicine*] (DAVI) ... BB
Blow in Door ... BID
Blow in Place ... BIP
Blow Me Down School/Public Library, Lark Harbour, Newfoundland [*Library symbol National Library of Canada*] (NLC) ... NFLHB
Blow Me Down School/Public Library, Lark Harbour, NF, Canada [*Library symbol Library of Congress*] (LCLS) ... CaNfLHB
Blow Molding [*Bottle manufacturing*] ... BM
Blow Molding System ... BMS
Blow Valve ... BV
Blowback ... BB
Blowdown [*Nuclear energy*] (NRCH) ... BD
Blowdown (NASA) ... BLDN
Blowdown [*Chemical engineering*] ... BLWDN
Blowdown/Emergency Core Cooling [*Nuclear energy*] (NRCH) ... BD/ECC
Blowdown Heat Transfer [*Nuclear energy*] ... BDHT
Blowdown Heat Transfer [*Nuclear energy*] (OA) ... BHT
Blowdown Suppression Tank [*Nuclear energy*] (NRCH) ... BST
Blow-Down Valve [*Railroad term*] ... BDV
Blower (IAA) ... B
Blower ... BL
Blower (KSC) ... BLO
Blower (NVT) ... BLR
Blower (KSC) ... BLWR
Blower Access Cover ... BAC
Blower Ramp Sensor [*Automotive air conditioning*] ... BRS
Blower Wheel Housing ... BWH
Blowing [*ICAO*] (FAAC) ... BL
Blowing Dust (BARN) ... BD
Blowing Dust [*ICAO*] (FAAC) ... BLDU
Blowing Rock, NC [*AM radio station call letters*] ... WVIO
Blowing Rock, NC [*AM radio station call letters*] (RBYB) ... WXIT-AM
Blowing Sand [*ICAO*] (FAAC) ... BLSA
Blowing Sand [*Meteorology*] (DNAB) ... BS
Blowing Snow [*Meteorology*] (DA) ... BLSN
Blowing Snow [*Meteorology*] (BARN) ... BS
Blowing Spray [*ICAO*] (FAAC) ... BY
Blowline ... BL
Blowoff ... BO
Blowout ... BLWT
Blowout (IAA) ... BO
Blowout Coil ... BOC
Blow-Out Emergency Team [*British government*] ... BET
Blowout Pipe System ... BPS
Blowout Preventer [*or Prevention*] ... BOP
Blowtorch ... BLWT
Blue [*Philately*] ... B
Blue (KSC) ... BL
Blue (VRA) ... bl
Blue (KSC) ... BLU
Blue ... Bu
Blue Affirmative Flag [*Navy British*] ... BF
Blue Airlines [*Zaire*] [*ICAO designator*] (FAAC) ... BUL
Blue Anchor, Inc. [*Formerly, CFE*] [*Later, BAI*] [*An association*] ... BA
Blue Anchor, Inc. [*An association*] (EA) ... BAI
[*The*] **Blue and the Gray** [*A publication*] ... BIG
Blue Army of Our Lady of Fatima [*Later, World Apostolate of Fatima - WAF*] (EA) ... BALF
Blue Bell [*Pennsylvania*] [*Airport symbol*] (OAG) ... BBX
Blue Blazes Irregulars (EA) ... BBI
Blue Bloaters [*Emphysema*] [*Slang Medicine*] (MAE) ... BB
Blue Bomber [*Valium tablet*] [*Slang*] ... BB
Blue Book [*Directory of proprietaries*] ... BB
Blue Card (EA) ... BC
Blue Chip [*Investment term*] ... BC
Blue Chip Computerware [*NASDAQ symbol*] (TTSB) ... BCHPE
Blue Chip Computerware, Inc. [*NASDAQ symbol*] (SAG) ... BCHP
Blue Chip Computerware, Inc. [*Associated Press*] (SAG) ... BlChip
Blue Chip Fund [*Associated Press*] (SAG) ... BlueChp
Blue Chip Value Fund [*NYSE symbol*] (SPSG) ... BLU
Blue Circle Industries [*British*] ... BCI
Blue Compact Galaxy [*Astronomy*] ... BCG
Blue Crescent [*Later, BCI*] [*An association*] (EAIO) ... BC
Blue Crescent International (EAIO) ... BCI
Blue Cross [*Health insurance plan*] ... BC
Blue Cross and Blue Shield [*Insurance plan*] (DAVI) ... BX BS
Blue Cross and Blue Shield Association [*Chicago, IL*] (EA) ... BCBSA
Blue Cross & Blue Shield of Colorado, Denver, CO [*Library symbol Library of Congress*] (LCLS) ... CoDBCS
Blue Cross & Blue Shield of North Carolina, Durham, NC [*Library symbol Library of Congress*] (LCLS) ... NcDurBC
Blue Cross and Blue Shield of Tennessee, Chattanooga, TN [*Library symbol Library of Congress*] (LCLS) ... TCBCS
Blue Cross Association [*Later, BCBSA*] (EA) ... BCA
Blue Cross Association, Chicago, IL [*Library symbol Library of Congress*] (LCLS) ... ICBC
Blue Cross/Blue Shield [*Health insurance plan*] ... BC/BS
Blue Cross/Blue Shield of Oregon, Portland, OR [*Library symbol*] [*Library of Congress*] (LCLS) ... OrPBC
Blue Cross Interim Payment [*Insurance*] ... BIP
Blue Cross Plan [*Health insurance*] ... BCP
Blue Diamond Energy [*Vancouver Stock Exchange symbol*] ... BED
Blue Diamond Growers [*An association*] (EA) ... BDG
Blue Diaper Syndrome [*Medicine*] (DMAA) ... BD
Blue Dolphin Energy [*NASDAQ symbol*] (TTSB) ... BDCO
Blue Dolphin Energy Co. [*NASDAQ symbol*] (SAG) ... BDCO
Blue Dolphin Energy Co. [*Associated Press*] (SAG) ... BluDolp
Blue Earth, MN [*AM radio station call letters*] ... KBEW
Blue Earth, MN [*FM radio station call letters*] ... KBEW-FM
Blue Earth, MN [*FM radio station call letters*] ... KJLY
Blue Earth, MN [*Location identifier FAA*] (FAAL) ... SBU
Blue Emerald Resources [*Vancouver Stock Exchange symbol*] ... BER
Blue Etch-Anodize (PDAA) ... BEA
Blue Flame Gas Association [*Nebraska*] (SRA) ... BFGA

Blue Force (DOMA) .... BLUFOR
Blue Force Data Link [*Military*] (CAAL) .... BFDL
Blue Gold Resources [*Vancouver Stock Exchange symbol*] .... BLQ
Blue Hill, ME [*FM radio station call letters*] .... WERU
Blue Hill Meteorological Observatory [*Harvard University*] (MCD) .... BHMO
Blue Hills Community School, Buffalo Head Prairie, Alberta [*Library symbol National Library of Canada*] (BIB) .... ABHPBS
Blue Hills Power Plant [*Nuclear energy*] (NRCH) .... BH
Blue Hills Station [*Nuclear energy*] (NRCH) .... BHS
Blue Horizon Travel Club [*ICAO designator*] (FAAC) .... BLH
Blue Horizontal Branch .... BHB
Blue Indicator Light .... BIL
Blue Island Public Library, Blue Island, IL [*Library symbol Library of Congress*] (LCLS) .... IBi
Blue Knights International Law Enforcement Motorcycle Club (EA) .... BK
Blue Laid [*Paper*] (DGA) .... BL
Blue Line (MCD) .... BL
Blue Line Copy .... BLC
Blue Line Print .... BLP
Blue Line Requisition .... BL REQ
Blue Military Damage Assessment .... BMDA
Blue Mountain [*Alaska*] [*Seismograph station code, US Geological Survey*] (SEIS) .... BLM
Blue Mountain College [*Mississippi*] .... BMC
Blue Mountain College, Blue Mountain, MS [*Library symbol Library of Congress*] (LCLS) .... MsBm
Blue Mountain Community College, Pendleton, OR [*Library symbol Library of Congress*] (LCLS) .... OrPeB
Blue Mountain Lake [*New York*] [*Seismograph station code, US Geological Survey Closed*] (SEIS) .... BML
Blue Mountain Lake, NY [*FM radio station call letters*] .... WXLH
Blue Mountain Seismological Observatory .... BMSO
Blue Mountains Array [*Oregon*] [*Seismograph station code, US Geological Survey Closed*] (SEIS) .... BMO
Blue Mountains Tourism Authority [*Australia*] .... BMTA
Blue Nile Bank Ltd. [*Sudan*] .... BNB
Blue Nose Minnow [*Ichthyology*] .... Bn
Blue Oyster Cult [*Rock music group*] .... BOC
Blue Pennant [*Navy British*] .... BL
Blue Print Files (NRCH) .... BPF
Blue Return [*Round trip fare*] [*British*] .... B
Blue Ribbon Coalition [*An association*] (EA) .... BRC
Blue Ribbon Defense Panel .... BRDP
Blue Ridge, GA [*FM radio station call letters*] .... WPPL
Blue Ridge Parkway [*National Park Service designation*] .... BLRI
Blue Ridge Railroad (IIA) .... BR
Blue Ridge Regional Library, Martinsville, VA [*Library symbol*] [*Library of Congress*] (LCLS) .... ViMv
Blue Ridge Resources Ltd. [*Vancouver Stock Exchange symbol*] .... BRG
Blue Ridge Technical Institute, Hendersonville, NC [*Library symbol Library of Congress*] (LCLS) .... NcHvH
Blue Ridge Township Public Library, Mansfield, IL [*Library symbol Library of Congress*] (LCLS) .... IMan
Blue Ridge, TX [*Location identifier FAA*] (FAAL) .... BUJ
Blue Rubber Bleb Nevus Syndrome [*Medicine*] (DMAA) .... BRBNS
Blue Second Hydrogen Line in the Solar Spectrum (BARN) .... F
Blue Shade [*Paper*] .... BS
Blue Shield [*Health insurance plan*] .... BS
Blue Shield Association [*Later, BCBSA*] (EA) .... BSA
Blue Shield Medical Care Plans [*Later, BSA*] [*An association*] .... BSMCP
Blue Sky (ROG) .... B
Blue Sky Carrier Co. Ltd. [*Poland ICAO designator*] (FAAC) .... BSC
Blue Sky Law Reporter [*Commerce Clearing House*] [*A publication*] (DLA) .... Blue Sky L Rep
Blue Sky Laws .... BSL
Blue Springs, MO [*AM radio station call letters*] .... KBEQ
Blue Springs, MO [*AM radio station call letters*] (RBYB) .... KOWW-AM
Blue Square Israel Ltd. [*Associated Press*] (SAG) .... BlueSq
Blue Square Israel Ltd. [*NYSE symbol*] (SAG) .... BSI
Blue Star Mothers of America (EA) .... BSM
Blue Steel [*Guns*] .... BS
Blue Stellar Object [*Astronomy*] .... BSO
Blue Straggler [*Star*] [*Astronomy*] .... BS
Blue Streak [*Military*] (SAA) .... BS
Blue Streak Request [*Military*] .... BSR
Blue Supergiant [*Astronomy*] .... BSG
Blue Tetrazolium [*A dye*] .... BT
Blue Tongue Virus [*Medicine*] (DMAA) .... BTV
Blue Tool Steel (MSA) .... BTS
Blue Water Bridge Authority .... BWBA
Blue/White Pottery Club (EA) .... BWPC
Blue Willow Collectors Society (EA) .... BWCS
Blue Wove [*Paper*] (DGA) .... BW
Blueberry Leaf Mottle Virus .... BBLMV
Blueberry Mottle Virus .... BBMV
Blueberry Red Ringspot Virus [*Plant pathology*] .... BRRV
Blueberry Shoestring Virus .... BBSSV
Blueberry Shoestring Virus [*Plant pathology*] .... BSSV
Bluebird [*Division of Victor*] [*Record label*] .... BB
Blue-Black .... BB
Blue-Collar Ethnic Catholic [*Political demography*] .... BCEC
Blue-Collar Guy [*Lifestyle classification*] .... BCG
Bluefield [*West Virginia*] [*Airport symbol*] (OAG) .... BLF
Bluefield College, Bluefield, VA [*Library symbol Library of Congress*] (LCLS) .... ViBluC
Bluefield Public Library, Bluefield, WV [*Library symbol Library of Congress*] (LCLS) .... WvBl
Bluefield State College [*West Virginia*] .... BSC
Bluefield State College, Bluefield, WV [*Library symbol Library of Congress*] (LCLS) .... WvBIS
Bluefield, VA [*FM radio station call letters*] .... WBDY
Bluefield, VA [*AM radio station call letters*] .... WHYS
Bluefield, WV [*FM radio station call letters*] .... WHAJ
Bluefield, WV [*AM radio station call letters*] .... WHIS
Bluefield, WV [*AM radio station call letters*] .... WKOY
Bluefield, WV [*Television station call letters*] .... WLFB
Bluefield, WV [*FM radio station call letters*] .... WPIB
Bluefield, WV [*Television station call letters*] .... WVVA
Bluefields [*Nicaragua*] [*ICAO location identifier*] (ICLI) .... MNBL
Bluegill [*Ichthyology*] .... BG
Bluegrass (WGA) .... BG
Bluegrass Army Depot .... BGAD
Bluegrass Depot Activity [*Army*] (AABC) .... BGDA
Bluegrass Petroleum, Inc. [*Vancouver Stock Exchange symbol*] .... BGS
Blue-Green Algae [*Water purification*] .... BGA
Blue-Green Algal Virus (OA) .... BGAV
Bluegreen Corp. [*Associated Press*] (SAG) .... Bluegreen
Bluegreen Corp. [*NYSE symbol*] (SAG) .... BXG
Bluegreen Corp. [*NYSE symbol*] (TTSB) .... BXG
Bluejacket's Manual [*Navy*] .... BJM
Blue-Laid [*Paper*] .... BLD
Blue-Line Drawing .... BLD
Blueprint .... BLUPRNT
Blueprint .... BP
Blueprint Analysis Report (MCD) .... BAR
Blueprints and Plans (MCD) .... B & P
Blues Foundation (EA) .... BF
Blues Heaven Foundation (EA) .... BHF
Bluesky Oil & Gas [*Toronto Stock Exchange symbol Vancouver Stock Exchange symbol*] .... BKY
Bluestone [*Inferior gin or whiskey*] [*Slang*] (ADA) .... BL/ST
Bluestone (ABBR) .... BS
Bluetick Breeders of America (EA) .... BBA
Blue-Tongue [*Medicine*] (DMAA) .... BT
Bluett's Advocate's Note Book, Isle Of Man [*1720-1846*] [*A publication*] (DLA) .... Blu
Bluett's Isle Of Man Cases [*A publication*] (DLA) .... Bluett
Blue-Visual [*Color index*] .... B-V
Blue-Whale-Unit [*Whaling industry*] .... BWU
Blue-Winged Olive [*Insect*] .... BWO
Blufete Industrial S.A. ADS [*NYSE symbol*] (TTSB) .... GBI
Bluff .... BLF
Bluff .... BLF
Bluff [*Commonly used*] (OPSA) .... BLF
Bluff [*Commonly used*] (OPSA) .... BLUF
Bluff [*Commonly used*] (OPSA) .... BLUFF
Bluff Creek Industries R. R. [*AAR code*] .... BCI
Bluffs [*Postal Service standard*] (OPSA) .... BLFS
Bluffs .... BLFS
Bluffs [*Commonly used*] (OPSA) .... BLUFFS
Bluffton College, Bluffton, OH [*OCLC symbol*] (OCLC) .... BLC
Bluffton College, Bluffton, OH [*Library symbol Library of Congress*] (LCLS) .... OBIC
Bluffton College, Mennonite Historical Library, Bluffton, OH [*Library symbol Library of Congress*] (LCLS) .... OBIC-M
Bluffton, IN [*FM radio station call letters*] .... WNUY
Bluffton, SC [*FM radio station call letters*] .... WLOW
Bluffton-Wells County Public Library, Bluffton, IN [*Library symbol Library of Congress*] (LCLS) .... InBlu
Bluffton-Wells County Public Library, Bluffton, IN [*OCLC symbol*] (OCLC) .... IWM
Bluie East [*US air bases in Greenland*] [*World War II*] .... BE
Bluie West [*US air bases in Greenland*] [*World War II*] .... BW
Bluish Green .... BG
Blume [*Germany ICAO aircraft manufacturer identifier*] (ICAO) .... BM
Blumenstiel on Bankruptcy [*A publication*] (DLA) .... Blum B'k'cy
Blunt Conical Model .... BCM
Blunt Conical Reentry Vehicle .... BCRV
Blunt End Forward (KSC) .... BEF
Blunt Leading Edge .... BLE
Blunt Trailing Edge .... BTE
Blunted Delta Wing .... BDW
Blunted Wedge .... BW
Blur Diameter [*Optics*] .... B/D
Blutkorpersenkung [*Blood Sedimentation Rate*] [*German Medicine*] .... BKS
Blydenburgh. Law of Usury [*1844*] [*A publication*] (DLA) .... Bly Us
B-Lymphoblastoid Cell Line [*Biochemistry*] .... BLCL
Blyn Mountain [*Washington*] [*Seismograph station code, US Geological Survey*] (SEIS) .... BLN
Blyth Holdings [*NASDAQ symbol*] (TTSB) .... BLYH
Blyth Holdings, Inc. [*NASDAQ symbol*] (NQ) .... BLYH
Blyth Holdings, Inc. [*Associated Press*] (SAG) .... Blyth
Blyth Industries [*NYSE symbol*] (TTSB) .... BTH
Blyth Industries, Inc. [*Associated Press*] (SAG) .... BlythInd
Blyth Industries, Inc. [*NYSE symbol*] (SAG) .... BTH
Blythe [*California*] [*Airport symbol*] (OAG) .... BLH
Blythe, CA [*FM radio station call letters*] .... KJMB
Blythe, CA [*Location identifier FAA*] (FAAL) .... RPY
Blytheville Air Force Base [*Arkansas*] [*ICAO location identifier*] (ICLI) .... KBYH
Blytheville, AR [*Location identifier FAA*] (FAAL) .... BYH

Blytheville, AR [*Location identifier FAA*] (FAAL) ..... GOJ
Blytheville, AR [*Location identifier FAA*] (FAAL) ..... HKA
Blytheville, AR [*FM radio station call letters*] ..... KHLS
Blytheville, AR [*AM radio station call letters*] ..... KLCN
Blythwood, SC [*AM radio station call letters*] ..... WBAJ
BlyvoorGold Mng ADR [*NASDAQ symbol*] (TTSB) ..... BLYVY
Blyvooruitzicht Gold [*NASDAQ symbol*] (SAG) ..... BLYD
Blyvooruitzicht Gold Mining Co. Ltd. [*NASDAQ symbol*] (NQ) ..... BLYV
Blyvooruitzicht Gold Mining Co. Ltd. [*Associated Press*] (SAG) ..... Blyvoor
BMA [*British Medical Association*] **Press Cuttings Database** [*Information service or system*] (IID) ..... BMAP
BMB Compuscience Canada Ltd. [*Toronto Stock Exchange symbol*] ..... BMB
BMC Industries [*NYSE symbol*] (TTSB) ..... BMC
BMC Industries, Inc. [*NYSE symbol*] (SPSG) ..... BMC
BMC Software [*NASDAQ symbol*] (TTSB) ..... BMCS
BMC Software, Inc. [*NASDAQ symbol*] (NQ) ..... BMCS
BMC Softwear [*Associated Press*] (SAG) ..... BMC Soft
BMC Softwear, Inc. [*Associated Press*] (SAG) ..... BMC Sf
BMC West [*NASDAQ symbol*] (SPSG) ..... BMCW
BMC West Corp. [*Associated Press*] (SAG) ..... BMC Wst
BMEWS [*Ballistic Missile Early Warning System*] **Operational Simulation System** (IAA) ..... BOSS
BMEWS [*Ballistic Missile Early Warning System*] **Performance Test Outline** ..... BPTO
BMEWS [*Ballistic Missile Early Warning System*] **Raid Input Generator** (IAA) ..... BRIG
BMEWS [*Ballistic Missile Early Warning System*] **Rearward Communications System** (AFM) ..... BRCS
BMEWS [*Ballistic Missile Early Warning System*] **Specification** (AFM) ..... BSP
BMEWS [*Ballistic Missile Early Warning System*] **System Program Office** (AFM) ..... BSPO
BMEWS [*Ballistic Missile Early Warning System*] **Test Procedure** (AFM) ..... BTP
BMEWS [*Ballistic Missile Early Warning System*] **Test Report** (AFM) ..... BTR
BMI Finance, Regina, Saskatchewan [*Library symbol National Library of Canada*] (NLC) ..... SRBMI
BMI Finance, Regina, SK, Canada [*Library symbol Library of Congress*] (LCLS) ..... CaSRBMI
BMJ Financial Corp. [*Associated Press*] (SAG) ..... BMJ
BMJ Financial Corp. [*NASDAQ symbol*] (NQ) ..... BMJF
BMMF [*Bible and Medical Missionary Fellowship*] **International** [*Later, IUSA*] (EA) ..... BMMFI
BMMF [*Bible and Medical Missionary Fellowship*] **International/USA** [*Later, IUSA*] (EA) ..... BMMFI/USA
BMO II Financial Corp. [*Toronto Stock Exchange symbol*] ..... BMF
BMO II Financial Pr [*Toronto Stock Exchange symbol*] ..... BMFPRA
BMO NT Financial Corp. [*Toronto Stock Exchange symbol*] ..... BMN
B-Mode Receiving Station [*Telecommunications*] (TEL) ..... BRS
BMP Technologies Ltd. [*Vancouver Stock Exchange symbol*] ..... BMP
BMT [*British Maritime Technology Ltd.*] **Abstracts Online** [*Wallsend, Tyne, and Wear, England*] [*Information service or system*] (IID) ..... BOATS
BMW [*Bavarian Motor Works*] **Automobile Club of America** (EA) ..... BMW-ACA
BMW [*Bavarian Motor Works*] **Car Club of America** (EA) ..... BMWCCA
BMW [*Bavarian Motor Works*] **Car Club of Canada** (EAIO) ..... BMW-CCC
BMW [*Bavarian Motor Works*] **Riders Association** (EA) ..... BMWRA
BMW [*Bavarian Motor Works*] **Rolls-Royce AeroEngines** [*Commercial firm*] (ECON) ..... BRRA
BMW [*Bavarian Motor Works*] **Vintage Club of America** (EA) ..... BMWVCA
B'nai Birth Canada [*Also, Children of the Convenant*] (AC) ..... BBC
B'nai B'rith [*Later, BBI*] (EA) ..... BB
B'nai B'rith Bulletin [*A publication*] (ADA) ..... BBB
B'nai B'rith Hillel Foundations (EA) ..... BBHF
B'nai B'rith International (EA) ..... BBI
B'nai B'rith International Commission on Adult Jewish Education [*Later, BBICCJE*] (EA) ..... BBICAJE
B'nai B'rith International Commission on Continuing Jewish Education (EA) ..... BBICCJE
B'nai B'rith International Senior Citizens Housing Committee (EA) ..... BBISCHC
B'nai B'rith Vocational Service [*Later, B'nai B'rith Career and Counseling Services*] (EA) ..... BBVS
B'nai B'rith Women (EA) ..... BBW
B'nai B'rith Youth Organization (EA) ..... BBYO
Bnai Israel (BJA) ..... BI
Bnai Zion (EA) ..... BZ
BNCCORP, Inc. [*Associated Press*] (SAG) ..... BNC
BNCCORP, Inc. [*NASDAQ symbol*] (SAG) ..... BNCC
Bnei Akiva (BJA) ..... BA
Bnei Akiva of North America (EA) ..... BA of NA
BNH Bancshares [*NASDAQ symbol*] (TTSB) ..... BNHB
BNH Bancshares, Inc. [*Associated Press*] (SAG) ..... BNH
BNH Bancshares, Inc. [*NASDAQ symbol*] (NQ) ..... BNHB
Bnos Agudath Israel (EA) ..... BAI
Bo [*Sierra Leone*] [*Airport symbol Obsolete*] (OAG) ..... KBS
Boa Vista [*Brazil*] [*Airport symbol*] (OAG) ..... BVB
Boa Vista [*Cape Verde Islands*] [*Airport symbol*] (OAG) ..... BVC
Boa Vista/Internacional [*Brazil ICAO location identifier*] (ICLI) ..... SBBV
Boaco [*Nicaragua*] [*Seismograph station code, US Geological Survey*] (SEIS) ..... BOA
Boalsburg, PA [*FM radio station call letters*] ..... WVCV
Boang [*Papua New Guinea*] [*Airport symbol*] (OAG) ..... BOV
Board ..... B
Board ..... BD
Board (VRA) ..... bd
Board ..... BD
Board (WDMC) ..... bd.
Board ..... BRD
Board and Care [*Medicine*] (DAVI) ..... B & C
Board and Care [*Medicine*] (DAVI) ..... Bd & C
Board Certified [*Physician*] (BARN) ..... BC
Board/Detached [*Bookselling*] (DGA) ..... BD/DET
Board Eligible (MEDA) ..... BE
Board Examined [*of a physician*] (BARN) ..... BE
Board, Family, and Associates [*Company stockholders*] ..... BFA
Board for Aviation Accident Research [*Army*] ..... BAAR
Board for Certification of Genealogists (EA) ..... BCG
Board for Coordination of Civil Aviation [*NATO*] ..... BOCCA
Board for Correction of Military Records ..... BCMR
Board for Correction of Naval Records ..... BCNR
Board for Engineers' Registration (ACII) ..... BER
Board for Fundamental Education (EA) ..... BFE
Board for International Broadcasting [*Independent government agency*] ..... BIB
Board for International Food and Agricultural Development [*Agency for International Development*] [*Washington, DC*] ..... BIFAD
Board for Mission and Unity [*Church of England*] ..... BMU
Board Information Terminal [*Automotive electronic displays*] ..... BIT
Board Level Computer (MHDI) ..... BLC
Board Measure [*Lumber*] ..... BM
Board Measurement Feet ..... BMF
Board of Action on Letter of Intent Conversion [*Navy*] ..... BALIC
Board of Action on Redetermination [*Navy*] ..... BOAR
Board of Airline Representatives in the United Kingdom ..... BARUK
Board of Appeals and Review [*Later, ARB*] [*Civil Service Commission*] (AFM) ..... BAR
Board of Architects of New South Wales [*Australia*] ..... BANSW
Board of Architects of Queensland [*Australia*] ..... BAQ
Board of Architectural Education [*British*] (BI) ..... BAE
Board of Assistance Appeals [*Environmental Protection Agency*] (GFGA) ..... BAA
Board of Australian Journals of Scientific Research ..... BAJSR
Board of Brethren Homes and Older Adult Ministries [*Later, BHOAM*] (EA) ..... BBHOAM
Board of Broadcast Governors [*Later, Canadian Radio-Television Commission*] ..... BBG
Board of Certification in Anesthesiology (EA) ..... BCA
Board of Certification in Pedorthics (EA) ..... BCP
Board of Certification in Surgery (EA) ..... BCS
Board of Certified Hazard Control Management (EA) ..... BCHCM
Board of Certified Product Safety Management (EA) ..... BCPSM
Board of Certified Safety Professionals (EA) ..... BCSP
Board of Contract Appeals [*Energy Research and Development Administration*] ..... BCA
Board of Contract Appeals Bar Association (AAGC) ..... BCABA
Board of Contract Appeals Bid Protest Decisions 1985-96 [*A publication*] (AAGC) ..... BPD
Board of Contract Appeals Decisions [*CCH*] [*A publication*] (AAGC) ..... BCA
Board of Contract Appeals Decisions [*Commerce Clearing House*] [*A publication*] (DLA) ..... Bd Cont App Dec
Board of Contract Appeals Judges Association (AAGC) ..... BCAJA
Board of Contract Appeals Lawyers Association [*Formerly ASCTLA*] (AAGC) ..... BCALA
Board of Control [*British*] (ROG) ..... BC
Board of Cooperative Educational Services (BOCES), Spencerport, NY [*Library symbol Library of Congress*] (LCLS) ..... NSpeB
Board of Cooperative Educational Services - Monroe I, Fairport, NY [*Library symbol Library of Congress*] (LCLS) ..... NFaiB
Board of Cooperative Educational Services, Nassau Education Resource Center, Westbury, NY [*Library symbol Library of Congress*] (LCLS) ..... NWeBE
Board of Cooperative Educational Services, Regional Resource Center, Mexico, NY [*Library symbol Library of Congress*] (LCLS) ..... NMxB
Board of Customs [*British*] (DAS) ..... BOC
Board of Customs and Excise [*British*] ..... BCE
Board of Customs and Excise [*British*] (ODBW) ..... BOCE
Board of Decorations and Medals [*Navy*] ..... BD D & M
Board of Deputies of British Jews ..... BDBJ
Board of Directors (NATG) ..... BOD
Board of Directors NATO Maintenance Supply Service System (NATG) ..... BDNMSSS
Board of Economic Warfare [*World War II*] ..... BEW
Board of Education ..... B of E
Board of Education ..... BE
Board of Education ..... BEd
Board of Education (AIE) ..... BOE
Board of Education ..... BOE
Board of Education, Cleveland, OH [*Library symbol Library of Congress*] (LCLS) ..... OCIBE
Board of Education for the Borough of East York [*UTLAS symbol*] ..... EYS
Board of Education for the City of Etobicoke [*UTLAS symbol*] ..... ETS
Board of Education for the City of York Library [*UTLAS symbol*] ..... CYS
Board of Education for the City of York, Schools, Toronto, ON, Canada [*Library symbol*] [*Library of Congress*] (LCLS) ..... CaOTYBES
Board of Educational Development [*University of California, Berkeley*] ..... BED
Board of Engineers for Rivers and Harbors [*Army*] ..... BERH
Board of Engineers for Rivers and Harbors Resident Scholar Program [*Fort Belvoir, VA*] [*Army*] ..... BERH-RSP
Board of Environmental Studies and Toxicology [*NRC*] ..... BEST
Board of Ethnic Affairs [*Queensland, Australia*] ..... BEA
Board of Examiners for Steam Engine Drivers and Boiler Attendants [*Victoria, Australia*] ..... BOESEDBA
Board of Examiners for the Foreign Service [*Department of State*] ..... BEX
Board of Examiners of Engineers and Overseers of Works to Local Authorities [*Australia*] ..... BOEEOWLA
Board of Examiners (Scaffolding) [*Victoria, Australia*] ..... BOE(S)

Board of Examiners (Welders of Boilers and Pressure Vessels) [*Victoria, Australia*] .... BOE(WBPV)
Board of Faculty of Dental Surgery [*British*] .... BFDS
Board of Fire Commissioners, New South Wales [*Australia*] .... BFCNSW
Board of Fire Underwriters of the Pacific [*Later, ISO*] .... BFUP
Board of Foreign Scholarships [*Department of State*] [*Washington, DC*] .... BFS
Board of General Purposes [*Freemasonry*] .... B of GP
Board of Geographic Names .... BGN
Board of Governors .... BG
Board of Governors [*Federal Reserve System*] .... BOG
Board of Governors, Federal Reserve System .... BGFRS
Board of Governors, Federal Reserve System, Washington, DC [*Library symbol Library of Congress*] (LCLS) .... DFR
Board of Green Cloth (ROG) .... BGC
Board of Guardians [*British*] (ROG) .... BG
Board of Health .... B of H
Board of Health (DAVI) .... BOH
Board of Home Missions of the National Association of Free Will Baptists (EA) .... BHMNAFWB
Board of Hospitals and Homes of the Methodist Church [*Later, National Association of Health and Welfare Ministries of the United Methodist Church*] (EA) .... BHHMC
Board of Immigration Appeals [*Department of Justice*] .... BIA
Board of Incorporated Engineers and Technicians [*British*] (EAIO) .... BIET
Board of Inland Revenue [*British*] .... BIR
Board of Inquiry (Army) Rules [*British military*] (DMA) .... BI(A)R
Board of Inspection and Survey [*Navy*] .... B/S
Board of Inspection and Survey [*Navy*] .... BIS
Board of Inspection and Survey [*Navy*] .... INSURV
Board of Inspection and Survey, Instructions [*Navy*] .... INSURVINST
Board of Inspection and Survey, Preliminary Evaluation [*Navy*] .... BISPE
Board of International Ministries (EA) .... BIM
Board of Investments [*Generic term*] .... BOI
Board of Medical Quality Assurance (DAVI) .... BMQA
Board of National Estimates [*Terminated*] [*CIA*] .... BNE
Board of National Ministries (EA) .... BNM
Board of Navy Commissioners [*1815-1842*] .... BNC
Board of Nephrology Examiners for Nursing and Technology .... BONENT
Board of Nurse Examiners .... BNE
Board of Nursing Studies [*Queensland, Australia*] .... BNS
Board of Optical Registration [*South Australia and Tasmania*] .... BOR
Board of Optometrical Registration [*New South Wales, Australia*] .... BOR
Board of Ordnance .... BO
Board of Parish Education, Lutheran Church in America (EA) .... BPE-LCA
Board of Parole [*Abolished, 1976, functions transferred to United States Parole Commission*] [*Department of Justice*] .... BP
Board of Patent Interferences [*of Patent Office*] .... BPI
Board of Professional Engineers of Queensland [*Australia*] .... BPEQ
Board of Public Works .... BPW
Board of Rabbis .... BR
Board of Realty Information Systems [*Professional Guidance Systems, Inc.*] [*Information service or system*] (IID) .... BORIS
Board of Registered Nursing .... BRN
Board of Registration of Medical Auxiliaries [*British*] .... BRMA
Board of Review [*Army*] .... BOR
Board of Review [*Army*] .... BR
Board of Review and Judicial Council of the Army (DLA) .... BR-JC (Army)
Board of Schools of Medical Technology [*Later, NAACLS*] (EA) .... BSMT
Board of Scientific Affairs .... BSA
Board of Secondary Studies .... BSS
Board of Standards Review [*American National Standards Institute*] .... BSR
Board of Supply, Executive Yuan [*Responsible for removing surplus US war material to China from Guam*] .... BOSEY
Board of Tax Appeals .... BTA
Board of Tax Appeals Decisions (Commerce Clearing House) [*A publication*] (DLA) .... BTACCH
Board of Tax Appeals Decisions (Prentice-Hall, Inc.) [*A publication*] (DLA) .... BTAPH
Board of Tax Appeals Memorandum Decisions (Prentice-Hall, Inc.) [*A publication*] (DLA) .... BTAM (P-H)
Board of Teacher Registration .... BTR
Board of the Army Council .... BAC
Board of Thoracic Surgery [*Later, American Board of Thoracic Surgery*] (EA) .... BTS
Board of Trade [*Shipping*] .... B of T
Board of Trade [*Shipping*] .... BOT
Board of Trade [*Shipping*] .... BT
Board of Trade Journal [*A publication*] (DLA) .... BOT Jo
Board of Trade of Kansas City [*Missouri*] .... B of TKC
Board of Trade of Kansas City, MO (EA) .... KCBT
Board of Trade of the City of Chicago .... B of TCC
Board of Trade of the Wholesale Seafood Merchants (EA) .... BTWSM
Board of Trade Unit [*British and Canadian*] [*Military*] .... BOTU
Board of Trade Unit [*British*] .... BTU
Board of Transport [*NATO*] (NATG) .... BOT
Board of Trustees .... BOT
Board of Underwriters of New York (EA) .... BUNY
Board of US Civil Service Examiners .... BCSE
Board of Veterans Appeals [*Veterans Administration*] .... BVA
Board of Veterinary Surgeons of New South Wales [*Australia*] .... BVSNSW
Board of Visitors (DOMA) .... BOV
Board of Vocational Education and Training [*New South Wales, Australia*] .... BVET
Board of War Communications [*World War II*] .... BWC
Board of Works [*British*] .... BW

Board of Zoning Adjustment .... BZA
Board on Army Science and Technology [*National Research Council, Academies of Science and Engineering, and Institute of Medicine*] .... BAST
Board on Geographic Names [*Defense Mapping Agency*] [*Washington, DC*] .... BGN
Board on Medicine [*of the National Academy of Sciences*] [*Later, IOM*] (EA) .... BOM
[*The*] **Board on Natural Disasters** [*National Research Council*] .... BOND
Board on Ocean Science Affairs [*National Academy of Science*] (MSC) .... BOSA
Board on Personnel Administration (AEBS) .... BPA
Board on Radioactive Waste Management (EA) .... BRWM
Board on Science and Technology for International Development [*National Academy of Sciences*] .... BOSTID
Board President .... B/P
Board Room (VRA) .... bdrm
Board Secretary .... BS
Board Test Language (PDAA) .... BTL
Board-Foot (MUGU) .... BD-FT
Board-Foot .... BF
Boarding [*Schools or pupils*] .... B
Boarding .... BRDNG
Boarding School Allowance [*Government scholarship*] [*British*] .... BSA
Boarding Schools Association (AIE) .... BSA
Boardman Public Library, Boardman, OR [*Library symbol Library of Congress*] (LCLS) .... OrBo
Boards .... BDS
Board's Minute [*Custom house*] [*British*] (ROG) .... BM
Boards of Cooperative Educational Services .... BOCES
Board's Order [*British*] (ROG) .... BO
Boardwalk Casino [*Associated Press*] (SAG) .... BoardC
Boardwalk Casino [*Associated Press*] (SAG) .... BoardCas
Boardwalk Casino [*NASDAQ symbol*] (SAG) .... BWLK
Boardwalk Casino Wrrt [*NASDAQ symbol*] (TTSB) .... BWLKW
Boat .... B
Boat (AABC) .... BT
Boat Allowance List [*Navy*] (CAAL) .... BAL
Boat and Aircraft (CAAL) .... B & A
Boat and Engine Repair Shop [*Coast Guard*] .... B & ERS
Boat & Motor Dealer [*A publication*] .... B & MD
Boat Club .... BC
Boat Foreman (DNAB) .... BF
Boat Group Commander [*Navy*] (NVT) .... BGC
Boat Harbor .... BHBR
Boat Information Book [*Navy*] (CAAL) .... BIB
Boat Inlet/High-Capacity [*Analytical combustion system*] .... BIHC
Boat Landing Team .... BLT
Boat Lanes .... BL
Boat Launching and Recovery Device (PDAA) .... BLARD
Boat Manufacturers Association [*Later, NMMA*] (EA) .... BMA
Boat Manufacturers' Association of Australia .... BMAA
Boat Operating and Repair Unit [*Navy*] .... BORU
Boat Operating Unit [*Navy*] .... BOU
Boat Owners Association of the United States (EA) .... BOAT/US
Boat Owners Association of the United States .... BOATS
Boat Owners Council of America [*Defunct*] .... BOCA
Boat Repair Unit [*Navy*] .... BRU
Boat Support Unit (CINC) .... BSU
Boat Trailer Manufacturers Association [*Later, TMA*] (EA) .... BTMA
Boat Wave .... BTW
Boating Accident Data Base [*Database*] [*Coast Guard*] .... BADB
Boating Accident Reports System [*Coast Guard Information service or system*] (IID) .... BARS
Boating Anti-Pollution Council (EA) .... BAC
Boating Industry Association [*Later, NMMA*] .... BIA
Boating Industry Association of New South Wales [*Australia*] .... BIANSW
Boating Industry Association of Queensland [*Australia*] .... BIAQ
Boating Industry Association of South Australia .... BIASA
Boating Industry Association of Western Australia .... BIAWA
Boating Safety Circular [*USCG*] (TAG) .... BSC
Boating Safety Detachment [*Coast Guard*] .... BOSDET
Boating Service Officer .... BSO
Boating Trades Association of Texas (SRA) .... BTAT
Boating While Intoxicated (BARN) .... BWI
Boating Writers International (EA) .... BWI
Boatinus de Mantua [*Deceased, 1300*] [*Authority cited in pre-1607 legal work*] (DSA) .... Boa
Boatinus de Mantua [*Deceased, 1300*] [*Authority cited in pre-1607 legal work*] (DSA) .... Boat
Boatmen's Bancshares [*NASDAQ symbol*] (TTSB) .... BOAT
Boatmen's Bankshares, Inc. [*NASDAQ symbol*] (NQ) .... BOAT
Boatmen's Bankshares, Inc. [*Associated Press*] (SAG) .... BoatBnc
Boatowners Unlimited [*An association*] (EA) .... BU
Boatswain .... B
Boatswain (KSC) .... BOSN
Boatswain .... BOSUN
Boatswain (AABC) .... BTSWN
Boatswain's Mate [*Navy rating*] .... BM
Boatswain's Mate, Chief [*Navy rating*] .... BMC
Boatswain's Mate, Construction Battalion, Boatswain [*Navy rating*] .... BMCBB
Boatswain's Mate, Construction Battalion, Stevedore [*Navy rating*] .... BMCBS
Boatswain's Mate, First Class [*Navy rating*] BM1
Boatswain's Mate, Master Chief [*Navy rating*] .... BMCM
Boatswain's Mate, Second Class [*Navy rating*] BM2
Boatswain's Mate, Senior Chief [*Navy rating*] .... BMCS
Boatswain's Mate, Ship Repair, Canvasman [*Navy rating*] .... BMSRS

Boatswain's Mate, Ship Repair, Crane Operator [Navy rating] .... BMSRC
Boatswain's Mate, Ship Repair, Rigger [Navy rating] .... BMSRR
Boatswain's Mate, Third Class [Navy rating] BM3
Boatswain's Mate-of-the-Watch (DNAB) .... BMOW
Boat-Tail [Bullet] (DICI) .... BT
Boatyard [British Waterways Board sign] .... B
Boavista, Boavista Island [Cape Verde] [ICAO location identifier] (ICLI) .... GVBA
Boaz, AL [AM radio station call letters] .... WBSA
Bob Dylan Fan Club (EA) .... BDFC
Bob Evans Farms [NASDAQ symbol] (TTSB) .... BOBE
Bob Evans Farms, Inc. [NASDAQ symbol] (NQ) .... BOBE
Bob Evans Farms, Inc. [Associated Press] (SAG) .... BobEvn
Bob Everhart Fan Club (EA) .... BEFC
Bob Hastings Fan Club [Inactive] (EA) .... BHFC
Bob Homan Fan Club (EA) .... BHFC
Bob Hope Theatre [British] .... BHT
Bob Jones University [South Carolina] .... BJU
Bob Jones University, Greenville, SC [Library symbol Library of Congress]
   (LCLS) .... ScGBJ
Bob Oscar Plenty [Character in "Dick Tracy" comic strip] .... BO
Bob Rumball Centre for the Deaf (AC) .... BRCD
Bobbie Brooks [NASDAQ symbol] (TTSB) .... BBKS
Bobbie Brooks, Inc. [NASDAQ symbol] (NQ) .... BBKS
Bobbie Brooks, Inc. [Associated Press] (SAG) .... BobBrk
Bobbin (KSC) .... BOB
Bobbin Coil Winder .... BCW
Bobby Bare Fan Club (EA) .... BBFC
Bobby Blue Fan Club [Defunct] (EA) .... BBFC
Bobby "C" Fan Club [Defunct] (EA) .... BCFC
Bobby Darin Fan Club (EA) .... BDFC
Bobby Fuller Four-Ever International Fan Club [Defunct] (EA) .... BFFEIFC
Bobby Goldsboro Fan Club (EA) .... BGFC
Bobby Vinton Booster Club (EA) .... BVBC
Bobby Vinton International Fan Club (EA) .... BVIFC
Bobcaygeon Branch, Victoria County Public Library, Ontario [Library
   symbol National Library of Canada] (BIB) .... OBV
Bobete [Lesotho] [ICAO location identifier] (ICLI) .... FXBB
Bobo Dioulass [Volta] [Airport symbol] (AD) .... BOY
Bobo-Dioulasso [Burkina Faso] [Airport symbol] (OAG) .... BOY
Bobo-Dioulasso [Burkina Faso] [ICAO location identifier] (ICLI) .... DHOO
Bobov in Israel [An association] (EA) .... BI
Bobs International [An association] (EAIO) .... BI
BOC Group [Associated Press] (SAG) .... BOC ADS
BOC Group [NYSE symbol] (SAG) .... BOX
Boca Chapare [Bolivia] [ICAO location identifier] (ICLI) .... SLBC
Boca Do Acre [Brazil ICAO location identifier] (ICLI) .... SBBA
Boca Naranjo [Costa Rica] [ICAO location identifier] (ICLI) .... MRBO
Boca Raton [Florida] [ICAO location identifier] (ICLI) .... KBCT
Boca Raton, FL [Location identifier FAA] (FAAL) .... BCT
Boca Raton, FL [FM radio station call letters] .... WKIS
Boca Raton, FL [Television station call letters] .... WPPB
Boca Raton, FL [AM radio station call letters] .... WSBR
Boca Raton Public Library, Boca Raton, FL [Library symbol Library of
   Congress] (LCLS) .... FBo
Boca Research [NASDAQ symbol] (TTSB) .... BOCI
Boca Research, Inc. [Associated Press] (SAG) .... BocaRs
Boca Research, Inc. [NASDAQ symbol] (SAG) .... BOCI
Bocanda [Ivory Coast] [ICAO location identifier] (ICLI) .... DIBC
Bocas Del Toro [Panama] [Airport symbol] (OAG) .... BOC
Bocas Del Toro [Panama] [ICAO location identifier] (ICLI) .... MPBO
Boccaccio [Italian author, 1313-1375] (ROG) .... BOCC
Bocce Federation of Australia .... BFA
BOCES [Boards of Cooperative Educational Services] Geneseo Migrant
   Center (EA) .... BGMC
BOCES [Boards of Cooperative Educational Services], Monroe 1, Penfield, NY
   [OCLC symbol] (OCLC) .... VBL
BOCES [Boards of Cooperative Educational Services], Monroe 2, Orleans,
   Spencerport, NY [OCLC symbol] (OCLC) .... VBM
Boch & Limoges [Vancouver Stock Exchange symbol] .... BLL
Bochum [Federal Republic of Germany] [Seismograph station code, US
   Geological Survey] (SEIS) .... BOC
Bochum - University [Federal Republic of Germany] [Seismograph station
   code, US Geological Survey] (SEIS) .... BUG
Bockus International Society of Gastroenterology (EA) .... BISG
Bodansky Unit [Clinical chemistry] .... BD
Bodansky Unit [Clinical chemistry] .... BOD
Bodansky Unit [Also, BD, BOD] [Clinical chemistry] (AAMN) .... BU
Bodaybo [Former USSR Seismograph station code, US Geological Survey]
   (SEIS) .... BOD
Bodaybo [Former USSR ICAO location identifier] (ICLI) .... UIKB
Boddam and Greenwood's Notanda Digest [A publication] (DLA) .... Not Dig
Boddie-Noell Properties [AMEX symbol] (TTSB) .... BNP
Boddie-Noell Properties, Inc. [AMEX symbol] (SPSG) .... BNP
Boddie-Noell Properties, Inc. [Associated Press] (SAG) .... Boddie
Bodega Marine Laboratory [University of California] [Research center]
   (RCD) .... BML
Boden [Sweden ICAO location identifier] (ICLI) .... ESPG
Bodenstein Number .... Bo
Bodhisattva (VRA) .... bodh
Bodily Injury [Insurance] .... BI
Bodily Injury and Property Damage [Insurance] .... BI/PD
Bodinumu [Papua New Guinea] [Airport symbol] (OAG) .... BNM
Bodleian Library (DAS) .... BL
Bodleian Library [British] (DGA) .... BOD
Bodleian Library [Oxford University] [British] (BARN) .... Bodl

Bodleian Library (DGA) .... BODL LIB
Bodmin [Municipal borough in England] .... BODM
Bodmin [British ICAO location identifier] (ICLI) .... EGLA
Bodo [Norway] [Airport symbol] (OAG) .... BOO
Bodo [Norway ICAO location identifier] (ICLI) .... ENBD
Bodo [Norway ICAO location identifier] (ICLI) .... ENBO
Bodo Oceanic [Norway ICAO location identifier] (ICLI) .... ENOB
Bodon [Former USSR Seismograph station code, US Geological Survey]
   (SEIS) .... BDN
Bodoni [Printing] (DGA) .... BOD
Body .... B
Body .... BDY
Body [Slang] (DSUE) .... BOD
Body Acceleration Synchronous with the Heartbeat [Cardiology] .... BASH
Body and Assembly Operation [Ford Motor Co.] .... B & AO
Body and Assembly Operations .... BAO
Body Armor System Individual Countermine Armor [Army] (INF) .... BASIC
Body Awareness Resource Network .... BARN
Body Axis Coordinate System (MCD) .... BACS
Body Belts [Medicine] (DAVI) .... B/B
Body Bound Bolts (MSA) .... BBB
Body Burden [of radiation] .... BB
Body/Caudal Fin [Ichthyology] .... BCF
Body Cell Mass .... BCM
Body Computer Module [General Motors' computer system] .... BCM
Body Control Module [Automotive engineering] .... BCM
Body Count [Military] (CINC) .... BC
Body Dysmorphic Disorder [Medicine] .... BDD
Body Electronics Area Network .... BEAN
Body Engineering Office .... BEO
Body Engineering Product Engineering .... BEPE
Body Engineering Product Engineering Office .... BEPEO
Body Flap (NASA) .... BDYFLP
Body Flap Control (MCD) .... BFC
Body Guard [Special Air Service] [British] .... BG
Body Heat Content .... BHC
Body Hematocrit-Venous Hematocrit Ratio (MAE) .... BH/VH
Body in White [Automotive manufacturing] .... BIW
Body in White .... BIW
Body Line [Typography] (WDMC) .... BL
Body Mass [Medicine] .... BM
Body Mass Index [Medicine] .... BMI
Body Mass Measurements Device (KSC) .... BMMD
Body Mounted (MCD) .... BM
Body Odor [Slang] .... BO
Body or Roof [Freight] .... BDY or RF
Body Part [Anatomy] (DAVI) .... BP
Body Point (MCD) .... BPT
Body Restraint System .... BRS
Body Rot of Papaya [Plant pathology] .... BR
Body Sensor Assembly [Military] .... BSA
Body Shell .... BS
Body Side Molding .... BSM
Body Station (MCD) .... BS
Body Support Cradle .... BSC
Body Surface Area .... BSA
Body Surface Burned [Medicine] .... BSB
Body Surface Potential Mapping [Dermatology] (DAVI) .... BSPM
Body Temperature [Medicine] .... BT
Body Temperature [Medicine] .... Tb
Body Temperature and Pressure [Medicine] (WDAA) .... BTP
Body Temperature Measuring System .... BTMS
Body Temperature, Pressure [Prevailing atmospheric], and Saturation [With
   water vapor] (DAVI) .... BTPS
Body Temperature, [Ambient] Pressure, Dry [Medicine] .... BTPD
Body Temperature, [Ambient] Pressure, Saturated [with water] [Medicine].... BTPS
Body Water [Medicine] .... BW
Body Weight .... BW
Body Whorl .... BW
Body Wing (KSC) .... BW
Body-Centered [Crystallography] .... BC
Body-Centered Cubic [Also, BCCUB] [Crystallography] .... BCC
Body-Centered Cubic [Also, BCC] [Crystallography] .... BCCUB
Body-Centered Cubic System [Crystallography] (IAA) .... BCCS
Body-Centered Tetragonal [Crystallography] .... BCT
Bodycolor (VRA) .... bdyco
Body-Cooling Garment [NASA] (MCD) .... BCG
Body-Fitted Coordinates [Computer science] .... BFC
Body-Mounted Accelerometer .... BMA
Body-Mounted Attitude Gyro (KSC) .... BMAG
Body-Mounted [Altitude] Gyroscope (SAA) .... BMG
Body-Mounted Radiator (SSD) .... BMR
Body-on-Chassis [Technical drawings] .... BOC
Body-over-Frame [Automotive engineering] .... BOF
Boehm Test of Basic Concepts [Psychology] .... BTBC
Boehringer Ingelheim Pharmaceuticals, Inc. [Commercial firm] (DAVI) .... BI
Boehringer Mannheim Biochemicals .... BMB
Boehringer Mannheim Corp. [Chemical industry supplier] .... BMC
Boehringer Mannheim Corp., Indianapolis, IN [OCLC symbol] (OCLC) .... IBL
Boehringer Mannheim GmbH, Mannheim, Germany [Library symbol Library
   of Congress] (LCLS) .... GyMB
Boeing Aerospace [or Aircraft] Corp. (MCD) .... BAC
Boeing Air Transport .... BAT
Boeing Airborne Instrumentation Equipment (SAA) .... BAI

Boeing Airplane Co. [*later, The Boeing Co.*] **Algebraic Interpretive Computing System** .... BACAIC
Boeing Applied Computing Service (SAA) .... BACS
Boeing Associated Products (MCD) .... BAP
Boeing Atlantic Test Center (KSC) .... BATC
Boeing Canada Dash-8 [*Airplane code*] Dh8
Boeing Commericial Airplane Group [*ICAO designator*] (FAAC) .... BOE
[*The*] **Boeing Co.** [*ICAO aircraft manufacturer identifier*] (ICAO) .... B
[*The*] **Boeing Co.** [*NYSE symbol*] (SPSG) .... BA
[*The*] **Boeing Co.** [*Associated Press*] (SAG) .... Boeing
[*The*] **Boeing Co., Aerospace Division, Technical Library, Kent, WA** [*Library symbol Library of Congress*] (LCLS) .... WaSBo-A
[*The*] **Boeing Co., Commercial Airplane Group, Technical Libraries, Seattle,WA** [*Library symbol Library of Congress*] (LCLS) .... WaSBo
Boeing Co., Technical Libraries, Bellevue, WA [*Library symbol*] [*Library of Congress*] (LCLS) .... WaSBo-B
Boeing Co., Technical Libraries, Kent, WA [*Library symbol*] [*Library of Congress*] (LCLS) .... WaSBo-K
[*The*] **Boeing Co., Wichita Division Library, Wichita, KS** [*Library symbol Library of Congress*] (LCLS) .... KWiB
Boeing Computer Services Co. [*Information service or system*] (IID) .... BCS
Boeing Data Entry System [*Boeing Computer Services*] (NITA) .... BDES
Boeing Dehavilland Canada [*ICAO designator*] (FAAC) .... DHC
Boeing Engineering Analog Computer (IEEE) .... BEAC
Boeing Engineering Co. (MCD) .... BEC
Boeing Engineering Thermal Analyzer (MCD) .... BETA
Boeing Field Test Unit [*NASA*] (IAA) .... BFTU
Boeing Flight Test Center [*NASA*] (IAA) .... BFTC
Boeing Ground Support (KSC) .... BGS
Boeing Gulf Test Section (SAA) .... BGTS
Boeing Infrared Missile Attack Simulation (MCD) .... BIRMAS
Boeing Intelligent Terminal System [*Boeing Computer Services Co.*] [*Information service or system*] (IID) .... BITS
Boeing Interface Surveillance Unit (KSC) .... BISU
Boeing Materials Specification .... BMS
Boeing Military Airplane Co. .... BMAC
Boeing Military Airplane Development Organization .... BMADO
Boeing Network Architecture [*Telecommunications*] (TSSD) .... BNA
Boeing of Canada Ltd., Arnprior, ON, Canada [*Library symbol*] [*Library of Congress*] (LCLS) .... CaOArBC
Boeing of Canada Ltd., Arnprior, Ontario [*Library symbol National Library of Canada*] (BIB) .... OARBC
Boeing on Dock .... BOD
Boeing Operational Supervisory System .... BOSS
Boeing Plastic Analysis Capability for Engines [*Computer science NASA*] .... BOPACE
Boeing Radiation Effect Laboratory .... BREL
Boeing Robotic Air Vehicles .... BRAVE
Boeing Scientific Research Laboratories .... BSRL
Boeing Services International, Inc. (MCD) .... BSI
Boeing Shaped Scan Correlator (MCD) .... BOSSCO
Boeing Small Research Module [*NASA*] .... BSRM
Boeing Systems Coordinator (MUGU) .... BSC
Boeing Test Support [*NASA*] (KSC) .... BTS
Boeing Wind Tunnel .... BWT
Boeing-Michigan Aeronautical Research Center .... BOMARC
Boeing-Vertol Division [*The Boeing Co.*] [*ICAO aircraft manufacturer identifier*] (ICAO) .... BV
Boeing-Vertol Division [*The Boeing Co.*] [*ICAO aircraft manufacturer identifier*] (ICAO) .... HV
Boeken van het Oude Testament [*Roermond/Maaseik*] [*A publication*] (BJA) .... BoekOT
Boende [*Zaire*] [*Airport symbol*] (OAG) .... BNB
Boende [*Zaire*] [*ICAO location identifier*] (ICLI) .... FZGN
Boere Weerstandsbeweging [*South Africa Political party*] (EY) .... BWB
Boeren Partij [*Farmers' Party*] [*Netherlands Political party*] (PPE) .... BP
Boerne, TX [*AM radio station call letters*] .... KBRN
Boevaya Mashina Pekhota [*Infantry Fighting Vehicle*] [*Russian*] .... BMP
Bofors Spent Acid Concentration [*Chemical industry*] .... BOSAC
Bogalusa, LA [*Location identifier FAA*] (FAAL) .... BXA
Bogalusa, LA [*Location identifier FAA*] (FAAL) .... VNL
Bogalusa, LA [*AM radio station call letters*] .... WBOX
Bogalusa, LA [*AM radio station call letters*] .... WIKC
Bogande [*Burkina Faso*] [*ICAO location identifier*] (ICLI) .... DHEB
Bogande [*Burkina Faso*] [*Airport symbol*] (OAG) .... XBG
Bogart-Brociner Associates [*Information service or system*] (IID) .... BBA
Bogazici Hava Tasimacilik AS [*Turkey*] [*ICAO designator*] (FAAC) .... BHT
Bogdanovka [*Former USSR Seismograph station code, US Geological Survey Closed*] (SEIS) .... BGD
Bogen [*Bow*] [*Music*] .... Bg
Bogen Communic Intl. [*AMEX symbol*] (TTSB) .... BGN
Bogen Communic Intl Unit [*AMEX symbol*] (TTSB) .... BGN.E
Bogen Communic Intl Wrrt [*AMEX symbol*] (TTSB) .... BGN.WS
Bogen Communications International [*AMEX symbol*] (SAG) .... BGN
Bogen Communications International [*Associated Press*] (SAG) .... Bogen
Bogen Communications International [*Associated Press*] (SAG) .... BogenC
Bogert on Trusts and Trustees [*A publication*] (DLA) .... Bogert Trusts
Boghazkoi-Sammlung des Berliner Museum (BJA) .... Bo
Boghazkoi-Studien [*Leipzig, 1916-1924*] [*A publication*] (BJA) .... BoSt
Boghazkoy [*Museum of the Ancient Orient, Istanbul*] (BJA) .... Bo
Bogie Fan Club [*Canada*] (EAIO) .... BFC
Bogle & Gates, Law Library, Seattle, WA [*Library symbol*] [*Library of Congress*] (LCLS) .... WaSBG
Bognor Regis [*British ICAO location identifier*] (ICLI) .... EGKC
Bogoliubov-Born-Green-Kirkwood-Yvon [*Plasma kinetic theory hierarchy*] .... BBGKY
Bogong [*Victoria*] [*Australia*] [*Seismograph station code, US Geological Survey*] [*Closed*] (SEIS) .... BOV
Bogoslovni Vestnik [*Ljubljana*] [*A publication*] (BJA) .... BogVest
Bogoslovska Smotra [*Zagreb*] [*A publication*] (BJA) .... BogSmot
Bogota [*Colombia*] [*Seismograph station code, US Geological Survey*] (SEIS) .... BOCO
Bogota [*Colombia*] [*Seismograph station code, US Geological Survey*] (SEIS) .... BOG
Bogota [*Colorado ICAO location identifier*] (ICLI) .... SKED
Bogota/Eldorado [*Colorado ICAO location identifier*] (ICLI) .... SKBO
Bogota Public Library, Bogota, NJ [*Library symbol Library of Congress*] (LCLS) .... NjBo
Bogue [*Mauritania*] [*ICAO location identifier*] (ICLI) .... GQNE
Bogus Check [*Banking*] .... BC
Bohairic Version of the Bible (BJA) .... Boh
Boheme, Butterfly, and Barber of Seville [*Frequently performed operas*] .... 3B's
Bohemia .... BOH
Bohemia Ragtime Society (EA) .... BRS
Bohemian [*Language, etc.*] (ROG) .... BOH
Bohemian [*Language, etc.*] (ROG) .... BOHEM
Bohemian Club (EA) .... BC
Bohemian Club, San Francisco, CA [*Library symbol Library of Congress*] (LCLS) .... CSfBo
Bohemian Free Thinking School Society (EA) .... BFTSS
Bohemian-Hungarian [*Slang*] .... BOHUNK
Bohemium [*Chemical element*] (MAE) .... Bo
Bohmer [*Germany ICAO location identifier*] (ICLI) .... EDIJ
Bohn's Artist's Library [*A publication*] .... BAL
Bohn's Philosophical Library [*A publication*] .... BPL
Bohn's Standard Library [*A publication*] .... BSL
Bohr and Mottleson Model [*of nuclear structure*] .... BMM
Bohr Frequency Condition .... BFC
Bohr Magneton [*Atomic physics*] .... BM
Bohr-Kramers-Slater [*Quantum theory*] .... BKS
Bohr-Sommerfeld Atom .... BSA
Bohr-Wheeler Theory .... BWT
Bohun. Ecclesiastical Jurisdiction [*A publication*] (DLA) .... Boh Eccl Jur
Bohun. English Lawyer [*A publication*] (DLA) .... Boh Eng L
Bohun. Practising Attorney [*A publication*] (DLA) .... Boh Att
Bohun. Privilegia Londini [*A publication*] (DLA) .... Boh Priv Lond
Bohun. Titles [*A publication*] (DLA) .... Boh Ti
Bohun's Cursus Cancellariae (ILCA) .... Boh Curs Can
Bohun's Cursus Cancellariae [*A publication*] (DLA) .... Bohun Curs Canc
Bohun's Declarations and Pleadings [*A publication*] (DLA) .... Boh Dec
Bohun's Election Cases [*England*] [*A publication*] (DLA) .... Bohun
Bohun's Institutio Legalis (ILCA) .... Boh Inst Leg
Bohun's Institutio Legalis [*A publication*] (DLA) .... Bohun Inst Leg
BOI [*Board of Investments*] **Unit for Industrial Linkage Development** (ECON) .... BUILD
Boiled [*Linseed*] **Oil** .... BO
Boiler .... B
Boiler (AAG) .... BLR
Boiler (DNAB) .... BOI
Boiler and Industrial Furnace [*Environmental Protection Agency*] .... BIF
Boiler and Machinery .... B & M
Boiler and Pressure Vessel [*Nuclear energy*] (NRCH) .... B + PV
Boiler and Pressure Vessel Committee [*Nuclear Regulatory Commission*] (GFGA) .... BPVC
Boiler and Pressure Vessel Manufacturers' Association of Australia .... BPVMAA
Boiler Blower Control (DNAB) .... BBC
Boiler Design and Performance .... BODEPE
Boiler Feed [*Technical drawings*] .... BF
Boiler Feed Compound Tank [*Technical drawings*] .... BFCT
Boiler Feed Pump [*Technical drawings*] .... BFP
Boiler Feed Water [*Technical drawings*] .... BFW
Boiler Horsepower .... BHP
Boiler Horsepower (IAA) .... BOHP
Boiler House [*Technical drawings*] .... BH
Boiler Information Data System [*Southwest Research Institute*] .... BIDS
Boiler Inspection and Insurance .... BI & I
Boiler Manufacturer (DS) .... BO
Boiler Plate .... BP
Boiler Pressure .... BOPRESS
Boiler Pressure .... BP
Boiler Room .... BR
Boiler Survey .... BS
Boiler Turbine Generator (IAA) .... BTG
Boiler Water .... BOWR
Boiler Water/Feedwater Test and Treatment Training (DNAB) .... BW/FWT & TT
Boilermaker [*Navy*] .... B
Boilermaker [*Military British*] .... BM
Boilermaker (MSA) .... BMKR
Boilermaker [*Navy rating*] .... BR
Boilermaker, Chief [*Navy rating*] .... BRC
Boilermaker, First Class [*Navy rating*] BR1
Boilermaker, Master Chief [*Navy rating*] .... BRCM
Boilermaker, Second Class [*Navy rating*] BR2
Boilermaker, Senior Chief [*Navy rating*] .... BRCS
Boilermaker, Ship Repair [*Navy rating*] .... BSR
Boilermaker, Third Class [*Navy rating*] BR3
Boilermaker/Welder .... BMW
Boilerman [*Navy rating*] .... BT
Boilerman, Chief [*Navy rating*] .... BTC

Boilerman, First Class [*Navy rating*] ... BT1
Boilerman, Master Chief [*Navy rating*] ... BTCM
Boilerman, Second Class [*Navy rating*] ... BT2
Boilerman, Senior Chief [*Navy rating*] ... BTCS
Boilerman, Third Class [*Navy rating*] ... BT3
Boilerplates Aerodynamic Test Vehicle (MCD) ... BATV
Boilerwater/Feedwater Test and Treatment ... BFWTT
Boiling ... BOG
Boiling Heavy Water Reactor ... BHWR
Boiling Light Water [*Nuclear energy*] ... BLW
Boiling Light Water Cooled Plutonium Burner [*Nuclear energy*] (NUCP) ... BLW (PB)
Boiling Liquid Expanding Vapor Explosion [*Chemical engineering*] ... BLEVE
Boiling Nuclear Superheat Critical Experiment (NRCH) ... BONUS-CX
Boiling Nuclear Superheat Reactor ... BONUS
Boiling Point ... BP
Boiling Point ... BPT
Boiling Point Elevation ... BPE
Boiling Point Margin [*Engineering*] ... BPM
Boiling Point Number [*Chemical engineering*] ... BPN
Boiling Point Rise ... BPR
Boiling Range ... BR
Boiling Reactor Experiments [*Nuclear energy*] ... BORAX
Boiling Springs, NC [*FM radio station call letters*] ... WGWG
Boiling Transition [*Nuclear energy*] (NRCH) ... BT
Boiling Water Reactor ... BWR
Boiling Water Reactor Owners Group [*Nuclear energy*] (NRCH) ... BWROG
Boil-Off ... B-O
Boil-Off Gas [*Petroleum product transportation*] ... BOG
Boils At ... B
BOIP [*Basis of Issue Plan*] **Feeder Data** [*DoD*] ... BOIPFD
BOIP [*Basis of Issue Plan*] **Retrieval Program** [*DoD*] ... BPPRM
Boise [*Diocesan abbreviation*] [*Idaho*] (TOCD) ... B
Boise [*Idaho*] [*Airport symbol*] (OAG) ... BOI
Boise [*Idaho*] [*Seismograph station code, US Geological Survey*] (SEIS) ... BSE
Boise Basin District Library, Idaho City, ID [*Library symbol*] [*Library of Congress*] (LCLS) ... Idlc
Boise Bible College, Boise, ID [*Library symbol*] [*Library of Congress*] (LCLS) ... IdBBC
Boise/Boise Air Terminal [*Idaho*] [*ICAO location identifier*] (ICLI) ... KBOI
Boise Cascade [*NYSE symbol*] (SAG) ... BCC
Boise Cascade 7.48% Dep Pfd [*NYSE symbol*] (TTSB) ... BCCPrG
Boise Cascade 9.40% Dep Pfd [*NYSE symbol*] (TTSB) ... BCCPrF
Boise Cascade Corp. [*Associated Press*] (SAG) ... BoisC
Boise Cascade Corp. [*Associated Press*] (SAG) ... BoiseC
Boise Cascade Corp. Library, Boise, ID [*Library symbol*] [*Library of Congress*] (LCLS) ... IdBBC
Boise Cascade Corp., Research Library, International Falls, MN [*Library symbol Library of Congress*] (LCLS) ... MnIfBC
Boise Cascade Office Products [*NYSE symbol*] (SAG) ... BCP
Boise Cascade Office Products [*Associated Press*] (SAG) ... BoisCOff
Boise Cascade Office Products [*NYSE symbol*] (SAG) ... BOP
Boise Cascade Office Products [*NYSE symbol*] (TTSB) ... BOP
Boise City, OK [*Location identifier FAA*] (FAAL) ... BCY
Boise Creek Resources [*Vancouver Stock Exchange symbol*] ... BOS
Boise, ID [*Television station call letters*] ... KAID
Boise, ID [*Television station call letters*] ... KBCI
Boise, ID [*AM radio station call letters*] ... KBOI
Boise, ID [*AM radio station call letters*] ... KBSU
Boise, ID [*FM radio station call letters*] ... KBSU-FM
Boise, ID [*AM radio station call letters*] ... KGEM
Boise, ID [*AM radio station call letters*] ... KIDO
Boise, ID [*FM radio station call letters*] ... KIZN
Boise, ID [*FM radio station call letters*] ... KJOT
Boise, ID [*AM radio station call letters*] ... KKIC
Boise, ID [*FM radio station call letters*] ... KLTB
Boise, ID [*FM radio station call letters*] ... KQFC
Boise, ID [*AM radio station call letters*] ... KSPD
Boise, ID [*Television station call letters*] ... KTVB
Boise Interagency Fire Center, Boise, ID [*OCLC symbol*] (OCLC) ... UDF
Boise Junior College [*Idaho*] ... BJC
Boise Peace Quilt Project (EA) ... BPQP
Boise Public Library, Boise, ID [*Library symbol Library of Congress*] (LCLS) ... IdB
Boise Senior High School, Boise, ID [*Library symbol*] [*Library of Congress*] (LCLS) ... IdBSH
Boise State College, Boise, ID [*Library symbol Library of Congress*] (LCLS) ... IdBB
Boise State University (GAGS) ... Boise St U
Boissevain and Morton Regional Library, Boissevain, Manitoba [*Library symbol National Library of Canada*] (NLC) ... MBOM
Boissevain and Morton Regional Library, Boissevain, MB, Canada [*Library symbol Library of Congress*] (LCLS) ... CaMBoM
Boissevain Health Centre, Manitoba [*Library symbol National Library of Canada*] (NLC) ... MBHC
Boissevain, MB [*AM radio station call letters*] ... CJRB
Boisterous (ABBR) ... BSTRU
Boisterous (ABBR) ... BSTRUS
Boisterously (ABBR) ... BSTRUSY
Boisterousness (ABBR) ... BSTRUSNS
Boite Postale [*Post Office Box*] [*French*] ... BP
Boite-a-Musique, Paris [*Record label*] [*France*] ... BaM
Bojnord [*Iran*] [*ICAO location identifier*] (ICLI) ... OIMN
BOK Financial [*NASDAQ symbol*] (TTSB) ... BOKF
BOK Financial Corp. [*Associated Press*] (SAG) ... BOK
BOK Financial Corp. [*NASDAQ symbol*] (SAG) ... BOKF
Bokada [*Zaire*] [*ICAO location identifier*] (ICLI) ... FZFG
Bokaro [*India*] [*Seismograph station code, US Geological Survey*] (SEIS) ... BOK
Bokaro [*India*] [*ICAO location identifier*] (ICLI) ... VEBK
Boke/Baralande [*Guinea*] [*ICAO location identifier*] (ICLI) ... GUOK
Bokenge [*Zaire*] [*ICAO location identifier*] (ICLI) ... FZGD
Bokepyin [*Myanmar*] [*ICAO location identifier*] (ICLI) ... VBBP
Bokhara (VRA) ... Bokh
Boko [*Zaire*] [*ICAO location identifier*] (ICLI) ... FZCO
Bokondini [*Indonesia*] [*ICAO location identifier*] (ICLI) ... WAJB
Bokoro [*Chad*] [*ICAO location identifier*] (ICLI) ... FTTK
Bokote/Basengele [*Zaire*] [*ICAO location identifier*] (ICLI) ... FZBW
Bokoudini [*Indonesia*] [*Airport symbol*] (OAG) ... BUI
Boku [*Papua New Guinea*] [*Airport symbol Obsolete*] (OAG) ... BOQ
Bokungu [*Zaire*] [*ICAO location identifier*] (ICLI) ... FZGF
Bol [*Chad*] [*ICAO location identifier*] (ICLI) ... FTTL
Bol [*Chad*] [*Airport symbol*] (AD) ... OTC
Bola De Oro [*Ecuador*] [*ICAO location identifier*] (ICLI) ... SEBD
Bolama [*Guinea-Bissau*] [*ICAO location identifier*] (ICLI) ... GGBO
Bold (ADA) ... BD
Bold (ADA) ... BLD
Bold Face [*Printing term*] ... BF
Bold Face Capitals [*Printing term*] ... BFC
Bolder Tech [*NASDAQ symbol*] (TTSB) ... BOLD
Boldface [*Typography*] (WDMC) ... bf
Bole [*Ghana*] [*ICAO location identifier*] (ICLI) ... DGLB
Bolero Resources, Inc. [*Vancouver Stock Exchange symbol*] ... BOR
Boletim de Bibliografia Portuguesa [*A bibliographic publication*] [*Portugal*] ... BBP
Boletim. Ministerio de Justica [*Portugal*] [*A publication*] (DLA) ... Bol Min Justica
Boletus Virus [*Plant pathology*] ... BOV
Boliche [*Ecuador*] [*ICAO location identifier*] (ICLI) ... SEBI
Bolingbroke, GA [*FM radio station call letters*] (RBYB) ... WDBS-FM
Bolinger Road [*California*] [*Seismograph station code, US Geological Survey*] (SEIS) ... BGC
Bolito [*Race of maize*] ... BOL
Bolivar [*Monetary unit*] [*Venezuela*] ... B
Bolivar [*Argentina ICAO location identifier*] (ICLI) ... SAZI
Bolivar County Library, Cleveland, MS [*Library symbol Library of Congress*] (LCLS) ... MsCle
Bolivar Free Library, Bolivar, NY [*Library symbol Library of Congress*] (LCLS) ... NBo
Bolivar Free Library, Bolivar, NY [*Library symbol*] [*Library of Congress*] (LCLS) ... NBoL
Bolivar, MO [*AM radio station call letters*] ... KYOO
Bolivar, TN [*Location identifier FAA*] (FAAL) ... BAV
Bolivar, TN [*AM radio station call letters*] ... WBOL
Bolivar, TN [*FM radio station call letters*] ... WMOD
Bolivar, TN [*FM radio station call letters*] ... WOJG
Bolivarian Society of the United States (EA) ... BSUS
Bolivia [*ANSI two-letter standard code*] (CNC) ... BO
Bolivia [*MARC country of publication code Library of Congress*] (LCCP) ... bo
Bolivia [*ANSI three-letter standard code*] (CNC) ... BOL
Bolivia (VRA) ... Bol
Bolivia [*MARC geographic area code Library of Congress*] (LCCP) ... s-bo--
Bolivian Air-Shower Joint Experiment ... BASJE
Bolivian Hemorrhagic Fever [*Medicine*] (DMAA) ... BHF
Boliviano [*Monetary unit*] [*Bolivia*] ... B
Boll Weevil Research Laboratory [*Department of Agriculture*] [*Mississippi State, MS*] [*Research center*] ... BWRL
Boll Weevil Research Unit [*Mississippi State, MS*] [*Agricultural Research Service*] [*Department of Agriculture*] (GRD) ... BWRU
Bollard [*Shipping*] [*British*] ... Bol
Bollard Pull [*Shipping*] [*British*] ... BP
Bollettino. Commissione Archeologica Comunale in Roma [*A publication*] (OCD) ... Boll Com Arch
Bollettino di Archeologia Cristiana [*A publication*] (BJA) ... BAC
Bollettino di Filologia Classica [*A publication*] (OCD) ... Boll Fil Class
Bollettino di Legislazione Comparata [*A publication*] (ILCA) ... BLC
Bollettino. Istituto di Diritto Romano [*A publication*] (OCD) ... Boll Ist Dir Rom
Bologna [*Italy*] [*Airport symbol*] (OAG) ... BLQ
Bologna [*Italy*] [*Seismograph station code, US Geological Survey*] (SEIS) ... BOL
Bologna/Borgo Panigale [*Italy ICAO location identifier*] (ICLI) ... LIPE
Bolometric Correction ... BC
Bolometric Voltage and Current [*Voltage measurement*] [*National Institute of Standards and Technology*] ... BOLOVAC
Bolshoi Alt-Azimuth Telescope [*Former USSR*] ... BAT
Bolshoi Ballet Academy [*Former USSR*] ... BA
Bolshoi Ballet Academy [*Moscow*] ... BBA
Bolster (KSC) ... BOLS
Bolt (MSA) ... BLT
Bolt ... BO
Bolt (ABBR) ... BT
Bolt Action [*British military*] (DMA) ... BA
Bolt and Bond Assembly ... BBA
Bolt and Nut ... BN
Bolt, Beranek & Newman, Inc. [*NYSE symbol*] (SPSG) ... BBN
Bolt, Beranek & Newman, Inc. [*Associated Press*] (SAG) ... BoltBer
Bolt Circle [*Technical drawings*] ... BC
Bolt Extrusion Thrust Termination (MCD) ... BETT
Bolt Installation and Removal Tool ... BIRT
Bolt, Nut, and Rivet Makers Association of Scotland [*A union*] ... BNRMAS
Bolt Out of the Blue [*Surprise nuclear attack*] ... BOOB
Bolt Removal Tool ... BRT
Bolt Technology Corp. [*Associated Press*] (SAG) ... BoltTch
Bolt Technology Corp. [*AMEX symbol*] (SAG) ... BTJ
Bolted Manhole Cover Plate [*Shipfitting*] ... BM

Bolted Plate [*Technical drawings*] ... BP
Bolted Repair [*Composite structures*] (MCD) ... BREPAIR
Bolted Separable Connector ... BSC
Bolted-on-Base ... BO/BS
Bolton [*Craniometric point*] ... BO
Bolton Environmental Sensing System (NOAA) ... BESS
Bolton Evening News, Bolton, United Kingdom [*Library symbol Library of Congress*] (LCLS) ... UkBoN
Bolton Institute for a Sustainable Future (EA) ... BISF
Bolt-On Intelligence [*Proposed use for the biochip*] ... BOI
Bolton Point [*Medicine*] (DMAA) ... B
Bolton Point [*Medicine*] (DMAA) ... BP
Bolton, VT [*FM radio station call letters*] (RBYB) ... WCMK
Bolton-Hunter Reagent-Labeled Eledoisin [*Analytical biochemistry*] ... BHE
Bolton-Hunter Reagent-Labeled Substance K [*Analytical biochemistry*] ... BHSK
Boltzmann Constant [*Symbol*] [*IUPAC*] ... k
Boltzmann Constant [*Statistical mechanics*] ... S
Boltzmann Function [*Physics*] (BARN) ... H
Boltzmann Transport Equation [*Physics*] ... BTE
Bolus [*Large Pill*] [*Pharmacy*] ... BOL
Bolworra [*Australia Airport symbol Obsolete*] (OAG) ... BCK
Bolzano [*Italy*] [*Seismograph station code, US Geological Survey*] (SEIS) ... BLZ
Bolzano [*Italy*] [*Airport symbol*] (AD) ... BZO
Bolzano [*Italy ICAO location identifier*] (ICLI) ... LIPB
Bom Jesus Da Lapa [*Brazil*] [*Airport symbol*] (OAG) ... LAZ
Bom Jesus Da Lapa [*Brazil ICAO location identifier*] (ICLI) ... SBLP
Boma [*Zaire*] [*ICAO location identifier*] (ICLI) ... FZAJ
Bomai [*Papua New Guinea*] [*Airport symbol*] (OAG) ... BMH
BOMARC [*Boeing-Michigan Aeronautical Research Center*] **Interceptor** ... BIN
BOMARC [*Boeing-Michigan Aeronautical Research Center*] **Prelaunch Output** (IAA) ... BPO
BOMARC [*Boeing-Michigan Aeronautical Research Center*] **SAGE Compatibility** [*Semiautomatic Ground Environment*] (IAA) ... BOSCO
BOMARC [*Boeing-Michigan Aeronautical Research Center*] **Squadron Simulator** ... BSS
BOMARC [*Boeing-Michigan Aeronautical Research Center*] **Unintegrated Guidance** (IAA) ... BUG
BOMARC [*Boeing-Michigan Aeronautical Research Center*] **Universal SAGE** [*Semiautomatic Ground Environment*] (IAA) ... BUS
Bomb (NG) ... B
Bomb (MUGU) ... BB
Bomb (DNAB) ... BOM
Bomb Alarm System [*Air Force*] ... BAS
Bomb and Mine Disposal Officer [*British military*] (DMA) ... BMDO
Bomb Assembly Spares (NG) ... BAS
Bomb Bay [*of an aircraft*] ... BB
Bomb Bay Ring Out (SAA) ... BBRO
Bomb Damage Assessment ... BDA
Bomb Damage Repair ... BDR
Bomb Damage Survey ... BDS
Bomb Data Center [*International Association of Chiefs of Police*] ... BDC
Bomb Director High-Speed Aircraft ... BDHSA
Bomb Director Set [*or System*] [*Army*] ... BDS
Bomb Disposal ... BD
Bomb, Dummy Unit (AFM) ... BDU
Bomb Fall Line [*Military*] (NVT) ... BFL
Bomb LASER Directed (MCD) ... BOLD
Bomb LASER Tracking (MCD) ... BOLT
Bomb Line (DNAB) ... BL
Bomb Line Unit (MCD) ... BLU
Bomb, Live Unit (AFM) ... BLU
Bomb Maintenance Spares ... BMS
Bomb Mine (MCD) ... BOMINE
Bomb Navigation Guidance System ... BNGS
Bomb Nose Fuze ... BNF
Bomb or Missile Optics (MCD) ... BOMO
Bomb Orbital Strategic System ... BOSS
Bomb Orbital Strategic System - Weapon Development Glide Entry ... BOSS-WEDGE
Bomb Pulsed Release Generator (DWSG) ... BPRG
Bomb Rack/Rocket Launcher (NG) ... BR/RL
Bomb Rack Unit ... BRU
Bomb, Radio, Longitudinal, Generator-Powered ... BRLG
Bomb, Radio, Transverse, Generator-Powered (IAA) ... BRTG
Bomb Release Angle Computer (MCD) ... BRAC
Bomb Release Distance [*Army*] (AABC) ... BRD
Bomb Release Line ... BRL
Bomb Run Insert (SAA) ... BRI
Bomb Safety Officer [*Navy*] ... BSO
Bomb Service ... BS
Bomb Service Truck (MUGU) ... BSTRK
Bomb Sight ... BS
Bomb Tail Fuse ... BTF
Bomb Targets Information Committee [*Air Ministry*] [*British World War II*] ... BTIC
Bomb Testing Device ... BTD
Bomb Thermal Battery (DNAB) ... BTB
Bomb-Aimer [*British military*] (DMA) ... B/A
Bombardier ... B
Bombardier ... BDR
Bombardier (AFM) ... BMBDR
Bombardier ... BMDR
Bombardier ... BOM
Bombardier [*British*] (ROG) ... BOMB
Bombardier ... BOMBDR
Bombardier [*British*] (ADA) ... BR
Bombardier, Inc. [*Toronto Stock Exchange symbol*] ... BBD
Bombardier Inc.Cl'B' [*TS Symbol*] (TTSB) ... BBD.B
Bombardier/Navigator (DOMA) ... BOMB/NAV
Bombardier-Navigator (MUGU) ... BN
Bombardier's Information File ... BIF
Bombardment (KSC) ... BBT
Bombardment ... BOMB
Bombardment Control Unit ... BCU
Bombardment Enhanced Etch Rate (IAA) ... BEE
Bombardment Enhanced Etch Rate ... BEER
Bombardment (Heavy) Wing [*Air Force*] ... BHW
Bombardment Liaison Officer [*Navy*] ... BLO
Bombardment (Medium) Wing [*Air Force*] ... BMW
Bombardment Rocket (KSC) ... BOMROC
Bombardment Squadron [*Air Force*] ... BMBSq
Bombardment Squadron [*Air Force*] ... BMS
Bombardment Wing [*Air Force*] ... BW
Bombardment-Induced Conductivity ... BIC
Bombardment-Induced Light Emission [*Physics*] ... BLE
Bombardon [*Musical instrument*] ... BOMB
Bombay [*India*] [*Seismograph station code, US Geological Survey*] (SEIS) ... BOM
Bombay [*India*] [*Later, ABG*] [*Geomagnetic observatory code*] ... BOM
Bombay [*India*] [*ICAO location identifier*] (ICLI) ... VABB
Bombay [*India*] [*ICAO location identifier*] (ICLI) ... VABF
Bombay, Baroda, and Central India Railway ... BB & CIRly
Bombay Cavalry [*British military*] (DMA) ... BC
Bombay Co. [*NYSE symbol*] (SPSG) ... BBA
Bombay Company [*NYSE symbol*] (TTSB) ... BBA
Bombay Co. [*Associated Press*] (SAG) ... Bombay
Bombay High Court Criminal Rulings [*India*] [*A publication*] (DLA) ... Bomb Cr Rul
Bombay High Court Printed Judgments [*1869-1900*] [*India*] [*A publication*] (DLA) ... BHCPJ
Bombay High Court Printed Judgments [*1869-1900*] [*India*] [*A publication*] (DLA) ... PJ
Bombay High Court Reports [*1862-75*] [*India*] [*A publication*] (DLA) ... BHC
Bombay High Court Reports [*1862-75*] [*India*] [*A publication*] (DLA) ... BHCR
Bombay High Court Reports [*1862-75*] [*India*] [*A publication*] (DLA) ... Bom
Bombay High Court Reports [*1862-75*] [*India*] [*A publication*] (DLA) ... Bom HCR
Bombay High Court Reports [*1862-75*] [*India*] [*A publication*] (DLA) ... Bomb H Ct
Bombay High Court Reports [*1862-75*] [*India*] [*A publication*] (DLA) ... Bomb HC
Bombay High Court Reports [*1862-75*] [*India*] [*A publication*] (DLA) ... Bomb Hg Ct
Bombay Horse Artillery [*British military*] (DMA) ... BHA
Bombay/Juhu [*India*] [*ICAO location identifier*] (ICLI) ... VAJJ
Bombay Law Journal [*India*] [*A publication*] (DLA) ... Bom LJ
Bombay Law Journal [*India*] [*A publication*] (DLA) ... Bombay LJ
Bombay Law Reporter [*India*] [*A publication*] (DLA) ... BLR
Bombay Law Reporter [*India*] [*A publication*] (DLA) ... Bom LR
Bombay Law Reporter [*India*] [*A publication*] (DLA) ... Bom LRJ
Bombay Law Reporter [*India*] [*A publication*] (DLA) ... Bomb LR
Bombay Law Reports [*India*] [*A publication*] (DLA) ... Bom L Rep
Bombay Light Cavalry [*British military*] (DMA) ... BLC
Bombay Port Trust Employees' Union [*India*] ... BPTEU
Bombay Reports, Appellate Juris [*India*] [*A publication*] (DLA) ... Bom AC
Bombay Reports, Crown Cases [*India*] [*A publication*] (ILCA) ... Bom Cr Cas
Bombay Reports, Crown Cases [*India*] [*A publication*] (DLA) ... Bomb Cr Cas
Bombay Reports, Oudh Cases [*India*] [*A publication*] (DLA) ... Bom OC
Bombay Sadr Diwani Adalat Reports [*A publication*] (DLA) ... Bellasis
Bombay Select Cases, Sadr Diwani Adalat [*India*] [*A publication*] (DLA) ... Bomb Sel Cas
Bombay Staff Corps [*British military*] (DMA) ... Bomb SC
Bombay Stock Exchange [*India*] ... BSE
Bombay Unreported Criminal Cases [*1862-98*] [*India*] [*A publication*] (DLA) ... Bom Unrep Cr C
Bombay Unreported Criminal Cases [*1862-98*] [*India*] [*A publication*] (DLA) ... Unrep Cr C
Bomb-Disposal Squad ... BDS
Bomb-Disposal Unit ... BDU
Bombenzielapparat [*Bomb sight*] [*German military - World War II*] ... BZA
Bombenzielgeraet [*Bomb sight*] [*German military - World War II*] ... BZG
Bomber [*Russian aircraft symbol*] ... AR
Bomber [*Designation for US military aircraft*] ... B
Bomber [*Russian aircraft symbol*] ... BB
Bomber [*Military*] ... BMB
Bomber [*Air Force*] (AFM) ... BMBR
Bomber ... BMBR
Bomber (AABC) ... BMR
Bomber [*Russian aircraft symbol*] ... B-SCH
Bomber [*Russian aircraft symbol*] ... DB
Bomber [*Russian aircraft symbol*] ... IL
Bomber [*Russian aircraft symbol*] ... SB-RK
Bomber [*Russian aircraft symbol*] ... ZKB
Bomber Activity Weekly Brief (MCD) ... BAWB
Bomber Air Relay System - Extension (MCD) ... BARS-X
Bomber Air Relay System - Fly Along (MCD) ... BARS-F
Bomber Command [*British military*] (DMA) ... B Cmd
Bomber Command ... BC
Bomber Command [*Army*] ... BOMCOM
Bomber Command Headquarters [*British military*] (DMA) ... BCH
Bomber Command Intelligence Report ... BCIR
Bomber Command Intelligence Summary ... BCIS
Bomber Command Liaison Officer (NATG) ... BCLO
Bomber Command Operational Order ... BCOO
Bomber Command Tactical Planning Committee ... BCTPC
Bomber Control Team [*Air Force*] (DOMA) ... BCT
Bomber Defence Training Flight [*British military*] (DMA) ... BDTF

Bomber Defense Missile [*Air Force*] ..... BDM
Bomber Field ..... B
Bomber Fighter Training System (MCD) ..... BFTS
Bomber (Intruder) [*British military*] (DMA) ..... B(I)
Bomber Operations [*Air Ministry*] [*British World War II*] ..... BOPS
Bomber Reconnaissance Aircraft ..... BR
Bomber Recovery Team [*Air Force*] (DOMA) ..... BRT
Bomber Replenishment Area [*Military*] ..... BRA
Bomber Support ..... BS
Bomber Support Development Unit ..... BSDU
Bomber Transport [*Air Force*] ..... BT
Bomber-Fighter Squadron [*Navy symbol*] ..... VBF
Bombesin [*Biochemistry*] ..... BB
Bombesin [*Biochemistry*] ..... BBS
Bombesin [*Biochemistry*] ..... Bn
Bombesin-Like Peptide [*Biochemistry*] ..... BLP
Bombesin-Releasing Immunoreactivity ..... BRI
Bombing [*JETDS nomenclature*] ..... B
Bombing (AABC) ..... BOM
Bombing Analysis Unit [*Supreme Headquarters, Allied Expeditionary Force*] [*World War II*] ..... BAU
Bombing and Gunnery Flight [*British military*] (DMA) ..... B & GF
Bombing and Gunnery Range ..... BGR
Bombing and Gunnery School [*British*] (DMA) ..... BAGS
Bombing and Gunnery School [*British*] ..... BGS
Bombing and Navigation Inertial Reference ..... BANIR
Bombing and Reconnaissance Navigation ..... BARN
Bombing Computer Set ..... BCS
Bombing Development Unit ..... BDU
Bombing Encyclopedia (CINC) ..... BE
Bombing Exercise [*Military*] (NVT) ..... BOMBEX
Bombing Landplane ..... BLP
Bombing/Navigation (NG) ..... B/N
Bombing/Navigation (DOMA) ..... BOMB/NAV
Bombing over the Horizon ..... BOTH
Bombing Plane [*Navy symbol*] ..... VB
Bombing RADAR Navigation Equipment ..... BRANE
Bombing Report [*Military*] ..... BOMREP
Bombing Report (NATG) ..... BOMREPT
Bombing Restriction Area [*British military*] (DMA) ..... BRA
Bombing Squadron ..... BOMRON
Bombing through Overcast [*By means of RADAR equipment*] ..... BTO
Bombing, Torpedo Plane [*Navy symbol*] ..... VBT
Bombing-Fighting Aircraft [*Navy symbol*] ..... VBF
Bombing-Navigation System (AFM) ..... BNS
Bombline ..... BL
Bombsight (AABC) ..... BOMST
Bomb-to-Warhead Conversion (MCD) ..... B/WC
Bomb-to-Warhead Conversion Components (CINC) ..... BWCC
Bombyx mori Nuclear Polyhedrosis Virus ..... BmNPV
BOMEX [*Barbados Oceanographic and Meteorological Experiment*] **Analysis Program** (NOAA) ..... BOMAP
Bomoen [*Norway ICAO location identifier*] (ICLI) ..... ENBM
Bon Accord Airways [*British ICAO designator*] (FAAC) ..... BON
Bon Accord, NB [*Television station call letters*] (RBYB) CBAT-1
Bon Accord, NB [*TV station call letters*] (RBYB) ..... CBAT-TV
Bon Accord Public Library, Alberta [*Library symbol National Library of Canada*] (NLC) ..... ABOA
Bon Accord Public Library, Bon Accord, AB, Canada [*Library symbol*] [*Library of Congress*] (LCLS) ..... CaABoa
Bon Chic, Bon Genre [*Good Style, Good Family*] [*Initialism used to denote French Yuppies*] [*Lifestyle classification*] ..... BCBG
Bon pour Francs [*Value in Francs*] [*French*] ..... BPF
Bon Secours Medical Library, Baltimore, MD [*Library symbol Library of Congress*] (LCLS) ..... MdBBS
Bona Fide [*In Good Faith*] [*Latin*] ..... BF
Bona Fide Occupational Qualification ..... BFOQ
Bona Fide Purchaser [*Legal term*] (DLA) ..... BFP
Bona Fide Purchaser for Value [*of a security, or other negotiable instrument*] [*Legal term*] ..... BFPV
Bonae Feminae [*To the Good Woman*] [*Latin*] ..... BF
Bonae Memoriae [*Of Happy Memory*] [*Latin*] ..... BM
Bonae Memoriae [*of Happy Memory*] [*Reference to a deceased person*] [*Latin*] (BARN) ..... Bon Mem
Bonaguida de Aretio [*Flourished, 1251-58*] [*Authority cited in pre-1607 legal work*] (DSA) ..... Bo
Bonaguida de Aretio [*Flourished, 1251-58*] [*Authority cited in pre-1607 legal work*] (DSA) ..... Bona
Bonaguida de Aretio [*Flourished, 1251-58*] [*Authority cited in pre-1607 legal work*] (DSA) ..... Bonag
Bonair Aviation Ltd. [*Canada ICAO designator*] (FAAC) ..... BNR
Bonaire [*Netherland Antilles*] [*Airport symbol*] (OAG) ..... BON
Bonaire Government Tourist Office (EA) ..... BGTO
Bonanza [*Nicaragua*] [*ICAO location identifier*] (ICLI) ..... MNBZ
Bonanza Airlines (MHDB) ..... BAL
Bonanza Oil & Gas Ltd. [*Toronto Stock Exchange symbol*] ..... BZO
Bonanza, OR [*FM radio station call letters*] (RBYB) ..... KAQX-FM
Bonanza Resources Ltd. [*Toronto Stock Exchange symbol*] ..... BNZ
Bonaparte Record-Republican, Bonaparte, IA [*Library symbol Library of Congress*] (LCLS) ..... IaBonR
Bonaparte Record-Republican, Bonaparte, IA [*Library symbol*] [*Library of Congress*] (LCLS) ..... IaBonRR
Bonar, Inc. [*Toronto Stock Exchange symbol*] ..... BON
Bonaventure [*Canada*] [*Airport symbol*] (OAG) ..... YVB
Bonavista Bay, NF [*AM radio station call letters*] ..... CBGY
Bonavista Bay, NF [*FM radio station call letters*] ..... CJOZ
Bonavista, NF [*Television station call letters*] ..... CJWB
Bonavista, NF [*ICAO location identifier*] (ICLI) ..... CWVA
Bonavista Public Library, Bonavista, NF, Canada [*Library symbol Library of Congress*] (LCLS) ..... CaNfBo
Bonavista Public Library, Newfoundland [*Library symbol National Library of Canada*] (NLC) ..... NFBO
Bonaza School, Alberta [*Library symbol National Library of Canada*] (BIB) ..... ABOS
Bond [*Investment term*] ..... B
Bond [*Investment term*] ..... BD
Bond (ROG) ..... BND
Bond Adjustment [*Finance*] ..... AB
Bond Air Services Ltd. [*Uganda*] [*ICAO designator*] (FAAC) ..... BOD
Bond and Allotment (DNAB) ..... B & A
Bond and Burglary ..... B & BU
Bond and Preferred [*Business term*] ..... BP
Bond and Share Society [*British*] (DBA) ..... BASS
Bond and Share Society (EA) ..... BSS
Bond Anticipation Note [*Banking*] ..... BAN
Bond Club of New York [*New York, NY*] (EA) ..... BCNY
Bond County Community Unit, School District 2, De Land, IL [*Library symbol Library of Congress*] (LCLS) ..... IDelanSD
Bond Dissociation Energy [*Chemistry*] ..... BDE
Bond Enabling Annual Retirement Savings (DFIT) ..... BEARS
Bond Equivalent (TDOB) ..... BE
Bond Equivalent Yield [*Business term*] (EMRF) ..... BEY
Bond Fund [*Finance*] ..... BF
Bond Helicopters Ltd. [*British ICAO designator*] (FAAC) ..... BND
Bond Index to the Determination of Inorganic Crystal Structures [*McMaster University, Canada*] ..... BIDICS
Bond International Gold, Inc. [*Toronto Stock Exchange symbol*] ..... BG
Bond Investors Guaranty Insurance ..... BIGI
Bond Law Review [*A publication*] ..... Bond LR
Bond Maturity [*Investment term*] ..... BM
Bond Molecular Orbitals ..... BMO
Bond Negative Resistor ..... BNR
Bond Number [*Chemistry*] ..... BN
Bond Number ..... Bo
Bond Public Library, Wenona, IL [*Library symbol Library of Congress*] (LCLS) ..... IWen
Bond Rating [*Investment term*] ..... BR
Bond Strength Model of Active Sites ..... BSMAS
Bond Test Device (MCD) ..... BTD
Bond Trade Analysis Program [*IBM Corp.*] ..... BTAP
Bond Valence Sum [*Physical chemistry*] ..... BVS
Bondage and Discipline [*or Domination*] ..... B & D
Bondage/Domination (WGA) ..... B/D
Bonded ..... B
Bonded (MSA) ..... BND
Bonded Double Cotton [*Wire insulation*] (KSC) ..... BDC
Bonded Double Paper [*Wire insulation*] (KSC) ..... BDP
Bonded Double Silk [*Wire insulation*] ..... BDS
Bonded Goods [*International trade*] ..... B/G
Bonded Laminates Profiled Ltd. [*British*] ..... BLP
Bonded Motors [*NASDAQ symbol*] (TTSB) ..... BMTR
Bonded Motors, Inc. [*NASDAQ symbol*] (SAG) ..... BMTR
Bonded Motors, Inc. [*Associated Press*] (SAG) ..... BondMot
Bonded Part [*Wire insulation*] (IAA) ..... BP
Bonded Phase Chromatography ..... BPC
Bonded Single Cotton [*Wire insulation*] (MSA) ..... BC
Bonded Single Paper [*Wire insulation*] (IAA) ..... BP
Bonded Single Silk [*Wire insulation*] (MSA) ..... BS
Bonded Spoon Type (DNAB) ..... BST
Bonded Warehouse ..... BW
Bonded Wine Cellar ..... BWC
Bonded Winery ..... BW
Bondell Industries, Inc. [*Vancouver Stock Exchange symbol*] ..... BLI
Bond-Energy Bond-Order [*Chemical kinetics*] ..... BEBO
Bonderize ..... BNDZ
Bondi-Metzner-Sachs [*Physics*] ..... BMS
Bonding ..... BNDG
Bonding ..... BO
Bonding Jig (MCD) ..... BJ
Bonding Tool (AAG) ..... BNTO
Bondo [*Zaire*] [*ICAO location identifier*] (ICLI) ..... FZKP
Bondoukou [*Ivory Coast*] [*Airport symbol*] (OAG) ..... BDK
Bondoukou/Soko [*Ivory Coast*] [*ICAO location identifier*] (ICLI) ..... DIBU
Bond's United States Circuit Reports [*A publication*] (DLA) ..... Bond
Bondsman ..... BNDSMN
Bone Age [*Medicine*] ..... BA
Bone and Joint [*Medicine*] ..... B & J
Bone and Joint [*Medicine*] ..... BJ
Bone Apposition Rate [*Physiology*] ..... BAR
Bone Care International, Inc. [*NASDAQ symbol*] (SAG) ..... BCII
Bone Care International, Inc. [*Associated Press*] (SAG) ..... BoneCre
Bone Care Intl. [*NASDAQ symbol*] (TTSB) ..... BCII
Bone Conduction [*Medicine*] ..... BC
Bone Dry ..... BD
Bone Dry-Weight Basis (IAA) ..... BDWB
Bone Formation ..... BF
Bone Formation Rate [*Medicine*] ..... BFR
Bone Fragment [*Orthopedics*] (DAVI) ..... BF
Bone Graft [*Orthopedics*] ..... BG
Bone Greater Than Air [*Conduction*] ..... B + A
Bone Haft and Scale Cutters Society [*A union*] [*British*] ..... BHSCS

Bone Injury [*Medicine*] .... BI
Bone Marker [*Aviation*] .... BM
Bone Marrow .... BM
Bone Marrow Arrest [*Medicine*] (DMAA) .... BMA
Bone Marrow Aspirate [*Hematology*] (DAVI) .... BMA
Bone Marrow Cell [*Cytology*] .... BMC
Bone Marrow Depression [*Hematology*] (AAMN) .... BMD
Bone Marrow Failure [*Medicine*] (DMAA) .... BMF
Bone Marrow Granulocyte Reserve [*Physiology*] .... BMGR
Bone Marrow Lymphocytosis [*Medicine*] (DMAA) .... BML
Bone Marrow Plasmacytosis [*Oncology*] .... BMPC
Bone Marrow Pressure [*Orthopedics and radiology*] (DAVI) .... BMP
Bone Marrow Prostatic Acid Phosphatase .... BMPAP
Bone Marrow Stem Cell [*Hematology*] .... BMSC
Bone Marrow Transplant [*Medicine*] .... BMT
Bone Marrow Transplant Unit [*Hematology*] (DAVI) .... BMTU
Bone Mineral Content [*Medicine*] .... BMC
Bone Mineral Content/Width [*Medicine*] .... BMC/W
Bone Mineral Densitrometry [*Medicine*] .... BMD
Bone Mineral Density [*Medicine*] .... BMD
Bone Morphogenetic Protein .... BMP
Bone Phosphate of Lime .... BPL
Bone. Precedents in Conveyancing [*1838-40*] [*A publication*] (DLA) .... Bone Prec
Bone Resorption .... BR
Bone-Derived Growth Factor [*Genetics*] .... BDGF
Bone-Dried Ton .... BDT
Bone-Marrow Derived [*Hematology*] .... B
Bone-Marrow Leucocyte [*Physiology*] .... BML
Bone-Marrow-Derived Cultured Mast Cell .... BMCMC
Bone-Marrow-Derived Lymphocyte [*Hematology*] .... BL
Bone-Marrow-Derived Macrophage [*Biochemistry*] .... BMM
Bone-Marrow-Derived Mast Cells [*Cytology*] .... BMMC
Bone-Marrow-Derived Suppressor Factor [*Immunology*] .... BDSF
Bone-Patellar Tendon-Tubercle Bone [*Graft*] .... BTB
Bone-Resorbing Factor [*Medicine*] (DMAA) .... BRF
Bones, Joints, and Examination [*Medicine*] (DAVI) .... BJE
Bones, Joints, Muscles [*Medicine*] .... BJM
Bones, Muscles, Joints [*Medicine*] (DMAA) .... BMJ
Bonesteel Public Library, Bonesteel, SD [*Library symbol Library of Congress*] (LCLS) .... SdBo
Bonfield Public Library, Bonfield, ON, Canada [*Library symbol*] [*Library of Congress*] (LCLS) .... CaOBONF
Bonfield Public Library, Ontario [*Library symbol National Library of Canada*] (NLC) .... OBONF
Bongao/Sanga-Sanga, Sulu [*Philippines*] [*ICAO location identifier*] (ICLI) .... RPWN
Bongimba [*Zaire*] [*ICAO location identifier*] (ICLI) .... FZBB
Bongor [*Chad*] [*ICAO location identifier*] (ICLI) .... FTTB
Bonham, TX [*AM radio station call letters*] .... KFYN
Bonham, TX [*FM radio station call letters*] .... KFYZ
Bonhomie & Hattiesburg Southern R. R. [*AAR code*] .... BHS
Bonifati [*Italy ICAO location identifier*] (ICLI) .... LIBW
Bonifay, FL [*FM radio station call letters*] .... WTBB
Bonifay Sand [*A soil type*] .... BS
Bonita Springs, FL [*FM radio station call letters*] .... WRXK
Bonn [*Germany Airport symbol*] (OAG) .... BNJ
Bonn (Bad Godesberg-Plittersdorf) [*Germany ICAO location identifier*] (ICLI) .... EDOJ
Bonn, Frankfurt Am Main [*Germany ICAO location identifier*] (ICLI) .... EDDA
Bonn/Hangelar [*Germany ICAO location identifier*] (ICLI) .... EDKB
Bonne Bay, NF [*Television station call letters*] CBYT-3
Bonne Terre, MO [*FM radio station call letters*] .... KDBB
Bonner Durchmusterung [*Star chart*] .... BD
Bonner General Hospital, Medical Library, Sandpoint, ID [*Library symbol*] [*Library of Congress*] (LCLS) .... IdSanH
Bonner Jahrbuecher [*A publication*] (OCD) .... Bonner Jahrb
Bonner-Bibel (BJA) .... BB
Bonners Ferry, ID [*AM radio station call letters*] .... KBFI
Bonners Ferry, ID [*FM radio station call letters*] .... KRBF
Bonnet (MSA) .... BNT
Bonnet Valve .... BV
Bonnetti's Italian Dictionary [*A publication*] (DLA) .... Bonnetti Ital Dict
Bonneville County District Library, Idaho Falls, ID [*Library symbol*] [*Library of Congress*] (LCLS) .... IdIfC
Bonneville Power Acquisition Guide [*A publication*] (AAGC) .... BAG
Bonneville Power Administration [*Department of Energy*] [*Portland, OR*] .... BPA
Bonneville Power Administration Acquisition [*A publication*] (AAGC) .... BAR
Bonneville Power Administration, Portland, OR [*Library symbol Library of Congress*] (LCLS) .... OrPB
Bonneville Power Administration Selective Dissemination of Information [*Department of the Interior*] .... BPA-SDI
Bonneville Regional Advisory Council [*Terminated, 1978*] [*Department of Energy*] (EGAO) .... BRAC
Bonneville, UT [*Location identifier FAA*] (FAAL) .... BVL
Bonney on Insurance [*A publication*] (DLA) .... Bon Ins
Bonney on Insurance [*A publication*] (DLA) .... Bonn Ins
Bonney-Fessenden Sociograph [*Psychology*] .... BFS
Bonney's Railway Carriers [*A publication*] (DLA) .... Bon RR Car
Bonney's Railway Carriers [*A publication*] (DLA) .... Bonn Car
Bonnie Hartle Fan Club (EA) .... BHFC
Bonnie Lou Bishop Fan Club (EA) .... BLBFC
Bonnyville, AB [*Television station call letters*] CBXFT-1
Bonnyville Municipal Library, Alberta [*Library symbol National Library of Canada*] (NLC) .... ABM
Bonray Drilling [*NASDAQ symbol*] (TTSB) .... BNRY
Bonray Drilling Corp. [*NASDAQ symbol*] (NQ) .... BNRY
Bonray Drilling Corp. [*Associated Press*] (SAG) .... Bonray
Bons Vivants [*An association*] (EA) .... BV
Bonsai and Orchid Association (EAIO) .... BOA
Bonsai Clubs International (EA) .... BCI
Bonsai Society of Australia .... BSA
Bonsai Society of Western Australia .... BSWA
Bonso Electronics [*Associated Press*] (SAG) .... Bonso
Bonso Electronics International, Inc. [*NASDAQ symbol*] (NQ) .... BNSO
Bonso Electronics International, Inc. [*NASDAQ symbol*] (SAG) .... BNSW
Bonso Electronics Intl. [*NASDAQ symbol*] (TTSB) .... BNSOF
Bonso Electrs Intl. Wrrt [*NASDAQ symbol*] (TTSB) .... BNSWF
Bontang [*Indonesia*] [*ICAO location identifier*] (ICLI) .... WRLC
Bonthe [*Sierre Leone*] [*Airport symbol*] (OAG) .... BTE
Bonthe [*Sierra Leone*] [*ICAO location identifier*] (ICLI) .... GFBN
Bontika [*Zaire*] [*ICAO location identifier*] (ICLI) .... FZBF
Bon-Ton Stores [*NASDAQ symbol*] (SPSG) .... BONT
Bon-Ton Stores [*NASDAQ symbol*] (TTSB) .... BONT
Bon-Ton Stores, Inc. [*Associated Press*] (SAG) .... BonTon
Bonum Factum [*A Good or Proper Act, Deed, or Decree*] [*Latin Legal term*] (DLA) .... BF
Bonum Publicum [*The Public Good*] [*Latin*] .... BP
Bonus (ADA) .... BNS
Bonus Aviation [*British*] [*FAA designator*] (FAAC) .... BPT
Bonus Delivery [*Shares*] .... Bnd
Bonus Expeditionary Force .... BEF
Bonus, Extension, and Reenlistment [*Army*] (INF) .... BEAR
Bonus Petroleum Corp. [*Vancouver Stock Exchange symbol*] .... BOU
Bonus Points .... BP
Bonus Vacation Days [*United Auto Workers*] .... BVD
Bony Intraorbital Distance [*Medicine*] (DMAA) .... BIOD
Boob and Bourgeoisie [*H. L. Mencken's portmanteau for the American middle class*] .... BOOBOISIE
BOOG [*British Osborne Owners Group*] **Information Exchange** (NITA) .... BOOGIE
Boogie Down Productions [*Rap recording group*] .... BDP
Book .... B
Book (WDMC) .... b
Book (WDMC) .... bk
Book (AAG) .... BK
Book (VRA) .... bk
Book About Me [*Psychological testing*] .... BAM
Book Acquisition and Bibliographic Service [*National Book Centre*] [*Canada*] .... BABS
Book Action for Nuclear Disarmament [*British*] .... BAND
Book and Periodical Circulation (DGA) .... BPC
Book & Periodical Council (AC) .... BPC
Book Arts Guild (EA) .... BAG
Book Association of Ireland (BARN) .... BAI
Book Auction Records [*A publication British*] .... BAR
Book Club Associates [*British*] .... BCA
Book Club of California, San Francisco, CA [*Library symbol Library of Congress*] (LCLS) .... CSfBk
Book Collector [*A publication*] (BRI) .... BC
Book Collectors' Society of Australia .... BCSA
Book Communications System [*Information service*] .... BCS
Book Designer [*MARC relator code*] [*Library of Congress*] (LCCP) .... bkd
Book Development Council [*British*] .... BDC
Book Edge Guilders' Trade Society (DGA) .... BEGTS
[*The*] **Book Guild Ltd.** [*British*] (ECON) .... BG
[*The*] **Book House** [*ACCORD*] [*UTLAS symbol*] .... BKH
Book House Training Centre [*British*] .... BHTC
Book Indexing .... BINDEX
Book Indexing with Context and Entry Points from Text [*Indexing method*] [*Computer science*] (DIT) .... BICEPT
Book Industry Communication [*British An association*] .... BIC
Book Industry Study Group (EA) .... BISG
Book Industry Systems Advisory Committee [*Book Industry Study Group*] [*New York, NY*] .... BISAC
Book Inventory Building and Library Oriented System (EDAC) .... BIBLIOS
Book Inventory Building Library Information Oriented System [*Orange County Public Library, California*] (NITA) .... BIBLIOS
Book Manufacturers Institute (EA) .... BMI
Book Marketing Council [*British*] .... BMC
Book Marketing Opportunities Database [*Ad-Lib Publications*] [*Information service or system*] (CRD) .... BMO
[*The*] **Book of a Thousand Poems** [*A publication*] .... BoTP
Book of Alternative Services [*Ecclesiastical*] .... BAS
[*The*] **Book of American Negro Poetry** [*A publication*] .... BANP
[*The*] **Book of American Poetry** [*A publication*] .... BAP
[*A*] **Book of American Verse** [*A publication*] .... BAV
[*The*] **Book of Canadian Poetry** [*A publication*] .... BoCaPo
[*A*] **Book of Children's Literature** [*A publication*] .... BoChLi
Book of Classic English Poetry [*A publication*] .... BCEP
Book of Common Prayer [*Episcopalian*] .... BCP
[*A*] **Book of Danish Ballads** [*A publication*] .... BoDaBa
Book of English Literature [*A publication*] .... BEL
[*The*] **Book of Friendship** [*A publication*] .... BoFr
Book of Heroic Verse [*A publication*] .... BHV
[*A*] **Book of Historical Poems** [*A publication*] .... BoHrPo
[*The*] **Book of Humorous Verse** [*A publication*] .... BoHV
[*The*] **Book of Joshua in Greek** [*A publication*] (BJA) .... BJG
Book of Jubilees [*Apocalyptic book*] .... BK JUB
Book of Judgments [*England*] [*A publication*] (DLA) .... Book of Judg
Book of Judgments, by Townshend [*A publication*] (DLA) .... Bk Judg
Book of Living Poems [*A publication*] .... BLP
[*The*] **Book of Living Verse** [*A publication*] .... BLV

[*The*] Book of Living Verse [*A publication*]	BOLiVe
[*A*] Book of Lullabies [*A publication*]	BoL
[*The*] Book of Modern English Poetry [*A publication*]	BMEP
Book of Moroni (AD)	Moro
Book of Mosiah (AD)	Mos
[*The*] Book of Nonsense [*A publication*]	BoN
Book of Omni (AD)	Om
[*A*] Book of Personal Poems [*A publication*]	BPP
Book of Reference	BR
[*A*] Book of Russian Verse [*A publication*]	BoR
[*A*] Book of Scottish Verse [*A publication*]	BSV
[*A*] Book of South African Verse [*A publication*]	BoSA
Book of the Season Scheme [*British*]	BOSS
Book of the Winter [*A publication*]	BoW
[*A*] Book of Treasured Poems [*A publication*]	BTP
Book Order	BO
Book Order and Record Document (PDAA)	BORD
Book Order and Selection [*Computer science*]	BOS
Book Order Register and Invoicing System [*British*] (NITA)	BORIS
Book Order System [*Computer science*] (NITA)	BOS
Book Ordering, Registering and Inventory System (PDAA)	BORIS
Book Packagers Association [*British*] (DBA)	BPA
Book Paper Manufacturers' Association (DGA)	BPMA
Book Prices Current [*1887-1956*] [*A publication British*]	BPC
Book Profit [*Investment term*]	BP
Book Promoters' Association of Canada (AC)	BPAC
Book Promotion Society [*Canada*]	BPS
Book Publisher's Association (NTCM)	BPA
Book Publishers' Association of Canada	BPAC
Book Publisher's Directory [*Later, PD*] [*A publication*]	BPD
Book Publishers Representatives' Association [*British*] (BI)	BPRA
Book Publishing	BP
Book Publishing Development Program [*Canada*]	BPDP
Book Publishing Record (DIT)	BPR
Book Rack (MSA)	BR
Book Records [*Record label*]	Book
Book Registration Number	BRN
Book Report [*A publication*] (BRI)	B Rpt
Book Review	BR
Book Review Editors File [*University Press of New England*] [*Information service or system*] (IID)	BREF
Book Review Index [*Gale Research, Inc.*] [*Detroit, MI*] [*Information service or system*] [*A publication*]	BRI
Book Review Index Annual Cumulation [*A publication*]	BRI-Cum
Book Review Index Master Cumulations [*A publication*]	BRI-MC
Book Review Index: Periodical Reviews, 1976-1984 [*A publication*]	BRI-PR
Book Review Index: Reference Books, 1965-1984 [*A publication*]	BRI-RB
Book Services International [*ACCORD*] [*UTLAS symbol*]	BSI
Book Shelf [*Technical drawings*] (DAC)	BK SH
Book Stacks Unlimited [*Networked bookseller*]	BSU
Book Trade Benevolent Society [*British*]	BTBS
Book Trade Employers' Federation (DGA)	BTEF
Book Trade Systems Network [*Publishers' Association*] [*British*]	BTSN
Book Value [*Business term*]	BV
Book World [*A publication*] (BRI)	BW
Bookbinder (DGA)	BKBNDR
Bookbinder	BKBNDR
Bookbinders' Charitable Society (DGA)	BCS
Bookbindery (DGA)	BDY
Bookbinding (DGA)	BKBNDG
Bookbinding	BKBNDNG
Bookbinding (ROG)	BOOKB
Bookbinding and Allied Trades Management Association (DGA)	BATMA
Bookbinding Cloth (DGA)	BDG CL
Bookbird [*A publication*] (BRI)	Bkbird
Bookcase (MSA)	BC
Bookcase [*s*] [*Freight*]	BK
Bookcliff Junior High School, Grand Junction, CO [*Library symbol Library of Congress*] (LCLS)	CoGjBoJ
Booker Aircraft Museum [*Wycombe Air Park, Booker, Buckinghamshire, England*]	BAM
Booker Gold Explorations [*Vancouver Stock Exchange symbol*]	BGE
Booker T. Washington Foundation (EA)	BTWF
Booker T. Washington National Monument	BOWA
Bookform Drawing (MSA)	BFD
Booking (WDAA)	BKG
Booking Agents Association of Great Britain Ltd. (BI)	BAA
Booking and Sampling for Indirect Standards [*British*]	BASIS
Booking Office [*British*] (ROG)	BO
Bookjacket Designer [*MARC relator code*] [*Library of Congress*] (LCCP)	bjd
Book-Keeper (ADA)	BK
Bookkeeper (WGA)	BKPR
Bookkeeper	BKPR
Bookkeeping	BKG
Bookkeeping (MUGU)	BKPG
Bookkeeping	BKPG
Bookkeeping (ROG)	BOOKK
Booklet (AFM)	BKLT
Booklet Category Test [*Brain dysfunction test*]	BCT
Booklet Pane [*Philately*]	BP
Booklet Pane Society [*Defunct*] (EA)	BPS
Book-Library-Management [*System*]	BLM
Bookline Alert: Missing Books and Manuscripts [*Information service or system A publication*]	BAMBAM
Booklist [*A publication*] (BRI)	BL

Bookmakers' Licensing Board [*South Australia*]	BLB
Bookmakers' Protection Association Ltd. (BI)	BPA
Bookmakers' Revision Committee [*New South Wales, Australia*]	BRC
Bookman's Price Index [*A reference publication listing rare books and their list prices*]	BPI
Book-of-the-Month Club (WDMC)	BOM
Book-of-the-Month Club, Inc.	BOMC
Book-on-Payment [*Travel industry*]	BOP
Book-Physical Inventory Difference [*AEC*]	B-PID
Bookplate [*Bibliography*]	B/PL
Bookplate (WGA)	BKP
Bookplate Designer [*MARC relator code*] [*Library of Congress*] (LCCP)	bpd
Bookplate Society [*London, England*] (EAIO)	BS
Bookplates [*A publication*]	BP
Books (WDAA)	BB
Books (DLA)	bks
Books A Million, Inc. [*NASDAQ symbol*] (SAG)	BAMM
Books A Million, Inc. [*Associated Press*] (SAG)	BookMill
Books & Culture [*A publication*] (BRI)	Bks & Cult
Books by Mail	BBM
Books for Bible Students [*A publication*]	BBS
Books for College Libraries [*A publication of ALA*]	BCL
Books for College Libraries [*UTLAS symbol*]	BCLT
Books for Equal Education [*An association Defunct*]	BEE
Books for Keeps [*A publication*] (BRI)	Bks Keeps
Books for Libraries [*Program*]	BFL
Books for Libraries Micropublications, Freeport, NY [*Library symbol Library of Congress*] (LCLS)	BFL
Books for Professionals/Miller Accounting Publications [*Harcourt, Brace, Jovanovich, Inc.*]	BFP/MAP
Books for the Heart [*A publication*]	BH
Books for the People Fund (EA)	BPF
Books for Your Children [*A publication*] (BRI)	BFYC
Books in Canada [*A publication*] (BRI)	BIC
Books in English (AIE)	BIE
Books in Print [*Bibliographic database*] [*R. R. Bowker Co.*] [*A publication*]	BIP
Books in Series [*A publication*]	BIS
Books Magazine [*A publication*] (BRI)	Books
Books of Regiam Majestatem [*Scotland*] [*A publication*] (DLA)	Reg Maj
Books of Sederunt [*A publication*] (DLA)	Books S
Books of Sederunt [*A publication*] (DLA)	Books Sed
Books on Egypt and Chaldea [*A publication*]	BEC
Books on Tape	BOT
Books-Across-the-Sea [*Project*]	BAS
Books-A-Million [*NASDAQ symbol*] (TTSB)	BAMM
Bookseller	BKSLLR
Bookseller [*MARC relator code*] [*Library of Congress*] (LCCP)	bsl
Booksellers Association of Great Britain and Ireland (EAIO)	BA
Booksellers' Association Service House [*British*]	BASH
Booksellers Clearing House [*Commercial firm British*]	BCH
Booksellers of Great Britain	BGB
Booksellers of Great Britain and Ireland (DGA)	BGD
Booksellers Order Distribution [*British*]	BOD
Bookseller's Order Service [*For-profit subsidiary of American Booksellers Association*] [*Defunct*]	BOS
Booksellers' Provident Institution [*British*] (DGA)	BPI
Booksellers' Provident Institution and Retreat [*British*] (DGA)	BPIR
Bookselling (ROG)	BOOKS
Bookshelf	BKSHLF
Books-on-Japan-in-English [*A publication*]	BJE
Bookstore	BKSTR
Bookwatch [*A publication*] (BRI)	BWatch
Boolarra Virus	BOV
Boole & Babbage [*NASDAQ symbol*] (TTSB)	BOOL
Boole & Babbage, Inc. [*NASDAQ symbol*] (NQ)	BOOL
Boole & Babbage, Inc. [*Associated Press*] (SAG)	BooleB
Boolean [*Mathematics*]	B
Boolean [*Mathematics*]	BOOL
Boolean Algebra [*Mathematics*]	BA
Boolean Approach for Bivalent Optimization [*Computer science*] (PDAA)	BABO
Boolean Array Identifier [*Mathematics*]	BAID
Boolean Assignment Statement [*Mathematics*]	BAS
Boolean Function Designator [*Mathematics*]	BFD
Boolean Function Identifier [*Mathematics*]	BFID
Boolean Logic And State Transfer (EECA)	BLAST
Boolean Normal Form [*Mathematics*]	BNF
Boolean Simple Variable [*Mathematics*]	BSV
Boolean Time Sequence [*Mathematics*]	BTS
Boom (DS)	BM
Boom Antenna (IAA)	BMANT
Boom Control Unit (MCD)	BCU
Boom Controller (MCD)	BC
Boom Defence [*Navy British*]	BD
Boom Defence Depot [*Navy British*]	BDD
Boom Defence Vessel [*Navy British*]	BDV
Boom Defense Officer	BDO
Boom Operator Part Task Trainer (MCD)	BOPTT
Boom Operator Part Task Training Simulator	BOPTTS
Boom Operator Trainer	BOT
Boom Patrol Boat [*British Marines' Special Forces*] [*World War II*]	BPB
Boom Time Remaining (NASA)	BTR
Boomerang Association of Australia	BAA
Boomerangs Disabled Association [*Australia*]	BDA
Boomsail [*Ship's rigging*] (ROG)	BMSL
Boomtown, Inc. [*NASDAQ symbol*] (SAG)	BMTN

Boomtown, Inc. [*Associated Press*] (SAG) ... Boomtwn
Boone and Crockett Club (EA) ... BCC
Boone County Courthouse, Boone, IA [*Library symbol Library of Congress*] (LCLS) ... IaBoCoC
Boone County Recorder's Office, Lebanon, IN [*Library symbol Library of Congress*] (LCLS) ... InLebCR
Boone, IA [*Location identifier FAA*] (FAAL) ... BNW
Boone, IA [*AM radio station call letters*] ... KFGQ
Boone, IA [*FM radio station call letters*] ... KFGQ-FM
Boone, IA [*FM radio station call letters*] (RBYB) ... KRKQ-FM
Boone, IA [*FM radio station call letters*] ... KRUU
Boone, IA [*AM radio station call letters*] ... KWBG
Boone Junior College [*Iowa*] ... BJC
Boone, NC [*FM radio station call letters*] ... WASU
Boone, NC [*AM radio station call letters*] ... WATA
Boone News-Republican, Boone, IA [*Library symbol Library of Congress*] (LCLS) ... IaBoNR
Boone on Corporations [*A publication*] (DLA) ... Boone Corp
Booneville, AR [*FM radio station call letters*] ... KEZU
Booneville, MS [*AM radio station call letters*] ... WBIP
Booneville, MS [*FM radio station call letters*] ... WBIP-FM
Booneville, MS [*FM radio station call letters*] ... WMAE
Booneville, MS [*Television station call letters*] ... WMAE-TV
Boonton Radio Corp. (IAA) ... BRC
Boonville, IN [*AM radio station call letters*] ... WBNL
Boonville, IN [*FM radio station call letters*] ... WBNL-FM
Boonville, MO [*FM radio station call letters*] ... KCLR
Boonville, MO [*AM radio station call letters*] ... KWRT
Boonville, MO [*Location identifier FAA*] (FAAL) ... VER
Boonville, NY [*AM radio station call letters*] ... WBRV
Boonville, NY [*FM radio station call letters*] ... WBRV-FM
Boonville Standard, Boonville, IN [*Library symbol Library of Congress*] (LCLS) ... InBooS
Boonville Warrick County Public Library, Boonville, IN [*Library symbol Library of Congress*] (LCLS) ... InBoo
Booraem's Reports [*6-8 California*] [*A publication*] (DLA) ... Boor
Booraem's Reports [*6-8 California*] [*A publication*] (DLA) ... Booraem
Boosey & Hawkes [*Record label*] [*Great Britain, USA*] (ADA) ... B & H
Boosey & Hawkes [*Record label*] [*Great Britain, USA*] ... BH
Boost Alcohol Consciousness Concerning the Health of University Students [*In association name BACCHUS of the US*] (EA) ... BACCHUS
Boost Discrimination and Track System ... BDTS
Boost Glide Reentry Vehicle [*Air Force*] ... BGRV
Boost, Insertion, and Abort [*Aerospace*] ... BIA
Boost Measurement and Analysis Program (MCD) ... BMAP
Boost Phase Intercept (AABC) ... BPHI
Boost Phase Intercept ... BPI
Boost Phase Track System ... BPTS
Boost Protective Cover [*Apollo*] [*NASA*] ... BPC
Boost Pump (MCD) ... BP
Boost Pump Start (MCD) ... BPS
Boost Stage Discharge Pressure (MCD) ... BSDP
Boost Surveillance and Tracking System [*Satellite*] [*Military*] ... BSTS
Boostan [*Iran*] [*ICAO location identifier*] (ICLI) ... OIAB
Boost-Controlled Decelerating Device ... BCDD
Boosted Kinetic Energy Penetrator [*Proposed submunition*] ... BKEP
Booster ... B
Booster (MUGU) ... BST
Booster [*Military*] (AFM) ... BSTR
Booster and Sustainer ... B & S
Booster Assembly Building [*NASA*] ... BAB
Booster Assembly Contractor [*NASA*] (NASA) ... BAC
Booster Battery ... BB
Booster Brake [*Automotive engineering*] ... B/BRK
Booster Burn-Out (IAA) ... BBO
Booster Change Assembly (MCD) ... BCA
Booster Cutoff Backup ... BCOB
Booster Development ... BD
Booster Dynamic Condition at Abort (SAA) ... BDCAA
Booster Engine [*Rocketry*] ... BE
Booster Engine Cutoff [*Rocketry*] ... BCO
Booster Engine Cutoff [*Rocketry*] ... BECO
Booster Exhaust Stream ... BES
Booster Exhaust Study Test [*NASA*] (NASA) ... BEST
Booster Flight-Acceptance Composite Test [*NASA*] ... B-FACT
Booster Fuel Jacket ... BFJ
Booster Gas Generator ... BGG
Booster Inertial Guidance System [*Aerospace*] ... BIGS
Booster Interstage Assembly [*Aerospace*] ... BIA
Booster Jettison ... BOJ
Booster Lift-Off Mass [*NASA*] (KSC) ... BLOM
Booster Lift-Off Weight [*NASA*] (KSC) ... BLOW
Booster Orbiter (MCD) ... B/O
Booster Press, Howell, NJ [*Library symbol Library of Congress*] (LCLS) ... NjHowB
Booster Pump [*Liquid gas carriers*] ... b
Booster Release Actuator (MCD) ... BRA
Booster Requirements Document ... BRD
Booster Separation Motors [*NASA*] (NASA) ... BSM
Booster Situation Indicator ... BSI
Booster Solid Rocket Motor [*NASA*] (NASA) ... BSRM
Booster Systems Engineer [*NASA*] (KSC) ... BSE
Booster Test Department [*NASA*] (KSC) ... BST
Booster Umbilical Assembly ... BUA
Booster Vacuum Pump ... BVP
Booster Vacuum Pump System ... BVPS
Booster-Distribution Amplifier ... BDA
Booster-Regulator [*NASA*] ... BR
Boot and Shoe Manufacturers' Association and Leather Trades Protection Society [*British*] (BI) ... BASMA
Boot and Shoe Travelers Association of New York (EA) ... BSTANY
Boot and Shoe Travelers Association of New York (SRA) ... BSTANY
Boot and Shoe Workers' Union [*Later, UFCWIU*] ... BSW
Boot and Shoe Workers' Union [*Later, UFCWIA*] (IIA) ... BSWU
Boot or Shoes, or Boot or Shoe Findings [*Freight*] ... BS BSF
Boote. Action at Law [*A publication*] (ILCA) ... Boote Act
Boote. Chancery Practice [*A publication*] (DLA) ... Boote Ch Pr
Bootes [*Constellation*] ... Boo
Bootes [*Constellation*] ... Boot
Boote's Suit at Law [*A publication*] (DLA) ... Boote
Boote's Suit at Law [*A publication*] (DLA) ... Boote SL
Booth American Shipping Corp. (MHDB) ... BASC
Booth. Indictable Offences [*A publication*] (DLA) ... Booth In Of
Booth Library On-Line Circulation [*Data processing system*] [*Eastern Illinois University Charleston, IL*] ... BLOC
Booth Memorial Hospital, Flushing, NY [*Library symbol Library of Congress*] (LCLS) ... NFB
Booth on Real Actions [*A publication*] (DLA) ... Boo R Act
Booth on Real Actions [*A publication*] (DLA) ... Booth R Act
Booth on Real Actions [*A publication*] (DLA) ... Booth Real Act
Booth on Real Actions [*A publication*] (DLA) ... BR Act
Boothbay Harbor, ME [*FM radio station call letters*] ... WCME
Boothby, Lovelace, Bulbulian [*Of Mayo Clinic*] **Unit** (DAVI) ... BLB
Bootheville, LA [*Location identifier FAA*] (FAAL) ... BVE
Booth-Henry-Gorin [*Equations for calculation of net charge and valence of molecule*] ... BHG
Booth's Law of Wills [*A publication*] (DLA) ... Booth Wills
Boots Contract Manufacturing ... BCM
Boots Pure Drug Co. [*Great Britain*] [*Research code symbol*] ... RD
Bootstap Confidence Level [*Mathematics*] ... BCL
Bootstrap [*Computer science*] ... BOOT
Bootstrap [*Computer science*] (HGAA) ... BTSP
Bootstrap (MSA) ... BTST
Bootstrap Combined Programming Language [*Computer science*] (CSR) ... BCPL
Bootstrap Commissioning Program [*Air Force*] ... BCP
Bootstrap Gyroscope (IAA) ... BSG
Bootstrap Protocol [*Telecommunications*] (ACRL) ... BOOTP
Booue [*Gabon*] [*Airport symbol*] (OAG) ... BGB
Booue [*Gabon*] [*ICAO location identifier*] (ICLI) ... FOGB
Booz, Allen & Hamilton, Inc., Chicago, IL [*Library symbol Library of Congress*] (LCLS) ... ICBAH
Booz, Allen & Hamilton Inc. Computer Utilization System (IAA) ... BACUS
Booz-Allen Applied Research, Inc. ... BAARINC
Boozing Urban-Rural Parasites [*Lifestyle classification*] ... BURPIES
Bop Air (Pty) Ltd. [*South Africa ICAO designator*] (FAAC) ... BOP
Bophuthatswana Democratic Party [*Political party*] (PPW) ... BDP
Bor [*Sudan*] [*ICAO location identifier*] (ICLI) ... HSBR
Bora Bora/Motu-Mute [*French Polynesia*] [*ICAO location identifier*] (ICLI) ... NTTB
Borabicyclononane [*Organic chemistry*] ... BBN
Bora-Bora [*French Polynesia*] [*Airport symbol*] (OAG) ... BOB
Bora-Bora [*Society Islands*] [*Airport symbol*] (AD) ... BOB
Boral Ltd ADS [*NASDAQ symbol*] (TTSB) ... BORAY
Borane Methyl Sulfide [*Organic chemistry*] ... BMS
Boras-Viared [*Sweden ICAO location identifier*] (ICLI) ... ESGX
Borate and Aluminum (IIA) ... BORAL
Borated Water Storage Tank [*Nuclear energy*] (NRCH) ... BWST
Borax and Carbon (IIA) ... BORON
Boray Ltd. [*NASDAQ symbol*] (SAG) ... BORA
Boray Ltd. [*Associated Press*] (SAG) ... Boral
Borazjan [*Iran*] [*ICAO location identifier*] (ICLI) ... OIBN
Borcan Resources [*Vancouver Stock Exchange symbol*] ... BOA
Bord Gais Eirecann [*Irish Gas Board*] (EY) ... BGE
Bord Telecom Eireann [*Nationalized industry*] [*Ireland*] (EY) ... BTE
Bordaire Ltd. [*Canada ICAO designator*] (FAAC) ... BOF
Bordano [*Italy*] [*Seismograph station code, US Geological Survey*] (SEIS) ... BORI
Bordeaux [*France*] [*Airport symbol*] (OAG) ... BOD
Bordeaux [*France ICAO location identifier*] (ICLI) ... LFBB
Bordeaux [*France ICAO location identifier*] (ICLI) ... LFXJ
Bordeaux Agents Association [*British*] (BI) ... BAA
Bordeaux/Merignac [*France ICAO location identifier*] (ICLI) ... LFBD
Bordeaux or Rouen [*Shipping*] (ROG) ... B/R
Bordeaux/Saucats [*France ICAO location identifier*] (ICLI) ... LFCS
Bordeaux/Souge [*France ICAO location identifier*] (ICLI) ... LFDO
Bordeaux-Hamburg Inclusive [*Shipping*] ... B/H
Bordeaux-Yvrac [*France ICAO location identifier*] (ICLI) ... LFDY
Borden Chem/Plastics L.P. [*NYSE symbol*] (TTSB) ... BCU
Borden Chemical & Plastics Ltd. [*NYSE symbol*] (SAG) ... BCU
Borden Chemical, Westhill, ON, Canada [*Library symbol Library of Congress*] (LCLS) ... CaOWesBC
Borden Chemical, Westhill, Ontario [*Library symbol National Library of Canada*] (NLC) ... OWESBC
Borden Chemicals & Plastics Ltd. [*Associated Press*] (SAG) ... BordCh
Borden, Inc. [*Wall Street slang name: "Moo Moo"*] [*Associated Press*] (SAG) ... Borden
Borden Museum, Borden, IN [*Library symbol Library of Congress Obsolete*] (LCLS) ... InBoM
Bordentown Historical Society, Bordentown, NJ [*Library symbol Library of Congress*] (LCLS) ... NjBorHi
Border (FAAC) ... BDR
Border Airways [*South Africa ICAO designator*] (FAAC) ... BDA
Border Boundary Police [*Thailand*] (CINC) ... BBP

Border Cargo Selectivity [*USTTA*] (TAG) ... BCS
Border Collie Club of Queensland [*Australia*] ... BCCQ
Border Detection Method [*Radiology*] (DAVI) ... BDM
Border Ecology Project [*Staff consists of Americans and Mexicans concerned with environmental issues*] (CROSS) ... BEP
Border Gateway Protocol [*Computer science*] (PCM) ... BGP
Border Leicester [*Sheep*] ... BL
Border Leicester Sheepbreeders' Association [*Australia*] ... BLSA
Border Leicester Sheepbreeders' Association of New South Wales [*Australia*] ... BLSANSW
Border Line ... BL
Border Mounted Rifles [*British military*] (DMA) ... BMR
Border Patrol ... BOPAT
Border Patrol ... BP
Border Patrol Academy ... BPA
Border Patrol Sector Headquarters ... BPSH
Border Regiment [*British*] ... BR
Border Security Police [*NATO*] (NATG) ... BSP
Border Surveillance [*Military*] ... BS
Border Terrier Club of America (EA) ... BTCA
Border Trade Alliance [*Mexico/US relations*] (CROSS) ... BTA
Border Union Agricultural Society [*British*] ... BUAS
Bordereau [*Statement*] [*French Business term*] ... BORD
Border-Fault System [*Geology*] ... BFS
Borderland Sciences Research Foundation (EA) ... BSRF
Borderline [*Biochemistry*] (DAVI) ... BOD
Borderline [*Biochemistry*] (DAVI) ... BORD
Borderline ... BRD
Borderline Dull [*Medicine*] ... BD
Borderline Glucose Tolerance Test [*Medicine*] (MAE) ... BGTT
Borderline Left-Axis Deviation [*Cardiology*] ... BLAD
Borderline Lepromatous [*Medicine*] ... BL
Borderline Personality Disorder [*Psychology*] ... BPD
Borderline Pumping Temperature [*Automotive engineering*] ... BPT
Borderline Tuberculoid [*Medicine*] ... BT
Borders Group [*NYSE symbol*] (TTSB) ... BGP
Borders Group, Inc. [*NYSE symbol*] (SAG) ... BGP
Borders Group, Inc. [*Associated Press*] (SAG) ... Borders
Bordetella [*Biochemistry*] (DAVI) ... B
Bordetella Pertussis Vaccine ... BPV
Bordet-Gengou [*Bacillus*] [*Microbiology*] ... BG
Bordier & Compagnie [*Bank*] [*Switzerland*] ... B & Cie
Bordj El Amri [*Tunisia*] [*ICAO location identifier*] (ICLI) ... DTTI
Bordj Mokhtar [*Algeria*] [*ICAO location identifier*] (ICLI) ... DATM
Bordj Omar Driss [*Algeria*] [*ICAO location identifier*] (ICLI) ... DAAW
Bordmechaniker [*Flight engineer*] [*German military - World War II*] ... BM
Bore [*Freight*] ... BRE
Bore Autonomic Tester ... BAT
Bore Erosion Gauge Reading ... BEGR
Borea Ecosystem-Atmosphere Study [*Marine science*] (OSRA) ... BOREAS
Boreal Ecosystem-Atmosphere Study (USDC) ... BOREAS
Boreal Institute for Northern Studies, University of Alberta, Edmonton, Alberta [*Library symbol National Library of Canada*] (NLC) ... AEUB
Boreal Northern Titles [*Database*] [*Boreal Institute for Northern Studies*] [*Information service or system*] (CRD) ... BNT
Borealis Technology Corp. [*Associated Press*] (SAG) ... Borealis
Borealis Technology Corp. [*NASDAQ symbol*] (SAG) ... BRLS
Bored Insitu Piles [*Camutek*] [*Software package*] (NCC) ... BPILE
Borehole ... BH
Borehole Capsule ... BHC
Borehole Compensated [*Sonic log*] ... BHC
Borehole Seismometer ... BHS
Borehole Televiewer [*Drilling technology*] ... BHTV
Borescope (MSA) ... BS
Boresight (MSA) ... BRSIT
Boresight (KSC) ... BS
Boresight ... BST
Boresight Adjustment System (PDAA) ... BAS
Boresight Axis ... BSA
Boresight Camera ... BC
Boresight Camera (MUGU) ... BSC
Boresight Collimator Test Set (DWSG) ... BSCTS
Boresight Datum Line [*Military*] ... BSDL
Boresight Error ... BSE
Boresight Error Slope ... BSES
Boresight Fixture (MCD) ... BSF
Boresight Reference Line (DNAB) ... BRL
Boresight Reticle Unit (MCD) ... BRU
Boresight Tower (MUGU) ... BST
Borg & Beck [*Automotive industry supplier*] ... BB
Borg Warner Security Corp. [*NYSE symbol*] (SAG) ... BOR
Borgarfjordur [*Iceland*] [*Airport symbol*] (OAG) ... BGJ
Borge Prien Prove [*Danish intelligence test*] ... BPP
Borger, TX [*Location identifier FAA*] (FAAL) ... BGD
Borger, TX [*FM radio station call letters*] ... KQFX
Borger, TX [*AM radio station call letters*] ... KQTY
Borgess Hospital, Medical Library, Kalamazoo, MI [*Library symbol Library of Congress*] (LCLS) ... MiKB
Borglanda [*Sweden ICAO location identifier*] (ICLI) ... ESMB
Borgninus Cavalcanus [*Flourished, 16th century*] [*Authority cited in pre-1607 legal work*] (DSA) ... Borgnin Cavalcan
Borgward Owners' Club (EA) ... BOC
Borg-Warner Automotive [*Associated Press*] (SAG) ... BorgWAu
Borg-Warner Automotive [*NYSE symbol*] (TTSB) ... BWA
Borg-Warner Automotive, Inc. [*NYSE symbol*] (SPSG) ... BWA
Borg-Warner Corp. [*NYSE symbol*] (SPSG) ... BOR
Borg-Warner Corp. ... BW
Borg-Warner Corp., B-J Electronics Division, Santa Ana, CA [*Library symbol Library of Congress*] (LCLS) ... CStaB-E
Borg-Warner Corp., Borg-Warner Chemicals Technical Center, Washington, WV [*Library symbol Library of Congress*] (LCLS) ... WvWaB
Borg-Warner Corp., Des Plaines, IL [*OCLC symbol*] (OCLC) ... IBW
Borg-Warner Corp., Ingersoll Research Center, Des Plaines, IL [*Library symbol Library of Congress*] (LCLS) ... IDesB
Borg-Warner Corp., York Division, York, PA [*Library symbol Library of Congress*] (LCLS) ... PYB
Borg-Warner Security [*NYSE symbol*] (TTSB) ... BOR
Borg-Warner Security Corp. [*Associated Press*] (SAG) ... BorWSc
Boric Acid [*Inorganic chemistry*] ... BA
Boric Acid [*Pharmacology*] (DAVI) ... H_3BO_3
Boric Acid Concentrator (NRCH) ... BAC
Boric Acid Injection Tank (IEEE) ... BIT
Boric Acid Mix Tank [*Nuclear energy*] (NRCH) ... BAMT
Boric Acid Storage Tank (IEEE) ... BAST
Boric Acid Tank [*Nuclear energy*] (NRCH) ... BAT
Boric Acid Transfer [*Nuclear energy*] (NRCH) ... BAT
Boric Acid Transfer Pump (IEEE) ... BATP
Boring Bar ... BOBR
Boring But Important Information [*Journalism*] (WDMC) ... BBI
Boring Fixture (MCD) ... BF
Boring Fixture (AAG) ... BOFX
Boring Institute (EA) ... BI
Boring Old Fart [*Slang*] (DSUE) ... BOF
Boring Party (EA) ... BP
Boris Becker Fan Club (EA) ... BBFC
Boris Becker of Leimen [*Acronym also refers to pretzel produced by German bakers in recognition of this tennis player*] ... BOBELE
Borjeson-Forssman-Lehmann Syndrome [*Medicine*] (DMAA) ... BFLS
Borkenberge [*Germany ICAO location identifier*] (ICLI) ... EDLB
Borkin Industries Corp. [*Vancouver Stock Exchange symbol*] ... BNI
Borkum [*Germany Airport symbol*] (OAG) ... BMK
Borkum [*Germany ICAO location identifier*] (ICLI) ... EDWR
Borland Database Engine [*Borland International, Inc.*] [*Computer science*] ... BDE
Borland Graphics Interface [*Borland International*] (BYTE) ... BGI
Borland International, Inc. [*NASDAQ symbol*] (SAG) ... BORL
Borland International, Inc. [*Associated Press*] (SAG) ... Borlnd
Borland Intl. [*NASDAQ symbol*] (TTSB) ... BORL
Borland Object Component Architecture [*Borland International, Inc.*] (PCM) ... BOCA
Borland Pascal 7 [*Borland International, Inc.*] [*Computer programming*] (PCM) ... BP7
Borlange [*Sweden*] [*Airport symbol*] (OAG) ... BLE
Borlange [*Sweden ICAO location identifier*] (ICLI) ... ESSD
Born ... B
Born (VRA) ... b
Born (WDMC) ... b
Born (ADA) ... BN
Born ... BO
Born Again Pagans (EA) ... BAP
Born before Arrival [*of mother at hospital*] [*Medicine*] ... BBA
Born Fool (DAS) ... BF
Born in Colony [*British*] (ADA) ... BC
Born in Japan ... BIJ
Born on Arrival [*of mother at hospital*] [*Medicine*] ... BOA
Born Out of Asepsis [*Neonatology and obstetrics*] (DAVI) ... BOA
Born Young [*An association*] (EA) ... BY
Borna Disease [*Medicine*] (PDAA) ... BD
Borna Disease Virus [*Veterinary medicine*] ... BDV
Born-Again Christian ... BAC
Borneo ... Bor
Borneo Island [*MARC geographic area code Library of Congress*] ... a-bn--
Born-Haber Cycle [*Physics*] ... BHC
Bornier Programmable (IAA) ... BP
Born-Infeld Theory [*Physics*] ... BIT
Born-Mayer Equation [*Physics*] ... BME
Born-Oppenheimer Method [*Physical chemistry*] ... BO
Born-Oppenheimer Method [*Physical chemistry*] ... BOM
Bornu Youth Movement - Action Group Alliance [*Nigeria*] ... BYM-AG
Borobudur (VRA) ... Boro
Borocarbon ... BC
Borocarbon Resistor (CET) ... BCR
Borok [*Former USSR Geomagnetic observatory code*] ... BOX
Boromo [*Burkina Faso*] [*ICAO location identifier*] (ICLI) ... DHCO
Boron [*Chemical element*] ... B
Boron [*Symbol is B*] [*Chemical element*] (ROG) ... BOR
Boron Fiber Reinforced Plastics (NASA) ... BFRP
Boron Fluoride-Ethyl Ether [*Organic chemistry*] ... BFEE
Boron Injection Tank [*Nuclear energy*] (NRCH) ... BIT
Boron Management System [*Nuclear energy*] (NRCH) ... BMS
Boron Measurement (System) [*Nuclear energy*] (NRCH) ... BM(S)
Boron Metal Fiber ... BMF
Boron Metals Plant (SAA) ... BMP
Boron Neutron Capture Therapy ... BNCT
Boron Nitride [*Inorganic fiber*] ... BN
Boron Nitride Fiber [*Inorganic fiber*] ... BNF
Boron Nitride Image Guide (PDAA) ... BNIG
Boron Plastic ... BP
Boron Potassium Nitrate ... $BKNO_3$
Boron Pyrolytic Graphite ... BPG
Boron Recycle System [*Nuclear energy*] (NRCH) ... BRS

Boron Storage Tank [*Nuclear energy*] (NRCH) ... BST
Boron Thermal Regeneration System [*Nuclear energy*] (NRCH) ... BTRS
Boron-Aluminum ... BORAL
Boronated Protoporphyrin [*Organic chemistry*] ... BOPP
Boron-Based Fuel ... BBF
Boronophenylalanine [*Organic chemistry*] ... BPA
Boron-Oxygen Hole Centre (PDAA) ... BOHC
Borosilicate Crown (MSA) ... BSC
Boro-Silicate Glass (PDAA) ... BSG
Borough (ROG) ... BGH
Borough ... BO
Borough ... BOR
Borough (ROG) ... BORO
Borough ... BORO
Borough Constituency ... BC
Borough Council ... BC
Borough Fiscal [*British*] (ROG) ... BF
Borough of Manhattan Community College, New York, NY [*Library symbol Library of Congress*] (LCLS) ... NNBMC
Borough of Manhattan Community College, New York, NY [*OCLC symbol*] (OCLC) ... XMC
Boroujen [*Iran*] [*ICAO location identifier*] (ICLI) ... OIFB
Boroujerd [*Iran*] [*ICAO location identifier*] (ICLI) ... OICJ
Borradaile's Civil Cases, Bombay [*1800-24*] [*India*] [*A publication*] (DLA) ... Borr
Borrego Springs [*California*] [*Airport symbol*] (OAG) ... BXS
Borrelia [*Biochemistry*] (DAVI) ... B
Borroloola [*Airport symbol*] ... BOX
Borromeo Seminary of Ohio, Wickliffe, OH [*Library symbol Library of Congress*] (LCLS) ... OWicB
Borror Corp. [*NASDAQ symbol*] (SAG) ... BORR
Borror Corp. [*Associated Press*] (SAG) ... Borror
Borrowed Light (DAC) ... Bit
Borrowed Light (KSC) ... BLT
Borrowed Military Manpower ... BMM
Borrower's Option for Notes and Underwritten Standby [*Finance*] ... BONUS
Borrowings [*Banking*] ... BOR
Borrows, S. A., Detroit, MI [*STAC*] ... BSA
Borthwick. Modes of Prosecuting for Libel [*1830*] [*A publication*] (DLA) ... Borth
Borzhomi [*Former USSR Seismograph station code, US Geological Survey Closed*] (SEIS) ... BOR
Borzoi Club of America (EA) ... BCOA
B.O.S. Better Online Sol Wrrt [*NASDAQ symbol*] (TTSB) ... BOSWF
B.O.S. Better Online Solutions [*NASDAQ symbol*] (TTSB) ... BOSCF
BOS Better Online Solutions Ltd. [*NASDAQ symbol*] (SAG) ... BOSC
BOS Better Online Solutions Ltd. [*Associated Press*] (SAG) ... BOSLtd
BOS Better Online Solutions Ltd. [*NASDAQ symbol*] (SAG) ... BOSW
BO-S-AIRE Corp. [*Air carrier designation symbol*] ... BOSX
Bosal International Management NV [*Belgium ICAO designator*] (FAAC) ... BOS
Bosanquet and Darby's Limitations [*A publication*] (DLA) ... Bos & D Lim
Bosanquet and Puller's English Common Pleas, Exchequer, and House of Lords Rep orts [*1796-1804*] [*A publication*] (DLA) ... B & P
Bosanquet and Puller's English Common Pleas Reports [*126, 127 English Reprint*] [*A publication*] (DLA) ... Bos & P
Bosanquet and Puller's English Common Pleas Reports [*126, 127 English Reprint*] [*A publication*] (DLA) ... Bos & P (Eng)
Bosanquet and Puller's English Common Pleas Reports [*126, 127 English Reprint*] [*A publication*] (DLA) ... Bos & Pu
Bosanquet and Puller's English Common Pleas Reports [*126, 127 English Reprint*] [*A publication*] (DLA) ... Bos & Pul
Bosanquet and Puller's New Reports, English Common Pleas [*1804-07*] [*A publication*] (DLA) ... B & PNR
Bosanquet and Puller's New Reports, English Common Pleas [*1804-07*] [*A publication*] (DLA) ... Bos & PNR
Bosanquet and Puller's New Reports, English Common Pleas [*1804-07*] [*A publication*] (DLA) ... Bos & PNR (Eng)
Bosanquet and Puller's New Reports, English Common Pleas [*1804-07*] [*A publication*] (DLA) ... Bos & Pul NR
Bosanquet and Puller's New Reports, English Common Pleas [*1804-07*] [*A publication*] (ILCA) ... Bos N R
Bosanquet and Puller's New Reports, English Common Pleas [*1804-07*] [*A publication*] (DLA) ... BPNR
Bosanquet and Puller's New Reports, English Common Pleas [*1804-07*] [*A publication*] (DLA) ... New Rep
Bosanquet and Puller's New Reports, English Common Pleas [*1804-07*] [*A publication*] (DLA) ... NR
Bosanquet's Rules of Pleading [*A publication*] (DLA) ... Bos Pl
Bosaso [*Somalia*] [*Airport symbol*] (OAG) ... BSA
Bosaso [*Somalia*] [*ICAO location identifier*] (ICLI) ... HCMF
Boscawen on Convictions [*A publication*] (DLA) ... Bosc Con
Boscombe Down [*British ICAO location identifier*] (ICLI) ... EGDM
Boscombe Down MOD/PE [*British ICAO designator*] (FAAC) ... BDN
Bose-Chaudhuri-Hocquenghem [*Cyclic codes*] [*Telecommunications*] (MCD) ... BCH
Bose-Einstein [*Statistics*] (IAA) ... BE
Bose-Einstein Condensation [*Cryogenius*] [*Physics*] ... BEC
Bose-Einstein Statistics ... BES
Bosler Free Library, Carlisle, PA [*Library symbol Library of Congress*] (LCLS) ... PCarl
Bosnaair [*Yugoslavia*] [*ICAO designator*] (FAAC) ... BAA
Bosnian Canadian Relief Association (AC) ... BCRA
Bosobe-Boshwe [*Zaire*] [*ICAO location identifier*] (ICLI) ... FZBK
Bosondjo [*Zaire*] [*ICAO location identifier*] (ICLI) ... FZGB
Bosphorus Hava Yollari Turizm Ve Ticaret AS [*Turkey*] [*ICAO designator*] (FAAC) ... BSP
Bosque Alegre [*Argentina*] [*Seismograph station code, US Geological Survey Closed*] (SEIS) ... BOS
Bosque Farms, NM [*FM radio station call letters*] (RBYB) ... KEXT
Bossangoa [*Central African Republic*] [*Airport symbol*] (AD) ... BSN
Bossangoa [*Central African Republic*] [*ICAO location identifier*] (ICLI) ... FEFS
Bossembele [*Central African Republic*] [*ICAO location identifier*] (ICLI) ... FEFL
Bossier Parish Library, Benton, LA [*Library symbol Library of Congress*] (LCLS) ... LBeB
Bost [*Afghanistan*] [*ICAO location identifier*] (ICLI) ... OABT
Boston [*Diocesan abbreviation*] [*Massachusetts*] (TOCD) ... BO
Boston [*Massachusetts*] [*Airport symbol*] ... BOS
Boston [*Massachusetts*] ... BOST
Boston [*Massachusetts*] [*ICAO location identifier*] (ICLI) ... KRBN
Boston Acoustics [*NASDAQ symbol*] (TTSB) ... BOSA
Boston Acoustics, Inc. [*NASDAQ symbol*] (NQ) ... BOSA
Boston Acoustics, Inc. [*Associated Press*] (SAG) ... BostAc
Boston & Albany Railroad ... B & A
Boston & Albany Railroad ... B & ARR
Boston & Albany Railroad [*AAR code*] ... BA
Boston & Fitchburg Railroad ... B & F
Boston & Maine Corp. ... B & M
Boston & Maine Corp. [*AAR code*] ... BM
Boston & Maine Railroad [*Later, Boston & Maine Corp.*] ... B & MRR
Boston Assesment of Severe Aphasia [*Medicine*] (DMAA) ... BASA
Boston Athenaeum, Boston, MA [*OCLC symbol*] (OCLC) ... BAT
Boston Athenaeum, Boston, MA [*Library symbol Library of Congress*] (LCLS) ... MBAt
Boston Bancorp. [*Associated Press*] (SAG) ... BostBc
Boston Bancorp [*Formerly, South Boston Savings Bank*] [*NASDAQ symbol*] (NQ) ... SBOS
Boston Bar Association, Boston, MA [*Library symbol Library of Congress*] (LCLS) ... MBBA
Boston Bar, BC [*FM radio station call letters*] ... CKGO-1
Boston Beer 'A' [*NYSE symbol*] (TTSB) ... SAM
Boston Beer Co. [*Associated Press*] (SAG) ... BostBeer
Boston Beer Co. [*Associated Press*] (SAG) ... BstBeer
Boston Beer Co. [*NYSE symbol*] (SAG) ... SAM
Boston Biomedica, Inc. [*NASDAQ symbol*] (SAG) ... BBII
Boston Biomedica, Inc. [*Associated Press*] (SAG) ... BostnBio
Boston Biomedical Library Consortium [*Library network*] ... BBLC
Boston Biomedical Research Institute [*Research center*] (RCD) ... BBRI
Boston Bruins Hockey Fan Club (EA) ... BBHFC
Boston Celtics [*NYSE symbol*] (SPSG) ... BOS
Boston Celtics Ltd. [*Associated Press*] (SAG) ... BCelts
Boston Celtics L.P. [*NYSE symbol*] (TTSB) ... BOS
Boston Chicken [*NASDAQ symbol*] (TTSB) ... BOST
Boston Chicken, Inc. [*NASDAQ symbol*] (SAG) ... BOST
Boston Chicken, Inc. [*Associated Press*] (SAG) ... BostChk
Boston College [*Chestnut Hill, MA*] ... BC
Boston College (GAGS) ... Boston C
Boston College, Chestnut Hill, MA [*OCLC symbol*] (OCLC) ... BXM
Boston College, Chestnut Hill, MA [*Library symbol Library of Congress*] (LCLS) ... MChB
Boston College Industrial and Commercial Law Review [*A publication*] (AAGC) ... BC Indus & Com L Rev
Boston College. Law Review [*A publication*] (DLA) ... Boston College L Rev
Boston College Law School, Newton, MA [*OCLC symbol*] (OCLC) ... BXL
Boston College Mathematics Institute [*Boston College*] [*Research center*] (RCD) ... BCMI
Boston College. Third World Law Journal [*A publication*] (DLA) ... BC Third World LJ
Boston College, Weston Observatory, Weston, MA [*Library symbol Library of Congress*] (LCLS) ... MChB-WO
Boston Communications Group, Inc. [*NASDAQ symbol*] (SAG) ... BCGI
Boston Communications Group, Inc. [*Associated Press*] (SAG) ... BostnCm
Boston Computer Exchange ... BCE
Boston Computer Exchange (CDE) ... BOCOEX
Boston Computer Society (EA) ... BCS
Boston Conservatory of Music ... BCM
Boston Consulting Group (ECON) ... BCG
Boston Consulting Group, Chicago, IL [*Library symbol Library of Congress*] (LCLS) ... ICBCG
Boston Diagnostic Aphasia Examination ... BDAE
Boston Diagnostic Inventory of Basic Skills [*Speech and language therapy*] (DAVI) ... BDIBS
Boston Edison [*NYSE symbol*] (TTSB) ... BSE
Boston Edison 7.75% Dep Ptd [*NYSE symbol*] (TTSB) ... BSEPrB
Boston Edison 8.25% Dep Pfd [*NYSE symbol*] (TTSB) ... BSEPrA
Boston Edison Co. [*Associated Press*] (SAG) ... BosE
Boston Edison Co. [*Associated Press*] (SAG) ... BostEd
Boston Edison Co. [*NYSE symbol*] (SPSG) ... BSE
Boston Exchange Automated Communication Order-Routing Network (DFIT) ... BEACON
Boston, GA [*FM radio station call letters*] ... WTUF
Boston Grain and Flour Exchange (EA) ... BGFE
Boston Hebrew College (BJA) ... BHC
Boston International Choreography Competition ... BICC
Boston Irish ... BI
Boston Law Reporter [*A publication*] (DLA) ... Bost Law Rep
Boston Law Reporter [*A publication*] (DLA) ... Bost LR
Boston Life Sciences [*NASDAQ symbol*] (TTSB) ... BLSI
Boston Life Sciences, Inc. [*NASDAQ symbol*] (SAG) ... BLSI
Boston Life Sciences, Inc. [*Associated Press*] (SAG) ... BostLfSci
Boston Life Sciences Wrrt [*NASDAQ symbol*] (TTSB) ... BLSIW

Boston/Logan International [*Massachusetts*] [*ICAO location identifier*] (ICLI) .... KBOS
Boston, MA [*Location identifier FAA*] (FAAL) .... DGU
Boston, MA [*Location identifier FAA*] (FAAL) .... LIP
Boston, MA [*Location identifier FAA*] (FAAL) .... LQN
Boston, MA [*Location identifier FAA*] (FAAL) .... MDC
Boston, MA [*Location identifier FAA*] (FAAL) .... NIK
Boston, MA [*Location identifier FAA*] (FAAL) .... NMF
Boston, MA [*Television station call letters*] .... WABU
Boston, MA [*FM radio station call letters*] .... WBCN
Boston, MA [*FM radio station call letters*] .... WBCS
Boston, MA [*FM radio station call letters*] .... WBMX
Boston, MA [*AM radio station call letters*] .... WBNW
Boston, MA [*FM radio station call letters*] .... WBUR
Boston, MA [*AM radio station call letters*] .... WBZ
Boston, MA [*Television station call letters*] .... WBZ-TV
Boston, MA [*Television station call letters*] .... WCVB
Boston, MA [*AM radio station call letters*] .... WEEI
Boston, MA [*FM radio station call letters*] .... WERS
Boston, MA [*AM radio station call letters*] .... WEZE
Boston, MA [*Television station call letters*] .... WFXT
Boston, MA [*FM radio station call letters*] .... WGBH
Boston, MA [*Television station call letters*] .... WGBH-TV
Boston, MA [*Television station call letters*] .... WGBX
Boston, MA [*Television station call letters*] .... WHDH
Boston, MA [*AM radio station call letters*] .... WILD
Boston, MA [*FM radio station call letters*] .... WJMN
Boston, MA [*AM radio station call letters*] .... WMEX
Boston, MA [*FM radio station call letters*] .... WMJX
Boston, MA [*AM radio station call letters*] (RBYB) .... WNRB
Boston, MA [*FM radio station call letters*] .... WODS
Boston, MA [*FM radio station call letters*] .... WRBB
Boston, MA [*AM radio station call letters*] .... WRKO
Boston, MA [*AM radio station call letters*] .... WROL
Boston, MA [*Television station call letters*] .... WSBK
Boston, MA [*FM radio station call letters*] .... WUMB
Boston, MA [*FM radio station call letters*] .... WZLX
Boston, MA [*Location identifier FAA*] (FAAL) .... ZBW
Boston Museum of Fine Arts .... BMFA
Boston Museum of Science, Boston, MA [*Library symbol Library of Congress*] (LCLS) .... MBN
Boston Naming Test [*Analysis of lexical processing disorders*] .... BNT
Boston, Nashua [*New Hampshire*] [*ICAO location identifier*] (ICLI) .... KZBW
Boston National Historic Sites Commission [*Government agency, discontinued, 1960*] .... BNHSC
Boston Naval Shipyard .... BNS
Boston Naval Shipyard .... BNSY
Boston Navy Yard [*Later, Boston Naval Shipyard*] .... BNYD
Boston, New York, Washington [*Proposed name for possible "super-city" formed by growth and mergers of other cities*] .... BOSNYWASH
Boston Ordnance District [*Military*] (AAG) .... BOD
Boston Police Court. Reports [*A publication*] (DLA) .... Bos Pol Rep
Boston Police Court. Reports [*A publication*] (DLA) .... Bost Pol Rep
Boston Private Bancorp [*Associated Press*] (SAG) .... BostPrv
Boston Private Bancorp [*NASDAQ symbol*] (SAG) .... BPBC
Boston Public Library and Eastern Massachusetts Regional Public Library System, Boston, MA [*Library symbol Library of Congress*] (LCLS) .... MB
Boston Records [*Record label*] .... Bo
Boston Red Sox [*Baseball team*] .... BOSOX
Boston Redevelopment Authority .... BRA
Boston Restaurant Assoc [*NASDAQ symbol*] (TTSB) .... BRAI
Boston Restaurant Assoc Wrrt [*NASDAQ symbol*] (TTSB) .... BRAIW
Boston Restaurant Associates [*Associated Press*] (SAG) .... BostRest
Boston Restaurant Associates [*Associated Press*] (SAG) .... BostRs
Boston Restaurant Associates [*NASDAQ symbol*] (SAG) .... BRAI
Boston Review [*A publication*] (BRI) .... Boston R
Boston School of Occupational Therapy [*Tufts University*] .... BSOT
Boston Scientific [*NYSE symbol*] (TTSB) .... BSX
Boston Scientific Corp. [*Associated Press*] (SAG) .... BostSc
Boston Scientific Corp. [*NYSE symbol*] (SPSG) .... BSX
Boston Shipping Association (EA) .... BSA
Boston Sickle Cell Center [*Boston City Hospital*] [*Research center*] (RCD) .... BSCC
Boston Star Trek Association (EA) .... BSTA
Boston State College, Boston, MA [*Library symbol Library of Congress*] (LCLS) .... MBSC
Boston State College Library, Boston, MA [*OCLC symbol*] (OCLC) .... BST
Boston Stock Exchange .... B
Boston Stock Exchange [*Massachusetts*] .... BSE
Boston Symphony Orchestra .... BSO
Boston Tea Party II [*An association*] (EA) .... BTPII
Boston Technology [*Associated Press*] (SAG) .... BostTech
Boston Technology [*NYSE symbol*] (SAG) .... BSN
Boston Technology [*NASDAQ symbol*] (SAG) .... BSTN
Boston Technology, Inc. [*Associated Press*] (SAG) .... BostTc
Boston Terminal Co. [*AAR code*] .... BTCO
Boston Terrier Club of America (EA) .... BTCA
Boston Test for Examining Aphasia [*Speech and language therapy*] (DAVI) .... BTEA
Boston Theological Institute (EA) .... BTI
Boston Theological Institute, Cambridge, MA [*OCLC symbol*] (OCLC) .... BTI
Boston Theological Institute, Learning Development Program, Boston, MA [*Library symbol Library of Congress*] (LCLS) .... MBTI
Boston Theological Institute Library [*Library network*] .... BTI
Boston to Washington [*Proposed name for possible "super-city" formed by growth and mergers between these two*] .... BOSWASH
Boston Transportation Authority (BARN) .... BTA
Boston University (GAGS) .... Boston U
Boston University [*Massachusetts*] .... BU
Boston University, Boston, MA [*OCLC symbol*] (OCLC) .... BOS
Boston University, Boston, MA [*Library symbol Library of Congress*] (LCLS) .... MBU
Boston University. International Law Journal [*A publication*] (DLA) .... BU Int'l LJ
Boston University Marine Program [*Boston University*] [*Research center*] .... BUMP
Boston University, School of Education, Boston, MA [*Library symbol Library of Congress*] (LCLS) .... MBU-E
Boston University School of Law (DLA) .... BUSL
Boston University, School of Law, Boston, MA [*Library symbol Library of Congress*] (LCLS) .... MBU-L
Boston University, School of Medicine, Boston, MA [*OCLC symbol*] (OCLC) .... MBU
Boston University, School of Medicine, Boston, MA [*Library symbol Library of Congress*] (LCLS) .... MBU-M
Boston University, School of Theology, Boston, MA [*OCLC symbol*] (OCLC) .... BZM
Boston University, School of Theology, Boston, MA [*Library symbol Library of Congress*] (LCLS) .... MBU-T
Boston Women's Health Book Collective .... BWHBC
Boston Wool Trade Association (EA) .... BWTA
BostonFed Bancorp [*AMEX symbol*] (TTSB) .... BFD
Bostonfed Bancorp, Inc. [*AMEX symbol*] (SAG) .... BFD
Bostonfed Bancorp, Inc. [*Associated Press*] (SAG) .... Bostnfd
Bostonian Society (EA) .... BS
Bostonian Society, Boston, MA [*Library symbol Library of Congress*] (LCLS) .... MBBS
Boston-to-Washington Corridor .... BOWASH
Bostwick, GA [*FM radio station call letters*] .... WMOQ
Boswell Enterprise, Boswell, IN [*Library symbol Library of Congress*] (LCLS) .... InBosE
Boswell, GA [*FM radio station call letters*] (RBYB) .... WTHA-FM
Boswell's Reports, Scotch Court of Sessions [*A publication*] (DLA) .... Bosw
Bosworth's New York Superior Court Reports [*A publication*] (DLA) .... Bos
Bosworth's New York Superior Court Reports [*A publication*] (DLA) .... Bosw
Botanic Garden .... BG
Botanic Gardens of Adelaide and State Herbarium [*Australia*] .... BGASH
Botanical .... BOTAN
Botanical Gardens Conservation Secretariat (GNE) .... BGCS
Botanical Origin .... BO
Botanical Society, London .... BSL
Botanical Society of America (EA) .... BSA
Botanical Society of the British Isles .... BSBI
Botanico-Periodicum-Huntianum [*Book title*] .... B-P-H
Botany [*or Botanist*] .... BOT
Botany Bay National Park [*Australia*] .... BBNP
Botany Bay Regional Planning and Development Committee [*Australia*] .... BBRPDC
Botany-Genetics Library, McGill University, Montreal, Quebec [*Library symbol National Library of Canada*] (BIB) .... QMMBG
Bote aus Zion (BJA) .... BoZ
Boteka [*Zaire*] [*ICAO location identifier*] (ICLI) .... FZGT
Botetourt-Rockbridge Regional Library, Lexington, VA [*Library symbol Library of Congress*] (LCLS) ViLx
Both (DAVI) .... B
Both Bones [*With reference to fractures*] [*Medicine*] .... BB
Both Dates Inclusive [*Business term*] .... BDI
Both Ends .... BENDS
Both Ends, All Time Saved [*Shipping*] .... BEATS
Both Eyes [*Pharmacy*] .... O^2
Both Faces [*Technical drawings*] .... BF
Both Hands [*Psychometrics*] .... BH
Both Lower Extremities [*Medicine*] .... BLE
Both Lower Extremities [*Neurology and orthopedics*] (DAVI) .... BLE's
Both of This Parish .... BOTP
Both Sideband .... BSB
Both Sides [*Technical drawings*] .... BS
Both Upper Extremities [*Medicine*] (DMAA) .... BUE
Both Upper Extremities [*Neurology and orthopedics*] (DAVI) .... BUE's
Both Way Trunk .... BWT
Both Ways [*Technical drawings*] .... BW
Bother (ABBR) .... BTHR
Bothered (ABBR) .... BTHRD
Bothered about Dungeons & Dragons [*Video game*] .... BADD
Bothering (ABBR) .... BTHRG
Bothersome (ABBR) .... BTHRSM
Both-to-Blame [*Shipping*] .... B/B
Botopasie [*Surinam*] [*Airport symbol*] (OAG) .... BTO
Botopasie [*Surinam*] [*ICAO location identifier*] (ICLI) .... SMBO
Botswana [*Aircraft nationality and registration mark*] (FAAC) A2
Botswana [*Spaceflight Tracking and Data Network*] [*NASA*] .... BOT
Botswana .... BOTS
Botswana (VRA) .... Botsw
Botswana [*MARC country of publication code Library of Congress*] (LCCP) .... bs
Botswana [*ANSI two-letter standard code*] (CNC) .... BW
Botswana [*ANSI three-letter standard code*] (CNC) .... BWA
Botswana [*MARC geographic area code Library of Congress*] (LCCP) .... f-bs--
Botswana [*IYRU nationality code*] (IYR) .... RB
Botswana Democratic Party [*Political party*] (PPW) .... BDP
Botswana Independence Party [*Political party*] (PPW) .... BIP
Botswana, Lesotho, Swaziland .... BLS
Botswana Liberal Party [*Political party*] (PPW) .... BLP
Botswana National Airways .... BNA

Botswana National Front [*Political party*] (PPW) ... BNF
Botswana National Productivity Centre ... BNPC
Botswana Notes and Records [*A publication*] ... BNR
Botswana People's Party [*Political party*] (PPW) ... BPP
Botswana Progressive Union ... BPU
Botswana Protectorate Federal Party ... BPFP
Botswana Renewable Energy Technology Project [*Ministry of Mineral Resources and Water Affairs in cooperation with United States Agency for International Development*] [*Research center*] ... BRET
Bottega (VRA) ... btga
Bottineau, ND [*FM radio station call letters*] ... KBTO
Bottle ... BOT
Bottle (MCD) ... BT
Bottle ... BTL
Bottle Cleaning/Charging Station ... BC/CS
Bottle Drainage ... BD
Bottle-Baby Meal [*Airline notation*] ... BBML
Bottled ... BOTLD
Bottled (ABBR) ... BTLD
Bottled in Bond [*Wines and spirits*] ... B/B
Bottled in Bond [*Wines and spirits*] ... BIB
Bottler ... BTTLR
Bottles per Minute (WGA) ... BPM
Bottling (ABBR) ... BTLG
Bottling ... BTLG
Bottom ... B
Bottom ... BO
Bottom (KSC) ... BOT
Bottom (VRA) ... bot
Bottom [*Commonly used*] (OPSA) ... BOT
Bottom [*Commonly used*] (OPSA) ... BOTTM
Bottom [*Commonly used*] (OPSA) ... BOTTOM
Bottom ... BTM
Bottom ... BTM
Bottom Bounce [*SONAR propogation mode*] [*Navy*] (NG) ... BB
Bottom Bounce/Omnidirectional Transmission [*Navy*] ... BB/ODT
Bottom Bounce/Track [*Navy*] ... BB/T
Bottom Center [*Valve position*] ... BC
Bottom Chord ... BC
Bottom Contour [*Navy British*] ... BC
Bottom Dead Center [*Engineering*] ... BDC
Bottom Dead Point ... BDP
Bottom Down (OA) ... BD
Bottom Dropped Out [*Investment term*] ... BDO
Bottom Environmental Sensing System ... BESS
Bottom Face [*Technical drawings*] ... BF
Bottom Finding Pinger ... BFP
Bottom Grille (OA) ... BG
Bottom Hole Assembly [*Well drilling technology*] ... BHA
Bottom Hole Circulating Temperature [*Oil well borehole*] ... BHCT
Bottom Hole Pressure [*Oil well borehole*] ... BHP
Bottom Hole Static Temperature [*Oil well borehole*] ... BHST
Bottom Hole Temperature [*Oil well borehole*] ... BHT
Bottom Hole (Treating) Pressure [*Oil well borehole*] ... BH(T)P
Bottom Layer [*Technical drawings*] ... BL
Bottom Lead Left (MSA) ... BTLL
Bottom Lead Right (MSA) ... BTLR
Bottom Left Side (MCD) ... BLS
Bottom Level ... BL
Bottom Ocean Monitor [*Marine science*] (MSC) ... BOM
Bottom of Active Fuel [*Nuclear energy*] (GFGA) ... BAF
Bottom of Conduit (NRCH) ... BOC
Bottom of Edge ... BOE
Bottom of Hole [*Geology*] ... BOH
Bottom Plane (MSA) ... BP
Bottom Pressure Fluctuation ... BPF
Bottom Pressure Recorder [*Marine science*] (OSRA) ... BPR
Bottom Pressure Recorder (USDC) ... BPR
Bottom Pumparound [*Drilling technology*] ... BPA
Bottom Reflection [*Navy*] (NVT) ... BR
Bottom Reflection Active SONAR System ... BRASS
Bottom Refraction Acoustic Telemetry System (MCD) ... BRATS
Bottom Register (OA) ... BR
Bottom Right Side (MCD) ... BRS
Bottom Sediment [*Maps and charts*] ... BS
Bottom Sediment and Water [*in crude oil*] ... BSW
Bottom Settlings [*of crude oil in storage*] ... BS
Bottom Simulating Reflector [*Oceanography*] ... BSR
Bottom SONAR Marker ... BSM
Bottom Topography Survey System [*Naval Oceanographic Office*] ... BOTOSS
Bottom Up ... BU
Bottom Value ... BOTVAL
Bottom Water Temperature [*Oceanography*] ... BWT
Bottom Withdrawal [*Tube*] ... BW
Bottomed (ABBR) ... BTMD
Bottoming (MSA) ... BOTMG
Bottoming (ABBR) ... BTMG
Bottomless (ABBR) ... BTMLS
Bottom-Loading Transfer Cask [*Nuclear energy*] (NRCH) ... BLTC
Bottom-Mounted Impact Locations System [*Missile technology*] ... BMILS
Bottom-Mounted Instrumentation System (MCD) ... BOMIS
Bottom-Oriented Shrimp Harvester ... BOSH
Bottom-Up Greedy ... BUG
Bottom-Up Modular Programming ... BUMP
Bottom-Up Review ... BUR
Bott's Poor Law Cases [*1560-1833*] [*England*] [*A publication*] (DLA) ... Bott PL Cas
Bott's Poor Law Cases [*1560-1833*] [*England*] [*A publication*] (DLA) ... Bott's PL
Bott's Poor Law Cases [*1560-1833*] [*England*] [*A publication*] (DLA) ... BPL
Bott's Poor Law Cases [*1560-1833*] [*England*] [*A publication*] (DLA) ... BPL Cas
Bott's Poor Law Cases [*1560-1833*] [*England*] [*A publication*] (DLA) ... BPL Cases
Bott's Poor Law Settlement Cases [*A publication*] (DLA) ... Bott
Bott's Poor Law Settlement Cases [*A publication*] (DLA) ... Bott Poor Law Cas
Bott's Poor Law Settlement Cases [*A publication*] (DLA) ... Bott Set Cas
Bott's Poor Laws [*A publication*] (DLA) ... Bott PL
Bott's Poor Laws, by Const [*1560-1833*] [*A publication*] (DLA) ... Const
Bott's Poor Laws, by Court [*A publication*] (DLA) ... Court
Bottu [*France*] [*Research code symbol*] ... BO
Botulinum Neurotoxin ... BoNT
Botulinum Toxin ... BOT
Botulism [*Medicine*] (ABBR) ... BTLM
Botulism Toxoid Pentavalent [*Biochemistry*] (DAVI) ... ABCDE
Botwood Public Library, Botwood, NF, Canada [*Library symbol Library of Congress*] (LCLS) ... CaNfBot
Botwood Public Library, Newfoundland [*Library symbol National Library of Canada*] (NLC) ... NFBOT
Bou Saada [*Algeria*] [*ICAO location identifier*] (ICLI) ... DAAD
Bou Sfer [*Algeria*] [*ICAO location identifier*] (ICLI) ... DAOE
Bouake [*Ivory Coast*] [*Airport symbol*] (OAG) ... BYK
Bouake [*Ivory Coast*] [*ICAO location identifier*] (ICLI) ... DIBK
Bouar [*Central African Republic*] [*Airport symbol*] (AD) ... BOP
Bouar [*Central African Republic*] [*ICAO location identifier*] (ICLI) ... FEFO
Boublik, Alder, Chen, Kreglewski Equation [*Physical chemistry*] ... BACK
Boucher's Instituts au Droit Maritime [*A publication*] (DLA) ... Bouch Ins Dr Mar
Boufarik [*Algeria*] [*ICAO location identifier*] (ICLI) ... DAAK
Bougainville Copper Ltd. [*Australia*] ... BCL
Bougainville Revolutionary Army [*Papua New Guinea*] [*Political party*] (EY) ... BRA
Bougair [*ICAO designator*] (AD) ... JX
Bought (WGA) ... BGHT
Bought (ROG) ... BGT
Bought ... BO
Bought ... BOT
Bought ... BT
Bought Book [*Tea trade*] (ROG) ... BB
Bought Ledger and Expenditure Analysis Package (PDAA) ... BLEAP
Bought Off (MCD) ... BO
Bougouni [*Mali*] [*ICAO location identifier*] (ICLI) ... GABG
Bouguer Corrected Free-Air Gradient [*Geophysics*] ... BCFAG
Bouillon Filtre [*Bouillon Filtrate*] ... BF
Boulangerie, Confiserie, Tabac [*Bakery, Confectionary, and Tobacco*] [*Canadian Union*] ... BCT
Boulay-Paty. Droit Commun [*A publication*] (DLA) ... Boul P Dr Com
Boulder [*Wyoming*] [*Seismograph station code, US Geological Survey*] (SEIS) ... BDW
Boulder [*Maps and charts*] ... Bld
Boulder [*Colorado*] [*Seismograph station code, US Geological Survey Closed*] (SEIS) ... BO1
Boulder [*Colorado*] [*Seismograph station code, US Geological Survey Closed*] (SEIS) ... BOU
Boulder [*Colorado*] [*Airport symbol*] (OAG) ... WBU
Boulder Atmospheric Observatory [*Army*] (OSRA) ... BAO
Boulder Atmospheric Observatory (USDC) ... BAO
Boulder City [*Nevada*] [*Seismograph station code, US Geological Survey Closed*] (SEIS) ... BCN
Boulder City Library, Boulder City, NV [*Library symbol Library of Congress*] (LCLS) ... NvBc
Boulder City, NV [*Location identifier FAA*] (FAAL) ... BLD
Boulder City, NV [*FM radio station call letters*] (RBYB) ... KQOL
Boulder, CO [*AM radio station call letters*] ... KBCO
Boulder, CO [*FM radio station call letters*] ... KBCO-FM
Boulder, CO [*AM radio station call letters*] (RBYB) ... KBVI
Boulder, CO [*FM radio station call letters*] ... KGNU
Boulder, CO [*FM radio station call letters*] ... KRKS
Boulder, CO [*Television station call letters*] ... KTVJ
Boulder Dam [*Arizona*] [*Seismograph station code, US Geological Survey Closed*] (SEIS) ... BDA
Boulder Junction, WI [*Location identifier FAA*] (FAAL) ... BDJ
Boulder Laboratory Macrosystem [*National Institute of Standards and Technology*] ... BOUMAC
Boulder Mountain Resources [*Vancouver Stock Exchange symbol*] ... BMR
Boulder Public Library, Boulder, CO [*Library symbol Library of Congress*] (LCLS) ... CoB
Boulder Valley School, Boulder, CO [*Library symbol*] [*Library of Congress*] (LCLS) ... CoBVS
Boulder Valley School District, Boulder, CO [*OCLC symbol*] (OCLC) ... BOA
Boulders [*Quality of the bottom*] [*Maps and charts*] ... Blds
Bouldin's Reports [*119 Alabama*] [*A publication*] (DLA) ... Bould
Boulevard (EY) ... BD
Boulevard (EY) ... BLD
Boulevard (EY) ... BLVD
Boulevard (VRA) ... blvd
Boulevard (DD) ... Blvd
Boulevard [*Postal Service standard*] (OPSA) ... BLVD
Boulevard ... BLVD
Boulevard (DD) ... boul
Boulevard ... BOUL
Boulevard [*Commonly used*] (OPSA) ... BOULEVARD
Boulevard [*Commonly used*] (OPSA) ... BOULV
Boulia [*Australia Airport symbol*] (OAG) ... BQL
Boulmer [*British ICAO location identifier*] (ICLI) ... EGQM

Boulnois' Reports [*Bengal*] [*A publication*] (DLA) .... Bouln
Boulnois' Reports [*Bengal*] [*A publication*] (DLA) .... Boulnois
Boulsa [*Burkina Faso*] [*ICAO location identifier*] (ICLI) .... DHEA
Bouna [*Ivory Coast*] [*Airport symbol*] (OAG) .... BQO
Bouna/Tehini [*Ivory Coast*] [*ICAO location identifier*] (ICLI) .... DIBN
Bouncing-Ball Generator .... BBG
Bound (ADA) .... B
Bound .... BD
Bound (WDMC) .... bd.
Bound Brook Chronicle, Bound Brook, NJ [*Library symbol Library of Congress*] (LCLS) .... NjBbC
Bound Brook Memorial Library, Bound Brook, NJ [*Library symbol Library of Congress*] (LCLS) .... NjBb
Bound/Free [*Ratio*] [*Biochemistry*] .... B/F
Bound Hepatitis Antibody [*Medicine*] (DMAA) .... BHA
Bound in Boards .... BDS
Bound in Boards [*Book production*] (WDMC) .... bds.
Bound Plasma Tryptophan (PDAA) .... BPT
Bound Seam (DNAB) .... BS
Bound Serum Iron [*Serology*] .... BSI
Bound to Stay Bound Books, Inc. .... BTSB
Bound With (ROG) .... BW
Boundary (WGA) .... BD
Boundary (AABC) .... BDRY
Boundary (KSC) .... BDY
Boundary (AFM) .... BNDRY
Boundary (DNAB) .... BNDY
Boundary, AK [*Location identifier FAA*] (FAAL) .... BYA
Boundary and Annexation Survey [*Bureau of the Census*] (GFGA) .... BAS
Boundary and Interior Layer (MCD) .... BAIL
Boundary County Library District, Bonners Ferry, ID [*Library symbol*] [*Library of Congress*] (LCLS) .... IdBnf
Boundary Element Analysis System [*Computational Mechanics Ltd.*] [*Software package*] (NCC) .... BEASY
Boundary Element Method (IAA) .... BEM
Boundary Element Tape [*Computational Mechanics Ltd.*] [*Software package*] (NCC) .... BET
Boundary Estimate Message [*Aviation code*] .... EST
Boundary Integral Equation (MCD) .... BIE
Boundary Intermediate System [*Computer science*] (TNIG) .... BIS
Boundary Layer .... BL
Boundary Layer Acoustic Monitor (MCD) .... BLAM
Boundary Layer Aerodynamic Technology [*Auto racing*] .... BLAT
Boundary Layer Control .... BLC
Boundary Layer Control Outlet [*Mitsubishi*] [*Aerodynamics*] [*Automotive engineering*] .... BLCO
Boundary Layer Control System [*Fluid mechanics*] (IAA) .... BLCS
Boundary Layer Flow .... BLF
Boundary Layer Induction Stack Suppressor (CAAL) .... BLISS
Boundary Layer Instrumentation Package [*Meteorology*] .... BLIP
Boundary Layer Instrumentation System [*Meteorology*] .... BLIS
Boundary Layer Integral Matrix Procedure (KSC) .... BLIMP
Boundary Layer LIDAR System (MCD) .... BLLS
Boundary Layer Model (MCD) .... BLM
Boundary Layer Profile [*Meteorology*] .... BLP
Boundary Layer Separation .... BLS
Boundary Layer Thrust Vector Control (MCD) .... BLTVC
Boundary Layer Zone .... BLZ
Boundary Light (IAA) .... BOL
Boundary Lights [*Aviation*] (DA) .... BO
Boundary Marker (MCD) .... BM
Boundary Monument [*Control point*] [*Nautical charts*] .... Bdy Mon
Boundary Museum, Grand Forks, BC, Canada [*Library symbol*] [*Library of Congress*] (LCLS) .... CaBGFBM
Boundary Museum, Grand Forks, British Columbia [*Library symbol National Library of Canada*] (NLC) .... BGFBM
Boundary Phase Plasticity (PDAA) .... BPP
Boundary Plasma Sheet .... BPS
Boundary Router [*Computer science*] (TNIG) .... BR
Boundary Stimulus [*To light*] .... BS
Boundary Trap .... BT
Boundary Value Analysis [*Computer program test*] .... BVA
Boundary Value Problem .... BVP
Boundary Waters Canoe Area [*Minnesota*] .... BWCA
Boundary-Condition .... BC
Boundary-Layer Sub-Programme Data Centre [*GARP Atlantic Tropical Experiment*] (MSC) .... BSDC
Boundary-Scan Test [*John Fluke Manufacturing Co., Inc.*] .... BST
Boundary-Spanning Activity (PDAA) .... BSA
Bounded Carry Inspection Adder (PDAA) .... BCIA
Bounded Cellular Space (PDAA) .... BCS
Bounded Error Navigation System (MCD) .... BENS
Bounded Right Context (MHDI) .... BRC
Bounded-Input Bounded-Output [*Computer science*] (MHDB) .... BIBO
Boundiali [*Ivory Coast*] [*Airport symbol*] (OAG) .... BXI
Boundiali [*Ivory Coast*] [*ICAO location identifier*] (ICLI) .... DIBI
Boundji [*Congo*] [*Airport symbol*] (OAG) .... BOE
Boundji [*Congo*] [*ICAO location identifier*] (ICLI) .... FCOB
Bountiful Peak [*Utah*] [*Seismograph station code, US Geological Survey Closed*] (SEIS) .... BPU
Bountiful, UT [*Location identifier FAA*] (FAAL) .... BTF
Bountiful, UT [*FM radio station call letters*] (RBYB) .... KURR-FM
Bountiful, UT [*FM radio station call letters*] .... KUTQ
Bounty Information Service (EA) .... BIS
Bouraq Indonesia Airlines (FEA) .... BIA
Bouraq Indonesia Airlines [*ICAO designator*] (AD) .... BO
Bouraq Indonesia Airlines PT [*ICAO designator*] (FAAC) .... BOU
Bourbon Public Library, Bourbon, IN [*Library symbol Library of Congress*] (LCLS) .... InBou
Bourdeaux Resources Ltd. [*Vancouver Stock Exchange symbol*] .... BDX
Bourdin on the Land Tax [*A publication*] (DLA) .... Bourd LT
Bourdon Tube Element .... BTE
Bourem [*Mali*] [*ICAO location identifier*] (ICLI) .... GABR
Bourg/Ceyreziat [*France ICAO location identifier*] (ICLI) .... LFHS
Bourgas [*Bulgaria*] [*Airport symbol*] (OAG) .... BOJ
Bourgeois [*Typography*] (DGA) .... BOURG
Bourges [*France ICAO location identifier*] (ICLI) .... LFLD
Bourke [*Australia Airport symbol*] (OAG) .... BRK
Bourke on the Indian Law of Limitations [*A publication*] (DLA) .... Bourke Lim
Bourke's Parliamentary Precedents [*1842-56*] [*England*] [*A publication*] (DLA) .... Bourke PP
Bourke's Reports, Calcutta High Court [*India*] [*A publication*] (DLA) .... Bourke
Bourn (Cambs) [*British ICAO location identifier*] (ICLI) .... EGSN
Bournemouth [*England*] [*Airport symbol*] (OAG) .... BOH
Bournemouth/Hurn [*British ICAO location identifier*] (ICLI) .... EGHH
Bourns Assist [*Medicine*] (DAVI) .... BA
Boussinesq Viscosity Model (MCD) .... BVM
Bousso [*Chad*] [*ICAO location identifier*] (ICLI) .... FTTS
Bousso [*Chad*] [*Airport symbol*] (AD) .... OUT
Boutilimit [*Mauritania*] [*ICAO location identifier*] (ICLI) .... GQNB
Boutilimit [*Mauritania*] [*Airport symbol*] (AD) .... OTL
Boutique .... BTQ
Boutwell's Manual of the United States Tax System [*A publication*] (DLA) .... Bout Man
Bouvet Island [*MARC country of publication code Library of Congress*] (LCCP) .... bv
Bouvet Island [*ANSI two-letter standard code*] (CNC) .... BV
Bouvet Island [*ANSI three-letter standard code*] (CNC) .... BVT
Bouvet Island [*MARC geographic area code Library of Congress*] (LCCP) .... lsbv--
Bouvier's Institutes of American Law [*A publication*] (DLA) .... Bou Inst
Bouvier's Institutes of American Law [*A publication*] (DLA) .... Bouv Inst
Bouvier's Law Dictionary [*A publication*] (DLA) .... Bou Dic
Bouvier's Law Dictionary [*A publication*] (DLA) .... Bouv
Bouvier's Law Dictionary [*A publication*] (DLA) .... Bouv L Dict
Bouvier's Law Dictionary [*A publication*] (DLA) .... Bouv Law Dict
Bouvier's Law Dictionary [*A publication*] (DLA) .... Bouvier
Bouygues Offshore SA [*Associated Press*] (SAG) .... Bouygs
Bouygues Offshore SA [*NYSE symbol*] (SAG) .... BWG
Bovey Public Library, Bovey, MN [*Library symbol*] [*Library of Congress*] (LCLS) .... MnBov
Bovie-Assisted Uvulopalatoplasty (DMAA) .... BAUP
Bovill's Patent Cases [*A publication*] (DLA) .... Bov Pat Ca
Bovine Albumin [*Physiology*] (MAE) .... BA
Bovine Albumin in Phosphate Buffer [*Medicine*] (DMAA) .... BAP
Bovine Albumin Phosphate Saline [*Physiology*] .... BAPS
Bovine Alimentary Papilloma Virus [*Medicine*] (DMAA) .... BAPV
Bovine Aortic Endothelium .... BAE
Bovine Artery Endothelial Cell [*Cytology*] .... BAEC
Bovine Beta-Lactoglobulin [*Biochemistry*] .... BBLG
Bovine Capillary Endothelial [*Cytology*] .... BCE
Bovine Carbonic Anhydrase [*An enzyme*] .... BCA
Bovine Chymotrypsin (DMAA) .... BCtr
Bovine Coronavirus [*Biochemistry*] .... BCV
Bovine Cutaneous Papilloma Virus [*Medicine*] (DMAA) .... BCPV
Bovine Derived Growth Factor [*Biochemistry*] .... BDGF
Bovine Embroyonic Spleen Cells [*Medicine*] (DMAA) .... BESP
Bovine Embryo Skeletal Muscle .... BESM
Bovine Embryonic Kidney Cells [*Medicine*] (DMAA) .... BEK
Bovine Embryonic Lung [*Medicine*] (DMAA) .... BEL
Bovine Enteritis [*Medicine*] (MAE) .... BE
Bovine Enterovirus .... BEV
Bovine Feces Virus [*Veterinary medicine*] (DAVI) .... BFV
Bovine Follicle-Stimulating Hormone [*Biochemistry*] .... BFSH
Bovine Follicular Fluid .... BFF
Bovine Gamma Globulin [*Immunology*] .... BGG
Bovine Growth Hormone [*Endocrinology*] .... BGH
Bovine Immunodeficiency Virus .... BIV
Bovine Immunodeficiency-Like Virus [*Immunology*] (DAVI) .... BIV
Bovine Leukemia Virus .... BLV
Bovine Lumpy Skin Disease [*Medicine*] (DMAA) .... BLSD
Bovine Lung Lipids [*Biochemistry*] .... BLL
Bovine Milk Lysozyme [*Biochemistry*] (OA) .... BML
Bovine Neutrophil Beta-Defensin [*Biochemistry*] .... BNBD
Bovine Pancreatic Polypeptide .... BPP
Bovine Pancreatic Trypsin Inhibitor [*Biochemistry*] .... BPTI
Bovine Papillomavirus [*Veterinary medicine*] .... BPV
Bovine Papillomavirus Vaccine [*Veterinary medicine*] .... BPV
Bovine Paragenital Papilloma Virus [*Medicine*] (DMAA) .... BPPV
Bovine Parathyroid Hormone [*Endocrinology*] .... bPTH
Bovine Pituitary Extract .... BPE
Bovine Plasma Albumin .... BPA
Bovine Protein Kinase C [*An enzyme*] .... bPKC
Bovine Pulmonary Artery Endothelium Cell [*Cell line*] .... BPEC
Bovine Red Blood Cell [*Hematology*] (MAE) .... BRBC
Bovine Research Center at Cornell [*Cornell University*] [*Research center*] (RCD) .... BRCC
Bovine Rhodopsin [*Physiology*] .... bRHOD
Bovine Serum Albumin [*Immunology*] .... BSA
Bovine Serum Amine Oxidase [*An enzyme*] .... BSAO
Bovine Somatotropin [*Endocrinology*] .... BST

Bovine Spinal Cord Protein [*Medicine*] (DMAA) ... BSCP
Bovine Spongiform Encephalopathy [*Veterinary medicine*] ... BSE
Bovine Substance K ... bSK
Bovine Thyroid-Stimulating Hormone [*Endocrinology*] ... BTSH
Bovine Thyrotropin [*Endocrinology*] (DAVI) ... BTSH
Bovine Trophoblast Protein [*Biochemistry*] ... BTP
Bovine Vaginitis Virus [*Veterinary medicine*] (MAE) ... BVV
Bovine Viral Diarrhea ... BVD
Bovine Viral Diarrhea Virus ... BVDV
Bow and Stern Thruster [*of a ship*] (DS) ... BS
Bow Buoyancy ... BBYCY
Bow Designation Light (IAA) ... BDLT
Bow Diving ... BDVG
Bow Door ... BDO
Bow Island Public Library, Alberta [*Library symbol National Library of Canada*] (NLC) ... ABI
Bow Island Public Library, Bow Island, AB, Canada [*Library symbol Library of Congress*] (LCLS) ... CaABi
Bow Light ... BWLT
Bow Plane ... BPLA
Bow Shock [*Astrophysics*] ... BS
Bow Thruster [*of a ship*] (DS) ... BT
Bow Tie Manufacturers Association (EA) ... BTMA
Bow Valley Naturalists (AC) ... BVN
Bow Valley Resource Services Ltd. [*Toronto Stock Exchange symbol*] ... BOW
Bowater Faculty of Business [*Deakin University*] [*Australia*] ... BFB
Bowater, Inc. [*NYSE symbol*] (SPSG) ... BOW
Bowater, Inc. [*Associated Press*] (SAG) ... Bowat
Bowater, Inc. [*Associated Press*] (SAG) ... Bowatr
Bowater Inc.'C'8.40% Dep Pfd [*NYSE symbol*] (TTSB) ... BOWPrC
Bowater Inc. Dep'B'7%'PRIDES' [*NYSE symbol*] (TTSB) ... BOWPrB
Bowden Pioneer Museum, Alberta [*Library symbol National Library of Canada*] (BIB) ... ABOM
Bowden Public Library, Alberta [*Library symbol National Library of Canada*] (NLC) ... ABOW
Bowdock [*Navy symbol*] ... YBD
Bowdoin College, Brunswick, ME [*OCLC symbol*] (OCLC) ... BBH
Bowdoin College, Brunswick, ME [*Library symbol Library of Congress*] (LCLS) ... MeB
Bowdon College, Bowdon, GA [*Library symbol Library of Congress Obsolete*] (LCLS) ... GBowdC
Bowdon Railway & Transportation (IIA) ... BR & T
Bowdon Railway Co. [*AAR code*] ... BODN
Bowel [*Medicine*] ... BO
Bowel Care of Choice [*Medicine*] (DMAA) ... BCOC
Bowel Impaction [*Gastroenterology*] (DAVI) ... BI
Bowel Injection ... BI
Bowel Movement [*Medicine*] ... BM
Bowel Obstruction [*Medicine*] ... BO
Bowel or Bladder [*Medicine*] (DAVI) ... BB
Bowel Sounds [*Medicine*] ... BS
Bowel Sounds Normal [*Medicine*] ... BSN
Bowel Sounds Normal and Active [*Medicine*] (AAMN) ... BSNA
Bowels [*Medicine*] (BARN) ... B
Bowels Not Open [*Medicine*] ... BNO
Bowels Opened [*Medicine*] ... BO
Bowels Opened Regularly [*Medicine*] (MAE) ... BOR
Bowen [*Queensland*] [*Airport symbol*] (AD) ... ZBO
Bowen [*Australia Airport symbol Obsolete*] (OAG) ... ZBO
Bowen Island, BC [*Television station call letters*] (RBYB) ... CHAN-2
Bowen Island Public Library, British Columbia [*Library symbol National Library of Canada*] (BIB) ... BBI
Bowen's Political Economy [*A publication*] (DLA) ... Bowen Pol Econ
Bowes Lyon Resources Ltd. [*Vancouver Stock Exchange symbol*] ... BWY
Bowhunters Who Care (EA) ... BWC
Bowie State College, Bowie, MD [*Library symbol Library of Congress*] (LCLS) ... MdBo
Bowie State College Library, Bowie, MD [*OCLC symbol*] (OCLC) ... BCM
Bowie State University (GAGS) ... Bowie St U
Bowie, TX [*Location identifier FAA*] (FAAL) ... GMZ
Bowie, TX [*AM radio station call letters*] ... KRJT
Bowie, TX [*FM radio station call letters*] ... KRJT-FM
Bowker Out of Print Books [*Source file*] [*UTLAS symbol*] ... BWK
Bowker's International Serials Database [*R. R. Bowker Co.*] [*Information service or system*] (IID) ... BISD
Bowker's Publisher Authority Database [*R. R. Bowker Co.*] [*Information service or system*] (CRD) ... BPAD
Bowl America, Inc. [*Associated Press*] (SAG) ... BowlA
Bowl America, Inc. [*AMEX symbol*] (SPSG) ... BWL
Bowl Vent [*Automotive engineering*] ... BV
Bowled [*Cricket*] ... B
Bowled Out ... B
Bowler and Bowers' United States Comptroller's Decisions [*2, 3*] [*A publication*] (DLA) ... B & B
Bowler and Bowers' United States Comptroller's Decisions [*2, 3*] [*A publication*] (DLA) ... Bow
Bowler's London Session Records [*1605-85*] [*A publication*] (DLA) ... Bow
Bowles Engineering Corp. ... BEC
Bowles on Libel [*A publication*] (DLA) ... Bowl Lib
Bowlin Outdoor Advertising & Travel Ctr., Inc. [*NASDAQ symbol*] (SAG) ... BWLN
Bowlin Outdoor Advertising & Travel Ctr., Inc. [*Associated Press*] (SAG) ... BwlOtdr
Bowling ... BOWL
Bowling Apparel Manufacturers of America (EA) ... BAM
Bowling Centers Association of Florida (SRA) ... BCAF
Bowling Centers Association of Michigan (SRA) ... BCAM
Bowling Club [*Generic term*] (WGA) ... BC
Bowling Green [*Ohio*] [*Seismograph station code, US Geological Survey*] (SEIS) ... BGO
Bowling Green [*Kentucky*] [*Airport symbol*] (AD) ... BWG
Bowling Green College of Commerce [*Later, a division of Western Kentucky State College*] ... BGCC
Bowling Green Elementary School, East Meadow, NY [*Library symbol Library of Congress*] (LCLS) ... NEmBGE
Bowling Green Elementary School, Westbury, NY [*Library symbol*] [*Library of Congress*] (LCLS) ... NWeBGE
Bowling Green Junior High School, Bowling Green, OH [*Library symbol*] [*Library of Congress*] (LCLS) ... OBgJH
Bowling Green, KY [*Location identifier FAA*] (FAAL) ... BWG
Bowling Green, KY [*AM radio station call letters*] ... WBGN
Bowling Green, KY [*Television station call letters*] ... WBKO
Bowling Green, KY [*FM radio station call letters*] ... WBVR
Bowling Green, KY [*FM radio station call letters*] ... WCVK
Bowling Green, KY [*FM radio station call letters*] ... WDNS
Bowling Green, KY [*AM radio station call letters*] ... WKCT
Bowling Green, KY [*Television station call letters*] ... WKGB
Bowling Green, KY [*Television station call letters*] ... WKNT
Bowling Green, KY [*FM radio station call letters*] ... WKYU
Bowling Green, KY [*Television station call letters*] ... WKYU-TV
Bowling Green, KY [*AM radio station call letters*] ... WLBJ
Bowling Green, KY [*FM radio station call letters*] ... WWHR
Bowling Green, MO [*AM radio station call letters*] ... KPCR
Bowling Green, MO [*FM radio station call letters*] ... KPCR-FM
Bowling Green, OH [*FM radio station call letters*] ... WBGU
Bowling Green, OH [*Television station call letters*] ... WBGU-TV
Bowling Green, OH [*AM radio station call letters*] ... WJYM
Bowling Green, OH [*FM radio station call letters*] ... WRQN
Bowling Green Senior High School, Bowling Green, OH [*Library symbol*] [*Library of Congress*] (LCLS) ... OBgSH
Bowling Green State University [*Ohio*] ... BGSU
Bowling Green State University (GAGS) ... Bowl Gr St U
Bowling Green State University, Bowling Green, OH [*OCLC symbol*] (OCLC) ... BGU
Bowling Green State University, Bowling Green, OH [*Library symbol Library of Congress*] (LCLS) ... OBgU
Bowling Green State University, Center for Archival Collections, Bowling Green, OH [*Library symbol Library of Congress*] (LCLS) ... OBgU-C
Bowling Green, VA [*Location identifier FAA*] (FAAL) ... APH
Bowling League of Ireland (EAIO) ... BLI
Bowling Proprietors' Association of America (EA) ... BPAA
Bowling Proprietors' Association of America - Duckpin Activities Department [*Defunct*] (EA) ... BPAA-DAD
Bowling Writers Association of America (EA) ... BWAA
Bowman [*South Carolina*] [*Seismograph station code, US Geological Survey*] (SEIS) ... BOW
Bowman Aviation, Inc. [*ICAO designator*] (FAAC) ... BMN
Bowman Gray School of Medicine, Winston-Salem, NC [*OCLC symbol*] (OCLC) ... NBG
Bowman, ND [*Location identifier FAA*] (FAAL) ... BOD
Bowman, ND [*AM radio station call letters*] ... KPOK
Bowman, SC [*FM radio station call letters*] ... WACJ
Bowman-Birk Soybean Inhibitor [*Medicine*] (DMAA) ... BBI
Bowman's Capsule (MAE) ... BC
Bowmanville Museum, Ontario [*Library symbol National Library of Canada*] (BIB) ... OBOM
Bowmar Canada Ltd., Ottawa, ON, Canada [*Library symbol Library of Congress*] (LCLS) ... CaOOBC
Bowmar Canada Ltd., Ottawa, Ontario [*Library symbol National Library of Canada*] (NLC) ... OOBC
Bowmar Instr $3.00 Cv Pfd [*AMEX symbol*] (TTSB) ... BOMPr
Bowmar Instrument [*AMEX symbol*] (TTSB) ... BOM
Bowmar Instrument Corp. [*AMEX symbol*] (SPSG) ... BOM
Bowmar Instrument Corp. [*Associated Press*] (SAG) ... Bowmr
Bowne & Co. [*AMEX symbol*] (TTSB) ... BNE
Bowne & Co., Inc. [*AMEX symbol*] (SPSG) ... BNE
Bowne & Co., Inc. [*Associated Press*] (SAG) ... Bowne
Bowne Information Systems (NITA) ... BIS
Bowstead on Agency [*1896-1951*] [*A publication*] (DLA) ... Bowstead
Bowstring ... BWSTRN
Bowtex Energy (Canada) Corp. [*Toronto Stock Exchange symbol*] ... BXE
Bowyer. Commentaries on the Constitutional Law of England [*2nd ed.*] [*1846*] [*A publication*] (DLA) ... Bow Cons Law
Bowyer. Commentaries on Universal Public Law [*1854*] [*A publication*] (DLA) ... Bow Com
Bowyer. Commentaries on Universal Public Law [*1854*] [*A publication*] (DLA) ... Bow Pub Law
Bowyer. Introduction to the Study and Use of the Civil Law [*1874*] [*A publication*] (DLA) ... Bow Int
Bowyer's Modern Civil Law [*A publication*] (DLA) ... Bow Civ Law
Bowyer's Modern Civil Law [*A publication*] (DLA) ... Bowyer Mod Civil Law
Box ... BX
Box (VRA) ... bx
Box Bark Strips [*Construction*] (BARN) ... BBS
Box Container [*Shipping*] (DS) ... bx
Box Core [*Marine geology*] ... BC
Box Culvert Association [*British*] (DBA) ... BCA
Box Diffusion [*Oceanography*] ... BD
Box Energy 'B' [*NASDAQ symbol*] (TTSB) ... BOXXB
Box Energy Corp. [*Associated Press*] (SAG) ... BoxEn

Box Energy Corp. [*NASDAQ symbol*] (SAG) ... BOXX
Box Energy'A' [*NASDAQ symbol*] (TTSB) ... BOXXA
Box External Data ... BED
Box Fin ... BXF
Box Manufacturers Association of Greater New York [*Defunct*] (EA) ... BMAGNY
Box Office [*Theatrical slang*] ... BO
Box Office [*Theater*] (WDMC) ... bo
Box Office Management International [*An association*] (EA) ... BOMI
Box Project (EA) ... BP
Box Van [*Shipping*] (DCTA) ... B
Boxboard (DGA) ... BXBD
Boxboard Research and Development Association (EA) ... BRDA
Boxcar Detector (MSA) ... BXDT
Boxcar Doppler Filter (PDAA) ... BDF
Boxed ... BXD
Boxed Edit [*Control*] [*Computer science*] (PCM) ... BEDIT
Boxed or Tanked ... BX/TK
Boxes, Barrels, or Packages [*Freight*] ... BBP
Boxes or Crates [*Freight*] ... BC
Boxford, MA [*FM radio station call letters*] ... WBMT
Boxing Authority of New South Wales [*Australia*] ... BANSW
Boxing Writers Association ... BWA
Box-Office Computer System ... BOCS
Box-Office Reservation and Information Service ... BORIS
Boxwood (VRA) ... bxwd
Boy Clerks Association [*A union*] [*British*] ... BCA
Boy Entrant [*British military*] (DMA) ... B/E
Boy Savior Youth Movement [*Defunct*] (EA) ... BSYM
Boy Scouts ... BS
Boy Scouts International Bureau ... BSIB
Boy Scouts of America (EA) ... BSA
Boy Scouts of America Alumni Family [*Defunct*] (EA) ... BSAAF
Boy Scouts World Bureau [*Later, WSB*] ... BSWB
Boyce and Hart Fan Club (EA) ... BHFC
Boyce, LA [*FM radio station call letters*] ... KBCE
Boyce Thompson Institute for Plant Research, Yonkers, NY [*Library symbol Library of Congress*] (LCLS) ... NYBT
Boyce's Delaware Supreme Court Reports [*1909-19*] [*A publication*] (DLA) ... Boyce
Boyce's Practice in the United States Courts [*A publication*] (DLA) ... Boyce US Pr
Boycott [*Legal shorthand*] (LWAP) ... BOY
Boycott Burger King Coalition [*Defunct*] (EA) ... BBKC
Boycott McDonald's Coalition (EA) ... BMC
Boyd Bros.Transport'n [*NASDAQ symbol*] (TTSB) ... BOYD
Boyd Brothers Transportation, Inc. [*NASDAQ symbol*] (SAG) ... BOYD
Boyd Brothers Transportation, Inc. [*Associated Press*] (SAG) ... BoydBros
Boyd Gaming [*NYSE symbol*] (SPSG) ... BYD
Boyd Gaming Corp. [*Associated Press*] (SAG) ... BoydGm
Boyd. Justice of the Peace [*A publication*] (DLA) ... Boyd Jus
Boyd. Merchant Shipping Laws [*1876*] [*A publication*] (DLA) ... Boyd Sh
Boyd's Admiralty Law [*Ireland*] [*A publication*] (DLA) ... Boyd Adm
Boyds Wheels [*NASDAQ symbol*] (TTSB) ... BYDS
Boyds Wheels, Inc. [*NASDAQ symbol*] (SAG) ... BYDS
Boyds Wheels, Inc. [*Associated Press*] (SAG) ... BydWhls
Boyertown, PA [*FM radio station call letters*] ... WBYN
Boyfriend [*Slang*] ... BF
Boykin Lodging Co. [*NYSE symbol*] (SAG) ... BOY
Boykin Lodging Co. [*Associated Press*] (SAG) ... BoykinL
Boyle. Charities [*1837*] [*A publication*] (DLA) ... Boy Char
Boyle. Charities [*1837*] [*A publication*] (DLA) ... Boyle Char
Boyle Public Library, Alberta [*Library symbol National Library of Canada*] (NLC) ... ABO
Boyle Public Library, Boyle, AB, Canada [*Library symbol*] [*Library of Congress*] (LCLS) ... CaABoy
Boyle-Conway Solution [*Neurophysiology*] ... BC
Boyle's Precis of an Action at Common Law [*A publication*] (DLA) ... Boyle Act
Boyne City, MI [*FM radio station call letters*] ... WBCM
Boyne City Public Library, Boyne City, MI [*Library symbol Library of Congress*] (LCLS) ... MiBoy
Boyne City Railroad Co. [*AAR code*] ... BCRR
Boyne Falls, MI [*Location identifier FAA*] (FAAL) ... BFA
Boyne Falls Public Library, Boyne Falls, MI [*Library symbol Library of Congress*] (LCLS) ... MiBoyf
Boyne Regional Library, Carman, Manitoba [*Library symbol National Library of Canada*] (NLC) ... MCB
Boyne Regional Library, Carman, MB, Canada [*Library symbol Library of Congress*] (LCLS) ... CaMCB
Boynton Beach, FL [*AM radio station call letters*] (RBYB) ... WJNA-AM
Boynton Beach, FL [*FM radio station call letters*] ... WRMB
Boynton Beach, FL [*AM radio station call letters*] ... WYFX
Boys' and Girls' Brigades of America (EA) ... BGBA
Boys and Girls International Floor Hockey (EA) ... BGIFH
Boys and Young Men's Apparel Manufacturers Association [*Defunct*] (EA) ... BAMA
Boys' Apparel Buyers Association (EA) ... BABA
[*The*] **Boy's Book of Verse** [*A publication*] ... BBV
Boys' Brigade [*British*] ... BB
Boys Club Professional Association [*Later, ABGCP*] (EA) ... BCPA
Boys' Club, St. John's, Newfoundland [*Library symbol National Library of Canada*] (NLC) ... NFSBC
Boy's Club, St. John's, NF, Canada [*Library symbol Library of Congress*] (LCLS) ... CaNfSBC
Boys' Clubs of America (EA) ... BCA
Boys Hope (EA) ... BH
Boy's Life Brigade ... BLB
Boys of Woodcraft Sportsmen's Clubs [*Later, Woodmen Rangers and Rangerettes*] (EA) ... BWSC
Boys on Coroners [*A publication*] (DLA) ... Boys Cor
[*The*] **Boy's Own Paper** [*Late nineteenth- and early twentieth-century periodical*] [*British*] ... BOP
Boys School [*British*] ... B
Boys Technical School [*British military*] (DMA) ... BTS
Boys Town Center for the Study of Youth Development, Omaha, NE [*OCLC symbol*] (OCLC) ... BTC
Boys Town Center for the Study of Youth Development, Omaha, NE [*Library symbol Library of Congress*] (LCLS) ... NbOB
Boys Town Jerusalem Foundation of America (EA) ... BTJFA
Boys' Towns of Italy (EA) ... BTI
Boysen Reservoir, WY [*Location identifier FAA*] (FAAL) ... BOY
Boyuibe [*Bolivia*] [*ICAO location identifier*] (ICLI) ... SLBY
Bozell, Jacobs, Kenyon & Eckhardt [*Advertising agency*] [*New York, NY*] ... BJK & E
Bozeman [*Montana*] [*Seismograph station code, US Geological Survey Closed*] (SEIS) ... BOZ
Bozeman [*Montana*] [*Seismograph station code, US Geological Survey Closed*] (SEIS) ... BZE
Bozeman [*Montana*] [*Seismograph station code, US Geological Survey Closed*] (SEIS) ... BZM
Bozeman [*Montana*] [*Airport symbol*] (OAG) ... BZN
Bozeman, MT [*Location identifier FAA*] (FAAL) ... AMD
Bozeman, MT [*FM radio station call letters*] ... KATH
Bozeman, MT [*FM radio station call letters*] ... KBMC
Bozeman, MT [*AM radio station call letters*] ... KBOZ
Bozeman, MT [*Television station call letters*] ... KCTZ
Bozeman, MT [*FM radio station call letters*] ... KGLT
Bozeman, MT [*AM radio station call letters*] ... KMMS
Bozeman, MT [*FM radio station call letters*] ... KMMS-FM
Bozeman, MT [*AM radio station call letters*] ... KOBB
Bozeman, MT [*Television station call letters*] ... KUSM
Bozeman, MT [*AM radio station call letters*] ... KZLO
Bozeman Pubic Library, Bozeman, MT [*Library symbol*] [*Library of Congress*] (LCLS) ... MtB
Bozoum [*Central African Republic*] [*ICAO location identifier*] (ICLI) ... FEGZ
Bozzel & Jacobs Corp., Information Center, Chicago, IL [*Library symbol*] [*Library of Congress*] (LCLS) ... ICBo
Bozzetto (VRA) ... boz
BP Canada, Inc. [*Toronto Stock Exchange symbol Vancouver Stock Exchange symbol*] ... BPC
BP Exploration Canada Ltd., Calgary, AB, Canada [*Library symbol*] [*Library of Congress*] (LCLS) ... CaACBPE
BP Exploration Canada Ltd., Calgary, Alberta [*Library symbol National Library of Canada*] (NLC) ... ACBPE
BP Exploration Information Resource Center, Anchorage, AK [*Library symbol*] [*Library of Congress*] (LCLS) ... AkABP
BP Flight Operations Ltd. [*British ICAO designator*] (FAAC) ... BPO
BP Prudhoe Bay Royalty [*NYSE symbol*] (SPSG) ... BPT
BP Prudhoe Bay Royalty Trust [*Associated Press*] (SAG) ... BP Pru
BPI ...A Growers Organization (EA) ... BPI
BPI Packaging Tech [*NASDAQ symbol*] (TTSB) ... BPIE
BPI Packaging Technologies, Inc. [*Associated Press*] (SAG) ... BPI
BPI Packaging Technologies, Inc. [*Associated Press*] (SAG) ... BPI Pkg
BPI Packaging Technologies, Inc. [*NASDAQ symbol*] (SAG) ... BPIE
BPI Pkg Tech 8.50%'A'Pfd [*NASDAQ symbol*] (TTSB) ... BPIEP
BPI Pkg Technologies Wrrt'B' [*NASDAQ symbol*] (TTSB) ... BPIEZ
BPI Resources Ltd. [*Vancouver Stock Exchange symbol*] ... BPY
Braathens Helicopter AS [*Norway ICAO designator*] (FAAC) ... BRH
Braathens SAFE Airtransport [*ICAO designator*] (AD) ... BU
Braathens South American & Far East Airtransport AS [*Norway*] [*ICAO designator*] (FAAC) ... BRA
Brabazon Aircraft [*British*] (DSUE) ... BRAB
Brabrook. Industrial and Provident Societies [*1869*] [*A publication*] (DLA) ... Bra Ind Soc
Brabrook's Law of Trade Unions [*A publication*] (DLA) ... Bra Tr Un
Bracciera [*Ship's rigging*] (ROG) ... BRA
Bracco Industria Chimica [*Italy*] [*Research code symbol*] ... H
Brace [*Medicine*] ... B
Brace (MSA) ... BRC
Brace Bit Makers Society [*A union*] [*British*] ... BBMS
Brace Resources Ltd. [*Vancouver Stock Exchange symbol*] ... BCE
Bracebridge, ON [*FM radio station call letters*] ... CFBG
Bracebridge Public Library, Bracebridge, ON, Canada [*Library symbol Library of Congress*] (LCLS) ... CaOBrac
Bracebridge Public Library, Ontario [*Library symbol National Library of Canada*] (NLC) ... OBRAC
Braced ... BRCD
Braced and Racked [*Freight*] ... BR
Brachial [*Medicine*] (DMAA) ... Brach
Brachial Arterial Pressure [*Medicine*] (MAE) ... Pba
Brachial Artery [*Pressure*] [*Cardiology*] (DAVI) ... BA
Brachial Artery [*Anatomy*] ... BRA
Brachial Artery Pressure [*Medicine*] ... BAP
Brachial Neuritis [*Medicine*] (MAE) ... BN
Brachial Plexus Neuropathy [*Medicine*] (DMAA) ... BPN
Brachio [*To the Arm*] [*Pharmacy*] ... BRACH
Brachiocephalic Artery [*Cardiology*] (DAVI) ... BCA
Brachioradialis Jerk [*Neurology and orthopedics*] (DAVI) ... BRJ
Brachium [*Neurology*] ... BC
Brachium Conjunctivum [*Neuroanatomy*] ... BC
Brachmann-De Lange Syndrome [*Medicine*] (DMAA) ... BDLS
Brachycardia [*Cardiology*] ... BC

Bracing (DAC) .... Brcg
Bracken Basic Concept Scale - Diagnostic Scale [Educational development test] .... BBCS-DIAG
Bracken Library, Queen's University, Kingston, Ontario [Library symbol National Library of Canada] (NLC) .... OKQH
Brackendale, BC [Television station call letters] (RBYB) CHAN-5
Brackenridge Field Laboratory [University of Texas at Austin] [Research center] (RCD) .... BFL
Brackenridge on the Law of Trusts [A publication] (DLA) ...... Brack Tr
Brackenridge's Miscellanies [A publication] (DLA) .... Brack Misc
Bracket .... BKT
Bracket (KSC) .... BRKT
Bracket and Linkage Assembly .... BLA
Bracknell [British ICAO location identifier] (ICLI) .... EGRR
Bracknell Resources Ltd. [Toronto Stock Exchange symbol] ...... BRK
Bracton. De Legibus Angliae [A publication] (DLA) .... Bra
Bracton. De Legibus et Consuetudinibus Angliae [England] [A publication] (DLA) .... Brac
Bracton. De Legibus et Consuetudinibus Angliae [England] [A publication] (DLA) .... Bract
Bracton. De Legibus et Consuetudinibus Angliae [England] [A publication] (DLA) .... Bracton
Bracton's Note Book, King's Bench [1217-40] [A publication] (DLA) .... Br NB
Bracton's Note Book, King's Bench [1217-40] [A publication] (DLA) .... Brac
Bracton's Note Book Tempore Henry III [A publication] (DLA) ..... BNB
Brada-Svejda [Tumor] [Medicine] .... BS
Bradbury International Equity [Vancouver Stock Exchange symbol] ...... BBE
Bradbury Wilkinson (DGA) .... BW
Bradbury's Pleading and Practice Reports [New York] [A publication] (DLA) .... Bradb
Bradby on Distresses [A publication] (DLA) .... Brad Dis
Braddock Heights, MD [FM radio station call letters] (RBYB) ...... WWVZ-FM
Braddock, PA [AM radio station call letters] .... WCXJ
Braddock, PA [FM radio station call letters] .... WRRK
Bradenton, FL [FM radio station call letters] .... WDUV
Bradenton, FL [Television station call letters] .... WFCT
Bradenton, FL [FM radio station call letters] .... WJIS
Bradenton, FL [AM radio station call letters] (RBYB) .... WWPR
Bradfield [England] .... BRADF
Bradford [Pennsylvania] [Airport symbol] (OAG) .... BFD
Bradford [England] [Airport symbol] (AD) .... BRF
Bradford Action on Teacher Shortages (AIE) .... BATS
Bradford College [Formerly, BJC] [Massachusetts] .... BC
Bradford Community Learning and Education Resource (AIE) ...... BE CLEAR
Bradford County Public Library, Starke, FL [Library symbol Library of Congress] (LCLS) .... FStaB
Bradford Durfee College of Technology [Later, Southeastern Massachusetts Technical Institute] .... BDCT
Bradford, IL [Location identifier FAA] (FAAL) .... BDF
Bradford Junior College [Later, BC] [Massachusetts] .... BJC
Bradford Junior College [Later, BC], Bradford, MA [Library symbol Library of Congress] (LCLS) .... MBradJ
Bradford, PA [FM radio station call letters] .... WBRR
Bradford, PA [AM radio station call letters] .... WESB
Bradford Public Library, Bradford, IL [Library symbol Library of Congress] (LCLS) .... IBra
Bradford Public Library, Bradford, IL [OCLC symbol] (OCLC) ...... IQX
Bradford Public Library, Bradford, ON, Canada [Library symbol Library of Congress] (LCLS) .... CaOBr
Bradford Public Library, Ontario [Library symbol National Library of Canada] (NLC) .... OBR
Bradford Science Technology and Commercial Services [Information service or system] (NITA) .... BRASTACS
Bradford University Research Ltd. [British] (IRUK) .... BURL
Bradford University Software Services Ltd. [British] (IRUK) ..... BUSS
Bradford's Iowa Supreme Court Reports [1839-41] [A publication] (DLA) .... Bradford
Bradford's New York Surrogate's Court Reports [A publication] (DLA) .... Brad
Bradford's New York Surrogate's Court Reports [A publication] (DLA) ...... Brad R
Bradford's New York Surrogate's Court Reports [A publication] (DLA) .... Brad Sur
Bradford's New York Surrogate's Court Reports [A publication] (DLA) ..... Bradf
Bradford's New York Surrogate's Court Reports [A publication] (DLA) .... Bradf Rep
Bradford's New York Surrogate's Court Reports [A publication] (DLA) .... Bradf Sur
Bradford's New York Surrogate's Court Reports [A publication] (DLA) .... Bradf Sur R
Bradford's New York Surrogate's Court Reports [A publication] (DLA) .... Bradford's R
Bradford's New York Surrogate's Court Reports [A publication] (DLA) .... Bradford's Sur R
Bradford's Proceedings in the Court of Star Chamber [Somerset Record Society Publications, Vol. 27] [A publication] (DLA) ...... Bradf
Bradford's Reports [1838-41] [Iowa] [A publication] (DLA) ...... Brad
Bradford's Reports [1838-41] [Iowa] [A publication] (DLA) ...... Bradf
Bradford's Somerset Star Chamber [A publication] (DLA) .... Brad
Bradlees, Inc. [NYSE symbol] (SPSG) .... BLE
Bradlees, Inc. [Associated Press] (SAG) .... Bradlee
Bradley Aberration Method .... BAM
Bradley Air (Charter) Services Ltd. [Canada ICAO designator] (FAAC) ...... BAR
Bradley Commander [Army] (INF) .... BC
Bradley Commander/Gunner Certification Test [Army] (INF) ...... BCGC
Bradley Commander Proficiency Course [Army] (INF) .... BCPC
Bradley Crew Evaluator [Army] (INF) .... BCE
Bradley Desktop Trainer [Military] .... BDT

Bradley Fighting Vehicle [Army] .... BFV
Bradley Fighting Vehicle Armament [Army] (RDA) .... BFVA
Bradley Fighting Vehicle Systems [Army] (RDA) .... BFVS
Bradley Fighting Vehicle Systems Command and Control Vehicle [Army] (RDA) BFVS-C2V
Bradley Fire Support Vehicle [Army] (INF) .... BFSV
Bradley Gunnery and Missile Target System [Army] (INF) ...... BGMTS
Bradley Gunnery Skills Test [Army] (INF) .... BGST
Bradley Infantry Fighting Vehicle [Army] (INF) .... BIFV
Bradley International Airport [FAA] (TAG) .... BDL
Bradley Memorial Hospital, Cleveland, TN [Library symbol Library of Congress] (LCLS) .... TCleB
Bradley Pharm Wrrt 'B' [NASDAQ symbol] (TTSB) .... BPRXZ
Bradley Pharm Wrrt 'D' [NASDAQ symbol] (TTSB) .... BPRXL
Bradley Pharm Wrrt 'A' [NASDAQ symbol] (TTSB) .... BPRXW
Bradley Pharmaceuticals, Inc. [NASDAQ symbol] (SAG) ...... BPRX
Bradley Pharmaceuticals, Inc. [Associated Press] (SAG) ...... BradP
Bradley Pharmaceuticals, Inc. [Associated Press] (SAG) ...... BradPhm
Bradley Pharmaceuticals, Inc. [Associated Press] (SAG) ...... BrdP
Bradley Pharmaceuticals 'A' [NASDAQ symbol] (TTSB) .... BPRXA
Bradley Real Estate [Formerly, Bradley Real Estate Trust] [Associated Press] (SAG) .... BradRE
Bradley Real Estate [Formerly, Bradley Real Estate Trust] [NYSE symbol] (SAG) .... BTR
Bradley Subcaliber Device [Army training device] (INF) .... BSCD
Bradley Table [Army] (INF) .... BT
Bradley University (GAGS) .... Bradley U
Bradley University, Peoria, IL [OCLC symbol] (OCLC) .... IBA
Bradley University, Peoria, IL [Library symbol Library of Congress] (LCLS) ...... IPB
Bradley, Voorhees, & Day [A brand name underwear] .... BVD
Bradley's Point Book [A publication] (DLA) .... Bradl PB
Bradley's Rhode Island Reports [A publication] (DLA) .... Bradl
Bradley's Rhode Island Reports [A publication] (DLA) ...... Bradl (RI)
BRADLEY-STINGER Fighting Vehicle-Enhanced [Army] .... BSFV-E
Bradner Resources Ltd. [Vancouver Stock Exchange symbol] ...... BRD
Bradshaw Field, Hawaii Island [Hawaii] [ICAO location identifier] (ICLI) ...... PHSF
Bradsue Resources [Vancouver Stock Exchange symbol] ...... BDU
Braduskill Intercept Concept .... BIC
Bradwell's Illinois Appellate Reports [A publication] (DLA) ...... App Ct Rep
Bradwell's Illinois Appellate Reports [A publication] (DLA) ...... Brad
Bradwell's Illinois Appellate Reports [A publication] (DLA) ...... Bradw
Brady [W. T.] Co. [Associated Press] (SAG) .... BradyW
Brady [W.H.] Co. [NASDAQ symbol] (NQ) .... BRCO
Brady, TX [Location identifier FAA] (FAAL) .... BBD
Brady, TX [FM radio station call letters] .... KIXV
Brady, TX [AM radio station call letters] .... KNEL
Brady, TX [FM radio station call letters] (RBYB) .... KNEL-FM
Brady, W.T. Co. Class A [Associated Press] (SAG) .... BrdyW
Bradycardia [Cardiology] (DAVI) .... brady
Bradycardia after Arteriovenous Fistula Occlusion [Cardiology] (DMAA) .... BAVFO
Bradykinin [Biochemistry] .... BK
Bradykinin Antagonist [Medicine] .... BKA
Bradykinin-Potentiating Factor [Biochemistry Medicine] (DMAA) .... BPF
Brady's English History [1648] [A publication] (DLA) .... Bra
Brady's Historical Treatise on Cities [A publication] (DLA) ...... Bra Cit
Brady's History of the Succession of the Crown of England [A publication] (DLA) .... Brad
Brady's Index, Arkansas Reports [A publication] (DLA) ...... Brady Ind
Brady's Treatise upon Cities and Boroughs [A publication] (DLA) .... Brady's Tr
Brady(W.H.)'A'non-vtg [NASDAQ symbol] (TTSB) .... BRCOA
Braga [Portugal ICAO location identifier] (ICLI) .... LPBR
Braganca [Portugal] [Airport symbol] (OAG) .... BGC
Braganca [Portugal ICAO location identifier] (ICLI) .... LPBG
Bragg Cell Receiver (MCD) .... BCR
Braham Middle School, Braham, MN [Library symbol] [Library of Congress] (LCLS) .... MnBhM
Brahma Resources, Inc. [Vancouver Stock Exchange symbol] ...... BMA
Braid (IAA) .... B
Braid (KSC) .... BRD
Braided Rug Manufacturers Association [Defunct] (EA) .... BRMA
Braided Trimming Manufacturers Association [Later, EFMCNTA] (EA) ...... BTMA
Braided Tube Bundle .... BTB
Braided Wire Armor (AAG) .... BW
Braidwood Station [Nuclear energy] (NRCH) .... BS
Braille and Talking Book Library (ADA) .... B & TBL
Braille Authority of North America (EA) .... BANA
Braille Institute (EA) .... BI
Braille Institute of America [Later, BI] (EA) .... BIA
Braille Institute of America, Los Angeles, CA [Library symbol Library of Congress] (LCLS) .... CLBraille
Braille Revival League (EA) .... BRL
Braille Technical Press [Defunct] (EA) .... BTP
Braille Time-Sharing System .... BTSS
Brain [Neurology] (DAVI) .... BRA
Brain .... BRN
Brain Dead [Medicine] (DAVI) .... BD
Brain Derived Growth Factor [Biochemistry] .... BDGF
Brain Edema [Medicine] (DMAA) .... BE
Brain Electrical Activity Mapping .... BEAM
Brain Evoked Potential [Neurophysiology] .... BEP
Brain Hormone [Endocrinology] .... BH
Brain Information Service (EA) .... BIS
Brain Injured (EDAC) .... BI
Brain Mapping Technique .... BRAMATEC
Brain Missile Wound [Medicine] .... BMW

Brain Natriuretic Peptide [*Biochemistry*] .... BNP
Brain Protein Solvent [*Biochemistry*] .... BPS
Brain Research Association [*British*] .... BRA
Brain Research Foundation (EA) .... BRF
Brain Research Institute [*UCLA*] [*Research center*] .... BRI
Brain Retraction Pressure [*Neurophysiology*] .... BRP
Brain Stem Auditory Evoked Response [*Neurology and otorhinolaryngology*] (DAVI) .... BSAER
Brain Stem Evoked Potential [*Neurology*] (DAVI) .... BEP
Brain Stem Evoked Potential [*Neurophysiology*] (DMAA) .... BSEP
Brain Stem Evoked Response Audiometry [*Neurology and otorhinolaryngology*] (DAVI) .... BERA
Brain Stimulation Reinforcement [*Electrophysiology*] .... BSR
Brain Stimulation Reinforcement [*Neurology*] (DAVI) .... BSS
Brain Tumor [*Medicine*] .... BT
Brain Tumor Research Center [*University of California, San Francisco*] [*Research center*] (RCD) .... BTRC
Brain Tumor Study Group [*National Cancer Institute*] .... BTSG
Brain Uptake Index [*Physiology*] .... BUI
Brain Water .... BW
Brain-Age Quotient [*Medicine*] (DMAA) .... BAQ
Brainard's Legal Precedents in Land and Mining Cases [*United States*] [*A publication*] (DLA) .... BLP L & M Cas
Brainard's Legal Precedents in Land and Mining Cases [*United States*] [*A publication*] (DLA) .... Brain LP
Brain-Computer Interface (DMAA) .... BCI
Brain-Derived Neurotrophic Factor [*Neurochemistry*] .... BDNF
Brainerd [*Minnesota*] [*Airport symbol*] (OAG) .... BRD
Brainerd Community College, Brainerd, MN [*Library symbol Library of Congress*] (LCLS) .... MnBrC
Brainerd High School, Brainerd, MN [*Library symbol*] [*Library of Congress*] (LCLS) .... MnBrHS
Brainerd International [*Associated Press*] (SAG) .... Brainerd
Brainerd International, Inc. [*NASDAQ symbol*] (NQ) .... BIRI
Brainerd, MN [*Location identifier FAA*] (FAAL) .... EEE
Brainerd, MN [*Television station call letters*] .... KAWB
Brainerd, MN [*FM radio station call letters*] .... KBPR
Brainerd, MN [*FM radio station call letters*] (RBYB) .... KFGI-FM
Brainerd, MN [*AM radio station call letters*] .... KLIZ
Brainerd, MN [*FM radio station call letters*] .... KLIZ-FM
Brainerd, MN [*AM radio station call letters*] .... KVBR
Brainerd, MN [*FM radio station call letters*] .... KVBR-FM
Brainerd, MN [*FM radio station call letters*] .... WJJY
Brainerd Public Library, Brainerd, MN [*Library symbol*] [*Library of Congress*] (LCLS) .... MnBr
Brain-Heart Infusion [*Growth medium*] .... BHI
Brain-Heart Infusion Agar [*Growth medium*] (OA) .... BHIA
Brain-Heart Infusion Blood Agar [*Growth medium*] .... BHIBA
Brain-Heart Infusion Supplemented [*Broth or agar*] [*Growth medium*] .... BHIS
Brain-Heart Infusion [*Broth*] **with Acetone** [*Growth medium*] .... BHI-Ac
Brains on Board [*Robot*] [*Androbot, Inc.*] .... BOB
Brainstem Auditory Evoked Potential [*Neurophysiology*] .... BAEP
Brainstem Auditory Evoked Response [*Neurophysiology*] .... BAER
Brainstem Transmission Time [*Neurophysiology*] .... BTT
Brainstem-Evoked Response [*Neurophysiology*] .... BSER
Brainstorm (ABBR) .... BRSTRM
Brainstorming (ABBR) .... BRSTRMG
Braintree [*Urban district in England*] .... BRAINT
Braintree Savings Bank [*Associated Press*] (SAG) .... Brantre
[*The*] **Braintree Savings Bank** [*NASDAQ symbol*] (NQ) .... BTSB
Braithwaite. Oaths in Chancery [*2nd ed.*] [*1864*] [*A publication*] (DLA) .... Braith Oaths
Braithwaite. Oaths in the Supreme Court [*4th ed.*] [*1881*] [*A publication*] (DLA) .... Braith Oaths
Braithwaite. Record and Writ Practice of the Court of Chancery [*1858*] [*A publication*] (DLA) .... Braith Pr
Braithwaite. Times of Procedure in Chancery [*1864*] [*A publication*] (DLA) .... Braith Chy
Braithwaite's Register [*A publication*] (DLA) .... Br Reg
Braj [*MARC language code Library of Congress*] (LCCP) .... bra
Brake (KSC) .... BK
Brake [*Automotive engineering*] .... BRK
Brake .... BRK
Brake Die .... BKDI
Brake Die (MCD) .... BRD
Brake Electromagnet .... BM
Brake Force Distributor [*Automotive engineering*] .... BFD
Brake Headquarters USA, Inc. [*NASDAQ symbol*] (SAG) .... BHQU
Brake Headquarters USA, Inc. [*Associated Press*] (SAG) .... BrkeHd
Brake Horsepower .... B
Brake Horsepower (IAA) .... BH
Brake Horsepower .... BHP
Brake Horsepower-Hour (AAG) .... BHP-HR
Brake Light Switch [*Automotive engineering*] .... BLS
Brake Mean Effective Pressure .... BMEP
Brake Mean Power .... BMP
Brake On/Off Sensor [*Automotive engineering*] .... BOO
Brake Rating Horsepower [*Automotive engineering*] .... BRHP
Brake Relay .... BR
Brake Release Gross Weight .... BRGW
Brake Skid Control [*or Controller*] (NASA) .... B/SC
Brake Specific Carbon Monoxide [*Automotive engineering*] .... BSCO
Brake Specific Fuel Consumption .... BSFC
Brake Specific Hydrocarbons [*Automotive engineering*] .... BSHC
Brake Specific Oxides of Nitrogen [*Exhaust emissions*] [*Automotive engineering*] .... BSNO
Brake Specific Oxides of Nitrogen [*Automotive engineering*] .... BSNOX
Brake System Parts Manufacturers Council (EA) .... BSPMC
Brake Temperature Monitoring System (MCD) .... BTMS
Brake Thermal Efficiency [*Automotive engineering*] .... BTE
Brake Thermal Efficiency .... BThE
Brakeband (MSA) .... BRKBD
Braked Servomotor .... BSM
Brakes Release Point (ADA) .... BRP
Brake-Transmission Shift Interlock [*Automotive engineering*] .... BTSI
Brake-Transmission Shift Interlock .... BTSI
Braking [*Aviation*] (FAAC) .... BRKG
Braking Action Fair [*Aviation*] (FAAC) .... BRAF
Braking Action Good [*Aviation*] (FAAC) .... BRAG
Braking Action Nil [*Aviation*] (FAAC) .... BRAN
Braking Action Poor [*Aviation*] (FAAC) .... BRAP
Braking Force Coefficient (PDAA) .... BFC
Brakpan [*South Africa*] [*ICAO location identifier*] (ICLI) .... FABB
Bralorne Pioneer Museum, Bralorne, BC, Canada [*Library symbol*] [*Library of Congress*] (LCLS) .... CaBBPM
Bralorne Pioneer Museum, British Columbia [*Library symbol National Library of Canada*] (NLC) .... BBPM
Bralorne Resources Ltd. [*Toronto Stock Exchange symbol*] .... BR
Bram Stoker Club [*Ireland*] (EAIO) .... BSC
Bram Stoker Memorial Association (EA) .... BSMA
Bram Stoker Society (EA) .... BSS
Bramalea Ltd. [*Toronto Stock Exchange symbol*] .... BCD
Bramalea Properties, Inc. [*Toronto Stock Exchange symbol*] .... BPR
Brame's Reports [*66-72 Mississippi*] [*A publication*] (DLA) .... Brame
Brampton [*British ICAO location identifier*] (ICLI) .... EGYB
Brampton Brick Ltd. [*Toronto Stock Exchange symbol*] .... BBL
Brampton Campus, Sheridan College, Brampton, Ontario [*Library symbol National Library of Canada*] (BIB) .... OBRASC
Brampton Island [*Australia Airport symbol*] (OAG) .... BMP
Brampton, ON [*FM radio station call letters*] .... CFNY
Brampton, ON [*AM radio station call letters*] .... CIAO
Brampton Public Library, Brampton, ON, Canada [*Library symbol Library of Congress*] (LCLS) .... CaOBra
Brampton Public Library, Ontario [*Library symbol National Library of Canada*] (NLC) .... OBRA
Bran and Multiple Vitamins and Minerals, B-Complex Vitamins, and Yogurt [*A nutritional plan*] .... BAMBY
Branch (IAA) .... B
Branch (ADA) .... BCH
Branch (EY) .... BR
Branch .... BR
Branch [*Postal Service standard*] (OPSA) .... BR
Branch [*Commonly used*] (OPSA) .... BRANCH
Branch (ADA) .... BRCH
Branch [*Commonly used*] (OPSA) .... BRNCH
Branch Address .... BRA
Branch Always [*Computer science*] .... BRA
Branch and Bound [*Algorithm*] .... BAB
Branch and Class (DNAB) .... BR & CL
Branch and Flow [*Diagram*] .... B & F
Branch and Link (CDE) .... BAL
Branch and Link (IAA) .... BRL
Branch and Store Instruction [*Computer science*] (MDG) .... BSI
Branch Arm Piping [*Nuclear energy*] (NRCH) .... BAP
Branch Arm Piping Enclosure [*Nuclear energy*] (NRCH) .... BAPE
Branch Arm Piping Shielding [*Nuclear energy*] (NRCH) .... BAPS
Branch Assistance Team [*Military*] (AABC) .... BAT
Branch Aviation Supply Office [*Navy*] .... BRASO
Branch Back and Load [*Computer science*] .... BBL
Branch Bill .... BB
Branch Circuit Protection Device .... BCPD
Branch City [*Databank terminology*] (NITA) .... BC
Branch Conditional (IAA) .... BC
Branch Conditional .... BRC
Branch Conditionally [*Computer science*] .... BCC
Branch County Library, Coldwater, MI [*Library symbol Library of Congress*] (LCLS) .... MiCwB
Branch Cultural Affairs Officer [*United States Information Service*] .... BCAO
Branch Exchange [*Telecommunications*] .... BX
Branch Head .... BH
Branch History Table [*Computer science*] .... BHT
Branch Hydrographic Office [*Navy*] .... BHO
Branch Hydrographic Office [*Navy*] .... BRANCHYDRO
Branch if Carry Set .... BCS
Branch if Less Than [*Computer science*] (NHD) .... BLT
Branch If Multiplexer .... BIM
Branch Immaterial .... BI
Branch Immaterial Officer Candidate Course .... BIOCC
Branch Information Processing System [*Computer science*] .... BIPS
Branch Intelligence Officer [*Military British*] .... BIO
Branch Liaison Team [*US Army Chemical School*] [*Fort McClellan, AL*] (RDA) .... BLT
Branch Library, Manitoba Veterinarian Services, Winnipeg, Manitoba [*Library symbol National Library of Canada*] (NLC) .... MWVS
Branch Line Society [*British*] .... BLS
Branch Manager (MCD) .... BM
Branch Material [*Military*] (AABC) .... BM
Branch Memorandum .... BM
Branch Navy Commissary Store (DNAB) .... BRNAVCOMMSTO

Branch No Group [*Computer science*] (MDG) .... BNG
Branch of Fall Zero .... BFZ
Branch of Full Minus (SAA) .... BFM
Branch Office .... BO
Branch Office, Boston [*Office of Naval Research*] (DNAB) .... BOB
Branch Office, Chicago [*Office of Naval Research*] (DNAB) .... BOC
Branch Office London [*ONR*] .... BOL
Branch Office, Military Intelligence Division [*Army*] .... BOMID
Branch Office, Office of Naval Research .... ONR BR
Branch Office, Pasadena [*Office of Naval Research*] (DNAB) .... BOP
Branch Officer Candidate Course [*DoD*] .... BOCC
Branch Officer, Inspector of Naval Material (DNAB) .... BRINSMAT
Branch Officer Roster [*Army*] .... BOR
Branch on Count (IAA) .... BCT
Branch on Left Minus (SAA) .... BLM
Branch on Minus .... BM
Branch on Nonzero .... BN
Branch on Right Minus (SAA) .... BRM
Branch Operating Instruction [*Air Force*] .... BOI
Branch Operating Instruction [*Air Force*] (AFM) .... BROI
Branch Output Interrupt [*Computer science*] (MDG) .... BOI
Branch Point Sequence [*Genetics*] .... BPS
Branch Prediction Unit [*Computer science*] (PCM) .... BPU
Branch Processing Unit [*Computer science*] .... BPO
Branch Public Affairs Officer [*United States Information Service*] .... BPAO
Branch Public Relations Office .... BPRO
Branch Report .... BR
Branch Retinal Artery Occlusion [*Ophthalmology*] (DAVI) .... BRAO
Branch Retinal Vein Occlusion [*Ophthalmology*] (DAVI) .... BrRvo
Branch Retinal Vein Occlusion [*Ophthalmology*] (CPH) .... BRVO
Branch Stack .... BS
Branch State [*Database terminology*] (NITA) .... BS
Branch System General License [*Information technology*] .... BSGL
Branch Target Buffer [*Computer science*] (PCM) .... BTB
Branch Technical Position [*Nuclear energy*] (NRCH) .... BTP
Branch to Subroutine [*Computer science*] .... BSR
Branch Training Team [*Army*] .... BTT
Branch Transportation Office [*or Officer*] [*Army*] .... BTO
Branch Unconditionally .... BRU
Branch Unit [*Computer science*] (PCM) .... BU
Branch Vein Occlusion [*Medicine*] (DMAA) .... BVO
Branch Warehouse Association (EA) .... BWA
Branch Zip Code [*Database Terminology*] (NITA) .... BZ
Branch-Bound Mixed Integer Programming [*Computer science*] .... BBMIP
Branche Africaine du Mouvement International des Etudiants Catholiques
   [*African International Movement of Catholic Students - AIMCS*] (EAIO) ...... MIEC
Branched Alkylbenzene [*Organic chemistry*] .... BAB
Branched Amino Acid (DMAA) .... BAA
Branched Ribonucleic Acid [*Genetics*] .... bRNA
Branched-Chain Amino Acid [*Biochemistry*] .... BAA
Branched-Chain Amino Acid [*Biochemistry*] .... BCAA
Branched-Chain Ketoacid [*Biochemistry*] .... BCKA
Branched-Chain Ketoacid Dehydrogenase [*Biochemistry*] .... BCKD
Branched-Chain Oxoacid Dehydrogenase [*An enzyme*] .... BCODH
Branchial Filament .... BRF
Branching Filter [*Telecommunications*] (TEL) .... BF
Branchioganglionic Neuron [*Neurology*] .... BGN
Branchio-Oto-Ureteral [*Syndrome*] [*Medicine*] (DMAA) .... BOU
Branch's Maxims [*A publication*] (DLA) .... Branch Max
Branch's Principia Legis et Equitatis [*Maxims*] [*A publication*] (DLA) ..... Branch Pr
Branch's Principia Legis et Equitatis [*Maxims*] [*A publication*]
   (DLA) .... Branch Princ
Branch's Reports [*1 Florida*] [*A publication*] (DLA) .... Branch
Branch-Target Address Cache [*Computer science*] .... BTAC
Branchville, SC [*FM radio station call letters*] .... WGFG
Brand Development [*Marketing*] (DOAD) .... BD
Brand Development Index (WDMC) .... BDI
Brand Name Contract (AABC) .... BNC
Brand Name Resale (AABC) .... BNR
Brand Names Foundation (EA) .... BNF
Brand Potential Index [*Marketing*] (DOAD) .... BPI
Brand Rating Index Corp. .... BRI
Branded Furniture Society [*British*] (BI) .... BFS
Branded Knitting-Wool Association Ltd. [*British*] (BI) .... BKWA
Brandeis - Bardin Institute (EA) .... BBI
Brandeis School, Lawrence, NY [*Library symbol*] [*Library of Congress*]
   (LCLS) .... NLawBS
Brandeis University (GAGS) .... Brandeis U
Brandeis University [*Waltham, MA*] (BJA) .... BU
Brandeis University, Waltham, MA [*OCLC symbol*] (OCLC) .... MBB
Brandeis University, Waltham, MA [*Library symbol Library of Congress*]
   (LCLS) .... MWalB
Brandenburg, KY [*AM radio station call letters*] .... WMMG
Brandenburg, KY [*FM radio station call letters*] .... WMMG-FM
Brandenburg's Bankruptcy Digest [*A publication*] (DLA) .... Brandenburg Bankr
Brandenburg's Bankruptcy Digest [*A publication*] (DLA) .... Brandenburg Dig
Brandenburg's Reports [*21 Opinions Attorneys-General*] [*A publication*]
   (DLA) .... Brand
Brande's Dictionary of Science, Etc. [*A publication*] (DLA) .... Brande
Brandevor Enterprises Ltd. [*Toronto Stock Exchange symbol Vancouver Stock Exchange symbol*] .... BVE
Brandl, H. R., Chicago IL [*STAC*] .... BHR
Brandon [*Canada*] [*Airport symbol*] (OAG) .... YBR
Brandon Call Fan Club (EA) .... BCFC
Brandon Films, Inc. .... BF

Brandon, FL [*AM radio station call letters*] .... WBDN
Brandon Free Public Library, Brandon, VT [*Library symbol Library of Congress*] (LCLS) .... VtBran
Brandon General Hospital, School of Nursing, Brandon, MB, Canada
   [*Library symbol Library of Congress*] (LCLS) .... CaMBGH
Brandon, MB [*Television station call letters*] CBWFT-10
Brandon, MB [*AM radio station call letters*] .... CKLQ
Brandon, MB [*AM radio station call letters*] .... CKX
Brandon, MB [*FM radio station call letters*] .... CKX-FM
Brandon, MB [*Television station call letters*] .... CKX-TV
Brandon, MB [*Television station call letters*] .... CKYB
Brandon, MB [*ICAO location identifier*] (ICLI) .... CYBR
Brandon Mental Health Centre, Brandon, MB, Canada [*Library symbol Library of Congress*] (LCLS) .... CaMBMH
Brandon Mental Health Centre, Manitoba [*Library symbol National Library of Canada*] (NLC) .... MBMH
Brandon, MS [*FM radio station call letters*] .... WRJH
Brandon, MS [*AM radio station call letters*] .... WRKN
Brandon on Foreign Attachment [*A publication*] (DLA) .... Brand F Attachm
Brandon on Foreign Attachment [*A publication*] (ILCA) .... Brand For Att
Brandon on Foreign Attachment [*A publication*] (DLA) .... Brand For Attachm
Brandon. Practice of the Mayor's Court [*1864*] [*A publication*]
   (DLA) .... Brand May Ct
Brandon Public School, Brandon, MN [*Library symbol*] [*Library of Congress*] (LCLS) .... MnBraS
Brandon Systems [*AMEX symbol*] (SPSG) .... BRA
Brandon Systems Corp. [*Associated Press*] (SAG) .... Brandn
Brandon University, Archives, Brandon, MB, Canada [*Library symbol Library of Congress*] (LCLS) .... CaMBCA
Brandon University, Brandon, MB, Canada [*Library symbol Library of Congress*] (LCLS) .... CaMBC
Brandon University, Department of Geography, Brandon, MB, Canada
   [*Library symbol Library of Congress*] (LCLS) .... CaMBCG
Brandon University Library [*UTLAS symbol*] .... BUL
Brandon University, Manitoba [*Library symbol National Library of Canada*]
   (NLC) .... MBC
Brandon, VT [*FM radio station call letters*] .... WADT
Brands and Their Companies [*Formerly, TND*] [*A publication*] .... BTC
Brandt on Suretyship and Guaranty [*A publication*] (DLA) .... Brandt Sur
Brandvlei [*South Africa*] [*ICAO location identifier*] (ICLI) .... FABV
Brandy and Benedictine (CDAI) .... B & B
Brandy and Dry Ginger (ADA) .... b & d
Brandy and Soda .... B and S
Brandy Resources [*Vancouver Stock Exchange symbol*] .... BYU
Brandywine College of Widener University, Wilmington, DE [*OCLC symbol*] (OCLC) .... DLB
Brandywine College, Wilmington, DE [*Library symbol Library of Congress*]
   (LCLS) .... DeWB
Brandywine Realty Trust [*Formerly, Linpro Specified Properties*] [*AMEX symbol*] (SPSG) .... BDN
Brandywine Realty Trust [*Associated Press*] (SAG) .... Brandyw
Brandywine Rlty Trust SBI [*AMEX symbol*] (TTSB) .... BDN
Braner Resources [*Vancouver Stock Exchange symbol*] .... BRJ
Branford Savings Bank [*Associated Press*] (SAG) .... BranfdSv
Branford Savings Bank [*NASDAQ symbol*] (NQ) .... BSBC
Branford Savings Bank(CT) [*NASDAQ symbol*] (TTSB) .... BSBC
Branford Steam Railroad [*AAR code*] .... BRFD
Braniff Airways, Inc. [*of Braniff International Corp.*] .... BA
Braniff Airways, Inc. [*of Braniff International Corp.*] [*ICAO designator*] (OAG) .... BN
Braniff International Airways (IIA) .... BI
Braniff International Corp. [*ICAO designator*] .... BNF
Braniff International Council [*Club for frequent flyers*] (EA) .... BIC
Brans-Dicke-Jordan [*Scalar-tensor theory*] .... BDJ
Branson, MO [*FM radio station call letters*] .... KLFC
Branson, MO [*AM radio station call letters*] .... KOMC
Branson, MO [*FM radio station call letters*] (RBYB) .... KOZO-FM
Branson, MO [*FM radio station call letters*] .... KRZK
Branson, MO [*Location identifier FAA*] (FAAL) .... PLK
Branson's Digest [*Bombay*] [*A publication*] (DLA) .... Brans Dig
Brant County Historical Museum, Brantford, ON, Canada [*Library symbol Library of Congress*] (LCLS) .... CaOBrtBM
Brant County Historical Museum, Brantford, Ontario [*Library symbol National Library of Canada*] (NLC) .... OBBM
Brantford, ON [*AM radio station call letters*] .... CKPC
Brantford, ON [*FM radio station call letters*] .... CKPC-FM
Brantford Public Library, Brantford, ON, Canada [*Library symbol Library of Congress*] (LCLS) .... CaOBrt
Brantford Public Library, Ontario [*Library symbol National Library of Canada*] (NLC) .... OBRT
Brantley Capital Corp. [*NASDAQ symbol*] (SAG) .... BBDC
Brantley Capital Corp. [*Associated Press*] (SAG) .... BrantCp
Brantly's Reports [*80-90 Maryland*] [*A publication*] (DLA) .... Brant
Brantly's Reports [*80-90 Maryland*] [*A publication*] (DLA) .... Brantly
Bras D'Or Mines [*Vancouver Stock Exchange symbol*] .... BRM
Brasair Transportes Aereos [*Brazil*] [*FAA designator*] (FAAC) .... BSI
Brascade Resources, Inc. [*Toronto Stock Exchange symbol*] .... BCA
Brascan Ltd. [*Toronto Stock Exchange symbol*] .... BL
Brascan Ltd. [*AMEX symbol*] (SPSG) .... BRS
Brascan Ltd. [*Associated Press*] (SAG) .... Brscn
Brascon Resources Ltd., Calgary, AB, Canada [*Library symbol Library of Congress*] (LCLS) .... CaACB
Brascon Resources Ltd., Calgary, Alberta [*Library symbol National Library of Canada*] (NLC) .... ACB
Brasenose College [*Oxford*] .... BNC
Brashear-Hastings Prism .... BHP

Brasil [*Portuguese spelling*] and Canada [*In company name "Brascan Ltd."*] .... BRASCAN
Brasil Gold Resources [*Vancouver Stock Exchange symbol*] .... BGZ
Brasil-Central Linhas Areas Regional SA [*Brazil*] [*ICAO designator*] (FAAC) .... BLC
Brasileia [*Brazil*] [*Airport symbol*] (AD) .... BZY
Brasilia [*Brazil*] [*Seismograph station code, US Geological Survey*] (SEIS) .... BAE
Brasilia [*Brazil*] [*Seismograph station code, US Geological Survey*] (SEIS) .... BDF
Brasilia [*Brazil*] [*Airport symbol*] (OAG) .... BSB
Brasilia [*Airplane code*] Em2
Brasilia [*Brazil ICAO location identifier*] (ICLI) .... SBBS
Brasilia Array [*Brazil*] [*Seismograph station code, US Geological Survey*] (SEIS) .... BAO
Brasilia/Gama [*Brazil ICAO location identifier*] (ICLI) .... SBGA
Brasilia/Internacional [*Brazil ICAO location identifier*] (ICLI) .... SBBR
Brass (WGA) .... B
Brass .... BR
Brass (KSC) .... BRS
Brass (VRA) .... bs
Brass and Bronze Ingot Institute (EA) .... BBII
Brass, Bronze, or Copper [*Freight*] .... BRBZC
Brass Divider Strip [*Technical drawings*] .... BDS
Brass Dressers Trade Society [*A union*] [*British*] .... BDTS
Brass or Bronze [*Top*] [*Freight*] .... B or B
Brass or Iron [*Freight*] .... B or I
Brass Pounders League [*Unit of American Radio Relay League*] .... BPL
Brass Ring Resources [*Vancouver Stock Exchange symbol*] .... BSG
Brass Ring Society (EA) .... BRS
Brassboard Configuration Model (MCD) .... BCM
Brassboard Fault Tolerant Spaceborne Computer (MCD) .... BFTSC
Brasschaat [*Belgium ICAO location identifier*] (ICLI) .... EBBT
Brasserie .... BRSSR
Brassey's Naval Record [*Brassey's Defence Publishers Ltd.*] [*No longer maintained*] [*Information service or system*] (IID) .... BNR
Brassie Golf Corp. [*Associated Press*] (SAG) .... BrassieG
Brassie Golf Corp. [*NASDAQ symbol*] (SAG) .... PUTT
Brassiere (DSUE) .... BRA
Brassiere (DSUE) .... BRAS
Brassiere (ABBR) .... BRSSIR
Brassiness (ABBR) .... BRSNS
Brassy (ABBR) .... BRSSY
Brassy (ABBR) .... BRSY
Braswell, J. V., Dallas TX [*STAC*] .... BJV
Bratislava [*Czechoslovakia*] [*Seismograph station code, US Geological Survey Closed*] (SEIS) .... BRA
Bratislava [*Former Czechoslovakia*] [*Airport symbol*] (OAG) .... BTS
Bratislava [*Czechoslovakia*] [*ICAO location identifier*] (ICLI) .... LKBB
Bratislava [*Czechoslovakia*] [*Seismograph station code, US Geological Survey*] (SEIS) .... ZST
Bratislava/Ivanka [*Former Czechoslovakia*] [*ICAO location identifier*] (ICLI) ..... LKIB
Bratschen [*Viola*] .... BR
Bratsk [*Former USSR Airport symbol*] (OAG) .... BTK
Bratsk [*Former USSR ICAO location identifier*] (ICLI) .... UIBB
Brattforsheden [*Sweden ICAO location identifier*] (ICLI) .... ESSM
Brattleboro, Vermont-Keene, New Hampshire [*Airport symbol*] (AD) .... EEN
Brattleboro, VT [*AM radio station call letters*] .... WKVT
Brattleboro, VT [*FM radio station call letters*] .... WKVT-FM
Brattleboro, VT [*AM radio station call letters*] .... WTSA
Brattleboro, VT [*FM radio station call letters*] .... WTSA-FM
Braun's Fashions [*NASDAQ symbol*] (TTSB) .... BFCI
Brauns Fashions Corp. [*NASDAQ symbol*] (SAG) .... BFCI
Braun's Fashions Corp. [*Associated Press*] (SAG) .... Brauns
Braunschweig [*Germany ICAO location identifier*] (ICLI) .... EDVB
Braunschweig [*Germany ICAO location identifier*] (ICLI) .... EDVE
Braunton [*England*] .... BRAUN
Bravado (ABBR) .... BRVDO
Bravais-Miller Indices [*Physics*] .... BMI
Brave (ABBR) .... BRV
Braved (ABBR) .... BRVD
Bravely (ABBR) .... BRVY
Braveness (ABBR) .... BRVNS
Braverman-Chevigny Auditory Projective Test [*Psychology*] .... BCAPT
Bravery Medal (ADA) .... BM
Braving (ABBR) .... BRVG
Bravo [*International phonetic alphabet*] (DSUE) .... B
Bravo Resources [*Vancouver Stock Exchange symbol*] .... BVO
Bravo Zone (SAA) .... BRZN
Bravo Zulu [*Signal for "job well done"*] [*Navy*] (DOMA) .... BZ
Brawdy [*British ICAO location identifier*] (ICLI) .... EGDA
Brawled (ABBR) .... BRWLD
Brawley, CA [*Location identifier FAA*] (FAAL) .... BWC
Brawley, CA [*AM radio station call letters*] .... KROP
Brawley, CA [*FM radio station call letters*] .... KSIQ
Brawley, CA [*FM radio station call letters*] .... KWST
Brawley Public Library, Brawley, CA [*Library symbol Library of Congress*] (LCLS) .... CBr
Brawling (ABBR) .... BRWLG
Bray Elementary School, Biwabik, MN [*Library symbol*] [*Library of Congress*] (LCLS) .... MnBiwE
Brayton Heat Exchanger Unit .... BHXU
Brayton Isotope Power System .... BIPS
Brayton Rotating Unit .... BRU
Brayton Turboelectric Engine .... BTE
Brayton Turboelectric Engine .... BTEE
Brayton's Reports [*Vermont*] [*A publication*] (DLA) .... Bray

Brayton's Reports [*Vermont*] [*A publication*] (DLA) .... Bray R
Brayton's Reports [*Vermont*] [*A publication*] (ILCA) .... Brayt
Brayton's Reports [*Vermont*] [*A publication*] (DLA) .... Brayt Rep
Brayton's Reports [*Vermont*] [*A publication*] (DLA) .... Brayton (VT)
Brayton's Reports [*Vermont*] [*A publication*] (DLA) .... Brayton's Rep
Braze .... BRZ
Brazed (VRA) .... braz
Brazed (ABBR) .... BRZD
Brazed Joint-Face Fed (DNAB) .... BF
Brazed Joint-Preinserted Ring (DNAB) .... BP
Brazen (ABBR) .... BRZN
Brazened (ABBR) .... BRZND
Brazening (ABBR) .... BRZNG
Brazier (MSA) .... BRAZ
Brazier (ABBR) .... BRZIR
Brazier Head .... BRAZH
Brazil [*IYRU nationality code*] [*MARC country of publication code Library of Congress*] (LCCP) .... bl
Brazil [*ANSI two-letter standard code*] (CNC) .... BR
Brazil [*ANSI three-letter standard code*] (CNC) .... BRA
Brazil .... BRAZ
Brazil (VRA) .... Braz
Brazil [*International civil aircraft marking*] (ODBW) .... PP
Brazil [*International civil aircraft marking*] (ODBW) .... PT
Brazil [*MARC geographic area code Library of Congress*] (LCCP) .... s-bl--
Brazil Democratic Movement [*Political party*] .... BDM
Brazil Fast Food [*NASDAQ symbol*] (TTSB) .... BOBS
Brazil Fast Food Corp. [*NASDAQ symbol*] (SAG) .... BOBS
Brazil Fast Food Corp. [*Associated Press*] (SAG) .... Brazil
Brazil Fast Food Corp. [*Associated Press*] (SAG) .... BrazlFst
Brazil Fast Food Wrrt'A' [*NASDAQ symbol*] (TTSB) .... BOBSW
Brazil Fast Food Wrrt'B' [*NASDAQ symbol*] (TTSB) .... BOBSZ
Brazil Fund [*NYSE symbol*] (TTSB) .... BZF
Brazil Fund, Inc. [*Associated Press*] (SAG) .... Brazil
Brazil Fund, Inc. [*NYSE symbol*] (SPSG) .... BZF
Brazil, IN [*AM radio station call letters*] .... WSDM
Brazil, IN [*FM radio station call letters*] .... WSDM-FM
Brazil Labor Information and Resource Center (EA) .... BLI
Brazil Nut Advertising Fund [*Defunct*] (EA) .... BNAF
Brazil Nut Association .... BNA
Brazil Philatelic Association (EA) .... BPA
Brazil Public Library, Brazil, IN [*Library symbol Library of Congress*] (LCLS) .... InBra
Brazil Times, Brazil, IN [*Library symbol Library of Congress*] (LCLS) .... InBraT
Brazil Tourism Office .... BTO
Brazilian Air Force [*ICAO designator*] (FAAC) .... BRS
Brazilian American Survey [*A publication*] .... BAS
Brazilian Angel [*Record label*] .... BrzA
Brazilian Army Aviation [*FAA designator*] (FAAC) .... EXB
Brazilian Center of New York (EA) .... BCNY
Brazilian Coffee Institute (EA) .... BCI
Brazilian Columbia [*Record label*] .... BrzC
Brazilian Continental [*Record label*] .... BrzCont
Brazilian Elite [*Record label*] .... BrzEli
Brazilian Equity Fund [*Associated Press*] (SAG) .... BrazilEF
Brazilian Equity Fund [*NYSE symbol*] (SPSG) .... BZL
Brazilian Expeditionary Force .... BEF
Brazilian Government Trade Bureau (EA) .... BGTB
Brazilian Infantry Division [*World War II*] .... BID
Brazilian International Airlines .... BIA
Brazilian MGM [*Record label*] .... BrzMGM
Brazilian Navy .... BN
Brazilian News Briefs [*A publication*] (EAAP) .... BNB
Brazilian Odeon [*Record label*] .... BrzOd
Brazilian Studies Association .... BRASA
Brazilian Thorium Sludge .... BTS
Brazilian Tourism Foundation (EA) .... BTF
Brazilian Victor [*Record label*] .... BrzV
Brazilian-American Chamber of Commerce (EA) .... BACC
Brazilian-American Cultural Institute (EA) .... BACI
Brazilian-American Society [*Defunct*] (EA) .... BAS
Brazil-US Business Council (EA) .... BUSBC
Brazing .... B
Brazing (KSC) .... BRZG
Brazing Accessory [*Tool*] (AAG) .... BZAC
Brazing Fixture .... BZFX
Brazoria County Library, Angleton, TX [*Library symbol Library of Congress*] (LCLS) .... TxAng
Brazoria, TX [*Location identifier FAA*] (FAAL) .... BZT
Brazos Petroleum [*Vancouver Stock Exchange symbol*] .... BRS
Brazos Santiago, TX [*Location identifier FAA*] (FAAL) .... PIL
Brazosport College, Lake Jackson, TX [*Library symbol Library of Congress*] (LCLS) .... TxLjB
Brazosport Junior College, Freeport, TX [*Library symbol Library of Congress*] (LCLS) .... TxFrB
Brazzaville [*People's Republic of the Congo*] [*Airport symbol*] (OAG) .... BZV
Brazzaville [*Congo*] [*ICAO location identifier*] (ICLI) .... FCBV
Brazzaville [*Congo*] [*ICAO location identifier*] (ICLI) .... FCCC
Brazzaville/Maya Maya [*Congo*] [*ICAO location identifier*] (ICLI) .... FCBB
BRC Holdings [*NASDAQ symbol*] (TTSB) .... BRCP
BRC Holdings, Inc. [*Associated Press*] (SAG) .... BRC Hld
BRC Holdings, Inc. [*NASDAQ symbol*] (SAG) .... BRCP
BRE Properties Cl A [*NYSE symbol*] (SPSG) .... BRE
BRE Properties, Inc. [*Associated Press*] (SAG) .... BRE
Breach [*Legal shorthand*] (LWAP) .... BR

Breach of Contract [*Legal term*] ... BOC
Breach of Peace [*FBI standardized term*] ... B of P
Breach of Peace ... BOP
Breach of Promise [*Legal term*] ... B of P
Breach of Promise [*Legal term*] (DLA) ... BRECH PROM
Breach of Warranty [*Insurance*] (AIA) ... BOW
Breaching (MSA) ... BRHG
Bread [*Dietetics*] ... Brd
Bread and Puppet Theater [*Vermont*] ... B and P
Bread and Roses (EA) ... B & R
Bread and Water ... B & W
[*The*] **Bread Board System** [*eSoft, Inc.*] [*Computer science*] (PCM) ... TBBS
Bread, Butter, and Marmalade [*Slang*] ... BBM
Bread Equivalent [*Medicine*] (DMAA) ... BE
Bread Exchange [*Dietetics*] ... Brd Ex
Bread for the World (EA) ... BFW
Bread Industry Authority [*Queensland, Australia*] ... BIA
Bread Industry Employees and Salespersons' Association of New South Wales [*Australia*] ... BIESANSW
Bread Loaf Writers Conference (EA) ... BLWC
Bread Manufacturers' Association of New South Wales [*Australia*] ... BMANSW
Bread Manufacturers' Association of South Australia ... BMASA
Bread Manufacturers' Association of Tasmania [*Australia*] ... BMAV
Bread Manufacturers' Association of Western Australia ... BMAWA
Bread Manufacturers' Industrial Association of Australia ... BMIAA
Bread Manufacturers of New South Wales [*Australia*] ... BMNSW
Bread Manufacturers of Queensland Union of Employers [*Australia*] ... BMQUE
Bread Research Institute of Australia ... BRIA
Breadalbane Fencibles [*British military*] (DMA) ... BF
Breadboard [*NASA*] (KSC) ... BB
Breadboard Kit [*NASA*] ... BBK
Breadboard of an Electrochemical Air Revitalization System [*NASA*] ... BEARS
Breadboard Terminal Landing System [*NASA*] (KSC) ... BTLS
Breadboard Verification Equipment [*NASA*] ... BVE
Breadboard Visual Reference System [*NASA*] ... BVRS
Breadth ... B
Breadth ... BRDTH
Breadth-Length ... BL
Break [*Electronics*] ... B
Break (IDOE) ... BK
Break (KSC) ... BRK
Break Bulk [*Shipping*] ... BB
Break Bulk Point [*Transportation*] ... BBP
Break Control Command Transducers (NASA) ... BCCT
Break Engage (CAAL) ... BK ENG
Break, Enter, and Steal (ADA) ... BE & S
Break Even Analysis [*Accounting*] ... BEA
Break in Overcast [*Meteorology*] ... BINOVC
Break Jaw (MSA) ... BJ
Break Line [*Printing*] (DGA) ... BK L
Break of Entry (NASA) ... BOE
Break of Inspection ... BOI
Break of Integrity (NASA) ... BOI
Break Over Diode [*Electronics*] (EECA) ... BOD
Break Pressure Tank (PDAA) ... BPT
Break Pulse Generator (CET) ... BPG
Break Request [*Computer science*] (MDG) ... BR
Break Request Signal [*Computer science*] ... BRS
Break Transmission (NVT) ... BT
Breakage (WGA) ... BKG
Break-Away Torque [*Automotive engineering*] ... BAT
Break-Before-Make ... BBM
Breakdown (MSA) ... BKDN
Breakdown [*Electronics*] ... BR
Breakdown Control Number (MCD) ... BCN
Breakdown Diode [*Electronics*] ... BKDNDIO
Breakdown Maintenance ... BM
Breakdown of Recoverable Items (MCD) ... BRI
Breakdown Pulse Noise (KSC) ... BPN
Breakdown Truck [*British*] ... BT
Breakdown Voltage [*Telecommunications*] (TEL) ... BDV
Breakdown Voltage ... BV
Breaker (KSC) ... BKR
Breaker ... BRKR
Breaker Block ... BB
Breaker End (MSA) ... BE
Breaker Failure (IAA) ... BF
Breakerless Electronic Ignition (DICI) ... BEI
Breakerless Ignition System [*Automotive engineering*] ... BIS
Breakers [*Freight*] ... BRKS
Break-Even Load Factor (IIA) ... BELF
Break-Even Point [*Accounting*] ... B/E
Breakfast (CDAI) ... B
Breakfast [*Classified advertising*] (ADA) ... B'FAST
Breakfast (DAVI) ... bkf
Breakfast ... bkfst
Breakfast ... bkft
Breakfast ... BRKF
Breakfast (CPH) ... brkt
Breakfast and Lunch [*Refers to a late morning or early afternoon meal*] ... BRUNCH
Breakfast Fed (MAE) ... BF
Breakfast Time [*Early morning television program*] [*BBC*] ... BT
Break-In (IDOE) ... BK
Break-In [*Telecommunications*] (TEL) ... BKI
Break-In Cycle (SAA) ... BI
Break-In Keying (IAA) ... BK
Break-In Relay ... BIR
Breaking [*FBI standardized term*] ... B
Breaking ... BRKG
Breaking Action (DNAB) ... B/A
Breaking and Entering ... B & E
Breaking and Entering and Auto Theft [*Police crime computer*] ... BEAT
Breaking and Entering in Nighttime and Petty Larceny ... B & ENT & PL
Breaking Capacity (IAA) ... BC
Breaking Strain [*Of fishing lines or casts*] ... BS
Breaking Strength (MAE) ... BS
Breaking Up (ADA) ... B/U
Break-Lock ECM [*Electronic Countermeasures*] **Training** [*Navy*] (ANA) ... BKLKTNG
Break-Loose Torque [*Automotive engineering*] ... BLT
Break-Off Altitude [*Aviation*] (AFM) ... BOA
Breakout (NASA) ... B/O
Breakout Box [*Computer service industry*] (MCD) ... BO
Breakout Box [*Computer service industry*] ... BOB
Breakout Procurement Center Representative (AAGC) ... BPCR
Breakover [*Electronics*] ... BO
Breakpoint [*Telecommunications*] (TEL) ... BP
Breakpoint ... BPT
Breakpoint Address Register (IAA) ... BPA
Breakpoint Cluster Region [*Genetics*] ... BCR
Break-Point Instruction ... BPI
Breaks Above ... BA
Breaks Below ... BB
Breaks in Higher Overcast [*NWS*] (FAAC) ... BRKHIC
Breakthrough ... BT
Breakthrough Bleeding [*Medicine*] ... BB
Breakthrough Bleeding [*Medicine*] ... BTB
Breakthrough Foundation (EA) ... BF
Breakthrough Foundation (EA) ... BTF
Break-Up Missile (MCD) ... BUM
Breakup Time [*Ophthalmology*] ... BUT
Breakwater ... BKW
Breakwater (WDAA) ... BRKWTR
Breakwater Resources Ltd. [*Toronto Stock Exchange symbol Vancouver Stock Exchange symbol*] ... BWR
Brealy Library, Sir Sandford Fleming College, Peterborough, Ont ario [*Library symbol National Library of Canada*] (NLC) ... OPETSF
Bream Fishermen Association ... BFA
Breast (ABBR) ... BRST
Breast Biopsy [*Medicine*] ... B Bx
Breast Biopsy [*Medicine*] ... BB
Breast Biopsy [*Gynecology*] (DAVI) ... br bx
Breast Cancer Advisory Center (EA) ... BCAC
Breast Cancer Detection Center [*University of Michigan*] [*Research center*] (RCD) ... BCDC
Breast Cancer Detection Demonstration Project [*NCI/ACS cosponsored project*] ... BCDDP
Breast Cancer, Ductal [*Medicine*] (DMAA) ... BRCD
Breast Cancer Estrogen-Inducible [*Medicine*] (DMAA) ... BCEI
Breast Cancer Information Clearinghouse ... BCIC
Breast Cancer Screening Indicator ... BCSI
Breast Cancer Task Force [*National Cancer Institute*] ... BCTF
Breast Care and Mastectomy Association (DBA) ... BCMA
Breast Examination (DAVI) ... BE
Breast Examination Bras, Inc. ... BEBI
Breast Examination through Simultaneous Temperature Evaluation ... BEST
Breast Exposure National Trends [*Study*] [*FDA*] ... BENT
Breast Fed [*Medicine*] ... BF
Breast Milk [*Neonatology and obstetrics*] (DAVI) ... BM
Breast Milk [*Neonatology and obstetrics*] (DAVI) ... BrM
Breast Needle Location [*Radiology*] (DAVI) ... BNL
Breast Self Exam [*Gynecology*] (DAVI) ... BSE
Breast Self-Examination [*for cancer*] [*Medicine*] ... BSE
Breast Tumor [*Medicine*] ... BT
Breast Tumor Frozen Section [*Medicine*] (DMAA) ... BTFS
Breastbone (ABBR) ... BRSTBN
Breast-Cyst Fluid Protein [*Immunochemistry*] ... BCFP
Breastplate (ABBR) ... BRSTPLT
Breath [*Medicine*] ... BR
Breath [*or Breathe*] (ABBR) ... BRTH
Breath Alcohol Concentration ... BAC
Breath Alcohol Ignition Interlock Device [*Automotive safety*] ... BAIID
Breath Hydrogen Test ... BHT
Breath Rate per Minute (MCD) ... BRPM
Breath Sounds [*Medicine*] ... BrS
Breath Sounds [*Medicine*] ... BS
Breath Test [*For determining whether or not an auto driver is legally drunk*] [*British*] ... B (Test)
Breath Test ... BT
Breath Units ... BU
Breathable Barrier Film [*Organic chemistry*] ... BBF
Breath-Alcohol Concentration [*Sobriety test*] ... BrAC
Breathe (MSA) ... BRTH
Breathe (ABBR) ... BRTHE
Breathe on Recirculation Ignition System (PDAA) ... BORIS
Breathed (ABBR) ... BRTHD
Breather (MSA) ... BRTHR
Breather Hose/Mouthpiece (MCD) ... BH/MP
Breathers for the Reduction of Atmospheric Hazards to the Environment [*Student legal action organization*] ... BREATHE

Breathers United to Stop Standing Time of Passenger-Buses [*Student legal action organization*] .... BUS STOP
Breath-Hold Diving .... BH
Breath-Hold Time .... BHT
Breathing (ABBR) .... BRTHG
Breathing Air (MCD) .... BA
Breathing Air (NASA) .... BAIR
Breathing Apparatus .... BA
Breathing Apparatus Self-Contained Compressed Air Search and Rescue (PDAA) .... BASAR
Breathing Frequency [*Medicine*] (DAVI) .... f
Breathing Metabolic Simulator [*IBM Corp.*] .... BMS
Breathing Reserve (ADA) .... BR
Breaths per Minute .... BPM
Breaths per Second .... BPS
Breathtaking (ABBR) .... BRTHTKG
Breaux Bridge, LA [*FM radio station call letters*] .... KFTE
Brecht Society of America [*Defunct*] (EA) .... BSA
Breckenridge, CO [*FM radio station call letters*] .... KSMT
Breckenridge Elementary School, Breckenridge, MN [*Library symbol*] [*Library of Congress*] (LCLS) .... MnBreE
Breckenridge High School, Breckenridge, MN [*Library symbol*] [*Library of Congress*] (LCLS) .... MnBreH
Breckenridge, MN [*AM radio station call letters*] .... KBMW
Breckenridge, MN [*FM radio station call letters*] .... KLTA
Breckenridge Public Library, Breckenridge, MN [*Library symbol*] [*Library of Congress*] (LCLS) .... MnBre
Breckenridge, TX [*Location identifier FAA*] (FAAL) .... BKD
Breckenridge, TX [*AM radio station call letters*] .... KBIL
Breckenridge, TX [*FM radio station call letters*] .... KROO
Brecknockshire [*Wales*] (BARN) .... Brec
Brecknockshire [*County in Wales*] (ROG) .... BRECK
Brecknockshire [*County in Wales*] (ROG) .... BRECONS
Brecknockshire [*County in Wales*] (ROG) .... BRK
Brecknockshire [*County in Wales*] .... BRKS
Brecon [*Welsh depot code*] .... BCN
Brecon and Merthyr Railway [*Wales*] .... BM
Breda News, Breda, IA [*Library symbol Library of Congress*] (LCLS) .... IaBreN
Bredasdorp [*South Africa*] [*ICAO location identifier*] (ICLI) .... FABR
Bredstedt [*Germany ICAO location identifier*] (ICLI) .... EDZS
Breech [*Obstetrics*] (DAVI) .... Br
Breech Loading Gun .... BLG
Breech Mechanism [*of a weapon*] .... BM
Breech-Loading [*Weapon*] .... BL
Breech-Loading Rifle .... BLR
Breech-Loading Rifled Guns .... BLRG
Breed Age Average [*Dairy science*] (OA) .... BAA
Breed of Sire .... BOS
Breed Technologies [*NYSE symbol*] (SPSG) .... BDT
Breed Technologies [*Associated Press*] (SAG) .... BredTch
Breeder .... BRDR
Breeder .... BRDR
Breeder Reactor .... BR
Breeder Reactor Corp. .... BRC
Breeders and Hatchermen's Association [*Australia*] .... BHA
Breeding .... BRDG
Breeding Bird Census (BARN) .... BBC
Breeding Bird Survey [*Department of the Interior*] .... BBS
Breeding Gain .... BG
Breeding Ratio [*Nuclear energy*] (NRCH) .... BR
Breema Rug Study Society [*Later, CRSS*] (EA) .... BRSS
Breen, CO [*AM radio station call letters*] .... KLLV
Breese Elementary District 12, Breese, IL [*Library symbol Library of Congress*] (LCLS) .... IBreD
Breese Public Library, Breese, IL [*Library symbol Library of Congress*] (LCLS) .... IBre
Breese's Illinois Reports [*1 Illinois*] [*A publication*] (DLA) .... Breese
Breese's Illinois Supreme Court Reports [*1 Illinois*] [*1819-31*] [*A publication*] (DLA) .... Breese
Breeze (ABBR) .... BRZ
Breeze Electron Ballistic Accelerometer (SAA) .... BEBA
Breezeway (ABBR) .... BRZWY
Breezier (ABBR) .... BRZIR
Breeziest (ABBR) .... BRZST
Breeziness (ABBR) .... BRZNS
Breezing [*Horse racing*] .... B
Breezy (ABBR) .... BRZY
Breezy Point, MN [*FM radio station call letters*] .... KLKS
Brefeldin A [*Antibiotic*] .... BFA
Breguet Cruise [*SST*] .... BC
Breguet-Dassault [*Societe Anonyme des Ateliers d'Aviation Louis Breguet*] [*France ICAO aircraft manufacturer identifier*] (ICAO) .... BG
Breiddalsvik [*Iceland*] [*Airport symbol*] (OAG) .... BXV
Breitkopf & Haertel [*Music*] .... B & H
Breitscheid/Dillkreis [*Germany ICAO location identifier*] (ICLI) .... EDGB
Breit-Wigner Formula .... BWF
Breit-Wigner-Fano [*Spectra interference*] .... BWF
Bremen [*Germany Airport symbol*] (OAG) .... BRE
Bremen [*Germany ICAO location identifier*] (ICLI) .... EDDW
Bremen [*Germany ICAO location identifier*] (ICLI) .... EDWW
Bremen [*Costa Rica*] [*ICAO location identifier*] (ICLI) .... MRBM
Bremen Demokratische Volkspartei [*Bremen Democratic People's Party*] [*Germany Political party*] (PPE) .... BDV
Bremen Enquirer, Bremen, IN [*Library symbol Library of Congress*] (LCLS) .... InBreE

Bremen, GA [*AM radio station call letters*] .... WGMI
Bremen, IN [*FM radio station call letters*] .... WYEZ
Bremen Port of Embarkation [*West Germany*] .... BPE
Bremer County Courthouse, Waverly, IA [*Library symbol Library of Congress*] (LCLS) .... IaWavCoC
Bremer County Historical Society, Plainsfield, IA [*Library symbol Library of Congress*] (LCLS) .... IaPlaBHi
Bremer County Historical Society, Waverly, IA [*Library symbol Library of Congress*] (LCLS) .... IaWavBHi
Bremer County Independent, Waverly, IA [*Library symbol Library of Congress*] (LCLS) .... IaWavI
Bremerhaven [*Germany Airport symbol*] (OAG) .... BRV
Bremerhaven [*Germany ICAO location identifier*] (ICLI) .... EDEO
Bremerhaven/Am Luneort [*Germany ICAO location identifier*] (ICLI) .... EDWB
Bremerton Freight Car Ferry [*AAR code*] .... BFCF
Bremerton, WA [*Location identifier FAA*] (FAAL) .... BER
Bremerton, WA [*Location identifier FAA*] (FAAL) .... CAN
Bremerton, WA [*AM radio station call letters*] .... KBRO
Bremerton, WA [*FM radio station call letters*] .... KRWM
Bremerton, WA [*Location identifier FAA*] (FAAL) .... PWT
Bremgarten [*Germany ICAO location identifier*] (ICLI) .... EDSG
Bremsstrahlung Isochromat Spectroscopy (MCD) .... BIS
Bren Del Win Centennial Library, Deloraine, Manitoba [*Library symbol National Library of Canada*] (NLC) .... MDB
Bren Del Win Centennial Library, Deloraine, MB, Canada [*Library symbol Library of Congress*] (LCLS) .... CaMDB
Bren Gun [*or Gunner*] [*British military*] (DMA) .... BG
Bren Gun Carrier [*British military*] (DMA) .... BGC
Brenair Ltd. [*British ICAO designator*] (FAAC) .... BNX
Brenau College, Gainsville, GA [*Library symbol Library of Congress*] (LCLS) .... GGaB
Brencham Air Charter Ltd. [*British ICAO designator*] (FAAC) .... BRE
Brenco, Inc. [*NASDAQ symbol*] (NQ) .... BREN
Brenco, Inc. [*Associated Press*] (SAG) .... Brenco
Brenda Lee Fan Club (EA) .... BLFC
Brenda Mines Ltd. [*Toronto Stock Exchange symbol Vancouver Stock Exchange symbol*] .... BND
Brendle's, Inc. [*NASDAQ symbol*] (NQ) .... BRDL
Brendle's, Inc. [*Associated Press*] (SAG) .... Brendle
Brenham, TX [*Location identifier FAA*] (FAAL) .... BNH
Brenham, TX [*FM radio station call letters*] .... KTTX
Brenham, TX [*FM radio station call letters*] .... KULF
Brenham, TX [*AM radio station call letters*] .... KWHI
Bren-Mar Resources [*Vancouver Stock Exchange symbol*] .... BML
Brent Resources Group Ltd. [*Vancouver Stock Exchange symbol*] .... BTG
Brenton Banks [*NASDAQ symbol*] (TTSB) .... BRBK
Brenton Banks, Inc. [*NASDAQ symbol*] (NQ) .... BRBK
Brenton Banks, Inc. [*Associated Press*] (SAG) .... BrentBk
Brentwood [*Urban district in England*] .... BRENTW
Brentwood, NY [*FM radio station call letters*] .... WXBA
Brentwood Public Library, Brentwood, MO [*Library symbol Library of Congress*] (LCLS) .... MoBr
Brentwood Public Library, Brentwood, NY [*Library symbol Library of Congress*] (LCLS) .... NBren
Brentwood, TN [*AM radio station call letters*] .... WYOR
Brenwest Mining [*Vancouver Stock Exchange symbol*] .... BWM
Brescia College, London, ON, Canada [*Library symbol*] [*Library of Congress*] (LCLS) .... CaOLBR
Brescia College, London, Ontario [*Library symbol National Library of Canada*] (NLC) .... OLBR
Brescia College, Owensboro, KY [*Library symbol Library of Congress*] (LCLS) .... KyOwB
Bresea Resources Ltd. [*Vancouver Stock Exchange symbol*] .... BSR
Breslau [*Wroclaw*] [*Poland*] [*Seismograph station code, US Geological Survey*] [*Closed*] (SEIS) .... BRE
Breslauer Philologische Abhandlungen [*A publication*] (OCD) .... Bresl Phil Abh
Breslich & Foss [*British*] .... B & F
Brest [*France*] [*Airport symbol*] (OAG) .... BES
Brest [*France ICAO location identifier*] (ICLI) .... LFRR
Brest [*France ICAO location identifier*] (ICLI) .... LFRX
Brest/Guipavas [*France ICAO location identifier*] (ICLI) .... LFRB
Brest Subarea, Channel [*NATO*] .... BRESTCHAN
Bret "Hit Man" Hart Fan Club (EA) .... BHMHFC
Brethren (ABBR) .... BRTHRN
Brethren Historical Library and Archives, Elgin, IL [*Library symbol Library of Congress*] (LCLS) .... IEIgB
Brethren Homes and Older Adult Ministries [*An association*] (EA) .... BHOAM
Brethren in Christ World Missions (EA) .... BICWM
Brethren/Mennonite Council for Lesbian and Gay Concerns (EA) .... BMC
Brethren of the White Cross [*Book written by James De Mille (1873)*] .... BOWC
Brethren Peace Fellowship [*Inactive*] (EA) .... BPF
Brethren Service Commission [*Later, World Ministries Commission*] (EA) ...... BSC
Brethren Volunteer Service (EA) .... BVS
Bretigny-Sur-Orge [*France ICAO location identifier*] (ICLI) .... LFPY
Breton [*MARC language code Library of Congress*] (LCCP) .... bre
Breton [*Language, etc.*] (ROG) .... BRET
Breton Municipal Library, Alberta [*Library symbol National Library of Canada*] (NLC) .... ABRM
Bretton Woods Committee (EA) .... BWC
Bretton Woods Fund (EA) .... BWF
Brett's Cases in Modern Equity [*A publication*] (DLA) .... Brett Ca Eq
Brevard College, Brevard, NC [*Library symbol Library of Congress*] (LCLS) .... NcBreC
Brevard Community College [*Florida*] (KSC) .... BCC
Brevard Community College, Cocoa, FL [*OCLC symbol*] (OCLC) .... EBC

Brevard Community College, Cocoa, FL [*Library symbol Library of Congress*] (LCLS) .... FCoaB
Brevard County Library System, Merritt Island, FL [*Library symbol Library of Congress*] (LCLS) .... FMiB
Brevard Engineering College [*Florida*] (KSC) .... BEC
Brevard, NC [*AM radio station call letters*] .... WGCR
Brevard, NC [*AM radio station call letters*] .... WRAQ
Brevard's Digest of the Public Statute Law, South Carolina [*A publication*] (DLA) .... Brev Dig
Brevard's South Carolina Reports [*1793-1816*] [*A publication*] (DLA) .... Brev
Brevet [*Military*] .... BREV
Brevet [*Military*] .... BT
Brevet [*Military*] .... BVT
Brevete [*Patent*] [*French*] .... BREV
Brevete [*Patent*] [*French*] .... BTE
Brevete sans Garantie du Gouvernement [*Patent without Government Guarantee*] [*French*] .... BSGDG
Breveted [*Military British*] (ROG) .... BREV
Brevetoxin-B [*Biochemistry*] .... BTX-B
Brevia Judicialia [*Judicial Writs*] [*Latin Legal term*] (DLA) .... Brev Ju
Brevia Selecta [*Choice Writs*] [*Latin Legal term*] (DLA) .... Brev Sel
Breviary (VRA) .... brev
Brevier .... BREV
Brevig Mission [*Alaska*] [*Airport symbol*] (OAG) .... KTS
Brevity (ABBR) .... BRVT
Brewarrina [*Australia Airport symbol*] (OAG) .... BWQ
Brewer (ABBR) .... BRWR
Brewer, ME [*FM radio station call letters*] .... WKIT
Brewer, ME [*AM radio station call letters*] .... WNSW
Brewer, ME [*FM radio station call letters*] .... WQCB
Brewer,C Homes'A' [*NASDAQ symbol*] (TTSB) .... CBHI
Breweries and Bottleyard Employees' Industrial Union of Workers of Western Australia .... BBEIUWWA
Breweries and Bottleyards Employees' Union [*Australia*] .... BBEU
Brewers Association of America (EA) .... BAA
Brewers Association of Canada, [*Association des Brasseurs du Canada*], Ott awa, Ontario [*Library symbol National Library of Canada*] (NLC) .... OOBA
Brewers' Association of New South Wales [*Australia*] .... BANSW
Brewers Hop Research Institute [*Later, USBA*] .... BHRI
Brewer's Reports [*19-26 Maryland*] [*A publication*] (DLA) .... Brew
Brewer's Reports [*19-26 Maryland*] [*A publication*] (DLA) .... Brew (MD)
Brewer's Reports [*19-26 Maryland*] [*A publication*] (DLA) .... Brewer
Brewer's Spent Grain .... BSG
Brewer's Spent Grain Bran .... BSGB
Brewers Yeast Council [*Later, Brewers Yeast and Grains Council*] [*Defunct*] (EA) .... BYC
Brewery .... BRWRY
Brewery and Bottling Engineers Association (PDAA) .... BBEA
Brewing (ROG) .... BREW
Brewing .... BRWNG
Brewing & Malting Barley Research Institute [*Institut de Recherche-Brassage et Orge de Maltage*] (AC) .... BMBRI
Brewing Industries Research Institute [*Defunct*] (EA) .... BIRI
Brewing Industry Research Foundation [*British*] .... BIRF
Brewing Research Foundation [*British*] .... BRF
Brewing Trade Review Law Reports [*A publication*] (DLA) .... BTRLR
Brewing Trade Review Licensing Law Reports [*England*] [*A publication*] (DLA) .... BTR
Brewmaster Systems Ltd. [*Vancouver Stock Exchange symbol*] .... BWE
Brewmeisters Anonymous (EA) .... BA
Brewster [*Unit*] [*Physics*] .... B
Brewster Angle Microscopy .... BAM
Brewster Elementary School, Brewster, MN [*Library symbol*] [*Library of Congress*] (LCLS) .... MnBrwES
Brewster Ladies Library, Brewster, MA [*Library symbol*] [*Library of Congress*] (LCLS) .... MBre
Brewster, NY [*AM radio station call letters*] .... WPUT
Brewster Public Library, Brewster, NY [*Library symbol Library of Congress*] (LCLS) .... NBre
Brewster Society (EA) .... BS
Brewsterite [*A zeolite*] .... BRE
Brewster's Pennsylvania Digest [*A publication*] (DLA) .... Brewst PA Dig
Brewster's Pennsylvania Reports [*A publication*] (DLA) .... Brews
Brewster's Pennsylvania Reports [*A publication*] (DLA) .... Brews (PA)
Brewster's Pennsylvania Reports [*A publication*] (DLA) .... Brewst
Brewster's Pennsylvania Reports [*A publication*] (DLA) .... Brewster
Brewton, AL [*AM radio station call letters*] .... WEBJ
Brewton, AL [*FM radio station call letters*] .... WKNU
Brewton-Parker College, Mount Vernon, GA [*Library symbol Library of Congress*] (LCLS) .... GMtvB
Bre-X Minerals Ltd. [*Associated Press*] (SAG) .... BreXMn
Bre-X Minerals Ltd. [*NASDAQ symbol*] (SAG) .... BXMN
Bria [*Central African Republic*] [*ICAO location identifier*] (ICLI) .... FEFR
Brian Head, UT [*FM radio station call letters*] .... KREC
Brian Nolan Spradlin International Fan Club Organization (EA) .... BNSIFCO
Briana Resources Ltd. [*Vancouver Stock Exchange symbol*] .... BIA
Briar Cliff College [*Sioux City, IA*] .... BCC
Briar Cliff College, Sioux City, IA [*Library symbol Library of Congress*] (LCLS) .... IaScB
Briar Cliff College, Sioux City, IA [*OCLC symbol*] (OCLC) .... IOB
Briar Pipe Trade Association [*British*] (DBA) .... BPTA
Briarcliff College, Briarcliff Manor, NY [*Library symbol Library of Congress*] (LCLS) .... NBmB
Briarcliff Manor, NY [*FM radio station call letters*] .... WRGX
Briarcliff Manor Public Library, Briarcliff Manor, NY [*Library symbol Library of Congress*] (LCLS) .... NBm
Briard Club of America (EA) .... BCA
Briare/Chatillon [*France ICAO location identifier*] (ICLI) .... LFEI
Bribery [*FBI standardized term*] .... BRBY
Bribery (DLA) .... BRIB
Bribery-Labor [*FBI undercover investigation*] .... BRILAB
Brican Resources [*Vancouver Stock Exchange symbol*] .... BRI
Brice Henderson Fan Club (EA) .... BHFC
Brice. Law Relating to Public Worship [*1875*] [*A publication*] (DLA) .... Bri Pub Wor
Brices Crossroads National Battlefield Site .... BRCR
Brice's Ultra Vires [*A publication*] (ILCA) .... Br Ult V
Brice's Ultra Vires [*A publication*] (DLA) .... Bri Ult V
Brice's Ultra Vires [*A publication*] (DLA) .... Brice Ult V
Brick (WGA) .... B
Brick [*Classified advertising*] (ADA) .... BK
Brick .... BRCK
Brick (VRA) .... bri
Brick (MSA) .... BRK
Brick and Tile (ADA) .... BT
Brick Association of North Carolina (SRA) .... BANC
Brick Association of South Carolina (SRA) .... BASC
Brick Brewing Co. Ltd. [*Toronto Stock Exchange symbol*] .... BRB
Brick Construction .... BR
Brick Development Association [*British*] (DBA) .... BDA
Brick Development Research Institute [*Australia*] .... BDRI
Brick Institute of America (EA) .... BIA
Brick Institute of California (SRA) .... BRIC
Brick of Bytes [*Computer software*] [*Army High-Performance Computing Research Center*] (RDA) .... BOB
Brick Piers (BARN) .... bp
Brick Protected [*Insurance classification*] .... BP
Brick Township, NJ [*FM radio station call letters*] .... WBGD
Brick Unprotected [*Insurance classification*] .... BU
Brick Veneered [*Insurance classification*] .... BV
Brickell's Digest [*Alabama*] [*A publication*] (DLA) .... Brick Ala Dig
Brickell's Digest [*Alabama*] [*A publication*] (DLA) .... Brick Dig
Bricklayers, Masons, and Plasterers' International of America [*Later, BAC*] .... BMP
Bricklayers, Masons Independent Union of Canada .... BMIU
Bricklin International (EA) .... BI
Brickmakers Society [*A union*] [*British*] .... BS
Bricks, Pottery, Glass, Cement [*Department of Employment*] [*British*] .... BPGC
Brickwork .... BWK
Bridal .... BRDL
Bridal and Bridesmaids Apparel Association (EA) .... BBAA
Bridal Industry Association (EA) .... BIA
Bridge [*Shipping*] .... B
Bridge [*Board on Geographic Names*] (KSC) .... BDG
Bridge (ADA) .... BDGE
Bridge [*Dentistry*] (DAVI) .... BR
Bridge [*Interconnects computer networks*] .... BR
Bridge (ROG) .... BRD
Bridge (KSC) .... BRDG
Bridge [*or Bridging*] [*Telecommunications*] (TEL) .... BRG
Bridge .... BRG
Bridge [*Postal Service standard*] (OPSA) .... BRG
Bridge .... BRI
Bridge [*Commonly used*] (OPSA) .... BRIDGE
Bridge Across the Pond Tom Jones Fan Club (EA) .... BATP
Bridge Amplifier .... BA
Bridge and Building Supply Association [*Defunct*] .... BBSA
Bridge and Structures Information Center [*University of Pittsburgh Department of Civil Engineering*] [*Information service or system*] (IID) .... BASIC
Bridge Construction Exercise [*Military*] (NVT) .... BRIDGEX
Bridge Control System (IAA) .... BCS
Bridge Cutoff (IEEE) .... BCO
Bridge Display Console .... BDC
Bridge Display Panel [*Navy*] (CAAL) .... BDP
Bridge Educational Trust Ltd. [*British*] .... BET
Bridge Erection Boat .... BEB
Bridge Excitation .... BRDGSCIT
Bridge/Forecastle [*of a ship*] (DS) .... BF
Bridge Grid Flooring Manufacturers Association (EA) .... BGFMA
Bridge Needs and Investment Process [*FHWA*] (TAG) .... BNIP
Bridge Plotting Room [*Navy*] .... BPR
Bridge Protocol Data Unit [*Telecommunications*] (ACRL) .... BPDU
Bridge Rating and Analysis Structural System (MCD) .... BRASS
Bridge Receiving Room [*Navy*] .... BRR
Bridge Relay Element [*Electronics*] (ACRL) .... BRE
Bridge Resources Ltd. [*Vancouver Stock Exchange symbol*] .... BGU
Bridge/Router [*Telecommunications*] (ACRL) .... B/R
Bridge View Bancorp [*Associated Press*] (SAG) .... BrdgVw
Bridge View Bancorp [*AMEX symbol*] (SAG) .... BVB
Bridge Wireless Officer [*British military*] (DMA) .... BWO
Bridged Frequency Ringing [*Telecommunications*] (TEL) .... BFR
Bridged Tap Isolator (IEEE) .... BTI
Bridge-Element Delay (IEEE) .... BED
Bridgehampton, NY [*FM radio station call letters*] .... WLIE
Bridgehead (MSA) .... BRGHD
Bridgehead (AABC) .... BRH
Bridgelayer [*British military*] (DMA) .... B/L
Bridgeport [*Connecticut*] [*Airport symbol*] (OAG) .... BDR
Bridgeport [*Diocesan abbreviation*] [*Connecticut*] (TOCD) .... BGP

Bridgeport [*Connecticut*] [*Seismograph station code, US Geological Survey Closed*] (SEIS) .... BPT
Bridgeport, AL [*AM radio station call letters*] .... WBTS
Bridgeport City Normal School, Bridgeport, CT [*Library symbol Library of Congress Obsolete*] (LCLS) .... CtBN
Bridgeport, CT [*AM radio station call letters*] .... WCUM
Bridgeport, CT [*AM radio station call letters*] .... WDJZ
Bridgeport, CT [*Television station call letters*] .... WEDW
Bridgeport, CT [*FM radio station call letters*] .... WEZN
Bridgeport, CT [*Television station call letters*] .... WHAI
Bridgeport, CT [*AM radio station call letters*] .... WICC
Bridgeport, CT [*FM radio station call letters*] .... WPKN
Bridgeport Engineering Institute [*Connecticut*] .... BEI
Bridgeport Machines [*NASDAQ symbol*] (TTSB) .... BPTM
Bridgeport Machines, Inc. [*NASDAQ symbol*] (SAG) .... BPTM
Bridgeport Machines, Inc. [*Associated Press*] (SAG) .... BptMach
Bridgeport, NY [*FM radio station call letters*] .... WTKW
Bridgeport Public Library, Bridgeport, CT [*OCLC symbol*] (OCLC) .... BPT
Bridgeport Public Library, Bridgeport, CT [*Library symbol Library of Congress*] (LCLS) .... CtB
Bridgeport Public Library, Bridgeport, MI [*Library symbol Library of Congress*] (LCLS) .... MiBrid
Bridgeport, TX [*Location identifier FAA*] (FAAL) .... BPR
Bridgeport, TX [*FM radio station call letters*] .... KBOC
Bridgeport, TX [*FM radio station call letters*] .... KBTT
Bridgeport, WV [*FM radio station call letters*] .... WDCI
Bridger Memorial Public Library, Bladenboro, NC [*Library symbol Library of Congress*] (LCLS) .... NcBl
Bridger Resources, Inc. [*Vancouver Stock Exchange symbol*] .... BDG
Bridges and Tunnels Crowd [*Derogatory reference to people who reach Manhattan via these routes*] .... B and T
Bridgeton Evening News, Bridgeton, NJ [*Library symbol Library of Congress*] (LCLS) .... NjBN
Bridgeton Free Public Library, Bridgeton, NJ [*Library symbol Library of Congress*] (LCLS) .... NjB
Bridgeton, NJ [*FM radio station call letters*] .... WNJB
Bridgeton, NJ [*AM radio station call letters*] .... WSNJ
Bridgeton, NJ [*FM radio station call letters*] .... WSNJ-FM
Bridgetown [*Barbados*] [*ICAO location identifier*] (ICLI) .... TBPO
Bridgetown/Grantley Adams Internacional [*Barbados*] [*ICAO location identifier*] (ICLI) .... TBPB
Bridgettines [*Roman Catholic religious order*] .... BRIDG
Bridge-Tunnel [*Proposed English Channel link between Britain and France*] .... BRUNNEL
Bridgeview Public Library, Bridgeview, IL [*Library symbol Library of Congress*] (LCLS) .... IBrv
Bridgeville Savings Bank FSB [*Pennsylvania*] [*NASDAQ symbol*] (SAG) ...... BREC
Bridgeville Savings Bank FSB [*Pennsylvania*] [*Associated Press*] (SAG) .... BridgvSv
Bridgeville Savings Bank FSB PA [*NASDAQ symbol*] (SAG) .... BRFC
Bridgeville Savings Bk [*NASDAQ symbol*] (TTSB) .... BRFC
Bridgewater College, Bridgewater, VA [*OCLC symbol*] (OCLC) .... VBC
Bridgewater College, Bridgewater, VA [*Library symbol Library of Congress*] (LCLS) .... ViBrC
Bridgewater, MA [*FM radio station call letters*] .... WBIM
Bridgewater, NJ [*AM radio station call letters*] .... WBRW
Bridgewater, NS [*AM radio station call letters*] .... CKBW
Bridgewater State College (GAGS) .... Bridgewater St C
Bridgewater State College, Bridgewater, MA [*OCLC symbol*] (OCLC) .... BDR
Bridgewater State College, Bridgewater, MA [*Library symbol Library of Congress*] (LCLS) .... MBridT
Bridgewater, VA [*Location identifier FAA*] (FAAL) .... VBW
Bridgewater, VA [*FM radio station call letters*] .... WAMM
Bridgewest Development [*Vancouver Stock Exchange symbol*] .... BWD
Bridgewire (NASA) .... BW
Bridgford Foods [*NASDAQ symbol*] (TTSB) .... BRID
Bridgford Foods Corp. [*NASDAQ symbol*] (NQ) .... BRID
Bridging [*Graphics*] .... BDG
Bridging and Routing Packet Control Facility [*Network Systems Corp.*] (PCM) .... BCF/PCF
Bridging Hepatic Necrosis [*Gastroenterology*] (DAVI) .... BHN
Bridging Key [*on Dial Assistance Switchboard*] (CET) .... BR
Bridging Truck [*British*] .... BT
Bridgman. Index to Equity Cases [*A publication*] (DLA) .... Bridg Eq Ind
Bridgman. Legal Bibliography [*1801*] [*A publication*] (DLA) .... Bridg Leg Bib
Bridgman, MI [*FM radio station call letters*] (RBYB) .... WYTZ
Bridgman on Conveyancing [*A publication*] (DLA) .... Bridg Conv
Bridgman Public Library, Bridgman, MI [*Library symbol Library of Congress*] (LCLS) .... MiBridm
Bridgman. Reflections on the Study of the Law [*1804*] [*A publication*] (DLA) .... Bridg Ref
Bridgman's Digested Index [*A publication*] (DLA) .... Bridg Dig Ind
Bridgman's Thesaurus Juridicus [*A publication*] (DLA) .... Bridg Thes
Bridle Arrester (MCD) .... B/A
Bridled with Rainbows [*A publication*] .... BrR
Bridlington [*Yorkshire resort town*] [*England*] (DSUE) .... BRID
Bridport [*Municipal borough in England*] .... BRIDP
Brief .... BF
Brief .... br
Brief .... BRF
Brief (FAAC) .... BRF
Brief Adaptive Psychotherapy [*Psychology*] .... BAP
Brief and Time [*Photography*] .... B & T
Brief, Bright, Brotherly [*Religion*] (DSUE) .... 3B's
Brief Carroll Depression Rating Scale [*Psychology*] (DMAA) .... BCDRS

Brief Cognitive Rating Scale [*Medicine*] (DMAA) .... BCRS
Brief Easy Editing Routine (ADA) .... BEER
Brief Entry .... BE
Brief Index of Adaptive Behavior [*Educational development test*] .... BIAB
Brief Intelligence Summary (NATG) .... BINSUM
Brief Introduction .... BI
Brief Maximal Effort [*Orthopedics and physical therapy*] (DAVI) .... BME
Brief Neuropsychological Mental Status Examination .... BNMSE
Brief of the Phi Delta Phi [*Menasha, Wisconsin*] [*A publication*] (DLA) .... Brief
Brief Psychiatric Rate Scale (DAVI) .... BPRS
Brief Psychiatric Rating Scale .... BPRS
Brief Psychiatric Reacting Scale (DAVI) .... BPRS
Brief Record Cataloging .... BRC
Brief Repetitive Isometric Maximal Exercise (DMAA) .... BRIME
Brief Short-Action Potential (MAE) .... BSAP
Brief, Small, Abundant Potential (MAE) .... BSAP
Brief Stimulus Therapy [*Psychology*] .... BST
Brief Stop for Ammunition Lift [*Military*] (NVT) .... BSA
Brief Stop for Cargo Lift [*or Delivery*] [*Military*] (NVT) .... BSC
Brief Stop for Embarking or Debarking Personnel [*Military*] (NVT) .... BSP
Brief Stop for Fuel [*Military*] (NVT) .... BSF
Brief Symptom Inventory [*Personality development test*] [*Psychology*] .... BSI
Brief Systems Test [*NASA*] (KSC) .... BST
Brief Task Description (AAG) .... BTD
Brief Task Outline (AAG) .... BTO
Brief Vestibular Disorientation Test .... BVDT
Briefcase Terminal [*Army*] (INF) .... BCT
Briefer .... BFR
Briefing (AABC) .... BFG
Briefing (KSC) .... BRFG
Briefing Centre, World University Services of Canada [*Centre de Ressources, Entraide Universitaire Mondiale du Canada*], Ottawa, Ontario [*Library symbol National Library of Canada*] (NLC) .... OOWU
Briefing Papers (AAGC) .... BP
[*The*] Briefing Papers Collection [*A publication*] (AAGC) .... BPC
Briefing Room [*Navy*] .... BR
Briefings/Issues/Projects/Programs (DNAB) .... BIPP
Brienne-Le-Chateau [*France ICAO location identifier*] (ICLI) .... LFFN
Brig [*Ship*] (ROG) .... BG
Brig .... BR
Brig [*Shipping*] (ROG) .... BRG
Brig [*Switzerland*] [*Seismograph station code, US Geological Survey Closed*] (SEIS) .... BRI
Brigadas Revolucionarias [*Revolutionary Brigades*] [*Portugal Political party*] (PPE) .... BR
Brigade (AABC) .... BDE
Brigade .... BGDE
Brigade (WGA) .... BR
Brigade .... BRIG
Brigade Administrative Area [*Military British*] .... BAA
Brigade Aeroportee Renforcee [*Reinforced Airborne Brigade*] [*Zaire*] (AF) ..... BAR
Brigade Air Support Officer [*Military British*] .... BASO
Brigade Air Support Operations Centre [*Military British*] .... BASOC
Brigade Airborne Alert Force [*Military*] .... BAAF
Brigade and Below Command and Control [*Military*] (RDA) B2C2
Brigade Artillery [*Army*] (INF) .... BRIGARTY
Brigade Artillery Intelligence Officer [*Military British*] .... BAIO
Brigade/Battalion Simulation [*Army*] (DOMA) .... BBS
Brigade/Battalion Simulations [*Army*] (INF) .... BBS
Brigade Battle Simulation [*Army*] .... BBS
Brigade Combat Team [*Army*] (INF) .... BCT
Brigade Data Center [*Military*] (AABC) .... BDC
Brigade Data Processing System .... BDPS
Brigade Electrical and Mechanical Engineer [*Military British*] .... BEME
Brigade Engineer Group [*Marine Corps*] (CINC) .... BEG
Brigade Headquarters [*Army*] .... BH
Brigade Headquarters [*Army*] .... BHQ
Brigade Headquarters [*Army*] .... BRIGHED
Brigade Landing Exercise [*Military*] (NVT) .... BRIGLEX
Brigade Landing Team [*Army*] (AABC) .... BDELT
Brigade Logistic Support Group [*Marine Corps*] (CINC) .... BLSG
Brigade Maintenance Area [*British military*] (DMA) .... BMA
Brigade Major (DAS) .... B Maj
Brigade Major [*Military*] .... Bde Maj
Brigade Major .... BM
Brigade Major of the Queen's Troops [*British*] (ROG) .... BMQT
Brigade Major, Royal Artillery [*British and Canadian*] .... BMRA
Brigade of Guards .... BOG
Brigade of Gurkhas [*British military*] (DMA) .... BG
Brigade Operations Display and After Action Review System [*Army*] (RDA) .... BODAS
Brigade Ordnance Officer [*British*] .... BOO
Brigade Ordnance Warrant Officer [*British*] .... BOWO
Brigade Quartermaster [*Marine Corps*] .... BRQM
Brigade Receiving Room .... BRR
Brigade Resources, Inc. [*Vancouver Stock Exchange symbol*] .... BGA
Brigade Rouge d'Occitanie [*Red Brigade of Occitania*] [*France*] (PD) .... BROC
Brigade Routine Order [*British*] .... BRO
Brigade Support Area [*Military*] (AABC) .... BSA
Brigade Tactical Operations Center .... BTOC
Brigade Transport Officer [*British*] .... BTO
Brigades Revolutionnaires Francaises [*Revolutionary French Brigades*] [*French*] (PD) .... BRF
Brigadier .... BDR
Brigadier [*British military*] (DMA) .... Br

Brigadier (EY) ... BRIG
Brigadier ... BRIG
Brigadier (ODBW) ... Brig
Brigadier General ... BG
Brigadier General ... BGEN
Brigadier General (AFM) ... BRIG GEN
Brigadier General ... BRIGEN
Brigadier General [*Air Force, Army, Marine Corps*] ... O7
Brigadier, General Staff [*Army British*] ... BGS
Brigadier, Royal Artillery [*British*] ... BRA
Brigadier, Royal Artillery (Antiaircraft Artillery) [*British and Canadian*] ... BRA(AA)
Brigantine [*Ship*] ... BGN
Brigantine [*Ship*] (ROG) ... BN
Brigantine [*Ship*] (ADA) ... B'TINE
Brigantine Times, Brigantine, NJ [*Library symbol Library of Congress*] (LCLS) ... NjBrigT
Brigate Rosse [*Red Brigades*] [*Italy*] (PD) ... BR
Brigford Foods Corp. [*Associated Press*] (SAG) ... BrdgF
Brigford Foods Corp. [*Associated Press*] (SAG) ... BrdgF
Briggs & Stratton [*NYSE symbol*] (TTSB) ... BGG
Briggs & Stratton Corp. ... B & S
Briggs & Stratton Corp. [*NYSE symbol*] (SPSG) ... BGG
Briggs & Stratton Corp. [*Associated Press*] (SAG) ... BrigSt
Briggs & Stratton Corp. [*Associated Press*] (SAG) ... BrigStrat
Brigg's General Railway Acts [*A publication*] (DLA) ... Briggs Ry Acts
Briggs, OH [*Location identifier FAA*] (FAAL) ... BSV
Briggs-Lawrence County Public Library, Ironton, OH [*Library symbol Library of Congress*] (LCLS) ... OIB
Brigham City, UT [*Location identifier FAA*] (FAAL) ... BMC
Brigham City, UT [*FM radio station call letters*] (RBYB) ... KLZX-FM
Brigham City, UT [*AM radio station call letters*] ... KSOS
Brigham City, UT [*FM radio station call letters*] ... KSOS-FM
Brigham Young Libraries Information Network [*Brigham Young University*] [*Provo, UT*] [*Information service or system*] (IID) ... BYLINE
Brigham Young University [*Utah*] ... BYU
Brigham Young University, Hawaii Campus, Laie, HI [*OCLC symbol*] (OCLC) ... BYU
Brigham Young University, Hawaii Campus, Laie, HI [*Library symbol Library of Congress*] (LCLS) ... HLaB
Brigham Young University, J. Reuben Clark Law Library, Provo, UT [*Library symbol Library of Congress*] (LCLS) ... UPB-L
Brigham Young University Press ... BYUP
Brigham Young University, Provo, UT [*Library symbol Library of Congress*] (LCLS) ... UPB
Brigham Young University, School of Library and Information Science, Provo, UT [*OCLC symbol*] (OCLC) ... UUB
Bright [*of stars*] (BARN) ... a
Bright (FAAC) ... BRGT
Bright (MSA) ... BRT
Bright Alphanumeric Display System (CAAL) ... BRANDS
Bright Alphanumeric Sub-System (PDAA) ... BANS
Bright [*T. G.*] **& Co. Ltd.** [*Toronto Stock Exchange symbol*] ... BRT
Bright Annealed (DAC) ... BA
Bright Belt Warehouse Association (EA) ... BBWA
Bright Cathode-Ray Tube (DEN) ... BCRT
Bright Display Equipment ... BDE
Bright Display RADAR Indicator ... BDRI
Bright Greenish Yellow [*Fluorescence*] [*A fungal metabolite property*] (OA) ... BGY
Bright Greenish Yellow Fluorescence [*A fungal metabolite property*] ... BGYF
Bright. Husband and Wife [*3rd ed.*] [*1849*] [*A publication*] (DLA) ... Bright H & W
Bright Object Sensor (MCD) ... BOS
Bright Old Thing [*A member of established society in Washington, DC*] ... BOT
Bright QUASAR Survey [*Astronomy*] ... BQS
Bright RADAR Indicator-Tower Equipment ... BRITE
Bright RADAR Tube Display (AAG) ... BRTD
Bright Red Blood [*Medicine*] ... BRB
Bright Red Blood per Rectum [*Medicine*] ... BRBPR
Bright Source Protection [*Optics*] ... BSP
Bright Two Sides [*Lumber*] (DAC) ... B2S
Bright Wire Goods Manufacturers Service Bureau [*Defunct*] (EA) ... BWGMSB
Bright Young Thing (DSUE) ... BYT
Brightly on the Law of Costs in Pennsylvania [*A publication*] (DLA) ... Bright Costs
Brightly's Analytical Digest of the Laws of the United States [*A publication*] (DLA) ... Bright Dig
Brightly's Analytical Digest of the Laws of the United States [*A publication*] (DLA) ... Bright US Dig
Brightly's Analytical Digest of the Laws of the United States [*A publication*] (DLA) ... Brightly Dig
Brightly's Annotated Bankrupt Law [*A publication*] (DLA) ... Bright Bank Law
Brightly's Digest [*Pennsylvania*] [*A publication*] (DLA) ... Bright Dig
Brightly's Digest [*New York*] [*A publication*] (DLA) ... Bright Dig
Brightly's Digest [*New York*] [*A publication*] (DLA) ... Brightly Dig
Brightly's Digest [*Pennsylvania*] [*A publication*] (DLA) ... Brightly Dig
Brightly's Edition of Purdon's Digest of Pennsylvania Laws [*A publication*] (DLA) ... Bright Pur Dig
Brightly's Edition of Purdon's Digest of Pennsylvania Laws [*A publication*] (DLA) ... Bright Purd
Brightly's Edition of Troubat and Haly's Practice [*A publication*] (DLA) ... Bright Tr & H Pr
Brightly's Equitable Jurisdiction [*Pennsylvania*] [*A publication*] (DLA) ... Bright Eq Jur
Brightly's Federal Digest [*A publication*] (DLA) ... Br Fed Dig
Brightly's Federal Digest [*A publication*] (DLA) ... Bright Fed Dig
Brightly's Leading Election Cases [*Pennsylvania*] [*A publication*] (DLA) ... Bright EC
Brightly's Leading Election Cases [*Pennsylvania*] [*A publication*] (DLA) ... Bright Elec Cas
Brightly's Leading Election Cases [*Pennsylvania*] [*A publication*] (DLA) ... Brightly El
Brightly's Leading Election Cases [*Pennsylvania*] [*A publication*] (DLA) ... Brightly El Cas
Brightly's Leading Election Cases [*Pennsylvania*] [*A publication*] (DLA) ... Brightly Elect Cas
Brightly's Leading Election Cases [*Pennsylvania*] [*A publication*] (DLA) ... Brightly Election Cas (PA)
Brightly's Leading Election Cases [*Pennsylvania*] [*A publication*] (DLA) ... Brightly's Elec Cas
Brightly's New York Digest [*A publication*] (DLA) ... Bright NY Dig
Brightly's Pennsylvania Digest [*A publication*] (DLA) ... Bright PA Dig
Brightly's Pennsylvania Nisi Prius Reports [*A publication*] (DLA) ... Bright
Brightly's Pennsylvania Nisi Prius Reports [*A publication*] (DLA) ... Bright NP
Brightly's Pennsylvania Nisi Prius Reports [*A publication*] (DLA) ... Bright (PA)
Brightly's Pennsylvania Nisi Prius Reports [*A publication*] (DLA) ... Brightly
Brightly's Pennsylvania Nisi Prius Reports [*A publication*] (DLA) ... Brightly NP
Brightly's Pennsylvania Nisi Prius Reports [*A publication*] (DLA) ... Brightly's Rep
Brightly's Pennsylvania Nisi Prius Reports [*A publication*] (DLA) ... PA NP
Brightness ... B
Brightness (KSC) ... BRI
Brightness (GAVI) ... BRT
Brightness Contrast ... BC
Brightness Contrast Value ... BCV
Brightness Merit ... BM
Brightness Modulation [*Ultrasound scanning*] [*Medicine*] (DAVI) ... B-Mode
Brighton [*County borough in England*] ... BRIGH
Brighton [*England*] [*Airport symbol*] (AD) ... BSH
Brighton (ROG) ... BTON
Brighton & South Coast Railway [*British*] (ROG) ... BSC
Brighton & South Coast Railway [*British*] (ROG) ... BSCR
Brighton City Library, Brighton, MI [*Library symbol Library of Congress*] (LCLS) ... MiBrig
Brighton, CO [*AM radio station call letters*] (RBYB) ... KLDC-AM
Brighton, CO [*AM radio station call letters*] ... KLTT
Brighton Community Hospital, Medical Library, Brighton, CO [*Library symbol Library of Congress*] (LCLS) ... CoBriH-M
Brighton Enterprise-News, Brighton, IA [*Library symbol*] [*Library of Congress*] (LCLS) ... IaBrBEN
Brighton Enterprise-News, Brighton, IA [*Library symbol Library of Congress*] (LCLS) ... IaBrEN
Brighton High School Library, Rochester, NY [*OCLC symbol*] (OCLC) ... RVS
Brighton MARC [*Machine-Readable Catalogue*] **Project** [*British*] (NITA) ... BRIMARC
Brighton Memorial Library, Brighton, IL [*Library symbol Library of Congress*] (LCLS) ... IBri
Brighton, NY [*FM radio station call letters*] (RBYB) ... WAQB-FM
Brighton Public Library, Ontario [*Library symbol National Library of Canada*] (BIB) ... OBRIG
Brighton Reading and Individualized Skills Continuum (EDAC) ... BRISC
Brightpoint, Inc. [*Associated Press*] (SAG) ... Brightpt
Brightpoint, Inc. [*NASDAQ symbol*] (SAG) ... CELL
Brightwells Barrow [*England*] ... BRIGHTW BAR
Brigitte Bardot [*French actress*] ... BB
Brigittine Monks (TOCD) ... OSsS
Brigittine Monks (TOCD) ... osss
Brigus Public Library, Brigus, NF, Canada [*Library symbol Library of Congress*] (LCLS) ... CaNfBri
Brigus Public Library, Newfoundland [*Library symbol National Library of Canada*] (NLC) ... NFBRI
Brill, C. D., Washington DC [*STAC*] ... BCD
Brillante [*Brilliantly*] [*Music*] ... BRILL
Brilliance (KSC) ... BRIL
Brilliance China Automotive [*NYSE symbol*] (SPSG) ... CBA
Brilliance China Automotive Holding Ltd. [*Associated Press*] (SAG) ... BrillChA
Brilliant [*Philately*] ... bril
Brilliant [*British Slang*] ... BRILL
Brilliant and Ivory [*Jewelry*] (ROG) ... B & I
Brilliant Anti-Armor Submunition [*Army*] (RDA) ... BAT
Brilliant Anti-Armor [*Submunition*] **Technology** ... BAT
Brilliant Anti-Tank System [*Army*] ... BAT
Brilliant Buff Finishing [*Metal finishing*] ... BBF
[*A*] **Brilliant Career** ... ABC
Brilliant Computer Products Co. (PCM) ... BCP
Brilliant Cresyl Blue [*Biological stain*] ... BCB
Brilliant Digital Entertainment, Inc. [*AMEX symbol*] (SAG) ... BDE
Brilliant Digital Entertainment, Inc. [*Associated Press*] (SAG) ... BrillDig
Brilliant Eyes ... BE
Brilliant Green [*An indicator*] [*Chemistry*] ... BG
Brilliant Green Agar (OA) ... BGA
Brilliant Green Bile [*Microorganism growth medium*] ... BGB
Brilliant Green Lactose Broth (MAE) ... BGLB
Brilliant Green Suphadiazine-Deoxycholate Agar (PDAA) ... BGSDA
Brilliant Pebbles ... BP
Brilliant Uncirculated [*Condition of coins*] [*Numismatics*] ... BU
Brillion, WI [*FM radio station call letters*] ... WEZR
Brillouin Scattering (PDAA) ... BS
Brillouin Zone [*Physics*] ... BZ
Brillouin-Wentzel-Kramers [*Physics*] ... BWK
Brimm Energy Corp. [*NASDAQ symbol*] (SAG) ... BRIM
Brimm Energy Corp. [*NASDAQ symbol*] (TTSB) ... BRIMF

Brimm Energy Corp. [*Associated Press*] (SAG) ... Brimm
Brimstone R. R. [*AAR code*] ... BRM
Brinco Ltd. [*Toronto Stock Exchange symbol*] ... BRN
Brindise/Casale [*Italy ICAO location identifier*] (ICLI) ... LIBR
Brindisi [*Italy*] [*Airport symbol*] (OAG) ... BDS
Brindisi [*Italy ICAO location identifier*] (ICLI) ... LIBB
Brindled (WGA) ... BD
Brine Chiller Test Stand (DWSG) ... BCTS
Brine Disposal Program [*Environmental Data and Information Service*] (MSC) ... BDP
Brine Shrimp Nauplii [*Ichthyology*] ... BSN
Brinell Hardness Number [*Also, BHN, BHNo, HB*] ... BH
Brinell Hardness Number [*Also, BH, BHNo, HB*] ... BHN
Brinell Hardness Number [*Also, BH, BHN, HB*] ... BHNo
Brinell Hardness Number [*Also, BH, BHN, BHNo*] ... HB
Bring Back Mark Lindsay Campaign (EA) ... BBMLC
Bring 'Em Back Alive [*AAA Holiday News Service*] ... BEBA
Bring Forward ... BF
Bring Your Own [*Liquor*] [*Party invitation notation*] ... BYO
Bring Your Own Beef [*Phrase popularized during 1973 beef shortage*] ... BYOB
Bring Your Own Boat ... BYOB
Bring Your Own Booze [*or Bottle*] [*Party invitation notation*] ... BYOB
Bring Your Own Girl (IIA) ... BYOG
Bring Your Own Grog [*British*] (ADA) ... BYOG
Bring Your Own TV ... BYOTV
Bring Your Own Vehicle ... BYOV
Bring Your Own Wine (ADA) ... BYOW
Bringham Memorial Library, Sharon, WI [*Library symbol Library of Congress*] (LCLS) ... WSha
Bring-Up Security Investigation [*Military*] ... BUSI
Brinker International [*Formerly, Chili's, Inc.*] [*Associated Press*] (SAG) ... Brinker
Brinker International [*Formerly, Chili's, Inc.*] [*NYSE symbol*] (SPSG) ... EAT
Brinker Intl. [*NYSE symbol*] (TTSB) ... EAT
Brinkley, AR [*Location identifier FAA*] (FAAL) ... BKZ
Brinkley, AR [*AM radio station call letters*] ... KBRI
Brinkley, AR [*FM radio station call letters*] ... KQMC
Brio Industries [*NASDAQ symbol*] (SAG) ... BRIO
Brio Industries [*NASDAQ symbol*] (TTSB) ... BRIOF
Brio Industries [*Associated Press*] (SAG) ... BrioInd
Brioude-Beaumont [*France ICAO location identifier*] (ICLI) ... LFHR
Briquet ... BQ
Briquette (ADA) ... BRIQ
Briquette ... BRQTT
Briquettes (VRA) ... briq
Brisa International [*Toronto Stock Exchange symbol*] ... BSA
Brisbane [*Australia ICAO location identifier*] (ICLI) ... ABBB
Brisbane [*Australia ICAO location identifier*] (ICLI) ... ABBN
Brisbane [*Australia ICAO location identifier*] (ICLI) ... ABBR
Brisbane [*Australia ICAO location identifier*] (ICLI) ... ABBX
Brisbane [*Australia ICAO location identifier*] (ICLI) ... ABEF
Brisbane [*Australia ICAO location identifier*] (ICLI) ... ABRF
Brisbane [*Australia Airport symbol*] (OAG) ... BNE
Brisbane [*Australia*] ... Bris
Brisbane [*Australia Seismograph station code, US Geological Survey*] (SEIS) ... BRS
Brisbane Amateur Winemakers' Club [*Australia*] ... BAWC
Brisbane/Archerfield [*Australia ICAO location identifier*] (ICLI) ... ABAF
Brisbane Basketball ... BB
Brisbane Biennial ... BB
Brisbane Bushwalkers Club ... BBC
Brisbane Forest Park Administration [*Australia*] ... BFPA
Brisbane Funeral Directors' Association [*Australia*] ... BFDA
Brisbane Jazz Club [*Australia*] ... BJC
Brisbane Latvian Club [*Australia*] ... BLC
Brisbane Market Trust [*Australia*] ... BMT
Brisbane Netball Association [*Australia*] ... BNA
Brisbane Night Tennis Association [*Australia*] ... BNTA
Brisbane Overseas Wharfowners' Association [*Australia*] ... BOWA
Brisbane Produce Merchants' Association [*Australia*] ... BPMA
Brisbane Sand and Gravel Producers' Association [*Australia*] ... BSGPA
Brisbane Sporting Car Club [*Australia*] ... BSCC
Brisbane Theosophical Society [*Australia*] ... BTS
Brisbane Tramway Museum Society [*Australia*] ... BTMS
Brisbane Warana Festival [*Australia*] ... BWF
Brisbane Women's Club [*Australia*] ... BWC
Brisbane Women's Hockey Association [*Australia*] ... BWHA
Brisbin's Reports [*1 Minnesota*] [*A publication*] (DLA) ... Brisb Minn
Brisbin's Reports [*1 Minnesota*] [*A publication*] (DLA) ... Brisbin
Brisk and Equal [*Medicine*] (DMAA) ... B&E
Brisket (ABBR) ... BRSKT
Briskly (ABBR) ... BRSKY
Bris-Myr Squibb,$2 Cv Pfd [*NYSE symbol*] (TTSB) ... BMYPr
Bristle (ABBR) ... BRSL
Bristled (ABBR) ... BRSLD
Bristling (ABBR) ... BRSLG
Bristol [*Board/paper*] ... B
Bristol [*France*] [*Research code symbol*] ... B
Bristol [*City and county borough in England*] (ROG) ... BRIS
Bristol [*England*] [*Airport symbol*] (OAG) ... BRS
Bristol [*City and county borough in England*] ... BRSTL
Bristol [*British ICAO location identifier*] (ICLI) ... EGRD
Bristol Aero Engines Ltd., Montreal, PQ, Canada [*Library symbol Library of Congress*] (LCLS) ... CaQMBAE
Bristol Aero Engines Ltd., Montreal, Quebec [*Library symbol National Library of Canada*] (NLC) ... QMBAE
Bristol Aeroplane Co. (MCD) ... BAC
Bristol Aerospace Ltd., Winnipeg, Manitoba [*Library symbol National Library of Canada*] (NLC) ... MWBA
Bristol and Birmingham Railway (ROG) ... B & BR
Bristol & Wessex Aeroplane Club Ltd. [*British ICAO designator*] (FAAC) ... FLP
Bristol BAE [*British ICAO designator*] (FAAC) ... GEM
Bristol Bay Oceanographic Processes ... B-BOP
Bristol Bay School, Media Center, Naknek, AK [*Library symbol*] [*Library of Congress*] (LCLS) ... AkNakBS
Bristol Centre for the Advancement of Architecture [*British*] (CB) ... BCAA
Bristol Channel [*British*] ... B/CH
Bristol Channel [*British*] ... BC
Bristol City Line [*Steamship*] (MHDW) ... BCL
Bristol Community College, Fall River, MA [*OCLC symbol*] (OCLC) ... BRC
Bristol Community College, Fall River, MA [*Library symbol Library of Congress*] (LCLS) ... MFB
Bristol County Law Library, Taunton, MA [*Library symbol Library of Congress*] (LCLS) ... MTaB
Bristol, CT [*AM radio station call letters*] ... WPRX
Bristol Evening Post, Bristol, United Kingdom [*Library symbol Library of Congress*] (LCLS) ... UkBrP
Bristol Fighter [*Aircraft*] [*World War I*] ... BF
Bristol Fighter [*British aircraft*] (DSUE) ... BRISFIT
Bristol/Filton [*British ICAO location identifier*] (ICLI) ... EGTG
Bristol Flying Centre Ltd. [*British ICAO designator*] (FAAC) ... CLF
Bristol Historical and Preservation Society, Bristol, RI [*Library symbol Library of Congress*] (LCLS) ... RBrHi
Bristol Hotel [*NYSE symbol*] (TTSB) ... BH
Bristol Hotel Co. [*NYSE symbol*] (SAG) ... BH
Bristol Hotel Co. [*Associated Press*] (SAG) ... BristHtl
Bristol Independent School District Library, Bristol, SD [*Library symbol Library of Congress*] (LCLS) ... SdBrS
Bristol Laboratories ... BL
Bristol Laboratories [*Research code symbol*] ... BL-H
Bristol Laboratories [*Research code symbol*] ... P
Bristol Laboratories, Library, Syracuse, NY [*OCLC symbol*] (OCLC) ... ZUD
Bristol Laboratories, Syracuse, NY [*Library symbol Library of Congress*] (LCLS) ... NSyBL
Bristol/Lulsgate [*British ICAO location identifier*] (ICLI) ... EGGD
Bristol Memorial Hospital, Bristol, TN [*Library symbol Library of Congress*] (LCLS) ... TBriH
Bristol Myers Squibb [*NYSE symbol*] (SAG) ... BMY
Bristol Myers Squibb [*Associated Press*] (SAG) ... BrMSq
Bristol Myers Squibb [*Associated Press*] (SAG) ... BrMySq
Bristol Owners' Club (EA) ... BOC
Bristol Owners Club, US Branch (EA) ... BOC
Bristol Polytechnic [*Bristol, England*] ... BP
Bristol, RI [*FM radio station call letters*] ... WQRI
Bristol Simplified Reheat [*Aircraft*] (NATG) ... BSR
Bristol Social Adjustment Guides [*Psychology*] ... BSAG
Bristol Steam Navigation Co. (MHDB) ... BSNC
Bristol Technology Systems, Inc. [*Associated Press*] (SAG) ... BristIT
Bristol Technology Systems, Inc. [*NASDAQ symbol*] (SAG) ... BTEC
Bristol, TN [*Location identifier FAA*] (FAAL) ... BON
Bristol, TN [*Location identifier FAA*] (FAAL) ... TRI
Bristol, TN [*AM radio station call letters*] ... WBCV
Bristol, TN [*FM radio station call letters*] ... WHCB
Bristol, TN [*FM radio station call letters*] ... WXBQ-FM
Bristol United Press Ltd., Bristol, United Kingdom [*Library symbol Library of Congress*] (LCLS) ... BUP
Bristol, VA [*Television station call letters*] ... WCYB
Bristol, VA [*AM radio station call letters*] ... WOPI
Bristol, VA [*AM radio station call letters*] ... WXBQ
Bristol, VA [*AM radio station call letters*] ... WZAP
Bristol-Myers Co. ... B-M
Bristol-Myers Co. [*Research code symbol*] ... NSC
Bristol-Myers Co. [*Research code symbol*] ... RP
Bristol-Myers Squibb [*NYSE symbol*] (TTSB) ... BMY
Bristol-Myers Squibb Co. [*NYSE symbol*] (SPSG) ... BMY
Bristol-Myers Squibb Co. [*Associated Press*] (SAG) ... BrMSq
Bristol-Myers Squibb Co. [*Associated Press*] (SAG) ... BrMySq
Bristol-Myers Squibb's ... BMS
Bristol-Washington Township Public Library (Bristol Public Library), Bristol, IN [*Library symbol Library of Congress*] (LCLS) ... InBri
Bristow Helicopters Group Ltd. [*British ICAO designator*] (FAAC) ... BHL
Bristow Masayu Helicopter PT [*Indonesia*] [*ICAO designator*] (FAAC) ... BMH
Bristow, OK [*FM radio station call letters*] ... KREK
Bristow Public Library, Bristow, OK [*Library symbol Library of Congress*] (LCLS) ... OkBr
Brit Chalutzim Datiyim (BJA) ... BACHAD
Brit Ivrit Olamit [*World Association for Hebrew Language and Culture*] (EAIO) ... BIO
Britain (ROG) ... BR
Britain [*or British*] ... BRIT
Britain (VRA) ... Brit
Britain-Australia Society (DBA) ... B-AS
Britain-China Friendship Association (BI) ... BCFA
Britair SA [*France ICAO designator*] (FAAC) ... BZH
Britannarium [*Of All the Britains*] [*Coin inscription*] (ROG) ... BRITT
Britannia ... BRIT
Britannia Airways [*Airline flight code*] (ODBW) ... BY
Britannia Airways Ltd. [*British ICAO designator*] (FAAC) ... BAL
Britannia Building Society [*British*] ... BBS
Britannia Petite Rabbit Fanciers Association [*Defunct*] (EA) ... BPRFA
Britannia Royal Naval College ... BritColl

Britannia Royal Naval College .... BRNC
Britannica .... BRIT
Britannica Junior Encyclopedia [*A publication*] .... BJE
Britannica Reading Achievement Center .... BRAC
Britcol Resource Development [*Vancouver Stock Exchange symbol*] .... BTO
Brite Voice System, Inc. [*NASDAQ symbol*] (NQ) .... BVSI
Brite Voice Systems [*NASDAQ symbol*] (TTSB) .... BVSI
Brite Voice Systems, Inc. [*Associated Press*] (SAG) .... BriteV
Brith Abraham (BJA) .... BA
Brith Abraham Foundation [*Later, BZ*] (EA) .... BAF
B'rith Christian Union [*Later, FSJ*] (EA) .... BCU
Brith Sholom (EA) .... BS
Brith Trumpeldor of America (EA) .... BTA
Britian Israel Public Affairs Centre .... BIPAC
Briticism (BARN) .... Brit
British .... B
British .... BR
British (DLA) .... BRIT
British (ROG) .... BRT
British .... BRTSH
British Ability Scales (EDAC) .... BAS
British Abrasive Federation (EAIO) .... BAF
British Absolute Unit .... BAU
British Academy .... BA
British Academy of Experts (DBA) .... BAE
British Academy of Film and Television Arts .... BAFTA
[*The*] **British Academy of Forensic Sciences** .... BAFS
British Academy of Songwriters, Composers, and Authors .... BASCA
British Accounting and Finance Association (PDAA) .... BAFA
British Accounting Association (DBA) .... BAA
British Acetylene Association (BI) .... BAA
British Acoustical Society .... BAS
British Action for Children's Television (AIE) .... BAC
British Activity Holiday Association (DBA) .... BAHA
British Actors' Equity Association [*A union*] (DCTA) .... BAEA
British Acupuncture Association and Register (DBA) .... BAA
British Acupuncture Association and Register (EA) .... BAAR
British Adhesive and Sealants Association .... BASA
British Admiralty .... BA
British Admiralty Delegation [*to Washington*] .... BAD
British Admiralty Establishment .... BAE
British Admiralty Maintenance and Supply Representative .... BAMSR
British Admiralty Repair Mission .... BARM
British Admiralty Signal RADAR Establishment .... B/ASRE
British Admiralty Technical Mission [*World War II*] .... BATM
British Advertising Gift Distributors' Association (DI) .... BAGDA
British Advisory Committee for Aeronautics .... BACA
British Aerial Transport Ltd. .... BAT
British Aerobatic Association (PDAA) .... BAeA
British Aeromedical Practitioners Association (DBA) .... BAMPA
British Aeromedical Practitioners Association (DA) .... BAPA
British Aeronautical Research Committee .... BARC
British Aerophilatelic Federation (DBA) .... BAeF
British Aerosol Manufacturers Association .... BAMA
British Aerospace Air Combat Maneuvering Instrumentation Range (DA) .... BAACMIR
British Aerospace Australia .... BAeA
British Aerospace Flying College Ltd. [*ICAO designator*] (FAAC) .... AYR
British Aerospace Jetstream 31 [*Airplane code*] J31
British Aerospace Ltd. .... BA
British Aerospace Ltd. .... BAe
British Aerospace PLC [*ICAO designator*] (FAAC) .... BAE
British Agencies for Adoption and Fostering (DI) .... BAAF
British Aggregate Construction Materials Industry .... BACMI
British Agricultural and Garden Machinery Association .... BAGMA
British Agricultural and Horticultural Plastics Association (PDAA) .... BAHPA
British Agricultural Export Council .... BAEC
British Agricultural History Society .... BAHS
British Agricultural Marketing Research Group .... BAMRG
British Agrochemicals Association .... BAA
British Air Commission [*Washington*] .... BAC
British Air Cushion Vehicle Safety Requirements (PDAA) .... BACVSR
British Air Ferries [*ICAO designator*] (AD) .... VF
British Air Ferries Ltd. [*ICAO designator*] (FAAC) .... BAF
British Air Force .... BAF
British Air Forces in France [*World War II*] .... BAFF
British Air Forces in Greece [*British military*] (DMA) .... BAFG
British Air Forces of Occupation [*Military*] .... BAFO
British Air Mail Society (BI) .... BAMS
British Air Ministry .... BAM
British Air Ministry Control Office .... BAMCO
British Air Survey Association (DBA) .... BASA
British Air Transport Association (DA) .... BATA
British Aircraft Corp. Ltd. [*ICAO aircraft manufacturer identifier*] (ICAO) .... BA
British Aircraft Corp. Ltd. .... BAC
British Aircraft Corp. Ltd. [*ICAO aircraft manufacturer identifier*] (ICAO) .... BR
British Aircraft Corp. Ltd. [*ICAO aircraft manufacturer identifier*] (ICAO) .... PE
British Aircraft Corp. Ltd. [*ICAO aircraft manufacturer identifier*] (ICAO) VC
British Aircraft Corp. Ltd. Commercial Habitat under the Sea .... BACCHUS
British Aircraft Preservation Council .... BAPC
British Airline Pilots Association .... BALPA
British Airport Rapid Control and Indication Systems (PDAA) .... BARCIS
British Airports Authority .... BAA
British Airports Information Retrieval [*System*] .... BAIR
British Airtours Ltd. [*Airline*] .... BA
British Airtours Ltd. [*British ICAO designator*] (ICDA) .... KT
British Airways [*British ICAO designator*] (ICDA) .... BA
British Airways [*ICAO designator*] (FAAC) .... BAW
British Airways [*Associated Press*] (SAG) .... BritAir
British Airways ADS [*NYSE symbol Toronto Stock Exchange symbol*] (SPSG) .... BAB
British Airways Board (AIA) .... BAB
British Airways Safety Information System (GAVI) .... BASIS
British Airways Shuttle [*ICAO designator*] (FAAC) .... SHT
British Airways Shuttle Services .... BASS
British Allergy Society .... BAS
British Alsatian Association (BI) .... BAA
British Aluminium Building Service (BI) .... BABS
British Aluminium Co. Ltd. .... BA
British Aluminium Co. Ltd. (ODBW) .... BACO
British Aluminium Foil Rollers Association (BI) .... BAFRA
British Amateur Athletic Board .... BAAB
British Amateur Baseball Federation .... BABF
British Amateur Electronics Club (PDAA) .... BAEC
British Amateur Gymnastics Association .... BAGA
British Amateur Press Association (BI) .... BAPA
British Amateur Radio Teleprinter Group (BI) .... BARTG
British Amateur Rugby League Association (DBA) .... BARLA
British Amateur Strand Pulling Association .... BASPA
British Amateur Tape Recording Society .... BATRS
British Amateur Television Club .... BATC
British Amateur Weight Lifters' Association .... BAWLA
British Amateur Wrestling Association (BI) .... BAWA
British America .... BA
British America (BARN) .... BR AM
British American Bank Note, Inc. [*Toronto Stock Exchange symbol Vancouver Stock Exchange symbol*] .... BAN
British American Educational Foundation (EA) .... BAEF
British American Minesweeper [*British military*] (DMA) .... BAMS
British American Repertory Company .... BARC
British American Scientific Research Association .... BASRA
British Amputee Sports Association (DBA) .... BASA
British Amusement Catering Trades Association (DBA) .... BACTA
British Anaerobic and Biomass Association (PDAA) .... BABA
British Anaerobic & Biomass Association Ltd. .... BABA LTD
British Anaesthetic and Respiratory Equipment Manufacturers Association (DBA) .... BAREMA
British and Colonial Prize Cases [*A publication*] (DLA) .... B & C Pr Cas
British and Colonial Prize Cases [*A publication*] (DLA) .... Br & Col
British and Colonial Prize Cases [*A publication*] (DLA) .... Br & Col Pr Cas
British and Colonial Prize Cases [*A publication*] (DLA) .... Brit & Col Pr Cas
British and Colonial Prize Cases [*A publication*] (DLA) .... PC
British and Colonial Prize Cases [*A publication*] (DLA) .... Trehern
British & Commonwealth [*Company*] .... B & C
British & Commonwealth Holdings [*Commercial firm*] (ECON) .... B & C
British and European Geranium Society (EAIO) .... BEGS
British and European Osteopathic Association [*Sutton, Surrey, England*] (EAIO) .... BEOA
British and Foreign Bible Society .... BFBS
British and Foreign Maritime Agencies (BARN) .... BAFMA
British and Foreign Schools Society (AIE) .... BFSS
British and International Addressing Post [*A publication*] .... BIA
British and Irish Association of Law Librarians (DLA) .... BIALL
British and Irish Basketball Federation (DBA) .... BIBF
British and Irish Communist Organization [*Irish*] .... B & ICO
British and Irish Skeptic (EAIO) .... BIS
British & Irish Steam Packet Co. (MHDB) .... B & I SPC
British and South African Forum .... BASAF
British and South Asian Trade Association [*British Overseas Trade Board*] (DS) .... BASATA
British Angular Rate Bombsight .... BARB
British Anodising Association .... BAA
British Antarctic Expedition .... BAE
British Antarctic Expedition [*1898-1900,1907-09,1910-13*] .... BrAE
British Antarctic Survey [*Research center*] (IRC) .... BAS
British Antarctic Territory .... BAT
British Anti-Common Market Campaign [*An association*] (DBA) .... BACMC
British Anti-Lewisite [*Also, DMP: Dimercapto, propanol*] [*Detoxicant*] .... BAL
British Antique Dealers' Association .... BADA
British Anti-Smoking Education Society .... BASES
British Antitank Bar Mine System (MCD) .... BATBAMS
British Anti-Zionist Organisation - Palestine Solidarity .... BAZO-PS
British Appaloosa Society (DBA) .... BApS
British Approvals Board for Telecommunications .... BABT
British Approvals for Fire Equipment .... BAFE
British Approvals Service for Electric Cables (PDAA) .... BASEC
British Approvals Service for Electrical Equipment in Flammable Atmospheres [*General Council of British Shipping*] [*Research center*] (DS) .... BASEEFA
British Approved Name .... BAN
British Aqueous Fusion Process (MCD) .... BAF
British Arabian Technical Cooperation (PDAA) .... BATC
British Archaeological Association .... BAA
British Archaeologists and Developers Liaison Group .... BADLG
British Architectural Library [*Royal Institute of British Architects*] [*Information service or system*] (IID) .... BAL
British Architectural Students' Association (BI) .... BASA
British Archives Council (DIT) .... BAC
British Armed Forces Special Vouchers [*British military*] (DMA) .... BAFSV

British Armed Forces Voucher [*Pronounced "baff"*] [*Paper money used on military bases*] (DSUE) .... BAFV
British Army .... BA
British Army Aid Group [*China*] [*World War II*] .... BAAG
British Army Equipment Exhibition (MCD) .... BAEE
British Army Forces Overseas .... BAFO
British Army Motoring Association [*British military*] (DMA) .... BAMA
British Army News Service [*British military*] (DMA) .... BANEWS
British Army of Occupation [*World War II*] .... BAO
British Army of the Rhine [*NATO/NORTHAG*] .... BAOR
British Army Post Office [*British military*] (DMA) .... BAPO
British Army Review [*A publication*] .... BAR
British Army Staff .... BAS
British Army Staff, Washington (MCD) .... BASW
British Army Training Liaison Staff, Kenya .... BATLSK
British Army Training Team .... BATT
British Army Training Unit, Suffield [*British military*] (DMA) .... BATUS
British Aromatic Compounds Manufacturers' Association (BI) .... BACMA
British Art Medal Society (DBA) .... BAMS
British Artists [*A publication*] .... BA
British Artists' Colour Manufacturers' Association (BI) .... BACMA
British Artists in Glass .... BAG
British Arts Festivals Association (DBA) .... BAFA
British Association for American Studies (EA) .... BAAS
British Association for Autogenic Training and Therapy (DBA) .... BAFATT
British Association for Brazing and Soldering .... BABS
British Association for Canadian Studies .... BACS
British Association for Cancer Research .... BACR
British Association for Cemeteries in South Asia .... BACSA
British Association for Chemical Specialities .... BACS
British Association for Commercial and Industrial Education (DCTA) .... BACIE
British Association for Construction Heads (AIE) .... BACH
British Association for Counselling .... BAC
[*The*] British Association for Early Childhood Education .... BAECE
British Association for Irish Studies .... BAIS
British Association for Language Teaching .... BALT
British Association for Local History .... BALH
British Association for Open Learning .... Baol
British Association for Perinatal Paediatrics (PDAA) .... BAPP
British Association for Psychopharmacology .... BAP
British Association for Rheumatology and Rehabilitation .... BARR
British Association for Romanian Studies (EAIO) .... BARS
British Association for Service to the Elderly (DBA) .... BASE
British Association for Shooting and Conservation .... BASC
British Association for Soviet, Slavonic, and East European Studies (DBA) .... BASSEES
British Association for the Advancement of Science (BI) .... BA
British Association for the Advancement of Science .... BAAS
British Association for the Control of Airport Noise .... BACAN
British Association for the Retarded .... BAR
British Association for the Study and Prevention of Child Abuse and Neglect (DI) .... BASPCAN
British Association for the Study of Community Dentistry .... BASCD
British Association in Forensic Medicine .... BAFM
British Association of Academic Phoneticians (DBA) .... BAAP
British Association of Accountants and Auditors (DBA) .... BAA
British Association of Advisers and Lecturers in Physical Education .... BAALPE
British Association of Aesthetic Plastic Surgeons (EAIO) .... BAAPS
British Association of Airport Equipment Manufacturers and Services (DA) .... BAAEMS
British Association of Applied Linguists [*British*] .... BAAL
British Association of Art Therapists Ltd. .... BAAT
British Association of Barbershop Singers (EAIO) .... BABS
British Association of Beauty Therapy and Cosmetology (DBA) .... BABTAC
British Association of Behavioural Psychotherapy (DBA) .... BABP
British Association of Behavioural Psychotherapy (DI) .... BABP
British Association of Bio-Fuel and Oil .... BABFO
British Association of Cancer United Patients .... BACUP
British Association of Canned and Preserved Food Importers and Distributors (DBA) .... BACFID
British Association of Canoe Traders (DBA) .... BACT
British Association of Chemists .... BAC
British Association of Chinese Studies (DBA) .... BACS
British Association of Clinical Anatomists .... BACA
British Association of Clothing Machinery Manufacturers (PDAA) .... BACMM
British Association of Colliery Management (DCTA) .... BACM
British Association of Community Physicians (DBA) .... BACP
British Association of Concert Agents .... BACA
British Association of Conference Towns .... BACT
British Association of Consultants in Agriculture and Horticulture (BI) .... BACAH
British Association of Consulting Engineers .... BACE
British Association of Cosmetic Surgeons .... BACS
British Association of Crystal Growth .... BACG
British Association of Dermatologists [*or Dermatology*] (EAIO) .... BAD
British Association of Electrolysists .... BAE
British Association of Electrolysists (DBA) .... BAE
British Association of Feed Supplement Manufacturers (DBA) .... BAFSM
British Association of Fitted Furniture Installers (DBA) .... BAFFI
British Association of Friends of Museums .... BAFM
British Association of Golf Course Architects (DBA) .... BAGCA
British Association of Grain, Seed Feed and Agricultural Merchants (PDAA) .... BASAM
British Association of Green Crop Driers (DBA) .... BAGCD
British Association of Helicopter Operators (PDAA) .... BAHO

British Association of Homoeopathic Pharmacists .... BAHP
British Association of Homoeopathic Veterinary Surgeons .... BAHVS
British Association of Hotel Accountants (DBA) .... BAHA
British Association of Immediate Care Schemes (PDAA) .... BASICS
British Association of Industrial Editors (EAIO) .... BAIE
British Association of Landscape Industries .... BALI
British Association of Lecturers in English for Academic Purposes (AIE) .... BALEAP
British Association of Leisure Parks, Piers, and Attractions (DBA) .... BALPPA
British Association of Lithographic Plate Manufacturers (DBA) .... BALPM
British Association of Machine Tool Merchants, Inc. (BI) .... BAMTM
British Association of Manipulative Medicine .... BAMM
British Association of Meat Wholesalers Ltd. (BI) .... BAMW
British Association of Myasthenics (DBA) .... BAM
British Association of Nature Conservationists .... BANC
British Association of Neurologists (DI) .... BAN
British Association of Numismatic Societies .... BANS
British Association of Occupational Therapists .... BAOT
British Association of Operating Department Assistants (DBA) .... BAODA
British Association of Oral and Maxillofacial Surgeons (DBA) .... BAOMS
British Association of Oral and Maxillo-Facial Surgeons (DBA) .... BAOS
British Association of Orthodontists .... BAO
British Association of Otolaryngologists .... BAO
British Association of Otolaryngologists (DBA) .... BAOL
British Association of Overseas Furniture Removers (BI) .... BAOFR
British Association of Paediatric Surgeons (EAIO) .... BAPS
British Association of Palestine-Israel Philatelists (BI) .... BAPIP
British Association of Paper Exporters (PDAA) .... BAPEX
British Association of Parascending Clubs (DBA) .... BAPL
British Association of Physical Medicine (BABM) .... BAPhysMed
British Association of Physical Medicine (BI) .... BAPM
British Association of Picture Libraries and Agencies (DBA) .... BAPLA
British Association of Pig Producers (BI) .... BAPP
British Association of Plastic Surgeons .... BAPS
British Association of Pool Table Operators (DBA) .... BAPTO
British Association of Professional Hairdressing Employers (DBA) .... BAPHE
British Association of Psychotherapists (DBA) .... BAP
British Association of Rally Doctors .... BARD
British Association of Rehabilitated Psychotherapy (DI) .... BARP
British Association of Removers (DBA) .... BAR
British Association of Residential Settlements (BI) .... BARS
British Association of Retired Persons (DI) .... BARP
British Association of Rose Breeders .... BARB
British Association of Seed Analysts .... BASA
British Association of Settlements and Social Action Centres .... BAS
British Association of Settlements and Social Action Centres .... BASSAC
British Association of Sewing Machine Manufacturers (PDAA) .... BASMM
British Association of Ship Suppliers (DBA) .... BASS
British Association of Ski Instructors (DI) .... BASI
British Association of Skin Camouflage (DBA) .... BASC
British Association of Social Psychiatry .... BASP
British Association of Social Workers .... BASW
British Association of Sound Collections (DBA) .... BASC
British Association of Sport Medicine .... BASM
British Association of Sports Ground and Landscape Contractors Ltd. (BI) .... BASLC
British Association of State Colleges in English Language Teaching (DBA) .... BASCELT
British Association of Surgical Oncology .... BASO
British Association of Symphonic Bands and Wind Ensembles (EAIO) .... BASBWE
British Association of Synthetic Rubber Manufacturers (PDAA) .... BASRM
British Association of Teachers of the Deaf (AIE) .... BATD
British Association of Teachers of the Deaf .... BATOD
British Association of the Hard of Hearing .... BAHOH
British Association of Tourism Officers (EAIO) .... BATO
British Association of Trade Computer Label Manufacturers (DBA) .... BATCLM
British Association of Trauma in Sport (DBA) .... BATS
British Association of Traumatology in Sport (DI) .... BATS
British Association of Urological Surgeons .... BAUS
British Association of Viewdata Information Providers .... BAVIP
British Association of Wheelchair Distributors (DBA) .... BAWD
British Association of Women Entrepreneurs (DBA) .... BAWE
British Association of Women Executives (DI) .... BAWE
British Association of Young Scientists (BI) .... BAYS
British Association Screw Thread .... BA
British Association Sovereign and Military Order of Malta (BI) .... BASMON
British Association Standard (IAA) .... BAS
British Association Unit (IAA) .... BAU
British Astronomical Association .... BAA
British Atlantic Committee (EAIO) .... BAC
British Atomic Committee .... BAC
British Atomic Energy Authority .... BAEA
British Atomic Energy Research Establishment .... B/AERE
British Audio Dealers Association (DBA) .... BADA
British Australian Settlers Society .... BASS
British Australian Wool Realization Association .... BAWRA
British Auto Racing Funatics [*An association*] .... BARF
British Automatic Sprinkler Association (DBA) .... BASA
British Automobile Manufacturers Association (EA) .... BAMA
British Automobile Manufacturers Association in Canada (PDAA) .... BAMAC
British Automobile Racing Club .... BARC
British Aviation Archaeological Council (DBA) .... BAAC
British Aviation Insurance Co. (AIA) .... BAIC
British Baby Carriage Manufacturers' Association (BI) .... BBCMA

British Bacon Curers' Federation (BI)	BBCF
British Baking Industries Research Association (PDAA)	BBIRA
British Ballet Organization	BBO
British Balloon and Airship Club	BBAC
British Bank of the Middle East	BBME
British Bankers' Association	BBA
British Baseball Federation (DBA)	BBF
British Bath Manufacturers' Association Ltd. (BI)	BBMA
British Bathroom Council	BBC
British Battery Makers' Society (BI)	BBMS
British Battery Manufacturers Association (DBA)	BBMA
British Bedding Plant Association (DBA)	BBPA
British Bee Keepers Association (BI)	BBKA
British Beer-Mat Collectors' Society (EA)	BB-CS
British Binders and Finishers Association (DBA)	BBFA
British Biophysical Society	BBS
British Biotech plc ADS [NASDAQ symbol] (TTSB)	BBIOY
British Bio-Technologies, Inc. [NASDAQ symbol] (SAG)	BBIO
British Bio-Technology Group [Associated Press] (SAG)	BritBio
British Bio-Technology Ltd. (IRC)	BBL
British Bird Breeders' Association (BI)	BBBA
British Blind and Shutter Association (DBA)	BBSA
British Bloodstock Agency	BBA
British Blue [A British sailor]	BB
British Board of Agreement [Department of the Environment] [Research center] (IRUK)	BBA
British Board of Film Censors (BI)	BBFC
British Board of Film Classification	BBFC
British Board of Quality Control	BBQC
British Bobsleigh [or Bobsled] Association (EAIO)	BBA
British Bombing Research Mission [World War II]	BBRM
British Bombing Survey Units [World War II]	BBSU
British Bone Society	BBS
British Bonsai Association (DBA)	BBA
British Books in Print [Whitaker & Sons, Ltd.] [Information service or system] (IID)	BBIP
British Boot, Shoe and Allied Trades Research Association (BI)	BBSATRA
British Borneo Civil Affairs Unit [World War II]	BBCAU
British Bottlers' Institute (DBA)	BBI
British Box and Packaging Association (DBA)	BB & PA
British Boxing Board of Control	BBBC
British Branded Hosiery Group [An association] (DBA)	BBHG
British Broadcasting Corp. [State-operated radio and television]	BBC
British Broadcasting Corp. Scottish Symphony Orchestra	BBCSSO
British Broadcasting Corp. Symphony Orchestra	BBCSO
British Broiler Growers' Association (BI)	BBGA
British Brush Manufacturers Association (PDAA)	BBMA
British Brush Manufacturers Research Association (IRUK)	BBMRA
British Bryological Society	BBS
British Buddy Holly Society (EAIO)	BBHS
British Building and Engineering Appliances	BB & EA
British Bulgarian Friendship Society (DBA)	BBFS
British Bureau of Non-Ferrous Metal Statistics (BI)	BNFMS
British Bureau of Television Advertising	BBTA
British Burma	BR BUR
British Burma (ILCA)	Brit Burm
British Burn Association (DBA)	BBA
British Business Association [Singapore] (DS)	BBA
British Business Graduates Society (DBA)	BBGS
British Businessmen's Associaton (DBA)	BBA
British Butterfly Conservation Society	BBCS
British Button Manufacturers Association (BI)	BBMA
British Button Society (DBA)	BBS
British Cable Makers Confederation (DBA)	BCMC
British Cable Services (NITA)	BCS
British Cactus and Succulent Society (DBA)	BCSS
British Calcium Carbonates Federation (DBA)	BCCF
British Caledonian Airways	B Cal
British Caledonian Airways [ICAO designator] (AD)	BCAL
British Caledonian Airways Ltd.	BCA
British Caledonian Airways Ltd. [ICAO designator] (OAG)	BR
British Calibration Service [Research center] (IRC)	BCS
British Camp Fire Girls (BI)	BCFG
British Campaign Against Book Piracy	BCABP
British Canadian Trade Association (BI)	BCTA
British Canoe Union	BCU
British Canoe Union International Canoeing Exhibition [British]	BCUICE
British Car Auctions	BCA
British Car Rental Association (BI)	BCRA
British Car Wash Association (DBA)	BCWA
British Caramel Manufacturers Association (DBA)	BCMA
British Caravanners Club (DBA)	BCC
British Cardiac Society (DBA)	BCS
British Cargo Ship	BAK
British Caribbean Airways Ltd. [ICAO designator] (FAAC)	BCL
British Caribbean Philatelic Study Group (EA)	BCPSG
British Caribbean Territory	BCT
British Carpet Classification Scheme (PDAA)	BCCS
British Carpet Manufacturers Association (PDAA)	BCMA
British Carpet Technical Centre (CB)	BCTC
British Cartographic Society	BCS
British Carton Association (BI)	BCA
British Casino Association (DBA)	BCA
British Caspian Trust	BCT
British Cast Iron Pressure Pipe Association (PDAA)	BCIPPA

British Cast Iron Research Association	BCIRA
British Catalogue of Audiovisual Materials [British Library] (NITA)	BCAVM
British Catalogue of Music [British National Bibliography]	BCM
British Cattle Veterinary Association (DBA)	BCVA
British Cave Research Association	BCRA
British Cement Association [Also, an information service or system] (IID)	BCA
British Central Africa [Pre-World War II]	BCA
British Central Office of Information	BCOI
British Ceramic Confederation (DBA)	BCC
British Ceramic Gift and Tableware Manufacturers' Association (DBA)	BCGTMA
British Ceramic Manufacturers' Federation (DBA)	BCMF
British Ceramic Plant and Machinery Manufacturers Association (PDAA)	BCPMMA
British Ceramic Research Association (PDAA)	BCeramRA
British Ceramic Research Association (PDAA)	BCRA
British Ceramic Research Ltd. [Research center] (IRC)	CERAM
British Ceramic Society	BCS
British Ceramic Tile Council Ltd. (BI)	BCTC
British Chain Manufacturers Association (DBA)	BCMA
British Chamber of Commerce (DS)	BCC
British Chamber of Commerce, Bangkok (DS)	BCCB
British Chamber of Commerce in Germany (DBA)	BCCG
British Chamber of Commerce in Japan (DBA)	BCCJ
British Chamber of Commerce in Turkey (DBA)	BCCT
British Channel Island Ferries	BCIE
British Channel Island Ferries	BCIF
British Charollais Sheep Society (DBA)	BCSS
British Charter [ICAO designator] (FAAC)	BCR
British Charter [British ICAO designator] (ICDA)	SE
British Chemical and Dyestuffs Traders' Association (BI)	BCDTA
British Chemical Distributors and Traders Association (DBA)	BCDTA
British Chemical Engineering Contractors Association (PDAA)	BCECA
British Chemical Plant Manufacturers' Association (BI)	BCPMA
British Cheque Collectors Society (DBA)	BCCS
British Chess Federation (BI)	BCF
British Chess Magazine	BCM
British Chicken Association Ltd. (BI)	BCA
British Chief Administrator	BCA
British Chiefs of Staff	BCOS
British Chiefs of Staff	BCS
British Children's Theatre Association	BCTA
British Chilean Chamber of Commerce (DBA)	BCCC
British China and Porcelain Artists Association (DBA)	BCPAA
British Chip Board Manufacturers' Association (BI)	BCMA
British Chiropody Association (DBA)	BChA
British Chiropractors' Association	BCA
British Christmas Tree Growers Association (DBA)	BCTGA
British Circus Ring (BI)	BCR
British Citizens' Band Council (DBA)	BCBC
British Civil Airworthiness Requirements	BCAR
British Civil Aviation Regulations (MCD)	BCAR
British Civil Uranium Procurement Directorate (NUCP)	BCUPO
British Clayware Land Drain Industry [An association] (DBA)	BCLDI
British Cleaning Council Exhibition (ITD)	BCCE
British Clock and Watch Manufacturers Association (PDAA)	BCWMA
British Clothing Industry Association (DBA)	BCIA
British Clothing Industry Productivity and Technology Centre (CB)	BCC
British Coal Enterprise	BCE
British Coal Utilisation Research Association	BCURA
British Code of Advertising Practice (ODBW)	BCAP
British Coke Research Association (PDAA)	BCRA
British College of Accountancy, Ltd.	BCA
British College of Acupuncture (DI)	BCA
British College of Aeronautics	B/C of A
British College of Naturopathy and Osteopathy	BCNO
British College of Ophthalmic Opticians (DBQ)	BCOO
British College of Optometrists (DBA)	BCO
British Colleges Sports Association	BCSA
British Colombia Ladies Curling Association (AC)	BCLCA
British Colombia Water & Wastewater Association (AC)	BCWWA
British Colonial Airlines, Inc.	BCA
British Colostomy Association (DBA)	BCA
British Colour Council	BCC
British Colour Makers' Association (DI)	BCMA
British Columbia [Canadian province] [Postal code]	BC
British Columbia [MARC country of publication code Library of Congress] (LCCP)	bcc
British Columbia (ILCA)	Br Col
British Columbia (DLA)	BRIT COL
British Columbia [MARC geographic area code Library of Congress] (LCCP)	n-cn-bc
British Columbia and Yukon Chamber of Mines, Vancouver, BC, Canada [Library symbol of Library of Congress] (LCLS)	CaBVaBY
British Columbia and Yukon Chamber of Mines, Vancouver, British Columbia [Library symbol National Library of Canada] (NLC)	BVABY
British Columbia Annual Law Lectures [Canada] [A publication] (DLA)	BCL Lectures
British Columbia Art Therapy Association (AC)	BCATA
British Columbia Association for Community Living [Formerly, British Columbians for Mentally Handicapped People] (AC)	BCACL
British Columbia Association for Community Living (AC)	BCACL
British Columbia Association of Broadcasters (AC)	BCAB
British Columbia Association of Community Care (AC)	BCACC
British Columbia Association of Health Care Auxiliaries (AC)	BCAHA

British Columbia Association of Medical Radiation Technologists (AC) ... BCAMRT
British Columbia Association of Optometrists (AC) ... BCAO
British Columbia Association of Podiatrists (AC) ... BCAP
British Columbia Association of Social Workers [*Association des Travailleurs Sociaux de la Colombie-Britannique*] (AC) ... BCASW
British Columbia Automobile Association (AC) ... BCAA
British Columbia Barkerville Restoration Advisory Committee, Victoria, BC, Canada [*Library symbol Library of Congress*] (LCLS) ... CaBViB
British Columbia Barkerville Restoration Advisory Committee, Victoria, British Columbia [*Library symbol National Library of Canada*] (NLC) ... BVIB
British Columbia Branch Lectures [*A publication*] (DLA) ... BC Branch Lectures
British Columbia Building Envelope Council [*Formerly, Building Envelope Council of British Columbia*] (AC) ... BCBEC
British Columbia Bureau of Economics and Statistics, Business-Finance Library, Victoria, BC, Canada [*Library symbol Library of Congress*] (LCLS) ... CaBViBE
British Columbia, Canada (ILCA) ... Brit Col (Can)
British Columbia Central Credit Union, Vancouver, British Columbia [*Library symbol National Library of Canada*] (NLC) ... BVACCU
British Columbia Chapter, American Foundrymen's Society Archives and Museum, Delta, British Columbia [*Library symbol National Library of Canada*] (NLC) ... BDEAF
British Columbia Coalition of People with Disabilities (AC) ... BCCPD
British Columbia Coast Terminals [*Canada*] ... BCCT
British Columbia College and Institute Library Services Clearinghouse for the Print Impaired (CILS), Vancouver, British Columbia [*Library symbol National Library of Canada*] (NLC) ... BVACILS
British Columbia College of Teachers (AC) ... BCCT
British Columbia Colleges Athletic Association (AC) ... BCCAA
British Columbia Council of Licensed Practical Nurses (AC) ... BCCLPN
British Columbia Dietitians' & Nutritionists' Association (AC) ... BCDNA
British Columbia Educational Association of Disabled Students (AC) ... BCEADS
British Columbia Energy Commission, Vancouver, BC, Canada [*Library symbol Library of Congress*] (LCLS) ... CaBVaEC
British Columbia Energy Commission, Vancouver, British Columbia [*Library symbol National Library of Canada*] (NLC) ... BVAEC
British Columbia Farm Machinery Museum, Fort Langley, BC, Canada [*Library symbol*] [*Library of Congress*] (LCLS) ... CaBFLFMM
British Columbia Farm Machinery Museum, Fort Langley, British Columbia [*Library symbol National Library of Canada*] (NLC) ... BFLFMM
British Columbia Federation of Agriculture (AC) ... BCFA
British Columbia Federation of Foster Parent Associations (AC) ... BCFFPA
British Columbia Federation of Labour [*Federation du travail de la Colombie-Britannique*] (AC) ... BCFL
British Columbia Ferry & Marine Workers' Union [*Syndicat des Travailleurs Marins et de Bacs de la Colombie-Britannique*] (AC) ... BCFMWU
British Columbia Ferry Corp., Victoria, British Columbia [*Library symbol National Library of Canada*] (NLC) ... BVIFC
British Columbia Floor Covering Association (AC) ... BCFCA
British Columbia Forest Museum, Duncan, BC, Canada [*Library symbol*] [*Library of Congress*] (LCLS) ... CaBDUFM
British Columbia Forest Museum, Duncan, British Columbia [*Library symbol National Library of Canada*] (NLC) ... BDUFM
British Columbia Forest Service, Victoria, BC, Canada [*Library symbol Library of Congress*] (LCLS) ... CaBViFS
British Columbia Forest Service, Victoria, British Columbia [*Library symbol National Library of Canada*] (NLC) ... BVIFS
British Columbia Forestry Association [*Formerly, Canadian Forestry Association of BC*] (AC) ... BCFA
British Columbia Government [*Canada ICAO designator*] (FAAC) ... BCG
British Columbia Health Association (AC) ... BCHA
British Columbia Heritage Conservation, Branch Resource Information Centre, Victoria, BC, Canada [*Library symbol*] [*Library of Congress*] (LCLS) ... CaBViHCR
[*The*] **British Columbia Humanist Association** [*Also, Humanist Association of BC*] [*Formerly, Humanist Association of Greater Vancouver*] (AC) ... BCHA
British Columbia Hydro and Power Authority [*Formerly, British Columbia Electric Co. Ltd.*] [*AAR code*] ... BCE
British Columbia Hydro and Power Authority, Surrey, BC, Canada [*Library symbol Library of Congress*] (LCLS) ... CaBSH
British Columbia Hydro and Power Authority, Surrey, British Columbia [*Library symbol National Library of Canada*] (NLC) ... BSH
British Columbia Hydro and Power Authority [*Formerly, British Columbia Electric C o. Ltd.*], Vancouver, BC, Canada [*Library symbol Library of Congress*] (LCLS) ... CaBVaH
British Columbia Hydro and Power Authority, Vancouver, British Columbia [*Library symbol National Library of Canada*] (NLC) ... BVAH
British Columbia Hydro Engineering Library, Vancouver, BC, Canada [*Library symbol Library of Congress*] (LCLS) ... CaBVaHE
British Columbia Hydro Engineering Library, Vancouver, British Columbia [*Library symbol National Library of Canada*] (NLC) ... BVAHE
British Columbia Institute of Technology [*Canada*] (ASF) ... BCIT
British Columbia Institute of Technology, Burnaby, BC, Canada [*Library symbol Library of Congress*] (LCLS) ... CaBBIT
British Columbia Institute of Technology, Burnaby, British Columbia [*Library symbol National Library of Canada*] (NLC) ... BBIT
British Columbia Institute of Technology Library [*UTLAS symbol*] ... BCI
British Columbia Institute of Technology Staff Society [*Societe du Personnel de l'Institut de la Technolgie de la Colombie-Britannique*] (AC) ... BCITSS
British Columbia Insulation Contractors Association (AC) ... BCICA
British Columbia Interior Curling Association (AC) ... BCICA
British Columbia Labour Relations Board Decisions [*Database*] [*Western Legal Publications Ltd.*] [*Information service or system*] (CRD) ... BCLRBD
British Columbia Law Notes [*A publication*] (DLA) ... BCL Notes
British Columbia Law Reports [*Canada*] [*A publication*] (DLA) ... BC
British Columbia Law Reports [*Canada A publication*] (DLA) ... BCLR
British Columbia Library Association [*Canada*] (AEBS) ... BCLA
British Columbia Library Network [*Canada*] (NITA) ... BCLN
British Columbia Library, New Westminster, BC, Canada [*Library symbol Library of Congress*] (LCLS) ... CaBNWB
British Columbia Library Services Branch, Audiobook Service to the Handicapped, Burnaby, BC, Canada [*Library symbol*] [*Library of Congress*] (LCLS) ... CaBBLA
British Columbia Library Trustees Association (AC) ... BCLTA
British Columbia Lumber Manufacturers' Association [*Canada*] (BI) ... BCLMA
British Columbia Medical Association (AC) ... BCMA
British Columbia Medical Library Service, Vancouver, BC, Canada [*Library symbol Library of Congress*] (LCLS) ... CaBVaM
British Columbia Medical Library Service, Vancouver, British Columbia [*Library symbol National Library of Canada*] (NLC) ... BVAM
British Columbia Microelectronics, Burnaby, BC, Canada [*Library symbol*] [*Library of Congress*] (LCLS) ... CaBBBCM
British Columbia Microelectronics, Burnaby, British Columbia [*Library symbol National Library of Canada*] (NLC) ... BBBCM
British Columbia Ministry of Attorney General, CLEU Library, Victoria, BC, Canada [*Library symbol Library of Congress*] (LCLS) ... CaBViAGC
British Columbia Ministry of Economic Development, Victoria, BC, Canada [*Library symbol Library of Congress*] (LCLS) ... CaBViED
British Columbia Ministry of Education [*UTLAS symbol*] ... VME
British Columbia Ministry of Education, Victoria, BC, Canada [*Library symbol Library of Congress*] (LCLS) ... CaBViDE
British Columbia Ministry of Education, Victoria, British Columbia [*Library symbol National Library of Canada*] (NLC) ... BVIDE
British Columbia Ministry of Energy, Mines and Petroleum Resources, Victoria, British Columbia [*Library symbol National Library of Canada*] (NLC) ... BVIM
British Columbia Ministry of Environment, Planning and Resource Management Division, Victoria, BC, Canada [*Library symbol*] [*Library of Congress*] (LCLS) ... CaBViEPR
British Columbia Ministry of Environment, Victoria, British Columbia [*Library symbol National Library of Canada*] (NLC) ... BVILFW
British Columbia Ministry of Forests, Victoria, British Columbia [*Library symbol National Library of Canada*] (NLC) ... BVIFO
British Columbia Ministry of Health, Health Information, Victoria, BC, Canada [*Library symbol Library of Congress*] (LCLS) ... CaBViHI
British Columbia Ministry of Health, Health Promotion Programmes, Victoria, BC, Canada [*Library symbol Library of Congress*] (LCLS) ... CaBViHPP
British Columbia Ministry of Health, Victoria, BC, Canada [*Library symbol Library of Congress*] (LCLS) ... CaBViHe
British Columbia Ministry of Health, Victoria, British Columbia [*Library symbol National Library of Canada*] (NLC) ... BVIHE
British Columbia Ministry of Highways and Public Works, Victoria, BC, Canada [*Library symbol Library of Congress*] (LCLS) ... CaBViH
British Columbia Ministry of Highways and Public Works, Victoria, British Columbia [*Library symbol National Library of Canada*] (NLC) ... BVIH
British Columbia Ministry of Human Resources, Staff Development Division, Victoria, BC, Canada [*Library symbol Library of Congress*] (LCLS) ... CaBViHRS
British Columbia Ministry of Human Resources, Vancouver, British Columbia [*Library symbol National Library of Canada*] (NLC) ... BVIHRS
British Columbia Ministry of Industry and Small Business Development, Victoria, British Columbia [*Library symbol National Library of Canada*] (NLC) ... BVIED
British Columbia Ministry of Labour, Victoria, BC, Canada [*Library symbol*] [*Library of Congress*] (LCLS) ... CaBViML
British Columbia Ministry of Labour, Victoria, British Columbia [*Library symbol National Library of Canada*] (NLC) ... BVIML
British Columbia Ministry of Lands, Parks, and Housing, Parks Library, Victoria,BC, Canada [*Library symbol Library of Congress*] (LCLS) ... CaBViLPHP
British Columbia Ministry of Mines and Petroleum Resources, Victoria, BC, Canada [*Library symbol Library of Congress*] (LCLS) ... CaBViM
British Columbia Ministry of Recreation and Conservation, Fish and Game Branch, Victoria, BC, Canada [*Library symbol Library of Congress*] (LCLS) ... CaBViRC
British Columbia Ministry of Social Services and Housing, Vancouver, British Columbia [*Library symbol National Library of Canada*] (NLC) ... BVIHRS
British Columbia Ministry of the Attorney General, Law Library, Victoria, BC, Canada [*Library symbol*] [*Library of Congress*] (LCLS) ... CaBViAGL
British Columbia Ministry of the Environment, Environmental Protection, Pollution Control Branch, Victoria, BC, Canada [*Library symbol Library of Congress*] (LCLS) ... CaBViEP
British Columbia Ministry of the Environment, Victoria, BC, Canada [*Library symbol Library of Congress*] (LCLS) ... CaBViLFW
British Columbia Motion Picture Association (AC) ... BCMPA
British Columbia Museum of Medicine, Vancouver, BC, Canada [*Library symbol*] [*Library of Congress*] (LCLS) ... CaBVaMUM
British Columbia Museum of Medicine, Vancouver, British Columbia [*Library symbol National Library of Canada*] (NLC) ... BVAMUM
British Columbia Museum of Mining, Britannia Beach, British Columbia [*Library symbol National Library of Canada*] (NLC) ... BBBM
British Columbia Museum, Vancouver, British Columbia [*Library symbol National Library of Canada*] (NLC) ... BVABSM
British Columbia Native Women's Society (AC) ... BCNWS
British Columbia Native Women's Society, Kamloops, British Columbia [*Library symbol National Library of Canada*] (NLC) ... BKNW
British Columbia Neurofibromatosis Foundation (AC) ... BCNF
British Columbia Nurses' Union [*Syndicat des Infirmieres de la Colombie-Britannique*] (AC) ... BCNU

British Columbia Orchard Archives Society, Delta, BC, Canada [*Library symbol*] [*Library of Congress*] (LCLS) .... CaBDEOA
British Columbia Orchard Archives Society, Delta, British Columbia [*Library symbol National Library of Canada*] (NLC) .... BDEOA
British Columbia Packers Ltd. [*Toronto Stock Exchange symbol*] .... BCK
British Columbia Packers Ltd. [*Vancouver Stock Exchange symbol*] .... BPQ
British Columbia Packers Ltd., Product Assurance and Development, Vancouver, BC, Canada [*Library symbol Library of Congress*] (LCLS) .... CaBVaPAD
British Columbia Paint Manufacturers' Association (AC) .... BCPMA
British Columbia Paraplegic Association (AC) .... BCPA
British Columbia Parkinson's Disease Association (AC) .... BCPDA
British Columbia Power and Hydro Authority [*Canada ICAO designator*] (FAAC) .... BCH
British Columbia Printing Industries Association (AC) .... BCPIA
British Columbia Provincial Museum, Ethnology Division, Victoria, BC, Canada [*Library symbol Library of Congress*] (LCLS) .... CaBViPME
British Columbia Provincial Museum, Victoria, BC, Canada [*Library symbol*] [*Library of Congress*] (LCLS) .... CaBViPM
British Columbia Provincial Museum, Victoria, British Columbia [*Library symbol National Library of Canada*] (NLC) .... BVIPM
British Columbia Rail, Corporate Information, Vancouver, BC, Canada [*Library symbol*] [*Library of Congress*] (LCLS) .... CaBVaBCR
British Columbia Railway Co. [*AAR code*] .... BCOL
British Columbia Railway Historical Association (AC) .... BCRHA
British Columbia Real Estate Association (AC) .... BCREA
British Columbia Recreation & Parks Association (AC) .... BCRPA
[*The*] British Columbia Regional Network [*Computer science*] [*Canada*] (TNIG) .... BCNET
British Columbia Reports [*A publication*] (DLA) .... BC Rep
British Columbia Reports [*A publication*] (DLA) .... BCC
British Columbia Reports [*A publication*] (DLA) .... BCR
British Columbia Research Council, Vancouver, BC, Canada [*Library symbol Library of Congress*] (LCLS) .... CaBVaR
British Columbia Research Council, Vancouver, British Columbia [*Library symbol National Library of Canada*] (NLC) .... BVAR
British Columbia Resources Investment Corp. [*Toronto Stock Exchange symbol Vancouver Stock Exchange symbol*] .... BCI
British Columbia Revised Statutes [*Canada*] [*A publication*] (DLA) .... BC Rev Stat
British Columbia Securities Commission, Vancouver, British Columbia [*Library symbol National Library of Canada*] (BIB) .... BVASEC
British Columbia Society of Artists [*1949-68, founded 1908 as BCSFA*] [*Canada*] (NGC) .... BCSA
British Columbia Society of Fine Arts [*1908, BCSA from 1949*] [*Canada*] (NGC) .... BCSFA
British Columbia Society of Landscape Architects (AC) .... BCSLA
British Columbia Special Olympics (AC) .... BCSO
British Columbia Sports Hall of Fame and Museum, Vancouver, British Columbia [*Library symbol National Library of Canada*] (NLC) .... BVABCS
British Columbia Sports Medicine Clinic [*University of British Columbia*] [*Research center*] (RCD) .... BCSMC
British Columbia Statutes [*Canada*] [*A publication*] (DLA) .... BC Stat
British Columbia Surgical Society (AC) .... BCSS
British Columbia Systems Corp., Victoria, British Columbia [*Library symbol National Library of Canada*] (NLC) .... BVISC
British Columbia Tax Reporter (Commerce Clearing House) [*A publication*] (DLA) .... BC Tax Rep (CCH)
British Columbia Teacher-Librarians' Association (AC) .... BCTLA
British Columbia Teachers' Federation [*Canada*] (AEBS) .... BC
British Columbia Teachers' Federation [*Federation des Enseignants de la Colombie-Britannique*] (AC) .... BCTF
British Columbia Teachers' Federation Resources Centre, Vancouver, BC, Canada [*Library symbol Library of Congress*] (LCLS) .... CaBVaTF
British Columbia Teachers' Federation Resources Centre, Vancouver, British Columbia [*Library symbol National Library of Canada*] (NLC) .... BVATF
British Columbia Telephone Co. [*Toronto Stock Exchange symbol Vancouver Stock Exchange symbol*] .... BCT
British Columbia Telephone Co., Burnaby, BC, Canada [*Library symbol Library of Congress*] (LCLS) .... CaBBT
British Columbia Telephone Co., Burnaby, British Columbia [*Library symbol National Library of Canada*] (NLC) .... BVABT
British Columbia Telephone Co., Vancouver, BC, Canada [*Library symbol Library of Congress*] (LCLS) .... CaBVaBT
British Columbia Telephone Ltd. [*Canada ICAO designator*] (FAAC) .... BCT
British Columbia Trade Union Group [*Canada*] (CROSS) .... TUG
British Columbia Trucking Association (AC) .... BCTA
British Columbia Union Catalogue, Burnaby, BC, Canada [*Library symbol Library of Congress*] (LCLS) .... CaBBUC
British Columbia Union Catalogue, Burnaby, British Columbia [*Library symbol National Library of Canada*] (NLC) .... BBUC
British Columbia Veterinary Medical Association (AC) .... BCVMA
British Columbia Water Polo Association (AC) .... BCWPA
British Columbia Watershed Protection Alliance (AC) .... BCWPA
British Columbian, New Westminster, British Columbia [*Library symbol National Library of Canada*] (NLC) .... BNWB
British Combustion Equipment Manufacturers Associaton (DBA) .... BCEMA
British Commerical Glasshouse Manufacturers Association (DBA) .... BCGMA
British Commissioner [*Salvation Army*] .... BC
British Committee for Map Information and Catalogue Systems (NITA) .... BRICMICS
British Committee for Standards in Haematology .... BCSH
British Commonwealth [*MARC geographic area code Library of Congress*] (LCCP) .... b----
British Commonwealth .... BC
British Commonwealth Air Training Plan [*World War II*] .... BCATP

British Commonwealth Alliance (ADA) .... BCA
British Commonwealth and Empire .... BCE
British Commonwealth Ex-Services League [*Formerly, British Empire Services League*] [*British*] .... BCEL
British Commonwealth Far East Strategic Reserve .... BCFESR
British Commonwealth Forces .... BCF
British Commonwealth Forces, Korea [*British military*] (DMA) .... BCFK
British Commonwealth Forest Translation Exchange .... BCFTE
British Commonwealth Geographical Liaison Office (PDAA) .... BCGLO
British Commonwealth International News Agency .... BCINA
British Commonwealth Korean Base [*British military*] (DMA) .... BCKB
British Commonwealth Occupation Force [*Military*] .... BCOF
British Commonwealth of Nations .... BCN
British Commonwealth Pacific Airlines Ltd. (ADA) .... BCP
British Commonwealth Pacific Airlines Ltd. .... BCPA
British Commonwealth Producers' Organization .... BCPO
British Commonwealth Scientific Office .... BCSO
British Commonwealth Scientific Office (North America) [*Washington, DC*] .... BCSO(NA)
British Commonwealth Sugar Agreement .... BCSA
British Commonwealth Union (ADA) .... BCU
British Comparative Education Society (AIE) .... BCES
British Compressed Air Society .... BCAS
British Compressed Gases Association (DBA) .... BCGA
British Computer Associated for the Blind (PDAA) .... BCAB
British Computer Society [*London*] .... BCS
British Computer Society Schools Committee (AIE) .... BCSSC
British Concrete Pumping Association (PDAA) .... BCPA
British Confectioners' Association (BI) .... BCA
British Conference and Exhibition Centres Export Council (DBA) .... BCECEC
British Conference on Automation and Computation .... BCAC
British Constructional Steelwork Association (PDAA) .... BCSA
British Consultants Bureau (CB) .... BCB
British Contact Lens Association .... BCLA
British Contract Furnishing Association (PDAA) .... BCFA
British Control Supply Mission [*World War II*] .... BCSM
British Cooking Industry Association (BI) .... BCIA
British Cookware Manufacturers Association (DBA) .... BCMA
British Co-Operative Clinical Group (BABM) .... BCCG
British Coordinating Committee for Biotechnology .... BCCB
British Copyright Council (ILCA) .... BCC
British Copyright Protection Association (PDAA) .... BCPA
British Corinthian Yacht Club (DI) .... BCYC
British Corp. .... BC
British Correspondence Chess Association (BI) .... BCCA
British Cotton Growing Association (BI) .... BCGA
British Cotton Industry Research Association (DI) .... BCIRA
British Council .... BC
British Council for Aid to Refugees .... BCAR
British Council for Rehabilitation of the Disabled (BI) .... BCRD
British Council for the Promotion of International Trade (BI) .... BCPIT
British Council in Australia .... BCA
British Council of Churches .... BCC
British Council of Productivity Association (PDAA) .... BCPA
British Council of Shopping Centres .... BCSC
British Council Undergraduate Fellowship Scheme (AIE) .... BRUFS
British Country Music Association .... BCMA
British Crafts Centre (CB) .... BCC
British Crayfish Marketing Association (DBA) .... BCMA
British Crime Survey (ECON) .... BCS
British Crop Protection Council .... BCPC
British [*or English*] Crown Cases [*A publication*] (DLA) .... Br CC
British [*or English*] Crown Cases [*A publication*] (DLA) .... Br Cr Ca
British [*or English*] Crown Cases [*A publication*] (DLA) .... Br Cr Cas
British [*or English*] Crown Cases [*A publication*] (DLA) .... Brit Cr Cas
British Crown Colony .... BCC
British Crown Green Bowling Association (DBA) .... BCGBA
British Cryogenics Council (DBA) .... BCC
British Cutlery and Silverware Association (EAIO) .... BCSA
British Cycling Federation .... BCF
British Cyclo-Cross Association (DBA) .... BCCA
British Dahlia Growers Association (DBA) .... BDGA
British Darts Organization (DBA) .... BDO
British Deaf and Dumb Association (BI) .... BDDA
British Deaf Association (DI) .... BDA
British Deaf Sports Council (DBA) .... BDSC
British Decorators Association (DBA) .... BDA
British Deer Farmers Association (DBA) .... BDFA
British Deer Producers' Association (DBA) .... BDPS
British Deer Society .... BDS
British Defence and Aid Fund for Southern Africa (EAIO) .... BDAFSA
British Defence Coordination Committee, Middle East (NATG) .... BDCC/ME
British Defence Directory [*Brassey's Defence Publishers Ltd.*] [*Information service or system*] (IID) .... BDD
British Defence Manufacturers Association (PDAA) .... BDMA
British Defence Staff .... BDS
British Defence Staff, Washington, DC [*Also, BDSWASHDC*] (NATG) .... BDSW
British Defence Staff, Washington, DC [*Also, BDSW*] (NATG) .... BDSWASHDC
British Deming Association (DBA) .... BDA
British Democratic Party [*Political party*] .... BDP
British Dental Association .... BDA
British Dental Health Foundation (DI) .... BDHF
British Dental Health Organisation (DI) .... BDHO
British Dental Hygienists Association (DI) .... BDHA
British Dental Institute (DI) .... BDI

British Dental Migraine Study Group [*An association*] (DBA)	BDMSG
British Dental Students' Association (BI)	BDSA
British Dental Trade Association (DBA)	BDTA
British Department of Transport	BDOT
British Destroyer Escort	BDE
British Diabetic Association (IRUK)	BDA
British Diamond Workers Trade Union	BDWTU
[*The*] British Dietetic Association	BDA
British Digestive Foundation (IRUK)	BDF
British Direct Mail Advertising Association (DI)	BDMAA
British Direct Marketing Association (DBA)	BDMA
British Disinfectant Manufacturers' Association (BI)	BDMA
British Display Society (BI)	BDS
British Disposable Products Association (PDAA)	BDPA
British Document Exchange	BDE
British Document Exchange	BRITDOC
British Doll Artists Association (DBA)	BDA
British Double Summer Time	BDST
British Drag Racing Association (BI)	BDRA
British Drama League (DI)	BDL
British Drilling Association (DBA)	BDA
British Driving Society (BI)	BDS
British Drug Houses Ltd. [*Research code symbol*]	BDH
British Dyslexia Association	BDA
British Eagle Airlines (IIA)	BE
British Earth Sheltering Association (DBA)	BESA
British East Africa	BEA
British East Africa Protectorate [*British government*]	BEAP
British Eastern Merchant Shippers' Association (BI)	BEMSA
British Ecological Society	BES
British Education and Training Technology Exhibition (ITD)	BETT
British Education Management and Administration Society (DBA)	BEMAS
British Educational Contractors Group (AIE)	BECG
British Educational Equipment Association (DS)	BEEA
British Educational Furniture Manufacturers Council (AIE)	BEFMC
British Educational Research Association	BERA
British Educational Suppliers Association (AIE)	BESA
British Effluent and Water Association [*Trade association*]	BEWA
British Egg Association (BI)	BEA
British Egg Information Service (DI)	BEIS
British Egg Marketing Board (DI)	BEMB
British Egg Products Association (DI)	BEPA
British Electric Cable Testing Organisation (MCD)	BECTO
British Electric Conduit Systems Manufacturers [*Later, British Electrical Systems Association*] (PDAA)	BECSM
British Electric Resistance Co. (IAA)	BERCO
[*The*] British Electric Traction Co. Ltd.	BET
British Electrical and Allied Industries Research Association (MCD)	BEAIRA
British Electrical and Allied Manufacturers Association	BEAMA
British Electrical Approvals Board	BEAB
British Electrical Conduit Manufacturers	BECM
British Electrical Development Association (DI)	BEDA
British Electrical Power Convention (MCD)	BEPC
British Electrical Systems Association (DBA)	BESA
British Electricity Authority	BEA
British Electro-Ceramic Manufacturers' Association (BI)	BECMA
British Electronic and Applied Research Association (MCD)	BEARA
British Electronics Week [*Trade show*] (ITD)	BEW
British Electrostatic Control Association (EAIO)	BECA
British Electrostatic Manufacturers Association (DBA)	BESMA
British Electrotechnical Approvals Board (NITA)	BEAB
British Electrotechnical Committee (BARN)	BEL
British Element	BE
British Embassy (DS)	B/E
British Embassy, Washington, DC [*Library symbol Library of Congress*] (LCLS)	DBE
British Emergency Air Medical Service (DA)	BEAMS
British Empire	BE
British Empire and Commonwealth	BE & C
British Empire and Commonwealth Games Federation	BECGF
British Empire and Commonwealth Weight-Lifting Council	BE & CWLC
British Empire Cancer Campaign for Research [*Later, Cancer Research Campaign*] (PDAA)	BECCR
British Empire Cancer Council	BECC
British Empire Forces	BEF
British Empire League	BEL
British Empire Leprosy Relief Association	BELRA
British Empire Medal	BEM
British Empire Naturalist Association	BENA
British Empire Series [*A publication*]	BES
British Empire Service League	BESL
British Empire Union	BEU
British Employers' Confederation	BEC
British Endodontic Society	BES
British Energy Management Systems	BEMS
British Engineering Standards Association	BESA
British Engineers Association	BEA
British Engineers Club	BEC
British English [*Language*] (WGA)	BrE
British Entertainment and Dancing Association (DBA)	BEDA
British Entomological and Natural History Society	BENHS
British Epilepsy Association	BEA
British Equestrian Federation (DBA)	BEF
British Equestrian Promotions, Ltd.	BEP
British Equestrian Trade Association (DBA)	BETA

British Equine Veterinary Association (DBA)	BEVA
British Esperanto Association, Inc. (BI)	BEA
British Essence Manufacturers' Association (BI)	BEMA
British European Airways Corp. [*Later, British Airways*]	BEA
British European Airways Corp. [*Later, British Airways*]	BEAC
British European Airways Corp. [*later, British Airways*] Computerized Office Network	BEACON
British Examining and Registration Board in Occupational Hygiene	BERBOH
British Executive Air Services	BEAS
British Executive Service Overseas [*Overseas Development Administration*] (DS)	BESO
British Exhibition Contractors Association (EAIO)	BECA
British Exhibition Venues Association	BEVA
British Exhibitors' Association (BI)	BEA
British Expeditionary Force	BEF
British Experimental Pile Operation [*Nuclear reactor*] (DEN)	BEPO
British Experimental Rotor Program	BERP
British Expertise in Science and Technology [*Longman Cartermill Ltd.*] [*Scotland*] [*Information service or system*] (IID)	BEST
British Export Board (PDAA)	BEB
British Export Houses' Association (DS)	BEHA
British Export Trade Research Organisation	BETRO
British Exporters Association (DBA)	BExA
British Exports Marketing Advisory Committee [*Defunct*]	BEMAC
British Ex-Services Association [*Australia*]	BESA
British Ex-Services Womens (United Kingdom) Association	BESW(UK)A
British Fabric Association (DBA)	BFA
British Facsimile Industry Consultative Committee (NITA)	BFICC
British Families Education Service	BFES
British Fantasy Society (DBA)	BFS
British Farm Produce Council (BI)	BFPC
British Federation of Aesthetics and Cosmetology (BI)	BFAC
British Federation of Brass Bands (DBA)	BFBB
British Federation of Business and Professional Women (ODBW)	BFBPW
British Federation of Care Home Proprietors (DBA)	BFCHP
British Federation of Commodity Associations (ODBW)	BFCA
British Federation of Film Societies	BFFS
British Federation of Hotel, Guest House, and Self-Catering Associations (DBA)	BFHGH & SC
British Federation of Iron and Steel Stockholders (BI)	BFISS
British Federation of Master Printers [*A union*]	BFMP
British Federation of Musical Festivals	BFMF
British Federation of Printing Machinery and Supplies	BFPMS
British Federation of Sand and Land Yacht Clubs	BFSLYC
British Federation of Textile Technicians (DCTA)	BFTT
British Federation of University Women	BFUW
British Federation of Young Choirs (DBA)	BFYC
British Fibreboard Packaging Association (DBA)	BFPA
British Field Hospital [*British military*] (DMA)	BFH
British Field Post Office [*World War II*]	BFPO
British Field [*Wireless*] Set [*British military*] (DMA)	BF Set
British Field Sports Society	BFSS
British Film and Television Producers' Association	BFTPA
British Film Designers Guild (DBA)	BFDG
British Film Fund Agency	BFFA
British Film Institute	BFI
British Fire Protection Systems Association (PDAA)	BFPSA
British Fire Services Association (PDAA)	BFSA
British Fireboard Packaging Employers' Association	BFPEA
British First Airborne Division	BFAD
British First Army	BFA
British Fishing and Small Vessel Equipment Association [*Later, BSSEA*] (PDAA)	BFSVEA
British Flat Roofing Council (DBA)	BFRC
British Flight Battalion	BFB
British Floorcovering Manufacturers Association (DBA)	BFMA
British Flower Industry Association (PDAA)	BFIA
British Flue and Chimney Manufacturers Association (DBA)	BFCMA
British Fluid Power Association (EAIO)	BFPA
British Fluid Power Distributors Association (DBA)	BFPDA
British Food Classification (BARN)	A
British Food Export Council (DS)	BFEC
British Food Manufacturing Industries Research Association (ARC)	BFMIRA
British Food Mission [*World War II*]	BFM
British Foods Action Group (DI)	BFAG
British Footwear Manufacturers' Federation	BFMF
British Forces (DMA)	BF
British Forces, Arabian Peninsula [*British military*] (DMA)	BFAP
British Forces Broadcasting Service [*or Station*]	BFBS
British Forces Broadcasting Unit (IAA)	BFBU
British Forces Germany [*NATO*]	BFG
British Forces Network	BFN
British Forces Post Office	BFPO
British Foreign and Colonial Corp. [*Finance*]	BFCC
British Foreign and State Papers [*A publication*] (DLA)	BFSP
British Foreign Legion [*British military*] (DMA)	BFL
British Forging Industry Association (EAIO)	BFIA
British Foundation for Age Research (IRUK)	BFAR
British Foundry Association (DBA)	BFA
British Franchise Association (DBA)	BFA
British Francophone Business Group [*An association*] (DBA)	BFBG
British Free Corps [*Corps formed by Germans among POW's and civil internees*] [*World War II*]	BFC
British Friction Materials Council (BI)	BFMC
British Friesian Cattle Society of Great Britain and Ireland	BFCS

British Frontier Service (BARN) ... BFS
British Frozen Food Federation (DBA) ... BFFF
British Fruit and Vegetable Canners Association (DBA) ... BF & VCA
British Fuchsia Society (BI) ... BFS
British Fulbright Scholars Association (PDAA) ... BFSA
British Fur Trade Association (DBA) ... BFTA
British Furniture Manufacturers' Federated Associations (BI) ... BFM
British Gallantry Medal ... BGM
British Gaming Association (BARN) ... BGA
British Gas (ECON) ... BG
British Gas ADS [*NYSE symbol*] (SPSG) ... BRG
British Gas Corp. ... BGC
British Gas Corp. [*Toronto Stock Exchange symbol*] ... BGS
British Gas Corporation Pension Scheme ... BGCPS
British Gas International ... BGI
British Gas Ltd. [*Associated Press*] (SAG) ... BritGas
British Gas Ltd. American Depository Receipts [*Toronto Stock Exchange symbol*] ... BGSR
British Gas Region ... BGR
British Gas Staff Association [*A union*] ... BGSA
British Gas Staff Pension Scheme ... BGSPS
British Gauge [*Metal industry*] ... BG
British Gear Manufacturers Association (MCD) ... BGMA
British Gelatine and Glue Research Association (DAVI) ... BGGRA
British General Hospital ... BGH
British Geological Survey ... BGS
British Geomorphological Research Group ... BGRG
British Geotechnical Society ... BGS
British Geotechnical Society ... BGTS
British Geriatrics Society ... BGS
British Glaciological Society (NOAA) ... BGS
British Gladiolus Society (BI) ... BGS
British Glass Industry Research Association [*Research center*] (IRC) ... BGIRA
British Glass Manufacturers Confederation (DBA) ... BGMC
British Gliding Association (MCD) ... BGA
British Go Association (DBA) ... BGA
British Goat Society ... BGS
British Golf Greenkeepers' Association (BI) ... BGGA
British Goose Producers Association (DBA) ... BGPA
British Graham Land Expedition [*1934-37*] ... BGLE
British Granite and Whinstone Federation (PDAA) ... BGWF
British Grassland Society ... BGS
British Grenadiers ... BG
British Ground Freezing Society (PDAA) ... BGFS
British Growers' Look Ahead International Exhibition (ITD) ... BGLA
British Guiana ... BG
British Guiana ... BGU
British Guiana (ILCA) ... Brit Gui
British Guiana Airways Ltd. [*A national airline*] ... BGAL
British Guiana Full Court Reports (Official Gazette) [*A publication*] (DLA) ... FC
British Guiana General Jurisdiction (Official Gazette) [*1899-*] [*A publication*] (ILCA) ... GJ
British Guiana Law Reports [*A publication*] (DLA) ... BG
British Guiana Law Reports (Old and New Series) [*A publication*] (DLA) ... BGLR
British Guiana Limited Jurisdiction (Official Gazette) [*1899-1955*] [*A publication*] (DLA) ... LJ
British Guiana Militia Artillery [*British military*] (DMA) ... BGMA
British Guiana Reports of Opinions [*A publication*] (DLA) ... RBG
British Guiana Supreme Court, Appellate Jurisdiction (DLA) ... AJ
British Guiana Volunteer Force [*British military*] (DMA) ... BGVF
British Guild of Flight Operations Officers (DA) ... BritGFO
British Hacksaw and Bandsaw Manufacturers' Association (DBA) ... BHBMA
British Handball Association (DBA) ... BHA
British Hang Glider Manufacturers Federation (PDAA) ... BHGMF
British Hang Gliding Association ... BHGA
British Hard Metal Association ... BHMA
British Hardmetal Association (DBA) ... BHA
British Hardware and Housewares Manufacturers Association (DBA) ... BHHMA
British Hardware Federation (DBA) ... BHF
British Hardware Promotion Council Ltd. (BI) ... BHPC
British Harness Racing Club (DBA) ... BHRC
British Hat Guild (DBA) ... BHG
British Hay and Straw Merchants' Association (DBA) ... BHSMA
British Headwear Industries Federation (DBA) ... BHIF
British Health Care Association (DBA) ... BHCA
British Health Food Trade Association (DBA) ... BHFTA
British Health-Care Export Council (DS) ... BHCEC
British Health-Care Export Council (EAIO) ... BHEC
British Heart Foundation (EAIO) ... BHF
British Heavy Steel Association (BI) ... BHSA
British Helicopter Advisory Board (AIA) ... BHAB
British Hellenic Chamber of Commerce (DBA) ... BHCC
British Herb Trade Association (DBA) ... BHTA
British Herbal Medicine Association ... BHMA
British Herdsmen's Club (BI) ... BHC
British Heritage Institute (Canada) Inc. (AC) ... BHIC
British Heritage Society (EA) ... BHS
British Herpetological Society ... BHS
British High Commissioner ... BHC
British Hire Cruiser Federation (DBA) ... BHCF
British Holiday and Home Parks Association (DBA) ... BH & HPA
British Holiday Fellowship Ltd. (BI) ... BHF
British Holistic Medical Association [*British*] ... BHMA
British Holistic Medical Society ... BHMS
British Holstein Society (DBA) ... BHS
British Home and Hospital for Incurables ... BHHI
British Home Furnishings Bureau (DBA) ... BHFB
British Home Stores [*Retail chain*] ... BHS
British Homeopathic Association ... BHA
British Honduras ... BH
British Honduras [*MARC country of publication code Library of Congress*] (LCCP) ... bh
British Honduras (ILCA) ... Brit Hond
British Honduras [*MARC geographic area code Library of Congress*] (LCCP) ... ncbh--
British Honey Importers and Packers Association (DBA) ... BHIPA
British Horological Institute ... BHI
British Horse Society (DI) ... BHS
British Horsepower ... BHP
British Hospital Equipment Display Centre (CB) ... BHEDC
British Hospitals Contributory Schemes Association (PDAA) ... BHCSA
British Hospitals Export Council [*Later, BHCEC*] (DS) ... BHEC
British Hosta and Hemerocallis Society (EAIO) ... BHHS
British Hotels and Restaurants Association (BI) ... BHRA
British Hotels Association (BARN) ... BHA
British Hotels, Restaurants, and Caterers Association ... BHRCA
British Housewives' League (DI) ... BHL
British Hovercraft ... BH
British Hovercraft Corp. ... BHC
British Humanist Association ... BHA
British Humanities Research Board (AIE) ... BHRB
British Hydromechanics Research Association [*Later, BHRA Ltd.*] ... BHRA
British Hypnosis Research [*An association*] (DBA) ... BHRE
British Hypnosis Research Association ... BHRA
British Hypnotherapy Association ... BHA
British Ice Hockey Association (DI) ... BIHA
British Ichthyological Society ... BIS
British Impact Treatment Association (DBA) ... BITA
British Imperial System ... BIS
British Import Union (DBA) ... BIU
British Importers' Confederation (DS) ... BIC
British Incoming Tour Operators Association (DBA) ... BITOA
British Independent Air Transport Association ... BIATA
British Independent Airways [*ICAO designator*] (FAAC) ... BXH
British Independent Airways [*ICAO designator*] (AD) ... RX
British Independent Factors Association (DBA) ... BIFA
British Independent Garages Association (DBA) ... BIGA
British Independent Grocers' Association (DBA) ... BIGA
British Independent Plastic Extruders Association (DBA) ... BIPEA
British Independent Steel Producers Association (PDAA) ... BISPA
British India ... BI
British India Steam Navigation Co. (IIA) ... BI
British India Steam Navigation Co. ... BISN
British India Steam Navigation Co. (ROG) ... BISNC
British Indian Ocean Territory [*MARC country of publication code Library of Congress*] (LCCP) ... bi
British Indian Ocean Territory ... BIOT
British Indian Ocean Territory [*MARC geographic area code Library of Congress*] (LCCP) ... i-bi--
British Indian Ocean Territory [*ANSI two-letter standard code*] (CNC) ... IO
British Indian Ocean Territory [*ANSI three-letter standard code*] (CNC) ... IOT
British Industrial Advertising Association (PDAA) ... BIAA
British Industrial and Scientific Film Association ... BISFA
British Industrial Biological Research Association (ARC) ... BIBRA
British Industrial Ceramic Manufacturers Association (DBA) ... BICMA
British Industrial Collaborative Exponential Program ... BICEP
British Industrial Development Office [*Through foreign branches, encourages investments in Britain from abroad*] ... BIDO
British Industrial Fasteners Federation (DBA) ... BIFF
British Industrial Furnace Construction Association (DBA) ... BIFCA
British Industrial Measuring and Control Apparatus Manufacturers' Association ... BIMCAM
British Industrial Plastics (ODBW) ... BIP
British Industrial Truck Association ... BITA
British Industries Fair ... BIF
British Industries Federation ... BIF
British Industry [*Vancouver Stock Exchange symbol*] ... BI
British Industry Committee on South Africa ... BICSA
British Informatics Society Ltd. (NITA) ... BISL
British Information Services ... BIS
British Information Services, New York, NY [*Library symbol Library of Congress*] (LCLS) ... NNBLI
British Information Technology Exhibition and Conference on Engineering Software [*Computational Mechanics Institute*] ... BRITEC
British Infrared Manufacturers Organization (PDAA) ... BIRMO
British Institute for Brain Injured Children ... BIBIC
British Institute of Agricultural Consultants (DBA) ... BIAC
British Institute of Architectural Technicians (EAIO) ... BIAT
[*The*] **British Institute of Cleaning Science** ... BICS
British Institute of Cleaning Science ... BICSC
British Institute of Dealers in Securities [*Defunct*] ... BIDS
British Institute of Electrical Engineers ... BIEE
British Institute of Embalmers ... BIE
British Institute of Energy Economics (DBA) ... BIEE
British Institute of Engineering Technology (DI) ... BIET
British Institute of Engineers (MCD) ... BIE
British Institute of Graphologists (DBA) ... BIG
British Institute of Hardwood Flooring Specialists (BI) ... BIHFS
British Institute of Human Rights (DLA) ... BIHR
British Institute of Industrial Art ... BIIA

British Institute of Industrial Therapy .... BIIT
British Institute of Innkeeping .... BII
British Institute of International and Comparative Law .... BIICL
British Institute of International and Comparative Law (EA) .... BRICLAW
British Institute of Jazz Studies (BI) .... BIJS
British Institute of Kitchen Architecture (DBA) .... BIKA
British Institute of Management .... BIM
British Institute of Management Secretariat for Overseas Countries (PDAA) .... BIMSOC
British Institute of Mental Handicap .... BIMH
British Institute of Non-Destructive Testing (PDAA) .... BINDT
British Institute of Non-Destructive Testing (EAIO) .... BInst NDT
British Institute of Organ Studies (DBA) .... BIOS
British Institute of Persian Studies (DBA) .... BIPS
British Institute of Practical Psychology .... IPP
British Institute of Practical Psychology Ltd. (BI) .... BIPP
British Institute of Professional Photography (AIE) .... BIPP
British Institute of Public Opinion .... BIPO
British Institute of Radio Engineers .... BIRE
British Institute of Radio Engineers (IAA) .... BRITIRE
British Institute of Radiology (DEN) .... BIR
British Institute of Recorded Sound .... BIRS
British Institute of Regulatory Affairs (DBA) .... BIRA
British Institute of Securities Laws (DBA) .... BISL
British Institute of Sewage Purification .... BISP
British Institute of Sports Coaches (DBA) .... BISC
British Institute of Surgical Technologists .... BIST
British Institute of Traffic Education Research (DBA) .... BITER
British Institution (ROG) .... BI
British Institution of Training Officers (PDAA) .... BITO
British Institutions Reflection Profiling Syndicate [*Seismic profiling*] .... BIRPS
British Insulated Cables .... BIC
British Insulated Callender's Cable .... BICC
British Insurance and Finance Union (DI) .... BIFU
British Insurance and Investment Brokers' Association .... BIIBA
British Insurance Association .... BIA
British Insurance Brokers' Association (DLA) .... BIBA
British Insurance Law Association (DLA) .... BILA
British Insurance Law Association. Bulletin [*A publication*] (DLA) .... BILA Bull
British Intelligence Objectives Subcommittee .... BIOS
British Interactive Broadcasting .... BIB
British Interactive Video Association [*Information service or system*] (IID) .... BIVA
British Interlining Manufacturers Association (DBA) .... BIMA
British Internal Combustion Engine Manufacturers' Association .... BICEMA
British Internal Combustion Engine Research Institute Ltd. [*Research center*] (IRUK) .... BICERI
British International Freight Association (EAIO) .... BIFA
British International Helicopters [*ICAO designator*] (AD) .... UR
British International Helicopters Ltd. [*ICAO designator*] (FAAC) .... BIH
British International Law Cases [*A publication*] (DLA) .... BILC
British International Law Society (DLA) .... BILS
British International Motorcycle Association (EA) .... BIMA
British International Postcard Exhibition .... BIPEX
British International Studies Association (DBA) .... BISA
British Interplanetary Society .... BIS
British Investment Casting Trade Association .... BICTA
British Investors Database .... BID
British Iris Society (EAIO) .... BIS
British Iron and Steel Consumers' Council .... BRISCC
British Iron and Steel Corp. .... BISC
British Iron and Steel Federation .... BISF
British Iron and Steel Industry Translation Service .... BISITS
British Iron and Steel Institute Translation Service (NITA) .... BISITS
British Iron and Steel Research Association .... BISRA
British Iron, Steel and Kindred Trades Association (BI) .... BISAKTA
British Ironfounders Association (BI) .... BIA
British Island Airways [*ICAO designator*] (AD) IV
British Island Airways Ltd. .... BIA
British Isles Bee Breeders Association (DBA) .... BIBBA
British Jewellers Association (PDAA) .... BJA
British Jewellery and Giftware Federation (DBA) .... BJGF
British Jewish Cockney .... BJC
British Jigsaw Puzzle Library [*An association*] (DBA) .... BJPL
British Joint Communications Board [*British military*] (DMA) .... BJCB
British Joint Communications Office (NATG) .... BJCO
British Joint Communications-Electronics Board [*Military*] .... BJCEB
British Joint Services .... BJS
British Joint Services Mission [*Later, SUKLO*] .... BJSM
British Joint Staff Mission [*World War II*] .... BJSM
British Journal for the Philosophy of Science [*A publication*] .... BJPS
British Journal of Administrative Law [*A publication*] (DLA) .... BJAL
British Journal of Administrative Law [*A publication*] (DLA) .... Brit J Adm L
British Journal of Administrative Law [*A publication*] (DLA) .... Brit J Admin Law
British Journal of International Law [*A publication*] (DLA) .... Brit J Int'l L
British Judo Association .... BJA
British Junior Chamber [*An association*] (DBA) .... BJC
British Junior Chambers of Commerce (BI) .... BJCC
British Jute Trade Research Association (PDAA) .... BJTRA
British Karate Board (DI) .... BKB
British Kidney Patient Association (DI) .... BKPA
British Kinematography, Sound, and Television Society .... BKSTS
British Knights [*Brand name of athletic shoe*] .... BK
British Knitting and Clothing Export Council (DBA) .... BKCEC
British Kodaly Academy (DBA) .... BKA
British Korfball Association (EAIO) .... BKA
British Laboratory Animals Veterinary Association (DBA) .... BLAVA
British Laboratory Ware Association Ltd. (BI) .... BLWA
British Lamp Blown Scientific Glassware Manufacturers' Association Ltd. (BI) .... BLSGMA
British Landrace Pig Society (BI) .... BLPS
British Laryngological, Rhinological, and Otological Association (MAE) .... BLROA
British Latin America Volunteers [*British military*] (DMA) .... BLAV
British Launderers Research Association (PDAA) .... BLRA
British Lawn Mower Racing Association (DBA) .... BLMRA
British League of Male Chauvinists (EAIO) .... BLMC
British Leather Confederation (IRUK) .... BLC
British Leather Fashion Council (DBA) .... BLFC
British Leather Federation (BI) .... BLF
British Leather Manufacturers Research Association .... BLMRA
British Leathergoods Manufacturers Association (DBA) .... BLMA
British Legal Association (DLA) .... BLA
British Legal Services Agency (DLA) .... BLSA
British Legion .... BL
British Legion Headquarters .... BLH
British Legion Village .... BLV
British Leprosy Relief Association (BI) .... BLRA
British Leprosy Relief Association (IRUK) .... LEPRA
British Leyland [*Later, BL Ltd., then Rover Group*] [*Auto manufacturing company*] .... BL
British Leyland Europe and Overseas [*Commercial firm*] .... BLEO
British Leyland Motor Corp. [*Auto manufacturing company*] .... BLMC
British Leyland Motor Holdings [*Auto manufacturing company*] .... BLMH
British Leyland Systems Ltd. (NITA) .... BLSL
British Liaison Officer .... BLO
British Liberation Army [*Later, British Army of the Rhine*] .... BLA
British Library [*Formerly, The British Museum Reading Room*] .... BL
British Library Association (BARN) .... BLA
British Library Automated Information Service [*European host database system*] (IID) .... BLAISE
British Library Bibliographic Services [*London, England*] .... BLBS
[*The*] **British Library Bibliographic Services Division** (NITA) .... BLBSD
British Library Catalog: Humanities and Social Sciences [*Information service or system*] (CRD) .... HSS
British Library, Development and Systems Office, London, England [*Library symbol*] [*Library of Congress*] (LCLS) .... Uk-D
British Library Document Supply Centre (CB) .... BLDSC
British Library General Catalogue of Printed Books [*A publication*] .... BLC
British Library Information Sciences Service .... BLISS
British Library Information Skills (AIE) .... BLIS
British Library Lending Division .... BLL
British Library Lending Division .... BLLD
British Library, London, England [*OCLC symbol*] (OCLC) .... BRI
British Library, London, United Kingdom [*Library symbol Library of Congress*] (LCLS) .... Uk
British Library of Political and Economic Science [*London School of Economics*] .... BLPES
British Library of Tape .... BLOT
British Library of Wildlife Sound .... BLOWS
[*The*] **British Library Reference Division** (NITA) .... BLRD
[*The*] **British Library Research and Development Department** (NITA) .... BLR & DD
British Library Research and Development Division (AIE) .... BLRDD
British Lichen Society (EAIO) .... BLS
British Life Assurance Trust .... BLAT
British Lift Association (DBA) .... BLA
British Light Aviation Center (MCD) .... BLAC
British Lighting Council [*Defunct*] .... BLC
British Limbless Ex-Service Men's Association .... BLESMA
British Limousin Cattle Society (DBA) .... BLCS
British Linen Bank .... BLB
British Linen Hire Association (PDAA) .... BLHA
British Lion [*Motion picture company*] .... BL
British List Brokers Association (DBA) .... BLBA
British Lubricants Federation (DBA) .... BLF
British Machine Guarding Authority .... BMGA
British Machine Vision Association .... BMVA
British Magical Society (DBA) .... BMS
British Mail Order Corp. (DGA) .... BMOC
British Maize Starch and Glucose Manufacturers Association (BI) .... BMSGMA
British Majorettes' Association (DI) .... BMA
British Malaysian Industry and Trade Association (DS) .... BMITA
British Malaysian Society (DBA) .... BMS
British Malleable Tube Fittings Association (BI) .... BMTFA
British Man-Made Fibres Federation (BI) .... BMFF
British Man-Made Fibres Federation .... BMMFF
British Mantle Manufacturers' Association (BI) .... BMMA
British Manufacture and Research .... BMS
British Manufacturers' Association Ltd. (BI) .... BMA
British Manufacturers of Malleable Tube Fittings Export Group .... BRIMAFEX
British Marine Aquarist Association .... BMAA
British Marine Equipment Association (DBA) .... BMEA
British Marine Equipment Council (DS) .... BMEC
British Marine Industries Federation (EAIO) .... BMIF
British Marine RADAR (IAA) .... BMR
British Maritime Law Association .... BMLA
British Maritime Technology Ltd. [*Research center*] (IRC) .... BMT
British Market Research Bureau Ltd. [*Information service or system*] (IID) .... BMRB
British Mass Transit Consultants [*Commercial firm*] .... BMTC

British Mat and Matting Manufacturers Association (BI) ... BMMMA
British Matchbox Label and Booklet Society ... BML-BS
British Materials Handling Federation (DBA) ... BMHF
British Mean Time (DAS) ... BMT
British Measurement and Testing Association (ACII) ... BMTA
British Measures Group ... BMG
British Mechanical Engineering Federation (DI) ... BMEF
British Medal (DI) ... BM
British Medical [*Vancouver Stock Exchange symbol*] ... BMD
British Medical Acupuncture Association (PDAA) ... BMAA
British Medical Acupuncture Society ... BMAS
British Medical Association ... BMA
British Medical Charter [*ICAO designator*] (FAAC) ... BMD
British Medical Council ... BMC
British Medical Data Systems (NITA) ... BMDS
British Medical Informatics Society (ACII) ... BMIS
British Medical Journal [*A publication*] ... BMJ
British Medical LASER Association ... BMLA
British Medical Representatives Association (BI) ... BMRA
British Medical Research Council ... BMRC
British Medical Students Association (BI) ... BMSA
British Medical Television ... BMTV
British Medical Ultrasound Society (EAIO) ... BMUS
British Mediterranean Airways Ltd. [*FAA designator*] (FAAC) ... LAJ
British Menswear Guild Ltd. (BI) ... BMG
British Merchant Banking and Securities Houses Association (EAIO) ... BMBA
British Merchant Navy ... BMN
British Merchant Shipping Mission ... BMSM
British Metal Castings Council (DBA) ... BMCC
British Metallurgical Plant Constructors Association (DBA) ... BMPCA
British Meteor Society (EAIO) ... BMS
British Meteorological Office (MCD) ... BMO
British Metrication Board ... BMB
British Mexican Society (DBA) ... BMS
British Micro Manufacturer Group ... BMMG
British Microcirculation Society (EAIO) ... BMS
British Microcomputer Manufacturers' Group (NITA) ... BMMG
British Micrographic Manufacturers Association (DBA) ... BMMA
British Microlight Aircraft Association (PDAA) ... BMAA
British Micropalaeontological Research Group ... BMRG
British Middle East Office ... BMEO
British Midland Airways [*ICAO designator*] (AD) ... BD
British Midland Airways Ltd. ... BM
British Midland Airways Ltd. [*ICAO designator*] (FAAC) ... BMA
British Military Administration ... BMA
British Military Administration, British Borneo ... BMA(BB)
British Military Authority ... BMA
British Military Government ... BMG
British Military Hospital ... BMH
British Military Mission ... BMM
British Military Supply Mission [*World War II*] ... BMSM
British Ministry of Information (DAS) ... BMI
British Ministry of Supply (AAG) ... B/MOS
British Ministry of Supply ... BMS
British Ministry of Supply Research and Development Establishment ... BMSRDE
British Ministry of War Transport [*World War II*] ... BMWT
British Model Soldier Society ... BMSS
British Morgan Horse Society ... BMHS
British Morgan Horse Society (DBA) ... BMHS
British Moth Boat Association (BI) ... BMBA
British Motor Corp. Ltd. ... BMC
British Motor Cycle Racing Club (DBA) ... BEMSEE
British Motor Heritage ... BMH
British Motor Holdings ... BMH
British Motor Racing Marshals Club (DBA) ... BMRMC
British Motor Racing Research Trust ... BMRRT
British Motor Ship Owners Association (DBA) ... BMSOA
British Motor Trade Association (BI) ... BMTA
British Mountaineering Council ... BMC
British Movement [*Political party*] ... BM
British Museum [*London*] ... BM
British Museum Catalogue ... BMC
British Museum Catalogue of Coins of the Roman Empire [*A publication*] (OCD) ... B M Coins Rom Emp
British Museum Expeditions to Middle Egypt [*London*] [*A publication*] (BJA) ... BME
British Museum Library [*London*] ... BML
British Museum (Natural History) [*London*] ... BMNH
British Museum - Sloan Herbarium [*London*] ... MB-SL
British Music Hall Society (BI) ... BMHS
British Music Information Centre (CB) ... BMIC
British Music Society ... BMS
British Musicians' Pensions Society (BI) ... BMPS
British Mycological Society ... BMS
British Narrow Fabrics Association (DBA) ... BNFA
British National Antarctic Expedition [*1901-04*] ... BrNAE
British National Association for Soviet and East European Studies (PDAA) ... BNASEES
British National Association of Perry Makers ... BNAPM
British National Bibliographical Staff Association ... BNBSA
British National Bibliography Research Fund ... BNBRF
British National Book Centre ... BNBC
British National Carnation Society (BI) ... BNCS
British National Committee for Electroheat (PDAA) ... BNCE
British National Committee for International Engineering Affairs (PDAA) ... BNCIEA
British National Committee for Non-Destructive Testing (ACII) ... BNCNDT
British National Committee of the International Chamber of Commerce (DS) ... BNC/ICC
British National Committee on Antarctic Research ... BNCAR
British National Committee on Data for Science and Technology (DIT) ... BNCDST
British National Committee on Materials ... BNCM
British National Committee on Ocean Engineering ... BNCOE
British National Committee on Research ... BNCOR
British National Committee on Space Research ... BNCSR
British National Committee on Surface Active Agents ... BNC
British National Committee on Surface Active Agents (BI) ... BNCSAA
British National Conference on Databases (NITA) ... BNCOD
British National Export Council ... BNEC
British National Film Catalogue (DIT) ... BNFC
British National Formulary [*A publication*] ... BNF
British National Institute of Oceanography ... BNIO
British National Oil Corp. [*Pronounced "bee-knock"*] [*Nationalized industry*] [*British*] ... BNOC
British National Opera Company ... BNOC
British National Party (PPW) ... BNP
British National Space Centre ... BNSC
British Natural Hygiene Society ... BNHS
British Naturalists' Association (BARN) ... BNA
British Naturopathic and Osteopathic Association ... BNOA
British Nautical Instrument Trade Association (DBA) ... BNITA
British Naval Air Service ... BNAS
British Naval Air Staff ... BNAS
British Naval Attache (NATG) ... BNA
British Naval Connector (CDE) ... BNC
British Naval Equipment Association (PDAA) ... BNEA
British Naval Gunnery Mission [*British military*] (DMA) ... BNGM
British Naval Liaison Officer ... BNLO
British Naval Liaison [*Office*] **US Navy** [*London*] ... BNLUS
British Naval Staff ... BNS
British Needlecrafts Council (DBA) ... BNC
British Neuropathological Society ... BNS
British New Guinea (ADA) ... BNG
British New Zealand Trade Council, Inc. (DBA) ... B-NZTC
British Non-Commissioned Officer [*British military*] (DMA) ... BNCO
British Non-Ferrous Abstracts [*A database*] [*British Non-Ferrous Metals Technology Centre*] (NITA) ... BNF ABS
British Non-Ferrous Metals Abstracts [*BNF Metals Technology Centre*] [*Information service or system*] (CRD) ... BNF
British Non-Ferrous Metals Federation (BI) ... BNFMF
British Non-Ferrous Metals Research Association ... BNFMRA
British Non-Ferrous Metals Research Association ... BNMRA
British Non-Ferrous Metals Technology Centre (EAIO) ... BNFMTC
British Nonwovens Manufacturers Association (DBA) ... BNMA
British North Africa Force ... BNAF
British North America ... BNA
British North America Philatelic Society (EA) ... BNAPS
British North American Act ... BNAA
British North Atlantic (DS) ... BNA
British North Borneo ... BNB
British Nuclear Ballistic Missile ... BNBM
British Nuclear Design and Construction ... BNDC
British Nuclear Energy Conference ... BNEC
British Nuclear Energy Society ... BNES
British Nuclear Export Executives [*Group to promote export of nuclear power stations of British design*] ... BNX
British Nuclear Forum ... BNF
British Nuclear Fuels Ltd. ... BNF
British Nuclear Fuels Ltd. ... BNFL
British Nuclear Test Veterans Association (DBA) ... BNTVA
British Nuclear Waste Ltd. (NUCP) ... BNWL
British Numerical Control Society (MCD) ... BNCS
British Numismatic Society ... BNS
British Numismatic Trade Association ... BNTA
British Nursery Goods Association (BI) ... BNGA
British Nursing Association (BI) ... BNA
British Nutrition Foundation ... BNF
British Oat and Barley Millers Association (DBA) ... BOBMA
British Occupational Hygiene Society (EAIO) ... BOHS
British Oceanographic Data Centre [*Marine science*] (OSRA) ... BODC
British Oceanographic Data Service ... BODS
British Office for Training Exchange ... BOTEX
British Office Systems and Stationery Federation (DBA) ... BOSSF
British Office Technology Manufacturers Alliance (NITA) ... BOTMA
British Officer [*British military*] (DMA) ... BO
British Offshore Equipment Association (DS) ... BOEA
British Offshore Support Vessels Association (DS) ... BOSVA
British Oil and Cake Mills ... BOCM
British Oil and Mineral ... BOM
British Oil Burner Manufacturers' Association (BI) ... BOBMA
British Oil Equipment Credits Ltd. ... BOEC
British Oil Spill Control Association (ASF) ... BOSCA
British Olympic Association ... BOA
British Oncological Association (DBA) ... BOA
British Oncology Data Managers (DBA) ... BODMA
British Onion Growers' Association (BI) ... BOGA
British Ophthalmic Lens Manufacturers and Distributors Association (DBA) ... BOLMADA

British Ophthalmic Mass Manufacturers Association (DBA) .... BOMMA
British Optical Association .... BOA
British Optical Association (Dispenser) (DI) .... BOA(Disp)
British Optical Association, London, United Kingdom [*Library symbol Library of Congress*] (LCLS) .... UkLBOA
British Order of Ancient Free Gardeners .... BOAFG
British Organ Donor Society (PDAA) .... BODY
British Organic Farmers .... BOF
British Organisation of Non-Parents (DBA) .... BON
British Organisation of Non-Parents (DI) .... BON-P
British Orienteering Federation (DBA) .... BOF
British Origami Society .... BOS
British Ornithologists' Club .... BOC
British Ornithologists' Union .... BOU
British Orthopaedic Association .... BOA
British Orthoptic Society .... BOS
British Osborne Owners Group [*A user group*] (NITA) .... BOOG
British Osteopathic Association .... BOA
British Other Ranks .... BOR
British Overseas Aid Group (DS) .... BOAG
British Overseas Airways Corp. [*Later, British Airways*] .... BOA
British Overseas Airways Corp. [*Humorously interpreted as "Better on a Camel"*] [*Later, British Airways*] .... BOAC
British Overseas Airways Corp. [*later, British Airways*] **Digital Information Computer for Electronic Automation** .... BOADICEA
British Overseas and Commonwealth Banks Association (DBA) .... BOCBA
British Overseas Citizenship .... BOC
British Overseas Media Bureau .... BOMB
British Overseas Mining Association (BI) .... BOMA
British Overseas Trade Advisory Committee .... BOTAC
British Overseas Trade Board .... BOTB
British Overseas Trade Group for Israel (DS) .... BOTGI
British Oxygen Co. [*Later, BOC Group*] .... BOC
British Pacific [*Vancouver Stock Exchange symbol*] .... BSH
British Pacific Financial, Inc. [*Formerly, British Pacific Resources, Inc.*] [*Vancouver Stock Exchange symbol*] .... BTF
British Pacific Fleet [*Obsolete*] .... BPF
British Pacific Fleet Intelligence Liaison Officer .... BPFILO
British Pacific Fleet Liaison Officer .... BPFLO
British Paediatric Association .... BPA
British Pantomime Association .... BPA
British Paper and Board Industry Federation (DGA) .... BPBIF
British Paper and Board Industry Research Association .... BPBIRA
British Paper and Board Makers' Association (DGA) .... BPBMA
British Paper Box Federation (DGA) .... BPBF
British Paper Box Manufacturers' Federation (DGA) .... BPBMF
British Paper Machinery Makers Association (DBA) .... BPMMA
British Parachute Association .... BPA
British Paraplegic Sports Society (DBA) .... BPSS
British Parking Association .... BPA
British Pasta Products Association (DBA) .... BPPA
British Patent .... BP
British Patent (IAA) .... BRITPAT
British Patent .... BRP
British Pattern Recognition Association (ACII) .... BPRA
British Pattern Recognition Association (NITA) .... BPRA
British Payroll Managers Association (DBA) .... BPMA
British Peace Assembly .... BPA
British Pediatric Association (BARN) .... BPA
British Penny [*Derived from Latin "denarius"*] .... d
British Percheron Horse Society (BI) .... BPHS
British Pest Control Association (EAIO) .... BPCA
British Petrol ADS [*NYSE symbol*] (TTSB) .... BP
British Petroleum Co. [*NYSE symbol Toronto Stock Exchange symbol*] (SPSG) .... BP
British Petroleum Co. (IIA) .... BPT
British Petroleum Co. Ltd. [*Associated Press*] (SAG) .... BritPt
British Petroleum Exploration [*Columbia*] [*FAA designator*] (FAAC) .... BPX
British Petroleum North America .... BPNA
British Pharmaceutical Code .... BPC
British Pharmaceutical Codex [*A publication in pharmacy*] .... BPC
British Pharmaceutical Students' Association (BI) .... BPSA
British Pharmacological Society .... BPS
British Pharmacopoeia [*A publication in pharmacy*] .... BP
British Pharmacopoeia [*A publication*] (MAE) .... BPh
British Pharmacopoeia (DAVI) .... PhB
British Pharmacopoeia (Veterinary) .... BP(Vet)
British Philatelic Association Ltd. (BI) .... BPA
British Philatelic Federation (DBA) .... BPF
British Philatelic Trust (DI) .... BPT
British Phonographic Industry .... BPI
British Phosphate Commission (FEA) .... BPC
British Photobiology Society .... BPS
British Photographic Association (DBA) .... BPA
British Photographic Export Group (DBA) .... BPEG
British Photographic Importers Association (DBA) .... BPIA
British Photographic Manufacturers Association (DGA) .... BPMA
British Phycological Society .... BPS
British Physical Laboratories Ltd. (NUCP) .... BPL
British Pilots Association [*A union*] .... BPA
British Pipe Organ Society (DBA) .... BPOS
British Plain Spirits .... BPS
British Plant Growth Regulator Group (EAIO) .... BPGRG
British Plastics Federation .... BPF
British Plastics Federation .... BPF
British Plastics Windows Group [*An association*] (DBA) .... BPWG
British Ploughing Association (BI) .... BPA
British Plumbing Fittings Manufacturers Association (DBA) .... BPFMA
British Poets of the Nineteenth Century [*A publication*] .... BPN
British Polarographic Research Institute .... BPRI
British Polarological Research Society (DBA) .... BPRS
British Polio Fellowship [*British*] .... BPF
British Polled Hereford Society Ltd. (BI) .... BPHS
British Polytechnics Sports Association (DBA) .... BPSA
British Ports Association (DS) .... BPA
British Ports Federation (DBA) .... BPF
British Post Office .... BPO
British Postal Chess Federation (BI) .... BPCF
British Poster Advertising Association (DGA) .... BPAA
British Postgraduate Medical Federation .... BPMF
British Postmark Society (EA) .... BPS
British Pottery Managers Association (DBA) .... BPMA
British Poultry Breeders and Hatcheries Association (DBA) .... BPBHA
British Poultry Federation (EAIO) .... BPF
British Poultry Meat Federation (EAIO) .... BPMF
British Pound [*Monetary unit*] .... BP
British Powder Metal Federation (DBA) .... BPMF
British Power Press Manufacturers Association (MCD) .... BPPMA
British Practice in International Law [*A publication*] (DLA) .... Brit Prac Int'l L
British Precast Concrete Federation (EAIO) .... BPCF
British Precision Pilots Association (DA) .... BPPA
British Pressure Gauge Manufacturers Association (BI) .... BPGMA
British Printing & Communication Corporations [*Later, MCC*] .... BPCC
British Printing Corp. [*Later, BPCC*] .... BPC
British Printing Industries' Federation (DCTA) .... BPIF
British Printing Ink Manufacturers (DGA) .... BPIM
British Printing Ink Society (DGA) .... BPIS
British Printing Machinery Association (DGA) .... BPMA
British Printing Society (DGA) .... BPS
British Production and Inventory Control Society (DBQ) .... BPICS
British Productivity Council .... BPC
British Professional Association (DBA) .... BPA
British Promotional Merchandise Association (DBA) .... BPMA
British Property Federation (DBA) .... BPF
British Psychoanalytical Society (EAIO) .... BPS
British Psychodrama Association (DBA) .... BPA
British Psychological Society (EAIO) .... BPS
British Pteridological Society (DBA) .... BPS
British Public [*Slang*] .... BP
British Public Schools Association of New South Wales [*Australia*] .... BPSANSW
British Public Works Association (EAIO) .... BPWA
British Pump Manufacturers Association (EAIO) .... BPMA
[*The*] **British Puppet and Model Theatre Guild** .... BPMTG
British Purchasing Commission .... BPC
British Pyrotechnists' Association (BI) .... BPA
British Quality Association (DBA) .... BQA
British Quality Awards Scheme (AIE) .... BQAS
British Quality Vegetable Salad Association (DBA) .... BQVSA
British Quarter Horse Association (DBA) .... BQHA
British Rabbit Council (BI) .... BRC
British Racing and Sport Car Club .... BRSCC
British Racing Drivers Club .... BRDC
British Racing Green (ADA) .... BRG
British Racing Motors .... BRM
British Racing Tobaggan Association (BI) .... BRTA
British Racketball Association (DBA) .... BRA
British Radiation Protection Association (DBA) .... BRadPA
British Radiesthesia Association (BI) .... BRA
British Radio and Electronic Equipment Manufacturers Association (DS) .... BREEMA
British Radio and Electronic Equipment Manufacturers Association [*Formerly, British Radio Equipment Manufacturers Association*] .... BREMA
British Radio Cabinet Manufacturers' Association (IAA) .... BRCMA
British Radio Communication (IAA) .... BRC
British Radio Valve Manufacturers' Association .... BRVMA
British Radiological Protection Association (DEN) .... BRPA
British Rail Engineering .... BRE
British Rail Hovercraft (PDAA) .... BRH
British Rail Property Board .... BRPB
British Railway Industry Export Group .... BRIEX
British Railway Modellers of North America [*Canada*] .... BRMNA
British Railwaymen's Touring Club (BI) .... BRTC
British Railways .... BR
British Railways Board .... BRB
British Rainwear Manufacturers Federation (BI) .... BRMF
British Rate and Data .... BRAD
British Raw Materials Mission [*World War II*] .... BRMM
British Ready Mixed Concrete Association (BI) .... BRMCA
British Receiving Station (IAA) .... BRS
British Record Society .... BRS
British Records Association .... BRA
British Red Cross Society .... BRCS
British Refrigeration Association (DBA) .... BRA
British Regional Television Association (BI) .... BRTA
British Reinforcement Manufacturers Association (DBA) .... BRMA
British Reports, Translations, and Theses [*A publication*] .... BRTT
British Research and Development Corp. (NUCP) .... BRDC
British Research Station .... BRS
British Resin Manufacturers Association (DBA) .... BResMA
British Resorts Association .... BRA

British Retail Consortium (EAIO) ... BRC
British Retail Florist's Association (DBA) ... BRFA
British Retail Footwear Market ... BRFM
British Retinitis Pigmentosa Society ... BRPS
British Revision [*of BNA*] [*Medicine*] ... BR
British Rheumatism and Arthritis Association (BI) ... BRA
British Rigid Urethane Foam Manufacturers Association ... BRUFMA
British Rivet Export Group (BI) ... BREG
British Road Federation Ltd. (BI) ... BRF
British Road Research Laboratory ... BRRL
British Road Services ... BRS
British Road Tar Association (BI) ... BRTA
British Robot Association Ltd. ... BRA
British Robotics Systems Ltd. (NITA) ... BRSL
British Roentgen Society (MAE) ... BRS
British Roll Tuners Trade Society [*A union*] (DCTA) ... BRTTS
British Roller Canary Association (BI) ... BRCA
British Roller Canary Club (BI) ... BRCC
British Romagnola Cattle Society (DBA) ... BRCS
British Romanian Friendship Association (DBA) ... BRFA
British Routing Liaison Officer [*World War II*] ... BRLO
British Routing Office ... BRO
British Royal Marine Corps (CINC) ... BRMC
British Rubber and Resin Adhesive Manufacturers' Association (BI) ... BRRAMA
British Rubber Manufacturers' Association (EAIO) ... BRMA
British Rubber Products Research Association (MCD) ... BRPRA
British Ruling Cases [*A publication*] (DLA) ... Br Rul Cas
British Ruling Cases [*A publication*] (DLA) ... BRC
British Ruling Cases [*A publication*] (DLA) ... Brit Rul Cas
British Safety Council ... BSC
British Sailors Society (BI) ... BSS
British Salonica Force ... BSF
British Samoyed Club (BI) ... BSC
British Sanitary Fireclay Association (BI) ... BSFA
British Satellite Beam (BARN) ... BSB
British Satellite Broadcasting [*Telecommunications*] ... BSB
British Savings Bond ... BSB
British School at Rome [*Italy*] ... BSR
British School of Archaeology in Jerusalem ... BSA
British School of Archeology at Athens (BARN) ... BSAA
British School of Egyptian Archaeology ... BSEA
British School of Motoring (DI) ... BSM
British School of Osteopathy ... BSO
British School Technology (NITA) ... BST
British Schools and Universities Club of New York (EA) ... BSUCNY
British Schools and Universities Foundation (EA) ... BSUF
British Schools Exploration Society ... BSES
British Science and Technology in Education (AIE) ... BSTF
British Science Fiction Association Ltd. ... BSFA
British Scientific Instrument Research Association ... BSIRA
British Scrap Federation (DBA) ... BSF
British Seafarers' Joint Council (DS) ... BSJC
British Seafarers' Union ... BSU
British Secondary Metals Association (DBA) ... BSMA
British Security Coordination [*World War II*] ... BSC
British Security Industry Association (EAIO) ... BSIA
British Seeds Council (DBA) ... BSC
British Sewage Plant Manufacturers Association (PDAA) ... BSPMA
British Sheep Dairying Association (DBA) ... BSDA
British Shell Collectors Club ... BSCC
British Shingon Buddhist Association (EAIO) ... BSBA
British Ship Adoption Society ... BSAS
British Ship Research Association [*Research center*] (IRC) ... BSRA
British Ship Research Council ... BSRC
British Shipbreakers' Association (BI) ... BSA
British Shipbuilders ... BS
British Shipbuilding Exports (BI) ... BSE
British Shipbuilding Hydrodynamics ... BSH
British Shipbuilding Integrated Production System (PDAA) ... BRITSHIPS
British Shipbuilding Research Association ... BSRA
British Shippers Council (DS) ... BSC
British Shipping Federation (DS) ... BSF
British Shipping Laws [*A publication*] (DLA) ... Brit Ship L
British Shoe Corp. ... BSC
British Shoe Repair Council (DBA) ... BSRC
British Shooting Sports Council (DBA) ... BSSC
British Shops and Stores Association (DBA) ... BSSA
British Show Jumping Association (DI) ... BSJA
British Show Pony Society (DBA) ... BSPS
British Sign Association (DBA) ... BSA
British Sign Language (DI) ... BSL
British Silbak Premier Mines [*Vancouver Stock Exchange symbol*] ... BSK
British Size (IAA) ... BS
British Sjogren's Syndrome Association (DBA) ... BSSA
British Skate Makers' Association (BI) ... BSMA
British Ski Club for the Disabled (DBA) ... BSCD
British Ski Federation (EAIO) ... BSF
British Sky Broadcasting [*Satellite-television consortium*] (ECON) ... BSkyB
British Sky Broadcasting Ltd. [*Associated Press*] (SAG) ... BritSky
British Sky Broadcasting Ltd. [*NYSE symbol*] (SAG) ... BSY
British Sky Broadcsting Gp ADS [*NYSE symbol*] (TTSB) ... BSY
British Slag Federation [*A union*] ... BSF
British Slot Car Racing Association (DBA) ... BSCRA
British Small Animal Veterinary Association (EAIO) ... BSAVA
British Snail Farmers Association (DBA) ... BSFA
British Social Attitudes [*Survey*] ... BSA
British Social Biology Council ... BSBC
British Social Hygiene Association ... BSHA
British Socialist Party ... BSP
British Societies Institute (BI) ... BSI
British Society for Agricultural Labour Science ... BSALS
British Society for Allergy and Clinical Immunology ... BSACI
British Society for Antimicrobial Chemotherapy ... BSAC
British Society for Cell Biology ... BSCB
British Society for Clinical Cytology ... BSCC
British Society for Dental Research (DBA) ... BSDR
British Society for Dermatopathology (EAIO) ... BSD
British Society for Developmental Biology ... BSDB
British Society for Digestive Endoscopy ... BSDE
British Society for Eighteenth Century Studies ... BSECS
British Society for Electronic Music ... BSEM
British Society for Experimental and Clinical Hypnosis (DBA) ... BSECH
British Society for Haematology ... BSH
[*The*] **British Society for Immunology** ... BSI
British Society for International Bibliography [*Later, Aslib*] ... BSIB
British Society for International Health Education (AEBS) ... BSIHE
British Society for International Understanding (BI) ... BSIU
British Society for Medical and Dental Hypnosis (DBA) ... BSMDH
British Society for Music Therapy ... BSMT
British Society for Mycopathology (DBA) ... BSM
British Society for Non-Destructive Testing (MCD) ... BSNDT
British Society for Parasitology (EAIO) ... BSP
[*The*] **British Society for Phenomenology** ... BSP
British Society for Plant Growth Regulation (EAIO) ... BSPGR
British Society for Plant Pathology ... BSPP
British Society for Research in Agricultural Engineering (BI) ... BSRAE
British Society for Research on Ageing (EAIO) ... BSRA
British Society for Rheology (DBA) ... BSR
British Society for Rheumatology (EAIO) ... BSR
British Society for Social Responsibility in Science ... BSSRS
British Society for Strain Measurement ... BSSM
British Society for the History of Mathematics (DBA) ... BSHM
British Society for the History of Pharmacy ... BSHP
[*The*] **British Society for the History of Science** ... BSHS
British Society for the Philosophy of Science ... BSPS
British Society for the Study of Mental Subnormality ... BSSMS
British Society for the Study of Orthodontics (BI) ... BSSO
British Society for the Study of Prosthetic Dentistry ... BSSPD
British Society of Aesthetics ... BSA
British Society of Allergy and Environmental Medicine (DBA) ... BSAEM
British Society of Animal Production ... BSAP
British Society of Audiology ... BSA
British Society of Audiology ... BSAUD
British Society of Australian Philately ... BSAP
British Society of Cinematographers (DBA) ... BSC
British Society of Commerce (BI) ... BSC
British Society of Dentistry for the Handicapped (DBA) ... BSDH
[*The*] **British Society of Dowsers** ... BSD
British Society of Flavourists ... BSF
British Society of Gastroenterology ... BSG
British Society of Gerontology (DBA) ... BSG
British Society of Hypnotherapists ... BSH
British Society of Master Glass Painters (BI) ... BSMGP
British Society of Nutritional Medicines ... BSNM
British Society of Oral Medicine (DBA) ... BSOM
British Society of Perfumers (DBA) ... BSP
British Society of Periodontology ... BSP
British Society of Plant Breeders (DBA) ... BSPB
British Society of Poster Designers ... BPD
British Society of Psychosomatic Obstetrics and Gynecology and Andrology (DBA) ... BSPOGA
British Society of Restorative Dentistry ... BSRD
British Society of Scientific Glassblowers ... BSSG
British Society of Social and Behavioural Gerontology ... BSSBG
British Society of Soil Science ... BSSS
British Society of Sports History (DBA) ... BSSH
British Society of Stamp Journalists (BI) ... BSSJ
British Society of Surgery of the Hand (DBA) ... BSSH
British Society of Toxicological Pathologists (DBA) ... BSTP
British Society of Underwater Photographers (DBA) ... BSoUP
British Sociological Associates ... BSOCA
[*The*] **British Sociological Association** ... BSA
British Soft Drinks Association (DBA) ... BSDA
British Software Factory (NITA) ... BSF
British Soil Classification System (NUCP) ... BSCS
British Solomon Islands [*MARC country of publication code Library of Congress*] (LCCP) ... bp
British Solomon Islands ... BSI
British Solomon Islands [*MARC geographic area code Library of Congress*] (LCCP) ... pobp--
British Solomon Islands Protectorate (ADA) ... BSIP
British Soluble Coffee Manufacturers Association (DBA) ... BSCMA
British Sound Recording Association (BI) ... BSRA
British [*formerly, Birmingham*] **Sound Reproduction** [*Initialism is now name of company and brand name of its products*] ... BSR
British South Africa ... BSA
British South Africa Co. (ROG) ... BSAC
British South Africa Corps ... BSAC
British South Africa Police ... BSAP
British South American Airways Corp. ... BSAA

British South American Airways Corp. [*Later absorbed by BOAC*] ... BSAAC
British Soviet Friendship Society (BI) ... BSFS
British Space Development Co. ... BSDC
British Spas Federation (DBA) ... BSF
British Special Ship Equipment Association (PDAA) ... BSSEA
British Spectacle Frame Makers Association (DBA) ... BSFMA
British Speedway Promoters Association (BI) ... BSPA
British Speleological Association (BI) ... BSA
British Spinners and Doublers Association (PDAA) ... BSDA
British Sporting Rifle Club (PDAA) ... BSRC
British Sports and Allied Industries Federation (DBA) ... BSAIF
British Sports Association for the Disabled ... BSAD
British Spotted Pony Society (DBA) ... BSpPS
British Standard (IAA) ... BRSTD
British Standard ... BS
British Standard Beam [*Engineering*] ... BSB
British Standard Black [*Ink*] (DGA) ... BS BLK
British Standard Channel (IAA) ... BSC
British Standard Code of Practice ... BSCP
British Standard Cycle (IAA) ... BSC
British Standard Data Code (BUR) ... BSDC
British Standard Dimension ... BSD
British Standard Fine Thread ... BSF
British Standard Four-Color Blue [*Ink*] (DGA) ... BS4B
British Standard Gauge [*Telecommunications*] (TEL) ... BSG
British Standard Handful [*Slang*] (DSUE) ... BSH
British Standard Number ... BSN
British Standard Pipe Thread ... BSP
British Standard Red [*Ink*] (DGA) ... BSR
British Standard Size [*Typography*] (DGA) ... BSS
British Standard Specification ... BSS
British Standard Three-Color Blue [*Ink*] (DGA) ... BS3B
British Standard Time (NATG) ... BST
British Standard Whitworth (MCD) ... BSW
British Standard Wire Gauge ... BSWG
British Standard Yellow [*Ink*] (DGA) ... BSY
British Standards Association ... BSA
British Standards Institution (ARC) ... BSI
British Standards Institution (DAVI) ... BSID
British Standards Society (DBA) ... BSS
British Starch Industry Association (DBA) ... BSIA
British Stationery and Office Equipment Association (BI) ... BSOEA
British Stationery Council (DGA) ... BSC
British Statistics Office ... BSO
British Steel ADS [*NYSE symbol*] (TTSB) ... BST
British Steel Castings Research Association [*Later, SCRATA*] (EA) ... BSCRA
British Steel Corp. ... BSC
British Steel Export Association (BI) ... BSEA
British Steel Ltd. [*Associated Press*] (SAG) ... BritStl
British Steel Ltd. [*NYSE symbol*] (CTT) ... BST
British Stickmakers Guild (DBA) ... BSG
British Stock Car Association ... BSCA
British Stone Federation (BI) ... BSF
British Structural Bearings Manufacturers Association (DBA) ... BSBMA
British Student Tuberculosis Foundation (BI) ... BSTF
British Students Sports Federation (DBA) ... BSSF
British Studies Intelligencer (EA) ... BSI
British Sub-Aqua Club (BI) ... BSAC
British Subject without Citizenship ... BSWC
British Sugar Beet Seed Producers Association (DBA) ... BSBSPA
British Sugar Corp. ... BSC
British Sugar Machinery Manufacturers Association (PDAA) ... BSMMA
British Sulphate of Ammonia Federation Ltd. (BI) ... BSAF
British Sulphate of Copper Association (Export) Ltd. (BI) ... BSCA
British Summer Time ... BST
British Supply Board [*Ottawa*] [*World War II*] ... BSB
British Supply Council ... BSC
British Supply Mission [*World War II*] ... BSM
British Supply Office ... BSO
British Surface Treatment Suppliers Association (DBA) ... BSTSA
British Surfing Association ... BSA
British Surgical Export Group (DBA) ... BSEG
British Surgical Support Suppliers Association (BI) ... BSSSA
British Surgical Trades Association (BI) ... BSTA
British Suzuki Institute (EAIO) ... BSI
British Tabulating Machinery Co. ... BTMC
British Tactical Air Force ... BTAF
British Tanning Extract Manufacturers' Association (BI) ... BTEMA
British Tarantula Society (DBA) ... BTS
British Tarpaviors Federation Ltd. (BI) ... BTF
British Tattoo Artists Federation (DBA) ... BTAF
British Tea Table Co. (ROG) ... BTT
British Technical Council [*of the Motor and Petroleum Industries*] ... BTC
British Technical Council of Motor and Petroleum Industries ... BTCMPI
British Technology Group [*Research center*] ... BTG
British Technology Index (AIE) ... BTI
British Telecom [*or Telecommunications*] [*Common carrier*] ... BT
British Telecom Action for Disabled Customers (NITA) ... BTADC
British Telecom Business Systems (NITA) ... BTBS
British Telecom Enterprises (NITA) ... BTE
British Telecom Enterprises' Value Added Systems and Services (NITA) ... BTE/Vass
British Telecom International (NITA) ... BTI
British Telecom Lempel Ziv (CDE) ... BTLZ
British Telecom Mobile Communications ... BTMC
British Telecom Phonecards [*Prepaid cards for use in noncoin pay telephones*] ... BTP
British Telecom Research Laboratories ... BTRL
British Telecom Unions Committee ... BTUC
British Telecommn ADR [*NYSE symbol*] (TTSB) ... BTY
British Telecommunications Ltd. [*Associated Press*] (SAG) ... BritTel
British Telecommunications Ltd. [*NYSE symbol Toronto Stock Exchange symbol*] (SPSG) ... BTY
British Telecommunications Systems Ltd. (TEL) ... BTS
British Temperance Society (BI) ... BTS
British Tenpin Bowling Association, Ltd. ... BTBA
British Tensional Strapping Association (PDAA) ... BTSA
British term for sonar (DOMA) ... ASDIC
British Tertiary Volcanic Province [*Geology*] ... BTVP
British Textile Confederation (DCTA) ... BTC
British Textile Employers' Association (EAIO) ... BTEA
British Textile Machinery Association (DS) ... BTMA
British Textile Technology Group (ECON) ... BTTG
British Theatre Association [*Defunct*] ... BTA
British Theatre Institute (EA) ... BTI
British Theatre Museum (BI) ... BTM
British Thermal Unit ... BTHU
British Thermal Unit ... BTU
British Thermal Units per Hour (MCD) ... BTU/h
British Thermal Units per Hour (DNAB) ... BTU/HR
British Thomson-Houston Co. ... BTH
British Thoracic and Tuberculosis Association ... BTTA
[*The*] **British Thoracic Society** ... BTS
British Throwsters Association (DBA) ... BTA
British Timber Merchants Association (DBA) ... BTMA
British Time (IAA) ... BRT
British Tin Box Manufacturers Federation (PDAA) ... BTBMF
British Tinnitus Association ... BTA
British Tire & Rubber Co. ... BTR
British Tissues, Ltd. ... BT
British Tobacco Industry ... BTI
British Touch for Health Association ... BTFHA
British Tourist Authority (EA) ... BTA
British Towing Tank Panel (MCD) ... BTTP
British Toxicology Society (DBA) ... BTS
British Toy and Hobby Association (EAIO) ... BTHA
British Toymakers' Guild (BI) ... BTG
British Tractor Pullers Association (DBA) ... BTPA
British Trade and Investment Office (EA) ... BTIO
British Trade Development Office [*Later, BTIO*] (EA) ... BTDO
British Trade Journal [*A publication*] (ROG) ... BTJ
British Trade Mission ... BTM
British Trades Union Congress [*TUC*] ... BKT
British Trampoline Federation (DBA) ... BTF
British Trans-Atlantic Air Mail Service (IAA) ... BRAMS
British Trans-Atlantic Air Mail Service ... BTAMS
British Transplantation Society ... BTS
British Transport Advertising ... BTA
British Transport Commission ... BTC
British Transport Commission Police ... BTCP
British Transport Docks Board ... BTDB
British Transport Hotels [*Commercial firm*] ... BTH
British Transport Officers Guild (DBA) ... BTOG
British Transport Staff College (BI) ... BTSC
British Travel and Holidays Association [*Later, British Travel Association*] ... BTHA
British Travel Association (BI) ... BTA
British Travel Survey (ECON) ... BTS
British Trawler Federation ... BTF
British Trawler Officers Federation [*A union*] ... BTOF
British Treaty Series [*A publication*] (DLA) ... Brit TS
British Trials and Rally Drivers Association ... BTRDA
British Triathlon Association (DBA) ... BTA
British Trolleybus Society (DCTA) ... BTS
British Troops, Austria [*World War II*] ... BTA
British Troops in Egypt [*World War II*] ... BTE
British Troops in Germany (DMA) ... BTG
British Troops in Iraq (DMA) ... BTI
British Troops in North Africa [*World War II*] ... BTNA
British Trout Association (DBA) ... BTA
British Truck Racing Association (DBA) ... BTRA
British Trust for Conservation Volunteers ... BTCV
British Trust for Ornithology ... BTO
British Tugowners Association (BI) ... BTA
British Turf Irrigation Association (DBA) ... BTIA
British Turkey Federation Ltd. (BI) ... BTF
British Turned-Parts Manufacturers Association (DBA) ... BTMA
British Tutorial Institute ... BTI
British Twinning and Bilingual Association (BI) ... BTBA
British Typewriter Manufacturers Association (PDAA) ... BTMA
British UFO Research Association (EAIO) ... BUFORA
British Ultimate Federation (DBA) ... BUF
British Underground Nuclear Test (MCD) ... BUNT
British Unemployment Resource Network (PDAA) ... BURN
British Unidentified Flying Objects Research Association ... BUFORA
British Union Catalogue of Periodicals [*A publication*] ... BUCOP
British Union for the Abolition of Vivisection ... BUAV
British Union of Fascists ... BUF
British United Airways ... BUA
British United Island Airways ... BUIA

British United Press ... BUP
British United Provident Association (DCTA) ... BUPA
British United Shoe Machinery [*Commercial firm*] ... BUSM
British United Traction Co. ... BUT
British Universities Accommodation Consortium ... BUAC
British Universities Association of Slavists ... BUAS
British Universities Film and Video Council [*Information service or system*] (IID) ... BUFVC
British Universities Industrial Relations Association ... BUIRA
British Universities North America Club (EA) ... BUNAC
British Universities Society of Arts ... BUSA
British Universities Sports Federation ... BUSF
British Universities Transatlantic Exchange Committee (AIE) ... BUTEC
British Urban and Regional Information System Association ... BURISA
British Urban Development ... BUD
British Urban Development Services Unit [*Department of Environment*] (DI) ... BUDSU
British Urethane Foam Contractors Association (DBA) ... BUFCA
British Vacuum Council (DBA) ... BVC
British Valve and Actuators Manufacturers Association (DBA) ... BVAMA
British Valve Manufacturers Association (PDAA) ... BVMA
British Vehicle Rental and Leasing Association (DBA) ... BVRLA
British Venture Capital Association (DBA) ... BVCA
British Veterinary Association ... BVA
British Veterinary Code ... BVC
British Veterinary Codex [*A publication*] ... BVetC
British Veterinary Hospitals Association (DBA) ... BVHA
British Veterinary Nursing Association (DBA) ... BVNA
British Veterinary Radiology Association (DBA) ... BVRA
British Veterinary Zoological Society (DBA) ... BVZS
British Vexillological Society ... BVS
British Videogram Association ... BVA
British Videogram Association (NITA) ... BVGA
British Vigilance Association (BI) ... BVA
British Virgin Island [*IYRU nationality code*] (IYR) ... KV
British Virgin Islands ... BVI
British Virgin Islands [*ANSI two-letter standard code*] (CNC) ... VG
British Virgin Islands [*ANSI three-letter standard code*] (CNC) ... VGB
British Virgin Islands Hotel and Commerce Association (EAIO) ... BVIHCA
British Visitor's Passport ... BVP
British Volunteer Programme ... BVP
British Volunteers, Latin America [*British military*] (DMA) ... BVLA
British War Cabinet ... BWC
British War Medal ... BWM
British War Relief Society [*in US*] ... BWRS
British War Supplies Committee [*Combined Production and Resources Board*] [*World War II*] ... BWSC
British War Veterans of America (EA) ... BWVA
British Warm Air Hand Drier Association (DBA) ... BWAHDA
British Warm-Blood Society (DBA) ... BWBS
British Waste Paper Association (PDAA) ... BWPA
British Waste Paper Utilisation Council (BI) ... BWPUC
British Watch and Clockmakers Guild (DBA) ... BWCMG
British Water and Effluent Treatment Plant Association (PDAA) ... BWETPA
British Water Colour Society (BI) ... BWS
British Water Industries Group (DBA) ... BWIG
British Water International ... BWI
British Water Ski Federation ... BWSF
British Waterfowl Association (BI) ... BWA
British Waterways [*State-owned company*] ... BW
British Waterways Board ... BWB
British Waterworks Association ... BWA
British Weed Control Council (BI) ... BWCC
British Welded Steel Tube Manufacturers Association (PDAA) ... BWSTMA
British Welding Research Association [*Later, WI*] (MCD) ... BWRA
British West Africa ... BWA
British West Indian Airways Ltd. [*ICAO designator*] (OAG) ... BW
British West Indian Airways Ltd. ... BWIA
British West Indies [*Later, WI*] ... BWI
British Wheat Starch Association (DBA) ... BWSA
British Wheel of Yoga [*An association*] (DBA) ... BWOY
British White Cattle Society of Australia ... BWCSA
British Whiting Federation (BI) ... BWF
British Wholesale Traders Association (DBA) ... BWTA
British Wildlife Appeal (EAIO) ... BWA
British Wind Energy Association (IRUK) ... BWEA
British Winter Time (IAA) ... BWT
British Wire Netting Manufacturers Association (DBA) ... BWNMA
British Wire Rod Rollers' Association (BI) ... BWRRA
British Wireless Marine Service (DEN) ... BWMS
British Withdrawal from Northern Ireland Campaign ... BWNIC
British Women Pilots Association (PDAA) ... BWPA
British Women's Temperance Association (BI) ... BWTA
British Wood Chipboard Manufacturers Association (PDAA) ... BWCMA
British Wood Preserving Association ... BWPA
British Wood Pulp Association (DBA) ... BWPA
British Wood Turners' Association ... BWTA
British Woodwork Manufacturers' Association (BI) ... BWMA
British Woodworking Federation (DBA) ... BWF
British Wool Federation ... BWF
British Wool Marketing Board ... BWMB
British Working Men's Club ... BWMC
British Workmen's Institute (BI) ... BWI
British World Airlines Ltd. [*FAA designator*] (FAAC) ... BWL
British Woven Wire Export Association (DBA) ... BWWEA
British Yard Motor Minesweepers ... BYMS
British Young Naturalists Association (BI) ... BYNA
British Youth Council (EAIO) ... BYC
British Yugoslav Society (DBA) ... BYS
British Zeolite Association ... BZA
British Zone Petroleum Coordinating Authority [*Post-World War II, Germany*] ... BZPCA
British-American Arts Association (EA) ... BAAA
British-American Business Association (EAIO) ... BABA
British-American Chamber of Commerce (EA) ... BACC
British-American Collectors' Club (EA) ... BACC
British-American Coordinating Committee [*Turkey*] ... BACC
British-American Light Opera Exchange ... BALOE
British-American Rhykenological Society [*Defunct*] (EA) ... B-ARS
British-American Scientific International Commercial English ... BASIC (English)
British-American Tobacco Co. ... BAT
British-American Tobacco Co. ... BATC
British-American Wrestling Association (DI) ... BAWA
British-Australian Heritage Society ... BAHS
British-Australian Studies Association ... BASA
British-Australian-New Zealand Antarctic Research Expedition [*1929-31*] ... BANZARE
British-Canadian Holstein-Friesian Association (BI) ... BCHFA
British-Central-European Chamber of Commerce (DAS) ... BCECC
British-Israel Chamber of Commerce (DBA) ... B-ICC
British-Israel World Federation ... BI
British-Israel World Federation ... BIWF
British-Kurdish Friendship Society ... BKFS
British-North American Committee (EA) ... BNAC
British-Romanian Association (EAIO) ... ACARDA
British-Soviet Chamber of Commerce (DS) ... BSCC
British-United States Agreement [*Signed May 17, 1943; formalized cooperation between the communications intelligence agencies of Great Britain and the United States*] ... BRUSA
British-United States Amateur Rocket Bureau ... BUSARB
British-United States Convoy Instructions ... BUSCI
British-United States Routing Agreement [*Shipping*] ... BUSRA
Briton ... Brit
Brits [*South Africa*] [*ICAO location identifier*] (ICLI) ... FABS
Britt Airways [*ICAO designator*] (AD) ... RU
Britt Airways, Inc. [*ICAO designator*] (FAAC) ... BTA
Britt Area Community Library, Britt, Ontario [*Library symbol National Library of Canada*] (NLC) ... OBRIT
Britt News-Tribune, Britt, IA [*Library symbol Library of Congress*] (LCLS) ... IaBriNT
Brittany Air International [*Airline*] [*France*] ... BRITAIR
Brittany Air International [*ICAO designator*] (AD) ... DB
Brittany Base Section [*World War II*] ... BBS
Brittany Oceanological Center ... BOC
Brittany Revolutionary Front [*France*] ... FLB
Britten Norman (Bembridge) Ltd. [*British ICAO aircraft manufacturer identifier*] (ICAO) ... BN
Brittle (ABBR) ... BRTL
Brittle Bone Society [*British*] ... BBS
Brittle Materials Design (MCD) ... BMD
Brittle Matrix Composite [*Materials science*] ... BMC
Britton & Koontz Capital Corp. [*NASDAQ symbol*] (SAG) ... BKBK
Britton & Koontz Capital Corp. [*Associated Press*] (SAG) ... Brt&Ktz
Britton, SD [*Location identifier FAA*] (FAAL) ... BTN
Britton's Ancient Pleas of the Crown [*A publication*] (DLA) ... Brit
Britton's Ancient Pleas of the Crown [*A publication*] (DLA) ... Britt
Brive/La Roche [*France ICAO location identifier*] (ICLI) ... LFBV
Brive-La-Gaillarde [*France*] [*Airport symbol*] (OAG) ... BVE
Brixton College [*London, England*] ... BC
Brize Norton [*British ICAO location identifier*] (ICLI) ... EGVN
Brize Norton, FTU [*British*] [*FAA designator*] (FAAC) ... BZN
Brno [*Former Czechoslovakia*] [*Airport symbol*] (OAG) ... BRQ
Brno-Enfield [*Machine gun*] ... BREN
BRO Resources Ltd. [*Vancouver Stock Exchange symbol*] ... BRO
Broach (MSA) ... BRCH
Broach (KSC) ... BRO
Broach Adapter ... BHAD
Broach Fixture ... BHFX
Broach Fixture (MCD) ... BRF
Broad [*Also, BR*] [*Spectral*] ... B
Broad (ADA) ... BD
Broad [*Also, B*] [*Spectral*] ... BR
Broad Absorption Line [*Quasar*] [*Astrophysics*] ... BAL
Broad Agency Announcement [*National automotive center*] (RDA) ... BAA
Broad Anatomy Marine [*See also HAM*] [*Slang term for female marines*] [*Bowdlerized version*] ... BAM
Broad Area Announcement ... BAA
Broad Audit Guidelines ... BAG
Broad Band Noise (DMAA) ... BBN
Broad Bean Mottle Virus [*Plant pathology*] ... BBMV
Broad Bean Necrosis Virus [*Plant pathology*] ... BBNV
Broad Bean Stain Virus [*Plant pathology*] ... BBSV
Broad Bean True Mosaic Virus [*Plant pathology*] ... BBTMV
Broad Bean Wilt Virus [*Plant pathology*] ... BBWV
Broad Economic Category ... BEC
Broad Emission Line [*Spectra*] ... BEL
Broad Field of View (MCD) ... BFOV
Broad Folio [*Typography*] (DGA) ... BRD FO
Broad Gage (IAA) ... BG
Broad Host Range [*Biochemistry*] ... BHR
Broad Measure (ADA) ... BM

Broad National Bancorp [*NASDAQ symbol*] (NQ) ... BNBC
Broad National Bancorp [*Associated Press*] (SAG) ... BroadN
Broad Natl Bancorp [*NASDAQ symbol*] (TTSB) ... BNBC
Broad Ocean Area ... BOA
Broad Ocean Area - Missile Impact Locating System [*Navy*] (NG) ... BOA-MILS
Broad Ocean Deployment ... BOD
Broad Ocean Development (MCD) ... BOD
Broad Ocean Scoring System [*Missiles*] ... BOSS
Broad Pass [*Alaska*] [*Seismograph station code, US Geological Survey Closed*] (SEIS) ... BDP
Broad Street Pneumonia [*Center for Disease Control*] ... BSP
Broad System of Ordering (MCD) ... BSO
Broadax Systems, Inc. (PCM) ... BSI
Broadband [*Communications channel description*] (IEEE) ... BB
Broadband Acoustic Array Section ... BAAS
Broadband Active Analyzer ... BAA
Broadband Analysis SONAR Surveillance (MCD) ... BASS
Broadband Antenna ... BBA
Broadband Antenna Kit ... BAK
Broadband Code Division Multiple Access [*Telecommunications*] (ACRL) ... B-CDMA
Broadband Communication Network (BUR) ... BCN
Broadband Conducted (IEEE) ... BBC
Broadband Connectionless Bearer Service [*Telecommunications*] (ACRL) ... BCLB
Broadband Connection-Oriented Bearer Service [*Telecommunications*] (ACRL) ... BCOB
Broadband Distributive Services [*Telecommunications*] ... BD
Broadband Exchange [*Western Union communication system*] ... BEX
Broadband Frequency ... BF
Broadband Integrated Glass Fibre Optical Network [*Project*] [*Federal Republic of Germany*] (NITA) ... BIGFON
Broadband Integrated Services Digital Network [*Telecommunications*] ... BISDN
Broadband Integrated Services Digital Network (ACRL) ... B-ISDN
Broadband Interface Controller [*Motorola, Inc.*] ... BIC
Broadband Interneuron [*Neuroanatomy*] ... BBI
Broadband ISDN [*Integrated Services Digital Network*] **User Part** [*Telecommunications*] (ACRL) ... B-ISUP
Broadband Isotropic Real-Time Electric Field Sensor (MCD) ... BIRES
Broadband Klystron Amplifier ... BKA
Broadband Latching Circulator ... BLC
Broadband Latching Switch ... BLS
Broadband Local Exchange [*Telecommunications*] (ACRL) ... B-LE
Broadband Microwave Power Amplifier ... BMPA
Broadband Network Operating System ... BNOS
Broadband Network Service [*Telecommunications*] (ACRL) ... BNS
Broadband Network Termination [*Telecommunications*] ... BNT
Broadband Packet Exchange [*Telecommunications*] (ACRL) ... BPX
Broadband Radiated (IEEE) ... BBR
Broadband Rectangular-to-Circular Transition [*Telecommunications*] (IAA) ... BRCT
Broadband Remote Line Unit [*Telecommunications*] (ACRL) ... BRLU
Broadband Remote Oculometer (KSC) ... BRO
Broadband Service Expert Group ... BSEG
Broadband Service Integration Multiplexer [*Telecommunications*] ... BSIM
Broadband Solid-State Preamplifier ... BSSP
Broadband Subsystem ... BRD
Broadband Switching Element [*Telecommunications*] ... BSE
Broadband Switching Network [*Telecommunications*] ... BSN
Broadband Switching System [*Telecommunications*] (ACRL) ... BSS
Broadband Switching Unit [*Telecommunications*] ... BSU
BroadBand Technologies [*NASDAQ symbol*] (TTSB) ... BBTK
BroadBand Technologies, Inc. [*NASDAQ symbol*] (SAG) ... BBTK
BroadBand Technologies, Inc. [*Associated Press*] (SAG) ... BrdbdTc
Broadband Terminal Adapter [*Telecommunications*] (ACRL) ... B-TA
Broadband Terminal Equipment [*Telecommunications*] (ACRL) ... B-TE
Broadband Trunk Module [*Telecommunications*] ... BTM
Broadband Unbalanced Transformer [*Telecommunications*] (OA) ... BUT
Broadband Waveguide Circulator ... BBWC
Broadband Waveguide Circulator ... BWC
Broadband X-Band Klystron ... BXK
Broadband X-Ray Telescope ... BBXRT
Broad-Based Consumption Tax (ADA) ... BBCT
Broad-Based Enhanced Savings Tax ... BEST
Broadbed and Furrow System (GNE) ... BBF
Broadcast [*FCC*] (NTCM) ... B
Broadcast (NATG) ... B/C
Broadcast (IDOE) ... BC
Broadcast ... bcst
Broadcast [*Information transmission*] (AFM) ... BCST
Broadcast ... BRDCST
Broadcast ... BRDSCT
Broadcast (MUGU) ... BRST
Broadcast Advertisers Reports [*Information service or system Defunct*] ... BAR
Broadcast Advertising Producers Society of America (NTCM) ... BAPSA
Broadcast Amplifier (IAA) ... BCAMPL
Broadcast and Television Receivers (MCD) ... BTR
Broadcast Band ... BCB
Broadcast Bureau [*of FCC*] ... BB
Broadcast Bureau of Measurement [*FCC*] (NTCM) ... BBM
Broadcast Cable Financial Management Association (EA) ... BCFMA
Broadcast Capital Fund, Inc. (NTCM) ... BROADCAP
Broadcast Communications System ... BCS
Broadcast Control ... BC
Broadcast Control Authority (NVT) ... BCA
Broadcast Control Center ... BCC
Broadcast Credit Association (EA) ... BCA
Broadcast Designers Association (EA) ... BDA
Broadcast Education Association (EA) ... BEA
Broadcast Educators Association of Canada (AC) ... BEAC
Broadcast Electronic Video Recording (IAA) ... BEVR
Broadcast Engineering Officer (ADA) ... BEO
Broadcast Exchange (IAA) ... BEX
Broadcast, Execute This Command [*Telecommunications*] [*Electronics*] (ECII) ... BETC
Broadcast Executives Society (AC) ... BES
Broadcast Fighter Control [*Military*] ... BROFICON
Broadcast Financial Management Association [*Later, BCFMA*] (EA) ... BFM
Broadcast Industry Automation System [*Data Communications Corp.*] [*Information service or system*] (IID) ... BIAS
Broadcast Information Bureau, Inc. ... BIB
Broadcast Institute of North America (NTCM) ... BINA
Broadcast Intercept (MCD) ... BI
Broadcast Interference [*Telecommunications*] ... BCI
Broadcast Keying Station (NVT) ... BKS
Broadcast Listener [*Amateur radio*] ... BCL
Broadcast Listening (IDOE) ... BCL
Broadcast Measurement Bureau (NTCM) ... BMB
Broadcast Music, Inc. (EA) ... BMI
Broadcast Net (NATG) ... BRN
Broadcast News Ltd. (NTCM) ... BNL
Broadcast News Service (NTCM) ... BNS
Broadcast Officer ... BOR
Broadcast Operator's Certificate of Proficiency ... BOCP
Broadcast Pioneers (EA) ... BP
Broadcast Pioneers Educational Fund, Inc. (NTCM) ... BPEF
Broadcast Pioneer's Library (NTCM) ... BPL
Broadcast Production Officer ... BPO
Broadcast Promotion and Marketing Executives (EA) ... BPME
Broadcast Radio Emergency Communication [*Air Force*] ... BRECOM
Broadcast Rating Council [*Later, EMRC*] ... BRC
Broadcast Requested (FAAC) ... BCREQ
Broadcast Satellite [*Japan*] ... BS
Broadcast Satellite International, Inc. [*Dallas, TX*] [*Telecommunications service*] (TSSD) ... BSI
Broadcast Satellite Service ... BSS
Broadcast Services for Windows (PCM) ... BSW
Broadcast Specialist Course [*Department of Defense Information School*] (DNAB) ... BSC
Broadcast Station (FAAC) ... BCSTN
Broadcast Television Systems Committee Recommendation [*FCC*] (NTCM) ... BTSC
Broadcast to Allied Merchant Ships ... BAMS
Broadcast Transmission Systems (MCD) ... BTS
Broadcast Unknown Server [*Telecommunications*] (ACRL) ... BUS
Broadcaster ... BCSTR
Broadcaster ... BRDCSTR
Broadcasters Audience Research Board [*British Information service or system*] ... BARB
Broadcasters Database [*Houston, TX*] [*Information service or system*] (IID) ... BDB
Broadcaster's Foundation, Inc. (NTCM) ... BFI
Broadcasters Nonprofit Satellite Service [*Ford Foundation*] ... BNS
Broadcasters' Promotion Association [*Later, BPME*] (EA) ... BPA
Broadcasting ... B
Broadcasting (MCD) ... BC
Broadcasting ... BCSTG
Broadcasting ... BRDSCTG
Broadcasting Amplitude Modulation ... BAM
Broadcasting and Entertainment Trades Alliance [*A union*] [*British*] (EAIO) ... BETA
Broadcasting and Film Commission [*Later, CC*] (EA) ... BFC
Broadcasting and Film Commission/National Council of the Churches of Christ in the USA (NTCM) ... BFC/NCC
Broadcasting Co. of America (NTCM) ... BCA
Broadcasting Complaints Commission [*British*] ... BCC
Broadcasting Corp. of China ... BCC
Broadcasting Corp. of New Zealand ... BCNZ
Broadcasting Corp. of the Bahamas ... BCB
Broadcasting Council [*Australia*] ... BC
Broadcasting Entertainment Cinematograph and Theatre Union [*British*] (EAIO) ... BECTU
Broadcasting for International Understanding (AC) ... BIU
Broadcasting Foundation of America [*Defunct*] (EA) ... BFA
Broadcasting in Australia [*A publication*] ... BIA
Broadcasting Maintenance District ... BMD
Broadcasting Operations Recording and Information System ... BORIS
Broadcasting Organizations of Non-Aligned Countries [*Belgrade, Yugoslavia*] (EAIO) ... BONC
Broadcasting Program [*Association of Independent Colleges and Schools specialization code*] ... BC
Broadcasting Reports [*Australia A publication*] ... BR
Broadcasting Satellite Experimental [*Japan*] (MCD) ... BSE
Broadcasting Squadron [*Air Force*] ... BRS
Broadcasting Station [*ITU designation*] (CET) ... BC
Broadcasting Station ... BS
Broadcasting Station, Television [*ITU designation*] ... BT
Broadcasting Support Services (AIE) ... BSS
Broadcast-Television Recording Engineers [*An association*] (NTCM) ... BTRE
Broadened Opportunities for Officer Selection and Training [*Navy*] (NVT) ... BOOST
Broader Term [*Cross-reference*] [*Indexing*] ... BT

Broad-Flanged Beam ... BFB
Broadland Noise Generator ... BNG
Broadlaw [*Scotland*] [*Seismograph station code, US Geological Survey*] (SEIS) ... EBL
Broad-Line Radio Galaxy [*Astrophysics*] ... BLRG
Broad-Line Region [*Spectra*] ... BLR
Broadside [*Paper*] (DGA) ... BS
Broadus, MT [*Location identifier FAA*] (FAAL) ... BDX
Broadus Public Library, Broadus, MT [*Library symbol*] [*Library of Congress*] (LCLS) ... MtBr
Broadview Public Library, Broadview, IL [*Library symbol Library of Congress*] (LCLS) ... IBrov
Broadview, SK [*ICAO location identifier*] (ICLI) ... CYDR
BroadVision, Inc. [*Associated Press*] (SAG) ... BroadVis
BroadVision, Inc. [*NASDAQ symbol*] (SAG) ... BVSN
Broadway [*A street name*] ... BDWY
Broadway [*A street name*] [*British*] ... BDY
Broadway ... BRDWY
Broadway [*A street name*] ... B'WAY
Broadway & Seymour [*NASDAQ symbol*] (SAG) ... BSIS
Broadway & Seymour, Inc. [*Associated Press*] (SAG) ... BdwySey
Broadway & Seymour Inc. [*NASDAQ symbol*] (TTSB) ... BSIS
Broadway Beverages [*Vancouver Stock Exchange symbol*] ... BEV
[*The*] **Broadway Book of English Verse** [*A publication*] ... BrBEV
Broadway Elementary School, Grand Junction, CO [*Library symbol*] [*Library of Congress*] (LCLS) ... CoBjBrE
Broadway Elementary School, Grand Junction, CO [*Library symbol Library of Congress*] (LCLS) ... CoGjBrE
Broadway Financial [*NASDAQ symbol*] (TTSB) ... BYFC
Broadway Financial Corp. [*Associated Press*] (SAG) ... BrdwyF
Broadway Financial Corp. [*NASDAQ symbol*] (SAG) ... BYFC
Broadway Stores [*Associated Press*] (SAG) ... Bdway
Broadway Stores [*Formerly, Carter Hawley, Hale*] [*NYSE symbol*] (SAG) ... BWY
Broadway Stores Wrrt [*NYSE symbol*] (TTSB) ... BWY.WS
Broadway, VA [*FM radio station call letters*] ... WLTK
Broadway-Timberville, VA [*AM radio station call letters*] ... WBTX
Broadwoodwidger [*England*] ... BROADWOODW
Brobeck, Phleger, and Harrison, San Francisco, CA [*Library symbol Library of Congress*] (LCLS) ... CSfBPH
Brobeck, Phleger & Harrison, San Francisco, CA [*Library symbol*] [*Library of Congress*] (LCLS) ... CSfBPH
Broca Index [*Medicine*] ... BI
Brocade (VRA) ... brcd
Brocades-Stheeman [*Netherlands*] [*Research code symbol*] ... BS
Broccoli Necrotic Yellows Virus [*Plant pathology*] ... BNYV
Brochet, MB [*ICAO location identifier*] (ICLI) ... CYBT
Brock Air Services Ltd. [*Canada ICAO designator*] (FAAC) ... BRD
Brock Control Systems, Inc. [*NASDAQ symbol*] (SAG) ... BROC
Brock Control Systems, Inc. [*Associated Press*] (SAG) ... BrockCS
Brock Exploration Corp. [*AMEX symbol*] (SPSG) ... BKE
Brock Exploration Corp. [*Associated Press*] (SAG) ... BrockCp
Brock Intl Inc. [*NASDAQ symbol*] (TTSB) ... BROC
Brock Township Public Library, Beaverton Branch, Beaverton, ON, Canada [*Library symbol*] [*Library of Congress*] (LCLS) ... CaOBEAB
Brock Township Public Library, Cannington Branch, Cannington, ON, Canada [*Library symbol*] [*Library of Congress*] (LCLS) ... CaOCAB
Brock Township Public Library, Sunderland, ON, Canada [*Library symbol Library of Congress*] (LCLS) ... CaOSunB
Brock Township Public Library, Sunderland, Ontario [*Library symbol National Library of Canada*] (NLC) ... OSUNB
Brock University, Department of Geography, Saint Catharines, ON, Canada [*Library symbol Library of Congress*] (LCLS) ... CaOStCBG
Brock University Library [*UTLAS symbol*] ... BCK
Brock University, Saint Catharines, ON, Canada [*Library symbol Library of Congress*] (LCLS) ... CaOStCB
Brock University, St. Catharines, Ontario [*Library symbol National Library of Canada*] (NLC) ... OSTCB
Brockenbrough and Holmes. Virginia Cases [*A publication*] (DLA) ... Brock & H
Brockenbrough and Holmes. Virginia Cases [*A publication*] (DLA) ... Brock & Ho
Brockenbrough and Holmes. Virginia Cases [*A publication*] (DLA) ... Brock & Hol
Brockenbrough and Holmes. Virginia Cases [*A publication*] (DLA) ... Brock & Hol Cas
Brockenbrough. Virginia Cases [*A publication*] (DLA) ... Brock Cas
Brockenbrough's Marshall's Decisions, United States Circuit Court [*A publication*] (DLA) ... Brock
Brockenbrough's Marshall's Decisions, United States Circuit Court [*A publication*] (DLA) ... Brock CC
Brockenbrough's Marshall's Decisions, United States Circuit Court [*A publication*] (DLA) ... Brock Marsh
Brocket Public Library, Alberta [*Library symbol National Library of Canada*] (NLC) ... ABRO
Brocklebank & Well Lines [*Steamship*] (MHDB) ... B & W
Brockport High School Library, Brockport, NY [*OCLC symbol*] (OCLC) ... RVT
Brockport, NY [*AM radio station call letters*] ... WASB
Brockport, NY [*FM radio station call letters*] ... WASB-FM
Brockport, NY [*FM radio station call letters*] ... WBSU
Brockton, MA [*AM radio station call letters*] ... WBET
Brockton, MA [*FM radio station call letters*] ... WCAV
Brockton, MA [*AM radio station call letters*] ... WMSX
Brockton Public Library, Brockton, MA [*Library symbol Library of Congress*] (LCLS) ... MBrock
Brockville [*Canada*] [*Airport symbol*] (OAG) ... XBR
Brockville, ON [*AM radio station call letters*] ... CFJR
Brockville, ON [*FM radio station call letters*] ... CHXL
Brockville Psychiatric Hospital, Library Resources and Informtion Centre, Brockville, ON, Canada [*Library symbol*] [*Library of Congress*] (LCLS) ... CaOBRPH
Brockville Public Library, Brockville, ON, Canada [*Library symbol Library of Congress*] (LCLS) ... CaOB
Brockville Public Library, Ontario [*Library symbol National Library of Canada*] (NLC) ... OB
Brockway, PA [*AM radio station call letters*] ... WVCQ
Brockway Standard Holdings, Inc. [*Associated Press*] (SAG) ... BrckwSt
Brockway Standard Holdings, Inc. [*NASDAQ symbol*] (SAG) ... BWAY
Brodart Co. [*ACCORD*] [*UTLAS symbol*] ... BRD
Broderbund Software [*NASDAQ symbol*] (TTSB) ... BROD
Broderbund Software, Inc. [*NASDAQ symbol*] (SPSG) ... BROD
Broderbund Software, Inc. [*Associated Press*] (SAG) ... BrodSft
Broderick and Freemantle's Ecclesiastical Cases [*1840-64*] [*A publication*] (DLA) ... Br & F Ecc
Broderick and Freemantle's Ecclesiastical Cases [*1840-64*] [*A publication*] (DLA) ... Br & Fr
Broderick and Freemantle's Ecclesiastical Cases [*1840-64*] [*A publication*] (DLA) ... Bro & F
Broderick and Freemantle's Ecclesiastical Cases [*1840-64*] [*A publication*] (DLA) ... Bro & Fr
Broderick and Freemantle's Ecclesiastical Cases [*1840-64*] [*A publication*] (DLA) ... Brod
Broderick and Freemantle's Ecclesiastical Cases [*1840-64*] [*A publication*] (DLA) ... Brod & F
Broderick and Freemantle's Ecclesiastical Cases [*1840-64*] [*A publication*] (DLA) ... Brod & F Ecc Cas
Broderick and Freemantle's Ecclesiastical Cases [*1840-64*] [*A publication*] (DLA) ... Brod & Fr
Broderick and Freemantle's Ecclesiastical Cases [*1840-64*] [*A publication*] (DLA) ... Brod & Fr Ecc Cas
Broderick and Freemantle's Ecclesiastical Cases [*1840-64*] [*A publication*] (DLA) ... Brod & Frem
Broderick and Freemantle's English Ecclesiastical Reports [*1840-64*] [*A publication*] (DLA) ... B & F
Broderip and Bingham's English Common Pleas Reports [*A publication*] (DLA) ... B & B
Broderip and Bingham's English Common Pleas Reports [*A publication*] (DLA) ... Br & B
Broderip and Bingham's English Common Pleas Reports [*A publication*] (DLA) ... Brod & B
Broderip and Bingham's English Common Pleas Reports [*129 English Reprint*] [*A publication*] (DLA) ... Brod & Bing
Brodhead Memorial Public Library, Brodhead, WI [*Library symbol Library of Congress*] (LCLS) ... WBro
Brodie Resource Library, Thunder Bay, ON, Canada [*Library symbol Library of Congress*] (LCLS) ... CaOTBBR
Brodie Resource Library, Thunder Bay, Ontario [*Library symbol National Library of Canada*] (NLC) ... OTBBR
Brodie's Notes and Supplement to Stair's Institutions [*Scotland*] [*A publication*] (DLA) ... Bro St
Brodie's Notes and Supplement to Stair's Institutions [*Scotland*] [*A publication*] (DLA) ... Bro Stair
Brodie's Notes and Supplement to Stair's Institutions [*Scotland*] [*A publication*] (DLA) ... Brod Stair
Brodix's American and English Patent Cases [*A publication*] (DLA) ... Brodix Am & E Pat Cas
Brodix's American and English Patent Cases [*A publication*] (DLA) ... Brodix Am & Eng Pat Cas
Brodmann's Areas [*Brain anatomy*] ... BA
Brodsky, David, New York NY [*STAC*] ... BDD
Brohm Resources, Inc. [*Toronto Stock Exchange symbol Vancouver Stock Exchange symbol*] ... BRH
Broiler and Egg Association of Minnesota (SRA) ... BEAM
Brokaw Hospital Medical Center, Normal, IL [*Library symbol Library of Congress*] (LCLS) ... INBH
Broke [*Rough finish of paper*] ... B
Broken ... B
Broken ... BKN
Broken [*Quality of the bottom*] [*Nautical charts*] ... brk
Broken ... BRKN
Broken Arrow, OK [*FM radio station call letters*] ... KNYD
Broken Arrow, OK [*FM radio station call letters*] (RBYB) ... KOAS
Broken as Designed [*Computer hacker terminology*] (NHD) ... BAD
Broken Bow Carnegie Library, Broken Bow, NE [*Library symbol Library of Congress*] (LCLS) ... NbBro
Broken Bow, NE [*Location identifier FAA*] (FAAL) ... BBW
Broken Bow, NE [*Location identifier FAA*] (FAAL) ... CUZ
Broken Bow, NE [*FM radio station call letters*] ... KBBN
Broken Bow, NE [*AM radio station call letters*] ... KCNI
Broken Bow, OK [*FM radio station call letters*] (RBYB) ... KCGX
Broken Bow, OK [*FM radio station call letters*] ... KKBI
Broken Clouds or Better (MUGU) ... BCOB
Broken Clouds or Better [*Meteorology*] (DA) ... BCOP
Broken Corn and Foreign Material [*Quality measure for grain*] ... BCFM
Broken Cubic Meter (DAC) ... BCM
Broken Cubic Yard (DAC) ... BCY
Broken Hill [*Australia ICAO location identifier*] (ICLI) ... AABH
Broken Hill [*Australia ICAO location identifier*] (ICLI) ... APBH
Broken Hill [*Kabwe*] [*Zambia*] [*Seismograph station code, US Geological Survey*] (SEIS) ... BHA
Broken Hill [*Australia Airport symbol*] (OAG) ... BHQ
Broken Hill Chamber of Commerce [*Australia*] ... BHCC

Broken Hill Municipal Library, Broken Hill, NSW, Australia [Library symbol Library of Congress] (LCLS) .... AuBh
Broken Hill Prop ADR [NYSE symbol] (TTSB) .... BHP
Broken Hill Proprietary ADR [NYSE symbol] (SPSG) .... BHP
Broken Hill Proprietary Co. Ltd. [Associated Press] (SAG) .... BOP
Broken Orange Pekoe [Tea] .... BOP
Broken Orange Pekoe Fannings [Tea] .... BOPF
Broken Paper (BARN) XXX
Broken Sea [Navigation] .... B
Broken Time Payment [US Olympic Committee] .... BTP
Broken-Case Price [Marketing] (DOAD) .... BCP
Brokenhead River Regional Library, Beausejour, Manitoba [Library symbol National Library of Canada] (NLC) .... MBBR
Brokenhead River Regional Library, Beausejour, MB, Canada [Library symbol Library of Congress] (LCLS) .... CaMBBR
Broker [London Stock Exchange] .... B
Broker [Business term] .... BKR
Broker .... BRKR
Broker (WDAA) .... BROK
Broker Management Council (EA) .... BMC
Broker Services, Inc. [Englewood, CO] [Information service or system] (IID) .... BSI
Brokerage .... BRKRGE
Brokerage (ROG) .... BROK
Brokerage Accounting Information System (SAA) .... BRAINS
Brokerage Accounting System Elements [IBM computer program] .... BASE
Broker-Dealer .... B/D
Broker-Dealer (DFIT) .... BD
Broker-Dealer-Investment Advisor Directory [Securities and Exchange Commission] (GFGA) .... BDA
Broker's Daily Statement .... BDS
Broker's Order [Finance] .... BO
Bromacetylcellulose [or Bromoacetycellulose] [Organic chemistry] .... BAC
Bromcresol Green [An indicator] [Chemistry] .... BCG
Bromcresol Purple [An indicator] [Chemistry] .... BCP
Brome County Historical Society, Knowlton, PQ, Canada [Library symbol Library of Congress] (LCLS) .... CaQKB
Brome County Historical Society, Knowlton, Quebec [Library symbol National Library of Canada] (NLC) .... QKB
Bromegrass Mosaic Virus .... BMV
Bromeliad Society (EA) .... BS
Bromeliad Society of New South Wales [Australia] .... BSNSW
Bromeliad Society of Victoria [Australia] .... BSV
Bromide [Chemistry] (ADA) .... BROM
Brominated Vegetable Oil [Soft drink additive] .... BVO
Bromine [Chemical element] .... Br
Bromine Efficiency Factor .... BEF
Bromine Pentafluoride [Corrosive compound] .... BPF
Bromine-Loading Potential [Atmospheric science] .... BLP
Bromma Flygskola/Cabair [Sweden ICAO designator] (FAAC) .... CVN
Bromo [As substituent on nucleoside] [Biochemistry] .... br
Bromoacetaldehyde Diethyl Acetal [Organic chemistry] .... BADEA
Bromoacetamidothymidine [Antineoplastic drug] .... BAT
Bromoacetone [War gas] .... BA
Bromoacetyl [Organic chemistry] .... BA
Bromoacetylcholine [Biochemistry] .... BAC
Bromoacetyl-DNP-Diamino-L-Butyric Acid [Biochemistry] .... BADB
Bromoacetyl-DNP-Ethylenediamine [Biochemistry] .... BADE
Bromoacetyl-DNP-L-Lysine [Biochemistry] .... BADL
Bromoacetyl-DNP-L-Ornithine [Biochemistry] .... BADO
Bromoacetylmono(azobenzenearsonic Acid)-L-tyrosine [Biochemistry] .... BAAT
Bromoamiloride [Biochemistry] .... Br-A
(Bromobenzoyl)methyladamantylamine [Biochemistry] .... BMA
Bromobenzyl Cyanide [Tear gas] .... BBC
Bromobenzylnitrile [Toxic compound] .... BBN
Bromochlorodifluoromethane [Fire extinguishing agent] [Organic chemistry] (ADA) .... BCF
Bromo(chloro)indolylphosphate [Organic chemistry] .... BCIP
Bromochlorophenol Blue [Organic chemistry] .... BCPB
Bromocresol Purple Desoxycholate [Agar] [Chemistry] (DAVI) .... BCP-D
Bromocriptine [Pharmacology] .... Br
Bromodeoxyuridine [Also, BDUR, BrDU] [Biochemistry] .... BDU
Bromodeoxyuridine [Also, BDU, BrDU] [Biochemistry] .... BDUR
Bromodeoxyuridine [Also, BDU, BDUR] [Biochemistry] .... BrDU
Bromodeoxyuridine [Also, BDU, BDUR] [Antineoplastic drug] (DAVI) .... BrdUrd
Bromodeoxyuridine [Antineoplastic drug] (DAVI) .... BUDU
Bromodiphenyl(ethylphenyl)ethylene [Endocrinology] .... BDPE
Bromoergocryptine [Organic chemistry] .... BEC
Bromoethanesulfonic Acid [Organic chemistry] .... BES
Bromoform-Triallyl Phosphate [Flame retardant] .... BAP
Bromoil Print (VRA) .... BRPT
Bromoisobutene Isoprene Rubber [Organic chemistry] .... BIIR
Bromoisovalerylurea [Pharmacology] .... BVU
Bromomercurihydroxypropane [Clinical chemistry] .... BMHP
Bromo-Methoxychalcone [Organic chemistry] .... BMC
(Bromomethyl)dimethyl Chlorosilane [Organic chemistry] .... BMDMCS
Bromo-Naphthyl-Beta-Galactosidase [An enzyme] (MAE) .... BNGase
Bromo-Naphthyl-Beta-Galactoside (MAE) .... BNG
Bromoperoxidase [An enzyme] .... BPO
Bromophenacyl Bromide [Organic chemistry] .... BPB
Bromophenol Blue [A pH indicator] [Organic chemistry] (DAVI) .... BPB
Bromopyrogallol Red [An indicator] [Chemistry] .... BPR
Bromosulfophthalein [Clinical chemistry] .... BSP
Bromothymol Blue Lactose [Medicine] (DMAA) .... BTBL
Bromotrifluoroethylene [Organic chemistry] .... BFE

Bromotrifluoromethane [Fire extinguishing agent] [Organic chemistry] (ADA) .... BTM
Bromouracil [Biochemistry] .... BU
Bromouracildeoxyriboside [Antineoplastic drug] .... BUdR
Bromouridine [One-letter symbol; see BrUrd] .... B
Bromouridine [Also, B] [A nucleoside] .... BrUrd
Bromovinyldeoxyuridine [Biochemistry] .... BVDU
(Bromovinyl)uracil [Antiviral compound] .... BVU
Brompheniramine Maleate [Antihistamine] .... BPM
Bromphenol [or Bromophenol] Blue [A dye] .... BPB
Brompton Park Military Hospital [British military] (DMA) .... BPMH
Bromthymol [or Bromothymol] Blue [A dye] .... BTB
Bronchial .... BRON
Bronchial Allergen Challenge [Immunology] .... BAC
Bronchial Artery Embolization [Cardiology] (DAVI) .... BAE
Bronchial Asthma [Medicine] .... BA
Bronchial Blood Flow [Medicine] (DMAA) .... BBF
Bronchial Carcinoid [Medicine] .... BC
Bronchial Carcinoma [Medicine] (DAVI) .... BC
Bronchial Drainage [Medicine] (DAVI) .... BD
Bronchial Lymph Node [Medicine] (MAE) .... BLN
Bronchial Provocation Test [Medicine] .... BPT
Bronchial Smooth Muscle Cell [Medicine] (DMAA) .... BSMC
Bronchiectasis, Eosinophilia, Asthma, Pneumonia [Medicine] (DMAA) .... BEAP
Bronchiectatic Cyst [Pulmonary medicine] .... BC
Bronchiolitis Obliterans-Organizing Pneumonia [Medicine] (DMAA) .... BOOP
Bronchitis [Medicine] .... BR
Bronchoalveolar Cells [Medicine] .... BAC
Bronchoalveolar Lavage [Medicine] .... BAL
Bronchoalveolar Lavage Fluid [Medicine] .... BALF
Bronchoalveolar Lavage Fluid .... BALF
Bronchoalveolar Wash Fluids [Medicine] .... BAW
Bronchodilation Following Deep Inspiration [Medicine] (DMAA) .... BFDI
Bronchodilator [Medicine] .... B
Bronchoesophagology [Medicine] .... BE
Bronchogenic Carcinoma [Medicine] (DMAA) .... BGCA
Bronchogenic Cyst .... BC
Bronchophony [Medicine] (DAVI) .... Brhp
Bronchopleural [Medicine] .... BP
Bronchopleural Fistula [Anatomy] .... BPF
Bronchopulmonary [Medicine] (DAVI) .... BP
Bronchopulmonary Dysplasia [Medicine] .... BPD
Bronchopulmonary Segmental Artery [Medicine] (DMAA) .... BPSA
Bronchopulmonary Segmental Drainage [Medicine] (DAVI) .... BPSD
Bronchoscopist [Medicine] (DAVI) .... bronch
Bronchoscopy [Medicine] (DAVI) .... BRO
Bronchoscopy [Medicine] .... BRON
Bronchoscopy [Medicine] .... BRONCH
Bronchoscopy [Medicine] (DAVI) .... broncho
Bronchospasm [Medicine] .... BSp
Bronchovascular Marking [Medicine] (MAE) .... BVM
Bronchovesicular [Breath sounds] [Medicine] .... BV
Bronchus Associated Lymphoid Tissue .... BALT
Bronco Petroleum Ltd. [Vancouver Stock Exchange symbol] .... BOP
Broneje Transporter [Soviet Armored Personnel Carrier] .... BTR
Bronevaya Mashina Destany [Soviet airborne combat vehicle] (INF) .... BMD
Bronfman Science Center [Williams College] [Research center] (RCD) .... BSC
Bronnoysund [Norway] [Airport symbol] (OAG) .... BNN
Bronnoysund/Bronnoy [Norway ICAO location identifier] (ICLI) .... ENBN
Bronson, MI [FM radio station call letters] .... WCVM
Bronsted Acid [Biochemistry] .... BA
Bronsted Base [Biochemistry] .... BB
Bronsweg [Surinam] [ICAO location identifier] (ICLI) .... SMBW
Bronte Society (EA) .... BS
Bronx [New York] (BARN) .... Bx
Bronx Community College [New York] .... BCC
Bronx Community College Library, Bronx, NY [OCLC symbol] (OCLC) .... VWB
Bronx Community College, New York, NY [Library symbol Library of Congress] (LCLS) .... NNBC
Bronxville Public Library, Bronxville, NY [Library symbol Library of Congress] (LCLS) .... NBron
Bronze .... BR
Bronze [Philately] .... brnz
Bronze (WGA) .... BRO
Bronze (KSC) .... BRZ
Bronze .... BZ
Bronze (VRA) .... bz
Bronze Age .... BA
Bronze Floors [On ships] .... BF
Bronze Medal .... BM
Bronze Service Star [Military decoration] (AFM) .... BSS
Bronze Star Medal [Military decoration] .... BSM
Broadband Inter-Carrier Interface [Telecommunications] .... BICI
Brooder [s] [Freight] .... BRD
Brook (WGA) .... BK
Brook (MCD) .... BRK
Brook .... BRK
Brook [Commonly used] (OPSA) .... BROOK
Brook College, Chicago, IL [Library symbol] [Library of Congress] (LCLS)... ICBCL
Brook Reaction Test [Medicine] (DMAA) .... BRT
Brookdale Community College, Lincroft, NJ [OCLC symbol] (OCLC) .... BCC
Brookdale Community College, Lincroft, NJ [Library symbol Library of Congress] (LCLS) .... NjLincB
Brooke Army Medical Center .... BAMC

Brooke General Hospital, Medical Library, Fort Sam Houston, TX [*Library symbol Library of Congress*] (LCLS) .... TxFshBH
Brooke Group Ltd. [*NYSE symbol*] (SPSG) .... BGL
Brooke Group Ltd. [*Associated Press*] (SAG) .... Brooke
Brooke on the Office of a Notary in England [*A publication*] (DLA) .... Bro Not
Brooke, VA [*Location identifier FAA*] (FAAL) .... BRV
Brooke's Abridgment [*England*] [*A publication*] (DSA) .... B
Brooke's Abridgment [*England*] [*A publication*] (DSA) .... Br
Brooke's Abridgment [*England*] [*A publication*] (DLA) .... Br Abr
Brooke's Abridgment [*England*] [*A publication*] (DLA) .... Bro Ab
Brooke's Abridgment [*England*] [*A publication*] (DLA) .... Bro Abr
Brooke's Abridgment [*England*] [*A publication*] (DLA) ...... Brook Abr
Brooke's Abridgment [*England*] [*A publication*] (DLA) ...... Brooke Abr
Brooke's Bibliotheca Legum Angliae [*A publication*] (DLA) .... Brooke Bib Leg
Brooke's Churchwarden's Guide [*A publication*] (DLA) .... Brooke Ch W
Brookes Deflection Potentiometer .... BDP
Brooke's Ecclesiastical Cases [*1850-72*] [*England*] [*A publication*] (DLA) .... Brooke
Brooke's Ecclesiastical Judgments [*A publication*] (DLA) .... Brooke Eccl Judg
Brooke's New Cases (Collected by Bellewe) [*A publication*] (DLA) .... Bell
Brooke's New Cases (Collected by Bellewe) [*A publication*] (DLA) .... Bell Cas T H VIII
Brooke's New Cases (Collected by Bellewe) [*A publication*] (DLA) .... Bellewe T H VIII
Brooke's New Cases, English King's Bench [*1515-58*] [*A publication*] (DLA) .... Bell Cas T Hen VIII
Brooke's New Cases, English King's Bench [*1515-58*] [*A publication*] (DLA) .... Bellewe's Ca Temp Hen VIII
Brooke's New Cases, English King's Bench [*1515-58*] [*A publication*] (DLA) .... BNC
Brooke's New Cases, English King's Bench [*1515-58*] [*A publication*] (DLA) .... Br N Cas
Brooke's New Cases, English King's Bench [*1515-58*] [*A publication*] (DLA) .... Br NC
Brooke's New Cases, English King's Bench [*1515-58*] [*A publication*] (DLA) .... Bro NC
Brooke's New Cases, English King's Bench [*1515-58*] [*A publication*] (DLA) .... Brook N Cas
Brooke's New Cases, English King's Bench [*1515-58*] [*A publication*] (DLA) .... Brooke
Brooke's New Cases, English King's Bench [*1515-58*] [*A publication*] (DLA) .... Brooke NC
Brooke's New Cases, English King's Bench [*1515-58*] [*A publication*] (DLA) .... Brooke (Petit)
Brooke's New Cases, English King's Bench [*1515-58*] [*A publication*] (DLA) .... Lit Brooke
Brooke's New Cases, English King's Bench [*1515-58*] [*A publication*] (DLA) .... Little Brooke
Brooke's New Cases (Petit Brooke) [*1515-58*] [*A publication*] (DLA) .... Pet Br
Brooke's Office and Practice of a Notary [*A publication*] (DLA) .... Br Not
Brooke's Office and Practice of a Notary [*A publication*] (DLA) .... Brooke Not
Brooke's Reading on the Statute of Limitations [*A publication*] (DLA) .... Bro Read
Brooke's Reading on the Statute of Limitations [*A publication*] (DLA) .... Brooke Lim
Brooke's Six Ecclesiastical Judgments [*A publication*] (DLA) .... Bro Ecc
Brooke's Six Ecclesiastical Judgments [*A publication*] (DLA) .... Brooke Eccl
Brooke's Six Ecclesiastical Judgments [*A publication*] (DLA) .... Brooke Six Judg
Brookfield [*Connecticut*] [*Seismograph station code, US Geological Survey*] (SEIS) .... BCT
Brookfield, CT [*AM radio station call letters*] .... WINE
Brookfield, CT [*FM radio station call letters*] .... WRKI
Brookfield Free Public Library, Brookfield, IL [*Library symbol Library of Congress*] (LCLS) .... IBro
Brookfield, MO [*Location identifier FAA*] (FAAL) .... BZK
Brookfield, MO [*AM radio station call letters*] .... KZBK
Brookfield, MO [*FM radio station call letters*] .... KZBK-FM
Brookfield, WI [*FM radio station call letters*] (RBYB) .... WFMI
Brookhaven Area Office [*Energy Research and Development Administration*] .... BAO
Brookhaven Beam Research Reactor .... BBRR
Brookhaven Energy System Optimization Model (MCD) .... BESOM
Brookhaven Free Library, Brookhaven, NY [*Library symbol Library of Congress*] (LCLS) .... NBroo
Brookhaven Graphite Research Reactor .... BGRR
Brookhaven Linac Isotope Producer [*Nuclear energy*] .... BLIP
Brookhaven Medical Reactor .... BMR
Brookhaven Medical Research Center .... BMRC
Brookhaven Medical Research Reactor (NRCH) .... BMRR
Brookhaven Memorial Hospital, Patchogue, NY [*Library symbol Library of Congress*] (LCLS) .... NPatBH
Brookhaven, MS [*Location identifier FAA*] (FAAL) .... BVV
Brookhaven, MS [*FM radio station call letters*] .... WBKN
Brookhaven, MS [*AM radio station call letters*] .... WCHJ
Brookhaven National Laboratory [*Department of Energy*] [*Upton, NY*] .... BNL
Brookhaven National Laboratory, Upton, NY [*OCLC symbol*] (OCLC) .... ZBN
Brookhaven Office [*AEC*] .... BH
Brookhaven Portable Cesium Developmental Irradiator Unit [*Nuclear energy*] .... BPCDI
Brookhaven Press, Washington, DC [*Library symbol Library of Congress*] (LCLS) .... BkP
Brookhaven Research Reactor .... BRR
Brookhaven Service Center [*IRS*] .... BSC
Brookhaven Town Hall, Historical Collection, Patchogue, NY [*Library symbol Library of Congress*] (LCLS) .... NPatB
Brookings [*South Dakota*] [*Airport symbol*] (OAG) .... BKX
Brookings Economics and Statistical Translator [*Computer science*] .... BEAST

Brookings Institution (EA) .... BI
Brookings Institution, Washington, DC [*Library symbol Library of Congress*] (LCLS) .... DBI
Brookings, OR [*Location identifier FAA*] (FAAL) .... BOK
Brookings, OR [*AM radio station call letters*] .... KURY
Brookings, OR [*FM radio station call letters*] .... KURY-FM
Brookings Public Library, Brookings, SD [*Library symbol Library of Congress*] (LCLS) .... SdBro
Brookings, SD [*AM radio station call letters*] .... KBRK
Brookings, SD [*FM radio station call letters*] .... KBRK-FM
Brookings, SD [*FM radio station call letters*] .... KESD
Brookings, SD [*Television station call letters*] .... KESD-TV
Brookings, SD [*FM radio station call letters*] .... KSDJ
Brook-Iroquois Public Library, Brook, IN [*Library symbol Library of Congress*] (LCLS) .... InBro
Brooklands [*British ICAO location identifier*] (ICLI) .... EGLB
Brookline, MA [*FM radio station call letters*] .... WBOS
Brookline, MA [*AM radio station call letters*] .... WUNR
Brooklyn .... BKLN
Brooklyn [*New York*] (BARN) .... Bklyn
Brooklyn [*Diocesan abbreviation*] [*New York*] (TOCD) .... BRK
Brooklyn Academy of Music .... BAM
Brooklyn Army Terminal .... BART
Brooklyn Avenue School, Valley Stream, NY [*Library symbol*] [*Library of Congress*] (LCLS) .... NVsBAE
Brooklyn Bancorp, Inc. [*Associated Press*] (SAG) .... BklynBc
Brooklyn Bancorp, Inc. [*NASDAQ symbol*] (SAG) .... BRKB
Brooklyn Botanic Garden [*Brooklyn, NY*] .... BBG
Brooklyn Botanic Garden, Brooklyn, NY [*Library symbol Library of Congress*] (LCLS) .... NBG
Brooklyn, Bronx, and Queens [*New York City slang for nightclub or restaurant that has fallen out of favor with the pacesetters*] .... BBQ
Brooklyn Business Library .... BBL
Brooklyn Center for the Performing Arts at Brooklyn College .... BCBC
Brooklyn Children's Museum, Brooklyn, NY [*Library symbol Library of Congress*] (LCLS) .... NBCMu
Brooklyn Chronicle, Brooklyn, IA [*Library symbol Library of Congress*] (LCLS) .... IaBroC
Brooklyn College, Brooklyn, NY [*Library symbol Library of Congress*] (LCLS) .... NBC
Brooklyn College, Brooklyn, NY [*OCLC symbol*] (OCLC) .... VDB
Brooklyn College of Pharmacy, Brooklyn, NY [*Library symbol Library of Congress*] (LCLS) .... NBCP
Brooklyn College of the City University of New York (GAGS) .... Brooklyn C (CUNY)
Brooklyn Daily Record [*A publication*] (DLA) .... Brookl Rec
Brooklyn Daily Record [*A publication*] (DLA) .... Brooklyn Daily Rec
Brooklyn Eastern District Terminal [*AAR code*] .... BEDT
Brooklyn Friends School, New York, NY [*Library symbol Library of Congress*] (LCLS) .... NBF
Brooklyn, IA [*FM radio station call letters*] .... KSKB
Brooklyn Institute of Arts and Sciences .... BIAS
Brooklyn Law School [*New York, NY*] .... BLS
Brooklyn Law School (GAGS) .... Brooklyn Law
Brooklyn Law School, Brooklyn, NY [*Library symbol Library of Congress*] (LCLS) .... NBL
Brooklyn Law School, Brooklyn, NY [*OCLC symbol*] (OCLC) .... ZBL
Brooklyn Local Economic Development Corp. .... BLEDCO
Brooklyn, MI [*AM radio station call letters*] .... WKHM
[*The*] Brooklyn Museum Aramaic Papyri [*A publication*] (BJA) .... BMAP
Brooklyn Museum, Brooklyn, NY [*Library symbol Library of Congress*] (LCLS) .... NBB
Brooklyn Museum, Wilbour Library of Egyptology, Brooklyn, NY [*Library symbol Library of Congress*] (LCLS) .... NBB-E
Brooklyn, NY [*Location identifier FAA*] (FAAL) .... NOP
Brooklyn, NY [*FM radio station call letters*] .... WKRB
Brooklyn Park, MN [*AM radio station call letters*] .... WLOL
Brooklyn Public Library [*New York, NY*] .... BPL
Brooklyn Public Library, Brooklyn, NY [*Library symbol Library of Congress*] (LCLS) .... NB
Brooklyn Public Library, Brooklyn, NY [*Library symbol*] [*Library of Congress*] (LCLS) .... NBPu
Brooklyn, Queens, Long Island [*Section of New York Times*] .... BQLI
Brooklyn Rapid Transit Co. [*A New York City subway line*] [*Became BMT*] .... BRT
Brooklyn Union Gas [*NYSE symbol*] (TTSB) .... BU
Brooklyn Union Gas Co. [*Associated Press*] (SAG) .... BklyUG
Brooklyn Union Gas Co. [*Wall Street slang name: "Bug"*] [*NYSE symbol*] (SPSG) .... BU
Brooklyn Union Gas Co. .... BUG
Brooklyn-Manhattan Transit Corp. [*A New York City subway line*] .... BMT
Brooklyn-Queens-Staten Island Health Sciences Group [*Library network*] .... BQSI
Brookmere Ventures [*Vancouver Stock Exchange symbol*] .... BKV
Brookneal, VA [*AM radio station call letters*] (RBYB) .... WODI-AM
Brookport, IL [*Location identifier FAA*] (FAAL) .... BDD
Brookport, IL [*AM radio station call letters*] .... WRIK
Brooks .... BRKS
Brooks [*Postal Service standard*] (OPSA) .... BRKS
Brooks [*Commonly used*] (OPSA) .... BROOKS
Brooks, AB [*AM radio station call letters*] .... CIBQ
Brooks Art Gallery, Memphis, TN [*Library symbol Library of Congress*] (LCLS) .... TMBA
Brooks Automation [*NASDAQ symbol*] (TTSB) .... BRKS
Brooks Automation, Inc. [*NASDAQ symbol*] (SAG) .... BRKS
Brooks Automation, Inc. [*Associated Press*] (SAG) .... BrooksA
Brooks Automation, Inc. [*Associated Press*] (SAG) .... BrooksAu

Brooks Bird Club (EA) ... BBC
Brooks Brothers [*Clothing store*] ... B^2
Brooks Fiber Properties [*NASDAQ symbol*] (TTSB) ... BFPT
Brooks Fiber Properties, Inc. [*NASDAQ symbol*] (SAG) ... BFPT
Brooks Fiber Properties, Inc. [*Associated Press*] (SAG) ... BrooksF
Brooks Free Library, Harwich, MA [*Library symbol*] [*Library of Congress*] (LCLS) ... MHar
Brooks Memorial Hospital Medical Center, Dunkirk, NY [*Library symbol Library of Congress*] (LCLS) ... NDunBH
Brooks Memorial Library, Brattleboro, VT [*Library symbol Library of Congress*] (LCLS) ... VtBrt
Brooks Public Library, Alberta [*Library symbol National Library of Canada*] (NLC) ... ABR
Brooks' Reports [*106-119 Michigan*] [*A publication*] (DLA) ... Brooks
Brooks Resources Corp. [*Vancouver Stock Exchange symbol*] ... BRC
Brookside Elementary School, Baldwin, NY [*Library symbol Library of Congress*] (LCLS) ... NBaldBE
Brookside Junior High School, North Merrick, NY [*Library symbol*] [*Library of Congress*] (LCLS) ... NNmBJ
Brookston, IN [*FM radio station call letters*] ... WEZV
Brookstone, Inc. [*NASDAQ symbol*] (SAG) ... BKST
Brookstone, Inc. [*Associated Press*] (SAG) ... Brookstn
Brooksville, FL [*Location identifier FAA*] (FAAL) ... BKV
Brooksville, FL [*AM radio station call letters*] ... WWJB
Brooksville, MS [*FM radio station call letters*] (RBYB) ... WAJV
Brooktree Corp. [*Associated Press*] (SAG) ... Brktree
Brooktree Corp. [*NASDAQ symbol*] (SPSG) ... BTRE
Brooktrout Technologies, Inc. [*NASDAQ symbol*] (SAG) ... BRKT
Brooktrout Technology [*NASDAQ symbol*] (TTSB) ... BRKT
Brooktrout Technology, Inc. [*Associated Press*] (SAG) ... Broktrt
Brookview Elementary School, Rockford, IL [*Library symbol*] [*Library of Congress*] (LCLS) ... IRoBrE
Brookville American, Brookville, IN [*Library symbol Library of Congress*] (LCLS) ... InBrkvA
Brookville Democrat, Brookville, IN [*Library symbol Library of Congress*] (LCLS) ... InBrkvD
Brookville, NY [*FM radio station call letters*] ... WCWP
Brookville, PA [*FM radio station call letters*] ... WMKX
Brookwood, AL [*Location identifier FAA*] (FAAL) ... OKW
Brookwood Reservoir [*California*] [*Seismograph station code, US Geological Survey*] (SEIS) ... BKC
Broom and Hadley's Blackstone [*A publication*] (DLA) ... B & H Black
Broom and Hadley's Commentaries on the Laws of England [*A publication*] (DLA) ... Br & Had
Broom and Hadley's Commentaries on the Laws of England [*A publication*] (DLA) ... Broom & H Com
Broom and Hadley's Commentaries on the Laws of England [*A publication*] (DLA) ... Broom & H Comm
Broom and Whisk Makers (MHDB) ... BWM
Broom Closet ... BCL
Broom. Common Law [*9th ed.*] [*1896*] [*A publication*] (DLA) ... Br Com
Broom. Constitutional Law [*3rd ed.*] [*1885*] [*A publication*] (DLA) ... Br Cons Law
Broom. Constitutional Law [*3rd ed.*] [*1885*] [*A publication*] (DLA) ... Broom Const L
Broom on Parties to Actions [*A publication*] (DLA) ... Broom Part
Broom. Philosophy of Law [*3rd ed.*] [*1883*] [*A publication*] (DLA) ... Br Phil Law
Broom. Philosophy of Law [*3rd ed.*] [*1883*] [*A publication*] (DLA) ... Broom Ph Law
Broome [*Australia ICAO location identifier*] (ICLI) ... APBR
Broome [*Australia Airport symbol*] (OAG) ... BME
Broome Regional Aboriginal Medical Service [*Australia*] ... BRAMS
Broome Technical Community College [*New York*] ... BTCC
Broome Technical Community College, Binghamton, NY [*Library symbol Library of Congress*] (LCLS) ... NBiBT
Broomfield, CO [*Television station call letters*] ... KBDI
Broom's Commentaries on the Common Law [*A publication*] (DLA) ... Bro Com
Broom's Commentaries on the Common Law [*A publication*] (DLA) ... Broom CL
Broom's Commentaries on the Common Law [*A publication*] (DLA) ... Broom Com Law
Broom's Legal Maxims [*A publication*] (DLA) ... Br Leg Max
Broom's Legal Maxims [*A publication*] (DLA) ... Br Max
Broom's Legal Maxims [*A publication*] (DLA) ... Bro Leg Max
Broom's Legal Maxims [*A publication*] (DLA) ... Bro Max
Broom's Legal Maxims [*A publication*] (DLA) ... Broom
Broom's Legal Maxims [*A publication*] (DLA) ... Broom Leg Max
Broom's Legal Maxims [*A publication*] (DLA) ... Broom Max
Brooten High School, Brooten, MN [*Library symbol*] [*Library of Congress*] (LCLS) ... MnBtH
Broth Filtrate [*Microbiology*] ... BF
Brothel (ABBR) ... BRTHL
Brother [*or Brotherhood*] ... B
Brother ... BR
Brother ... BRO
Brother (DMAA) ... bro
Brother ... BRO
Brother (ROG) ... BROR
Brother to Brother International (EA) ... BBI
Brotherhood (ILCA) ... Bhd
Brotherhood ... BRTHD
Brotherhood Association of Military Airmen ... BAMA
Brotherhood Commission (EA) ... BC
Brotherhood of Anglican Churchmen [*Canada*] ... BAC
Brotherhood of Associated Book Travelers (EA) ... BABT
Brotherhood of Book Travelers [*Later, ABT*] (EA) ... BBT
Brotherhood of Knights of the Black Pudding Tasters (EA) ... BKBPT
Brotherhood of Locomotive Engineers ... B of LE
Brotherhood of Locomotive Engineers State Legislative Board, Illinois (SRA) ... BLESLB-IL
Brotherhood of Locomotive Firemen and Enginemen [*Later, United Transportation Union*] [*AFL-CIO*] ... BLFE
Brotherhood of Locomotive Firemen and Enginemen [*Later, United Transportation Union*] [*AFL-CIO*] ... LFE
Brotherhood of Maintenance of Way Employes (EA) ... BMWE
[*The*] **Brotherhood of Man under the Fatherhood of God** [*Journalistic slang for political platitudes; said to be taken from a speech by Hubert H. Humphrey*] ... BOMFOG
Brotherhood of Marine Engineers [*Later merged with MEBA*] ... BME
Brotherhood of Marine Officers (EA) ... BMO
Brotherhood of Painters, Decorators, and Paperhangers of America [*Later, IBPAT*] (EA) ... B of PDPH of A
Brotherhood of Painters, Decorators, and Paperhangers of America [*Later, IBPAT*] ... BPDP
Brotherhood of Railroad Signalmen (EA) ... B of RS
Brotherhood of Railroad Signalmen (EA) ... BRS
Brotherhood of Railroad Trainmen [*Later, United Transportation Union*] (EA) ... BRT
Brotherhood of Railway, Airline, and Steamship Clerks; Freight Handlers; Expressand Station Employees ... BRASC
Brotherhood of Railway, Airline, and Steamship Clerks; Freight Handlers; Expressand Station Employes (EA) ... BRAC
Brotherhood of Railway and Steamship Clerks, Freight Handlers, Express and Station Employees [*Later, BRAC*] (EA) ... BRSC
Brotherhood of Railway Carmen of America [*Later, BRC of US & C*] [*AFL-CIO*] ... BRC
Brotherhood of Railway Carmen of America [*Later, BRC of US & C*] [*AFL-CIO*] (EA) ... BRC of A
Brotherhood of Railway Carmen of the United States and Canada [*AFL-CIO*] (EA) ... BRC of US & C
Brotherhood of Saint Andrew (EA) ... BSA
Brotherhood of Shoe and Allied Craftsmen (EA) ... BSAC
Brotherhood of Sleeping Car Porters (IIA) ... BSCP
Brotherhood of Sleeping Car Porters [*Later, BRAC*] (EA) ... SCP
Brotherhood of the American Lutheran Church [*Later, American Lutheran Church Men*] (EA) ... BALC
Brotherhood of the Holy Cross [*Anglican religious community*] ... BHC
Brotherhood of the Holy Name ... BHN
Brotherhood of the Holy Trinity ... BHT
Brotherhood of the Jungle Cock (EA) ... BJC
Brotherhood of the Knights of the Vine (EA) ... BKV
Brotherhood of Traveling Jewelers (EA) ... BTJ
Brotherhood of Utility Workers of New England (EA) ... BUWNE
Brotherhood of Utility Workers of New England (EA) ... UWNE
[*A*] **Brotherhood Towards Education** ... ABATE
Brother-in-Law (ADA) ... BIL
Brotherly (ABBR) ... BRY
Brotherly Love, Relief, and Truth [*Freemasonry*] ... BLRT
Brothers ... BROS
Brothers (ODBW) ... Bros
Brothers and Sisters in Christ [*An association*] (EA) ... BASIC
Brother's Brother Foundation (EA) ... BBF
Brothers Gourmet Coffees [*NASDAQ symbol*] (SAG) ... BEAN
Brothers Gourmet Coffees [*Associated Press*] (SAG) ... BroGour
Brothers of Charity (TOCD) ... FC
Brothers of Charity (TOCD) ... fc
Brothers of Charity of Spokane [*Roman Catholic religious order*] ... BCS
Brothers of Christian Instruction (TOCD) ... FIC
Brothers of Christian Instruction (TOCD) ... flc
Brothers of Christian Service (TOCD) ... BCS
Brothers of Mercy (TOCD) ... FMM
Brothers of Mercy (TOCD) ... fmm
Brothers of Our Lady, Mother of Mercy [*Netherlands*] (EAIO) ... BOLMM
Brothers of Our Lady, Mother of Mercy (TOCD) ... CFMM
Brothers of Our Lady of Mercy [*Roman Catholic religious order*] ... CFMM
Brothers of Our Lady of Providence (TOCD) ... olc
Brothers of Our Lady of Providence (TOCD) ... OLP
Brothers of St. Francis Xavier (TOCD) ... CFX
Brothers of St. Francis Xavier (TOCD) ... cfx
Brothers of St. Patrick (TOCD) ... fsp
Brothers of St. Patrick (TOCD) ... FSP
Brothers of Saint Pius X (TOCD) ... cspx
Brothers of St. Pius X [*Roman Catholic religious order*] ... CSPX
Brothers of the Christian Schools (TOCD) ... fsc
Brothers of the Christian Schools (TOCD) ... FSC
Brothers of the Congregation of Holy Cross (TOCD) ... CSC
Brothers of the Congregation of Our Lady of the Holy Rosary (TOCD) ... fsr
Brothers of the Congregation of Our Lady of the Holy Rosary (TOCD) ... FSR
Brothers of the Good Shepherd [*Roman Catholic religious order*] ... BGS
Brothers of the Holy Eucharist (TOCD) ... FSE
Brothers of the Holy Eucharist (TOCD) ... fse
Brothers of the Immaculate Heart of Mary (TOCD) ... ihm
Brothers of the Immaculate Heart of Mary (TOCD) ... IHM
Brothers of the Poor of St. Francis (TOCD) ... cfmm
Brothers of the Poor of St. Francis (TOCD) ... cfp
Brothers of the Sacred Heart (TOCD) ... SC
Brothers of the Sacred Heart (TOCD) ... sc
Brothers to All Men [*An association*] ... BAM
Brothers to All Men International (EA) ... BAMI
Brothers United for Future Foreskins (EA) ... BUFF
Brothers-in-Law (ABBR) ... BRSNLW
Brough [*British ICAO location identifier*] (ICLI) ... EGNB
Brough's Law of Elections [*A publication*] (DLA) ... Brough Elec

Brought (ADA) ... BROT
Brought ... BRT
Brought Down [*Horse racing*] ... B
Brought Down [*Accounting*] ... BD
Brought Forward [*Business term*] ... BF
Brought in by Police Department [*Emergency medicine*] (DAVI) ... BIBPD
Brought in Dead [*Medicine*] ... BID
Brought into Service [*Telecommunications*] (TEL) ... BIS
Brought on Charge (MCD) ... BOC
Brought Over [*Business term*] ... B/O
Brought Over (ROG) ... OB
Brought-in-By (HGAA) ... BIB
Broughton [*Canada*] [*Airport symbol*] (OAG) ... YVM
Broughton Hospital, Staff Library, Morganton, NC [*Library symbol Library of Congress*] (LCLS) ... NcMoBH
Broughton Island, NT [*ICAO location identifier*] (ICLI) ... CYVM
Broughton's Indian Civil Procedure [*A publication*] (DLA) ... Bro Civ Proc
Broughton's Indian Civil Procedure [*A publication*] (DLA) ... Brough Civ Pro
Broulan Resources, Inc. [*Toronto Stock Exchange symbol*] ... BNR
Broun's Reports, Scotch Justiciary Court [*1842-45*] [*A publication*] (DLA) ... Bro Just
Broun's Reports, Scotch Justiciary Court [*1842-45*] [*A publication*] (DLA) ... Broun
Broun's Reports, Scotch Justiciary Court [*1842-45*] [*A publication*] (DLA) ... Broun Just
Brouwer General Perturbations Differential Correction Program (MCD) ... BGPDC
Brouwer-Lyddane Orbit Generation Routine ... BROWRO
Broward Community College, Fort Lauderdale, FL [*OCLC symbol*] (OCLC) ... EDB
Broward Community College, Fort Lauderdale, FL [*Library symbol Library of Congress*] (LCLS) ... FFIB
Broward County Libraries Division, Fort Lauderdale, FL [*Library symbol Library of Congress*] (LCLS) ... FFIBL
Broward County Libraries Division, Pompano Beach, FL [*OCLC symbol*] (OCLC) ... FBR
Browbeat (ABBR) ... BRWBT
Browbeaten (ABBR) ... BRWBTN
Browbeating (ABBR) ... BRWBTG
Brower Exploration, Inc. [*Vancouver Stock Exchange symbol*] ... BRE
Browerville, MN [*FM radio station call letters*] ... KXDL
Browerville Public School, Browerville, MN [*Library symbol*] [*Library of Congress*] (LCLS) ... MnBvP
Brown ... BR
Brown [*Thoroughbred racing*] ... BR
Brown (KSC) ... BRN
Brown (VRA) ... brn
Brown ... BRWN
Brown [*Telecommunications*] (TEL) ... BWN
Brown Adipose Tissue [*Physiology*] ... BAT
Brown. Agency and Trusts [*1868*] [*A publication*] (ILCA) ... Bro Ag
Brown Ale and Mild Bitters [*British*] (DSUE) ... B and M
Brown Algorithm Simulator and Animator [*Framework for software construction*] [*Brown University*] (NITA) ... BALSA
Brown & Bigelow ... B & B
Brown and Hemingway's Reports [*53-58 Mississippi*] [*A publication*] (DLA) ... Bro & H
Brown and Hemingway's Reports [*53-58 Mississippi*] [*A publication*] (DLA) ... Brown & H
Brown and Hemingway's Reports [*53-58 Mississippi*] [*A publication*] (DLA) ... Brown & Hemingway
Brown and McCall's Yorkshire Star Chamber [*Yorkshire Archaeological Society Record, Series 44, 45, 51, 70*] [*A publication*] (DLA) ... Bro & M
Brown and Rader's Reports [*137 Missouri*] [*A publication*] (DLA) ... Br & R
Brown and Rader's Reports [*137 Missouri*] [*A publication*] (DLA) ... Brown & R
Brown & Root, Inc., Technical Library, Houston, TX [*Library symbol Library of Congress*] (LCLS) ... TxHBR
Brown & Root International (ECON) ... BRI
Brown & Root-Northrop ... BRN
Brown and Sharpe [*Wire gauge*] ... B & S
Brown and Sharpe Gauge ... B & SG
Brown & Sharpe Manufacturing Co. [*NYSE symbol*] (SPSG) ... BNS
Brown & Sharpe Manufacturing Co. [*Associated Press*] (SAG) ... BwnSh
Brown & Sharpe Mfg'A' [*NYSE symbol*] (TTSB) ... BNS
Brown & Williamson Tobacco Corp. ... B & W
Brown & Williamson Tobacco Corp., Research Department Library, Louisville, KY [*Library symbol Library of Congress*] (LCLS) ... KyLoBW
Brown Bag Institute (EA) ... BBI
Brown, Boveri & Co. Ltd. [*Switzerland*] ... BBC
Brown, Boveri-Krupp Reaktorbau [*Germany*] ... BB/KR
Brown Brothers Harriman (ECON) ... BBH
Brown City Public Library, Brown City, MI [*Library symbol Library of Congress*] (LCLS) ... MiBrc
Brown County Democrat, Nashville, IN [*Library symbol Library of Congress*] (LCLS) ... InNasD
Brown County Historical Society, Nashville, IN [*Library symbol Library of Congress*] (LCLS) ... InNasBHi
Brown County Hospital, Green Bay, WI [*Library symbol Library of Congress*] (LCLS) ... WGrBC
Brown County Library, Green Bay, WI [*OCLC symbol*] (OCLC) ... GZG
Brown County Library, Green Bay, WI [*Library symbol Library of Congress*] (LCLS) ... WGr
Brown County Public Library, Nashville, IN [*Library symbol Library of Congress*] (LCLS) ... InNas
Brown County Recorder's Office, Nashville, IN [*Library symbol Library of Congress*] (LCLS) ... InNasCR
Brown, Durbin, and Evans [*Statisticians*] ... BDE
Brown Engineering Co. (KSC) ... BEC
Brown Engineering Co. (KSC) ... BECO
Brown Forman, Inc. [*NYSE symbol*] (SAG) ... BF
Brown Forman, Inc. [*Associated Press*] (SAG) ... BrnF
Brown Forman, Inc. [*Associated Press*] (SAG) ... BrwnFA
Brown Forman, Inc. [*Associated Press*] (SAG) ... BrwnFB
Brown Group [*NYSE symbol*] (TTSB) ... BG
Brown Group, Inc. [*NYSE symbol*] (SPSG) ... BG
Brown Group, Inc. [*Associated Press*] (SAG) ... BrwnGp
Brown [*Alex*], Inc. [*Associated Press*] (SAG) ... AlexBrn
Brown [*Tom*], Inc. [*Associated Press*] (SAG) ... BrTom
Brown [*Tom*], Inc. [*NASDAQ symbol*] (SAG) ... TMBR
Brown, James H., Atlanta GA [*STAC*] ... BJH
Brown. Limitations as to Real Property [*1869*] [*A publication*] (DLA) ... Bro Lim
Brown. Limitations as to Real Property [*1869*] [*A publication*] (DLA) ... Bro RPL
Brown Line Positive ... BR/L
Brown Lung Association (EA) ... BLA
Brown Norway [*Rat variety*] ... BN
Brown Oil of Vitriol ... BOV
Brown on Agency and Trust [*A publication*] (DLA) ... Bro Ag
Brown on Fixtures [*A publication*] (DLA) ... Bro Fix
Brown on Forestalling, Regrating, and Monopolizing, with Cases [*A publication*] (DLA) ... Bro For
Brown Planthopper [*Entomology*] ... BPH
Brown Public Library, Northfield, VT [*Library symbol Library of Congress*] (LCLS) ... VtN
Brown Sedge Growth with Brown Sedge [*Ecology*] ... BB
Brown Stem Rot [*Plant pathology*] ... BSR
Brown Stock Washer [*Pulp and paper technology*] ... BSW
Brown Strachan Associates, Vancouver, BC, Canada [*Library symbol*] [*Library of Congress*] (LCLS) ... CaBVaBS
Brown Strachan Associates, Vancouver, British Columbia [*Library symbol National Library of Canada*] (NLC) ... BVABS
Brown Swiss Cattle Breeders Association of the USA (EA) ... BSCBA
Brown. Treatise on Law of Sale [*Scotland*] [*A publication*] (DLA) ... Bro Sal
Brown Trout Club (EA) ... BTC
Brown University (GAGS) ... Brown U
Brown University [*Rhode Island*] ... BU
Brown University, Annmary Brown Memorial Library, Providence, RI [*Library symbol Library of Congress*] (LCLS) ... RPAB
Brown University Display for Working Set References ... BUDWSR
Brown University Graphic System ... BUGS
Brown University Interpreter [*Computer science*] ... BRUIN
Brown University, John Hay Library of Rare Books annd Special Collections, Providence, RI [*Library symbol Library of Congress*] (LCLS) ... RPB-JH
Brown University, Providence, RI [*OCLC symbol*] (OCLC) ... RBN
Brown University, Providence, RI [*Library symbol Library of Congress*] (LCLS) ... RPB
Brown University, Sciences Library, Providence, RI [*Library symbol Library of Congress*] (LCLS) ... RPB-S
Brown Wrapping Paper (OA) ... BWP
Browndale Community Library, Browndale, AB, Canada [*Library symbol*] [*Library of Congress*] (LCLS) ... CaABrC
Browne. Actions at Law [*1843*] [*A publication*] (DLA) ... Bro Ac
Browne. Actions at Law [*1843*] [*A publication*] (DLA) ... Bro Act
Browne. Actions at Law [*1843*] [*A publication*] (DLA) ... Browne Act
Browne and Gray's Reports [*A publication*] (DLA) ... Browne & G
Browne and Gray's Reports [*A publication*] (DLA) ... Browne & Gray
Browne and MacNamara. Railway Cases [*A publication*] (DLA) ... B & Macn
Browne and MacNamara's English Railway and Canal Cases [*A publication*] (DLA) ... Browne & MacN
Browne and MacNamara's Railway Cases [*A publication*] (DLA) ... B & M
Browne and MacNamara's Railway Cases [*A publication*] (DLA) ... B & Mac
Browne and MacNamara's Railway Cases [*A publication*] (DLA) ... Bro & M
Browne and MacNamara's Railway Cases [*A publication*] (DLA) ... Bro & Mac
Browne and MacNamara's Railway Cases [*A publication*] (DLA) ... Brown & MacN
Browne and Theobald. Railways [*4th ed.*] [*1911*] [*A publication*] (DLA) ... Browne & Th Railw
Browne, Bortz & Coddington, Inc. [*Denver, CO*] [*Telecommunications*] (TSSD) ... BBC
Browne. Georgia Pleading and Practice and Legal Forms, Annotated [*A publication*] (DLA) ... Brown GA Pl & Pr Anno
Browne. Law of Carriers [*1873*] [*A publication*] (DLA) ... Bro Car
Browne. Law of Rating of Hereditaments [*2nd ed.*] [*1886*] [*A publication*] (DLA) ... Bro Hered
Browne on Carriers [*A publication*] (DLA) ... Browne Car
Browne on the Companies' Acts [*A publication*] (DLA) ... Bro Co Act
Browne on the Statute of Frauds [*A publication*] (DLA) ... Bro Fr
Browne on the Statute of Frauds [*A publication*] (DLA) ... Bro St Fr
Browne on the Statute of Frauds [*A publication*] (DLA) ... Browne Fr
Browne on the Statute of Frauds [*A publication*] (DLA) ... Browne St Frauds
Browne on Trade Markets [*A publication*] (DLA) ... Bro Tr M
Browne on Trade Markets [*A publication*] (DLA) ... Browne Tr M
Browne on Usages and Customs [*A publication*] (DLA) ... Browne Us
Browne. Practice in Divorce and Matrimonial Causes [*11th ed.*] [*1931*] [*A publication*] (DLA) ... Browne Div Pr
Browned-Off Passed-Over (SAA) ... BOPO
Browne's Civil and Admiralty Law [*A publication*] (DLA) ... Bro C & AL
Browne's Civil and Admiralty Law [*A publication*] (DLA) ... Bro Civ Law
Browne's Civil and Admiralty Law [*A publication*] (DLA) ... Browne Civ L
Browne's Civil and Admiralty Law [*A publication*] (DLA) ... Browne Civ Law

Browne's Civil Procedure Reports [*New York*] [*A publication*] (DLA) .... Browne
Browne's Digest of Decisions on Divorce and Alimony [*A publication*] (DLA) .... Bro Dig Div
Browne's Divorce Court Practice [*A publication*] (DLA) .... Bro Div Pr
Browne's Divorce Court Practice [*A publication*] (DLA) .... Browne Div
Browne's Judicial Interpretation of Common Words and Phrases [*A publication*] (DLA) .... Browne Jud Interp
Browne's Law of Usages and Customs [*A publication*] (DLA) .... Bro Us & Cus
Browne's Medical Jurisprudence of Insanity [*A publication*] (DLA) .... Bro Ins
Browne's National Bank Cases [*A publication*] (DLA) .... Bro NB Cas
Browne's National Bank Cases [*A publication*] (DLA) .... Browne Bank Cas
Browne's National Bank Cases [*A publication*] (DLA) .... Browne NBC
Browne's New Abridgment of Cases in Equity [*A publication*] (DLA) .... Bro Abr in Eq
Browne's Parliamentary and Municipal Registration Act [*A publication*] (DLA) .... Bro Reg Act
Browne's Patent Office Practice [*A publication*] (DLA) .... Bro Pat Pr
Browne's Pennsylvania Reports [*1801-14*] [*A publication*] (DLA) .... Bro PA
Browne's Practice of the High Court of Chancery [*A publication*] (DLA) .... Bro Ch Pr
Browne's Probate Practice [*A publication*] (DLA) .... Bro Prob Pr
Browne's Probate Practice [*A publication*] (ILCA) .... Browne Prob
Browne's Probate Practice [*A publication*] (DLA) .... Browne Prob Pr
Browne's Reports [*Ceylon*] [*A publication*] (DLA) .... Br R
Browne's Reports [*Pennsylvania*] [*A publication*] (DLA) .... Bro
Browne's Reports [*Sri Lanka*] [*A publication*] (DLA) .... Bro
Browne's Reports [*Sri Lanka*] [*A publication*] (DLA) .... Browne
Browne's Reports [*Massachusetts*] [*A publication*] (DLA) .... Browne
Browne's Reports [*Pennsylvania*] [*A publication*] (DLA) .... Browne
Browne's Reports [*Pennsylvania*] [*A publication*] (DLA) .... Browne (PA)
Browne's Reports [*Pennsylvania*] [*A publication*] (DLA) .... Browne PA R
Browne's Reports [*Pennsylvania*] [*A publication*] (DLA) .... Browne's Rep
Browne's Reports [*Pennsylvania*] [*A publication*] (DLA) .... Brown's (Penn)
Browne's Reports [*Pennsylvania*] [*A publication*] (DLA) .... Brown's Penn Rep
Browne's Reports [*Pennsylvania*] [*A publication*] (DLA) .... PA Browne R
Browne's Reports (Pennsylvania) [*A publication*] (DLA) .... PA Browne (PA)
Brownfield Public Library, Alberta [*Library symbol National Library of Canada*] (NLC) .... ABROW
Brownfield, TX [*Location identifier FAA*] (FAAL) .... BFE
Brownfield, TX [*AM radio station call letters*] .... KKUB
Brownfield, TX [*FM radio station call letters*] .... KLZK
Brown-Forman [*NYSE symbol*] (SPSG) .... BF
Brown-Forman Cl'B' [*NYSE symbol*] (TTSB) .... BFB
Brown-Forman, Inc. [*Associated Press*] (SAG) .... BrnF
Brown-Forman Inc. 4% Pfd [*NYSE symbol*] (TTSB) .... BFPr
Brown-Forman'A' [*NYSE symbol*] (TTSB) .... BFA
Browning Aircraft Machine Gun .... BAMG
Browning and Lushington on Marriage and Divorce [*A publication*] (DLA) .... Bro & Lush M & D
Browning and Lushington on Marriage and Divorce [*A publication*] (DLA) .... Brown & Lush M & D
Browning and Lushington's English Admiralty Reports [*1863-65*] [*A publication*] (DLA) .... B & L
Browning and Lushington's English Admiralty Reports [*1863-65*] [*A publication*] (DLA) .... Br & L
Browning and Lushington's English Admiralty Reports [*1863-65*] [*A publication*] (DLA) .... Br & Lush
Browning and Lushington's English Admiralty Reports [*1863-65*] [*A publication*] (DLA) .... Bro & L
Browning and Lushington's English Admiralty Reports [*1863-65*] [*A publication*] (DLA) .... Bro & Lush
Browning and Lushington's English Admiralty Reports [*1863-65*] [*A publication*] (DLA) .... Brown & L
Browning and Lushington's English Admiralty Reports [*1863-65*] [*A publication*] (DLA) .... Brown & L (Eng)
Browning and Lushington's English Admiralty Reports [*1863-65*] [*A publication*] (DLA) .... Brown & Lush
Browning Automatic Rifle .... BAR
Browning Ferris [*NYSE symbol*] (SAG) .... BFE
Browning Ferris [*NYSE symbol*] (SAG) .... BFI
Browning Ferris [*Associated Press*] (SAG) .... BrnFAC
Browning Ferris [*Associated Press*] (SAG) .... BrwnFr
Browning Institute (EA) .... BI
Browning Machine Gun .... BMG
Browning on Marriage and Divorce [*A publication*] (DLA) .... Bro M & D
Browning on Marriage and Divorce [*A publication*] (DLA) .... Brown M & D
Browning-Ferris 7.25% 'ACES' [*NYSE symbol*] (TTSB) .... BFE
Browning-Ferris Indus [*NYSE symbol*] (TTSB) .... BFI
Browning-Ferris Industries, Inc. [*NYSE symbol*] (SPSG) .... BFI
Browning-Ferris Industries, Inc. [*Associated Press*] (SAG) .... BrwnFr
Browning's Divorce Court Practice [*A publication*] (DLA) .... Brown Div Pr
Brownish [*Philately*] .... brnsh
Brownish-Black .... BB
Brownlow and Goldesborough's English Common Pleas Reports [*A publication*] (DLA) .... Br & G
Brownlow and Goldesborough's English Common Pleas Reports [*A publication*] (DLA) .... Br & Gold
Brownlow and Goldesborough's English Common Pleas Reports [*A publication*] (DLA) .... Bro & G
Brownlow and Goldesborough's English Common Pleas Reports [*A publication*] (DLA) .... Brown
Brownlow and Goldesborough's English Common Pleas Reports [*A publication*] (DLA) .... Brown & G (Eng)
Brownlow and Goldesborough's English Common Pleas Reports [*A publication*] (DLA) .... Brown & Gold
Brownlow and Goldesborough's English Common Pleas Reports [*A publication*] (DLA) .... Brownl
Brownlow and Goldesborough's English Common Pleas Reports [*A publication*] (DLA) .... Brownl & G
Brownlow and Goldesborough's English Common Pleas Reports [*A publication*] (DLA) .... Brownl & Gold
Brownlow and Goldesborough's Nisi Prius Reports [*1569-1624*] [*England*] [*A publication*] (DLA) .... B & G
Brownlow's Brevia Judicialia, Etc. [*1662*] [*A publication*] (DLA) .... Br Brev Jud
Brownlow's Brevia Judicialia, Etc. [*1662*] [*A publication*] (DLA) .... Br Brev Jud & Ent
Brownlow's Brevia Judicialia, Etc. [*1662*] [*A publication*] (DLA) .... Brow Brev
Brownlow's Brevia Judicialia, Etc. [*1662*] [*A publication*] (DLA) .... Brownl Brev
Brownlow's Entries [*A publication*] (DLA) .... Br Ent
Brownlow's Entries [*A publication*] (DLA) .... Brown Ent
Brownlow's Entries [*A publication*] (DLA) .... Brownl Ent
Brownlow's Latine Redivivus [*or Entries*] [*A publication*] (DLA) .... Bro Ent
Brownlow's Latine Redivivus [*or Entries*] [*A publication*] (DLA) .... Brownl Redv
Brown-Roberts-Wells [*Computerized tomographic stereotaxic guide*] [*Radiology*] (DAVI) .... BRW
Brown's Cases in Parliament [*A publication*] (DLA) .... BPC
Brown's Cases in Parliament [*A publication*] (DLA) .... Bro Parl Cas
Brown's Chancery Cases [*England*] [*A publication*] (DLA) .... BC Rep
Brown's Chancery Cases [*England*] [*A publication*] (DLA) .... BCC
Brown's Chancery Cases [*England*] [*A publication*] (DLA) .... BCR
Brown's Chancery Cases [*England*] [*A publication*] (DLA) .... Br CC
Brown's Chancery Cases [*England*] [*A publication*] (DLA) .... Br PC
Brown's Chancery Cases Tempore Lord Thurlow [*England*] [*A publication*] (DLA) .... Brown Ch
Brown's Chancery Cases Tempore Lord Thurlow [*England*] [*A publication*] (DLA) .... Brown Ch C
Brown's English Chancery Cases [*or Reports*] [*A publication*] (DLA) .... Bro CC
Brown's English Chancery Cases [*or Reports*] [*A publication*] (DLA) .... Brown C
Brown's English Chancery Cases [*or Reports*] [*A publication*] (DLA) .... Brown CC
Brown's English Chancery Reports [*28, 29 English Reprint*] [*A publication*] (DLA) .... Bro
Brown's English Chancery Reports [*28, 29 English Reprint*] [*A publication*] (DLA) .... Bro Ch
Brown's English Chancery Reports [*28, 29 English Reprint*] [*A publication*] (DLA) .... Bro Ch Cas
Brown's English Chancery Reports [*28, 29 English Reprint*] [*A publication*] (DLA) .... Bro Ch R
Brown's English Chancery Reports [*28, 29 English Reprint*] [*A publication*] (DLA) .... Brown
Brown's English Ecclesiastical Reports [*A publication*] (DLA) .... Brown Ecc
Brown's English Nisi Prius Cases [*A publication*] (DLA) .... Bro NP
Brown's English Nisi Prius Cases [*A publication*] (DLA) .... Brown NP Cas
Brown's English Parliamentary Cases [*A publication*] (DLA) .... Bro PC
Brown's English Parliamentary Cases [*A publication*] (DLA) .... Brown
Brown's Entries [*A publication*] (DLA) .... Bro Ent
Brown's Epitome and Analysis of Savigny's Treatise on Obligations in Roman Law [*A publication*] (DLA) .... Brown's Roman Law
Browns Ferry Nuclear Plant (NRCH) .... BFNP
Browns Ferry Nuclear Power Plant (NRCH) .... BFNPP
Brown's Formulae Bene Placitandi [*A publication*] (DLA) .... Bro Form
Brown's Formulae Bene Placitandi [*A publication*] (ILCA) .... Form Pla
Brown's Forum [*A publication*] (DLA) .... Bro For
Brown's House of Lords Cases [*England*] [*A publication*] (DLA) .... Brown Parl
Brown's House of Lords Cases [*England*] [*A publication*] (DLA) .... Brown Parl Cas
Brown's House of Lords Cases [*England*] [*A publication*] (DLA) .... Brown PC
Brown's Law Dictionary [*A publication*] (DLA) .... Bro Law Dic
Brown's Law Dictionary [*A publication*] (DLA) .... Brown
Brown's Law Dictionary [*A publication*] (DLA) .... Brown Dict
Brown's Law Dictionary and Institute [*1874*] [*A publication*] (DLA) .... Brown
Brown's Michigan Nisi Prius Reports [*A publication*] (DLA) .... Bro
Brown's Michigan Nisi Prius Reports [*A publication*] (DLA) .... Bro NP
Brown's Michigan Nisi Prius Reports [*A publication*] (DLA) .... Brown
Brown's Michigan Nisi Prius Reports [*A publication*] (DLA) .... Brown NP
Brown's Michigan Nisi Prius Reports [*A publication*] (DLA) .... Brown NP (Mich)
Brown's Michigan Nisi Prius Reports [*A publication*] (DLA) .... Mich Nisi Prius
Brown's Michigan Nisi Prius Reports [*A publication*] (DLA) .... Mich NP
Brown's Modus Intrandi [*A publication*] (DLA) .... Mod Int
Brown's Parliamentary Cases [*England*] [*A publication*] (DLA) .... Bro
Brown's Parliamentary Reports [*England*] [*A publication*] (DLA) .... BPR
Brown's Parties to Actions [*A publication*] (DLA) .... Br Par
Brown's Practice (Praxis) [*or Precedents*] **in Chancery** [*A publication*] (DLA) .... Bro Prac
Brown's Practice (Praxis) [*or Precedents*] **in Chancery** [*A publication*] (DLA) .... Prax
Brown's Reports [*53-65, 80-136 Missouri*] [*A publication*] (DLA) .... Bro
Brown's Reports [*53-65 Mississippi*] [*A publication*] (DLA) .... Brown
Brown's Reports [*80-137 Missouri*] [*A publication*] (DLA) .... Brown
Brown's Reports [*4-25 Nebraska*] [*A publication*] (DLA) .... Brown
Brown's Scotch Reports [*A publication*] (DLA) .... Brown
Brown's Supplement to Morison's Dictionary of Decisions, Scotch Court of Sessions [*A publication*] (DLA) .... Bro Sup to Mor
Brown's Supplement to Morison's Dictionary of Decisions, Scotch Court of Sessions [*A publication*] (DLA) .... BS
Brown's Supplement to Morison's Dictionary, Scotch Court of Sessions [*A publication*] (DLA) .... Br Sup
Brown's Supplement to Morison's Dictionary, Scotch Court of Sessions [*A publication*] (DLA) .... Bro Supp
Brown's Supplement to Morison's Dictionary, Scotch Court of Sessions [*A publication*] (DLA) .... Brown Sup

Brown's Supplement to Morison's Dictionary, Scotch Court of Sessions [*A publication*] (DLA) .... Brown Sup Dec
Brown's Synopsis of Decisions, Scotch Court of Sessions [*1540-1827*] [*A publication*] (DLA) .... Br Syn
Brown's Synopsis of Decisions, Scotch Court of Sessions [*1540-1827*] [*A publication*] (DLA) .... Bro Syn
Brown's Synopsis of Decisions, Scotch Court of Sessions [*1540-1827*] [*A publication*] (DLA) .... Bro Synop
Brown's Synopsis of Decisions, Scotch Court of Sessions [*1540-1827*] [*A publication*] (DLA) .... Brown Syn
Brown's United States Admiralty Reports [*A publication*] (DLA) .... Bro Adm
Brown's United States Admiralty Reports [*A publication*] (DLA) .... Brown
Brown's United States Admiralty Reports [*A publication*] (DLA) .... Brown Adm
Brown's United States Admiralty Reports (Appendix) [*A publication*] (DLA) .... Brown's Adm App
Brown's United States District Court Reports [*A publication*] (DLA) .... Brown
Brown's United States District Court Reports (Admiralty and Revenue Cases) [*A publication*] (DLA) .... Bro A & R
Brown's United States District Court Reports (Admiralty and Revenue Cases) [*A publication*] (DLA) .... Brown A & R
Brown's Vade Mecum [*A publication*] (DLA) .... Bro VM
Brownsburg Guide, Brownsburg, IN [*Library symbol Library of Congress*] (LCLS) .... InBrbG
Brownsburg, IN [*FM radio station call letters*] .... WQFE
Brownsburg Public Library, Brownsburg, IN [*Library symbol Library of Congress*] (LCLS) .... InBrb
Brownshall [*England*] .... BROWNS
Brownstone Revival Committee (EA) .... BRC
Brownstown Banner, Brownstown, IN [*Library symbol Library of Congress*] (LCLS) .... InBrtB
Brownstown Community School District No. 201, Brownstown, IL [*Library symbol Library of Congress*] (LCLS) .... IBrowSD
Brownstown Public Library, Brownstown, IN [*Library symbol Library of Congress*] (LCLS) .... InBrt
Brownsville [*Texas*] [*Airport symbol*] (OAG) .... BRO
Brownsville [*Diocesan abbreviation*] [*Texas*] (TOCD) .... BWN
Brownsville Historical Association, Brownsville, TX [*Library symbol Library of Congress*] (LCLS) .... TxBHi
Brownsville/International [*Texas*] [*ICAO location identifier*] (ICLI) .... KBRO
Brownsville, OR [*FM radio station call letters*] (RBYB) .... KEHK-FM
Brownsville, OR [*FM radio station call letters*] .... KLRF
Brownsville, PA [*AM radio station call letters*] .... WASP
Brownsville, TN [*AM radio station call letters*] .... WNWS
Brownsville, TN [*FM radio station call letters*] .... WTBG
Brownsville, TX [*FM radio station call letters*] .... KBNR
Brownsville, TX [*AM radio station call letters*] .... KBOR
Brownsville, TX [*FM radio station call letters*] .... KKPS
Brownsville, TX [*FM radio station call letters*] .... KTEX
Brownsville, TX [*Television station call letters*] .... KVEO
Brownsville, TX [*Location identifier FAA*] (FAAL) .... MIH
Brownton Public Schools, Brownton, MN [*Library symbol*] [*Library of Congress*] (LCLS) .... MnBroPS
Browntown Public Library, Browntown, MN [*Library symbol*] [*Library of Congress*] (LCLS) .... MnBro
Brownvale Community Library, Alberta [*Library symbol National Library of Canada*] (NLC) .... ABC
Brownwood [*Texas*] [*Airport symbol*] (OAG) .... BWD
Brownwood Public Library, Brownwood, TX [*Library symbol Library of Congress*] (LCLS) .... TxBrd
Brownwood, TX [*AM radio station call letters*] .... KBWD
Brownwood, TX [*FM radio station call letters*] .... KOXE
Brownwood, TX [*FM radio station call letters*] .... KPSM
Brownwood, TX [*AM radio station call letters*] .... KXYL
Brownwood, TX [*FM radio station call letters*] .... KXYL-FM
Brows, Lids, and Lashes [*Anatomy*] (DAVI) .... BLL
Browse (ABBR) .... BRWS
Browsed (ABBR) .... BRWSD
Browsing (ABBR) .... BRWSG
Browsing On-Line with Selective Retrieval .... BROWSER
Broxton, GA [*FM radio station call letters*] .... WULS
Broye-Les-Pesmes [*France ICAO location identifier*] (ICLI) .... LFYH
BRT Realty Trust [*Associated Press*] (SAG) .... BRT
BRT Realty Trust SBI [*NYSE symbol*] (SPSG) .... BRT
BRT Realty Trust SBI [*NYSE symbol*] (TTSB) .... BRT
Bruccoli-Clark Publishers .... BCP
Bruce and Williams. Admiralty Jurisdiction [*A publication*] (DLA) .... Bru & Wil Adm
Bruce Boxleitner Fan Club (EA) .... BBFC
Bruce County Museum, Southampton, Ontario [*Library symbol National Library of Canada*] (BIB) .... OSOM
Bruce County Public Library, Port Elgin, ON, Canada [*Library symbol Library of Congress*] (LCLS) .... CaOPteB
Bruce County Public Library, Port Elgin, Ontario [*Library symbol National Library of Canada*] (NLC) .... OPEB
Bruce Maximum Stress Test [*Medicine*] (DMAA) .... BMST
Bruce Mines & Plummer Additional Union Public Library, Bruce Mines, ON, Canada [*Library symbol*] [*Library of Congress*] (LCLS) .... CaOBMP
Bruce Mines and Plummer Additional Union Public Library, Bruce Mines, Ontario [*Library symbol National Library of Canada*] (NLC) .... OBMP
Bruce Peel Special Collections Library, University of Alberta, Edmonton, Alberta [*Library symbol National Library of Canada*] (NLC) .... AEUS
Bruce, Principia Juris Feudalis [*A publication*] (DLA) .... Bru Princip
Bruce Trail Association (EA) .... BTA
Brucella [*Bacteriology*] .... B
Brucella [*Bacteriology*] (AAMN) .... BR
Brucella Agglutinins [*Bacteriology*] (DAVI) .... BRUCL
Brucella Ring Test [*Dairy science*] (OA) .... BRT
Brucella, Vitamin K Blood Agar [*Bacteriology*] (DAVI) .... BRBA
Brucellosis Information System [*Department of Agriculture*] (GFGA) .... BIS
Brucellus Abortus [*Bacteriology*] .... BA
Bruce's Military Law [*A publication*] (DLA) .... Bru ML
Bruce's Scotch Court of Session Reports [*1714-15*] [*A publication*] (DLA) .... Br
Bruce's Scotch Court of Session Reports [*1714-15*] [*A publication*] (DLA) .... Bru
Bruce's Scotch Court of Session Reports [*1714-15*] [*A publication*] (DLA) .... Bruce
Bruckner Society of America (EA) .... BSA
Bruder [*Brother*] [*Freemasonry*] [*German*] (ROG) .... B
Bruderheim Municipal Library, Alberta [*Library symbol National Library of Canada*] (NLC) .... ABRUM
Bruderheim Municipal Library, Bruderheim, AB, Canada [*Library symbol*] [*Library of Congress*] (LCLS) .... CaABruM
Brudzinski, Oppenheim, Chaddock, and Gullaird [*Reflexes and signs*] [*Neurology*] (DAVI) .... BOCG
Bruedern [*Brethren*] [*Freemasonry*] [*German*] .... B'n
Bruggemeyer Memorial Library, Monterey Park Public Library, Monterey Park, CA [*Library symbol*] [*Library of Congress*] (LCLS) .... CMp
Bruggen [*Germany ICAO location identifier*] (ICLI) .... EDUR
Bruininks-Oseretsky Balance Subtest [*Occupational therapy*] .... BOBS
Bruininks-Oseretsky Test of Motor Proficiency [*Occupational therapy*] .... BOTMP
Bruise (ABBR) .... BRUS
Bruised (ABBR) .... BRUSD
Bruiser (ABBR) .... BRUSR
Bruising (ABBR) .... BRUSG
Brule, WI [*FM radio station call letters*] .... WHSA
Brumado [*Brazil*] [*Airport symbol*] (OAG) .... BMS
Brunauer-Emmett-Teller [*Adsorption equation*] .... BET
Brunauer-Emmett-Teller Isotherm [*Adsorption isotherm equation*] .... BET Isotherm
Bruncor, Inc. [*Toronto Stock Exchange symbol*] .... BRR
Bruneau District Library, Bruneau, ID [*Library symbol*] [*Library of Congress*] (LCLS) .... IdBr
Brunei [*MARC geographic area code Library of Congress*] .... a-bx--
Brunei (BARN) .... B
Brunei [*International vehicle registration*] (ODBW) .... BRU
Brunei .... BRUN
Brunei [*MARC country of publication code Library of Congress*] (LCCP) .... bx
Brunei Broadcasting Service .... BBS
Brunei Darussalam [*ANSI two-letter standard code*] (CNC) .... BN
Brunei Darussalam [*ANSI three-letter standard code*] (CNC) .... BRN
Brunei Darussalam [*Aircraft nationality and registration mark*] (FAAC) V8
Brunei, Indonesia, Malaysia, Philippines [*International trade*] .... BIMP
Brunei, Indonesia, Malaysia, Philippines East Asian Growth Area [*International trade*] .... BIMP-EAGA
Brunei/International [*Brunei*] [*ICAO location identifier*] (ICLI) .... WBSB
Brunei National Democratic Party [*Political party*] (FEA) .... BNDP
Brunei National United Party [*Political party*] (EY) .... BNUP
Brunei People's Independence Front [*Political party*] (FEA) .... BPIF
Brunei Town [*Brunei*] [*Airport symbol*] (AD) .... BTN
Brunel Institute for Bioengineering [*Brunel University*] [*Information service or system*] (IID) .... BIB
Brunel Institute of Computational Mathematics [*Research center British*] (IRUK) .... BICOM
Brunet (ABBR) .... BRUT
Brunett Downs [*Northern Territory, Australia*] [*Airport symbol*] (AD) .... BTD
Brunker's Irish Common Law Digest [*A publication*] (DLA) .... Brunk Ir Dig
Brunner's Collected Cases [*United States*] [*A publication*] (DLA) .... Brun Col Cas
Brunner's Collected Cases [*United States*] [*A publication*] (DLA) .... Brunn Col Cas (F)
Brunner's Collected Cases [*United States*] [*A publication*] (DLA) .... Brunn Coll Cas
Brunner's Collected Cases [*United States*] [*A publication*] (DLA) .... Brunner Col Cas
Brunner's Selected Cases [*United States*] [*A publication*] (DLA) .... Brun Sel Cas
Brunner's Selected Cases [*United States*] [*A publication*] (DLA) .... Brunn Sel Cas
Brunner's Selected Cases, United States Circuit Courts [*A publication*] (DLA) .... Brunner Sel Cas
Bruno Elementary School, Bruno, MN [*Library symbol*] [*Library of Congress*] (LCLS) .... MnBruE
Bruno's, Inc. [*NASDAQ symbol*] (NQ) .... BRNO
Brunskill's Land Cases [*Ireland*] [*A publication*] (DLA) .... Bruns LC
Brunskill's Land Cases [*Ireland*] [*A publication*] (DLA) .... Brunskill
Brunswick [*Record label*] [*Great Britain*] .... B
Brunswick [*Georgia*] [*Airport symbol*] (OAG) .... BQK
Brunswick [*Georgia*] [*Airport symbol*] (AD) .... SSI
Brunswick/Brunswick Naval Air Station [*Maryland*] [*ICAO location identifier*] (ICLI) .... KNHZ
Brunswick Corp. [*NYSE symbol*] (SPSG) .... BC
Brunswick Corp. [*Associated Press*] (SAG) .... Brnwk
Brunswick, GA [*Location identifier FAA*] (FAAL) .... BQK
Brunswick, GA [*Location identifier FAA*] (FAAL) .... SSI
Brunswick, GA [*FM radio station call letters*] (RBYB) .... WAQC-FM
Brunswick, GA [*Television station call letters*] .... WBSG
Brunswick, GA [*AM radio station call letters*] .... WGIG
Brunswick, GA [*AM radio station call letters*] .... WMOG
Brunswick, GA [*AM radio station call letters*] .... WPIQ
Brunswick, GA [*FM radio station call letters*] .... WSEG
Brunswick, GA [*FM radio station call letters*] (RBYB) .... WSOL-FM
Brunswick, GA [*FM radio station call letters*] .... WWIO
Brunswick, GA [*FM radio station call letters*] (RBYB) .... WWRD
Brunswick, GA [*FM radio station call letters*] (RBYB) .... WWRR-FM
Brunswick General Hospital, Amityville, NY [*Library symbol Library of Congress*] (LCLS) .... NAmiGH

Brunswick/Glynco Naval Air Station [*Georgia*] [*ICAO location identifier*] (ICLI) ... KNEA
Brunswick Junior College, Brunswick, GA [*Library symbol Library of Congress*] (LCLS) ... GBruJC
Brunswick, MD [*AM radio station call letters*] ... WTRI
Brunswick, ME [*Location identifier FAA*] (FAAL) ... NBT
Brunswick, ME [*Location identifier FAA*] (FAAL) ... NHZ
Brunswick, ME [*Location identifier FAA*] (FAAL) ... NMU
Brunswick, ME [*FM radio station call letters*] ... WBOR
Brunswick, ME [*AM radio station call letters*] ... WCLZ
Brunswick, ME [*FM radio station call letters*] ... WCLZ-FM
Brunswick Mining & Smelting Corp. Ltd. [*Toronto Stock Exchange symbol*] ... BMS
Brunswick Regional Library, Brunswick, GA [*Library symbol Library of Congress*] (LCLS) ... GBru
Brunswick Steam Electric Plant (NRCH) ... BSEP
Brunswick Technical College, Supply, NC [*Library symbol Library of Congress*] (LCLS) ... NcSupB
Brunswick-Greensville Regional Library, Lawrenceville, VA [*Library symbol Library of Congress*] (LCLS) ... ViLaw
Brush (MSA) ... BR
Brush (VRA) ... bru
Brush Beryllium Co. (MCD) ... BBC
Brush Border [*of intestinal epithelial cell*] [*Cell physiology*] ... BB
Brush Border Endopeptidase [*Medicine*] (DMAA) ... BBEP
Brush Border Membrane [*Medicine*] (DMAA) ... BBM
Brush Border Myosin [*Biology*] ... BBMI
Brush, CO [*AM radio station call letters*] ... KSIR
Brush, CO [*FM radio station call letters*] ... KSIR-FM
Brush Creek Mining & Development [*Associated Press*] (SAG) ... BrushCrk
Brush Creek Mining & Development Co., Inc. [*NASDAQ symbol*] (NQ) ... BCMD
Brush Creek Mining/Dvlp [*NASDAQ symbol*] (TTSB) ... BCMD
Brush Holder ... BRH
Brush Holder (IAA) ... BRHLR
Brush Owner's Association [*Defunct*] (EA) ... BOA
Brush Public Library, Brush, CO [*Library symbol Library of Congress*] (LCLS) ... CoBru
Brush Style [*Computer science*] (PCM) ... BS
Brush Wellman [*NYSE symbol*] (TTSB) ... BW
Brush Wellman, Inc. [*Associated Press*] (SAG) ... BrshWl
Brush Wellman, Inc. [*NYSE symbol*] (SPSG) ... BW
Brushless Torque Motor ... BTM
Brushmakers of Scotland Protection Association [*A union*] ... BSPA
Brush-Off [*Slang*] ... BRO
Brushware Manufacturers' Association of Australia ... BMAA
Brusly, LA [*FM radio station call letters*] ... KRVE
Brusque (ABBR) ... BRSQ
Brusquely (ABBR) ... BRSQY
Brusqueness (ABBR) ... BRSQNS
Brussels [*Belgium*] [*Airport symbol*] (OAG) ... BRU
Brussels [*Belgium ICAO location identifier*] (ICLI) ... EBBB
Brussels [*Belgium ICAO location identifier*] (ICLI) ... EBBS
Brussels [*Belgium ICAO location identifier*] (ICLI) ... EBBU
Brussels [*Belgium ICAO location identifier*] (ICLI) ... EBBV
Brussels [*Belgium ICAO location identifier*] (ICLI) ... EBMI
Brussels [*Belgium ICAO location identifier*] (ICLI) ... EBUM
Brussels [*Belgium ICAO location identifier*] (ICLI) ... EBUR
Brussels [*Belgium ICAO location identifier*] (ICLI) ... EBVA
Brussels [*Belgium ICAO location identifier*] (ICLI) ... EBWM
Brussels Community High School District 37, Brussels, IL [*Library symbol Library of Congress*] (LCLS) ... IBrusSD
Brussels/Grimbergen [*Belgium ICAO location identifier*] (ICLI) ... EBGB
Brussels/National [*Belgium ICAO location identifier*] (ICLI) ... EBBR
Brussels Nomenclature [*Standard customs nomenclature published by the Customs Cooperation Council*] ... BN
Brussels Sprouts Marketing Program (EA) ... BSMP
Brussels Tariff Nomenclature (ILCA) ... BNT
Brussels Tariff Nomenclature [*See also CCCN*] [*EEC Belgium*] ... BTN
Brussels Tariff Nomenclature for the Latin American Free Trade Association (BARN) ... NABLOC
Brussels Treaty Organization [*Later, Western European Union*] ... BTO
Brussels Treaty Permanent Commission (NATG) ... BTPC
Brussels-Richwood Community Consolidated School District 41, Brussels, IL [*Library symbol Library of Congress*] (LCLS) ... IBrusRSD
Brutal (ABBR) ... BRTL
Brutality (ABBR) ... BRTLT
Brutalize (ABBR) ... BRTLZ
Brutalized (ABBR) ... BRTLZD
Brutalizing (ABBR) ... BRTLZG
Brutally (ABBR) ... BRTLY
Brute (ABBR) ... BRT
Brute Force and Ignorance [*Computer science Slang*] (WDMC) ... BFI
Brute Force Gyro ... BFG
Brute Force [*Unregulated*] **Supply** (IEEE) ... BFS
Brutish (ABBR) ... BRTSH
Brutish (ABBR) ... BRUTH
Brutishly (ABBR) ... BRTSHY
Brutishness (ABBR) ... BRTSHNS
Bruton's Tyrosine Kinase [*An enzyme*] ... Btk
Bruttoregistertonne [*Gross Registered Ton*] [*German*] ... BRT
Brutus [*of Plutarch*] [*Classical studies*] (OCD) ... Brut
Brutus or De Claris Oratoribus [*of Cicero*] [*Classical studies*] (OCD) ... Brut
Bruxelles [*Belgium*] [*City in Belgium*] (ROG) ... BRUX
Bruzual [*Venezuela*] [*Airport symbol*] (AD) ... BRZ
Bruzual, Apure [*Venezuela ICAO location identifier*] (ICLI) ... SVBZ
BRX Mining & Petroleum [*Vancouver Stock Exchange symbol*] ... BXG
Bryan [*Texas*] [*Airport symbol*] (AD) ... CFD
Bryan Adams Fan Club (EA) ... BAFC
Bryan/Coulter Field [*Texas*] [*ICAO location identifier*] (ICLI) ... KCFD
Bryan, OH [*Location identifier FAA*] (FAAL) ... BWB
Bryan, OH [*Location identifier FAA*] (FAAL) ... BYN
Bryan, OH [*FM radio station call letters*] (RBYB) ... WAOX
Bryan, OH [*FM radio station call letters*] ... WBNO
Bryan, OH [*FM radio station call letters*] (RBYB) ... WGBE-FM
Bryan, OH [*AM radio station call letters*] ... WQCT
Bryan Public Library, Bryan, TX [*Library symbol Library of Congress*] (LCLS) ... TxBry
Bryan, TX [*Location identifier FAA*] (FAAL) ... CFD
Bryan, TX [*AM radio station call letters*] ... KAGC
Bryan, TX [*FM radio station call letters*] ... KBMA
Bryan, TX [*Television station call letters*] ... KBTX
Bryan, TX [*FM radio station call letters*] ... KKYS
Bryan, TX [*FM radio station call letters*] ... KORA
Bryan, TX [*AM radio station call letters*] ... KTAM
Bryan, TX [*Television station call letters*] ... KYLE
Bryan-Bennett Public Library, Salem, IL [*Library symbol Library of Congress*] (LCLS) ... ISal
Bryansk [*Former USSR ICAO location identifier*] (ICLI) ... UUBP
Bryant and Stratton. Commercial Law [*A publication*] (DLA) ... Bry & Str Com L
Bryant College (GAGS) ... Bryant C
Bryant College, Smithfield, RI [*OCLC symbol*] (OCLC) ... BRB
Bryant College, Smithfield, RI [*Library symbol Library of Congress*] (LCLS) ... RSmB
Bryant Library, Roslyn, NY [*Library symbol Library of Congress*] (LCLS) ... NRosl
Bryce Canyon National Park ... BRCA
Bryce Canyon, UT [*Location identifier FAA*] (FAAL) ... BCE
Bryce. Registration of Trade Marks [*A publication*] (DLA) ... Bryce Tr M
Bryce's Study of the Civil Law [*A publication*] (DLA) ... Bryce Civ L
Bry-Lin Hospital, Buffalo, NY [*Library symbol Library of Congress*] (LCLS) ... NBuBLH
Brymon Airways [*British*] ... BA
Brymon Airways [*ICAO designator*] (AD) ... BC
Brymon Airways [*Airline flight code*] (ODBW) ... BC
Brymon Airways [*British*] ... BR
Brymon European Airway [*British ICAO designator*] (FAAC) ... BRY
Bryn Mawr Bank [*NASDAQ symbol*] (TTSB) ... BMTC
Bryn Mawr Bank Corp. [*NASDAQ symbol*] (NQ) ... BMTC
Bryn Mawr Bank Corp. [*Associated Press*] (SAG) ... BrynMw
Bryn Mawr College [*Pennsylvania*] ... BMC
Bryn Mawr College (GAGS) ... Bryn Mawr C
Bryn Mawr College, Bryn Mawr, PA [*OCLC symbol*] (OCLC) ... BMC
Bryn Mawr College, Bryn Mawr, PA [*Library symbol Library of Congress*] (LCLS) ... PBm
Bryne Library Consulting, Richmond, VA [*Library symbol*] [*Library of Congress*] (LCLS) ... ViRBL
Bryology ... BRY
Bryology (ROG) ... BRYOL
Bryson City, NC [*AM radio station call letters*] ... WBHN
Brystol-Myers Pharmaceuticals R & D, Buffalo, NY [*Library symbol*] [*Library of Congress*] (LCLS) ... NBuBM
BSB Bancorp [*Associated Press*] (SAG) ... BSB Bcp
BSB Bancorp [*NASDAQ symbol*] (TTSB) ... BSBN
BSB Bancorp, Inc. [*NASDAQ symbol*] (NQ) ... BSBN
BSL Airlines [*Ukraine*] [*FAA designator*] (FAAC) ... BSL
BT Financial [*NASDAQ symbol*] (TTSB) ... BTFC
BT Financial Corp. [*Associated Press*] (SAG) ... BT Fin
BT Financial Corp. [*NASDAQ symbol*] (NQ) ... BTFC
BT Office Prod Intl. [*NYSE symbol*] (TTSB) ... BTF
BT Office Products International, Inc. [*Associated Press*] (SAG) ... BT Off
BT Office Products International, Inc. [*NYSE symbol*] (SAG) ... BTF
BT Shipping Ltd. [*Associated Press*] (SAG) ... BT Shp
BT Shipping Ltd. [*NASDAQ symbol*] (NQ) ... BTBT
BT Shipping Ltd ADR [*NASDAQ symbol*] (TTSB) ... BTBTY
BTG, Inc. [*Associated Press*] (SAG) ... BTG Inc
BTG, Inc. [*NASDAQ symbol*] (SAG) ... BTGI
BTG Inc. [*NASDAQ symbol*] (TTSB) ... BTGI
BTI Computer Systems [*Formerly, Basic Timesharing, Inc.*] ... BTI
BTL Corp. [*Formerly, Butler Brothers*] ... BTL
BTL [*Bell Telephone Laboratories*] **Furnished Equipment** (MCD) ... BFE
B-Track Initiator (SAA) ... BTI
BTU International [*NASDAQ symbol*] (TTSB) ... BTUI
BTU International, Inc. [*Associated Press*] (SAG) ... BTU Int
BTU International, Inc. [*NASDAQ symbol*] (CTT) ... BTUI
Bua [*Fiji*] [*Airport symbol Obsolete*] (OAG) ... BVF
Bua [*Fiji*] [*ICAO location identifier*] (ICLI) ... NFNU
Buattifel [*Libya*] [*ICAO location identifier*] (ICLI) ... HLFL
Buayan/General Santos, Cotabato (South) [*Philippines*] [*ICAO location identifier*] (ICLI) ... RPWB
Bubaque [*Guinea-Bissau*] [*ICAO location identifier*] (ICLI) ... GGBU
Bubble (KSC) ... BUB
Bubble Bath Detector (OA) ... BBD
Bubble Chamber ... BC
Bubble Chamber Experiment ... BCE
Bubble Column [*Engineering*] ... BC
Bubble Column Slurry Reactor [*Chemical engineering*] ... BCSR
Bubble Curtain [*Pisciculture*] ... BC
Bubble Domain Memory ... BDM
Bubble Electromagnetic Pulse ... BEMP
Bubble Growth (PDAA) ... BUBGRO
Bubble Interfacial Microlayer Sampler [*Oceanography*] (MSC) ... BIM

Bubble Interfacial Microlayer Sampler [*Oceanography*] ... BIMS
Bubble Lattice File [*Computer science*] (HGAA) ... BLF
Bubble Memory [*Data storage device*] [*Computer science*] (BUR) ... BM
Bubble Memory [*Data storage device*] [*Computer science*] (MSA) ... BUBMEM
Bubble Memory Controller [*Computer science*] ... BMC
Bubble Memory Device [*Computer science*] ... BMD
Bubble Position Register [*Computer science*] (IAA) ... BPR
Bubble Pulse (IAA) ... BP
Bubble Pulse Period ... BPP
Bubble-Gum Brigade [*Preteens*] ... BGB
Bubble-Up Initiation [*Automotive project management*] ... BI
Bubbling Fluidized Bed Combustion ... BFBC
Bucak [*Turkey*] [*Seismograph station code, US Geological Survey*] (SEIS) ... BCK
Bucaramanga [*Colombia*] [*Seismograph station code, US Geological Survey*] (SEIS) ... BCR
Bucaramanga [*Colombia*] [*Airport symbol*] (OAG) ... BGA
Bucaramanga/Palo Negro Sur [*Colorado ICAO location identifier*] (ICLI) ... SKBG
Buccal [*Pertaining to the cheek*] ... B
Buccal [*Dentistry*] (DAVI) ... Buc
Buccal Cartilage [*Dentistry*] ... BC
Buccal Commissure [*Dentistry*] ... BC
Buccal Ganglion [*Dentistry*] ... BUG
Buccal Mass [*Dentistry*] ... BM
Buccaneer ... BCCNR
Buccaneer Aircraft [*"Banana Bomber"*] [*British*] (DSUE) ... BUCC
Buccaneer National Class Association (EA) ... BNCA
Buccoaxial [*Dentistry*] ... BA
Buccoaxiocervical [*Dentistry*] ... BAC
Buccoaxiogingival [*Dentistry*] ... BAG
Buccocervical [*Dentistry*] ... BC
Buccodistal [*Dentistry*] ... BD
Buccogingival [*Dentistry*] ... BG
Buccolingual [*Dentistry*] ... BL
Buccomesial [*Dentistry*] ... BM
Bucco-Occlusal [*Dentistry*] ... BO
Buccopulpal [*Dentistry*] ... BP
Buchan [*Australia Seismograph station code, US Geological Survey Closed*] (SEIS) ... BUV
Buchan [*British ICAO location identifier*] (ICLI) ... EGQN
Buchanan [*Liberia*] [*ICAO location identifier*] (ICLI) ... GLBU
Buchanan [*Liberia*] [*ICAO location identifier*] (ICLI) ... GLLB
Buchanan [*Liberia*] [*Airport symbol*] (AD) ... UCN
Buchanan. Cape Colony Court of Appeal Reports [*South Africa*] [*A publication*] (DLA) ... AC
Buchanan. Cape Colony Court of Appeal Reports [*South Africa*] [*A publication*] (DLA) ... App Ca
Buchanan County Courthouse, Independence, IA [*Library symbol*] [*Library of Congress*] (LCLS) ... IaIndpBC
Buchanan County Courthouse, Independence, IA [*Library symbol Library of Congress*] (LCLS) ... IaIndpCoC
Buchanan, MI [*FM radio station call letters*] ... WSMK
Buchanan's Appeal Court Reports, Cape Of Good Hope [*A publication*] (DLA) ... BAC
Buchanan's Appeal Court Reports, Cape Of Good Hope [*A publication*] (DLA) ... Buch AC
Buchanan's Appeal Court Reports, Cape Of Good Hope [*A publication*] (DLA) ... Buch App Cas
Buchanan's Appeal Court Reports, Cape Of Good Hope [*A publication*] (DLA) ... Buch Ct Ap Cape GH
Buchanan's Appeal Court Reports, Cape Of Good Hope [*A publication*] (ILCA) ... Buch Ct App Cape G H
Buchanan's Cape Of Good Hope Reports [*A publication*] (DLA) ... Buch
Buchanan's Cape Of Good Hope Reports [*A publication*] (DLA) ... Buch E Cape GH
Buchanan's Cape Of Good Hope Reports [*A publication*] (DLA) ... Buch Rep
Buchanan's Court of Session [*1800-13*] [*Scotland*] [*A publication*] (DLA) ... Buch
Buchanan's New Jersey Equity Reports [*A publication*] (DLA) ... Buch
Buchanan's New Jersey Equity Reports [*A publication*] (DLA) ... Buch Eq (NJ)
Buchanan's New Jersey Equity Reports [*A publication*] (DLA) ... Buchan
Buchanan's Precedents of Pleading [*A publication*] (DLA) ... Buch Pr Pl
Buchanan's Remarkable Criminal Cases [*Scotland*] [*A publication*] (DLA) ... Buch Cas
Buchanan's Remarkable Criminal Cases [*Scotland*] [*A publication*] (DLA) ... Buch Tr
Buchanan's Reports, Cape Of Good Hope [*A publication*] (DLA) ... Buch J Cape GH
Buchanan's Reports, Court of Session and Justiciary [*Scotland*] [*A publication*] (DLA) ... Buchanan
Buchanan's Reports of the Court of Appeal, Cape [*1880-1910*] [*South Africa*] [*A publication*] (ILCA) ... A
Buchanan's Supreme Court Reports [*Cape Colony*] [*A publication*] (DLA) ... Buch
Buchanan's Supreme Court Reports, Cape Of Good Hope [*1868-79*] [*South Africa*] [*A publication*] (DLA) ... B
Buchanan's Supreme Court Reports, Cape Of Good Hope [*1868-79*] [*South Africa*] [*A publication*] (DLA) ... Buch SC Rep
Buchan's California Lien Laws [*A publication*] (DLA) ... Buch Lien Law
Buchans Public Library, Buchans, NF, Canada [*Library symbol Library of Congress*] (LCLS) ... CaNfBu
Buchans Public Library, Newfoundland [*Library symbol National Library of Canada*] (NLC) ... NFBU
Bucharest [*Romania*] [*Seismograph station code, US Geological Survey*] (SEIS) ... BUC
Bucharest [*Romania*] [*Seismograph station code, US Geological Survey*] (SEIS) ... BUC1
Bucharest [*Romania*] [*Seismograph station code, US Geological Survey*] (SEIS) ... BUC2
Bucharest [*Romania*] [*Airport symbol*] (OAG) ... BUH
Bucharest [*Romania*] **Banesa Airport** [*Airport symbol*] (OAG) ... BBU
Buchberg [*Switzerland*] [*Seismograph station code, US Geological Survey*] (SEIS) ... BUB
Buchel [*Germany ICAO location identifier*] (ICLI) ... EDSB
Buchtel, OH [*AM radio station call letters*] ... WAIS
Buciclovir Triphosphate [*Antiviral*] ... BCVTP
Buck Island Reef National Monument ... BUIS
Buck Memory Element (MCD) ... BME
Buck Owens Fan Club [*Defunct*] (EA) ... BOFC
Buck-a-Day (PDAA) ... BAD
Buck-Boost Transformer ... BBT
Bucket ... BCKT
Bucket ... BKT
Bucket Wheel Excavator (DICI) ... BWE
Bucket-Brigade Device [*Electronics*] ... BBD
Buckeye ... BCKEYE
Buckeye Airways International [*Air carrier designation symbol*] ... BAIX
Buckeye Association of School Administrators [*Ohio*] (SRA) ... BASA
Buckeye, AZ [*Location identifier FAA*] (FAAL) ... BXK
Buckeye, AZ [*FM radio station call letters*] ... KMJK
Buckeye Cellulose [*NYSE symbol*] (TTSB) ... BKI
Buckeye Cellulose Corp. [*NYSE symbol*] (SAG) ... BKI
Buckeye Cellulose Corp. [*Associated Press*] (SAG) ... BuckCel
Buckeye Cellulose Corp., Technical Division Library, Memphis, TN [*Library symbol Library of Congress*] (LCLS) ... TMBC
Buckeye Partners Ltd. [*Associated Press*] (SAG) ... Buckeye
Buckeye Partnership [*NYSE symbol*] (SPSG) ... BPL
Buckeye Ptnrs L.P. [*NYSE symbol*] (TTSB) ... BPL
Buckeye Public Library, Buckeye, AZ [*Library symbol Library of Congress*] (LCLS) ... AzBu
Buckham Memorial Library, Faribault, MN [*Library symbol Library of Congress*] (LCLS) ... MnF
Buckhannon, WV [*FM radio station call letters*] ... WBTQ
Buckhannon, WV [*AM radio station call letters*] ... WBUC
Buckhannon, WV [*FM radio station call letters*] ... WBUC-FM
Buckhannon, WV [*FM radio station call letters*] ... WVPW
Buckhannon, WV [*FM radio station call letters*] ... WVWC
Buckhead America [*NASDAQ symbol*] (TTSB) ... BUCK
Buckhead America Corp. [*NASDAQ symbol*] (SAG) ... BUCK
Buckhead America Corp. [*Associated Press*] (SAG) ... BuckAm
Buckhorn, California [*Spaceflight Tracking and Data Network*] [*NASA*] ... BUC
Bucking Current Generator ... BCG
Bucking Signal ... BS
Buckingham [*Electrostatic measure*] ... B
Buckingham [*Municipal borough in England*] ... BUCK
Buckingham Palace [*British*] ... BP
Buckingham Palace Press Office [*British*] ... BPPO
Buckinghamshire [*County in England*] ... BUCKS
Buckinghamshire [*County in England*] (ODBW) ... Bucks
Buckland [*Alaska*] [*Airport symbol*] (OAG) ... BKC
Buckland [*England*] ... BUCK
Buckle (ROG) ... BKLE
Buckle, Inc. [*NASDAQ symbol*] (SAG) ... BKLE
Buckle, Inc. [*Associated Press*] (SAG) ... Buckle
Buckled Zone (SAA) ... BZ
Buckley on the Companies Acts [*1873-1949*] [*A publication*] (DLA) ... Buck Comp Act
Buckley on the Companies Acts [*1873-1949*] [*A publication*] (DLA) ... Buckl
Buckley Public Library, Poteau, OK [*Library symbol Library of Congress*] (LCLS) ... OkPot
Buckley-Loda Community Unit School District, Buckley, IL [*Library symbol*] [*Library of Congress*] (LCLS) ... IBucSD
Buckling of Shells of Revolution [*Computer program*] [*NASA*] (MCD) ... BOSOR
Buckman Laboratories, Inc., Memphis, TN [*Library symbol Library of Congress*] (LCLS) ... TMBL
Buckminster Fuller Institute (EA) ... BFI
Bucknall Steamship Lines Ltd. (ROG) ... BSL
Bucknell Computer Services [*Bucknell University*] [*Research center*] (RCD) ... BCS
Bucknell University (GAGS) ... Bucknell U
Bucknell University, Lewisburg, PA [*OCLC symbol*] (OCLC) ... PBU
Bucknell University, Lewisburg, PA [*Library symbol Library of Congress*] (LCLS) ... PLeB
Buckner's Decisions [*in Freeman's Mississippi Chancery Reports, 1839-43*] [*A publication*] (DLA) ... Buck Dec
Bucknill. Care of the Insane [*1880*] [*A publication*] (DLA) ... Buck Ins
Bucknill on Lunacy [*A publication*] (DLA) ... Buck Lun
Bucknill's Cooke's Cases of Practice, Common Pleas [*England*] [*A publication*] (DLA) ... Buck Cooke
Buckram (ADA) ... BKM
Buckram [*Fabric*] ... BUCK
Bucks County Community College, Newtown, PA [*OCLC symbol*] (OCLC) ... BUC
Bucks County Community College, Newtown, PA [*Library symbol Library of Congress*] (LCLS) ... PNtB
Bucks County Free Library, Doylestown, PA [*OCLC symbol*] (OCLC) ... DPB
Bucks County Free Library, Doylestown, PA [*Library symbol Library of Congress*] (LCLS) ... PDoB
Bucks County Historical Society, Doylestown, PA [*Library symbol Library of Congress*] (LCLS) ... PDoBHi
Bucks County Law Reporter [*Pennsylvania*] [*A publication*] (DLA) ... Bucks
Bucks County Law Reporter [*Pennsylvania*] [*A publication*] (DLA) ... Bucks Co L Rep
Bucks County Law Reporter [*Pennsylvania*] [*A publication*] (DLA) ... Bucks Co LR (PA)
Buck's English Cases in Bankruptcy [*1816-20*] [*A publication*] (DLA) ... Buck

Buck's English Cases in Bankruptcy [1816-20] [A publication] (DLA) .... Buck Bankr (Eng)

Buck's English Cases in Bankruptcy [1816-20] [A publication] (DLA) ..... Buck Cas

Buck's Massachusetts Ecclesiastical Law [A publication] (DLA) ...... Buck Eccl Law

Buck's Reports [7-8 Montana] [A publication] (DLA) .... Buck

Buckskin (VRA) .... bcksk

Bucksport, SC [FM radio station call letters] .... WGTR

Bucky [Cassette film in Potter-Bucky Diaphragm] [Radiology] (DAVI) .... B

BUCS [Backup Control System] Self Test (MCD) .... BUCS/ST

Bucuresti [Romania] [ICAO location identifier] (ICLI) .... LRBB

Bucuresti/Baneasa [Romania] [ICAO location identifier] (ICLI) .... LRBS

Bucuresti/Otopeni [Romania] [ICAO location identifier] (ICLI) .... LROP

Bucyrus Intl. [NASDAQ symbol] (TTSB) .... BCYR

Bucyrus, OH [AM radio station call letters] .... WBCO

Bucyrus, OH [FM radio station call letters] .... WQEL

Bucyrus-Erie Co. [NASDAQ symbol] (SAG) .... BCYR

Bucyrus-Erie Co. .... BE

Bucyrus-Erie Co. [Associated Press] (SAG) .... BucyEr

Bud Collins' Modern Encyclopedia of Tennis [A publication] .... BCMET

Budakeszi [Hungary] [Later, TYH] [Geomagnetic observatory code] .... BUZ

Budapest [Hungary] [Airport symbol] (OAG) .... BUD

Budapest [Hungary] [Seismograph station code, US Geological Survey] (SEIS) .... BUD

Budapest (BARN) .... Budpst

Budapest [Hungary] [ICAO location identifier] (ICLI) .... LHAA

Budapest [Hungary] [ICAO location identifier] (ICLI) .... LHCC

Budapest/Ferihegy [Hungary] [ICAO location identifier] (ICLI) .... LHBP

Budd Canada, Inc. [Toronto Stock Exchange symbol] .... BUD

Budd Co., Fort Washington, PA [Library symbol Library of Congress] (LCLS) .... PFwB

Budd-Chiari Syndrome [Medicine] .... BCS

Buddhism .... BUDD

Buddhist Center of the United States of America (EA) .... BCUSA

Buddhist Churches of America Federation of Buddhist Women's Associations (EA) .... BCAFBWA

Buddhist Council for Refugee Rescue and Resettlement (EA) .... BCRRR

Buddhist Era .... BE

Buddhist Foundation of Victoria [Australia] .... BFV

Buddhist Peace Fellowship (EA) .... BPF

Buddhist Publication Society [Multinational association based in Sri Lanka] (EAIO) .... BPS

[The] Buddhist Society [British] (EAIO) .... TBS

Buddhist Society of Compassionate Wisdom [Canada] (EAIO) .... BSCW

Buddhist Society of New South Wales [Australia] .... BSNSW

Buddhist Society of Queensland [Australia] .... BSQ

Buddhist Text Translation Society (EA) .... BTTS

Buddhist Union of Europe (EAIO) .... BUE

Buddhist Vihara Society (EA) .... BVS

Buddhists Concerned for Animals [Defunct] (EA) .... BCA

Budding Uninhibited by Benzimidazole [Cytology] .... BUB

Buddy .... BDDY

Buddy Clark Fan Club [Defunct] (EA) .... BCFC

Buddy DeFranco Appreciation Society (EA) .... BDAS

Buddy Holly and the Crickets Fan Club (EAIO) .... BHCFC

Buddy Holly Memorial Society (EA) .... BHMS

Buddy Max Fan Club (EA) .... BMFC

Buddy Rich Fan Club (EA) .... BRFC

Buddy Secondary Life Support System [Aerospace] .... BSLSS

Bude, MS [FM radio station call letters] .... WMAU

Bude, MS [Television station call letters] .... WMAU-TV

Budgerigar (ODBW) .... budgie

Budgerigar Society [British] (DBA) .... BS

Budgerigar Society of Australia .... BSA

Budget (DLA) .... B

Budget .... BGT

Budget (ODBW) .... bud

Budget (AFM) .... BUD

Budget, Accounting, and Finance (AFM) .... BA & F

Budget Accounting Information System [IBM Corp.] .... BACIS

Budget Activity [Navy] .... BA

Budget Activity Account [Army] (AABC) .... BAA

Budget Adjustment Request .... BAR

Budget Advisory Board (SAA) .... BAB

Budget Advisory Committee [Army] .... BAC

Budget Allocation Notice (MCD) .... BAN

Budget Allocation Sheets (MCD) .... BAS

Budget Allocation Summary (MCD) .... BAS

Budget Analysis and Review Committee [American Library Association] ..... BARC

Budget Analysis Reporting System (MCD) .... BARS

Budget and Accounting Officer [Military] .... BAO

Budget and Finance Division [NATO] (NATG) .... BUDFIN

Budget and Forecast Calendarization [Accounting] .... BFC

Budget and Manpower Guidance [Military] (AABC) .... BMG

Budget and Program Resources Review [Army] .... BAPRR

Budget and Reporting (NRCH) .... B & R

Budget at Completion (MCD) .... BAC

Budget at Completion Variance (MCD) .... BACV

Budget Authority [Office of Management and Budget] .... BA

Budget Authorization [Air Force] (AFM) .... BA

Budget Authorization Account Number [Air Force] (AFM) .... BAAN

Budget Authorization and Updating Form (MCD) .... BAUF

Budget Center (MCD) .... BC

Budget Change Document [Accounting] (SSD) .... BCD

Budget Change Proposal [Accounting] .... BCP

Budget Change Request [Accounting] (MCD) .... BCR

Budget Classification Code (NVT) .... BCC

Budget Code [Air Force] (AFIT) .... BC

Budget/Cost Account Plan (MCD) .... BCAP

Budget Division [Environmental Protection Agency] (GFGA) .... BD

Budget Enactment Instruction .... BEI

Budget Enforcement Act [1990] .... BEA

Budget Enhancement Act (AAGC) .... BEA

Budget Estimate Guidance [Military] .... BEG

Budget Estimate Submission [DoD] .... BES

Budget Estimates Presentation Instructions (AFM) .... BEPI

Budget Execution [Army] (AABC) .... BEXEC

Budget Execution Appropriation Maintenance System [Military] .... BEAMS

Budget Execution Code .... BEC

Budget Execution Plan [Army] .... BEP

Budget Execution Review [Army] (AABC) .... BER

Budget Executives Institute [Later, PEI] (EA) .... BEI

Budget Fiscal Year .... BFY

Budget Formulation [Army] (AABC) .... BFORM

Budget Formulation and Appropriation Model (MCD) .... BFAM

Budget Formulation Directive [Military] (AABC) .... BFD

Budget Formulation Office, Office of the Director of the Army Budget .... BFOODAB

Budget Furniture Forum [Later, ROFF] (EA) .... BFF

Budget Increment Package [DoD] .... BIP

Budget Information for the States [Office of Management and Budget] (GFGA) .... BIS

Budget Information Form (OICC) .... BIF

Budget Line Item Number (MCD) .... BLIN

Budget Management System .... BMS

Budget Obligation [or Overlay] (NRCH) .... B/O

Budget Office [Army] .... BUD

Budget Office, Department of the Army (AAGC) .... BUD

Budget Office, War Department [World War II] .... BOWD

Budget Preparation System Master File [Office of Management and Budget] (GFGA) .... BPS

Budget Program [DoD] (GFGA) .... BP

Budget Program Activity Code .... BPAC

Budget Program Activity Code Material Program Code (MCD) .... BPAC/MPC

Budget Program Estimate (MCD) .... BPE

Budget Project [Navy] (CAAL) .... BP

Budget Project Account [Military] (AABC) .... BPA

Budget Project Number [Navy] .... BPN

Budget Project Officer [Navy] (DNAB) .... BPO

Budget Project Symbol Number (AFM) .... BPSN

Budget Related Papers .... BRP

Budget Review Committee .... BRC

Budget Review Group (IAA) .... BRG

Budget System .... BUSY

Budget Tracking System .... BTS

Budget Workload Analysis Report [Navy] (NG) .... BWAR

Budget Workload Indicators .... BWI

Budget Year (AFM) .... BY

Budgetaire, Comptable, et Financier [Budget, Accounting, and Finance - BA & F] .... BCF

Budgetary and Planning (NASA) .... B & P

Budgetary and Planning Quotations (MCD) .... BPQ

Budgetary and Scheduling Information System (MCD) .... BASIS

Budgetary Control (DCTA) .... BC

Budgetary Cost Information [Accounting] .... BCI

Budgetary Policy .... BP

Budgeted Actual Cost .... BAC

Budgeted Cost (ADA) .... BC

Budgeted Cost at Completion (AAGC) .... BAC

Budgeted Cost for Work Performed .... BCWP

Budgeted Cost for Work Scheduled .... BCWS

Budget-Funded Agency .... BFA

Budhana Ligo Esperantista [Buddhist League of Esperantists - BLE] [Germany] (EAIO) .... BLE

Budingen [Germany ICAO location identifier] (ICLI) .... EDEP

Budkov [Czechoslovakia] [Geomagnetic observatory code] .... BDV

Budleigh [England] .... BUDL

Budoia [Papua New Guinea] [Seismograph station code, US Geological Survey] (SEIS) .... BDO

Bueckeburg [Germany ICAO location identifier] (ICLI) .... EDCB

Buecker Flugzeugbau GmbH & Hagglund-Soner [Germany ICAO aircraft manufacturer identifier] (ICAO) .... BC

Buehlerhoehe [Federal Republic of Germany] [Seismograph station code, US Geological Survey] (SEIS) .... BUH

Buena Hora [Bolivia] [ICAO location identifier] (ICLI) .... SLBH

Buena Park, CA [FM radio station call letters] .... KBPK

Buena Park Library District Library, Buena Park, CA [Library symbol Library of Congress] (LCLS) .... CBp

Buena Vista [Guatemala] [Seismograph station code, US Geological Survey] (SEIS) .... BVA

Buena Vista [Bolivia] [ICAO location identifier] (ICLI) .... SLBW

Buena Vista, CO [AM radio station call letters] .... KDMN

Buena Vista College [Storm Lake, IA] .... BVC

Buena Vista College, Storm Lake, IA [Library symbol Library of Congress] (LCLS) .... IaSIB

Buena Vista College, Storm Lake, IA [OCLC symbol] (OCLC) .... IOE

Buena Vista Public Library, Buena Vista, CO [Library symbol Library of Congress] (LCLS) .... CoBue

Buena Vista, VA [FM radio station call letters] .... WREL

Buenaventura [Colombia] [Airport symbol] (AD) .... BUN

Buenaventura [Colorado ICAO location identifier] (ICLI) .... SKBU

Buenavista, Agusan [*Philippines*] [*ICAO location identifier*] (ICLI) .... RPWV
Buenos Aires [*Argentina*] .... BA
Buenos Aires [*Argentina*] [*Seismograph station code, US Geological Survey*] (SEIS) .... BAA
Buenos Aires [*Argentina*] [*Airport symbol*] (OAG) .... BUE
Buenos Aires [*Costa Rica*] [*ICAO location identifier*] (ICLI) .... MRBA
Buenos Aires [*Argentina ICAO location identifier*] (ICLI) .... SABA
Buenos Aires/Aeroparque, Jorge Newbery [*Argentina ICAO location identifier*] (ICLI) .... SABE
Buenos Aires/Don Torcuato [*Argentina ICAO location identifier*] (ICLI) ... SADD
Buenos Aires (Edificio Condor) [*Argentina ICAO location identifier*] (ICLI) .... SABC
Buenos Aires Embotell'a [*NYSE symbol*] (SPSG) .... BAE
Buenos Aires Embotell'a ADS [*NYSE symbol*] (TTSB) .... BAE
Buenos Aires Embotelladora [*Commercial firm Associated Press*] (SAG) ... BAEmb
Buenos Aires [*Argentina*] Ezeiza [*Airport symbol*] (OAG) .... EZE
Buenos Aires [*Argentina*]/Ezeiza [*Argentina ICAO location identifier*] (ICLI) .... SAEZ
Buenos Aires [*Argentina*] Jorge Newbery Airport [*Airport symbol*] (OAG) .... AEP
Buenos Aires (Servicio Meteorologico Nacional) [*Argentina ICAO location identifier*] (ICLI) .... SABM
Buergerinitiative Parlament [*Citizens' Parliamentary Initiative*] [*Austria Political party*] (EY) .... BIP
Buergerinitiativen [*Citizens' action groups*] [*Germany*] .... BI's
Buergerpartei [*Citizens' Party*] [*Germany Political party*] (PPE) .... BP
Buergerpartei [*Citizens' Party*] [*Germany Political party*] (PPW) .... BPa
Buestenhalter [*Brassiere*] [*German slang*] .... BH
Bufete Industrial [*Associated Press*] (SAG) .... Bufete
Bufete Industrial SA [*NYSE symbol*] (SPSG) .... GBI
Buff and Polishing Wheel Manufacturers Association [*Defunct*] .... BPWMA
Buff Polish [*Optics*] .... BP
Buffalo (WDAA) .... BFO
Buffalo [*New York*] [*Seismograph station code, US Geological Survey Closed*] (SEIS) .... BUF
Buffalo [*Rat variety*] .... BUF
Buffalo [*New York*] [*Airport symbol*] .... BUF
Buffalo .... BUFF
Buffalo Airways [*ICAO designator*] (FAAC) .... BVA
Buffalo Airways Ltd. [*Canada ICAO designator*] (FAAC) .... BFL
Buffalo and Erie County Historical Society, Buffalo, NY [*Library symbol Library of Congress*] (LCLS) .... NBuHi
Buffalo and Erie County Public Library, Buffalo, NY [*Library symbol Library of Congress*] (LCLS) .... NBu
Buffalo and Erie County Public Library, Buffalo, NY [*Library symbol*] [*Library of Congress*] (LCLS) .... NBuBE
Buffalo and Erie County Public Library, Buffalo, NY [*OCLC symbol*] (OCLC) .... VHB
Buffalo Bill Historical Center (EA) .... BBHC
Buffalo Bill Museum, Cody, WY [*Library symbol Library of Congress*] (LCLS) .... WyCoB
Buffalo Center Tribune, Buffalo Center, IA [*Library symbol Library of Congress*] (LCLS) .... IaBucCT
Buffalo City School District, Buffalo, NY [*Library symbol*] [*Library of Congress*] (LCLS) .... NBuSD
Buffalo Color Corp., Buffalo, NY [*Library symbol Library of Congress*] (LCLS) .... NBuCo
Buffalo Columbus Hospital, Buffalo, NY [*Library symbol*] [*Library of Congress*] (LCLS) .... NBuCoH
[*The*] Buffalo Creek Railroad Co. [*Absorbed into Consolidated Rail Corp.*] [*AAR code*] .... BCK
Buffalo Express Airlines, Inc. [*ICAO designator*] (FAAC) .... BRX
Buffalo Gap, VA [*FM radio station call letters*] (RBYB) .... WZXI
Buffalo General Hospital, Buffalo, NY [*Library symbol Library of Congress*] (LCLS) .... NBuGH
Buffalo General Hospital, School of Nursing, Buffalo, NY [*Library symbol Library of Congress*] (LCLS) .... NBuGH-N
Buffalo/Greater Buffalo International [*New York*] [*ICAO location identifier*] (ICLI) .... KBUF
Buffalo Head Prairie School, Alberta [*Library symbol National Library of Canada*] (BIB) .... ABHPS
Buffalo Intermediate School, Buffalo, MN [*Library symbol*] [*Library of Congress*] (LCLS) .... MnBfI
Buffalo Junior High School, Buffalo, MN [*Library symbol*] [*Library of Congress*] (LCLS) .... MnBfJ
Buffalo, KY [*AM radio station call letters*] .... WXAM
Buffalo - Larkin [*New York*] [*Seismograph station code, US Geological Survey Closed*] (SEIS) .... BFF
Buffalo Memorial Hospital, Medical Library, Buffalo, MN [*Library symbol*] [*Library of Congress*] (LCLS) .... MnBfH
Buffalo, MN [*AM radio station call letters*] .... KRWC
Buffalo, MO [*FM radio station call letters*] .... KBFL
Buffalo Narrows [*Canada*] [*Airport symbol Obsolete*] (OAG) .... YVT
Buffalo Narrows Public Library, Buffalo Narrows, SK, Canada [*Library symbol*] [*Library of Congress*] (LCLS) .... CaSBuN
Buffalo Narrows Public Library, Saskatchewan [*Library symbol National Library of Canada*] (NLC) .... SBN
Buffalo Narrows, SK [*ICAO location identifier*] (ICLI) .... CYVT
Buffalo, NY [*Location identifier FAA*] (FAAL) .... GBI
Buffalo, NY [*AM radio station call letters*] .... WBEN
Buffalo, NY [*FM radio station call letters*] .... WBFO
Buffalo, NY [*FM radio station call letters*] .... WBNY
Buffalo, NY [*FM radio station call letters*] .... WDCX
Buffalo, NY [*FM radio station call letters*] (RBYB) .... WEDG
Buffalo, NY [*FM radio station call letters*] .... WFBF
Buffalo, NY [*AM radio station call letters*] .... WGR
Buffalo, NY [*FM radio station call letters*] .... WGRF
Buffalo, NY [*Television station call letters*] .... WGRZ

Buffalo, NY [*AM radio station call letters*] .... WHTT
Buffalo, NY [*FM radio station call letters*] .... WHTT-FM
Buffalo, NY [*Television station call letters*] .... WIVB
Buffalo, NY [*FM radio station call letters*] .... WJYE
Buffalo, NY [*Television station call letters*] .... WKBW
Buffalo, NY [*FM radio station call letters*] .... WMJQ
Buffalo, NY [*AM radio station call letters*] .... WNED
Buffalo, NY [*FM radio station call letters*] .... WNED-FM
Buffalo, NY [*Television station call letters*] .... WNED-TV
Buffalo, NY [*Television station call letters*] .... WNEQ
Buffalo, NY [*Television station call letters*] .... WNYB
Buffalo, NY [*TV station call letters*] (RBYB) .... WNYO-TV
Buffalo, NY [*FM radio station call letters*] (RBYB) .... WSJZ-FM
Buffalo, NY [*Television station call letters*] .... WUTV
Buffalo, NY [*AM radio station call letters*] .... WWKB
Buffalo, NY [*AM radio station call letters*] .... WWWS
Buffalo, NY [*FM radio station call letters*] .... WYRK
Buffalo, OK [*Location identifier FAA*] (FAAL) .... BFK
Buffalo Organization for Social and Technological Innovation (EA) .... BOSTI
Buffalo Organization for Social and Technological Innovation, Inc. (BOSTI), Buffalo, NY [*Library symbol Library of Congress*] (LCLS) .... NBuBO
Buffalo Orphan Prototype [*Medicine*] (MAE) .... BOP
Buffalo Primary Library, Buffalo, MN [*Library symbol*] [*Library of Congress*] (LCLS) .... MnBfP
Buffalo Psychiatric Center, Buffalo, NY [*Library symbol Library of Congress*] (LCLS) .... NBuPC
Buffalo Public Library, Buffalo, MN [*Library symbol*] [*Library of Congress*] (LCLS) .... MnBf
Buffalo Range [*Zimbabwe*] [*Airport symbol*] (OAG) .... BFO
Buffalo Rat Liver [*Cytology*] .... BRL
Buffalo Resources [*Vancouver Stock Exchange symbol*] .... BUF
Buffalo Ridge Baptist Academy, Lake Benton, MN [*Library symbol*] [*Library of Congress*] (LCLS) .... MnLbBa
Buffalo, Rochester & Pittsburg Railway [*Terminated*] .... BR & PRY
Buffalo, Rochester & Pittsburgh Railroad .... BR & P
Buffalo Sabres Booster Club (EA) .... BSBC
Buffalo, SD [*Location identifier FAA*] (FAAL) .... BUA
Buffalo Senior High School, Buffalo, MN [*Library symbol*] [*Library of Congress*] (LCLS) .... MnBfS
Buffalo Society of Natural Sciences, Buffalo Museum of Science, Buffalo, NY [*Library symbol Library of Congress*] (LCLS) .... NBuB
Buffalo, Union-Carolina Railroad (IIA) .... BUC
Buffalo, WY [*Location identifier FAA*] (FAAL) .... BYG
Buffalo, WY [*AM radio station call letters*] .... KBBS
Buffalo, WY [*FM radio station call letters*] .... KLGT
Buffelsfontein Gold Mines Ltd. [*NASDAQ symbol*] (SAG) .... BLGM
Buffelsfontein Gold Mines Ltd. [*Associated Press*] (SAG) .... Buff ADR
Buffelsfontein Gold Mining Co. [*Associated Press*] (SAG) .... Buffels
Buffelsfontein Gold Mining Co. Ltd. [*NASDAQ symbol*] (NQ) .... BFEL
Buffer [*Computer science*] (TEL) .... B
Buffer [*Computer science*] (MSA) .... BFR
Buffer [*Computer science*] .... BUF
Buffer (NASA) .... BUFF
Buffer Access Card [*Computer science*] (NASA) .... BAC
Buffer Address Array [*Computer science*] (IAA) .... BAA
Buffer Address Register [*Computer science*] .... BAR
Buffer Amplifier [*Computer science*] .... BA
Buffer Base (MAE) .... BB
Buffer Cell (IAA) .... BC
Buffer Control Junction Switch [*Computer science*] .... BCJS
Buffer Control Register (NITA) .... BCR
Buffer Control Unit [*Computer science*] (CET) .... BCU
Buffer Control Word [*Computer science*] .... BCW
Buffer Cycle (IAA) .... BC
Buffer Index [*Computer science*] .... BI
Buffer Input/Output Processor [*Computer science*] (NITA) .... BIOP
Buffer Input-Output Memory [*Computer science*] .... BIOM
Buffer Interface Unit [*Computer science*] (NASA) .... BIU
Buffer Map [*Computer science*] (NASA) .... BMAP
Buffer Mark [*Computer science*] (IAA) .... BM
Buffer Memory .... BM
Buffer Module [*Computer science*] .... BM
Buffer/Multiplexer [*Computer science*] (CET) .... B/M
Buffer Register [*Computer science*] .... BR
Buffer Register Under Computer Edict [*Computer science*] (PDAA) .... BRUCE
Buffer Stock Financing Facility [*International Monetary Fund*] .... BSFF
Buffer Word Counter [*Computer science*] .... BWC
Buffered [*Medicine*] .... BF
Buffered Azide Glucose Glycerol [*Broth*] [*Microbiology*] .... BAGG
Buffered Block Channel (MCD) .... BBC
Buffered Communications Adapter [*Computer science*] (IAA) .... BCA
Buffered Data and Control Bus .... BDCB
Buffered Data Transmission Simulator .... BDTS
Buffered Deoxycholate Glucose [*Broth*] [*Microbiology*] .... BDG
Buffered Desoxycholate Glucose [*Agar or broth*] [*Biochemistry*] (DAVI) ...... BDG
Buffered Direct Injection (IAA) .... BDI
Buffered Distilled Water [*Chemistry*] .... BDW
Buffered Emitter Follower .... BEF
Buffered FET [*Field Effect Transistor*] Logic [*Integrated circuitry*] .... BFL
Buffered Filtered Seawater .... BFSW
Buffered Flip-Flop [*Computer science*] .... BFF
Buffered Input/Output [*Computer science*] (NITA) .... BIO
Buffered Magnetic Tape Transfer [*Computer science*] (NITA) .... BMTT
Buffered Magnetic Tape Transport [*Computer science*] (OA) .... BMTT
Buffered Printing .... BP

Buffered Pyrophosphatase Activity [*Chemistry*] ... BPA
Buffered Remote Interactive Search Console (PDAA) ... BRISC
Buffered Ringer's Solution [*Medicine*] ... BFR
Buffered Ringer's Solution [*Medicine*] (CPH) ... BFR Sol
Buffered Saline Solution (AAMN) ... BSS
Buffered Selector Channel ... BSELCH
Buffered Send/Receive ... BSR
Buffered Terminal Multiplexer [*Computer science*] (IAA) ... BTM
Buffered-Saline/Glucose [*Clinical chemistry*] ... BSG
Buffet and Bull [*Slang for a political dinner*] ... B & B
Buffets, Inc. [*NASDAQ symbol*] (NQ) ... BOCB
Buffets, Inc. [*Associated Press*] (SAG) ... Buffets
Buffing (MSA) ... BFG
Buffoons of America (EA) ... BA
Buffton Corp. [*AMEX symbol*] (SPSG) ... BFX
Buffton Corp. [*Associated Press*] (SAG) ... Buffton
Buford, GA [*FM radio station call letters*] ... WLKQ
Buford, GA [*AM radio station call letters*] ... WXEM
Buford's Boosters Fan Club (EA) ... BBFC
Bug (DSUE) ... B
Bug Off [*Slang*] ... BO
Bugaboo Creek Steak House [*Associated Press*] (SAG) ... BugCreek
Bugaboo Creek Steak House [*NASDAQ symbol*] (SAG) ... RARE
Bugatti [*Automobile*] ... BUG
Bug-Eyed Monster [*Science fiction or fantastic literature which makes great use of monsters in its storyline or illustrations*] ... BEM
Bugger All [*Slang British*] (DSUE) ... BA
Buginarium [*Nasal Bougie*] [*Pharmacy*] ... BUGINAR
Buglemaster [*Navy*] ... BGM
Buglemaster ... BGMSTR
Bugler [*British military*] (DMA) ... B
Bugler ... BGLR
Bugler ... BR
Bugler [*Navy*] ... BUG
Buhasa [*United Arab Emirates*] [*ICAO location identifier*] (ICLI) ... OMAB
Buhl, MN [*FM radio station call letters*] (RBYB) ... WIRN-FM
Buhl Public Library, Buhl, ID [*Library symbol*] [*Library of Congress*] (LCLS) ... IdBuh
Buhl Public Library, Buhl, MN [*Library symbol*] [*Library of Congress*] (LCLS) ... MnBul
Buia [*Italy*] [*Seismograph station code, US Geological Survey*] (SEIS) ... BUII
BUIC [*Backup Interceptor Control*] **NOPAD Control Center** ... BNCC
Buick Club of America (EA) ... BCA
Buick Collector's Club of America [*Defunct*] ... BCCA
Buick Compact Club [*Defunct*] (EA) ... BCC
Buick Compact Club of America [*Later, BCC*] (EA) ... BCCA
Buick GS [*Gran Sport*] **Club of America** (EA) ... BGSCA
Buick Motor Division [*General Motors Corp.*] ... BMD
Buick-Oldsmobile-Cadillac Group [*General Motors Corp.*] ... BOC
Buick-Oldsmobile-Pontiac [*General Motors Corp.*] ... BOP
Buie's Creek, NC [*FM radio station call letters*] ... WCCE
Build (DNAB) ... BLD
Build Absolutely Nothing Anywhere Near Anything [*Facetious successor to NIMBY*] ... BANANA
Build Ada Main Program [*Computer science*] ... BAMP
Build and Blood Pressure Study [*Society of Actuaries*] ... BBPS
Build, Operate, Transfer [*Business term*] ... BOT
Build Options, Renew Norms, Free Roles through Educational Equity [*National project to help students choose appropriate future careers*] ... BORN FREE
Build Out Capacitor [*Telecommunications*] (TEL) ... BOC
Build Out Lattice [*Telecommunications*] (TEL) ... BOL
Build, Own, Operate [*Property development*] ... BOO
Build, Own, Operate, Transfer [*Property development*] ... BOOT
Build, Own, Transfer [*Property development*] ... BOT
Builder ... BLDR
Builder (VRA) ... bldr
Builder ... BLDR
Builder [*Navy rating*] ... BU
Builder, Concrete [*Navy rating*] ... BUR
Builder, Constructionman (DNAB) ... BUCN
Builder, First Class [*Navy rating*] ... BU1
Builder, Heavy [*Navy rating*] ... BUH
Builder, Light [*Navy rating*] ... BUL
Builder, Second Class [*Navy rating*] ... BU2
Builder, Third Class [*Navy rating*] ... BU3
Builder's and Sponsor's Profit and Risk Allowance [*Department of Housing and Urban Development*] (GFGA) ... BSPRA
Builders Association of Minnesota (SRA) ... BAM
Builders Association of Missouri (SRA) ... BAM
Builders' Benevolent Institution [*British*] (BI) ... BBI
Builders' Exchange Association of Texas (SRA) ... BX
Builders Exchange of Detroit and Michigan (EA) ... BEDM
Builders' Hardware Manufacturers Association (EA) ... BHMA
Builders Hardware Manufacturers Association, Inc. (AAGC) ... BHMA
Builders Hardware Manufacturers Association of Canada [*Association Canadienne des Fabricants de Quincaillerie de Batiment*] (AC) ... BHMAC
Builders of Greater Britain [*A publication*] ... BGB
Builders Old Measurement ... BOM
Builders' Registration Board of Western Australia [*Australia*] ... BRBWA
Builder's Risk [*Insurance*] ... BR
Builders Supply Association of West Virginia (SRA) ... BSA-WV
Builders Transport [*NASDAQ symbol*] (TTSB) ... TRUK
Builders Transport, Inc. [*Associated Press*] (SAG) ... BuildT
Builders Transport, Inc. [*NASDAQ symbol*] (NQ) ... TRUK
Builder's Trials [*Shipbuilding*] ... BT
Builders Warehouse Assn [*NASDAQ symbol*] (TTSB) ... BWAI
Builders Warehouse Association, Inc. [*Associated Press*] (SAG) ... BldrWr
Builders Warehouse Association, Inc. [*NASDAQ symbol*] (SAG) ... BWAI
Building (ADA) ... B
Building (ADA) ... BDG
Building (NATG) ... BLD
Building (AFM) ... BLDG
Building (DD) ... bldg
Building ... BLDG
Building ... BLG
Building (ROG) ... BUILD
Building Access Card [*Issued to Senate staff members to ensure security in the Capitol*] ... BAC
Building Advisor [*Red Cross Disaster Services*] ... BA
Building Advisory Committee ... BAC
Building Advisory Service [*British*] (BI) ... BAS
Building and Civil Engineer [*British*] ... B & CE
Building and Construction Contracts [*A publication*] (DLA) ... Bldg Contr
Building and Construction Council, New South Wales [*Australia*] ... BCCNSW
Building and Construction Industry Council [*Australia*] ... BCIC
Building and Construction Industry Long Service Leave Board [*Australia*] ... BCILSB
Building and Construction Law [*Australia A publication*] ... BCL
Building and Construction Trades Council - North Dakota (SRA) ... BCTC-ND
Building and Construction Trades Council of Delaware (SRA) ... BCTCD
Building and Construction Trades Department [*AFL-CIO*] ... BCTD
Building and Contents [*Insurance*] ... B & C
Building and Engineering [*British*] ... B & E
Building and Engineering Journal [*A publication*] ... Building & Eng J
Building and Loan ... B & L
Building and Loan Association (DLA) ... B & L
Building and Monument Workers Association of Scotland [*A union*] ... BMWAS
Building and Repair [*Red Cross Disaster Services*] ... B and R
Building and Safety Engineering ... BSE
Building and Service Industry ... B & SI
Building and Social Housing Foundation [*British*] ... BSHF
Building Better Boards for Community Organizations Project [*American Association of Community and Junior Colleges*] (EDAC) ... BBB
Building Block (KSC) ... BB
Building Block Concept [*Army-ROAD concept*] ... BBC
Building Block Monochromator ... BBM
Building Block Oriented Language [*Computer science*] (PDAA) ... BBOL
Building Block Principle ... BBP
Building Block Signal Processor [*Computer science*] (MHDI) ... BBSP
Building Block System ... BBS
Building Board Manufacturers Association (PDAA) ... BBMA
Building Center Trust (PDAA) ... BCT
Building Code (DAC) ... BC
Building Conservation Trust [*An association*] (DBA) ... BCT
Building Construction Materials and Equipment [*A publication*] (ADA) ... BCME
Building Contractors Association of New Jersey (SRA) ... BCANJ
Building Control Accreditation Authority [*Victoria, Australia*] ... BCAA
Building Control Qualifications Board [*Victoria, Australia*] ... BCQB
Building Control Technical Advisory Council [*Victoria, Australia*] ... BCTAC
Building Cost Information Service [*Royal Institute of Chartered Surveyors*] [*Information service or system*] (IID) ... BCIS
Building Density (SAA) ... BD
Building Description Language ... BDL
Building Design Association of South Australia ... BDASA
Building Design System [*Applied Research of Cambridge Ltd.*] [*Software package*] (NCC) ... BDS
Building Disputes Tribunal [*Australia*] ... BDT
Building Distribution Frame [*Telecommunications*] (NITA) ... BDF
Building Economic Alternatives [*Co-Op America*] [*A publication*] ... BEA
Building Employers' Confederation [*A union*] [*British*] ... BEC
Building Energy Performance Standards ... BEPS
Building Energy Systems Analysis Project [*Public Works Canada*] ... BESA
Building Energy Utilization Laboratory [*Iowa State University*] [*Research center*] (RCD) ... BEUL
Building Engineer (HGAA) ... BIDGE
Building Engineer ... Bldg E
Building Envelope Council of Ottawa Region (AC) ... BECOR
Building Equipment Accessories and Materials [*Program*] [*Canada*] ... BEAM
Building Fire Safety Committee [*South Australia*] ... BFSC
Building Industry Advisory Council [*Australia*] ... BIAC
Building Industry Association (ECON) ... BI
Building Industry Association (SRA) ... BIA
Building Industry Association of Hawaii (SRA) ... BIA-HI
Building Industry Association of Washington (SRA) ... BIAW
Building Industry Consulting Service [*Telecommunications*] (TEL) ... BICS
Building Industry Consulting Service International [*Tampa, FL*] [*Telecommunications service*] ... BICSI
Building Industry Development Services ... BIDS
Building Industry Employers of New York State (SRA) ... BIENYS
Building Information Centre [*Cauldon College of Further and Higher Education*] [*British*] (CB) ... BIC
Building Integrated Timing Supply (ACRL) ... BITS
Building Item Name Directory [*A publication*] ... BIND
Building Liaison Officer (ADA) ... BLO
Building Line [*Technical drawings*] ... BL
Building Loads Analysis and System Thermodynamics [*Computer program*] ... BLAST
Building Maintenance Employers Association [*Later, SEA*] (EA) ... BMEA
Building Maintenance Information Ltd. (DBA) ... BMI

Building Management Authority of Western Australia ... BMAWA
Building Management System (ACII) ... BMS
Building Management Systems (NITA) ... BMS
Building Material Exhibitors Association [*Defunct*] (EA) ... BMEA
Building Material Series [*National Institute of Standards and Technology*] ... BMS
Building Materials and Structures (SAA) ... BMS
Building Materials Export Group [*British*] (DS) ... BMEG
Building Merchants' Federation [*British*] ... BMF
Building Monitoring System (ADA) ... BMS
Building Officials and Code Administrators International (EA) ... BOCA
Building Officials Conference of America, Inc. ... BOCA
Building Optimization Program [*Computer science*] ... BOP
Building Out Section ... BOS
Building Owners and Managers Association International (EA) ... BOMA
Building Owners and Managers Association International ... BOMAI
Building Owners and Managers' Association of Australia ... BOMAA
Building Owners Federation of Mutual Insurance Companies [*Defunct*] (EA) ... BOF
Building Products Executives Conference ... BPEC
Building Products Ltd., Montreal, PQ, Canada [*Library symbol Library of Congress*] (LCLS) ... CaQMBP
Building Products Ltd., Montreal, Quebec [*Library symbol National Library of Canada*] (NLC) ... QMBP
Building Products Register [*American Institute of Architects*] ... BPR
Building Registration Board of Queensland [*Australia*] ... BRBQ
Building Regulation Review Task Force ... BRRTF
Building Regulations Advisory Committee [*British*] ... BRAC
Building Related Illness ... BRI
Building Renovating Association ... BRA
Building Research Advisory Board [*Later, ABBE*] [*National Academy of Sciences*] ... BRAB
Building Research Advisory Service [*Building Research Establishment*] [*Department of Industry*] [*British*] (DS) ... BRAS
Building Research Board (EA) ... BRB
Building Research Energy Conservation Support Unit [*British*] ... BRECSU
Building Research Energy Conservation Support Unit (AIE) ... BRESCU
Building Research Establishment [*Research center British*] (IRC) ... BRE
Building Research Establishment ... BRE
Building Research Institute [*Later, BRAB, ABBE*] (EA) ... BRI
Building Research Laboratory [*Ohio State University*] [*Research center*] (RCD) ... BRL
Building Research Station [*British*] ... BRS
Building Research Station News [*A publication*] ... BRS
Building Restriction Line [*FAA*] (TAG) ... BRL
Building Science Series [*National Institute of Standards and Technology*] ... BSS
Building Service Contractors Association International (EA) ... BSCA
Building Service Contractors Association International (EAIO) ... BSCAI
Building Service Employees' International Union [*Later, SEIU*] (EA) ... BSE
Building Service League [*Later, SEA*] (EA) ... BSL
Building Services Authority [*Queensland, Australia*] ... BSA
Building Services Calculations [*Amazon Computers*] [*Software package*] (NCC) ... BSC
Building Services Estimating [*Tipdata Ltd.*] [*Software package*] (NCC) ... BSE
Building Services Programs [*Amazon Computers*] [*Software package*] (NCC) ... BSP
Building Services Research and Information Association [*Information service or system*] (IID) ... BSRIA
Building Societies Act [*British*] ... BSA
Building Societies Association [*British*] ... BSA
Building Societies' Commission [*British*] ... BSC
Building Societies Database [*British*] ... BSD
Building Societies' Institute (BARN) ... BSI
Building Societies Members Association [*British*] (DBA) ... BSMA
Building Societies Ombudsman Scheme [*British*] ... BSOS
Building Society (ODBW) ... BS
Building Space Requirement (DAC) ... BSR
Building Stone Institute (EA) ... BSI
Building Supply Institute of Technology [*Canada*] ... BSIT
Building Systems Division [*Washington, DC Department of Energy*] (GRD) ... BSD
Building Systems Institute (EA) ... BSI
Building Thermal Envelope Systems and Materials ... BTESM
Building Trades Employers Association (SRA) ... BTEA
Building Use Studies [*Research firm*] [*British*] ... BUS
Building Utility Design System (MHDI) ... BUDS
Building Wake Factor [*Nuclear energy*] (NRCH) ... BWF
Building Waterproofers Association [*Defunct*] (EA) ... BWA
Building Woodwork [*Freight*] ... BLDG WDWRK
Building Workers' Industrial Union [*British*] ... BWIU
Building Workers' Industrial Union of Australia ... BWIUA
Building-Energy Management System ... BEMS
Buildings and Community Systems (EG) ... BCS
Buildings and Equipment Section [*Library Administration and Management Association*] ... BES
Buildings, Antennas, Spans, and Earth Formations [*Fixed-object parachuting*] ... BASE
Buildings Control Officer ... BUCO
Buildings Energy Technology Transfer Program [*Canada*] ... BETT
Buildings for College and University Libraries Committee [*Library Administration and Management Association*] [*American Library Association*] ... BCUL
Build-to-Order [*Compaq Computer Corp.*] [*Computer science*] ... BTO
Buildup (FAAC) ... BLDUP
Buildup (KSC) ... BU
Build-Up Control Organization [*Established to supervise flow of personnel and equipment to the Continent, immediately following Normandy invasion*] [*British World War II*] ... BUCO
Built (DAC) ... Bit
Built ... BLT
Built (BARN) ... blt
Built (ROG) ... BT
Built for British [*As suffix to plane designation*] ... B
Built on Mask [*Microlithography*] ... BOM
Built-Down [*Military*] (INF) ... BD
Built-In [*Classified advertising*] (ADA) ... B/I
Built-In ... BLTIN
Built-In Bit Error Rate [*Computer science*] ... BER
Built-In Breathing System ... BIBS
Built-In Cleaning Systems Institute [*Defunct*] (EA) ... BCSI
Built-In Diagnostic Equipment [*Analytical chemistry*] ... BIDE
Built-In Hold [*of countdown*] [*NASA*] (KSC) ... BIH
Built-In Light Beacon ... BILB
Built-In Logic Block Observer [*Computer science*] (MHDB) ... BILBO
Built-In Orderly Organized Knowledge [*Learning device*] ... BOOK
Built-In Self-Test ... BIST
Built-In Test [*or Testing*] [*Computer science*] ... BIT
Built-In Test/Built-In Test Equipment [*Military*] (RDA) ... BIT/BITE
Built-In Test Equipment ... BITE
Built-In Test System [*Military*] (CAAL) ... BITS
Built-In Unit (SSD) ... BIU
Built-In Variance (MCD) ... BIV
Built-in-Place Component [*Electronics*] ... BIPCO
Built-Up Cast Iron Propeller [*of a ship*] (DS) ... BCP
Built-Up Cast Steel Propeller [*of a ship*] (DS) ... BCSP
Built-Up Edge (MCD) ... BUE
Built-Up Low-Cost Advanced Titanium Structures (MCD) ... BLATS
Built-Up Roofing ... BUR
Buin [*Papua New Guinea*] [*Airport symbol*] (OAG) ... UBI
Buisson Ardent [*The Burning Bush*] [*Freemasonry*] ... BA
Bujumbura [*Burundi*] [*Airport symbol*] (OAG) ... BJM
Bujumbura [*Burundi*] [*ICAO location identifier*] (ICLI) ... HBBA
Buka Island [*Papua New Guinea*] [*Airport symbol*] (OAG) ... BUA
Bukavu [*Zaire*] [*Airport symbol*] (OAG) ... BKY
Bukavu/Kavumu [*Zaire*] [*ICAO location identifier*] (ICLI) ... FZMA
Bukhara [*Former USSR Airport symbol*] (OAG) ... BHK
Bukoba [*Tanzania*] [*Airport symbol*] (OAG) ... BKZ
Bukoba [*Tanzania*] [*ICAO location identifier*] (ICLI) ... HTBU
Bul Bul Academy of Fine Arts [*Dacca, Pakistan*] ... BAFA
Bula [*Indonesia*] [*ICAO location identifier*] (ICLI) ... WAPB
Bulan, Sorsogon [*Philippines*] [*ICAO location identifier*] (ICLI) ... RPUU
Bulape [*Zaire*] [*ICAO location identifier*] (ICLI) ... FZUL
Bulawayo [*Zimbabwe*] [*Seismograph station code, US Geological Survey*] (SEIS) ... BUL
Bulawayo [*Zimbabwe*] [*Airport symbol*] (OAG) ... BUQ
Bulawayo/Bulawayo [*Zimbabwe*] [*ICAO location identifier*] (ICLI) ... FVBU
Bulawayo/Induna [*Zimbabwe*] [*ICAO location identifier*] (ICLI) ... FVIN
Bulb ... B
Bulb and Time [*Photography*] ... B & T
Bulb Angle [*Shipfitting*] ... BA
Bulb Distributors' Association [*British*] (DBA) ... BDA
Bulbocavernosus [*Muscle group*] ... BC
Bulbocavernosus Activity [*Physiology*] ... BCA
Bulbocavernosus Reflex [*Medicine*] (DAVI) ... BCR
Bulbus Chordae [*Cardiology*] (DAVI) ... BC
Bulchi [*Ethiopia*] [*ICAO location identifier*] (ICLI) ... HABU
Bulford/Salisbury Plain [*British ICAO location identifier*] (ICLI) ... EGDS
Bulgaria [*ANSI two-letter standard code*] (CNC) ... BG
Bulgaria [*ANSI three-letter standard code*] (CNC) ... BGR
Bulgaria [*MARC country of publication*] [*Library of Congress*] (LCCP) ... bu
Bulgaria [*IYRU nationality code*] ... BU
Bulgaria (WDAA) ... BUL
Bulgaria ... BULG
Bulgaria (VRA) ... Bulg
Bulgaria [*MARC geographic area code Library of Congress*] (LCCP) ... e-bu--
Bulgaria [*License plate code assigned to foreign diplomats in the US*] ... QM
Bulgarian [*MARC language code Library of Congress*] (LCCP) ... bul
Bulgarian Agrarian Party [*Political party*] (PPW) ... BAP
Bulgarian Agrarian People's Party [*Political party*] (PPW) ... BAPP
Bulgarian Agrarian People's Union - Nikola Petkov [*Political party*] ... BAPU-NP
Bulgarian Agrarian People's Union-United [*Political party*] (EY) ... BAPU
Bulgarian Agrarian Union [*Political party*] ... BAU
Bulgarian Air Cargo [*ICAO designator*] (FAAC) ... BCA
Bulgarian Communist Party [*Bulgarska Komunisticheska Partiia*] [*Political party*] (PPW) ... BCP
Bulgarian Flying Cargo [*FAA designator*] (FAAC) ... BFB
Bulgarian Liberal Party [*Political party*] ... BLP
Bulgarian Lucky Flight [*ICAO designator*] (FAAC) ... BLF
Bulgarian National Committee (EA) ... BNC
Bulgarian National Front (EA) ... BNF
Bulgarian Socialist Labor Federation [*Defunct*] (EA) ... BSLF
Bulgarian Socialist Party [*Political party*] (EY) ... BSP
Bulgarian Telegraph Agency [*News agency*] ... BTA
Bulgarian Turkish Association of Australia ... BTAA
Bulgarska Komunisticheska Partiia [*Bulgarian Communist Party*] [*Political party*] (PPE) ... BKP
Bulgarska Rabotnicheska Partiia [*Bulgarian Workers Party*] [*Political party*] (PPE) ... BRP
Bulgarska Socialdemokraticheska Partiia [*Bulgarian Social Democratic Party*] [*Political party*] (PPE) ... BSDP

Bulgarska Telegrafna Agentsiya [*Bulgarian News Agency*] .... BTA
Bulgarski Naroden Zemedelski Suiuz [*Bulgarian National Agrarian Union*]
  (PPE) .... BNZS
Bulgarski Zemedelski Naroden Soyuz [*Bulgarian Agrarian People's Union-
  United*] [*Political party*] (EY) .... BZNS
Bulgarus de Bulgarinis [*Deceased, 1166*] [*Authority cited in pre-1607 legal
  work*] (DSA) .... B
Bulgarus de Bulgarinis [*Deceased, 1166*] [*Authority cited in pre-1607 legal
  work*] (DSA) .... Bu
Bulgarus de Bulgarinis [*Deceased, 1166*] [*Authority cited in pre-1607 legal
  work*] (DSA) .... Bul
Bulgarus de Bulgarinis [*Deceased, 1166*] [*Authority cited in pre-1607 legal
  work*] (DSA) .... Bulg
Bulimba [*Australia Airport symbol Obsolete*] (OAG) .... BIP
Bulimia, Anorexia Self-Help .... BASH
Bulimia Cognitive Distortions Scale [*Psychology*] (DMAA) .... BCDS
Bulimia Nervosa [*Medicine*] .... BN
Bulimia Test [*Personality development test*] [*Psychology*] .... BULIT
Bulimic Investigatory Test [*Psychology*] (DMAA) .... BITE
Bulk .... BLK
Bulk [*Substrate*] [*Electron device*] (MSA) .... BU
Bulk Acoustic Wave [*Physics*] .... BAW
Bulk Airmail .... BAM
Bulk Biomass Model [*Pisciculture*] .... BBM
Bulk Burning (IEEE) .... BB
Bulk Carrier [*Shipping*] (DS) .... BLK CAR
Bulk Carrier of 26,000 Deadweight Tons [*Shipping*] (DS) .... B 26
Bulk Carrier of 30,000 Deadweight Tons [*Shipping*] (DS) .... B 30
Bulk Carriers Conference, Arlington VA [*STAC*] .... BLK
Bulk/Common Items List (MCD) .... BCIL
Bulk Containers [*Shipping*] (DCTA) .... BK
Bulk Continuous Filament [*Textile science*] .... BCF
Bulk Copy Program [*Computer science*] (PCM) .... BCP
Bulk Core (MHDI) .... BC
Bulk Current Injection [*Electronics*] .... BCI
Bulk Data Processing (IAA) .... BDP
Bulk Data Switching .... BDS
Bulk Data Transfer Subsystem [*Telecommunications*] (TEL) ...... BDTS
Bulk Density (IAA) .... BD
Bulk Direct Mail Service (ADA) .... BDMS
Bulk Electronic Clearance System .... BECS
Bulk Filtering Acquisition and Tracking System (MCD) .... BATS
Bulk Freight Containers [*Shipping*] (DCTA) .... BU
Bulk Fuel Tank Assembly (MCD) .... BFTA
Bulk Function Transfer (PDAA) .... BFT
Bulk Grains Queensland [*An association Australia*] .... BGQ
Bulk Head .... BH
Bulk in Barrels [*Freight*] .... BLK B
Bulk Inland Petroleum, Oil, and Lubrication Transport (NATG) .. BIPOLT
Bulk Issue (ADA) .... BI
Bulk Items List .... BIL
Bulk Mail .... BM
Bulk Mail Center [*Postal Service*] .... BMC
Bulk Material Length (NRCH) .... BML
Bulk Media Conversion .... BMC
Bulk Modulus of Elasticity [*Symbol*] (DEN) .... k
Bulk Molding Compound .... BMC
Bulk Molding Compound [*Plastics technology*] .... BMMC
Bulk Negative Conductance [*Electronics*] (IAA) .... BNC
Bulk Negative Differential Conductivity [*Electronics*] (IAA) ...... BNDC
Bulk Oil Temperature (PDAA) .... BOT
Bulk Packaging and Containerization Institute [*Later, CII*] (EA) ... BPCI
Bulk Packed on Pallets [*Paper*] (DGA) .... BPOP
Bulk Packed on Pallets [*Paper*] (DGA) .... BPP
Bulk Petrol Co. [*British and Canadian*] [*Military*] .... BPC
Bulk Petroleum Facilities and Systems .... BPFS
Bulk Petroleum Management System .... BPMS
Bulk Petroleum Products .... BPP
Bulk Pharmaceutical Chemical [*Manufacturing*] .... BPC
Bulk Pharmaceutical Chemical [*Manufacturing Plant*] .... BPC
Bulk Polymerization Process [*Plastics technology*] .... BPP
Bulk Presorted Mail (ADA) .... BPSM
Bulk Rate Business Mail .... BBM
Bulk Resistance (IAA) .... BR
Bulk Semiconductor Limiter .... BSL
Bulk Shielding Facility [*ORNL*] .... BSF
Bulk Shielding Reactor .... BSR
Bulk Silicate Earth [*Biology*] .... BSE
Bulk Storage Device (IEEE) .... BSD
Bulk Storage System .... BSS
Bulk Store Memory Device (MCD) .... BSMD
Bulk Supply Tariff (MHDB) .... BST
Bulk Tainers [*Shipping*] (DS) .... Bk
Bulk Tape Degausser .... BTD
Bulk Tape Eraser .... BTE
Bulk Transfer Facility .... BTF
Bulk Transfer Hose .... BTH
Bulk Verification Services [*British*] .... BVS
Bulk Wet Density .... BWD
Bulk-Channel Charge-Coupled Device [*Electronics*] (TEL) .... BCCD
Bulk-Cohesion-Dipolarity-Elasticity [*Factor analysis of physical property data
  of liquid compounds*] .... BCDE
Bulked Continuous Fiber [*or Filament*] [*Textile*] .... BCF
Bulkhead (AAG) .... BHD
Bulkhead .... Bkhd

Bulkhead (MUGU) .... BLKD
Bulkhead (KSC) .... BLKHD
Bulkhead Connector .... BC
Bulkhead Jack .... BHJ
Bulkhead Jack .... BJ
Bulkhead Receptacle .... BHR
Bulkhead Receptacle .... BR
Bulky Mechanical [*Paper*] (DGA) .... BM
Bulky Mechanical Newsprint (DGA) .... BMN
Bull & Bear Group, Inc. [*NASDAQ symbol*] (NQ) .... BNBG
Bull & Bear Group, Inc. [*Associated Press*] (SAG) .... BullBear
Bull & Bear Group'A' [*NASDAQ symbol*] (TTSB) .... BNBGA
Bull & Bear Municipal Income Fund, Inc. [*AMEX symbol*] (SAG) .... BBM
Bull & Bear US Government Securities Fund [*AMEX symbol*] (SAG) ...... BBG
Bull Baffles Brains [*Bowdlerized version*] (DSUE) .... 3B's
Bull Elephants (EA) .... BE
Bull General Electric .... BGE
Bull HN [*Honeywell and NEC*] Information Systems Inc. [*Billerica, MA*]
  (CDE) .... Bull HN
Bull Nose .... BN
Bull Run Corp. [*NASDAQ symbol*] (NQ) .... BULL
Bull Run Corp. [*Associated Press*] (SAG) .... Bull Run
Bull Session [*Slang for a random conversation*] .... BS
Bull Terrier Club of America (EA) .... BTCA
Bullard and Curry's Louisiana Digest [*A publication*] (DLA) .... Bull & C Dig
Bullard and Curry's Louisiana Digest [*A publication*] (DLA) .... Bull & Cur Dig
Bullard-Sanford Public Library, Vassar, MI [*Library symbol Library of
  Congress*] (LCLS) .... MiVa
Bulldog Club of America (EA) .... BCA
Bulldozer [*Freight*] .... BDOZER
Bulldozer (MSA) .... BDZR
Bulldozing .... BLLDZG
Bulleid Pacific Preservation Society [*British*] (BI) .... BPPS
Bullen and Leake's Pleadings on Actions in King's Bench Decisions
  [*A publication*] (DLA) .... Bull & L
Bullen and Leake's Precedents of Pleading [*A publication*] (ILCA) .... B & L
Bullen and Leake's Precedents of Pleading [*A publication*] (DLA) .... B & L Pr
Bullen and Leake's Precedents of Pleading [*A publication*] (DLA) ..... Bull & L Pr
Buller and Bund's Manual of Bankruptcy [*A publication*] (DLA) .... Bull & B Bank
Buller's Law of Distress for Rent [*A publication*] (DLA) .... Bull Dis
Buller's Law of Nisi Prius [*England*] [*A publication*] (DLA) .... BNP
Buller's Law of Nisi Prius [*England*] [*A publication*] (DLA) ..... Bull NP
Buller's Law of Nisi Prius [*England*] [*A publication*] (DLA) .... Bull NP (Eng)
Buller's Law of Nisi Prius [*England*] [*A publication*] (DLA) .... Buller NP
Bullet .... BLLT
Bullet Dispersion Indicator .... BDI
Bullet Drop Compensator (DICI) .... BDC
Bullet Group, Inc. [*Formerly, Bullet Energy Ltd.*] [*Vancouver Stock Exchange
  symbol*] .... BUL
Bullet Hit Indicator (MCD) .... BHI
Bullet Path [*Ballistics*] .... BP
Bullet Sports International, Inc. [*Associated Press*] (SAG) .... BulletSp
Bullet Sports International, Inc. [*NASDAQ symbol*] (SAG) .... PARR
Bullet Sports Intl [*NASDAQ symbol*] (TTSB) .... PARR
Bulletin .... B
Bulletin .... BLLTN
Bulletin (WGA) .... BU
Bulletin (AFM) .... BUL
Bulletin .... BULL
Bulletin [*News*] [*Advertising*] (WDMC) .... bull
Bulletin (NTCM) .... BUN
Bulletin. American Academy of Psychiatry and the Law [*A publication*]
  (DLA) .... Bull Am Acad Psych & L
Bulletin. American Patent Law Association [*A publication*] (DLA) ...... APLA Bull
Bulletin. Anglo-Soviet Law Association [*A publication*] (DLA) ..... Bull Anglo-Sov LA
Bulletin Articles Information Subsystem [*Computer science*] .... BAIS
Bulletin. Association of the Bar of the City of New York [*A publication*]
  (DLA) .... New York City BA Bul
Bulletin. Association of the Bar of the City of New York [*A publication*]
  (DLA) .... NYCBA Bull
Bulletin. Australian Society of Legal Philosophy [*A publication*] .... BASLP
Bulletin Board [*Computer online message system*] .... BB
Bulletin Board (PCM) .... BB
Bulletin Board [*Technical drawings*] .... BBD
Bulletin Board for Libraries [*British*] .... BUBL
Bulletin Board Note Manager [*Prodigy offline reader*] .... BBNM
Bulletin Board Service .... BBS
Bulletin Board Systems [*Personal computer message network system*] ...... BBS
Bulletin. Committee on Criminal Courts' Law and Procedure. Association
  of the B ar. City of New York [*A publication*] (DLA) .... CCC Bull
Bulletin. Comparative Law Bureau [*A publication*] (DLA) .... Bulletin Comp L
Bulletin d'Epigraphie Semitique [*A publication*] (BJA) .... BES
Bulletin des Arrets de la Chambre Criminelle de la Cour de Cassation
  [*A publication*] (ILCA) .... Bull Crim
Bulletin des Assurances [*A publication*] (ILCA) .... BA
Bulletin Francais. Societe Internationale de Musique [*A publication*] ...... BSIM
Bulletin. Geological Survey of South Australia
  [*A publication*] .... Bull Geol Survey Sth Aust
Bulletin. Industrial Law Society [*A publication*] (DLA) .... Indust L Soc Bull
Bulletin. Institut Intermediaire International [*A publication*] (DLA) ...... Bull III
Bulletin. International Association of Law Libraries [*A publication*]
  (DLA) .... IALL Bull
Bulletin. International Bar Association [*A publication*] (DLA) .... Bull IBA
Bulletin. International Commission of Jurists [*A publication*] (DLA) ...... Bull ICJ

Bulletin International des Sciences Sociales [*A publication*] (DLA) ... Bull Int Sc Soc
Bulletin. International Law Association [*1936-38*] [*A publication*] (DLA) ... Int'l L Ass'n Bull
Bulletin. International Seismological Centre [*A publication*] ... BISC
Bulletin. John Rylands Library [*A publication*] (OCD) ... Bull Rylands Libr
Bulletin. Judge Advocate General of the Army [*United States*] [*A publication*] (DLA) ... Bull JAG
Bulletin Legislatif Dalloz [*A publication*] (ILCA) ... BLD
Bulletin. National Tax Association [*A publication*] (DLA) ... Bull Nat Tax Assoc
Bulletin. National Tax Association [*A publication*] (DLA) ... Bull NTA
Bulletin of Canadian Welfare Law [*A publication*] (DLA) ... Bull Can Welfare Law
Bulletin of Comparative Labour Relations [*A publication*] (DLA) ... Bull Comp Lab Rel
Bulletin of Czechoslovak Law [*A publication*] (DLA) ... Bull Czech L
Bulletin of Experimental Biology and Medicine [*A publication*] ... BEBIM
Bulletin of Law, Science, and Technology [*A publication*] (DLA) ... Bull L Science & Tech
Bulletin of Legal Developments [*A publication*] (DLA) ... Bull Leg Dev
Bulletin of Legal Developments [*A publication*] (DLA) ... Bull Legal Devel
Bulletin of Medieval Canon Law [*A publication*] (DLA) ... Bull Mediev Canon L
Bulletin of the Atomic Scientists [*A publication*] (BRI) ... BAS
Bulletin of the Judge Advocate General of the Army [*Now LAAWS BBS*] (AAGC) ... Bull JAGA
Bulletin of the National Research Council [*A publication*] (BARN) ... BNRC
Bulletin of the Philosophical Society of Washington [*A publication*] (BARN) ... BPSW
Bulletin Officiel des Annonces des Marches Publics [*Direction des Journaux Officiels*] [*Database*] ... BOAMP
Bulletin. Quebec Society of Criminology [*A publication*] (DLA) ... Bull Que Soc Crim
Bulletin. Societe "Union Musicologique" [*A publication*] ... BUM
Bulletin. Sydney Division. Institution of Engineers of Australia [*A publication*] ... Bull Syd Div Instn Eng Aust
Bulletin. United States Trademark Association Series [*A publication*] (DLA) ... Trademark Bull
Bulletin Usuel des Lois et Arretes [*A publication*] (ILCA) ... Bull Us
Bulletin with Newsweek [*A publication*] (APTA) ... B/N
Bulletin-Press, Sioux Rapids, IA [*Library symbol*] [*Library of Congress*] (LCLS) ... IaSrBP
Bulletins and Orders (NUCP) ... B and O
Bulletins and Orders Task Force [*Nuclear Regulatory Commission*] (NRCH) ... B & OTF
Bulletins of Ordnance Information ... BOI
Bulletproof [*Army*] (AABC) ... BPRF
Bullet-Trap Rifle Grenade [*Army*] (INF) ... BTRG
Bullhead City, AZ [*AM radio station call letters*] ... KBAS
Bullhead City, AZ [*AM radio station call letters*] ... KFLG
Bullhead City, AZ [*FM radio station call letters*] ... KFLG-FM
Bullhead City [*Arizona*]/Laughlin [*Nevada*] [*Airport symbol*] (OAG) ... BHC
Bulliat [*Let It Boil*] [*Pharmacy*] ... BULL
Bullientis [*Boiling*] [*Pharmacy*] (ROG) ... BULLIENT
Bulling the Market [*Investment term*] ... BTM
Bullingbroke's Ecclesiastical Law [*A publication*] (DLA) ... Bull Eccl
Bullion (ROG) ... BLLN
Bullion (ROG) ... BLN
Bullion Range Exploration [*Vancouver Stock Exchange symbol*] ... BIN
Bullnose Morris Club (EA) ... BMC
Bullock Ridge Splitting [*Agriculture*] ... BL
Bullocks Harbour/Great Harbour Cay, Berry Island [*Bahamas*] [*ICAO location identifier*] (ICLI) ... MYBG
Bullous Pemphigoid [*Medicine*] ... BP
Bullous Pemphigoid Antigen [*Immunology*] ... BPA
Bullous Pemphigoid Antigen [*Medicine*] (DMAA) ... BPAG
Bullpup All-Weather Guidance System [*Naval Ordnance Systems Command*] ... BAGS
Bullseye Cancel Collectors Club ... BCCC
Bullseye Class Association (EA) ... BCA
Bullseye Engineering and Technical Services (DNAB) ... BETS
Bullsling [*or Bullslinger*] [*Bowdlerized version*] ... BS
Bulolo [*Papua New Guinea*] [*Airport symbol*] (OAG) ... BUL
Bulolo [*New Guinea*] [*Airport symbol*] (AD) ... BUL
Bulonge-Kigogo [*Zaire*] [*ICAO location identifier*] (ICLI) ... FZMK
Bulstrode's English King's Bench Reports [*1610-25*] [*A publication*] (DLA) ... Buls
Bulstrode's English King's Bench Reports [*1610-25*] [*A publication*] (DLA) ... Bulst
Bulstrode's English King's Bench Reports [*1610-25*] [*A publication*] (DLA) ... Bulstr
Bulwark ... BWK
Bum Boy [*Slang British*] (DSUE) ... BB
BUM International, Inc. [*Associated Press*] (SAG) ... BUM Int
BUM International, Inc. [*NASDAQ symbol*] (SAG) ... BUMM
Bumba [*Zaire*] [*Airport symbol*] (OAG) ... BMB
Bumba [*Zaire*] [*ICAO location identifier*] (ICLI) ... FZFU
Bum-Fodder [*Toilet paper*] [*Slang British*] (DSUE) ... BUMF
Bump. Federal Procedure [*A publication*] (DLA) ... Bump Fed Pr
Bump on Bankruptcy [*A publication*] (DLA) ... Bump B'k'cy
Bump on Composition in Bankruptcy [*A publication*] (DLA) ... Bump Comp
Bump on Fraudulent Conveyances [*A publication*] (DLA) ... Bump Fr Conv
Bump on Fraudulent Conveyances [*A publication*] (DLA) ... Bump Fraud Conv
Bump Protection Hat ... BPH
Bump, Squeak, and Rattle [*Automotive characterization*] ... BSR
Bump. United States Stamp Laws [*A publication*] (DLA) ... Bump St L
Bumped [*Bookselling*] (DGA) ... BMP
Bumper [*Automotive engineering*] ... BMPR
Bumper Impulse Detector ... BID
Bumper Lift Jack ... BLJ
Bumper Limiter/Protective Plates (MCD) ... BL/PP
Bumper Recycling Association of North America (EA) ... BRANA
Bumper to Back of Cab [*Automotive engineering*] ... BBC
Bumper to Bumper ... BTB
Bump's Internal Revenue Laws [*A publication*] (DLA) ... Bump Int Rev
Bump's Internal Revenue Laws [*A publication*] (DLA) ... Bump's Int Rev Law
Bump's Law of Patents, Trade-Marks, Etc. [*A publication*] (DLA) ... Bump Pat
Bump's Notes on Constitutional Decisions [*A publication*] (DLA) ... Bump Const Dec
Bump's Notes on Constitutional Decisions [*A publication*] (DLA) ... Bump NC
Bumpstead [*England*] ... BUMP
Bunbury [*Australia Airport symbol*] (OAG) ... BUY
Bunbury. English Exchequer Reports [*145 English Reprint*] [*A publication*] (DLA) ... Bunb
Bunbury Institute of Advanced Education [*Australia*] ... BIAE
Bunch (WGA) ... BCH
Bunch (DNAB) ... BH
[*A*] **Bunch of Guys Seated around a Table Method** [*Facetious description of a decision-making process*] ... BOGSAT
[*A*] **Bunch of Guys Sitting around a Table Method** [*Facetious description of a decision-making process*] ... BOGSAAT
[*A*] **Bunch of Jewish Kids** [*Slang*] (BJA) ... ABOJK
Bunching (MSA) ... BCHG
Bunching Block (MSA) ... BB
Bundaberg [*Australia ICAO location identifier*] (ICLI) ... ABBU
Bundaberg [*Australia Airport symbol*] (OAG) ... BDB
Bund-Communist Party [*Political party*] (BJA) ... BCP
Bundelkund Legion [*British military*] (DMA) ... BL
Bundesamt fuer Militarflugplatze [*Switzerland ICAO designator*] (FAAC) ... BAMF
Bundesamt fuer Verfassungsschutz [*Federal Office for the Protection of the Constitution*] [*West German counterintelligence agency*] ... BfV
Bundesamt fur Militarflugplatze [*Switzerland ICAO designator*] (FAAC) ... SUI
Bundesamt fur Statistik [*Federal Statistical Office*] [*Information service or system*] (IID) ... BFS
Bundesanstalt fuer Materialforschung und -Pruefung [*Federal Institute for Materials Research and Testing*] [*Database producer*] [*Germany Information retrieval*] (IID) ... BAM
Bundesanstalt fuer Materialprufung Unter den Eichen [*International Association for Structural Mechanics in Reactor Technology*] (EAIO) ... BAM
Bundesanwalt [*Public Prosecutor or Attorney General*] [*German*] (ILCA) ... BA
Bundesanwaltschaft [*The Office of Public Prosecutor*] [*German*] (ILCA) ... BA
Bundesanzeiger Verlagsgesellschaft, mbH, Koln, Germany [*Library symbol*] [*Library of Congress*] (LCLS) ... GyKoB
Bundesarbeitsgericht [*Federal Supreme Labour Court*] [*German*] (DLA) ... BAG
Bundesarbeitsgericht [*Federal Labor Court*] [*German*] (ILCA) ... BArbG
Bundesaufsichtsamt fur das Kreditwesen [*Federal Supervisory Office for Credit*] [*Germany*] ... BAK
Bundesfinanzhof [*Federal Supreme Fiscal Court*] [*German*] (DLA) ... BFH
Bundesforschungsanstalt fuer Fischerei [*Database producer*] [*Germany*] ... BFF
Bundesgericht [*Federal Supreme Court*] [*German*] (DLA) ... BG
Bundesgerichtshof [*Federal Supreme Court*] [*German*] (DLA) ... BGH
Bundesgesetz [*Federal Act or Statute*] [*German*] (ILCA) ... BdG
Bundesgesetz [*Federal Act or Statute*] [*German*] (ILCA) ... BdGes
Bundesgesetz [*Federal Act or Statute*] [*German*] (ILCA) ... BG
Bundesgesundheitsamt [*Database producer*] ... BGA
Bundesgrenzschutz [*Germany ICAO designator*] (FAAC) ... BGS
Bundesgrenzschutz [*West Germany*] [*Military*] (NATG) ... BGS
Bundesinstitut fuer Sportwissenschaft [*Federal Institute for Sports Science*] [*Germany*] (IID) ... BISp
Bundeskanzler [*Federal Chancellor*] [*German*] (ILCA) ... BK
Bundeskanzleramt [*Federal Chancery*] [*German*] (ILCA) ... BK
Bundeskartellamt [*Federal Cartel Office*] [*German*] (ILCA) ... BKA
Bundeskriminalamt [*Federal Criminal Police Bureau*] [*Germany*] ... BKA
Bundesminister der Justiz [*Federal Minister of Justice*] [*German*] (ILCA) ... BMJ
Bundesministerium fuer Forschung und Technologie [*Ministry for Research and Technology*] [*Information service or system Germany*] (IID) ... BMFT
Bundesnachrichtendienst [*Federal Intelligence Service*] [*Germany*] ... BND
Bundesrepublik Deutschland [*Federal Republic of Germany*] ... BRD
Bundesrueckerstattungsgesetz [*A publication*] (BJA) ... BRuG
Bundessozialgericht [*Federal Supreme Social Security Court*] [*German*] (DLA) ... B Soz G
Bundessozialgericht [*Federal Court of Social Security*] [*German*] (ILCA) ... BSG
Bundesstelle fuer Aussenhandelsinformation [*Federal Office of Foreign Trade Information*] [*German Ministry of Economics*] (IID) ... BfAi
Bundesverband der Deutschen Industrie [*Federation of German Industries*] ... BDI
Bundesvereinigung Deutscher Apothekerverbande [*German Pharmaceutical Association Research Institute*] [*Information service or system*] (IID) ... ABDA
Bundesverfassungsgericht [*Federal Constitutional Court*] [*German*] (DLA) ... B Verf G
Bundesverwaltungsgericht [*Federal Supreme Administrative Court*] [*German*] (DLA) ... B Verw G
Bundi [*Papua New Guinea*] [*Airport symbol*] (OAG) ... BNT
Bundle (MCD) ... BD
Bundle (WDMC) ... bd.
Bundle ... BDL
Bundle ... BDLE
Bundle ... BNDL
Bundle Assembly (SAA) ... BA
Bundle Branch Block [*Cardiology*] ... BBB
Bundle Controlled Expansion ... BCEX
Bundle Drawing Process [*Metal fiber technology*] ... BDP

Bundle of His [*Cardiology*] (DAVI) ... BH
Bundle-Branch [*Cardiology*] (DAVI) ... BB
Bundle-Branch Heart Block [*Cardiology*] (DAVI) ... BBHB
Bundle-Forming Pili [*Microbiology*] ... BFP
Bundles ... BDLS
Bungalow [*Classified advertising*] (ADA) ... BUNG
Bungarotoxin [*Also, BTX, BuTx*] [*Biochemistry*] ... BGT
Bungarotoxin [*Also, BGT, BuTx*] [*Biochemistry*] ... BTX
Bungarotoxin [*Also, BGT, BTX*] [*Biochemistry*] ... BuTx
Bung-Hole [*i.e., cheese*] [*British slang*] ... BH
Bungo Tebo/Pasir Mayang [*Indonesia*] [*ICAO location identifier*] (ICLI) ... WIPI
Bungoma [*Kenya*] [*ICAO location identifier*] (ICLI) ... HKBU
Bunia [*Zaire*] [*Airport symbol*] (OAG) ... BUX
Bunia [*Zaire*] [*Airport symbol*] (AD) ... BUX
Bunia [*Zaire*] [*ICAO location identifier*] (ICLI) ... FZKA
Bunia-Ruampara [*Zaire*] [*Geomagnetic observatory code*] ... BNA
Bunion [*Orthopedics and podiatry*] (DAVI) ... BUN
Bunker Adjustment Factor [*Business term*] ... BAF
Bunker Defeat Munition [*Army*] (INF) ... BDM
Bunker Fuel Oil (DS) ... BFO
Bunker Hill Mining [*Vancouver Stock Exchange symbol*] ... BNH
Bunker Hill Public Library, Bunker Hill, IL [*Library symbol Library of Congress*] (LCLS) ... IBun
Bunkie, LA [*FM radio station call letters*] ... KEZP
Bunkum [*Nonsense*] [*Slang*] (DSUE) ... BUNK
Bunnie Mills Fan Club (EA) ... BMFC
Bunno Bedele [*Ethiopia*] [*ICAO location identifier*] (ICLI) ... HABB
Bunnythorpe [*New Zealand*] [*Seismograph station code, US Geological Survey Closed*] (SEIS) ... BUN
Buno-Bonnevaux [*France ICAO location identifier*] (ICLI) ... LFFB
Bunt [*Baseball*] (BARN) ... b
Buntok/Sanggau [*Indonesia*] [*ICAO location identifier*] (ICLI) ... WRBU
Bunyon. Domestic Law [*1875*] [*A publication*] (DLA) ... Buny Dom L
Bunyon. Fire Insurance [*7th ed.*] [*1923*] [*A publication*] (DLA) ... Buny Fire Ins
Bunyon. Life Insurance [*5th ed.*] [*1914*] [*A publication*] (DLA) ... Buny Life Ins
Bunyon on Life Assurance [*A publication*] (DLA) ... Buny Life Ass
Bunzl Flexpack Ltd. [*British*] ... BFL
Buoni del Tesoro Poliennali [*Italy*] (ECON) ... BTP
Buonmethuot/Chung Duc [*Viet Nam*] [*ICAO location identifier*] (ICLI) ... VVBM
Buoy Boat ... BU
Buoy Boat, Stern Loading ... BUSL
Buoy Integrated Antenna Submarine [*or System*] (MCD) ... BIAS
Buoy Messenger ... BMSS
Buoy Power Supply ... BPS
Buoy Tender [*Coast Guard symbol*] (DNAB) ... WYTM
Buoy Underwater Sound Signal (NG) ... BUSS
Buoyancy ... B
Buoyancy Compensator Device ... BCD
Buoyancy Compensators ... BC
Buoyancy Induced Dispersion (GFGA) ... BID
Buoyancy Transport Vehicle (MCD) ... BTV
Buoyancy-Actuated Launch and Retrieval Elevator (PDAA) ... BALARE
Buoyant (MSA) ... BYNT
Buoyant Ballistic Inertial Missile (MCD) ... BBIM
Buoyant Capsule (MCD) ... BC
Buoyant Line and Point Source Model [*Environmental Protection Agency*] (GFGA) ... BLP
Buoyant Venus Station [*NASA*] ... BVS
Buprenorphine [*Analgesic*] ... BUP
Bur Oak Library System [*Library network*] ... BOLS
Bura [*Kenya*] [*ICAO location identifier*] (ICLI) ... HKBR
Buraimi [*Oman*] [*ICAO location identifier*] (ICLI) ... OOBR
Burao [*Somalia*] [*Airport symbol*] (OAG) ... BUO
Burao [*Somalia*] [*ICAO location identifier*] (ICLI) ... HCMV
Buras, LA [*FM radio station call letters*] (RBYB) ... KMRL
Burbank [*California*] [*Airport symbol*] ... BUR
Burbank, CA [*AM radio station call letters*] ... KRCK
Burbank/Hollywood-Burbank [*California*] [*ICAO location identifier*] (ICLI) ... KBUR
Burbank Public Library, Burbank, CA [*Library symbol Library of Congress*] (LCLS) ... CBb
Burchardus Wormatiensis [*Deceased, 1025*] [*Authority cited in pre-1607 legal work*] (DSA) ... B
Burda-MarketingInfoSystem [*Burda GmbH, Marketing Service Department*] [*Information service or system*] (IID) ... MADIS
Burdekin Agricultural College [*Australia*] ... BAC
Burdekin River Irrigation Area Advisory Committee [*Queensland, Australia*] ... BRIAAC
Burdekin River Irrigation Area Technical Advisory Committee [*Queensland, Australia*] ... BRIATAC
Burden Center ... BC
Burden of Going Forward [*Legal shorthand*] (LWAP) ... BOGF
Burden of Proof [*Legal shorthand*] (LWAP) ... BOP
Burden Rate Adjustment (MCD) ... BRA
Burdett Resources Ltd. [*Vancouver Stock Exchange symbol*] ... BDT
Burdick [*Suction*] [*Surgery*] (DAVI) ... BURD
Burdick Suction [*Medicine*] (BABM) ... Burd
Burdick's Law of Crime [*A publication*] (DLA) ... Burdick Crime
Burdick's Principles of Roman Law [*A publication*] (DLA) ... Burdick Roman Law
Burdock Yellows Virus [*Plant pathology*] ... BUYV
Bureau (AABC) ... BU
Bureau (AFM) ... BUR
Bureau ... BUR
Bureau (WDMC) ... bur
Bureau Arabe de Presse et de Publications [*Paris*] (BJA) ... BAPP
Bureau Canadien de l'Education Internationale [*Canadian Bureau for International Education - CBIE*] ... BCEI
Bureau Central de Compensation [*Central Bureau of Compensation - CBC*] (EAIO) ... BCC
Bureau Central des Renseignements et d'Action [*French Resistance organization*] ... BCRA
Bureau Control Activity Number ... BCAN
Bureau Control Number ... BCN
Bureau County Historical Society, Princeton, IL [*Library symbol Library of Congress*] (LCLS) ... IPriHi
Bureau d'Amenagement du Nouvel Aeroport International de Montreal [*New Montreal International Airport Project Office - NMIAPO*] [*Canada*] ... BANAIM
Bureau de la Baie James et du Nord Quebecois, Ste.-Foy, PQ, Canada [*Library symbol Library of Congress*] (LCLS) ... CaQQBJNQ
Bureau de la Baie James et du Nord Quebecois, Ste.-Foy, Quebec [*Library symbol National Library of Canada*] (NLC) ... QQBJNQ
Bureau de la Cooperation et du Developpement International [*Office for International Cooperation & Development*] (AC) ... BCDI
Bureau de la Science et de la Technologie, Quebec, PQ, Canada [*Library symbol Library of Congress*] (LCLS) ... CaQQBST
Bureau de la Statistique du Quebec, Quebec, PQ, Canada [*Library symbol Library of Congress*] (LCLS) ... CaQQBS
Bureau de la Statistique du Quebec, Quebec, Quebec [*Library symbol National Library of Canada*] (NLC) ... QQBS
Bureau de l'Assistance Technique [*Technical Assistance Bureau*] ... BAT
Bureau de Liaison de l'Information Religieuse dans l'Ocean Indien [*Indian Ocean Religious Information Liaison Office*] (AF) ... BLIROI
Bureau de Liaison des Industries du Caoutchouc de la CEE [*Rubber Industries Liaison Bureau of the EEC*] [*Belgium*] ... BLIC
Bureau de Liaison des Syndicats Europeens (CEE) des Produits Aromatiques [*Liaison Bureau of the European and EEC Unions of Aromatic Products*] (EAIO) ... BLA
Bureau de Recherche et de Consultation en Education [*Bureau of Research and Consultation in Education*] [*Canada*] ... BRCE
Bureau de Recherches Geologiques et Minieres [*Bureau of Geological and MiningResearch*] [*Burkina Faso*] [*Information service or system*] (IID) ... BRGM
Bureau de Traduction, Gouvernement du Nouveau-Brunswick [*Translation Bureau, Governement of New Brunswick*] **Fredericton, New Brunswick** [*Library symbol National Library of Canada*] (NLC) ... NBFT
Bureau d'Education Ibero-Americain ... BEIA
Bureau des Jeux Olympiques d'Hiver de 1988, Gouvernement du Canada [*Office of the 1988 Winter Olympic Games, Government of Canada*] ... BJOH
Bureau des Plans de Vol Repetitifs [*FAA designator*] (FAAC) ... ZBZ
Bureau d'Etudes Industrielles et de Cooperation, Institut Francais du Petrole [*Office of Industrial Studies and Cooperation, French Institute of Petroleum*] [*Canada*] ... BEICIP
Bureau d'Information et de Presse [*Circulated Allied propaganda in France and informed Allies of resistance activities*] [*World War II*] ... BIP
Bureau d'Informations et de Previsions Economiques [*Office of Economic Information and Forecasting*] [*Information service or system*] (IID) ... BIPE
Bureau d'Interventions Cliniques et Communautaires [*Office of Clinical and Communal Operations*] [*Canada*] ... BICC
Bureau d'Investissement en Afrique [*Office of Investments in Africa*] [*France*] (AF) ... BIA
Bureau du Coordonnateur, Reforme de la Reglementation [*Office of the Coordinator, Regulatory Reform*] [*Canada*] ... BCRR
Bureau du Verificateur General du Canada [*Office of the Auditor-General of Canada*] ... BVG
Bureau Electr Pubg Wrrt [*NASDAQ symbol*] (TTSB) ... BEPIW
Bureau Electronics Equipment Model [*Navy*] (MCD) ... BEEM
Bureau Equipment List (MCD) ... BEL
Bureau Europeen de Controle et d'Etudes Generales ... BECEG
Bureau Europeen de Coordination des Organisations Internationales de Jeunesse [*European Coordination Bureau for International Youth Organizations - ECB*] (EAIO) ... BEC
Bureau Europeen de la Jeunesse et de l'Enfance ... BEJE
Bureau Europeen de l'Education Populaire [*European Bureau of Adult Education - EBAE*] (EAIO) ... BEEP
Bureau Europeen des Unions de Consommateurs [*European Bureau of Consumers' Unions*] (EAIO) ... BEUC
Bureau Federal d'Examen des Evaluations Environnementales [*Federal Environmental Assessment Review Office*] [*Canada*] ... BFEEE
Bureau for Adult Thalidomide Victims [*West Germany*] ... BATV
Bureau for Africa and Europe [*AID*] ... BAE
Bureau for Careers in Jewish Service [*Defunct*] (EA) ... BCJS
[*The*] **Bureau for Excellence in Durham Region** (AC) ... BEDR
Bureau for Latin America [*Agency for International Development*] ... BLA
Bureau for Overseas Medical Service [*British*] (CB) ... BOMS
Bureau for Policy and Program Support [*United Nations*] (ECON) ... BPPS
Bureau for Private Enterprise ... PRE
Bureau for Reference and Loan Services [*Library network*] ... R & L
Bureau for the Advancement of Independent Retailing (EA) ... BAIR
Bureau Hydrographique International [*International Hydrographic Organization*] (EAIO) ... BHI
Bureau Inlichtingen [*Netherlands Information Office*] [*World War II*] ... BI
Bureau, Institute, and Division [*National Institutes of Health*] ... BID
Bureau Interafricain de Developpement et de Cooperation [*Inter-African Development and Cooperation Office*] (AF) ... BIDC
Bureau Interafricain des Sols [*Inter-African Soils Office*] (AF) ... BIS
Bureau Interafricain des Sols et de l'Economie Rurale [*Inter-African Bureau of Soils and Rural Economy*] ... BIS
Bureau Interafricain des Sols et de l'Economie Rurale [*Inter-African Soils and Rural Economy Office*] (AF) ... BISER
Bureau International Afghanistan (EA) ... BIA

Bureau International Catholique de l'Enfance [*International Catholic Child Bureau - ICCB*] [*Geneva, Switzerland*] (EA) .... BICE

Bureau International d'Anthropologie Differentielle [*International Bureau of Differential Anthropology*] .... BIAD

Bureau International d'Audiophonologie [*International Office for Audiophonology - IOA*] [*Brussels, Belgium*] (EA) .... BIAP

Bureau International de Documentation des Chemins de Fer [*International Office of Railway Documentation*] .... BDC

Bureau International de la Chaussure et du Cuir .... BIC

Bureau International de la Recuperation [*International Bureau of Recuperation*] [*Brussels, Belgium*] (EA) .... BIR

Bureau International de l'Edition Mecanique .... BIEM

Bureau International de l'Heure [*International Time Bureau*] (EAIO) .... BIH

Bureau International de Recherche sur les Implications Sociales du Progres Technique .... BIRISPT

Bureau International d'Education [*International Bureau of Education - IBE*] (EAIO) .... BIE

Bureau International des Containers [*International Container Bureau*] [*Paris, France*] (EAIO) .... BIC

Bureau International des Expositions [*International Bureau of Exhibitions*] (EAIO) .... BIE

Bureau International des Poids et Mesures [*International Bureau of Weights and Measures*] [*Sevres, France*] (EA) .... BIPM

Bureau International des Producteurs d'Assurances et de Reassurances [*International Association of Insurance and Reinsurance Intermediaries - IAIRI*] [*Paris, France*] (EAIO) .... BIPAR

Bureau International des Universites .... BIU

Bureau International d'Information des Chambres de Commerce .... BIICC

Bureau International du Beton Manufacture [*International Bureau for Precast Concrete*] (EAIO) .... BIBM

Bureau International du Cinema [*International Cinematograph Bureau*] .... BIC

Bureau International du Film des Chemins de Fer [*International Railway Film Bureau*] .... BFC

Bureau International du Scoutisme .... BIS

Bureau International du Tourisme Social [*International Bureau of Social Tourism - IBST*] (EAIO) .... BITS

Bureau International du Travail [*International Labour Office*] [*French*] .... BIT

Bureau International Permanent de Chimie Analytique pour les Matieres Destinees a l'Alimentation de l'Homme et des Animaux [*Permanent International Bureau of Analytical Chemistry of Human and Animal Food*] .... BIPCA

Bureau International pour la Standardisation de la Rayonne et des Fibres Synthetiques [*International Bureau for the Standardisation of Manmade Fibres*] (EAIO) .... BISFA

Bureau International pour le Tourisme et les Echanges de la Jeunesse [*International Bureau for Youth Tourism and Exchanges*] (EAIO) .... BITEJ

Bureau International Technique de l'ABS [*Acronitrile-Butadiene-Styrene*] [*of the European Council of Chemical Manufacturers' Federations*] (EAIO) .... BITL

Bureau International Technique des Gelatines (EAIO) .... BITG

Bureau International Technique des "Inorganic Feed Phosphates" [*Inorganic Feed Phosphates International Technical Bureau - IFPITB*] (EAIO) .... BITIFP

Bureau International Technique des Polyesters (EAIO) .... BITP

Bureau International Technique des Polyesters Insatures [*of the European Council of Chemical Manufacturers' Federations*] (EAIO) .... BITPI

Bureau International Technique du Methanol [*European Council of Chemical Manufacturers' Federations*] [*Belgium*] (EAIO) .... BITM

Bureau Issues Association (EA) .... BIA

Bureau Local d'Intervention Traitant du Sida (AC) .... BLITS

Bureau Marcel van Dijk, SA [*Information service or system*] (IID) .... BMvD

Bureau Militaire de Standardisation [*Military Agency for Standardization*] [*NATO*] .... BMS

Bureau National de l'Information Scientifique et Technique [*National Scientific and Technical Information Bureau*] [*France Information service or system*] (IID) .... BNIST

Bureau National des Donnees Oceaniques [*National Bureau for Ocean Data*] [*European host database system*] [*France*] [*Information service or system*] (IID) .... BNDO

Bureau Number [*Database terminology*] (NITA) .... BN

Bureau Number [*Aircraft identification*] [*Obsolete Navy*] .... BUNO

Bureau of Accounts [*Department of the Treasury*] .... BA

Bureau of Accreditation and School Improvement Studies [*University of Michigan*] [*Research center*] (RCD) .... BASIS

Bureau of Administrative Management and Budget [*United Nations Development Program*] .... BAMB

Bureau of Adult, Vocational, and Technical Education (OICC) .... BAVTE

Bureau of Advertising [*American Newspaper Publishers Association*] (NTCM) .... B of A

Bureau of Aeronautics [*Later, Naval Air Systems Command*] .... B/A

Bureau of Aeronautics [*Later, Naval Air Systems Command*] .... BAR

Bureau of Aeronautics [*Later, Naval Air Systems Command*] [*Obsolete*] .... BUAER

Bureau of Aeronautics General Representative [*Obsolete Navy*] .... BAGR

Bureau of Aeronautics General Representative, Eastern District [*Obsolete Navy*] .... BAGRED

Bureau of Aeronautics General Representative, Western District [*Obsolete Navy*] .... BAGRWD

Bureau of Aeronautics Industrial Reserve [*Obsolete Navy*] .... BAIR

Bureau of Aeronautics Maintenance Repair Officer [*Obsolete Navy*] .... BAMRO

Bureau of Aeronautics Maintenance Representative [*Obsolete Navy*] .... BAMR

Bureau of Aeronautics Maintenance Resident Representative Office [*Obsolete Navy*] .... BAMRRO

Bureau of Aeronautics Material Officer [*Obsolete Navy*] .... BAMO

Bureau of Aeronautics Representative [*Obsolete Navy*] .... BAR

Bureau of Aeronautics Resident Representative [*Obsolete Navy*] .... BARR

Bureau of Aeronautics Shipment Order [*Obsolete Navy*] .... BASO

Bureau of Aeronautics Training Unit [*Obsolete Navy*] .... BARTU

Bureau of African Affairs [*Department of State*] .... BAA

Bureau of Agricultural and Industrial Chemistry [*Department of Agriculture*] .... BAIC

Bureau of Agricultural Economics [*Functions dispersed, 1953*] [*Department of Agriculture*] .... BAE

Bureau of Air Commerce [*Later, Civil Aeronautics Authority*] .... BAC

Bureau of Air Commerce Type Certificate .... ACTC

Bureau of Air Pollution Sciences .... BAPS

Bureau of Air Traffic Management .... BATM

Bureau of Alcohol, Tobacco, and Firearms [*Department of the Treasury*] .... ATF

Bureau of Alcohol, Tobacco, and Firearms [*Department of the Treasury*] .... BATF

Bureau of Alcohol, Tobacco, and Firearms Laboratory, Washington, DC [*OCLC symbol*] (OCLC) .... ATF

Bureau of American Ethnology [*of the Smithsonian Institution*] .... BAE

Bureau of Analyzed Samples [*British*] .... BAS

Bureau of Animal Industry [*Department of Agriculture*] .... BAI

Bureau of Animal Welfare [*Victoria, Australia*] .... BAW

Bureau of Applied Social Research [*Columbia University*] (IID) .... BASR

Bureau of Apprenticeship and Training [*Department of Labor*] .... BAT

Bureau of Automotive Regulation .... BAR

Bureau of Aviation Medicine (KSC) .... BAM

Bureau of Biological Research [*Rutgers University*] [*Research center*] (RCD) .... BBR

Bureau of Biologics [*Also, BOB*] [*FDA*] .... BB

Bureau of Biologics [*Also, BB*] [*FDA*] .... BOB

Bureau of Broadcast Measurement [*Canada*] (NTCM) .... BBM

Bureau of Business and Economic Research [*Old Dominion University*] [*Norfolk, VA*] [*Research center*] (RCD) .... BBER

Bureau of Business Research [*University of Texas, Austin*] [*Information service or system*] (IID) .... BBR

Bureau of Catholic Indian Missions (EA) .... BCIM

Bureau of Child Welfare (BARN) .... BCW

Bureau of Commercial Fisheries [*Later, National Marine Fisheries Service*] .... BCF

Bureau of Commercial Fisheries [*Later, National Marine Fisheries Service*] (MCD) .... BOCF

Bureau of Commerical Fisheries [*Now National Marine Fisheries Service*] (USDC) .... BSF

Bureau of Community Corrections (OICC) .... BCC

Bureau of Community Environmental Management [*Terminated, 1973*] [*HEW*] .... BCEM

Bureau of Community Health Services [*Health Services Administration*] .... BCHS

Bureau of Competitive Assessment and Business Policy [*Department of Commerce*] .... BCABP

Bureau of Construction and Repair [*Until 1940*] [*Navy*] .... BUC & R

Bureau of Construction and Repair [*Until 1940*] [*Navy*] .... BUCON

Bureau of Construction and Repair [*Until 1940*] [*Navy*] .... C & R

Bureau of Consultation [*Federal Trade Commission*] .... BC

Bureau of Contract Information [*Defunct*] (EA) .... BCI

Bureau of Co-Ordination of Arabization (EA) .... BCA

Bureau of Crime Statistics and Research [*New South Wales, Australia*] .... BCSR

Bureau of Criminal Investigation (BARN) .... BCI

Bureau of Criminal Statistics (BARN) .... BCS

Bureau of Customs [*Later, US Customs Service*] [*Department of the Treasury*] .... BC

Bureau of Customs [*Later, US Customs Service*] [*Department of the Treasury*] .... BOC

Bureau of Dairy Industry [*Department of Agriculture*] [*Functions transferred to ARS, 1953*] .... BDI

Bureau of Dangerous Drugs [*Canada*] .... BDD

Bureau of Data Management and Strategy [*Department of Health and Human Services*] (GFGA) .... BDMS

Bureau of Data Processing and Accounts [*Social Security Administration*] .... BDPA

Bureau of Disability Insurance [*Social Security Administration*] .... BDI

Bureau of Disease Prevention and Environmental Control .... BDPEC

Bureau of Domestic Business Development [*Department of Commerce*] .... BDBD

Bureau of Domestic Commerce [*Formerly, Business and Defense Services Administration and Office of Field Services*] [*Department of Commerce Terminated, 1977, functions transferred to Domestic and International Business Administration*] .... BDC

Bureau of Drug Abuse Control [*Absorbed by Bureau of Narcotics and Dangerous Drugs of Department of Justice*] .... BDAC

Bureau of Drugs [*Later, Center for Drugs and Biologics*] [*FDA*] .... BD

Bureau of East Asian and Pacific Affairs [*Formerly, Bureau of Far Eastern Affairs*] [*Department of State*] .... BEAPA

Bureau of East-West Trade [*Department of Commerce*] .... BEWT

Bureau of Economic Affairs [*Later, Bureau of Economic and Business Affairs*] [*Department of State*] .... BEA

Bureau of Economic Analysis [*Department of Commerce*] [*Washington, DC*] (IID) .... BEA

Bureau of Economic and Business Affairs [*Formerly, Bureau of Economic Affairs*] [*Department of State*] .... BEBA

Bureau of Economic and Business Research [*University of Florida*] [*Gainesville*] [*Information service or system*] (IID) .... BEBR

Bureau of Economic and Business Research [*University of Delaware*] [*Research center*] (RCD) .... BEBR

Bureau of Economic Regulation [*of CAB*] .... BER

Bureau of Economic Research and Development [*Virginia State University*] [*Research center*] (RCD) .... BERD

Bureau of Economics [*Federal Trade Commission*] .... BE

Bureau of Education for Fair Trade .... BEFT

Bureau of Education for the Handicapped [*Office of Education*] [*Later, SEP*] .... BEH

Bureau of Educational and Cultural Affairs [*Later Known as USIA, then as ICA or USICA, then again as USIA*] ... BECA
Bureau of Educational Evaluation [*Research center*] (RCD) ... BEE
Bureau of Educational Personnel Development [*HEW*] ... BEPD
Bureau of Educational Research and Evaluation [*Mississippi State University*] [*Research center*] (RCD) ... BERE
Bureau of Educational Research and Service [*Memphis State University*] [*Research center*] (RCD) ... BERS
Bureau of Educational Research and Service [*University of Tennessee at Knoxville*] [*Research center*] (RCD) ... BERS
Bureau of Elec Pub [*NASDAQ symbol*] (TTSB) ... BEPI
Bureau of Electronic Publishing, Inc. [*NASDAQ symbol*] (SAG) ... BEPI
Bureau of Electronic Publishing, Inc. [*Associated Press*] (SAG) ... BurEl
Bureau of Electronic Publishing, Inc. [*Associated Press*] (SAG) ... BurElP
Bureau of Elementary and Secondary Education [*Office of Education*] ... BESE
Bureau of Employees' Compensation [*Later, OWCP*] [*Department of Labor*] ... BEC
Bureau of Employment Security [*Later, US Employment Service*] [*Department of Labor*] ... BES
Bureau of Enforcement ... BOE
Bureau of Engineering [*Obsolete Navy*] ... BUENG
Bureau of Engraving and Printing [*Department of the Treasury*] ... BEP
Bureau of Entomology and Plant Quarantine [*Department of Agriculture*] [*Functions transferred to ARS, 1953*] ... BEPQ
Bureau of Equipment and Recruiting [*Abolished, 1914*] [*Navy*] ... BER
Bureau of European Affairs [*Department of State*] ... BEA
Bureau of European Designers Associations (EA) ... BEDA
Bureau of Evaluative Studies and Testing [*Indiana University*] [*Research center*] (RCD) ... BEST
Bureau of Executive Manpower [*Civil Service Commission*] ... BEM
Bureau of Explosives [*Later, HMS (BOE)*] ... BE
Bureau of Explosives [*A publication*] (EAAP) ... BOE
Bureau of Export Administration [*Department of Commerce*] ... BXA
Bureau of Export Development [*Department of Commerce*] ... BED
Bureau of Facilities and Material (AAGC) ... BFM
Bureau of Family Services [*of SSA*] ... BFS
Bureau of Far Eastern Affairs [*Department of State*] ... BFEA
Bureau of Federal Credit Unions [*Later, NCUA*] [*Social Security Administration*] ... BFCU
Bureau of Federal Supply (AAGC) ... BFS
Bureau of Finance and Administration [*US Postal Service*] (MCD) ... BFA
Bureau of Fisheries and Aquatic Resources [*Phillippines*] [*Marine science*] (OSRA) ... BFAR
Bureau of Flight Standards (KSC) ... BFS
Bureau of Flora and Fauna [*Australia*] ... BFF
Bureau of Foods Irradiated Foods Committee [*Food and Drug Administration*] ... BFIFC
Bureau of Foods, Pesticides, and Product Safety [*FDA*] ... BFPPS
Bureau of Foreign and Domestic Commerce [*Functions later dispersed*] [*Department of Commerce*] ... BFDC
Bureau of Foreign Commerce [*Abolished, 1961*] [*Department of Commerce*] ... BFC
Bureau of Freelance Photographers [*British*] (CB) ... BFP
Bureau of Government Financial Operations [*Department of Treasury*] ... BGFO
Bureau of Governmental Research [*University of California*] [*Research Center*] (AEBS) ... BGR
Bureau of Governmental Research and Service [*University of Oregon*] [*Research center*] (RCD) ... BGRS
Bureau of Health Care Delivery and Assistance [*Department of Health and Human Services*] ... BHCDA
Bureau of Health Insurance [*Social Security Administration*] ... BHI
Bureau of Health Manpower [*Later, Health Resources Administration*] [*HEW*] ... BHM
Bureau of Health Manpower Education [*National Institutes of Health*] ... BHME
Bureau of Health Planning and Resource Development [*Later, Bureau of Health Planning*] [*HEW*] ... BHPRD
Bureau of Health Professions [*Department of Health and Human Services*] (DAVI) ... BHPr
Bureau of Health Professions Education and Manpower Training [*HEW*] ... BEMT
Bureau of Health Services [*Public Health Service*] ... BHS
Bureau of Hearings and Appeals [*Social Security Administration*] ... BHA
Bureau of Higher Education [*Later, Bureau of Higher and Continuing Education*] [*Office of Education*] ... BHE
Bureau of Human Nutrition and Home Economics [*Department of Agriculture*] [*Functions transferred to ARS, 1953*] ... BHNHE
Bureau of Hygiene and Tropical Diseases [*Database producer*] ... BHTD
Bureau of Immigration Research Advisory Committee [*Australia*] ... BIRAC
Bureau of Independent Publishers and Distributors (EA) ... BIPAD
Bureau of Indian Affairs [*Department of the Interior*] ... BIA
Bureau of Indian Affairs [*Better known as BIA*] [*Department of the Interior*] (MCD) ... BOIA
Bureau of Indian Affairs Procurement Regulation [*A publication*] (AAGC) ... BIAPR
Bureau of Industrial Costs and Prices [*India*] (ECON) ... BICP
Bureau of Industrial Economics [*Department of Commerce*] ... BIE
Bureau of Inspection and Survey ... BIS
Bureau of Institutional Development [*Office of Education*] ... BID
Bureau of Insular Affairs [*Originally, part of War Department; functions transferred to Department of Interior, 1939*] ... BIA
Bureau of Intelligence and Research [*Department of State*] ... BIR
Bureau of Intelligence and Research [*Department of State*] ... INR
Bureau of Inter-American Affairs [*Department of State*] ... BIAA
Bureau of Intergovernmental Personnel Programs ... BIPP
Bureau of Inter-Industrial Statistics and Multiple Regression Analysis (MCD) ... BISMRA
Bureau of Internal Affairs ... BIA
Bureau of Internal Revenue [*Department of the Treasury*] [*Later, Internal Revenue Service*] ... BIR
Bureau of International Affairs (MCD) ... BIA
Bureau of International Business Operations [*Department of Commerce*] [*Abolished, 1963*] ... BIBO
Bureau of International Commerce [*Department of Commerce*] [*Functions transferred to Domestic and International Business Administration*] ... BIC
Bureau of International Economic Policy and Research [*Department of Commerce*] ... BIEPR
Bureau of International Labor Affairs [*Department of Labor*] ... BILA
Bureau of International Labor Affairs [*Department of Labor*] ... ILAB
Bureau of International Organization Affairs [*Department of State*] ... BIOA
Bureau of International Programs [*Department of Commerce*] ... BIP
Bureau of International Scientific and Technological Affairs [*Department of State*] ... BISTA
Bureau of International Whaling Statistics (BARN) ... BIWS
Bureau of Investigation [*Federal Trade Commission*] ... BI
Bureau of Jewish Education ... BJE
Bureau of Justice Assistance ... BJA
Bureau of Justice Statistics [*Department of Justice*] [*Also, an information service or system*] (IID) ... BJS
Bureau of Labor - Management Relations and Cooperative Programs [*Department of Labor*] ... BLMRCP
Bureau of Labor - Management Reports [*Department of Labor*] ... BLMR
Bureau of Labor Standards [*Absorbed by OSHA*] [*Department of Labor*] [*Washington, DC*] ... BLS
Bureau of Labor Statistics [*Department of Labor*] [*Washington, DC*] ... BLS
Bureau of Labor Statistics. Bulletin [*A publication*] (DLA) ... BLS Bull
Bureau of Land Management [*Department of the Interior*] ... BLM
Bureau of Land Management [*Department of the Interior*] (MCD) ... BOLM
Bureau of Land Management, Billings, MT [*Library symbol Library of Congress*] (LCLS) ... MtBilB
Bureau of Land Management, Billings, MT [*OCLC symbol*] (OCLC) ... UBD
Bureau of Land Management, Boise District Office, Boise, ID [*OCLC symbol*] (OCLC) ... UDL
Bureau of Land Management, Boise, ID [*Library symbol Library of Congress*] (LCLS) ... IdBLM-B
Bureau of Land Management, Denver, Denver, CO [*OCLC symbol*] (OCLC) ... UDD
Bureau of Land Management, Library, New Orleans, New Orleans, LA [*OCLC symbol*] (OCLC) ... UDQ
Bureau of Laundry and Dry Cleaning Standards (EA) ... BLDCS
Bureau of Libraries and Educational Technology [*Later, BLLR*] [*HEW*] ... BLET
Bureau of Libraries and Learning Resources [*Formerly, BLET*] [*HEW*] ... BLLR
Bureau of Litigation [*Federal Trade Commission*] ... BL
Bureau of Management Consulting, Department of Supply and Services [*Bureau des Conseillers en Gestion, Ministere des Approvisionnements et Services*] **Ottawa, Ontario** [*Library symbol National Library of Canada*] (NLC) ... OOBMC
Bureau of Manpower Utilization [*World War II*] ... BMU
Bureau of Medical Devices [*Food and Drug Administration*] ... BMD
Bureau of Medical Devices and Diagnostic Products [*FDA*] ... BMDDP
Bureau of Medical Services [*Public Health Service*] ... BMS
Bureau of Medicine [*of FDA*] ... BM
Bureau of Medicine and Supply Integrated Allowance List ... BM & SIAL
Bureau of Medicine and Surgery [*Later, Naval Medical Command*] [*Navy*] ... BMS
Bureau of Medicine and Surgery [*Navy*] ... BUM & S
Bureau of Medicine and Surgery [*Obsolete Navy*] ... BUMED
Bureau of Medicine and Surgery [*Navy*] ... M & S
Bureau of Medicine and Surgery Hospital Corps Publication [*Later, NAVMED*] [*Navy*] ... NMSHC
Bureau of Medicine and Surgery Instructions [*Navy*] ... BUMEDINST
Bureau of Medicine and Surgery Publications [*Navy*] ... NM & S
Bureau of Meteorology ... BOM
Bureau of Meteorology Research Center [*Marine science*] (OSRA) ... BMRC
Bureau of Meteorology Research Center (USDC) ... BMRC
Bureau of Meteorology Research Centre ... BMRC
Bureau of Meteorology Training Centre ... BMTC
Bureau of Military Application of Scientific Research (NATG) ... BMASR
Bureau of Mines [*Department of the Interior*] ... B of M
Bureau of Mines [*Department of the Interior*] ... BM
Bureau of Mines [*Department of the Interior*] ... BOM
Bureau of Mines [*Department of the Interior*] ... BuM
Bureau of Mines [*Department of the Interior*] ... BUMINES
Bureau of Mines. Information Circular [*Department of the Interior A publication*] ... BMIC
Bureau of Mines, Pittsburg (MCD) ... BMP
Bureau of Mines Technical Paper ... BMTP
Bureau of Motor Carrier Safety [*Department of Transportation*] ... BMCS
Bureau of Motor Carriers [*ICC*] ... BMC
Bureau of Municipal Research [*Canada*] (IRC) ... BMR
Bureau of Narcotics [*Department of the Treasury*] [*Absorbed by BNDD of Department of Justice*] ... BN
Bureau of Narcotics and Dangerous Drugs [*Formerly, Bureau of Narcotics and Bureau of Drug Abuse Control; later, Drug Enforcement Administration*] [*Department of Justice*] ... BNDD
Bureau of National Affairs (EA) ... BNA
Bureau of National Capital Airports [*of FAA*] ... BNCA
Bureau of Natural Gas [*of FPC*] ... BNG
Bureau of Naval Personnel [*Also, BUPERS, NAVPERS*] ... BNP
Bureau of Naval Personnel [*Also, BNP, NAVPERS*] ... BUPERS
Bureau of Naval Personnel [*Also, BNP, BUPERS*] ... NAVPERS

Bureau of Naval Personnel Circular Letters .... BNPCL
Bureau of Naval Personnel Controlled Instructor Billets .... BUPERSCONINSTRBIL
Bureau of Naval Personnel Instruction .... NAVPERSINST
Bureau of Naval Personnel Manual .... BNPM
Bureau of Naval Personnel - Personnel Research Division .... NAVPERS-PRD
Bureau of Naval Ships [*Obsolete*] (MCD) .... BNS
Bureau of Naval Weapons [*Obsolete*] .... BNW
Bureau of Naval Weapons [*Obsolete*] .... BUWEPS
Bureau of Naval Weapons (AAGC) .... BUWEPS
Bureau of Naval Weapons [*Obsolete*] .... NAVWEPS
Bureau of Naval Weapons Branch Representative [*Obsolete*] (MCD) .... BWBR
Bureau of Naval Weapons Fleet Readiness [*Obsolete*] (MCD) .... BUWEPS FR
Bureau of Naval Weapons Fleet Readiness Representative [*Obsolete*] (MCD) .... BUWEPSFLEREADREP
Bureau of Naval Weapons Fleet Readiness Representative [*Obsolete*] (MUGU) .... BUWEPSFLTREADREP
Bureau of Naval Weapons Fleet Readiness Representative [*Obsolete*] (MCD) .... BWFRR
Bureau of Naval Weapons Fleet Readiness Representative, Atlantic [*Obsolete*] (MCD) .... BUWEPSFLEREADREPLANT
Bureau of Naval Weapons Fleet Readiness Representative, Atlantic [*Obsolete*] (MUGU) .... BWFRRLANT
Bureau of Naval Weapons Fleet Readiness Representative, Central [*Obsolete*] (MCD) .... BUWEPSFLEREADREPCEN
Bureau of Naval Weapons Fleet Readiness Representative, Central [*Obsolete*] (MUGU) .... BWFRRCEN
Bureau of Naval Weapons Fleet Readiness Representative, Pacific [*Obsolete*] (MCD) .... BUWEPSFLEREADREPPAC
Bureau of Naval Weapons Fleet Readiness Representative, Pacific [*Obsolete*] (MUGU) .... BWFRRPAC
Bureau of Naval Weapons Instruction [*Obsolete*] (MCD) .... BUWEPSINST
Bureau of Naval Weapons Notice [*Obsolete*] .... BUWEPSNOTE
Bureau of Naval Weapons Representative [*Obsolete*] (MCD) .... BUWEPSREP
Bureau of Naval Weapons Representative [*Obsolete*] .... BWR
Bureau of Naval Weapons Representatives (AAGC) .... BUWEPSREPS
Bureau of Naval Weapons Resident Representative [*Obsolete*] .... BUWEPSRESREP
Bureau of Naval Weapons Resident Representative [*Obsolete*] (MUGU) .... BWRR
Bureau of Naval Weapons Support Representative, Naval Air Training Command [*Obsolete*] (MUGU) .... BWSRT
Bureau of Naval Weapons Technical Liaison Office [*Obsolete*] (MUGU) .... BUWEPSTLO
Bureau of Naval Weapons Technical Representative [*Obsolete*] (MUGU) .... BUWEPSTECHREP
Bureau of Navigation [*Later, Bureau of Naval Personnel*] [*Navy*] .... BUNAV
Bureau of Navy Yards and Docks [*Later, NFEC*] .... BNYD
Bureau of Near Eastern and South Asian Affairs [*Department of State*] .... BNESAA
Bureau of Occupational and Adult Education [*Office of Education*] .... BOAE
Bureau of Oceans and International Enviromental and Scientific Affairs/ Scientific and Technological Affairs [*Department of State*] (MSC) .... OES/SCI
Bureau of Oceans and International Environmental and Scientific Affairs [*Department of State*] .... OES
Bureau of Oceans and International Environmental and Scientific Affairs/ Environmental and Population Affairs [*Department of State*] (MSC) .... OES/ENP
Bureau of Oceans and International Environmental and Scientific Affairs/ Ocean and Fishery Affairs [*Department of State*] (MSC) .... OES/OFA
Bureau of Oceans, Fisheries, and Scientific Affairs [*Department of State*] .... BOFSA
Bureau of Old-Age and Survivors Insurance [*Social Security Administration*] .... BOASI
Bureau of Operating Rights [*ICC*] .... BOR
Bureau of Operations and Programming [*United Nations Development Program*] .... BOP
Bureau of Ordnance [*Functions transferred to Bureau of Naval Weapons, 1960, and later to Naval Ordnance Systems Command*] [*Navy*] .... BO
Bureau of Ordnance [*Functions transferred to Bureau of Naval Weapons, 1960, and later to Naval Ordnance Systems Command*] [*Navy*] .... BUORD
Bureau of Ordnance and Hydrography [*Obsolete Navy*] .... BOH
Bureau of Ordnance Design Unit [*Obsolete Navy*] .... BODU
Bureau of Ordnance Fleet Test Equipment [*Obsolete Navy*] .... B of TE
Bureau of Ordnance Instructions [*Later, NAVORDINST*] .... BUORDINST
Bureau of Ordnance Publication [*Later, NAVORD*] [*Navy*] .... NORD
Bureau of Ordnance Shipment Order [*Obsolete Navy*] .... BOSO
Bureau of Outdoor Recreation [*Terminated, 1978, functions transferred to Heritage Conservation and Recreation Service*] [*Department of the Interior*] (MCD) .... BOOR
Bureau of Outdoor Recreation [*Terminated, 1978, functions transferred to Heritage Conservation and Recreation Service*] [*Department of the Interior*] .... BOR
Bureau of Pension Advocates [*Canada*] .... BPA
Bureau of Plant Industry [*Later, BPISAE*] [*Department of Agriculture*] .... BPI
Bureau of Plant Industry, Soils, and Agricultural Engineering [*Formerly, BPI*] [*Functions transferred to ARS, 1953 Department of Agriculture*] .... BPISAE
Bureau of Postsecondary Education [*Later, Bureau of Higher and Continuing Education*] [*Office of Education*] .... BPE
Bureau of Power [*of FPC*] .... BP
Bureau of Prisons [*Department of Justice*] .... BP
Bureau of Prisons Acquisition Regulation [*A publications*] (AAGC) .... BPAR
Bureau of Product Safety [*FDA*] .... BPS
Bureau of Professional Education of the American Osteopathic Association (EA) .... BPEAOA
Bureau of Provisions and Clothing [*See also BSA*] [*Navy*] .... BPC
Bureau of Public Administration [*University of Tennessee at Knoxville*] [*Research center*] (RCD) .... BPA
Bureau of Public Assistance [*Later, BFS*] [*Social Security Administration*] .... BPA
Bureau of Public Inquiries .... BPI
Bureau of Public Relations [*War Department*] [*World War II*] .... BPR
Bureau of Public Roads [*Department of Transportation*] .... BPR
Bureau of Public Roads Transport Highway Mobilization [*Federal emergency order*] .... BPR-THM
Bureau of Quality Assurance [*HEW*] .... BQA
Bureau of Quality Control [*Department of Health and Human Services*] (GFGA) .... BQC
Bureau of Radiation Protection (NRCH) .... BRP
Bureau of Radiological Health [*FDA*] .... BRH
Bureau of Radiological Health / Division of Electronics Products [*FDA*] (PDAA) .... BRH/DEP
Bureau of Radiological Health / Division of Environmental Radiation [*FDA*] (PDAA) .... BRH/DER
Bureau of Radiological Health / Division of Medical Radiation Exposure [*FDA*] (PDAA) .... BRH/DMRE
Bureau of Radiological Health / Northeastern Radiological Health Laboratory [*FDA*] (PDAA) .... BRH/NERHL
Bureau of Radiological Health / Office of Regional Operations [*FDA*] (PDAA) .... BRH/ORO
Bureau of Radiological Health, Rockville, MD [*OCLC symbol*] (OCLC) .... BRH
Bureau of Radiological Health / Southeastern Radiological Health Laboratory [*FDA*] (PDAA) .... BRH/SERHL
Bureau of Radiological Health / Southwestern Radiological Health Laboratory [*FDA*] (PDAA) .... BRH/SWRHL
Bureau of Railroad Safety [*Department of Transportation*] .... BRS
Bureau of Railway Economics [*Later, AAR*] .... BRE
Bureau of Raw Materials for American Vegetable Oils and Fats Industries (EA) .... BORM
Bureau of Reclamation [*Later, WPRS*] [*Department of the Interior*] (MCD) .... BOR
Bureau of Reclamation [*Later, WPRS*] [*Department of the Interior*] .... BR
Bureau of Reclamation [*Later, WPRS*] [*Department of the Interior*] .... BUREC
Bureau of Recruiting and Examining [*Civil Service Commission*] .... BRE
Bureau of Research and Community Services [*Duquesne University*] [*Research center*] (RCD) .... BORACS
Bureau of Research and Development (KSC) .... BRAD
Bureau of Research and Development Center [*FAA*] (AAG) .... BRDC
Bureau of Research and Engineering [*US Postal Service*] .... BRE
Bureau of Resource Assessment and Land Use Planning .... BRALUP
Bureau of Resources and Trade Assistance [*Department of Commerce*] .... BRTA
Bureau of Retirement and Insurance [*Civil Service Commission*] .... BRI
Bureau of Retirement Survivors Insurance [*Social Security Administration*] .... BRSI
Bureau of Safety and Supply Radio Services .... BSSRS
Bureau of Safety Regulations (SAA) .... BSR
Bureau of Salesmen's National Associations (EA) .... BSNA
Bureau of School Systems [*Office of Education*] .... BSS
Bureau of Ships [*Later, Naval Sea Systems Command*] .... BS
Bureau of Ships [*Later, Naval Sea Systems Command*] .... BUSHIPS
Bureau of Ships Analog Computer [*Obsolete Navy*] .... BUSAC
Bureau of Ships Journal [*Obsolete Navy*] .... BSJ
Bureau of Ships Publications [*Obsolete Navy*] .... NBS
Bureau of Social Sciences Research, Inc. (MCD) .... BSSR
Bureau of Soils and Water Management [*Department of Agriculture*] .... BSWM
Bureau of Solid Waste Management [*Environmental Protection Agency*] .... BSWM
Bureau of Sport Fisheries and Wildlife [*Superseded by US Fish and Wildlife Service*] [*Department of the Interior*] (MCD) .... BOSFW
Bureau of Sport Fisheries and Wildlife [*Superseded by US Fish and Wildlife Service*] [*Department of the Interior*] .... BSFW
Bureau of Sport Fisheries and Wildlife, Eastern Fish Disease Laboratory, Kearneysville, WV [*Library symbol Library of Congress*] (LCLS) .... WvKeFW
Bureau of Standards .... B of S
Bureau of Standards .... BS
Bureau of Standards .... BUSTDS
Bureau of State Security [*Later, Department of National Security*] [*South Africa*] .... BOSS
Bureau of State Services [*of Public Health Service*] .... BSS
Bureau of Statistics, Alberta Treasury, Edmonton, Alberta [*Library symbol National Library of Canada*] (NLC) .... AETBS
Bureau of Steam Engineering [*Navy*] .... BSE
Bureau of Student Support [*Office of Education*] .... BSS
Bureau of Supplies and Accounts [*Later, NSUPSC*] [*Navy*] .... BSA
Bureau of Supplies and Accounts [*Later, NSUPSC*] [*Navy*] .... BUSANDA
Bureau of Supplies and Accounts [*Later, NSUPSC*] [*Navy*] .... NAVSANDA
Bureau of Supplies and Accounts [*Later, NSUPSC*] [*Navy*] .... S & A
Bureau of Supplies and Accounts Shipment Order [*Obsolete Navy*] .... SANDASO
Bureau of Technical Assistance Operations [*UN*] .... BTAO
Bureau of Technical Information (SAA) .... BTI
Bureau of the Budget [*Later, OMB*] .... BB
Bureau of the Budget [*Later, OMB*] .... BOB
Bureau of the Budget [*Later, OMB*] .... BuB
Bureau of the Budget [*Later, OMB*] .... BUBUD
Bureau of the Budget Approval [*Obsolete*] .... BBA
Bureau of the Budget in Exile Unrequited Marching and Chowder Society (EA) .... BBEUMCS
Bureau of the Census [*Department of Commerce*] (MCD) .... BC
Bureau of the Census, Field Division Library, Washington, DC [*OCLC symbol*] (OCLC) .... CBW
Bureau of the Census, Washington, DC [*OCLC symbol*] (OCLC) .... CBU
Bureau of the Mint [*Department of the Treasury*] .... BM
Bureau of the Public Debt [*Department of the Treasury*] .... BPD
Bureau of Trade Regulation [*Department of Commerce*] .... BTR

Bureau of Transport and Communications Economics [*Austria Also, an information service or system*] (IID) .... BTCE
Bureau of Transport Economics and Statistics [*ICC*] .... BTE & S
Bureau of Transportation and International Services [*US Postal Service*] (MCD) .... BTIS
Bureau of Transportation Statistics [*BTS*] [*OFR*] (TAG) ...... BTS
Bureau of Transportation Statistics (USGC) .... BTS
Bureau of University Travel [*Defunct*] .... BUT
Bureau of Veterans Reemployment Rights [*Department of Labor*] .... BVRR
Bureau of Veterinary Medicine [*FDA*] .... BVM
Bureau of Vital Statistics (AFM) .... BVS
Bureau of Vocational Rehabilitation (OICC) .... BVR
Bureau of War Risk Litigation .... BWRL
Bureau of Water Carriers .... BWC
Bureau of Weapons [*Navy*] .... BUWEAPS
Bureau of Work-Training Programs [*Terminated, 1969*] [*Department of Labor*] .... BWTP
Bureau of Yards and Docks [*Later, NFEC*] [*Washington, DC*] [*Navy*] ...... BUDOCKS
Bureau of Yards and Docks [*Later, NFEC*] [*Navy*] .... BUY & D
Bureau of Yards and Docks [*Later, NFEC*] [*Navy*] (KSC) .... BUYARD
Bureau of Yards and Docks [*Later, NFEC*] [*Navy*] ...... BUYDSDOCKS
Bureau of Yards and Docks [*Later, NFEC*] [*Navy*] (MCD) ...... BYD
Bureau of Yards and Docks [*Later, NFEC*] [*Navy*] .... Y & D
Bureau of Yards and Docks Publications [*Obsolete Navy*] .... NAVDOCKS
Bureau of Yards and Docks Publications [*Obsolete Navy*] .... NAVDOCSP
Bureau on Agriculture and Renewable Resources .... BARR
Bureau on Jewish Employment Problems (EA) .... BJEP
Bureau Permanent Interafricain de la Tse-Tse et de la Trypanosomiase .... BPITT
Bureau Permanent International des Constructeurs d'Automobiles [*International Permanent Bureau of Motor Manufacturers*] (EAIO) .... BPICA
Bureau Permanent International des Constructeurs de Motocycles [*Permanent International Bureau of Motorcycle Manufacturers*] (EAIO) ..... BPICM
Bureau Planned Procurement Guide [*Navy*] .... BPPG
Bureau Politique National [*National Political Bureau*] (AF) .... BPN
Bureau Regional d'Action Sida (AC) .... BRAS
Bureau Regional de l'UNESCO pour la Science et la Technologie en Afrique [*UNESCO Regional Office for Science and Technology in Africa - UNESCO-ROSTA*] [*Nairobi, Kenya*] (EAIO) .... BRUSTA
Bureau Regional de Science et de Technologie pour l'Europe et l'Amerique du Nord [*Regional Office for Science and Technology for Europe and North America*] (EAIO) .... SC/ROSTENA
Bureau Socialiste International [*Brussels*] .... BSI
Bureau Township Consolidated School District 250, Princeton, IL [*Library symbol Library of Congress*] (LCLS) .... IPriBSD
Bureau [*of Naval Personnel*] Unit Identification Code .... BUIC
Bureau +van Dijk, SA (IID) .... BvD
Bureau Veritas [*International register for the classification of shipping and aircraft*] .... BV
Bureau Veritas SA [*France ICAO designator*] (ICDA) .... XD
Bureau Veritas SA [*France ICAO designator*] (FAAC) .... XDA
Bureau voor de Industriele Eigendom, Bibliotheek Octrooiraad, The Hague, Netherlands [*Library symbol Library of Congress*] (LCLS) .... NeHB
Bureau Voucher [*Army*] (AABC) .... BV
Bureau Weather Control .... BWC
Bureaucratic Syndrome [*In book title "B.S.: The Bureaucratic Syndrome"*] .... BS
Bureaux Internationaux Reunis pour la Protection de la Propriete Intellectuelle [*United International Bureau for the Protection of Intellectual Property*] [*Later, WIPO*] .... BIRPI
Bureta [*Fiji*] [*Airport symbol*] (OAG) .... LEV
Bureta [*Fiji*] [*ICAO location identifier*] (ICLI) .... NFNB
Burford Public Library, Ontario [*Library symbol National Library of Canada*] (BIB) .... OBUR
Burford's Reports [*6-18 Oklahoma*] [*A publication*] (DLA) ...... Burf
Burg .... BG
Burg .... BG
Burg [*Commonly used*] (OPSA) .... BURG
Burg Eltz [*Federal Republic of Germany*] [*Seismograph station code, US Geological Survey*] (SEIS) .... BGG
Burg Feuerstein [*Germany ICAO location identifier*] (ICLI) .... EDQE
Burgan Bank [*Kuwait*] .... BB
Burgas [*Bulgaria*] [*Airport symbol*] (AD) .... BOJ
Burgas [*Bulgaria*] [*ICAO location identifier*] (ICLI) ...... LBBG
Burgaw, NC [*FM radio station call letters*] .... WKXB
Burgaw, NC [*AM radio station call letters*] .... WVBS
Burge on Appellate Jurisdiction [*1841*] [*A publication*] (DLA) ...... Burge App
Burge on Colonial and Foreign Law [*A publication*] (DLA) .... Burg Col & For Law
Burge on Colonial and Foreign Law [*A publication*] (DLA) .... Burge Col Law
Burge on Maritime International Law [*A publication*] (DLA) .... Burge Mar Int L
Burge on Suretyship [*A publication*] (DLA) .... Burge Sur
Burge on the Conflict of Laws [*A publication*] (DLA) .... Burge Confl Law
Burgeo Public Library, Newfoundland [*Library symbol National Library of Canada*] (NLC) .... NFBUR
Burger .... BGR
Burger King Corp. .... BK
Burgerlijk Wetboek [*Civil Code*] [*Netherlands*] (DLA) .... B
Burgerlijk Wetboek [*Civil Code*] [*Netherlands*] (ILCA) ...... BW
Burgersdorp [*South Africa*] [*ICAO location identifier*] (ICLI) .... FABD
Burgess .... BURG
Burgess' Reports [*16-49 Ohio*] [*A publication*] (DLA) ...... Burgen
Burgess' Reports [*16-49 Ohio*] [*A publication*] (DLA) ...... Burgess
Burgess-Manning Co., Dallas, TX [*Library symbol Library of Congress*] (LCLS) .... TxDaBM
Burgher (ROG) .... BURG
Burglar Alarm .... BA
Burglary .... BU

Burglary .... Burg
Burglary (DLA) .... BURGL
Burgomaster .... BM
Burgomaster (ROG) .... BURG
Burgos [*Spain ICAO location identifier*] (ICLI) .... LEBG
Burgs .... BGS
Burgs [*Postal Service standard*] (OPSA) .... BGS
Burgs [*Commonly used*] (OPSA) .... BURGS
Burgwyn's Digest Maryland Reports [*A publication*] (DLA) ...... Burg Dig
Burgwyn's Digest Maryland Reports [*A publication*] (DLA) .... Burgw MD Dig
Buried (ROG) .... B
Buried (ROG) .... BD
Buried (ROG) .... BU
Buried .... BUR
Buried Coarctate Mesa [*LASER diode technology*] (NITA) ...... BCM
Buried Distribution Wire [*Telecommunications*] (TEL) .... BDW
Buried Heterostructure (IAA) .... BH
Buried History: Quarterly Journal of the Australian Institute of Archaeology [*A publication*] (APTA) .... BH
Buried Injector Logic (IAA) .... BIL
Buried Line Intrusion Sensor [*Military*] (LAIN) .... BLIS
Buried Tape Armor [*Telecommunications*] (TEL) .... BT
Buried Trench Weapons System (MCD) .... BTWS
Buried Wire [*Telecommunications*] (TEL) .... BW
Buried-BIT [*Binary Digit*] Line [*Computer science*] (IAA) ...... BBL
Buried-Oxide Metal-Oxide Semiconductor (IAA) .... BOMOS
Burien-Seattle, WA [*AM radio station call letters*] .... KGNW
Burin Public Library, Burin, NF, Canada [*Library symbol Library of Congress*] (LCLS) .... CaNfBuri
Burin Public Library, Newfoundland [*Library symbol National Library of Canada*] (NLC) .... NFBURI
Burkburnett, TX [*FM radio station call letters*] .... KYYI
Burke. Copyright [*1842*] [*A publication*] (DLA) .... Burke Cop
Burke. Criminal Law [*2nd ed.*] [*1845*] [*A publication*] (DLA) .... Burke Cr L
Burke. International Copyright [*1852*] [*A publication*] (DLA) .... Burke Int Cop
Burke Mills [*NASDAQ symbol*] (TTSB) .... BMLS
Burke Mills, Inc. [*NASDAQ symbol*] (NQ) .... BMLS
Burke Mills, Inc. [*Associated Press*] (SAG) .... Burke
Burke on the Law of Public Schools [*A publication*] (DLA) .... Burke Pub Sch
Burke Public Library, Burke, SD [*Library symbol Library of Congress*] (LCLS) .... SdBu
Burke's Celebrated Trials [*A publication*] (DLA) .... Burke Cel Tr
Burke's Celebrated Trials [*A publication*] (DLA) .... Burke Tr
Burke's Celebrated Trials [*A publication*] (DLA) .... Cel Tr
Burkesville, KY [*AM radio station call letters*] .... WKYR
Burkesville, KY [*FM radio station call letters*] .... WKYR-FM
Burketown [*Australia Airport symbol*] (OAG) .... BUC
Burkina Faso [*ANSI two-letter standard code*] (CNC) ...... BF
Burkina Faso [*ANSI three-letter standard code*] (CNC) .... BFA
Burkitt's Lymphoma [*Medicine*] .... BL
Burks' Behavior Rating Scale [*Psychology*] (DAVI) .... BBRS
Burks Falls, Armour & Ryerson Union Library, Burks Falls, ON, Canada [*Library symbol*] [*Library of Congress*] (LCLS) .... CaOBfAR
Burks Falls, Armour, and Ryerson Union Library, Burks Falls, Ontario [*Library symbol National Library of Canada*] (NLC) .... OBFAR
Burks' Reports [*91-98 Virginia*] [*A publication*] (DLA) .... Burks
Burl (VRA) .... br
Burlamaqui's Natural and Political Law [*A publication*] (DLA) .... Burl Nat
Burlamaqui's Natural and Political Law [*A publication*] (DLA) .... Burl Natural & Pol Law
Burlamaqui's Natural and Political Law [*A publication*] (DLA) .... Burlamaqui
Burlap .... BRLP
Burlap (VRA) .... bur
Burlap and Jute Association (EA) .... BJA
Burleigh-Anstruther and Chandos Union Public Library, Apsley, Ontario [*Library symbol National Library of Canada*] (BIB) .... OABA
Burlesque (ROG) .... BURL
Burlesque Historical Society (EA) .... BHS
Burley and Dark Leaf Tobacco Export Association (EA) ...... BDLTEA
Burley Auction Warehouse Association (EA) .... BAWA
Burley, ID [*Location identifier FAA*] (FAAL) .... BYI
Burley, ID [*AM radio station call letters*] .... KBAR
Burley, ID [*FM radio station call letters*] .... KZDX
Burley Leaf Tobacco Dealers Association (EA) .... BLTDA
Burley Public Library, Burley, ID [*Library symbol*] [*Library of Congress*] (LCLS) .... IdBur
Burley Stabilization Corp. (EA) .... BSC
Burley Tobacco Growers Cooperative Association (EA) .... BTGCA
Burley-Rupert [*Idaho*] [*Airport symbol*] (AD) .... BYI
Burlingame Public Library, Burlingame, CA [*Library symbol Library of Congress*] (LCLS) .... CBu
Burlingame Research Center (MCD) .... BRC
Burlington [*Iowa*] [*Airport symbol*] (OAG) .... BRL
Burlington [*Vermont*] [*Airport symbol*] (OAG) .... BTV
Burlington [*Vermont*] [*Seismograph station code, US Geological Survey Closed*] (SEIS) .... BUR
Burlington Air Express [*ICAO designator*] (AD) .... BAX
Burlington Area Office [*Energy Research and Development Administration*] .... BAO
Burlington Association for Nuclear Disarmament (AC) .... BAND
Burlington Atmospheric Density Model Evaluation Program [*IBM Corp.*] .... BADMEP
Burlington Autosport Club (AC) .... BAC
Burlington, Cedar Rapids & Minnesota Railroad .... BCR & M
Burlington, Cedar Rapids & Northern Railway .... BCR & N
Burlington, CO [*AM radio station call letters*] .... KNAB

Burlington, CO [*FM radio station call letters*] .... KNAB-FM
Burlington Coat Factory [*NYSE symbol*] (TTSB) .... BCF
Burlington Coat Factory Warehouse Corp. [*NYSE symbol*] (SPSG) .... BCF
Burlington Coat Factory Warehouse Corp. [*Associated Press*] (SAG) .... BurlCoat
Burlington County Area Reference Library, Mount Holly, NJ [*Library symbol Library of Congress*] (LCLS) .... NjMhB
Burlington County Clerk, Mount Holly, NJ [*Library symbol Library of Congress*] (LCLS) .... NjMhCoC
Burlington County College, Pemberton, NJ [*Library symbol Library of Congress*] (LCLS) .... NjPeB
Burlington County Herald, Mount Holly, NJ [*Library symbol Library of Congress*] (LCLS) .... NjMhH
Burlington County Historical Society, Burlington, NJ [*Library symbol Library of Congress*] (LCLS) .... NjBuHi
Burlington County Lyceum [*Mount Holly Public Library*], Mount Holly, NJ [*Library symbol Library of Congress*] (LCLS) .... NjMhL
Burlington County Prison Museum, Mount Holly, NJ [*Library symbol Library of Congress*] (LCLS) .... NjMhPM
Burlington County Times, Willingboro, NJ [*Library symbol Library of Congress*] (LCLS) .... NjWiT
Burlington Free Public Library, Burlington, IA [*Library symbol Library of Congress*] (LCLS) .... IaB
Burlington, IA [*AM radio station call letters*] .... KBUR
Burlington, IA [*AM radio station call letters*] .... KCPS
Burlington, IA [*FM radio station call letters*] .... KDMG
Burlington, IA [*FM radio station call letters*] .... KGRS
Burlington, IA [*Television station call letters*] .... KJMH
Burlington, IA [*FM radio station call letters*] .... KKMI
Burlington Industries [*NYSE symbol*] (TTSB) .... BUR
Burlington Industries, Inc. [*NYSE symbol*] (SPSG) .... BUR
Burlington Industries, Inc. [*Formerly, Burlington Industries Equity*] [*Associated Press*] (SAG) .... BurlInds
Burlington Industries, Inc., Information Services Library, Greensboro, NC [*Library symbol Library of Congress*] (LCLS) .... NcGBI
Burlington Industries, Inc., Information Services Library, Greensboro, NC [*Library symbol Library of Congress*] (LCLS) .... NcGBur
Burlington/International [*Vermont*] [*ICAO location identifier*] (ICLI) .... KBTV
Burlington, KS [*FM radio station call letters*] .... KSNP
Burlington Liars Club (EA) .... BLC
Burlington Magazine [*A publication*] (BRI) .... BM
Burlington, NC [*Location identifier FAA*] (FAAL) .... BUY
Burlington, NC [*Television station call letters*] .... WAAP
Burlington, NC [*AM radio station call letters*] .... WBBB
Burlington, NC [*FM radio station call letters*] .... WPCM
Burlington, NJ [*Television station call letters*] .... WGTW
Burlington Northern, Inc. [*AAR code*] .... BN
Burlington Northern, Inc. [*NYSE symbol*] (SPSG) .... BNI
Burlington Northern (Manitoba) Limited [*AAR code*] .... BNML
Burlington Northern Santa Fe [*NYSE symbol*] (TTSB) .... BNI
Burlington Northern Santa Fe Corp. [*Associated Press*] (SAG) .... BNSF
Burlington Northern Santa Fe Corp. [*Associated Press*] (SAG) .... BurlNSF
Burlington, ON [*FM radio station call letters*] .... CING
Burlington Public Library [*UTLAS symbol*] .... BUR
Burlington Public Library, Burlington, CO [*Library symbol Library of Congress*] (LCLS) .... CoBur
Burlington Public Library, Burlington, ON, Canada [*Library symbol Library of Congress*] (LCLS) .... CaOBU
Burlington Public Library, Burlington, WI [*Library symbol Library of Congress*] (LCLS) .... WBur
Burlington Public Library, Ontario [*Library symbol National Library of Canada*] (NLC) .... OBU
Burlington Randomized Controlled Trial [*Criterion for medical evaluation*] .... BRCT
Burlington Res CoalSeamGasRty [*NYSE symbol*] (TTSB) .... BRU
Burlington Resources [*NYSE symbol*] (TTSB) .... BR
Burlington Resources Coal Seam Gas Royalty Trust [*NYSE symbol*] (SAG) .... BRU
Burlington Resources Coal Seam Gas Royalty Trust [*Associated Press*] (SAG) .... BurlRsCl
Burlington Resources, Inc. [*NYSE symbol*] (SPSG) .... BR
Burlington Resources, Inc. [*Associated Press*] (SAG) .... BrlRsc
Burlington Township Library, Burlington, MI [*Library symbol Library of Congress*] (LCLS) .... MiBurl
Burlington, VT [*Television station call letters*] .... WCAX
Burlington, VT [*Television station call letters*] .... WETK
Burlington, VT [*FM radio station call letters*] .... WEZF
Burlington, VT [*Television station call letters*] (RBYB) .... WFFF-TV
Burlington, VT [*AM radio station call letters*] .... WJOY
Burlington, VT [*AM radio station call letters*] .... WKDR
Burlington, VT [*FM radio station call letters*] .... WOKO
Burlington, VT [*FM radio station call letters*] .... WRUV
Burlington, VT [*AM radio station call letters*] .... WVMT
Burlington, VT [*Television station call letters*] .... WVNY
Burlington, VT [*FM radio station call letters*] .... WVPS
Burlington, WA [*Location identifier FAA*] (FAAL) .... BTA
Burlington, WI [*Location identifier FAA*] (FAAL) .... BUU
Burlington, WI [*FM radio station call letters*] .... WBSD
Burlington-Graham, NC [*AM radio station call letters*] .... WBAG
Burlington-Graham, NC [*FM radio station call letters*] (RBYB) .... WRSN-FM
Burlington-Graham, NC [*FM radio station call letters*] .... WZZU
Burlington-Rock Island Railroad Co. .... B-RI
Burma [*MARC geographic area code Library of Congress*] (LCCP) .... a-br--
Burma [*IYRU nationality code*] [*MARC country of publication code Library of Congress*] (LCCP) .... br
Burma [*ANSI two-letter standard code*] (CNC) .... BU
Burma [*ANSI three-letter standard code*] (CNC) .... BUR
Burma (WDAA) .... BURM
Burma [*International civil aircraft marking*] (ODBW) .... XY
Burma Airways Corp. [*Rangoon*] (EY) .... BAC
Burma Airways Corp. [*Myanmar*] [*ICAO designator*] (ICDA) .... UB
Burma Communist Party [*"White Flag" party*] [*Political party*] (PD) .... BCP
Burma Defense Army [*Later, BNA*] [*World War II*] .... BDA
Burma Frontier Force [*British military*] (DMA) .... BFF
Burma Independence Army [*Fighting on the side of the Japanese*] [*World War II*] .... BIA
Burma Law Institute. Journal [*A publication*] (DLA) .... BLIJ
Burma Law Institute. Journal [*A publication*] (DLA) .... Burma L Inst J
Burma Law Institute. Journal [*A publication*] (DLA) .... Burma Law Inst J
Burma Law Journal [*A publication*] (DLA) .... BLJ
Burma Law Journal [*A publication*] (DLA) .... Bur LJ
Burma Law Journal [*A publication*] (DLA) .... Burm LJ
Burma Law Reports [*A publication*] (DLA) .... Bur LR
Burma Law Reports [*A publication*] (DLA) .... Burm LR
Burma Law Reports [*A publication*] (DLA) .... Burma LR
Burma Law Times [*A publication*] (DLA) .... BLT
Burma Law Times [*A publication*] (DLA) .... Bur LT
Burma Law Times [*A publication*] (DLA) .... Burm LT
Burma Military Police [*British military*] (DMA) .... BMP
Burma National Army [*Formerly, BDA*] .... BNA
Burma Socialist Programme Party [*Political party*] (PPW) .... BSPP
Burma Trade Union Congress .... BTUC
Burma-America Buddhist Association (EA) .... BABA
Burmac Energy Corp. [*Vancouver Stock Exchange symbol*] .... BUS
Burmah Castrol Ltd. [*NASDAQ symbol*] (SAG) .... BURM
Burmah Castrol Ltd. [*Associated Press*] (SAG) .... BurmhC
Burmah Castrol plc ADR [*NASDAQ symbol*] (TTSB) .... BURMY
Burman Aviation (Charter) Ltd. [*British*] [*FAA designator*] (FAAC) .... BMM
Burmese [*MARC language code Library of Congress*] (LCCP) .... bur
Burmese Air Force .... BAF
Burmese Army (CINC) .... BA
Burmese Navy (CINC) .... BN
Burn Depth Indicator [*A video camera*] [*Medicine*] (DAVI) .... BDI
Burn Index [*Medicine*] .... BI
Burn on Stock Jobbing [*A publication*] (DLA) .... Burn St Job
Burn Rate .... BR
Burn Time [*NASA*] .... BT
Burn Time Remaining (MCD) .... BTR
Burn to Depletion [*NASA*] (KSC) .... BTD
Burn Unit [*Medicine*] .... BU
Burnable Poison Rod [*Nuclear energy*] (NRCH) .... BPR
Burnable Poison Rod Assembly [*Nuclear energy*] (NRCH) .... BPRA
Burnable Poison Water Reactor (IEEE) .... BPWR
Burnaby Art Gallery, British Columbia [*Library symbol National Library of Canada*] (NLC) .... BBA
Burnaby Art Gallery, Burnaby, BC, Canada [*Library symbol Library of Congress*] (LCLS) .... CaBBA
[*The*] **Burnaby Association for the Mentally Handicapped** .... BAMH
Burnaby Public Library, British Columbia [*Library symbol National Library of Canada*] (NLC) .... BB
Burnaby Public Library, Burnaby, BC, Canada [*Library symbol Library of Congress*] (LCLS) .... CaBB
Burnaby Public Library, Kingsway Branch, Kingsway, BC, Canada [*Library symbol*] [*Library of Congress*] (LCLS) .... CaBBK
Burnaby Village Museum, British Columbia [*Library symbol National Library of Canada*] (NLC) .... BBVM
Burn-Bash-Bury [*Australian trash disposal policy in Vietnam*] (VNW) .... B-B-B
Burndale Resources Ltd. [*Vancouver Stock Exchange symbol*] .... BDL
Burn-Dressing Change [*Medicine*] .... BDC
Burndy Corp., Technical Library, Norwalk, CT [*Library symbol Library of Congress*] (LCLS) .... CtNowaB
Burned [*Ecology*] .... B
Burned Area [*Ecology*] .... BA
Burned, Shaded [*Ecology*] .... BS
Burner (MSA) .... BNR
Burner .... BRNR
Burners Out of Service [*Combustion emission control*] .... BOOS
Burnet. Criminal Law of Scotland [*A publication*] (DLA) .... Burn Cr L
Burnet, Duckworth & Palmer, Calgary, Alberta [*Library symbol National Library of Canada*] (BIB) .... ACBDP
Burnet. Manuscript Decisions, Scotch Court of Session [*A publication*] (DLA) .... Burnet
Burnet, TX [*Location identifier FAA*] (FAAL) .... BMQ
Burnet, TX [*FM radio station call letters*] .... KBLK
Burnet, TX [*AM radio station call letters*] .... KHLB
Burnet, TX [*FM radio station call letters*] .... KHLB-FM
Burnett Elementary School, Houston, TX [*Library symbol*] [*Library of Congress*] (LCLS) .... TxHBE
Burnettown, SC [*AM radio station call letters*] (RBYB) .... WKRU-AM
Burnettown, SC [*AM radio station call letters*] .... WVAA
Burnett's Reports [*20-22 Oregon*] [*A publication*] (DLA) .... Burnett
Burnett's Wisconsin Reports [*A publication*] (DLA) .... Burn
Burnett's Wisconsin Reports [*A publication*] (DLA) .... Burnett
Burnett's Wisconsin Reports [*A publication*] (DLA) .... Burnett (Wis)
Burnett's Wisconsin Reports [*A publication*] (DLA) .... Burnett's Rep
Burnett's Wisconsin Supreme Court Reports [*1841-43*] [*A publication*] (DLA) .... Bur
Burney, CA [*Location identifier FAA*] (FAAL) .... BNY
Burney, CA [*FM radio station call letters*] .... KARZ
Burney, CA [*AM radio station call letters*] .... KAVA
Burney, CA [*FM radio station call letters*] .... KIBC
Burney, CA [*FM radio station call letters*] .... KNCA

Burnham [*England*] .... BURN
Burnham City Hospital, Champaign, IL [*Library symbol Library of Congress*] (LCLS) .... IChamBH
Burnham, J. B., Chicago IL [*STAC*] .... BJB
Burnham, PA [*FM radio station call letters*] .... WVNW
Burnham Pacific Prop [*NYSE symbol*] (TTSB) .... BPP
Burnham Pacific Properties [*NYSE symbol*] (SPSG) .... BPP
Burnham Pacific Properties [*Associated Press*] (SAG) .... BurnPP
Burnie High School [*Tasmania*] [*Seismograph station code, US Geological Survey*] (SEIS) .... BNE
Burnie-Wynward [*Tasmania*] [*Airport symbol*] (AD) .... WNY
Burn-In/Aging Tester .... BIAT
Burn-In Screening .... BIS
Burning .... BRNG
Burning .... BRNNG
Burning Anomaly Rate Factor (MCD) .... BARF
Burning Bush [*Freemasonry*] .... BB
Burning Bush Museum, Pictou, Nova Scotia [*Library symbol National Library of Canada*] (BIB) .... NSPBB
Burning Bush Museum, Pictou, NS, Canada [*Library symbol*] [*Library of Congress*] (LCLS) .... CaNSPBB
Burning Feet Syndrome [*Medicine*] (DMAA) .... BF
Burning Rate Extraction Technique (MCD) .... BRET
Burning Surface Area of Propellant [*Symbol*] [*Aerospace*] .... A
Burnish (KSC) .... BNH
Burnish (MSA) .... BNSH
Burnished (VRA) .... burn
Burnisher (MSA) .... BRNSHR
Burnishing Tool .... BITO
Burnout (KSC) .... BO
Burnout Missile Configuration [*Military*] .... BMC
Burnout Proof .... BOP
Burnout Safety Factor (SAA) .... BOSF
Burnout Velocity .... BOV
Burns & Laird Line [*Steamship*] (MHDW) .... B & L
Burns and McDonnell Engineering Co., Kansas City, MO [*Library symbol Library of Congress*] (LCLS) .... MoKBM
Burns & Roe, Inc., Branch Library, Hempstead, NY [*Library symbol Library of Congress*] (LCLS) .... NHemB
Burns & Roe, Inc., Oradell, NJ [*Library symbol Library of Congress*] (LCLS) .... NjOrdB
Burns and Schreiber Comedy Hour [*Television program*] [*Obsolete*] .... BS
Burns' Annotated Statutes [*Indiana*] [*A publication*] (DLA) .... Burns' Ann St
Burns' Annotated Statutes [*Indiana*] [*A publication*] (DLA) .... Burns' Rev St
Burn's Attorney's Practice [*A publication*] (DLA) .... Burn Att Pr
Burns. Conveyancing Practice [*Scotland*] [*A publication*] (DLA) .... Burns Pract
Burn's Ecclesiastical Law [*A publication*] (DLA) .... B Ecc L
Burn's Ecclesiastical Law [*A publication*] (DLA) .... Burn Ecc Law
Burn's Ecclesiastical Law [*A publication*] (DLA) .... Burn Eccl
Burn's Ecclesiastical Law [*A publication*] (DLA) .... Burn's Ecc Law
Burns Elementary School, Hicksville, NY [*Library symbol Library of Congress*] (LCLS) .... NHickBE
Burns Federation [*Scotland*] (EAIO) .... BA
Burns' Indiana Administrative Rules and Regulations [*A publication*] (DLA) .... Ind Admin R
Burns' Indiana Statutes, Annotated Code Edition [*A publication*] (DLA) .... Ind Code Ann
Burn's Justice of the Peace [*England*] [*A publication*] (DLA) .... B Just
Burn's Justice of the Peace [*England*] [*A publication*] (DLA) .... Burn JP
Burn's Justice of the Peace [*England*] [*A publication*] (DLA) .... Burn's JP (Eng)
Burns Lake, BC [*AM radio station call letters*] .... CFLD
Burns Lake Public Library, British Columbia [*Library symbol National Library of Canada*] (NLC) .... BBUL
Burn's Law Dictionary [*A publication*] (DLA) .... Burn Dict
Burn's Law Dictionary [*A publication*] (DLA) .... Burn Law Dict
Burn's Marine Insurance [*A publication*] (DLA) .... Burn Mar Ins
Burns, OR [*Location identifier FAA*] (FAAL) .... BNO
Burns, OR [*Location identifier FAA*] (FAAL) .... ILR
Burns, OR [*FM radio station call letters*] (RBYB) .... KQHC-FM
Burns, OR [*AM radio station call letters*] .... KZZR
Burns, Philip, & Co. [*Steamship*] (MHDW) .... BP & CO
Burns Society of the City of New York (EA) .... BSCNY
Burns United Support Group (EA) .... BUSG
Burns, WY [*FM radio station call letters*] .... KMUS
Burnside, KY [*FM radio station call letters*] .... WJDJ
Burnside, KY [*AM radio station call letters*] .... WKEQ
Burnside-Ott Aviation Training Center [*Florida*] .... BATC
Burnsville, NC [*AM radio station call letters*] .... WKYK
Burnt (ROG) .... BNT
Burnt [*Philately*] .... brnt
Burnt (ROG) .... BT
Burnt Island Gold Ltd. (NPL) [*Vancouver Stock Exchange symbol*] .... BUR
Burnt Out But Opulent .... BOBO
Burnthills [*ICAO designator*] (AD) .... KB
Burnthrough (NVT) .... BT
Burnup .... BU
Burnup Fraction [*of fuel in plasma*] (MCD) .... BF
Burr Junior High School, Commack, NY [*Library symbol*] [*Library of Congress*] (LCLS) .... NCoBJ
Burr Oak Township Library, Burr Oak, MI [*Library symbol Library of Congress*] (LCLS) .... MiBar
Burr Oak Township Library, Burr Oak, MI [*Library symbol*] [*Library of Congress*] (LCLS) .... MiBur
Burrard Inlet Environmental Action Program (AC) .... BIEAP
Burr-Brown Corp. [*NASDAQ symbol*] (NQ) .... BBRC

Burr-Brown Corp. [*Associated Press*] (SAG) .... BurrBr
Burrell-Lawrence-Kennedy [*Vacuum milking device*] .... BLK
Burrell's Admiralty Cases [*1584-1839*] [*A publication*] (DLA) .... Burr Adm
Burrell's Reports, Admiralty, Edited by Marsden [*167 English Reprint*] [*A publication*] (DLA) .... Burrell
Burrell's Reports, Admiralty, Edited by Marsden [*167 English Reprint*] [*A publication*] (DLA) .... Burrell (Eng)
Burrill on Assignments [*A publication*] (DLA) .... Burr Ass
Burrill on Assignments [*A publication*] (DLA) .... Burrill Assignm
Burrill on Circumstantial Evidence [*A publication*] (DLA) .... Bur Circ Ev
Burrill on Circumstantial Evidence [*A publication*] (DLA) .... Burr Circ Ev
Burrill on Circumstantial Evidence [*A publication*] (DLA) .... Burrill Circ Ev
Burrill on Voluntary Assignments [*A publication*] (DLA) .... Bur Ass
Burrill on Voluntary Assignments [*A publication*] (DLA) .... Burrill Ass
Burrill's Forms [*A publication*] (DLA) .... Bur Forms
Burrill's Forms [*A publication*] (DLA) .... Burr Forms
Burrill's Law Dictionary [*A publication*] (DLA) .... Bur Law Dic
Burrill's Law Dictionary [*A publication*] (DLA) .... Burr Dict
Burrill's Law Dictionary [*A publication*] (DLA) .... Burr Law Dict
Burrill's Law Dictionary [*A publication*] (DLA) .... Burrill
Burrill's New York Practice [*A publication*] (DLA) .... Bur Pr
Burrill's New York Practice [*A publication*] (DLA) .... Burr Pr
Burrill's Practice [*A publication*] (DLA) .... Burrill Pr
Burring Cutter .... BUCU
Burro Club [*Democratic political organization*] [*Defunct*] (EA) .... BC
Burro Red Blood Cells .... BRBC
Burroughs Advanced Statistical Inquiry System [*Computer science*] (BUR) .... BASIS
Burroughs Algebraic Compiler (IEEE) .... BALGOL
Burroughs and Gresson's Irish Equity Pleader [*A publication*] (DLA) .... Bur & Gres Eq Pl
Burroughs and Gresson's Irish Equity Pleader [*A publication*] (DLA) .... Burr & Gr Eq Pl
Burroughs and Sperry Information Systems [*Suggested name for the corporation formed by the Burroughs/Sperry merger*] .... BASIS
Burroughs Bibliophiles (EA) .... BB
Burroughs Common Language [*Computer science*] (BUR) .... BCL
Burroughs Computer Output to Microfilm (IEEE) .... BCOM
Burroughs Corp. .... BC
Burroughs Corp. (AAG) .... BRC
Burroughs Corp., Western Region Central Technical Library, Pasadena, CA [*Library symbol Library of Congress*] (LCLS) .... CPB-E
Burroughs Current Mode Logic .... BCML
Burroughs Data Link Control [*Computer science*] (BUR) .... BDLC
Burroughs Distribution Scheduling System [*Computer science*] (BUR) .... BURDS
Burroughs Electrographic Printer-Plotter for Ordnance Computing .... BEPOC
Burroughs Electronic Accounting Machine (BUR) .... BEAM
Burrough's History of the Chancery [*A publication*] (DLA) .... Bur Chy
Burroughs' History of the Chancery [*A publication*] (DLA) .... Burr Ch
Burroughs Hospital Administrative System [*Computer science*] (BUR) .... BHAS
Burroughs Input and Display Terminal (IAA) .... BIDS
Burroughs Inventory Control System [*Computer science*] (BUR) .... BICS
Burroughs Inventory Planning Analysis and Simulation System [*Computer science*] (BUR) .... BIPASS
Burroughs on Public Securities [*A publication*] (DLA) .... Burr Pub Sec
Burroughs on Taxation [*A publication*] (DLA) .... Bur Tax
Burroughs on Taxation [*A publication*] (DLA) .... Burr Tax
Burroughs Optical Lens Docking System (MCD) .... BOLDS
Burroughs Programming Language (IAA) .... BPL
Burroughs Scientific Processor [*Computer science*] (BUR) .... BSP
Burroughs, UNIVAC, NCR, Control Data, Honeywell [*IBM competitors in computer manufacture*] .... BUNCH
Burroughs Wellcome & Co. .... BW
Burroughs Wellcome & Co., Greenville, NC [*Library symbol Library of Congress*] (LCLS) .... NcDurW-Gv
Burroughs Wellcome & Co., Kirkland, Quebec [*Library symbol National Library of Canada*] (NLC) .... QKBW
Burroughs Wellcome & Co., Research Triangle Park, NC [*OCLC symbol*] (OCLC) .... NRT
Burroughs Wellcome Fund .... BWF
Burroughs Wellcome, Inc., Kirkland Lake, ON, Canada [*Library symbol*] [*Library of Congress*] (LCLS) .... CaQKIBW
Burroughs Wellcome Research Institute [*Great Britain*] [*Research code symbol*] .... BW
Burrow. English King's Bench Reports [*A publication*] (DLA) .... Bur
Burrow. English King's Bench Reports Tempore Lord Mansfield [*97, 98 English Reprint*] [*A publication*] (DLA) .... Burr
Burrow. English King's Bench Reports Tempore Lord Mansfield [*97, 98 English Reprint*] [*A publication*] (DLA) .... Burr (Eng)
Burrow's English Settlement Cases [*A publication*] (DLA) .... Bur SC
Burrow's English Settlement Cases [*A publication*] (DLA) .... Burr S Cas
Burrow's English Settlement Cases [*A publication*] (DLA) .... Burr S Cases
Burrow's English Settlement Cases [*A publication*] (DLA) .... Burr SC
Burrow's English Settlement Cases [*A publication*] (DLA) .... Burr Sett Cas
Burrow's English Settlement Cases [*A publication*] (DLA) .... Burr Sett Cas (Eng)
Burrow's English Settlement Cases [*A publication*] (DLA) .... Burrow Sett Cas
Burrow's English Settlement Cases [*A publication*] (DLA) .... Sett Cas
Burrow's Reports, English King's Bench [*A publication*] (DLA) .... Burrow
Burrow's Reports Tempore Mansfield [*England*] (DLA) .... B Monr
Burrow's Reports Tempore Mansfield [*England*] [*A publication*] (DLA) .... BM
Burrow's Reports Tempore Mansfield [*England*] [*A publication*] (DLA) .... Bur M
Burrow's Reports Tempore Mansfield [*England*] [*A publication*] (DLA) .... Burr TM
Burrows Trail Arts Council (AC) .... BTAC
Burr's Lane Junior High School, Dix Hills, NY [*Library symbol Library of Congress*] (LCLS) .... NDxhBJ

Burr's Trial, Reported by Robertson [*A publication*] (DLA) .... Burr Tr
Burr's Trial, Reported by Robertson [*A publication*] (DLA) .... Burr Tr Rob
Burry Port [*Welsh depot code*] .... BP
Burry Port & Gwendraeth Valley Railway [*Wales*] .... BPGV
Bursa [*Turkey*] [*Airport symbol Obsolete*] (OAG) .... BTZ
Bursa [*Turkey ICAO location identifier*] (ICLI) .... LTBE
Bursa Airlines, Inc. [*Turkey ICAO designator*] (ICDA) .... FB
Bursa Cells [*Of thymus or lymph nodes*] .... B
Bursa Equivalent Lymphocyte (MAE) .... B-L
Bursa Hava Yollari [*ICAO designator*] (AD) .... WL
Bursal Dependent [*Cells*] [*Immunology*] .... BD
Bursal Lymphomas [*Oncology*] .... BLYM
Bursar (ABBR) .... BRSR
Bursar .... BRSR
Bursar .... BURS
Bursary (ABBR) .... BRSRY
Bur-Sin (BJA) .... BS
Bursitis [*Medicine*] .... B
Bursitis (ABBR) .... BRSTS
Burst .... BRST
Burst (IAA) .... BST
Burst and Synchronous BIT [*Binary Digit*] **Generator** [*Computer science*] (IAA) .... BSBG
Burst and Transient Source Experiment [*Gamma Ray Observatory satellite data collection*] .... BATSE
Burst Cartridge Detection .... BCD
Burst Cladding Detection System [*Nuclear energy*] (NUCP) .... BCD
Burst Communications Systems (MCD) .... BCS
Burst Delay Timer (MCD) .... BDT
Burst EDO [*Extended Data Out*] [*Computer science*] .... BEDO
Burst Error Correction [*Encoder/decoder*] (MCD) .... BEC
Burst Error Detection and Correlation .... BEDAC
Burst Height Compensator [*Military*] (CAAL) .... BHC
Burst Limit Switch (MCD) .... BLS
Burst Measuring System .... BMS
Burst Multiplexer Channel [*Telecommunications*] .... BMC
Burst of Ventricular Pacing [*Medicine*] (DMAA) .... BVP
Burst Position Locator .... BPL
Burst Slug Detection .... BSD
Burst Time Indicator (MCD) .... BTI
Burst Time Plan (LAIN) .... BTP
Burst Tolerance [*Telecommunications*] (ACRL) .... BT
Burst Transmission Group .... BTG
Burst Trapping (MHDI) .... BT
Burst Waveform .... BWF
Burster .... BRSTR
Burst-Error Channel (IAA) .... BEC
Burster-Trimmer-Stacker [*Printing*] (DGA) .... BTS
Burst-Forming Unit .... BFU
Burst-Forming Unit erythroid [*Hematology*] .... BFUe
Burst-Height Indicator .... BHI
Bursting (ABBR) .... BRSTG
Bursting Charge [*Military*] .... BC
Bursting Pacemaker Potential [*Electrophysiology*] .... BPP
Burst-on-Target (MCD) .... BOT
Burst-Promoting Activity [*Cytology*] .... BPA
Burst-Promoting Factor [*Endocrinology; hematology*] .... BPF
Bursts with Memory [*Physics*] .... BWM
Burt Reynolds Fan Club (EA) .... BRFC
Burton and Bitter [*Drink served in British public houses*] .... BB
Burton. Cases and Opinions [*A publication*] (DLA) .... Cas Op
Burton. Manual of the Laws of Scotland [*A publication*] (DLA) .... Burt Man
Burton on Bankruptcy [*A publication*] (DLA) .... Burt Bank
Burton on Real Property [*A publication*] (DLA) .... Burt Real Prop
Burton on Real Property [*A publication*] (DLA) .... Burt RP
Burton Public Library, Burton, OH [*OCLC symbol*] (OCLC) .... BVP
Burton Public Library, Burton, OH [*Library symbol Library of Congress*] (LCLS) .... OBur
Burton-On-Trent Public Library, Burton-On-Trent, United Kingdom [*Library symbol Library of Congress*] (LCLS) .... UkBot
Burton's Collection of Cases and Opinions [*England*] [*A publication*] (DLA) .... Burt Cas
Burton's Parliamentary Diary [*A publication*] (DLA) .... Burt Parl
Burton's Scotch Trials [*A publication*] (DLA) .... Burt Sc Tr
Burtonwood [*British ICAO location identifier*] (ICLI) .... EGOB
Burundi [*Aircraft nationality and registration mark*] (FAAC) 9U
Burundi [*MARC country of publication code Library of Congress*] (LCCP) .... bd
Burundi [*ANSI three-letter standard code*] (CNC) .... BDI
Burundi [*ANSI two-letter standard code*] (CNC) .... BI
Burundi (VRA) .... Buru
Burundi [*MARC geographic area code Library of Congress*] (LCCP) .... f-bd--
Burwash, YT [*ICAO location identifier*] (ICLI) .... CYDB
Burwell, NE [*Location identifier FAA*] (FAAL) .... BUB
Bury Cooper Whitehead Ltd. [*British*] (IRUK) .... BCW
Burying (ABBR) .... BRYG
Bus [*Computer science*] .... B
Bus Access Module .... BAM
Bus Acknowledgement [*Computer science*] (TEL) .... BUSAK
Bus and Coach Association of New South Wales .... BCANSW
Bus and Coach Council [*British*] .... BCC
Bus Arbitration Module [*Motorola, Inc.*] .... BAM
Bus Association of New York State (SRA) .... BANY
Bus Automation [*Computer science*] (ODBW) .... BA
Bus Available [*Computer science*] .... BA
Bus Block Transfer .... BBLT
Bus Compatible (IAA) .... BC
Bus Configuration Table (MCD) .... BCT
Bus Control Card [*Electronics*] (ACRL) .... BCC
Bus Control Electronics (MCD) .... BCE
Bus Control Element (MCD) .... BCE
Bus Control Interface Unit (MCD) .... BCIU
Bus Control Unit (KSC) .... BCU
Bus Controller (MCD) .... BC
Bus Coupler [*Computer science*] (MCD) .... BC
Bus Differential [*Electronics*] (IAA) .... BDF
Bus Direction [*Computer science*] (TEL) .... BDIR
Bus Driver [*Electronics*] (IAA) .... BD
Bus Duct [*Electronics*] (IAA) .... BD
Bus Enable [*Computer science*] (MHDI) .... BEN
Bus for Data Output (IAA) .... BDO
Bus Grant (IAA) .... BG
Bus History Association (EA) .... BHA
Bus Interface [*Computer science*] .... B/I
Bus Interface Adapter (SSD) .... BIA
Bus Interface Circuit [*Computer science*] (MDG) .... BIC
Bus Interface Controller [*Computer science*] (NITA) .... BIC
Bus Interface Module .... BIM
Bus Interface Unit [*Computer science*] .... BIU
Bus Interrupter Module [*Motorola, Inc.*] .... BIM
Bus Ion Mass Spectrometer [*Space science instrumentation*] .... BIMS
Bus Link (IAA) .... BL
Bus Master Interface Controller [*Computer science*] (PCM) .... BMIC
Bus Monitor Unit (MCD) .... BMU
Bus Multiplexer .... BM
Bus Neutral Mass Spectrometer [*Space science instrumentation*] .... BNMS
Bus Out Register [*Computer science*] .... BOR
Bus Proprietors' Association, Victoria [*Australia*] .... BPAV
Bus Request [*Computer science*] (IAA) .... BR
Bus Request [*Computer science*] (TEL) .... BUSRQ
Bus Selector [*Computer science*] .... BSLR
Bus Service Management System [*FTA*] (TAG) .... BSMS
Bus Terminal Unit (MCD) .... BTU
Bus Tie [*Technical drawings*] .... BT
Bus Tie Breaker .... BTB
Bus Tie Contractor (MCD) .... BTC
Bus Tie Relay (MCD) .... BTS
Bus Transfer (AAG) .... BTR
Bus Unit [*Computer science*] .... BU
Bus Workers' Protection Society [*A union*] [*British*] .... BWPS
Busala [*Zaire*] [*ICAO location identifier*] (ICLI) .... FZCR
Busan [*South Korea ICAO location identifier*] (ICLI) .... RKPP
Bus-Bar Layout Drawing [*Computer science*] (TEL) .... BB
Busbee's Criminal Digest [*North Carolina*] [*A publication*] (DLA) .... Busb Cr Dig
Busbee's North Carolina Equity Reports [*A publication*] (DLA) .... Bus Eq
Busbee's North Carolina Equity Reports [*A publication*] (DLA) .... Busb Eq
Busbee's North Carolina Equity Reports [*A publication*] (DLA) .... Busbee Eq (NC)
Busbee's North Carolina Law Reports [*A publication*] (DLA) .... BNC
Busbee's North Carolina Law Reports [*A publication*] (DLA) .... Busb
Busbee's North Carolina Law Reports [*A publication*] (DLA) .... Busb L
Busboy (ABBR) .... BSBY
Busch Grand National [*Auto racing*] .... BGN
Buschke Memory Test [*Psychology*] (DAVI) .... BMT
Bus-Earth Tracking Station Link [*NASA*] .... BEL
Buses and Trucks .... BAT
Buses International Association (EA) .... BIA
Buses Worldwide [*British*] [*An association*] (DBA) .... BWW
Bush Boake Allen [*NYSE symbol*] (TTSB) .... BOA
Bush, Boake Allen, Inc. [*NYSE symbol*] (SAG) .... BOA
Bush Boake Allen, Inc. [*Associated Press*] (SAG) .... Bush BA
Bush Church Aid Society [*Australia*] .... BCA
Bush Church Aid Society of Australia .... BCASA
Bush Fire Board of Western Australia .... BFBWA
Bush Fire Council of the Northern Territory [*Australia*] .... BFCNT
Bush Fires Board [*Western Australia*] .... BFB
Bush Indus Cl'A' [*NYSE symbol*] (TTSB) .... BSH
Bush Industries [*NYSE symbol*] (SAG) .... BSH
Bush Industries [*Associated Press*] (SAG) .... BushInd
Bush Pilots Airways [*ICAO designator*] (AD) .... QN
Bush Pilots Airways Ltd. [*Australia*] (ADA) .... BPA
Bush Terminal R. R. [*AAR code*] .... BUSH
Bushby. Parliamentary Elections [*5th ed.*] [*1880*] [*A publication*] (DLA) .... Bush Elec
Bushed (ABBR) .... BSHD
Bushehr [*Iran*] [*Airport symbol*] (OAG) .... BUZ
Bushehr [*Iran*] [*ICAO location identifier*] (ICLI) .... OIBT
Bushehr/Bushehr [*Iran*] [*ICAO location identifier*] (ICLI) .... OIBB
Bushel (ROG) .... BSH
Bushel (ABBR) .... BSHL
Bushel .... BU
Bushel .... BUS
Bushel .... BUSH
Bushfires Council of the Northern Territory [*Australia*] .... BCNT
Bushier (ABBR) .... BSHR
Bushiest (ABBR) .... BSHST
Bushiness (ABBR) .... BSHNS
Bushing (MSA) .... BSHG
Bushing (MSA) .... BUSH
Bushing Current Transformer (KSC) .... BCT
Bushing Potential Device (MSA) .... BPD
Bushire [*Iran*] [*Airport symbol*] (AD) .... BUZ

Bushmaster Aircraft Corp. [*ICAO aircraft manufacturer identifier*] (ICAO) .... BU
Bushnell, FL [*AM radio station call letters*] .... WKFL
Bushnell, IL [*FM radio station call letters*] .... WLMD
Bush's Digest of Florida Laws [*A publication*] (DLA) .... Bush Dig
Bush's Kentucky Reports [*64-77 Kentucky*] [*A publication*] (DLA) .... Bush
Bush's Kentucky Reports [*64-77 Kentucky*] [*A publication*] (DLA) .... Bush (KY)
Bushveldt Carabineers [*British military*] (DMA) .... BVC
Bushwaster Armored Turret (MCD) .... BAT
Bushwhack (ABBR) .... BSHWHK
Bushwhacker (ABBR) .... BSHWHKR
Busia [*Kenya*] [*ICAO location identifier*] (ICLI) .... HKBA
Busily (ABBR) .... BSLY
Business [*Slang*] (DSUE) .... BIZ
Business [*As in show biz*] (WDMC) .... biz
Business (ABBR) .... BSNS
Business (AFM) .... BUS
Business (DD) .... bus
Business .... BUS
Business (BARN) .... Busn
Business Account Number File [*IRS*] .... BANF
Business/Accounts Reporting Operating Network [*Computer science*] (PDAA) .... BARON
Business Acronyms [*A publication*] .... BA
Business Administration [*A publication*] .... Bus Admin
Business Administration, Management, and/or Marketing Programs [*Association of Independent Colleges and Schools specialization code*] .... BS
Business Advisory Committee on Procurement [*DoD*] .... BACP
Business Advisory Council [*Later, Business Council*] .... BAC
Business Air AG [*Switzerland ICAO designator*] (FAAC) .... BUR
Business Air Ltd. [*British ICAO designator*] (FAAC) .... GNT
Business Air Service Ltd. [*Airline*] [*Canada*] .... BAS
Business Air Services (Toronto) Ltd. [*Canada ICAO designator*] (FAAC) .... BAM
Business Air Taxi [*Switzerland ICAO designator*] (FAAC) .... BUT
Business Air Transport Service .... BATS
Business Aircraft Users' Association [*British*] .... BAUA
Business Alert to Nuclear War (EA) .... BANW
Business Alliance on Government Competition [*Defunct*] (EA) .... BAGC
Business Analyst Skills Evaluation [*Test*] .... BUSAN
Business and Commerce [*A publication*] (DLA) .... Bus & Com
Business and Consumer Affairs (WDAA) .... BACA
Business and Defense Services Administration [*Later, BDC*] [*Department of Commerce*] .... BDSA
Business and Economic Research Center [*Middle Tennessee State University*] [*Research center*] (RCD) .... BERC
Business and Engineering Enriched FORTRAN [*Programming language*] [*Sperry UNIVAC*] .... BEEF
Business and Farm [*IRS*] .... B & F
Business and Financial Manager [*Military*] (DOMA) .... BFM
Business and Government Services (ACRL) .... BGS
Business and Industrial Development Corporation [*Generic term for a for-profit investment company*] .... BIDCO
Business and Industrial Development Institute [*Saginaw Valley State College*] [*Database search service*] (OLDSS) .... BIDI
Business and Industry Advisory Committee [*NATO*] (NATG) .... BIAC
Business and Industry Association of New Hampshire (SRA) .... BIA
Business and Industry Management Abstracts [*A publication*] .... BIMA
Business and Industry Nongovernment Organization .... BINGO
Business and Institutional Furniture Manufacturers Association (EA) .... BIFMA
Business and Investments Centre [*British*] .... BIC
Business and Law [*A publication*] (DLA) .... Bus & L
Business and Law Review [*Corporate Agents, Inc.*] [*Information service or system*] (CRD) .... BLR
Business and Professional Software [*Software publisher*] .... BPS
Business and Professional Women's Club [*Australia*] .... BPWC
Business and Professional Women's Club of Perth [*Australia*] .... BPWCP
Business and Professional Women's Foundation .... BPW
Business and Professional Women's Foundation (EA) .... BPWF
Business and Professions [*A publication*] (DLA) .... Bus & Prof
Business and Professions Code (DLA) .... Bus & Prof C
Business and Residence Centrex Services [*Telecommunications*] (ACRL) .... BRCS
Business and Society [*A publication*] (BRI) .... Bus Soc
Business and Technician Education Council [*British*] .... BTEC
Business and Technician Education Council (ACII) .... BTECH
Business and Technology Center [*Control Data Corp.*] [*British*] .... BTC
Business and Technology Education Council National Certificate (AIE) .... BTECNC
Business Application Language .... BAL
Business Applications Performance Corp. (CDE) .... BAPC
Business Applications Programming Guide (MCD) .... BAPG
Business Archives Council [*British*] .... BAC
Business as Usual .... BAU
Business Assessment Study and Evaluation (PDAA) .... BASE
Business Association of Latin American Studies (EA) .... BALAS
Business Automobile Policy [*Insurance*] .... BAP
Business Aviation AS [*Denmark ICAO designator*] (FAAC) .... BUA
Business Book Review [*A publication*] (BRI) .... Bus Bk R
Business Card Collectors International (EA) .... BCCI
Business Census .... BC
Business Class [*Also, J*] [*Airline fare code*] C
Business Class [*Also, C*] [*Airline fare code*] .... J
Business Clearance Memorandum (AAGC) .... BCM
Business Clearance Reviewing Authority (AAGC) .... BCRA
Business Coalition for Fair Competition (EA) .... BCFC
Business Committee for the Arts (EA) .... BCA
Business Communications Co., Inc. [*Norwalk, CT*] [*Information service or system Telecommunications*] (TSSD) .... BCC
Business Communications Service [*British Telecommunications International*] [*London*] (TSSD) .... BCS
Business Communications Systems [*Telecommunications*] (TEL) .... BCS
Business Competitive Intelligence .... BCI
Business Comptuer Systems Ltd. [*Later, Business Computer Systems PLC*] [*British*] (NITA) .... BCL
Business Computer (IAA) .... BC
Business Computer Network, Inc. [*San Antonio, TX*] [*Telecommunications*] (TSSD) .... BCN
Business Computers Ltd. [*British*] (NITA) .... BCL
Business Computers Users Association (MHDB) .... BCUA
Business Control System .... BCS
Business Cooperation Center [*EC*] (ECED) .... BCC
Business Corporation Board .... BCB
Business Corp. Law [*A publication*] .... BCL
Business Council (EA) .... BC
Business Council for Effective Literacy [*Defunct*] (EA) .... BCEL
Business Council for Fair Trade (AC) .... BCFT
Business Council for Improved Transport Policies (EA) .... BCITP
Business Council for International Understanding (EA) .... BCIU
Business Council for the United Nations (EA) .... BCUN
Business Council on National Issues [*Canadian research and lobbying organization*] (CROSS) .... BCNI
Business Council on the Reduction of Paperwork (EA) .... BCORP
Business Customer Services [*Telecommunications*] (TEL) .... BCS
Business Cycle Developments [*Bureau of the Census*] [*A publication*] .... BCD
Business Data Processing .... BDP
Business Data Processing Operation .... BDPO
Business Dateline Database [*Information service or system*] (IT) .... BDD
Business Definition Language [*Computer science*] (IAA) .... BDL
Business Definition System (MHDI) .... BDS
Business Development Consultants International, Ltd. [*British*] .... BDC
Business Development Group .... BDG
Business Development Report [*Department of Commerce*] (GFGA) .... BDR
Business Development Report System [*Department of Commerce*] [*Database*] .... BDRS
Business Development Specialist (DOMA) .... BDS
Business Directory International (ACII) .... BDI
Business Directory of Registered Plumbers [*A publication*] .... BDRP
Business Division [*Census*] (OICC) .... BUS
Business EDP [*Electronic Data Processing*] **Systems Technique** [*NCR Corp.*] (IEEE) .... BEST
Business Education Adminstrators Association [*Defunct*] (EA) .... BEAA
Business Education Connection (OICC) .... BEC
Business Education Council .... BEC
Business Education Council General Award (AIE) .... BGen
Business Education Research Foundation (EA) .... BERF
Business Education Research of America [*Hato Rey, PR*] (EA) .... BERA
Business Efficiency Exhibition [*British*] (DIT) .... BEE
Business Efficiency Exhibition [*Business Equipment Association of South Africa*] .... BEXA
Business Electronics Computer [*Used in training*] .... BEC
Business Emergency Plan .... BEP
Business Energy Investment Tax Credit [*IRS*] .... BEITC
Business, Engineering, Appropriate Technology, and Skilled Trades [*Peace Corps program*] .... BEAST
Business English Test [*Vocational guidance test*] .... BET
Business Enterprise Center [*Australia*] .... BEC
Business Environment Risk Information [*Information service or system*] (IID) .... BERI
Business Equipment .... BE
Business Equipment and Information Technology Association [*British*] .... BEITA
Business Equipment Digest [*British*] [*A publication*] (NITA) .... BED
Business Equipment Manufacturers Association [*Later, CBEMA*] .... BEMA
Business Equipment Software Techniques [*Computer science*] .... BEST
Business Equipment Trade Association [*London, England*] .... BETA
Business Espionage Controls and Countermeasures Association (EA) .... BECCA
Business European Airways Ltd. [*British*] [*FAA designator*] (FAAC) .... MIN
Business Executives for National Security (EA) .... BENS
Business Executives for National Security Education Fund (EA) .... BENS/ED
Business Executives Move for New National Priorities [*An association*] (EA) .... BEM
Business Executives Move for Peace [*An association*] (VNW) .... BEM
Business Expansion Scheme [*British*] .... BES
Business Expenditure Research and Development .... BERD
Business Experience Training (BARN) .... BET
Business Express [*ICAO designator*] (FAAC) .... GAA
Business Express [*ICAO designator*] (AD) .... HQ
Business Express Delivery Ltd. [*Canada ICAO designator*] (FAAC) .... EXP
Business Firms Master Index [*A publication*] .... BFMI
Business Flight Service [*Denmark ICAO designator*] (FAAC) .... BSF
Business Flights Ltd. [*Canada ICAO designator*] (FAAC) .... BFA
Business for Social Responsibility .... BSR
Business Forecasting (MCD) .... BIZFORC
Business Forms Institute [*Defunct*] .... BFI
Business Forms Management Association (EA) .... BFMA
Business Funding Scheme .... BFS
Business Grant Services [*Information service or system*] .... BGS
Business Group for Latin America [*Later, COA*] .... BGLA
Business Health Assessment Program .... BHAP
Business/Higher Education Round Table .... BHERT
Business History Conference (EA) .... BHC
Business History Foundation [*Defunct*] (EA) .... BHF

Business History Review [*A publication*] (BRI) .... BHR
Business Hours .... BH
Business Improvement Area .... BIA
Business Improvement Services (AIE) .... BIS
Business in the Community [*British*] .... BIC
Business Industry Community College Coalition (EDAC) .... BICCC
Business/Industry Data Center [*Bureau of the Census*] (GFGA) .... BIDC
Business Information Analysis and Integration Technique [*Computer science*] .... BIAT
Business Information Centre, Bank of Montreal, Toronto, Ontario [*Library symbol National Library of Canada*] (BIB) .... OTBMBI
Business Information Centre/SVP [*Information service or system*] (IID) .... BIC/SVP
Business Information Desk Reference [*A publication*] .... BIDR
Business Information Exchange Network [*Databank*] [*Canada*] .... BIEN
Business Information Group [*Information service or system*] (IID) .... BIG
Business Information Network [*Billboard Publications, Inc.*] [*New York, NY Telecommunications*] (TEL) .... BIN
Business Information Processing .... BIP
Business Information Service [*Financial Times Business Information Ltd.*] [*British Information service or system*] (IID) .... BIS
Business Information Services [*Control Data Corp.*] [*Information service or system*] (IID) .... BIS
Business Information System/Trunks and Special Services [*Telecommunications*] (TEL) .... BISTSS
Business Information Systems [*Bell System*] .... BIS
Business Information Systems Analysis and Design [*Bell System*] (DIT) .... BISAD
Business Information Systems Communications [*Bell System*] .... BISCOM
Business Information Systems Customer Service [*Bell System*] .... BISCUS
Business Information Systems Customer Service/Facilities Assignment and Control System [*Bell System*] (MCD) .... BISCUS/FACS
Business Information Systems Management [*Mountain View, CA*] [*Telecommunications service*] (TSSD) .... BISM
Business Information Systems Modeling and Planning System [*Bell System*] .... BISMAPS
Business Information Systems Programs [*Bell System*] .... BISP
Business Information Technology .... BIT
Business Information Terminal [*Computer science*] (HGAA) .... BIT
Business Information Wire [*Database*] [*The Canadian Press*] [*Information service or system*] (CRD) .... BIW
Business Input/Output Rerun [*UNIVAC compiling system*] [*Computer science*] .... BIOR
Business Instruction Set [*Computer science*] (IAA) .... BIS
Business Insurance Trust (DLA) .... BIT
Business Intelligence .... BI
Business Intelligence Center [*SRI International*] [*Information service or system*] (IID) .... B-I-C
Business Intelligence Program Research Catalog [*SRI International*] [*Information service or system*] (IID) .... B-I-P
Business Intelligence Services Ltd. [*British*] .... BIS
Business International Corp. .... BI
Business International Country Assessment Service [*Business Intern ational Corp.*] [*Defunct Information service or system*] (CRD) .... BI/CAS
Business International Non-Governmental Organization (MHDB) .... BINGO
Business Interruption [*Insurance*] .... BI
Business Interruption Insurance .... BII
Business Inventory Management System (HGAA) .... BIM
Business Investment Game .... BIG
Business Jets [*ICAO designator*] (AD) .... BQ
Business Law Journal (DLA) .... Bus LJ
Business Law Journal (DLA) .... Business LJ
Business Law Reports (DLA) .... Bus L Rep
Business Lead Identification System [*Timeplace, Inc.*] [*Database*] .... BLIS
Business Leader Group [*Washington, DC*] (EA) .... BLG
Business Library Review [*A publication*] (BRI) .... BusLR
Business Library, Saskatchewan Department of Tourism and Small Business, Regina,Saskatchewan [*Library symbol National Library of Canada*] (NLC) .... SRTSB
Business Licence [*British*] (ADA) .... BL
Business License Information Service .... BLIS
Business Machine .... BM
Business Machine Computer .... BISMAC
Business Machine Computer (MHDI) .... BIZMAC
Business Machines Group [*Burroughs Corp.*] .... BMG
Business Mail Foundation [*Later, DMMA*] (EA) .... BMF
Business Management (DD) .... BusMgmt
Business Management Control System [*Computer science*] (IAA) .... BMCS
Business Management Control System Research Project (IAA) .... BMCSRP
Business Management Game .... BMG
Business Management System (BUR) .... BMS
Business Management System Team [*Air Force*] (MCD) .... BMST
Business Manager (MCD) .... BM
Business Manager (WDAA) .... BUS MGR
Business Master File [*OMB*] .... BMF
Business Men's League of the United States (EA) .... BMLUS
Business Modeling Language (MCD) .... BML
Business Name and Address File [*IRS*] .... BNAF
Business Name and Address Key Index File [*IRS*] .... BKIF
Business Objects ADS [*NASDAQ symbol*] (TTSB) .... BOBJY
Business Objects SA [*NASDAQ symbol*] (SAG) .... BOBJ
Business Objects SA [*Associated Press*] (SAG) .... BusinObj
Business Objects SA [*Associated Press*] (SAG) .... BusnObj
Business Office Force Administration Data System [*Bell System*] .... BOFADS
Business Office Must [*Copy that must be printed*] [*Publishing*] .... BOM
Business Office Supervisor [*Telecommunications*] (TEL) .... BOS
Business Operations Support Services [*British*] [*FAA designator*] (FAAC) .... GEN
Business Opportunities Sourcing System [*Information service or system Canada*] .... BOSS
Business Opportunity Bank [*Institute for New Enterprise Development*] .... BOB
Business Organization Climate Index (MHDB) .... BOCI
Business Organizations, Agencies, and Publications Directory [*Formerly, BOAD*] [*A publication*] .... BOAPD
Business Organizations and Agencies Directory [*Later, BOAPD*] [*A publication*] .... BOAD
Business Organizer Scheduling System .... BOSS
Business Partnership for Peace (EA) .... BPP
Business Passenger's Extra Option [*Proposed*] [*Travel industry*] .... BPEX
Business People, Inc. [*Minneapolis, MN*] [*Telecommunications service*] (TSSD) .... BPI
Business Periodicals Circulation Services [*Harcourt Brace Jovanovich*] .... BPCS
Business Periodicals Directory [*A publication*] .... BPD
Business Periodicals Ondisc [*UMI/Data Courier*] [*Information service or system*] (CRD) .... BPO
Business Plan System .... BPS
Business Planning Board [*Later, BTPB*] (EA) .... BPB
Business Planning Language [*Computer science*] (MHDI) .... BPL
Business Press International (DGA) .... BPI
Business Process Analysis .... BPA
Business Process Improvement (AAGC) .... BPI
Business Process Readiness [*GSA*] (AAGC) .... BPR
Business Process Re-Engineering (ECON) .... BPR
Business Products Standards Association (NITA) .... BPSA
Business/Professional Advertising Association [*New York, NY*] (EA) .... B/PAA
Business Professionals of America .... BPOA
Business Publications Audit (DGA) .... BPC
Business Publications Audit of Circulation (EA) .... BPA
Business Publications Index and Abstracts [*A publication*] .... BPIA
Business Publishers, Inc. [*Silver Spring, MD*] [*Information service or system*] (IID) .... BPI
Business Radio Service .... BRS
Business Rankings Annual [*A publication*] .... BRA
Business Record, Des Moines, IA [*Library symbol*] [*Library of Congress*] (LCLS) .... IaDmBR
Business Records Holding Corp. [*NASDAQ symbol*] (SPSG) .... BRCP
Business Records Holding Corp. [*Associated Press*] (SAG) .... BusnRc
Business Records Manufacturers Association [*Later, ABPM*] (EA) .... BRMA
Business Recovery Service (ACRL) .... BRS
Business Reference and Services Section [*American Library Association*] .... BRASS
Business Regulation (DLA) .... Bus Reg
Business Regulation Law Report [*A publication*] (DLA) .... Bus Reg L Rep
Business Reply Card [*Advertising*] .... BRC
Business Reply Envelope [*Advertising*] .... BRE
Business Reply Mail [*Advertising*] .... BRM
Business Reply Mail Accounting System [*US Postal Service*] .... BRMAS
Business Reply Post [*British*] (ADA) .... BRP
Business Research Corp. [*Boston, MA*] [*Information service or system*] (IID) .... BRC
Business Research Management Center [*Wright-Patterson Air Force Base, OH*] .... BRMC
Business Resource Group [*NASDAQ symbol*] (SAG) .... BRGP
Business Resource Group [*Associated Press*] (SAG) .... BusnRs
Business Risk and Value of Operation in Space [*NASA*] (NASA) .... BRAVO
Business Risks International, Inc. [*Database producer*] (IID) .... BRI
Business Roundtable (EA) .... BR
Business Roundtable .... BRT
Business School .... B (School)
Business Science Experts [*NOMOS Datapool*] [*Germany Information service or system*] (CRD) .... WEX
Business Service Center (USGC) .... BSC
Business Service Center .... BSC
Business Service Unit [*Telecommunications*] (TEL) .... BSU
Business Services and Defense Administration [*Department of Commerce*] (BARN) .... BSDA
Business Services on the Net .... BSN
Business Software Alliance [*Formerly, Business Software Association*] (EA) .... BSA
Business Software Database [*Information Sources, Inc.*] [*Information service or system*] (CRD) .... BSD
Business Start-Up Scheme [*British*] .... BSS
Business Statistics Office [*Department of Trade and Industry*] [*Information service or system*] (IID) .... BSO
Business Strategy Group [*of ABT Associates, Inc.*] [*Cambridge, MA*] [*Telecommunications service*] (TSSD) .... BSG
Business Strategy Panel [*Military*] .... BSP
Business Studies (DD) .... BusStudies
Business System Planning .... BSP
Business Systems and Security Marketing Association (EA) .... BSSMA
Business Systems Services (MCD) .... BSS
Business Systems Technology, Inc. .... BST
Business Taxpayer Information File [*IRS*] .... BTIF
Business Technology Association [*Kansas City, MO*] [*An association*] (CDE) .... BTA
Business Technology Research, Inc. [*Telecommunications service*] (TSSD) .... BTR
Business Telecommunications Corp. [*Chicago, IL*] (TSSD) .... BTC
Business Telecommunications Equipment [*Canada*] .... BTE
Business Telecommunications Services (ADA) .... BTS
Business Television (WDMC) .... BTV
Business Terminal Equipment [*Telecommunications*] (TEL) .... BTE

Business The Real-Time Operating System Nucleus [Computer science] (NITA) ... B TRON
Business Training College ... BTC
Business Transfer Tax [Proposed] [Canada] ... BTT
Business Travel Accident [Insurance] ... BTA
Business Traveler Hotel Guide [National Association of Business Travel Agents] [A publication] ... BTHG
Business Traveler Magazine [National Association of Business Travel Agents] [A publication] ... BT
Business Trend Analysts, Inc. [Commack, NY] [Information service or system] (IID) ... BTA
Business Turnover Tax (IMH) ... BTT
Business User Group [Computer science] ... BUG
Business Vehicle Survey ... BVS
Business Venture Profiles [TECHSTART International, Inc.] [Information service or system] (CRD) ... BVP
Business Visit [Program] [United States Travel Service] ... BUSIVISIT
Business Visitors Memorandum [British Overseas Trade Board] (DS) ... BVM
Business Volunteers for the Arts [NFD] ... BVA
Business Week [A publication] (BRI) ... Bus W
Business Week [A publication] (AAGC) ... Bus Wk
Business Week [A publication] ... BW
Business Who's Who of Australia [Database] [R.G. Riddell Pty. Ltd.] ... BUWA
[The] Business World [A publication] ... TBW
Business-Higher Education Forum [Washington, DC] (EA) ... B-HEF
Business-Industry Political Action Committee (EA) ... BIPAC
Business-Industry-Education [Days] [Usually sponsored by chambers of commerce] ... BIE
Businesslike (ABBR) ... BSNSLK
Businessman ... bsman
Businessman (ABBR) ... BSNSMN
Business-Oriented Search Service [Information service or system] (IID) ... BOSS
Business-Oriented Software System [Digital Equipment Corp.] [Computer science] (BUR) ... BOSS
Businessowners Policy [Insurance] ... BOP
Business-to-Business [Advertising] (WDMC) ... B-B
Business-to-Business [Advertising] (WDMC) ... B-to-B
Businesswoman (ABBR) ... BSNSWMN
Businesswomen (ABBR) ... BSNSWMEN
Busiris [of Isocrates] [Classical studies] (OCD) ... Bus
Buskin (ABBR) ... BSKN
Buskirk. Indiana Practice [A publication] (DLA) ... Busk Pr
Buss Durkee Hostility Inventory (EDAC) ... BDHI
Bust (ADA) ... B
Bust Bodice [Early name for brassiere] ... BB
Busted Aristocrat [A cadet officer reduced to the ranks] [Military slang] ... BA
Bustle (ABBR) ... BSTL
Bustled (ABBR) ... BSTLD
Bustling (ABBR) ... BSTLG
Bus-to-Bus Access Circuit [Bell System] ... BBAC
Busulfan [Also, BUS] [Antineoplastic drug] ... BSF
Busulfan [Antineoplastic drug] (CDI) ... BU
Busulfan [Also, BSF] [Antineoplastic drug] ... BUS
Buswell and Wolcott. Massachusetts Practice [A publication] (DLA) ... Busw & Wol Pr
Busy ... BSY
Busy [Telecommunications] (TEL) ... BY
Busy Bee of Norway AS [ICAO designator] (FAAC) ... BEE
Busy BIT [Binary Digit] [Computer science] (IAA) ... BB
Busy Flash [Telecommunications] (NITA) ... BFL
Busy Hour (IAA) ... BH
Busy Hour Call [Telecommunications] (TEL) ... BHC
Busy Hour Call Attempts [Telecommunications] ... BHCA
Busy Hour Call Completions [Telecommunications] (ACRL) ... BHCC
Busy Hour Load [Telecommunications] (TEL) ... BHL
Busy Hour Model [Computer science] ... BHM
Busy Lamp Field [Phone console] [Bell System] ... BLF
Busy Season Busy Hour [Telecommunications] (ACRL) ... BSBH
Busy Tax Practitioner's Digest [Australia A publication] ... BTPD
Busy Tone [Telecommunications] (TEL) ... BT
Busy Tone Multiple-Access [Telecommunications] (MHDB) ... BTMA
Busy Tone Trunk [Telecommunications] ... BTT
Busy Tone Trunks [Telecommunications] (TEL) ... BOTTS
Busy Verification [Telecommunications] (TEL) ... BV
Busybody (ABBR) ... BSYBDY
Busying (ABBR) ... BSYG
Busy-Tone Start Lead ... BTST
But Less Than ... BLT
But Not ... BN
But Not Exceeding ... BNE
But Not Over ... BNOV
Buta [Zaire] [Airport symbol] (OAG) ... BZU
Buta Zega [Zaire] [ICAO location identifier] (ICLI) ... FZKJ
Butacaine [Topical anesthetic] ... BC
Butadiene Extraction [Chemical engineering] ... BTX
Butadiene Rubber ... BR
Butane (MSA) ... BUTN
Butane Buzzard Aviation Corp. [British ICAO designator] (FAAC) ... BZZ
Butane Secondary Refrigerant ... BSR
Butane-Butene Fraction ... B-B
Butanediol [Organic chemistry] ... BDO
Butanediol Diacetate [Organic chemistry] ... BDDA
Butanediol Diglycidyl Ether [Organic chemistry] ... BDGE
Butanediol Succinate [Organic chemistry] ... BDS
Butanetetracarboxylic Acid [Organic chemistry] ... BTCA

Butanetriol Trinitrate [An explosive] ... BTTN
Butanol [Organic chemistry] ... BUT
Butanol/Acetic Acid/Water [Solvent system] ... BAW
Butanol/Ethanol/Water [Solvent system] ... BEW
Butanol-Extractable Iodine [Clinical chemistry] ... BEI
Butare [Rwanda] [Airport symbol] (AD) ... BQR
Butare [Astrida] [Rwanda] [Seismograph station code, US Geological Survey] [Closed] (SEIS) ... BTR
Butare [Rwanda] [ICAO location identifier] (ICLI) ... HRYI
Butaritari [Kiribati] [Airport symbol] (OAG) ... BBG
Butaritari [Kiribati] [ICAO location identifier] (ICLI) ... NGTU
Butazolidin [Pharmacology] (DAVI) ... BTZ
Butcher [Navy] ... B
Butcher (ABBR) ... BTCHR
Butcher ... BTCHR
Butcher (MSA) ... BTCR
Butchery (ABBR) ... BTCHRY
Bute Resources [Vancouver Stock Exchange symbol] ... BTA
Butec International Chemical Corp. [Formerly, Tay River Petroleum Ltd.] [Vancouver Stock Exchange symbol] ... BIC
Butembo [Zaire] [Seismograph station code, US Geological Survey] (SEIS) ... BTC
Butembo [Zaire] [ICAO location identifier] (ICLI) ... FZMB
Buteshire [County in Scotland] (BARN) ... Bute
Buthionine Sulfoximine [Biochemistry] ... BSO
Buthylethylmagnesium [Organic chemistry] ... BEM
Butler (ABBR) ... BTLR
Butler ... BTLR
Butler Air Transport Ltd. ... BAT
Butler, AL [Location identifier FAA] (FAAL) ... BCZ
Butler, AL [AM radio station call letters] ... WPRN
Butler, AL [FM radio station call letters] ... WQGL
Butler Area Librarians [Library network] ... BAL
Butler Bulletin, Butler, IN [Library symbol Library of Congress] (LCLS) ... InBuB
Butler Carnegie Library, Butler, IN [Library symbol Library of Congress] (LCLS) ... InBu
Butler College, Tyler, TX [Library symbol Library of Congress] (LCLS) ... TxTyB
Butler County Courthouse, Allison, IA [Library symbol Library of Congress] (LCLS) ... IaAlnBCo
Butler County Historical Society, Hamilton, OH [Library symbol Library of Congress] (LCLS) ... OHaBHi
Butler County Legal Journal [Pennsylvania] [A publication] (DLA) ... Butler
Butler County Tribune-Journal, Allison, IA [Library symbol Library of Congress] (LCLS) ... IaAlnTJ
Butler Health Center, Providence, RI [Library symbol Library of Congress] (LCLS) ... RPBH
Butler High School, Augusta, GA [Library symbol Library of Congress] (LCLS) ... GAuBH
Butler International [Formerly, North American Ventures, Inc.] [NASDAQ symbol] (SPSG) ... BUTL
Butler International, Inc. [Associated Press] (SAG) ... Butler
Butler Manufacturing [NYSE symbol] (SAG) ... BBR
Butler Manufacturing [Associated Press] (SAG) ... ButlerMfg
Butler Manufacturing Co. [NASDAQ symbol] (NQ) ... BTLR
Butler Manufacturing Co. [Associated Press] (SAG) ... ButlrMf
Butler Mfg [NASDAQ symbol] (TTSB) ... BTLR
Butler, MO [Location identifier FAA] (FAAL) ... BUM
Butler, MO [AM radio station call letters] ... KMAM
Butler, MO [FM radio station call letters] ... KMOE
Butler Mountain Minerals [Vancouver Stock Exchange symbol] ... BMM
Butler National Corp. [NASDAQ symbol] ... BUKS
Butler National Corp. [Associated Press] (SAG) ... ButlrNt
Butler Natl [NASDAQ symbol] (TTSB) ... BUKS
Butler, PA [Location identifier FAA] (FAAL) ... BTP
Butler, PA [Location identifier FAA] (FAAL) ... GXO
Butler, PA [AM radio station call letters] ... WBUT
Butler, PA [AM radio station call letters] ... WISR
Butler, PA [FM radio station call letters] ... WLER
Butler Public Library, Butler, PA [Library symbol Library of Congress] (LCLS) ... PBut
Butler University (GAGS) ... Butler U
Butler University, College of Pharmacy, Indianapolis, IN [Library symbol Library of Congress] (LCLS) ... InIB-P
Butler University, Indianapolis, IN [OCLC symbol] (OCLC) ... IIB
Butler University, Indianapolis, IN [Library symbol Library of Congress] (LCLS) ... InIB
Butler's Horae Juridicae [A publication] (DLA) ... Butler Hor Jur
Butler's Lawyer and Client [A publication] (DLA) ... But Law & Cl
Butler's Notes to Coke on Littleton [A publication] (DLA) ... Butler Co Litt
Butler's Wharf [Shipping] [British] (ROG) ... BW
Butoxyacetanilide [Pharmacology] ... BOA
Butoxycarbonyl [Also, Boc] [Organic chemistry] ... BOC
Butoxycarbonyl [or t-BOC] [Biochemistry] ... t-Boc
Butoxycarbonylethyl Polysulfide [Organic chemistry] ... BCEPS
Butropium Bromide [Pharmacology] ... BHB
Butt Line [Technical drawings] ... BL
Butt Plane ... BP
Butt Splice (MCD) ... BUSP
Butt Weld (DNAB) ... BW
Butt Welded ... BTWLD
Butt Welded (IAA) ... BW
Butt Welded Filter ... BWF
Butt Welded Joint ... BWJ
Butte [Montana] [Airport symbol] (OAG) ... BTM
Butte [Montana] [Seismograph station code, US Geological Survey] (SEIS) ... BUT
Butte, Anaconda & Pacific Railway Co. [AAR code] ... BAP

Butte Aviation, Inc. [*FAA designator*] (FAAC) .... PPS
Butte County Historical Society, Oroville, CA [*Library symbol*] [*Library of Congress*] (LCLS) .... COroBHi
Butte County Library, Oroville, CA [*Library symbol Library of Congress*] (LCLS) .... COroB
Butte Free Public Library, Butte, MT [*Library symbol Library of Congress*] (LCLS) .... MtBu
Butte, MT [*Location identifier FAA*] (FAAL) .... BEY
Butte, MT [*Location identifier FAA*] (FAAL) .... CPN
Butte, MT [*FM radio station call letters*] .... KAAR
Butte, MT [*FM radio station call letters*] (RBYB) .... KAPC-FM
Butte, MT [*AM radio station call letters*] .... KBOW
Butte, MT [*FM radio station call letters*] .... KMSM
Butte, MT [*FM radio station call letters*] .... KOPR
Butte, MT [*FM radio station call letters*] .... KQUY
Butte, MT [*Television station call letters*] .... KTVM
Butte, MT [*Television station call letters*] .... KWYB
Butte, MT [*Television station call letters*] .... KXLF
Butte, MT [*AM radio station call letters*] .... KXTL
Butter [*Phonetic alphabet*] [*Royal Navy World War I*] (DSUE) .... B
Butter (AAMN) .... BUT
Butter .... BUTR
Butter Fat (MAE) .... BF
Butter Information Council [*British*] .... BIC
Butter, Lard, and Salt Provisions .... BL & SP
Butter Marketing Board [*Queensland, Australia*] .... BMB
Butterfly (MSA) .... BTFL
Butterfly [*Stroke*] [*Swimming*] .... BUFLY
Butterfly and Moth Stamp Society (EA) .... BMSS
Butterfly Lovers International (EA) .... BLI
Butterfly Spread [*Investment term*] .... BS
Butterfly Valve (DAC) .... BV
Buttermilk [*Freight*] .... BTRMLK
Butterworth [*Malaysia*] [*ICAO location identifier*] (ICLI) .... WMKB
Butterworth's Co. Law Bulletin [*Australia A publication*] .... BCLB
Butterworth's Current Law [*A publication*] (DLA) .... B Current L
Butterworths Proprietory Ltd., Chatswood, NSW, Australia [*Library symbol Library of Congress*] (LCLS) .... AuBut
Butterworth's Rating Appeals [*1913-31*] [*England*] [*A publication*] (DLA) .... BRA
Butterworth's Rating Appeals [*1913-31*] [*England*] [*A publication*] (DLA) .... Butt RA
Butterworth's Rating Appeals [*1913-31*] [*England*] [*A publication*] (DLA) .... Butt Rat App
Butterworth's South African Law Review [*A publication*] (DLA) .... Butt SA Law Rev
Butterworth's South African Law Review [*A publication*] (DLA) .... Butterworth's SA Law Review
Butterworth's South African Law Review [*A publication*] (DLA) .... Butterworth's South Afr L Rev
Butterworths Tax Guide [*A publication*] .... BTG
Butterworth's Weekly Tax Bulletin [*Australia A publication*] .... BWT Bull
Butterworth's Workmen's Compensation Cases [*A publication*] (DLA) .... Butt WCC
Butterworth's Workmen's Compensation Cases [*A publication*] (DLA) .... Butt Work Comp Cas
Butterworth's Workmen's Compensation Cases [*A publication*] (DLA) .... BWCC
Butterworth's Workmen's Compensation Cases [*A publication*] (DLA) .... BWCC (Eng)
Buttock [*Shipfitting*] .... BTK
Buttock [*Slang*] (DSUE) .... BUTT
Buttock Line [*Engineering*] .... BL
Button (AAG) .... BTN
Button .... BUT
Button .... BUTN
Button at Right Bottom [*Telephone touch-tone dial*] .... BARB
Button Cell Battery .... BCB
Button Head .... BTNHD
Button Switch .... BS
Buttons and Bows [*Magazine in Judith Krantz's novel "I'll Take Manhattan"*] .... B & B
Buttress (VRA) .... butr
Buttrey Food & Drug Stores [*NASDAQ symbol*] (TTSB) .... BTRY
Buttrey Food & Drug Stores Co. [*NASDAQ symbol*] (SAG) .... BTRY
Buttrey Food & Drug Stores Co. [*Associated Press*] (SAG) .... Butrey
Butts Army Airfield [*Fort Carson, CO*] .... BAAF
Butts' Edition of Shower's English King's Bench Reports [*A publication*] (DLA) .... Butts Sh
Butts Master [*British and Canadian*] [*World War II*] .... BM
Butt-Treated Cedar (IAA) .... BTC
Butt-Treated Lodgepole Pine (IAA) .... BTLP
Buttwil [*Switzerland ICAO location identifier*] (ICLI) .... LSZU
Butuan [*Philippines*] [*Seismograph station code, US Geological Survey Closed*] (SEIS) .... BTN
Butuan [*Philippines*] [*Airport symbol*] (OAG) .... BXU
Butuan, Agusan [*Philippines*] [*ICAO location identifier*] (ICLI) .... RPWE
Butut [*Monetary unit*] [*Gambia*] .... B
Butyl [*Organic chemistry*] .... Bu
Butyl Acrylate [*Organic chemistry*] .... BA
Butyl Benzyl Phthalate [*Organic chemistry*] .... BBP
Butyl Carbitol Piperonylate [*Organic chemistry*] .... BCP
Butyl (Chlorophenyl)carbamate [*Organic chemistry*] .... BCPC
Butyl Di-Iodohydroxybenzoate [*Organic chemistry*] (DAVI) .... DIB
Butyl Ethyl Ketene [*Organic chemistry*] .... BEK
Butyl Glycidyl Ether [*Organic chemistry*] .... BGE
Butyl Hydroperoxide [*Organic chemistry*] .... BHP
Butyl Isocyanate [*Organic chemistry*] .... BIC
Butyl Methacrylate [*Organic chemistry*] .... BMA
Butyl Phenyl Ether [*Organic chemistry*] .... BPE
Butyl Phthalyl Butyl Glycolate [*Organic chemistry*] .... BPBG
Butyl Vinyl Ether [*Organic chemistry*] .... BVE
Butylacetanilide [*Organic chemistry*] .... BAA
Butylated Hydroxyanisole [*Antioxidant*] .... BHA
Butylated Hydroxyanisole [*Antioxidant*] (WGA) .... BTA
Butylated Hydroxytoluene [*Also, DBPC*] [*Antioxidant*] .... BHT
Butylated Hydroxytolulene [*Antioxidant*] (BABM) .... BTH
Butylazo(hydroxy)(methyl)hexane [*Organic chemistry*] .... BHMH
Butyldiethanolamine [*Organic chemistry*] .... BDEA
Butylene Dimethacrylate [*Organic chemistry*] .... BDMA
Butylene Glycol [*Organic chemistry*] .... BG
Butylene Glycol Dinitrate [*Organic chemistry*] .... BGDN
Butyl-ethyl-propanediol [*Organic chemistry*] .... BEPD
Butyl(hydroxybutyl)nitrosamine [*Organic chemistry*] .... BHBN
Butylisonitrile (DMAA) .... BIN
Butyl(methoxy)azobenzene [*Organic chemistry*] .... BMAB
Butylnitrosobenzene [*Organic chemistry*] .... BNB
Butyl(octyl)magnesium [*Organic chemistry*] .... BOM
Butylpyridinium Chloride [*Organic chemistry*] .... BPC
Butyrolactone [*Organic chemistry*] .... BLO
Butyrum [*Butter*] [*Pharmacy*] (ROG) .... BUT
Butyrylcholinesterase [*An enzyme*] .... BuChE
Butzbach (Schloss) [*Germany ICAO location identifier*] (ICLI) .... EDIO
Butzweilerhof [*Germany ICAO location identifier*] (ICLI) .... EDCU
BUWEPS [*Bureau of Naval Weapons, now obsolete*] **Aviation Clothing and Survival Equipment Bulletin** (MCD) .... BACSEB
BUWEPS [*Bureau of Naval Weapons, now obsolete*] **Evaluation** .... BWE
BUWEPS [*Bureau of Naval Weapons, now obsolete*] **- Industry Material Reliability Advisory Board** .... BIMRAB
Buxom Belles, International (EA) .... BBI
Buxton's Reports [*123-129 North Carolina*] [*A publication*] (DLA) .... Buxton
Buxton's Reports [*123-129 North Carolina*] [*A publication*] (DLA) .... Buxton (NC)
Buy a Car [*Slogan during automobile sales slump of 1974-75*] .... BAC
Buy American Act (AAGC) .... BAA
Buy Back [*Investment term*] .... BB
Buy Here - Pay Here [*Used car sales*] .... BHPH
Buy Order [*Investment term*] .... BO
Buy Our Spares Smart [*Program*] (AAGC) .... BOSS
Buy per Drawing (SAA) .... BPD
Buy per Manufacturing Specification (SAA) .... BPMS
Buy Support Objective (AFIT) .... BSO
Buy United States Here [*Program to procure US-made supplies from overseas subsidiaries of US firms*] (AFM) .... BUSH
Buy-Build-Operate (AAGC) .... BBO
Buydown (TDOB) .... BD
Buydown Mortgage [*Business term*] (EMRF) .... BD
Buyer .... B
Buyer .... BUYR
Buyer Attitudes and Sales Experiences [*LIMRA*] .... BASE
Buyer Designated Equipment (MCD) .... BDE
Buyer Furnished Equipment (MCD) .... BFE
Buyer Has Seven Days to Take Up [*Securities brokerage*] [*Investment term*] B7D
Buyer has Seven Days to Take Up [*Investment term*] (MHDW) .... BSD
Buyer Protection Plan [*Sales*] .... BPP
Buyers .... BYRS
Buyer's Fashion Outlet [*Retailing*] .... BFO
Buyers Health Care Action Group [*Minnesota*] .... BHCAG
Buyers Laboratory, Inc. .... BLI
Buyers' Market [*Investment term*] .... BM
Buyer's Option [*Business term*] .... BO
Buyer's Option to Double (ROG) .... BOD
Buyers Screening Guide .... BSG
Buying [*Rate*] [*Value of the English pound*] .... BG
Buying Activity [*Air Force*] (AFM) .... BUYAC
Buying on Margin [*Investment term*] .... BOM
Buying Power Index .... BPI
Buying, Receiving, and Accounts Payable Integrated Data (MCD) .... BRAID
Buy-It-Yourself .... BIY
Buy-Off .... B-O
Buy-Off Date .... BOD
Buys Ballot Law .... BBL
Buzz Attenuation Device (CAAL) .... BAD
Buzz Word Quotient [*Computer science*] (NHD) .... BWQ
Buzzer (IEEE) .... BU
Buzzer (MSA) .... BUZ
Buzzer [*Electronics*] (IAA) .... BZ
Buzzer (FAAC) .... BZR
Buzzworm's Earth Journal [*A publication*] .... Buzz E J
BVBA Lucorp [*Belgium*] [*FAA designator*] (FAAC) .... LIM
Bvbalia, MS [*FM radio station call letters*] (RBYB) .... WYLT-FM
BVD Co. [*Initials stand for Bradley, Voorhies, and Day, organizers of the company*] .... BVD
BVL [*Bowlers' Victory Legion*] **Fund** (EA) .... BVL
BVR Technologies Ltd. [*Associated Press*] (SAG) .... BVR
BVR Technologies Ltd. [*NASDAQ symbol*] (SAG) .... BVRT
BVR Technologies Ltd [*NASDAQ symbol*] (TTSB) .... BVRTF
BW Air Services Ltd. [*British ICAO designator*] (FAAC) .... BWO
BW/IP Inc. [*NASDAQ symbol*] (TTSB) .... BWIP
BWAY Corp. [*NASDAQ symbol*] (TTSB) .... BWAY
BWAY Corp. [*Associated Press*] (SAG) .... BWAY
BWAY Corp. [*NYSE symbol*] (SAG) .... BY
BWIA International [*ICAO designator*] (AD) .... BW
BWIP Holding, Inc. [*Associated Press*] (SAG) .... BWIP
BWIP, Inc. [*NYSE symbol*] (SAG) .... BWF

BWIP, Inc. [*NASDAQ symbol*] (SAG) .... BWIP
By (ROG) .... B
By [*As in 9 x 12*] X
By Any Means Necessary .... BAMN
By Direction (NVT) .... BYDIR
By Direction of the President .... DP
By Mouth [*Pharmacy*] (DAVI) .... OS
By Other Means (NVT) .... BOM
By Procuration [*In power of attorney*] [*Legal term*] .... BP
By the Way [*Internet language*] [*Computer science*] .... BTW
By The Way [*Internet language*] [*Computer science*] .... btw
Byblian (BJA) .... Byb
Byblos Librairie Bookshop, Beirut, Lebanon [*Library symbol Library of
  Congress*] (LCLS) .... ByB
Bycatch Reduction Device [*Fishing technology*] .... BRD
Bydgoszcz [*Poland*] [*Airport symbol Obsolete*] (OAG) .... BZG
Bye [*Cricket*] .... B
By-Election [*Politics*] .... b/e
Byelorussia [*Belarus*] (BARN) .... Bye
Byelorussian Congress Committee of America (EA) .... BCCA
Byelorussian Democratic Bloc [*Political party*] .... BDB
Byelorussian Institute of Arts and Science (EA) .... BIAS
Byelorussian Liberation Front [*Defunct*] (EA) .... BLF
Byelorussian Literary Association (EA) .... BLA
Byelorussian Popular Front [*Political party*] .... BPF
Byelorussian Soviet Socialist Republic .... BelSSR
Byelorussian Soviet Socialist Republic .... BSSR
Byelorussian Soviet Socialist Republic [*ISO two-letter standard code*]
  (CNC) .... BY
Byelorussian Soviet Socialist Republic [*ISO three-letter standard code*]
  (CNC) .... BYS
Byelorussian Youth Association of America [*Later, BAYO*] (EA) .... BYAA
Byelorussian-American Veteran Association (EA) .... BAVA
Byelorussian-American Women Association (EA) .... BAWA
Byelorussian-American Youth Organization (EA) .... BAYO
Byers, Casgrain, Montreal, Quebec [*Library symbol National Library of
  Canada*] (BIB) .... QMBC
Byesville, OH [*FM radio station call letters*] .... WILE
BYG Natural Resources, Inc. [*Toronto Stock Exchange symbol*] .... BYG
Byggvaruregistret [*Building Commodity File*] [*Swedish Building Center
  Stockholm*] [*Information service or system*] (IID) .... BVR
Byhalia, MS [*FM radio station call letters*] .... WHLE
Byholma [*Sweden ICAO location identifier*] (ICLI) .... ESFY
Byk-Gulden Lomberg [*Germany*] [*Research code symbol*] C
Byk-Gulden Lomberg [*Germany*] [*Research code symbol*] ..... Do
Byles' Law of Exchange [*A publication*] (DLA) .... Byl Exch
Byles on Bills of Exchange [*A publication*] (DLA) .... Byl Bills
Byles on Bills of Exchange [*A publication*] (DLA) .... Byles
Byles on the Usury Laws [*A publication*] (DLA) .... Byl Us L
By-Line [*Publishing*] .... BL
Byng, OK [*FM radio station call letters*] .... KYKC
Bynkershoek's Law of War [*A publication*] (DLA) .... Byn War
Bypass .... BP
Bypass (KSC) .... BYP
Bypass .... BYP
Bypass [*Commonly used*] (OPSA) .... BYPA
Bypass [*Commonly used*] (OPSA) .... BYPAS
Bypass [*Commonly used*] (OPSA) .... BYPASS

Bypass [*Commonly used*] (OPSA) .... BYPS
Bypass Capacitor [*Electronics*] (IAA) .... BYPCAP
Bypass Condenser [*Electronics*] (IAA) .... BYPCOND
Bypass Electronic Emergency Fuel System .... BEEFS
Bypass Flow Module [*Nuclear energy*] (NRCH) .... BPFM
Bypass Graft (DAVI) .... BPH
Bypass Isolation Switch .... BIS
Bypass Isolation Transfer Switch .... BITS
Bypass Label Processing [*Computer science*] .... BLP
Bypass Monochrome Signal .... BMS
Bypass Ratio .... BPR
Bypass Turbojet Engine Noise .... BTJE
Bypass Valve (NRCH) .... BPV
Bypass Valve (MCD) .... BV
Byrd [*Antarctica*] [*Seismograph station code, US Geological Survey Closed*]
  (SEIS) .... BSA
Byrd [*Antarctica*] [*Seismograph station code, US Geological Survey Closed*]
  (SEIS) .... BYR
Byrd Antarctic Expedition [*1928-30, 1933-35*] .... ByrdAE
Byrd Polar Research Center [*Ohio State University*] [*Information service or
  system*] (IID) .... BPRC
Byrd - Stanford Research Institute [*Antarctica*] [*Seismograph station code,
  US Geological Survey Closed*] (SEIS) BY1
Byrd Station, Antarctica .... BYA
Byrne. Bills of Sale [*2nd ed.*] [*1870*] [*A publication*] (DLA) .... Byrne BS
Byrne on Patents [*A publication*] (DLA) .... Byrne Pat
Byron Bay, NT [*ICAO location identifier*] (ICLI) .... CYUK
Byron, GA [*FM radio station call letters*] .... WPWB
Byron Resources, Inc. [*Vancouver Stock Exchange symbol*] .... BYN
Byron Society (EA) .... BS
Byron Station (NRCH) .... BS
Bystander Dominates Initial Dominant [*Sociology*] .... BDID
Byte [*Usually 8 BITS*] [*Computer science*] .... B
Byte [*Computer science*] (IAA) .... BT
Byte Control Protocol [*Computer science*] .... BCP
Byte Count Register [*Computer science*] (MHDI) .... BCR
BYTE Information Exchange [*Electronic conferencing system provided by
  McGraw-Hill's Byte magazine*] .... BIX
Byte Input Control [*Computer science*] .... BIC
Byte Machine [*Computer science*] (IAA) .... BM
Byte Multiplexer Mode [*Computer science*] (IAA) .... BM
Byte Output Control [*Computer science*] .... BOC
Byte Stream Protocol [*Telecommunications*] (OSI) .... BSP
Byte-Multiplexer Channel .... BYMUX
Bytes per Inch [*Computer science*] .... BPI
Bytes per Second [*Computer science*] (BUR) .... BPS
Bythewood. Precedents in Conveyancing [*4th ed.*] [*1884-90*] [*A publication*]
  (DLA) .... Byth Conv
Bythewood. Precedents in Conveyancing [*4th ed.*] [*1884-90*] [*A publication*]
  (DLA) .... Byth Prec
Bythotrephes Cederstroemi [*Zoology*] .... BC
Bytom [*Poland*] [*Seismograph station code, US Geological Survey*] (SEIS) .... BYT
Byzantine .... BYZ
Byzantine (VRA) .... Byz
Byzantine .... Byzan
Byzantinische Zeitschrift [*A publication*] (OCD) .... Byz Zeitschr
Byzantinisch-Neugriechische Jahrbucher [*A publication*]
  (OCD) .... Byz und Neugr Jahrb

C
By Meaning

C (100) Call Seconds [Telecommunications] (NITA) .... CCS
C. A Pippy Jr. Medical Library, Grace General Hospital, St. John's, Newfoundland [Library symbol National Library of Canada] (NLC) .... NFSGGH
C & M Aviation, Inc. [ICAO designator] (FAAC) .... TIP
C & W [Cable & Wireless North America, Inc.] Network Services [Dallas, TX] [Telecommunications] (TSSD) .... CWNS
C. Berger & Co., Wheaton, IL [Library symbol] [Library of Congress] (LCLS) .... IWB
C Brewer Homes [NASDAQ symbol] (SAG) .... CBHI
C Brewer Homes [Associated Press] (SAG) .... CBrewer
C. F. Braun & Co., Alhambra, CA [Library symbol Library of Congress] (LCLS) .... CAlhB
C. H. Boehringer Sohn, Ingelheim [Germany] [Research code symbol] .... Ad
C. H. Boehringer Sohn, Ingelheim [Germany] [Research code symbol] .... FH
C. H. Boehringer Sohn, Ingelheim [Germany] [Research code symbol] .... Ko
C. H. Boehringer Sohn, Ingelheim [Germany] [Research code symbol] .... KSD
C. H. Boehringer Sohn, Ingelheim [Germany] [Research code symbol] .... KSW
C. H. Boehringer Sohn, Ingelheim [Germany] [Research code symbol] .... Me
C. H. Boehringer Sohn, Ingelheim [Germany] [Research code symbol] .... St
C. H. Boehringer Sohn, Ingelheim [Germany] [Research code symbol] .... Th
C. Howard Marcy State Hospital, Pittsburgh, PA [OCLC symbol] (OCLC) ...... PHY
C. Hurst & Co. [Publisher] [British] .... CH
C L & P Capital Ltd. [NYSE symbol] (SAG) .... CPM
"C" Message Weighting [Telecommunications] (TEL) .... CMSG
C. S. Draper Laboratory, Inc. Cambridge, MA [OCLC symbol] (OCLC) .... CSD
C. S. [Charles Sanders] Peirce Society (EA) .... CSPS
C. Stroemgren, Sorel, Quebec [Library symbol National Library of Canada] (NLC) .... QSOCS
C. W. Post Campus of Long Island University (GAGS) .... C W Post (LIU)
C. W. - Tariff Agency, Inc., Lansing MI [STAC] .... CWA
C³ [Command, Control, and Communications] Countermeasures [Pronounced "see-cubed see-m"] .... C³CM
CAA Calibration Flight [British ICAO designator] (FAAC) .... CLB
CAA Flight Examiners [British ICAO designator] (FAAC) .... EXM
CAA Flying Unit [British ICAO designator] (FAAC) .... CFU
CAA Flying Unit [British ICAO designator] (ICDA) .... MC
CAA [Civil Aeronautics Authority] High-Altitude Remote Monitoring .... CHARM
CAA Training Standards [British ICAO designator] (FAAC) .... SDS
CAAA Air Martinique [France ICAO designator] (FAAC) .... MTQ
Caaf Ho Nandi [Fiji] [ICAO location identifier] (ICLI) .... NFHO
Caara Ventures, Inc. [Vancouver Stock Exchange symbol] .... CVZ
Cab Alongside Engine [Automotive engineering] .... CAE
Cab Behind Engine [Automotive engineering] .... CBE
CAB [Commonwealth Agricultural Bureaux] International Bureau of Animal Breeding and Genetics (EAIO) .... CBABG
CAB [Commonwealth Agricultural Bureaux] International Institute of Entomology [British] (IRUK) .... CIE
CAB [Commonwealth Agricultural Bureaux] International Mycological Institute [British] (IRUK) .... CMI
Cab Over Engine [Type of truck] .... COE
Cab Over [Engine] Heavy, High [Mobility Multipurpose Wheeled] Vehicle [Army] .... COHHV
Cab Research Bureau [Later, ITA] (EA) .... CRB
Cab to Axle [GSA] (TAG) .... CA
Cab Trade Council [A union] [British] .... CTC
Cab Tyred Sheathed (PDAA) .... CTS
Cababe and Ellis' Queen's Bench Reports [1882-85] [England] [A publication] (DLA) .... C & E
Cababe and Ellis' Queen's Bench Reports [1882-85] [England] [A publication] (DLA) .... Cab & E
Cababe and Ellis' Queen's Bench Reports [1882-85] [England] [A publication] (DLA) .... Cab & El
Cababe and Ellis' Queen's Bench Reports [1882-85] [England] [A publication] (DLA) .... Cab & El (Eng)
Cababe and Ellis' Queen's Bench Reports [1882-85] [England] [A publication] (DLA) .... Cab & Ell
Cababe. Interpleader and Attachment of Debts [1900] [A publication] (ILCA) .... Cab Int
Cabalistic (ROG) .... CAB
Caballero [Cavalier] [Spanish] (DSUE) .... CAB
Caballococha [Peru] [ICAO location identifier] (ICLI) .... SPBC
Cabanatuan, Nueva Ecija [Philippines] [ICAO location identifier] (ICLI) .... RPUC
Cabano, PQ [FM radio station call letters] CFVD-1
Cabano, PQ [AM radio station call letters] .... CJAF
Cabaret .... CBRT
Cabaret, Hotel, Restaurant and Retailers Association [Alaska] (SRA) .... CHARR

Cabarien [Cuba] [Airport symbol] (AD) .... CBN
Cabarrus County Health Department, Concord, NC [Library symbol Library of Congress] (LCLS) .... NcCoCH
Cabarrus County Library, Concord, NC [Library symbol] [Library of Congress] (LCLS) .... NcCoC
Cabbage Looper [Entomology] CL
Cabbage Patch Kids .... CPK
Cabell-Huntington Public Library [Western Counties Regional Library], Huntington, WV [Library symbol Library of Congress] (LCLS) .... WvHu
CABI [Commonwealth Agricultural Bureaux International] Institute of Biological Control [Research center British] (IRC) .... CIBC
CABI [Commonwealth Agricultural Bureaux International] Institute of Parasitology [Research center British] (IRC) .... CIP
Cabin (MSA) .... CAB
Cabin .... CBN
Cabin Address System [Aviation] (AIA) .... CAS
Cabin Air Manifold Pressure [Aviation] .... CAMP
Cabin Air Temperature [Aviation] (NG) .... CAT
Cabin Air Temperature Valve [Aviation] .... CATV
Cabin Atmosphere Monitoring System [NASA] .... CAMS
Cabin Bleed Valve [Aviation] (MCD) .... CBV
Cabin/Cockpit Temperature Control Systems [Aviation] .... CTCS
Cabin Communications System [Aviation] .... CCS
Cabin Discrepancy Report [Report for airline log] .... CDR
Cabin Display Unit [Aviation] .... CDU
Cabin Equipment Interface [Aviation] .... CEI
Cabin Gas Analysis Unit [Aviation] (NASA) .... CGAU
Cabin Heat Exchanger [Aviation] (MCD) .... CHX
Cabin Humidity Control Subsystem [Aviation] (NASA) .... CHCS
Cabin Pressure Control System [Aviation] .... CPCS
Cabin Pressure Controller [Aviation] (MCD) .... CPC
Cabin Pressure Relief Valve [Aviation] (KSC) .... CPRV
Cabin Service/Management System [Aviation] .... CSMS
Cabin Telecommunications Unit [Telecommunications] (PCM) .... CTU
Cabinda [Angola] [Airport symbol] (OAG) .... CAB
Cabinda [Angola] [ICAO location identifier] (ICLI) .... FNCA
Cabinet [Technical drawings] (NFPA) C
Cabinet (KSC) .... CAB
Cabinet .... CABNT
Cabinet .... CABT
Cabinet .... CBNT
Cabinet (WGA) .... CBT
Cabinet Card (VRA) .... CABN
Cabinet Casemakers' Union [British] .... CCU
Cabinet Committee for Economic Policy [Later, CEP] .... CCEP
Cabinet Committee on Economic and Regional Development [Canada] .... CCERD
Cabinet Committee on International Narcotics Control [Terminated, 1977] .... CCINC
Cabinet Council on Commerce and Trade [Reagan administration] .... CCCT
Cabinet Council on Economic Affairs [Reagan administration] .... CCEA
Cabinet Council on Management and Administration [Executive Office of the President] (GFGA) .... CCMA
Cabinet File (CDE) .... CAB file
Cabinet Lawyer, by John Wade [England] [A publication] (DLA) .... Cab Lawy
Cabinet Makers' Society [A union] [British] .... CMS
Cabinet Office [New South Wales] [Australia] .... CO
Cabinet Office Briefing Room [British] .... COBRA
Cabinet Offices Cypher Office [British World War II] .... COCO
Cabinet Pressurization System .... CPS
Cabinet War Room .... CWR
Cabinetmaker .... CABMKR
Cabinetmakers' Association of Western Australia .... CMAWA
Cable C
Cable (MSA) .... CA
Cable .... CABL
Cable (AAG) .... CBL
Cable Access Cover .... CAC
Cable Access Point [Telecommunications] (TSSD) .... CAP
Cable Activity System [Telecommunications] (TEL) .... CAS
Cable & Co. Worldwide, Inc. [Associated Press] (SAG) .... CableCo
Cable & Co. Worldwide, Inc. [Associated Press] (SAG) .... CbleCo
Cable & Co. Worldwide, Inc. [NASDAQ symbol] (SAG) .... CCWW
Cable and Satellite Television (NITA) .... CAST
Cable and Telegraph Operators' Association [A union] [British] .... CTOA
Cable & Wireless AD [NYSE symbol] (TTSB) .... CWP

Cable and Wireless Ltd. [*Telecommunications*] (TEL) ... C & W
Cable & Wireless Ltd. [*Associated Press*] (SAG) ... CablWire
Cable and Wireless Ltd. [*Telecommunications*] (IAA) ... CAW
Cable & Wireless Ltd. ADS [*NYSE symbol*] (SPSG) ... CWP
Cable Antenna Television (IAA) ... CATV
Cable Arts Foundation, Inc. (NTCM) ... CAF
Cable Assembly ... CA
Cable Assembly Set (KSC) ... CAS
Cable Authority [*British*] ... CA
Cable Avoiding Tool (PDAA) ... CAT
Cable Car Beverage [*NASDAQ symbol*] (TTSB) ... DRNK
Cable Car Beverage Corp. [*Associated Press*] (SAG) ... CblCar
Cable Car Beverage Corp. [*NASDAQ symbol*] (NQ) ... DRNK
Cable Communications Resource Center (EA) ... CRC
Cable Connector (IAA) ... CC
Cable Connector Panel ... CCP
Cable Delay Line ... CDL
Cable Design Technologies [*Associated Press*] (SAG) ... CblDsgn
Cable Design Technologies [*NASDAQ symbol*] (SAG) ... CDTC
Cable Distribution Frame (NASA) ... CDF
Cable Distribution Head ... CDH
Cable Distribution Unit [*Aerospace*] (AAG) ... CDU
Cable Duct (MSA) ... CD
Cable End Sealing Kit ... CESK
Cable Firing [*or Fuzing*] (NG) ... CF
Cable FM [*Radio*] (NTCM) ... CAFM
Cable, Functional ... CF
Cable Health Network [*Cable-television system*] [*Viacom International, Inc.*] ... CHN
Cable Households Using Television [*Cable television ratings*] (NTCM) ... CHUT
Cable in the Classroom [*An association*] (ECON) ... CIC
Cable Integrity Group (NASA) ... CIG
Cable Interconnection Diagram (KSC) ... CID
Cable Interface Unit (DGA) ... CIU
Cable Jacket Zipper ... CJZ
Cable Jointing [*Section of the British Royal Navy*] ... J
Cable Launch Control System (SAA) ... CLCS
Cable Laying Ship ... CLS
Cable Link [*Telecommunications*] (OA) ... CL
Cable Maintenance Center [*Telecommunications*] (TEL) ... CMC
Cable Makers' Association [*British*] (BI) ... CMA
Cable Marking System ... CMS
Cable Monitoring and Rating System (MHDI) ... CMARS
Cable Multiplexer [*Electronics*] (IAA) ... CMX
Cable Network Engineering Program [*Bell System*] ... CNEP
Cable Network Joint Committee ... CNJC
Cable News Network [*Facetious translation: Chicken Noodle Network*] [*Cable-television system*] ... CNN
Cable On-Line Data Exchange [*Nielson Media Research*] [*Information service or system*] ... CODE
Cable Operated Zero Impedence Decoupler (MCD) ... COZID
Cable Orderwire Unit (MCD) ... COU
Cable Pair Identification [*Telecommunications*] (TEL) ... CPI
Cable Pressure Monitoring System [*Bell System*] ... CPMS
Cable Pressurization Equipment ... CPE
Cable Program Providers Group [*British*] (DBA) ... CPPG
Cable Programming Resource Directory [*A publication*] (TSSD) ... CPRD
Cable Rack (KSC) ... CR
Cable Reed ... CBLRD
Cable Reinforcement Set (MCD) ... CRS
Cable Relay Service [*or Station*] [*Television transmission*] ... CARS
Cable Repairing Ship [*Navy symbol*] ... ARC
Cable Routing Rotation (MCD) ... CRN
Cable Running Sheets ... CRS
Cable Satellite Public Affairs Network [*Cable-television system*] ... C-SPAN
Cable Ship [*Followed by name of cable-laying ship*] ... CS
Cable/Show Cause [*FCC*] (NTCM) ... CSC
Cable/Special Relief [*FCC*] (NTCM) ... CSR
Cable/Special Temporary Authority [*FCC*] (NTCM) ... CSTA
Cable Splicing Kit ... CSK
Cable Spreading Room [*Nuclear energy*] (NRCH) ... CSR
Cable Subscription Television ... CSTV
Cable Systems International ... CSI
Cable Systems International ... CSI
Cable Systems International ... CSI
Cable Telemetry System ... CTS
Cable Television [*Later, CTV*] ... CATV
Cable Television [*Formerly, CATV*] ... CTV
Cable Television Administration and Marketing Society (EA) ... CTAM
Cable Television Association [*British*] (NITA) ... CTA
Cable Television Cable Makers Association [*British*] (NITA) ... CATVCMA
Cable Television Cable Makers Association (PDAA) ... CATVCMA
Cable Television Construction Ltd. [*British*] (NITA) ... CTVC
Cable Television Information Center [*Defunct*] (EA) ... CTIC
Cable Television Relay (NTCM) ... CAR
Cable Television Technical Advisory Committee [*FCC*] (NTCM) ... CTAC
Cable Terminal Section [*Telecommunications*] (TEL) ... CTS
Cable Termination Equipment (CET) ... CTE
Cable Termination Network ... CTN
Cable, Test ... CT
Cable Test Set (MCD) ... CTS
Cable Testing Meter ... CTM
Cable Transfer [*of funds*] ... C/T
Cable Transfer Machine [*Nuclear energy*] (NRCH) ... CTM
Cable Tray (KSC) ... C/T
Cable Trays Vertical Chase [*Nuclear energy*] (NRCH) ... CTVC
Cable Trouble Ticket [*Telecommunications*] (TEL) ... CTT
Cable Turning Section [*Telecommunications*] (TEL) ... CTS
Cable Turning System [*Telecommunications*] (NITA) ... CTS
Cable Twist ... CT
Cable Twist Angle ... CTA
Cable Untwist ... CU
Cable Value Network [*Television*] ... CVN
Cable-Controlled Underwater Research Vehicle ... CURV
Cable-Controlled Unmanned Recovery Vehicle (MCD) ... CURV
Cable-Harness Analyzer ... CHA
Cableman (IAA) ... CBLMN
CableMaxx Holdings, Inc. [*Associated Press*] (SAG) ... Cablmax
Cablemaxx, Inc. [*NASDAQ symbol*] (SAG) ... CMAX
Cables [*Business term*] ... CAB
Cable-Satellite Public Affairs Network [*Washington, D.C.*] (WDMC) ... C-Span
Cableshare, Inc. [*Toronto Stock Exchange symbol*] ... CSH
Cabletel Communications [*AMEX symbol*] (TTSB) ... TTV
Cabletel Communications Corp. [*Associated Press*] (SAG) ... Cabeltel
Cabletel Communications Corp. [*Associated Press*] (SAG) ... Cabletel
Cabletel Communications Corp. [*AMEX symbol*] (SAG) ... TTV
Cabletelevision Advertising Bureau [*New York, NY*] (EA) ... CAB
Cabletron Systems [*NYSE symbol*] (TTSB) ... CS
Cabletron Systems, Inc. [*Associated Press*] (SAG) ... Cabltrn
Cabletron Systems, Inc. [*NYSE symbol*] (SPSG) ... CS
Cablevision Sys'A' [*AMEX symbol*] (TTSB) ... CVC
CableVision Systems Corp. [*Associated Press*] (SAG) ... Cablvsn
Cablevision Systems Corp. [*AMEX symbol*] (SPSG) ... CVC
CablevisionSys 8.50% Dep Cv Ex Pfd [*AMEX symbol*] (TTSB) ... CVCPr
Cabline ... CBL
Cabling Data ... CD
Cabling Diagram ... CAD
Cabling Interface Drawing (MCD) ... CID
Cabo Frio [*Costa Rica*] [*Seismograph station code, US Geological Survey*] (SEIS) ... AR7
Cabo Rojo [*Dominican Republic*] [*ICAO location identifier*] (ICLI) ... MDCR
Cabo Rojo, PR [*AM radio station call letters*] ... WEKO
Cabo Rojo, PR [*FM radio station call letters*] ... WMIO
Cabo Velas [*Costa Rica*] [*ICAO location identifier*] (ICLI) ... MRCV
Cabochon (VRA) ... cabo
Cabool, MO [*FM radio station call letters*] ... KOZX
Cabool, MO [*Location identifier FAA*] (FAAL) ... TVB
Caboose [*Freight*] ... CBSE
Caborca [*Mexico*] [*Seismograph station code, US Geological Survey*] (SEIS) ... CBS
Cabot, AR [*AM radio station call letters*] ... KBBL
Cabot, AR [*FM radio station call letters*] ... KBBL-FM
Cabot, AR [*FM radio station call letters*] (RBYB) ... KKRN-FM
Cabot Archives, Neil's Harbour, Nova Scotia [*Library symbol National Library of Canada*] (NLC) ... NSNHC
Cabot Archives, Neil's Harbour, NS, Canada [*Library symbol*] [*Library of Congress*] (LCLS) ... CaNSNhC
Cabot Corp. [*Associated Press*] (SAG) ... Cabot
Cabot Corp. [*NYSE symbol*] (SPSG) ... CBT
Cabot Corp., Stellite Division, Kokomo, IN [*Library symbol Library of Congress*] (LCLS) ... InKoC
Cabot Corp., Stellite Division, Kokomo, IN [*OCLC symbol*] (OCLC) ... ISD
Cabot Corp., Technical Information Center, Billerica, MA [*Library symbol Library of Congress*] (LCLS) ... MBilC
Cabot Institute of Applied Arts and Technology, St. John's, Newfoundland [*Library symbol National Library of Canada*] (NLC) ... NFSCT
Cabot Oil & Gas [*Associated Press*] (SAG) ... CbtOG
Cabot Oil & Gas [*NYSE symbol*] (SPSG) ... COG
Cabot Oil & Gas'A' [*NYSE symbol*] (TTSB) ... COG
Cabramurra [*Australia Seismograph station code, US Geological Survey Closed*] (SEIS) ... CAB
Cabre Corp. [*NASDAQ symbol*] (SAG) ... CABR
Cabre Corp. [*Associated Press*] (SAG) ... Cabre
Cabre Exploration Ltd. [*Toronto Stock Exchange symbol*] ... CBE
Cabrillo College, Aptos, CA [*Library symbol Library of Congress*] (LCLS) ... CApC
Cabrillo National Monument ... CABR
Cabrini College, Library, Radnor, PA [*OCLC symbol*] (OCLC) ... PAB
Cabriolet (ROG) ... CAB
Cab-to-Rear Axle [*Automotive engineering*] ... CA
Cacao Necrosis Virus [*Plant pathology*] ... CNV
Cacao Swollen Shoot Virus [*Plant pathology*] ... CSSV
Cacao Yellow Mosaic Virus [*Plant pathology*] ... CYMV
Caceres [*Brazil*] [*Airport symbol*] (OAG) ... CCX
Cache Bay Public Library, Ontario [*Library symbol National Library of Canada*] (NLC) ... OCB
Cache Bus Interface [*Computer science*] (BYTE) ... CBI
Cache County Public Library, Logan, UT [*Library symbol Library of Congress*] (LCLS) ... ULC
Cache/Disk System [*A storage device*] [*Computer science*] (NITA) ... C/DS
Cache d'Or Resources [*Vancouver Stock Exchange symbol*] ... CCI
Cache DRAM [*Dynamic Random Access Memory*] (CDE) ... CDRAM
Cache Enable [*Computer science*] (PCM) ... CE
Cache, Inc. [*NASDAQ symbol*] (NQ) ... CACH
Cache, Inc. [*Associated Press*] (SAG) ... Cache
Cache/Memory Management Unit (BYTE) ... CAMMU
Cache Memory Management Unit [*Computer science*] (BYTE) ... CMMU
Cache Valley Historical Society, Logan, UT [*Library symbol Library of Congress*] (LCLS) ... ULCHi
Cachimbo [*Brazil ICAO location identifier*] (ICLI) ... SBCC
Cachipo, Monagas [*Venezuela ICAO location identifier*] (ICLI) ... SVCI
Cachoeira do Sul [*Brazil*] [*Airport symbol*] (AD) ... CCQ

Cachucha Ranch [*New Mexico*] [*Seismograph station code, US Geological Survey Closed*] (SEIS) .... CCN
CACI Int'l [*NASDAQ symbol*] (TTSB) .... CACI
Cacia International [*Associated Press*] (SAG) .... CACI
Cacia International, Inc. [*NASDAQ symbol*] (NQ) .... CACI
Cacine [*Guinea-Bissau*] [*ICAO location identifier*] (ICLI) .... GGCC
Cacolo [*Angola*] [*ICAO location identifier*] (ICLI) .... FNCC
Cacquot Kite Balloon .... CKB
Cactoblastis [*South American moth brought to Australia to destroy the prickly pear*] (DSUE) .... CACTO
Cactus [*Horticulture*] C
Cactus and Succulent Society of America (EA) .... CSSA
Cactus and Succulent Society of the Australian Capital Territory .... CSSACT
Cactus Virus 2 [*Plant pathology*] CV2
Cactus Virus X [*Plant pathology*] CVX
Cactus West Explorations Ltd. [*Vancouver Stock Exchange symbol*] .... CWE
Cacwhuacintle [*Race of maize*] .... CAC
CAD/CAM [*Computer-Aided Design/Computer-Aided Manufacturing*] **Systems** .... CCS
CAD/CAM [*Computer-Aided Design/Computer-Aided Manufacturing*] **Systems** (MCD) .... CCSYS
CAD [*Computer-Aided Design*] **for VLSI** [*Very Large Scale Integrati on*] **System** [*Electronics*] (NITA) .... CVS
CAD [*Computer-Aided-Design*] **Programming Language** (PCM) .... CPL
Cadarache [*France*] [*Seismograph station code, US Geological Survey*] (SEIS) .... CDR
Cadastral and Land-Use Mapping Information System (PDAA) .... CLUMIS
Cadaver [*Medicine*] .... Cad
Cadaver [*Medicine*] (ROG) .... CADAV
Cadaver Donor [*Medicine*] .... CD
Cadaveric Donor Renal Transplantation [*Medicine*] .... CDRTx
Cadbury [*England*] .... CADB
Cadbury Schwep LP 8.625%'QUIPS' [*NYSE symbol*] (TTSB) .... CSDPrA
Cadbury Schweppes ADS [*NYSE symbol*] (TTSB) .... CSG
Cadbury Schweppes Delaware LP [*Associated Press*] (SAG) .... CadScD
Cadbury Schweppes Delaware LP [*NYSE symbol*] (SAG) .... CSD
Cadbury Schweppes Ltd. [*NASDAQ symbol*] .... CADB
Cadbury Schweppes PLC (MHDW) .... CADBY
Cadbury Schwepps Ltd. [*Associated Press*] (SAG) .... CadbyS
Cadbury Schwepps PLC [*NYSE symbol*] (SAG) .... CSG
Caddev Industry, Inc. [*Vancouver Stock Exchange symbol*] .... CJH
Caddo [*MARC language code Library of Congress*] (LCCP) .... cad
Caddo Mills, TX [*Location identifier FAA*] (FAAL) .... MII
Caddo Parish Library, Shreveport, LA [*Library symbol Library of Congress*] (LCLS) .... LShCa
Cade Industries [*NASDAQ symbol*] (TTSB) .... CADE
Cade Industries, Inc. [*NASDAQ symbol*] (NQ) .... CADE
Cade Industries, Inc. [*Associated Press*] (SAG) .... CadeIn
Cadeguomycin Deazaguanosine [*Antineoplastic drug*] .... CDM
Cadena Azul de Radiodifusion [*Radio network*] [*Spain*] .... CAR
Cadena Garcia Valseca [*Press agency*] [*Mexico*] .... CGV
Cadena Radial Ecuatoriana (EY) .... CRE
Cadence Design Sys [*NYSE symbol*] (TTSB) .... CDN
Cadence Design Systems [*NYSE symbol*] (SPSG) .... CDN
Cadence Design Systems, Inc. [*Associated Press*] (SAG) .... Cadence
Cadence Design Systems, Inc. (MHDW) .... CDNC
Cadenza [*Cadence*] [*Music*] .... CAD
Cadet [*British military*] (DMA) C
Cadet .... CAD
Cadet [*British military*] (DMA) .... Cdt
Cadet .... CDT
Cadet Administrative Management Information System [*Air Force*] (GFGA) .... CAMIS
Cadet Battalion [*British military*] (DMA) .... CB
Cadet Captain CC
Cadet Corps [*British military*] (DMA) CC
Cadet Forces Medal [*British military*] (DMA) .... CFM
Cadet Practice Squadron .... CADETRON
Cadet Troop Leader Training (MCD) .... CTLT
Cadets Norfolk Artillery [*British military*] (DMA) .... CNA
Cadger (ROG) .... CAD
Cadillac & Lake City Railway Co. [*AAR code*] .... CLK
Cadillac Convertible Owners of America (EA) .... CCOA
Cadillac Fairview Corp. Ltd. [*Toronto Stock Exchange symbol Vancouver Stock Exchange symbol*] .... CFV
Cadillac, MI [*Location identifier FAA*] (FAAL) .... CAD
Cadillac, MI [*AM radio station call letters*] .... WATT
Cadillac, MI [*FM radio station call letters*] .... WCKC
Cadillac, MI [*Television station call letters*] .... WCMV
Cadillac, MI [*Television station call letters*] .... WGKI
Cadillac, MI [*AM radio station call letters*] .... WKJF
Cadillac, MI [*FM radio station call letters*] .... WKJF-FM
Cadillac, MI [*FM radio station call letters*] .... WLXV
Cadillac, MI [*FM radio station call letters*] .... WOLW
Cadillac, MI [*Television station call letters*] .... WWTV
Cadillac Motor Car Division [*General Motors Corp.*] .... CMCD
Cadillac Public School, Cadillac, MI [*Library symbol*] [*Library of Congress*] (LCLS) .... MiCadCS
Cadillac-Larder Lake [*Geology*] .... CLDZ
Cadillac-LaSalle Club (EA) CLC
Cadillac-Wexford Public Library, Cadillac, MI [*Library symbol Library of Congress*] (LCLS) .... MiCad
Cadiz, KY [*AM radio station call letters*] .... WKDZ
Cadiz, KY [*FM radio station call letters*] .... WKDZ-FM
Cadiz Land [*NASDAQ symbol*] (TTSB) CLCI
Cadiz Land Co., Inc. [*Associated Press*] (SAG) .... Cadiz
Cadiz Land Co., Inc. [*NASDAQ symbol*] (SAG) CLCI
Cadiz, OH [*Location identifier FAA*] (FAAL) .... CFX
Cadiz, OH [*FM radio station call letters*] .... WCDK
Cadiz Public Library, Cadiz, OH [*Library symbol Library of Congress*] (LCLS) .... OCad
Cadiz Railroad Co. [*AAR code*] .... CAD
Cadkey Object Developer [*Computer science*] .... COD
Cadmium [*Chemical symbol is Cd*] (KSC) .... CAD
Cadmium [*Chemical element*] .... Cd
Cadmium Association [*British*] (EAIO) .... CA
Cadmium Binding Protein .... CdBP
Cadmium Bronze .... CB
Cadmium Bronze Connector .... CBC
Cadmium Council (EA) CC
Cadmium Mercury Telluride [*Solid state chemistry*] .... CMT
Cadmium Oxide - Ethylenediamine [*Cellulose solvent*] .... CADOXEN
Cadmium Pigments Association (EAIO) .... CPA
Cadmium Plate [*Technical drawings*] .... CDPL
Cadmium Red Line .... CRL
Cadmium Sulfide [*Inorganic chemistry*] (WGA) .... CdS
Cadmium, Zinc, and Telluride .... CZT
Cadmium-Sulfide Cell .... CSC
Cadmus Communication [*NASDAQ symbol*] (TTSB) .... CDMS
Cadmus Communications Corp. [*NASDAQ symbol*] (NQ) .... CDMS
Cadmus Communicatons Corp. [*Associated Press*] (SAG) .... Cadmus
Cadmus Group, Inc. (GAAI) .... CADMUS
CADO [*Computer Access Device Output*] **Actions-Terminal** (IAA) .... CAT
Cadotte Lake School, Alberta [*Library symbol National Library of Canada*] (BIB) .... ACALS
Cadre .... CDR
Cadre Weather Team (MCD) .... CWT
Cadus Pharmaceutical Corp. [*Associated Press*] (SAG) .... CadusPh
Cadus Pharmaceutical Corp. [*NASDAQ symbol*] (SAG) .... KDUS
Cadwalader's Cases, United States District Court, Eastern District of Pennsylva nia [*A publication*] (DLA) .... Cadwalader
Cadwalader's Digest of Attorney-General's Opinions [*A publication*] (DLA) .... Cadw Dig
Cady Mountains [*California*] [*Seismograph station code, US Geological Survey Closed*] (SEIS) .... CAD
CAE Electronics Ltd., Montreal, Quebec [*Library symbol National Library of Canada*] (NLC) .... QMCAE
CAE Industries Ltd. [*Toronto Stock Exchange symbol*] .... CAE
Caecum C
Caecum Ligation and Puncture [*Medicine*] .... CLP
Caeharris [*Cardiff*] [*Welsh depot code*] .... CH
Caelebs [*Unmarried*] [*Latin*] (ROG) .... CAEL
Caelum [*Constellation*] .... Cae
Caelum [*Constellation*] .... Cael
Caen [*France*] [*Airport symbol*] (OAG) .... CFR
Caen/Carpiquet [*France ICAO location identifier*] (ICLI) .... LFRK
Caenorhabditis [*Nematode*] **Genetics Center** .... CGC
Caere Corp. [*NASDAQ symbol*] (NQ) .... CAER
Caere Corp. [*Associated Press*] (SAG) .... Caere
Caernarvonshire [*Wales*] (BARN) .... Caern
Caernarvonshire [*County in Wales*] .... Caerns
Caerulcus [*Blue*] [*Pharmacy*] (ROG) .... CAERL
Caeruleus [*Dark Blue, Dark Green*] [*Pharmacy*] (DAVI) .... caerul
Caesar [*of Plutarch*] [*Classical studies*] (OCD) .... Caes
Caesar Contardus [*Deceased, 1585*] [*Authority cited in pre-1607 legal work*] (DSA) .... Caes Contar
Caesar Resources Ltd. [*Vancouver Stock Exchange symbol*] .... CER
Caesarean [*or Cesarean*] [*Section Obstetrics*] (DAVI) C
Caesarean [*or Cesarean*] **Birth** [*Obstetrics*] (DAVI) .... CB
Caesarean Delivered [*Medicine*] .... CD
Caesarean [*or Cesarean*] **Section** [*Obstetrics*] (DAVI) .... C Sect
Caesarean Section [*Medicine*] .... C (Section)
Caesarean Section [*Medicine*] .... CS
Caesarean Support Network [*British*] (DBA) .... CSN
Caesarean-Originated, Barrier-Sustained [*Rodent breeding*] .... COBS
Caesium Beam Frequency Standard (IAA) .... CBFS
Caeteris Paribus [*Other Things Being Equal*] [*Latin*] (ROG) .... CAET PAR
Cafe-au-Lait Macules (DMAA) .... CALM
Cafeteria (BARN) .... caf
Cafeteria .... CAFTRA
Cafeteria Benefits [*Health insurance*] (GHCT) .... CB
Caffeic Acid [*Organic chemistry*] .... CA
Caffeine .... CAF
Caffeine, Alcohol, Pepper, and Aspirin [*As in CAPA-free diet*] [*Medicine*] (DAVI) .... CAPA
Caffeine, Alcohol, Pepper, Peppermint, and Alcohol [*As in CAPPA-free diet*] (DAVI) .... CAPPA
Caffeine, Alcohol, Pepper, Spicy Foods [*Nutrition*] .... CAPS
Caffeine Halothane Challenge Test [*Clinical chemistry*] .... CHCT
Caffeine Sodium Benzoate [*Chemistry*] (DAVI) .... CSB
Cagayan De Oro [*Philippines*] [*Airport symbol*] (OAG) .... CGY
Cagayan De Oro, Misamis Oriental [*Philippines*] [*ICAO location identifier*] (ICLI) .... RPWL
Cage (MSA) .... CG
Cage Container (DCTA) C
Cage Inventory Record [*Shipping*] (DS) .... CIR
CAGE [*Computerized Aerospace Ground Equipment*] **Test Language** [*Computer science*] (KSC) .... CTL
Caging Amplifier Assembly .... CAA
Caging Retainer and Boresight [*Air Force*] .... CRAB

Cagle's, Inc. [*Associated Press*] (SAG) .... Cagle
Cagle's, Inc. [*AMEX symbol*] (SPSG) .... CGL
Cagle's Inc. 'A' [*AMEX symbol*] (TTSB) .... CGLA
Cagliari [*Italy*] [*Airport symbol*] (OAG) .... CAG
Cagliari/Elmas [*Italy ICAO location identifier*] (ICLI) .... LIEE
Cagney and Lacey [*Television series*] .... C & L
Caguas [*Puerto Rico*] [*Seismograph station code, US Geological Survey*] (SEIS) .... CAG
Caguas [*Diocesan abbreviation*] [*Puerto Rico*] (TOCD) .... CGS
Caguas, PR [*Television station call letters*] .... WLII
Caguas, PR [*AM radio station call letters*] .... WNEL
Caguas, PR [*Television station call letters*] .... WUJA
Caguas, PR [*AM radio station call letters*] .... WVJP
Caguas, PR [*FM radio station call letters*] .... WVJP-FM
Cahiers de Droit Compare [*A publication*] (ILCA) .... CDC
Cahiers de Droit Familial [*A publication*] (ILCA) .... CDF
Cahiers de Droit Fiscal International [*A publication*] (DLA) .... Cahier Dr Fiscal
Cahiers. Faculte de Droit et des Sciences Economiques de Nancy [*A publication*] (DLA) .... Cah de la Fac de Droit Nancy
Cahill's Illinois Statutes [*A publication*] (DLA) .... Cahill's Ill St
Cahners Advertising Research Reports [*A publication*] .... CARR
Cahners Books International, Inc. [*Later, CBI Publishing Co., Inc.*] .... CBI
Cahners Exposition Group [*Telecommunications service*] (TSSD) .... CEG
Cahokia Community Unit School District 187, Cahokia, IL [*Library symbol Library of Congress*] (LCLS) .... ICahSD
Cahokia Public Library, Cahokia, IL [*Library symbol Library of Congress*] (LCLS) .... ICah
Cahors/Lalbenque [*France ICAO location identifier*] (ICLI) .... LFCC
CAI [*Compagnia Aeronautica Italiana SpA*] [*Italy ICAO designator*] (FAAC) .... KVY
CAI Wireless Systems [*NASDAQ symbol*] (TTSB) .... CAWS
CAI Wireless Systems, Inc. [*Associated Press*] (SAG) .... CAI Wre
CAI Wireless Systems, Inc. [*NASDAQ symbol*] (SAG) .... CAWS
Caibarien [*Cuba ICAO location identifier*] (ICLI) .... MUCB
Caicara [*Venezuela*] [*Airport symbol*] (OAG) .... CXA
Caicara de Orinoco [*Venezuela*] [*Airport symbol*] (AD) .... CXA
Caicara De Orinoco, Bolivar [*Venezuela ICAO location identifier*] (ICLI) .... SVCD
Caile Ferate Romane [*Romanian Railways Board*] [*Department of Railways*] .... CFR
Caines and Leigh. Crown Cases [*England*] [*A publication*] (DLA) .... C & LCC
Caines' Cases [*New York*] [*A publication*] (DLA) .... Cai Ca
Caines' Cases [*New York*] [*A publication*] (DLA) .... Cains C
Caines' Lex Mercatoria Americana [*A publication*] (DLA) .... Cai Lex Mer
Caines' New York Cases in Error [*A publication*] (DLA) .... Cai
Caines' New York Cases in Error [*A publication*] (DLA) .... Cai Cas
Caines' New York Cases in Error [*A publication*] (DLA) .... Cai Cas Err
Caines' New York Cases in Error [*A publication*] (DLA) .... Cai R
Caines' New York Cases in Error [*A publication*] (DLA) .... Cain
Caines' New York Cases in Error [*A publication*] (DLA) .... Cain Cas in Error
Caines' New York Cases in Error [*A publication*] (DLA) .... Cain CE
Caines' New York Cases in Error [*A publication*] (DLA) .... Cain E
Caines' New York Cases in Error [*A publication*] (DLA) .... Caines
Caines' New York Cases in Error [*A publication*] (DLA) .... Caines Ca in E
Caines' New York Cases in Error [*A publication*] (DLA) .... Caines' Ca in Er
Caines' New York Cases in Error [*A publication*] (DLA) .... Caines Cas
Caines' New York Cases in Error [*A publication*] (DLA) .... Caines' Cas in Er
Caines' New York Cases in Error [*A publication*] (DLA) .... Caines (NY)
Caines' New York Cases in Error [*A publication*] (DLA) .... Cas Err
Caines' New York Cases in Error [*A publication*] (DLA) .... CCE
Caines' New York Cases in Error [*A publication*] (DLA) .... NY Cas Err
Caines' New York Cases in Error [*A publication*] (DLA) .... NY Cas in Error
Caines' Practical (New York) Forms [*A publication*] (DLA) .... Cai Forms
Caines' Practice [*A publication*] (DLA) .... Cai Pr
Caines' Reports [*New York*] [*A publication*] (DLA) .... Cai (NY)
Caines' Reports [*New York*] [*A publication*] (DLA) .... Caine R
Caines' Reports [*New York*] [*A publication*] (DLA) .... Caines' R
Caines' Reports [*New York*] [*A publication*] (DLA) .... Caines Rep
Caines' Reports [*New York*] [*A publication*] (DLA) .... Cains R
Caines' Reports, New York Supreme Court [*A publication*] (DLA) .... Cai
Caines' Reports, New York Supreme Court [*A publication*] (DLA) .... Cai Cas
Caines' Reports, New York Supreme Court [*A publication*] (DLA) .... Cai R
Caines' Reports, New York Supreme Court [*A publication*] (DLA) .... Cain
Caines' Reports, New York Supreme Court [*A publication*] (DLA) .... Caines
Caines' Reports, New York Supreme Court [*A publication*] (DLA) .... Caines Cas
Caines' Reports, New York Supreme Court [*A publication*] (DLA) .... Caines (NY)
Caines' Term Reports [*New York*] [*A publication*] (DLA) .... NYT Rep
Caines' Term Reports [*New York*] [*A publication*] (DLA) .... TR
Caines' Term Reports [*New York*] [*A publication*] (DLA) .... TR (NY)
Caines' Term Reports, New York Supreme Court [*A publication*] (DLA) .... Cai
Caines' Term Reports, New York Supreme Court [*A publication*] (DLA) .... Cai Cas
Caines' Term Reports, New York Supreme Court [*A publication*] (DLA) .... Cai R
Caines' Term Reports, New York Supreme Court [*A publication*] (DLA) .... Cai TR
Caines' Term Reports, New York Supreme Court [*A publication*] (DLA) .... Cain
Caines' Term Reports, New York Supreme Court [*A publication*] (DLA) .... Caines
Caines' Term Reports, New York Supreme Court [*A publication*] (DLA) .... Caines Cas
Caines' Term Reports, New York Supreme Court [*A publication*] (DLA) .... Caines (NY)
Caines' Term Reports, New York Supreme Court [*A publication*] (DLA) .... Caines Term Rep (NY)
Cain-Levine Social Competency Scale [*Psychology*] .... C-L
Cain-Levine Social Competency Scale [*Psychology*] .... CLSCS
CAINS [*Carrier/Aircraft Inertial Navigation System*] **Covert Data Link** (MCD) .... CCDL
C-Air [*Former USSR*] [*FAA designator*] (FAAC) .... CEE
Cairensis Gnosticus [*Nag Hammadi Codices*] (BJA) .... CG
Cairine Wilson Secondary School, Gloucester, Ontario [*Library symbol National Library of Canada*] (BIB) .... OGCW
Cairn Energy USA [*NASDAQ symbol*] (TTSB) .... CEUS
Cairn Energy USA, Inc. [*Associated Press*] (SAG) .... Cairn
Cairn Energy USA, Inc. [*NASDAQ symbol*] (SAG) .... CEUS
Cairn Terrier Club of America (EA) .... CTCA
Cairngorm [*Type of quartz*] (ROG) .... CGM
Cairns [*Australia ICAO location identifier*] (ICLI) .... ABCS
Cairns [*Australia Airport symbol*] (OAG) .... CNS
Cairns Agricultural, Pastoral, and Mining Association [*Australia*] .... CAPMA
Cairns and District Historic Vehicle Club [*Australia*] .... CHHVC
Cairns. Decisions in the Albert Arbitration (Reilly) [*1871-75*] [*England*] [*A publication*] (DLA) .... Cairns Dec
Cairo [*Egypt*] [*Airport symbol*] (OAG) .... CAI
Cairo [*Illinois*] [*Airport symbol*] (AD) .... CIR
Cairo [*Egypt*] [*ICAO location identifier*] (ICLI) .... HECC
Cairo Air Transport Co. [*Egypt*] [*ICAO designator*] (FAAC) .... CCE
Cairo Documents of the Damascus Covenanters [*A publication*] (BJA) .... CDC
Cairo, GA [*Location identifier FAA*] (FAAL) .... CYR
Cairo, GA [*AM radio station call letters*] .... WGRA
Cairo, GA [*FM radio station call letters*] .... WSLE
Cairo Geniza (BJA) .... CG
Cairo, IL [*Location identifier FAA*] (FAAL) .... CIR
Cairo, IL [*AM radio station call letters*] .... WKRO
Cairo/International [*Egypt*] [*ICAO location identifier*] (ICLI) .... HECA
Cairo Public Library, Cairo, IL [*Library symbol Library of Congress*] (LCLS) .... ICa
Cairo Public Library, Cairo, IL [*Library symbol*] [*Library of Congress*] (LCLS) .... ICaL
Caisse Commune d'Epargne et d'Investissement [*Finance institutions*] [*Cameroon*] (EY) .... CCEI
Caisse de Depot de Placement du Quebec, Montreal, PQ, Canada [*Library symbol Library of Congress*] (LCLS) .... CaQMCDP
Caisse de Depot et Placement du Quebec, Montreal, Quebec [*Library symbol National Library of Canada*] (NLC) .... QMCDP
Caisse Generale d'Epargne et de Retraite [*State-owned bank*] [*Belgium*] (EY) .... CGER
Caisse Nationale de Credit Agricole du Burkina (EY) .... CNCAB
Caisse Primaire d'Assurance Maladie [*French*] (DLA) .... CPAM
Caithness [*County in Scotland*] (ROG) .... CAI
Caithness County [*Scotland*] (BARN) .... caith
Caithness Paperweight Collectors Society [*Perth, Scotland*] (EAIO) .... CPCS
Caius (ROG) C
Caius College [*Cambridge University*] (ROG) CC
Cajabamba/Pampa Grande [*Peru*] [*ICAO location identifier*] (ICLI) .... SPJB
Cajal Club (EA) CC
Cajamarca [*Peru*] [*Airport symbol*] (OAG) .... CJA
Cajamarca/Mayor General FAP Armando Revoredo Iglesias [*Peru*] [*ICAO location identifier*] (ICLI) .... SPJR
Cajazeiras [*Brazil*] [*Airport symbol*] (AD) .... CJZ
Cajun Nike [*US Navy missile*] .... CAN
Cake .... CK
Cake and Biscuit Alliance [*British*] .... CBA
Cal Aviation SA [*Greece*] [*ICAO designator*] (FAAC) CLV
Cal Denver Resources [*Vancouver Stock Exchange symbol*] .... CEV
Cal Dynamics Corp. [*Vancouver Stock Exchange symbol*] .... CYE
Cal Fed Bancorp [*NYSE symbol*] (TTSB) .... CAL
Cal Fed Bk 7.75% CvPfd'A' [*NYSE symbol*] (TTSB) .... CALPr
Cal Graphite Corp. [*Vancouver Stock Exchange symbol*] .... CGP
Cal Owner's Association [*Defunct*] (EA) .... COA
Cal Sierra [*ICAO designator*] (AD) .... QS
Calabar [*Nigeria*] [*Airport symbol*] (OAG) .... CBQ
Calabar [*Nigeria*] [*ICAO location identifier*] (ICLI) .... DNCA
Calabozo [*Venezuela*] [*Airport symbol*] (OAG) .... CLZ
Calabozo, Guarico [*Venezuela ICAO location identifier*] (ICLI) .... SVCL
Calais [*France*] [*Airport symbol*] (AD) .... CQF
Calais/Dunkerque [*France ICAO location identifier*] (ICLI) .... LFAC
Calais, ME [*FM radio station call letters*] .... WMED
Calais, ME [*Television station call letters*] .... WMED-TV
Calais, ME [*AM radio station call letters*] .... WQDY
Calais, ME [*FM radio station call letters*] .... WQDY-FM
Calais Resources Ltd. [*Toronto Stock Exchange symbol*] .... CLJ
Calama [*Chile*] [*Seismograph station code, US Geological Survey*] (SEIS) .... CAC
Calama [*Chile*] [*Airport symbol*] (OAG) .... CJC
Calama/El Loa [*Chile*] [*ICAO location identifier*] (ICLI) .... SCCF
Calamocha [*Spain ICAO location identifier*] (ICLI) .... LECH
Calamus Length CL
Calamus Length Index CLI
Calando [*Dying Away*] [*Music*] .... Cal
Calapan, Oriental Mindoro [*Philippines*] [*ICAO location identifier*] (ICLI) .... RPUK
Calaveras County Free Library, San Andreas, CA [*Library symbol Library of Congress*] (LCLS) .... CSadC
Calaveras County Museum & Archives Library, San Andreas, CA [*Library symbol*] [*Library of Congress*] (LCLS) .... CSadM
Calaveras Reservoir [*California*] [*Seismograph station code, US Geological Survey*] (SEIS) .... CVR
Calavo Growers of California (EA) .... CGC
Calbayog [*Philippines*] [*Airport symbol*] (OAG) .... CYP
Calbayog, Western Samar [*Philippines*] [*ICAO location identifier*] (ICLI) .... RPVC
Calcareous [*Quality of the bottom*] [*Nautical charts*] .... Ca
Calcarine Sulcus [*Medicine*] (DMAA) .... CAS
Calcasieu Parish Public Library, Lake Charles, LA [*Library symbol Library of Congress*] (LCLS) LLcC
Calced Carmelites (TOCD) .... OCarm
Calcein Blue Acetoxymethyl Ester [*Organic chemistry*] .... CBAM
Calcific Aortic Stenosis [*Medicine*] (DMAA) .... CAS

Calcified Alluvium [*Archeology*]	Cala
Calcified Bone Mineral Density	CBMD
Calcified Pea Gravel [*Archeology*]	cpg
Calcifying Epithelial Odontogenic Tumor [*Medicine*] (DMAA)	CEOT
Calcined Gross Fission Product	CGFP
Calcined Waste Packaging Cell [*Nuclear energy*] (NRCH)	CWPC
Calcineurin [*Biochemistry*]	CaN
Calcineurin [*Biochemistry*]	CN
Calcinosis Cutis, Raynaud's Phenomenon, Sclerodactyly, and Telangiectasia [*A medical syndrome*]	CRST
Calcinosis, Raynaud's Phenomenon, Esophageal Dysfunction, Sclerodactyly, and Telangiectasia [*A medical syndrome*]	CREST
Calcinosis, Raynaud's Phenomenon, Esophageal Dysmotility [*or Dysfunction*],Sclerodactyly, and Telangiectasia [*Syndrome*] [*Rheumatology*] (DAVI)	CREST
Calcite [*CIPW classification*] [*Geology*]	cc
Calcite Compensation Depth [*Oceanography*]	CCD
Calcitonin [*Also, TCA, TCT*] [*Endocrinology*]	CT
Calcitonin Gene Related Peptide Receptor [*Medicine*] (DMAA)	CGRPR
Calcitonin Gene-Related Peptide [*Endocrinology*]	CGRP
Calcitonin Receptor [*Endocrinology*]	CTR
Calcium [*Chemical element*]	Ca
Calcium [*Symbol is Ca*] [*Chemical element*] (ROG)	CAL
Calcium [*Test*] [*Dentistry*] (DAVI)	CAL
Calcium Activated Neutral Protease [*An enzyme*]	CANP
Calcium Alginate [*Swab*] [*Medicine*] (DAVI)	CALGI
Calcium Aluminate Cement [*PDAA*]	CAC
Calcium- and Magnesium-Free	CMF
Calcium- and Magnesium-Free Synthetic Seawater	CMFSW
Calcium Binding Protein [*Biochemistry*]	CaBP
Calcium Bone Index [*Medicine*] (DAVI)	CaBI
Calcium Carbonate [*Pharmacology*] (DAVI)	CACB
Calcium Carbonate [*Pharmacology*] (DAVI)	CaCO3
Calcium Carbonate Deposition Test [*Organic chemistry*] (DICI)	CCDT
Calcium Channel Blocker [*Medicine*] (CPH)	CCB
Calcium Chloride [*Pharmacology*] (DAVI)	CaCl2
Calcium Chloride Hexahydrate	CCH
Calcium Chloride Institute [*Defunct*] (EA)	CCI
Calcium Cyanamide Citrated [*or Citrated Calcium Carbimide*] [*Pharmacology*]	CCC
Calcium Cyclamate [*Sweetener*]	CC
Calcium Diethylene-Triamine-Pentaacetic Acid (PDAA)	CDTPA
Calcium Disodium Ethylenediaminetetraacetate [*Chelating agent*]	CaEDTA
Calcium Entry Blocking [*Agent*] [*Physiology*]	CEB
Calcium Excretion [*Medicine*] (DMAA)	CaE
Calcium, Ferrous, Magnesium, Aluminum, Silicon [*Oxide system in geology*]	CFMAS
Calcium Hydroxide [*Inorganic chemistry*] (OA)	CH
Calcium in the Solar Spectrum [*Astronomy*] (BARN)	K
Calcium Influx Factor [*Neurobiology*]	CIF
Calcium Intake Score [*Medicine*]	CS
Calcium, Ionized [*Organic chemistry*] (DAVI)	CA ION
Calcium Lanthanum Silicate Oxyapatite (IEEE)	CaLaSOAP
Calcium, Lime, Rust Remover [*Cleaning product*]	CLR
Calcium Magnesium Acetate	CMA
Calcium, Magnesium, Aluminum, Silicon [*Oxide system in geology*]	CMAS
Calcium Methanearsonate [*Herbicide*]	CMA
Calcium Nutrient Agar [*Medicine*] (DMAA)	CNA
Calcium Oxalate [*Organic chemistry*] (AAMN)	CA OX
Calcium Oxalate [*Organic chemistry*]	COX
Calcium Oxide [*Organic chemistry*] (DAVI)	CaO
Calcium Phosphate [*Organic chemistry*] (DAVI)	CAPC
Calcium Pyrophosphate [*Organic chemistry*] (DAVI)	CAPR
Calcium Pyrophosphate Deposition [*Medicine*]	CPPD
Calcium Pyrophosphate Deposition Disease [*Rheumatology*] (DAVI)	CPDD
Calcium Pyrophosphate Dihydrate [*Inorganic chemistry*]	CaPDi
Calcium Pyrophosphate Dihydrate [*Inorganic chemistry*]	CPPD
Calcium Silicate Hydrate [*Inorganic chemistry*]	CSH
Calcium Tolerance Test [*Medicine*] (DMAA)	CATT
Calcium Urine Spot [*Test*] [*Biochemistry*] (DAVI)	CA-SP
Calcium-Activated Factor [*Meat science*]	CAF
Calcium-Activated Sarcoplasmic Factor [*A proteolytic enzyme*]	CASF
Calcium-Aluminum-Rich Inclusion [*Meteorite composition*]	CAI
Calcium-Ammonium Nitrate [*Fertilizer*]	CAN
Calcium-Based Minerals [*Inorganic chemistry*]	CBM
Calcium-Binding Modulator Protein	CMP
Calcium-Binding Para-Albumin [*Biochemistry*]	CPA
Calcium-Boron-Aluminum [*Glasses*]	CABAL
Calcium-Dependent Adenosine Triphophatase (PDAA)	Ca-ATPase
Calcium-Dependent Protease Small Subunit [*Medicine*] (DMAA)	CDPS
Calcium-Dependent Protein Kinase [*An enzyme*]	CDPK
Calcium-Induced Calcium Release [*Biochemistry*]	CICR
Calcium-Ion Dependent Regulator [*Biochemistry*]	CDR
Calcium-Magnesium Silicate (OA)	CMS
Calcium-Reduced Skim Milk	CRSM
Calcium-Reduced Skim Milk Powder (OA)	CRSMP
Calcium-to-Phosphorus [*Molar ratio*] (DAVI)	Ca/P
Calcofluor White [*A cotton whitener*]	CFW
Calcraft [*Hangman*] [*Slang British*] (DSUE)	CAL
Calcrete [*Geology*]	cAL
Calculate [*or Calculated*]	CALC
Calculated (ADA)	CALCD
Calculated Access Method (PDAA)	CAM
Calculated Air Speed (MSA)	CAS
Calculated Altitude	CALALT

Calculated Area under the Curve [*Statistics*]	CAUC
Calculated Average Life (AAG)	CAL
Calculated Cetane Index [*Fuel technology*]	CCI
Calculated Colloidal Osmotic Pressure [*Clinical chemistry*]	cCOP
Calculated Date of Confinement [*Obstetrics*] (DAVI)	CDC
Calculated Error Probable	CEP
Calculated Estimated Time of Departure [*Aviation*] (DA)	CETD
Calculated Estimated Time of Overflight [*Aviation*] (DA)	CETO
Calculated Landing Time [*FAA*] (TAG)	CLT
Calculated Particulate Organic Carbon [*Oceanography*]	CPOC
Calculated Protein Efficiency Ration [*Nutrition*]	C-PER
Calculated Time of Arrival (DA)	CTA
Calculated Weight Report	CWR
Calculated Zenith Distance	CZD
Calculation (IAA)	CALCN
Calculation/Experiment (NRCH)	C/E
Calculation Link Processing System [*Military*] (CAAL)	CLIPS
Calculation of Drilling Coordinates (MCD)	CADRIC
Calculation of Indirect Resources and Conversion to Unit Staff [*Computer science*]	CIRCUS
Calculation of Inertia (IAA)	CAIN
Calculation of Miss Distance Between Objects [*Naval Research Laboratory*] (PS)	COMBO
Calculations of Reactor Accident Consequences (NRCH)	CRAC
Calculator (WDAA)	CALC
Calculator (MDG)	CC
Calculator Collectors Club [*British*] (DBA)	CCC
Calculator on Substrate (IAA)	COS
Calculator Printing (IAA)	CP
Calculator-Aware Number [*Project*] (AIE)	CAN
Calculator-Oriented Processor (MHDB)	COP
Calculus (MAE)	C
Calculus (WDAA)	CALC
Calculus of Variation [*NASA*]	COV
Calculus Rate Problem Solver (PDAA)	CARPS
Calculus Removal (MAE)	CR
Calcutta [*India*] [*Seismograph station code, US Geological Survey*] (SEIS)	CAL
Calcutta [*India*] (ROG)	CALC
Calcutta [*India*] [*Airport symbol*] (OAG)	CCU
Calcutta [*India*] [*ICAO location identifier*] (ICLI)	VECC
Calcutta [*India*] [*ICAO location identifier*] (ICLI)	VECF
Calcutta (Behala) [*India*] [*ICAO location identifier*] (ICLI)	VEBA
Calcutta Computers [*Software manufacturing company*] [*India*] (ECON)	CC
Calcutta Law Journal [*A publication*] (DLA)	Calc LJ
Calcutta Law Journal (DLA)	Calcutta LJ
Calcutta Law Journal [*A publication*] (DLA)	CLJ
Calcutta Law Journal Reports [*A publication*] (DLA)	Cal LJ
Calcutta Law Reporter [*A publication*] (DLA)	Cal LR
Calcutta Law Reporter [*A publication*] (DLA)	CLR
Calcutta Legal Adviser [*India*] [*A publication*] (DLA)	Cal Leg Adv
Calcutta Legal Observer [*A publication*] (DLA)	Cal Leg Obs
Calcutta Light Horse [*British military*] (DMA)	CLH
Calcutta Port Shramik Union [*India*]	CPSU
Calcutta Reports of Cases in Appeal [*A publication*] (DLA)	Sevestre
Calcutta Sadr Diwani Adalat Reports [*India*] [*A publication*] (DLA)	Cal SDA
Calcutta Series, Indian Law Reports [*A publication*] (DLA)	Cal Ser
Calcutta Series, Indian Law Reports [*A publication*] (DLA)	Calc Ser
Calcutta Volunteer Guards [*British military*] (DMA)	VCG
Calcutta Volunteer Lancers [*British military*] (DMA)	CVL
Calcutta Weekly Notes [*A publication*] (DLA)	Cal WN
Calcutta Weekly Notes [*A publication*] (DLA)	Calc WN
Calcutta Weekly Notes [*A publication*] (DLA)	Calcutta WN
Calcutta Weekly Notes [*A publication*] (DLA)	CWN
Calcutta Weekly Notes [*A publication*] (DLA)	WN
Calcutta Weekly Notes [*A publication*] (DLA)	WN (Calc)
Calcutta Weekly Reporter [*A publication*] (DLA)	Cal WR
Calcyclin [*Medicine*] (DMAA)	CACY
Caldarium (VRA)	caldm
Caldecott's English Settlement Cases [*1776-85*] [*A publication*] (DLA)	Cal
Caldecott's Magistrates' and Settlement Cases [*1776-85*] [*England*] [*A publication*] (DLA)	Cald
Caldecott's Magistrates' and Settlement Cases [*1776-85*] [*England*] [*A publication*] (DLA)	Cald (Eng)
Caldecott's Magistrates' and Settlement Cases [*1776-85*] [*England*] [*A publication*] (DLA)	Cald JP
Caldecott's Magistrates' and Settlement Cases [*1776-85*] [*England*] [*A publication*] (DLA)	Cald M Cas
Caldecott's Magistrates' and Settlement Cases [*1776-85*] [*England*] [*A publication*] (DLA)	Cald Mag Cas
Caldecott's Magistrates' and Settlement Cases [*1776-85*] [*England*] [*A publication*] (DLA)	Cald SC
Caldecott's Magistrates' and Settlement Cases [*1776-85*] [*England*] [*A publication*] (DLA)	Cald Set Cas
Caldecott's Magistrates' and Settlement Cases [*1776-85*] [*England*] [*A publication*] (DLA)	Cald Sett Cas
Caldera [*Chile*] [*Seismograph station code, US Geological Survey Closed*] (SEIS)	CLD
Caldera Mines Ltd. [*Vancouver Stock Exchange symbol*]	CMM
Calderdale Information Service [*Library cooperative*] [*British*] (NITA)	CALDIS
Calderon [*Spanish dramatist, 1600-1682*] (ROG)	CALD
Caldor Corp. [*Associated Press*] (SAG)	Caldor
Caldor Corp. [*NYSE symbol*] (SPSG)	CLD
Caldwell. Arbitration [*2nd ed.*] [*1825*] [*A publication*] (DLA)	Cald Arb
Caldwell College, Caldwell, NJ [*Library symbol Library of Congress*] (LCLS)	NjCalC

Caldwell College for Women [*New Jersey*] .... CCW
Caldwell College for Women, Caldwell, NJ [*OCLC symbol*] (OCLC) .... CAL
Caldwell Community College and Technical Institute, Lenoir, NC [*Library symbol Library of Congress*] (LCLS) .... NcLeCT
Caldwell County Public Library, Lenoir, NC [*Library symbol Library of Congress*] (LCLS) .... NcLeC
Caldwell Free Public Library, Caldwell, NJ [*Library symbol Library of Congress*] (LCLS) .... NjCal
Caldwell, ID [*FM radio station call letters*] (RBYB) .... KARO
Caldwell, ID [*AM radio station call letters*] .... KBGN
Caldwell, ID [*FM radio station call letters*] .... KBXL
Caldwell, ID [*AM radio station call letters*] .... KCID
Caldwell, ID [*FM radio station call letters*] .... KCID-FM
Caldwell, ID [*Television station call letters*] .... KHDT
Caldwell, ID [*TV station call letters*] (RBYB) .... KNIN-TV
Caldwell, ID [*FM radio station call letters*] .... KTSY
Caldwell, NJ [*Location identifier FAA*] (FAAL) .... CDW
Caldwell, OH [*FM radio station call letters*] .... WWKC
Caldwell Parish Library, Columbia, LA [*Library symbol Library of Congress*] (LCLS) .... LColC
Caldwell Progress, Caldwell, NJ [*Library symbol Library of Congress*] (LCLS) .... NjCalP
Caldwell Public Library, Caldwell, ID [*Library symbol Library of Congress*] (LCLS) .... IdCa
Caldwell Public Library, Caldwell, OH [*Library symbol Library of Congress*] (LCLS) .... OCal
Caldwell Township Public Library, Verner, Ontario [*Library symbol National Library of Canada*] (NLC) .... OVCT
Caldwell's Reports [*25-36 West Virginia*] [*A publication*] (DLA) .... Cald
Caledon Information & Community Services [*Formerly, Bolton Contact Centre*] [*Formerly, Caledon Information Centre*] (AC) .... CICS
Caledon Public Libraries, Bolton, ON, Canada [*Library symbol Library of Congress*] (LCLS) .... CaOBolC
Caledon Public Libraries, Bolton, Ontario [*Library symbol National Library of Canada*] (NLC) .... OBOLC
Caledonia [*Scotland*] (ROG) .... CAL
Caledonia [*Scotland*] .... CALED
Caledonia [*Panama*] [*Airport symbol*] (OAG) .... CDE
Caledonia [*Costa Rica*] [*ICAO location identifier*] (ICLI) .... MRCD
Caledonia MacBrayne [*Commercial firm British*] .... CALMAC
Caledonia Mining [*Associated Press*] (SAG) .... Caledon
Caledonia Mining [*NASDAQ symbol*] (SAG) .... CALV
Caledonia Mining [*NASDAQ symbol*] (TTSB) .... CALVF
Caledonia, MN [*Location identifier FAA*] (FAAL) .... CHU
Caledonia, MN [*FM radio station call letters*] .... KSOF
Caledonia, NS [*Television station call letters*] CJCH-6
Caledonia Resources Ltd. [*Vancouver Stock Exchange symbol*] .... CLN
Caledonia-Mumford Junior/Senior High School Library, Caledonia, NY [*OCLC symbol*] (OCLC) .... RVU
Caledonian [*Railway*] [*Scotland*] (ROG) C
Caledonian Airways Ltd. [*British ICAO designator*] (FAAC) .... CKT
Caledonian Railway [*Scotland*] .... CR
Caledonian Society [*Australia*] .... CS
Calefactus [*Made Warm*] [*Pharmacy*] (ROG) .... CALEFACT
Calefiat [*Warm It*] [*Pharmacy*] .... CALEF
Calendae [*Calends*] [*The First Day of the Month*] [*Latin*] C
Calendae [*Calends*] [*The First Day of the Month*] [*Latin*] (ROG) .... CAL
Calendar .... CAL
Calendar (VRA) .... cal
Calendar (WDMC) .... cal
Calendar Day (AFM) .... CD
Calendar Marketing Agreement .... CMA
Calendar Marketing Association (EA) .... CMA
Calendar of Charter Rolls [*British*] .... CChR
Calendar of Close Rolls [*British*] .... CCR
Calendar of Coroners Rolls of the City of London [*A publication*] (DLA) .... Sharpe
Calendar of Liberate Rolls [*British*] .... CLR
Calendar of Literary Facts [*A publication*] .... CLF
Calendar of Patent Rolls [*British*] .... CPR
Calendar of Proceedings in Chancery Tempore Elizabeth [*1827-32*] [*A publication*] (DLA) .... Cal Ch
Calendar of Proceedings in Chancery Tempore Elizabeth [*1827-32*] [*A publication*] (DLA) .... Cal P Ch
Calendar of State Papers [*British*] (ROG) .... CSP
Calendar Process [*Telecommunications*] (TEL) .... CP
Calendar Reform Foundation [*Defunct*] (EA) .... CRF
Calendar Reform Political Action Group [*Defunct*] (EA) .... CRPAG
Calendar Time .... CT
Calendar Variations Analysis .... CVA
Calendar Year (TEL) .... CY
Calendarium Rotulorum Patentium [*Calendar of the Patent Rolls*] [*Latin*] .... CAL ROT PAT
Calendarium Rotulorum Patentum [*Calendar of the Patent Rolls*] [*Latin*] .... CRP
Calendars of the Proceedings in Chancery, Record Commission [*A publication*] (DLA) .... Cal
Calendered Paper (BARN) .... Cal
Calendrier Republicain [*Republican Calendar*] [*French*] .... CR
Calenergy Co., Inc. [*Associated Press*] (SAG) .... Calenergy
Calenergy Co., Inc. [*NYSE symbol*] (SAG) .... CE
CalEngery Co. [*NYSE symbol*] (TTSB) .... CE
Calera, AL [*AM radio station call letters*] .... WBYE
Caleta Josefina [*Chile*] [*Airport symbol*] (AD) .... WCJ
Calexico, CA [*Location identifier FAA*] (FAAL) CXL
Calexico, CA [*AM radio station call letters*] .... KICO
Calexico, CA [*FM radio station call letters*] .... KQVO

Calexico, CA [*FM radio station call letters*] .... KUBO
Calexico/International [*California*] [*ICAO location identifier*] (ICLI) .... KCXL
Calexico Public Library, Calexico, CA [*Library symbol Library of Congress*] (LCLS) .... CCal
Calf .... CF
Calf [*Calfskin*] [*Bookbinding*] (WDMC) .... cf
Calf Certifying Officer [*Ministry of Agriculture, Fisheries, and Food*] [*British*] .... CCO
Calf Intestinal Phosphatase [*An enzyme*] .... CIP
Calf Lung Surfactant Extract [*Medicine*] (DMAA) .... CLSE
Calf Pulmonary Artery Endthelial [*Cell line*] .... CPAE
Calf Serum [*Biochemistry*] (DAVI) .... CS
Calf Thymus Extract [*Medicine*] (DMAA) .... CTE
Calfskin [*Book cover material*] (NTCM) .... CALF
Calgary [*Canada*] (ROG) .... CALG
Calgary [*Canada*] [*Airport symbol*] (OAG) .... YYC
Calgary, AB [*AM radio station call letters*] .... CBR
Calgary, AB [*FM radio station call letters*] .... CBR-FM
Calgary, AB [*Television station call letters*] .... CBRT
Calgary, AB [*AM radio station call letters*] .... CFAC
Calgary, AB [*Television station call letters*] .... CFCN-TV
Calgary, AB [*AM radio station call letters*] .... CFFR
Calgary, AB [*AM radio station call letters*] .... CFXL
Calgary, AB [*FM radio station call letters*] .... CHFM
Calgary, AB [*AM radio station call letters*] .... CHQR
Calgary, AB [*Television station call letters*] .... CICT
Calgary, AB [*FM radio station call letters*] .... CJAY
Calgary, AB [*FM radio station call letters*] .... CJSW
Calgary, AB [*FM radio station call letters*] .... CKIK
Calgary, AB [*FM radio station call letters*] (RBYB) .... CKIS-FM
Calgary, AB [*AM radio station call letters*] (RBYB) .... CKMX
Calgary, AB [*FM radio station call letters*] .... CKRY
Calgary, AB [*FM radio station call letters*] CKUA-1
Calgary Air Conditioning & Sheet Metal Association (AC) .... CASMA
Calgary & District Labour Council (AC) .... CDLC
Calgary Board of Education, Acquisition and Technical Services [*UTLAS symbol*] .... CBE
Calgary Board of Education, Professional Library [*UTLAS symbol*] .... CBP
Calgary Board of Education Professional Library, Alberta [*Library symbol National Library of Canada*] (NLC) .... ACBEP
Calgary Branch Library, Alberta Research Council, Alberta [*Library symbol National Library of Canada*] (NLC) .... ACRC
Calgary Centre Holdings Ltd. [*Toronto Stock Exchange symbol*] .... CGY
Calgary Construction Association (AC) .... CCA
Calgary Early Music Society (AC) .... CEMS
Calgary Field Naturalists' Society [*Societe des Champs Etat de Nature de Calgary*] [*Formerly, Calgary Bird Club*] (AC) .... CFNS
Calgary General Hospital, Alberta [*Library symbol National Library of Canada*] (NLC) .... ACGH
Calgary Herald, Alberta [*Library symbol National Library of Canada*] (NLC) .... ACCH
Calgary Herald, Calgary, AB, Canada [*Library symbol Library of Congress*] (LCLS) .... CaACCH
Calgary Immigrant Aid Society (AC) .... CIAS
Calgary/International, AB [*ICAO location identifier*] (ICLI) .... CYYC
Calgary Library Service Centre, Alberta [*Library symbol National Library of Canada*] (NLC) .... ACCL
Calgary Library Service Centre, Calgary, AB, Canada [*Library symbol Library of Congress*] (LCLS) .... CaACCL
Calgary Milk Producers' Association [*Formerly, United Milk & Cream Producers*] (AC) .... CMPA
Calgary Olympic Organizing Committee [*Calgary, AB*] (EAIO) .... COOC
Calgary Photographic Historical Society (AC) .... CPHS
Calgary Police Association [*Association de la Police de Calgary*] (AC) .... CPA
Calgary Power Ltd., Calgary, AB, Canada [*Library symbol Library of Congress*] (LCLS) .... CaACPow
Calgary Public Library [*UTLAS symbol*] .... CPL
Calgary Public Library, Alberta [*Library symbol National Library of Canada*] (NLC) .... AC
Calgary Public Library, Calgary, AB, Canada [*Library symbol Library of Congress*] (LCLS) .... CaAC
Calgary Public Library Government Documents [*Information service or system*] (IID) .... CALDOC
Calgary Public School Board, Calgary, AB, Canada [*Library symbol Library of Congress*] (LCLS) .... CaACLS
Calgary Research Center, Calgary, AB, Canada [*Library symbol*] [*Library of Congress*] (LCLS) .... CaACR
Calgary Research Centre, Alberta [*Library symbol National Library of Canada*] (NLC) .... ACR
Calgary Research Centre Library, Shell Canada Ltd., Alberta [*Library symbol National Library of Canada*] (NLC) .... ACSCL
Calgary Round-Up Band Association (AC) .... CRUB
Calgene, Inc. [*Associated Press*] (SAG) .... Calgene
Calgene, Inc. [*NASDAQ symbol*] (NQ) .... CGNE
Calgon Carbon [*NYSE symbol*] (SAG) CCC
Calgon Carbon [*NYSE symbol*] (TTSB) CCC
Calgon Carbon [*NYSE symbol*] (SAG) .... COC
Calgon Carbon Corp. [*Associated Press*] (SAG) .... Calgon
Calgon Carbon Corp. (MHDW) .... CRBN
Calgon Corp., Pittsburgh, PA [*OCLC symbol*] (OCLC) .... PCA
Calgranulin A (DMAA) .... CAGA
Calgranulin B (DMAA) .... CAGB
Calhoun Community Unit, School District 40, Hardin, IL [*Library symbol Library of Congress*] (LCLS) .... IHardCSD
Calhoun County Historical Society, Rockwell City, IA [*Library symbol Library of Congress*] (LCLS) .... IaRcCHi

Calhoun County Public Library, St. Matthews, SC [Library symbol] [Library of Congress] (LCLS) .... ScStm
Calhoun Falls [South Carolina] [Seismograph station code, US Geological Survey] (SEIS) .... CHF
Calhoun, GA [Location identifier FAA] (FAAL) .... CZL
Calhoun, GA [AM radio station call letters] .... WEBS
Calhoun, GA [AM radio station call letters] .... WJTH
Calhoun, TN [FM radio station call letters] .... WCLE
Cali [Colombia] [Airport symbol] (OAG) .... CLO
Cali/Alfonso Bonilla Aragon [Colorado ICAO location identifier] (ICLI) .... SKCL
Cali Realty [NYSE symbol] (TTSB) CLI
Cali Realty Corp. [Associated Press] (SAG) .... CaliRlty
Cali Realty Corp. [Associated Press] (SAG) .... CaliRty
Cali Realty Corp. [NYSE symbol] (SAG) CLI
Caliber (AFM) .... CAL
Caliber (DMAA) .... Cal
Caliber System [NYSE symbol] (TTSB) .... CBB
Caliber Systems, Inc. [Associated Press] (SAG) ..... Caliber
Caliber Systems, Inc. [NYSE symbol] (SAG) .... CBB
Calibrate .... CAB
Calibrate (CET) .... CAL
Calibrate (AAG) .... CALIB
Calibrated Air Speed .... CAS
Calibrated Airborne Measurements Program (MCD) .... CAMP
Calibrated Airborne Multispectral Scanner [Instrumentation] ...... CAMS
Calibrated Airborne Special Infrared Measurement Systems (PDAA) ...... CASIMS
Calibrated Altitude [Navigation] .... CA
Calibrated Angle of Attack (MCD) .... AOAC
Calibrated Armor Vehicle Simulator (MCD) .... CAVS
Calibrated Engine Testing .... CET
Calibrated Focal Length (MSA) .... CFL
Calibrated Magnification (MSA) .... CM
Calibrated Optical and Near Infrared Imaging System (MCD) ...... CONIRIS
Calibrated Pressure Switch (KSC) .... CALIPS
Calibrated Probability Density Distribution .... CPDD
Calibrated Sweep Delay .... CSD
Calibrating, Amplitude-Variation, and Level-Correcting Analog-Digital Equipment (DEN) ...... CAVALCADE
Calibrating Work Center (AFIT) .... CWC
Calibration (MSA) .... CAL
Calibration (AABC) .... CALBR
Calibration (AAG) .... CALIBN
Calibration .... CALIBR
Calibration .... CLBR
Calibration and Certification (IAA) .... CAC
Calibration and Checkout (IAA) .... CAC
Calibration and Measurement Summaries [Air Force] (AFIT) ...... CMS
Calibration and Repair Center .... CRC
Calibration and Tracking Visible Sensor (MCD) ...... CTVS
Calibration Blank [Spectroscopy] .... CALBLK
Calibration/Certification (SAA) .... CAL/CERT
Calibration Check Compound CCC
Calibration Curve Data .... CCD
Calibration Cycle (AFIT) CC
Calibration Device (KSC) .... CD
Calibration Equipment [Military] .... CAL-E
Calibration Factor .... CF
Calibration Marker .... CM
Calibration/Measurement Requirements Summary ...... CMRS
Calibration Procedure .... CP
Calibration Procedure .... CPC
Calibration Procedure Status Report [Polaris missile] ...... CPSR
Calibration Recall Information Systems (KSC) .... CRIS
Calibration Recall System [Army] .... CRS
Calibration, Repair, and Return .... CR & R
Calibration Requirements List (NG) .... CARL
Calibration Requirements List (MCD) .... CRL
Calibration Requirements Summary .... CRS
Calibration Rocket [NASA] .... CALROC
Calibration Signal Generator .... CSG
Calibration Sphere (MCD) .... CALSPHERE
Calibration Team .... CT
Calibration Technician (KSC) .... CT
Calibration Test Box .... CTB
Calibration Validation Unit [Instrumentation] .... CVU
Calibration Verification Sample [Spectroscopy] ...... CVS
Calibration Vibration Exciter .... CVE
Calibre-Radius Head [of projectile] [British] .... CRH
Calicivirus [Medicine] (DMAA) .... CaCV
Calico Printers' Association (DGA) .... CPA
Calicut [India] [ICAO location identifier] (ICLI) .... VOCL
Calidus [Warm] [Pharmacy] (ROG) .... CALID
Caliente Resources Ltd. [Vancouver Stock Exchange symbol] ...... CIT
Calif Amplifier [NASDAQ symbol] (TTSB) .... CAMP
Calif Bancshares [NASDAQ symbol] (TTSB) .... CABI
Calif Culinary Academy [NASDAQ symbol] (TTSB) .... COOK
Calif Fed'l Bk10.625%'B'Pfd [NYSE symbol] (TTSB) .. CALPrB
Calif Finl Hldg [NASDAQ symbol] (TTSB) .... CFHC
Calif Micro Devices [NASDAQ symbol] (TTSB) .... CAMD
Calif Microwave [NASDAQ symbol] (TTSB) .... CMIC
Calif Pro Sports [NASDAQ symbol] (TTSB) .... CALP
Calif REIT SBI [NYSE symbol] (TTSB) .... CT
Calif Water Svc [NYSE symbol] (TTSB) .... CWT
California [Postal code] .... CA
California .... CAL

California .... Cali
California (AFM) .... CALIF
California (ODBW) .... Calif
California [MARC country of publication code Library of Congress] (LCCP) ...... cau
California [MARC geographic area code Library of Congress] (LCCP) ...... n-us-ca
California Academic Libraries Lists of Serials (EDAC) ...... CALLS
California Academy of Family Physicians (SRA) ...... CAFP
California Academy of General Dentistry (SRA) ...... CAGD
California Academy of Physician Assistants (SRA) ... CAPA
California Academy of Sciences .... CAS
California Academy of Sciences, San Francisco, CA [Library symbol Library of Congress] (LCLS) ...... CSfA
California Achievement Test .... CAT
California Administrative Code [A publication] (DLA) ...... Cal Adm Code
California Administrative Code [A publication] (DLA) ...... Cal Admin Code
California Administrative Register [A publication] (DLA) ...... Cal Admin Reg
California Advance Legislative Service (Deering) [A publication] (DLA) ...... Cal Adv Legis Serv
California Agricultural Aircraft Association (EA) ...... CAAA
California Agricultural Production Consultants Association (SRA) ...... CAPCA
California Agricultural Teachers Association (SRA) .. CATA
California Agriculture Code [A publication] (DLA) ... Cal Agric Code
California Air Resources Board .... CARB
California Alarm Association (SRA) .... CAA
California Almond Growers Exchange [Later, BDG] (EA) ...... CAGE
California Ambulance Association (SRA) .... CAA
California Amplifier, Inc. [Associated Press] (SAG) ... CalAmp
California Amplifier, Inc. [NASDAQ symbol] (NQ) ..... CAMP
California Analysis Centers, Inc. [A management consulting company] [Arlington, Virginia] (WDMC) ...... CACI
California and Mexico (IIA) .... CALEXICO
California Apartment Association (SRA) .... CAA
California Apparel Industries Association [Later, CFC] (EA) ...... CAIA
California Appellate Decisions [A publication] (DLA) ... Cal App Dec
California Appellate Reports [A publication] (DLA) .. CA
California Appellate Reports [A publication] (DLA) .. CA A
California Appellate Reports [A publication] (DLA) .. Cal App
California Appellate Reports, Second Series [A publication] (DLA) ...... CA 2d
California Appellate Reports, Second Series [A publication] (DLA) ...... CA A 2d
California Appellate Reports, Second Series [A publication] (DLA) ...... Cal App 2d
California Appellate Reports, Second Series, Supplement [A publication] (DLA) ...... CA 2d Supp
California Appellate Reports, Second Series, Supplement [A publication] (DLA) ...... Cal App 2d Supp
California Appellate Reports, Supplement [A publication] (DLA) ...... CA Supp
California Appellate Reports, Supplement [A publication] (DLA) ...... Cal App Supp
California Appellate Reports, Third Series [A publication] (DLA) ...... CA 3d
California Appellate Reports, Third Series [A publication] (DLA) ...... CA A 3d
California Appellate Reports, Third Series [A publication] (DLA) ...... Cal App 3d
California Appellate Reports, Third Series, Supplement [A publication] (DLA) ...... CA 3S
California Appellate Reports, Third Series, Supplement [A publication] (DLA) ...... Cal App 3d Supp
California Applicants Attorney Association (SRA) .... CAAA
California Apricot Advisory Board (EA) .... CAAB
California Aqueduct Control System .... CACS
California Arabian Standard Oil Co. .... CASOC
California, Arizona, Florida, and Texas .... CAFT
California Artichoke Advisory Board (EA) .... CAAB
California Asparagus Advisory Board [Defunct] (EA) .. CAAB
California Associated Truckers (SRA) .... CAT
California Association for Adult Day Services (SRA) .. CAADS
California Association for Bilingual Education (SRA) .. CABE
California Association for Counseling and Development (SRA) ...... CACD
California Association for Health, Physical Education, Recreation, and Dance (SRA) ...... CAHPERD
California Association for Health Services at Home (SRA) ...... CAHSAH
California Association for Local Economic Development (SRA) ...... CALED
California Association for Medical Laboratory Technology (SRA) ...... CAMLT
California Association of Acupuncture and Oriental Medicine (SRA) ...... CAAOM
California Association of Alcoholic Recovery Homes (SRA) ...... CAARH
California Association of Catholic Hospitals (SRA) ... CACH
California Association of Children's Homes (SRA) .... CCH
California Association of Collectors (SRA) .... CAC
California Association of College Stores (SRA) ...... CACS
California Association of Community Managers (SRA) . CACM
California Association of Employers (SRA) .... CAE
California Association of Flower Growers and Shippers (SRA) ...... CAFG&S
California Association of Health Facilities (SRA) .... CAHF
California Association of Hearing Instrument Specialists (SRA) ...... CAHIS
California Association of Highway Patrolmen (SRA) .. CAHP
California Association of Homes and Services for the Aging (SRA) ...... CAHSA
California Association of Independent Business (SRA) . CAIB
California Association of Independent Insurance Adjusters (SRA) ...... CAIIA
California Association of Licensed Investigators (SRA) .. CALI
California Association of Life Underwriters (SRA) .... CALU
California Association of Local Agency Formation Commissions (SRA) ...... CALAFCO
California Association of Long Distance Telephone Companies (SRA) .... CALTEL
California Association of Marriage and Family Therapists (SRA) ...... CAMFT
California Association of Medical Products Suppliers (SRA) ...... CAMPS
California Association of Mortgage Brokers (SRA) .... CAMB
California Association of Nonprofits (SRA) .... CAN
California Association of Nurse Anesthetists (SRA) .. CANA
California Association of Nurserymen (SRA) .... CAN

California Association of Ophthalmology (SRA) .... CAO
California Association of Parking Controllers (EA) .... CAPC
California Association of Pet Professionals (EA) .... CAPP
California Association of Photocopiers and Process Servers (SRA) .... CAPPS
California Association of Port Authorities (SRA) .... CAPA
California Association of Public Cemeteries (SRA) .... CAPC
California Association of Public Hospitals (SRA) .... CAPH
California Association of Realtors (SRA) .... CAR
California Association of Resourse Conservation Districts (SRA) .... CARCD
California Association of Sanitation Agencies (SRA) .... CASA
California Association of School Psychologists (SRA) .... CASP
California Association of Student Councils (BARN) .... CASC
California Association of Teachers of English to Speakers of Other Languages (EDAC) .... CATESOL
California Association of Temporary and Staffing Services (SRA) .... CATSS
California Association of Thrift and Loan Companies (SRA) .... CATLC
California Association of Tiger-Owners (EA) .... CAT
California Association of Wheat Growers (SRA) .... CAWG
California Association of Window Manufacturers (SRA) .... CAWM
California Association of Winegrape Growers (EA) .... CAWG
California Autobody Association (SRA) .... CAA
California Automotive Wholesalers' Association (SRA) .... CAWA
California Aviation Business Association (SRA) .... CABA
California Aviation Education Association .... CAEA
California Avocado Advisory Board [*Later, CAC*] .... CAAB
California Avocado Commission (EA) .... CAC
California Avocado Society (EA) .... CAS
California Bancshares, Inc. [*NASDAQ symbol*] (SAG) .... CABI
California Bancshares, Inc. [*Associated Press*] (SAG) .... CalBnc
California Bankers Association (SRA) .... CBA
California Baptist Theological Seminary .... CBTS
California Bearing Ratio [*Aviation*] .... CBR
California Beer and Beverage Distributors (SRA) .... CBBD
California Beet Growers Association (SRA) .... CBGA
California Beverage Merchants (SRA) .... CBM
California Biotechnology, Inc.[*Later, Scios, Inc.*] .... CAL-BIO
California Brandy Advisory Board [*Defunct*] (EA) .... CBAB
California Brief Life History Inventory [*Personality development test*] [*Psychology*] .... CBLHI
California Broadcasters Association (SRA) .... CBA
California Building Industry Association (SRA) .... CBIA
California Building Material Dealers Association (SRA) .... CBMDA
California Business Education Association (SRA) .... CBEA
California Business Properties Association (SRA) .... CBPA
California Cable Television Association (SRA) .... CCTA
California Cactus Growers Association (EA) .... CCGA
California Canning Peach Association (EA) .... CCPA
California Carvers Guild (EA) .... CCG
California Cast Metals Association (SRA) .... CCMA
California Cattlemen's Association (SRA) .... CCA
California Celery Research Advisory Board (SRA) .... CCRAB
California Central Airlines .... CCA
California Certified Organic Farmers .... CCOF
California Chamber of Commerce (SRA) CCC
California Chicano News Media Association (SRA) .... CCNMA
California Children's Hospital Association (SRA) .... CCHA
California Chiropractic Association (SRA) .... CCA
California Christmas Tree Growers (SRA) .... CCTG
California Citrus Mutual (SRA) .... CCM
California Civil Rights Initiative (ECON) .... CCRI
California Cling Peach Advisory Board .... CCPAB
California Cling Peach Advisory Board (EA) .... CPAB
California Cling Peach Growers Advisory Board (SRA) .... CCPGAB
California Code of Regulations [*Also CCR*] [*A publication*] (AAGC) .... Cal Code Regs
California Code of Regulations [*A publication*] (AAGC) .... CCR
California College of Arts and Crafts (GAGS) .... Cal C Arts & Crafts
California College of Arts and Crafts [*Oakland*] .... CCAC
California College of Arts and Crafts, Oakland, CA [*Library symbol Library of Congress*] (LCLS) .... COC
California College of Arts and Crafts, Oakland, CA [*Library symbol*] [*Library of Congress*] (LCLS) .... COCAC
California College of Chiropody CCC
California Commun Bancshs [*NASDAQ symbol*] (TTSB) .... CCBC
California Community Bancshares Corp. [*Associated Press*] (SAG) .... CalCmB
California Community Bancshares Corp. [*NASDAQ symbol*] (SAG) .... CCBC
California Compensation Cases [*A publication*] (DLA) .... Cal Comp Cases
California Compensation Cases [*A publication*] (DLA) CC
California Computer Products, Inc. (MCD) .... CALCOMP
California Concordia College, Oakland, CA [*Library symbol Library of Congress*] (LCLS) .... COCC
California Conference of Machinists (SRA) .... CCM
California Conference of Mason Contractor Associations (SRA) .... CCMCA
California Connections [*Information service or system*] (CRD) .... CALCON
California Constitution [*A publication*] (DLA) .... Cal Const
California Contract Cities Association (SRA) .... CCCA
California Contract Show [*Western Merchandise Mart*] (TSPED) .... CALICON
California Cooperative Oceanic Fisheries Investigations [*Also, CALCOFI*] (MSC) .... CCOFI
California Cooperative Oceanic Fishery Investigations [*Also, CCOFI*] .... CALCOFI
California Correctional Peace Officers Association (SRA) .... CCPOA
California Cosmetology Association (SRA) .... CCA
California Council for Interior Design Certification (SRA) .... CCIDC
California Council for International Trade (SRA) .... CCIT
California Council of Police and Sheriffs (SRA) .... CAL-COPS
California Court Clerks Association (SRA) .... CCCA
California Credit Union League (SRA) .... CCUL
California Crop Improvement Association (SRA) .... CCIA
California Culinary Academy, Inc. [*Associated Press*] (SAG) .... CalifCul
California Culinary Academy, Inc. [*NASDAQ symbol*] (SAG) .... COOK
California Current System [*Oceanography*] .... CCS
California Dairy Herd Improvement Association (SRA) .... CDHIA
California Data Network [*Claremont McKenna College, Rose Institue of State and Local Government*] [*Information service or system*] (IID) .... CDN
California Date Administrative Committee (EA) .... CDAC
California Date Growers Association [*Defunct*] (EA) .... CDGA
California Debris Commission [*Army*] .... CDC
California Decisions [*A publication*] (DLA) .... Cal Dec
California Defense Counsel (SRA) .... CDC
California Dental Association (SRA) .... CDA
California Department of Forestry Firefighters Association (SRA) .... CDFFA
California Department of Parks and Recreation, Sacramento Area State Parks, Sacramento, CA [*Library symbol Library of Congress*] (LCLS) .... CSPR
California Department of Transportation [*BTS*] (TAG) .... CALTRANS
California Depopulation Commission [*Defunct*] (EA) .... CALDEPOP
California Dietetic Association (SRA) .... CDA
California Distance Table Bureau, San Francisco CA [*STAC*] .... CDB
California Distributors Association (SRA) .... CDA
California District Attorneys Association (SRA) .... CDAA
California Dried Fig Advisory Board [*Later, CFAB*] .... CDFAB
California Dried Fruit Export Association (EA) .... CDFEA
California Dry Bean Advisory Board (EA) .... CDBAB
California Dump Truck Owners Association (SRA) .... CDTOA
California Eastern Airways .... CEA
[*The*] **California Education & Research Federation Network** [*Computer science*] (TNIG) .... CERFnet
California Educational Computing Consortium (EA) .... CECC
California Elementary School, Uniondale, NY [*Library symbol Library of Congress*] (LCLS) .... NUnCE
California Encephalitis [*Medicine*] .... CE
California Energy Co. [*Associated Press*] (SAG) .... CalEng
California Energy Co., Inc. [*NYSE symbol*] (SPSG) .... CE
California Engineering Foundation (EA) .... CEF
California Environmental Quality Act (DOGT) .... CEQA
California Escrow Association (SRA) .... CEA
California Fashion Creators (EA) .... CFC
California Federal Bank [*NYSE symbol*] (SPSG) .... CAL
California Federal Bank [*Associated Press*] (SAG) .... CalFd
California Federal Bank [*Associated Press*] (SAG) .... CalFdCt
California Federal Bank [*Associated Press*] (SAG) .... CalFedl
California Federal Bank [*Associated Press*] (SAG) .... CalFSecCt
California Federal Bank [*NASDAQ symbol*] (SAG) .... CALG
California Fertilizer Association (SRA) .... CFA
California Fig Advisory Board (EA) .... CFAB
California Fig Institute (EA) .... CFI
California Financial Holding Co. [*Associated Press*] (SAG) .... CalFncl
California Financial Holding Co. [*NASDAQ symbol*] (NQ) .... CFHC
California Fish Canners Association [*Later, TRF*] (EA) .... CFCA
California Fisheries Information Network [*Marine science*] (OSRA) .... CALFIN
California Fisheries Information Network (USDC) .... CALFIN
California Flyers School of Aeronautics .... CFSA
California Forestry Association (SRA) .... CFA
California Freezers Association [*AFFI*] [*Absorbed by*] (EA) .... CFA
California Fruit Exchange [*Later, BAI*] (EA) .... CFE
California General Corporation Law [*A publication*] (DLA) .... CA GCL
California Geotechnical Engineers Association (SRA) .... CGEA
California Glass Association (SRA) .... CGA
California Gold Mines Ltd. [*Toronto Stock Exchange symbol Vancouver Stock Exchange symbol*] .... CFA
California Grain annd Feed Association (SRA) .... CGFA
California Grape and Tree Fruit League (EA) .... CG & TFL
California Grocers Association (SRA) .... CGA
California Groundwater Association (SRA) .... CGA
California Guaranteed Student Loans (EDAC) .... CGSL
California Health Federation (SRA) .... CHF
California Health Information Association (SRA) .... CHIA
California Healthcare Association (SRA) .... CHA
California Highway Patrol [*Acronym used as title of TV series*] .... CHiPS
California Historical Society, San Francisco, CA [*Library symbol Library of Congress*] (LCLS) .... CHi
California Hotel and Motel Association (SRA) .... CH&MA
California Housing Council (SRA) .... CHC
California Hungarian American Cultural Foundation (EA) .... CHACF
California Iceberg Lettuce Commission (EA) CILC
California Independant Bancorp [*Associated Press*] (SAG) .... Califlnd
California Independant Bancorp [*NASDAQ symbol*] (SAG) .... CIBN
California Independent Petroleum Association (SRA) .... CIPA
California Industrial Accident Commission, Compensation Cases [*A publication*] (DLA) .... Cal IACCC
California Industrial Accident Decisions [*A publication*] (DLA) .... Cal IAC Dec
California Industrial Accident Decisions [*A publication*] (DLA) .... Cal Ind Acci Dec
California Information Network [*Library network*] .... CALINET
California Institute of Asian Studies [*An evening graduate school*] (EA) .... CIAS
California Institute of Asian Studies, San Francisco, CA [*Library symbol Library of Congress*] (LCLS) .... CSfCI
California Institute of Biological Research [*La Jolla*] .... CIBR
California Institute of Social Welfare .... CISW
California Institute of Technology (GAGS) .... Cal Tech
California Institute of Technology [*Also, CALT, CALTECH, CIT*] [*Pasadena*] (MCD) .... CALIT

California Institute of Technology [Also, CALIT, CALTECH, CIT] [Pasadena] ... CALT
California Institute of Technology [Also, CALIT, CALT, CIT] [Pasadena] ... CALTECH
California Institute of Technology [Also, CALIT, CALT, CALTECH] ... CIT
California Institute of Technology, Pasadena, CA [Library symbol Library of Congress] (LCLS) ... CPT
California Institute of the Arts [Valencia, CA] ... CalArts
California Institute of the Arts [Valencia] [OCLC symbol] (OCLC) ... CIA
California Institute of the Arts, Valencia [Library symbol Library of Congress] (LCLS) ... CValA
[The] California Institute of the Sisters of the Most Holy and Immaculate Heart of the Blessed Virgin Mary (TOCD) ... IHM
California Institution for Women ... CIW
California Jurisprudence [A publication] (DLA) ... Cal Jur
California Jurisprudence, Second Edition [A publication] (DLA) ... Cal Jur 2d
California Jury Instructions, Civil [A publication] (DLA) ... CAJI
California Jury Instructions, Criminal [A publication] (DLA) ... CAJC
California Jury Instructions, Criminal [A publication] (DLA) ... Cal JIC
California Kamchatka Companies (ECON) ... CKC
California Kiwifruit Commission (EA) ... CKC
California Labor Federation AFL-CIO Library, San Francisco, CA [Library symbol Library of Congress] (LCLS) ... CSfSFL
California Law Enforcement Telecommunications System ... CLETS
California Law Journal [A publication] (DLA) ... Cal LJ
California Law Journal [A publication] (DLA) ... CLJ
California Law Journal and Literary Review [A publication] (DLA) .... CLJ & Lit Rev
California League Enlisting Action Now [Antiobscenity group] ... CLEAN
California League of Food Processors (SRA) ... CLFP
California League of Middle Schools (SRA) ... CLMS
California Legal Record [A publication] (DLA) ... C Leg Rec
California Legal Record [A publication] (DLA) ... Cal Leg Rec
California Legislative Service (West) [A publication] (DLA) ... Cal Legis Serv
California Library Authority for Systems and Services [Library network].... CLASS
California Library Services Act Statewide Data Base [California Library Services Board] [Information service or system] (IID) ... CLSA-DB
California Licensed Foresters Association (SRA) ... CLFA
California Life Goals Evaluation Schedules [Psychology] ... CLGES
California Line Source Model [Environmental Protection Agency] (GFGA) ... CALINE
California Loans to Assist Students (EDAC) ... CLAS
California Lodging Industry Association (SRA) ... CLIA
California Low-Emission Vehicle [Automotive industry] ... CALLEV
California Lutheran College, Thousand Oaks, CA [OCLC symbol] (OCLC) .... CCT
California Lutheran College, Thousand Oaks, CA [Library symbol Library of Congress] (LCLS) ... CToL
California Lutheran University (GAGS) ... Cal Luth U
California Macadamia Society (EA) ... CMS
California Manufacturers Register [Database Publishing] [Information service or system] (CRD) ... CMR
California Marine Mammal Center [Research center] (RCD) ... CMMC
California Maritime Academy [Vallejo] ... CMA
California Maritime Academy, Vallejo, CA [Library symbol Library of Congress] (LCLS) ... CVM
California Marriage Readiness Evaluation [Psychology] ... CMRE
California Mastitis Test [Medicine] (DMAA) ... CM
California Mastitis Test ... CMT
California, MD [FM radio station call letters] ... WRFK
California Medical Survey [Psychology] ... CMS
California Melon Research Board (EA) ... CMRB
California Mental Health Analysis [Testing] ... CMHA
California Micro Devices Corp. [Associated Press] (SAG) ... CalMicr
California Micro Devices Corp. [NASDAQ symbol] (SAG) ... CAMD
California Microfilm Co., Fresno, CA [Library symbol Library of Congress] (LCLS) ... CmC
California Microwave, Inc. [Associated Press] (SAG) ... CalMic
California Microwave, Inc. [NASDAQ symbol] (NQ) ... CMIC
California Milk Producers (SRA) ... CMP
California, MO [FM radio station call letters] (RBYB) ... KATI
California, MO [AM radio station call letters] (RBYB) ... KREL
California Narcotics Officers Association (SRA) ... CNOA
California National Fuchsia Society [Later, NFS] ... CNFS
California Natural Diversity Data Base [California State Department of Fish and Game] [Information service or system] (IID) ... CNDDB
California Natural Gas Association ... CNGA
California Network [US Geological Survey] ... CALNET
California Nurses Association (SRA) ... CNA
California Occupational Preference Inventory [Psychology] (DAVI) ... COPI
California Occupational Preference Survey ... COPS
California Olive Association (EA) ... COA
California Olive Industry News ... COIN
California Optometric Association (SRA) ... COA
California Orthopaedic Association (SRA) ... COA
California, PA [FM radio station call letters] ... WVCS
California Palace of the Legion of Honor [San Francisco] ... CPLN
California Palace of the Legion of Honor, San Francisco, CA [Library symbol Library of Congress] (LCLS) ... CSfLH
California Penal Code [A publication] (DLA) ... Cal Penal Code
California Persimmon Growers Association (EA) ... CPGA
California Personality [or Psychological] Inventory ... CPI
California Pistachio Association (EA) ... CPA
California Pistachio Commission (EA) ... CPC
California Podiatric Medical Association (SRA) ... CPMA
California Polytechnic State University (PDAA) ... CPSU

California Polytechnic State University, Pomona, CA [OCLC symbol] (OCLC) ... CPO
California Polytechnic State University, Pomona, CA [Library symbol Library of Congress] (LCLS) ... CPomCP
California Polytechnic State University, San Luis Obispo, CA [OCLC symbol] (OCLC) ... CPS
California Polytechnic State University, San Luis Obispo, CA [Library symbol Library of Congress] (LCLS) ... CSluSP
California Poultry Industry Federation (SRA) ... CPIF
California Practice [A publication] (DLA) ... Cal Prac
California Preschool Scale of Social Competence (EDAC) ... CPSSC
California Primate Research Center [Research center] (RCD) ... CPRC
California Pro Sports, Inc. [NASDAQ symbol] (SAG) ... CALP
California Pro Sports, Inc. [Associated Press] (SAG) ... CalPro
California Pro Sports Wrrt [NASDAQ symbol] (TTSB) ... CALPW
California Probation, Parole, and Correctional Association ... CPPCA
California Prune Advisory Board [Later, CPB] ... CPAB
California Prune and Apricot Growers Association [Later, Sunsweet Growers] ... CPAGA
California Prune Board (EA) ... CPB
California Public Administrator, Public Guardian, and Public Conservator Association (SRA) ... CPAPGPCA
California Public Employees' Retirement System ... CalPERS
California Public Employees Retirement System [Pension fund] ... CalPERS
California Q-Set [Psychology] ... CQS
California Railroad Commission Digest of Decisions [A publication] (DLA) ... Cal RC Dec
California Railroad Commission Digest of Decisions [A publication] (DLA) ... Cal RC Dec Dig
California Railroad Commission Digest of Decisions [A publication] (DLA) ... CRC
California Raisin Advisory Board (EA) ... CALRAB
California Raisin Advisory Board (EA) ... CRAB
California Rare Fruit Growers (EA) ... CRFG
California Real Estate Investment Trust [Associated Press] (SAG) ... CalRE
California Real Estate Investment Trust SBI [NYSE symbol] (SPSG) ... CT
California Redwood Association (EA) ... CRA
California Regulatory Notice Register [A publication] (AAGC).... Cal Reg Notice Reg
California Relative Value Studies [Medicine] (DHSM) ... CRVS
California Reporter [A publication] (DLA) ... CA R
California Reporter (West) [A publication] (DLA) ... Cal Rptr
California Reports [A publication] (DLA) ... C
California Reports [A publication] (DLA) ... Cal
California Reports [A publication] (DLA) ... Cal Rep
California Reports [A publication] (DLA) ... Calif
California Reports, Second Series [A publication] (DLA) ... Cal 2d
California Reports, Third Series [A publication] (DLA) ... Cal 3d
California Research and Education Network [Computer science] (TNIG) ... CALREN
California Research Corp., Richmond, CA [Library symbol Library of Congress] (LCLS) ... CRicCR
California Resources Agency, Sacramento, CA [Library symbol Library of Congress] (LCLS) ... CSRes
California Rug Study Society (EA) ... CRSS
California Rural Legal Assistance (BARN) ... CRLA
California School Boards Association (SRA) ... CSBA
California School Employees Association (SRA) ... CSEA
California School of Fine Arts ... CSFA
California School of Professional Psychology ... CSPP
California School of Professional Psychology, Fresno, CA [Library symbol Library of Congress] (LCLS) ... CFSP
California Self-Insurers Association (SRA) ... CSIA
California Service Station and Automotive Repair Association (SRA) .... CSSARA
California Society for Healthcare Attorneys (SRA) ... CSHA
California Society of Addiction Medicine (SRA) ... CSAM
California Society of Certified Public Accountants (SRA) ... CSCPA
California Society of Enrolled Agents (SRA) ... CSEA
California Society of Pathologists (SRA) ... CSP
California Society of Periodontists (SRA) ... CSP
California Society of Professional Engineers (SRA) ... CSPE
California Society of Radiologic Technologists (SRA) ... CSRT
California Solar Energy Industries Association (SRA) ... CAL-SEIA
California Spanish Language Data Base [Information service or system] (IID) ... CSLDB
California Spanish Language Data Base, Oakland, CA [Library symbol] [Library of Congress] (LCLS) ... COCSL
California Special Districts Association (SRA) ... CSDA
California State Automobile Association (ACRL) ... CSAA
California State Bank [Associated Press] (SAG) ... CalSBk
California State Bank [NASDAQ symbol] (NQ) ... CSTB
California State Bar Journal [A publication] (DLA) ... Cal SBJ
California State Bar Journal [A publication] (DLA) ... Calif SBJ
California State College at Fresno ... CSCF
California State College, Bakersfield, CA [OCLC symbol] (OCLC) ... CBA
California State College, Bakersfield, CA [Library symbol Library of Congress] (LCLS) ... CBaS
California State College, California, PA [OCLC symbol] (OCLC) ... CSC
California State College, California, PA [Library symbol Library of Congress] (LCLS) ... PCalS
California State College, Dominguez Hills [Later, California State University, Dominguez Hills], Dominguez Hills, CA [Library symbol Library of Congress] (LCLS) ... CDhS
California State College, San Bernardino (PDAA) ... CSCSB
California State College, San Bernardino, San Bernardino, CA [OCLC symbol] (OCLC) ... CSB

California State College, San Bernardino, San Bernardino, CA [*Library symbol Library of Congress*] (LCLS) .... CSbC
California State College, Sonoma, Rohnert Park, CA [*Library symbol Library of Congress*] (LCLS) .... CRpS
California State College, Stanislaus, Turlock, CA [*OCLC symbol*] (OCLC) .... CTU
California State College, Stanislaus, Turlock, CA [*Library symbol Library of Congress*] (LCLS) .... CTurS
California State Department of Fish and Game, Marine Technical Information Center, San Pedro, CA [*Library symbol Library of Congress*] (LCLS) .... C-F
California State Department of Mental Hygiene, Metropolitan State Hospital Professional Staff Library, Norwalk, CA [*Library symbol Library of Congress*] (LCLS) .... CNwMH
California State Division of Mines, San Francisco, CA [*Library symbol Library of Congress*] (LCLS) .... CSfCSM
California State Employee's Association (SRA) .... CSEA
California State Firefighters Association (SRA) .... CSFA
California State [*University*], Hayward [*California*] [*Seismograph station code, US Geological Survey*] (SEIS) .... CSH
California State Horseman's Association (SRA) .... CSHA
California State Law Library, Sacramento, CA [*Library symbol Library of Congress*] (LCLS) .... C-L
California State Library, Sacramento, CA [*Library symbol Library of Congress*] (LCLS) C
California State Library, Sutro Branch, San Francisco, CA [*Library symbol Library of Congress*] (LCLS) .... C-S
California State Managers and Supervisors (SRA) .... CSMSA
California State Polytechnic College [*Later, California Polytechnic State University*] .... CSPC
California State Polytechnic University at Pomona (GAGS) .... Cal St Poly U (Pomona)
California State Polytechnic University at San Luis Obispo (GAGS) .... Cal St Poly U (San Luis Obispo)
California State Polytechnic University of Pomona (MCD) .... CSPUP
California State Psychological Association .... CSPA
California State Supervisors (SRA) .... CSS
California State University [*Formerly, San Francisco State College*] .... CSU
California State University and Colleges [*System*] .... CSUC
California State University and Colleges, Tape Profile, Long Beach, CA [*OCLC symbol*] (OCLC) .... CAC
California State University at Chico (GAGS) .... Cal St U (Chico)
California State University at Dominguez Hills (GAGS) .... Cal St U (Dominguez Hills)
California State University at Fresno (GAGS) .... Cal St U (Fresno)
California State University at Fullerton (GAGS) .... Cal St U (Fullerton)
California State University at Hayward (GAGS) .... Cal St U (Hayward)
California State University at Long Beach (GAGS) .... Cal St U (Long Beach)
California State University at Los Angeles (GAGS) .... Cal St U (LA)
California State University at Northridge (GAGS) .... Cal St U (Northridge)
California State University at Sacramento (GAGS) .... Cal St U (Sacramento)
California State University at San Bernardino (GAGS) .... Cal St U (San Bernardino)
California State University at Stanislaus (GAGS) .... Cal St U (Stanislaus)
California State University, Chico .... CSUC
California State University, Chico, Chico, CA [*OCLC symbol*] (OCLC) .... CCH
California State University, Chico, Chico, CA [*Library symbol Library of Congress*] (LCLS) .... CChiS
California State University, Dominguez Hills, Carson, CA [*OCLC symbol*] (OCLC) .... CDH
California State University, Fresno (PDAA) .... CSUF
California State University, Fresno, Fresno, CA [*Library symbol Library of Congress OCLC symbol*] (LCLS) .... CFS
California State University, Fullerton, Fullerton, CA [*OCLC symbol*] (OCLC) .... CFI
California State University, Fullerton, Fullerton, CA [*Library symbol Library of Congress*] (LCLS) .... CFIS
California State University, Hayward, Hayward, CA [*Library symbol Library of Congress*] (LCLS) .... CHS
California State University, Hayward, Hayward, CA [*OCLC symbol*] (OCLC) .... CSH
California State University, Long Beach .... CSULB
California State University, Long Beach, Long Beach, CA [*OCLC symbol*] (OCLC) .... CLO
California State University, Long Beach, Long Beach, CA [*Library symbol Library of Congress*] (LCLS) .... CLobS
California State University, Los Angeles, Los Angeles, CA [*OCLC symbol*] (OCLC) .... CLA
California State University, Los Angeles, Los Angeles, CA [*Library symbol Library of Congress*] (LCLS) .... CLS
[*The*] **California State University Network** [*Computer science*] (TNIG) .... CSUnet
California State University, Northridge .... CSUN
California State University, Northridge, Northridge, CA [*OCLC symbol*] (OCLC) .... CNO
California State University, Northridge, Northridge, CA [*Library symbol Library of Congress*] (LCLS) .... CNoS
California State University, Sacramento .... CSUS
California State University, Sacramento, Sacramento, CA [*OCLC symbol*] (OCLC) .... CSA
California State University, Sacramento, Sacramento, CA [*Library symbol Library of Congress*] (LCLS) .... CSS
California Strawberry Advisory Board (EA) .... CSAB
California Student Opportunity and Access Program (EDAC) .... CAL-SOAP
California Superior Court, Reports of Cases in Appellate Departments [*A publication*] (DLA) .... Cal Sup
California Superior Court, Reports of Cases in Appellate Departments [*A publication*] (DLA) .... Cal Sup (Cal)
California Supplement [*A publication*] (DLA) .... Cal Sup
California Supreme Court Reports [*A publication*] (DLA) C
California Supreme Court Reports, Second Series [*A publication*] (DLA) C2d
California Supreme Court Reports, Third Series [*A publication*] (DLA) C3d
California Supreme Court, San Francisco, CA [*Library symbol Library of Congress*] (LCLS) .... C-SC
California Sweet Potato Growers (SRA) .... CSPG
California Table Grape Commission (EA) .... CTGC
California Teachers Association, Burlingame, CA [*Library symbol Library of Congress*] (LCLS) .... CBuCTA
California Terms [*Grain shipping*] .... CT
California Test Bureau [*McGraw Hill, Inc.*] [*Psychology*] .... CTB
California Test of Basic Skills [*Education*] .... CTBS
California Test of Mental Maturity .... CTMM
California Test of Personality [*Psychology*] .... CTP
California Texas Oil Co. .... CALTEX
California Tomorrow [*An association*] (EA) .... CT
California Traffic Safety Foundation [*Defunct*] (EA) .... CTSF
California Travel Industry Association (SRA) .... CALTIA
California Trial Lawyers Journal [*A publication*] (DLA) .... CTLJ
California Tumor Registry .... CTR
California Ultra-Low-Emission Vehicle [*Automotive industry*] .... CALULEV
California Undersea Aqueduct Reconnaissance-Oceanography Study [*Department of the Interior*] (GFGA) .... CUARO
California Union List of Periodicals [*Cooperative Library Agency for Systems and Services*] [*Database*] .... CULP
California Union of Safety Employees (SRA) .... CAUSE
California Universities Council on Space Sciences .... CUCOSS
California University Cyclotron .... CALUTRON
California University of Pennsylvania (GAGS) .... Cal U (Pa)
California Unreported Cases [*1855-1910*] [*A publication*] (DLA) .... CA U
California Unreported Cases [*1855-1910*] [*A publication*] (DLA) .... Cal Unrep
California Unreported Cases [*1855-1910*] [*A publication*] (DLA) .... Cal Unrep Cas
California Unreported Cases [*1855-1910*] [*A publication*] (DLA) .... Cal Urep
California Unreported Cases [*1855-1910*] [*A publication*] (DLA) .... CU
California Veterinary Diagnostic Laboratory System .... CVDLS
California Warehouse Association (SRA) .... CWA
California Water Association (SRA) .... CWA
California Water Service Co. [*Associated Press*] (SAG) .... CalWtr
California Water Service Co. [*NYSE symbol*] (SAG) .... CWT
California Western Railroad [*AAR code*] .... CWR
California Western School of Law (GAGS) .... Cal West Sch of Law
California Western School of Law Library, San Diego, CA [*OCLC symbol*] (OCLC) .... CWE
California Western School of Law, San Diego, CA [*Library symbol*] [*Library of Congress*] (LCLS) .... CSdCWL
California Wheelchair Aviators (EA) .... CWA
California Wilderness Survival League (EA) .... CWSL
California Yoga Teachers Association (EA) .... CYTA
California-Arizona Citrus League (SRA) .... CACL
Californian Rabbit Specialty Club (EA) .... CRSC
California-Nevada Conference of Operating Engineers (SRA) .... CNCOE
California's Wine Wonderland [*A publication*] (EAAP) .... CWW
Californium [*Chemical element*] .... Cf
Californium-252 Plasma Desorption Mass Spectrometry .... CFPDMS
Califronia Association of Alcoholism and Drug Abuse Counselors (SRA) .... CAADAC
Caligula [*the Poisoner*] [*the Hun the Emperor Initials that form the name of the villain in "Captain Marvel" comic strip and indicate the sources of his power*] .... IBAC
Caliop [*France ICAO designator*] (FAAC) .... IOP
Calipatria, CA [*Location identifier FAA*] (FAAL) .... CLR
Calipatria, CA [*FM radio station call letters*] .... KSSB
Caliper (MSA) .... CLPR
Caliper .... CLPR
Caliper Disk Brake .... CDB
Calistoga [*California*] [*Seismograph station code, US Geological Survey Closed*] (SEIS) .... CLS
Calistoga Free Public Library, Calistoga, CA [*Library symbol Library of Congress*] (LCLS) .... CCali
Calix [*Anatomy*] (MAE) .... K
Calix Society (EA) .... CS
Call (IAA) C
Call Accounting Reconciliation Process [*Telecommunications*] (TEL) .... CARP
Call Accounting System [*or Subsystem*] [*Telecommunications*] .... CAS
Call Accounting System for Hotels [*Telecommunications*] (IAA) .... CASH
Call Address Code [*Telecommunications*] (ECII) .... CDC
Call Aircraft Co. .... CAL
Call Attempts per Second [*Telecommunications*] (TEL) .... CAPS
Call Back [*Word processing*] .... CB
Call Box Discrimination [*Telecommunications*] (TEL) .... CBD
Call Box Station (MSA) .... CBS
Call Charge Record (ADA) .... CCR
Call Check [*Telecommunications*] (NITA) CC
Call Contract CC
Call Control Processing [*Telecommunications*] (TEL) .... CCP
Call Control Systems [*San Clemente, CA*] [*Telecommunications*] (TSSD) .... CCS
Call Count Meter [*Telecommunications*] (NITA) .... CCM
Call Deflection [*Telecommunications*] (DOM) .... CD
Call Description Language [*Computer science*] (PDAA) .... CDL
Call Detail Recording [*Telecommunications*] (TEL) .... CDR
Call Detector (IAA) .... CD
Call Directing Character (IAA) .... CDC
Call Directing Code .... CDC
Call Director (SAA) .... CD

Call Director Unit ... CDU
Call Disconnect [*Telecommunications*] (ACRL) ... CD
Call Dispatch (IAA) ... CD
Call Diverter (NITA) ... CADI
Call Failed [*or Failure*] [*Telecommunications*] (TEL) ... CFL
Call Failure Detection Equipment [*Telecommunications*] (NITA) ... CFDE
Call Finder [*Telecommunications*] ... CF
Call for Action [*An association*] (NTCM) ... CFA
Call for Action, Inc. (EA) ... CFAI
Call Forward Directive [*World War II*] ... CFD
Call Forwarding Busy [*Telecommunications*] (DOM) ... CFB
Call Forwarding No Reply [*Telecommunications*] (DOM) ... CFNR
Call Forwarding Unconditional [*Telecommunications*] (DOM) ... CFU
Call Handler for Advanced Telephone Services [*Telecommunications*] (NITA) ... CHATS
Call Hold [*Telecommunications*] (DOM) ... HOLD
Call Hold and Trace [*Telecommunications*] (TEL) ... CHT
Call Holding Time [*Telecommunications*] (TEL) ... CHT
Call Identification Line [*Telecommunications*] (NITA) ... CIL
Call Indicator [*Computer science*] ... CI
Call Information Logging [*Telecommunications*] (NITA) ... CIL
Call Information Logging Equipment [*Computer science*] (PDAA) ... CILE
Call Key [*Telecommunications*] ... CK
Call Level Interface [*Computer science*] ... CLI
Call Loan [*Banking*] ... CL
Call Management Language [*Telecommunications*] (ACRL) ... CAMEL
Call Management System [*Accounting package*] (CDE) ... CMS
Call Money [*Investment term*] ... CM
Call Monitor (NOAA) ... CALM
Call Net Enterprises [*Associated Press*] (SAG) ... CallNet
Call Net Enterprises [*NASDAQ symbol*] (SAG) ... CNEB
Call Number [*Online database field identifier*] ... CN
Call Number Identification (IAA) ... CNI
Call of More [*Stock exchange term British*] (ROG) ... C/M
Call Option [*Investment term*] ... CO
Call Originate Status [*Telecommunications*] (HGAA) ... COS
Call Paid [*Telecommunications*] (ADA) ... CP
Call Process [*Telecommunications*] (NITA) ... CP
Call Processing/Voice Messaging (BTTJ) ... CP/VM
Call Processor [*Computer science*] ... CP
Call Progress Indicator [*Telecommunications*] (TEL) ... CPI
Call Protocol Message [*Telecommunications*] (TEL) ... CPM
Call Quickly Distress [*International telegrapher's signal for an emergency*] (WDMC) ... CQD
Call Reference Value [*Telecommunications*] (ACRL) ... CRV
Call Request [*Telecommunications*] ... CR
Call Request [*Telecommunications*] (TEL) ... CRQ
Call Routine Display Panel (IAA) ... CDP
Call Sign [*or Signal*] [*Radio*] ... CS
Call Signs and/or Address Group Remain Same (MUGU) ... CADSAME
Call Store [*Telecommunications*] (TEL) ... CS
Call Supervision Module [*Telecommunications*] (TEL) ... CSM
Call Time Adjustor [*Military communications*] ... CTA
Call to Australia [*Political party*] ... CTA
Call to Australia - Democratic Labor Party Coalition [*Political party*] ... CTA-DLP
Call To Quarter [*Wire-service jargon for correction*] (WDMC) ... cq
Call to Quarters [*General call preceding transmission of radio signals*] ... CQ
Call Waiting [*Telephone communication*] ... CW
Call Waiting Indication [*Telecommunications*] (TEL) ... CWI
Callable Bond [*Investment term*] ... CA
Callable Bond [*Investment term*] ... CB
Callahan, FL [*AM radio station call letters*] ... WELX
Callahan, FL [*FM radio station call letters*] (RBYB) ... WPLA
Callahan, FL [*FM radio station call letters*] (RBYB) ... WPLA-FM
Callan's Military Laws of the United States [*A publication*] (DLA) ... Cal Mil Laws
Callan's Military Laws of the United States [*A publication*] (DLA) ... Call Mil L
Callao Caves [*Philippines*] [*Seismograph station code, US Geological Survey*] (SEIS) ... CVP
Callaway Elementary School, Callaway, MN [*Library symbol*] [*Library of Congress*] (LCLS) ... MnCalE
Callaway, FL [*FM radio station call letters*] ... WDRK
Callaway Golf [*NYSE symbol*] (TTSB) ... ELY
Callaway Golf Co. [*Associated Press*] (SAG) ... CallGolf
Callaway Golf Co. [*NYSE symbol*] (SAG) ... ELY
Callaway Mills Co., Technical Library, LaGrange, GA [*Library symbol Library of Congress*] (LCLS) ... GLagCM
Callaway Plant (NRCH) ... CP
Call-Detail Routing [*Telecommunications*] (TSSD) ... CDR
Call-Detail-Recording/Station-Message-Detail-Recording [*Telecommunications*] ... CDR/SMDR
Calle ... CLL
Called [*In stock listings of newspapers*] [*Business term*] ... CLD
Called Game [*Baseball*] ... Cg
Called Line (ECII) ... CLD
Called Output Image ... COI
Called Subscriber Answer [*Telecommunications*] (TEL) ... CSA
Called Subscriber Busy [*Telecommunications*] (NITA) ... CSB
Called Subscriber Held [*Telecommunications*] (TEL) ... CSH
Called to See Patient [*Medicine*] (CPH) ... CTSP
Called to the Bar [*British*] (ROG) ... B
Callex Enterprises Ltd. [*Vancouver Stock Exchange symbol*] ... CLS
Callex Mineral Exploration [*Vancouver Stock Exchange symbol*] ... CXX
Callier Center for Communication Disorders, Dallas, TX [*Library symbol Library of Congress*] (LCLS) ... TxDaCCD
Calligrapher [*MARC relator code*] [*Library of Congress*] (LCCP) ... cll
Calligrapher ... CLLGRPHR
Calligraphy (VRA) ... calig
Calligraphy Society of Victoria [*Australia*] ... CSV
Callimachus [*Third century BC*] [*Classical studies*] (OCD) ... Callim
Call-In Time [*Military communications*] ... CIT
Calling (ROG) ... CALLG
Calling (DEN) ... CLG
Calling Card Service [*Bell System*] ... CCS
Calling Device [*Telecommunications*] ... CD
Calling for Orders [*Shipping*] ... CFO
Calling Lake School, Alberta [*Library symbol National Library of Canada*] (BIB) ... ACALLS
Calling Line (ECII) ... CLG
Calling Line Identification [*or Identity*] [*Telecommunications*] (TEL) ... CLI
Calling Line Identification [*Telecommunications*] (ACRL) ... CLID
Calling Line Identification Presentation [*Telecommunications*] (DOM) ... CLIP
Calling Line Identification Restriction [*Telecommunications*] (DOM) ... CLIR
Calling Number Display [*Telecommunications*] ... CND
Calling Party Cannot Hear [*Telecommunications*] (TEL) ... CPCH
Calling Party Forced Release [*Telecommunications*] (TEL) ... CPFR
Calling Party Number [*Telecommunications*] ... CPN
Calling Party's Category [*Telecommunications*] (TEL) ... CPC
Calling Processing Subsystem [*Telecommunications*] (TEL) ... CPS
Calling Tone [*Computer science*] ... CNG
Calling-On [*Railroad signal arm*] [*British*] ... C
Callington [*England*] ... CALL
Callis on Sewers [*A publication*] (DLA) ... Cal Sew
Callis on Sewers [*A publication*] (DLA) ... Call Sew
Callis on Sewers [*A publication*] (DLA) ... Callis
Callis on Sewers [*A publication*] (DLA) ... Callis Sew
Callisthenic Association of South Australia ... CASA
Callisthenics Victoria [*Australia*] ... CV
Callistratus [*Flourished, 3rd century*] [*Authority cited in pre-1607 legal work*] (DSA) ... Calis
Callitrichid Hepatitis Virus ... CHV
Callitype (VRA) ... calit
Callman on Unfair Competition and Trade Marks [*A publication*] (DLA) ... Callman Unfair Comp
Call-Net Enterprises'B' [*NASDAQ symbol*] (TTSB) ... CNEBF
Callon Petroleum [*NASDAQ symbol*] (TTSB) ... CLNP
Callon Petroleum Co. [*Associated Press*] (SAG) ... CallonP
Callon Petroleum Co. [*NASDAQ symbol*] (SAG) ... CLNP
Callon Petroleum Cv Exch 'A' Pfd [*NASDAQ symbol*] (TTSB) ... CLNPP
Callose Platelets [*Botany*] ... CP
Calloway's Nursery [*NASDAQ symbol*] (SPSG) ... CLWY
Calloways Nursery, inc. [*Associated Press*] (SAG) ... Caloway
CallPath Services Architecture (CDE) ... CSA
Calls for Service Signal [*Telecommunications*] (TEL) ... CFS
Calls per Day (IAA) ... CD
Calls per Day [*Telecommunications*] (IAA) ... CPD
Calls per Minute [*Telecommunications*] (IAA) ... CPM
Calls per Second [*Telecommunications*] (TEL) ... CS
Calls Underwritten by Swanbrook [*Investment term*] (DFIT) ... CUBS
Call's Virginia Reports [*5-10 Virginia*] [*1797-1825*] [*A publication*] (DLA) ... Call
Call's Virginia Reports [*5-10 Virginia*] [*1797-1825*] [*A publication*] (DLA) ... Call (VA)
Callus [*Medicine*] (DAVI) ... CAL
Call-Us, Inc. ... CU
Call-Waiting Identification [*Telecommunications service*] ... CWID
Calm [*i.e., no wind*] ... C
Calm Air [*Canada ICAO designator*] (FAAC) ... CAV
Calm Air International [*ICAO designator*] (AD) ... MO
Calm Water Line ... CWL
Calmar Public Library, Alberta [*Library symbol National Library of Canada*] (NLC) ... ACALM
CalMat Co. [*Associated Press*] (SAG) ... Calmat
CalMat Co. [*NYSE symbol*] (SPSG) ... CZM
Calmato [*More Calm*] [*Music*] ... CALM
Calmodulin [*Also, CaM*] [*Biochemistry*] ... CalM
Calmodulin [*Also, CalM*] [*Biochemistry*] ... CaM
Calmodulin Binding Protein [*Biochemistry*] ... CaM-BP
Calmodulin-Dependent Protein Kinase [*An enzyme*] ... CAM-PK
Calnetics Corp. [*NASDAQ symbol*] (NQ) ... CALN
Calnetics Corp. [*Associated Press*] (SAG) ... Calnetcs
Calnexin (DMAA) ... CANX
Calnor Resources Ltd. [*Vancouver Stock Exchange symbol*] ... CUU
Calomel [*Pharmacy*] (ROG) ... CAL
Calomel, Rhubarb, Colocynth [*Medicine*] ... CRC
Calopezzati [*Italy ICAO location identifier*] (ICLI) ... LICM
Caloric Heat Unit ... CHU
Caloric Restriction ... CR
Calorie ... C
Calorie [*Small Calorie*] [*Dietetics*] (DAVI) ... c
Calorie (MSA) ... CAL
Calorie (IDOE) ... cal
Calorie Control Council (EA) ... CCC
Calories Don't Count [*Title of a 1961 book by Dr. Herman Taller; initialism referred to the diet and diet capsules promoted by the book*] ... CDC
Calorific Power (IAA) ... CP
Calorific Recovery Anaerobic Process [*Inc*] ... CRAP
Calorific Value [*of a fuel*] ... CV
Calorimetry Conference (EA) ... CC
Calotype (VRA) ... CALOT
Caloundra [*Australia Airport symbol*] (OAG) ... CUD
Calpetro Resources, Inc. [*Vancouver Stock Exchange symbol*] ... COZ

Calpine Corp. [*Associated Press*] (SAG) .... Calpine
Calpine Corp. [*NYSE symbol*] (SAG) .... CPN
Calpine Resources, Inc. [*Vancouver Stock Exchange symbol*] .... CLP
Calprop Corp. [*Associated Press*] (SAG) .... Calprop
Calprop Corp. [*AMEX symbol*] (SPSG) .... CPP
Calpurnius Siculus [*First century AD*] [*Classical studies*] (OCD) .... Calp
CALS [*Customs Acts Legislation Service*] **Information Bulletin** [*Australia A publication*] .... CIB
Calsequestrin (DMAA) .... CASQ
Calspan Corp. [*Formerly, Cornell Aeronautical Laboratory*] .... CAL
Calspan On-Line Information Service [*Calspan Corp.*] [*Information service or system*] (IID) .... COINS
Caltech Data Ltd. [*Vancouver Stock Exchange symbol*] .... KAL
Caltech Political Military Exercise [*International relations simulation game*] .... PME
Caltech Population Program [*Agency for International Development*] (IID) .... CPP
Caltex Pacific Indonesia .... CPI
Calthrop on Copyholds [*A publication*] (DLA) .... Calth Copyh
Calthrop's City of London Cases, King's Bench [*England*] [*A publication*] (DLA) .... Calth
Calthrop's City of London Cases, King's Bench [*England*] [*A publication*] (DLA) .... Calth (Eng)
Calthrop's City of London Cases, King's Bench [*England*] [*A publication*] (DLA) .... Calthr
Calthrop's English King's Bench Reports [*80 English Reprint*] [*A publication*] (DLA) .... Cal
Calthrop's English King's Bench Reports [*80 English Reprint*] [*A publication*] (DLA) .... Cal Rep
Calthrop's English King's Bench Reports [*80 English Reprint*] [*A publication*] (DLA) .... Calth
Calthrop's English King's Bench Reports [*80 English Reprint*] [*A publication*] (DLA) .... Calth (Eng)
Calthrop's English King's Bench Reports [*80 English Reprint*] [*A publication*] (DLA) .... Calthr
Calton, Inc. [*Associated Press*] (SAG) .... Calton
Calton, Inc. [*AMEX symbol*] (SPSG) .... CN
Calument City Public Library, Calumet City, IL [*Library symbol*] [*Library of Congress*] (LCLS) .... ICcP
Calumet Bancorp [*NASDAQ symbol*] (SAG) .... CBCI
Calumet Bancorp, Inc. [*Associated Press*] (SAG) .... Calumet
Calumet City Public Library, Calumet City, IL [*Library symbol Library of Congress*] (LCLS) ICc
Calumet College, Whiting, IN [*OCLC symbol*] (OCLC) ICC
Calumet College, Whiting, IN [*Library symbol Library of Congress*] (LCLS) .... InWhC
Calumet, MI [*TV station call letters*] (RBYB) .... WBKP-TV
Calumet Public Library, Calumet, MN [*Library symbol*] [*Library of Congress*] (LCLS) .... MnCm
Calumet Public-School Library, Calumet, MI [*Library symbol Library of Congress*] (LCLS) .... MiCal
Calvada Resources [*Vancouver Stock Exchange symbol*] .... CVH
Calvarium and Scalp [*Anatomy*] (DAVI) .... C & S
Calvary Baptist School of Theology, Lansdale, PA [*Library symbol Library of Congress*] (LCLS) .... PLdaC
Calvary Christian School, Worthington, MN [*Library symbol*] [*Library of Congress*] (LCLS) .... MnWoCCS
Calvert City, KY [*FM radio station call letters*] .... WCCK
Calvert Cliffs Nuclear Power Plant (NRCH) .... CCNPP
Calvert Gas & Oils Ltd. [*Toronto Stock Exchange symbol*] .... CVT
Calverton, NY [*Location identifier FAA*] (FAAL) CCC
Calverton, NY [*Location identifier FAA*] (FAAL) .... CTO
Calverton, NY [*Location identifier FAA*] (FAAL) .... PIC
Calvert's Parties to Suits in Equity [*A publication*] (DLA) .... Calv Par
Calvert's Parties to Suits in Equity [*A publication*] (DLA) .... Calv Parties
Calvi [*Corsica*] [*Airport symbol*] (OAG) .... CLY
Calvi [*Corsica*] [*Seismograph station code, US Geological Survey*] (SEIS) .... CVF
Calvi/Sainte-Catherine, Corse [*France ICAO location identifier*] (ICLI) .... LFKC
Calviac [*France*] [*Seismograph station code, US Geological Survey*] (SEIS) .... CAF
Calvin and Hobbes [*Comic strip*] .... C & H
Calvin College and Seminary, Grand Rapids, MI [*OCLC symbol*] (OCLC) .... EXC
Calvin College and Seminary, Grand Rapids, MI [*Library symbol Library of Congress*] (LCLS) .... MiGrC
Calvin Coolidge Memorial Foundation (EA) .... CCMF
Calvin Klein [*Fashion designer, 1942-*] .... CK
Calvinia [*South Africa*] [*ICAO location identifier*] (ICLI) .... FACV
Calwer Bibellexikon (BJA) .... CBL
Calwestern Automated Clearing House Association (MHDB) .... CACHA
Calypso Development Ltd. [*Vancouver Stock Exchange symbol*] .... CYS
Calypte Biomedical Corp. [*NASDAQ symbol*] (SAG) .... CALY
Calypte Biomedical Corp. [*Associated Press*] (SAG) .... Calypte
Calyx [*Botany*] (ROG) C
Calyx Lateral Lobe Length [*Botany*] CLLL
Calyx Lateral Lobe Shape [*Botany*] .... CLLS
Calyx Lateral Lobe Width [*Botany*] .... CLLW
Calyx Tube Length [*Botany*] .... CTBL
Cam Action Wheel .... CAW
Cam Air Management Ltd. [*British ICAO designator*] (FAAC) .... CMR
Cam Box .... CBX
Cam Case .... CMCS
CAM Control Block [*Computer science*] .... CCB
CAM Data Systems [*NASDAQ symbol*] (SAG) .... CADA
CAM Data Systems, Inc. [*Associated Press*] (SAG) .... CAM Dt
Cam Designs [*NASDAQ symbol*] (TTSB) .... CMDA
Cam Designs Co. [*Associated Press*] (SAG) .... CamDs
Cam Designs Co. [*Associated Press*] (SAG) .... CampDsg
Cam Designs Co. [*NASDAQ symbol*] (SAG) .... CMDA
Cam Designs Wrrt [*NASDAQ symbol*] (TTSB) .... CMDAW
Cam Follower .... CMFLR
CAM [*Central American Mission*] **International** (EA) .... CAM
Cam Limit Switch .... CLS
Cam Plate Readout .... CPR
Cam Pocket .... CMPKT
Cam Ranh Bay [*Vietnam*] .... CRB
Cam Roller .... CMRLR
Cam Timing Contact .... CTC
Cam Wedge Clamp .... CWC
Cam Wedge Power Clamp .... CWPC
CAMA [*Centralized Automatic Message Accounting*] **Operator Position Exercise** (PDAA) .... COPE
Camabatela [*Angola*] [*ICAO location identifier*] (ICLI) .... FNCM
CAMAC [*Computer-Aided Measurement and Control*] **Input-Output Processor** [*Computer*] .... CIOP
Camaguey [*Cuba*] [*Airport symbol*] (OAG) .... CMW
Camaguey/Ignacio Agramonte [*Cuba ICAO location identifier*] (ICLI) .... MUCM
Camair [*Division of Cameron Iron Works, Inc.*] [*ICAO aircraft manufacturer identifier*] (ICAO) .... CM
Camaldolese Benedictine Sisters (TOCD) .... OSBCam
Camaldolese Hermits (TOCD) .... osbcam
Camaldolese Hermits (TOCD) .... OSBCam
Camaldolese Hermits of the Congregation of Monte Corona (TOCD) .... ErCam
Camaldolese Hermits of the Congregation of Monte Corona (TOCD) .... ercam
Camana [*Peru*] [*ICAO location identifier*] (ICLI) .... SPAM
Camanachd Association (EA) .... CA
Cam-and-Claw [*Pulldown mechanism in a camera or projector*] .... CAM
Camara Brasileira do Livro [*Brazilian Chamber of Publishing*] (EAIO) .... CBL
Camargo Township Library, Villa Grove, IL [*Library symbol Library of Congress*] (LCLS) .... IVg
Camargue Air Transport [*France ICAO designator*] (FAAC) .... CMG
Camarillo, CA [*FM radio station call letters*] .... KMRO
Camarillo, CA [*FM radio station call letters*] (RBYB) .... KOCP
Camarillo State Hospital, Camarillo, CA [*Library symbol Library of Congress*] (LCLS) .... CCamarH
Camaro Owners of America [*Defunct*] (EA) .... COA
Camas County District Library, Fairfield, ID [*Library symbol*] [*Library of Congress*] (LCLS) .... IdFa
Camas Prairie [*Railroad*] (MHDW) .... CAP
Camas Prairie Railroad Co. (IIA) .... CAP
Camas Prairie Railroad Co. [*AAR code*] .... CSP
Camas Public Library, Camas, WA [*Library symbol*] [*Library of Congress*] (LCLS) .... WaCa
Camas Resources Ltd. [*Vancouver Stock Exchange symbol*] .... KMS
Camas, WA [*FM radio station call letters*] (RBYB) .... KNRK
Camaxilo [*Angola*] [*ICAO location identifier*] (ICLI) .... FNCX
Camber [*Aerospace engineering*] .... CAM
Cambex Corp. [*Associated Press*] (SAG) .... Cambex
Cambex Corp. [*NASDAQ symbol*] .... CBEX
Cambior, Inc. [*Associated Press*] (SAG) .... Camb
Cambior, Inc. [*Associated Press*] (SAG) .... Cambior
Cambior, Inc. [*AMEX symbol*] (SAG) .... CBJ
Cambistry [*Finance*] .... CAMB
Cambodia [*Democratic Kampuchea*] [*MARC geographic area code Library of Congress*] (LCCP) .... a-cb--
Cambodia (WDAA) .... CAMB
Cambodia (VRA) .... Camb
Cambodia [*Democratic Kampuchea*] [*MARC country of publication code Library of Congress*] (LCCP) .... cb
Cambodia [*ANSI two-letter standard code*] (CNC) .... KH
Cambodia [*ANSI three-letter standard code*] (CNC) .... KHM
Cambodia Crisis Center [*Defunct*] (EA) CCC
Cambodia-IRRI [*International Rice Research Institute*]-Australia Project .... CIAP
Cambodian [*MARC language code Library of Congress*] (LCCP) .... cam
Cambodian Advisory Council of Australia .... CACA
Cambodian Appeal [*Defunct*] (EA) .... CA
Cambodian Association of Victoria [*Australia*] .... CAV
Cambodian Buddhist Association of Victoria [*Australia*] .... CBAV
Cambodian Buddhist Society (EA) .... CBS
Cambodian Community Welfare Centre [*Australia*] .... CCWC
Cambodian Crisis Committee (EA) CCC
Cambodian Investment Board (ECON) .... CIB
Cambodian People's Party [*Political party*] (ECON) .... CPP
Cambodian Women's Association of New South Wales [*Australia*] .... CWANSW
Camborne [*Urban district in England*] .... CAMB
Camborne School of Metalliferous Mining [*British*] .... CSMM
Camborne School of Mines [*British*] (IRUK) .... CSM
Cambourne Resources [*Vancouver Stock Exchange symbol*] .... KAV
Cambrai/Epinoy [*France ICAO location identifier*] (ICLI) .... LFQI
Cambrai/Niergnies [*France ICAO location identifier*] (ICLI) .... LFYG
Cambrex Corp. [*Associated Press*] (SAG) .... Cambrx
Cambrex Corp. [*AMEX symbol*] (SPSG) .... CBM
Cambria & Indiana Railroad Co. [*AAR code*] CI
Cambria, CA [*FM radio station call letters*] .... KOTR
Cambria County Legal Journal [*Pennsylvania*] [*A publication*] (DLA) .... Cambria
Cambria County Legal Journal [*Pennsylvania*] [*A publication*] (DLA) .... Cambria Co LJ
Cambria County Legal Journal [*Pennsylvania*] [*A publication*] (DLA) .... Cambria Co (PA)
Cambria County Library System, Johnstown, PA [*OCLC symbol*] (OCLC) .... JOC
Cambria County Library System, Johnstown, PA [*Library symbol Library of Congress*] (LCLS) .... PJo
Cambria County Reports [*Pennsylvania*] [*A publication*] (DLA) .... Camb Co LJ
Cambria Resources Ltd. [*Vancouver Stock Exchange symbol*] .... KMR

Cambrian [*Period, era, or system*] [*Geology*] ... CAMB
Cambrian Airways Ltd. ... CAS
Cambrian College, Sudbury, ON, Canada [*Library symbol*] [*Library of Congress*] (LCLS) ... CaOSUC
Cambrian College, Sudbury, Ontario [*Library symbol National Library of Canada*] (NLC) ... OSUC
Cambrian Railway [*British*] ... CAM R
Cambrian Railway [*British*] (ROG) ... CR
Cambrian Society of Victoria [*Australia*] ... CSV
Cambridge [*Municipal borough in England*] ... C
Cambridge [*Municipal borough in England*] ... CAM
Cambridge [*Massachusetts*] [*Seismograph station code, US Geological Survey Closed*] (SEIS) ... CAM
Cambridge [*Record label*] ... Camb
Cambridge [*Municipal borough in England*] ... CAMB
Cambridge [*England*] [*Airport symbol Obsolete*] (OAG) ... CBG
Cambridge [*British ICAO location identifier*] (ICLI) ... EGSC
Cambridge Acoustical Associates, Inc. (MCD) ... CAA
Cambridge Algebraic System [*Programming language*] [*1975*] (CSR) ... CAMAL
Cambridge Analog Simulator for Predicting Atomic Reactions [*British*] (DIT) ... CASPAR
Cambridge Ancient History [*1st edition, 1923-39*] [*A publication*] (OCD) ... CAH
Cambridge Ancient History [*2nd edition*] [*A publication*] (OCD) ... CAH^2
Cambridge Automatic Digital Computer (IEEE) ... CADC
Cambridge Bay [*Canada*] [*Geomagnetic observatory code*] ... CBB
Cambridge Bay [*Canada*] [*Airport symbol*] (OAG) ... YCB
Cambridge Bay, NT [*ICAO location identifier*] (ICLI) ... CYCB
Cambridge Bible [*A publication*] (BJA) ... CambB
[*The*] **Cambridge Bible Commentary: New English Bible** [*A publication*] (BJA) ... CBC
Cambridge Bible Commentary: New English Bible [*A publication*] (BJA) ... CNEB
Cambridge Bible for Schools and Colleges [*A publication*] (BJA) ... CaB
Cambridge Bible for Schools and Colleges [*A publication*] (BJA) ... CBSC
[*The*] **Cambridge Bibliography of English Literature** [*A publication*] ... CBEL
Cambridge Bicycle Club [*British*] ... CBC
Cambridge Biological Series [*A publication*] ... CBS
Cambridge BioScience Corp. ... CBS
[*The*] **Cambridge Book of Poetry for Children** [*A publication*] ... CBPC
Cambridge Buddhist Association (EA) ... CBA
Cambridge City Public Library, Cambridge City, IN [*Library symbol Library of Congress*] (LCLS) ... InCc
Cambridge Communication Corp. (MCD) ... CCC
Cambridge Community College, Cambridge, MN [*Library symbol*] [*Library of Congress*] (LCLS) ... MnCaCC
Cambridge Conference on School Mathematics [*National Science Foundation*] ... CCSM
Cambridge Consultants Ltd.[*Arthur D. Little Ltd.*] [*Research center British*] (IRUK) ... CCL
Cambridge Crystallographic Data Centre [*University of Cambridge*] [*Information service or system*] (IID) ... CCDC
Cambridge Crystallographic Data File [*Database*] ... CCDF
Cambridge Crystallographic Database [*England*] ... CCD
Cambridge Crystallography Subroutine Library [*Database*] ... CCSL
Cambridge Display Technology [*British*] ... CDT
Cambridge District Library, Cambridge, ID [*Library symbol*] [*Library of Congress*] (LCLS) ... IdCm
Cambridge Econometrics [*British*] ... CE
Cambridge Economic Policy Group [*British*] ... CEPG
Cambridge Education Consultants Ltd. [*British*] ... CEC
Cambridge Electron Accelerator ... CEA
Cambridge Electron Accelerator Laboratories [*Massachusetts Institute of Technology*] ... CEAL
Cambridge Electronic Industries [*British*] ... CEI
Cambridge Electronic Research Laboratory (KSC) ... CERL
Cambridge Elementary School, Media Center, Cambridge, MN [*Library symbol*] [*Library of Congress*] (LCLS) ... MnCaES
Cambridge Energy Research Group [*University of Cambridge*] [*British*] (IRUK) ... CERG
Cambridge English Classics [*A publication*] ... CEC
Cambridge Geographical Series [*A publication*] ... CGS
Cambridge Graphic Systems [*Computer science*] (HGAA) ... CGS
[*The*] **Cambridge Greek Testament** [*A publication*] (BJA) ... CGT
Cambridge Greek Testament Commentary [*A publication*] (BJA) ... CGTC
Cambridge Greek Testament for Schools and Colleges [*A publication*] (BJA) ... CGTSC
Cambridge Heart, Inc. [*Associated Press*] (SAG) ... CambHrt
Cambridge Heart, Inc. [*NASDAQ symbol*] (SAG) ... CAMH
Cambridge High School, Media Center, Cambridge, MN [*Library symbol*] [*Library of Congress*] (LCLS) ... MnCaHS
Cambridge Higher Local Examination [*British*] (ROG) ... CHL
Cambridge Historical Series [*A publication*] ... CHS
Cambridge History of English Literature ... CHEL
Cambridge Instrument Co. PLC (MHDW) ... CAMBY
Cambridge International Dictionary of English [*A publication*] ... CIDE
Cambridge Junior College [*Massachusetts*] ... CJC
Cambridge Language Research Unit ... CLRU
Cambridge Life Sciences [*British*] ... CLS
Cambridge, MA [*FM radio station call letters*] ... WHRB
Cambridge, MA [*AM radio station call letters*] ... WJIB
Cambridge, MA [*Television station call letters*] ... WLVI
Cambridge, MA [*FM radio station call letters*] ... WMBR
Cambridge Manuals of Science and Literature [*A publication*] ... CMSL
Cambridge Mathematical Series [*A publication*] ... CMS
Cambridge, MD [*Location identifier FAA*] (FAAL) ... CGE
Cambridge, MD [*AM radio station call letters*] ... WCEM
Cambridge, MD [*FM radio station call letters*] ... WCEM-FM
Cambridge, MD [*FM radio station call letters*] ... WFBR
Cambridge Memorial Hospital, Health Sciences Library, Cambridge, MN [*Library symbol*] [*Library of Congress*] (LCLS) ... MnCaH
Cambridge Memorial Hospital, Ontario [*Library symbol National Library of Canada*] (BIB) ... OCCMH
Cambridge Memories, Inc. ... CMI
Cambridge Middle School, Media Center, Cambridge, MN [*Library symbol*] [*Library of Congress*] (LCLS) ... MnCaM
Cambridge Military Library, Halifax, Nova Scotia [*Library symbol National Library of Canada*] (NLC) ... NSHC
Cambridge Military Library, Halifax, NS, Canada [*Library symbol*] [*Library of Congress*] (LCLS) ... CaNSHC
Cambridge Military Library, Halifax, NS, Canada [*Library symbol Library of Congress*] (LCLS) ... DaNSHC
Cambridge, MN [*Location identifier FAA*] (FAAL) ... CBG
Cambridge, MN [*FM radio station call letters*] ... WREV
Cambridge Modern History [*A publication*] (ROG) ... CMH
Cambridge Monitor System ... CMS
Cambridge Natural Science Manuals [*A publication*] ... CNSM
Cambridge, NE [*Location identifier FAA*] (FAAL) ... CSB
Cambridge NeuroScience [*NASDAQ symbol*] (TTSB) ... CNSI
Cambridge NeuroScience, Inc. [*Associated Press*] (SAG) ... CambNe
Cambridge NeuroScience, Inc. [*NASDAQ symbol*] (SAG) ... CNSI
Cambridge, NY [*Location identifier FAA*] (FAAL) ... CAM
Cambridge, OH [*Location identifier FAA*] (FAAL) ... CDI
Cambridge, OH [*FM radio station call letters*] ... WCMJ
Cambridge, OH [*AM radio station call letters*] ... WILE
Cambridge, OH [*FM radio station call letters*] ... WOUC
Cambridge, OH [*Television station call letters*] ... WOUC-TV
Cambridge, ON [*AM radio station call letters*] ... CIAM
Cambridge Optical Aperture Synthesis Telescope ... Coast
Cambridge Optical Aperture Synthesis Telescope ... COAST
Cambridge, Oxford & Southern Secondary Examinations Council [*British*] (AIE) ... COSSEC
Cambridge Physical Series [*A publication*] ... CPS
Cambridge Public Library, Cambridge, MA [*Library symbol Library of Congress*] (LCLS) ... MC
Cambridge Public Library, Cambridge, ON, Canada [*Library symbol Library of Congress*] (LCLS) ... CaOGal
Cambridge Public Library, Ontario [*Library symbol National Library of Canada*] (NLC) ... OGAL
Cambridge Pulsar (IIA) ... CP
Cambridge Radio Observatory Committee ... CAMROC
Cambridge Reports, Inc. [*Database producer*] (IID) ... CRI
Cambridge Research Biochemicals [*British*] ... CRB
Cambridge Research Center [*Air Force*] ... CRC
Cambridge Research Institute, Inc., Cambridge, MA [*Library symbol Library of Congress*] (LCLS) ... MCRI
Cambridge Research Laboratory ... CRL
Cambridge Scientific Abstracts [*Information service or system*] (IID) ... CSA
Cambridge Series for Schools and Training Colleges [*A publication*] ... CSSTC
Cambridge Seventh Day Adventist Library, Cambridge, MN [*Library symbol*] [*Library of Congress*] (LCLS) ... MnCaSD
Cambridge Shopping Centres Ltd. [*Toronto Stock Exchange symbol*] ... CBG
Cambridge SoundWorks [*NASDAQ symbol*] (TTSB) ... HIFI
Cambridge Soundworks, Inc. [*Associated Press*] (SAG) ... CambSnd
Cambridge Soundworks, Inc. [*NASDAQ symbol*] (SAG) ... HIFI
Cambridge State Hospital, Staff Library, Cambridge, MN [*Library symbol*] [*Library of Congress*] (LCLS) ... MnCaSH
Cambridge Structural Database [*Genetics*] ... CSD
Cambridge Technology, Inc. ... CTI
Cambridge Technology Partners [*Associated Press*] (SAG) ... CambTch
Cambridge Technology Partners [*NASDAQ symbol*] (SAG) ... CATP
Cambridge Technology Partners [*Associated Press*] (SAG) ... CmbTch
Cambridge Technology Ptnrs [*NASDAQ symbol*] (TTSB) ... CATP
Cambridge Training and Development [*British*] (AIE) ... CTAD
Cambridge University [*England*] ... CAMB
Cambridge University [*England*] ... CU
Cambridge University Air Squadron [*British*] (DI) ... CUAS
Cambridge University, Cambridge, United Kingdom [*Library symbol Library of Congress*] (LCLS) ... UkCU
Cambridge University Conservative Association (ECON) ... CUCA
Cambridge University Department of Education [*British*] (AIE) ... CUDE
Cambridge University Library [*British*] (DLA) ... CUL
Cambridge University Mission ... CUM
Cambridge University Officer Training Corps [*British military*] (DMA) ... CUOTC
Cambridge University Press ... CUP
Cambridge University Press Limited Editions ... CUPLE
Cambridge University Rifles [*British military*] (DMA) ... CUR
Cambridgeshire [*County in England*] ... CAMBS
Cambridgeshire [*County in England*] (ODBW) ... Cambs
Cambridgeshire College of Arts and Technology [*British*] (AIE) ... CCAT
Cambridgeshire Rifle Volunteer Corps [*British military*] (DMA) ... CRVC
Cambyses (BJA) ... Camb
Camco Financial [*NASDAQ symbol*] (TTSB) ... CAFI
Camco Financial Corp. [*NASDAQ symbol*] (SAG) ... CAFI
Camco Financial Corp. [*Associated Press*] (SAG) ... CamcoFn
Camco, Inc. [*Toronto Stock Exchange symbol*] ... COC
Camco International [*NYSE symbol*] (SPSG) ... CAM
Camco International [*Associated Press*] (SAG) ... Camco
Camden [*Australia ICAO location identifier*] (ICLI) ... ASCN
Camden [*Division of Victor*] [*Record label*] ... Cam
Camden [*Diocesan abbreviation*] [*New Jersey*] (TOCD) ... CAM
Camden [*Arkansas*] [*Airport symbol*] (OAG) ... CDH

Camden, AL [*Location identifier FAA*] (FAAL) .... IWE
Camden, AL [*AM radio station call letters*] .... WCOX
Camden, AL [*FM radio station call letters*] .... WYVC
Camden, AR [*AM radio station call letters*] .... KAMD
Camden, AR [*FM radio station call letters*] (RBYB) .... KAMD-FM
Camden, AR [*FM radio station call letters*] .... KCAC
Camden, AR [*FM radio station call letters*] .... KCXY
Camden, AR [*FM radio station call letters*] (RBYB) .... KMGC
Camden, AR [*AM radio station call letters*] .... KOSG
Camden Council for International Cooperation [*British*] CCIC
Camden County College, Blackwood, NJ [*Library symbol Library of Congress*] (LCLS) .... NjBlaC
Camden County College, Voorhees, NJ [*OCLC symbol*] (OCLC) .... NCK
Camden County Historical Society, Camden, NJ [*Library symbol Library of Congress*] (LCLS) .... NjCaHi
Camden County Library, Voorhees, NJ [*OCLC symbol*] (OCLC) .... NCL
Camden County Times, Collingswood, NJ [*Library symbol Library of Congress*] (LCLS) .... NjCoT
Camden County Times, Westmont, NJ [*Library symbol Library of Congress*] (LCLS) .... NjWemT
Camden East Branch, Lennox and Addington County Library, Ontario [*Library symbol National Library of Canada*] (NLC) .... OCELAC
Camden Free Public Library, Camden, NJ [*Library symbol Library of Congress*] (LCLS) .... NjCa
Camden Library [*A publication*] .... CLA
Camden, ME [*FM radio station call letters*] .... WQSS
Camden News, Camden, NJ [*Library symbol Library of Congress*] (LCLS) .... NjCaN
Camden, NJ [*FM radio station call letters*] .... WKDN
Camden, NJ [*Television station call letters*] .... WNJS
Camden, NJ [*AM radio station call letters*] .... WSSJ
Camden, NJ [*AM radio station call letters*] .... WTMR
Camden Property Trust [*Associated Press*] (SAG) .... CamdnP
Camden Property Trust [*NYSE symbol*] (SPSG) .... CPT
Camden, SC [*Location identifier FAA*] (FAAL) .... CDN
Camden, SC [*AM radio station call letters*] (RBYB) .... WAME
Camden, SC [*AM radio station call letters*] .... WCAM
Camden, SC [*FM radio station call letters*] .... WPUB
Camden, TN [*AM radio station call letters*] .... WFWL
Camden, TN [*FM radio station call letters*] .... WRJB
Camden Township Library, Camden, MI [*Library symbol Library of Congress*] (LCLS) .... MiCam
Camden-Gloucester Newspapers, Blackwood, NJ [*Library symbol Library of Congress*] (LCLS) .... NjBlaCG
Camden-Jackson Township Public Library, Camden, IN [*Library symbol Library of Congress*] (LCLS) .... InCam
Camden's Britannia [*A publication*] (DLA) .... Cam Brit
Camden's Britannia [*A publication*] (DLA) .... Camd Brit
Camden's Britannia [*A publication*] (DLA) .... Camden
Camdenton, MO [*FM radio station call letters*] .... KCVO
Came Free (ADA) .... CF
Cameco Corp. [*Associated Press*] (SAG) .... Cameco
Cameco Corp. [*NYSE symbol*] (SAG) .... CCJ
Cameco Corp. [*NYSE symbol*] (TTSB) .... CCJ
Cameco Corp. 1st Installment [*NYSE symbol*] (TTSB) .... CCJPP
Cameco Research Center, Ottawa, Ontario [*Library symbol National Library of Canada*] (NLC) .... OOEN
Camegie Group [*NASDAQ symbol*] (TTSB) .... CGIX
CAMEL [*Critical Aeronautical Material and Equipment List*] **Gate Field Effe ct Transistors** (MCD) .... CAMFET
Camel Oil & Gas Ltd. [*Toronto Stock Exchange symbol*] .... CEG
Camelford [*Rural district in England*] .... CAMELF
Camelopardalis [*Constellation*] .... Cam
Camelopardalis [*Constellation*] .... Caml
Camelot Corp. [*Associated Press*] (SAG) .... Camelot
Camelot Corp. [*NASDAQ symbol*] (NQ) .... CAML
Camembe [*Angola*] [*ICAO location identifier*] (ICLI) .... FNCB
Cameo (VRA) .... cmo
Camera (VRA) .... cam
Camera (KSC) .... CAM
Camera .... CAM
Camera (MSA) .... CAMR
Camera (ABBR) .... CMRA
Camera and Recorder .... Camcorder
Camera Concealment and Deception (DWSG) .... CCD
Camera Control System (KSC) .... CCS
Camera Control Unit .... CCU
Camera Copy [*or Camera-Ready Copy*] CC
Camera de Comercio Mexico-Estados Unidos [*United States-Mexico Chamber of Commerce*] (EAIO) .... CCMEU
Camera Ducata [*Duchy Chamber*] [*Latin Legal term*] (DLA) .... Cam Duc
Camera Electronic Unit (MCD) .... CEU
Camera Europea degli Arbitri Stragiudiziali e dei Periti Esperti Consulenti Tecnici [*European Chamber of Extra-Judicial Adjudicators and Expert Technical Advisors*] (EAIO) .... CEASPECT
Camera Gun .... CG
Camera Industries of West Germany [*Defunct*] .... CIWG
Camera Model System (MCD) .... CMS
Camera Obscura (VRA) .... cam obs
Camera Override Control System [*NASA*] (KSC) .... COCS
Camera Processor Viewer (NITA) .... CPV
Camera Quality (MUGU) .... CQ
Camera Ready [*Publishing*] (WDMC) .... CR
Camera Rehearsal .... CR
Camera Repairman [*Navy rating*] .... CR
Camera Scaccari [*Exchequer Chamber*] [*Latin Legal term*] (DLA) .... CAM SCAC
Camera Scaccarii [*Exchequer Chamber*] [*Latin Legal term*] (DLA) .... Cam Scacc
Camera Site [*NASA*] (KSC) .... CS
Camera Stellate [*Star Chamber*] [*Latin Legal term*] (DLA) .... Cam Stell
Camera, Timing, and Control (NASA) .... CTC
Camera Timing Indicator .... CTI
Camera-Ready Art [*Publishing*] .... CRA
Camera-Ready Copy [*Publishing*] .... CRC
Camera-Ready Mechanical .... CRM
Cameri [*Italy ICAO location identifier*] (ICLI) .... LIMN
Camerino [*Italy*] [*Seismograph station code, US Geological Survey Closed*] (SEIS) .... CMR
Cameron and Norwood's North Carolina Conference Reports [*A publication*] (DLA) .... C & N
Cameron and Norwood's North Carolina Conference Reports [*A publication*] (DLA) .... Cam & N
Cameron and Norwood's North Carolina Conference Reports [*1800-04*] [*A publication*] (DLA) .... Cam & Nor
Cameron and Norwood's North Carolina Conference Reports [*A publication*] (DLA) .... CN Conf
Cameron Ashley [*Associated Press*] (SAG) .... CamrnAsh
Cameron Ashley Bldg Prod [*NASDAQ symbol*] (TTSB) .... CABP
Cameron Ashley Building Products, Inc. [*NASDAQ symbol*] (SAG) .... CABP
Cameron College, Medical Library Resource Center, Lawton, OK [*Library symbol Library of Congress*] (LCLS) .... OkLC-M
Cameron Financial [*NASDAQ symbol*] (TTSB) .... CMRN
Cameron Financial Corp. [*Associated Press*] (SAG) .... CamrnF
Cameron Financial Corp. [*NASDAQ symbol*] (SAG) .... CMRN
Cameron. Intestate Succession in Scotland [*A publication*] (DLA) .... Cam Int Suc
Cameron Iron Works, Inc., Houston, TX [*Library symbol Library of Congress*] (LCLS) .... TxHCI
Cameron, MO [*AM radio station call letters*] .... KMRN
Cameron, MO [*FM radio station call letters*] .... KNOZ
Cameron on Joint Stock Companies [*Scotland*] [*A publication*] (DLA) .... Cam JS Comp
Cameron Parish Library, Cameron, LA [*Library symbol Library of Congress*] (LCLS) .... LCaC
Cameron. Reports, Upper Canada Queen's Bench [*A publication*] (DLA) .... Cam
Cameron State Agricultural College [*Oklahoma*] .... CSAC
Cameron Station [*Virginia*] [*Army*] (AABC) .... CAMSTA
Cameron, TX [*FM radio station call letters*] .... KHLR
Cameron, TX [*FM radio station call letters*] .... KJKS
Cameron, TX [*AM radio station call letters*] .... KMIL
Cameron University, Lawton, OK [*OCLC symbol*] (OCLC) .... OKC
Cameron University, Lawton, OK [*Library symbol Library of Congress*] (LCLS) .... OkLC
Cameron's Legal Opinions [*Toronto*] [*A publication*] (DLA) .... Cam Op
Cameron's Practice [*Canada*] [*A publication*] (DLA) .... Cameron Pr
Cameron's Practice [*Canada*] [*A publication*] (DLA) .... Cameron Pr (Can)
Cameron's Privy Council Decisions [*1832-1929*] [*Canada*] [*A publication*] (DLA) .... CAM
Cameron's Supreme Court Cases [*Canada*] [*A publication*] (DLA) .... CAM
Cameron's Supreme Court Cases [*Canada*] [*A publication*] (DLA) .... Cam Cas
Cameron's Supreme Court Cases [*Canada*] [*A publication*] (DLA) .... Cam SC
Cameron's Supreme Court Cases [*Canada*] [*A publication*] (DLA) .... Cameron
Cameron's Supreme Court Cases [*Canada*] [*A publication*] (DLA) .... Cameron (Can)
Cameron's Supreme Court Cases [*Canada*] [*A publication*] (DLA) .... Cameron Cas (Can)
Cameron's Supreme Court Cases [*Canada*] [*A publication*] (DLA) .... Cameron SC
Cameron's Supreme Court Cases [*Canada*] [*A publication*] (DLA) .... SCC
Cameron's Supreme Court Practice [*Canada*] [*A publication*] (DLA) .... Cam Prac
Cameroon (WDAA) .... CAM
Cameroon .... Camer
Cameroon [*MARC country of publication code Library of Congress*] (LCCP) .... cm
Cameroon [*ANSI two-letter standard code*] (CNC) .... CM
Cameroon [*ANSI three-letter standard code*] (CNC) .... CMR
Cameroon [*MARC geographic area code Library of Congress*] (LCCP) .... f-cm--
Cameroon [*Aircraft nationality and registration mark*] (FAAC) .... TJ
Cameroon Airlines [*ICAO designator*] (AD) .... UY
Cameroon Airlines [*ICAO designator*] (FAAC) .... UYC
Cameroon National Union [*Political party*] .... CNU
Cameroon People's National Congress .... CPNC
Cameroon Protestant College .... CPC
Cameroon Tribune [*A publication*] .... CT
Cameroon United Congress [*Political party*] .... CUC
Camfrey Resources Ltd. [*Vancouver Stock Exchange symbol*] .... CFB
Camiare [*Bolivia*] [*ICAO location identifier*] (ICLI) .... SLCM
Camilla, GA [*Location identifier FAA*] (FAAL) .... CXU
Camilla, GA [*FM radio station call letters*] .... WQVE
Camillian Fathers and Brothers (TOCD) .... oscam
Camillus [*of Plutarch*] [*Classical studies*] (OCD) .... Cam
Camillus Plautius [*Flourished, 1533-66*] [*Authority cited in pre-1607 legal work*] (DSA) .... Camil Plaut
Camillus Salernus [*Flourished, 16th century*] [*Authority cited in pre-1607 legal work*] (DSA) .... Cam Sal
Camillus Salernus [*Flourished, 16th century*] [*Authority cited in pre-1607 legal work*] (DSA) .... Cam Salern
Camillus Salernus [*Flourished, 16th century*] [*Authority cited in pre-1607 legal work*] (DSA) .... CS
Camindex Mines Ltd. [*Toronto Stock Exchange symbol*] .... CXM
Caminhos de Ferro Portugueses [*Railway*] [*Portugal*] (EY) .... CP
Caminito .... CMT
Camino .... CAM
Camino Energy Corp. [*Vancouver Stock Exchange symbol*] .... CIY
Camino, Placerville & Lake Tahoe Railroad Co. [*AAR code*] .... CPLT
Camino Resources Ltd. [*Vancouver Stock Exchange symbol*] .... CWM

Camiri [*Bolivia*] [*Airport symbol*] (OAG) ... CAM
Camiri [*Bolivia*] [*ICAO location identifier*] (ICLI) ... SLCA
Camisole (DSUE) ... CAM
Camisole (DSUE) ... CAMI
Cammed-Gear Speed Variator ... CSV
Cammooweal [*Queensland*] [*Airport symbol*] (AD) ... CML
Cam-Net Communic Ntwk [*NASDAQ symbol*] (TTSB) ... CWKTF
Cam-Net Communications Network, Inc. [*Vancouver Stock Exchange symbol*] ... CWK
Cam-Net Communications Network, Inc. [*NASDAQ symbol*] (NQ) ... CWKT
Cam-Net Communicatoins Network [*Associated Press*] (SAG) ... CamNt
Camoens [*Portuguese poet, 1524-1579*] (ROG) ... CAM
Cam-Operated Plunger ... COP
Camosun College Library [*UTLAS symbol*] ... CAM
Camosun College, Victoria, BC, Canada [*Library symbol Library of Congress*] (LCLS) ... CaBViC
Camosun College, Victoria, British Columbia [*Library symbol National Library of Canada*] (NLC) ... BVIC
Camouflage (AFM) ... CAM
Camouflage ... CAMO
Camouflage (MSA) ... CAMOF
Camouflage, Concealment, and Deception (MCD) ... CCD
Camouflage Critical [*Designation*] [*Army*] (RDA) ... CC
Camouflage Detection [*Often, in regard to a special photographic film, as, "CD film"*] [*Military*] ... CD
Camouflage Effectiveness Assessment Office [*Army*] (RDA) ... CEAO
Camouflage Mobile Field Kitchen [*Military*] (MCD) ... CMFK
Camouflage Officer [*British*] ... CO
Camouflage Signature Measurement [*Army*] (RDA) ... CSM
Camouflage Technology Center [*Battelle Columbus Division, OH*] ... CAMTEC
Camouflage Unit [*Military*] ... CU
Camouflage-Sensitive [*Designation*] [*Army*] (RDA) ... CS
CAMP [*Commonly used*] (OPSA) ... CAMP
Camp (ABBR) ... CMP
Camp ... CP
Camp ... CP
Camp Atterbury, IN [*Location identifier FAA*] (FAAL) ... XAY
Camp Avenue Elementary School, North Merrick, NY [*Library symbol*] [*Library of Congress*] (LCLS) ... NNmCE
Camp Beverly Hills [*California clothing store*] ... CBH
Camp Century [*Greenland*] [*Seismograph station*] ... CC
Camp Century [*Greenland*] [*Seismograph station code, US Geological Survey Closed*] (SEIS) ... CCG
Camp Chair ... CC
Camp Coles Signal Laboratory [*Army*] (MCD) ... CCSL
Camp Commandant ... CC
Camp De Bitche [*France ICAO location identifier*] (ICLI) ... LFXG
Camp De Canjuers [*France ICAO location identifier*] (ICLI) ... LFHK
Camp De Caylus [*France ICAO location identifier*] (ICLI) ... LFXT
Camp De Coetquidan [*France ICAO location identifier*] (ICLI) ... LFXQ
Camp De La Courtine [*France ICAO location identifier*] (ICLI) ... LFXS
Camp De Mourmelon [*France ICAO location identifier*] (ICLI) ... LFXE
Camp De Sissonne [*France ICAO location identifier*] (ICLI) ... LFXP
Camp De Suippes [*France ICAO location identifier*] (ICLI) ... LFXK
Camp Douglas, WI [*Location identifier FAA*] (FAAL) ... VOK
Camp Du Larzac [*France ICAO location identifier*] (ICLI) ... LFXW
Camp Du Valdahon [*France ICAO location identifier*] (ICLI) ... LFXH
Camp Elliot [*California*] [*Seismograph station code, US Geological Survey*] (SEIS) ... CPE
Camp Evans Signal Laboratory [*Army*] ... CESL
Camp Fire Boys and Girls (EA) ... CFBG
Camp Fire Club of America (EA) ... CFCA
Camp Fire Conservation Fund (EA) ... CFCF
Camp Fire Girls [*Later, CFBG*] (EA) ... CFG
Camp Fire, Inc. (AEE) ... CFI
Camp Gagetown Canadian Forces Base, NB [*ICAO location identifier*] (ICLI) ... CYCX
Camp Hill Hospital, Halifax, Nova Scotia [*Library symbol National Library of Canada*] (NLC) ... NSHCH
Camp Hill Hospital, Halifax, NS, Canada [*Library symbol Library of Congress*] (LCLS) ... CaNSHCH
Camp Horsemanship Association (EA) ... CHA
Camp Lejeune [*North Carolina*] [*Marine Corps*] ... CAMLEJ
Camp Lejeune, NC [*AM radio station call letters*] (RBYB) ... WCTJ-AM
Camp Lejeune, NC [*AM radio station call letters*] ... WWOF
Camp Lejeune Railroad Co. [*AAR code*] ... CPLJ
Camp Manufacturing Co., Franklin, VA [*Library symbol Library of Congress*] (LCLS) ... ViFraC
Camp Military Police [*British military*] (DMA) ... CMP
Camp New Amsterdam [*Netherlands*] ... CNA
Camp Newspaper Service ... CNS
Camp of Israel [*Freemasonry*] (ROG) ... COI
Camp Okavango [*Botswana*] [*ICAO location identifier*] (ICLI) ... FBCO
Camp Parks, CA [*Location identifier FAA*] (FAAL) ... PNY
Camp Parks Communication Annex [*California*] (MCD) ... CPCA
Camp Pendleton [*California*] [*Marine Corps*] ... CAMPEN
Camp Pendleton [*California*] [*Seismograph station code, US Geological Survey*] (SEIS) ... CPT
Camp Pohakuloa, HI [*Location identifier FAA*] (FAAL) ... BSF
Camp Quartermasters Store [*British military*] (DMA) ... CQMS
Camp Reception Station [*A kind of field hospital*] [*British*] ... CRS
Camp Ripley/Little Falls, MN [*Location identifier FAA*] (FAAL) ... MTK
Camp Sentinel RADAR [*Military*] (RDA) ... CRS
Camp Springs/Andrews Air Force Base [*Maryland*] [*ICAO location identifier*] (ICLI) ... KADW
Camp Springs, MD [*Location identifier FAA*] (FAAL) ... ADW
Camp Springs, MD [*Location identifier FAA*] (FAAL) ... MXK
Camp Springs, MD [*Location identifier FAA*] (FAAL) ... NSF
Camp Springs, MD [*Location identifier FAA*] (FAAL) ... RWS
Camp Strike Force [*Military*] (VNW) ... CSF
Camp Williams [*Utah*] [*Seismograph station code, US Geological Survey*] (SEIS) ... CWU
Campagne Elementary School, Bethpage, NY [*Library symbol Library of Congress*] (LCLS) ... NBetCaE
Campaign ... CMPGN
Campaign Against Arms Trade [*British*] (EAIO) ... CAAT
Campaign Against Book Piracy [*British*] (NITA) ... CABP
Campaign Against Censorship [*British*] (DBA) ... CAC
Campaign Against Council Corruption [*British*] (DBA) ... CAMACC
Campaign Against Health Fraud [*British*] (DBA) ... CAHF
Campaign Against Investment in South Africa [*Defunct*] (EA) ... CAISA
Campaign Against Lead in Petrol [*British*] ... CALIP
Campaign Against Lorry Menace [*British*] ... CALM
Campaign Against Marijuana Planting ... CAMP
Campaign Against Nuclear War (EA) ... CANW
Campaign Against Pollution ... CAP
Campaign Against Pornography [*British*] ... CAP
Campaign Against Racial Discrimination [*British*] ... CARD
Campaign Against Racism and Fascism [*British*] (DI) ... CARF
Campaign Against Racism in the Media [*British*] (DI) ... CRAM
Campaign Against Secret Records on Schoolchildren (AIE) ... CASROS
Campaign Against US Military Bases in the Philippines (EA) ... CAB
Campaign Brief [*A publication*] ... CB
Campaign Communications Institute [*Telemarketing*] (WDMC) ... CCI
Campaign for a British Referendum (ECON) ... CBR
Campaign for Action on Navigation and Locks [*British*] (DI) ... CANAL
Campaign for All Employees to Reduce Errors (SAA) ... CARE
Campaign for Comprehensive Education [*British*] (DI) ... CCE
Campaign for Democratic Socialism [*British*] ... CDS
Campaign for Economic Democracy ... CED
Campaign for Homosexual Equality [*British*] (DBA) ... CHE
Campaign for Human Development (EA) ... CHD
Campaign for Independent Financial Advice [*British*] (ECON) ... CAMIFA
Campaign for Independent Financial Advice [*British*] ... CIFA
Campaign for Justice in Divorce [*British*] (DI) ... CJD
Campaign for Labour Party Democracy [*British*] ... CLPD
Campaign for Lead-Free Air [*British*] ... CLEAR
Campaign for Nuclear Disarmament ... CND
Campaign for Peace and Democracy/East and West (EA) ... CPD/EW
Campaign for Pesticide Reform [*Environmental Protection Agency*] (GFGA) ... CPR
Campaign for Political Rights [*Defunct*] (EA) ... CPR
Campaign for Press and Broadcasting Freedom [*British*] (DI) ... CPBF
Campaign for Prosperity (EA) ... CP
Campaign for Real Ale ... CAMRA
Campaign for Real Ice Cream [*British*] (DI) ... CAFRIC
Campaign for Space Political Action Committee [*Defunct*] (EA) ... CSPAC
Campaign for State-Supported Alternative Schools (AIE) ... CSSAS
Campaign for Surplus Rosaries [*Defunct*] (EA) ... CSR
Campaign for the Advancement of State Education [*British*] ... CASE
Campaign for the Creation of the National Youth Advisor (EA) ... CCNYA
Campaign for the Defence of the Turkish Peace Movement [*British*] ... CDTPM
Campaign for the Homeless and Rootless [*British*] (DI) ... CHAR
Campaign for the Mentally Handicapped [*British*] ... CMH
Campaign for the Protection of Rural Wales [*See also YDCW*] (EAIO) ... CPRW
Campaign for the Restoration of the National Anthem and Flag [*British*] (DBA) ... CRNAF
Campaign for UN Reform (EA) ... CUNR
Campaign for World Government (EA) ... CWG
Campaign Fund for Republican Women [*Defunct*] (EA) ... CFRW
Campaign on Use and Restriction of Barbiturates [*British*] (DI) ... CURB
Campaign Poster Award [*British*] ... CPA
Campaign to Impede Sex Stereotyping in the Young [*British*] (DI) ... CISSY
Campaign to Oppose Bank Loans to South Africa [*Defunct*] (EA) ... COBLSA
Campaign to Re-Elect Mrs. [*Margaret*] **Thatcher** [*British Obsolete*] ... CREET
Campaign to Remove US Bases from the Philippines [*Later, CAB*] (EA) ... CRUSBP
Campaign to Save Native Forests, Western Australia ... CSNFWA
Campaign to Save the People of Palestine (EA) ... CSPP
Campaign to Stop Government Spying [*Later, CPR*] (EA) ... CSGS
Campana de Solidaridad con Nicaragua [*Nicaragua Solidarity Campaign*] (EAIO) ... CSN
Campanian ... CAMP
Campanile (VRA) ... cmpnl
Campbell Army Airfield [*Fort Campbell, Kentucky*] ... CAAF
Campbell College, Buies Creek, NC [*Library symbol Library of Congress*] (LCLS) ... NcBuC
Campbell Colpitts Bridge [*Electronics*] ... CCB
Campbell County Public Library, Gilete, WY [*Library symbol*] [*Library of Congress*] (LCLS) ... WyG
Campbell Foundation, Memphis, TN [*Library symbol Library of Congress*] (LCLS) ... TMCF
Campbell, Godfrey & Lewtas, Toronto, ON, Canada [*Library symbol Library of Congress*] (LCLS) ... CaOTCGL
Campbell, Godfrey & Lewtas, Toronto, Ontario [*Library symbol National Library of Canada*] (NLC) ... OTCGL
Campbell Island [*New Zealand*] [*Seismograph station code, US Geological Survey*] (SEIS) ... CBZ
Campbell Island [*New Zealand*] [*ICAO location identifier*] (ICLI) ... NZCA
Campbell. Mercantile Law [*3rd ed.*] [*1904*] [*A publication*] (DLA) ... Camp Merc L

Campbell. Negligence [*2nd ed.*] [*1878*] [*A publication*] (DLA) ... Camp Neg
Campbell, OH [*AM radio station call letters*] ... WASN
Campbell on Citation and Diligence [*A publication*] (DLA) ... Camp Cit
Campbell on Executors and Administrators in Pennsylvania [*A publication*] (DLA) ... Camp Ex
Campbell Reproductions Ltd., Ottawa, ON, Canada [*Library symbol Library of Congress*] (LCLS) ... CamR
Campbell Resources [*NYSE symbol*] (TTSB) ... CCH
Campbell Resources, Inc. [*Formerly, Campbell Chibougamau Mines Ltd.*] [*NYSE symbol Toronto Stock Exchange symbol*] (SPSG) ... CCH
Campbell Resources, Inc. [*Formerly, Campbell Chibougarnau Mines Ltd.*] [*Associated Press*] (SAG) ... CmpR
Campbell River [*Canada*] [*Airport symbol*] (OAG) ... YBL
Campbell River, BC [*AM radio station call letters*] ... CFWB
Campbell River, BC [*Television station call letters*] ... CHEK-5
Campbell River, BC [*ICAO location identifier*] (ICLI) ... CYBL
Campbell River Museum and Archives, British Columbia [*Library symbol National Library of Canada*] (NLC) ... BCRM
Campbell. Sale of Goods and Commercial Agency [*2nd ed.*] [*1891*] [*A publication*] (DLA) ... Camp Sale
Campbell Soup [*NYSE symbol*] (TTSB) ... CPB
Campbell Soup Co. [*Associated Press*] (SAG) ... CampSp
Campbell Soup Co. [*NYSE symbol*] (SPSG) ... CPB
Campbell Soup Co. Ltd. [*Toronto Stock Exchange symbol*] ... CSC
Campbell University (GAGS) ... Campbell U
Campbell University, Law Library, Buies Creek, NC [*Library symbol*] [*Library of Congress*] (LCLS) ... NcBuC-L
Campbell-Ewald Co. [*Advertising agency*] ... C-E
Campbellford Branch, Northumberland County Public Library, Ontario [*Library symbol National Library of Canada*] (NLC) ... OCA
Campbellford Public Library, Campbellford, ON, Canada [*Library symbol Library of Congress*] (LCLS) ... CaOCam
Campbell-Johnston Associates [*Commercial firm British*] ... CJA
Campbell-Larsen Potentiometer ... CLP
Campbellpore [*Pakistan*] [*Airport symbol*] (AD) ... CWP
Campbellpur [*Pakistan*] [*Seismograph station code, US Geological Survey*] (SEIS) ... CBP
Campbell's Compendium of Roman Law [*A publication*] (DLA) ... Camp
Campbell's Compendium of Roman Law [*A publication*] (DLA) ... Camp Rom L
Campbell's Compendium of Roman Law [*A publication*] (DLA) ... Camp Rom L Comp
Campbell's Compendium of Roman Law [*A publication*] (DLA) ... Campb
Campbell's Compendium of Roman Law [*A publication*] (DLA) ... Campbell
Campbell's Creek R. R. [*AAR code*] ... CCK
Campbell's English Nisi Prius Cases [*A publication*] (DLA) ... CNPC
Campbell's English Nisi Prius Reports [*A publication*] (DLA) ... Camp
Campbell's English Nisi Prius Reports [*A publication*] (DLA) ... Camp NP
Campbell's English Nisi Prius Reports [*A publication*] (DLA) ... Campb
Campbell's English Nisi Prius Reports [*A publication*] (DLA) ... Campb (Eng)
Campbell's English Nisi Prius Reports [*A publication*] (DLA) ... Campbell
Campbell's Legal Gazette Reports [*Pennsylvania*] [*A publication*] (DLA) ... Camp
Campbell's Legal Gazette Reports [*Pennsylvania*] [*A publication*] (DLA) ... Camp LG
Campbell's Legal Gazette Reports [*Pennsylvania*] [*A publication*] (DLA) ... Campb
Campbell's Legal Gazette Reports [*Pennsylvania*] [*A publication*] (DLA) ... Campb (PA)
Campbell's Legal Gazette Reports [*Pennsylvania*] [*A publication*] (DLA) ... Campbell
Campbell's Legal Gazette Reports [*Pennsylvania*] [*A publication*] (DLA) ... Leg Gaz R
Campbell's Legal Gazette Reports [*Pennsylvania*] [*A publication*] (ILCA) ... Leg Gaz Re
Campbell's Legal Gazette Reports [*Pennsylvania*] [*A publication*] (DLA) ... Leg Gaz Rep
Campbell's Lives of the Chief Justices [*A publication*] (DLA) ... Camp Ch Jus
Campbell's Lives of the Chief Justices [*A publication*] (DLA) ... Campbell
Campbell's Lives of the Lord Chancellors [*A publication*] (DLA) ... Camp Ld Ch
Campbell's Lives of the Lord Chancellors [*A publication*] (DLA) ... Camp Lives Ld Ch
Campbell's Lives of the Lord Chancellors [*A publication*] (DLA) ... Campbell
Campbell's Reports [*27-58 Nebraska*] [*A publication*] (DLA) ... Camp
Campbell's Reports [*27-58 Nebraska*] [*A publication*] (DLA) ... Campb
Campbell's Reports [*27-58 Nebraska*] [*A publication*] (DLA) ... Campbell
Campbell's Reports of Taney's United States Circuit Court Decisions [*A publication*] (DLA) ... Camp
Campbell's Reports of Taney's United States Circuit Court Decisions [*A publication*] (DLA) ... Camp Dec
Campbell's Reports of Taney's United States Circuit Court Decisions [*A publication*] (DLA) ... Campb
Campbell's Reports of Taney's United States Circuit Court Decisions [*A publication*] (DLA) ... Campb Dec
Campbell's Reports of Taney's United States Circuit Court Decisions [*A publication*] (DLA) ... Campbell
Campbell's Ruling Cases [*England*] [*A publication*] (DLA) ... Rul Cas
Campbellsville College, Campbellsville, KY [*Library symbol Library of Congress*] (LCLS) ... KyCambC
Campbellsville, KY [*Location identifier FAA*] (FAAL) ... AAS
Campbellsville, KY [*FM radio station call letters*] (RBYB) ... WAPD-FM
Campbellsville, KY [*FM radio station call letters*] ... WCKQ
Campbellsville, KY [*Television station call letters*] ... WGRB
Campbellsville, KY [*AM radio station call letters*] ... WTCO
Campbell-Tintah Elementary School, Campbell, MN [*Library symbol*] [*Library of Congress*] (LCLS) ... MnCamE
Campbell-Tintah High School, Campbell, MN [*Library symbol*] [*Library of Congress*] (LCLS) ... MnCamH
Campbellton Centennial Public Library, Campbellton, NB, Canada [*Library symbol Library of Congress*] (LCLS) ... CaNBCa
Campbellton Centennial Public Library, New Brunswick [*Library symbol National Library of Canada*] (NLC) ... NBCA
Campbellton, NB [*Television station call letters*] ... CBAT-4
Campbellton, NB [*Television station call letters*] ... CKCD
Campbellton, NB [*AM radio station call letters*] ... CKNB
Campbeltown [*Scotland*] [*Airport symbol*] (OAG) ... CAL
Campden [*England*] ... CAMP
Campden Food Preservation Research Association [*British*] (DBA) ... CFPRA
Campeau Corp. [*Toronto Stock Exchange symbol*] ... CMP
Campeche [*Mexico*] (BARN) ... Camp
Campeche [*Mexico*] [*Airport symbol*] (OAG) ... CPE
Campeche [*Mexico*] [*Airport symbol*] (AD) ... CPE
Campeche [*Mexico ICAO location identifier*] (ICLI) ... MMCP
Camper ... CMPR
Camper Alert Team [*for missile sites*] [*Air Force*] ... CAT
Campers and Caravanners' Association of New South Wales [*Australia*] ... CCANSW
Campership Outdoor Program of Education [*Federal antipoverty program*] ... COPE
Campground ... CMPGRND
Camphora [*Camphor*] [*Pharmacy*] (ROG) ... CAMPH
Camphorsulfonic Acid [*Organic chemistry*] ... CSA
Campina Grande [*Brazil*] [*Airport symbol*] (OAG) ... CPV
Campina Grande/Joao Suassuna [*Brazil ICAO location identifier*] (ICLI) ... SBKG
Campinas [*Brazil*] [*Airport symbol*] (OAG) ... CPQ
Camping ... CMPNG
Camping and Outdoor Leisure Association [*British*] (DBA) ... COLA
Camping Club Youth [*British*] ... CCY
Camping Council of Great Britain and Ireland, Ltd. ... CCGBI
Camping Products Division [*of Industrial Fabrics Association International*] (EA) ... CPD
Camping Trade Association of Great Britain Ltd. (BI) ... CTA
Camping Trailer Manufacturers Association [*Later, RVIA*] ... CTMA
Camping Women (EA) ... CW
Campionati Sciistici della Truppe Alpini [*Alpini Ski Championships*] [*Italian*] ... CaSTA
Campo Alegre [*Brazil*] [*Airport symbol*] (OAG) ... CMP
Campo, CA [*Location identifier FAA*] (FAAL) ... CZZ
Campo De Francia/Enrique A. Jimenez [*Panama*] [*ICAO location identifier*] (ICLI) ... MPCF
Campo Electr Appliances/Comp [*NASDAQ symbol*] (TTSB) ... CMPO
Campo Electronics, Appliances & Computers, Inc. [*Associated Press*] (SAG) ... CampoEl
Campo Electronics, Appliances & Computers, Inc. [*NASDAQ symbol*] (SAG) ... CMPO
Campo Grande [*Brazil*] [*Airport symbol*] (OAG) ... CGR
Campo Grande [*Brazil ICAO location identifier*] (ICLI) ... SBCD
Campo Grande/Internacional [*Brazil ICAO location identifier*] (ICLI) ... SBCG
Campobasso [*Italy ICAO location identifier*] (ICLI) ... LIBS
Campobello Public Library, Campobello, NB, Canada [*Library symbol*] [*Library of Congress*] (LCLS) ... CaNBCAM
Campobello Public Library, New Brunswick [*Library symbol National Library of Canada*] (BIB) ... NBCAM
Campomelic Dysplasia [*Medicine*] ... CD
Camp-On [*Telecommunications*] (TEL) ... CMP
Campos [*Brazil*] [*Airport symbol*] (OAG) ... CAW
Campos/Bartolomeu Lisandro [*Brazil ICAO location identifier*] (ICLI) ... SBCP
Campos/Plataforma PNA-1 [*Brazil ICAO location identifier*] (ICLI) ... SBGP
Campos/Plataforma SS-17 [*Brazil ICAO location identifier*] (ICLI) ... SBEN
Camp's Reports [*1 North Dakota*] [*A publication*] (DLA) ... Camp
Campsite ... CMPST
Campton, NH [*FM radio station call letters*] ... WVFM
Camptothecin [*Antineoplastic drug*] (CDI) ... CPT
Camptothecin Sodium [*Biochemistry*] (AAMN) ... CS
Campulung [*Romania*] [*Seismograph station code, US Geological Survey*] (SEIS) ... CMP
Campus ... CAM
Campus (ABBR) ... CMPS
Campus ... CMPS
Campus 1, Champlain Regional College, St.-Lambert, Quebec [*Library symbol National Library of Canada*] (NLC) ... QSLCR
Campus Action Network [*Defunct*] (EA) ... CAN
Campus Americans for Democratic Action [*Defunct*] (EA) ... CADA
Campus Chemical Instrument Center [*Ohio State University*] [*Research center*] (RCD) ... CCIC
Campus Conference Network [*Services by Satellite, Inc.*] [*Washington, DC*] [*Telecommunications*] (TSSD) ... CCN
Campus Crusade for Christ International (EA) ... CCC
Campus Crusade for Christ International (EA) ... CCCI
Campus Liaison Officer [*Military*] (DNAB) ... CLO
Campus Ministries of America (EA) ... CMA
Campus Ministry Women (EA) ... CMW
Campus Notre-Dame de Foy, Cap-Rouge, PQ, Canada [*Library symbol Library of Congress*] (LCLS) ... CaQCRCN
Campus Notre-Dame-De-Foy, Cap-Rouge, Quebec [*Library symbol National Library of Canada*] (NLC) ... QCRCN
Campus Outreach Opportunity League (EA) ... COOL
Campus Safety Association [*of the National Safety Council*] (EA) ... CSA
Campus Safety Association of the National Safety Council (EA) ... CSANSC
Campus Studies Institute (EA) ... CSI
Campus-Based Information System [*National Science Foundation*] ... CBIS
Campus-Free College ... CFC
Campus-Wide Information Systems [*Internet*] ... CWIS

Campylobacter-Like Organism (PDAA) .... CLO
Camreco, Inc. [Toronto Stock Exchange symbol] .... CMR
Camrose, AB [AM radio station call letters] .... CFCW
Camrose International Institute [L'Institut International de Camrose] [Formerly, Camrose One World Institute] (AC) CII
Camrose Lutheran College, Alberta [Library symbol National Library of Canada] (NLC) .... ACAL
Camrose Lutheran College, Camrose, AB, Canada [Library symbol Library of Congress] (LCLS) .... CaACAL
Camrose Public Library, Alberta [Library symbol National Library of Canada] (NLC) .... ACA
Camshaft [Automotive engineering] .... CAM
Camshaft (MSA) .... CMSHFT
Camshaft Profile Switching [Automotive engine design] .... CPS
Camuy, PR [AM radio station call letters] .... WCHQ
Camuy, PR [FM radio station call letters] .... WCHQ-FM
Can [Buoy] [Maps and charts] C
Can .... CN
Can Am Gold Resources [Vancouver Stock Exchange symbol] .... CAZ
CAN [Controller Area Network] Application Layer (ACII) .... CAL
Can Do It [Temporary-help agency] .... CDI
Can Go Over [Newspapers] .... CGO
Can Go Over (WDMC) .... cgo
Can Go Over (WDMC) .... CGO
Can Manufacturers Institute (EA) .... CMI
Can You Come and See Me .... UCM
Cana/Bohicon [Benin] [ICAO location identifier] (ICLI) .... DBBC
Canaan, VT [FM radio station call letters] .... WXMX
Canaanite (BJA) .... Can
Canaanite Myths and Legends [A publication] (BJA) .... CML
Canacord Resources, Inc. [Toronto Stock Exchange symbol] .... CQD
Canada C
Canada [ANSI two-letter standard code] (CNC) .... CA
Canada [ANSI three-letter standard code] (CNC) .... CAN
Canada (VRA) .... Can
Canada (ODBW) .... Can
Canada (WGA) .... CANAD
Canada .... CDA
Canada [MARC country of publication code Library of Congress] (LCCP) .... cn
Canada [IYRU nationality code] (IYR) .... KC
Canada [MARC geographic area code Library of Congress] (LCCP) .... n-cn--
Canada Academy & Association of Chinese Acupuncture/Medicine (AC) .... CACA
Canada & Gulf Terminal Railway (MHDB) .... C & GTR
[The] Canada & Gulf Terminal Railway Co. [AAR code] .... CGT
Canada Arctic Gas Study Ltd., Toronto, ON, Canada [Library symbol Library of Congress] (LCLS) .... CaOTCAG
Canada Arctic Gas Study Ltd., Toronto, Ontario [Library symbol National Library of Canada] (NLC) .... OTCAG
Canada Art Council [Conseil des Arts du Canada] .... CAC
Canada Art Council, Ottawa, ON, Canada [Library symbol Library of Congress] (LCLS) .... CaOOCAC
Canada Asia Working Group .... CAWG
Canada Assistance Plan .... CAP
Canada, Australia and New Zealand .... CANZ
Canada Awards for Business Excellence .... ACAE
Canada Bottle Water Federation [Federation Canadienne des Eaux Embouteillees] (AC) .... CBWF
Canada Brush, Broom & Mop Manufacturers Association [Association Candienne des Fabricants de Brosses, Balais et Vadrouilles] (AC) ...... CBBMMA
Canada Business Opportunity Centre [1986] .... CBOC
Canada Cement Co. Ltd., Montreal, PQ, Canada [Library symbol Library of Congress] (LCLS) .... CaQMCC
Canada Cement Co., Montreal, Quebec [Library symbol National Library of Canada] (NLC) .... QMCC
Canada Cement Lafarge Ltd. [Toronto Stock Exchange symbol] ...... CCT
Canada Cement Lafarge Ltd., Belleville, ON, Canada [Library symbol Library of Congress] (LCLS) .... CaOBCCL
Canada Cement Lafarge Ltd., Belleville, Ontario [Library symbol National Library of Canada] (NLC) .... OBCCL
Canada Centre for Inland Waters .... CCIW
Canada Centre for Inland Waters [Centre Canadien des Eaux Interieures], Burlington, Ontario [Library symbol National Library of Canada] (NLC) ...... OBUC
Canada Centre for Mineral and Energy Technology [Department of Energy, Mines, and Resources] [Ottawa, ON] .... CANMET
Canada Centre for Remote Sensing, Energy, Mines and Resources Canada [Centre Canadien de Teledetection, Energie, Mines et Ressources Canada] Ottawa, Ontario [Library symbol National Library of Canada] (NLC) .... OOCCR
Canada Centre for Remote Sensing Library [UTLAS symbol] .... EMC
Canada Centre for Space Science [National Research Council of Canada] [Research center] (RCD) .... CCSS
Canada Club of Victoria [Australia] CCV
Canada Coast Guard College, Sydney, NS, Canada [Library symbol Library of Congress] (LCLS) .... CaNSSCG
Canada College Library, Redwood City, CA [OCLC symbol] (OCLC) .... CCG
Canada Committee on Agricultural Engineering .... CCAE
Canada Committee on Ecological (Biophysical) Land Classification G2 [See also CCCET] .... CCELC
Canada Committee on Plant Gene Resources .... CCPGR
Canada Committee on Socio-Economic Services [See also CCSSE] .... CCSES
Canada Community Services Projects .... CCSP
Canada Council (EAIO) CC
Canada Council [Conseil des Arts du Canada] Ottawa, Ontario [Library symbol National Library of Canada] (NLC) .... OOCAC
Canada Criminal Acts, Taschereau's Edition [A publication] (DLA) ..... Can Cr Acts

Canada Criminal Cases, Annotated [A publication] (DLA) .... Can CC
Canada Department of Agriculture, Animal Diseases Research Institute (West), Lethbridge, AB, Canada [Library symbol Library of Congress] (LCLS) .... CaALADR
Canada Department of Agriculture, Canadian Farm Management Data System, Guelph, ON, Canada [Library symbol Library of Congress] (LCLS) .... CaOGCF
Canada Department of Agriculture, Canadian Grain Commission, Winnipeg, MB, Canada [Library symbol Library of Congress] (LCLS) .... CaMWGR
Canada Department of Agriculture, Economics Branch, Regina, SK, Canada [Library symbol Library of Congress] (LCLS) .... CaSRAgE
Canada Department of Agriculture, Entomological Society of British Columbia Library, Vancouver, BC, Canada [Library symbol Library of Congress] (LCLS) .... CaBVaAg
Canada Department of Agriculture, Experimental Farm, La Pocatiere, PQ, Canada [Library symbol Library of Congress] (LCLS) ..... CaQPAg
Canada Department of Agriculture, Experimental Farm, L'Assomption, PQ, Canada [Library symbol Library of Congress] (LCLS) .... CaQAsAg
Canada Department of Agriculture, Lethbridge, AB, Canada [Library symbol Library of Congress] (LCLS) .... CaALAg
Canada Department of Agriculture, Ottawa, ON, Canada [Library symbol Library of Congress] (LCLS) .... CaOOAg
Canada Department of Agriculture, Research Institute, Belleville, ON, Canada [Library symbol Library of Congress Obsolete] (LCLS) .... CaOBP
Canada Department of Agriculture, Research Institute, London, ON, Canada [Library symbol Library of Congress] (LCLS) .... CaOLAg
Canada Department of Agriculture, Research Station, Agassiz, BC, Canada [Library symbol Library of Congress] (LCLS) .... CaBAgAg
Canada Department of Agriculture, Research Station, Beaverlodge, AB, Canada [Library symbol Library of Congress] (LCLS) .... CaABeAg
Canada Department of Agriculture, Research Station, Brandon, MB, Canada [Library symbol Library of Congress] (LCLS) .... CaMBAg
Canada Department of Agriculture, Research Station, Charlottetown, PE, Canada [Library symbol Library of Congress] (LCLS) .... CaPCAg
Canada Department of Agriculture, Research Station, Delhi, ON, Canada [Library symbol Library of Congress] (LCLS) .... CaODeAg
Canada Department of Agriculture, Research Station, Fredericton, NB, Canada [Library symbol Library of Congress] (LCLS) .... CaNBFAg
Canada Department of Agriculture, Research Station, Harrow, ON, Canada [Library symbol Library of Congress] (LCLS) .... CaOHarAg
Canada Department of Agriculture, Research Station, Kamloops, BC, Canada [Library symbol Library of Congress] (LCLS) .... CaBKAg
Canada Department of Agriculture, Research Station, Kentville, NS, Canada [Library symbol Library of Congress] (LCLS) .... CaNSKR
Canada Department of Agriculture, Research Station, Lacombe, AB, Canada [Library symbol Library of Congress] (LCLS) .... CaALaAg
Canada Department of Agriculture, Research Station, Morden, MB, Canada [Library symbol Library of Congress] (LCLS) .... CaMMoAg
Canada Department of Agriculture, Research Station, Regina, SK, Canada [Library symbol Library of Congress] (LCLS) .... CaSRAgR
Canada Department of Agriculture, Research Station, Saanichton, BC, Canada [Library symbol Library of Congress] (LCLS) .... CaBSAg
Canada Department of Agriculture, Research Station, Ste.-Foy, PQ, Canada [Library symbol Library of Congress] (LCLS) .... CaQSFAg
Canada Department of Agriculture, Research Station, St. John's, NF, Canada [Library symbol Library of Congress] (LCLS) .... CaNfsAg
Canada Department of Agriculture, Research Station, Saint-Jean, PQ, Canada [Library symbol Library of Congress] (LCLS) .... CaQStJAg
Canada Department of Agriculture, Research Station, Saskatoon, SK, Canada [Library symbol Library of Congress] (LCLS) .... CaSSAgR
Canada Department of Agriculture, Research Station, Summerland, BC, Canada [Library symbol Library of Congress] (LCLS) .... CaBSuAg
Canada Department of Agriculture, Research Station, Swift Current, SK, Canada [Library symbol Library of Congress] (LCLS) .... CaSSCAg
Canada Department of Agriculture, Research Station, Vineland Station, ON, Canada [Library symbol Library of Congress] (LCLS) .... CaOVAgR
Canada Department of Agriculture, Research Station, Winnipeg, MB, Canada [Library symbol Library of Congress] (LCLS) .... CaMWAG
Canada Department of Agriculture, Winnipeg, MB, Canada [Library symbol Library of Congress] (LCLS) .... CaMWA
Canada Department of Communications, Central Region Information Resources Center, Winnipeg, MB, Canada [Library symbol Library of Congress] (LCLS) .... CaMWCCIR
Canada Department of Communications, Communications Research Centre, Ottawa, ON, Canada [Library symbol Library of Congress] (LCLS) .... CaOORPL
Canada Department of Communications, Ottawa, ON, Canada [Library symbol Library of Congress] (LCLS) .... CaOOCO
Canada Department of Consumer and Corporate Affairs, Ottawa, ON, Canada [Library symbol Library of Congress] (LCLS) .... CaOOCI
Canada Department of Energy, Mines, and Resources, Canada Centre for Remote Sensing, Ottawa, ON, Canada [Library symbol Library of Congress] (LCLS) .... CaOOCCR
Canada Department of Energy, Mines, and Resources, Earth Physics Branch, Ottawa,ON, Canada [Library symbol Library of Congress] (LCLS) .... CaOOO
Canada Department of Energy, Mines, and Resources, Energy Development Sector, Ottawa, ON, Canada [Library symbol Library of Congress Obsolete] (LCLS) .... CaOOEME
Canada Department of Energy, Mines, and Resources, Map Library, Ottawa, ON, Canada [Library symbol Library of Congress] (LCLS) .... CaOOSMM
Canada Department of Energy, Mines, and Resources, Physical Metallurgy Division,Ottawa, ON, Canada [Library symbol Library of Congress] (LCLS) .... CaOOMP

Canada Department of Energy, Mines, and Resources, Resources Economic Library, Ottawa, ON, Canada [*Library symbol Library of Congress*] (LCLS) .... CaOOMR

Canada Department of Energy, Mines, and Resources, Surveys and Mapping Branch, Ottawa, ON, Canada [*Library symbol Library of Congress*] (LCLS) .... CaOOSM

Canada Department of External Affairs, Legal Branch, Ottawa, ON, Canada [*Library symbol Library of Congress*] (LCLS) .... CaOOELB

Canada Department of External Affairs, Ottawa, ON, Canada [*Library symbol Library of Congress*] (LCLS) .... CaOOE

Canada Department of Finance, Ottawa, ON, Canada [*Library symbol Library of Congress*] (LCLS) .... CaOOF

Canada Department of Fisheries and Ocean, St. John's, NF, Canada [*Library symbol*] [*Library of Congress*] (LCLS) .... CaNfSF

Canada Department of Fisheries and Oceans, Institute of Ocean Studies, Sidney, BC, Canada [*Library symbol Library of Congress*] (LCLS) .... CaBSIOS

Canada Department of Fisheries and Oceans, St. Johns, NF, Canada [*Library symbol Library of Congress*] (LCLS) .... CaNfSEC

Canada Department of Fisheries and Oceans, Vancouver, BC, Canada [*Library symbol Library of Congress*] (LCLS) .... CaBVaFi

Canada Department of Fisheries and the Environment, Fisheries and Marine Service, Quebec, PQ, Canada [*Library symbol Library of Congress*] (LCLS) .... CaQQPSM

Canada Department of Indian Affairs and Northern Development, Battleford National HistoricPark, Battleford, SK, Canada [*Library symbol*] [*Library of Congress*] (LCLS) .... CaSBIN

Canada Department of Indian Affairs and Northern Development, Inuvik Research Laboratory, Inuvik, NT, Canada [*Library symbol Library of Congress*] (LCLS) .... CaNWII

Canada Department of Indian Affairs and Northern Development, Ottawa, ON, Canada [*Library symbol*] [*Library of Congress*] (LCLS) .... CaOORD

Canada Department of Indian Affairs and Northern Development, Parks Canada, Atlantic Regional Office, Halifax, NS, Canada [*Library symbol*] [*Library of Congress*] (LCLS) .... CaNSHIAP

Canada Department of Indian Affairs and Northern Development, Parks Canada, Ontario Regional Office, Cornwall, ON, Canada [*Library symbol*] [*Library of Congress*] (LCLS) .... CaOGIAP

Canada Department of Indian Affairs and Northern Development, Parks Canada, Quebec Regional Office, Ste-Foy, Quebec, PQ, Canada [*Library symbol Library of Congress*] (LCLS) .... CaQQIAP

Canada Department of Indian Affairs and Northern Development, Parks Canada, Western Regional Office, Calgary, AB, Canada [*Library symbol Library of Congress*] (LCLS) .... CaACIA

Canada Department of Indian Affairs and Northern Development, Point Pelee National Park, Leamington, ON, Canada [*Library symbol Library of Congress*] (LCLS) .... CaOLeI

Canada Department of Indian and Northern Affairs, Prince Albert, SK, Canada [*Library symbol Library of Congress*] (LCLS) .... CaSPAIN

Canada Department of Indian and Northern Affairs, Yellowknife, NT, Canada [*Library symbol Library of Congress*] (LCLS) .... CaNWYIM

Canada Department of Industry, Ottawa, ON, Canada [*Library symbol Library of Congress Obsolete*] (LCLS) .... CaOOI

Canada Department of Industry, Trade, and Commerce, Ottawa, ON, Canada [*Library symbol Library of Congress*] (LCLS) .... CaOOTC

Canada Department of Insurance, Ottawa, ON, Canada [*Library symbol Library of Congress*] (LCLS) .... CaOOIn

Canada Department of Justice, Edmonton, AB, Canada [*Library symbol Library of Congress*] (LCLS) .... CaAEJ

Canada Department of Justice [*Ministere de la Justice*] Edmonton, Alberta [*Library symbol National Library of Canada*] (NLC) .... AEJ

Canada Department of Justice [*Ministere de la Justice*] Halifax, Nova Scotia [*Library symbol National Library of Canada*] (NLC) .... NSHJ

Canada Department of Justice, Halifax, NS, Canada [*Library symbol Library of Congress*] (LCLS) .... CaNSHJ

Canada Department of Justice, Montreal, PQ, Canada [*Library symbol Library of Congress*] (LCLS) .... CaQMJM

Canada Department of Justice [*Ministere de la Justice*] Montreal, Quebec [*Library symbol National Library of Canada*] (NLC) .... QMJM

Canada Department of Justice, Occupational Analysis Library, Ottawa, ON, Canada [*Library symbol Library of Congress Obsolete*] (LCLS) .... CaOOOA

Canada Department of Justice, Ottawa, ON, Canada [*Library symbol Library of Congress*] (LCLS) .... CaOOJ

Canada Department of Justice, Toronto, ON, Canada [*Library symbol Library of Congress*] (LCLS) .... CaOTJ

Canada Department of Justice, Vancouver, BC, Canada [*Library symbol Library of Congress*] (LCLS) .... CaBVaJ

Canada Department of Justice [*Ministere de la Justice*] Vancouver, British Columbia [*Library symbol National Library of Canada*] (NLC) .... BVAJ

Canada Department of Justice [*Ministere de la Justice*] Winnipeg, Manitoba [*Library symbol National Library of Canada*] (NLC) .... MWJ

Canada Department of Justice, Winnipeg, MB, Canada [*Library symbol Library of Congress*] (LCLS) .... CaMWJ

Canada Department of Labour, Occupational Safety and Health Branch, Ottawa, ON, Canada [*Library symbol Library of Congress*] (LCLS) ...... CaOOLAP

Canada Department of Labour, Ottawa, ON, Canada [*Library symbol Library of Congress*] (LCLS) .... CaOOL

Canada Department of Manpower and Immigration, Halifax, NS, Canada [*Library symbol Library of Congress Obsolete*] (LCLS) .... CaNSHMI

Canada Department of Manpower and Immigration, Prince Albert, SK, Canada [*Library symbol Library of Congress Obsolete*] (LCLS) .... CaSPAMI

Canada Department of Manpower and Immigration, Winnipeg, MB, Canada [*Library symbol Library of Congress*] (LCLS) .... CaMWMI

Canada Department of Mines and Resources, Centre for Inland Waters, Burlington, ON, Canada [*Library symbol Library of Congress*] (LCLS) .... CaOBUC

Canada Department of National Defence, Canadian Forces Staff School, Toronto, ON, Canada [*Library symbol Library of Congress*] (LCLS) ..... CaOTRCS

Canada Department of National Defence, Defence Research Establishment, Esquimalt, BC, Canada [*Library symbol Library of Congress*] (LCLS) .... CaBEPN

Canada Department of National Defence, Defence Research Establishment, Ottawa, ON, Canada [*Library symbol Library of Congress*] (LCLS) ...... CaOODRC

Canada Department of National Defence, Defence Research Establishment Suffield, Ralston, AB, Canada [*Library symbol*] [*Library of Congress*] (LCLS) .... CaARS

Canada Department of National Defence, Headquarters Mobile Command, St. Hubert, PQ, Canada [*Library symbol Library of Congress*] (LCLS) .... CaQStHuM

Canada Department of National Defence, Northern Region Information System, [*NORIS*], Yellowknife, NT, Canada [*Library symbol Library of Congress*] (LCLS) .... CaNWYND

Canada Department of National Defence, Ottawa, ON, Canada [*Library symbol Library of Congress Obsolete*] (LCLS) .... CaOOAM

Canada Department of National Defence, Quality Assurance Division, Ottawa, ON, Canada [*Library symbol Library of Congress*] (LCLS) .... CaOOQA

Canada Department of National Defence, Reference and Recreational Library [*Stadacona*], Halifax, NS, Canada [*Library symbol Library of Congress*] (LCLS) .... CaNSHND

Canada Department of National Defence Research Establishment Atlantic, Dartmouth, NS, Canada [*Library symbol Library of Congress*] (LCLS) .... CaNSHN

Canada Department of National Health and Welfare, Food and Drug Directorate, Ottawa, ON, Canada [*Library symbol Library of Congress*] (LCLS) .... CaOOFD

Canada Department of National Health and Welfare, Health Protection Branch, Laboratory Centre for Disease Control, Ottawa, ON, Canada [*Library symbol*] [*Library of Congress*] (LCLS) .... CaOONHL

Canada Department of National Health and Welfare, Health Protection Branch, Montreal, PQ, Canada [*Library symbol Library of Congress*] (LCLS) .... CaQMNHH

Canada Department of National Health and Welfare, Health Protection Branch, Toronto, ON, Canada [*Library symbol*] [*Library of Congress*] (LCLS) .... CaOTNHH

Canada Department of National Health and Welfare, Health Protection Branch, Vancouver, BC, Canada [*Library symbol Library of Congress*] (LCLS) .... CaBVaNH

Canada Department of National Revenue, Customs and Excise Division, Ottawa, ON, Canada [*Library symbol Library of Congress*] (LCLS) .... CaOONR

Canada Department of National Revenue, Taxation Division, Ottawa, ON, Canada [*Library symbol Library of Congress*] (LCLS) .... CaOONRT

Canada Department of Public Works, Capital Region Library, Ottawa, ON, Canada [*Library symbol Library of Congress*] (LCLS) .... CaOOPWC

Canada Department of Public Works, Office of the Dominion Fire Commissioner, Ottawa, ON, Canada [*Library symbol Library of Congress Obsolete*] (LCLS) .... CaOOPWD

Canada Department of Public Works, Ottawa, ON, Canada [*Library symbol Library of Congress*] (LCLS) .... CaOOPW

Canada Department of Public Works, Research and Development Laboratories, Ottawa, ON, Canada [*Library symbol Library of Congress*] (LCLS) .... CaOOPWR

Canada Department of Regional Economic Expansion, Moncton, NB, Canada [*Library symbol Library of Congress*] (LCLS) .... CaNBMoRE

Canada Department of Regional Economic Expansion, Ottawa, ON, Canada [*Library symbol Library of Congress*] (LCLS) .... CaOOREx

Canada Department of Regional Economic Expansion, Prairie Farm Rehabilitation Administration, Regina, SK, Canada [*Library symbol Library of Congress*] (LCLS) .... CaSRREE

Canada Department of Regional Economic Expansion, Reference and Enquiries Unit, Ottawa, ON, Canada [*Library symbol Library of Congress Obsolete*] (LCLS) .... CaOORExR

Canada Department of Regional Economic Expansion, St. John's, NF, Canada [*Library symbol Library of Congress*] (LCLS) .... CaNfSREx

Canada Department of Regional Economic Expansion, Toronto, ON, Canada [*Library symbol Library of Congress*] (LCLS) .... CaOTREx

Canada Department of Regional Industrial Expansion [*Ministere de l'Expansion Industrielle Regionale*] Moncton, New Brunswick [*Library symbol National Library of Canada*] (NLC) .... NBMORE

Canada Department of Regional Industrial Expansion [*Ministere de l'Expansion Industrielle Regionale*] Montreal, Quebec [*Library symbol National Library of Canada*] (NLC) .... QMREX

Canada Department of Regional Industrial Expansion [*Ministere de l'Expansion Industrielle Regionale*] St. John's, Newfoundland [*Library symbol National Library of Canada*] (NLC) .... NFSREX

Canada Department of Regional Industrial Expansion [*Ministere de l'Expansion Industrielle Regionale*] Saskatoon, Saskatchewan [*Library symbol National Library of Canada*] (NLC) .... SSREX

Canada Department of Regional Industrial Expansion [*Ministere de l'Expansion Industrielle Regionale*] Toronto, Ontario [*Library symbol National Library of Canada*] (NLC) .... OTREX

Canada Department of Revenue, Canada Customs and Excise, Scientific and Technical Information Centre, Laboratory and Scientific Services Division, Ottawa, ON, Canada [*Library symbol Library of Congress*] (LCLS) .... CaOOSTI

Canada Department of Supply and Services, Bureau of Management and Consulting, Ottawa, ON, Canada [*Library symbol Library of Congress*] (LCLS) .... CaOOBMC

Canada Department of Supply and Services, Compensation Branch, Superannuation Division, Ottawa, ON, Canada [*Library symbol Library of Congress*] (LCLS) .... CaOODPS

Canada Department of Supply and Services, Ottawa, ON, Canada [*Library symbol Library of Congress*] (LCLS) .... CaOODP

Canada Department of the Environment, Atmospheric Environment Service, Atlantic Region, Halifax, NS, Canada [*Library symbol Library of Congress*] (LCLS) .... CaNSHW

Canada Department of the Environment, Atmospheric Environment Service, Toronto, ON, Canada [*Library symbol Library of Congress*] (LCLS) .... CaOTM

Canada Department of the Environment, Bedford Institute of Oceanography, Dartmouth, NS, Canada [*Library symbol Library of Congress*] (LCLS) .... CaNSDB

Canada Department of the Environment, Canadian Wildlife Service, Edmonton, AB, Canada [*Library symbol Library of Congress*] (LCLS) .... CaAEECW

Canada Department of the Environment, Canadian Wildlife Service, Ottawa, ON, Canada [*Library symbol Library of Congress*] (LCLS) ..... CaOOECW

Canada Department of the Environment, Canadian Wildlife Service, Prairie Migratory Bird Research Centre, Saskatoon, SK, Canada [*Library symbol Library of Congress*] (LCLS) .... CaSSECW

Canada Department of the Environment, Canadian Wildlife Service, Sackville, NB, Canada [*Library symbol Library of Congress*] (LCLS) .... CaNBSaCW

Canada Department of the Environment, Environmental Protection Service, Vancouver, BC, Canada [*Library symbol Library of Congress*] (LCLS) .... CaBVaEP

Canada Department of the Environment, Environmental Protection Services, Montreal, PQ, Canada [*Library symbol*] [*Library of Congress*] (LCLS) .... CaQMEE

Canada Department of the Environment, Fisheries and Marine Service, Halifax, NS, Canada [*Library symbol*] [*Library of Congress*] (LCLS) .... CaNSHF

Canada Department of the Environment, Fisheries and Marine Service, Research and Development Directorate Biological Station, St. Andrews, NB, Canada [*Library symbol*] [*Library of Congress*] (LCLS).... CaNBAB

Canada Department of the Environment, Fisheries and Marine Service, Research andDevelopment Directorate, Pacific Biological Station, Nanaimo, BC, Canada [*Library symbol Library of Congress*] (LCLS) .... CaBNP

Canada Department of the Environment, Fisheries and Marine Service, Research andDevelopment Directorate, Vancouver Laboratory, Vancouver, BC, Canada [*Library symbol Library of Congress*] (LCLS).... CaBVaF

Canada Department of the Environment, Fisheries and Marine Service, Ste.-Anne-De-Bellevue, PQ, Canada [*Library symbol Library of Congress*] (LCLS) .... CaQMFR

Canada Department of the Environment, Fontaine Branch Library, Ottawa, ON, Canada [*Library symbol Library of Congress*] (LCLS) .... CaOOEF

Canada Department of the Environment, Forest Fire Research Institute, Ottawa, ON, Canada [*Library symbol Library of Congress*] (LCLS) .... CaOOFFR

Canada Department of the Environment, Forest Products Laboratory, Ottawa, ON, Canada [*Cl osed*] [*Library symbol*] [*Library of Congress*] (LCLS) .... CaOOFP

Canada Department of the Environment, Forest Products Laboratory, Vancouver, BC,Canada [*Library symbol Library of Congress*] (LCLS) .... CaBVaFP

Canada Department of the Environment, Forest Research Laboratory, Quebec, PQ, Canada [*Library symbol Library of Congress*] (LCLS) .... CaQQMF

Canada Department of the Environment, Forest Research Laboratory, Victoria, BC, Canada [*Library symbol Library of Congress*] (LCLS) .... CaBViF

Canada Department of the Environment, Institute of Ocean Sciences, Victoria, BC,Canada [*Library symbol Library of Congress*] (LCLS) .... CaBViEM

Canada Department of the Environment, Maritimes Forest Research Centre, Fredericton, NB, Canada [*Library symbol Library of Congress*] (LCLS) .... CaNBFE

Canada Department of the Environment, Northern Forest Research Centre, Edmonton,AB, Canada [*Library symbol Library of Congress*] (LCLS) .... CaAEF

Canada Department of the Environment, Ottawa, ON, Canada [*Library symbol Library of Congress*] (LCLS) .... CaOOFF

Canada Department of the Environment, Pacific Environment Institute, Vancouver, BC, Canada [*Library symbol Library of Congress*] (LCLS) .... CaBVaPE

Canada Department of the Environment, Petawawa Forest Experiment Station, Chalk River, ON, Canada [*Library symbol Library of Congress*] (LCLS) .... CaOCkE

Canada Department of the Environment, Quebec Region, Ste.-Foy, Quebec, PQ, Canada [*Library symbol Library of Congress*] (LCLS) .... CaQQE

Canada Department of the Environment, Research Station, Sault Ste. Marie, ON, Canada [*Library symbol Library of Congress*] (LCLS) .... CaOStMF

Canada Department of the Environment, Resource and Environmental Law Library, Ottawa, ON, Canada [*Library symbol Library of Congress Obsolete*] (LCLS) .... CaOOERE

Canada Department of the Environment, Sea Lamprey Control Centre, Sault Ste. Marie, ON, Canada [*Library symbol Library of Congress*] (LCLS) .... CaOStMEF

Canada Department of the Secretary of State, Ottawa, ON, Canada [*Library symbol Library of Congress*] (LCLS) .... CaOOSS

Canada Department of the Secretary of State, Translation Bureau, Montreal, PQ, Canada [*Library symbol Library of Congress*] (LCLS) .... CaQMBD

Canada Department of the Secretary of State, Translation Bureau, Multilingual Services Division, Ottawa, ON, Canada [*Library symbol Library of Congress Obsolete*] (LCLS) .... CaOOSST

Canada Department of the Secretary of State, Translation Bureau, Terminology Centre Library, Ottawa, ON, Canada [*Library symbol Library of Congress*] (LCLS) .... CaOOSSTT

Canada Department of the Solicitor General, Ottawa, ON, Canada [*Library symbol Library of Congress*] (LCLS) .... CaOOSG

Canada Department of Veterans Affairs, Ottawa, ON, Canada [*Library symbol Library of Congress*] (LCLS) .... CaOOV

Canada Deposit Insurance Corp. .... CDIC

Canada Development Corp. [*Toronto Stock Exchange symbol Vancouver Stock Exchange symbol*] .... CDC

Canada Development Investment Corp. [*Corp. de Developpement des Inve stissements du Canada*] .... CDIC

Canada East .... CE

Canada Emergency Measures Organization [*Civil defense*] .... CEMO

Canada Employment and Immigration Advisory Council (EDAC) .... CEIAC

Canada Employment and Immigration Commission .... CEIC

Canada Employment and Immigration Department, Ottawa, ON, Canada [*Library symbol Library of Congress*] (LCLS) .... CaOOMI

Canada Employment and Immigration Department, Quebec Regional Office, Montreal, PQ, Canada [*Library symbol Library of Congress*] (LCLS) .... CaQMMIQ

Canada Employment and Immigration Department, Toronto, ON, Canada [*Library symbol Library of Congress*] (LCLS) .... CaOTMIO

Canada Employment and Immigration Department, Vancouver, BC, Canada [*Library symbol Library of Congress*] (LCLS) .... CaBVaMI

Canada Employment and Immigration Union .... CEIU

Canada Employment Centre .... CEC

Canada Exchequer Court Reports [*1875-1922*] [*A publication*] (DLA) .... Ex CR

Canada [*or Canadian*] **Farm Building Plan Service** .... CFBPS

Canada Farm Labor Pool .... CFLP

Canada Federal Court Reports [*A publication*] (DLA) .... Can FCR

Canada Fortnightly Law Journal [*A publication*] (DLA) .... FLJ

Canada Gazette (Regulations) [*A publication*] (DLA) .... Can Gaz

Canada Geographic Information System [*Canada Land Data Systems Division*] [*Environment Canada*] [*Information service or system*] (IID) .... CGIS

Canada Geological Survey, Vancouver, BC, Canada [*Library symbol Library of Congress*] (LCLS) .... CaBVaG

Canada, Hungary, Indonesia, and Poland [*Countries comprising the International Commission of Control and Supervision, charged with supervising the cease-fire in Vietnam, 1973*] .... CHIP

Canada in World Affairs [*A publication*] (DLA) .... Can in Wld Aff

Canada Income Plus Fund 1986 Trust Units [*Toronto Stock Exchange symbol*] .... CNFUN

Canada Income Plus Fund 1987 Trust Units [*Toronto Stock Exchange symbol*] .... CUF

Canada Income Plus Fund Trust Units [*Toronto Stock Exchange symbol*] .... CIB

Canada Institute for Scientific and Technical Information [*National Research Council of Canada*] (IID) .... CISTI

Canada Institute for Scientific and Technical Information, Administration Building Library, Ottawa, ON, Canada [*Library symbol Library of Congress*] (LCLS) .... CaOONAB

Canada Institute for Scientific and Technical Information, Aeronautical and Mechanical Engineering Branch, Ottawa, ON, Canada [*Library symbol Library of Congress*] (LCLS) .... CaOONAM

Canada Institute for Scientific and Technical Information, Chemistry Library, Ottawa, ON, Canada [*Library symbol Library of Congress*] (LCLS) .... CaOONC

Canada Institute for Scientific and Technical Information, Division of Building Research, Ottawa, ON, Canada [*Library symbol Library of Congress*] (LCLS) .... CaOONBR

Canada Institute for Scientific and Technical Information, National Research Council (CISTI) [*Institut Canadien de l'Information Scientifique et Technique, Conseil National de Recherches (ICIST)*] **Ottawa, Ontario** [*Library symbol National Library of Canada*] (NLC) .... OON

Canada Institute for Scientific and Technical Information, National Research Council, Ottawa, ON, Canada [*Library symbol Library of Congress*] (LCLS) .... CaOON

Canada Institute for Scientific and Technical Information, Radio and Electrical Engineering Division, Ottawa, ON, Canada [*Library symbol Library of Congress*] (LCLS) .... CaOONRE

Canada Institute for Scientific and Technical Information, Sussex Library, Ottawa, ON, Canada [*Library symbol Library of Congress*] (LCLS) .... CaOONS

Canada Institute for Scientific and Technical Information, Uplands Library, Ottawa, ON, Canada [*Library symbol Library of Congress*] (LCLS) .... CaOONU

Canada Labour Relations Board .... CLRB

Canada Labour Relations Board, Ottawa, ON, Canada [*Library symbol Library of Congress*] (LCLS) .... CaOOLRB

Canada Labour Relations Board [*Conseil Canadien des Relations de Travail*] **Ottawa, Ontario** [*Library symbol National Library of Canada*] (NLC) .... OOLRB

Canada Land Data System .... CLDS

Canada Land Inventory CLI

Canada Land Surveyor .... CLS

Canada Law Journal [*A publication*] (DLA) .... Can LJ

Canada Law Journal [*A publication*] (DLA) .... CLJ

Canada Law Journal, New Series [*A publication*] (DLA) .... Can LJ NS

Canada Law Journal, Old Series [*A publication*] (DLA) .... UCLJ OS

Canada Law Reform Commission (DLA) .... CLRC

Canada Law Reports [*A publication*] (DLA) .... CLR

Canada Law Reports, Exchequer Court [*A publication*] (DLA) .... Can Ex

Canada Law Reports, Exchequer Court [*A publication*] (DLA) .... Can Ex CR

Canada Law Reports, Exchequer Court [*A publication*] (DLA) .... Can Ex R

Canada Law Reports, Exchequer Court [*A publication*] (DLA) .... Can Exch

Canada Law Reports, Exchequer Court [*A publication*] (DLA) .... ECR

Canada Law Reports, Exchequer Court [*A publication*] (DLA) .... Ex CR

Canada Law Reports, Exchequer Court [*A publication*] (DLA) .... Exch C

Canada Law Reports, Exchequer Court [*A publication*] (DLA) .... Exch Can

Canada Law Reports, Exchequer Court [*A publication*] (DLA) .... Exch CR

Canada Law Reports, Exchequer Court [*A publication*] (DLA) .... Exch Ct (Can)

Canada Law Reports, Exchequer Court and Supreme Court [*A publication*] (DLA) .... Can LR

Canada Law Reports, Exchequer Court and Supreme Court [*A publication*] (DLA) .... CLR (Can)

Canada Law Reports, Federal Court [*A publication*] (DLA) .... FC

Canada Law Reports, Supreme Court [*A publication*] (DLA) ...... Can S Ct
Canada Lease Financing Ltd. [*Toronto Stock Exchange symbol*] ...... CQF
Canada Legal News [*A publication*] (DLA) ...... Can Leg N
Canada Malting Co. Ltd. [*Toronto Stock Exchange symbol*] ...... CMG
Canada Manpower Centre ...... CMC
Canada Manpower Industrial Training ...... CMIT
Canada Manpower Mobility Program ...... CMMP
Canada Manpower Training Program ...... CMTP
Canada Marketing Assistance Program ...... CANMAP
Canada Medal ...... CM
Canada Ministry of State for Science and Technology, Ottawa, ON, Canada [*Library symbol Library of Congress*] (LCLS) ...... CaOOMSS
Canada Ministry of State for Urban Affairs, Ottawa, ON, Canada [*Library symbol Library of Congress*] (LCLS) ...... CaOOMUA
Canada Ministry of the Solicitor General, Penitentiary, Federal Training Centre,Laval, PQ, Canada [*Library symbol Library of Congress*] (LCLS) ...... CaQLASGPT
Canada Ministry of Transport, Canadian Air Transportation Administration, Ontario Region, Toronto, ON, Canada [*Library symbol Library of Congress*] (LCLS) ...... CaOTTOA
Canada Ministry of Transport, Marine Library, Halifax, NS, Canada [*Library symbol Library of Congress*] (LCLS) ...... CaNSHMT
Canada Ministry of Transport Training Institute, Ottawa, ON, Canada [*Library symbol Library of Congress*] (LCLS) ...... CaOOTI
Canada Ministry of Transport, Transportation Development Agency, Montreal, PQ, Canada [*Library symbol Library of Congress*] (LCLS) ...... CaQMTD
Canada Ministry of Transport, Waterways Development, Montreal, PQ, Canada [*Library symbol Library of Congress*] (LCLS) ...... CaQMTR
Canada Mink Breeders Association [*Association des Eleveurs de Visions du Canada*] (AC) ...... CMBA
Canada Mortgage and Housing Corp. [*Government agency*] ...... CMHC
Canada Network [*Computer science*] (TNIG) ...... CAnet
Canada News-Wire [*Database*] [*Canada News-Wire Service*] [*Information service or system*] (CRD) ...... CNW
Canada Northwest Energy Ltd. [*Toronto Stock Exchange symbol*] ...... CNW
Canada Oil and Gas Lands Administration ...... COGLA
Canada Oil Low Acid [*Variety of rapeseed*] ...... CANOLA
Canada Oil Substitution Program ...... COSP
Canada Olympic Park [*Calgary, AB*] ...... COP
Canada Orient Resources [*Vancouver Stock Exchange symbol*] ...... CDO
Canada Packers Ltd., Toronto, Ontario [*Library symbol National Library of Canada*] (NLC) ...... OTCP
Canada Pension Plan ...... CPP
Canada Permanent Mortgage Corp. [*Toronto Stock Exchange symbol*] ...... CDP
Canada Plan Service ...... CPS
Canada Post Corporation Library [*UTLAS symbol*] ...... CPC
Canada Post [*Postes Canada*] **Ottawa, Ontario** [*Library symbol National Library of Canada*] (NLC) ...... OOPO
Canada Privy Council Office, Management Information, Ottawa, ON, Canada [*Library symbol Library of Congress*] (LCLS) ...... CaOOPC
Canada Publishing Corp., Agincourt, ON, Canada [*Library symbol*] [*Library of Congress*] (LCLS) ...... CaOAgCP
Canada Publishing Corp., Agincourt, Ontario [*Library symbol National Library of Canada*] (BIB) ...... OACP
Canada Railway Cases [*A publication*] (DLA) ...... Can Ry Cas
Canada Regional Industrial Expansion [*Expansion Industrielle Regionale*], Prince Albert, Saskatchewan [*Library symbol National Library of Canada*] (BIB) ...... SPAREX
Canada Remote Systems Ltd. [*Information service or system*] (IID) ...... CRS
Canada Road [*California*] [*Seismograph station code, US Geological Survey*] (SEIS) ...... CDC
Canada Safety Council (AC) ...... CSC
Canada Safety Council, Ottawa, ON, Canada [*Library symbol*] [*Library of Congress*] (LCLS) ...... CaOOCSC
Canada Safety Council [*Conseil Canadien de la Securite*] **Ottawa, Ontario** [*Library symbol National Library of Canada*] (NLC) ...... OOCSC
Canada Safeway Ltd. [*Toronto Stock Exchange symbol*] ...... CNS
Canada Savings Bond [*Investment term*] ...... CSB
Canada Southern Petroleum Ltd. [*Associated Press*] (SAG) ...... CanSoPt
Canada Southern Petroleum Ltd. [*NASDAQ symbol*] (SAG) ...... CSPL
Canada Southern Petroleum Ltd. [*Toronto Stock Exchange symbol*] ...... CSW
Canada Southern Railway [*Penn Central*] [*AAR code*] ...... CASO
Canada South'n Petrol [*NASDAQ symbol*] (TTSB) ...... CSPLF
Canada Standard Size [*Of Clothing*] (BARN) ...... CSS
Canada Starch Co. ...... CASCO
Canada Steamship Lines ...... CSL
Canada Steamship Lines [*AAR code*] ...... CSSL
Canada Student Loans Program ...... CSLP
Canada Studies Foundation [*See also FEC*] ...... CSF
Canada Supreme Court (DLA) ...... Can SC
Canada Supreme Court (DLA) ...... CSC
Canada Supreme Court Reports [*A publication*] (DLA) ...... Can S Ct
Canada Supreme Court Reports [*A publication*] (DLA) ...... Can SC
Canada Supreme Court Reports [*A publication*] (DLA) ...... Can SC Rep
Canada Supreme Court Reports [*A publication*] (DLA) ...... Can SCR
Canada Supreme Court Reports [*A publication*] (DLA) ...... Can Sup Ct
Canada Systems Group [*Database producer*] [*Ottawa, ON*] [*Information service or system*] ...... CSG
Canada Systems Group, Mississauga, ON, Canada [*Library symbol Library of Congress*] (LCLS) ...... CaOMCSG
Canada Systems Group, Mississauga, Ontario [*Library symbol National Library of Canada*] (NLC) ...... OMCSG
Canada Tax Appeal Board Cases [*A publication*] (DLA) ...... Can Tax App Bd
Canada Tax Appeal Board Cases [*A publication*] (DLA) ...... Tax ABC
Canada Tax Cases [*A publication*] (DLA) ...... Can Tax Cas

Canada Tax Cases [*A publication*] (DLA) ...... CTC
Canada Tax Cases, Annotated [*A publication*] (DLA) ...... Can Tax Cas Ann
Canada Tax Cases, Annotated [*A publication*] (DLA) ...... Cas Tax
Canada Taxation Publications [*Database*] (IID) ...... CTP
Canada - Transport Canada [*Canada ICAO designator*] (ICDA) ...... GO
Canada Treaty Series [*A publication*] (DLA) ...... Can TS
Canada Trust Income Investments [*Toronto Stock Exchange symbol*] ...... CNN
Canada Trustco Mortgage Co. [*Toronto Stock Exchange symbol*] ...... CT
Canada Tungsten Mining Corp. Ltd. [*Toronto Stock Exchange symbol*] ...... CTM
Canada/United States Region (NATG) ...... CUSR
Canada VM Users Group (EAIO) ...... CVMUG
Canada Water [*Canada*] [*A database*] (NITA) ...... CWA
Canada West ...... CW
Canada West Air Ltd. [*ICAO designator*] (FAAC) ...... CWA
Canada West Gold Rush Museum, Surrey, British Columbia [*Library symbol National Library of Canada*] (NLC) ...... BSURCW
Canada West Universities Athletic Association [*Association Sportive Universitaire de l'Ouest Canadien*] [*Formerly, Western Canadian Intercollegiate Athletic Union*] (AC) ...... CWUAA
Canada Wire & Cable Co. Ltd., Montreal, PQ, Canada [*Library symbol Library of Congress*] (LCLS) ...... CaQMCW
Canada Wire & Cable Co. Ltd., Montreal, Quebec [*Library symbol National Library of Canada*] (NLC) ...... QMCW
Canada Wire & Cable Co. Ltd., Toronto, ON, Canada [*Library symbol Library of Congress*] (LCLS) ...... CaOTCW
Canada Wire & Cable Co. Ltd., Toronto, Ontario [*Library symbol National Library of Canada*] (NLC) ...... OTCW
Canada World Youth (AC) ...... CWY
Canada-Arab Business Council (AC) ...... CABC
Canada-Australia Trade Agreement ...... CANATA
Canada-California Chamber of Commerce (SRA) CCCC
Canada-Caribbean-Central America Policy Alternatives [*An association*] (AC) ...... CAPA
Canada-Cuba Sports & Fitness Cultural Festivals (AC) ...... CCS&FCF
Canada-France Redshift Survey [*Astronomy*] ...... CFRS
Canada-France-Hawaii Telescope [*Mauna Kea, Hawaii*] ...... CFHT
Canada-France-Hawaii Telescope Corp. Kamuela, HI [*Library symbol*] [*Library of Congress*] (LCLS) ...... HKamCF
Canadain Native Friendship Centre (AC) ...... CNFC
Canada-India Reactor ...... CIR
Canadair Ltd. [*Canada ICAO aircraft manufacturer identifier*] (ICAO) CL
Canadair Ltd., Engineering Library, Montreal, PQ, Canada [*Library symbol Library of Congress*] (LCLS) ...... CaQMCa
Canadair Ltd., Missiles and Systems Library, Montreal, PQ, Canada [*Library symbol Library of Congress*] (LCLS) ...... CaQMCam
Canadair Regional Jet ...... CRJ
Canada-Israel Foundation for Academic Exchanges [*Foundation Canada-Israel pour les Exchanges Universitaires*] (AC) ...... CIFAE
Canada-Latin American Resource Centre (AC) ...... CLARC
Canada-Ontario Rideau-Trent-Severn Study Committee ...... CORTS
Canada-Pakistan Business Council [*Conseil de Commerce Canada Pakistan*] [*Formerly, Canada-Parkistan Trade & Economic Committee*] (AC) ...... CPBC
Canada-Russia Business Council (AC) ...... CRBC
Canada-Taiwan Business Association (AC) ...... CTBA
Canada-Taiwan Friendship Association (AC) ...... CTFA
Canada-Transport Canada [*ICAO designator*] (FAAC) ...... TGO
Canada-United Kingdom ...... CAN-UK
Canada-United Kingdom Chamber of Commerce (DS) ...... CUKCC
Canada-United Kingdom-Joint Communications Electronics Committees ...... CAN-UK JCEC
Canada-United Kingdom-United States [*Agreement*] ...... CANUKUS
Canada-United Kingdom-United States Cryptographic Systems General Publications (MCD) ...... CCG
Canada-United Kingdom-United States Joint Communications-Electronics Committees ...... CANUKUS JCECS
Canada-United States (AFM) ...... CAN-US
Canada-United States Environmental Council (EA) ...... CUSEC
Canada-United States Regional Planning Group [*NATO*] ...... CUSRPG
Canadex Resources Ltd. [*Toronto Stock Exchange symbol*] ...... CDX
Canadian (ROG) ...... CAN
Canadian (ODBW) ...... Can
Canadian ...... CANDN
Canadian (NATG) ...... CDN
Canadian (DD) ...... Cdn
Canadian ...... CNDN
Canadian (FAAC) ...... CNDN
Canadian Abortion Rights Action League ...... CARAL
Canadian Abridgment [*A publication*] (DLA) ...... Can Abr
Canadian Abridgment [*2nd ed.*] [*A publication*] (DLA) ...... Can Abr (2d)
Canadian Academic Accounting Association [*See also ACPC*] ...... CAAA
Canadian Academic Centre in Italy ...... CACI
Canadian Academic Decathlon Associations (AC) ...... CADA
Canadian Academic Research Libraries ...... CARL
Canadian Academy of Endodontics (EAIO) ...... CAE
Canadian Academy of Engineering (EAIO) ...... CAE
Canadian Academy of Facial Plastic & Reconstructive Surgery [*Academie Canadienne de Chirurgie Plastique et Reconstructive Faciale*] [*Formerly, Canadian Institute of Facial Plastic Surgery*] (AC) ...... CAFPRS
Canadian Academy of Oral Radiology [*Academie Canadienne de Radiologie Buccale*] (AC) ...... CAOR
Canadian Academy of Podiatric Sports Medicine ...... CAPSM
Canadian Academy of Recording Arts and Sciences ...... CARAS
Canadian Academy of Sport Medicine [*See also CCMS*] ...... CASM
Canadian Academy of Sport Medicine (AC) ...... CASM
Canadian Academy of the History of Pharmacy [*Academie Canadienne d'Histoire de la Pharmacie*] (AC) ...... CAHP

Canadian Accredited Insurance Broker (DD) ... CAIB
Canadian Achievement Test in English [*Education*] (AEBS) ... CATE
Canadian Achievement Test in French [*Education*] (AEBS) ... CATF
Canadian Achievement Test in Mathematics [*Education*] (AEBS) ... CATM
Canadian Achievement Test in Technical and Commercial Mathematics [*Education*] (AEBS) ... CATTCM
Canadian Acoustical Association ... CAA
Canadian Action for Nicaragua (AC) ... CAN
Canadian Actors' Equity Association [*Canada*] (WWLA) ... CAEA
Canadian Addiction Foundation, Addictions Librarians Special Interest Section ... CAFALSIS
Canadian Administrative Housekeepers Association (AC) ... CAHA
Canadian Advanced Industrial Materials Forum [*Forum Canadien des Materiaux Industriels de Haute Qualite*] (AC) ... CAIMAF
Canadian Advanced Technology Association [*Association Canadienne de Technologie de Pointe*] (AC) ... CATA
Canadian Advanced Technology Association [*Ottawa, ON*] [*Telecommunications service*] ... CATA
Canadian Advertising Advisory Board ... CAAB
Canadian Advertising and Sales Association ... CASA
Canadian Advertising Foundation ... CAF
Canadian Advertising Rates and Data ... CARD
Canadian Advertising Rates and Data ... CARD
Canadian Advertising Research Foundation [*Founded 1949*] ... CARF
Canadian Advisory Committee on Programming Languages ... CAC/PL
Canadian Advisory Council on the Status of Women (AC) ... CACSW
Canadian Advisory Council on the Status of Women, Documentation Centre, Ottawa, ON, Canada [*Library symbol*] [*Library of Congress*] (LCLS) ... CaOOCACSW
Canadian Aeronautical Institute (IAA) ... CAEI
Canadian Aeronautical Institute ... CAI
Canadian Aeronautics and Space Institute ... CASI
Canadian Aerophilatelic Society (AC) ... CAS
Canadian African Newcomer Aid Centre of Toronto (AC) ... CANACT
Canadian Agency for International Development [*Defunct*] ... CAID
Canadian Aging Research Network [*University of Toronto*] [*Research center*] (RCD) ... CARNET
Canadian Agricultural Chemics Association ... CACA
Canadian Agricultural Economics and Farm Management Society ... CAEFMS
Canadian Agricultural Economics Society ... CAES
Canadian Agricultural Export Corp. ... CANAGREX
Canadian Agricultural Market Development Fund ... CAMDF
Canadian Agricultural Research Council ... CARC
Canadian Agricultural Services Coordinating Committee ... CASCC
Canadian Air Cushion Technology Society (AC) ... CACTS
Canadian Air Defence Identification Zone ... CADIZ
Canadian Air Division (MCD) ... CAD
Canadian Air Division Headquarters [*Allied Air Forces in Europe*] ... CANAIRDIV
Canadian Air Force [*1920-1923*] ... CAF
Canadian Air Group (MCD) ... CAG
Canadian Air Line Dispatchers' Association [*See also ACRV*] ... CALDA
Canadian Air Line Flight Attendants Association ... CALFAA
Canadian Air Lines Employees Association ... CALEA
Canadian Air Mail Collectors Club (EA) ... CAMCC
Canadian Air Publication ... CAP
Canadian Air/Sea Transportable Combat Group ... CAST
Canadian Air Traffic Control Association ... CATCA
Canadian Air Training Command Headquarters ... CANAIRTRAIN
Canadian Air Transport Board ... CATB
Canadian Air Transport Command (MUGU) ... CATC
Canadian Air Transportation Administration ... CATA
Canadian Airborne Regiment (MCD) ... CAR
Canadian Aircraft Insurance Group ... CAIG
Canadian Air-Ground Environment ... CAGE
Canadian Airline Pilots Association ... CALPA
Canadian Airlines [*TS Symbol*] (TTSB) ... CA
Canadian Airlines International Ltd. [*Canadian Pacific Airlines Ltd. and Pacific Western Airlines Ltd.*] [*Formed by a merger of*] ... CAI
Canadian Airlines International Ltd. [*Canadian Pacific Airlines Ltd. and Pacific Western Airlines Ltd.*] [*Formed by a merger of*] ... CAIL
Canadian Airlines International Ltd. [*ICAO designator*] (FAAC) ... CDN
Canadian Airports Council [*Conseil des Aeroports du Canada*] (AC) ... CAC
Canadian Airspace Reservation Unit [*Aviation*] (FAAC) ... CARU
Canadian Airways Ltd. ... CAL
Canadian Alarm & Security Association [*Association Canadienne de l'Alarme et de la Securite*] (AC) ... CANASA
Canadian Alliance Against Software Theft [*Alliance Canadienne Contre le vol de Logiciels*] (AC) ... ACCVOL
Canadian Alliance Against Software Theft [*Alliance Canadienne Contre le vol de Logiciels*] (AC) ... CAAST
Canadian Alliance in Solidarity with the Native People (EA) ... CASNP
Canadian Alliance of Black Educators [*See also ACEN*] ... CABE
Canadian All-Terrain Vehicle Distributors Council [*Conseil Canadien des Distributeurs de Vehicules Tout Terrain*] (AC) ... CATV
Canadian Almanac and Directory [*A publication*] ... CAD
Canadian Altitude Sensing Experiment Package (MCD) ... CASEP
Canadian Amateur Cowboys Association ... CACA
Canadian Amateur Diving Association Inc. [*Association Candienne du Plongeon Amateur Inc.*] (AC) ... CADA
Canadian Amateur Football Association ... CAFA
Canadian Amateur Hockey Association ... CAHA
Canadian Amateur Musicians (EAIO) ... CAMMAC
Canadian Amateur Radio Federation (PDAA) ... CARF
Canadian Amateur Radio Teletype Group (HGAA) ... CART
Canadian Amateur Speed Skating Association ... CASA
Canadian Amateur Speed Skating Association ... CASSA
Canadian Amateur Sports Federation ... CASF
Canadian Amateur Synchronized Swimming Association ... CASSA
Canadian Amateur Wrestling Association [*Association Canadienne de Lutte Amateur*] (AC) ... CAWA
Canadian Amenian Business Council Inc. [*Conseil Commercial Canadien-Armenien Inc.*] (AC) ... CABC
Canadian American Business Association (AC) ... CABA
Canadian Amputee Sports Association [*Association Canadienne des Sports Pour Amputes*] (AC) ... CASA
Canadian Amputee Sports Association ... CASA
Canadian Anaesthetists Society ... CAS
Canadian and Catholic Confederation of Labour ... CCCL
Canadian Angus Resources [*Vancouver Stock Exchange symbol*] ... AGB
Canadian Animal Health Institute [*Institut Canadien de la Sante Animale*] (AC) ... CAHI
Canadian Animation Producers Association ... CAPA
Canadian Annual Digest [*A publication*] (DLA) ... CAD
Canadian Anti-Acoustic Torpedo Gear [*World War II*] ... CAT
Canadian Antique Dealers Association (AC) ... CADA
Canadian Anti-Racism Education & Research Society (AC) ... CAERS
Canadian Anti-Soviet Action Committee (EAIO) ... CASAC
Canadian Apparel Federation [*Federation Canadienne du Vetement*] (AC) ... CAF
Canadian Apparel Manufacturers Institute (EAIO) ... CAMI
Canadian Appeal Cases [*A publication*] (DLA) ... Can App Cas
Canadian Appliance Manufacturers Association (AC) ... CAMA
Canadian Applied Mathematics Society (MCD) ... CAMS
Canadian Aquaculture Producers' Council [*Conseil Canadien des Aquiculteurs*] (AC) ... CAPC
Canadian Arab Federation [*Federation Canado-Arabe*] (AC) ... CAF
Canadian Arab Friendship Association ... CAFA
Canadian Arab Friendship Society of Toronto (AC) ... CAFS
Canadian Archaeological Association [*SA ACA*] ... CAA
Canadian Arctic Gas Pipeline Ltd. ... CAGPL
Canadian Arctic Island ... CAI
Canadian Arctic Petroleum [*Vancouver Stock Exchange symbol*] ... CAK
Canadian Arctic Resources Committee [*Ottawa, ON*] [*Research center*] ... CARC
Canadian Arctic Resources Committee, Ottawa, ON, Canada [*Library symbol Library of Congress*] (LCLS) ... CaOOCAR
Canadian Arctic Resources Committee, Ottawa, Ontario [*Library symbol National Library of Canada*] (NLC) ... OOCAR
Canadian Armament Research and Development Establishment ... CARDE
Canadian Armed Forces ... CAF
Canadian Armed Forces [*ICAO designator*] (FAAC) ... CFC
Canadian Armed Forces Institute of Environmental Medicine (PDAA) ... CFIEM
Canadian Armoured Brigade ... CAB
Canadian Armoured Corps ... CAC
Canadian Army ... CA
Canadian Army (NATG) ... CANA
Canadian Army Active Service Force ... CAASF
Canadian Army Dental Corps (DMA) ... CADC
Canadian Army Liaison Executive ... CALE
Canadian Army Medical Corps ... CAMC
Canadian Army (Militia) ... CA(M)
Canadian Army Operational Research Establishment ... CAORE
Canadian Army Operational Research Group (DMA) ... CAORG
Canadian Army Orders ... CAO
Canadian Army Pay Corps (DMA) ... CAPC
Canadian Army Post Office (DMA) ... CAPO
Canadian Army (Regular) ... CA(R)
Canadian Army Service Corps [*British military*] (DMA) ... CASC
Canadian Army Signals Engineering Establishment (IAA) ... CASEE
Canadian Army Trophy ... CAT
Canadian Army Veterinary Corps (DMA) ... CAVC
Canadian Arrow Mines Ltd. [*Toronto Stock Exchange symbol*] ... CGR
Canadian Arsenals Limited ... CAL
Canadian Arsenals Ltd. [*Arsenaux Canada Ltee.*], Le Gardeur, Quebec [*Library symbol National Library of Canada*] (BIB) ... QLAR
Canadian Art Club, Toronto [*1907-15*] (NGC) ... CAC
Canadian Art Libraries ... CARLIS
Canadian Art Museum Directors Organization ... CAMDO
Canadian Art Therapy Association-Eastern Chapter (AC) ... CATA
Canadian Arthritis and Rheumatism Society ... CARS
Canadian Artists' Representation ... CAR
Canadian Artists' Representation/Front des Artistes Canadiens ... CARFAC
Canadian Artists' Representation Manitoba [*Also, CARFAC Manitoba*] (AC) ... CARMAN
Canadian Artists' Representation Ontario [*Front des Artistes Canadiens del'Ontario*] (AC) ... CARO
Canadian Artists Selected by You [*Music award alternative to the Canadian Juno Award*] [*Established 1985*] ... CASBY
Canadian Arts Presenters Association [*Association Candienne des Organismes Artistiques*] (AC) ... CAPACOA
Canadian Asbestos Information Centre, Montreal, PQ, Canada [*Library symbol*] [*Library of Congress*] (LCLS) ... CaQMCAI
Canadian Asbestos Information Centre [*Centre Canadien d'Information sur l'Amiante*] **Montreal, Quebec** [*Library symbol National Library of Canada*] (NLC) ... QMCAI
Canadian Asian Studies Association [*See also ACEA*] ... CASA
Canadian Associate for Humane Trapping (AC) ... CAHT
Canadian Associated Air Balance Council (AC) ... AABC
Canadian Associated School of Karate-Doh ... CASK
Canadian Association Against Sexual Harassment in Higher Education [*Association Canadienne Contre le Harcelement Sexuel en Milieu d'Ensignement Superieur*] (AC) ... CAASHHE

Canadian Association for Adult Education .... CAAE
Canadian Association for Adult Education, Toronto, ON, Canada [*Library symbol Library of Congress*] (LCLS) .... CaOTCAE
Canadian Association for American Studies (EA) .... CAAS
Canadian Association for Business Economics .... CABE
Canadian Association for Business Forms Management .... CABFM
Canadian Association for Children of Alcoholics (AC) .... CACOA
Canadian Association for Children with Learning Disabilities .... CACLD
Canadian Association for Clinical Microbiology & Infectious Diseases [*Association Canadienne de Microbiologie Clinique et des Maladies Contagieuses*] (AC) .... CACMID
Canadian Association for Commonwealth Literature and Language Studies [*See also ACELLC*] .... CACLALS
Canadian Association for Community Living (EAIO) .... CACL
Canadian Association for Community Living .... CACL
Canadian Association for Composite Structures & Materials (AC) .... CACSMA
Canadian Association for Co-Operative Education [*Association Canadienne de l'Enseignement Cooperatif*] (AC) .... CACE
Canadian Association for Disable Skiing [*Association Canadienne des Sports pour Skieurs Handicapes*] (AC) .... CADS
Canadian Association for Distance Education .... CADE
Canadian Association for Enterostomal Therapy (AC) .... CAET
Canadian Association for Environmental Analytical Laboratories (AC) .... CAEAL
Canadian Association for Free Expression .... CAFE
Canadian Association for Future Studies .... CAFS
Canadian Association for Graduate Studies (AC) .... CAGS
Canadian Association for Health, Physical Education, and Recreation .... CAHPER
Canadian Association for Health, Physical Education, Recreation & Dance [*Association Canadienne pour la Sante, l'Education Physique, les Loisirs et la Danse*] (AC) .... CAHPERD
Canadian Association for Information Science [*Ottawa, ON*] .... CAIS
Canadian Association for Information Science/Association Canadienne des Sciencesde l'Information (IID) .... CAIS/ACSI
Canadian Association for Irish Studies .... CAIS
Canadian Association for Israel Philately .... CAFIP
Canadian Association for Japanese Language Education (AC) .... CAJLE
Canadian Association for Laboratory Animal Science .... CALAS
Canadian Association for Labour Israel (AC) .... CALI
Canadian Association for Music Therapy .... CAMT
Canadian Association for Nursing Law (AC) .... CANL
Canadian Association for Pastoral Education (AC) .... CAPE
Canadian Association for Peace in the Middle East .... CAFPME
Canadian Association for Physical Anthropology .... CAPA
Canadian Association for Production and Inventory Control .... CAPIC
Canadian Association for Quality in Health Care [*Association Canadienne pour la Qualite dans les Services de Sante*] (AC) .... CAQHC
Canadian Association for Research in Home Economics [*See also ACREF*] .... CARHE
Canadian Association for Research in Nondestructive Evaluation (AC) .... CARNDE
Canadian Association for Scottish Studies [*See also ACEE*] .... CASS
Canadian Association for South Asian Studies .... CASAS
Canadian Association for Sport Heritage [*Association Canadienne pour l'Heritage Sportif*] (AC) .... CASH
Canadian Association for Studies in Cooperation [*See also ACEC*] .... CASC
Canadian Association for Suicide Prevention [*L'Association Canadienne pour la Prevention du Suicide*] (AC) .... CASP
Canadian Association for Teacher Education (AC) .... CATE
Canadian Association for the Advancement of Netherlandic Studies G2 [*See also ACAEN*] .... CAANS
Canadian Association for the Advancement of Women & Sport & Physical Activity [*Association Canadienne pour l'Avancement des Femmes du Sport et de l'Activite Physique*] (AC) .... CAAWS
Canadian Association for the History of Nursing (AC) .... CAHN
Canadian Association for the Mentally Retarded .... CAMR
Canadian Association for the Practical Study of Law in Education [*Association Canadienne pour une Etude Pratique de la Loi Dan le Systeme Educatif*] (AC) .... CAPSLE
Canadian Association for the Social Studies .... CASS
Canadian Association for the Study of Adult Education [*See also ACEEA*] .... CASAE
Canadian Association for the Study of International Development [*L'Association Canadienne d'Etudes du Developpement International*] (AC) .... CASID
Canadian Association for the Treatment of Offenders .... CATO
Canadian Association for University Continuing Education .... CAUCE
Canadian Association for Vocational Evaluation & Work Adjustment [*Association Canadienne des Evaluateur de Capacites de Travail*] (AC) .... CAVEWA
Canadian Association for Young Children .... CAYC
Canadian Association in Support of the Native Peoples, Toronto, ON, Canada [*Library symbol Library of Congress*] (LCLS) .... CaOTCAS
Canadian Association in Support of the Native Peoples, Toronto, Ontario [*Library symbol National Library of Canada*] (NLC) .... OTCAS
Canadian Association of Administrators of Labour Legislation .... CAALL
Canadian Association of Advertising Agencies (NTCM) .... CAAA
Canadian Association of African Studies [*See also ACEA*] .... CAAS
Canadian Association of Amateur Oarsmen .... CAAO
Canadian Association of Anatomists (AC) .... CAA
Canadian Association of Animal Breeders [*Association Canadienne des Eleveus de Betail*] (AC) .... CAAB
Canadian Association of Animal Health Technologists & Technicians (AC) .... CAAHTT
Canadian Association of Applied Linguistics .... CAAL
Canadian Association of Applied Social Research [*See also ACRSA*] .... CAASR
Canadian Association of Artists Managers (AC) .... CAAM
Canadian Association of Basketball Officials .... CABO
Canadian Association of British Manufacturers and Agencies .... CABMA
Canadian Association of Broadcasters .... CAB
Canadian Association of Broadcasters [*Association Canadienne des Radiodiffuseurs*] **Ottawa, Ontario** [*Library symbol National Library of Canada*] (NLC) .... OOCAB
Canadian Association of Burn Nurses (AC) .... CABN
Canadian Association of Business Valuators .... CABV
Canadian Association of Captioning Consumers (AC) .... CACC
Canadian Association of Cardio-Pulmonary Technologists (AC) .... CACPT
Canadian Association of Certified Executive Accountants [*Formerly, Association of Cost & Executive Acconants in Canada*] (AC) .... CACEA
Canadian Association of Certified Planning Tecnicians (AC) .... CACPT
Canadian Association of Chairmen of English Departments .... CACE
Canadian Association of Chemical Distributors [*Association Canadienne des Distributeurs de Produits Chimiques*] (AC) .... CACD
Canadian Association of Chiefs of Police .... CACP
Canadian Association of Children's Librarians .... CACL
Canadian Association of College and University Libraries .... CACUL
Canadian Association of College and University Student Services .... CACUSS
Canadian Association of Communications & Allied Workers [*Association Canadienne des Employes de Communications et Travailleurs Connexes*] (AC) .... CACAW
Canadian Association of Critical Care Nurses [*Association Canadienne des Infirmieres et Infirmiers de Soins Intensifs*] [*Formerly, National Society of Critical Care Nurses*] (AC) .... CACCN
Canadian Association of Data and Professional Service Organizations [*Information service or system*] (IID) .... CADAPSO
Canadian Association of Data Processing Organizations (IAA) .... CADAPSO
Canadian Association of Data Processing Service Organizations (NITA) .... CADAPSO
Canadian Association of Deans and Directors of Education .... CADDE
Canadian Association of Drilling Engineers (AC) .... CADE
Canadian Association of Education Development Officers .... CAEDO
Canadian Association of Educational Development Officers (NFD) .... CAEDO
Canadian Association of Electroencephalograph Technologists .... CAET
Canadian Association of Elizabeth Fry Societies [*Association Canadienne des Societes Elizabeth Fry*] (AC) .... CAEFS
Canadian Association of Emergency Physicians .... CAEP
Canadian Association of Energy Service Companies (AC) .... CAESCO
Canadian Association of Ethnic (Radio) [*Association Canadienne des Radiodiffuseurs Ethniques*] (AC) .... CAEB
Canadian Association of Exhibitions [*Association des Expositions du Canada*] (AC) .... CAE
Canadian Association of Exposition Managers .... CAEM
Canadian Association of Family Enterprise [*Association Canadienne des Enterprises Familiales*] (AC) .... CAFE
Canadian Association of Fire Chiefs .... CAFC
Canadian Association of Firefighters [*Association Canadienne des Pompiers*] (AC) .... CAFF
Canadian Association of Fish Exporters (AC) .... CAFE
Canadian Association of Food Banks [*Association Canadienne des Banques Alimentaires*] (AC) .... CAFB
Canadian Association of Footwear Importers Inc. (AC) .... CAFI
Canadian Association of Former International Civil Servants [*Association Canadienne des Anciens Fonctionnaires Internationaux*] (AC) .... CAFICS
Canadian Association of Foundations of Education .... CAFE
Canadian Association of General Surgeons .... CAGS
Canadian Association of Geographers .... CAG
Canadian Association of Geographers/Association Canadienne des Geographes .... CAG/ACG
Canadian Association of Geophysical Contractors (AC) .... CAGC
Canadian Association of Gift Planners (NFD) .... CAGP
Canadian Association of Gift Planners .... CAGP
Canadian Association of Health-Care Auxiliaries [*Associations des Auxiliaires Benevoles des Etablissements de Sante du Canada*] [*Formerly, Canadian Association of Hospital Auxiliaries*] (AC) .... CAHA
Canadian Association of Hispanists [*See also ACH*] .... CAH
Canadian Association of Home Inspectors (AC) .... CAHI
Canadian Association of Housing and Renewal Officials .... CAHRO
Canadian Association of Hungarian Studies [*See also ACEH*] .... CAHS
Canadian Association of Immersion Teachers (AC) .... CAIT
Canadian Association of Independent Living Centres (AC) .... CAILC
Canadian Association of Independent Schools (EAIO) .... CAIS
Canadian Association of Industrial, Mechanical, and Allied Workers .... CAIMAW
Canadian Association of Investment Clubs .... CAIC
Canadian Association of Japanese Automovbile Dealers (AC) .... CAJAD
Canadian Association of Journalists [*L'Association Canadienne des Journalistes*] (AC) .... CAJ
Canadian Association of Labour Media .... CALM
Canadian Association of Latin American and Caribbean Studies .... CALACS
Canadian Association of Latin American Studies .... CALAS
Canadian Association of Law Libraries .... CALL
Canadian Association of Law Teachers [*See also ACPD*] .... CALT
Canadian Association of Legal Assistants (AC) .... CALA
Canadian Association of Legal Support Staff (AC) .... CALSS
Canadian Association of Library Schools .... CALS
Canadian Association of Logistics Management (EAIO) .... CALM
Canadian Association of Management Consultants .... CAMC
Canadian Association of Manufacturers of Medical Devices .... CAMMD
Canadian Association of Marketing Research Organization [*Association Canadienne des Organisms de Recherche en Marketing*] (AC) .... CAMRO
Canadian Association of Medical Biochemists (AC) .... CAMB

Canadian Association of Medical Microbiologists [*Association Canadienne des Medecins Microbiologistes*] (AC) .... CAMM
Canadian Association of Medical Radiation Technologists (EAIO) .... CAMRT
Canadian Association of Medical Radiation Technologists, Ottawa, Ontario [*Library symbol National Library of Canada*] (BIB) .... OOCAM
Canadian Association of Medical Record Librarians .... CAMRL
Canadian Association of Medical Students and Interns .... CAMSI
Canadian Association of Members of Public Utility Tribunals (AC) .... CAMPUT
Canadian Association of Message Exchanges, Inc. [*Association Canadienne d'Echange de Messages, Inc.*] (AC) .... CAM-X
Canadian Association of Metal Finishers .... CAMF
Canadian Association of Mining Equipment & Services for Export (AC) .... CAMESE
Canadian Association of Moldmakers [*Formerly, Windsor Association of Moldmakers*] (AC) .... CAMM
Canadian Association of Motion Picture and Electronic Recording Artists .... CAMERA
Canadian Association of Motion Picture Producers .... CAMPP
Canadian Association of Municipal Administrators (AC) .... CAMA
Canadian Association of Music Libraries .... CAML
Canadian Association of Mutual Insurance Companies (AC) .... CAMIC
Canadian Association of Neuroscience Nurses [*Association Canadienne des infirmieres el Infirmiers en Sciences Neurologiques*] (AC) .... CANN
Canadian Association of Nordic Ski Instructors (AC) .... CANSI
Canadian Association of Numismatic Dealers (AC) .... CAND
Canadian Association of Nurse Administrators (AC) .... CANA
Canadian Association of Nurses in AIDS Care (AC) .... CANAC
Canadian Association of Occupational Therapists [*Association Canadienne des Ergotherapeutes*] (AC) .... CAOT
Canadian Association of Occupational Therapy (HGAA) .... CAOP
Canadian Association of Oilwell Drilling Contractors .... CAODC
Canadian Association of Orthodontists [*Association Canadienne des Orthodontists*] (AC) .... CAO
Canadian Association of Palynologists [*Association Canadienne des Palynologues*] (AC) .... CAP
Canadian Association of Pathologists .... CAP
Canadian Association of Pediatric Nurses (AC) .... CAPN
Canadian Association of Pension Supervisory Authorities [*Association Canadienne des Organismes de Controle des Regimes de Retraite*] (AC) .... CAPSA
Canadian Association of Petroleum Producers (IID) .... CAPP
Canadian Association of Pharmacy Technicians (AC) .... CAPT
Canadian Association of Photographers & Illustrators in Communications [*Association Canadienne de Photographes et Illustrateurs de Publicite*] (AC) .... CAPIC
Canadian Association of Physical Medicine and Rehabilitation (EAIO) .... CAPM & R
Canadian Association of Physicists (MCD) .... CAP
Canadian Association of Plastic Surgery (HGAA) .... CAPIS
Canadian Association of Poison Control Centres .... CAPCC
Canadian Association of Police Boards (AC) .... CAPB
Canadian Association of Practical Nursing Assistants .... CAPNA
Canadian Association of Prawn Producers [*Association Canadienne des Producteurs de Crevette*] (AC) .... CAPP
Canadian Association of Principals (AC) .... CAP
Canadian Association of Profession Radio Operators [*Association Canadienne des Professionnels de l'Exploitation Radio*] (AC) .... CAPRO
Canadian Association of Professional Conservators .... CAPC
Canadian Association of Professional Dance Organizations (AC) .... CADPO
Canadian Association of Professional Heritage Consultants [*Association Canadienne des Consultants Patrimoine*] (AC) .... CAPHC
Canadian Association of Professors of Education .... CAPE
Canadian Association of Prosthetists and Orthotists .... CAPO
Canadian Association of Psychoanalytic Child Therapists (AC) .... CAPCT
Canadian Association of Public Libraries .... CAPL
Canadian Association of Publishers' Educational Representatives .... CAPER
Canadian Association of Purchasing Agents (HGAA) .... CAPA
Canadian Association of Quality Assurance Professionals .... CAQAP
Canadian Association of Radiation Oncologists [*Association Canadienne des Radio-Oncologues*] (AC) .... CARO
Canadian Association of Radio and Television Broadcasters .... CARTB
Canadian Association of Radiologists .... CAR
Canadian Association of Recycling Industries (AC) .... CARI
Canadian Association of Regulated Importers [*Association Canadienne des Importateurs Reglementes*] (AC) .... CARI
Canadian Association of Rehabilitation Personnel .... CARP
Canadian Association of Research Libraries [*Also, ABRC*] .... CARL
Canadian Association of Retail Travel Agents (AC) .... CARTA
Canadian Association of Retired Persons [*Association Canadienne des Individus Retraites*] (AC) .... CARP
Canadian Association of Rhodes Scholars .... CARS
Canadian Association of Rural Studies .... CARS
Canadian Association of SAS Users (AC) .... CASU
Canadian Association of School Administrators (AC) .... CASA
Canadian Association of School Social Workers & Attendance Counsellors (AC) .... CASSWAC
Canadian Association of Schools of Social Work [*See also ACESS*] .... CASSW
Canadian Association of Second Language Teachers (AC) .... CASLT
Canadian Association of Senior Travellers (AC) .... CAST
Canadian Association of Sexual Assault Centres [*Association Canadienne des Centres Contre le Viol*] (AC) .... CASAC
Canadian Association of Slavists [*See also ACS*] .... CAS
Canadian Association of Smelter and Allied Workers .... CASAW

Canadian Association of Social Work Administrators in Health Facilities [*Associations Canadienne des Administrateurs de Services Sociaux en Milieu de Sante*] (AC) .... CASWAHF
Canadian Association of Social Workers [*See also ACTS*] .... CASW
Canadian Association of Special Libraries (EAIO) .... CASL
Canadian Association of Special Libraries and Information Services (HGAA) .... CASLIS
Canadian Association of Specialty Foods [*L'Association Canadienne des Aliments Fins*] [*Formerly, Canadian Specialty Food Association*] (AC) .... CASF
Canadian Association of Speech-Language Pathologists & Audiologists [*Association Canadienne des Orthophonistes et Audiologistes*] (AC) ...... CASLPA
Canadian Association of Sports Sciences .... CASS
Canadian Association of Statutory Human Rights Agencies [*Association Canadienne des Organismes Statutaires pour la Protection des Droits de la Personne*] (AC) .... CASHRA
Canadian Association of Teachers of Community Health [*Association Canadienne des Professeurs de Sante Communautaire*] (AC) .... CATCH
Canadian Association of Teachers of Technical Writing .... CATTW
Canadian Association of Textile Colourists and Chemists (HGAA) .... CATCC
Canadian Association of the Deaf (EAIO) .... CAD
Canadian Association of Token Collectors .... CATC
Canadian Association of Toy Libraries and Parent Resource Centers (EAIO) .... CATL
Canadian Association of Toy Libraries and Parent Resource Centers (EAIO) .... TLRC
Canadian Association of University Business Officers .... CAUBO
Canadian Association of University Research Administrators [*See also ACARU*] .... CAURA
Canadian Association of University Schools of Music .... CAUSM
Canadian Association of University Schools of Nursing [*See also ACEUN*] .... CAUSN
Canadian Association of University Schools of Rehabilitation (AC) .... CAUSR
Canadian Association of University Student Personnel Services .... CAUSPS
Canadian Association of University Teachers .... CAUT
Canadian Association of University Teachers of German .... CAUTG
Canadian Association of Volunteer Bureaux Centres (AC) .... CAVB
Canadian Association of Warehousing & Distribution Services [*Association Canadienne des Entreposeurs et des Distributeurs*] [*Formerly, Canadian Warehousing Association*] (AC) .... CAWDS
Canadian Association of Women Executives & Entrepreneurs [*Association Canadienne des Femmes Cadres et Entrepreneurs*] (AC) .... CAWEE
Canadian Association of Wooden Money Collectors (AC) .... CAWMC
Canadian Association of Youth Orchestras .... CAYO
Canadian Association of Zoological Parks & Aquariums (AC) .... CAZPA
Canadian Association on Charitable Gift Annuities (NFD) .... CACGA
Canadian Association on Gerontology [*Association Canadienne de Gerontologie*] (AC) .... CAG
Canadian Association on Water Pollution Research and Control (EAIO) .... CAWPRC
Canadian Association on Water Quality [*Also, Canadian National Committee of the International Association on Water Quality*] [*Formerly, Canadian Association on Water Pollution Research & Control*] (AC) .... CAWQ
Canadian Astronautical Society .... CAS
Canadian Astronautics, Ottawa, Ontario [*Library symbol National Library of Canada*] (NLC) .... OOCAA
Canadian Astronomical Society .... CAS
Canadian Atherosclerosis Society [*Societe Canadienne d'Atherosclerose*] (AC) .... CAS
Canadian Athletic Therapists Association .... CATA
Canadian Atlantic Fisheries Scientific Advisory Committee (ASF) .... CAFSAC
Canadian Atlantic Storms Program [*Meteorology*] .... CASP
Canadian Atlantic Subarea [*Canadian Navy*] .... CANLANT
Canadian Australian Line .... CASCO
Canadian Authors Association .... CAA
Canadian Auto Workers Union .... CAW
Canadian Automated Air Traffic System .... CAATS
Canadian Automated Buildings Association [*Association Canadienne pour l'Automatisation des Batiments*] (AC) .... CABA
Canadian Automated Pilot Selection System .... CAPSS
Canadian Automatic Merchandising Association (AC) .... CAMA
Canadian Automatic Sprinkler Association (AC) .... CASA
Canadian Automobile Association .... CAA
Canadian Automobile Association, Ottawa, Ontario [*Library symbol National Library of Canada*] (BIB) .... OOCAAS
Canadian Automobile Dealers Association [*Formerly, Federation of Automobile Dealer Associations of Canada*] (AC) .... CADA
Canadian Automobile Sports Club .... CASC
Canadian Automobile Workers Union, Willowdale, Ontario [*Library symbol National Library of Canada*] (BIB) .... OWCA
Canadian Automotive Electric Association .... CAEA
Canadian Automotive Historians (AC) .... CAH
Canadian Automotive Trade [*A publication*] .... CAT
Canadian Avalanche Association [*Also, Canadian Avalanche Centre*] (AC)..... CAA
Canadian Aviation Electronics .... CAE
Canadian Aviation Electronics, Montreal, PQ, Canada [*Library symbol Library of Congress*] (LCLS) .... CaQMCAE
Canadian Aviation Historical Society (AC) .... CAHS
Canadian Aviation Safety Board .... CASB
Canadian Aviation Safety Board [*Bureau Canadien de la Securite Aerienne*] Ottawa, Ontario [*Library symbol National Library of Canada*] (NLC) .... OOTAS
Canadian Bacterial Diseases Network (AC) .... CBDN
Canadian Badminton Association .... CBA
Canadian Badminton Coaches Association .... CBCA
Canadian Band Association (EAIO) .... CBA
Canadian Bankers Association .... CBA

Canadian Bankruptcy Reports, Annotated [*A publication*] (DLA) ..... Can Bankr Ann
Canadian Bankruptcy Reports, Annotated [*A publication*] (DLA) ..... CBR
Canadian Bankruptcy Reports, Annotated, New Series [*A publication*] (DLA) ..... Can Bankr Ann (NS)
Canadian Bankruptcy Reports, Annotated, New Series [*A publication*] (DLA) ..... CBR (NS)
Canadian Baptist Archives, McMaster Divinity College, McMaster University, Hamilton, Ontario [*Library symbol National Library of Canada*] (NLC) ..... OHMDBA
Canadian Baptist International Ministries (EAIO) ..... CBIM
Canadian Baptist Overseas Mission Board ..... CBOMB
Canadian Bar Association ..... CBA
Canadian Bar Association. Journal [*A publication*] (DLA) ..... Can BAJ
Canadian Bar Association. Proceedings [*A publication*] (DLA) ..... Can BA
Canadian Bar Association. Year Book [*A publication*] (DLA) ..... Can B Ass'n YB
Canadian Bar Insurance Association [*Association d'Assurance du Barreau Canadien*] (AC) ..... CBIA
Canadian Barranca Corp. [*Vancouver Stock Exchange symbol*] ..... CBR
Canadian Battery Association (AC) ..... CBA
Canadian Beaver Resources [*Vancouver Stock Exchange symbol*] ..... CBV
Canadian Bible College, Regina, Saskatchewan [*Library symbol National Library of Canada*] (NLC) ..... SRCB
Canadian Bible College, Regina, SK, Canada [*Library symbol Library of Congress*] (LCLS) ..... CaSRCB
Canadian Biochemical Society (HGAA) ..... CBS
Canadian Bison Association [*Association Canadienne du Bison*] (AC) ..... CBA
Canadian Board of Marine Underwriters ..... CBMU
Canadian Boiler and Machinery Underwriters Association ..... CBMUA
Canadian Boiler Society [*Societe Canadienne de Manufacturiers Chaudieres*] (AC) ..... CBS
Canadian Book and Periodical Development Council ..... CBPDC
Canadian Book Exchange Centre (IID) ..... CBEC
Canadian Book Information Centre ..... CBIC
Canadian Book Manufacturing Association ..... CBMA
Canadian Book Marketing Centre [*Formerly, Canadian Book Information Centre*] (AC) ..... CBMC
Canadian Book Publishers' Council ..... CBPC
Canadian Book Review Annual [*A publication*] (BRI) ..... CBRA
Canadian Bookbinders & Book Artist Guild [*Guide Canadienne des Relieurs et des Artisans du Livre*] (AC) ..... CBBAG
Canadian Bookbinders and Book Artists Guild ..... CBBG
Canadian Booksellers Association ..... CBA
Canadian Botanical Association ..... CBA
Canadian Bridge Federation ..... CBF
Canadian British Consultants Ltd., Halifax, Nova Scotia [*Library symbol National Library of Canada*] (NLC) ..... NSHCBC
Canadian British Consultants Ltd., Halifax, NS, Canada [*Library symbol Library of Congress*] (LCLS) ..... CaNSHCBC
Canadian Broadcast Program Development Fund ..... CBPDF
Canadian Broadcasting Corp. [*Ottawa, ON*] [*Also facetiously translated as Casual Broadcasting Corp. and Communist Broadcasting Corp.*] [*Telecommunications*] ..... CBC
Canadian Broadcasting Corp., Engineering Headquarters Library, Montreal, PQ, Canada [*Library symbol Library of Congress*] (LCLS) ..... CaQMCBE
Canadian Broadcasting Corp., Montreal, PQ, Canada [*Library symbol Library of Congress*] (LCLS) ..... CaQMCB
Canadian Broadcasting Corp. [*Societe Radio-Canada*] **Montreal, Quebec** [*Library symbol National Library of Canada*] (NLC) ..... QMCB
Canadian Broadcasting Corp., Music and Record Library, Halifax, NS, Canada [*Library symbol Library of Congress*] (LCLS) ..... CaNSHCB
Canadian Broadcasting Corp., Music and Record Library, Winnipeg, MB, Canada [*Library symbol Library of Congress*] (LCLS) ..... CaMWC
Canadian Broadcasting Corp., Music Library, Montreal, PQ, Canada [*Library symbol*] [*Library of Congress*] (LCLS) ..... CaQMCBM
Canadian Broadcasting Corp., Ottawa, ON, Canada [*Library symbol Library of Congress*] (LCLS) ..... CaOOAR
Canadian Broadcasting Corp. [*Societe Radio-Canada*] **Ottawa, Ontario** [*Library symbol National Library of Canada*] (NLC) ..... OOAR
Canadian Broadcasting Corp., Program Archives, Toronto, ON, Canada [*Library symbol Library of Congress*] (LCLS) ..... CaOTBCP
Canadian Broadcasting Corp., Toronto, ON, Canada [*Library symbol Library of Congress*] (LCLS) ..... CaOTBC
Canadian Broadcasting Corp. [*Societe Radio-Canada*] **Toronto, Ontario** [*Library symbol National Library of Canada*] (NLC) ..... OTBC
Canadian Broadcasting Corp., VTR Library, Vancouver, BC, Canada [*Library symbol*] [*Library of Congress*] (LCLS) ..... CaBVaCBV
Canadian Broadcasting League ..... CBL
Canadian Broadcasting Winnipeg [*Canadian Broadcasting Co. record series pref ix*] ..... CBW
Canadian Brotherhood of Railway Employees and Other Transport Workers ..... CBRE
Canadian Brotherhood of Railway Transport and General Workers ..... CBRT
Canadian Bureau for International Education [*See also BCEI*] ..... CBIE
Canadian Bureau for the Advancement of Music (AC) ..... BAM
Canadian Bus Association [*Association Canadienne de l'Autobus*] [*Formerly, Canadian Motor Coach Association*] (AC) ..... CBA
Canadian Business Aircraft Association (EAIO) ..... CBAA
Canadian Business and Current Affairs [*Micromedia Ltd.*] [*Information service or system*] (CRD) ..... CBCA
Canadian Business Equipment Manufacturers Association (HGAA) ..... CBEMA
Canadian Business Forms Association (DGA) ..... CBFA
Canadian Business Manufacturers Association (MCD) ..... CBMA
Canadian Business Press ..... CBP
Canadian Business Telecommunications Alliance (AC) ..... CBTA
Canadian Business Travel Association [*Association Canadienne des Charges de Voyages*] (AC) ..... CBTA
Canadian Cable Television Association ..... CCTA
Canadian Camping Association (AC) ..... CCA
Canadian Cancer Society (BARN) ..... CCS
Canadian Canners Ltd., Burlington, ON, Canada [*Library symbol Library of Congress*] (LCLS) ..... CaOBUCC
Canadian Canners Ltd., Burlington, Ontario [*Library symbol National Library of Canada*] (NLC) ..... OBUCC
Canadian Canoe Association ..... CCA
Canadian Canoe, Single Person (ADA) C1
Canadian Canoe, Two Person (ADA) C2
Canadian Canon Law Society (AC) ..... CCLS
Canadian Car Demurrage Bureau, The, Montreal PQ CDA [*STAC*] ..... CCD
Canadian Carbonization Research Association (AC) ..... CCRA
Canadian Cardiovascular Society (EAIO) ..... CCS
Canadian Career Information Association (AC) ..... CCIA
Canadian Cariboo Resources Ltd. [*Vancouver Stock Exchange symbol*] CCV
Canadian Carpet Institute (EAIO) CCI
Canadian Cartographic Association [*Association Canadienne de Cartographie*] (AC) ..... CCA
Canadian Casualty Assembly Centre (DMA) ..... CCAC
Canadian Cat Association ..... CCA
Canadian Cataloguing in Publication ..... CCIP
Canadian Catholic Conference CCC
Canadian Catholic Historical Association [*See also SCHEC*] ..... CCHA
Canadian Catholic School Trustees' Association [*Association Canadienne des Commissaires d'Ecoles Catolique*] (AC) ..... CCSTA
Canadian Cattle Breeders' Association (AC) ..... CCBA
Canadian Cattlemen's Association ..... CCA
Canadian Celanese Ltd., Drummondville, PQ, Canada [*Library symbol Library of Congress*] (LCLS) ..... CaQDC
Canadian Celiac Association [*Association Canadienne de la Maladie Coeliaque*] [*Also, Celiac Canada*] (AC) ..... CCA
Canadian Center for Occupational Safety and Health (IID) ..... CCOSH
Canadian Centre for Architecture ..... CCA
Canadian Centre for Architecture, New York, NY [*Library symbol*] [*Library of Congress*] (LCLS) ..... NNCCA
Canadian Centre for Creative Technology [*Centre Canadien de Technologie Creative*] (AC) ..... CCCT
Canadian Centre for Drug-Free Sport [*Centre Candien Sur le Dopage Sportif*] (AC) ..... CCDS
Canadian Centre for Films on Art, Ottawa, ON, Canada [*Library symbol Library of Congress*] (LCLS) ..... CaOOCCFA
Canadian Centre for Films on Art [*Centre Canadien du Film sur l'Art*] **Ottawa, Ontario** [*Library symbol National Library of Canada*] (NLC) ..... OOCCFA
Canadian Centre for Fisheries Innovation [*Centre Canadien d'Innovations des Peches*] [*Formerly, Centre for Fisheries Innovation*] (AC) ..... CCFI
Canadian Centre for Global Security [*Centre Canadien pour la Securite Mondiale*] [*Formerly, The Arms Control Centre*] (AC) ..... CCGS
Canadian Centre for Information and Documentation on Archives [*National Archives of Canada*] ..... CCIDA
Canadian Centre for Learning Systems [*Research center*] (RCD) ..... CCLS
Canadian Centre for Occupational Health and Safety [*Ministry of Labour*] ..... CCOHS
Canadian Centre for Occupational Health & Safety [*Centre Canadien d'Hygiene et de Securite au Travail*] (AC) ..... CCOHS
Canadian Centre for Occupational Health and Safety, Hamilton, ON, Canada [*Library symbol Library of Congress*] (LCLS) ..... CaOHOHS
Canadian Centre for Occupational Health and Safety [*Centre Canadien d'Hygieneet de Securite au Travail*] **Hamilton, Ontario** [*Library symbol National Library of Canada*] (NLC) ..... OHOHS
Canadian Centre for Philanthropy, Toronto, ON, Canada [*Library symbol Library of Congress*] (LCLS) ..... CaOTCCP
Canadian Centre for Philanthropy, Toronto, Ontario [*Library symbol National Library of Canada*] (NLC) ..... OTCCP
Canadian Centre for Policy Alternatives (EAIO) ..... CCPA
Canadian Centre for Remote Sensing [*See also CCT*] ..... CCRS
Canadian Centre for Toxicology [*Research center*] (RCD) ..... CCT
Canadian Centre for Victims of Torture [*Formerly, Canadian Centre for Investigation & Prevention of Torture*] (AC) ..... CCVT
Canadian Centre on Substance Abuse (AC) ..... CCSA
Canadian Ceramic Society (AC) ..... CCS
Canadian Cerebral Palsy Sports Association [*Association Canadienne Sports de Paralysie Cerebrale*] (AC) ..... CCPSA
Canadian Certified General Accountants' Association ..... CCGAA
Canadian Certified Reference Materials Project (PDAA) ..... CCRMP
Canadian Chapter of the International Council of Community Churches [*Section Canadienne du Conseil International des Eglises Communautaires*] (AC) CCICCC
Canadian Charolais Association ..... CCA
Canadian Chemical Association (HGAA) ..... CCA
Canadian Chemical Producers Association ..... CCPA
Canadian Chicken Marketing Agency [*Office Canadien de Commercialisation des Poulets*] (AC) ..... CCMA
Canadian Chiefs of Staff Committee ..... COSC
Canadian Child and Youth Drama Association ..... CCYDA
Canadian Child Care Federation [*Formerly, Canadian Child Day Care Federation*] (AC) ..... CCCF
Canadian Children's Literature [*A publication*] (BRI) ..... Can CL
Canadian Children's Multimedia Foundation (AC) ..... CCMF
Canadian Children's Opera Chorus (AC) ..... CCOC
Canadian Children's Project, Inc. ..... CCP
Canadian Chiropractic Association ..... CCA

Canadian Circulation Management Association [*Association Canadienne des Chefs de Tirage*] (AC) .... CCMA
Canadian Circulations Audit Board [*Founded 1937*] (IRC) .... CCAB
Canadian Circumpolar Institute [*University of Alberta*] (IRC) CCI
Canadian Civil Liberties Association .... CCLA
Canadian Civil Liberties Union .... CCLU
Canadian Classification and Dictionary of Occupations [*A publication*] .... CCDO
Canadian Classification Research Group [*International Federation for Documentation*] .... CCRG
Canadian Clean Air Act (GNE) .... CCAA
Canadian Clearinghouse for Ongoing Research in Nursing [*University of Alberta*] (IID) .... CORN
Canadian Climate Center CCC
Canadian Clinical Nurse Specialist Interest Group (AC) .... CCNSIG
Canadian Club [*A whiskey*] CC
Canadian Club of New York (EA) .... CCNY
Canadian Coalition for Ecology, Ethics & Religion (AC) .... CCEER
Canadian Coalition for High Blood Pressure Prevention & Control [*Coalition Canadienne pour la Prevention et le Controle de l'Hypertension Arterielle*] (AC) .... CCHBPPC
Canadian Coalition for Nuclear Responsibility .... CCNR
Canadian Coast Guard .... CCG
Canadian Coast Guard [*ICAO designator*] (FAAC) .... CTG
Canadian Coast Guard College [*College de la Garde Cotiere Canadienne*] Sydney, Nova Scotia [*Library symbol National Library of Canada*] (NLC) .... NSSCG
Canadian Coast Guard, Quebec, PQ, Canada [*Library symbol*] [*Library of Congress*] (LCLS) .... CaQQTCG
Canadian Coast Guard [*Garde Cotiere Canadienne*] Quebec, Quebec [*Library symbol National Library of Canada*] (NLC) .... QQTCG
Canadian Coast Guard [*Garde Cotiere Canadienne*] St. John's, Newfoundland [*Library symbol Obsolete National Library of Canada*] (NLC) .... NFSTCG
Canadian Coast Guard Service .... CCGS
Canadian Coastal Zone Atlantic .... CCZA
Canadian Coastal Zone Pacific .... CCZP
Canadian Cognitive Abilities Test [*Academic achievement and aptitude test*] .... CCAT
Canadian College of Health Service Executives [*College Canadien des Directeurs de Services de Sante*] (AC) .... CCHSE
Canadian College of Medical Geneticists [*College Canadien de Geneticiens Medicaux*] (AC) .... CCMG
Canadian College of Organists .... CCO
Canadian College of Physicists in Medicine [*College Canadien des Physiciens en Medecine*] (AC) .... CCPM
Canadian College of Teachers [*See also CCE*] .... CCT
Canadian Colleges Athletic Association .... CCAA
Canadian Colonial Airways .... CCA
Canadian Command Active Sonobuoy System (PDAA) .... CANCASS
Canadian Commander, Army, Pacific (CINC) .... CANCOMARPAC
Canadian Commercial Bank .... CCB
Canadian Commercial Bank [*Toronto Stock Exchange symbol*] .... CCU
Canadian Commercial Corp. [*Government-owned*] (RDA) CCC
Canadian Commercial Law Guide (Commerce Clearing House) [*A publication*] (DLA) .... Can Com L Guide (CCH)
Canadian Commercial Law Reports [*1901-05*] [*A publication*] (DLA) .... Can Com Cas
Canadian Commercial Law Reports [*1901-05*] [*A publication*] (DLA) .... Can Com LR
Canadian Commercial Law Reports [*1901-05*] [*A publication*] (DLA) .... Can Com R
Canadian Commission for UNESCO, Ottawa, Ontario [*Library symbol National Library of Canada*] (BIB) .... OOCCU
Canadian Committee for Industrial Organization .... CCIO
Canadian Committee for the International Biological Programme .... CCIBP
Canadian Committee of Scientists & Scholars [*Comite Canadien des Savants et Scientifiques*] (AC) .... CCSS
Canadian Committee on Cataloguing [*Librarianship*] CCC
Canadian Committee on Financing University Research .... CCFUR
Canadian Committee on MARC .... CCM
[The] Canadian Committee to Protect Journalists (AC) .... CPJ
Canadian Commonwealth Association .... CCA
Canadian Communicable Disease Center .... CCDC
Canadian Communication Association .... CCA
Canadian Communications and Transportation Commission .... CCTC
Canadian Communications Foundation .... CCF
Canadian Communications Law Review [*A publication*] (DLA) .... Can Com L Rev
Canadian Communist League (Marxist-Leninist) .... CCL(ML)
Canadian Communist Party [*Political party*] .... KKP
Canadian Community Law Journal [*A publication*] (DLA) .... Can Com LJ
Canadian Community Newspapers Association [*Founded 1919*] .... CCNA
Canadian Community of Computer Educators (AC) .... CCCE
Canadian Comparative Literature Association [*See also ACLC*] .... CCLA
Canadian Comprehensive Auditing Foundation (HGAA) .... CCAF
Canadian Computer Complex (NITA) CCC
Canadian Computer Conference (MCD) CCC
Canadian Computer Dealer Association (EAIO) .... CCDA
Canadian Computer Graphics Association (AC) .... CCGA
Canadian Computer Show .... CCS
Canadian Computer-Based Reference Service [*National Library of Canada*] [*Information service or system*] (IID) .... CAN/CRS
Canadian Concerned Fathers Action Committee .... CCFAC
Canadian Concrete Masonry Producers' Association (EAIO) .... CCMPA
Canadian Concrete Pipe Association (AC) .... CCPA
Canadian Condominium Institute-National Chapter (AC) CCI
Canadian Conference of Catholic Bishops .... CCCB

Canadian Conference of the Arts .... CCA
Canadian Conference of Tourism Officials .... CCTO
Canadian Congress for Learning Opportunities for Women .... CCLOW
Canadian Congress of Applied Mechanics (PDAA) .... CANCAM
Canadian Congress of Applied Mechanics (HGAA) .... CCAM
Canadian Congress of Labour CCL
Canadian Congress of Neurological Sciences [*Congres Canadien des Sciences Neurologiques*] (AC) .... CCNS
Canadian Conservation Institute [*See also ICC*] [*National Museums of Canada*] [*Research center*] (RCD) CCI
Canadian Conservation Institute, National Museums of Canada [*Institut Canadien de Conservation, Musees Nationaux du Canada*] **Ottawa, Ontario** [*Library symbol National Library of Canada*] (NLC) .... OONMCC
Canadian Conservative Centre (EAIO) CCC
Canadian Consortium for Social Research (IID) .... CCSR
Canadian Construction Association .... CCA
Canadian Consulate General Library, New York, NY [*Library symbol*] [*Library of Congress*] (LCLS) .... NNCCG
Canadian Consultative Council on Multiculturalism .... CCCM
Canadian Consulting Agrologists Association [*L'Assiciation Canadienne des Agronomes-Conseils*] (AC) .... CCAA
Canadian Continental Oil [*Vancouver Stock Exchange symbol*] .... CBO
Canadian Control System [*For convoys in Canadian Coastal Zone*] .... CANCON
Canadian Cooperative Applications Satellite (HGAA) .... CAS
Canadian Co-Operative Association (AC) .... CCA
Canadian Cooperative Credit Society .... CCCS
Canadian Co-Ordinating Council on Deafness .... CCCD
Canadian Copper and Brass Development Association .... CCBDA
Canadian Copper Refiners Ltd., Montreal, PQ, Canada [*Library symbol Library of Congress*] (LCLS) .... CaQMCR
Canadian Copper Refiners Ltd., Montreal, Quebec [*Library symbol National Library of Canada*] (NLC) .... QMCR
Canadian Copyright Institute CCI
Canadian Corporate Management Co. Ltd. [*Toronto Stock Exchange symbol*] .... CCM
Canadian Corporate Names [*Canada Systems Group*] [*Information service or system*] (IID) .... CNAM
Canadian Corporate Shareholder Services Association [*Association Canadienne des Services aux Actionnaires*] (AC) .... CCSSA
Canadian Corporations [*Micromedia Ltd.*] [*Canada Information service or system*] (CRD) .... CanCorp
Canadian Corps Heavy Artillery [*World War I*] .... CCHA
Canadian Correspondence Art Gallery .... CCAG
Canadian Cosmetic, Toiletry & Fragrance Association [*Association Canadienne des Cosmetiques, Produit de Toilette et Parfums*] (AC) .... CCTFA
Canadian Cosmetics Careers Association .... CCCA
Canadian Council Cardiovascular Nurses [*Conseil Canadien des Infirmieres en Nursing Cardiovasculaire*] (AC) .... CCCN
[The] Canadian Council for Accreditation of Pharmacy Programs [*Le Conseil Canadien de l'Agrement des Programmes de Pharmacie*] (AC) .... CCAPP
Canadian Council for European Affairs [*Conseil Canadien des Affairs Europeenes*] (AC) .... CCEA
Canadian Council for Fisheries Research (ASF) .... CCFFR
Canadian Council for Human Resources in the Environment Industry [*Le Conseil Canadien des Ressources Humaines de l'Industrie de L'Environnement*] (AC) .... CCHREI
Canadian Council for International Business [*Conseil Canadien pour le Commerce International*] [*Also, Canadian Secretariat ICC/BIAC*] (AC) .... CCIB
Canadian Council for International Cooperation CCIC
Canadian Council for Multicultural & Intercultural Education (AC) .... CCMIE
Canadian Council for Non-Destructive Technology (HGAA) .... CCNDT
Canadian Council for Racial Harmony (AC) .... CCRH
Canadian Council for Refugees [*Conseil Canadien pour les Refugies*] [*Formerly, Standing Conference of Organizations Concerned for Refugees*] (AC) .... CCR
Canadian Council for Research in Education .... CCRE
Canadian Council for Research in Education, Ottawa, ON, Canada [*Library symbol Library of Congress Obsolete*] (LCLS) .... CaOORE
Canadian Council for Southeast Asian Studies [*Carleton University*] [*Research center*] (RCD) .... CCSEAS
Canadian Council for the Advancement of Education .... CCAE
Canadian Council for the Advancement of Education [*Le Conseil Canadien pour l'Avancement de l'Education*] (AC) .... CCAE
Canadian Council for the Advancement of Education (NFD) .... CCAE
Canadian Council of Archives [*Conseil Canadien des Archives*] (AC) .... CCA
Canadian Council of Better Business Bureaus [*Conseil Canadien des Bureaux d'Ethique Commerciale*] (AC) .... CCBBB
Canadian Council of Christian Charities (AC) CCCC
[The] Canadian Council of Christians & Jews [*Conseil Canadien des Chretiens et des Juifs*] (AC) .... CCCJ
Canadian Council of Churches (EAIO) CCC
Canadian Council of Engineering Students .... CCES
Canadian Council of Grocery Distributors [*Conseil Canadien de la Distribution Alimentaire*] (AC) .... CCDA
Canadian Council of Grocery Distributors [*Conseil Canadien de la Distribution Alimentaire*] (AC) .... CCGD
Canadian Council of Independent Laboratories [*Conseil Canadien des Laboratoires Independents*] (AC) CCIL
Canadian Council of Land Surveyors [*See also CCAG*] .... CCLS
Canadian Council of Library Schools [*Conseil Canadien des Ecoles de Bibliotheconomie*] (AC) .... CCLS
Canadian Council of Management Associations (HGAA) .... CCMA
Canadian Council of Motor Transport Administrators [*Conseil Canadien des Administrateurs en Transport Motorise*] (AC) .... CCMTA

Canadian Council of Professional Engineers .... CCPE
Canadian Council of Resource and Environment Ministers .... CCREM
Canadian Council of Resource Ministers, Montreal, PQ, Canada [*Library symbol Library of Congress*] (LCLS) .... CaQMCCR
Canadian Council of Resource Ministers [*Conseil Canadien des Ministres des Ressources*] **Montreal, Quebec** [*Library symbol National Library of Canada*] (NLC) .... QMCCR
Canadian Council of Teachers of English .... CCTE
Canadian Council of Teachers of English & Language Arts (AC) .... CCTELA
Canadian Council of Technicians & Technologists [*Conseil Canadien des Techniciens et Technologues*] (AC) .... CCTT
Canadian Council of the Blind .... CCB
Canadian Council of University Biology Chairs (AC) .... CCUBC
Canadian Council on Animal Care .... CCAC
Canadian Council on Children and Youth [*Research center*] (RCD) .... CCCY
Canadian Council on Health Facilities Accreditation .... CCHFA
Canadian Council on Hospital Accreditation (HCT) .... CCHA
Canadian Council on International Law [*Conseil Canadien de Droit International*] (AC) CCII
Canadian Council on Rehabilitation & Work [*Le Conseil Canadien de la Readaptation et du Travail*] (AC) .... CCRT
Canadian Council on Rehabilitation & Work (AC) .... CCRW
Canadian Council on Smoking and Health .... CCSH
Canadian Council on Social Development .... CCSD
Canadian Council on Social Development, Ottawa, ON, Canada [*Library symbol Library of Congress*] (LCLS) .... CaOOCW
Canadian Council on Social Development [*Conseil Canadien de Developpement Social*] **Ottawa, Ontario** [*Library symbol National Library of Canada*] (NLC) .... OOCW
Canadian Council on Urban and Regional Research (EA) .... CCURR
Canadian Country Music Association [*Association de la Musique Country Canadienne*] (AC) .... CCMA
Canadian Court Martial Appeal Reports [*1957-*] [*A publication*] (DLA) .... CMAR
Canadian Cowboys Association .... CCA
Canadian Craft & Hobby Association (AC) .... CCHA
Canadian Crafts Council CCC
Canadian Creative Music Collective [*Jazz group*] .... CCMC
Canadian Credit Institute CCI
Canadian Credit Management Association [*Formerly, Creditel of Canada Ltd.*] .... CREDITEL
Canadian Crew Energy [*Vancouver Stock Exchange symbol*] .... KNC
Canadian Criminal Cases [*A publication*] (DLA) .... Can Cr Cas
Canadian Criminal Cases [*Law Book, Inc.*] [*Information service or system*] CCC
Canadian Criminal Cases, Annotated [*A publication*] (DLA) .... Can Crim Cas
Canadian Criminal Cases, Annotated [*A publication*] (DLA) .... Can Crim Cas Ann
Canadian Criminal Cases, New Series [*A publication*] (DLA) .... Can Crim Cas (NS)
Canadian Criminal Justice Association [*Association Canadienne de Justice Penale*] (AC) .... CCJA
Canadian Criminal Reports [*A publication*] (DLA) .... Can Cr R
Canadian Criminology and Corrections Association .... CCCA
Canadian Critical care Society [*Societe Canadienne de Soins Intensifs*] (AC) .... CCCS
Canadian Crossroads International CCI
Canadian Culinary Institute (AC) CCI
Canadian Curtiss-Wright Ltd. [*Toronto Stock Exchange symbol*] .... CCW
Canadian Custom Bonded .... CCB
Canadian Cycling Association .... CCA
Canadian Cystic Fibrosis Foundation .... CCFF
Canadian Daily Newspaper Publishers Association .... CDNPA
Canadian Daily Newspapers Association .... CDNA
Canadian Dairy & Food Industries Supply Association [*Association Canadienne des Fournisseurs des Industries Laitierie et de l'Alimentation*] (AC) .... CDFISA
Canadian Dairy Commission .... CDC
Canadian Dance Teachers Association [*Association Canadienne des Professeurs de Danse*] (AC) .... CDTA
Canadian Data Processing Service Organisation (PDAA) .... CDAPSO
Canadian Deaf & Hard of Hearing Forum (AC) .... CDHHF
Canadian Deaf Sports Association [*Association des Sports des Sourds du Canada*] (AC) .... CDSA
Canadian Deafblind & Rubella Association [*Association Canadienne de la Surdi-Cecite et de la Rubeole*] (AC) .... CDBRA
Canadian Deafness Research & Training Institute [*Institut Canadien de Recherche et de Formation sur la Surdite*] (AC) .... CDRTI
Canadian Decorating Products Association [*Association Canadienne de l'Industrie de Decoration*] (AC) .... CDPA
Canadian Defence Education Establishment (PDAA) .... CDEE
Canadian Defence Liaison Staff (Washington) (AFM) .... CDLS(W)
Canadian Defence Research Board .... CDRB
Canadian Defense Preparedness Association .... CDPA
Canadian Dental Assistants Association (AC) .... CDAA
Canadian Dental Association .... CDA
Canadian Dental Association, Ottawa, ON, Canada [*Library symbol Library of Congress*] (LCLS) .... CaOOCDA
Canadian Dental Association, Ottawa, Ontario [*Library symbol National Library of Canada*] (NLC) .... OOCDA
Canadian Dental Hygenists' Association [*Association Canadienne des Hygienistes Denteurs*] (AC) .... CDHA
Canadian Dental Research Foundation (HGAA) .... CDRF
Canadian Department of Agriculture .... CDA
Canadian Department of Defence Production .... CDDP
Canadian Department of Fisheries and Oceans, Marine Fish Division [*Research center*] (RCD) .... MFD
Canadian Department of Industry, Trade, and Commerce (DLA) .... Canada Commerce
Canadian Department of National Defence .... CDND
Canadian Department of Supply and Services (MCD) .... CDSS
Canadian Depository for Securities .... CDS
Canadian Dermatology Association (EAIO) .... CDA
Canadian Destroyers Atlantic .... CANDESLANT
Canadian Destroyers Far East .... CANDESFE
Canadian Destroyers Pacific .... CANDESPAC
Canadian Deuterium Reactor (GAAI) .... CANDU
Canadian Deuterium Uranium [*Family of nuclear reactors developed in Canada*] .... CANDU
Canadian Deuterium Uranium Boiling Light-Water [*Nuclear reactor*] .... CANDU BLW
Canadian Development Institute (AC) .... CDI
Canadian Dexter Cattle Association (AC) .... CDCA
Canadian Diabetic Association .... CDA
Canadian Diamond Drilling Association .... CDDA
Canadian Dietetic Association .... CDA
Canadian Direct Mail Association .... CDMA
Canadian Direct Mail/Marketing Association .... CDMMA
Canadian Direct Marketing Association .... CDMA
Canadian Directory of Completed Master's Theses in Nursing [*University of Alberta*] [*Information service or system*] (IID) .... CAMN
Canadian Disability Rights Council (AC) .... CDRC
Canadian Disaggregated Interdepartmental Economic Model .... CANDIDE
Canadian Disarmament Information Service .... CANDIS
Canadian Disc Jockey Association (AC) .... CDJA
Canadian Documentation [*National Research Council*] (NITA) .... CANDOC
Canadian Documentation Centre, Fitness and Sport, Ottawa, ON, Canada [*Library symbol Library of Congress*] (LCLS) .... CaOOFS
Canadian Dollar [*Monetary unit*] .... CD
Canadian Dollar [*Vancouver Stock Exchange symbol*] .... XCD
Canadian Dollar Investments (Bermuda) Ltd. [*Toronto Stock Exchange symbol*] .... CDI
Canadian Donkey & Mule Association (AC) .... CDMA
[*The*] **Canadian Doukhobor Society** (AC) .... CDS
Canadian Down Syndrome Society .... CDSS
Canadian Dressage Owners and Riders Association .... CADORA
Canadian Drilling Association [*Also, Canadian Diamond Drilling Association*] (AC) .... CDA
Canadian Drilling Research Association (HGAA) .... CDRA
Canadian Driver and Safety Educators Association .... CDSA
Canadian Drug Manufactures Association (AC) .... CDMA
Canadian Dun's Market Identifiers [*Dun & Bradstreet Canada Ltd.*] [*Information service or system*] (CRD) .... CDMI
Canadian Eagle Aviation Ltd. [*ICAO designator*] (FAAC) .... HIA
Canadian Earth Energy Association [*Association Canadienne de l'Energie du Sol*] (AC) .... CEEA
Canadian Economics Association [*See also ACE*] .... CEA
Canadian Education Association .... CEA
Canadian Education Association, Toronto, ON, Canada [*Library symbol Library of Congress*] (LCLS) .... CaOTCEA
[*The*] **Canadian Education Association** [*L'Association Canadienne d'Education*] **Toronto, Ontario** [*Library symbol National Library of Canada*] (NLC) .... OTCEA
Canadian Educational Researchers Association [*See also ACCE*] .... CERA
Canadian Educational Standards Institute (AC) .... CESI
Canadian Efficiency Decoration [*Military*] (DD) .... ED
Canadian Egg Marketing Agency .... CEMA
Canadian Egg Producers Council .... CEPC
Canadian Electrical Association .... CEA
Canadian Electrical Code .... CEC
Canadian Electrical Distributors Association, Inc. .... CEDA
Canadian Electrical Manufacturers' Association .... CEMA
Canadian Electronic & Appliance Service Association [*Organisation Canadienne de Service d'Appareils Domestique*] (AC) .... CEASA
Canadian Electronic Sales Representatives .... CESR
Canadian Embassy, Washington, DC [*Library symbol Library of Congress*] (LCLS) .... DCaE
Canadian Encyclopedic Digest [*A publication*] (DLA) .... CED
Canadian Energy Pipeline Association (AC) .... CEPA
Canadian Energy Research Institute [*University of Calgary*] [*Research center*] (RCD) .... CERI
Canadian Energy Services Ltd. [*Toronto Stock Exchange symbol*] .... CE
Canadian Engineering Manpower Council .... CEMC
Canadian Engineering Standards Association [*Later, Canadian Standards Association*] .... CESA
Canadian Engineers (DMA) .... CE
Canadian Environment [*Database*] [*WATDOC*] [*Information service or system*] (CRD) .... CENV
Canadian Environment Industry Association [*Association Canadienne des Industries de l'Environnement*] (AC) .... CEIA
Canadian Environmental Assessment Research Council .... CEARC
Canadian Environmental Auditing Association (AC) .... CEAA
Canadian Environmental Defence Fund (AC) .... CEDF
Canadian Environmental Exposition [*Heating, Refrigerating, and Air Conditioning Institute of Canada*] (TSPED) .... CEX
Canadian Environmental Law Association .... CELA
Canadian Environmental Law Association. Newsletter [*A publication*] (DLA) .... CELA Newsletter
Canadian Environmental Law News [*A publication*] (DLA) .... C Environ LN
Canadian Environmental Law News [*A publication*] (DLA) .... Can Env L News
Canadian Environmental Law News [*A publication*] (DLA) .... Can Environ LN
Canadian Environmental Law Reports [*A publication*] (DLA) .... CELR
Canadian Environmental Law Research Foundation (GNE) .... CELRF
Canadian Environmental Network (GNE) .... CEN

Canadian Environmental Protection Act ... CEPA
Canadian Equestrian Federation [*Federation Equestre Canadienne*] (AC) ... CEF
Canadian Equestrian Team ... CET
Canadian Estate Land Corp. [*Vancouver Stock Exchange symbol*] ... CZY
Canadian Ethnic Studies Association ... CESA
Canadian Evaluation Society [*Societe Canadienne l'Evaluation*] (AC) ... CES
Canadian Executive Service Organization ... CESO
Canadian Expedition to Study the Alpha Ridge [*1983*] ... CESAR
Canadian Expeditionary Forces ... CEF
Canadian Export Association ... CEA
Canadian Export Association, Montreal, PQ, Canada [*Library symbol Library of Congress*] (LCLS) ... CaQMCEA
Canadian Export Association [*Association Canadienne d'Exportation*] **Montreal, Quebec** [*Library symbol National Library of Canada*] (NLC) ... QMCEA
Canadian Exporters' Association [*Association des Exportateurs Canadiens*] (AC) ... CEA
Canadian Express Ltd. [*Toronto Stock Exchange symbol Vancouver Stock Exchange symbol*] ... XE
Canadian Familial Polyposis Registry (DMAA) ... CFPR
Canadian Farm and Industrial Equipment Institute ... CFIEI
Canadian Farm Management Data System, Agriculture Canada [*Systeme Canadien deDonnees sur la Gestion Agricole, Agriculture Canada*] **Guelph, Ontario** [*Library symbol National Library of Canada*] (NLC) ... OGCF
Canadian Farmworkers Union (AC) ... CFU
Canadian Federal Corporations and Directors [*Canada Systems Group*] [*Information service or system*] (IID) ... CFCD
Canadian Federal Warning Center ... CFWC
Canadian Federation for the Humanities [*See also FCEH*] [*Research center*] (RCD) ... CFH
Canadian Federation of Agriculture ... CFA
Canadian Federation of Biological Societies ... CFBS
Canadian Federation of Business and Professional Women's Clubs [*Established 1930*] ... CFBPWC
Canadian Federation of Chefs & Cooks [*Federation Canadienne des Chefs et Cuisiniers*] (AC) ... CFCC
Canadian Federation of Communications Workers [*See also FCC*] ... CFCW
Canadian Federation of Deans of Management & Administrative Studies [*Federation Canadienne des Doyens de Gestion et d'Administration*] (AC) ... CFDMAS
Canadian Federation of Engineers and Scientists ... CFES
Canadian Federation of Film Societies ... CFFS
Canadian Federation of Friends of Museums (AC) ... CFFM
Canadian Federation of Humane Societies [*Federation des Societes Candiennes d'Assistance aux Animaux*] (AC) ... CFHS
Canadian Federation of Independent Business ... CFIB
Canadian Federation of Independent Business, Willowdale, Ontario [*Library symbol National Library of Canada*] (BIB) ... OWCF
Canadian Federation of Independent Grocers [*Federation Canadienne des Epiciers Independants*] (AC) ... CFIG
Canadian Federation of Insurance Agents and Brokers ... CFIAB
Canadian Federation of Labour ... CFL
Canadian Federation of Mayors and Municipalities ... CFMM
Canadian Federation of Music Teachers' Associations ... CFMTA
Canadian Federation of Students ... CFS
Canadian Federation of University Women ... CFUW
Canadian Feed Industry Association [*Association Canadienne des Industries de l'Alimentation Animale*] (AC) ... CFIA
Canadian Feed Information Centre (AC) ... CFIC
Canadian Feed the Children (AC) ... CFTC
Canadian Fencing Association ... CFA
Canadian Fencing Federation [*Federation Canadienne d'Escrime*] (AC) ... CFF
Canadian Fertility & Andrology Society [*Societe Canadienne de Fertilite et d'Andrologie*] (AC) ... CFAS
Canadian Fiber Foods [*Vancouver Stock Exchange symbol*] ... CKF
Canadian Fibreboard Manufacturers' [*Association Canadienne des Manufacturiers d'Isolant de Fibre de Bois*] (AC) ... CFMA
Canadian Field Artillery ... CFA
Canadian Field Hockey Association ... CFHA
Canadian Field Hockey Council ... CFHC
Canadian Figure Skating Association ... CFSA
Canadian Film and Television Association ... CFTA
Canadian Film & Television Production Association [*Association Canadienne de Production de Film et Television*] (AC) ... CFTPA
Canadian Film and Videotape Certification Office ... CFVCO
Canadian Film Centre [*Centre Canadien du Film*] [*Formerly, Canadian Centre for Advanced Film Studies*] (AC) ... CFC
Canadian Film Development Corp. ... CFDC
Canadian Film Editors Guild ... CFEG
Canadian Film Group ... CFG
Canadian Film Institute [*See also ICF*] ... CFI
Canadian Film Institute, Ottawa, ON, Canada [*Library symbol Library of Congress*] (LCLS) ... CaOOCF
Canadian Film Institute [*Institut Canadien du Film*] **Ottawa, Ontario** [*Library symbol National Library of Canada*] (NLC) ... OOCF
Canadian Film-Makers Distribution Centre ... CFDC
Canadian Film-Makers Distribution Centre ... CFMDC
Canadian Finance & Leasing Association (AC) ... CFLA
Canadian Financial Database [*The Globe and Mail*] [*Toronto, ON*] [*Information service or system*] (IID) ... CFD
Canadian Fire Safety Association (AC) ... CFSA
Canadian Fire Underwriters' Association [*Later, Canadian Underwriters' Association*] ... CFUA
Canadian Fitness & Lifestyle Research Institute [*Institut Canadien de la Recherche sur la Condition Physique et le Mode de Vie*] (AC) ... CFLRI
Canadian Flexible Foam Manufacturers' Association (AC) ... CFFMA
Canadian Flight Experiment [*NASA*] ... CANEX
Canadian Fluid Power Association [*Association Canadienne d'Energie Fluide*] (AC) ... CFPA
Canadian Folk Music Society ... CFMS
Canadian Food and Allied Workers ... CFAW
Canadian Food Brokers Association [*Association Canadienne des Courtiers en Alimentation*] (AC) ... CFBA
Canadian Food Processors Association ... CFPA
Canadian Food Products Development Center, Portage La Prairie, Manitoba [*Library symbol National Library of Canada*] (NLC) ... MPCFP
Canadian Food Products Development Center, Portage La Prairie, MB, Canada [*Library symbol Library of Congress*] (LCLS) ... CaMPCFP
Canadian Food Service Executives Association ... CFSEA
Canadian Food Service Supervisors Association ... CFSSA
Canadian Foodgrains Bank Association Inc. [*Association de la Banque Candienne de Grains Inc.*] (AC) ... CFGB
Canadian Football League ... CFL
Canadian Football League Players' Association [*Association des Joueurs de la Ligue de Football Canadienne*] (AC) ... CFLPA
Canadian Force Communications System ... CFCS
Canadian Forces (AABC) ... CF
Canadian Forces Administrative Order ... CFAO
Canadian Forces Aerospace and Navigation School, Canadian Forces Base Winnipeg, Westwin, Manitoba [*Library symbol National Library of Canada*] (NLC) ... MWCF
Canadian Forces Air Defense Command [*ICAO designator*] (FAAC) ... CFADC
Canadian Forces Air Navigation School ... CFANS
Canadian Forces Attache ... CFA
Canadian Forces Auxiliary Vessels [*Military*] ... CFAV
Canadian Forces Base (NATG) ... CFB
Canadian Forces Base Barrington, Stone Horse, Nova Scotia [*Library symbol National Library of Canada*] (NLC) ... NSSHCF
Canadian Forces Base Barrington, Stone Horse, NS, Canada [*Library symbol*] [*Library of Congress*] (LCLS) ... CaNSShCF
Canadian Forces Base, Cornwallis, Nova Scotia [*Library symbol National Library of Canada*] (NLC) ... NSCCF
Canadian Forces Base, Cornwallis, NS, Canada [*Library symbol*] [*Library of Congress*] (LCLS) ... CaNSCoCF
Canadian Forces Base, Ensign, Cornwallis, NS, Canada [*Library symbol*] [*Library of Congress*] (LCLS) ... CaNSCoCFE
Canadian Forces Base, Gagetown, NB, Canada [*Library symbol Library of Congress*] (LCLS) ... CaNBGACF
Canadian Forces Base, Gagetown, New Brunswick [*Library symbol National Library of Canada*] (NLC) ... NBGACF
Canadian Forces Base, Greenwood, NS, Canada [*Library symbol*] [*Library of Congress*] (LCLS) ... CaNSGCFA
Canadian Forces Base Halifax, Ships Recreational Library, Halifax, NS, Canada [*Library symbol*] [*Library of Congress*] (LCLS) ... CaNSHNS
Canadian Forces Base, Ottawa, Ontario [*Library symbol National Library of Canada*] (BIB) ... OOCFB
Canadian Forces Base, Royal Canadian Army Museum, Shilo, MB, Canada [*Library symbol Library of Congress*] (LCLS) ... CaMShCFAM
Canadian Forces Base St. Jean [*Base des Forces Canadiennes St.-Jean*], Quebec [*Library symbol National Library of Canada*] (NLC) ... QSTJCF
Canadian Forces Base Winnipeg, Canadian Forces Aerospace and Navigation School, Westwin, MB, Canada [*Library symbol*] [*Library of Congress*] (LCLS) ... CaMWCF
Canadian Forces College Library [*UTLAS symbol*] ... CFL
Canadian Forces College, Toronto, ON, Canada [*Library symbol Library of Congress*] (LCLS) ... CaOTRC
Canadian Forces College, Toronto, Ontario [*Library symbol National Library of Canada*] (NLC) ... OTRC
Canadian Forces Communication Command (NATG) ... CFCC
Canadian Forces Decoration ... CD
Canadian Forces Exchange [*Military*] ... CANEX
Canadian Forces Headquarters [*NATO*] (NATG) ... CANFORCEHED
Canadian Forces Headquarters [*NATO*] ... CFHQ
Canadian Forces Hospital ... CFH
Canadian Forces in Europe (NATG) ... CFE
Canadian Forces Institute of Aviation Medicine (PDAA) ... CFIAM
Canadian Forces Low Level Air Defense System [*Military*] ... CFLLADS
Canadian Forces Maritime Warfare School [*Canadian Navy*] ... CFMWFS
Canadian Forces Postal System ... CFPS
Canadian Forces Project Management Office (HGAA) ... CFPMO
Canadian Forces Publication ... CFP
Canadian Forces Recruiting Centre ... CFRC
Canadian Forces School of Communications and Electronics, Kingston, Ontario [*Library symbol National Library of Canada*] (BIB) ... OKC
Canadian Forces - Second Career Assistance Network ... CF-SCAN
Canadian Forces Special Projects Laboratory (HGAA) ... CFSPL
Canadian Forces Staff School, Canada Department of National Defence [*College d'Etat-Major des Forces Canadiennes, Ministere de la Defense Nationale*] **Toronto, Ontario** [*Library symbol National Library of Canada*] (NLC) ... OTRCS
Canadian Forces Station ... CFS
Canadian Forces Supplementary Order ... CFSO
Canadian Forces Supply System (MCD) ... CFSS
Canadian Forces Supply System Upgrade ... CFSSU
Canadian Forces Technical Orders (MCD) ... CFTO
Canadian Foremost Ltd. [*Toronto Stock Exchange symbol*] ... CFT
Canadian Foresters Life Insurance Society (EA) ... CFLIS
Canadian Forestry Association [*See also AFC*] ... CFA
Canadian Forestry Association of British Columbia ... CFABC
Canadian Forestry Corps [*World War I*] ... CFC
Canadian Forestry Service ... CFS

Canadian Forum [*A publication*] (BRI) .... CF
Canadian Foundation Co. Ltd. [*Toronto Stock Exchange symbol*] .... CDF
Canadian Foundation for AIDS Research [*Fondation Canadienne de Recherche sur le SIDA*] (AC) .... CanFar
Canadian Foundation for Economic Education [*Fondation d'Education Economique*] (AC) .... CFEE
Canadian Foundation for the Advancement of Pharmacy [*Fondation Canadienne pour l'Avancement de la Pharmacie*] [*Also, Canadian Foundation for Pharmacy*] (AC) .... CFP
Canadian Foundation for the Study of Infant Deaths [*Fondation Canadienne sur l'Etude de la Mortalite Infantile*] (AC) .... CFSID
Canadian Foundation for World Development (AC) .... CFWD
Canadian Foundation on Alcohol and Drug Dependencies .... CFADD
Canadian Foundation on Compulsive Gambling (AC) .... CFCG
Canadian Foundry Association [*Association des Fonderies Canadiennes*] (AC) .... CFA
Canadian Fourteenth Air Training Group Headquarters, Winnipeg..... CANAIRPEG
Canadian Fraternal Association [*Association Canadienne des Societes Fraternelles*] (AC) .... CFA
Canadian Free Trade Agreement (ECON) .... CFTA
Canadian Freight Association .... CFA
Canadian French [*Language*] (BARN) .... Can Fr
Canadian Friends of Mine (EA) .... CFM
Canadian Friends Service Committe [*Also, Religious Society of Friends*] (AC) .... CFSC
Canadian Fusion Fuels Technology Project .... CFFTP
Canadian Futurity Oils Ltd. [*Toronto Stock Exchange symbol*] .... CAF
Canadian Garrison Artillery .... CGA
Canadian Garrison Regiment (DMA) .... CGR
Canadian Gas Association .... CGA
Canadian Gas Processors Association (AC) .... CGPA
Canadian Gas Research Institute [*Canadian Gas Association*] (IRC) .... CGRI
Canadian Gas Research Institute, Don Mills, ON, Canada [*Library symbol Library of Congress*] (LCLS) .... CaOTCGR
Canadian Gas Research Institute, Don Mills, Ontario [*Library symbol National Library of Canada*] (NLC) .... OTCGR
Canadian General Capital [*Associated Press*] (SAG) .... CdnGn
Canadian General Capital [*NYSE symbol*] (SAG) .... CGG
Canadian General Electric Co. Ltd. [*Toronto Stock Exchange symbol*] .... CGE
Canadian General Electric Co. Ltd., Peterborough, ON, Canada [*Library symbol Library of Congress*] (LCLS) .... CaOPeTCG
Canadian General Electric Co. Ltd., Peterborough, Ontario [*Library symbol National Library of Canada*] (NLC) .... OPETCG
Canadian General Electric Co. Ltd., Toronto, ON, Canada [*Library symbol Library of Congress*] (LCLS) .... CaOTGE
Canadian General Investments Ltd. [*Toronto Stock Exchange symbol*] .... CGI
Canadian General Standards Board [*Formerly, Canadian Government Specifications Board*] .... CGSB
Canadian Genetic Diseases Network (AC) .... CGDN
Canadian Genl Cp 9.125%'TOPrS' [*NYSE symbol*] (TTSB) .... CGGPrT
Canadian Geographic [*A publication*] (BRI) .... CG
Canadian Geographical Society (BARN) .... CGS
Canadian Geophysical Union .... CGU
Canadian Geophysics Congress (AC) .... CGC
Canadian Geoscience Council [*Conseil Geoscientifique Canadien*] (AC) .... CGC
Canadian Geotechnical Society .... CGS
Canadian Geriatrics Research Society .... CGRS
Canadian Geriatrics Research Society, Toronto, Ontario [*Library symbol National Library of Canada*] (NLC) .... OTOGR
Canadian Gerontological Nursing Association (AC) .... CGNA
Canadian Giant Explorations [*Vancouver Stock Exchange symbol*] .... CEG
Canadian Give the Gift of Literacy Foundation (AC) .... CGGLF
Canadian Goat Society .... CGS
Canadian Gold Resources [*Vancouver Stock Exchange symbol*] .... CGO
Canadian Golf Superintendents Association [*Association Canadienne des Surintendants de Golf*] (AC) .... CGSA
Canadian Good Roads Association .... CGRA
Canadian Government Expositions Centre, Department of Supply and Services [*Centre des Expositions du Gouvernement Canadien, Ministere des Approvisionnements et Services*] Ottawa, Ontario [*Library symbol National Library of Canada*] (NLC) .... OOGE
Canadian Government Office of Tourism .... CGOT
Canadian Government Photo Centre .... CGPC
Canadian Government Purchasing Service (PDAA) .... CGPS
Canadian Government Travel Bureau, Reference Library, Ottawa, ON, Canada [*Library symbol Library of Congress*] (LCLS) .... CaOOTB
Canadian Grain Commission, Agriculture Canada [*Commission Canadienne des Grains, Agriculture Canada*] Winnipeg, Manitoba [*Library symbol National Library of Canada*] (NLC) .... MWGR
Canadian Graphite [*Vancouver Stock Exchange symbol*] .... CDT
Canadian Green Bag [*A publication*] (DLA) .... Can Green Bag
Canadian Ground Water Association [*Association Canadienne des Eaux Souterraine*] [*Formerly, Canadian Water Well Contractors Association*] [*Formerly, Canadian Water Well Association*] (AC) .... CGWA
Canadian Group of Painters [*1933-69*] (NGC) .... CGP
Canadian Group Psychotherapy Association (AC) .... CGPA
Canadian Guard Association [*Association Canadienne des Gardiens*] (AC)..... CGA
Canadian Guidance and Counselling Association .... CGCA
Canadian Guidance & Counselling Foundation (AC) .... CGCF
Canadian Guide Dogs for the Blind (AC) .... CGDB
Canadian Hail Underwriters Association .... CHUA
Canadian Handball Association [*Federation de Balle au mur du Canada*] (AC) .... CHA
Canadian Hard of Hearing Association .... CHHA

Canadian Hardware & Housewares Manufacturers' Association [*Association Canadienne des Fabricants en Quincaillerie et Article Menagers*] (AC) .... CHHMA
Canadian Hardwood Plywood Association (AC) .... CHPA
Canadian Head Injury Coalition (AC) .... CHIC
Canadian Health Alliance to Stop Therapist Exploitation Now (AC) ...... CHASTEN
Canadian Health Association .... CHA
Canadian Health Economics Research Association [*See also ACRES*] .... CHERA
Canadian Health Education Specialists Society .... CHESS
Canadian Health Food Association .... CHFA
Canadian Health Insurance Association .... CHIA
Canadian Health Libraries Association .... CHLA
Canadian Health Record Association .... CHRA
Canadian Hearing Society (AC) .... CHS
Canadian Heat Exchange & Vessel Manufacturers Association (AC) ..... CHEVMA
Canadian Helicopters [*ICAO designator*] (FAAC) .... WSR
Canadian Hemochromatosis Society [*Societe Canadienne de l'Hemochromatose*] (AC) .... CHS
Canadian Hemophilia Society [*Societe Canadienne de l'Hemophilie*] (AC) ...... CHS
Canadian Heritage Information Network [*National Museums of Canada*] [*Ottawa, ON*] [*Information service or system*] (IID) .... CHIN
Canadian Heritage River System [*NPPAC*] .... CHRS
Canadian High Technology Week [*Trade show*] (ITD) .... CHTW
Canadian Highland Cattle Society [*Societe Canadienne des Eleveurs de Bovins Highland*] .... CHCS
Canadian Historical Association [*See also SHC*] .... CHA
Canadian Historical Production/Injection File [*Petroleum Information Corp.*] [*Information service or system*] (CRD) .... CHST
Canadian Historical Review [*A publication*] (BRI) .... Can Hist R
Canadian Holistic Medicine Association .... CHMA
Canadian Holistic Nurses Association (AC) .... CHNA
Canadian Holocust Remembrance Association (AC) .... CHRA
Canadian Home & School & Parent-Teacher Federation [*Federation Canadienne des Associations Foyer-Ecole et Parents-Maitres*] (AC) ... CHSPTF
Canadian Home Builders' Association .... CHBA
Canadian Home Care Association [*Association Canadienne de Soins et Services a Domicile*] (AC) .... CHCA
Canadian Home Economics Association [*Association Canadienne d'Economie Familiale*] (AC) .... CHEA
Canadian Home Economics Association Foundation [*Fondation de l'Association Canadienne d'Economie Familiale*] (AC) .... CHEAF
Canadian Home Fitness Test [*Medicine*] .... CHFT
Canadian Home Insulation Plan .... CHIP
Canadian Home Renovation Program .... CHRP
Canadian Home Shopping Club .... CHSC
Canadian Home Shopping Network [*Television*] .... CHSN
Canadian Home Shopping Network Ltd. [*Toronto Stock Exchange symbol*] .... CWS
Canadian Horticultural Council [*Conseil Canadien de l'Horticulture*] (AC) .... CHC
Canadian Horticultural Council [*Conseil Canadien de l'Horticulture*], Ottawa, Ontario [*Library symbol National Library of Canada*] (BIB) .... OOCHC
Canadian Hospital Association .... CHA
Canadian Hospital Association [*Association des Hopitaux du Canada*] Ottawa,Ontario [*Library symbol National Library of Canada*] (NLC) .... OOCHA
Canadian Hospital Association, Toronto, ON, Canada [*Library symbol Library of Congress*] (LCLS) .... CaOTCHA
Canadian Hospital Association [*Association des Hopitaux du Canada*] Toronto, Ontario [*Library symbol National Library of Canada*] (NLC) ...... OTCHA
Canadian Hospital Engineering Society .... CHES
Canadian Hotel Marketing & Sales Executive (AC) .... CHMSE
Canadian Housing & Renewal Association (AC) .... CHRA
Canadian Housing Design Council [*CMHC*] .... CHDC
Canadian Housing Information Centre, Canada Mortgage and Housing Corp. [*Centre Canadien de Documentation sur l'Habitation, Societe Canadienne d'Hypotheques et de Logement*] Ottawa, Ontario [*Library symbol National Library of Canada*] (NLC) .... OOCM
Canadian Human Rights Commission [*See also CCDP*] .... CHRC
Canadian Human Rights Commission, Ottawa, ON, Canada [*Library symbol Library of Congress*] (LCLS) .... CaOOCHR
Canadian Human Rights Commission [*Commission Canadienne des Droits de la Personne*] Ottawa, Ontario [*Library symbol National Library of Canada*] (NLC) .... OOCHR
Canadian Human Rights Reporter [*A publication*] (DLA) .... Can Human Rights Rep
Canadian Humanist Publications (AC) .... CHP
Canadian Hunger Foundation [*Fondation Canadienne Contre la Faim*] (AC).... CHF
Canadian Hunter Exploration Ltd., Calgary, AB, Canada [*Library symbol Library of Congress*] (LCLS) .... CaACHE
Canadian Hunter Exploration Ltd., Calgary, Alberta [*Library symbol National Library of Canada*] (NLC) .... ACHE
Canadian Hydrocarbons Ltd. [*Toronto Stock Exchange symbol*] (SPSG) .... CDH
Canadian Hydrographic Association [*Association Canadienne d'Hydrographie*] (AC) .... CHA
Canadian Hydrographic Service (MCD) .... CHS
Canadian Hydrological Operational Multipurpose Subprogramme [*Environment Canada*] [*Information service or system*] (CRD) .... CHOMS
Canadian Hypertension Society [*Societe Canadienne d'Hypertension Arterielle*] (AC) .... CHS
Canadian Icelandic Horse Federation (AC) .... CIHF
Canadian Image Processing and Pattern Recognition Society .... CIPPRS
Canadian Imperial Bank of Commerce .... CIBC
Canadian Imperial Bank of Commerce [*Toronto Stock Exchange symbol Vancouver Stock Exchange symbol*] .... CM
Canadian Imperial Bank of Commerce, Toronto, ON, Canada [*Library symbol Library of Congress*] (LCLS) .... CaOTCIB

Canadian Imperial Bank of Commerce, Toronto, Ontario [*Library symbol National Library of Canada*] (NLC) .... OTCIB
Canadian Imperial Bk [*TS, exchange symbol*] (TTSB) .... CM
Canadian Imperial Ginseng Products Ltd. [*Associated Press*] (SAG) .... CdnIGin
Canadian Imperial Ginseng Products Ltd. [*NASDAQ symbol*] (SAG) .... IGPF
Canadian Implant Association (EAIO) .... CIA
Canadian Import Tribunal [*QL Systems Ltd.*] [*Information service or system*] (CRD) .... CIT
Canadian Importers Association .... CIA
Canadian Income Plus Fund 1986 Trust Units [*Toronto Stock Exchange symbol*] .... CNF
Canadian Independent Adjusters Conference .... CIAC
Canadian Independent Record Producers Association .... CIRPA
Canadian Independent Record Production Association (AC) .... CIRPA
Canadian Independent Recording Artists in Concert [*Pronounced "kerrack"*] .... CIRAC
Canadian Independent Telephone Association .... CITA
Canadian Index of Computer Literature [*A publication*] CICL
Canadian Indian/Native Studies Association .... CINSA
Canadian Industrial Innovation Centre (AC) CIIC
Canadian Industrial Innovation Centre/Waterloo [*University of Waterloo*] [*Research center*] (RCD) .... CIIC/W
Canadian Industrial Minerals Corp. [*Vancouver Stock Exchange symbol*] .... CIJ
Canadian Industrial Preparedness Association (HGAA) .... CIPA
Canadian Industrial Relations Association [*See also ACRI*] .... CIRA
Canadian Industrial Renewal Board [*Montreal, PQ*] .... CIRB
Canadian Industrial Renewal Program .... CIRP
Canadian Industrial Safety Association (PDAA) .... CISA
Canadian Industrial Sweetener Users (AC) .... CISU
Canadian Industrial Traffic League .... CITL
Canadian Industries Ltd. CIL
Canadian Industries Ltd., Central Research Laboratory, McMasterville, PQ, Canada [*Library symbol Library of Congress*] (LCLS) .... CaQMCILR
Canadian Industries Ltd., Legal Department, Montreal, PQ, Canada [*Library symbol Library of Congress*] (LCLS) .... CaQMCILL
Canadian Industries Ltd., Montreal, PQ, Canada [*Library symbol Library of Congress*] (LCLS) .... CaQMCIL
Canadian Industry Program for Energy Conservation .... CIPEC
Canadian Infantry Association [*Association Canadienne de l'Infanterie*] (AC) .... CIA
Canadian Infantry Brigade (DMA) .... CIB
Canadian Infantry Brigade Group [*British military*] (DMA) .... CIBG
Canadian Infantry Corps CIC
Canadian Infantry Holding Unit .... CIHU
Canadian Infectious Disease Society [*Societe Canadienne de Maladies Infectieuses*] (AC) .... CIDS
Canadian Information and Image Management Society [*Information service or system*] (IID) .... CIIMS
Canadian Information Industry Association [*Information service or system Defunct*] (IID) .... CIIA
Canadian Information Processing Society [*Toronto, ON*] .... CIPS
Canadian Information Sharing Service .... CISS
Canadian Injured Workers Alliance [*L'Alliance Canadienne des Victimes d'Accidents et de Maladies du Travail*] (AC) .... CIWA
Canadian Injury Prevention Foundation (AC) .... CIPF
Canadian In-Line & Roller Skating Association (AC) .... CIRSA
Canadian Insolvency Practitioner (DD) .... CIP
Canadian Insolvency Practitioners Association [*Association Canadienne des Professionnels de l'Insolvabilite*] (AC) .... CIPA
Canadian Institue for the Admistration of Justice (AC) .... CIAJ
Canadian Institue of Hypnotism (AC) .... CIH
Canadian Institute for Advanced Research .... CIAR
Canadian Institute for Conflict Resolution [*Institute Canadien pour la Resolution des Conflits*] (AC) .... CICR
Canadian Institute for Development Management (AC) .... CIDM
Canadian Institute for Energy Training Inc. [*L'Institut Canadien de Formation de l'Energie*] (AC) .... CIET
Canadian Institute for Environmental Law and Policy .... CIELP
Canadian Institute for Historical Microreproductions [*Source file*] [*UTLAS symbol*] .... CHM
Canadian Institute for Historical Microreproductions .... CIHM
Canadian Institute for Historical Microreproductions, Ottawa, ON, Canada [*Library symbol*] [*Library of Congress*] (LCLS) .... CaOOCIHM
Canadian Institute for Historical Microreproductions [*Institut Canadien de Microreproductions Historiques*] Ottawa, Ontario [*Library symbol National Library of Canada*] (NLC) .... OOCIHM
Canadian Institute for International Peace and Security [*UTLAS symbol*] ..... CPS
Canadian Institute for International Peace and Security [*Institut Canadien pour la Paix et la Securite Mondiales*] Ottawa, Ontario [*Library symbol National Library of Canada*] (NLC) .... OOCIIPS
Canadian Institute for Organization Management (AC) .... CIOM
Canadian Institute for Radiation Safety [*Institut Canadien de Radioprotection*] (AC) .... CAIRS
Canadian Institute for Radiation Safety, Ottawa, Ontario [*Library symbol National Library of Canada*] (NLC) .... OOCIRS
Canadian Institute for Research .... CIR
Canadian Institute for Research in Atmospheric Chemistry [*York University*] .... CIRAC
Canadian Institute for Scientific and Technical Information - CISTI [*UTLAS symbol*] .... CIS
Canadian Institute for Synchrotron Radiation .... CISR
Canadian Institute for Telecommunications Research [*Research center*] (RCD) .... CITR
Canadian Institute for Theatre Technology (AC) .... CITT

Canadian Institute for Theoretical Astrophysics [*University of Toronto*] [*Research center*] (RCD) .... CITA
Canadian Institute of Academic Medicine [*Institut Canadien de Medecine Academique*] (AC) .... CIAM
Canadian Institute of Actuaries .... CIA
Canadian Institute of Adult Education, Montreal, PQ, Canada [*Library symbol Library of Congress*] (LCLS) .... CaQMICE
Canadian Institute of Adult Education [*Institut Canadien d'Education des Adultes*] Montreal, Quebec [*Library symbol National Library of Canada*] (NLC) .... QMICE
Canadian Institute of Biotechnology [*Institut Canadien de la Biotechnologie*] (AC) .... CIB
Canadian Institute of Certified Administrative Managers (AC) .... CICAM
Canadian Institute of Chartered Accountants .... CICA
Canadian Institute of Chartered Business Valuators [*Formerly, Canadian Association of Business Valuators*] (AC) .... CICBV
Canadian Institute of Child Health .... CICH
Canadian Institute of Energy (AC) .... CIE
Canadian Institute of Fisheries Technology [*Technical University of Nova Scotia*] [*Research center*] (RCD) .... CIFT
Canadian Institute of Forestry .... CIF
Canadian Institute of Geomatics [*Association Canadienne des Sciences Geomatiques*] (AC) .... CIG
Canadian Institute of Guided Ground Transport [*Queen's University at Kingston*] [*Research center*] (RCD) .... CIGGT
Canadian Institute of Guided Ground Transport, Queen's University, Kingston, Ontario [*Library symbol National Library of Canada*] (NLC) ..... OKQCI
Canadian Institute of International Affairs .... CIIA
Canadian Institute of International Affairs, Toronto, ON, Canada [*Library symbol Library of Congress*] (LCLS) .... CaOTCIA
Canadian Institute of International Affairs [*Institut Canadien des Affaires Internationales*] Toronto, Ontario [*Library symbol National Library of Canada*] (NLC) .... OTCIA
Canadian Institute of Management [*Institut Canadien de Gestion*] (AC) .... CIM
Canadian Institute of Marketing [*Institut Canadien du Marketing*] (AC) .... CIM
Canadian Institute of Metalworking [*McMaster University*] [*Research center*] (RCD) .... CIM
Canadian Institute of Mining .... CIM
Canadian Institute of Mining and Metallurgy .... CIMM
Canadian Institute of Mining and Metallurgy, Montreal, PQ, Canada [*Library symbol Library of Congress*] (LCLS) .... CaQMCIM
Canadian Institute of Mining and Metallurgy [*Institut Canadien des Mines et de la Metallurgie*] Montreal, Quebec [*Library symbol National Library of Canada*] (NLC) .... QMCIM
Canadian Institute of Personalized Education Inc. (AC) .... CIPE
Canadian Institute of Planners (PDAA) .... CIP
Canadian Institute of Plumbing & Heating [*L'Institut Canadien de Plomberie et de Chauffage*] (AC) .... CIPH
Canadian Institute of Public Affairs .... CIPA
Canadian Institute of Public Health Inspectors [*Institut Canadien des Inspecteurs en Hygiene Publique*] (AC) .... CIPHI
Canadian Institute of Resources Law [*University of Calgary*] [*Research center*] (RCD) .... CIRL
Canadian Institute of Science and Technology Ltd. .... CIST
Canadian Institute of Steel Construction .... CISC
Canadian Institute of Strategic Studies (EAIO) .... CISS
Canadian Institute of Surveying .... CIS
Canadian Institute of Surveying and Mapping (EAIO) .... CISM
Canadian Institute of Surveying and Photogrammetry .... CIS & P
Canadian Institute of Technology for the Environment (AC) .... CITE
Canadian Institute of Traffic and Transportation .... CITT
Canadian Institute of Travel Counsellors .... CITC
Canadian Institute of Treated Wood .... CITW
Canadian Institute of Ukrainian Studies [*Institut Canadien d'Etudes Ukrainiennes*] (AC) .... CIUS
Canadian Institute on Pollution Control .... CIPC
Canadian Insulock [*Vancouver Stock Exchange symbol*] .... CIK
Canadian Insurance Claims Managers Association .... CICMA
Canadian Intelligence Corps .... C Int C
Canadian Intelligence Corps (DMA) CIC
Canadian Interagency Forest Fire Centre [*ICAO designator*] (FAAC) .... TKR
Canadian Intercollegiate Athletic Union .... CIAU
Canadian Intercollegiate Sailing Association .... CISA
Canadian Intergovernmental Conference Secretariat .... CICS
Canadian International Development Agency [*Formerly, External Aid Office*] .... CIDA
Canadian International Development Agency, Ottawa, ON, Canada [*Library symbol Library of Congress*] (LCLS) .... CaOOCD
Canadian International Development Agency [*Agence Canadienne de DeveloppementInternational*] Ottawa, Ontario [*Library symbol National Library of Canada*] (NLC) .... OOCD
Canadian International DX Radio Club (AC) .... CIDX
Canadian International Footwear Exposition (ITD) .... CIFE
Canadian International Freight Forwarders Association, Inc. (AC) .... CIFFA
Canadian International Grains Institute .... CIGI
Canadian International Institute of Applied Negotiation [*L'Institut International Canadien de la Negociation Pratique*] (AC) .... CIIAN
Canadian International Network Association (AC) .... CINA
Canadian International Paper Co. .... CIP
Canadian International Trade Association (AC) .... CITA
Canadian International Trade Tribunal [*Tribunal Canadien du Commerce Exterieur*], Ontario [*Library symbol National Library of Canada*] (BIB) ..... OOCITT
Canadian International Water and Energy Consultants .... Ciwec
Canadian Intravenous Nurses Association (EAIO) .... CINA

Canadian Inventory of Historic Building [*Environment Canada*] [*Information service or system*] (IID) .... CIHB
Canadian Investor Relations Institute [*Institut Canadien de Relations Avec les Investisseurs*] [*Formerly, National Investor Relations Institute Canada*] (AC) .... CIRI
Canadian Iris Society .... CIS
Canadian Italian Business & Professional Association Inc. [*Association des Gens d'Affaires & Professionnels Italo-Canadiens Inc.*] (AC) .... CIBPA
Canadian Italian Business & Professional Association of British Columbia [*Formerly, Italian Canadian Business & Professional Association of British Columbia*] (AC) .... CIBPA
Canadian Italian Business and Professional Men's Association .... CIBPA
Canadian Jewellers Institute .... CJI
Canadian Jewish Congress [*Congres Juif Canadien*] (AC) .... CJC
Canadian Jewish Congress Library, Montreal, PQ, Canada [*Library symbol Library of Congress*] (LCLS) .... CaQMCJ
Canadian Jewish Congress [*Congres Juif Canadien*] **Montreal, Quebec** [*Library symbol National Library of Canada*] (NLC) .... QMCJ
Canadian Jewish Historical Society [*See also SCHJ*] .... CJHS
Canadian Jobs Strategy [*Employment and Immigration Canada program launched in 1986*] .... CJS
Canadian Joint Staff .... CJS
Canadian Jorex Ltd. [*Toronto Stock Exchange symbol*] .... CJX
Canadian Journal of Corrections [*A publication*] (ILCA) .... Can J Correct
Canadian Journal of Criminology [*A publication*] (DLA) .... Can J Criminol
Canadian Journal of Information Science [*A publication*] (NITA) .... CJIS
Canadian Journal of Law and Society/Revue Canadienne de Droit et Societe [*A publication*] .... CJLS/RCDS
Canadian Journal of Political and Social Theory [*A publication*] .... CJPST
Canadian Journalism Data Base [*University of Western Ontario*] (IID) .... CJD
Canadian Journalism Foundation [*La Fondation pour le Journalisme Canadien*] (AC) .... CJF
Canadian Kennel Club .... CKC
Canadian Kitchen Cabinet Association (AC) .... CKCA
Canadian L and Surface Scheme .... CLASS
Canadian Laboratory for Integrated Spatial Information Research and Engineering [*University of New Brunswick*] [*Research center*] (RCD) .... CanLabINSPIRE
Canadian Labour Arbitration Summaries [*Canada Law Book, Inc.*] [*Information service or system*] (CRD) .... CLAS
Canadian Labour Congress CLC
Canadian Labour Congress, Ottawa, ON, Canada [*Library symbol Library of Congress*] (LCLS) .... CaOOCLC
Canadian Labour Congress [*Congres du Travail du Canada*] **Ottawa, Ontario** [*Library symbol National Library of Canada*] (NLC) .... OOCLC
Canadian Labour Defence League .... CLDL
Canadian Labour Force Development Board [*La Commission Canadienne de Mise en Valeur de la Main-d'Oeuvre*] (AC) .... CLFDB
Canadian Labour Law Cases [*A publication*] (DLA) CLLC
Canadian Labour Market & Productivity Centre [*Centre Canadien du Marche du Travail et de la Productivite*] (AC) .... CLMPC
Canadian Labour Market and Productivity Centre [*Centre Canadien du Marche du Travail et de la Productivite*], Ottawa, Ontario [*Library symbol National Library of Canada*] (NLC) .... OOCLM
Canadian Labour Party .... CLP
Canadian Labour Relations Board Reports [*A publication*] (DLA) .... Can LRBR
Canadian Labour Union .... CLU
Canadian Lacrosse Association (AC) .... CLA
Canadian Lacrosse Hall of Fame, New Westminster, British Columbia [*Library symbol National Library of Canada*] (NLC) .... BNWLH
Canadian Ladies Association of Shooting Sports .... CLASS
Canadian Ladies' Golf Association [*Association Canadienne des Golfeuses*] (AC) .... CLGA
Canadian Ladies Lawn Bowling Council .... CLLBC
Canadian Lake & Ocean Salvage Team [*Commercial firm*] .... CLOST
Canadian Land Forces Command and Staff College, Kingston, ON, Canada [*Library symbol Library of Congress*] (LCLS) .... CaOKF
Canadian Latvian Business & Professional Association (AC) .... CLBPA
Canadian Law and Society Association [*See also ACDS*] .... CLSA
Canadian Law Information Council [*Information service or system*] (IID) CLIC
Canadian Law Review [*A publication*] (DLA) .... Can L Rev
Canadian Law Review and Corporation Legal Journal [*A publication*] (DLA) .... CLR
Canadian Law Times [*A publication*] (DLA) .... Can L Times
Canadian Law Times [*A publication*] (DLA) .... Can LT
Canadian Law Times [*A publication*] (DLA) .... Canada LT
Canadian Law Times [*A publication*] (DLA) .... CLT
Canadian Law Times. Occasional Notes [*A publication*] (DLA) .... Can LT Occ N
Canadian Law Times. Occasional Notes [*A publication*] (DLA) .... CLT Occ N
Canadian Lawn Bowling Council .... CLBC
Canadian Lawyers Insurance Association [*Association d'Assurances des Juristes Canadiens*] (AC) .... CLIA
Canadian League for the Liberation of Ukraine .... CLLU
Canadian League of Composers CLC
Canadian Learning Materials Centre .... CLMC
Canadian Legal Advocacy Information and Research Association of the Disabled .... CLAIR
Canadian Legal Information Centre (EAIO) CLIC
Canadian Legal Studies [*A publication*] (DLA) .... Can Leg Stud
Canadian Legal Studies [*A publication*] (DLA) .... Can Leg Studies
Canadian Legal Studies [*A publication*] (ILCA) .... Can LS
Canadian Lencourt Mines Ltd. [*Toronto Stock Exchange symbol*] .... CLE
Canadian Lesbian and Gay Rights Coalition .... CLGRC
Canadian Library Association [*Also known as ACB and CLA*] .... CANLA
Canadian Library Association [*Also known as ACB and CANLA*] .... CLA
Canadian Library Association, Ottawa, ON, Canada [*Library symbol Library of Congress*] (LCLS) .... CanLA
Canadian Library Association, Ottawa, ON, Canada [*Library symbol*] [*Library of Congress*] (LCLS) .... CaOOCLA
Canadian Library Association, Ottawa, Ontario [*Library symbol National Library of Canada*] (BIB) .... OOCLA
Canadian Library Exhibitors' Association .... CLEA
Canadian Library Trustees' Association .... CLTA
Canadian Life & Health Insurance Association Inc. [*Association Canadienne des Compagnies d'Assurances de Personnes Inc.*] [*Formerly, Canadian Life Insurance Association*] (AC) .... CLHIA
Canadian Life Insurance Medical Officers Association [*Association Canadienne des Directeurs Medicaux en Assurance-Vie*] (AC) .... CLIMOA
Canadian Lifeboat Institution Inc. (AC) CLI
Canadian Light Rail Vehicle .... CLRV
Canadian Linguistic Association [*See also ACL*] .... CLA
Canadian Literary Periodical Index [*Information service or system*] (IID) .... CLPI
Canadian Literature [*A publication*] (BRI) .... Can Lit
Canadian Liver Foundation [*Fondation Canadienne du Foie*] (AC) .... CLF
Canadian Livestock Feed Board .... CLFB
Canadian Livestock Feed Board [*Office Canadien des Provendes*] **Montreal, Quebec** [*Library symbol National Library of Canada*] (NLC) .... QMOCP
Canadian Livestock Records Corporation [*Societe Canadienne d'Enregistrement des Animaux*] (AC) .... CLRC
Canadian Long Distance Riding Association (AC) .... CaLDRA
Canadian Long Term Care Assciation [*Association Canadienne de Soins a Long Terme*] (AC) .... CLS
Canadian Longhorn Petroleum [*Vancouver Stock Exchange symbol*] .... CHN
Canadian Lumber Size (DAC) .... CLS
Canadian Lumbermen's Association .... CLA
Canadian Lung Association [*Association Pulmonaire du Canada*] (AC) .... CLA
Canadian Machine Gun Corps [*World War I*] .... CMGC
Canadian Machine Tool Distributors' Association (AC) .... CMTDA
Canadian Machine Tool Show (ITD) .... CMTS
Canadian Machine-Readable Cataloguing [*National Library of Canada*] [*Information service or system*] .... CAN/MARC
Canadian Magazine Index [*Micromedia Ltd.*] [*Information service or system*] (IID) .... CMI
Canadian Magazine Publishers Association [*Formerly, Canadian Periodical Publisher's Association*] (AC) .... CMPA
Canadian Maine-Anjou Association (AC) .... CMAA
Canadian Major Junior Hockey League .... CMJHL
Canadian Management Associates for Global Development (AC) .... CAMDEV
Canadian Managing Editors' Conference .... CMEC
Canadian Man-Computer Communications Society .... CMCS
Canadian Manoir Industries Ltd. [*Toronto Stock Exchange symbol*] .... CMQ
Canadian Manufacturers Association .... CMA
Canadian Manufacturers of Chemical Specialties Association (EAIO) .... CMCS
Canadian Manufacturers of Chemical Specialties Association .... CMCSA
Canadian MARC [*Machine-Readable Cataloging*] [*Source file*] [*UTLAS symbol*] .... CAN
Canadian Marconi [*AMEX symbol*] (TTSB) .... CMW
Canadian Marconi Co. [*Aerospace*] .... CMA
Canadian Marconi Co. [*Associated Press*] (SAG) .... CMarc
Canadian Marconi Co. [*Toronto Stock Exchange symbol*] .... CMC
Canadian Marconi Co. [*AMEX symbol Toronto Stock Exchange symbol*] (SPSG) .... CMW
Canadian Marconi Co., Kanata, Ontario [*Library symbol National Library of Canada*] (NLC) .... OKCM
Canadian Marconi Co., Montreal, PQ, Canada [*Library symbol Library of Congress*] (LCLS) .... CaQMCM
Canadian Marconi Co., Montreal, Quebec [*Library symbol National Library of Canada*] (NLC) .... QMCM
Canadian Marine Trade Exhibition and Congress [*SHOWBEX*] (TSPED) .... CAMTEC
Canadian Marine Transportation Administration .... CMTA
Canadian Maritime Command .... CANMARCOM
Canadian Maritime Commander, Atlantic (NATG) .... CANCOMARLANT
Canadian Maritime Industries Association [*Association Canadienne des Industries Maritimes*] [*Formerly, Canadian Shipbuilding & Ship Repairing Association*] (AC) .... CMIA
Canadian Maritime Rescue Auxiliary (PDAA) .... CMRA
Canadian Maritime Union (BARN) .... CMU
Canadian Masonry Contractors' Association (AC) .... CMCA
Canadian Massage Therapist Alliance [*Alliance Candienne de Massotherapeutes*] (AC) .... CMTA
Canadian Master Athlete Federation (AC) .... CMAF
Canadian Masters Cross-Country Ski Association [*Association Canadienne des Maitres en Ski de Fond*] (AC) .... CMCSA
Canadian Mathematical Society [*Societe Mathematique du Canada*] (AC) .... CMS
Canadian Mathematics Achievement Test [*Education*] (AEBS) .... CMAT
Canadian Meat Council [*Conseil des Viandes du Canada*] [*Formerly, Meat Packers Council of Canada*] (AC) .... CMC
Canadian Meat Importers Committee (AC) .... CMIC
Canadian Mechanized Brigade Group (MCD) .... CMBG
Canadian Media Guild [*La Guilde Canadienne des Medias*] (AC) .... CMG
Canadian Medical and Biological Engineering Society .... CMBES
Canadian Medical Association .... CMA
Canadian Medical Association, Ottawa, ON, Canada [*Library symbol Library of Congress*] (LCLS) .... CaOOCMA
Canadian Medical Association, Ottawa, Ontario [*Library symbol National Library of Canada*] (NLC) .... OOCMA
Canadian Medical Discovery Fund .... CMDF
Canadian Medical Malpractice Prevention Association (AC) .... CMMPA
Canadian Medical Protective Association .... CMPA

Canadian Mediterranean Institute [*Research center*] (RCD) .... CMI
Canadian Member, Canadian Joint Staff, Washington, DC .... CANAVUS
Canadian Memorial Chiropractic College, Toronto, ON, Canada [*Library symbol Library of Congress*] (LCLS) .... CaOTCMC
Canadian Memorial Chiropractic College, Toronto, Ontario [*Library symbol National Library of Canada*] (NLC) .... OTCMC
Canadian Mennonite Bible College .... CMBC
Canadian Mennonite Bible College, Winnipeg, Manitoba [*Library symbol National Library of Canada*] (NLC) .... MWCM
Canadian Mennonite Bible College, Winnipeg, MB, Canada [*Library symbol Library of Congress*] (LCLS) .... CaMWCM
Canadian Mental Health Association .... CMHA
Canadian Mental Health Association, Toronto, Ontario [*Library symbol National Library of Canada*] (BIB) .... OTCMHA
Canadian Merchant Navy Association Inc. [*Association de la Marine Marchande Canadienne Inc.*] (AC) .... CMNA
Canadian Merchant Service Guild .... CMSG
Canadian Metal Mining Association .... CMMA
Canadian Meteorological and Oceanographic Society .... CMOS
Canadian Meteorological Centre [*Marine science*] (MSC) .... CMC
Canadian Metric Association .... CMA
Canadian Microcool Corp. [*Vancouver Stock Exchange symbol*] .... CQO
Canadian Microfilming Co. Ltd. [*Societe Canadienne du Microfilm, Inc.*] **Montreal, Quebec** [*Library symbol National Library of Canada*] (NLC) .... QMSCM
Canadian Microfilming Co., Montreal, PQ, Canada [*Library symbol Library of Congress*] (LCLS) .... CanM
Canadian Micrographic Society .... CMS
Canadian Military Electronics Standards Agency (MCD) .... CAMESA
Canadian Military Headquarters (DMA) .... CMHQ
Canadian Military Pattern (DMA) .... CMP
Canadian Militia .... CM
Canadian Mineral Analysts [*Analystes des Mineraux Canadiens*] (AC) .... CMA
Canadian Mineral Occurrence Index [*Department of Energy, Mines, and Resources*] [*Information service or system*] (IID) .... CANMINDEX
Canadian Mineral Processors (HGAA) .... CMP
Canadian Mineworkers Union .... CMU
Canadian Minimum Navigation Performance Specification Airspace [*FAA*] (TAG) .... CMNPS
Canadian Mobile Home Association .... CMHA
Canadian Modern Rhythmic Gymnastics Federation .... CMRGF
Canadian Morgan Horse Association Inc. [*Association des Chevaux Morgan Canadien Inc.*] (AC) .... CMHA
Canadian Motion Picture Distributors Association .... CMPDA
Canadian Motor Machine Gun [*World War I*] .... CMMG
Canadian Motor Machine Gun Brigade (DMA) .... CMMGB
Canadian Motor Vehicle Arbitration Program .... CAMVAP
Canadian Motor Vehicle Safety Standard .... CMVSS
Canadian Motor Vehicle Safety Standard .... CMVSS
Canadian Motor Vehicle Tyre Safety Standard (PDAA) .... CMVTSS
Canadian Motorcycle Association [*Association Motocycliste Canadienne*] (AC) .... CMA
Canadian Mounted Rifles .... CMR
Canadian Municipal Journal [*A publication*] (DLA) .... Can Mun J
Canadian Municipal Journal [*A publication*] (DLA) .... CMJ
Canadian Museum Association, Ottawa, ON, Canada [*Library symbol*] [*Library of Congress*] (LCLS) .... CaOOCANM
Canadian Museum Association [*Association des Musees Canadiens*], Ottawa, Ontario [*Library symbol National Library of Canada*] (NLC) .... OOCANM
Canadian Museum of Civilization, National Museums of Canada [*Musee Canadien des Civilisations, Musees Nationaux du Canada*] **Ottawa, Ontario** [*Library symbol National Library of Canada*] (NLC) .... OONMM
Canadian Museum of Contemporary Photography .... CMCP
Canadian Museum of Flight and Transportation .... CMFT
Canadian Museums Association .... CMA
Canadian Music Centre .... CMC
Canadian Music Council [*Defunct*] (EAIO) .... CMC
Canadian Music Educators' Association .... CMEA
Canadian Music Library Association, Toronto, ON, Canada [*Library symbol Library of Congress*] (LCLS) .... CaOTCMLA
Canadian Music Library Association [*Association Canadienne des Bibliotheques Musicales*] **Toronto, Ontario** [*Library symbol National Library of Canada*] (NLC) .... OTCMLA
Canadian Music Publishers Association [*See also ACEM*] .... CMPA
Canadian Music Research Council .... CMRC
Canadian Music Therapy Association .... CMTA
Canadian Musical Heritage Society [*Societe pour le Patrimoine Musical Canadien*] (AC) .... CMHS
Canadian Musical Reproduction Rights Agency .... CMRRA
Canadian Mutual Aid Board [*World War II*] .... CMAB
Canadian National Asbestos Council [*Formerly, The Canadian Chapter of the National Asbestos Council*] (AC) .... CANNAC
Canadian National/Canadian Pacific Telecommunications (NITA) .... CN/CPT
Canadian National Committee for Earthquake Engineering .... CANCEE
Canadian National Committee for Mental Hygiene (BARN) .... CNCMH
Canadian National Committee for the International Association on the Properties of Steam (PDAA) .... CNC/IAPS
Canadian National Committee for the International Federation of Automatic Control (EAIO) .... CNC-IFAC
Canadian National Committee - International Peat Society .... CNC-IPS
Canadian National Committee of the International Committee on Water Pollution Research and Control (EAIO) .... CNC/IAWPRC
Canadian National Committee, World Energy Conference .... CANWEC
Canadian National Energy Forum .... CNEF
Canadian National Exhibition [*Held annually in Toronto*] .... CNE
Canadian National Federation of Independent Unions [*See also FCNSI*] .... CNFIU
Canadian National Institute for the Blind .... CNIB
Canadian National Institute for the Blind, National Library Division, Toronto, ON, Canada [*Library symbol*] [*Library of Congress*] (LCLS) .... CaOTBNL
Canadian National Library (BARN) .... CNL
Canadian National Packaging Exposition [*Packaging Association of Canada*] (TSPED) .... PAC-EX
Canadian National Power Alcohol Conference .... CANPAC
Canadian National Railway Co. [*Associated Press*] (SAG) .... CdnNRy
Canadian National Railway Co. [*Associated Press*] (SAG) .... CdnRy
Canadian National Railway Co. [*NYSE symbol*] (SAG) .... CNI
Canadian National Railways [*AAR code*] .... CN
Canadian National Railways [*Facetious translation: Certainly No Rush*] .... CNR
Canadian National Railways, Chemical Library, Montreal, PQ, Canada [*Library symbol Library of Congress*] (LCLS) .... CaQMCNC
Canadian National Railways, Montreal, PQ, Canada [*Library symbol Library of Congress*] (LCLS) .... CaQMCN
Canadian National Railways [*Chemins de fer Nationaux du Canada*] **Montreal, Quebec** [*Library symbol National Library of Canada*] (NLC) .... QMCN
Canadian National Railways Pension Trust Fund [*Montreal-based pension fund*] .... CNRPTF
Canadian National Recreation Association .... CNRA
Canadian National Seismograph Network .... CNSN
Canadian National Steamships (MHDW) .... CNS
Canadian National Steamships [*AAR code*] .... CNSS
Canadian National Telecommunications .... CNT
Canadian National Telecommunications [*Canada ICAO designator*] (ICDA) .... XN
Canadian National Telecommunications [*FAA designator*] (FAAC) .... XNC
Canadian National Telephone Co. (NITA) .... CNT
Canadian National Yellow Pages Service .... CANYPS
Canadian National-Canadian Pacific Railway .... CNCP
Canadian Native Arts Foundation (AC) .... CNAF
Canadian Native Law Reporter. Native Law Centre. University of Saskatchewan [*A publication*] (DLA) .... Can Native L Rep
Canadian Natl Railway [*NYSE symbol*] (TTSB) .... CNI PP
Canadian Natural Deuterium Uranium Pressurized Heavy-Water [*Nuclear reactor*] .... CANDU PHW
Canadian Natural Resources Ltd. [*Toronto Stock Exchange symbol*] .... CNQ
Canadian Nature Federation [*Federation Canadienne de la Nature*] [*Formerly, Canadian Audubon Society*] (AC) .... CNF
Canadian Naturopathic Association [*Association Canadienne de Naturopathie*] (AC) .... CNA
Canadian Nautical Research Society [*Societe Canadienne pour la Recherche Nautique*] (AC) .... CNRS
Canadian Naval Air Station .... CANAS
Canadian Naval Board .... CNB
Canadian Naval Commander Newfoundland .... CANCOMNEW
Canadian Naval Electronic Warfare System .... CANEWS
Canadian Naval Mission Overseas .... CNMO
Canadian Naval Modifications .... CANAVMODS
Canadian Naval Service .... CNS
Canadian Navigation Society (AC) .... CNS
[*The*] **Canadian Network for Environmental Education & Communication** [*Reseau Canadien d'Education et de Communication Relatives a l'Environnement*] (AC) .... EECOM
Canadian Network for Sampling Precipitation .... CANSAP
Canadian Network for Space Research (AC) .... CNSR
Canadian Network for the Advancement of Research, Industry and Education (IID) .... CANARIE
Canadian Network of Toxicology Centres (AC) .... CNTC
Canadian Neurological Society [*Societe Canadienne de Neurologie*] (AC) .... CNS
Canadian News Index [*Micromedia Ltd.*] [*Information service or system A publication*] .... CNI
Canadian News Service .... CNS
Canadian Newspaper Unit .... CNU
Canadian NORAD Region [*Aviation*] (FAAC) .... CANR
Canadian Northeast Wideband Systems [*Air Force*] (MCD) .... CNEWS
Canadian Northern Pacific Railway .... CNP
Canadian Northern Railway .... CNoR
Canadian Northern Railway (ROG) .... CNR
Canadian Northstar Corp. [*Toronto Stock Exchange symbol*] .... CNX
Canadian Northwest Atlantic Area .... CNA
Canadian Nuclear Association .... CNA
Canadian Nuclear Society (NUCP) .... CNS
Canadian Numismatic Association [*Association Canadienne de Numismatique*] (AC) .... CNA
Canadian Numismatic Research Society .... CNRS
Canadian Nurse Educators Association .... CNEA
Canadian Nursery Trades Association (AC) .... CNTA
Canadian Nurses' Association [*See also AIC*] .... CNA
Canadian Nurses' Association, Ottawa, ON, Canada [*Library symbol Library of Congress*] (LCLS) .... CaOOCN
Canadian Nurses' Association [*Association Canadienne des Infirmieres*] **Ottawa, Ontario** [*Library symbol National Library of Canada*] (NLC) .... OOCN
Canadian Nurses Foundation [*Fondation des Infirmieres et Infirmiers du Canada*] (AC) .... CNF
Canadian Nurses Protective Society (AC) .... CNPS
Canadian Nurses Respiratory Society (AC) .... CNRS
Canadian Nut Council [*Conseil Canadien des Noix*] (AC) .... CNC
Canadian Obstetric, Gynecologic & Neonatal Nurses (AC) .... COGNN
Canadian Occidental Petrol [*AMEX symbol*] (TTSB) .... CXY
Canadian Occidental Petroleum Ltd. [*Associated Press*] (SAG) .... CdnOc
Canadian Occidental Petroleum Ltd. [*AMEX symbol*] (SPSG) .... CXY

Canadian Occidental Petroleum Ltd., Calgary, Alberta [*Library symbol National Library of Canada*] (NLC) .... ACCOP
Canadian Occupational Forecasting Program (EDAC) .... COFOR
Canadian Occupational Health Nurses Association [*Formerly, National Association of Occupational Health Nurses*] (AC) .... COHNA
Canadian Occupational Interest Inventory [*Vocational test*] .... COII
Canadian Ocean Data System .... CODS
Canadian Ocean Escort Vessel .... COEV
Canadian Oceanographic Data Centre [*Later, MEDS*] .... CODC
Canadian Oceanographic Identification Center (HGAA) .... COIC
Canadian Office Employees Union [*See also SCEB*] .... COEU
Canadian Office Machine Dealers Association (HGAA) .... COMDA
Canadian Office Products Association .... COPA
Canadian Officers Training Corps .... COTC
Canadian Offshore Resources Exposition (ITD) .... CORE
Canadian Oil and Gas Handbook [*A publication*] (DLA) .... Can Oil & Gas
Canadian Oldtimers Hockey Association .... COHA
Canadian Olympic Association .... COA
Canadian Olympic Regatta at Kingston .... CORK
Canadian Online Enquiry System [*Pronounced "can-olay"*] [*National Research Council of Canada Ottawa, ON*] .... CAN/OLE
Canadian On-Line Record Database .... CORD
Canadian Opera Company .... COC
Canadian Operating Statistics [*Database*] [*Statistics Canada*] [*Information service or system*] (CRD) .... COPS
Canadian Operational Research Society .... CORS
Canadian Ophthalmological Society (DAVI) .... COS
Canadian Oral History Association [*See also SCHO*] .... COHA
Canadian Order of Foresters [*Later, CFLIS*] (EA) .... COF
Canadian Organic Growers .... COG
Canadian Organisation for the Promotion of Education Inc. [*Organization Canadienne pour la Promotion de l'Education Inc.*] (AC) .... COPE
Canadian Organization for Advancement of Computers in Health (EAIO) .... COACH
Canadian Organization for Campus Activities .... COCA
Canadian Organization for Development through Education .... CODE
Canadian Organization for the Rights of Prostitutes (AC) .... CORP
Canadian Organization for the Simplification of Trade Procedures .... COSTPRO
Canadian Organization of Public Housing Tenants .... COPHT
Canadian Organization of Small Business Inc. [*Also, The Voice of Business*] (AC) .... COSBI
Canadian Orienteering Federation .... COF
Canadian Ornamental Plant Foundation [*Fondation Canadienne des Plantes Ornementales*] (AC) .... COPF
Canadian Orthopaedic Association (DAVI) .... COA
Canadian Orthopaedic Nurses' Association .... CONA
Canadian Osteopathic Aid Society (AC) .... COAS
Canadian Otolaryngological Society (PDAA) .... COS
Canadian Outdoor Measurement Bureau .... COMB
Canadian Outrigger Racing Association (AC) .... CORA
Canadian Overseas Exploration [*Vancouver Stock Exchange symbol*] CVC
Canadian Overseas Military Railway Construction Corps [*World War I*] .... CORCC
Canadian Overseas Telecommunications Corp. .... COTC
Canadian Over-the-Counter Automated Trading System .... COATS
Canadian Owners and Pilots Association .... COPA
Canadian Ownership and Control Determination .... COCD
Canadian Pacer Petroleum [*Vancouver Stock Exchange symbol*] .... CDP
Canadian Pacific Airlines [*ICAO designator*] (AD) .... CP Air
Canadian Pacific Airlines Ltd. [*Facetious translations: Can't Possibly Arrive, Come Push Along*] .... CPA
Canadian Pacific Airlines Ltd. .... CPAir
Canadian Pacific Airlines Ltd. .... CPAL
Canadian Pacific Express and Transport .... CPET
Canadian Pacific Ltd. [*Associated Press*] (SAG) .... CdnPc
Canadian Pacific Ltd. [*NYSE symbol Toronto Stock Exchange symbol Vancouver Stock Exchange symbol*] (SPSG) .... CP
Canadian Pacific Ltd. [*Le Canadien Pacifique*] Montreal, Quebec [*Library symbol National Library of Canada*] (NLC) .... QMCP
Canadian Pacific, Ord [*NYSE symbol*] (TTSB) .... CP
Canadian Pacific Police Association [*Association des Policiers du Canadien Pacifique*] (AC) .... CPPA
Canadian Pacific Railroad (MHDB) .... CP Rail
Canadian Pacific Railway [*Facetious translations: Can't Pay Rent, Can't Promise Returns*] .... CPR
Canadian Pacific Railway Co., Montreal, PQ, Canada [*Library symbol Library of Congress*] (LCLS) .... CaQMCP
Canadian Pacific Steamships (MHDB) .... CP Ships
Canadian Paediatric Society (EAIO) .... CPS
Canadian Paint and Wallpaper Dealers' Association .... CPWDA
Canadian Palliative Care Association (AC) .... CPCA
Canadian Paper Box Manufacturers' Association Inc. [*Association Canadienne des Fabricants de Boites en Cartons*] (AC) .... CPBMA
Canadian Paper Money Society .... CPMS
Canadian Paper Trade Association (AC) .... CPTA
Canadian Paperworkers Union .... CPU
Canadian Paralympic Committee [*Comite Paralympique du Canada*] [*Formerly, Canadian Federation of Sport Organizations for the Disabled*] (AC) .... CPC
Canadian Paraplegic Association [*Ontario*] (AC) .... CPA
Canadian Paraplegic Association (AC) .... CPA
Canadian Paraplegic Association Nova Scotia (AC) .... CPA-NS
Canadian Parents for French (AC) .... CPF
Canadian Park Service, Environment Canada [*Service Canadien des Parcs, Environnement Canada*], Canmore, Alberta [*Library symbol National Library of Canada*] (BIB) .... ACACP

Canadian Park Service, Environment Canada [*Service Canadien des Parcs, Environnement Canada*], Cornwall, Ontario [*Library symbol National Library of Canada*] (NLC) .... OCN
Canadian Park Service, Environment Canada [*Service Canadien des Parcs, Environnement Canada*], Quebec, Quebec [*Library symbol National Library of Canada*] (NLC) .... QQPCQ
Canadian Parks & Wilderness Society [*Societe pour la Protection des Parcs et des Sites Naturales du Canada*] (AC) .... CPAWS
Canadian Parks Partnership [*Partenaires des Parcs Canadiens*] (AC) .... CPP
Canadian Parks/Recreation Association [*Association Canadienne des Loisirs/Parcs*] (AC) .... CP/RA
Canadian Particleboard Association [*Canada*] (EAIO) .... CPA
Canadian Passenger Transportation Corp. [*Proposed*] .... CPTC
Canadian Patent (IAA) .... CANPAT
Canadian Patent Office. Record [*A publication*] (DLA) .... Can Pat Off Rec
Canadian Patent Report, Second Series [*A publication*] (DLA) .... CPR (2d)
Canadian Patents and Developments Ltd. .... CPDL
Canadian Patrol Frigate [*Military*] .... CPF
Canadian Patrol Frigates Program [*Canadian Navy*] .... CPFP
Canadian Pawnee Oil [*Vancouver Stock Exchange symbol*] .... CPW
Canadian Payments Association .... CPA
Canadian Payments Association, Ottawa, Ontario [*Library symbol National Library of Canada*] (BIB) .... OOCPA
Canadian Payroll Association [*Association Canadienne de la Paie*] (AC) .... CPA
Canadian Peace Alliance [*Alliance Canadienne pour la Paix*] (AC) .... CPA
Canadian Peace Research and Education Association [*See also ACREP*] .... CPREA
Canadian Peace Research Institute .... CPRI
Canadian Peace Research Institute, London, Ontario [*Library symbol National Library of Canada*] (NLC) .... OLCPR
Canadian PEN Center (EAIO) .... CPENC
Canadian Penitentiary Service .... CPS
Canadian Pension Commission .... CPC
Canadian Pension Commission [*Commission Canadienne des Pensions*], Charlottetown, Prince Edward Island [*Library symbol National Library of Canada*] (BIB) .... PCCP
Canadian People's [*Citizens and Residents*] Defence Committee .... CPDC
Canadian Performance Distributors .... CPD
Canadian Periodical Index [*The Globe and Mail*] [*Information service or system*] (CRD) .... CPI
Canadian Periodical Publishers Association .... CPPA
Canadian Periodical Reference Services, Ottawa, ON, Canada [*Library symbol Library of Congress Obsolete*] (LCLS) .... CaOOCAP
Canadian Permanent Army Service Corps (DMA) .... CPASC
Canadian Permanent Committee on Geographical Names .... CPCGN
Canadian Permanent Signal Corps [*British military*] (DMA) .... CPSC
Canadian Perspectives on International Law and Organization [*A publication*] (DLA) .... Can Persp
Canadian Pest Management Society [*Societe Canadienne de Lutte Contre les Organismes Nuisibles*] [*Formerly, Agricultural Pesticide Society*] (AC) .... CPMS
Canadian Petroleum Association .... CPA
Canadian Petroleum Association, Calgary, AB, Canada [*Library symbol Library of Congress*] (LCLS) .... CaACCP
Canadian Petroleum Association, Calgary, Alberta [*Library symbol National Library of Canada*] (NLC) .... ACCP
Canadian Petroleum Association Statistics [*Information service or system*] (CRD) .... CPASTATS
Canadian Petroleum Products Institute [*Institut Canadien des Produits Petroliers*] [*Formerly, Petroleum Association for Conservation of the Canadian Environment*] (AC) .... CPPI
Canadian Petroleum Writers Association (AC) .... CPWA
Canadian Pharmaceutical Association (MCD) .... CPA
Canadian Pharmaceutical Association (EAIO) .... CPhA
Canadian Philosophical Association .... CPA
Canadian Philosophical Reviews [*A publication*] (BRI) .... CPR
Canadian Photo Video Trade Association [*Formerly, Canadian Photographic Trade Association*] (AC) .... CPVTA
Canadian Physicians for Aid & Relif (AC) .... CPAR
Canadian Physiological Society [*Societe Canadienne de Physiologie*] (AC) .... CPS
Canadian Physiotherapy Association .... CPA
Canadian Physiotherapy Cardio-Respiratory Society (AC) .... CPCRS
Canadian Phytopathological Society Inc. [*Societe Canadienne de Phytopathologie*] (AC) .... CPS
Canadian Picture Pioneers (AC) .... CPP
Canadian Pinzgauer Association (AC) .... CPA
Canadian Plains Research Center [*University of Regina*] [*Information service or system*] (IID) .... CPRC
Canadian Plastics Institute [*Institut Canadien du Plastique*] (AC) .... CPI
Canadian Play Therapy Association (AC) .... CPTA
Canadian Podiatric Sports Medicine Academy .... CPSMA
Canadian Poetry Association [*Also, London Regional Literary Society*] (AC) .... CPA
Canadian Poetry in English [*A publication*] .... CaP
Canadian Police Association .... CPA
Canadian Police College, Royal Canadian Mounted Police, Ottawa, ON, Canada [*Library symbol Library of Congress*] (LCLS) .... CaOOCPC
Canadian Police Information Centre .... CPIC
Canadian Political Memorabilia Club (AC) .... CPMC
Canadian Political Science Association .... CPSA
Canadian Polystyrene Recycling Association (AC) .... CPRA
Canadian Population Society [*See also SCP*] .... CPS
Canadian Pork Council [*Formerly, Canadian Swine Council*] (AC) .... CPC
Canadian Port & Harbour Association [*Association des Ports et Havres du Canada*] (AC) .... CPHA

Canadian Portland Cement Association [*Association Canadienne du Ciment Portland*] (AC) .... CPCA
Canadian Postal Corps [*Later, RCPC*] .... CPC
Canadian Postmasters and Assistants Association .... CPAA
Canadian Postmaster's Association .... CPA
Canadian Post-MD Education Registry [*Systeme Informatise sur les Stagiaires Post-MD en Formation Clinique*] (AC) .... CAPER
Canadian Posture and Seating Centre [*Research center*] (RCD) .... CPSC
Canadian Potash Producers Association .... CPPA
Canadian Potato Chip/Snack Food Association [*Association Canadienne des Fabricants de Chips/Grignotines*] (AC) .... CPC/SFA
Canadian Poultry & Egg Processors Council [*Formerly, Canadian Produce Council*] (AC) .... CPEPC
Canadian Power Squadrons [*Boating*] .... CPS
Canadian Premium Resources Corp. [*Vancouver Stock Exchange symbol*] .... CIP
Canadian Press .... CP
Canadian Press Information Network (IID) .... CPIN
Canadian Press Newstex [*The Canadian Press*] [*Information service or system*] (IID) .... CPN
Canadian Prestressed Concrete Institute [*See also ICBP*] .... CPCI
Canadian Print Marketers Association [*Association Canadienne des Courtiers en Imprimerie*] (AC) .... CPMA
Canadian Print Measurement Bureau (NITA) .... PMB
Canadian Printing Industries Association (EAIO) .... CPIA
Canadian Produce Marketing Association [*Association Canadienne de la Distribution de Fruite et Legumes*] [*Formerly, Canadian Fruit Wholesalers Association*] (AC) .... CPMA
Canadian Professional Logistics Institute [*Institut Canadien Professionnel Logistique*] [*Formerly, Professional Logistics Institute of Canada*] (AC) .... CPLI
Canadian Professional Sales Association [*Association Canadienne des Professionnels de la Vente*] [*Formerly, Commercial Travellers Association of Canada*] (AC) .... CPSA
Canadian Professional Soccer League .... CPSL
Canadian Professors for Peace in The Middle East (AC) .... CPPME
Canadian Programming Service [*Service Canadien de Programmation*] (AC) .... CPS
Canadian Psoriasis Foundation [*Fondation Canadienne du Psoriasis*] (AC) .... CPF
Canadian Psychiatric Association .... CPA
Canadian Psychological Association (MCD) .... CPA
Canadian Psychological Association - Interest Group on Women and Psychology .... CPA-IGWAP
Canadian Public Administration [*A publication*] (DLA) .... Can Pub Ad
Canadian Public Health Association .... CPHA
Canadian Public Personnel Management Association .... CPPMA
Canadian Public Relations Society .... CPRS
Canadian Public Relations Society .... CPRS
Canadian Public Relations Society [*Societe Canadienne des Relations Publiques*], Ottawa, Ontario [*Library symbol National Library of Canada*] (BIB) .... OOCPR
Canadian Pulp and Paper Association [*See also ACPPP*] .... CPPA
Canadian Pulp and Paper Association, Montreal, PQ, Canada [*Library symbol Library of Congress*] (LCLS) .... CaQMNA
Canadian Pulp and Paper Asssociation [*Association Canadienne des Producteurs dePates et Papiers*] Montreal, Quebec [*Library symbol National Library of Canada*] (NLC) .... QMNA
Canadian Quaternary Association .... CANQUA
Canadian Quilters Association (AC) .... CQA
Canadian Racquetball Association .... CRA
Canadian Radio Broadcasting Commission [*Later, Canadian Broadcasting Corp.*] .... CRBC
Canadian Radio Relay League (PDAA) .... CRRL
Canadian Radio Technical Planning Board (NTCM) .... CRTPB
Canadian Radio-Direction Finder (MCD) .... CRDF
Canadian Radio-Television and Telecommunications Commission [*Conseil de la Radiodiffusion et des Telecommunications Canadiennes*] [*Ottawa, ON*] [*Telecommunications*] .... CRTC
Canadian Radio-Television and Telecommunications Commission, Ottawa, ON, Canada [*Library symbol Library of Congress*] (LCLS) .... CaOORT
Canadian Radio-Television and Telecommunications Commission [*Conseil de la Radiodiffusion et des Telecommunications Canadiennes*] Ottawa, Ontario [*Library symbol National Library of Canada*] (NLC) .... OORT
Canadian Railroad Historical Association .... CRHA
Canadian Railway and Transport Cases [*A publication*] (DLA) .... Can Ry & T Cas
Canadian Railway and Transport Cases [*A publication*] (DLA) .... CRTC
Canadian Railway Cases [*A publication*] (DLA) .... Can R Cas
Canadian Railway Cases [*A publication*] (DLA) .... CRC
Canadian Railway Commission .... CRC
Canadian Railway Labour Association .... CRLA
Canadian Railway Labour Executives' Association .... CRLEA
Canadian Railway Troops [*World War I*] .... CRT
Canadian Real Estate Association .... CREA
Canadian Recording Industry Association .... CRIA
Canadian Recreational Canoeing Association .... CRCA
Canadian Recreational Vehicle Association (EAIO) .... CRVA
Canadian Red Cross Committee (HGAA) .... CRCC
Canadian Red Cross Society, Ottawa, ON, Canada [*Library symbol Library of Congress*] (LCLS) .... CaOOCRC
Canadian Red Cross Society [*Societe Canadienne de la Croix-Rouge*] Ottawa, Ontario [*Library symbol National Library of Canada*] (NLC) .... OOCRC
Canadian Refrigeration & Air Conditioning Contractors Association (AC) .... CRACCA
Canadian Regional Science Association [*See also ACSR*] .... CRSA
Canadian Regulatory Reporter [*Database*] [*Canadian Law Information Council*] [*Information service or system*] (CRD) .... CRR
Canadian Rehabilitation Council for the Disabled .... CRCD

Canadian Religious Conference .... CRC
Canadian Remote Sensing Society (EAIO) .... CRSS
Canadian Renewable Fuels Association (AC) .... CRFA
Canadian Reports, Appeal Cases [*1828-1913*] [*A publication*] (DLA) .... AC
Canadian Reports, Appeal Cases [*1828-1913*] [*A publication*] (DLA) .... Can App
Canadian Reports, Appeal Cases [*1828-1913*] [*A publication*] (DLA) .... Can R App Cas
Canadian Reports, Appeal Cases [*1828-1913*] [*A publication*] (DLA) .... Can RAC
Canadian Reports, Appeal Cases [*1828-1913*] [*A publication*] (DLA) .... CR
Canadian Reports, Appeal Cases [*1828-1913*] [*A publication*] (DLA) .... CRAC
Canadian Reprography Collective .... CRC
Canadian Research and Education Network [*Computer science*] (TNIG) .... CDNnet
Canadian Research Institute for the Advancement of Women [*Research center*] (RCD) .... CRIAW
Canadian Research Institute for the Advancement of Women, Ottowa, ON, Canada [*Library symbol*] [*Library of Congress*] (LCLS) .... CaOOCRI
Canadian Research Institute for the Avancement of Women [*Institut Canadien deRecherches sur les Femmes*] Ottawa, Ontario [*Library symbol National Library of Canada*] (NLC) .... OOCRI
Canadian Reserve File [*Petroleum Information Corp.*] [*Information service or system*] (CRD) .... CNDN
Canadian Resort Development [*Formerly, Canadian Resort & Recreational Development Association*] (AC) .... CRDA
Canadian Resources for Enterprise Development Organization (AC) .... CREDO
Canadian Restaurant and Foodservices Association .... CR & FA
Canadian Restaurant & Foodservices Association [*Association Canadienne des Restaurateurs et des Services Alimentaires*] (AC) .... CRFA
Canadian Restaurant Association .... CRA
Canadian Restricted [*Broadcasting term*] .... CR
Canadian Retail Hardware Association (PDAA) .... CRHA
Canadian Retransmission Collective (AC) .... CRC
Canadian Retransmission Right Association (AC) .... CRRA
Canadian Rheumatism Association (HGAA) .... CRA
Canadian Rhythmic Sportive Gymnastic Federation [*Federation Canadienne de Gymnastique Rythmique Sportive*] [*Formerly, Canadian Modern Rhythmic Gymnastic Federation*] (AC) .... CRSGF
Canadian Rights and Liberties Federation, Ottawa, ON, Canada [*Library symbol Library of Congress*] (LCLS) .... CaOOCRLF
Canadian Rights and Liberties Federation, Ottawa, Ontario [*Library symbol National Library of Canada*] (NLC) .... OOCRLF
Canadian Risk Manager (DD) .... CRM
Canadian Rock Art Research Associates .... CRARA
Canadian Rock Mechanics Association [*Association Candienne de Mechanique des Roches*] (AC) .... CARMA
Canadian Roofing Contractors' Association .... CRCA
Canadian Rose Society [*Formerly, Rose Society of Ontario*] (AC) .... CRS
Canadian Roxy Petroleum Ltd. [*Toronto Stock Exchange symbol*] .... CNR
Canadian Royal Mint, Ottawa, ON, Canada [*Library symbol Library of Congress*] (LCLS) .... CaOOCRM
Canadian Royal Mint [*Monnaie Royale Canadienne*] Ottawa, Ontario [*Library symbol National Library of Canada*] (NLC) .... OOCRM
Canadian Sailfish Corp. [*See also OCPS*] .... CSFC
Canadian Sales Finance Long Form Report .... CANSAF
Canadian Sales Tax Reporter (Commerce Clearing House) [*A publication*] (DLA) .... Can Sales Tax Rep (CCH)
Canadian Sanitation Standards Association .... CSSA
Canadian Sanitation Supply Association [*Association Canadienne des Fournisseurs de Produits Sanitaires*] [*Formerly, Canadian Sanitation Standards Association*] (AC) .... CSSA
Canadian Satellite Communications, Inc. [*Mississauga, ON*] [*Telecommunications*] (TSSD) .... CANCOM
Canadian Satellite Communications, Inc. [*Toronto Stock Exchange symbol*] .... SAT
Canadian Saturday Night [*A publication*] .... CSN
Canadian Save the Children Fund .... CANSAVE
Canadian Schizophrenia Foundation (EA) .... CSF
Canadian Scholarship Trust Foundation [*Fondation Fiduciaire Canadienne de Bourses d'Etudes*] [*Formerly, CST Foundation*] (AC) .... CST
Canadian School Boards Association [*Association Canadienne des Commissions/Conseils Scolaires*] [*Formerly, Canadian School Trustees' Association*] (AC) .... CSBA
Canadian School Library Association .... CSLA
Canadian School of Missions and Ecumenical Institute, Toronto, ON, Canada [*Library symbol Library of Congress*] (LCLS) .... CaOTCM
Canadian School of Missions and Ecumenical Institute, Toronto, Ontario [*Library symbol National Library of Canada*] (NLC) .... OTCM
Canadian Science & Technology Historical Association (AC) .... CSTHA
Canadian Science Film Association .... CSFA
Canadian Science Writers' Association [*Association Canadienne des Redacteurs Sceintifiques*] (AC) .... CSWA
Canadian Scientific Liaison Office (HGAA) .... CSLO
Canadian Scientific Ship (BARN) .... CSS
Canadian Seamen's Union .... CSU
Canadian Search and Rescue Association .... CASARA
Canadian Section International Association of Penal Law (EAIO) .... CSIAPL
[*The*] Canadian Securities [*Institut Canadien des Valeurs Mobilieres*] (AC) .... CSI
Canadian Security and Intelligence Service .... CSIS
Canadian Security and Intelligence Service [*UTLAS symbol*] .... SIS
Canadian Seed Growers Association (HGAA) .... CSGA
Canadian Seed Trade Association (AC) .... CSTA
Canadian Selection, Toronto, Ontario [*Library symbol National Library of Canada*] (NLC) .... OTCSE
Canadian Semiotic Association [*See also ACS*] .... CSA
Canadian Seniors Packaging Advisory Council [*Conseil Consultatif Canadien pour l'Adaptation de l'Emballage aux Besoins des Aines*] (AC) .... CASPAC

Canadian Service for Overseas Students and Trainees ... CSOST
Canadian Service for the Selective Dissemination of Information [*National Research Council of Canada*] [*Information service or system*] (IID) ... CAN/SDI
Canadian Services College ... CANSERVCOL
Canadian Sewing & Needlecraft Association [*Association Canadienne des Travaux d'Aiguilles*] [*Formerly, Canadian Home Sewing & Needlecraft Association*] (AC) ... CSNA
Canadian Sheet Steel Building Institute [*Institut Canadien de la tole d'Acier pour le Batiment*] (AC) ... CSSBI
Canadian Shipbuilding and Ship Repairing Association ... CSSRA
Canadian Shipowners Association (EAIO) ... CSA
Canadian Shipping Act [*1970*] (MSC) ... CSA
Canadian Shooting Sports Foundation [*La Fondation des Sports de Tir*] (AC) ... CSSF
Canadian Shopcraft Union ... CSU
Canadian Siberian Expeditionary Force ... CSEF
Canadian Ski Association ... CSA
Canadian Ski Instructors' Alliance ... CSIA
Canadian Ski Marathon [*Marathon Canadien de Ski*] (AC) ... CSM
Canadian Ski Patrol System [*Organisation de la Patrouille Canadienne de Ski*] (AC) ... CSPS
Canadian Sleep Society (AC) ... CSS
Canadian Slovak League ... CSL
Canadian Snowbird Association (AC) ... CSA
Canadian Soccer Association ... CSA
Canadian Social Science Abstracts [*York University*] [*Canada*] [*A database*] (NITA) ... CSSA
Canadian Society for Aesthetic (Cosmetic) Plastic Surgery (EAIO) ... CSACPS
Canadian Society for Aesthetics (AC) ... CSA
Canadian Society for Aesthetics ... CSAC
Canadian Society for Asian Studies ... CSAS
Canadian Society for Chemical Engineering ... CSChE
Canadian Society for Chemical Engineers [*Also, CSChe*] ... CSCE
Canadian Society for Chemical Technology (EAIO) ... CSCT
Canadian Society for Chemistry (EAIO) ... CSC
Canadian Society for Civil Engineering ... CSCE
Canadian Society for Clinical Investigation [*Societe Canadienne de Recherches Cliniques*] (AC) ... CSCI
Canadian Society for Clinical Pharmacology [*Societe Canadienne de Pharmacologie Clinique*] (AC) ... CSCP
Canadian Society for Colour in Art, Industry, and Science (EAIO) ... CSC
Canadian Society for Cultural and Intellectual History ... CSCIH
Canadian Society for Education through Art [*1951*] (NGC) ... CSEA
Canadian Society for Education through Art (AC) ... CSEA
Canadian Society for Eighteenth-Century Studies (AC) ... CSECS
Canadian Society for Electrical and Computer Engineering (EAIO) ... CSECE
Canadian Society for Electrical Engineers (MCD) ... CSEE
Canadian Society for Engineering Management [*Societe Canadienne de Gestion en Ingeniere*] [*Formerly, EIC General Members Society*] (AC) ... CSEM
Canadian Society for Exercise Physiology [*Formerly, Canadian Association of Sport Sciences*] (AC) ... CSEP
Canadian Society for Horticultural Science (AC) ... CSHS
Canadian Society for Industrial Heritage (AC) ... CSIH
Canadian Society for Industrial Security ... CSIS
Canadian Society for International Health [*Societe Canadienne pour la Sante International*] [*Formerly, Canadian Society for Tropical Medicine & International Health*] (AC) ... CSIH
Canadian Society for Italian Studies ... CSIS
Canadian Society for Mechanical Engineering ... CSME
Canadian Society for Medical Mycology [*Societe Canadienne de Mycologie Medicale*] (AC) ... CSMM
Canadian Society for Mesopotamian Studies [*Societe Canadienne des Etudes Mesopotamiens*] [*Formerly, Society for Mesopotamian Studies*] (AC) ... CSMS
Canadian Society for Musical Traditions (EAIO) ... CSMT
Canadian Society for Musical Traditions [*Societe Canadienne pour les Traditions Musicales*] [*Formerly, Canadian Folk Music Society*] (AC) ... CSTM
Canadian Society for Non-Destructive Testing ... CSNDT
Canadian Society for Professional Engineers (AC) ... CSPE
Canadian Society for Psychomotor Learning and Sport Psychology (EDAC) ... CSPLSP
Canadian Society for Renaissance Studies [*See also SCER*] ... CSRS
Canadian Society for the Advancement of Legal Technology [*Association Canadienne pour l'Advancement de l'Informatique Juridique*] (AC) ... CSALT
Canadian Society for the Comparative Study of Civilizations [*See also SCECC*] ... CSCSC
Canadian Society for the History and Philosophy of Mathematics [*See also SCHPM*] ... CSHPM
Canadian Society for the History and Philosophy of Science [*See also SCHPS*] ... CSHPS
Canadian Society for the History of Medicine [*See also SCHM*] ... CSHM
Canadian Society for the History of Rhetoric [*See also SCHR*] ... CSHR
Canadian Society for the Prevention of Cruelty to Animals (BARN) ... CSPCA
Canadian Society for the Prevention of Cruelty to Children ... CSPCC
Canadian Society for the Study of Education [*See also SCEE*] [*University of Ottawa*] [*Research center*] (RCD) ... CSSE
Canadian Society for the Study of Higher Education [*See also SCEES*] ... CSSHE
Canadian Society for the Study of Names [*See also SCEN*] ... CSSN
Canadian Society for the Study of Religion [*See also SCER*] ... CSSR
Canadian Society for Titanic Education & Preservation (AC) ... CANSTEP
Canadian Society for Transfusion Medicine [*Societe Canadienne de Medecine Transfusionnelle*] [*Formerly, Canadian Association of Immunohematologists*] (AC) ... CSTM
Canadian Society of Aerospace Medicine [*Societe Medicale Aeronautique du Canada*] (AC) ... CSAM
Canadian Society of Agricultural Engineering ... CSAE
Canadian Society of Agronomy ... CSA
Canadian Society of Allergy & Clinical Immunology [*Societe Canadienne d'Allergie et d'Immunologie Clinique*] (AC) ... CSACI
Canadian Society of Animal Science ... CSAS
Canadian Society of Applied Art [*1905, founded 1903 as Society of Arts and Crafts of Canada*] (NGC) ... CSAP
Canadian Society of Association Executives ... CSAE
Canadian Society of Association Executives [*Formerly, Institute of Canadian Trade Association Executives*] (AC) ... CSAE
Canadian Society of Association Executives (NFD) ... CSAE
Canadian Society of Biblical Studies [*See also SCEB*] ... CSBS
Canadian Society of Children's Authors, Illustrators, and Performers ... CANSCAIP
Canadian Society of Church History [*See also SCHE*] ... CSCH
Canadian Society of Cinematographers ... CSC
Canadian Society of Clinical Chemists [*Societe Canadienne des Clinico-Chimistes*] (AC) ... CSCC
Canadian Society of Clinical Neurophysiologists [*Societe Canadienne de Neurophsiologistes Cliniques*] (AC) ... CSCN
Canadian Society of Computational Studies of Intelligence (IAA) ... CSCI
Canadian Society of Computational Studies of Intelligence ... CSCSI
Canadian Society of Copyright Consumers [*Societe Canadienne des Consommaters Copyright*] [*Formerly, Musical Protective Society of Canada*] (AC) ... CSCC
Canadian Society of Corporate Secretaries (AC) ... CSCS
Canadian Society of Cytology ... CSC
Canadian Society of Decorative Arts [*Cercle Canadien des Arts Decoratifs*] (AC) ... CSDA
Canadian Society of Diagnostic Medical Sonographers (AC) ... CSDMS
Canadian Society of Environmental Biologists [*La Societe Canadienne des Biologistes de l'Environnement*] (AC) ... CSEB
Canadian Society of Exploration Geophysicists (AC) ... CSEG
Canadian Society of Extension ... CSE
Canadian Society of Forensic Science (AC) ... CSFS
Canadian Society of Forest Engineers (HGAA) ... CSFE
Canadian Society of Fund Raising Executives ... CSFRE
Canadian Society of Fund Raising Executives (NFD) ... CSFRE
Canadian Society of Graphic Art [*1923-76, founded c.1903 as GAC, SGA from 1912*] (NGC) ... CSGA
Canadian Society of Hospital Pharmacists ... CSHP
Canadian Society of Internal Medicine [*Societe Canadienne de Medecine Interne*] (AC) ... CSIM
Canadian Society of Laboratory Technologists (EAIO) ... CSLT
Canadian Society of Landscape Architects ... CSLA
Canadian Society of Landscape Architects and Town Planners (HGAA) ... CSLATP
Canadian Society of Magazine Editors (AC) ... CSME
Canadian Society of Marine Artists ... CSMA
Canadian Society of Microbiologists (EAIO) ... CSM
Canadian Society of Military Medals and Insignia ... CSMMI
Canadian Society of New York (EA) ... CSNY
Canadian Society of Orthopaedic Technologists (EAIO) ... CSOT
Canadian Society of Otolaryngology - Head and Neck Surgery (EAIO) ... CSO-HNS
Canadian Society of Painters in Water Color (AC) ... CSPWC
Canadian Society of Painters in Water Colour [*1925*] (NGC) ... CSPWC
Canadian Society of Patristic Studies [*See also ACEP*] ... CSPS
Canadian Society of Petroleum Geologists (DD) ... CSPG
Canadian Society of Petroleum Geologists [*Formerly, Alberta Society of Petroleum Geologists*] (AC) ... CSPG
Canadian Society of Plant Physiologists (AC) ... CSPP
Canadian Society of Plastic Surgeons [*Societe Canadienne des Chirurgiens Plasticiens*] (AC) ... CSPS
Canadian Society of Public Health Dentists [*Association Canadienne des Dentistes en Sante Publique*] (AC) ... CSPHD
Canadian Society of Radiological Technicians ... CSRT
Canadian Society of Respiratory Therapists (AC) ... CSRT
Canadian Society of Rural Extension ... CSRE
Canadian Society of Safety Engineering ... CSSE
Canadian Society of Scientific Photography [*Societe Canadienne de la Photographie Scientifique*] (AC) ... CSSP
Canadian Society of Soil Science [*Societe Canadienne de la Science du Sol*] (AC) ... CSSS
Canadian Society of Surgical Oncology [*Societe Canadienne d'Oncologie Chirurgicale*] (AC) ... CSSO
Canadian Society of Wildlife and Fishery Biologists ... CSWFB
Canadian Socio-Economic Information Management System [*Statistics Canada*] [*Database Ottawa, ON*] (IID) ... CANSIM
Canadian Sociology and Anthropology Association [*See also ACSA*] ... CSAA
Canadian Soft Drink Association [*Association Canadeinne de l'Industrie des Boissons Gazeuses*] [*Formerly, Canadian Association of Carbonated Beverages*] (AC) ... CSDA
Canadian Soil Information System [*Land Resource and Research Institute*] [*Ottawa, ON*] [*Information service or system*] (IID) ... CanSIS
Canadian Soil Science Society (MCD) ... CSSS
Canadian Solar Industries Association ... CSIA
Canadian Solar Industries Association Inc. [*Association des Industries Solaires du Canada Inc.*] (AC) ... CanSIA
Canadian Space Agency ... CSA
Canadian Speech Association ... CSA
Canadian Spice Association (AC) ... CSA
Canadian Spooner Resources, Inc. [*Toronto Stock Exchange symbol*] ... CSF
Canadian Sport & Fitness Administration Centre [*Centre Canadien d'Administration du Sport et de la Condition Physique*] (AC) ... CSFAC

Canadian Sport Parachuting Association (EA) .... CSPA
Canadian Sporting Goods Association [Association Canadienne d'Article Sport] (AC) .... CSGA
Canadian Sports & Fitness Marketing Inc. [Le Marketing Canadien du Sport et de la Condition Physique] (AC) .... CSFM
Canadian Sprinkler Risk Pool .... CSRP
Canadian Stamp Dealers' Association .... CSDA
Canadian Standard Freeness [Drainage rate of synthetic pulps] .... CSF
Canadian Standardbred Horse Society (AC) .... CSHS
Canadian Standardized Test of Fitness .... CSTF
Canadian Standards [Standards Council of Canada] [Information service or system] (CRD) .... CANSTAN
Canadian Standards Approval .... CSA
Canadian Standards Association .... CSA
Canadian Standards Association, Rexdale, Ontario [Library symbol National Library of Canada] (NLC) .... OTCSA
Canadian Standards Association, Toronto, ON, Canada [Library symbol Library of Congress] (LCLS) .... CaOTCSA
Canadian Statistical Society .... CSS
Canadian Steel Can Recycling Council (AC) .... CSCRC
Canadian Steel Construction Council .... CSCC
Canadian Steel Environmental Association [Association Environnemental de la Siderurgie Canadienne] (AC) .... AESC
Canadian Steel Environmental Association [Association Environnemental de la Siderurgie Canadienne] (AC) .... CSEA
Canadian Steel Industries Construction Council (HGAA) .... CSICC
Canadian Steel Industry Research Association .... CSIRA
Canadian Steel Producers Association (AC) .... CSPA
Canadian Stock Options [Toronto Stock Exchange] [Canada Information service or system] (CRD) .... CDNOPT
Canadian Street Rod Association .... CSRA
Canadian String Teachers' Association .... CSTA
Canadian Student Debating Federation .... CSDF
Canadian Student Pugwash .... CSP
Canadian Sugar Beet Producers' Association (AC) .... CSBPA
Canadian Sugar Factories Ltd. .... CSF
Canadian Sugar Institute [Institut Canadien du Sucre] (AC) .... CSI
Canadian Superior Oil Ltd., Calgary, AB, Canada [Library symbol Library of Congress] (LCLS) .... CaACCS
Canadian Swimming Pool Association .... CANSPA
Canadian Switched Network .... CSN
Canadian Table Tennis [Association Canadienne de Tennis de Table] (AC) .... CTTA
Canadian Tactical Air Command Headquarters .... CANAIRTAC
Canadian Talent Library .... CTL
Canadian Task Force on the Periodic Health Examination .... CTFPHE
Canadian Tax Cases [A publication] (DLA) .... C Tax C
Canadian Tax Foundation (AC) .... CTF
Canadian Tax Foundation. Conference Report [A publication] (DLA) .... Can Tax Found
Canadian Tax Foundation. Report of Proceedings of the Tax Conference [A publication] (DLA) .... Can Tax Found Rep Proc Tax Conf
Canadian Tax Foundation, Toronto, ON, Canada [Library symbol Library of Congress] (LCLS) .... CaOTCT
Canadian Tax Foundation [Association Canadienne d'Etudes Fiscales] Toronto, Ontario [Library symbol National Library of Canada] (NLC) .... OTCT
Canadian Tax Law Journal [A publication] (DLA) .... Can Tax LJ
Canadian Tax Reporter (Commerce Clearing House) [A publication] (DLA) .... Can Tax Rep (CCH)
Canadian Taxpayers Federation (AC) .... CTF
Canadian Teachers Federation .... CTF
Canadian Teachers Federation, Ottawa, ON, Canada [Library symbol Library of Congress] (LCLS) .... CaOOCT
Canadian Teachers Federation, Ottawa, Ontario [Library symbol National Library of Canada] (NLC) .... OOCT
Canadian Team Handball Federation .... CTHF
Canadian Technical Asphalt Association (EAIO) .... CTAA
Canadian Technical Awareness Programme (HGAA) .... CAN/TAP
Canadian Technology Satellite (MCD) .... CTS
Canadian Telebook Agency [ACCORD] [Source file] [UTLAS symbol] .... CTA
Canadian Telebook Agency, Toronto, ON, Canada [Library symbol Library of Congress] (LCLS) .... CaOTCTA
Canadian Telebook Agency, Toronto, Ontario [Library symbol National Library of Canada] (NLC) .... OTCTA
Canadian Telecommunications Carriers Association .... CTCA
Canadian Telecommunications Consultants Association (AC) .... CTCA
Canadian Telefunken [Record label] .... CanT
Canadian Telephone Employees' Association [See also ACET] .... CTEA
Canadian Television Network .... CTV
Canadian Television Producers and Directors Association .... CTPDA
Canadian Test Centre Inc. (AC) .... CTC
Canadian Test of Basic Skills [Education] .... CTBS
Canadian Test of General Information [Education] (AEBS) .... CTGI
Canadian Testing Association .... CTA
Canadian Textbook Publishers' Institute .... CTPI
Canadian Textile and Chemical Union .... CTCU
Canadian Textiles Institute (EAIO) .... CTI
Canadian Textiles Institute [Institut Canadien des Textiles], Ottawa, Ontario [Library symbol National Library of Canada] (BIB) .... OOCTI
Canadian Theatre Critics Association [Association des Critiques de Theatre du Canada] (AC) .... CTCA
Canadian Theatre Critics Association [Canada] (WWLA) .... CTCA
Canadian Theological College .... CTC
Canadian Theological Seminary .... CTS
Canadian Theological Society [See also SCT] .... CTS

Canadian Thoracic Society [Societe Canadienne de Thoracologie] (AC) .... CTS
Canadian Thoroughbred Horse Society [Societe Canadienne du Cheval Thoroughbred] (AC) .... CTHS
Canadian Tire Corp. Ltd. [Toronto Stock Exchange symbol] .... CTR
Canadian Tire Coupon Collectors Club [Club de Collectionneurs de Coupons Canadian Tire] (AC) .... CTCCC
Canadian Tobacco Manufacturers' Council .... CTMC
Canadian Tobacco Manufacturers' Council, Montreal, PQ, Canada [Library symbol Library of Congress] (LCLS) .... CaQMCTM
Canadian Tobacco Manufacturers' Council [Conseil Canadien des Fabricants des Produits du Tabac] Montreal, Quebec [Library symbol National Library of Canada] (NLC) .... QMCTM
Canadian Tooling Manufacturers' Association [Association Canadienne des Fabricants d'Outillage] (AC) .... CTMA
Canadian Towed Array SONAR System .... CANTASS
Canadian Toy Testing Council .... CTTC
Canadian Trace Minerals Ltd. [Vancouver Stock Exchange symbol] .... CTJ
Canadian Trade and Tariffs Committee .... CTTC
Canadian Trade Index [Canada Systems Group] [Information service or system] (IID) .... CTIX
Canadian Trade Marks [Canada Systems Group] [Information service or system] (IID) .... TMRK
Canadian Training Division [Canadian Navy] .... CANTRAINDIV
Canadian Training Squadron [Canadian Navy] .... CANTRAINRON
Canadian Trakehner Horse Society (AC) .... CTHS
Canadian Transatlantic Telephone Cable [Between Canada and England] .... CANTAT
Canadian Transport Commission .... CTC
Canadian Transport Commission, Air Transport Committee, Ottawa, ON, Canada [Library symbol Library of Congress Obsolete] (LCLS) .... CaOOAT
Canadian Transport Commission, Ottawa, ON, Canada [Library symbol Library of Congress] (LCLS) .... CaOOTT
Canadian Transport Tariff Bureau Association .... CTTBA
Canadian Transport Workers Union [Syndicat Canadien des Travailleurs du Transport] (AC) .... CTWU
Canadian Transportation Documentation System [Database] [Transport Canada Library and Information Center] [Information service or system] (CRD) .... CTDS
Canadian Transportation Equipment Association .... CTEA
Canadian Transportation Research Forum .... CTRF
Canadian Transportation Research Information Service .... CTRIS
Canadian Transtech Industries [Vancouver Stock Exchange symbol] .... CDA
Canadian Trotting Association .... CTA
Canadian Trucking Association .... CTA
Canadian Trucking Association (AC) .... CTA
Canadian Tuberculosis and Respiratory Disease Association .... CTRDA
Canadian Tuberculosis Association (DAVI) .... CTA
Canadian Turkey Marketing Agency [Office Canadien de Commercialisation du Dindon] (AC) .... CTMA
Canadian Turnaround Management Association [Association Canadienne de Restructuration d'Entreprises] (AC) .... CTMA
Canadian, TX [Location identifier FAA] (FAAL) .... HHF
Canadian, TX [FM radio station call letters] .... KRBG
Canadian, TX [FM radio station call letters] (RBYB) .... KYEG-FM
Canadian Ukrainian Youth Association .... CYMK
Canadian Underwriters Association .... CUA
Canadian Union Catalogue of Books [National Library of Canada] [Information service or system] (IID) .... UCB
Canadian Union Catalogue of Library Materials for the Handicapped [National Library of Canada] [Information service or system] (IID) .... CANUC:H
Canadian Union Catalogue of Serials [National Library of Canada] [Information service or system] (IID) .... UCS
Canadian Union College .... CUC
Canadian Union College, College Heights, AB, Canada [Library symbol Library of Congress] (LCLS) .... CaAChCU
Canadian Union College, College Heights, Alberta [Library symbol National Library of Canada] (NLC) .... ACHCU
Canadian Union of Base Metal Workers .... CUBMW
Canadian Union of Educational Workers .... CUEW
Canadian Union of Jewish Students .... CUJS
Canadian Union of Operating Engineers and General Workers .... CUOE
Canadian Union of Postal Workers .... CUPW
Canadian Union of Professional and Technical Employees .... CUPTE
Canadian Union of Public Employees .... CUPE
Canadian Union of Students .... CUS
Canadian Union of Transportation Employees .... CUTE
Canadian Unitarian Council .... CUC
Canadian United Minerals [Vancouver Stock Exchange symbol] .... CUN
Canadian Unity Information Centre, Ottawa, ON, Canada [Library symbol Library of Congress] (LCLS) .... CaOOCUI
Canadian Unity Information Office [Centre d'Information sur l'Unite Canadienne] Ottawa, Ontario [Library symbol National Library of Canada] (NLC) .... OOCUI
Canadian Universities' Reciprocal Insurance Exchange .... CURIE
Canadian University & College Conference Officers Association (AC) .... CUCCOA
Canadian University & College Counselling Association [Association Canadienne de Counselling Universitaire et Collegial] [Formerly, University Counselling & Placement Association] (AC) .... CUCCA
Canadian University Computer Network (MCD) .... CANUNET
Canadian University Music Society [See also SMUC] .... CUMS
Canadian University Press (DGA) .... CUP
Canadian University Service Overseas .... CUSO
Canadian University Service Overseas, Ottawa, ON, Canada [Library symbol Library of Congress] (LCLS) .... CaOOCUS

Canadian University Teachers of Home Economics [*See also PEDUC*] .... CUTHE
Canadian Urban Institute [*Institut Urbain du Canada*] (AC) .... CUI
Canadian Urban Transit Association .... CUTA
Canadian Urethane Manufacturers Association (HGAA) .... CUMA
Canadian Urological Surgeons .... CUA
Canadian Utilities Ltd. [*Toronto Stock Exchange symbol*] .... CU
Canadian Utilities Ltd., Edmonton, AB, Canada [*Library symbol*] [*Library of Congress*] (LCLS) .... CaAECU
Canadian Utilities Ltd., Edmonton, Alberta [*Library symbol National Library of Canada*] (NLC) .... AECU
Canadian Vegans for Animal Rights (AC) .... C-VAR
Canadian Vent Corp. [*Vancouver Stock Exchange symbol*] .... CVB
Canadian Veterinary Medical Association (EAIO) .... CVMA
Canadian Vintage Wireless Association [*Defunct*] (EA) .... CVWA
Canadian Vocational Association (AC) .... CVA
Canadian Voice of Women for Peace [*See also VFCP*] .... VOW
Canadian Volunteers in Corrections Training Project .... CaVIC
Canadian War Museum, Ottawa, ON, Canada [*Library symbol Library of Congress*] (LCLS) .... CaOONMC
Canadian War Museum [*Musee de Guerre du Canada*] **Ottawa, Ontario** [*Library symbol National Library of Canada*] (NLC) .... OONMC
Canadian War Narrative Section [*World War I*] .... CWNS
Canadian War Office (DMA) .... CWO
Canadian War Records Office [*World War I*] .... CWRO
Canadian War Supplies Assignment Board [*World War II*] .... CWSAB
Canadian Warplane Heritage, Inc. .... CWH
Canadian Warplane Heritage Museum [*ICAO designator*] (FAAC) .... CWH
Canadian Waste Technology, Inc., Toronto, Ontario [*Library symbol National Library of Canada*] (NLC) .... OTCWT
Canadian Water & Wastewater Association (AC) .... CWWA
Canadian Water Quality Association [*Association Canadienne pour la Qualite de l'Eau*] (AC) .... CWQA
Canadian Water Resources Association (EAIO) .... CWRA
Canadian Water Ski Association .... CWSA
Canadian Water Supply Energy Loop .... CANWEL
Canadian Weekly Newspapers Association (DGA) .... CWNA
Canadian Weightlifting Federation/Halterophile Canadienne .... CWFHC
Canadian Welding Development Institute, Toronto, ON, Canada [*Library symbol Library of Congress*] (LCLS) .... CaOTCWB
Canadian Well Logging Society .... CWLS
Canadian Western Amateur Bodybuilding Association .... CWABBA
Canadian Western Approaches .... CWA
Canadian Western Bank [*Toronto Stock Exchange symbol*] .... CWB
Canadian Western Natural Gas Co. Ltd. [*Toronto Stock Exchange symbol*] .... CWN
Canadian Westinghouse Library, Hamilton, ON, Canada [*Library symbol Library of Congress*] (LCLS) .... CaOHW
Canadian Wheat Board .... CWB
Canadian Wheat Board Library [*UTLAS symbol*] .... CWB
Canadian Wheat Board [*Commission Canadienne du Ble*] **Winnipeg, Manitoba** [*Library symbol National Library of Canada*] (NLC) .... MWCWB
Canadian Wheat Board, Winnipeg, MB, Canada [*Library symbol Library of Congress*] (LCLS) .... CaMWCWB
Canadian Wheelchair Sports Association .... CWSA
Canadian Wholesale Drug Association [*Association des Grossistes en Medicaments du Canada*] (AC) .... CWDA
Canadian Wildlife Federation [*Federation Canadienne de la Fuane*] (AC) .... CWF
Canadian Wildlife Service, Environment Canada [*Service Canadien de la Faune, Environnement Canada*] **Ottawa, Ontario** [*Library symbol National Library of Canada*] (NLC) .... OOECW
Canadian Wildlife Service, Environment Canada [*Service Canadien de la Faune, Environnement Canada*] **Sackville, New Brunswick** [*Library symbol National Library of Canada*] (NLC) .... NBSACW
Canadian Wildlife Service, Environment Canada [*Service Canadien de la Faune, Environnement Canada*] **Winnipeg, Manitoba** [*Library symbol National Library of Canada*] (NLC) .... MWECW
Canadian Wildlife Service, Environment Canada [*Service Canadien de la Faune, Environnement Canada*] **Yellowknife, Northwest Territories** [*Library symbol National Library of Canada*] (NLC) .... NWYECW
Canadian Wildlife Service, Quebec Region [*Environment Canada*] [*Research center*] .... CWS
Canadian Wind Energy Association Inc. [*Association Canadienne d'Energie Ecolienne*] (AC) .... CANWEA
Canadian Wind Engineering Association .... CWEA
Canadian Window and Door Manufacturers Association .... CWDMA
Canadian Women in Radio & Television (AC) .... CWRT
Canadian Women of Note [*Database*] [*York University*] [*Defunct*] [*Information service or system*] (CRD) .... CWON
Canadian Women's Army Corps .... CWAC
Canadian Women's Intercollegiate Athletic Union .... CWIAU
Canadian Women's Press Club [*Later, Media Club of Canada*] .... CWPC
Canadian Women's Sailboat Racing Association .... CWSRA
Canadian Women's Studies Association [*See also ACEF*] .... CWSA
Canadian Wood Council .... CWC
Canadian Wood Council, Ottawa, ON, Canada [*Library symbol*] [*Library of Congress*] (LCLS) .... CaOOCWC
Canadian Wood Council [*Conseil Canadien du Bois*] **Ottawa, Ontario** [*Library symbol National Library of Canada*] (NLC) .... OOCWC
Canadian Wood Energy Institute .... CWEI
Canadian Wood Pallet and Container Association (EAIO) .... CWPCA
Canadian Wood Preservers Bureau [*Bureau Canadien de la Preservation du Bois*] (AC) .... CWPB
Canadian Woodmen of the World (EA) .... CWW
Canadian Workplace Automation Research Centre [*Department of Communications*] (IRC) .... CWARC
Canadian Workplace Automation Research Centre, Laval, PQ, Canada [*Library symbol*] [*Library of Congress*] (LCLS) .... CaQLaCW
Canadian Workplace Automation Research Centre [*Centre Canadien de Recherche sur l'Informatisation du Travail*] **Laval, Quebec** [*Library symbol National Library of Canada*] (NLC) .... QLACW
Canadian Worldwide Energy Ltd. [*Toronto Stock Exchange symbol*] .... CWW
Canadian Writers and Illustrators of British Columbia [*Canada*] (WWLA) .... CWILLBC
Canadian Yachting Association .... CYA
Canadian Youth for Peace .... CYP
Canadian Youth Foundation (AC) .... CYF
Canadian Youth Hostels Association .... CYHA
Canadian Zionist Federation [*La Federation Sioniste Canadienne*] (AC) .... CZF
Canadiana Acquisitions, National Library of Canada [*Acquisitions pour Canadiana, Bibliotheque Nationale du Canada*] **Ottawa, Ontario** [*Library symbol National Library of Canada*] (NLC) .... OONLC
Canadiana/Cataloguing Subsystem .... CAN/CAT
Canadiana Department, Royal Ontario Museum, Toronto, Ontario [*Library symbol National Library of Canada*] (NLC) .... OTRMC
Canadian-American Center [*University of Maine at Orono*] [*Research center*] (RCD) .... CAN-AM
Canadian-American Challenge Cup Series [*Auto racing*] .... CAN-AM
Canadian-American Committee (EA) .... CAC
Canadian-American Free Trade Area .... CAFTA
Canadian-American Law Journal [*A publication*] (DLA) .... Cam Am LJ
Canadian-American Merchant Shipping Instructions .... CAMSI
Canadian-American Motor Carriers Association (EA) .... CAMCA
Canadian-American Women's Association, American Section (EA) .... CAWAAS
Canadian-Controlled Private Corp. .... CCPC
Canadian-English Achievement Test [*Education*] (AEBS) .... CEAT
Canadians Against Drunk Driving [*Canadiens Contre l'Alcool au Volant*] (AC) .... CADD
Canadians Concerned About Violence in Entertainment (AC) .... C-CAVE
Canadians for Accessible Governmetn & Equal Employment Inc. (AC) .... CAGEE
Canadians for Decency (AC) .... CFD
Canadians for Ethical Treatment of Food Animals (AC) .... CETFA
Canadians for Health Research [*Canadiens pour la Recherche Medicale*] (AC) .... CHR
Canadians for Responsible Government (EAIO) .... CFRG
Canadians Jewellers Association (AC) .... CJA
Canadian-Scandinavian Foundation (AC) .... CSF
Canadian-Tech Industries, Inc. [*Vancouver Stock Exchange symbol*] .... KT
Canadian-United States Eastern Power Complex .... CANUSE
Canadien Society of Customs Brokers [*Societe Canadienne des Coutiers en Douane*] (AC) .... CSCB
Canadina Institute of Mining, Metallurgy & Petroleum [*Institut Canadien des Mines, de la Metallurgie et du Petrole*] [*Formerly, Canadian Institute of Mining & Metallurgy*] (AC) .... CIM
Canadore College, North Bay, Ontario [*Library symbol National Library of Canada*] (NLC) .... ONBCC
Canady, J. G., Charlotte NC [*STAC*] .... CJG
Canaima [*Venezuela*] [*Airport symbol*] (OAG) .... CAJ
Canaima, Bolivar [*Venezuela ICAO location identifier*] (ICLI) .... SVCN
CanAir [*Canada*] [*FAA designator*] (FAAC) .... CWW
Canair Cargo [*Canada ICAO designator*] (FAAC) .... TDR
Canajoharie, NY [*FM radio station call letters*] .... WCAN
Canakkale [*Turkey ICAO location identifier*] (ICLI) .... LTBH
Canal (ROG) .... CAN
Canal [*Board on Geographic Names*] .... CNL
Canal .... CNL
Canal and Lake .... C and L
Canal and Rail [*Transportation*] .... C & R
Canal Defense Light .... CDL
Canal Flats, BC [*Television station call letters*] CBUBT-1
Canal Fulton Public Library, Canal Fulton, OH [*Library symbol Library of Congress*] (LCLS) .... OCnf
Canal, Lake, and Rail .... CL & R
Canal, River, and Dock Watchmen's Association [*A union*] [*British*] .... CRDWA
Canal Safe Transit System .... CASTS
Canal Society of New York State (EA) .... CSNYS
Canal Transport Marketing Board [*British*] (BI) .... CTMB
Canal Zone [*MARC country of publication code Library of Congress*] (LCCP) .... cz
Canal Zone [*Postal code*] (AFM) .... CZ
Canal Zone [*MARC geographic area code Library of Congress*] (LCCP) .... nccz--
Canal Zone [*ANSI three-letter standard code Obsolete*] (CNC) .... PCZ
Canal Zone [*ANSI two-letter standard code Obsolete*] (CNC) .... PZ
Canal Zone Biological Area [*A preserve administered by the Smithsonian Institution*] [*Later, Smithsonian Tropical Research Institute*] .... CZBA
Canal Zone Code [*A publication*] (DLA) .... CZ Code
Canal Zone Code [*A publication*] (DLA) .... CZC
Canal Zone Government [*Superseded by Panama Canal Commission*] .... CZG
Canal Zone Junior College .... CZJC
Canal Zone Merit System (MHDB) .... CZMS
Canal Zone Reports, Supreme and District Courts [*A publication*] (DLA) .... CZ Rep
Canal Zone Study Group (EA) .... CZSG
Canal Zone Supreme Court Reports [*A publication*] (DLA) .... Canal Zone Sup Ct
Canalicular Liver Plasma Membrane [*Anatomy*] .... CLPM
Canam Industry Corp. [*Vancouver Stock Exchange symbol*] .... CAR
Canam Manac Group, Inc. [*Toronto Stock Exchange symbol*] .... CAM
Canamax Resources, Inc. [*Toronto Stock Exchange symbol*] .... CMX
Canamera Explorations, Inc. [*Vancouver Stock Exchange symbol*] .... CXT
Canamin Resources [*Vancouver Stock Exchange symbol*] .... CA
Canandaigua, NY [*AM radio station call letters*] .... WCGR

Canandaigua, NY [*FM radio station call letters*] .... WCIY
Canandaigua, NY [*FM radio station call letters*] .... WLKA
Canandaigua, NY [*FM radio station call letters*] (RBYB) .... WMHX-FM
Canandaigua Veterans Administration Medical Center Library, Canandaigua, NY [*OCLC symbol*] (OCLC) .... VQC
Canandaigua Wine Cl'A' [*NASDAQ symbol*] (TTSB) .... WINEA
Canandaigua Wine Cl'B' [*NASDAQ symbol*] (TTSB) .... WINEB
Canandaigua Wine Co., Inc. [*Associated Press*] (SAG) .... CWine
Canandaigua Wine Co., Inc. [*NASDAQ symbol*] (SAG) .... WINE
Cananea [*Mexico*] [*Airport symbol*] (AD) .... CNA
Cananea [*Mexico ICAO location identifier*] (ICLI) .... MMCA
Canarc Resources [*Vancouver Stock Exchange symbol*] .... CCM
Canarchon Holdings Ltd. [*Toronto Stock Exchange symbol*] .... CAH
Canarctic Ventures [*Vancouver Stock Exchange symbol*] .... CTV
Canard Homing Antimaterial Projectile .... CHAMP
Canari Airlines [*Israel*] [*ICAO designator*] (FAAC) .... CRI
Canarias [*Canary Islands*] [*ICAO location identifier*] (ICLI) .... GCCC
Canarias [*Formerly, Tenerife*] [*Spain*] [*Geomagnetic observatory code*] .... TEN
Canarsie, NY [*Location identifier FAA*] (FAAL) .... CRI
Canary Islands (KSC) .... CYI
Canary Islands [*MARC geographic area code Library of Congress*] (LCCP) .... lnca--
Canas [*Costa Rica*] [*ICAO location identifier*] (ICLI) .... MRCA
Canasia Industries Corp. [*Vancouver Stock Exchange symbol*] .... CAJ
Canasil Resources, Inc. [*Vancouver Stock Exchange symbol*] .... CLZ
CanAtom Ltd., Montreal, PQ, Canada [*Library symbol Library of Congress*] (LCLS) .... CaQMCL
CanAtom Ltd., Montreal, Quebec [*Library symbol National Library of Canada*] (NLC) .... QMCL
Canaustra Gold Explorations [*Vancouver Stock Exchange symbol*] .... CZX
Canavaninosuccinic Acid [*Organic chemistry*] (MAH) .... CSA
Canaveral [*Obsolete NASA*] (KSC) .... CAN
Canaveral Administration Complex [*NASA*] (SAA) .... CAC
Canaveral Council of Technical Societies .... CCTS
Canaveral District Office [*Obsolete NASA*] (KSC) .... CANDO
Canaveral Test Report .... CTR
Canaveral-Mila [*Military*] .... CNM
Canavieiras [*Brazil*] [*Airport symbol*] (OAG) .... CNV
Canbec Resources [*Vancouver Stock Exchange symbol*] .... CCS
Canberra [*Australia ICAO location identifier*] (ICLI) .... ASCA
Canberra [*Australia ICAO location identifier*] (ICLI) .... ASCB
Canberra [*Australia ICAO location identifier*] (ICLI) .... ASCO
Canberra [*Australia ICAO location identifier*] (ICLI) .... ASMO
Canberra [*Australia Geomagnetic observatory code*] .... CAA
Canberra [*Australia Seismograph station code, US Geological Survey*] (SEIS) .... CAN
Canberra [*Australia Airport symbol*] (OAG) .... CBR
Canberra and District Home Care [*Australia*] .... CDHC
Canberra Archaeological Society [*Australia*] .... CAS
Canberra Blind Society [*Australia*] .... CBS
Canberra Bonsai Society [*Australia*] .... CBS
Canberra Bridge Club [*Australia*] .... CBC
Canberra Bushwalkers' Club [*Australia*] .... CBC
Canberra Business Council [*Australia*] .... CBC
Canberra Canoe Club [*Australia*] CCC
Canberra Chamber of Commerce [*Australia*] CCC
Canberra Children's Choir [*Australia*] CCC
Canberra Churches Centre [*Australia*] CCC
Canberra Civil Rehabilitation Committee [*Australia*] .... CCRC
Canberra Classical Association [*Australia*] .... CCA
Canberra Consumers Incorporated [*Australia*] CC
Canberra Craft Bookbinders' Guild [*Australia*] .... CCBG
Canberra Development Board [*Australia*] .... CDB
Canberra Entertainment Centre [*Australia*] .... CEC
Canberra Ex-Servicewomen's Association [*Australia*] .... CESA
Canberra Historical Journal [*A publication*] .... Can HJ
Canberra Historical Journal [*A publication*] .... Canberra Hist J
Canberra Horticultural Society [*Australia*] .... CHS
Canberra Income Tax Circular Memorandum [*Australia A publication*] .... CITCM
Canberra Income Tax Circular Memorandum [*A publication*] .... CM
Canberra Institute of Technology [*Australia*] .... CIT
Canberra Institute of the Arts [*Australia*] .... CIA
Canberra Kennel Club [*Australia*] .... CKC
Canberra Philharmonic Society [*Australia*] .... CPS
Canberra Skeptics [*Australia*] .... CS
Canberra Times [*A publication*] .... Can T
Canbra Foods Ltd. [*Toronto Stock Exchange symbol*] .... CBF
Canby Community Hospital, Canby, MN [*Library symbol*] [*Library of Congress*] (LCLS) .... MnCanH
Canby High School, Canby, MN [*Library symbol*] [*Library of Congress*] (LCLS) .... MnCanHS
Canby Public Library, Canby, MN [*Library symbol*] [*Library of Congress*] (LCLS) .... MnCan
Canby Public Library, Canby, OR [*Library symbol Library of Congress*] (LCLS) .... OrCan
Canby Union High School, Canby, OR [*Library symbol Library of Congress*] (LCLS) .... OrCanHS
Cancapital Corp. [*Toronto Stock Exchange symbol*] .... CJC
Cancel (AABC) .... CAN
Cancel [*Publishing*] (WDMC) .... can
Cancel [*Computer science*] (BARN) .... CNCL
Cancel [*or Cancellation*] (AFM) .... CNL
Cancel (NVT) .... CNX
Cancel [*or Cancelled*] (CINC) CX
Cancel Approved Arrival [*Aviation*] (FAAC) .... CXA
Cancel Approved Departure [*Aviation*] (FAAC) .... CXD
Cancel Back Order .... CBO
Cancel Character [*Keyboard*] [*Computer science*] .... CAN
Cancel/Clarify Message (SSD) .... CCM
Cancel Flight Plan (FAAC) .... CNLFP
Cancel Launch in Progress [*Air Force*] .... CLIP
Cancel on Back [*Deltiology*] .... C/B
Cancel on Face [*Deltiology*] .... C/F
Cancel Previous Order (DI) .... CPO
Cancelable (ABBR) .... CNCLB
Cancelation Clause [*Business term*] CC
Canceled C
Canceled (WDMC) .... can
Canceled .... CANC
Canceled (ABBR) .... CNCLD
Canceled Check [*Banking*] CC
Canceled or Postponed .... COP
Canceled to Order [*Philately*] .... CTO
Canceled Transmission (CET) .... CANTRAN
Canceler (ABBR) .... CNCLR
Canceling (DCTA) .... CANCL
Canceling .... CANCLG
Canceling (ABBR) .... CNCLG
Canceling Former Order .... CFO
Cancellation .... CANC
Cancellation (ROG) .... CANCLN
Cancellation (ABBR) .... CNCLAN
Cancellation (ABBR) .... CNCLN
Cancellation Addendum Sales Order (NASA) .... CASO
Cancellation of Amplitude Modulation (MCD) .... CAM
Cancellation of Instruments [*Legal term*] (DLA) .... CANC INSTR
Cancelled (BARN) .... CLD
Cancelled CXL
Cancelling (IAA) .... CLG
Cancer C
Cancer [*or Carcinoma*] [*Medicine*] .... CA
Cancer [*Oncology*] (DAVI) .... Can
Cancer [*Constellation*] .... CAN
Cancer [*Constellation*] .... Canc
Cancer [*Constellation*] .... Cnc
Cancer (ABBR) .... CNCR
Cancer Aftercare and Rehabilitation Society [*British*] (DBA) .... CARE
Cancer Aid Listening Line [*British*] (DI) .... CALL
Cancer and Leukemia, Group B [*Medicine*] .... CALGB
Cancer Attitude Survey [*Oncology and psychiatry*] (DAVI) .... CAS
Cancer Breaking Factor [*Antineoplastic drug*] .... CBF
Cancer Care (EA) CC
Cancer Care, Inc. (EA) CCI
Cancer Checking Lipid [*Oncology*] CCL
Cancer Chemotherapy National Service Center [*National Institutes of Health*] .... CCNSC
Cancer Control Agency of British Columbia (PDAA) .... CCABC
Cancer Control Agency of British Columbia, Vancouver, British Columbia [*Library symbol National Library of Canada*] (NLC) .... BVACCA
Cancer Control Science Associates Program [*National Cancer Institute*] .... CCSAP
Cancer Control Society (EA) .... CCS
Cancer Council, New South Wales [*Australia*] .... CCNSW
Cancer Cytology Foundation of America [*Later, National Cancer Cytology Center*] .... CCF
Cancer Cytology Foundation of America [*Later, National Cancer Cytology Center*] .... CCFA
Cancer Detection Centre [*British*] .... CDC
Cancer Dose (NUCP) .... CD
Cancer Family Syndrome [*Oncology*] (DAVI) .... CFS
Cancer Federation, Inc. (EA) .... CFI
Cancer Free [*Medicine*] .... CF
Cancer Fund of America .... CFA
Cancer Genetics Studies Consortium .... CGSC
Cancer Genome Anatomy Project [*A Cooperative database*] .... CGAP
Cancer Guidance Institute (EA) .... CGI
Cancer Hazards Ranking and Information System .... CHRIS
Cancer Hopefuls United for Mutual Support [*Defunct*] (EA) .... CHUMS
Cancer Hot Line [*of Cancer Connection*] (EA) .... CH
Cancer Information Clearinghouse [*National Cancer Institute*] [*Database*] CIC
Cancer Information Dissemination and Analysis Center .... CIDAC
Cancer Information Service [*HEW*] .... CIS
Cancer International Research Cooperative .... CANCIRCO
Cancer Literature [*National Cancer Institute*] [*Information service or system*] .... CANCERLIT
Cancer Multistep Therapy [*Medicine*] (DMAA) .... CMT
Cancer of Prostate [*Oncology and urology*] (DAVI) .... CAP
Cancer of the Cervix [*Medicine*] .... CACX
Cancer Patients' Assistance Society of New South Wales [*Australia*] .... CPASNSW
Cancer Patients, Weight Losing .... CWL
Cancer Patients, Weight Stable .... CWS
Cancer Potential Index .... CPI
Cancer Prevention Benefit Program [*National Cancer Institute*] .... CPBP
Cancer Prevention Fellowship Program [*NCI*] .... CPFP
Cancer Proneness Phenotype [*Medicine*] (DMAA) .... CPP
Cancer Rehabilitation Evaluation System [*Medicine*] (DMAA) .... CARES
Cancer Relief Macmillan Fund [*British*] (DBA) .... CRMF
Cancer Research Campaign [*British*] .... CRC
Cancer Research Center [*Research center*] (RCD) .... CRC
Cancer Research Emphasis Grants .... CREG

Cancer Research Projects [*National Cancer Intitute*] [*Information service or system Defunct*] .... CANCERPROJ
Cancer Research Society Inc. [*Societe de Recherche sur le Cancer Inc.*] (AC) .... CRS
Cancer Research Unit [*Flinders University*] [*Australia*] .... CRU
Cancer Risk-Assessment Verification Endeavor .... CRAVE
Cancer Serum Index .... CSI
Cancer Therapy Evaluation Program [*Bethesda, MD*] [*National Cancer Institute*] [*Department of Health and Human Services*] (GRD) .... CTEP
Cancer Therapy Facility .... CTF
Cancer Treatment Advisory Committee [*HEW*] (EGAO) .... CTAC
Cancer Treatment Hldgs [*ECM symbol*] (TTSB) .... CTHEC
Cancer Treatment Holdings, Inc. [*Associated Press*] (SAG) .... CancTr
Cancer Treatment Holdings, Inc. [*AMEX symbol*] (SAG) .... CTH
Cancer-Associated Polypeptide Antigen [*Medicine*] (DMAA) .... CAPA
Cancer-Free White Mouse [*Medicine*] (MEDA) .... CFW
Cancer-Free White Mouse [*Medicine*] (MAE) .... CFWM
Cancer-Free White Mouse (DMAA) .... CFWM
Cancer-Potency Factor [*Environmental chemistry*] .... CPF
Cancom Industries, Inc. [*Vancouver Stock Exchange symbol*] CCX
CANCOM [*Canadian Satellite Communications, Inc.*] **Teleconference Network, Inc.** [*Telecommunications service*] (TSSD) .... CTN
Cancorp Enterprises [*Vancouver Stock Exchange symbol*] .... CEE
Cancrinite [*A zeolite*] .... CAN
Cancun [*Mexico*] [*Airport symbol*] (OAG) .... CUN
Cancun [*Mexico ICAO location identifier*] (ICLI) .... MMUN
Cancun Avioturismo SA [*Mexico ICAO designator*] (FAAC) .... CAU
Candala [*Somalia*] [*ICAO location identifier*] (ICLI) .... HCMC
Candela [*Formerly, Candlepower*] [*See also cd*] (MDG) C
Candela [*Formerly, Candlepower*] [*Symbol SI unit of luminous intensity*] .... cd
Candela Corp. [*NASDAQ symbol*] (TTSB) .... CLZR
Candela Corp. Wrrt [*NASDAQ symbol*] (TTSB) .... CLZRW
Candela Laser Corp. [*Associated Press*] (SAG) .... Candela
Candela Laser Corp. [*Associated Press*] (SAG) .... Candla
Candela Laser Corp. [*NASDAQ symbol*] (NQ) .... CLZR
Candela per Square Inch (WDAA) .... CD/IN^2
Candela per Square Meter (WDAA) .... CD/M^2
Candela per Steradian .... CD/SR
Candela Resources Ltd. [*Vancouver Stock Exchange symbol*] .... CDD
Candelabra Edison Screw (IAA) .... CES
Candelabra Prefocused .... CPREF
Candelabra Screw (IAA) .... CANDSC
Candelas per Square Foot .... CD/FT^2
Candelas per Square Meter (IDOE) .... cd/m^2
Candida [*Genus of fungi*] (AAMN) .... CAN
Candida Albicans Skin Test Antigen [*Immunology*] .... CASTA
Candida Cylindracea [*A yeast*] CCL
Candida Rugosa Lipase [*An enzyme*] .... CRL
Candida Yeast [*Biochemistry*] (DAVI) .... CANDID
Candidate (AFM) .... CAND
Candidate Density Function (MCD) .... CDF
Candidate Environmental Impact Statement (MCD) .... CEIS
Candidate Evaluation .... CE
Candidate for Disposal (MCD) .... CFD
Candidate in Philosophy .... Fil Kand
Candidate Item File .... CIF
Candidate Material .... CM
Candidate/Nominee Protective Division [*US Secret Service*] .... CNPD
Candidate of Historical Sciences .... CSc
Candidate of Pharmacy .... Cand Pharm
Candidate of Science .... C Sc
Candidate of Technical Science .... Cand Techn Sci
Candidate of Theology .... C Th
Candidate of Theology (IIA) .... CT
Candidate of Theology .... Th C
Candidate Pass Generator [*NASA*] .... CPG
Candidate Repair Parts Redistribution Report .... CRPRR
Candidate Selection [*Army*] .... CS
Candidates Reply Date Agreement [*Education*] .... CRDA
Candidatus [*Academic degree*] [*Latin*] C
Candidatus Juris [*Doctor of Law*] [*Latin*] (WDAA) .... CAND JUR
Candidatus Magisterii [*Academic Degree*] [*Latin*] .... CMG
Candies, Inc. [*NASDAQ symbol*] (SAG) .... CAND
Candies, Inc. [*Associated Press*] (SAG) .... Candi
Candies, Inc. [*Associated Press*] (SAG) .... Candies
Candies Inc. Wrrt'B' [*NASDAQ symbol*] (TTSB) .... CANDL
Candies Inc. Wrrt'C' [*NASDAQ symbol*] (TTSB) .... CANDN
Candilejas [*Colombia*] [*Airport symbol*] (OAG) .... CJD
Candle [*Illumination*] C
Candle (IDOE) c
Candle .... Ca
Candle [*Illumination*] .... CD
Candle, AK [*Location identifier FAA*] (FAAL) .... CDL
Candle Foot [*Illumination*] (IAA) .... CF
Candle Manufacturers Association [*Later, NCA*] (EA) .... CMA
Candle Power (IDOE) .... cp
Candle Power/Square Foot (KSC) .... CPSF
Candle-Hour [*Illumination*] .... CH
Candle-Hour [*Illumination*] (AAG) .... C-HR
Candlelight .... CNDLLGHT
Candlelighters Childhood Cancer Foundation (EA) .... CCCF
Candlelighters Childhood Cancer Foundation (EA) .... CF
Candlelighters Childhood Cancer Foundation Canada [*Fondation des Eclaireurs pour le Cancer dans l'Enfance Canada*] [*Also, Candlelighters Canada*] (AC) .... CCCFC
Candlepower [*Physics*] .... CP
Candlepower Hour (IAA) .... CPH
Candles per Square Meter [*Optics*] .... c/m^2
Candlewood Hotel Co., Inc. [*NASDAQ symbol*] (SAG) .... CNDL
Candlewood Hotel Co., Inc. [*Associated Press*] (SAG) .... Cndlewd
Cando Public Library, Cando, ND [*Library symbol Library of Congress*] (LCLS) .... NdCan
Candol Developments Ltd. [*Toronto Stock Exchange symbol*] .... CJD
Candorado Mines Ltd. [*Vancouver Stock Exchange symbol*] .... COM
Candover Investments [*Finance British*] CI
CANDU Owners Group (AC) .... COG
Candy .... CNDY
Candy Apple [*Bowdlerized version*] .... CA
Candy Brokers Association of America [*Later, NCBSA*] (EA) .... CBA
Candy, Chocolate and Confectionery Institute (EA) CCCI
Candy. Mayor's Court Practice [*1879*] [*A publication*] (DLA) .... Candy MC
Cane and Leigh. Crown Cases Reserved [*England*] [*A publication*] (DLA) .... Cane & L
Cane Invert Syrup [*Food sweetener*] .... CIS
Cane Medium Invert Syrup [*Food sweetener*] .... CMIS
Cane, Wicker, and Perambucot Operatives' Society [*A union*] [*British*] .... CWPOS
CANEBSCO Subscription Service Ltd. [*ACCORD*] [*UTLAS symbol*] .... EBS
Canebsco Subscription Service Ltd., Toronto, ON, Canada [*Library symbol*] [*Library of Congress*] (LCLS) .... CaOTCSS
CANEBSCO Subscription Service Ltd., Toronto, Ontario [*Library symbol National Library of Canada*] (NLC) .... OTCSS
Caneco Audio-Publishers, Inc. [*Vancouver Stock Exchange symbol*] .... CPB
Canertech, Inc., Winnipeg, Manitoba [*Library symbol National Library of Canada*] (NLC) .... MWCI
Canertech, Inc., Winnipeg, MB, Canada [*Library symbol*] [*Library of Congress*] (LCLS) .... CaMWCI
Canes Venatici [*Constellation*] .... CVen
Canes Venatici [*Constellation*] .... CVn
Canet Nordenfelt Gun .... CN
Canever English History Club .... CEHC
Canewdon [*England*] .... CANEW
Can-Ex Resources Ltd. [*Vancouver Stock Exchange symbol*] .... CXZ
Caney, KS [*FM radio station call letters*] .... KEOJ
Cane-Zebiak [*Marine science*] (OSRA) .... CZ
Canfic Resources Ltd. [*Vancouver Stock Exchange symbol*] .... CNM
Canfield Centre for Logistics and Transportation .... CCLT
Canfield Instructional Styles Inventory [*Teacher evaluation test*] .... CIS
Canfield Learning Styles Inventory [*Educational test*] .... CLS
Canfield, Rodeman, Adams, and Preller [*Philadelphia law firm in Spiro Agnew's book, "The Canfield Decision"*] .... CRAP
Canfor Capital Ltd. [*Toronto Stock Exchange symbol*] .... CCP
Canfor Corp. [*Toronto Stock Exchange symbol Vancouver Stock Exchange symbol*] .... CFP
Canguard Health Technologies, Inc. [*Vancouver Stock Exchange symbol*] .... CGD
Canhorn Mining Corp. [*Toronto Stock Exchange symbol*] .... CNH
Canifair Aviation, Inc. [*Canada ICAO designator*] (FAAC) .... CNF
Canine [*Deciduous*] [*Dentistry*] C
Canine [*K9 Corps - Army Dogs*] [*World War II*] K9
Canine Adenovirus [*Veterinary medicine*] .... CAV
Canine Behavior Institute (EA) .... CBI
Canine Companions for Independence (EA) CCI
Canine Control Council [*Australia*] CCC
Canine Defense Fund (EA) .... CDF
Canine Distemper [*Veterinary medicine*] .... CD
Canine Distemper Encephalitis [*A disease*] .... CDE
Canine Distemper Virus [*Veterinary medicine*] .... CDV
Canine Dose [*Veterinary medicine*] .... CD
Canine Eye Registration Foundation [*Defunct*] (EA) .... CERF
Canine Gastric Dilatation-Volvulus [*Veterinary medicine*] .... CGDV
Canine Good Citizen [*Purebred canine award*] .... CGC
Canine Home Protection System [*Acronym is title of 1979 movie*] .... CHOMPS
Canine Kidney [*Physiology*] .... CK
Canine Livestock Animals Welfare Service [*Australia*] .... CLAWS
Canine Parovirus .... CPV
Canine Pulmonary Surfactant .... CPSA
Canine Quarterly: a Parody of the World's Most Elegant Magazine for Men [*A publication*] .... CQ
Canine X-Linked Muscular Dystrophy .... CXMD
Canis Major [*Constellation*] .... CMa
Canis Major [*Constellation*] .... CMaj
Canis Minor [*Constellation*] .... CMi
Canis Minor [*Constellation*] .... CMin
Canisco Resources [*NASDAQ symbol*] (TTSB) .... CANRQ
Canisius College (GAGS) .... Canisius C
Canisius College, Buffalo, NY [*Library symbol Library of Congress*] (LCLS) .... NBuCC
Canisius College, Buffalo, NY [*OCLC symbol*] (OCLC) .... VKC
Canister (AAG) .... CAN
Canister .... CN
Canister (KSC) .... CSTR
Canister Harpoon Control and Launch System (MCD) .... CHCLS
Canister/Interceptor .... C/I
Canister/Launcher [*Strategic Defense Initiative*] .... C/L
Canister/Launcher Electronic Equipment .... CLEE
Canister/Launcher Electronics .... CLE
Canister Purge [*Automotive engineering*] .... CP
Canister Purge Regulator Valve [*Automotive engineering*] .... CPRV
Canister Purge Solenoid [*Automotive engineering*] .... CANP
Canister Return Purge Valve [*Automotive engineering*] .... CRPV
Canister Treatment Cell [*Nuclear energy*] (NUCP) .... CTC

Canlan Investment Corp. [*Vancouver Stock Exchange symbol*] ... CAI
Can-Mac Exploration Ltd. [*Vancouver Stock Exchange symbol*] ... CXB
CANMARC [*Canadian Machine-Readable Cataloging*] **English Authority File** [*Source file*] [*UTLAS symbol*] ... CAE
CANMARC [*Canadian Machine-Readable Cataloging*] **French Authority File** [*Source file*] [*UTLAS symbol*] ... CAF
Canmax, Inc. [*Associated Press*] (SAG) ... Canmax
Canmax, Inc. [*NASDAQ symbol*] (SAG) ... CNMX
CANMET [*Canada Centre for Mineral and Energy Technology*] **Library** [*Canada Energy, Mines, and Resources*] [*UTLAS symbol*] ... EMM
CANMET [*Canada Centre for Mineral and Energy Technology*] **Library, Energy, Mines, and Resources Canada , Devon, Alberta** [*Bibliotheque CANMET, Energie, Mines, et Ressources Canada*] [*Library symbol National Library of Canada*] (NLC) ... ADEMRCM
CANMET [*Canada Centre for Mineral and Energy Technology*] **Library, Energy, Mines, and Resources Canada , Ottawa, Ontario** [*Bibliotheque CANMET, Energie, Mines, et Ressources Canada*] [*Library symbol National Library of Canada*] (NLC) ... OOM
CANMET [*Canada Centre for Mineral and Energy Technology*] **Library, Western Research Laboratory, Energy, Mines, and Resources Canada , Sherwood Park, Alberta** [*Bibliotheque CANMET, Laboratoire de Recherche de l'Ouest, Energie, Mines, et Ressources Canada*] [*Library symbol National Library of Canada*] (NLC) ... ASPEMRCM
Canmore, AB [*AM radio station call letters*] ... CFHC
Canmore Municipal Library, Alberta [*Library symbol National Library of Canada*] (NLC) ... ACAM
Canmore Municipal Library, Canmore, AB, Canada [*Library symbol Library of Congress*] (LCLS) ... CaACaM
Canna Yellow Mottle Virus [*Plant pathology*] ... CAYMV
Cannabidiol [*Organic chemistry*] ... CBD
Cannabidiolic Acid [*Organic chemistry*] ... CBDA
Cannabinol [*A component of marijuana*] ... CBN
Cannabis Action Network (EA) ... CAN
Cannan Electric Co., Los Angeles, CA [*Library symbol Library of Congress*] (LCLS) ... CLCan
Canned and Cooked Meat Importers Association (EA) ... CCMIA
Canned Antiair Warfare Exercise (NVT) ... CAAWEX
Canned Chop Suey Foods Industry [*Defunct*] ... CCSFI
Canned Food Information Council (EA) ... CFIC
Canned Food Marketing Committee (EA) ... CFMC
Canned Salmon Institute [*Later, SI*] (EA) ... CSI
Cannelton, IN [*FM radio station call letters*] ... WLME
Cannelton Public Library, Cannelton, IN [*Library symbol Library of Congress*] (LCLS) ... InCan
Cannery ... CAN
Cannery Board [*Queensland*] [*Australia*] ... CB
Cannes [*France*] [*Airport symbol*] (AD) ... CEQ
Cannes/Mandelieu [*France ICAO location identifier*] (ICLI) ... LFMD
Cannet Des Maures [*France*] [*Seismograph station code, US Geological Survey Closed*] (SEIS) ... CMF
Cannibalistic Humanoid Underground Dwellers [*or Contaminated Hazard Underground Disposal*] [*Acronym used as title of movie*] ... CHUD
Cannibalization Point [*Supply and Maintenance*] [*Military*] ... CP
Cannibalize (MCD) ... K-BALL
Canning ... CNNNG
Canning Machinery and Supplies Association [*Later, FPM & SA*] (EA) ... CMSA
Canning, NS [*Television station call letters*] ... CJCH-1
Canning Rvier Wetlands Conservation Society [*Australia*] ... CRWCS
Cannington Branch, Brock Township Public Library, Ontario [*Library symbol National Library of Canada*] (BIB) ... OCAB
Cannon (WDAA) ... CAN
Cannon [*Freight*] ... CANN
Cannon Artillery Weapon Systems (MCD) ... CAWS
Cannon Beach, OR [*FM radio station call letters*] (RBYB) ... KCBZ
Cannon Express [*NASDAQ symbol*] (TTSB) ... CANX
Cannon Express, Inc. [*Associated Press*] (SAG) ... CannEx
Cannon Express, Inc. [*Associated Press*] (SAG) ... CannExp
Cannon Express, Inc. [*NASDAQ symbol*] (NQ) ... CANX
[*The*] **Cannon Group, Inc.** (MHDW) ... CAN
Cannon House Office Building ... CHOB
Cannon Hunters Association of Seattle [*Defunct*] (EA) ... CHAOS
Cannon Maintenance Trainer ... CMT
Cannon Memorial YMCA Public Library, Kannapolis, NC [*Library symbol Library of Congress*] (LCLS) ... NcKa
Cannon Minerals Ltd. [*Vancouver Stock Exchange symbol*] ... CN
Cannon Nonlaunched Guided Projectile ... CNLGP
Cannon Street Investments [*Finance British*] ... CSI
Cannon Street Station [*London*] (ROG) ... C
Cannondale Corp. [*NASDAQ symbol*] (SAG) ... BIKE
Cannondale Corp. [*Associated Press*] (SAG) ... Canondle
Cannonical Correlation Analysis (PDAA) ... CCA
Cannon-Launched Beam Rider Projectile (MCD) ... CLBRP
Cannon-Launched Guided Projectile ... CLGP
Cannon-Launched Precision Guided Munition (MCD) ... CL-PGM
Cannons Regular of the Immaculate Conception (TOCD) ... crlc
Cannonsburg, KY [*AM radio station call letters*] ... WOKT
Cannot Comply (NVT) ... CANTCO
Cannot Duplicate (MCD) ... CND
Cannot Find ... CF
Cannot Hear Of [*Bookselling*] ... C/H/O
Canobie [*Australia Airport symbol Obsolete*] (OAG) ... CBY
CanOcean Resources Ltd., New Westminster, BC, Canada [*Library symbol Library of Congress*] (LCLS) ... CaBNWCR
CanOcean Resources Ltd., New Westminster, British Columbia [*Library symbol National Library of Canada*] (NLC) ... BNWCR
Canoe ... C
Canoe South Australia ... CSA
Canoe-Camping Club [*British*] (BI) ... CCC
Canoga Park Area Office [*AEC*] (MCD) ... CPAO
Canoga Test Laboratory [*NASA*] (NASA) ... CTL
Canon ... C
Canon ... CAN
Canon ... CN
Canon Auto Tuning [*Photography*] (OA) ... CAT
Canon City, CO [*AM radio station call letters*] ... KRLN
Canon City, CO [*FM radio station call letters*] ... KRLN-FM
Canon City, CO [*FM radio station call letters*] ... KSTY
Canon City Public Library, Canon City, CO [*Library symbol Library of Congress*] (LCLS) ... CoCc
Canon, Inc. [*NASDAQ symbol*] (NQ) ... CANN
Canon, Inc. (MHDW) ... CANNY
Canon, Inc. [*Associated Press*] (SAG) ... Canonl
Canon Law Society of America (EA) ... CLS
Canon Law Society of America (EA) ... CLSA
Canon Printer System Language [*Computer application*] (PCM) ... CaPSL
Canon-Caliber Electromagnetic Launcher ... CCEML
Canonesses Regular of St. Augustine [*Roman Catholic women's religious order*] ... CRA
Canonical Correlation Analysis [*Mathematics*] ... CCA
Canonical Correspondence Analysis [*Statistical analysis*] ... CANOCO
Canonical Molecular Orbital [*Physical chemistry*] ... CMO
Canonical Unit of Length ... CUL
Canonical Unit of Time ... CUT
Canonical Variates Analysis [*Mathematics*] ... CVA
Canonici Regulares Immaculate Conceptionis [*Canons Regular of the Immaculate Conception*] [*Roman Catholic men's religious order*] ... CRIC
Canonici Regulares Lateranenses [*Canons Regular of the Lateran*] ... CRL
Canonici Regulares Ordinis Sanctae Crucis [*Canons Regular of the Order of the Holy Cross*] [*Crosier Fathers*] [*Roman Catholic religious order*] ... OSC
Canonicorum [*England*] ... CAN
Canons Enacted under King Edgar [*A publication*] (DLA) ... Edg C
Canons of Aelfric [*A publication*] (DLA) ... Aelf C
Canons Regular of Premontre (TOCD) ... OPraem
Canons Regular of Premontre, Premonstratensians, Norbetines (TOCD) ... opraem
Canons Regular of the Immaculate Conception (TOCD) ... CRIC
Canons Regular of the Lateran (TOCD) ... CRL
Canons Regular of the Lateran (TOCD) ... crl
Canons Regular of the Order of the Holy Cross, Crosier Fathers (TOCD) ... osc
Canonsburg, PA [*AM radio station call letters*] ... WWCS
Canopus Acquisition Gate [*NASA*] ... CAG
Canopus Probe near Limb of Venus Angle [*NASA*] ... CPV
Canopy (MSA) ... CAN
Canopy Cover [*Ecology*] ... CNPY
Canopy Removal System [*for helicopters*] (RDA) ... CRS
Canopy Smoke Grenade (DWSG) ... CSG
Canossian Daughters of Charity (TOCD) ... FdCC
Canova Public Library, Canova, SD [*Library symbol Library of Congress*] (LCLS) ... SdCan
Canova Resources Ltd. [*Vancouver Stock Exchange symbol*] ... CVD
Canpax-Air AG [*Switzerland ICAO designator*] (FAAC) ... CAX
Canreos Minerals [*Vancouver Stock Exchange symbol*] ... CSL
Canron, Inc. [*Toronto Stock Exchange symbol*] ... CL
Cans or Cartons [*Freight*] ... CC
Canso Historical Society, Canso, NS, Canada [*Library symbol*] [*Library of Congress*] (LCLS) ... CaNSCaH
Canso Historical Society, Nova Scotia [*Library symbol National Library of Canada*] (NLC) ... NSCH
Canstar Oil Sands Ltd., Calgary, Alberta [*Library symbol National Library of Canada*] (NLC) ... ACCOS
Canstar Sports, Inc. [*Toronto Stock Exchange symbol*] ... HKY
Canstat Petroleum Corp. [*Vancouver Stock Exchange symbol*] ... CPT
CanSurmount (EA) ... CS
Cant [*or Canting*] [*Heraldry*] ... CA
Can't Add, Doesn't Even Try [*Computer science*] ... CADET
Can't Be Called [*Telecommunications*] (TEL) ... CBC
Can't Be Heard [*Telecommunications*] (TEL) ... CBH
Can't Break Dial Tone [*Telecommunications*] (TEL) ... CBDT
Can't Call - No Dial Tone [*Telecommunications*] (TEL) ... CC-NDT
Can't Hear [*Telecommunications*] (TEL) ... CH
Can't Manage a Rifle [*Formed by reversing the initials of Royal Army Medical Corps*] [*World War I*] [*British*] ... CMAR
Can't Say Good-By ... CSG
Can't Tell What [*Accounting slang*] ... CTW
Cantab Pharmaceuticals ADS [*NASDAQ symbol*] (TTSB) ... CNTBY
Cantab Pharmaceuticals Ltd. [*Associated Press*] (SAG) ... Cantab
Cantab Pharmaceuticals Ltd. [*NASDAQ symbol*] (SAG) ... CNTB
Cantabile [*Flowing Style*] [*Music*] ... CANT
Cantabile [*Flowing Style*] [*Music*] ... CANTAB
Cantabrigiensis [*Of Cambridge University*] [*Latin*] (ROG) ... CANT
Cantabrigiensis [*Of Cambridge University*] [*Latin*] ... CANTAB
Cantando [*In a Singing Manner*] [*Music*] (ROG) ... CANTO
Cantate Domino [*Sing Unto the Lord*] [*Music*] ... CAND
Cantchungo [*Guinea-Bissau*] [*ICAO location identifier*] (ICLI) ... GGCG
Canted Fuselage Station (MCD) ... CFS
Canteen for Extreme Climate [*Army*] ... CEC
Cantel Industries [*NASDAQ symbol*] (TTSB) ... CNTI
Cantel Industries, Inc. [*Associated Press*] (SAG) ... Cantel
Cantel Industries, Inc. [*NASDAQ symbol*] (SAG) ... CNTL

Canter Background Interference Procedure [*For the Bender Gestalt Test*] [*Psychology*] (DAVI) .... CBIP
Canter Background Interference Procedure for Bender Gestalt [*Test*] [*Psychology*] (DAVI) .... CBIPBG
Canterbury [*City in England*] .... CANT
Canterbury [*Record label*] .... Cant
Canterbury [*City and county borough in England*] .... CANTERB
Canterbury Corporate Services [*Associated Press*] (SAG) .... Cantbry
Canterbury Corporate Services [*NASDAQ symbol*] (SAG) .... XCEL
Canterbury Corporate Svcs [*NASDAQ symbol*] (TTSB) .... XCEL
Canterbury Park Holdings [*Associated Press*] (SAG) .... CantbrPk
Canterbury Park Holdings [*Associated Press*] (SAG) .... CantP
Canterbury Park Holdings [*Associated Press*] (SAG) .... CntPk
Canterbury Park Holdings [*NASDAQ symbol*] (SAG) .... TRAK
Canterbury Pk Hldg Corp. [*NASDAQ symbol*] (TTSB) .... TRAK
Canterbury Pk Hldg Wrrt [*NASDAQ symbol*] (TTSB) .... TRAKW
Canterbury Resources, Inc. [*Vancouver Stock Exchange symbol*] .... CYZ
Canterbury Yeomanry Cavalry [*British military*] (DMA) .... CYC
Canterra Energy Ltd. [*Toronto Stock Exchange symbol*] .... CEN
Canterra Energy Ltd., Calgary, Alberta [*Library symbol National Library of Canada*] (NLC) .... ACCE
Cantetech, Inc., Winnipeg, MB, Canada [*Library symbol Library of Congress*] (LCLS) .... CaMWCA
Cantharides [*Spanish Fly*] [*Pharmacy*] (ROG) .... CANTHA
Cantharides [*Spanish Fly*] [*Pharmacy*] (ROG) .... CANTHARD
Cantho [*Viet Nam*] [*ICAO location identifier*] (ICLI) .... VVCT
Canthomeatal Line [*Anatomy*] .... CML
Cantiague Elementary School, Jericho, NY [*Library symbol*] [*Library of Congress*] (LCLS) .... NJerCE
Canticle of Canticles [*Old testament book*] [*Douay version*] .... CANT
Canticles [*Song of Solomon*] [*Old Testament book*] .... Cant
Canticles [*Song of Solomon*] [*Old Testament book*] (BJA) .... Ct
Cantilever .... CANT
Cantilever (MSA) .... CANTIL
Cantilevered Elevated Causeway [*Army*] .... CANTELCAS
Canto (ROG) C
Canto [*Melody*] [*Music*] .... CAN
Canto [*Melody*] [*Music*] .... CANT
Canto Primo [*First Soprano*] [*Music*] C1O
Canto Primo [*First Soprano*] [*Music*] (ROG) .... CO 1MO
Canto Primo [*First Soprano*] [*Music*] CO1O
Canton [*City in China*] (ROG) .... CAN
Canton [*China*] [*Airport symbol*] (AD) .... CAN
Canton [*Republic of China*] [*Seismograph station code, US Geological Survey*] (SEIS) .... CNT
Canton & Carthage Railroad (IIA) .... C & C
Canton and Enderbury Islands [*MARC country of publication code Library of Congress*] (LCCP) .... cp
Canton and Enderbury Islands [*ANSI two-letter standard code*] (CNC) .... CT
Canton and Enderbury Islands [*ANSI three-letter standard code*] (CNC) .... CTE
Canton and Enderbury Islands [*MARC geographic area code Library of Congress*] (LCCP) .... pocp--
Canton Carnegie Public Library, Canton, SD [*Library symbol Library of Congress*] (LCLS) .... SdCa
Canton Free Library, Canton, NY [*Library symbol Library of Congress*] (LCLS) .... NCa
Canton Free Library, Canton, NY [*Library symbol*] [*Library of Congress*] (LCLS) .... NCaL
Canton, GA [*AM radio station call letters*] .... WCHK
Canton, GA [*FM radio station call letters*] .... WGST
Canton, IL [*Location identifier FAA*] (FAAL) .... CTK
Canton, IL [*AM radio station call letters*] .... WBYS
Canton, IL [*FM radio station call letters*] .... WBYS-FM
Canton Island [*Phoenix Islands*] [*Airport symbol*] (AD) .... CIS
Canton Island [*Phoenix Islands*] [*ICAO location identifier*] (ICLI) .... PCIS
Canton Island Range Communications Control Center [*Military*] (MCD) .... CRCCC
Canton, MO [*FM radio station call letters*] (RBYB) .... KRRY
Canton, MS [*AM radio station call letters*] .... WMGO
Canton, MS [*AM radio station call letters*] .... WONG
Canton, NC [*AM radio station call letters*] .... WPTL
Canton, NC [*AM radio station call letters*] .... WWIT
Canton, NJ [*FM radio station call letters*] .... WNNN
Canton, NY [*AM radio station call letters*] .... WNYS
Canton, NY [*FM radio station call letters*] .... WSLU
Canton, NY [*FM radio station call letters*] .... WVNC
Canton, NY [*FM radio station call letters*] .... WXQZ
Canton, OH [*AM radio station call letters*] .... WCER
Canton, OH [*Television station call letters*] .... WDLI
Canton, OH [*AM radio station call letters*] .... WHBC
Canton, OH [*FM radio station call letters*] .... WHBC-FM
Canton, OH [*AM radio station call letters*] .... WINW
Canton, OH [*Television station call letters*] .... WOAC
Canton, OH [*AM radio station call letters*] .... WRCW
Canton, OH [*FM radio station call letters*] .... WRQK
Canton, OH [*FM radio station call letters*] .... WTOF
Canton, PA [*FM radio station call letters*] .... WHGL
Canton Public Library Association, Canton, OH [*Library symbol Library of Congress*] (LCLS) .... OCan
Canton Public Library, Canton, MS [*Library symbol Library of Congress*] (LCLS) .... MsCa
Canton Railroad Co. [*AAR code*] .... CTN
Canton, SD [*FM radio station call letters*] (RBYB) .... KIXK
Cantonese .... CANT
Cantonment .... CNTNMNT
Cantonment, FL [*AM radio station call letters*] .... WNVY
Cantonments [*Military*] (ROG) .... CANTON
Cantor .... CANT
Cantor .... CANTR
Cantoris [*Of the Cantor*] [*Music*] .... CAN
Cantors Assembly (EA) .... CA
Cantors Assembly of America [*Later, CA*] (EA) .... CAA
Cantor's Traumatic Medicine and Surgery for the Attorney [*A publication*] (DLA) .... Cantor Med & Surg
Cantrell and Cochrane [*Initials used as brand name of soft drink*] .... C & C
Cantrell Resources [*Vancouver Stock Exchange symbol*] .... CLJ
Cantuaria [*Canterbury*] [*Latin*] .... CANTUAR
Cantuariensis [*of Canterbury*] [*Latin*] (BARN) .... Cantaur
Cantuariensis [*Of Canterbury*] [*Latin*] (ILCA) .... Cantuar
Cantus [*Record label*] [*Sweden*] .... Cus
Cantus Firmus [*Plain Chant*] [*Music*] .... CF
Cantwell's Cases on Tolls and Customers [*Ireland*] [*A publication*] (DLA) .... Cantwell
Canuck Engineering Ltd., Calgary, AB, Canada [*Library symbol*] [*Library of Congress*] (LCLS) .... CaACCEL
Canuck Engineering Ltd., Calgary, Alberta [*Library symbol National Library of Canada*] (NLC) .... ACCEL
Canuck Resources Corp. [*Vancouver Stock Exchange symbol*] .... CKC
Canuck Resources, Inc. [*Toronto Stock Exchange symbol*] .... CNC
Canus Laboratories Ltd. [*Vancouver Stock Exchange symbol*] .... CZL
Canusa Financial Corp. [*Vancouver Stock Exchange symbol*] .... CZF
Canutama [*Brazil*] [*Airport symbol*] (AD) .... CUJ
Canute [*King of England, Denmark, and Norway, 994-1035*] (ILCA) .... Can
Canvas (VRA) c
Canvas (DAC) .... Can
Canvas .... CANV
Canvas .... CANV
Canvas Awning Institute [*Later, American Canvas Institute*] (EA) .... CAI
Canvas Covers [*Shipping*] (DS) CC
Canvas Products Association International [*Later, IFAI*] (EA) .... CPAI
Canvasback Society (EA) .... CS
Canvas-Covered Wire-Rope Handrail [*Aerospace*] (AAG) .... CC WR HDR
Canvas-Covered Wire-Rope Handrail [*Aerospace*] (MSA) .... CCWRH
Canwest Global Communications Corp. [*Associated Press*] (SAG) .... Canwst
Canwest Global Communications Corp. [*NYSE symbol*] (SAG) .... CWG
Canwest Trustco [*Vancouver Stock Exchange symbol*] .... CWX
Canyon [*Commonly used*] (OPSA) .... CANYN
Canyon [*Commonly used*] (OPSA) .... CANYON
Canyon [*Commonly used*] (OPSA) .... CNYN
Canyon [*Commonly used*] (OPSA) .... CYN
Canyon .... CYN
Canyon .... CYN
Canyon City, OR [*FM radio station call letters*] (RBYB) .... KJDY-FM
Canyon Country, CA [*AM radio station call letters*] .... KBET
Canyon de Chelly National Monument .... CACH
Canyon Diablo Troilite [*Geophysics*] .... CDT
Canyon Junction [*Wyoming*] [*Seismograph station code, US Geological Survey Closed*] (SEIS) .... CJW
Canyon Research Group, Inc., Westlake Village, CA [*Library symbol Library of Congress*] (LCLS) .... CWlvC
Canyon Resources [*Associated Press*] (SAG) .... CanyonRs
Canyon Resources [*AMEX symbol*] (SAG) .... CAU
Canyon Resources [*NASDAQ symbol*] (TTSB) .... CYNR
Canyon Resources Corp. [*Associated Press*] (SAG) .... Cany
Canyon Resources Corp. [*Associated Press*] (SAG) .... CanyRs
Canyon Resources Corp. [*NASDAQ symbol*] (NQ) .... CYNR
Canyon, TX [*FM radio station call letters*] .... KPUR-FM
Canyon, TX [*FM radio station call letters*] .... KWTS
Canyon, TX [*AM radio station call letters*] (RBYB) .... KZRK
Canyon, TX [*FM radio station call letters*] (RBYB) .... KZRK-FM
Canyon View Group Home, East Wenatchee, WA [*Library symbol Library of Congress*] (LCLS) .... WaEawC
Canyonlands Field Institute [*An association*] (EA) .... CFI
Canyonlands National Park .... CANY
Caobang [*Viet Nam*] [*ICAO location identifier*] (ICLI) .... VVCB
Cap and Gown; a Treasury of College Verse [*A publication*] .... CAG
Cap Haitien [*Haiti*] [*Airport symbol*] (OAG) .... CAP
Cap Haitien Internacional [*Haiti*] [*ICAO location identifier*] (ICLI) .... MTCH
CAP PA Gutierrez [*Hernando R.*] **Ordonez** [*Mexico ICAO designator*] (FAAC) .... ORD
Cap Rlty Inv TaxExFdL P1 [*AMEX symbol*] (TTSB) .... CRA
Cap Rlty Inv TaxExFdLP II [*AMEX symbol*] (TTSB) .... CRB
Cap Rlty Inv TaxExFdLP III [*AMEX symbol*] (TTSB) .... CRL
Cap Screw and Special Threaded Products Bureau [*Defunct*] (EA) .... CSSTPB
Cap Skirring [*Senegal*] [*Airport symbol*] (OAG) .... CSK
Cap Skirring [*Senegal*] [*ICAO location identifier*] (ICLI) .... GOGS
Capabilities and Procedures .... C & P
Capabilities Data (SAA) .... CD
Capabilities Engineering Data Report System (MCD) .... CEDRS
Capabilities Live Fire Exercise [*Military*] .... CALFEX
Capability (KSC) .... CAPAB
Capability and Proficiency Evaluation .... CAPE
Capability Categories (RDA) .... CAPCATS
Capability Design Specifications (AABC) .... CDS
Capability Evaluation Plan .... CEP
Capability Exercise .... CAPEX
Capability Inspection [*Air Force*] (AFM) CI
Capability Maturity Model .... CMM
Capability Objective Package (MCD) .... COP
Capability Password Level [*Telecommunications*] (TEL) .... CPL
Capability Support Plan .... CASP

Capable [or Capability] (AFM) .... CPBL
Capacitance [Symbol] [IUPAC] C
Capacitance (IDOE) c
Capacitance (IDOE) .... cap
Capacitance (DEN) .... CAP
Capacitance as a Function of Voltage (IEEE) .... C(V)
Capacitance Decode Box .... CDB
Capacitance Diaphragm Gauge [Instrumentation] .... CDG
Capacitance Discharge Vaporization [Nuclear energy] (NRCH) .... CDV
Capacitance Electronic Disk .... CED
Capacitance Grid [Electronics] (IAA) .... CG
Capacitance Grid Plate [Electronics] (IAA) .... CGP
Capacitance Hole Probe .... CHP
Capacitance Proximity Sensor (PDAA) .... CPS
Capacitance Voltage Measurements (MCD) .... CVM
Capacitative Discharge [Voltage source] .... CD
Capacitive Loss Factor (IEEE) .... CLF
Capacitive Position Sensing Transducer (PDAA) .... CPST
Capacitive Pressure Transducer [Engineering] (IAA) .... CPT
Capacitive Reactance Xc
Capacitive Read-Only Memory [Computer science] (IEEE) .... CROM
Capacitive Voltage Divider .... CVD
Capacitively Coupled Microwave Plasma .... CMP
Capacitor (CET) C
Capacitor (IAA) .... CA
Capacitor (MSA) .... CAP
Capacitor (IDOE) .... cap
Capacitor Bank .... CB
Capacitor Coupled Logic [Electronics] (NITA) CCL
Capacitor Diode .... CD
Capacitor Diode FET [Field Effect Transistor] Logic [Electronics] (NITA) .... CDFL
Capacitor Diode Gate [Electronics] (NITA) .... CDG
Capacitor Discharge [Automotive engineering] .... CD
Capacitor Discharge Ignition [Automotive technology] .... CDI
Capacitor Flashgun [Photography] .... CAPFG
Capacitor Input Filter .... CIF
Capacitor Leakage Indicator CLI
Capacitor Qualification Test .... CQT
Capacitor Rate-Integrating Gyroscope .... CRIG
Capacitor Read-Only Storage [Computer science] .... CROS
Capacitor Resonance Frequency .... CRF
Capacitor Start and Run (IAA) .... CAPSTAR
Capacitor Test Program .... CTP
Capacitor-Diode Logic (MSA) .... CDL
Capacitor-Resistor (IAA) .... CAPRISTOR
Capacitor-Resistor Diode .... CRD
Capacitor-Start [Motor] [Electricity] .... CAPST
Capacity [Medicine] c
Capacity [Electricity] (DAS) C
Capacity (AFM) .... CAP
Capacity [Insurance; Finance; Transportation] .... CAPY
Capacity (FAAC) .... CPTY
Capacity (ADA) .... CY
Capacity (AAG) .... K
Capacity Activated Transducer [Electronics] (NITA) .... CAT
Capacity Assurance Plan [Environmental regulation] .... CAP
Capacity Coupling CC
Capacity Factor (IAA) .... CAPF
Capacity Factor (IAA) .... CF
Capacity Limiting Constituents (GNE) CLC
Capacity Loading and Schedule System .... CLASS
Capacity Planning and Operations Sequencing System [IBM Corp.] .... CAPOSS
Capacity Planning and Operations Sequencing System - Extended [IBM Corp.] .... CAPOSS-E
Capacity Planning System (IAA) .... CPS
Capacity Planning Volume .... CPV
Capacity Requirements Planning (MCD) .... CRP
Capacity Selector Valve (MCD) .... CSV
Capacity Ships Force .... CAPSHIPFOR
Capco Automotive Products [Formerly, Clark Automotive Products] [NYSE symbol] (SAG) .... CAB
Capco Automotive Products [Formerly, Clark Automotive Products] [Associated Press] (SAG) .... CapcoA
Cape [Maps and charts] C
Cape .... CA
Cape [Commonly used] (OPSA) .... CAPE
Cape [Commonly used] (OPSA) .... CPE
Cape .... CPE
Cape .... CPE
Cape and Orange Free State Native Appeal Court, Selected Decisions [A publication] (DLA) .... NAC & O
Cape Ann Historical Association, Gloucester, MA [Library symbol Library of Congress] (LCLS) .... MGlHi
Cape Ballet [South Africa] .... CB
Cape Breton Development Corp., Sydney, Nova Scotia [Library symbol National Library of Canada] (NLC) .... NSSCBD
Cape Breton Hospital, Sydney, Nova Scotia [Library symbol National Library of Canada] (NLC) .... NSSCBH
Cape Breton Island .... CB
Cape Breton Island [Nova Scotia] (BARN) .... CBT
Cape Breton Post, Sydney, Nova Scotia [Library symbol National Library of Canada] (NLC) .... NSSCB
Cape Breton Post, Sydney, NS, Canada [Library symbol] [Library of Congress] (LCLS) .... CaNSSCB

Cape Breton Regional Library, Sydney, Nova Scotia [Library symbol National Library of Canada] (NLC) .... NSSC
Cape Breton Regional Library, Sydney, NS, Canada [Library symbol Library of Congress] (LCLS) .... CaNSSC
Cape Canaveral [Florida] .... CNV
Cape Canaveral Air Force Station (NASA) .... CCAFS
Cape Canaveral Air Station .... CCAS
Cape Canaveral Auxiliary Air Force Base [Obsolete] (AAG) .... CCAAFB
Cape Canaveral, FL [Location identifier FAA] (FAAL) .... XMR
Cape Canaveral Forecast Facility [NASA] (NASA) .... CCFF
Cape Canaveral Missile Test Annex [Later, KSC] .... CCMTA
Cape Canaveral Missile Test Center [Later, KSC] .... CCMTC
Cape Canaveral Public Library, Cape Canaveral, FL [Library symbol Library of Congress] (LCLS) .... FCa
Cape Canaveral Reference Atmosphere [NASA] (NASA) .... CCRA
Cape Canaveral Test Annex [Obsolete Aerospace] (AAG) .... CCTA
Cape Central Airways, Inc. [ICAO designator] (FAAC) .... SEM
Cape Charles, VA [Location identifier FAA] (FAAL) CCV
Cape Charles, VA [FM radio station call letters] .... WROX
Cape Chelyuskin [Former USSR Geomagnetic observatory code] .... CCS
Cape Cod Bank & Trust [Associated Press] (SAG) .... CCBT
Cape Cod Bank & Trust Co. [NASDAQ symbol] (NQ) .... CCBT
Cape Cod Central Railroad CCC
Cape Cod Community College [West Barnstable, MA] CCCC
Cape Cod Community College, West Barnstable, MA [Library symbol Library of Congress] (LCLS) .... MWebaC
Cape Cod Direction Center [Air Force] .... CCDC
Cape Cod Experiment [Oceanography] .... CCE
Cape Cod Museum of Natural History, Brewster, MA [Library symbol] [Library of Congress] (LCLS) .... MBreC
Cape Cod National Seashore [National Park Service designation] .... CACO
Cape Cod System [Air Force] .... CCS
Cape Colony [British Empire] CC
Cape Colony Cyclist Corps [British military] (DMA) CCCC
Cape Colony Supreme Court Reports [A publication] (DLA) .... SCR
Cape Communications Control [NASA] CCC
Cape Coral, FL [Television station call letters] .... WFTX
Cape Coral, FL [FM radio station call letters] .... WXKB
Cape Corps [British military] (DMA) CC
Cape Croker Public Library, Wiarton, ON, Canada [Library symbol] [Library of Congress] (LCLS) .... CaOWCC
Cape Croker Public Library, Wiarton, Ontario [Library symbol National Library of Canada] (NLC) .... OWCC
Cape Decision, AK [Location identifier FAA] (FAAL) .... CDE
Cape Dorset [Canada] [Airport symbol] (OAG) .... YTE
Cape Dorset, NT [Canada] [ICAO location identifier] (ICLI) .... CYTE
Cape Douglas [Alaska] [Seismograph station code, US Geological Survey] (SEIS) .... CDA
Cape Dyer, NT [ICAO location identifier] (ICLI) .... CYVN
Cape Eleuthera, Eleuthera Island [Bahamas] [ICAO location identifier] (ICLI) .... MYEC
Cape Fear Railways, Inc. [AAR code] .... CF
Cape Fear Technical Institute [Wilmington, NC] (ASF) .... CFTI
Cape Fear Technical Institute, Wilmington, NC [Library symbol Library of Congress] (LCLS) .... NcWCF
Cape Fear Valley Hospital, Medical Library, Fayetteville, NC [Library symbol Library of Congress] (LCLS) .... NcFayCFH
Cape Garrison Artillery [British military] (DMA) .... CGA
Cape Giradeau, MO [AM radio station call letters] (RBYB) .... KGIR-AM
Cape Girardeau [Missouri] [Airport symbol] (OAG) .... CGI
Cape Girardeau [Missouri] [Seismograph station code, US Geological Survey] (SEIS) .... CGM
Cape Girardeau, MO [AM radio station call letters] .... KAPE
Cape Girardeau, MO [Television station call letters] .... KBSI
Cape Girardeau, MO [AM radio station call letters] .... KCGQ
Cape Girardeau, MO [FM radio station call letters] .... KEZS
Cape Girardeau, MO [Television station call letters] .... KFVS
Cape Girardeau, MO [FM radio station call letters] .... KGMO
Cape Girardeau, MO [FM radio station call letters] .... KRCU
Cape Girardeau, MO [AM radio station call letters] .... KZIM
Cape Girardeau Public Library, Cape Girardeau, MO [Library symbol Library of Congress] (LCLS) .... MoCg
Cape Gloucester [Papua New Guinea] [Airport symbol] (OAG) .... CGC
Cape Hatteras National Seashore [National Park Service designation] .... CAHA
Cape Henry (GAAI) .... HEN
Cape Kennedy [NASA] (KSC) .... CK
Cape Kennedy Air Force Station .... CKAFS
Cape Kennedy Forecast Facility [NASA] (KSC) .... CKFF
Cape Kennedy Missile Test Annex [NASA] (KSC) .... CKMTA
Cape Kennedy Precipitation Experiment [Marine science] (OSRA) .... CAPE
Cape Kennedy Precipitation Experiment [USDC] .... CAPE
Cape Kennedy Range Safety Officer [NASA] (KSC) .... CKRSO
Cape Kennedy Reference Atmosphere [Later, CCRA] [NASA] (NASA) .... CKRA
Cape Kennedy Space Network, Inc. [NASA] .... CKSNI
Cape Law Journal [South Africa] [A publication] (DLA) .... Cape Law J
Cape Law Journal [South Africa] [A publication] (DLA) .... Cape LJ
Cape Law Journal [South Africa] [A publication] (DLA) .... CLJ
Cape Law Reports [South Africa] [A publication] (DLA) .... CLR
Cape Lisburne [Alaska] [Airport symbol] (OAG) .... LUR
Cape Lisburne Air Force Station [Alaska] [ICAO location identifier] (ICLI) .... PALU
Cape Lookout National Seashore [National Park Service designation] .... CALO
Cape May [New Jersey] [Airport symbol] (OAG) .... WWD
Cape May County Clerk, Cape May Court House, NJ [Library symbol Library of Congress] (LCLS) .... NjCmCoC

Cape May County Gazette, Cape May Court House, NJ [*Library symbol Library of Congress*] (LCLS) ... NjCmG
Cape May County Library, Cape May Court House, NJ [*Library symbol Library of Congress*] (LCLS) ... NjCmCo
Cape May County Times and Seven Mile Beach Reporter, Sea Isle City, NJ [*Library symbol Library of Congress*] (LCLS) ... NjSicTR
Cape May Court House, NJ [*FM radio station call letters*] ... WBNJ
Cape May Court House, NJ [*FM radio station call letters*] (RBYB) ... WNJZ-FM
Cape May, NJ [*Location identifier FAA*] (FAAL) ... NMK
Cape May, NJ [*FM radio station call letters*] ... WSJL
Cape Medical Staff Corps [*British military*] (DMA) ... CMSC
Cape Monze [*Pakistan*] [*ICAO location identifier*] (ICLI) ... OPKA
Cape Mounted Police [*British*] (ROG) ... CMP
Cape Mounted Rifles [*British*] ... CMR
Cape Mounted Rifles, Left Wing [*British*] ... CMRLW
Cape Mounted Rifles, Right Wing [*British*] ... CMRRW
Cape Mounted Yeomanry [*British military*] (DMA) ... CMY
Cape Newenham [*Alaska*] [*Airport symbol*] (OAG) ... EHM
Cape Newenham Air Force Station [*Alaska*] [*ICAO location identifier*] (ICLI) ... PAEH
Cape of Good Hope [*South Africa*] ... C of GH
Cape of Good Hope [*South Africa*] [*Seismograph station code, US Geological Survey Closed*] (SEIS) ... CGH
Cape Of Good Hope Reports [*South Africa*] [*A publication*] (DLA) ... SC
Cape Palmas [*Liberia*] [*Airport symbol*] (OAG) ... CPA
Cape Parry, NT [*ICAO location identifier*] (ICLI) ... CZUE
Cape Peninsular Rifles [*British military*] (DMA) ... CPR
Cape Province [*of South Africa*] ... CP
Cape Provincial Division Reports [*South Africa*] [*A publication*] (DLA) ... C
Cape Provincial Division Reports [*South Africa*] [*A publication*] (DLA) ... Cape P Div
Cape Provincial Division Reports [*South Africa*] [*A publication*] (DLA) ... CPD
Cape Reinga [*New Zealand*] [*Seismograph station code, US Geological Survey*] (SEIS) ... CRZ
Cape Resources, Inc. [*Vancouver Stock Exchange symbol*] ... CKT
CAPE [*Capability and Proficiency Evaluation*] **Review Period** ... CRP
Cape Rodney [*Papua New Guinea*] [*Airport symbol*] (OAG) ... CPN
Cape Romanzof [*Alaska*] [*Seismograph station code, US Geological Survey Closed*] (SEIS) ... CPR
Cape Romanzof [*Alaska*] [*Airport symbol*] (OAG) ... CZF
Cape Romanzof Air Force Station [*Alaska*] [*ICAO location identifier*] (ICLI) ... PACZ
Cape Romanzof, AK [*Location identifier FAA*] (FAAL) ... CZF
Cape Sable Historical Society, Barrington, Nova Scotia [*Library symbol National Library of Canada*] (NLC) ... NSBCSH
Cape Sable Historical Society, Barrington, NS, Canada [*Library symbol*] [*Library of Congress*] (LCLS) ... CaNSBaCSH
Cape St. George Public Library, Newfoundland [*Library symbol National Library of Canada*] (NLC) ... NFCSG
Cape St. Jacques [*South Vietnam*] [*Airport symbol*] (AD) ... CSJ
Cape San Juan [*Puerto Rico*] [*Seismograph station code, US Geological Survey*] (SEIS) ... CSJ
Cape Sarichef [*Alaska*] [*Seismograph station code, US Geological Survey Closed*] (SEIS) ... CSA
Cape Sarichef Air Force Station [*Alaska*] [*ICAO location identifier*] (ICLI) ... PACS
Cape Seppings, AK [*Location identifier FAA*] (FAAL) ... XCS
Cape Shipunski [*Former USSR Seismograph station code, US Geological Survey*] (SEIS) ... SPN
Cape Shore Public Library, St. Brides, Newfoundland [*Library symbol National Library of Canada*] (NLC) ... NFSBCS
Cape Shore Public Library, St. Brides, NF, Canada [*Library symbol Library of Congress*] (LCLS) ... CaNfSbCS
Cape Smyth Air [*ICAO designator*] (FAAC) ... CMY
Cape Spencer, AK [*Location identifier FAA*] (FAAL) ... CSP
Cape Support Coordinator [*NASA*] (KSC) ... CSC
Cape Times [*A publication*] (DLA) ... CT
Cape Times Common Law Reports [*South Africa*] [*A publication*] (DLA) ... CTCLR
Cape Times Law Reports, Edited by Shiel [*A publication*] (DLA) ... Shiel
Cape Times Supreme Court Reports, Cape Of Good Hope [*South Africa*] [*A publication*] (DLA) ... Cape TR
Cape Times Supreme Court Reports, Cape Of Good Hope [*South Africa*] [*A publication*] (DLA) ... CTR
Cape Town [*South Africa*] (ROG) ... CAPETN
Cape Town [*South Africa*] [*Airport symbol*] (OAG) ... CPT
Cape Town [*South Africa*] [*Later, HER*] [*Geomagnetic observatory code*] ... CTO
Cape Town [*South Africa*] [*ICAO location identifier*] (ICLI) ... FACT
Cape Town Cavalry [*British military*] (DMA) ... CTC
Cape Verde [*ANSI three-letter standard code*] (CNC) ... CPV
Cape Verde [*ANSI two-letter standard code*] (CNC) ... CV
Cape Verde [*Islands*] [*MARC country of publication code Library of Congress*] (LCCP) ... cv
Cape Verde [*Aircraft nationality and registration mark*] (FAAC) ... D4
Cape Verde [*Islands*] [*MARC geographic area code Library of Congress*] (LCCP) ... lncv--
Cape Verde Escudo (ODBW) ... CV Esc
Cape Verde Islands ... C Verd Isls
Cape Verde Islands ... CVI
Cape Verde Islands [*International civil aircraft marking*] (ODBW) ... D4
Cape Vincent, NY [*FM radio station call letters*] ... WKGG
Cape Vincent, NY [*FM radio station call letters*] ... WMHI
Cape Vogel [*Papua New Guinea*] [*Airport symbol*] (OAG) ... CVL
Cape Volunteer Bearer Corps [*British military*] (DMA) ... CVBC
Cape Young, NT [*ICAO location identifier*] (ICLI) ... CYUI
Capel-Cure Myers [*Stockbrokers*] [*British*] ... CCM
Capella [*Chapel*] [*Latin*] (BARN) ... capel
Capella Resources Ltd. [*Vancouver Stock Exchange symbol*] ... CAL
Capetown Performing Arts Board ... CAPAB
CAP-Gemini-Sogeti [*Software manufacturer*] ... CGS
Capiantur [*Let Them Be Taken*] [*Pharmacy*] (ROG) ... CAPIANT
Capias ad Respondendum [*That You Take to Answer*] [*A judicial writ*] [*Latin*] [*Legal term*] (ROG) ... CA RESP
Capias ad Respondendum [*That You Take to Answer*] [*A judicial writ*] [*Latin*] [*Legal term*] (ADA) ... CARE
Capias ad Satisfaciendum [*A writ of execution*] [*Latin Legal term*] (ROG) ... CA SA
Capiat [*Let the Patient Take*] [*Pharmacy*] ... CAP
Capiat [*Let the Patient Take*] [*Pharmacy*] (ROG) ... CAPT
Capiat [*Let the Patient Take*] [*Pharmacy*] (ROG) ... CPT
Capiat Quantum Vult [*Let the Patient Take as Much as He Will*] [*Pharmacy*] ... CAP QUANT VULT
Capiendus [*To Be Taken*] [*Pharmacy*] ... CAPIEND
Capilano College Media Centre [*UTLAS symbol*] ... CAP
Capilano College, Vancouver, BC, Canada [*Library symbol Library of Congress*] (LCLS) ... CaBVaC
Capilano College, Vancouver, British Columbia [*Library symbol National Library of Canada*] (NLC) ... BVAC
Capilano Resources, Inc. [*Vancouver Stock Exchange symbol*] ... CUZ
Capillary (AAMN) ... c
Capillary (MSA) ... CPLRY
Capillary Action Shaping Technique (MCD) ... CAST
Capillary Agglutination Test [*Medicine*] (DMAA) ... CAT
Capillary Array Electrophoresis [*Analytical biochemistry*] ... CAE
Capillary Blood [*Medicine*] (DAVI) ... C
Capillary Blood Flow [*Medicine*] (MAE) ... CBF
Capillary Blood Gas [*Biochemistry*] (DAVI) ... CBG
Capillary Blood Gases [*Medicine*] (DAVI) ... CPG
Capillary Blood Glucose [*Biochemistry*] (DAVI) ... CBG
Capillary Blood Volume (DAVI) ... Qc
Capillary Column Gas Chromatography ... CCGC
Capillary Column Usage ... CCU
Capillary Diffusion Capacity [*Medicine*] (DMAA) ... CDC
Capillary Electrochromatography [*Computer science*] ... CEC
Capillary Electrophoresis [*Physical chemistry*] ... CE
Capillary Electrophoresis System [*In CES I, manufactured by Dionex Corp.*] [*Analytical biochemistry*] ... CES
Capillary Electrophoresis-Single Cell Biosensor [*Analytical biochemistry*] ... CE-SCB
Capillary Filtration Coefficient (IEEE) ... CFC
Capillary Free Zone [*Medicine*] (DMAA) ... CFZ
Capillary Gas Chromatograph ... CGC
Capillary Gel Electrophoresis ... CGE
Capillary Isoelectric Focusing ... CIEF
Capillary Isotachophoresis [*Biochemistry*] ... CITP
Capillary Osmotic Pressure [*Physiology*] ... COP
Capillary Pressure [*Physiology*] ... CP
Capillary Suction Times ... CST
Capillary Volume [*Clinical chemistry*] (AAMN) ... VC
Capillary Whole Blood True Sugar [*Medicine*] (AAMN) ... CWBTS
Capillary Zone Electrophoresis [*Physical chemistry*] ... CZE
Capillary Zone Electrophoresis - Mass Spectrometry [*Analytical chemistry*] ... CZE-MS
Capistrano [*Hazardous test facility*] ... CAPO
Capistrano Test Site ... CTS
Capita [*Chapters*] [*Latin*] ... CC
Capita Preferred Trust [*Associated Press*] (SAG) ... Capita
Capita Preferred Trust [*NYSE symbol*] (SAG) ... TCC
Capital (WDMC) ... cap
Capital (EY) ... CAP
Capital (VRA) ... cap
Capital ... Capit
Capital [*Accounting; Finance; Economics*] (ROG) ... CAPL
Capital ... CPTAL
Capital [*Factor of production*] ... K
Capital Account [*Finance*] ... CA
Capital Accumulation [*Business term*] ... CA
Capital Acquisition Deduction [*Business term*] ... CAD
Capital Adequacy, Asset Quality, Management, Earnings, Liquidity [*Formula used by the Federal Deposit Insurance Corp. to evaluate banks*] ... CAMEL
Capital Adequacy Directive [*European Union*] (ECON) ... CAD
Capital Adequacy Ratio ... CAR
Capital Air Service, Inc. [*ICAO designator*] (FAAC) ... CPX
Capital Airlines [*ICAO designator*] (AD) ... BZ
Capital Airlines, Inc. ... CA
Capital Airlines, Inc. [*ICAO designator*] (FAAC) ... CAP
Capital American Financial [*NYSE symbol*] (SPSG) ... CAF
Capital American Financial Co. [*Associated Press*] (SAG) ... CapAm
Capital & Counties [*Property development company*] [*British*] ... C & C
Capital & Counties [*Property development company*] [*British*] ... CAPCO
Capital and Lower Case (WDMC) ... c & lc
Capital and Lower Case (WDMC) ... clc
Capital and Small Capitals (WDMC) ... c&sc
Capital Appreciation [*Business term*] ... CA
Capital Appropriation Request (TDOB) ... CAR
Capital Area, Personnel Service Office (Navy) ... CAPSO-N
Capital Area Regional Library, Raymond, MS [*Library symbol Library of Congress*] (LCLS) ... MsR
Capital Area Support Center [*Military*] ... CASC
Capital Asset ... CA
Capital Assets Review Board ... CARB
Capital Associates [*NASDAQ symbol*] (TTSB) ... CAII

Capital Associates, Inc. [*NASDAQ symbol*] (NQ) .... CAII
Capital Authorization Request .... CAR
Capital Aviation Services Ltd. [*Canada ICAO designator*] (FAAC) .... VEN
Capital Bancorp [*NASDAQ symbol*] (SPSG) .... CABK
Capital Bancorp $2 Dep'C'Pfd [*NASDAQ symbol*] (TTSB) .... CABKZ
Capital Bancorp (Florida) [*Associated Press*] (SAG) .... CapBFL
Capital Bancorp (Florida) [*NASDAQ symbol*] (SAG) .... CBCP
Capital Bancorp, Inc. [*Associated Press*] (SAG) .... CapAsc
Capital Bancorp, Inc. [*Associated Press*] (SAG) .... CapBn
Capital Bancorp, Inc. [*Associated Press*] (SAG) .... CapBnc
Capital Brands [*NASDAQ symbol*] (TTSB) .... CAASD
Capital Brands, Inc. [*NASDAQ symbol*] (SAG) .... CAAS
Capital Brands, Inc. [*Associated Press*] (SAG) .... CapBrnd
Capital Builder Account [*Merrill Lynch & Co., Inc.*] [*Finance*] .... CBA
Capital Cities/ABC, Inc. [*Associated Press*] (SAG) .... CapCities
Capital Cities/ABC, Inc. [*NYSE symbol*] (SPSG) .... CCB
Capital Cities Communications, Inc. CCCI
Capital Commitment Request (DNAB) .... CCR
Capital Construction Fund [*FHWA*] (TAG) .... CCF
Capital Consumption Adjustment [*or Allowance*] [*Accounting*] .... CCA
Capital Corp. of the West [*Associated Press*] (SAG) .... CapWest
Capital Corp. of the West [*NASDAQ symbol*] (SAG) .... CCOW
Capital Corp. of the West [*NASDAQ symbol*] (TTSB) .... CCOW
Capital Cost Allowance [*Accounting*] .... CCA
Capital Development Fund [*United Nations*] .... CDF
Capital District Library Council for Reference and Research Resources [*Latham, NY*] [*Library network*] .... CDLC
Capital District Library Council, Schenectady, NY [*Library symbol Library of Congress*] (LCLS) .... NScHLC
Capital District Library Council, Troy, NY [*OCLC symbol*] (OCLC) .... VYD
Capital Dynamics [*Vancouver Stock Exchange symbol*] .... CAP
Capital Equipment (AFIT) .... CE
Capital Equipment Corp. [*Burlington, MA*] .... CEC
Capital Expenditure [*Accounting*] .... CE
Capital Expenditure Price Index .... CEPI
Capital Expenditure Proposal .... CEP
Capital Expenditure Request .... CER
Capital Expenditure Review (DHSM) .... CER
Capital Expenditure Threshold (DMAA) .... CET
Capital Factors Holding, Inc. [*NASDAQ symbol*] (SAG) .... CAPF
Capital Factors Holding, Inc. [*Associated Press*] (SAG) .... CapFact
Capital Formation [*Later, NCCD*] (EA) .... CF
Capital Formation Counselors [*Service mark of Capital Formation Counselors, Inc.*] .... CFC
Capital Gain [*Accounting*] .... CG
Capital Gains Tax .... CGT
Capital Goods [*Finance*] .... CAPG
Capital Goods [*Business term*] .... CG
Capital Guaranteed [*Business term*] .... CG
Capital Guaranty Corp. [*Associated Press*] (SAG) .... CapGty
Capital Guaranty Corp. [*NYSE symbol*] (SPSG) .... CGY
Capital Guaranty Insurance .... CGI
Capital Improved Value (ADA) CIV
Capital Improvements Program .... CIP
Capital Intensive [*Finance*] CI
Capital Investment Analysis [*Business term*] .... CIA
Capital Investment Computer Program [*Economics*] .... CICP
Capital Investment Discard .... CID
Capital Investment Goal Programming .... CIGP
Capital Investment Model [*Navy*] .... CIM
Capital Investment Plan [*FAA*] (TAG) .... CIP
Capital Investment Program .... CIP
Capital Issues Committee [*British*] (BARN) CIC
Capital Legal Foundation (EA) .... CLF
Capital Letter [*Typography*] (WDAA) .... CAP
Capital Library Cooperative, Mason, MI [*OCLC symbol*] (OCLC) .... EEJ
Capital Library Wholesale [*ACCORD*] [*UTLAS symbol*] .... CLW
Capital Library Wholesale, Ottawa, Ontario [*Library symbol National Library of Canada*] (NLC) .... OOCL
Capital Loss [*Accounting*] CL
Capital Maintenance and Rental Funds (DNAB) .... CMRF
Capital Maintenance Fund .... CMF
Capital Market Statistics .... CMS
Capital Marketers Assurance Corporation (TDOB) .... CapMAC
Capital Markets Report [*Dow Jones & Co., Inc.*] [*Information service or system*] (CRD) .... CMR
Capital Media Group Ltd. [*Associated Press*] (SAG) .... CapMdia
Capital Media Group Ltd. [*NASDAQ symbol*] (SAG) .... CPMG
Capital Military Assistance Command (AABC) .... CMAC
Capital Military District [*Vietnam*] .... CMD
Capital Military Region .... CMR
Capital Needs Analysis [*Finance*] .... CNA
Capital One Financial [*NYSE symbol*] (TTSB) .... COF
Capital One Financial Corp. [*Associated Press*] (SAG) .... CapOne
Capital One Financial Corp. [*NYSE symbol*] (SAG) .... COF
Capital Pacific Hldgs [*AMEX symbol*] (TTSB) .... CPH
Capital Pacific Holdings [*Associated Press*] (SAG) .... CapPcHl
Capital Pacific Holdings [*AMEX symbol*] (SAG) .... CPH
Capital PC [*Personal Computer*] **User Group** (EA) .... CPCUG
Capital Planning Information Ltd. [*Information service or system*] (IID) .... CPI
Capital Press Club (EA) .... CPC
Capital Property Accounting and Control (MCD) .... CAPPRO
Capital Punishment Project (EA) .... CPP
Capital Re [*NYSE symbol*] (TTSB) .... KRE
Capital Re Corp. [*Associated Press*] (SAG) .... CapRe
Capital Re Corporation1 [*NYSE symbol*] (SAG) .... KRE
Capital Re LLC'MIPS' [*NYSE symbol*] (TTSB) .... KREPrL
Capital Real Estate [*NYSE symbol*] (SPSG) .... KRE
Capital Realty Investment Tax Exempt Fund Ltd. [*AMEX symbol*] (SPSG) .... CRA
Capital Realty Investment Tax Exempt Fund Ltd. [*AMEX symbol*] (SPSG) .... CRB
Capital Realty Investment Tax Exempt Fund Ltd. [*AMEX symbol*] (SPSG) .... CRL
Capital Realty Investors Tax Exempt Fund Ltd. [*Associated Press*] (SAG) CapRI2
Capital Realty Investors Tax Exempt Fund Ltd. [*Associated Press*] (SAG) CapRI3
Capital Realty Investors Tax Exempt Ltd. [*Associated Press*] (SAG) .... CapRtyI
Capital Recovery Factor .... CRF
Capital Recovery Schedule .... CRS
Capital Region Centre for the Hearing Impaired [*Centre de la Region de la Capitale pour les Personnes a Deficience Auditive*] (AC) .... CRCHI
Capital Region Library, Public Works Canada [*Bibliotheque de la Region de la Capitale, Travaux Publics Canada*] **Ottawa, Ontario** [*Library symbol National Library of Canada*] (NLC) .... OOPWC
Capital Research Center .... CRC
Capital ROK [*Republic of Korea*] **Infantry Division** .... CRID
Capital Savings Bancorp [*NASDAQ symbol*] (SAG) .... CAPS
Capital Savings Bancorp [*Associated Press*] (SAG) .... CapSvgs
Capital Secure [*Finance*] .... CS
Capital Ship [*Bomb*] .... CS
Capital Southwest [*NASDAQ symbol*] (TTSB) .... CSWC
Capital Southwest Corp. [*Associated Press*] (SAG) .... CapSw
Capital Southwest Corp. [*NASDAQ symbol*] (NQ) .... CSWC
Capital Speakers Club (EA) .... CSC
Capital Special Zone [*Saigon, Vietnam*] (VNW) .... CSZ
Capital Stock .... CS
Capital Stock Model [*Congressional Budget Office*] (GFGA) .... CSM
Capital Stock Tax Ruling, Internal Revenue Bureau [*United States*] [*A publication*] (DLA) .... CST
Capital Systems Group, Inc. [*Information service or system*] (IID) .... CSG
Capital Trading Aviation Ltd. [*British ICAO designator*] (FAAC) .... EGL
Capital Transfer Tax [*British*] .... CTT
Capital Type Rehabilitation Facility (MCD) .... CTR
Capital University (GAGS) .... Capital U
Capital University, Columbus, OH [*OCLC symbol*] (OCLC) .... CAU
Capital University, Columbus, OH [*Library symbol Library of Congress*] (LCLS) .... OCoC
Capital University, Columbus, OH [*Library symbol*] [*Library of Congress*] (LCLS) .... OCoCU
Capital University, Law Library, Columbus, OH [*OCLC symbol*] (OCLC) .... CAV
Capital University, School of Law, Columbus, OH [*Library symbol Library of Congress*] (LCLS) .... OCoC-L
Capital Work Order (NRCH) .... CWO
Capital-Asset Pricing Model .... CAPM
Capitalisation .... cap
Capitalization [*Real estate*] .... CAP
Capitals [*Printing*] C
Capitals [*Printing*] .... CAPS
Capitals and Lower Case [*Printing*] .... C & LC
Capitals and Small Capitals [*Printing*] .... C & SC
Capitation .... CAP
Capiteq Ltd., Trading as Air North Regional [*Australia*] [*FAA designator*] (FAAC) .... ANO
Capitol [*Record label*] .... Cap
Capitol .... CAP
Capitol .... CPTOL
Capitol [*Record label*] [*Great Britain*] .... DCap
Capitol Air Express [*ICAO designator*] (FAAC) .... CEX
Capitol Air Lines .... CAL
Capitol Air Service [*ICAO designator*] (AD) .... RX
Capitol American Financial Cp. [*NYSE symbol*] (SAG) .... CAF
Capitol American Financial Cp. [*Associated Press*] (SAG) .... CapAm
Capitol American Finl [*NYSE symbol*] (TTSB) .... CAF
Capitol Area Health Consortium Libraries [*Library network*] .... CAHCL
Capitol Area Library Consortium, Inc. [*Library network*] .... CALCO
Capitol Area Motion Pictures Education Organization [*Washington, DC*] .... CAMEO
Capitol Bancorp Ltd. [*Associated Press*] (SAG) .... CaptlBc
Capitol Bancorp Ltd. [*NASDAQ symbol*] (NQ) .... CBCL
Capitol Consortium Network [*of CUMWA*] [*Information service or system*] .... CAPCON
Capitol Consortium Network, Washington, DC [*OCLC symbol*] (OCLC) .... TPU
Capitol Consortium Network, Washington, DC [*OCLC symbol*] (OCLC) .... TPV
Capitol Hill Burro Club (EA) .... CHBC
Capitol Hill Restoration Society (EA) .... CHRS
Capitol Hill Women's Political Caucus (EA) .... CHWPC
Capitol Historical Society [*Washington, DC*] .... CHS
Capitol Information Association (EA) .... CIA
Capitol International Airways (MCD) .... CAP
Capitol International Airways [*Air carrier designation symbol*] .... CAPX
Capitol International Airways [*ICAO designator*] (AD) CL
Capitol Line-Up [*A publication*] (EAAP) .... CLU
Capitol Multimedia [*NASDAQ symbol*] (TTSB) .... CDIM
Capitol MultiMedia, Inc. [*Associated Press*] (SAG) .... CapMl
Capitol MultiMedia, Inc. [*Associated Press*] (SAG) .... CapMult
Capitol MultiMedia, Inc. [*NASDAQ symbol*] (SAG) .... CDIM
Capitol Multimedia Wrrt 'A' [*NASDAQ symbol*] (TTSB) .... CDIMW
Capitol Peak [*Washington*] [*Seismograph station code, US Geological Survey*] (SEIS) .... CPW
Capitol Publications, Inc. [*Information service or system*] (IID) .... CPI
Capitol Publishing Group [*Information service or system*] (IID) .... CPG

Capitol Radio Engineering Institute [*Now known only by initialism*] ..... CREI
Capitol Reef National Monument ..... CARE
Capitol Region Library Council [*Library network*] ..... CRLC
Capitol Services, Inc. [*Database producer*] [*Information service or system*] (IID) ..... CSI
Capitol Transamerica [*Associated Press*] (SAG) ..... CapTrns
Capitol Transamerica [*NASDAQ symbol*] (TTSB) ..... CATA
Capitol Transamerica Corp. [*NASDAQ symbol*] (NQ) ..... CATA
Capitol Wireless, Inc. [*Telecommunications service*] (TSSD) ..... CAPWIRE
Capitola, CA [*AM radio station call letters*] (RBYB) ..... KMBY
Capitol-Cetra [*Record label*] ..... CCet
Capitolo [*Chapter*] [*Italian*] (ILCA) ..... Cap
Capitular Degrees [*Freemasonry*] (ROG) ..... CAP D
Capitular Masonry [*Freemasonry*] (ROG) ..... CM
Capitulo [*Chapter*] [*Latin*] (ROG) ..... CALO
Capitulum [*Chapter*] [*Latin*] (ROG) C
Capitulum [*Chapter*] [*Latin*] ..... CAP
CapMAC Holdings [*Associated Press*] (SAG) ..... CapMAC
CapMAC Holdings [*NYSE symbol*] (SAG) ..... KAP
CapMAC Holdings [*NYSE symbol*] (TTSB) ..... KAP
Capo [*The Beginning*] [*Music*] C
Capo Bellavista [*Italy ICAO location identifier*] (ICLI) ..... LIEB
Capo Caccia [*Italy ICAO location identifier*] (ICLI) ..... LIEH
Capo Carbonara [*Italy ICAO location identifier*] (ICLI) ..... LIEC
Capo Frasca [*Italy ICAO location identifier*] (ICLI) ..... LIEF
Capo Mele [*Italy ICAO location identifier*] (ICLI) ..... LIMU
Capo Palinuro [*Italy ICAO location identifier*] (ICLI) ..... LIQK
Capo S. Lorenzo [*Italy ICAO location identifier*] (ICLI) ..... LIEL
Capo Spartivento [*Italy ICAO location identifier*] (ICLI) ..... LICH
Capodimonte [*Italy*] [*Seismograph station code, US Geological Survey Closed*] (SEIS) ..... CAP
Capoverso [*Paragraph*] [*Italian*] (ILCA) ..... Capv
Cappadocian (BJA) ..... Capp
Capped (MSA) ..... CPPD
Capped Argon Bubbling [*Steelmaking*] ..... CAB
Capper Military Occupational Specialty [*Army*] (AABC) ..... CMOS
Capreol Public Library, Ontario [*Library symbol National Library of Canada*] (NLC) ..... OCAP
Capreomycin [*An antibiotic*] (MAE) ..... CM
Capri [*Italy*] [*Geomagnetic observatory code*] ..... CPI
Capri [*Italy ICAO location identifier*] (ICLI) ..... LIQC
Capri [*Italy*] [*Airport symbol*] (AD) ..... PRJ
Capri Class Association (EA) ..... CCA
Capri Resources Ltd. [*Vancouver Stock Exchange symbol*] ..... CPI
Capricorn Conservation Council [*Australia*] CCC
Capricorn Resources Ltd. [*Vancouver Stock Exchange symbol*] ..... CAX
Capricornia Wildlife Welfare Association [*Australia*] ..... CWWA
Capricornus [*Constellation*] ..... Cap
Capricornus [*Constellation*] ..... Capr
Caprine Arthritis Encephalitis Virus [*Veterinary medicine*] ..... CAEV
Caprine Arthritis-Encephalitis [*Veterinary medicine*] ..... CAE
Caprine Placental Lactogen [*Medicine*] (DMAA) ..... CPL
Caprock Energy Ltd. [*Vancouver Stock Exchange symbol*] ..... CYG
Caps and Small Caps (IIA) ..... C & SC
Capscrew [*Technical drawings*] ..... CAPSCR
Capsid-Targeted Viral Inactivation [*Immunlogy*] ..... CTVI
Capstan ..... CPSN
Capstar Hotel Co. [*Associated Press*] (SAG) ..... Capstar
Capstar Hotel Co. [*NYSE symbol*] (SAG) ..... CHO
Capstead Mortgage [*NYSE symbol*] (SPSG) ..... CMO
Capstead Mortgage Corp. [*Associated Press*] (SAG) ..... CapM
Capstead Mortgage Corp. [*Associated Press*] (SAG) ..... Capstd
Capstead Mtge $1.26 cm Cv Pfd [*NYSE symbol*] (TTSB) ..... CMOPrB
Capstead Mtge $1.60cm Cv Pfd [*NYSE symbol*] (TTSB) ..... CMOPrA
Capstone Capital [*NYSE symbol*] (TTSB) ..... CCT
Capstone Capital Trust, Inc. [*Associated Press*] (SAG) ..... CapsCT
Capstone Capital Trust, Inc. [*Associated Press*] (SAG) ..... CapstCT
Capstone Capital Trust, Inc. [*NYSE symbol*] (SAG) ..... CCT
Capstone Material Fielding Plan [*Army*] ..... CMFP
Capstone Pharmacy Services, Inc. [*Associated Press*] (SAG) ..... CapsPh
Capstone Pharmacy Services, Inc. [*Associated Press*] (SAG) ..... CapsPhm
Capstone Pharmacy Services, Inc. [*NASDAQ symbol*] (SAG) ..... DOSE
Capstone Pharmacy Svc [*NASDAQ symbol*] (TTSB) ..... DOSE
Capstone Pharmacy Svcs Wrrt [*NASDAQ symbol*] (TTSB) ..... DOSEW
Capsula [*Capsule*] [*Pharmacy*] ..... CAP
Capsula [*Capsule*] [*Pharmacy*] ..... CAPS
Capsula [*Capsule*] [*Pharmacy*] (DAVI) ..... capsul
Capsula Amylacea [*A Cachet*] [*Pharmacy*] ..... CAPS AMYLAC
Capsula Gelatina [*A Gelatine Capsule*] [*Pharmacy*] ..... CAPS GELAT
Capsula Mollis [*Soft Capsule*] [*Pharmacy*] ..... CAP MOLL
Capsular Antigen [*Immunology*] (MAE) ..... K
Capsular Polysaccharide [*Biochemistry*] ..... CPS
Capsular Polysaccharide Complex [*Biochemistry*] ..... CPC
Capsule ..... CAPS
Capsule (MSA) ..... CPSL
Capsule Assembly Machine (MCD) ..... CAM
Capsule Cartilage Articular Preservation [*Orthopedics*] (DAVI) ..... CCAP
Capsule Communications [*or Communicator*] [*NASA*] ..... CAPCOM
Capsule Communications [*or Communicator*] [*NASA*] CC
Capsule Communications [*or Communicator*] [*NASA*] (IAA) ..... CPCOM
Capsule Control [*NASA*] (KSC) ..... CAPCON
Capsule Drive Core [*Aerospace*] ..... CDC
Capsule Elapsed Time [*Aerospace*] ..... CET
Capsule End Cover [*Aerospace*] ..... CEC
Capsule Escape and Survival Applied Research [*Aerospace*] ..... CESAR
Capsule Integrated Test Equipment [*Aerospace*] ..... CITE
Capsule Internal Programmer [*Aerospace*] ..... CIP
Capsule Mechanical Training Model [*Aerospace*] (MCD) ..... CMTM
Capsule Observation Panel [*Aerospace*] ..... COP
Capsule Positioning Mechanism [*Aerospace*] ..... CPM
Capsule Separation [*Aerospace*] (AAG) ..... CAPSEP
Capsule Systems Advanced Development [*Aerospace*] (MCD) ..... CSAD
Capsule Systems Test [*NASA*] ..... CST
Capsule/Tablet [*Medicine*] ..... Caplet
Capsule Technology Group, Inc. [*Toronto Stock Exchange symbol*] ..... TKG
Capsule Technology International Ltd. ..... CTIL
Capsule Test Conductor [*NASA*] (KSC) ..... CTC
Capsule Test Unit [*Aerospace*] ..... CTU
Capsule-Orbiting Bus Link [*NASA*] ..... COL
Capsure Holdings [*Associated Press*] (SAG) ..... Capsure
Capsure Holdings [*NYSE symbol*] (SPSG) ..... CSH
Captain C
Captain [*Worn on captain's uniform*] [*Hockey*] C
Captain ..... CAP
Captain (ROG) ..... CAPN
Captain (AAG) ..... CAPT
Captain (DD) ..... Capt
Captain ..... CAPT
Captain (ODBW) ..... Capt
Captain [*Military*] ..... CPT
Captain [*Air Force, Army, Marine Corps*] O3
Captain [*Navy*] O6
Captain, Coastal Forces [*Navy British*] ..... CCF
Captain, Coastal Forces, Eastern Theater [*Navy*] ..... CCFET
Captain Consolidated Resources [*Vancouver Stock Exchange symbol*] ..... CTC
Captain Cook [*Hawaii*] [*Seismograph station code, US Geological Survey*] (SEIS) ..... CPH
Captain Cook Study Unit [*American Topical Association*] (EA) ..... CCSU
Captain [*Commanding*] **Escort Forces** [*Navy*] ..... CEF
Captain, Fishery Protection Squadron [*NATO*] ..... CFPS
Captain James Smith Memorial Foundation (EA) ..... CJSMF
Captain John Curtis Memorial Library, Brunswick, ME [*Library symbol*] [*Library of Congress*] (LCLS) ..... MeBC
Captain (Naval) ..... Capt (N)
Captain, Naval Operations Command Systems [*British military*] (DMA) ..... CNOCS
Captain of Gun [*British military*] (DMA) ..... CG
Captain of Horse [*British*] ..... CH
Captain of Royal Marines [*Military British*] ..... RMC
Captain of the Dockyard [*Obsolete British*] ..... CD
Captain of the Fleet [*Navy British*] ..... COF
Captain of the Guard [*Freemasonry*] ..... CG
Captain of the Host [*Freemasonry*] (ROG) ..... CH
Captain of the Parish [*British*] (ROG) ..... CP
Captain of the Port [*Coast Guard*] ..... COTP
Captain of the Yeoman of the Guard [*British*] (ROG) ..... CYG
Captain, Surface Weapons Acceptance [*British military*] (DMA) ..... CSWA
Captain Theodore C. Freeman Memorial Library, Houston, TX [*Library symbol Library of Congress*] (LCLS) ..... TxHF
Captain-General [*British military*] (DMA) ..... Capt-Gen
Captain-General ..... CG
Captain-General and President (ROG) ..... CGP
Captain-General of the Religious and Military Order of the Temple for Scotland [*Freemasonry*] (ROG) ..... CGR & MOT for S
Captain-Instructor [*Navy British*] CI
Captain's Imperfect Entry [*Shipping*] ..... CIE
Caption (ADA) ..... CAPT
Caption Code (DNAB) CC
Caption Sheet [*Television*] [*Publishing*] (WDMC) ..... cap sheet
Captive Air Spacecraft (MCD) ..... CASC
Captive Airborne Training Missile (DOMA) ..... CATM
Captive Animals Protection Society [*British*] (DI) ..... CAPS
Captive Boresight Harmonization Kit (MCD) ..... CBHK
Captive Carrier Test [*Military*] ..... CCT
Captive European Nations (NATG) ..... CEN
Captive Firing Test Set [*Aerospace*] (AAG) ..... CFTS
Captive Flight (MUGU) ..... C/FLT
Captive Flight Model [*Military*] (CAAL) ..... CFM
Captive Flight Test Missiles (MCD) ..... CFTM
Captive Flight Trainer ..... CFT
Captive Installation Function [*Telecommunications*] (TEL) ..... CIF
Captive Insurance Companies Association (EA) ..... CICA
Captive Nations Committee (EA) ..... CNC
Captive Nations' Council of New South Wales [*Australia*] ..... CNCNSW
Captive Power Plant ..... CPP
Captive Reset Ignitor (NASA) ..... CAPRI
Captive Simulation (NASA) ..... CAPSIM
Captive Test ..... CT
Captive Test Unit (MCD) ..... CTU
Captive Test Vehicle ..... CTV
Captive Trainer ..... CT
Captive Trajectory System [*Air Force*] ..... CTS
Captivi [*of Plautus*] [*Classical studies*] (OCD) ..... Capt
Captopril [*Also, CPT*] [*Antihypertensive drug*] ..... CP
Captopril [*Antihypertensive drug*] ..... CPT
Captopril Prevention Project [*Study*] [*Medicine*] (DMAA) ..... CAPP
Capture ..... CAP
Capture (AABC) ..... CPTR
Capture/Compare [*Electronics*] [*Automotive engineering*] ..... CAPCOM
Capture Orbit Vehicle Assembly Mode ..... COVAM
Captured Air Bubble (MCD) ..... CAB

Captured Air Bubble Boat [*Navy*] .... CABB
Captured Air Bubble Over Water Vehicle [*Military*] (IAA) .... CABOWV
Captured Enemy Documents [*Military*] (AFM) .... CED
Captured Enemy Documents Organization (NATG) .... CEDO
Captured Enemy Equipment [*Military*] (AFM) .... CEE
Captured Enemy Material [*Military*] .... CEM
Captured Enemy Signal Equipment [*Military*] (MCD) .... CESE
Captured Gamma Ray .... CGR
Captured in Action [*Military*] .... CIA
Captured Steam Bubble Nuclear .... CSBN
Capture-Mark-Recapture [*Demography*] .... CMR
Capuchin Franciscan Friary .... CFF
[*The*] **Capuchin Friars** (TOCD) .... OFMCap
[*The*] **Capuchin Friars, Franciscan Fathers** (TOCD) .... ofmcap
Capuchin Poor Clares (TOCD) .... CPC
Capuchin Poor Clares (TOCD) .... OSCCap
Capuchin Sisters (Spain) (TOCD) .... CDP
Capuchin Theological Seminary, Garrison, NY [*Library symbol Library of Congress*] (LCLS) .... NGaC
Capuchin-Franciscans (Province of St. Joseph) (EA) .... CFPSJ
Capulin Mountain National Monument [*National Park Service designation*] .... CAMO
Caput [*Head*] [*Latin*] C
Caput [*Head*] [*Latin*] .... CAP
Caquetania [*Colombia*] [*Airport symbol*] (OAG) .... CQT
Caquiaviri [*Bolivia*] [*ICAO location identifier*] (ICLI) .... SLHY
Car Accountant .... CA
Car and Motorcycle Drivers Association Ltd. [*British*] (BI) .... CAMDA
Car and Truck Renting and Leasing Association (EA) .... CATRALA
Car Assembly .... CA
Car Audio Specialists Association (EA) .... CASA
Car Care Council (EA) CCC
Car Craft [*A publication*] CC
Car Deck .... CD
Car Department Officers Association (EA) .... CDOA
Car Float [*Non-self-propelled*] [*Navy symbol*] .... YCF
Car Handling Automation for Fail-Safe European Roadway .... CHAUFFEUR
Car Information and Navigation System [*Compact disc technology*] .... CARIN
Car Nicobar [*India*] [*ICAO location identifier*] (ICLI) .... VECX
Car of the Year .... COTY
Car of the Year .... COY
Car Park (ADA) .... CP
Car Pricing .... CP
Car Return (ECII) .... CR
Car Service [*Railroads*] .... CS
Car Service Department .... CSD
Car Service Order .... CSO
Car Service Section [*Railroads*] .... CSS
Car Wash Owners and Suppliers Association (EA) .... COSA
Cara [*Dear One*] [*Latin*] .... K
Cara Operations Ltd. [*Toronto Stock Exchange symbol*] .... CAO
Caracas [*Venezuela*] [*Seismograph station code, US Geological Survey*] (SEIS) .... CAR
Caracas [*Venezuela*] [*Airport symbol*] (OAG) .... CCS
Caracas Ciudad Distrito Federal [*Venezuela ICAO location identifier*] (ICLI) .... SVCC
Caracas/Generelisimo Francisco De Miranda Base Aerea La Carlota, Miranda [*Venezuela ICAO location identifier*] (ICLI) .... SVFM
Caracas/Internacional del Centro Miranda [*Venezuela ICAO location identifier*] (ICLI) .... SVCS
Caracas Maiquetia Distrito Federal [*Venezuela ICAO location identifier*] (ICLI) .... SVCA
Caracas/Metropolitano Internacional, Miranda [*Venezuela ICAO location identifier*] (ICLI) .... SVMP
Caracas/Simon Bolivar Internacional Maiquetia Distrito Federal [*Venezuela ICAO location identifier*] (ICLI) .... SVMI
Caraco Pharm Labs [*NASDAQ symbol*] (TTSB) .... CARA
Caraco Pharm Labs Wrrt [*NASDAQ symbol*] (TTSB) .... CARAW
Caraco Pharmaceutical Labs [*NASDAQ symbol*] (SAG) .... CARA
Caraco Pharmaceutical Labs [*Associated Press*] (SAG) .... Caraco
Caraffa Di Catanzaro [*Italy ICAO location identifier*] (ICLI) .... LIBK
Caranavi [*Bolivia*] [*ICAO location identifier*] (ICLI) .... SLVI
Caransebes/Caransebes [*Romania*] [*ICAO location identifier*] (ICLI) .... LRCS
Carapace Length [*Pisciculture*] CL
Carapace Width .... CW
Caraquet, NB [*AM radio station call letters*] .... CJVA
Carat [*Unit of measure for precious stones or gold*] C
Carat [*Unit of measure for precious stones or gold*] .... CAR
Carat [*Unit of measure for precious stones or gold*] .... CT
Carat [*Unit of measure for precious stones or gold*] .... K
Carat Assembled Logical Loader (IAA) .... CALL
Carat, Metric .... CM
Caratage, Color, Clarity, and Shape [*Factors in determining the value of a diamond*] .... CCCS
Carate [*Costa Rica*] [*ICAO location identifier*] (ICLI) .... MRCE
Carauari [*Brazil*] [*Airport symbol*] (AD) .... CAF
Carauari [*Brazil ICAO location identifier*] (ICLI) .... SBUI
Caraustar Industries [*NASDAQ symbol*] (TTSB) .... CSAR
Caraustar Industries, Inc. [*Associated Press*] (SAG) .... Caraustr
Carauster Industries, Inc. [*NASDAQ symbol*] (SAG) .... CSAR
Caravan America-China [*Defunct*] (EA) .... CAC
Caravan and Camping Industry Association of New South Wales [*Australia*] .... CCIANSW
Caravan and Camping Industry Association of South Australia [*Australia*] .... CCIASA
Caravan House [*An association*] (EA) .... CH
Caravan of East and West (EA) .... CEW
Caravan Sites Act [*Town planning*] [*British*] .... CSA
Caravan Trade and Industries Association of Queensland [*Australia*] .... CTIAQ
Caravela [*Guinea-Bissau*] [*ICAO location identifier*] (ICLI) .... GGCV
Caravelas [*Brazil*] [*Airport symbol*] (AD) .... CRV
Caravelas [*Brazil ICAO location identifier*] (ICLI) .... SBCV
Caraveli [*Peru*] [*Seismograph station code, US Geological Survey Closed*] (SEIS) .... CRV
Caraveli [*Peru*] [*ICAO location identifier*] (ICLI) .... SPVL
Caraz [*Peru*] [*ICAO location identifier*] (ICLI) .... SPAA
Carbachol [*Cholinergic*] .... CCh
Carbamazepine [*Also, CBZ*] [*An analgesic*] .... CARB
Carbamazepine [*Pharmacology*] (DAVI) .... CARBAM
Carbamazepine [*Also, CARB*] [*An analgesic*] .... CBZ
Carbamazepine-Epoxide [*An analgesic*] .... CBZ-E
Carbamoylcyclopropene [*Organic chemistry*] .... CCP
Carbamoyldihydropyridine [*Organic chemistry*] .... CDHP
Carbamyl Phosphate [*Also, CP*] [*Organic chemistry*] .... CAP
Carbamyl Phosphate [*Also, CAP*] [*Organic chemistry*] .... CP
Carbamyl Phosphate Synthetase (PDAA) .... CPSase
Carbamylcholine [*Organic chemistry*] CC
Carbamylmethyl [*Biochemistry*] .... Cam
Carbamyl-Phosphate Synthetase [*An enzyme*] .... CPS
Carbazilquinone [*Antineoplastic drug*] .... CQ
Carbazopropionyl - Phosphatidyl Ethanolamine [*Organic chemistry*] .... CPA-PE
Carben Energy, Inc. [*Vancouver Stock Exchange symbol*] .... CBZ
Carbenicillin [*Bactericide*] .... CB
Carbenicillin [*Bactericide*] .... CBC
Carbenicillin [*Medicine*] (DMAA) .... CBCN
Carberry/North Cypress Library, Carberry, Manitoba [*Library symbol National Library of Canada*] (NLC) .... MCNC
Carbide .... CARB
Carbide (MSA) .... CBD
Carbide Diamond Abrasive (IAA) .... CDA
Carbide/Graphite Group [*NASDAQ symbol*] (TTSB) .... CGGI
[*The*] **Carbide/Graphite Group, Inc.** [*Associated Press*] (SAG) .... CarGrpt
[*The*] **Carbide/Graphite Group, Inc.** [*NASDAQ symbol*] (SAG) .... CGGI
Carbide-Forming Element [*Metal treating*] .... CFE
Carbimazole [*Pharmacology*] (DAVI) .... CGI
Carbine (AABC) .... CBN
Carbinol Reduction Potential [*Chemistry*] .... CRP
Carbo Ceramics [*NASDAQ symbol*] (TTSB) .... CRBO
Carbo Ceramics, Inc. [*Associated Press*] (SAG) .... CarboCe
Carbo Ceramics, Inc. [*NASDAQ symbol*] (SAG) .... CRBO
Carbobenzoxy [*Also, CBZ*] [*Organic chemistry*] .... Cb
Carbobenzoxy [*Also, Cb*] [*Organic chemistry*] .... CBZ
Carbobenzoxychloride [*Organic chemistry*] (DAVI) .... CBz
Carbodiimide [*Organic chemistry*] .... CDI
Carbodiimide Residue [*As substituent on nucleoside*] [*Biochemistry*] .... cms
Carbohydrate [*Dietetics*] C
Carbohydrate [*Dietetics*] .... Car
Carbohydrate [*Dietetics*] .... CARB
Carbohydrate [*Dietetics*] .... CARBO
Carbohydrate [*Organic chemistry*] .... CHO
Carbohydrate .... COH
Carbohydrate Antigen [*A tumor marker*] (CDI) .... CA
Carbohydrate Antigen 125 [*Immunology*] (DAVI) .... CA 125
Carbohydrate Craver [*Nutrition*] CC
Carbohydrate Metabolism Index [*Biochemistry*] .... CMI
Carbohydrate Recognition Domain [*Biochemistry*] .... CRD
Carbohydrate Research Institute [*Queen's University at Kingston*] [*Canada Research center*] (RCD) .... CRI
Carbohydrate-Craving Obesity [*Medicine*] .... CCO
Carbohydrate-Induced Hyperglyceridemia [*Medicine*] .... CIH
Carbohydrate-Recognition Domain [*Cytology*] .... CRD
Carbolfuchsin [*A dye*] .... CF
Carbolic Methylene Blue [*Clinical chemistry*] .... CMB
Carboline Carboxylic Acid Ester [*Medicine*] (DMAA) .... CCE
Carbon [*Chemical element*] C
Carbon .... CARB
Carbon 13 Nuclear Magnetic Resonance [*Informations system Karls rube*] (NITA) C13-NMR
Carbon Absorption Bio-oxidation System (PDAA) .... CABOS
Carbon Absorption Unit (GFGA) .... CAU
Carbon Adsorber Tube (PDAA) .... CAT
Carbon Adsorption/Absorption [*for vapor recovery*] .... CAA
Carbon and Quartz/Phenolic .... CQ/P
Carbon Arc Brazing .... CAB
Carbon Arc Cutting [*Welding*] .... CAC
Carbon Arc Welding .... CAW
Carbon Black Export (EA) .... CBE
Carbon Black Feedstock .... CBFS
Carbon Black Producers Traffic Committee .... CBPTC
Carbon Bond [*Chemistry*] .... CB
Carbon Bond Mechanism - Version 4 [*Air pollution*] CB4
Carbon Copy CC
Carbon Copy for Windows [*Symantec Corp.*] (PCM) .... CCW
Carbon County Railway Co. [*AAR code*] .... CBC
Carbon Design Partnership .... CDP
Carbon Dioxide (CDAI) .... CO_2
Carbon Dioxide Concentrating [*or Concentrator*] **Module** .... CDCM
Carbon Dioxide Economizer .... CDE
Carbon Dioxide Equivalent [*Environmental science*] .... CDE
Carbon Dioxide Exchange Rate [*Plant biochemistry*] .... CER

Carbon Dioxide Information and Analysis Center [*Department of Energy Information service or system*] (IID) .... CDIAC
Carbon Dioxide Information Center [*Department of Energy*] [*Oak Ridge, TN Database*] .... CDIC
Carbon Dioxide LASER .... CDL
Carbon Dioxide LASER Beam (MCD) .... CDLB
Carbon Dioxide LASER Rangefinder [*Army*] .... CO2 LRF
Carbon Dioxide Observational Platform System [*NASA*] .... CO-OPS
Carbon Dioxide Production [*Medicine*] (DAVI) .... VCO$_2$
Carbon Dioxide Reduction [*Factor for metabolism*] .... CDR
Carbon Dioxide Reduction Subsystem (NASA) .... CRS
Carbon Dioxide Research Division [*Oak Ridge National Laboratory*] .... CDRD
Carbon Dioxide System [*of a ship*] (DS) .... CAR DI SYS
Carbon Dioxide Tension [*in blood gases*] (DAVI) .... PCO$_2$
Carbon Dioxide Therapy .... CDT
Carbon Electrode Equipment .... CEE
Carbon Equilibrium Loop .... CEL
Carbon Equivalent [*Chemical engineering*] .... CE
Carbon Equivalent Value (PDAA) .... CEV
Carbon Fiber .... CF
Carbon Fiber Reinforced Composite .... CFC
Carbon Fiber Reinforced Plastic .... CFRP
Carbon Fiber Reinforced Thermoplastic [*Plastics technology*] .... CFRTP
Carbon Fiber-Reinforced Glass (PDAA) .... CFRG
Carbon Fiber-Reinforced Glass-Ceramic (PDAA) .... CFRGC
Carbon Fiber-Reinforced Polymer (PDAA) .... CFRP
Carbon Film .... CF
Carbon Filtered .... CF
Carbon from Dissolved Carbonates .... CDC
Carbon Furnace .... CF
Carbon, Hydrogen, Nitrogen .... CHN
Carbon, Hydrogen, Nitrogen, Oxygen, Phosphorus, and Sulfur [*Compounds*] .... CHNOPS
Carbon, Hydrogen, Oxygen, Nitrogen [*Composition of interstellar dust*] .... CHON
Carbon Magnetic Resonance [*Also, CNMR*] .... CMR
Carbon Micro-Fiber [*Materials science*] .... CMF
Carbon Molecular Sieve [*Adsorption technology*] .... CMS
Carbon Molybdenum Steel (MSA) .... CMOS
Carbon Monofluoride [*Inorganic chemistry*] .... CMF
Carbon Monoxide .... CO
Carbon Monoxide [*Endogenous production*] [*Medicine*] (DAVI) .... V$_{co}$
Carbon Monoxide Concentration .... COC
Carbon Monoxide Dehydrogenase [*An enzyme*] .... CODH
Carbon Monoxide Emission Index [*Automotive engineering*] .... COEI
Carbon Monoxide Mass [*Automotive engineering*] .... COM
Carbon Monoxide Measuring System .... CMMS
Carbon Monoxide Pollution Experiment [*NASA/General Electric*] .... COPE
Carbon Monoxide Tension (DAVI) .... P$_{co}$
Carbon Municipal Library, Alberta [*Library symbol National Library of Canada*] (NLC) .... ACARM
Carbon Municipal Library, Carbon, AB, Canada [*Library symbol Library of Congress*] (LCLS) .... CaACarM
Carbon Paper and Inked Ribbon Association [*Defunct*] (EA) .... CPIRA
Carbon Paste .... CP
Carbon Paste Electrode [*Electrochemistry*] .... CPE
Carbon/Phenolic .... C/P
Carbon Preference Index [*Organic geochemistry*] .... CPI
Carbon Rod Atomizer [*Spectroscopy*] .... CRA
Carbon, Rust, and Undesirable Dirt [*Facetious interpretation of what collects on objects left unprotected*] [*Automotive engineering*] .... CRUD
Carbon Shell System .... CSS
Carbon Star [*Astronomy*] (BARN) .... N
Carbon Stars [*Astronomy*] (BARN) .... R
Carbon Steel .... CS
Carbon Tetrachloride (GNE) .... CCL$_4$
Carbon Tetrachloride [*Also, CTC*] [*Organic chemistry*] .... CT
Carbon Tetrachloride [*Also, CT*] [*Organic chemistry*] .... CTC
Carbon to Nitrogen Ratio .... C/N
Carbon to Oxygen [*Ratio*] .... C/O
Carbon Usage Rate [*Environmental Protection Agency*] .... CUR
Carbon Vacuum Deoxidized .... CVD
Carbon Zinc Battery .... CZB
Carbon-13 Nuclear Magnetic Resonance [*Also, CMR*] .... CNMR
Carbon-13 Nuclear Magnetic Resonance Search System [*Netherlands Information Combine*] [*Database*] .... CNMR
Carbonaceous Biochemical Oxygen Demand [*Environmental chemistry*] .... CBOD
Carbonaceous Chondrite CC
Carbonaceous Chondrite Fission [*Geophysics*] .... CCF
Carbonaceous Chondrite Fission Xenon [*Geophysics*] .... CCFXe
Carbonaceous Chondrite Reference Standard [*Geophysics*] .... CCRS
Carbonate .... CARB
Carbonate CO3
Carbonate (GNE) .... CO$_3$
Carbonate (MSA) .... CRBNT
Carbonate Accumulation [*Archeology*] .... ca
Carbonate Compensation Depth [*Oceanography*] .... CCD
Carbonate Compensation Level [*Oceanography*] CCL
Carbonate Crust [*Archeology*] CC
Carbonate Dehydratase [*An enzyme*] (MAE) .... CD
Carbonate Hydroxy Fluorapatite [*Inorganic chemistry*] .... CHFA
Carbonate Nodule [*Archeology*] .... cn
Carbonate of Flake [*Archeology*] .... cf
Carbonate Platform [*Archaeology*] .... CP
Carbonated .... CARB
Carbonated .... CRBNATD

Carbonated Beverage Can Makers Committee [*Division of CBCMA*] (EA) .... CBCMC
Carbonated Beverage Container Manufacturers Association [*Later, CMI*] (EA) .... CBCMA
Carbonated Beverage Institute (EA) .... CBI
Carbon-Bonded Carbon Fiber .... CBCF
Carbon-Carbon (NASA) .... C-C
Carbon-Carbon Data Base [*Battelle Columbus Laboratories*] [*Database*] .... CCDB
Carbon-Chloroform Extract (PDAA) .... CCE
Carbondale [*Illinois*] [*Airport symbol*] (OAG) .... MDH
Carbondale, CO [*Location identifier FAA*] (FAAL) .... CQL
Carbondale, CO [*FM radio station call letters*] .... KDNK
Carbondale, IL [*AM radio station call letters*] .... WCIL
Carbondale, IL [*FM radio station call letters*] .... WCIL-FM
Carbondale, IL [*FM radio station call letters*] (RBYB) .... WDBX-FM
Carbondale, IL [*FM radio station call letters*] .... WSIU
Carbondale, IL [*Television station call letters*] .... WSIU-TV
Carbondale Middle School, Carbondale, CO [*Library symbol*] [*Library of Congress*] (LCLS) .... CoCaCM
Carbondale Mining Technology Center [*Department of Energy*] (GRD) .... CMTC
Carbondale/Murphysboro, IL [*Location identifier FAA*] (FAAL) .... MDH
Carbondale, PA [*AM radio station call letters*] .... WCDL
Carbondale, PA [*FM radio station call letters*] .... WSGD
Carbonear General Hospital, Carbonear, NF, Canada [*Library symbol Library of Congress*] (LCLS) .... CaNfCGH
Carbonear General Hospital, Newfoundland [*Library symbol National Library of Canada*] (NLC) .... NFCGH
Carbonear, NF [*AM radio station call letters*] .... CHVO
Carbonear Public Library, Carbonear, NF, Canada [*Library symbol Library of Congress*] (LCLS) .... CaNfC
Carbonear Public Library, Newfoundland [*Library symbol National Library of Canada*] (NLC) .... NFC
Carbon-Equivalent, Liquidus (OA) .... CEL
Carbon-Equivalent-Difference (PDAA) .... CED
Carbon-Fibre Electrode .... CFE
Carbon-Film Resistor .... CFR
Carbon-Free Medium [*Cytology*] .... CFM
Carbonic Anhydrase [*An enzyme*] .... CA
Carbonic Anhydrase II [*Analytical chemistry*] .... CAII
Carbonic Dichloride [*Phosgene*] [*Poison gas Army symbol*] .... CG
Carbon-in-Column [*Gold ore processing*] CIC
Carbon-in-Leach [*Gold ore processing*] CIL
Carbon-in-Pulp [*Gold ore processing*] .... CIP
Carbonless Copying Paper (IAA) .... CCP
Carbon-Nitrogen-Oxygen [*Galactic molecular formation cycle*] .... CNO
Carbonprint (VRA) .... CBPT
Carbonyl Sulphide (PDAA) .... COS
Carbonyl Value [*Food science*] CV
Carbonylcyanide-meta-chlorophenylhydrazone [*Also, CCP*] [*Organic chemistry*] .... CCCP
Carbonylcyanide-meta-chlorophenylhydrazone [*Also, CCCP*] [*Organic chemistry*] .... CCP
Carbonyldiimidazole [*Organic chemistry*] .... CDI
Carboplatin [*Antineoplastic drug*] (CDI) .... CBDCA
Carboplatin, Doxorubicin, Cytoxan [*Antineoplastic drug*] (CDI) .... CDC
Carborundum (VRA) .... carbor
Carborundum Co., Niagara Falls, NY [*Library symbol Library of Congress*] (LCLS) .... NNiaCa
Carboxamidomethyl [*Organic chemistry*] .... CAM
(Carboxamidophenyl)dimethyltriazene [*Biochemistry*] .... CADT
Carboxy Nitroso Rubber [*Organic chemistry*] .... CNR
Carboxy Terminus of Propressophysin [*Laboratory*] (DAVI) .... CPP
Carboxyamidoimidazole [*Organic chemistry*] .... CAI
Carboxyarabitol Bisphosphate [*Biochemistry*] .... CABP
(Carboxybenzoyl)quinolinecarboxaldehyde [*Organic chemistry*] .... CBQCA
Carboxyfluorescein [*Fluorophore*] .... CF
Carboxyfluorescein Diacetate [*Organic chemistry*] .... CFDA
Carboxyhemoglobin [*Biochemistry*] .... COHB
Carboxyhemoglobin [*Biochemistry*] (AAMN) .... COHgB
Carboxyhemoglobin A [*Biochemistry*] .... COHbA
Carboxyl Terminal (DMAA) .... Ct
Carboxylation Efficiency [*Botany*] .... CE
Carboxyl-Ester Lipase (DMAA) .... CEL
Carboxylesterase [*An enzyme*] .... CE
Carboxylic Acid Reductase [*An enzyme*] .... CAR
Carboxyl-Terminal Domain [*Genetics*] .... CTD
Carboxyl-Terminated Butadiene-Acrylonitrile [*Organic chemistry*] .... CTBN
Carboxyl-Terminated Polybutadiene Binder [*Organic chemistry*] .... CTPB
Carboxyl-Terminated Polyester Propellant (MCD) .... CTPE
Carboxymethyl [*Also, Cm, Cme*] [*Biochemistry*] .... CM
Carboxymethyl [*Also, CM, Cm*] [*Biochemistry*] .... Cme
Carboxymethyl Cyclodextrin [*University of Arizona, Tucson*] .... CMCD
Carboxymethyl Hydroxyethyl Cellulose [*Organic chemistry*] .... CMHEC
Carboxymethyl Starch [*Organic chemistry*] .... CMS
Carboxymethylcellulose [*Organic chemistry*] .... CMC
[*Sodium*] Carboxymethylcellulose (BARN) .... CMC-CT
Carboxymethylcellulose (DMAA) .... COMC
Carboxymethylcysteine [*Biochemistry*] .... CMC
Carboxymethyldextran [*Organic chemistry*] .... CMD
Carboxymuconolactone Decarboxylase [*An enzyme*] .... CMD
Carboxymyoglobin [*Biochemistry*] .... COMb
Carboxypeptidase A [*An enzyme*] .... CPA
Carboxypeptidase B [*An enzyme*] .... CPB
Carboxypeptidase E [*An enzyme*] .... CPE
Carboxypeptidase Inhibitor [*in potatoes*] .... CPI

Carboxypeptidase Y [*An enzyme*] ... CPY
(Carboxyphenyl)benzoyl-Aminopenicillanic Acid [*Biochemistry*] ... CBAP
Carboxypolymethylene [*Organic chemistry*] ... CARBOPOL
Carboxypyridine Disulfide [*Biochemistry*] ... CPDS
Carboxyribitol Bisphosphate [*Biochemistry*] ... CRBP
Carboy (MCD) ... CB
Carboy ... CBY
Carburetor (MSA) ... CARB
Carburetor ... CARBTR
Carburetor Air Temperature [*Aviation*] ... CAT
Carburetor Bowl Vent [*Automotive engineering*] ... CBV
Carburetor Deceleration Combustion Controlled Valve [*Automotive engineering*] ... CDCCV
Carburized, Quenched, and Tempered [*Steel heat treatment*] (IIA) ... CQT
Carcano Rifle ... CARC
Carcass Weight [*Animal husbandry*] ... CW
Carcassonne [*France*] [*Airport symbol*] (OAG) ... CCF
Carcassonne/Salvaza [*France ICAO location identifier*] (ICLI) ... LFMK
Carcinoembryonic Antigen [*Immunochemistry*] ... CEA
Carcinoembryonic Antigen [*Medicine*] (CDI) ... CEA
Carcinoembryonic Antigen-Like [*Protein*] [*Medicine*] (DMAA) ... CEAL
Carcinogen Assessment Group [*Environmental Protection Agency*] ... CAG
Carcinogen Bioassay in Small Rodents ... CBSR
Carcinogen Information Program (EA) ... CIP
Carcinogenesis Bioassay Data System [*National Cancer Institute*] (IID) ... CBDS
Carcinogenic Activity Indicator (FFDE) ... CAI
Carcinogenic Index ... CI
Carcinogenic Potency Database [*Toxicology*] ... CPOB
Carcinogenic Potency Factor (FFDE) ... CPF
Carcinoid Syndrome [*Oncology*] (DAVI) ... CS
Carcinoma ... CA
Carcinoma Cell Line [*Cytology*] ... CCL
Carcinoma In Situ [*Oncology*] ... CIS
Carcinoma of Undetermined Primary [*A cancer condition*] (CDI) ... CUP
Carcinoma-Bearing Animal (AAMN) ... CBA
Carcinomatous Meningitis [*Oncology*] ... CM
Card [*Manuscript descriptions*] ... C
Card (MSA) ... CD
Card (VRA) ... cd
Card Agglutination Trypanosomiasis Test [*Clinical chemistry*] ... CATT
Card Alert [*Database terminology*] (NITA) ... CA
Card and Light Gun Input (SAA) ... CLI
Card and Printer Remote Interface ... CAPRI
Card Assembly Program ... CAP
Card Automated Reproduction and Distribution System (ECII) ... CARD
Card Automatic Code System [*IBM Corp.*] (IEEE) ... CARDCODER
Card Capacitor Read-Only Storage [*Computer science*] (IEEE) ... CCROS
Card Clothing Manufacturers Association [*Defunct*] (EA) ... CCMA
Card Code ... CC
Card Column ... CC
Card Computer Interface [*Computer science*] (IID) ... CCI
Card Count [*Computer science*] ... CC
Card Deck (IAA) ... CD
Card Distribution ... CD
Card Distribution Service [*Library of Congress*] ... CDS
Card Error [*Computer science*] (IAA) ... CE
Card Feed [*Computer science*] (IAA) ... CF
Card Format Identifier (NASA) ... CFI
Card Identification Code [*DoD*] (AFIT) ... CIC
Card Image Correction [*Computer science*] ... CIMCO
Card Image Manipulator for Large Entities [*Computer science*] (PDAA) ... CIMPLE
Card Information Structure [*Computer science*] ... CIS
Card Input [*Computer science*] (BUR) ... CI
Card Input Editor [*Computer science*] (SAA) ... CIED
Card Input-Preliminary Processing (SAA) ... CCP
Card Inventory Control ... CIC
Card Module Tester ... CMT
Card Operating System (IAA) ... COS
Card Packet System (AABC) ... CARDPAC
Card Pick Up (DCTA) ... CPU
Card Print Processor [*Computer science*] (IAA) ... CPP
Card Programmable Hand-Held Calculator/Computer (MCD) ... CPHHC
Card Programmed Calculator [*IBM Corp. - late 1940's*] [*Computer science*] ... CPC
Card Programmed Computer (IAA) ... CPC
Card Programming System [*Computer science*] (CMD) ... CPS
Card Punch [*Computer science*] (BUR) ... CP
Card Punch and Reader [*Computer science*] ... CP/R
Card Punching Printer [*Computer output device*] [*Computer science*] (BUR) ... CPP
Card Random-Access Memory [*NCR Corp.*] [*Computer science*] ... CRAM
Card Reader [*Computer science*] ... CDR
Card Reader [*Computer science*] (NVT) ... CR
Card Reader [*Computer science*] ... CRD
Card Reader/Punch [*Computer science*] ... CRP
Card Reader Unit [*Computer science*] ... CRU
Card Reader-Punch Interpreter [*Computer science*] (DNAB) ... CRPI
Card Ready [*Computer science*] (SAA) ... CR
Card Reproducer [*Computer science*] (IAA) ... CR
Card Security Number [*Banking*] ... CSN
Card Service [*Computer science*] (PCM) ... CS
Card Service/Socket Service [*Computer science*] (PCM) ... CS/SS
Card Setting Machine Tenters' Society [*A union*] [*British*] (DCTA) ... CSMTS
Card Socket [*Electronics*] (IAA) ... CS
Card Station [*Computer science*] (BUR) ... CS
Card Stock (VRA) ... cdst
Card Store Control [*Computer science*] (IAA) ... CSC
Card to Printer (IAA) ... CP
Card Type (DNAB) ... CT
Card-Automated Reproduction and Distribution System [*Library of Congress*] ... CARDS
Cardboard (MAE) ... cb
Cardboard (ADA) ... CDBD
Cardboard (VRA) ... cdbd
Cardboard Film Holder Without Intensifying Screens [*Radiology*] (DAVI) ... cb
Cardboard Illustrative Aid to Computation [*Bell Telephone Co.*] [*Computer science*] ... CARDIAC
Cardboard Illustrative Aid to Computation [*Computer science*] (PDAA) ... CARIAC
Carded for Record Only ... CRO
Carded Packaging Institute (EA) ... CPI
Carded Yarn Association [*Later, AYSA*] (EA) ... CYA
Cardiac ... CRDC
Cardiac Accelerator Center [*Physiology*] ... CAC
Cardiac Adjustment Scale [*Psychology*] ... CAS
Cardiac Ambulatory Monitoring Unit [*Cardiology*] (DAVI) ... CAMU
Cardiac Arrest [*Medicine*] ... CA
Cardiac Arrest Code [*Medicine*] ... CAC
Cardiac Arrhythmia Suppression Trial [*National Heart, Lung, and Blood Institute*] ... CAST
Cardiac Care Registered Nurse (WGA) ... CCRN
Cardiac Care Unit [*Medicine*] ... CCU
Cardiac Catheterization [*Cardiology*] (DAVI) ... CC
Cardiac Cycle [*Medicine*] ... CC
Cardiac Defects, Abnormal Facies, Thymic Hypoplasia, Cleft Palate, and Hypocalcemia from Deletions in Chromosome 22 [*Medical syndrome*] ... CATCH-22
Cardiac Disease [*Medicine*] ... CD
Cardiac Dullness [*Physiology*] ... CD
Cardiac Emergency [*Medicine*] (MAE) ... CE
Cardiac Enlargement [*Medicine*] ... CE
Cardiac Failure [*Medicine*] ... CF
Cardiac Filling Pressure [*Cardiology*] ... CFP
Cardiac Index [*Physiology*] ... CI
Cardiac Inhibition Center [*Physiology*] ... CIC
Cardiac Insufficiency [*Medicine*] (MAE) ... CI
Cardiac Intensive Care Unit [*of a hospital*] (AAMN) ... CICU
Cardiac Inward Rectifier [*Biochemistry*] ... CIR
Cardiac Magnetic Resonance Imaging [*Cardiology*] ... CMRI
Cardiac Minute Output [*Physiology*] ... CMO
Cardiac Monitor [*Medicine*] (MAE) ... CM
Cardiac Observation Unit [*Cardiology*] (DAVI) ... COU
Cardiac Output [*Cardiology*] ... CO
Cardiac Output (DAVI) ... Q
Cardiac Output [*Cardiology*] (DAVI) ... QT
Cardiac Output by Thermodilution [*Cardiology*] (DMAA) ... COTD
Cardiac Output Recorder [*Physiology*] ... COR
Cardiac Pathways Corp. [*Associated Press*] (SAG) ... CardPth
Cardiac Pathways Corp. [*NASDAQ symbol*] (SAG) ... CPWY
Cardiac Pulmonary Reserve [*Physiology*] ... CPR
Cardiac Reconditioning Center [*Rehabilitation*] (DAVI) ... CRC
Cardiac Rehabilitation (DAVI) ... CR
Cardiac Rehabilitation Unit [*Cardiology*] (DMAA) ... CRU
Cardiac Resuscitation Team [*Medicine*] ... CRT
Cardiac Society of Great Britain and Ireland (DAVI) ... CSGBI
Cardiac Stress Test [*Medicine*] (MAE) ... CST
Cardiac Surgery [*Medicine*] (MAE) ... CAS
Cardiac Surgical Intensive Care Unit [*Medicine*] ... CSICU
Cardiac Surveillance Unit (DAVI) ... CSU
Cardiac/Thoracic Intensive Care Unit [*Medicine*] (DAVI) ... CTIU
Cardiac/Thoracic Unit [*Medicine*] ... CTU
Cardiac Troponin C [*Biochemistry*] ... CTnC
Cardiac Type ... CT
Cardiac Work [*Physiology*] ... CW
Cardiac Work Index [*Physiology*] ... CWI
Cardiac-Recurrent Nerve [*Medicine*] (PDAA) ... CRN
Cardiff [*Welsh depot code*] ... CDF
Cardiff [*Wales*] [*Airport symbol*] (OAG) ... CWL
Cardiff [*British ICAO location identifier*] (ICLI) ... EGFF
Cardiff City [*British ICAO location identifier*] (ICLI) ... EGRG
Cardiff East Docks [*Welsh depot code*] ... CED
Cardiff Railway [*Wales*] ... CAR R
Cardiff/Tremorfa [*British ICAO location identifier*] (ICLI) ... EGFC
Cardiff University Industry Centre [*British*] (IRUK) ... CUIC
Cardiff Valleys [*Welsh depot code*] ... CV
Cardigan (DSUE) ... CARDI
Cardigan [*City and county in Wales*] (ROG) ... CDG
Cardigan Welsh Corgi Club of America (EA) ... CWCCA
Cardiganshire [*County in Wales*] (ROG) ... CARD
Cardiganshire [*County in Wales*] (ROG) ... CARDIGS
Cardiganshire [*County in Wales*] ... CARDS
Cardinal ... CA
Cardinal ... CARD
Cardinal ... CARD
Cardinal ... CDL
Cardinal Airlines (MHDB) ... CD
Cardinal Bancshares [*NASDAQ symbol*] (TTSB) ... CARD
Cardinal Bancshares, Inc. [*NASDAQ symbol*] (SAG) ... CARD
Cardinal Bancshares, Inc. [*Associated Press*] (SAG) ... CardBnc
Cardinal Club (EA) ... CC
Cardinal Health [*NYSE symbol*] (TTSB) ... CAH
Cardinal Health, Inc. [*NYSE symbol*] (SAG) ... CAH
Cardinal Health, Inc. [*Associated Press*] (SAG) ... CardinlH

Cardinal Health, Inc. [*Associated Press*] (SAG) .... CardnHlt
Cardinal Leger & His Endeavours (AC) .... CLE
[*Le*] **Cardinal Leger et Ses Oeuvres** (AC) .... CLO
Cardinal Mindszenty Foundation (EA) .... CMF
Cardinal Mineral Corp. Ltd. [*Vancouver Stock Exchange symbol*] .... CDB
Cardinal Mooney High School Library, Rochester, NY [*OCLC symbol*] (OCLC) .... RVV
Cardinal Point (ROG) .... CP
Cardinal Public Library, Cardinal, ON, Canada [*Library symbol*] [*Library of Congress*] (LCLS) .... CaOCARD
Cardinal Public Library, Ontario [*Library symbol National Library of Canada*] (BIB) .... OCARD
Cardinal Realty Services, Inc. [*Associated Press*] (SAG) .... CardRit
Cardinal Realty Services, Inc. [*Associated Press*] (SAG) .... CardRlty
Cardinal Realty Services, Inc. [*NASDAQ symbol*] (SAG) .... CRSI
Cardinal Realty Svcs [*NASDAQ symbol*] (TTSB) .... CRSI
Cardinal Stritch College (GAGS) .... Card Stritch C
Cardinal Stritch College [*Wisconsin*] .... CSC
Cardinal Stritch College, Milwaukee, WI [*Library symbol Library of Congress*] (LCLS) .... WMCSC
Cardinal Virtues [*Freemasonry*] (ROG) CV
Cardinalis [*Authority cited in pre-1607 legal work*] (DSA) .... Car
Cardinalis [*Authority cited in pre-1607 legal work*] (DSA) .... Card
Cardinalis [*Authority cited in pre-1607 legal work*] (DSA) .... Cardi
Cardinalis Florentinus [*Franciscus Zabarella*] [*Deceased, 1417*] [*Authority cited in pre-1607 legal work*] (DSA) .... Card Flor
Cardinalis Florentinus (Franciscus Zabarella) [*Deceased, 1417*] [*Authority cited in pre-1607 legal work*] (DSA) .... Card Zabarel
Cardington Atmospheric Boundary Layer Experiment (PDAA) .... CABLE
Cardioacceleratory Peptide [*Biochemistry*] .... CAP
Cardiodilatin [*Biochemistry*] .... CDD
Cardioesophageal [*Junction*] [*Gastroenterology*] (DAVI) .... CE
Cardioesophageal Junction [*Gastroenterology*] (DAVI) .... CEJ
CardioGenesis Corp. [*Associated Press*] (SAG) .... CardGen
CardioGenesis Corp. [*NASDAQ symbol*] (SAG) .... CGCP
CardioGenesis Corp. [*NASDAQ symbol*] (TTSB) .... CGCP
Cardiogenic Pulmonary Edema [*Cardiology*] (DAVI) .... CPE
Cardiogenic Shock [*Cardiology*] (DMAA) .... CGS
Cardiogenic Shock .... CS
Cardiographic .... CRDGRPHC
Cardio-Green (Dye) [*Trademark*] .... CG
Cardiokymograph (BARN) .... CKG
Cardiolipin [*Immunochemistry*] CL
Cardiolipin Complement Fixation [*Immunochemistry*] (DAVI) .... CCF
Cardiolipin Microflocculation Test [*Medicine*] (DMAA) .... CMFT
Cardiolipin Natural Lecithin [*Immunochemistry*] (MAE) .... CNL
Cardiolipin Synthetic Lecithin [*Biochemistry*] (MAE) .... CSL
Cardiology (MAE) .... card
Cardiology .... CARDIO
Cardiology .... cardiol
Cardiology .... CRDLGY
Cardiology (DAVI) .... Ventricular Rhythm
Cardiology Research Center [*Russian*] .... CRC
Cardiology Technologists' Association of British Columbia (AC) .... CTABC
Cardiology Transcription Unit [*Medicine*] .... CTU
Cardiometrics, Inc. [*Associated Press*] (SAG) .... Cardiom
Cardiometrics, Inc. [*NASDAQ symbol*] (SAG) .... CFLO
Cardiomyography [*Cardiology*] .... CM
Cardiomyopathy [*Medicine*] .... CM
Cardiomyopathy [*Medicine*] (MAE) .... CMP
Cardion Electronics, Woodbury, NY [*Library symbol Library of Congress*] (LCLS) .... NWbC
Cardiopulmonary .... CARDPLMNRY
Cardiopulmonary [*Medicine*] .... CP
Cardiopulmonary Arrest [*Medicine*] (CPH) .... CPA
Cardiopulmonary Bypass [*Medicine*] .... CPB
Cardiopulmonary Cerebral Resuscitation [*Medicine*] (DMAA) .... CPCR
Cardiopulmonary Corp. [*Associated Press*] (SAG) .... Cardpul
Cardiopulmonary Corp. [*NASDAQ symbol*] (SAG) .... CPCP
Cardiopulmonary Exercise Testing [*Medicine*] .... CPX
Cardiopulmonary Research Institute (DAVI) .... CAPRI
Cardiopulmonary Resuscitation [*Medicine*] .... CPR
Cardiopulmonary-Cerebral Resuscitation (DAVI) .... CPCR
Cardiorespiratory [*Medicine*] .... CR
Cardiorespirogram [*Medicine*] (DAVI) .... CRG
Cardiotachometer [*Medicine*] .... CTM
Cardiotech International, Inc. [*Associated Press*] (SAG) .... Cardtch
Cardiotech International, Inc. [*AMEX symbol*] (SAG) .... CTE
Cardiothoracic Intensive Care Unit .... CTICU
Cardiothoracic Ratio [*Medicine*] .... CT
Cardiothoracic Ratio [*Medicine*] .... CTR
Cardiothoracic Research and Education Foundation (EA) .... CREF
Cardiothoracic Systems [*NASDAQ symbol*] (TTSB) .... CTSI
CardioThoracic Systems, Inc. [*Associated Press*] (SAG) .... CardioTh
CardioThoracic Systems, Inc. [*NASDAQ symbol*] (SAG) .... CTSI
Cardiotocography [*Gynecology*] .... CTG
Cardiotronics Inc. [*NASDAQ symbol*] (TTSB) .... CDIO
Cardiovascular .... CRDVSCLR
Cardiovascular [*Medicine*] CV
Cardiovascular Accident [*Medicine*] (DMAA) .... CVA
Cardiovascular and Interventional Radiology Society of Europe (EA) .... CIRSE
Cardiovascular Computerized Tomography [*Scanner*] [*Cardiology*] (DAVI) .... CVCT
Cardiovascular Conditioning Suit [*Medicine*] .... CVCS
Cardiovascular Credentialing International (EA) CCI
Cardiovascular Data Analysis by Machine Processing (AEBS) .... CARDAMAP
Cardiovascular Deconditioning [*Medicine*] (MEDA) .... CD
Cardiovascular Diagnostics [*NASDAQ symbol*] (TTSB) .... CVDI
Cardiovascular Diagnostics, Inc. [*Associated Press*] (SAG) .... CardiDiag
Cardiovascular Diagnostics, Inc. [*NASDAQ symbol*] (SAG) .... CVDI
Cardiovascular Disease [*Medicine*] .... CD
Cardiovascular Disease [*Medicine*] .... CVD
Cardiovascular Disease Study [*British*] .... CVDS
Cardiovascular Dynamics, Inc. [*Associated Press*] (SAG) .... CardiDy
Cardiovascular Dynamics, Inc. [*NASDAQ symbol*] (SAG) .... CCVD
Cardiovascular In-Patient Care Unit .... CICU
Cardiovascular Institute [*Boston University*] [*Research center*] (RCD) CVI
Cardiovascular Monitor [*Medicine*] .... CVM
Cardiovascular Pulmonary Laboratory [*Medicine*] (MAE) .... CVPlab
Cardiovascular Reflex Conditioning [*Medicine*] .... CRC
Cardiovascular Reflex Conditioning System [*Medicine*] .... CRCS
Cardiovascular Renal Disease [*Medicine*] .... CVRD
Cardiovascular Research and Training Center [*University of Alabama in Birmingham*] [*Research center*] (RCD) .... CVRTC
Cardiovascular Research Institute [*University of California, San Francisco*] [*Research center*] (RCD) .... CVRI
Cardiovascular Respiratory Disease [*Medicine*] .... CVRD
Cardiovascular Respiratory System [*Medicine*] .... CVR
Cardiovascular Studies Unit [*University of Pennsylvania*] [*Research center*] (RCD) .... CVSU
Cardiovascular Surgery [*Medicine*] .... CVS
Cardiovascular Surgery Unit (DAVI) .... CSU
Cardiovascular System [*Medicine*] .... CVS
Cardiovascular Technologist (DAVI) .... CT
Cardiovascular Technologist (HCT) .... CVT
Cardiovascular Thoracic Intensive Care Unit (DAVI) .... CVT-ICU
Cardiovascular Thoracic Post-Intensive Care Unit (DAVI) .... CVTP-ICU
Cardiovascular-Renal [*Medicine*] .... CVR
Cardiovascular-Thoracic Surgery (DAVI) .... CVT S
Cards per Day [*Computer science*] (BUR) .... CPD
Cards per Hour [*Computer science*] .... C/H
Cards per Hour [*Computer science*] .... CPH
Cards per Minute [*Computer science*] .... CM
Cards per Minute [*Computer science*] (IAA) .... CMIN
Cards per Minute [*Computer science*] .... CPM
Cards per Second [*Computer science*] .... CPS
Card-Select Number [*Computer science*] (PCM) .... CSN
Cardston Public Library, Alberta [*Library symbol National Library of Canada*] (NLC) .... ACAR
Card-to-Magnetic Tape Conversion System [*Computer science*] (DIT) .... CTS
Card-to-Tape Converter [*Computer science*] (IAA) .... CTC
Card-to-Tape Tape [*Computer science*] .... CTT
Care .... K
Care about the Strays (EA) .... CATS
Care Aggregated Module .... CAM
Care and Maintenance [*British military*] (DMA) .... C & M
Care and Maintenance [*British military*] (IAA) .... CAM
Care and Maintenance Instruction [*Nuclear energy*] (NRCH) .... CMI
Care and Preservation [*Army*] (AABC) .... C & P
Care Canada, Ottawa, Ontario [*Library symbol National Library of Canada*] (BIB) .... OOCARE
Care Custody and Control CCC
Care for Life [*An association*] (EA) .... CFL
Care for the Wild [*An association British*] (EAIO) .... CW
Care Group [*NASDAQ symbol*] (TTSB) .... CARE
[*The*] **Care Group, Inc.** [*NASDAQ symbol*] (NQ) .... CARE
Care Group, Inc. [*Associated Press*] (SAG) .... CareGp
Care How Others Keep the Environment [*An association*] .... CHOKE
Care Logic Module (NASA) .... CLM
Care Of [*Correspondence*] .... C/O
Care Of (WDMC) .... co
Care of County (WDMC) .... C/O
Care of Ship Checkoff List (DNAB) .... CSCL
Care of Supplies in Storage [*Military*] (AABC) .... COSIS
Care Point Medical Centres Ltd. [*Vancouver Stock Exchange symbol*] .... CPJ
Care Unit Program [*Chemical dependency*] (DAVI) .... CUP
Care Vet Pharmacy [*Vancouver Stock Exchange symbol*] .... VET
Care-Cure Coordination [*Medicine*] (DMAA) CCC
Career .... CAR
Career Ability Placement Survey [*Vocational guidance test*] .... CAPS
Career Adaptive Behavior Inventory [*Vocational guidance test*] .... CAB
Career Advancement Network (EA) .... CAN
Career Airmen Reenlistment Reservation System [*Air Force*] .... CAREERS
Career Analysis Procedure [*LIMRA*] .... CAP
Career Apparel Institute (EA) .... CAI
Career Area Rotation Model [*Air Force*] .... CAROM
Career Assessment Inventory [*Vocational guidance test*] .... CAI
Career Assistance Counseling [*Air Force*] (AFM) .... CAC
Career Assistance Program [*Department of Labor*] .... CAP
Career Awareness Inventory [*Vocational guidance test*] .... CAI
Career Control (AFM) CC
Career Counselor [*Military*] (AABC) .... CARCSLR
Career Criminal Apprehension Unit (LAIN) .... CCAU
Career Decision Scale (EDAC) .... CDS
Career Development (WYGK) .... CD
Career Development Center (EA) .... CDC
Career Development Center, Shaker Heights, OH [*OCLC symbol*] (OCLC) .... SKS
Career Development Course (AFM) .... CDC
Career Development Program (OICC) .... CDP
Career Development Review [*Australia*] .... CDR

Career Development Scheme	CDS
Career Education Association of Victoria [Australia]	CEAV
Career Employment Experience [Office of Youth Programs] [Department of Labor]	CEE
Career Employment Group [British military] (DMA)	CEG
Career Executive Force [Air Force]	CEF
Career Exploration Profile [Vocational guidance test]	CEP
Career Exploration Series [Vocational guidance test]	CES
Career Factor Checklist (EDAC)	CFC
Career Horizons [NYSE symbol] (TTSB)	CHZ
Career Horizons, Inc. [Associated Press] (SAG)	CareerHz
Career Horizons, Inc. [NASDAQ symbol] (SAG)	CARH
Career Information and Counseling [Air Force]	CIAC
Career Information Center (DNAB)	CARINFOCEN
Career Information Center (OICC)	CIC
Career Information Delivery System (OICC)	CIDS
Career Information Resource Advisory Group [Canada]	CIRAG
Career Information System [National Career Information System] [Eugene, OR] [Information service or system] (IID)	CIS
Career Information Unit (OICC)	CIU
Career Interest Test [Vocational guidance test]	CIT
Career Intern Program (MCD)	CIP
Career is Over [Business term] (MHDB)	CIO
Career Laboratories Utilizing Experience (OICC)	CLUE
Career Limiting Move (MCD)	CLM
Career Management and Assignment [Department of State]	CMA
Career Management Field [Military] (AABC)	CMF
Career Management Individual Files [Military] (INF)	CMIF
Career Management Information File [Military] (AABC)	CMIF
Career Maturity Inventory [Vocational guidance test]	CMI
Career Minister [Department of State]	CM
Career Motivation (AFM)	CM
Career Motivation and Achievement Planning Inventory (EDAC)	C-MAP
Career Officer Candidate Development Course [Air Force]	COCDC
Career Opportunities and Planning for Employment Center [Public library service]	COPE
Career Opportunities for Youth (SAA)	COY
Career Opportunities Program [Office of Education] (EA)	COP
Career Orientation Placement and Evaluation Survey [Vocational guidance test]	COPES
Career Orientation Program [LIMRA]	COP
Career Oriented Modules to Explore Topics in Science (EDAC)	COMETS
Career Placement Registry, Inc. [Database producer] [Information service or system] (IID)	CPR
Career Planning and Adult Development Network (EA)	CPADN
Career Planning Board [Navy] (NVT)	CPB
Career Planning Program [Vocational guidance test]	CPP
Career Program [Army] (RDA)	CP
Career Program Manager (MCD)	CPM
Career Progression Military Occupational Specialty (MCD)	CPMOS
Career Recruiter Force (DNAB)	CRF
Career Reenlistment Objectives [Navy]	CREO
Career Reserve Status [Air Force]	CRS
Career Resources Information [JA Micropublishing, Inc.] [Information service or system] (IID)	CRI
Career Retrieval Search System [Pittsburgh University] (NITA)	CARESS
Career Structure Review [Australia]	CSR
Career Technologies Corp. [Database producer] (IID)	CTC
Career Trainee (BARN)	ct
Career Training Foundation (EA)	CTF
Career Vitae [Job applications] (DCTA)	CV
Career Woman [A publication]	Car Wom
Career Women's Forum (EAIO)	CWF
Career-Oriented Preparation for Employment [Federal antipoverty program]	COPE
Careers	CARS
Careers and Occupational Information Centre (IID)	COIC
Careers and Occupational Information Unit (AIE)	COIU
Careers and the Disabled [A publication]	Car Dis Ab
Careers' Association of New South Wales [Australia]	CANSW
Careers Education and Guidance (AIE)	CEG
Careers, Education, and Training Advice Centre [British] (CB)	CETAC
Careers Guidance Observed (AIE)	CARGO
Careers Literature and Information Prescription Service (AIE)	CLIPS
Careers Office Management and Public Appraisal System (AIE)	COMPAS
Careers on the Move for Engineers of Tomorrow [An association]	COMET
Careers Research and Advisory Centre [British]	CRAC
Careers Service Branch [Department of Employment] [British] (AIE)	CSB
Careers Services [Navy British]	CS
Career-Shortening Gesture	CSG
Careerware Reference Centre, STM Systems Corp., Ottawa, Ontario [Library symbol National Library of Canada] (BIB)	OOSTM
Careless and Negligent Driving [Traffic offense charge]	CN
Caremark International [NYSE symbol] (SPSG)	CK
Caremark International, Inc. [Associated Press] (SAG)	Caremk
Carematrix Corp. [Associated Press] (SAG)	Caremtx
Carematrix Corp. [AMEX symbol] (SAG)	CMD
Carena-Bancorp, Inc. [Toronto Stock Exchange symbol]	CAR
Care-Oriented Medical Record [University of Alabama]	COMREC
Caretenders Healthcorp. [Associated Press] (SAG)	Caretnd
Caretenders Healthcorp. [NASDAQ symbol] (SPSG)	CTND
Carey Foster Bridge [Electronics]	CFB
Carga Aerea Dominicana [Dominican Republic] [ICAO designator] (FAAC)	CDM
Carga Aerea Venezolana Caraven SA [Venezuela] [ICAO designator] (FAAC)	CCR

Carga del Caribe SA de CV [Mexico] [FAA designator] (FAAC)	CDC
Cargill Branch, Bruce County Public Library, Ontario [Library symbol National Library of Canada] (NLC)	OCAR
Cargill Information Center, Wayzata, MN [OCLC symbol] (OCLC)	CAR
Cargill Instructional Center, Wayzata, MN [Library symbol Library of Congress] (LCLS)	MnWayC
Cargill Technical Services, Ltd. [British] [Commercial firm]	CTS
Cargo (WGA)	C
Cargo (MSA)	CAR
Cargo (AABC)	CGO
Cargo	CRG
Cargo Accounts Settlement System [IATA] (DS)	CASS
Cargo Agents Reservation Airwaybill Insurance and Tracking System (DA)	CARAT
Cargo Air Lines [Israel] (BJA)	CAL
Cargo Aircraft Mine Laying (MCD)	CAML
Cargo Airline Evaluation Model (PDAA)	CAEM
Cargo Allocation and Load Control [Aviation]	CALC
Cargo and Loading Analysis [Shipping]	C & LA
Cargo & Passenger Air Services Ltd. [Switzerland ICAO designator] (FAAC)	CPS
Cargo & Passenger Air Services Ltd. [Switzerland ICAO designator] (FAAC)	CPZ
Cargo and Rescue Aircraft	CARA
Cargo Apparent Good Order [Shipping]	CAGO
Cargo Bay Module Personnel Provisions [NASA] (KSC)	CBMPP
Cargo Bay Stowage Assembly (NASA)	CBSA
Cargo Capacity [Shipping] (DCTA)	CC
Cargo Center of Gravity (MSA)	CCG
Cargo Container (KSC)	CACON
Cargo Control	CC
Cargo Data Interchange System (MCD)	CARDIS
Cargo Data Standards Board [IATA] (DS)	CDSB
Cargo Delivery Receipt [Shipping]	CDR
Cargo Delivery System [Shipping]	CDS
Cargo Disposition Instructions [Shipping]	CDI
Cargo Dor Ltd. [Ghana] [ICAO designator] (FAAC)	CDO
Cargo Drop Reel (NVT)	CDR
Cargo Glider [Military]	CG
Cargo Handling and Port Group [Navy] (NVT)	CHAPGRU
Cargo Handling and Storage Facility	CHSF
Cargo Handling Battalion [Obsolete Army]	CHB
Cargo Handling Charge [Shipping] (DS)	CHC
Cargo Handling Cooperative Program [MARAD] (TAG)	CHCP
Cargo Handling Equipment [Army]	CHE
Cargo Handling Rig (RDA)	CHR
Cargo Hazardous Servicing Facility (MCD)	CHSF
Cargo Helicopter (AABC)	CH
Cargo Increment Number (DOMA)	CIN
Cargo Information Message Procedures [IATA] (DS)	IMP
Cargo Information System [Aviation] (DA)	CIS
Cargo Integration Control Center (MCD)	CICC
Cargo Integration Review (MCD)	CIR
Cargo Integration Test Equipment (NASA)	CITE
Cargo Interface Verification Test (MCD)	CIVT
Cargo Investigation Panel [IATA] (DS)	CIP
Cargo Left Trailer (KSC)	CLT
Cargo Loaded on Vehicles [MTMC] (TAG)	VEHCAR
Cargo Lunar Excursion Module	CLEM
Cargo Management (MCD)	CM
Cargo Module (MCD)	CAM
Cargo Oil (DS)	co
Cargo Operations [NASA] (MCD)	co
Cargo Orbit Transfer Vehicle (MCD)	COTV
Cargo Outturn Report (AABC)	COR
Cargo Outturn Reporting System	CORS
Cargo Performance Overview System [BTS] (TAG)	CAPOS
Cargo Preference Year [MARAD] (TAG)	CPY
Cargo Processing Contract (MCD)	CPC
Cargo Processing Facility [Shipping] (NASA)	CPF
Cargo Processing Technician (NASA)	CPT
Cargo Program [or Projects] Office [NASA] (MCD)	CP
Cargo Projects - Program Control Office [NASA] (NASA)	CP-PCO
Cargo Propulsion Module [NASA] (KSC)	CPM
Cargo Reinsurance Association [New York, NY] (EA)	CRA
Cargo Security Advisory Standards [Department of Transportation]	CSAS
Cargo Services Conference [IATA] (DS)	CSC
Cargo Ship [of any type] [Navy symbol]	AK
Cargo Ship	CA
Cargo Ship [Military Sea Transportation Service] (CINC)	TAK
Cargo Ship and Aircraft Ferry [Navy symbol]	AKV
Cargo Ship and Aircraft Ferry [Military Sea Transportation Service] (CINC)	TAKV
Cargo Ship, Dock [Navy symbol]	AKD
Cargo Ship, Merchant Marine Manned	XAK
Cargo Submarine [Navy symbol Obsolete]	AK(SS)
Cargo Submarine [Navy symbol Obsolete]	ASSA
Cargo Submarine [Navy symbol Obsolete]	SSA
Cargo Systems and Procedures Committee [IATA] (DS)	CSPC
Cargo Tank [Shipping] (DS)	CT
Cargo Tank Center (DS)	CTC
Cargo Tank Common [of a ship] (DS)	CTX
Cargo Tank Wing [of a ship] (DS)	CTW
Cargo/Tanker Branch (DNAB)	C/TB
Cargo Technical Evaluation Task Force [IATA] (DS)	CTETF

Cargo Three, Inc. [*Panama*] [*FAA designator*] (FAAC) .... CTW
Cargo Traffic Analysis (MCD) .... CTA
Cargo Traffic Procedures Committee [*IATA*] (DS) .... CTPC
Cargo/Transport [*Designation for all US military aircraft*] C
Cargo/Transport Aircraft - Experimental CX
Cargo/Transport Aircraft Experimental - Heavy Logistics System
   (KSC) .... CX-HLS
Cargo Variant [*LSD 41 variant*] (DOMA) CV
Cargojet [*Formerly, Yugoslav Republic*] [*FAA designator*] (FAAC) .... CRJ
Cargolux Airline International [*Luxembourg*] [*ICAO designator*] (FAAC) CLX
Cargoman [*Oman*] [*ICAO designator*] (FAAC) .... CGM
Cargo's Proportion of (General) Average [*Shipping*] .... CGA
Cargosur [*Spain ICAO designator*] (FAAC) .... OWS
Cariana International Industries, Inc. [*Vancouver Stock Exchange symbol*] ..... CIA
Carib [*MARC language code Library of Congress*] (LCCP) .... car
Carib Aviation Ltd. [*Antigua and Barbuda*] [*FAA designator*] (FAAC) .... DEL
Carib Express [*Barbados*] [*FAA designator*] (FAAC) .... BCB
Caribair [*Airlines*] (OAG) .... CB
Caribbean .... CAR
Caribbean (AFM) .... CARIB
Caribbean .... CRBBN
Caribbean Action Lobby (EA) .... CAL
Caribbean Air Cargo [*Barbados*] [*ICAO designator*] (FAAC) .... DCC
Caribbean Air Cargo Ltd. [*Barbados*] (EY) .... CARICARGO
Caribbean Air Command [*Air Force*] .... CAC
Caribbean Air Command [*Air Force*] .... CAIRC
Caribbean Air Transport [*ICAO designator*] (AD) XC
Caribbean Air Transport Co., Inc. [*Netherlands ICAO designator*] (FAAC) .... CLT
Caribbean Airways [*ICAO designator*] (AD) .... IQ
Caribbean Airways [*Barbados*] [*ICAO designator*] (FAAC) .... IQQ
Caribbean American Intercultural Organization (EA) .... CAIO
Caribbean Amphibious Ready Group [*Navy*] (NVT) .... CARG
Caribbean Area [*Services to the Armed Forces*] [*Red Cross*] .... CA
Caribbean Area [*MARC geographic area code Library of Congress*]
   (LCCP) .... cc----
Caribbean Area Small Craft Project .... CASCP
Caribbean Association for the Rehabilitation of the Disabled [*Defunct*]
   (EAIO) .... CARD
Caribbean Association of Rehabilitation Therapists [*Guyana*] (EAIO) .... CART
Caribbean Atlantic Airlines [*Puerto Rico*] .... CARIBAIR
Caribbean Atlantic Airlines [*Puerto Rico*] [*ICAO designator*] .... CBA
Caribbean Australian Association .... CAA
Caribbean Basin Business Information Center (IMH) .... CBIC
Caribbean Basin Corrections Association [*Cayman Islands*] (EAIO) .... CBCA
Caribbean Basin Economic Recovery Act .... CBERA
Caribbean Basin Information Network [*Caribbean/Central American Action*]
   [*Information service or system*] (IID) .... CBIN
Caribbean Basin Initiative [*Financial aid package proposed by President
   Reagan for Central American and Caribbean countries*] .... CBI
Caribbean Broadcasting Corp. .... CaBC
Caribbean Broadcasting Union .... CBU
Caribbean Cane Farmers' Association [*Kingston, Jamaica*] [*Inactive*]
   (EAIO) .... CCFA
Caribbean/Central American Action (EA) .... C/CAA
Caribbean Cigar Co. [*Associated Press*] (SAG) .... CaribCig
Caribbean Cigar Co. [*NASDAQ symbol*] (SAG) .... CIGR
Caribbean Cigar Co. [*Associated Press*] (SAG) .... CribCig
Caribbean Coastal Marine Productivity [*Marine science*] (OSRA) .... CARICOMP
Caribbean Command [*Military*] .... CARIBCOM
Caribbean Commission [*Later, Caribbean Organization*] CC
Caribbean Common Market Standards Council [*Georgetown, Guyana*]
   (EAIO) .... CCMSC
Caribbean Community [*or Common Market*] [*Barbados, Jamaica, Trinidad-
   Tobago, Guyana, Belize, Dominica, Grenada, St. Kitts-Nevis-Anguilla, St.
   Lucia, St. Vincent Guyana*] .... CARICOM
Caribbean Conference of Churches (EAIO) CCC
Caribbean Congress of Labor CCL
Caribbean Conservation Association [*St. Michael, Barbados*] .... CCA
Caribbean Conservation Corp. (EA) CCC
Caribbean Consumers Union [*Antigua-Barbuda*] (EAIO) .... CCU
Caribbean Defense Command [*or Commander*] .... CDC
Caribbean Development and Cooperation Committee [*Economic
   Commission for Latin America*] .... CDCC
Caribbean Development Bank .... CARIBANK
Caribbean Development Bank [*St. Michael, Barbados*] .... CDB
Caribbean Division [*Navy*] (DNAB) .... CARIBDIV
Caribbean Division Naval Facilities Engineering
   Command .... CARIBNAVFACENGCOM
Caribbean Division Naval Facilities Engineering Command .... DIRCARIBDOCKS
Caribbean Economic Community .... CEC
Caribbean Educational Service .... CES
Caribbean Employers Confederation [*Trinidad and Tobago*] (EAIO) .... CEC
Caribbean Energy Information System [*UNESCO*] (DUND) .... CEIS
Caribbean Environment Program [*Marine science*] (OSRA) .... CEP
Caribbean Environment Program (USDC) .... CEP
Caribbean Examinations Council [*St. Michael, Barbados*] (EAIO) CXC
Caribbean Express, Inc. [*ICAO designator*] (FAAC) .... TLC
Caribbean Family Planning Affiliation (EAIO) .... CFPA
Caribbean Federation of Aeroclubs (EA) .... CFA
Caribbean Fishery Management Council [*National Oceanic and Atmospheric
   Administration*] (GFGA) .... CFMC
Caribbean Food Corp. [*An association*] (EAIO) .... CFC
Caribbean Food Crops Society [*Isabela, Puerto Rico*] (EAIO) .... CFCS
Caribbean Free Trade Association .... CARIFTA
Caribbean Gamefishing Association .... CGA

Caribbean Group for Cooperation in Economic Development (EA) .... CGED
Caribbean Hotel Association (EA) .... CHA
Caribbean Industrial Research Institute [*Trinidad and Tobago*] [*Research
   center*] (IRC) .... CARIRI
Caribbean Industrial Research Institute .... CIRI
Caribbean Information System for Economic and Social Planning [*ECLAC*]
   [*United Nations*] (DUND) .... CARISPLAN
Caribbean Institute for Meteorology and Hydrology [*Caribbean Meteorologic
   al Institute*] [*Acronym is based on former name,*] (EAIO) .... CMI
Caribbean International [*ICAO designator*] (AD) .... XQ
Caribbean Law Journal [*A publication*] (DLA) .... Carib LJ
Caribbean Law Journal [*A publication*] (DLA) .... Caribbean LJ
Caribbean Marine Biological Institute (BARN) .... CMBI
Caribbean Meteorological Institute [*Marine science*] (OSRA) .... CMI
Caribbean Meteorological Organisation [*Formerly, Caribbean Meteorological
   Service*] (EA) .... CMO
Caribbean Meteorological Organization [*Marine science*] (OSRA) .... CMO
Caribbean Natural Resources Institute (EAIO) .... CANARI
Caribbean Network of Educational Innovation for Development [*UNESCO*]
   [*United Nations*] (DUND) .... CARNEID
Caribbean Organization [*An international governmental body, of which the US
   was a member*] [*Terminated, 1965*] .... CO
Caribbean Organization of Tax Administrators (EAIO) .... COTA
Caribbean Planning for Adaptation to Global Climate in the Caribbean.... CPACC
Caribbean Plant Protection Commission [*Trinidad and Tobago*] (EAIO) .... CPPC
Caribbean Press Association (NTCM) .... CPA
Caribbean Primate Research Center [*University of Puerto Rico*] [*Research
   center*] (RCD) .... CPRC
Caribbean Public Services Association [*Barbados*] (EAIO) .... CPSA
Caribbean Region [*USTTA*] (TAG) .... CAR
Caribbean Regional Badminton Confederation [*Aruba*] (EAIO) .... CAREBACO
Caribbean Regional Council for Adult Education [*University of the West
   Indies*] (EAIO) .... CARAE
Caribbean Regional Council for Adult Education [*Barbados*] (EAIO) .... CARCAE
Caribbean Research Institute [*College of the Virgin Islands*] .... CRI
Caribbean Resources Corp. [*Vancouver Stock Exchange symbol*] .... CBC
Caribbean Sea Frontier [*Navy*] .... CARIBSEAFRON
Caribbean Sea Frontier [*Navy*] .... CSF
Caribbean Studies Association (EA) .... CSA
Caribbean Super Station [*Satellite television system*] .... CSS
Caribbean Tourism Association [*Later, Caribbean Tourism Organization*]
   (EA) .... CTA
Caribbean Tourism Organization (EAIO) .... CTO
Caribbean Tourism Research and Development Centre [*Later, Caribbean
   Tourism Organization*] (EAIO) .... CTRC
Caribbean Writers Series [*Heinemann Educational Books Ltd.*] [*British*] .... CWS
Caribbeana Council [*Defunct*] (EA) CC
Caribe Petroleums [*Vancouver Stock Exchange symbol*] .... CBP
Caribiner International [*NYSE symbol*] (TTSB) .... CWC
Caribiner Intl., Inc. [*Associated Press*] (SAG) .... Caribinr
Caribiner Intl., Inc. [*NYSE symbol*] (SAG) .... CWC
Caribintair SA [*Haiti*] [*ICAO designator*] (FAAC) .... CRT
Caribjet, Inc. [*Antigua and Barbuda*] [*ICAO designator*] (FAAC) .... CBJ
Cariboo College, Kamloops, BC, Canada [*Library symbol Library of
   Congress*] (LCLS) .... CaBKCC
Cariboo College, Kamloops, British Columbia [*Library symbol National
   Library of Canada*] (NLC) .... BKCC
Cariboo College Library [*UTLAS symbol*] .... CAR
Cariboo Lumber Manufacturers' Association (AC) .... CLMA
Cariboo Tourist Association (AC) .... CTA
Cariboo-Chilcotin Archives, Williams Lake, British Columbia [*Library symbol
   National Library of Canada*] (NLC) .... BWLC
Cariboo-Thompson Nicola Library System, Kamloops, BC, Canada [*Library
   symbol Library of Congress*] (LCLS) .... CaBKCT
Cariboo-Thompson Nicola Library System, Kamloops, British Columbia
   [*Library symbol National Library of Canada*] (NLC) .... BKCT
Caribou [*Maine*] [*Seismograph station code, US Geological Survey*] (SEIS) ..... CBM
Caribou [*Maine*] [*ICAO location identifier*] (ICLI) .... KCAR
Caribou, ME [*Location identifier FAA*] (FAAL) .... CAR
Caribou, ME [*FM radio station call letters*] .... WCXU
Caribou, ME [*AM radio station call letters*] .... WFST
Caribou Performance Test .... CPT
Carica [*A Fig*] [*Pharmacology*] (ROG) .... CARIC
Caricature [*or Caricaturist*] .... caric
Caricaturists Society of America (EA) .... CSA
Carina [*Constellation*] .... Car
Carina [*Constellation*] .... Cari
Carina Minerals Resources Ltd. [*Vancouver Stock Exchange symbol*] .... CIM
Caring Relationship Inventory [*Psychology*] .... CRI
Carissimus [*Dearest*] [*Latin*] .... K
Caritas Internationalis [*International Confederation of Catholic Organizations
   for Charitable and Social Action*] [*Vatican City, Vatican City State*] (EAIO) CI
Carl Duisberg Society [*Later, CDSI*] (EA) .... CDS
Carl Gustav [*King of Sweden*] .... CG
Carl H. Pforzheimer Library, New York, NY [*Library symbol Library of
   Congress*] (LCLS) .... NNPf
Carl Hanser Verlag [*Publisher*] .... CHV
Carl Karcher Enterprises .... CKE
Carl Perkins Fan Club [*Defunct*] (EA) .... CPFC
Carl Perkins Vocational Education Act [*1984*] (OICC) .... CPVEA
Carl Reiner, Sheldon Leonard, Dick Van Dyke, Danny Thomas [*Acronym is
   name of production company of TV series "The Dick Van Dyke
   Show"*] .... CALVADA
Carl Sandburg Birthplace Association, Galesburg, IL [*Library symbol Library
   of Congress*] (LCLS) .... IGS

Carl Sandburg College, Galesburg, IL [*Library symbol Library of Congress*] (LCLS) ... IGSC
Carl Sandburg College, LRC, Galesburg, IL [*OCLC symbol*] (OCLC) ... IHR
Carl Schurz Memorial Foundation [*Later, NCSA*] (EA) ... CSMF
Carl Vinson Nuclear Powered Carrier [*DoD*] ... CVN
Carla Riggs-Hall International Fan Club (EA) ... CRHIFC
Carle Foundation Hospital, Urbana, IL [*Library symbol Library of Congress*] (LCLS) ... IUrCH
Carle Place High School, Carle Place, NY [*Library symbol*] [*Library of Congress*] (LCLS) ... NCpHS
Carleton and Regiment [*British military*] (DMA) ... CYR
Carleton Board of Education, Ottawa, ON, Canada [*Library symbol Library of Congress*] (LCLS) ... CaOOCBE
Carleton Board of Education, Ottawa, Ontario [*Library symbol National Library of Canada*] (NLC) ... OOCBE
Carleton Board of Education, Sir Wilfrid Laurier High School Library, Ottawa, ON, Canada [*Library symbol*] [*Library of Congress*] (LCLS) ... CaOOWLS
Carleton College, Northfield, MN [*OCLC symbol*] (OCLC) ... MNN
Carleton College, Northfield, MN [*Library symbol Library of Congress*] (LCLS) ... MnNC
Carleton County Historical Society, Upper Woodstock, New Brunswick [*Library symbol National Library of Canada*] (NLC) ... NBUWH
Carleton Library System [*Carleton University*] [*Information service or system*] (IID) ... CLS
Carleton Memorial Hospital, Woodstock, New Brunswick [*Library symbol National Library of Canada*] (BIB) ... NBWH
Carleton, MI [*Location identifier FAA*] (FAAL) ... CRL
Carleton Place Public Library, Carleton Place, ON, Canada [*Library symbol Library of Congress*] (LCLS) ... CaOCp
Carleton Place Public Library, Ontario [*Library symbol National Library of Canada*] (NLC) ... OCP
Carleton, PQ [*Television station call letters*] ... CHAU
Carleton, PQ [*FM radio station call letters*] (RBYB) ... CIEU
Carleton University Academic Staff Association [*Association du Personnel Enseignant de l'Universite Carleton*] (AC) ... CUASA
Carleton University, Department of Art History, Ottawa, ON, Canada [*Library symbol Library of Congress*] (LCLS) ... CaOOCCAH
Carleton University, Geography Department, Ottawa, ON, Canada [*Library symbol Library of Congress*] (LCLS) ... CaOOCCG
Carleton University Library [*UTLAS symbol*] ... CTN
Carleton University, Ottawa, ON, Canada [*Library symbol Library of Congress*] (LCLS) ... CaOOCC
Carleton University, Ottawa, Ontario [*Library symbol National Library of Canada*] (NLC) ... OOCC
Carleton University, Social Sciences Division, Ottawa, ON, Canada [*Library symbol Library of Congress Obsolete*] (LCLS) ... CaOOCCSS
Carleton's New Brunswick Reports [*A publication*] (DLA) ... Carl
Carleton's New Brunswick Reports [*A publication*] (DLA) ... NBR Carl
Carletonville [*South Africa*] [*ICAO location identifier*] (ICLI) ... FACR
Carlin Resources Corp. [*Vancouver Stock Exchange symbol*] ... CLM
Carline Assignment Model [*General Motors Corp.*] ... CLAM
Carlinville, IL [*FM radio station call letters*] ... WCNL
Carlinville, IL [*FM radio station call letters*] ... WIBI
Carlinville, IL [*FM radio station call letters*] (RBYB) ... WTSG-FM
Carlinville Public Library, Carlinville, IL [*Library symbol Library of Congress*] (LCLS) ... ICarl
Carlisle [*England*] [*Airport symbol*] (OAG) ... CAX
Carlisle [*British ICAO location identifier*] (ICLI) ... EGNC
Carlisle Citizen, Carlisle, IA [*Library symbol Library of Congress*] (LCLS) ... IaCarlC
Carlisle Companies [*Associated Press*] (SAG) ... Carlisle
Carlisle Companies [*NYSE symbol*] (SPSG) ... CSL
Carlisle, KY [*FM radio station call letters*] ... WCAK
Carlisle, PA [*FM radio station call letters*] ... WDCV
Carlisle, PA [*AM radio station call letters*] ... WHYL
Carlisle, PA [*FM radio station call letters*] ... WHYL-FM
Carlisle, PA [*AM radio station call letters*] ... WIOO
Carlisle Plastics Cl'A' [*NYSE symbol*] (TTSB) ... CPA
Carlisle Plastics, Inc. [*Associated Press*] (SAG) ... CarlisIP
Carlisle Plastics, Inc. [*NYSE symbol*] (SAG) ... CPA
Carlisle Public Library, Carlisle, IA [*Library symbol Library of Congress*] (LCLS) ... IaCarl
Carlisle Public Library, Carlisle, IN [*Library symbol Library of Congress*] (LCLS) ... InCa
Carlisle Public Library, Carlisle, IN [*Library symbol*] [*Library of Congress*] (LCLS) ... InCaL
Carlo Erba [*Italy*] [*Research code symbol*] ... I
Carlo Erba [*Italy*] [*Research code symbol*] ... K
Carload ... CL
Carload (WDMC) ... cl
Carload Lot [*Commerce*] ... CL
Carloading ... CRLDNG
Carloforte [*Sardinia*] [*Seismograph station code, US Geological Survey Closed*] (SEIS) ... CRL
Carlos Cervantes del Rio [*Mexico ICAO designator*] (FAAC) ... CCD
Carlos Elementary School, Carlos, MN [*Library symbol*] [*Library of Congress*] (LCLS) ... MnCarE
Carlotn High School, Carlton, MN [*Library symbol*] [*Library of Congress*] (LCLS) ... MnCtH
Carlow [*County in Ireland*] (ROG) ... CAR
Carlow College, Our Lady of Mercy Academy, Pittsburgh, PA [*Library symbol Library of Congress*] (LCLS) ... PPiCa-O
Carlow College, Pittsburgh, PA [*OCLC symbol*] (OCLC) ... CRC
Carlow College, Pittsburgh, PA [*Library symbol Library of Congress*] (LCLS) ... PPiCa
Carlsbad [*California*] [*Airport symbol*] (OAG) ... CLD
Carlsbad [*New Mexico*] [*Seismograph station code, US Geological Survey*] (SEIS) ... CLN
Carlsbad [*New Mexico*] [*Airport symbol*] (OAG) ... CNM
Carlsbad, CA [*Location identifier FAA*] (FAAL) ... CRQ
Carlsbad, CA [*Location identifier FAA*] (FAAL) ... EKG
Carlsbad, CA [*FM radio station call letters*] (RBYB) ... KUPR
Carlsbad/Cavern City Air Terminal [*New Mexico*] [*ICAO location identifier*] (ICLI) ... KCNM
Carlsbad Caverns National Park ... CACA
Carlsbad City Library, Carlsbad, CA [*Library symbol Library of Congress*] (LCLS) ... CCarl
Carlsbad City Library, Carlsbad, CA [*OCLC symbol*] (OCLC) ... CCP
Carlsbad, NM [*Location identifier FAA*] (FAAL) ... CNM
Carlsbad, NM [*AM radio station call letters*] ... KAMQ
Carlsbad, NM [*AM radio station call letters*] ... KATK
Carlsbad, NM [*FM radio station call letters*] ... KATK-FM
Carlsbad, NM [*AM radio station call letters*] ... KCCC
Carlsbad, NM [*FM radio station call letters*] ... KCDY
Carlsbad, NM [*Television station call letters*] ... KOCT
Carlsbad Public Library, Carlsbad, NM [*Library symbol Library of Congress*] (LCLS) ... NmC
Carlsbad Ventures [*Vancouver Stock Exchange symbol*] ... KVI
Carlsberg Automated Meridian Circle [*Astronomy*] ... CAMC
Carlson Elementary School, Rockford, IL [*Library symbol*] [*Library of Congress*] (LCLS) ... IRoCaE
Carlson Mines Ltd. [*Vancouver Stock Exchange symbol*] ... CLX
Carlson Psychological Survey [*Test*] ... CPS
Carlton and United Breweries [*Australia*] ... CUB
Carlton Communications [*NYSE symbol*] (SPSG) ... CCM
Carlton Communications Ltd. [*Associated Press*] (SAG) ... CarlCm
Carlton Communications Ltd. [*Associated Press*] (SAG) ... CarltCm
Carlton Communications Ltd. [*NASDAQ symbol*] (SAG) ... CCTV
Carlton Commun'X-CAPS' [*NYSE symbol*] (TTSB) ... CCMPr
Carlton County Historical Society, Cloquet, MN [*Library symbol*] [*Library of Congress*] (LCLS) ... MnClHi
Carlton Public Library, Carlton, MN [*Library symbol*] [*Library of Congress*] (LCLS) ... MnCt
Carlyle Barton Laboratory (MCD) ... CBL
Carlyle Energy Ltd. [*Toronto Stock Exchange symbol*] ... CYD
Carlyle Golf, Inc. [*NASDAQ symbol*] (SAG) ... CRLG
Carlyle Golf, Inc. [*Associated Press*] (SAG) ... CrlyGl
Carlyle Golf, Inc. [*Associated Press*] (SAG) ... CrlyleGlf
Carlyle Golf Wrrt [*NASDAQ symbol*] (TTSB) ... CRLGW
Carlyle School, Carlyle, IL [*Library symbol Library of Congress*] (LCLS) ... ICarlyS
Carma Developers Ltd. [*Toronto Stock Exchange symbol*] ... CDV
Carma Ltd. [*Toronto Stock Exchange symbol*] ... CVP
Carmac Resources [*Vancouver Stock Exchange symbol*] ... CMA
Carmanguay Public Library, Alberta [*Library symbol National Library of Canada*] (NLC) ... ACARMA
Carmanville Public Library, Carmanville, NF, Canada [*Library symbol Library of Congress*] (LCLS) ... CaNfCa
Carmanville Public Library, Newfoundland [*Library symbol National Library of Canada*] (NLC) ... NFCA
Carmarthen [*Welsh depot code*] ... CARM
Carmarthenshire [*County in Wales*] ... CARM
Carmarthenshire [*County in Wales*] (ROG) ... CARMARTHS
Carmarthenshire [*County in Wales*] ... CARMS
Carmel, CA [*FM radio station call letters*] (RBYB) ... KBOQ
Carmel, CA [*AM radio station call letters*] ... KRML
Carmel, CA [*FM radio station call letters*] (RBYB) ... KXDC
Carmel Clay Schools, Carmel IN [*Library symbol*] [*Library of Congress*] (LCLS) ... InCarS
Carmel Community [*Roman Catholic women's religious order*] ... CC
Carmel Container Sys [*AMEX symbol*] (TTSB) ... KML
Carmel Container Systems Ltd. [*Associated Press*] (SAG) ... Carmel
Carmel Container Systems Ltd. [*AMEX symbol*] (SPSG) ... KML
Carmel de Montreal, Montreal, PQ, Canada [*Library symbol Library of Congress*] (LCLS) ... CaQMACAR
Carmel de Montreal, Quebec [*Library symbol National Library of Canada*] (NLC) ... QMCAR
Carmel, IN [*FM radio station call letters*] ... WHJE
Carmel News Journal, Carmel, IN [*Library symbol Library of Congress*] (LCLS) ... InCarNJ
Carmel, NY [*Location identifier FAA*] (FAAL) ... CMK
Carmel Public Library, Carmel, IN [*Library symbol Library of Congress*] (LCLS) ... InCar
Carmel Valley, CA [*AM radio station call letters*] ... KIEZ
Carmelita [*Guatemala*] [*ICAO location identifier*] (ICLI) ... MGCR
Carmelita Petroleum [*Vancouver Stock Exchange symbol*] ... CFH
Carmelitae Divini Cordis Jesu [*Carmelite Sisters of the Divine Heart of Jesus*] [*Roman Catholic religious order*] ... DCJ
Carmelitas del Sagrado Corazon (TOCD) ... OCD
Carmelite ... CARM
Carmelite Brothers of the Holy Eucharist [*Roman Catholic religious order*] ... CFSE
Carmelite Community of the Word (TOCD) ... CCW
Carmelite Fathers and Brothers (TOCD) ... OCarm
Carmelite Fathers and Brothers (TOCD) ... ocarm
Carmelite Missionaries [*Rome, Italy*] (EAIO) ... CM
Carmelite Missionaries of St. Theresa [*Roman Catholic women's religious order*] ... CMST
Carmelite Nuns of the Ancient Observance (TOCD) ... OCarm
Carmelite Sisters (Corpus Christi) (TOCD) ... OCarm
Carmelite Sisters for Aged and Infirm (TOCD) ... OCarm
Carmelite Sisters of Charity (TOCD) ... Cach

Carmelite Sisters of St. Teresa (TOCD) .... CSST
Carmelite Sisters of St. Therese of the Infant Jesus [Roman Catholic religious order] .... CST
Carmelite Sisters of the Divine Heart of Jesus (TOCD) .... CarmelDCJ
Carmelite Sisters of the Eucharist (TOCD) .... CSE
Carmelite Sisters of the Most Sacred Heart of Los Angeles (TOCD) .... OCD
Carmelite Third Order [Rome, Italy] (EAIO) .... CTO
Carmelite Vietnamese of Our Lady of Mt. Carmel (TOCD) .... OCA
Carmelites of Mary Immaculate (TOCD) .... CMI
Carmelites of Mary Immaculate (TOCD) .... cmi
Carmen Arvale [of Calpurnius Siculus] [Classical studies] (OCD) .... Carm Arv
Carmen de Bello Aegyptiaco sive Actiaco [of Ausonius] [Classical studies] (OCD) .... B Aegypt
Carmen de Patagones [Argentina] [Airport symbol] (AD) .... CPG
Carmen Division of the Brotherhood of Railway, Airline and Steamship Clerks, Freight Handlers, Express and Station Employes (EA) .... CD/BRAC
Carmen Saeculare [of Horace] [Classical studies] (OCD) .... Carm Saec
Carmen Saliare [of Calpurnius Siculus] [Classical studies] (OCD) .... Carm Sal
Carmi, IL [Location identifier FAA] (FAAL) .... CUL
Carmi, IL [AM radio station call letters] .... WROY
Carmi, IL [FM radio station call letters] .... WRUL
Carmichael, CA [AM radio station call letters] .... KFIA
Carmike Cinemas, Inc. [Columbus, GA] [Associated Press] (SAG) .... Carmik
Carmike Cinemas Inc. [NYSE symbol] (SPSG) .... CKE
Carmike Cinemas 'A' [NYSE symbol] (TTSB) .... CKE
Carmina [or Odes] [of Sidonius Apollinaris] [Classical studies] (OCD) .... Carm
Carmina Epigraphica [of Calpurnius Siculus] [Classical studies] (OCD) .... Carm Epigr
Carmina Latina Epigraphica [A publication] (OCD) .... Carm Epigr
Carmina Popularia [of Calpurnius Siculus] [Classical studies] (OCD) .... Carm Pop
Carminative [Expelling Wind] [Pharmacy] (ROG) .... CAR
Carmine (ROG) .... CAR
Carmody-Wait. Cyclopedia of New York Practice [A publication] (DLA) .... Carmody-Wait NY Prac
Carnal Knowledge [FBI standardized term] .... CK
Carnal Knowledge of Female Child [FBI standardized term] .... CK of FC
Carnarvon [Australia ICAO location identifier] (ICLI) .... APCR
Carnarvon [Australia Airport symbol] (OAG) .... CVQ
Carnarvon [Western Australia] [Airport symbol] (AD) .... CVQ
Carnarvon Township Public Library, Mindemoya, Ontario [Library symbol National Library of Canada] (NLC) .... OMCT
Carnarvon Tracking Station [NASA] .... CRO
Carnarvonshire [County in Wales] .... CARN
Carnarvonshire [County in Wales] (ROG) .... CARNARVS
Carnarvonshire [County in Wales] (ROG) .... CARNS
Carnasaw Mountain - Lookout Tower [Oklahoma] [Seismograph station code, US Geological Survey] (SEIS) .... CRO
Carnation (DSUE) .... CARN
Carnation Cryptic Virus [Plant pathology] .... CARCV
Carnation Etched Ring Virus .... CERV
Carnation Instant Breakfast [Nestle Beverage Co.] [Tradename] (DAVI) .... CIB
Carnation Italian Ringspot Virus [Plant pathology] .... CIRSV
Carnation Latent Virus [Plant pathology] CLV
Carnation Mottle Virus .... CaMoV
Carnation Mottle Virus .... CarMV
Carnation Necrotic Fleck Virus .... CNFV
Carnation Research Laboratories, Van Nuys, CA [Library symbol Library of Congress] (LCLS) .... CVnCR
Carnation Ringspot Virus .... CRSV
Carnation Vein Mottle Virus [Plant pathology] .... CVMV
Carnation Yellow Stripe Virus [Plant pathology] .... CYSV
Carnegie Bancorp [Associated Press] (SAG) .... CarnB
Carnegie Bancorp [Associated Press] (SAG) .... CarnegBc
Carnegie Bancorp [NASDAQ symbol] (SAG) .... CBNJ
Carnegie Bancorp Wrrt [NASDAQ symbol] (TTSB) .... CBNJW
Carnegie Bookmobile Library, Grafton, ND [Library symbol Library of Congress] (LCLS) .... NdGrC
Carnegie Center for Transnational Studies .... CCTS
Carnegie City Library, Little Falls, MN [Library symbol] [Library of Congress] (LCLS) .... MnLf
Carnegie Commission on Higher Education .... CCHE
Carnegie Commission on Science, Technology, and Government (EA) .... CCSTG
Carnegie Corp. of New York (EA) .... CCNY
Carnegie Corp. of New York, New York, NY [ICAO symbol Library of Congress] (LCLS) .... NNCar
Carnegie Council of Policy Studies in Higher Education [Defunct] (EA) .... CCPSHE
Carnegie Council on Adolescent Development (EA) .... CCAD
Carnegie Council on Ethics and International Affairs (EA) .... CCEIA
Carnegie Ellsworth Public Library, Iowa Falls, IA [Library symbol Library of Congress] (LCLS) .... Ialf
Carnegie Endowment for International Peace (EA) .... CEIP
Carnegie Endowment for International Peace, New York, NY [Library symbol Library of Congress] (LCLS) .... NNCE
Carnegie Forum on Education and the Economy (EA) .... CFEE
Carnegie Foundation for the Advancement of Teaching (EA) .... CFAT
Carnegie Free Library, Beaver Falls, PA [Library symbol Library of Congress] (LCLS) .... PBf
Carnegie Free Library, Braddock, PA [Library symbol Library of Congress] (LCLS) .... PBra
Carnegie Free Library of McKeesport, McKeesport, PA [Library symbol Library of Congress] (LCLS) .... PMck
Carnegie Group, Inc. [Associated Press] (SAG) .... Carnegie
Carnegie Group, Inc. [NASDAQ symbol] (SAG) .... CGIX
Carnegie Hall - Jeunesses Musicales [Defunct] (EA) .... CH-JM

Carnegie Hero Fund Commission (EA) .... CHFC
Carnegie Institute [New York] CI
Carnegie Institute of Technology [Later, Carnegie-Mellon University] [Pennsylvania] .... CIT
Carnegie Institution of Washington .... CIW
Carnegie Institution of Washington [District of Columbia] [Seismograph station code, US Geological Survey Closed] (SEIS) .... DTM
Carnegie Institution of Washington, Department of Terrestrial Magnetism, Washington, DC [Library symbol Library of Congress] (LCLS) .... DCI-T
Carnegie Institution of Washington, Geophysical Laboratory, Washington, DC [Library symbol Library of Congress] (LCLS) .... DCI-G
Carnegie Institution of Washington, Washington, DC [Library symbol Library of Congress] (LCLS) .... DCI
Carnegie Interest Inventory [Medicine] (DMAA) CII
Carnegie Library, Dawson, MN [Library symbol] [Library of Congress] (LCLS) .... MnDaw
Carnegie Library of Parkersburg and Wood County, Parkersburg, WV [Library symbol Library of Congress] (LCLS) .... WvP
Carnegie Library of Pittsburgh, Allegheny Regional Branch, Monroeville, PA [Library symbol Library of Congress] (LCLS) .... PPi-A
Carnegie Library of Pittsburgh, Pittsburgh, PA [OCLC symbol] (OCLC) .... CPL
Carnegie Library of Pittsburgh, Pittsburgh, PA [Library symbol Library of Congress] (LCLS) .... PPi
Carnegie Library, Rockport, MA [Library symbol Library of Congress] (LCLS) .... MRp
Carnegie Library, Rome, GA [Library symbol Library of Congress] (LCLS) .... GR
Carnegie Mellon University (GAGS) .... Carnegie Mellon U
Carnegie Multi-Mini Processor .... CMMP
Carnegie Museum of Natural History [Pittsburgh, PA] .... CM
Carnegie, PA [AM radio station call letters] .... WPLW
Carnegie Public Library, Angola, IN [OCLC symbol] (OCLC) .... IIA
Carnegie Public Library, Angola, IN [Library symbol Library of Congress] (LCLS) .... InAng
Carnegie Public Library, Bradford, PA [Library symbol Library of Congress] (LCLS) .... PBr
Carnegie Public Library, Browns Valley, MN [Library symbol] [Library of Congress] (LCLS) .... MnBrv
Carnegie Public Library, Clarksdale, MS [Library symbol Library of Congress] (LCLS) .... MsCld
Carnegie Public Library, Conneaut, OH [Library symbol] [Library of Congress] (LCLS) .... OConCL
Carnegie Public Library District, Fortville, IN [Library symbol Library of Congress] (LCLS) .... InFtv
Carnegie Public Library, Las Vegas, NM [OCLC symbol] (OCLC) .... LVN
Carnegie Public Library of Corning, Corning, CA [Library symbol Library of Congress] (LCLS) .... CCorn
Carnegie Public Library, Union, OR [Library symbol Library of Congress] (LCLS) .... OrUn
Carnegie Public Library, Washington Court House, OH [Library symbol Library of Congress] (LCLS) .... OWas
Carnegie Public Library, Washington, IN [Library symbol Library of Congress] (LCLS) .... InWas
Carnegie Southern Observatory [Later, Las Campanas Observatory] .... CARSO
Carnegie United Kingdom Trust (BARN) .... CUKT
Carnegie-Mellon University [Pittsburgh, PA] .... CMU
Carnegie-Mellon University, Hunt Institute for Botanical Documentation, Pittsburgh, PA [Library symbol Library of Congress] (LCLS) .... PPiHB
Carnegie-Mellon University, Mellon Institute, Pittsburgh, PA [Library symbol Library of Congress] (LCLS) .... PPiM
Carnegie-Mellon University, Pittsburgh, PA [OCLC symbol] (OCLC) .... PMC
Carnegie-Mellon University, Pittsburgh, PA [Library symbol Library of Congress] (LCLS) .... PPiC
Carnegie-Mellon University-Design Automation (MCD) .... CMU-DA
Carnegie-Stout Free Public Library, Dubuque, IA [Library symbol Library of Congress] (LCLS) .... IaDu
Carnelian (VRA) .... carnl
Carnelian Bay, CA [FM radio station call letters] .... KODS
Carnes Creek Explorations [Vancouver Stock Exchange symbol] .... CSK
Carney, William L., Bresman IN [STAC] .... CWL
Carnian [Geology] C
Carnicobar [India] [ICAO location identifier] (ICLI) .... VOCX
Carnival .... CARN
Carnival (DSUE) .... CARNI
Carnival Air [ICAO designator] (FAAC) .... CAA
Carnival Corp 'A' [NYSE symbol] (TTSB) CCL
Carnival Corp. [Formerly, Carnival Cruise] [Associated Press] (SAG) .... CarnCp
Carnival Corp. [Associated Press] (SAG) .... CarnvCp
Carnival Corp. [NYSE symbol] (SAG) CCL
Carnmarth [England] .... CARNM
Carnot [Central African Republic] [Airport symbol] (AD) .... CRF
Carnow, Coninleas & Associates, Ltd., Chicago, IL [Library symbol] [Library of Congress] (LCLS) .... ICCaC
Caro, MI [FM radio station call letters] .... WIDL
Caro, MI [AM radio station call letters] .... WKYO
Carol Burnett Fund for Responsible Journalism (EA) .... CBFRJ
Carol Lawrence National Fan Club (EA) .... CLFC
Carol P&L $5 cm Pfd [AMEX symbol] (TTSB) .... CPLPr
Carolan Systems International, Inc. [Toronto Stock Exchange symbol] .... CSJ
Carolin Mines Ltd. [Toronto Stock Exchange symbol Vancouver Stock Exchange symbol] CLL
Carolina [United States] [Obsolete] (ROG) .... CAR
Carolina [Brazil] [Airport symbol] (AD) .... CLN
Carolina [South Africa] [ICAO location identifier] (ICLI) .... FACL
Carolina [Brazil ICAO location identifier] (ICLI) .... SBCI
Carolina Air Transit, Inc. [ICAO designator] (FAAC) .... CTX

Carolina & North Western [Railroad] (MHDB)	C & NW
Carolina & Northwestern Railroad (IIA)	C & NW
Carolina & Northwestern Railway Co. [AAR code]	CRN
Carolina Asphalt Pavement Association (SRA)	CAPA
Carolina Association of Professional Insurance Agents (SRA)	CAPIA
Carolina Beach, NC [FM radio station call letters]	WLGX
Carolina Beach, NC [AM radio station call letters]	WMYT
Carolina, Clinchfield & Ohio [Railway] (MHDB)	CCL
Carolina Discipliana Library, Wilson, NC [Library symbol Library of Congress] (LCLS)	NcWilC
Carolina Fincorp., Inc. [Associated Press] (SAG)	CaroFin
Carolina Fincorp., Inc. [NASDAQ symbol] (SAG)	CFNC
Carolina First Corp. [NASDAQ symbol] (NQ)	CAFC
Carolina First Corp. [Associated Press] (SAG)	CaroF
Carolina First Corp. [Associated Press] (SAG)	CaroFst
Carolina First Corp. [Associated Press] (SAG)	CaroFt
Carolina Freight Corp. [NYSE symbol] (SPSG)	CAO
Carolina Gold [Vancouver Stock Exchange symbol]	CJE
Carolina Institute for Research on Early Education for the Handicapped (EDAC)	CIREEH
Carolina Law Journal [A publication] (DLA)	Car LJ
Carolina Law Journal [A publication] (DLA)	Carolina LJ
Carolina Law Repository [North Carolina] [A publication] (DLA)	Car L Rep
Carolina Law Repository [North Carolina] [A publication] (DLA)	Car LlA Repos
Carolina Law Repository [North Carolina] [A publication] (DLA)	Carolina L Repos
Carolina Law Repository [North Carolina] [A publication] (DLA)	Law Repos
Carolina Law Repository (Reprint) [North Carolina] [A publication] (DLA)	Car L Repos
Carolina Law Repository (Reprint) [North Carolina] [A publication] (DLA)	Car LR
Carolina Law Repository (Reprint) [North Carolina] [A publication] (DLA)	L Rep
Carolina Law Repository (Reprint) [North Carolina] [A publication] (DLA)	N Car Law Rep
Carolina Library Services, Inc. (IID)	CLS
Carolina Population Center [University of North Carolina] [Research center] (IID)	CPC
Carolina Power & Light Co. [Associated Press] (SAG)	CaroP
Carolina Power & Light Co. [Associated Press] (SAG)	CaroPw
Carolina Power & Light Co. [Associated Press] (SAG)	CarP8.55
Carolina Power & Light Co. [NYSE symbol] (SAG)	CPD
Carolina Power & Light Co. [NYSE symbol] (SPSG)	CPL
Carolina Power & Light Co., Technical Library, Raleigh, NC [Library symbol Library of Congress] (LCLS)	NcRCPL
Carolina, PR [FM radio station call letters]	WAHQ
Carolina, PR [Television station call letters]	WDZE
Carolina, PR [AM radio station call letters]	WIDA
Carolina, PR [FM radio station call letters]	WIDA-FM
Carolina Pwr & Lt [NYSE symbol] (TTSB)	CPL
Carolina Pwr & Lt 8.55%'QUICS' [NYSE symbol] (TTSB)	CPD
Carolina Quarterly [A publication] (BRI)	CQ
Carolina Record of Individual Behavior (EDAC)	CRIB
Carolina Regina [Queen Caroline] [Latin]	CR
Carolina Southern Bank [Associated Press] (SAG)	CaroSth
Carolina Southern Bank [NASDAQ symbol] (NQ)	CSBK
Carolina Southern Railway Co. [AAR code]	CRS
Carolina Southern Railway Co. (IIA)	CS
Carolina Sthrn Bk Spartn SC [NASDAQ symbol] (TTSB)	CSBK
Carolina Western [AAR code]	CARW
Carolinas Association of Chamber of Commerce Executives (SRA)	CACCE
Carolinas Concrete Masonry Association (SRA)	CCMA
Carolinas Electrical Contractors Association (SRA)	CECA
Carolinas Independent Automobile Dealers Association (SRA)	CIADA
Carolinas-Virginia Nuclear Power Associates, Inc.	CVNPA
Carolinas-Virginia Tube Reactor	CVTR
Caroline Chisholm School of Nursing [Monash University] [Australia]	CCSN
Caroline Chisholm Society [Australia]	CCS
Caroline County Public Library, Denton, MD [Library symbol Library of Congress] (LCLS)	MdD
Caroline G. Atkinson Elementary School, Freeport, NY [Library symbol] [Library of Congress] (LCLS)	NFreeAtE
Caroline Islands [Diocesan abbreviation] (TOCD)	CI
Caroline Islands [MARC geographic area code Library of Congress] (LCCP)	poci--
Caroline Islands (VRA)	TT
Caroline Public Library, Alberta [Library symbol National Library of Canada] (NLC)	ACARO
Carolus [Charles] [Numismatics] (ROG)	CAR
Carolus Cordell, Catholicae Academicae Duacenae Alumnus [Pseudonym used by Charles Cordell]	CCCADA
Carolus Molinaeus [Deceased, 1566] [Authority cited in pre-1607 legal work] (DSA)	Caro Molin
Carolus Molinaeus [Deceased, 1566] [Authority cited in pre-1607 legal work] (DSA)	Carol Molin
Carolus Rex [King Charles] [Latin]	CR
Caronport, SK [FM radio station call letters] (RBYB)	CJOS
Carora, Lara [Venezuela ICAO location identifier] (ICLI)	SVCO
Carotene [Biochemistry] (DAVI)	CAROT
Carotid Artery [Anatomy] (DAVI)	CA
Carotid Artery Occlusion [Medicine]	CAO
Carotid Artery System [Medicine]	CAS
Carotid Audiofrequency Analysis [Medicine] (DMAA)	CAA
Carotid Bodies Resected [Medicine] (AAMN)	CBR
Carotid Cavernous Fistula [Medicine]	CCF
Carotid Chemoreceptor Activation [Medicine]	CCRA
Carotid Compression Tomography [Medicine]	CCT
Carotid Endarterectomy [Medicine]	CE

Carotid Endarterectomy [Cardiology] (DAVI)	CEA
Carotid Phonoangiography [Medicine]	CPA
Carotid Photoangiography [Cardiology] (DAVI)	CPA
Carotid Pulse Tracing [Cardiology] (DAVI)	CPT
Carotid Sheath [Cardiology] (DAVI)	CS
Carotid Sinus [Cardiology] (DAVI)	CS
Carotid Sinus Hypersensitivity [Cardiology] (DAVI)	CSH
Carotid Sinus Massage [Cardiology]	CSM
Carotid Sinus Nerve [Cardiology] (AAMN)	CSN
Carotid Sinus Nerve Stimulation [or Stimulator] [Cardiology] (AAMN)	CSNS
Carotid Sinus Pressure [Cardiology] (CPH)	CSP
Carotid Sinus Stimulation [Cardiology]	CSS
Carotid Sinus Transmural Pressure [Cardiology]	CSTMP
Carotid Tracing [Medicine]	CT
Carotis Pulse Curve [Cardiology]	CPC
Carousel Transfer Tube	CTT
Carp Lake Township Library, White Pine, MI [Library symbol Library of Congress] (LCLS)	MiWp
Carpal Tunnel [Medicine]	CT
Carpal Tunnel Decompression [Medicine]	CTD
Carpal Tunnel Release [Medicine] (DMAA)	CTR
Carpal Tunnel Syndrome [Medicine]	CTS
Carpathian Mountains (BARN)	Carp
Carpatho-Russian Benevolent Association Liberty (EA)	CRBAL
Carpel [Botany] (BARN)	cpl
Carpentaria (ROG)	CARP
Carpentaria Community Services [Australia]	CCS
Carpenter [Navy British] (ROG)	CAR
Carpenter [or Carpentry]	CARP
Carpenter [Theater] [Slang] (WDMC)	carp
Carpenter	CARPTR
Carpenter (MSA)	CPNTR
Carpenter (AABC)	CPTR
Carpenter Lake Resources [Vancouver Stock Exchange symbol]	CTA
Carpenter Technology [NYSE symbol] (TTSB)	CRS
Carpenter Technology Corp. [Associated Press] (SAG)	CarpTech
Carpenter Technology Corp. [Formerly, Carpenter Steel Co.] [Associated Press] (SAG)	CarTec
Carpenter Technology Corp. [Formerly, Carpenter Steel Co.] [NYSE symbol] (SPSG)	CRS
Carpenters and Joiners of America (MHDB)	CJA
Carpenters and Joiners Protection Society [A union] [British]	CJPS
Carpenters' Co. (EA)	CC
Carpenters' Co., Philadelphia, PA [Library symbol Library of Congress] (LCLS)	PPCC
Carpenter's Mate [Navy]	CM
Carpenter's Mate, Construction Battalion [Navy]	CMCB
Carpenter's Mate, Construction Battalion, Builder [Navy]	CMCBB
Carpenter's Mate, Construction Battalion, Draftsman [Navy]	CMCBD
Carpenter's Mate, Construction Battalion, Excavation Foreman [Navy]	CMCBE
Carpenter's Mate, Ship Repair [Navy]	CMSR
Carpenter's Mate, Ship Repair, Boatbuilder-Wood [Navy]	CMSRB
Carpenter's Mate, Ship Repair, Carpenter [Navy]	CMSRC
Carpenter's Mate, Ship Repair, Caulker-Boat [Navy]	CMSRK
Carpenter's Mate, Ship Repair, Cement Worker-Concrete [Navy]	CMSRN
Carpenter's Mate, Ship Repair, Joiner [Navy]	CMSRJ
Carpenter's Mate, Ship Repair, Shipwright [Navy]	CMSRS
Carpenter's Reports [52-53 California] [A publication] (DLA)	Carp
Carpenter's Reports [52-53 California] [A publication] (DLA)	Carpenter
Carpentras [France ICAO location identifier] (ICLI)	LFNH
Carpentry	CRPNTRY
Carpentry and Joinery	C & J
Carpet [MSA]	CARP
Carpet [Classified advertising] (ADA)	CPT
Carpet (VRA)	cpt
Carpet	CPT
Carpet [Classified advertising] (ADA)	CRPT
Carpet and Rug Industry Consumer Action Panel [Defunct]	CRICAP
Carpet and Rug Institute (EA)	CRI
Carpet and Upholstery Cleaning Association [Australia]	CUCA
Carpet Cleaners Institute of the Northwest (SRA)	CCINW
Carpet Cushion Council (EA)	CCC
Carpet Information Network [Tapistree Group, Inc.] [Information service or system] (IID)	C-LINE
Carpet Institute of Australia	CIA
Carpet Manufacturers Marketing Association (EA)	CMMA
Carpet Wool Council [Defunct]	CWC
Carpeting Mats or Rugs [Freight]	CPTNG MATS RGS
Carpets and Curtains (ADA)	C & C
Carpinteria, CA [FM radio station call letters]	KSBL
Carpinteria Valley Historical Association, Carpinteria, CA [Library symbol] [Library of Congress] (LCLS)	CCarpHi
Carpita Corp. [Toronto Stock Exchange symbol]	CYY
Carpmael's Patent Cases [1602-1842] [England] [A publication] (DLA)	Carp
Carpmael's Patent Cases [1602-1842] [England] [A publication] (DLA)	Carp Pat Cas
Carpmael's Patent Cases [1602-1842] [England] [A publication] (DLA)	Carp PC
Carpometacarpal [Anatomy]	CMC
Carpometacarpal Joint [Medicine] (DMAA)	CMCJ
Carpometacarpal Joint [Anatomy] (DAVI)	CMJ
Carr America Realty Corp. [Associated Press] (SAG)	CarrAmR
Carr America Realty Corp. [NYSE symbol] (SAG)	CRE
Carr Gottstein Foods [Associated Press] (SAG)	CarGot
Carr Gottstein Foods [Associated Press] (SAG)	CarrGott
Carr Gottstein Foods [NYSE symbol] (SAG)	CGF

Carr Realty [*Associated Press*] (SAG) ... CarrRlty
Carr Realty Corp. [*NYSE symbol*] (SPSG) ... CRE
CarrAmerica Realty [*NYSE symbol*] (TTSB) ... CRE
Carran's Summary Cases [*India*] [*A publication*] (DLA) ... Carr Cas
Carrasco [*Montevideo, Uruguay*] [*Airport symbol*] (AD) ... CSO
Carrau's Edition of Summary Cases [*Bengal*] [*A publication*] (DLA) ... Carrau
Carre (DD) ... car
Carrefour Canadien International [*Canadian Crossroads International*] (EAIO) ... CCI
Carrefour des Agents de Pastorale en Monde Ouvrier [*Crossroads of Pastoral Agents and Workers of the World*] [*Canada*] ... CAPMO
Carrefour des Employees de Secretariat [*Crossroads of Secretariat Employees*] [*Canada*] ... CES
Carrel-Dakin [*Fluid*] ... CD
Carrer Development and Assessment Center for Librarians (EDAC) ... CDACL
Carretera ... CARR
Carr-Gottstein Foods [*NYSE symbol*] (TTSB) ... CGF
Carr-Gottstein Foods, Inc. [*NYSE symbol*] (SPSG) ... CGF
Carriacou [*Windward Islands*] [*Airport symbol*] (OAG) ... CRU
Carriage (ROG) ... CARR
Carriage ... CARR
Carriage ... CGE
Carriage (MSA) ... CRG
Carriage and Insurance Paid to Named Point [*Shipping*] (DS) ... CIP
Carriage and Packing [*Shipping*] (ADA) ... C & P
Carriage and Wagon Work [*British railroad term*] ... C and W
Carriage Association of America (EA) ... CAA
Carriage Control ... CC
Carriage Control Character [*Computer science*] ... CCC
Carriage Forward [*Finance*] (ODBW) ... carr fwd
Carriage, Insurance, and Freight ... CIF
Carriage of Explosives Regulations ... CER
Carriage of Goods [*by sea*] [*Shipping*] ... C of G
Carriage of Goods by Sea Act [*Shipping*] ... COGSA
Carriage Paid ... CP
Carriage Reset (WDMC) ... CR
Carriage Return ... CR
Carriage Return Contact ... CRC
Carriage Return/Line Feed [*Computer science*] ... CR/LF
Carriage Services, Inc. [*Associated Press*] (SAG) ... CarrSrv
Carriage Services, Inc. [*NASDAQ symbol*] (SAG) ... CRSV
Carriage Tape Simulator [*Computer science*] (IAA) ... CTS
Carribean Basin Radar Network [*Military*] (DOMA) ... CBRN
Carrie Palmer Weber Junior High School, Port Washington, NY [*Library symbol*] [*Library of Congress*] (LCLS) ... NPtwWJ
Carried (ADA) ... CARR
Carried Down [*Bookkeeping*] ... CD
Carried Forward (WGA) ... C/F
Carried Forward [*Bookkeeping*] (ODBW) ... cd fwd
Carried Forward [*Bookkeeping*] (ODBW) ... cf
Carried Forward [*Finance*] (DFIT) ... CF
Carried Over [*Accounting*] ... CO
Carrier [*JETDS nomenclature*] ... C
Carrier (CINC) ... CAR
Carrier [*Telecommunications*] (AFM) ... CARR
Carrier [*Telecommunications*] (CET) ... CX
Carrier [*Telecommunications*] ... CXR
Carrier Access Billing System [*Telecommunications*] (ACRL) ... CABS
Carrier Air Group [*Navy*] ... CAG
Carrier Air Group [*Canadian military*] ... CANCARAIRGRP
Carrier Air Group [*Navy*] ... CARAIRGROUP
Carrier Air Group ... CARG
Carrier Air Group [*Navy*] (MUGU) ... CVG
Carrier Air Traffic Control ... CATOC
Carrier Air Traffic Control Center [*Navy*] ... CATCC
Carrier Air Traffic Control Center [*Navy*] (DOMA) ... CATCC
Carrier Air Traffic Control Center - Direct Altitude Identity Readout [*Navy*] (MCD) ... CATCC-DAIR
Carrier Air Traffic Control Officer [*Navy*] ... CATCO
Carrier Air Traffic Controller (MCD) ... CATC
Carrier Air Wing [*Navy*] ... CAW
Carrier Air Wing Reserve [*Navy*] ... CAWR
Carrier Airborne Early Warning Squadron [*Navy*] ... CARAEWRON
Carrier Airborne Early Warning Squadron [*Navy symbol*] (NVT) ... VAW
Carrier Airborne Early Warning Training Squadron [*Navy*] (DNAB) ... CARAEWTRARON
Carrier Airborne Early Warning Wing [*Navy*] (NVT) ... CAEWW
Carrier Aircraft (MCD) ... CA
Carrier Aircraft Deck Operations Control System [*Navy*] (NG) ... CADOCS
Carrier Aircraft Equipment ... CAE
Carrier Aircraft [*or Alignment*] **Inertial Navigation System** (MCD) ... CAINS
Carrier Aircraft Maintenance Support Improvement (DNAB) ... CAMSI
Carrier Aircraft Modification (NASA) ... CAM
Carrier Aircraft Operational Compatibility System [*Navy*] ... CAOCS
Carrier Aircraft Service Detachment [*Marine Corps*] ... CASD
Carrier Aircraft Service Division [*Navy*] ... CASD
Carrier Aircraft Service Division [*Navy*] ... CASDIV
Carrier Aircraft Service Unit [*Navy*] ... CASU
Carrier Aircraft Squadron Effectiveness Evaluation ... CASEE
Carrier Aircraft Support Study [*Navy*] (NG) ... CASS
Carrier All-Weather Flying ... CAWF
Carrier and Bit Timing Recovery [*Computer science*] (LAIN) ... CBTR
Carrier and Field Service Unit (NVT) ... CAFSU
Carrier and Sideband (IAA) ... CBS
Carrier and Sideband (DA) ... CSB
Carrier Antisubmarine Air Group [*Navy*] ... COMCARANTISUBAIRGRU
Carrier Antisubmarine Air Group [*Navy*] (NVT) ... CVSG
Carrier Antisubmarine Warfare Group [*Navy*] (DNAB) ... CARANTISUBGRU
Carrier Balloon/Omegasonde System [*National Center for Atmospheric Research*] ... CBO
Carrier Balloon System (MCD) ... CBS
Carrier Battle Group [*Navy*] ... CVBG
Carrier Bombs Light Store [*Military*] (PDAA) ... CBLS
Carrier Color Signal ... CCS
Carrier Common Line [*Telecommunications*] (IT) ... CCL
Carrier Common Line Charge [*Computer science*] (TNIG) ... CCLC
Carrier Controlled Approach [*Aircraft carrier RADAR landing system*] ... CCA
Carrier Corp., Library, Syracuse, NY [*OCLC symbol*] (OCLC) ... ZUE
Carrier Corp., Syracuse, NY [*Library symbol Library of Congress*] (LCLS) ... NSyC
Carrier Current (IAA) ... CC
Carrier Detect [*Electronics*] (ECII) ... CD
Carrier Detector (BUR) ... CD
Carrier Division [*Navy*] ... CARDIV
Carrier Elimination Filter ... CEF
Carrier Evaluation and Reporting System ... CERS
Carrier Frequency [*Radio*] ... CF
Carrier Frequency (IDOE) ... f_c
Carrier Frequency Alarm [*Telecommunications*] (TEL) ... CFA
Carrier Frequency Pulse ... CFP
Carrier Frequency Shift ... CFS
Carrier Frequency Telephone Repeater [*Telecommunications*] ... CRF
Carrier Gas Fusion [*Chemistry*] ... CGF
Carrier Group Alarm [*Telecommunications*] ... CGA
Carrier Identification Code ... CIC
Carrier Input (MSA) ... CIN
Carrier Insertion Oscillator [*Telecommunications*] (EECA) ... CIO
Carrier Instrument Landing System [*Navy*] (CAAL) ... CILS
Carrier Landing-Aid Stabilization System [*Navy*] ... CLASS
Carrier Liaison Committee [*An association*] (EA) ... CLC
Carrier Mills, IL [*FM radio station call letters*] ... WBVN
Carrier Noise Level ... CNL
Carrier of Iron (Ferrum) (MAE) ... Cf
Carrier Onboard Delivery [*Naval aviation*] ... COD
Carrier Overhaul (MCD) ... COH
Carrier Performance Rating (AABC) ... CPR
Carrier Power Supply, Transistorized [*Telecommunications*] (TEL) ... CST
Carrier Qualification [*Navy*] (NG) ... CARQUAL
Carrier Qualification [*Navy*] (CAAL) ... CQ
Carrier Qualification Training Unit ... CQTU
Carrier Removal Rate (PDAA) ... CRR
Carrier Replacement Air Group [*Navy*] ... CRAG
Carrier Replacement Air Wing [*Navy*] ... CRAW
Carrier Return Character [*Computer science*] ... CRC
Carrier Route (WGA) ... CAR-RT
Carrier Route Information System [*Postal Service*] [*United States*] (WDMC) ... CRIS
Carrier Route Sort [*Postal Service*] [*United States*] (WDMC) ... Car-rt-sort
Carrier Route Sort [*Postal Service*] [*United States*] (WDMC) ... CR-RT SORT
Carrier Sense Collision Detection (SSD) ... CSCD
Carrier Sense Multiple Access [*Telecommunications service*] (BARN) ... CSM
Carrier Sense Multiple Access [*Telecommunications*] ... CSMA
Carrier Sense Multiple Access with Collision Avoidance [*Networking technique*] ... CSMA/CA
Carrier Sense Multiple Access with Collision Detection [*Networking technique*] ... CSMA/CD
Carrier Sense Multiple Access with Collision Prevention [*Telecommunications*] (OSI) ... CSMA/CP
Carrier Serving Area [*Telecommunications*] (ACRL) ... CSA
Carrier Stability ... CS
Carrier State ... CARSTAT
Carrier Striking Force [*Tactical Air Command*] (NATG) ... CARSTRIKFOR
Carrier Striking Force [*Tactical Air Command*] ... CSF
Carrier Striking Group [*NATO*] ... CARSTRIKGRU
Carrier Suitability ... CARSUIT
Carrier Suitability (DNAB) ... CS
Carrier Supply (MSA) ... CS
Carrier Suppression Filter (IAA) ... CSF
Carrier System for Control Approach of Naval Aircraft ... C-SCAN
Carrier Tactical Control Zone [*Military*] (NVT) ... CTCZ
Carrier Task Force [*Navy*] ... CARTASKFOR
Carrier Telegraph Receiver ... CTR
Carrier Telephone Channel ... CT
Carrier Terminal Information Services (DNAB) ... CTIS
Carrier Test Switch (IEEE) ... CTS
Carrier Tracking Loop ... CTL
Carrier Transfer Station ... CTS
Carrier Transmission Maintenance System [*Bell System*] ... CTMS
Carrier Vehicle [*Military*] ... CV
Carrier Vessel Reactor ... CVR
Carrier Virtual Circuit [*Telecommunications*] ... CVC
Carrier Wave [*A form of radio transmission in code*] (KSC) ... CRW
Carrier Wave [*A form of radio transmission in code*] ... CW
Carrier Wave Oscillator [*Radio transmission device*] (IAA) ... CWO
Carrier Wave Telegraphy (IAA) ... CWT
Carrier Wave Transmission (IAA) ... CWT
Carrierband MODEM [*Motorola, Inc.*] ... CBM
Carrier-Based ... CB
Carrier-Based Airborne Tactical Control System (SAA) ... CB/ATCS
Carrier-Based Airborne Tactical Data System (MCD) ... CB/ATDS
Carrier-Based Antisubmarine Warfare Module [*Navy*] (CAAL) ... CV-ASWM

Carrier-Based Tactical Support Center [*Navy*] (NVT) .... CVTSC
Carrier-Borne Air Liaison Section [*Navy*] .... CBALS
Carrier-Borne Air Liaison Section [*Navy*] .... CBLS
Carrier-Borne Ground Liaison Officer [*Military British*] .... CBGLO
Carrier-Bound [*Ferrum Iron*] (DAVI) .... CF-Fe
Carrier-Controlled Approach System .... CCAS
Carrier-Controlled Intercept (DNAB) CCI
Carrier-Free [*Radioisotope*] .... CF
Carrier-Free Radar (LAIN) .... CFR
Carrierless Amplitude/Phase Modulation (ACRL) .... CAP
Carrier-on-Deck [*Navy carrier-based aircraft*] .... COD
Carrier-Operated Device, Antinoise [*Radio*] .... CODAN
Carrier-Operated Noise Suppression .... CONS
Carrier-Operated Relay .... COR
Carriers Haulage [*Shipping*] (DS) .... CH
Carriers, Pacific Fleet [*Navy*] .... CARPAC
Carrier's Risk [*Shipping*] .... CR
Carrier's Tax (DLA) .... CT
Carrier's Tax Ruling [*IR Bulletin*] [*A publication*] (DLA) .... CT
Carrier-Specific T-Helper [*Cell*] [*Medicine*] (DMAA) .... CTh
Carrier-to-Interference Ratio [*Computer science*] .... C/I
Carrier-to-Interference Ratio [*Computer science*] .... CIR
Carrier-to-Noise [*Ratio*] .... C/N
Carrier-to-Noise Density .... C/No
Carrier-to-Noise Density, Downlink .... C/No/d
Carrier-to-Noise Density, Intermodulation .... C/No/im
Carrier-to-Noise Density, Total .... C/No/t
Carrier-to-Noise Density, Uplink .... C/No/u
Carrier-to-Noise, Downlink .... C/N/d
Carrier-to-Noise, Intermodulation .... C/N/im
Carrier-to-Noise Ratio [*Telecommunications*] (OSI) .... C/N
Carrier-to-Noise Ratio .... CNR
Carrier-to-Noise Temperature, Downlink .... C/T/d
Carrier-to-Noise Temperature, Intermodulation .... C/T/im
Carrier-to-Noise Temperature, Total .... C/T/t
Carrier-to-Noise Temperature, Uplink .... C/T/u
Carrier-to-Noise, Total .... C/N/t
Carrier-to-Noise, Uplink .... C/N/u
Carries Ampholytes [*Chemistry*] .... CA
Carrigan Industries Ltd. [*Vancouver Stock Exchange symbol*] .... CCG
Carrigan Industries Ltd. [*Vancouver Stock Exchange symbol*] .... CRN
Carrillo [*Costa Rica*] [*ICAO location identifier*] (ICLI) .... MRCR
Carrington and Kirwan's English Nisi Prius Reports [*174, 175 English Reprint*] [*A publication*] (DLA) .... C & K
Carrington and Kirwan's English Nisi Prius Reports [*174, 175 English Reprint*] [*A publication*] (DLA) .... Car & K
Carrington and Kirwan's English Nisi Prius Reports [*174, 175 English Reprint*] [*A publication*] (DLA) .... Car & K (Eng)
Carrington and Kirwan's English Nisi Prius Reports [*174, 175 English Reprint*] [*A publication*] (DLA) .... Car & Kir
Carrington and Marshman's English Nisi Prius Reports [*1840-42*] [*A publication*] (DLA) .... C & M
Carrington and Marshman's English Nisi Prius Reports [*1840-42*] [*A publication*] (DLA) .... C & Mar
Carrington and Marshman's English Nisi Prius Reports [*1840-42*] [*A publication*] (DLA) .... C & Marsh
Carrington and Marshman's English Nisi Prius Reports [*1840-42*] [*A publication*] (DLA) .... Car & M
Carrington and Marshman's English Nisi Prius Reports [*1840-42*] [*A publication*] (DLA) .... Car & M (Eng)
Carrington and Marshman's English Nisi Prius Reports [*1840-42*] [*A publication*] (DLA) .... Car & Mar
Carrington and Marshman's English Nisi Prius Reports [*1840-42*] [*A publication*] (DLA) .... Carr & M
Carrington and Payne's English Nisi Prius Reports [*1823-41*] [*A publication*] (DLA) .... C & P
Carrington and Payne's English Nisi Prius Reports [*1823-41*] [*A publication*] (DLA) .... Car & P
Carrington and Payne's English Nisi Prius Reports [*1823-41*] [*A publication*] (DLA) .... Car & P (Eng)
Carrington Cotton Corporation [*Australia*] CCC
Carrington. Criminal Law [*3rd ed.*] [*1828*] [*A publication*] (DLA) .... Car Cr L
Carrington Laboratories [*NASDAQ symbol*] (TTSB) .... CARN
Carrington Laboratories, Inc. (MHDW) .... CARN
Carrington Labs [*Associated Press*] (SAG) .... Caringtn
Carrington Labs [*NASDAQ symbol*] (SAG) .... CARN
Carrington, ND [*FM radio station call letters*] (RBYB) .... KANG-FM
Carrington, ND [*AM radio station call letters*] .... KDAK
Carrizal [*Costa Rica*] [*ICAO location identifier*] (ICLI) .... MRCZ
Carrizo [*California*] [*Seismograph station code, US Geological Survey*] (SEIS) .... CRR
Carrizo Springs, TX [*Location identifier FAA*] (FAAL) .... CZT
Carrizo Springs, TX [*Location identifier FAA*] (FAAL) .... DMD
Carrizo Springs, TX [*AM radio station call letters*] .... KBEN
Carrizo Springs, TX [*FM radio station call letters*] .... KCZO
Carroll Air Service, Inc. [*ICAO designator*] (FAAC) .... ULS
Carroll Aircraft Corp. PLC [*British ICAO designator*] (FAAC) .... FBO
Carroll Center for the Blind (EA) .... CCB
Carroll College, Helena, MT [*Library symbol Library of Congress*] (LCLS) .... MtHC
Carroll College, Library, Helena, MT [*OCLC symbol*] (OCLC) .... MTC
Carroll College, Waukesha, WI [*OCLC symbol*] (OCLC) .... GZB
Carroll College, Waukesha, WI [*Library symbol Library of Congress*] (LCLS) .... WWauC
Carroll County Comet, Delphi, IN [*Library symbol Library of Congress*] (LCLS) .... InDelCC
Carroll County Heritage Center, Berryville, AR [*Library symbol Library of Congress*] (LCLS) .... ArBerC
Carroll County Historical Museum, Delphi, IN [*Library symbol Library of Congress*] (LCLS) .... InDelCHi
Carroll County Historical Society Museum, Carroll, IA [*Library symbol Library of Congress*] (LCLS) .... IaCarCH
Carroll County Historical Society, Westminister, MD [*Library symbol*] [*Library of Congress*] (LCLS) .... MdWemHi
Carroll County Public Library, Westminster, MD [*Library symbol Library of Congress*] (LCLS) .... MdWem
Carroll County Recorder's Office, Delphi, IN [*Library symbol Library of Congress*] (LCLS) .... InDelCR
Carroll, IA [*Location identifier FAA*] (FAAL) .... CIN
Carroll, IA [*AM radio station call letters*] .... KCIM
Carroll, IA [*FM radio station call letters*] .... KKRL
Carroll, McEntee & McGinley [*Commercial firm*] .... CM & M
Carroll Public Library, Carroll, IA [*Library symbol Library of Congress*] (LCLS) .... IaCar
Carroll Publishing Co. [*Information service or system*] (IID) .... CPC
Carroll Shelby Experimental [*Automobile model*] .... CSX
Carrollton, AL [*FM radio station call letters*] (RBYB) .... WALN
Carrollton, AL [*AM radio station call letters*] .... WRAG
Carrollton, AL [*FM radio station call letters*] (RBYB) .... WZBQ
Carrollton Bancorp [*Associated Press*] (SAG) .... CarrollB
Carrollton Bancorp [*NASDAQ symbol*] (SAG) .... CRRB
Carrollton Community Unit, District 1, Carrollton, IL [*Library symbol Library of Congress*] (LCLS) .... ICarrCD
Carrollton, GA [*Location identifier FAA*] (FAAL) .... CTJ
Carrollton, GA [*Location identifier FAA*] (FAAL) .... GPQ
Carrollton, GA [*FM radio station call letters*] .... WBTR
Carrollton, GA [*AM radio station call letters*] .... WLBB
Carrollton, GA [*AM radio station call letters*] .... WPPI
Carrollton, GA [*FM radio station call letters*] .... WWGC
Carrollton, KY [*FM radio station call letters*] .... WIKI
Carrollton, MI [*FM radio station call letters*] .... WTCF
Carrollton, MO [*AM radio station call letters*] .... KAOL
Carrollton, MO [*FM radio station call letters*] .... KMZU
Carrollton, OH [*Location identifier FAA*] (FAAL) .... TSO
Carrollton Press, Inc., Washington, DC [*Library symbol Library of Congress*] (LCLS) .... CarP
Carrollton Public Library, Carrollton, IL [*Library symbol Library of Congress*] (LCLS) .... ICarr
[*The*] **Carrollton Railroad** [*AAR code*] .... CARR
Carronade .... CAR
Carrot Latent Virus [*Plant pathology*] .... CALV
Carrot Mottle Dwarf Virus .... CMDV
Carrot Mottle Virus [*Plant pathology*] .... CMOTV
Carrot Red Leaf Virus [*Plant pathology*] .... CARLV
Carrot Thin Leaf Virus [*Plant pathology*] .... CTLV
Carrot Yellow Leaf Virus [*Plant pathology*] .... CYLV
Carrots in Oil [*Health food capsules*] [*British*] .... CIO
Carrow and Oliver's English Railway and Canal Cases [*A publication*] (DLA) .... C & OR Cas
Carrow Auditory-Visual Abilities Test .... CAVAT
Carrow Elicited Language Inventory [*Education*] .... CELI
Carrow, Hamerton, and Allen's New Sessions Cases [*1844-51*] [*England*] [*A publication*] (DLA) .... Car H & A
Carrow, Hamerton, and Allen's New Sessions Cases [*1844-51*] [*England*] [*A publication*] (DLA) .... Carr Ham & Al
Carrow, Hamerton, and Allen's New Sessions Cases [*1844-51*] [*England*] [*A publication*] (DLA) .... CH & A
Carrow Test for Auditory Comprehension [*Speech and language pathology*] (DAVI) .... CTAC
Carr-Purcell Spin-Echo .... CPSE
Carr-Purcell-Meiboom-Gill [*Radiologic instrumentation*] .... CPMG
Carry C
Carry .... CA
Carry .... CY
Carry Flag [*Computer science*] (PCM) .... CF
Carry Flip-Flop [*Computer science*] (IAA) .... CFF
Carry Forward [*Accounting*] (MUGU) .... C/F
Carry Lookahead (MHDI) .... CLA
Carry Out Remainder Basic Orders .... CARBASORD
Carry Propagate Adder [*Computer*] .... CPA
Carry Register (NITA) .... CR
Carry Ripple Adder [*Computer science*] (IAA) .... CRA
Carrying (MSA) .... CRYG
Carrying [*Freight*] .... CRYNG
Carrying a Dangerous Weapon [*Police term*] .... CDW
Carrying Capacity (EA) CC
Carrying Capacity [*Genetics*] (DAVI) .... K
Carrying Concealed Deadly Weapon [*Police term*] .... CCDW
Carrying Concealed Weapon [*Police term*] .... CCW
Carrying Nuclear-Strike Cruiser .... CNSC
Carry-On Box .... COB
Carry-On Laboratory [*NASA*] .... COL
Carry-On Oxygen System (MCD) .... COS
Carryover from Previous Log [*Aviation*] (FAAC) .... CFPL
Carry-Save Adder [*Computer science*] (IAA) .... CSA
Cars & Concepts [*Auto industry supplier*] .... C & C
[*The*] **Cars Fan Club** (EA) .... TCFC
Cars of the Past [*An association Defunct*] (EA) .... CP
Carshaltown's Court Rolls [*England*] [*A publication*] (DLA) .... Carsh
Carson and Staughton [*Inventors of a teargas*] (BARN) .... CS
Carson City [*Nevada*] [*Mint mark, when appearing on US coins*] [*Obsolete*] CC

Carson City, NV [*FM radio station call letters*] ... KBUL
Carson City, NV [*FM radio station call letters*] ... KNIS
Carson City, NV [*AM radio station call letters*] ... KPTL
Carson City, NV [*FM radio station call letters*] ... KTHX-FM
Carson City, NV [*FM radio station call letters*] ... KWNZ
Carson City Public Library, Carson City, MI [*Library symbol Library of Congress*] (LCLS) ... MiCc
Carson Gold Corp. [*Vancouver Stock Exchange symbol*] ... CQG
Carson Hill [*California*] [*Seismograph station code, US Geological Survey*] (SEIS) ... CRH
Carson, Inc. [*Associated Press*] (SAG) ... Carson
Carson, Inc. [*NYSE symbol*] (SAG) ... CIC
Carson Pirie Scott [*NYSE symbol*] (TTSB) ... CRP
Carson Pirie Scott & Co. [*Associated Press*] (SAG) ... CarsPir
Carson Pirie Scott & Co. [*NYSE symbol*] (SAG) ... CRP
Carson Times, Carson, IA [*Library symbol Library of Congress*] (LCLS) ... IaCarsT
Carson-Newman College [*Tennessee*] ... CNC
Carson-Newman College, Jefferson City, TN [*OCLC symbol*] (OCLC) ... TCN
Carson-Newman College, Jefferson City, TN [*Library symbol Library of Congress*] (LCLS) ... TJefC
Carson's Rule Bandwidth ... CRBW
CARSTAB Corp., Research Library, Cincinnati, OH [*Library symbol*] [*Library of Congress*] (LCLS) ... OCC
Carstairs Public Library, Alberta [*Library symbol National Library of Canada*] (NLC) ... ACARS
Carswell [*Texas*] [*ICAO location identifier*] (ICLI) ... KAWN
Carta [*Music*] ... CAR
Carta [*Music*] ... CART
Cartage [*Shipping*] ... CART
Cartage ... CTG
Cartage [*Shipping*] ... CTGE
Cartagena [*Colombia*] [*Airport symbol*] (OAG) ... CTG
Cartagena/Rafael Nunez [*Colorado ICAO location identifier*] (ICLI) ... SKCG
Cartago [*Colombia*] [*Airport symbol*] (OAG) ... CRC
Cartago, CA [*FM radio station call letters*] ... KWTY
Carte Blanche [*Credit card*] ... CB
Carte Blanche [*Freedom of Action*] [*French*] ... CBL
Carte de Visite [*Visiting Card*] [*French*] ... C de V
Carte de Visite [*Visiting Card*] [*French*] ... CDV
Carted Luggage (ROG) ... CL
Carte-de-Visite (VRA) ... CDVT
Cartel. Review of Monopoly, Developments, and Consumer Protection [*London, England*] [*A publication*] (DLA) ... Cartel
Cartel Suisse des Associations de Jeunesse [*Switzerland*] ... CSAJ
Carter & Burgess, Inc., Fort Worth, TX [*Library symbol Library of Congress*] (LCLS) ... TxFCB
Carter Family Fan Club (EA) ... CFFC
Carter-Atkinson Lurmann Mechanism [*Air pollution*] ... CAL
Cartercar Registry (EA) ... CR
Carteret Bancorp, Inc. (MHDW) ... CBC
Carteret Technical Institute, Morehead City, NC [*Library symbol Library of Congress*] (LCLS) ... NcMcC
Carter's Adaptation Procesor to Aid Interception (SAA) ... CAPTAIN
Carters Dam [*Georgia*] [*Seismograph station code, US Geological Survey*] (SEIS) ... CDG
Carter's English Common Pleas Reports [*1664-76*] [*A publication*] (DLA) ... Cart
Carter's English Common Pleas Reports Tempore Orlando Bridgman [*A publication*] (DLA) ... Carter
Carter's English Common Pleas Reports Tempore Orlando Bridgman [*A publication*] (DLA) ... Rep T O Br
Carter's Reports [*1, 2 Indiana*] [*A publication*] (DLA) ... Cart
Carter's Reports [*1, 2 Indiana*] [*A publication*] (DLA) ... Carter
Cartersville, GA [*AM radio station call letters*] ... WBHF
Cartersville, GA [*FM radio station call letters*] ... WCCV
Cartersville, GA [*AM radio station call letters*] ... WYXC
Carterville, IL [*FM radio station call letters*] ... WXLT
Carter-Wallace [*NYSE symbol*] (TTSB) ... CAR
Carter-Wallace, Inc. ... C/W
Carter-Wallace, Inc. [*NYSE symbol*] (SPSG) ... CAR
Carter-Wallace, Inc. [*Associated Press*] (SAG) ... CartWal
Cartesian Coordinate Grid (NVT) ... CCG
Cartesian Mapping Function ... CMF
Cartesian to Polar ... C-P
Cartesian-to-Polar Converter (SAA) ... CPC
Carthage ... CARTH
Carthage (VRA) ... Carth
Carthage College, Kenosha, WI [*OCLC symbol*] (OCLC) ... GZC
Carthage College, Kenosha, WI [*Library symbol Library of Congress*] (LCLS) ... WKenC
Carthage, IL [*AM radio station call letters*] ... WCAZ
Carthage, IL [*FM radio station call letters*] ... WCAZ-FM
Carthage, IL [*FM radio station call letters*] (RBYB) ... WZBN
Carthage, MO [*AM radio station call letters*] ... KDMO
Carthage, MO [*FM radio station call letters*] ... KMXL
Carthage, MS [*AM radio station call letters*] ... WSSI
Carthage, MS [*FM radio station call letters*] ... WSSI-FM
Carthage, NY [*FM radio station call letters*] ... WTOJ
Carthage, NY [*Television station call letters*] ... WWNY
Carthage Public Library, Carthage, IL [*Library symbol Library of Congress*] (LCLS) ... ICart
Carthage Public Library, Carthage, SD [*Library symbol Library of Congress*] (LCLS) ... SdCar
Carthage, TN [*AM radio station call letters*] ... WRKM
Carthage, TN [*FM radio station call letters*] ... WUCZ
Carthage, TX [*AM radio station call letters*] ... KGAS
Carthage, TX [*FM radio station call letters*] ... KGAS-FM
Carthage, TX [*FM radio station call letters*] ... KTUX
Carthaginia (ROG) ... CARTH
Carthew's English King's Bench Reports [*1686-1701*] [*A publication*] (DLA) ... Cart
Carthew's English King's Bench Reports [*1686-1701*] [*A publication*] (DLA) ... Carth
Carthew's English King's Bench Reports [*1686-1701*] [*A publication*] (DLA) ... Carth (Eng)
Carthusian ... CARTH
Carti [*Panama*] [*Airport symbol*] (OAG) ... CTE
Cartier Public Library, Ontario [*Library symbol National Library of Canada*] (NLC) ... OCART
Cartier Resources, Inc. [*Toronto Stock Exchange symbol*] ... CTE
Cartilage Induction Factor [*Biochemistry*] (DAVI) ... CIF
Cartilage Matrix Protein [*Medicine*] (DMAA) ... CRTM
Cartilage Oligomeric Matrix Protein [*Biology*] ... COMP
Cartilage Residue [*Orthopedics*] (DAVI) ... CR
Cartilage-Derived Growth Factor [*Biochemistry*] ... CDGF
Cartilage-Derived Inhibitor [*To vascularization*] [*Biochemistry*] ... CDI
Cartilage-Hair Hypoplasia [*Medicine*] (MAE) ... CHH
Carting to Shipside [*Shipping*] ... C to S
Cartmell's Trade Mark Cases [*1876-92*] [*England*] [*A publication*] (DLA) ... Cartm
Cartographer [*or Cartography*] (AFM) ... CRTOG
Cartographer [*Navy rating*] ... CT
Cartographer [*MARC relator code*] [*Library of Congress*] (LCCP) ... ctg
Cartographic and Geodetic Processing Squadron [*Air Force*] (AFM) ... CGPSq
Cartographic Assistant [*Ministry of Agriculture, Fisheries, and Food*] [*British*] ... CA
Cartographic Automatic Mapping (PDAA) ... CAM
Cartographic Conversion Station (MCD) ... CCS
Cartographic Geodetic Squadron [*Air Force*] ... CGEOSq
Cartographic Information Systems Research Group [*Hull University*] [*British*] (NITA) ... CISRG
Cartographic Materials [*International Federation of Library Associations*] ... CM
Cartographic Test Standard [*Air Force*] ... CTS
Cartographic Users Advisory Council [*American Library Association*] ... CUAC
Cartography ... CART
Cartography (MUGU) ... CARTOG
Cartoid Sinus Nerve Stimulation [*Medicine*] (DMAA) ... CSNS
Cartoid Ultrasound [*Neurology*] (CPH) ... CUS
Carton ... C
Carton [*Packaging*] ... CRTN
Carton (MCD) ... CT
Carton ... CTN
Carton (WDMC) ... ctn
Carton Communic ADS [*NASDAQ symbol*] (TTSB) ... CCTVY
Cartoon (VRA) ... crtn
Cartoon Conservation Scales [*Educational test*] ... CCS
Cartoon/Fantasy Organization [*Defunct*] (EA) ... C/FO
Cartoonists Guild (EA) ... CG
Carto-Philatelists (EA) ... CP
Cartophilic Society of Great Britain ... CSGB
Cartotheque, Departement de Geographie, Universite de Montreal, Quebec [*Library symbol National Library of Canada*] (NLC) ... QMUGC
Cartotheque, Departement de Geographie, Universite de Sherbrooke, Quebec [*Library symbol National Library of Canada*] (NLC) ... QSHERUGC
Cartotheque, Departement de Geographie, Universite du Quebec, Trois-Rivieres, Quebec [*Library symbol National Library of Canada*] (NLC) ... QTUGC
Cartotheque, INRS-Urbanisation, Montreal, Quebec [*Library symbol National Library of Canada*] (NLC) ... QMUQIC
Cartotheque, Institut de Geologie, Universite de Montreal, Quebec [*Library symbol National Library of Canada*] (NLC) ... QMUGL
Cartotheque, Universite du Quebec, Chicoutimi, Quebec [*Library symbol National Library of Canada*] (NLC) ... QCUGC
Cartotheque, Universite du Quebec, Montreal, Quebec [*Library symbol National Library of Canada*] (NLC) ... QMUQC
Cartotheque, Universite du Quebec, Rimouski, Quebec [*Library symbol National Library of Canada*] (NLC) ... QRUC
Cartotheque, Universite Laval, Quebec, Quebec [*Library symbol National Library of Canada*] (NLC) ... QQLACA
Cartouche (VRA) ... crtch
Car-Tours in Europe, Inc. ... CTE
Cartridge ... CART
Cartridge (MSA) ... CRTG
Cartridge (AABC) ... CTG
Cartridge Access Controller-to-Update System [*Primary Rate, Inc.*] ... CACTUS
Cartridge Assembly Test (NG) ... CAT
Cartridge Direct Memory Access ... CDMA
Cartridge Disk Unit [*Computer science*] (MHDI) ... CDU
Cartridge Magnetic Tape Unit ... CMTU
Cartridge Module Drive (PDAA) ... CMD
Cartridge Storage Case ... CSC
Cartridge Tape (NTCM) ... CT
Cartridge Tape Unit [*Telecommunications*] (TEL) ... CTU
Cartridge-Actuated Compaction Press (PDAA) ... CACP
Cartridge-Actuated Device [*Military*] (NVT) ... CAD
Cartridge-Actuated Flame System [*Terminated Military*] (MCD) ... CAFS
Cartuja [*Granada*] [*Spain*] [*Seismograph station code, US Geological Survey*] (SEIS) ... CRT
Cartularium Saxonicum [*A publication*] (ILCA) ... Cart Sax
Cartwright, NF [*ICAO location identifier*] (ICLI) ... CYCA
Cartwright Public Library, Newfoundland [*Library symbol National Library of Canada*] (BIB) ... NFCW
Cartwright's Cases [*Canada*] [*A publication*] (DLA) ... Cart Cas (Can)
Cartwright's Cases [*Canada*] [*A publication*] (DLA) ... Cartwr Cas

Cartwright's Cases on the British North America Act [*Canada*] [*A publication*] (DLA) .... Cart
Cartwright's Constitutional Cases [*1868-96*] [*Canada*] [*A publication*] (DLA) .... Cart BNA
Cartwright's Constitutional Cases [*1868-96*] [*Canada*] [*A publication*] (DLA) .... Cartw CC
Carupano [*Venezuela*] [*Airport symbol*] (OAG) .... CUP
Carupano/Gral. en Jefe Jose Francisco Bermudez, Sucre [*Venezuela ICAO location identifier*] (ICLI) .... SVCP
Carus .... K
Carus Chemical Co., Inc., LaSalle, IL [*Library symbol Library of Congress*] (LCLS) .... ILasC
Caruscan Corp. [*Toronto Stock Exchange symbol*] .... CAR
Caruther's History of a Lawsuit. Cases in Chancery [*A publication*] (DLA) .... Car Laws
Caruthersville, MO [*AM radio station call letters*] .... KCRV
Caruthersville, MO [*FM radio station call letters*] .... KLOW
Carved (VRA) .... crv
Carver Corp. [*Associated Press*] (SAG) .... Carver
Carver Corp. [*NASDAQ symbol*] (NQ) .... CAVR
Carver County Library, Chaska, MN [*Library symbol Library of Congress*] (LCLS) .... MnCh
Carver Federal Savings Bank [*Associated Press*] (SAG) .... CarverFS
Carver Federal Svgs Bank [*NASDAQ symbol*] (TTSB) .... CARV
Carver FSB [*NASDAQ symbol*] (SAG) .... CARV
Carver, J. C., Neptune NJ [*STAC*] .... CJC
Carver's Treatise on the Law Relating to the Carriage of Goods by Sea [*1885-1957*] [*A publication*] (DLA) .... Carv Carr
Carver's Treatise on the Law Relating to the Carriage of Goods by Sea [*1885-1957*] [*A publication*] (DLA) .... Carver
Carwash Operators Association (EA) .... COA
Carworth Farm Mice (Webster strain) [*Research*] (DAVI) .... CFWM
Carworth Farm Mouse, Webster Strain [*Medicine*] (DMAA) .... CFW
Cary Memorial Library, Lexington, MA [*OCLC symbol*] (OCLC) .... LEX
Cary Memorial Library, Lexington, MA [*Library symbol Library of Congress*] (LCLS) .... MLex
Cary on Juries [*A publication*] (DLA) .... Cary Jur
Cary. Partnership [*1827*] [*A publication*] (ILCA) .... Cary Part
Carya cardioformis [*Butternut hickory tree*] Cc
Carya glabra [*Pignut hickory*] .... Cg
Carya ovata [*Shagbark hickory*] .... Co
Carya pecan [*Pecan tree*] .... Cp
Caryatid (VRA) .... crytd
Cary's Commentary on Littleton's Tenures [*A publication*] (DLA) .... Cary Lit
Cary's English Chancery Reports [*1537-1604*] [*A publication*] (DLA) .... Cary
Carzinophilin [*Antineoplastic drug*] (DAVI) .... CZ
CASA [*Construcciones Aeronauticas Sociedad Anonima*] [*Spain ICAO aircraft manufacturer identifier*] (ICAO) .... HA
Casa Editrice Dott. A. Milani [*Italian publisher*] .... CEDAM
Casa El Salvador (EA) .... CES
Casa Grande, AZ [*Location identifier FAA*] (FAAL) .... CGZ
Casa Grande, AZ [*Location identifier FAA*] (FAAL) .... CZG
Casa Grande, AZ [*AM radio station call letters*] .... KFAS
Casa Grande, AZ [*FM radio station call letters*] (RBYB) .... KLVA
Casa Grande, AZ [*AM radio station call letters*] .... KWLL
Casa Grande Engineering & Mines [*Vancouver Stock Exchange symbol*] .... CGZ
Casa Grande Public Library, Casa Grande, AZ [*Library symbol Library of Congress*] (LCLS) .... AzCg
Casa Grande Ruins National Monument [*National Park Service designation*] .... CAGR
Casa Ole Restaurants, Inc. [*NASDAQ symbol*] (SAG) .... CASA
Casa Ole Restaurants, Inc. [*Associated Press*] (SAG) .... CasaOle
Casa Ole-Restaurants [*NASDAQ symbol*] (TTSB) .... CASA
Casablanca [*Morocco*] [*Airport symbol*] (OAG) .... CAS
Casablanca [*Morocco*] [*ICAO location identifier*] (ICLI) .... GMMM
Casablanca/ANFA [*Morocco*] [*ICAO location identifier*] (ICLI) .... GMMC
Casablanca/Mohamed V [*Morocco*] [*ICAO location identifier*] (ICLI) .... GMMN
Casablanca/Tit-Mellil [*Morocco*] [*ICAO location identifier*] (ICLI) .... GMMT
Casablanca-Mohamed V [*Morocco*] [*Airport symbol*] (OAG) .... CMN
Casamari [*Italy*] [*Seismograph station code, US Geological Survey Closed*] (SEIS) .... CAS
Casamicciolo [*Isola D'Ischia*] [*Italy*] [*Seismograph station code, US Geological Survey*] [*Closed*] (SEIS) .... CSM
Casamino Acids [*Biochemistry*] .... CAA
Casanova, VA [*Location identifier FAA*] (FAAL) .... CSN
Casau Explorations Ltd. [*Vancouver Stock Exchange symbol*] .... CUX
Cascade (MSA) .... CAS
Cascade .... CASC
Cascade [*Meteorology*] (FAAC) .... CASCD
Cascade Access Method [*Computer science*] (NITA) .... CAM
Cascade Activity Numbering (PDAA) .... CAN
Cascade Airways [*ICAO designator*] (AD) .... CZ
Cascade Amplifier (DEN) .... CA
Cascade Bancorp [*NASDAQ symbol*] (SAG) .... CACB
Cascade Bancorp [*Associated Press*] (SAG) .... CascBcp
Cascade Charge Coupled Device [*Electronics*] C3D
Cascade College, Portland, OR [*Library symbol Library of Congress*] (LCLS) .... OrPC
Cascade Communications [*Associated Press*] (SAG) .... CascCm
Cascade Communications [*NASDAQ symbol*] (SAG) .... CSCC
Cascade Corp. [*NYSE symbol*] (SAG) .... CAE
Cascade Corp. [*NASDAQ symbol*] (NQ) .... CASC
Cascade Corp. [*Associated Press*] (SAG) .... Cascde
Cascade Corp. [*Associated Press*] (SAG) .... CascdeCp
Cascade Filtration [*Medicine*] (DMAA) .... CF
Cascade Financial Corp [*Washington*] [*Associated Press*] (SAG) .... CascFin
Cascade Financial Corp. [*Washington*] [*NASDAQ symbol*] (SAG) .... CASB
Cascade Holistic Economic Consultants (EA) .... CHEC
Cascade Impactor Data Reduction System [*Environmental Protection Agency*] (GFGA) .... CIDRS
Cascade Improvement Program [*AEC*] .... CIP
Cascade Junior High School, Bend, OR [*Library symbol*] [*Library of Congress*] (LCLS) .... OrBeCJ
Cascade Locks, OR [*Location identifier FAA*] (FAAL) .... CZK
Cascade Microfilm Systems, Inc., Portland, OR [*Library symbol Library of Congress*] (LCLS) .... CmI
Cascade Natural Gas [*NYSE symbol*] (TTSB) .... CGC
Cascade Natural Gas Corp. [*Associated Press*] (SAG) .... CascNG
Cascade Natural Gas Corp. [*NYSE symbol*] (SPSG) .... CGC
Cascade Nozzle [*Aviation*] (OA) .... CN
Cascade Orificial Restrictive Device (MCD) .... CORD
Cascade Pioneer-Advertiser, Cascade, IA [*Library symbol Library of Congress*] (LCLS) .... IaCasPA
Cascade Public Library, Cascade, ID [*Library symbol*] [*Library of Congress*] (LCLS) .... IdCs
Cascade Uprating Program [*AEC*] .... CUP
Cascade Variable Conductance Heat Pipe (PDAA) .... CVCHP
Cascade-Failure Analysis (IEEE) .... CFA
Cascades [*NWS*] (FAAC) .... CASDS
Cascades, Inc. [*Toronto Stock Exchange symbol*] .... CAS
Cascades Volcano Observatory [*US Geological Survey*] .... CVO
Cascadia Juvenile Diagnostic Center, Tacoma, WA [*Library symbol Library of Congress*] (LCLS) .... WaTCJ
Cascadia Mines [*Vancouver Stock Exchange symbol*] .... CAC
Cascading Style Sheets [*Computer science*] .... CSS
Cascading Stylesheets [*Computer science*] .... CSS
Cascais [*Portugal ICAO location identifier*] (ICLI) .... LPCS
Cascara [*A cathartic*] [*Pharmacy*] (DAVI) .... casc
Cascavel [*Brazil*] [*Airport symbol*] (OAG) .... CAC
Cascavel [*Brazil ICAO location identifier*] (ICLI) .... SBCA
Case C
Case [*Legal term*] (ILCA) .... Ca
Case .... CS
Case (WDMC) .... cs
Case Aide [*Red Cross*] .... CA
Case Assignment Control File [*IRS*] .... CACF
Case at Bar [*Legal shorthand*] (LWAP) .... CAB
Case Center for Complex Flow Measurements [*Case Western Reserve University*] [*Research center*] (RCD) C3FM
Case Center for Electrochemical Sciences [*Case Western Reserve University*] [*Research center*] (RCD) .... CCES
Case Collectors Club (EA) CCC
Case Copy [*Computer science*] .... CY
Case Corp. [*Formerly, Case Equipment*] [*Associated Press*] (SAG) .... CaseCp
Case Corp. [*Formerly, Case Equipment*] [*NYSE symbol*] (SAG) .... CSE
CASE [*Computer-Aided Software Engineering*] **Data Interchange Format** (CDE) .... CDIF
Case Data System [*Computer science*] (PDAA) .... CDS
Case Development Inspection .... CDI
Case Fatality Ratio [*Medicine*] .... CFR
Case Handling Information Processing System [*National Labor Relations Board*] .... CHIPS
Case Harden [*Metal*] [*Technical drawings*] .... CH
Case Informant [*Criminology*] (LAIN) CI
Case Institute of Technology [*Later, Case Western Reserve University*] [*Ohio*] .... CIT
Case Makers Association [*British*] (DBA) .... CMA
Case Management Organization (WYGK) .... CMO
Case Management System [*Department of Justice*] (GFGA) .... CMS
Case Mix Grouping .... CMG
Case Monitoring [*Air Force*] (AFIT) .... CM
Case Of (AAG) .... C/O
Case of Need .... CN
Case of the City of Chester on Quo Warranto [*A publication*] (DLA) .... Chest Ca
Case Officer [*Criminology*] (LAIN) .... CO
Case Oil .... C/O
Case on Appeal (DLA) .... AC
Case Packaging [*Shipping*] (DS) C
Case Postale (DD) .... CP
Case Preparation .... CP
Case Project [*IRS*] .... C/P
Case Project Master File [*IRS*] .... CPMF
Case Review Section [*Social Security Administration*] (OICC) .... CRS
Case Study and Justification Folder .... CSJF
Case Supervisor [*Red Cross*] [*Services to the Armed Forces; Disaster Services*] .... CS
Case Western Reserve University (GAGS) .... Case West Res U
Case Western Reserve University [*Cleveland, OH*] .... CWRU
Case Western Reserve University, Cleveland Health Sciences Library, Cleveland, OH [*Library symbol Library of Congress*] (LCLS) .... OCIW-H
Case Western Reserve University, Cleveland, OH [*OCLC symbol*] (OCLC) .... CWR
Case Western Reserve University, Cleveland, OH [*Library symbol Library of Congress*] (LCLS) .... OCIW
Case Western Reserve University Law Library, Cleveland, OH [*OCLC symbol*] (OCLC) .... CWL
Case Western Reserve University, Law Library, Cleveland, OH [*Library symbol*] [*Library of Congress*] (LCLS) .... OCIW-L
Case Western Reserve University, School of Applied Social Science, Cleveland, OH [*Library symbol Library of Congress*] (LCLS) .... OCIW-SS

Case Western Reserve University, School of Library Science, Cleveland, OH [*Library symbol Library of Congress*] (LCLS) .... OCIW-LS
Case Western Reserve University, Sears Library, Cleveland, OH [*Library symbol Library of Congress*] (LCLS) .... OCIW-S
Case-Based Reasoning .... CBR
Cased Telescoped [*Type of ammunition*] (DOMA) .... CT
Case-Halstead Library, Carlyle, IL [*Library symbol Library of Congress*] (LCLS) .... ICarly
Casein .... CAS
Casein (VRA) .... cas
Casein Glue Manufacturers Association [*British*] (BI) .... CGMA
Casein Hydrolyzate [*Cell growth medium*] .... CH
Casein Importers Association (EA) .... CIA
Casein Kinase (DMAA) .... CSNK
Casein Plastic [*Organic chemistry*] .... CS
Casein Yeast Lactate [*Media*] [*Biochemistry*] (DAVI) .... CYL
Caseinomacropeptide [*Biochemistry*] .... CMP
Caseless Ammunition Aerial Gun System (MCD) .... CAAGS
Caseless Round Gun Program [*Military*] (MCD) .... CRGP
Casement [*Technical drawings*] .... CSMT
Casement Aviation [*ICAO designator*] (FAAC) .... CMT
Casement Projected Transom [*Technical drawings*] .... CPT
Case-Mix Index [*Medicare*] (DHSM) .... CMI
Case-Oriented Studies Information Retrieval System [*Later, TISCA*] [*Navy*] .... COSIRS
Caserio .... CA
Cases and Cabinets [*JETDS nomenclature*] [*Military*] (CET) .... CY
Cases and Opinions in Law, Equity, and Conveyancing [*A publication*] (DLA) .... Cas Eq
Cases and Resolutions (of Settlements; not Holt's King's Bench Reports) [*England*] [*A publication*] (DLA) .... Cas BR Holt
Cases Argued and Decreed in Chancery, English [*A publication*] (DLA) .... Cas Arg & Dec
Cases at Nisi Prius [*A publication*] (DLA) .... CNP
Cases at the End of Popham's Reports [*A publication*] (DLA) .... Poph (2)
Cases Banco Regis Tempore William III [*12 Modern Reports*] [*A publication*] (DLA) .... Cas BR
Cases in Chancery [*England*] [*A publication*] (DLA) .... Cas Ch
Cases in Chancery [*England*] [*A publication*] (DLA) .... Cas in C
Cases in Chancery [*England*] [*A publication*] (DLA) .... Cas in Ch
Cases in Chancery [*England*] [*A publication*] (DLA) CC
Cases in Chancery [*England*] [*A publication*] (DLA) .... Ch Ca
Cases in Chancery [*England*] [*A publication*] (DLA) .... Ch Cas
Cases in Chancery [*England*] [*A publication*] (DLA) .... Ch Cas (Eng)
Cases in Chancery [*England*] [*A publication*] (DLA) .... Chan Cas
Cases in Chancery Tempore Car. II [*A publication*] (DLA) .... Cas Ch 1 2 3
Cases in Chancery Tempore George II [*England*] [*A publication*] (DLA) .... Temp Geo II
Cases in Chancery Tempore King [*25 English Reprint*] [*1724-33*] [*A publication*] (DLA) .... Ca Temp King
Cases in Chancery Tempore King, King's Bench [*1724-33*] [*England*] [*A publication*] (DLA) .... Ca Temp K
Cases in Chancery Tempore Plunkett [*1834-39*] [*Ireland*] [*A publication*] (DLA) .... Ca T Plunk
Cases in Chancery Tempore Talbot, King's Bench [*1734-38*] [*England*] [*A publication*] (DLA) .... Ca Temp Talb
Cases in Crown Law [*England*] [*A publication*] (DLA) .... Cas CL
Cases in Equity Abridged [*1667-1744*] [*England*] [*A publication*] (DLA) .... Cas Eq Abr
Cases in Equity, Gilbert's Reports [*A publication*] (DLA) .... Cas Eq
Cases in Gold Coast Law [*A publication*] (DLA) .... Danquah
Cases in King's Bench [*7-10 George II Tempore*] [*A publication*] (DLA) .... Ann
Cases in King's Bench [*8 Modern Reports*] [*England*] [*A publication*] (DLA) .... Cas KB
Cases in King's Bench Tempore Hardwicke [*1733-38*] [*England*] [*A publication*] (DLA) .... BRH
Cases in King's Colorado Civil Practice [*A publication*] (DLA) .... King Cas
Cases in Law and Equity [*10 Modern Reports*] [*A publication*] (DLA) .... Ca T Mac
Cases in Law and Equity [*10 Modern Reports*] [*A publication*] (DLA) .... Cas L Eq
Cases in Parliament [*A publication*] (DLA) .... Ca P
Cases in Parliament [*A publication*] (DLA) .... Cas P
Cases in Parliament [*A publication*] (DLA) .... Cas Parl
Cases in Parliament (Shower) [*1694-99*] [*A publication*] (DLA) .... Ca Parl
Cases in the Eastern District's Local Division of the Supreme Court [*1910-46*] [*South Africa*] [*A publication*] (DLA) .... E
Cases in the Griqualand West Local Division of the Supreme Court [*1910-46*] [*South Africa*] [*A publication*] (DLA) .... GLD
Cases in the Griqualand West Local Division of the Supreme Court [*1910-46*] [*South Africa*] [*A publication*] (DLA) .... GW
Cases in the House of Lords [*England*] [*A publication*] (DLA) .... Cas HL
Cases in the Supreme Court, Cape Of Good Hope [*A publication*] (DLA) .... Cas SC (Cape GH)
Cases of Appeal to the House of Lords [*A publication*] (DLA) .... Cas App
Cases of Contested Elections [*A publication*] (DLA) .... C of CE
Cases of Contested Elections [*A publication*] (DLA) .... CCE
Cases of Practice, English Common Pleas [*Cooke's Reports*] [*A publication*] (DLA) .... Cas Pr CP
Cases of Practice, English Common Pleas [*1702-27*] [*A publication*] (DLA) .... Cas Pra CP
Cases of Practice, English Common Pleas [*1702-27*] [*A publication*] (DLA) .... Cas Prac CP
Cases of Practice, English King's Bench [*A publication*] (DLA) .... Cas Pr
Cases of Practice, English King's Bench [*A publication*] (DLA) .... Cas Pr KB
Cases of Practice, English King's Bench [*A publication*] (DLA) .... Cas Pra KB
Cases of Practice, English King's Bench [*A publication*] (DLA) .... Cas Prac KB
Cases of Settlement, King's Bench [*1713-15*] [*England*] [*A publication*] (DLA) .... Cas SM
Cases of Settlements and Removals [*1710-42*] [*England*] [*A publication*] (DLA) .... Ca Sett
Cases of Settlements and Removals [*1710-42*] [*England*] [*A publication*] (DLA) .... Cas Sett
Cases on the Six Circuits [*1841-43*] [*Ireland*] [*A publication*] (DLA) .... Cas Six Cir
Cases on the Six Circuits [*1841-43*] [*Ireland*] [*A publication*] (DLA) .... Six Circ
Cases per Officer [*Term used by crime laboratories*] .... CPO
Cases Taken and Adjudged [*First Edition of Reports in Chancery*] [*England*] [*A publication*] (DLA) .... Cas Tak & Adj
Cases Temporary [*Legal term British*] .... CAT
Cases Tempore Charles 2 [*A publication*] (DLA) .... Ca T Ch 2
Cases Tempore Charles II [*A publication*] (DLA) .... Cas T Ch II
Cases Tempore Finch, English Chancery [*1673-81*] [*23 English Reprint*] [*A publication*] (DLA) .... Ca Temp F
Cases Tempore Finch, English Chancery [*1673-81*] [*23 English Reprint*] [*A publication*] (DLA) .... Cas T F
Cases Tempore Finch, English Chancery [*1673-81*] [*23 English Reprint*] [*A publication*] (DLA) .... Cas T Finch (Eng)
Cases Tempore Finch, English Chancery [*1673-81*] [*23 English Reprint*] [*A publication*] (DLA) .... Cas Temp F
Cases Tempore Finch, English Chancery [*1673-81*] [*23 English Reprint*] [*A publication*] (DLA) .... Rept T Finch
Cases Tempore George I, English Chancery [*8, 9 Modern Reports*] [*A publication*] (DLA) .... Cas T Geo I
Cases Tempore Hardwicke [*A publication*] (DLA) .... Cas Temp Hardw
Cases Tempore Hardwicke, by Lee [*England*] [*A publication*] (DLA) .... Cas T Hard by Lee
Cases Tempore Hardwicke, by Lee [*England*] [*A publication*] (DLA) .... Hardw
Cases Tempore Hardwicke, by Lee [*England*] [*A publication*] (DLA) .... Hardw (Eng)
Cases Tempore Hardwicke, by Lee and Hardwicke [*A publication*] (DLA) .... Hardw Cas Temp
Cases Tempore Hardwicke, by Ridgeway [*England*] [*A publication*] (DLA) .... Hardw
Cases Tempore Hardwicke, by Ridgeway [*England*] [*A publication*] (DLA) .... Hardw (Eng)
Cases Tempore Hardwicke, English King's Bench [*95 English Reprint*] [*1733-38*] [*A publication*] (DLA) .... Ca T Hard
Cases Tempore Hardwicke, English King's Bench [*95 English Reprint*] [*1733-38*] [*A publication*] (DLA) .... Ca Temp H
Cases Tempore Hardwicke, English King's Bench [*95 English Reprint*] [*1733-38*] [*A publication*] (DLA) .... Ca Temp Hard
Cases Tempore Hardwicke, English King's Bench [*95 English Reprint*] [*1733-38*] [*A publication*] (DLA) .... Ca TH
Cases Tempore Hardwicke, English King's Bench [*95 English Reprint*] [*1733-38*] [*A publication*] (DLA) .... Cas Temp H
Cases Tempore Hardwicke, English King's Bench (Ridgway, Lee, or Annaly) [*1733-38*] [*A publication*] (DLA) .... Cas T H
Cases Tempore Hardwicke, English King's Bench (Ridgway, Lee, or Annaly) [*1733-38*] [*A publication*] (DLA) .... Cas T Hardw
Cases Tempore Hardwicke (W. Kelynge's English King's Bench Reports) [*A publication*] (DLA) .... Cas KBT Hard
Cases Tempore Hardwicke (W. Kelynge's English King's Bench Reports) [*A publication*] (DLA) .... Cas KBTH
Cases Tempore Holt [*11 Modern Reports*] [*88 English Reprint 1702-10*] [*A publication*] (DLA) .... Ca T Holt
Cases Tempore Holt [*11 Modern Reports*] [*88 English Reprint 1702-10*] [*A publication*] (DLA) .... Ca T QA
Cases Tempore Holt [*11 Modern Reports*] [*88 English Reprint 1702-10*] [*A publication*] (DLA) .... Ca TH
Cases Tempore Holt, English King's Bench [*A publication*] (DLA) .... Ca Temp Holt
Cases Tempore Holt, English King's Bench [*A publication*] (DLA) .... Cas T H
Cases Tempore Holt, English King's Bench [*A publication*] (DLA) .... Cas T Holt
Cases Tempore Holt, English King's Bench [*A publication*] (DLA) .... Rept T Holt
Cases Tempore King, Chancery [*A publication*] (DLA) .... Ca T King
Cases Tempore King, Chancery [*A publication*] (DLA) .... Ca TK
Cases Tempore King, Chancery [*A publication*] (DLA) .... CTK
Cases Tempore Lee [*1752-58*] [*A publication*] (DLA) .... Ca T Lee
Cases Tempore Lee (English Ecclesiastical) [*A publication*] (DLA) .... Cas Temp Lee
Cases Tempore Macclesfield [*10 Modern Reports*] [*1710-25 England*] [*A publication*] (DLA) .... Cas T Mac
Cases Tempore Macclesfield [*10 Modern Reports*] [*1710-25 England*] [*A publication*] (DLA) .... Cas T Maccl
Cases Tempore Northington [*Eden's English Chancery Reports*] [*A publication*] (DLA) .... CTN
Cases Tempore Queen Anne [*11 Modern Reports*] [*1702-30 England*] [*A publication*] (DLA) .... Cas T Q Anne
Cases Tempore Queen Anne [*11 Modern Reports*] [*1702-30 England*] [*A publication*] (DLA) .... Cas T QA
Cases Tempore Sugden, Irish Chancery [*A publication*] (DLA) .... Cas T Sugd
Cases Tempore Talbot [*A publication*] (DLA) .... Ca Temp Talbot
Cases Tempore Talbot [*A publication*] (DLA) .... Cas T Talb
Cases Tempore Talbot [*A publication*] (DLA) .... Cas Temp Talb
Cases Tempore Talbot, English Chancery [*1734-38*] [*A publication*] (DLA) .... C T T
Cases Tempore Talbot, English Chancery [*1734-38*] [*A publication*] (DLA) .... Ca T Talb
Cases Tempore Talbot, English Chancery [*1734-38*] [*A publication*] (DLA) .... Cas T Tal
Cases Tempore Talbot, English Chancery [*1734-38*] [*A publication*] (DLA) .... Tal
Cases Tempore Talbot, English Chancery [*1734-38*] [*A publication*] (DLA) .... Talb
Cases Tempore Talbot, English Chancery (Forrester) [*A publication*] (DLA) .... Cas FT

Cases Tempore William 3 [*12 Modern Reports*] [*A publication*] (DLA) .... Ca T Wm 3
Cases Tempore William III [*12 Modern Reports*] [*A publication*] (DLA) .... Cas CR
Cases Tempore William III [*12 Modern Reports*] [*A publication*] (DLA) .... Cas T Wm III
Cases under Sugden's Act [*1838*] [*England*] [*A publication*] (DLA) .... Cooke
Cases with Opinions by Eminent Counsel [*1700-75*] [*A publication*] (DLA) .... Cas w Op
Casework [*or Caseworker*] .... CW
Casework Supervisor [*Red Cross*] .... CWS
Casey [*Australia Geomagnetic observatory code*] .... CSY
Casey Community Unit School District, Casey, IL [*Library symbol*] [*Library of Congress*] (LCLS) .... ICasSD
Casey, IL [*Location identifier FAA*] (FAAL) .... CZB
Casey, IL [*FM radio station call letters*] .... WCBH
Casey, IL [*AM radio station call letters*] .... WKZI
Casey Jones Railroad Unit (EA) .... CJRRU
Casey Township Library, Casey, IL [*Library symbol Library of Congress*] (LCLS) .... ICas
Casey's General Stores, Inc. [*Associated Press*] (SAG) .... Caseys
Casey's General Stores, Inc. [*NASDAQ symbol*] (NQ) .... CASY
Casey's Reports [*25-36 Pennsylvania*] [*A publication*] (DLA) .... Cas
Casey's Reports [*25-36 Pennsylvania*] [*A publication*] (DLA) .... Cas R
Casey's Reports [*25-36 Pennsylvania*] [*A publication*] (DLA) .... Casey
Caseyville Public Library, Caseyville, IL [*Library symbol Library of Congress*] (LCLS) .... ICasv
Cash [*Stock exchange term*] (SPSG) C
Cash (DCTA) .... CSH
Cash Account [*Banking*] .... CA
Cash Advance (DCTA) .... CADV
Cash Against Disbursement [*Sales*] (MHDW) .... CAD
Cash Against Documents [*Sales*] (ADA) .... C/D
Cash Against Documents [*Sales*] .... CAD
Cash Against Policy [*Insurance*] .... CAP
Cash Amer Intl [*NYSE symbol*] (TTSB) .... PWN
Cash America International, Inc. [*Associated Press*] (SAG) .... CashAm
Cash America International, Inc. [*NYSE symbol*] (SPSG) .... PWN
Cash and Carry (IIA) .... C & C
Cash before Delivery .... CBD
Cash Book .... CB
Cash by Return Mail [*Business term*] (IAA) .... CBRM
Cash by Return Mail [*Business term*] .... CRM
Cash by Return Steamer [*Business term*] .... CRS
Cash Clothing Allowance .... CCA
Cash Collection Voucher CCV
Cash Commodity [*Business term*] CC
Cash Concentration and Disbursement .... CCD
Cash Credit [*British*] CC
Cash Disbursements Journal [*Accounting*] .... CDJ
Cash Discount [*Sales*] .... CD
Cash Discount (WDMC) .... cd
Cash Dispenser [*Banking*] (BUR) .... CD
Cash Dispensing Machine [*Banking*] .... CDM
Cash Earnings [*Business term*] .... CE
Cash Flow .... CF
Cash Flow Component .... CFC
Cash Flow Return on Investment .... CFROI
Cash Free America [*An association*] (EA) .... CFA
Cash in Advance .... CIA
Cash in Fist .... CIF
Cash Index Participation [*Investment term*] (DFIT) .... CIP
Cash Item [*Accounting*] CI
Cash Letter [*Banking*] .... C/L
Cash Management Account [*Merrill Lynch*] .... CMA
Cash Management Institute (EA) .... CMI
Cash Management Practitioners Association [*Later, NCCMA*] (EA) .... CMPA
Cash Management System (IAA) .... CMS
Cash Management Trust (ADA) .... CMT
Cash [*or Collect*] **on Delivery** [*Business term*] .... COD
Cash on Delivery Service .... CDS
Cash on Receipt .... COR
Cash On Receipt (WDMC) .... cor
Cash Operating Profits after Tax (DICI) .... COPAT
Cash or Deferred Arrangement .... CODA
Cash Order [*Business term*] .... CO
Cash Order (WDMC) .... co
Cash Purchasing Agent (AFM) .... CPA
Cash Receipts Journal [*Accounting*] .... CRJ
Cash Register Tape .... CRT
Cash Reserve [*Business term*] .... CR
Cash Sale [*Business term*] (ADA) .... C/S
Cash Surrender Value [*Insurance*] .... Csv
Cash Surrender Value of Life Insurance .... CSVLI
Cash Terminals Systems [*Commercial firm*] (NITA) .... CTS
Cash Trade [*Investment term*] .... CT
Cash Transaction Report [*Finance*] .... CTR
Cash Value Life Insurance CVLI
Cash Versus Documents .... CVD
Cash with Order [*Business term*] .... CWO
Cashel [*City in Ireland*] (ROG) .... CASH
Cashel Mercy Sisters (TOCD) .... CMS
Cashew Nutshell Liquid .... CNSL
Cash-Flow Accounting .... CFA
Cashier (ROG) .... CAS
Cashier .... CAS
Cashier .... CASH
Cashier .... CASHR
Cashier and Accountant [*British*] (ROG) .... CA
Cashiers' Automatic Processing System (DIT) .... CAPS
Cashier's Check CC
Cashmere (VRA) .... cashm
Cashmere, WA [*FM radio station call letters*] .... KZPH
Cash-on-Hand [*Banking*] (MHDW) .... COH
Cash-on-Shipment .... COS
Cash-To-Futures Basis [*Business term*] (EMRF) .... CFB
Cashtown, PA [*AM radio station call letters*] .... WFKJ
Casigua [*Venezuela*] [*Airport symbol*] (AD) .... CUV
Casimir, Jennings, and Appleby Public Library, St. Charles, Ontario [*Library symbol National Library of Canada*] (NLC) .... OSCCJA
Casina [*of Plautus*] [*Classical studies*] (OCD) .... Cas
Casing (WGA) .... CAS
Casing (KSC) .... CSG
Casing Cooling Tank Level (IEEE) .... CCTL
Casino [*Australia Airport symbol*] (OAG) .... CSI
Casino Advisory Committee [*Tasmania*] [*Australia*] .... CAC
Casino America [*NASDAQ symbol*] (TTSB) .... CSNO
Casino America, Inc. [*Associated Press*] (SAG) .... CasinoAm
Casino America, Inc. [*NASDAQ symbol*] (SAG) .... CSNO
Casino Chips and Gaming Tokens Collectors Club (EA) .... CC & GTCC
Casino Data Systems [*Commercial firm Associated Press*] (SAG) .... CasinoD
Casino Data Systems [*NASDAQ symbol*] (SAG) .... CSDS
Casino Magic [*NASDAQ symbol*] (TTSB) .... CMAG
Casino Magic Corp. [*Associated Press*] (SAG) .... CasMagic
Casino Magic Corp. [*NASDAQ symbol*] (SAG) .... CMAG
Casino Resource [*NASDAQ symbol*] (TTSB) .... CSNR
Casino Resource Corp. [*Associated Press*] (SAG) .... CasnRsc
Casino Resource Corp. [*Associated Press*] (SAG) .... CasRs
Casino Resource Corp. [*NASDAQ symbol*] (SAG) .... CSNR
Casino Resource Wrrt 'A' [*NASDAQ symbol*] (TTSB) .... CSNRW
Casino Silver Mines [*Vancouver Stock Exchange symbol*] .... CSV
Casinos Czechoslovakia (ECON) CC
Casitas Dam [*California*] [*Seismograph station code, US Geological Survey*] (SEIS) .... BCD
Casitas Lake [*California*] [*Seismograph station code, US Geological Survey Closed*] (SEIS) .... BCL
Cask .... CK
Cask .... CSK
Cask Decontamination Pit [*Nuclear energy*] (NRCH) .... CDP
Cask Decontamination Station [*Nuclear energy*] (NRCH) .... CDS
Cask Loading Station [*Nuclear energy*] (NRCH) .... CLS
Cask Support Structure [*Nuclear energy*] (NRCH) .... CSS
Cask Tilting Fixture [*Nuclear energy*] (NRCH) .... CTF
Cask Transfer Tunnels [*Nuclear energy*] (NRCH) .... CTT
Cask Unloading Cell [*Nuclear energy*] (NRCH) .... CUC
Cask Unloading Pool [*Nuclear energy*] (NRCH) .... CUP
Cask Unloading Warm Shop [*Nuclear energy*] (NRCH) .... CUWS
Casket .... CSKT
Casket Manufacturers Association of America (EA) .... CMA
Casks .... CSKS
Caslan Public Library, Alberta [*Library symbol National Library of Canada*] (NLC) .... ACAS
Caslan Public Library, Caslan, AB, Canada [*Library symbol*] [*Library of Congress*] (LCLS) .... CaACas
Caslon Old Face [*Typeface*] (DGA) .... COF
Casma [*Peru*] [*ICAO location identifier*] (ICLI) .... SPSA
Casomorphin [*Biochemistry*] .... CM
Caspair Ltd. [*Kenya*] [*ICAO designator*] (FAAC) .... SAL
Casper [*Wyoming*] [*Airport symbol*] (OAG) .... CPR
Casper Air Service, Inc. [*ICAO designator*] (FAAC) .... CSP
Casper College, Casper, WY [*Library symbol Library of Congress*] (LCLS) .... WyCaC
Casper, WY [*Location identifier FAA*] (FAAL) .... CPR
Casper, WY [*Location identifier FAA*] (FAAL) .... HAD
Casper, WY [*FM radio station call letters*] (RBYB) .... KASS
Casper, WY [*FM radio station call letters*] .... KCSP
Casper, WY [*Television station call letters*] .... KFNB
Casper, WY [*Television station call letters*] .... KGWC
Casper, WY [*FM radio station call letters*] .... KMGW
Casper, WY [*FM radio station call letters*] .... KQLT
Casper, WY [*FM radio station call letters*] .... KTRS
Casper, WY [*AM radio station call letters*] .... KTWO
Casper, WY [*Television station call letters*] .... KTWO-TV
Casper, WY [*AM radio station call letters*] .... KVOC
Casper, WY [*Location identifier FAA*] (FAAL) .... SYD
Casper's Forensic Medicine [*A publication*] (DLA) .... Casp For Med
Caspian Sea and Area [*MARC geographic area code Library of Congress*] (LCCP) .... ak----
Cass County Court House, Fargo, ND [*Library symbol Library of Congress*] (LCLS) .... NdFC
Cass County Extension Office, Walker, MN [*Library symbol*] [*Library of Congress*] (LCLS) .... MnWalC
Cass County Historical Society Museum Library, Logansport, IN [*Library symbol Library of Congress*] (LCLS) .... InLogCHi
Cass County Historical Society, Walker, MN [*Library symbol*] [*Library of Congress*] (LCLS) .... MnWalHi
Cass County Library, Cassopolis, MI [*Library symbol Library of Congress*] (LCLS) .... MiCassC
Cass County Public Library, Harrisonville, MO [*Library symbol Library of Congress*] (LCLS) .... MoHarC
Cass Lake Community Library, Lake, MN [*Library symbol*] [*Library of Congress*] (LCLS) .... MnCas

Cass Lake Elementary School, Cass Lake, MN [Library symbol] [Library of Congress] (LCLS) .... MnCasE
Cass Lake High School, Cass Lake, MN [Library symbol] [Library of Congress] (LCLS) .... MnCasHS
Cassagnes-Begonhes [France ICAO location identifier] (ICLI) .... LFIG
Cassandra: Radical Feminist Nurses Network (EA) .... CRFNN
Cassanova Brown Streak Disease [Plant pathology] .... CBSD
Cassatie [Appeal to High Court of Justice] [Netherlands] (ILCA) .... Cass
Cassava Common Mosaic Virus [Plant pathology] .... CSCMV
Cassava Latent Virus [Plant pathology] .... CALV
Cassava Vein Mosaic Virus [Plant pathology] .... CAVMV
Cassegrain Feed System .... CFS
Cassegrain Reflector Antenna .... CRA
Cassel Group Level of Aspiration Test [Psychology] .... CGLAT
Cassel. Procedure in the Court of Canada [A publication] (DLA) .... Cas Proc
Cassel. Procedure in the Court of Canada [A publication] (DLA) .... Cass Proc
Cassel Psychotherapy Progress Record [Psychology] .... CPPR
Cassell's Anthology of English Poetry [A publication] .... CaAEP
Cassells' Family Magazine [A publication] (ROG) .... CFM
Cassel's Digest [Canada] [A publication] (DLA) .... Cass Dig
Cassel's Practice Cases [Canada] [A publication] (DLA) .... Cass Prac
Cassel's Practice Cases [Canada A publication] (DLA) .... Cass Prac Cas
Cassel's Supreme Court Decisions [A publication] (DLA) .... Cass SC
Cassel's Supreme Court Digest [Canada] [A publication] (DLA) .... SC Dig
Cassel's Supreme Court Practice [2nd ed., by Masters] [A publication] (DLA) .... Cass Sup C Prac
Cassenne [France] [Research code symbol] C
Cassenne [France] [Research code symbol] .... CS
Cassette (MSA) .... CASS
Cassette .... CASSTT
Cassette Camera Recorder (BARN) .... CCR
Cassette Information Services .... CIS
Cassette Magnetic Tape .... CMT
Cassette Magnetic Tape Operating System [Computer science] (PDAA) .... CMTOS
Cassette Operating Executive (MHDI) .... COPE
Cassette Operating Monitor .... COM
Cassette Operating System (NITA) .... COS
Cassette Programming System [Digital Equipment Corp.] .... CAPS
Cassette Single [Trademark of IRS Records] .... Cassingle
Cassette Tape .... CT
Cassette Tape Controller (IAA) .... CTC
Cassette Tape Loader .... CTL
Cassette Tape Operating System (IEEE) .... CTOS
Cassette Tape / Selectric Typewriter (HGAA) .... CT/ST
Cassette Transport System .... CTS
Cassette User Tape System .... CUTS
Cassette-Operated System (MSA) .... COS
Cassia Petroleum [Vancouver Stock Exchange symbol] .... CAU
Cassiar Mining Corp. [Toronto Stock Exchange symbol] .... CSQ
Cassidy Class (EA) CC
Cassidy Resources Ltd. [Vancouver Stock Exchange symbol] .... CYT
Cassidy's Ltd. [Toronto Stock Exchange symbol] .... CYL
Cassilandia [Brazil] [Airport symbol] (OAG) .... CSS
Cassiodori Variarum [A publication] (DLA) .... Cassiod Var
Cassiodorus [Sixth century AD] [Classical studies] (OCD) .... Cassiod
Cassiopeia [Constellation] .... Cas
Cassiopeia [Constellation] .... Cass
Cassiopeia A [Constellation] .... CasA
Cassiopeium [An early name for the chemical element lutetium] .... Cp
Cassite (BJA) .... Cass
Casson's Local Government Board Decisions [1902-16] [England] [A publication] (DLA) .... Cass LGB
Cassopolis, MI [AM radio station call letters] (RBYB) .... WGTO
Cassovia Air [Slovakia] [ICAO designator] (FAAC) CVI
Cassville, MO [FM radio station call letters] .... KRLK
Cast (AAG) C
Cast (VRA) .... cst
Cast Aluminum Structure .... CAS
Cast Aluminum Structure Technology .... CAST
Cast Arrested Repeating Persons [Fictitious fishing term] .... CARP
Cast Brass .... CB
Cast Brass .... CBR
Cast Bronze (IIA) .... CB
Cast Bronze Bearings Institute [Later, NFFS] .... CBBI
Cast Bronze Institute [Defunct] (EA) .... CBI
Cast Bullet Association (EA) .... CBA
Cast Carbon Steel .... CCS
Cast Coated [Paper] (DGA) CC
Cast Copper CC
Cast Double Base .... CDB
Cast Enamel [Classified advertising] (ADA) .... CE
Cast Iron CI
Cast Iron Maintenance Optimization System [for gas distribution mains] [A trademark] .... CIMOS
Cast Iron Pipe Research Association [Later, DIPRA] (EA) .... CIPRA
Cast Iron Seat Collectors Association (EA) .... CISCA
Cast Iron Soil Pipe Foundation [Defunct] (EA) .... CISPF
Cast Iron Soil Pipe Institute (EA) .... CISPI
Cast Metal Part .... CMP
Cast Metals Association (EA) .... NFA
Cast Metals Federation [Later, NFA] (EA) .... CMF
Cast Number [In urinalysis] [Biochemistry] (DAVI) .... CASTNO
Cast Off, to X-Ray [Performed with the cast off] [Orthopedics] (DAVI) .... COTX
CAST [Computerized Automatic System Tester] Programming Language .... CPL
Cast Removed, Take to X-Ray [Orthopedics] (DAVI) .... CRTX

Cast Steel .... CS
Cast Stone (AAG) .... CS
Cast Stone [Technical drawings] .... CST
Castable Smoke Mix Grenade (MCD) .... CSMG
Castalia Foundation [Defunct] (EA) .... CF
Castalia, OH [FM radio station call letters] .... WGGN
Castanospermine [Biochemistry] .... CST
Castaway [Fiji] [Airport symbol] (OAG) .... CST
CasTech Aluminum Group [NYSE symbol] (TTSB) .... CTA
Castech Aluminum Group, Inc. [Associated Press] (SAG) .... Castech
Castech Aluminum Group, Inc. [NYSE symbol] (SAG) .... CTA
Castel Tesino [Italy] [Geomagnetic observatory code] .... CTS
Castellate .... CSTL
Castelle [NASDAQ symbol] (TTSB) .... CSTL
Castello Resources Ltd. [Vancouver Stock Exchange symbol] .... CZH
Castelnaudary/Villeneuve [France ICAO location identifier] (ICLI) .... LFMW
Castelnau-Magnoac [France ICAO location identifier] (ICLI) .... LFDQ
Castelsarrasin/Moissac [France ICAO location identifier] (ICLI) .... LFCX
Caster and Floor Truck Manufacturers Association [Later, ICM] .... CFT
Caster and Floor Truck Manufacturers Association [Later, ICM] (EA) .... CFTMA
Casters and Towbar .... CT
Castilejo-Dalitz-Dyson .... CDD
Castilho/Urubupunga [Brazil ICAO location identifier] (ICLI) .... SBUP
Castillejos, Zambales [Philippines] [ICAO location identifier] (ICLI) .... RPUJ
Castillo de San Marcos National Monument .... CASA
Castinet .... CAST
Casting .... CAST
Casting (KSC) .... CSTG
Casting Division .... CD
Casting Industry Suppliers Association (EA) .... CISA
Casting Society of America (WDMC) .... CSA
Casting Up [Printing] (DGA) .... CU
Cast-in-Place Concrete [Technical drawings] .... CIPC
Cast-Iron Pipe [Technical drawings] .... CIP
Cast-Iron Soil Pipe (DNAB) .... CISP
Castle C
Castle (MSA) .... CAS
Castle .... CAST
Castle .... CASTL
Castle AM & Co. [Associated Press] (SAG) .... CastlAM
Castle [A. M.] & Co. [AMEX symbol] (SPSG) .... CAS
Castle [A. M.] & Co. [Associated Press] (SAG) .... CastleAM
Castle & Cooke [Associated Press] (SAG) .... CastCk
Castle & Cooke [NYSE symbol] (SAG) .... CCS
Castle & Cooke Inc. [NYSE symbol] (TTSB) .... CCS
Castle Aviation, Inc. [ICAO designator] (FAAC) .... CSJ
Castle Clinton National Monument .... CACL
Castle Convert Fund [AMEX symbol] (TTSB) .... CVF
Castle Convertible Fund, Inc. [Associated Press] (SAG) .... CasFd
Castle Convertible Fund, Inc. [AMEX symbol] (SPSG) .... CVF
Castle Energy Corp. [Associated Press] (SAG) .... CastleEn
Castle Energy Corp. [NASDAQ symbol] (NQ) .... CECX
Castle Hill Museum, Cobham, VA [Library symbol Library of Congress] (LCLS) .... ViCoC
Castle Mountain [California] [Seismograph station code, US Geological Survey] (SEIS) .... CTM
Castle on Rating [4th ed.] [1903] [A publication] (DLA) .... Cast Rat
Castle Rock [California] [Seismograph station code, US Geological Survey] (SEIS) .... CRC
Castle Rock [New York] [Seismograph station code, US Geological Survey] (SEIS) .... CTR
Castle Rock, CO [FM radio station call letters] (RBYB) .... KJMN-FM
Castle Rock, CO [FM radio station call letters] (RBYB) .... KNRX
Castle Rock, CO [Television station call letters] .... KWHD
Castle Rock, WA [FM radio station call letters] .... KAZL
Castle Rock, WA [FM radio station call letters] (RBYB) .... KRQT-FM
Castlecrag Conservation Society [Australia] .... CCS
Castlegar [Canada] [Airport symbol] (OAG) .... YCG
Castlegar and District Public Library, Castlegar, British Columbia [Library symbol National Library of Canada] (NLC) .... BCD
Castlegar, BC [AM radio station call letters] .... CKQR
Castlegar, BC [ICAO location identifier] (ICLI) .... CYCG
Castleman's Disease [Oncology] .... CD
Castlepoint [New Zealand] [Seismograph station code, US Geological Survey] (SEIS) .... CAZ
Castles Association (EA) .... CA
Castle's Law of Commerce in Time of War [A publication] (DLA) .... Cast Com
Castleton State College, Castleton, VT [Library symbol Library of Congress] (LCLS) .... VtCasT
Castleton, VT [FM radio station call letters] .... WIUV
Cast-Off X-Ray [Performed with the cast off] [Orthopedics] (DAVI) .... COX
Castor Oil .... CO
Castor Public Library, Alberta [Library symbol National Library of Canada] (NLC) .... ACAST
Castoreum [Castor] [Pharmacy] (ROG) .... CASTOR
Cast-Out-Nines .... CON
Castrate .... CAST
Castres/Mazamet [France ICAO location identifier] (ICLI) .... LFCK
Castries/Vigie [St. Lucia] [ICAO location identifier] (ICLI) .... TLPC
Castro [Chile] [Airport symbol] (AD) .... WCA
Castro/Gamboa [Chile] [ICAO location identifier] (ICLI) .... SCST
Castroville, TX [Location identifier FAA] (FAAL) .... CVB
Castrovirreyna [Peru] [Seismograph station code, US Geological Survey] (SEIS) .... CST
Casual .... CAS

Casual ... CSL
Casual Disability Exclusion [*Insurance*] ... CDEX
Casual Payment ... CASPMT
Casual Payments Book [*British*] (ADA) ... CPB
Casual-Associative Network [*for medical applications*] [*Computer science*] ... CASNET
Casualties Union (EA) ... CU
Casualty [*Insurance*] ... C
Casualty (AFM) ... CAS
Casualty ... CSLTY
Casualty Actuarial Society (EA) ... CAS
Casualty Air Evacuation Unit [*RAF*] [*British*] ... CAEU
Casualty Analysis for Determining Weapon System Effectiveness [*Army*] (AABC) ... CAWSE
Casualty and Damage Assessment (MCD) ... CDA
Casualty Assessment System [*Army*] ... CAS
Casualty Assistance Calls and Funeral Honors Support Program [*Military*] (DNAB) ... CAC/FHS
Casualty Assistance Calls Officer ... CACO
Casualty Assistance Calls Program (CINC) ... CACP
Casualty Assistance Control Officer [*Navy*] (DOMA) ... CACO
Casualty Assistance Officer [*Army*] (ADDR) ... CAO
Casualty Branch [*BUPERS*] ... CB
Casualty Canceled [*Navy*] ... CASCAN
Casualty Clearing Station [*Military*] ... CCS
Casualty Collecting-Post (NATG) ... CCP
Casualty Collection Point [*Army*] (INF) ... CCP
Casualty Control Panel (CAAL) ... CCP
Casualty Control Station [*Military*] (DNAB) ... CASCON
Casualty Corrected [*Navy*] ... CASCOR
Casualty Correction Report ... CASCOR
Casualty Department [*British police*] ... CD
Casualty Estimation Study [*Military*] ... CES
Casualty Evacuation ... CASEVAC
Casualty Evacuation and Control Ship [*Navy*] (NVT) ... CECS
Casualty Evacuation Officer ... CEO
Casualty Evacuation Train [*British*] ... CET
Casualty Firing Panel ... CFP
Casualty Information Support System [*Military*] (DNAB) ... CASINFOSUPPSYS
Casualty Information Support System [*Military*] (DNAB) ... CISS
Casualty Information System (MCD) ... CIS
Casualty Insurance Logistics Automated (PDAA) ... CILA
Casualty Mode [*Military*] (CAAL) ... CM
Casualty Officer [*Military*] (DAVI) ... CO
Casualty Procedure ... CASPRO
Casualty Receiving Hospital [*British*] ... CRH
Casualty Report [*Navy*] ... CASREP
Casualty Report [*Navy*] ... CASREPT
Casualty Situation Report ... CASSIT
Casualty Staging Facility [*Military*] (AFM) ... CSF
Casualty Staging Unit [*Military*] (AFM) ... CSU
Casualty Surgeons Association [*British*] ... CSA
Casualty Underwriting Manual [*Insurance*] ... CUM
Casualty Vulnerability Number ... CVN
Casualty Weapon Director ... CWD
Casualty Weapon Director Panel ... CWDP
Caswall. Copyholds [*3rd ed.*] [*1841*] [*A publication*] (DLA) ... Casw Cop
Cat Allergen [*Immunology*] ... CA
Cat Association of the Northern Territory [*Australia*] ... CANT
Cat Aviation, AG [*Switzerland ICAO designator*] (FAAC) ... CAZ
Cat Cay [*Bahamas*] [*Airport symbol*] (OAG) ... CXY
Cat Collectors [*Commercial firm*] (EA) ... CC
Cat Eye Syndrome [*Medicine*] ... CES
Cat Fanciers' Association (EA) ... CFA
Cat Fanciers' Federation (EA) ... CFF
Cat Fancy [*A publication*] (BRI) ... Cat Fan
Cat Fund (EA) ... CF
Cat Island [*Bahamas*] [*Airport symbol*] (AD) ... CAT
Cat Kargo Hava Tasima, AS [*Turkey*] [*FAA designator*] (FAAC) ... KET
Cat Pack [*"Women's Wear Daily" slang for jetsetters*] ... CP
Cat Protection Society of New South Wales [*Australia*] ... CPSNSW
Cat Protection Society of Victoria [*Australia*] ... CPSV
Cat Scratch [*Medicine*] (AAMN) ... CS
Cat Scratch Disease [*Medicine*] ... CSD
Cat Scratch Disease Bacillus [*Medicine*] (DMAA) ... CSDB
Cata SACIFI [*Argentina ICAO designator*] (FAAC) ... CTZ
Catabolite Activator Protein [*Biochemistry, genetics*] ... CAP
Catabolite Gene Activator [*Medicine*] (DMAA) ... CGA
Catabolite Gene Activator Protein [*Biochemistry, genetics*] ... CAP
Catacamas [*Honduras*] [*ICAO location identifier*] (ICLI) ... MHCA
Cataclysmic Binary [*Computer science*] ... CB
Cataclysmic Variable [*Astronomy, physics*] ... CV
Catacomb (VRA) ... ctmb
Catadioptric [*Optics*] ... CAT
Catadioptric-Herschelian Telescope (PDAA) ... CHT
Catafalque ... CAT
Catahoula Parish Library, Harrisonburg, LA [*Library symbol Library of Congress*] (LCLS) ... LHarC
Catalan [*MARC language code Library of Congress*] (LCCP) ... cat
Catalan [*Language, etc.*] ... CAT
Catalan Solidarity [*Political party*] (PPW) ... SC
Catalase [*Also, CTS*] [*An enzyme*] ... CAT
Catalase [*An enzyme*] ... CTS
Catalase B (DMAA) ... CATB
Catalepton [*of Vergil*] [*Classical studies*] (OCD) ... Catal
Catalina 22 National Sailing Association (EA) ... CTNSA
Catalina 25 National Association (EA) ... CTNA
Catalina Airlines [*ICAO designator*] (AD) ... KG
Catalina Flying Boats, Inc. [*FAA designator*] (FAAC) ... CBT
Catalina Island [*California*] [*Airport symbol*] (OAG) ... AVX
Catalina Island [*California*] [*Seismograph station code, US Geological Survey*] (SEIS) ... CIS
Catalina Island [*California*] [*Airport symbol Obsolete*] (OAG) ... TWH
Catalina Island [*California*] **Airport in the Sky** [*Airport symbol*] (OAG) ... CIB
Catalina Lighting [*Associated Press*] (SAG) ... Cata ILt
Catalina Lighting [*NYSE symbol*] (SAG) ... LTG
Catalina Marine Science Center [*University of Southern California*] [*Research center*] ... CMSC
Catalina Marketing [*NYSE symbol*] (TTSB) ... POS
Catalina Marketing Corp. [*Associated Press*] (SAG) ... CatMkt
Catalina Marketing Corp. [*NYSE symbol*] (SPSG) ... POS
Catalog ... C
Catalog (KSC) ... CAT
Catalog (VRA) ... cat
Catalog (WDMC) ... cat
Catalog ... CATA
Catalog (ROG) ... CATAL
Catalog (BUR) ... CATLG
Catalog ... CATLG
Catalog Access System [*Project for automated library systems*] ... CATS
Catalog Card Corporation of America (NITA) ... 3C
Catalog Card Corp. of America [*Information service or system*] (IID) ... CCC
Catalog Data Activity [*Army*] ... CDA
Catalog Data Agency (MCD) ... CDA
Catalog Events [*Exhibition of US company product catalogs, etc., in foreign markets*] [*Department of Commerce*] ... CE
Catalog for Information Exchange and Message Standards (MCD) ... CIEMS
Catalog Input Transmittal (DNAB) ... CIT
Catalog Management Data Notification [*Army*] (AABC) ... CMDN
Catalog Master Data File ... CMDF
Catalog Number ... CANO
Catalog of American Portraits [*Smithsonian Institution*] [*Washington, DC*] ... CAP
Catalog of Approved Requirement Documents [*Army*] (RDA) ... CARDS
Catalog of Available and Standard Hardware [*NASA*] ... CASH
Catalog of Federal Domestic Assistance [*A publication*] ... CFDA
Catalog of Material Improvement Cards (MCD) ... CMIC
Catalog of Museum Publications and Media [*A publication*] ... CMPM
Catalog of Navy Training Courses (NVT) ... CANTRAC
Catalog of Programs ... CAPR
Catalog of the New York Public Library ... CATNYP
Catalog of the Public Documents [*A bibliographic publication*] ... CPD
Catalog of Virginia Library Resources (EDAC) ... CAVALIR
Catalog On-Line [*National Library of Medicine*] [*Bibliographic database*] ... CATLINE
Catalog Online Tool [*DoD*] ... COLT
Catalog Recovery Area [*Computer science*] ... CRA
Catalog Services Association [*Defunct*] (EA) ... CSA
Catalog Support System [*UTLAS International Canada*] [*Information service or system*] ... CATSS
Catalog Typing Worksheet [*for MT/ST typist*] ... CWS
Cataloging and Classification Section [*of ALA*] ... CCS
Cataloging and Classification Section's Descriptive Cataloging Committee [*of ALA*] ... CCS/DCC
Cataloging and Indexing Number [*Later, AGRICOLA*] [*National Agricultural Library Database*] ... CAIN
Cataloging and Provisioning System (MCD) ... CPS
Cataloging and Standardization Center [*Air Force*] ... CASC
Cataloging and Standardization Office [*Air Force*] (AFIT) ... CASO
Cataloging Code Revision Committee [*of ALA*] ... CCRC
Cataloging Distribution Service [*Library of Congress*] [*Washington, DC*] ... CDS
Cataloging in Publication [*Pronounced "sip"*] [*Formerly, CIS Library science*] ... CIP
Cataloging in Source [*Later, CIP*] [*Library science*] ... CIS
Cataloging Management Data [*Army*] ... CMD
Cataloging Management Team [*American Library Association*] ... CMT
Cataloging Responsibility Code ... CRC
Cataloging Services Department, OCLC [*Online Computer Library Center*], Inc., Columbus, OH [*OCLC symbol*] (OCLC) ... SER
Catalogo Colectivo de Publicaciones Periodicas [*Database*] [*Ministerio de Cultura*] [*Spanish*] [*Information service or system*] (CRD) ... CPUP
Catalogo Italiano Riviste su Calcolatore Elettronico [*Database*] [*Editrice Bibliografica*] [*Italian*] [*Information service or system*] (CRD) ... CIRCE
Catalogue ... CTLG
Catalogue Collectif des Periodiques [*A bibliographic publication*] ... CCP
Catalogue de l'Edition Francaise ... CEF
Catalogue des Textes Hittites [*Paris*] (BJA) ... CTH
Catalogue des Theses de Doctorat [*A bibliographic publication*] [*France*] ... CTD
Catalogue General des Antiquites Egyptiennes du Musee du Caire (BJA) ... CG
Catalogue Interoperability Experiment [*Marine science*] (OSRA) ... CINTEX
Catalogue Interoperability Experiment (USDC) ... CINTEX
Catalogue Magazine ... CATAZINE
Catalogue of Approved Scientific and Technical Intelligence Tasks (MCD) ... CAST
Catalogue of Oriental Manuscripts in Danish Collections (BJA) ... COMDC
Catalogue of Printed Music [*A publication*] ... CPM
Catalogue of the Babylonian Section [*University Museum, Philadelphia*] [*Formerly, CBM*] (BJA) ... CBS
Catalogue of the Greek Coins of Palestine [*A publication*] (BJA) ... CGCP
Catalogue of the Greek Papyri in the John Rylands Library at Manchester [*A publication*] (OCD) ... P Ryl

Catalogue of the Literary Papyri in the British Museum [*A publication*] (OCD) ... Cat Lit Pap
Catalogued ... CD
Catalogues on Microfiche (AIE) ... COM
Cataloguing and Classification Quarterly [*A publication*] ... CCQ
Cataloguing in Advance of Publication [*British Library Bibliographic Services Division*] (NITA) ... CAP
Catalogus Codicum Astrologorum Graecorum [*A publication*] (OCD) ... CCAG
Catalogus Codicum Orientalium [*The Netherlands*] [*A publication*] (BJA) ... CCON
Catalonian [*Language, etc.*] (ROG) ... CAT
Catalysed Signal Amplification [*Analytical biochemistry*] ... CSA
Catalyst ... C
Catalyst (WGA) ... CAT
Catalyst (MSA) ... CTLST
Catalyst International, Inc. [*Associated Press*] (SAG) ... Catalyst
Catalyst International, Inc. [*NASDAQ symbol*] (SAG) ... CLYS
Catalyst Intl. [*NASDAQ symbol*] (TTSB) ... CLYS
Catalyst Oriented Packing [*Chemical engineering*] ... COP
Catalyst Pass Fraction ... CPF
Catalyst Resource on the Work Force and Women [*Catalyst Information Center*] [*Information service or system*] (IID) ... CRWF
Catalyst Resources for Women [*A database*] [*Bibliographic Retrieval Service*] (NITA) ... CRFW
Catalyst Semiconductor [*NASDAQ symbol*] (TTSB) ... CATS
Catalyst Semiconductor, Inc. [*Associated Press*] (SAG) ... CatalSem
Catalyst Semiconductor, Inc. [*NASDAQ symbol*] (SAG) ... CATS
Catalytic [*Automotive engineering*] ... CATA
Catalytic Coal Gasification [*Fuel technology*] ... CCG
Catalytic Coal Liquefaction ... CCL
Catalytic Construction Co. ... CATCO
Catalytic Construction Co. (MCD) ... CCC
Catalytic Construction Co. (KSC) ... CCCO
Catalytic Converter [*Automotive engineering*] ... CC
Catalytic Cracker [*Chemical engineering*] ... CC
Catalytic Cracking Unit [*Chemical engineering*] ... CCU
Catalytic Dehydrogenative Polycondensation [*Organic chemistry*] ... CDHP
Catalytic Dewaxing [*Petroleum refining*] ... CDW
Catalytic Extraction Process [*Engineering*] ... CEP
Catalytic Extraction Processing [*Recycling*] ... CEP
Catalytic Flame Ionization Detector ... CFID
Catalytic Membrane Reactor [*Chemical engineering*] ... CMR
Catalytic Optimum Profit-Sharing ... COPS
Catalytic Oxidation ... CAT-OX
Catalytic Reforming (IAA) ... CR
Catalytic Reforming Unit [*Petroleum refining*] ... CRU
Catalytic Research Unit (SSD) ... CRU
Catalytic Rich Gas ... CRG
Catalytic Transfer Hydrogenation ... CTH
Catalytica, Inc. [*Associated Press*] (SAG) ... Catalyt
Catalytica, Inc. [*NASDAQ symbol*] (SAG) ... CTAL
Catalytically Cracked Clarified Oil [*Petroleum technology*] ... CCCO
Catalytic-Dow (KSC) ... C-D
Catalyzed Electrolytic Plutonium Oxide Dissolution [*Chemistry*] ... CEPOD
Catamaran (ADA) ... cat
Catamaran Mine Disposal System (MCD) ... CATMDV
Catamarca [*Argentina*] [*Airport symbol*] (OAG) ... CTC
Catamarca [*Argentina ICAO location identifier*] (ICLI) ... SANC
Catamenia [*Menstruation*] (CPH) ... cta
Catania [*Italy*] [*Seismograph station code, US Geological Survey*] (SEIS) ... CAT
Catania [*Italy*] [*Airport symbol*] (OAG) ... CTA
Catania/Fontanarossa [*Italy ICAO location identifier*] (ICLI) ... LICC
Cataphyll [*Botany*] ... Ct
Catapilco [*Chile*] [*Seismograph station code, US Geological Survey*] (SEIS) ... CTP
Cataplasma [*Poultice*] [*Pharmacy*] ... CAT
Cataplasma [*Poultice*] [*Pharmacy*] (ROG) ... CATAPL
Cataplasma [*Poultice*] [*Pharmacy*] (ROG) ... CATAPLAS
Cataplasma [*Poultice*] [*Pharmacy*] ... CATAPLSM
Cataplus [*of Lucian*] [*Classical studies*] (OCD) ... Catapl
Catapult (NG) ... CAT
Catapult Aircraft Merchantship [*Used by British RAF to catapult Hurricane fighter planes from ships to defend convoys from enemy bombers*] [*World War II*] ... CAM
Catapult and Arresting Gear [*Aviation*] (DNAB) ... CAG
Catapult and Arresting Gear Pool [*Navy*] ... CAP
Catapult Arresting Gear and Landing Aids Maintenance [*Aviation*] (NG) ... CALM
Catapult Bulletin (MCD) ... CB
Catapult Data Acquisition System (DNAB) ... CDAS
Catapult Hookup and Launch Surveillance ... CAHALS
Catapult Launched Fuel Air Expendable Round (DWSG) ... CATFAE
Catapult Lighter [*Navy symbol*] ... YVC
Catapult-Assisted Takeoff ... CATO
Cataract [*Ophthalmology*] ... Cat
Cataract-Microcephaly-Arthrogryposis-Kyphosis [*Syndrome*] [*Medicine*] (DMAA) ... CAMAK
Catarama [*Ecuador*] [*ICAO location identifier*] (ICLI) ... SECA
Catarman [*Philippines*] [*Airport symbol*] (OAG) ... CRM
Catarman, Northern Samar [*Philippines*] [*ICAO location identifier*] (ICLI) ... RPVF
Catarrhal Colds [*Medicine*] ... C (Colds)
Catastrophic Failure Rate ... CFR
Catastrophic Health Expense Protection Plan [*Insurance*] ... CHEPP
Catastrophic Health Insurance (GFGA) ... CHI
Catastrophic Sexual Transmutation Theory [*Plant genetics*] ... CSTT
Catawba Area Mental Health Center, Hickory, NC [*Library symbol*] [*Library of Congress*] (LCLS) ... NcHyCM
Catawba College, Salisbury, NC [*Library symbol Library of Congress*] (LCLS) ... NcSalC
Catawba County Library, Newton, NC [*Library symbol Library of Congress*] (LCLS) ... NcNt
Catawba Memorial Hospital, Northwest AHEC Library at Hickory, Hickory, NC [*Library symbol*] [*Library of Congress*] (LCLS) ... NcHyCH
Catawba Nuclear Station (NRCH) ... CNS
Catawba Valley Technical Institute, Hickory, NC [*Library symbol Library of Congress*] (LCLS) ... NcHyC
Catboat Association (EA) ... CA
Catch [*Pisciculture*] ... C
Catch a Horse and Ride [*Fictitious railroad initialism used to indicate one of the most reliable modes of rural transportation*] ... CH & R
Catch All Phaults [*Quality control*] ... CAP
Catch Basin [*Technical drawings*] ... CB
Catch per Angler [*Pisciculture*] ... CA
Catch per Hour [*Pisciculture*] ... CPH
Catch per Standard Day of Fishing [*Fishery management*] (MSC) ... CPSDF
Catch per Unit Effort [*Pisciculture*] ... C/E
Catch per Unit Effort [*Pisciculture*] (MSC) ... CPUE
Catch per Unit Effort [*Pisciculture*] ... CUE
Catch Phrase ... CP
Catch Society of America [*Defunct*] (EA) ... CSA
Catcher [*Baseball*] ... C
Catchment Area Management [*Army medical term*] ... CAM
Catchment Management Advisory Committee [*Australia*] ... CMAC
Catch-per-Effort [*Fishing*] ... CPE
Catchword ... CWD
Catchword and Trade Name Index [*A publication*] ... CATNI
Catear Resources Ltd. [*Vancouver Stock Exchange symbol*] ... CAA
Catechism ... C
Catechism ... CAT
Catechol Methyltransferase (DMAA) ... CCMT
Catecholamine [*or Catecholaminergic*] [*Biochemistry*] ... CA
Catecholamine [*Biochemistry*] ... CAT
Catecholamine Club (EA) ... CC
Catecholamines Radioenzymic Assay Kit [*Clinical chemistry*] [*Acronym is trademark*] ... CAT-A-KIT
Catechol-O-Methyltransferase [*An enzyme*] ... CCMT
Catechol-O-Methyltransferase [*An enzyme*] (MAE) ... CMT
Catechol-O-Methyltransferase [*An enzyme*] ... COMT
Categoriae [*of Aristotle*] [*Classical studies*] (OCD) ... Cat
Categorical Grammar ... CG
Category ... CA
Category (AFM) ... CAT
Category ... CATEG
Category (FAAC) ... CTGY
Category Assignment Responsibility List (MCD) ... CARL
Category B Flying Accident [*British military*] (DMA) ... BFA
Category Code [*Online database field identifier*] ... CC
Category Codes and Nomenclature (MCD) ... CCN
Category Development Index (WDMC) ... CDI
Category E Flying Accident [*British military*] (DMA) ... EFA
Category Stimulus [*To light*] ... CS
Category Switch [*Electronics*] (IAA) ... CATS
Catellus Development [*NYSE symbol*] (TTSB) ... CDX
Catellus Development Corp. [*Associated Press*] (SAG) ... Catelu
Catellus Development Corp. [*Associated Press*] (SAG) ... Catelus
Catellus Development Corp. [*NYSE symbol*] (SPSG) ... CDX
Catellus Dvlp $3.75'A'Cv Pfd [*NYSE symbol*] (TTSB) ... CDXPrA
Catenarian Arch [*Freemasonry*] (ROG) ... CA
Catenary Anchor Leg Mooring ... CALM
Caterer [*Military British*] ... CA
Caterer ... CATR
Cateret County Public Library, Beaufort, NC [*Library symbol Library of Congress*] (LCLS) ... NcBea
Catering ... CARG
Catering Accountant [*British military*] (DMA) ... CA
Catering Equipment Distributors Association [*British*] (DBA) ... CEDA
Catering Equipment Manufacturers' Association [*British*] (BI) ... CEMA
Catering Managers Association of Great Britain and Northern Ireland (BI) ... CMA
Catering Officer [*British military*] (DMA) ... CT O
Catering Teachers Association [*British*] ... CTA
Catering Wages Commission [*British*] (DAS) ... CWC
Caterpillar Club (EA) ... CC
Caterpillar, Inc. [*Wall Street slang name: "Cat"*] [*NYSE symbol*] (SPSG) ... CAT
Caterpillar, Inc. [*Wall Street slang name: "Cat"*] [*Associated Press*] (SAG) ... Caterp
Caterpillar Micro Oxidation Test [*Automotive lubricant*] ... CMOT
Caterpillar Tractor Co. [*NYSE symbol; later, CAT*] [*Wall Street slang name: "Cat"*] (SPSG) ... CTR
Caterpillar Tractor Co., Business Library, Peoria, IL [*Library symbol Library of Congress*] (LCLS) ... IPCT
Caterpillar Tractor Co., Peoria, IL [*OCLC symbol*] (OCLC) ... IDX
Caterpillar Tractor Co., Technical Information Center, Peoria, IL [*Library symbol Library of Congress*] (LCLS) ... IPCT-T
Caterpillar Tractor Co., Technical Information Center, Peoria, IL [*OCLC symbol*] (OCLC) ... ISH
Caterpillar Truck Engine Owners Club ... CTEOC
Cates' Reports [*109-127 Tennessee*] [*A publication*] (DLA) ... Cates
Catex Compagnie [*France ICAO designator*] (FAAC) ... TEX
Catfish ... CTFSH
Catfish Farmers of America (EA) ... CFA
Catfish Institute [*An association*] (EA) ... CI

Catfish Pond [New Jersey] [Seismograph station code, US Geological Survey Closed] (SEIS) ..... CNJ
Catgut Acoustical Society (EA) ..... CAS
Catgut Suture [Medicine] ..... CGS
Cathartic [Pharmacy] ..... CATH
Cathartic Compound (IIA) CC
Cathartica [Cathartic] [Pharmacy] (ROG) ..... CATHART
Cathay Bancorp [NASDAQ symbol] (TTSB) ..... CATY
Cathay Bancorp, Inc. [Associated Press] (SAG) ..... CathBcp
Cathay Bancorp, Inc. [NASDAQ symbol] (SAG) ..... CATY
Cathay Pacific Airways [ICAO designator] (AD) CX
Cathay Pacific Airways Ltd. [British ICAO designator] (FAAC) ..... CPA
Cathays [Cardiff] [Welsh depot code] ..... CYS
Cathedral ..... CATH
Cathedral (VRA) ..... cath
Cathedral ..... CATHDRL
Cathedral ..... CATHL
Cathedral ..... CD
Cathedral ..... CTHDL
Cathedral Architects Association [British] (DBA) ..... CAA
Cathedral City, CA [AM radio station call letters] ..... KWXY
Cathedral City, CA [FM radio station call letters] ..... KWXY-FM
Cathedral Gold Corp. [Toronto Stock Exchange symbol] ..... CAT
Cathedral of Saint John the Divine, New York, NY [Library symbol Library of Congress] (LCLS) ..... NNSJD
Cathedral Organists' Association (EA) ..... COA
Cathedral Peace Institute (EA) ..... CPI
Cathedral Priory ..... CDPR
Cathedral Series [A publication] ..... CS
Cathedrals Advisory Committee [Church of England] ..... CAC
Cathepsin S (DMAA) ..... CTSS
Catherine Booth Hospital, Montreal, PQ, Canada [Library symbol] [Library of Congress] (LCLS) ..... CaQMCBH
Catherine Booth Hospital, Montreal, Quebec [Library symbol National Library of Canada] (NLC) ..... QMCBH
[St.] Catherine's College [Oxford University] (BARN) ..... Cath
Catherines Stores [NASDAQ symbol] (TTSB) ..... CATH
Catherines Stores Corp. [NASDAQ symbol] (SPSG) ..... CATH
Catherines Stores Corp. [Associated Press] (SAG) ..... CathStr
Catheter [Medicine] ..... CATH
Catheter Balloon Valvuloplasty [Medicine] (CPH) ..... CBT
Catheter Specimen of Urine [Medicine] ..... CSU
Catheterization [or Catheterize] [Cardiology and urology] (DAVI) ..... CATH
Catheterized Bladder [Urology] (DAVI) ..... CB
Catheter-Related Infection [Medicine] ..... CRI
Cathodal Closure Clonus [Medicine] ..... CC Cl
Cathodal Closure Clonus [Medicine] (DMAA) CCCl
Cathodal Closure Contraction [Also, CCC] [Physiology] ..... CaCC
Cathodal Closure Contraction [Also, CaCC] [Physiology] CCC
Cathodal Closure Tetanus [Physiology] ..... CCT
Cathodal Closure Tetanus [Physiology] ..... CCTE
Cathodal Duration [Medicine] (DMAA) ..... KD
Cathodal Duration Tetanus [Physiology] ..... CaDTe
Cathodal Opening [Medicine] (ROG) ..... CO
Cathodal Opening Clonus [Physiology] (MAE) ..... COC
Cathodal Opening Clonus [Physiology] ..... COCL
Cathodal Opening Clonus [Medicine] (DMAA) ..... COCl
Cathodal Opening Contraction [Also, COC] [Physiology] ..... CaOC
Cathodal Opening Contraction [Also, CaOC] [Physiology] ..... COC
Cathodal Opening Tetanus [Physiology] ..... COT
Cathodal Opening Tetanus [Physiology] ..... COTe
Cathode [or Cathodal] [Radiology] (DAVI) C
Cathode ..... CA
Cathode (MSA) ..... CATH
Cathode [Electron device] (MSA) ..... K
Cathode [Electron device] (AAMN) ..... Ka
Cathode Current Efficiency [Electrochemistry] ..... CCE
Cathode Dark Space ..... CDS
Cathode Electrodeposited Paint [Environmental science] ..... CEP
Cathode Flicker Effect ..... CFE
Cathode Follower (IAA) ..... CATHFOL
Cathode Follower ..... CF
Cathode Follower Mixer ..... CFM
Cathode Heating Time ..... CHT
Cathode Potential Stabilized ..... CPS
Cathode Pulse Modulation ..... CPM
Cathode Ray ..... CR
Cathode Ray Setter (DGA) ..... CRS
Cathode Ray Tube Controller (NITA) ..... CRTC
Cathode Ray Tube Operating System (NITA) ..... CRTOS
Cathode Reaction ..... CR
Cathode Resistance (IDOE) ..... R$_K$
Cathode-Grid Capacitance ..... CGC
Cathode-Ray Direction Finder [RADAR] ..... CRDF
Cathode-Ray Electron Tube ..... CRET
Cathode-Ray Furnace ..... CRF
Cathode-Ray Lamp ..... CRL
Cathode-Ray Oscillator ..... CO
Cathode-Ray Oscilloscope [or Oscillograph] ..... CRO
Cathode-Ray Screen [Air Force] ..... C-SCOPE
Cathode-Ray Terminal ..... CRT
Cathode-Ray Tube ..... CRT
Cathode-Ray Tube (IDOE) ..... crt
Cathode-Ray Tube Automatic Direction Finding (IEEE) ..... CADF
Cathode-Ray Tube Controller ..... CRTC

Cathode-Ray Tube Indicators [JETDS nomenclature] [Military] (CET) ..... IP
Cathode-Ray Tube Oscillograph ..... CRTO
Cathode-Ray Tube Shield ..... CRTS
Cathode-Ray Tube Tester ..... CRTT
Cathode-Ray Typesetting ..... CRT
Cathodic Arc Plasma Deposition [Coating technology] ..... CAPD
Cathodic Dichromate (PDAA) ..... CDC
Cathodic Protection [Metallurgy] ..... CP
Cathodic Protection by Automatically-Controlled Impressed Current (PDAA) ..... CAPAC
Cathodic Protection Equipment ..... CPE
Cathodic Protection Index (PDAA) ..... CPI
Cathodic Protection Industry Association (EA) ..... CPIA
Cathodic Protection Survey Kit ..... CPSK
Cathodic Stripping Voltammetry [Analytical chemistry] ..... CSV
Cathodic Survey Kit ..... CSK
Cathodic Voltametry Stripping [Marine science] (OSRA) ..... CVS
Cathodic Voltametry Stripping (USDC) ..... CVS
Cathodochromic [Cathode-ray tube] CC
Cathodochromic Cathode Ray Tube (PDAA) ..... CCRT
Cathodoluminescence [Geophysics] CL
Cathodoluminescence/Energy Dispersive Spectroscopy ..... CL/EDS
Cathodoluminescence Microscope Attachment ..... CMA
Catholic C
Catholic (ADA) ..... CAT
Catholic ..... CATH
Catholic ..... CATH
Catholic ..... CATHOL
Catholic Accountants Guild (EA) ..... CAG
Catholic Action ..... CA
Catholic Actors Guild of America (EA) ..... CAG
Catholic Actors Guild of America (EA) ..... CAGA
Catholic Aid Association (EA) ..... CAA
Catholic Alumni Clubs International (EA) ..... CACI
Catholic Anthropological Association [Defunct] (EA) ..... CAA
Catholic Anthropological Conference ..... CAC
Catholic Apostolate of Radio, Television, and Advertising (NTCM) ..... CARTA
Catholic Archdiocese of Detroit, Archives, Detroit, MI [Library symbol] [Library of Congress] (LCLS) ..... MiDAA
Catholic Archdiocese of Melbourne Schools' Provident Fund [Australia] ..... CAMSPF
Catholic Archdiocese of Seattle, Archives, Seattle, WA [Library symbol Library of Congress] (LCLS) ..... WaSAA
Catholic Art Association [Defunct] (EA) ..... CAA
Catholic Association for International Peace [Defunct] (EA) ..... CAIP
Catholic Association of Foresters (EA) ..... CAOF
Catholic Association of Persons with Visual Impairment (EA) ..... CAPVI
Catholic Audio-Visual Educators Association (EA) ..... CAVE
Catholic Aviation League of Our Lady of Loreto [Defunct] (EA) ..... CALOLL
Catholic Bible Society of America (EA) ..... CBSA
Catholic Biblical Association of America (EA) ..... CBA
Catholic Biblical Association of Canada [Formerly, Canadian Catholic Biblical Association] (AC) ..... CBAC
Catholic Biblical Encyclopedia. New Testament [A publication] (BJA) ..... CBENT
Catholic Biblical Encyclopedia. Old Testament [A publication] (BJA) ..... CBEOT
Catholic Big Brothers (EA) ..... CBB
Catholic Bishops' Conference of England and Wales (EAIO) ..... CBCEW
Catholic Book Publishers [Later, CBPA] (EA) ..... CBP
Catholic Book Publishers Association (EA) ..... CBPA
Catholic Book Week ..... CBW
Catholic Broadcasters Association (EA) ..... CBA
Catholic Bushwalking Club [Australia] ..... CBC
Catholic Business Education Association [Later, NCBEA] (EA) ..... CBEA
Catholic Campus Ministry Association (EA) ..... CCMA
Catholic Central High School, London, ON, Canada [Library symbol Library of Congress] (LCLS) ..... CaOLC
Catholic Central High School, London, Ontario [Library symbol National Library of Canada] (NLC) ..... OLC
Catholic Central Union [Later, COF] ..... CCU
Catholic Central Union of America (EA) ..... CCUA
Catholic Central Union of America, St. Louis, MO [Library symbol Library of Congress] (LCLS) ..... MoSV
Catholic Central Youth Union of America (EA) ..... CCYUA
Catholic Charismatic Renewal Movement ..... CCRM
Catholic Charities USA (EA) ..... CCUSA
Catholic Church, Archdiocese of Kingston, Archives, Kingston, ON, Canada [Library symbol Library of Congress] (LCLS) ..... CaOKCAA
Catholic Church, Archdiocese of Vancouver, Archives, Vancouver, BC, Canada [Library symbol Library of Congress] (LCLS) ..... CaBVaCAA
Catholic Church Development Fund [Australia] ..... CCDF
Catholic Church Extension Society of the United States of America (EA) ..... CCESUSA
Catholic Church Extension Society of the USA (EA) ..... CCES
Catholic Civics Clubs of America [Defunct] (EA) ..... CCCA
Catholic Clergyman CC
Catholic College Admissions and Information Center (EA) ..... CCAIC
Catholic College of Oklahoma for Women, Guthrie, OK [Library symbol Library of Congress Obsolete] (LCLS) ..... OkGuC
Catholic Commission on Intellectual and Cultural Affairs (EA) ..... CCICA
Catholic Committee for Refugees (EA) ..... CCR
Catholic Committee of Appalachia (EA) ..... CCA
Catholic Committee on Scouting [Later, NCCS] ..... CCS
Catholic Committee on Urban Ministry (EA) ..... CCUM
Catholic Communications Foundation (NTCM) ..... CCF

Catholic Community Services Inc. [*Services Communautaires Catholiques Inc.*] (AC) .... CCS
Catholic Confraternity Version [*1941, 1952*] (BJA) CC
Catholic Construction Workers of America (EA) .... CCWA
Catholic Council on Civil Liberties [*Defunct*] (EA) CCCL
Catholic Council on Working Life (EA) .... CCWL
Catholic Curate CC
Catholic Daughters of the Americas (EA) .... CDA
Catholic Douay Version [*of the Bible*] [*1609*] (BJA) .... Dy
Catholic Economic Association [*Later, ASE*] (EA) .... CEA
Catholic Education Aboriginal Advisory Committee [*Australia*] .... CEAAC
Catholic Education Office, Melbourne [*Australia*] .... CEOM
Catholic Education Office of Western Australia .... CEOWA
Catholic Educational Exhibitors Association [*Later, NCEE*] .... CEEA
Catholic Enquiry Centre [*Australia*] .... CEC
Catholic Epistles (BJA) .... CathEp
Catholic Evidence Guild [*Defunct*] (EA) .... CEG
Catholic Evidence Guild of New York [*Defunct*] (EA) .... CEGNY
Catholic Family Life Insurance (EA) .... CFLI
Catholic Family Missionary Alliance [*Later, MEW*] (EA) .... CFMA
Catholic Fine Arts Society (EA) .... CFAS
Catholic Foreign Mission Society of America (EA) .... CFMSA
Catholic Fund for Overseas Development [*British*] .... CAFOD
Catholic Golden Age (EA) .... CGA
Catholic Guardian Society (EA) .... CGS
Catholic Guild for All the Blind [*Later, CCB*] (EA) .... CGFAB
Catholic Health Association of Alberta [*Formerly, Catholic Health Care Conference of Alberta*] (AC) .... CHAA
Catholic Health Association of British Columbia (AC) .... CHABC
Catholic Health Association of Canada .... CHAC
Catholic Health Association of Canada [*Association Catholique Canadienne de la Sante*], Ottawa, Ontario [*Library symbol National Library of Canada*] (NLC) .... OOCHAC
Catholic Health Association of Manitoba (AC) .... CHAM
Catholic Health Association of Ontario (AC) .... CHAO
Catholic Health Association of Saskatchewan (AC) .... CHAS
Catholic Health Association of the United States (EA) .... CHA
Catholic Health Association of the United States (EA) .... CHA-US
Catholic Health Care Association of New South Wales [*Australia*] .... CHCNSW
Catholic High Schools Athletic Association .... CHSAA
Catholic Historical Review [*A publication*] (BRI) .... CHR
Catholic Homiletic Society [*Later, CPC*] (EA) .... CHS
Catholic Hospital Association [*Canada*] .... CHA
Catholic Hospital Association of Canada .... CHAC
Catholic Housing Aid Society [*British*] (DBA) .... CHAS
Catholic Information Society [*Defunct*] (EA) .... CIS
Catholic Institute for International Relations [*British*] (EAIO) .... CIIR
Catholic Institute of the Food Industry (EA) .... CIFI
Catholic Institute of the Press [*Later, Catholic Alliance for Communications*] (EA) .... CIP
Catholic Inter-American Cooperation Program [*Defunct*] .... CICOP
Catholic Intercontinental Press .... CIP
Catholic International Education Office [*Belgium*] .... CIEO
Catholic International Federation for Physical and Sports Education [*See also FICEP*] [*Paris, France*] (EAIO) .... CIFPSE
Catholic International Union for Social Service .... CIUSS
Catholic Interracial Council of Chicago (EA) CICC
Catholic Interracial Council of New York (EA) CIC
Catholic Interracial Council of New York (EA) .... CICNY
Catholic Irish Attorneys [*Fictional organization*] .... CIA
Catholic Journalist [*A publication*] (EAAP) .... CJ
Catholic Knights Insurance Society (EA) .... CKIS
Catholic Knights of America (EA) .... CKA
Catholic Knights of St. George (EA) .... CKSG
Catholic Kolping Society of America (EA) .... CKSA
Catholic Ladies Aid Society .... CLAS
Catholic Ladies of Columbia CLC
Catholic Lay Mission Corps (EA) .... CLMC
Catholic League for Religious and Civil Rights (EA) .... CLRCR
Catholic League for Religious Assistance to Poland (EA) .... CLRAP
Catholic Library Association .... CATLA
Catholic Library Association (EA) .... CLA
Catholic Library World [*A publication*] (BRI) .... CLW
Catholic Life Insurance Union (EA) .... CLIU
Catholic Listener Library [*Later, Maynard Listener Library*] (EA) CLL
Catholic Major Markets Newspaper Association (EA) .... CMMNA
Catholic Media Council [*Aachen, Federal Republic of Germany*] (EAIO) .... CaMeCo
Catholic Medical Center of Brooklyn & Queens, Inc., Jamaica, NY [*Library symbol*] [*Library of Congress*] (LCLS) .... NJMI
Catholic Medical Mission Board (EA) .... CMMB
Catholic Messenger, Davenport, IA [*Library symbol Library of Congress*] (LCLS) .... IaDaCM
Catholic Microfilm Center [*Defunct*] .... CMC
Catholic Microfilm Center, Berkeley, CA [*Library symbol Library of Congress Obsolete*] (LCLS) .... CathMC
Catholic Mission Sisters of St. Francis Xavier (TOCD) .... XS
Catholic Missionary Society .... CMS
Catholic Near East Welfare Association (EA) .... CNEWA
Catholic Negro-American Mission Board (EA) .... CNAMB
Catholic One Parent Organization (EA) .... COPO
Catholic Order of Foresters (EA) .... COF
Catholic Pamphlet Society of the United States (EA) .... CPS
Catholic Peace Fellowship (EA) .... CPF
Catholic Poetry Society of America [*Defunct*] (EA) .... CPSA
Catholic Press Association (EA) .... CPA

Catholic Press Features .... CPF
Catholic Press Office [*British*] .... CPO
Catholic Record Society (EA) .... CRS
Catholic Relief Services [*Later, CRS-USCC*] .... CRS
Catholic Relief Services - National Catholic Welfare Conference [*Later, CRS-USCC*] (EA) .... CRS-NCWC
Catholic Relief Services - US Catholic Conference (EA) .... CRS-USCC
Catholic Renascence Society [*Defunct*] (EA) .... CRS
Catholic Russian Center, San Francisco, CA [*Library symbol Library of Congress*] (LCLS) .... CSfCR
Catholic Scholarships for Negroes [*Defunct*] (EA) .... CSN
Catholic School Commission, Montreal, PQ, Canada [*Library symbol Library of Congress*] (LCLS) .... CaQMCEC
Catholic School Commission [*Commission des Ecoles Catholiques*] **Montreal, Quebec** [*Library symbol National Library of Canada*] (NLC) .... QMCEC
Catholic School Press Association [*Defunct*] (EA) .... CSPA
Catholic Schools Office [*Australia*] .... CSO
Catholic Slovak Brotherhood .... CSB
Catholic Sokol Printing Co., Passaic, NJ [*Library symbol Library of Congress*] (LCLS) .... NjPasCS
Catholic Solo Parents [*Australia*] .... CSP
Catholic Star Herald, Camden, NJ [*Library symbol Library of Congress*] (LCLS) .... NjCaSH
Catholic Students' Mission Crusade [*Defunct*] .... CSMC
Catholic Tape Recorders, International (EA) .... CTRI
Catholic Teachers College [*Rhode Island*] .... CTC
Catholic Teachers Federation [*British*] (DBA) .... CTF
Catholic Telecommunications Network of America [*Staten Island, NY*] (TSSD) .... CTNA
Catholic Television Network [*Cable-television system*] .... CTN
Catholic Theological Society of America (EA) .... CTSA
Catholic Theological Union [*Australia*] .... CTU
Catholic Theological Union, Chicago, IL [*Library symbol Library of Congress*] (LCLS) .... ICTU
Catholic Theological Union, Chicago, IL [*OCLC symbol*] (OCLC) .... IDJ
Catholic Total Abstinence Union .... CTAU
Catholic Total Abstinence Union of America (EA) .... CTAUA
Catholic Traditionalist Movement (EA) .... CTM
Catholic Truth Society [*British*] (BI) .... CTS
Catholic University .... CU
[*The*] Catholic University of America (GAGS) .... Catholic U
Catholic University of America [*Washington, DC*] .... CUA
Catholic University of America, Clementine Library, Washington, DC [*Library symbol Library of Congress*] (LCLS) .... DCU-C
Catholic University of America, Hyvernat Collection, Washington, DC [*Library symbol Library of Congress*] (LCLS) .... DCU-H
Catholic University of America, Ibero-American Collection, Washington, DC [*Library symbol Library of Congress*] (LCLS) .... DCU-IA
Catholic University of America Law School (DLA) .... CUALS
Catholic University of America, Washington, DC [*OCLC symbol*] (OCLC) .... CUA
Catholic University of America, Washington, DC [*Library symbol Library of Congress*] (LCLS) .... DCU
Catholic University of Puerto Rico (GAGS) .... Catholic U of PR
Catholic University of Puerto Rico .... CUPR
Catholic University of Puerto Rico, Law Library, Ponce, Puerto Rico [*Library symbol*] [*Library of Congress*] (LCLS) .... PrPCU-L
Catholic Walking Club of Victoria [*Australia*] .... CWCV
Catholic War Veterans of the USA (EA) .... CWV
Catholic War Veterans of the USA Auxiliary (EA) .... CWVUSAA
Catholic War Veterans of the USA Ladies Auxiliary [*Later, CWVUSAA*] (EA) .... CWVA
Catholic Weekly [*A publication*] .... Catholic Wkly
Catholic White Anglo-Saxon Protestant .... CWASP
Catholic Women for the ERA (EA) .... CWERA
Catholic Women's Benevolent Legion (EA) .... CWBL
Catholic Women's League (BARN) .... CWL
Catholic Women's League of Australia [*An association*] .... CWLA
Catholic Women's Seminary Fund [*Defunct*] (EA) .... CWSF
Catholic Worker Movement (EA) .... CWM
Catholic Workman (EA) .... CW
Catholic World [*A publication*] (BRI) .... Cath W
Catholic Writers Guild of America (EA) .... CWGA
Catholic Young Men's Society [*Ireland*] (BI) .... CYMS
Catholic Youth Adoration Society [*Defunct*] (EA) .... CYA
Catholic Youth Association [*Lithuania*] (EAIO) .... CYA
Catholic Youth Council [*Belgium*] (EAIO) .... CYC
Catholic Youth Organization .... CYO
Catholicarum Universitatum Federatio [*Federation of Catholic Universities*] .... CUF
Catholics for a Free Choice .... CFFC
Catholics for Christian Political Action [*Defunct*] (EA) .... CCPA
Catholics for Latin America .... CFLA
Catholics Speak Out [*Quixote Center*] (EA) .... CSO
Catholics United for Life (EA) .... CUL
Catholics United for Spiritual Action (EA) .... CUSA
Catholics United for the Faith (EA) .... CUF
Cathy Buchanan Fan Club (EA) .... CBFC
Caticlan, Aklan [*Philippines*] [*ICAO location identifier*] (ICLI) .... RPVE
Catio [*Guinea-Bissau*] [*ICAO location identifier*] (ICLI) .... GGCT
Cation Exchange Chromography (NUCP) .... CEC
Cation-Exchange Capacity [*Chemical technology*] .... CEC
Cation-Exchange Resin [*Chemical technology*] .... CER
Cationic Asphalt-Neoprene Emulsion [*Dust control*] .... CANE
Cationic Flocculant Producers Association [*Defunct*] (EA) .... CFPA
Cationized Ferritin [*Biochemistry*] .... CF
Cation-Responsive Electrode .... CRE

Catlettsburg, KY [*FM radio station call letters*] (RBYB) ... WRVC-FM
Catlin Public Library, Catlin, IL [*Library symbol Library of Congress*] (LCLS) ... ICat
Catlow Resources Ltd. [*Vancouver Stock Exchange symbol*] ... CTW
Catlow/Whitney Family Organization (EA) ... CWFO
[*The*] **Cato Corp.** [*NASDAQ symbol*] (NQ) ... CACO
Cato Corp. [*Associated Press*] (SAG) ... CatoCp
Cato Corp.'A' [*NASDAQ symbol*] (TTSB) ... CACOA
Cato Institute (EA) ... CI
Cato Maior [*of Plutarch*] [*Classical studies*] (OCD) ... Cat Mai
Cato Minor [*of Plutarch*] [*Classical studies*] (OCD) ... Cat Min
Cato Township Public Library, Lakeview, MI [*Library symbol Library of Congress*] (LCLS) ... MiLakv
Catoctin Mountain Park [*National Park Service designation*] ... CATO
Catonsville Community College, Baltimore, MD [*OCLC symbol*] (OCLC) ... CAT
Catonsville Community College, Learning Resources Division, Baltimore, MD [*Library symbol Library of Congress*] (LCLS) ... MdBCC
Catonsville, MD [*FM radio station call letters*] ... WQSR
Cats and Dogs [*i.e., low selling items or speculative stock*] [*Slang Business term*] ... C & D
Cats in Industry [*British*] (DI) ... CII
Cats on Stamps Study Unit [*American Topical Association*] (EA) ... CSSU
Cats Protection League [*British*] (DBA) ... CPL
C.ATS Software [*NASDAQ symbol*] (TTSB) ... CATX
CATS Software, Inc. [*Associated Press*] (SAG) ... CATS
CATS Software, Inc. [*NASDAQ symbol*] (SAG) ... CATX
Catskill Airways [*ICAO designator*] (AD) ... KF
Catskill Airways, Inc. [*FAA designator*] (FAAC) ... MOW
Catskill Financial [*NASDAQ symbol*] (TTSB) ... CATB
Catskill, NY [*AM radio station call letters*] ... WCKL
Catskill, NY [*FM radio station call letters*] ... WCTW
Catskills (FAAC) ... CTSKLS
Catskills/Sullivan County [*New York*] [*Airport symbol Obsolete*] (OAG) ... MSV
Cattaraugus-Allegany School Library System, Olean, NY [*Library symbol*] [*Library of Congress*] (LCLS) ... NoISL
Cattell Infant Intelligence Scale [*Psychology*] (DAVI) ... CIIS
Cattermole Memorial Library, Fort Madison, IA [*Library symbol Library of Congress*] (LCLS) ... IaFm
Cattle (ROG) ... C
Cattle ... CAT
Cattle ... CTL
Cattle ... CTTL
Cattle Containers (DCTA) ... CT
Cattle Hide ... CATLHD
Cattle on Feed (GFGA) ... COF
Cattlemans, Inc. [*Associated Press*] (SAG) ... Catleman
Cattlemans, Inc. [*NASDAQ symbol*] (SAG) ... CTLO
Cattlemans Inc. [*NASDAQ symbol*] (TTSB) ... CTLO
Cattle-Plague (ROG) ... CP
Catullus [*First century BC*] [*Classical studies*] (OCD) ... Catull
Catwalk [*Technical drawings*] (DAC) ... CATW
Catwalk ... CTWALK
Cauayan [*Philippines*] [*Airport symbol*] (OAG) ... CYZ
Cauayan, Isabela [*Philippines*] [*ICAO location identifier*] (ICLI) ... RPUY
Caucasia [*Colombia*] [*Airport symbol*] (OAG) ... CAQ
Caucasian ... C
Caucasian [*MARC language code Library of Congress*] (LCCP) ... cau
Caucasian (AFM) ... CAU
Caucasian (MAE) ... Cauc
Caucasian Except as Otherwise Indicated [*Army*] ... CAUEOI
Caucasian Female ... CF
Caucasian Male ... CM
Caucasus [*MARC geographic area code Library of Congress*] (LCCP) ... e-urk-
Cauchy Boundary Condition [*Mathematics*] ... CBC
Cauchy Convergence Test [*Mathematics*] ... CCT
Cauchy-Riemann Equation [*Mathematics*] ... CRE
Caucus for a New Political Science (EA) ... CNPS
Caucus for Producers, Writers, and Directors (EA) ... CPWD
Caucus for Women in Statistics (EA) ... CWS
Caudal [*Anatomy*] ... C
Caudal [*Anatomy*] (DAVI) ... CAUD
Caudal [*Anatomy*] ... CD
Caudal [*Medicine*] (DMAA) ... cd
Caudal Magnocellular [*Nuclei*] [*Neuroanatomy*] ... CM
Caudal Mediastinal Node [*Medicine*] (DMAA) ... CMN
Caudal Photoreceptor [*Biology*] ... CPR
Caudality Scale [*Psychology*] ... Ca
Caudate Nucleus [*Anatomy*] ... CN
Caudate Putamen [*Neuroanatomy*] ... CP
Caudate Putamen (DMAA) ... CPU
Caudate-Caudate to Outer Table (Ratio) [*Neuroradiology*] ... CC/OT
Caudate-Putamen Complex [*Anatomy*] ... CPU
Caudill, Rowlett & Scott [*Architectural firm*] ... CRS
Caudodorsal Cell Hormone [*Zoology*] ... CDCH
Caudodorsal Cells [*Anatomy*] ... CDC
Caudodorsal Cells Autotransmitter [*Zoology*] ... CDCA
Caught [*by*] [*In cricket*] ... C
Caught ... CAT
Caught ... CT
Caught and Bowled [*Cricket*] ... C & B
Caught Out ... C
Caught Stealing [*Baseball*] ... CS
Caulfield Resources Ltd. [*Vancouver Stock Exchange symbol*] ... CXI
Cauliflower (DSUE) ... CAULI
Cauliflower Mosaic Virus [*Also, CLMV*] ... CaMV
Cauliflower Mosaic Virus [*Also, CaMV*] ... CLMV
Caulked Joint ... CAJ
Caulked Joint ... CLKJ
Caulking (MSA) ... CLKG
Caulking Seam (DAC) ... CS
Causa [*Case or Cause*] ... C
Causa [*Decretum Gratiani*] [*A publication*] (DSA) ... Ca
CAUSA Institute (EA) ... CI
Causa Mortis [*On Occasion of Death*] [*Latin*] ... CM
Causal Factors Analysis [*Engineering*] ... CFA
Causal Tree Method [*Engineering*] ... CTM
Causapscal, PQ [*AM radio station call letters*] ... CJBM
Causation ... CAUS
Causative (BJA) ... Caus
Cause ... C
Cause Consequence Diagram Method [*Engineering*] ... CCDM
Cause for Concern [*Defunct*] (EA) ... CC
Cause of Action (MHDB) ... CA
Cause of Action [*Legal shorthand*] (LWAP) ... COA
Cause of Death [*Medicine*] ... COD
Cause of Failure [*Telecommunications*] (TEL) ... COF
Cause of Failure, Effect, and Correction (SAA) ... COFF
Cause Undetermined [*Medicine*] (DAVI) ... CUD
Cause Unknown [*Medicine*] (DAVI) ... CU
Cause-Effect Graph Language [*Computer science*] (IBMDP) ... CEGL
Cause-Effect Logic Diagram [*Engineering*] ... CELD
Cause-Related Marketing [*Finance*] ... CRM
Causes Celebres [*Quebec Provincial Reports*] [*A publication*] (DLA) ... Ca Celeb
Causes Celebres [*Quebec Provincial Reports*] [*A publication*] (DLA) ... CC
Causeway [*Commonly used*] (OPSA) ... CAUSEWAY
Causeway [*Commonly used*] (OPSA) ... CAUSWAY
Causeway ... CSWAY
Causeway ... CSWY
Causeway (KSC) ... CSWY
Causeway Section, Nonpowered [*Navy*] (ANA) ... CSNP
Caustic Boundary Layer [*Acoustics*] ... CBL
Cauterization [*Medicine*] (DMAA) ... caut
Cauterize [*or Cauterization*] (CPH) ... CAUT
Caution (AFM) ... CAUT
Caution ... CTN
Caution Advised Until Further Notice [*Aviation*] (FAAC) ... CAUFN
Caution Against Dangerous Exports [*Shipping*] ... CADE
Caution and Warning [*Aerospace*] (KSC) ... C & W
Caution and Warning Advisory Panel (MCD) ... CWAP
Caution and Warning Advisory Panel Indicators (MCD) ... CWAPI
Caution and Warning Advisory Signals (MCD) ... CWAS
Caution and Warning Annunciator (MCD) ... CWA
Caution and Warning Electronics (NASA) ... CWE
Caution and Warning Electronics Assembly [*Apollo*] [*NASA*] ... CWEA
Caution and Warning Electronics Unit (MCD) ... CWEU
Caution and Warning Equipment [*NASA*] (KSC) ... CWE
Caution and Warning/Fire Suppression Panel (MCD) ... CWFSP
Caution and Warning Limit Module [*NASA*] (NASA) ... CWLM
Caution and Warning Status (MCD) ... CWS
Caution and Warning Status Unit [*NASA*] (NASA) ... CWSU
Caution and Warning System [*NASA*] (KSC) ... C & WS
Caution and Warning Unit (MCD) ... CWU
Cautious Hawk [*Description of President Reagan's position on foreign affairs, used in book "Gambling with History: Reagan in the White House"*] ... CAWK
Cavalier [*Knight title*] ... CAV
Cavalier Homes [*NYSE symbol*] (TTSB) ... CAV
Cavalier Homes [*Associated Press*] (SAG) ... CavalrH
Cavalier Homes Co. [*NYSE symbol*] (SAG) ... CAV
Cavalier Homes Co. [*Associated Press*] (SAG) ... CavallrH
Cavalier King Charles Spaniel Club of America (EA) ... CKCSC
Cavalier, ND [*FM radio station call letters*] (RBYB) ... KAOC
Cavalry [*British military*] (DMA) ... C
Cavalry ... CAV
Cavalry ... CLVRY
Cavalry Brigade ... CB
Cavalry Brigade (Air Attack) [*Army*] ... CB(AA)
Cavalry Division [*Army*] ... CD
Cavalry Fighting Vehicle ... CFV
Cavalry Mobile Veterinary Section [*British military*] (DMA) ... CMVS
Cavalry Navigation System (MCD) ... CAVNAVS
Cavalry Replacement Training Center ... CRTC
Cavalry Transport [*Navy ship symbol*] [*Obsolete*] ... APC
Cavan [*County in Ireland*] (ROG) ... CA
Cavan [*County in Ireland*] (ROG) ... CAV
Cavanagh's Law of Money Securities [*A publication*] (DLA) ... Cav Mon Sec
Cavco Indus [*NASDAQ symbol*] (TTSB) ... CVCO
Cavco Industries, Inc. [*Associated Press*] (SAG) ... Cavco
Cavco Industries, Inc. [*NASDAQ symbol*] (NQ) ... CVCO
CAVDA [*Citizens Alliance for Venereal Disease Awareness*]-Citizens AIDS Project (EA) ... CAP
Cave (ROG) ... CV
Cave Automatic Virtual Environment [*Virtual reality*] ... CAVE
Cave City, AR [*FM radio station call letters*] ... KZIG
Cave City, KY [*FM radio station call letters*] ... WHHT
Cave Creek, AZ [*AM radio station call letters*] ... KCCF
Cave Creek Public Library, Cave Creek, AZ [*Library symbol Library of Congress*] (LCLS) ... AzCc
Cave Exploration Group [*Australia*] ... CEG
Cave Junction, OR [*FM radio station call letters*] ... KCNA
Cave Junction, OR [*Location identifier FAA*] (FAAL) ... SSB

Cave Rescue Organization [*British*] (PDAA) .... CRO
Cave Research Associates (EA) .... CRA
Cave Research Foundation (EA) .... CRF
Cave Research Group of Great Britain (BI) .... CRG
Caveat [*Let Him Beware*] [*A judicial writ*] [*Latin Legal term*] .... CAV
Caveat [*Let Him Beware*] [*A judicial writ*] [*Latin Legal term*] (ROG) .... CAVT
Caveat Emptor [*Let the Buyer Beware*] [*Latin*] .... CE
Caveat Emptor Consumer Report [*A publication*] (AAGC) .... Caveat Emptor
Cavedale Road [*California*] [*Seismograph station code, US Geological Survey*] (SEIS) .... CRD
Cavei Avir Lemitanim [*Israel*] [*ICAO designator*] (FAAC) ICL
Cavender's Debates on Canada [*A publication*] (DLA) .... Cav Deb Can
Cavendish Public Library (G. Galloway), Ontario [*Library symbol National Library of Canada*] (BIB) .... OGALL
Cavendish's Debates, House of Commons [*A publication*] (DLA) .... Cav Deb
Cavern (ROG) C
Cavern (ROG) .... CAV
Cavernous Sinus Thrombosis [*Medicine*] .... CST
Cavernous Sinus Thrombosis [*Medicine*] .... CVT
Cavinas [*Bolivia*] [*ICAO location identifier*] (ICLI) .... SLCJ
Cavinas [*Bolivia*] [*ICAO location identifier*] (ICLI) .... SLCV
Cavitation .... CAV
Cavitation Intensity Meter .... CIM
Cavitation Tendency Ratio .... CTR
Cavitron Ultrasonic Surgical Aspirator [*Medicine*] .... CUSA
Cavity [*Dentistry*] (DAVI) .... cav
Cavity (MSA) .... CAV
Cavity Alternated Phase Shift (MCD) .... CAPS
Cavity Nester [*Ornithology*] .... CN
Cavity Rim Cup [*A contraceptive device*] .... CRC
Cavity Ringdown LASER Absorption Spectroscopy .... CRLAS
Cavity Transfer Mixer [*Chemical engineering*] .... CTM
Cavity Tuned Oscillator .... CTO
Cavity Turnable Filter .... CTF
Cavity Wall .... CW
Cavum Septum Pellucidum (DAVI) .... CSP
Cawcaw Swamp [*South Carolina*] [*Seismograph station code, US Geological Survey*] (SEIS) .... CCS
Cawkell Information & Technology Services, Ltd. [*Telecommunications*] (IID) .... CITECH
Cawley's Laws Concerning Jesuits, Etc. [*1680*] [*A publication*] (DLA) .... Cawl
Caxias [*Brazil*] [*Airport symbol*] (AD) .... CXS
Caxias do Sul [*Brazil*] [*Airport symbol*] (AD) .... CXJ
Cay Sal [*Bahamas*] [*ICAO location identifier*] (ICLI) .... MYCS
Cayajabo [*Cuba ICAO location identifier*] (ICLI) .... MUCY
Cayana [*Surinam*] [*ICAO location identifier*] (ICLI) .... SMCA
Cayce, SC [*FM radio station call letters*] .... WHKZ
Cayce, SC [*AM radio station call letters*] .... WTGH
Cayce, SC [*FM radio station call letters*] .... WYFV
Cayenne [*French Guiana*] [*Airport symbol*] (OAG) .... CAY
Cayenne/Rochambeau [*French Guiana*] [*ICAO location identifier*] (ICLI) .... SOCA
Cayenne Software, Inc. [*Associated Press*] (SAG) .... CayenneSf
Cayenne Software, Inc. [*NASDAQ symbol*] (SAG) .... CAYN
Cayes [*Haiti*] [*ICAO location identifier*] (ICLI) .... MTCA
Cayey [*Puerto Rico*] [*Seismograph station code, US Geological Survey*] (SEIS) .... SJCC
Cayey, PR [*AM radio station call letters*] .... WLEY
Cayley-Klein Parameter [*Mathematics*] .... CKP
Cayman Airways [*ICAO designator*] (AD) .... KX
Cayman Airways [*Airline flight code*] (ODBW) .... KX
Cayman Airways Ltd. [*British ICAO designator*] (FAAC) .... CAY
Cayman Brac [*West Indies*] [*Airport symbol*] (OAG) .... CYB
Cayman Brac/Gerrard Smith [*Cayman Islands*] [*ICAO location identifier*] (ICLI) .... MWCB
Cayman Islands CI
Cayman Islands [*MARC country of publication code Library of Congress*] (LCCP) .... cj
Cayman Islands [*ANSI three-letter standard code*] (CNC) .... CYM
Cayman Islands [*ANSI two-letter standard code*] (CNC) .... KY
Cayman Islands [*MARC geographic area code Library of Congress*] (LCCP) .... nwcj--
Cayman Islands [*International civil aircraft marking*] (ODBW) .... VR-C
Cayman Islands Department of Tourism (EA) .... CIDT
Cayman Water Co. Ltd. [*Associated Press*] (SAG) .... CayWtr
Cayman Water Co. Ltd. [*NASDAQ symbol*] (SAG) .... CWCO
Cayman Water Co. Ltd [*NASDAQ symbol*] (TTSB) .... CWCOF
Cayo Largo Del Sur [*Cuba ICAO location identifier*] (ICLI) .... MUCL
Cayo Mambi [*Cuba*] [*Airport symbol*] (AD) .... CMV
Cayo Mambi [*Cuba ICAO location identifier*] (ICLI) .... MUBI
Cay's Abridgment, or the English Statutes [*A publication*] (DLA) .... Cay Abr
Cayuga County Community College, Auburn, NY [*Library symbol Library of Congress*] (LCLS) .... NAuC
Cayuga County Historical Society, Auburn, NY [*Library symbol Library of Congress*] (LCLS) .... NAuHi
Cayuga Herald News, Cayuga, IN [*Library symbol Library of Congress*] (LCLS) .... InCayHN
Cazador Explorations [*Vancouver Stock Exchange symbol*] .... CAZ
Cazaux [*France ICAO location identifier*] (ICLI) .... LFBC
Cazenovia College, Cazenovia, NY [*Library symbol Library of Congress*] (LCLS) .... NCazC
Cazenovia College, Witherill Learning Center, Cazenovia, NY [*OCLC symbol*] (OCLC) .... ZCZ
Cazenovia, NY [*FM radio station call letters*] .... WITC
Cazombo [*Angola*] [*ICAO location identifier*] (ICLI) .... FNCZ
CB Bancorp [*NASDAQ symbol*] (TTSB) .... CBCO
CB Bancorp, Inc. [*Associated Press*] (SAG) .... CB Bcp
CB Bancorp, Inc. [*NASDAQ symbol*] (SAG) .... CBCO
CB Bancshares [*NASDAQ symbol*] (TTSB) .... CBBI
CB Bancshares, Inc. [*Associated Press*] (SAG) .... CB Bnc
CB Bancshares, Inc. [*NASDAQ symbol*] (SAG) .... CBBI
CB Commercial Real Estate Services Group, Inc. [*Associated Press*] (SAG) .... CB CoRl
CB Commercial Real Estate Services Group, Inc. [*NASDAQ symbol*] (SAG) .... CBCG
CB Exective Helicopters [*British ICAO designator*] (FAAC) .... CBH
CB Pak, Inc. [*Toronto Stock Exchange symbol*] .... CBK
CB [*Citizens Band*] **Radio Patrol of American Federation of Police** (EA) .... CBRP
CBA Engineering Ltd., Vancouver, BC, Canada [*Library symbol Library of Congress*] (LCLS) .... CaBVaCBA
CBA Engineering Ltd., Vancouver, British Columbia [*Library symbol National Library of Canada*] (NLC) .... BVACBA
C-Band [*3900-6200 MHz*] .... C/B
C-Band [*3900-6200 MHz*] (NASA) .... C-BD
C-Band Checkout System (KSC) .... CBCS
C-Band Communications Transponder .... CCT
C-Band Frequency Converter .... CFC
C-Band Monopulse Feed .... CMF
C-Band RADAR Transponder .... CRT
C-band Scatterometer [*Marine science*] (OSRA) .... C-SCAT
C-Band Scatterometer (USDC) .... C-SCAT
C-Band Sensitivity Improvement [*Navy*] (MCD) .... CSI
C-Band Temperature .... CTF
C-Band Tracking RADAR .... CTR
C-Band Transponder [*Radio*] .... CBX
C-Band Transponder Antenna [*Radio*] (CET) .... CBA
C-Battery .... CB
CBI Industries, Inc. [*Formerly, Chicago Bridge & Iron Co.*] [*Associated Press*] (SAG) .... CBI
CBL & Associates Prop [*NYSE symbol*] (TTSB) .... CBL
CBL & Associates Properties [*NYSE symbol*] (SPSG) .... CBL
CBL & Associates Properties [*Associated Press*] (SAG) .... CBL Asc
CBN University, Virginia Beach, VA [*Library symbol*] [*Library of Congress*] (LCLS) .... ViVbC
CBNU Learning Resources Center, Virginia Beach, VA [*OCLC symbol*] (OCLC) .... VCB
CBO Resources Corp. [*Vancouver Stock Exchange symbol*] .... CBU
CBPO [*Consolidated Base Personnel Office*] **Strength Summary Card** (AFM) .... CSS
CBPO [*Consolidated Base Personnel Office*] **Strength Summary Card** (AFM) .... CSSC
CBS, Inc. [*Formerly, Columbia Broadcasting System, Inc.*] [*NYSE symbol*] (SPSG) .... CBS
CBS, Inc. [*Formerly, Columbia Broadcasting System, Inc.*] [*Associated Press*] (SAG) .... CBS
CBT Corp. [*Associated Press*] (SAG) .... CBT Cp
CBT Corp. [*NASDAQ symbol*] (SAG) .... CBTC
CBT Group ADS [*NASDAQ symbol*] (TTSB) .... CBTSY
CBT Group PLC [*Associated Press*] (SAG) .... CBT
CBT Group PLC [*Associated Press*] (SAG) .... CBT Gp
CBT Group PLC [*NASDAQ symbol*] (SAG) .... CBTS
C.C. Enrique Cuahonte Delgado, Marta Amezcua de Cuahonte [*Mexico*] [*FAA designator*] (FAAC) .... CUO
CCA Industries [*NASDAQ symbol*] (TTSB) .... CCAM
CCA Industries, Inc. [*Associated Press*] (SAG) .... CCA
CCA Industries, Inc. [*NASDAQ symbol*] (NQ) .... CCAM
CCAIR, Inc. [*Associated Press*] (SAG) .... CCAIR
CCAIR, Inc. [*NASDAQ symbol*] (NQ) .... CCAR
CCAir, Inc. [*ICAO designator*] (FAAC) .... CDL
CCATS [*Communications, Command, and Telemetry Systems*] **Command Controller** [*NASA*] CCC
CCATS [*Communications, Command, and Telemetry Systems*] **Telemetry Controller** [*NASA*] .... CTC
CCB Financial [*NYSE symbol*] (SAG) .... CCB
CCB Financial [*NASDAQ symbol*] (TTSB) .... CCBF
CCB Financial Co. [*Associated Press*] (SAG) .... CCB Fn
CCB Financial Corp. [*NASDAQ symbol*] (NQ) .... CCBF
CCC Coded Communications [*Vancouver Stock Exchange symbol*] .... CCE
CCC Information Services Group, Inc. [*Associated Press*] (SAG) .... CCC Info
CCC Information Services Group, Inc. [*NASDAQ symbol*] (SAG) .... CCCG
CCCO [*Central Committee for Conscientious Objectors*]/An Agency for Military and Draft Counseling (EA) .... CCCO
CCD [*Charge-Coupled Device*] **Transit Instrument** [*Telescope*] .... CTI
CCF Holding [*NASDAQ symbol*] (TTSB) .... CCFH
CCF Holding Co. [*Associated Press*] (SAG) .... CCF
CCF Holding Co. [*NASDAQ symbol*] (SAG) .... CCFH
CCH FAR Archives [*Historical FARs on CD-ROM*] (AAGC) .... FARchives
CCH, Inc. [*Associated Press*] (SAG) .... CCH
CCH, Inc. [*NASDAQ symbol*] (SAG) .... CCHI
CCH [*Commerce Clearing House*] **Publications Index** (ADA) .... CCHP
CCITT [*Consultative Committee on International Telegraphy and Telephony*] **High-Level Language** [*Telecommunications*] (TEL) .... CHILL
CCL Industries, Inc. [*Toronto Stock Exchange symbol*] .... CCQ
CCMS [*Checkout, Control and Monitor Systems*] **Application Program** .... CAP
CCMS [*Checkout, Control, and Monitor Subsystem*] **Application Programs** [*NASA*] (NASA) .... CAP
CCNU [*Lomustine*], Adriamycin, Bleomycin, Streptozotocin [*Antineoplastic drug regimen*] .... CABS
CCNU [*Lomustine*], Adriamycin, Vinblastine [*Antineoplastic drug regimen*] .... CAVe
CCNU [*Lomustine*], Bleomycin, Vinblastine, Dexamethasone [*Antineoplastic drug regimen*] .... CBVD

CCNU [*Lomustine*], Cyclophosphamide, Adriamycin, Vincristine, VP-16 [*Antineoplastic drug regimen*] (DAVI) .... CCAVV
CCNU [*Lomustine*], Cyclophosphamide, Methotrexate, Adriamycin [*Antineoplastic drug regimen*] (DAVI) .... CCMA
CCNU [*Lomustine*], Cyclophosphamide, Oncovin , Bleomycin [*Vincristine*] [*Antineoplastic drug regimen*] (DAVI) .... CCOB
CCNU [*Lomustine*], Cyclophosphamide, Vincristine [*Antineoplastic drug regimen*] (DAVI) CCV
CCNU [*Lomustine*], Cyclophosphamide, Vincristine, Alternating with Adriamycin, Vincristine [*Antineoplastic drug regimen*] .... CCV-AV
CCNU [*Lomustine*], Cyclophosphamide, Vincristine, Bleomycin [*Antineoplastic drug regimen*] (DAVI) .... CCVB
CCNU [*Lomustine*], Cyclophosphamide, Vincristine, Procarbazine, Prednisone [*Antineoplastic drug regimen*] .... CCVPP
CCNU [*Lomustine*], Etoposide, Prednimustine [*Antineoplastic drug regimen*] .... CEP
CCNU [*Lomustine*], Etoposide, Vindesine, Dexamethasone [*Antineoplastic drug regimen*] .... CEVD
CCNU [*Lomustine*], Ifosfamide, Adriamycin [*Antineoplastic drug regimen*] .... CIA
CCNU Lomustine, Oncovin [*Vincristine*], Prednisone [*Antineoplastic drug regimen*] (DAVI) .... CCNU-OP
CCNU [*Lomustine*], Methotrexate, Procarbazine [*Antineoplastic drug regimen*] (DAVI) .... CMP
CCNU [*Lomustine*], Oncovin , Methotrexate, Procarbazine [*Vincristine*] [*Antineoplastic drug regimen*] .... COMP
CCNU [*Lomustine*], Oncovin , Prednisone, Adriamycin, Cyclophosphamide [*Vincristine*] [*Antineoplastic drug regimen*] .... COPAC
CCNU [*Lomustine*], Oncovin , Procarbazine, Prednisone [*Vincristine*] [*Antineoplastic drug regimen*] .... COPP
CCNU [*Lomustine*], Procarbazine, Methotrexate [*Antineoplastic drug regimen*] .... CPM
CCNU [*Lomustine*], Vinblastine, Bleomycin [*Antineoplastic drug regimen*] .... CVB
CCNU [*Lomustine*], Vinblastine, Prednisone, Procarbazine [*Antineoplastic drug regimen*] .... CVPP
CCOR Electronics, Inc. [*Associated Press*] (SAG) .... C COR
C-COR Electronics, Inc. [*NASDAQ symbol*] (NQ) .... CCBL
C-COR Electrs [*NASDAQ symbol*] (TTSB) .... CCBL
Ccos (Keeling) Islands Cooperative Society [*Australia*] .... C(K)ICS
C-CUBE Microsystems [*Associated Press*] (SAG) .... C-CUBE
C-CUBE Microsystems [*NASDAQ symbol*] (SAG) .... CUBE
CCW System Ltd. [*Vancouver Stock Exchange symbol*] .... CWI
CD [*Compact Disc*] **Data Report** [*Langley Publications*] [*Information service or system A publication*] (IID) .... CDDR
CD [*Compact Disk*] **- Erasable** (CDE) .... CD-E
CD Radio, Inc. [*Associated Press*] (SAG) .... CDRad
CD Radio, Inc. [*Associated Press*] (SAG) .... CDRadio
CD Radio, Inc. [*NASDAQ symbol*] (SAG) .... CDRD
CD Radio Inc. Wrrt [*NASDAQ symbol*] (TTSB) .... CDRDW
CD Warehouse, Inc. [*Associated Press*] (SAG) .... CD Wrhs
CD Warehouse, Inc. [*NASDAQ symbol*] (SAG) .... CDWI
CDI Corp. [*NYSE symbol*] (SPSG) .... CDI
CDIS Software, Inc. [*Vancouver Stock Exchange symbol*] .... CIS
CDK (Cyclin Dependent Kinae) Activating Kinae [*An enzyme*] .... CAK
CDOS [*Customer Data and Operations System*] **Integration and Test Facility** (SSD) .... CITF
CDR Discrepancy Notice [*NASA*] (MCD) .... CDN
CDR Discrepancy Notice Record .... CDNR
CDR Resources [*Vancouver Stock Exchange symbol*] .... CDR
CD-ROM [*Compact Disk Read-Only Memory*] **Continuous Information Service** [*International Data Group - IDG*] [*Information service or system*] (IID) .... CIS
CDS Application Support Programs [*NASA*] (NASA) .... CASP
CDS [*Carl Duisberg Society*] **International** (EA) .... CDSI
CDW Computer Centers [*Associated Press*] (SAG) .... CDW Cpt
CDW Computer Centers [*NASDAQ symbol*] (TTSB) .... CDWC
CDW Computer Centers, Inc. [*NASDAQ symbol*] (SAG) .... CDWC
CE Franklin Ltd. [*Associated Press*] (SAG) .... CE Frnk
CE Franklin Ltd. [*AMEX symbol*] (SAG) .... CFK
CE Franklin Ltd [*AMEX symbol*] (TTSB) .... CFK
CE Software Hldgs [*NASDAQ symbol*] (TTSB) .... CESH
CE Software Holdings, Inc. [*Associated Press*] (SAG) .... CE Soft
CE Software Holdings, Inc. [*NASDAQ symbol*] (SAG) .... CESH
Cease and Desist [*Legal shorthand*] (LWAP) .... C & D
Cease and Desist Order [*Legal shorthand*] (LWAP) .... CDO
Ceased Breathing [*Medicine*] (DAVI) .... CB
Ceased to Breathe [*Medicine*] .... CTB
Cebu [*Philippines*] [*Later, DAV*] [*Geomagnetic observatory code*] .... CCP
Cebu [*Philippines*] [*Airport symbol*] (OAG) .... CEB
Cebu City [*Philippines*] [*Seismograph station code, US Geological Survey*] (SEIS) .... CCP
Cebu/Lahug, Cebu [*Philippines*] [*ICAO location identifier*] (ICLI) .... RPMC
Cebu Stevedores Association [*Philippines*] .... CSA
CEC [*Council for Exceptional Children*] **Pioneers Division** (PAZ) .... CEC-PD
CEC Resources [*AMX*] (TTSB) .... CGS
CEC Resources Ltd. [*Associated Press*] (SAG) .... CEC
CEC Resources Ltd. [*AMEX symbol*] (SAG) .... CGS
Cecchetti Council of America (EA) .... CCA
Cechoslovakische Statistik [*Czechoslovakia*] .... CS
Cecil Aviation Ltd. [*ICAO designator*] (FAAC) CIL
Cecilia Lee International Fan Club (EA) .... CLIFC
Cecils Junior College, Asheville, NC [*Library symbol*] [*Library of Congress*] (LCLS) .... NcAC
Ceco Environmental [*NASDAQ symbol*] (SAG) .... CECE
Ceco Environmental [*Associated Press*] (SAG) .... CecoEnv
CECOM Flight Test Activity [*Lakehurst, NJ*] [*Later, AERA*] [*Army*] (GRD) .... CFTA
CECOS International, Buffalo, NY [*Library symbol Library of Congress*] (LCLS) .... NBuCEC
Cedalion Systems, Inc., Information Resources, Charlotte, NC [*Library symbol*] [*Library of Congress*] (LCLS) .... NcCCed
Cedar .... CEDR
Cedar Bluff, VA [*FM radio station call letters*] .... WBBY
Cedar Bluff, VA [*AM radio station call letters*] .... WYRV
Cedar Breaks National Monument .... CEBR
Cedar City [*Utah*] [*Seismograph station code, US Geological Survey*] (SEIS) .... CCU
Cedar City [*Utah*] [*Airport symbol*] (OAG) .... CDC
Cedar City, UT [*AM radio station call letters*] .... KBRE
Cedar City, UT [*FM radio station call letters*] .... KBRE-FM
Cedar City, UT [*Television station call letters*] .... KSGI
Cedar City, UT [*FM radio station call letters*] .... KSSD
Cedar City, UT [*AM radio station call letters*] .... KSUB
Cedar City, UT [*FM radio station call letters*] .... KSUU
Cedar County Courthouse, Tipton, IA [*Library symbol*] [*Library of Congress*] (LCLS) .... IaTipCoC
Cedar County Historical Society, Clarence, IA [*Library symbol Library of Congress*] (LCLS) .... IaClarCHi
Cedar Creek, FL [*FM radio station call letters*] .... WKSG
Cedar Creek Youth Camp, Littlerock, WA [*Library symbol Library of Congress*] (LCLS) .... WaLrC
Cedar Crest and Muhlenberg Colleges, Allentown, PA [*OCLC symbol*] (OCLC) .... EVI
Cedar Crest College [*Pennsylvania*] CCC
Cedar Crest College, Allentown, PA [*Library symbol Library of Congress*] (LCLS) .... PAtC
Cedar Fair Ltd. [*Associated Press*] (SAG) .... CedrFr
Cedar Fair LP [*NYSE symbol*] (SAG) .... FUN
Cedar Falls Historical Society, Cedar Falls, IA [*Library symbol Library of Congress*] (LCLS) .... IaCfHi
Cedar Falls, IA [*AM radio station call letters*] (RBYB) .... KCNZ
Cedar Falls, IA [*FM radio station call letters*] .... KHKE
Cedar Falls, IA [*FM radio station call letters*] .... KKCV
Cedar Falls, IA [*FM radio station call letters*] .... KUNI
Cedar Falls Public Library, Cedar Falls, IA [*Library symbol Library of Congress*] (LCLS) .... IaCf
Cedar Falls Record, Cedar Falls, IA [*Library symbol Library of Congress*] (LCLS) .... IaCfR
Cedar Group [*NASDAQ symbol*] (TTSB) .... CGMV
Cedar Group, Inc. [*Associated Press*] (SAG) .... CedarGp
Cedar Group, Inc. [*NASDAQ symbol*] (SAG) .... CGMV
Cedar Grove Public Library, Cedar Grove, NJ [*Library symbol Library of Congress*] (LCLS) .... NjCg
Cedar Income Fund [*NASDAQ symbol*] (TTSB) .... CEDR
Cedar Income Fund Ltd. [*Associated Press*] (SAG) .... Cedarl
Cedar Income Fund Ltd. [*NASDAQ symbol*] (NQ) .... CEDR
Cedar Key, FL [*Location identifier FAA*] (FAAL) .... CDK
Cedar Key, FL [*FM radio station call letters*] (RBYB) .... WCQQ
Cedar Key, FL [*FM radio station call letters*] (RBYB) .... WRGO-FM
Cedar Mill Community Library, Portland, OR [*Library symbol Library of Congress*] (LCLS) .... OrPCM
Cedar Mt. Elementary School, Franklin, MN [*Library symbol*] [*Library of Congress*] (LCLS) .... MnFrnCES
Cedar Mountain School, Morgan, MN [*Library symbol*] [*Library of Congress*] (LCLS) .... MnMnCMS
Cedar Rapids & Iowa City [*Railway*] (MHDB) .... CRANDIC
Cedar Rapids & Iowa City Railway Co. [*AAR code*] CIC
Cedar Rapids Area Library Consortium [*Library network*] .... CRALC
Cedar Rapids Gazette, Cedar Rapids, IA [*Library symbol Library of Congress*] (LCLS) .... IaCrG
Cedar Rapids, IA [*FM radio station call letters*] .... KCCK
Cedar Rapids, IA [*AM radio station call letters*] .... KCRG
Cedar Rapids, IA [*Television station call letters*] .... KCRG-TV
Cedar Rapids, IA [*FM radio station call letters*] (RBYB) .... KDAT
Cedar Rapids, IA [*Television station call letters*] (RBYB) .... KFXA
Cedar Rapids, IA [*Television station call letters*] .... KGAN
Cedar Rapids, IA [*FM radio station call letters*] .... KHAK-FM
Cedar Rapids, IA [*AM radio station call letters*] .... KMRY
Cedar Rapids, IA [*FM radio station call letters*] .... KTOF
Cedar Rapids, IA [*Television station call letters*] .... KTVC
Cedar Rapids, IA [*FM radio station call letters*] (RBYB) .... KXMX
Cedar Rapids, IA [*Location identifier FAA*] (FAAL) .... RRU
Cedar Rapids, IA [*AM radio station call letters*] .... WMT
Cedar Rapids, IA [*FM radio station call letters*] .... WMT-FM
Cedar Rapids/Iowa City [*Iowa*] [*Airport symbol*] (OAG) .... CID
Cedar Rapids Public Library, Cedar Rapids, IA [*Library symbol Library of Congress*] (LCLS) .... IaCr
Cedar Rapids Public Library, Cedar Rapids, IA [*OCLC symbol*] (OCLC) .... IWR
Cedar Road Elementary School, Commack, NY [*Library symbol*] [*Library of Congress*] (LCLS) .... NCoCE
Cedar Shake and Shingle Bureau (EA) .... CSSB
Cedar Springs [*California*] [*Seismograph station code, US Geological Survey Closed*] (SEIS) .... CED
Cedar Springs [*California*] [*Seismograph station code, US Geological Survey*] (SEIS) .... CSP
Cedar Valley Times, Vinton, IA [*Library symbol*] [*Library of Congress*] (LCLS) .... IaVinT
Cedar Waxwing [*Ornithology*] .... CW
Cedarbrae Branch, Scarborough Public Library, Ontario [*Library symbol National Library of Canada*] (NLC) .... OTSPC
Cedaredge Public Library, Cedaredge, CO [*Library symbol Library of Congress*] (LCLS) .... CoCe
Cedarholm, Bland, Havens, and Townes [*Ether drift experiment*] (MUGU) .... CBHT
Cedarhurst Elementary School, Lawrence, NY [*Library symbol Library of Congress*] (LCLS) .... NLawChE

Cedars of Lebanon Hospital (MCD) ... CLH
Cedars-Sinai Medical Center [*Los Angeles, CA*] ... CS
Cedars-Sinai Medical Center, Los Angeles, CA [*Library symbol Library of Congress*] (LCLS) ... CLCLH
Cedartown, GA [*AM radio station call letters*] ... WGAA
Cedartown, GA [*FM radio station call letters*] ... WJCK
Cedarville College, Cedarville, OH [*OCLC symbol*] (OCLC) ... CDC
Cedarville College, Cedarville, OH [*Library symbol Library of Congress*] (LCLS) ... OCedC
Cedarville, OH [*FM radio station call letters*] ... WCDR
Cedi [*Monetary unit*] [*Ghana*] ... C
Cedrol ... CDRL
Ceduna [*Australia ICAO location identifier*] (ICLI) ... AACD
Ceduna [*Australia ICAO location identifier*] (ICLI) ... APCD
Ceduna [*Australia Airport symbol*] (OAG) ... CED
Ceeta-Kel Air [*France ICAO designator*] (FAAC) ... CET
Cefazolin [*Antibacterial compound*] ... CEZ
Cefazolin (DMAA) ... CEZ
Cefazolin [*An antibiotic*] ... CZ
Cefi Aviation SRL [*Italy ICAO designator*] (FAAC) ... IFC
Cefmenoxime (DMAA) ... CMX
Cefotaxime [*An antibiotic*] ... CTX
Cefoxitin Cyclosterine Fructose Agar [*Medium*] [*Microbiology*] (DAVI) ... CCFA
Cefoxitin Cyclosterine Fructose Agar Medium [*Medicine*] (BABM) ... CCFA
Cefpodoxime (DMAA) ... CPDX
Ceftriaxone (DMAA) ... CTRX
Cefuroxime [*Antibacterial drug*] ... CXM
Cefuzonam [*Antibacterial*] ... CZON
Cega Aviation Ltd. [*British ICAO designator*] (FAAC) ... CEG
CEGEP [*College d'Enseignement General et Professionnel*] **de Hauterive, BaieComeau, Quebec** [*Library symbol National Library of Canada*] (NLC) ... QHAC
CEGEP [*College d'Enseignement General et Professionnel*] **de La Pocatiere, Quebec** [*Library symbol National Library of Canada*] (NLC) ... QPCE
Cegep de Levis-Lauzon, Lauzon, PQ, Canada [*Library symbol*] [*Library of Congress*] (LCLS) ... CaQLCLL
CEGEP [*College d'Enseignement General et Professionnel*] **de Levis-Lauzon, Lauzon, Quebec** [*Library symbol National Library of Canada*] (BIB) ... QLCLL
CEGEP [*College d'Enseignement General et Professionnel*] **de Limoilou, Quebec, PQ, Canada** [*Library symbol Library of Congress*] (LCLS) ... CaQQCE
CEGEP [*College d'Enseignement General et Professionnel*] **de Limoilou, Quebec, Quebec** [*Library symbol National Library of Canada*] (NLC) ... QQCE
CEGEP [*College d'Enseignement General et Professionnel*] **de l'Outaouais, Heritage Campus, Hull, PQ, Canada** [*Library symbol Library of Congress*] (LCLS) ... CaQHCH
CEGEP [*College d'Enseignement General et Professionnel*] **de l'Outaouais, Hull, Quebec** [*Library symbol National Library of Canada*] (NLC) ... QHC
CEGEP [*College d'Enseignement General et Professionnel*] **de Rimouski, Quebec** [*Library symbol National Library of Canada*] (NLC) ... QRIC
CEGEP [*College d'Enseignement General et Professionnel*] **de Riviere-Du-Loup, Quebec** [*Library symbol National Library of Canada*] (BIB) ... QRLC
CEGEP [*College d'Enseignement General et Professionnel*] **de St.-Jerome, Quebec** [*Library symbol National Library of Canada*] (BIB) ... QSTJEC
CEGEP [*College d'Enseignement General et Professionnel*] **de Sept-Iles, Quebec** [*Library symbol National Library of Canada*] (BIB) ... QSIC
CEGEP [*College d'Enseignement General et Professionnel*] **de Shawinigan, Quebec** [*Library symbol National Library of Canada*] (NLC) ... QSHC
CEGEP [*College d'Enseignement General et Professionnel*] **de Shawinigan, Shawinigan, PQ, Canada** [*Library symbol Library of Congress*] (LCLS) ... CaQSHC
CEGEP [*College d'Enseignement General et Professionnel*] **F. X. Garneau, Sillery, Quebec** [*Library symbol National Library of Canada*] (NLC) ... QQCFX
CEGEP [*College d'Enseignement General et Professionnel*] **John Abbott College Library** [*UTLAS symbol*] ... JAC
CEGEP [*College d'Enseignement General et Professionnel*] **Montmorency, Laval, Quebec** [*Library symbol National Library of Canada*] (NLC) ... QLAC
CEGEP [*College d'Enseignement General et Professionnel*] **Montmorency-Chomedy, Laval, PQ, Canada** [*Library symbol Library of Congress*] (LCLS) ... CaQLAC
CEGEP [*College d'Enseignement General et Professionnel*], Trois-Rivieres, Bibliotheque [*EDUCATSS*] [*UTLAS symbol*] ... EUG
CEGEP [*College d'Enseignement General et Professionnel*], Trois-Rivieres, PQ, Canada [*Library symbol Library of Congress*] (LCLS) ... CaQTCE
CEGEP [*College d'Enseignement General et Professionnel*], Trois-Rivieres, Quebec [*Library symbol National Library of Canada*] (NLC) ... QTCE
Ceiba, PR [*AM radio station call letters*] ... WFAB
Ceiling [*Hazard limit*] ... C
Ceiling [*Aviation*] ... CEIL
Ceiling (VRA) ... ceil
Ceiling (DA) ... CIG
Ceiling [*Aviation*] (KSC) ... CLG
Ceiling and Visibility Unrestricted [*or Unlimited*] [*Aviation*] (MCD) ... CAVU
Ceiling Grille [*Technical drawings*] (DAC) ... CG
Ceiling Height (OA) ... CH
Ceiling Height [*Technical drawings*] ... CHT
Ceiling Joist ... CJ
Ceiling Level ... CL
Ceiling Limit Value [*Investment term*] (MHDW) ... CLV
Ceiling Price Regulation (DLA) ... CPR
Ceiling Register (OA) ... CR
Ceilings and Interior Systems Construction Association (EA) ... CISCA
CEIP [*Communications-Electronics Implementation Plan*] **Implementation Directive** [*Air Force*] (CET) ... CID
Ceja Corp., Tulsa, OK [*Library symbol Library of Congress*] (LCLS) ... OkTC
CEL Industry Ltd. [*Vancouver Stock Exchange symbol*] ... CKL
Celadon (VRA) ... cel
Celadon Group [*Associated Press*] (SAG) ... Celadon
Celadon Group [*NASDAQ symbol*] (SAG) ... CLDN
Celanese Canada [*TS Symbol*] (TTSB) ... CCL
Celanese Canada, Inc. [*Toronto Stock Exchange symbol*] ... CCL
Celanese Canada Ltd., Montreal, PQ, Canada [*Library symbol Library of Congress*] (LCLS) ... CaQMCE
Celanese Canada Ltd., Montreal, Quebec [*Library symbol National Library of Canada*] (NLC) ... QMCE
Celanese Corp., Clarkwood, TX [*Library symbol Library of Congress*] (LCLS) ... TxClwC
Celanese Corp., Narrows, VA [*Library symbol Library of Congress*] (LCLS) ... ViNarC
Celanese Engineering Resins Division [*Celanese Corp.*] ... CER
Celanese Fibers Co., Technical Information Center, Charlotte, NC [*Library symbol Library of Congress*] (LCLS) ... NcCCel
Celaya [*Race of maize*] ... CEL
Celaya [*Mexico ICAO location identifier*] (ICLI) ... MMCY
Celebrated ... CEL
Celebrity ... CLBRTY
Celebrity Engineering [*Vancouver Stock Exchange symbol*] ... CEC
Celebrity Entertainment [*NASDAQ symbol*] (TTSB) ... CLER
Celebrity Entertainment, Inc. [*Associated Press*] (SAG) ... CelebEn
Celebrity Entertainment, Inc. [*NASDAQ symbol*] (SAG) ... CLEB
Celebrity, Inc. [*Associated Press*] (SAG) ... CelebInc
Celebrity, Inc. [*NASDAQ symbol*] (SAG) ... FLWR
Celendin [*Peru*] [*ICAO location identifier*] (ICLI) ... SPLD
Celeritek Inc. [*NASDAQ symbol*] (TTSB) ... CLTK
Celery and Parsley Cross [*Genetics*] ... CxP
Celery Mosaic Virus [*Plant pathology*] ... CEMV
Celescope Optical Package (KSC) ... COP
Celesta [*Music*] ... CEL
Celeste Resources [*Vancouver Stock Exchange symbol*] ... CST
Celestial (AFM) ... CEL
Celestial (FAAC) ... CLST
Celestial Atomic Trajectile ... CAT
Celestial Canopy [*Freemasonry*] ... CC
Celestial Equator ... CE
Celestial Infrared Mapping [*Air Force*] (MCD) ... CIRM
Celestial Infrared Measurement System ... CIRMS
Celestial Mapping Program [*Air Force*] (MCD) ... CMP
Celestial Mechanics ... CM
Celestial Moving Target Indicator ... CMTI
Celestial Navigation (FAAC) ... CELNAV
Celestial Navigation Trainer ... CNT
Celestial North Pole (DNAB) ... CNP
Celestial Research Corp. (KSC) ... CELESCO
Celestial Seasonings [*NASDAQ symbol*] (TTSB) ... CTEA
Celestial Seasonings, Inc. [*Associated Press*] (SAG) ... Celestial
Celestial Seasonings, Inc. [*NASDAQ symbol*] (SAG) ... CTEA
Celestial Telescope [*OAO*] ... CELESCOPE
Celestial Telescope [*OAO*] (DNAB) ... CELSCOPE
Celestial Training Device (MCD) ... CTD
Celex Group [*NASDAQ symbol*] (TTSB) ... CLXG
Celex Group, Inc. [*Associated Press*] (SAG) ... Celex
Celex Group, Inc. [*NASDAQ symbol*] (SAG) ... CLXG
Celgene Corp. [*NASDAQ symbol*] (NQ) ... CELG
Celgene Corp. [*Associated Press*] (SAG) ... Celgene
Celiac Axis [*Anatomy*] ... CA
Celiac Disease Foundation (EA) ... CDF
Celiac Sprue [*Medicine*] (DAVI) ... CS
Celiac Sprue Association/United States of America (EA) ... CSA/USA
Celiac, Superior Mesenteric Artery [*Anatomy*] ... CSMA
Celiac, Superior Mesenteric Vein [*Anatomy*] ... CSMV
Celibate ... CEL
Celico Resources [*Vancouver Stock Exchange symbol*] ... CEL
Celina, OH [*Location identifier FAA*] (FAAL) ... CQA
Celina, OH [*AM radio station call letters*] ... WCSM
Celina, OH [*FM radio station call letters*] ... WCSM-FM
Celina, OH [*FM radio station call letters*] ... WKKI
Celina, TN [*FM radio station call letters*] ... WVFB
Celktic Council of Australia ... CCA
Cell ... C
Cell Adhesion Factor [*Cytochemistry*] ... CAF
Cell Adhesion Molecule [*Cytology*] ... CAM
Cell Adhesion Regulator [*Genetics*] ... CAR
Cell Affinity Chromatography ... CAC
Cell Analysis System [*Microscopy*] ... CAS
Cell Antiviral Factor [*Immunochemistry*] ... CAF
Cell Associating Molecule [*Cytology*] ... CAM
Cell Atmosphere Processing System [*Nuclear energy*] (NRCH) ... CAPS
Cell Attached [*Microbiology*] ... CA
Cell Attachment Protein [*Cytochemistry*] ... CAP
Cell Cap [*Botany*] ... CC
Cell Cover Arming Unit (MCD) ... CCAU
Cell Culture [*Cytology*] ... CC
Cell Culture and Nitrogen Fixation Laboratory [*Department of Agriculture*] ... CC & NF
Cell Current Density ... CCD
Cell Cycle Analyzer [*Instrumentation*] ... CCA
Cell Cycle Nonspecific [*Antitumor agent*] ... CCNS
Cell Cycle Specific [*Antitumor agent*] ... CCS
Cell Delay Variation Tolerance [*Telecommunications*] (ACRL) ... CDVT
Cell Division Cycle [*Cytology*] ... CDC
Cell Division Cycle Kinases [*Genetics*] (DOG) ... cdc kinases

Cell Factor [*Biology*] .... CF
Cell Free Extract [*Microbiology*] .... CFE
Cell Genesys [*NASDAQ symbol*] (TTSB) .... CEGE
Cell Genesys, Inc. [*NASDAQ symbol*] (SAG) .... CEGE
Cell Genesys, Inc. [*Associated Press*] (SAG) .... CellGens
Cell Hemoglobin Concentration [*Biochemistry, medicine*] .... CHC
Cell Hemoglobin Concentration Mean [*Biochemistry, medicine*] .... CHCM
Cell Host Computer .... CHC
Cell Interaction [*Immunology*] CI
Cell Kinetics Society (EA) .... CKS
Cell Line [*Cytology*] CL
Cell Loss Priority [*Computer science*] .... CLP
Cell Management Language [*Software*] (BYTE) .... CML
Cell Matrix Adhesion Regulator [*Medicine*] (DMAA) .... CMAR
Cell [*or Cellular*]-Mediated Immunity [*Immunochemistry*] .... CMI
Cell Membrane .... CM
Cell Multiplication Inhibition .... CMI
Cell Pack [*Horticulture*] .... CP
Cell Processor System (MCD) .... CPS
Cell Research Institute [*University of Texas at Austin*] [*Research center*] (RCD) .... CRI
Cell Scanning System [*Cytology*] (SAA) .... CELESCAN
Cell Separation [*Cytology*] .... Cel Sep
Cell Simulation [*Programming language*] [*1973*] (CSR) .... CELLSIM
Cell Surface Antigens [*Immunology*] .... CSA
Cell Surface Fibronectin [*Biochemistry*] .... CSFN
Cell Surface Protein [*Also known as LETS protein*] [*Cytochemistry*] .... CSP
Cell Transport Integral Calculation (PDAA) .... CELTIC
Cell Volume [*Hematology*] CV
Cell Volume Profile [*Hematology*] .... CVP
Cell Wall .... CW
Cell Wall Constituent (OA) .... CWC
Cell Wall Defective [*Microbiology*] .... CWD
Cell Wall Material [*Biochemistry*] .... CWM
Cell Wall Skeleton [*Cytology*] .... CWS
Cell Wall-Deficient Bacterial Form [*Microbiology*] (MAE) .... CWDF
Cell Water Removal Mechanism .... CWRM
Cell-Cell Adhesion Molecules [*Genetics*] (DOG) .... CAMs
Cell-Cycle Box [*Genetics*] .... CCB
Cell-Cycle Box Factor [*Genetics*] .... CCBF
Cell-Cycle Element [*Cytology*] .... CCE
Cell-Directed Inhibitor [*Medicine*] (DMAA) .... CDI
Celle [*Germany ICAO location identifier*] (ICLI) .... EDCL
Celle/Arloh [*Germany ICAO location identifier*] (ICLI) .... EDVC
Cellegy Pharmaceutical [*NASDAQ symbol*] (TTSB) .... CLGY
Cellegy Pharmaceuticals [*Associated Press*] (SAG) .... Cellegy
Cellegy Pharmaceuticals [*Associated Press*] (SAG) .... CellegyPh
Cellegy Pharmaceuticals [*Associated Press*] (SAG) .... Cellgy
Cellegy Pharmaceuticals [*NASDAQ symbol*] (SAG) .... CLGY
Cellegy Pharmaceuticals Wrrt [*NASDAQ symbol*] (TTSB) .... CLGYW
Cellex Biosciences [*NASDAQ symbol*] (TTSB) CLXX
Cellex Biosciences, Inc. [*Associated Press*] (SAG) .... CellexB
Cellex Biosciences, Inc. [*Associated Press*] (SAG) .... Cellx
Cellex Biosciences, Inc. [*Associated Press*] (SAG) .... CllxBio
Cellex Biosciences, Inc. [*NASDAQ symbol*] (SAG) CLXX
Cellex Biosciences Wrrt 2000 [*NASDAQ symbol*] (TTSB) .... CLXXZ
Cell-Free Elicitor Preparation [*Plant pathology*] .... CFEP
Cell-Junctional Molecule [*Embryology*] .... CJM
Cell-Mediated Cytolysis .... CMC
Cell-Mediated Immune Response [*Immunology*] (AAMN) .... CMIR
Cell-Mediated Immunity (DOG) .... CMI
Cell-Mediated Lympholysis [*Immunology*] .... CML
CellNet Data Systems, Inc. [*Associated Press*] (SAG) .... CellNet
CellNet Data Systems, Inc. [*NASDAQ symbol*] (SAG) .... CNDS
Cellobiohydrolase [*An enzyme*] .... CBH
Cellophane (DGA) .... C/PHANE
Cellophane (VRA) .... celph
Cellophane (AAG) .... K
CellPro, Inc. [*Associated Press*] (SAG) .... CellPro
CellPro, Inc. [*NASDAQ symbol*] (SPSG) .... CPRO
Cells in Frames [*Telecommunications*] (ACRL) .... CIF
Cells per Colony [*Microbiology*] .... CPC
Cellstar Corp. [*Associated Press*] (SAG) .... Cellstar
Cellstar Corp. [*NASDAQ symbol*] (SAG) .... CLST
Cell-Substrate Attachment [*Immunology*] .... CSAT
Celltech Media, Inc. [*NASDAQ symbol*] (SAG) .... CTMI
Celltropin [*Biochemistry*] .... CTP
Cellular .... CELL
Cellular .... CELLUL
Cellular [*Freight*] .... CEUR
Cellular Absorbed Dose Spectrometer .... CADS
Cellular and Molecular Basis of Disease [*Program*] [*National Institutes of Health*] .... CMBD
Cellular and Molecular Biology .... CMB
Cellular and Molecular Life Sciences [*A publication*] [*Formerly Experientia*] .... CMLS
Cellular and Molecular Pharmacology (GNE) .... CMP
Cellular Array Processor [*Computer science*] (NITA) .... CAP
Cellular Automation [*Computer science*] (IAA) .... CA
Cellular Cellulose Acetate [*Organic chemistry*] .... CCA
Cellular Commun Intl [*NASDAQ symbol*] (TTSB) CCIL
Cellular Commun P.R. [*NASDAQ symbol*] (TTSB) .... CCPR
Cellular Communications, Inc. [*Associated Press*] (SAG) .... CelCmA
Cellular Communications, Inc. [*NASDAQ symbol*] (NQ) .... COMM

Cellular Communications Industry Association [*Telecommunications*] (EA) .... CCIA
Cellular Communications International, Inc. [*NASDAQ symbol*] (SAG) CCIL
Cellular Communications International, Inc. [*Associated Press*] (SAG) .... Cell Intl
Cellular Communications Puerto Rico [*NASDAQ symbol*] (SAG) .... CCPR
Cellular Communications Puerto Rico [*Associated Press*] (SAG) .... CelCmPR
Cellular Concrete Association (EA) .... CCA
Cellular Data Link Control [*Communications protocol*] .... CDLC
Cellular Digital Packet Data [*Computer science*] (PCM) .... CDPD
Cellular Directions, Inc. [*Telecommunications service*] (TSSD) .... CDI
Cellular Envelope [*Embryology*] .... CE
Cellular General Purpose Computer .... CGPC
Cellular Geographic Serving Area [*Telecommunications*] .... CGSA
Cellular Immunity Deficiency Syndrome [*Medicine*] .... CIDS
Cellular, Inc. [*Telecommunications service*] (TSSD) CI
Cellular Intercarrier Billing Exchange Record .... CIBER
Cellular Intercarrier Billing Exchange Roamer Record [*A publication*] (TSSD) .... CIBER
Cellular Logic Image Processor [*Telecommunications*] (TEL) .... CLIP
Cellular Logic Operation [*Telecommunications*] (IAA) .... CLO
Cellular Logic-In Memory [*Telecommunications*] (IAA) .... CLIM
Cellular Management System [*Stratus Computer, Inc.*] .... CMS
Cellular Mobile Carrier .... CMC
Cellular Mobile Telephone .... CMT
Cellular Mobile Telephone Service .... CMTS
Cellular Natural Killing (PDAA) .... CNK
Cellular Neoprene Rubber .... CNR
Cellular Radio .... CR
Cellular Radio Communications Association [*Later, CCIA*] (EA) .... CRCA
Cellular Radio Ltd. [*British*] (NITA) .... CRL
Cellular Radio Switching Office [*Telecommunications*] .... CRSO
Cellular Remote Access Bulletin Board [*Cellular Communications Industry Association*] [*Information service or system*] (IID) .... CRABB
Cellular Retinoic Acid-Binding Protein [*Biochemistry*] .... CRABP
Cellular Retinol-Binding Protein [*Biochemistry*] .... CRBP
Cellular Sales & Marketing [*Creative Communications*] [*Information service or system*] (IID) .... CS & M
Cellular Size Volume .... CSV
Cellular Slime Mold [*Biology*] .... CSM
Cellular Surface Area [*Cytology*] .... CSA
Cellular Technical Services [*Associated Press*] (SAG) .... CellrTch
Cellular Technical Services [*NASDAQ symbol*] (SAG) .... CTSC
Cellular Technical Svcs [*NASDAQ symbol*] (TTSB) .... CTSC
Cellular Telecommunications Industry Association (EA) .... CTIA
Cellular Telephone Service (HGAA) .... CTS
Cellular Therapy [*Medicine*] .... CT
Cellular Ventures, Inc. [*Atlanta, GA*] [*Telecommunications*] (TSSD) CV
Cellular-Automata Machine [*Computer science*] (BARN) .... CAM
CellularCommunications'A' [*NASDAQ symbol*] (TTSB) .... COMMA
CellularVision USA [*NASDAQ symbol*] (TTSB) .... CVUS
CellularVision USA, Inc. [*Associated Press*] (SAG) .... CellVisin
CellularVision USA, Inc. [*NASDAQ symbol*] (SAG) .... CVUS
Cellules Combattantes Communistes [*Communist Combatant Cells*] [*Belgium*] CCC
Cellules Communistes Combattantes [*Terrorist organization*] [*Belgium*] (EY) CCC
Celluloid .... CEL
Celluloid [*Dentistry*] (DAVI) .... Cell
Cellulolytic Enzyme Biodegradability [*Biochemistry*] .... CEB
Cellulose [*Botany*] .... CEL
Cellulose Acetate [*Organic chemistry; plastics*] .... CA
Cellulose Acetate Butyrate [*Organic chemistry*] .... CAB
Cellulose Acetate Diethylaminoacetate (OA) .... CADA
Cellulose Acetate Electrophoresis [*Organic chemistry*] (MAE) .... CAE
Cellulose Acetate Methacrylate .... CAM
Cellulose Acetate Phthalate [*Organic chemistry*] (MAE) .... CAP
Cellulose Acetate Propionate [*Organic chemistry*] .... CAP
Cellulose Ester [*Organic chemistry*] .... CE
Cellulose Industry Standards Enforcement Program (EA) .... CISEP
Cellulose Insulation Manufacturers Association of Canada (AC) .... CIMAC
Cellulose Manufacturers Association (EA) .... CMA
Cellulose Nitrate (PDAA) .... CLN
Cellulose Nitrate [*Organic chemistry*] .... CN
Cellulose Nitrate with Hydrophobic Edge [*Membrane filtration*] .... CN(h)
Cellulose Paper .... CP
Cellulose Polyethylene [*Organic chemistry*] .... CPE
Cellulose Propionate Plastic [*Organic chemistry*] .... CP
Cellulose Research Institute [*Syracuse University*] .... CRI
Cellulose Sodium Phosphate [*Organic chemistry*] .... CSP
Cellulose Sponge Institute [*Defunct*] (EA) .... CSI
Cellulose Synthase Activator [*Biochemistry*] .... CSA
Cellulose Triacetate [*Organic chemistry*] .... CTA
Cellulose Trinitrate [*Organic chemistry*] .... CTN
Cellulose-Binding Domain [*Genetics*] .... CBD
Celmar Servicios Aereos SA de CV [*Mexico ICAO designator*] (FAAC) .... CER
Celotex (VRA) .... celtx
Celox Laboratories [*NASDAQ symbol*] (TTSB) .... CELX
Celox Laboratories, Inc. [*Associated Press*] (SAG) .... CeloxLab
Celox Laboratories, Inc. [*NASDAQ symbol*] (SAG) .... CELX
Celo-Zongo [*Zaire*] [*ICAO location identifier*] (ICLI) .... FZAD
Cel-Sci Corp. [*NASDAQ symbol*] (NQ) .... CELI
Cel-Sci Corp. [*Associated Press*] (SAG) .... CelSc
Cel-Sci Corp. [*Associated Press*] (SAG) .... CelSci
Cel-Sci Corp. Wrrt [*NASDAQ symbol*] (TTSB) .... CELIW
Celsius [*Centigrade*] [*Temperature scale*] C

Celsius [*Centigrade*] [*Temperature scale*] .... CEL
Celsius (ROG) .... CELS
Celsius Heat Unit (ADA) .... CHU
Celsius Temperature [*Symbol*] [*IUPAC*] .... t
Celsus, De Medicina [*First century AD*] [*Classical studies*] (OCD) .... Celsus Med
Celtic (ROG) C
Celtic .... CEL
Celtic .... CELT
Celtic Club Melbourne [*Australia*] .... CCM
Celtic Group [*MARC language code Library of Congress Obsolete*] (LCCP) .... cel
Celtic Inernational Ltd. [*British ICAO designator*] (FAAC) CIC
Celtic Investment [*NASDAQ symbol*] (TTSB) .... CELT
Celtic Investment, Inc. [*NASDAQ symbol*] (SAG) .... CELT
Celtic Investment, Inc. [*Associated Press*] (SAG) .... CelticInv
Celtic League [*Peel, Isle of Man, England*] (EAIO) CL
Celtic League, American Branch (EA) .... CLAB
Celtic Resources Ltd. [*Vancouver Stock Exchange symbol*] CLI
Celtrix Pharmaceuticals [*Associated Press*] (SAG) .... Celtrx
Celtrix Pharmaceuticals [*NASDAQ symbol*] (SAG) .... CTRX
CEM Corp. [*Associated Press*] (SAG) .... CEM
CEM Corp. [*NASDAQ symbol*] (NQ) .... CEMX
Cembalo [*Cymbals*] [*Music*] (ROG) .... CEMB
Cembratriene-diol [*Organic chemistry*] .... CBT
Cement (KSC) .... CEM
Cement (VRA) .... cem
Cement .... CEM
Cement .... CEMT
Cement [*Classified advertising*] (ADA) .... CMT
Cement Admixtures Association (EAIO) .... CAA
Cement Aggregate Mixture (OA) .... CAM
Cement and Concrete Association [*British Research center*] (IRUK) .... C & CA
Cement and Concrete Association [*British Research center*] .... CCA
Cement Base [*Technical drawings*] .... CB
Cement Conduit [*Telecommunications*] (TEL) .... CEM
Cement Employers Association (EA) .... CEA
Cement Finish (DAC) .... Cem Fin
Cement Floor [*Technical drawings*] (DAC) .... Cem Fl
Cement Floor [*Technical drawings*] .... CF
Cement Gland [*Embryology*] .... CG
Cement, Lime, Gypsum, and Allied Workers Division (EA) .... CLGAWD
Cement Mortar [*Technical drawings*] (DAC) .... Cem Mort
Cement or Concrete [*Freight*] .... CMT CONC
Cement Plaster [*Technical drawings*] (DAC) .... Cem Plas
Cement Plaster (AAG) .... CPL
Cement Render .... CR
Cement Riverine Assault Boat [*Navy*] (MCD) .... CRAB
Cement Squeeze Simulator [*For testing well drilling material*] .... CSS
Cement Tile [*Classified advertising*] (ADA) .... CT
Cement Water Ratio (IAA) .... CW
Cement-Asbestos Board (DAC) .... CAB
Cement-Asbestos Board (DAC) .... Cem Ab
Cement-Coated Heavy Epoxy .... CCHEP
Cement-Coated Single Epoxy .... CCSEP
Cement-Coated Triple Epoxy .... CCTEP
Cemented Carbide Producers Association (EA) .... CCPA
Cemented Only [*Of envelopes*] .... CO
Cement-Enamel Junction [*Dentistry*] .... CEJ
Cementex [*Research code symbol*] .... N
Cementitious Barrier Coat [*Anticorrosive coating*] .... CBC
Cement-Modified Soil (PDAA) .... CMS
Cement-Plaster Ceiling [*Technical drawings*] .... CPC
Cement-Sand-Molasses (PDAA) .... CSM
Cement-Treated Base .... CTB
Cemetery (AABC) .... CEM
Cemetery (ROG) .... CEMET
Cemetery (VRA) .... cemet
Cemetery (ABBR) .... CMTRY
Cemetery .... CNTRY
Cemetery & Crematorium Association of British Columbia (AC) .... CCABC
Cemetery Consumer Service Council (EA) .... CCSC
Cemetery Supply Association [*Later, ICSA*] (EA) .... CSA
CEMR [*Canada Energy Mines and Resources*] **Headquarters Library** [*UTLAS symbol*] .... EME
Ceneast Airlines Ltd. [*Kenya*] [*ICAO designator*] (FAAC) .... CEL
CENELEC [*Comite Europeen de Normalisation Electrotechnique*] **Electronic Components Committee** (DS) .... CECC
CENFED Financial [*NASDAQ symbol*] (TTSB) .... CENF
Cenfed Financial Corp. [*NASDAQ symbol*] (SAG) .... CENF
Cenfed Financial Corp. [*Associated Press*] (SAG) .... Cenfed
Cenior Services Ltd., Calgary, AB, Canada [*Library symbol*] [*Library of Congress*] (LCLS) .... CaACCES
Cenit Bancorp [*Associated Press*] (SAG) .... CenitBcp
Cenit Bancorp [*NASDAQ symbol*] (SAG) .... CNIT
Cenlor Services Ltd., Calgary, Alberta [*Library symbol National Library of Canada*] (NLC) .... ACCES
Cenomanian [*Paleontology*] C
Cenomanian/Turonian [*Geological boundary zone*] .... C/T
Cenomanian Turonian Black Shale Horizon [*Nuclear energy*] (NUCP) .... CTBSH
Cenozoic [*Period, era, or system*] [*Geology*] .... CEN
Cenral Alberta AIDS Network Society (AC) .... CAANS
Cenral Nova Tourist Association (AC) .... CNTA
Censo de Archivos [*Database*] [*Ministerio de Cultura*] [*Spanish*] [*Information service or system*] (CRD) .... CARC
Censo de Bibliotecas [*Database*] [*Ministerio de Cultura*] [*Spanish*] [*Information service or system*] (CRD) .... CBIB
Censo de Museos de Espana [*Database*] [*Ministerio de Cultura*] [*Spanish*] [*Information service or system*] (CRD) .... CMUS
Censor (ROG) C
Censor [*or Censorship*] (AFM) .... CENS
Censor [*MARC relator code*] [*Library of Congress*] (LCCP) .... cns
Censorship of Publications Board [*Ireland*] .... CPB
Censorship Policy Board [*World War II*] .... CPB
Censorship Records and Information Middle East [*Military*] .... CRIME
Census .... CS
Census Access System [*Urban Decision Systems, Inc.*] [*Information service or system Defunct*] (CRD) .... CENSAC
Census Agglomeration [*Canada*] .... CA
Census and Data Users Services [*Illinois State University*] [*Information service or system*] (IID) .... CADUS
Census and Economic Information Center [*Montana State Department of Commerce*] [*Helena*] [*Information service or system*] (IID) .... CEIC
Census Awareness and Products Program [*Bureau of the Census*] (GFGA) .... CAPP
Census Awareness and Products Staff [*Bureau of the Census*] (GFGA) .... CAPS
Census Bureau [*Department of Commerce*] .... CB
Census Bureau Software Package (GFGA) .... CENSPAC
Census Community Awareness Program [*Bureau of the Census*] (GFGA) .... CCAP
Census Community Communications Council [*US Census Bureau*] C4
Census Control System [*Bureau of the Census*] (GFGA) .... CCS
Census County Division [*Bureau of Census*] .... CCD
Census Data [*Database*] .... CDATA
Census Designated Place [*Bureau of the Census*] (GFGA) .... CDP
Census Grievance Committee [*Vietnam*] .... CGC
Census Library, Statistics Canada [*Bibliotheque du Recensement, Statistique Canada*] **Ottawa, Ontario** [*Library symbol National Library of Canada*] (NLC) .... OOSCL
Census Map Library, Statistics Canada [*Cartotheque du Recensement, Statistique Canada*] **Ottawa, Ontario** [*Library symbol National Library of Canada*] (NLC) .... OOSCM
Census Metropolitan Area [*Canada*] .... CMA
Census of Australian Vascular Plants .... CAVP
Census of Graduate Medical Trainees .... CGMT
Census Projections [*Database*] (IT) .... CENPRO
Census Promotion Office [*Bureau of the Census*] (GFGA) .... CPO
Census Registration Working Party [*US Military Government, Germany*] .... CRWP
Census Servomechanism and Tape Handler .... CENSER
Census Transportation Planning Package [*BTS*] (TAG) .... CTPP
Census User Guide .... CUG
Cent [*Monetary unit*] C
Cent [*Monetary unit*] .... CT
Cent Call Seconds [*Telecommunications*] .... CCS
Centacare Australia .... CA
Cental [*Short hundredweight*] [*British*] (WGA) C
Cental [*Short hundredweight*] [*British*] (ROG) .... CENT
Cental [*Short hundredweight*] [*British*] (ROG) .... CT
Cental [*Short hundredweight*] [*British*] (ROG) .... CTL
Centare [*Unit of area in metric system*] .... CA
Centaur [*Rocket*] [*NASA*] (KSC) .... CEN
Centaur [*Rocket*] [*NASA*] (KSC) .... CENT
Centaur Integrated Support Structure (MCD) .... CISS
Centaur Resources Ltd. [*Vancouver Stock Exchange symbol*] .... KNL
Centaur Standard Shroud [*NASA*] .... CSS
Centaurus [*Constellation*] .... Cen
Centaurus [*Constellation*] .... Cent
Centaurus Distant Supercluster [*Astronomy*] .... CDS
Centavo [*Monetary unit in many Spanish-American countries*] C
Centavo [*Cent*] [*Monetary unit in many Spanish-American countries*] .... CTVO
Cente de Prevention du Suicide (AC) .... CPS
Cente d'Information et de Recherche en Consommation de Charlevoix-Ouest (AC) .... CIRCCO
Cente d'Inspection et de Prevention Automobile de l'Estrie (AC) .... CIPAE
Cente for Research-Action on Race Relations (AC) .... CRARR
Cente Francophone ASSITEJ Canada (AC) .... ASSITEJ Canada
Cente International de Documentation et d'Echanges de la Francophonie (AC) .... CIDES
Cente Patronal de l'Environnement du Quebec (AC) .... CPEQ
Centenary [*or Centennial*] .... Cent
Centenary College for Women, Hackettstown, NJ [*Library symbol Library of Congress*] (LCLS) .... NjHaC
Centenary College of Louisiana [*Shreveport*] CCL
Centenary College of Louisiana, Magale Library, Shreveport, LA [*OCLC symbol*] (OCLC) .... CEN
Centenary College of Louisiana, Shreveport, LA [*Library symbol Library of Congress*] (LCLS) .... LShC
Centennial (ROG) .... CEN
Centennial .... CENT
Centennial [*Spain ICAO designator*] (FAAC) .... CNA
Centennial Airlines, Inc. [*ICAO designator*] (FAAC) .... CNL
Centennial Bancorp [*NASDAQ symbol*] (SAG) .... CEBC
Centennial Bancorp [*Associated Press*] (SAG) .... CentlBc
Centennial Branch, Nepean Public Library, Ontario [*Library symbol National Library of Canada*] (NLC) .... ONCB
Centennial Cellular 'A' [*NASDAQ symbol*] (TTSB) .... CYCL
Centennial Cellular Corp. [*Associated Press*] (SAG) .... CentCel
Centennial Cellular Corp. [*NASDAQ symbol*] (SAG) .... CYCL
Centennial Centre of Science and Technology .... CCST
Centennial College of Applied Arts and Technology, Scarborough, ON, Canada [*Library symbol Library of Congress*] (LCLS) .... CaOTARC
Centennial College of Applied Arts and Technology, Scarborough, Ontario [*Library symbol National Library of Canada*] (NLC) .... OTARC

Centennial Collegiate Vocational Institute, Guelph, ON, Canada [Library symbol] [Library of Congress] (LCLS) .... CaOGC
Centennial Collegiate Vocational Institute, Guelph, Ontario [Library symbol National Library of Canada] (NLC) .... OGC
Centennial Elementary School, Roosevelt, NY [Library symbol] [Library of Congress] (LCLS) .... NRoosCE
Centennial Flight Centre [Canada ICAO designator] (FAAC) .... CNS
Centennial Legion of Historic Military Commands (EA) .... CLHMC
Centennial Minerals [Toronto Stock Exchange symbol Vancouver Stock Exchange symbol] .... CTN
Centennial Museum, Vancouver, BC, Canada [Library symbol Library of Congress] (LCLS) .... CaBVaCM
Centennial Museum, Vancouver, British Columbia [Library symbol National Library of Canada] (NLC) .... BVACM
Centennial Park Trust [Australia] .... CPT
Centennial Secondary School, Welland, ON, Canada [Library symbol Library of Congress] (LCLS) .... CaOWeC
Centennial Secondary School, Welland, Ontario [Library symbol National Library of Canada] (NLC) .... OWEC
Centennial Secondary School, Windsor, ON, Canada [Library symbol Library of Congress] (LCLS) .... CaOWC
Centennial Secondary School, Windsor, Ontario [Library symbol National Library of Canada] (NLC) .... OWC
Centennial Technologies [AMEX symbol] (TTSB) .... CTN
Centennial Technologies, Inc. [Associated Press] (SAG) .... CentenT
Centennial Technologies, Inc. [Associated Press] (SAG) .... CentTc
Centennial Technologies, Inc. [AMEX symbol] (SAG) .... CTN
Center [A position in football, lacrosse, basketball] C
Center [or Central] (AFM) .... CEN
Center [Commonly used] (OPSA) .... CENT
Center [Commonly used] (OPSA) .... CENTER
Center [Commonly used] (OPSA) .... CENTR
Center [Commonly used] (OPSA) .... CENTRE
Center [Commonly used] (OPSA) .... CNTER
Center .... CNTR
Center (DS) .... CR
Center (AAG) .... CTR
Center (WDMC) .... ctr
Center .... CTR
Center Accessory Compartment (MCD) .... CAC
Center Ad Hoc Data Review Team [NASA] (KSC) .... CAHDRT
Center Aiming Disc (NATG) .... CAD
Center Airman Record File [Air Force] .... CARF
Center Aisle Connector Bracket (MCD) .... CACB
Center Apollo Data Manager [NASA] (KSC) .... CADM
Center Apollo Document Description Standards [NASA] (KSC) .... CADDS
Center Apollo Documentation Administration Instructions [NASA] (KSC) .... CADAI
Center Apollo Program Offices [NASA] (KSC) .... CAPO
Center Back [Soccer] .... CB
Center Back Stage [A stage direction] .... CBS
Center Bancorp, Inc. [NASDAQ symbol] (SAG) .... CNBC
Center Bancorp, Inc. [Associated Press] (SAG) .... CntBncp
Center Banks [NASDAQ symbol] (SAG) .... CTBK
Center Banks [Associated Press] (SAG) .... CtrBnk
Center Beam One Side [Lumber] (DAC) CB1S
Center Beam Two Sides [Lumber] (DAC) CB2S
Center City Report [A publication] (EAAP) .... CCR
Center City Transportation Program .... CCTP
Center Console Panel (MCD) .... CCP
Center Data Descriptions Catalog (KSC) .... CDDC
Center Director [John F. Kennedy Space Center Directorate] [NASA] (NASA) .... CD
Center Distance (MSA) .... CD
Center Engine Cutoff [NASA] (KSC) .... CECO
Center Field [or Fielder] [Baseball] .... CF
Center Financial [NASDAQ symbol] (TTSB) .... CFCX
Center Financial Corp. (Connecticut) [Associated Press] (SAG) .... CenterFn
Center Financial Corp. (Connecticut) [NASDAQ symbol] (SAG) .... CFCX
Center Fire .... CF
Center Focus [Binoculars] .... CF
Center for a New Democracy (EA) .... CND
Center for a Voluntary Society [Defunct] (EA) .... CVS
Center for a Woman's Own Name [An association Defunct] (EA) .... CWON
Center for Academic & Administrative Computing [George Washington University] [Research center] (RCD) .... CAAC
Center for Academic Ethics (EA) .... CAE
Center for Academic Precocity [Arizona State University] [Research center] (RCD) .... CAP
Center for Accelerator Technology and Applied Sciences [University of Texas at Arlington] [Research center] (RCD) .... CATAS
Center for Accountability to the Public (EA) .... CAP
Center for Acquisition Education, Training, and Research [Military] (RDA) .... CAETR
Center for Acquisition Management Policy [DSMC] (AAGC) .... CAMP
Center for Action on Endangered Species (EA) .... CAES
Center for Adhesives, Sealants, and Coatings [Case Western Reserve University] [Research center] (RCD) .... CASC
Center for Administrative Justice [Later, NCAJ] (EA) .... CAJ
Center for Advanced Biotechnology and Medicine [Rutgers University] [Research center] (RCD) .... CABM
Center for Advanced Decision Support for Water and Environmental Systems [University of Colorado at Boulder] [Research center] (RCD) .... CADSWES
Center for Advanced Digital Applications [New York University School of Continuing Education] .... CADA

Center for Advanced Feminist Studies [University of Minnesota] [Research center] (RCD) .... CAFS
Center for Advanced Food Technology [Rutgers University] .... CAFT
Center for Advanced Heart Research .... CAHR
Center for Advanced Macrostructures and Devices [Louisiana State University] .... CAMD
Center for Advanced Management Programs [University of Houston at Clear Lake] [Research center] (RCD) .... CAMP
Center for Advanced Manufacturing and Production [Southern Illinois University at Edwardsville] [Research center] (RCD) .... CAMP
Center for Advanced Materials [Lawrence Berkeley Laboratory] [Berkeley, CA] [Department of Energy] (GRD) .... CAM
Center for Advanced Materials [Pennsylvania State University] [Research center] (RCD) .... CAM
Center for Advanced Materials Processing [Clarkson University] [Research center] (RCD) .... CAMP
Center for Advanced Professional Education [Canada] .... CAPE
Center for Advanced Purchasing Studies [Arizona State University] [Research center] (RCD) .... CAPS
Center for Advanced Rehabilitation Engineering [University of Texas at Arlington] [Research center] (RCD) .... CARE
Center for Advanced Research in Biotechnology [Jointly sponsored by the US National Bureau of Standards and the University of Maryland] .... CARB
Center for Advanced Research in Phenomenology [Defunct] (EA) .... CARP
Center for Advanced Studies in International Business .... CASIB
Center for Advanced Studies in Telecommunications [Ohio State University] (TSSD) .... CAST
Center for Advanced Study in Education [City University of New York] [Research center] (RCD) .... CASE
Center for Advanced Study in the Behavioral Sciences (EA) .... CASBS
Center for Advanced Study in the Behavioral Sciences, Stanford, CA [Library symbol Library of Congress] (LCLS) .... CStC
Center for Advanced Study in Theatre Arts [City University of New York] [Research center] (RCD) .... CASTA
Center for Advanced Study of International Development [Michigan State University] [Research center] (RCD) .... CASID
Center for Advanced Technologies [Focus: HOPE] .... CAT
Center for Advanced Technology for Large Structural Systems [Lehigh University] [Research center] (RCD) .... ATLSS
Center for Advanced Technology in Telecommunications [Polytechnic Institute of New York] [Brooklyn] [Telecommunications service] (TSSD) ..... CATT
Center for Advanced Television Studies [British] (NTCM) .... CATS
Center for Advanced Visual Studies [Massachusetts Institute of Technology] [Research center] (RCD) .... CAVS
Center for Aerospace Doctrine, Research, and Education [Air University] [Research center] (RCD) .... CADRE
Center for Aerospace Information (AAGC) .... CASI
Center for Aerospace Technology [Weber State College] [Research center] (RCD) .... CAST
Center for Affective Disorders [University of Wisconsin, Madison] [Research center] (RCD) .... CAD
Center for Afro-American and African Studies [University of Michigan] [Research center] (RCD) .... CAAS
Center for Afro-American Studies [University of California, Los Angeles] [Research center] (RCD) .... CAAS
Center for Aging Research .... CAR
Center for Agricultural and Rural Development [Iowa State University] [Research center] (RCD) .... CARD
Center for Agricultural Meteorology and Climatology [University of Nebraska - Lincoln] [Research center] (RCD) .... CAMAC
Center for Agricultural Molecular Biology [Rutgers University] [Research center] (RCD) .... AgBioTech
Center for AIDS Prevention Studies [University of California, San Francisco] [Research center] (RCD) .... CAPS
Center for AIDS Research [National Institutes of Health] .... CFAR
Center for Air Environment Studies [Pennsylvania State University] [Research center] (RCD) .... CAES
Center for Air Pollution Impact and Trend Analysis [Washington University] [Research center] (RCD) .... CAPITA
Center for Alcohol Research [University of Florida] [Research center] (RCD) .... CAR
Center for Alcohol Studies (EA) .... CAS
Center for Alternative Living Medicine .... CALM
Center for Alternative Mining Development Policy (EA) .... CAMDP
Center for Alternative Sentencing and Employment Services [Research center] (RCD) .... CASES
Center for Alternatives to Animal Testing [At Johns Hopkins] .... CAAT
Center for American Archeology (EA) .... CAA
Center for American History [University of Texas, Austin] [Research center] (RCD) .... CAH
Center for Analysis and Prediction of Storms [University of Oklahoma] [Research center] (RCD) .... CAPS
Center for Analysis of Developing Economies [University of Pennsylvania] [Research center] (RCD) .... CADE
Center for Analysis of Environmental Change [Oregon State University] [Research center] (RCD) .... CAEC
Center for Analytic Research in Economics and the Social Sciences [University of Pennsylvania] [Research center] (RCD) .... CARESS
Center for Animals and Public Policy (GNE) .... CAPP
Center for Anthropometric Research Data (IID) .... CARD
Center for Anti-Fratricide Technology [Army] (DOMA) .... CAFT
Center for Application of Sciences and Technology .... CAST
Center for Applications of Psychological Type (EA) .... CAPT
Center for Applications of Remote Sensing [Oklahoma State University] [Research center] (RCD) .... CARS

Center for Applied Isotope Studies [*University of Georgia*] [*Research center*] (RCD) .... CAIS

Center for Applied Linguistics (EA) .... CAL

Center for Applied Linguistics, Arlington, VA [*Library symbol Library of Congress*] (LCLS) .... ViArAL

Center for Applied Linguistics, Washington, DC [*Library symbol Library of Congress*] (LCLS) .... DCAL

Center for Applied Mathematics [*University of Georgia*] [*Research center*] (RCD) .... CAM

Center for Applied Microbiology [*University of Texas at Austin*] [*Research center*] (RCD) .... CAM

Center for Applied Parallel Processing [*University of Colorado, Boulder*] [*Research center*] (RCD) .... CAPP

Center for Applied Polymer Research [*Case Western Reserve University*] [*Research center*] (RCD) .... CAPRI

Center for Applied Research in the Apostolate (EA) .... CARA

Center for Applied Research in the Apostolate [*CARA*], African Research andInformation Center, Washington, DC [*Library symbol Library of Congress*] (LCLS) .... DARI

Center for Applied Research in the Language Arts [*Texas Tech University*] [*Research center*] (RCD) .... CARLA

Center for Applied Social Science [*Boston University*] [*Research center*] (RCD) .... CASS

Center for Applied Special Technology .... CAST

Center for Applied Studies in International Negotiations [*Switzerland*] (EAIO) .... CASIN

Center for Applied Thermodynamic Studies [*University of Idaho*] [*Research center*] (RCD) .... CATS

Center for Aquatic Plant Research and Technology [*Army*] .... CAPRT

Center for Arab-Islamic Studies (EA) .... CAIS

Center for Archaeological Investigations [*Southern Illinois University at Carbondale*] [*Research center*] (RCD) .... CAI

Center for Architectural Research [*Rensselaer Polytechnic Institute*] [*Research center*] (RCD) .... CAR

Center for Architecture and Urban Planning Research [*University of Wisconsin - Milwaukee*] [*Research center*] (RCD) .... CAUPR

Center for Army Leadership [*Fort Leavenworth, KS*] (INF) .... CAL

Center for Army Lessons Learned (INF) .... CALL

Center for Arts Information [*Defunct*] (EA) .... CAI

Center for Aseptic Processing and Packaging Studies [*North Carolina State University*] [*Research center*] (RCD) .... CAPPS

Center for Assessment and Demographic Studies [*Gallaudet College*] [*Research center*] (RCD) .... CADS

Center for Assessment and Training [*Peace Corps*] .... CAST

Center for Astronomical Data [*Academy of Sciences of the USSR*] [*Information service or system*] (IID) .... CAD

Center for Astrophysical Research in Antarctica [*National Science Foundation*] .... CARA

Center for Astrophysics [*Harvard-Smithsonian*] .... CA

Center for Astrophysics [*Harvard-Smithsonian*] .... CFA

Center for Astrophysics and Space Sciences [*University of California, San Diego*] [*Research center*] (RCD) .... CASS

Center for Athletes' Rights and Education [*Defunct*] (EA) .... CARE

Center for Atmospheric and Space Sciences [*Utah State University*] [*Research center*] (RCD) .... CASS

Center for Atmospheric Theory and Analysis [*Research center*] (RCD) .... CATA

Center for Atomic Radiation Studies (EA) .... CARS

Center for Attitudinal Healing (EA) .... CAH

Center for Auditory and Speech Sciences [*Gallaudet University*] [*Research center*] (RCD) .... CASS

Center for Austrian Studies (EA) .... CAS

Center for Auto Safety (EA) .... CAS

Center for Automation and Intelligent Systems Research [*Case Western Reserve University*] [*Research center*] (RCD) .... CAISR

Center for Automation Research [*University of Maryland*] [*Research center*] (RCD) .... CfAR

Center for Automotive Research [*Wayne State University*] [*Research center*] (RCD) .... CAR

Center for Autonomous and Man-Controlled Robotic and Sensing Systems [*Research center*] (RCD) .... CAMRSS

Center for Bibliographical Services [*Modern Language Association*] (BARN) .... CBS

Center for Bigfoot Studies [*An association*] (EA) .... CBS

Center for Bilingual Research and Second Language Education [*Later, CLEAR*] (GRD) .... CBSLE

Center for Bioanalytical Research [*University of Kansas*] .... CBAR

Center for Biochemical and Biophysical Studies [*Northern Illinois University*] [*Research center*] (RCD) .... CBBS

Center for Biochemical Engineering Research [*New Mexico State University*] [*Research center*] (RCD) .... CBER

Center for Biofilm Engineering [*Montana State University*] .... CBE

Center for Biological Macromolecules [*State University of New York at Albany*] [*Research center*] (RCD) .... CBM

Center for Biologics Evaluation and Research [*FDA*] .... CBER

Center for Biomedical and Toxicological Research [*Florida State University*] [*Research center*] (RCD) .... CBTR

Center for Biomedical Design [*University of Utah*] [*Research center*] (RCD) .... CBD

Center for Blood Research [*Research center*] (RCD) .... CBR

Center for Book Arts (EA) .... CBA

Center for Borderline History (EA) .... CBH

Center for Brain Research [*University of Rochester*] [*Research center*] (RCD) .... CBR

Center for Building Technology [*Gaithersburg, MD*] [*National Institute of Standards and Technology*] .... CBT

Center for Built Environment Research [*Morgan State University*] [*Research center*] (RCD) .... CEBER

Center for Business and Economic Development [*Auburn University at Montgomery*] [*Research center*] (RCD) .... CBED

Center for Business and Economic Research [*University of Alabama*] [*University, AL*] [*Information service or system*] (IID) .... CBER

Center for Business & Economics Research [*University of Nevada - Las Vegas*] [*Research center*] (RCD) .... CBER

Center for Business Information [*Information service or system*] (IID) .... CBI

Center for Canadian Historical Horticultural Studies [*Hamilton, ON*] .... CCHHS

Center for Carburization Heat Treatment Studies [*Worchester Polytechnic Institute*] [*Research center*] (RCD) .... CCHTS

Center for Cereals Research [*Pennsylvania State University*] [*Research center*] (RCD) .... CCR

Center for Chemical Process Safety (EA) .... CCPS

Center for Children and Technology [*Bank Street College of Education*] [*Research center*] (RCD) .... CCT

Center for Children's Books. Bulletin [*A publication*] (BRI) .... CCB-B

Center for Chinese Research Materials (EA) .... CCRM

Center for Chinese Research Materials, Washington, DC [*Library symbol Library of Congress*] (LCLS) .... DCCRM

Center for Chinese Studies [*University of Michigan*] [*Research center*] (RCD) .... CCS

Center for Christian Studies (EA) .... CCS

Center for Clean Air Policy (EA) .... CCAP

Center for Climate System Research [*Marine science*] (OSRA) .... CCSR

Center for Climate System Research (USDC) .... CCSR

Center for Climatic and Environmental Assessment [*National Oceanic and Atmospheric Administration*] (IID) .... CCEA

Center for Climatic Research [*University of Wisconsin - Madison*] [*Research center*] (RCD) .... CCR

Center for Coastal Studies [*University of California, San Diego*] [*Research center*] (RCD) .... CCS

Center for Cold Regions Engineering, Science, and Technology [*State University of New York at Buffalo*] [*Research center*] (RCD) .... CREST

Center for Command, Control, Communications, and Intelligence [*George Mason University*] [*Research center*] (RCD) C3I

Center for Communication Programs (EA) .... CCP

Center for Communications Media [*University of Massachusetts-Boston*] [*Telecommunications service*] (TSSD) .... CCM

Center for Communications Ministry [*Formerly, NSCS*] [*Defunct*] (EA) .... CCM

Center for Communications Systems [*CADPL*] [*Army*] (RDA) .... CENCOMS

Center for Community and Regional Research [*University of Minnesota, Duluth*] [*Research center*] (RCD) .... CCRR

Center for Community Change (EA) CCC

Center for Community Development [*Humboldt State University*] [*Research center*] (RCD) .... CCD

Center for Community Economic Development .... CCED

Center for Community Education Facility Planning [*Inactive*] (EA) .... CCEFP

Center for Community Justice (EA) .... CCJ

Center for Community Planning [*HEW*] .... CCP

Center for Community Study [*University of Rochester*] [*Research center*] (RCD) .... CCS

Center for Comparative Sociology .... CCS

Center for Compatible Economic Development [*Leesburg, VA*] .... CCED

Center for Compliance Information (EA) CCI

Center for Composite Materials [*University of Delaware*] [*Research center*] (RCD) .... CCM

Center for Computational Seismology [*Berkeley, CA*] [*Lawrence Berkeley Laboratory*] [*Department of Energy*] (GRD) .... CCS

Center for Computer Aided Design [*University of Iowa*] [*Research center*] (RCD) .... CCAD

Center for Computer Aids for Industrial Productivity [*Rutgers University*] [*Research center*] (RCD) .... CAIP

Center for Computer and Information Services [*Rutgers University, The State University of New Jersey*] [*Information service or system*] (IID) .... CCIS

Center for Computer Integrated Engineering and Manufacturing [*University of Tennessee at Knoxville*] [*Research center*] (RCD) .... CCIEM

Center for Computer/Law (EA) CCL

Center for Computer Research in Music and Acoustics [*Pronounced "karma"*] [*Stanford University*] .... CCRMA

Center for Computer Sciences and Technology [*Later, ICST*] [*National Institute of Standards and Technology*] .... CCST

Center for Computer Systems Design [*Washington University*] [*Research center*] (RCD) .... CCSD

Center for Computer-Assisted Legal Instruction (EA) .... CCALI

Center for Computer-Based Behavioral Studies [*Research center*] (RCD).... CCBS

Center for Conscious Evolution (EA) .... CCE

Center for Constitutional Rights (EA) .... CCR

Center for Consumer Affairs, University of Wisconsin-Milwaukee (EA) .... CCA-UWM

Center for Consumer Product Safety [*National Institute of Standards and Technology*] .... CCPS

Center for Consumer Product Technology [*National Institute of Standards and Technology*] (GRD) .... CCPT

Center for Contemporary Arab Studies [*Georgetown University*] [*Research center*] (RCD) .... CCAS

Center for Contemporary Opera (EA) .... CCO

Center for Continuing Education for Women .... CCEW

Center for Continuing Study of the California Economy [*Information service or system*] (IID) .... CCSCE

Center for Control Science and Dynamical Systems [*University of Minnesota*] [*Research center*] (RCD) .... CSDS

Center for Corporate Economics and Strategy [*Defunct*] (EA) .... CCES

Center for Corporate Public Involvement (EA) .... CCPI

Center for Craniofacial Anomalies [*University of Illinois at Chicago*] [*Research center*] (RCD) ... CCFA
Center for Creative Imaging [*Camden, Maine*] [*Computer art training*] ... CCI
Center for Creative Leadership (EA) ... CCL
Center for Creative Leadership, Greensboro, NC [*Library symbol Library of Congress*] (LCLS) ... NcGCL
Center for Cross-Cultural Studies [*University of Alaska, Fairbanks*] [*Research center*] (RCD) ... CXCS
Center for Cuban Studies (EA) ... CCS
Center for Curriculum Design [*Information service or system Defunct*] (IID) ... CCD
Center for Cybernetic Studies [*University of Texas at Austin*] [*Research center*] (RCD) ... CCS
Center for Cybernetic Studies [*University of Texas*] (PDAA) ... CS
Center for Cybernetics Systems Synergism ... CYSYS
Center for Dance Medicine (EA) ... CDM
Center for Data Systems and Analysis [*Montana State University*] [*Research center*] (RCD) ... CDSA
Center for Death Education and Research (EA) ... CDER
Center for Defense Information (EA) ... CDI
Center for Democracy and Technology ... CDT
Center for Democratic Alternatives [*Defunct*] (EA) ... CDA
Center for Democratic Policy (EA) ... CDP
Center for Democratic Renewal (EA) ... CDR
Center for Demographic and Population Genetics [*University of Texas*] [*Research center*] (RCD) ... CDPG
Center for Demographic Studies [*Census*] (OICC) ... CDS
Center for Demography and Ecology [*University of Wisconsin - Madison*] [*Research center*] (RCD) ... CDE
Center for Design Planning (EA) ... CDP
Center for Development Planning, Projections, and Policies [*United Nations*] ... CDPPP
Center for Development Policy [*Later, ICDP*] (EA) ... CDP
Center for Development Research, Koobenhavn, Denmark [*Library symbol Library of Congress*] (LCLS) ... DnKDR
Center for Development Studies ... CDS
Center for Developmental Change [*University of Kentucky*] [*Research center*] (RCD) ... CDC
Center for Devices and Radiological Health [*FDA*] ... CDRH
Center for Discrete Mathematics and Theoretical Computer Science [*Rutgers University*] [*Research center*] (RCD) ... DIMACS
Center for Disease Control and Prevention (DHSM) ... CDCP
Center for Disease Control, Atlanta, GA [*OCLC symbol*] (OCLC) ... HNC
Center for Disease Control, Family Planning Evaluation Division, Atlanta, GA [*Library symbol Library of Congress*] (LCLS) ... GACDC-FP
Center for Disease Control, Main Library, Atlanta, GA [*Library symbol Library of Congress*] (LCLS) ... GACDC
Center for Dispute Settlement (EA) ... CDS
Center for Documentation and Communication Research [*Case Western Reserve University*] ... CDCR
Center for Documentation on Refugees [*United Nations High Commission for Refugees*] [*Switzerland Information service or system*] (IID) ... CDR
Center for Drug Evaluation and Research [*Food and Drug Administration*] ... CDER
Center for Drugs and Biologics [*FDA*] ... CDB
Center for Early Adolescence (EA) ... CEA
Center for Earth Observations and Remote Sensing [*Boulder, CO*] [*Cooperative Institute for Research in Environmental Sciences*] [*National Oceanic and Atmospheric Administration*] (GRD) ... CEORS
Center for Earthquake Research and Information [*Memphis State University*] [*Research center*] (RCD) ... CERI
Center for Econometrics and Decision Sciences [*University of Florida*] [*Research center*] (RCD) ... CEDS
Center for Economic and Management Research [*University of Oklahoma*] [*Norman*] [*Information service or system*] (IID) ... CEMR
Center for Economic Conversion (EA) ... CEC
Center for Economic Development and Business Research [*Wichita State University*] [*Kansas*] [*Information service or system*] (IID) ... CEDBR
Center for Economic Renewal and Technology Transfer [*Montana State University*] ... CERTT
Center for Economic Research [*University of Texas at Austin*] [*Research center*] (RCD) ... CER
[*The*] **Center for Economic Research and Graduate Education** [*Prague*] (ECON) ... CERGE
Center for Economic Studies [*Washington, DC Department of Commerce*] (GRD) ... CES
Center for Editions of American Authors [*Later, CSE*] ... CEAA
Center for Education and Research in Free Enterprise [*College Station, TX*] (EA) ... CERFE
Center for Education Improvement [*U.S. Department of Education*] (EDAC) ... CEI
Center for Education in International Management [*Canada*] ... CEI
Center for Education Statistics [*Washington, DC Department of Education Also, an information service or system*] (IID) ... CES
Center for Educational Change [*University of California, Berkeley*] ... CEC
Center for Educational Development [*University of Illinois at Chicago*] [*Research center*] (RCD) ... CED
Center for Educational Experimentation, Development, and Evaluation [*University of Iowa*] [*Research center*] (RCD) ... CEEDE
Center for Educational Policy and Management [*Department of Education*] (GRD) ... CEPM
Center for Educational Policy Studies (EA) ... CEPS
Center for Educational Reform (EA) ... CER
Center for Educational Research and Development [*University of Maryland*] [*Research center*] (RCD) ... CERD
Center for Educational Technology [*Florida State University*] [*Research center*] ... CET
Center for Electromechnics [*University of Texas at Austin*] [*Research center*] (RCD) ... CEM
Center for Electron Optics [*Michigan State University*] [*Research center*] (RCD) ... CEO
Center for Electronic Warfare/Reconnaissance, Surveillance, and Target Acquisit ion [*Fort Monmouth, NJ*] [*United States Army Communications-Electronics Command*] (GRD) ... EW/RSTA
Center for Endocrinology, Metabolism, and Nutrition [*Northwestern University*] ... CEMN
Center for Energy and Economic Development [*US Bureau of Mines*] ... CEED
Center for Energy and Environmental Information [*Department of Energy*] (GRD) ... CEEI
Center for Energy and Environmental Policy Research [*Formerly, Center for Energy Policy and Research*] ... CEEPR
Center for Energy and Environmental Research [*University of Puerto Rico*] ... CEER
Center for Energy and Environmental Studies [*Carnegie-Mellon University*] [*Research center*] (RCD) ... CEES
Center for Energy and Mineral Resources [*Texas A & M University*] [*Research center*] ... CEMR
Center for Energy Information [*Defunct*] ... CEI
Center for Energy Policy and Research (EA) ... CEPR
Center for Energy Studies [*University of Texas at Austin*] [*Research center*] (RCD) ... CES
Center for Energy Studies [*Louisiana State University*] [*Information service or system*] (IID) ... CES
Center for Energy Systems [*General Electric Information Services Co.*] (NITA) ... CFES
Center for Engineering Applications of Radioisotopes [*North Carolina State University*] [*Research center*] (RCD) ... CEAR
Center for Engineering Development and Research [*University of South Florida*] [*Research center*] (RCD) ... CEDAR
Center for Engineering Plants for Resistance Against Pathogens [*University of California*] [*Research center*] (RCD) ... CEPRAP
Center for Engineering Systems Advanced Research [*Oak Ridge National Laboratory*] [*Oak Ridge, TN*] [*Department of Energy*] ... CESAR
Center for Entrepreneurial Development [*Carnegie-Mellon University*] ... CED
Center for Entrepreneurial Development, Advancement, Research, and Support [*University of Texas, El Paso*] [*Research center*] (RCD) ... CEDAR
Center for Entrepreneurial Management [*New York, NY*] (EA) ... CEM
Center for Entrepreneurial Studies [*New York University*] [*Research center*] (RCD) ... CES
Center for Entrepreneurship and Economic Development [*Pan American University*] [*Research center*] (RCD) ... CEED
Center for Environmental and Estuarine Studies [*University of Maryland*] [*Research center*] ... CEES
Center for Environmental Assessment Services [*National Oceanic and Atmospheric Administration Information service or system*] (IID) ... CEAS
Center for Environmental Design Education and Research [*University of Colorado*] [*Research center*] (RCD) ... CEDER
Center for Environmental Education [*Research center*] (EA) ... CEE
Center for Environmental Health [*Atlanta, GA*] [*Department of Health and Human Services*] (GRD) ... CEH
Center for Environmental Health and Injury Control [*Atlanta, GA*] [*Centers for Disease Control*] [*Department of Health and Human Services*] (GRD) ... CEHIC
Center for Environmental Information, Inc. [*Information service or system*] (IID) ... CEI
Center for Environmental Intern Programs (EA) ... CEIP
Center for Environmental Research Education [*State University of New York College, Buffalo*] [*Research center*] (RCD) ... CERE
Center for Environmental Research Information [*Environmental Protection Agency*] (EPA) ... CERI
Center for Environmental Sciences [*University of Colorado at Denver*] [*Research center*] (RCD) ... CES
Center for Environmental Studies [*Arizona State University*] [*Research center*] (RCD) ... CES
Center for Environmental Studies [*Williams College*] [*Research center*] (RCD) ... CES
Center for Environmental Toxicology [*Michigan State University*] [*Research center*] (RCD) ... CET
Center for Epidemiologic Studies - Depression Scale [*Personality development test*] [*Psychology*] ... CES-D
Center for Equine Health ... CEH
Center for Evaluative Clinical Sciences ... CECS
Center for Experiment Design and Data Analysis [*National Oceanic and Atmospheric Administration*] ... CEDDA
Center for Experimental Studies in Business [*University of Minnesota*] ... CESB
Center for Exposure Assessment Modeling [*Athens, GA*] [*Environmental Protection Agency*] (GRD) ... CEAM
Center for Faith Development [*Later, CRFMD*] (EA) ... CFD
Center for Family Business [*Cleveland, OH*] (EA) ... CFB
Center for Family Support (EA) ... CFS
Center for Fast Kinetics Research [*University of Texas at Austin*] [*Research center*] (RCD) ... CFKR
Center for Federal Policy Review (EA) ... CFPR
Center for Fertility and Reproductive Research [*Vanderbilt University*] [*Research center*] (RCD) ... C-FARR
Center for Field Research (EA) ... CFR
Center for Financial Freedom and Accuracy in Financial Reporting (EA) ... CFFAFR
Center for Food Safety and Applied Nutrition [*Washington, DC Department of Health and Human Services*] (GRD) ... CFSAN
Center for Foreign Journalists (EA) ... CFJ
Center for Foreign Policy Development (EA) ... CFPD

Center for Global Education (EA) .... CGE
Center for Government Service [*Rutgers University*] [*Research center*] (RCD) .... CGS
Center for Governmental Research, Inc. [*Research center*] (RCD) .... CGR
Center for Governmental Research Inc. (EA) .... CGRI
Center for Governmental Research Library, Rochester, NY [*OCLC symbol*] (OCLC) .... VQD
Center for Great Lakes and Aquatic Sciences [*University of Michigan*] .... CGLAS
Center for Great Lakes Studies [*University of Wisconsin - Milwaukee*] [*Research center*] (RCD) .... CGLS
Center for Growth Alternatives [*Defunct*] (EA) .... CGA
Center for Hazardous Materials Research (EA) .... CHMR
Center for Health Action (EA) .... CHA
Center for Health Administration Studies [*University of Chicago*] [*Research center*] (RCD) .... CHAS
Center for Health and Advanced Policy Studies [*Boston University*] [*Research center*] (RCD) .... CHAPS
Center for Health Applications of Aerospace Related Technologies .... CHAART
Center for Health Policy Research [*University of Florida*] [*Research center*] (RCD) .... CHPR
Center for Health Promotion and Education [*Atlanta, GA*] [*Department of Health and Human Services*] (GRD) .... CHPE
Center for Health Promotion Research and Development [*University of Texas*] [*Research center*] (RCD) .... CHPRD
Center for Health Research [*Wayne State University*] [*Research center*] (RCD) .... CHR
Center for Health Resources Planning Information [*National Institutes of Health*] .... CHRPI
Center for Health Services and Policy Research [*Northwestern University*] [*Research center*] (RCD) .... CHSPR
Center for Health Services Research [*University of Iowa*] [*Research center*] (RCD) .... CHSR
Center for Hellenic Studies, Harvard University, Washington, DC [*Library symbol Library of Congress*] (LCLS) .... DCHS
Center for High Angular Resolution Astronomy [*Georgia State University*] [*Research center*] .... CHARA
Center for History of Chemistry [*Later, NFHC*] (EA) .... CHOC
Center for Holistic Resource Management (EA) .... CHRM
Center for Holocaust Studies (EA) .... CHS
Center for Hospitality Research and Service (EA) .... CHRS
Center for Housing, Building, and Planning [*United Nations*] .... UNCHBP
Center for Human Environments Associates, Inc. [*City University of New York*] [*Research center*] (RCD) .... CHE INC
Center for Human Growth and Develoment [*University of Michigan*] [*Research center*] (RCD) .... CHGD
Center for Human Information Processing [*Research center*] (RCD) .... CHIP
Center for Human Radiobiology .... CHR
Center for Human Resource Research [*Ohio State University*] [*Research center*] (RCD) .... CHRR
Center for Human Resources [*Rutgers University*] [*Research center*] (RCD) .... CHR
Center for Human Rights and Responsibilities [*British*] .... CHRR
Center for Human Services (EA) .... CHS
Center for Human Toxicology [*University of Utah*] [*Research center*] (RCD).... CHT
Center for Humane Options in Childbirth Experiences (EA) .... CHOICE
Center for Hydrogen Embrittlement of Electroplated Fasteners [*Worchester Polytechnic Institute*] [*Research center*] (RCD) .... CHEEF
Center for Image Processing and Integrated Computing [*University of California at Davis*] [*Research center*] (RCD) .... CIPIC
Center for Imaging Science [*University of Chicago*] [*Research center*] (RCD) .... CIS
Center for Immigrants Rights (EA) .... CIR
Center for Immigration Studies (CROSS) .... CIS
Center for Immunity Enhancement in Domestic Animals [*Iowa State University of Science and Technology*] [*Research center*] (RCD) .... CIEDA
Center for Improving Mountain Living [*Western Carolina University*] [*Research center*] (RCD) .... CIML
Center for Independent Action (EA) .... CFIA
Center for Independent Education [*Later, Cato Institute*] (EA) .... CIE
Center for Independent Living [*Rehabilitation*] (DAVI) CIL
Center for Independent Living Services .... CILS
Center for Industrial and Engineering Technology [*Central Connecticut University*] [*Research center*] (RCD) .... CIET
Center for Industrial Development [*European Economic Community/African, Caribbean, and Pacific States*] (DS) .... CID
Center for Industrial Research and Service .... CIRAS
Center for Infectious Diseases [*Department of Health and Human Services*] (GRD) .... CID
Center for Information and Immigration Studies [*Mexico*] (CROSS) .... CIEM
Center for Information and Numerical Data Analysis and Synthesis [*West Lafayette, IN*] [*Department of Commerce*] (MCD) .... CINDAS
Center for Information on America [*Defunct*] (EA) .... CIOA
Center for Information Research [*Research center*] (IID) .... CIR
Center for Information Sciences (KSC) .... CIS
Center for Information Systems Research [*Massachusetts Institute of Technology*] [*Research center*] (RCD) .... CISR
Center for Information Systems Security [*DoD*] (DOMA) .... CISS
Center for Information Technology [*Stanford University*] [*Stanford, CA*] (CSR) .... CIT
Center for Information Technology Integration [*University of Michigan*] [*Research center*] (RCD) .... CITI
Center for Inherited Disease Research [*Genotyping facility, Maryland*] .... CIDER
Center for Inherited Disease Research [*Baltimore*] [*National Institutes of Health and Johns Hopkins University*] .... CIDR
Center for Innovation Management Studies [*Lehigh University*] [*Information service or system*] (IID) .... CIMS
Center for Innovative Diplomacy [*Defunct*] (EA) .... CID
Center for Inquiry and Discovery [*Washington, DC, museum*] .... CID
Center for Institutional Reform and the Informal Sector [*University of Maryland*] (ECON) .... IRIS
Center for Instructional and Research Computing Activities [*University of Florida*] [*Research center*] (RCD) .... CIRCA
Center for Instructional Services [*Purdue University*] [*Research center*] (RCD) .... CIS
Center for Instructional Services and Research [*Memphis State University*] [*Research center*] (RCD) .... CISR
Center for Integral Medicine [*Defunct*] (EA) .... CIM
Center for Integrated Electronics [*Rensselaer Polytechnic Institute*] [*Research center*] (RCD) .... CIE
Center for Integrated Facility Engineering [*Stanford University*] [*Research center*] (RCD) .... CIFE
Center for Integrated Manufacturing Studies [*Rochester Institute of Technology*] [*Research center*] (RCD) .... CIMS
Center for Integrated Systems [*Stanford University*] [*Research center*] (RCD) .... CIS
Center for Intelligence Studies (EA) .... CIS
Center for Intelligent Computing Studies [*Washington University*] [*Research center*] (RCD) .... CICS
Center for Intelligent Machines and Robotics [*University of Florida*] [*Research center*] (RCD) .... CIMAR
Center for Intelligent Vision and Information Systems .... CIVIS
Center for Interactive Computer Graphics [*Rensselaer Polytechnic Institute*] [*Research center*] (RCD) .... CICG
Center for Interactive Programs [*University of Wisconsin-Extension*] [*Madison*] [*Information service or system*] [*Telecommunications*] (TSSD) .... CIP
Center for Interactive Technology, Applications, and Research [*University of South Florida*] [*Research center*] (RCD) .... CITAR
Center for Inter-American and Border Studies [*University of Texas, El Paso*] [*Research center*] (RCD) .... CIABS
Center for Inter-American and Border Studies [*University of Texas, El Paso*] [*Research center*] (RCD) .... CIBS
Center for Inter-American Relations (EA) .... CIAR
Center for Inter-American Relations .... CIR
Center for Interdisciplinary Research in Computer-Based Learning [*University of Delaware*] [*Research center*] (RCD) .... CIRCL
Center for Interdisciplinary Research on Immunologic Diseases [*Department of Health and Human Services*] (GRD) .... CIRID
Center for Interdisciplinary Study of Science and Technology [*Northwestern University*] [*Research center*] (RCD) .... CISST
Center for Interest Measurement [*University of Minnesota*] [*Research center*] (RCD) .... CIMR
Center for International Affairs [*Harvard University*] [*Research center*] (RCD) .... CFIA
Center for International and Strategic Affairs [*Research center*] (RCD) .... CISA
Center for International Business Cycle Research [*Columbia University*] [*New York, NY Research center*] (RCD) .... CIBCR
Center for International Business Studies [*Research center*] (RCD) .... CIBS
Center for International Community Health Studies [*University of Connecticut*] [*Research center*] (RCD) .... CICHS
Center for International Economic Growth [*Defunct*] (EA) .... CIEG
Center for International Education and Research in Accounting [*University of Illinois, Urbana-Champaign*] [*Research center*] (RCD) .... CIERA
Center for International Environment Information [*Later, WEC*] (EA) .... CIEI
Center for International Financial Analysis and Research, Inc. [*Princeton, NJ*] [*Information service or system*] (IID) .... CIFAR
Center for International Forestry Research .... CIFOR
Center for International Higher Education Documentation (EDAC) .... CIHED
Center for International Policy (EA) .... CIP
Center for International Private Enterprise [*Washington, DC*] (EA) .... CIPE
Center for International Programs and Studies [*University of Missouri - Rolla*] [*Research center*] (RCD) .... CIPAS
Center for International Relations [*University of California, Los Angeles*] [*Research center*] (RCD) .... CIR
Center for International Research [*Bureau of the Census*] [*Information service or system*] (IID) .... CIR
Center for International Security [*Defunct*] (EA) .... CIS
Center for International Studies, Albany, NY [*Library symbol Library of Congress*] (LCLS) .... NAICI
Center for International Systems Research .... CISR
Center for International Trade Development [*Oklahoma State University*] [*Research center*] (RCD) .... CITD
Center for International Trade in Forest Products [*University of Washington*] .... CINTRAFOR
Center for Interreligious Affairs .... CIA
Center for Investigative Reporting (EA) .... CIR
Center for Irrigation Technology [*California State University, Fresno*] [*Research center*] (RCD) .... CIT
Center for Japanese Studies [*University of Michigan*] [*Research center*] (RCD) .... CJS
Center for Judicial Studies (EA) .... CJS
Center for Labor and Industrial Relations [*New York Institute of Technology*] [*Research center*] (RCD) .... CLIR
Center for Labor Education and Research [*University of Hawaii*] [*Research center*] (RCD) .... CLEAR
Center for Labor Education and Research [*University of Alabama at Birmingham*] [*Research center*] (RCD) .... CLEAR
Center for Labor Education and Research [*University of Colorado*] .... CLEAR
Center for Labor Research and Studies [*Florida International University*] [*Research center*] (RCD) .... CLRS

Center for Lake Erie Area Research [*Ohio State University*] ... CLEAR
Center for Lake Superior Environmental Studies [*Universtiy of Wisconsin - Superior*] [*Research center*] (RCD) ... CLSES
Center for Language Education and Research [*Los Angeles, CA*] [*Department of Education*] (GRD) ... CLEAR
Center for Latin American and Iberian Studies [*Vanderbilt University*] [*Research center*] (RCD) ... CLAIS
Center for Law and Education (EA) ... CLE
Center for Law and Religious Freedom (EA) ... CLRF
Center for Law and Social Policy (EA) ... CLASP
Center for Law and Social Policy (EPA) ... CLSP
Center for Law in the Public Interest (EA) ... CLIPI
Center for Leadership Development (EA) ... CLD
Center for Learning and Telecommunications [*American Association for Higher Education*] [*Information service or system*] (IID) ... CLT
Center for Lesbian and Gay Studies (EA) ... CLAGS
Center for Libertarian Studies (EA) ... CLS
Center for Life Cycle Software Engineering [*Communications-Electronics Command*] [*Army*] ... CLCSE
Center for Lifelong Education [*Ball State University*] [*Research center*] (RCD) ... CLLE
Center for Living Democracy (EA) ... CLD
Center for Local Government Technology [*Oklahoma State University*] [*Research center*] (RCD) ... CLGT
Center for Local Tax Research (EA) ... CLTR
Center for Loss in Multiple Birth ... CLIMB
Center for Loss in Multiple Birth (EA) ... CLMB
Center for Low-Intensity Conflict [*Army*] ... CLIC
Center for Machine Intelligence [*Research center*] (RCD) ... CMI
Center for Magnetic Recording Research [*University of California, San Diego*] [*Research center*] (RCD) ... CMRR
Center for Management Development [*American Management Association*] (EA) ... CMD
Center for Management Effectiveness [*Pacific Palisades, CA*] (EA) ... CME
Center for Management Systems (EA) ... CMS
Center for Management Technology [*Commercial firm*] (EA) ... CMT
Center for Manufacturing Productivity and Technology Transfer [*Rensselaer Polytechnic Institute*] [*Research center*] (RCD) ... CMP
Center for Manufacturing Systems [*New Jersey*] ... CMS
Center for Marine Affairs [*Scripps Institution of Oceanography*] ... CMA
Center for Marine Conservation (EA) ... CMC
Center for Marine Exploration (GNE) ... CME
Center for Marine Resources [*National Oceanic and Atmospheric Administration*] ... CMR
Center for Maritime Studies [*Later, MRD*] [*Webb Institute of Naval Architecture*] [*Research center*] (EA) ... CMS
Center for Market and Trade Development [*China*] ... CMTD
Center for Marketing Communications [*Later, Advertising Research Foundation*] (EA) ... CMC
Center for Marxist Research [*Defunct*] (EA) ... CMR
Center for Mass Communication [*Columbia University*] ... CMC
Center for Mass Communications Research and Policy [*University of Denver*] [*Research center*] (RCD) ... CMCRP
Center for Massachusetts Data [*Information service or system*] (IID) ... CMD
Center for Materials Research [*Johns Hopkins University*] [*Research center*] (RCD) ... CMR
Center for Materials Research [*Stanford University*] [*Research center*] (RCD) ... CMR
Center for Materials Science [*Los Alamos, NM*] [*Los Alamos National Laboratory*] [*Department of Energy*] (GRD) ... CMS
Center for Materials Science and Engineering [*MIT*] [*Research center*] (RCD) ... CMSE
Center for Measurement Science (BARN) ... CMS
Center for Media and Public Affairs (EA) ... CMPA
Center for Media Education ... CME
Center for Medical Consumers and Health Care Information (EA) ... CMC
Center for Medical Consumers and Health Care Information (EA) ... CMCHCI
Center for Medical Manpower Studies [*Northeastern University*] [*Research center*] (RCD) ... CMMS
Center for Medieval and Early Renaissance Studies (EA) ... CEMERS
Center for Medieval and Renaissance Studies (EA) ... CMRS
Center for Mental Health Services (USGC) ... CMHS
Center for Metals Production [*Carnegie Mellon University*] [*Research center*] (RCD) ... CMP
Center for Metric Education [*Western Michigan University*] ... CME
Center for Metropolitan Studies [*University of Missouri - Saint Louis*] [*Research center*] (RCD) ... CMS
Center for Microcontamination Control [*Research center*] ... CMC
Center for Middle Eastern Studies [*Harvard University*] [*Research center*] (RCD) ... CMES
Center for Middle Eastern Studies [*University of California, Berkeley*] [*Research center*] (RCD) ... CMES
Center for Migration Studies of New York (EA) ... CMS
Center for Modern Dance Education [*Hackensack, NJ*] ... CMDE
Center for Molecular and Genetic Medicine [*Stanford University*] [*Research center*] ... CMGM
Center for Molecular Medicine [*Germany*] ... CMM
Center for Multinational Studies [*Defunct*] (EA) ... CMS
Center for National Policy (EA) ... CNP
Center for National Policy Review [*Defunct*] (EA) ... CNPR
Center for National Security Studies (EA) ... CNSS
Center for Nationalist Studies (EA) ... CNS
Center for Natural Areas (EA) ... CNA
Center for Naval Analyses [*Alexandria, VA*] [*Navy*] ... CNA
Center for Naval Analysis [*Marine science*] (OSRA) ... CNA
Center for Near Eastern and North African Studies [*University of Michigan*] [*Research center*] (RCD) ... CNENAS
Center for Neighborhood Technology (EA) ... CNT
Center for Neo-Hellenic Studies (EA) ... CNHS
Center for Networked Information Discovery and Retrieval ... CNIDR
Center for Neuroscience [*Rutgers University*] ... CNS
Center for Neuroscience, University of Pittsburgh ... CNUP
Center for New Corporate Priorities [*Defunct*] (EA) ... CNCP
Center for New Creation (EA) ... CNC
Center for New National Security (EA) ... CNNS
Center for New Schools (EA) ... CNS
Center for Night Vision and Electro-Optics [*Fort Belvoir, VA*] [*Army*] (INF) ... CNVEO
Center for Non-Broadcast Television [*Defunct*] (EA) ... CNB-TV
Center for Nonlinear Studies [*Los Alamos, NM*] [*Department of Energy*] (GRD) ... CNLS
Center for Nonprofit Organizations [*Defunct*] (EA) ... CNO
Center for Nonviolent Alternatives [*Defunct*] (EA) ... CNVA
Center for Nonviolent Communication (EA) ... CNC
Center for Nonviolent Studies [*An association*] (EA) ... CNS
Center for Northern Studies [*Research center*] (RCD) ... CNS
Center for Nuclear Studies [*Memphis State University*] [*Research center*] (RCD) ... CNS
Center for Numerical Analysis [*University of Texas at Austin*] [*Research center*] (RCD) ... CNA
Center for Nursing Education, Spokane, WA [*Library symbol Library of Congress*] (LCLS) ... WaSpCN
Center for Nursing Research [*Ohio State University*] [*Research center*] (RCD) ... CNR
Center for Nursing Research and Evaluation [*University of Wisconsin - Milwaukee*] [*Research center*] (RCD) ... CNRE
Center for Occupational Hazards (EA) ... COH
Center for Occupational Health and Safety [*University of Waterloo*] [*Research center*] (RCD) ... COHS
Center for Occupational Research and Development [*Research center*] (RCD) ... CORD
Center for Ocean Analysis and Prediction [*Monterey, CA*] [*NOAA*] ... COAP
Center for Ocean Climate Chemistry [*Canada*] [*Marine science*] (OSRA) ... COCC
Center for Oceanic Analysis and Prediction [*Monterey, CA*] [*National Oceanic and Atmospheric Administration*] ... COAP
Center for Ocean-Land-Atmosphere Studies [*Marine science*] (OSRA) ... COLA
Center for Oceans Law and Policy (EA) ... COLP
Center for Office Technology (EA) ... COT
Center for Oil Spill, Oil Spill Public Information Center, Anchorage, AK [*Library symbol*] [*Library of Congress*] (LCLS) ... AkAOS
Center for Operations Research [*MIT*] (MCD) ... COR
Center for Optics Manufacturing (RDA) ... COM
Center for Optics, Photonics, and LASERS [*Laval University*] [*Research center*] (RCD) ... COPL
Center for Optimum Environments (EA) ... COE
Center for Oral Health Research [*University of Pennsylvania*] [*Research center*] (RCD) ... COHR
Center for Organ Recovery and Education [*Medicine*] ... CORE
Center for Organizational and Community Development (EA) ... COCD
Center for Overseas Program Analysis [*Department of State*] ... COPA
Center for Packaging Education (EA) ... CPE
Center for Parapsychological Research [*Defunct*] (EA) ... CPR
Center for Particle Theory [*University of Texas at Austin*] [*Research center*] (RCD) ... CPT
Center for Peace Studies (EA) ... CPS
Center for Philosophy and Public Policy [*Later, IPPP*] (EA) ... CPPP
Center for Philosophy, Law, Citizenship (EA) ... CPLC
Center for Philosophy of Science [*University of Pittsburgh*] [*Research center*] (RCD) ... CPS
Center for Plant Conservation (EA) ... CPC
Center for Plutonium Production [*France*] (NRCH) ... CPP
Center for Policy Alternatives (EA) ... CPA
Center for Policy and Law in Education [*University of Miami*] [*Research center*] (RCD) ... CPLE
Center for Policy Process [*Defunct*] ... CPP
Center for Policy Research (EA) ... CPR
Center for Policy Research in Education [*New Brunswick, NJ*] [*Department of Education*] (GRD) ... CPRE
Center for Political Research [*Later, Government Research Corp.*] ... CPR
Center for Popular Economics (EA) ... CPE
Center for Popular Music, Middle Tennessee State University, Murfreesboro, TN [*Library symbol*] [*Library of Congress*] (LCLS) ... TMurS-M
Center for Population and Family Health [*Columbia University*] [*Research center*] (RCD) ... CPFH
Center for Population Options (EA) ... CPO
Center for Population Options' Media Project (EA) ... CPOMP
Center for Population Research and Census [*Portland State University*] [*Oregon*] [*Information service or system*] (IID) ... CPRC
Center for Population Research - National Institute of Child Health and Human Development [*Bethesda, MD*] [*Department of Health and Human Services*] (GRD) ... CPR-NICHD
Center for Preservation Research ... CPR
Center for Prevention of Premature Arterial Sclerosis ... CPPA
Center for Prevention Services [*Department of Health and Human Services*] (GFGA) ... CPS
Center for Process Analytical Chemistry [*University of Washington*] [*Research center*] (RCD) ... CPAC
Center for Process Studies (EA) ... CPS
Center for Produce Quality ... CPQ

Center for Professional Development [*University of Kentucky*] [*Research center*] (RCD) .... CPD
Center for Professional Development and Training [*University of Texas at Austin*] (RDA) .... CPDT
Center for Propellant and Missile Completion [*France*] .... CAPE
Center for Public Administration and Policy [*Virginia Polytechnic Institute and State University*] [*Research center*] (RCD) .... CPAP
Center for Public Affairs [*Arizona State University*] [*Research center*] (RCD) .... CPA
Center for Public Dialogue (EA) .... CPD
Center for Public Health Studies [*Portland State University*] [*Research center*] (RCD) .... CPHS
Center for Public Integrity .... CPI
Center for Public Justice (EA) .... CPJ
Center for Public Policy, Union Institute (EA) .... CPPUI
Center for Public Representation (EA) .... CPR
Center for Public Resources (EA) .... CPR
Center for Radiation Research [*National Institute of Standards and Technology*] .... CRR
Center for Radiophysics and Space Research [*Cornell University*] [*Research center*] .... CRSR
Center for Rate Controlled Recordings [*Defunct*] (EA) .... CRCR
Center for Reflection on the Second Law (EA) .... CFRSL
Center for Reformation Research (EA) .... CRR
Center for Reformation Research, St. Louis, MO [*Library symbol Library of Congress*] (LCLS) .... MoSCRR
Center for Rehabilitation Technology [*Georgia Institute of Technology*] [*Research center*] (RCD) .... CRT
Center for Religion, Ethics, and Social Policy [*Cornell University*] [*Research center*] (RCD) .... CRESP
Center for Remote Sensing and Cartography [*University of Utah Research Institute*] [*Research center*] (RCD) .... CRSC
Center for Renewable Resources (EA) .... CRR
Center for Reproduction of Endangered Wildlife [*Research center*] (RCD) .... CREW
Center for Reproductive and Sexual Health [*Defunct*] (EA) .... CRASH
Center for Reproductive Law and Policy (EA) .... CRLP
Center for Research and Development in Masonry, Calgary, AB, Canada [*Library symbol*] [*Library of Congress*] (LCLS) .... CaACRDM
Center for Research and Documentation on the European Community [*American University*] [*Research center*] (RCD) .... CERDEC
Center for Research and Documentation on the European Community [*American University*] [*Research center*] .... CRDEC
Center for Research and Education in Sexuality [*San Francisco State University*] [*Research center*] (RCD) .... CERES
Center for Research and Evaluation in Applications of Technology in Education [*Palo Alto, CA*] .... CREATE
Center for Research Animal Resources [*Cornell University*] [*Research center*] (RCD) .... CRAR
Center for Research for Mothers and Children [*National Institutes of Health*] (GRD) .... CRMC
Center for Research in Ambulatory Health Care Administration (EA) .... CRAHCA
Center for Research in College Instruction of Science and Mathematics (EA) .... CRICISAM
Center for Research in Computing Technology [*Harvard University*] [*Research center*] (RCD) .... CRCT
Center for Research in Electro-Optics and Lasers [*University of Central Florida*] [*Research center*] (RCD) .... CREOL
Center for Research in Engineering Science [*University of Kansas*] .... CRES
Center for Research in Faith and Moral Development (EA) .... CRFMD
Center for Research in Innovative Services for the Communicatively Impaired [*Memphis State University*] [*Research center*] (RCD) .... CRISCI
Center for Research in Integrated Manufacturing [*University of Michigan*] [*Research center*] (RCD) .... CRIM
Center for Research in Management Science [*University of California*] (MCD) .... CRMS
Center for Research in Oral Biology [*University of Washington*] [*Research center*] (RCD) .... CROB
Center for Research in Scientific Communication [*Johns Hopkins University*] (IID) .... CRSC
Center for Research in Security Prices [*University of Chicago*] [*Chicago, IL Information service or system*] (IID) .... CRSP
Center for Research in Social Behavior [*University of Missouri - Columbia*] [*Research center*] (RCD) .... CRSB
Center for Research in Social Change [*Emory University, Atlanta, GA*] .... CRSC
Center for Research in Social Systems [*American University*] (MCD) .... CRESS
Center for Research in Social Systems of the American University (IEEE) .... CRESS/AU
Center for Research in Surface Science and Submicron Analysis [*Montana State University*] [*Research center*] (RCD) .... CRISS
Center for Research in the Hospitality Service Industries (EA) .... CRHSI
Center for Research in Water Resources [*University of Texas at Austin*] [*Research center*] (RCD) .... CRWR
Center for Research Initiatives and Strategies for the Communicatively Impaired [*Memphis State University*] [*Research center*] (RCD) .... CRISCI
Center for Research Libraries [*Library network*] (EA) .... CRL
Center for Research Libraries, Chicago, IL [*Inactive*] [*OCLC symbol*] (OCLC) .... CRL
Center for Research Libraries, Chicago, IL [*Library symbol Library of Congress*] (LCLS) .... ICRL
Center for Research on Economic Development [*University of Michigan*] [*Research center*] (RCD) .... CRED
Center for Research on Educational Accountability and Teacher Evaluation [*Western Michigan University*] [*Research center*] (RCD) .... CREATE
Center for Research on Effective Schooling for Disadvantaged Students [*Johns Hopkins University*] [*Research center*] (RCD) .... CDS
Center for Research on Evaluation, Standards, and Student Testing [*Los Angeles, CA*] [*Department of Education*] (GRD) .... CRESST
Center for Research on Industrial Strategy and Policy [*Illinois Institute of Technology*] [*Research center*] (RCD) .... CRISP
Center for Research on Judgment and Policy [*University of Colorado - Boulder*] [*Research center*] (RCD) .... CRJP
Center for Research on Language and Language Behavior [*University of Michigan*] .... CRLLB
Center for Research on Learning and Teaching [*University of Michigan*] [*Research center*] (RCD) .... CRLT
Center for Research on Multi-Ethnic Education [*University of Oklahoma*] [*Research center*] (RCD) .... CRME
Center for Research on Occupational and Environmental Toxicology [*Oregon Health Sciences University*] [*Research center*] (RCD) .... CROET
Center for Research on Social Organization [*University of Michigan*] [*Research center*] (RCD) .... CRSO
Center for Research on Utilization of Scientific Knowledge [*University of Michigan*] .... CRUSK
Center for Research on Women [*Duke University*] [*Research center*] (RCD) .... CROW
Center for Research on Women [*Stanford University*] (RCD) .... CROW
Center for Resource Development in Adult Education [*University of Missouri - Kansas City*] [*Research center*] (RCD) .... CRD
Center for Respect of Life and Environment (GNE) .... CRLE
Center for Responsive Design [*Defunct*] (EA) .... CRD
Center for Responsive Governance (EA) .... CRG
Center for Responsive Politics (EA) .... CRP
Center for Responsive Psychology (EA) .... CRP
Center for Robotic Systems in Microelectronics [*Research center*] (RCD) .... CRSM
Center for Rural Affairs (EA) .... CRA
Center for Rural Studies [*University of Vermont*] [*Research center*] (RCD) ...... CRS
Center for Russian and East European Jewry [*Later, CREEJ*] (EA) .... CFRJ
Center for Russian and East European Jewry (EA) .... CREEJ
Center for Russian and East European Studies [*University of Michigan*] [*Research center*] (RCD) .... CREES
Center for Russian and East European Studies [*University of Pittsburgh*] [*Research center*] (RCD) .... REES
Center for Safety in the Arts (PAZ) .... CSA
Center for Scholarly Editions [*Formerly, CEAA*] (EA) .... CSE
Center for Science and International Affairs [*Harvard University*] [*Research center*] .... CSIA
Center for Science in the Public Interest (EA) .... CSPI
Center for Science in the Public Interest (GNE) .... CSPI
Center for Science Information (EA) .... CSI
Center for Scientific Anomalies Research [*Ann Arbor, MI*] .... CSAR
Center for Scientific Information on Vivisection (EA) .... CIVITAS
Center for Seafarers' Rights (EA) .... CSR
Center for Security Policy (EA) .... CSP
Center for Self-Sufficiency (EA) .... CSS
Center for Separation Science [*University of Arizona*] .... CSS
Center for Short-Lived Phenomena [*Cambridge, MA*] .... CFSLP
Center for Short-Lived Phenomena (EA) .... CSLP
Center for Sickle Cell Disease (EA) .... CSCD
Center for Signals Warfare [*Warrenton, VA*] [*Army*] (GRD) .... CSW
Center for Slavic and East European Studies [*University of Connecticut*] [*Research center*] (RCD) .... CSEES
Center for Social Analysis [*State University of New York at Binghamton*] [*Research center*] (RCD) .... CSA
Center for Social and Behavior Science Research [*Research center*] (RCD) .... CSBSR
[*The*] **Center for Social Gerontology** (EA) .... TCSG
Center for Social Organization of Schools [*Department of Education*] [*Research center*] (GRD) .... CSOS
Center for Social Organization Studies [*University of Chicago*] [*Research center*] (RCD) .... CSOS
Center for Social Research [*Stanford University*] [*Research center*] (RCD) ..... CSR
Center for Social Research [*City University of New York*] [*Research center*] (RCD) .... CSR
Center for Social Research and Education (EA) .... CSRE
Center for Social Science Research and Documentation for the Arab Region [*UNESCO*] [*Information service or system*] (IID) .... ARCSS
Center for Social Studies Education (EA) .... CSSE
Center for Socialist History (EA) .... CSH
Center for Software Engineering [*Army*] .... CSE
Center for Solid State Electronics [*Arizona State University*] [*Research center*] (RCD) .... CSSER
Center for South and Southeast Asian Studies [*University of Michigan*] [*Research center*] (RCD) .... CSSEAS
Center for Southern Folklore (EA) .... CSF
Center for Soviet and East European Studies [*University of Connecticut*] [*Research center*] (RCD) .... CSEES
Center for Soviet-American Dialogue (EA) .... CSAD
Center for Space Policy, Inc. [*Cambridge, MA*] [*Telecommunications*] (TSSD) .... CSP
Center for Space Research [*Massachusetts Institute of Technology*] [*Research center*] (RCD) .... CSR
Center for Space Research and Applications [*University of Texas at Austin*] [*Research center*] (RCD) .... CSR
Center for Space Structures and Controls [*University of Colorado at Boulder*] [*Research center*] (RCD) .... CSSC
Center for Sports Sponsorship (EA) .... CSS
Center for Standards .... CFS

Center for State Employment Security Automated Systems ... CSESAS

Center for Statistics [*Later, CES*] [*Department of Education*] (IID) ... CS

Center for Strategic and International Studies [*Georgetown University*] ... CSIS

Center for Strategy Research, Inc. [*Information service or system*] (IID) ... CSR

Center for Student Testing, Evaluation, and Standards [*Later, CRESST*] [*Department of Education*] (GRD) ... CSTES

Center for Studies in Criminal Justice (EA) ... CSCJ

Center for Studies in Criminology and Criminal Law [*Later, SCSCCL*] (EA) ... CSCCL

Center for Studies in Demography and Ecology [*University of Washington*] [*Research center*] (RCD) ... CSDE

Center for Studies in Education and Human Development [*Gallaudet College*] [*Research center*] (RCD) ... CSEHD

Center for Studies in Language and Communication [*Gallaudet College*] [*Research center*] (RCD) ... CSLC

Center for Studies in Music Technology [*Yale University*] [*Research center*] (RCD) ... CSMT

Center for Studies of Ethnicity and Race in America [*University of Colorado at Boulder*] [*Research center*] (RCD) ... CSERA

Center for Studies of Mental Health of the Aging [*National Institute of Mental Health*] (GRD) ... CSMHA

Center for Studies of Nonlinear Dynamics [*Research center*] (RCD) ... CSND

Center for Studies of Suicide Prevention [*National Institute of Mental Health*] ... CSSP

Center for Study of Federalism [*Temple University*] [*Research center*] (RCD) ... CSF

Center for Study of Higher and Postsecondary Education [*University of Michigan*] [*Research center*] (RCD) ... CSHPE

Center for Study of Multiple Birth (EA) ... CSMB

Center for Study of Responsive Law (EA) ... CSRL

Center for Substance Abuse Prevention [*Department of Health and Human Services*] ... CSAP

Center for Substance Abuse Treatment [*Department of Health and Human Services*] ... CSAT

Center for Supercomputing Research and Development [*University of Illinois*] [*Urbana*] [*Information service or system*] (IID) ... CSRD

Center for Supplying Services by Redemptorists for North America ... CSSRNA

Center for Surface Coatings Research [*Lehigh University*] ... CSCR

Center for Surrogate Parenting (EA) ... CSP

Center for Survey Methods Research [*Bureau of the Census*] (GFGA) ... CSMR

Center for Survey Research [*University of Massachusetts*] [*Research center*] (RCD) ... CSR

Center for Sustainable Agriculture (EA) ... CSA

Center for Sustainable Transportation (EA) ... CST

Center for Systems Engineering and Integration [*Army*] (GRD) ... CENSEI

Center for Tactical Computer Systems [*CADPL*] [*Army*] (MCD) ... CENTACS

Center for Talented Youth [*Johns Hopkins University*] (PAZ) ... CTY

Center for Teaching about China (EA) ... CTAC

Center for Teaching Effectiveness [*University of Texas at Austin*] [*Research center*] (RCD) ... CTE

Center for Teaching International Relations ... CTIR

Center for Technical Services [*Air Force*] ... CTS

Center for Technology and Administration [*American University*] [*Research center*] (RCD) ... CTA

Center for Technology, Environment, and Development [*Clark University*] ... CENTED

Center for Telecommunications Management [*UCLA*] (TSSD) ... CTM

Center for Telecommunications Research [*Columbia University*] [*New York, NY Telecommunications service*] (TSSD) ... CTR

Center for Telecommunications Studies [*Formerly, Broadcast Research Center*] [*Ohio University*] [*Research center*] (RCD) ... CTS

Center for Telephone Information [*Laguna Hills, CA*] [*Telecommunications*] (TSSD) ... CTI

Center for the Advanced Study of Educational Administration ... CASEA

Center for the Advancement of Human Co-Operation (EA) ... CAHC

Center for the Advancement of Human Service Practice (EA) ... CAHSP

Center for the American Woman and Politics (EA) ... CAWP

Center for the Analysis of Public Issues [*Princeton, NJ*] ... CAPI

Center for the Applied Behavioral Sciences [*St. Louis University*] [*Research center*] (RCD) ... CABS

Center for the Biology of Natural Systems [*Washington University*] ... CBNS

Center for the Book in the Library of Congress (EA) ... CBLC

Center for the Coordination of Foreign Manuscript Copying [*Library of Congress*] ... CCFMC

Center for the Defense of Free Enterprise [*Bellevue, WA*] (EA) ... CDFE

Center for the Development of Human Resources in Rural Asia (EAIO) ... CENDHRRA

Center for the Environment and Man, Inc. [*Research center*] (RCD) ... CEM

Center for the Exploitation of Science and Techology [*British*] ... CEST

Center for the History of American Needlework (EA) ... CHAN

Center for the Humanities [*State University of New York at Albany*] [*Research center*] (RCD) ... CHUM

Center for the Improvement of Reasoning in Early Childhood (EA) ... CIREC

Center for the Ministry of Teaching (EA) ... CMT

Center for the New Leadership (EA) ... CTNL

Center for the Progress of Peoples (EAIO) ... CPP

Center for the Rights of Campus Journalists (EA) ... CRCJ

Center for the Rights of the Terminally Ill (EA) ... CRTI

Center for the Social Sciences [*Columbia University*] [*Research center*] (RCD) ... CSS

Center for the Study of Aging (EA) ... CSA

Center for the Study of Beadwork [*An association*] (EA) ... CSB

Center for the Study of Commercialism (EA) ... CSC

Center for the Study of Data Processing [*Washington University*] [*Research center*] (RCD) ... CSDP

Center for the Study of Democratic Institutions [*Later, Robert Maynard HutchinsCenter for the Study of Democratic Institutions*] (EA) ... CSDI

Center for the Study of Democratic Societies (EA) ... CSDS

Center for the Study of Development and Aging [*University of Detroit*] [*Research center*] (RCD) ... CSDA

Center for the Study of Drug Development [*Tufts University*] [*Research center*] (RCD) ... CSDD

Center for the Study of Drug Policy [*NORML*] [*Absorbed by*] (EA) ... CSDP

Center for the Study of Earth from Space [*University of Colorado*] [*National Oceanic and Atmospheric Administration Research center*] (GRD) ... CSES

Center for the Study of Economics [*Columbia, MD*] (EA) ... CSE

Center for the Study of Ethics in the Professions [*Illinois Institute of Technology*] [*Research center*] (RCD) ... CSEP

Center for the Study of Evaluation [*Department of Education*] (GRD) ... CSE

Center for the Study of Evolution and the Origin of Life [*University of California at Los Angeles*] [*Research center*] (RCD) ... CSEOL

Center for the Study of Foreign Affairs (EA) ... CSFA

Center for the Study of Human Rights (EA) ... CSHR

Center for the Study of Information and Education [*Syracuse University*] (IID) ... CSIE

Center for the Study of Instruction [*of NEA*] ... CSI

Center for the Study of Language and Information [*Stanford University*] [*Research center*] (RCD) ... CSLI

Center for the Study of Law and Politics (EA) ... CSLP

Center for the Study of Law and Society [*University of California, Berkeley*] [*Research center*] (RCD) ... CSLS

Center for the Study of Learning [*Pittsburgh, PA*] [*Department of Education*] (GRD) ... CSL

Center for the Study of Legal Authority and Mental Patient Status (EA) ... LAMP

Center for the Study of Liberal Education for Adults (EA) ... CSLEA

Center for the Study of Multiple Gestation [*Later, CSMB*] (EA) ... CSMG

Center for the Study of Non-Medical Drug Use [*Later, CSDP*] (EA) ... CSNMDU

Center for the Study of Parent Involvement (EA) ... CSPI

Center for the Study of Parental Acceptance and Rejection [*University of Connecticut*] [*Research center*] (RCD) ... CSPAR

Center for the Study of Pharmacy and Therapeutics for the Elderly (EA) ... CSPTE

Center for the Study of Political Graphics [*An association*] ... CSPG

Center for the Study of Power [*Later, SPI*] (EA) ... CSP

Center for the Study of Race, Crime, and Social Policy [*Cornell University*] [*Research center*] (RCD) ... CSRCSP

Center for the Study of Reading [*Later, RREC*] [*Department of Education*] (GRD) ... CSR

Center for the Study of Responsive Law (GNE) ... CSRL

Center for the Study of Sensory Integrative Dysfunction [*American Occupational Therapy Association*] ... CSSID

Center for the Study of Social Policy (EA) ... CSSP

Center for the Study of the American Family Farm (EA) ... CSAFF

Center for the Study of the College Fraternity (EA) ... CSCF

Center for the Study of the Evaluation of Instructional Programs ... CSEIP

Center for the Study of the Future (EA) ... CSF

Center for the Study of the Presidency (EA) ... CSP

Center for the Study of Writing [*Berkeley, CA*] [*Department of Education*] (GRD) ... CSW

Center for the Survival of Western Democracies (EA) ... CSWD

Center for the Utilization of Federal Technology [*National Technical Information Service*] [*Springfield, VA*] ... CUFT

Center for the Well-Being of Health Professionals (EA) ... CWBHP

Center for Theoretical Studies [*University of Miami*] [*Research center*] (RCD) ... CTS

Center for Third World Organizing (EA) ... CTWO

Center for Tissue Trauma Research and Education (EA) ... CTTRE

Center for Total Access [*Army*] ... CTA

Center for Trace Characterization [*Texas A & M University*] [*Research center*] (RCD) ... CTC

Center for Training, Experimentation, and Research on Education (IID) ... CPEIP

Center for Transportation Research [*University of Texas at Austin*] [*Research center*] (RCD) ... CTR

Center for Transportation Studies [*Morgan State University*] [*Research center*] (RCD) ... CTS

Center for Transportation Training and Research [*Texas Southern University*] [*Research center*] (RCD) ... CTTR

Center for Tropical Agriculture [*University of Florida*] [*Research center*] (RCD) ... CTA

Center for Tropical and Subtropical Architecture Planning and Construction [*University of Florida*] [*Research center*] (RCD) ... TROPARC

Center for Tropical Animal Health [*Texas A & M University*] [*Research center*] (RCD) ... CTAH

Center for UFO [*Unidentified Flying Object*] **Studies** [*Information service or system*] (IID) ... CUFOS

Center for Ulcer Research and Education [*University of California, Los Angeles*] [*Research center*] (RCD) ... CURE

Center for UN Reform Education (EA) ... CUNRE

Center for UN Reform Education (EA) ... CURE

Center for UN Studies (EAIO) ... CUNS

Center for Urban Affairs and Community Services [*North Carolina State University*] [*Research center*] (RCD) ... CUACS

Center for Urban and Regional Affairs [*University of Minnesota*] [*Research center*] (RCD) ... CURA

Center for Urban and Regional Studies (EA) ... CURS

Center for Urban Black Studies (EA) ... CUBS

Center for Urban Economics Development [*University of Illinois at Chicago*] [*Research center*] (RCD) ... CUED

Center for Urban Education [*Research center*] (RCD) ... CUE

Center for Urban Environmental Studies (EA) ... CUES

Center for Urban Policy [*Loyola University of Chicago*] [*Research center*] (RCD) .... CUP
Center for Urban Programs [*St. Louis University*] [*Research center*] (RCD) .... CUP
Center for Urban Programs and Research [*St. Louis University*] [*Research center*] (RCD) .... CUPR
Center for Urban Studies [*University of Chicago*] [*Research center*] (RCD) ..... CUS
Center for Urban Studies [*Wayne State University*] [*Research center*] (RCD) .... CUS
Center for US Capital Markets (EA) .... CUSCM
Center for US-USSR Initiatives (EA) .... CUSUSSRI
Center for US-USSR Initiatives (EAIO) .... CUUI
Center for Venture Research (EA) .... CVR
Center for Veterinary Medicine [*Food and Drug Administration*] .... CVM
Center for Vietnamese Studies [*Southern Illinois University at Carbondale*] [*Research center*] (RCD) .... CVS
Center for Visual Science [*University of Rochester*] [*Research center*] (RCD) .... CVS
Center for Vocational and Technical Education, Ohio State University, Columbus, OH [*Inactive*] [*OCLC symbol*] (OCLC) .... CVT
Center for Vocational and Technical Education, Ohio State University, Columbus, OH [*Library symbol Library of Congress*] (LCLS) .... OCoV
Center for Vocational, Technical, and Adult Education [*University of Wisconsin - Stout*] [*Research center*] (RCD) .... CVTAE
Center for War, Peace, and the News Media (EA) .... CWPNM
Center for War/Peace Studies (EA) .... CW/PS
Center for Waste Reduction Technologies (EA) .... CWRT
Center for Water and Environment [*University of Minnesota*] .... CWE
Center for Water Policy [*International Ground Water Modeling Center*] .... CWP
Center for Water Resources Research [*University of Nevada*] .... CWRR
Center for Welding Research [*Ohio State University*] [*Research center*] (RCD) .... CWR
Center for Women and Sport [*Defunct*] (EA) .... CWS
Center for Women Policy Studies (EA) .... CWPS
Center for Women's Studies and Services (EA) .... CWSS
Center for Wooden Boats (EA) .... CWB
Center for World Christian Interaction (EA) .... CWCI
Center for World Thanksgiving (EA) .... CWT
Center for Youth and Social Development [*India*] (EAIO) .... CYSD
Center for Zoroastrian Research (EA) .... CZR
Center Forward [*Soccer*] .... CF
Center Frequency .... CF
Center Frequency (MSA) .... CTRF
Center Frequency Modulation .... CFM
Center Frequency Stabilization [*Radio*] .... CFS
Center Groove Two Edges [*Lumber*] (DAC) CG2E
Center Halfback [*Soccer*] .... CH
Center Halfback [*Soccer*] .... CHB
Center High-Mounted Stop Lamp [*Pronounced "chimsel"*] [*Automotive engineering*] .... CHMSL
Center (Hospital and Domiciliary) [*Veterans Administration*] .... C(H & D)
Center Housing Rotating Assembly [*Automotive engineering*] .... CHRA
Center Information Network [*Support servicing center*] (SSD) .... CIN
Center International de Vol Libre [*Aguessac, France*] (EAIO) CIVL
Center International des Civilisations Bantu (EAIO) .... CICB
Center Island [*Nuclear energy*] (NRCH) CI
Center Island Vessel [*Nuclear energy*] (NRCH) CIV
Center Landing Gear (MCD) .... CLG
Center Launch and Flight Instrumentation Center [*NASA*] (KSC) .... CLFIC
Center Left [*Theatrical term*] (WDMC) CL
Center Light [*Aviation*] (DA) .... C/L
Center Line CL
Center Line Average .... CLA
Center Line Bend (MSA) .... CLB
Center Line Block [*Philately*] .... CLB
Center Line of Occupant .... CLO
Center Matched [*Technical drawings*] .... CM
Center Materials Representative [*NASA*] (NASA) .... CMR
Center Moriches Free Public Library, Center Moriches, NY [*Library symbol Library of Congress*] (LCLS) .... NCm
Center of Advanced Technology in Electronic Imaging Systems [*New York State Science and Technology Foundation*] (RDA) .... CAT-EIS
Center of Buoyancy .... CB
Center of Concern (EA) CC
Center of Effort [*Sailing*] .... CE
Center of Experimentation in the Pacific Ocean (BARN) .... CEP
Center of Figure [*Topographical coordinate system*] .... COF
Center of Filtering and Plotting (NATG) .... CFP
Center of Flotation .... CF
Center of Fruiting Period [*Ecology*] .... CFP
Center of Genetic Diversity .... CGD
Center of Gravity .... C of G
Center of Gravity .... CG
Center of Gravity .... COG
Center of Gravity above Keel (MCD) .... KG
Center of Impact CI
Center of Influence [*Military*] .... COI
Center of International Studies [*MIT*] [*Research center*] (MCD) .... CIS
Center of Lateral Resistance (IAA) .... CLR
Center of Lift CL
Center of Marine Biology [*University of Maryland*] .... COMB
Center of Marine Biotechnology [*Marine science*] (OSRA) .... COMB
Center of Mass .... C of M
Center of Mass [*Atomic physics*] .... CM
Center of Mass [*Coordinate system*] (MCD) .... COM
Center of Military History (AABC) .... CMH

Center of Nuclear Image (DMAA) .... CNI
Center of Pillar .... CPLR
Center of Pressure .... CP
Center of Pressure Back (DIT) .... CPB
Center of Programmed Instruction (DIT) .... CPI
Center of Research in Administrative Sciences [*University of Moncton*] [*Research center*] (RCD) .... CRSA
Center of Resistance .... CR
Center of Rotation .... COR
Center of Science and Industry [*Ohio*] (AEBS) .... COSI
Center of Technical Excellence [*Army*] (RDA) .... CTX
Center on Aging [*University of Maryland*] [*Research center*] (RCD) .... COA
Center on Budget and Policy Priorities (EA) .... CBPP
Center on Destructive Cultism (EA) .... CDC
Center on Human Policy (EA) .... CHP
Center on International Race Relations [*University of Denver*] .... CIRR
Center on Law and Pacifism [*Defunct*] (EA) .... CLP
Center on National Labor Policy (EA) .... CNLP
Center on Religion and Society (EA) .... CRS
Center on Social Welfare Policy and Law (EA) .... CSWPL
Center on Technology and Society, Inc. [*Research center*] (RCD) .... CTS
Center on the Consequences of Nuclear War (EA) .... CCNW
Center on Transnational Corporations [*United Nations*] .... CTC
Center on War and the Child (EA) .... CWC
Center Operations Area .... COA
Center Operations Directorate (MCD) .... COD
Center Overage Pending Assignment (MCD) .... COPA
Center Pivot Irrigation System .... CPIS
Center po Atomn. i Jadernum Dannym [*Center for Nuclear Structure and Reaction Data*] [*USSR State Committee on the Utilization of Atomic Energy*] [*Information service or system*] (IID) .... CAJAD
Center Point, TX [*Location identifier FAA*] (FAAL) .... CSI
Center pour les Droits de l'Homme [*Center for Human Rights*] [*Switzerland*] (EAIO) .... CDH
Center Pressure Index .... CPI
Center Program Director [*NASA*] (KSC) .... CPD
Center Program Manager [*NASA*] (KSC) .... CPM
Center Punch (MSA) .... CP
Center Range Control Station [*NASA*] (KSC) .... CRCS
Center (Regional Office and Hospital) [*Veterans Administration*] .... C(RO & H)
Center (Regional Office and Insurance) [*Veterans Administration*] .... C(RO & INS)
Center Right [*Theatrical term*] (WDMC) .... CR
Center Right [*Theater*] (WDMC) .... CR
Center Science Assessment Team [*NASA*] .... CSAT
Center Section .... CS
Center Special Slotted Container [*Packaging*] .... CSSC
Center Stage [*A stage direction*] .... CS
Center Stage Back [*A stage direction*] .... CSB
Center Stage Front [*A stage direction*] .... CSF
Center Standards Officer [*Job Corps*] .... CSO
Center Street Elementary School, Williston Park, NY [*Library symbol*] [*Library of Congress*] (LCLS) .... NWpCsE
Center Tap [*Technical drawings*] .... CT
Center Thickness [*Optics*] .... CT
Center to Center [*Technical drawings*] .... C to C
Center to Center .... C-C
Center to End .... C to E
Center to Prevent Handgun Violence (EA) .... CPHV
Center to Study Human-Animal Relationships and Environments [*University of Minnesota*] [*Research center*] (RCD) .... CENSHARE
Center Tracon Automation System [*FAA*] (PS) .... CTAS
Center Traffic Management Advisor [*FAA*] (TAG) .... CTMA
Center, TX [*Location identifier FAA*] (FAAL) .... CZJ
Center, TX [*AM radio station call letters*] .... KDET
Center, TX [*FM radio station call letters*] .... KDET-FM
Center Vee One Side [*Lumber*] (DAC) CV1S
Center Vee Two Sides [*Lumber*] (DAC) CV2S
Center Weather Advisory [*FAA*] (TAG) .... CWA
Center Weather Service Unit [*FAA*] (TAG) .... CWSU
Center Work System [*NASA*] (KSC) .... CWS
Centerboard (MSA) .... CNTBRD
Center-Clipping Echo Suppressor (MCD) .... CCES
Center-Cracked Tension (MCD) .... CCT
Centering .... CTRG
Centerior Energy [*NYSE symbol*] (SAG) CX
Centerior Energy Corp. [*Associated Press*] (SAG) .... CentEn
Centerless Ground (DNAB) .... CG
Centerline (WDMC) C
Centerline (FAAC) .... CNTRLN
Centerline Light [*Aviation*] (DA) CL
Centerline Lighting Will be Provided [*Aviation*] (DA) CLL
Centerline of Occupant [*Automotive engineering*] .... CLO
Center-Line Plotting (MCD) .... CLPLOT
Centerline Vertical Keel .... CVK
Centerns Kvinnoforbund [*Women's Association of the Centre Party*] [*Sweden Political party*] (EAIO) .... CKF
Center-of-Gravity Locator .... CGL
Center-of-Inertia System .... CIS
Centerpartiet [*Center Party*] [*Sweden Political party*] (PPE) .... CP
CenterPoint Properties [*AMEX symbol*] (SPSG) .... CNT
Centerpoint Properties Corp. [*Associated Press*] (SAG) .... CentrpPr
Centers [*Commonly used*] (OPSA) .... CENTERS
Centers [*Postal Service standard*] (OPSA) .... CTRS
Centers .... CTRS
Centers and Regional Associations (EA) .... CARA

Centers for Disease Control [Formerly, Communicable Disease Center] [Department of Health and Human Services Atlanta, GA] ...... CDC
Centers for Disease Control and Prevention ...... CDC
Centers for Education and Research in Therapeutics [FDA] ...... CERT
Centers for Health, Education, and Social Systems Studies [Formerly, Center for H ealth and Social Systems Research] [Research center] (RCD) ...... CHESS
Centers for Radiological Physics ...... CRP
Centers for the Analysis of Science and Technical Information (NITA) ..... CASTI
Centers for the Commercial Development of Space ...... CCDS
Centers of Excellence [Army] (RDA) ...... COE
Centers of Excellence [Marine science] (OSRA) ...... COEs
Centers of Excellence (USDC) ...... COEs
Centerville and Center Township Library, Centerville, IN [Library symbol Library of Congress] (LCLS) ...... InCe
Centerville Community College [Iowa] CCC
Centerville, IA [AM radio station call letters] ...... KCOG
Centerville, IA [FM radio station call letters] ...... KMGO
Centerville, IN [AM radio station call letters] ...... WHON
Centerville, OH [FM radio station call letters] ...... WCWT
Centerville Public Library, Centerville, MA [Library symbol] [Library of Congress] (LCLS) ...... MCen
Centerville, TN [Location identifier FAA] (FAAL) ...... GHM
Centerville, TN [AM radio station call letters] ...... WNKX
Centerville, TN [FM radio station call letters] ...... WNKX-FM
Centerville, UT [FM radio station call letters] ...... KCPX
Centerville, UT [AM radio station call letters] (RBYB) ...... KCPX-AM
Centerville, UT [FM radio station call letters] ...... KUMT
Centesimo [or Centimo] [Monetary unit in many Spanish-American countries] ...... CTMO
Centex Construction Prod [NYSE symbol] (TTSB) ...... CXP
Centex Construction Products [Associated Press] (SAG) ...... CentxCn
Centex Construction Products [NYSE symbol] (SAG) ...... CXP
Centex Corp. [Associated Press] (SAG) ...... Centex
Centex Corp. [NYSE symbol] (SPSG) ...... CTX
Centex Corp. [NYSE symbol] (TTSB) ...... CTX
Centi [A prefix meaning divided by 100] [SI symbol] c
Centibar ...... CB
Centibels [Telecommunications] ...... Cb
Centified Professional Public Buyer (AAGC) ...... CPPB
Centigrade [Celsius] [Temperature scale] C
Centigrade [Celsius] [Temperature scale] (KSC) ...... CENT
Centigrade [Celsius] [Temperature scale] (ROG) ...... CENTIG
Centigrade Heat Unit ...... CHU
Centigrade Thermal Unit ...... CTU
Centigram C
Centigram ...... Cg
Centigram ...... CGM
Centigram Communications [NASDAQ symbol] (SPSG) ...... CGRM
Centigram Communications Corp. [Associated Press] (SAG) ...... Centgrm
Centigrams (ROG) CC
Centigray [Radiation therapy] (ADDR) ...... CGY
Centiliter (GPO) CL
Centime [Monetary unit] [France] C
Centime [Monetary unit] [France] ...... CENT
Centimes [Monetary unit] [France] (GPO) ...... ces
Centimeter C
Centimeter (MAE) ...... cent
Centimeter (GPO) ...... cm
Centimeter Height-Finder [RADAR] ...... CMH
Centimeter per Second [Measurement] (DAVI) ...... cm/s
Centimeter-Candle ...... CM C
Centimeter-Gram-Second [System of units] (AAG) ...... CGS
Centimeter-Gram-Second (IDOE) ...... cgs
Centimeter-Gram-Second Unit ...... CGSU
Centimeter-Gram-Second-Biot [System of units] ...... cm-g-s-Bi
Centimeter-Gram-Second-Electromagnetic ...... CGSM
Centimeter-Gram-Second-Electrostatic ...... CGSE
Centimeter-Gram-Second-Franklin [System of units] ...... cm-g-s-Fr
Centimeters of Water [Cuff pressure] [Medicine] (DAVI) CmH2O
Centimeters of Water Pressure [Measurement] (DAVI) ...... CWP
Centimeters per Second [Telecommunications] (TEL) ...... CM/SEC
Centimeters per Second ...... CMPS
Centimeters per Second (DMAA) ...... cmps
Centimetric Early Warning RADAR (IAA) ...... CEWR
Centimorgan [Unit of genetic map distance] ...... cM
Centimorgan [Unit of genetic map distance] (MAE) ...... cMo
Centipoise [Unit of viscosity] ...... CP
Centipoise [Unit of viscosity] ...... CPS
Centipoise (BARN) ...... cpse
Centissime (ROG) C
Centistere [Metric] ...... CS
Centistoke (BARN) ...... ck
Centistoke [Also, cSt] [Unit of kinematic viscosity] ...... cs
Centistoke [Also, cs] [Unit of kinematic viscosity] ...... cSt
Centistokes [Unit of kinematic viscosity] ...... CKS
Centl Hispano Cap 10.50% Pref [NYSE symbol] (TTSB) ...... HCLPr
Centl Hispano Intl9.875% 'MIPS' [NYSE symbol] (TTSB) ...... HPNPr
Cento [Composition compiled from other works] C
CENTO [Central Treaty Organization] Institute of Nuclear Science (EY) .... CINS
CENTO [Central Treaty Organization] Military Communications System (MCD) ...... CMCS
Cento Nuptialis [of Ausonius] [Classical studies] (OCD) ...... Cent Nupt
Centocelle [Italy ICAO location identifier] (ICLI) ...... LIRC
Centocor, Inc. [Associated Press] (SAG) ...... Centocor

Centocor, Inc. [NASDAQ symbol] (NQ) ...... CNTO
Centraide, Montreal, PQ, Canada [Library symbol Library of Congress] (LCLS) ...... CaOMCCS
Centraide, Montreal, PQ, Canada [Library symbol] [Library of Congress] (LCLS) ...... CaQMCCS
Centraide, Montreal, Quebec [Library symbol National Library of Canada] (NLC) ...... QMCCS
Central C
Central (SSD) ...... CE
Central [Alaska] [Airport symbol] (OAG) ...... CEM
Central ...... CENT
Central (AAGC) ...... Cent
Central (ROG) ...... CENTR
Central ...... CNTL
Central (VRA) ...... cntr
Central (MSA) ...... CTL
Central ...... CTRL
Central ...... CTRL
Central [Wisconsin] [Airport symbol] (AD) ...... WIS
Central Abstracting and Indexing Service [American Petroleum Institute] [Information service or system] (IID) ...... CAIS
Central Access Monitor Program (NITA) ...... CAMP
Central Accounting Office [Military] (AFM) ...... CAO
Central Action Office [Army] ...... CAO
Central Acts, India [A publication] (DLA) ...... India Cen Acts
Central Address Memory [Computer science] ...... CAM
Central Administrative Support Center [Marine science] (OSRA) ...... CASC
Central Administrative Support Center (USDC) ...... CASC
Central Advisory Committee [British] ...... CAC
Central Advisory Council for Science and Technology [British] ...... CACST
Central Aero-Hydrodynamical Institute [Former USSR] ...... CAHI
Central Aerospace Rescue and Recovery Center [Air Force] ...... CARRC
Central Africa ...... CAfr
Central Africa Party [Southern Rhodesia] ...... CAP
Central Africa Protectorate [British government] ...... CAP
Central African Airways Corp. ...... CAA
Central African Empire [Later, CAR] ...... CAE
Central African Federation [Disbanded Dec. 31, 1963] ...... CAF
Central African Mineral Resources Development Centre [Congo] (EAIO) ...... CAMRDC
Central African Regiment [British military] (DMA) ...... CAR
Central African Republic [ANSI three-letter standard code] (CNC) ...... CAF
Central African Republic ...... CAfrRep
Central African Republic ...... CAR
Central African Republic (WDAA) ...... CEN AFR REP
Central African Republic (VRA) ...... Cent Afr Rep
Central African Republic [ANSI two-letter standard code] (CNC) ...... CF
Central African Republic [MARC country of publication code Library of Congress] (LCCP) cx
Central African Republic [MARC geographic area code Library of Congress] (LCCP) ...... f-cx--
Central African Republic [International civil aircraft marking] (ODBW) ...... TL
Central After Care Association [British] ...... CACA
Central Agramonte [Cuba ICAO location identifier] (ICLI) ...... MUAG
Central Air Conditioning [Classified advertising] (CDAI) ...... C/A
Central Air Conditioning [Classified advertising] ...... CAC
Central Air Data Computer ...... CADC
Central Air Data Computer / Central Computer (PDAA) ...... CADC/CC
Central Air Data Computer Test Set ...... CADCTS
Central Air Data System [Air Force] ...... CADS
Central Air Defense Force ...... CADF
Central Air Documents Office [Air Force] ...... CADO
Central Air Materiel Area, Europe ...... CAMAE
Central Air Procurement District ...... CEAPD
Central Air Transport ...... CATR
Central Airborne Performance Analyzer (MCD) ...... CAPA
Central Aircraft Dispatch ...... CAD
Central Aircrew Medical Review Board [Military] (AFM) ...... CAMRB
Central Airlines, Inc. ...... CEN
Central Airlines, Inc. ...... CN
Central Airlines, Inc. [ICAO designator] (FAAC) ...... CTL
Central Airlines Ltd. [Nigeria] [ICAO designator] (ICDA) ...... HU
Central Airways [Medicine] (DMAA) ...... CAW
Central Airways Corp. ...... CA
Central Airways Corp. [Canada ICAO designator] (FAAC) ...... CEN
Central Alarm Station (IEEE) ...... CAS
Central Alarm System (NUCP) ...... CARS
Central Alarm System (NRCH) ...... CAS
Central Altitude Reservation Facility [or Function] ...... CARF
Central Altitude Reservation Function [FAA] (TAG) ...... CARF
Central Amancio Rodriguez [Cuba ICAO location identifier] (ICLI) ...... MUFC
Central America ...... CA
Central America ...... CENTAM
Central America [MARC geographic area code Library of Congress] (LCCP) ...... nc----
Central America and Panama (IID) ...... CAP
Central America Information Center [An association] (EA) ...... CAIC
Central America Information Office [Defunct] (EA) ...... CAMINO
Central America Peace Campaign [Defunct] (EA) ...... CAPC
Central America Research Institute (EA) ...... CARIN
Central America Resource Center (EA) ...... CARC
Central America Task Force (EA) ...... CATF
Central America Week ...... CAW
Central American (VRA) ...... Cent Am
Central American Airways [Air carrier designation symbol] ...... CAAX

Central American and Caribbean Sports Organization (EAIO) .... CACSO
Central American and Mexico Coniferous Resources Cooperative (GNE) .... CAMCORE
Central American Association of Families of Disappeared Persons [*See also ACAFADE*] [*San Jose, Costa Rica*] (EAIO) .... CAAFDP
Central American Bank for Economic Integration .... CABEI
Central American Club of New York (EA) .... CAC
Central American Committee for Human Rights [*British*] (EAIO) .... CACHR
Central American Common Market (BARN) .... CACM
Central American Common Market .... CACOM
Central American Confederation of Workers (EAIO) .... CACW
Central American Development Coordination Council .... CADCC
Central American Economics Association .... CAEA
Central American Energy Commission (EAIO) .... CAEC
Central American Free Trade Area .... CAFTA
Central American Human Rights Committee [*British*] .... CAHRC
Central American Indian [*MARC language code Library of Congress*] (LCCP) .... cai
Central American International [*Air carrier designation symbol*] .... CAIX
Central American Monetary Council .... CAMC
Central American Refugee Center (EA) .... CARECEN
Central American Society of Pharmacology [*Panama*] (EAIO) .... CASP
Central American Tropical [*In CATHOUSES, a reference to temporary US Army barracks in Honduras, 1984*] .... CAT
Central Ammunition Depot (NATG) .... CAD
Central Ammunition Management Office - Pacific [*Army*] (MCD) .... CAMO-P
Central Ammunition Management Office - Pacific [*Army*] (AABC) .... CAMO-PAC
Central Ammunition Supply Status Point .... CASSP
Central Amplifier Station [*Telecommunications*] (OA) .... CAS
Central Analog Data Distributing and Computing System (KSC) .... CADDAC
Central and East European Studies Association of Canada [*See also AEECEEC*] .... CEESAC
Central and Eastern Europe .... CEE
Central and Eastern European Country (ECON) .... CEEC
Central and Local Trades Committees [*Australia*] .... CLTC
Central & So. West [*NYSE symbol*] (TTSB) .... CSR
Central and South African Basic Encyclopedia [*A publication*] .... CSABE
Central & South West Corp. [*Associated Press*] (SAG) .... CenSoWst
Central & South West Corp. [*NYSE symbol*] (SPSG) .... CSR
Central & Southern Holding [*NASDAQ symbol*] (TTSB) .... CSBC
Central & Southern Holding Co. [*NASDAQ symbol*] (NQ) .... CSBC
Central & Southern Holding Co. [*Associated Press*] (SAG) .... CtlSou
Central and Southern Line Islands [*gb (Gilbert Islands) used in records cataloged after October 1978*] [*MARC country of publication code Library of Congress*] (LCCP) .... ln
Central and Southern Line Islands [*MARC geographic area code Library of Congress*] (LCCP) .... poln--
Central & Southern Motor Freight Tariff Association, Inc. .... CSMFTA
Central & Southern Motor Freight Tariff Association, Inc., Louisville KY [*STAC*] .... CSA
Central Annunciator Display Panel (MCD) .... CADP
Central Apollo Data Index [*NASA*] (MCD) .... CADI
Central Apparatus Room (DEN) .... CAR
Central Applications Office [*Ireland*] .... CAO
Central Arbitration Committee [*British*] (ILCA) .... CAC
Central Arbitration Control Point (BYTE) .... CACP
Central Arbitration Point [*Computer science*] (PCM) .... CAP
Central Archives for the History of the Jewish People [*Jerusalem*] [*A publication*] (BJA) .... CAHJP
Central Archives of Fiji, Suva, Fiji [*Library symbol Library of Congress*] (LCLS) .... Fj-Ar
Central Archives of the Jewish People [*Jerusalem*] [*A publication*] (BJA) .... CAJP
Central Area .... CA
Central Area, Military Traffic Management and Terminal Service (AABC) .... CAMTMTS
Central Area Power Coordination Group [*Nuclear Regulatory Commission*] (GFGA) .... CAPCO
Central Area Training Aboriginal Resource Accounting Committee [*Australia*] .... CATARAC
Central Arizona College, Instructional Materials Center, Coolidge, AZ [*Library symbol Library of Congress*] (LCLS) .... AzCoC
Central Arizona Project [*Federal water-and-power project, similar to TVA*] .... CAP
Central Arizona Project Association (EA) .... CAPA
Central Arkansas Library System, Little Rock, AR [*OCLC symbol*] (OCLC) .... AKD
Central [*European*] **Army Group** [*NATO*] .... CENTAG
Central Asian States (ECON) .... CAS
Central Asian-American Enterprise Fund [*Commercial firm*] [*Republic of Kazakstan*] .... CAAEF
Central Assets Account [*Finance*] .... CAA
Central Associated Engineers, Inc. [*Versailles, KY*] [*Telecommunications service*] (TSSD) .... CAE
Central Association of Agricultural Valuers [*British*] .... CAAV
Central Association of Irish Schoolmistresses (BI) .... CAISM
Central Association of Obstetricians and Gynecologists (PDAA) .... CAOG
Central Association of Science and Mathematics Teachers [*Later, SSMA*] .... CASMT
Central Association of the Miraculous Medal (EA) .... CAMM
Central Atlantic Regional Ecological Test Site [*Department of the Interior*] .... CARETS
Central Atlantic Regional Educational Laboratory .... CAREL
Central Atmosphere Monitoring System [*Military*] (CAAL) .... CAMS
Central Auditory Nervous System (DMAA) .... CANS
Central Aural Warning System (MCD) .... CAW
Central Aural Warning System (MCD) .... CAWS
Central Australian Aboriginal Legal Aid Scheme .... CAALAS
Central Australian Folk Society .... CAFS
Central Australian Motels Association .... CAMA
Central Australian Show Society .... CASS
Central Australian Tourism Industry Association .... CATIA
Central Autentica Nacionalista [*Nationalist Authentic Central*] [*Guatemala*] [*Political party*] (PPW) .... CAN
Central Automated Inventory and Referral Activity [*Organization for operation of CAIRS*] [*Air Force*] .... CAIRA
Central Automated Inventory and Referral System [*Air Force*] .... CAIRS
Central Automated Personnel Security Transaction or Notification Exchange [*DoD*] .... CAPSTONE
Central Automated Replenishment Technique (IEEE) .... CART
Central Automated Support System (DNAB) .... CASS
Central Automatic Digital Data Encoder [*NASA*] .... CADDE
Central Automatic Message Accounting System (CET) .... CAMAS
Central Automatic Reliability Tester (IEEE) .... CART
Central Aviation, Inc. [*ICAO designator*] (FAAC) .... YOG
Central Bank [*Philippines*] (IMH) .... CB
Central Bank Money .... CBM
Central Bank of China .... CBoC
Central Bank of Malta .... CBM
Central Baptist Seminary and Bible College, Toronto, Ontario [*Library symbol National Library of Canada*] (NLC) .... OTCBS
Central Baptist Theological Seminary, Kansas City, KS [*Library symbol Library of Congress*] (LCLS) .... KKcB
Central Battery (NATG) .... CB
Central [*Common*] **Battery Alarm Signaling** [*Electronics*] .... CBAS
Central [*Common*] **Battery Apparatus** [*Electronics*] .... CBA
Central Battery Exchange [*Electronics*] (IAA) .... CBE
Central Battery Signaling (NATG) .... CBS
Central [*Common*] **Battery Supply** [*Electronics*] .... CBS
Central [*Common*] **Battery Switchboard** [*Electronics*] .... CBS
Central [*Common*] **Battery System** [*Electronics*] .... CBS
Central Battery Telephone [*Telecommunications*] .... CBT
Central Battery Telephone Apparatus [*Telecommunications*] .... CBTA
Central Battery Telephone Set [*Telecommunications*] .... CBTS
Central Battle Manager .... CBM
Central Bible College, Springfield, MO [*Library symbol Library of Congress*] (LCLS) .... MoSpCB
Central Bible Institute [*Missouri*] .... CBI
Central Bibliographic System [*Library of Congress*] .... CBS
Central Bidder's List .... CBL
Central Black Soil Region, RSFSR [*MARC geographic area code Library of Congress*] (LCCP) .... e-urc-
Central Blood Laboratories Authority [*British*] .... CBLA
Central Blood Volume [*Medicine*] .... CBV
Central Board .... CB
Central Board of Health [*South Australia*] [*Australia*] .... CBH
Central Bomber Establishment [*British military*] (DMA) .... CBE
Central Borrowing Authorities .... CBA
Central Branch, Nepean Public Library, Ontario [*Library symbol National Library of Canada*] (NLC) .... ON
Central Brasil [*Cuba ICAO location identifier*] (ICLI) .... MUNU
Central British Fund for World Jewish Relief (EAIO) .... CBF
Central Broadcasting Administration [*China*] .... CBA
Central Bureau, Catholic Central Union of America (EA) .... CBCCUA
Central Bureau for Astronomical Telegrams (EA) .... CBAT
Central Bureau for Educational Visits and Exchanges .... CBEVE
Central Bureau for the Jewish Aged (EA) .... CBJA
Central Bureau of Compensation [*See also BCC*] [*Belgium*] (EAIO) .... CBC
Central Bureau of Identification (WDAA) .... CBI
Central Bureau of Nuclear Measurements [*European Atomic Energy Community*] .... CBNM
Central Bureau of Statistics [*Information service or system*] (IID) .... CBS
Central Business District .... CBD
Central California Traction Co. [*AAR code*] .... CCT
Central Canada Broadcasting Association .... CCBA
Central Canada Exhibition Association .... CCEA
Central Canada University Geological Conference .... CCUGC
Central Canal [*Anatomy*] CC
Central Capital Corp. [*Toronto Stock Exchange symbol*] .... CEH
Central Cardiac Monitoring System .... CCMS
Central Carolina Technical Institute, Sanford, NC [*Library symbol Library of Congress*] (LCLS) .... NcSaC
Central Certificate Service [*Stock exchange automation program*] .... CCS
Central Cervical Spinal Cord Syndrome [*Medicine*] (DMAA) .... CCSCS
Central Charging Panel [*Navy*] .... CCP
Central Circulating Blood Volume [*Physiology*] .... CCBV
Central Citizens' Defence Committee [*Northern Ireland*] .... CCDC
Central Citroen Club [*Defunct*] (EA) CCC
Central Citrus Council of Western Australia .... CCCWA
Central City, KY [*Location identifier FAA*] (FAAL) .... CCT
Central City, KY [*AM radio station call letters*] .... WMTA
Central City, KY [*AM radio station call letters*] .... WNES
Central City, KY [*FM radio station call letters*] .... WQXQ
Central City, NE [*FM radio station call letters*] .... KZEN
Central City, PA [*FM radio station call letters*] .... WYSN
Central Civilian Personnel Office [*Military*] .... CCPO
Central Classification Committee [*International Federation for Documentation*] CCC
Central Clearance Facility [*Military*] (GFGA) .... CCF
Central Clock Generator [*Telecommunications*] (ACRL) .... CCG
Central Coast (ADA) CC
Central Coast Country Music Association .... CCCMA

Central Coast Gruens [*Political party Australia*] ..... CCG
Central College of Kentucky ..... CCK
Central College, Pella, IA [*Library symbol Library of Congress*] (LCLS) ..... IaPeC
Central College, Pella, IA [*OCLC symbol*] (OCLC) ..... IOP
Central Collegiate Hockey Association (EA) ..... CCHA
Central Colorado Regional Library Service System [*Library network*] ..... CCLS
Central Command [*Persian Gulf War*] ..... CENTCOM
Central Command Decoder [*Spacecraft assembly*] (MCD) ..... CCD
Central Command Network ..... CCN
Central Commission for the Navigation of the Rhine [*France*] (EAIO) ..... CCNR
Central Commissioning Detail [*Navy*] ..... CCD
Central Committee CC
Central Committee for Forest Ownership in the EEC (EAIO) ..... CCFOE
Central Committee for Hospital Medical Services [*British*] (DAVI) ..... CCHMS
Central Committee for the Architectural Advisory Panels [*British*] ..... CCAAP
Central Committee of Lithuanian Jurists (EA) ..... CCLJ
Central Committee on Communications Facilities ..... CCCF
Central Communications Controller CCC
Central Communications Region [*Air Force*] ..... CCOMMRGN
Central Communications Region [*Air Force*] (MCD) ..... CCR
Central Communications Region [*Air Force*] (AFM) ..... CENCOMMRGN
Central Composite Design [*Statistical design of experiments*] ..... CCD
Central Computational Computer CCC
Central Computer CC
Central Computer Accounting ..... CCA
Central Computer Accounting Corp. ..... CCAC
Central Computer Agency [*Civil Service Department*] [*British*] (NITA) ..... CCA
Central Computer and Display Facility [*Air Force*] (CET) ..... CC & DF
Central Computer and Sequencer [*NASA*] ..... CC & S
Central Computer and Sequencer [*NASA*] (IAA) ..... CCAS
Central Computer and Telecommunications Agency [*British*] ..... CCTA
Central Computer Center CCC
Central Computer Center (AABC) ..... CCMPTC
Central Computer Complex CCC
Central Computer Station ..... CCS
Central Computer Unit ..... CCU
Central Computing Facility [*NASA*] ..... CCF
Central Computing Site (IAA) ..... CCS
Central Computing System [*Computer science*] ..... CCS
Central Conference of American Rabbis (EA) ..... CCAR
Central Configuation Management ..... CCM
Central Connecticut State College [*Later, Central Connecticut State University*] [*New Britain*] ..... CCSC
Central Connecticut State College, New Britain, CT [*Library symbol Library of Congress*] (LCLS) ..... CtNbT
Central Connecticut State University (GAGS) ..... Cent Conn St U
Central Console CC
Central Contract Management Region [*Air Force*] ..... CCMR
Central Control (KSC) CC
Central Control and Display Console ..... CCDC
Central Control and Monitoring System [*for managing buildings' heating, ventilation, and security needs*] ..... CCMS
Central Control Channel Command (MCD) CC
Central Control Computer System ..... CCCS
Central Control Evaluation and Warning Team (CINC) ..... CCEWT
Central Control Facility [*Military*] (AABC) ..... CCF
Central Control Function [*Aviation*] (DA) ..... CCF
Central Control Indicator (MCD) CCI
Central Control Point (AAGC) ..... CCP
Central Control Room (DEN) ..... CCR
Central Control Section (NASA) ..... CCS
Central Control Ship [*Navy*] (NVT) ..... CCS
Central Control Station (MCD) ..... CCS
Central Control Unit ..... CCU
Central Coolant Supply Station (MCD) ..... CCSS
Central Co-Operative Bank [*NASDAQ symbol*] (NQ) ..... CEBK
Central Cooperative Bank [*Associated Press*] (SAG) ..... CtrCOp
Central Cooperative Society [*United Arab Republic*] ..... CCS
Central Co-Operative Society Council [*Rangoon, Burma*] (EY) ..... CCS
Central Coordinating Staff, Canada (AFM) ..... CCS-C
Central Corporate Design ..... CCD
Central Council for Agricultural and Horticultural Co-Operation [*British*] ..... CCAC
Central Council for British Naturism (BI) ..... CCBN
Central Council for Education and Training in Social Work [*British*] ..... CCETSW
Central Council for Health Education [*British*] (AEBS) ..... CCHE
Central Council of Ceylon Trade Unions ..... CCCTU
Central Council of Church Bell Ringers [*British*] ..... CCCBR
Central Council of National Retail Associations (EA) ..... CCNRA
Central Council of Physical Recreation [*British*] ..... CCPR
Central Counteradaptive Change (AAMN) CCC
Central Criminal Court [*Old Bailey*] [*British*] CCC
Central Criminal Court Cases [*1834-1913*] [*England*] [*A publication*] (DLA) ..... CC Ct Cas
Central Criminal Court Cases, Sessions Papers [*1834-1913*] [*England*] [*A publication*] (DLA) ..... CCC Cas
Central Criminal Court Cases, Sessions Papers [*1834-1913*] [*England*] [*A publication*] (DLA) ..... CCC Sess Pap
Central Criminal Court Cases, Sessions Papers [*1834-1913*] [*England*] [*A publication*] (DLA) ..... Cent Crim C Cas
Central Criminal Court Cases, Sessions Papers [*1834-1913*] [*England*] [*A publication*] (DLA) ..... Centr Cr Ct R
Central Criminal Court Cases, Sessions Papers [*1834-1913*] [*England*] [*A publication*] (ILCA) ..... Sess Pap CC
Central Criminal Court Cases, Sessions Papers [*1834-1913*] [*England*] [*A publication*] (DLA) ..... Sess Pap CCC
Central Criminal Court Reports [*England*] [*A publication*] (DLA) ..... Cent Crim CR
Central Criminal Court Reports [*England*] [*A publication*] (ILCA) ..... Centr Cr Ct R
Central Crude Ltd. [*Vancouver Stock Exchange symbol*] CLC
Central Cultural Movement [*China*] ..... CCM
Central Data Acquisition System ..... CDAS
Central Data Analysis Area (KSC) ..... CDAA
Central Data and Cataloging Center (AFM) ..... CD & CC
Central Data and Switching Center [*NASA*] (KSC) ..... CD & SC
Central Data Bank ..... CDB
Central Data Bank, EUROCONTROL [*Belgium ICAO location identifier*] (ICLI) ..... EBBD
Central Data Base Server (DOMA) ..... CDBS
Central Data Buffer [*Computer science*] (MCD) ..... CDB
Central Data Collection Point [*Army*] ..... CDCP
Central Data Collection System (AFM) ..... CDCS
Central Data Display ..... CDD
Central Data Distribution Facility [*National Oceanic and Atmospheric Administration*] ..... CDDF
Central Data Facility [*NASA*] (NASA) ..... CDF
Central Data Flow Control ..... CFC
Central Data Management (NRCH) ..... CDM
Central Data Processing Center ..... CDPC
Central Data Processing Computer ..... CDPC
Central Data Processing Facility [*NASA*] ..... CDPF
Central Data Recording ..... CDR
Central Data Station ..... CDS
Central Data System [*or Subsystem*] (MCD) ..... CDS
Central Database Administrator (GFGA) ..... CDBA
Central Database System (DA) ..... CDBS
Central Data-Conversion Equipment ..... CDCE
Central Datum ..... CEN
Central Daylight Saving Time ..... CDST
Central Daylight Time ..... CDT
Central Defence Staff [*British*] ..... CDS
Central Demand Data Base Supply [*Army*] ..... CDDB
Central Dental Laboratories [*Army*] ..... CDL
Central Design Activity (MCD) ..... CDA
Central Design Group ..... CDG
Central Development Unit ..... CDU
Central Developmental Groove [*Medicine*] (DMAA) ..... CDG
Central Differential Analyzer Control ..... CEDAC
Central Digital Computer ..... CDC
Central Directed Audit [*Military*] ..... CDA
Central Directorate on Environmental Protection [*British*] (DCTA) ..... CDEP
Central Disc [*of flowers*] [*Botany*] ..... CD
Central Dispatching Organization of the Interconnected Power Systems [*Former Czechoslovakia*] (EAIO) ..... CDOIPS
Central Display Generator (MCD) ..... CDG
Central Display Unit ..... CDU
Central Distribution Center [*Army*] (DOMA) ..... CDC
Central Distribution Frame (CDE) ..... CDF
Central Distribution Panel ..... CDP
Central Distribution Point ..... CDP
Central Distribution Programmer (IAA) ..... CDP
Central Distribution System [*Publications*] [*Navy*] ..... CDS
Central District ..... CD
Central Districts Airlines [*Former USSR*] [*FAA designator*] (FAAC) ..... CDS
Central Dockyard Laboratory [*British*] ..... CDL
Central Document Control [*Jet Propulsion Laboratory, NASA*] ..... CDC
Central Drafting Officer [*Navy*] ..... CENDRAFT
Central Dredging Association (EA) ..... CEDA
Central Drug Research Institute [*India*] [*Research code symbol*] X
Central Drugs and Illegal Immigration Intelligence Unit [*British*] (DI) ..... CDIIIU
Central DuPage Hospital, Medical Library, Winfield, IL [*Library symbol*] [*Library of Congress*] (LCLS) ..... IWinfC
Central Dynamic Store (PDAA) ..... CDS
Central East Coast ..... CEC
Central East Pacific [*Region*] ..... CEP
Central Eastern Personnel Organization [*Computerized scouting combine for professional football teams*] ..... CEPO
Central Economic Committee ..... CEC
Central Economic Information Service [*British*] ..... CEIS
Central Economic Zone ..... CEZ
Central Education Network [*Des Plaines, IL*] [*Telecommunications service*] (TSSD) ..... CEN
Central Electric Railfans' Association (EA) ..... CERA
Central Electricity Authority [*British*] ..... CEA
Central Electricity Board [*British*] ..... CEB
Central Electricity Generating Board [*British*] ..... CEGB
Central Electricity Research Laboratories [*British*] ..... CERL
Central Electrochemical Research Institute ..... CERI
Central Electron Microscopy Laboratory [*University of Georgia*] [*Research center*] (RCD) ..... CEML
Central Electronic Management System ..... CEMS
Central Electronics System (KSC) ..... CES
Central Elementary School, Bemidji, MN [*Library symbol*] [*Library of Congress*] (LCLS) ..... MnBemCE
Central Elementary School, Bethpage, NY [*Library symbol Library of Congress*] (LCLS) ..... NBetCE
Central Elementary School, Lawrence, NY [*Library symbol Library of Congress*] (LCLS) ..... NLawCE
Central Elementary School, Worthington, MN [*Library symbol*] [*Library of Congress*] (LCLS) ..... MnWoCES
Central Emergency Government Headquarters (MCD) ..... CEG
Central Engine [*Galactic radio source*] ..... CE

Central Engine Room Control .... CERC
Central Engineering (IIA) .... CE
Central Engineering Projects Office [*NATO*] (NATG) ...... CEPO
Central England Temperature [*Record since 1659*] .... CET
Central England Winter Temperature (PDAA) .... CEWT
Central Episiotomy [*Obstetrics*] (DAVI) .... CE
Central Episiotomy and Repair [*Obstetrics*] (DAVI) .... CE & R
Central Equatorial Pacific Experiment [*Marine science*] (OSRA) ..... CEPEX
Central Equatorial Pacific Experiment (USDC) .... CEPEX
Central Equipment Group [*Military*] (CAAL) .... CEG
Central Equipment Management and Inventory Control System (MCD) .... CEMICS
Central Error Module (CAAL) .... CEM
Central Euro Media Enter'A' [*NASDAQ symbol*] (TTSB) ... CETV
Central Europe (NATG) .... CE
Central Europe Inland Waterways Transport [*NATO*] (NATG) ... CE/IWT
Central Europe Joint Emergency Defense Plan [*NATO*] (NATG) .... CEJEDP
Central Europe Operating Agency [*Versailles, France*] [*NATO*] ... CEOA
Central Europe Pipeline Agency [*Later, CEOA*] [*NATO*] (NATG) ... CEPA
Central Europe Pipeline Office [*NATO*] .... CEPO
Central Europe Pipeline Policy Committee [*NATO*] .... CEPPC
Central Europe Pipeline System [*NATO*] (NATG) .... CEPS
Central Europe Railroad Transport [*NATO*] (NATG) .... CE/RRT
Central Europe Road Transport [*NATO*] (NATG) .... CE/RT
Central European (AFM) .... CENEUR
Central European Air Defense Sector .... CEADS
Central European Airlines [*Czechoslovakia*] [*ICAO designator*] (FAAC) ..... CMA
Central European Communication Region [*Air Force*] (MCD) ..... CECR
Central European Development Corp. .... CEDC
Central European Encephalitis Virus [*Medicine*] (MAE) ... CEEV
Central European Eq Fd [*NYSE symbol*] (TTSB) .... CEE
Central European Equity Fund [*NYSE symbol*] (SAG) ..... CEE
Central European Equity Fund [*Associated Press*] (SAG) ... CentEur
Central European Federal Youth Movement .... CEFYM
Central European Federation of Christian Trade Unions (EA) ..... CEFCTU
Central European Forces Distribution Agency [*NATO*] (NATG) ..... CEFDA
Central European History [*A publication*] (BRI) .... CEH
Central European Line [*Oil pipeline*] .... CEL
Central European Media Enterprises .... CME
Central European Media Enterprises Ltd. [*NASDAQ symbol*] (SAG) ... CETV
Central European Media Enterprises Ltd. [*Associated Press*] (SAG) ... CEurMda
Central European Time (DEN) .... CET
Central European Treaty Organization (MCD) .... CENTO
Central European University [*Hungary*] .... CEU
Central Evidence of Research and Development Reports .. CERD
Central Exchange .... CENTREX
Central Exchange CX
Central Exchange Area [*Telecommunications*] (NITA) ..... CXA
Central [*Nervous System*] **Excitatory State** .... CES
Central Executive System .... CES
Central Executive Unit (DA) .... CEU
Central Experimental and Proving Establishment [*Canada*] (MCD) ... CEPE
Central External Liaison Department [*Chinese Secret Service*] ... CELD
Central Facilities Area .... CFA
Central Facilities - National Reactor Test Station (SAA) ... CF-NRTS
Central Fibrous Body [*Medicine*] (DMAA) .... CFB
Central Fidelity Bank [*Associated Press*] (SAG) .... CFidBk
Central Fidelity Banks [*NASDAQ symbol*] (TTSB) .... CFBS
Central Fidelity Banks, Inc. [*NASDAQ symbol*] (NQ) ..... CFBS
Central Field [*Ophthalmology*] (CPH) .... CF
Central Fighter Establishment [*British*] .... CFE
Central Fighter Weapons Instructor School (NATG) .... CFWIS
Central File Document Control .... CFDC
Central Files .... CF
Central Files Repository .... CFR
Central Film Library [*British*] .... CFL
Central Financial Acceptance Corp. [*Associated Press*] (SAG) ... CenFAcc
Central Financial Acceptance Corp. [*NASDAQ symbol*] (SAG) ... CFAC
Central Financial Management Activities [*Military*] (AABC) ... CFMA
Central Fire Brigades Advisory Council [*British*] .... CFBAC
Central Fire Control [*Military*] .... CFC
Central Firing Unit .... CFU
Central Flight Instructor Course [*Military*] .... CFIC
Central Flight Status Selection Board [*Air Force*] .... CFSSB
Central Florida Community College, Ocala, FL [*Library symbol Library of Congress*] (LCLS) ... FOcC
Central Florida Information Research Service, Inc. [*Information service or system*] (IID) ... CFIRS
Central Florida Library Consortium, Sanford, FL [*Library symbol*] [*Library of Congress*] (LCLS) ... FsanLC
Central Florida Regional Library, Ocala, FL [*Library symbol Library of Congress*] (LCLS) ... FOc
Central Florida Research Park .... CFRP
Central Flow Control Facility [*or Function*] (MCD) .... CFCF
Central Flow Weather Service Unit [*FAA*] (TAG) .... CFMWP
Central Flow Weather Service Unit (FAAC) .... CFWSU
Central Flying School [*RAF*] [*British Australia*] .... CFS
Central Flying Training Command [*AAFCFTC*] .... CFTC
Central Food Preparation Facility [*Military*] (AABC) .... CFPF
Central Food Preparation System [*Military*] (AABC) ..... CFPS
Central Food Technology Research Institute [*India*] ...... CFTRI
Central Forecast Office (DA) .... CFO
Central Forecasting Station (IAA) .... CFS
Central Forms Committee [*Defunct*] (EA) .... CFC
Central Freight Association .... CFA

Central Freight Bureau (DS) .... CFB
Central Freight Tariff Bureau .... CFTB
Central Frequency Synthesizer .... CFS
Central Fuel Injection [*Automotive engineering*] .... CFI
Central Fund of Canada Ltd. [*AMEX symbol Toronto Stock Exchange symbol*] ... CEF
Central Fund of Canada Ltd. [*Associated Press*] (SAG) ... CFCda
Central Fund,Cda'A' [*AMEX symbol*] (TTSB) .... CEF
Central Garden & Pet [*NASDAQ symbol*] (TTSB) .... CENT
Central Garden & Pet Co. [*Associated Press*] (SAG) ...... CenGardn
Central Garden & Pet Co. [*NASDAQ symbol*] (SAG) ...... CENT
Central Gear Box (MCD) .... CGB
Central General Hospital, Plainview, NY [*Library symbol Library of Congress*] (LCLS) ... NPICH
Central Georgia Associated Libraries [*Library network*] ... CGAL
Central German Administrative Department [*Economic*] **Committee** [*US Military Government, Germany*] ... CADM
Central Gland [*of the prostate*] .... CG
Central Gliding School [*British military*] (DMA) .... CGS
Central Government Borrowing Requirement [*British*] ... CGBR
Central Grant Aid [*British*] .... CGA
Central Graphics Processor [*Computer science*] (NITA) ... CGP
Central Gray [*Brain anatomy*] .... CG
Central Gray Matter [*Physiology*] .... CGM
Central Grounding Point (NASA) .... CGP
Central Group of Forces (MCD) .... CGF
Central Guaranty Trustco Ltd. [*Toronto Stock Exchange symbol*] ... CGA
Central Guatemala [*Cuba ICAO location identifier*] (ICLI) ... MUPS
Central Gunnery School [*British military*] (DMA) .... CGS
Central Gyro Reference System .... CGRS
Central Heading System (SAA) .... CHS
Central Headquarters (DCTA) .... CHQ
Central Health Services Council (AIE) .... CHSC
Central Health Services Executive [*British*] (DI) .... CHSE
Central Heating .... CH
Central Heating Plant (KSC) .... CHP
Central Hemorrhagic Necrosis [*Medicine*] (MAE) .... CHN
Central High School, Crookston,MN [*Library symbol*] [*Library of Congress*] (LCLS) ... MnCrCH
Central High School, Duluth, MN [*Library symbol*] [*Library of Congress*] (LCLS) ... MnDuCH
Central High School, Grand Junction, CO [*Library symbol Library of Congress*] (LCLS) ... CoGjCeH
Central Hispano Cap 9.43% Pref [*NYSE symbol*] (TTSB) ... HCLPrB
Central Hispano Capital Ltd. [*Associated Press*] (SAG) ... CHisC
Central Hispano Capital Ltd. [*NYSE symbol*] (SAG) .... HCL
Central Hispano International, Inc. [*Associated Press*] (SAG) ... CHisIn
Central Hispano International, Inc. [*NYSE symbol*] (SAG) ... HPN
Central Hockey League .... CHL
Central Hole in Pintle [*Diesel engineering*] .... CHIP
Central Hudson Gas & Electric Corp. [*Associated Press*] (SAG) ... CenHud
Central Hudson Gas & Electric Corp. [*NYSE symbol*] (SPSG) ... CNH
Central Hudson Gas&El [*NYSE symbol*] (TTSB) .... CNH
Central [*Atom*] **Hyperfine Structure** .... CHFS
Central I11 Lt4 1/2% cm Pfd [*NYSE symbol*] (TTSB) .... CERPr
Central Identification, Friend or Foe [*DoD*] .... CIFF
Central Identification Laboratory [*Hawaii*] [*Army*] CIL
Central Identification Laboratory - Hawaii [*Army*] .... CIL-HI
Central Illinois Light Co. [*NYSE symbol*] (SAG) .... CER
Central Illinois Light Co. [*Associated Press*] (SAG) .... CnILt
Central Illinois Light Co., Resource Center, Peoria, IL [*Library symbol Library of Congress*] (LCLS) ... IPCL
Central Imagery Office [*DoD*] .... CIO
Central Imagery Office [*Formerly, NRO; changed in 1992*] [*DoD*] (DOMA) ... CIO
Central Independent Television [*British*] (DI) .... CIT
Central Independiente de Obreros Agricolas y Campesinos [*Member of RMALC*] [*Mexico*] (CROSS) ... CIOAC
Central Index File .... CIF
Central Index File - Europe (NATG) .... CIFE
Central India Horse [*British military*] (DMA) .... CIH
Central Indiana Railroad (IIA) CI
Central Indiana Railway Co. [*Absorbed into Consolidated Rail Corp.*] [*AAR code*] ... CIND
Central Industrial Applications Center [*Southeastern Oklahoma State University*] [*Information service or system*] (IID) ... CIAC
Central Inertial Guidance Test Facility [*Air Force*] .... CIGTF
Central Inertial Reference Instrumentation System (MCD) ... CIRIS
Central Infantile Hypotonic Syndrome [*Medicine*] (DMAA) ... CIHS
Central Information Dispatch [*Genesis Electronics Corp.*] [*Folsom, CA*] [*Telecommunications*] (TSSD) ... CINDI
Central Information Exchange [*Community Service Council of Broward County, Inc.*] [*Information service or system*] (IID) ... CIE
Central Information File .... CIF
Central Information Processor (MCD) .... CIP
Central Information Reference and Control (DIT) .... CIRC
Central Information Reference and Control On-Line System (MCD) ... CIRCOL
Central Information Retrieval and Cartridge Update System [*Computer science*] (NITA) ... CIRCUS
Central Information Service [*The British Council*] (IID) ... CIS
Central Information Service [*University of London*] (IID) ... CIS
Central Inhibitory State [*Neurology*] (DAVI) .... CIS
Central Initial Zone [*in inflorescence*] [*Botany*] .... CIZ
Central Input-Output Multiplexer [*Computer science*] ... CIO
Central Inspectorate of Vehicles [*British military*] (DMA) ... CIV
Central Installation Supply [*Air Force*] .... CIS

Central Institute for Industrial Research (AAG) .... CIIR
Central Institute for the Deaf (MCD) .... CID
Central Institute of Foreign Affairs Research .... CIFAR
Central Institution [*Scotland*] (AIE) CI
Central Instructor School .... CIS
Central Instrument Warning System [*Aviation*] (DA) .... CIWS
Central Instrumentation Control and Data (MCD) .... CICADA
Central Instrumentation Department [*David W. Taylor Naval Ship Research and Development Center*] [*Bethesda, MD*] .... CID
Central Instrumentation Facility [*NASA*] .... CIF
Central Integrated Checkout System .... CICS
Central Integrated Test System .... CITS
Central Integrated Test System Multiplex (PDAA) .... CITS-Mux
Central Integrated Traffic Control (PDAA) .... CITRAC
Central Integration Facility .... CIF
Central Integration Site (NASA) .... CIS
Central Intelligence Agency [*Acronym has been facetiously translated "Casey in Action," a reference to the agency's former director*] .... CIA
Central Intelligence Agency, Atlantic (MCD) .... CIALANT
Central Intelligence Agency / Counter-Terrorism Center (LAIN) .... CIA/C-TC
Central Intelligence Agency, McLean, VA [*Library symbol Library of Congress*] (LCLS) .... ViMcC
Central Intelligence Agency Retirement and Disability System .... CIARDS
Central Intelligence Board .... CIB
Central Intelligence Group (LAIN) .... CIG
Central Intelligence Organizations [*South Vietnam*] .... CIO
Central Intelligence Retirees Association (EA) .... CIRA
Central Intelligence Retrieval Center (MCD) .... CIRC
Central Intercollegiate Athletic Association (EA) .... CIAA
Central Interface Converter Unit .... CICU
Central Interior Logging Association (AC) .... CILA
Central Interpretation Unit [*Military*] .... CIU
Central Interval CI
Central Inventory of Production Equipment Records [*Army*] .... CIPER
Central Investment Program [*Army*] (MCD) .... CIP
Central Iowa Railway Co. [*AAR code*] .... CIRC
Central Iowa Regional Library [*Library network*] .... CIRL
Central Iowa Regional Library System, Des Moines, IA [*Library symbol*] [*Library of Congress*] (LCLS) .... IaDmCI
Central Iron and Steel Research Institute [*China*] .... CISRI
Central Ironmoulders Association of Scotland [*A union*] .... CIAS
Central Islip Public Library, Central Islip, NY [*Library symbol Library of Congress*] (LCLS) .... NCi
Central Islip State Hospital, Central Islip, NY [*Library symbol Library of Congress*] (LCLS) .... NCiSH
Central Issue Facility [*Military*] (AABC) .... CIF
Central Jersey Financial Corp. [*Associated Press*] (SAG) .... CJerFin
Central Jersey Financial Corp. [*NASDAQ symbol*] (NQ) .... CJFC
Central Jersey Finl [*NASDAQ symbol*] (TTSB) .... CJFC
Central Joint Advisory Committee on Tutoral Classes [*British*] .... CJAC
Central Junior High School, Alexandria, MN [*Library symbol*] [*Library of Congress*] (LCLS) .... MnAleCJ
Central Junior High School, Grand Forks, MN [*Library symbol*] [*Library of Congress*] (LCLS) .... MnEgfJ
Central Juvenile Index .... CJI
Central Kalgoorlie Gold [*Australia*] .... CKG
Central Kansas Library System [*Library network*] .... CKLS
Central Kansas Library System, Book Processing Center, Great Bend, KS [*OCLC symbol*] (OCLC) .... KKV
Central Kansas Library System, Great Bend, KS [*Library symbol Library of Congress*] (LCLS) .... KGbLS
Central Kansas Medical Center, Great Bend, KS [*Library symbol Library of Congress*] (LCLS) .... KGbMC
Central La Elec [*NYSE symbol*] (TTSB) .... CNL
Central Labor Relations Commission [*Japan*] .... CLRC
Central Laboratory CL
Central Laboratory Equipment Management (MCD) .... CLEM
Central Labour College [*Railroad*] [*British*] (ROG) CLC
Central Lake Township Library, Central Lake, MI [*Library symbol Library of Congress*] (LCLS) .... MiCenl
Central Latinamericana de Trabajadores [*Latin American Central of Workers*] (EA) .... CLAT
Central Law Journal [*A publication*] (DLA) .... Cent Law J
Central Law Journal [*A publication*] (DLA) .... Cent LJ
Central Law Journal [*A publication*] (DLA) .... Centr LJ
Central Law Journal [*A publication*] (DLA) .... Central LJ
Central Law Journal [*A publication*] (DLA) .... CLJ
Central Law Monthly [*A publication*] (DLA) .... Cent L Mo
Central Leather Research Institute [*British*] .... CLRI
Central Library, Albright & Wilson Americas, Islington, Ontario [*Library symbol National Library of Canada*] (NLC) .... OIE
Central Library and Documentation Branch [*International Labor Organization*] (IEEE) .... CLD
Central Library, C-I-L, Inc., North York, Ontario [*Library symbol National Library of Canada*] (NLC) .... OTCIL
Central Library, Dow Chemical of Canada Ltd., Fort Saskatchewan, Alberta [*Library symbol National Library of Canada*] (NLC) .... AFSD
Central Library Network [*Library network*] .... CLN
Central Library, North York, ON, Canada [*Library symbol Library of Congress*] (LCLS) .... CaOTCe
Central Library, North York, Ontario [*Library symbol National Library of Canada*] (NLC) .... OTCE
Central Light Loss (OA) CLL
Central Limit Theorem [*Statistics*] .... CLT
Central Line CL
Central Liquidity Facility [*National Credit Union Administration*] .... CLF
Central Load Dispatching Office [*US Military Government, Germany*] .... CLDO
Central Locking [*Automotive accessory*] CL
Central Logic Bus [*Computer science*] .... CLB
Central Logic Control [*Computer science*] CLC
Central Logic Rack [*Telecommunications*] (TEL) .... CLR
Central Logic Unit [*Computer science*] .... CLU
Central Logistics Command [*Republic of Vietnam Armed Forces*] CLC
Central Logistics Management Center (NASA) .... CLMC
Central London Underground Railway .... CLR
Central Louisiana Electric Co., Inc. [*Associated Press*] (SAG) .... CenLAEl
Central Louisiana Electric Co., Inc. [*NYSE symbol*] (SPSG) .... CNL
Central Louisiana State Hospital, Medical Library, Pineville, LA [*Library symbol Library of Congress*] (LCLS) .... LPiC
Central Lutheran Theological Seminary, Fremont, NE [*Library symbol Library of Congress*] (LCLS) .... NbFC
Central Machine Gun .... CMG
Central Magistrates' Court Committee [*British*] .... CMCC
Central Magnetic Tape Exchange [*Computer science*] (ADA) .... CEMTEX
Central Mail Exchange [*British*] (ADA) .... CME
Central Main Interactive Telecommunications System (EDAC) .... CMITS
Central Maine Power [*NYSE symbol*] (TTSB) .... CTP
Central Maine Power Co. [*Associated Press*] (SAG) .... CeMP
Central Maine Power Co. [*Associated Press*] (SAG) .... CeMPw
Central Maine Power Co. [*Associated Press*] (SAG) .... CenM
Central Maine Power Co. [*AMEX symbol*] (SAG) .... CTP
Central Maine Power Co. [*NYSE symbol*] (SPSG) .... CTP
Central Maine Pwr 7.875% Pfd [*NYSE symbol*] (TTSB) .... CTPPrA
Central Maine Pwr,3 1/2% Pfd [*AMEX symbol*] (TTSB) .... CTPPr
Central Maintenance Computer (GAVI) .... CMC
Central Maintenance Facility (NRCH) .... CMF
Central Management Army Commissaries (AABC) .... CMAC
Central Management Staff Record (PDAA) .... CMSR
Central Marine Chamber of Commerce [*Defunct*] (EA) .... CMCC
Central Massachusetts Regional Public Library System [*Library network*] .... CMRLS
Central Master Control (MCD) .... CMC
Central Material Section [*Medicine*] (DAVI) .... CMS
Central Material Supply [*Medicine*] (DAVI) .... CMS
Central Materiel Service Team [*Military*] .... CMS
Central Meat Processing Facility [*Army*] (AABC) .... CMPF
Central Mechanical Engineering Research Institute (MCD) .... CMERI
Central Medical Board (BARN) .... CMB
Central Medical Establishment, Aviation [*Air Force*] .... CMEA
Central Mediterranean Area [*NATO*] .... MEDCENT
Central Mediterranean Force [*Later, AAI*] [*British World War II*] .... CMF
Central Memory [*Computer science*] (BUR) .... CM
Central Memory Access Priority [*Computer science*] .... CMAP
Central Memory Extension [*Computer science*] .... CME
Central Meridian Distance [*NASA*] .... CMD
Central Meridian Longitude [*Planetary science*] .... CML
Central Mesabi Medical Center, Hibbing, MN [*Library symbol*] [*Library of Congress*] (LCLS) .... MnHibM
Central Meteorological Observatory [*Japan*] .... CMO
Central Methodist College, Fayette, MO [*Library symbol Library of Congress*] (LCLS) .... MoFC
Central Michigan Library System [*Library network*] .... CMLS
Central Michigan University (GAGS) .... Cent Mich U
Central Michigan University [*Mount Pleasant*] .... CMU
Central Michigan University, Mount Pleasant, MI [*OCLC symbol*] (OCLC) .... EZC
Central Michigan University, Mount Pleasant, MI [*Library symbol Library of Congress*] (LCLS) .... MiMtpT
Central Microfilm Service Corp., St. Louis, MO [*Library symbol Library of Congress*] (LCLS) .... CeM
Central Midwest Regional Educational Laboratory .... CEMREL
Central Midwest Regional Educational Laboratory (AEBS) .... CMREL
Central Midwives Board .... CMB
Central Military Commission [*China*] .... CMC
Central Milk Distributive Committee [*British*] .... CMDC
Central Mine Data Systems .... CMDS
Central Minnesota Christian School, Prinsburg, MN [*Library symbol*] [*Library of Congress*] (LCLS) .... MnPrbMCS
Central Minnesota Educational Cooperative Service Unit, St. Cloud, MN [*Library symbol*] [*Library of Congress*] (LCLS) .... MnStclEC
Central Minnesota Educational Research and Development Council, Film Library, St. Cloud, MN [*Library symbol*] [*Library of Congress*] (LCLS) .... MnStclER
Central Minnesota Seismic Array [*Minnesota*] [*Seismograph station code, US Geological Survey*] (SEIS) CM6
Central Mississippi Library Council [*Library network*] .... INFO PASS
Central Missouri State College [*Later, Central Missouri State University*] .... CMSC
Central Missouri State University (GAGS) .... Cent Mo St U
Central Missouri State University .... CMSU
Central Missouri State University, Warrensburg, MO [*OCLC symbol*] (OCLC) .... MCW
Central Missouri State University, Warrensburg, MO [*Library symbol Library of Congress*] (LCLS) .... MoWarbT
Central Molecular Zone [*Galactic science*] .... CMZ
Central Monitor and Control System (MCD) .... CMACS
Central Monitoring Position (IAA) .... CMP
Central Mortgage and Housing Corp. [*Canada*] (BARN) .... CMHC
Central Mortgage & Housing Corp., Children's Environments Advisory Service, Ottawa, ON, Canada [*Library symbol Library of Congress*] (LCLS) .... CaOOCMC

Central Mortgage & Housing Corp., Ottawa, ON, Canada [*Library symbol Library of Congress*] (LCLS) .... CaOOCM
Central Mortgage & Housing Corp., Standards Information Centre, Ottawa, ON, Canada [*Library symbol Library of Congress*] (LCLS) .... CaOOCMS
Central Mountain Air Ltd. [*Canada ICAO designator*] (FAAC) .... GLR
Central Naval Ordnance Management Information System .... CENO
Central Naval Ordnance Management Information System Office (DNAB) .... CENOMISO
Central Navigation Computer .... CNC
Central Navigation School .... CNS
Central Nervous System [*Physiology*] .... CNS
Central Neurogenic Hyperpnea [*Medicine*] (DAVI) .... CNH
Central Neurogenic Hyperventilation [*Medicine*] .... CNH
Central Neurogenic Hyperventilation [*Medicine*] .... CNHV
Central Neuropsychiatric Association (EA) .... CNA
Central Nevada Field Laboratory [*University of Nevada - Reno*] [*Research center*] (RCD) .... CNFL
Central New Brunswick Woodmen's Museum, Boiestown, New Brunswick [*Library symbol National Library of Canada*] (NLC) .... NBBWM
Central New York Library Resources Council [*Syracuse, NY*] [*Library network*] .... CENTRO
Central New York Library Resources Council, Syracuse, NY [*OCLC symbol*] (OCLC) .... SRR
Central New York Railroad Corp. [*AAR code*] .... CNYK
Central New York Union List of Serials, Syracuse, NY [*OCLC symbol*] (OCLC) .... ZUA
Central Newfoundland Hospital, Grand Falls, Newfoundland [*Library symbol National Library of Canada*] (NLC) .... NFGFH
Central Newfoundland Hospital, Grand Falls, NF, Canada [*Library symbol Library of Congress*] (LCLS) .... CaNfGfH
Central News Agency (DGA) .... CNA
Central Newspapers, Inc. Class A [*NYSE symbol*] (SPSG) .... ECP
Central Newspapers 'A' [*NYSE symbol*] (TTSB) .... ECP
Central Night Vision Training School [*Military British*] .... CNVTS
Central, NM [*FM radio station call letters*] (RBYB) .... KNUW-FM
Central Noel Fernandez [*Cuba ICAO location identifier*] (ICLI) .... MUCS
Central Nonprofit Agency (AAGC) .... CNA
Central Normal College, Danville, IN [*Library symbol Library of Congress Obsolete*] (LCLS) .... InDanN
Central Norseman Gold Corp. Ltd. [*Australia*] .... CNG
Central North Carolina Regional Library, Burlington, NC [*Library symbol Library of Congress*] (LCLS) .... NcBur
Central North Pacific [*Aviation*] (FAAC) .... CENPAC
Central North Pacific .... CNP
Central North Pacific Ocean .... CNP
Central NOTAM [*Notice to Airmen*] Facility [*Military*] .... CNF
Central Nova Therapeutic Riding Association (AC) .... CENTRA
Central Obesity Index [*Medicine*] (DMAA) .... COI
Central of Georgia Railroad Co. .... C of GA
Central of Georgia Railroad Co. .... CG
Central of Georgia Railroad Co. [*AAR code*] .... CGA
Central of Georgia Railroad Co. .... CGARY
Central Off-Equatorial Pacific Upper Layer Temperature [*Oceanography*] .... CULT
Central Office .... CO
Central Office Connection [*Telecommunications*] (TSSD) .... COC
Central Office Equipment [*Bell System*] .... COE
Central Office Equipment Estimation System [*Bell System*] .... COEES
Central Office Executives Association of National Panhellenic Conference (EA) .... COEA/NPC
Central Office for Environmental Protection [*Basle, Switzerland*] .... COEP
Central Office Line Tester (IAA) .... COLT
Central Office - Local Area Network .... CO-LAN
Central Office Local Area Network (BTTJ) .... CO-LAN
Central Office Maintenance Management System [*Telecommunications*] (TEL) .... COMMS
Central Office Maintenance Management System - Preventive Maintenance [*Telecommunications*] (TEL) .... COMMS-PM
Central Office Maintenance Printout Analysis and Suggestion System [*Computer science*] (MHDB) .... COMPASS
Central Office of Information [*London, England*] .... COI
Central Office of Record [*DoD*] .... COR
Central Office of South Vietnam [*North Vietnamese high command in the South*] .... COSVN
Central Office of the Industrial Tribunal [*Department of Employment*] [*British*] .... COIT
Central Office Signaling Panel [*Telecommunications*] (TEL) .... COSP
Central Office Systems Analyst [*Computer science*] .... COSA
Central Office Terminal [*Telecommunications*] (TEL) .... COT
Central Office to Central Office [*Bell System*] .... CO-CO
Central Office-based Local Area Network [*Telecommunications*] (ACRL) .... COLAN
Central Officers' Training School .... COTS
Central Ohio Fibrositis Association (EA) .... COFA
Central Ohio Interlibrary Network [*Library network*] .... COIN
Central Oil Identification Laboratory [*Groton, CT*] [*Coast Guard*] (MSC) .... COIL
Central Okanagan Foundation (AC) .... COF
Central Oncology Group (DAVI) .... COG
Central Ontario Mopar Owners Association (AC) .... COMOA
Central Ontario Regional Library, Richmond Hill, ON, Canada [*Library symbol Library of Congress*] (LCLS) .... CaORhCO
Central Ontario Regional Library, Richmond Hill, Ontario [*Library symbol National Library of Canada*] (NLC) .... ORCO
Central Opera Service (EA) .... COS
Central Operating Agency (NATG) .... COA
Central Operations System (PDAA) .... COS
Central Operator Panel (IAA) .... COP

Central Orchid Society [*British*] (DBA) .... COS
Central Ordering Point (IAA) .... COP
Central Oregon Community College, Bend, OR [*Library symbol Library of Congress*] (LCLS) .... OrBeC
Central Oregon Community College, Library, Bend, OR [*OCLC symbol*] (OCLC) .... CEO
Central Oregon District Hospital, Medical Library, Redmond, OR [*Library symbol Library of Congress*] (LCLS) .... OrRedDH
Central Organization for Jewish Education (EA) .... COJE
Central Organization of Liaison for Allocation of Circuit (NATG) .... COLAC
Central Organization of Trade Unions .... COTU
Central Overseas Recruiting and Rotation Office [*Military*] .... CORRO
Central Pac Minerals NL [*NASDAQ symbol*] (TTSB) .... CPMINY
Central Pacific Area [*Navy*] .... CENPAC
Central Pacific Area [*Hawaiian area*] [*World War II*] .... CPA
Central Pacific Base Command [*Navy*] .... CENTPACBACOM
Central Pacific Base Command [*Hawaiian Islands*] [*World War II*] .... CPBC
Central Pacific Combat Air Transport Service .... CENCATS
Central Pacific Communications Instructions .... CENTCOM
Central Pacific Fisheries Research Center [*National Oceanic and Atmospheric Administration*] .... CPFRC
Central Pacific Forces .... CENPACFOR
Central Pacific Hurricane Center [*Honolulu*] [*National Weather Service*] (NOAA) .... CPHC
Central Pacific Minerals [*Associated Press*] (SAG) .... CPcMn
Central Pacific Minerals NL [*NASDAQ symbol*] (NQ) .... CPMN
Central Pacific Search and Rescue Coordinator [*Coast Guard*] (DNAB) .... CENPACSARCOORD
Central Pain Syndrome [*Medicine*] .... CPS
Central Parking [*NYSE symbol*] (TTSB) .... PK
Central Parking Corp. [*Associated Press*] (SAG) .... CentPkg
Central Parking Corp. [*NYSE symbol*] (SAG) .... PK
Central Pastry Kitchen [*Army*] (AABC) .... CPK
Central Patch and Test [*Facility*] .... CENPAT
Central Patents Index [*A publication*] .... CPI
Central Path Method [*Computer science*] .... CPM
Central Pattern Generator [*Neurochemistry*] .... CPG
Central Pay Accounts Division [*Navy*] .... CPAD
Central Pay Office (AIE) .... CPO
Central Paying and Transfer Agent [*Business term*] (EMRF) .... CPTA
Central Pennsylvania District Library Center, Bellefonte, PA [*OCLC symbol*] (OCLC) .... PCB
Central Pennsylvania Medical Librarians [*Library network*] .... CPHSLA
Central Pennsylvania Youth Ballet .... CPYB
Central Perfusion Pressure [*Medicine*] .... CPP
Central Personnel Data File [*Office of Personnel Management*] [*Washington, DC*] .... CPDF
Central Personnel Directorate [*British*] .... CPD
Central Personnel Security Clearance Facility [*Army*] (MCD) .... CCF
Central Personnel Security Clearance Index [*Nuclear energy*] (NRCH) .... CPSCI
Central Physical Evaluation Board [*Navy*] (NVT) .... CPEB
Central Piedmont Community College, Charlotte, NC [*Library symbol Library of Congress*] (LCLS) .... NcCCP
Central Plains Experimental Range (GNE) .... CPER
Central Plains Turfgrass Foundation [*Later, KTF*] (EA) .... CPTF
Central Planning Center (NASA) .... CPC
Central Planning Office [*NASA*] (KSC) .... CPO
Central Planning Team (NATG) .... CPT
Central Plasma Sheet .... CPS
Central Point .... CP
Central Point Anti-Virus [*Central Point Software, Inc.*] [*Computer science*] (PCM) .... CPAV
Central Point Recuperator [*Computer program*] (PCM) .... CPR
Central Policy Review Staff [*British*] .... CPRS
Central Pontine Myelinolysis [*Medicine*] .... CPM
Central Port Call Office [*Army*] (AABC) .... CPCO
Central Post Fund [*Army*] .... CPF
Central Post, South Brunswick, NJ [*Library symbol Library of Congress*] (LCLS) .... NjSobC
Central Postal Directory [*Army*] (AABC) .... CPD
Central Posterior Curve [*Ophthalmology*] .... CPC
Central Poststroke Pain [*Medicine*] (DMAA) .... CPSP
Central Power Supply .... CPS
Central Power System .... CPS
Central Powerhouse .... CPH
Central Premonitions Registry (EA) .... CPR
Central Press .... CP
Central Primero De Enero [*Cuba ICAO location identifier*] (ICLI) .... MUVA
Central Problem [*Psychometrics*] .... CP
Central Processing Area (ADA) .... CPA
Central Processing Console [*NBDS*] .... CPC
Central Processing Element [*Computer science*] .... CPE
Central Processing Element BIT Slice [*Computer science*] (NITA) .... CPEBS
Central Processing Facility (MCD) .... CPF
Central Processing Modules [*Computer science*] (MCD) .... CPM
Central Processing Point [*Computer science*] .... CPP
Central Processing Subsystem [*Computer science*] .... CPSS
Central Processing System [*Computer science*] .... CPS
Central Processing Unit [*Computer science*] .... CPU
Central Processing Unit (DMAA) .... CPU
Central Processing Unit Diagnostic Program .... CPUD
Central Processing Unit Identification Number [*Computer science*] .... CPUID
Central Processor [*Computer science*] .... CP
Central Processor (IDOE) .... cp
Central Processor Memory Address [*Computer science*] .... CPMA

Central Processor Molecules (NITA) ... CPM
Central Processor Subunit [*Computer science*] ... CPSU
Central Processor System (NITA) ... CPS
Central Processor Test Console [*Computer science*] ... CPTC
Central Procurement [*or Centrally Procured*] (AFM) ... CP
Central Procurement Accounting System [*Air Force*] (GFGA) ... CPAS
Central Procurement Division [*Marine Corps*] ... CPD
Central Procurement Office (AABC) ... CPO
Central Production Unit [*Publishing services*] [*American Library Association*] ... CPU
Central Professional Hockey League ... CPHL
Central Programmer and Evaluator ... CPE
Central Project Office [*of ARS, Department of Agriculture*] ... CPO
Central Property Control ... CPC
Central Property Control System (MCD) ... CPCS
Central Provident Fund [*Singapore*] (ECON) ... CPF
Central Provinces [*Later, Madhya Pradesh, India*] ... CP
Central Provinces, India (DLA) ... CP Ind
Central Provinces Law Reports [*India*] [*A publication*] (DLA) ... Cent Prov LR
Central Provinces Law Reports [*India*] [*A publication*] (DLA) ... CPLR
Central Provision Office [*World War II*] ... CPO
Central Psi Research Institute (EA) ... CPRI
Central Public Health Laboratory [*British*] (IRUK) ... CPHL
Central Pulmonary Vessels Enlargement [*Medicine*] ... CVE
Central Pulse Amplifier (MCD) ... CPA
Central Pulse Distributor [*Telecommunications*] (TEL) ... CPD
Central Purchasing Authority [*Military*] (NVT) ... CPA
Central Purchasing Organization ... CPO
Central Queensland Articled Law Clerks' Association [*Australia*] ... CQALCA
Central Queensland Consumers Association [*Australia*] ... CQCA
Central Queensland Egg Marketing Board [*Australia*] ... CQEMB
Central Queensland Grain Sorghum Marketing Board [*Australia*] ... CQGSMB
Central Queensland Speleological Society [*Australia*] ... CQSS
Central Queensland University [*Australia*] ... CQU
Central R. R. of Pennsylvania [*AAR code*] ... CRP
Central Radio Office [*Telecommunications*] (TEL) ... CRO
Central Radio Propagation Laboratory [*Later, ITS*] ... CRPL
Central Railroad Co. of New Jersey [*Absorbed into Consolidated Rail Corp.*] [*AAR code*] ... CNJ
Central Railroad Co. of New Jersey [*Absorbed into Consolidated Rail Corp.*] ... CRR of NJ
Central Railway [*British*] (ROG) ... CR
Central Rappahannock Regional Library, Fredericksburg, VA [*Library symbol Library of Congress*] (LCLS) ... ViFre
Central Ray, Pella, IA [*Library symbol Library of Congress*] (LCLS) ... IaPeCR
Central Real Estate Office [*Military*] ... CREO
Central Receiver Test Facility [*Department of Energy*] ... CRTF
Central Reconnaissance Establishment [*British military*] (DMA) ... CRE
Central Record, Medford, NJ [*Library symbol Library of Congress*] (LCLS) ... NjMedR
Central Recorder Subsystem [*NASA*] ... CR
Central Recorder Subsystem [*NASA*] ... CRS
Central Records Control Area (SAA) ... CRCA
Central Records Depository ... CRD
Central Records Facility, United States Army Intelligence Center ... CRFUSAIC
Central Records Library, Newfoundland Light and Power Co. Ltd., St. John's, Newfoundland [*Library symbol National Library of Canada*] (NLC) ... NFSLP
Central Records Office ... CRO
Central Records, Ontario Hydro, Toronto, Ontario [*Library symbol National Library of Canada*] (NLC) ... OTOHCR
Central Recruiting Division [*Military*] ... CRD
Central Reference Library [*British*] (DIT) ... CRL
Central Reference Room Bulletin (SAA) ... CRRB
Central Reference Supply ... CRS
Central Region Cultural Authority [*South Australia*] ... CRCA
Central Region Headquarters, Atmospheric Environment Service, Environment Canada[*Quartier-General de la Region Centrale, Service de l'Environnement Atmosphe rique, Environnement Canada*] **Winnipeg, Manitoba** [*Library symbol National Library of Canada*] (NLC) ... MWEAE
Central Region Information Resources Center, Canada Department of Communications[*Centre de Documentation Region du Centre, Ministere des Communications*] **Winnipeg, Manitoba** [*Library symbol National Library of Canada*] (NLC) ... MWCCIR
Central Region Interface Working Group [*NATO*] (NATG) ... CRIWG
Central Region Libraries, Grand Falls, Newfoundland [*Library symbol National Library of Canada*] (NLC) ... NFGFC
Central Region Libraries, Grand Falls, NF, Canada [*Library symbol Library of Congress*] (LCLS) ... CaNfGfC
Central Region, RSFSR [*MARC geographic area code Library of Congress*] (LCCP) ... e-url-
Central Region SEATO [*Southeast Asia Treaty Organization*] **Field Forces** (CINC) ... CRSFF
Central Regional Automated Funds Transfer System ... CRAFTS
Central Regional Laboratory [*Environmental Protection Agency*] (GFGA) ... CRL
Central Regional Library, Transport Canada [*Bibliotheque Regionale du Centre,Transports Canada*], Winnipeg, Manitoba [*Library symbol National Library of Canada*] (NLC) ... MWTCR
Central Register and Clearing House [*British*] ... CRACH
Central Registration Depository [*Investment term*] ... CRD
Central Registry [*of the Ordnance Survey*] [*British*] ... CR
Central Registry of Charities [*British*] ... CRC
Central Registry of Magazine Subscription Solicitors [*Defunct*] (EA) ... CRMSS
Central Registry of War Criminals and Security Suspects [*World War II*] ... CROWCASS
Central Registry of World Dancers (EA) ... CROWD
Central Regulatory Electronic Stenographic System (NRCH) ... CRESS
Central Religious Advisory Committee [*British*] ... CRAC
Central Repair Depot (NATG) ... CRD
Central Repair Facility (MCD) ... CRF
Central Repeater System (MCD) ... CRS
Central Reporter [*A publication*] (DLA) ... Cent
Central Reporter [*Pennsylvania*] [*A publication*] (DLA) ... Cent R (PA)
Central Reporter [*A publication*] (DLA) ... Cent Rep
Central Reporter [*A publication*] (DLA) ... CR
Central Requirements Committee ... CRC
Central Research Agency [*Cuc Nghien-Chu Trung-Uong*] [*North Vietnamese intelligence agency*] ... CRA
Central Research and Support Establishment [*Information service or system*] (IID) ... CRSE
Central Research Establishment [*Home Office Forensic Science Service*] [*British Information service or system*] (IID) ... CRE
Central Research Laboratory of Tashiba ... CRLT
Central Reserve Air Fleet ... CRAF
Central Reserve Life [*NASDAQ symbol*] (SAG) ... CRLC
Central Reserve Life Corp. [*Associated Press*] (SAG) ... CRsLfe
Central Resource Centre, Carleton Roman Catholic School Board, Nepean, Ontario [*Library symbol National Library of Canada*] (NLC) ... ONCRC
Central Resource Centre, Prairie View School Division No. 74, Milestone, Saskatchewan [*Library symbol National Library of Canada*] (NLC) ... SMPVS
Central Retinal Artery [*Ophthalmology*] ... CRA
Central Retinal Artery Occlusion [*Ophthalmology*] ... CRAO
Central Retinal Vein [*Ophthalmology*] ... CRV
Central Retinal Vein Occlusion [*Ophthalmology*] ... CRVO
Central Retransmission Facility (IAA) ... CRF
Central Rhine Commission [*Post-World War II*] ... CRC
Central Rice Research Institute (GNE) ... CRRI
Central Rivers Search and Rescue Coordinator [*Coast Guard*] (DNAB) ... CENRIVSARCOORD
Central Rural Construction Command [*Military*] (CINC) ... CRCC
Central School (ADA) ... CS
Central Sec$2cmCv D Pfd [*AMEX symbol*] (TTSB) ... CETRrD
Central Secondary Item Stratification [*Military*] (AFIT) ... CSIS
Central Securities [*AMEX symbol*] (TTSB) ... CET
Central Securities Corp. [*Associated Press*] (SAG) ... CentSE
Central Securities Corp. [*AMEX symbol*] (SPSG) ... CET
Central Securities Corp. [*Associated Press*] (SAG) ... CnS
Central Security Control [*Military*] (AFM) ... CSC
Central Security Service [*National Security Agency*] [*Obsolete*] (AABC) ... CSS
Central Selling Organization [*London diamond exchange*] ... CSO
Central Senior High School, Valley Stream, NY [*Library symbol Library of Congress*] (LCLS) ... NVsCSH
Central Sephardic Jewish Community of America (EA) ... CSJCA
Central Serous Chorioretinopathy [*or Choroidopathy*] [*Ophthalmology*] ... CSC
Central Serous Retinopathy [*Medicine*] (CPH) ... CSP
Central Service [*Medicine*] (DHSM) ... CS
Central Service Facility (NRCH) ... CSF
Central Service Point [*DoD*] (AFIT) ... CSP
Central Services Organization ... CSO
Central Services Unit for University Careers and Appointments Services [*British*] ... CSU
Central Servicing Development Establishment (MCD) ... CSDE
Central Ships Alignment Console [*Navy*] (NG) ... CSAC
Central Sierra Snow Laboratory [*Norden, CA*] ... CSSL
Central Sign Off (AAG) ... CSO
Central Signal Processor ... CSP
Central Signals Establishment [*Military British*] ... CSE
Central Site ... C/S
Central Skyport, Inc. [*ICAO designator*] (FAAC) ... CSI
Central Society for Clinical Research (EA) ... CSCR
Central Solar Heating Plant with Seasonal Storage [*Pronounced "chips"*] [*Thermal technology*] (PS) ... CSHPSS
Central Source Data File (MCD) ... CSDF
Central South Africa Railway (ROG) ... CSA
Central Sprinkler [*NASDAQ symbol*] (TTSB) ... CNSP
Central Sprinkler Corp. [*NASDAQ symbol*] (NQ) ... CNSP
Central Sprinkler Corp. [*Associated Press*] (SAG) ... CnSprn
Central Standard Summer Time ... CSST
Central Standard Time ... CST
Central Standards Office (OICC) ... CSO
Central State College [*Ohio, Oklahoma*] ... CSC
Central State Hospital, Waupun, WI [*Library symbol Library of Congress*] (LCLS) ... WWpC
Central State University [*Wilberforce, OH*] ... CSU
Central State University, Edmond, OK [*Library symbol Library of Congress*] (LCLS) ... OkEdT
Central State University, Edmond, OK [*OCLC symbol*] (OCLC) ... OKX
Central State University, Wilberforce, OH [*OCLC symbol*] (OCLC) ... CNC
Central State University, Wilberforce, OH [*Library symbol Library of Congress*] (LCLS) ... OWibfC
Central States [*An association*] (EA) ... CS
Central States Anthropological Society (EA) ... CSAS
Central States College Association [*Defunct*] ... CSCA
Central States Football League ... CSFL
Central States Motor Freight Bureau ... CSMFB
Central States Motor Freight Bureau, Chicago IL [*STAC*] ... CMB
Central States Pension Fund ... CSPF
Central States Roller Canary Breeders Association (EA) ... CSRCBA
Central States Speech Association (AEBS) ... CSSA
Central Station [*NASA*] ... C/S

Central Station Alarm Association (EA) .... CSAA
Central Station Electrical Protection Association [Later, CSAA] (EA) .... CSEPA
Central Statistical Board [Functions taken over by Bureau of the Budget, 1940] ...... CSB
Central Statistical Office [British Information service or system] (IID) .... CSO
Central Statistical Unit [of VLRL] ...... CSU
Central Statistics Bureau [British Columbia Ministry of Industry and Small Business Development] [Information service or system] (IID) ...... CSB
Central Sterile Supply [Medicine] (CPH) ...... CSS
Central Sterile Supply Department [Medicine] (DAVI) ...... CSSD
Central Sterile Supply Unit [Medicine] (DMAA) ...... CSSU
Central Still-Photo Depository (DNAB) ...... CSPD
Central Structure Storage [Computer science] (BYTE) ...... CSS
Central Subarea, Atlantic [NATO] ...... CENTLANT
Central Suffolk Hospital, Riverhead, NY [Library symbol Library of Congress] (LCLS) ...... NRvCH
Central Sugar Cane Prices Board [Queensland] [Australia] ...... CSCPB
Central Supplies Agency (NATG) ...... CSA
Central Supply (KSC) ...... CS
Central Supply Association [Later, ASA] (EA) ...... CSA
Central Supply Facility (MCD) ...... CSF
Central Supply Room ...... CSR
Central Supply Support Activity ...... CSSA
Central Support Services [Marine science] (OSRA) ...... CSS
Central Support Services [National Weather Service] (USDC) ...... CSS
Central Switching Center [Telecommunications] (TEL) ...... CSC
Central Switching Concept (KSC) ...... CSC
Central Switching Facility ...... CSF
Central Switching Unit ...... CSU
Central System Maintenance Support (NATG) ...... CSMS
Central Systems Design Agency ...... CSDA
Central Tactical System [RAF] (MCD) ...... CTS
Central Tactical Unit [Drug Enforcement Administration] ...... CENTAC
Central Tap [Electronics] (ECII) ...... CT
Central Target Director [Military] (CAAL) ...... CTD
Central Target Simulator [Navy] (MCD) ...... CTS
Central Task Force ...... CTF
Central Technical Authority (MCD) ...... CTA
Central Technical Community College, Hastings, NE [Library symbol Library of Congress] (LCLS) ...... NbHCC
Central Technical Doctrine Officer (DNAB) ...... CTDO
Central Technical Documents Office [Naval Ordnance Systems Command] [Information service or system] (IID) ...... CTDO
Central Technical Institute [Netherlands] ...... CTI
Central Technical Library, Cominco Ltd., Trail, British Columbia [Library symbol National Library of Canada] (NLC) ...... BTC
Central Technical Manual Management Activity [Navy] (NVT) ...... CTMMA
Central Technical Order Control [or Coordination] Unit (MCD) ...... CTOCU
Central Technical Order Coordination Unit ...... CTOC
Central Technical Support Facility [Army] ...... CTSF
Central Telegraph Exchange [British] ...... CTE
Central Telegraph Male Superintending Officers' Association [A union] [British] ...... CTMSOA
Central Telegraph Office [British] (ROG) ...... CTO
Central Telegraph Superintending Officers' Association [A union] [British] ...... CTSOA
Central Telephone and Utilities Corp. (NITA) ...... CTU
Central Telephone Operator [British] (ROG) ...... CTO
Central Terminal of Wilson (DAVI) ...... CTW
Central Terminal Signaling Interface [Telecommunications] (TEL) ...... CTSI
Central Terminal Unit [Telecommunications] ...... CTU
Central Territory Railroad Tariff Bureau ...... CTR
Central Test Site for Personnel and Training Evaluation Program [Military] (DNAB) ...... CTSPTEP
Central Test Site for Personnel and Training Evaluation Program Detachment [Military] (DNAB) ...... CTSPTEPDET
Central Test Technology Coordinating Office [Army] (RDA) ...... CTTCO
Central Texas College, Killeen, TX [Library symbol Library of Congress] (LCLS) ...... TxKiC
Central Texas Library System [Library network] ...... CTLS
Central Time (GPO) ...... CT
Central Time and Frequency Control ...... CTFC
Central Timing and Data Distribution System (SAA) ...... CT & DDS
Central Timing Equipment ...... CTE
Central Timing Signal Generator [Air Force] (MCD) ...... CTSG
Central Timing System ...... CTS
Central Timing Unit (KSC) ...... CTU
Central Tire Inflation System [Automotive engineering] ...... CTIS
Central TMDE [Test, Measuring, and Diagnostic Equipment] Activity [Army] (MCD) ...... CTA
Central to Peripheral Ratio [Anatomy] ...... C/P
Central Tool Room ...... CTR
Central Torpedo Office ...... CTO
Central Tracing Bureau [Post-World War II] ...... CTB
Central Tracing Policy Board [Post-World War II] ...... CTPB
Central Track Store Locator (MCD) ...... CTSL
Central Track Stores Index (MCD) ...... CTSX
Central Tracking Center (IAA) ...... CTC
Central Tractor Farm & Country [NASDAQ symbol] (TTSB) ...... CTFC
Central Tractor Farm & Country, Inc. [NASDAQ symbol] (SAG) ...... CTFC
Central Tractor Farm & Country, Inc. [Associated Press] (SAG) ...... CtrlTrac
Central Trade Test Board [British] ...... CTTB
Central Trades' Union [British] ...... CTU
Central Traffic Control ...... CTC
Central Train Control (IAA) ...... CTC

Central Training Council [Department of Employment] [British] ...... CTC
Central Training Facility (MCD) ...... CTF
Central Training Section [Air Force] (AFM) ...... CTS
Central Trans Rental Gp ADS [NYSE symbol] (TTSB) ...... TPH
Central Transfer Point ...... CTP
Central Translation Evidence ...... CTE
Central Transport Authority (ADA) ...... CTA
Central Transport Consultative Committee [British] ...... CTCC
Central Transport Rental Group Ltd. [Formerly, Tiphook Ltd. ADS] [Associated Press] (SAG) ...... CnTrnRtl
Central Transport Rental Group Ltd. [Formerly, Tiphook Ltd. ADS] [NYSE symbol] (SAG) ...... TPH
Central Treaty Organization [Also, CTO] [Formerly, Baghdad Pact] ...... CENTO
Central Treaty Organization [Also, CENTO] [Formerly, Baghdad Pact] ...... CTO
Central Treaty Organization Allied Military Publication ...... CENTAMP
Central Trunk Terminal ...... CTT
Central Trust Co. [Toronto Stock Exchange symbol] ...... CET
Central Trust of China ...... CTC
Central Tuber Crops Research Institute ...... CTCRI
Central Tumor Registry [Medicine] (BARN) ...... CTR
Central Union for Child Welfare [Finland] (EAIO) ...... CUCW
Central Unit [Computer science] (IAA) ...... CU
Central Unit for Scientific Photography [Royal Aircraft Establishment] [British] ...... CUSP
Central Unit on Environmental Pollution [British] ...... CUEP
Central Unit-Buffer (IAA) ...... CUB
Central United States Registry [Army] ...... CUSR
Central Unit-Memory (MCD) ...... CUM
Central Unit-Memory Programmer (MCD) ...... CUMP
Central Utah Project [Federal aqueduct-and-reservoir plan] ...... CUP
Central Vacuum Loading System ...... CVLS
Central Valley, CA [FM radio station call letters] ...... KNNN
Central Valley Project [California] (ECON) ...... CVP
Central Vancouver Island Multicultural Society (AC) ...... CVIMS
Central Vehicle Index [Record of cars lost or stolen in London] CVI
Central Vehicle Monitoring [Automotive engineering] ...... CVM
Central Vein [or Venous] [Anatomy] CV
Central Vein Occlusion [Medicine] (DMAA) ...... CVO
Central Venous Catheter [Medicine] CVC
Central Venous Pressure [Medicine] ...... CVP
Central Verband der Siebenburger Sachsen of the United States [Later, Alliance of Transylvanian Saxons] (EA) ...... CVSSUS
Central Vermillion County Schools Cooperative, Danville, IL [Library symbol] [Library of Congress] (LCLS) ...... IDanviCS
Central Vermont Public Service Corp. [NYSE symbol] (SPSG) CV
Central Vermont Public Service Corp. [Associated Press] (SAG) ...... CVtPS
Central Vermont Railway, Inc. [AAR code] CV
Central Vermont Railway, Inc. ...... CVT
Central Veterinary Laboratory [Research center British] (IRC) CVL
Central Virginia Bankshares [Associated Press] (SAG) ...... CtrlVA
Central Virginia Bankshares [NASDAQ symbol] (SAG) ...... CVBK
Central Virginia Community College, Lynchburg, VA [Library symbol Library of Congress] (LCLS) ViLCV
Central Visual Field [Optics] ...... CVF
Central Volunteer Bureau of Ottawa-Carleton [Bureau Central des Benevoles d'Ottawa-Carleton] Ottawa, Ontario [Library symbol National Library of Canada] (BIB) ...... OOCVB
Central Volunteer Headquarters [Military British] ...... CVHQ
Central VT Pub Svc [NYSE symbol] (TTSB) CV
Central Washington Hospital, Health Sciences Library, Wenatchee, WA [Library symbol Library of Congress] (LCLS) ...... WaWeC
Central Washington State College, Ellensburg, WA [Library symbol Library of Congress] (LCLS) ...... WaEIC
Central Washington University (GAGS) ...... Cent Wash U
Central Waste Disposal Facility [Oak Ridge National Laboratory] ...... CWDF
Central Weather Bureau [Taiwan] [Marine science] (OSRA) ...... CWB
Central Weather Bureau [Taiwan] (USDC) ...... CWB
Central Weather Processor [FAA] (TAG) ...... CWP
Central Weather Service Unit [Marine science] (OSRA) ...... CWSU
Central Weather Service Unit [FAA] (USDC) ...... CWSU
Central Weather Service Unit (FAAC) ...... CWSU
Central Welsh Board ...... CWB
Central Wesleyan College, Central, SC [Library symbol] [Library of Congress] (LCLS) ...... ScCenW
Central Western Law Society [Australia] ...... CWLS
Central Western Region ...... CWR
Central Wholesalers Association (EA) ...... CWA
Central Winter Time (IAA) ...... CWT
Central Wireless Station [Air Force British] ...... CWS
Central Wisconsin Colony, Staff Library, Madison, WI [Library symbol Library of Congress] (LCLS) ...... WMaC
Central Wisconsin Colony, Staff Library, Madison, WI [Library symbol] [Library of Congress] (LCLS) ...... WMaCW
Central Wyoming Community College, Riverton, WY [Library symbol Library of Congress] (LCLS) ...... WyRiC
Central Yiddish (BJA) ...... CY
Central Yiddish Culture Organization (EA) ...... CYCO
Central YMCA Community College, Chicago, IL [Library symbol Library of Congress] (LCLS) ...... ICCYM
Central Youth Employment Executive [Department of Employment] [British] ...... CYEE
Centrala Filmarkivet Ab, Stockholm, Sweden [Library symbol Library of Congress] (LCLS) ...... CeF
Central-Anzeiger fuer Juedische Litteratur [A publication] (BJA) ...... CAJL

Centrale Bemiddeling bij Medefinanciering Ontuikkelingsprogramma's [*Netherlands*] .... CEBEMO
Centrale de l'Enseignement du Quebec [*Quebec Teaching Congress*] (AC) .... CEQ
Centrale de l'enseignment du Quebec [*Canada An association*] (CROSS) ...... CEQ
Centrale de Livraison de Valeurs Mobilieres .... CEDEL
Centrale des Bibliotheques, Centre Documentaire, Montreal, PQ, Canada [*Library symbol Library of Congress*] (LCLS) .... CaQMCD
Centrale des Bibliotheques, Services Documentaires Multimedia, Inc., Montreal, Quebec [*Library symbol National Library of Canada*] (NLC)..... QMECB
Centrale des Professionnelles et Professionnels de la Sante (AC) .... CPS
Centrale des Syndicats Democratiques [*Congress of Democratic Unions*] ..... CSD
Centrale Nucleaire Europeenne a Neutrons Rapides SA [*France*] (PDAA) .... NERSA
Centralforbundet for Alkohol- och Narkotikaupplysning [*Swedish Council for Information on Alcohol and Other Drugs*] [*Information service or system*] (IID) .... CAN
Centralia College, Centralia, WA [*Library symbol Library of Congress*] (LCLS) .... WaCeC
Centralia Correctional Center, Centralia, IL [*Library symbol Library of Congress*] (LCLS) .... ICenC
Centralia District High School, District 200, Centralia, IL [*Library symbol Library of Congress*] (LCLS) .... ICenHS
Centralia, IL [*Location identifier FAA*] (FAAL) .... ENL
Centralia, IL [*AM radio station call letters*] .... WILY
Centralia, IL [*FM radio station call letters*] .... WRXX
Centralia, MO [*FM radio station call letters*] .... KMFC
Centralia Public Library, Centralia, IL [*Library symbol Library of Congress*] (LCLS) .... ICen
Centralia Township Junior College [*Illinois*] .... CTJC
Centralia, WA [*FM radio station call letters*] .... KCED
Centralia, WA [*Television station call letters*] .... KCKA
Centralia, WA [*FM radio station call letters*] .... KMNT
Centralia-Chehalis, WA [*AM radio station call letters*] .... KELA
Centralia-Chehalis, WA [*AM radio station call letters*] .... KITI
Centralinstitut for Nordisk Asienforskning [*Scandinavian Institute of Asian Studies*] [*Later, NIAS*] (EAIO) .... CINA
Centralis Lateralis [*Neuroanatomy*] CL
Centralization of Supply Management Operations [*DoD*] .... COSMOS
Centralized Accounting and Billeting [*Military*] (DNAB) .... CAB
Centralized Accounting and Billing (MCD) .... CAB
Centralized Accounting and Polling Software [*Computer science*] (PCM) .... CAPS
Centralized Accounting for Local Management [*Veterans Administration*].... CALM
Centralized Administrative Systems Control and Design (PDAA) .... CASCADE
Centralized Air Defense System (SAA) .... CADS
Centralized Alarm and Control System [*Telecommunications*] (TEL) .... CACS
Centralized Army Passenger Port Call System (AABC) .... CAPPS
Centralized Asset Visibility and Management Program for Vietnam [*Army*] (RDA) .... CAVAMP-V
Centralized Assignment Procedures [*Military*] (INF) .... CAP
Centralized Assignment Procedures Computer System [*Military*] .... CAP III
Centralized Attendants Service [*Bell System*] .... CAS
Centralized Authorized File [*IRS*] .... CAF
Centralized Automated Military Pay System .... CAMPS
Centralized Automated Pay System .... CAPS
Centralized Automatic Loop Reporting System [*Telecommunications*] (TEL) .... CALRS
Centralized Automatic Message Accounting [*Bell System*] .... CAMA
Centralized Automatic Message Accounting - Computerized [*Bell System*] (TEL) .... CAMA-C
Centralized Automatic Message Accounting - Operator Number Identification [*Telecommunications*] (TEL) .... CAMA-ONI
Centralized Automatic Recorder and Tester .... CART
Centralized Automatic Recording on Trunks [*Bell System*] .... CAROT
Centralized Automatic Test System [*Navy*] (MCD) .... CATES
Centralized Automatic Test System [*Navy*] (MCD) .... CATS
Centralized Automatic Testing .... CAT
Centralized Automatic Toll Ticketing [*Telecommunications*] (TEL) .... CATT
Centralized Automatic Trouble-Locating and Analysis System [*AT & T*] (TEL) .... CATLAS
Centralized Automotive Reporting System [*DARCOM*] (MCD) .... CARS
Centralized Branch Exchange [*Telecommunications*] (TEL) .... CBE
Centralized Branch Exchange [*Telecommunications*] (NITA) .... CBX
Centralized Cancer Patient Data System .... CCPDS
Centralized COMINT Communications Center [*National Security Agency*]..... CCCC
Centralized Command Selection System (MCD) .... CCSS
Centralized Computing Services .... CCS
Centralized Control Facility .... CENTCON
Centralized Correspondence Study [*Alaska*] (EDAC) .... CC/S
Centralized Data Base (RDA) .... CDB
Centralized Data Processing (IEEE) .... CDP
Centralized Dealer Inventory Control System (MHDB) .... CDICS
Centralized Digital Control System [*Computer science*] (PDAA) .... CDCS
Centralized Digital Telecommunications System [*Telecommunications*] (HGAA) .... CDTS
Centralized Electrification and Traffic Control (MCD) .... CETC
Centralized Electronic Control [*Navy*] .... CEC
Centralized Employment Program .... CEP
Centralized Environmental Facility .... CEF
Centralized Excess Personal Property [*Department of Agriculture*] (GFGA) .... CEPO
Centralized Expenditure/Reimbursement Processing System (NVT) .... CERPS
Centralized Flow Management Unit (DA) .... CFMU
Centralized Information Reference and Control .... CIRC
Centralized Input/Output System (DNAB) .... CINOS

Centralized Integrated System Compiler (MCD) .... CISIL
Centralized Integrated Systems for International Logistics .... CISIL
Centralized Integrated Technical Information System (DIT) .... CITIS
Centralized Intercept Bureau [*Bell System*] .... CIB
Centralized Intermediate Logistics Concept (MCD) CILC
Centralized Intermediate Logistics System (MCD) .... CILS
Centralized Intermediate Repair Facility .... CIRF
Centralized Library Information Processor [*United States Computer Corp.*] [*Information service or system*] (IID) .... CLIP
Centralized Lighting System [*Automotive engineering*] .... CLS
Centralized Lubrication [*Automotive engineering*] CL
Centralized Mail Remittance [*Telecommunications*] (TEL) .... CMR
Centralized Maintenance System [*Telecommunications*] .... CMS
Centralized Materials Section .... CMS
Centralized Message Data System [*Bell System*] .... CMDS
Centralized Munitions Systems [*USARPAC*] (MCD) .... CMS
Centralized Operating System (IAA) .... COS
Centralized or Distributed Integrated Access Control [*Computer science*] .... CODIAC
Centralized Payroll System (ADA) .... CPS
Centralized Personnel Record System [*Telecommunications*] (TEL) .... CPRS
Centralized Receiving Point .... CRP
Centralized Records Business Office [*Telecommunications*] (TEL) .... CRBO
Centralized Referral Activity [*Military*] (AFM) .... CRA
Centralized Referral System [*Military*] (AFM) .... CRS
Centralized Reliability Data Organization [*Nuclear Regulatory Commission*] (GFGA) .... CREDO
Centralized Repair Activity [*Air Force*] (AFIT) .... CRA
Centralized Repair Service Attendants [*Telecommunications*] (TEL) .... CRSA
Centralized Requisitioning Accounting and Billing .... CRAB
Centralized Results System [*Telecommunications*] (TEL) .... CRS
Centralized Service Observation [*Telecommunications*] (TEL) .... CSO
Centralized Ships Force Management System .... CSFMS
Centralized Status, Alarm, and Control System [*Bell System*] .... CSACS
Centralized Supervisory and Control (BUR) .... CSC
Centralized Support Base [*Military*] .... CSB
Centralized Theater Surveillance Database (MCD) .... CTSDB
Centralized Ticket Investigation [*Telecommunications*] .... CTI
Centralized Traffic Control [*TRB*] (TAG) .... CTC
Centralized Train Central (GAVI) .... CTC
Centralized Training [*Material management subsystem*] (MCD) .... CENTRA
Centralized Transient Accounting System (MCD) .... CTAS
Centralized Translation System [*Communications*] .... CTS
Centrally Funded (AFM) .... CF
Centrally Funded Second Destination Transportation [*Army*] .... CFSDT
Centrally Funded Short Course Program .... CFSCP
Centrally Planned Economy .... CPE
Centrally Procured Items (MCD) .... CPI
Centrally Reportable Equipment (AAGC) .... CRE
Centralny Osrodek Informacji Normalizacyjnej i Metrologicznej [*Center for Information on Standardization and Metrology*] [*Poland*] (EAIO) .... COINIM
Centralverein-Zeitung [*A publication*] (BJA) .... CVZ
Centre Academique Canadien en Italie [*Canadian Academic Centre in Italy*] .... CACI
Centre Acadien, Universite Sainte-Anne, Church Point, Nova Scotia [*Library symbol National Library of Canada*] (BIB) .... NSCSA
Centre Africain de Formation et de Recherche Administratives pour la Developpement [*African Training and Research Center in Administration for Development*] (IID) .... CAFRAD
Centre Africain de Recherche Appliquee et de Formation en Matiere de Developpement Social [*African Center for Applied Research and Training in Social Development - ACARTSD*] (EAIO) .... CAFRADES
Centre Africaine d'Etudes Monetaires [*African Centre for Monetary Studies*] [*Senegal*] (EAIO) .... CAEM
Centre Afro-Americain du Travail [*Afro-American Labor Center*] (AF) .... CAAT
Centre Against Apartheid [*United Nations*] (DUND) .... CAA
Centre Airlines, Inc. [*ICAO designator*] (FAAC) .... DTV
Centre, AL [*AM radio station call letters*] .... WAGC
Centre, AL [*AM radio station call letters*] .... WEIS
Centre, AL [*FM radio station call letters*] .... WRHY
Centre Alliance Students' Association [*Australia*] .... CASA
Centre Antonien, Quebec, PQ, Canada [*Library symbol Library of Congress*] (LCLS) .... CaQQCA
Centre Canadien d'Architecture [*Canadian Centre for Architecture*] Montreal, Quebec [*Library symbol National Library of Canada*] (NLC) .... QMCCA
Centre Canadien de Lutte Contre l'Alcoolisme et les Toxicomanies (AC) .... CCLAT
Centre Canadien de Recherche en Politiques de Rechange [*Canadian Centre for Policy Alternatives*] (EAIO) .... CCRPR
Centre Canadien de Teledetection [*Canadian Centre for Remote Sensing - CCRS*] .... CCT
Centre Canadien d'Etudes et de Cooperation Internationale, Montreal, Quebec [*Library symbol National Library of Canada*] (NLC) .... QMCECI
Centre Canadien d'Etudes et de Cooperation Internationle, Montreal, PQ, Canada [*Library symbol Library of Congress*] (LCLS) .... CaQMCECI
Centre Canadien d'Hygiene et de Securite au Travail [*Canadian Centre for Occupational Health and Safety - CCOHS*] .... CCHST
Centre Catholique International pour l'UNESCO [*France*] CCIC
Centre College of Kentucky, Danville, KY [*OCLC symbol*] (OCLC) .... KCC
Centre College of Kentucky, Danville, KY [*Library symbol Library of Congress*] (LCLS) .... KyDC
Centre Commun de Recherches Nucleaires [*Joint Nuclear Research Center*] [*EURATOM*] .... CCRN
Centre Commun d'Etudes de Television et de Telecommunications [*Videotex research center*] [*France*] .... CCETT

Centre County Court House, Bellefonte, PA [*Library symbol Library of Congress*] (LCLS) ... PBelC
Centre County Legal Journal [*Pennsylvania*] [*A publication*] (DLA) ... CCLJ
Centre County Library, Bellefonte, PA [*Library symbol Library of Congress*] (LCLS) ... PBel
[*Le*] **Centre Culturel Francophone de Vancouver** [*Vancouver French Cultural Centre*] (AC) ... CCFV
Centre Culturel, Verdun, PQ, Canada [*Library symbol Library of Congress*] (LCLS) ... CaQVeC
Centre d'Accueil Domremy-Montreal, Ste.-Genevieve, Quebec [*Library symbol National Library of Canada*] (NLC) ... QMCADM
Centre d'Action Europeenne Federaliste [*European Center for Federalist Action*] ... AEF
Centre d'Adaptation de la Main-d'Oeuvre Aerospatiale du Quebec (AC) ... CAMAQ
Centre d'Analyse et de Recherche Documentaires pour l'Afrique Noire ... CARDAN
Centre d'Analyse et de Recherche Operationnelle [*Operational Research and Analysis Establishment*] [*Canadian Department of National Defense*] ... CARO
Centre d'Analyse et de Traitement Automatique de la Bible [*Centre of Analysis and Automatic Treatment of the Bible*] [*Canada*] ... CATAB
Centre d'Animation de Developpement et de Recherche en Education (AC) ... CADRE
Centre d'Animation, de Developpement, et de Recherche en Education, Montreal, PQ, Canada [*Library symbol Library of Congress*] (LCLS) ... CaQMCAD
Centre d'Animation, de Developpement, et de Recherche en Education, Montreal, Quebec [*Library symbol National Library of Canada*] (NLC) ... QMCAD
Centre d'Animation des Femmes de Hull (AC) ... CAF
Centre d'Animation Pedagogique, Conseil des Ecoles Separees Catholiques d'Ottawa, Ontario [*Library symbol National Library of Canada*] (BIB) ... OOCESC
Centre d'Arbitrage Commerical National et International du Quebec [*Quebec National & International Commerical Arbitration Centre*] (AC) ... CACNIQ
Centre de Compilation de Donnees Neutroniques [*Neutron Data Compilation Center*] [*France Information service or system*] (IID) ... CCDN
Centre de Conditionnement Pre-Natal [*Pre-Natal Conditions Centre*] [*Canada*] ... CCPN
Centre de Controle Mixte [*Joint Control Center*] [*NATO*] (NATG) ... CCM
Centre de Controle Tactique Aerien [*Air Tactical Control Center*] [*NATO*] (NATG) ... CCTA
Centre de Cooperation pour les Recherches Scientifiques Relatives au Tabac [*Cooperation Center for Scientific Research Relative to Tobacco*] [*Paris, France*] (EA) ... CORESTA
Centre de Creation Industrielle [*Center for Industrial Creation*] [*Information service or system*] (IID) ... CCI
Centre de Danse International [*France*] ... CDI
Centre de Documentation, APO Quebec, Montreal, PQ, Canada [*Library symbol*] [*Library of Congress*] (LCLS) ... CaQMAPO
Centre de Documentation, APO Quebec, Montreal, Quebec [*Library symbol National Library of Canada*] (NLC) ... QMAPO
Centre de Documentation, Assurance-Vie Desjardins, Levis, Quebec [*Library symbol National Library of Canada*] (NLC) ... QLAVD
Centre de Documentation Astrologique (AC) ... CDA
Centre de Documentation, Banque Nationale du Canada, Montreal, Quebec [*Library symbol National Library of Canada*] (NLC) ... QMBAN
Centre de Documentation, Bureau de la Protection Civile du Quebec, Ste.-Foy, Quebec [*Library symbol National Library of Canada*] (BIB) ... QSFPC
Centre de Documentation, Bureau des Economies d'Energie du Quebec, Mont real, Quebec [*Library symbol National Library of Canada*] (NLC) ... QMBE
Centre de Documentation, Centrale de l'Enseignement du Quebec, Ste.-Foy, Quebec [*Library symbol National Library of Canada*] (NLC) ... QSTFCE
Centre de Documentation, Centre de Recherche Informatique de Montreal, Quebec [*Library symbol National Library of Canada*] (BIB) ... QMCRIM
Centre de Documentation, Centre de Services Sociaux de Quebec, Quebec [*Library symbol National Library of Canada*] (BIB) ... QQCSS
Centre de Documentation, Centre Hospitalier Anna-Laberge, Chateauguay, Quebec [*Library symbol National Library of Canada*] (BIB) ... QCAL
Centre de Documentation, Centre Hospitalier des Laurentides et Centre d'Accueil et de Readaptation des Hautes-Vallees, L'Annonciation, Quebec [*Library symbol National Library of Canada*] (BIB) ... QACHL
Centre de Documentation, Centre Hospitalier Fleury, Montreal, PQ, Canada [*Library symbol*] [*Library of Congress*] (LCLS) ... CaQMCHF
Centre de Documentation, Centre Hospitalier Fleury, Montreal, Quebec [*Library symbol National Library of Canada*] (NLC) ... QMCHF
Centre de Documentation, Centre Hospitalier Pierre Boucher, Longueuil, Quebec [*Library symbol National Library of Canada*] (NLC) ... QLOPB
Centre de Documentation, Centre Hospitalier Regional de Rimouski, Quebec [*Library symbol National Library of Canada*] (NLC) ... QRCH
Centre de Documentation, CGI [*Conseillers en Gestion et Informatique*], I nc., Quebec [*Library symbol National Library of Canada*] (NLC) ... QQCGI
Centre de Documentation, Charette, Fortier, Hawey, Touche, Ross, Montreal, Quebec [*Library symbol National Library of Canada*] (NLC) ... QMCFH
Centre de Documentation, CLSC de Hull, Quebec [*Library symbol National Library of Canada*] (NLC) ... QHCL
Centre de Documentation, CLSC de l'Aquilon, Baie-Comeau, Quebec [*Library symbol National Library of Canada*] (BIB) ... QBCCL
Centre de Documentation, Commission d'Acces a l'Information, Quebec, Quebec [*Library symbol National Library of Canada*] (NLC) ... QQCAI
Centre de Documentation, Commission de la Fonction Publique du Quebec, Quebec, Quebec [*Library symbol National Library of Canada*] (BIB) ... QQCFP
Centre de Documentation, Commission des Normes du Travail, Quebec [*Library symbol National Library of Canada*] (NLC) ... QQCDT
Centre de Documentation, Commission Rochon, Ste.-Foy, Quebec [*Library symbol National Library of Canada*] (BIB) ... QSFCRO
Centre de Documentation, Conseil de la Science et de la Technologie du Quebec, Ste.-Foy, Quebec [*Library symbol National Library of Canada*] (NLC) ... QQCPS
Centre de Documentation, Conseil de la Science et de la Technologie, Quebec [*Library symbol National Library of Canada*] (NLC) ... QQST
Centre de Documentation, Conseil des Colleges du Quebec, Quebec, Quebec [*Library symbol National Library of Canada*] (BIB) ... QQCC
Centre de Documentation, Conseil Superieur de l'Education du Quebec, Ste.-Foy, Quebec [*Library symbol National Library of Canada*] (BIB) ... QSFCSE
Centre de Documentation de la Direction Generale de l'Energie du Ministere des Richesses Naturelles du Quebec, Quebec, PQ, Canada [*Library symbol Library of Congress Obsolete*] (LCLS) ... CaQQRNC
Centre de Documentation de la Mecanique [*Documentation Center for Mechanics*] [*Technical Center for Mechanical Industries*] [*Information service or system*] (IID) ... CDM
Centre de Documentation de la Regie du Logement, Montreal, PQ, Canada [*Library symbol Library of Congress*] (LCLS) ... CaQMRL
Centre de Documentation de la Regie du Logement, Montreal, PQ, Canada [*Library symbol Library of Congress*] (LCLS) ... CaQQCRS
Centre de Documentation, Departement de Sante Communautaire, Centre Hospitalier,Universite Laval, Quebec [*Library symbol National Library of Canada*] (NLC) ... QQLACHC
Centre de Documentation, Departement de Sante Communautaire de Lanaudiere, Joliette, Quebec [*Library symbol National Library of Canada*] (BIB) ... QJCH
Centre de Documentation, Departement de Sante Communautaire du Haut-Richelieu, St.-Jean, Quebec [*Library symbol National Library of Canada*] (NLC) ... QSTJSC
Centre de Documentation, Departement de Sante Communautaire, Hopital du Saint-Sacrement, Quebec, Quebec [*Library symbol National Library of Canada*] (BIB) ... QQHSSC
Centre de Documentation - DGTI [*Direction Generale des Technologies de l'Information*], Ministere des Communications du Quebec, Ste.-Foy, Quebec [*Library symbol National Library of Canada*] (BIB) ... QQCOC
Centre de Documentation, Directeur General des Elections du Quebec, Ste.-Foy, Quebec [*Library symbol National Library of Canada*] (BIB) ... QSFE
Centre de Documentation, Direction de l'Environnement, Hydro-Quebec, Montreal, Quebec [*Library symbol National Library of Canada*] (NLC) ... QMHDE
Centre de Documentation, Direction Generale de la Planification, Ministere de laMain-d'Oeuvre et de la Securite du Revenu du Quebec, Quebec [*Library symbol National Library of Canada*] (BIB) ... QQMSRP
Centre de Documentation, Direction Generale de l'Enseignement et de la RechercheUniversitaires, Ministere de l'Enseignement Superieur et de la Science du Quebe c, Quebec, Quebec [*Library symbol National Library of Canada*] (BIB) ... QQESE
Centre de Documentation, Direction Generale des Medias, Ministere des Communications du Quebec, Quebec, Quebec [*Library symbol National Library of Canada*] (BIB) ... QQCOM
Centre de Documentation, Direction Generale des Ressources Informationnelles, Ministere de la Main d'Oeuvre et de la Securite du Revenu du Quebec, Quebec, Quebec [*Library symbol National Library of Canada*] (NLC) ... QQMSRD
Centre de Documentation DSC, Hotel-Dieu de Riviere-Du-Loup, Quebec [*Library symbol National Library of Canada*] (BIB) ... QRLH
Centre de Documentation du 200, Ministere de l'Agriculture, des Pecheries, et del'Alimentation, Quebec, Quebec [*Library symbol National Library of Canada*] (NLC) ... QQAG
Centre de Documentation du Personnel, Hopital de Convalescents Julius Richardson[*Staff Library, Julius Richardson Convalescent Hospital, Inc.*], Montreal, Quebec [*Library symbol National Library of Canada*] (NLC) ... QMHJR
Centre de Documentation, Ecole Secondaire de Plantagenet [*Documentation Centre, Plantagenet Secondary School*], Ontario [*Library symbol National Library of Canada*] (BIB) ... OPES
Centre de Documentation en Theatre Quebecois, Trois-Rivieres, PQ, Canada [*Library symbol Library of Congress*] (LCLS) ... CaQTUTH
Centre de Documentation en Theatre Quebecois, Trois-Rivieres, Quebec [*Library symbol National Library of Canada*] (NLC) ... QTUTH
Centre de Documentation et d'Audio-Visuel, Hopital d'Youville de Sherbrooke, Quebec [*Library symbol National Library of Canada*] (NLC) ... QSHERY
Centre de Documentation et d'Information Interuniversitaire en Sciences Sociales[*Interuniversity Documentation and Information Center for the Social Science s*] [*Information service or system*] (IID) ... CENDIS
Centre de Documentation, Hotel-Dieu d'Arthabaska, Quebec [*Library symbol National Library of Canada*] (BIB) ... QAHD
Centre de Documentation, Hydro-Quebec International, Montreal, Quebec [*Library symbol National Library of Canada*] (BIB) ... QMHI
Centre de Documentation, INRS [*Institut National de la Recherche Scientifique*]-Eau, Quebec, Quebec [*Library symbol National Library of Canada*] (NLC) ... QQUIE
Centre de Documentation, INRS [*Institut National de la Recherche Scientifique*]-Energie, Varennes, Quebec [*Library symbol National Library of Canada*] (NLC) ... QVAI
Centre de Documentation, INRS [*Institut National de la Recherche Scientifique*]-Georessources, Ste.-Foy, Quebec [*Library symbol National Library of Canada*] (NLC) ... QSFIG
Centre de Documentation, INRS [*Institut National de la Recherche Scientifique*]-Sante, Montreal, Quebec [*Library symbol National Library of Canada*] (NLC) ... QMUQIS
Centre de Documentation INRS [*Institut National de la Recherche Scientifique*]-Urbanisation, Montreal, Quebec [*Library symbol National Library of Canada*] (NLC) ... QMUQIU

Centre de Documentation, Institut de Recherche Appliquee sur le Travail, Montreal, Quebec [*Library symbol National Library of Canada*] (NLC) .... QMRAD
Centre de Documentation, Institut de Technologie Agro-Alimentaire de La Pocatiere, Quebec [*Library symbol National Library of Canada*] (NLC) ..... QPES
Centre de Documentation, Institut Raymond-Dewar, Montreal, Quebec [*Library symbol National Library of Canada*] (NLC) ..... QMISM
Centre de Documentation Internationale des Industries Utilisatrices de Produits Agricoles [*International Documentation Center for Industries Using Agricultural Products*] [*Database producer*] [*Information service or system*] (IID) ..... CDIUPA
Centre de Documentation, La Presse Ltee., Montreal, Quebec [*Library symbol National Library of Canada*] (NLC) ..... QMLP
Centre de Documentation, Laurentienne Mutuelle d'Assurance, Quebec, Quebec [*Library symbol National Library of Canada*] (BIB) ..... QQLM
Centre de Documentation, le Verificateur General du Quebec, Quebec, Quebec [*Library symbol National Library of Canada*] (BIB) ..... QQV
Centre de Documentation, Loto-Quebec, Montreal, Quebec [*Library symbol National Library of Canada*] (NLC) ..... QMLQ
Centre de Documentation, Ministere de la Main-d'Oeuvre et de la Securite du Revenu du Quebec, Montreal, Quebec [*Library symbol National Library of Canada*] (NLC) ..... QMMSR
Centre de Documentation, Ministere de l'Agriculture, des Pecheries, et de l'Alimentation, Ste.-Foy, Quebec [*Library symbol National Library of Canada*] (NLC) ..... QSTFAG
Centre de Documentation, Ministere de l'Education du Quebec, Quebec, Quebec [*Library symbol National Library of Canada*] (BIB) ..... QQED
Centre de Documentation, Ministere de l'Enseignement Superieur et de la Science du Quebec, Ste.-Foy, Quebec [*Library symbol National Library of Canada*] (NLC) ..... QQBST
Centre de Documentation, Ministere des Affaires Municipales du Quebec, Quebec, Quebec [*Library symbol National Library of Canada*] (NLC) .... QQAM
Centre de Documentation, Ministere des Transports du Quebec, Montreal, Quebec [*Library symbol National Library of Canada*] (NLC) ..... QMTRA
Centre de Documentation, Ministere des Transports - Rue Dorchester, Quebec [*Library symbol National Library of Canada*] (NLC) ..... QQTRD
Centre de Documentation, Ministere du Commerce Exterieur et du Developpement Technologique du Quebec, Montreal, Quebec [*Library symbol National Library of Canada*] (BIB) ..... QMCED
Centre de Documentation, Ministere du Travail du Quebec, Montreal, Quebec [*Library symbol National Library of Canada*] (NLC) ..... QMTMO
Centre de Documentation, Ministere du Travail du Quebec, Quebec [*Library symbol National Library of Canada*] (BIB) ..... QQTQ
Centre de Documentation, Musee Beaulne, Coaticook, Quebec [*Library symbol National Library of Canada*] (NLC) ..... QCMB
Centre de Documentation, Musee de la Civilisation, Quebec [*Library symbol National Library of Canada*] (BIB) ..... QQMUC
Centre de Documentation, Musee Laurier, Arthabaska, Quebec [*Library symbol National Library of Canada*] (NLC) ..... QAML
Centre de Documentation, Office de Planification et de Developpement du Quebe c, Trois-Rivieres, Quebec [*Library symbol National Library of Canada*] (NLC) ..... QTOPDQ
Centre de Documentation, Office de Planification et de Developpement du Quebec, Montreal, Quebec [*Library symbol National Library of Canada*] (BIB) ..... QMOP
Centre de Documentation, Office des Professions du Quebec, Quebec [*Library symbol National Library of Canada*] (NLC) ..... QQEDOP
Centre de Documentation, Pavillon St.-Joseph, Centre Hospitalier Regional de Beauceville, Quebec [*Library symbol National Library of Canada*] (BIB) ..... QBCH
Centre de Documentation, Peches Maritimes, Ministere de l'Agriculture, des Pe cheries, et de l'Alimentation du Quebec, Gaspe, Quebec [*Library symbol National Library of Canada*] (NLC) ..... QGAP
Centre de Documentation pour le Sport [*Sport Information Resource Centre*] [*Coaching Association of Canada*] ..... CDS
Centre de Documentation, Programme de Recherche sur l'Amiante, Universite de Sherbrooke, Quebec [*Library symbol National Library of Canada*] (NLC) ..... QSHERURA
Centre de Documentation, Projet Archipel de Montreal, Quebec [*Library symbol National Library of Canada*] (NLC) ..... QMPA
Centre de Documentation, Redaction et Terminologie, Hydro-Quebec, Montreal, Quebec [*Library symbol National Library of Canada*] (BIB) .... QMHRT
Centre de Documentation, Regie de la Securite dans les Sports du Quebec, Trois-Rivieres, Quebec [*Library symbol National Library of Canada*] (NLC) ..... QTRRSS
Centre de Documentation, Roche Associes Ltee., Ste.-Foy, Quebec [*Library symbol National Library of Canada*] (NLC) ..... QSTFRA
Centre de Documentation Sciences Humaines [*Documentation Center for Human Sciences*] [*France*] [*Information service or system*] (IID) ..... CDSH
Centre de Documentation, Secretariat a la Condition Feminine du Quebec, Quebec, Quebec [*Library symbol National Library of Canada*] (BIB) .... QQSCF
Centre de Documentation, Secretariat aux Affaires Autochtones, Quebec [*Library symbol National Library of Canada*] (BIB) ..... QQSAA
Centre de Documentation, Secteur Affaires Sociales, Association pour la Sante etla Securite du Travail, Montreal, Quebec [*Library symbol National Library of Canada*] (NLC) ..... QMASSAS
Centre de Documentation, Societe d'Habitation du Quebec, Montreal, Quebec [*Library symbol National Library of Canada*] (BIB) ..... QMSHQ
Centre de Documentation, Societe d'Habitation du Quebec, Quebec [*Library symbol National Library of Canada*] (BIB) ..... QQSHQ
Centre de Documentation, SOGIC [*Societe Generale des Industries Culturelles du Quebec*], Montreal, Quebec [*Library symbol National Library of Canada*] (BIB) ..... QMSDI
Centre de Documentation, Syndicat de Professionnels et de Professionnelles du Gouvernement du Quebec, Quebec [*Library symbol National Library of Canada*] (BIB) ..... QQSP
Centre de Documentation, Verification Generale, Hydro-Quebec, Montreal, Quebec [*Library symbol National Library of Canada*] (BIB) ..... QMHVG
Centre de Documentation-Energie, Ministere de l'Energie et des Ressources du Quebec, Quebec, Quebec [*Library symbol National Library of Canada*] (NLC) ..... QQERE
Centre de Documentation-Mines, Ministere de l'Energie et des Ressources du Quebec, Quebec, Quebec [*Library symbol National Library of Canada*] (NLC) ..... QQERM
Centre de Documentation-Terres et Forets, Ministere de l'Energie et des Ressources du Quebec, Quebec, Quebec [*Library symbol National Library of Canada*] (NLC) ..... QQERT
Centre de Donnees Stellaires [*Stellar Data Center*] [*France Information service or system*] (IID) ..... CDS
Centre de Formation et de Recyclage des Enseignants des Droits de l'Homme [*France*] ..... CIFREDH
Centre de Gravite Verticale [*Vertical Center of Gravity*] [*Shipping*] [*French*] .... CGV
Centre de l'Abitibi-Temiscamingue, Archives Nationales du Quebec, Rouyn-Noranda,Quebec [*Library symbol National Library of Canada*] (BIB) ..... QRAAT
Centre de Liaison des Industries de Traitement des Algues Marines de la CEE [*Liaison Center of the Industries for the Treatment of Seaweeds in the European Economic Community*] ..... CLITAM
Centre de Liaison des Industries Transformatrices de la CEE [*Liaison Center of the Meat Processing Industries of the EEC*] [*Belgium*] .... CLITRAVI
Centre de Liaison International des Marchands de Machines Agricoles et Reparateurs [*International Liaison Center for Agricultural Machinery Distributors and Maintenance*] [*Common Market*] ..... CLIMMAR
Centre de Maintenance, VIA Rail, Montreal, Quebec [*Library symbol National Library of Canada*] (BIB) ..... QMVRM
Centre de Preparation Documentaire a la Traduction [*Center for Translation Documentation*] [*Information service or system*] (IID) ..... CPDT
Centre de Promotion du Logiciel Quebecois (AC) ..... CPLQ
Centre de Protection de l'Enfance et de la Jeunesse de l'Outaouais (AC) ..... CPEJO
Centre de Readaptation Constance-Lethbridge [*Constance Lethbridge Rehabilition Centre*] (AC) ..... CRCL
Centre de Readaptation le Jeunes de l'Outaouais (AC) ..... CRJO
Centre de Recherche, Centre Hospitalier, Universite Laval, Quebec, Quebec [*Library symbol National Library of Canada*] (BIB) ..... QQLACHR
Centre de Recherche de Mathematiques Appliquees [*University of Montreal*] [*Research center*] (RCD) ..... CRMA
Centre de Recherche Documentaire [*Documentary Research Center*] [*Information service or system*] (IID) ..... CREDOC
Centre de Recherche en Biologie Marine [*Marine Biology Research Center*] [*Research center*] (RCD) ..... CRBM
Centre de Recherche en Civilisation Canadienne-Francaise [*Center for Research in French Canadian Civilisation*] ..... CRCCF
Centre de Recherche en Civilisation Canadienne-Francaise, Universite d'Ottawa [*Centre for Research on French Canadian Culture, University of Ottawa*], Ontario [*Library symbol National Library of Canada*] (BIB) .... OOURC
Centre de Recherche en Developpement Humain [*Centre for Research in Human Development*] [*Concordia University*] [*Canada*] [*Research center*] (RCD) ..... CRDH
Centre de Recherche en Droit Public [*Center for Research in Public Law*] [*Canada*] (IRC) ..... CRDP
Centre de Recherche en Litterature Quebecoise [*Universite Laval, Quebec*] [*Canada*] ..... CRELIQ
Centre de Recherche en Sciences Neurologiques [*Center for Research in Neurological Sciences*] [*Canada*] (IRC) ..... CRSN
Centre de Recherche et d'Etudes sur les Societes Mediterraneennes [*Center forResearch and Studies on Mediterranean Societies*] [*Information service or system*] (IID) ..... CRESM
Centre de Recherche et Developpement en Economique (AC) ..... CRDE
Centre de Recherche Industrielle du Quebec [*Industrial Research Center of Quebec*] [*Information service or system*] (IID) ..... CRIQ
Centre de Recherche Industrielle du Quebec, Montreal, PQ, Canada [*Library symbol*] [*Library of Congress*] (LCLS) ..... CaQMCRI
Centre de Recherche Industrielle du Quebec, Montreal, Quebec [*Library symbol National Library of Canada*] (NLC) ..... QMCRI
Centre de Recherche Industrielle du Quebec, Ste.-Foy, Quebec [*Library symbol National Library of Canada*] (NLC) ..... QSFCR
Centre de Recherche sur la Croissance Humaine [*University of Montreal*] [*Research center*] (RCD) ..... CRCH
Centre de Recherche sur l'Amerique Latine et le Tiers-Monde [*France*] ..... CETRAL
Centre de Recherche sur l'Enseignement du Francais [*St. Anne University*] [*Canada Research center*] (RCD) ..... CREF
Centre de Recherche sur les Transports [*Center for Transport Research*] [*University of Montreal*] [*Research center*] (RCD) ..... CRT
Centre de Recherche, Tourbieres Premier Ltee., Riviere-Du-Loup, Quebec [*Library symbol National Library of Canada*] (BIB) ..... QRLP
Centre de Recherches en Amenagement et en Developpement [*Laval University*] [*Canada Research center*] (RCD) ..... CRAD
Centre de Recherches en Relations Humaines, Montreal, PQ, Canada [*Library symbol Library of Congress*] (LCLS) ..... CaQMRH
Centre de Recherches en Relations Humaines, Montreal, Quebec [*Library symbol National Library of Canada*] (NLC) ..... QMRH
Centre de Recherches et de Documentation des Institutions Chretiennes [*Christian Institutions Research and Documentation Center*] [*France*] [*Information service or system*] (IID) ..... CERDIC
Centre de Recherches et Investigations Eridermiques et Sensorielles [*The Epidermal and Sensory Research and Investigation Center*] [*Funded by Chanel*] [*France*] ..... CERIES
Centre de Recherches Forestieres des Laurentides [*Laurentian Forest Research Center*] [*Canada*] (ARC) ..... CRFL

Centre de Recherches Industrielles en Afrique Centrale .... CRIAC
Centre de Recherches pour le Developpement International [*International Development Research Centre*] [*Canada*] .... CIID
Centre de Recherches Scientifiques et Techniques de l'Industrie des FabricationsMetalliques [*Center for Scientific and Technical Research for the Metal Manu facturing Industry*] [*Information service or system*] (IID) ..... CRIF
Centre de Recherches sur l'Afrique Mediterraneenne .... CRAM
Centre de Recherches sur les Communications [*Sherbrooke University*] [*Canada Research center*] (RCD) .... CRCS
Centre de Recherches sur l'Opinion Publique [*Research Centre on Public Opinion*] [*Canada*] .... CROP
Centre de Reflexion sur le Monde Non Occidental [*Center for the Study of the Non-Occidental World*] (EA) .... CRM
Centre de Regroupement Africain [*Center for African Regroupment*] [*Congo - Leopoldville*] .... CEREA
Centre de Rencontres et d'Echanges Internationaux du Pacifique [*Center of International Cultural and Linguistic Exchanges in the Pacific*] [*Noumea, New Caledonia*] (EAIO) .... CREIPAC
Centre de Reperage des Debouches du Canada [*Canada Business Opportunity Centre - CBOC*] .... CRDC
Centre de Ressources, Ecole Secondaire Algonquin, North Bay, Ontario [*Library symbol National Library of Canada*] (NLC) .... ONBA
Centre de Sensibilisation au Developpement International (AC) .... CSDI
Centre de Service Social Ville-Marie [*Ville-Marie Social Service Centre*] **Montreal, Quebec** [*Library symbol National Library of Canada*] (NLC) .... QMSVM
Centre de Services Sociaux Richelieu, Longueuil, Quebec [*Library symbol National Library of Canada*] (NLC) .... QLOCSS
Centre de Services Sociaux, Trois-Rivieres, PQ, Canada [*Library symbol Library of Congress*] (LCLS) .... CaQTCSS
Centre de Services Sociaux, Trois-Rivieres, Quebec [*Library symbol National Library of Canada*] (NLC) .... QTCSS
Centre de Toxicologie, Centre Hospitalier, Universite Laval, Quebec, Quebec [*Library symbol National Library of Canada*] (BIB) .... QQLACHT
Centre de Traitement de l'Information [*Data Processing Center*] [*Ministry of Economic Affairs*] [*Belgium*] [*Information service or system*] (IID) .... CTI
Centre de Transit [*International routing term*] [*Telecommunications*] (NITA) .... CT
Centre de Valorisation du Patrimoine Vivant (AC) .... CVPV
Centre d'Ecologie et de Toxicologie de l'Industrie Chimique Europeenne [*European Chemical Industry Ecology and Toxicology Center - ECETOC*] (EAIO) .... CETICE
Centre d'Education et d'Action des Femmes de Montreal (AC) .... CEAF
Centre d'Education Interculturelle et de Comprehension Internationale [*Centre for Intercultural Education & International Understanding*] (AC) ...... CEICI
Centre Democratique [*Democratic Center*] [*Later, Center of Social Democrats*] [*France*] [*Political party*] (PPE) .... CD
Centre des Auteurs Dramatiques (AC) .... CEAD
Centre des Democrates Sociaux [*Center of Social Democrats*] [*France Political party*] (PPW) .... CDS
Centre des Dossiers et de Documentation, Direction de Montreal, Ministere des Affaires Culturelles du Quebec [*Library symbol National Library of Canada*] (BIB) .... QMACM
Centre des Hautes Etudes Administratives sur l'Afrique et l'Asie Modernes [*Center for Advanced Administrative Studies on Modern Africa and Asia*] [*French*] (AF) .... CHEAM
Centre des Hautes Etudes Americaines [*Paris*] .... HEA
Centre des Medias, CEGEP [*College d'Enseignement General et Professionnel*]de Ste.-Foy, Quebec [*Library symbol National Library of Canada*] (NLC) .... QSFC
Centre des Nations Unies pour les Etablissements Humains [*United Nations Centre for Human Settlements*] [*French*] (DUND) .... CNUEH
Centre des Recherches Historiques, Quebec, PQ, Canada [*Library symbol Library of Congress Obsolete*] (LCLS) .... CaQQCRH
Centre des Technologies Textiles (AC) .... CTT
Centre d'Essaies Vehicule Automobile [*Motor Vehicle Test Center*] [*French*] .... CEVA
Centre d'Essais en Vol [*France ICAO designator*] (FAAC) .... CEV
Centre d'Essais Regional Europeen [*European Regional Test Center*] [*NATO*] (NATG) .... CERE
Centre d'Etude de l'Energie Nucleaire/Studiecentrum voor Kernenergie [*Belgium*] (EY) .... CEN/SCK
Centre d'Etude des Supports Publicitaires [*Center for the Study of Advertising Support*] [*Database producer Paris, France*] .... CESP
Centre d'Etude du Polymorphisme Humain [*Paris, France*] (ECON) .... CEPH
Centre d'Etude et de Cooperation International [*International Study and Cooperation Centre*] [*Canada*] .... CECI
Centre d'Etudes Anti-Imperialistes [*France*] .... CEDETIM
Centre d'Etudes de l'Asie de l'Est [*University of Montreal*] [*Research center*] (RCD) .... CEAE
Centre d'Etudes des Consequences Generales des Grands Techniques Nouvelles [*Center for the Study of the General Results of New Technologies*] (EA) .... CTN
Centre d'Etudes des Problemes d'Outre-Mer [*Center for the Study of Overseas Problems*] [*France*] (AF) .... CEPOM
Centre d'Etudes des Systemes d'Information des Administrations [*Center for the Study on Information Systems in Government*] [*Information service or system*] (IID) .... CESIA
Centre d'Etudes en Administration Internationale [*Canada*] .... CETAI
Centre d'Etudes en Geographie Tropicale [*Centre of Studies in Tropical Geography*] [*France*] .... CEGET
Centre d'Etudes en Relations Humaines [*Centre of Studies in Human Relations*] [*Canada*] .... CERHU
Centre d'Etudes et de Documentation d'Amerique Latine (AC) .... CEDAL
Centre d'Etudes et de Documentation Europeennes [*Montreal*] .... CEDE
Centre d'Etudes et de Recherches de Biologie et d'Oceanographie Medicale .... CERBOM
Centre d'Etudes et de Recherches Documentaires sur l'Afrique Centrale .... CERDAC
Centre d'Etudes et de Recherches sur les Qualifications (AIE) .... CEREQ
Centre d'Etudes et d'Experimentation du Machinisme Agricole Tropical [*Center for the Study and Experimentation of Tropical Agriculture Machinery*] [*International Cooperation Center of Agricultural Research for Development*] [*Information service or system*] [*France*] (IID) .... CEEMAT
Centre d'Etudes Franco-Canadiennes de l'Ouest [*Centre of Studies of French-Canadians of Western Canada*] .... CEFCO
Centre d'Etudes Industrielles [*Center for education in international management*] [*Switzerland*] (DCTA) .... CEI
Centre d'Etudes Internationales de la Propriete Industrielle .... CEIPI
Centre d'Etudes Nord-Americaines, Aix-En-Provence, France [*Library symbol Library of Congress*] (LCLS) .... FrAipNA
Centre d'Etudes Politiques et Administratives du Quebec [*University of Quebec*] [*Research center*] (RCD) .... CEPAQ
Centre d'Etudes Scientifiques et Techniques d'Aquitaine [*France*] .... CESTA
Centre d'Etudes sur la Langue, les Arts, et les Traditions Populaires des Francophones en Amerique du Nord [*Laval University*] [*Canada Research center*] (RCD) .... CELAT
Centre d'Etudes Theoriques de la Detection et des Communications .... CETHEDEC
Centre d'Etudis Historics Internationals [*Center for International Historical Studies*] (EA) .... CEHI
Centre d'Excellence pour le Developpement de la Technologie Telidon [*Telidon Technology Development Center*] [*Polytechnical School of Montreal Quebec*] [*Information service or system*] (IID) .... CDT
Centre d'Histoire de l'Aeronautique et de l'Espace [*Aeronautics and Space Historical Center - ASHC*] (EAIO) .... CHAE
Centre d'Information de Presse [*Press agency*] [*Belgium*] .... CIP
Centre d'Information des Chemins de Fer Europeens [*Information Center of the European Railways*] .... CICE
Centre d'Information des Nations Unies .... CINU
Centre d'Information Documentaire Come-Saint-Germain, Drummondville, Quebec [*Library symbol National Library of Canada*] (NLC) .... QDM
Centre d'Information en Temps Reel pour l'Europe [*European Center for Information in Real Time*] [*France*] [*Information service or system*] (IID) .... CITERE
Centre d'Information et de Documentation Atlantique [*Brussels, Belgium*] .... CIDA
Centre d'Information, IST [*Industriel Services Techniques*], Montreal, Quebec [*Library symbol National Library of Canada*] (BIB) .... QMIST
Centre d'Information sur la Sante de l'Enfant, Hopital Sainte-Justine, Montreal,Quebec [*Library symbol National Library of Canada*] (NLC) ..... QMSTJ
Centre d'Information Textile Habillement [*Textile and Clothing Information Center*] [*Information service or system*] (IID) .... CITH
Centre d'Informations Catholiques pour la France et l'Etranger CIC
Centre d'Informations Spectroscopiques [*Spectroscopic Information Center*] [*Group for the Advancement of Spectroscopic Methods and Physicochemical Analysis*] [*Information service or system*] (IID) .... CIS
Centre d'Informatique Appliquee au Developpement et a l'Agriculture Tropicale [*Center for Informatics Applied to Development and Tropical Agriculture*] [*Royal Museum of Central Africa*] [*Information service or system*] (IID) .... CIDAT
Centre d'Informatique et Documentation Automatique [*Center for Automated Information and Documentation*] [*France*] [*Information service or system*] (IID) .... CIDA
Centre d'Ingenierie Nordique [*University of Montreal*] [*Research center*] (RCD) .... CINEP
Centre d'Inter-Action Culturelle [*Center for Inter-Cultural Action*] (EAIO) .... CIAC
Centre d'Intervention et de Prevention en Toxicomanie de l'Outaouais (AC) .... CIPTO
Centre d'Intervention et de Recherche pour l'Amelioration des Situations de Travail [*University of Quebec at Rimouski*] [*Research center*] (RCD) .... CIRAST
Centre Documentaire, Centrale des Bibliotheques, Montreal, Quebec [*Library symbol National Library of Canada*] (NLC) .... QMCD
Centre du Commerce International [*International Trade Center - ITC*] [*Geneva, Switzerland*] [*French*] (EAIO) CCI
Centre Ecologique Albert Schweitzer [*Albert Schweitzer Ecological Centre*] [*Switzerland*] (EAIO) .... CEAS
Centre Economique de Secours Europeens [*European Economic Relief Committee*] [*NATO*] (NATG) .... CESE
Centre Elementary School, East Rockaway, NY [*Library symbol Library of Congress*] (LCLS) .... NErCE
Centre European de Recherches Nucleaires [*Switzerland*] (USDC) .... CERN
Centre Europeen d'Aviation Agricole .... CEAA
Centre Europeen de Documentation et de Compensation .... CEDEC
Centre Europeen de Formation des Statisticiens Economistes des Pays en Voie de Developpement [*European Center for Training Statisticians and Economists from Developing Countries*] .... CESD
Centre Europeen de Formation et de Recherche en Action Sociale [*European Centre for Social Welfare Training and Research - ECSWTR*] [*United Nations*] (EAIO) .... CEFRAS
Centre Europeen de la Culture [*European Cultural Centre - ECC*] (EAIO) .... CEC
Centre Europeen de l'Entreprise Publique [*European Center of Public Enterprise - ECPE*] (EAIO) .... CEEP
Centre Europeen de Recherche et de Documentation Parlementaires [*European Centre for Parliamentary Research and Documentation - ECPRD*] [*Luxembourg*] (EAIO) .... CERDP
Centre Europeen de Recherches Mauvernay [*France*] [*Research code symbol*] .... CERM
Centre Europeen de Recherches sur l'Investissement (EAIO) .... CERI

Centre Europeen de Traduction [*European Translation Center*] ..... CET
Centre Europeen de Traitement de l'Information Scientifique [*EURATOM*] ..... CETIS
Centre Europeen des Parents de l'Ecole Publique (AIE) ..... CEPEP
Centre Europeen des Silicones [*of the European Council of Chemical Manufacturers' Federations*] (EAIO) ..... CES
Centre Europeen d'Etudes de l'Acide Sulfurique [*European Center for Studies of Sulfuric Acid*] (EAIO) ..... CEEAS
Centre Europeen d'Etudes de Population [*European Center for Population Studies*] ..... CEEP
Centre Europeen du Commerce de Detail [*European Center of the Retail Trade*] [*Common Market*] ..... CECODE
Centre Europeen pour la Promotion de la Formation Milieu Agricole et Rural [*European Training and Development Centre for Farming and Rural Life - ETDCFRL*] (EAIO) ..... CEPFAR
Centre Europeen pour le Developpement de la Formation Professionnelle [*European Centre for the Development of Vocational Training*] (EAIO) ..... CEDEFOP
Centre Europeen pour l'Enseignement Superieur [*European Centre for Higher Education*] (EAIO) ..... CEPES
Centre Europeen pour les Loisirs et l'Education [*European Centre for Leisure and Education - ECLE*] (EAIO) ..... CLE
Centre Europe-Tiers Monde [*Switzerland*] ..... CETIM
Centre for Aboriginal and Islander Studies [*Northern Territory*] [*Australia*] ..... CAIS
Centre for Advanced Land Use Studies [*College of Estate Management*] [*British*] (CB) ..... CALUS
Centre for Advanced Materials Technology [*Monash University*] [*Australia*] ..... CAMT
Centre for Advanced Numerical Computation in Engineering and Science [*Australia*] ..... CANCES
Centre for Advanced Study in the Developmental Sciences [*British*] ..... CASDS
Centre for Advanced Technology Education [*Ryerson Polytechnical Institute*] [*Canada Research center*] (RCD) ..... CATE
Centre for Advancement in Work & Living (AC) ..... CAWL
Centre for Advancement of Counselling [*British*] ..... CAC
Centre for African Family Studies [*Kenya*] (EAIO) ..... CAFS
Centre for African Studies [*International Planned Parenthood Federation*] (ECON) ..... CAFS
Centre for Aging Studies [*Flinders University*] [*Australia*] ..... CAS
Centre for Agricultural Commerce [*University of New England*] [*Australia*] ..... CAC
Centre for Agricultural Publications and Documents, Wageningen, Netherlands [*OCLC symbol*] (OCLC) ..... NET
Centre for Agricultural Strategy [*University of Reading*] [*British*] (CB) ..... CAS
Centre for Alcohol and Road Safety Education [*British*] (AIE) ..... CARSE
Centre for Alternative Industrial and Technological Systems [*British*] (CB) ..... CAITS
Centre for Alternative Technology [*British*] (CB) ..... CAT
Centre for American and Commonwealth Arts and Studies [*British*] (CB) ..... AmCAS
Centre for Applied Health Studies [*University of Ulster at Coleraine*] [*British*] (CB) ..... CAHS
Centre for Applied Language Studies [*Carleton University*] [*Canada Research center*] (RCD) ..... CALS
Centre for Applied Linguistics, University of South Australia ..... CALUSA
Centre for Applied Microbiology and Research [*Public Health Laboratory Service*] [*British*] ..... CAMR
Centre for Applied Research and Engineering Design [*McMaster University, Hamilton, ON*] ..... CARED
Centre for Applied Research in Education [*University of East Anglia*] [*British*] (CB) ..... CARE
Centre for Applied Social Research [*Macquarie University*] [*Australia*] ..... CASR
Centre for Architectural Research and Development Overseas [*University of Newcastle upon Tyne*] [*British*] (CB) ..... CARDO
Centre for Arid Zone Studies [*University College of North Wales*] [*British*] (CB) ..... CAZS
Centre for Astrophysical Research in Antarctica (ECON) ..... CARA
Centre for Atmospheric Science ..... CAS
Centre for Australian Languages and Linguistics [*Batchelor College*] ..... CALL
Centre for Brain Injury Rehabilitation and Development [*British*] (CB) ..... BIRD
Centre for Business Research [*Manchester Business School*] [*British*] (CB) ..... CBR
Centre for Business Systems Analysis [*City University*] [*British*] (CB) ..... CBSA
Centre for Canadian Population Studies ..... CCPS
Centre for Career Development, Revenue Canada - Taxation [*Centre de Developpement Professionnel, Revenu Canada - Impot*] **Ottawa, Ontario** [*Library symbol National Library of Canada*] (NLC) ..... OONRTC
Centre for Catalogue Research [*University of Bath*] [*British*] (CB) ..... CCR
Centre for Cell and Tissue Research [*University of York*] [*Research center British*] (CB) ..... CCTR
Centre for Child Study [*University of Birmingham*] [*British*] (CB) ..... CCS
Centre for Chiropractic and Osteopathy [*Macquarie University*] [*Australia*] ..... CCO
Centre for Chiropractic and Osteopathy [*Macquarie University*] [*Australia*] ..... CPO
Centre for Clinical Epidemiology and Biostasis [*University of Newcastle*] [*Australia*] ..... CCEB
Centre for Cold Ocean Resources Engineering [*Memorial University of Newfoundland*] [*Research center*] (RCD) ..... C-CORE
Centre for Comparative Literature and Cultural Studies [*Monash University*] [*Australia*] ..... CCLCS
Centre for Computers in Education and Training [*University of Salford*] [*British*] (CB) ..... CCET
Centre for Conflict Resolution [*Macquarie University*] [*Australia*] ..... CCR
Centre for Conservation Farming [*Charles Sturt University*] [*Australia*] ..... CCF
Centre for Construction Market Information Ltd. [*British*] (CB) ..... CCMT
Centre for Contemporary Cultural Studies [*University of Birmingham*] [*British*] (CB) ..... CCCS
Centre for Contemporary Studies [*British*] (CB) ..... CCS
Centre for Continuing Education in the Building Industry [*Polytechnic of the South Bank*] [*British*] (CB) ..... CCEBI
Centre for Criminological Research [*University of Alberta*] [*Canada*] (IRC) ..... CCR
Centre for Criminology and the Social and Philosophical Study of Law [*University of Edinburgh*] [*British*] (CB) ..... CCSPSL
Centre for Curriculum Renewal and Educational Development Overseas ..... CREDO
Centre for Deafness Studies and Research [*Griffith University*] [*Research center Australia*] ..... CDSR
Centre for Developing-Area Studies [*McGill University*] [*Canada*] (IRC) ..... CDAS
Centre for Development and Population Activities (EA) ..... CEDPA
Centre for Development of Instructional Technology ..... CENDIT
Centre for Development Studies [*Flinders University*] [*Australia*] ..... CDS
Centre for Distance Learning [*University of Central Queensland*] [*Australia*] ..... CDL
Centre for Documentation on Refugees [*UNHCR*] [*Information service or system*] (IID) ..... CDR
Centre for Earth Resources Research [*Memorial University of Newfoundland*] [*Research center*] (RCD) ..... CERR
Centre for Economic and Environmental Development [*British*] (CB) ..... CEED
Centre for Economic and Social Information [*United Nations*] ..... CESI
Centre for Economic Cooperation (AC) ..... CEC
Centre for Economic Forecasting [*London Business School*] [*British*] (CB) ..... CEF
Centre for Economic Policy Research [*Australian National University*] [*Economics Australia*] ..... CEPR
Centre for Economic Policy Research [*British*] (ECON) ..... CEPR
Centre for Editing Early Canadian Texts ..... CEECT
Centre for Educational Development and Training [*Manchester Polytechnic*] [*British*] (CB) ..... CEDAT
Centre for Educational Development, Appraisal and Research [*University of Warwick*] [*British*] (AIE) ..... CEDAR
Centre for Educational Development Overseas ..... CEDO
Centre for Educational Research and Innovation (EAIO) ..... CERI
Centre for Educational Sociology [*University of Edinburgh*] [*British*] (CB) ..... CES
Centre for Educational Studies [*King's College, London*] [*British*] (CB) ..... CES
Centre for Educational Television Overseas [*British*] ..... CETO
Centre for Electronics in Agriculture [*University of New England*] [*Australia*] ..... CEA
Centre for Employment Initiatives Ltd. [*British*] (CB) ..... CEI
Centre for Endangered Reptiles [*Centre Pour Reptiles Menaces*] [*Formerly, The Reptile Breeding Foundation*] (AC) ..... CER
Centre for Energy Studies [*Technical University of Nova Scotia*] [*Research center*] (RCD) ..... CES
Centre for English Cultural Tradition and Language [*University of Sheffield*] [*British*] (CB) ..... CECTAL
Centre for English Language Teaching [*University of Stirling*] [*British*] (CB) ..... CELT
Centre for Environmental Education [*British*] (AIE) ..... CCE
Centre for Environmental Interpretation [*Manchester Polytechnic*] [*British*] (CB) ..... CEI
Centre for Environmental Management [*University of Newcastle*] [*Australia*] ..... CEM
Centre for Environmental Studies [*British*] ..... CES
Centre for Ergonomics and Human Factors [*Australia*] ..... CEHF
Centre for European Agricultural Studies [*British*] (ARC) ..... CEAS
Centre for European Industrial Studies [*University of Bath*] [*British*] (CB) ..... CEIS
Centre for European Legal Studies [*University of Exeter*] [*British*] (CB) ..... CELS
Centre for European Policy Studies (ECON) ..... CEPS
Centre for European Security and Cooperation [*Netherlands*] ..... CESC
Centre for European Studies [*Monash University*] [*Australia*] ..... CES
Centre for Exploitation of Science and Technology [*British*] (ECON) ..... CEST
Centre for Fiscal Studies [*University of Bath*] [*British*] (CB) ..... CFS
Centre for Foreign Policy Studies [*Dalhousie University*] [*Canada*] (IRC) ..... CFPS
Centre for Frontier Engineering Research [*University of Alberta*] [*Canada*] (IRC) ..... C-FER
Centre for Habilitation Education and Research [*University of Waterloo*] [*Research center*] (RCD) ..... CHER
Centre for Health Services Management [*Leicester Polytechnic*] [*British*] (CB) ..... CHSM
Centre for Higher Education Policy Studies [*British*] (AIE) ..... CHEPS
Centre for Human Development [*British*] (CB) ..... CHD
Centre for Human Ecology and Health Advancement [*University of Newcastle*] [*Australia*] ..... CHEHA
Centre for Human Relations and Community Studies [*Concordia University*] [*Canada Research center*] (RCD) ..... CHRCS
Centre for Image Analysis [*Charles Sturt University*] [*Australia*] ..... CIA
Centre for Independent Living in Toronto (AC) ..... CILT
Centre for Industrial Control [*Concordia University*] [*Canada Research center*] (RCD) CIC
Centre for Industrial Control Science [*University of Newcastle*] [*Australia*] ..... CICS
Centre for Industrial Innovation [*British*] (ARC) CII
Centre for Information and Advice on Educational Disadvantage [*British*] ..... CED
Centre for Information and Documentation [*EURATOM*] (MCD) ..... CID
Centre for Information and Technical Assistance, Institute of Man and Resources,Charlottetown, Prince Edward Island [*Library symbol National Library of Canada*] (NLC) ..... PCIMR
Centre for Information Media and Technology [*British*] (EAIO) ..... CIMTECH
Centre for Information on Language Teaching and Research [*Regent's College*] [*British*] (CB) ..... CILT
Centre for Information on Language Teaching and Research [*British*] (AIE) ..... CILT
Centre for Information on Language Training [*British*] ..... CILT
Centre for Information on Standardization and Metrology [*Information service or system*] (IID) ..... CIS

Centre for Information Services [*Council for Scientific and Industrial Research - CSIR*] [*South Africa*] [*Information service or system*] (IID) ... CIS
Centre for Information Technology and Communications [*Queensland*] [*Australia Information service or system*] ... CITC
Centre for Institutional Studies [*North East London Polytechnic*] [*British*] (CB) ... CIS
Centre for Integrated Rural Development for Asia and the Pacific ... CIRDAP
Centre for Interdisciplinary Studies in Chemical Physics [*University of Western Ontario*] [*Canada*] (IRC) ... CCP
Centre for Interfirm Comparison [*British*] ... CIFC
Centre for International and Strategic Studies [*York University*] [*Research center*] (RCD) ... CISS
Centre for International Education [*Netherlands*] (EAIO) ... CEVNO
Centre for International Studies [*Canada*] (CROSS) ... CIS
Centre for Internationalising the Study of English ... CIE
Centre for Japanese Business Language [*Australia*] ... CJBL
Centre for Japanese Economic Studies [*Macquarie University*] [*Australia*] ... CJES
Centre for Journalism Studies [*British*] (CB) ... CJS
Centre for Language Studies [*University of Newcastle*] [*Australia*] ... CLS
Centre for Latin American Linguistic Studies [*University of St. Andrews*] [*British*] (CB) ... CLALS
Centre for Learning and Development [*British*] (AIE) ... CLD
Centre for Library and Information Management [*Loughborough University of Technology*] [*British Information service or system*] (IID) ... CLAIM
Centre for Literacy and Linguistic Computing [*University of Newcastle*] [*Australia*] ... CLLC
Centre for Local Economic Strategies Ltd. [*British*] (CB) ... CLES
Centre for Machine Condition Monitoring [*Monash University*] [*Australia*] ... CMCM
Centre for Manufacturing Renewal [*University of Warwick*] [*British*] (CB) ... CMR
Centre for Mass Communication Research [*University of Leicester*] [*British*] (CB) ... CMCR
Centre for Measurement and Information in Medicine [*City University*] [*British*] (CB) ... CMIM
Centre for Medicines Research [*British*] (CB) ... CMR
Centre for Medieval Studies [*University of Toronto*] [*Canada*] (IRC) ... CMS
Centre for Mennonite Brethren Studies in Canada, Winnipeg, Manitoba [*Library symbol National Library of Canada*] (NLC) ... MWCMS
Centre for Middle Eastern and Islamic Studies [*University of Durham*] [*British*] (CB) ... CMEIS
Centre for Molecular Biology and Medicine [*Monash University*] [*Australia*] ... CMBM
Centre for Molecular Structure and Function [*Australian National University*] ... CMSF
Centre for Monitoring the Indian Economy (ECON) ... CMIE
Centre for Multicultural Education [*University of London Institute of Education*] [*British*] (CB) ... CME
Centre for Multicultural Studies [*Flinders University*] [*Australia*] ... CMS
Centre for Natural Resources, Energy, and Transport [*United Nations*] ... CNRET
Centre for Neuroscience [*University College, London*] [*British*] (CB) ... CNS
Centre for Nonlinear Studies [*University of Leeds*] [*British*] (CB) ... CNLS
Centre for North-West Regional Studies [*University of Lancaster*] [*British*] (CB) ... CNWRS
Centre for Nuclear Magnetic Resonance [*University of Warwick*] [*British*] (CB) ... NMR
Centre for Nursing and Health Care Practices [*Southern Cross University*] [*Medicine Australia*] ... CFN&HCP
Centre for Ocean Technology [*Canada*] (IRC) ... COT
Centre for Offshore and Remote Medicine [*Memorial University of Newfoundland*] [*Research center*] (RCD) ... MEDICOR
Centre for Overseas Pest Research [*England*] ... COPR
Centre for Pastoral Work in Europe [*See also CPE*] (EAIO) ... CPWE
Centre for Personal Construct Psychology [*British*] (CB) ... PCP
Centre for Pest Management [*Simon Fraser University*] [*Canada Research center*] (RCD) ... CPM
Centre for Petroleum and Mineral Law Studies [*University of Dundee*] [*British*] (CB) ... CPMLS
Centre for Petrology and Lithospheric Studies [*Macquarie University*] [*Australia*] ... CPLS
Centre for Plant Molecular Biology [*McGill University*] [*Canada*] (IRC) ... CPMB
Centre for Policy on Ageing (EAIO) ... CPA
Centre for Policy Studies [*Monash University*] [*Australia*] ... CPS
Centre for Policy Studies [*British*] ... CPS
Centre for Precision Technology [*Australia*] ... CPT
Centre for Protein and Enzyme Technology [*La Trobe University*] [*Australia*] ... CPET
Centre for Public Sector Research [*University of Canberra*] [*Australia*] ... CPSR
Centre for Regional Economic Analysis [*Australia*] ... CREA
Centre for Remote Sensing [*Imperial College of Science and Technology*] [*British*] (CB) ... CRS
Centre for Remote Sensing [*James Cook University*] [*Australia*] ... CRS
Centre for Research & Development in Masonry [*Centre de Recherche et de Developpement en Maconnerie*] **Calgary, Alberta** [*Library symbol National Library of Canada*] (NLC) ... ACRDM
Centre for Research and Education on Gender [*University of London*] [*British*] (AIE) ... CREG
Centre for Research in Comparative Medicine [*Canada*] (IRC) ... CRCM
Centre for Research in Education and Work [*Macquarie University*] [*Australia*] ... CREW
Centre for Research in Ethnic Relations [*University of Warwick*] [*British*] (CB) ... CRER
Centre for Research in Experimental Space Science [*York University*] [*Canada Research center*] (RCD) ... CRESS
Centre for Research in Finance [*University of New South Wales*] [*Information service or system*] (IID) ... CRIF
Centre for Research in Industrial Democracy and Participation [*University of Glasgow*] [*British*] (CB) ... CRIDP
Centre for Research in Librarianship [*University of Toronto*] [*Research center*] (RCD) ... CRL
Centre for Research in Philosophy and Literature [*University of Warwick*] [*British*] (CB) ... CRPL
Centre for Research into Communist Economies [*Research center British*] (IRC) ... CRCE
Centre for Research Into Economics and Finance in South Africa [*London School of Economic and Political Science*] (ECON) ... CREFSA
Centre for Research into Public Health and Nursing [*La Trobe University*] [*Australia*] ... CRPHN
Centre for Research into Strategic Information Systems [*University of Bath*] [*British*] ... CRSIS
Centre for Research on Atoms and Molecules [*Laval University*] [*Canada Research center*] (RCD) ... CRAM
Centre for Research on European Women [*Belgium*] (EAIO) ... CREW
Centre for Research on Latin America and the Caribbean [*York University*] [*Canada Research center*] (RCD) ... CERLAC
Centre for Research on Perception and Cognition [*University of Sussex*] [*British*] (CB) ... CRPC
Centre for Research on User Studies [*University of Sheffield*] [*England*] [*Information service or system*] (IID) ... CRUS
Centre for Resource and Environmental Studies ... CRES
Centre for Resource Studies [*Queen's University at Kingston*] [*Canada Research center*] (RCD) ... CRS
Centre for Rural Research Management [*University of New England*] [*Australia*] ... CRRM
Centre for Rural Social Research [*Charles Sturt University*] [*Australia*] ... CRSR
Centre for Rural Transport [*St. David's University College*] [*British*] (CB) ... CRT
Centre for Russian and East European Studies [*University of Birmingham*] [*British*] (CB) ... CREES
Centre for Russian and East European Studies [*University of Toronto*] [*Canada*] (IRC) ... CREES
Centre for Science and Mathematics Education [*British*] (AIE) ... CSME
Centre for Scientific and Technological Information [*Council for Scientific and Industrial Research*] [*Pretoria, South Africa*] ... CSTI
Centre for Social Development and Humanitarian Affairs [*United Nations*] (EAIO) ... CSDHA
Centre for Socio-Legal Studies [*British*] (CB) ... CSLS
Centre for Software Engineering Ltd. [*British*] (CB) ... CSE
Centre for Software Reliability [*City University*] [*British*] (IRUK) ... CSR
Centre for South Australian Economic Studies [*Flinders University*] [*Australia*] ... CSAES
Centre for Southeast Asian Studies [*Monash University*] [*Australia*] ... CSAS
Centre for Southern African Studies [*University of York*] [*British*] (CB) ... CSAS
Centre for Speech Technology Research [*British*] (CB) ... CSTR
Centre for Studies in Money, Banking, and Finance [*Macquarie University*] [*Australia*] ... CSMBF
Centre for Studies in Science and Mathematical Education [*University of Leeds*] [*British*] (CB) ... CSSME
Centre for Studies on Integration in Education [*British*] (CB) ... CSIE
Centre for Study of Education in Developing Countries [*Netherlands*] (EAIO) ... CSEDC
Centre for Study of Insurance Operations (AC) ... CSIO
Centre for Teaching and Learning Services [*McGill University*] [*Canada Research center*] (RCD) ... CTLS
Centre for Technology and Social Change (EERA) ... TASC
Centre for Telecommunications Development [*ITU*] [*United Nations*] (DUND) ... CTD
Centre for the Advancement and Study of the European Currency [*France*] (EAIO) ... CASEC
Centre for the Advancement of Mathematical Education in Technology [*Loughborough University of Technology*] [*Research center British*] (CB) ... CAMET
Centre for the Analysis of Conflict [*Research center British*] (IRC) ... CAC
Centre for the Analysis of Social Policy [*University of Bath*] [*British*] (CB) ... CASP
Centre for the Independence of Judges and Lawyers [*See also CIMA*] [*Geneva, Switzerland*] (EAIO) ... CIJL
Centre for the Study of Arms Control and International Security [*University of Lancaster, Fylde College*] [*British*] (CB) ... CSACIS
Centre for the Study of Communication and Culture [*British*] (CB) ... CSCC
Centre for the Study of Community and Race Relations [*Brunel University*] [*British*] (CB) ... CSCRR
Centre for the Study of Comprehensive Schools [*Wentworth College, University of York*] [*British*] (CB) ... CSCS
Centre for the Study of Developing Societies [*Information service or system*] (IID) ... CSDS
Centre for the Study of Economics and Religion [*Fraser Institute*] [*Canada*] (IRC) ... CSER
Centre for the Study of Human Learning [*Brunel University*] [*British*] (CB) ... CSHL
Centre for the Study of International Economic Relations [*University of Western Ontario*] [*Canada*] (IRC) ... CSIER
Centre for the Study of Mental Retardation [*Canada*] ... CSMR
Centre for the Study of Public Policy [*University of Strathclyde*] [*British*] (CB) ... CSPP
Centre for the Study of Regulated Industries [*McGill University*] [*Canada Research center*] (RCD) ... CSRI
Centre for Trade Policy and Law [*Established to promote greater public understanding of trade policies*] [*Canada*] (CROSS) ... CTPL
Centre for Transport Engineering Practice [*Loughborough University of Technology*] [*British*] (CB) ... CTEP

Centre for Transportation Studies [*University of British Columbia*] [*Canada*] (IRC) .... CTS

Centre for Tropical Veterinary Medicine [*Overseas Development Administration*] [*British*] (DS) .... CTVM

Centre for Urban and Community Studies [*University of Toronto*] [*Research center*] (RCD) .... CUCS

Centre for Urban and Regional Development Studies [*University of Newcastle upon Tyne*] [*British*] (CB) .... CURDS

Centre for Visual Arts [*University of New England*] [*Australia*] .... CVA

Centre for Water Policy Research [*University of New England*] [*Australia*].... CWPR

Centre for Women's Development Studies [*India*] (EAIO) .... CWDS

Centre for Women's Health Studies [*Cumberland College of Health Sciences*] [*Australia*] .... CWHS

Centre for World Development Education [*Regent's College*] [*British*] (CB) .... CWDE

Centre Francais de la Couleur [*Online service*] .... CFC

Centre Francois Charron, Quebec, Quebec [*Library symbol National Library of Canada*] (BIB) .... QQCF

Centre Franco-Ontarien de Folklore [*Formerly, Institut de Folklore*] [*Research center*] (RCD) .... CFOF

Centre Franco-Ontarien de Ressources Pedagogiques (AC) .... CFORP

Centre Francophone de Recherche en Informatisation des Organisations (AC) .... CEFRIO

Centre Hospitalier Christ-Roi, Quebec, Quebec [*Library symbol National Library of Canada*] (BIB) .... QQCR

Centre Hospitalier Cooke, Trois-Rivieres, Quebec [*Library symbol National Library of Canada*] (NLC) .... QTCHC

Centre Hospitalier de Charlevoix, Baie St. Paul, PQ, Canada [*Library symbol*] [*Library of Congress*] (LCLS) .... CaQBSPH

Centre Hospitalier de Charlevoix, Baie St.-Paul, Quebec [*Library symbol National Library of Canada*] (BIB) .... QBSPH

Centre Hospitalier de Gatineau, Gatineau, PQ, Canada [*Library symbol*] [*Library of Congress*] (LCLS) .... CaQGatCH

Centre Hospitalier de Gatineau, Quebec [*Library symbol National Library of Canada*] (NLC) .... QGCH

Centre Hospitalier de Lachine, Montreal, PQ, Canada [*Library symbol Library of Congress*] (LCLS) .... CaQMCHL

Centre Hospitalier de Lachine, Montreal, Quebec [*Library symbol National Library of Canada*] (NLC) .... QMCHL

Centre Hospitalier de l'Universite Laval, Quebec, Quebec [*Library symbol National Library of Canada*] (NLC) .... QQLACH

Centre Hospitalier de Verdun, Montreal, PQ, Canada [*Library symbol Library of Congress*] (LCLS) .... CaQMHGC

Centre Hospitalier de Verdun, Quebec [*Library symbol National Library of Canada*] (NLC) .... QMHGC

Centre Hospitalier du Sacre-Coeur, Hull, PQ, Canada [*Library symbol Library of Congress*] (LCLS) .... CaQHSC

Centre Hospitalier Hotel-Dieu, Sherbrooke, PQ, Canada [*Library symbol Library of Congress*] (LCLS) .... CaQSherHD

Centre Hospitalier Hotel-Dieu, Sherbrooke, Quebec [*Library symbol National Library of Canada*] (NLC) .... QSHERHD

Centre Hospitalier Jacques Viger, Montreal, PQ, Canada [*Library symbol Library of Congress*] (LCLS) .... CaQMHM

Centre Hospitalier Jacques Viger, Montreal, Quebec [*Library symbol National Library of Canada*] (NLC) .... QMHM

Centre Hospitalier Jeffery Hale, Quebec, Quebec [*Library symbol National Library of Canada*] (BIB) .... QQCHJH

Centre Hospitalier Le Gardeur, Repentigny, PQ, Canada [*Library symbol*] [*Library of Congress*] (LCLS) .... CaQRECHL

Centre Hospitalier Le Gardeur, Repentigny, Quebec [*Library symbol National Library of Canada*] (NLC) .... ORECHL

Centre Hospitalier Pierre Boucher, Longueuil, PQ, Canada [*Library symbol*] [*Library of Congress*] (LCLS) .... CaQLoPB

Centre Hospitalier Pierre Janet, Hull, PQ, Canada [*Library symbol Library of Congress*] (LCLS) .... CaQHPJ

Centre Hospitalier Pierre Janet, Hull, Quebec [*Library symbol National Library of Canada*] (NLC) .... QHPJ

Centre Hospitalier Regional de La Mauricie, Shawinigan, Quebec [*Library symbol National Library of Canada*] (NLC) .... QSHCH

Centre Hospitalier Regional de Lanaudiere, Joliette, Quebec [*Library symbol National Library of Canada*] (NLC) .... QJH

Centre Hospitalier Regional de l'Outaouais, Hull, Quebec [*Library symbol National Library of Canada*] (NLC) .... QHSC

Centre Hospitalier Robert Giffard, Beauport, Quebec [*Library symbol National Library of Canada*] (NLC) .... QBRG

Centre Hospitalier Robert Giffard, Quebec, PQ, Canada [*Library symbol Library of Congress*] (LCLS) .... CaQBRG

Centre Hospitalier Rouyn-Noranda, Noranda, PQ, Canada [*Library symbol Library of Congress*] (LCLS) .... CaQNCHRN

Centre Hospitalier Rouyn-Noranda, Noranda, Quebec [*Library symbol National Library of Canada*] (NLC) .... QNCHRN

Centre Hospitalier St.-Augustin, Beauport, Quebec [*Library symbol National Library of Canada*] (BIB) .... QBSA

Centre Hospitalier St.-Vincent-De-Paul, Sherbrooke, PQ, Canada [*Library symbol Library of Congress*] (LCLS) .... CaQSherSV

Centre Hospitalier St.-Vincent-De-Paul, Sherbrooke, Quebec [*Library symbol National Library of Canada*] (NLC) .... QSHERSV

Centre Informatique Geologique [*Geological Information Centre*] [*Canada*] .... CIG

Centre Interafricain pour le Developpement de la Formation Professionnelle [*Inter-African Center for the Development of Professional Training*] [*Abidjan, Ivory Coast*] (EAIO) .... CIADFOR

Centre Interamericain d'Education Rurale .... CIER

Centre Interculturel Monchanin, Montreal, Quebec [*Library symbol National Library of Canada*] (NLC) .... QMCICM

Centre Intergouvernemental de Documentation sur l'Habitat et l'Environnement [*Intergovernmental Center for Documentation on Dwellings and the Environment*] (PDAA) .... CIDHEC

Centre Internacional Escarre per a les Minories Etniques i Nacionalitats (EAIO) .... CIEMEN

Centre International d'Alcoologie / Toxixomanies [*International Center of Alcohol/Drug Addiction*] (PDAA) .... CIATO

Centre International d'Aviation Agricole [*International Agricultural Aviation Center*] .... CIAA

Centre International de Conferences de Geneve [*International Conference Center of Geneva*] [*Switzerland*] (PDAA) .... CICG

Centre International de Coordination pour la Celebration des Anniversaires .... CICCA

Centre International de Criminologie Comparee [*International Center for Comparative Criminology - ICCC*] [*Montreal, PQ*] (EA) CICC

Centre International de Developpement de l'Aluminium .... CIDA

Centre International de Documentation [*International Center for Documentation*] .... CID

Centre International de Documentation Arachnologique [*International Centre for Arachnological Documentation*] (EAIO) .... CIDA

Centre International de Documentation Concernant les Expressions Plastiques .... CIDEP

Centre International de Documentation de l'Inspection Technique des Vehicules Automobiles .... CIDITVA

Centre International de Documentation Economique et Sociale Africaine [*International Center for African Social and Economic Documentation*]..... CIDESA

Centre International de Documentation et d'Information .... CIDI

Centre International de Documentation Parlementaire [*International Center for Parliamentary Documentation*] (EAIO) .... CIDP

Centre International de Formation Europeenne [*France*] .... CIFE

Centre International de Gerontologie Sociale [*International Center of Social Gerontology - ICSG*] [*Paris, France*] [*Defunct*] .... CIGS

Centre International de Hautes Etudes Agronomiques Mediterraneennes .... CIHEAM

Centre International de la Tapisserie Ancienne et Moderne [*Switzerland*] .... CITAM

Centre International de l'Actualite Fantastique et Magique .... CIAFMA

Centre International de l'Eau et l'Assainissement [*IRC International Water and Sanitation Centre*] (EAIO) .... CIR

Centre International de l'Enfance [*International Children's Centre*] [*Paris, France*] (EAIO) .... CIE

Centre International de Liaison des Ecoles de Cinema et de Television [*International Liaison Centre for Film and Television Schools*] (EAIO) .... CILECT

Centre International de Mathematiques Pures et Appliquees [*International Center for Pure and Applied Mathematics - ICPAM*] [*United Nations*] (EA) .... CIMPA

Centre International de Phenomenologie Clinique (EAIO) .... CIPC

Centre International de Recherche, de Creation, et d'Animation [*France*] .... CIRCA

Centre International de Recherche en Amenagement Linguistique (AC) .... CIRAL

Centre International de Recherches et d'Etudes en Management [*International Centre for Research and Studies in Management*] [*Canada*] .... CIREM

Centre International de Recherches sur l'Anarchisme [*International Research Center on Anarchism*] [*Geneva, Switzerland*] (EAIO) .... CIRA

Centre International de Recherches sur le Bilinguisme [*International Center for Research on Bilingualism*] [*Universite Laval, Quebec*] [*Canada*] .... CIRB

Centre International de Recherches sur le Bilinguisme, Universite Laval, Quebec,Quebec [*Library symbol National Library of Canada*] (NLC) .... QQLACI

Centre International de Recherches sur les Communautes Cooperatives Rurales [*International Research Center on Rural Cooperative Communities*] .... CIRCOM

Centre International de Solidarite Ouvriere (AC) .... CISO

Centre International d'Enseignement Superieur de Journalisme [*UNESCO*] (NTCM) .... CIESJ

Centre International des Antiparasitaires .... CIA

Centre International des Civilisations Bantu [*International Center for the Bantu Civilizations*] [*Gabon*] [*Research center*] (IRC) .... CICIBA

Centre International des Engrais Chimiques [*International Center of Fertilizers*] .... CIEC

Centre International des Etudes de la Musique Ancienne [*International Center of Studies on Early Music*] .... CIEMA

Centre International des Marees Terrestres [*International Centre for Earth Tides*] (EAIO) .... CIMT

Centre International des Sciences Mecaniques .... CISM

Centre International des Syndicalistes Libres en Exil [*International Center of Free Trade Unionists in Exile*] [*Defunct*] .... CISLE

Centre International d'Etude des Textiles Anciens [*International Center for the Study of Ancient Textiles*] [*France*] (SLS) .... CIETA

Centre International d'Etudes des Textiles Anciens [*International Center for the Study of Ancient Textiles*] [*Lyon, France*] .... CIETA

Centre International d'Etudes du Lindane [*International Research Centre on Lindane - IRCL*] (EAIO) .... CIEL

Centre International d'Etudes et de Recherches en Socio-Economie de la Sante [*International Health Centre of Socioeconomics, Researches and Studies - IHCSERS*] [*Lailly En Val, France*] (EAIO) .... CIERSES

Centre International d'Exploitation des Oceans [*See also ICOD*] [*Canada*] .... CIEO

Centre International d'Information de la Mutualite .... CIIM

Centre International d'Information et de Recherche sur la Formation Professionnelle .... CIRF

Centre International d'Information sur le Gaz Naturel et tous Hydrocarbures Ga zeux [*International Information Center on Natural Gas and Gaseous Hydrocarbons*] [*France*] (PDAA) .... CEDIGAZ

Centre International d'Informations de Securite et d'Hygiene du Travail [*International Occupational Safety and Health Information Center*] [*International Labour Office*] (IID) .... CIS

Centre International du Commerce de Gros [*International Center for Wholesale Trade*] .... CICG

Centre International du Film pour l'Enfance et la Jeunesse [*International Center of Films for Children and Young People*] .... CIFEJ

Centre International Humanae Vitae [*International Centre Humanae Vitae*] [*Paris, France*] (EAIO) .... CIHV

Centre International pour Education Artistique [*International Centre for Art Education*] (EAIO) .... CIEA

Centre International pour la Coordination des Recherches en Agriculture .... CICRA

Centre International pour la Formation et les Echanges Geologiques [*International Center for Training and Exchanges in the Geosciences*] (EAIO) .... CIFEG

Centre International pour la Terminologie des Sciences Sociales [*France*] (EAIO) .... CITSS

Centre International pour le Developpement [*International Center for Development*] [*French*] (AF) .... CID

Centre International pour le Reglement des Differends Relatifs aux Investissements [*International Center for Settlement of Investment Disputes*] .... CIRDI

Centre International pour les Etudes Chimiques [*International Center for Chemical Studies - ICCS*] (EAIO) .... CIEC

Centre International pour l'Etude de la Marionnette Traditionnelle [*International Center for Research on Traditional Marionettes*] .... CIPEMAT

Centre International Provisoire de Calcul .... CIPC

Centre Interuniversitaire d'Etudes Europeennes [*Interuniversity Centre for European Studies*] [*Canada*] .... CIEE

Centre Islamique pour le Developpement du Commerce [*Islamic Center for Development of Trade - ICDT*] [*Casablanca, Morocco*] (EAIO) .... CIDC

Centre Left [*Australian Labor Party*] [*Political party*] CL

Centre Marin, Shippagan, NB, Canada [*Library symbol Library of Congress*] (LCLS) .... CaNBShCM

Centre Marin, Shippagan, New Brunswick [*Library symbol National Library of Canada*] (NLC) .... NBSCM

Centre Meteorologique de Concentration et de Diffusion, French Air Force [*France ICAO location identifier*] (ICLI) .... LFYF

Centre Mondial d'Information sur l'Education Bilingue [*World Information Centre for Bilingual Education - WICBE*] (EAIO) .... CMIEB

Centre National de Documentation [*National Documentation Center*] [*Morocco*] [*Information service or system*] (IID) .... CND

Centre National de Documentation Pedagogique [*National Center for Pedagogical Documentation*] [*Ministry of Education*] [*Information service or system*] (IID) .... CNDP

Centre National de Documentation Scientifique et Technique [*National Scientific and Technical Documentation Center*] [*Royal Library of Belgium Belgium*] [*Information service or system*] (IID) .... CNDST

Centre National de la Recherche Scientifique [*France*] [*Marine science*] (OSRA) .... CNRS

Centre National de l'Information Chimique [*National Center for Chemical Information*] [*Information service or system*] (IID) .... CNIC

Centre National de Prevention et de Traitement des Intoxications [*National Poison Control Center*] [*Information service or system*] (IID) .... CNPTI

Centre National de Recherches Meteorologiques [*Toulouse, France*] [*Marine science*] (OSRA) .... CNRM

Centre National des Documents du Personnel [*National Personnel Records Center - NPRC*] .... CNDP

Centre National des Expositions et Concours Agricoles .... CENECA

Centre National des Independants [*National Center of Independents*] [*France Political party*] (PPE) .... CNI

Centre National des Independants et des Paysans [*National Centre of Independents and Peasants*] (EAIO) .... CNI

Centre National des Independants et des Paysans [*National Center of Independents and Peasants*] [*France Political party*] (PPW) .... CNIP

Centre National des Republicains Sociaux [*National Center of Social Republicans*] [*France Political party*] (PPE) .... CNRS

Centre National d'Etudes des Telecommunications [*France ICAO designator*] (FAAC) .... CNET

Centre National d'Etudes des Telecommunications [*France ICAO designator*] (FAAC) .... CNT

Centre National d'Etudes et d'Experimentation du Machinisme Agricole .... CNEEMA

Centre National d'Etudes Spatiales [*National Center for Space Studies*] [*France*] .... CNES

Centre National d'Information et de Recherche sur l'Aide Juridique [*National Legal Aid Research Centre*] [*Canada*] .... CNIRA

Centre of Advanced European Studies and Research [*Germany*] .... CAESAR

Centre of Christian Spirituality [*Australia*] .... CCS

Centre of Criminology, University of Toronto, Ontario [*Library symbol National Library of Canada*] (NLC) .... OTUCR

Centre of European Governmental Studies [*University of Edinburgh*] [*British*] (CB) .... CEGS

Centre of Films for Children and Young People [*British*] (DI) .... CFCYP

Centre of Forensic Sciences, Ontario Solicitor General, Toronto, ON, Canada [*Library symbol Library of Congress*] (LCLS) .... CaOTCF

Centre of Gravity Factor [*Yachting*] .... CGF

Centre of Indian Trade Unions .... CITU

Centre of Information Resource & Technology, Singapore [*Information service or system*] (IID) .... CIRTS

Centre of Latin American Studies [*University of Cambridge*] [*British*] (CB) .... CLAS

Centre of Management in Agriculture [*British*] (CB) .... CMA

Centre of Polish Research [*Institute of Comparative Civilizations*] [*Canada*] (IRC) .... CPR

Centre of South-East Asian Studies [*University of Hull*] [*British*] (CB) .... SEAS

Centre of West African Studies [*University of Birmingham*] [*British*] (CB) ..... CWAS

Centre on Environment for the Handicapped [*British*] (CB) .... CEH

Centre on Scientific and Technical Information [*Israel*] (NITA) .... COST

Centre pour Democratie et Progres [*Center for Democracy and Progress*] [*Later, Center of Social Democrats*] [*France*] [*Political party*] (PPE) .... CDP

Centre pour l'Avancement des Associations du Quebec (AC) .... CEPAQ

Centre pour le Developpement Industriel [*Centre for the Development of Industry*] (EAIO) .... CDI

Centre pour l'Independance des Magistrats et des Avocats [*Centre for the Independence of Judges and Lawyers - CIJL*] (EA) .... CIMA

Centre Quebecois de Relations Internationales [*Quebec Center for International Relations*] [*Canada*] (IRC) .... CQRI

Centre Quebecois des Sciences de l'Eau, Universite du Quebec, Quebec, Quebec [*Library symbol National Library of Canada*] (NLC) .... QQQE

Centre Quebecois du Droit de l'Environnement [*Quebec Environmental Law Centre*] (AC) .... CQDE

Centre Quebecois du PEN [*Poets, Playwrights, Editors, and Novelists*] International [*Canada*] (EAIO) .... CQPEN

Centre Regional Africain de Conception et de Fabrication Techniques [*African Regional Centre for Engineering Design and Manufacturing - ARCEDEM*] (EAIO) .... CRAFT

Centre Regional Africain de Technologie [*African Regional Centre for Technology - ARCT*] (EA) .... CRAT

Centre Regional de Documentation Pedagogique, Commission Scolaire de Le Gardeur, Repentigny, Quebec [*Library symbol National Library of Canada*] (BIB) .... QRECS

Centre Regional de Formation aux Techniques des Leves Aeriens [*Regional Center for Training in Aerial Surveys - RECTAS*] (EAIO) .... CRFTLA

Centre Regional de la Cote-Nord, Archives Nationales du Quebec, Sept-Iles, Quebec [*Library symbol National Library of Canada*] (BIB) .... QSIA

Centre Regional de l'Estrie, Archives Nationales du Quebec, Sherbooke, Quebec [*Library symbol National Library of Canada*] (NLC) .... QSHERAN

Centre Regional de l'Outaouais, Archives Nationales du Quebec, Hull, Quebec [*Library symbol National Library of Canada*] (BIB) .... QHQAR

Centre Regional de Montreal, Archives Nationales du Quebec, Quebec [*Library symbol National Library of Canada*] (NLC) .... QMQAR

Centre Rennais d'Information pour le Developpement et la Liberation des Peuples [*France*] .... CRIDEV

Centre Technique de Cooperation Agricole et Rural [*Technical Centre for Agricultural and Rural Cooperation*] (EAIO) .... CTA

Centre Technique des Industries de la Fonderie [*Database producer*] .... CTIF

Centre Technique International de l'Embouteillage [*International Technical Center of Bottling*] .... CETIE

Centre Terry Fox de la Jeunesse Canadienne [*Terry Fox Canadian Youth Centre*] .... CTFJC

Centre Universitaire de Shippagan, New Brunswick [*Library symbol National Library of Canada*] (NLC) .... NBSCU

Centre Universitaire de Shippagan, Shippagan, NB, Canada [*Library symbol Library of Congress*] (LCLS) .... CaNBSCU

Centre Universitaire Saint-Louis Maillet, Edmundston, New Brunswick [*Library symbol National Library of Canada*] (NLC) .... NBESLM

Centre Wellington District High School, Fergus, ON, Canada [*Library symbol*] [*Library of Congress*] (LCLS) .... CaOFerC

Centre Wellington District High School, Fergus, Ontario [*Library symbol National Library of Canada*] (NLC) .... OFERC

Centreboard Factor [*IOR*] .... CBF

Centred' Etudes de la Navigation Aerienne [*France*] (GAVI) .... CENA

Centreline Air Services Ltd. [*British ICAO designator*] (ICDA) .... HG

Centres Biblio-Culturels de Montreal-Nord, Quebec [*Library symbol National Library of Canada*] (NLC) .... QMN

[Les] Centres Jeunesse de Quebec (AC) .... CJQ

Centres of Excellence in Molecular and Interfacial Dynamics [*Research center*] (RCD) .... CEMAID

Centreville, AL [*Location identifier FAA*] (FAAL) .... CKL

Centreville, AL [*AM radio station call letters*] .... WBIB

Centreville, MS [*FM radio station call letters*] (RBYB) .... WPAE-FM

Centreville Public Library, Centreville, NF, Canada [*Library symbol Library of Congress*] (LCLS) .... CaNfCe

Centreville Public Library, Newfoundland [*Library symbol National Library of Canada*] (NLC) .... NFCE

Centreville Township Hospital, East St. Louis, IL [*Library symbol Library of Congress*] (LCLS) .... IEsCTH

Centrex Central Office [*Telecommunications*] (TEL) .... CTXCO

Centrex Customer [*Telecommunications*] (TEL) .... CTXCU

Centrex System Number [*Bell System*] [*Telecommunications*] (TEL) .... CTX

Centri Elettronici Reteconnessi Valutazione Elaborazione Dati [*Central Electronic Network for Data Processing and Analysis*] [*Information service or system*] (IID) .... CERVED

Centric Jaw Relationship [*Dentistry*] (DAVI) .... CJR

Centric Occlusion [*Dentistry*] .... CO

Centric Relation [*Dentistry*] .... CR

Centric Relation Occlusion [*Dentistry*] .... CRO

Centrifugal C

Centrifugal (KSC) .... CENT

Centrifugal .... CENTF

Centrifugal (MSA) .... CNTFGL

Centrifugal (AABC) .... CNTRF

Centrifugal [*Freight*] .... CNTRFUGL

Centrifugal Barrel Finishing [*of metal surfaces*] .... CBF

Centrifugal Charging Pump (IEEE) .... CCP

Centrifugal Coating CC

Centrifugal Countercurrent Chromatography CCCC

Centrifugal Electrostatic Focusing [*Engineering*] (IAA) .... CEF

Centrifugal Fast Analyzer [*Analytical chemistry*] .... CFA

Centrifugal Fault Display System .... CFDS
Centrifugal Fluidized Bed [*Chemical engineering*] .... CFB
Centrifugal Force .... CF
Centrifugal Liquid Extraction [*Chemistry*] .... CLE
Centrifugal Lockup Converter [*Automotive engineering*] CLC
Centrifugal Partition Chromatography .... CPC
Centrifugal Photosedimentation .... CP
Centrifugal Spray Deposition [*Steelmaking*] .... CSD
Centrifugal Spraying .... CS
Centrifugal Throwout [*Automotive engineering*] .... C/T
Centrifugal Urine Separator Assembly [*Aerospace*] (MCD) .... CUSA
Centrifugation Extractable Fluid .... CEF
Centrifugation Interaction CI
Centrifugation-Sugar Flotation [*Soil testing*] .... CSF
Centrifuge Moisture Equivalent .... CME
Centrifuge Plant Demonstration Facility [*Department of Energy*] .... CPDF
Centrilobular Emphysema [*Medicine*] (MAE) .... CLE
Centripetal Force .... CF
Centripetal Rub [*Medicine*] .... CPR
Centristas de Cataluna [*Political party Spain*] (EY) CC
Centro Academico da Democracia Crista [*Academic Center for Christian Democracy*] [*Portugal Political party*] (PPE) .... CADC
Centro Agronomico Tropical Investigacion y Ensenanza [*Tropical Agricultural Research and Training Center*] [*Turrialba, Costa Rica*] (EAIO) .... CATIE
Centro Anglo-Espanol (EA) .... CAE
Centro Argentino de Informacion Cientifica y Tecnologica [*Argentine Center for Scientific and Technological Information*] [*Information service or system*] (IID) .... CAICYT
Centro Calculo Sabadell [*Sabadell Computing Center*] [*Information service or system*] (IID) .... CCS
Centro Catolico Portugues [*Portuguese Catholic Center*] [*Political party*] (PPE) .... CCP
Centro Coordinador de Proyectos Ecumenicos [*Promotes exchanges between Mexico, US, and Canada*] (CROSS) .... CECOPE
Centro de Analisis e Investigacion Economica [*Participant in the Inter-American Bank Research Network*] [*Mexico*] (CROSS) .... CAIE
Centro de Apoyo para Mujeres Violadas [*An association Mexico*] (EAIO) .... CAMVAC
Centro de Arte y Communicacion [*Center of Art and Communication*] [*Argentina*] (EAIO) .... CAYC
Centro de Calculo Electronico Universidad Nacional Autonoma de Mexico [*National Autonomous University of Mexico, Data Processing Center*] [*Mexico*] .... CCE
Centro de Comercio Internacional [*International Trade Center - ITC*] [*Spanish*] CCI
Centro de Documentacao Cientifica e Tecnica [*Scientific and Technical Documentation Center*] [*Portugal*] [*Information service or system*] (IID) .... CDCT
Centro de Encuentros y Dialogos [*Member of RMALC*] (CROSS) .... CED
Centro de Epidemiologia Molecular, Network for Epidemiologic Tracking [*An international alliance of hospitals that track drug resistance*] .... CEM/NET
Centro de Esploro kaj Dokumentado pri la Monda Lingvo-Problemo [*Center for Research and Documentation on International Language Problems*] (EAIO) .... CED
Centro de Estudios Democraticos de America Latina .... CEDAL
Centro de Estudios Economicos y Sociales del Tercer Mundo [*Center for Economic and Social Studies of the Third World*] [*Canada*] .... CEESTEM
Centro de Estudios Estrategicos [*Center for Strategic Studies*] [*Mexico*] (CROSS) .... CEE
Centro de Estudios Interplanetarios [*Spain*] (EAIO) .... CEI
Centro de Estudios Monetarios Latinoamericanos [*Center for Latin American Monetary Studies*] [*Mexico City, Mexico*] (EAIO) .... CEMLA
Centro de Estudios para el Cambio del campo en Mexico [*A Mexican think tank which works on policies and training for growers*] (CROSS) .... CECCAM
Centro de Estudios Puertorriquenos, New York, NY [*Library symbol Library of Congress*] (LCLS) .... NNCEP
Centro de Estudios Puertorriquenos, New York, NY [*OCLC symbol*] (OCLC) .... VXY
Centro de Estudos Franciscanos e Pastorais para a America Latina .... CEFEPAL
Centro de Informacao e Documentacao Amilcar Cabral [*Portugal*] .... CIDAC
Centro de Informacion Cientifica y Humanistica [*Center for Scientific and Humanistic Information*] [*Mexico*] [*Information service or system*] (IID) .... CICH
Centro de Informacion de Medicamentos [*Spanish Drug Information Center*] [*Information service or system*] (IID) .... CINIME
Centro de Informacion, Documentacion, y Analisis Latinoamericano .... CIDAL
Centro de Informacion Tecnica [*Technical Information Center*] [*University of Puerto Rico*] [*Information service or system*] (IID) .... CIT
Centro de Informacion y Solidaridad con el Paraguay [*Switzerland*] .... CISP
Centro de Informacoes Nucleares [*Center for Nuclear Information*] [*Brazil*] [*Information service or system*] (IID) .... CIN
Centro de Informativo y Documentacion [*Press agency*] [*Argentina*] .... CID
Centro de Investigacion Laboral y Asesoria Sindical [*Member of RMALC*] [*Mexico*] (CROSS) .... CILAS
Centro de Investigacion para el Desarrollo [*Mexican government funded political and economic research center*] (CROSS) .... CIDAC
Centro de Investigacion y de Estudios Avanzados, Instituto Politecnico Nacional,Mexico City, Mexico [*Library symbol Library of Congress*] (LCLS) .... MxMC
Centro de Investigacion y Docencia Economica [*Institute which focuses on Mexica n/US relations*] (CROSS) .... CIDE
Centro de Investigaciones sobre Estados Unidos de America [*Mexico/US relations*] [*Member of UNAM*] (CROSS) .... CISEUA
Centro de las Naciones Unidas para los Asentamientos Humanos [*United Nations Centre for Human Settlements*] [*Spanish*] (DUND) .... CNUAH
Centro de Utilizacion y Promocion de Productos Forestales [*Forestry project*] [*Honduras*] .... CUPRFOR
Centro Democratico de Macau [*Macao Democratic Center*] (PPW) .... CDM
Centro Democratico y Social [*Democratic and Social Center*] [*Spain Political party*] (PPE) .... CDS
Centro di Azione e Documentazione sull'America Latina .... CADAL
Centro di Documentazione Umberto Nobile, Museo Storico, Rome, Italy [*Library symbol*] [*Library of Congress*] (LCLS) .... ItRUN
Centro di Riferimento Italiano DIANE [*Italian Reference Center for EURONET DIANE*] [*National Research Council*] [*Information service or system*] (IID) .... CRID
Centro di Studi Nucleari Enrico Fermi [*Nuclear Engineering Institute - Enrico Fermi Nuclear Center*] [*Italy*] (NRCH) .... CESNEF
Centro Economico Italia Africa [*Italian-African Economic Center*] (AF) .... CEIA
Centro Filatelico Internazionale .... CFI
Centro Gerontologico Latino [*An association*] (EA) .... CGL
Centro Hispano Catolico [*Catholic Spanish Center*] (EA) .... CHC
Centro Interamericano de Administracion del Trabajo [*Inter-American Center for Labor Administration*] [*Lima, Peru*] (EAIO) .... CIAT
Centro Interamericano de Administradores Tributarios [*Inter-American Center of Tax Administrators*] (EAIO) .... CIAT
Centro Interamericano de Documentacion e Informacion Agricola [*Inter-American Center for Documentation and Agricultural Information*] [*Inter-American Institute for Cooperation on Agriculture*] [*Information service or system*] (IID) .... CIDIA
Centro Interamericano de Ensenanza de Estadistica .... CIENES
Centro Interamericano de Fotointerpretacion [*Bogota, Colombia*] .... CIAF
Centro Interamericano de Investigacion y Documentacion sobre Formacion Profesional [*Inter-American Centre for Research and Documentation on Vocational Training - IACRDVT*] (EAIO) .... CINTERFOR
Centro Interamericano de Libros Academicos [*Inter-American Scholarly Book Center*] .... CILA
Centro Interamericano de Promocion de Exportaciones [*Inter-American Export Promotion Center*] .... CIPE
Centro Interamericano de Vivienda .... CINVA
Centro Interamericano para el Desarrollo Regional [*Inter-American Center for Regional Development*] [*Venezuela*] (EAIO) .... CINDER
Centro Intercultural de Documentacion [*Center for Intercultural Documentation*] [*Cuernavaca, Mexico*] .... CIDOC
Centro Internacional de Agricultura Tropical [*International Center for Tropical Agriculture*] [*Colombia*] .... CIAT
Centro Internacional de Arreglo de Diferencias Relativas a Inversiones [*International Center for Settlement of Investment Disputes*] .... CIADI
Centro Internacional de Educacion y Desarrollo [*Venezuela*] .... CIED
Centro Internacional de Estudios Superiores de Periodisma para America Latina [*Press agency*] [*Ecuador*] .... CIESPAL
Centro Internacional de Formacion en Ciencias Ambientales para Paises de Habla Espanol [*International Center for the Preparation of Personnel in Environmental Sciences in Spanish-Speaking Countries*] [*Spain*] .... CIFCA
Centro Internacional de Informacion Economica .... CIDIE
Centro Internacional de Informacion sobre Seguridad e Higiene del Trabajo [*International Occupational Safety and Health Information Center*] [*Spain*] .... CIS
Centro Internacional de Investigaciones sobre el Cancer [*International Agency for Research on Cancer*] CIIC
Centro Internacional de la Infancia [*International Children's Center*] CII
Centro Internacional de la Papa [*International Potato Center*] [*ICSU*] (EAIO).... CIP
Centro Internacional de Mejoramiento de Maiz y Trigo [*International Maize and Wheat Improvement Center*] [*ICSU*] (EAIO) .... CIMMYT
Centro Internazionale di Fisica Teorica [*International Center for Theoretical Physics - ICTP*] (EAIO) .... CIFT
Centro Internazionale di Studi sui Trasporti [*International Center for Transportation Studies - ICTS*] (EAIO) .... CIST
Centro Internazionale di Studi sull'Economia Turistica [*International Center of Studies on the Tourist Economy*] [*University of Venice*] [*Italy*] .... CISET
Centro Internazionale Radio-Medico [*International Radio Medical Center; gives emergency medical advice to ships at sea*] .... CIRM
Centro Latinoamericana de Demografia [*Latin American Demographic Center*] [*Economic Commission for Latin America and the Caribbean Chile*] [*United Nations*] .... CELADE
Centro Latinoamericano de Administracion para el Desarrollo [*Latin American Center for Development Administration*] [*Research center Venezuela*] (IRC) .... CLAD
Centro Latinoamericano de Ciencias Biologicas [*Latin American Center of Biological Sciences*] [*Research center Venezuela*] (IRC) .... CLAB
Centro Latinoamericano de Documentacion Economica y Social [*Latin American Center for Economic and Social Documentation*] [*Economic Commission for Latin America and the Caribbean*] [*United Nations*] [*Information service or system*] (IID) .... CLADES
Centro Latinoamericano de Quimica [*Latin American Center for Chemistry*] (PDAA) .... CLAQ
Centro Nacional de Desenvolvimento do Gerenciamento da Informacao [*National Center for Information Management Development*] [*Brazil Information service or system*] (IID) .... CENADEM
Centro Nacional de Informacao Documental Agricola [*National Center for Agricultural Documentary Information*] [*Ministry of Agriculture Brazil*] [*Information service or system*] (IID) .... CENAGRI
Centro Nacional de Informacion y Documentacion [*National Center for Information and Documentation*] [*Chile*] [*Information service or system*].... CENID
Centro Nacional de Informacion y Documentacion [*National Information and Documentation Center*] [*Ministry of Labour*] [*Information service or system*] (IID) .... CNID
Centro Nacional de Informacion y Documentacion en Salud [*National Center for Health Information and Documentation*] [*Mexico*] [*Information service or system*] (IID) .... CENIDS

Centro Nacional de Informaciones [*National Information Center*] [*Supersedes DINA Chile*] .... CNI
Centro Nacional de Microfilm, Madrid, Spain [*Library symbol Library of Congress*] (LCLS) .... CnM
Centro Nacionalista [*Nationalist Center*] [*Bolivia*] [*Political party*] (PPW) .... CEN
Centro Nazionale Universitario di Calcalo Electronico [*National University Center for Electronic Calculation*] [*Italy*] (NITA) .... CNUCE
Centro Panamericano de Estudios e Investigaciones Geograficas [*Pan American Center for Geographical Studies and Research - PACGSR*] (EAIO) .... CEPEIGE
Centro Panamericano de Fiebre Aftosa [*South American Commission for the Control of Foot-and-Mouth Disease*] (EAIO) .... COSALFA
Centro Panamericano de Ingenieria Sanitaria y Ciencias del Ambiente [*Pan American Center for Sanitary Engineering and Environmental Sciences*] [*Peru*] [*Research center*] (IRC) .... CEPIS
Centro para la Independencia de Jueces y Abogados [*Switzerland*] .... CIJA
Centro Regional de Educacion de Adultos y Alfabetizacion Funcional para America Latina [*Regional Center for Adult Education and Functional Literacy for Latin America*] [*Mexico*] (EAIO) .... CREFAL
Centro Regional de Sismologia para America del Sur [*Regional Seismology Center for South America*] [*Peru*] [*Research center*] (IRC) .... CERESIS
Centro Regional de Sismologia para America del Sur [*Regional Center for Seismology for South America - RCSSA*] (EAIO) .... CRSAS
Centro Regional para el Fomento del Libro en America Latina .... CERLAL
Centro Regional para la Educacion Superior en America Latina y el Caribe [*Regional Center for Higher Education in Latin America and the Caribbean-Venezuela*] [*United Nations*] (IID) .... CRESALC
Centro Ricerche Interdisciplinari sul Suicidio [*Interdisciplinary Research Center on Suicide*] [*Italy*] (EAIO) .... CRIS
Centro Studi Politica Economica [*of the Italian Communist Party*] .... CESPE
Centro Studi Terzo Mondo [*Study Center for the Third World*] [*Italy*] (EAIO) .... CSTM
Centro Televisivo Vaticano [*Vatican Television Center*] [*1984*] .... CTV
Centroblastic/Centrocytic [*Biochemistry*] .... CB-CC
Centroid Moment Tensor Solutions [*A publication*] .... CMTS
Centroid-Moment Tensor [*Seismology*] .... CMT
Centrolateral [*Nucleus of thalamus*] [*Neuroanatomy*] CL
Centromere Protein (DMAA) .... CENP
Centromeric Indices [*Chromosomes*] CI
Centrum Partii [*Center Party*] [*Netherlands Political party*] (EY) .... CP
Centrum voor de Studie van het Onderwijs in Ontwikkelingslanden [*Centre for Study of Education in Developing Countries*] [*Netherlands*] (EAIO) .... CESO
Centrum voor Informatie Beleid [*Netherlands Center for Information Policy*] [*The Hague*] [*Information service or system*] (IID) .... CIB
Centrum voor Informatie en Documentatie [*Center for Information and Documentation*] [*Netherlands Organization for Applied Scientific Research Delft*] [*Information service or system*] (IID) .... CID
Centrum voor Landbouwpublikaties en Landbouwdocumentatie [*Center for Agricultural Publishing and Documentation*] [*Ministry of Agriculture and Fisheries*] [*Information service or system*] (IID) .... PUDOC
Centrum voor Postoraal in Europa [*Centre for Pastoral Work in Europe*] (EAIO) .... CPE
Centrum-Demokraterne [*Center Democrats*] [*Denmark Political party*] (PPE) ..... CD
Cents per Available Seat Statute Mile [*Aviation*] .... C/ASSM
Cents per Kilometer (ADA) .... CPK
Cents Per Litre .... cpl
Cents per Share (ODBW) .... CPS
Cents-Off Coupon [*Advertising*] .... C/O
Centum [*Hundred*] C
Centum [*Hundred*] .... CENT
Centum [*Hundred*] .... CT
Centum Call-Seconds [*Telecommunications*] (PCM) .... CCS
Centum Milia [*One Hundred Thousand*] [*Latin*] C
Centum Weight [*Hundredweight*] [*Latin*] (GPO) .... CWT
Centura Banks [*NYSE symbol*] (SPSG) .... CBC
Centura Banks [*Associated Press*] (SAG) .... CentBk
Centura Software Corp. [*Associated Press*] (SAG) .... CenturaSft
Centura Software Corp. [*NASDAQ symbol*] (SAG) .... CNTR
Centuries CC
Centurion COLIDAR [*Coherent Light Detecting and Ranging*] System .... CCS
Centurion Gold Ltd. [*Vancouver Stock Exchange symbol Toronto Stock Exchange symbol*] .... CEU
Centurion LASER Range-Finder .... CLR
Centurion Mines [*NASDAQ symbol*] (SAG) .... CTMC
Centurion Mines Corp. [*Associated Press*] (SAG) .... CntMne
Century C
Century (VRA) c
Century .... CEN
Century .... CEN
Century .... CENT
Century (BARN) .... centy
Century Airlines [*ICAO designator*] (AD) .... QX
Century Aluminum [*NASDAQ symbol*] (TTSB) .... CENX
Century Aluminum Co. [*Associated Press*] (SAG) .... CentAl
Century Aluminum Co. [*NASDAQ symbol*] (SAG) .... CENX
Century Association, New York, NY [*Library symbol Library of Congress*] (LCLS) .... NNCenC
Century Aviation International Ltd. [*Canada*] [*FAA designator*] (FAAC) .... HAI
Century Aviation, SA de CV [*Mexico*] [*FAA designator*] (FAAC) .... URY
Century BanCorp, Inc. [*NASDAQ symbol*] (NQ) .... CNBK
Century Bancorp, Inc. [*Associated Press*] (SAG) .... CntyBc
Century Bancorp(MA) [*NASDAQ symbol*] (TTSB) .... CNBKA
Century Bible [*A publication*] .... CB
Century Bible [*A publication*] (BJA) .... CentB
Century Casinos [*NASDAQ symbol*] (TTSB) .... CNTY

Century Casinos, Inc. [*Associated Press*] (SAG) .... CentC
Century Casinos, Inc. [*Associated Press*] (SAG) .... CentCas
Century Casinos, Inc. [*NASDAQ symbol*] (SAG) .... CNTY
Century Casinos Wrrt [*NASDAQ symbol*] (TTSB) .... CNTYW
Century Communic'ns'A' [*NASDAQ symbol*] (TTSB) .... CTYA
Century Dictionary [*A publication*] (ROG) .... CD
Century Dictionary [*A publication*] (DLA) .... Cent Dict
Century Dictionary and Cyclopedia [*A publication*] (DLA) .... Cent Dict and Cyc
Century Dictionary and Encyclopedia [*A publication*] (DLA) .... Cent Dict & Ency
Century Edition of the American Digest System (West) [*A publication*] (DLA) .... CD
Century Edition of the American Digest System (West) [*A publication*] (DLA) .... Cent Dig
Century Financial Corp. [*Associated Press*] (SAG) .... CentFin
Century Financial Corp. [*NASDAQ symbol*] (SAG) .... CYFN
Century, FL [*FM radio station call letters*] .... WKGT
Century, FL [*FM radio station call letters*] (RBYB) .... WPFL-FM
Century Hutchinson [*Publisher*] [*British*] .... CH
Century Minerals and Mining [*Australia*] .... CMM
[A] Century of Excavation in Palestine [*A publication*] (BJA) .... CEP
[A] Century of Humorous Verse [*A publication*] .... CenHV
[A] Century of Lyrics [*A publication*] .... CenL
Century Publishing Co. .... CPC
Century Research Center Corp. [*Information service or system*] (IID) .... CRC
Century South Banks [*NASDAQ symbol*] (TTSB) .... CSBI
Century South Banks, Inc. [*NASDAQ symbol*] (SAG) .... CSBI
Century South Banks, Inc. [*Associated Press*] (SAG) .... CtrySo
Century Sports Network .... CSN
Century Stand [*Filmmaking*] (WDMC) .... C-stand
Century Tel Enterp [*NYSE symbol*] (TTSB) .... CTL
Century Telecommunications [*Associated Press*] (SAG) .... CntyCm
Century Telecommunications [*NASDAQ symbol*] (SAG) .... CTYA
Century Telephone Co. [*Associated Press*] (SAG) .... CntyTl
Century Telephone Enterprises, Inc. [*NYSE symbol*] (SPSG) .... CTL
Century Village, Lang, ON, Canada [*Library symbol*] [*Library of Congress*] (LCLS) .... CaOLgCV
Century Village, Lang, Ontario [*Library symbol National Library of Canada*] (BIB) .... OLCV
Centus [*Constellation*] .... Cet
Centus [*Constellation*] .... Ceti
Cephalic (ROG) .... CEPH
Cephalic Artery .... CA
Cephalic Index CI
Cephalic Sinus .... CS
Cephalic Vasomotor Response [*Medicine*] (DMAA) .... CVR
Cephalic-Phase Insulin Release [*Medicine*] (DMAA) .... CPIR
Cephalin Cholesterol Antigen [*Immunochemistry*] .... CCA
Cephalin Flocculation [*Clinical chemistry*] (AAMN) .... CEPH-FLOC
Cephalin-Cholesterol Flocculation [*Clinical chemistry*] .... CCF
Cephalo Pedal Sinus .... CPS
Cephalo-Facial Deformity [*Medicine*] (DMAA) .... CFD
Cephalon, Inc. [*NASDAQ symbol*] (SPSG) .... CEPH
Cephalon, Inc. [*Associated Press*] (SAG) .... Cephln
Cephalopelvic Disproportion [*Gynecology*] .... CPD
Cephalosporin [*Pharmacology*] (DAVI) .... CEPH
Cephalosporium gramineum [*Plant pathology*] .... Cg
Cephalosporium Stripe [*of wheat*] [*Plant pathology*] .... Cs
Cephalothin [*Medicine*] (CPH) .... CF
Cepheus [*Constellation*] .... Cep
Cepheus [*Constellation*] .... Ceph
Cepi Corpus [*Latin Legal term*] (DLA) CC
Cepi Corpus [*I Have Taken the Body*] [*Latin Legal term*] (DLA) .... CE C
Cepi Corpus and Bail Bond [*Legal term*] (DLA) .... CC & BB
Cepi Corpus and Committitur [*Legal term*] (ILCA) .... CC & C
Cepu/Ngloram [*Indonesia*] [*ICAO location identifier*] (ICLI) .... WRSC
Ceradyne, Inc. [*Associated Press*] (SAG) .... Cerdyn
Ceradyne, Inc. [*NASDAQ symbol*] (NQ) .... CRDN
Ceramic (MSA) .... CER
Ceramic (ROG) .... CERAM
Ceramic .... CRMC
Ceramic and Allied Trade Union [*British*] (DCTA) .... CATU
Ceramic and Alloy [*NASA*] .... CERAMAL
Ceramic and Graphite Information Center [*Air Force*] (MCD) .... C & G
Ceramic Arts Federation International (EA) .... CAFI
Ceramic Audio Tone Transducer (PDAA) .... CATT
Ceramic Awareness Bulletin [*Defense Ceramic Information Center*] [*A publication*] .... CAB
Ceramic Beam Pentode .... CBP
Ceramic Capacitor (IAA) CC
Ceramic Chip Carrier C3
Ceramic Delay Line .... CDL
Ceramic DIP [*Dual In-line Package*] (CDE) .... CERDIP
Ceramic Disk Capacitor .... CDC
Ceramic Dual In-Line Package .... CER-DIP
Ceramic Educational Council (EA) .... CEC
Ceramic Engineer .... Cer E
Ceramic Fiber Optics .... CFO
Ceramic Foam Insulation .... CFI
Ceramic [*or Clear*] Glazed Structural Facing Units [*Technical drawings*] .... CGSFU
Ceramic [*or Clear*] Glazed Structural Unit Base [*Technical drawings*] .... CGSUB
Ceramic Glazed Unit [*Technical drawings*] .... CGU
Ceramic Gold Coating .... CGC
Ceramic Gravitational Containment Vessel [*i.e., cup*] [*Slang*] .... CGCV
Ceramic Hotform Die (MCD) .... CHFD
Ceramic Insulated Wire .... CIW

Ceramic Leaded Chip Carrier (NITA) ... CLCC
Ceramic Manufacturers' Association of Australia ... CMAA
Ceramic Manufacturers' Association of New South Wales [*Australia*] ... CMANSW
Ceramic Matrix Composite [*Materials science*] ... CMC
Ceramic Metal Element [*NASA*] ... CERMET
Ceramic Metal Fuel [*NASA*] (IAA) ... CERMET
Ceramic Metal Terminal [*NASA*] (IAA) ... CERAMETERM
Ceramic Mosaic Tile [*Technical drawings*] ... CMT
Ceramic Oceanographic Buoy ... COB
Ceramic Package [*NASA*] (IAA) ... CERPACK
Ceramic Planar Tube ... CPT
Ceramic Printed Circuit (IAA) ... CPC
Ceramic Refraction Coating ... CRC
Ceramic Reusable Surface Insulation (NASA) ... CRSI
Ceramic Silicone Foam [*Chemistry*] ... CSF
Ceramic Tile [*Technical drawings*] ... CT
Ceramic Tile Contractors & Industry Association of British Columbia (AC) ... CTCIA
Ceramic Tile Distributors Association (EA) ... CTDA
Ceramic Tile Institute of America (EA) ... CTIOA
Ceramic Tile Marketing Federation [*Defunct*] (EA) ... CTMF
Ceramic Tube Fabrication ... CTF
Ceramic Vacuum Relay ... CVR
Ceramic-Based Microcircuit ... CBM
Ceramic-Heated Tunnel [*Langley Research Center*] ... CHT
Ceramics (VRA) ... cer
Ceramics Advanced Manufacturing Development Engineering Center [*Defunct*] (EA) ... CAMDEC
Ceramics and Graphite Branch [*Air Force*] ... CGB
Ceramics and Graphite Information Center [*Air Force*] ... CGIC
Ceramics Applications in Reciprocating Engines [*Research group*] [*British*] ... CARE
Ceramics Distributors of America (EA) ... CDA
Ceramics, Glass, and Solid State Science Division [*National Institute of Standards and Technology*] (GRD) ... CGSS
Ceramics Industry Training Organisation [*British*] (AIE) ... CITO
Ceramics Information Analysis Center (IID) ... CIAC
Ceramics International Association [*Defunct*] (EA) ... CIA
Ceramics Monthly [*A publication*] (BRI) ... Ceram Mo
Ceramic-Tile Base [*Technical drawings*] ... CTB
Ceramic-Tile Floor [*Technical drawings*] ... CTF
Ceramic-to-Metal Seal ... CERMET
Ceramic-to-Metal Seal ... CTMS
Ceramic-Wafer Printed Circuit ... CPC
Ceramide [*Biochemistry*] ... Cer
Ceramide Activated Protein Phosphatase [*An enzyme*] ... CAPP
Ceramide Dihexoside [*Biochemistry*] ... CDH
Ceramide Monohexoside [*Biochemistry*] ... CMH
Ceramide Trihexosides [*Biochemistry*] ... CTH
Ceramide-Activated Protein [*Biochemistry*] ... CAP
Ceratobasidium Anastomosis Group [*Phytopathology*] ... CAG
Ceratum [*Wax Ointment*] [*Pharmacy*] ... CERAT
CERBCO, Inc. [*NASDAQ symbol*] (NQ) ... CERB
Cerbco, Inc. [*Associated Press*] (SAG) ... Cerbco
Cercarienhullen Reaktion [*Medicine*] ... CHR
CERCLA [*Comprehensive Environmental Response, Compensation, and Liability Act*] **Enforcement Division** [*Environmental Protection Agency*] (GFGA) ... CED
CERCLA Information System ... CERCLIS
Cercle Culturel Camerounais ... CCC
Cercle de la Finance Internationale de Montreal (AC) ... CEFIM
Cercle Populaire Europeen [*European Popular Circle - EPC*] (EAIO) ... CPE
Cercle pour le Renoveau et le Progres [*Gabon*] [*Political party*] (EY) ... CRP
Cerdas [*Bolivia*] [*ICAO location identifier*] (ICLI) ... SLCS
Cereal Agar ... CER
Cereal Chlorotic Mottle Virus [*Plant pathology*] ... CECMV
Cereal Cyst Nematode [*Medicine*] ... CCN
Cereal Institute [*Defunct*] (EA) ... CI
Cereal Municipal Library, Alberta [*Library symbol National Library of Canada*] (NLC) ... ACERM
Cereal Municipal Library, Cereal, AB, Canada [*Library symbol Library of Congress*] (LCLS) ... CaACerM
Cereal Rust Laboratory [*Department of Agriculture*] (GRD) ... CRL
Cereal Ryegrowers' Association [*Australia*] ... CRA
Cereal Tillering Disease Virus [*Plant pathology*] ... CTDV
Cerebellar Model Articulation Control [*System*] [*National Institute of Standards and Technology*] ... CMAC
Cerebellar Purkinje Cell [*Medicine*] (DMAA) ... CPC
Cerebellopontine [*Anatomy*] (AAMN) ... CP
Cerebellopontine Angle [*Brain anatomy*] ... CPA
Cerebellum [*Brain anatomy*] ... CB
Cerebral Amyloid Angiopathy [*Medicine*] ... CAA
Cerebral Aqueduct [*Brain anatomy*] ... CA
Cerebral Arteriosclerosis [*Medicine*] (MAE) ... CAS
Cerebral Autosomal Dominant Arteriopathy with Subcortical Infarcts and Leukoencephalopathy [*Medicine*] ... CADASIL
Cerebral Blood Flow [*Medicine*] ... CBF
Cerebral Blood Flow Autoregulation ... CBFA
Cerebral Blood Flow Laboratories [*Research center*] (RCD) ... CBF Labs
Cerebral Blood Flow Studies [*Cardiology*] (DAVI) ... CBFS
Cerebral Blood Flow Velocity [*Cardiology*] (DAVI) ... CBFV
Cerebral Commissure [*Brain anatomy*] ... CC
Cerebral Cortex Perfusion Rate [*Medicine*] (MAE) ... CPR
Cerebral Edema [*Medicine*] (CPH) ... CE
Cerebral Function Monitor (PDAA) ... CFM
Cerebral Ganglion [*Medicine*] ... CG
Cerebral Glucose Oxygen Quotient [*Medicine*] (MAE) ... CG/OQ
Cerebral Infarction [*Medicine*] ... CI
Cerebral Lipidosis [*Medicine*] (AAMN) ... CLIP
Cerebral Malaria [*Medicine*] ... CM
Cerebral Metabolic Rate [*Medicine*] ... CMR
Cerebral Metabolic Rate for Oxygen ... $CMRO_2$
Cerebral Metabolic Rate of Glucose [*Also, CMRglc*] [*Biochemistry*] ... CMRG
Cerebral Metabolic Rate of Glucose [*Also, CMRG*] [*Biochemistry*] ... CMRglc
Cerebral Metabolic Rate of Lactate [*Medicine*] (DMAA) ... CMRI
Cerebral Metabolic Rate of Oxygen [*Biochemistry*] (DAVI) ... CMRO
Cerebral Motor Dysfunction [*Medicine*] ... CMD
Cerebral Palsy [*Medicine*] ... CP
Cerebral Palsy Association of Quebec, Inc., Quebec, PQ, Canada [*Library symbol Library of Congress*] (LCLS) ... CaQQAPC
Cerebral Palsy Association of Quebec, Inc. [*L'Association de Paralysie Cerebrale du Quebec, Inc.*] **Quebec, Quebec** [*Library symbol National Library of Canada*] (NLC) ... QQAPC
Cerebral Palsy Clinic ... CPC
Cerebral Palsy International Sports and Recreation Association [*Arnhem, Netherlands*] (EAIO) ... CPISRA
Cerebral Palsy Ireland (EAIO) ... CPI
Cerebral Palsy Sports Association of British Columbia (AC) ... CPSA-BC
Cerebral Peduncle [*Brain anatomy*] ... CP
Cerebral Performance Category ... CPC
Cerebral Perfusion Pressure [*Medicine*] ... CPP
Cerebral Ridge [*Medicine*] ... CR
Cerebral Subarachnoid Venous Pressure [*Medicine*] (DMAA) ... CSAVP
Cerebral Thrombosis [*Medicine*] ... CT
Cerebral Tissue Perfusion Pressure [*Medicine*] (DMAA) ... CTPP
Cerebral Tumor [*Medicine*] ... CT
Cerebral Vascular Profile Study [*Cardiology*] (DAVI) ... C-Vasc
Cerebral Venous Sinus Thrombosis [*Medicine*] ... CVST
Cerebral-Pedal Regulator [*Neurobiology*] ... CPR
Cerebriform Intradermal Nevus [*Medicine*] (AAMN) ... CIN
Cerebro-Buccal Commissure [*Medicine*] ... CBC
Cerebrocostomandibular Syndrome [*Medicine*] (DMAA) ... CCM
Cerebrohepatorenal Syndrome [*Medicine*] ... CHRS
Cerebro-Oculo-Facial-Skeletal Syndrome [*Medicine*] (DMAA) ... COFS
Cerebrooculomuscular Syndrome [*Medicine*] (DMAA) ... COMS
Cerebro-Pedal Commissure [*Medicine*] ... CPC
Cerebropontine [*Angle*] [*Neurosurgery*] (DAVI) ... CP
Cerebrospinal [*Medicine*] ... CS
Cerebrospinal Fluid [*Medicine*] (AAMN) ... C
Cerebrospinal Fluid [*Medicine*] ... CSF
Cerebrospinal Fluid Leukocyte Particle Counter [*Instrumentation*] ... CSFLpc
Cerebrospinal Fluid Pressure [*Medicine*] (AAMN) ... CSFP
Cerebrospinal Fluid Protein [*Biochemistry*] (DAVI) ... CFP
Cerebrospinal Fluid-Wassermann Reaction [*Medicine*] (AAMN) ... CSF-WR
Cerebrospinal Meningitis [*Medicine*] ... CSM
Cerebrotendinous Xanthomatosis [*Medicine*] ... CTX
Cerebrovascular [*Medicine*] ... CV
Cerebrovascular Accident [*Medicine*] ... CVA
Cerebrovascular Amyloid [*Medicine*] ... CA
Cerebrovascular Disease [*Medicine*] (DMAA) ... CBVD
Cerebrovascular Disease [*Neurology and psychiatry*] (DAVI) ... CVD
Cerebrovascular Episode [*Medicine*] (CPH) ... CVE
Cerebrovascular Insufficiency [*Medicine*] ... CVI
Cerebrovascular Obstructive Disease (MAE) ... CVOD
Cerebrovascular Profile [*Cardiology*] (DAVI) ... CVP
Cerebrovascular Resistance [*Medicine*] ... CVR
Ceremony ... CRMNY
Ceremony of Installation [*Freemasonry*] (ROG) ... C of I
Cereolus [*An urethral bougie*] [*Pharmacy*] ... CEREOL
Ceres [*South Africa*] [*Seismograph station code, US Geological Survey*] (SEIS) ... CER
Ceres [*Argentina ICAO location identifier*] (ICLI) ... SANW
Ceres, CA [*FM radio station call letters*] ... KBES
Ceres, CA [*TV station call letters*] (RBYB) ... KBSV-TV
Ceres, CA [*AM radio station call letters*] ... KLOC
Ceric Ammonium Nitrate [*Inorganic chemistry*] ... CAN
Ceridian Corp. [*Formerly, Control Data Corp.*] [*NYSE symbol*] (SPSG) ... CEN
Ceridian Corp. [*Associated Press*] (SAG) ... Ceridian
Ceridian Corp. [*Associated Press*] (SAG) ... Ceridn
Ceridian Cp Cv Ex Dep Pfd [*NYSE symbol*] (TTSB) ... CENPr
Cerion Technologies, Inc. [*NASDAQ symbol*] (SAG) ... CEON
Cerion Technologies, Inc. [*Associated Press*] (SAG) ... CerionT
Cerise [*Philately*] ... cer
Cerium [*Chemical element*] ... Ce
Cerium Magnesium Nitrate [*Inorganic chemistry*] ... CMN
Cerknica [*Yugoslavia*] [*Seismograph station code, US Geological Survey*] (SEIS) ... CEY
CERMET [*Ceramic Metal Element*] **Hybrid Integrated Circuit** ... CHIC
CERMET [*Ceramic Metal Element*] **Resistor Network** ... CRN
CERN [*Conseil European pour la Recherche Nucleaire*]-Dortmund-Heidelberg-Saclay Collaboration ... CDHS
CERN [*Conseil Europeen pour la Recherche Nucleaire*] **Linear Collider** [*Particle physics*] ... CLIC
Cerner Corp. [*NASDAQ symbol*] (NQ) ... CERN
Cerner Corp. [*Associated Press*] (SAG) ... Cerner
Cerplex Group [*Associated Press*] (SAG) ... Cerplex
Cerplex Group [*NASDAQ symbol*] (SAG) ... CPLX
Cerprobe Corp. [*Associated Press*] (SAG) ... Cerprbe
Cerprobe Corp. [*NASDAQ symbol*] (NQ) ... CRPB
Cerrada ... CER

Cerre Les Noroy [*France*] [*Seismograph station code, US Geological Survey Closed*] (SEIS) .... CNF
Cerritos Junior College, Artesia, CA [*Library symbol Library of Congress*] (LCLS) .... CArtC
Cerro Catedral [*Argentina ICAO location identifier*] (ICLI) .... SAZK
Cerro De Punta [*Puerto Rico*] [*Seismograph station code, US Geological Survey*] (SEIS) .... CDP
Cerro Del Durzno [*New Mexico*] [*Seismograph station code, US Geological Survey*] (SEIS) .... CDN
Cerro La Pandura [*Puerto Rico*] [*Seismograph station code, US Geological Survey*] (SEIS) .... CPD
Cerro Sombrero [*Chile*] [*Airport symbol*] (AD) .... SMB
Cerro Tololo Interamerican Observatory [*Astronomy*] .... CTIO
Cerro-Negro [*Argentina*] [*Seismograph station code, US Geological Survey*] (SEIS) .... CEN
Cerro-Tololo Inter-American Observatory [*Chile*] [*National Science Foundation*] .... CTIO
Certain (ROG) .... CERTN
Certain Borough [*British*] .... CB
Certain Submarine [*Navy*] (NVT) .... CERTSUB
[*A*] Certainty .... CERT
Certainty Equivalent Coefficient [*Finance*] .... CE
Certainty Equivalent of Revenues [*Business term*] .... CEOR
Certainty Factor [*Mathematics*] (BARN) .... CF
Certificado de Abono Tributario [*Tax Credit Certificate*] [*Spanish*] .... CAT
Certificant, Canadian Board of Occupational Medicine (DD) .... CCBOM
Certificat d'Aptitude Professionelle [*Certificate of Professional Ability*] [*French*] (BARN) .... CAP
Certificate (DD) .... Cert
Certificate [*or Certification*] (AFM) .... CERT
Certificate (ROG) .... CERTC
Certificate .... CERTIF
Certificate [*Stock exchange term*] (SPSG) .... CT
Certificate .... CTF
Certificate as a Qualified Social Worker [*British*] .... CQSW
Certificate Depository [*New York Stock Exchange*] .... CEDE
Certificate for Amortizing Revolving Debts [*Salomon Brothers*] [*Accounting*] .... CARD
Certificate for Automobile Receivables [*Investment term*] (DFIT) .... CAR
Certificate For Automobile Receivables [*Business term*] (EMRF) .... CARS
Certificate for Physical Education [*British*] (ROG) .... CPE
Certificate for Vocational Preparation Tutors (AIE) .... CVPT
Certificate in Advanced Social Research (PGP) .... CASR
Certificate in Advanced Standing (GAGS) .... CAS
Certificate in Advanced Study in Business (GAGS) .... CAGSB
Certificate in Applied Linguistics (PGP) .... CAL
Certificate in Architectural Drafting .... CertArchDraft
Certificate in Art .... CertArt
Certificate in Art Studies .... CertArtStud
Certificate in Astrology .... CertAst
Certificate in Basic Health Sciences (PGP) .... CBHS
Certificate in Business Administration [*Academic degree*] (AIE) .... CBA
Certificate in Business Management .... CertBusMan
Certificate in Business Studies .... CertBusStud
Certificate in Communication, Advertising, and Marketing (ODBW) .... Cert CAM
Certificate in Community Development .... CertComDev
Certificate in Community Health (PGP) .... CCH
Certificate in Computer Programming [*Designation awarded by Institute for the Certification of Computer Professionals*] .... CCP
Certificate in Counselling .... CertCouns
Certificate in Criminal Justice Administration (PGP) .... CCJA
Certificate in Data Education (BUR) .... CDE
Certificate in Data Processing [*Designation awarded by Institute for Certification of Computer Professionals*] .... CDP
Certificate in Dietetics .... CertDiet
Certificate in Early Childhood Teacher Education .... CertECTEd
Certificate in Education (ODBW) .... Cert Ed
Certificate in Education [*British*] (DBQ) .... CertEd
Certificate in Electrical Engineering .... CertElecEng
Certificate in Electronic Data Processing Auditing (IAA) .... CEDPA
Certificate in Electronics and Communication .... CertElecComm
Certificate in Family Systems Studies .... CertFSStud
Certificate in Fine Arts .... CertFA
Certificate in Gerontology (PGP) .... CG
Certificate in Health Services Management [*Academic degree*] (AIE) .... CertHSM
Certificate in Higher Education .... CertHEd
Certificate in History and Philosophy of Science .... CertHisPhilSc
Certificate in Home Health Nursing (PGP) .... CHHN
Certificate in Horticulture .... CertHort
Certificate in Human Resources Management (DD) .... CHRM
Certificate in Industrial Relations .... CI Rel
Certificate in International Finance (PGP) .... CIF
Certificate in Journalism .... CertJourn
Certificate in Library Science (BARN) .... CIs
Certificate in Lieu [*of*] CIL
Certificate in Management .... CIM
Certificate in Management Accounting [*Institute of Man agement Accounting of the National Association of Accountants*] [*Designation awarded by*] .... CMA
Certificate in Marketing Management .... CertMarkMan
Certificate in Marriage and Family Therapy .... CertMFTh
Certificate in Medical Humanities (PGP) .... CMH
Certificate in Medical Parasitology (ADA) .... CMP
Certificate in Ministerial Studies (PGP) .... CMS
Certificate in Music Studies (PGP) .... CMS
Certificate in Nonprofit Management (PGP) .... CNM

Certificate in Pacific Administration .... CertPacAdm
Certificate in Performance (PGP) .... CP
Certificate in Planning Information (PGP) .... CPI
Certificate in Professional Counseling (PGP) .... CPC
Certificate in Professional Writing and Editing .... CertProWriEd
Certificate in Psychotherapy .... CertPsychTh
Certificate in Public Administration .... CP Adm
Certificate in Public Health [*British*] .... CPH
Certificate in Public Management (PGP) .... CPM
Certificate in Public Relations .... CertPR
Certificate in Publications and Communications (PGP) .... CPC
Certificate in Residential Social Work [*British*] (DI) .... CRSW
Certificate in Sales Engineering .... CS En
Certificate in Social Service [*British*] (DBQ) .... CSS
Certificate in Spiritual Direction (PGP) .... CSD
Certificate in Systems Analysis (IAA) .... CSA
Certificate in Teaching .... CertTeach
Certificate in Teaching English as a Second Language .... CertTESL
Certificate in Teaching English to Speakers of Other Languages [*Australia*] .... CertTesol
Certificate in Textiles .... CertText
Certificate in the Residential Care of Children and Young People [*British*] (DI) .... CRCCYP
Certificate in the Teaching of Handicapped Children (ADA) .... CTHC
Certificate in Tourism .... CertTour
Certificate in Transport Administration .... CertTransAdm
Certificate in Tropical Community Medicine and Health [*British*] (DI) .... CTCM and H
Certificate in University Education .... CertUniEd
Certificate in Urban and Regional Planning (PGP) .... CURP
Certificate Issuing System (ACRL) .... CIS
Certificate of Accrual on Treasury Securities [*Salomon Brothers*] [*Finance*] .... CATS
Certificate of Advanced Educational Specialization (PGP) .... CAES
Certificate of Advanced Graduate Study .... CAGS
Certificate of Advanced Librarianship (PGP) .... CAL
Certificate of Advanced Management Studies (PGP) .... CAMS
Certificate of Advanced Professional Studies (PGP) .... CAPS
Certificate of Advanced Study (WGA) .... CAS
Certificate of Advanced Study in Public Administration (PGP) .... CASPA
Certificate of Airworthiness .... C of A
Certificate of Airworthiness .... CA
Certificate of Analysis .... C of A
Certificate of Assignment of Quarters [*Navy*] .... C/Q
Certificate of Authority .... COA
Certificate of Bank Deposit .... CBD
Certificate of Beneficial Ownership .... CBO
Certificate of Clinical Competence CCC
Certificate of Clinical Competence in Audiology .... CCC-A
Certificate of Clinical Competence in Speech .... CCC-S
Certificate of Competency [*Education*] .... C of C
Certificate of Competency [*Small Business Administration*] .... COC
Certificate of Compliance [*FCC*] (NTCM) .... COC
Certificate of Conformance [*DoD*] .... COC
Certificate of Consignment/Origin [*Shipping*] (DS) .... CC/O
Certificate of Damage [*Tea trade*] (ROG) .... C/D
Certificate of Delivery .... C/D
Certificate of Deposit [*Banking*] .... C of D
Certificate of Deposit [*Banking*] .... CD
Certificate of Deposit [*Banking*] .... CDS
Certificate of Deposit [*Banking*] .... COD
Certificate of Designer of the Royal College of Art [*British*] (DBQ) .... CertDesRCA
Certificate of Destruction (AFM) .... CD
Certificate of Disability for Discharge [*Military*] .... CDD
Certificate of Disposal (ADA) .... CD
Certificate of Disposition of Classified Documents (AAG) .... CDCD
Certificate of Distribution .... CD
Certificate of Eligibility [*Navy*] .... COE
Certificate of Exemption .... C of E
Certificate of Experience (DA) .... C of E
Certificate of Extended Education [*British*] (DI) .... CEE
Certificate of Flight Readiness [*NASA*] (NASA) .... COFR
Certificate of Flight Worthiness [*NASA*] (KSC) .... COFW
Certificate of Gameness [*Purebred canine award*] .... CG
Certificate of General Education .... CGE
Certificate of Graduate Studies (PGP) .... CGS
Certificate of Health Education [*British*] (DI) .... CertHE
Certificate of Incorporation [*Business law*] .... COI
Certificate of Indebtedness [*Finance*] .... C/I
Certificate of Indebtedness [*Finance*] .... COI
Certificate of Individual Theological Studies (PGP) .... CITS
Certificate of Industrial Health .... CIH
Certificate of Insurance CI
Certificate of Insurance (HCT) .... COI
Certificate of Internal Auditing (TDOB) .... CIA
Certificate of Library and Information Science (PGP) .... CLIS
Certificate of Merit .... C of M
Certificate of Need .... C of N
Certificate of Need .... CON
Certificate of Need .... CON
Certificate of Neo-Natal Intensive Care Nursing .... CertNNICU
Certificate of Occupancy [*Business term*] (EMRF) .... CO
Certificate of Office Studies [*Academic degree*] (AIE) .... COS
Certificate of Origin [*International trade*] .... C/O
Certificate of Origin [*Investment term*] (DFIT) .... CO

Certificate of Origin and Consignment [*Shipping*] (DS) .... C/OC
Certificate of Participation .... COP
Certificate of Posting [*Post Office receipt*] [*British*] .... COP
Certificate of Pre-Vocational Education [*Academic degree*] (AIE) .... CPVE
Certificate of Prior Submission [*Navy*] .... CPS
Certificate of Professional and Vocational Education [*British*] .... CPVE
Certificate of Professional Competence [*British*] (DI) .... CPC
Certificate of Professional Studies (PGP) .... CPS
Certificate of Proficiency in English [*Cambridge*] [*British*] (AIE) .... CPE
Certificate of Public Convenience and Necessity .... CPC & N
Certificate of Qualification (KSC) .... COQ
Certificate of Reasonable Value [*Veterans Administration*] .... CRV
Certificate of Registration (ADA) .... C of R
Certificate of Retirement (MUGU) .... C/R
Certificate of Sanitary Science [*British*] .... CSS
Certificate of Secondary Education [*British*] .... CSE
Certificate of Secondary Education (BARN) .... CSE
Certificate of Security Clearance (NATG) .... CSC
Certificate of Service [*Military*] (MCD) .... CS
Certificate of Sixth Year Studies [*Scotland*] (DBQ) .... CSYS
Certificate of Special Studies (PGP) .... CSS
Certificate of Tax Deposit [*British*] .... CTD
Certificate of the College of Family Physicians of Canada (DD) .... CCFP
Certificate of the Royal College of Physicians [*British*] .... CRCP
Certificate of the Royal College of Surgeons [*British*] .... CRCS
Certificate of Theological Studies (PGP) .... CTS
Certificate of Title .... CT
Certificate of Value (DS) .... C/V
Certificate of Value and Origin (DS) .... CVO
Certificate of Vocational Preparation (AIE) .... VOC
Certificate of War Necessity [*World War II*] .... CWN
Certificate Revocation List (ACRL) .... CRL
Certificate Signing Unit (ACRL) .... CSU
Certificated Associate of the Institute of Bankers [*British*] (DI) .... CertAIB
Certificated Bailiffs Association [*British*] (DBA) .... CBA
Certificated Master [*or Mistress*] [*British*] .... CM
Certificated Teacher [*British*] .... CT
Certificates [*in bond listings of newspapers*] [*Investment term*] .... CF
Certificates for Amortizing Revolving Debts [*Finance*] (DFIT) .... CARDS
Certificates of Automobile Receivables [*Salomon Bros.*] .... CAR's
Certificati del Tesoro in Euroscudi [*Italy*] (ECON) .... CTE
Certificati di Credito del Tesoro [*Italy*] (ECON) .... CCT
Certification .... CTRFCTN
Certification Analysis Network (NASA) .... CAN
Certification Approval Request (NASA) .... CAR
Certification as Professional Contract Manager (RDA) .... CPCM
Certification Authority (ACRL) .... CA
Certification Authority for Reinforcing Steels (PDAA) .... CARES
Certification Board for Music Therapists (EA) .... CBMT
Certification Body (IAA) .... CB
Certification Committee [*American National Standards Institute*] (IEEE) .... CERTICO
Certification Control Number (MCD) .... CCN
Certification Data (AFIT) .... CD
Certification Division [*Environmental Protection Agency*] (GFGA) .... CD
Certification Evaluation Review .... CER
Certification for Emergency Nursing .... CEN
Certification for Issue (MCD) .... CFI
Certification Inspection (MCD) CI
Certification of Air Moving Equipment [*British*] (IRUK) .... CAME
Certification of Completion .... COC
Certification of Equipment Completion (SAA) .... CEC
Certification of Equivalency [*Air Force*] .... COE
Certification of Nonavailability [*DoD*] .... C/NA
Certification of Purchase .... CP
Certification Office [*Trade union regulation*] [*British*] .... CO
Certification Reciprocity Consortium/Alcoholism and Other Drug Abuse [*Later, NCRC/AODA*] (EA) .... CRC/AODA
Certification Requirement (MCD) .... CR
Certification Short Test [*Exhaust emissions testing*] [*Automotive engineering*] .... CST
Certification Status Report (NASA) .... CSR
Certification Test Network [*NASA*] (KSC) .... CTN
Certification Test Requirement [*NASA*] .... CTR
Certification Test Specification [*NASA*] (KSC) .... CTS
Certification Test System (MCD) .... CERTS
Certification Unit .... CU
Certified (AAG) C
Certified .... CERT
Certified .... CERTD
Certified (ROG) .... CERTFD
Certified Acupuncturist [*Medicine*] (DAVI) .... CA
Certified Acupuncturist [*Medicine*] .... CA
Certified Administrative Manager [*Administrative Manag ement Society*] [*Designation awarded by*] .... CAM
Certified Advertising Agency Practitioner .... CAAP
Certified Aircraft Dispatch, Inc. [*ICAO designator*] (FAAC) .... XAD
Certified Alfalfa Seed Council (EA) .... CASC
Certified American Indian Lineage Specialist .... CAILS
Certified American Lineage Specialist .... CALS
Certified Arbitrator [*Canada*] (DD) .... CArb
Certified Assistant Export Manager [*American Society of International Executives*] [*Designation awarded by*] .... CAEM
Certified Associate Contracts Manager [*Exam*] (AAGC) .... CACM
Certified Associate of the Institute of Bankers (ODBW) .... CAIB
Certified Associate of the Institute of Bankers [*Canada*] (DD) .... CAIB
Certified Association Executive [*American Society of A ssociation Executives*] [*Designation awarded by*] .... CAE
Certified Athletic Trainer (DAVI) .... ATC
Certified Automotive Repairmen's Society [*Defunct*] (EA) .... CARS
Certified Ballast Manufacturers Association (EA) .... CBM
Certified Ballast Manufacturers Association .... CBMA
Certified Bank Examiner .... CBE
Certified Biomedical Equipment Technician (RDA) .... CBET
Certified Building Code Official [*Canada*] (AAGC) .... CBCO
Certified Building Society Executive [*Canada*] (DD) .... CBSE
Certified Business Appraiser [*Institute of Business Appraisers*] [*Designation awarded by*] .... CBA
Certified Business Solutions .... CBS
Certified by the Association for Healthcare Philanthropy (NFD) .... CAHP
Certified Cash Manager [*National Corporate Cash Management Association*] [*Designation awarded by*] .... CCM
Certified Cell Line [*ATCC*] CCL
Certified Chamber Executive [*American Chamber of Comme rce Executives*] [*Designation awarded by*] .... CCE
Certified Check [*Banking*] CC
Certified Chemical Engineer .... CChE
Certified Claims Professional .... CCP
Certified Claims Professional Accreditation Council (EA) .... CCPAC
Certified Clinic Account Manager [*American Guild of Patient Account Manag ement*] [*Designation awarded by*] .... CCAM
Certified Clinical Nutritionist [*Medicine*] .... CCN
Certified Club Manager [*Club Managers Association of America*] [*Designation awarded by*] .... CCM
Certified Cold Fur Storage Association (EA) .... CCFSA
Certified Collateral Corp. (IID) CCC
Certified Color Manufacturers Association (EA) .... CCMA
Certified Commercial Investment Member [*Realtors Natio nal Marketing Institute of the National Association of Realtors*] [*Designation awarded by*] .... CCIM
Certified Configuration Manager .... CCM
Certified Configuration Specialist .... CCS
Certified Construction Specifier [*Construction Specifications Institute*] [*Automotive engineering*] .... CCS
Certified Consultants International [*Defunct*] (EA) CCI
Certified Consumer Credit Executive [*International Con sumer Credit Association*] [*Designation awarded by*] .... CCCE
Certified Corporate Travel Executive [*National Passenger Traffic Associat ion*] [*Designation awarded by*] .... CCTE
Certified Corrective Therapist .... CCT
Certified Cost Estimator/Analyst (AAGC) .... CCE/A
Certified Credit Bureau Executive [*Society of Certified Consumer Credit E xecutives*] [*Designation awarded by*] .... CCBE
Certified Data Educator (HGAA) .... CDE
Certified Data Manager .... CDM
Certified Data Processing Auditor [*EDP Auditors Foundation*] [*Designation awarded by*] .... CDPA
Certified Data Processor (DD) .... CDP
Certified Data Specialist .... CDS
Certified Decal Manufacturers (EA) .... CDM
Certified Dental Assistant .... CDA
Certified Dental Technician .... CDT
Certified Diabetes Educator (MEDA) .... CDE
Certified Diploma in Accounting and Finance [*British*] (DBQ) .... CDipAF
Certified Direct Marketing Practitioner [*Direct Marketing Association Ins urance Council*] [*Designation awarded by*] .... CDMP
Certified Documentary Specialist [*Designation awarded by American Society of International Executives, Inc.*] .... CDS
Certified Employee Benefit Specialist [*Trademark of the International Foundation of Employee Benefit Plans, Inc.*] .... CEBS
Certified Engineering Geologist [*Environmental science*] .... CEG
Certified Engineering Operations Executive [*American Hotel and Motel Asso ciation*] [*Designation awarded by*] .... CEOE
Certified Engineering Technologist [*Environmental science*] .... CET
Certified Environmental Auditor [*Environmental science*] .... CEA
Certified Environmental Professional [*Environmental science*] .... CEP
Certified Environmental Trainer .... CET
Certified Exchangor [*International Exchangors Association*] [*Designation awarded by*] .... CE
Certified Exchangors [*An association*] (EA) .... CE
Certified Exhibit Specialist (WDMC) .... CES
Certified Exposition Manager [*National Association of Exposition Managers , Inc.*] [*Designation awarded by*] .... CEM
Certified Financial Consultant [*Canada*] (DD) .... CHFC
Certified Financial Examiner [*Society of Financial Examiners*] [*Designation awarded by*] .... CFE
Certified Financial Planner [*College of Financial Planning*] [*Designation awarded by Business term*] .... CFP
Certified Fitness Appraiser [*Canadian Association of Sports Sciences*] .... CFA
Certified Flight Instructor [*Aviation*] .... CFI
Certified Flight Instructor, Instrument [*Aviation*] .... CFII
Certified Food and Beverage Executive [*Educational Institute of the Ameri can Hotel and Motel Association*] [*Designation awarded by*] .... CFBE
Certified Fraud Examiner [*Canada*] (DD) .... CFE
Certified From [*or Certified To*] [*Legal term*] (DLA) .... cert
Certified Fund-Raising Executive .... CFRE
Certified Gastrointestinal Clinician (MEDA) .... CGC
Certified Genealogical Instructor .... CGI
Certified Genealogical Lecturer .... CGL
Certified Genealogical Record Searcher .... CGRS
Certified Genealogist .... CG

Certified General Accountant .... CGA
Certified Graphoanalyst .... CGA
Certified Guitar Player [*Monogram used by Chet Atkins*] .... CGP
Certified Hardware List (MCD) .... CHL
Certified Hazardous Materials Manager [*Environmental science*] .... CHMM
Certified Hemodialysis Nurse (MEDA) .... CHN
Certified Herbalist .... CH
Certified Hospital Admission Program (DAVI) .... CHAP
Certified Hospitality Housekeeping Executive [*Educational Institute of th e American Hotel and Motel Association*] [*Designation awarded by*] .... CHHE
Certified Hotel Administrator [*Educational Institute of the American Hote l and Motel Association*] [*Designation awarded by*] .... CHA
Certified Human Resources Professional [*Canada*] (DD) .... CHRP
Certified Hypnotherapist [*Medicine*] .... CHt
Certified in Education for Public Relations [*Public Relations Society of America*] [*New York, NY*] (WDMC) .... CEPR
Certified Incentive Travel Executive [*Society of Incentive Travel Executi ves*] [*Designation awarded by*] .... CITE
Certified Industrial Hygienist .... CIH
Certified Industrial Manager .... CIM
Certified Infection Control (MEDA) CIC
Certified Information Systems Auditor [*EDP Auditors Foundation*] [*Designation awarded by*] .... CISA
Certified Institution for the Mental Defective [*British*] .... CIMD
Certified Insurance Counselor [*Society of Certified Insurance Counselors*] [*Designation awarded by*] CIC
Certified Internal Auditor [*The Institute of Internal Auditors, Inc.*] [*Designation awarded by*] .... CIA
Certified International Executive [*American Society of International Exec utives*] [*Designation awarded by*] .... CIE
Certified International Executive - Air Forwarding [*Am erican Society of International Executives, Inc.*] [*Designation awarded by*] .... CIE-AF
Certified International Executive - Export Management [*American Society of International Executives, Inc.*] [*Designation awarded by*] .... CIE-EM
Certified International Executive - Forwarding [*Americ an Society of International Executives, Inc.*] [*Designation awarded by*] .... CIE-F
Certified International Executive - Traffic Management [*American Society of International Executives, Inc.*] [*Designation awarded by*] .... CIE-TM
Certified International Traffic Manager [*American Society of Internationa l Executives, Inc.*] [*Designation awarded by*] .... CITM
Certified Kitchen Designer .... CKD
Certified Kosher [*Food labeling*] (IIA) .... CK
Certified Kosher [*Food labeling*] .... K
Certified Laboratory Assistant (WGA) .... CLA
Certified Laundry Manager .... CLM
Certified Legal Assistant .... CLA
Certified Lenders Program [*Small Business Administration*] .... CLP
Certified Life Underwriter [*Insurance*] .... CLU
Certified Livestock Marketing Association [*Later, Livestock Marketing Association*] .... CLMA
Certified Management Accountant (DD) .... CMA
Certified Management Consultant [*Institute of Management Consultants, Inc .*] [*Designation awarded by*] .... CMC
Certified Manufacturing Engineer (DD) .... CMgE
Certified Market Technician (DD) .... CMT
Certified Marketing Director [*International Council of Shopping Centers*] [*Designation awarded by*] .... CMD
Certified Master [*British*] .... CM
Certified Material Test Report [*Nuclear energy*] (NRCH) .... CMRT
Certified Medical Assistant .... CMA
Certified Medical Assistant-Administrative (WGA) .... CMA-A
Certified Medical Assistant-Administrative and Clinical (WGA) .... CMA-AC
Certified Medical Assistant-Clinical .... CMA-C
Certified Medical Electroencephalographic Technician (WGA) .... CMET
Certified Medical Representative (MAE) .... CMR
Certified Medical Representatives Institute (EA) .... CMRI
Certified Medical Transcriptionist .... CMT
Certified Member, American Society of Traffic and Transportation [*America n Society of Transportation and Logistics*] [*Designation awarded by*] .... CM-ASTT
Certified Member of AHP [*Association of Healthcare Philanthropy*] .... CAHP
Certified Member of the Institute of Wood Science [*British*] (DBQ) .... CMIWSc
Certified Metrication Specialist (DICI) .... CMS
Certified Midwife .... CM
Certified Milk Producers Association of America (EA) .... CMPAA
Certified Navy Twill (DNAB) .... CNT
Certified NetWare Engineer [*Novell, Inc.*] [*Computer science*] (PCM) .... CNE
Certified Neuroscience Registered Nurse (MEDA) .... CNRN
Certified Nuclear Medicine Technologist (MAE) .... CNMT
Certified Nurse Midwife .... CNM
Certified Nurse Midwife [*Medicine*] .... CNM
Certified Nurse, Operating Room (MEDA) .... CNOR
Certified Nurse's Aide .... CNA
Certified Nutrition Support Nurse (MEDA) .... CNSN
Certified Nutritionist [*Medicine*] .... CN
Certified Occupational Therapy Assistant .... COTA
Certified Office Administrator .... COA
Certified Official Government Business .... COGB
Certified Operating Room Technician .... CORT
Certified Ophthalmic Medical Assistant (DAVI) .... COMT
Certified Orthotist .... CO
Certified Park Operators Program (EA) .... CPOP
Certified Patient [*British*] .... CP
Certified Patient Account Manager [*American Guild of Patient Account Mana gement*] [*Designation awarded by*] .... CPAM
Certified Pediatric Nurse Practitioner/Associate (MEDA) .... CPNP/A
Certified Pediatric Worker (BARN) .... CPW
Certified Pedorthist .... CPed
Certified Personnel Consultant [*Designation awarded by National Association of Personnel Consultants*] .... CPC
Certified Post-Anesthesia Nurse (MEDA) .... CPAN
Certified Professional Bureau Executive [*Medical-Dental-Hospital Bureaus of America*] [*Designation awarded by*] .... CPBE
Certified Professional Chemist .... CPC
Certified Professional Contracts Manager [*Exam*] (AAGC) .... CPCM
Certified Professional Geologist .... CPG
Certified Professional in Quality Assurance (HCT) .... CPQA
Certified Professional Insurance Woman [*National Association of Insurance Women*] [*Designation awarded by*] .... CPIW
Certified Professional Insurance Women's Association [*Canada*] (DD) .... CPIW
Certified Professional Logistician (MCD) .... CPL
Certified Professional Purchaser [*Canada*] (DD) .... CPP
Certified Professional Secretary [*Institute for Certifying Secretaries*] [*Designation awarded by*] .... CPS
Certified Professional Soil Scientist [*Environmental science*] .... CPSS
Certified Program Generator (IAA) .... CPG
Certified Project Officer [*Environmental Protection Agency*] (GFGA) .... CPO
Certified Property Manager [*Institute of Real Estate Management*] [*Designation awarded by*] .... CPM
Certified Prosthetist .... CP
Certified Prosthetist and Orthotist .... CPO
Certified Protection Professional [*American Society for Industrial Securi ty*] [*Designation awarded by*] .... CPP
Certified Psychologist [*Canada*] (DD) .... CPsych
Certified Public Accountant .... CPA
Certified Public Purchasing Officer [*Canadian*] .... CPPO
Certified Public Secretary .... CPS
Certified Purchasing Manager [*National Association of Purchasing Manageme nt, Inc.*] [*Designation awarded by*] .... CPM
Certified Radio Marketing Consultant (NTCM) .... CRMC
Certified Raw Milk (MEDA) .... CRM
Certified Real Estate Appraiser [*National Association of Real Estate Appr aisers*] [*Designation awarded by*] .... CREA
Certified Real Estate Securities Member [*Real Estate Securities and Syndi cation Institute of the National Association of Realtors*] [*Designation awarded by*] .... CRSM
Certified Real Estate Securities Sponsor [*Real Estate Securities and Synd ication Institute of the National Association of Realtors*] [*Designation awarded by*] .... CRSS
Certified Record Librarian .... CRL
Certified Records Manager [*Institute of Certified Records Managers*] [*Designation awarded by*] (MCD) .... CRM
Certified Reference Librarian (BARN) .... CRL
Certified Reference Materials .... CRM
Certified Registered Nurse Anesthetist .... CRNA
Certified Registered Nurse of Infusion .... CRNI
Certified Registered Nurse Practioner (DAVI) .... CRNP
Certified Rehabilitation Counselor .... CRC
Certified Rehabilitation Registered Nurse .... CRRN
Certified Reliability Data Shell [*Computer science*] (PDAA) .... CRDS
Certified Remodeller .... CR
Certified Residential Broker [*Realtors National Marketing Institute of th e National Association of Realtors*] [*Designation awarded by*] .... CRB
Certified Residential Specialist [*Realtors National Marketing Institute o f the National Association of Realtors*] [*Designation awarded by*] .... CRS
Certified Respiratory Therapy Technician (DAVI) .... CRRT
Certified Respiratory Therapy Technician .... CRTT
Certified Retinal Angiographer .... CRA
Certified Review Appraiser [*Finance*] (EMRF) .... CRA
Certified Rooms Division Executive [*Educational Institute of the American Hotel and Motel Association*] [*Designation awarded by*] .... CRDE
Certified Round Assembly Facility [*Military*] .... CRAF
Certified Safety Professional [*Designation awarded by Board of Certified Safety Professionals*] .... CSP
Certified School Nurse (MEDA) .... CSN
Certified Security and Safety Professional [*Environmental science*] .... CSSP
Certified Shopping Center Manager [*International Council of Shopping Cent ers*] [*Designation awarded by*] .... CSM
Certified Shorthand Reporter .... CSR
Certified Social Worker .... CSW
Certified Speaking Professional .... CSP
Certified Surgical Technologist (HCT) .... CST
Certified Systems Engineer (CDE) .... CSE
Certified Systems Professional (CDE) .... CSP
Certified Systems Professional [*Institute for Certification of Computer P rofessionals*] [*Designation awarded by*] .... CSP
Certified Tax Specialist (PGP) .... CTS
Certified Test Data .... CTD
Certified Test Record (IAA) .... CTR
Certified Test Results (NRCH) .... CTR
Certified Tool List (AAG) .... CTL
Certified Traffic Manager .... CTM
Certified Travel Counselor [*Institute of Certified Tra vel Agents*] [*Designation awarded by*] .... CTC
Certified Tumor Registrar [*Medicine*] (BARN) .... CTR
Certified Urological Registered Nurse (MEDA) .... CURN
Certified Vendor Information (NRCH) CVI
Certify (DLA) .... cert
Certify (FAAC) .... CRTFY
Certiorari [*Legal term*] (DLA) .... CERT

Certiorari [*To be certified*] [*A writ from a superior to an inferior court*] [*Latin*] (AAGC) ... cert
Certiorari Denied [*Legal term*] (DLA) ... cert den
Certiorari Denied by United States Supreme Court [*Legal term*] (DLA) ... US Cert Den
Certiorari Dismissed [*Legal term*] (DLA) ... cert dis
Certiorari Dismissed by United States Supreme Court [*Legal term*] (DLA) ... US Cert Dis
Certiorari Granted [*Legal term*] (DLA) ... CERT GR
Certron Corp. [*Associated Press*] (SAG) ... Certron
Certron Corp. [*NASDAQ symbol*] (NQ) ... CRTN
Cerulein [*Biochemistry*] ... CRL
Cerulein and Secretin (Test) [*Clinical chemistry*] ... CS
Ceruloplasmin [*Biochemistry*] (DAVI) ... CERULO
Ceruloplasmin [*Biochemistry*] ... Cp
Cervia [*Italy ICAO location identifier*] (ICLI) ... LIPC
Cervical [*Medicine*] ... C
Cervical and Thoracic Vertebrae [*Medicine*] (DMAA) ... CTV
Cervical Compression Overloading Test [*Medicine*] (DMAA) ... CCOT
Cervical Connective [*Neuroanatomy*] ... CC
Cervical Internal Cartoid Artery [*Medicine*] (DMAA) ... CICA
Cervical Intraepithelial Neoplasia [*Medicine*] ... CIN
Cervical Laminectomy [*Neurology and orthopedics*] (DAVI) ... C LAM
Cervical Lymph Node [*Anatomy*] ... CLN
Cervical Mediastinal Exploration (AAMN) ... CME
Cervical Motion Tenderness [*Medicine*] (DAVI) ... CMT
Cervical Motion Tenderness [*Gynecology*] (DAVI) ... CxMT
Cervical Mucous Basal Body Temperature [*Gynecology and obstetrics*] (DAVI) ... CMBBT
Cervical Mucous Solution [*Gynecology*] (DAVI) ... CMS
Cervical Mucus [*Obstetrics*] ... CM
Cervical Orthosis [*Medicine*] ... CO
Cervical Prevertebral Soft Tissue Measurement [*Medicine*] (DMAA) ... CSTM
Cervical Range of Motion [*Medicine*] (DMAA) ... CROM
Cervical Spine [*Neurology and orthopedics*] (DAVI) ... CS
Cervical Stimulation [*Neurology and orthopedics*] (DAVI) ... CS
Cervical Traction [*Neurology, orthopedics, and physical therapy*] (DAVI) ... CT
Cervical Vertebra [*Medicine*] ... CV
Cervico [*Vertical*] [*Medicine*] (ROG) ... CV
Cervicoaxial [*Dentistry*] ... CA
Cervicoaxial [*Dentistry*] (DAVI) ... CO
Cervicolinguoaxial [*Dentistry*] ... CLA
Cervicothoracic Orthosis [*Also, CTO*] [*Medicine*] ... CER
Cervicothoracic Orthosis [*Also, CER*] [*Medicine*] ... CTO
Cervicothoracolumbar Orthosis [*Medicine*] ... CTLO
Cervicothoracolumbosacral Orthosis [*Medicine*] ... CTLSO
Cervix [*Anatomy*] ... CERV
Cervix [*Gynecology*] (DMAA) ... cerv
Cervix [*Anatomy*] ... CX
Cervus [*Deer*] (ROG) ... C
[*The*] **Cesarean Connection** (EA) ... TCC
Cesarean Prevention Movement (EA) ... CPM
Cesarean-Delivered [*Obstetrics*] (MAE) ... CD
Cesareans/Support, Education, and Concern [*An association*] (EA) ... C/SEC
Cesium [*Chemical element*] ... Cs
Cesium Atomic Beam Tube (IAA) ... CABT
Cesium Beam Time Standard ... CBTS
Cesium Beam Tube ... CBT
Cesium Bombardment Engine ... CBE
Cesium Chloride ... CsCl
Cesium Chloride Polymerizable [*Analytical chemistry*] ... CCP
Cesium Contact Engine ... CCE
Cesium Contact Thruster ... CCT
Cesium Dihydrogen Arsenate ... CDA
Cesium Feed System ... CFS
Cesium Implant [*Oncology and radiation therapy*] (DAVI) ... CI
Cesium Iodide ... CSI
Cesium Ion Emission ... CIE
Cesium Ion Propulsion System ... CIPS
Cesium Ion Source ... CIS
Cesium Time Standard ... CTS
Cesium Trifluoroacetate [*Reagent*] ... CsTFA
Cesium Vapor Cathode ... CVC
Cesium Vapor Feed System ... CVFS
Cesium-137 ... Cs-137
Ceskoslovenska Bioklimatologicka Spolecnost [*Czechoslovak Bioclimatological Society*] [*Multinational association*] (EAIO) ... CSBkS
Ceskoslovenska Socialnedemokraticka Strana Delnicka [*Czechoslovak Social Democratic Workers' Party*] (PPE) ... CSSD
Ceskoslovenska Socialni Demokracie v Exilu [*Czechoslovak Social Democratic Party*] (EAIO) ... CSDE
Ceskoslovenska Strana Lidova [*Czechoslovak People's Party*] (PPE) ... CSL
Ceskoslovenska Strana Socialisticka [*Czechoslovak Socialist Party*] (PPE) ... CSS
Ceskoslovenska Tiskova Kancelar [*Czechoslovak News Agency*] ... CTK
Ceskoslovenske Aerolinie [*Czechoslovakia*] [*ICAO designator*] (FAAC) ... CSA
Cessford Community Library, Alberta [*Library symbol National Library of Canada*] (NLC) ... ACC
Cessford Community Library, Cessford, AB, Canada [*Library symbol Library of Congress*] (LCLS) ... CaACeC
Cessna [*Airplane code*] ... Cna
Cessna Aircraft Co. [*ICAO aircraft manufacturer identifier*] (ICAO) ... C
Cessna Aircraft Co. ... CAC
Cessna Airmaster Club (EA) ... CAC
Cessna Owners Organization (EA) ... COO
Cessna Pilots Association (EA) ... CPA
Cessnock [*Australia Airport symbol*] (OAG) ... CES
Cesspits (ROG) ... CP
Cesspool (AAG) ... CP
C'Est-a-Dire [*That Is to Say*] [*French*] ... C-A-D
Cestriensis [*Signature of the Bishops of Chester*] (ROG) ... CESTR
Cestriensis [*Signature of the Bishops of Chester*] (ROG) ... CESTRIEN
CET Environmental Services [*Associated Press*] (SAG) ... CET EnvS
CET Environmental Services [*Associated Press*] (SAG) ... CET ES
CET Environmental Services [*AMEX symbol*] (SAG) ... ENV
CET Environmental Svcs [*AMEX symbol*] (TTSB) ... ENV
Cetacean and Turtle Assessment Program [*University of Rhode Island*] [*Research center*] (RCD) ... CETAP
Cetacean Society International (EA) ... CSI
Cetane [*Organic chemistry*] ... Cet
Cetane Index [*Fuel technology*] ... CI
Cetane Number [*Fuel technology*] ... CN
Cetec Engineering Co., Inc. [*Vancouver Stock Exchange symbol*] ... CEK
Ceteris Paribus [*Other Things Being Equal*] [*Latin*] ... CET PAR
Cetfa SA [*Spain ICAO designator*] (FAAC) ... CTF
Cetra [*Record label*] [*Italy*] ... Cet
Cetrimonium Bromide [*Organic chemistry*] (DAVI) ... CTBA
Cetus [*Whale constellation*] [*Latin*] (BARN) ... Cet
Cetyl Trimethylammonium Tosylate [*Organic chemistry*] ... CTAT
Cetyldimethylbenzylammonium Chloride [*A surfactant*] ... CDAC
Cetyl(dimethyl)ethylammonium Bromide [*A surfactant*] ... CDEA
Cetylpyridinium Bromide [*Medicine*] (DMAA) ... CPB
Cetylpyridinium Chloride [*Organic chemistry*] ... CPC
Cetyltrimethylammonium [*Organic chemistry*] ... CTA
Cetyltrimethylammonium Bromide [*Also, CTAB, CTBM*] [*Antiseptic*] ... CETAB
Cetyltrimethylammonium Bromide [*Also, CETAB, CTBM*] [*Antiseptic*] ... CTAB
Cetyltrimethylammonium Bromide [*Also, CETAB, CTAB*] [*Antiseptic*] (AAMN) ... CTBM
Cetyltrimethylammonium Chloride [*Organic chemistry*] ... CTACl
Cetyltrimethylammonium Cyanide [*Organic chemistry*] ... CTACN
Cetyltrimethylammonium Toluenesulfonate [*Organic chemistry*] ... CETATS
Ceuta Unida [*Political party*] (EY) ... CEU
CevionTechnologies [*NASDAQ symbol*] (TTSB) ... CEON
Ceylon [*Sri Lanka*] [*MARC geographic area code Library of Congress*] (LCCP) ... a-ce--
Ceylon [*Sri Lanka*] [*MARC country of publication code Library of Congress*] (LCCP) ... ce
Ceylon ... Cey
Ceylon (VRA) ... Ceyl
Ceylon [*Sri Lanka*] ... CL
Ceylon [*Sri Lanka*] (ROG) ... CY
Ceylon and Mauritius Royal Garrison Artillery [*British military*] (DMA) ... CMRGA
Ceylon Army Service Corps [*British military*] (DMA) ... CASC
Ceylon Civil Service [*Obsolete*] ... CCS
Ceylon Corps of Military Police [*British military*] (DMA) ... CCMP
Ceylon Criminal Appeal Reports [*A publication*] (DLA) ... Ceyl Cr App R
Ceylon Federation of Labor [*Obsolete*] ... CFL
Ceylon Labor Union [*Obsolete*] ... CLU
Ceylon Labour Law Journal [*A publication*] (DLA) ... Cey Lab LJ
Ceylon Law Journal [*A publication*] (DLA) ... Ceyl LJ
Ceylon Law Journal [*A publication*] (DLA) ... CLJ
Ceylon Law Recorder [*A publication*] (DLA) ... Ceyl L Rec
Ceylon Law Recorder [*A publication*] (DLA) ... Ceyl LR
Ceylon Law Recorder [*A publication*] (DLA) ... Ceylon Law Rec
Ceylon Law Recorder [*A publication*] (DLA) ... Law Rec
Ceylon Law Reports [*A publication*] (DLA) ... CLR
Ceylon Law Review [*A publication*] (DLA) ... Ceyl L Rev
Ceylon Law Review and Reports [*A publication*] (DLA) ... Ceylon LR
Ceylon Law Society. Journal [*A publication*] (DLA) ... Ceylon L Soc J
Ceylon Law Weekly [*A publication*] (DLA) ... Ceyl LW
Ceylon Law Weekly [*A publication*] (ILCA) ... CLW
Ceylon Legal Miscellany [*A publication*] (DLA) ... Ceyl Leg Misc
Ceylon Lines [*Steamship*] (MHDW) ... CL
Ceylon Mercantile Union [*Obsolete*] ... CMU
Ceylon Plantation Workers' Union [*Obsolete*] ... CPWU
Ceylon Railway Clerical Service Union [*Obsolete*] ... CRCSU
Ceylon Tamil Association [*Victoria*] [*Australia*] ... CTA
Ceylon Tourist Board (EAIO) ... CTB
Ceylon Trade Union Federation [*Sri Lanka*] (FEA) ... CTUF
Ceylon Weekly Reporter [*A publication*] (ILCA) ... CWR
Ceylonese Welfare Organisation [*Australia*] ... CWO
CF Bancorp [*Associated Press*] (SAG) ... CF Bcp
CF Bancorp [*NASDAQ symbol*] (SAG) ... CFBC
CFB Bancorp [*NASDAQ symbol*] (TTSB) ... CFBN
CFB Bancorp, Inc. [*Associated Press*] (SAG) ... CFB Bcp
CFB Bancorp, Inc. [*NASDAQ symbol*] (SAG) ... CFBN
CFC Financial Communications [*An association*] (EA) ... CFC
CFC International, Inc. [*NASDAQ symbol*] (SAG) ... CFCI
CFC International, Inc. [*Associated Press*] (SAG) ... CFCIntl
CFC Intl. [*NASDAQ symbol*] (TTSB) ... CFCI
CFCF, Inc. [*Toronto Stock Exchange symbol*] ... CF
CFI Industries [*Associated Press*] (SAG) ... CFI Ind
CFI Industries [*NASDAQ symbol*] (NQ) ... CFIB
CFI ProServices [*NASDAQ symbol*] (TTSB) ... PROI
CFI Proservices, Inc. [*Associated Press*] (SAG) ... CFI Pro
CFI Proservices, Inc. [*NASDAQ symbol*] (SAG) ... PROI
CFM Technologies, Inc. [*Associated Press*] (SAG) ... CFM T
CFM Technologies, Inc. [*NASDAQ symbol*] (SAG) ... CFMT
CFS Group, Inc. [*Toronto Stock Exchange symbol*] ... CFZ
CFSB Bancorp [*NASDAQ symbol*] (TTSB) ... CFSB
CFSB Bancorp, Inc. [*NASDAQ symbol*] (SAG) ... CFSB

CFU [*Croatian Fraternal Union of America*] **Junior Cultural Federation** (EA) ... CFUJCF
CFW Communications [*NASDAQ symbol*] (TTSB) ... CFWC
CFW Communications Co. [*Associated Press*] (SAG) ... CFW Cm
CFW Communications Co. [*NASDAQ symbol*] (SAG) ... CFWC
CFX Corp. [*Formerly, Chesire Financial*] [*AMEX symbol*] (SAG) ... CFX
CFX Corp. [*Formerly, Cheshire Financial*] [*Associated Press*] (SAG) ... CFX Cp
CGA - Canada Research Foundation (AC) ... CGARF
CGC, Inc. [*Toronto Stock Exchange symbol*] ... GYP
CH Financial Co. [*Vancouver Stock Exchange symbol*] ... CFQ
C.H. Reinhard School, Bellmore, NY [*Library symbol*] [*Library of Congress*] (LCLS) ... NBellmR
CH2M Hill Library, Boise, ID [*Library symbol*] [*Library of Congress*] (LCLS) ... IdBCH
Chabazite [*A zeolite*] ... CHA
Chablis Resources Ltd. [*Vancouver Stock Exchange symbol*] ... CHK
Chabot College, Hayward, CA [*Library symbol Library of Congress*] (LCLS) ... CHC
Chabot Observatory, Oakland, CA [*Library symbol Library of Congress*] (LCLS) ... COCh
Chabua [*India*] [*Airport symbol*] (AD) ... CHU
Chacarita [*Argentina*] [*Seismograph station code, US Geological Survey Closed*] (SEIS) ... CCR
Chacarita [*Costa Rica*] [*ICAO location identifier*] (ICLI) ... MRCH
Chachapoyas [*Peru*] [*ICAO location identifier*] (ICLI) ... SPPY
Chachoengsao/Phanom Sarakhan [*Thailand*] [*ICAO location identifier*] (ICLI) ... VTBF
Chachro [*Pakistan*] [*ICAO location identifier*] (ICLI) ... OPCR
Chaco Canyon National Monument ... CHCA
Chad [*MARC country of publication code Library of Congress*] (LCCP) ... cd
Chad [*MARC geographic area code Library of Congress*] (LCCP) ... f-cd--
Chad [*ANSI three-letter standard code*] (CNC) ... TCD
Chad [*ANSI two-letter standard code*] (CNC) ... TD
Chad [*International civil aircraft marking*] (ODBW) ... TT
Chad Therapeutics [*AMEX symbol*] (TTSB) ... CTU
Chad Therapeutics, Inc. [*Associated Press*] (SAG) ... ChadThr
Chad Therapeutics, Inc. [*AMEX symbol*] (SAG) ... CTU
Chadashoth Archeologioth [*Israel*] [*A publication*] (BJA) ... ChadArch
Chadbourn, NC [*AM radio station call letters*] ... WVOE
Chadbourne & Parke, New York, NY [*Library symbol*] [*Library of Congress*] (LCLS) ... NNCh
Chadron [*Nebraska*] [*Airport symbol*] (OAG) ... CDR
Chadron, NE [*Location identifier FAA*] (FAAL) ... HIN
Chadron, NE [*FM radio station call letters*] (RBYB) ... KALG
Chadron, NE [*FM radio station call letters*] ... KCNE
Chadron, NE [*AM radio station call letters*] ... KCSR
Chadron, NE [*FM radio station call letters*] ... KQSK
Chadron Public Library, Chadron, NE [*Library symbol Library of Congress*] (LCLS) ... NbCh
Chadron State College (GAGS) ... Chadron St C
Chadron State College, Chadron, NE [*Library symbol Library of Congress*] (LCLS) ... NbChS
Chadron State College, Chadron, NE [*OCLC symbol*] (OCLC) ... NCC
Chadwell, Kayser, Ruggles, McGee & Hasting, Chicago, IL [*Library symbol Library of Congress*] (LCLS) ... ICCK
Chadwell, Kayser, Ruggles, McGee & Hastings, Chicago, IL [*OCLC symbol*] (OCLC) ... ILQ
Chadwick-Goldhaber Effect [*Physics*] ... CGE
Chadwyck-Healey Ltd., Bishops Stortford, Herts., United Kingdom [*Library symbol Library of Congress*] (LCLS) ... ChaH
Chaff/Delivery (SAA) ... C/D
Chaff Dispensing System [*or Subsystem*] (MCD) ... CDS
Chaff/Flare (MCD) ... C/F
Chaff/Flare Countermeasures Dispenser System (PDAA) ... CMDS
Chaff Rocket [*Military*] (NVT) ... CHAFFROC
Chaffee, MO [*FM radio station call letters*] ... KYRX
Chaffey College, Alta Loma, CA [*Library symbol Library of Congress*] (LCLS) ... CAltaC
Chafford [*England*] ... CHAF
Chagan-Uzun [*Former USSR Seismograph station code, US Geological Survey*] (SEIS) ... CUR
Chagrin Falls Public Library, Chagrin Falls, OH [*Library symbol Library of Congress*] (LCLS) ... OCf
Chah Bahar/Konarak [*Iran*] [*ICAO location identifier*] (ICLI) ... OIZC
Chah-Bahar [*Iran*] [*Airport symbol*] (OAG) ... ZBR
Chai Na Ta Corp. [*NASDAQ symbol*] (SAG) ... CCCF
Chai Na Ta Corp. [*Associated Press*] (SAG) ... ChaiNT
Chaillotine Air Service [*France ICAO designator*] (FAAC) ... CIS
Chain ... CH
Chain (WDMC) ... ch
Chain ... CHN
Chain [*Measure*] ... CHN
Chain [*Symbol*] [*A part of the immunoglobulin molecular structure*] (DAVI) ... J
Chain Arrester Gear (MCD) ... CHAG
Chain Block Character [*Computer science*] (NITA) ... CBC
Chain Break [*Broadcasting*] (WDMC) ... CB
Chain Command Flag (IAA) ... CCF
Chain Crossing Model [*Semiconductor technology*] (OA) ... CCM
Chain Delivery [*Press*] (DGA) ... CD
Chain Grate (MSA) ... CG
Chain Handling Automated Overlay System (SAA) ... CHAOS
Chain Home [*Aviation*] ... CH
Chain Home Beamed [*Aviation*] ... CHB
Chain Home Extra Low [*Aviation*] ... CHEL
Chain Home High [*Aviation*] ... CHH
Chain Home Low [*Aviation*] ... CHL
Chain Ignition Hazard ... CIH
Chain Index (ADA) ... CI
Chain Input Pointing [*Computer science*] ... CHIP
Chain Link Fence Manufacturers Institute (EA) ... CLFMI
Chain Makers' and Strikers' Association [*A union*] [*British*] ... CMSA
Chain Makers' Providential Association [*A union*] [*British*] ... CMPA
Chain of Command (IAA) ... CC
Chain of Command ... CHACOM
Chain of Custody ... COC
Chain Operator (AAG) ... CO
Chain Overseas [*Aviation*] ... CO
Chain Overseas Extremely Low [*Aviation*] ... COEL
Chain Overseas Low [*Aviation*] ... COL
Chain Procedure [*Indexing*] (NITA) ... CP
Chain RADAR System ... CRS
Chain Saw Manufacturers Association [*Later, PPEMA*] (EA) ... CSMA
Chain Store Renovation and Maintenance, Materials, Modernization ... CRAMMM
Chain Testers Association of Great Britain (BI) ... CTA
Chai-Na-Ta Corp. [*NASDAQ symbol*] (TTSB) ... CCCFF
Chai-Na-Ta Ginsing Products Ltd. [*Associated Press*] (SAG) ... ChaiNaTa
Chai-Na-Ta-Ginseng [*Vancouver Stock Exchange symbol*] ... CJG
Chained File Management System [*IBM Corp.*] ... CFMS
Chained Sequential Operation ... CSO
Chain-Extended Polyethylene (PDAA) ... CEPE
Chaining Data [*Computer science*] (IAA) ... CD
Chain-Transfer Agent [*Organic chemistry*] ... CTA
Chair ... CH
Chair ... CHR
Chair and Bed Rest [*Medical directive*] (CPH) ... C & B
Chair Frame Manufacturers' Association [*British*] (BI) ... CFMA
Chair of the Board (DD) ... chr
Chair Shower [*Medical rehabilitation*] (DAVI) ... C-Sh
Chaired ... CHRD
Chairmakers' Protection Society [*A union*] [*British*] ... CPS
Chairman [*or Chairwoman or Chairperson*] ... C
Chairman ... CH
Chairman (EY) ... CHAIR
Chairman ... CHM
Chairman ... CHMAN
Chairman (AFM) ... CHMN
Chairman (ROG) ... CHN
Chairman ... CHRM
Chairman ... CHRMN
Chairman ... CHRMN
Chairman, Communications-Electronics Committee [*NATO*] (NATG) ... CCEC
Chairman, Joint Chiefs of Staff (AFM) ... CJCS
Chairman, Military Committee Memorandum [*NATO*] ... CMCM
Chairman of Defense Committee (NATG) ... CODEF
Chairman of Military Committee (NATG) ... COMIL
Chairman of the Board ... CB
Chairman of the Office of Savings Associations ... COSA
Chairman of Volunteers [*Red Cross*] ... CV
Chairman, Operational Planners Group [*Military*] ... COPG
Chairman, Special Studies Group [*Joint Chiefs of Staff*] ... CSSG
Chairman's Guidance (DOMA) ... CG
Chairman's Memorandum ... CM
Chairman's Net Assesment of Strategic Planning (DOMA) ... CNASP
Chairman's Program Assessment [*Joint Chiefs of Staff*] (DOMA) ... CPA
Chairman's Staff Group [*DoD*] ... CSG
Chairperson (BARN) ... Chpr
Chairperson ... CHRPRSN
Chairperson ... CHRPRSN
Chairwoman ... CHRWMN
Chaiten [*Chile*] [*Airport symbol*] (AD) ... WCH
Chaiten/Chaiten [*Chile*] [*ICAO location identifier*] (ICLI) ... SCTN
Chaitya (VRA) ... chya
Chaix Hill [*Alaska*] [*Seismograph station code, US Geological Survey*] (SEIS) ... CHX
Chaiyaphum [*Thailand*] [*ICAO location identifier*] (ICLI) ... VTUC
Chaiyaphum/Phu Khieo [*Thailand*] [*ICAO location identifier*] (ICLI) ... VTUG
Chajangni [*South Korea ICAO location identifier*] (ICLI) ... RKSI
Chakcharan [*Afghanistan*] [*Airport symbol Obsolete*] (OAG) ... CCN
Chakhamenu Zikhronam Livrakhah [*A publication*] (BJA) ... CHaZaL
Chakhcharan [*Afghanistan*] [*ICAO location identifier*] (ICLI) ... OACC
Chakulia [*India*] [*ICAO location identifier*] (ICLI) ... VECK
Chala [*Peru*] [*Seismograph station code, US Geological Survey Closed*] (SEIS) ... CLA
Chala [*Peru*] [*ICAO location identifier*] (ICLI) ... SPHC
Chalais [*France ICAO location identifier*] (ICLI) ... LFIH
Chalan Kanoa [*Diocesan abbreviation*] (TOCD) ... CHK
Chalcedon Foundation (EA) ... CF
Chalcedony (VRA) ... chldy
Chalcone Isomerase [*An enzyme*] ... CHI
Chalcone Synthase [*An enzyme*] ... CHS
Chaldaeisches Woerterbuch ueber die Targumim [*A publication*] (BJA) ... CWbT
Chaldea (ROG) ... CH
Chaldea [*or Chaldean or Chaldaic*] ... CHALD
Chaldron [*Unit of measure*] [*Obsolete*] ... CH
Chaldron [*Unit of measure*] [*Obsolete*] ... CHAL
Chaldron [*Unit of measure*] [*Obsolete*] ... CHD
Chaldron [*Unit of measure*] [*Obsolete*] (ROG) ... CHL
Chaleur Environment Protection Association (AC) ... CEPA
Chaleur Library Region, Campbellton, NB, Canada [*Library symbol Library of Congress*] (LCLS) ... CaNBCaC

Chaleur Library Region, Campbellton, New Brunswick [*Library symbol National Library of Canada*] (NLC) .... NBCAC
Chalgrove [*British ICAO location identifier*] (ICLI) .... EGLJ
Chalice Mining, Inc. [*Vancouver Stock Exchange symbol*] .... CLG
Chalk [*Quality of the bottom*] [*Nautical charts*] .... Ck
Chalk (VRA) .... ck
Chalk Board [*Technical drawings*] .... CHBD
Chalk Quarrying Association [*British*] (BI) .... CQA
Chalk River Bibliographic Data Information System [*Atomic Energy of Canada Ltd.*] (NITA) .... CHARIBDIS
Chalk River Nuclear Laboratories [*Atomic Energy of Canada Ltd.*] [*Information service or system Research center*] (IID) .... CRNL
Chalk River Public Library, Ontario [*Library symbol National Library of Canada*] (BIB) .... OCK
Chalk River Unidentified Deposit [*Nuclear energy*] (GFGA) .... CRUD
Chalk's International Airline [*ICAO designator*] (AD) .... BK
Chalky [*Philately*] .... chlk
Chalkyitsik [*Alaska*] [*Airport symbol*] (OAG) .... CIK
Challanger International Ltd. [*Associated Press*] (SAG) .... ChalInt
Challengair [*Belgium*] [*FAA designator*] (FAAC) .... CHG
Challenge (AABC) .... CHAL
Challenge Air Cargo, Inc. [*ICAO designator*] (FAAC) .... CWC
Challenge Air Transport, Inc. [*ICAO designator*] (FAAC) .... OFF
Challenge Aviation Pty Ltd. [*Australia ICAO designator*] (FAAC) .... CHS
Challenge Certificate [*In dog shows*] (BARN) CC
Challenge Handshake Authentication Protocol [*Telecommunications*] (PCM) .... CHAP
Challenge Position [*Dancing*] .... CH-P
Challenge Test Plan .... CTP
Challenge Virus Strain .... CVS
Challenger Armored Repair and Recovery Vehicle [*British*] .... CARRV
Challenger Armored Repair and Recovery Vehicle [*British*] .... CR-ARRV
Challenger Communications Consultants Ltd. [*British Telecommunications service*] (TSSD) CCC
Challenger International [*NASDAQ symbol*] (SAG) .... ICOM
Challenger International Ltd. [*Formerly, Coastal International Ltd.*] [*Toronto Stock Exchange symbol*] .... CTT
Challenger School, Pasadena, TX [*Library symbol*] [*Library of Congress*] (LCLS) .... TxPCS
Challenger Society for Marine Science [*British*] (EAIO) .... CSMS
Challenging Adults to Read Effectively (EDAC) .... CARE
Challis, ID [*Location identifier FAA*] (FAAL) .... LLJ
Challis on Real Property [*1885-1911*] [*A publication*] (DLA) .... Challis
Challis Public Library, Challis, ID [*Library symbol*] [*Library of Congress*] (LCLS) .... IdCha
Challock [*British ICAO location identifier*] (ICLI) .... EGKE
Chalmers' Colonial Opinions [*England*] [*A publication*] (DLA) .... Ch
Chalmers' Colonial Opinions [*England*] [*A publication*] (DLA) .... Ch Col Op
Chalmers on Bills of Exchange [*1878-1952*] [*A publication*] (DLA) .... Chalmers
Chalmers' Opinions, Constitutional Law [*1669-1809*] [*England*] [*A publication*] (DLA) .... Chal Op
Chalmette National Historical Park .... CHAL
Chalna [*Bangladesh*] [*Airport symbol*] (AD) .... CHL
Chalon/Champforgeuil [*France ICAO location identifier*] (ICLI) .... LFLH
Chalone Wine Group [*NASDAQ symbol*] (NQ) .... CHLN
Chalone Wine Group Ltd. [*Associated Press*] (SAG) .... Chalone
Chalons/Ecury-Sur-Coole [*France ICAO location identifier*] (ICLI) .... LFQK
Chalons/Vatry [*France ICAO location identifier*] (ICLI) .... LFOK
Chalous [*Iran*] [*ICAO location identifier*] (ICLI) .... OINC
Chalqueno [*Race of maize*] .... CHL
Chalumeau [*Reed*] [*Music*] .... CHAL
Chalumeau [*Reed*] [*Music*] (ROG) .... CHALM
Chama [*New Mexico*] [*Seismograph station code, US Geological Survey Closed*] (SEIS) .... CNM
Chama Cha Mapinduzi [*Revolutionary Party*] [*Tanzania*] [*Political party*] (PPW) .... CCM
Chamaeleon [*Constellation*] .... Cha
Chamaeleon [*Constellation*] .... Cham
Chamber (ADA) .... CH
Chamber .... Cha
Chamber (MSA) .... CHAMB
Chamber (VRA) .... chbr
Chamber (AAG) .... CHM
Chamber (MSA) .... CHMBR
Chamber .... CHMBR
Chamber Coolant Valve (NASA) CCV
Chamber Coolant Valve Actuator (MCD) .... CCVA
Chamber Flow-Field Code (MCD) .... CFC
Chamber Music America (EA) .... CMA
Chamber Music Society of Lincoln Center .... CMS/LC
Chamber of Automotive Industries of New South Wales [*Australia*] .... CAINSW
Chamber of Coal Traders [*British*] (DBA) .... CCT
Chamber of Commerce .... C of C
Chamber of Commerce CC
Chamber of Commerce .... COC
Chamber of Commerce and Industry of South Australia .... CCISA
Chamber of Commerce and Industry of Western Australia .... CCIWA
Chamber of Commerce of the Apparel Industry (EA) .... CCAI
Chamber of Commerce of the United States (EA) .... CCUS
Chamber of Commerce of the United States (EA) .... COCUSA
Chamber of Commerce of the United States, Washington, DC [*Library symbol Library of Congress*] (LCLS) .... DCC
Chamber of Deputies (DAS) .... COD
Chamber of Destination of Ships .... CDS
Chamber of Mineral Resources of Nova Scotia (AC) .... CMRNS
Chamber of Mines and Energy of Western Australia .... CMEWA
Chamber of Mines, Metals, and Extractive Industries [*Australia*] .... CMMEI
Chamber of Mines of Western Australia .... CMWA
Chamber of Shipping (DAS) .... COS
Chamber Orchestra of Europe .... COE
Chamber Pressure .... CP
Chamber Reports, Upper Canada [*A publication*] (DLA) .... Chamber
Chamber Reports, Upper Canada [*A publication*] (DLA) .... Chr Rep
Chamberlain [*California*] [*Seismograph station code, US Geological Survey*] (SEIS) .... CBC
Chamberlain (ROG) .... CHAMB
Chamberlain Public Library, Chamberlain, SD [*Library symbol Library of Congress*] (LCLS) .... SdCh
Chamberlin's American Commercial Law [*A publication*] (DLA) .... Cham Com Law
Chambers .... CHAS
Chambers (ROG) .... CHRS
Chambers and Parsons' Railroad Laws [*A publication*] (DLA) .... Cham & PRR
Chambers and Pretty. Cases on Finance Act [*1909-10*] [*England*] [*A publication*] (DLA) .... Ch & P
Chambers' Chancery Jurisdiction as to Infants [*A publication*] (DLA) .... Cham Chy Jur
Chambers' Common Law [*Upper Canada*] [*A publication*] (DLA) .... CL Chamb
Chambers' Common Law [*Upper Canada*] [*A publication*] (DLA) .... CL Chambers
Chambers. Commons and Open Spaces [*1877*] [*A publication*] (DLA) .... Cham Com
Chambers' Digest of Public Health Cases [*A publication*] (DLA) .... Chamb Dig PHC
Chambers. Estates and Tenures [*A publication*] (DLA) .... Cham Est
Chambers. Landlord and Tenant [*1823*] [*A publication*] (DLA) .... Cha L & T
Chambers. Landlord and Tenant [*1823*] [*A publication*] (DLA) .... Cham L & T
Chambers. Leases [*1819*] [*A publication*] (DLA) .... Cham Leas
Chambers of Commerce and Industry [*ASEAN*] (DS) CCI
Chambers of Commerce of Ireland (EAIO) CCI
Chambers Practice [*A publication*] (DLA) .... Cham Pr
Chambers. Rates and Rating [*2nd ed.*] [*1889*] [*A publication*] (DLA) .... Cham Rat
Chambers' Upper Canada Reports [*1849-82*] [*A publication*] (DLA) .... Cham
Chambers' Upper Canada Reports [*1849-82*] [*A publication*] (DLA) .... Cham Rep
Chambers' Upper Canada Reports [*1849-82*] [*A publication*] (DLA) .... Chamb
Chambersburg, PA [*Location identifier FAA*] (FAAL) .... EQB
Chambersburg, PA [*AM radio station call letters*] .... WCBG
Chambersburg, PA [*AM radio station call letters*] .... WCHA
Chambersburg, PA [*FM radio station call letters*] .... WIKZ
Chambers's Encyclopaedia [*A publication*] (ROG) .... Chamb Ency
Chambery [*France*] [*Airport symbol*] (OAG) .... CMF
Chambery/Aix-Les-Bains [*France ICAO location identifier*] (ICLI) .... LFLB
Chambery/Challes-Les-Eaux [*France ICAO location identifier*] (ICLI) .... LFLE
Chambon-La-Foret [*France*] [*Seismograph station code, US Geological Survey Closed*] (SEIS) .... CLF
Chambre d'Appel [*French Legal term*] (DLA) .... Ch App
Chambre de Commerce du Sud-Ouest de l'Ile de Montreal (AC) .... CCSOIM
Chambre de Commerce et d'Industrie de Paris [*Paris Chamber of Commerce and Industry*] [*France*] [*Information service or system*] (IID) .... CCIP
Chambre de Commerce Internationale [*The International Chamber of Commerce - ICC*] [*Paris, France*] (EAIO) CCI
Chambre de Compensation de l'Afrique de l'Ouest [*West African Clearing House - WACH*] (EAIO) .... CCAO
Chambre de Compensation des Instruments Financiers de Paris .... CCIFP
Chambre Europeenne pour le Developpement du Commerce, de l'Industrie, et des Finances [*European Chamber for the Development of Trade, Industry, and Finances*] [*Brussels, Belgium*] (EAIO) .... CECIF
Chambre Immobiliere de la Haute Yamaska Inc. [*Haute Yamaska Real Estate Board*] (AC) .... CIHY
Chambre Islamique de Commerce, d'Industrie et d'Echange des Marchandises [*Islamic Chamber of Commerce, Industry, and Commodity Exchange - ICCICE*] [*Karachi, Pakistan*] (EAIO) .... CICIEM
Chambre Syndicale des Fabricants de Papiers a Cigarettes et Autres Papiers Minces (EAIO) .... CSFPCPM
Chameleon Micro Implementation Language [*1978*] [*Computer science*] (CSR) .... CHAMIL
Chamfer [*Design engineering*] (IAA) .... CH
Chamfer [*Design engineering*] .... CHAM
Chamizal National Memorial .... CHAM
Chamois [*Philately*] .... cham
Chamois Contagious Ecthyma [*Medicine*] (DMAA) .... CCE
Chamomile [*Pharmacology*] (ROG) .... CHAM
Champ Du Feu [*France*] [*Seismograph station code, US Geological Survey*] (SEIS) .... CDF
Champagne (ROG) .... CHAM
Champagne d'Argent Federation (EA) .... CDF
Champagne Gift Service [*De Courcy Pere et Fils*] [*British*] .... CGS
Champagne News and Information Bureau (EA) .... CNIB
Champagne Resources Ltd. [*Vancouver Stock Exchange symbol*] .... CPG
Champagne-Mumm Admiral's Cup [*Yacht racing*] .... C-MAC
Champagnole/Crotenay [*France ICAO location identifier*] (ICLI) .... LFGX
Champaign [*Illinois*] [*Airport symbol*] (OAG) .... CMI
Champaign, IL [*FM radio station call letters*] .... WBGL
Champaign, IL [*Television station call letters*] .... WCIA
Champaign, IL [*AM radio station call letters*] .... WDWS
Champaign, IL [*FM radio station call letters*] .... WEFT
Champaign, IL [*FM radio station call letters*] .... WHMS
Champaign, IL [*Television station call letters*] .... WICD
Champaign, IL [*FM radio station call letters*] .... WIXY
Champaign, IL [*FM radio station call letters*] .... WLRW
Champaign, IL [*FM radio station call letters*] .... WPCD
Champaign Public Library, Champaign, IL [*Library symbol Library of Congress*] (LCLS) .... ICham

Champaign Public Library, Champaign, IL [*OCLC symbol*] (OCLC) ... IKG
Champaign/Urbana, IL [*Location identifier FAA*] (FAAL) ... CMI
Champerty and Maintenance [*A publication*] (DLA) ... Champ
Champion [*Dog show term*] ... CH
Champion (DSUE) ... CHAMP
Champion ... CHAMP
Champion Aircraft Co. ... CAC
Champion Enterprises [*NYSE symbol*] (SAG) ... CHB
Champion Enterprises [*NYSE symbol*] (TTSB) ... CHB
Champion Enterprises [*Associated Press*] (SAG) ... ChmpE
Champion Enterprises, Inc. [*AMEX symbol*] (SPSG) ... CHB
Champion Enterprises, Inc. [*Associated Press*] (SAG) ... ChpEn
Champion Fleet Owners Association (EA) ... CFOA
Champion Healthcare [*AMEX symbol*] (TTSB) ... CHC
Champion Healthcare Corp. [*AMEX symbol*] (SAG) ... CHC
Champion Healthcare Corp. [*Associated Press*] (SAG) ... ChmpH
Champion Industries [*NASDAQ symbol*] (TTSB) ... CHMP
Champion Industries, Inc. [*NASDAQ symbol*] (SAG) ... CHMP
Champion Industries, Inc. [*Associated Press*] (SAG) ... ChmpIn
Champion International Corp. [*NYSE symbol*] (SPSG) ... CHA
Champion International Corp. (MHDW) ... CHAP
Champion International Corp. [*Associated Press*] (SAG) ... ChmpIn
Champion Intl. [*NYSE symbol*] (TTSB) ... CHA
Champion Oil & Gas [*Vancouver Stock Exchange symbol*] ... CHP
Champion Papers, Inc., Pasadena, TX [*Library symbol Library of Congress*] (LCLS) ... TxPC
Champion Parts [*NASDAQ symbol*] (TTSB) ... CREB
Champion Parts Rebuilders, Inc. [*Associated Press*] (SAG) ... ChmpPr
Champion Parts Rebuilders, Inc. [*NASDAQ symbol*] (NQ) ... CREB
Champion Public Library, Alberta [*Library symbol National Library of Canada*] (NLC) ... ACHAM
Champion Road Machinery [*NASDAQ symbol*] (TTSB) ... CRMLE
Champion Road Machinery Ltd. [*Associated Press*] (SAG) ... ChpRM
Champion Road Machinery Ltd. [*Associated Press*] (SAG) ... ChRM
Champion Road Machinery Ltd. [*NASDAQ symbol*] (SAG) ... CRML
Champion Tracker ... CT
Champion's Cases, Wine and Beer-Houses Act [*England*] [*A publication*] (DLA) ... Champ
Championship ... CHP
Championship Association of Mechanics (EA) ... CAM
Championship Auto Racing Teams (EA) ... CART
Championship Drivers Licensing Group [*Automobile racing*] ... CDLG
Champlain College, Burlington, VT [*Library symbol Library of Congress*] (LCLS) ... VtBC
Champlain College, Plattsburgh, NY [*Library symbol Library of Congress Obsolete*] (LCLS) ... NPlaC
Champlain Enterprises, Inc. [*ICAO designator*] (FAAC) ... UCA
Champlain, NY [*AM radio station call letters*] ... WCHP
Champlain Regional College, Campus 1, St.-Lambert, PQ, Canada [*Library symbol Library of Congress*] (LCLS) ... CaQSICR
Champlain Society (EA) ... CS
Champlain Valley Physicians Hospital, Plattsburgh, NY [*Library symbol Library of Congress*] (LCLS) ... NPlaP
Champlain Valley School of Nursing, Plattsburgh, NY [*Library symbol Library of Congress*] (LCLS) ... NPlaCN
Champleve (VRA) ... champ
Champps Entertainment, Inc. [*Associated Press*] (SAG) ... Champps
Champps Entertainment, Inc. [*NASDAQ symbol*] (SAG) ... CHPP
CHAMPUS [*Civilian Health and Medical Program of the Uniformed Services*] **Reform Initiative** (GFGA) ... CRI
CHAMPUS [*Civilian Health and Medical of the Uniformed Services*] **Regional Review System** ... CRRS
Chan Hills Military Police [*British military*] (DMA) ... CHMP
Chanaral [*Chile*] [*Seismograph station code, US Geological Survey*] (SEIS) ... CAA
Chanaral [*Chile*] [*Airport symbol*] (AD) ... CNR
Chance (FAAC) ... CHC
Chance Failure Rate (IAA) ... CFR
Chance on Powers [*1831*] [*Supplement, 1841*] [*A publication*] (DLA) ... Chanc Pow
[*A*] **Chance to Grow** (EA) ... ACTG
Chance Vought Aircraft, Inc. [*Obsolete*] ... CVA
Chance-Constrained Programming (PDAA) ... CCP
Chancellor ... C
Chancellor (ADA) ... CH
Chancellor (DLA) ... Chan
Chancellor ... CHANC
Chancellor ... CHANCLLR
Chancellor ... Chllr
Chancellor Broadcstg'A' [*NASDAQ symbol*] (TTSB) ... CBCA
Chancellor Corp. [*NASDAQ symbol*] (SAG) ... CBCA
Chancellor Corp. [*Associated Press*] (SAG) ... Chncellr
Chancellor Energy Resources, Inc. [*Toronto Stock Exchange symbol*] ... CHC
Chancellor of the Duchy of Lancaster [*British*] ... CDL
Chancellor of the Exchequer [*British*] ... CE
Chancellor of the Exchequer [*British*] (DLA) ... Chanc Ex
Chancellor's Court [*England*] (DLA) ... Ch
Chancery ... C
Chancery [*British*] ... CH
Chancery ... CHAN
Chancery (ROG) ... CHANC
Chancery ... CHY
Chancery Appeal Cases [*1865-75*] [*A publication*] (DLA) ... LR Ch App
Chancery Appeal Cases, English Law Reports [*A publication*] (DLA) ... CA
Chancery Appeal Cases, English Law Reports [*A publication*] (DLA) ... Ch App Cas
Chancery Appeal Cases, English Law Reports [*A publication*] (DLA) ... Cha App
Chancery Cases [*2 Notes of King's Bench Cases*] [*England*] [*A publication*] (DLA) ... Keny Ch
Chancery Cases Chronicle [*Ontario*] [*A publication*] (DLA) ... CC Chr
Chancery Cases Chronicle [*Ontario*] [*A publication*] (DLA) ... CC Chron
Chancery Cases Tempore Talbot [*England*] [*A publication*] (DLA) ... Forester
Chancery Chambers [*Upper Canada*] (DLA) ... Ch Chamb
Chancery Chambers [*Upper Canada*] (DLA) ... Ch Chamb (Can)
Chancery Chambers Reports, Ontario [*A publication*] (DLA) ... Chamb Rep
Chancery Chambers Reports, Upper Canada [*1857-72*] [*A publication*] (DLA) ... Chan Chamb
Chancery Court (DLA) ... Chan Ct
Chancery Division ... CD
Chancery Divisional Court [*England*] (DLA) ... Ch Div'l Ct
Chancery Practice [*A publication*] (DLA) ... Ch Pr
Chancery Proceedings [*British*] (ROG) ... CHAN PROC
Chancery Reports Tempore Car. I to Queen Anne [*A publication*] (DLA) ... CR
Chancery Sentinel [*New York*] [*A publication*] (DLA) ... Ch Sent
Chancery Sentinel [*New York*] [*A publication*] (DLA) ... Ch Sent (NY)
Chancery Sentinel [*New York*] [*A publication*] (DLA) ... Chan Sentinel
Chancery Sentinel [*New York*] [*A publication*] (DLA) ... NY Ch
Chances Accepted [*Baseball*] ... CA
Chandalar [*Alaska*] [*Airport symbol*] (OAG) ... WCR
Chandalar Lake, AK [*Location identifier FAA*] (FAAL) ... CQR
Chandalar Lake, AK [*Location identifier FAA*] (FAAL) ... WCR
Chandeleur Bay [*Vancouver Stock Exchange symbol*] ... CYJ
Chandigarh [*India*] [*Airport symbol*] (OAG) ... IXC
Chandigarh [*India*] [*ICAO location identifier*] (ICLI) ... VICG
Chandler ... CHANL
Chandler and Price Letterpress Printing Press (WDMC) ... C&P press
Chandler, AZ [*Location identifier FAA*] (FAAL) ... AMS
Chandler, AZ [*Location identifier FAA*] (FAAL) ... CHD
Chandler, AZ [*Location identifier FAA*] (FAAL) ... HAN
Chandler, AZ [*FM radio station call letters*] ... KMLE
Chandler, AZ [*Location identifier FAA*] (FAAL) ... UTE
Chandler Evans Corp. ... CECO
Chandler, IN [*FM radio station call letters*] ... WNTC
Chandler Insurance Co. Ltd. [*NASDAQ symbol*] ... CHAN
Chandler Insurance Co. Ltd. [*Associated Press*] (SAG) ... ChanIn
Chandler Insurance Ltd. (MHDW) ... CHANF
Chandler, OK [*Location identifier FAA*] (FAAL) ... CQB
Chandler Public Library, Chandler, AZ [*Library symbol Library of Congress*] (LCLS) ... AzCh
Chandler/Williams Air Force Base [*Arizona*] [*ICAO location identifier*] (ICLI) ... KCHD
Chandler-Lake Wilson High School, Chandler, MN [*Library symbol*] [*Library of Congress*] (LCLS) ... MnChaHS
Chandler's American Criminal Trials [*A publication*] (DLA) ... Chand Cr T
Chandler's American Criminal Trials [*A publication*] (DLA) ... Chand Crim Tr
Chandler's Reports [*20, 38-44 New Hampshire*] [*A publication*] (DLA) ... Chand
Chandler's Reports [*20, 38-44 New Hampshire*] [*A publication*] (DLA) ... Chand (NH)
Chandler's Reports [*20, 38-44 New Hampshire*] [*A publication*] (DLA) ... Chandl
Chandler's Wisconsin Reports [*1849-52*] [*A publication*] (DLA) ... Chand
Chandler's Wisconsin Reports [*1849-52*] [*A publication*] (DLA) ... Chand R
Chandler's Wisconsin Reports [*1849-52*] [*A publication*] (DLA) ... Chand (Wis)
Chandler's Wisconsin Reports [*1849-52*] [*A publication*] (DLA) ... Chandl
Chandler's Wisconsin Reports [*1849-52*] [*A publication*] (DLA) ... Chandler
Chandler's Wisconsin Reports [*1849-52*] [*A publication*] (DLA) ... Chandler Wis
Chandpur [*Bangladesh*] [*Airport symbol*] (AD) ... CDP
Chandragarhi [*Nepal*] [*ICAO location identifier*] (ICLI) ... VNCG
Chanduy [*Ecuador*] [*ICAO location identifier*] (ICLI) ... SEUY
Chane Bedoya [*Bolivia*] [*ICAO location identifier*] (ICLI) ... SLHN
Chaney's Digest, Michigan Reports [*A publication*] (DLA) ... Ch Dig
Chaney's Digest, Michigan Reports [*A publication*] (DLA) ... Cha Dig
Chaney's Michigan Reports [*37-58 Michigan*] [*A publication*] (DLA) ... Chan
Chaney's Michigan Reports [*37-58 Michigan*] [*A publication*] (DLA) ... Chaney
Chaney's Michigan Reports [*37-58 Michigan*] [*A publication*] (DLA) ... Chaney (Mich)
Chang Conjunctiva Cells [*Medicine*] (DMAA) ... CHANG C
Chang Liver Cells [*Medicine*] (DMAA) ... CHANG L
Changalane [*Mozambique*] [*Seismograph station code, US Geological Survey*] (SEIS) ... CNG
Changan Airlines [*China*] [*FAA designator*] (FAAC) ... CGN
Changchu International Symposium on Analytical Chemistry [*1990*] ... CISAC
Changchun [*China*] [*Airport symbol*] (OAG) ... CGQ
Changchun [*Republic of China*] [*Seismograph station code, US Geological Survey*] (SEIS) ... CNH
Changchun [*China*] [*ICAO location identifier*] (ICLI) ... ZYCC
Changchun Institute of Applied Chemistry [*China*] ... CIAC
Change [*Used in combinations only*] [*Army*] (AABC) ... C
Change (AABC) ... CH
Change (AAG) ... CHG
Change [*Telecommunications*] (TEL) ... CHN
Change (MSA) ... CHNG
Change ... CHNG
Change [*A publication*] (BRI) ... Cng
Change Administration ... CA
Change Administration Conference ... CAC
Change Administration Cover Sheet ... CA/CS
Change Agent Questionnaire [*Interpersonal skills and attitudes test*] ... CAQ
Change Agent Research (PDAA) ... CAR
Change Analysis Board ... CAB
Change Analysis Commitment (SAA) ... CAC
Change Analysis Group ... CAG
Change Analysis Section ... CAS

Change Board (MCD)	CB
Change Board Analysis Record (SAA)	CBAR
Change Board Comment Record	CBCR
Change Board Register	CBR
Change Bulletin	CB
Change Code (MCD)	CC
Change Column Measure [Typesetting] (WDMC)	cc
Change Commitment Record (SAA)	CCR
Change Control Board [Social Security Administration]	CCB
Change Control Board [NASA] (KSC)	CHGCB
Change Control Board Directive [NASA] (MCD)	CCBD
Change Control Board Summary [NASA] (MCD)	CCBS
Change Control Determine (MCD)	CCD
Change Control Engineer	CCE
Change Control Sub-Board (DNAB)	CCSB
Change Control System	CCS
Change Course	CC
Change Design Order [Navy] (NG)	CDO
Change Diameter (MCD)	CD
Change Directive (AAG)	CD
Change Directory [Computer science]	CD
Change Directory [Computer science]	CHDIR
Change Directory Extended [Computer science] (PCM)	CDX
Change Display [Utility]	CHAD
Change Evaluation (NASA)	CE
Change Evaluation Board [NASA] (SSD)	CEB
Change Evalution/Analysis [Engineering]	CE/A
Change Facilitator Stages of Concern Questionnaire [Educational test]	CFSOCQ
Change Film Frame (SAA)	CFF
Change Flight Plan	CFP
Change Font [Typesetting] (WDMC)	cf
Change for Children [An association] (EA)	CC
Change for Children Association (AC)	CFCA
Change for Good [An association] (EA)	CFG
Change for Good (EA)	CG
Change Identification Control Number	CIC
Change Identification Control Schedule Analysis	CICSA
Change Identification Control Schedule Summary	CIC-SS
Change Identification Number (NASA)	CIN
Change Impact Board (NASA)	CIB
Change Impact Summary (NASA)	CIS
Change Implementation Board [NASA] (GFGA)	CIB
Change in Design	CID
Change in Drawing Authorization (MCD)	CIDA
Change in Drawing Notice	CIDN
Change in Formula	CF
Change Incorporation Notice [Business law]	CIN
Change Indicator (SSD)	CI
Change Indicator Code (SAA)	CIC
Change Initiation Request (KSC)	CIR
Change Instrumentation Notice	CIN
Change Islands Public Library, Newfoundland [Library symbol National Library of Canada] (NLC)	NFCI
Change Leading [Typography] (WDMC)	CL
Change Leading [Typesetting] (WDMC)	cl
Change Letter Control (NASA)	CLC
Change List	CL
Change Management/Tracking [IBM Corp.]	CM/T
Change My Operation Order [Military]	CHORD
Change My Operation Plan [Military] (AABC)	CHOPLN
Change My Operation Schedule [Military] (MUGU)	CHSKED
Change Notice	CN
Change Notice Card (AFIT)	CNC
Change Notice Request (MCD)	CNR
Change of Address [Postal term] [United States] (WDMC)	C/A
Change of Address (WDMC)	CA
Change of Address [Direct marketing] (WDMC)	CHAD
Change of Address	COA
Change of Appointing Office (FAAC)	CAO
Change of Assignment	COA
Change of Command	COC
Change of Contract [Business law] (AAG)	COC
Change of Course [Aviation]	C/C
Change of Initial Condition (MCD)	CIC
Change of Operational Control [Military]	CHOP
Change of Operational Control of Air Cover [Military] (NVT)	CHOPAIR
Change of Operational Control Summary [Military] (NVT)	CHOPSUM
Change of Personal Particulars (ADA)	COPP
Change of Plaster [Medicine]	COP
Change of Quarters (DNAB)	CQ
Change of Rating	C/R
Change of Speed (DNAB)	C/S
Change of Status (NASA)	CS
Change of Subscribers (TEL)	COS
Change Operations Directive (MCD)	COD
Change Order (NG)	C/O
Change [of] Order	CO
Change Order Account (AFM)	COA
Change Order (Aircraft)	CO(A)
Change Order Board (AAG)	COB
Change Order Conference (AAG)	COC
Change Order (Electronic)	CO(E)
Change Order Modification (KSC)	COM
Change Order Request (DNAB)	COR

Change Order Work Sheet (DNAB)	COWS
Change Over	CHGOV
Change Over (DEN)	CO
Change Package (AAG)	CP
Change Package Identification	CPI
Change Package Identification Number	CPIN
Change Pages (MCD)	CP
Change Planning Group (NASA)	CPG
Change Point [Surveying]	CP
Change Process Authorization (MCD)	CPA
Change Processing Station (AAG)	CPS
Change Proposal (KSC)	CP
Change Recommendation (AFM)	CR
Change Record Sheet (MCD)	CRS
Change Release [Military]	CR
Change Request	CR
Change Request Directive (MCD)	CR/DIR
Change Request Disposition (MCD)	CRD
Change Request Forms	CRF
Change Request Material (AAG)	CRM
Change Request Review Board [Marine science] (OSRA)	CRRB
Change Request Review Board (USDC)	CRRB
Change Review Board [NASA] (KSC)	CRB
Change Review Committee [Military] (AABC)	CRCOM
Change Review Group [NASA] (GFGA)	CRG
Change Routing Indicator (MCD)	CRI
Change Schedule Chart	CSC
Change Seeker Index	CSI
Change Sheet [Marine Corps]	CS
Change Status Page (MCD)	CSP
Change Status Report (MCD)	CSR
Change to Approach Control (FAAC)	CAC
Change to Initial Release (MCD)	CIR
Change to Lower Grade [Army]	CLG
Change to Navy Regulations	CNR
Change Transfer Device (MCD)	CTD
Change Verification Notice	CVN
Change Verification Record	CVR
Change Weight Manifest [Aviation] (FAAC)	CWM
Changeable Message Sign [Highway engineering]	CMS
Changeable Type-Plate Style	CT-PS
Changed (WGA)	CHGD
Changed Number Interception [Telecommunications] (TEL)	CNI
Changeout (NASA)	C/O
Changeover [Aviation] (FAAC)	CHOV
Changeover (AAG)	CHOVR
Change-Over Delay (AEBS)	COD
Changeover Panel (NATG)	COP
Changeover Switch (NATG)	COS
Changes and Specifications	C & S
Changes Being Effected [Food and Drug Administration]	CBE
Changes in Global National Security Environment (DOMA)	CGNSE
Changes in Itinerary to Proceed to Additional Places [Military]	CIPAP
Changes in Law (MCD)	CIL
Changes Islands Public Library, Changes Islands, NF, Canada [Library symbol Library of Congress] (LCLS)	CaNfCI
Changes per Inch (IAA)	CPI
Change-Transfer-to-Solvent [Physical chemistry]	CTTS
Changing Men [A publication] (BRI)	Cha Men
Changing Over (FAAC)	CHGO
Changing Path of Operation	CPO
Changing Radio Automatic Frequency Transmission	CRAFT
Changing Role of the Secondary Head [Project] (AIE)	CROSH
Changsha [China] [Airport symbol] (OAG)	CSX
Changsha/Datuopu [China] [ICAO location identifier] (ICLI)	ZGCS
Changuinola [Panama] [Airport symbol] (OAG)	CHX
Changuinola/Cap. Manuel Nino [Panama] [ICAO location identifier] (ICLI)	MPCH
Changzhi [China] [Airport symbol] (OAG)	CIH
Chania [Greece] [Airport symbol] (OAG)	CHQ
Channel	CH
Channel (WDMC)	ch
Channel (WDMC)	chan
Channel [Computer science] (AABC)	CHAN
Channel (NASA)	CHL
Channel [Electrical transmission] (AFM)	CHNL
Channel	CHNNL
Channel 4 [Television] [British]	C4
Channel Adapter [Computer science] (IBMDP)	CA
Channel Address [Military]	CAD
Channel Address Register [Computer science]	CAR
Channel Address Word [Computer science]	CAW
Channel Allocation and Routing Data (IEEE)	CARD
Channel Amplitude Class [Electrical engineering]	CAC
Channel and Isolation Supervision [Telecommunications] (TEL)	CIS
Channel and Technical Control Facility [In a tape-relay station in the AIRCOMNET]	CTCF
Channel and Traffic Control Agency [of AACS]	CTCA
Channel and Traffic Control Unit [Subordinate unit of the Channel and Traffic Control Agency]	CTCU
Channel Associated Signaling [Telecommunications] (ACRL)	CAS
Channel Aviation Ltd. [British ICAO designator] (FAAC)	GID
Channel Aviation Ltd. [British] [FAA designator] (FAAC)	GJD
Channel Bank (ACRL)	CB
Channel Base Section [World War II]	CBS
Channel Catfish Virus	CCV

Channel Command [*Refers to English Channel*] [*Military*] CC
Channel Command [*or Control*] **Block** [*Computer science*] (IAA) .... CCB
Channel Command [*or Control*] **Entry** [*Computer science*] (IAA) .... CCE
Channel Command or Control [*Computer science*] (IAA) CCC
Channel Command [*or Control*] **Register** [*Computer science*] (IAA) .... CCR
Channel Command [*or Control*] **Word** [*Computer science*] .... CCW
Channel Committee [*NATO*] (NATG) .... CHANCOM
Channel Committee [*NATO*] (NATG) .... CHANCOMTEE
Channel Committee Secretary [*NATO*] (NATG) .... CHANSEC
Channel Control (BUR) .... CHC
Channel Control Check [*Electronics*] (IAA) CCC
Channel Control Check [*Electronics*] (OA) .... CCK
Channel Control Field [*Telecommunications*] (ECII) .... CCF
Channel Control Orderwire (CAAL) .... CCOW
Channel Control Processor [*Computer science*] (NITA) .... CCP
Channel Control Reconfiguration [*Computer science*] (MHDI) .... CCR
Channel Control Unit (CMD) .... CCU
Channel Control Unit .... CHCU
Channel Controller (MCD) CC
Channel Coordinator [*Telecommunications*] (NITA) CC
Channel Data Check .... CDK
Channel Definition Format [*Microsoft Corp.*] [*Computer science*] .... CDF
Channel Definition Format [*Computer science*] .... CDF
Channel Down [*Biochemistry*] (DAVI) .... CD
Channel Electron Multiplier (MCD) .... CEM
Channel Electron Multiplier Array (MCD) .... CEMA
Channel End (OA) .... CE
Channel End (BUR) .... CHE
Channel Evaluation and Call (IEEE) .... CHEC
Channel Express (Air Services) Ltd. [*British ICAO designator*] (FAAC) .... EXS
Channel Extension Unit .... CEU
Channel Flow Control .... CFC
Channel Flying [*ICAO designator*] (AD) .... IH
Channel for Orders [*Business term*] .... CFO
Channel Frequency Class [*Electrical engineering*] .... CFC
Channel Handicap System [*Yacht racing*] .... CHS
Channel Identification (CET) .... CID
Channel Indirect Data Addressing (IBMDP) .... CIDA
Channel Interface .... CHIF
Channel Interface Bus (NITA) .... CIB
Channel Interface Processor [*Telecommunications*] (ACRL) .... CIP
Channel Island Aviation [*ICAO designator*] (FAAC) .... CHN
Channel Island Ferries [*British*] .... CIF
Channel Islands CI
Channel Islands National Monument .... CHIS
Channel Level Control (MCD) CLC
Channel Multiplier Array .... CMA
Channel Navigation Information Service [*British Coast Guard*] (PDAA) .... CNIS
Channel One [*French television station*] TF1
Channel Oscilloscope .... C/O
Channel/Port Aux Basques Public Library, Channel/Port Aux Basques, NF, Canada [*Library symbol Library of Congress*] (LCLS) .... CaNfCP
Channel/Port Aux Basques Public Library, Newfoundland [*Library symbol National Library of Canada*] (NLC) .... NFCP
Channel Port Index .... CPI
Channel Processor .... CHP
Channel Program Area [*Computer science*] (IAA) .... CPA
Channel Program Block [*Computer science*] .... CPB
Channel Program Commands .... CPC
Channel Reference Tone (MCD) .... CRT
Channel Request-High Priority (MHDB) .... CR-HI
Channel Request-Low Priority (MHDB) .... CR-LO
Channel Request-Medium Priority (MHDB) .... CR-MED
Channel Resources Ltd. [*Vancouver Stock Exchange symbol*] .... CHU
Channel Response Time (IAA) .... CRT
Channel Select Register [*Telecommunications*] (NITA) .... CSR
Channel Service Unit [*Telecommunications*] (TEL) .... CSU
Channel Service Unit/Data Service Unit .... CSU/DSU
Channel Signaling System No. 7 [*Computer science*] (TNIG) CSS7
Channel State Feedback (PDAA) .... CSFB
Channel Status .... CS
Channel Status Byte [*Computer science*] (IAA) .... CBS
Channel Status Field [*Electronics*] (ECII) .... CSF
Channel Status Indicator [*Computer science*] (MDG) .... CST
Channel Status Table [*Computer science*] (IAA) .... CST
Channel Status Word [*Computer science*] (BUR) .... CSW
Channel Swimming Association [*British*] (EAIO) .... CSA
Channel Synchronizer Unit [*Computer science*] .... CSU
Channel Television [*Channel Islands network*] .... CTV
Channel Terminal Bay .... ChTB
Channel Terminator (HGAA) .... CT
Channel Testing Unit [*Telecommunications*] (OA) .... CTU
Channel to Channel Adapter [*Computer science*] (IBMDP) .... CTCA
Channel to Interference Ratio [*Telecommunications*] (OSI) .... C/I
Channel Traffic Control (IAA) .... CTC
Channel Translating Equipment [*Telecommunications*] (TEL) .... CTE
Channel Transmission and Engineering Activation .... CTEA
Channel Tunnel [*Joint British-French project in English Channel*] .... CHUNNEL
[*The*] **Channel Tunnel Association** [*British*] .... CTA
Channel Tunnel Group [*British*] .... CTG
Channel Unit Signal Controller (IAA) .... CUSC
Channel Verification Signal Generator .... CVSG
Channel Word (IAA) .... CW
Channel Work Area Expansion [*Computer science*] (ECII) .... CWAE
Channel-Check Handler [*Japan*] (MCD) .... CCH
Channeled-Substrate-Planar [*Materials science*] .... CSP
Channel-Forming Integral Protein [*Biochemistry*] .... CHIP
Channeling Effect Factor .... CEF
Channell Commercial Corp. [*Associated Press*] (SAG) .... Channell
Channell Commercial Corp. [*NASDAQ symbol*] (SAG) .... CHNL
Channelled Narrow Stripe [*LASER diode technology*] (NITA) .... CNS
Channels of English Literature [*A publication*] .... CEL
Channels Ratio .... CR
Channel-to-Channel (MCD) .... CTC
Channel-to-Channel Adapter [*Computer science*] .... CCA
Chanson [*Song*] [*Music*] .... CHANS
Chant du Monde [*Record label*] [*France*] .... CdM
Chantal Pharmaceutical [*NASDAQ symbol*] (TTSB) .... CHTL
Chantal Pharmaceutical Corp. [*Associated Press*] (SAG) .... Chantal
Chantal Pharmaceutical Corp. [*NASDAQ symbol*] (NQ) .... CHTL
Chanthaburi [*Thailand*] [*ICAO location identifier*] (ICLI) .... VTBC
Chantry Certificates [*British*] (ROG) .... CHANT CERT
Chanute Air Force Base [*Illinois*] (SAA) .... CAFB
Chanute Air Force Base [*Illinois*] (AAG) .... CHAFB
Chanute, KS [*Location identifier FAA*] (FAAL) .... CNU
Chanute, KS [*AM radio station call letters*] .... KKOY
Chanute, KS [*FM radio station call letters*] .... KKOY-FM
Chanute Technical Training Center [*Air Force*] .... CTTC
Cha-Pa [*Vietnam*] [*Geomagnetic observatory code*] .... CPA
Chapacura [*Bolivia*] [*ICAO location identifier*] (ICLI) .... SLCH
Chapais, PQ [*AM radio station call letters*] .... CFED
Chapalote [*Race of maize*] .... CHP
Chaparral [*Colombia*] [*Airport symbol*] (AD) .... CPL
Chaparral Airlines [*ICAO designator*] (FAAC) .... CPL
Chaparral Airlines [*ICAO designator*] (AD) .... FC
Chaparral/Forward Area Alert RADAR [*Military*] (RDA) .... CHAP/FAAR
Chaparral Resources [*NASDAQ symbol*] (TTSB) .... CHAR
Chaparral Resources, Inc. [*Associated Press*] (SAG) .... Chapral
Chaparral Resources, Inc. [*NASDAQ symbol*] (NQ) .... CHAR
Chaparral Steel Co. [*Associated Press*] (SAG) .... ChpStl
Chaparral Steel Co. [*NYSE symbol*] (SPSG) .... CSM
Chaparral Vulcan [*Army*] CV
Chapeau, PQ [*Television station call letters*] .... CIVP
Chapeco [*Brazil ICAO location identifier*] (ICLI) .... SBCH
Chapeco [*Brazil*] [*Airport symbol*] (OAG) .... XAP
Chapel C
Chapel .... CHAP
Chapel (VRA) .... cpl
Chapel .... CPL
Chapel Hill [*North Carolina*] [*Seismograph station code, US Geological Survey*] (SEIS) .... CEH
Chapel Hill [*North Carolina*] [*Seismograph station code, US Geological Survey Closed*] (SEIS) .... CHC
Chapel Hill, NC [*AM radio station call letters*] .... WCHL
Chapel Hill, NC [*AM radio station call letters*] .... WRTP
Chapel Hill, NC [*FM radio station call letters*] .... WUNC
Chapel Hill, NC [*Television station call letters*] .... WUNC-TV
Chapel Hill, NC [*FM radio station call letters*] .... WXYC
Chapel Hill Public Library, Chapel Hill, NC [*Library symbol Library of Congress*] (LCLS) .... NcCh
Chapel of Ease [*Church of England*] .... CHE
Chapel Resources, Inc. [*Vancouver Stock Exchange symbol*] .... CPL
Chapelco [*Argentina*] [*Airport symbol*] (OAG) .... CPC
Chapelry [*Geographical division*] [*British*] .... CHAP
Chapin Memorial Library, Myrtle Beach, SC [*Library symbol*] [*Library of Congress*] (LCLS) .... ScMb
Chapin Social Insight Test [*Psychology*] .... CSIT
Chaplain (AFM) .... CH
Chaplain .... CHAP
Chaplain .... CHAP
Chaplain .... CHAPL
Chaplain .... CHPLN
Chaplain Area Representative [*Air Force*] .... CHAPAR
Chaplain Corps .... CHC
Chaplain General [*British*] (DAS) .... CGen
Chaplain of His Holiness .... CHH
Chaplain of the Fleet [*Navy British*] .... C of F
Chaplain of the Fleet [*Navy British*] .... CF
Chaplain of the Fleet [*Navy British*] .... CH of F
Chaplain of the Fleet [*Navy British*] .... ChF
Chaplain of the Order of St. John of Jerusalem .... Ch St J
Chaplain of the Order of St. John of Jerusalem .... Chap St J
Chaplain of the Order of St. John of Jerusalem .... CHSTJJ
Chaplain of the Order of St Lazarus of Jerusalem [*Australia*] .... CHLJ
Chaplain of the Territorial Army [*British*] .... CTA
Chaplain Service Personnel [*Air Force*] .... CSP
Chaplain to Foreign Immigrants [*British*] (DI) .... CFI
Chaplain to the Forces [*British*] .... CF
Chaplain to the Forces - Emergency Commission [*British*] .... CF(EC)
Chaplain to the Forces (Jewish) [*British*] .... CF(J)
Chaplain to the Forces - Reserve of Officers [*British*] .... CF(R of O)
Chaplain to the Forces (Territorial Army) [*British*] .... CF(TA)
Chaplain to the Territorial Forces [*British*] .... CTF
Chaplain-General to the Forces [*British*] (ROG) .... CHAP-GEN
Chaplain-in-Chief [*British*] .... CH-in-C
Chaplains' Aid Association [*Later, CAA/SEF*] (EA) .... CAA
Chaplains' Aid Association/Seminary Education Fund (EA) .... CAA/SEF
Chaplains' Relevance to the Emerging Drug Order [*Navy*] .... CREDO
Chapleau [*Canada*] [*Airport symbol*] (OAG) .... YLD
Chapleau, ON [*ICAO location identifier*] (ICLI) .... CYLD

Chapleau Public Library, Ontario [*Library symbol National Library of Canada*] (NLC) .... OCHAP

Chapleau Resources Ltd. [*Vancouver Stock Exchange symbol*] .... CHI

Chaplin [*Connecticut*] [*Seismograph station code, US Geological Survey Closed*] (SEIS) .... CPL

Chapman [*One who sells in a cheaping or market*] [*Said to be origin of "chap," meaning "fellow"*] .... CHAP

Chapman & Cutter, Law Library, Chicago, IL [*Library symbol*] [*Library of Congress*] (LCLS) .... ICChC

Chapman Chemical Co., Memphis, TN [*Library symbol Library of Congress*] (LCLS) .... TMCC

Chapman College Library, Orange, CA [*OCLC symbol*] (OCLC) CCX

Chapman College, Orange, CA [*Library symbol Library of Congress*] (LCLS) .... COrC

Chapman Freeborn [*British*] [*FAA designator*] (FAAC) .... CFO

Chapman. Practice of the Court of King's Bench [*2nd ed.*] [*1831*] [*A publication*] (DLA) .... Cha Pr

Chapman University (GAGS) .... Chapman U

Chapman-Jouquet [*Pressures*] (MCD) .... CJ

Chapman's Addenda [*A publication*] (DLA) .... Cha Add

Chappaqua Library, Chappaqua, NY [*Library symbol Library of Congress*] (LCLS) .... NChap

Chappell [*Record label*] [*Great Britain*] .... Chap

Chappell and Shoard. Copyright [*1863*] [*A publication*] (DLA) .... Chap & Sh

Chappell, NE [*Location identifier FAA*] (FAAL) .... CNP

Chappel-Perry Medium [*Microbiology*] .... CP

Chapter C

Chapter .... CH

Chapter (AAGC) .... Ch

Chapter (WDMC) .... ch

Chapter (WDMC) .... chap

Chapter (AFM) .... CHAP

Chapter (VRA) .... chpt

Chapter .... CHPTR

Chapter .... CP

Chapter Director .... CD

Chapter House [*British*] (ROG) .... CH

Chapter House [*British*] (ROG) .... CHAP HO

Chapter House (VRA) .... chpt hs

Chapter Illuminators of Sweden [*Freemasonry*] (ROG) .... CHAP I of S

Chapter Liaison Officer .... CLO

Chapter Relations Committee [*American Library Association*] .... CRC

Chapters (WGA) CC

Chapters of Instruction [*Freemasonry*] (ROG) CI

Chara Corallina Virus [*Plant pathology*] CCV

Charabanc [*Bus used for sightseeing trips*] [*Slang British*] (DSUE) .... CHARA

Characato [*Formerly, Arequipa*] [*Peru Later, FRD*] [*Geomagnetic observatory code*] .... ARE

Character (BUR) C

Character [*Computer science*] (BUR) .... CH

Character (KSC) .... CHAR

Character .... CHAR

Character [*or Characteristic*] [*Computer science*] (IAA) .... CHARAC

Character (BUR) .... CHR

Character Address Module [*Computer science*] (PDAA) .... CAM

Character Allocated Transfer Channel [*Computer science*] (IAA) .... CATCH

Character and Pattern Telephone Access Information Network System [*Viewdata system*] [*Japan*] .... CAPTAINS

Character Assemble/Disassemble .... CAD

Character Assignment Table [*Computer science*] (IAA) .... CAT

Character Background Generator [*Television*] (WDMC) .... Dubner CBG

Character Block Transfer (BYTE) .... CBLT

Character Buffer Unit [*Computer science*] (ECII) .... CBU

Character, Capacity, Capital [*Accounting*] .... 3C's

Character, Capacity, Capital, Collateral, and Conditions [*Credit evaluation*] [*Banking*] .... 5C's

Character Control Block [*Computer science*] (IBMDP) .... CCB

Character Controlled Protocol (HGAA) .... CCP

Character Count [*Typography*] CC

Character Count Protocol (HGAA) .... CCP

Character Delete [*Computer science*] (WDMC) .... char del

Character Disorder Sign [*Psychology*] .... CdS

Character Education Institute (EA) .... CEI

Character Education Partnership [*An association*] .... CEP

Character Error Rate Test .... CERT

Character Generator [*Telecommunications*] .... CG

Character Generator [*Computer science*] (NITA) .... CHRGN

Character Guidance [*Army*] (AABC) .... CHARGUID

Character Instruction Set (IEEE) .... CIS

Character Manipulation Procedures .... CHAMP

Character Mode Communications Adapter .... CMCA

Character Multiplexer [*Telecommunications*] .... CMX

Character Position in Frame .... CPIF

Character Printer [*Computer science*] .... CP

Character Reader [*Computer science*] (IAA) .... CR

Character Recognition Circuit (IAA) .... CRC

Character Register .... CHR

Character Scan Command [*Computer science*] .... CSCN

Character Scan or Alternate [*Computer science*] .... CSA

Character Scan or Fail [*Computer science*] .... CSF

Character Sequence Detector (MCD) .... CSD

Character Set Computer Development .... CSCD

Character Shape Player (PCM) .... CSP

Character Start-Stop .... CSS

Character String Scanner [*Computer program*] .... CSS

Character-Based User Interface [*Computer science*] .... CUI

Character-Error Correcting Convolutional Self-Orthogonal Code (PDAA) .... CCSOC

Characteres [*of Theophrastus*] [*Classical studies*] (OCD) .... Char

Character-Generated [*Refers to electronically produced text*] (WDMC) .... CG

Characteristic (AABC) .... CHAR

Characteristic (MSA) .... CHRST

Characteristic Distortion Compensation [*Telecommunications*] (TEL) .... CDC

Characteristic Event Hypothesis [*For earthquake occurence*] .... CEH

Characteristic Frequency [*Acoustics*] .... CF

Characteristic Function Estimator .... CFE

Characteristic Impedance (IDOE) .... Z

Characteristic Independence CI

Characteristic Instants of Restitution [*Telecommunications*] (OA) .... CIR

Characteristic Item Description (MCD) .... CID

Characteristic Loss Spectroscopy .... CLS

Characteristic Relief .... CR

Characteristic Slope .... CS

Characteristic Standard .... CS

Characteristic Statistical Value .... CSV

Characteristic Storage and Retrieval (EDAC) .... CSAR

Characteristics of Business Owners [*Bureau of the Census*] (GFGA) .... CBO

Characteristics of Materials (KSC) .... COMAT

Characteristics of Transportation Resources File .... CHSTR

Characteristics of Urban Transportation Demand (MCD) .... CUTD

Characteristics Properties Code [*NASA*] (NASA) .... CPC

Characterization and Assessment Division [*Environmental Protection Agency*] (GFGA) .... CAD

Character-Mode Data Terminal Equipment [*Computer science*] (PDAA) .... C-DTE

Character-Oriented Input-Output Processor [*Computer science*] (IAA) .... CHIO

Character-Oriented Message (RDA) .... COM

Characters in 19th Century Literature [*A publication*] .... CNCL

Characters in Twentieth-Century Literature [*A publication*] .... CTCL

Characters per Column [*Typesetting*] .... CPC

Characters per Hour [*Computer science*] .... CPH

Characters Per Hour (WDMC) .... cph

Characters per Inch [*Computer science*] (CMD) .... CHPI

Characters per Inch [*Typesetting*] .... CPI

Characters Per Inch [*Typesetting*] (WDMC) .... cpi

Characters Per Line [*Typesetting*] (WDMC) .... cpl

Characters per Line [*Typesetting*] .... CPL

Characters per Millimeter [*Typesetting*] (IAA) .... CPMM

Characters per Minute [*Computer science*] .... CPM

Characters Per Minute [*Typesetting*] (WDMC) .... cpm

Characters Per Pica [*Typesetting*] (WDMC) .... CPP

Characters per Second [*Computer science*] (IAA) .... CHARSEC

Characters per Second [*Computer science*] (CMD) .... CHPS

Characters per Second [*Computer science*] (IAA) .... CHS

Characters per Second [*Computer science*] (IAA) .... CHSEC

Characters per Second [*Computer science*] .... CPS

Characters per Second [*Computer science*] .... cps

Characters Per Second [*Computer science*] (WDMC) .... cps

Character-to-Date [*Microsoft Corp. FoxPro function*] (PCM) .... CTOD

Charactron Tube [*Electronics*] .... CHT

Charactron Tube [*Electronics*] .... CRT

Charagua [*Bolivia*] [*ICAO location identifier*] (ICLI) .... SLCG

Charan Industries, Inc. [*Toronto Stock Exchange symbol*] .... CHN

Charana [*Bolivia*] [*ICAO location identifier*] (ICLI) .... SLCN

Charbonneau Connection (EA) CC

Charburjak [*Afghanistan*] [*ICAO location identifier*] (ICLI) .... OACB

Charcoal [*Automotive advertising*] .... CH

Charcoal .... CHAR

Charcoal (VRA) .... chl

Charcoal .... CHRCL

Charcoal Accumulation Rate [*Ecology*] .... CHAR

Charcoal Canister (GNE) CC

Charcoal Hemoperfusion [*Medicine*] .... CH

Charcoal Inhalation Tester (PDAA) .... CIT

Charcoal, Ink, Oil, Pencil, and Watercolor [*Acronym is used as title of 1931 volume containing art works by e.e. cummings*] .... CIOPW

Charcoal Treated .... CT

Charcoal Viral Transport [*Medium*] [*Microbiology*] .... CVTR

Charcoal Yeast Extract [*Agar medium*] [*Microbiology*] .... CYE

Charcot-Marie Tooth 1B [*Medicine*] CMT1B

Charcot-Marie-Tooth [*Atrophy*] [*Medicine*] .... CMT

Charcot-Marie-Tooth Disease [*Medicine*] (DMAA) .... CMTD

Charcot-Marie-Tooth Syndrome [*Medicine*] (DMAA) .... CMTS

Charcot-Marie-Tooth, X-Linked [*Medicine*] [*Syndrome*] (DMAA) .... CMTX

Chardon du Dol et de la Fraude [*A publication*] (DLA) .... Chard

Chardon, OH [*Location identifier FAA*] (FAAL) .... CXR

Chardon, OH [*AM radio station call letters*] .... WATJ

Charette, Fortier, Hawey, Touche, Ross, Centre de Documentation, Montreal, PQ, Canada [*Library symbol*] [*Library of Congress*] (LCLS) .... CaQMCFH

Charge (ROG) C

Charge .... CGE

Charge (KSC) .... CHG

Charge .... CHGE

Charge (AFM) .... CHRG

Charge .... CHRG

Charge Account Bankers Association [*Later, ABA*] .... CABA

Charge Air-Temperature Sensor [*Automotive engineering*] .... CAS

Charge Amplifier (NRCH) .... CA

Charge Capacitance Probe (NASA) .... CCP

Charge Composition Explorer [*Spacecraft*] .... CCE

Charge Conjugation [*Atomic physics*] C
Charge Conjugation - Parity - Time-Reversal [*Theorem*] [*Atomic physics*] ..... CPT
Charge Conveyor [*Electronics*] (EECA) CC
Charge Coupled (IAA) CC
Charge Coupled Diode Array [*Liquid chromatography*] ..... CCDA
Charge d'Affaires [*Foreign Service*] ..... CA
Charge d'Affaires [*Foreign Service*] ..... CHG
Charge Data System [*Equal Employment Opportunity Commission*] (GFGA) ..... CDS
Charge/Discharge (IAA) ..... CD
Charge Exchange ..... CEX
Charge Exchange Cross Section ..... CECS
Charge Exchange Excitations [*Physics*] ..... CXE
Charge Exchange Neutralo Analyzer (MCD) ..... CENA
Charge for Service ..... CS
Charge Generation Layer (MCD) ..... CGL
Charge Imaging Matrix [*Electronics*] ..... CIM
Charge Injection Transistor Memory [*Electronics*] (NITA) ..... CITM
Charge Material Allocation Processor ..... CMAP
Charge Motion Oriented Process ..... CMOP
Charge Number Grouping (MCD) ..... CNG
Charge Number of a Cell Reaction [*Symbol*] [*Electrochemistry*] ..... z
Charge Nurse [*Medicine*] ..... CN
Charge of Quarters [*Army*] ..... CQ
Charge Parity [*Atomic physics*] ..... CP
Charge, Parity, and Time Coordinates [*Physics*] ..... CPT
Charge Priming Device [*Video technology*] ..... CPD
Charge Pumping Logic (IAA) ..... CPL
Charge Routing Network (IAA) ..... CRN
Charge Spotting Bomb Unit ..... CXU
Charge Storage Junction Field Effect Transistor (IAA) ..... CSJFET
Charge Transfer Efficiency [*In photodetectors*] ..... CTE
Charge Transfer Inefficiency [*in Photodetectors*] (IAA) ..... CTI
Charge Transfer Light Modulator [*Instrumentation*] ..... CTLM
Charge Transforming Operator (IEEE) ..... CTO
Charge Transforming Parameter (IEEE) ..... CTP
Charge Transport Layer (MCD) ..... CTL
Chargeable Downtime [*Navy*] ..... CDT
Chargeable Time (DGA) ..... CT
Chargeable Time Clock [*Telecommunications*] (NITA) ..... CTC
Chargeable to Accidents (MCD) ..... CA
Chargeable to Crew (MCD) CC
Chargeable to Hardware ..... CH
Chargeable to Manuals (MCD) ..... CM
Chargeable to Support Equipment (MCD) ..... CSE
Charge-Air Cooling [*Automotive engineering*] ..... CAC
Charge-Amplified Sample and Hold (PDAA) ..... CASH
Charge-Coupled Area Imaging Device (PDAA) ..... CCAID
Charge-Coupled Device [*Data storage device*] ..... CCD
Charge-Coupled Imager CCI
Charge-Coupled Infrared Information Device (PDAA) ..... CCIRID
Charge-Coupled Memory [*Computer science*] (IAA) ..... CCM
Charge-Coupled Photodiode Array ..... CCPD
Charged (ROG) ..... CHGD
Charged Current [*Physics*] CC
Charged Droplet Scrubber ..... CDS
Charged Particle Activation ..... CPA
Charged Particle Activation Analysis [*Analytical chemistry*] ..... CPAA
Charged Particle Analyzer ..... CPA
Charged Particle Beam [*Weapon*] [*DoD*] ..... CPB
Charged Particle Beam Weapon [*Computer science*] (PDAA) ..... CPBW
Charged Particle Electrostatic Thruster ..... CPET
Charged Particle Equilibrium (DEN) ..... CPE
Charged Particle Lunar Environment Experiment [*NASA*] ..... CPLEE
Charged Particle Telescope ..... CPT
Charged Particles Information Center [*ORNL*] ..... CPIC
Charged Pigment Xerography (IEEE) ..... CPX
Charged Tape Detection [*Fuel-failure monitor*] [*Nuclear energy*] (NRCH) ..... CTD
Charged-Drop Precipitator (PDAA) ..... CDP
Charge-Density Wave [*Physics*] ..... CDW
Charge-Flow Transistor (PDAA) ..... CFT
Charge-Free Anticontamination System ..... CFAS
Charge-Induced Voltage Alteration [*Electronics*] ..... CIVA
Charge-Injection Device [*Electronics*] ..... CID
Charger (MSA) ..... CHGR
Charger Battery Relay (MCD) ..... CBR
Charger Resources Ltd. [*Vancouver Stock Exchange symbol*] ..... CHJ
Charger-Battery-Regulator Module [*NASA*] ..... CBRM
Charge-Recombination [*Physical chemistry*] ..... CR
Charges ..... CHGS
Charges Collect [*Business term*] CC
Charges Forward (DS) ..... Ch Fwd
Charges Prepaid (WDAA) ..... CH PPD
Charge-Separation [*Physical chemistry*] ..... CS
Charge-Transfer [*Intermolecular electron transfer*] ..... CT
Charge-Transfer Device [*Electronics*] ..... CTD
Charge-Transfer Photography ..... CTP
Charge-Transfer Spectrum ..... CTS
Charging Electrical Effects Analyzer (MCD) ..... CEEA
Charging Order (DCTA) ..... CO
Charging Pump (IEEE) ..... CHGP
Charging Pump (NRCH) ..... CP
Charing Cross, Euston & Highgate (Underground) Railway [*British*] (ROG) ..... CCE & HR
Charing Cross Station [*England*] (ROG) CX
Charismatic Renewal Services (EA) ..... CRS
Charitable ..... CHRTBL
Charitable / Employee Stock Ownership Plan [*Tax plan*] (MHDW) ..... CHEPSOP
Charitable/Employee Stock Ownership Plan [*Tax plan*] ..... CHESOP
Charitable Lead Trust ..... CLT
Charitable Organizations of the US [*A publication*] ..... COUS
Charitable Remainder Annuity Trust (NFD) ..... CRAT
Charitable Remainder Trust ..... CRT
Charitable Remainder Unitrust (NFD) ..... CRUT
Charitable Trust for Vietnam War Art (EA) ..... CTVWA
Charities Aid Foundation [*Information service or system*] (IID) ..... CAF
Charities Aid Fund [*British*] ..... CAF
Charities Deposit Fund [*Finance British*] ..... CDF
Charities Information Bureaux [*British*] (CB) ..... CIB
Charities Official Investment Fund [*Finance British*] ..... COIF
Chariton Herald-Patriot, Chariton, IA [*Library symbol Library of Congress*] (LCLS) ..... IaChHP
Chariton, IA [*Location identifier FAA*] (FAAL) ..... CNC
Chariton, IA [*FM radio station call letters*] ..... KELR
Chariton Leader, Chariton, IA [*Library symbol Library of Congress*] (LCLS) ..... IaChL
Charity ..... CHAR
Charity ..... CHY
Charity Christmas Card Council [*British*] (DI) CCCC
Charity Commission [*British*] CC
[*The*] **Charity Forum** [*British*] (EAIO) ..... TCF
Charity Organization Society [*British*] ..... COS
Charlemagne Resources [*Vancouver Stock Exchange symbol*] ..... CHG
Charleroi/Gosselies [*Belgium ICAO location identifier*] (ICLI) ..... EBCI
Charleroi, PA [*AM radio station call letters*] ..... WESA
Charleroi, PA [*FM radio station call letters*] ..... WESA-FM
Charles A. Janeway Child Health Centre, St. John's, NF, Canada [*Library symbol Library of Congress*] (LCLS) ..... CaNfSCJ
Charles A. Lindbergh Association [*Defunct*] (EA) ..... CALA
Charles A. Lindbergh Collectors Club (EA) ..... CALCC
Charles A. Lindbergh Collectors Club (EA) LCC
Charles A. Lindbergh Fund [*An association*] (EA) ..... CALF
Charles A. Ransom Public Library, Plainwell, MI [*Library symbol Library of Congress*] (LCLS) ..... MiPl
Charles Babbage Institute for the History of Information Processing (EA) ..... CBI
Charles Bruning Reproduction Processes ..... CB
Charles Camsell Hospital, Peter Wilcock Library, Edmonton, AB, Canada [*Library symbol Library of Congress*] (LCLS) ..... CaAECCH
Charles City, IA [*Location identifier FAA*] (FAAL) ..... CCY
Charles City, IA [*AM radio station call letters*] ..... KCHA
Charles City, IA [*FM radio station call letters*] ..... KCHA-FM
Charles City Press, Charles City, IA [*Library symbol Library of Congress*] (LCLS) ..... IaChcP
Charles City Public Library, Charles City, IA [*Library symbol Library of Congress*] (LCLS) ..... IaChc
Charles City Western Railway Co. [*AAR code*] ..... CCW
Charles County Community College [*La Plata, MD*] CCCC
Charles County Community College, La Plata, MD [*Library symbol Library of Congress*] (LCLS) ..... MdLapC
Charles Crane Memorial Library, University of British Columbia, Vancouver, British Columbia [*Library symbol National Library of Canada*] (NLC) ..... BVAUCC
Charles Curtis [*Genotype of Phlox paniculata*] C
Charles Curtis Memorial Hospital, International Grenfell Association, St. Anthony, Newfoundland [*Library symbol National Library of Canada*] (NLC) ..... NFSAIC
Charles Curtis Memorial Hospital, International Grenfell Association, St. Anthony, NF, Canada [*Library symbol Library of Congress*] (LCLS) ..... CaNfSaIC
Charles Darwin Foundation for the Galapagos Isles (EA) ..... CDFGI
Charles Darwin Research Station [*Santa Cruz, Galapagos Islands*] ..... CDRS
Charles De Gaulle Airport [*France*] ..... CDG
Charles E. Frosst & Co., Montreal, PQ, Canada [*Library symbol Library of Congress*] (LCLS) ..... CaQMCF
Charles E. Merriam Center for Public Administration, Merriam Center Library, Chicago, IL [*Library symbol Library of Congress*] (LCLS) ..... ICMer
Charles E. Schwarting Elementary School, Massapequa, NY [*Library symbol*] [*Library of Congress*] (LCLS) ..... NMassSE
Charles E. Stevens American Atheist Library and Archives, Inc., Austin, TX [*Library symbol Library of Congress*] (LCLS) ..... TxAuA
Charles Edison Memorial Youth Fund [*Later, FAS*] (EA) ..... CEMYF
Charles F. Kettering Foundation, Dayton, OH [*OCLC symbol*] (OCLC) ..... OKK
Charles F. Kettering Foundation, Kettering, OH [*Library symbol Library of Congress*] (LCLS) ..... OKetK
Charles F. Kettering Foundation, Research Laboratory Library, Yellow Springs, OH [*Library symbol Library of Congress*] (LCLS) ..... OYesK
Charles, [*J. W.*] Financial Services [*Associated Press*] (SAG) ..... CharlsFS
Charles, [*J. W.*] Financial Services [*NASDAQ symbol*] (SAG) ..... KORP
Charles H. Roth High School Library, Henrietta, NY [*OCLC symbol*] (OCLC) ..... RVW
Charles H. Stone Memorial Library, Pilot Mountain, NC [*Library symbol Library of Congress*] (LCLS) ..... NcPm
Charles H. Taylor Memorial Library, Hampton, VA [*Library symbol Library of Congress*] (LCLS) ..... ViHa
Charles Homer Haskins Society (EA) ..... CHHS
Charles Howard & Associates, Winnipeg, Manitoba [*Library symbol National Library of Canada*] (NLC) ..... MWCHA
Charles Howard & Associates, Winnipeg, MB, Canada [*Library symbol Library of Congress*] (LCLS) ..... CaMWCHA
Charles Ives Society (EA) ..... CIS
Charles J. Colgan & Associates, Inc. [*FAA designator*] (FAAC) ..... CJC
Charles (JW) Finl Svcs [*NASDAQ symbol*] (TTSB) ..... KORP

Charles Lamb Society [*British*] ... CLS
Charles Lindbergh Elementary School, Little Falls, MN [*Library symbol*] [*Library of Congress*] (LCLS) ... MnLfCL
Charles M. Shields Centennial Library, South Porcupine, Ontario [*Library symbol National Library of Canada*] (BIB) ... OSPCS
Charles Pfizer & Co. [*Research code symbol*] ... CP
Charles Rennie Mackintosh Society (EAIO) ... CRMS
Charles River Associates Library, Boston, MA [*OCLC symbol*] (OCLC) ... CRA
Charles River Breeding Laboratories ... CRBL
Charles River Data Systems, Inc. (NITA) ... CRDS
Charles S. Peirce Society (EA) ... CPS
Charles Simkins and Rachel Hawthorne Family Association (EA) ... CSRHFA
Charles Stark Draper Laboratory, Inc. [*MIT*] [*Research center*] (NASA) ... CSDL
Charles Stark Draper Laboratory, Inc., Technical Information Center, Cambridge, MA [*Library symbol Library of Congress*] (LCLS) ... MCCSD
Charles Stewart Mott Community College [*Formerly, Genesee Community College*] [*Flint, MI*] ... CSMCC
Charles Stuart Calverley [*19th-century British parodist*] ... CSC
Charles Sturt University - Mitchell at Bathurst [*Australia*] ... CSU-MB
Charles Sturt University - Murray, at Albury Wodonga [*Australia*] ... CSU-MAW
Charles Town, WV [*AM radio station call letters*] ... WXVA
Charles Town, WV [*FM radio station call letters*] ... WXVA-FM
Charles Williams Society [*British*] (EAIO) ... CWS
Charlesbourg [*Quebec*] [*Seismograph station code, US Geological Survey*] (SEIS) ... CHQ
Charleston [*Diocesan abbreviation*] [*South Carolina*] (TOCD) ... CHR
Charleston [*South Carolina*] [*Airport symbol*] ... CHS
Charleston [*West Virginia*] [*Airport symbol*] (AD) ... CHW
Charleston [*West Virginia*] [*Airport symbol*] (OAG) ... CRW
Charleston Air Force Base [*South Carolina*] ... CAFB
Charleston & Western Carolina Railway Co. [*Seaboard Coast Line Railroad*] ... C & WC
Charleston & Western Carolina Railway Co. [*Seaboard Coast Line Railroad*] [*AAR code*] ... CWC
Charleston Area Cooperative Film Library, Charleston, IL [*Library symbol*] [*Library of Congress*] (LCLS) ... ICharF
Charleston Army Depot [*South Carolina*] [*Closed*] (AABC) ... CHAD
Charleston Carnegie Public Library, Charleston, IL [*Library symbol Library of Congress*] (LCLS) ... IChar
Charleston Community Memorial Hospital, Charleston, IL [*Library symbol Library of Congress*] (LCLS) ... ICharH
Charleston Community Unit School District, Charleston, IL [*Library symbol*] [*Library of Congress*] (LCLS) ... ICarSD
Charleston Community Unit School District, Charleston, IL [*Library symbol*] [*Library of Congress*] (LCLS) ... ICharSD
Charleston County Library, Charleston, SC [*Library symbol Library of Congress*] (LCLS) ... ScCF
Charleston Diocesan Archives, Roman Catholic Church, Charleston, SC [*Library symbol Library of Congress*] (LCLS) ... ScCRC
Charleston General Hospital, Charleston, WV [*Library symbol Library of Congress*] (LCLS) ... WvCGH
Charleston, IL [*AM radio station call letters*] ... WEIC
Charleston, IL [*FM radio station call letters*] ... WEIU
Charleston, IL [*Television station call letters*] ... WEIU-TV
Charleston, IL [*FM radio station call letters*] ... WHQQ
Charleston Library Society, Charleston, SC [*Library symbol Library of Congress*] (LCLS) ... ScC
Charleston, MO [*Location identifier FAA*] (FAAL) ... CHQ
Charleston, MO [*AM radio station call letters*] ... KCHR
Charleston, MO [*FM radio station call letters*] ... KWKZ
Charleston, MS [*FM radio station call letters*] ... WTGY
Charleston/Municipal and Air Force Base [*South Carolina*] [*ICAO location identifier*] (ICLI) ... KCHS
Charleston Museum Library, Charleston, SC [*Library symbol Library of Congress*] (LCLS) ... ScCMu
Charleston Naval Shipyard [*South Carolina*] (DNAB) ... CHANSY
Charleston Naval Shipyard [*South Carolina*] ... CHASNAVSHIPY
Charleston Naval Shipyard [*South Carolina*] ... CHNSY
Charleston Naval Shipyard ... CNS
Charleston Naval Shipyard (DOGT) ... CNS
Charleston Naval Shipyard [*South Carolina*] ... CNSY
Charleston Naval Shipyard [*South Carolina*] ... CNSYD
Charleston Naval Station [*South Carolina*] ... CNAVSTA
Charleston Naval Weapons Annex [*South Carolina*] ... CNWA
Charleston, NC [*AM radio station call letters*] ... WQSC
Charleston Resources [*Vancouver Stock Exchange symbol*] ... CNJ
Charleston, SC [*Location identifier FAA*] (FAAL) ... CCI
Charleston, SC [*Location identifier FAA*] (FAAL) ... JZI
Charleston, SC [*Location identifier FAA*] (FAAL) ... NAO
Charleston, SC [*Television station call letters*] (RBYB) ... WBNU
Charleston, SC [*Television station call letters*] ... WCBD
Charleston, SC [*Television station call letters*] ... WCIV
Charleston, SC [*Television station call letters*] ... WCSC
Charleston, SC [*FM radio station call letters*] ... WEZL
Charleston, SC [*FM radio station call letters*] ... WFCH
Charleston, SC [*Television station call letters*] ... WITV
Charleston, SC [*FM radio station call letters*] (RBYB) ... WJZK-FM
Charleston, SC [*AM radio station call letters*] ... WPAL
Charleston, SC [*AM radio station call letters*] (RBYB) ... WQNT-AM
Charleston, SC [*FM radio station call letters*] ... WSCI
Charleston, SC [*FM radio station call letters*] ... WSSX
Charleston, SC [*FM radio station call letters*] ... WSUY
Charleston, SC [*Television station call letters*] ... WTAT
Charleston, SC [*AM radio station call letters*] ... WTMA
Charleston, SC [*AM radio station call letters*] ... WUJM
Charleston, SC [*AM radio station call letters*] ... WXTC
Charleston, SC [*FM radio station call letters*] ... WXTC-FM
Charleston Submarine Training Center [*South Carolina*] ... CSTC
Charleston Training Center [*South Carolina*] ... CTC
Charleston, WV [*Location identifier FAA*] (FAAL) ... CRW
Charleston, WV [*AM radio station call letters*] ... WCAW
Charleston, WV [*AM radio station call letters*] ... WCHS
Charleston, WV [*Television station call letters*] ... WCHS-TV
Charleston, WV [*AM radio station call letters*] ... WCZR
Charleston, WV [*Television station call letters*] ... WKRP
Charleston, WV [*FM radio station call letters*] ... WKWS
Charleston, WV [*AM radio station call letters*] ... WQBE
Charleston, WV [*FM radio station call letters*] ... WQBE-FM
Charleston, WV [*FM radio station call letters*] ... WVAF
Charleston, WV [*Television station call letters*] ... WVAH
Charleston, WV [*FM radio station call letters*] ... WVPN
Charleston, WV [*AM radio station call letters*] ... WVSR
Charleston, WV [*FM radio station call letters*] ... WVSR-FM
Charlestown/Newcastle [*Nevis Island*] [*ICAO location identifier*] (ICLI) ... TKPN
Charlestown Township Public Library, Charlestown, IN [*Library symbol Library of Congress*] (LCLS) ... InCha
Charleswood Public Library, Winnipeg, Manitoba [*Library symbol National Library of Canada*] (NLC) ... MWCHD
Charleswood Public Library, Winnipeg, MB, Canada [*Library symbol*] [*Library of Congress*] (LCLS) ... CaMWCHD
Charleville [*Australia ICAO location identifier*] (ICLI) ... ABCV
Charleville [*Australia Airport symbol*] (OAG) ... CTL
Charleville/Mezieres [*France ICAO location identifier*] (ICLI) ... LFQV
Charlevoix, MI [*Location identifier FAA*] (FAAL) ... CVX
Charlevoix, MI [*FM radio station call letters*] ... WKHQ
Charlevoix, MI [*AM radio station call letters*] ... WMKT
Charlevoix Public Library, Charlevoix, MI [*Library symbol Library of Congress*] (LCLS) ... MiChv
Charley [*Nevada*] [*Seismograph station code, US Geological Survey Closed*] (SEIS) ... NYC
Charley Pride Fan Club (EA) ... CPFC
Charley's Chamber Cases [*1875-76*] [*England*] [*A publication*] (DLA) ... Char Cham Cas
Charley's Chamber Cases [*1875-76*] [*England*] [*A publication*] (DLA) ... Charl Cha Cas
Charley's Chamber Cases [*1875-76*] [*England*] [*A publication*] (DLA) ... Charley Ch Cas
Charley's Pleading under the Judicature Acts [*A publication*] (DLA) ... Charl Pl
Charley's Practice Cases [*1875-81*] [*England*] [*A publication*] (DLA) ... Char Pr Cas
Charley's Practice Cases [*1875-81*] [*England*] [*A publication*] (DLA) ... Charl Pr Cas
Charley's Practice Cases [*1875-81*] [*England*] [*A publication*] (DLA) ... Charley Pr Cas
Charley's Real Property Statutes [*A publication*] (DLA) ... Charl RP Stat
Charlie [*Phonetic alphabet*] [*International since 1956*] (DSUE) ... C
Charlie Daniels Band ... CDB
Charlie Daniels Fan Club (EA) ... CDFC
Charlie Daniels Fan Club Volunteers (EA) ... CDFCV
Charlie Hammonds Flying Service, Inc. [*FAA designator*] (FAAC) ... HMD
Charlie Hodge Fan Club Internationale (EA) ... CHFCI
Charlie O Beverage [*Vancouver Stock Exchange symbol*] ... CJV
Charlie Rich Fan Club (EA) ... CRFC
Charlie/Victor/Yankee [*Military*] (CAAL) ... CVY
Charlim Explorations [*Vancouver Stock Exchange symbol*] ... CHO
Charlo [*Canada*] [*Airport symbol*] (OAG) ... YCL
Charlo, NB [*ICAO location identifier*] (ICLI) ... CYCL
Charlotte [*North Carolina*] [*Mint mark, when appearing on US coins*] ... C
Charlotte [*Diocesan abbreviation*] [*North Carolina*] (TOCD) ... CHL
Charlotte [*North Carolina*] [*Airport symbol*] (OAG) ... CLT
Charlotte Amalie, St. Thomas, VI [*Location identifier FAA*] (FAAL) ... TMN
Charlotte Amalie, VI [*Location identifier FAA*] (FAAL) ... STT
Charlotte Amalie, VI [*AM radio station call letters*] ... WGOD
Charlotte Amalie, VI [*FM radio station call letters*] ... WGOD-FM
Charlotte Amalie, VI [*FM radio station call letters*] ... WIVI
Charlotte Amalie, VI [*FM radio station call letters*] ... WIYC
Charlotte Amalie, VI [*AM radio station call letters*] ... WSTA
Charlotte Amalie, VI [*Television station call letters*] ... WTJX
Charlotte Amalie, VI [*FM radio station call letters*] ... WVGN
Charlotte Amalie, VI [*FM radio station call letters*] ... WVNX
Charlotte Amalie, VI [*AM radio station call letters*] ... WVWI
Charlotte Amalie, VI [*Television station call letters*] ... WVXF
Charlotte County Historical Society, Inc., St. Andrews, NB, Canada [*Library symbol Library of Congress*] (LCLS) ... CaNBACCH
Charlotte County Historical Society, Inc., St. Andrews, New Brunswick [*Library symbol National Library of Canada*] (NLC) ... NBACCH
Charlotte Junior/Senior High School Library, Rochester, NY [*OCLC symbol*] (OCLC) ... RVX
Charlotte, MI [*AM radio station call letters*] ... WLCM
Charlotte, MI [*FM radio station call letters*] ... WMMQ
Charlotte Motor Speedway [*Auto racing*] ... CMS
Charlotte, NC [*Location identifier FAA*] (FAAL) ... BQC
Charlotte, NC [*Location identifier FAA*] (FAAL) ... DQG
Charlotte, NC [*Location identifier FAA*] (FAAL) ... PEP
Charlotte, NC [*AM radio station call letters*] ... WBAV
Charlotte, NC [*AM radio station call letters*] ... WBT
Charlotte, NC [*Television station call letters*] ... WBTV
Charlotte, NC [*Television station call letters*] ... WCCB
Charlotte, NC [*Television station call letters*] ... WCNC
Charlotte, NC [*FM radio station call letters*] ... WEDJ
Charlotte, NC [*FM radio station call letters*] ... WFAE
Charlotte, NC [*AM radio station call letters*] (RBYB) ... WFNZ

Charlotte, NC [*AM radio station call letters*] ... WGSP
Charlotte, NC [*AM radio station call letters*] ... WHVN
Charlotte, NC [*AM radio station call letters*] ... WIST
Charlotte, NC [*FM radio station call letters*] (RBYB) ... WNKS-FM
Charlotte, NC [*AM radio station call letters*] (RBYB) ... WNMX-AM
Charlotte, NC [*AM radio station call letters*] ... WOGR
Charlotte, NC [*FM radio station call letters*] ... WSOC
Charlotte, NC [*Television station call letters*] ... WSOC-TV
Charlotte, NC [*FM radio station call letters*] ... WSSS
Charlotte, NC [*Television station call letters*] ... WTVI
Charlotte, NC [*FM radio station call letters*] (RBYB) ... WWSN
Charlotte, NC [*AM radio station call letters*] ... WYFQ
Charlotte, NC [*FM radio station call letters*] ... WYHC
Charlotte, NC Air National Guard [*FAA designator*] (FAAC) ... CGD
Charlotte Ordnance Missile Plant ... COMP
Charlotte Public Library, Charlotte, MI [*Library symbol Library of Congress*] (LCLS) ... MiChar
Charlotte-Glades Library System, Port Charlotte, FL [*Library symbol Library of Congress*] (LCLS) ... FPoCG
Charlotte-Mecklenburg School District ... CMS
Charlotte-Mecklenburg Schools, Staff Development Center, Charlotte, NC [*Library symbol Library of Congress*] (LCLS) ... NcCS
Charlottesville [*Virginia*] [*Airport symbol*] (OAG) ... CHO
Charlottesville [*Virginia*] [*Seismograph station code, US Geological Survey Closed*] (SEIS) ... CLT
Charlottesville [*Virginia*] [*Seismograph station code, US Geological Survey Closed*] (SEIS) ... CTV
Charlottesville [*Virginia*] [*Seismograph station code, US Geological Survey*] (SEIS) ... CVV
Charlottesville, VA [*Location identifier FAA*] (FAAL) ... AZS
Charlottesville, VA [*AM radio station call letters*] ... WCHV
Charlottesville, VA [*Television station call letters*] ... WHTJ
Charlottesville, VA [*AM radio station call letters*] ... WINA
Charlottesville, VA [*AM radio station call letters*] ... WKAV
Charlottesville, VA [*FM radio station call letters*] ... WLJL
Charlottesville, VA [*FM radio station call letters*] (RBYB) ... WNRN-FM
Charlottesville, VA [*FM radio station call letters*] ... WQMZ
Charlottesville, VA [*FM radio station call letters*] ... WTJU
Charlottesville, VA [*FM radio station call letters*] ... WUVA
Charlottesville, VA [*Television station call letters*] ... WVIR
Charlottesville, VA [*FM radio station call letters*] ... WVTU
Charlottesville, VA [*FM radio station call letters*] (RBYB) ... WVTW-FM
Charlottesville, VA [*FM radio station call letters*] ... WWWV
Charlottetown [*Canada*] [*Airport symbol*] (OAG) ... YYG
Charlottetown Area Tourism Industry Association (AC) ... CATIA
Charlottetown, PE [*Television station call letters*] ... CBCT
Charlottetown, PE [*FM radio station call letters*] ... CBCT-FM
Charlottetown, PE [*AM radio station call letters*] ... CFCY
Charlottetown, PE [*FM radio station call letters*] ... CHLQ
Charlottetown, PE [*AM radio station call letters*] ... CHTN
Charlottetown, PE [*FM radio station call letters*] (RBYB) ... CIMN
Charlottetown, PE [*Television station call letters*] ... CKCW-1
Charlottetown, PE [*ICAO location identifier*] (ICLI) ... CYYG
Charlton Kings [*Urban district in England*] ... CHARL
Charlton, MA [*FM radio station call letters*] ... WBPV
Charm [*Jewelry*] (ROG) ... CHM
Charm Bracelet Polymer [*Organic chemistry*] ... CBP
Charmed (Quark) [*Atomic physics*] ... c
Charmides [*of Plato*] [*Classical studies*] (OCD) ... Chrm
Charming Shoppes [*NASDAQ symbol*] (TTSB) ... CHRS
Charming Shoppes, Inc. [*Associated Press*] (SAG) ... ChmSh
Charming Shoppes, Inc. [*Associated Press*] (SAG) ... ChrmSh
Charming Shoppes, Inc. [*NASDAQ symbol*] (NQ) ... CHRS
Charnes Organizational Diagnosis Survey [*Medicine*] (DMAA) ... CODS
Charnwood Forest [*England*] [*Seismograph station code, US Geological Survey*] (SEIS) ... CWF
Charoen Pokphand [*Thai business conglomerate*] (ECON) ... CP
Char-Oil-Energy-Development [*Process*] [*Project of Office of Coal Research*] ... COED
Charolais Society of Australia ... CSA
Charpy V-Notch [*Nuclear energy*] (NRCH) ... CVN
Charring Ablation Program [*NASA*] ... CHAP
Charriot Resources [*Vancouver Stock Exchange symbol*] ... CIO
Char-Swiss Breeders Association (EA) ... CSBA
Chart ... CH
Chart ... CT
Chart Comparison Unit ... CCU
Chart Distribution Data ... CDD
Chart House Enterpr [*NYSE symbol*] (TTSB) ... CHT
Chart House Enterprises [*NYSE symbol*] (SPSG) ... CHT
Chart House Enterprises [*Associated Press*] (SAG) ... ChtHou
Chart Industries [*Associated Press*] (SAG) ... Chart
Chart Industries [*NYSE symbol*] (SPSG) ... CTI
Chart Maker [*Computer Design*] [*Software package*] (NCC) ... CM
Chart Not Available [*Medicine*] (DAVI) ... CNA
Chart Updating Manual [*Air Force*] ... CHUM
Charta [*Paper*] [*Pharmacy*] ... CHART
Charta Bibula [*Blotting Paper*] [*Latin*] ... CHART BIB
Charta Cerata [*Waxed Paper*] [*Pharmacy*] ... CHART CERAT
Charta de Foresta [*Charter of the Forest*] [*Latin A publication*] (DLA) ... Chart Forest
Charta de Foresta [*Charter of the Forest*] [*Latin A publication*] (DLA) ... Chart Foresta
Charta Mercatoria [*Latin A publication*] (DLA) ... Char Merc
Chartae Antiquae [*A publication*] (DLA) ... Chart Antiq
Chartair, Inc. [*ICAO designator*] (FAAC) ... SJN
Charted Visual Flight Procedure Approach [*FAA*] (TAG) ... CVFP
Charter ... CHAR
Charter ... CHRTR
Charter (FAAC) ... CHTR
Charter Air Ges. MbH & Co. Kg [*Austria*] [*FAA designator*] (FAAC) ... CHW
Charter Bancshares [*NASDAQ symbol*] (SPSG) ... SAIL
Charter Bancshares, Inc. [*Associated Press*] (SAG) ... ChtBnc
Charter Bank SB [*Associated Press*] (SAG) ... ChrtBk
Charter Bank Shares, Inc. [*NASDAQ symbol*] (SAG) ... CBSB
Charter Cruise Air Ltd. [*Australia*] ... CCA
Charter Federal Savings & Loan Virginia [*Associated Press*] (SAG) ... ChartFdl
Charter Federal Savings & Loan Virginia [*NASDAQ symbol*] (NQ) ... CHFD
Charter Financial [*NQS*] (TTSB) ... CBSB
Charter Long Term ... CHLT
Charter Medical Corp. [*Associated Press*] (SAG) ... ChrtMed
Charter Medical Corp. [*AMEX symbol*] (SPSG) ... CMD
Charter Oak Times, Charter Oak, IA [*Library symbol Library of Congress*] (LCLS) ... IaChoT
Charter of Economic Rights and Duties of States [*United Nations*] ... CERDS
Charter Oil Co. Ltd. [*Toronto Stock Exchange symbol*] ... CHR
Charter One Financial, Inc. [*Associated Press*] (SAG) ... ChtOneF
Charter One Financial, Inc. [*NASDAQ symbol*] (SAG) ... COFI
Charter One Finl [*NASDAQ symbol*] (TTSB) ... COFI
Charter Party [*Transportation*] ... CP
Charter Power Systems [*Associated Press*] (SAG) ... ChtPwr
Charter Power Systems [*NASDAQ symbol*] (SAG) ... CHTR
Charter Rolls [*British*] ... CH
Charter, Rural, and Intercity Bus Survey [*Bureau of the Census*] (GFGA) ... CRIBS
Charterair [*ICAO designator*] (AD) ... HO
Chartered ... CHRTRD
Chartered Accountant ... CA
Chartered Accountant ... CHARTAC
Chartered Accountant in Australia [*A publication*] ... Ch Acc Aust
Chartered Accountant in Australia [*A publication*] ... Chart Acc Aust
Chartered Accountant Students' Society [*Australia*] ... CASS
Chartered Administrator (DD) ... CAdm
Chartered Agent [*Business term*] ... C/A
Chartered Association of Certified Accountants [*British*] (EAIO) ... CACA
Chartered Auctioneers' and Estate Agents' Institute [*British*] (BI) ... CAEAI
Chartered Building Societies Institute [*British*] (DBA) ... CBSI
Chartered Business Valuator [*Canada*] (DD) ... CBV
Chartered Cartographer ... CC
Chartered Chemist [*British*] ... CChem
Chartered Colorist (DD) ... CCol
Chartered Colourist [*British*] (DBQ) ... CCol
Chartered Electrical Engineer [*British*] (DAS) ... CEE
Chartered Engineer [*British*] ... C Eng
Chartered Engineer [*British*] ... CE
Chartered Engineer [*A publication*] ... Chart Engr
Chartered Financial Analyst [*Institute of Chartered Fi nancial Analysts*] [*Designation awarded by*] ... CFA
Chartered Financial Consultant (MHDB) ... CFC
Chartered Financial Consultant [*The American College*] [*Designation awarded by*] ... ChFC
Chartered Financial Counselor (DFIT) ... CFC
Chartered Financial Planner ... CFP
Chartered Financial Planner [*Insurance*] ... ChFP
Chartered Financial Underwriter ... CFU
Chartered Institute of Arbitrators [*British*] (DBA) ... CIArb
Chartered Institute of Bankers [*London, England*] (EAIO) ... CIB
Chartered Institute of Building [*British Research center*] (DI) ... CIOB
Chartered Institute of Loss Adjusters [*British*] (BI) ... CILA
Chartered Institute of Management Accountants [*British*] (EAIO) ... CIMA
Chartered Institute of Marine Engineers ... CIME
Chartered Institute of Marketing [*British*] (EAIO) ... CIM
Chartered Institute of Marketing Management of Ontario (AC) ... CIMMO
Chartered Institute of Patent Agents [*British*] (BI) ... CIPA
Chartered Institute of Public Finance and Accountancy [*Formerly, IMTA*] [*British*] ... CIPFA
Chartered Institute of Secretaries [*British*] (BI) ... CIS
Chartered Institute of Transport (EAIO) ... CIT
Chartered Institute of Transport in Australia ... CITA
Chartered Institute of Transport in Canada [*Institut Agree des Transports du Canada*] (AC) ... CIT in Canada
Chartered Institution of Building Service (EAIO) ... CIBS
Chartered Institution of Building Services Engineers (EAIO) ... CIBSE
Chartered Insurance Broker ... CIB
Chartered Insurance Institute [*British*] ... CII
Chartered Investment Counsel (MHDB) ... CIC
Chartered Investment Counsellor [*Canada*] (DD) ... CIC
Chartered Librarian [*British*] ... CL
Chartered Life Underwriter [*Solomon S. Huebner School of CLU Studies, The American College*] [*Designation awarded by*] ... CLU
Chartered Life Underwriter (AAGC) ... CLU
Chartered Loss Adjuster (DD) ... CLA
Chartered Patent Agent ... CPA
Chartered Property and Casualty Underwriter [*Designation awarded by American Institute for Property and Liability Underwriters*] ... CPCU
Chartered Public Accountant ... CPA
Chartered Secretary [*A publication*] ... Ch Sec
Chartered Secretary [*A publication*] ... Chart Secretary
Chartered Shorthand Reporters' Association of Ontario (AC) ... CSRAO
Chartered Society of Designers [*British England*] (EAIO) ... CSD
Chartered Society of Massage and Medical Gymnastics (DAVI) ... CSMMG
Chartered Society of Physiotherapy [*British*] ... CSP

Chartered Stenographic Reporter ... CSR
Chartered Surveyor (ODBW) ... CS
Chartered Surveyors' Institution [*British*] (DAS) ... CSI
Charterers Pay Dues (WGA) ... CPD
Charterhall Oil Canada [*Vancouver Stock Exchange symbol*] ... CHL
Charters Towers [*Australia Seismograph station code, US Geological Survey*] (SEIS) ... CTA
Charters Towers [*Australia Seismograph station code, US Geological Survey*] (SEIS) ... CTAO
Charters Towers [*Australia Airport symbol*] (OAG) ... CXT
Chartier Family Association (EA) ... CFA
Charting (AFM) ... CHTG
Charting and Geodetic Services Office [*National Oceanic and Atmospheric Administration*] (PDAA) ... C & GS
Chartres/Champhol [*France ICAO location identifier*] (ICLI) ... LFOR
Chartula [*A Small Paper*] [*Pharmacy*] ... CHARTUL
Chartwell Leisure, Inc. [*Associated Press*] (SAG) ... ChartwellL
Chartwell Leisure, Inc. [*NASDAQ symbol*] (SAG) ... CHRT
Chartwell Re Corp. [*Associated Press*] (SAG) ... ChartwllRe
Chartwell Re Corp. [*NYSE symbol*] (SAG) ... CWL
Chartwell Re Corp. [*NASDAQ symbol*] (TTSB) ... CWLR
Charwoman [*Slang British*] (DSUE) ... CHAR
Charybdotoxin [*Biochemistry*] ... CTX
Chase Aircraft Co. ... CAC
Chase Brass Indus [*NYSE symbol*] (TTSB) ... CSI
Chase Brass Industries, Inc. [*Associated Press*] (SAG) ... ChaseBr
Chase Brass Industries, Inc. [*Associated Press*] (SAG) ... ChaseBrs
Chase Brass Industries, Inc. [*NYSE symbol*] (SAG) ... CSI
Chase City, VA [*Location identifier FAA*] (FAAL) ... CXE
Chase City, VA [*FM radio station call letters*] ... WFXQ
Chase City, VA [*AM radio station call letters*] ... WMEK
Chase Corp. [*AMEX symbol*] (SAG) ... CCF
Chase Corp. [*Associated Press*] (SAG) ... ChaseCp
Chase Econometrics Associates, Inc. [*Information service or system*] (IID) ... CEAI
Chase Econometrics/Interactive Data Corp. [*Database vendor*] ... CE/IDC
Chase Federal Bank [*NASDAQ symbol*] (TTSB) ... CHFB
Chase Manhattan [*NYSE symbol*] (TTSB) ... CMB
Chase Manhattan 10 1/2%'A'Pfd [*NYSE symbol*] (TTSB) ... CMBPrA
Chase Manhattan 7.50% Dep Pfd [*NYSE symbol*] (TTSB) ... CMBPfK
Chase Manhattan 7.58% Dep Pfd [*NYSE symbol*] (TTSB) ... CMBPrJ
Chase Manhattan 7.92% Dep Ptd [*NYSE symbol*] (TTSB) ... CMBPrI
Chase Manhattan 8.32%'F'Pfd [*NYSE symbol*] (TTSB) ... CMBPrF
Chase Manhattan 8.40% M Pfd [*NYSE symbol*] (TTSB) ... CMBPrM
Chase Manhattan 8.50%'E'Pfd [*NYSE symbol*] (TTSB) ... CMBPrE
Chase Manhattan 9.08%'D'Pfd [*NYSE symbol*] (TTSB) ... CMBPrD
Chase Manhattan 9.76%'B'Pfd [*NYSE symbol*] (TTSB) ... CMBPrB
Chase Manhattan 10.84%'C'Pfd [*NYSE symbol*] (TTSB) ... CMBPrC
Chase Manhattan 10.96% Pfd [*NYSE symbol*] (TTSB) ... CMBPrG
Chase Manhattan 8.375% Pfd [*NYSE symbol*] (TTSB) ... CMBPrH
Chase Manhattan Adj N Pfd [*NYSE symbol*] (TTSB) ... CMBPrN
Chase Manhattan Adj Rt'L'Pfd [*NYSE symbol*] (TTSB) ... CMBPrL
Chase Manhattan Bank, New York, NY [*OCLC symbol*] (OCLC) ... ZCB
[*The*] **Chase Manhattan Corp.** [*Associated Press*] (SAG) ... Chase
[*The*] **Chase Manhattan Corp.** [*Associated Press*] (SAG) ... Chse
[*The*] **Chase Manhattan Corp.** [*New York, NY NYSE symbol*] (SPSG) ... CMB
Chase Manhattan Wrrt [*NYSE symbol*] (TTSB) ... CMB.WS
Chase on Stephens' Digest of Evidence [*A publication*] (DLA) ... Chase Steph Dig Ev
Chase Preferred Capital Corp. [*Associated Press*] (SAG) ... ChsePC
Chase Preferred Capital Corp. [*NYSE symbol*] (SAG) ... CMB
Chase Public Library, Chase, MI [*Library symbol Library of Congress*] (LCLS) ... MiCha
Chase Ranch [*California*] [*Seismograph station code, US Geological Survey*] (SEIS) ... CSR
Chase Resources [*Vancouver Stock Exchange symbol*] ... CQS
Chase World Information Corp. [*Information service or system*] (IID) ... CWIC
Chase's Blackstone [*A publication*] (DLA) ... Ch Black
Chase's Blackstone [*A publication*] (DLA) ... Chase's Bl
Chase's Statutes at Large [*Ohio*] [*A publication*] (DLA) ... Chase's St
Chase's Trial (Impeachment) by the United States Senate [*A publication*] (DLA) ... Chase Tr
Chase's United States Circuit Court Decisions [*A publication*] (DLA) ... Chase
Chase's United States Circuit Court Decisions [*A publication*] (DLA) ... Chase Dec
Chase's United States Circuit Court Decisions, Edited by Johnson [*A publication*] (DLA) ... John
Chase's United States Circuit Court Decisions, Edited by Johnson [*A publication*] (DLA) ... Johns
Chasing (VRA) ... cha
Chasmogamous [*Botany*] ... CH
Chassemaree [*Ship's rigging*] (ROG) ... CH
Chassis ... CHA
Chassis (MSA) ... CHAS
Chassis Compound-Control System [*Automotive engineering*] ... CCS
Chassis Marking Kit ... CMK
Chasti Osobogo Naznacheniia [*Elements of Special Designation*] [*Political police units attached to the armed forces (1918-1924)*] [*Former USSR*] ... ChON
Chasuble (VRA) ... chsbl
ChatCom [*NASDAQ symbol*] (SAG) ... CHAT
ChatCom [*Associated Press*] (SAG) ... ChatCom
ChatCom Inc. [*NASDAQ symbol*] (TTSB) ... CHAT
Chateau [*New Zealand*] [*Seismograph station code, US Geological Survey*] (SEIS) ... CNZ
Chateau Properties [*Associated Press*] (SAG) ... ChateauP
Chateau Properties [*NYSE symbol*] (SPSG) ... CPJ
Chateau Stores of Canada Ltd. [*Toronto Stock Exchange symbol*] ... CTU
Chateau-Arnoux/Saint-Auban [*France ICAO location identifier*] (ICLI) ... LFMX
Chateaugay, NY [*FM radio station call letters*] ... WYUL
Chateauguay Valley English-Speaking Peoples' Association (AC) ... CVESPA
Chateauneuf-Sur-Cher [*France ICAO location identifier*] (ICLI) ... LFFU
Chateauquay, PQ [*FM radio station call letters*] (RBYB) ... CHAI-FM
Chateauroux/Deols [*France ICAO location identifier*] (ICLI) ... LFLX
Chateauroux/Villers [*France ICAO location identifier*] (ICLI) ... LFEJ
Chateau-Thierry-Belleau [*France ICAO location identifier*] (ICLI) ... LFFH
Chatelaine [*Jewelry*] (ROG) ... CHATNE
Chatellerault/Targe [*France ICAO location identifier*] (ICLI) ... LFCA
Chatfield College, St. Martin, OH [*Library symbol Library of Congress*] (LCLS) ... OStmaC
Chatfield Elementary School, Clifton, CO [*Library symbol Library of Congress*] (LCLS) ... CoCfCE
Chatham [*Canada*] [*Airport symbol*] (OAG) ... YCH
Chatham, AK [*Location identifier FAA*] (FAAL) ... CYM
Chatham Canadian Forces Base, NB [*ICAO location identifier*] (ICLI) ... CYCH
Chatham College, Pittsburgh, PA [*OCLC symbol*] (OCLC) ... HHC
Chatham College, Pittsburgh, PA [*Library symbol Library of Congress*] (LCLS) ... PPiCC
Chatham Courier, Chatham, NJ [*Library symbol Library of Congress*] (LCLS) ... NjCC
Chatham Division Royal Marines [*Military unit*] [*British*] ... CDRM
Chatham House (DAS) ... CH
Chatham House Foundation (EA) ... CHF
Chatham Island/Tuuta [*New Zealand*] [*ICAO location identifier*] (ICLI) ... NZCI
Chatham Island/Waitangi [*New Zealand*] [*ICAO location identifier*] (ICLI) ... NZWA
Chatham Islands [*New Zealand*] [*Seismograph station code, US Geological Survey*] (SEIS) ... CIZ
Chatham, MA [*Location identifier FAA*] (FAAL) ... CHH
Chatham, MA [*FM radio station call letters*] ... WFCC
Chatham, NJ [*Location identifier FAA*] (FAAL) ... CAT
Chatham, ON [*AM radio station call letters*] ... CFCO
Chatham, ON [*Television station call letters*] ... CICO-59
Chatham, ON [*FM radio station call letters*] ... CKSY
Chatham Public General Hospital, Chatham, ON, Canada [*Library symbol Library of Congress*] (LCLS) ... CaOChaH
Chatham Public General Hospital, Ontario [*Library symbol National Library of Canada*] (NLC) ... OCHAH
Chatham Public Library, Chatham, NJ [*Library symbol Library of Congress*] (LCLS) ... NjC
Chatham Public Library, Chatham, NY [*Library symbol Library of Congress*] (LCLS) ... NCha
Chatham Public Library, Chatham, ON, Canada [*Library symbol Library of Congress*] (LCLS) ... CaOCha
Chatham Public Library, Chatman, NY [*Library symbol*] [*Library of Congress*] (LCLS) ... NChaL
Chatham Public Library, Ontario [*Library symbol National Library of Canada*] (NLC) ... OCHA
Chatham Township Echoes, Chatham, NJ [*Library symbol Library of Congress*] (LCLS) ... NjCE
Chatham, VA [*AM radio station call letters*] ... WKBY
Chatham-Kent Museum, Chatham, ON, Canada [*Library symbol Library of Congress*] (LCLS) ... CaOChaK
Chatham-Kent Museum, Chatham, Ontario [*Library symbol National Library of Canada*] (NLC) ... OCHAK
Chatillon-Sur-Seine [*France ICAO location identifier*] (ICLI) ... LFQH
Chatom, AL [*FM radio station call letters*] (RBYB) ... WFOW-FM
Chator-Lea Sidecar [*Early motorcars*] (ROG) ... CL
Chatra [*Nepal*] [*Seismograph station code, US Geological Survey*] (SEIS) ... CHA
Chatsworth, GA [*Television station call letters*] ... WCLP
Chatsworth, GA [*FM radio station call letters*] ... WQMT
Chattahoochee, FL [*FM radio station call letters*] ... WBCD
Chattahoochee, FL [*AM radio station call letters*] ... WTCL
Chattahoochee Industrial Railroad [*AAR code*] ... CIRR
Chattahoochee Valley Railway Co. [*AAR code*] ... CHV
Chattahoochee Valley Regional Library, Columbus, GA [*OCLC symbol*] (OCLC) ... GCV
Chattanooga [*Tennessee*] [*Airport symbol*] ... CHA
Chattanooga/Lovell [*Tennessee*] [*ICAO location identifier*] (ICLI) ... KCHA
Chattanooga State Technical Community College, Chattanooga, TN [*Library symbol Library of Congress*] (LCLS) ... TCST
Chattanooga State Technical Institute [*Tennessee*] ... CSTI
Chattanooga, TN [*Location identifier FAA*] (FAAL) ... CGW
Chattanooga, TN [*Location identifier FAA*] (FAAL) ... CQN
Chattanooga, TN [*AM radio station call letters*] ... WDEF
Chattanooga, TN [*FM radio station call letters*] ... WDEF-FM
Chattanooga, TN [*Television station call letters*] ... WDEF-TV
Chattanooga, TN [*AM radio station call letters*] ... WDOD
Chattanooga, TN [*FM radio station call letters*] ... WDOD-FM
Chattanooga, TN [*Television station call letters*] ... WDSI
Chattanooga, TN [*FM radio station call letters*] ... WDYN
Chattanooga, TN [*AM radio station call letters*] ... WGOW
Chattanooga, TN [*AM radio station call letters*] ... WJOC
Chattanooga, TN [*AM radio station call letters*] ... WLMR
Chattanooga, TN [*FM radio station call letters*] ... WMBW
Chattanooga, TN [*AM radio station call letters*] ... WNOO
Chattanooga, TN [*Television station call letters*] ... WRCB
Chattanooga, TN [*FM radio station call letters*] ... WSKZ
Chattanooga, TN [*Television station call letters*] ... WTCI
Chattanooga, TN [*Television station call letters*] ... WTVC
Chattanooga, TN [*FM radio station call letters*] ... WUTC
Chattanooga-Hamilton County Bicentennial Library, Chattanooga, TN [*Library symbol Library of Congress*] (LCLS) ... TC

Chattanooga-Hamilton County Bicentennial Library, Chattanooga, TN [*Library symbol Library of Congress*] (LCLS) ..... TCHCB
Chattanooga-Hamilton County Bicentennial Library, Chattanooga, TX [*OCLC symbol*] (OCLC) ..... TCH
Chattel [*Legal shorthand*] (LWAP) ..... CHAT
Chattel Mortgage [*Legal term*] (DLA) ..... C/M
Chattem Drug and Chemical Co., Chattanooga, TN [*Library symbol Library of Congress*] (LCLS) ..... TCCDC
Chattem, Inc. [*Associated Press*] (SAG) ..... Chattm
Chattem, Inc. [*NASDAQ symbol*] (NQ) ..... CHTT
Chatterbox Recording Club [*British*] (EAIO) ..... CRC
Chatteris [*Urban district in England*] ..... CHATT
Chatterji's Non-Language Preference [*Vocational guidance test*] ..... CNPR
Chatterton Elementary School, Merrick, NY [*Library symbol*] [*Library of Congress*] (LCLS) ..... NMerk CE
Chatto, Bodley Head, and Jonathan Cape Group [*Publishers*] [*British*] ..... CBC
Chatwood Resources [*Vancouver Stock Exchange symbol*] ..... CHW
Chaucer [*Fourteenth century English poet*] (ROG) ..... CHAUC
Chaudiere Branch, Departmental Library, Environment Canada [*Succursale Chaudiere, Bibliotheque du Ministere, Environnement Canada*] **Ottawa, Ontario** [*Library symbol National Library of Canada*] (NLC) ..... OOPAC
Chauffair Ltd. [*British ICAO designator*] (FAAC) ..... CFR
Chauffeur [*Army*] ..... Cfr
Chauffeur (DSUE) ..... CHAUFF
Chauffeur ..... CHFFR
Chaumont-La Vendue [*France ICAO location identifier*] (ICLI) ..... LFSY
Chauncey, GA [*FM radio station call letters*] ..... WQIL
Chaurjahari [*Nepal*] [*Airport symbol*] (OAG) ..... CJR
Chaus [*Bernard*], Inc. [*Associated Press*] (SAG) ..... Chaus
Chaus [*Bernard*], Inc. [*NYSE symbol*] (SPSG) ..... CHS
Chaussure ..... CHSSR
Chautauqua Airlines [*ICAO designator*] (FAAC) ..... CHQ
Chautauqua County Board of Cooperative Educational Services, Fredonia, NY [*Library symbol*] [*Library of Congress*] (LCLS) ..... NFredCB
Chautauqua County Historical Society, Westfield, NY [*Library symbol Library of Congress*] (LCLS) ..... NWefHi
Chautauqua Literary and Scientific Circle (EA) ..... CLSC
Chautauqua-Cattaraugus Library System [*Library network*] ..... CCLS
Chautauqua-Cattaraugus Library System, Jamestown, NY [*Library symbol Library of Congress*] (LCLS) ..... NJamC
Chautauqua-Cattaraugus Library System, Jamestown, NY [*OCLC symbol*] (OCLC) ..... VXU
Chauvco Resources Ltd. [*Toronto Stock Exchange symbol*] ..... CHA
Chauvigny [*France ICAO location identifier*] (ICLI) ..... LFDW
Chauvin Municipal Library, Alberta [*Library symbol National Library of Canada*] (BIB) ..... ACHM
Chavenay/Villepreux [*France ICAO location identifier*] (ICLI) ..... LFPX
Chaves [*Portugal ICAO location identifier*] (ICLI) ..... LPCH
Chavin of Canada [*Vancouver Stock Exchange symbol*] ..... CHX
Chavis, KY [*Location identifier FAA*] (FAAL) ..... DUF
Chazuta [*Peru*] [*ICAO location identifier*] (ICLI) ..... SPZT
CHC Helicopter [*NASDAQ symbol*] (SAG) ..... FLYA
CHC Helicopter Cl'A' [*NASDAQ symbol*] (TTSB) ..... FLYAF
CHC Helicopter Corp. [*Associated Press*] (SAG) ..... CHCHel
CHC Helicopter Corp. [*Toronto Stock Exchange symbol*] ..... FLY
Cheap Access Terminal [*Computer science*] (MHDI) ..... CHAT
Cheap Analyzer of Demographic Data [*Term coined by William F. Doescher, publisher of "D & B Reports"*] ..... Cadd
Cheap Money [*Banking*] ..... CM
Cheap Reprint (DGA) ..... CH RPT
Cheap Trick International (EA) ..... CTI
Cheasapeake, VA [*FM radio station call letters*] ..... WFOS
Cheatham Dam [*TVA*] ..... CD
Cheb [*Eger*] [*Czechoslovakia*] [*Seismograph station code, US Geological Survey*] [*Closed*] (SEIS) ..... CHE
Cheboygan Area Public Library, Cheboygan, MI [*Library symbol Library of Congress*] (LCLS) ..... MiChe
Cheboygan, MI [*AM radio station call letters*] ..... WCBY
Cheboygan, MI [*FM radio station call letters*] ..... WGFM
Cheboygan, MI [*Television station call letters*] ..... WTOM
Chechen [*MARC language code Library of Congress*] (LCCP) ..... che
Check ..... CH
Check (KSC) ..... CHK
Check (WDMC) ..... chk
Check ..... CHK
Check (WDMC) ..... ck
Check (AFM) ..... CK
Check and Store ..... CHST
Check Area Airports (FAAC) ..... CARA
Check Authorization Method ..... CAM
Check Authorization Record (IBMDP) ..... CAR
Check Bit ..... CHKB
Check Coil ..... CHC
Check Collectors Round Table [*Later, ASCC*] (EA) ..... CCRT
Check Correct (ECII) ..... CD
Check Digit [*IRS*] ..... CD
Check Digit [*Computer science*] (EECA) ..... CKDIG
Check Digit Verification (CMD) ..... CDV
Check Digit Verifier ..... CDG
Check Disk [*Computer science*] ..... CHKDSK
Check Express, Inc. [*Associated Press*] (SAG) ..... ChckExp
Check Express, Inc. [*Associated Press*] (SAG) ..... ChkEx
Check Express, Inc. [*NASDAQ symbol*] (SAG) ..... CHXS
Check Fixture (MCD) ..... CKF
Check Form [*Tool*] (AAG) ..... CKFM
Check Gauge [*Tool*] (AAG) ..... CKGA
Check Issued ..... CKI
Check List Question (CAAL) ..... CLQ
Check Not OK [*Telecommunications*] (TEL) ..... CN
Check OK [*Telecommunications*] (TEL) ..... CO
Check Okay (FAAC) ..... CHOK
Check Open [*Nuclear energy*] (NRCH) ..... CO
Check Operator (DEN) ..... CKO
Check Out [*Medicine*] (DAVI) ..... C/O
Check Parity (SAA) ..... CP
Check Plus Minus Subroutine ..... CPMS
Check Point Software Technologies Ltd. [*NASDAQ symbol*] (SAG) ..... CHKP
Check Point Software Technologies Ltd. [*Associated Press*] (SAG) ..... ChkPnt
Check Processing Control System [*IBM Corp.*] (BUR) ..... CPCS
Check Received ..... CKR
Check Register Against Bounds [*Computer science*] ..... CHK
Check Reporting Service ..... CRS
Check Signal Return (NASA) ..... CSR
Check Signal Unit [*Telecommunications*] (TEL) ..... CSU
Check Sorter ..... CS
Check Status Reply (KSC) ..... CSR
Check Surface (IAA) ..... CS
Check Technology [*NASDAQ symbol*] (TTSB) ..... CTCO
Check Technology Corp. [*Associated Press*] (SAG) ..... ChkTch
Check Technology Corp. [*NASDAQ symbol*] (NQ) ..... CTCQ
Check Template ..... CKT
Check Template (MCD) ..... CT
Check Test (MCD) ..... CT
Check Valve (KSC) ..... CHV
Check Valve CV
Checker (MSA) ..... CHKR
Checker Car Club of America (EA) ..... CCCA
Checker Club (EA) CC
Checkerboard Immunoblotting Technique [*Immunology*] ..... CBIB
Checkered (WGA) ..... CH
Checkered [*Navigation markers*] ..... CHEC
Checkers Drive In Restaurants [*Associated Press*] (SAG) ..... Checkers
Checkers Drive-In Restaurants [*NASDAQ symbol*] (SPSG) ..... CHKR
Checkers Drive-In Restr [*NASDAQ symbol*] (TTSB) ..... CHKR
Checkfree Corp. [*Associated Press*] (SAG) ..... Chkfree
Checkfree Corp. [*NASDAQ symbol*] (SAG) ..... CKFR
Checking ..... CHKG
Checking, Accounting and Reporting for Member Firm [*Banking*] (IAA) ..... CHARM
Checking, Accounting, and Reporting for Member Firms [*London Stock Exchange*] (MHDW) ..... CHARM
Checklist (KSC) ..... C/L
Checklist Question (CAAL) ..... CQ
Checkmate ..... CHM
Checkmate Electronics [*NASDAQ symbol*] (TTSB) ..... CMEL
Checkmate Electronics, Inc. [*Associated Press*] (SAG) ..... Checkmte
Checkmate Electronics, Inc. [*NASDAQ symbol*] (SAG) ..... CMEL
Checkmate Resources [*Vancouver Stock Exchange symbol*] ..... CKM
Checkout ..... CKOUT
Checkout (KSC) ..... CO
Checkout and Automatic Monitoring (MSA) ..... CAM
Checkout and Fault Isolation [*NASA*] (KSC) ..... COFI
Checkout and Maintenance ..... CAM
Checkout Command Decoder (NASA) ..... CCD
Checkout Control and Monitor Subsystem [*NASA*] (NASA) ..... CCMS
Checkout/Control and Monitor Subsystem Interface [*NASA*] (NASA) ..... CMSI
Checkout Data Processor [*RADAR*] ..... CDP
Checkout Equipment for Onboard Automatic Maintenance ..... CEFOAM
Checkout Interpreter Module (MCD) ..... COIM
Checkout Language [*NASA*] (NASA) ..... COL
Checkout Operating System ..... COSY
Checkout Operations Manual (AAG) ..... COM
Check-Out Procedure (CAAL) ..... CHOP
Checkout, Servicing, and Maintenance [*Airlock equipment*] (SSD) ..... COSM
Checkout Station (MCD) ..... CS
Checkout Tape [*Computer science*] (IAA) ..... CT
Checkout Techniques Test Bed (NASA) ..... CTTB
Checkout Test Language [*Computer science*] ..... CTL
Checkout Test Set (AAG) ..... COTS
Checkout Time ..... COT
Checkout Valve ..... COV
Checkout-Oriented Language [*Computer science*] (IEEE) ..... COOL
Checkpoint [*A publication*] ..... Check
Checkpoint [*Computer science*] (BUR) ..... CHKPT
Checkpoint (MCD) ..... CKPT
Checkpoint ..... CP
Checkpoint Sys [*NYSE symbol*] (TTSB) ..... CKP
Checkpoint Systems, Inc. [*Associated Press*] (SAG) ..... ChkPt
Checkpoint Systems, Inc. [*NYSE symbol*] (SAG) ..... CKP
Checks Anonymous ..... CA
Checks Fragmentation [*Computer science*] (PCM) ..... CHKFRAG
Checksum Error (MCD) ..... CS
Checkup X-Ray [*Radiology*] (DAVI) ..... CUX
Checkwriting Redemptions [*Business term*] ..... CWR
Chediak-Higashi Disease [*Medicine*] ..... CHD
Chediak-Higashi Syndrome [*Medicine*] (DMAA) ..... CH
Chediak-Higashi Syndrome [*Medicine*] ..... CHS
Chedong [*South Korea ICAO location identifier*] (ICLI) ..... RKPD
Cheektowaga, NY [*AM radio station call letters*] ..... WECK
Cheers International [*Vancouver Stock Exchange symbol*] ..... CHR

Cheese (ROG) ... CH
Cheese ... CHES
Cheese Importers Association of America (EA) ... CIAA
Cheese Whey Powder ... CWP
Cheesecake Factory [*NASDAQ symbol*] (TTSB) ... CAKE
[*The*] **Cheesecake Factory, Inc.** [*NASDAQ symbol*] (SAG) ... CAKE
[*The*] **Cheesecake Factory, Inc.** [*Associated Press*] (SAG) ... Cheeseck
Cheever's Medical Jurisprudence for India [*A publication*] (DLA) ... Cheev Med Jur
Chef der Zivilverwaltung [*Chief of Civil Affairs Section*] [*German military - World War II*] ... CDZ
Chef des Generalstabs des Heeres [*Chief of General Staff of the Army*] [*German military - World War II*] ... CGS
Chefornak [*Alaska*] [*Airport symbol*] (OAG) ... CYF
Chefornak, AK [*Location identifier FAA*] (FAAL) ... CFZ
Chefornak, AK [*Location identifier FAA*] (FAAL) ... CYF
Chefs de Cuisine Association of America (EA) ... CCAA
Chefs de Cuisine Association of America ... CDCA
Chefs International, Inc. [*NASDAQ symbol*] (NQ) ... CHEF
Chefs International, Inc. [*Associated Press*] (SAG) ... ChefsInt
Chefs Intl. [*NASDAQ symbol*] (TTSB) ... CHEF
Cheguitti [*Mauritania*] [*Airport symbol*] (OAG) ... CGT
Chehalis, WA [*Location identifier FAA*] (FAAL) ... CLS
Chehalis, WA [*FM radio station call letters*] ... KACS
Cheju [*South Korea*] [*Airport symbol*] (OAG) ... CJU
Cheju/International [*South Korea ICAO location identifier*] (ICLI) ... RKPC
Cheju/Mosulpo [*South Korea ICAO location identifier*] (ICLI) ... RKPM
Chekiang Province [*China, Mainland*] [*MARC geographic area code Library of Congress*] (LCCP) ... a-cc-ch
Chekok [*Alaska*] [*Seismograph station code, US Geological Survey*] (SEIS) ... CKK
Chelan Butte [*Washington*] [*Seismograph station code, US Geological Survey*] (SEIS) ... CBW
Chelan Resources, Inc. [*Vancouver Stock Exchange symbol*] ... CJN
Chelan, WA [*AM radio station call letters*] ... KOZI
Chelan, WA [*FM radio station call letters*] ... KOZI-FM
Chelating Agent - Diethylenetriaminepentaacetic Acid (PDAA) ... Ca-DTPA
Chelation-Enhanced Fluorescence [*Chemistry*] ... CHEF
Chelation-Enhanced Quenching [*Chemistry*] ... CHEQ
Chelik Resources, Inc. [*Vancouver Stock Exchange symbol*] ... CKV
Chelinda [*Malawi*] [*ICAO location identifier*] (ICLI) ... FWCD
Chelkar [*Former USSR ICAO location identifier*] (ICLI) ... UATR
Chelles/Le Pin [*France ICAO location identifier*] (ICLI) ... LFPH
Chelmsford [*City in England*] ... CHELM
Chelmsford [*City in England*] (ROG) ... CHELMSF
Chelmsford (ODBW) ... CM
Chelmsford Branch, Rayside-Balfour Public Library, Chelmsford, Ontario [*Library symbol National Library of Canada*] (NLC) ... OCHERB
Chelmsford Library, Chelmsford, United Kingdom [*Library symbol Library of Congress*] (LCLS) ... UkCh
Chelsea [*A publication*] (BRI) ... Chel
Chelsea GCA Realty [*NYSE symbol*] (TTSB) ... CCG
Chelsea GCA Realty [*Associated Press*] (SAG) ... ChelGCA
Chelsea GCA Realty [*NYSE symbol*] (SAG) ... COG
Chelsea, London, Islington, Office [*Denoting a location where a manuscript was written*] [*Acronym used as pseudonym of Joseph Addison, British author, 1672-1719*] ... CLIO
Chelsea Public Library, Chelsea, MA [*Library symbol Library of Congress*] (LCLS) ... MChels
Chelsea Resources [*Vancouver Stock Exchange symbol*] ... CHD
Cheltenham [*Typeface*] (DGA) ... CHELT
Cheltenham [*City in England*] ... CHELT
Cheltenham [*City in England*] (ROG) ... CHELTM
Cheltenham [*Maryland*] [*Seismograph station code, US Geological Survey Closed*] (SEIS) ... CLH
Cheltenham and Gloucester [*A British Building Society*] (ECON) ... C & G
Cheltenham Annex [*Military*] (DNAB) ... CAX
Cheltenham-Gloucester [*England*] [*Airport symbol*] (AD) ... GLO
Chelyabinsk Air Enterprise [*Former USSR*] [*FAA designator*] (FAAC) ... CHB
Chem. Fabr. Tempelhof [*Germany*] [*Research code symbol*] ... CFT
Chem International, Inc. [*Associated Press*] (SAG) ... ChemIntl
Chem International, Inc. [*Associated Press*] (SAG) ... ChmInt
Chem International, Inc. [*NASDAQ symbol*] (SAG) ... CXIL
CHEM Singly Indexed Substances [*DIALOG Information Services, Inc.*] [*Database*] ... CHEMSIS
Chem. Werke Albert [*Germany*] [*Research code symbol*] ... HA
Chemagro, Kansas City, MO [*Library symbol Library of Congress*] (LCLS) ... MoKChe
Chemcell Ltd., Montreal, PQ, Canada [*Library symbol Library of Congress*] (LCLS) ... CaQMCh
Chemech Aviation Ltd. [*Pakistan*] [*FAA designator*] (FAAC) ... CMC
Chemed Corp. [*NYSE symbol*] (SPSG) ... CHE
Chemed Corp. [*Associated Press*] (SAG) ... Chemed
Chemehuevi Mountains [*California*] [*Seismograph station code, US Geological Survey*] (SEIS) ... CMH
Chemeketa Community College, Salem, OR [*OCLC symbol*] (OCLC) ... CHK
Chemeketa Community College, Salem, OR [*Library symbol Library of Congress*] (LCLS) ... OrSaC
Chemeketa Cooperative Regional Library Service [*Library network*] ... CCRLS
Chemetics International Ltd., Vancouver, BC, Canada [*Library symbol Library of Congress*] (LCLS) ... CaBVaCI
Chemetics International Ltd., Vancouver, British Columbia [*Library symbol National Library of Canada*] (NLC) ... BVACI
Chemfab Corp. [*Associated Press*] (SAG) ... Chmfab
Chemfab Corp. [*NASDAQ symbol*] (NQ) ... CMFB
Chemi Trol Chem [*NASDAQ symbol*] (TTSB) ... CTRL
Chemical (NFPA) ... C
Chemical [*or Chemistry*] (AFM) ... CHEM
Chemical (ROG) ... CHEML
Chemical ... CHEML
Chemical [*Freight*] ... CHM
Chemical (AABC) ... CML
Chemical Abstract Searching Terminal (NITA) ... CAST
Chemical Abstracts Condensates [*A publication*] (IID) ... CAC
Chemical Abstracts Condensates [*Database*] ... CACON
Chemical Abstracts, Even-Numbered Issue ... CAE
Chemical Abstracts Integrated Subject File [*Chemical Abstracts Service*] [*Database*] [*A publication*] (IID) ... CAISF
Chemical Abstracts, Odd-Numbered Issue ... CAO
Chemical Abstracts, Ohio State University, Columbus, OH [*Library symbol Library of Congress*] (LCLS) ... OUCA
Chemical Abstracts Reference (NITA) ... CR
Chemical Abstracts Selective Dissemination of Information (NITA) ... CHEMSDI
Chemical Abstracts Service [*American Chemical Society*] [*Columbus, OH Database producer*] ... CAS
Chemical Abstracts Service, Columbus, OH [*OCLC symbol*] (OCLC) ... CAS
Chemical Abstracts Service Document Delivery Service [*American Chemical Society*] (NITA) ... CAS DDS
Chemical Abstracts Service Registry Number [*Medicine*] (DMAA) ... CAS-REGN
Chemical Abstracts Service Registry Number ... CASRN
Chemical Abstracts Service Source Index [*American Chemical Society*] [*Information service or system*] ... CASSI
Chemical Abstracts Subject Index Alert [*Database*] [*A publication*] ... CASIA
Chemical Abuse Addiction Treatment Outcome Registry ... CATOR
Chemical Accident/Incident Control (MCD) ... CAIC
Chemical Accident/Incident Control Officer [*Military*] (AABC) ... CAICO
Chemical Activity Status Report [*Chemical Information Systems, Inc.*] [*Information service or system*] (CRD) ... CASR
Chemical Addiction Certification (BARN) ... CAC
Chemical Addition and Sampling System [*Nuclear energy*] (NRCH) ... CA
Chemical Addition Tank (NRCH) ... CAT
Chemical Advertisers Group of New York [*Inactive*] (EA) ... CAGNY
Chemical Age Project File [*Pergamon ORBIT InfoLine Inc.*] [*Information service or system*] ... CAPF
Chemical Agent Alarm ... CAA
Chemical Agent Casualty Assessment System (MCD) ... CACAS
Chemical Agent Decontamination Simulant (MCD) ... CADS
Chemical Agent Detection Network ... CADNET
Chemical Agent Disclosure Solution [*Toxicology*] ... CADS
Chemical Agent Identification Training Set ... CAITS
Chemical Agent Monitor [*Military*] (RDA) ... CAM
Chemical Agent Munition Disposal System [*Army*] ... CAMDS
Chemical Agent Resistant Coating [*A paint*] ... CARC
Chemical Algorithm for Reticulation Linearization (NITA) ... CARL
Chemical Analysis Detection Instrumentation Control ... CADIC
Chemical Analysis Facility (NRCH) ... CAF
Chemical and Allied Industries [*Department of Employment*] [*British*] ... CAI
Chemical and Biological [*Warfare*] [*Formerly, CBR, CEBAR*] [*Military*] ... CB
Chemical and Biological Accident and Incident Control [*Army*] (AABC) ... CBAIC
Chemical and Biological Accident and Incident Control Plan [*Army*] (AABC) ... CBAICP
Chemical and Biological Agent Delivery System (MCD) ... CBADS
Chemical and Biological Defense Command [*Army*] (RDA) ... CBDCOM
Chemical and Biological Information Handling [*National Institutes of Health*] ... CBIH
Chemical and Biological Warfare [*Military*] ... CBW
Chemical and Biological Weapons [*Military*] ... CBW
Chemical and Coating Laboratory [*Army*] (MCD) ... CCL
Chemical and Industrial Consultants Association (DBA) ... CICA
Chemical and Insulating ... C + I
Chemical & Petroleum Division (ACII) ... CHEMPID
Chemical and Radiological Laboratories [*Army*] ... CRLR
Chemical and Statistical Policy Division [*Environmental Protection Agency*] (GFGA) ... CSPD
Chemical and Volume Control [*Nuclear energy*] (NRCH) ... CVC
Chemical and Volume Control System [*Nuclear energy*] (NRCH) ... CVCS
Chemical Applications of Nuclear Explosions (PDAA) ... CANE
Chemical Assembly Fuel Element Exchange (NUCP) ... CAFEE
Chemical Attack Warning Transmission System (MCD) ... CAWTS
Chemical Automated Search Terminal [*Computer Corp. of America*] [*Information service or system*] (IID) ... CAST
Chemical Awareness and Emergency Response [*Program for handling hazards*] ... CAER
Chemical/Bacterial/Nuclear [*Military*] (MCD) ... CBN
Chemical Banking Corp. [*Associated Press*] (SAG) ... ChBk
Chemical Banking Corp. [*NYSE symbol*] (SPSG) ... CHL
Chemical Banking Corp. [*Associated Press*] (SAG) ... ChmBnk
Chemical Beam Epitaxy [*Solid state physics*] ... CBE
Chemical Binding Effect ... CBE
Chemical, Biological, and Radiological [*Warfare*] [*Later, CB*] [*Military*] ... CBR
Chemical, Biological, and Radiological Center [*Military*] ... CBRC
Chemical, Biological, and Radiological Element [*Military*] (AABC) ... CBRE
Chemical, Biological, and Radiological Protection (DNAB) ... CBRP
Chemical, Biological, and Radiological Section [*Military*] ... CBRS
Chemical Biological Defense Agency [*Army*] ... CBDA
Chemical/Biological Incident Response Force [*Marine Corps*] ... CBIRF
Chemical, Biological, Radiological Agency [*Military*] ... CBRA
Chemical, Biological, Radiological, and Nuclear [*Army*] (AABC) ... CBRN
Chemical, Biological, Radiological Control Center [*Military*] (AABC) ... CBRCC
Chemical, Biological, Radiological Officer [*Army*] ... CBRO
Chemical, Biological, Radiological Warfare [*Later, CB*] [*Military*] ... CEBAR
Chemical/Biological Unit (DWSG) ... CBU

Chemical Blowing Agent [*Plastics technology*] .... CBA
Chemical Bond Approach .... CBA
Chemical Bond Approach Study .... CBAS
Chemical Business NewsBase [*Royal Society of Chemistry*] [*Information service or system*] .... CBNB
Chemical Carcinogenesis Research Information System [*National Library of Medicine*] [*Information service or system*] .... CCRIS
Chemical Cleaning Building [*Nuclear energy*] (NRCH) .... CCB
Chemical Closet CC
Chemical Coaters Association (EA) .... CCA
Chemical Collection/Request Tracking System [*Environmental Protection Agency*] (ERG) .... CC/RTS
Chemical Collection System / Request Tracking [*Online database*] [*Environmental Protection Agency*] .... CCS/RTS
Chemical Communications Association (EA) .... CCA
Chemical Composition [*Of precious stones*] CC
Chemical Composition Distribution .... CCD
Chemical Compound Registry (System) (DIT) .... CCR(S)
Chemical Control Division [*Environmental Protection Agency*] (GFGA) .... CCD
Chemical Control Procedure [*Nuclear energy*] (NRCH) .... CCP
Chemical Coordination Staff [*Environmental Protection Agency*] (GFGA) .... CCS
Chemical Corps [*Army*] (GFGA) CC
Chemical Corps [*Army*] (RDA) .... CM
Chemical Corps (AAGC) .... CML
Chemical Corps [*Army*] .... CMLC
Chemical Corps Biological Laboratories [*Army*] .... CMLCBL
Chemical Corps Engineering Command [*Army*] .... CMLCENCOM
Chemical Corps Historical Office [*Army*] .... CMLHO
Chemical Corps Material Command [*Army*] .... CMLCMATCOM
Chemical Corps Proving Ground [*Army*] .... CCPG
Chemical Corps Research and Development Command [*Army*] (AAG) .... CCRDC
Chemical Corps Research and Development Command [*Army*] .... CMLCRDCOM
Chemical Corps Research and Engineering Command [*Army*] .... CMLCRECOM
Chemical Corps Technical Command [*Army*] (MCD) .... CCTC
Chemical Corps Training Command [*Army*] .... CMLCTNGCOM
Chemical Data Center, Inc. [*Information service or system*] (IID) .... CDC
Chemical Data System .... CDS
Chemical Decontamination Training Facility [*Military*] .... CDTF
Chemical Defence Establishment [*British*] .... CDE
Chemical Defence Experimental Establishment [*British*] .... CDEE
Chemical Defence Experimental Station [*British World War II*] .... CDES
Chemical Defence Research Establishment [*British*] .... CDRE
Chemical Defense .... CMLDEF
Chemical Defense Equipment [*Military*] (INF) .... CDE
Chemical Defense Program (MCD) .... CDP
Chemical Delivery System [*Medicine*] .... CDS
Chemical Demilitarization [*Military*] (RDA) .... CHEM DEMIL
Chemical Demilitarization and Installation Restoration (MCD) .... CDIR
Chemical Dependency (OICC) .... ChemDep
Chemical Detection and Alarm Training Simulator (MCD) .... CDATS
Chemical Development Corp. [*Geneva, Switzerland*] .... CDC
Chemical Dictionary On-Line [*National Library of Medicine*] [*Bethesda, MD Database*] .... CHEMLINE
Chemical Discriminator System .... CDS
Chemical Diversion and Trafficking Act [*1988*] .... CDTA
Chemical Downwind Message [*Military*] (INF) .... CDM
Chemical Economics Handbook [*SRI International*] [*Database*] .... CEH
Chemical Education for Public Understanding Program [*University of California, Berkley*] .... CEPUP
Chemical Education Material Study [*American Chemical Society*] (AEE) .... CHEMS
Chemical Education Planning and Coordinating Committee [*American Chemical Society*] .... CEPACC
Chemical Effects Information Center [*Department of Energy*] (IID) .... CEIC
Chemical Effects Information Task Group [*Department of Energy Information service or system*] (IID) .... CEITG
Chemical Element Balance (GFGA) .... CEB
Chemical Emergency Planning and Response Commission .... CEPRC
Chemical Emergency Preparedness Plan (GNE) .... CEPP
Chemical Emergency Preparedness Program [*Environmental Protection Agency*] .... CEPP
Chemical Energy .... CE
Chemical Engineer .... CE
Chemical Engineer .... Ch E
Chemical Engineer .... Chem E
Chemical Engineer .... Chem Eng
[*The*] Chemical Engineer [*A publication*] .... TCE
Chemical Engineering Abstracts [*Royal Society of Chemistry*] [*Information service or system*] .... CEA
Chemical Engineering and Biotechnology Abstracts [*A publication*] .... CEABA
Chemical Engineering and Mining Review [*A publication*] .... Chem Engng Mining Rev
Chemical Engineering Catalog [*A publication*] .... CEC
Chemical Engineering Database .... CHERUB
Chemical Engineering Information Processing System .... CHIPS
Chemical Engineering Investigation of Reaction Paths [*Computer science*] .... CHIRP
Chemical Engineering Modular Instruction [*Project*] .... CHEMI
Chemical Engineering Operations [*MIT*] (MCD) .... CEO
Chemical Evaluation Search and Retrieval System [*Michigan Department of Natural Resources*] [*Information service or system*] (CRD) .... CESARS
Chemical Exchange Directory SA [*Information service or system*] (IID) .... CED
Chemical Fabrics and Film Association (EA) .... CFFA
Chemical Financial [*NASDAQ symbol*] (TTSB) .... CHFC
Chemical Financial Corp. [*NASDAQ symbol*] (NQ) .... CHFC
Chemical Financial Corp. [*Associated Press*] (SAG) .... ChmFin

Chemical Force Microscope .... CFM
Chemical Gas (MCD) .... CG
Chemical Hazard Communication Policy [*Stanford University*] .... CHCP
Chemical Hazard Information Profile [*Environmental Protection Agency*] .... CHIP
Chemical Hazards .... CH
Chemical Hazards and Emergency Management Unit [*Queensland*] [*Australia*] .... CHEMU
Chemical Hazards in Industry [*Royal Society of Chemistry*] [*Information service or system*] (IID) .... CHI
Chemical Hazards Response Information System [*Coast Guard Information service or system*] .... CHRIS
Chemical Hazards Response Information System/Hazard Assessment Computer System [*Coast Guard*] (ERG) .... CHRIS/HACS
Chemical Heat Pipe [*Energy storage*] .... CHP
Chemical Heritage Foundation [*Formerly, NFHC*] .... CHF
Chemical Hygiene Plan [*Occupational Safety and Health Administration*] .... CHP
Chemical Identification File [*National Library of Medicine*] [*Information service or system*] (IID) .... ChemID
Chemical Index [*Database*] .... CHEMDEX
Chemical Industries Association .... CIA
Chemical Industries Association's Safety and Health Council [*British*] .... CISHEC
Chemical Industry Council CIC
Chemical Industry Data Exchange [*Computer science*] (ACRL) .... CIDX
Chemical Industry for Minorities in Engineering (EA) .... ChIME
Chemical Industry in Basle .... CIBA
Chemical Industry Institute of Toxicology (EA) .... CIIT
Chemical Industry institute of Toxicology, Durham, NC [*Library symbol*] [*Library of Congress*] (LCLS) .... NcDurIT
Chemical Information and Data System [*Army*] .... CIDS
Chemical Information and Tracking System (GNE) .... CHEMTRACK
Chemical Information Center [*Indiana University*] CIC
Chemical Information Management, Inc. [*Information service or system*] (IID) .... CIMI
Chemical Information On-Line [*Ministry of Labour*] [*Hamilton, ON*] [*Information service or system*] (IID) .... CIOL
Chemical Information Retrieval System [*Army*] (IID) .... CIRS
Chemical Information Services [*Stanford Research Institute*] (IID) .... CIS
Chemical Information Systems, Inc. [*Fein-Marquart Associates*] [*Information service or system*] (IID) .... CIS
Chemical Information Systems Operators [*Later, EUSIDIC*] .... CHEOPS
Chemical Injection [*Nuclear energy*] (NRCH) CI
Chemical Injection (System) [*Nuclear energy*] (NRCH) .... CI(S)
Chemical Inspectorate [*British*] CI
Chemical Institute of Canada CIC
Chemical Instrumentation Test and Evaluation [*Marine science*] (OSRA) .... CITE
Chemical Instrumentation Test and Evaluation [*NASA*] (USDC) .... CITE
Chemical International Finance & Consulting [*Belgium*] .... CHEMFICO
Chemical International Information Center CIIC
Chemical Ion Generator (AAG) .... CIG
Chemical Ionization [*Spectrometry*] CI
Chemical Ionization/Electron Impact [*Spectroscopy*] .... CI/EI
Chemical Ionization Mass Spectrometry .... CIMS
Chemical Journal of the Association of Official Analytical Chemists [*Association of Official Analytical Chemists*] [*Information service or system*] (CRD) .... CJAOAC
Chemical Journals of John Wiley & Sons [*John Wiley & Sons, Inc.*] [*Information service or system*] (CRD) .... CJWILEY
Chemical Journals of the American Chemical Society [*Information service or system*] (CRD) .... CJACS
Chemical Journals of the Royal Society of Chemistry [*British Information service or system*] (CRD) .... CJRSC
Chemical Journals Online [*American Chemical Society*] [*Database*] .... CJO
Chemical Kinetics Information Center [*National Institute of Standards and Technology*] .... CKIC
Chemical Laboratory CL
Chemical Laboratory Analysis and Scheduling System [*Computer science*] .... CLASS
Chemical Laboratory Technician [*or Technology*] [*Navy*] .... LBT
Chemical LASER (MCD) CL
Chemical LASER Analysis Program (MCD) .... CLAP
Chemical LASER Analytical System Program (MCD) .... CLASP
Chemical LASER Mode Control .... CLMC
Chemical LASER Study [*or System*] .... CLS
Chemical LASER System Code (MCD) .... CLASYC
Chemical Library, Canadian National Railways [*Bibliotheque Chimique, Chemins de fer Nationaux du Canada*] **Montreal, Quebec** [*Library symbol Obsolete National Library of Canada*] (NLC) .... QMCNC
Chemical List Index and Processing System [*Environmental Protection Agency*] (ERG) .... CLIPS
Chemical Literature [*A publication*] CL
Chemical Literature Data Extraction .... CLIDE
Chemical Low-Altitude Missile [*Air Force program*] .... CLAM
Chemical Low-Altitude Missile Puny [*Air Force program*] (MCD) .... CLAMP
Chemical Machining [*Factory automation*] (BTTJ) .... CHM
Chemical Machining Template (MCD) .... CMT
Chemical Machining Template Line (MCD) .... CMTL
Chemical Manufacture [*Department of Employment*] [*British*] .... CM
Chemical Manufacturers Association (EA) .... CMA
Chemical Market Associates, Inc. [*Information service or system*] (IID) .... CMAI
Chemical Marketing and Economics .... CM & E
Chemical Marketing and Economics .... CMEC
Chemical Marketing Research Association (EA) .... CMRA
Chemical Mass Balance .... CMB
Chemical Material Study Model [*Military*] (AFIT) .... CMSM
Chemical Materials Catalog .... CMC

Chemical Mechanical Polishing [*Engineering*] .... CMP
Chemical Metallurgical Reporting .... CMR
Chemical Milling (MSA) .... CM
Chemical Milling Machine .... CMM
Chemical Modeling Laboratory [*NIH/EPA Chemical Information System*] [*Database*] .... CHEMLAB
Chemical Monograph Referral Center [*Consumer Product Safety Commission*] [*Information service or system*] (IID) .... CHEMRIC
Chemical Name Dictionary [*Dialog Information Services, Inc.*] [*Database*] .... CHEMNAME
Chemical Network [*Chemical Transportation Emergency Center*] (ERG) .... CHEMNET
Chemical Neutron Activation Analysis .... CNAA
Chemical Nomenclature Advisory Service (PDAA) .... CNAS
Chemical On-Line Data Analyzer [*Interactive Elements, Inc.*] .... CODA
Chemical Operations [*Army*] (AABC) .... CMLOPS
Chemical Operations System .... CHEOPS
Chemical Orbit-to-Orbit Shuttle [*NASA*] .... COOS
Chemical Oxygen Demand .... COD
Chemical Oxygen Iodine LASER (MCD) .... COIL
Chemical/Petroleum Engineering (DD) .... Chem/PetEng
Chemical Pigment Co., Metals Division, Baltimore, MD [*Library symbol Library of Congress*] (LCLS) .... MdBCPM
Chemical Polish .... CP
Chemical Practitioner (DAS) .... CP
Chemical Preparation (OA) .... CP
Chemical Process Industry .... CPI
Chemical Process Quantitative Risk Assessment [*Chemical engineering*] .... CPQRA
Chemical Process Synthesis [*Chemical engineering*] .... CPS
Chemical Processing Cell [*Nuclear energy*] (NUCP) .... CPC
Chemical Processing Facility [*Nuclear energy*] (NUCP) .... CPF
Chemical Propulsion .... CP
Chemical Propulsion Abstracts [*Database*] [*Chemical Propulsion Information Agency*] [*Information service or system*] (CRD) .... CPA
Chemical Propulsion Division [*NASA*] (KSC) .... CPD
Chemical Propulsion Information Agency [*Laurel, MD*] [*DoD*] .... CPIA
Chemical Propulsion Technology Reviews [*Chemical Propulsion Information Agency*] (MCD) .... CPTR
Chemical Protective Clothing .... CPC
Chemical Protective Overgarment [*Army*] (DOMA) .... CPO
Chemical Protective Overgarment [*Military*] (INF) .... CPOG
Chemical Public Relations Association [*Later, CCA*] (EA) .... CPRA
Chemical Pulp .... CP
[*A*] **Chemical Radical** (DOG) .... R
Chemical, Radiological, Biological Warfare [*NATO*] (NATG) .... CRB
Chemical Reaction Engineering .... CRE
Chemical Reaction Interface Mass Spectrometry .... CRIMS
Chemical Reactions Documentation Service [*Derwent Publications Ltd.*] [*Bibliographic database*] (IID) .... CRDS
Chemical Recovery Association [*British*] (DBA) .... CRA
Chemical Referral Center (EA) .... CRC
Chemical Regulations and Guidelines System [*CRC Systems, Inc.*] [*Information service or system*] (IID) .... CRGS
Chemical Release and Radiation Effects Satellite [*NASA*] .... CRRES
Chemical Release Module (MCD) .... CRM
Chemical Remanent Magnetization [*Geophysics*] .... CRM
Chemical Report .... CR
Chemical Research and Development Center [*Aberdeen Proving Ground, MD*] [*Army*] (RDA) .... CRDC
Chemical Research and Development Laboratories [*Edgewood Arsenal, MD*] [*Army*] .... CRDL
Chemical Research Applied to World Need [*IUPAC*] .... CHEMRAWN
Chemical Research Consultants, Inc. .... CRC
Chemical Research, Development, and Engineering Center [*Aberdeen Proving Ground, MD*] [*Army*] (RDA) .... CRDEC
Chemical Research Laboratory, CIL, Inc., Mississauga, Ontario [*Library symbol National Library of Canada*] (NLC) .... OMCILCR
Chemical Research Project [*Military*] .... CRP
Chemical Resistant Coating .... CRC
Chemical Rubber Co. .... CRC
Chemical Rust-Inhibiting .... CRI
Chemical Safety and Hazardous Investigation Board [*Environmental Protection Agency*] .... CSHIB
Chemical Science and Technology Laboratory [*National Institute of Standards and Technology*] .... CSTL
Chemical Screening Battery (DAVI) .... CSB
Chemical Selection Working Group [*National Cancer Institute*] .... CSWG
Chemical Shielding Anisotropy [*Physics*] .... CSA
Chemical Shift [*Physical chemistry*] .... CS
Chemical Shift Anisotropy [*Physical chemistry*] .... CSA
Chemical Shift Selective [*Medicine*] (DMAA) .... CHESS
Chemical Short-Range Order (MCD) .... CSRO
Chemical Societies of the Nordic Countries (EAIO) .... CSNC
Chemical Society [*Later, RSC*] [*British*] .... CS
Chemical Society, London, United Kingdom [*Library symbol Library of Congress*] (LCLS) .... UkLC
Chemical Society of Japan .... CSJ
Chemical Society Research Unit in Information Dissemination and Retrieval [*British*] (DIT) .... CSRUIDR
Chemical Sources Association (EA) .... CSA
Chemical Special Emphasis Program [*Occupational Safety and Health Administration*] .... ChemSEP
Chemical Specialties Manufacturers Association (EA) .... CSMA
Chemical Species Balance (GFGA) .... CSB
Chemical Spray Deposition (PDAA) .... CSD
Chemical Stimulation of the Brain (WGA) .... CSB
Chemical Stockpile Disposal [*Military*] (RDA) .... CSD
Chemical Stockpile Disposal Program [*Military*] (DOMA) .... CSDP
Chemical Stockpile Emergency Preparedness [*Military*] (RDA) .... CSEP
Chemical Storage Area (NRCH) .... CSA
Chemical Structure Analysis Routine .... ChemSTAR
Chemical Structure and Nomenclature System [*Environmental Protection Agency*] .... CSNS
Chemical Structure Association (EAIO) .... CSA
Chemical Substances Information Network [*No longer exists*] [*Environmental Protection Agency Information service or system*] .... CSIN
Chemical Substances Inventory [*Environmental Protection Agency*] (GFGA) .... CSI
Chemical Substructure Index [*Trademark*] .... CSI
Chemical Surety Material (MCD) .... CSM
Chemical Sympathectomy [*Neurology*] (DAVI) .... CS
Chemical System Laboratory, Aberdeen Proving Grounds, MD [*OCLC symbol*] (OCLC) .... ADE
Chemical Systems Division [*NASA*] (NASA) .... CSD
Chemical Systems Laboratory [*Later, CRDC*] [*Army*] (RDA) .... CSL
Chemical Technicians Curriculum [*Project*] .... ChemTeC
Chemical Temperature Resistant [*Automotive engineering*] .... CTR
Chemical Test (MCD) .... CT
Chemical Testing and Assessment Research Commission (GNE) .... CTARC
Chemical Therapy [*or Chemotherapy*] [*Pharmacology*] (DAVI) .... Kemo Tx
Chemical Thermodynamics and Energy Hazard Evaluation [*American Society for Testing and Materials*] .... CHETAH
Chemical Thermodynamics Data Center [*National Institute of Standards and Technology*] .... CTDC
Chemical Toilet Association (EA) .... CTA
Chemical Transfer (MCD) .... CT
Chemical Transport and Deposition (MCD) .... CTD
Chemical Transport Reaction .... CTR
Chemical Transportation Emergency Center [*Chemical Manufacturers Association*] .... CHEMTREC
Chemical Transportation Industry Advisory Committee .... CTIAC
Chemical Treatment Pond (IEEE) .... CTP
Chemical Underwater Explosive (PDAA) .... CUE
Chemical Vapor Deposition [*Coating technology*] .... CVD
Chemical Vapor Infiltration [*Materials science*] CVI
Chemical Vapor Phase Oxidization (EECA) .... CVPO
Chemical Vapor Plating .... CVP
Chemical Vapor Transport .... CVT
Chemical Vehicle Vulnerability Analysis Model (MCD) .... CHEMVVAM
Chemical Warfare .... CW
Chemical Warfare - Bacteriological Warfare .... CWBW
Chemical Warfare/Chemical Biological Defense (RDA) .... CW/CBD
Chemical Warfare/Chemical Biological Defense Information Analysis Center [*DoD*] .... CBIAC
Chemical Warfare Defense .... CWD
Chemical Warfare Defense Equipment .... CWDE
Chemical Warfare Directional Detector [*Military*] (CAAL) .... CWDD
Chemical Warfare Laboratories [*Army Chemical Center, MD*] (MCD) .... CWL
Chemical Warfare/Nuclear, Biological, and Chemical (RDA) .... CW/NBC
Chemical Warfare Service [*Army*] .... CWS
Chemical Warfare Service Officer [*Army*] .... CWSO
Chemical Warfare Specialist, Medical [*Navy rating*] .... CWT
Chemical Warfare Technical Committee .... CWTC
Chemical Waste Program [*Stanford University*] .... CWP
Chemical Waste Transportation Council [*Washington, DC*] (EA) .... CWTC
Chemical Waste Transportation Institute .... CWTI
Chemical Weapons .... CW
Chemical Weapons Convention [*Proposed treaty*] .... CWC
Chemical Weapons Working Group [*A coalition of groups living near chemical weapons incinerators*] .... CWWG
Chemical Wood [*Paper*] (DGA) .... CW
Chemical Workers' Union .... CWU
Chemical World Index Key .... CWIK
Chemical-Atomic-Biological (BARN) .... CAB
Chemical-Biological Activities [*Information service or system A publication*] .... CBAC
Chemical-Biological Computer System .... CBCS
Chemical-Biological Coordination Center [*NAS/NRC*] .... CBCC
Chemical-Biological Defense [*Military*] .... CBD
Chemical-Biological Munitions (AFM) .... CBM
Chemical-Biological-Radiological Engineering Group [*Army*] (MCD) .... CBREG
Chemically [*Freight*] .... CHEMLY
Chemically Active Fluidized Bed [*Fuel gas*] .... CAFB
Chemically Active Material Ejected in Orbit (MCD) .... CAMEO
Chemically and Biologically Protected Shelter [*Army*] .... CBPS
Chemically Benign [*Medicine*] .... CB
Chemically Bonded Ceramic [*Materials science*] .... CBC
Chemically Contaminated Biological Mask (MCD) .... CCBM
Chemically Defined Medium [*Microbiology*] .... CDM
Chemically Diabetic [*Endocrinology*] .... CD
Chemically Enhanced Primary Treatment [*Water treatment*] .... CEPT
Chemically Induced Dynamic Electron Polarization [*Spectrometry*] .... CIDEP
Chemically Induced Dynamic Nuclear Polarization [*Spectrometry*] .... CIDNP
Chemically Initiated Electron Exchange Luminescence .... CIEEL
Chemically Malignant [*Medicine*] .... CM
Chemically Modified Electrode [*Electrochemistry*] .... CME
Chemically Perturbed Region [*Meteorology*] .... CPR
Chemically Pure [*Chemistry*] .... CP
Chemically Pure Ethylamine (PDAA) .... CPEA
Chemically Recuperated Intercooled Steam-Injected Gas Turbine .... CRISTIG

Chemically Rigidized Space Structure ... CRSS
Chemically Sensitive Field Effect Transistor ... CHEMFET
Chemically Sensitive Semiconductor Devices ... CSSD
Chemically Stable Oxide ... CSO
Chemically Treated Steel (DICI) ... CTS
Chemically-Assisted Field Evaporation [*Materials science*] ... CAFE
Chemically-Assisted Ion Beam Etching (MCD) ... CAIBE
Chemically-Bound Residue [*Medicine*] (DMAA) ... CBR
Chemically-Induced Mutants [*Genetics*] ... CM
Chemically-Modified Carbon Paste [*Electrode*] ... CMCP
Chemically-Powered Interorbital Space Shuttle (MCD) ... CIS
Chemically-Stimulated Rubber (PDAA) ... CSR
Chemical-Related Data Estimation Subroutines [*Environmental science*] ... CRDES
Chemicals and Polymers Group [*British*] ... C & P
Chemicals Control Order [*Australia*] ... CCO
Chemicals in Commerce Information System [*Environmental Protection Agency*] ... CICIS
Chemicals Notation Association [*British*] ... CNA
Chemicals on Reporting Rules Database [*Environmental Protection Agency*] ... CORR
Chemicals, Plastic Research ... CPR
Chemicals, Runoff, and Erosion from Agricultural Management Systems [*Agricultural Research Service*] ... CREAMS
Chemicals Selected for Equal, Analogous, or Related Character (DIT) ... CHEMSEARCH
Chemico-Viscous Remanent Magnetization [*Geophysics*] ... CVRM
Chemie Gruenenthal GmbH [*Germany*] [*Research code symbol*] ... CG
Chemie-Information und Dokumentation Berlin [*Chemical Information and Documentation - Berlin*] [*Information service or system German*] (IID) ... CIDB
Chemiewerke Homburg [*Germany*] [*Research code symbol*] ... D
Chemiluminescence ... CL
Chemiluminescence Depletion [*Chemical kinetics*] ... CD
Chemiluminescence Detector ... CLD
Chemiluminescence Immunoassay (OA) ... CIA
Chemi-Mechanical Pulp ... CMP
Chemin (DD) ... ch
Chemische Technik [*A database*] (NITA) ... CT
Chemischer Ingenieur [*Chemical Engineer*] [*German*] ... Chem Ing
Chemist ... CHEM
Chemist ... CHEM
Chemist and Druggist ... C & D
Chemistry [*Secondary school course*] [*British*] ... C
Chemistry (DD) ... Chem
Chemistry and Biology Research Institute [*Agriculture Canada Research Branch*] [*Research center*] (RCD) ... CBRI
Chemistry and Health Physics (GFGA) ... C & HP
Chemistry and Physics Study Unit (EA) ... CPSU
Chemistry Associates [*Australia*] ... CA
Chemistry Consortium (EA) ... CC
Chemistry Department, St. Francis Xavier University, Antigonish, Nova Scotia [*Library symbol National Library of Canada*] (NLC) ... NSASC
Chemistry Library, Canada Institute for Scientific and Technical Information [*Division de Chimie, Institut Canadien de l'Information Scientifique et Technique*] **Ottawa, Ontario** [*Library symbol National Library of Canada*] (NLC) ... OONC
Chemistry of High Elevation Fog Project [*Environment Canada*] ... CHEF
Chemistry Records and Grading System [*Computer science*] ... CRAGS
Chemistry Study Unit [*Later, CPSU*] (EA) ... CSU
Chemistry Teaching Information Processing System ... CHEMTIPS
Chemistry Test Item Collection (ADA) ... CHEMTIC
Chemists' Club [*New York*] (SRA) ... CC
Chemists' Club [*Formerly, Mining Club*] (EA) ... MC
Chemists' Club, New York, NY [*Library symbol Library of Congress*] (LCLS) ... NNCC
Chemists' Club - of New York (EA) ... CCNY
Chemists' Defence Association [*British*] (BI) ... CDA
Chemist's Personal Software Series ... CPSS
Chemithermomechanical Pulp [*Papermaking*] ... CTMP
Chemi-Trol Chemical Co. [*Associated Press*] (SAG) ... ChemTrl
Chemi-Trol Chemical Co. [*NASDAQ symbol*] (SAG) ... CTRL
Chemoglobulin [*Biochemistry*] (DAVI) ... cg
Chemogram (VRA) ... CHGR
Chemonucleolysis [*Surgery*] ... CNL
Chemoreceptor Trigger Zone ... CTZ
Chemotactic Factor [*Immunology*] ... CF
Chemotactic Factor Inactivator [*Immunology*] ... CFI
Chemotactic Index [*Immunology*] ... CMI
Chemotaxis-Generating Factor ... CGF
Chemotherapeutic Index [*Medicine*] ... CI
Chemotherapy [*Medicine*] (MAE) ... Chem
Chemotherapy [*Medicine*] (WDAA) ... CHEMO
Chemotherapy [*Medicine*] ... CT
Chemotherapy Foundation (EA) ... CF
Chemotherapy of Leprosy Program [*of the World Health Organization*] (DAVI) ... THELEP
Chemotherapy of Leprosy Program [*World Health Organization*] (BABM) ... THELEP
Chemotherapy Research Bulletin ... CRIB
Chemotherapy-Induced Nausea and Emesis [*Medicine*] (DMAA) ... CINE
Chempower, Inc. [*NASDAQ symbol*] (NQ) ... CHEM
Chempower, Inc. [*Associated Press*] (SAG) ... Chmpwr
Chemstrand Research Center, Inc., Durham, NC [*Library symbol Library of Congress*] (LCLS) ... NcDurCR
ChemTrak, Inc. [*Associated Press*] (SAG) ... ChmTrk
Chemtrak, Inc. [*NASDAQ symbol*] (SAG) ... CMTR
Chemtronics, Inc., Swannanoa, NC [*Library symbol*] [*Library of Congress*] (LCLS) ... NcSwC
Chemung County Historical Society, Elmira, NY [*Library symbol Library of Congress*] (LCLS) ... NElmHi
Chena Hot Springs, AK [*Location identifier FAA*] (FAAL) ... CEX
Chenango Bridge, NY [*FM radio station call letters*] (RBYB) ... WYOS-FM
Cheney, WA [*FM radio station call letters*] ... KEWU
Cheney, WA [*FM radio station call letters*] ... KEYF
Chengchow [*China*] [*Airport symbol*] (AD) ... CGO
Chengdu [*Republic of China*] [*Seismograph station code, US Geological Survey*] (SEIS) ... CNU
Chengdu [*China*] [*Airport symbol*] (OAG) ... CTU
Chengdu [*China*] [*ICAO location identifier*] (ICLI) ... ZUUU
Cheni Gold Mines, Inc. [*Toronto Stock Exchange symbol Vancouver Stock Exchange symbol*] ... CZG
Chenodeoxycholic Acid [*Also, CDC, CDCA, CHENIC*] [*Biochemistry*] ... CDA
Chenodeoxycholic Acid [*Also, CDA, CDCA, CHENIC*] [*Biochemistry*] ... CDC
Chenodeoxycholic Acid [*Also, CDA, CDC, CHENIC*] [*Biochemistry*] ... CDCA
Chenodeoxycholic Acid [*Also, CDA, CDC, CDCA*] [*Biochemistry*] ... CHENIC
Cheongokri [*South Korea ICAO location identifier*] (ICLI) ... RKSC
Chepes [*Argentina ICAO location identifier*] (ICLI) ... SACP
Cheque [*British*] (ROG) ... CHE
Cheque [*British*] (ROG) ... CHEQ
Cheque [*British*] ... CHQ
Cheque Account [*British Banking*] (ADA) ... C/A
Cheque Book [*British*] (DAS) ... C Bk
Cheque Reconciliation and Information System [*Australia*] ... CHRIS
Cheques [*British*] (ROG) ... CHEX
Cheragas [*Algeria*] [*ICAO location identifier*] (ICLI) ... DAAX
Cheraw, SC [*Location identifier FAA*] (FAAL) ... CQW
Cheraw, SC [*AM radio station call letters*] ... WCRE
Cheraw, SC [*FM radio station call letters*] ... WJMX
Cherbourg [*France*] [*Airport symbol*] (OAG) ... CER
Cherbourg [*France ICAO location identifier*] (ICLI) ... LFRY
Cherbourg/Maupertus [*France ICAO location identifier*] (ICLI) ... LFRC
Cher'd Interest [*Fan club*] (EA) ... CI
Cherished Numbers Dealers Association [*British*] (DBA) ... CNDA
Chernofski Harbor, AK [*Location identifier FAA*] (FAAL) ... KCN
Chernovtsy [*Former USSR Seismograph station code, US Geological Survey Closed*] (SEIS) ... CRA
Chernovtsy [*Former USSR Seismograph station code, US Geological Survey Closed*] (SEIS) ... CRB
Cherokee [*MARC language code Library of Congress*] (LCCP) ... chr
Cherokee Case [*A publication*] (DLA) ... Cher Ca
Cherokee County Courthouse, Cherokee, IA [*Library symbol Library of Congress*] (LCLS) ... IaCheCoC
Cherokee County Historical Society, Cherokee, IA [*Library symbol Library of Congress*] (LCLS) ... IaCheCHi
Cherokee County Public Library, Gaffney, SC [*Library symbol Library of Congress*] (LCLS) ... ScGa
Cherokee Group [*NASDAQ symbol*] (NQ) ... CHKE
Cherokee, IA [*Location identifier FAA*] (FAAL) ... CKP
Cherokee, IA [*AM radio station call letters*] ... KCHE
Cherokee, IA [*FM radio station call letters*] ... KCHE-FM
Cherokee, Inc. [*Associated Press*] (SAG) ... Cheroke
Cherokee Inc. [*NASDAQ symbol*] (TTSB) ... CHKE
Cherokee Leasing, Inc. [*ICAO designator*] (FAAC) ... CBM
Cherokee National Historical Society (EA) ... CNHS
Cherokee Nuclear Station (NRCH) ... CNS
Cherokee, OK [*Location identifier FAA*] (FAAL) ... CKA
Cherokee Pilots Association [*Commercial firm*] (EA) ... CPA
Cherokee Public Library, Cherokee, IA [*Library symbol Library of Congress*] (LCLS) ... IaChe
Cherokee Village, AR [*Location identifier FAA*] (FAAL) ... CVK
Cherokee Village, AR [*FM radio station call letters*] ... KFCM
Cherokee, WY [*Location identifier FAA*] (FAAL) ... CKW
Cherry (VRA) ... che
Cherry ... CHRY
Cherry Central Cooperative (EA) ... CCC
Cherry Corp. [*NASDAQ symbol*] (NQ) ... CHER
Cherry Corp. [*Associated Press*] (SAG) ... Cherry
Cherry Corp. 'A' [*NASDAQ symbol*] (TTSB) ... CHERA
Cherry Corp.'B' [*NASDAQ symbol*] (TTSB) ... CHERB
Cherry Creek Schools, Englewood, CO [*Library symbol*] [*Library of Congress*] (LCLS) ... COEnCS
Cherry Growers and Industries Foundation (EA) ... CGIF
Cherry Hill Free Public Library, Cherry Hill, NJ [*OCLC symbol*] (OCLC) ... CHF
Cherry Hill Free Public Library, Cherry Hill, NJ [*Library symbol Library of Congress*] (LCLS) ... NjCh
Cherry Hill Medical Center, Cherry Hill, NJ [*Library symbol Library of Congress*] (LCLS) ... NjChM
Cherry Hill, NJ [*FM radio station call letters*] (RBYB) ... WSJI-FM
Cherry Hospital, Learning Resource Center, Goldsboro, NC [*Library symbol Library of Congress*] (LCLS) ... NcGoCH
Cherry Lane Elementary School, Carle Place, NY [*Library symbol*] [*Library of Congress*] (LCLS) ... NCpCE
Cherry Lane Fashion [*Vancouver Stock Exchange symbol*] ... CFG
Cherry Leafroll Virus [*Plant pathology*] ... CLRV
Cherry Marketing Institute (EA) ... CMI
Cherry Point [*North Carolina*] [*Seismograph station code, US Geological Survey Closed*] (SEIS) ... CPC
Cherry Point Marine Corps Air Station [*North Carolina*] [*ICAO location identifier*] (ICLI) ... KNKT
Cherry Point, NC [*Location identifier FAA*] (FAAL) ... NJF

Cherry Point, NC [*Location identifier FAA*] (FAAL) .... NKT
Cherry Point, North Carolina [*Marine Corps Air Station*] .... CPNC
Cherry Processors' Cooperative [*Australia*] .... CPC
Cherry Public School, Iron, MN [*Library symbol*] [*Library of Congress*]
    (LCLS) .... MnIrCS
Cherry Rasp Leaf Virus [*Plant pathology*] .... CRLV
Cherry Red Spot Myoclonus [*Medicine*] (DMAA) .... CRSM
Cherry School District 92, Cherry, IL [*Library symbol Library of Congress*]
    (LCLS) .... ICherSD
Cherry Valley Elementary School, Cherry Valley, IL [*Library symbol*] [*Library of Congress*] (LCLS) .... IChevE
Cherry Valley, NY [*FM radio station call letters*] .... WJIV
Cherry-Crandall Unit (MAE) .... CCU
Cherryville, NC [*AM radio station call letters*] .... WCSL
Chervonets [*Monetary unit; 1922-1947*] [*Russian*] .... ch
Cheryl Hale Fan Club [*Defunct*] (EA) .... CHFC
Cheryl K. Warner Fan Club (EA) .... CKWFC
Cheryl Resources, Inc. [*Vancouver Stock Exchange symbol*] .... CYU
Cheryl Roth International Fan Club (EA) .... CRIFC
Chesaning Public Library, Chesaning, MI [*Library symbol Library of Congress*] (LCLS) .... MiChes
Chesapeake Air Services [*ICAO designator*] (FAAC) .... CAB
Chesapeake and Ohio Canal National Monument .... CHOH
Chesapeake and Ohio Historical Society (EA) .... COHS
[*The*] Chesapeake & Ohio Railway Co. [*Later, Chessie System, Inc.*] .... C & O
[*The*] Chesapeake & Ohio Railway Co. (Pere Marquette District) [*AAR code*] .... PM
Chesapeake Automotive Wholesalers Association (SRA) .... CAWA
Chesapeake Bay [*Virginia and Maryland*] .... CHES
Chesapeake Bay Agreement (GNE) .... CBA
Chesapeake Bay Annex [*Navy*] .... CBA
Chesapeake Bay Center for Environmental Studies [*Smithsonian Institution*] .... CBCES
Chesapeake Bay Detachment [*Washington, DC Navy*] (GRD) .... CBD
Chesapeake Bay Foundation [*Marine science*] (OSRA) .... CBF
Chesapeake Bay Foundation (USDC) .... CBF
Chesapeake Bay Group [*Navy*] (DNAB) .... CHESBAYGRU
Chesapeake Bay Institute [*Johns Hopkins University*] .... CBI
Chesapeake Bay Observing System [*Marine science*] (OSRA) .... CBOS
Chesapeake Bay Observing System (USDC) .... CBOS
Chesapeake Bio Labs 'A' [*ECM, Symbol*] (TTSB) .... PHD.EC
Chesapeake Biological Laboratories [*University of Maryland*] .... CBL
Chesapeake Biological Laboratories, Inc. [*Associated Press*] (SAG) .... ChesBio
Chesapeake Biological Laboratories, Inc. [*AMEX symbol*] (SAG) .... PHD
Chesapeake Computer [*Vancouver Stock Exchange symbol*] .... CKR
Chesapeake Corp. [*Associated Press*] (SAG) .... Chspk
Chesapeake Corp. [*NYSE symbol*] (SPSG) .... CSK
Chesapeake Division Naval Facilities Engineering Command [*Washington, DC*] .... CHES/NAVFAC
Chesapeake Division Naval Facilities Engineering Command (DNAB) .... CHESDIVNAVFACENGCOM
Chesapeake Division Naval Facilities Engineering Command [*Washington, DC*] .... CHESNAVFACENGCOM
Chesapeake Division Naval Facilities Engineering Command .... DIRCHESDOCKS
Chesapeake Division Support Facility [*Navy*] (DNAB) .... CHESDIVSUPPAC
Chesapeake Energy [*NYSE symbol*] (TTSB) .... CHK
Chesapeake Energy Corp. [*Associated Press*] (SAG) .... ChesEn
Chesapeake Energy Corp. [*NYSE symbol*] (SAG) .... CHK
Chesapeake Highway Advisories Routing Traffic .... CHART
Chesapeake Information Retrieval Service (IID) .... CIRS
Chesapeake, OH/Huntington, WV [*Location identifier FAA*] (FAAL) .... HTW
Chesapeake Public Library, Chesapeake, VA [*Library symbol*] [*Library of Congress*] (LCLS) .... ViChe
Chesapeake Research Consortium .... CRC
Chesapeake Seafood Packers Association (EA) .... CSPA
Chesapeake Utilities [*NYSE symbol*] (SPSG) .... CPK
Chesapeake Utilities Corp. [*Associated Press*] (SAG) .... ChesUtl
Chesapeake, VA [*AM radio station call letters*] .... WJQI
Chesapeake, VA [*FM radio station call letters*] (RBYB) .... WKOC
Chesapeake Western Railway [*AAR code*] .... CHW
Chesapeake Western Railway (IIA) .... CW
Chesbar Resources, Inc. [*Toronto Stock Exchange symbol*] .... CBI
Chesbro Reservoir [*California*] [*Seismograph station code, US Geological Survey*] (SEIS) .... CBO
Chesham [*Urban district in England*] .... CHES
Cheshire [*County in England*] .... CHES
Cheshire [*County in England*] (ODBW) .... Ches
Cheshire [*County in England*] (ROG) .... CHESH
Cheshire Achievement of Scientific Skills in Schools [*British*] (AIE) .... CHASSIS
Cheshire Air Training School [*British ICAO designator*] (FAAC) .... CHZ
Cheshire Experiment in Educational Software [*British*] (AIE) .... CHEESE
Cheshire Lines Committee Railway [*British*] (ROG) CLC
Cheshire Lines Committee Railway [*British*] (ROG) .... CLCR
Chesley Branch, Bruce County Public Library, Ontario [*Library symbol National Library of Canada*] (NLC) .... OCH
Chesnut Fencing Manufacturers Society [*British*] (DBA) .... CFRMS
Chess .... CHSS
Chess Association of New South Wales [*Australia*] .... CANSW
Chess Association of Queensland [*Australia*] .... CAQ
Chess Club CC
Chess Collectors Association [*Defunct*] (EA) .... CCA
Chess Collectors International (EA) CCI
Chess Federation of Canada .... CFC
Chess Journalists of America (EA) .... CJA
Chess Life [*A publication*] .... Chess L

Chess on Stamps Unit [*Defunct*] (EA) .... CSU
Chessminster Group Ltd. [*Vancouver Stock Exchange symbol*] .... CRG
Chest [*Medicine*] C
Chest [*Tea trade*] (ROG) C
Chest [*Medicine*] .... CH
Chest (DMAA) .... ch
Chest [*Shipping*] .... CHT
Chest [*Anatomy*] (DAVI) V
Chest and Heart Association [*British*] (BI) .... CHA
Chest and Left Arm [*Cardiology*] CL
Chest and Right Arm [*Cardiology*] .... CR
Chest Circumference [*Neonatology and pediatrics*] (DAVI) cc
Chest Complaint [*Medicine*] (ADA) CC
Chest, Heart, and Stroke Association [*British*] .... CHSA
Chest Incision [*Medicine*] CI
Chest of Drawers .... CDWR
Chest Pain [*Medicine*] (MAE) .... CP
Chest Pain Emergency Room .... CPER
Chest Pain of Unknown Etiology [*Medicine*] .... CPUE
Chest Physiotherapy [*Medicine*] .... CPT
Chest Physiotherapy and Physical Drainage [*Medicine*] .... CPPD
Chest Pysician (BABM) .... ChP
Chest Roentgenogram [*Radiology*] .... CR
Chest Strap [*Medicine*] .... CS
Chest, Training [*Parachute*] .... CT
Chest Tube [*Medicine*] .... CT
Chest Tube Drainage [*Medicine*] (DAVI) .... CTD
Chest Tube Out [*Medicine*] .... CTO
Chest Tube Under Water-Seal Drainage [*Medicine*] (MEDA) .... CTUWSD
Chest Wall [*Medicine*] .... CW
Chest Wall Stimulation [*Medicine*] .... CWS
Chest X-Ray [*Medicine*] CX
Chest X-Ray [*Medicine*] .... CXR
Chestatee Regional Library [*Library network*] .... NGAL
Chestatee Regional Library System, Gainsville, GA [*Library symbol*] [*Library of Congress*] (LCLS) .... GGaCL
Chest-Back [*Medicine*] .... CB
Chester [*England*] [*Airport symbol*] (AD) .... CEG
Chester [*City in England*] (ROG) .... CHEST
Chester [*British depot code*] .... CHS
Chester Alan Arthur [*US president, 1829-1886*] .... CAA
Chester Bancorp, Inc. [*Associated Press*] (SAG) .... ChestrBc
Chester Bancorp, Inc. [*NASDAQ symbol*] (SAG) .... CNBA
Chester Beatty Research Institute [*Great Britain*] [*Research code symbol*] .... CB
Chester, CA [*Location identifier FAA*] (FAAL) .... CBD
Chester, CA [*FM radio station call letters*] .... KCMT
Chester County District Library Center, Exton, PA [*OCLC symbol*] (OCLC) .... PWC
Chester County District Library Center, West Chester, PA [*Library symbol Library of Congress*] (LCLS) .... PWcC
Chester County Historical Society, West Chester, PA [*Library symbol Library of Congress*] (LCLS) .... PWcHi
Chester County Library, Chester, SC [*Library symbol*] [*Library of Congress*] (LCLS) .... ScCh
Chester County Reports [*Pennsylvania*] [*A publication*] (DLA) .... Ches Co
Chester County Reports [*Pennsylvania*] [*A publication*] (DLA) .... Ches Co Rep
Chester County Reports [*Pennsylvania*] [*A publication*] (DLA) .... Chest Co
Chester County Reports [*Pennsylvania*] [*A publication*] (DLA) .... Chest Co (PA)
Chester County Reports [*Pennsylvania*] [*A publication*] (DLA) .... Chest Co Rep
Chester County Reports [*Pennsylvania*] [*A publication*] (DLA) .... Chester
Chester County Reports [*Pennsylvania*] [*A publication*] (DLA) .... Chester Co (PA)
Chester County Reports [*Pennsylvania*] [*A publication*] (DLA) .... Chester Co Rep
Chester Free Public Library, Chester, NJ [*Library symbol Library of Congress*] (LCLS) .... NjChe
Chester Hldgs Ltd [*NASDAQ symbol*] (TTSB) .... CHES
Chester, IL [*AM radio station call letters*] .... KSGM
Chester, MA [*Location identifier FAA*] (FAAL) .... CTR
Chester, PA [*FM radio station call letters*] .... WDNR
Chester, PA [*AM radio station call letters*] .... WPWA
Chester, PA [*AM radio station call letters*] .... WVCH
Chester Palatine Courts [*1811*] [*England*] [*A publication*] (DLA) .... Booth
Chester Park Elementary School, Duluth, MN [*Library symbol*] [*Library of Congress*] (LCLS) .... MnDuCPE
Chester, SC [*Location identifier FAA*] (FAAL) .... DCM
Chester, SC [*AM radio station call letters*] (RBYB) .... WBT-FM
Chester, VA [*FM radio station call letters*] .... WDYL
Chester, VA [*AM radio station call letters*] .... WGGM
Chester Valley Bancorp [*Associated Press*] (SAG) .... ChestrV
Chester Valley Bancorp [*NASDAQ symbol*] (TTSB) .... CVAL
Chester Valley Bancorp, Inc. [*NASDAQ symbol*] (SAG) .... CVAL
Chester White Swine Record Association (EA) .... CWSRA
Chesterfield County Library, Chesterfield, SC [*Library symbol*] [*Library of Congress*] (LCLS) .... ScChf
Chesterfield Inlet, NT [*ICAO location identifier*] (ICLI) .... CYCS
Chesterfield Kings [*An association*] (EA) .... CK
Chesterfield, SC [*Location identifier FAA*] (FAAL) .... CTF
Chesterfield, SC [*FM station call letters*] (RBYB) .... WVSZ-FM
Chesterfield, VA [*Location identifier FAA*] (FAAL) .... CFU
Chesterfield, VA [*Location identifier FAA*] (FAAL) .... HYU
Chesterfield-Marlboro Technical College, Cheraw, SC [*Library symbol Library of Congress*] (LCLS) .... ScChwC
Chesterton [*England*] .... CHEST
Chesterton, IN [*FM radio station call letters*] (RBYB) .... WAJW
Chesterton, IN [*FM radio station call letters*] .... WDSO

Chesterton Tribune, Chesterton, IN [*Library symbol Library of Congress*] (LCLS) .... InCheT
Chestertown, MD [*AM radio station call letters*] .... WCTR
Chesterville Branch, Stormont, Dundas, and Glengarry County Public Library, Ontario [*Library symbol National Library of Canada*] (BIB) .... OCHSDG
Chestnut [*Horse racing*] .... CH
Chestnut (ROG) .... CHES
Chestnut [*Philately*] .... chnt
Chestnut [*Horse racing*] .... CHSTNT
Chestnut (VRA) .... chstnt
Chestnut .... CHSTNT
Chestnut Hill College [*Pennsylvania*] .... CHC
Chestnut Hill College, Philadelphia, PA [*OCLC symbol*] (OCLC) .... CHE
Chestnut Hill College, Philadelphia, PA [*Library symbol Library of Congress*] (LCLS) .... PPCCH
Chestnut Ridge Railway Co. [*AAR code*] .... CHR
Cheswick & Harmar [*AAR code*] .... CHH
Cheswick Historical Society (EA) .... CHS
Chet Atkins Appreciation Society (EA) .... CAAS
Chet Atkins Guitar Society [*British*] (EAIO) .... CAGS
Chetco Community Public Library, Brookings, OR [*Library symbol Library of Congress*] (LCLS) .... OrBroo
Chetek, WI [*FM radio station call letters*] .... WVXD
Cheticamp, NS [*Television station call letters*] CBHFT-4
Cheticamp, NS [*Television station call letters*] CBIT-2
Cheticamp, NS [*FM radio station call letters*] (RBYB) .... CKJM-FM
Chetumal [*Mexico*] [*Airport symbol*] (OAG) .... CTM
Chetumal [*Mexico ICAO location identifier*] (ICLI) .... MMCM
Chetwynd [*British Columbia*] [*Seismograph station code, US Geological Survey Closed*] (SEIS) .... CTC
Chetwynd Public Library, British Columbia [*Library symbol National Library of Canada*] (NLC) .... BCHE
Cheung Chau [*Hong Kong*] [*ICAO location identifier*] (ICLI) .... VHCH
Cheung Kong Infrastructure .... CKI
Chevak [*Alaska*] [*Airport symbol*] (OAG) .... VAK
Chevak, AK [*FM radio station call letters*] .... KCUK
Chevalier [*Knight title*] .... CHEV
Chevalier (DD) .... Chev
Cheval-Vapeur [*Horsepower*] [*French*] .... CH-V
Cheval-Vapeur [*Horsepower*] [*French*] CV
Cheveley [*England*] .... CHEV
Cheves' South Carolina Equity Reports [*1839-1940*] [*A publication*] (DLA) .... Chev Ch
Cheves' South Carolina Equity Reports [*1839-1940*] [*A publication*] (DLA) .... Chev Eq
Cheves' South Carolina Equity Reports [*1839-1940*] [*A publication*] (DLA) .... Cheves Eq (SC)
Cheves' South Carolina Equity Reports [*1839-1940*] [*A publication*] (DLA) .... Cheves L (SC)
Cheves' South Carolina Law Reports [*1839-1940*] [*A publication*] (DLA) .... Chev
Cheves' South Carolina Law Reports [*1839-1940*] [*A publication*] (DLA) .... Cheves
Chevet (VRA) .... chvt
Chevrolet [*Automotive engineering*] .... CHEV
Chevrolet .... CHEVY
Chevrolet Car Club of Victoria [*Australia*] CCCV
Chevrolet Motor Division [*General Motors Corp.*] .... CMD
Chevrolet Nomad Association (EA) .... CNA
Chevrolet-Pontiac-Canada Group [*General Motors Corp.*] .... CPC
Chevron .... CHEV
Chevron Canada Resources Ltd., Calgary, Alberta [*Library symbol National Library of Canada*] (NLC) .... ACHS
Chevron Corp. [*Associated Press*] (SAG) .... Chevron
Chevron Corp. [*Vancouver Stock Exchange symbol NYSE symbol*] (SPSG) .... CHV
Chevron Oil Field Research Co. .... COFRC
Chevron Oil Field Research Co., La Habra, CA [*Library symbol Library of Congress*] (LCLS) .... CLhC
Chevron Research Co., Technical Information Center, Richmond, CA [*Library symbol Library of Congress*] (LCLS) .... CRicC
Chevron Standard Ltd., Calgary, AB, Canada [*Library symbol Library of Congress*] (LCLS) .... CaACHS
Chevy Chase Preferred Capital Corp. [*NYSE symbol*] (SAG) .... CCP
Chevy Chase Preferred Capital Corp. [*Associated Press*] (SAG) .... ChevyC
Chevy Development Corp. [*Vancouver Stock Exchange symbol*] .... CDY
Chevy Oil Corp. [*Vancouver Stock Exchange symbol*] .... CVO
Chewing, Sucking, Swallowing [*Medicine*] .... CSS
Chewings Fescue and Creeping Red Fescue Commission (EA) .... CFCRFC
CHExchange Network [*An association*] (EA) .... CN
Cheyenne [*City in Wyoming*] (ROG) .... CHEY
Cheyenne [*MARC language code Library of Congress*] (LCCP) .... chy
Cheyenne [*Diocesan abbreviation*] [*Wyoming*] (TOCD) .... CHY
Cheyenne [*Wyoming*] [*Airport symbol*] (OAG) .... CYS
Cheyenne [*Wyoming*] [*ICAO location identifier*] (ICLI) .... KCYS
Cheyenne Airways, Inc. [*ICAO designator*] (FAAC) .... CYA
Cheyenne Mountain Air Force Software Support [*Army*] .... CMAFSS
Cheyenne Mountain Air Force Station .... CMAFS
Cheyenne Mountain Complex [*NORAD*] (MCD) .... CMC
Cheyenne Mountain Upgrade .... CMU
Cheyenne, OK [*Television station call letters*] .... KWET
Cheyenne Petroleums [*Vancouver Stock Exchange symbol*] .... CYP
Cheyenne Software [*AMEX symbol*] (TTSB) .... CYE
Cheyenne Software, Inc. (MHDW) .... CHEY
Cheyenne Software, Inc. [*Associated Press*] (SAG) .... CheySoft
Cheyenne Software, Inc. [*AMEX symbol*] (SPSG) .... CYE
Cheyenne, WY [*Location identifier FAA*] (FAAL) .... CYS
Cheyenne, WY [*Location identifier FAA*] (FAAL) .... FEW
Cheyenne, WY [*AM radio station call letters*] .... KFBC
Cheyenne, WY [*FM radio station call letters*] .... KFBQ
Cheyenne, WY [*Television station call letters*] .... KGWN
Cheyenne, WY [*FM radio station call letters*] (RBYB) .... KIGN-FM
Cheyenne, WY [*AM radio station call letters*] (RBYB) .... KJJL-AM
Cheyenne, WY [*FM radio station call letters*] .... KKAZ
Cheyenne, WY [*Television station call letters*] .... KKTU
Cheyenne, WY [*FM radio station call letters*] .... KLEN
Cheyenne, WY [*Television station call letters*] .... KLWY
Cheyenne, WY [*AM radio station call letters*] .... KRAE
Cheyenne, WY [*FM radio station call letters*] (RBYB) .... KRRR-FM
Cheyenne, WY [*AM radio station call letters*] .... KSHY
Cheyne-Stokes Respiration [*Medicine*] .... CSR
Cheyney State College, Cheyney, PA [*OCLC symbol*] (OCLC) .... PCH
Cheyney State College, Cheyney, PA [*Library symbol Library of Congress*] (LCLS) .... PCheS
Chi Square .... CS
Chian Federation of America (EA) .... CFA
Chiang Ching-kuo [*Son of Nationalist Chinese leader Chiang Kai-shek*] .... CCK
Chiang Kai-shek .... CKS
Chiang Mai [*Thailand*] [*Seismograph station code, US Geological Survey*] (SEIS) .... CHG
Chiang Mai [*Thailand*] [*Seismograph station code, US Geological Survey*] (SEIS) .... CHTO
Chiang Mai [*Thailand*] [*Airport symbol*] (OAG) .... CNX
Chiang Mai [*Thailand*] [*ICAO location identifier*] (ICLI) .... VTCC
Chiang Rai [*Thailand*] [*Airport symbol*] (OAG) .... CEI
Chiang Rai [*Thailand*] [*ICAO location identifier*] (ICLI) .... VTCR
Chiang Rai/Ban Chiang Kham [*Thailand*] [*ICAO location identifier*] (ICLI) .... VTCB
Chiang Rai/Chiang Khong [*Thailand*] [*ICAO location identifier*] (ICLI) .... VTCA
Chiari-Frommel (Syndrome) [*Medicine*] .... CF
Chiaroscuro (VRA) .... chiaro
Chiasma [*Genetics*] (AAMN) .... Xa
Chiasma [*Anatomy*] (DAVI) .... Xta
Chiavari [*Italy*] [*Seismograph station code, US Geological Survey Closed*] (SEIS) .... CHV
Chiayi [*Republic of China*] [*Seismograph station code, US Geological Survey*] (SEIS) .... CHY
Chiayi [*Taiwan*] [*Airport symbol*] (OAG) .... CYI
Chibcha [*MARC language code Library of Congress*] (LCCP) .... chb
Chibougamau [*Canada*] [*Airport symbol*] (OAG) .... YMT
Chibougamau, PQ [*AM radio station call letters*] .... CJMD
Chic By HIS, Inc. [*Associated Press*] (SAG) .... ChicBy
Chic by HIS, Inc. [*NYSE symbol*] (SPSG) .... JNS
Chicago [*Illinois*] (ROG) .... CH
Chicago [*Illinois*] .... CHGO
Chicago [*Illinois*] [*Airport symbol*] (OAG) .... CHI
Chicago [*Illinois*] .... CHIC
Chicago [*Illinois*] [*Seismograph station code, US Geological Survey Closed*] (SEIS) .... CHK
Chicago [*Branch in the Federal Reserve regional banking system*] (BARN) .... G
Chicago [*Illinois*] [*ICAO location identifier*] (ICLI) .... KRGC
Chicago Academic Library Council [*Library network*] .... CALC
Chicago Academy of Fine Arts .... CAFA
Chicago Academy of Science .... CAS
Chicago Academy of Sciences, Matthew Laflin Memorial Library, Chicago, IL [*Library symbol Library of Congress*] (LCLS) .... ICCAS
Chicago Air, Inc. [*ICAO designator*] (FAAC) .... CGO
Chicago & Alton Railroad Co. [*Also known as Alton*] .... C & A
Chicago & Eastern Illinois Railroad Co. [*Absorbed into Missouri Pacific System*] .... C & EI
Chicago & Eastern Illinois Railroad Co. [*Absorbed into Missouri Pacific System*] .... CEI
Chicago & Erie Railroad Co. .... C & E
Chicago & Illinois Midland Railway Co. .... C & IM
Chicago & Illinois Midland Railway Co. [*AAR code*] .... CIM
Chicago & Illinois Western Railroad [*AAR code*] .... CIW
Chicago and Midwest Envelope Manufacturers Association [*Defunct*] .... CMEMA
Chicago & Northern Pacific Railroad .... C & NPRR
Chicago and South Consortium [*Library network*] .... C & SC
Chicago & West Michigan Railroad .... C & WM
Chicago & Western Indiana Railroad Co. [*AAR code*] .... CWI
Chicago Area Computer Hobbyist Exchange .... CACHE
Chicago Area Geographic Information Study [*University of Illinois at Chicago*] [*Also, an information service or system*] (IID) .... CAGIS
Chicago Area Transportation Study .... CATS
Chicago Assyrian Dictionary [*A publication*] (BJA) .... CAD
Chicago, Aurora [*Illinois*] [*ICAO location identifier*] (ICLI) .... KZAU
Chicago, Aurora & Elgin Railroad Corp. [*AAR code*] .... CAE
Chicago Bar Association. Record [*A publication*] (DLA) .... Chi BA Rec
Chicago Bar Record [*A publication*] (DLA) .... Chi B Record
Chicago Board of Trade [*Chicago, IL*] (EAIO) .... CBOT
Chicago Board of Trade [*A futures exchange*] [*Investment term*] .... CBT
Chicago Board of Trade, Chicago, IL [*OCLC symbol*] (OCLC) .... IEY
Chicago Board Options Exchange [*Chicago, IL*] (EA) .... CBOE
Chicago Book Clinic .... CBC
Chicago Botanic Gardens, Glencoe, IL [*Library symbol*] [*Library of Congress*] (LCLS) .... IGlcB
Chicago Bridge & Iron Co. [*Later, CBI Industries*] .... CB & I
Chicago Bridge & Iron Co., Oak Brook, IL [*Library symbol Library of Congress*] (LCLS) .... IObC
Chicago, Burlington & Quincy Railroad [*Also known as Burlington Route*] .... CB & Q
Chicago, Burlington & Quincy Railroad [*Also known as Burlington Route*] [*AAR code*] .... CBQ

Chicago, Burlington & Quincy Railroad [*Also known as Burlington Route*] [*Slang*] ... Q
Chicago/Chicago Midway [*Illinois*] [*ICAO location identifier*] (ICLI) ... KMDW
Chicago, Cincinnati & Louisville Railway ... CC & L
Chicago City Ballet ... CCB
Chicago City College [*Illinois*] (AEBS) ... CCC
Chicago City Junior College [*Illinois*] ... CCJC
Chicago Clinical Chemist [*A publication*] ... CCC
Chicago Cluster of Theological Schools [*Library network*] ... CCTS
Chicago College of Osteopathic Medicine ... CCOM
Chicago College of Osteopathic Medicine, Chicago, IL [*Library symbol Library of Congress*] (LCLS) ... ICCO
Chicago Daily Tribune, Chicago, IL [*Library symbol Library of Congress*] (LCLS) ... ICDT
Chicago Dance Arts Coalition ... CDAC
Chicago Dock & Canal Trust [*Associated Press*] (SAG) ... ChDock
[*The*] **Chicago Dock & Canal Trust** [*NASDAQ symbol*] (NQ) ... DOCK
Chicago Dock & Canal Trust [*NASDAQ symbol*] (TTSB) ... DOCKS
Chicago Evangelistic Institute ... CEI
Chicago Fan Club (EA) ... CFC
Chicago Gorilla [*Slang for a desperado gunman*] ... CHICAGORILLA
Chicago Great Western Railroad (IIA) ... CGW
Chicago Great Western Railway ... C & GWRY
Chicago Heights Free Public Library, Chicago Heights, IL [*Library symbol Library of Congress*] (LCLS) ... ICh
Chicago Heights Free Public Library, Chicgo Heights, IL [*Library symbol*] [*Library of Congress*] (LCLS) ... IChL
Chicago Heights, IL [*Location identifier FAA*] (FAAL) ... CGT
Chicago Heights, IL [*AM radio station call letters*] ... WCFJ
Chicago Heights, IL [*AM radio station call letters*] ... WCGO
Chicago Heights Terminal Transfer Railroad Co. [*AAR code*] ... CHTT
Chicago Helicopter Airways, Inc. [*ICAO designator Obsolete*] ... CH
Chicago Helicopter Airways, Inc. ... CHA
Chicago Helicopter Airways, Inc. [*Air carrier designation symbol*] ... CHP
Chicago Historical Society, Chicago, IL [*Library symbol Library of Congress*] (LCLS) ... ICHi
Chicago, IL [*Location identifier FAA*] (FAAL) ... FJU
Chicago, IL [*Location identifier FAA*] (FAAL) ... HKH
Chicago, IL [*Location identifier FAA*] (FAAL) ... HNA
Chicago, IL [*Location identifier FAA*] (FAAL) ... IAC
Chicago, IL [*Location identifier FAA*] (FAAL) ... IDN
Chicago, IL [*Location identifier FAA*] (FAAL) ... JAV
Chicago, IL [*Location identifier FAA*] (FAAL) ... LQQ
Chicago, IL [*Location identifier FAA*] (FAAL) ... MED
Chicago, IL [*Location identifier FAA*] (FAAL) ... MXT
Chicago, IL [*Location identifier FAA*] (FAAL) ... NOH
Chicago, IL [*Location identifier FAA*] (FAAL) ... OHA
Chicago, IL [*Location identifier FAA*] (FAAL) ... PHA
Chicago, IL [*Location identifier FAA*] (FAAL) ... PYN
Chicago, IL [*Location identifier FAA*] (FAAL) ... RVG
Chicago, IL [*Location identifier FAA*] (FAAL) ... RXZ
Chicago, IL [*Location identifier FAA*] (FAAL) ... TSL
Chicago, IL [*AM radio station call letters*] ... WBBM
Chicago, IL [*FM radio station call letters*] ... WBBM-FM
Chicago, IL [*Television station call letters*] ... WBBM-TV
Chicago, IL [*FM radio station call letters*] ... WBEZ
Chicago, IL [*FM radio station call letters*] ... WBHI
Chicago, IL [*Television station call letters*] ... WCFC
Chicago, IL [*Television station call letters*] ... WCIU
Chicago, IL [*AM radio station call letters*] ... WCRW
Chicago, IL [*FM radio station call letters*] ... WCRX
Chicago, IL [*FM radio station call letters*] ... WCYC
Chicago, IL [*AM radio station call letters*] ... WEDC
Chicago, IL [*AM radio station call letters*] ... WEJM
Chicago, IL [*Television station call letters*] ... WFLD
Chicago, IL [*FM radio station call letters*] ... WFMT
Chicago, IL [*AM radio station call letters*] ... WGCI
Chicago, IL [*FM radio station call letters*] ... WGCI-FM
Chicago, IL [*AM radio station call letters*] ... WGN
Chicago, IL [*Television station call letters*] ... WGN-TV
Chicago, IL [*FM radio station call letters*] ... WHPK
Chicago, IL [*AM radio station call letters*] ... WIND
Chicago, IL [*AM radio station call letters*] ... WJJD
Chicago, IL [*FM radio station call letters*] ... WJMK
Chicago, IL [*FM radio station call letters*] ... WKKC
Chicago, IL [*FM radio station call letters*] ... WKQX
Chicago, IL [*FM radio station call letters*] (RBYB) ... WKXK-FM
Chicago, IL [*FM radio station call letters*] ... WLIT
Chicago, IL [*AM radio station call letters*] ... WLS
Chicago, IL [*FM radio station call letters*] ... WLS-FM
Chicago, IL [*Television station call letters*] ... WLS-TV
Chicago, IL [*FM radio station call letters*] ... WLUP
Chicago, IL [*FM radio station call letters*] ... WLUW
Chicago, IL [*AM radio station call letters*] (RBYB) ... WLXX
Chicago, IL [*AM radio station call letters*] ... WMAQ
Chicago, IL [*Television station call letters*] ... WMAQ-TV
Chicago, IL [*AM radio station call letters*] ... WMBI
Chicago, IL [*FM radio station call letters*] ... WMBI-FM
Chicago, IL [*AM radio station call letters*] ... WMVP
Chicago, IL [*FM radio station call letters*] ... WNIB
Chicago, IL [*FM radio station call letters*] ... WNUA
Chicago, IL [*FM radio station call letters*] ... WOUI
Chicago, IL [*FM radio station call letters*] ... WPNT
Chicago, IL [*FM radio station call letters*] ... WRCX
Chicago, IL [*AM radio station call letters*] ... WSBC
Chicago, IL [*AM radio station call letters*] ... WSCR
Chicago, IL [*Television station call letters*] ... WSNS
Chicago, IL [*FM radio station call letters*] ... WSSD
Chicago, IL [*Letters stand for "Windows to the World"*] [*Television station call letters*] ... WTTW
Chicago, IL [*FM radio station call letters*] ... WUSN
Chicago, IL [*FM radio station call letters*] ... WXRT
Chicago, IL [*Television station call letters*] ... WYCC
Chicago, IL [*FM radio station call letters*] ... WZRD
Chicago, IL [*Location identifier FAA*] (FAAL) ... ZAU
Chicago, Indianapolis & Louisville [*Louisville & Nashville Railroad Co.*] [*AAR code*] ... CIL
Chicago Institute for the Study of Learning Disabilities [*Research center*] (RCD) ... CHILD
Chicago International Antiques Show (ITD) ... CIAS
Chicago International Art Exhibition (ITD) ... CIAE
Chicago International Boat Show (ITD) ... CIBS
Chicago, Kalamazoo & Saginaw Railway [*AAR code*] ... CKS
Chicago LASER Systems, Inc. (NITA) ... CLS
Chicago Law Bulletin [*A publication*] (DLA) ... Chi LB
Chicago Law Bulletin [*A publication*] (DLA) ... Chic LB
Chicago Law Bulletin [*A publication*] (DLA) ... Chicago LB
Chicago Law Institute, Chicago, IL [*Library symbol Library of Congress*] (LCLS) ... ICLaw
Chicago Law Journal [*A publication*] (DLA) ... Chi LJ
Chicago Law Journal [*A publication*] (DLA) ... Chic LJ
Chicago Law Journal [*A publication*] (DLA) ... Chicago LJ
Chicago Law Journal [*A publication*] (DLA) ... CLJ
Chicago Law Record [*Illinois*] [*A publication*] (DLA) ... Chi LR
Chicago Law Record [*Illinois*] [*A publication*] (DLA) ... Chic LR
Chicago Law Record [*Illinois*] [*A publication*] (DLA) ... Chicago L Rec
Chicago Law Record [*Illinois*] [*A publication*] (DLA) ... Chicago L Record (Ill)
Chicago Law Times [*A publication*] (DLA) ... Chi LT
Chicago Law Times [*A publication*] (DLA) ... Chic LT
Chicago Law Times [*A publication*] (DLA) ... Chicago LT
Chicago Legal News [*Illinois*] [*A publication*] (DLA) ... Chi Leg N
Chicago Legal News [*Illinois*] [*A publication*] (DLA) ... Chic Leg N
Chicago Legal News [*Illinois*] [*A publication*] (ILCA) ... Chicago Leg News
Chicago Legal News [*Illinois*] [*A publication*] (DLA) ... Chicago Leg News (Ill)
Chicago Legal News [*Illinois*] [*A publication*] (DLA) ... CLN
Chicago Library Services for the Blind and Physically Handicapped (Subregional),Chicago Public Library, Chicago, IL [*Library symbol Library of Congress*] (LCLS) ... IC-CBPH
Chicago Library System [*Chicago Public Library*] [*Chicago, IL Library network*] ... CLS
Chicago Linear Music Language ... CLML
Chicago Livestock Exchange ... CLE
Chicago - Loyola [*Illinois*] [*Seismograph station code, US Geological Survey*] (SEIS) ... CHI
Chicago Lutheran Theological Seminary ... CLTS
Chicago Lying-In Hospital ... CLIH
Chicago Map Society (EA) ... CMS
Chicago Medical School ... CMS
Chicago [*Illinois*] **Meigs Field** [*Airport symbol*] (OAG) ... CGX
Chicago Mercantile Exchange (EA) ... CME
Chicago Mercantile Exchange, Chicago, IL [*Library symbol Library of Congress*] (LCLS) ... ICMen
Chicago Mercantile Exchange, Chicago, IL [*OCLC symbol*] (OCLC) ... IHU
Chicago/Metropolitan Area [*Illinois*] [*ICAO location identifier*] (ICLI) ... KCHI
Chicago [*Illinois*] **Midway** [*Airport symbol*] (OAG) ... MDW
Chicago Midway Laboratory [*Army*] (MCD) ... CML
Chicago, Milwaukee & Gary Railroad [*Nickname: Cold, Miserable, and Grouchy*] ... CM & G
Chicago, Milwaukee & Puget Sound Railroad ... CM & PS
Chicago, Milwaukee & St. Paul Railway ... CM & StP
Chicago, Milwaukee, St. Paul & Pacific Railroad (IIA) ... CMSP & P
Chicago, Milwaukee, St. Paul & Pacific Railroad Co. ... CM ST P & P
Chicago, Milwaukee, St. Paul & Pacific Railroad Co. [*AAR code*] ... MILW
Chicago Miniature Lamp [*NASDAQ symbol*] (TTSB) ... CHML
Chicago Miniature Lamp, Inc. [*Associated Press*] (SAG) ... ChiMini
Chicago Miniature Lamp, Inc. [*NASDAQ symbol*] (SAG) ... CHML
Chicago Municipal Reference Library, Chicago, IL [*OCLC symbol*] (OCLC) ... IBF
Chicago Municipal Reference Library, Chicago, IL [*Library symbol Library of Congress*] (LCLS) ... ICMR
Chicago Natural History Museum ... CNHM
Chicago North Shore & Milwaukee R. R. [*AAR code*] ... CNSM
Chicago/O'Hare [*Illinois*] [*ICAO location identifier*] (ICLI) ... KORD
Chicago [*Illinois*] **O'Hare Airport** [*Derived from former name: Orchard Field*] [*Airport symbol*] ... ORD
Chicago Open Board of Trade [*Later, MIDAM*] ... COBT
Chicago Operations and Regional Office [*Department of Energy*] (GRD) ... CORO
Chicago Operations Office [*Energy Research and Development Administration*] ... COO
Chicago Osteopathic Medical Center ... COMC
Chicago Outer Belt R. R. [*AAR code*] ... EJE
Chicago Pile [*Nuclear reactor*] ... CP
Chicago Pile-5 [*Nuclear heavy-water-research reactor*] ... CP-5
Chicago Piza & Brewery, Inc. [*Associated Press*] (SAG) ... ChiPizza
Chicago Pizza & Brewery, Inc. [*NASDAQ symbol*] (SAG) ... CHGO
Chicago Pizza & Brewery, Inc. [*Associated Press*] (SAG) ... ChiPza
Chicago Playing Card Collectors (EA) ... CPCC
Chicago Produce Terminal Co. [*Later, CPTC*] [*AAR code*] ... CPT
Chicago Produce Terminal Co. [*Formerly, CPT*] [*AAR code*] ... CPTC
Chicago Public Library, Chicago, IL [*OCLC symbol*] (OCLC) ... CGP

Chicago Public Library, Chicago, IL [*Library symbol Library of Congress*] (LCLS) IC
Chicago Railroad Terminal Information System [*Pronounced "Curtis"*] .... CRTIS
Chicago Reactor (NRCH) .... CR
Chicago Religious Task Force on Central America (EA) .... CRTFCA
Chicago Research & Trading Bank (ECON) .... CRT
Chicago Review Press [*Publisher*] .... CRP
Chicago Rice and Cotton Exchange (EA) .... CRCE
Chicago Ridge Public Library, Chicago Ridge, IL [*Library symbol Library of Congress*] (LCLS) .... ICr
[*The*] Chicago River & Indiana Railway Co. [*Absorbed into Consolidated Rail Corp.*] .... CR & I
[*The*] Chicago River & Indiana Railway Co. [*Absorbed into Consolidated Rail Corp.*] [*AAR code*] .... CRI
Chicago Rivet & Mach [*AMEX symbol*] (TTSB) .... CVR
Chicago Rivet & Machine Co. [*Associated Press*] (SAG) .... ChiRv
Chicago Rivet & Machine Co. [*Associated Press*] (SAG) .... ChiRv
Chicago Rivet & Machine Co. [*AMEX symbol*] (SPSG) .... CVR
Chicago, Rock Island & Pacific Railroad Co. [*Nickname: The Baby Road*] .... CRI & P
Chicago, Rock Island & Pacific Railroad Co. (MHDB) .... RI
Chicago, St. Paul & Kansas City Railway .... CStP & KC
Chicago, St. Paul, Minneapolis & Omaha R. R. [*AAR code*] .... CMO
Chicago, St. Paul, Minneapolis & Omaha Railway .... CStPM & O
Chicago School of Professional Psychology, Chicago, IL [*Library symbol Library of Congress*] (LCLS) .... ICCSP
Chicago School of Professional Psychology, Chicago, IL [*OCLC symbol*] (OCLC) .... JAX
Chicago Short Line Railway Co. [*AAR code*] .... CSL
Chicago South Shore & South Bend Railroad [*AAR code*] .... CSS
Chicago Standbys Fan Club (EA) .... CSFC
Chicago State University (GAGS) .... Chicago St U
Chicago State University, Chicago, IL [*OCLC symbol*] (OCLC) .... IAA
Chicago State University, Chicago, IL [*Library symbol Library of Congress*] (LCLS) .... ICSU
Chicago Stock Exchange (SRA) .... CHX
Chicago Suburban Motor Carriers Association, Inc., Homewood IL [*STAC*] .... CHS
Chicago Sun-Times and Chicago Daily News, Chicago, IL [*Library symbol Library of Congress*] (LCLS) .... ICSN
Chicago Symphony Orchestra .... CSO
Chicago Teachers College [*Later, Chicago State University*] .... CTC
Chicago Technical College .... CTC
Chicago Technology Park .... CTP
Chicago, Terre Haute & Southeastern R. R. [*AAR code*] .... CTSE
Chicago Theological Seminary .... CTS
Chicago Theological Seminary, Chicago, IL [*Library symbol Library of Congress*] (LCLS) .... ICT
Chicago Theological Seminary, Chicago, IL [*OCLC symbol*] (OCLC) .... IDG
Chicago Transit Authority .... CTA
Chicago Transit Authority, Chicago, IL [*OCLC symbol*] (OCLC) .... IBB
Chicago Transit Authority, Chicago, IL [*Library symbol Library of Congress*] (LCLS) .... ICTA
Chicago Tribune [*A publication*] (BARN) .... Chi Trib
Chicago Tribune [*A publication*] .... CT
Chicago Union Station Co. [*AAR code*] .... CUST
Chicago/West Chicago, IL [*Location identifier FAA*] (FAAL) .... DPA
Chicago, West Pullman & Southern Railroad Co. [*AAR code*] .... CWP
Chicago/Wheeling, IL [*Location identifier FAA*] (FAAL) .... PWK
Chicago White Sox [*Baseball team*] .... CHISOX
Chicago-Argonne Resonant Ionization Spectrometer for Microanalysis [*Astronomy*] .... CHARISMA
Chicago-Joliet Livestock Marketing Center (EA) .... CJLMC
Chicago-Kent College of Law .... CKCL
Chicago-Pittsburgh [*Proposed name for possible "super-city" formed by growth and mergers of other cities*] .... CHIPITTS
Chicago-University of Illinois [*RADAR system*] .... CHILL
Chicana Research and Learning Center (EA) .... CRLC
Chicana Rights Project [*Defunct*] (EA) .... CRP
Chicano Education Project [*Defunct*] (EA) .... CEP
Chicano Employment Committee (DICI) .... CEC
Chicano Family Center (EA) .... CFC
Chicano Humanities and Arts Council (EDAC) .... CHAC
Chicano Press Association (EA) .... CPA
Chicano Studies Research Center [*University of California, Los Angeles*] [*Research center*] (RCD) .... CSRC
Chicano Training Center (EA) .... CTC
Chicanos Against Military Intervention in Latin America [*Promotes understanding between Mexico and the US at the grassroots level*] (CROSS) .... CAMILA
Chichen Itza [*Mexico*] [*Airport symbol*] (OAG) .... CZA
Chichester [*City in England*] (ROG) .... CESTR
Chichester [*City in England*] (ROG) .... CHICH
Chichester/Goodwood [*British ICAO location identifier*] (ICLI) .... EGHR
Chichibu [*Japan*] [*Seismograph station code, US Geological Survey*] (SEIS) .... CHJ
Chichijima [*Bonin Islands*] [*Seismograph station code, US Geological Survey*] (SEIS) .... CBI
Chichijima [*Japan ICAO location identifier*] (ICLI) .... RJAO
Chick Cell Agglutination [*Vaccine potency test*] .... CCA
Chick Cell Agglutination Test (DMAA) .... CCAT
Chick Embryo Extract [*Culture media*] .... CEE
Chick Embryo Fibroblast .... CEF
Chick Embryo Kidney [*Medicine*] (DMAA) .... CEK
Chick Embryo Origin .... CEO
Chick Embryonic Skin .... CES

Chick Fibroblast [*Cytology*] .... CF
Chick Heart Fibroblast [*Cytology*] .... CHF
Chick Infective Dose (MAE) .... CID
Chick Muscle Extract [*Embryology*] .... CMX
Chick Neurotropic Factor [*Neurochemistry*] .... CNTF
Chick Red Blood Cells .... CRBC
Chickamauga and Chattanooga National Military Park .... CHCH
Chickamauga Dam [*TVA*] .... CMD
Chickasaw, AL [*FM radio station call letters*] .... WDLT
Chickasaw County Historical Society, Ionia, IA [*Library symbol Library of Congress*] (LCLS) .... IaIonCHi
Chickasaw County Historical Society, Nashua, IA [*Library symbol*] [*Library of Congress*] (LCLS) .... IaNasCHi
Chickasaw Horse Association (EA) .... CHA
Chickasaw Library System, Ardmore, OK [*OCLC symbol*] (OCLC) .... CKL
Chickasaw Library System, Ardmore, OK [*Library symbol Library of Congress*] (LCLS) .... OkArC
Chickasha, OK [*Location identifier FAA*] (FAAL) .... CHK
Chickasha, OK [*AM radio station call letters*] .... KWCO
Chickasha, OK [*FM radio station call letters*] .... KXXK
Chicken .... CHICK
Chicken .... CHKN
Chicken, AK [*Location identifier FAA*] (FAAL) .... CKX
Chicken Anaemia Agent [*Australia*] .... CAA
Chicken Embryo .... CE
Chicken Embryo Fibroblast [*Cell line*] .... CEF
Chicken Embryo Fibroblast [*Cytology*] .... CHEF
Chicken Embryo Lethal Orphan [*Virus*] .... CELO
Chicken Gamma-Globulin [*Immunology*] .... CGG
Chicken Hepatic Lectin .... CHL
Chicken Kidney .... CK
Chicken Lactose-Lectin [*Biochemistry*] CLL
Chicken Meat Industry Committee [*Queensland*] [*Australia*] .... CMIC
Chicken Meat Research and Development Council [*Australia*] .... CMRDC
Chicken Neural Cell Adhesion Molecule .... ChNCAM
Chicken Ovalbumin Upstream Promoter [*Genetics*] .... COUP
Chicken Ovalbumin Upstream Promoter Transcription Factor [*Genetics*] .... COUP-TF
Chicken Progesterone Receptor [*Genetics*] .... CPR
Chicken Red Blood Cell [*Medicine*] (DMAA) .... ChRBC
Chicken Thymidine Kinase [*An enzyme*] .... ChTK
Chicken Vitellogenin .... cVit
Chickenpox [*Also, Cp*] [*Medicine*] .... CHPX
Chickenpox [*Also, CHPX*] [*Medicine*] .... Cp
Chickering House, Dover, MA [*Library symbol Library of Congress*] (LCLS) .... MDovC
Chick-Martin [*Test*] [*Microbiology*] .... CM
Chiclayo [*Peru*] [*Airport symbol*] (OAG) CIX
Chiclayo/Cap. Jose Abelardo Quinones Gonzalez [*Peru*] [*ICAO location identifier*] (ICLI) .... SPHI
Chico [*California*] [*Seismograph station code, US Geological Survey*] (SEIS) .... CCO
Chico [*California*] [*Airport symbol*] (OAG) CIC
Chico, CA [*FM radio station call letters*] .... KCHO
Chico, CA [*Television station call letters*] .... KCPM
Chico, CA [*FM radio station call letters*] .... KFMF
Chico, CA [*FM radio station call letters*] .... KHAP
Chico, CA [*Television station call letters*] .... KHSL-TV
Chico, CA [*FM radio station call letters*] .... KLRS
Chico, CA [*FM radio station call letters*] (RBYB) .... KMXI
Chico, CA [*AM radio station call letters*] (RBYB) .... KNSN
Chico, CA [*AM radio station call letters*] .... KPAY
Chico, CA [*FM radio station call letters*] .... KZFR
Chico Public Library, Chico, CA [*Library symbol Library of Congress*] (LCLS) .... CChi
Chicopee Falls, MA [*Location identifier FAA*] (FAAL) .... CEF
Chicopee Falls, MA [*Location identifier FAA*] (FAAL) .... GWJ
Chicopee Falls, MA [*Location identifier FAA*] (FAAL) .... GWT
Chicopee Falls/Westover Air Force Base [*Massachusetts*] [*ICAO location identifier*] (ICLI) .... KCEF
Chicopee, MA [*AM radio station call letters*] .... WACE
Chicopee Public Library, Chicopee, MA [*Library symbol Library of Congress*] (LCLS) .... MChi
Chicory Yellow Mottle Virus [*Plant pathology*] .... CHYMV
Chico's FAS [*NASDAQ symbol*] (TTSB) .... CHCS
Chicos Fas, Inc. [*NASDAQ symbol*] (SAG) .... CHCS
Chicos Fas, Inc. [*Associated Press*] (SAG) .... Chicos
Chicoutimi, PQ [*AM radio station call letters*] .... CBJ
Chicoutimi, PQ [*FM radio station call letters*] .... CBJE-FM
Chicoutimi, PQ [*Television station call letters*] .... CBJET
Chicoutimi, PQ [*FM radio station call letters*] .... CBJ-FM
Chicoutimi, PQ [*Television station call letters*] CIVV
Chicoutimi, PQ [*FM radio station call letters*] .... CJAB
Chicoutimi, PQ [*Television station call letters*] .... CJPM
Chido [*Antibodies*] [*Immunology*] (DAVI) .... Ch
Chidren's Wonderland Unit [*NASDAQ symbol*] (TTSB) .... CWICU
Chief C
Chief (AFM) .... CH
Chief (WDMC) .... ch
Chief .... CHF
Chief .... CHF
Chief Accountant .... CA
Chief Accountant Officer [*RAF*] [*British*] .... CAO
Chief Activation Engineer .... CAE
Chief Administrative Engineer .... CAE
Chief Administrative Medical Officer [*British*] .... CAMO

Chief Administrative Officer ... CAO
Chief Advisor ... CA
Chief, Aerial Reconnaissance Coordination, All Hurricanes [*National Hurricane Center*] ... CARCAH
Chief Aerographer [*Navy rating Obsolete*] ... CAER
Chief Aerographer [*Navy rating Obsolete*] ... CHAER
Chief Aerographer's Mate [*Navy rating Obsolete*] ... CAERM
Chief Agency Officer [*Insurance*] ... CAO
Chief, Air Doctrine and Operations (MCD) ... CADO
Chief Air Fitter [*British military*] (DMA) ... CAF
Chief, Air Force Advisory Group ... CHAFAG
Chief, Air Force Modernization Coordination Office (MCD) ... CAFMCO
Chief, Air Force Section (CINC) ... CHAFSEC
Chief Aircraft Artificer [*British military*] (DMA) ... CAA
Chief Aircraft Communicator [*British military*] (IAA) ... CACOM
Chief, Aircraft Maintenance ... CAM
Chief Aircraft Mechanician [*British military*] (DMA) ... CAMN
Chief Aircrew Survival Equipmentman [*Formerly, Chief Parachute Rigger*] [*Navy rating*] ... PRC
Chief Airship Rigger [*Navy rating Obsolete*] ... CAR
Chief Airways Technical District Office ... CATDO
Chief Airways Technical Field Office ... CATFO
Chief Ancient Philosophies [*A publication*] ... CAP
Chief and Assistant Chief Fire Officers' Association [*British*] ... CACFOA
Chief, Army Reserve (AABC) ... CAR
Chief, Army Reserve and Reserve Officers Training Corps Affairs ... CARROTC
Chief Artificer Engineer [*Navy British*] (ROG) ... CH AE
Chief Artillery Controller (NATG) ... CAC
Chief Aviation Boatswain's Mate, Handler [*Navy rating*] (DNAB) ... ABHC
Chief Aviation Machinist's Mate (Reciprocating) [*Navy rating*] ... ADC
Chief Aviation Maintenance Technician (DNAB) ... CHAVMAINTECH
Chief Aviation Pilot [*Navy, Coast Guard*] ... CAP
Chief Baron [*British*] ... CB
Chief Baron of the Exchequer [*British*] (ROG) ... CB EX
Chief Baron of the Exchequer [*British*] (DLA) ... Ch B Ex
Chief Benefits Director [*Department of Veterans Affairs*] ... CBD
Chief Boatswain [*Navy rating Obsolete*] ... CHBOSN
Chief Boatswain's Mate [*Navy rating Obsolete*] ... CBM
Chief Boatswain's Mate, A [*Master-at-Arms*] [*Navy rating Obsolete*] ... CBMM
Chief Boatswain's Mate, Acting [*Navy rating Obsolete*] ... CBMA
Chief Boatswain's Mate, Construction Battalion, Boatswain [*Navy rating Obsolete*] ... CBMCBB
Chief Boatswain's Mate, Construction Battalion, Stevedore [*Navy rating Obsolete*] ... CBMCBS
Chief Boatswain's Mate, Ship Repair, Canvasman [*Navy rating Obsolete*] ... CBMSRS
Chief Boatswain's Mate, Ship Repair, Crane Operator [*Navy rating Obsolete*] ... CBMSRC
Chief Boatswain's Mate, Ship Repair, Rigger [*Navy rating Obsolete*] ... CBMSRR
Chief Boilermaker [*Navy rating Obsolete*] ... CB
Chief Boilermaker [*Coast Guard*] ... CBMKR
Chief Boilermaker, Ship Repair [*Navy*] ... CBSR
Chief Bombardment Liaison Officer [*Navy*] ... CBLO
Chief Buglemaster [*Navy*] ... CBgmstr
Chief Bug-O-Nay-Ge-Shig Library, Cass Lake, MN [*Library symbol*] [*Library of Congress*] (LCLS) ... MnCasCB
Chief Builder [*Navy rating*] ... BUC
Chief Cable Censor [*Navy rating Obsolete*] ... CCC
Chief Carpenter [*Navy rating Obsolete*] ... CHCARP
Chief Carpenter's Mate [*Navy rating Obsolete*] ... CCM
Chief Carpenter's Mate, Construction Battalion, Builder [*Navy rating Obsolete*] ... CCMCBB
Chief Carpenter's Mate, Construction Battalion, Draftsman [*Navy rating Obsolete*] ... CCMCBD
Chief Carpenter's Mate, Construction Battalion, Excavation Foreman [*Navy rating Obsolete*] ... CCMCBE
Chief Carpenter's Mate, Construction Battalion, Surveyor [*Navy rating Obsolete*] ... CCMCBS
Chief Carpenter's Mate, Ship Repair, Boatbuilder, Wood [*Navy rating Obsolete*] ... CCMSRB
Chief Carpenter's Mate, Ship Repair, Joiner [*Navy rating Obsolete*] ... CCMSRJ
Chief Central Security Service ... CHCSS
Chief Chemical Officer [*Army*] ... CCMLO
Chief Chemical Officer [*Army*] ... CCO
Chief Civil Affairs Officer [*Navy*] ... CCAO
Chief Civil Affairs Officer (Burma) [*British*] ... CCAO(B)
Chief Clerk ... CC
Chief Clerk (BARN) ... Ch Clk
Chief Clerk of the Admiralty [*British*] ... CCA
Chief, Command Naval Air Systems [*Later, NAVAIR*] ... CHCOMNAVAIRSYS
Chief Commanding Officer ... CCO
Chief Commissary Steward [*Navy rating Obsolete*] ... CCS
Chief Commissary Steward [*Navy rating Obsolete*] ... CCSTD
Chief Commissaryman [*Later, MSC*] [*Navy rating*] ... CSC
Chief Commissioner of Police (DAS) ... CCP
Chief Communications Yeoman [*British military*] (DMA) ... CCY
Chief Complaint [*Medicine*] ... CC
Chief Consol Mining [*NASDAQ symbol*] (TTSB) ... CFCM
Chief Consolidated Mining Co. [*NASDAQ symbol*] (NQ) ... CFCM
Chief Consolidated Mining Co. [*Associated Press*] (SAG) ... ChfCon
Chief Constable [*Scotland Yard*] ... CC
Chief, Construction and Properties, Library, Department of National Defence [*Bibliotheque, Chef - Construction et Immeubles, Ministere de le Defense Nationale*] **Ottawa, Ontario** [*Library symbol National Library of Canada*] (NLC) ... OONDCP
Chief Construction Engineer (OA) ... CCE
Chief, Contracting Office (AAGC) ... CCO
Chief Control Electrical Artificer [*British military*] (DMA) ... CCEA
Chief Control Electrical Mechanician [*British military*] (DMA) ... CCEMN
Chief Control Electrician [*British military*] (DMA) ... CCEL
Chief Controller (NATG) ... CC
Chief Controller ... CCNT
Chief Controller (FAAC) ... CCTLR
Chief Cook [*Navy rating Obsolete*] ... CCK
Chief Cook [*Navy rating Obsolete*] ... CHCK
Chief Cook (Baker) [*Navy rating Obsolete*] ... CCK(B)
Chief Cook (Commissary) [*Navy rating Obsolete*] ... CCK(C)
Chief, Corps of Engineers [*Army*] ... CCE
Chief Counsel (KSC) ... CC
Chief Court [*Freemasonry*] (ROG) ... CC
Chief Court of Cochin, Select Decisions [*A publication*] (DLA) ... Coch Ch Ct
Chief Damage Controlman [*Navy*] ... DCC
Chief Data Processing Technician [*Formerly, MAC*] [*Navy rating*] ... DPC
Chief Decision Makers ... CDM
Chief, Defense Liaison Group (CINC) ... CHDLG
Chief, Defense Liaison Group-Indonesia (DNAB) ... CHDLG-INDO
Chief Development Officer (NFD) ... CDO
Chief Directorate to the Council of Ministries for the Utilisation of Atomic Energy [*British*] (NUCP) ... GLAVATOM
Chief Draftsman (MCD) ... CD
Chief Draftsman Office Memorandum (SAA) ... CDOM
Chief Draftsman's Instructions (MCD) ... CDI
Chief Education Officer (AIE) ... CEO
Chief Elected Official (OICC) ... CEO
Chief Electoral Officer [*Canada*] ... CEO
Chief Electrical Artificer [*British military*] (DMA) ... CEA
Chief Electrical Mechanician [*British military*] (DMA) ... CELMN
Chief Electrician [*Navy rating Obsolete*] ... CHELEC
Chief Electrician (Air) [*British military*] (DMA) ... CEL(A)
Chief Electrician (Air Weapon) [*British military*] (DMA) ... CEL(AW)
Chief Electrician's Mate [*Navy rating Obsolete*] ... CEM
Chief Electrician's Mate, Construction Battalion, Communications [*Navy rating Obsolete*] ... CEMCBC
Chief Electrician's Mate, Construction Battalion, Draftsman [*Navy rating Obsolete*] ... CEMCBD
Chief Electrician's Mate, Construction Battalion, General [*Navy rating Obsolete*] ... CEMCBG
Chief Electrician's Mate, Construction Battalion, Line and Station [*Navy rating Obsolete*] ... CEMCBL
Chief Electrician's Mate, Ship Repair, General Electrician [*Navy rating Obsolete*] ... CEMSRG
Chief Electrician's Mate, Ship Repair, IC Repairman [*Navy rating Obsolete*] ... CEMSRT
Chief Electrician's Mate, Ship Repair, Shop Electrician [*Navy rating Obsolete*] ... CEMSRS
Chief Electronics Technician (DNAB) ... CHELECTECH
Chief Engine Room Artificer [*British military*] (DMA) ... CERA
Chief Engineer [*Navy*] ... CE
Chief Engineer [*British military*] (DMA) ... Ch E
Chief Engineer and Superintendent of Armaments Design [*British military*] (DMA) ... CEAD
Chief Engineer Port Construction [*British military*] (DMA) ... CEPC
Chief Engineer's Office (SAA) ... CEO
Chief Enlisted Manager ... CEM
Chief Executive ... CE
Chief Executive Dockyard [*Navy British*] ... CED
Chief Executive Officer ... CEO
Chief Executive Officer [*Also, CEO*] ... Ch Ex Off
Chief Executives Forum [*Later, CEO*] ... CEF
Chief Executives of Large Public Libraries of Ontario (AC) ... CELPLO
Chief Executives Organization (EA) ... CEO
Chief Financial Officer [*Business term*] ... CFO
Chief Financial Officer Act of 1990 ... CFOA
Chief Financial Official (AAGC) ... CFO
Chief Fire Controlman [*Navy rating Obsolete*] ... CFC
Chief Fire Controlman, Operator [*Navy rating Obsolete*] ... CFCO
Chief Fire Controlman, Submarines [*Navy rating Obsolete*] ... CFCS
Chief Fire Officer [*British*] (ADA) ... CFO
Chief Flight Operator (AAGC) ... CFO
Chief Flying Instructor [*RAF*] [*British*] ... CFI
Chief Ground Instructor [*British military*] (DMA) ... CGI
Chief Gunner [*Navy rating Obsolete*] ... CHGUN
Chief Gunner's Mate [*Navy rating Obsolete*] ... CGM
Chief Gunner's Mate, Construction Battalion, Armorer [*Navy rating Obsolete*] ... CGMCBG
Chief Gunner's Mate, Construction Battalion, Powderman [*Navy rating Obsolete*] ... CGMCBP
Chief Gunner's Mate, Technician [*Navy rating*] ... GMTC
Chief Gunnery Instructor [*British military*] (DMA) ... CGI
Chief Illustrator Draftsman [*Navy rating*] ... DMC
Chief Immigration Officer (DS) ... CIO
Chief Industrial Property ... CIP
Chief Information Officer [*Business term*] ... CIO
Chief Inspector ... CI
Chief Inspector of Armaments ... CIA
Chief Inspector of Engineering and Signal Stores [*Military British*] ... CIESS
Chief Inspector of Land Service Ammunition (NATG) ... CILSA
Chief Inspector of Machinery [*Navy British*] (ROG) ... CHIM
Chief Inspector of Machinery [*Navy British*] (ROG) ... CIM
Chief Inspector of Naval Ordnance [*British*] ... CINO

Chief Inspector of Royal Engineer Stores [*British military*] (DMA) ... CIRES
Chief Inspector of Supplementary Transport [*British military*] (DMA) ... CIST
Chief Instructor ... CI
Chief Instrumentman [*Navy rating*] ... IMC
Chief, Intelligence Corps ... CINTC
Chief Intendent-General [*Freemasonry*] (ROG) ... CIG
Chief Intercept Director ... CIND
Chief Japanese Maritime Staff Office (CINC) ... CMSO
Chief, Joint United States Military Advisory Group [*Followed by name of country*] (CINC) ... CHJUSMAG
Chief Journalist [*Navy rating*] ... JOC
Chief Judge [*Sports*] ... CJ
Chief Judge in Bankruptcy (DLA) ... CJB
Chief Justice [*British*] (ROG) ... CHJ
Chief Justice [*Various supreme courts*] ... CJ
Chief Justice of the Common Pleas [*British*] (DLA) ... CHCP
Chief Justice of the Common Pleas [*British*] (ROG) ... CHJCP
Chief Justice of the Common Pleas (DLA) ... CJCP
Chief Justice of the Common (Upper) Bench (DLA) ... CJUB
Chief Justice of the King's Bench (DLA) ... CJKB
Chief Justice of the Queen's Bench (DLA) ... CHQB
Chief Justice of the Queen's Bench (DLA) ... CJQB
Chief Justice of the Upper Bench [*British*] (ROG) ... CHJUB
Chief, Korea Military Assistance Group ... CHKMAG
Chief Labour Management Officer [*Ministry of Supply*] [*British*] ... CLMO
Chief Launch Vehicle Test Conductor [*NASA*] (KSC) ... CLTC
Chief Leisure Officers Association [*British*] (DBA) ... CLOA
Chief Lithographer [*Navy rating*] ... LIC
Chief, Logistics Data Management Office [*Army*] ... C/LDMO
Chief Machine Accountant [*Later, DPC*] [*Navy rating*] ... MAC
Chief Machinist [*Navy rating Obsolete*] ... CHMACH
Chief Machinist's Mate [*Navy rating Obsolete*] ... CMM
Chief Machinist's Mate, Construction Battalion, Equipment Operator [*Navy rating Obsolete*] ... CMMCBE
Chief Machinist's Mate, Industrial Gas Generating Mechanic [*Navy rating Obsolete*] ... CMMG
Chief Machinist's Mate, Refrigeration [*Navy rating Obsolete*] ... CMMR
Chief Machinist's Mate, Ship Repair, Outside Machinist [*Navy rating Obsolete*] ... CMMSRO
Chief Machinist's Mate, Shop [*Navy rating Obsolete*] ... CMMS
Chief Mailman [*Navy rating Obsolete*] ... CMAM
Chief Maintenance Officer ... CMO
Chief Marine Engineering Artificer [*British military*] (DMA) ... CMEA
Chief Marine Engineering Mechanic [*British military*] (DMA) ... CMEM
Chief Marine Gunner [*Navy rating*] ... CMG
Chief Marketing Officer [*Insurance*] ... CMO
Chief Master at Arms [*Navy rating*] ... CMAA
Chief Master Sergeant ... CMSGT
Chief Master Sergeant [*Air Force*] ... E9
Chief Master Sergeant of the Air Force (AFM) ... CMSAF
Chief Mechanic ... CM
Chief Mechanical and Electrical Engineer [*Air Force British*] ... CMEE
Chief Mechanical Engineer [*Military British*] ... CME
Chief Medical Adviser ... CMA
Chief Medical Director [*Department of Veterans Affairs*] ... CMD
Chief Medical Officer [*Military*] ... CMO
Chief Medical Technician [*British military*] (DMA) ... CMT
Chief Merchanist's Mate [*Navy British*] ... CMM
Chief Mess Management Specialist [*Formerly, CSC, CST, SDC*] [*Navy rating*] ... MSC
Chief Metalsmith [*Navy rating Obsolete*] ... CM
Chief Metalsmith, Ship Repair, Blacksmith [*Navy rating Obsolete*] ... CMSRB
Chief Metalsmith, Ship Repair, Coppersmith [*Navy rating Obsolete*] ... CMSRC
Chief Metalsmith, Ship Repair, Sheet Metal Worker [*Navy rating Obsolete*] ... CMSRS
Chief, Military Assistance Advisory Group [*Followed by name of country*] (CINC) ... CHMAAG
Chief, Military Assistance Advisory Group, Korea (Provisional) (CINC) ... CHPROVMAAGK
Chief, Military Equipment Delivery Team (CINC) ... CHMEDT
Chief, Military Planning Office (CINC) ... CHMPO
Chief, Military Technical Advisory Group (CINC) ... CHMILTAG
Chief Minister's Department [*Australian Capital Territory*] [*Australia*] ... CMD
Chief Motor Boatman [*British military*] (DMA) ... CMB
Chief Motor Machinist's Mate [*Navy rating Obsolete*] ... CMOMM
Chief Motor Machinist's Mate, Ship Repair, Diesel Engineering Mechanic [*Navy rating Obsolete*] ... CMOMSRD
Chief Motor Machinist's Mate, Ship Repair, Gasoline Engineering Mechanic [*Navy rating Obsolete*] ... CMOMSRG
Chief Motor Mechanic [*British military*] (DMA) ... CMM
Chief Moulder [*Navy rating Obsolete*] ... CML
Chief Musician [*Navy rating Obsolete*] ... CMUS
Chief, National Guard Bureau [*Army*] ... CNGB
Chief, Naval Advanced Air Training ... CNAAT
Chief Naval Adviser [*British*] ... CNA
Chief, Naval Advisory Group ... CHNAVADGP
Chief, Naval Advisory Group [*Followed by name of country*] (CINC) ... CHNAVADGRU
Chief, Naval Advisory Group ... CHNAVGP
Chief [*or Commander*], Naval Advisory Group (DNAB) ... CNAG
Chief, Naval Air Basic Training ... CNABT
Chief, Naval Air Basic Training (DNAB) ... CNABTRA
Chief, Naval Airships Training ... CHNAVAIRSHIPTRA
Chief Naval Censor [*Navy rating Obsolete*] ... CNC
Chief Naval Engineering Officer [*British*] ... CNEO
Chief Naval Judge Advocate [*British*] ... CNJA
Chief, Naval Mission ... CHNAVMIS
Chief, Naval Ordnance Management Information System Office (DNAB) ... CHNOMISO
Chief Naval Representative [*British*] ... CNR
Chief, Naval Reserve Forces ... CNRF
Chief, Naval Reserve Training ... CNRT
Chief Naval Supply and Secretariat Officer [*British*] ... CNSSO
Chief Navy Disbursing Officer ... CNDO
Chief, Navy Section (CINC) ... CHNAVSEC
Chief, Navy Section, Joint United States Military Advisory Group, Thailand (DNAB) ... CHNAVSECJUSMAGTHAI
Chief, Navy Section, Military Assistance Advisory Group ... CHNAVSECMAAG
Chief, Navy Section, Military Training Mission (DNAB) ... CHNAVSECMTM
Chief, Navy Section, United States Military Group (DNAB) ... CHNAVSECUSMILGP
Chief, Navy-Marine Corps Military Affiliate Radio Station (DNAB) ... CHNAVMARCORMARS
Chief Nursing Officer [*British*] ... CNO
Chief, Nursing Services (DAVI) ... CNS
Chief Observer [*Navy*] (NVT) ... CHOBS
Chief of Air Corps [*World War II*] ... C of AC
Chief of Air Corps [*World War II*] ... CAC
Chief of Air Defense ... CAD
Chief of Air Force Chaplains ... C of AFCH
Chief of Air Force Chaplains ... COFAFCH
Chief of Air Staff [*World War II*] ... C of AS
Chief of Air Staff [*World War II*] ... CAS
Chief of Army Audit Agency ... CAAA
Chief of Army Aviation ... CAA
Chief of Budget and Finance Division [*Supreme Headquarters Allied Powers Europe*] (NATG) ... CBUDFIN
Chief of Budget and Finance Division [*Supreme Headquarters Allied Powers Europe*] (NATG) ... CCM
Chief of Cavalry ... C of CAV
Chief of Chaplains [*Later, CCH*] [*Army*] ... C of CH
Chief of Chaplains [*Later, CCH*] [*Army*] ... CC
Chief of Chaplains [*Formerly, CC, C of CH, COFCH*] [*Army*] (AABC) ... CCH
Chief of Chaplains [*Navy*] ... COC
Chief of Chaplains [*Later, CCH*] [*Army*] ... COFCH
Chief of Civil Affairs [*Army*] ... CCA
Chief of Civil Engineers [*Army*] (DNAB) ... CHCIVENG
Chief of Civil Engineers [*Army*] ... CHCIVENGS
Chief of Coast Artillery ... C of CA
Chief of Combined Operations [*British Army*] [*World War II*] ... CCO
Chief of Communications - Electronics ... CCE
Chief of Defence Procurement [*British*] (RDA) ... CDP
Chief of Defence Staff [*British*] (NATG) ... CDS
Chief of Defense (NATG) ... CHOD
Chief of Defense Force Staff (MCD) ... CDFS
Chief of Detectives ... CD
Chief of Division ... CD
Chief of Engineers [*Later, COE*] [*Army*] ... C of E
Chief of Engineers [*Later, COE*] [*Army*] ... C of ENGRS
Chief of Engineers [*Army*] (SAA) ... C of Engs
Chief of Engineers [*Later, COE*] [*Army*] ... CE
Chief of Engineers [*Formerly, CE, C of E, C of ENGRS, COFENGS*] [*Army*] (AABC) ... COE
Chief of Engineers (MCD) ... COFENGRS
Chief of Engineers [*Later, COE*] [*Army*] ... COFENGS
Chief of Engineers (Assistant Chief of Engineers) [*Military*] ... COE(ACE)
Chief of Establishments and Research [*British*] ... CER
Chief of Field Artillery ... CFA
Chief of Finance [*Army*] ... C of F
Chief of Finance [*Army*] ... CF
Chief of Finance [*Army*] ... COFF
Chief of Finance and Accounting [*Army*] (AABC) ... CF & A
Chief of Fleet Support [*Navy British*] ... CFS
Chief of Government ... COG
Chief of Information [*Also, CINFO*] [*Navy*] ... CHINFO
Chief of Information [*Army*] ... CI
Chief of Information [*Also, CHINFO*] [*Navy*] ... CINFO
Chief of Legislative Liaison [*Army*] ... CLL
Chief of Military History [*Army*] ... CMH
Chief of Mission Operations [*NASA*] ... CMO
Chief of Naval Air ... CNA
Chief of Naval Air Advanced Training [*Also, CNAVANTRA*] [*Formerly, CNAOPTRA, CNAOT*] ... CNAADTRA
Chief of Naval Air Advanced Training [*Also, CNAADTRA*] ... CNAVANTRA
Chief of Naval Air Basic Training ... CNABATRA
Chief of Naval Air Intermediate Training [*Later, CNABATRA*] ... CNAINTERMTRA
Chief of Naval Air Intermediate Training [*Later, CNABATRA*] ... CNAIT
Chief of Naval Air Operational Training [*Later, CNAADTRA, CNAVANTRA*] ... CNAOPTRA
Chief of Naval Air Operational Training [*Later, CNAADTRA, CNAVANTRA*] ... CNAOT
Chief of Naval Air Pacific (MCD) ... CNAP
Chief of Naval Air Primary Training [*Later, CNARFSTRA*] ... CNAPRIMTRA
Chief of Naval Air Primary Training [*Later, CNARFSTRA*] ... CNAPT
Chief of Naval Air Primary Training ... CNARFSTRA
Chief of Naval Air Reserve Training ... CNARESTRA
Chief of Naval Air Services [*British*] ... CNAS
Chief of Naval Air Technical Training ... CNATECHTRA
Chief of Naval Air Technical Training ... CNATT
Chief of Naval Air Training ... CNAT
Chief of Naval Air Training ... CNATRA

Chief of Naval Airships Training and Experimentation .... CNATE
Chief of Naval Aviation Logistics (MCD) .... CNAL
Chief of Naval Communications [Formerly, DNC] .... CNC
Chief of Naval Development (DNAB) .... CHNAVDEV
Chief of Naval Development .... CND
Chief of Naval Education and Training (MCD) .... CNET
Chief of Naval Information [Obsolete British] .... CNI
Chief of Naval Intelligence .... CNI
Chief of Naval Material (MCD) .... CHNAVMAT
Chief of Naval Material .... CNM
Chief of Naval Material Emergency Relocation Site Commander
    (DNAB) .... CHNAVMAT ERS
Chief of Naval Operational Requirement and Plans .... CNORP
Chief of Naval Operations [Also, CNO] .... CNAVOP
Chief of Naval Operations [Also, CNAVOP] [Washington, DC] .. CNO
Chief of Naval Operations (AAGC) .... OPNAV
Chief of Naval Operations Budget Office .... CNOBO
Chief of Naval Operations Command/Management Information
    System .... CNOCOM/MIS
Chief of Naval Operations Communications Center (MCD) ...... CNOCC
Chief of Naval Operations Memorandum .... CNOM
Chief of Naval Operations Memorandum and Commandant of the Marine
    Corps Memorandum [Joint] .... CNOM/CMCM
Chief of Naval Operations Reserve Affairs Advisory Board (DNAB) .. CNO/RAAB
Chief of Naval Personnel (NVT) .... CHNAVPERS
Chief of Naval Personnel [The Second Sea Lord] [British] .... CNP
Chief of Naval Research .... CNR
Chief of Naval Reserve (DOMA) .... CHNAVRES
Chief of Naval Reserve (DOMA) .... CNR
Chief of Naval Technical Services [Canada] .... CNTS
Chief of Naval Technical Training (NVT) .... CNTT
Chief of Naval Training .... CHNAVTRA
Chief of Naval Training (AAGC) .... CNATRA
Chief of Naval Training .... CNT
Chief of Naval Transportation Service .... CNTS
Chief of Navy Technical Training (DNAB) .... CNTECHTRA
Chief of Office of Research and Inventions [Navy] .... CHORI
Chief of Operations .... CHOPS
Chief of Operations Analysis (MCD) .... COA
Chief of Ordnance [Army] .... C of ORD
Chief of Ordnance [Army] .... CO
Chief of Ordnance [Army] .... COFORD
Chief of Ordnance [Army] .... CORD
Chief of Outpost [CIA officer in charge of a field office] .... COO
Chief of Personnel and Logistics [Navy British] .... CPL
Chief of Police .... COP
Chief of Police .... CP
Chief of Public Affairs (AABC) .... CPA
Chief of Public Information [Army] .... CPI
Chief of Public Information Division [NATO] (NATG) .... CPUBINFO
Chief of Research and Development [Army] .... CR & D
Chief of Research and Development [Army] .... CRD
Chief of Research, Development, and Acquisition [Army] (RDA) .. CRDA
Chief of Reserve Components [Army] .... CRC
Chief of Rocket Troops and Artillery (MCD) .... CRTA
Chief of Section .... C of S
Chief of Section .... COS
Chief of Section .... CS
Chief of Staff [Military] .... C of S
Chief of Staff [Military] .... COFS
Chief of Staff [Military] .... COS
Chief of Staff [Medicine] (DAVI) .... COS
Chief of Staff [Military] .... CS
Chief of Staff Air Force Memorandum (AFM) .... CSAFM
Chief of Staff, Army Memorandum [Air Force] .... CSAM
Chief of Staff Memorandum [Military] (AABC) .... CSM
Chief of Staff, Military Intelligence Committee (NATG) .... COSMIC
Chief of Staff Regulations .... CSR
Chief of Staff Supreme Headquarters [British] .... CSSH
Chief of Staff to Supreme Allied Commander [Europe] [World War II] .. COSSAC
Chief of Staff, United States Air Force (NATG) .... COFSAF
Chief of Staff, United States Air Force .... CSAF
Chief of Staff, United States Army [Later, CSA] .... C of SA
Chief of Staff, United States Army [Later, CSA] .... COFSA
Chief of Staff, United States Army [Formerly, COFSA, C of SA] .. CSA
Chief of State .... COS
Chief of Station [CIA country team] .... COS
Chief of Supplies and Transport [Navy British] .... CST
Chief of Support Services [Army] (AABC) .... C of SptS
Chief of Support Services [Army] .... COFSPTS
Chief of Support Services [Army] .... CSS
Chief of Tariff Bureau .... CTB
Chief of the Army Air Forces [World War II] .... C of AAF
Chief of the Army Air Forces [World War II] .... CAAF
Chief of the Bureau of Aeronautics [Obsolete Navy] .... CHBUAER
Chief of the Bureau of Medicine and Surgery [Navy] .... CHBUMED
Chief of the Bureau of Naval Personnel .... CHBUPERS
Chief of the Bureau of Ordnance [Obsolete Navy] .... CHBUORD
Chief of the Bureau of Ships [Obsolete Navy] .... CHBUSHIPS
Chief of the Bureau of Supplies and Accounts [Obsolete Navy] .... CHBUSANDA
Chief of the Bureau of Yards and Docks [Obsolete Navy] .... CHBUDOCKS
Chief of the Chemical Warfare Service [World War II] .... C of CWS
Chief of the Chemical Warfare Service [World War II] .... CCWS
Chief of the General Staff [in the field] [Formerly, CIGS] [Military] [British] .. CGS
Chief of the Imperial General Staff [Later, CGS] [British] .... CIGS

Chief of the Joint General Staff [Vietnam] .... CJGS
Chief of the Naval Staff [Canada] .... CNS
Chief of the Purchasing Office (AAGC) .... CPO
Chief of the Tabernacle [Freemasonry] (ROG) .... C of T
Chief of Transportation [Army] .... C of T
Chief of Transportation [Army] .... COFT
Chief of Transportation [Army] .... CT
Chief, Office of Personnel Operations [Army] .... COPO
Chief, Office of Reserve Components [Army] (AABC) .... CORC
Chief Officer [Women's Royal Naval Service] [British] .... C/O
Chief Officers of State Library Agencies (EA) .... COSLA
Chief Operating Area Coordinator (DNAB) .... COAC
Chief Operating Officer .... COO
Chief Operating Officer of Business Affairs [Proposed alternative to the
    hiring of a baseball commissioner] .... COOBA
Chief Operator (NVT) .... CHOP
Chief Operator (NRCH) .... CO
Chief Opticalman [Navy rating] .... OMC
Chief Ordnance Electrical Artificer [British military] (DMA) ..... COEA
Chief Ordnance Electrical Mechanician [British military] (DMA) .. COEMN
Chief Ordnance Electrician [British military] (DMA) .... COEL
Chief Ordnance Mechanical Engineer [British] (ADA) .... COME
Chief Ordnance Officer .... COO
Chief Ordnance Officer .... CORDO
Chief Painter [Navy rating Obsolete] .... CPTR
Chief Painter, Aircraft [Navy rating Obsolete] .... CPTRV
Chief Parachute Rigger [Navy] .... CPR
Chief Parliamentary Counsel's Office [Victoria] [Australia] ..... CPCO
Chief Patriarch .... CP
Chief Patrol Inspector [Immigration and Naturalization Service] .. CPI
Chief Patternmaker [Navy rating Obsolete] .... CPM
Chief Patternmaker [Navy rating] .... PMC
Chief Pay Clerk [Navy rating Obsolete] .... CHPCLK
Chief Pay Clerk [Navy rating Obsolete] .... CPC
Chief, Perry, IA [Library symbol Library of Congress] (LCLS) .. IaPerC
Chief Personnelman [Navy rating] .... PNC
Chief Petty Officer [Navy] .... CPO
Chief Petty Officer [Navy] E7
Chief Petty Officer Air Technical Aircraft [Military Australia] ... CPO ATA
Chief Petty Officer Air Technical Communication [Military Australia] .. CPO ATC
Chief Petty Officer, Aircrewman [British military] (DMA) .... CPOACMN
Chief Petty Officer, Caterer [British military] (DMA) .... CPOCA
Chief Petty Officer Clearance Diver [Military Australia] .... CPO CD
Chief Petty Officer, Cook [British military] (DMA) .... CPOCK
Chief Petty Officer Coxswain [Military Australia] .... CPO COX
Chief Petty Officer Dental [Military Australia] .... CPO DEN
Chief Petty Officer Electrical Technical Power [Military Australia] ... CPO ETP
Chief Petty Officer Electrical Technical Weapons [Military Australia] .. CPO ETW
Chief Petty Officer Electronic Technical Communications [Military
    Australia] .... CPO ETC
Chief Petty Officer Electronic Warfare [Military Australia] .... CPO EW
Chief Petty Officer Fire Control [Military Australia] .... CPO FC
Chief Petty Officer Firefighter [Military Australia] .... CPO FF
Chief Petty Officer, First Class [Canadian] [Navy] C1
Chief Petty Officer Marine Technical Hull [Military Australia] ... CPO MTH
Chief Petty Officer Marine Technical Propulsion [Military Australia] .. CPO MTP
Chief Petty Officer, Master [Navy] (WGA) .... CPOM
Chief Petty Officer Medical [Military Australia] .... CPO MED
Chief Petty Officer, Medical Assistant [British military] (DMA) . CPOMA
Chief Petty Officer Meteorology [Military Australia] .... CPO MET
Chief Petty Officer Mine Warfare [Military Australia] .... CPO MW
Chief Petty Officer Motor Transport Driver [Military Australia] . CPO MTD
Chief Petty Officer Musician [Military Australia] .... CPO MUSN
Chief Petty Officer of the Command [Navy] (DNAB) .... CPOC
Chief Petty Officer of the Watch [Navy] .... CPOW
Chief Petty Officer Photography [Military Australia] .... CPO PH
Chief Petty Officer, Physical Trainer [British military] (DMA) ... CPOPT
Chief Petty Officer Quartermaster Gunner [Military Australia] . CPO QMG
Chief Petty Officer Radio Operator [Military Australia] .... CPO RO
Chief Petty Officer Radio Plotter [Military Australia] .... CPO RP
Chief Petty Officer, Second Class [Canadian] [Navy] C2
Chief Petty Officer, Senior [Navy] (WGA) .... CPOS
Chief Petty Officer Signalman [Military Australia] .... CPO SIG
Chief Petty Officer, Steward [British military] (DMA) .... CPOSTD
Chief Petty Officer, Stores Accountant [British military] (DMA) CPOSA
Chief Petty Officer Stores Naval [Military Australia] .... CPO SN
Chief Petty Officer Stores Victualling [Military Australia] .... CPO SV
Chief Petty Officer Survey Recorder [Military Australia] .... CPO SR
Chief Petty Officer Survival Equipment [Military Australia] ...... CPO SE
Chief Petty Officer Underwater Control [Military Australia] ...... CPO UC
Chief Petty Officer Work Study [Military Australia] .... CPO WS
Chief Petty Officer, Writer [British military] (DMA) .... CPOWTR
Chief Petty Officer-in-Charge [Navy] (DNAB) .... CPOIC
Chief Pharmacist [Navy rating Obsolete] .... CHPHAR
Chief Pharmacist's Mate [Navy rating Obsolete] .... CPHM
Chief Pharmacist's Mate, Dental Prosthetic Technician [Navy rating
    Obsolete] .... CPHMDP
Chief Pharmacist's Mate (Radium Plaque Adaptometer Operator) [Navy
    rating Obsolete] .... CPHM(RPA)
Chief Photographer [Navy rating Obsolete] .... CHPHOT
Chief Photographer [Navy rating Obsolete] .... CPHO
Chief Photographer's Mate [Navy rating Obsolete] .... CPHOM
Chief Photographer's Mate [Navy rating] .... PHC
Chief Photographic Intelligenceman [Navy rating] .... PTC
Chief Pilot .... CP

Chief Planning and Control Staff [*Coast Guard*] ..... CPC
Chief Plumber [*British military*] (DMA) ..... CPLMB
Chief Polaris Executive [*Missiles*] ..... CPE
Chief Political Officer [*British Military Administration*] ..... CPO
Chief Post Office [*British*] (ADA) ..... CPO
Chief Postal Clerk [*Navy rating*] ..... PCC
Chief Postal Inspector [*US Postal Service*] ..... CPI
Chief Preventive Officer [*Customs*] [*British*] (ROG) ..... CPO
Chief Printer [*Navy rating Obsolete*] ..... CPRTR
Chief Printer, Lithographer [*Navy rating Obsolete*] ..... CPRTRL
Chief Printer, Offset Process [*Navy rating Obsolete*] ..... CPRTRM
Chief Procurement Officer (AAGC) ..... CPO
Chief Program Engineer [*NASA*] (NASA) ..... CPE
Chief Programmer Team [*Computer science*] ..... CPT
Chief Programmer Team Organization [*Computer science*] (MHDI) ..... CPTO
Chief Quality Officer [*Business term*] (ECON) ..... CQO
Chief Quartermaster [*Navy rating Obsolete*] ..... CQM
Chief Quartermaster [*Navy rating*] ..... QMC
[*The*] **Chief Quartermaster** [*Military*] ..... TCQM
Chief Quartermaster Clerk [*Coast Guard*] ..... CHQMCLK
Chief Quartermaster Clerk [*Navy rating Obsolete*] ..... CQMC
Chief RADARman [*Navy rating Obsolete*] ..... CRDM
Chief RADARman [*Navy rating*] ..... RDC
Chief Radio Electrical Artificer [*British military*] (DMA) ..... CREA
Chief Radio Electrical Mechanician [*British military*] (DMA) ..... CREMN
Chief Radio Electrician [*Navy rating Obsolete*] ..... CHRELE
Chief Radio Electrician [*Navy rating Obsolete*] ..... CRE
Chief Radio Electrician [*British military*] (DMA) ..... CREL
Chief Radio Supervisor (Special) [*British military*] (DMA) ..... CRS(S)
Chief Radio Supervisor (Warfare) [*British military*] (DMA) ..... CRS(W)
Chief Radio Technician [*Navy rating Obsolete*] ..... CRT
Chief Radioman [*Navy rating Obsolete*] ..... CRM
Chief Radioman [*Navy rating*] ..... RMC
Chief Railway Construction Engineer [*British military*] (DMA) ..... CRCE
Chief Ranger ..... CR
Chief Recruiting Officer [*British military*] (DMA) ..... CRO
Chief Registrar's Reports [*England*] [*A publication*] (DLA) ..... CRR
Chief Regulating Officer [*Southwest Pacific Area, World War II*] [*Army*] ..... CREGO
Chief, Research and Development [*Department of National Defence*] [*Canada*] ..... CRAD
Chief Resource Officer ..... CRO
Chief Sailmaker [*British military*] (DMA) ..... CSLMR
Chief Scientific Adviser [*British*] (RDA) ..... CSA
Chief Scientific Officer [*Also, CSO*] [*Ministry of Agriculture, Fisheries, and Food*] [*British*] ..... CScO
Chief Scientific Officer [*Also, CScO*] [*Ministry of Agriculture, Fisheries, and Food*] [*British*] ..... CSO
Chief Scientist [*Marine science*] (OSRA) ..... CS
Chief Scientist [*National Oceanic and Atmospheric Administration*] (USDC) ..... CS
Chief Scientist (Royal Air Force) [*British*] ..... CS(RAF)
Chief Scientist's Directorate [*Nature Conservancy Council*] [*British*] ..... CSD
Chief, SEATO [*Southeast Asia Treaty Organization*] **Military Planning Office** (CINC) ..... CMPO
Chief Secretary (ADA) ..... CS
Chief Sector Control [*Aviation*] (OA) ..... CSC
Chief, Security Assistance Management and Staff [*Military*] (DNAB) ..... CHSAMS
Chief Shipfitter [*Navy rating Obsolete*] ..... CSF
Chief Shipfitter [*Navy rating*] ..... SFC
Chief Shipfitter, Construction Battalion, Mechanical Draftsman [*Navy rating Obsolete*] ..... CSFCBM
Chief Shipfitter, Construction Battalion, Pipe Fitter and Plumber [*Navy rating Obsolete*] ..... CSFCBP
Chief Shipfitter, Construction Battalion, Rigger [*Navy rating Obsolete*] ..... CSFCBR
Chief Shipfitter, Construction Battalion, Steel Worker [*Navy rating Obsolete*] ..... CSFCBS
Chief Shipfitter, Construction Battalion, Welder [*Navy rating Obsolete*] ..... CSFCBW
Chief Shipfitter, Ship Repair [*Navy rating Obsolete*] ..... CSFSR
Chief Shipfitter, Ship Repair, Pipe Fitter and Plumber [*Navy rating Obsolete*] ..... CSFSRP
Chief Shipfitter, Ship Repair, Welder [*Navy rating Obsolete*] ..... CSFSRW
Chief Ship's Clerk [*Navy rating Obsolete*] ..... CHSCLK
Chief Ship's Clerk [*Navy rating Obsolete*] ..... CSCLK
Chief Ship's Service Man [*Navy rating Obsolete*] ..... CSSM
Chief Ship's Service Man, Barber [*Navy rating Obsolete*] ..... CSSMB
Chief Ship's Service Man, Cobbler [*Navy rating Obsolete*] ..... CSSMC
Chief Ship's Service Man, Laundryman [*Navy rating Obsolete*] ..... CSSML
Chief Ship's Service Man, Tailor [*Navy rating Obsolete*] ..... CSSMT
Chief Ship's Serviceman [*Navy rating*] ..... SHC
Chief Sick Berth Attendant [*British military*] (DMA) ..... CSBA
Chief Signal Boatswain [*Navy British*] (ROG) ..... CHSB
Chief, Signal Corps [*Army*] ..... CSIGC
Chief Signal Officer [*Army*] ..... CSIGO
Chief Signal Officer [*Army*] ..... CSO
Chief Signalman [*Navy rating Obsolete*] ..... CSM
Chief Signalman [*Navy rating*] ..... SMC
Chief Skipper [*Navy British*] ..... ChSkr
Chief SONAR Technician [*Navy rating*] ..... STC
Chief SONARman [*Navy rating Obsolete*] ..... CSOM
Chief SONARman [*Navy rating Obsolete*] ..... SOC
Chief SONARman, Harbor Defense [*Navy rating Obsolete*] ..... CSOMH
Chief Special Artificer [*Navy rating Obsolete*] ..... CSA
Chief Special Artificer, Instruments [*Navy rating Obsolete*] ..... CSAI
Chief Special Artificer, Instruments, Typewriter and Office Equipment Repairman [*Navy rating Obsolete*] ..... CSAITR
Chief Special Artificer, Instruments, Watch Repairman [*Navy rating Obsolete*] ..... CSAIWR
Chief Special Artificer, Optical [*Navy rating Obsolete*] ..... CSAO
Chief Special Artificer, Synthetic Training Devices [*Navy rating Obsolete*] ..... CSAD
Chief Specialist [*Navy rating Obsolete*] ..... CSP
Chief Specialist, All Designators [*Navy rating Obsolete*] ..... CSPX
Chief Specialist, Chaplain's Assistant [*Navy rating Obsolete*] ..... CSPW
Chief Specialist, Control Tower Operator [*Navy rating Obsolete*] ..... CSPY
Chief Specialist, Identification [*Navy rating Obsolete*] ..... CSPR
Chief Specialist, Laboratory [*Navy rating Obsolete*] ..... CSPPLB
Chief Specialist, Link Trainer Instructor [*Navy rating Obsolete*] ..... CSPTLT
Chief Specialist, Motion Picture Production [*Navy rating Obsolete*] ..... CSPMP
Chief Specialist, Personnel Supervisor [*Navy rating Obsolete*] ..... CSPS
Chief Specialist, Petroleum Inspector [*Navy rating Obsolete*] ..... CSPO
Chief Specialist, Photogrammetry [*Navy rating Obsolete*] ..... CSPPPG
Chief Specialist, Physical Training Instructor [*Navy rating Obsolete*] ..... CSPA
Chief Specialist, Recruiter [*Navy rating Obsolete*] ..... CSPR
Chief Specialist, Shore Patrol and Security [*Navy rating Obsolete*] ..... CSPS
Chief Specialist, Teacher [*Navy rating Obsolete*] ..... CSPT
Chief Specialist, Transport Airman [*Navy rating Obsolete*] ..... CSPV
Chief Specialist, V-Mail [*Navy rating Obsolete*] ..... CSPPVM
Chief Staff Officer ..... CSO
Chief State School Officer (AEE) ..... CSSO
Chief Steelworker [*Navy rating*] ..... SWC
Chief Steward [*Later, MSC*] [*Navy rating*] ..... CST
Chief Steward [*Later, MSC*] [*Navy rating*] ..... SDC
Chief Storekeeper [*Navy rating Obsolete*] ..... CSK
Chief Storekeeper, Aviation [*Navy rating Obsolete*] ..... CSKV
Chief Storekeeper, Construction Battalion, Stevedore [*Navy rating Obsolete*] ..... CSKCB
Chief Storekeeper, Disbursing [*Navy rating Obsolete*] ..... CSKD
Chief Storekeeper, Technical [*Navy rating Obsolete*] ..... CSKT
Chief Superintendent (ADA) ..... CS
Chief Superintendent of Hydrographic Supplies ..... CSHS
Chief Superintendent of Juvenile Templars [*Order of Good Templars*] [*Freemasonry*] (ROG) ..... CS of JT
Chief Superintendent of Naval Meteorology [*British*] ..... CSNM
Chief Superintendent of Ordnance Factories [*British World War II*] ..... CSOF
Chief, Superintendent Range Operations [*NASA*] (KSC) ..... CSRO
Chief Superintendent, Research Department [*British military*] (DMA) ..... CSRD
Chief Systems Engineer (SSD) ..... CSE
Chief Technical Officer [*British*] (ADA) ..... CTO
Chief, Technical Services ..... CTS
Chief Telegrapher [*Navy rating Obsolete*] ..... CT
Chief Test Conductor (NASA) ..... CTC
Chief Testboard Man [*Telecommunications*] (TEL) ..... CTBM
Chief Torpedoman [*Navy rating Obsolete*] ..... CHTORP
Chief Torpedoman [*Navy rating Obsolete*] ..... CTORP
Chief Torpedoman's Mate [*Navy rating Obsolete*] ..... CTM
Chief Torpedoman's Mate [*Navy rating*] ..... TMC
Chief Torpedoman's Mate, Aviation [*Navy rating Obsolete*] ..... CTMV
Chief Torpedoman's Mate, Electrical [*Navy rating Obsolete*] ..... CTME
Chief TRADEVMAN [*Training Devices Man*] [*Navy rating*] ..... TDC
Chief Turret Captain [*Obsolete Navy*] ..... CTC
Chief, United States Army Overseas Supply Agency, San Francisco (CINC) ..... CHUSAOSASF
Chief, United States Army Reserve and Reserve Officers Training Corps Affairs ..... CUSARROTC
Chief, United States Defense Liaison Group (DNAB) ..... CHUSDLG
Chief, United States Military Supply Mission, India (CINC) ..... CHUSMSI
Chief, United States Naval Mission (DNAB) ..... CHUSNAVMIS
Chief Value CV
Chief Veterinary Officer [*Ministry of Agriculture, Fisheries, and Food*] [*British*] ..... CVO
Chief Warrant and Warrant Officers Association, United States Coast Guard (EA) ..... CW & WOA
Chief Warrant and Warrant Officers Association, United States Coast Guard ..... CWOA
Chief Warrant Officer [*Military rank*] ..... CW
Chief Warrant Officer [*Army*] (GPO) ..... CWO
Chief Warrant Officer 2 [*Army*] CW2
Chief Warrant Officer 3 [*Army*] CW3
Chief Warrant Officer 4 [*Army*] CW4
Chief Warrant Officer, W-2 [*Army*] (AABC) CWO-2
Chief Warrant Officer, W-3 [*Army*] (AABC) CWO-3
Chief Warrant Officer, W-4 [*Army*] (AABC) CWO-4
Chief Watch Officer [*Navy*] ..... CWO
Chief Water Tender [*Navy rating Obsolete*] ..... CWT
Chief, Western Pacific Transportation Office (CINC) ..... CHWTO
Chief WREN [*Women's Royal Naval Service*] **Air Fitter** [*British military*] (DMA) ..... CWRENAF
Chief WREN [*Women's Royal Naval Service*] **Cinema Operator** [*British military*] (DMA) ..... CWRENCINE
Chief WREN [*Women's Royal Naval Service*] **Cook** [*British military*] (DMA) ..... CWRENCK
Chief WREN [*Women's Royal Naval Service*] **Dental Hygienist** [*British military*] (DMA) ..... CWRENDHYG
Chief WREN [*Women's Royal Naval Service*] **Dental Surgery Assistant** [*British military*] (DMA) ..... CWRENDSA
Chief WREN [*Women's Royal Naval Service*] **Education Assistant** [*British military*] (DMA) ..... CWRENEDUC
Chief WREN [*Women's Royal Naval Service*] **Meteorological Observer** [*British military*] (DMA) ..... CWRENMET

Chief WREN [*Women's Royal Naval Service*] **Photographer** [*British military*] (DMA) .... CWRENPHOT
Chief WREN [*Women's Royal Naval Service*] **Quarters Assistant** [*British military*] (DMA) .... CWRENQA
Chief WREN [*Women's Royal Naval Service*] **(RADAR)** [*British military*] (DMA) .... CWREN(R)
Chief WREN [*Women's Royal Naval Service*] **Radio Electrician** [*British military*] (DMA) .... CWRENREL
Chief WREN [*Women's Royal Naval Service*] **Radio Supervisor (Morse)** [*British military*] (DMA) .... CWRENRS(M)
Chief WREN [*Women's Royal Naval Service*] **Regulating** [*British military*] (DMA) .... CWRENREG
Chief WREN [*Women's Royal Naval Service*] **Steward** [*British military*] (DMA) .... CWRENSTD
Chief WREN [*Women's Royal Naval Service*] **Stores Accountant** [*British military*] (DMA) .... CWRENSA
Chief WREN [*Women's Royal Naval Service*] **Stores Assistant (Clothes)** [*British military*] (DMA) .... CWRENS(C)
Chief WREN [*Women's Royal Naval Service*] **Stores Assistant (Victualling)** [*British military*] (DMA) .... CWRENS(V)
Chief WREN [*Women's Royal Naval Service*] **Telephonist** [*British military*] (DMA) .... CWRENTEL
Chief WREN [*Women's Royal Naval Service*] **Training Support Assistant** [*British military*] (DMA) .... CWRENTSA
Chief WREN [*Women's Royal Naval Service*] **Weapon Analyst** [*British military*] (DMA) .... CWRENWA
Chief WREN [*Women's Royal Naval Service*] **Welfare Worker** [*British military*] (DMA) .... CWRENWW
Chief WREN [*Women's Royal Naval Service*] **Writer (General)** [*British military*] (DMA) .... CWRENWTR(G)
Chief WREN [*Women's Royal Naval Service*] **Writer (Pay)** [*British military*] (DMA) .... CWRENWTR(P)
Chief Yeoman [*Navy rating Obsolete*] .... CY
Chiefland, FL [*AM radio station call letters*] .... WLQH
Chiefland, FL [*FM radio station call letters*] .... WLQH-FM
Chiefland, FL [*FM radio station call letters*] .... WTBH
Chiefs of Staff Committee [*Australia*] .... CSC
Chiefs of Staff, Mediterranean [*Military*] .... COSMED
Chiefs of Staff, Washington [*Military*] .... COS(W)
Chieftain (ROG) .... CHFTN
Chieftain Airways PLC [*British ICAO designator*] (FAAC) .... PQC
Chieftain Aviation PC [*South Africa ICAO designator*] (FAAC) .... LNP
Chieftain International [*Associated Press*] (SAG) .... Chief
Chieftain International [*AMEX symbol Toronto Stock Exchange symbol*] (SPSG) .... CID
Chieftain International Fund [*Associated Press*] (SAG) .... ChfInt
Chieftain International Fund [*AMEX symbol*] (SPSG) .... GSS
Chieftain Intl. [*AMEX symbol*] (TTSB) .... CID
Chieftain Intl Fd $1.8125 Cv Pfd [*AMEX symbol*] (TTSB) .... GSSPr
Chievres [*Belgium ICAO location identifier*] (ICLI) .... EBCV
Chifeng [*China*] [*Airport symbol*] (OAG) .... CIF
Chiffonier .... CH
Chignik, AK [*Location identifier FAA*] (FAAL) .... KCG
Chignik, AK [*Location identifier FAA*] (FAAL) .... KCL
Chigorodo [*Colombia*] [*Airport symbol*] (OAG) .... IGO
Chigwell [*Urban district in England*] .... CHIGW
Chihuahua [*Mexico*] [*Seismograph station code, US Geological Survey*] (SEIS) .... CHH
Chihuahua [*Mexico*] (BARN) .... Chic
Chihuahua [*Mexico*] [*Airport symbol*] (OAG) .... CUU
Chihuahua Club of America (EA) .... CCA
Chihuahua/Internacional [*Mexico ICAO location identifier*] (ICLI) .... MMCU
Chihuahuan Desert Research Institute (EA) .... CDRI
Chikungunya Virus CV
Chilas [*Pakistan*] [*ICAO location identifier*] (ICLI) .... OPCL
Chilchota Taxi Aereo SA de CV [*Mexico ICAO designator*] (FAAC) .... CCH
Chilcotin Caribou Aviation [*Canada ICAO designator*] (FAAC) .... DES
Child C
Child [*or Children*] .... CH
Child (DMAA) .... ch
Child (ROG) .... CHD
Child (ADA) .... CHIL
Child Abuse and Neglect .... CA/N
Child Abuse and Neglict Reprint and Inquiry Systems (EDAC) .... CANRIS
Child Abuse Institute of Research (EA) .... CAIR
Child Abuse Listening Mediation (EA) .... CALM
Child Abuse Prevention, Adoption, and Family Services Act of 1988 .... CAPAFSA
Child Abuse Prevention and Treatment Act .... CAPTA
Child Abuse Protection Board [*Tasmania*] [*Australia*] .... CAPB
Child Abuse Victims' Rights Act of 1986 .... CAVRA
Child Amputee Program [*Canada*] .... CHAMP
Child and Adolescent Adjustment Profile [*Child development test*] [*Psychology*] .... CAAP
Child and Youth Centered Information Systems .... CYCIS
Child Anxiety Scale [*Child development test*] [*Psychology*] .... CAS
Child Attitudes Survey [*Education*] .... CAS
Child Behavior and Characteristics .... CBC
Child Behavior Checklist .... CBCL
Child Behavior Rating Scale [*Devereaux*] [*Psychology*] .... CBRS
Child Behavior Therapy Special Interest Group [*Defunct*] (EA) .... CBTSIG
Child Care (ADA) CC
Child Care Action Campaign (EA) .... CCAC
Child Care Advocacy Association of Canada [*Association Canadienne pour la Promotion des Services de Garde a l'Enfance*] [*Formerly, Canadian Day Care Advocacy Association*] (AC) .... CCAAC
Child Care Assistance .... CCA
Child Care Association of Illinois (SRA) .... CCA
Child Care Centres Association, Victoria [*Australia*] .... CCCAV
Child Care Employee Project (EA) .... CCEP
Child Care Food Program [*Washington, DC*] .... CCFP
Child Care Law Center (EA) CCLC
Child Care Resource and Referral Program (WYGK) .... CCR&R
Child Care Worker .... CCW
Child Development Associate [*National certificate*] (OICC) .... CDA
Child Development Associate Consortium [*CDANCP*] [*Superseded by*] (EA) .... CDAC
Child Development Associate National Credentialing Program (EA) .... CDANCP
Child Development Center .... CDC
Child Development Center Q-Sort [*Personality development test*] [*Psychology*] .... CDCQ
Child Development Consultant .... CDC
Child Development Programme [*British*] .... CDP
Child Development Questionnaire (EDAC) .... CDQ
Child Development Research (BARN) .... CDR
Child Development Research Unit [*Nigeria*] .... CDRU
Child Education Foundation, New York, NY [*Library symbol Library of Congress Obsolete*] (LCLS) .... NNCEF
Child Evangelism Fellowship (EA) .... CEF
Child Evangelism Fellowship International [*Later, CEF*] (EA) .... CEFI
Child Evangelism Fellowship of Australia .... CEFA
Child Find [*Later, CFA*] [*An association*] (EA) .... CF
Child Find Alberta [*Formerly, Friends of Child Find Society*] (AC) .... CFA
Child Find of America (EA) .... CFA
Child Find PEI Inc. (AC) .... CEPEI
Child Growth Foundation [*British*] (DBA) .... CGF
Child Health Assessment Program .... CHAP
Child Health Centre [*Australia*] .... CHC
Child Health Services Research .... CHSR
Child [*or Children*] **in Need of Service** [*Pediatrics and social services*] (DAVI) .... CHINS
Child Keyppers' International (EA) .... CKI
Child Language Ability Measures [*Child development test*] .... CLAM
Child Life Council (EA) CLC
Child Migrants Trust .... CMT
Child Neurology .... CHN
Child Neurology Society (EA) .... CNS
Child Nutrition .... CN
Child Nutrition Forum (EA) .... CNF
Child Of [*Genealogy*] .... CH/O
Child of Upwardly Mobile Professionals [*Lifestyle classification*] .... Chump
Child Poverty Action Group [*British*] (BI) .... CPAG
Child Protection and Family Crisis Service [*New South Wales*] [*Australia*] .... CPFCS
Child Protection Council [*New South Wales*] [*Australia*] .... CPC
Child Protection Report [*A publication*] .... CPR
Child Psychiatry [*Medical specialty*] (DHSM) .... CHP
Child Psychiatry .... CP
Child Psychology .... CP
Child Report of Parent Behavior Inventory (EDAC) .... CRPBI
Child Resistant .... CR
Child Restraint and Air Bag Information [*Automotive safety*] .... CRABI
Child Safety Council [*Later, NCSC*] (EA) .... CSC
Child Safety Seat Questionnaire [*Auto safety research*] .... CSSQ
Child Service Demonstration Center [*Department of Education*] .... CSDC
Child Sexual Abuse Accommodation Syndrome .... CSAAS
Child Sexual Assault Program [*Australia*] .... CSAP
Child Study Association of America (BARN) .... CSA
Child Study Association of America [*Defunct*] (EA) .... CSAA
Child Study Association of America, New York, NY [*Library symbol Library of Congress*] (LCLS) .... NNCS
Child Study Center [*Brown University*] [*Research center*] (RCD) .... CSC
Child Study Team [*Education*] .... CST
Child Support Agency [*British*] (ECON) .... CSA
Child Support Enforcement [*Department of Health and Human Services*] .... CSE
Child Support Network [*Defunct*] (EA) .... CSN
Child Support Resistance (EA) .... CSR
Child Support Rulings [*Australian Taxation Office*] [*A publication*] .... CS
Child Survival Assistance Program [*Agency for International Development*] .... CSAP
Child Trends (EA) .... CT
Child Welfare .... CW
Child Welfare Center [*British*] (DAS) .... CWC
Child Welfare Information Services/Non-Profit Computer Services [*Information service or system*] (IID) .... CWIS/NPC
Child Welfare Institute (EA) .... CWI
Child Welfare League (BARN) .... CWL
Child Welfare League of America (EA) .... CWLA
Child Welfare League of Canada [*La Ligue pour la Protection de l'Enfance du Canada*] (AC) .... CWLC
Child Welfare Service .... CWS
Child, Youth, and Family Education Network [*Online resource*] (PAZ) .... CYFERNET
Childbearing Hips .... CBH
Childbirth and Parenting Association of Victoria [*Australia*] .... CPAV
Childbirth Education Association of Australia .... CEAA
Childbirth Education Foundation (EA) .... CEF
Childbirth without Pain .... CWOP
Childbirth without Pain (MAE) .... CWP
Childbirth without Pain Education Association [*Also known as Lamaze Birth without Pain Education Association*] (EA) .... CWPEA

Child-Centered Experience-Based Learning [*An association Canada*] .... CEL
Childhelp USA, Inc. (EA) .... CUI
Childhood .... CHILDHD
Childhood Aphasia, Neurological Disorders, Landau-Klefner, and Epilepsy .... CANDLE
Childhood Celiac Disease [*Medicine*] (DMAA) .... CCD
Childhood Disability Benefits [*Social Security Administration*] (OICC) .... CDB
Childhood Disease (HGAA) .... CD
Childhood Disease [*Medicine*] .... CHD
Childhood Education [*A publication*] (BRI) .... CE
Childhood in Poetry [*A publication*] .... CIP
Childhood in Poetry Supplement [*A publication*] .... CIPS
Childhood Muscular Dystrophy .... CMD
Childhood Polycystic Disease (PAZ) .... CPD
Childhood Polycystic Kidney Disease [*Medicine*] .... CPKD
Childhood Sensuality Circle (EA) .... CSC
Childless by Choice [*An association*] .... CBC
Child-Operated Mobile Electric Transport .... COMET
Children (ROG) .... CHDN
Children .... CHLD
Children [*Genealogy*] .... CHN
Children Against Smoking [*British*] .... CAS
Children and Adults with Attention Deficit Disorder (PAZ) .... CHADD
Children and Young Persons Act [*British*] .... CYPA
Children and Youth .... C & Y
Children as the Peacemakers (EA) .... CTP
Children before Dogs (EA) .... CBD
Children by Choice [*Australia*] .... CBC
Children Have a Potential [*Program for handicapped or disturbed children of Air Force personnel*] (AFM) .... CHAP
Children in Hospitals .... CIH
Children in Need of Assistance (OICC) .... CHINA
Children in Need of Supervision [*Classification for delinquent children*] (OICC) .... CHINS
Children in Need of Supervision .... CINS
Children in Residential Institutions Program [*Australia*] .... CRI
Children, Inc. [*An association*] (EA) CI
Children of Ageing Parents (EA) .... CAPS
Children of Alcoholic .... COA
Children of Alcoholic Parents [*An association*] (EA) .... CAP
Children of Alcoholics .... CoA
Children of Alcoholics Foundation (EA) .... CAF
Children of Auschwitz - Nazis' Deadly Lab Experiments Survivors [*Acronym is used as name of associaton*] (EA) .... CANDLES
Children of Deaf Adults (EA) .... CODA
Children of Gay Parentage (EA) .... CGP
Children of Gays/Lesbians [*Later, CGP*] (EA) .... CGL
Children of High Intellectual Potential .... CHIP
Children of High Intellectual Potential Foundation [*Australia*] .... CHIPF
Children of Light [*Freemasonry*] (ROG) .... C of L
Children of Prisoners Support Group [*Australia*] .... CPSG
Children of the Americas (EA) .... CA
Children of the Americas (EA) .... COA
Children of the Confederacy (EA) .... C of C
Children of the Green Earth (EA) .... CGE
Children of the Night (EA) .... CN
Children of the Universe [*Defunct*] (EA) .... CU
Children of War [*An association*] (EA) .... CW
Children Today [*A publication*] (BRI) .... CT
Children with Attention-Deficit Disorders (EA) .... ChADD
Children with Behavioral and Emotional Difficulty .... CBED
Children with Learning Disabilities .... CLD
Children with Special Health Care Needs .... CSHCN
Children's .... CHILD
Children's Action Network [*Defunct*] (EA) .... CAN
Children's Adaptive Behavior Report [*Child development test*] [*Psychology*] .... CABR
Children's Advocacy Center (EA) .... CAC
Children's Affective Reading Scale .... CARS
Children's Aid International (EA) .... CAI
Children's Aid Society (BARN) .... CAS
Children's Aid Society of Ottawa-Carleton, Ottawa, Ontario [*Library symbol National Library of Canada*] (NLC) .... OOCAS
Children's Aid Society, Ottawa, ON, Canada [*Library symbol*] [*Library of Congress*] (LCLS) .... CaOOCAS
Children's Alliance for Protection of the Environment (EA) .... CAPE
Children's and Adults' Library, St. John's, Newfoundland [*Library symbol National Library of Canada*] (NLC) .... NFSCA
Children's and Adults' Library, St. John's, NF, Canada [*Library symbol Library of Congress*] (LCLS) .... CaNfSCA
Children's and Young Adult Services .... CAYAS
Children's Apparel Manufacturers' Association [*Canada*] .... CAMA
Children's Apperception Test [*Psychology*] .... CAT
Children's Apperception Test [*Child development test*] [*Psychology*] .... CAT-A
Children's Apperception Test - Human Figures [*Child development test*] [*Psychology*] .... CAT-H
Children's Apperception Test - Supplement [*Child development test*] [*Psychology*] .... CAT-S
Children's Art Foundation (EA) .... CAF
Children's Assertiveness Behavior Scale .... CABS
Children's Associative Responding Test (EDAC) .... CART
Children's Asthma Research Institute and Hospital [*Denver, CO*] .... CARIH
Children's Attitude toward Reading Test .... CHART
Children's Attribution of Responsibility and Locus of Control (EDAC) .... CARALOC

Children's Attributional Style Questionnaire .... CASQ
Children's Authors and Illustrators [*A publication*] .... CAI
Children's Behavior Checklist .... CBC
Children's Behavior Inventory [*Medicine*] (DMAA) .... CBI
Children's Blood Foundation (EA) .... CBF
Children's Book Action Group [*National Book League*] [*British*] .... CBAG
Children's Book Circle [*British*] .... CBC
Children's Book Council (EA) .... CBC
Children's Book News [*A publication*] (BRI) .... Ch Bk News
Children's Book of the Year [*British*] .... CBY
Children's Book Review Service [*A publication*] (BRI) .... CBRS
Children's Book Week .... CBW
Children's Book Writers' Group [*Australia*] .... CBWG
Children's Bookwatch [*A publication*] (BRI) .... Ch BWatch
Children's Brittle Bone Foundation .... CBBF
Children's Broadcast Institute [*Canada*] .... CBI
Children's Broadcasting [*NASDAQ symbol*] (TTSB) .... AAHS
Childrens Broadcasting Corp. [*NASDAQ symbol*] (SAG) .... AAHS
Childrens Broadcasting Corp. [*Associated Press*] (SAG) .... ChldBrd
Children's Bureau [*of SSA*] .... CB
Children's Campaign for a Positive Future (EA) .... CCPF
Children's Campaign for Nuclear Disarmament (EA) .... CCND
Children's Cancer Fund of America [*Defunct*] (EA) .... CCFA
Childrens Cancer Group .... CCG
Children's Cancer Study Group [*National Institutes of Health*] .... CCSG
Children's Checking Test (EDAC) .... CCT
Children's Cognitive Style Assessment Instrument (EDAC) .... CCSA
Children's Committee 10 (EA) CC
Children's Comp Svcs [*NASDAQ symbol*] (TTSB) .... KIDS
Childrens Comprehensive Services [*Associated Press*] (SAG) .... ChldCmp
Children's Comprehensive Services [*NASDAQ symbol*] (SAG) .... KIDS
Children's Computer Workshop .... CCW
Children's Country Holiday Fund [*British*] .... CCHF
Children's Court [*Australia*] CC
Children's Court (DLA) .... Child Ct
Children's Court Advisory Committee [*Australia*] .... CCAC
Children's Creative Response to Conflict Program (EA) .... CCRC
Children's Defense Fund (EA) .... CDF
Children's Depression Inventory [*Personality development test*] [*Psychology*] .... CDI
Children's Depression Rating Scale .... CDRS
Children's Depression Rating Scale for Classrooms (EDAC) .... CDRSC
Children's Depression Scale .... CDS
Children's Diagnostic Inventory .... CDI
Childrens Discovery Centers [*NASDAQ symbol*] (TTSB) .... CDCR
Childrens Discovery Centers of America [*Associated Press*] (SAG) .... ChildDis
Children's Discovery Centers of America, Inc. [*NASDAQ symbol*] (NQ) .... CDCR
Children's Dress, Cotton Dress, and Sportswear Contractors Association [*Later, MAAA*] (EA) .... CDCDSCA
Children's Embedded Figures Test [*Psychology*] .... CEFT
Children's Emotions Anonymous (EA) .... CEA
Children's Environments Advisory Service, Canada Mortgage and Housing Corp. [*Service Consultatif sur l'Environnement de l'Enfant, Societe Canadienne d'Hypotheques et de Logement*] Ottawa, Ontario [*Library symbol National Library of Canada*] (NLC) .... OOCMC
Children's Express Foundation (EA) .... CEF
Children's Eye Care Foundation [*Later, NCECF*] (EA) .... CECF
Childrens Fashion Group [*British*] (BI) .... CFG
Children's Fear Survey Schedule [*Psychology*] (EDAC) .... CESS
Children's Film and Television Center of America (EA) .... CFTCA
Children's Film and Television Foundation [*British*] .... CFTF
Children's Film Foundation Ltd. [*British*] (BI) .... CFF
Children's Film Theatre [*Later, Media Center for Children*] .... CFT
[*The*] Children's Foundation .... TCF
Children's Friendship Project for Northern Ireland (EA) .... CFPNI
[*The*] Children's Garland [*A publication*] .... CG
Children's Health and Fitness Fund .... CHeaFF
Children's Health, Education, and Safety Services [*Australia*] .... CHESS
Children's Health Information about Liver Disease .... CHILD
Children's Health Services Division [*HEW*] .... CHSD
Children's Healthcare Is a Legal Duty .... CHILD
Children's Heart Association for Support & Education (AC) .... CHASE
Children's Heart Fund (EA) .... CHF
Children's Home of Kingston, Kingston, NY [*Library symbol Library of Congress*] (LCLS) .... NKiC
Children's Home-Based Education Association [*British*] (DBA) .... CHEA
Children's Hospice International (EA) .... CHI
Children's Hospital [*Philadelphia, PA*] .... CH
Children's Hospital Automated Medical Program (DMAA) .... CHAMP
Children's Hospital, Buffalo, NY [*Library symbol Library of Congress*] (LCLS) .... NBuCH
Children's Hospital, Los Angeles, CA .... CHLA
Children's Hospital Medical Center [*Ohio*] .... CHMC
Children's Hospital, Medical Library, Denver, CO [*Library symbol Library of Congress*] (LCLS) .... CoDCH-M
Children's Hospital of Eastern Ontario [*Hopital pour Enfants de l'Est de l'Ontario*] Ottawa, Ontario [*Library symbol National Library of Canada*] (NLC) .... OOCHEO
Children's Hospital of Michigan .... CHM
Children's Hospital of Michigan, Detroit, MI [*Library symbol Library of Congress*] (LCLS) .... MiDCh
Children's Hospital of Pittsburgh, Pittsburgh, PA [*OCLC symbol*] (OCLC) .... PHC
Children's Hospital, Ottawa, ON, Canada [*Library symbol Library of Congress*] (LCLS) .... CaOOCH
Children's Hospital Research Foundation [*Research center*] (RCD) .... CHRF

Children's Hospital Research Foundation, Research Library, Cincinnati, OH [*Library symbol Library of Congress*] (LCLS) .... OCCH
Children's Hospital, St. Paul, MN [*Library symbol Library of Congress*] (LCLS) .... MnSCH
Children's Hospital Society, Doctor's Library, Los Angeles, CA [*Library symbol Library of Congress*] (LCLS) .... CLCH
Children's Hypnotic Susceptibility Scale [*Psychology*] .... CHSS
Children's Intensive Care Unit (ADA) .... CICU
Children's Interaction Matrix [*Child development test*] [*Psychology*] .... CIM
Children's Interests Bureau [*South Australia*] .... CIB
Children's International Summer Villages International Association [*Newcastle-Upon-Tyne, England*] (EAIO) .... CISV
Children's Legal Centre (EAIO) CLC
Children's Legal Foundation (EA) .... CLF
Children's Legal Rights Information and Training [*An association*] (EA) .... CLRIT
Children's Legal Rights Journal [*A publication*] (DLA) .... Child Legal Rts J
Children's Leukemia and Cancer Foundation [*Australia*] .... CLCF
Children's Literature [*A publication*] (BRI) .... Child Lit
Children's Literature Association (EA) .... ChLA
Children's Literature Association Quarterly [*A publication*] (BRI) .... ChLAQ
Children's Literature in Education [*A publication*] (BRI) .... Ch Lit Ed
Children's Liver Foundation (EA) .... CLF
Children's Manifest Anxiety Scale [*Psychology*] (AEBS) .... CMAS
Children's Medical Center of Israel [*Tel Aviv*] .... CMCI
Children's Medical Relief International [*Defunct*] .... CMRI
Children's Medical Research .... CMR
Children's Medical Research Institute [*Australia*] .... CMRI
Children's Memorial Hospital, Joseph Brennemann Medical Library, Chicago, IL [*Library symbol Library of Congress*] (LCLS) .... ICChH
Children's Mercy Hospital, Kansas City, MO [*Library symbol Library of Congress*] (LCLS) .... MoKCH
Children's Miracle Network [*Medicine*] .... CMN
Children's Miracle Network Telethon .... CMNT
Children's Miracle Network Television .... CMNT
Children's Museum of Indianapolis, Indianapolis, IN [*OCLC symbol*] (OCLC) .... IIM
Children's Museum of Indianapolis, Indianapolis, IN [*Library symbol Library of Congress*] (LCLS) .... InICM
Children's Nutrition Laboratory [*Baylor College of Medicine*] .... CNL
Children's Oncology Care of Ontario Inc. [*Also, Ronald McDonald House*] (AC) .... COCO
Children's Organ Replacement Program Special Medical Alert Network .... CORPSMAN
Children's Organ Transplant Association .... COTA
Children's Organization for Peace and Brotherhood [*Defunct*] (EA) .... COPB
Children's Orientation and Amnesia Test [*Medicine*] (DMAA) .... COAT
Children's Orthopedic Hospital and Medical Center, Seattle, WA [*Library symbol Library of Congress*] (LCLS) .... WaSCO
Children's Own Garden International [*See also BjBI*] (EAIO) .... COGI
Children's Peace Union [*Defunct*] (EA) .... CPU
Children's Perceived Self-Control Scale .... CPSCS
Children's Perceived Self-Control Scale - Usually That's Me .... CPSCS-UTM
Children's Personality Questionnaire [*Psychology*] .... CPQ
Children's Picture Information Test [*Psychology*] (AEBS) .... CPIT
Children's PKU [*Phenylketonuria*] **Network** (PAZ) .... CPN
Children's Play Activities Ltd. [*British*] (BI) .... CPA
Children's Plea for Peace [*Later, World Pen Pals*] .... CPP
Children's Psychiatric Research Institute, Ontario Ministry of Community and Social Services, London, Ontario [*Library symbol National Library of Canada*] (NLC) .... OLCSSCP
Children's Public Policy Network [*Later, CAN*] (EA) .... CPPN
Children's Radio Network (NTCM) .... CRN
Children's Reading Round Table .... CRRT
Children's Reading Service (AEBS) .... CRS
Children's Record Guild [*Record label*] .... CRG
Children's Rehabilitation Centre, St. John's, Newfoundland [*Library symbol National Library of Canada*] (NLC) .... NFSCR
Children's Rehabilitation Centre, St. John's, NF, Canada [*Library symbol Library of Congress*] (LCLS) .... CaNfSCR
Children's Reinforcement Survey Schedule .... CRSS
Children's Relief International [*British*] (BI) .... CRI
Children's Research Unit [*Market research company*] [*British*] .... CRU
Children's Rights Group [*Defunct*] (EA) .... CRG
Children's Rights, Inc. [*CFC*] [*Superseded by*] (EA) .... CRI
Children's Rights of America (EA) .... CRA
Children's Rights Report [*A publication*] (DLA) .... Chil Rts Rep
Children's Self-Conceptions Test .... CSC
Children's Service Council [*Australian Capital Territory*] .... CSC
Children's Services Division [*American Library Association*] [*Later, ALSC*] (EA) .... CSD
Children's Services Planning Committee [*Australia*] .... CSPC
Children's Services Support Unit of Western Australia .... CSSUWA
Children's Special Health Care Needs Program [*Social Security Administration (SSA)*] (PAZ) .... CSHCN
Children's Special Service Mission [*British*] .... CSSM
Children's Strategies Assessment System (EDAC) .... CSAS
Children's Stressful Life Events Scale .... CSLES
Children's Television Workshop (EA) .... CTW
Children's Theatre Association of America [*Formerly, CTC*] (EA) .... CTA
Children's Theatre Association of America [*Formerly, CTC*] (EA) .... CTAA
Children's Theatre Conference (EA) .... CTC
Children's Transplant Association (EA) .... CTA
Children's Treatment Center, Madison, WI [*Library symbol Library of Congress*] (LCLS) .... WMaCT
Children's Vaccine Initiative [*Coalition of international donors*] CVI
Children's Version/Family Environment Scale [*Child development test*] [*Psychology*] .... CV/FES
Children's Village, USA [*of International Orphans Inc.*] [*Later, CVC*] (EA) .... CVUSA
Children's Ward [*of a hospital*] .... CW
Children's Wear Association (EA) .... CWA
Children's Wish Foundation International (EA) .... CWFI
Children's Wonderland [*NASDAQ symbol*] (TTSB) .... CWIC
Childrens Wonderland, Inc. [*Associated Press*] (SAG) .... ChldWn
Childrens Wonderland, Inc. [*Associated Press*] (SAG) .... ChldWon
Childrens Wonderland, Inc. [*NASDAQ symbol*] (SAG) .... CWIC
Children's Wonderland Wrrt [*NASDAQ symbol*] (TTSB) .... CWICW
Childrenswear Manufacturers Association (EA) .... CMA
Child-Resistant Closure [*Medicine containers, etc.*] .... CRC
Childress [*Texas*] [*Seismograph station code, US Geological Survey*] (SEIS) .... CEC
Childress [*Texas*] [*Seismograph station code, US Geological Survey*] (SEIS) .... CNE
Childress [*Texas*] [*Seismograph station code, US Geological Survey*] (SEIS) .... CNO
Childress [*Texas*] [*Seismograph station code, US Geological Survey*] (SEIS) .... CNW
Childress [*Texas*] [*Seismograph station code, US Geological Survey*] (SEIS) .... CSE
Childress [*Texas*] [*Seismograph station code, US Geological Survey*] (SEIS) .... CSW
Childress [*Texas*] [*Seismograph station code, US Geological Survey*] (SEIS) .... CWT
Childress [*Texas*] [*ICAO location identifier*] (ICLI) .... KCDS
Childress, TX [*Location identifier FAA*] (FAAL) .... CDS
Childress, TX [*AM radio station call letters*] .... KCTX
Childress, TX [*FM radio station call letters*] .... KSRW
Childrobics, Inc. [*Associated Press*] (SAG) .... Childr
Childrobics, Inc. [*Associated Press*] (SAG) .... Childrbc
Childrobics, Inc. [*NASDAQ symbol*] (SAG) .... CHLD
Childrobics Inc. Wrrt [*NASDAQ symbol*] (TTSB) .... CHLDW
Child's Fare [*Airline fare code*] .... CH
Child's Report of the Impact of Separation by Parents (EDAC) .... CRISP
[A] Child's Wish Come True (EA) .... CWCT
Childsave Project [*Defunct*] (EA) .... CP
Childtime Learning Centers [*NASDAQ symbol*] (TTSB) .... CTIM
Childtime Learning Centers, Inc. [*Associated Press*] (SAG) .... Chldtime
Childtime Learning Centers, Inc. [*NASDAQ symbol*] (SAG) .... CTIM
Chile .... CHIL
Chile [*ANSI three-letter standard code*] (CNC) .... CHL
Chile [*ANSI two-letter standard code*] (CNC) CL
Chile [*MARC country of publication code Library of Congress*] (LCCP) cl
Chile [*International vehicle registration*] (ODBW) .... RCH
Chile [*MARC geographic area code Library of Congress*] (LCCP) .... s-cl--
Chile [*IYRU nationality code*] (IYR) X
Chile Alert [*Defunct*] (EA) .... CA
Chile Chico [*Chile*] [*Airport symbol*] (AD) .... CCH
Chile Chico/Chile Chico [*Chile*] [*ICAO location identifier*] (ICLI) .... SCCC
Chile Committee for Human Rights [*Institute for Policy Studies*] (EA) .... CCHR
Chile Democratico (EA) .... ChD
Chile Fund, Inc. [*NYSE symbol*] (SPSG) .... CH
Chile Fund, Inc. [*Associated Press*] (SAG) .... Chile
Chile Legislative Center [*An association*] (EA) CLC
Chile Resource Center and Clearinghouse (EA) .... CRCCH
Chile Solidarity Campaign (EAIO) .... CSC
Chile-American Association (EA) .... CAA
Chilean Communist Party [*Political party*] .... CCP
Chilean Iodine Educational Bureau [*Defunct*] (EA) .... CIEB
Chilean National Committee of the International Association on Water Pollution Research and Control (EAIO) .... CNCIAWPRC
Chilean Odeon [*Record label*] .... ChOd
Chilean Victor [*Record label*] .... ChV
Chilecito [*Argentina*] [*Seismograph station code, US Geological Survey Closed*] (SEIS) .... CCT
Chilecito [*Argentina ICAO location identifier*] (ICLI) .... SANO
Chileka [*Malawi*] [*Seismograph station code, US Geological Survey*] (SEIS) .... CLK
Chiles [*Ecuador*] [*ICAO location identifier*] (ICLI) .... SECL
Chilford [*England*] .... CHILF
Chilgener SA [*NYSE symbol*] (SAG) .... CHR
Chilgener S.A. ADS [*NYSE symbol*] (TTSB) .... CHR
Chili Appreciation Society International (EA) .... CASI
Chilianus Koenig [*Deceased, 1526*] [*Authority cited in pre-1607 legal work*] (DSA) .... Chil Kon
Chilianus Koenig [*Deceased, 1526*] [*Authority cited in pre-1607 legal work*] (DSA) .... Chilian
Chilik [*Former USSR Seismograph station code, US Geological Survey Closed*] (SEIS) .... CHL
Chillagoe [*Australia Airport symbol Obsolete*] (OAG) .... LLG
Chillan/Gral, Bernardo O'Higgins [*Chile*] [*ICAO location identifier*] (ICLI) .... SCCH
Chilldown [*NASA*] (KSC) .... CD
Chilldown Flow Meter .... CFM
Chilled (MSA) .... CHLD
Chilled Drinking Water [*Aerospace*] (AAG) .... CDW
Chilled Drinking Water Return [*Aerospace*] .... CDWR
Chilled Foods Association (EA) .... CFA
Chilled Sea Water [*Pisciculture*] .... CSW
Chilled Water [*Aerospace*] (AAG) .... CHW
Chilled Water [*Aerospace*] (DNAB) .... CW
Chilled Water Supply [*Aerospace*] (AAG) .... CWS
Chillicothe and Ross County Public Library, Chillicothe, OH [*Library symbol Library of Congress*] (LCLS) .... OCh
Chillicothe, IL [*FM radio station call letters*] (RBYB) .... WKZW
Chillicothe, MO [*Location identifier FAA*] (FAAL) .... CHT
Chillicothe, MO [*AM radio station call letters*] .... KCHI

Chillicothe, MO [*FM radio station call letters*] ... KCHI-FM
Chillicothe, MO [*FM radio station call letters*] ... KRNW
Chillicothe, OH [*Location identifier FAA*] (FAAL) ... RZT
Chillicothe, OH [*AM radio station call letters*] ... WBEX
Chillicothe, OH [*AM radio station call letters*] ... WCHI
Chillicothe, OH [*FM radio station call letters*] ... WFCB
Chillicothe, OH [*FM radio station call letters*] ... WKKJ
Chillicothe, OH [*FM radio station call letters*] ... WOHC
Chillicothe, OH [*FM radio station call letters*] ... WOUH
Chillicothe, OH [*FM radio station call letters*] ... WVXC
Chillicothe, OH [*Television station call letters*] ... WWHO
Chillicothe Township Free Public Library, Chillicothe, IL [*Library symbol Library of Congress*] (LCLS) ... IChil
Chillicothe Township Free Public Library, Chillicothe, IL [*OCLC symbol*] (OCLC) ... ISI
Chilliwack Aviation Ltd. [*Canada ICAO designator*] (FAAC) ... CAD
Chilliwack, BC [*Television station call letters*] (RBYB) ... CHAN-1
Chilliwack, BC [*AM radio station call letters*] ... CHWK
Chilliwack, BC [*FM radio station call letters*] ... CKSR
Chilliwack, BC [*ICAO location identifier*] (ICLI) ... CYCW
Chilliwack Museum, British Columbia [*Library symbol National Library of Canada*] (NLC) ... BCHM
Chilliwack Public Library, British Columbia [*Library symbol National Library of Canada*] (NLC) ... BCH
Chilliwack Public Library, Chilliwack, BC, Canada [*Library symbol Library of Congress*] (LCLS) ... CaBCh
Chilpancingo [*Mexico ICAO location identifier*] (ICLI) ... MMCH
[*The*] **Chilswell Book of English Poetry** [*A publication*] ... CBE
Chiltern Airways [*British ICAO designator*] (FAAC) ... CHA
Chilton, WI [*AM radio station call letters*] ... WMBE
Chilworth Technology Ltd. [*British*] (IRUK) ... CTL
Chimachoy [*Guatemala*] [*Seismograph station code, US Geological Survey*] (SEIS) ... CIM
Chimaeric Virus Particles [*Biochemistry*] ... CVP
Chimbote [*Peru*] [*Airport symbol Obsolete*] (OAG) ... CHM
Chimbote [*Peru*] [*ICAO location identifier*] (ICLI) ... SPEO
Chimera Resources Ltd. [*Vancouver Stock Exchange symbol*] ... CMZ
Chimeric Receptor ... CR
Chimkent [*Former USSR Seismograph station code, US Geological Survey Closed*] (SEIS) ... CHM
Chimkent [*Former USSR ICAO location identifier*] (ICLI) ... UAII
Chimney [*Technical drawings*] (DAC) ... Chim
Chimney ... CHMNY
Chimney ... CHY
Chimney Safety Institute of America (EA) ... CSIA
Chimney Sweep Guild [*Later, NCSG*] (EA) ... CSG
Chimoio [*Mozambique*] [*ICAO location identifier*] (ICLI) ... FQCH
Chimpanzee Coryza Agent [*A virus*] ... CCA
Chimpanzee Infectious Dose for Half the Population ... CID_{50}
Chin National Army [*Myanmar*] [*Political party*] (EY) ... CNA
Chin National Front [*Myanmar*] [*Political party*] (EY) ... CNF
Chin National Organization [*Burma*] ... CNO
China [*IYRU nationality code*] (ROG) ... CH
China ... CHI
China ... CHIN
China [*ANSI three-letter standard code*] (CNC) ... CHN
China [*ANSI two-letter standard code*] (CNC) ... CN
China Aero-Space Corp. (ECON) ... CASC
China Air Cargo [*ICAO designator*] (FAAC) ... CHY
China Airlines [*Taiwan*] [*ICAO designator*] (FAAC) ... CAL
China Airlines [*ICAO designator*] (AD) ... CI
China Airlines [*Airline flight code*] (ODBW) ... CI
China Airlines (GAVI) ... CI
China American Petrochemical Co. Ltd. [*Taiwan*] ... CAPCO
China and Glass Retailers Association [*British*] (DBA) ... CGRA
China Association for Science and Technology ... CAST
China Association of Plant Engineering (EAIO) ... CAPE
China Association of Standardization [*INFOTERM*] ... CAS
China Book Information Letter [*A publication*] ... CBIL
China Building Technology Development Centre [*Beijing*] [*Information service or system*] (IID) ... CBTDC
China Business Resources Co. Ltd. (ECON) ... CBR
China Business Review [*A publication*] ... CBR
China Center for Advanced Science and Technology ... CCAST
China Central Television [*The national Chinese network*] ... CCTV
China Christian Council ... CCC
China Clay Producers Trade Association (EA) ... CCP
China Container Holdings ... CCHL
China Council [*An association*] (EA) ... CC
China Council for the Promotion of International Trade (PDAA) ... CCPIT
China Defense Supplies, Inc. ... CDS
China Democratic Socialist Party [*Political party*] (EY) ... CDSP
China Eastern Airlines [*ICAO designator*] (FAAC) ... CES
China Eastern Airlines [*ICAO designator*] (AD) ... MU
China Economic & Technology Alliance [*Sponsored by international chemical firms*] ... CETA
China Education and Research Network [*Computer science*] ... CERnet
China Environmental Research Network ... CERN
China Europe International Business School ... CEIBS
China Europe International Business School ... CEIBS
China External Trade Development Council [*Taiwan*] ... CETDC
China First Capital [*Vancouver Stock Exchange symbol*] ... CWF
China Flying Dragon Aviation Co. [*FAA designator*] (FAAC) ... CFA
[*The*] **China Fund** [*Associated Press*] (SAG) ... ChinaFd
China Fund [*NYSE symbol*] (SPSG) ... CHN
China General Aviation Corp. [*ICAO designator*] (FAAC) ... CGAC
China General Aviation Corp. [*ICAO designator*] (FAAC) ... CTH
China, Glass, and Giftware Association (EA) ... CGGA
China, Glass, and Pottery Association of America [*Later, CGGA*] (EA) ... CGPAA
China, Glass, Giftware Board of Trade [*Later, CGGA*] (EA) ... CGGBT
China Grove, NC [*AM radio station call letters*] ... WRNA
China, India, Burma ... CIB
China Industrial Group [*Associated Press*] (SAG) ... ChinaIndl
China Industrial Group [*Associated Press*] (SAG) ... ChinI
China Industrial Group [*NASDAQ symbol*] (SAG) ... CIND
China Industrial Grp Wrrt'A' [*NASDAQ symbol*] (TTSB) ... CINDW
China Industrial Grp Wrrt'B' [*NASDAQ symbol*] (TTSB) ... CINDZ
China Inland Mission ... CIM
China Inland Mission Overseas Missionary Fellowship [*Later, Overseas MissionaryFellowship*] (EA) ... CIM-OMF
China Institute in America (EA) ... CI
China Institute in America (EA) ... CIA
China Institute of New Jersey, Montclair State College, Upper Montclair, NJ [*Library symbol Library of Congress*] (LCLS) ... NjUpM-C
China International Center for Technical and Economic Exchange ... CICTEE
China International Cultural Exchange Organization ... CICEO
China International Foundation [*Later, TIF*] (EA) ... CIF
China International Travel Service ... CITS
China International Trust Investment Corp. ... CITIC
China Investment Bank ... CIB
China Lake [*California*] [*Seismograph station code, US Geological Survey*] (SEIS) ... CLC
China Lake, CA [*FM radio station call letters*] ... KSSI
China Law and Business Update [*A publication*] ... CLBU
China Law Review [*A publication*] (DLA) ... China L Rev
China Law Review [*A publication*] (DLA) ... China Law Rev
China, Mainland [*MARC geographic area code Library of Congress*] (LCCP) ... a-cc--
China Man-Made Fiber Corp. [*Taiwan*] ... CMFC
China Market Intelligence [*National Council for US-China Trade*] [*A publication*] ... CMI
China Medical Board of New York (EA) ... CMBNY
China Merchant Holdings (ECON) ... CMH
China National Aviation Corps ... CNAC
China National Cereals Oils & Foodstuffs Import & Export Corp. ... COFCO
China National Oceanographic Data Center [*Marine science*] (OSRA) ... CNODC
China News Service ... CNS
China Northern Airlines [*FAA designator*] (FAAC) ... CBF
China Northwest Airlines [*ICAO designator*] (FAAC) ... CNW
China Northwest Airlines [*ICAO designator*] (AD) ... WH
China Ocean Helicopter Corp. [*ICAO designator*] (FAAC) ... CHC
China Ocean Helicopter Corp. [*ICAO designator*] (FAAC) ... COHC
China Ocean Shipping Co. ... COSCO
China Pacific [*NASDAQ symbol*] (TTSB) ... CHNA
China Philatelic Study Group [*Defunct*] (EA) ... CPSG
China Policy Study Group [*British*] ... CPSG
China Pottery and Glassware Association (EA) ... CPGA
China, Republic of [*Taiwan*] [*MARC geographic area code Library of Congress*] (LCCP) ... a-ch--
China, Republic of [*Taiwan*] [*MARC country of publication code Library of Congress*] (LCCP) ... ch
China Research Associates ... CRA
China Resource Dvlmt [*NASDAQ symbol*] (TTSB) ... CHRB
China Resources Development, Inc. [*Associated Press*] (SAG) ... ChinRs
China Resources Development, Inc. [*NASDAQ symbol*] (SAG) ... CHRB
China Review International ... Ch Rev Int
China Review International [*A publication*] (BRI) ... Ch Rev Int
China Sea Resources Corp. [*Vancouver Stock Exchange symbol*] ... CHQ
China Securities Regulatory Commission (ECON) ... CSRC
China Service Medal [*Military decoration*] ... CHSM
China Shipbuilding Corp. ... CSBC
China Society for International Professionals Exchange and Development (EAIO) ... CSRIPPED
China Society of America (EA) ... CSA
China Solidarity Committee [*An association Defunct*] (EA) ... CSC
China Southern Airlines [*FAA designator*] (FAAC) ... CSN
China Southwest Airlines [*ICAO designator*] (FAAC) ... CXN
China Southwest Airlines [*ICAO designator*] (AD) ... SZ
China Spring (EA) ... CS
China Stamp Society (EA) ... CSS
China Surface-to-Surface Experimental Number 4 [*Rocket*] ... CSS-X-4
China Technical Consultants, Inc. ... CTCI
China Television Co. (EY) ... CTV
China Theater [*World War II*] ... CT
China Theater of Operations [*World War II*] ... CTO
China Tire Holdings Ltd. [*Associated Press*] (SAG) ... ChinTire
China Tire Holdings Ltd. [*NYSE symbol*] (SPSG) ... TIR
China Today [*A publication*] ... China T
China Tourist Hotel Association (EAIO) ... CTHA
China Travel Service (ECON) ... CTS
China Treasure, Inc. [*Associated Press*] (SAG) ... ChinaTr
China Treasure, Inc. [*NASDAQ symbol*] (SAG) ... CHNA
China United Airlines [*ICAO designator*] (FAAC) ... CUA
China Xinhua Airlines [*FAA designator*] (FAAC) ... CXH
China Yuchai International Ltd. [*Associated Press*] (SAG) ... ChiYuc
China Yuchai International Ltd. [*NYSE symbol*] (SAG) ... CYD
China Yuchai Intl. [*NYSE symbol*] (TTSB) ... CYD
China-Burma-India Hump Pilots Association (EA) ... CBIHPA
China-Burma-India Theater [*World War II*] ... CBI
China-Burma-India Theater [*World War II*] ... CBIT

China-Burma-India Veterans Association (EA) .... CBIVA
China-Europe Management Institute .... CEMI
Chinandega/German Pomares [*Nicaragua*] [*ICAO location identifier*] (ICLI) .... MNCH
China's Travel Information Database [*Information service or system*] (IID) .... CTIDB
China-United States Physics Examination and Application Program .... CUSPEA
Chinch Bug [*Entomology*] .... CB
Chincha [*Peru*] [*ICAO location identifier*] (ICLI) .... SPHA
Chinchilla [*Australia Airport symbol*] CCL
Chinchilla Fur Breeders' Association [*British*] (BI) .... CFBA
Chinchilla Pelt Marketing Association Ltd. [*British*] (BI) .... CPMA
Chinchina [*Colombia*] [*Seismograph station code, US Geological Survey*] (SEIS) .... CHN
Chincoteague Island, VA [*Location identifier FAA*] (FAAL) .... VWU
Chincoteague, VA [*Location identifier FAA*] (FAAL) .... WAL
Chinese .... Ch
Chinese [*MARC language code Library of Congress*] (LCCP) .... chi
Chinese [*Language, etc.*] (ROG) .... CHIN
Chinese .... CHIN
Chinese Academy of Geological Science .... CAGS
Chinese Academy of Sciences .... CAS
Chinese Academy of Space Technology .... CAST
Chinese Air Force [*Nationalist*] .... CAF
Chinese Air Task Force .... CATF
Chinese Alliance for Democracy (EA) .... CS
Chinese American Arts Council (EA) .... CAAC
Chinese American Association of Commerce (EA) .... CAAC
Chinese American Citizens Alliance (EA) .... CACA
Chinese American Civic Council (EA) .... CACC
Chinese American Food Society (EA) .... CAFS
Chinese American Forum (EA) .... CAF
Chinese American Medical Society (EA) .... CAMS
Chinese American Restaurant Association (EA) .... CARA
Chinese Army (CINC) .... CA
Chinese Army in India .... CAI
Chinese Art Society of America [*Later, AS*] (EA) .... CASA
Chinese Association for the Advancement of Science .... CAAS
Chinese Association of Victoria [*Australia*] .... CAV
Chinese Atmospheric Nuclear Test (MCD) .... CANT
Chinese Banknote Collectors Society [*Defunct*] (EA) .... CBCS
Chinese Biopharmaceutical Association .... CBA
Chinese Canadian Information Processing Professionals (EAIO) .... CCIPP
Chinese Canadian National Council [*Conseil National des Canadiens Chinois*] [*Also, Chinese Canadian National Council for Equality*] (AC) .... CCNC
Chinese Canadian National Council for Equality .... CCNCE
Chinese Chamber of Commerce of Hawaii (SRA) .... CCCH
Chinese Christian Mission (EA) .... CCM
Chinese Communist .... CHICOM
Chinese Communist Air Force .... CCAF
Chinese Communist Army (CINC) .... CCA
Chinese Communist Forces .... CCF
Chinese Communist Navy (CINC) .... CCN
Chinese Communist Party [*Political party*] (PD) .... CCP
Chinese Communist Party [*Political party*] .... KKP
Chinese Consolidated Benevolent Association (EA) .... CCBA
Chinese Coordination Centre of World Evangelism (North America) (EA) .... CCCOWE-NA
Chinese Culture Association (EA) .... CCA
Chinese Culture Foundation of San Francisco (EA) .... CCFSF
Chinese Development Council (EA) .... CDC
Chinese Digital Seismograph Network .... CDSN
Chinese Educational Resources Information System [*Database*] [*National Taiwan Normal University Library*] [*Information service or system*] (CRD) .... CERIS
Chinese Exclusion Act .... CEA
Chinese Expeditionary Force .... CEF
Chinese Export Commodities Fair .... CECF
Chinese Federation of Labor [*Nationalist China*] .... CFL
Chinese for Affirmative Action (EA) .... CAA
Chinese Foreign Missionary Union (EA) .... CFMU
Chinese Freedom Party [*Political party*] (EY) .... CFP
Chinese Hamster [*Medicine*] (DMAA) .... CHN
Chinese Hamster Embryo Fibroblast [*Cytology*] .... CHEF
Chinese Hamster Lung [*Cell line*] .... CHL
Chinese Hamster Ovarian [*or Ovary*] [*Cytology*] .... CHO
Chinese Historical Society of America (EA) .... CHHS
Chinese Historical Society of America (EA) .... CHSA
Chinese Industrial Standards .... CIS
Chinese Institute of Engineers - USA (EA) .... CIE-USA
Chinese, Japanese, and Korean [*Library of Congress computer system*] .... CJK
Chinese Language Computer Society (EA) .... CLCS
Chinese Language Encoder .... CHICODER
Chinese Language Teachers Association (EA) .... CLTA
Chinese Laundry Association (EA) .... CLA
Chinese Librarians Association (EA) .... CLA
Chinese Linguistics Bibliography on Computer [*Cambridge University Press*] [*England*] .... CLIBOC
Chinese Masonic Society [*Australia*] .... CMS
Chinese Materials and Research Aids Service Center, Inc., Taipei, Taiwan, China [*Library symbol Library of Congress*] (LCLS) .... CiTCM
Chinese Medicine & Acupunture Association Canada [*L'Association de Medecine Chinoise et d'Acupuncture du Canada*] (AC) .... CMAAC
Chinese Merchants Association (EA) .... CMA
Chinese Music Society of North America (EA) .... CMSNA
Chinese Musical and Theatrical Association (EA) .... CMTA
Chinese Nationalist .... CHINAT
Chinese Nationalist Air Force .... CNAF
Chinese Navy (CINC) .... CN
Chinese People's Political Consultative Conference .... CPPCC
Chinese People's Republic .... CPR
Chinese Pharmacopoeia [*A publication*] .... Chin P
Chinese Refugee Relief [*Defunct*] (EA) .... CRR
Chinese Republican Party [*Political party*] (EY) .... CRP
Chinese Restaurant Asthma [*Medicine*] .... CRA
Chinese Restaurant Syndrome [*Monosodium glutamate sensitivity*] [*Medicine*] .... CRS
Chinese School of Table Tennis [*France*] (EAIO) .... CSTT
Chinese Scientific and Technological Periodical Abstracts [*Information service or system*] (IID) .... STADB
Chinese Shar-Pei Club of America (EA) .... CSPCA
Chinese Taipei [*IYRU nationality code*] (IYR) .... TA
Chinese Television System (EY) .... CTS
Chinese University Language Translation [*Human-aided machine translation*] [*Hong Kong*] (NITA) .... CULT
Chinese Urban Professional [*Hong Kong Yuppie*] [*Lifestyle classification*] .... Chuppie
Chinese Women's Association (EA) .... CWA
Chinese Women's Benevolent Association (EA) .... CWBA
Chinese World, San Francisco, CA [*Library symbol Library of Congress*] (LCLS) .... CSfCWL
Chinese Youth Council [*Later, CDC*] (EA) .... CYC
Chinese-American Composite Wing [*Air Force*] .... CACW
Chinese-American Educational Foundation (EA) .... CAEF
Chinese-American Librarians Association (EA) .... CALA
Chinese-English Translation Assistance Group (EA) .... CETA
Chinese-Oriented Antiballistic Missile System (AABC) .... C-ABM
Ching Chuan Kang Air Base [*Vietnam*] .... CCK
Chinguacousy Township Public Library, Bramalea, ON, Canada [*Library symbol Library of Congress*] (LCLS) .... CaOBram
Chinguacousy Township Public Library, Bramalea, Ontario [*Library symbol National Library of Canada*] (NLC) .... OBRAM
Chinhae [*South Korea ICAO location identifier*] (ICLI) .... RKPE
Chinle, AZ [*FM radio station call letters*] (RBYB) .... KFXR
Chinle High School Library, Chinle, AZ [*Library symbol Library of Congress*] (LCLS) .... AzCH
Chino, CA [*Location identifier FAA*] (FAAL) .... CHJ
Chino, CA [*Location identifier FAA*] (FAAL) .... CNO
Chinoiserie (VRA) .... Chino
Chinook Jargon [*MARC language code Library of Congress*] (LCCP) .... chn
Chinook, MT [*FM radio station call letters*] .... KRYK
Chinook Regional Library, Swift Current, Saskatchewan [*Library symbol National Library of Canada*] (NLC) .... SCR
Chinook Regional Library, Swift Current, SK, Canada [*Library symbol Library of Congress*] (LCLS) .... CaSCR
Chinsali [*Zambia*] [*ICAO location identifier*] (ICLI) .... FLCS
Chintheche [*Malawi*] [*ICAO location identifier*] (ICLI) .... FWCC
Chios [*Greece*] [*Airport symbol*] (OAG) .... JKH
Chios Societies of America (EA) .... CSA
Chip Carrier [*Electronics*] (EECA) CC
Chip Detector Sensor (MCD) .... CDS
Chip Enable [*Computer science*] (NITA) .... CE
Chip Enable [*Computer science*] (MHDI) .... CHE
Chip Enable Input [*Computer science*] .... CE
Chip Enable Input [*Computer science*] (MHDI) .... CEI
Chip Enable Output [*Computer science*] .... CEO
Chip Hermeticity in Plastic [*Electronics*] (MDG) .... CHIP
Chip Operational Multifunction Auxiliary Computer (MCD) .... COMFAX
Chip Performance Index [*Computer science*] .... CPI
Chip Select .... CSE
Chip Select Input [*Computer science*] .... CS
Chip Selection [*Electronics*] (ECII) .... CS
Chipata [*Zambia*] [*Airport symbol*] (OAG) .... CIP
Chipata [*Zambia*] [*ICAO location identifier*] (ICLI) .... FLCP
Chipewyan Lake School, Wabasca, Alberta [*Library symbol National Library of Canada*] (BIB) .... AWACS
Chipinge [*Zimbabwe*] [*ICAO location identifier*] (ICLI) .... FVCH
Chipley, FL [*AM radio station call letters*] .... WBGC
Chipman on the Law of Contracts [*A publication*] (DLA) .... Chip Cont
Chipman's New Brunswick Manuscript Reports [*A publication*] (DLA) .... Chip Ms
Chipman's New Brunswick Reports [*1825-35*] [*A publication*] (DLA) .... Chip
Chipman's New Brunswick Reports [*1825-35*] [*A publication*] (DLA) .... Chip W
Chipman's New Brunswick Reports [*1825-35*] [*A publication*] (DLA) .... NBR Chip
Chipman's Principles of Government [*A publication*] (DLA) .... Chip Gov
Chipola Junior College [*Marianna, FL*] .... CJC
Chipola Junior College, Marianna, FL [*Library symbol Library of Congress*] (LCLS) .... FMaC
Chippewa Air Commuter, Inc. [*ICAO designator*] (FAAC) .... CPW
Chippewa County Library System, Montevideo, MN [*Library symbol Library of Congress*] (LCLS) .... MnMov
Chippewa County-Montevideo Hospital, Montevideo, MN [*Library symbol*] [*Library of Congress*] (LCLS) .... MnMovCH
Chippewa Falls Public Library, Chippewa Falls, WI [*Library symbol Library of Congress*] (LCLS) .... WCf
Chippewa Falls Public Library, Chippewa Falls, WI [*Library symbol Library of Congress Obsolete*] (LCLS) .... WCh
Chippewa Falls, WI [*AM radio station call letters*] .... WAYY
Chippewa Falls, WI [*FM radio station call letters*] .... WCFW
Chippewa Falls, WI [*Television station call letters*] .... WEUX
Chippewa Library League [*Library network*] CLL

Chippewa Library League, Mt. Pleasant, MI [*Library symbol Library of Congress*] (LCLS) .... MiMtpC
Chippewa Resource Center, Muncey, ON, Canada [*Library symbol*] [*Library of Congress*] (LCLS) .... CaOMuCR
Chippewa Resource Centre, Muncey, Ontario [*Library symbol National Library of Canada*] (NLC) .... OMCR
Chippewa Valley Museum, Eau Claire, WI [*Library symbol Library of Congress*] (LCLS) .... WECV
Chippewa-Ottawa Treaty Fishery Management Authority .... COTFMA
Chipping Sodbury [*England*] .... CHIPSODB
Chips and Technologies, Inc. [*Associated Press*] (SAG) .... ChipsTc
Chips & Technologies, Inc. [*NASDAQ symbol*] (NQ) .... CHPS
Chips/Technologies [*NASDAQ symbol*] (TTSB) .... CHPS
Chiquita Br Intl $2.875 Cv'A'Pfd [*NYSE symbol*] (TTSB) .... CQBPrA
Chiquita Brands International [*Associated Press*] (SAG) .... Chiq
Chiquita Brands International [*Associated Press*] (SAG) .... Chiquta
Chiquita Brands International [*NYSE symbol*] (SPSG) .... CQB
Chiquita Brands Intl. [*NYSE symbol*] (TTSB) .... CQB
Chiral Chromatography CC
Chiral Stationary Phase [*Chemical separation technique*] .... CSP
Chirat [*Pakistan*] [*ICAO location identifier*] (ICLI) .... OPCT
Chiredzi [*Rhodesia*] [*Seismograph station code, US Geological Survey*] (SEIS) .... CIR
Chiredzi/Buffalo Range [*Zimbabwe*] [*ICAO location identifier*] (ICLI) .... FVCV
ChiRex, Inc. [*Associated Press*] (SAG) .... ChiRex
ChiRex, Inc. [*NASDAQ symbol*] (SAG) .... CHRX
ChiRex Inc. [*NASDAQ symbol*] (TTSB) .... CHRX
Chiricahua National Monument and Fort Bowie National Historic Site .... CHIR
ChiroClec Resolves .... CR
Chiron Corp. [*NASDAQ symbol*] (NQ) .... CHIR
Chiron Corp. [*Associated Press*] (SAG) .... Chiron
Chiropodists' Registration Board of Victoria [*Australia*] .... CRBV
Chiropody Bibliographical Research Society .... CBRS
Chiropody Board of South Australia [*Medicine*] .... CBSA
Chiropractic .... CHIROPRCTC
Chiropractic Advancement Association [*British*] .... CAA
Chiropractic Association of Louisiana (SRA) .... CAL
Chiropractic Association of Oklahoma (SRA) .... CAO
Chiropractic Association of Oregon (SRA) .... CAO
Chiropractic Board of the Australian Capital Territory [*Medicine*] .... CBACT
Chiropractic Information Centre Ltd. [*British*] (CB) CIC
Chiropractor .... CHIRO
Chiropractors' and Osteopaths' Board of Queensland [*Australia*] .... COBQ
Chiropractors' Association of Australia .... CAA
Chiropractors' Association of Australia, Australian Capital Territory .... CAAACT
Chiropractors' Board of South Australia [*Medicine*] .... CBSA
Chiropractors' Registration Board [*Australia*] .... CRB
Chiropractors'and Osteopaths' Registration Board [*Victoria*] [*Australia*] .... CORB
Chiroptical Discrimination [*Steroisomeric chemistry*] .... CD
Chiro-Xylographic [*Type of block book*] .... CHX
Chirp (IAA) C
Chirp Duration [*Entomology*] .... CD
Chirp Period [*Entomology*] .... CP
Chirp Rate [*Entomology*] .... CR
Chirped Pulse Amplification [*Physics*] .... CPA
Chirp-Z-Transform .... CZT
Chirurgia [*Surgery*] [*Latin*] .... CH
Chirurgiae Baccalaureus [*Bachelor of Surgery*] .... CB
Chirurgiae Baccalaureus [*Bachelor of Surgery*] .... Ch B
Chirurgiae Baccalaureus [*Bachelor of Surgery*] [*Latin*] (BARN) .... Chit B
Chirurgiae Doctor [*Doctor of Surgery*] .... ChD
Chirurgiae Doctor [*Doctor of Surgery*] .... Chir Doct
Chirurgiae Doctor [*Doctor of Surgery*] [*Latin*] (NADA) .... ChirDoc
Chirurgiae Doctor [*Doctor of Surgery*] .... D Ch
Chirurgiae Magister [*Master of Surgery*] .... Ch M
Chirurgiae Magister [*Master of Surgery*] [*Latin*] .... CM
Chirurgicalis [*Surgical*] [*Pharmacy*] .... CHIRURG
Chirurgiese Navorsingsvereniging van Suidelike Afrika [*Surgical Research Society of Southern Africa*] (EAIO) .... CNSA
Chisago Lakes Area Junior High School, Lindstrom, MN [*Library symbol*] [*Library of Congress*] (LCLS) .... MnLiJ
Chisago Lakes Primary School, Chisago City, MN [*Library symbol*] [*Library of Congress*] (LCLS) .... MnCgP
Chisago Lakes Senior High School, Lindstrom, MN [*Library symbol*] [*Library of Congress*] (LCLS) .... MnLiS
Chisana [*Alaska*] [*Airport symbol*] (OAG) .... CZN
Chisana, AK [*Location identifier FAA*] (FAAL) .... CZN
Chisholm Junior High School, Chisholm, MN [*Library symbol*] [*Library of Congress*] (LCLS) .... MnChiJ
Chisholm Public Library, Chisholm, MN [*Library symbol*] [*Library of Congress*] (LCLS) .... MnChi
Chisholm Resources [*Vancouver Stock Exchange symbol*] .... CHZ
Chisholm Senior High School, Chisholm, MN [*Library symbol*] [*Library of Congress*] (LCLS) .... MnChiSH
Chi-Squared Automatic Interaction Detector .... CHAID
Chi-Squared Function .... CSF
Chi-Squared Test [*Statistics*] (DAVI) .... X_2t
Chistochina, AK [*Location identifier FAA*] (FAAL) .... CZO
Chita [*USSR*] [*Airport symbol*] (AD) .... CHT
Chita [*Former USSR Seismograph station code, US Geological Survey*] (SEIS) .... CIT
Chita/Kadala [*Former USSR ICAO location identifier*] (ICLI) .... UIAA
Chitaavia [*Former USSR*] [*FAA designator*] (FAAC) .... CHF
Chitarrone [*Large Guitar*] [*Music*] .... CHIT
Chitato [*Angola*] [*ICAO location identifier*] (ICLI) .... FNCH
Chitato [*Angola*] [*Airport symbol Obsolete*] (OAG) .... PGI
Chitina, AK [*Location identifier FAA*] (FAAL) CXC
Chitipa [*Malawi*] [*Airport symbol*] (AD) CII
Chitipa [*Malawi*] [*ICAO location identifier*] (ICLI) .... FWCT
Chitral [*Pakistan*] [*Airport symbol Obsolete*] (OAG) .... CJL
Chitral [*Pakistan*] [*ICAO location identifier*] (ICLI) .... OPCH
Chittagong [*Bangladesh*] [*Airport symbol*] (OAG) .... CGP
Chittagong [*Bangladesh*] [*Seismograph station code, US Geological Survey*] (SEIS) .... CHT
Chittagong [*Bangladesh*] [*ICAO location identifier*] (ICLI) .... VGEG
Chittenden Corp. [*Associated Press*] (SAG) .... Chittend
Chittenden Corp. [*NASDAQ symbol*] (NQ) .... CNDN
Chitty and Hulme on Bills of Exchange [*A publication*] (DLA) .... Chit & H Bills
Chitty and Mew's Supplement to Fisher's English Digest [*A publication*] (DLA) .... Chit & M Dig
Chitty and Patell's Supreme Court Appeals [*India*] [*A publication*] (DLA) .... Chitt & Pat
Chitty and Temple on Carriers [*A publication*] (DLA) .... Chit & T Car
Chitty, Junior, on Bills [*A publication*] (DLA) .... Chit Jun B
Chitty. Law of Nations [*1812*] [*A publication*] (DLA) .... Chit L of N
Chitty. Law of Nations [*1812*] [*A publication*] (DLA) .... Chit Nat
Chitty on Bills [*A publication*] (DLA) .... Ch Bills
Chitty on Bills [*A publication*] (DLA) .... Chit Bills
Chitty on Bills [*A publication*] (DLA) .... Chitty
Chitty on Commercial Law [*A publication*] (ILCA) .... Chit Com L
Chitty on Commercial Law [*A publication*] (DLA) .... Chit Com Law
Chitty on Commercial Law [*A publication*] (DLA) .... Chitty Com Law
Chitty on Contracts [*A publication*] (DLA) .... Chit Con
Chitty on Contracts [*A publication*] (DLA) .... Chit Cont
Chitty on Medical Jurisprudence [*A publication*] (DLA) .... Chit Med Jur
Chitty on Pleading [*A publication*] (DLA) .... Ch Pl
Chitty on Pleading [*A publication*] (DLA) .... Chit Pl
Chitty on the Game Laws [*A publication*] (DLA) .... Chit GL
Chitty on the Law of Descents [*A publication*] (DLA) .... Chit Des
Chitty's Commercial and General Lawyer [*A publication*] (DLA) .... Chit Lawy
Chitty's Criminal Law [*A publication*] (DLA) .... Ch Cr L
Chitty's Criminal Law [*A publication*] (DLA) .... Chit Cr L
Chitty's Criminal Law [*A publication*] (DLA) .... Chit Cr Law
Chitty's Criminal Law [*A publication*] (DLA) .... Chit Crim Law
Chitty's Edition of Archbold's Practice [*A publication*] (DLA) .... Chit Arch Pr
Chitty's Edition of Archbold's Practice [*A publication*] (DLA) .... Chit Archb Pr
Chitty's Edition of Blackstone's Commentaries [*A publication*] (DLA) .... Ch Black
Chitty's Edition of Blackstone's Commentaries [*A publication*] (DLA) .... Chi Black
Chitty's Edition of Blackstone's Commentaries [*A publication*] (DLA) .... Chit Bl
Chitty's Edition of Blackstone's Commentaries [*A publication*] (DLA) .... Chit Bl Comm
Chitty's Edition of Blackstone's Commentaries [*A publication*] (DLA) .... Chitty Bl Comm
Chitty's Edition of Burn's Justice [*A publication*] (DLA) .... Ch Burn's J
Chitty's Edition of Burn's Justice [*A publication*] (DLA) .... Chit Burn's J
Chitty's English Bail Court Reports [*1770-1822*] [*A publication*] (DLA) .... Chit
Chitty's English Bail Court Reports [*1770-1822*] [*A publication*] (DLA) .... Chit BC
Chitty's English Bail Court Reports [*1770-1822*] [*A publication*] (DLA) .... Chit R
Chitty's English Bail Court Reports [*1770-1822*] [*A publication*] (DLA) .... Chitt
Chitty's English Bail Court Reports [*1770-1822*] [*A publication*] (DLA) .... Chitty BC
Chitty's English Bail Court Reports [*1770-1822*] [*A publication*] (DLA) .... Chitty BC (Eng)
Chitty's English King's Bench Forms [*A publication*] (DLA) .... Chit F
Chitty's English King's Bench Practice Reports [*1819-20*] [*A publication*] (DLA) .... Chit
Chitty's English King's Bench Reports [*A publication*] (DLA) .... Ch R
Chitty's Equity Digest [*A publication*] (DLA) .... Chit Eq Dig
Chitty's Equity Index [*A publication*] (DLA) .... Chit Eq Ind
Chitty's Equity Index [*A publication*] (DLA) .... Chitty Eq Ind
Chitty's General Practice [*A publication*] (DLA) .... Chit Gen Pr
Chitty's General Practice [*A publication*] (DLA) .... Chit Pr
Chitty's Law Journal [*A publication*] (DLA) .... Chitt LJ
Chitty's Law of Apprentices [*A publication*] (DLA) .... Chit Ap
Chitty's Precedents in Pleading [*A publication*] (DLA) .... Chit Prec
Chitty's Prerogatives of the Crown [*A publication*] (DLA) .... Chit Prer
Chitty's Stamp Act [*A publication*] (DLA) .... Chit St A
Chitty's Statutes of Practical Utility [*1235-1948*] [*England*] [*A publication*] (DLA) .... Chit St
Chitty's Statutes of Practical Utility [*1235-1948*] [*England*] [*A publication*] (DLA) .... Chit Stat
Chitty's Summary of the Practice of the Superior Courts [*A publication*] (DLA) .... Chit Sum P
Chitty's Treatise on Carriers [*A publication*] (DLA) .... Chit Car
Chivalry (ROG) .... CHIV
Chivenor [*British ICAO location identifier*] (ICLI) .... EGDC
Chivenor FTU [*British ICAO designator*] (FAAC) .... CHV
Chloral Hydrate [*Pharmacology*] (DAVI) .... HYDRAT
Chlor-Alkali-Market Model .... CAMM
Chlorambucil [*Also, CHL, CMB*] [*Antineoplastic drug*] C
Chlorambucil [*Antineoplastic drug*] .... CHL
Chlorambucil [*Antineoplastic drug*] .... CLB
Chlorambucil [*Antineoplastic drug*] (CDI) .... CLB
Chlorambucil [*Antineoplastic drug*] .... CMB
Chlorambucil and Prednisone [*Antineoplastic drug regimen*] (DAVI) .... CHL + PRED
Chlorambucil, Vinblastine, Procarbazine, Prednisone [*Antineoplastic drug regimen*] .... CHL VPP
Chlorambucil, Vinblastine, Procarbazine, Prednisone [*Antineoplastic drug regimen*] .... CIVPP
Chlorambucil, Vinblastine, Vincristine, Prednisone [*Antineoplastic drug regimen*] (DAVI) .... LVVP

Chloramphenicol [*Antimicrobial compound*] C
Chloramphenicol [*Antimicrobial compound*] .... CAM
Chloramphenicol [*Antimicrobial compound*] .... CAP
Chloramphenicol [*Antimicrobial compound*] (MAE) .... CHL
Chloramphenicol [*Antimicrobial compound*] .... CM
Chloramphenicol [*Antimicrobial compound*] .... CMC
Chloramphenicol [*Antimicrobial compound*] .... CMP
Chloramphenicol Acetyltransferase [*An enzyme*] .... CAT
Chloramphenicol-Amended Potato Dextrose Agar [*Microbiology*] .... CPDA
Chloramphenicol-Sensitive Microsomal Protein (DMAA) .... CSMP
Chloramphetamine [*Neurochemistry*] .... CA
Chloranil [*Organic chemistry*] .... CA
Chloraromatic Compound [*Organic chemistry*] .... CAP
Chlorate Oxygen Candle .... COC
Chlordan [*or Chlordane*] [*Insecticide*] .... CD
Chlordecone (Kepone) [*Pesticide*] .... CD
Chlordiazepoxide [*Librium*] [*Sedative*] .... CDE
Chlordimeform [*Insecticide*] .... CDF
Chlordimeform [*Expectorant*] .... CDM
Chlorella International Union [*Later, MIU*] .... CIU
Chlorendic Acid [*Organic chemistry*] .... CA
Chlorendic Aldehyde [*Organic chemistry*] .... CEA
Chlorendic Anhydride [*Also, CAN*] [*Organic chemistry*] .... CA
Chlorendic Anhydride [*Also, CA*] [*Organic chemistry*] .... CAN
Chloride [*Chemistry*] (ADA) .... CHLO
Chloride [*Chemistry*] (ROG) .... CHLOR
Chloride (DAVI) Cl
Chloride Channel (DMAA) .... CLCN
Chloride Industrial Batteries [*Manufacturer*] [*British*] .... CIB
Chloride Leak Detector (IEEE) .... CLD
Chloride Test [*Dentistry*] (BABM) .... CLR
Chlorinated [*Freight*] .... CHLOR
Chlorinated Aromatic Compound [*Organic chemistry*] .... CAC
Chlorinated Dibenzofuran [*Organic chemistry*] (FFDE) .... CDBF
Chlorinated Dibenzofuran [*Organic chemistry*] .... CDF
Chlorinated Dibenzo-para-dioxin [*Organic chemistry*] .... CDD
Chlorinated Fluorocarbon (GAAI) .... CFC
Chlorinated Hydrocarbon .... CHC
Chlorinated Methane [*Organic chemistry*] .... CM
Chlorinated Naphthalene [*Organic chemistry*] .... CN
Chlorinated Organics in Wastewater .... COW
Chlorinated Paraffin [*Organic chemistry*] .... CP
Chlorinated Paraffins Industry Association (EA) .... CPIA
Chlorinated Polyethylene [*Organic chemistry*] .... CPE
Chlorinated Poly(vinyl Chloride) [*Organic chemistry*] .... CPVC
Chlorinated Synthetic Rubber .... CSR
Chlorine [*Chemical element*] Cl
Chlorine Efficiency Factor .... CEF
Chlorine Emergency Plan [*Chlorine Institute*] .... CHLOREP
Chlorine Institute (EA) Cl
Chlorine Pentafluoride [*Inorganic chemistry*] (MCD) .... CLPF
Chlorine Pentafluoride [*Inorganic chemistry*] .... CPF
Chlorine Trifluoride [*Inorganic chemistry*] .... CTF
Chlorine-Catalyzed Oxidative-Pyrolysis [*Chemical engineering*] .... CCOP
Chloris Striate Mosaic Virus [*Plant pathology*] .... CSMV
Chlorite [*A mineral*] .... CHL
Chlorite (VRA) .... chlr
Chlorite [*A mineral*] Cl
Chlorite-Iodide-Malonic-Acid [*Chemical reaction*] .... CIMA
Chlormerodrin Accumulation Test [*Medicine*] (MAE) .... CAT
Chlornaltrexamine [*Narcotic antagonist*] [*Pharmacochemistry*] .... CNA
Chloro [*As substituent on nucleoside*] [*Biochemistry*] cl
Chloroacetaldehyde Diethyl Acetal [*Organic chemistry*] .... CADEA
Chloroacetaldehyde Dimethyl Acetal [*Organic chemistry*] .... CADMA
Chloroacetatedinitrophenylhydrazone [*Fungicide*] .... CADNPH
Chloroacetate Esterase [*An enzyme*] .... CAE
Chloroacetophenone [*Also, CN*] [*Tear gas*] .... CAP
Chloroacetophenone [*Also, CAP*] [*Tear gas Army symbol*] (AAG) .... CN
Chloroacetophenone in Chloroform (PDAA) .... CNbr
Chloroacetyl [*Organic chemistry*] (DAVI) .... ClAc
Chloroacetyl Chloride [*Organic chemistry*] .... CAC
Chloroallyl Diethyldithiocarbamate [*Herbicide*] .... CDEC
Chlorobenzalmalononitrile [*Tear gas*] [*Army symbol*] .... CS
Chlorobenzine Producers Association (EA) .... CPA
Chlorobenzoic Acid [*Organic acid*] .... CBA
Chlorobenzotrifluoride [*Organic chemistry*] .... CBTF
Chlorobiphenyl [*Chemistry*] .... CB
Chlorobromide Print Process (VRA) .... CHBR
Chlorobromoethane [*Organic chemistry*] .... CBE
Chlorobromomethane [*Also, CBM*] [*Organic chemistry*] (MCD) .... CB
Chlorobromomethane [*Also, CB*] [*Organic chemistry*] .... CBM
Chlorobutanol [*Pharmacology*] (DAVI) .... Chlb
Chlorocetophenone Solution (AAG) .... CNS
Chlorocholine Chloride [*Organic chemistry*] CCC
Chlorodeoxyadenosine [*Biochemistry*] .... CDA
Chloro-deoxy-glucose [*Biochemistry*] .... CDG
Chlorodeoxylincomycin (MAE) .... CDL
Chlorodiallylacetamide [*Herbicide*] .... CDAA
Chlorodifluoroethylene [*Organic chemistry*] .... CDF
Chlorodihydroxybenzopyranone [*Organic chemistry*] .... CDBP
Chlorodinitrobenzene [*Organic chemistry*] .... CDNB
Chloroethane Phosphoric Acid [*Organic chemistry*] (DAVI) .... CEPA
(Chloroethyl)cyclohexylnitrosourea [*Lomustine*] [*Antineoplastic drug regimen*] .... CCNU

Chloroethyl-Cyclohexyl-Nitrosoures [*Also called Lomustine*] [*Antineoplastic drug*] (DAVI) .... CEENU
(Chloroethyl)deoxycytidine [*Antiviral*] .... CEDC
(Chloroethyl)deoxyuridine [*Biochemistry*] .... CEDU
Chloroethylnitrosourea [*A class of antineoplastic agents*] .... CENU
Chloroethylphosphonic Acid [*Maturation compound for fruits*] .... CEPA
Chlorofluorocarbon [*Organic chemistry*] .... CFC
Chlorofluoromethane [*Propellant*] .... CFM
Chloroform [*Organic chemistry*] (WGA) .... CHL
Chloroform [*Organic chemistry*] (ADA) .... CHLO
Chloroform [*Organic chemistry*] (ROG) .... CHLOR
Chloroform and Ether [*Mixture*] .... CE
Chloroform Fumigation-Incubation Technique .... CFI
Chlorogenic Acid [*Organic chemistry*] .... CA
Chlorogenic Acid [*Organic chemistry*] .... CGA
Chloroisatoic Anhydride [*Organic chemistry*] .... CIA
Chloroisobutene Isoprene Rubber .... CIIR
Chloromercuribenzoate [*Biochemistry*] .... ClHgBzO
Chloromercuribenzoic [*Organic chemistry*] .... CMB
Chloromethyl Chloroformate [*Organic chemistry*] (DAVI) .... K stoff
Chloromethyl Ether [*Organic chemistry*] .... CME
Chloromethyl Ketone [*Medicine*] (DMAA) .... CMK
Chloromethyl Methyl Ether [*Organic chemistry*] .... CMME
Chloromethyldimethylchlorosilane [*Organic chemistry*] .... CMDMS
Chloromethyldioxolane [*Organic chemistry*] .... CMDO
Chloromethylfurfuraldehyde [*Organic chemistry*] .... CMF
Chloro(methyl)phenol [*Organic chemistry*] .... CMP
((Chloro(methyl)phenoxy))propionic Acid [*Herbicide*] .... CMPP
Chloro(methyl)(ribityl)isoalloxazine [*Biochemistry*] .... CMRI
Chloronitroaniline [*Organic chemistry*] .... CNA
Chloro(nitro)phenol [*Organic chemistry*] .... CNP
Chloroperbenzoic Acid [*Organic acid*] .... CPBA
Chlorophenoxyacetic Acid [*Plant growth hormone*] .... CPA
(Chlorophenoxy)butanoic Acid [*Biochemistry*] .... CPBA
Chlorophenoxyisobutyrate [*Pharmacology*] .... CPIB
(Chlorophenoxy)propionic Acid [*Biochemistry*] .... CPPA
Chlorophenyl Red [*A dye*] .... CPR
Chlorophenylalanine [*Biochemistry*] .... CPA
Chlorophenyldimethylurea [*Herbicide*] .... CMU
(Chlorophenyl)methylcarbamate [*Organic chemistry*] .... CPMC
Chlorophyll .... ChL
Chloropicolinic Acid [*Organic chemistry*] .... CPA
Chloropicrin [*Poison gas*] [*Army symbol*] .... PS
Chloropicrin Stannic Chloride [*Inorganic chemistry*] .... NC
Chloroplast DNA [*Deoxyribonucleic Acid*] [*Genetics*] (DOG) .... chDNA
Chloroplasts, Ferredoxin, and Hydrogenase [*Photoreactant system*] .... CFH
Chloroplasts to Nuclei per Cell [*Botany*] .... C/N
Chloroprene Rubber .... CR
Chloroprocaine [*A local anesthetic*] .... CP
(Chloropropyl)deoxyuridine [*Antiviral*] .... CPDU
Chloropurine [*Antineoplastic drug*] (AAMN) .... CP
Chloroquine [*Antimalarial drug*] .... CQ
Chloroquine and Primaquine [*Antimalarial drugs*] (AAMN) .... CP
Chloroquine Mustard (MAE) .... CQM
Chloroquine, Pyrimethamine, Sulfisoxazole (MAE) .... CPS
Chloroquine Resistance [*Chemoprophylaxis*] .... CQR
Chloroquine-Mepacrine [*Antimalarial drugs*] (MAE) .... CM
Chloroquine-Quinine [*Antimalarial drug*] [*Pharmacology*] (DAVI) .... CQ
Chloroquine-Resistant [*Genetics*] .... CQR
Chloroquine-Resistant Plasmodium Falciparum [*Chemoprophylaxis*] .... CRPF
Chloroquine-Susceptible [*Genetics*] .... CQS
Chloroquinol [*Medicine*] (DMAA) .... CHQ
Chloroquinoxaline Sulfonamide [*Antineoplastic drug*] .... CQS
Chlorosulfonic Acid [*Organic chemistry*] .... CSA
Chlorosulfonyl Isocyanate [*Organic chemistry*] .... CSI
(Chlorosulfonyl)dicyclohexylamine [*Antineoplastic drug*] .... CSD
Chlorosulphonated Polyethlene .... CSP
Chlorosulphonated Polyethylene .... CSPE
Chlorothiazide [*Diuretic*] .... CHTZ
Chlorothiazide [*Diuretic*] .... CT
Chlorothiazide [*Diuretic*] (MAE) .... CTZ
Chlorotrifluoroethylene [*Organic chemistry*] .... CFE
Chlorotrifluoroethylene [*Organic chemistry*] .... CTFE
Chlorotrifluorethane [*Organic chemistry*] .... CTF
Chloroxymorphamine [*Narcotic agonist*] [*Pharmacochemistry*] .... COA
Chlorozotocin [*Antineoplastic drug*] (CDI) .... CLZ
Chlorozotocin [*Antineoplastic drug*] .... CZT
Chlorozotocin [*Organic chemistry*] (DAVI) .... DCNU
Chlorpheniramine [*Pharmacology*] .... CH
Chlorpheniramine Maleate [*Antihistamine*] .... CPM
Chlorpromazine [*Sedative*] .... CPZ
Chlorpropamide-Alcohol Flushing [*Medicine*] .... CPAF
Chlortetracycline [*Antibiotic*] .... CTC
Chlorthalidone [*Diuretic*] .... CHLT
Chlorthalidone (DMAA) .... CTHD
Chlortrimeton [*Antihistamine*] [*Trademark of Schering-Plough Corp.*] .... CTM
Chlorzotocin [*Organic chemistry*] (DAVI) .... CZN
Choay [*France*] [*Research code symbol*] .... CY
Chocha [*Zambia*] [*ICAO location identifier*] (ICLI) .... FLCO
Chochma, Bina, Daat [*Wisdom, Understanding, Knowledge*] [*Philosophy of the Lubavitch Movement, a Hasidic sect*] .... CHABAD
Chock Full O'Nuts [*NYSE symbol*] (TTSB) .... CHF
Chock Full O'Nuts Corp. [*Wall Street slang name: "Nuts"*] [*NYSE symbol*] (SPSG) .... CHF

Chock Full O'Nuts Corp. [*Wall Street Slang Name: "Nuts"*] [*Associated Press*] (SAG) .... ChkFull
Chocktaw, Oklahoma & Gulf Railroad .... CO & G
Chocolate .... ch
Chocolate .... CHOC
Chocolate .... CHOC
Chocolate Blood [*Agar*] [*Biochemistry*] (MAE) .... CB
Chocolate Manufacturers Association of the USA (EA) .... CMA
Chocolate Milk Foundation [*Defunct*] (EA) .... CMF
Chocolate-Coated [*Pharmacy*] CC
Chocolate-Coated [*or Covered*] Tablet [*Pharmacy*] .... CCT
Choctaw [*MARC language code Library of Congress*] (LCCP) .... cho
Choctaw Nation Multi-County Library, McAlester, OK [*OCLC symbol*] (OCLC) .... OKI
Choctaw Nation Multi-County Library, McAlester, OK [*Library symbol Library of Congress*] (LCLS) .... OkMcC
Choctawhatchee Regional Library [*Library network*] .... CRL
Choephori [*of Aeschylus*] [*Classical studies*] (OCD) .... Cho
Chofu [*Japan ICAO location identifier*] (ICLI) .... RJTF
Choice (ADA) .... CH
Choice .... CHCE
Choice Drug Systems, Inc. [*NASDAQ symbol*] (NQ) .... DOSE
Choice Hotels International, Inc. [*NYSE symbol*] (SAG) .... CHH
Choice Hotels International, Inc. [*Associated Press*] (SAG) .... ChoiceH
Choice in Dying .... CID
Choice Magazine Listening [*An "aural magazine" for the blind and visually handicapped*] .... CML
Choice Old Marsala .... COM
Choice Reaction Time (PDAA) .... CRT
Choice-in-Currency Research Institute (EA) .... CNCRI
Choir (ROG) .... CH
Choir .... CHOR
Choir Organ .... CH
Choir Organ (ROG) .... CO
Choir Screen (VRA) .... chr scrn
Choirmaster [*Music*] .... Choirm
Choirmaster [*Music*] .... CM
Choiseul Bay [*Solomon Islands*] [*Airport symbol*] (OAG) .... CHY
Choke (MSA) .... CH
Choke Breaker [*Automotive engineering*] .... CB
Choke Coil CC
Choke Coil (AAG) .... CHC
Choking Gas [*US Chemical Corps symbol*] .... CG
Chokio-Alberta High School, Alberta, MN [*Library symbol*] [*Library of Congress*] (LCLS) .... MnAlbeCH
Chokio-Alberto Elementary School, Chokio, MN [*Library symbol*] [*Library of Congress*] (LCLS) .... MnChoE
Chol Chol Foundation for Human Development (EA) .... CCFHD
Cholame Valley [*California*] [*Seismograph station code, US Geological Survey*] (SEIS) CVC
(Cholamidopropyl)dimethylammonio(hydroxy) Propanesulfonate [*Organic chemistry*] .... CHAPSO
((Cholamidopropyl)dimethylammonio)propanesulfonate [*Biochemistry*] .... CHAPS
Cholamine (PDAA) .... CA
Chole Packet (ACRL) .... CHO
Cholecalciferol [*Organic chemistry*] (DAVI) .... D
Cholecystectomy [*Medicine*] (MAE) .... chole
Cholecystogram [*Radiology*] (DAVI) .... CCG
Cholecystokinin [*Also, PZ*] [*Endocrinology*] .... CCK
Cholecystokinin Octapeptide [*Biochemistry*] (DAVI) .... CCK-OP
Cholecystokinin-Brain Type Receptor .... CCK-B
Cholecystokinin-Gallbladder [*Medicine*] (MEDA) .... CCK-GB
Cholecystokinin-Pancreozymin [*Endocrinology*] .... CCK-PZ
Cholecystokinin-Releasing Peptide [*Biochemistry*] .... CCKRP
Choledochoduodenal Junction [*Anatomy*] .... CDJ
Choledocwo-Caval Shunt [*Medicine*] .... CCS
Cholera Research Laboratory [*Bangladesh*] .... CRL
Cholera Toxin [*Medicine*] .... CT
Cholera Toxin [*Medicine*] .... ctx
Cholera Toxin B [*Medicine*] .... CHB
Cholera Toxin B [*Medicine*] .... CTB
Cholera Vaccine [*Medicine*] .... CHO/VAC
Cholera Vaccine Immunization [*Medicine*] CVI
Cholestatic Liver Disease [*Medicine*] .... CLD
Cholestech Corp. [*Associated Press*] (SAG) .... Cholest
Cholestech Corp. [*NASDAQ symbol*] (SAG) .... CTEC
Cholesteric Analysis Profile Test [*Thermography*] [*Radiology*] (DAVI) .... CAP
Cholesteric Liquid Crystal (PDAA) CLC
Cholesterol [*Also, Ch, Cho, CHOL*] [*Biochemistry*] (AAMN) C
Cholesterol [*Also, C, Cho, CHOL*] [*Biochemistry*] .... Ch
Cholesterol [*Also, C, Ch, CHOL*] [*Biochemistry*] .... Cho
Cholesterol [*Also, C, Ch, Cho*] [*Biochemistry*] .... CHOL
Cholesterol Binding Protein [*Biochemistry*] .... CBP
Cholesterol Epoxide [*Biochemistry*] .... CAE
Cholesterol Ester [*Clinical chemistry*] (MAE) .... Chol Est
Cholesterol Ester Storage Disease [*Medicine*] .... CESD
Cholesterol Ester Transport Protein [*Biochemistry*] .... CETP
Cholesterol Esters [*Clinical chemistry*] .... CE
Cholesterol Esters [*Organic chemistry*] (MAH) .... CHOL E
Cholesterol Esters [*Clinical chemistry*] (CPH) .... chol est
Cholesterol Gallstones [*Medicine*] .... CGS
Cholesterol Lowering Lipid [*Biochemistry*] CLL
Cholesterol Oxidase [*An enzyme*] .... CHOD
Cholesterol/Phospholipid Ratio [*Clinical chemistry*] .... C/P
Cholesterol Saturation Index [*Clinical chemistry*] .... CSI

Cholesterol/Triglyceride Ratio [*Clinical chemistry*] (AAMN) .... C/TG
Cholesterol-Esterifying Activity [*Biochemistry Medicine*] (DMAA) .... CEA
Cholesterol-Lecithin Flocculation (DAVI) .... CLF
Cholesterol-Lecithin Test [*Medicine*] (MAE) CL
Cholesterol-Lowering Atherosclerosis Study [*National Heart, Lung, and Blood Institute - NHLBI*] .... CLAS
Cholesteryl Erucyl Carbonate (PDAA) .... CEC
Cholesteryl Ester Transfer Protein [*Biochemistry*] .... CETP
Cholesteryl Iopanoate [*Biochemistry*] CI
Cholesteryl Oleate-Triglyceride [*Biochemistry*] .... COT
Cholet/Le Pontreau [*France ICAO location identifier*] (ICLI) .... LFOU
Cholic Acid [*Biochemistry*] (AAMN) .... CA
Choline [*Also, Cho*] [*Biochemistry*] .... Ch
Choline [*Also, Ch*] [*Biochemistry*] .... Cho
Choline Acetyl Transferase [*Also, ChA, ChAc, ChAT*] [*An enzyme*] .... CAT
Choline Acetylase [*Also, CAT, ChAc, ChAT*] [*An enzyme*] .... ChA
Choline Acetylase [*Also, CAT, ChA, ChAT*] [*An enzyme*] .... ChAc
Choline Acetyl-Transferase [*Also, CAT, ChA, ChAc*] [*An enzyme*] .... ChAT
Choline Glycerophosphatide (MAE) .... CGP
Choline Kinase [*An enzyme*] .... CK
Choline Magnesium Trisalicylate [*Pharmacy*] .... CMT
Choline Oxidase [*An enzyme*] .... CO
Choline-Adrenalin [*Test*] [*Medicine*] .... CA
Cholinesterase [*An enzyme*] .... ChE
Cholinesterase [*An enzyme*] .... CHS
Cholorquinine-Resistant Malaria .... CRPM
Choluteca [*Honduras*] [*ICAO location identifier*] (ICLI) .... MHCH
Choma [*Zambia*] [*ICAO location identifier*] (ICLI) .... FLCH
Chon Buri/Bang Phra [*Thailand*] [*ICAO location identifier*] (ICLI) .... VTBT
Chon Buri/Sattahip [*Thailand*] [*ICAO location identifier*] (ICLI) .... VTBS
Chonco [*Nicaragua*] [*Seismograph station code, US Geological Survey*] (SEIS) .... CNR
Chondritic Porous [*Aggregate*] [*Inorganic chemistry*] .... CP
Chondritic Uniform Reservoir [*Geology*] .... CHUR
Chondrocalcinosis [*Orthopedics*] (DAVI) CC
Chondrocyte Growth Factor [*Biochemistry*] .... CGF
Chondrodysplasia Punctata, Rhizomelic [*Medicine*] (DMAA) .... CDPR
Chondrodysplasia Punctata, X-Linked Dominant [*Medicine*] (DMAA) .... CPXD
Chondrodysplasia Punctata, X-Linked Recessive [*Medicine*] (DMAA) .... CPXR
Chondrodystrophia Foetalis [*Medicine*] (DMAA) .... CDF
Chondroectodermal Dysplasia [*Medicine*] (DMAA) .... CED
Chondroitin Sulfate [*Biochemistry*] .... CS
Chondroitin Sulfate A [*Biochemistry*] .... CSA
Chondromalacia [*Medicine*] (MAE) .... CM
Chondromalacia/Patella [*Medicine*] .... CH/P
Chondromalacia Patella [*Orthopedics*] (DAVI) .... CMP
Chondromalacia Patellae [*Orthopedics*] (DAVI) .... CMP
Chondromyxoid Fibroma [*Medicine*] .... CMF
Chondrosoma Permeation Pattern [*Oncology*] .... CPP
Chone [*Ecuador*] [*ICAO location identifier*] (ICLI) .... SECH
Chongqing [*China*] [*Airport symbol*] (OAG) .... CKG
Chongqing [*China*] [*ICAO location identifier*] (ICLI) .... ZUCK
Chopp Computer Corp. [*Vancouver Stock Exchange symbol*] .... CRP
Chopped Meat [*Medium*] [*Microbiology*] .... CM
Chopped Meat Carbohydrate [*Medium*] [*Microbiology*] .... CMC
Chopped Meat Glucose [*Medium*] [*Microbiology*] .... CMG
Chopped Meat Glucose Broth with Digoxin [*Medium*] [*Microbiology*] .... CMCD
Chopped Meat-Glucose-Starch Medium [*Medicine*] (DMAA) .... CMGS
Chopped Nylon Phenolic (SAA) .... CNP
Chopped Strand Mat (PDAA) .... CSM
Chopped Strand Mat .... CSM
Chopper (MSA) .... CHP
Chopper Mines Ltd. [*Vancouver Stock Exchange symbol*] .... COR
Chopper Stabilized Amplifier .... CSA
Choppy, Short, or Cross Sea [*Navigation*] C
Choral .... CHO
Choral .... CHOR
Choral Conductors Guild (EA) .... CCG
Chorale Book [*Music*] (ROG) .... CB
Chord .... CD
Chord (KSC) .... CHD
Chord Plane Line (MCD) .... CPL
Chorda Chirurgicalis [*Surgical Catgut*] [*Pharmacy*] .... CHORD CHIRURG
Chorda Tympani [*Neuroanatomy*] .... CT
Chore [*Pakistan*] [*ICAO location identifier*] (ICLI) .... OPKE
Choreograph .... CHOR
Choreographers Guild (EA) .... CG
Choreographers Theatre (EA) .... CG
Choreography .... CHGPH
Choreography .... Choreog
Choreti [*Bolivia*] [*ICAO location identifier*] (ICLI) .... SLCT
Chorioallantoic Membrane [*Embryology*] [*Assay for chemical irritability*] .... CAM
Choriocarcinoma [*Oncology*] CC
Choriocarcinoma [*Oncology*] .... CCA
Chorionic Biopsy [*Also, Chorionic Villus Sampling*] [*Medicine*] (PAZ) .... CVS
Chorionic Gonadotrophin [*Endocrinology*] .... CG
Chorionic Gonadotrophin Hormone [*Endocrinology*] (AAMN) .... CGH
Chorionic Gonadotrophin, Human [*Endocrinology*] .... CGH
Chorionic Gonadotropin [*Endocrinology*] (DAVI) .... APL
Chorionic Gonadotropin [*Endocrinology*] (MAE) .... CGT
Chorionic Gonadotropin in Pregnant Mare's Serum [*Veterinary medicine*] (DAVI) .... PMS
Chorionic Growth Hormone - Prolactin [*Also, HCS, HPL*] [*Endocrinology*] .... CGP
Chorionic Somatomammotrophin [*Endocrinology*] .... CS
Chorionic Villi Biopsy [*Medicine*] .... CVB

Chorionic Villi Sampling [*Medicine*] ... CVS
Chorioretinopathy and Pituitary Dysfunction [*Medicine*] ... CPD
Chorismic Acid [*Biochemistry*] ... Chr
Choristers Guild (EA) ... CG
Choroid Plexus Papilloma [*Medicine*] ... CPP
Choroidal Neovascularization [*Opthalmology*] ... CNV
Choroideremia [*Ophthalmology*] ... CHM
Chorus [*Music*] ... Cho
Chorus ... CHOR
Chorus Object-Oriented Layer [*Computer science*] ... COOL
Chorzow [*Poland*] [*Seismograph station code, US Geological Survey*] (SEIS) ... CHZ
Chose ... CHS
Chosen Coefficient of Variation [*Statistics*] ... CCV
Chosen People Ministries (EA) ... CPM
Choshi [*Japan*] [*Seismograph station code, US Geological Survey*] (SEIS) ... CHO
Chosin Few (EA) ... CF
Chosmadal [*Argentina ICAO location identifier*] (ICLI) ... SAHC
Chota [*Peru*] [*ICAO location identifier*] (ICLI) ... SPCT
Chota Nagpur Regiment [*British military*] (DMA) ... CN Regt
Choteau, MT [*Location identifier FAA*] (FAAL) ... CHX
Chouteau County Free Library, Fort Benton, MT [*Library symbol*] [*Library of Congress*] (LCLS) ... MtFb
Chow Chow Club (EA) ... CCC
Chowan College, Murfreesboro, NC [*Library symbol Library of Congress*] (LCLS) ... NcMfC
Chowchilla, CA [*FM radio station call letters*] (RBYB) ... KLVN
Chowiet Island [*Alaska*] [*Seismograph station code, US Geological Survey*] (SEIS) ... CHW
Choya [*Argentina*] [*Seismograph station code, US Geological Survey*] (SEIS) ... CYA
Choyce's Cases in Chancery [*1557-1606*] [*England*] [*A publication*] (DLA) ... CCC
Choyce's Cases in Chancery [*1557-1606*] [*England*] [*A publication*] (DLA) ... Ch Ca Ch
Choyce's Cases in Chancery [*1557-1606*] [*England*] [*A publication*] (DLA) ... Ch Cas Ch
Choyce's Cases in Chancery [*1557-1606*] [*England*] [*A publication*] (DLA) ... Ch Cas in Ch
Choyce's Cases in Chancery [*1557-1606*] [*England*] [*A publication*] (DLA) ... Cho Ca Ca
Choyce's Cases in Chancery [*1557-1606*] [*England*] [*A publication*] (DLA) ... Cho Ca Ch
Choyce's Cases in Chancery [*1557-1606*] [*England*] [*A publication*] (DLA) ... Choyce Cas Ch
Choyce's Cases in Chancery [*1557-1606*] [*England*] [*A publication*] (DLA) ... Choyce Cas (Eng)
Chreod International, Ottawa, Ontario [*Library symbol National Library of Canada*] (NLC) ... OOCHI
Chreschtlech-Sozial Vollekspartei [*Christian Social Party*] [*Luxembourg*] [*Political party*] (PPW) ... CSV
Chrestomathy (BARN) ... chr
Chretiens pour la Liberation du Peuple Guadeloupeen [*Guadeloupe*] (PD) ... CLPG
Chretiens pour Une Eglise Populaire [*Christians for One Common Church*] [*Canada*] ... CEP
Chrezvychainaya Komissiya po Borbe s Kontrrevolutisiei i Sabotazhem [*Extraordinary Commission for Combating Counterrevolution and Sabotage; Soviet secret police organization, 1917-1921*] ... CHEKA
Chripa [*Costa Rica*] [*Seismograph station code, US Geological Survey*] (SEIS) ... AR6
Chris LeDoux International Fan Club (EA) ... CLIFC
Chris-Craft Antique Boat Club (EA) ... CCABC
Chris-Craft Ind,$1 Pr Pfd [*NYSE symbol*] (TTSB) ... CCNPrA
Chris-Craft Ind,$1.40 Cv Pfd [*NYSE symbol*] (TTSB) ... CCNPrB
Chris-Craft Indus [*NYSE symbol*] (TTSB) ... CCN
Chris-Craft Industries, Inc. [*NYSE symbol*] (SPSG) ... CCN
Chris-Craft Industries, Inc. [*Associated Press*] (SAG) ... ChCft
Chris-Craft Industries, Inc. [*Associated Press*] (SAG) ... ChrisCr
Chrisman Public Library, Chrisman, IL [*Library symbol Library of Congress*] (LCLS) ... IChr
Christ (WDAA) ... C
Christ ... CH
Christ [*or Christian*] ... CHR
Christ ... CHRST
Christ ... XT
Christ Alongside (EA) ... CA
Christ Church College [*Oxford University*] (ROG) ... C CH COLL
Christ for the Nations (EA) ... CFN
Christ Hospital Institute of Medical Research, Research Library, Cincinnati, OH [*Library symbol Library of Congress*] (LCLS) ... OCCIM
Christ Hospital, Oak Lawn, IL [*Library symbol Library of Congress*] (LCLS) ... IOIC
Christ in Action Ministries (EA) ... CAM
Christ Seminary-Seminex, St. Louis, MO [*Library symbol Library of Congress*] (LCLS) ... MoSCEx
Christ the King ... CHK
Christ the King Foundation [*Defunct*] (EA) ... CKF
Christ the King School, Browerville, MN [*Library symbol*] [*Library of Congress*] (LCLS) ... MnBvC
Christ the King Seminary, East Aurora, NY [*Library symbol Library of Congress*] (LCLS) ... NEAuC
Christ the King Seminary, East Aurora, NY [*OCLC symbol*] (OCLC) ... VYK
Christ Truth Ministries (EA) ... CTM
Christadelphian Auxiliary Lecturing Society [*British*] (BI) ... CALS
Christchurch [*New Zealand*] [*Airport symbol*] (OAG) ... CHC
Christchurch [*New Zealand*] [*Later, EYR*] [*Geomagnetic observatory code*] ... CHR
Christchurch [*New Zealand*] [*ICAO location identifier*] (ICLI) ... NZCO
Christchurch [*New Zealand*] [*ICAO location identifier*] (ICLI) ... NZZC
Christchurch Chromosome [*Genetics*] (DAVI) ... CH
Christchurch Chromosome ... Ch[1]c
Christchurch/International [*New Zealand*] [*ICAO location identifier*] (ICLI) ... NZCH
Christchurch/International [*New Zealand*] [*ICAO location identifier*] (ICLI) ... NZDF
Christel, Bean & Linihan, Buffalo, NY [*Library symbol*] [*Library of Congress*] (LCLS) ... NBuCBL
Christelijk-Democratische Unie [*Christian Democratic Union*] [*Netherlands*] (PPE) ... CDU
Christelijke Bond voor de Ondergrondse Kerk/Action Chretienne pour l'Eglise du Silence [*Belgium*] ... CBOK-ACES
Christelijke Vervoerarbeiders en Diamantbewerkers [*Christian Trade Union of Transport and Diamond Workers*] [*Belgium*] (EAIO) ... CVD
Christelijke Volkspartij [*Christian Social Party*] [*Also, PSC*] [*Belgium*] [*Political party*] (PPW) ... CVP
Christelijk-Historische Unie [*Christian-Historical Union*] [*Netherlands Political party*] (PPW) ... CHU
Christen Democratisch Appel [*Christian Democratic Appeal*] [*Netherlands Political party*] (PPW) ... CDA
Christened ... CHR
Christened (ADA) ... CHRIS
Christensen Canadian African Line [*Steamship*] (MHDW) ... CCAL
Christentum und Wissenschaft [*A publication*] (BJA) ... ChrW
Christentum und Wissenschaft [*A publication*] (BJA) ... CHuW
Christian ... C
Christian ... Chr
Christian ... CHRSTN
Christian ... CHRSTN
Christian (VRA) ... Xian
Christian ... XN
Christian ... XTIAN
Christian (ROG) ... XTN
Christian Action Council (EA) ... CAC
Christian Action for Development in the Caribbean [*Caribbean Conference of Churches*] ... CADEC
Christian Action for the Abolition of Torture [*Defunct*] (EA) ... ACAT
Christian Action, Research, and Education [*British*] ... CARE
Christian Addiction Rehabilitation Association (EA) ... CARA
Christian Aid for Romania (EA) ... CAR
Christian Aid Mission (EA) ... CAM
Christian AIDS Services Alliance (EA) ... CASA
Christian Airmen's Fellowship International [*Defunct*] (EA) ... CAS
Christian Alliance of Women and Girls [*British*] (BI) ... CAWG
Christian Amateur Radio Fellowship [*Defunct*] (EA) ... CARF
Christian Amendment Movement [*Later, CGM*] (EA) ... CAM
Christian and Missionary Alliance ... CMA
Christian Anti-Communism Crusade (EA) ... CACC
Christian Anti-Jewish Party (BJA) ... CAJP
Christian Anti-Narcotic Association [*Later, SFM*] ... CANA
Christian Appalachian Project ... CAP
Christian Army (ROG) ... CA
Christian Assembly of New South Wales [*Australia*] ... CANSW
Christian Association for Adult and Continuing Education [*British*] ... CAACE
Christian Association for Psychological Studies (EA) ... CAPS
Christian Association of Business Executives [*British*] ... CABE
Christian Beacon, Collingswood, NJ [*Library symbol Library of Congress*] (LCLS) ... NjCoB
Christian Blind Mission International [*Bensheim, Federal Republic of Germany*] (EAIO) ... CBMI
Christian Boaters Association (EA) ... CBA
Christian Bodybuilding Association (EA) ... CBA
Christian Book Distributors [*An association*] ... CBD
Christian Book Selling Association of Australia ... CBSAA
Christian Booksellers Association (EA) ... CBA
Christian Bookstall Managers Association (EA) ... CBMA
Christian Brethren Assemblies [*Australia*] ... CBA
Christian Brethren Church in the Province of Quebec [*l'Eglise des Freres Chretiens dans la Province du Quebec*] [*Also, Plymouth Brethren*] (AC) ... CBCPQ
Christian Brethren Schools [*Australia*] ... CBS
Christian Brethren Youth Hostel [*Australia*] ... CBYH
Christian Broadcasting Association (EA) ... CBA
Christian Broadcasting Network [*Cable-television system*] ... CBN
Christian Brothers' Association of Australia ... CBA
Christian Brothers Boys Association (EA) ... CBBA
Christian Brothers College [*Tennessee*] ... CBC
Christian Brothers College, Memphis, TN [*Library symbol Library of Congress*] (LCLS) ... TMCBC
Christian Brothers Conference (EA) ... CBC
Christian Brothers Education Association [*Later, RECCB*] (EA) ... CBEA
Christian Brothers School [*Ireland*] ... CBS
Christian Business Men of Canada ... CBMC
Christian Business Men's Committee International [*Later, CBMC*] (EA) ... CBMCI
Christian Business Men's Committee of USA (EA) ... CBMC
Christian Business Men's Committees Australia ... CBMCA
Christian Businessman [*Christian Business Men's Committee of United States of America*] [*A publication*] ... CB
Christian Businessman's Committees [*Australia*] ... CBC
Christian Camping International [*Later, CCI/USA*] (EA) ... CCI
Christian Camping International/USA (EA) ... CCI/USA
Christian Century [*A publication*] (BRI) ... CC
Christian Century Foundation (EA) ... CCF
Christian Chamber of Commerce (EA) ... CCC
Christian Chaplain Services (EA) ... CCS

Christian Children's Fund (EA) ... CCF
Christian Children's Fund, Richmond, VA [*Library symbol*] [*Library of Congress*] (LCLS) ... ViRCCF
Christian Chiropractors Association (EA) ... CCA
Christian Church (Disciples of Christ) in Canada [*Formerly, All-Canada Committee of the Christian Church (Disciples of Christ)*] (AC) ... DISCAN
Christian Citizens' Crusade (EA) ... CCC
Christian City Church [*Australia*] ... CCC
Christian Classic Bikers Association [*Later, ICCM*] (EA) ... CCBA
Christian Classic Bikers Association International [*Later, ICCM*] (EA) ... CCBAI
Christian Coalition (EA) ... CC
Christian College Coalition (EA) ... CCC
Christian College, Columbia, MO [*Library symbol Library of Congress*] (LCLS) ... MoCoC
Christian College Consortium (EA) ... CCC
Christian College of the Southwest, Dallas, TX [*Library symbol Library of Congress*] (LCLS) ... TxDaCC
Christian Comic Arts Society (EA) ... CCAS
Christian Committee for Human Rights in Latin America [*Canada*] (EAIO) ... CCHRLA
Christian Communications, Inc. (EA) ... CCI
Christian Community Church [*Australia*] ... CCC
Christian Community Concern [*Australia*] ... CCC
Christian Community High School [*Australia*] ... CCHS
Christian Community School, Willmar, MN [*Library symbol*] [*Library of Congress*] (LCLS) ... MnWilCS
Christian Community Schools [*Australia*] ... CCS
Christian Computer Users [*Defunct*] (EA) ... CCU
Christian Computer Users Association (EA) ... CCUA
Christian Conference of Asia (EA) ... CCA
Christian Crusade (EA) ... CC
Christian Dance Federation of Australia ... CDFA
Christian Defense League (EA) ... CDL
Christian Democrat International (EAIO) ... CDI
Christian Democrat Party [*Australia Political party*] ... CDP
Christian Democratic Action for Social Justice [*Namibia*] [*Political party*] (EY) ... CDA
Christian Democratic Labour Party [*Grenada*] [*Political party*] (EY) ... CDLP
Christian Democratic Movement [*Former Czechoslovakia*] [*Political party*] (EY) ... CDM
Christian Democratic Organisation of America [*Venezuela*] (EAIO) ... CDOA
Christian Democratic Party [*Italy Political party*] ... CDP
Christian Democratic People's Party [*Hungary Political party*] (EY) ... CDPP
Christian Democratic Union [*Germany*] [*Political party*] ... CDU
Christian Democratic Union [*Czechoslavakia*] [*Political party*] (ECON) ... KDU
Christian Democratic Union of Central Europe [*Former Czechoslovakia*] (EAIO) ... CDUCE
Christian Democratic World Union (EA) ... CDWU
Christian Democrats [*European political movement*] (ECON) ... CD
Christian Democrats (EY) ... ChrDem
Christian Dental Society (EA) ... CDS
Christian Dior [*Couturier*] ... CD
Christian Doctors Sodality (EA) ... CDS
Christian Economic and Social Research Foundation [*British*] (DI) ... CESRF
Christian Education Movement [*British*] ... CEM
Christian Education Publications [*Australia*] ... CEP
Christian Educators Association International (EAIO) ... CEAI
Christian Educators Fellowship [*Later, CEAI*] (EA) ... CEF
Christian Endeavor (IIA) ... CE
Christian Endeavor Union ... CEU
Christian Era ... CE
Christian European Visual Media Association (EAIO) ... CEVMA
Christian Evidence Society [*British*] (DBA) ... CES
Christian Family Life (EA) ... CFL
Christian Family Movement (EA) ... CFM
Christian Family Renewal (EA) ... CFR
Christian Farmers Federation of Ontario [*Federation des Agriculteurs Chretien de l'Ontario*] (AC) ... CFFO
Christian Feminists (EA) ... CF
Christian Film Distributors Association (NTCM) ... CFDA
Christian Focus on Government (EA) ... CFG
Christian Forum Research Foundation [*Later, CC*] (EA) ... CFRF
Christian Foundation for Children and Aging (EA) ... CFCA
Christian Freedom Foundation (EA) ... CFF
Christian Friends of Israel [*British*] (BI) ... CFI
Christian Government Movement [*Defunct*] (EA) ... CGM
Christian Herald Association (EA) ... CHA
Christian Heritage Center (EA) ... CHC
Christian Heritage College [*El Cajon, CA*] ... CHC
Christian Heritage Library, El Cajon, CA [*Library symbol Library of Congress*] (LCLS) ... CEcajC
Christian Heritage Party of Canada [*Parti d'Heritage du Canada*] (AC) ... CHP
Christian Heritage Year [*1984*] [*British*] ... CHY
Christian Holiness Association (EA) ... CHA
Christian Home Educators Association (EA) ... CHEA
Christian Homesteading Movement (EA) ... CHM
Christian Instrumental Directors Association (EA) ... CIDA
Christian Ireland Ministries (EA) ... CIM
Christian Israelite Church [*Australia*] ... CIC
Christian Jail Workers (EA) ... CJW
Christian Knowledge Society [*Also known as Society for Promoting Christian Knowledge*] ... CKS
Christian Labor Association of the USA (EA) ... CLA
Christian Labour Association of Canada ... CLAC
Christian Law Association (EA) ... CLA
Christian Law Institute (EA) ... CLI
Christian Leaders for Responsible Television (NTCM) ... CLeaR-TV
Christian League for the Handicapped (EA) ... CLH
Christian Legal Society (EA) ... CLS
Christian Librarians' Fellowship (EA) ... CLF
Christian Life and Ministry [*Canada*] ... CLM
Christian Life Centre [*Australia*] ... CLC
Christian Life Commission of the Southern Baptist Convention (EA) ... CLCSBC
Christian Life Communities [*English Canada*] (AC) ... CLC
Christian Life Movement ... CLM
Christian Literacy Associates (EA) ... CLA
Christian Literature and Bible Center (EA) ... CLBC
Christian Literature Crusade [*British*] ... CLC
Christian Literature Crusade (International) [*Australia*] ... CLC(I)
Christian Macintosh Users Group (EA) ... CMUG
Christian Management Association (EA) ... CMA
Christian Management Report [*Christian Ministries Management Association*] [*A publication*] ... CMR
Christian Maternity Home Association (EA) ... CMHA
Christian Medical and Dental Society (EA) ... CMDS
Christian Medical Commission (EA) ... CMC
Christian Medical Council [*Defunct*] (EA) ... CMC
Christian Medical Fellowship [*British*] (DAVI) ... CMF
Christian Medical Foundation International (EA) ... CMF
Christian Medical Society [*Later, CMDS*] (EA) ... CMS
Christian Methodist Episcopal Church ... CME
Christian Methodist Episcopal Church ... CMEC
Christian Military Fellowship (EA) ... CMF
Christian Ministries Management Association [*Later, CMA*] (EA) ... CMMA
Christian Ministry Centre [*Australia*] ... CMC
[*A*] **Christian Ministry in the National Parks** (EA) ... ACMNP
Christian Mission (EA) ... CM
Christian Mission for the Deaf (EA) ... CMD
Christian Mission for the Deaf (EA) ... CMFD
Christian Mission to Buddhists [*See also NKB*] [*Arhus, Denmark*] (EAIO) ... CMB
Christian Mission to the Communist World [*Australia*] ... CMCW
Christian Mission to the Communist World [*Australia*] ... CMTTCW
Christian Missionary Fellowship (EA) ... CMF
Christian Missions in Many Lands (EA) ... CMML
Christian Missions to the Communist World (EA) ... CMCW
Christian Motorcyclist Association (EA) ... CMA
Christian Movement for Peace [*See also MCP*] [*Brussels, Belgium*] (EAIO) ... CMP
Christian Nationals' Evangelism Council [*Australia*] ... CNEC
Christian Organisations Research and Advisory Trust [*Church of England*] ... CORAT
Christian Outdoorsman Association (EA) ... COA
Christian Overcomers [*An association*] (EA) ... CO
Christian Palestinian Aramaic (BJA) ... CPA
Christian Parent-Controlled Schools [*Australia*] ... CPCS
Christian Patriot Association (EA) ... CPA
Christian Peace Conference [*See also CCP*] [*Prague, Czechoslovakia*] (EAIO) ... CPC
[*The*] **Christian People's Party - Progressive and Fishing Industry Party** [*Kristiligi Folkaflokkurin, Foroya Framburds- og Fiskivinnuflokkurin*] [*The Faroe Islands*] [*Political party*] (EY) ... CPP-PFIP
Christian Pharmacists Fellowship International (EA) ... CPFI
Christian Pilots Association (EA) ... CPA
Christian Preaching Conference [*Defunct*] (EA) ... CPC
Christian Projects [*Australia*] ... CP
Christian Psychological Services [*Australia*] ... CPS
Christian Publicity Organisation [*British*] ... CPO
Christian Record Benevolent Association [*Later, CRBF*] ... CRBA
Christian Record Braille Foundation [*Later, CRS*] (EA) ... CRBF
Christian Record Services (EA) ... CRS
Christian Reformed Church ... CRC
Christian Reformed Church in North America (AC) ... CRCNA
Christian Reformed Church World Literature Ministries (EA) ... CRCWLM
Christian Reformed World Relief Committee (EA) ... CRWRC
Christian Renewal Ministry (EA) ... CRM
Christian Renewal Outreach [*Australia*] ... CRO
Christian Republican Party [*Bulgaria*] [*Political party*] ... CRP
Christian Rescue Effort for the Emancipation of Dissidents [*Acronym now used as organization name*] (EA) ... CREED
Christian Research (EA) ... CR
Christian Research Institute (EA) ... CRI
Christian Response International (EA) ... CRI
Christian Restoration Association (EA) ... CRA
Christian Revival Fellowship [*Australia*] ... CRF
Christian Road Safety League [*British*] (BI) ... CRSL
Christian Rural Fellowship [*Defunct*] (EA) ... CRF
Christian Rural Overseas Program [*Acronym is now the official name of organization*] (EA) ... CROP
Christian Schools' Association [*Australia*] ... CSA
Christian Schools International (EA) ... CSI
Christian Science ... CS
Christian Science Monitor [*A publication*] (BRI) ... CSM
Christian Science Publishing Society (EA) ... CSPS
Christian Science Reading Room, Cleveland, OH [*Library symbol Library of Congress*] (LCLS) ... OClCh
Christian Science Reading Room, Montreal, PQ, Canada [*Library symbol Library of Congress*] (LCLS) ... CaQMCS
Christian Science Reading Room, Montreal, Quebec [*Library symbol National Library of Canada*] (NLC) ... QMCS
Christian Science Visiting Nurse Service New South Wales [*Australia*] ... CSVNSNSW

Christian Scientist ... SC
Christian Service Brigade (EA) ... CSB
Christian Service Club (EA) ... CSC
Christian Service Corps [*Defunct*] (EA) ... CSC
Christian Services for the Blind [*Australia*] ... CSB
Christian Services for the Hearing Impaired [*Australia*] ... CSHI
[*The*] **Christian Sisters (Pious Union)** (TOCD) ... CS
Christian Social Union [*Germany*] ... CSU
Christian Socialist (EY) ... ChrSoc
Christian Solidarity International [*Zurich, Switzerland*] (EAIO) ... CSI
Christian Syndrome [*Medicine*] (DMAA) ... CHRS
Christian Television Association of New South Wales [*Australia*] ... CTVANSW
Christian Television Association of South Australia ... CTASA
Christian Television Mission (EA) ... CTM
Christian Temperance Council for the Nordic Countries (EA) ... CTCNC
Christian Theological Seminary, Indianapolis, IN [*Library symbol Library of Congress*] (LCLS) ... InIT
Christian Theological Seminary, Indianapolis, IN [*OCLC symbol*] (OCLC) ... IXT
Christian Union [*University student group*] [*British*] ... CU
Christian Voice (EA) ... CV
Christian Volunteer Ministries (EA) ... CVM
Christian Welfare and Social Relief Organization [*Sierra Leone*] (EAIO) ... CWASRO
Christian Welfare Hospital, East St. Louis, IL [*Library symbol Library of Congress*] (LCLS) ... IEsCH
Christian Witness International [*British*] ... CWI
Christian Women's Fellowship (EA) ... CWF
Christian Women's Movement [*Bulgaria*] [*Political party*] ... CWM
Christian Women's National Concerns [*Defunct*] (EA) ... CWNC
Christian Workers Fellowship [*Sri Lanka*] (EAIO) ... CWF
Christian Workers Party [*Malta*] [*Political party*] (PPE) ... CWP
Christian Yellow Pages [*A publication*] ... CYP
Christian Youth Travel Association [*Australia*] ... CYTA
Christiana [*City in South Africa*] (ROG) ... CR
Christiana Companies, Inc. [*Associated Press*] (SAG) ... Christn
[*The*] **Christiana Companies, Inc.** [*NYSE symbol*] (SPSG) ... CST
Christiana, DE [*FM radio station call letters*] ... WXHL
Christian-Albrechts-Universitat Kiel, Kiel, Germany [*Library symbol Library of Congress*] (LCLS) ... GyKiU
Christianburg, VA [*FM radio station call letters*] ... WBNK
Christiane Fabre de Morlhon [*Information service name CFM Documentazione*] (IID) ... CFM
Christianity ... XNTY
Christianity ... XTY
Christianity Today [*A publication*] (BRI) ... Ch Today
Christian-Muslim Dialogue Committee (EA) ... CMDC
Christians Associated for Relationships with Eastern Europe (EA) ... CAREE
Christian's Bankrupt Law [*A publication*] (DLA) ... Chris BL
Christian's Charges to Grand Juries [*A publication*] (DLA) ... Chr Ch
Christians Concerned for Israel [*Superseded by NCLCI*] (EA) ... CCI
Christians for Socialism in the United States (EA) ... CFS
Christians in Crisis (EA) ... CC
Christians in Futures [*Defunct*] (EA) ... CF
Christians in Government (EA) ... CG
Christians in the Arts Networking (EA) ... CAN
Christians' Israel Public Action Campaign (EA) ... CIPAC
Christians United for Responsible Entertainment (EA) ... CURE
Christiansburg, VA [*AM radio station call letters*] (RBYB) ... WNNI
Christianshab [*Greenland*] [*ICAO location identifier*] (ICLI) ... BGCH
Christianskii Wostok [*A publication*] (BJA) ... ChrWo
Christiansted National Historic Site ... CHRI
Christiansted, St. Croix, VI [*Location identifier FAA*] (FAAL) ... STX
Christiansted, VI [*FM radio station call letters*] ... WAVI
Christiansted, VI [*FM radio station call letters*] ... WIVH
Christiansted, VI [*FM radio station call letters*] ... WJKC
Christiansted, VI [*AM radio station call letters*] ... WSTX
Christiansted, VI [*FM radio station call letters*] ... WSTX-FM
Christiansted, VI [*Television station call letters*] ... WSVI
Christiansted, VI [*FM radio station call letters*] ... WVIQ
Christiansted, VI [*FM radio station call letters*] ... WVIS
Christic Institute (EA) ... CI
Christie, Atkins, Munch-Peterson Test [*Bacteriology*] ... CAMP
Christie Home Historical Society, Long Prairie, MN [*Library symbol*] [*Library of Congress*] (LCLS) ... MnLpCHi
Christie Township Public Library, Parry Sound, Ontario [*Library symbol National Library of Canada*] (NLC) ... OPSCT
Christie's Contemporary Art [*Reproductions*] [*London, England*] ... CCA
Christie's Precedents of Wills [*A publication*] (DLA) ... Chr Pr W
Christina Exploration [*Vancouver Stock Exchange symbol*] ... KRX
Christlich Demokratische Union/Christlich Soziale Union [*Christian Democratic Union/Christian Social Union*] [*Germany Political party*] (PPE) ... CDU/CSU
Christlich Soziale Partei [*Christian Social Party*] [*Liechtenstein*] [*Political party*] (PPW) ... CSP
Christlich-Demokratische Union [*Christian Democratic Union*] [*Germany Political party*] (PPW) ... CDU
Christlichdemokratische Volkspartei der Schweiz [*Christian Democratic Party of Switzerland*] [*Political party*] (PPE) ... CVP
Christliche Bayerische Volkspartei - Bayerische Patriotenbewegung [*Christian Bavarian People's Party - Movement of Bavarian Patriots*] [*Germany Political party*] (PPW) ... CBV
Christliche Volkspartei [*Christian People's Party*] [*Pre-1945 Germany*] [*Political party*] (PPE) ... CVP
Christliche Waehlerunion Bayern [*Christian Voters' Union of Bavaria*] [*Germany Political party*] (PPW) ... CWU
Christliche-Sozialistiche Arbeitsgemeinschaft [*Christian Social-Workers' Community*] [*Lithuania*] [*Political party*] (PPE) ... CSA
Christlich-Nationaler Gewerkschaftsbund der Schweiz [*Swiss Federation of National-Christian Trade Unions*] ... CNGS
Christlich-Soziale Union [*Political party in Bavaria connected with the CDU*] [*West Germany*] ... CSU
Christlich-Soziale Waehler Union im Saarland [*Christian Social Voters' Union in Saarland*] [*Germany Political party*] (PPW) ... CSWU
Christman Air System [*ICAO designator*] (FAAC) ... CAS
Christman Air System [*ICAO designator*] (AD) ... SX
Christmas ... XM
Christmas ... XMAS
Christmas and Easter [*Refers to Church of England members who attend church only on those days*] (DSUE) ... C and E
Christmas Bird Count [*National Audubon Society*] ... CBC
Christmas Club (EA) ... CC
Christmas Factor [*Also, PTC*] [*Hematology*] ... CF
Christmas, FL [*AM radio station call letters*] ... WORL
Christmas Island [*Australia ICAO location identifier*] (ICLI) ... APXM
Christmas Island [*ANSI two-letter standard code*] (CNC) ... CX
Christmas Island [*Kiribati*] [*Airport symbol*] (OAG) ... CXI
Christmas Island [*ANSI three-letter standard code*] (CNC) ... CXR
Christmas Island [*Indian Ocean*] [*MARC geographic area code Library of Congress*] (LCCP) ... i-xa--
Christmas Island [*Indian Ocean*] [*MARC country of publication code Library of Congress*] (LCCP) ... xa
Christmas Island [*Airport symbol*] ... XCH
Christmas Island [*Seismograph station code, US Geological Survey*] (SEIS) ... XMI
Christmas Island Administration and Assembly [*Australia*] ... CIAA
Christmas Island Arbitrator ... CIA
Christmas Island Services Corp. ... CISC
Christmas Island Station [*Military*] (SAA) ... CIS
Christmas Philatelic Club (EA) ... CPC
Christmas Seal and Charity Stamp Society (EA) ... CS & CSS
Christmas Study Unit [*American Topical Association*] (EA) ... CSU
[*A*] **Christmas Trains and Trucks Program** [*Marine Corps program in Vietnam*] ... ACTT
Christmas Tree Pattern ... CTP
Christopher Burns, Inc. [*Also, an information service or system*] (IID) ... CBI
Christopher Columbus Philatelic Society (EA) ... CCPS
Christopher Davies [*Publisher*] [*British*] ... CD
Christopher, IL [*FM radio station call letters*] ... WUEZ
Christopher Morley Knothole Association (EA) ... CMKA
Christopher Newport College, Newport News, VA [*OCLC symbol*] (OCLC) ... VCN
Christopher Newport College, Newport News, VA [*Library symbol Library of Congress*] (LCLS) ... ViNeC
Christopher Robinson's English Admiralty Reports [*165 English Reprint*] [*A publication*] (DLA) ... C Rob
Christopher Robinson's English Admiralty Reports [*165 English Reprint*] [*A publication*] (DLA) ... C Rob Adm
Christopher Robinson's English Admiralty Reports [*165 English Reprint*] [*A publication*] (DLA) ... C Rob (Eng)
Christopher Robinson's English Admiralty Reports [*165 English Reprint*] [*A publication*] (DLA) ... Chr Rob
Christophorus Lanfranchinus [*Deceased, 1490*] [*Authority cited in pre-1607 legal work*] (DSA) ... Christ Lanfran
Christos Lavatus [*An association*] (EA) ... CL
Christ's College [*Cambridge University*] (ROG) ... CH COLL
Christ's College (Cambridge University) (ROG) ... CCC
Christschall [*Record label*] [*Austria*] ... Chr
Christus [*Christ*] [*Latin*] ... X
Christus [*Christ*] [*Latin*] ... XPC
Christus [*Christ*] [*Latin*] ... XS
Christus Dominus [*Decree on the Bishops' Pastoral Office in the Church*] [*Vatican II document*] ... CD
Chritiania Bank og Kreditkasse [*Bank*] [*Norway*] ... K
Chroma Time Compressed Multiplex (NTCM) ... CTCM
Chromacom Proof Recorder (DGA) ... CPR
Chromaffin Granule Amine Transporter [*Biochemistry*] ... CGAT
Chromate (MSA) ... CRMT
Chromate Sensitivity [*Immunology*] ... CS
Chromated Copper Arsenate [*Wood preservative*] ... CCA
Chromated Zinc Chloride [*Wood preservative*] ... CZC
Chromatic Aberration-Free [*Optics*] ... CF
Chromatics Color Sci Wrrt [*NASDAQ symbol*] (TTSB) ... CCSIW
Chromatics Color Sciences [*NASDAQ symbol*] (TTSB) ... CCSI
Chromatics Color Sciences International, Inc. [*NASDAQ symbol*] (SAG) ... CCSI
Chromatics Color Sciences International, Inc. [*Associated Press*] (SAG) ... ChmCS
Chromatics Color Sciences International, Inc. [*Associated Press*] (SAG) ... ChromCS
Chromatid Interchange (PDAA) ... CI
Chromatin Assembly Factor [*Genetics*] ... CAF
Chromatin Protein [*Biochemistry*] ... CP
Chromatofocusing [*Analytical biochemistry*] ... CRF
Chromatogram Automatic Soaking, Scanning, and Digital Recording Apparatus ... CASSANDRA
Chromatographia [*A publication*] ... Chromia
Chromatographic Optimization Function [*Analytical chemistry*] ... COF
Chromatographic Response Factor ... CRF
Chromatographic Separation ... CGS
Chromatographic Specialties Ltd., Brockville, ON, Canada [*Library symbol*] [*Library of Congress*] (LCLS) ... CaOBCS
Chromatographic Specialties Ltd., Brockville, Ontario [*Library symbol National Library of Canada*] (NLC) ... OBCS

Chromatography Control Module [*Instrumentation*] ..... CCM
Chromatography Laboratory Automatic Software ..... CLAS
Chromatography Signal Interface ..... CSI
Chromatopyrography [*for polymer characterization*] ..... CPG
Chromcraft Revington [*NYSE symbol*] (TTSB) ..... CRC
Chromcraft Revington, Inc. [*Associated Press*] (SAG) ..... Chrcft
Chromcraft Revington, Inc. [*NYSE symbol*] (SAG) ..... CRC
Chrome (ROG) ..... CHR
Chrome (VRA) ..... chr
Chrome (MSA) ..... CRM
Chrome and Nickel Plating Logistics Automated Test Electronics System (MCD) ..... CANPLATES
Chrome Card Collectors Club [*Later, D of A*] (EA) CCCC
Chrome Plated [*Freight*] ..... CHRO PLTD
Chrome Plated ..... CP
Chrome Vanadium ..... CRV
Chrome Vanadium ..... CRVAN
Chrome Wire Wheels [*Automotive accessory*] ..... CWW
Chromemoly ..... CroMo
Chromex Nickel Mines Ltd. [*Vancouver Stock Exchange symbol*] ..... CXN
Chromic Acid [*Inorganic chemistry*] (OA) ..... CA
Chrominance [*Video monitor*] C
Chromite [*CIPW classification*] [*Geology*] ..... cm
Chromium [*Chemical symbol is Cr*] (MSA) ..... CHR
Chromium [*Chemical symbol is Cr*] ..... CHROM
Chromium [*Chemical element*] ..... Cr
Chromium Oxalate [*Organic chemistry*] ..... CROX
Chromium Plate [*Metallurgy*] ..... CRPL
Chromium Release Assay [*Clinical chemistry*] ..... CRA
Chrom-Moly (MCD) ..... CM
Chromobacterium (MAE) ..... Chr
Chromogenic (WGA) ..... CH
Chromogenic Systems Analyzer ..... CSA
Chromogranin [*Biochemistry*] ..... Cg
Chromogranin A [*Biochemistry*] ..... CGA
Chromographic Mode Sequencing [*Chromatography*] ..... CMS
Chromolithograph (VRA) ..... chlith
Chromolithograph (DSUE) ..... CHRO
Chromolithograph (ROG) ..... CHROMO
Chromophore-Assisted LASER Inactivation [*Analytical biochemistry*] ..... CALI
Chromosomal Expression Vector [*Genetics*] ..... CEV
Chromosomal Fraction ..... CF
Chromosomal Gonadal Dysgenesis [*Genetics*] (AAMN) ..... CGD
Chromosomal In Situ Suppression [*Genetics*] ..... CISS
Chromosomally-Mediated Resistant Neisseria Gonorrhoeae [*Medicine*] ..... CMRNG
Chromosome [*Genetics*] ..... Chrom
Chromosome Distribution Pattern [*Genetics*] ..... CDP
Chromosome Information System [*Genetics*] ..... CIS
Chromosome Interphase Staining [*Medicine*] ..... CHIPS
Chromosome Modification Site [*Genetics*] (DAVI) ..... CMS
Chromosome-Mediated Gene Transfer [*Biochemistry*] ..... CMGT
Chromotropic Acid (MAE) ..... CTA
Chrondroitin Sulfate Proteoglycans [*Biochemistry*] ..... CSPG
Chronic [*Medicine*] ..... CH
Chronic [*Medicine*] (DMAA) ..... ch
Chronic [*Medicine*] ..... CHR
Chronic [*Medicine*] (AAMN) ..... chron
Chronic Abdominal Tympany [*Medicine*] (AAMN) ..... CAT
Chronic, Acquired, Pure Red Cell Aplasia [*Medicine*] (DMAA) ..... CAPRCA
Chronic Active Autoimmune Hepatitis [*Medicine*] (DMAA) ..... CAAH
Chronic Active Hepatitis [*Medicine*] ..... CAH
Chronic Active Hepatitis Type B [*Medicine*] ..... CAHB
Chronic Active Liver Disease [*Medicine*] ..... CALD
Chronic Affliction Serum Hepatitis [*Medicine*] ..... CASH
Chronic Aggressive Hepatitis [*Medicine*] (MEDA) ..... CAH
Chronic Airflow Limitation [*Medicine*] ..... CAL
Chronic Airway Obstruction [*Medicine*] ..... CAO
Chronic Ambulatory Peritoneal Dialysis [*Medicine*] ..... CAPD
Chronic Anovulation Syndrome [*Medicine*] (MEDA) ..... CAS
Chronic Atrophic Gastritis [*Medicine*] ..... CAG
Chronic Bed Rest [*Medicine*] ..... CBR
Chronic Benign Mucous Membrane Pemphigoid [*Medicine*] ..... CBMMP
Chronic Benign Neutropenia [*Hematology*] (DAVI) ..... CBN
Chronic Beryllium Disease [*Medicine*] (MCD) ..... CBD
Chronic Brain Syndrome [*Medicine*] ..... CBS
Chronic Brain Syndrome [*Medicine*] ..... CHRBRSYN
Chronic Bronchitis [*Medicine*] ..... CB
Chronic Bronchitis and Asthma [*Medicine*] ..... CBA
Chronic Bullous Disease of Children [*Medicine*] (DMAA) ..... CBDC
Chronic Calcific Pancreatitis [*Medicine*] ..... CCP
Chronic Calculous Cholecystitis [*Medicine*] (MAE) CCC
Chronic Cerebellar Stimulation [*Medicine*] ..... CCS
Chronic Cerebrovascular Disease [*Medicine*] (DMAA) ..... CCVD
Chronic Cholestatic Liver Disease [*Medicine*] ..... CCLD
Chronic Complainer [*Medicine*] (DMAA) CC
Chronic Coronary Insufficiency [*Medicine*] CCI
Chronic Cutaneous (Discoid) Lupus Erythematosus [*Medicine*] ..... CCLE
Chronic Daily Headache [*Neurology*] (DAVI) ..... CDH
Chronic Diffuse Interstitial Lung Disease [*Medicine*] (DMAA) ..... CDILD
Chronic Disabling Dermatoses [*Medicine*] ..... CDD
Chronic Discoid Lupus Erythematosus [*Medicine*] (DMAA) ..... CDLE
Chronic Disease Facility [*Medicine*] ..... CDF
Chronic Ectopic Atrial Tachycardia [*Medicine*] (DMAA) ..... CEAT
Chronic Endstage Renal Disease [*Nephrology*] ..... CERD
Chronic Enthusiasm Disorder [*Medicine*] (MEDA) ..... CED
Chronic Epstein-Barr Virus [*Medicine*] ..... CEBV
Chronic Ethanolism [*Chemical dependency*] (DAVI) ..... Chr Etoh
Chronic False Positive [*Test*] [*Medicine*] ..... CFP
Chronic Fatigue Immune Dysfunction Syndrome [*Medicine*] ..... CFIDS
Chronic Fatigue Immune Dysfunction Syndrome Association (EA) ..... CFIDSA
Chronic Fatigue Syndrome [*Medicine*] ..... CFS
Chronic Fatigue Syndrome Society, International (EA) ..... CFSS
Chronic Gastrointestinal [*Tract*] **Bleeding** [*Gastroenterology*] (DAVI) ..... CGB
Chronic Glomerulonephritis [*Medicine*] ..... CG
Chronic Glomerulonephritis [*Medicine*] ..... CGN
Chronic Glomerulonephritis [*Nephrology*] (DAVI) ..... Ch GN
Chronic Gonadotropin, Beta-Unit [*Medicine*] (DMAA) ..... CGB
Chronic Graft-Versus-Host Disease [*Medicine*] ..... CGVHD
Chronic Granulocytic Leukemia [*Medicine*] ..... CGL
Chronic Granulomatous Disease [*Medicine*] ..... CGD
Chronic Heart Failure [*Cardiology*] (DAVI) ..... CHF
Chronic Hemodialysis [*Nephrology*] ..... CHD
Chronic Hemolytic Anemia [*Medicine*] ..... CHA
Chronic Hepatitis B [*Medicine*] ..... CHB
Chronic Hepatitis B [*Medicine*] (DMAA) ..... CHB
Chronic Hypoxic Lung Disease [*Medicine*] (DMAA) ..... CHLD
Chronic Idiopathic Anhidrosis [*Medicine*] (DAVI) ..... CIA
Chronic Idiopathic Intesinal Pseudo-Obstruction Syndrome [*Medicine*] (DMAA) ..... CIIPS
Chronic Idiopathic Thrombocytopenic Purpura [*Medicine*] ..... CITP
Chronic Idiopathic Ulcerative Colitis [*Gastroenterology*] ..... CIUC
Chronic Idiopathic Urticaria [*Dermatology*] (DAVI) ..... CIU
Chronic Infantile Neurological Cutaneous and Auricular [*Syndrome*] [*Medicine*] (DMAA) ..... CINCA
Chronic Infectious Neuropathic Agents [*Medicine*] ..... CHINA
Chronic Inflammatory Bowel Disease [*Medicine*] ..... CIBD
Chronic Inflammatory Demyelinating Polyradiculoneuropathy [*Neurology*] (DAVI) ..... CIDP
Chronic Inflammatory Polyneuropathy [*Medicine*] (DMAA) ..... CIPN
Chronic Interstitial Nephritis [*Medicine*] (MAE) ..... CIN
Chronic Intractable Benign Pain [*Medicine*] (DMAA) ..... CIBP
Chronic Intractable Benign Pain Syndrome [*Medicine*] (DMAA) ..... CIBPS
Chronic Leukemia [*Hematology and oncology*] (DAVI) CL
Chronic Liver Disease [*Medicine*] ..... CLD
Chronic Lobular Hepatitis [*Medicine*] (MAE) ..... CLH
Chronic Low Back Pain [*Medicine*] (DMAA) ..... CLBP
Chronic Lung Disease [*Medicine*] ..... CLD
Chronic Lymphatic [*or Lymphocytic*] **Leukemia** [*Medicine*] CLL
Chronic Lymphocytic Thyroiditis [*Medicine*] ..... CLT
Chronic Lymphosarcoma Cell Leukemia [*Medicine*] (MAE) ..... CLSL
Chronic Megakaryocytic Granulocytic Myelosis [*Medicine*] ..... CMGM
Chronic Membranoproliferative Glomerulonephritis [*Immunology*] ..... CMPGN
Chronic Membranous Glomerulonephritis [*Medicine*] (MAE) ..... CMGN
Chronic Mental Defective [*British*] (ADA) ..... CMD
Chronic Mesenteric Ischemia [*Medicine*] ..... CMI
Chronic Monoblastic Leukemia [*Hematology and oncology*] (DAVI) ..... CMoL
Chronic Monocytic Leukemia [*Medicine*] (MAE) ..... CMoL
Chronic Mucocutaneous Candidiasis [*Medicine*] ..... CMC
Chronic Mucocutaneous Candidiasis [*Medicine*] (DMAA) ..... CMCC
Chronic Mucocutaneous Moniliasis [*Medicine*] (DAVI) ..... CMC
Chronic Myelocytic [*or Myeloid or Myelogenous*] **Leukemia** [*Oncology*] ..... CML
Chronic Myelomonocytic Leukemia [*Oncology*] ..... CMML
Chronic Myelomonocytic Leukemia in Transition [*Oncology*] ..... CMMLIT
Chronic Myeloproliferative Disorder [*Medicine*] (DMAA) ..... CMPD
Chronic Nerve Irritation [*Medicine*] (DMAA) ..... CNI
Chronic Nervous Exhaustion [*Medicine*] ..... CNE
Chronic Nervous Exhaustion Syndrome [*Medicine*] (DMAA) ..... CNES
Chronic Nodular Fibrositis [*Medicine*] (DMAA) ..... CNF
Chronic Nonspecific Diarrhea [*Medicine*] ..... CNSD
Chronic Nonspecific Lung Disease (CPH) ..... CNSLD
Chronic Nonvalvular Atrial Fibrillation [*Medicine*] (DMAA) ..... CNAF
Chronic Obstruction of Biliary Tract [*Medicine*] ..... COBT
Chronic Obstructive Airflow Limitation [*Medicine*] (DMAA) ..... COAL
Chronic Obstructive Airway Disease [*Medicine*] ..... COAD
Chronic Obstructive Arterial Disease [*Cardiology*] (DAVI) ..... COAD
Chronic Obstructive Bronchitis [*Medicine*] (DMAA) ..... COB
Chronic Obstructive Lung Disease [*Medicine*] ..... COLD
Chronic Obstructive Outflow Disease [*Medicine*] ..... COOD
Chronic Obstructive Pulmonary Disease [*Medicine*] ..... COPD
Chronic Obstructive Pulmonary Emphysema [*Medicine*] ..... COPE
Chronic Obstructive Respiratory Disease [*Medicine*] ..... CORD
Chronic Open Angle Glaucoma [*Ophthalmology*] ..... COAG
Chronic Organic Brain Syndrome [*Medicine*] ..... COBS
Chronic Otitis Media [*Medicine*] ..... COM
Chronic Pain (DAVI) ..... CP
Chronic Pain Anonymous [*Self-help program*] ..... CPA
Chronic Pain Support Group (EA) ..... CPSG
Chronic Pancreatic Insufficiency [*Medicine*] ..... CPI
Chronic Pancreatitis [*Medicine*] (PDAA) ..... CP
Chronic Passive Congestion [*Medicine*] ..... CPC
Chronic Pelvic Inflammatory Disease [*Gynecology*] (DAVI) ..... CPID
Chronic Persistent Hepatitis [*Medicine*] ..... CPH
Chronic Polyneuropathy [*Medicine*] (AAMN) ..... CPN
Chronic Post-Traumatic Headache [*Neurology*] (DAVI) ..... CPTH
Chronic Progressive [*Medicine*] ..... CP
Chronic Progressive Coccidioidal Pneumonitis [*Medicine*] ..... CPCP
Chronic Progressive External Ophthalmoplegia [*Ophthalmology*] ..... CPEO
Chronic Progressive Multiple Sclerosis [*Medicine*] (DMAA) ..... CPMS
Chronic Progressive Renal Disease [*Medicine*] (CPH) ..... CPRD

Chronic Proliferative Glomerulonephritis [*Immunology*] ... CPGN
Chronic Pulmonary Disease (BARN) ... CPD
Chronic Pulmonary Emphysema [*Medicine*] ... CPE
Chronic Pulmonary Insufficiency of Prematurity [*Medicine*] (DMAA) ... CPIP
Chronic Pyelonephritis [*Urology*] ... CP
Chronic Pyelonephritis [*Urology*] ... CPN
Chronic Reactive Lymphadenopathy Syndrome [*Medicine*] ... CRLS
Chronic Rejection [*Medicine*] ... CR
Chronic Renal Disease [*Medicine*] ... CRD
Chronic Renal Failure [*Medicine*] ... CRF
Chronic Respiratory Disease [*Medicine*] ... CRD
Chronic Respiratory Failure [*Medicine*] (DAVI) ... CRF
Chronic Restrictive Pulmonary Disease [*Medicine*] (DMAA) ... CRPD
Chronic Schizophrenia (AAMN) ... CS
Chronic Serous Otitis Media [*Otorhinolaryngology*] (DAVI) ... CSOM
Chronic Simple Glaucoma [*Ophthalmology*] (CPH) ... CSG
Chronic Spinal Muscular Atrophy [*Medicine*] (DMAA) ... CSMA
Chronic Stasis Leg Ulcer [*Medicine*] (AAMN) ... CSLU
Chronic Subclinical Scurvy [*Medicine*] ... CSS
Chronic Subdural Hematoma [*Medicine*] ... CSH
Chronic Suppurative Otitus Media [*Otolaryngology*] ... CSOM
Chronic Ulcerative Colitis [*Medicine*] ... CUC
Chronic Undifferentiated Schizophrenia [*Psychiatry*] (DAVI) ... CUS
Chronic Urticaria [*Immunology*] ... CU
Chronic Uterine Inflammation [*Medicine*] ... CUI
Chronic Villous Arthritis [*Medicine*] (DMAA) ... CVA
Chronica [*of St. Jerome*] [*Classical studies*] (OCD) ... Chron
Chronica Juridicalia [*A publication*] (DLA) ... Chron Jur
Chronically Mentally Ill [*Medicine*] ... CMI
Chronicle ... CHRNCL
Chronicle ... CHRON
Chronicle of Higher Education [*A publication*] (BRI) ... CHE
Chronicles [*Old Testament book*] (BJA) ... Ch
Chronicles [*Old Testament book*] ... Chr
Chronicles [*Old Testament book*] ... Chron
Chronicles Concerning Early Babylonian Kings [*A publication*] (BJA) ... CCEBK
Chronicles of the Divorce Courts [*A publication*] (DLA) ... Chron Div Cts
Chronik der Christlichen Welt [*A publication*] (BJA) ... ChChW
Chronimed, Inc. [*NASDAQ symbol*] (SAG) ... CHMD
Chronimed, Inc. [*Associated Press*] (SAG) ... Chronimd
Chronium (ROG) ... C
Chronocoulometry [*Electrochemistry*] ... CC
Chronological ... CHRON
Chronological (AFM) ... CHRONO
Chronological Age [*Psychology*] ... CA
Chronology ... chron
Chronology of African-American History [*A publication*] ... CAAH
Chronology of Hispanic-American History [*A publication*] ... CHAH
Chronology of Native North American History [*A publication*] ... CNNAH
Chronology of Twentieth-Century Eastern European History [*A publication*] ... CTCEEH
Chronology of Womens's History [*A publication*] ... CWH
Chronometer ... CHRON
Chronometer (ROG) ... CHRONTER
Chronometer ... CRNMTR
Chronometer Correction [*Navigation*] ... CC
Chronometer Error [*Navigation*] ... CE
Chronometer Time [*Navigation*] ... C
Chronometer Time [*Navigation*] (IAA) ... CT
Chronometer Time Minus Watch Time [*Navigation*] ... C-W
Chronometric ... CRNMTC
Chronopotentiometric Stripping Analysis [*Analytical electrochemistry*] ... CPSA
Chrostwaite's Pennsylvania Municipal Law Reporter [*A publication*] (DLA) ... Mun L Rep
Chrysanthemum [*Horticulture*] (DSUE) ... CHRYSANT
Chrysanthemum [*Horticulture*] ... Mum
Chrysanthemum Chlorotic Mottle Viroid ... ChCMV
Chrysanthemum Stunt Viroid ... CSV
Chrysanthemum Virus B [*Plant pathology*] ... CVB
Chrysler ... CHRYSLR
Chrysler Art Museum, Jean Outland Chrysler Library, Norfolk, VA [*Library symbol Library of Congress*] (LCLS) ... ViNC
Chrysler Car Club Council (EA) ... CCCC
Chrysler Collision Detection [*Automotive safety and electronics*] ... C2D
Chrysler Corp. [*NYSE symbol Toronto Stock Exchange symbol*] (SPSG) ... C
Chrysler Corp. ... CC
Chrysler Corp. ... CHRY
Chrysler Corp. [*Associated Press*] (SAG) ... Chryslr
Chrysler Corp., Engineering Division, Detroit, MI [*Library symbol Library of Congress*] (LCLS) ... MiDChryE
Chrysler Corporation Missile Division (MCD) ... CCMD
Chrysler Corporation Space Division (KSC) ... CCSD
Chrysler de Mexico SA [*Chrysler Corp.*] ... CdM
Chrysler Financial Corp. ... CFC
Chrysler Historical Foundation ... CHF
Chrysler Improved Numerical Differencing Analyzer [*Computer science*] ... CINDA
Chrysler Improved Numerical Differencing Analyzer for Third-Generation Computers [*Computer science*] ... CINDA-3G
Chrysler Information Resources Center [*Pronounced "serk"*] ... CIRC
Chrysler LASER Atlas Satellite System [*Automotive engineering*] ... CLASS
Chrysler Optical Processing Scanner ... COPS
Chrysler Performance Parts Association (EA) ... CPPA
Chrysler Product Owners Club (EA) ... CPOC
Chrysler Products Restorers Club [*Later, CRC*] (EA) ... CPRC
Chrysler Restorers Club [*Formerly, CPRC*] (EA) ... CRC
Chrysler Town and Country Owners Registry (EA) ... CTCOR
Chrysler Town and Country Owners Registry (EA) ... CTCR
Chrysler Town and Country Owners Registry (EA) ... TCOR
Chrysoberyl [*Jewelry*] (ROG) ... CHRS
Chrysoberyl [*Jewelry*] (ROG) ... CS
Chrysolite [*Jewelry*] (ROG) ... CRY
CHS Aviation Ltd. [*Kenya*] [*ICAO designator*] (FAAC) ... HSA
CHS Electronics [*NASDAQ symbol*] (TTSB) ... CHSE
CHS Electronics, Inc. [*Associated Press*] (SAG) ... CHS El
CHS Electronics, Inc. [*NASDAQ symbol*] (SAG) ... CHSE
Chualar, CA [*FM radio station call letters*] ... KHDC
Chuan Hup Canada [*Vancouver Stock Exchange symbol*] ... CJU
Chub Cay [*Bahamas*] [*Airport symbol*] (OAG) ... CCZ
Chub Cay, Berry Island [*Bahamas*] [*ICAO location identifier*] (ICLI) ... MYBC
[*The*] **Chubb Corp.** [*NYSE symbol*] (SPSG) ... CB
[*The*] **Chubb Corp.** [*Associated Press*] (SAG) ... Chubb
Chubbuck, ID [*AM radio station call letters*] ... KRCD
Chubbuck, ID [*FM radio station call letters*] ... KRSS
Chuchupate [*California*] [*Seismograph station code, US Geological Survey Closed*] (SEIS) ... CHP
Chuck Jaws [*Tools*] ... CCJW
Chuck Jennings Fan Club [*Defunct*] (EA) ... CJFC
Chuck Norris International Fan Club (EA) ... CNIFC
Chuian-Garon [*Former USSR Seismograph station code, US Geological Survey Closed*] (SEIS) ... CGT
Chukchi Sea Circulation Study [*Marine science*] (OSRA) ... CSCS
Chukchi Sea Circulation Study (USDC) ... CSCS
Chukyo University [*UTLAS symbol*] ... CUL
Chula Vista Public Library, Chula Vista, CA [*Library symbol Library of Congress*] (LCLS) ... CChu
Chulman [*Former USSR ICAO location identifier*] (ICLI) ... UELL
CHUM Ltd. [*Toronto Stock Exchange symbol*] ... CHM
Chumleigh [*England*] ... CHUM
Chumpon [*Thailand*] [*ICAO location identifier*] (ICLI) ... VTSD
Chums, Inc. [*An association*] (EA) ... CI
Chunchon [*South Korea ICAO location identifier*] (ICLI) ... RKNC
Chung Wah Association [*Australia*] ... CWA
Chung Wah Society [*Northern Territory*] [*Australia*] ... CWS
Chung-Hau Min Kuo [*Republic of China*] ... CHMK
Chungju [*South Korea ICAO location identifier*] (ICLI) ... RKTC
Chungking [*China*] [*Airport symbol*] (AD) ... CKG
Chunya [*Tanzania*] [*ICAO location identifier*] (ICLI) ... HTCH
Chun-ying [*Leung*] [*Hong Kong politician*] ... CY
Chur [*Coire*] [*Switzerland*] [*Seismograph station code, US Geological Survey*] [*Closed*] (SEIS) ... CHU
Church ... C
Church ... CH
Church (VRA) ... ch
Church [*Alaska*] [*Seismograph station code, US Geological Survey*] (SEIS) ... CHB
Church (ROG) ... CHCH
Church (MCD) ... CHR
Church ... CHU
Church Action with the Unemployed [*Church of England*] ... CAWTU
Church Aircraft Ltd. [*ICAO designator*] (FAAC) ... CHU
Church & Dwight [*NYSE symbol*] (TTSB) ... CHD
Church & Dwight Co., Inc. [*NYSE symbol*] (SPSG) ... CHD
Church & Dwight Co., Inc. [*Associated Press*] (SAG) ... ChrDwt
Church and Peace [*Schoeffengrund, Federal Republic of Germany*] (EAIO) ... CaP
Church and Synagogue Library Association (EA) ... CSLA
Church Architectural Guild of America [*Later, IFRAA*] (EA) ... CAGA
Church Army [*An association*] (EA) ... CA
Church Army Society (EA) ... CAS
Church Assembly Measure (DLA) ... CAM
Church Association [*British*] ... CA
Church Association for Seamen's Work [*Later, SCI*] (EA) ... CASW
Church Building Society [*British*] ... CBS
Church Center for the United Nations (EA) ... CCUN
Church Coalition for Human Rights in the Philippines (EA) ... CCHRP
Church Committee for Human Rights in Asia (EA) ... CCHRA
Church Council on Justice and Correction [*Conseil des Eglises pour la Justiceet la Criminologie*], Ottawa, Ontario [*Library symbol National Library of Canada*] (BIB) ... OOCCJ
Church Council on Justice & Corrections [*Conseil des Eglises pour la Justice et la Criminologie*] (AC) ... CCJC
Church Defence Institution [*British*] ... CDI
Church Elementary School, Rockford, IL [*Library symbol*] [*Library of Congress*] (LCLS) ... IRoChE
Church Employed Women (EA) ... CEW
Church Evangelism Association [*Later, Masterkey Association*] (EA) ... CEA
Church Executive Development Board ... CEDB
Church Extension Association [*British*] ... CEA
Church Family Newspaper [*A publication*] (ROG) ... CFN
Church Fenton [*British ICAO location identifier*] (ICLI) ... EGXG
Church Furniture Manufacturers Association [*Defunct*] (EA) ... CFMA
Church Growth Center (EA) ... CGC
Church Guilds Union [*British*] ... CGU
Church Heritage [*A publication*] (APTA) ... CH
Church Hill, TN [*AM radio station call letters*] ... WMCH
Church Historical Society [*Later, HSEC*] (EA) ... CHS
Church Historical Society, Austin, TX [*Library symbol Library of Congress*] (LCLS) ... TxAuCH
Church History [*A publication*] (BRI) ... CH
Church Information Office [*British*] ... CIO

Church Jesus Christ of Latter-Day Saints, Genealogical Society Library, Cleveland Branch, Westlake, OH [*Library symbol*] [*Library of Congress*] (LCLS) .... OWIGS
Church Lads and Church Girls Brigade [*British*] [*An association*] (DBA) .... CL & CGB
Church Lads' Brigade [*Church of England*] .... CLB
Church League of America [*Defunct*] (EA) .... CLA
Church Literature Association [*British*] (BI) .... CLA
Church Missionary (IIA) .... CM
Church Missionary College [*Church of England*] .... CMCOLL
Church Missionary Society [*British*] .... CMS
Church Missionary Society of Australia .... CMSA
Church Missionary Union [*British*] .... CMU
Church Monuments Society (EA) .... CMS
Church Music Association [*British*] .... CMA
Church Music Association of America (EA) .... CMAA
Church Music Publishers Association (EA) .... CMPA
Church Music Trust [*British*] (BI) .... CMT
Church of Christ CC
Church of Christ, Scientist .... CCS
Church of England .... C of E
Church of England .... CE
Church of England .... COE
Church of England Boys' School in Tasmania [*Australia*] .... CEBST
Church of England Children's Society .... CECS
Church of England Historical Society (ADA) .... CEHS
Church of England Historical Society [*Australia*] .... COEHS
Church of England Men's Society .... CEMS
Church of England Newspaper .... CEN
Church of England School [*British*] .... E
Church of England Soldiers', Sailors', and Airmen's Club .... CESSA
Church of England Soldiers', Sailors', and Airmen's Clubs .... CESSAC
Church of England Sunday School Institute .... CESSI
Church of England Temperance Society .... CETS
Church of England Women's Help Society [*British*] .... CEWHS
Church of England Working Men's Society .... CEWMS
Church of England Young Men's Society .... CEYMS
Church of England Young People's Assembly [*British*] .... CEYPA
Church of England Youth Council (BI) .... CEYC
Church of England Zenana Missionary Society [*British*] .... CEZMS
Church of God, Men International (EA) .... CGMI
Church of God Peace Fellowship (EA) .... CGPF
Church of Ireland .... C of I
Church of Ireland .... C of IRE
Church of Ireland Young Men's Society .... CIYMS
Church of Jesus Christ of Latter-Day Saints, Genealogical Society Library, Adelaide Stake Branch, Firle, SA, Australia [*Library symbol Library of Congress*] (LCLS) .... AuFirGS
Church of Jesus Christ of Latter-Day Saints, Genealogical Society Library, AftonBranch, Afton, WY [*Library symbol Library of Congress*] (LCLS) .... WyAGS
Church of Jesus Christ of Latter-Day Saints, Genealogical Society Library, Albany New York Stake Branch, Loudonville, NY [*Library symbol Library of Congress*] (LCLS) .... NLouvGS
Church of Jesus Christ of Latter-Day Saints, Genealogical Society Library, Albuquerque Branch, Albuquerque, NM [*Library symbol Library of Congress*] (LCLS) .... NmAGS
Church of Jesus Christ of Latter-Day Saints, Genealogical Society Library, Anaheim Branch, Anaheim, CA [*Library symbol Library of Congress*] (LCLS) .... CAnaGS
Church of Jesus Christ of Latter-Day Saints, Genealogical Society Library, Anchorage Branch, Anchorage, AK [*Library symbol Library of Congress*] (LCLS) .... AkAGS
Church of Jesus Christ of Latter-Day Saints, Genealogical Society Library, Annandale Branch, Annandale, VA [*Library symbol Library of Congress*] (LCLS) .... ViAnGS
Church of Jesus Christ of Latter-Day Saints, Genealogical Society Library, Arvada Branch, Arvada, CO [*Library symbol Library of Congress*] (LCLS) .... CoArGS
Church of Jesus Christ of Latter-Day Saints, Genealogical Society Library, Auckland Branch, Auckland, New Zealand [*Library symbol Library of Congress*] (LCLS) .... NzAGS
Church of Jesus Christ of Latter-Day Saints, Genealogical Society Library, Augusta Branch, Farmingdale, ME [*Library symbol Library of Congress*] (LCLS) .... MeFarGS
Church of Jesus Christ of Latter-Day Saints, Genealogical Society Library, Austin Branch, Austin, TX [*Library symbol Library of Congress*] (LCLS) .... TxAuGS
Church of Jesus Christ of Latter-Day Saints, Genealogical Society Library, Bakersfield Branch, Bakersfield, CA [*Library symbol Library of Congress*] (LCLS) .... CBaGS
Church of Jesus Christ of Latter-Day Saints, Genealogical Society Library, Barstow Branch, Barstow, CA [*Library symbol Library of Congress*] (LCLS) .... CBarGS
Church of Jesus Christ of Latter-Day Saints, Genealogical Society Library, BatonRouge Branch, Baton Rouge, LA [*Library symbol Library of Congress*] (LCLS) .... LBrGS
Church of Jesus Christ of Latter-Day Saints, Genealogical Society Library, Bear Lake Branch, Montpelier, ID [*Library symbol Library of Congress*] (LCLS) .... IdMonGS
Church of Jesus Christ of Latter-Day Saints, Genealogical Society Library, Beaumont Branch, Vidor, TX [*Library symbol Library of Congress*] (LCLS) .... TxVidGS
Church of Jesus Christ of Latter-Day Saints, Genealogical Society Library, Beaver Branch, Beaver, UT [*Library symbol Library of Congress*] (LCLS) .... UBeGS
Church of Jesus Christ of Latter-Day Saints, Genealogical Society Library, Beaverton Branch, Beaverton, OR [*Library symbol Library of Congress*] (LCLS) .... OrBGS
Church of Jesus Christ of Latter-Day Saints, Genealogical Society Library, Bellevue Branch, Bellevue, WA [*Library symbol Library of Congress*] (LCLS) .... WaBGS
Church of Jesus Christ of Latter-Day Saints, Genealogical Society Library, Billings Branch, Billings, MT [*Library symbol Library of Congress*] (LCLS) .... MtBilGS
Church of Jesus Christ of Latter-Day Saints, Genealogical Society Library, Blackfoot West Branch, Stake Center, Blackfoot, ID [*Library symbol Library of Congress*] (LCLS) .... IdBfGS
Church of Jesus Christ of Latter-Day Saints, Genealogical Society Library, Bloomfield Hills Branch, Bloomfield Hills, MI [*Library symbol Library of Congress*] (LCLS) .... MiBloGS
Church of Jesus Christ of Latter-Day Saints, Genealogical Society Library, Boston Branch, Weston, MA [*Library symbol Library of Congress*] (LCLS) .... MWestonGS
Church of Jesus Christ of Latter-Day Saints, Genealogical Society Library, Boulder Stake Branch, Boulder, CO [*Library symbol Library of Congress*] (LCLS) .... CoBGS
Church of Jesus Christ of Latter-Day Saints, Genealogical Society Library, Brigham City South Branch, Brigham City, UT [*Library symbol Library of Congress*] (LCLS) .... UBcGS
Church of Jesus Christ of Latter-Day Saints, Genealogical Society Library, Burley Branch, Burley, ID [*Library symbol Library of Congress*] (LCLS) .... IdBurGS
Church of Jesus Christ of Latter-Day Saints, Genealogical Society Library, ButteStake Branch, Dillon Chapel, Dillon, MT [*Library symbol Library of Congress*] (LCLS) .... MtDiGS
Church of Jesus Christ of Latter-Day Saints, Genealogical Society Library, CacheBranch, Logan, UT [*Library symbol Library of Congress*] (LCLS) .... ULGS
Church of Jesus Christ of Latter-Day Saints, Genealogical Society Library, Caldwell Branch, Summit, NJ [*Library symbol Library of Congress*] (LCLS) .... NjSGS
Church of Jesus Christ of Latter-Day Saints, Genealogical Society Library, Calgary Branch, Calgary, AB, Canada [*Library symbol Library of Congress*] (LCLS) .... CaACCJC
Church of Jesus Christ of Latter-Day Saints, Genealogical Society Library, Canterbury Branch, Christchurch, New Zealand [*Library symbol Library of Congress*] (LCLS) .... NzCGS
Church of Jesus Christ of Latter-Day Saints, Genealogical Society Library, Cardston Branch, Cardston, AB, Canada [*Library symbol Library of Congress*] (LCLS) .... CaACaCJC
Church of Jesus Christ of Latter-Day Saints, Genealogical Society Library, Casper Branch, Casper, WY [*Library symbol Library of Congress*] (LCLS) .... WyCaGS
Church of Jesus Christ of Latter-Day Saints, Genealogical Society Library, Champaign Stake Branch, Champaign, IL [*Library symbol Library of Congress*] (LCLS) .... IChamGS
Church of Jesus Christ of Latter-Day Saints, Genealogical Society Library, Charlotte North Carolina Branch, Charlotte, NC [*Library symbol Library of Congress*] (LCLS) .... NcCGS
Church of Jesus Christ of Latter-Day Saints, Genealogical Society Library, Cheyenne Branch, Cheyenne, WY [*Library symbol Library of Congress*] (LCLS) .... WyCGS
Church of Jesus Christ of Latter-Day Saints, Genealogical Society Library, Chicago Heights Branch, Chicago Heights, IL [*Library symbol Library of Congress*] (LCLS) .... IChGS
Church of Jesus Christ of Latter-Day Saints, Genealogical Society Library, ChicoBranch, Stake Center, Chico, CA [*Library symbol Library of Congress*] (LCLS) .... CChiGS
Church of Jesus Christ of Latter-Day Saints, Genealogical Society Library, Cincinnati Branch, Cincinnati, OH [*Library symbol Library of Congress*] (LCLS) .... OCGS
Church of Jesus Christ of Latter-Day Saints, Genealogical Society Library, Cleveland Branch, Westlake, OH [*Library symbol Library of Congress*] (LCLS) .... OWIGS
Church of Jesus Christ of Latter-Day Saints, Genealogical Society Library, Cody Branch, Cody, WY [*Library symbol Library of Congress*] (LCLS) .... WyCoGS
Church of Jesus Christ of Latter-Day Saints, Genealogical Society Library, Colonia Juarez Branch, Chihuahua, Mexico [*Library symbol Library of Congress*] (LCLS) .... MxChGS
Church of Jesus Christ of Latter-Day Saints, Genealogical Society Library, Colorado Springs Branch, Colorado Springs, CO [*Library symbol Library of Congress*] (LCLS) .... CoCGS
Church of Jesus Christ of Latter-Day Saints, Genealogical Society Library, Columbia Branch, Columbia, SC [*Library symbol Library of Congress*] (LCLS) .... ScCoGS
Church of Jesus Christ of Latter-Day Saints, Genealogical Society Library, Columbia Missouri Branch, Columbia, MO [*Library symbol Library of Congress*] (LCLS) .... MoCoGS
Church of Jesus Christ of Latter-Day Saints, Genealogical Society Library, Columbus Branch, Columbus, OH [*Library symbol Library of Congress*] (LCLS) .... OCoGS
Church of Jesus Christ of Latter-Day Saints, Genealogical Society Library, Coos Bay Stake Branch, North Bend, OR [*Library symbol Library of Congress*] (LCLS) .... OrNbGS
Church of Jesus Christ of Latter-Day Saints, Genealogical Society Library, Corpus Christi Branch, Corpus Christi, TX [*Library symbol Library of Congress*] (LCLS) .... TxCcGS

Church of Jesus Christ of Latter-Day Saints, Genealogical Society Library, Corvallis Branch, Corvallis, OR [*Library symbol Library of Congress*] (LCLS) .... OrCGS
Church of Jesus Christ of Latter-Day Saints, Genealogical Society Library, Covina Branch, Covina, CA [*Library symbol Library of Congress*] (LCLS) .... CCovGS
Church of Jesus Christ of Latter-Day Saints, Genealogical Society Library, Dallas Branch, Dallas, TX [*Library symbol Library of Congress*] (LCLS) .... TxDaGS
Church of Jesus Christ of Latter-Day Saints, Genealogical Society Library, Dayton Ohio Branch, Dayton, OH [*Library symbol Library of Congress*] (LCLS) .... ODaGL
Church of Jesus Christ of Latter-Day Saints, Genealogical Society Library, Dearborn Stake Branch, LDS Chapel, Dearborn, MI [*Library symbol Library of Congress*] (LCLS) .... MiDbGS
Church of Jesus Christ of Latter-Day Saints, Genealogical Society Library, Denver Branch, Stake Center, Denver, CO [*Library symbol Library of Congress*] (LCLS) .... CoDGL
Church of Jesus Christ of Latter-Day Saints, Genealogical Society Library, Denver North Branch, Northglenn, CO [*Library symbol Library of Congress*] (LCLS) .... CoNgGS
Church of Jesus Christ of Latter-Day Saints, Genealogical Society Library, Des Moines Branch, West Des Moines, IA [*Library symbol Library of Congress*] (LCLS) .... IaWdmGS
Church of Jesus Christ of Latter-Day Saints, Genealogical Society Library, Driggs Branch, Driggs, ID [*Library symbol Library of Congress*] (LCLS) .... IdDrGS
Church of Jesus Christ of Latter-Day Saints, Genealogical Society Library, Duchesne Branch, Stake Center, Duchesne, UT [*Library symbol Library of Congress*] (LCLS) .... UDucGS
Church of Jesus Christ of Latter-Day Saints, Genealogical Society Library, Durango Stake Branch, Cortez, CO [*Library symbol Library of Congress*] (LCLS) .... CoCoGS
Church of Jesus Christ of Latter-Day Saints, Genealogical Society Library, East Brunswick Stake Branch, East Brunswick, NJ [*Library symbol Library of Congress*] (LCLS) .... NjEbGS
Church of Jesus Christ of Latter-Day Saints, Genealogical Society Library, Edmonton Branch, Edmonton, AB, Canada [*Library symbol Library of Congress*] (LCLS) .... CaAECJC
Church of Jesus Christ of Latter-Day Saints, Genealogical Society Library, El Paso Branch, El Paso, TX [*Library symbol Library of Congress*] (LCLS) .... TxEGS
Church of Jesus Christ of Latter-Day Saints, Genealogical Society Library, Ely Branch, Ely, NV [*Library symbol Library of Congress*] (LCLS) .... NvElGS
Church of Jesus Christ of Latter-Day Saints, Genealogical Society Library, Eugene Branch, Eugene, OR [*Library symbol Library of Congress*] (LCLS) .... OrEGS
Church of Jesus Christ of Latter-Day Saints, Genealogical Society Library, Eureka Branch, Eureka, CA [*Library symbol Library of Congress*] (LCLS) .... CEGS
Church of Jesus Christ of Latter-Day Saints, Genealogical Society Library, Evanston Branch, Evanston, WY [*Library symbol Library of Congress*] (LCLS) .... WyEvGS
Church of Jesus Christ of Latter-Day Saints, Genealogical Society Library, Everett, Washington Stake Branch, Everett, WA [*Library symbol Library of Congress*] (LCLS) .... WaEGS
Church of Jesus Christ of Latter-Day Saints, Genealogical Society Library, Fairbanks Alaska District Branch, Fairbanks, AK [*Library symbol Library of Congress*] (LCLS) .... AkFGS
Church of Jesus Christ of Latter-Day Saints, Genealogical Society Library, Fallon Branch, Fallon, NV [*Library symbol Library of Congress*] (LCLS) .... NvFGS
Church of Jesus Christ of Latter-Day Saints, Genealogical Society Library, Farmington Branch, Farmington, NM [*Library symbol Library of Congress*] (LCLS) .... NmFGS
Church of Jesus Christ of Latter-Day Saints, Genealogical Society Library, Flagstaff Branch, Flagstaff, AZ [*Library symbol Library of Congress*] (LCLS) .... AzFGS
Church of Jesus Christ of Latter-Day Saints, Genealogical Society Library, Fort Collins Branch, Fort Collins, CO [*Library symbol Library of Congress*] (LCLS) .... CoFGS
Church of Jesus Christ of Latter-Day Saints, Genealogical Society Library, Fort Wayne Branch, Fort Wayne, IN [*Library symbol Library of Congress*] (LCLS) .... InFwGS
Church of Jesus Christ of Latter-Day Saints, Genealogical Society Library, Fort Worth Branch, North Richland Hills, Fort Worth, TX [*Library symbol Library of Congress*] (LCLS) .... TxFGS
Church of Jesus Christ of Latter-Day Saints, Genealogical Society Library, Fresno Branch, Fresno, CA [*Library symbol Library of Congress*] (LCLS) .... CFGS
Church of Jesus Christ of Latter-Day Saints, Genealogical Society Library, Gettysburg Branch, York, PA [*Library symbol Library of Congress*] (LCLS) .... PYGS
Church of Jesus Christ of Latter-Day Saints, Genealogical Society Library, GrandJunction Branch, Stake Center, Grand Junction, CO [*Library symbol Library of Congress*] (LCLS) .... CoGjGS
Church of Jesus Christ of Latter-Day Saints, Genealogical Society Library, GreatFalls Branch, Great Falls, MT [*Library symbol Library of Congress*] (LCLS) .... MtGrGS
Church of Jesus Christ of Latter-Day Saints, Genealogical Society Library, Gresham Branch, Gresham, OR [*Library symbol Library of Congress*] (LCLS) .... OrGrGS
Church of Jesus Christ of Latter-Day Saints, Genealogical Society Library, Gridley Branch, Gridley, CA [*Library symbol Library of Congress*] (LCLS) .... CGrlGS
Church of Jesus Christ of Latter-Day Saints, Genealogical Society Library, Hartford Branch, Manchester, CT [*Library symbol Library of Congress*] (LCLS) .... CtManGS
Church of Jesus Christ of Latter-Day Saints, Genealogical Society Library, Helena Branch, Helena, MT [*Library symbol Library of Congress*] (LCLS) .... MtHGS
Church of Jesus Christ of Latter-Day Saints, Genealogical Society Library, Holbrook Branch, Holbrook, AZ [*Library symbol Library of Congress*] (LCLS) .... AzHGS
Church of Jesus Christ of Latter-Day Saints, Genealogical Society Library, Houston Branch, Houston, TX [*Library symbol Library of Congress*] (LCLS) .... TxHGS
Church of Jesus Christ of Latter-Day Saints, Genealogical Society Library, Houston East Branch, Houston, TX [*Library symbol Library of Congress*] (LCLS) .... TxHGS-E
Church of Jesus Christ of Latter-Day Saints, Genealogical Society Library, Huntsville Branch, Huntsville, AL [*Library symbol Library of Congress*] (LCLS) .... AHGS
Church of Jesus Christ of Latter-Day Saints, Genealogical Society Library, IdahoFalls Branch, Idaho Falls, ID [*Library symbol Library of Congress*] (LCLS) .... IdIfGS
Church of Jesus Christ of Latter-Day Saints, Genealogical Society Library, Indianapolis Branch, Indianapolis, IN [*Library symbol Library of Congress*] (LCLS) .... InIGS
Church of Jesus Christ of Latter-Day Saints, Genealogical Society Library, Ithaca Branch, Vestal, NY [*Library symbol Library of Congress*] (LCLS) .... NVeGS
Church of Jesus Christ of Latter-Day Saints, Genealogical Society Library, Jacksonville Branch, Jacksonville, FL [*Library symbol Library of Congress*] (LCLS) .... FJGS
Church of Jesus Christ of Latter-Day Saints, Genealogical Society Library, Kalispell Branch, Kalispell, MT [*Library symbol Library of Congress*] (LCLS) .... MtKGS
Church of Jesus Christ of Latter-Day Saints, Genealogical Society Library, KanabBranch, Stake Center, Kanab, UT [*Library symbol Library of Congress*] (LCLS) .... UKaGS
Church of Jesus Christ of Latter-Day Saints, Genealogical Society Library, Kaneohe Stake Branch, Kaneohe, HI [*Library symbol Library of Congress*] (LCLS) .... HKGS
Church of Jesus Christ of Latter-Day Saints, Genealogical Society Library, Kansas City Branch, Kansas City, MO [*Library symbol Library of Congress*] (LCLS) .... MoKGS
Church of Jesus Christ of Latter-Day Saints, Genealogical Society Library, Knoxville Branch, Knoxville, TN [*Library symbol Library of Congress*] (LCLS) .... TKGS
Church of Jesus Christ of Latter-Day Saints, Genealogical Society Library, La Grande Branch, La Grande, OR [*Library symbol Library of Congress*] (LCLS) .... OrLgGS
Church of Jesus Christ of Latter-Day Saints, Genealogical Society Library, Laie Branch, Laie, HI [*Library symbol Library of Congress*] (LCLS) .... HLaGS
Church of Jesus Christ of Latter-Day Saints, Genealogical Society Library, LaJara Branch, Stake Center, LaJara, CO [*Library symbol Library of Congress*] (LCLS) .... CoLjaGS
Church of Jesus Christ of Latter-Day Saints, Genealogical Society Library, Lansing Branch, Stake Center, Lansing, MI [*Library symbol Library of Congress*] (LCLS) .... MiLGS
Church of Jesus Christ of Latter-Day Saints, Genealogical Society Library, Las Vegas Branch, Las Vegas, NV [*Library symbol Library of Congress*] (LCLS) .... NvLGS
Church of Jesus Christ of Latter-Day Saints, Genealogical Society Library, Lethbridge Branch, Stake Center, Lethbridge, AB, Canada [*Library symbol Library of Congress*] (LCLS) .... CaALCJC
Church of Jesus Christ of Latter-Day Saints, Genealogical Society Library, Lewiston Branch, Stake Center, Lewiston, ID [*Library symbol Library of Congress*] (LCLS) .... IdLGS
Church of Jesus Christ of Latter-Day Saints, Genealogical Society Library, Littleton Branch, Littleton, CO [*Library symbol Library of Congress*] (LCLS) .... CoLiGS
Church of Jesus Christ of Latter-Day Saints, Genealogical Society Library, Long Beach East Branch, Stake Center, Long Beach, CA [*Library symbol Library of Congress*] (LCLS) .... CLobGS
Church of Jesus Christ of Latter-Day Saints, Genealogical Society Library, Longview Branch, Gilmer, TX [*Library symbol Library of Congress*] (LCLS) .... TxGilGS
Church of Jesus Christ of Latter-Day Saints, Genealogical Society Library, Longview Stake Branch, Longview, WA [*Library symbol Library of Congress*] (LCLS) .... WaLoGS
Church of Jesus Christ of Latter-Day Saints, Genealogical Society Library, Los Angeles East Branch, Los Angeles, CA [*Library symbol Library of Congress*] (LCLS) .... CLGLE
Church of Jesus Christ of Latter-Day Saints, Genealogical Society Library, Los Angeles Temple, Los Angeles, CA [*Library symbol Library of Congress*] (LCLS) .... CLGL
Church of Jesus Christ of Latter-Day Saints, Genealogical Society Library, Lovell Branch, Lovell, WY [*Library symbol Library of Congress*] (LCLS) .... WyLoGS
Church of Jesus Christ of Latter-Day Saints, Genealogical Society Library, MaconBranch, Columbus, GA [*Library symbol Library of Congress*] (LCLS) .... GColuGS
Church of Jesus Christ of Latter-Day Saints, Genealogical Society Library, MaladStake Branch, Malad City, ID [*Library symbol Library of Congress*] (LCLS) .... IdMaGS
Church of Jesus Christ of Latter-Day Saints, Genealogical Society Library, Medford Branch, Medford, OR [*Library symbol Library of Congress*] (LCLS) .... OrMeGS

Church of Jesus Christ of Latter-Day Saints, Genealogical Society Library, Melbourne Branch, Northcote, V, Australia [*Library symbol Library of Congress*] (LCLS) .... AuNocGS

Church of Jesus Christ of Latter-Day Saints, Genealogical Society Library, Memphis Branch, Memphis, TN [*Library symbol Library of Congress*] (LCLS) .... TMGS

Church of Jesus Christ of Latter-Day Saints, Genealogical Society Library, Mesa Branch, Mesa, AZ [*Library symbol Library of Congress*] (LCLS) ..... AzMGS

Church of Jesus Christ of Latter-Day Saints, Genealogical Society Library, Mexico City Branch, Mexico City, Mexico [*Library symbol Library of Congress*] (LCLS) .... MxMGS

Church of Jesus Christ of Latter-Day Saints, Genealogical Society Library, MiamiBranch, Miami, FL [*Library symbol Library of Congress*] (LCLS) ..... FMGS

Church of Jesus Christ of Latter-Day Saints, Genealogical Society Library, Midland Stake Branch, Midland, MI [*Library symbol Library of Congress*] (LCLS) .... MiMidGS

Church of Jesus Christ of Latter-Day Saints, Genealogical Society Library, Milwaukee Branch, Hales Corners, WI [*Library symbol Library of Congress*] (LCLS) .... WHcGS

Church of Jesus Christ of Latter-Day Saints, Genealogical Society Library, Minneapolis Branch, Minneapolis, MN [*Library symbol Library of Congress*] (LCLS) .... MnMGS

Church of Jesus Christ of Latter-Day Saints, Genealogical Society Library, Missoula Branch, Missoula, MT [*Library symbol Library of Congress*] (LCLS) .... MtMisGS

Church of Jesus Christ of Latter-Day Saints, Genealogical Society Library, Modesto, CA [*Library symbol Library of Congress*] (LCLS) .... CMG

Church of Jesus Christ of Latter-Day Saints, Genealogical Society Library, Monterey Branch, Seaside, CA [*Library symbol Library of Congress*] (LCLS) .... CSeaGS

Church of Jesus Christ of Latter-Day Saints, Genealogical Society Library, MooreBranch, Lost River Stake Center, Moore, ID [*Library symbol Library of Congress*] (LCLS) .... IdMoGS

Church of Jesus Christ of Latter-Day Saints, Genealogical Society Library, MosesLake Branch, Moses Lake, WA [*Library symbol Library of Congress*] (LCLS) .... WaMlGS

Church of Jesus Christ of Latter-Day Saints, Genealogical Society Library, MountPleasant Branch, Stake Center, Mount Pleasant, UT [*Library symbol Library of Congress*] (LCLS) .... UMpGS

Church of Jesus Christ of Latter-Day Saints, Genealogical Society Library, MountVernon Branch, Mount Vernon, WA [*Library symbol Library of Congress*] (LCLS) .... WaMtvGS

Church of Jesus Christ of Latter-Day Saints, Genealogical Society Library, Naperville Branch, Naperville, IL [*Library symbol Library of Congress*] (LCLS) .... INapGS

Church of Jesus Christ of Latter-Day Saints, Genealogical Society Library, New York Branch, New York, NY [*Library symbol Library of Congress*] (LCLS) .... NNGS

Church of Jesus Christ of Latter-Day Saints, Genealogical Society Library, Norfolk Virginia Stake Branch, Virginia Beach, VA [*Library symbol Library of Congress*] (LCLS) .... ViVbGS

Church of Jesus Christ of Latter-Day Saints, Genealogical Society Library, NyssaBranch, Nyssa, OR [*Library symbol Library of Congress*] (LCLS) .... OrNyGS

Church of Jesus Christ of Latter-Day Saints, Genealogical Society Library, Oakland Branch, Oakland, CA [*Library symbol Library of Congress*] (LCLS) .... COGS

Church of Jesus Christ of Latter-Day Saints, Genealogical Society Library, Odessa Stake Branch, Odessa, TX [*Library symbol Library of Congress*] (LCLS) .... TxOGS

Church of Jesus Christ of Latter-Day Saints, Genealogical Society Library, OgdenBranch, Ogden, UT [*Library symbol Library of Congress*] (LCLS) .... UOGS

Church of Jesus Christ of Latter-Day Saints, Genealogical Society Library, Oklahoma City Branch, Oklahoma City, OK [*Library symbol Library of Congress*] (LCLS) .... OkOkGS

Church of Jesus Christ of Latter-Day Saints, Genealogical Society Library, Olympia Branch, Olympia, WA [*Library symbol Library of Congress*] (LCLS) .... WaOGS

Church of Jesus Christ of Latter-Day Saints, Genealogical Society Library, OmahaBranch, Omaha, NE [*Library symbol Library of Congress*] (LCLS) .... NbOGS

Church of Jesus Christ of Latter-Day Saints, Genealogical Society Library, Orlando Branch, Orlando, FL [*Library symbol Library of Congress*] (LCLS) .... FOGS

Church of Jesus Christ of Latter-Day Saints, Genealogical Society Library, PascoBranch, Pasco, WA [*Library symbol Library of Congress*] (LCLS) .... WaPaGS

Church of Jesus Christ of Latter-Day Saints, Genealogical Society Library, Pensacola Branch, Pensacola, FL [*Library symbol Library of Congress*] (LCLS) .... FPeGS

Church of Jesus Christ of Latter-Day Saints, Genealogical Society Library, Philadelphia Branch, Broomall, PA [*Library symbol Library of Congress*] (LCLS) .... PBroGS

Church of Jesus Christ of Latter-Day Saints, Genealogical Society Library, Phoenix Arizona North Branch, Phoenix, AZ [*Library symbol Library of Congress*] (LCLS) .... AzPhGS

Church of Jesus Christ of Latter-Day Saints, Genealogical Society Library, Phoenix Arizona West Branch, Phoenix, AZ [*Library symbol Library of Congress*] (LCLS) .... AzPhWGS

Church of Jesus Christ of Latter-Day Saints, Genealogical Society Library, Plainview Branch, Plainview, NY [*Library symbol Library of Congress*] (LCLS) .... NPlGS

Church of Jesus Christ of Latter-Day Saints, Genealogical Society Library, Pocatello Branch, Pocatello, ID [*Library symbol Library of Congress*] (LCLS) .... IdPGS

Church of Jesus Christ of Latter-Day Saints, Genealogical Society Library, Portland Branch, Portland, OR [*Library symbol Library of Congress*] (LCLS) .... OrPGS

Church of Jesus Christ of Latter-Day Saints, Genealogical Society Library, Portland East Branch, Portland, OR [*Library symbol Library of Congress*] (LCLS) .... OrPGSE

Church of Jesus Christ of Latter-Day Saints, Genealogical Society Library, Prescott Branch, Prescott, AZ [*Library symbol Library of Congress*] (LCLS) .... AzPrGS

Church of Jesus Christ of Latter-Day Saints, Genealogical Society Library, PriceBranch, Price, UT [*Library symbol Library of Congress*] (LCLS) ...... UPrGS

Church of Jesus Christ of Latter-Day Saints, Genealogical Society Library, Quincy Branch, Quincy, WA [*Library symbol Library of Congress*] (LCLS) .... WaQGS

Church of Jesus Christ of Latter-Day Saints, Genealogical Society Library, Raleigh Branch, Raleigh, NC [*Library symbol Library of Congress*] (LCLS) .... NcRGS

Church of Jesus Christ of Latter-Day Saints, Genealogical Society Library, Redding Branch, Redding, CA [*Library symbol Library of Congress*] (LCLS) .... CRedGS

Church of Jesus Christ of Latter-Day Saints, Genealogical Society Library, Reno Branch, Reno, NV [*Library symbol Library of Congress*] (LCLS)..... NvRGS

Church of Jesus Christ of Latter-Day Saints, Genealogical Society Library, Richfield Branch, Richfield, UT [*Library symbol Library of Congress*] (LCLS) .... URifGS

Church of Jesus Christ of Latter-Day Saints, Genealogical Society Library, Richland Branch, Richland, WA [*Library symbol Library of Congress*] (LCLS) .... WaRiGS

Church of Jesus Christ of Latter-Day Saints, Genealogical Society Library, Richmond Stake Branch, Richmond, VA [*Library symbol Library of Congress*] (LCLS) .... ViRGS

Church of Jesus Christ of Latter-Day Saints, Genealogical Society Library, Riverside Branch, Riverside, CA [*Library symbol Library of Congress*] (LCLS) .... CRivGS

Church of Jesus Christ of Latter-Day Saints, Genealogical Society Library, Riverside West Branch, Riverside, CA [*Library symbol Library of Congress*] (LCLS) .... CRivGS-W

Church of Jesus Christ of Latter-Day Saints, Genealogical Society Library, Rochester Branch, Rochester, NY [*Library symbol Library of Congress*] (LCLS) .... NRGS

Church of Jesus Christ of Latter-Day Saints, Genealogical Society Library, Sacramento Branch, Sacramento, CA [*Library symbol Library of Congress*] (LCLS) .... CSGS

Church of Jesus Christ of Latter-Day Saints, Genealogical Society Library, Safford Branch, Safford, AZ [*Library symbol Library of Congress*] (LCLS) .... AzSafGS

Church of Jesus Christ of Latter-Day Saints, Genealogical Society Library, St. David Arizona Stake Branch, St. David, AZ [*Library symbol Library of Congress*] (LCLS) .... AzStdGS

Church of Jesus Christ of Latter-Day Saints, Genealogical Society Library, St. George Branch, St. George, UT [*Library symbol Library of Congress*] (LCLS) .... UStgGS

Church of Jesus Christ of Latter-Day Saints, Genealogical Society Library, St. Johns Branch, Stake Center, St. Johns, AZ [*Library symbol Library of Congress*] (LCLS) .... AzSjGS

Church of Jesus Christ of Latter-Day Saints, Genealogical Society Library, St. Louis Branch, St. Louis, MO [*Library symbol Library of Congress*] (LCLS) .... MoSGS

Church of Jesus Christ of Latter-Day Saints, Genealogical Society Library, SalemBranch, Salem, OR [*Library symbol Library of Congress*] (LCLS) .... OrSaGS

Church of Jesus Christ of Latter-Day Saints, Genealogical Society Library, Salmon Branch, Salmon River Stake Center, Salmon, ID [*Library symbol Library of Congress*] (LCLS) .... IdSulGS

Church of Jesus Christ of Latter-Day Saints, Genealogical Society Library, Salt Lake City, UT [*Library symbol Library of Congress*] (LCLS) .... USlGS

Church of Jesus Christ of Latter-Day Saints, Genealogical Society Library, San Antonio Branch, San Antonio, TX [*Library symbol Library of Congress*] (LCLS) .... TxSaGS

Church of Jesus Christ of Latter-Day Saints, Genealogical Society Library, San Bernardino Branch, San Bernardino, CA [*Library symbol Library of Congress*] (LCLS) .... CSbGS

Church of Jesus Christ of Latter-Day Saints, Genealogical Society Library, San Diego Branch, San Diego, CA [*Library symbol Library of Congress*] (LCLS) .... CSdGS

Church of Jesus Christ of Latter-Day Saints, Genealogical Society Library, San Jose Branch, San Jose, CA [*Library symbol Library of Congress*] (LCLS) .... CSjGS

Church of Jesus Christ of Latter-Day Saints, Genealogical Society Library, San Luis Obispo Branch, San Luis Obispo, CA [*Library symbol Library of Congress*] (LCLS) .... CSluGS

Church of Jesus Christ of Latter-Day Saints, Genealogical Society Library, SandySprings Georgia Branch, Dunwoody, GA [*Library symbol Library of Congress*] (LCLS) .... GDunGS

Church of Jesus Christ of Latter-Day Saints, Genealogical Society Library, SantaBarbara Branch, Goleta, CA [*Library symbol Library of Congress*] (LCLS) .... CGoGS

Church of Jesus Christ of Latter-Day Saints, Genealogical Society Library, SantaClara Branch, Santa Clara, CA [*Library symbol Library of Congress*] (LCLS) .... CStclGS

Church of Jesus Christ of Latter-Day Saints, Genealogical Society Library, SantaMaria Branch, Lompoc, CA [*Library symbol Library of Congress*] (LCLS) ... CLomGS
Church of Jesus Christ of Latter-Day Saints, Genealogical Society Library, Santaquin Stake Branch, Santaquin, UT [*Library symbol Library of Congress*] (LCLS) ... USanGS
Church of Jesus Christ of Latter-Day Saints, Genealogical Society Library, Seattle North Branch, Seattle, WA [*Library symbol Library of Congress*] (LCLS) ... WaSGS
Church of Jesus Christ of Latter-Day Saints, Genealogical Society Library, Show Low Branch, Show Low, AZ [*Library symbol Library of Congress*] (LCLS) ... AzShGS
Church of Jesus Christ of Latter-Day Saints, Genealogical Society Library, Silver Spring Branch, Silver Spring, MD [*Library symbol Library of Congress*] (LCLS) ... MdSsGS
Church of Jesus Christ of Latter-Day Saints, Genealogical Society Library, Snowflake Branch, Snowflake, AZ [*Library symbol Library of Congress*] (LCLS) ... AzSnGS
Church of Jesus Christ of Latter-Day Saints, Genealogical Society Library, Spokane Branch, Spokane, WA [*Library symbol Library of Congress*] (LCLS) ... WaSpGL
Church of Jesus Christ of Latter-Day Saints, Genealogical Society Library, Springville Branch, Springville, UT [*Library symbol Library of Congress*] (LCLS) ... USpGS
Church of Jesus Christ of Latter-Day Saints, Genealogical Society Library, Stockton Branch, Stockton, CA [*Library symbol Library of Congress*] (LCLS) ... CStoGS
Church of Jesus Christ of Latter-Day Saints, Genealogical Society Library, Sydney Branch, Sydney, NSW, Australia [*Library symbol Library of Congress*] (LCLS) ... AuSGS
Church of Jesus Christ of Latter-Day Saints, Genealogical Society Library, Sydney South Branch, Sutherland Ward Chapel, Kirrawee, NSW, Australia [*Library symbol Library of Congress*] (LCLS) ... AuKirGS
Church of Jesus Christ of Latter-Day Saints, Genealogical Society Library, Tacoma Branch, Tacoma, WA [*Library symbol Library of Congress*] (LCLS) ... WaTGS
Church of Jesus Christ of Latter-Day Saints, Genealogical Society Library, TampaBranch, Tampa, FL [*Library symbol Library of Congress*] (LCLS) ... FTGS
Church of Jesus Christ of Latter-Day Saints, Genealogical Society Library, Temple View Branch, Temple View, New Zealand [*Library symbol Library of Congress*] (LCLS) ... NzTvGS
Church of Jesus Christ of Latter-Day Saints, Genealogical Society Library, Tennessee South District Branch, Tullahoma, TN [*Library symbol Library of Congress*] (LCLS) ... TTuGS
Church of Jesus Christ of Latter-Day Saints, Genealogical Society Library, Toronto Branch, Etobicoke, ON, Canada [*Library symbol Library of Congress*] (LCLS) ... CaOTCJC
Church of Jesus Christ of Latter-Day Saints, Genealogical Society Library, Tucson Branch, Tucson, AZ [*Library symbol Library of Congress*] (LCLS) ... AzTGS
Church of Jesus Christ of Latter-Day Saints, Genealogical Society Library, TulsaBranch, Tulsa, OK [*Library symbol Library of Congress*] (LCLS) ... OkTGS
Church of Jesus Christ of Latter-Day Saints, Genealogical Society Library, Twin Falls Branch, Twin Falls, ID [*Library symbol Library of Congress*] (LCLS) ... IdTfGS
Church of Jesus Christ of Latter-Day Saints, Genealogical Society Library, Uintah Basin Branch, Vernal, UT [*Library symbol Library of Congress*] (LCLS) ... UVGS
Church of Jesus Christ of Latter-Day Saints, Genealogical Society Library, Utah Valley Branch, Provo, UT [*Library symbol Library of Congress*] (LCLS) ... UPGS
Church of Jesus Christ of Latter-Day Saints, Genealogical Society Library, Vancouver Branch, Stake Center, Burnaby, Vancouver, BC, Canada [*Library symbol Library of Congress*] (LCLS) ... CaBBCJC
Church of Jesus Christ of Latter-Day Saints, Genealogical Society Library, Ventura Branch, Ventura, CA [*Library symbol Library of Congress*] (LCLS) ... CVtGS
Church of Jesus Christ of Latter-Day Saints, Genealogical Society Library, Wellington Stake Branch, Wellington, New Zealand [*Library symbol Library of Congress*] (LCLS) ... NzWGS
Church of Jesus Christ of Latter-Day Saints, Genealogical Society Library, Wichita Branch, Wichita, KS [*Library symbol Library of Congress*] (LCLS) ... KWiGS
Church of Jesus Christ of Latter-Day Saints, Genealogical Society Library, Wilmette Branch, Wilmette, IL [*Library symbol Library of Congress*] (LCLS) ... IWilGS
Church of Jesus Christ of Latter-Day Saints, Genealogical Society Library, Wisconsin East District Branch, Shawano, WI [*Library symbol Library of Congress*] (LCLS) ... WShawGS
Church of Jesus Christ of Latter-Day Saints, Genealogical Society Library, Yakima Branch, Yakima, WA [*Library symbol Library of Congress*] (LCLS) ... WaYGS
Church of Jesus Christ of Latter-Day Saints, Genealogical Society Library, Yuma Branch, Yuma, AZ [*Library symbol Library of Congress*] (LCLS) ... AzYGS
Church of Jesus Christ of Latter-Day Saints, Historian's Office, Salt Lake City,UT [*Library symbol Library of Congress*] (LCLS) ... USIC
Church of Jesus Christ of Latter-Day-Saints, Genealogical Society Library, Ridgecrest [*Library symbol*] [*Library of Congress*] (LCLS) ... CRidGS
Church of Monday Night Football (EA) ... CMNFB
Church of Scientology ... CoS
Church of Scientology of California (EA) ... CSC
Church of Scotland ... C of S
Church of Scotland ... C of SCOT
Church of Scotland and Free Churches [*British military*] (DMA) ... CSFC
Church of Scotland and Free Churches Chaplain [*Navy British*] ... CSFCh
Church of Scotland Chaplain [*British military*] (DMA) ... C of S Ch
Church of South India ... CSI
Church of Spiritual Discovery (EA) ... CSD
[*The*] **Church of the Brethren Homes and Hospitals Association** [*Later, BHOAM*] (EA) ... CBHHA
Church of the Lutheran Confession ... CLC
Church of the Movement for Spiritual Inner Awareness (ECON) ... MSIA
Church of What's Happening Now (EA) ... CWHN
Church Pastoral Aid Society [*British*] ... CPAS
Church Peace Union [*Later, CRIA*] ... CPU
Church Penitentiary Association [*British*] ... CPA
Church Pennant [*Navy British*] ... CH
Church Pension Fund (EA) ... CPF
Church Pensions Conference (EA) ... CPC
Church Periodical Club (EA) ... CPC
Church Planting International (EA) ... CPI
Church Record [*Genealogy*] ... CR
Church Research and Information Projects ... CRIPS
Church Scene [*A publication*] (APTA) ... CS
Church Schools Company Ltd. [*British*] (BI) ... CSC
Church Slavic [*MARC language code Library of Congress*] (LCCP) ... chu
Church Society for College Work (EA) ... CSCW
Church Sunday School Union [*British*] ... CSSU
Church Union [*British*] (DAS) ... CU
Church Universal and Triumphant (EA) ... CUT
Church Women United (EA) ... CWU
Church Women's Missionary Association [*Episcopalian*] ... CWMA
Church World Service [*Later, CWSW*] (EA) ... CWS
Church World Service Aids for the Horn of Africa (EA) ... CWSAHA
Church World Service and Witness (EA) ... CWSW
Church World Service, Immigration and Refugee Program (EA) ... CWSIRP
Churches at Bosra and Samaria-Sebaste [*A publication*] (BJA) ... CBSS
Churches' Center for Theology and Public Policy (EA) ... CCTPP
Churches Commission on Overseas Students (EAIO) ... CCOS
[*The*] **Churches' Committee for Supplementing Religious Education Among Men in HM Forces** [*British military*] (DMA) ... CCMF
Churches' Committee for Voter Registration-Education (EA) ... CCVRE
Churches Committee for Work Among Women Serving with HM Forces [*British military*] (DMA) ... CWWF
Churches' Committee on Migrants in Europe (EAIO) ... CCME
Churches' Council on Alcohol and Drugs [*Church of England*] ... CCOAD
Churches Speak [*A publication*] ... CHU
Churches Speak [*A publication*] ... CS
Churchill [*Canada*] [*Airport symbol*] (OAG) ... YYQ
Churchill and Bruce. Office and Duties of Sheriff [*2nd ed.*] [*1882*] [*A publication*] (DLA) ... Church & Br Sh
Churchill Downs, Inc. [*NASDAQ symbol*] (SAG) ... CHDN
Churchill Downs, Inc. [*Associated Press*] (SAG) ... ChrchllD
Churchill Elementary School, Cloquet, MN [*Library symbol*] [*Library of Congress*] (LCLS) ... MnClCE
Churchill Falls [*Canada*] [*Airport symbol*] (OAG) ... ZUM
Churchill Falls, NF [*FM radio station call letters*] ... CFLC
Churchill Falls Public Library, Churchill Falls, NF, Canada [*Library symbol Library of Congress*] (LCLS) ... CaNfCF
Churchill Falls Public Library, Newfoundland [*Library symbol National Library of Canada*] (NLC) ... NFCF
Churchill, MB [*AM radio station call letters*] ... CHFC
Churchill, MB [*ICAO location identifier*] (ICLI) ... CYYQ
Churchill Public Library, Churchill, MB, Canada [*Library symbol Library of Congress*] (LCLS) ... CaMCh
Churchill Public Library, Manitoba [*Library symbol National Library of Canada*] (NLC) ... MCH
Churchill Research Range [*Air Force*] ... CRR
Churchill Technology [*Associated Press*] (SAG) ... ChchTch
Churchill Technology [*NASDAQ symbol*] (TTSB) ... CHUR
Churchill Technology, Inc. [*NASDAQ symbol*] (NQ) ... CHUR
Churchman Associates (EA) ... CA
Churchman Publishing [*British*] ... CP
Churchman's Library [*A publication*] ... CL
Churchmen's Commission for Decent Publications [*Defunct*] (EA) ... CCDP
ChurchNews International [*Database*] [*Resources for Communication*] [*Information service or system*] (CRD) ... CNI
Church's Ministry among Jews [*Church of England*] ... CMJ
Churchville, VA [*FM radio station call letters*] ... WBOP
Churchville, VA [*AM radio station call letters*] ... WNLR
Churchville-Chili Senior High School Library, Rochester, NY [*OCLC symbol*] (OCLC) ... RVY
Churchwarden ... C
Churchwarden ... CHWDN
Churchwarden ... CW
Churchyard ... CHYD
Churdan City Library, Churdan, IA [*Library symbol Library of Congress*] (LCLS) ... IaChu
Churubusco, IN [*FM radio station call letters*] (RBYB) ... WEJE
Chusal [*Former USSR Seismograph station code, US Geological Survey Closed*] (SEIS) ... CHS
Chute ... CH
Chute (KSC) ... CHT
Chute's Equity under the Judicature Act [*A publication*] (DLA) ... Chute Eq
Chutine Resources Ltd. [*Vancouver Stock Exchange symbol*] ... CHS
Chutty [*Chewing gum*] [*Slang British*] (DSUE) ... CHUT
Chutz La'aretz (BJA) ... CL
Chuvash [*MARC language code Library of Congress*] (LCCP) ... chv
Chylomicron Remnant [*Physiology*] ... CR
Chymohelizyme [*Biochemistry*] ... CHZ

Chymotrypsin [*An enzyme*] ... ChTr
Chymotrypsin [*An enzyme*] ... CT
Chymotrypsin Inhibitor Activity ... CIA
Chymotrypsin Unit ... CU
Chymotrypsin Units Inhibited ... CUI
Chymotrypsin-Like [*Protease*] (DMAA) ... CTRL
Chymotrypsinogen [*Biochemistry*] ... ChTg
Chymotrypsinogen B [*Biochemistry*] ... CTRB
Chyron Corp. [*NYSE symbol*] (SPSG) ... CHY
Chyron Corp. [*Associated Press*] (SAG) ... Chyron
Ciao Cucina Corp. [*Associated Press*] (SAG) ... CiaoCuc
Ciao Cucina Corp. [*NASDAQ symbol*] (SAG) ... CIAU
Ciatti's, Inc. [*NASDAQ symbol*] (NQ) ... CIAT
Ciatti's, Inc. [*Associated Press*] (SAG) ... Ciattis
Ciba Co. Ltd., Montreal, PQ, Canada [*Library symbol Library of Congress*] (LCLS) ... CaQMCi
Ciba/Geigy Canada Ltd., Mississauga, ON, Canada [*Library symbol Library of Congress*] (LCLS) ... CaOMCG
Ciba/Geigy Canada Ltd., Mississauga, Ontario [*Library symbol National Library of Canada*] (NLC) ... OMCG
Ciba Pharmaceutical Co., Research Library, Summit, NJ [*Library symbol Library of Congress*] (LCLS) ... NjSC
Cibachrome (VRA) ... CIBCH
Cibachrome-Print [*Color photography*] ... CCP
Ciba-Geigy [*France*] [*Research code symbol*] ... AP
Ciba-Geigy AG [*Switzerland*] [*Research code symbol*] ... Ba
Ciba-Geigy AG [*Switzerland*] [*Research code symbol*] ... C
Ciba-Geigy AG [*Switzerland*] [*Research code symbol*] ... G
Ciba-Geigy AG [*Switzerland*] [*Research code symbol*] ... GP
Ciba-Geigy Canada Ltd., Dorval, PQ, Canada [*Library symbol Library of Congress*] (LCLS) ... CaQMCG
Ciba-Geigy Corp. [*Research code symbol*] ... GPA
Ciba-Geigy Corp. [*Research code symbol*] ... Su
Ciba-Geigy Corp., Biotechnology Library, Durham, NC [*Library symbol*] [*Library of Congress*] (LCLS) ... NcDurCG
CIBA-GEIGY Corp., Corporate Library, Ardsley, NY [*Library symbol*] [*Library of Congress*] (LCLS) ... NArdCG
Ciba-Geigy Corp., Technical Information Service, Greensboro, NC [*Library symbol Library of Congress*] (LCLS) ... NcGCG
Ciber, Inc. [*Associated Press*] (SAG) ... CIBER
Ciber, Inc. [*NASDAQ symbol*] (SAG) ... CIBR
Ciborium (VRA) ... cibr
Cibus [*Meal*] [*Latin*] ... C
Cibus [*Meal*] [*Latin*] ... CIB
CICAR [*Cooperative Investigation of the Caribbean and Adjacent Regions*] **Data Inventory** [*Marine science*] (MSC) ... CICARDI
CICAR [*Cooperative Investigation of the Caribbean and Adjacent Regions*] **Intercalibration Experiment** [*Marine science*] (MSC) ... CINTEX
Cicatricial Ocular Pemphigoid [*Ophthalmology*] (DAVI) ... COP
Cicatricial Pemphigoid [*Medicine*] ... CP
Cicero [*of Plutarch*] [*Classical studies*] (OCD) ... Cic
Cicero [*Marcus Tullius, Roman orator and author, 106-43BC*] [*Classical studies*] ... CIC
Cicero, IL [*AM radio station call letters*] ... WCEV
Cicero, IL [*AM radio station call letters*] ... WVON
Cicero Public Library, Cicero, IL [*Library symbol Library of Congress*] (LCLS) ... ICic
Cicero's De Oratore [*A publication*] (DLA) ... De Orat
Cicia [*Fiji*] [*Airport symbol*] (OAG) ... ICI
Ciclopirox Olamine [*Antifungal agent*] ... CO
CICS [*Customer Information Control System*] **Queue Command Facility** [*Computer science*] (HGAA) ... CQCF
CID [*Consortium on International Development*] **Information Network** ... CIDNET
Cidco, Inc. [*NASDAQ symbol*] (SAG) ... CDCO
Cidco, Inc. [*Associated Press*] (SAG) ... Cidco
Cider Association of North America (EA) ... CANA
Cidra, PR [*FM radio station call letters*] ... WBRQ
Cie. Internationale des Wagons-Lits et du Tourisme [*International Sleeping Car Co.*] ... CIWLT
CIE [*Communications Interface Equipment*] **Test Unit** ... CTU
Ciego De Avila [*Cuba ICAO location identifier*] (ICLI) ... MUCA
Ciego De Avila Norte [*Cuba ICAO location identifier*] (ICLI) ... MUCN
Cienfuegos [*Cuba*] [*Airport symbol Obsolete*] (OAG) ... CFG
Cienfuegos [*Cuba ICAO location identifier*] (ICLI) ... MUCF
Ciesta Gold Exploration Ltd. [*Vancouver Stock Exchange symbol*] ... CI
Ciga Hotels Aviation SpA [*Italy ICAO designator*] (FAAC) ... CHO
Cigar ... CG
Cigar Association of America (EA) ... CAA
Cigar Box Makers' and Paperers' Trade Union [*British*] ... CBMPTU
Cigar Box Manufacturers [*Defunct*] (EA) ... CBM
Cigar Institute of America [*Later, CAA*] (EA) ... CIA
Cigar Makers' International Union of America (EA) ... CMIU of A
Cigar Makers' Mutual Association [*A union*] [*British*] ... CMMA
Cigar Manufacturers Association of America [*Later, CAA*] (EA) ... CMA
Cigar Manufacturers Association of America [*Later, CAA*] ... CMAA
Cigar Smokers of America [*Defunct*] (EA) ... CSA
Cigarette ... CIG
Cigarette Advertising Code, Inc. (EA) ... CAC
Cigarette Advertising Normally Directed to Youth [*Student legal action organization*] ... CANDY
Cigarette [*or Cigar*] **Lighter** [*Automotive engineering*] ... C/LTR
Cigarette Lighter Manufacturers Association (EA) ... CLMA
Cigarette Machine Operators' Society [*A union*] [*British*] ... CMOS
Cigarette Makers' and Tobacco Cutters' Union [*British*] ... CMTCU
Cigarette Pack Collectors Association (EA) ... CPCA
Cigarette Smoke [*or Smoker*] (DAVI) ... CS
Cigarette Smoke Condensate ... CSC
Cigarettes per Day [*Medicine*] ... C/d
CIGNA Corp. [*NYSE symbol*] (SPSG) ... CI
CIGNA Corp. [*Associated Press*] (SAG) ... CIGNA
CIGNA High Income Shares [*Associated Press*] (SAG) ... CIGHi
CIGNA High Income Shares [*NYSE symbol*] (SPSG) ... HIS
CIGNA High Income Shs [*NYSE symbol*] (TTSB) ... HIS
Ciguatera Fish Poisoning [*Medicine*] ... CFP
Ciguatoxin ... CT
Ciguatoxin [*Agent in fish poisoning*] ... CTX
C-I-L, Inc. [*Toronto Stock Exchange symbol*] ... CIL
Cilacap/Tunggul Wulung [*Indonesia*] [*ICAO location identifier*] (ICLI) ... WIIL
Cilag-Chemie AG [*Switzerland*] [*Research code symbol*] ... C
Cilag-Chemie AG [*Switzerland*] [*Research code symbol*] ... R
Cilco, Sanford, NC [*Library symbol*] [*Library of Congress*] (LCLS) ... NcSaCi
Cilcorp [*NYSE symbol*] (SAG) ... CER
CILCORP ,Inc. [*NYSE symbol*] (TTSB) ... CER
Cilcorp., Inc. [*Associated Press*] (SAG) ... Cilcorp
Cilgener SA [*Associated Press*] (SAG) ... Chilgener
Ciliary Dyskinesia Activity (PDAA) ... CDA
Ciliary Ganglion [*Neurology*] ... CG
Ciliary Neurotrophic Factor [*Biochemistry*] ... CNTF
Ciliary Particle Transport Activity ... CPTA
Ciliated Epithelial Cells [*Medicine*] ... CEC
Ciliated Groove to Mouth ... CGM
Ciliated Groove to Ventral Sac ... CGVS
Cilicap [*Indonesia*] [*Airport symbol*] (OAG) ... CXP
Ciliocytopathoria [*Medicine*] ... CCP
Cilium [*Zoology*] ... CL
Cilla's Circle of Fans (EAIO) ... CCF
CIM High Yield Sec [*AMEX symbol*] (TTSB) ... CIM
CIM High Yield Securities [*AMEX symbol*] (SPSG) ... CIM
CIM High Yield Securities [*Associated Press*] (SAG) ... CIM
CIMA Labs [*NASDAQ symbol*] (TTSB) ... CIMA
CIMA Labs, Inc. [*NASDAQ symbol*] (SAG) ... CIMA
CIMA Labs, Inc. [*Associated Press*] (SAG) ... CIMA Lb
Cima Resources Ltd. [*Vancouver Stock Exchange symbol*] ... CIU
Cimarron, NM [*Location identifier FAA*] (FAAL) ... CIM
Cimarron Petroleum Ltd. [*Toronto Stock Exchange symbol*] ... CIR
Cimatron Ltd [*NASDAQ symbol*] (TTSB) ... CIMTF
Cimbalom [*Music*] ... CIMB
Cimber Air [*ICAO designator*] (AD) ... QI
Cimber Air, Sonderjyllands Flyveselskab [*Denmark ICAO designator*] (FAAC) ... DQI
Cimbr Air, AS [*Denmark*] [*FAA designator*] (FAAC) ... CIM
CIMCO, Inc. [*NASDAQ symbol*] (NQ) ... CIMC
Cimco, Inc. [*Associated Press*] (SAG) ... Cimco
Cimetidine [*Pharmacology*] ... C
Cimetidine [*Pharmacology*] ... CI
Cimex [*Genus of microorganisms*] (MAH) ... C
Cimitarra [*Colombia*] [*Airport symbol*] (OAG) ... CIM
Cimon [*of Plutarch*] [*Classical studies*] (OCD) ... Cim
Cinar Films Cl'B' [*NASDAQ symbol*] (TTSB) ... CINRF
Cinar Films, Inc. [*Associated Press*] (SAG) ... CinarF
Cinar Films, Inc. [*NASDAQ symbol*] (SAG) ... CINR
CINC [*Commander in Chief*] **Command Center** (DOMA) ... CCC
CINC [*Commander-in-Chief*] **Initiative Fund** [*DoD*] ... CIF
CINC [*Commander in Chief*] **Strategic Preparedness Assessment Report** (DOMA) ... CSPAR
CINCFLEETWOC [*British ICAO location identifier*] (ICLI) ... EGWX
Cinchona [*Quinine*] [*Pharmacology*] (ROG) ... Cinch
Cincinnati [*Ohio*] ... CIN
Cincinnati [*Ohio*] (WGA) ... Cinn
Cincinnati [*Ohio*] [*Seismograph station code, US Geological Survey Closed*] (SEIS) ... CNN
Cincinnati [*Ohio*] [*Airport symbol*] (OAG) ... CVG
Cincinnati Area Health Sciences Library Association [*Library network*] ... CAHSLA
Cincinnati Art Museum, Cincinnati, OH [*Library symbol Library of Congress*] (LCLS) ... OCA
Cincinnati Bar Association. Journal [*A publication*] (DLA) ... Cin B Ass'n J
Cincinnati Bell [*NYSE symbol*] (TTSB) ... CSN
Cincinnati Bell, Inc. [*Associated Press*] (SAG) ... CinnBel
Cincinnati Bell, Inc. [*NYSE symbol*] (SPSG) ... CSN
Cincinnati Bible Seminary, Cincinnati, OH [*OCLC symbol*] (OCLC) ... BSC
Cincinnati Bible Seminary, Cincinnati, OH [*Library symbol Library of Congress*] (LCLS) ... OCB
Cincinnati Board of Trade [*Defunct*] (EA) ... CBT
Cincinnati [*Ohio*] **- Covington** [*Kentucky*] [*Airport symbol*] ... CVG
Cincinnati Electronics Corp. [*Information service or system Defunct*] (IID) ... CE
Cincinnati Electronics Corporation, Cincinnati, OH [*Library symbol Library of Congress*] (LCLS) ... OCEleC
Cincinnati Financial [*NASDAQ symbol*] (TTSB) ... CINF
Cincinnati Financial Corp. [*NASDAQ symbol*] (NQ) ... CINF
Cincinnati Financial Corp. [*Associated Press*] (SAG) ... CinnFin
Cincinnati G & E,4% Pfd [*NYSE symbol*] (TTSB) ... CINPrA
Cincinnati G & El 4 3/4% Pfd [*NYSE symbol*] (TTSB) ... CINPrB
Cincinnati G&E 7.375% Pfd [*NYSE symbol*] (TTSB) ... CINPrG
Cincinnati G&E 7.875% Pfd [*NYSE symbol*] (TTSB) ... CINPrI
Cincinnati G&E8.28%JrSubDebs [*NYSE symbol*] (TTSB) ... JRL
Cincinnati Gas & Electric [*NYSE symbol*] (SAG) ... JRL
Cincinnati Gas & Electric Co. [*NYSE symbol*] (SPSG) ... CIN
Cincinnati Gas & Electric Co. [*Associated Press*] (SAG) ... CinG
Cincinnati General Hospital, Medical Library, Cincinnati, OH [*Library symbol Library of Congress*] (LCLS) ... OCG

Cincinnati/Greater Cincinnati [Ohio] [ICAO location identifier] (ICLI) .... KCVG
Cincinnati Historical Society, Cincinnati, OH [Library symbol Library of Congress] (LCLS) .... OCHP
Cincinnati, Indiana & Western Railway .... CI & W
Cincinnati Law Bulletin [A publication] (DLA) .... Cin L Bull
Cincinnati Law Bulletin [A publication] (DLA) .... Cin Law Bul
Cincinnati Law Bulletin [A publication] (DLA) .... Cinc L Bul
Cincinnati Law Library Association, Cincinnati, OH [Library symbol Library of Congress] (LCLS) .... OCLaw
Cincinnati Masonic Temple, Cincinnati, OH [Library symbol Library of Congress] (LCLS) .... OCM
Cincinnati Microwave [NASDAQ symbol] (TTSB) .... CNMW
Cincinnati Microwave, Inc. [Associated Press] (SAG) .... CinMic
Cincinnati Microwave, Inc. .... CMI
Cincinnati Microwave, Inc. [NASDAQ symbol] (NQ) .... CNMW
Cincinnati Microwave Wrrt [NASDAQ symbol] (TTSB) .... CNMWW
Cincinnati Milacron [NYSE symbol] (TTSB) .... CMZ
Cincinnati Milacron, Inc. [Associated Press] (SAG) .... CinMil
Cincinnati Milacron, Inc. [NYSE symbol] (SPSG) .... CMZ
Cincinnati Milacron, Inc., Corporate Information Center, Cincinnati, OH [OCLC symbol] (OCLC) .... CML
Cincinnati Milacron, Inc., Corporate Information Center, Cincinnati, OH [Library symbol] [Library of Congress] (LCLS) .... OCMilC
Cincinnati Milacron, Inc., Research Library, Cincinnati, OH [Library symbol Library of Congress] (LCLS) .... OCMil
Cincinnati Milacron, Inc., Technical Information Center, Cincinnati, OH [Library symbol Library of Congress] (LCLS) .... OCMil-T
Cincinnati Municipal Decisions [A publication] (DLA) .... Cin Mun Dec
Cincinnati/Municipal-Lunken Field [Ohio] [ICAO location identifier] (ICLI) ..... KLUK
Cincinnati, New Orleans & Texas Pacific Railroad (MHDB) .... CNO & TPR
Cincinnati, New Orleans & Texas Pacific Railway Co. .... CNO & TP
Cincinnati, New Orleans & Texas Pacific Railway Co. [AAR code] .... CNTP
Cincinnati/New Orleans City Ballet .... C/NOCB
Cincinnati Northern [AAR code] .... CNOR
Cincinnati, OH [Location identifier FAA] (FAAL) .... LUK
Cincinnati, OH [Location identifier FAA] (FAAL) .... MDE
Cincinnati, OH [FM radio station call letters] .... WAKW
Cincinnati, OH [AM radio station call letters] .... WAOZ
Cincinnati, OH [FM radio station call letters] (RBYB) .... WAZU-FM
Cincinnati, OH [Television station call letters] .... WCET
Cincinnati, OH [AM radio station call letters] .... WCIN
Cincinnati, OH [AM radio station call letters] .... WCKY
Cincinnati, OH [Television station call letters] .... WCPO
Cincinnati, OH [FM radio station call letters] .... WEBN
Cincinnati, OH [AM radio station call letters] .... WGUC
Cincinnati, OH [FM radio station call letters] .... WJVS
Cincinnati, OH [Television station call letters] .... WKRC-TV
Cincinnati, OH [FM radio station call letters] .... WKRQ
Cincinnati, OH [AM radio station call letters] .... WLW
Cincinnati, OH [Television station call letters] .... WLWT
Cincinnati, OH [FM radio station call letters] .... WRRM
Cincinnati, OH [AM radio station call letters] .... WSAI
Cincinnati, OH [Television station call letters] .... WSTR
Cincinnati, OH [AM radio station call letters] .... WTSJ
Cincinnati, OH [AM radio station call letters] .... WUBE
Cincinnati, OH [FM radio station call letters] .... WUBE-FM
Cincinnati, OH [FM radio station call letters] .... WVXU
Cincinnati, OH [FM radio station call letters] .... WWNK
Cincinnati Service Center [IRS] .... CSC
Cincinnati Stock Exchange [Ohio] .... CSE
Cincinnati Superior Court Decisions [Ohio] [A publication] (DLA) .... Hosea's Rep
Cincinnati Superior Court Reporter [Ohio] [A publication] (DLA) .... Cin Sup Ct R
Cincinnati Superior Court Reporter [Ohio] [A publication] (DLA) .... Cin Super Ct
Cincinnati Superior Court Reporter [Ohio] [A publication] (DLA) .... Cinc Sup Ct Rep
Cincinnati Superior Court Reporter [Ohio] [A publication] (DLA) .... Cinc Super
Cincinnati Superior Court Reporter [Ohio] [A publication] (DLA) .... CSCR
Cincinnati Superior Court Reports [Ohio] [A publication] (DLA) .... Cin R
Cincinnati Superior Court Reports [Ohio] [A publication] (DLA) .... Cin Rep
Cincinnati Superior Court Reports [Ohio] [A publication] (DLA) .... Cin SC Rep
Cincinnati Superior Court Reports [Ohio] [A publication] (DLA) .... Cin SCR
Cincinnati Superior Court Reports [Ohio] [A publication] (DLA) .... Cin Sup Ct
Cincinnati Superior Court Reports [Ohio] [A publication] (DLA) .... Cin Sup Ct Rep
Cincinnati Superior Court Reports [Ohio] [A publication] (DLA) .... Cin Super Ct Rep'r
Cincinnati Superior Court Reports [Ohio] [A publication] (DLA) .... Cin Super (Ohio)
Cincinnati Superior Court Reports [Ohio] [A publication] (DLA) .... Cinc (Ohio)
Cincinnati Symphony Orchestra (BARN) .... CSO
Cincinnati Technical College, Cincinnati, OH [Library symbol Library of Congress OCLC symbol] (LCLS) .... OCT
Cincinnati Uplink, Inc. [Cincinnati, OH] [Telecommunications] (TSSD) .... CUI
Cincinnati, Washington & Baltimore Railroad .... CW & B
Cincinnati Weekly Law Bulletin [A publication] (DLA) .... Weekly Cin Law Bull
Cincinnatus Society [Defunct] (EA) .... CS
CINCPAC [Commander-in-Chief, Pacific] Operation Center (CINC) .... COC
CINCPAC [Commander-in-Chief, Pacific] Route Slip (CINC) .... CPRS
CINCPAC [Commander-in-Chief, Pacific] Supplement to DoD Basic Planning [Department of Defense] (CINC) .... CSBPD
CINCPAC [Commander-in-Chief, Pacific] Supplement to the Military Assistance Manual (CINC) .... CSMAM
CINCPAC [Commander-in-Chief, Pacific] Teletype Automated Net (NVT) .... CTAN
CINCPAC Voice Alert Net (MCD) .... CVN
CINCPAC [Commander-in-Chief, Pacific] Voice Automated Net (NVT) .... CVAN
CINCPACAF [Commander-in-Chief, Pacific Air Force] Integrated Decision Support System .... CIDSS
CINC's [Commander in Chief's] Strategic Priorities Assessment (DOMA) ..... CSPA

Cinder-Block on Concrete Slab [Construction] .... CBS
Cinderella Softball Leagues (EA) .... CSL
Cinders [Quality of the bottom] [Nautical charts] .... Cn
Cine [Turkey] [Seismograph station code, US Geological Survey] (SEIS) .... CIN
Cinegraphic Scoring System (MCD) .... CSS
Cinema (NTCM) .... CINE
Cinema .... CINE
Cinema (WDMC) .... cine
Cinema Advertising Association [British] .... CAA
Cinema and Television Benevolent Fund [British] .... CTBF
Cinema Board [Tasmania] [Australia] .... CB
Cinema Center Films .... CCF
Cinema Digital Sound .... CDS
Cinema Industry Benevolent Fund of Victoria [Australia] .... CIBFV
Cinema Organ Society [British] .... COS
Cinema Ride [Associated Press] (SAG) .... CineRide
Cinema Ride [Associated Press] (SAG) .... CinRd
Cinema Ride [NASDAQ symbol] (SAG) .... MOVE
Cinema Ride Inc. [NASDAQ symbol] (TTSB) .... MOVE
Cinema Ride Wrrt [NASDAQ symbol] (TTSB) .... MOVEW
Cinema Television Digest .... CTVD
Cinema Theatre Association [British] .... CTA
Cinemas [Public-performance tariff class] [British] C
Cinemascope .... CS
Cinemastar Luxry Theaters Wrrt [NASDAQ symbol] (TTSB) .... LUXYW
Cinemastar Luxury Theaters [NASDAQ symbol] (TTSB) .... LUXY
CinemaStar Luxury Theaters, Inc. [Associated Press] (SAG) .... CinStar
CinemaStar Luxury Theaters, Inc. [Associated Press] (SAG) .... CinStr
CinemaStar Luxury Theaters, Inc. [NASDAQ symbol] (SAG) .... LUXY
Cinematheque Quebecoise, Montreal, Quebec [Library symbol National Library of Canada] (BIB) .... QMCQ
Cinematheque Scientifique Internationale [International Scientific Film Library] .... CSI
Cinematografia [Ministerio de Cultura] [Spain Information service or system] (CRD) .... CINE
Cinematograph Exhibitioners' Association of Great Britian and Ireland ...... CEA
Cinematograph Exhibitors' Association [Australia] .... CEA
Cinematograph Films Council [British] .... CFC
Cinematograph Operators' Board [Victoria] [Australia] .... COB
Cinematographic (MSA) .... CINE
Cinemax [Cable television channel] .... MAX
Cinemists 63 (EA) C63
Cineplex Odeon [NYSE symbol] (TTSB) .... CPX
Cineplex Odeon Corp. [Associated Press] (SAG) .... CineOd
Cineplex Odeon Corp. [NYSE symbol Toronto Stock Exchange symbol] .... CPX
Cinequity Corp. [Toronto Stock Exchange symbol] .... CEQ
Cinergi Pictures Entertain [NASDAQ symbol] (TTSB) .... CINE
Cinergi Pictures Entertainment, Inc. [NASDAQ symbol] (SAG) .... CINE
Cinergi Pictures Entertainment, Inc. [Associated Press] (SAG) .... Cinergi
CINergy Corp. [NYSE symbol] (SAG) .... CIN
CINergy Corp. [Associated Press] (SAG) .... CINergy
Cinetheodolite Orientation Target Array .... COTA
Cingulate Sulcus (DMAA) .... CiS
Cinnabar Resources Ltd. [Vancouver Stock Exchange symbol] .... CBS
Cinnamic Acid [Organic chemistry] (OA) .... CA
Cinnaminson Little Paper, Cinnaminson, NJ [Library symbol Library of Congress] (LCLS) .... NjCiL
Cinnamomum [Cinnamon] [Pharmacology] (ROG) .... Cinnam
Cinnamon Rabbit Breeders Association (EA) .... CRBA
Cinnamyl Alcohol Dehydrogenase [An enzyme] .... CAD
Cinque Ports Artillery Volunteers [British military] (DMA) .... CPAV
Cinque Ports Rifle Volunteers [British military] (DMA) .... CPRV
Cinram Ltd. [Toronto Stock Exchange symbol] .... CRW
Cinram Ltd [NASDAQ symbol] (TTSB) .... CNRMF
Cintas Corp. [Associated Press] (SAG) .... Cintas
Cintas Corp. [NASDAQ symbol] (NQ) .... CTAS
Cinus de Pistoia [Deceased, 1336] [Authority cited in pre-1607 legal work] (DSA) Ci
CIP Research Ltd., Hawkesbury, Ontario [Library symbol National Library of Canada] (NLC) .... OHKC
Cipher and Telephony Equipment [Military] .... CIPHONY
Cipher Block Chaining [Computer science] (HGAA) .... CBC
Cipher Feedback .... CFB
Cipher Text [Telecommunications] (MCD) .... CT
Cipher Text Auto Key [Computer science] .... CTAK
Cipolletti [Argentina] [Seismograph station code, US Geological Survey Closed] (SEIS) .... CIP
Ciprico, Inc. [Associated Press] (SAG) .... Ciprico
Ciprico, Inc. [NASDAQ symbol] (NQ) .... CPCI
CIPSCO, Inc. [NYSE symbol] (SPSG) .... CIP
CIPSCO, Inc. [Associated Press] (SAG) .... CIPSCO
CIRC [Central Information Reference and Control] Online Experiment .... COLEX
Circa [or Circiter or Circum] [About (used with dates denoting approximate time)] [Latin] (GPO) c
Circa [or Circiter or Circum] [About (used with dates denoting approximate time)] [Latin] .... ca
Circa [About, Approximately] [Latin] .... cca
Circa [or Circiter or Circum] [About (used with dates denoting approximate time)] [Latin] .... CIR
Circa [or Circiter or Circum] [About (used with dates denoting approximate time)] [Latin] .... CIRC
Circadian Data System (MCD) .... CDS
Circadian Pacemaker [Neurophysiology] .... CP
Circadian Periodicity Experiment [Skylab] [NASA] .... CPE
Circadian Quotient (MAE) .... CQ

Circadian Time [*Physiology*] .... CT
Circeo [*Italy ICAO location identifier*] (ICLI) .... LIQT
Circimus [*Constellation*] .... Cir
Circimus [*Constellation*] .... Circ
Circle [*Freemasonry*] (ROG) C
Circle .... CIR
Circle (DD) .... Cir
Circle (WDMC) .... cir
Circle .... CIR
Circle (WDMC) .... circ
Circle .... CIRC
Circle [*Commonly used*] (OPSA) .... CIRCL
Circle [*Commonly used*] (OPSA) .... CIRCLE
Circle (ROG) .... CR
Circle [*Commonly used*] (OPSA) .... CRCL
Circle [*Commonly used*] (OPSA) .... CRCLE
Circle [*Alaska*] [*Airport symbol*] (OAG) .... IRC
Circle, AK [*Location identifier FAA*] (FAAL) .... CRC
Circle Bed [*Medicine*] .... CB
Circle Card Test [*For syphilis*] .... CT
Circle Cutting .... CCT
Circle/Dashed Circle (MCD) .... CIR/CIRD
Circle End Point .... CEP
Circle Financial Corp. [*Associated Press*] (SAG) .... CircFn
Circle Financial Corp. [*NASDAQ symbol*] (SAG) .... CRCL
Circle Finl [*NASDAQ symbol*] (TTSB) .... CRCL
Circle Hot Springs [*Alaska*] [*Airport symbol Obsolete*] (OAG) .... CHP
Circle Income Shares [*Associated Press*] (SAG) .... CircInc
Circle Income Shares, Inc. [*NASDAQ symbol*] (NQ) .... CINS
Circle K Corp. [*Associated Press*] (SAG) .... CircleK
Circle K Corp. [*NYSE symbol*] (SAG) .... CRK
Circle K International (EA) .... CKI
Circle, MT [*Location identifier FAA*] (FAAL) .... CRR
Circle of Companions [*Defunct*] (EA) .... COC
Circle of Equal Probability .... CEP
Circle of State Librarians [*British*] .... CSL
Circle Repertory Theater Company .... CRTC
Circle Track [*A publication*] .... CT
Circles [*Commonly used*] (OPSA) .... CIRCLES
Circles [*Postal Service standard*] (OPSA) .... CIRS
Circles .... CIRS
Circles Effect Research Group [*British*] (DBA) .... CERES
Circles of Exchange [*Later, COE*] [*An association*] (EA) .... CE
Circles of Exchange (EA) .... COE
Circleville, OH [*Location identifier FAA*] (FAAL) .... CYO
Circleville, OH [*FM radio station call letters*] .... WAHC
Circleville, OH [*AM radio station call letters*] .... WNRJ
Circleville, OH [*Location identifier FAA*] (FAAL) .... XUB
Circling [*Approach and landing charts*] [*Aviation*] C
Circling Guidance Light [*Aviation*] (FAAC) .... CGL
Circo Craft Co., Inc. [*Toronto Stock Exchange symbol*] CCC
CircOlectric Bed [*A trademark*] [*Medicine*] .... COL
Circon Corp. [*NASDAQ symbol*] (NQ) .... CCON
Circon Corp. [*Associated Press*] (SAG) .... Circon
Circuit C
Circuit (NATG) .... CCT
Circuit (AFM) .... CIR
Circuit .... CIRC
Circuit (DD) .... Circt
Circuit (AAG) .... CKT
Circuit (KSC) .... CRCT
Circuit .... CRCT
Circuit .... CT
Circuit Access Point [*Telecommunications*] (TEL) .... CAP
Circuit Activation Order .... CAO
Circuit Analysis [*Computer science*] .... CIRCAL
Circuit Analyzer - Fault Isolation Generator (PDAA) .... CAFIG
Circuit Assurance Block (SSD) .... CAB
Circuit Board [*Automotive engineering*] .... C/BRD
Circuit Board (DWSG) .... CB
Circuit Board Assembly (MCD) .... CBA
Circuit Board Card .... CBC
Circuit Board Card Tester .... CBCT
Circuit Board Design System [*IBM Corp.*] .... CBDS
Circuit Board Extractor .... CBE
Circuit Board Holder .... CBH
Circuit Board Rack .... CBR
[*The*] Circuit Board Thermometer [*Computer science*] .... TCBT
Circuit Break/Alternating Current .... CB/ac
Circuit Breaker (NTCM) .... BKR
Circuit Breaker .... CB
Circuit Breaker [*Technical drawings*] (DAC) .... CIR BKR
Circuit Breaker (MSA) .... CKT BKR
Circuit Breaker/Direct Current .... CB/dc
Circuit Card Assembly (MCD) .... CCA
Circuit Cellar Intelligent Serial EPROM Programmer [*Computer science*] .... CCSP
Circuit Check [*Electronics*] (IAA) .... CK
Circuit City Stores [*NYSE symbol*] (TTSB) CC
Circuit City Stores, Inc. [*NYSE symbol*] (SPSG) CC
Circuit City Stores, Inc. [*Associated Press*] (SAG) .... CirCty
Circuit Closing CC
Circuit Concentration Bay (IEEE) .... CCB
Circuit Condition Indicator CCI
Circuit Continuity Tester [*Electronics*] (IAA) .... CCT
Circuit Control .... C/C

Circuit Control Office [*Automatic Digital Information Network*] (CET) .... CCO
Circuit Court CC
Circuit Court (DLA) .... Cir
Circuit Court Decisions [*A publication*] (DLA) .... Cir Ct Dec
Circuit Court Decisions [*Ohio*] [*A publication*] (DLA) .... Cir Ct Dec (Ohio)
Circuit Court Library, Birmingham, AL [*Library symbol Library of Congress*] (LCLS) .... ABCC
Circuit Court of Appeals (GPO) .... CCA
Circuit Court of Appeals (DLA) .... Cir
Circuit Court of Appeals (DLA) .... Cir Ct App
Circuit Court of Appeals (United States) [*A publication*] (DLA) .... CCA (US)
Circuit Court of the United States (DLA) .... CCUS
Circuit Court Reports [*A publication*] (DLA) .... Cir Ct R
Circuit Court Reports [*Ohio*] [*A publication*] (DLA) .... Cir Ct R
Circuit Data Sheet .... CDS
Circuit Decisions [*A publication*] (DLA) .... CD
Circuit Defense Counsel .... CDC
Circuit Description (MSA) .... CD
Circuit Descriptive Language .... CDL
Circuit Design Fabrication (NASA) .... CDF
Circuit Design, Fabrication, and Test Data Systems (NASA) .... CDF & TDS
Circuit Design System (MCD) .... CDS
Circuit Diagrams .... CD
Circuit Directory Maintenance (IAA) .... CDM
Circuit Distribution Assembly [*Ground Communications Facility, NASA*] .... CDA
Circuit Distribution Assembly [*Ground Communications Facility, NASA*] .... CDSA
Circuit Edges [*Bookbinding*] (DGA) .... CE
Circuit Edges [*Bookbinding*] (DGA) .... CIRC E
Circuit Emulation Service [*Electronics*] (ACRL) .... CES
Circuit Finder .... CF
Circuit Finder (MSA) .... CKTF
Circuit Group [*Telecommunications*] (TEL) .... CGRP
Circuit Group Congestion [*Telecommunications*] (TEL) .... CGC
Circuit Group Congestion Signal [*Telecommunications*] (IAA) .... CGS
Circuit Identification [*Telecommunications*] (TEL) .... CKT-ID
Circuit Interrupter (MCD) CI
Circuit Judge (DLA) .... CJ
Circuit Layout [*AT & T*] CL
Circuit Layout, Automated Scheduling and Production (PDAA) .... CLASP
Circuit Layout Record Card [*Telecommunications*] (TEL) .... CLRC
Circuit Line Up .... CLU
Circuit Maintenance System [*AT & T*] .... CMS
Circuit Master (MSA) .... CM
Circuit Master Tape [*Computer science*] (IAA) .... CMT
Circuit Modeller [*Seasim Engineering Software Ltd.*] [*Software package*] (NCC) .... CM
Circuit Modeller Plus [*Seasim Engineering Software Ltd.*] [*Software package*] (NCC) .... CMP
Circuit Net Loss .... CNL
Circuit Order Layout Record [*Telecommunications*] (TEL) .... COLR
Circuit Order Preparation [*or Processing*] System [*AT & T*] .... COPS
Circuit Package (MSA) .... CP
Circuit Package Schematic (MSA) .... CPS
Circuit Protection Device .... CPD
Circuit Provision System [*AT & T*] .... CPS
Circuit Quality Monitoring System .... CQMS
Circuit Reliability Improvement .... CRI
Circuit Requirement Table (MSA) .... CRT
Circuit Research [*Associated Press*] (SAG) .... CircRsh
Circuit Research Laboratories, Inc. [*NASDAQ symbol*] (NQ) .... CRLI
Circuit Resh Labs [*NASDAQ symbol*] (TTSB) .... CRLI
Circuit Simulation [*Electronics*] (IAA) .... CCTSIM
Circuit Simulator (MHDB) .... CIRCUS
Circuit Switched Data [*Telecommunications*] .... CSD
Circuit Switched Data Network (NITA) .... CSDN
Circuit Switched Digital Capability [*AT & T*] .... CSDC
Circuit Switched Line [*Telecommunications*] (MCD) .... CSL
Circuit Switched Multiplexer [*Telecommunications*] .... CS-MUX
Circuit Switched Public Data Network [*Telecommunications*] .... CSPDN
Circuit Switched Voice [*Telecommunications*] .... CSV
Circuit Switching [*Telecommunications*] .... CS
Circuit Switching Center [*Telecommunications*] (TEL) .... CSC
Circuit Switching Magnetic Tape [*Telecommunications*] (AFM) .... CSMT
Circuit Switching Network [*Telecommunications*] .... CSN
Circuit Switching Station [*Telecommunications*] (CET) .... CSS
Circuit Switching Unit [*Telecommunications*] (CET) .... CSU
Circuit Systems [*NASDAQ symbol*] (TTSB) .... CSYI
Circuit Systems, Inc. [*Associated Press*] (SAG) .... CircSy
Circuit Systems, Inc. [*NASDAQ symbol*] (NQ) .... CSYI
Circuit Technology (IAA) .... CT
Circuit Terminal Unit [*Mercury Communications Ltd.*] [*British*] .... CTU
Circuit Terminating Arrangement .... CTA
Circuit Test Set [*Electricity*] .... CTS
Circuit Theory [*Electricity*] (MCD) .... CT
Circuit Transient Analysis Program (IAA) .... CTAP
Circuit Trial Counsel .... CTC
Circuit under Test [*Electricity*] (IEEE) .... CUT
Circuit Unit Assembly .... CUA
Circuitless Electron Beam Amplifier (MCD) .... CEBA
Circuitry Adapter [*Electronics*] (IAA) .... CA
Circuits and Systems [*IEEE*] (MCD) .... CAS
Circuit-Switched Digital [*or Data*] Network [*Telecommunications*] (IAA) .... CSDN
Circuit-Switched Digital Services [*Telecommunications*] (HGAA) .... CSDS
Circuit-Switched Exchange [*Telecommunications*] (IAA) .... CSE
Circuit-to-Specification (IAA) .... CTS

CircuitWriter Network [*Information service or system*] (IID) ... CWN
Circular ... C
Circular (AABC) ... CIR
Circular (WDMC) ... cir
Circular (WDMC) ... circ
Circular (AFM) ... CIRC
Circular ... CIRCL
Circular ... CRCLR
Circular Active Reflector Antenna (PDAA) ... CARA
Circular Antenna [*Electromagnetism*] (IAA) ... CIRANT
Circular Aperture Antenna ... CAA
Circular Arc [*Aviation*] ... CA
Circular Arc ... CIRCARC
Circular Area Method ... CAM
Circular Crystal Facet ... CCF
Circular Cylindrical Shell ... CCS
Circular Date Stamp [*Postmark of a stamp cancellation*] ... CDS
Circular Dichroism [*Optics*] ... CD
Circular Diffraction Grating ... CDG
Circular Dispersion ... CD
Circular Electric Mode ... CEM
Circular Electric Wire ... CEW
Circular Error [*Military*] ... CE
Circular Error Average [*Military*] ... CEA
Circular Error Probability [*Military*] ... CEP
Circular Error Probability [*Military*] (DNAB) ... CIREP
Circular Error Probable (AAGC) ... CEP
Circular Exhaust Cloud (PDAA) ... CEC
Circular Hollow Section [*Metal industry*] ... CHS
Circular Intensity Difference [*Spectrometry*] ... CID
Circular Letter ... CILET
Circular Letter [*Military*] ... CIRCLTR
Circular Letter ... CL
Circular Magnetic Wave ... CMW
Circular Mail ... CM
Circular Map Accuracy Standard (PDAA) ... CMAS
Circular Measure ... CM
Circular Mil (IDOE) ... cir mil
Circular Mil [*Wire measure*] (IAA) ... CIRMIL
Circular Mil [*Wire measure*] ... CM
Circular Mil (IDOE) ... cm
Circular Mil [*Wire measure*] (MSA) ... CMIL
Circular Mil Area ... CMA
Circular Mil Foot ... CMF
Circular Mils, Thousands ... MCM
Circular Muscle [*Anatomy*] ... CM
Circular Note [*Business term*] ... CN
Circular of Requirements ... COR
Circular Orders, Northwestern Provinces [*India*] [*A publication*] (ILCA) ... Cir Od NWP
Circular Orders, Northwestern Provinces [*India*] [*A publication*] (DLA) ... Cir Ord NWP
Circular Parking Orbit [*Aerospace*] (AAG) ... CPO
Circular Permutation Analysis [*Genetics*] ... CPA
Circular Pitch [*Technical drawings*] ... CP
Circular Polarization [*Optics*] ... CP
Circular Polarization Ratio [*Physics*] ... CPR
Circular Polarized Light [*Physics*] ... CPL
Circular Probable Error ... CPE
Circular Radio Beacon ... RC
Circular Sequential Access Memory ... CSAM
Circular Standard Deviation [*Statistics*] ... CSD
Circular Tank System [*Pisciculture*] ... CT
Circular Terminal Orbit [*Aerospace*] (AAG) ... CTO
Circular Variable Filter [*Instrumentation*] ... CVF
Circular Variable Filter Spectrometer ... CVFS
Circular Vection [*Optics*] ... CV
Circular Velocity ... VC
Circular-Arc-Toothed Cylindrical (PDAA) ... CATC
Circularization Burn [*Orbital Maneuvering Subsystem 2*] [*NASA*] (NASA) ... CIRC
Circularly Disposed Antenna Array [*Radio receiver*] ... CDAA
Circularly Polarized Antenna [*or Array*] ... CPA
Circularly Polarized Fluorescence [*Physics*] ... CPF
Circularly Polarized Luminescence [*Spectroscopy*] ... CPL
Circularly Polarized-Electron Nuclear Double Resonance [*Spectroscopy*] ... CP-ENDOR
Circulate (MSA) ... CRCLT
Circulate (FAAC) ... CRLC
Circulating Anticoagulant [*Medicine*] (MEDA) ... CAC
Circulating Blood Volume [*Medicine*] ... CBV
Circulating Copy ... CC
Circulating Fluid Bed [*Chemical engineering*] ... CFB
Circulating Fuel Reactor Experiment [*Nuclear energy*] ... CFRE
Circulating Granulocyte Pool [*Hematology*] ... CGP
Circulating Immune Complexes [*Medicine*] ... CIC
Circulating Nurse (HGAA) ... CN
Circulating Plasma Volume [*Hematology*] ... CPV
Circulating Platelet Aggregate [*Hematology*] ... CPA
Circulating Reflux [*Chemical engineering*] ... CR
Circulating Shift Register (IAA) ... CSR
Circulating Water [*Nuclear energy*] (NRCH) ... CW
Circulating Water Pump ... CWP
Circulating Water Pumphouse [*Nuclear energy*] (NRCH) ... CWPH
Circulating Water System [*Nuclear energy*] (NRCH) ... CWS
Circulation (ADA) ... CIR
Circulation (WDMC) ... cir
Circulation (EY) ... CIRC
Circulation Bed Combustor [*Chemical engineering*] ... CBC
Circulation Control Point (AABC) ... CCP
Circulation Control Rotor [*Navy*] ... CCR
Circulation Control Wing (MCD) ... CCW
Circulation Council of DMA [*Direct Marketing Association*] [*New York, NY*] (EA) ... CC
Circulation Input Recording Center [*Data processing system*] ... CIRC
Circulation Library Automated System for Inventory Control [*Cincinnati Electronics Corp.*] [*Discontinued*] [*Information service or system*] (IID) ... CLASSIC
Circulation Lift Limit ... CLL
Circulation Manager (IIA) ... CM
Circulation, Motion, and Sensation (HGAA) ... CMS
Circulation, Motor Ability, Sensation, and Swelling [*Medicine*] ... CMSS
Circulation Pump ... CP
Circulation, Sensation [*or Sensory*], Movement [*or Motion*] [*Neurology and orthopedics*] (DAVI) ... CSM
Circulation System [*Computer science*] (NITA) ... CIRC
Circulation System (ADA) ... CIRSYS
Circulation Time [*Cardiology*] ... CT
Circulation Time Distribution [*Chemical engineering*] ... CTD
Circulator Outlet Gas Duct (OA) ... COGD
Circulatory [*Medicine*] (DAVI) ... Circ
Circulatory Assist Device (PDAA) ... CAD
Circulatory Collapse [*Cardiology*] ... CC
Circulo de Escritores y Poetas Iberoamericanos [*An association*] (EA) ... CEPI
Circulo Espanol de Amigos de Europa [*Spanish Circle of Friends of Europe*] (PD) ... CEDADE
Circum ... C
Circumambulation [*Freemasonry*] (ROG) ... CIRCUM
Circum-Atlantic Project [*Marine science*] (OSRA) ... CAO
Circumcaribbean [*MARC geographic area code Library of Congress*] (LCCP) ... cr----
Circumcision [*Medicine*] ... CIRC
Circumcision [*Urology*] (DAVI) ... circum
Circumference ... C
Circumference (WDMC) ... cir
Circumference (WDMC) ... circ
Circumference ... CIRC
Circumference (ROG) ... CIRCFCE
Circumference ... CIRCM
Circumference (KSC) ... CIRCUM
Circumference (MSA) ... CRCMF
Circumference of Head [*Medicine*] ... C of H
Circumferential Pneumatic Compression [*Medicine*] ... CPC
Circumferential Pneumatic Compression Suit [*Medicine*] (DMAA) ... CPCS
Circumferential Selectable Aim Warhead ... CSAW
Circumflex [*Coronary artery*] [*Cardiology*] (DAVI) ... CFX
Circumflex Coronary Artery [*Medicine*] (MEDA) ... CCA
Circumflex Coronary Artery [*Anatomy*] ... CIRC
Circumjacent (ROG) ... CIRCUMJAC
Circumlocution [*Used in correcting manuscripts, etc.*] ... C
Circumlunar Mission (KSC) ... CLM
Circumnavigators Club (EA) ... CC
Circum-Pacific Council for Energy and Mineral Resources (EA) ... CPCEMR
Circum-Pacific Energy and Mineral Resources Conference ... CPEMRC
Circumpolar Deep Water [*Oceanography*] ... CDW
Circumpolar Deep Water [*Also, CDW*] [*Oceanography*] ... CPDW
Circumpolar Water [*Oceanography*] ... CPW
Circumscribing Circle Diameter (MCD) ... CCD
Circumsporozoite [*Protozoology*] ... CS
Circumsporozoite Precipitation [*Clinical chemistry*] ... CSP
Circumstance (AABC) ... CIRC
Circumstance ... CIRCE
Circumstances [*Slang*] (DSUE) ... CIRCS
Circumstances Undetermined Pending Police Investigation ... CUPPI
Circumstellar Matter [*Astrophysics*] ... CSM
Circus ... CIR
Circus (WDAA) ... CIRC
Circus ... CRCS
Circus Circus Enterp [*NYSE symbol*] (TTSB) ... CIR
Circus Circus Enterprises, Inc. [*NYSE symbol*] (SPSG) ... CIR
Circus Circus Enterprises, Inc. [*Associated Press*] (SAG) ... Circus
Circus Clown Friends Club [*British*] ... CCFC
Circus Education Specialists [*In association name, CES, Inc.*] (EA) ... CES
Circus Fans Association of America (EA) ... CFA
Circus Historical Society (EA) ... CHS
Circus Model Builders, International (EA) ... CMB
Circus Movement Tachycardia [*Medicine*] (DMAA) ... CMT
Circus Saints and Sinners Club of America (EA) ... CSSCA
Circus World Museum, Baraboo, WI [*Library symbol Library of Congress*] (LCLS) ... WBaraC
Circuses [*Public-performance tariff class*] [*British*] ... K
Cirebon [*Indonesia*] [*Airport symbol*] (OAG) ... CBN
Cirebon/Panggung [*Indonesia*] [*ICAO location identifier*] (ICLI) ... WIIC
Cirencester [*Urban district in England*] ... CIRENC
Ciro Alegria [*Peru*] [*ICAO location identifier*] (ICLI) ... SPAC
Cirque ... CRQ
Cirque Energy Ltd. [*NASDAQ symbol*] (SAG) ... CIRQ
Cirque Energy Ltd. [*Associated Press*] (SAG) ... CirqueE
Cirque Energy Ltd [*NASDAQ symbol*] (TTSB) ... CIRQF
Cirrhosis [*Medicine*] ... Ci
Cirrhosis [*Medicine*] ... CIR

Cirripedia [*Quality of the bottom*] [*Nautical charts*] ... Cir
Cirrocumulus [*Meteorology*] ... CC
Cirrocumulus [*Meteorology*] ... CICU
Cirrostratus [*Meteorology*] ... CS
Cirrus [*Meteorology*] ... C
Cirrus [*Meteorology*] ... CI
Cirrus Air, Inc. [*ICAO designator*] (FAAC) ... NTS
Cirrus Logic [*NASDAQ symbol*] (TTSB) ... CRUS
Cirrus Logic, Inc. [*Associated Press*] (SAG) ... Cirrus
Cirrus Logic, Inc. [*NASDAQ symbol*] (NQ) ... CRUS
Ciruelas [*Costa Rica*] [*ICAO location identifier*] (ICLI) ... MRCI
Cis Anti-Repression Sequence [*Genetics*] ... CAR
Cis Repressor Sequence [*Genetics*] ... CRS
C.I.S. Technologies [*NASDAQ symbol*] (TTSB) ... CISI
CIS Technologies, Inc. [*Vancouver Stock Exchange symbol*] ... CIH
CIS Technologies, Inc. [*Associated Press*] (SAG) ... CIS Tch
CIS Technologies, Inc. [*NASDAQ symbol*] (NQ) ... CISI
cis-Aconityl [*Organic radical*] ... CA
cis-Acting REV-Responsive Sequence [*Genetics*] ... CAR
Cis-Air [*Czechoslovakia*] [*ICAO designator*] (FAAC) ... CSR
Cisco Certified Internetwork Expert (CDE) ... CCIE
Cisco Enterprise Accounting [*Computer science*] ... CEA
Cisco Junior College [*Texas*] ... CJC
Cisco Junior College, Cisco, TX [*Library symbol Library of Congress*] (LCLS) ... TxCiC
Cisco Resources [*Vancouver Stock Exchange symbol*] ... CCO
Cisco Router Module [*Cisco Systems, Inc.*] [*Computer science*] ... CRM
Cisco Systems [*NASDAQ symbol*] (SAG) ... CSCO
Cisco Systems, Inc. [*Associated Press*] (SAG) ... Cisco
cis-Diamminadichloroplatinum [*Cisplatin*] [*Also, cis-DDP, CPDD, CPT, DDP, P*] [*Antineoplastic drug*] ... CDDP
cis-Diamminodichloroplatinum [*Cisplatin*] [*Also, CDDP, CPDD, CPT, DDP, P*] [*Antineoplastic drug*] ... cis-DDP
Ciskei International Airways Corp. [*South Africa ICAO designator*] (FAAC) ... COK
Ciskei People's Rights Protection Party [*South Africa*] [*Political party*] (EY) ... CPRP
Cislunar Space ... CLS
Cisplatin [*Antineoplastic drug*] (DAVI) ... CACP
Cisplatin [*or Cis-platinum*] [*Antineoplastic drug*] (DAVI) ... CP
Cisplatin [*Also, cis-DDP, CDDP, CPDD, DDP, P*] [*Antineoplastic drug*] ... CPT
Cisplatin [*Antineoplastic drug*] (DAVI) ... DDP
Cisplatin, Adriamycin, Cyclophosphamide, CCNU [*Lomustine*], Oncovin [*Vincristine*] [*Antineoplastic drug regimen*] ... PACCO
Cisplatin, Cyclophosphamide, Adriamycin [*Antineoplastic drug regimen*] ... CISCA
Cisplatin, Fluorouracil [*Antineoplastic drug*] (CDI) ... CF
Cisplatin, Fluorourncil, Leucovorin Calcium [*Antineoplastic drug*] (CDI) ... CFL
Cisplatin, Methotrexate, Bleomycin, Oncovin (Vincristine) [*Antineoplastic drug regimen*] ... CABO
Cisplatin, Oncovin [*Vincristine*], Bleomycin [*Antineoplastic drug regimen*] (DAVI) ... COB
Cisplatin, Oncovin, Bleomycine [*Antineoplastic drug*] (CDI) ... COB
Cisplatin, VePesid [*Antineoplastic drug*] (CDI) ... CV
Cisplatin, Vinblastine, Etoposide, Bleomycin [*Antineoplastic drug*] (CDI) ... CVEB
Cisplatin, Vindesine, Dacarbazine [*Antineoplastic drug regimen*] ... CiViDiC
cis-Platinum [*Cisplatin*] [*Also, cis-DDP, CDDP, CPDD, CPT, DDP*] [*Antineoplastic drug*] ... P
cis-Platinum [*Cisplatin*], Adriamycin, Cyclophosphamide [*Antineoplastic drug regimen*] ... PAC
cis-Platinum Diammine Dichloride [*Cisplatin*] [*Also, CDDP, cis-DDP, CPT, DDP, P*] [*Antineoplastic drug*] ... cPDD
Cis-Platinum, Methotrexate, Bleomycin [*Antineoplastic drug regimen*] (DAVI) ... PMB
Cis-Platinumdiamminedichloride [*Also called Cisplatin and Platinol*] [*Antineoplastic drug*] (DAVI) ... CPE
Cisplatis, VePesid, Ifosfamide [*Antineoplastic drug*] (CDI) ... CVI
Cissna Park Community Unit School District, Cissna Park, IL [*Library symbol*] [*Library of Congress*] (LCLS) ... ICipSD
Cistellaria [*of Plautus*] [*Classical studies*] (OCD) ... Cist
Cistercian Fathers (TOCD) ... OCist
Cistercian Fathers (TOCD) ... ocist
Cistercian Monks of the Strict Observance (TOCD) ... socist
Cistercian Monks of the Strict Observance (TOCD) ... SOCist
[*The*] **Cistercians Order of the Strict Observance, Trappists** (TOCD) ... ocso
Cisterdan Nuns (TOCD) ... OCist
Cistern Cay, Berry Island [*Bahamas*] [*ICAO location identifier*] (ICLI) ... MYBT
CISTI [*Canada Institute for Scientific and Technical Information*] **Serials** [*Information service or system*] (CRD) ... CISTISER
Citadel (ROG) ... CIT
Citadel Capital Corp. [*Toronto Stock Exchange symbol*] ... CZJ
Citadel, Charleston, SC [*Library symbol Library of Congress*] (LCLS) ... ScCCit
Citadel, Daniel Library, Charleston, SC [*OCLC symbol*] (OCLC) ... SCN
Citadel Gold Mines, Inc. [*Toronto Stock Exchange symbol*] ... CIG
Citadel Holding [*AMEX symbol*] (TTSB) ... CDL
Citadel Holding Corp. [*AMEX symbol*] (SPSG) ... CDL
Citadel Holding Corp. [*Associated Press*] (SAG) ... Citadel
Citation (AFM) ... CIT
Citation (WDMC) ... cit
Citation (AABC) ... CITA
Citation Abstract Procurement ... CAP
CITATION Computer Sys [*NASDAQ symbol*] (TTSB) ... CITA
Citation Computer Systems [*NASDAQ symbol*] (SAG) ... CITA
Citation Computer Systems [*Associated Press*] (SAG) ... CitatnCpt
Citation Corp. [*NASDAQ symbol*] (TTSB) ... CAST
Citation Corp. Alabama [*NASDAQ symbol*] (SAG) ... CAST
Citation Corp. Alabama [*Associated Press*] (SAG) ... Citation
Citation in Examiner's Decision [*Legal term*] (DLA) ... Ex
Citation Insurance [*NASDAQ symbol*] (TTSB) ... CITIN
Citation Number [*Database terminology*] (NITA) ... CN
Citato [*Cited*] [*Latin*] (ADA) ... CIT
Citator [*or Cited In or Citing*] [*Legal term*] (DLA) ... cit
Citator and Indian Law Journal [*1908-14*] [*A publication*] (DLA) ... Cit
Citco Growth Investment [*Vancouver Stock Exchange symbol*] ... CGW
CITE Augmentation Support System (MCD) ... CASS
Cite de la Sante de Laval, Laval, PQ, Canada [*Library symbol Library of Congress*] (LCLS) ... CaQLACS
Cite de la Sante de Laval, Quebec [*Library symbol National Library of Canada*] (NLC) ... QLACS
Cited (DLA) ... C
Cited (WDMC) ... cit
Cited Authors [*Database terminology*] (NITA) ... CA
Cited Pages [*Database terminology*] (NITA) ... CP
Cited Reference [*Online database field identifier*] ... CR
Cited Volume [*Database terminology*] (NITA) ... CV
Citfed Bancorp [*NASDAQ symbol*] (TTSB) ... CTZN
CitFed Bancorp, Inc. [*Associated Press*] (SAG) ... CitFed
CitFed Bancorp, Inc. [*NASDAQ symbol*] (SAG) ... CTZN
Citi Bancshares, Inc. [*Associated Press*] (SAG) ... CitiBnc
Citi Bancshares, Inc. [*NASDAQ symbol*] (SAG) ... CNBL
Citi-Bancshares [*NASDAQ symbol*] (TTSB) ... CNBL
Citibank Economic Database [*Citibank, NA*] [*New York, NY*] [*Information service or system*] (IID) ... CITIBASE
Citibank NA [*ICAO designator*] (FAAC) ... XCX
CITIBASE-Weekly [*Citicorp Database Services*] [*Information service or system*] (IID) ... CBW
Citicasters, Inc. [*NASDAQ symbol*] (SAG) ... CITI
Citicasters, Inc. [*Associated Press*] (SAG) ... Citicast
Citicasters Inc.'A' [*NASDAQ symbol*] (TTSB) ... CITI
Citicorp [*NYSE symbol*] (SPSG) ... CCI
Citicorp [*Associated Press*] (SAG) ... Citcp
Citicorp [*Associated Press*] (SAG) ... Citicorp
Citicorp [*Toronto Stock Exchange symbol*] ... CTI
Citicorp 7.50% Dep Pfd [*NYSE symbol*] (TTSB) ... CCIPrF
Citicorp 7.75% Dep Sr 22 Pfd [*NYSE symbol*] (TTSB) ... CCIPrK
Citicorp 8.00% Dep Pfd [*NYSE symbol*] (TTSB) ... CCIPrE
Citicorp 8.30% Dep Pfd [*NYSE symbol*] (TTSB) ... CCIPrI
Citicorp 8.50% Dep Pfd [*NYSE symbol*] (TTSB) ... CCIPrJ
Citicorp 9.08% Dep Pfd [*NYSE symbol*] (TTSB) ... CCIPrD
Citicorp Adj Rt 2nd Pfd [*NYSE symbol*] (TTSB) ... CCIPr
Citicorp Adj Rt 3rd Pfd [*NYSE symbol*] (TTSB) ... CCIPrA
Citicorp Adj Rt Dep Pfd [*NYSE symbol*] (TTSB) ... CCIPrG
Citicorp Adj Rt Dep'H'Pfd [*NYSE symbol*] (TTSB) ... CCIPrH
Citicorp Economic Report [*Database*] [*Citicorp Information Services*] [*Information service or system*] (CRD) ... CER
Citicorp Economic Services [*Information service or system*] (IID) ... CES
Citicorp Investment Bank Ltd. [*England*] ... CIBL
Citicorp Scrimgeour Vickers [*Commercial firm British*] (ECON) ... CSV
Citicorp Venture Capital Fund [*Investment term*] ... CVCF
Cities in Schools (EA) ... CIS
Cities in Schools [*An association*] (EA) ... CS
[*The*] **Cities of the Eastern Roman Provinces** [*A publication*] (OCD) ... Cities E Rom Prov
Cities of the United States [*A publication*] ... CUS
Cities of the World [*A publication*] ... CIW
Cities of the World [*A publication*] ... CW
Cities Service Co., Corporate Library, New York, NY [*Library symbol Library of Congress*] (LCLS) ... NNCit
Cities Service Co., Energy Resources Group, E & P Library, Tulsa, OK [*Library symbol Library of Congress*] (LCLS) ... OkTCS
Cities Service Co., Technical Center - Energy Resources Group, Research Library,Tulsa, OK [*OCLC symbol*] (OCLC) ... OCS
CitiSave Financial [*AMEX symbol*] (TTSB) ... CZF
Citisave Financial Corp. [*Associated Press*] (SAG) ... Citisave
Citisave Financial Corp. [*AMEX symbol*] (SAG) ... CZF
Citiz Util Tr 5%'EPPICS' [*NYSE symbol*] (TTSB) ... CZNPr
Citizen (AFM) ... CIT
Citizen ... CITZN
Citizen Action Fund (EA) ... CAF
Citizen Action Group [*Defunct*] (EA) ... CAG
Citizen Diplomacy (EA) ... CD
Citizen Education Association [*Defunct*] (EA) ... CEA
Citizen Exchange Council (EA) ... CEC
Citizen Initiated Referendum Alliance [*Australia Political party*] ... CIRA
Citizen Initiated Referendums [*Political party Australia*] ... CIR
Citizen Involvement Training Program (EA) ... CITP
Citizen/Labor Energy Coalition [*Defunct*] (EA) ... C/LEC
Citizen Military Forces [*New Guinea*] ... CMF
Citizen Mobilization Campaign [*Defunct*] (EA) ... CMC
Citizen of Morris County, Denville, NJ [*Library symbol Library of Congress*] (LCLS) ... NjDeC
Citizen Radio [*Telecommunications*] (IAA) ... CR
Citizen Radio Service [*Telecommunications*] (IAA) ... CRS
Citizen Soldier (EA) ... CS
Citizen Utility Board Campaign [*Defunct*] (EA) ... CUBC
Citizens' Advice Bureau [*British*] ... CAB
Citizens' Advice Bureau, Adelaide [*Australia*] ... CABA
Citizen's Advice Bureau, Australian Capital Territory ... CABACT
Citizens' Advice Bureau, Brisbane [*Australia*] ... CABB
Citizens' Advice Bureaux [*British*] (ILCA) ... CABx
Citizens' Advice Notes [*British*] (DI) ... CANS
Citizen's Advisory Board (OICC) ... CAB

Citizens Advisory Committee on Environmental Quality ... CACEQ
Citizens' Advisory Council on the Status of Women ... CACSW
Citizens Advocacy ... CA
Citizens Advocate Center [*Antipoverty organization*] [*Defunct*] ... CAC
Citizens Against a Radioactive Environment [*An association*] (ECON) ... CARE
Citizens Against Airport Environment Association ... CAAEA
Citizens Against Bad Law (AC) ... CABL
Citizens Against Crime Association [*Australia*] ... CACA
Citizens Against Foreign Control of America (EA) ... CAFCA
Citizens Against Government Waste (EA) ... CAGW
Citizens Against Lawyer Abuse (EA) ... CALA
Citizens Against Legalized Murder [*Opposes death penalty for criminals*] [*Defunct*] ... CALM
Citizens Against Military Injustice [*Defunct*] (EA) ... CAMI
Citizens Against Noise ... CAN
Citizens Against Nuclear War [*Defunct*] (EA) ... CAN
Citizens Against PAC's [*Political Action Committees*] [*Defunct*] (EA) ... CAP
Citizens Against Pornography (EA) ... CAP
Citizens Against Rationing Health [*An association*] ... CARH
Citizens Against the Concorde Here ... CATCH
Citizens Against Tobacco Smoke (EA) ... CATS
Citizens Against UFO [*Unidentified Flying Object*] **Secrecy** (EA) ... CAUS
Citizens Against Unneccessary Tax Increases and Other Nonsense [*St. Louis organization*] ... CAUTION
Citizens Alarm System (MCD) ... CAS
Citizens Alliance for Self-Help (EA) ... CASH
Citizens Alliance for VD [*Venereal Disease*] **Awareness** (EA) ... CAVDA
Citizens & Southern Corp. ... C & S
Citizens Assessment Administration ... CAA
Citizens Association for Sound Energy (EA) ... CASE
Citizens Association for the Care of Animals (EA) ... CACA
Citizens Bancorp [*NASDAQ symbol*] (NQ) ... CIBC
Citizens Bancorp [*Associated Press*] (SAG) ... CtzBcp
Citizens Bancshares [*NASDAQ symbol*] (TTSB) ... CICS
Citizens Bancshares, Inc. [*NASDAQ symbol*] (SAG) ... CICS
Citizens Bancshares, Inc. [*Associated Press*] (SAG) ... CtzBnch
Citizens Band [*A radio frequency band for limited-range, two-way voice communications by persons without technical training or standard operator licenses*] ... CB
Citizens Band Operating Area ... CBOA
Citizens Band Radio (IAA) ... CBR
Citizens Banking [*NASDAQ symbol*] (TTSB) ... CBCF
Citizens Banking Corp. [*NASDAQ symbol*] (NQ) ... CBCF
Citizens Banking Corp. [*Associated Press*] (SAG) ... CitizBkg
Citizens Bar Association (EA) ... CBA
Citizen's Call (EA) ... CC
Citizen's Choice [*Defunct*] (EA) ... CC
Citizens' Civic Action Association [*Canada*] (BARN) ... CCAA
Citizen's Clearinghouse for Hazardous Wastes (EA) ... CCHW
Citizens' Clearinghouse on Waste Management (AC) ... CCWM
Citizens Coalition for Rational Traffic Laws [*Later, NMA*] (EA) ... CCRTL
Citizens' Commission on AIDS [*Acquired Immune Deficiency Syndrome*] (EA) ... CCA
Citizens' Commission on Civil Rights (EA) ... CCCR
Citizens Committee for a Free Cuba ... CCFC
Citizens' Committee for Children of New York (EA) ... CCC
Citizens Committee for Constitutional Liberties [*Defunct*] ... CCCL
Citizens' Committee for Immigration Reform [*Defunct*] (EA) ... CCIR
Citizens Committee for the Right to Keep and Bear Arms (EA) ... CCRKBA
Citizens Committee for Victim Assistance (EA) ... CCVA
Citizens Committee on Future Directions for the Peace Corps [*Defunct*] (EA) ... CCFDPC
Citizens Committee on Natural Resources [*Defunct*] (EA) ... CCNR
Citizens Committee on the El Salvador Crisis (EA) ... CCESC
Citizens Committee on the Fair Labor Standards Act (EA) ... CCFLSA
Citizens Communication Center (NTCM) ... CCC
Citizens Communication Center of the Institute for Public Representation [*Later, CCCPIPR*] (EA) ... CCCIPR
Citizens Communications Center Project of the Institute for Public Representation (EA) ... CCCPIPR
Citizens Concerned About Free Trade [*Canadian organization opposed to the US/Canadian free trade agreement*] (CROSS) ... CCAFT
Citizens Conference on State Legislatures [*Later, Legis 50/The Center for Legislative Improvement*] ... CCSL
Citizens Corp. [*Associated Press*] (SAG) ... CtznCp
Citizens Corp. [*NYSE symbol*] (SPSG) ... CZC
Citizens' Council Forum [*Defunct*] (EA) ... CCF
Citizens Council of America for Segregation [*Defunct*] (EA) ... CCAS
Citizens' Council on Civic Development [*Canada*] ... CCCD
Citizens' Councils of America (EA) ... CCA
Citizens Crusade Against Poverty [*Absorbed by Center for Community Change*] ... CCAP
Citizens' Defense Corps ... CDC
Citizens Democracy Corps [*An association*] (EA) ... CDC
Citizens Educational Advisory Committee ... CEAC
Citizens Electoral Council [*Political party Australia*] ... CEC
Citizens Energy Corp. [*Nonprofit*] ... CEC
Citizen's Energy Council (EA) ... CEC
Citizens' Energy Project [*Defunct*] (EA) ... CEP
Citizens Environment Alliance of Southwestern Ontario (AC) ... CEA
Citizens Federal Bank, a Federal Savings Bank [*NASDAQ symbol*] (SAG) ... CFBK
Citizens Federal Bank, FSB [*Associated Press*] (SAG) ... CtzFBk
Citizens Financial Corp. [*Associated Press*] (SAG) ... CitzFnCp
Citizens Financial Corp. [*NASDAQ symbol*] (SAG) ... CNFL
Citizens Finl Kentucky [*NASDAQ symbol*] (TTSB) ... CNFL
Citizens First Financial Corp. [*AMEX symbol*] (SAG) ... CBK
Citizens First Financial Corp. [*Associated Press*] (SAG) ... CitFFin
Citizens First Finl [*AMEX symbol*] (TTSB) ... CBK
Citizens' Flag Alliance [*An association*] ... CFA
Citizens for a Balanced Budget (EA) ... CBB
Citizens for a Better America (EA) ... CBA
Citizens for a Better Environment (EA) ... CBE
Citizens for a Competitive America (EA) ... CCA
Citizens for a Debt Free America (EA) ... CDFA
Citizens for a Drug Free America (EA) ... CDFA
Citizens for a Lakeshore Greenway (AC) ... CFLAG
Citizens for a Lebanon-Grenada National Memorial [*Defunct*] (EA) ... CLGNM
Citizens for a Nuclear Freeze [*Defunct*] (EA) ... CNF
Citizens for a Quieter City [*New York City*] [*Defunct*] (EA) ... CQC
Citizens for a Safe Environment (AC) ... CSE
Citizens for a Sound Economy [*Washington, DC*] (EA) ... CSE
Citizens for Alternatives to Trident and ELF [*Extremely Low Frequency System*] [*Defunct*] (EA) ... CATE
Citizens for America [*Later, CFAEF*] (EA) ... CFA
Citizens for America Educational Foundation (EA) ... CFAEF
Citizens for an Alternative Tax System (EA) ... CATS
Citizens for Animals [*Defunct*] (EA) ... CA
Citizens for Animals, Resources, and Environment (EA) ... CARE
Citizens for Better Care in Nursing Homes, Homes for the Aged, and Other After- Care Facilities (EA) ... CBC
Citizens for Better Driving Records [*Later, CSD*] (EA) ... CBDR
Citizens for Cable Awareness (NTCM) ... CCA
Citizens for Civil Justice Reform ... CCJR
Citizens for Clean Air ... CCA
Citizens for Common Sense [*Defunct*] (EA) ... CCS
Citizens for Constitutional Concerns (EA) ... CCC
Citizens for Decency through Law [*Later, CLF*] (EA) ... CDL
Citizens for Decent Literature [*Later, Citizens for Decency through Law*] (EA) ... CDL
Citizens for Educational Freedom (EA) ... CEF
Citizens for Energy Conservation and Solar Development ... CECSD
Citizens for Eye Research (EA) ... CER
Citizens for Eye Research to Prevent Blindness [*Defunct*] (EA) ... CERPB
Citizens for Farm Labor [*Defunct*] (EA) ... CFL
Citizens for Foreign Aid Reform [*Canada*] ... CFAR
Citizens for Foreign Aid Reform Inc. (AC) ... C-FAR
Citizens for Free Kuwait [*Defunct*] (EA) ... CFK
Citizens for Good Government [*Political fund of Ling-Temco-Vought, Inc.*] ... CITIGO
Citizens for Governmental Restraint (EA) ... CGR
Citizens for Health ... CFH
Citizens for Highway Safety [*Defunct*] (EA) ... CHS
Citizens for Improved Education ... CIE
Citizens for Informed Choices on Marijuana (EA) ... CICOM
Citizens for Law and Order (DICI) ... CLO
Citizens for Media Responsibility without Law (EA) ... CMRWL
Citizens for Ocean Law (EA) ... COL
Citizens for Proportional Representation (EA) ... CPR
Citizens for Public Justice (AC) ... CPJ
Citizens for Reagan (EA) ... CFR
Citizens for Safe Drivers [*Formerly, CBDR*] (EA) ... CSD
Citizens for Sensible Control of Acid Rain [*Defunct*] (EA) ... CSCAR
Citizens for Social Justice (EA) ... CSJ
Citizens for Social Reponsibility [*Citoyen pour la Conscience Sociale*] [*Formerly, Citizens for Nuclear Responsibility*] (AC) ... CFSR
Citizens for Space Demilitarization (EA) ... CFSD
Citizens for Tax Justice (EA) ... CTJ
Citizens for the Republic (EA) ... CFTR
Citizens for the Treatment of High Blood Pressure (EA) ... CTHBP
Citizens Foreign Aid Committee [*Defunct*] (EA) ... CFAC
Citizens Forum on Self-Government/National Municipal League [*Information service or system*] (IID) ... CF/NML
Citizens Forum on Self-Government/National Municipal League [*Information service or system*] (IID) ... CFSG/NML
Citizens Freedom Foundation (EA) ... CFF
Citizens Global Action (EA) ... CGA
Citizens Honest Elections Foundation ... CHEF
Citizens in Defense of Civil Liberties [*Defunct*] (EA) ... CDCL
Citizens in Politics [*Defunct*] (EA) ... CIP
Citizens, Inc. [*AMEX symbol*] (SAG) ... CIA
Citizens, Inc. [*Associated Press*] (SAG) ... CitizInc
Citizens Inc.'A' [*AMEX symbol*] (TTSB) ... CIA
Citizen's Internet Empowerment Coalition [*Sponsored by CDT - Center for Democracy and Technology*] ... CIEC
Citizens Law and Research Association [*Defunct*] (EA) ... CLARA
Citizens Leadership Foundation [*Defunct*] (EA) ... CLF
Citizens League Against the Sonic Boom [*Defunct*] ... CLASB
Citizens Legal Protective League [*Defunct*] (EA) ... CLPL
Citizen's Library of Economics [*A publication*] ... CLE
Citizens Library, Washington, PA [*Library symbol Library of Congress*] (LCLS) ... PW
Citizen's Library, Washington, PA [*OCLC symbol*] (OCLC) ... WWC
Citizens Military Training Corps (AABC) ... CMTC
Citizens Network for Foreign Affairs (EA) ... CNFA
Citizens Network on Waste Management (AC) ... CNWM
Citizens of the United Kingdom and Commonwealth ... CUKC
Citizens' Organisation for a Sane World [*British*] (DI) ... COSW
Citizens Organized to Defend the Environment ... CODE
Citizens Organized to Restore an Effective Corporate Tax (EA) ... CORECT

Citizens' Parliamentary Club [*Poland*] [*Political party*] ... OKP
Citizens Participation Project/the Missing Half [*Defunct*] (EA) ... CPP/TMH
Citizen's Party (EA) ... CIP
Citizen's Party [*Defunct*] (EA) ... CP
Citizens Protection Society [*British*] ... CPS
Citizens Radio UFO [*Unidentified Flying Object*] **Network** ... CRUFON
Citizens Research and Investigative Committee [*California*] ... CRIC
Citizens' Research Foundation (EA) ... CRF
Citizens Responsible Action for Safety on the Highways ... CRASH
Citizens' Rights Movement [*Israel*] [*Political party*] (ECON) ... CRM
Citizens' Scholarship Foundation of America (EA) ... CSFA
Citizens Security Group, Inc. [*NASDAQ symbol*] (NQ) ... CSGI
Citizens Security Group, Inc. [*Associated Press*] (SAG) ... CtzSec
Citizens Security Grp [*NASDAQ symbol*] (TTSB) ... CSGI
Citizens' Service Corps ... CSC
Citizens' Stamp Advisory Committee [*US Postal Service*] (EA) ... CSAC
Citizens to End Animal Suffering and Exploitation (EA) ... CEASE
Citizens to Reduce Airline Smoking Hazards [*Student legal action organization*] ... CRASH
Citizens' Training Corps ... CTC
Citizens United for Bear ... CUB
Citizens United for Racial Equality ... CURE
Citizens United for Rehabilitation of Errants (EA) ... CURE
Citizens United for Research and Education (EA) ... CURE
Citizens United for Responsible Energy (EA) ... CURE
Citizens United for Safety and Justice [*Canada*] ... CUSJ
Citizens Util 'B' [*NYSE symbol*] (TTSB) ... CZN.B
Citizens Util'A' [*NYSE symbol*] (TTSB) ... CZN.A
Citizens Utilities [*Associated Press*] (SAG) ... CitzUt
Citizens Utilities Co. [*NYSE symbol*] (SAG) ... CZN
Citizens Utilities Trust [*Associated Press*] (SAG) ... CitzUt
Citizens Utility Board ... CUB
Citizens Welfare Service, Drummond Street Centre [*Australia*] ... CWSDSC
Citizens Welfare Service of Victoria [*Australia*] ... CWSV
Citizenship Automated System [*Australia*] ... CAS
Citizenship Clearing House ... CCH
Citizenship of British Dependent Territories ... CBDT
CITL [*Crew-in-the-Loop*] **Encapsulated Methodology** [*Army*] ... CEM
CITL [*Crew-in-the-Loop*] **Encapsulation Template** [*Army*] ... CET
CitnIns [*NASDAQ symbol*] (SAG) ... CITN
CitnIns [*Associated Press*] (SAG) ... CitnIns
Cito Dispensetur [*Dispense Quickly*] [*Pharmacy*] ... CITO DISP
Citraconic Anhydride [*Organic chemistry*] ... CTA
Citrate ... CIT
Citrate Synthase [*An enzyme*] ... CS
Citrated Calcium Cyanamide (IIA) ... CCC
Citrate-Extractable Heavy Metal ... cxHM
Citrate-Phosphate-Dextrose [*Anticoagulant*] [*Hematology*] ... CPD
Citrate-Phosphate-Dextrose-Adenine [*Anticoagulant*] [*Hematology*] ... CPDA
Citric Acid Fermentation (DMAA) ... CAF
Citric Acid Fermenter [*Microbiology*] ... CAF
Citriculture ... CITRIC
Citrix Systems [*NASDAQ symbol*] (TTSB) ... CTXS
Citroen Car Club (EA) ... CCC
Citroen Quarterly Car Club (EA) ... CQCC
Citron [*Philately*] ... cit
Citronelle, AL [*FM radio station call letters*] ... WHXT
Citrovorum Factor [*Biochemistry*] ... CF
Citrovorum Rescue Factor [*Medicine*] (MEDA) ... CRF
Citrovorum-Factor Rescue [*Cancer treatment*] ... CFR
Citrulline [*An amino acid*] ... Cit
Citrus ... CTRS
Citrus Administrative Committee [*Florida*] (SRA) ... CAC
Citrus Bacterial Canker Disease [*Plant pathology*] ... CBCD
Citrus Board of South Australia ... CBSA
Citrus College, Azusa, CA [*Library symbol Library of Congress*] (LCLS) ... CAzC
Citrus College, Azusa, CA [*OCLC symbol*] (OCLC) ... CCI
Citrus Crinkly Leaf Virus [*Plant pathology*] ... CICLV
Citrus Exocortis Viroid ... CEV
Citrus Junior College [*California*] ... CJC
Citrus Label Society (EA) ... CLS
Citrus Leaf Rugose Virus [*Plant pathology*] ... CILRV
Citrus Mealybug [*Plant pest*] ... CMLB
Citrus Tatter Leaf Virus [*Plant pathology*] ... CITLV
Citrus Tristeza Virus ... CTV
Citrus Variegation Virus [*Plant pathology*] ... CVV
Citty Taxi Aereo Nacional SA de CV [*Mexico ICAO designator*] (FAAC) ... CCT
City [*Maps and charts*] ... C
City ... CTY
City (MCD) ... CY
City Administrative Office ... CAO
City Air Bus Ltd. [*British*] [*FAA designator*] (FAAC) ... CYB
City Air Defense Evaluation Tool ... CADET
City Air Ltd. [*British ICAO designator*] (FAAC) ... ISY
City Air Terminal (IAA) ... CAT
City and Guilds [*of London*] **Institute** (BARN) ... CGI
City and Guilds of London [*British*] ... C & G
City and Guilds of London Insignia Award [*British*] ... CGIA
City & Guilds of London Institute (ACII) ... C&GLI
City and Guilds of London Institute [*British*] (AIE) ... CGLI
City and Regional Magazine Association (EA) ... CRMA
City and South London Railway [*"The Tube"*] (ROG) ... C & SLR
City and South London Railway [*"The Tube"*] (ROG) ... CSLR
City and State Directories in Print [*A publication*] ... C & S DIP
City and State Directories in Print [*A publication*] ... CSDIP
City Art Museum of St. Louis, St. Louis, MO [*Library symbol Library of Congress*] (LCLS) ... MoSR
City Bank, North America, New York, NY [*Library symbol*] [*Library of Congress*] (LCLS) ... NNCBN
City Business System [*British Telecom*] (NITA) ... CBS
City Center Arts [*A publication*] ... CCA
City [*or County*] **Civil Defense Director** ... CCD
City College of City University of New York ... CCCUNY
City College of City University of New York, New York, NY [*Library symbol Library of Congress*] (LCLS) ... NNR
City College of New York [*Later, City University of New York*] ... CCNY
City College of New York [*New York*] [*Seismograph station code, US Geological Survey*] (SEIS) ... CNY
City College of New York, New York, NY [*OCLC symbol*] (OCLC) ... ZXC
City College of San Francisco [*California*] ... CCSF
City College of San Francisco, San Francisco, CA [*OCLC symbol*] (OCLC) ... CCS
City College of San Francisco, San Francisco, CA [*Library symbol Library of Congress*] (LCLS) ... CSfCiC
City College of The City University of New York (GAGS) ... CCNY (CUNY)
City Communications Centre [*British*] (CB) ... CCC
City Corp. [*of London*] ... CC
City Council [*or Councillor*] ... CC
City Court (DLA) ... CC
City Court (DLA) ... City Ct
City Court Reports [*A publication*] (DLA) ... CCR
City Court Reports [*New York*] [*A publication*] (DLA) ... City Ct R
City Court Reports [*New York*] [*A publication*] (DLA) ... City Ct Rep
City Court Reports, Supplement [*New York*] [*A publication*] (DLA) ... CC Supp
City Court Reports, Supplement [*New York*] [*A publication*] (DLA) ... City Ct R Supp
City Court Reports, Supplement [*New York*] [*A publication*] (DLA) ... City Ct Rep Supp
City Court Reports, Supplement [*New York*] [*A publication*] (DLA) ... City Ct Supp (NY)
City Demonstration Agency ... CDA
City Development Board (OICC) ... CDB
City Express [*ICAO designator*] (AD) ... OU
City Facts and Abstracts [*EDIC*] [*Ringmer Near Lewes, East Sussex, England*] [*Information service or system*] (IID) ... CFA
City Flug [*ICAO designator*] (AD) ... VG
City Hall Branch, Gloucester Public Library, Ontario [*Library symbol National Library of Canada*] (NLC) ... OGO
City Hall Recorder [*New York City*] [*A publication*] (DLA) ... City Hall Rec (NY)
City Hall Recorder (Rogers) [*New York City*] [*A publication*] (DLA) ... CH Rec
City Hall Reporter (Lomas) [*New York City*] [*A publication*] (DLA) ... CH Rep
City Hall Reporter (Lomas) [*New York City*] [*A publication*] (DLA) ... City H Rep
City Hall Reporter (Lomas) [*New York City*] [*A publication*] (DLA) ... City Hall Rep
City Hall Reporter (Lomas) [*New York City*] [*A publication*] (DLA) ... City Hall Rep (NY)
City Holding [*NASDAQ symbol*] (TTSB) ... CHCO
City Holding Co. [*NASDAQ symbol*] (NQ) ... CHCO
City Holding Co. [*Associated Press*] (SAG) ... CtyHld
City Hospital at Elmhurst, Elmhurst, NY [*Library symbol Library of Congress*] (LCLS) ... NElmhC
City Hostess International (EA) ... CHI
City Imperial Volunteers [*Military unit*] [*British*] ... CIV
City Industry Task Force [*Confederation of British Industry*] ... CITF
City Investing Co. Liquidating Trust [*NASDAQ symbol*] (NQ) ... CNVL
City Investing Co. Liquidating Trust [*Associated Press*] (SAG) ... CtyLTr
City Investing Liq Tr [*NASDAQ symbol*] (TTSB) ... CNVLZ
City Investment Centres [*British*] ... CIC
City Jet [*Ireland*] (FAAC) ... BCY
City Limits [*In outdoor advertising*] (WDMC) ... C/
City Merchant Developers [*British*] ... CMD
City Merchant Developers Development Coordination [*British*] ... CMDDC
City National [*NYSE symbol*] (TTSB) ... CYN
City National Corp. [*Associated Press*] (SAG) ... CityNC
City National Corp. [*NYSE symbol*] (SPSG) ... CYN
City Normal School, Syracuse, NY [*Library symbol Library of Congress Obsolete*] (LCLS) ... NSyN
City of Adelaide Planning Commission [*Australia*] ... CAPC
City of Alamosa-Southern Peaks Library, Alamosa, CO [*Library symbol Library of Congress*] (LCLS) ... CoAl
City of Bangor, Maine [*FAA designator*] (FAAC) ... XBG
City of Birmingham Symphony Orchestra [*British*] ... CBSO
City of Calgary Electric System, Resource Centre, Calgary, AB, Canada [*Library symbol Library of Congress*] (LCLS) ... CaACES
City of David Archaeological Project ... CODAP
City of Edmonton Archives, Alberta [*Library symbol National Library of Canada*] (NLC) ... AEEA
City of Edmonton Archives, Edmonton, AB, Canada [*Library symbol Library of Congress*] (LCLS) ... CaAEEA
City of Etobicoke Archives, Etobicoke, ON, Canada [*Library symbol*] [*Library of Congress*] (LCLS) ... CaOEA
City of Hope (EA) ... CH
City of Hope Medical Center, Duarte, CA [*Library symbol Library of Congress*] (LCLS) ... CDuH
City of Hope Medical Center, Duarte, CA [*OCLC symbol*] (OCLC) ... CHM
City of Houston Legal Department, Houston, TX [*Library symbol Library of Congress*] (LCLS) ... TxHLD
City of Lincoln Public Library, Lincoln, United Kingdom [*Library symbol Library of Congress*] (LCLS) ... UkLin
City of London [*British*] ... C of L
City of London [*British*] ... CL

City of London Engineers [*British military*] (DMA) .... CLE
City of London National Guard [*British military*] (DMA) .... CLNG
City of London Police (ROG) .... CLP
City of London Rifles [*British*] .... CLR
City of London Yeomanry [*Military British*] (ROG) .... C of LY
City of Memphis Hospital, Memphis, TN [*Library symbol Library of Congress*] (LCLS) .... TMCH
City of Ottawa Archives, Ontario [*Library symbol National Library of Canada*] (NLC) .... OOOA
City of Prineville Railway [*AAR code*] .... COP
City of Refuge National Historic Park .... CIRE
City of Savannah, Municipal Research Library, Savannah, GA [*Library symbol*] [*Library of Congress*] (LCLS) .... GSM
City of Sydney Cultural Centre [*Australia*] .... CSCC
City of Sydney Public Library, Sydney, NSW, Australia [*Library symbol Library of Congress*] (LCLS) .... AuS
City of Toronto, Division of Records and Archives, Toronto, ON, Canada [*Library symbol*] [*Library of Congress*] (LCLS) .... CaOTCTAR
City of Tucson, Department of Planning, Tucson, AZ [*Library symbol*] [*Library of Congress*] (LCLS) .... AzTDP
City of White Rock Museum and Archives, British Columbia [*Library symbol National Library of Canada*] (NLC) .... BWRM
City of Winnipeg Metro Planning Division, Manitoba [*Library symbol National Library of Canada*] (NLC) .... MWMP
City of York Community & Agency Social Planning Council (AC) .... Y-CASP
City of York Public Library, Toronto, Ontario [*Library symbol National Library of Canada*] (NLC) .... OTYP
City Planning Commission (WDAA) .... CPC
City Police Commissioner (DAS) .... CPC
City Police Court [*British*] (DAS) .... CPC
City Reference File [*Bureau of the Census*] (GFGA) .... CRF
City Resources (Canada) Ltd. [*Vancouver Stock Exchange symbol Toronto Stock Exchange symbol*] .... CIZ
City Technology Colleges [*British*] .... CTC
City University Business School [*London, England*] .... CUBS
City University Library Resource Center, Bellevue, WA [*Library symbol*] [*Library of Congress*] (LCLS) .... WaBC
City University of New York (CDAI) .... CUNY
City University of New York, Central Office, New York, NY [*Library symbol*] [*Library of Congress*] (LCLS) .... NNCU-C
City University of New York, Division of Teacher Education, New York, NY [*Library symbol Library of Congress*] (LCLS) .... NNCU-T
City University of New York (Graduate Center) (GAGS) .... CUNY (Grad Cent)
City University of New York, Graduate Center, New York, NY [*Library symbol Library of Congress*] (LCLS) .... NNCU-G
City University of New York, Graduate School, New York, NY [*OCLC symbol*] (OCLC) .... ZGM
City University of New York, Law School, Flushing, NY [*Library symbol Library of Congress*] (LCLS) .... NNCU-L
City Urban Renewal Management Corp. [*New York City*] .... CURMCO
City-County Memorial Library, Bay St. Louis, MS [*Library symbol Library of Congress*] (LCLS) .... MsBs
City-County Public Library, Moundsville, WV [*Library symbol Library of Congress*] (LCLS) .... WvMo
Cityflyer Express [*British ICAO designator*] (FAAC) .... CFE
City-Jet Luftverklehrsges, GmbH [*Austria ICAO designator*] (FAAC) .... CIT
City-Link Airlines Ltd. [*Nigeria*] [*ICAO designator*] (FAAC) .... CRG
Cityscape Financial [*NASDAQ symbol*] (TTSB) .... CTYS
Cityscape Financial Corp. [*NASDAQ symbol*] (SAG) .... CTYS
Cityscape Financial Corp. [*Associated Press*] (SAG) .... Ctyscape
Ciudad Acuna [*Mexico ICAO location identifier*] (ICLI) .... MMCC
Ciudad Bolivar [*Venezuela*] [*Airport symbol*] (OAG) .... CBL
Ciudad Bolivar, Bolivar [*Venezuela ICAO location identifier*] (ICLI) .... SVCB
Ciudad de Valles [*Mexico*] [*Airport symbol*] (AD) .... VAE
Ciudad Del Carmen [*Mexico*] [*Airport symbol*] (OAG) .... CME
Ciudad Del Carmen [*Mexico ICAO location identifier*] (ICLI) .... MMCE
Ciudad Juarez [*Mexico*] [*Airport symbol*] (OAG) .... CJS
Ciudad Juarez/Abraham Gonzalez Internacional [*Mexico ICAO location identifier*] (ICLI) .... MMCS
Ciudad Mante [*Mexico*] [*Airport symbol*] (AD) .... MMC
Ciudad Mante [*Mexico ICAO location identifier*] (ICLI) .... MMDM
Ciudad Obregon [*Mexico*] [*Airport symbol*] (OAG) .... CEN
Ciudad Obregon [*Mexico ICAO location identifier*] (ICLI) .... MMCN
Ciudad Presidente Stroessner [*Paraguay*] [*ICAO location identifier*] (ICLI) .... SGPS
Ciudad Victoria [*Mexico*] [*Airport symbol*] (OAG) .... CVM
Ciudad Victoria [*Mexico ICAO location identifier*] (ICLI) .... MMCV
Civic CVC
Civic Action .... CA
Civic Action Centers [*Military*] (CINC) .... CAC
Civic Action Group [*Military*] (CINC) .... CAG
Civic Action Group [*Military*] (CINC) .... CIVACTGP
Civic Action Institute [*Defunct*] (EA) .... CAI
Civic Action Team [*Navy*] (VNW) .... CATS
Civic Bancorp [*NASDAQ symbol*] (SAG) CIVC
Civic Bancorp [*Associated Press*] (SAG) .... CivicBc
Civic Catering Association [*British*] (BI) .... CCA
Civic Club of Philadelphia, Philadelphia, PA [*Library symbol Library of Congress Obsolete*] (LCLS) .... PPCiC
Civic Democratic Alliance [*Former Czechoslovakia*] [*Political party*] (EY) .... CDA
Civic Democratic Party [*Former Czechoslovakia*] [*Political party*] (EY) .... CDP
Civic Democratic Party - Public Against Violence [*Former Czechoslovakia*] [*Political party*] (EY) .... CDU-PAV
Civic Development Movement [*Sierra Leone*] [*Political party*] (EY) .... CDEM
Civic Entertainment Officers' Association [*British*] (BI) .... CEOA
Civic Information & Techniques Exchange [*Citizens Forum on Self-Government/National Municipal League*] [*Information service or system*] (IID) .... CIVITEX
Civic Issues Voluntary Information Council [*Michigan*] CIVIC
Civic Movement [*Former Czechoslovakia*] [*Political party*] (EY) .... CM
Civic Square, Information and Reference, Sudbury Public Library, Ontario [*Library symbol National Library of Canada*] (NLC) .... OSUCS
Civic Trust (DCTA) .... CT
Civic United Front [*Tanzania*] [*Political party*] .... CUF
Civil [*Legal term*] (DLA) c
Civil (AFM) CIV
Civil (MSA) CVL
Civil CVL
Civil Action Detachment [*Military*] (DNAB) .... CAD
Civil Action Team (AFM) .... CAT
Civil Administration Committee [*US Military Government, Germany*] .... CAC
Civil Administrator (CINC) .... CIVAD
Civil Advanced Gas-Cooled Reactor (NUCP) .... CAGR
Civil Aeromedical Institute [*FAA*] .... CAI
Civil Aeromedical Institute [*FAA*] .... CAMI
Civil Aeromedical Research Institute [*FAA*] .... CARI
Civil Aeronautical Regulation (MCD) .... CAR
Civil Aeronautics Administration [*Later, part of FAA*] .... CAA
Civil Aeronautics Administration Manual .... CAAM
Civil Aeronautics Administration Type Certificate .... CAATC
Civil Aeronautics Authority (AAGC) .... CAA
Civil Aeronautics Authority Journal [*A publication*] (AAGC) .... CAAJ
Civil Aeronautics Authority Opinions [*A publication*] (DLA) .... CAA Op
Civil Aeronautics Authority Reports [*A publication*] (DLA) .... CAA
Civil Aeronautics Board [*Independent government agency*] [*Terminated, 1984, functions transferred to Department of Transportation*] .... CAB
Civil Aeronautics Board Air Transport Mobilization Standby Order .... CAB-ATM
Civil Aeronautics Board Reports [*A publication*] (DLA) .... CAB
Civil Aeronautics Bulletin .... CAB
Civil Aeronautics Manual .... CAM
Civil Affairs .... CA
Civil Affairs (DOMA) .... CA
Civil Affairs Association (EA) .... CAA
Civil Affairs Division [*Military*] .... CAD
Civil Affairs Group [*Military*] (DNAB) .... CAG
Civil Affairs Inland Depot [*for relief supplies to liberated territory*] [*British World War II*] .... CAID
Civil Affairs/Military Government .... CA/MG
Civil Affairs Mobile Training Team [*Military*] (CINC) .... CAMTT
Civil Affairs Officer [*Navy*] .... CAO
Civil Affairs Officer [*Army*] (AABC) S5
Civil Affairs Police Officer [*British World War II*] .... CAPO
Civil Affairs Section .... CAS
Civil Affairs Section [*of an Army division or brigade general staff; the officer in charge of this section*] G-5
Civil Affairs Service (Burma) [*British*] .... CAS(B)
Civil Affairs Service (Malaya) [*British*] .... CAS(M)
Civil Affairs Staff Center [*Wimbledon, England*] .... CCSC
Civil Affairs Staff Officer [*British*] .... CASO
Civil Affairs Staging Area [*World War II*] .... CASA
Civil Affairs Summary [*Navy*] .... CASUM
Civil Affairs Team .... CAT
Civil Affairs Training Center [*World War II*] .... CATC
Civil Affairs Training School [*Navy*] .... CATS
Civil Affairs Unit [*British*] .... CAU
Civil Agency .... CA
Civil Air Attache [*British*] .... CAA
Civil Air Branch [*Air Force*] .... CAB
Civil Air Carrier Turbojet (FAAC) .... CACT
Civil Air Defense Identification Zone (MCD) .... CADIZ
Civil Air Defense Services .... CADS
Civil Air Defense Warning [*System*] .... CADW
Civil Air Guard [*British*] .... CAG
Civil Air Movement .... CAM
Civil Air Patrol (EA) .... CAP
Civil Air Patrol Coastal Patrol [*Wartime*] .... CAPCP
Civil Air Patrol Guard .... CAPG
Civil Air Publication [*British*] (DEN) .... CAP
Civil Air Regulation [*FAA*] .... CAR
Civil Air Rescue Emergency Services (AC) .... CARES
Civil Air Rescue Emergency Services - AAC Project [*Also, Alberta Aviation Council Project*] (AC) .... CARES
Civil Air Reserve (AAG) .... CAR
Civil Air Search & Rescue Association (AC) .... CASARA
Civil Air Surgeon [*of FAA*] .... CAS
Civil Air Traffic Operations (AIA) .... CATO
Civil Air Training Academy [*Australia*] .... CATA
Civil Air Transport [*Free China's international airline*] .... CAT
Civil Air Transport Industry Training Board (MCD) .... CATITB
Civil Aircraft Airworthiness Data Recording Program [*British*] (MCD) .... CAADRP
Civil Aircraft Control Advisory Committee [*British*] (AIA) .... CACAC
Civil Aircraft Inspection Procedure (DA) .... CAIP
Civil Aircraft Notification Procedure (PDAA) .... CANP
Civil and Commercial Code [*A publication*] (DLA) .... C Com C
Civil and Commercial Code [*A publication*] (DLA) .... C Comm C
Civil and Criminal Law Series [*India*] [*A publication*] (DLA) .... Civ & Cr LS
Civil and Defense Mobilization Board [*Military*] (SAA) .... CDMB
Civil and Environmental Engineering .... CEE
Civil and Environmental Engineering Development Office [*Tyndall Air Force Base, FL*] .... CEEDO

Civil and Mining Engineer ... C & ME
Civil and Public Services Association [*British*] ... CPSA
Civil and Sanitary Engineering (MCD) ... CSE
Civil Appeals [*A publication*] (DLA) ... Civ
Civil Appeals, Texas [*A publication*] (DLA) ... CA TX
Civil Assistant Personal Services [*Navy British*] ... CAPS
Civil Assistant to Medical Director-General [*Navy British*] ... CAMDG
Civil Authorities [*Army*] ... C Auth
Civil Authorities ... CA
Civil Aviation ... CA
Civil Aviation Administration [*Marine science*] (OSRA) ... CAA
Civil Aviation Administration (USDC) ... CAA
Civil Aviation Administration of China ... CAAC
Civil Aviation Administration of Korea [*North Korea*] ... CAAK
Civil Aviation Administration of Vietnam ... CAAV
Civil Aviation Advisory [*or Assistance*] **Group** [*FAA*] ... CAAG
Civil Aviation Authority [*British*] ... CAA
Civil Aviation Authority of China (GAVI) ... CAAC
Civil Aviation Authority of New Zealand [*ICAO designator*] (FAAC) ... CIV
Civil Aviation Authority - War Training Service ... CAA-WTS
Civil Aviation Branch, Canadian Air Transportation Administration, Transport Canada [*Direction Generale de l'Aviation Civile, Administration Canadienne des Transports Aeriens, Transports Canada*] **Edmonton, Alberta** [*Library symbol National Library of Canada*] (NLC) ... AEMTCA
Civil Aviation Chaplains International (EAIO) ... CACI
Civil Aviation Communication Center [*Canada*] ... CACC
Civil Aviation Flying Unit [*British*] (AIA) ... CAFU
Civil Aviation Historical Society [*Australia*] ... CAHS
Civil Aviation Information Circular [*British*] (AIA) ... CAIC
Civil Aviation Inspectorate of the Czech Republic [*ICAO designator*] (FAAC) ... CBA
Civil Aviation Licensing Act (DLA) ... CALA
Civil Aviation Medical Association (EA) ... CAMA
Civil Aviation Medical Institute (MCD) ... CAMI
Civil Aviation Meteorological Facsimile Network (PDAA) ... CAMFAX
Civil Aviation Order ... CAO
Civil Aviation Packet Switching Integrated Network (DA) ... CAPSIN
Civil Aviation Planning Committee (AFM) ... CAPC
Civil Aviation Purchasing Service [*ICAO*] (DA) ... CAPS
Civil Aviation Research and Development [*NASA*] ... CARD
Civil Aviation Signal Training Establishment (IAA) ... CASTE
Civil Aviation Statistics Programme [*ICAO*] [*United Nations*] (DUND) ... CASP
Civil Budget Committee [*NATO*] (NATG) ... CBC
Civil Censorship Division [*US Military Government, Germany*] ... CCD
Civil Censorship Study Group (EA) ... CCSG
Civil Code [*A publication*] (DLA) ... CC
Civil Code of Louisiana [*A publication*] (DLA) ... Code LA
Civil Code of Practice [*A publication*] (DLA) ... Civ Code Prac
Civil Code of Quebec [*A publication*] (DLA) ... CCQ
Civil Commotion ... CC
Civil Communication Planning Committee [*Military*] (NATG) ... CCPC
Civil Communications Element [*Military*] (NATG) ... CCE
Civil Communications-Electronics Working-Group [*Military*] (NATG) ... CCEWG
Civil Contingency Unit [*Cabinet Office*] [*British*] (DI) ... CCU
Civil Cooperation Bureau [*South African covert-operations team*] (ECON) ... CCB
Civil Coordination Detachment [*General Air Traffic Element at Operational Traffic and Defense Centers*] [*NATO*] ... CCD
Civil Coordination Detachment General [*NATO*] (NATG) ... CCDG
Civil Court ... CC
Civil Court (DLA) ... Civ Ct
Civil Court of Record (DLA) ... Civ Ct Rec
Civil Damage Assessment Program [*Army*] (AABC) ... CDAP
Civil Defence ... CIVDEF
Civil Defence Force [*British military*] (DMA) ... CDF
Civil Defence Legion [*British military*] (DMA) ... CDL
Civil Defense ... CD
Civil Defense Adult Education [*Program*] ... CDAE
Civil Defense Adult Education Program ... CDAEP
Civil Defense Advisory Council ... CDAC
Civil Defense Agency ... CDA
Civil Defense Ambulance Service (WDAA) ... CDAS
Civil Defense Career Development Program ... CDCDP
Civil Defense Committee (NATG) ... CDC
Civil Defense Coordinator (AAG) ... CDC
Civil Defense Countermeasures System ... CDCS
Civil Defense Director/Coordinator ... CD D/C
Civil Defense Education Program ... CDEP
Civil Defense Emergency Operations System ... CDEOS
Civil Defense Exercise ... CDEX
Civil Defense Management ... CDM
Civil Defense Organization [*United Nations*] ... CDO
Civil Defense Quality Check Program [*Military*] (DNAB) ... CDQCP
Civil Defense Receiver ... CDR
Civil Defense Report ... CIDERE
Civil Defense Research Associates ... CDRA
Civil Defense Support Detachments (AABC) ... CDSD
Civil Defense, United States of America [*Home study course*] ... CD-USA
Civil Defense University Extension Program ... CDUEP
Civil Defense Warning ... CDW
Civil Defense Warning System ... CDWS
Civil Direction of Shipping (NVT) ... CDS
Civil Direction of Shipping Organization (MCD) ... CDSORG
Civil Director of Economics ... CDE
Civil Disobedience ... CD
Civil District Court (DLA) ... Civ D Ct
Civil Disturbance Group [*Department of Justice intelligence unit*] ... CDG
Civil Disturbance Readiness Conditions [*Army*] (AABC) ... CIDCON
Civil Disturbance Status Reporting [*Army*] (AABC) ... CIDSTAT
Civil Effects Exercise [*NASA*] (KSC) ... CEX
Civil Effects Experiments [*DASA and AEC*] ... CEX
Civil Effects Test Group [*DASA and AEC*] ... CETG
Civil Effects Test Operations [*DASA and AEC*] ... CETO
Civil Emergency Information Room [*NATO*] (NATG) ... CEIR
Civil Emergency Planning [*NATO*] (NATG) ... CEP
Civil Emergency Planning Bureau [*NATO*] (NATG) ... CEPB
Civil Emergency Planning Committee [*US/Canada*] ... CEPC
Civil Engineer ... CE
Civil Engineer (FAAC) ... CENGR
Civil Engineer Automated Specification Retrieval System [*Air Force*] ... CEASRS
Civil Engineer Construction Operations Group [*Air Force*] (AFM) ... CECOGp
Civil Engineer Corps [*Army*] ... CEC
Civil Engineer Corps, Engineer-in-Training [*Army*] (DNAB) ... CEC EIT
Civil Engineer Corps Officer's School [*Army*] (DNAB) ... CECOFFSCOL
Civil Engineer Corps Officer's School [*Army*] (DNAB) ... CECOS
Civil Engineer Corps, Professional Engineer [*Army*] (DNAB) ... CEC PE
Civil Engineer Corps, Registered Architect [*Army*] (DNAB) ... CEC RA
Civil Engineer Management System (AFM) ... CEMS
Civil Engineer Preventive Maintenance [*Air Force*] ... CEPM
Civil Engineer Support Equipment [*Army*] ... CESE
Civil Engineer Support Management Information System [*Military*] (DNAB) ... CESMIS
Civil Engineer Support Office [*Navy*] ... CESO
Civil Engineer Support Plan ... CESP
Civil Engineering ... CIVENG
Civil Engineering and Evaluation Laboratory [*Navy*] (MCD) ... CEREL
Civil Engineering and Services Management Evaluation Team [*Military*] ... CESMET
Civil Engineering Computer Laboratory [*MIT*] (MCD) ... CECL
Civil Engineering Computing System (PDAA) ... CECS
Civil Engineering Field Activities Center ... CEFAC
Civil Engineering File (DOMA) ... CEF
Civil Engineering Flight [*Military*] ... CEF
Civil Engineering Flight, Heavy Repair [*Military*] ... CEFHR
Civil Engineering Group [*Air Force*] ... CEG
Civil Engineering Laboratory [*Also, CIVENGRLAB*] [*Port Hueneme, CA*] [*Navy*] (MCD) ... CEL
Civil Engineering Laboratory [*Navy*] (DNAB) ... CIVENGLAB
Civil Engineering Laboratory [*Also, CEL*] [*Navy*] (MUGU) ... CIVENGRLAB
Civil Engineering Maintenance, Inspection, Repair, and Training Team [*Air Force*] ... CEMIRT
Civil Engineering Operations Squadron [*Air Force*] ... CEOS
Civil Engineering Package (IEEE) ... CEP
Civil Engineering Problems ... CEPS
Civil Engineering Program Applications (MCD) ... CEPA
Civil Engineering Report ... CER
Civil Engineering Report of Performance (AFM) ... CERP
Civil Engineering Research Association ... CERA
Civil Engineering Squadron [*Air Force*] ... CES
Civil Engineering Squadron [*Air Force*] ... CIVENGSq
Civil Engineering Squadron, Heavy Repair [*Air Force*] ... CESHR
Civil Engineering Support Flight [*Military*] ... CESF
Civil Engineering Support Plan Generator (DOMA) ... CESPG
Civil Engineering Support Squadron [*Air Force*] ... CESS
Civil Engineering Systems Laboratory [*University of Illinois*] ... CESL
Civil Engineers Corps Officers School [*Navy*] ... CECOS
Civil Enterprise [*Publishing program*] ... CE
Civil Fast Reactor (PDAA) ... CFR
Civil Guard [*Air Force*] (MCD) ... CG
Civil Imprisonment ... CI
Civil Industrial Technologies Cooperation Plan [*Framework agreement for conducting cooperative global research*] ... CITCP
Civil Information and Education Section of Allied Headquarters [*World War II*] ... CIANDE
Civil Investigative Demand [*Department of Justice*] ... CID
Civil Jet Transport ... CJT
Civil Justice Quarterly [*A publication*] (DLA) ... Civ Just Q
Civil Labour Control Unit [*British*] ... CLCU
Civil Law ... CL
Civil Liability Convention [*British*] ... CLC
Civil Liaison Division [*Army*] ... CLD
Civil Liaison Officer [*Army*] (AABC) ... CLO
Civil Liberties (ILCA) ... CL
Civil Liberties Action Security Project [*Canada*] ... CLASP
Civil Liberties and Police [*Germany*] ... CILIP
Civil Liberties Bureau [*Forerunner of the American Civil Liberties Union*] ... CLB
Civil Liberties Docket (DLA) ... Civ Lib Dock
Civil Liberties Educational Foundation [*Defunct*] (EA) ... CLEF
Civil Liberties Legal Defense Fund (EA) ... CLLDF
Civil Liberties Union (IIA) ... CLU
Civil Liberty (DLA) ... CIV LIB
Civil Litigation Reporter [*A publication*] (DLA) ... Civ Litigation Rep
Civil Mediator Organisation [*British*] (DA) ... CASOR
Civil Member for Development and Production [*British*] ... CMDP
Civil Military Exercise (MCD) ... CIMEX
Civil Monetary Penalties [*Medicaid program*] (GFGA) ... CMP
Civil Navigation Aids System ... CNAS
Civil Number [*Docket number*] (AAGC) ... Civ No
Civil Nursing Reserve (DAVI) ... CNR
Civil Operations for Rural Development Support [*Army*] ... CORDS
Civil Operations Revolutionary Development Support [*Army*] (AABC) ... CORDS

Civil Parish [*British*] ..... CP
Civil Pilots for Regulatory Reform (EA) ..... CPRR
Civil Post Office (AFM) ..... CPO
Civil Power ..... CP
Civil Practice Act [*New York*] (DLA) ..... CPA
Civil Practice Law and Rules [*A publication*] (DLA) ..... Civ Prac
Civil Practice Law and Rules [*New York, NY*] ..... CPLR
Civil Preparedness Guide [*Civil Defense*] ..... CPG
Civil Procedure [*Legal term*] (DLA) ..... Civ Proc
Civil Procedure [*Legal term*] ..... CP
Civil Procedure Reports [*New York*] [*A publication*] (DLA) ..... Civ Pr
Civil Procedure Reports [*New York*] [*A publication*] (DLA) ..... Civ Pr Rep
Civil Procedure Reports [*New York*] [*A publication*] (DLA) ..... Civ Pro
Civil Procedure Reports [*New York*] [*A publication*] (DLA) ..... Civ Pro R
Civil Procedure Reports [*New York*] [*A publication*] (DLA) ..... Civ Pro Reports
Civil Procedure Reports [*New York*] [*A publication*] (DLA) ..... Civ Proc R
Civil Procedure Reports [*New York*] [*A publication*] (DLA) ..... Civ Proc Rep
Civil Procedure Reports [*New York*] [*A publication*] (DLA) ..... Civil Pro R
Civil Procedure Reports [*New York*] [*A publication*] (DLA) ..... CP
Civil Procedure Reports [*New York*] [*A publication*] (DLA) ..... NY Civ Proc Rep
Civil Procedure Reports [*New York*] [*A publication*] (DLA) ..... NYCP
Civil Procedure Reports, New Series [*1908-13*] [*New York*] [*A publication*] (DLA) ..... Civ Pro R (NS)
Civil Procedure Reports, New Series [*1908-13*] [*New York*] [*A publication*] (DLA) ..... Civ Proc (NS)
Civil Procedure Reports, New Series [*1908-13*] [*New York*] [*A publication*] (DLA) ..... Civ Proc R (NS)
Civil Procedure Reports, New Series [*1908-13*] [*New York*] [*A publication*] (DLA) ..... Civ Proc Rep NS
Civil Procedure Reports, New Series [*1908-13*] [*New York*] [*A publication*] (DLA) ..... CPR (NS)
Civil Procedure Reports, New Series [*1908-13*] [*New York*] [*A publication*] (DLA) ..... CPRC (NS)
Civil Procedures, Quebec ..... CPQ
Civil Rail Lines Important to National Defense [*BTS*] (TAG) ..... CRLIND
Civil Readjustment Officer [*Military*] ..... CRO
Civil Reserve Air Field [*Department of Commerce*] (MCD) ..... CRAF
Civil Reserve Air Fleet [*Department of Commerce*] ..... CRAF
Civil Reserve Air Fleet Summary Report [*Department of Commerce*] ..... CRAFREP
Civil Reserve Air Tanker [*Department of Commerce*] (MCD) ..... CRAT
Civil Reserve Aircraft Fleet [*OST*] (TAG) ..... CRAF
Civil Reserve Airlift Fleet (DOMA) ..... CRAF
Civil Reserve Auxiliary Fleet Ships (DOMA) ..... CRAFTS
Civil Resettlement Unit [*British*] (DAS) ..... CRU
Civil Rights (DLA) ..... CIV R
Civil Rights ..... CR
Civil Rights Act [*1957, 1964, 1968*] ..... CRA
Civil Rights Act Compliance Log (OICC) ..... CRACL
Civil Rights and Law Reform [*Australia*] ..... CRLR
Civil Rights Commission [*Federal government*] ..... CRC
Civil Rights Division [*Department of Justice*] ..... CRD
Civil Rights of Institutionalized Persons Act of 1980 (EDAC) ..... CRIPA
Civil Rights Office, Education Department (OICC) ..... CROED
Civil Rights Party [*South Korea Political party*] (PPW) ..... CRP
Civil Rights-Civil Liberties (DLA) ..... CR-CL
Civil Rotorcraft IFR [*Instrument Flight Rules*] **Terminal-Area Technology Enhancement Research** (GAVI) ..... CRITTER
Civil Servant (DLA) ..... CS
Civil Service (DLA) ..... CIV S
Civil Service (DLA) ..... Civ Serv
Civil Service ..... CS
Civil Service and Post Office Sanitorium Society [*British*] (DI) ..... CSSS
Civil Service Arbitration Awards (DLA) ..... CSAA
Civil Service Arbitration Awards (DLA) ..... CSAB
Civil Service Arbitration Tribunal [*British*] ..... CSAT
Civil Service Association of Canada ..... CSAC
Civil Service Benevolent Fund [*British*] ..... CSBF
Civil Service Board (AAG) ..... CSB
Civil Service Building Society [*British*] ..... CSBS
Civil Service Cadet Battalion [*British military*] (DMA) ..... CSCB
Civil Service Catering Organization [*British*] ..... CISCO
Civil Service Clerical Association [*Later, CPSA*] [*British*] (DI) ..... CSCA
Civil Service Club [*British*] ..... CSC
Civil Service College [*British*] ..... CSC
Civil Service Commission [*Later, MSPB*] ..... CSC
Civil Service Commission - Investigations ..... CSC-I
Civil Service Commission of Canada (BARN) ..... CSCC
Civil Service Commission of Ontario, Toronto, ON, Canada [*Library symbol Library of Congress*] (LCLS) ..... CaOTCSC
Civil Service Commission of Ontario, Toronto, Ontario [*Library symbol National Library of Canada*] (NLC) ..... OTCSC
Civil Service Cooperative Society [*British*] ..... CSCS
Civil Service Council for Further Education [*British*] ..... CSCFE
Civil Service Department [*British*] ..... CSD
Civil Service Employees Association (EA) ..... CSEA
Civil Service Foreign Service Allowances Committee [*British*] ..... CSFSAC
Civil Service Forum (EA) ..... CSF
Civil Service Housing Association [*British*] ..... CSHA
Civil Service Insurance Society [*British*] ..... CSIS
Civil Service Legal Society [*British*] ..... CSLS
Civil Service Motoring Association [*British*] (BI) ..... CSMA
Civil Service National Whitley Council [*British*] ..... CSNWC
Civil Service Pay Research Unit (DLA) ..... CSPRU
Civil Service Pensioners Alliance [*British*] ..... CSPA
Civil Service Reform Act [*1978*] (RDA) ..... CSRA
Civil Service Reserve [*British*] (ROG) ..... CSR
Civil Service Retirement ..... CSR
Civil Service Retirement and Disability Fund ..... CSRDF
Civil Service Retirement Fellowship [*British*] ..... CSRF
Civil Service Retirement System (MCD) ..... CSRS
Civil Service Rifle Volunteers [*British*] ..... CSRV
Civil Service Rule ..... CSR
Civil Service Selection Board [*Pronounced "sissby"*] [*British*] ..... CSSB
Civil Service Sports Council [*British*] (DI) ..... CSSC
Civil Service Supply Association [*British*] ..... CSSA
Civil Service Typists' Association [*A union*] [*British*] ..... CSTA
Civil Service Union [*British*] ..... CSU
Civil Service Working Party [*US Military Government, Germany*] ..... CSWP
Civil Situation Reporting System (NATG) ..... CIVSITREP
Civil Society (EA) ..... CS
Civil Space Technology Initiative [*NASA*] (GFGA) ..... CSTI
Civil Surgeon (DAS) ..... CS
Civil Tilt Rotor [*Aviation*] (DA) ..... CTR
Civil War Centennial Association ..... CWCA
Civil War Centennial Commission [*Terminated, 1966*] ..... CWCC
Civil War Philatelic Society [*Later, AHPS*] (EA) ..... CWPS
Civil War Press Corps (EA) ..... CWPC
Civil War Round Table Associates (EA) ..... CWRTA
Civil War Society (EA) ..... CWS
Civil War Times Illustrated [*A publication*] ..... CWTI
Civil War Token Society (EA) ..... CWTS
Civil Works [*Assistant Secretary of the Army*] ..... CW
Civil Works Administration [*1933-1934*] ..... CWA
Civil Works Program ..... CWP
Civile [*Civil*] [*Latin*] (DLA) Civ
Civilian (AFM) CIV
Civilian Acquired Skills Program [*Military*] ..... CASP
Civilian Acquisition Management Branch [*Army*] (RDA) ..... CAMB
Civilian Acquisition Position List [*Army*] (RDA) ..... CAPL
Civilian Actress Technician [*Term for professional actresses who worked under Army Special Services Division in soldier shows*] [*World War II*] ..... CAT
Civilian Affairs Supports for Echelon above Corps [*Military*] ..... CASEAC
Civilian Agency Acquisition Council (AAGC) ..... CAAC
Civilian Air Navigation School ..... CANS
Civilian Air Transport ..... CAT
Civilian Anti-Aircraft Co-Operation Unit [*British military*] (DMA) ..... CAACU
Civilian Appellation Review Agency [*Army*] (MCD) ..... CARA
Civilian Application of the Results of Military Research and Development (PDAA) ..... CARMAND
Civilian Armed Force Geographical Units [*Paramilitary security force*] [*Philippines*] (ECON) ..... CAGFU
Civilian Authority for the Protection of Everybody, Regardless [*Crime-fighting unit in TV series "The Kids From C.A.P.E.R."*] ..... CAPER
Civilian Aviation Advisory Committee [*Air Defense Planning Board*] (AAG) ..... CAAC
Civilian Bachelor Quarters [*Air Force*] (AFM) ..... CBQ
Civilian Budgeting System [*Military*] ..... CBS
Civilian Career Management Center [*Military*] (DNAB) ..... CCMC
Civilian Career Management Field Agency (MCD) ..... CCMFA
Civilian Casualty Fund (EA) ..... CCF
Civilian Clothing ..... CIVCLO
Civilian Clothing Maintenance Allowance [*Army*] (AABC) ..... CCMA
Civilian Complaint Review Board ..... CCRB
Civilian Confinement [*Military*] (DNAB) ..... CIV CONF
Civilian Congress (EA) CC
Civilian Conservation Centers [*Job Corps*] CCC
Civilian Conservation Corps [*Created, 1937; liquidated, 1943*] CCC
Civilian Control Agency ..... CCA
Civilian Defense Volunteer Office ..... CDVO
Civilian Education Level [*Military*] (INF) ..... CEL
Civilian Electronics Technician Afloat [*Navy*] (NVT) ..... CETA
Civilian Employee (MCD) ..... CIVEMP
Civilian Employee Health Service ..... CEHS
Civilian Employee Welfare and Recreation Committee [*Military*] (DNAB) ..... CEWRC
Civilian Employment Level Plan [*DoD*] ..... CELP
Civilian Employment Projection (MCD) ..... CEP
Civilian Engineering Technical Service [*Navy*] (NVT) ..... CETS
Civilian Enterprise ..... CE
Civilian Executive Management Board [*Military*] (DNAB) ..... CEMB
Civilian Extraction [*Nuclear energy*] ..... CIVEX
Civilian Goods (Supply) Committee [*British World War II*] ..... CG(S)C
Civilian Health and Medical Program of the Uniformed Services [*Military*] ..... CHAMPUS
Civilian Health and Medical Program of the Veterans Administration [*Military*] ..... CHAMPVA
Civilian Information Management System (AFIT) ..... CIMS
Civilian Information Manpower Management System [*Navy*] ..... CIMMS
Civilian Instruction Program (MUGU) ..... CIP
Civilian Internee [*Military*] (INF) CI
Civilian Irregular Defense Group [*Military*] ..... CIDG
Civilian Jeep ..... CJ
Civilian Labor Force [*DoD*] ..... CLF
Civilian Labor Group (MCD) ..... CLG
Civilian Labor Group Center [*Army*] (AABC) ..... CLGC
Civilian Labor Group Special Orders [*Army*] (AABC) ..... CLGSO
Civilian Maimed and Limbless Association of Western Australia ..... CMLAWA
Civilian Manpower Management Guides [*Navy*] (NG) ..... CMMG
Civilian Manpower Management Instruction [*Navy*] (NG) ..... CMMI
Civilian Manpower Management Letters [*Navy*] (NG) ..... CMML

Civilian Man-Years [*Military*] (AABC) .... CMY
Civilian Marine Emergency Volunteers .... CMEV
Civilian Marine Personnel Instructions [*Navy*] .... CMPI
Civilian Marksmanship Program (MCD) .... CMP
Civilian Material Assistance (EA) .... CMA
Civilian Military Cooperation (NATG) .... CIMIC
Civilian/Military Liaison Committee .... CMLC
Civilian Military Training Camp (DNAB) .... CMTC
Civilian Mobilization Manpower Allocation/Requirements Plan .... CIV-M-MARP
Civilian Occupational Specialty .... COS
Civilian Orientation Cruise (DNAB) .... COC
Civilian Payroll Circular .... CPRC
Civilian Personnel Accounting System [*Military*] (MCD) .... CPAS
Civilian Personnel Administration Services Record System [*Military*]
   (DNAB) .... CIVPERSADMSYS
Civilian Personnel Advisor [*Military*] .... CPA
Civilian Personnel and Payroll Letter [*Military*] .... CPPL
Civilian Personnel Branch [*BUPERS*] .... CPB
Civilian Personnel Career Plan [*Air Force*] .... CPCP
Civilian Personnel Circular [*Army*] .... CPC
Civilian Personnel Directorate [*Military*] (GFGA) .... CPD
Civilian Personnel Division [*Coast Guard*] .... PC
Civilian Personnel/Equal Employment Opportunity Directives System
   [*Military*] (DNAB) .... CIVPERS/EEODIRSYS
Civilian Personnel Information System [*Army*] .... CIVPERSINS
Civilian Personnel Letter .... CPL
Civilian Personnel Letters and Dispatches .... CPL & D
Civilian Personnel Management Center [*Air Force*] (DOMA) .... CPMC
Civilian Personnel Management Information System (MCD) .... CPMIS
Civilian Personnel Modernization Project [*Military*] .... CPMP
Civilian Personnel Occupational Standards [*Military*] (AABC) .... CPOS
Civilian Personnel Office [*or Officer*] .... CPO
Civilian Personnel Pamphlet [*Military*] .... CPP
Civilian Personnel Procedures Manual [*Military*] .... CPPM
Civilian Personnel Records [*Military*] .... CPR
Civilian Personnel Reduction Plan (MCD) .... CPRP
Civilian Personnel Regulation [*Military*] .... CPR
Civilian Pilot Training [*Became War Training Service*] [*World War II*] .... CPT
Civilian Population (MCD) .... CP
Civilian Position Control Number .... CPCN
Civilian Position File (MCD) .... CPF
Civilian Production Administration [*Became part of Office of Temporary
   Controls, 1946*] .... CPA
Civilian Property Agent .... CPA
Civilian Public Service .... CPS
Civilian Radioactive Waste Management [*Department of Energy*]
   (NUCP) .... CRWM
Civilian Radioactive Waste Management System--Management and
   Operating [*Contractor*] (GAAI) .... CRWMS-M&O
Civilian Repair Organization [*Aircraft*] .... CRO
Civilian Repair Unit [*British military*] (DMA) .... CRU
Civilian Research and Development Foundation [*An organization formed to
   retain former FSU scientists in civilian research*] .... CRDF
Civilian Research and Development Foundation for the Independent States
   of the FSU [*former Soviet Union*] .... CRDF
Civilian Research, Interplanetary Flying Objects .... CRIFO
Civilian Science Systems Administration [*Proposed for National Science
   Foundation*] .... CSSA
Civilian Screening Center .... CSC
Civilian Service Unit (AFM) .... CSU
Civilian Skill Code (MCD) .... CSC
Civilian Substitution Program [*Navy*] (NVT) .... CIVSUB
Civilian Supervisory Selection Battery [*Military*] (AFM) .... CSSB
Civilian Supply Branch [*Army Service Forces*] [*World War II*] .... CSB
Civilian Supply Division [*Allied Military Government*] [*World War II*] .... CSD
Civilian Support Operation [*Military*] (INF) .... CSO
Civilian Technology Corporation (AAGC) .... CTC
Civilian Training, Education, and Development (MCD) .... CTED
Civilian War Casualties (VNW) .... CWC
Civilian War Dead .... CWD
Civilian Wartime Injuries .... CWTI
Civilian Welfare and Recreation Committee (MUGU) .... CWRC
Civilian Welfare Fund (AABC) .... CWF
Civilian-Military Contingency Hospital System [*DoD*] .... CMCHS
Civilians in Foreign Communications Operations [*Military*] .... CIFCO
Civilisations [*A publication*] CIV
Civilization (ROG) CIV
Civilization As We Know It [*An association British*] .... CAWKI
Civil-Military Affairs .... CMA
Civil-Military Integration (AAGC) .... CMI
Civil-Military Operations (AABC) .... CMO
Civil-Society Organizations .... CSOs
Civis Romanus [*Roman Citizen*] [*Latin*] .... CR
Civitan International (EA) CI
Civitavecchia [*Italy ICAO location identifier*] (ICLI) .... LIQJ
CKE Restaurants [*Associated Press*] (SAG) .... CKE Rst
CKE Restaurants [*NYSE symbol*] (TTSB) .... CKR
CKE Restaurants Ltd. [*Formerly, Carl Karcher Enterprise*] [*NYSE symbol*]
   (SAG) .... CKR
CKF Bancorp [*NASDAQ symbol*] (TTSB) .... CKFB
CKF Bancorp, Inc. [*Associated Press*] (SAG) .... CKF Bc
CKF Bancorp, Inc. [*NASDAQ symbol*] (SAG) .... CKFB
CKS Group [*NASDAQ symbol*] (TTSB) .... CKSG
CKS Group, Inc. [*Associated Press*] (SAG) .... CKS Gr
CKS Group, Inc. [*NASDAQ symbol*] (SAG) .... CKSG

CL & P Capital LP [*Associated Press*] (SAG) .... CL & P
CL & P Capital LP [*Associated Press*] (SAG) .... CL & P
Clackamas Community College Library, Oregon City, OR [*OCLC symbol*]
   (OCLC) .... CCK
Clackamas Community College, Oregon City, OR [*Library symbol Library of
   Congress*] (LCLS) .... OrOCC
Clackamas Cooperative County-Wide Library Services [*Library
   network*] .... CCCLS
Clackamas County Public Library, Oregon City, OR [*Library symbol Library
   of Congress*] (LCLS) .... OrOC
Clackamas High School, Media Center, Milwaukie, OR [*Library symbol
   Library of Congress*] (LCLS) .... OrMiCHS
Clackamas, OR [*Location identifier FAA*] (FAAL) .... CWY
Clackmannan [*Town and county in Scotland*] (ROG) CLC
Clackmannanshire [*County in Scotland*] .... CLACK
Clad Controlled Expansion .... CCEX
Clad Failure Detection [*Nuclear energy*] (NUCP) .... CFD
Cladosporium [*A fungus*] .... Clad
Cladosporium Herbarum [*A fungus*] .... Ch
Claflin College, Orangeburg, SC [*OCLC symbol*] (OCLC) .... CFC
Claflin College, Orangeburg, SC [*Library symbol Library of Congress*]
   (LCLS) .... ScOrC
Claiborne [*Liz*], Inc. [*Associated Press*] (SAG) .... LizClab
Claiborne Industries Ltd. [*Toronto Stock Exchange symbol*] .... CIB
Claim (WGA) CL
Claim .... CLM
Claim Account Number [*Social Security Administration*] (GFGA) .... CAN
Claim Agent [*Insurance*] .... CA
Claimant (WGA) .... CLT
Claimant Advisory Service Program [*Unemployment insurance*] .... CLASP
Claimant Procurement Planning Officer .... CPPO
Claimants and Unemployed Workers' Union (AIE) .... CUWU
Claimer Resources [*Vancouver Stock Exchange symbol*] .... CJL
Claiming (WGA) .... CLMG
Claiming Race [*Horse racing*] .... CLM
Claims (DLA) .... Clms
Claims (DLA) .... Cls
[*United States*] Claims Court [*Now Court of Federal Claims*] (AAGC) .... Cl Ct
Claims Court Reporter [*West*] [*A publication*] (AAGC) .... Cl Ct
Claims, Defense (CAAL) .... CD
Claims Inquiry Form (MEDA) .... CIF
Claims Manual [*Social Security Administration*] (OICC) .... CM
Claims Representative Exam for Social Security [*Federal job exam*] .... CRESS
Clairborne Parish Library, Homer, LA [*Library symbol Library of Congress*]
   (LCLS) .... LHoC
Claire's Stores [*Associated Press*] (SAG) .... ClairStr
Claire's Stores [*NYSE symbol*] (TTSB) .... CLE
Claire's Stores, Inc. [*Associated Press*] (SAG) .... ClairSt
Claire's Stores, Inc. [*NYSE symbol*] (SPSG) .... CLE
Clallam Bay Correctional Center, Clallam Bay, WA [*Library symbol*] [*Library
   of Congress*] (LCLS) .... WaCbC
Clamp (MSA) .... CLP
Clamped Dielectric Constant .... CDC
Clamped Homogeneous Electric Field .... CHEF
Clamped Speed Regulator .... CSR
Clamping Fixture (MCD) .... CF
Clamshell Alliance (EA) .... CA
Clan Grant No. 17, Order of Scottish Clans (EA) .... OSC
Clan McGillivray Society, Australia .... CMcGSA
Clan Napier in North America [*An association*] .... CNNA
Clan Sinclair Association (USA) (EA) .... CSAUSA
Clancy's Treatise of the Rights, Duties, and Liabilities of Husband and
   Wife [*A publication*] (DLA) .... Clancy Husb & W
Clancy's Treatise of the Rights, Duties, and Liabilities of Husband and
   Wife [*A publication*] (DLA) .... Clancy Rights
Clandestine Fission Explosive [*Nuclear energy*] (NRCH) .... CFE
Clandestine Intelligence (LAIN) CI
Clandestine Lodges [*Freemasonry*] (ROG) CL
Clandestine Underwater Nuclear Explosion .... CUNE
CL&P Capital LP.9.30%'MIPS' [*NYSE symbol*] (TTSB) .... CPMPrA
Clann Ltd., Sydney, NSW, Australia [*OCLC symbol*] (OCLC) .... CLN
Clans and Scottish Societies of Canada .... CSSC
Clanton, AL [*Location identifier FAA*] (FAAL) .... GGY
Clanton, AL [*FM radio station call letters*] .... WEZZ
Clanton, AL [*AM radio station call letters*] .... WKLF
Clanwilliam [*South Africa*] [*ICAO location identifier*] (ICLI) .... FACW
Clapeyron-Clausius Equation [*Physics*] .... CCE
Clapham [*England*] .... CLAP
Clapham Notre Dame Association [*British*] (BI) .... CNDA
Clapper [*Electricity*] .... CLPR
Clara Cell-Specific Protein (DMAA) .... CCSP
Clara City Public Library, Clara City, MN [*Library symbol*] [*Library of
   Congress*] (LCLS) .... MnClc
Clara City Public Schools, Clara City, MN [*Library symbol*] [*Library of
   Congress*] (LCLS) .... MnClcPS
Clara H. Carlson Elementary School, Elmont, NY [*Library symbol*] [*Library of
   Congress*] (LCLS) .... NElmoCCE
Clara Peak [*New Mexico*] [*Seismograph station code, US Geological Survey*]
   (SEIS) .... CLP
Clara Rios [*Bolivia*] [*ICAO location identifier*] (ICLI) .... SLCI
Clarcor, Inc. [*Associated Press*] (SAG) .... Clarcor
CLARCOR, Inc. [*NYSE symbol*] (SPSG) CLC
CLARCOR Inc. [*NYSE symbol*] (TTSB) CLC
Clare [*C.P.*] Corp. [*Associated Press*] (SAG) .... Clare
Clare [*C.P.*] Corp. [*NASDAQ symbol*] (SAG) .... CPCL

Clare Hall [*Cambridge University*] (ROG) .... CL H
Clare, MI [*FM radio station call letters*] .... WCFX
Claremont & Concord Railway Co., Inc. [*AAR code*] .... CLCO
Claremont, CA [*FM radio station call letters*] .... KSPC
Claremont Economics Institute [*Information service or system*] (IID) .... CEI
Claremont Graduate School (GAGS) .... Claremont Grad Sch
Claremont Men's College [*California*] .... CMC
Claremont Men's College, Claremont, CA [*OCLC symbol*] (OCLC) .... HDC
Claremont, NC [*AM radio station call letters*] .... WCXN
Claremont, NH [*Location identifier FAA*] (FAAL) .... CNH
Claremont, NH [*FM radio station call letters*] .... WHDQ
Claremont, NH [*AM radio station call letters*] .... WTSV
Claremont Public Library, Claremont, SD [*Library symbol Library of Congress*] (LCLS) .... SdCla
[*The*] **Claremont Ras Shamra Tablets** [*A publication*] (BJA) .... CRST
Claremont Technology Group, Inc. [*Associated Press*] (SAG) .... ClareTch
Claremont Technology Group, Inc. [*NASDAQ symbol*] (SAG) .... CLMT
Claremont, VA [*AM radio station call letters*] (RBYB) .... WVNS
Claremore, OK [*Television station call letters*] .... KRSC
Claremore, OK [*FM radio station call letters*] (RBYB) .... KRSC-FM
Claremore, OK [*FM radio station call letters*] .... KTFR
Claremore, OK [*AM radio station call letters*] .... KTRT
Clarence Bain, Andros Island [*Bahamas*] [*ICAO location identifier*] (ICLI) .... MYAB
Clarenden Press (DAS) .... CP
Clarendon [*Type*] (ROG) .... CLAR
[*The*] **Clarendon & Pittsford Railroad Co.** [*AAR code*] .... CLP
Clarendon College, Clarendon, TX [*Library symbol Library of Congress*] (LCLS) .... TxClaC
Clarendon County Public Library, Manning, SC [*Library symbol*] [*Library of Congress*] (LCLS) .... ScMan
Clarendon Hills Public Library, Clarendon Hills, IL [*Library symbol Library of Congress*] (LCLS) .... IClh
Clarendon Hills Public Library, Clarendon Hills, IL [*Library symbol*] [*Library of Congress*] (LCLS) .... IClhP
Clarendon Laboratory [*Oxford University*] (MCD) CL
Clarendon, PA [*FM radio station call letters*] (RBYB) .... WKNB
Clarendon, TX [*Location identifier FAA*] (FAAL) .... CNZ
Clarendon-Miller Branch, Frontenac County Library, Plevna, Ontario [*Library symbol National Library of Canada*] (NLC) .... OPFRC
Clarendon's Parliamentary Chronicle [*A publication*] (DLA) .... Clar Parl Chr
Clarenville, NF [*FM radio station call letters*] (RBYB) .... CJKK-FM
Clarenville, NF [*FM radio station call letters*] .... CKCV
Clarenville, NF [*AM radio station call letters*] .... CKVO
Clarenville Public Library, Clarenville, NF, Canada [*Library symbol Library of Congress*] (LCLS) .... CaNfCl
Clarenville Public Library, Newfoundland [*Library symbol National Library of Canada*] (NLC) .... NFCL
Clarepine Industries, Inc. [*Toronto Stock Exchange symbol*] .... DRS
Claresholm Public Library, Alberta [*Library symbol National Library of Canada*] (NLC) .... ACLAR
Claret [*Philately*] cl
Claretian Fathers Library, Washington, DC [*Library symbol Library of Congress*] (LCLS) .... DCF
Claretian Missionaries (TOCD) .... CMF
Claretian Missionaries, Missionary Sons of the Immaculate Heart of Mary (TOCD) .... cmf
Claretian Missionary Sisters (TOCD) .... RMI
Clarification [*or Clarify*] (AFM) .... CLAR
Clarification Request (AAGC) .... CR
Clarify (FAAC) .... CFY
Clarify, Inc. [*Associated Press*] (SAG) .... Clarify
Clarify, Inc. [*NASDAQ symbol*] (SAG) .... CLFY
Clarinda Herald-Journal, Clarinda, IA [*Library symbol Library of Congress*] (LCLS) .... IaCladHJ
Clarinda, IA [*Location identifier FAA*] (FAAL) ICL
Clarinda, IA [*FM radio station call letters*] .... KKBZ
Clarinda Public Library, Clarinda, IA [*Library symbol Library of Congress*] (LCLS) .... IaClad
Clarinet CL
Clarinet .... CLAR
Clarinetist (BARN) .... Clst
Clarinette Basse [*Bass Clarinet*] [*Music*] .... Cl B
Clarinette Contre Basse [*Contrabass Clarinet*] [*Music*] .... Cl CB
Clarinetto [*Clarinet*] [*Music*] (ROG) .... CLARTTO
Clarino [*Clarion*] [*Music*] (ROG) .... CLAR
Clarino [*Clarion*] [*Music*] .... CLARO
Clarion Free Library, Clarion, PA [*Library symbol Library of Congress*] (LCLS) .... PCl
Clarion, IA [*Location identifier FAA*] (FAAL) .... CAV
Clarion, IA [*FM radio station call letters*] .... KIAQ
Clarion Music Society (EA) .... CMS
Clarion, PA [*Location identifier FAA*] (FAAL) .... CIP
Clarion, PA [*FM radio station call letters*] .... WCCR
Clarion, PA [*FM radio station call letters*] .... WCUC
Clarion, PA [*AM radio station call letters*] .... WWCH
Clarion Public Library, Clarion, IA [*Library symbol Library of Congress*] (LCLS) .... IaCla
Clarion State College, Clarion, PA [*Library symbol Library of Congress*] (LCLS) .... PClS
Clarion State College, Clarion, PA [*OCLC symbol*] (OCLC) .... REC
Clarion State College, Oil City, PA [*Library symbol Library of Congress*] (LCLS) .... POC
Clarion State College, School of Library Media, Clarion, PA [*OCLC symbol*] (OCLC) .... CSI
Clarion University of Pennsylvania (GAGS) .... Clarion U
Claris Dynamic Markup Language [*Computer science*] .... CDML
Clarissa Elementary School, Clarissa, MN [*Library symbol*] [*Library of Congress*] (LCLS) .... MnClaE
Clarissa High School, Clarissa, MN [*Library symbol*] [*Library of Congress*] (LCLS) .... MnCLaH
Clarissima Femina [*Most Illustrious Woman*] [*Latin*] .... CF
Clarissima Puella [*Most Illustrious Maiden*] [*Latin*] .... CP
Clarissimi Viri [*Illustrious Men*] [*Latin*] (BARN) CCVV
Clarissimus Vir [*Most Illustrious Man*] [*Latin*] CLV
Claritas Corp. [*Information service or system*] (IID) CLC
Clarity, Brevity, Sharpness [*Objectives of good editing, as set forth in Barry Tarshis' book "How to Write without Pain"*] .... CBS
Clark Air Base, Pampanga [*Philippines*] [*ICAO location identifier*] (ICLI) .... RPMK
Clark and Finnelly's English House of Lords Cases [*1831-46*] [*A publication*] (DLA) .... Cl & F
Clark and Finnelly's English House of Lords Cases [*1831-46*] [*A publication*] (DLA) .... Cl & Fin
Clark and Finnelly's English House of Lords Cases [*1831-46*] [*A publication*] (DLA) .... Clark & Fin
Clark and Finnelly's English House of Lords Cases, New Series [*A publication*] (DLA) .... Clark & F (NS) Eng
Clark and Finnelly's English House of Lords Reports [*6-8 English Reprint*] [*A publication*] (DLA) .... C & F
Clark and Finnelly's English House of Lords Reports [*6-8 English Reprint*] [*A publication*] (DLA) .... Clark & F
Clark and Finnelly's English House of Lords Reports [*6-8 English Reprint*] [*A publication*] (DLA) .... Clark & F (Eng)
Clark and Finnelly's English House of Lords Reports, New Series [*9-11 English Reprint*] [*1847-66*] [*A publication*] (DLA) .... Clark & F (NS)
Clark and Finnelly's English House of Lords Reports, New Series [*9-11 English Reprint*] [*1847-66*] [*A publication*] (DLA) .... Clark & Fin (NS)
Clark Atlanta University (GAGS) .... Clark Atl U
Clark Aviation Corp. [*ICAO designator*] (FAAC) .... CLK
Clark, Cobb, and Irwin's Code [*Georgia*] [*A publication*] (DLA) .... Irwin's Code
Clark College, Atlanta, GA [*OCLC symbol*] (OCLC) CLC
Clark College, Atlanta, GA [*Library symbol Library of Congress*] (LCLS) .... GAC
Clark College, Library, Vancouver, WA [*OCLC symbol*] (OCLC) CCV
Clark College, Vancouver, WA [*Library symbol Library of Congress*] (LCLS) .... WaVC
Clark. Colonial Law [*1834*] [*A publication*] (ILCA) .... Clark Col Law
Clark County Community College, North Las Vegas, NV [*Library symbol Library of Congress*] (LCLS) .... NvNolC
Clark County Library, Las Vegas, NV [*Library symbol Library of Congress*] (LCLS) .... NvLC
Clark County Public Library, Winchester, KY [*Library symbol Library of Congress*] (LCLS) .... KyWn
Clark County Technical Institute, Springfield, OH [*Library symbol Library of Congress*] (LCLS) .... OSC
Clark Dietz Engineers, Urbana, IL [*Library symbol*] [*Library of Congress*] (LCLS) .... IUrCD
Clark Equipment Co. (MCD) .... CEC
Clark Free Public Library, Clark, NJ [*Library symbol Library of Congress*] (LCLS) .... NjCl
Clark Hill Reservoir [*Georgia*] [*Seismograph station code, US Geological Survey*] (SEIS) CH5
Clark Hill Reservoir [*Georgia*] [*Seismograph station code, US Geological Survey*] (SEIS) CH6
Clark Lake Radio Observatory [*University of Maryland*] [*Research center*] (RCD) .... CLRO
Clark Memorial College [*Mississippi*] .... CMC
Clark Public Library, Clark, SD [*Library symbol Library of Congress*] (LCLS) .... SdCl
Clark Road Secondary School, London, ON, Canada [*Library symbol Library of Congress*] (LCLS) .... CaOLCR
Clark Road Secondary School, London, Ontario [*Library symbol National Library of Canada*] (NLC) .... OLCR
Clark Technical College, Library Resource Center, Springfield, OH [*OCLC symbol*] (OCLC) .... CLT
Clark University (GAGS) .... Clark U
Clark University, Worcester, MA [*OCLC symbol*] (OCLC) .... CKM
Clark University, Worcester, MA [*Library symbol Library of Congress*] (LCLS) .... MWC
Clarke and Hall's Cases of Contested Elections in Congress [*1789-1834*] [*United States*] [*A publication*] (DLA) .... C & H Elec Cas
Clarke and Hall's Cases of Contested Elections in Congress [*1789-1834*] [*United States*] [*A publication*] (DLA) .... Cl & H
Clarke and Hall's Cases of Contested Elections in Congress [*1789-1834*] [*United States*] [*A publication*] (DLA) .... Clarke & H Elec Cas
Clarke and Scully's Drainage Cases [*Canada*] [*A publication*] (DLA) .... C & S
Clarke and Scully's Drainage Cases [*Canada*] [*A publication*] (DLA) .... Cl & Sc Dr Cas
Clarke and Scully's Drainage Cases [*Canada*] [*A publication*] (DLA) .... Clarke & S Dr Cas
Clarke College (GAGS) .... Clarke C
Clarke College, Dubuque, IA [*Library symbol Library of Congress*] (LCLS) .... IaDuCl
Clarke College, Dubuque, IA [*OCLC symbol*] (OCLC) .... IOC
Clarke County Courthouse, Osceola, IA [*Library symbol*] [*Library of Congress*] (LCLS) .... IaOscCoC
Clarke Courier, Dubuque, IA [*Library symbol Library of Congress*] (LCLS) .... IaDuCo
Clarke Institute of Psychiatry [*Research center*] (RCD) .... CIP
Clarke Institute of Psychiatry, University of Toronto, Ontario [*Library symbol National Library of Canada*] (NLC) .... OTUDP
Clarke Memorial College, Newton, MS [*Library symbol Library of Congress*] (LCLS) .... MsNeC

Clarke Memorial Museum, Eureka, CA [*Library symbol*] [*Library of Congress*] (LCLS) ... CECM
Clarke, Nichols & Co. [*British*] (ROG) ... CLARNICO
Clarke on Bills and Notes [*Canada A publication*] (DLA) ... Cl Bills
Clarke on Bills and Notes [*Canada A publication*] (DLA) ... Clarke B
Clarke on Extradition [*A publication*] (DLA) ... Cl Extr
Clarke on Extradition [*A publication*] (DLA) ... Clarke Extr
Clarke on Law of Insurance [*Canada A publication*] (DLA) ... Cl Ins
Clarke, W. H., New York NY [*STAC*] ... CWH
Clarke's Admiralty Practice [*A publication*] (DLA) ... Clarke Adm Pr
Clarke's Bibliotheca Legum [*A publication*] (DLA) ... Clarke Bib Leg
Clarke's Canada Insolvent Acts [*A publication*] (DLA) ... Cl Can Ins
Clarke's Constable's Manual [*Canada A publication*] (DLA) ... Clarke Const
Clarke's Criminal Law [*Canada A publication*] (DLA) ... Clarke Cr L
Clarke's Early Roman Law [*A publication*] (DLA) ... Cl RL
Clarke's Early Roman Law [*A publication*] (DLA) ... Clarke Rom L
Clarke's Edition of 1-8 Iowa [*A publication*] (DLA) ... Clarke
Clarke's Edition of 1-8 Iowa [*A publication*] (DLA) ... Clarke (IA)
Clarke's Insolvent Acts [*Canada A publication*] (DLA) ... Clarke Insol
Clarke's Insurance Law [*Canada A publication*] (DLA) ... Clarke Insur
Clarke's New York Chancery Reports [*A publication*] (DLA) ... Cl Ch
Clarke's New York Chancery Reports [*A publication*] (DLA) ... Cl R
Clarke's New York Chancery Reports [*A publication*] (DLA) ... Clarke
Clarke's New York Chancery Reports [*A publication*] (DLA) ... Clarke Ch
Clarke's New York Chancery Reports [*A publication*] (DLA) ... Clarke Ch (NY)
Clarke's New York Chancery Reports [*A publication*] (DLA) ... Clarke CR
Clarke's New York Chancery Reports [*A publication*] (DLA) ... Clarke's Chy (NY)
Clarke's Notes of Cases [*Bengal*] [*A publication*] (DLA) ... Clarke
Clarke's Notes of Cases, in His "Rules and Orders" [*Bengal*] [*A publication*] (DLA) ... Clarke Not
Clarke's Notes of Cases, in His "Rules and Orders" [*Bengal*] [*A publication*] (DLA) ... Clarke R & O
Clarke's Pennsylvania Reports [*5 vols.*] [*A publication*] (DLA) ... Clarke
Clarke's Pennsylvania Reports [*5 vols.*] [*A publication*] (DLA) ... Clarke (PA)
Clarke's Reports [*19-22 Michigan*] [*A publication*] (DLA) ... Clarke
Clarke's Reports [*19-22 Michigan*] [*A publication*] (DLA) ... Clarke (Mich)
Clarkesville, GA [*AM radio station call letters*] ... WCHM
Clarkesville, GA [*FM radio station call letters*] ... WMJE
Clarkia District Library, Clarkia, ID [*Library symbol*] [*Library of Congress*] (LCLS) ... IdCl
Clark's Appeal Cases, House of Lords [*England*] [*A publication*] (DLA) ... Cl App
Clark's Appeal Cases, House of Lords [*England*] [*A publication*] (DLA) ... Clark App
Clark's Colonial Laws [*A publication*] (DLA) ... Cl Col
Clark's Digest, House of Lords Reports [*A publication*] (DLA) ... Clark Dig
Clark's House of Lords Cases [*1847-66*] [*England*] [*A publication*] (DLA) ... Ho L Cas
Clark's House of Lords Cases [*1847-66*] [*England*] [*A publication*] (DLA) ... Ho Lords C
Clark's House of Lords Cases [*1847-66*] [*England*] [*A publication*] (DLA) ... Ho Lords Cas
Clark's Pennsylvania Law Journal Reports [*A publication*] (DLA) ... Clark (PA)
Clark's Pennsylvania Law Journal Reports [*A publication*] (DLA) ... PA LJR
Clarks Point [*Alaska*] [*Airport symbol*] (OAG) ... CLP
Clarks Point, AK [*Location identifier FAA*] (FAAL) ... CLP
Clark's Reports [*58 Alabama*] [*A publication*] (DLA) ... Clark
Clark's Reports [*58 Alabama*] [*A publication*] (DLA) ... Clark (Ala)
Clark's Summary of American Law [*A publication*] (DLA) ... Clark's Summary
Clark's Treatise on Elections [*A publication*] (DLA) ... Cl Elec
Clarksburg [*West Virginia*] [*Airport symbol*] (OAG) ... CKB
Clarksburg Public Library, Clarksburg, WV [*Library symbol Library of Congress*] (LCLS) ... WvCl
Clarksburg, WV [*Location identifier FAA*] (FAAL) ... CKB
Clarksburg, WV [*Television station call letters*] ... WBOY
Clarksburg, WV [*FM radio station call letters*] (RBYB) ... WFBY-FM
Clarksburg, WV [*AM radio station call letters*] ... WHAR
Clarksburg, WV [*FM radio station call letters*] ... WKJL
Clarksburg, WV [*FM radio station call letters*] ... WKKW
Clarksburg, WV [*Television station call letters*] ... WLYJ
Clarksburg, WV [*AM radio station call letters*] ... WOBG
Clarksburg, WV [*AM radio station call letters*] ... WPDX
Clarksburg, WV [*FM radio station call letters*] ... WPDX-FM
Clarksburg, WV [*FM radio station call letters*] ... WVHF
Clarksdale, MS [*Location identifier FAA*] (FAAL) ... CKM
Clarksdale, MS [*FM radio station call letters*] ... WAID
Clarksdale, MS [*FM radio station call letters*] ... WKDJ
Clarksdale, MS [*AM radio station call letters*] ... WROX
Clarksdale, MS [*FM radio station call letters*] ... WWUN
Clarkson College of Technology [*Potsdam, NY*] ... CCT
Clarkson College of Technology, Potsdam, NY [*Library symbol Library of Congress*] (LCLS) ... NPotC
Clarkson College of Technology, Potsdam, NY [*OCLC symbol*] (OCLC) ... VYT
Clarkson, Gordon & Co.: Woods, Gordon & Co., Toronto, ON, Canada [*Library symbol Library of Congress*] (LCLS) ... CaOTCGW
Clarkson Gordon Library, Calgary, Alberta [*Library symbol National Library of Canada*] (BIB) ... ACCG
Clarkson Gordon, London, Ontario [*Library symbol National Library of Canada*] (BIB) ... OLCG
Clarkson, Gordon, Woods, Gordon, Montreal, Quebec [*Library symbol National Library of Canada*] (NLC) ... QMCGW
Clarkson, Gordon, Woods, Gordon, Toronto, Ontario [*Library symbol National Library of Canada*] (NLC) ... OTCGW
Clarkson University (GAGS) ... Clarkson U
Clarkston, WA [*FM radio station call letters*] ... KCLK
Clarkston, WA [*FM radio station call letters*] (RBYB) ... KNWV-FM
Clarkston, WA [*FM radio station call letters*] (RBYB) ... KVAB-FM
Clarksville [*Tennessee*] [*Airport symbol*] (OAG) ... CKV
Clarksville, AR [*Location identifier FAA*] (FAAL) ... CZE
Clarksville, AR [*AM radio station call letters*] ... KLYR
Clarksville, AR [*FM radio station call letters*] ... KLYR-FM
Clarksville, AR [*FM radio station call letters*] ... KXIO
Clarksville Branch Office [*AEC*] ... CBO
Clarksville Memorial Hospital, Clarksville, TN [*Library symbol*] [*Library of Congress*] (LCLS) ... TCIH
Clarksville Memorial Hospital, Clarksville, TN [*Library symbol Library of Congress*] (LCLS) ... TCIH
Clarksville Star, Clarksville, IA [*Library symbol Library of Congress*] (LCLS) ... IaCkvS
Clarksville Star, Clarksville, IA [*Library symbol Library of Congress*] (LCLS) ... IaClvS
Clarksville, TN [*Location identifier FAA*] (FAAL) ... CKV
Clarksville, TN [*FM radio station call letters*] ... WAPX
Clarksville, TN [*AM radio station call letters*] ... WCTZ
Clarksville, TN [*AM radio station call letters*] ... WDXN
Clarksville, TN [*AM radio station call letters*] ... WJZM
Clarksville, TX [*AM radio station call letters*] ... KCAR
Clarksville, TX [*FM radio station call letters*] ... KGAP
Clarksville, VA [*FM radio station call letters*] ... WLCQ
Claro [*Light-colored cigar*] ... CCC
Clarsach Society (EAIO) ... CS
Clasp ... CLP
Class [*Used with number for Navy rating as: 1c; i.e., first class*] ... C
Class (AFM) ... CL
Class (WDMC) ... cl
Class [*Freight*] ... CLA
Class ... CLAS
Class A Airspace [*Aviation*] (FAAC) ... CAAS
Class "A" Preferred or Common Stock [*Investment term*] ... A
Class Action Reports [*A publication*] (DLA) ... Class Act Rep
Class Action Study and Survey [*Student legal action organization*] ... CLASS
Class Activities Questionnaire [*Teacher evaluation test*] ... CAQ
Class and Kind Made in Canada [*Business term*] ... CKMIC
Class and Kind Not Made in Canada [*Business term*] ... CKNMIC
Class B Airspace [*Aviation*] (FAAC) ... CBAS
Class "B" Preferred or Common Stock [*Investment term*] ... B
Class B Surface Area [*Aviation*] (FAAC) ... CBSA
CLass Based Queuing [*Computer science*] ... CBQ
Class C Airspace [*Aviation*] (FAAC) ... CCAS
Class "C" Preferred or Common Stock [*Investment term*] ... C
Class C Surface Area [*Aviation*] (FAAC) ... CCSA
Class Code [*Database terminology*] (NITA) ... CC
Class Code, Assignee, Index Method, Search [*IFI/Plenum Data Co.*] [*Patent database*] (NITA) ... CLAIMS
Class Code, Assignee, Index, Method, Search/Chemistry [*Patent database*] [*IFI/Plenum Data Co. Arlington, VA*] ... CLAIMS/CHEM
Class Code, Assignee, Index Method, Search/Classification [*Patent database*] (NITA) ... CLAIMS/CLASS
Class Code, Assignee, Index Method, Search/General [*IFI/Plenum Data Co.*] [*Patent database*] (NITA) ... CLAIMS/GEN
Class Code, Assignee, Index, Method, Search/General, Electrical, Mechanical [*Patent database*] [*IFI/Plenum Data Co. Arlington, VA*] ... CLAIMS/GEM
Class Code, Assignee, Index Method, Search/US Patent Abstracts (NITA) ... CLAIMS/US Pats Abs
Class Convening ... CLCON
Class Convening ... CLCVN
Class D Airspace [*Aviation*] (FAAC) ... CDAS
Class D Surface Area [*Aviation*] (FAAC) ... CDSA
Class Determination and Finding ... CD & F
Class Determination and Finding ... CDF
Class E Airspace [*Aviation*] (FAAC) ... CEAS
Class E Surface Area [*Aviation*] (FAAC) ... CESA
Class Featuring Information Compression (PDAA) ... CLAFIC
Class for Retarded in Mental Development ... CRMD
Class G Airspace [*Aviation*] (FAAC) ... CGAS
Class II-Associated Invariant Chain Peptides [*Biochemistry*] ... CLIP
Class Improvement Plan [*Navy*] ... CIP
Class Interval [*Statistics*] ... i
Class IX Study ... CLIXS
Class Life Asset Depreciation Range [*Insurance*] (DICI) ... CLADR
Class Marks [*Telecommunications*] (TEL) ... CM
Class Music Teaching (AIE) ... CMT
Class of Blue Copper Proteins [*Crystallography*] ... CBP
Class of Material (MCD) ... CM
Class of Service [*Telecommunications*] (TEL) ... COS
Class of Service [*Telecommunications*] (TEL) ... CS
Class of Supply [*Military*] ... CS
Class Queue Management (IAA) ... CQM
Class Rate [*Business term*] ... CR
Class Responsibility Collaboration Card (CDE) ... CRC card
Class Room ... CR
Class Work Planning Document [*Navy ship overhauls*] ... CWPD
Classic (ROG) ... CLASS
Classic (WDMC) ... class
Classic [*Record label*] [*France*] ... Clc
Classic ... CLSC
Classic Air AG [*Switzerland ICAO designator*] (FAAC) ... CLC
Classic AMX Club International (EA) ... CACI
Classic Bancshares [*NASDAQ symbol*] (TTSB) ... CLAS
Classic Bicycle and Whizzer Club of America (EA) ... CBWCA

Classic Car Club of America (EA) .... CCCA
Classic Chevy Club International (EA) CCCI
Classic Comet Club of America (EA) .... CCA
Classic Comet Club of America (EA) .... CCCA
Classic Desk Accessories [*Apple Computer, Inc.*] [*Utility program*] [*Computer science*] .... CDA
Classic Editions [*Record label*] .... CEd
Classic English Detective Novel .... CEDN
Classic Form of Kaposi Sarcoma [*Medicine*] (DMAA) .... CKS
Classic Jaguar Association (EA) .... CJA
Classic Motorcycle Club of Victoria [*Australia*] .... CMCV
Classic Racing Motorcycle Club [*Defunct*] (EA) .... CRMC
Classic Record Club [*Record label*] .... ACC
Classic Stage Company .... CSC
Classic Technique [*Surgery*] (DAVI) .... CT
Classic Thunderbird Association (EA) .... CTA
Classic Thunderbird Club International (EA) .... CTCI
Classic Vehicle Club's Committee [*British*] (DBA) CVCC
Classic Yacht Association (EA) .... CYA
Classical C
Classical CL
Classical .... class
Classical America (EA) .... CA
Classical Analytic Technique .... CAT
Classical Anaphylatoxin [*Immunology*] .... CAT
Classical and Medieval Literature Criticism [*A publication*] .... CMLC
Classical and Modern Literature [*A publication*] (BRI) .... CML
Classical Association (EAIO) .... CA
Classical Association of Canada [*See also SCEC*] .... CAC
Classical Association of New England (EDAC) .... CANE
Classical Association of Victoria [*Australia*] .... CAV
Classical Conditioning CC
Classical General Linear Model [*Statistics*] .... CGLM
Classical Journal [*A publication*] (BRI) .... CJ
Classical Latin (BARN) Cl
Classical Latin [*Language, etc.*] (ROG) .... CL L
Classical Latin (BARN) .... Cl Lat
Classical Mechanics [*Physics*] .... CM
Classical Music [*Radio station format*] (WDMC) CL
Classical Music [*Radio station format*] (WDMC) .... Clas
Classical Music Lovers' Exchange (EA) .... CMLE
Classical Outlook [*A publication*] (BRI) .... Class Out
Classical Philology [*A publication*] (OCD) .... CPhil
Classical Philosophy .... CP
Classical Receptive Field [*Biochemistry*] .... CRF
Classical Review [*A publication*] (BRI) .... Class R
Classical Scattering Aerosol Spectrometer [*Aerosol measurement device*] .... CSASP
Classical Scattering Spectrometer Probe [*Aerosol measurement device*] .... CSSP
Classical Strain [*Of RNA*] Cl
Classical Swine Fever Virus .... CSFV
Classical T Tauri Stars [*Astronomy*] .... CTTS
Classical World [*A publication*] (BRI) .... CW
Classical Writers [*A publication*] .... CW
Classics (ADA) CL
Classics International Entertainment, Inc. [*NASDAQ symbol*] (SAG) .... CIEI
Classics International Entertainment, Inc. [*Associated Press*] (SAG) .... Classics
Classics Intl. Entertainment [*NASDAQ symbol*] (TTSB) .... CIEI
Classics of Art [*A publication*] .... CA
Classification CL
Classification (WDMC) cl
Classification [*or Classified*] (DNAB) .... CLAS
Classification (AFM) .... CLASS
Classification (WDMC) .... class
Classification .... CLASS
Classification .... CLASSIF
Classification .... CLASSN
Classification and Audit (AFM) .... C & A
Classification and Classified List of Occupations .... CCLO
Classification and Compensation Society (EA) .... CCS
Classification and Index [*Air Force*] (AFM) .... C & I
Classification and Labelling of Explosives Regulations .... CLER
Classification and Rating Administration [*For movies*] .... CARA
Classification and Ratings Administration [*Motion Picture Association of America*] (WDMC) .... CARA
Classification and Regression Trees .... CART
Classification and Research Support Information System (AAGC) .... CASSIS
Classification and Search Support Information System [*Patent and Trademark Office*] [*Information service or system*] .... CASSIS
Classification and Testing [*Air Force*] (AFM) .... C & T
Classification Change Notice (KSC) .... CCN
Classification Code [*IRS*] [*Online database field identifier*] CC
Classification Code (NITA) CL
Classification Decimale Universelle [*Universal Decimal Classification*] .... CDU
Classification Document Index (DNAB) .... CDI
Classification Group [*Database terminology*] (NITA) CL
Classification, Hazard Information and Packaging [*British*] .... CHIP
Classification Inventory [*Military*] CI
Classification List [*Military*] CL
Classification Management (DNAB) .... CLAM
Classification of Characteristics [*Navy*] (NG) CC
Classification of Defects (AAG) .... CD
Classification of Galactic Nebulae Between Elliptical and Spiral Types Having a Bright Nucleus and Dark Bands of Matter But No Distinguishable Arms [*Astronomy*] (BARN) .... SBO
Classification of Identification of Covert Satellites .... CLASSICS
Classification of Instructional Programs [*Department of Education*] (OICC) .... CIP
Classification of Occupations and Directory of Occupational Titles [*Formerly, MOLOC*] [*British*] .... CODOT
Classification of Publications Board [*South Australia*] .... CPB
Classification of Secondary School Courses [*National Center for Education Statistics*] (EDAC) .... CSSC
Classification on Science and Technology .... CST
Classification Order Watch Service [*Research Publications, Inc.*] .... COWS
Classification, Packaging and Labelling [*Toxicology*] .... CPL
Classification Research .... CR
Classification Research Group [*British*] .... CRG
Classification Review Area [*Environmental Protection Agency*] (GFGA) .... CRA
[*The*] **Classification Society** (EA) .... TCS
Classification Society of North America (EA) .... CSNA
Classification Test Battery [*Aptitude and skills test*] .... CTB
Classification Type pour le Commerce International [*Standard International Trade Classification*] [*French*] .... CTCI
Classified (WDMC) .... class
Classified Abstract Archive of the Alcohol Literature .... CAAAL
Classified Advertisement Management Program [*British*] (DGA) .... CAMP
Classified Advertising Manager (IIA) .... CAM
Classified Anaphylatoxin [*Pharmacology*] (DAVI) .... CAT
Classified Area Term Pass (AAG) .... CATP
Classified by Association (DNAB) .... CBA
Classified Control Clerk [*Army*] CCC
Classified Control Officer .... CCO
Classified Defense Information [*Military*] .... CDI
Classified Document Control .... CDC
Classified Entries in Lateral Transposition [*Indexing*] .... CELT
Classified Information Procedures Act [*1980*] .... CIPA
Classified Information-Handling System [*Department of State*] (GFGA) .... CIHS
Classified Job Accountability Record (MCD) .... CJAR
Classified Mail Address .... CMA
Classified Material Control Officer (AFIT) .... CMCO
Classified Material Receipt .... CMR
Classified Materials System (LAIN) .... CMS
Classified Materials Systems (DOMA) .... CMS
Classified Matter Control Center (AAG) .... CMCC
Classified Message .... CM
Classified Military Information (MCD) .... CMI
Classified Ministry Lists of Types of Educational Establishments [*British*] .... CMLTEE
Classified Register (AAG) .... CR
Classified Restricted Data (DNAB) .... CRD
Classified Scientific and Technical Aerospace Reports [*NASA*] .... CSTAR
Classifier Overflow (IAA) .... CO
Classify (AFM) .... CLAS
Classify (WDMC) .... class
Classify (MSA) .... CLS
Classify, Locate, and Avoid Wind Shear [*National Center for Atmospheric Research*] .... CLAWS
Classless Inter-Domain Routing (CDE) .... CIDR
Class-Oriented Ring-Associative Language [*Computer science*] .... CORAL
Classroom (BARN) .... Clrm
Classroom Adjustment Code .... CAC
Classroom Adjustment Rating Scale .... CARS
Classroom Business Venture (EDAC) .... CBV
Classroom Climate Questionnaire (EDAC) .... CCQ
Classroom Environment Index [*Student attitude test*] .... CEI
Classroom Environment Scale [*Teacher evaluation test*] .... CES
Classroom Instruction Program [*Dialog Information Services, Inc.*] .... CIP
Classroom Management Improvement Study (EDAC) .... CMIS
Classroom Management Observation Scale (EDAC) .... CMOS
Classroom Observations Keyed for Effectiveness Research (EDAC) .... COKER
Classroom Periodical Publishers Association [*Later, CPA*] (EA) .... CPPA
Classroom Publishers Association (EA) .... CPA
Classroom Reading Inventory (EDAC) .... CRI
Classroom Teaching (OICC) .... C/T
Classroom Trainer (MCD) .... CRT
Classroom Trainer (MCD) .... CT
Classroom-Aided Dynamic Educational Time-Sharing System (IEEE) .... CADETS
Clastogenic Factor [*Medicine*] .... CF
Clathan Literary Institute [*British*] .... CLT
Clathrin Heavy Chain [*Genetics*] .... CHC
Clathrin-Associated Protein [*Cytology*] .... CAP
Clatsop Community College, Astoria, OR [*Library symbol Library of Congress*] (LCLS) .... OrAstC
Claude Dornier [*German aircraft designer, 1884-1969*] .... CD
Claude Resources, Inc. [*Toronto Stock Exchange symbol*] .... CRJ
Claude, TX [*FM radio station call letters*] .... KARX
Claudianus [*Fourth century AD*] [*Classical studies*] (OCD) .... Claud
Claus Oxygen-Based Process Expansion [*Petroleum technology*] .... COPE
Clause CL
Clause (WDMC) cl
Clausen, Miller, Gorman, Caffrey & Witous, Chicago, IL [*Library symbol Library of Congress*] (LCLS) .... ICCMG
Clausen, Miller, Gorman, Caffrey & Witous, Chicago, IL [*OCLC symbol*] (OCLC) .... ILP
Clauses (ADA) CLL
Clauses (DLA) .... Cls
Clauson Rolling Platform .... CRP
Clausthal [*Federal Republic of Germany*] [*Seismograph station code, US Geological Survey*] (SEIS) .... CLZ
Claustrum [*Neuroanatomy*] .... Clau

Clavering [*England*] ... CLAV
Clavibacter Xyli Cynodontis [*Microbiology*] ... Cxc
Clavichord [*Music*] ... Clav
Clavichord [*Music*] ... Clavi
Clavichord [*Music*] ... CLVCHD
Clavichord [*Music*] ... CLVD
Clavicle [*Anatomy*] ... CL
Clavicle [*Anatomy*] (DHSM) ... CLAV
Clavicle [*Medicine*] (DMAA) ... clav
Clavicular [*Medicine*] (ROG) ... CLAVR
Clavier [*Keyboard*] [*Music*] ... CLAV
Clavieruebung [*Music*] ... CU
Clavis Patrum Graecorum (BJA) ... CPG
Clavis Patrum Latinorum (BJA) ... CPL
Claw Plate [*Technical drawings*] ... CP
Claw Resources Ltd. [*Vancouver Stock Exchange symbol*] ... KLW
Claxton, GA [*AM radio station call letters*] ... WCLA
Claxton, GA [*FM radio station call letters*] ... WCLA-FM
Clay [*Quality of the bottom*] [*Nautical charts*] ... Cl
Clay (VRA) ... cl
Clay Bird Shooting Association [*British*] (DI) ... CBSA
Clay Brick and Paver Association of New South Wales [*Australia*] ... CBPANSW
Clay Brick and Paver Institute of South Australia ... CBPISA
Clay Brick Association of Canada [*Association Canadienne de Brique d'Argile Cuite*] [*Formerly, Canadian Structural Clay Asssociation*] (AC) ... CBAC
Clay Brick Association of Queensland [*Australia*] ... CBAQ
Clay Brick Manufacturers' Association of Western Australia ... CBMAWA
Clay Center, KS [*Location identifier FAA*] (FAAL) ... CYW
Clay Center, KS [*FM radio station call letters*] ... KCLY
Clay City News, Clay City, IN [*Library symbol Library of Congress*] (LCLS) ... InClcN
Clay County Historical Society, Brazil, IN [*Library symbol Library of Congress*] (LCLS) ... InBraCHi
Clay County Historical Society, Library and Archives, Moorhead, MN [*Library symbol*] [*Library of Congress*] (LCLS) ... MnMohHi
Clay County Public Library, Green Cove Springs, FL [*Library symbol Library of Congress*] (LCLS) ... FGcC
Clay County Public Library, Manchester, KY [*Library symbol Library of Congress*] (LCLS) ... KyMan
Clay Flue Lining Institute [*Defunct*] (EA) ... CFLI
Clay Minerals Society (EA) ... CMS
Clay or Terra Cotta [*Freight*] ... CLY T C
Clay Pigeon Shooting Association [*British*] ... CPSA
Clay Pigmented Organic Coating ... CPOC
Clay Pipe [*Technical drawings*] ... CP
Clay Pipe Development Association [*British*] (DBA) ... CPDA
Clay Pipe Institute (EA) ... CPI
Clay Products Association (EA) ... CPA
Clay Products Haulers Bureau, Inc., Worthington OH [*STAC*] ... CPH
Clay Products Technical Bureau [*British*] ... CPTB
Clay Roofing Tile Council [*British*] (DBA) ... CRTC
Clay Sewer Pipe Association (EA) ... CSPA
Claydon [*England*] ... CLAY
Claydon. Landlord and Tenant [*A publication*] (DLA) ... Clay L & T
Clay-Mill Technical Systems, Inc. [*Toronto Stock Exchange symbol*] ... CLY
Claymont Public Library, Claymont, DE [*Library symbol Library of Congress*] (LCLS) ... DeC
Claymore Resources [*Vancouver Stock Exchange symbol*] ... CYA
Claypool, AZ [*FM radio station call letters*] ... KIKO
Clay's Digest of Laws of Alabama [*A publication*] (DLA) ... Clay's Dig
Clayton College, Denver, CO [*Library symbol Library of Congress*] (LCLS) ... CoDC
Clayton County Register, Elkader, IA [*Library symbol Library of Congress*] (LCLS) ... IaElkCR
Clayton, GA [*AM radio station call letters*] ... WGHC
Clayton, GA [*FM radio station call letters*] ... WQXJ
Clayton Homes [*Associated Press*] (SAG) ... ClaytH
Clayton Homes [*NYSE symbol*] (TTSB) ... CMH
Clayton Homes, Inc. [*Associated Press*] (SAG) ... ClaytHm
Clayton Homes, Inc. [*NYSE symbol*] (SPSG) ... CMH
Clayton Junior College, Morrow, GA [*Library symbol*] [*Library of Congress*] (LCLS) ... GMorC
Clayton, MO [*AM radio station call letters*] ... KFUO
Clayton, MO [*FM radio station call letters*] ... KFUO-FM
Clayton, MO [*AM radio station call letters*] ... KSIV
Clayton, MO [*FM radio station call letters*] ... KWUR
Clayton, NC [*AM radio station call letters*] (RBYB) ... WHPY
Clayton, NM [*Location identifier FAA*] (FAAL) ... CAO
Clayton, NM [*AM radio station call letters*] (RBYB) ... KLMX-AM
Clayton on Conveyancing [*A publication*] (DLA) ... Clay Conv
Clayton, W. G., III, Buffalo NY [*STAC*] ... CWG
Clayton Williams Energy [*NASDAQ symbol*] (TTSB) ... CWEI
Clayton Williams Energy, Inc. [*Associated Press*] (SAG) ... ClayEng
Clayton Williams Energy, Inc. [*NASDAQ symbol*] (SAG) ... CWEI
Clayton's English Reports, York Assizes [*A publication*] (DLA) ... Clay
Clayton's English Reports, York Assizes [*A publication*] (DLA) ... Clayt
Clayton's English Reports, York Assizes [*A publication*] (DLA) ... Clayton
Clayton's English Reports, York Assizes [*A publication*] (DLA) ... Clayton (Eng)
Clayton's English Reports, York Assizes [*A publication*] (DLA) ... Rep Ass Y
Clayton's English Reports, York Assizes [*A publication*] (DLA) ... Rep York Ass
Clayton's English Reports, York Assizes [*A publication*] (DLA) ... York Ass
Clean ... C
Clean (MSA) ... CLN
Clean ... CLN
Clean Air Act [*1963, 1990*] ... CAA
Clean Air Act Amendment ... CAAA
Clean Air Car Race ... CACR
Clean Air Delivery Rate [*of air purifiers*] ... CADR
Clean Air Movement ... CAM
Clean Air Package ... CAP
Clean Air Projector ... CAP
Clean Air Scientific Advisory Committee [*Environmental Protection Agency Washington, DC*] ... CASAC
Clean Air Scientific Advisory Committee ... CASAC
Clean Air Society [*Australia*] ... CAS
Clean Air Transport [*Commercial firm Sweden*] ... CAT
Clean Air Working Group [*An association Defunct*] (EA) ... CAWG
Clean and Sober [*Slang*] ... C and S
Clean and Tight [*Publishing*] ... C/T
Clean Annapolis River Project (AC) ... CARP
Clean Arithmetic with Decimal Base and Controlled Precision (MCD) ... CADAC
Clean Assembly Facility ... CAF
Clean Ballast Tanks [*Transportation*] ... CBT
Clean Car Initiative ... CCI
Clean Catch [*of urine*] [*Medicine*] ... CC
Clean Catch Midstream Urine [*Medicine*] ... CCMS
Clean Catch Midstream Urine [*Medicine*] ... CCMSU
Clean Coal Coalition [*Defunct*] (EA) ... CCC
Clean Coal Technology Demonstration Program [*Department of Energy*] ... CCTDP
Clean Coal Technology Program (GNE) ... CCTP
Clean Community System [*Waste management program*] ... CCS
Clean Diesel Technologies [*NASDAQ symbol*] (TTSB) ... CDTI
Clean Draft [*Business term*] ... DFT/C
Clean Energy Research Institute [*University of Miami*] [*Research center*] ... CERI
Clean Fleet Vehicle [*VDOT*] (TAG) ... CFV
Clean Fuel Fleet [*VDOT*] (TAG) ... CFF
Clean Fuel Oil Tank (MSA) ... CFT
Clean Fuel Vehicle ... CFV
Clean Fuels Development Coalition (EA) ... CFDC
Clean Harbors [*NASDAQ symbol*] (TTSB) ... CLHB
Clean Harbors Cooperative (EA) ... CHC
Clean Harbors, Inc. [*Associated Press*] (SAG) ... CleanH
Clean Harbors, Inc. [*NASDAQ symbol*] (NQ) ... CLHB
Clean Intermittent Catherization [*Medicine*] ... CIC
Clean Letter of Credit [*Banking*] ... CLOC
Clean Liquid Radioactive Waste System (NRCH) ... CLRWS
Clean Liquid RADwater [*Nuclear energy*] (IEEE) ... CLR
Clean Lube Oil (AAG) ... CLO
Clean Midstream Urinalysis [*Medicine*] (DAVI) ... CMSUA
[*The*] **Clean Nova Scotia Foundation** (AC) ... CNSF
Clean Ocean Action (GNE) ... COA
Clean RADWASTE [*Radioactive waste*] [*Nuclear energy*] (NRCH) ... CRW
Clean Report of Findings [*Societe Generale de Surveillance SA*] (DS) ... CRF
Clean Room Kit ... CRK
Clean Shelter Area [*Army*] (ADDR) ... CSA
Clean Sites, Inc. (EA) ... CSI
Clean Sweep Generator (NVT) ... CSG
Clean Tanks, Gas Free (NVT) ... CTGF
Clean Up Buck (MCD) ... CUB
Clean Up TV Campaign [*Defunct*] (EA) ... CUTVC
Clean Urban River Environments [*Project*] ... CURE
Clean Urban Vehicle ... CUV
Clean Voided [*Specimen*] [*Biochemistry*] (DAVI) ... CL VOID
Clean Voided Specimen [*Medicine*] ... CVS
Clean Water (IEEE) ... CW
Clean Water Act [*Environmental Protection Agency*] ... CWA
Clean Water Action [*An association*] (EA) ... CWA
Clean Water Action Project [*Later, CWA*] (EA) ... CWAP
Clean Water Fund [*An association*] (EA) ... CWF
Clean Waters Advisory Committee [*New South Wales*] [*Australia*] ... CWAC
Clean Work Area [*NASA*] (NASA) ... CWA
Clean World International [*Brighton, East Sussex, England*] (EAIO) ... CWI
Clean-Catch-Midstream Urinalysis [*Medicine*] (MEDA) ... CCMSUA
Cleaned in Transit ... CIT
Cleaner [*Automotive engineering*] ... CL
Cleaner (NASA) ... CLNR
Cleaner ... CLNR
Cleaner Air System [*Automotive engineering*] ... CAS
Cleaner/Lubricant/Preservation [*for firearms*] (MCD) ... CLP
Cleaning ... CLNG
Cleaning ... CLNG
Cleaning and De-Icing System (MCD) ... CDS
Cleaning and Support Services Association [*British*] (EAIO) ... CSSA
Cleaning Contractors' Association of Western Australia ... CCAWA
Cleaning, Decontamination Request (MCD) ... CDR
Cleaning Equipment Manufacturers Association [*Later, CETA*] (EA) ... CEMA
Cleaning Equipment Trade Association (EA) ... CETA
Cleaning Gear Locker ... CGLKR
Cleaning, Lubrication, and Adjustment [*Camera repair*] ... CLA
Cleaning Management Institute (EA) ... CMI
Cleaning Management Station ... CMS
Cleaning-in-Place [*Microbiology*] ... CIP
Cleanliness Identification [*Label*] [*Aerospace*] (AAG) ... CID
Cleanly Designed Cigar ... CDC
Cleanout (AAG) ... CO
Clean-Out Door (OA) ... COD
Cleanout Flush with Finished Floor ... FCO
Cleanser ... CLNSR
Cleansing Officers' Guild [*British*] (BI) ... COG
Clean-Up System (IEEE) ... CUS

Clear [*Calculators*] ... C
Clear ... CL
Clear [*Biochemistry*] (DAVI) ... CLER
Clear [*Alaska*] [*Airport symbol*] (AD) ... CLF
Clear [*Alaska*] [*BMEWS Site 1*] (MCD) ... CLR
Clear (WDMC) ... clr
Clear [*Alaska*] [*ICAO location identifier*] (ICLI) ... PACL
Clear Above [*Aviation*] (FAAC) ... CA
Clear Air Dot Angle ... CADA
Clear Air Mass ... CLAM
Clear Air Temperature ... CAT
Clear Air Turbulence [*Aviation*] ... CAT
Clear, AK [*Location identifier FAA*] (FAAL) ... CLF
Clear All Channels ... CAC
Clear and Add ... CA
Clear and Add (SAA) ... CAD
Clear and Add ... CLA
Clear and Add Clock (SAA) ... CAC
Clear and Add Magnitude (IAA) ... CAM
Clear and Secure [*Military*] (VNW) ... C and S
Clear and Smooth [*NWS*] (FAAC) ... CLRS
Clear and Subtract (IEEE) ... CLS
Clear and Subtract ... CS
Clear and Subtract (IAA) ... CSU
Clear Aperture (MSA) ... CA
Clear Back [*Telecommunications*] (TEL) ... CB
Clear Both [*Computer science*] ... CLB
Clear, Cancel, or Complete (MCD) ... CCC
Clear Carry ... CLC
Clear Channel Broadcasting Service (EA) ... CCBS
Clear Channel Commun [*NYSE symbol*] (TTSB) ... CCU
Clear Channel, Inc. [*NYSE symbol*] (SAG) ... CCU
Clear Channel, Inc. [*Associated Press*] (SAG) ... ClearC
Clear Channel, Inc. [*Associated Press*] (SAG) ... ClearCh
Clear, Creamy Layer at Top [*Biochemistry*] (DAVI) ... CCT
Clear Creek Butte [*Alaska*] [*Seismograph station code, US Geological Survey Closed*] (SEIS) ... CCB
Clear Flight Level ... CFL
Clear Forward [*Telecommunications*] (TEL) ... CLF
Clear Forward Signal [*Telecommunications*] (NITA) ... CLF
Clear Glass ... CG
Clear Glazed Structural Facing Units [*Technical drawings*] ... CLGSFU
Clear Glazed Structural Unit Base [*Technical drawings*] ... CLGSUB
Clear Ice [*Aviation*] (DA) ... CLA
Clear Indicating Light (MSA) ... CIL
Clear Interrupt [*PC instruction*] (PCM) ... CLI
Clear Lake City [*Texas*] [*Airport symbol*] (OAG) ... CLC
Clear Lake City, TX [*Location identifier FAA*] (FAAL) ... CLC
Clear Lake, IA [*FM radio station call letters*] ... KLKK
Clear Lake Public Library, Clear Lake, IA [*Library symbol Library of Congress*] (LCLS) ... IaCII
Clear Lane Marking System [*Army*] (RDA) ... CLAMS
Clear Language for Expressing Orders [*Computer science*] (IEEE) ... CLEO
Clear Line-of-Sight (MCD) ... CLOS
Clear Liquid [*Medicine*] ... CL
Clear Liquid (BABM) ... Cl liq
Clear Liquid [*Dietetics*] (DAVI) ... cl liq
Clear Memory (IAA) ... CM
Clear Mews [*Alaska*] [*Seismograph station code, US Geological Survey Closed*] (SEIS) ... CMA
Clear Mines Ltd. [*Vancouver Stock Exchange symbol*] ... CEE
Clear, No Creamy Layer [*Biochemistry*] (DAVI) ... CNC
Clear of Clouds [*Aviation*] (FAAC) ... CCLDS
Clear Only if Known [*Buzz words, acronyms, etc., that are clear in context only if already known to the reader*] ... COIK
Clear or Scattered Clouds and Visibility Greater than Ten, Remainder of Report Missing [*NWS*] (FAAC) ... DCAVU
Clear over Base [*System of paint finishing*] [*Automotive engineering*] ... COB
Clear Record [*Telecommunications*] (TEL) ... CR
Clear Round [*Show jumping*] (ADA) ... CR
Clear Screen [*Computer science*] ... CLS
Clear Status (MCD) ... CS
Clear Stream Avenue Elementary School, Valley Stream, NY [*Library symbol*] [*Library of Congress*] (LCLS) ... NVsCSE
Clear to Auscultation [*Medicine*] (DAVI) ... CTA
Clear to Send [*Telecommunications*] ... CTS
Clear to Send/Request to Send [*Telecommunications*] (NITA) ... CTS/RTS
Clear to Send/Request to Send ... CTSRTS
Clear To Stand [*Telecommunications*] (EECA) ... CTS
Clear to Zero [*Computer science*] ... CLR
Clear Wire Glass [*Technical drawings*] ... CLWG
Clear Write Condition ... CWC
Clearance ... C
Clearance (MSA) ... CL
Clearance [*Broadcasting*] (WDMC) ... cl
Clearance (KSC) ... CLN
Clearance (AFM) ... CLNC
Clearance [*Physiology*] ... Cx
Clearance Array (MSA) ... CLA
Clearance Diver's Breathing Apparatus ... CDBA
Clearance Diving [*Navy British*] ... CD
Clearance Diving Tender ... CDT
Clearance Dock Club [*A union*] [*British*] ... CDC
Clearance Group [*Customs*] (DS) ... CG
Clearance Rate [*Renal*] [*Nephrology*] (DAVI) ... C
Clearance Required [*Civil Service*] ... CR
Clearance Void if Not Off [*Aviation*] (FAAC) ... CVINO
Clearbrook Public School, Clearbrook, MN [*Library symbol*] [*Library of Congress*] (LCLS) ... MnCleS
Clear-Cell Carcinoma of Endometrium [*Medicine*] ... CCE
Clear-Channel Station [*Telecommunications*] (LAIN) ... CCS
Cleared ... CLD
Cleared Altitude (IAA) ... CALT
Cleared as Planned (FAAC) ... CLRAP
Cleared Bidder's List ... CBL
Cleared Customs (FAAC) ... CCUS
Cleared for Approach [*Aviation*] ... CFA
Cleared for Approach [*Aviation*] (FAAC) ... CFAP
Cleared Land Explosion Widening and Proofing (MCD) ... CLEWP
Cleared V-8 Juice Agar [*Microbiology*] ... CV-8A
Cleared V-8 Juice Broth [*Microbiology*] ... CV-8B
Cleared without Examination [*Business term*] ... CWE
Clear-Entry [*Calculators*] ... CE
Clearfield Chronicle, Clearfield, IA [*Library symbol Library of Congress*] (LCLS) ... IaClfC
Clearfield, PA [*AM radio station call letters*] ... WCPA
Clearfield, PA [*Television station call letters*] ... WPSX
Clearfield, PA [*FM radio station call letters*] ... WQYX
Clearing (MSA) ... CLRG
Clearing ... CLRNG
Clearing House Accession Number [*Online database field identifier*] ... CHAN
Clearing House Code [*Database terminology*] (NITA) ... CH
Clearing House Electronic Subregister System [*Australian Stock Exchange*] ... CHESS
Clearing House for Education and Social Studies/Social Science [*Department of Education*] (NITA) ... ChESS
Clearing House Interbank Payment System (BUR) ... CHIPS
Clearinghouse [*Banking*] ... CH
Clearinghouse and Laboratory for Census Data [*Defunct*] ... CLCD
Clearinghouse Announcements in Science and Technology [*of CFSTI*] [*Later, WGA*] ... CAST
Clearinghouse Automated Payments System [*Banking*] [*London*] ... CHAPS
Clearinghouse Committee for Information on the Arts and Humanities ... CCIAH
[*The*] **Clearinghouse Directory** [*A publication*] ... CD
Clearinghouse for Augmenting Resources for Training [*DoD*] ... CHART
Clearinghouse for Community Based Free Standing Educational Institutions (EA) ... CBFSEI
Clearinghouse for Federal Scientific and Technical Information [*Later, NTIS*] [*National Institute of Standards and Technology*] ... CFSTI
Clearinghouse for Innovation in Scientific Communication ... CISC
Clearinghouse for Library and Information Sciences ... CLIS
Clearinghouse for Network Information and Discovery and Retrieval [*Computer science*] ... CNIDR
Clearinghouse for Occupational Safety and Health Information [*HEW*] (IID) ... COSHI
Clearinghouse for Research in Child Life [*Federal Security Administration*] ... CRCL
Clearinghouse for Scientific and Technical Information [*Later, NTIS*] [*National Institute of Standards and Technology*] ... CSTI
Clearing-House for Specialized Media and Technology ... CSMT
Clearinghouse International of the Women's Forum (EA) ... CIWF
Clearinghouse on Business Coalitions for Health Action [*Defunct*] (EA) ... CBCHA
Clearinghouse on Child Abuse and Neglect Information (EA) ... CCANI
Clearinghouse on Computer Accommodation [*General Services Administration*] ... COCA
Clearinghouse on Counseling and Personnel Services [*ERIC*] ... CAPS
Clearinghouse on Development Communication (EA) ... CDC
Clearinghouse on Disability Information (EA) ... CDI
Clearinghouse on Educational Administration [*ERIC*] ... CEA
Clearinghouse on Educational Facilities [*ERIC*] ... CEF
Clearinghouse on Election Administration [*Federal Election Commission*] ... CEA
Clearinghouse on Health Indexes [*Public Health Service*] [*Information service or system*] (IID) ... CHI
Clearinghouse on Rural Education and Small Schools [*ERIC*] ... CRESS
Clearinghouse on Women's Issues (EA) ... CWI
Clearinghouse on Women's Issues in Congress [*Later, CWI*] (EA) ... CWIC
Clearinghouse on Women's Studies (EA) ... CWS
Clearinghouse Review [*A publication*] (AAGC) ... Clearinghouse Rev
Clearlink Network Control System [*AT & T Tridom*] ... CNCS
Clearly Canadian Beverage [*NASDAQ symbol*] (TTSB) ... CLCDF
Clearly Canadian Beverage Corp. [*NASDAQ symbol*] (SAG) ... CLCD
Clearly Canadian Beverage Corp. [*Associated Press*] (SAG) ... ClerCd
Clearnet Communic 'A' [*NASDAQ symbol*] (TTSB) ... CLNTF
Clearnet Communications, Inc. [*Associated Press*] (SAG) ... Clearnet
Clearnet Communications, Inc. [*NASDAQ symbol*] (SAG) ... CLNT
Clearport Petroleum Ltd. [*Vancouver Stock Exchange symbol*] ... CPR
Clear-Type Exterior Trim [*Weyerhaeuser Co.*] ... CTX
Clearview Elementary School, Clear lake, MN [*Library symbol*] [*Library of Congress*] (LCLS) ... MnClkE
Clearwater, BC [*AM radio station call letters*] ... CHNL-1
Clearwater Christian College, Clearwater, FL [*Library symbol*] [*Library of Congress*] (LCLS) ... FCICC
Clearwater Correctional Center, Resident Library, Forks, WA [*Library symbol Library of Congress*] (LCLS) ... WaForC-R
Clearwater Correctional Center, Staff Library, Forks, WA [*Library symbol Library of Congress*] (LCLS) ... WaForC
Clearwater, FL [*Location identifier FAA*] (FAAL) ... CLW
Clearwater, FL [*Television station call letters*] ... WCLF
Clearwater, FL [*FM radio station call letters*] ... WMTX

Clearwater, FL [*AM radio station call letters*] .... WTAN
Clearwater, FL [*FM radio station call letters*] .... WXTB
Clearwater, KS [*FM radio station call letters*] .... KSPG
Clearwater Memorial Public Library, Orofino, ID [*Library symbol*] [*Library of Congress*] (LCLS) .... IdOr
Clearwater Public Library, Clearwater, FL [*Library symbol Library of Congress*] (LCLS) .... FCl
Clearwater Publishing Co., Inc., New York, NY [*Library symbol Library of Congress*] (LCLS) .... CpCo
Clearwater, SC [*FM radio station call letters*] .... WSLT
Clearwater-St. Petersburg [*Florida*] [*Airport symbol*] (AD) .... PIE
Clearway [*Aviation code*] .... CWY
Cleary College, Ypsilanti, MI [*Library symbol Library of Congress*] (LCLS) .... MiYCC
Cleary's Registration Cases [*England*] [*A publication*] (DLA) .... Cleary RC
Cleary's Registration Cases [*Ireland*] [*A publication*] (DLA) .... Cleary Reg Cas
Cleat .... CLT
Cleavage and Polyadenylation Specificity Factor [*Biochemistry*] .... CPSF
Cleavage of Lateral Epitaxial Film for Transfer [*Photovoltaic energy systems*] .... CLEFT
Cleaveland on the Banking System [*A publication*] (DLA) .... Cleve Bank
Cleaveland's Banking Laws of New York [*A publication*] (DLA) .... Cleav Bank L
Clebsch-Gordan Coefficients [*Mathematics*] .... CGC
Cleburne Public Library, Cleburne, TX [*Library symbol Library of Congress*] (LCLS) .... TxCle
Cleburne, TX [*AM radio station call letters*] .... KCLE
Cleft Lip and Cleft Palate [*Medicine*] (MAE) .... CL/CP
Cleft Lip and Palate [*Medicine*] (DAVI) .... CL & P
Cleft Lip and Palate Association [*British*] (DI) .... CLAPA
Cleft Palate [*Medicine*] .... CL PAL
Cleft Palate [*Medicine*] .... CP
Cleft Palate and Lip Society [*Australia*] .... CPLS
Cleft Palate-Lateral Synechia Syndrome [*Medicine*] (DMAA) .... CPLS
Cleidocranial Dysostosis [*Medicine*] (DMAA) .... CLCD
Cleidocranial Dysplasia [*Medicine*] .... CCD
Cleistogamous [*Botany*] CL
CLEM [*Closed-Loop Ex-Vessel Machine*] **Maintenance Pit** [*Nuclear energy*] (NRCH) .... CMP
CLEM [*Closed-Loop Ex-Vessel Machine*] **Transporter** [*Nuclear energy*] (NRCH) .... CT
Clemency Review Board [*for Vietnam War draft dodgers and defectors*] .... CRB
Clemens Alexandrinus [*First century AD*] [*Classical studies*] (OCD) .... Clem Al
Clemens on Corporate Securities [*A publication*] (DLA) .... Clem Corp Sec
Clemens' Reports [*57-59 Kansas*] [*A publication*] (DLA) .... Clem
Clement of Alexandria (BJA) .... Clem
Clemente Global Gr [*NYSE symbol*] (TTSB) .... CLM
Clemente Global Growth Fund, Inc. [*Associated Press*] (SAG) .... ClemGlb
Clemente Global Growth Fund, Inc. [*NYSE symbol*] (SPSG) .... CLM
Clementina [*Ecuador*] [*ICAO location identifier*] (ICLI) .... SECM
Clementinae Constitutiones [*A publication*] (DSA) .... Cle
Clementinae Constitutiones [*A publication*] (DSA) .... Clem
Clemson Hydraulics Laboratory [*Clemson University*] [*Research center*] (RCD) .... CHL
Clemson, SC [*Location identifier FAA*] (FAAL) .... CEU
Clemson, SC [*AM radio station call letters*] .... WCCP
Clemson, SC [*FM radio station call letters*] .... WCCP-FM
Clemson, SC [*FM radio station call letters*] .... WSBF
Clemson University (GAGS) .... Clemson U
Clemson University, Clemson, SC [*Library symbol Library of Congress*] (LCLS) .... ScCleU
Clemson University, Clemson, SC [*OCLC symbol*] (OCLC) .... SEA
Cleobury, Mortimer, and Ditton Prior Light Railway [*Wales*] .... CMDP
Cleomenes [*of Plutarch*] [*Classical studies*] (OCD) .... Cleom
Cleopatra [*Queen of Egypt, 69-30BC*] (ROG) .... CLEOP
Clerestory (VRA) .... clst
Clergy CL
Clergy .... CLER
Clergy .... CLER
Clergy Against Nuclear Arms [*British*] [*An association*] (DBA) .... CANA
Clergy and Laity Concerned (EA) .... CALC
Clergy and Laity Concerned About Vietnam [*An association*] (VNW) CLCV
Clergy and Laymen Concerned about Vietnam [*Later, CALC*] (EA) .... CALCAV
Clergy Counseling Service for Problem Pregnancies [*Defunct*] (EA) .... CCSPP
Clergy Couples of the Presbyterian Family [*Defunct*] (EA) .... CCPF
Clergy Economic Education Foundation [*Later, EEFC*] .... CEEF
Clergy Mutual Assurance Society [*British*] .... CMAS
Clergy Orphan Corp. [*British*] .... COC
Clergy Orphan Schools [*British*] (ROG) .... CO
Clergy Pensions Institution [*Church of England*] .... CPI
Clergyman .... CLERG
Cleric (BARN) Cl
Clerical .... CLER
Clerical Administration .... CLAD
Clerical, Administrative, and Fiscal [*Used with number, as, CAF-6, to indicate grade of position*] [*Civil Service*] .... CAF
Clerical Administrative Class (ADA) .... CAC
Clerical and Administrative Workers Union [*British*] .... CAWU
Clerical and Allied Service Employees (DICI) .... CASE
Clerical Aptitude [*Test*] .... CA
Clerical Aptitude Area (AABC) CL
Clerical Aptitude Test .... CAT
Clerical Assistant [*Civil Service*] [*British*] .... CA
Clerical Medical [*Insurance firm*] [*British*] .... CM
Clerical Medical International [*British*] .... CMI
Clerical Officer [*Civil Service*] [*British*] .... CO
Clerical Perception [*On General Aptitude Test Battery*] (DAVI) .... Q
Clerical Support .... CLS
Clerical Technician, Medical [*Navy*] .... CLT
Clerical Test [*Military*] .... CLER
Clerical Work Data (MHDI) .... CWD
Clerical Work Evaluation [*British*] .... CWE
Clerical Work Improvement Program [*British*] .... CWIP
Clerical Work Measurement (MHDI) .... CWM
Clerici Regulares Congregationis Somaschae [*Somaschi Fathers*] [*Roman Catholic religious order*] .... CRCS
Clerici Regulares Matris Dei [*Clerics Regular of the Mother of God*] [*Roman Catholic religious order*] .... CRMD
Clerici Regulares Ministrantes Infirmis [*Clerics Regular Attendant on the Sick, Camillini, Camilliani*] [*Roman Catholic religious order*] .... CRMI
Clerici Regulares Minores [*Clerics Regular Minor*] [*Adorno Fathers*] [*Roman Catholic religious order*] .... CRM
Clerici Regulares Pauperum Matris Dei Scholarum Piarum [*Clerics Regular of the Poor Men of the Mother of God for Pious Schools*] [*Piarists*] [*Roman Catholic religious order*] .... CRSP
Clerici Regulares Sancti Pauli [*Clerics Regular of St. Paul*] [*Barnabites Also, Barn*] [*Roman Catholic men's religious order*] .... CRSP
Clerici Regulares Theatini [*Theatines*] [*Roman Catholic religious order*] .... CRT
Clerici Sancti Viatoris [*Clerics of St. Viator*] [*Viatorian Fathers*] [*Roman Catholic religious order*] .... CSV
Clericorum Regularium Somaschensium [*Clerics Regular of Somasca*] [*Somascan Fathers*] [*Roman Catholic religious order*] .... CRS
Clerics of St. Viator (TOCD) .... CSV
Clerics of St. Vistor, Viatorian Fathers (TOCD) .... csv
Clerics Regular of St. Paul (TOCD) .... CRSP
Clerics Regular of St. Paul, Barnabite Fathers (TOCD) .... crsp
Clericus Parliamentariorum [*Clerk of Parliaments*] [*British*] (ROG) .... CLER PARL
Clerk (ROG) .... CK
Clerk CL
Clerk (AFM) .... CLK
Clerk .... CLRK
Clerk and Steward [*British*] .... C & S
Clerk Home's Decisions, Scotch Court of Session [*1735-44*] [*A publication*] (DLA) .... C Home
Clerk Home's Decisions, Scotch Court of Session [*1735-44*] [*A publication*] (DLA) .... Clerk Home
Clerk Home's Decisions, Scotch Court of Session [*1735-44*] [*A publication*] (DLA) .... Home (Cl)
Clerk Home's Scotch Session Cases [*A publication*] (DLA) .... Cl Home
Clerk in Orders [*Church of England*] .... CLKO
Clerk of Monmouth County, Freehold, NJ [*Library symbol Library of Congress*] (LCLS) .... NjFrCoC
Clerk of Petty Sessions [*British*] (ADA) .... CPS
Clerk of Sessions [*British*] (ROG) .... CS
Clerk of State Papers [*British*] (ROG) .... CSP
Clerk of the Chapel [*Unions*] [*British*] (DGA) CC
Clerk of the Chapel [*Unions*] [*British*] (DGA) .... COC
Clerk of the Crown [*British*] CC
Clerk of the House of Commons [*British*] (ROG) .... CL HO COM
Clerk of the House of Lords [*British*] (ROG) .... CL HL
Clerk of the Peace [*British*] (ROG) .... CL of P
Clerk of the Peace [*British*] .... CP
Clerk of the Privy Council [*British*] CC
Clerk of the Privy Council [*British*] .... CPC
Clerk of the Works (DAC) .... C/W
Clerk (Pay and Records) [*British military*] (DMA) .... CPR
Clerk to Guardians [*British*] (ROG) .... C to G
Clerk to Magistrates [*British*] (ROG) .... CL to MAGS
Clerk to the House of Commons (DLA) .... CHC
Clerk to the Signet [*British*] .... CS
Clerk to Vestry [*British*] (ROG) .... CL to VEST
Clerke and Brett on Conveyancing, Etc. [*A publication*] (DLA) .... Clerke & Br Conv
Clerke's American Law and Practice [*A publication*] (DLA) .... Clerke Am L
Clerke's Digest [*New York*] [*A publication*] (DLA) .... Clerke Dig
Clerke's Praxis Curiae Admiralitatis [*A publication*] (DLA) .... Clerke Pr
Clerke's Praxis Curiae Admiralitatis [*A publication*] (DLA) .... Clerke Prax
Clerk's Magazine [*A publication*] (DLA) .... Clk's Mag
Clerks of Court [*Legal term*] (DLA) .... CLK CT
Clerks Regular, Ministers of the Sick [*Rome, Italy*] (EAIO) .... CRMS
Clermont [*Australia Airport symbol*] (OAG) .... CMQ
Clermont County Public Library, Batavia, OH [*Library symbol Library of Congress*] (LCLS) .... OBat
Clermont, FL [*Television station call letters*] .... WKCF
Clermont, FL [*FM radio station call letters*] (RBYB) .... WLAZ-FM
Clermont General and Technical College, Batavia, OH [*Library symbol Library of Congress*] (LCLS) .... OBatC
Clermont Mercy Hospital, Batavia, OH [*Library symbol Library of Congress*] (LCLS) .... OBatH
Clermont-Ferrand [*France*] [*Airport symbol*] (OAG) .... CFE
Clermont-Ferrand [*France*] [*Seismograph station code, US Geological Survey*] (SEIS) .... CFF
Clermont-Ferrand/Aulnat [*France ICAO location identifier*] (ICLI) .... LFLC
CLEU Library, British Columbia Ministry of Attorney General, Victoria, British Columbia [*Library symbol National Library of Canada*] (NLC) .... BVIAGC
Cleve [*Australia Seismograph station code, US Geological Survey*] (SEIS) CLV
Cleve Trust Realty SBI [*NASDAQ symbol*] (TTSB) .... CTRIS
Cleveland [*Ohio*] [*Airport symbol*] .... CLE
Cleveland [*Ohio*] [*Seismograph station code, US Geological Survey*] (SEIS) .... CLE
Cleveland [*District in Yorkshire, England*] (ROG) .... CLEV
Cleveland (BARN) .... Cleve
Cleveland (BARN) CLV
Cleveland [*Branch in the Federal Reserve regional banking system*] (BARN) .... D

Cleveland [*Postcode*] (ODBW) .... TS
Cleveland Area Metropolitan Library System [*Library network*] .... CAMLS
Cleveland Bay Association of America [*Later, Cleveland Bay Society of America*] (EA) .... CBAA
Cleveland Bay Horse Society of America (EA) .... CBHSA
Cleveland Bay Society of America (EA) .... CBSA
Cleveland [*Ohio*] **Burke Lakefront** [*Airport symbol*] (OAG) .... BKL
Cleveland, Cincinnati, Chicago & St. Louis Railway .... CCC & StL
Cleveland, Cincinnati, Chicago & St. Louis Railway [*AAR code*] CCCL
Cleveland/Cleveland-Hopkins International [*Ohio*] [*ICAO location identifier*] (ICLI) .... KCLE
Cleveland Cliffs, Inc. Holding Co. [*NYSE symbol*] (SAG) .... CLF
Cleveland Cliffs, Inc. Holding Co. [*Associated Press*] (SAG) .... ClvClf
Cleveland Clinic Educational Foundation, Cleveland, OH [*Library symbol Library of Congress*] (LCLS) .... OCIC
Cleveland County Memorial Library, Shelby, NC [*Library symbol Library of Congress*] (LCLS) .... NcSh
Cleveland County Technical Institute, Shelby, NC [*Library symbol Library of Congress*] (LCLS) .... NcShC
Cleveland Diesel Engine Division [*GM Corp.*] .... CDED
Cleveland Elec Ill $7.56 Pfd [*NYSE symbol*] (TTSB) .... CVXPrB
Cleveland Elec Ill Adj L Pfd [*NYSE symbol*] (TTSB) .... CVXPrL
Cleveland Elec Ill'93 Sr'A'Dep Pfd [*NYSE symbol*] (TTSB) .... CVXPrT
Cleveland Electric Illuminating Co. [*Associated Press*] (SAG) .... ClvEl
Cleveland Electric Illuminating Co. [*NYSE symbol*] (SAG) CVX
Cleveland Elementary School, Fergus Falls, MN [*Library symbol*] [*Library of Congress*] (LCLS) .... MnFfCE
Cleveland, GA [*FM radio station call letters*] .... WAZX
Cleveland, GA [*AM radio station call letters*] .... WRWH
Cleveland Graphite [*American Cleveland Graphite Corp.*] [*Automotive parts supplier*] .... CLEVITE
Cleveland Health Sciences Library, Cleveland, OH [*OCLC symbol*] (OCLC) .... CHS
Cleveland Heights, OH [*AM radio station call letters*] .... WJMO
Cleveland Heights, OH [*FM radio station call letters*] .... WZJM
Cleveland Heights-University Heights Public Library, Cleveland Heights, OH [*Library symbol Library of Congress*] (LCLS) .... OClh
Cleveland Heights-University Heights Public Library, Cleveland Heights, OH [*OCLC symbol*] (OCLC) .... OZC
Cleveland Hockey Booster Club (EA) .... CHBC
Cleveland Institute of Art, Cleveland, OH [*OCLC symbol*] (OCLC) .... OAC
Cleveland Institute of Art, Cleveland, OH [*Library symbol Library of Congress*] (LCLS) .... OClSA
Cleveland Institute of Electronics [*Ohio*] .... CIE
Cleveland Institute of Music [*Record label*] .... CIM
Cleveland Institute of Music, Cleveland, OH [*Library symbol Library of Congress*] (LCLS) .... OClCIM
Cleveland Law Record [*Ohio*] [*A publication*] (DLA) .... CL Rec
Cleveland Law Record [*Ohio*] [*A publication*] (DLA) .... Clev L Rec
Cleveland Law Record [*Ohio*] [*A publication*] (DLA) .... Cleve L Rec
Cleveland Law Record [*Ohio*] [*A publication*] (DLA) .... Cleve L Rec (Ohio)
Cleveland Law Record [*Ohio*] [*A publication*] (DLA) .... Cleve Law Rec
Cleveland Law Record [*Ohio*] [*A publication*] (DLA) .... CLR
Cleveland Law Register [*Ohio*] [*A publication*] (DLA) .... CL Reg
Cleveland Law Register [*Ohio*] [*A publication*] (DLA) .... Clev L Reg
Cleveland Law Register [*Ohio*] [*A publication*] (DLA) .... Cleve L Reg
Cleveland Law Register [*Ohio*] [*A publication*] (DLA) .... Cleve L Reg (Ohio)
Cleveland Law Register [*Ohio*] [*A publication*] (DLA) .... Cleve Law Reg
Cleveland Law Reporter [*Ohio*] [*A publication*] (DLA) .... CL Rep
Cleveland Law Reporter [*Ohio*] [*A publication*] (DLA) .... Clev L Rep
Cleveland Law Reporter [*Ohio*] [*A publication*] (DLA) .... Cleve L Rep
Cleveland Law Reporter [*Ohio*] [*A publication*] (DLA) .... Cleve Law R
Cleveland Law Reporter [*Ohio*] [*A publication*] (DLA) .... Cleve Law Rep
Cleveland Law Reporter (Ohio) [*A publication*] (ILCA) .... Cleve LR (Ohio)
Cleveland Law Reporter (Reprint) [*Ohio*] [*A publication*] (DLA) .... Clev Law Rep
Cleveland Law Reporter (Reprint) [*Ohio*] [*A publication*] (DLA) .... Clev R
Cleveland Law Reporter (Reprint) [*Ohio*] [*A publication*] (DLA) .... Cleve Rep
Cleveland Metropolitan General Hospital, Cleveland, OH [*Library symbol Library of Congress*] (LCLS) .... OClMGH
Cleveland, MS [*Location identifier FAA*] (FAAL) .... RNV
Cleveland, MS [*AM radio station call letters*] .... WCLD
Cleveland, MS [*AM radio station call letters*] (RBYB) .... WCLD-AM
Cleveland, MS [*FM radio station call letters*] .... WCLD-FM
Cleveland, MS [*FM radio station call letters*] .... WDFX
Cleveland, MS [*AM radio station call letters*] (RBYB) .... WDSK
Cleveland, MS [*FM radio station call letters*] .... WDTL
Cleveland, MS [*FM radio station call letters*] .... WMJW
Cleveland Museum of Art, Cleveland, OH [*Library symbol Library of Congress*] (LCLS) .... OClMA
Cleveland Museum of Natural History, Cleveland, OH [*Library symbol Library of Congress*] (LCLS) .... OClMN
Cleveland, Oberlin [*Ohio*] [*ICAO location identifier*] (ICLI) .... KZOB
Cleveland, OH [*Location identifier FAA*] (FAAL) .... BFT
Cleveland, OH [*Location identifier FAA*] (FAAL) .... CEE
Cleveland, OH [*Location identifier FAA*] (FAAL) .... CGF
Cleveland, OH [*Location identifier FAA*] (FAAL) .... DJB
Cleveland, OH [*Location identifier FAA*] (FAAL) .... HPI
Cleveland, OH [*Location identifier FAA*] (FAAL) .... LVJ
Cleveland, OH [*Location identifier FAA*] (FAAL) .... SQF
Cleveland, OH [*AM radio station call letters*] .... WABQ
Cleveland, OH [*FM radio station call letters*] .... WCLV
Cleveland, OH [*FM radio station call letters*] .... WCPN
Cleveland, OH [*FM radio station call letters*] .... WCRF
Cleveland, OH [*FM radio station call letters*] .... WCSB
Cleveland, OH [*FM radio station call letters*] .... WDOK
Cleveland, OH [*FM radio station call letters*] .... WENZ
Cleveland, OH [*AM radio station call letters*] .... WERE
Cleveland, OH [*Television station call letters*] .... WEWS
Cleveland, OH [*FM radio station call letters*] .... WGAR
Cleveland, OH [*AM radio station call letters*] .... WHK
Cleveland, OH [*Television station call letters*] .... WJW
Cleveland, OH [*AM radio station call letters*] .... WKNR
Cleveland, OH [*Television station call letters*] .... WKYC
Cleveland, OH [*FM radio station call letters*] .... WLTF
Cleveland, OH [*AM radio station call letters*] (RBYB) .... WMIH
Cleveland, OH [*FM radio station call letters*] .... WMJI
Cleveland, OH [*FM radio station call letters*] .... WMMS
Cleveland, OH [*FM radio station call letters*] .... WNCX
Cleveland, OH [*FM radio station call letters*] .... WQAL
Cleveland, OH [*Television station call letters*] .... WQHS
Cleveland, OH [*AM radio station call letters*] .... WRMR
Cleveland, OH [*FM radio station call letters*] .... WRUW
Cleveland, OH [*AM radio station call letters*] (RBYB) .... WTAM-AM
Cleveland, OH [*Television station call letters*] .... WVIZ
Cleveland, OH [*AM radio station call letters*] .... WWWE
Cleveland, OH [*FM radio station call letters*] .... WZAK
Cleveland, OH [*Location identifier FAA*] (FAAL) .... ZOB
Cleveland, OK [*Location identifier FAA*] (FAAL) .... EVL
Cleveland Open Cup [*Flash point determination*] .... COC
Cleveland Public Library, Cleveland, OH [*OCLC symbol*] (OCLC) .... CLE
Cleveland Public Library, Cleveland, OH [*Library symbol Library of Congress*] (LCLS) .... OCl
Cleveland Public Library, Cleveland, TN [*Library symbol Library of Congress*] (LCLS) .... TCle
Cleveland Public [*Charles O. Austin Memorial*] **Library, Cleveland, TX** [*Library symbol Library of Congress*] (LCLS) .... TxClv
Cleveland State Community College, Cleveland, TN [*Library symbol Library of Congress*] (LCLS) .... TCleC
Cleveland State Law Journal [*A publication*] (DLA) .... Cleveland SLJ
Cleveland State University (GAGS) .... Cleve St U
Cleveland State University, Cleveland, OH [*OCLC symbol*] (OCLC) .... CSU
Cleveland State University, Cleveland, OH [*Library symbol Library of Congress*] (LCLS) .... OClU
Cleveland, TN [*Location identifier FAA*] (FAAL) .... HDI
Cleveland, TN [*FM radio station call letters*] .... WALV
Cleveland, TN [*AM radio station call letters*] .... WBAC
Cleveland, TN [*AM radio station call letters*] .... WCLE
Cleveland, TN [*Television station call letters*] .... WFLI
Cleveland, TN [*FM radio station call letters*] .... WUSY
Cleveland Trust Co. .... CTC
Cleveland, TX [*FM radio station call letters*] (RBYB) .... KOND-FM
Cleveland, WI [*FM radio station call letters*] .... WKTT
Cleveland-Cliffs [*NYSE symbol*] (TTSB) .... CLF
Cleveland-Cliffs, Inc. [*NYSE symbol*] (SPSG) .... CLF
Cleveland-Cliffs, Inc. [*Associated Press*] (SAG) .... ClvClf
ClevelandElec $7.40 cm A Pfd [*NYSE symbol*] (TTSB) .... CVXPr
Cleveland-Marshall College of Law, Cleveland, OH [*OCLC symbol*] (OCLC) .... LMC
Cleveland-Marshall College of Law, Cleveland State University, Cleveland, OH [*Library symbol Library of Congress*] (LCLS) .... OClU-L
Clevenger's Medical Jurisprudence of Insanity [*A publication*] (DLA) .... Clev Insan
Cleverness Factor [*Psychology*] C
Clevetrust Realty [*NASDAQ symbol*] (SAG) .... CTRI
Clevetrust Realty Investors [*Associated Press*] (SAG) .... ClevtRt
Clevis [*Metal shackle*] (KSC) CLV
Clewiston, FL [*AM radio station call letters*] .... WAFC
Clewiston, FL [*FM radio station call letters*] .... WAFC-FM
Cliche Verre (VRA) .... CLVR
Client (ROG) .... CLT
Client Assistance Program [*Department of Education Department of Health and Human Services*] (GFGA) .... CAP
Client Behavior Inventory [*Psychology*] (AEBS) .... CBI
Client Information Control System (ECII) .... CICS
Client Liaison Officer .... CLO
Client Owned and Maintained (ECII) .... COAM
Client Server Architecture (CDE) .... CSA
Client/Server Open Development Environment [*Computer architecture*] (PCM) .... CODE
Client Service Agent (OSI) .... CSA
Client Services Review [*Australia*] .... CSR
Client-Centered Counseling Progress Record [*Psychology*] .... CCCPR
Client-Employee Management Information System (MHDB) .... CEMIS
Client-Oriented Data Acquisition Process [*FDA*] .... CODAP
Clients Lifetime Advisory Service Program [*Insurance*] .... CLASP
Cliff (ROG) C
Cliff .... CLF
Cliff .... CLF
Cliff [*Commonly used*] (OPSA) .... CLIFF
Cliff Leader [*British military*] (DMA) CL
Cliff Resources Corp. [*Toronto Stock Exchange symbol*] .... CFK
Cliff Richard Fan Club of America (EA) .... CRFCA
Cliff Richard Movement - USA [*Later, CRFCA*] (EA) .... CRM-USA
Clifford and Richard's English Locus Standi Reports [*1873-84*] [*A publication*] (DLA) .... C & R
Clifford and Richard's English Locus Standi Reports [*1873-84*] [*A publication*] (DLA) .... Clif & R
Clifford and Richard's English Locus Standi Reports [*1873-84*] [*A publication*] (DLA) .... Clif & Rich

Clifford and Richard's English Locus Standi Reports [*1873-84*] [*A publication*] (DLA) .... Cliff & Rich
Clifford and Stephens' English Locus Standi Reports [*1867-72*] [*A publication*] (DLA) .... C & S
Clifford and Stephens' English Locus Standi Reports [*1867-72*] [*A publication*] (DLA) .... Clif & St
Clifford and Stephens' English Locus Standi Reports [*1867-72*] [*A publication*] (DLA) .... Clif & Steph
Clifford and Stephens' English Locus Standi Reports [*1867-72*] [*A publication*] (DLA) .... Cliff & Steph
Clifford and Stephens' English Locus Standi Reports, Appendix [*A publication*] (ILCA) .... C & S App
Clifford & Wills [*Commercial firm*] .... CW
Clifford, Arlington, Buckingham, Ashley, Lauderdale [*Ministers of Charles II of England*] [*Some claim that the word "cabal" is derived from this acronym; others, that it comes from the Hebrew "cabala"*] .... CABAL
Clifford's English Southwick Election Cases [*1796-97*] [*A publication*] (DLA) .... Clif El
Clifford's English Southwick Election Cases [*1796-97*] [*A publication*] (DLA) .... Clif El Cas
Clifford's English Southwick Election Cases [*1796-97*] [*A publication*] (DLA) .... Clif South El
Clifford's English Southwick Election Cases [*1796-97*] [*A publication*] (DLA) .... Clif South El Cas
Clifford's English Southwick Election Cases [*1796-97*] [*A publication*] (DLA) .... Cliff
Clifford's English Southwick Election Cases [*1796-97*] [*A publication*] (DLA) .... Cliff El Cas
Clifford's Probate Guide [*A publication*] (DLA) .... Clif Prob
Clifford's United States Circuit Court Reports, First Circuit [*A publication*] (DLA) .... Clif
Clifford's United States Circuit Court Reports, First Circuit [*A publication*] (DLA) .... Cliff
Clifford's United States Circuit Court Reports, First Circuit [*A publication*] (DLA) .... Cliff (CC)
Cliffs (MCD) .... CLFS
Cliffs .... CLFS
Cliffs [*Commonly used*] (OPSA) .... CLIFFS
Cliffs Drilling [*NASDAQ symbol*] (TTSB) .... CLDR
Cliffs Drilling Co. [*NASDAQ symbol*] (NQ) .... CLDR
Cliffs Drilling Co. (MHDW) .... CLDRV
Cliffs Drilling Co. [*Associated Press*] (SAG) .... ClfDr
Cliffs Drilling Co. [*Associated Press*] (SAG) .... ClifDr
Cliffside [*Montana*] [*Seismograph station code, US Geological Survey Closed*] (SEIS) .... CFM
Cliffside Park Public Library, Cliffside Park, NJ [*Library symbol Library of Congress*] (LCLS) .... NjClp
Cliffside Railroad Co. [*AAR code*] .... CLIF
Clifton Assessment Procedures for the Elderly [*Personality development test*] [*Psychology*] .... CAPE
Clifton, AZ [*AM radio station call letters*] .... KCUZ
Clifton, AZ [*FM radio station call letters*] (RBYB) .... KWRQ
Clifton Elementary School, Clifton, CO [*Library symbol Library of Congress*] (LCLS) .... CoCfCfE
Clifton Forge, VA [*AM radio station call letters*] .... WXCF
Clifton Forge, VA [*FM radio station call letters*] .... WXCF-FM
Clifton Herbarium [*British*] .... CFN
Clifton Hills [*Australia Airport symbol Obsolete*] (OAG) .... CFH
Clifton Independent Prospector, Clifton, NJ [*Library symbol Library of Congress*] (LCLS) .... NjClifI
Clifton Leader, Clifton, NJ [*Library symbol Library of Congress*] (LCLS) .... NjClifL
Clifton Park, NY [*FM radio station call letters*] .... WWCP
Clifton Public Library, Clifton, NJ [*Library symbol Library of Congress*] (LCLS) .... NjClif
Clifton Publishing Co., Clifton, NJ [*Library symbol Library of Congress*] (LCLS) .... NjClifP
Clifton Resources Ltd. [*Vancouver Stock Exchange symbol*] .... CLF
Clifton Star Resources, Inc. [*Vancouver Stock Exchange symbol*] .... CFD
Clifton, TX [*FM radio station call letters*] .... KWOW
Clifton-Essex-Franklin Library [*Library network*] .... C-E-F L
Clifton-Morenci, AZ [*Location identifier FAA*] (FAAL) .... CFT
Clift's Entries [*1719*] [*England*] [*A publication*] (DLA) .... Clift
Climate .... CLIMAT
Climate Action Network [*An alliance of groups that includes Greenpeace, the World Wide Fund for Nature, and The Natural Resources Defense Council*] .... CAN
Climate - Altitude Chamber .... CAC
Climate Analysis Center [*National Weather Service*] .... CAC
Climate and Global Change Program (USDC) .... C&GC
Climate and Global Change Program [*National Oceanic and Atmospheric Administration*] (USDC) .... CGCP
Climate and Global Change Program [*Marine science*] (OSRA) .... CGCP
Climate and Globe Change Program [*Marine science*] (OSRA) .... C&GC
Climate and Remote Sensing Group [*University of California, San Diego*] [*Research center*] (RCD) .... CARS
Climate Assessment Data Base [*National Meteorological Center*] [*Database*] .... CADB
Climate Change Detection Project [*Marine science*] (OSRA) .... CCDP
Climate Change Information Exchange CCIX
Climate Computing [*Marine science*] (OSRA) .... CLICOM
Climate Computing (USDC) .... CLICOM
Climate Control International [*Auto industry supplier*] CCI
Climate Data Service for West Africa [*Marine science*] (OSRA) .... WACLIM
Climate Diagnostics Center [*Marine science*] (OSRA) .... CDC
Climate Diagnostics Center [*Environmental Research Laboratories*] (USDC) .... CDC
Climate Impact Assessment Division [*National Enviromental Satellite, Data, and Information Service*] (USDC) .... CIAD
Climate Impact Assessment Division [*Marine science*] (OSRA) .... CIAD
Climate: Long-Range Investigation, Mapping, and Prediction [*National Science Foundation*] .... CLIMAP
Climate Modeling Prediction (USDC) .... CLIMAP
Climate Monitoring and Diagnostics Laboratory [*National Oceanic and Atmospheric Administration*] .... CMDL
Climate Pay [*British military*] (DMA) .... CP
Climate Prediction Center .... CPC
Climate Research Data Center [*Project*] [*Marine science*] (OSRA) .... CRDC
Climate Research Data Center [*Project*] (USDC) .... CRDC
Climate Research Data Tools (USDC) .... CRDtools
Climate Research Data Tools [*Marine science*] (OSRA) .... CRDTools
Climate Research Project [*Boulder, CO*] [*Department of Commerce*] (GRD) .... CRP
Climate System Monitoring [*Marine science*] (OSRA) .... CSM
Climate Test Chamber .... CTC
Climate Variability and Predictability Study .... CLIVAR
Climate Variability and Prediction [*Program*] (USDC) .... CLIVAR
Climate Variability and Prediction [*Program*] [*Marine science*] (OSRA) .... CLIVAR
Climate, Vegetation, Productivity .... CVP
Climates of the States [*A publication*] .... C of S
Climatic (AFM) .... CLIM
Climatic Data Analysis Program .... CDAP
Climatic Data for the World [*A publication*] .... W
Climatic Impact Assessment Program [*for high altitude aircraft*] .... CIAP
Climatic Impact Committee [*National Academy of Sciences - National Academy of Engineering*] CIC
Climatic Impacts Centre CIC
Climatic Implications of Atmospheric Pollution .... CIAP
Climatic Laboratory [*Military*] CL
Climatic Laboratory Instrumentation System (MCD) .... CLINS
Climatic Research Unit .... CRU
Climatic Wind Tunnel [*Automotive testing*] .... CWT
Climatological (AABC) .... CLTGL
Climatological Data, National Summary (NOAA) .... CDNS
Climatological Data Sheet [*Air Force*] .... CDS
Climatological Dispersion Model [*Environmental Protection Agency*] (GFGA) .... CDM
Climatology .... CLIMATOL
Climatology and Persistence .... CLIPER
Climatology Mission Success Indicators (MCD) .... CMSI
Climax Mine [*Nevada*] [*Seismograph station code, US Geological Survey Closed*] (SEIS) .... NYM
Climax Molybdenum Co., Technical Library, Climax, CO [*Library symbol Library of Congress*] (LCLS) .... CoCxC
Climax Public Library, Climax, MN [*Library symbol*] [*Library of Congress*] (LCLS) .... MnClim
Climax-Shelly School, Climax, MN [*Library symbol*] [*Library of Congress*] (LCLS) .... MnClimS
Climb (FAAC) .... CLB
Climb [*or Climbing*] [*Aviation*] (FAAC) .... CMB
Climb and Cross [*Aviation*] (FAAC) .... CATX
Climb and Cruise [*Aviation*] (FAAC) .... CCRZ
Climb at Pilot's Discretion [*Aviation*] (FAAC) .... CAPD
Climb Detent of the Thrust Levers (GAVI) .... CLB
Climb en Route [*Aviation*] (FAAC) .... CER
Climb Immediately [*Aviation*] (FAAC) .... CLBI
Climb on Course [*Aviation*] (FAAC) .... COC
Climb So as to Cross [*Aviation*] (FAAC) .... CSATX
Climb So as to Reach [*Aviation*] (FAAC) .... CSATR
Climb to and Cross [*Aviation*] (FAAC) .... CTAX
Climb to and Maintain [*Aviation*] (FAAC) .... CTAM
Climb Well to Right [*Aviation*] (FAAC) .... CWTR
Climb Well to Right of Course [*Aviation*] (FAAC) .... CWRC
Climbing Fiber [*Cytology*] .... CF
Clin-Byla [*France*] [*Research code symbol*] .... CB
Clin-Byla [*France*] [*Research code symbol*] .... FH
Clinch River Breeder Reactor .... CRBR
Clinch River Breeder Reactor Plant [*Department of Energy*] .... CRBRP
Clinch River Breeder Reactor Program Office [*Nuclear Regulatory Commission*] (GFGA) .... CRBRPO
Clinch River Breeder Reactor Project [*Department of Energy*] (NUCP) .... CRBRP
Clinch River Mile [*Energy Research and Development Administration*] .... CRM
Clinch Valley College of the University of Virginia, Wise, VA [*OCLC symbol*] (OCLC) VCV
Clinch Valley College of the University of Virginia, Wise, VA [*Library symbol Library of Congress*] (LCLS) .... ViWisC
Clinchco, VA [*AM radio station call letters*] .... WDIC
Clinchco, VA [*FM radio station call letters*] .... WDIC-FM
Clinchfield Railroad Co. [*AAR code*] .... CCO
Clindamycin [*Antibacterial compound*] CC
Cline Development Corp. [*Vancouver Stock Exchange symbol*] .... CND
Clinic CI
Clinic [*Medicine*] (WDAA) .... CLIN
Clinic .... CLNC
Clinical .... CLIN
Clinical .... CLINIC
Clinical Academic Staff Salaries Committee [*Committee of Vice Chancellors and Principals*] (AIE) .... CASSC
Clinical Analysis Questionnaire .... CAQ
Clinical and Administrative Record [*System*] .... CARE

Clinical Applications and Prevention Program [*Bethesda, MD*] [*National Heart, Lung, and Blood Institute*] [*Department of Health and Human Services*] (GRD) .... CAPP
Clinical Articulation Profile [*Speech evaluation test*] .... CAP
Clinical Behavior Therapy Review [*A publication*] .... CBTR
Clinical Breast Examination [*Medicine*] (DMAA) .... CBE
Clinical Care Management System [*Medicine*] (DMAA) .... CCMS
Clinical Center [*National Institutes of Health*] (GRD) CC
Clinical Center Blood Bank .... CCBB
Clinical Chemistry Lookout [*Medical Information Centre*] [*Defunct Information service or system*] (CRD) CCL
Clinical Course [*Medicine*] CC
Clinical Data Abstraction Center [*Medicine*] (DMAA) .... CDAC
Clinical Decision Making [*Medicine*] (DMAA) .... CDM
Clinical Decision Support System (MAE) .... CDSS
Clinical Dementia Rating .... CDR
Clinical Education and Assessment Center [*Medicine*] (DMAA) .... CEAC
Clinical Efficacy Assessment Project [*Medicine*] (DMAA) .... CEAP
Clinical Emphysema [*Medicine*] (MAE) .... CE
Clinical Evaluation Exercise [*Medicine*] (DMAA) .... CEX
Clinical Evaluation of Language Functions [*Speech evaluation test*] .... CELF
Clinical Fellow Year (BARN) .... CFY
Clinical Full-Time [*Medicine*] (MAE) .... CFT
Clinical Gene Therapy Branch .... CGTB
Clinical General Impression [*Psychiatric testing*] .... CGI
Clinical Genetical Society [*British*] .... CGS
Clinical Global Impression of Change .... CGIC
Clinical Global Impression [*Scale*] **PY** (DAVI) .... CGI
Clinical Hyaline Membrane Disease [*Medicine*] (AAMN) .... CHMD
Clinical Immunology Society (EA) .... CIS
Clinical Information System (MCD) .... CIS
Clinical Information Was Not Provided [*Medicine*] .... CIWNP
Clinical Investigation [*Medicine*] (MAE) CI
Clinical Investigation Center [*Oakland, CA*] CIC
Clinical Investigation Control Center [*Military*] (DNAB) CICC
Clinical Journal [*A publication*] (ROG) .... CLIN JL
Clinical Laboratory (DAVI) CL
Clinical Laboratory Assistant (American Society of Clinical Pathologists) (DAVI) .... CLA(ASCP)
Clinical Laboratory Automated System (PDAA) .... CLAS
Clinical Laboratory Data Acquisition System [*Computer science*] .... CLDAS
Clinical Laboratory for Evaluation and Assessment of Noxious Substances [*Environmental Protection Agency*] (GFGA) .... CLEANS
Clinical Laboratory for Evaluation and Validation of Epidemiologic Research [*Environmental Protection Agency*] (GFGA) .... CLEVER
Clinical Laboratory Improvement Act .... CLIA
Clinical Laboratory Management Association (EA) .... CLMA
Clinical Laboratory Management System [*Computer science*] .... CLMS
Clinical Laboratory of Evaluation and Assessment of Tox Substances (GNE) .... CLEATS
Clinical Laboratory Scientist (MAE) .... CLS
Clinical Laboratory Specialist (MEDA) .... CLSP
Clinical Laboratory Technician .... CLT
Clinical Laboratory Test Database [*Computer science*] .... CLTDB
Clinical Ligand Assay Society (EA) .... CLAS
Clinical Literature Untoward Effects [*Service published by International Information Institute*] .... CLUE
Clinical Medical Librarian .... CML
Clinical Medical Officer [*British*] .... CMO
Clinical Microbiology Laboratory .... CML
Clinical Modification .... CM
Clinical Neurology Information Center .... CNIC
Clinical Notes On-Line [*IRCS Medical Science*] [*Ceased operation*] [*Information service or system*] (IID) .... CNOL
Clinical Nurse Specialist .... CNS
Clinical Nursing .... CN
Clinical Nutrition Research Unit [*Medical College of Georgia*] [*Research center*] (RCD) .... CNRU
Clinical Nutrition Research Unit [*Birmingham, AL*] [*Department of Health and Human Services*] (GRD) .... CNRU
Clinical Orthopedic Society (EA) .... COS
Clinical Pastoral Education .... CPE
Clinical Pathology (DAVI) .... Clin Path
Clinical Pathology .... CLP
Clinical Pathology [*Medicine*] (DMAA) .... CIP
Clinical Pathology .... CP
Clinical Pathology Conference .... CPC
Clinical Performance Score [*Medicine*] (MAE) .... CPS
Clinical Pharmacokinetics Team [*Pharmacology*] (DAVI) .... CPT
Clinical Practice Guidelines .... CPG
Clinical Probes of Articulation Consistency [*Speech evaluation test*] .... C-PAC
Clinical Procedure [*Medicine*] (DAVI) .... Clin Proc
Clinical Protocols [*National Cancer Institute*] [*Information service or system*] .... CLINPROT
Clinical Record [*Medicine*] .... CR
Clinical Record Cover Sheet [*Army medical*] .... CRCS
Clinical Research [*Medicine*] (DAVI) .... CR
Clinical Research Center [*University of Utah*] [*Research center*] (RCD) .... CRC
Clinical Research Center [*University of Rochester*] [*Research center*] (RCD) .... CRC
Clinical Research Center [*Case Western Reserve University*] [*Research center*] (RCD) .... CRC
Clinical Research Center [*Massachusetts Institute of Technology*] [*Research center*] (RCD) .... CRC
Clinical Research Center [*Medical Research Institute of Delaware*] [*Research center*] .... CRC
Clinical Research Center [*UCLA*] [*Research center*] .... CRC
Clinical Research Center [*University of Tennessee*] [*Research center*] (RCD) .... CRC
Clinical Research Center for Periodontal Disease [*University of Minnesota*] .... CRCPD
Clinical Research Center for Periodontal Disease [*University of Florida*] [*Research center*] (RCD) .... PDRC
Clinical Research Centre [*British*] (CB) .... CRC
Clinical Research Institute of Montreal [*University of Montreal*] [*Research center*] (RCD) .... CRIM
Clinical Research Unit .... CRU
Clinical Sleep Society [*Neurology*] (DAVI) .... CCS
Clinical Society of Genito-Urinary Surgeons (EA) .... CSGUS
Clinical Sociology Association [*Later, SPA*] (EA) .... CSA
Clinical Specialist (PGP) .... CS
Clinical Staging [*Oncology*] .... CS
Clinical State .... CS
Clinical Supplies and Inventory System [*Medicine*] (DMAA) .... CSIS
Clinical Target Volume [*Medicine*] (DMAA) .... CTV
Clinical Treatment Failure .... CTF
Clinical Trial Certificate [*Medicine*] (DMAA) .... CTC
Clinical Trials and Treatments Advisory Committee [*Australia*] .... CTTAC
Clinical Trials Monitoring System .... CTMS
Clinical Unit .... CU
Clinical Unit Coordinator .... CUC
Clinical-Diagnostic Staging of Cancer [*Oncology*] (DAVI) .... cTNM
Clinically Undetectable Primary Malignancy [*Oncology*] .... CUPM
Clinician Full Time [*Chiropody*] [*British*] .... CF
Clinician Interview Based Impression .... CI-BI
Clinician's Interview Based Impression of Change .... CIBIC
Clinicorp, Inc. [*AMEX symbol*] (SPSG) .... BAK
Clinique d'Aide a l'Enfance, Ste.-Foy, PQ, Canada [*Library symbol Library of Congress*] (LCLS) .... CaQSFCAE
Clinique d'Aide a l'Enfance, Ste.-Foy, Quebec [*Library symbol National Library of Canada*] (NLC) .... QSFCAE
Clinitest [*Miles Inc.*] [*Endocrinology*] (DAVI) .... clini
Clinitest and Acitest [*Trademarked clinical laboratory tests*] .... C & A
Clinitron Air Fluidized Therapy [*Medicine*] (DAVI) .... CAFT
Clinoenstatite [*A mineral*] .... CE
Clinohypersthene [*Inorganic chemistry*] .... Chp
Clinometer [*Engineering*] .... CLN
Clinopyroxene [*A mineral*] .... CPX
Clint Ritchie Official Fan Club [*Defunct*] (EA) .... CROFC
Clinton [*Iowa*] [*Airport symbol*] (OAG) .... CWI
Clinton, AR [*AM radio station call letters*] .... KGFL
Clinton, AR [*FM radio station call letters*] .... KHPQ
Clinton Community College, Clinton, IA [*Library symbol Library of Congress*] (LCLS) .... IaCliCC
Clinton Community College, Plattsburgh, NY [*Library symbol Library of Congress*] (LCLS) .... NPlaCC
Clinton Community College, Plattsburgh, NY [*OCLC symbol*] (OCLC) .... YLC
Clinton Corn Processing Co., Clinton, IA [*Library symbol Library of Congress*] (LCLS) .... IaCliC
Clinton Corners Reading Center, Clinton Corners, NY [*Library symbol Library of Congress*] (LCLS) .... NClinc
Clinton County Historical Society, Clinton, IA [*Library symbol Library of Congress*] (LCLS) .... IaCliCHi
Clinton Engineer Works (SAA) .... CEW
Clinton Gas System [*NASDAQ symbol*] (TTSB) .... CGAS
Clinton Gas Systems, Inc. [*NASDAQ symbol*] (NQ) .... CGAS
Clinton Gas Systems, Inc. [*Associated Press*] (SAG) .... ClintGs
Clinton Health Security Plan [*Medicine*] .... CHSP
Clinton Herald, Clinton, IA [*Library symbol Library of Congress*] (LCLS) .... IaCliH
Clinton, IA [*Location identifier FAA*] (FAAL) .... CWI
Clinton, IA [*Location identifier FAA*] (FAAL) .... FNO
Clinton, IA [*FM radio station call letters*] .... KCLN
Clinton, IA [*AM radio station call letters*] .... KLNT
Clinton, IA [*FM radio station call letters*] .... KMXG
Clinton, IA [*AM radio station call letters*] .... KROS
Clinton, IL [*AM radio station call letters*] .... WHOW
Clinton, IL [*FM radio station call letters*] .... WHOW-FM
Clinton Junior College, Rock Hill, SC [*Library symbol*] [*Library of Congress*] (LCLS) .... ScRhM
Clinton, LA [*FM radio station call letters*] .... WQCK
Clinton Memorial Hospital, Health Resource Center, Wilmington, OH [*Library symbol Library of Congress*] (LCLS) .... OWilmH
Clinton, MO [*Location identifier FAA*] (FAAL) .... GLY
Clinton, MO [*AM radio station call letters*] .... KDKD
Clinton, MO [*FM radio station call letters*] .... KDKD-FM
Clinton, MO [*FM radio station call letters*] .... KLRQ
Clinton, MS [*FM radio station call letters*] .... WHJT
Clinton, MS [*AM radio station call letters*] .... WTWZ
Clinton Museum, British Columbia [*Library symbol National Library of Canada*] (NLC) .... BCLM
Clinton Museum, Clinton, BC, Canada [*Library symbol*] [*Library of Congress*] (LCLS) .... CaBCLM
Clinton, NC [*Location identifier FAA*] (FAAL) .... CTZ
Clinton, NC [*AM radio station call letters*] .... WCLN
Clinton, NC [*FM radio station call letters*] .... WCLN-FM
Clinton, NC [*AM radio station call letters*] .... WRRZ
Clinton Nuclear Power Plant (NRCH) .... CNPP
Clinton, NY [*FM radio station call letters*] .... WHCL
Clinton, OK [*Location identifier FAA*] (FAAL) .... BFV

Clinton, OK [*Location identifier FAA*] (FAAL) .... BZF
Clinton, OK [*Location identifier FAA*] (FAAL) .... CLK
Clinton, OK [*Location identifier FAA*] (FAAL) .... CSM
Clinton, OK [*FM radio station call letters*] .... KCLI
Clinton, OK [*AM radio station call letters*] (RBYB) ...... KCLI-AM
Clinton, OK [*FM radio station call letters*] (RBYB) ..... KQMX-FM
Clinton, OK [*FM radio station call letters*] .... KSWR
Clinton, OK [*AM radio station call letters*] .... KXOL
Clinton Point, NT [*ICAO location identifier*] (ICLI) ...... CYUH
Clinton Power Station [*Nuclear energy*] (GFGA) .... CPS
Clinton Public Library, Clinton, IA [*Library symbol Library of Congress*]
  (LCLS) .... IaCli
Clinton Public Library, Clinton, IN [*Library symbol Library of Congress*]
  (LCLS) .... InCli
Clinton Public Library, Clinton, MI [*Library symbol Library of Congress*]
  (LCLS) .... MiClin
Clinton Public Library, Clinton, OK [*Library symbol Library of Congress*]
  (LCLS) .... OkCl
Clinton, SC [*AM radio station call letters*] .... WPCC
Clinton, TN [*FM radio station call letters*] .... WDVX
Clinton, TN [*FM radio station call letters*] .... WYFC
Clinton, TN [*AM radio station call letters*] .... WYSH
Clinton-Essex-Franklin Library, Plattsburgh, NY [*OCLC symbol*] (OCLC) .... VZC
Clinton-Essex-Franklin Library System, Plattsburgh, NY [*Library symbol
  Library of Congress*] (LCLS) .... NPlaCEF
Clinton-Graceville High School, Graceville, MN [*Library symbol*] [*Library of
  Congress*] (LCLS) .... MnGraCHS
Clinton's Digest [*New York*] [*A publication*] (DLA) .... Clin Dig
Clintonville, WI [*Location identifier FAA*] (FAAL) CLI
Clintonville, WI [*AM radio station call letters*] .... WFCL
Clintonville, WI [*FM radio station call letters*] .... WJMQ
Clintrials Research [*NASDAQ symbol*] (SAG) .... CCRO
Clintrials Research, Inc. [*Associated Press*] (SAG) .... Clintrials
Clio: A Journal of Literature, History and the Philosophy of History
  [*A publication*] (BRI) .... Clio
Clip (MSA) CL
Clip-On Unit (DCTA) .... COU
Clip-on-Board [*Instrumentation*] .... COB
Clipped [*Ecology*] C
Clipped and Ash [*Ecology*] .... CA
Clipped and Burned [*Ecology*] .... CB
Clipped and Nitrogen Added [*Ecology*] .... CN
Clipped, Torched [*Ecology*] .... CT
Clipper .... CLPPR
Clipper Club [*Pan American Airlines' club for frequent flyers*] (EA) CC
Clipper Negative .... CLN
Clipper Positive .... CLP
Clipping [*Medicine*] .... Clip
Clipping Amplifier .... CA
Clips per Day [*Photocopying, microfilming*] .... CPD
Clips per Year [*Photocopying, microfilming*] .... CPY
CLIRA [*Closed-Loop In-Reactor Assembly*] Backup Plug Tool [*Nuclear
  energy*] (NRCH) .... CBPT
CLIRA [*Closed-Loop In-Reactor Assembly*] Holddown Assembly Tool [*Nuclear
  energy*] (NRCH) .... CHAT
Clitoria Yellow Vein Virus [*Plant pathology*] .... CYVV
Clive Public Library, Alberta [*Library symbol National Library of Canada*]
  (NLC) .... ACLI
Cloak and Suit Trucking Association (EA) .... CSTA
Clock C
Clock .... CK
Clock .... CLCK
Clock (AAG) .... CLK
Clock and Watch Manufacturers Association of America [*Defunct*] .... CWMAA
Clock Assemblers and Importers Association (EA) .... CAIA
Clock Coercion .... C/C
Clock Coercion Signal .... CCS
Clock Control (IAA) CC
Clock Delay .... CDL
Clock Driver .... CD
Clock Generator Random-Access Memory [*Computer science*] (OA) .... CGRAM
Clock Hour (KSC) .... CH
Clock Manufacturers and Marketing Association (EA) .... CMMA
Clock Oscillator .... CO
Clock Phase .... CP
Clock, Programming, and Timing [*NASA*] (KSC) .... CPT
Clock Pulse .... CP
Clock Pulse (IAA) .... CPS
Clock Pulse Generator .... CPG
Clock Pulse Interval .... CPI
Clock Pulse Repeater .... CPR
Clock Pulsed Control .... CPC
Clock Start Command .... CSC
Clock Subsystem (CET) .... CSS
Clock Synchronization .... CS
Clock Time .... CT
Clocked CMOS [*Complementary Metal-Oxide Semiconductor*] Logic
  [*Electronics*] (IAA) CCL
Clocked Complementary Metal Oxide Semiconductor [*Electronics*]
  (IAA) .... CCMOS
Clock-Sync Receiver Assembly [*Deep Space Instrumentation Facility,
  NASA*] .... CSR
Clockwise C
Clockwise (ADA) .... CKW
Clockwise (ADA) .... CLKW

Clockwise .... CLKWS
Clockwise (AFM) .... CLKWZ
Clockwise (IAA) .... CLW
Clockwise .... CLWS
Clockwise .... CW
Clockwise (AAG) .... CWS
Clockwise Bottom Angular Down (OA) .... CWBAD
Clockwise Bottom Angular Up (OA) .... CWBAU
Clockwise Down Blast (OA) .... CWDB
Clockwise Orbit [*Aviation*] (FAAC) .... CLKOB
Clockwise Top Angular Down (OA) .... CWTAD
Clockwise Top Angular Up (OA) .... CWTAU
Clockwise Top Horizontal (OA) .... CWTH
Clockwise Up Blast (OA) .... CWUB
Clode's Martial Law [*A publication*] (DLA) .... Clode ML
Clodius [*of Scriptores Historiae Augustae*] [*Classical studies*] (OCD) .... Clod
Clofibrate (DMAA) .... CLOF
Clogher [*Town in Northern Ireland*] (ROG) .... CLOGH
Cloisonne (VRA) .... clois
Cloisonne Collectors Club (EA) CCC
Cloister (DSUE) .... CLOI
Cloister (VRA) .... clstr
Clomiphene Citrate [*Fertility drug*] CC
Clomipramine [*Medicine*] (DMAA) CI
Clomipramine [*An antidepressant*] [*Medicine*] .... CMI
Clonal Apple Rootstock Liner .... CRL
Clonal Seed Orchard .... CSO
Clonazepam [*Antiepileptic drug*] .... CZP
Cloncurry [*Australia Airport symbol*] (OAG) .... CNJ
Clone CI
Clonfert [*Village in Ireland*] (ROG) .... CLONF
Clonidine (DMAA) .... CLON
Clonidine Displacing Substance [*Biochemistry*] .... CDS
Cloning Inhibiting Factor .... CIF
Cloning Inhibitory Factor [*Medicine*] (DMAA) .... CLIF
Clonorchis [*A liver fluke*] [*Gastroenterology*] (DAVI) .... Clon
Clonus C
Clonus Index (MAE) CI
Cloquet Middle School, Cloquet, MN [*Library symbol*] [*Library of Congress*]
  (LCLS) .... MnCIM
Cloquet, MN [*Location identifier FAA*] (FAAL) .... COQ
Cloquet, MN [*AM radio station call letters*] .... WKLK
Cloquet, MN [*FM radio station call letters*] .... WKLK-FM
Cloquet, MN [*FM radio station call letters*] .... WSCN
Cloquet Public Library, Cloquet, MN [*Library symbol Library of Congress*]
  (LCLS) .... MnCl
Cloquet Senior High School, Cloquet, MN [*Library symbol*] [*Library of
  Congress*] (LCLS) .... MnCISH
Clorinda [*Argentina ICAO location identifier*] (ICLI) .... SATC
Clorox Co. [*Associated Press*] (SAG) .... Clorox
Clorox Co. [*NYSE symbol*] (SPSG) CLX
Close (AAG) CL
Close .... CLO
Close [*Computer science*] (BUR) .... CLS
Close Air Support .... CAIRS
Close Air Support [*Military*] .... CAS
Close Air Support Aircraft [*Military*] .... CASA
Close Air Support Aircraft Design Alternative [*Military*] .... CASADA
Close Air Support/Battlefield Air Interdiction (DOMA) .... CAS/BAI
Close Air Support/Battlefield Air Interdiction .... CAS/BAT
Close Air Support Control [*Military*] (NVT) .... CASCON
Close Air Support Exercise [*Military*] (NVT) .... CASEX
Close Air Support Gun Program [*Military*] (MCD) .... CASGP
Close Air Support Gun System [*Military*] (MCD) .... CASGS
Close Air Support Missile [*Military*] (MCD) .... CASM
Close Air Support Request Processing [*Military*] .... CASRP
Close Air Support Standoff Munition (MCD) .... CASSCM
Close Air Support Survivability Enhancement System [*Military*] (MCD) ..... CASSE
Close Air Support System [*Military*] .... CLASS
Close Air Support Weapon [*Military*] (MCD) .... CASW
Close Air Support Weapon [*Military*] (MCD) .... CLAW
Close Air Support Weapon System [*Military*] (MCD) .... CASWS
Close Annealed [*Metal industry*] .... CA
Close Approach Indicator (IEEE) .... CAI
Close Assault Weapon (INF) .... CAW
Close Boundary Sentry [*Military*] (AFM) .... CBS
Close Combat Antiarmor Task Force (MCD) .... CCAATF
Close Combat Antiarmor Weapon System (MCD) .... CCAAWS
Close Combat Anti-Armor Weapon System [*Army*] (RDA) .... CCAWS
Close Combat Armament Center [*Dover, NJ*] [*Army*] (GRD) .... CCAC
Close Combat, Engineering, and Mine Warfare Directorate [*Army*] .... CCEMWD
Close Combat, Heavy .... CCH
Close Combat LASER Assault Weapon .... C-CLAW
Close Combat LASER Assault Weapon [*Military*] (PDAA) .... C-LAW
Close Combat Tactical Trainer .... CCTT
Close Combat Training System [*Army*] .... CCTS
Close Combat Vehicle [*Military*] CCV
Close Combat Vehicle Integration Diagnostic [*Army*] (RDA) .... CCVID
Close Combat Vehicle - Light [*Army*] CCVL
Close Combat Weapon System [*Army*] (MCD) .... CCW
Close Combat Weapon System [*Marine Corps*] .... CCWS
Close Confinement Mesa [*Electronics*] (NITA) .... CCM
Close Contact Annealing (MCD) .... CCA
Close Control Bombing [*Air Force*] .... CCB
Close Doublet (SAA) .... CD

Close Encounter [*with a UFO*] ..... CE
Close Encounters of the Third Kind [*Movie title*] CE3
Close Focus Lens ..... CFL
Close Lunar Satellite ..... CLS
Close Medium Shot [*A photograph or motion picture sequence taken from a relatively short distance*] ..... CMS
Close of Business [*With date*] ..... COB
Close Order Drill (DNAB) ..... COD
Close Packed (MSA) ..... CP
Close Range Analytical Bundle System (PDAA) ..... CRABS
Close Range Missile System (PDAA) ..... CRMS
Close Ratio [*Automotive engineering*] ..... CR
Close Reconnaissance Zone [*Army*] (AABC) ..... CRZ
Close Rolls [*British*] CL
Close Shot [*Photography*] ..... CS
Close Space Vapor Transport [*Photovoltaic energy systems*] ..... CSVT
Close Station March Order (MCD) ..... CSMO
Close Support [*Army*] ..... CS
Close Support Area [*Military*] (CAAL) ..... CSA
Close Support Artillery Rocket System (MCD) ..... CSARS
Close Support Artillery Weapon System (MCD) ..... CSAWS
Close Support Assault Weapon [*Obsolete Navy*] (MCD) ..... CSAW
Close Support Gun (DNAB) ..... CSG
Close Support Missile [*Air Force*] (MCD) ..... CSM
Close Surveillance Contractor List [*DoD*] ..... CSCL
Close Talking Microphone ..... CTM
Close This Office (FAAC) ..... CLOTO
Close to Shoulder (MSA) ..... CTS
Close Tolerance ..... CT
Close Triplet (SAA) ..... CT
Close Type Control Circuit Contact (MSA) ..... CTCCC
Close-Assault Weapon System ..... CAWS
Close-Binding-Intimate [*Biochemistry*] ..... CBI
Close-Coupled [*Electricity*] CC
Closed C
Closed (AAG) ..... CLSD
Closed Angle Glaucoma [*Ophthalmology*] (CPH) ..... COG
Closed Area Security System (MCD) ..... CASS
Closed at All Times (Except When in Actual Use) [*Ship's fittings classification*] X
Closed at Sea (for High Degree of Emergency Readiness) [*Ship's fittings classification*] ..... Y
Closed Bladder Drainage [*Medicine*] ..... CBD
Closed Bomb Data Reduction Program (MCD) ..... CBRED
Closed Brayton Cycle [*Thermodynamics*] ..... CBC
Closed Breech Scavenging System (MCD) ..... CBSS
Closed Captioned [*Refers to captioning of television programs for the deaf*] CC
Closed Chest Cardiac Massage and Mouth-to-Mouth Resuscitation [*Medicine*] (AABC) ..... CCCMMM
Closed Chest Cardiac Resuscitation [*Medicine*] ..... CCCR
Closed Circuit [*Transmission*] (DEN) CC
Closed Circuit Loop (MCD) CCL
Closed Circuit Radio Transmitter (NTCM) ..... CCRT
Closed Circuit Television (AIE) ..... CCTV
Closed Circuit Television / Large Screen Display (MHDI) ..... CCTV/LSD
Closed Circuit Television Manufacturers Association (EA) ..... CCTMA
Closed Condensation Nuclei (MCD) ..... CCN
Closed Cone at Maturity [*Botany*] ..... CLCONE
Closed Container [*Packaging*] (DCTA) CC
Closed Cooling Water [*Nuclear energy*] (NRCH) ..... CCW
Closed Cooling Water System [*Nuclear energy*] (NRCH) ..... CCWS
Closed Corporation [*Business term*] (MHDB) ..... CO LTD
Closed Craniocerebral Trauma [*Medicine*] (DMAA) ..... CCCT
Closed Cycle ADCAP [*Advanced Capability*] **Propulsion System** [*Mk48 torpedo improvement*] (DOMA) ..... CCAPS
Closed Ecological Life Support System [*NASA*] ..... CELSS
Closed Ecological System ..... CES
Closed End ..... CLE
Closed Entry Socket Insulator ..... CESI
Closed Flux Memory [*Computer science*] ..... CFM
Closed Head Injury [*Medicine*] ..... CHI
Closed Head Trauma [*Emergency medicine*] (DAVI) ..... CHT
Closed Head Unit [*Neurology*] (DAVI) ..... CHU
Closed Line Assembly for Single Particles (IEEE) ..... CLASP
Closed Loop (KSC) CL
Closed Loop Accounting for Stores Sales (IEEE) ..... CLASS
Closed Loop Artillery Simulation System [*Army*] ..... CLASS
Closed Mouth [*Doll collecting*] ..... CM
Closed Numbering Area [*Telecommunications*] ..... CNA
Closed Pack Ice Zone [*Oceanography*] ..... CPIZ
Closed Pore Insulation ..... CPI
Closed Position [*Dancing*] ..... CP
Closed Reduction [*Osteology*] (AAMN) ..... CR
Closed Roller Chock [*Shipfitting*] ..... CRC
Closed Routine (SAA) ..... CR
Closed Shell ..... CS
Closed Shelter Deck [*Shipping*] (DS) ..... CSD
Closed System Respirator Evaluator (KSC) ..... CSRE
Closed Throttle [*Automotive engineering*] ..... CT
Closed Timelike Curve [*Time travel*] ..... CTC
Closed Tracheal Suction System [*Medicine*] (DMAA) ..... CTSS
Closed Transition Transfer Switch ..... CTTS
Closed User Group [*Communications*] ..... CUG
Closed Vitrectomy [*Ophthalmology*] (DAVI) CV
Closed Waveguide ..... CWG
Closed, Well-Formed Formula [*Logic*] ..... CWFF
Closed-Circuit Radio ..... CCR
Closed-Circuit Saturation Diving System [*Navy*] (CAAL) ..... CCSDS
Closed-Circuit Television ..... CCTV
Closed-Circuit Television System (IAA) ..... CCTVS
Closed-Cycle Cooler CCC
Closed-Cycle Cryogenic Equipment ..... CCCE
Closed-Cycle Gas Turbine (PDAA) ..... CCGT
Closed-Cycle Gas-Cooled Reactor (DEN) ..... CCGCR
Closed-Cycle Refrigerator ..... CCR
Closed-End Fund [*Investment term*] ..... CEF
Closed-End Investment Company [*Business term*] ..... CEIC
Closed-Fist Injury ..... CFI
Closed-Form Solutions Applied to a Mesh-Point-Field [*Mathematics*] ..... CLAMP
Closed-Loop Adaptive Single Parameter (MCD) ..... CLASP
Closed-Loop Aiming Mechanism Prototype ..... CLAMP
Closed-Loop Approach Control ..... CLAC
Closed-Loop Bandwidth ..... CLBW
Closed-Loop Boresight Alignment (MCD) ..... CLBA
Closed-Loop Condensate [*Nuclear energy*] (NRCH) CLC
Closed-Loop Continuity Check [*Aerospace*] (AAG) CLCC
Closed-Loop Control [*Automotive engineering*] CLC
Closed-Loop Control and Instrumentation System [*Nuclear energy*] (NRCH) ..... CLCIS
Closed-Loop Control System [*Nuclear energy*] (IAA) ..... CLCS
Closed-Loop Cooling Water [*Nuclear energy*] (NRCH) ..... CLCW
Closed-Loop Cover Gas Monitor [*Nuclear energy*] (NRCH) ..... CLCGM
Closed-Loop Dynamic Stability Test (NASA) ..... CLDST
Closed-Loop Ecological Cycle [*Aerospace*] (AAG) ..... CLEC
Closed-Loop Environmental Control System ..... CECS
Closed-Loop Evaluation and Reporting System (MCD) ..... CLEAR
Closed-Loop Ex-Vessel Machine [*Formerly, EVHM*] [*Nuclear energy*] (NRCH) ..... CLEM
Closed-Loop Fire Control [*Army*] (MCD) ..... CLFC
Closed-Loop Gain ..... CLG
Closed-Loop In-Reactor Assembly [*Nuclear energy*] (NRCH) ..... CLIRA
Closed-Loop Jumper Assembly [*Nuclear energy*] (NRCH) ..... CLJA
Closed-Loop, Lock-In Compensation CLIC
Closed-Loop Stripping Analysis [*Analytical chemistry*] ..... CLSA
Closed-Loop Support [*Army*] (AABC) ..... CLS
Closed-Loop Support Extended [*Army*] (AABC) ..... CLSX
Closed-Loop System [*Chemical engineering*] [*Nuclear energy*] (NRCH) ..... CLS
Closed-Loop System Melt-Down Accident [*Nuclear energy*] (NRCH) ..... CLSMDA
Closed-Loop Telemetry ..... CLT
Closed-Loop Television ..... CLTV
Closed-Loop Test (NASA) ..... CLT
Closed-Loop Trainer Aid (MCD) ..... CLA
Close-Fitting Mask [*Medicine*] (DMAA) ..... CFM
Close-In CI
Close-In Automatic Route Restoral System [*NORAD*] ..... CARRS
Close-In Improvement Program [*to increase torpedo effectiveness*] (MCD) ..... CLIP
Close-In Support [*Military*] (AFM) ..... CIS
Close-In Weapon System (NATG) ..... CIWS
Closely Spaced Basing [*Proposed plan for protecting MX missiles from enemy attack*] ..... CSB
Close-Open ..... CO
Close-Open-Close (NASA) ..... COC
Closeout Door System (MCD) ..... CDS
Closeout System Installation (NASA) ..... COSI
Close-Packed Hexagonal [*Metallography*] ..... CPH
Close-Packed Structure ..... CPS
Close-Pair Interstitial Atom ..... CPIA
Close-Quarter Battle [*British military*] (DMA) ..... CQB
Closer Economic Relations (ADA) ..... CER
Closest Approach [*Aerospace*] ..... CA
Closest Approach Time (SAA) ..... CAT
Closest Point of Approach [*Navigation*] ..... CPA
Closet CL
Closet (MSA) ..... CLO
Closet ..... CLOS
Closet Accordion Players of America ..... CAPA
Close-Up [*A photograph or motion picture sequence taken from a short distance*] ..... CU
Close-Up (WDMC) ..... cu
Closing (AAG) ..... CLSG
Closing ..... CLSNG
Closing Abductory Wedge Osteotomy [*Orthopedics*] (DAVI) ..... CAWA
Closing Agreement Program (WYGK) ..... CAP
Closing Capacity CC
Closing Coil CC
Closing Date ..... CD
Closing Date ..... CLODA
Closing Order (ROG) ..... CO
Closing Pressure [*Medicine*] ..... CP
Closing Price [*Business term*] ..... CP
Closing Purchase [*Business term*] ..... CP
Closing Sale [*Business term*] ..... CS
Closing the Gap [*An association*] (PAZ) ..... CTG
Closing Volume [*Physiology*] CV
Clostridium [*Genus of microorganism*] (CPH) C
Clostridium [*Genus of microorganisms*] Cl
Clostridium [*Medicine*] (DMAA) ..... Clostr
Clostridium Difficile Disease [*Medicine*] ..... CDD
Clostridium Difficile-Associated Diarrhea [*Medicine*] ..... CDAD
Closure [*Medicine*] C

Closure [*Physiology*] ... CL
Closure (MSA) ... CLOS
Closure [*Technical drawings*] ... CLS
Closure (AAG) ... CLSR
Closure Manufacturers Association (EA) ... CMA
Closure Medical Corp. [*Associated Press*] (SAG) ... ClosMed
Closure Medical Corp. [*NASDAQ symbol*] (SAG) ... CLSR
Closure of Semilunar Valves [*Gastroenterology*] (DAVI) ... SC
Closure/Post-Closure ... C/PC
Clot Lysis [*Hematology*] (DAVI) ... CL LYS
Clot Lysis Time [*Hematology*] ... CLT
Clot Retraction [*Medicine*] ... CR
Cloth ... CL
Cloth [*Bookbinding*] (ROG) ... CLO
Cloth (VRA) ... cth
Cloth Assistance Factor [*Textiles*] ... CAF
Cloth Boards [*Bookbinding*] (ROG) ... CL BDS
Cloth Elongation Factor [*Textiles*] ... CEF
Cloth Extra [*Bookbinding*] (ROG) ... CL EX
Cloth Gilt [*Bookbinding*] (ROG) ... CL GT
Cloth Limp [*Bookbinding*] (ROG) ... CL LP
Cloth Pressers' Society [*A union*] [*British*] (DCTA) ... CPS
Cloth, Rollers, and Varnished [*Maps*] (ROG) ... CRV
Cloth Sides [*Bookbinding*] ... CS
Clothes ... CLTH
Clothes ... CLTHS
Clothes Drier ... CD
Clothes Time, Inc. [*Associated Press*] (SAG) ... Cloth
Clothes Time Inc. [*NASDAQ symbol*] (TTSB) ... CTMEO
Clothes Washer ... CW
Clothespin Manufacturers of America (EA) ... CMA
Clothestime, Inc. [*NASDAQ symbol*] (NQ) ... CTME
Clothier ... CLTHR
Clothing (AABC) ... CLO
Clothing ... CLOTH
Clothing (MSA) ... CLTHG
Clothing ... CLTHNG
Clothing Allowance [*British military*] (DMA) ... CA
Clothing and Allied Products Industry Training Board (AIE) ... CAPITB
Clothing and Equipage ... C & E
Clothing and Equipment Development Branch [*Army Natick Laboratories, MA*] ... C/ED
Clothing and Equipment Test Facility [*Army*] (RDA) ... CETF
Clothing and Footwear [*Department of Employment*] [*British*] ... CF
Clothing and Footwear Institute [*British*] (EAIO) ... CFI
Clothing and Housing Research Division [*of ARS, Department of Agriculture*] ... CH
Clothing and Individual Equipment [*Army*] (RDA) ... CIE
Clothing and Life Support Equipment [*Military*] ... C & LSE
Clothing and Organic Materials [*Army*] (MCD) ... C & OM
Clothing and Organic Materials Laboratory [*Army Natick Laboratories, MA*] ... C/OM
Clothing and Personal Life Support Equipment Laboratory [*Army Natick Laboratories, MA*] ... C/PLSEL
Clothing and Small Stores [*Military*] (DNAB) ... C & SS
Clothing and Small Stores Account [*Military*] ... CSSA
Clothing and Small Stores Fund [*Military*] ... CSSF
Clothing and Survival Equipment Bulletin (MCD) ... CSEB
Clothing and Survival Equipment Change [*Naval Air Systems Command*] (NG) ... CSC
Clothing and Survival Equipment Change [*Naval Air Systems Command*] ... CSEC
Clothing and Textile Materiel [*Army*] (AABC) ... C & TM
Clothing and Textiles ... C & T
Clothing Articles Require Explanation [*Student legal action organization*] ... CARE
Clothing, Equipment, and Materials Engineering Laboratory [*Army Natick Research and Development Laboratories, MA*] (RDA) ... CEMEL
Clothing Export Council [*British*] (DS) ... CEC
Clothing Initial Issue Point [*Military*] (AABC) ... CIIP
Clothing Maintenance Allowance [*Military*] ... CMA
Clothing Maintenance [*or Monetary*] **Allowance, Basic** [*Army*] ... CMAB
Clothing Maintenance Allowance, Standard [*Air Force*] ... CMAS
Clothing Maintenance Allowance System [*Military*] ... CMAS
Clothing Manufacturers Association of the USA (EA) ... CMA
Clothing Monetary Allowance ... CLMA
Clothing Monetary Allowance, Initial Issue [*Army*] ... CMAIISS
Clothing Monetary Allowance, Initial (Women's Army Corps) ... CMAIWAC
Clothing Monetary Allowance List [*Military*] (AFM) ... CMAL
Clothing Monetary Allowance, Standard [*Army*] ... CMAS
Clothing Monetary Maintenance Allowance [*Military*] (AABC) ... CMMA
Clothing Pattern Repository [*DoD*] ... CPR
Clothing Sales Store (AABC) ... CSS
Clothing Store Operating Budgets [*Air Force*] (AFIT) ... CSOB
Clothing Store Operating Programs [*Air Force*] (AFIT) ... CSOP
Clothing Supply Office [*Military*] ... CSO
Clot-Promoting Factor (MAE) ... CPF
Clotrimazole [*Antifungal agent*] ... CT
Clottable Protein [*Medicine*] (MAE) ... CP
Clotted [*Biochemistry*] (DAVI) ... CLT
Clotting [*or Coagulation*] **Time** [*Hematology*] ... CT
Cloud ... CLD
Cloud and Radiation Testbed [*Network*] [*Department of Energy*] (OSRA) ... CART
Cloud and Radiation Testbed Network [*Department of Energy*] (USDC) ... CART
Cloud and the Earth's Radiant Energy System ... CERES
Cloud and Visibility Okay [*NWS*] (FAAC) ... CAVOK
Cloud Base Recorder (PDAA) ... CBR
Cloud Camera Multiplexer ... CCM
Cloud Chamber [*Physics*] ... CC
Cloud Chamber Analysis ... CCA
Cloud Chamber Photographic Analysis ... CCPA
Cloud Condensation Nuclei [*Fog*] ... CCN
Cloud Cover (KSC) ... CC
Cloud Depiction and Forecast System [*Marine science*] (OSRA) ... CDFC
Cloud Depiction and Forecast System (USDC) ... CDFC
Cloud Height Remote Indicating System (PDAA) ... CHRIS
Cloud in Cell ... CIC
Cloud LIDAR System (MCD) ... CLS
Cloud Model with Explicit Microphysics [*Marine science*] (OSRA) ... CM-XMP
Cloud Model with Explicit Microphysics (USDC) ... CM-XMP
Cloud Nine [*Manufacturer of remote control devices for home electronics*] [*Company founded by Stephen Wozniak*] ... CL9
Cloud Physics Observatory [*University of Hawaii*] ... CPO
Cloud Physics Radiometer ... CPR
Cloud Point [*Petroleum characteristic*] ... CP
Cloud Processing Equipment (AABC) ... CPE
Cloud Radiation Feedback [*Marine science*] (OSRA) ... CRF
Cloud Radiation Feedback (USDC) ... CRF
Cloud Radiative Forcing [*Climatology*] ... CRF
Cloud Shadow (DNAB) ... CS
Cloud to Ground [*Marine science*] (OSRA) ... CG
Cloud to Ground (USDC) ... CG
Cloud Top Scanner (MCD) ... CTS
Cloud Water Project [*A cooperative ecosystem study*] ... CWP
Cloud-Croft Radiation Measurement ... CRM
Cloud-Free Line of Sight ... CFLOS
Cloudiness-Temperature [*Hypothesis*] [*Meteorology*] ... C-T
Cloud-to-Ground Lightning [*Meteorology*] ... CG
Cloud-to-Ground Lightning [*Meteorology*] (KSC) ... CGLTG
Cloud-Top Altitude Radiometer ... CAR
Cloud-Topped Boundary Layer [*Meterology*] ... CTBL
Cloud-Topped Marine Boundary Layer [*Marine science*] (OSRA) ... CTMBL
Cloud-Topped Marine Boundary Layer (USDC) ... CTMBL
Cloudy [*Meteorology*] ... C
Cloudy [*Biochemistry*] (DAVI) ... cl
Cloudy ... CLDY
Cloudy Cornea Syndrome [*Medicine*] (DMAA) ... CCS
Clove [*Seven pounds*] [*Unit of weight*] [*British*] (ROG) ... CL
Clover Bar Branch, Alberta Research Council, Edmonton, Alberta [*Library symbol National Library of Canada*] (NLC) ... AERC
Clover Blotch Virus [*Plant pathology*] ... CBV
Clover Primary Leaf Necrosis Virus [*Plant pathology*] ... CPLNV
Clover Yellow Mosaic Virus [*Plant pathology*] ... CLYMV
Clover Yellow Mosaic Virus ... CYMV
Clover Yellow Vein Virus [*Plant pathology*] ... CLYVV
Clover Yellow Vein Virus ... CYVV
Clover Yellows Virus [*Plant pathology*] ... CYV
Cloverdale Public Library, Cloverdale, CA [*Library symbol Library of Congress*] (LCLS) ... CCl
Cloverland Processing Center, Escanaba, MI [*OCLC symbol*] (OCLC) ... EZB
Clovis [*New Mexico*] [*Airport symbol*] (OAG) ... CVN
Clovis, CA [*Television station call letters*] ... KGMC
Clovis, CA [*AM radio station call letters*] ... KOQO
Clovis/Cannon Air Force Base [*New Mexico*] [*ICAO location identifier*] (ICLI) ... KCVS
Clovis, NM [*Location identifier FAA*] (FAAL) ... CRY
Clovis, NM [*Location identifier FAA*] (FAAL) ... CVN
Clovis, NM [*Location identifier FAA*] (FAAL) ... CVS
Clovis, NM [*Location identifier FAA*] (FAAL) ... GLO
Clovis, NM [*FM radio station call letters*] (RBYB) ... KAQF-FM
Clovis, NM [*AM radio station call letters*] ... KCLV
Clovis, NM [*FM radio station call letters*] ... KCLV-FM
Clovis, NM [*AM radio station call letters*] ... KICA
Clovis, NM [*FM radio station call letters*] (RBYB) ... KSMX
Clovis, NM [*FM radio station call letters*] ... KTQM
Clovis, NM [*Television station call letters*] ... KVIH
Clovis, NM [*AM radio station call letters*] ... KWKA
Clovis, NM [*FM radio station call letters*] ... KWUA
Clovis-Carver Public Library, Clovis, NM [*OCLC symbol*] (OCLC) ... CVC
Clovis-Carver Public Library, Clovis, NM [*Library symbol Library of Congress*] (LCLS) ... NmCl
Clown Club of America [*Later, CAI*] (EA) ... CCA
Clowns of America [*Later, CAI*] (EA) ... CA
Clowns of America International (EA) ... CAI
Clow's Leading Cases on Torts [*A publication*] (DLA) ... Clow LC on Torts
Cloyne Branch, Frontenac County Library, Ontario [*Library symbol National Library of Canada*] (BIB) ... OCFC
Clozapine [*Organic chemistry*] ... CLOZ
Clozapine [*A drug*] ... CLZ
CLSC Albert Samson, Coaticook, Quebec [*Library symbol National Library of Canada*] (NLC) ... QCCL
CLSC de Hull, Centre de Documentation, Hull, PQ, Canada [*Library symbol*] [*Library of Congress*] (LCLS) ... CaQHCL
Club ... C
Club ... CLB
Club ... CLB
Club [*Commonly used*] (OPSA) ... CLUB
Club Air Europe Ltd. [*British ICAO designator*] (FAAC) ... CLU
Club & Institute Union Ltd. [*British*] (BI) ... CIU
Club Anri [*Commercial firm*] (EA) ... CA
Club Aquarius (EA) ... CA
Club Cricket Conference [*British*] (BI) ... CCC

Club de las Americas [Defunct] (EA) .... CLA
Club de Petanque d'Adelaide [Australia] .... CdePA
Club Delahaye [An association France] (EAIO) .... CD
Club d'Electricite du Quebec Inc. (AC) .... CEleQ
Club des Ornithologues de Quebec Inc. (AC) .... COQ
Club Elite of North America (EA) .... CE
Club for Philately in Gerontology [Defunct] (EA) .... CPG
Club Ford [Class of racing cars] .... CF
Club Francais d'Amerique (EA) .... CFA
Club Francais du Disque [Record label] [France] .... CFD
Club Francais du Livre [French Book Club] .... CFL
Club International des Jeunes Naturistes [Paris, France] (EAIO) .... CIJN
Club Magazine [Generic term for a publication covering the activities of a science-fiction fan club] .... CLUBZINE
Club Management [Club Managers Association of America] [A publication] .... CM
Club Managers' Association [Australia] .... CMA
Club Managers Association of America (EA) .... CMAA
Club Mediterranee (EA) .... CM
Club National du Disque [Record label] [France] .... CND
Club of Channel Islands Collectors (EA) CCIC
Club of Printing Women of New York (EA) .... CPW
Club of the Friends of Ancient Smoothing Irons (EA) .... CFASI
Club Royale d'Automobile du Canada [Royal Automobile Club of Canada] .... CRAC
Club Safety Officer (DNAB) .... CSO
Clubair [ICAO designator] (AD) .... CG
Clubbing, Cyanosis, or Edema [Medicine] .... CCE
Clubhouse .... CLBHS
Clubs [Public-performance tariff class] [British] .... J
CluckCorp International, Inc. [Associated Press] (SAG) .... ClkCorp
CluckCorp International, Inc. [NASDAQ symbol] (SAG) .... ROTI
Clue Computing Co. [British] CCC
Cluj [Kolozvar] [Romania] [Seismograph station code, US Geological Survey] [Closed] (SEIS) .... CLU
Cluj-Napoca [Romania] [Airport symbol] (OAG) .... CLJ
Cluj-Napoca/Someseni [Romania] [ICAO location identifier] (ICLI) .... LRCL
Clumber Spaniel Club of America (EA) .... CSCA
Clumped [Biochemistry] (DAVI) .... CLMP
Clumping Inducing Agent [Bacteriology, genetics] .... CIA
Cluny [Queensland] [Airport symbol] (AD) .... CZY
Cluskey's Political Text Book [A publication] (DLA) .... Clusk Pol TB
Cluster (NASA) CL
Cluster [Programming language] [1973] (CSR) .... CLU
Cluster Activation Systems Specialist [NASA] .... CAS
Cluster Activation Systems Specialist [NASA] (KSC) .... CASS
Cluster Analysis [Data analysis] .... CA
Cluster Bomb [Military] .... CLSTBB
Cluster Bomb Unit [Military] .... CBU
Cluster Compression Algorithm (MCD) .... CCA
Cluster Control Unit .... CCU
Cluster Controller CC
Cluster Controller Node (IAA) .... CCN
Cluster Designation [Immunology] .... CD
Cluster Effects Bomblet .... CEB
Cluster Headache [Neurology] (DAVI) .... CH
Cluster Maintenance Facility [Military] .... CMF
Cluster Mission Simulator (KSC) .... CLMS
Cluster of Differentiation [Immunology] .... CD
Cluster of Stones [Jewelry] (ROG) .... CLUS
Cluster Significance Analysis [Data Analysis] .... CSA
Cluster Systems Description Document (KSC) .... CSDD
Cluster Variation Method [Physics] .... CVM
Cluster-Bethe-Lattice Method (MCD) .... CBLM
Cluster-Catalyzed Reactivity [Physics] .... CCR
Clustered Airfield Defeat Munition (MCD) .... CADM
Clustered Airfield Depot Munition (MCD) .... CADM
Clustered Atomic Warhead .... CLAW
Clusterin (DMAA) .... CLU
Clutch (MSA) CL
Clutch .... CLTCH
Clutch Drive [on a ship] (DS) .... CD
Clutch Release Bearing .... CRB
Clutter (MSA) .... CLTR
Clutter Acquisition .... CLA
Clutter Automatic Gain Control .... CAGC
Clutter Discriminating Fuze (MCD) .... CDF
Clutter Doppler Error (MCD) .... CDE
Clutter Gate .... CG
Clutter Gate Amplifier (MCD) .... CGA
Clutter Map (MSA) .... CLTRM
Clutter Map Update [Military] .... CMUP
Clutter Mapper Card .... CMC
Clutter on Target (MCD) .... COT
Clutter Reject Band (MCD) .... CRB
Clutter Rejection RADAR .... CRR
Clutter Threshold Detector (CET) .... CTD
Clutter-Locked Airborne Moving Target Indicator [Air Force] .... CLAMTI
Clutter-Operated Anticlutter .... COAC
Clyde Bowling Fan Club [Defunct] (EA) .... CBFC
Clyde Cablevision [Commercial firm] [British] (NITA) CCV
Clyde Mood Scale [Psychology] .... CMS
Clyde, NY [FM radio station call letters] .... WECQ
Clyde, NY [FM radio station call letters] (RBYB) .... WLLW-FM
Clyde, OH [FM radio station call letters] .... WHVT
Clyde, OH [FM radio station call letters] .... WNCG

Clyde River [Canada] [Airport symbol] (OAG) .... YCY
Clyde River, NT [ICAO location identifier] (ICLI) .... CYCY
Clyde Shipping Co. (MHDW) .... CSC
Clyde Surveys Ltd. [British ICAO designator] (FAAC) .... CLY
Clyde Yacht Clubs Association [British] (DBA) .... CYCA
Clydesdale [Valley in Scotland] (ROG) .... CLD
Clydesdale Bank [British] .... CB
Clydesdale Breeders Association of the United States [Later, CBUS] (EA) .... CBA
Clydesdale Breeders of the United States (EA) .... CBUS
Clydesdale Horse Society [British] (DBA) .... CHS
Clydesdale Runner's Association [Defunct] (EA) .... CRA
Clymer System .... CS
CM: A Reviewing Journal of Canadian Materials for Young People [A publication] (BRI) .... Can Mat
CM Preference Corp. [Toronto Stock Exchange symbol] .... ZCM
CMAC Computer Systems Ltd. [Vancouver Stock Exchange symbol] .... CMB
CMAC Investment [NYSE symbol] (TTSB) .... CMT
CMAC Investment Corp. [Associated Press] (SAG) .... CMAC
CMAC Investment Corp. [NYSE symbol] (SPSG) .... CMT
CMC Industries [NASDAQ symbol] (TTSB) .... CMCI
CMC Industries, Inc. [Associated Press] (SAG) .... CMC Ind
CMC Industries, Inc. [NASDAQ symbol] (NQ) .... CMCI
CME Capital, Inc. [Toronto Stock Exchange symbol] .... CME
CMG Info Services [NASDAQ symbol] (TTSB) .... CMGI
CMG Information Services [Associated Press] (SAG) .... CMG Inf
CMG Information Services [NASDAQ symbol] (SAG) .... CMGI
CMI Corp. [Associated Press] (SAG) .... CMI Cp
CMI Corp. [NYSE symbol] (SAG) .... CMX
CMI Corp. CI'A' [NYSE symbol] (TTSB) .... CMX
CML Group [NYSE symbol] (TTSB) .... CML
CML Group, Inc. [NYSE symbol] (SPSG) .... CML
CML Group, Inc. [Associated Press] (SAG) .... CML Gp
CML Industries Ltd. [Toronto Stock Exchange symbol] .... CNO
CMOS [Complementary Metal Oxide Semiconductor] Compact Cell Logic [Electronics] (NITA) CCCL
CMOS Idustrial Microcomputer (NITA) .... CIM
CMS Energy [Associated Press] (SAG) .... CMS
CMS Energy [NYSE symbol] (SAG) .... CPG
CMS Energy CI'G' [NYSE symbol] (TTSB) .... CPG
CMS Energy Corp. [NYSE symbol] (SPSG) .... CMS
CMS Energy Corp. [Associated Press] (SAG) .... CMS Eng
CMV [Cucumber Mosaic Virus] Associated Ribonucleic Acid [Biochemistry, genetics] .... CARNA
CN Biosciences, Inc. [Associated Press] (SAG) .... CN Biosc
CN Biosciences, Inc. [NASDAQ symbol] (SAG) .... CNBI
CNA Financial [NYSE symbol] (TTSB) .... CNA
CNA Financial Corp. [NYSE symbol] (SPSG) .... CNA
CNA Financial Corp. [Associated Press] (SAG) .... CNA Fn
CNA Financial Corp., Chicago, IL [Library symbol Library of Congress] (LCLS) .... ICCNA
CNA Financial Corp., Library, Chicago, IL [Inactive] [OCLC symbol] (OCLC) .... IBG
CNA Income Shares [NYSE symbol] (TTSB) .... CNN
CNA Income Shares, Inc. [Associated Press] (SAG) .... CNAI
CNA Income Shares, Inc. [NYSE symbol] (SPSG) .... CNN
CNARESTRA [Chief of Naval Air Reserve Training] Fleet Operating Squadrons .... CFOS
CNB Bancshares [NYSE symbol] (TTSB) .... BNK
CNB Bancshares, Inc. [NYSE symbol] (SAG) .... BNK
CNB Bancshares, Inc. [Associated Press] (SAG) .... CNB
CNB Bancshares, Inc. [Associated Press] (SAG) .... CNB Bcsh
CNB Bancshares, Inc. [NASDAQ symbol] (NQ) .... CNBE
CNB Financial Corp NY [Associated Press] (SAG) .... CNB Fn
CNB Financial Corp. [New York] [NASDAQ symbol] (SAG) .... CNBF
CNB Financial(NY) [NASDAQ symbol] (TTSB) .... CNBF
Cneius (ABBR) .... CN
Cnel. Suarez [Argentina ICAO location identifier] (ICLI) .... SAZC
CNI-Computer Networks International Ltd. [Vancouver Stock Exchange symbol] .... CUW
CNO [Chief of Naval Operations] Advisory Board .... CAB
CNO [Chief of Naval Operations] Evaluation Board .... CEB
CNO [Chief of Naval Operations] Executive Board .... CEB
CNO [Chief of Naval Operations] Industry Advisory Committee for Telecommunications [DoD] (EGAO) .... CIACT
CNO [Chief of Naval Operations] Policy and Planning Guidance .... CPPG
CNO [Chief of Naval Operations] Program Analysis Memorandum .... CPAM
CNO [Chief of Naval Operations] Program Fiscal Guidance [Navy] (CAAL) .... CPFG
CNP Resource Centre, Energy, Mines, and Resources Canada [Centre d'Information EESP, Energie, Mines, et Ressources Canada] Ottawa, Ontario [Library symbol National Library of Canada] (NLC) .... OOCNP
CNR [Christian News Report] Ministries (EA) .... CNRM
CNS Bancorp, Inc. [Associated Press] (SAG) .... CNS Bcp
CNS Bancorp, Inc. [NASDAQ symbol] (SAG) .... CNSB
CNS, Inc. [Associated Press] (SAG) .... CNS
CNS, Inc. [NASDAQ symbol] (NQ) .... CNXS
Cntrolled Slip Clutch .... CSC
CNW Corp. [NYSE symbol] (SPSG) .... CNW
CO_2 LASER Technology [Military] .... COLT
Coach .... CH
Coach [Airline fare code] .... Y
Coach and Bus First Aid Association [British] (DBA) .... CABFAA
Coach and Independent Bus Sector [British] (DI) .... CIBS
Coach Builder (ROG) .... CB
Coach House .... CH

Coach Lace Institute [*Defunct*] (EA) CLI
Coach USA [*NASDAQ symbol*] (TTSB) ..... TOUR
Coachella [*California*] [*Seismograph station code, US Geological Survey*] (SEIS) ..... COA
Coachella, CA [*AM radio station call letters*] ..... KCLB
Coachella, CA [*FM radio station call letters*] ..... KCLB-FM
Coachella Municipal Public Library, Coachella, CA [*Library symbol Library of Congress*] (LCLS) ..... CCoac
Coaches [*Freight*] ..... COCH
Coaches Association of PEI (AC) ..... CAPEI
Coaching Association of Canada ..... CAC
Coaching Club (EA) CC
Coachmen Indus [*NYSE symbol*] (TTSB) ..... COA
Coachmen Industries, Inc. [*NYSE symbol*] (SPSG) ..... COA
Coachmen Industries, Inc. [*Associated Press*] (SAG) ..... Coachm
Coadjutor (ROG) ..... COAD
Coadjutor (ROG) ..... COADJ
Coadjutor Bishop (ROG) ..... COADJ BP
Coady International Institute (AC) CII
Coagulase [*An enzyme*] C
Coagulase [*An enzyme*] ..... coag
Coagulase-Negative Staphylococci [*Medicine*] (DMAA) ..... CNST
Coagulase-Reacting Factor [*Biochemistry*] (MAE) ..... CRF
Coagulation [*Test*] ..... CA
Coagulation ..... CoA
Coagulation ..... COAG
Coagulation Profile - Diagnosis [*Hematology*] (DAVI) ..... COAG PD
Coagulation Profile - Presurgery [*Hematology*] (DAVI) ..... COAG PP
Coahoma Junior College [*Clarksdale,MS*] ..... CJC
Coahoma, TX [*FM radio station call letters*] ..... KBYG
Coahuila & Zacatecas Railway [*AAR code*] ..... CZ
Coal and Coke ..... C & C
Coal and Mining ..... C & M
Coal and Petroleum Products [*Department of Employment*] [*British*] ..... CPP
Coal and Shale Mine Workers' Superannuation Tribunal [*Australia*] ..... COSMWST
Coal and Steel (NATG) ..... CS
Coal and Steel Planning Committee [*NATO*] (NATG) ..... CSPC
Coal and Technology Export Program (AAGC) ..... CTEP
[*The*] **Coal Association of Canada** (AC) ..... CAC
Coal Aston [*British ICAO location identifier*] (ICLI) ..... EGCA
Coal Bug One [*Microbe used to remove sulfur from coal*] CB1
Coal City, IL [*FM radio station call letters*] ..... WKBM
Coal Combustion Technology ..... CCT
Coal, Conservation, and Nuclear [*Energy substitutes for oil*] [*British*] ..... Co-Co-Nuke
Coal Contractors Ltd. [*British*] CCL
Coal Corporation of Victoria [*Australia Commercial firm*] CCV
Coal Data Base [*International Energy Agency*] [*British*] (NITA) ..... CDB
Coal Development Establishment [*British*] (BI) ..... CDE
Coal Division, Denison Mines Ltd., Vancouver, British Columbia [*Library symbol National Library of Canada*] (BIB) ..... BVADC
Coal Employment Project (EA) ..... CEP
Coal Equivalent ..... CE
Coal Experts Committee [*Allied German Occupation Forces*] ..... CEC
Coal Exporters Association of the United States (EA) ..... CEA
Coal Extraction and Utilization Research Center [*Southern Illinois University at Carbondale*] [*Research center*] (RCD) ..... CEURC
Coal Fluid Flow Facility ..... CFFF
Coal Fuel Mixtures Association (EA) ..... CFMA
Coal [*into*] **Gas** [*Process*] ..... COGAS
Coal Grove, OH [*FM radio station call letters*] ..... WBVB
Coal Handling Plant ..... CHP
Coal Industry Advisory Board ..... CIAB
Coal Industry Social Welfare Organisation [*British*] ..... CISWO
Coal Industry Society [*British*] (BI) ..... CIS
Coal Merchants Federation [*British*] (DBA) ..... CMF
Coal Mine Roof Rating [*US Bureau of Mines*] ..... CMRR
Coal Mine Workers' Pension Tribunal [*Victoria*] [*Australia*] ..... CMWPT
Coal Miners' Industrial Union of Workers [*Australia*] ..... CMIUW
Coal Mines Board (DAS) ..... CMB
Coal Mining and Quarrying ..... CMQ
Coal Mining Institute of America [*Later, PCMIA*] (EA) ..... CMIA
Coal Mining Qualifications Board [*New South Wales*] [*Australia*] ..... CMQB
Coal Mining Research Centre [*Canada*] ..... CMRC
Coal Operators' Industrial Organisation of Employers, Queensland [*Australia*] ..... COIOEQ
Coal Preparation Plant Association [*British*] (EAIO) ..... CPPA
Coal Research Establishment [*British*] (IRUK) ..... CRE
Coal Research Projects [*IEA Coal Research*] [*Database*] ..... COALPRO
Coal Store (OA) ..... CS
Coal Supply and Transportation Model [*Department of Energy*] (GFGA) ..... CSTM
Coal Tar Pitch Emulsion Council [*Defunct*] (EA) ..... CTPEC
Coal Tar Pitch Volatile [*Organic chemistry*] ..... CTPV
Coal Tar Research Association [*British*] (BI) ..... CTRA
Coal Technology Information Centre [*Alberta Research Council*] [*Information service or system*] (IID) ..... CTIC
Coal Traffic Manager ..... CTM
Coal Utilisation Council [*British*] ..... CUC
Coal Workers' Pneumoconiosis [*Black lung*] [*Medicine*] ..... CWP
Coaldale, NV [*Location identifier FAA*] (FAAL) ..... OAL
Coaldale Public Library, Alberta [*Library symbol National Library of Canada*] (NLC) ..... ACO
Coalesce ..... CLSC
Coal-Fired Power Plant ..... CFPP
Coal-Gas Atmosphere (MCD) ..... CGA
Coalicion de Liberacion Nacional [*Panama*] [*Political party*] (EY) ..... COLINA
Coalicion del Centro Democratico [*Nicaragua*] [*Political party*] (EY) ..... CD
Coalicion Democratica [*Democratic Coalition*] [*Spain Political party*] (PPE) ..... CD
Coalicion Galega [*Spain Political party*] (EY) ..... CG
Coalicion Institucionalista Democratica [*Democratic Institutional Coalition*] [*Ecuador*] [*Political party*] (PPW) ..... CID
Coalicion Nacional Republicana [*Ecuador*] [*Political party*] (EY) ..... CNR
Coalicion Nacionalista [*Spain*] [*Political party*] (ECED) ..... CN
Coalicion Popular [*Popular Coalition*] [*Spain Political party*] (PPW) ..... CP
Coaling Station [*As part of a symbol*] ..... CS
Coalinga, CA [*Location identifier FAA*] (FAAL) ..... CLG
Coalinga, CA [*AM radio station call letters*] ..... KKFO
Coalinga, CA [*FM radio station call letters*] ..... KNGS
Coalinga Unified School District Library, Coalinga, CA [*Library symbol Library of Congress*] (LCLS) ..... CCoa
Coaliquid, Inc. (MCD) CLI
Coalition (ADA) ..... COAL
Coalition Advocating for Disability Refoerm in Education ..... CADRE
Coalition Against Anti-Asian Violence (EA) ..... CAAAV
Coalition Against Black Exploitation (EA) ..... CABE
Coalition Against Dangerous Exports ..... CADE
Coalition Against Double Taxation [*Defunct*] (EA) ..... CADT
Coalition Against Noneffective Lightning Protection Technologies (EA) ..... CANT
Coalition Against Pipeline Pollution (EA) ..... CAP
Coalition Against Regressive Taxation (EA) ..... CART
Coalition Against Sexist-Racist Hiring [*Student legal action organization*] ..... CASH
Coalition Against Unsolicited Commercial Email [*An association*] [*Computer science*] ..... CAUCE
Coalition Canadienne pour les Droits des Lesbiennes et des Gais [*Canadian Lesbian and Gay Rights Coalition*] ..... CCDLG
Coalition Concerned with Developmental Disabilities [*American Occupational Therapy Association*] ..... CCDD
Coalition, Coordination, Communications, and Integration Center (DOMA) ..... C³IC
Coalition de l'Opposition Democratique [*Togo*] [*Political party*] (EY) ..... COD
Coalition des Gauches [*Left Unity*] [*Transnational party group in the European Parliament*] (ECED) ..... CG
Coalition des Organismes Communautaires Quebecois de Lutte Contre le Sida (AC) ..... COCQ-SIDA
Coalition for a Decent USA [*Defunct*] (EA) ..... CDUSA
Coalition for a Democratic Majority (EA) ..... CDM
Coalition for a National Health System (EA) ..... CNHS
Coalition for a New Foreign Policy [*Defunct*] (EA) ..... CNFP
Coalition for a Non-Nuclear World [*Defunct*] (EA) ..... CNNW
Coalition for a Nuclear Free Harbor (EA) ..... CNFH
Coalition for Advertising Supported Information and Entertainment ..... CASIE
Coalition for Affordable Health Care ..... CAHC
Coalition for Alternatives in Jewish Education (EA) ..... CAJE
Coalition for Asian Peace and Security (EA) ..... CAPS
Coalition for Auto Repair Choice [*Defunct*] (EA) ..... CARC
Coalition for Auto Repair Equality [*Automotive aftermarket parts lobbying group*] ..... CARE
Coalition for Better Television ..... CBTV
[*The*] **Coalition for Brand Equity** [*An organization of advertisers, agencies, and media*] ..... CBE
Coalition for Children and Youth [*American Occupational Therapy Association*] ..... CCY
Coalition for Common Courtesy [*Defunct*] (EA) CCC
Coalition for Common Sense in Government Procurement [*Later, CGP*] [*Washington, DC*] (EA) ..... CCSGP
Coalition for Constitutional Justice and Security (EA) ..... CCJS
Coalition for Consumer Health and Safety (EA) ..... CCHS
Coalition for Consumer Justice [*Defunct*] (EA) ..... CCJ
Coalition for Corporate Responsibility [*Defunct*] (EA) ..... CCR
Coalition for Decency [*Later, NFF*] (EA) ..... CFD
Coalition for Drug-Free Horse Racing (EA) ..... CDFHR
Coalition for Economic Survival (EA) ..... CES
Coalition for Environmentally-Responsible Economies (EA) ..... CERES
Coalition for Food Irradiation [*Defunct*] (EA) ..... CFI
Coalition for Free and Open Elections (EA) ..... COFOE
Coalition for Government Procurement (EA) ..... CGP
Coalition for Handicapped Children's Education (DAVI) ..... CHANCE
Coalition for Harmony of Races in the US (EA) ..... CHORUS
Coalition for Health and the Environment (EA) ..... CHE
Coalition for Health Funding (EA) ..... CHF
Coalition for Hypertension Education and Control ..... CHEC
Coalition for Indian Education (EA) ..... CIA
Coalition for Information Access for Print Handicapped Readers [*An association*] ..... CIAPHR
Coalition for International Cooperation and Peace (EA) ..... CICP
Coalition for International Trade Equity ..... CITE
Coalition for Jobs, Peace, and Freedom in America (EA) ..... CJPFA
Coalition for Justice in the Maquiladoras (CROSS) ..... CJM
Coalition for Lesbian & Gay Right in Ontario [*Coalition pour les Droits des Lesbiennes et Personnes Gaies en Ontario*] [*Formerly, Coalition for Gay Rights in Ontario*] (AC) ..... CLGRO
Coalition for Life for All Mollusks ..... CLAM
Coalition for Literacy (EA) CL
Coalition for Manufacturing Performance through Technology ..... COMPETE
Coalition for National Dance Week (EA) ..... CNDW
Coalition for Networked Information [*Computer science*] (TNIG) ..... CNI
Coalition for Non-Violent Food (EA) ..... CNVF
Coalition for Peace through Strength [*Later, CCNS*] (EA) ..... CPTS
Coalition for Prompt Pay (EA) ..... CPP
Coalition for Public Information (AC) ..... CPI
Coalition for Religious Freedom (EA) ..... CRF

Coalition for Responsible Genetic Research (HGAA)	CRGR
Coalition for Responsible Mining Law [Defunct] (EA)	CRML
Coalition for Responsible Waste Incineration (EA)	CRWI
Coalition for Retirement Income Security (EA)	CRIS
Coalition for Safe and Efficient Transportation [MTMC] (TAG)	CSET
Coalition for Safe Food [Defunct] (EA)	CSF
Coalition for Safety of Abortion Clinics [Defunct] (EA)	CSAC
Coalition for Scenic Beauty [Later, SA] (EA)	CSB
Coalition for Sound Money (EA)	CSM
Coalition for State Prompt Pay (EA)	CSPP
Coalition for Strategic Stability in the Middle East (EA)	CSSME
Coalition for the Abolition of Marijuana Prohibition (EA)	CAMP
Coalition for the Advancement of Foreign Languages and International Studies	CAFLIS
Coalition for the Advancement of Jewish Education (EA)	CAJE
Coalition for the Apostolic Ministry [Later, ECM] (EA)	CAM
Coalition for the Education and Support of Attention Deficit Disorder (PAZ)	Co-ADD
Coalition for the Medical Rights of Women [Defunct] (EA)	CMRW
Coalition for the Peaceful Uses of Space (EA)	CPUS
Coalition for the Strategic Defense Initiative (EA)	CSDI
Coalition for Uniform Product Liability Law (EA)	CUPLL
Coalition for Vocational Home Economics Education (EA)	CVHEE
Coalition for Women in International Development (EA)	CWID
Coalition for Women in the Humanities and Social Sciences [Defunct] (EA)	CWHSS
Coalition for Women's Appointments (EA)	CWA
Coalition for Workplace Technology [Defunct] (EA)	CWT
Coalition Government of Democratic Kampuchea	CGDK
Coalition Internationale pour l'Action au Developpement [International Coalition for Development Action - ICDA] (EAIO)	CIAD
Coalition Mondiale pour l'Abolition de la Vivisection [World Coalition for the Abolition of Vivisection]	CMAV
Coalition Nationale pour les Droits des Homosexuals [National Gay Rights Coalition] [Canada]	CNDH
Coalition of Adult Education Organizations (EA)	CAEO
Coalition of America to Save the Economy (EA)	CASE
Coalition of American Pro-Life University Students [Later, ACL] (EA)	CAMPUS
Coalition of American Public Employees	CAPE
Coalition of Apparel Industries in California (SRA)	CAIC
Coalition of Asians to Nix Charlie Chan (EA)	CAN Charlie Chan
Coalition of Automotive Associations [Defunct] (EA)	CAA
Coalition of Black Trade Unionists (EA)	CBTU
Coalition of Digestive Disease Organizations (EA)	CDDO
Coalition of Eastern Native Americans [Defunct] (EA)	CENA
Coalition of Essential Schools (EA)	CES
Coalition of Higher Education Assistance Organizations (EA)	CHEAO
Coalition of Higher Education Assistance Organizations (EA)	COEAO
Coalition of Holistic Health Organizations [Defunct] (EA)	CHHO
Coalition of Indian Controlled School Boards (EDAC)	CICSB
Coalition of Labor Union Women (EA)	CLUW
Coalition of Labor Union Women Center for Education and Research (EA)	CLUWCER
Coalition of Minority Policy Professionals (EA)	CoMPP
Coalition of Minority Women in Business [Washington, DC] (EA)	CMWB
Coalition of Municipalities to Ban Animal Trafficking (EA)	COMBAT
Coalition of National Agreement [Croatia] [Political party]	CNA
Coalition of National Voluntary Organizations (DICI)	CONVO
Coalition of National Voluntary Organizations [Also, National Voluntary Organizations] (AC)	NVO
Coalition of Non-Postal Media [Defunct] (EA)	CNPM
Coalition of Northeastern Governors (EPA)	CNG
Coalition of Northeastern Governors	CONEG
Coalition of Public Employee Organizations (EA)	CPEO
Coalition of Publicly Traded Limited Partnerships [Later, CoPTP] (EA)	CPTLP
Coalition of Publicly Traded Partnerships (EA)	CoPTP
Coalition of Service Industries [Washington, DC] (EA)	CSI
Coalition of Spanish Speaking Mental Health Organizations [Later, NCHHSO] (EA)	COSSMHO
Coalition of Steel-Using Manufacturers	CASUM
Coalition of Women in National and International Business [Boston, MA] (EA)	CWNIB
Coalition of Women's Art Organizations (EA)	CWAO
Coalition on Block Grants and Human Needs (EA)	CBGHN
Coalition on Government Information (EA)	CGI
Coalition on Resource Recovery and the Environment (EA)	CORRE
Coalition on Sensible Transport	COST
Coalition on Sexuality and Disability (EA)	CSD
Coalition on Smoking or Health (EA)	CSH
Coalition on Southern Africa (EA)	CSA
Coalition on Temporary Shelter	COTS
Coalition on Women and Religion (EA)	CWR
Coalition on Women and the Budget [Defunct] (EA)	CWB
Coalition Opposed to Signal Theft (EA)	COST
Coalition Sida des Sourds du Quebec (AC)	CSSQ
Coalition to Abolish the Draize Rabbit Blinding Tests (EA)	CADRBT
Coalition to End Grand Jury Abuse [Later, CEGJA] (EA)	CEGJA
Coalition to Free Petkus and Gajauskas [Defunct] (EA)	CFPG
Coalition to Free Soviet Jews (EA)	CFSJ
Coalition to Halt Auto Theft (EA)	CHAT
Coalition to Keep Alaska Oil (EA)	CKAO
Coalition to Preserve the American Copyright [Defunct] (EA)	CPAC
Coalition to Promote America's Trade [Washington, DC] (EA)	CPAT
Coalition to Protect Animals in Entertainment (EA)	CPAE
Coalition to Protect Animals in Parks and Refuges (EA)	CPAPR
Coalition to Protect Social Security (EA)	SOS
Coalition to Save America's Music (EA)	CSAM
Coalition to Save Our Documentary Heritage [Defunct] (EA)	CSDH
Coalition to Stop Draize Rabbit Blinding Tests [Later, CADRBT] (EA)	CSDRBT
Coalition to Stop Food Irradiation [Later, NCSFWI] (EA)	CSFI
Coalition to Stop Government Waste (EA)	CSGW
Coalition to Stop Gun Violence (EA)	CSGV
Coalition to Support Cuban Detainees [Defunct] (EA)	CSCD
Coalition United for Bear	CUB
Coalition Unity Party [British]	CoU
Coalitions for America (EA)	CA
Coalitions for Health Care (EA)	CHC
Coal-Methane Mixture	CMM
Coal-Methanol-Water [Fuel]	CMW
Coalmont, TN [FM radio station call letters]	WSGM
Coal-Oil Dispersion [Fuel technology]	COD
Coal-Oil Mixture	COM
Coal-Oil-Gas [Fuel mixture]	COG
Coal-Oil-Water [Fuel mixture]	COW
Coal-Oil-Water Mixture [Fuel]	COWM
Coalville, UT [FM radio station call letters]	KCUA
Coal-Water [Fuel mixture]	CW
Coal-Water Mixture Fuel	CWF
Coal-Water Mixture Fuel	CWM
Coal-Water Slurry [Fuel]	CWS
Coal-Water Slurry Fuel	CWSF
Coaming [Naval architecture]	COAM
Coamo [Puerto Rico] [Seismograph station code, US Geological Survey] (SEIS)	CCA
Coamo, PR [AM radio station call letters]	WCPR
COAR [Comunidad Oscar A. Romero] Peace Mission (EA)	COAR
Coarctation [Cardiology]	COARC
Coarctation of the Aorta [Medicine] (DMAA)	CA
Coarctation of the Aorta [Cardiology] (DAVI)	CoA
Coari [Brazil] [Airport symbol] (AD)	CZA
Coariolanus [Shakespearean drama] (BARN)	Coriol
Coarse [Appearance of bacterial colony]	C
Coarse [Agronomy]	C
Coarse (AAG)	CRS
Coarse Acquisition Code [Computer science] (RDA)	C/A
Coarse Aim Positioning	CAP
Coarse Alignment	CA
Coarse Alignment Servo	CAS
Coarse Alignment Subsystem	CASS
Coarse Alignment Unit	CAU
Coarse Bearing Servo	CBS
Coarse Control [Nuclear energy] (NRCH)	CC
Coarse Control Damper [Nuclear energy] (NRCH)	CCD
Coarse Diffraction Pattern Analysis (MCD)	CDPA
Coarse Element Refinement (IAA)	CER
Coarse Erection	CE
Coarse Glass Frit	CGF
Coarse Grain (DAC)	CG
Coarse Optical Alignment Sight (NASA)	COAS
Coarse Particulate Matter [Pisciculture]	CPM
Coarse Particulate Organic Matter	CPOM
Coarse Pointing System (SSD)	CPS
Coarse Rales [On chest auscultation] [Medicine] (DAVI)	RL
Coarse-Fine/Pulse Code Modulator	C-F/PCM
Coarse-Grained Material (MCD)	CGM
Coarsely Granular [Organic chemistry] (DAVI)	CGRN
Coarticulation Assessment in Meaningful Language [Speech evaluation test]	CAML
Coast	CO
Coast [Board on Geographic Names]	CST
Coast	CST
Coast African People's Union [Kenya]	CAPU
Coast Air KS [Norway ICAO designator] (FAAC)	CST
Coast Air Ltd. [Kenya] [ICAO designator] (FAAC)	CQA
Coast Alliance [Defunct] (EA)	CA
Coast and Antiaircraft Experimental Establishment [British World War II]	CAAEE
Coast and Geodetic Magnetic Observatory	CGMO
Coast and Geodetic Survey [Later, NOAA] [Rockville, MD]	C & GS
Coast and Geodetic Survey [Later, NOAA] [Rockville, MD] (AFM)	CGS
Coast and Geodetic Tide Station	CGTS
Coast and Wetlands Society [New South Wales] [Australia]	CWS
Coast Artillery	CA
Coast Artillery Antiaircraft	CAAA
Coast Artillery Corps [Army]	CAC
Coast Artillery Reserve Corps	CARC
Coast Artillery School [British]	CAS
Coast Artillery Training Battalion	CATB
Coast Artillery Training Centre [British military] (DMA)	CATC
Coast Community College District, Orange Coast College, Costa Mesa, CA [OCLC symbol] (OCLC)	CRG
Coast Defense	CD
Coast Defense Study Group (EA)	CDSG
Coast Distribution Sys [AMEX symbol] (TTSB)	CRV
Coast Distribution Systems [Associated Press] (SAG)	CoastD
Coast Distribution Systems [AMEX symbol] (SPSS)	CRV
Coast Earth Station [INMARSAT]	CES
Coast for Orders [Chartering]	CFO
Coast Guard	CG

Coast Guard .... COGARD
Coast Guard Academy .... CGA
Coast Guard Achievement Medal [*Military decoration*] .... CGAM
Coast Guard Activities Europe .... CGACTEUR
Coast Guard Aids to Navigation Facility (DNAB) .... COGARDANFAC
Coast Guard Aids to Navigation Team (DNAB) .... COGARDANT
Coast Guard Air Base .... CGAB
Coast Guard Air Detachment .... CGAIRDET
Coast Guard Air Station .... CGAS
Coast Guard Aircraft Program Office (DNAB) .... COGARDACFTPROGOFF
Coast Guard Aircraft Repair and Supply Center (DNAB) .... COGARDARSC
Coast Guard Assistance Instruction Data .... COGAID
Coast Guard Auxiliary .... CGA
Coast Guard Aviation Detachment (DNAB) .... COGARDAVDET
Coast Guard Aviation Technical Training Center
 (DNAB) .... COGARDAVTECHTRACEN
Coast Guard Aviation Training Center (DNAB) .... COGARDAVTC
Coast Guard Base .... CGBASE
Coast Guard Board of Contract Appeals [*A publication*] (AAGC) ..... CGBCA
Coast Guard Boating Safety Team (DNAB) .... COGARDBST
Coast Guard Captain of the Port Office (DNAB) .... COGARDCOTP
Coast Guard Coastal Search and Rescue Facility (DNAB) ...... COGARDCOSARFAC
Coast Guard Combat Veterans Association (EA) .... CGCVA
Coast Guard Commandant .... COMDTCOGARD
Coast Guard Commendation Medal [*Military decoration*] .... CGCM
Coast Guard Communications Station (DNAB) .... COGARDCOMMSTA
Coast Guard Court-Martial Manual [*A publication*] (DLA) .... CGCMM
Coast Guard Cutter .... CGC
Coast Guard Depot (DNAB) .... COGARDEP
Coast Guard Detachment National Data Buoy Office (DNAB) ...... COGARDETNDBO
Coast Guard District .... CGD
Coast Guard District .... CGDIST
Coast Guard District Office .... CGDO
Coast Guard Docket .... CGD
Coast Guard Electronic Shop (DNAB) .... COGARDES
Coast Guard Electronic Shop Minor (DNAB) .... COGARDESM
Coast Guard Electronics Engineering Center (DNAB) ...... COGARDEECEN
Coast Guard Electronics Shop Major Telephone and Teletype
 (DNAB) .... COGARDEST
Coast Guard Electronics Shop Minor Telephone and Teletype
 (DNAB) .... COGARDESMT
Coast Guard Fire and Safety Test Detachment (DNAB) ...... COGARDFSTD
Coast Guard Good Conduct Medal .... CGGCM
Coast Guard Institute (DNAB) .... COGARDINST
Coast Guard International Ice Patrol (NOAA) .... CGIIP
Coast Guard Law Bulletin [*A publication*] (DLA) .... CGL Bull
Coast Guard League (EA) .... CGL
Coast Guard Liaison Officer, Commander Fleet Training Group
 (DNAB) .... COGARDLOCOMFLETRAGRU
Coast Guard Liaison Officer, Eastern Pacific Intelligence Center
 (DNAB) .... COGARDLOEPIC
Coast Guard Liaison Officer Representative (DNAB) ...... COGARDLOREP
Coast Guard Lifeboat Station .... CGLBSTA
Coast Guard Light Attendant Station .... CGLASTA
Coast Guard Light Station .... CGLTSTA
Coast Guard Light Station (DNAB) .... COGARDLTSTA
Coast Guard LORAN [*Long-Range Aid to Navigation*] Monitor Station
 (DNAB) .... COGARDLORMONSTA
Coast Guard LORAN [*Long-Range Aid to Navigation*] Station ...... CGLS
Coast Guard LORAN [*Long-Range Aid to Navigation*] Station
 (DNAB) .... COGARDLORSTA
Coast Guard LORAN [*Long-Range Aid to Navigation*] Transmitting
 Station .... CGLORSTA
Coast Guard Maintenance Repair Detachment (DNAB) ...... COGARDMRDET
Coast Guard Marine Inspection Detachment (DNAB) ...... COGARDMID
Coast Guard Marine Inspection Office (DNAB) .... COGARDMIO
Coast Guard Marine Safety Detachment (DNAB) .... COGARDMSD
Coast Guard Marine Safety Office (DNAB) .... COGARDMSO
Coast Guard National Data Buoy Office (DNAB) .... COGARDNDBO
Coast Guard National Motor Lifeboat School (DNAB) .... COGARDNMLBS
Coast Guard National Strike Force (DNAB) .... COGARDNSF
Coast Guard National Strike Force, Atlantic (DNAB) ...... COGARDNSFLANT
Coast Guard National Strike Force, Pacific (DNAB) ...... COGARDNSFPAC
Coast Guard Oceanographic Unit .... CGOU
Coast Guard Oil Identification Laboratory [*Groton, CT*] ...... COIL
Coast Guard Omega Navigation Systems Office Detachment
 (DNAB) .... COGARDONSOD
Coast Guard Omega Station (DNAB) .... COGARDOMSTA
Coast Guard Operating Base .... CGOB
Coast Guard Operations Computer Center (DNAB) ...... COGARDOCC
Coast Guard Operations Data Analysis Center (DNAB) ...... COGARDOPDAC
Coast Guard Ordnance Support Facility (DNAB) .... COGARDORDSUPPFAC
Coast Guard Patrol Cutter .... CGPC
Coast Guard Pension [*British*] (ROG) .... CGP
Coast Guard Port Safety Detachment (DNAB) .... COGARDPSDET
Coast Guard Port Safety Station (DNAB) .... COGARDPSSTA
Coast Guard Procurement Regulations .... CGPR
Coast Guard Publication [*Formerly, NCG*] .... NAVCG
Coast Guard Publication [*Later, NAVCG*] .... NCG
Coast Guard Radio (NOAA) .... CGRDO
Coast Guard Radio Liaison Station (PDAA) .... CRLS
Coast Guard Radio Station .... CGRADSTA
Coast Guard Radio Station (DNAB) .... COGARDRADSTA
Coast Guard Records Depot (DNAB) .... COGARDRECDEP
Coast Guard Recruiting Office (DNAB) .... COGARDCRUITOFF

Coast Guard Recruiting Station .... CGCRUITSTA
Coast Guard Regulations [*A publication*] (DLA) .... CGR
Coast Guard Representative, Naval Regional Medical Center
 (DNAB) .... COGARDREPNAVREGMEDCEN
Coast Guard Representative, Student Records (DNAB) ...... COGARDREPSTUDREC
Coast Guard Representative, Tripler Army Medical Center
 (DNAB) .... COGARDREPTAMC
Coast Guard Representative, United States Air Force Hospital
 (DNAB) .... COGARDREPUSAFH
Coast Guard Representative, United States Public Health Service
 Hospital (DNAB) .... COGARDREPUSPHS
Coast Guard Research and Development Center [*Groton, CT*] .... CGR/DC
Coast Guard Reserve .... CGR
Coast Guard Reserve Center (DNAB) .... COGARDRESCEN
Coast Guard Reserve Training Center (DNAB) .... COGARDRESTRACEN
Coast Guard Resident Inspecting Officer (DNAB) ...... COGARDRIO
Coast Guard, Shelburne, Nova Scotia [*Library symbol National Library of Canada*] (NLC) .... NSSCO
Coast Guard, Shelburne, NS, Canada [*Library symbol*] [*Library of Congress*]
 (LCLS) .... CaNSSheCO
Coast Guard Ship [*When precedes vessel classification*] [*Navy symbol*] ..... W
Coast Guard Ship Introduction Unit (DNAB) .... COGARDSIU
Coast Guard Specification .... CGS
Coast Guard Station .... CGSTA
Coast Guard Station (DNAB) .... COGARDSTA
Coast Guard Station, Washington [*District of Columbia*] [*ICAO location identifier*] (ICLI) .... KNMH
Coast Guard Stock Inventory Control Point (DNAB) ...... COGARDSICP
Coast Guard Supplement to Manual for Courts-Martial [*A publication*]
 (DLA) .... CGSMCM
Coast Guard Supply Center .... CGSUPCEN
Coast Guard Supply Center (DNAB) .... COGARDSUPCEN
Coast Guard Support Center (DNAB) .... COGARDSUPRTCEN
Coast Guard Support Facility (DNAB) .... COGARDSUPRTFAC
Coast Guard Teletype (NOAA) .... CGTEL
Coast Guard Training Center (DNAB) .... COGARDTRACEN
Coast Guard Training Station .... CGTRASTA
Coast Guard Training Station .... CGTS
Coast Guard Vessel Traffic System (DNAB) .... COGARDVTS
Coast Guard Yard .... CGYD
Coast Independent Hi-Tech [*Vancouver Stock Exchange symbol*] ..... KIH
Coast Lines [*Steamship*] (MHDW) CL
Coast Orbital Insertion (MCD) .... COI
Coast Phase Control System [*Army*] (AABC) .... CPCS
Coast Protection Act [*Town planning*] [*British*] .... CPA
Coast Protection Board [*South Australia*] .... CPB
Coast RADAR Station [*Maps and charts*] .... RA
Coast Range Resources Ltd. [*Vancouver Stock Exchange symbol*] ...... CSG
Coast Savings Financial, Inc. [*Associated Press*] (SAG) ..... CoastSv
Coast Savings Financial, Inc. [*NYSE symbol*] (SPSG) ...... CSA
Coast Star, Manasquan, NJ [*Library symbol Library of Congress*] (LCLS) .... NjManS
Coast Station [*ITU designation*] (CET) .... FC
Coast Survey Marine Observation System .... COSMOS
Coast Svgs Finl [*NYSE symbol*] (TTSB) .... CSA
Coast Torpedo Boat [*Navy symbol Obsolete*] .... CTB
Coast Waiter [*Coast Guard British*] (ROG) .... CW
Coastair [*Denmark ICAO designator*] (FAAC) .... CSX
Coastal .... CSTL
Coastal .... CSTL
Coastal Aerial Photo-LASER Survey (PDAA) .... CAPS
Coastal Air Force [*British*] .... CAF
Coastal Air Navigation Supplement (MCD) .... CANS
Coastal Air Transport [*St. Croix*] [*ICAO designator*] (FAAC) ..... CXT
Coastal Air Transport [*ICAO designator*] (AD) .... DQ
Coastal Airways [*ICAO designator*] (FAAC) .... CNG
Coastal Airways [*ICAO designator*] (AD) .... PN
Coastal America Partnership [*US Army Corps of Engineers*] ...... CAP
Coastal AMOS [*Automated Meteorological Observing Station*]
 Experiment .... CAMEX
Coastal and Arctic Research Division [*Formerly, Marine Services Research Division*] [*Marine science*] (OSRA) .... CARD
Coastal and Arctic Research Division [*Formerly, Marine Service Research Division*] (USDC) .... CARD
Coastal and Continental Shelf Zone [*Oceanography*] ..... CCSZ
Coastal and Estuarine Regimes [*Oceanography*] (MSC) ..... CER
Coastal and Hydraulics Laboratory [*U.S. Army Engineer Waterways Experiment Station*] .... CHL
Coastal Antimissile System (MCD) .... CAMS
Coastal Anti-Pollution League [*British*] .... CAPL
Coastal Area Management Act [*1974*] (MSC) .... CAMA
Coastal Bancorp [*NASDAQ symbol*] (SAG) .... CBSA
Coastal Bancorp [*Associated Press*] (SAG) .... CstBn
Coastal Bancorp [*Associated Press*] (SAG) .... CstBncp
Coastal Bancorp 9% 'A' Pfd [*NASDAQ symbol*] (TTSB) ...... CBSAP
Coastal Barrier Resources System [*Department of the Interior*] ...... CBRS
Coastal Base Section [*Name changed to Continental Advance Section*] [*World War II*] .... CBS
Coastal Buoy Tender [*Coast Guard symbol*] (DNAB) ...... WLM
Coastal Buoy Tender Replacement Vessel [*USCG*] (TAG) ...... WLMR
Coastal Carolina Community College, Jacksonville, NC [*Library symbol Library of Congress*] (LCLS) .... NcJaC
Coastal Command [*Air Force British*] (DMA) .... C Cmd
Coastal Command [*Air Force British*] CC
Coastal Command Defence Unit [*British*] .... CCDU
Coastal Command Development Unit [*British*] .... CCDU

Coastal Command Fighter Affiliation Training Unit [*British military*] (DMA) ... CCFATU
Coastal Command Flying Instructors School [*British military*] (DMA) ... CCFIS
Coastal Confluence Region (DNAB) ... CCR
Coastal Confluence Zone [*Aviation*] (DA) ... CCZ
Coastal Conservation Association (EA) ... CCA
[*The*] **Coastal Corp.** [*Formerly, Coastal States Gas Producing Co.*] [*NYSE symbol*] (SPSG) ... CGP
[*The*] **Coastal Corp.** [*Formerly, Coastal State Gas Producing Co.*] [*Associated Press*] (SAG) ... Coastal
[*The*] **Coastal Corp.** [*Formerly, Coastal State Gas Producing Co.*] [*Associated Press*] (SAG) ... Coastl
[*The*] **Coastal Corp.** [*Formerly, Coastal State Gas Producing Co.*] [*Associated Press*] (SAG) ... Cstl
Coastal Corp. $1.19 Cv A Pfd [*NYSE symbol*] (TTSB) ... CGPPrA
Coastal Corp. $1.83 Cv B Pfd [*NYSE symbol*] (TTSB) ... CGPPrB
Coastal Corp.$2.125 cm Pfd [*NYSE symbol*] (TTSB) ... CGPPrH
Coastal Courier, Glace Bay, Nova Scotia [*Library symbol National Library of Canada*] (NLC) ... NSGCC
Coastal Courier, Glace Bay, NS, Canada [*Library symbol*] [*Library of Congress*] (LCLS) ... CaNSGbCC
Coastal Defense RADAR (MUGU) ... CD
Coastal Defense RADAR for Detecting U-Boats ... CDU
Coastal District Surveillance Center [*Military*] ... CDSC
Coastal Division [*Navy*] (DNAB) ... COSDIV
Coastal Ecology Laboratory [*Louisiana State University*] [*Research center*] (RCD) ... CEL
Coastal Energy Impact Program [*National Oceanic and Atmospheric Administration*] ... CEIP
Coastal Energy Impact Program (USDC) ... CIEP
Coastal Engineering Education Program [*U.S. Army Engineer Waterways Experiment Station*] ... CEEP
Coastal Engineering Information Analysis Center [*Vicksburg, MS*] [*DoD*] (GRD) ... CEIAC
Coastal Engineering Manual [*A publication Army*] ... CEM
Coastal Engineering Research Board [*Vicksburg, MS*] [*Army*] (AABC) ... CERB
Coastal Engineering Research Center [*Vicksburg, MS*] [*Army*] (AABC) ... CERC
Coastal Engineering Research Council (EA) ... CERC
Coastal Engineering Research Office (SAA) ... CERO
Coastal Environmental Management Plan [*Advisory Committee on Pollution of the Sea*] ... CEMP
Coastal Escort [*Ship symbol*] (NATG) ... PC
Coastal Escort Medium [*200-500 tons*] [*Ship symbol*] (NATG) ... PCM
Coastal Financial Corp. [*NASDAQ symbol*] (SAG) ... CFCP
Coastal Financial Corp. [*Associated Press*] (SAG) ... CstlFncl
Coastal Finl Del [*NASDAQ symbol*] (TTSB) ... CFCP
Coastal Fisheries Institute [*Louisiana State University*] ... CFI
Coastal Flotilla [*Navy*] (DNAB) ... COSFLOT
Coastal Frontier [*Military*] ... CF
Coastal Frontier [*Coast Guard*] ... COFRON
Coastal Georgia Historical Society, St. Simons Island, GA [*Library symbol*] [*Library of Congress*] (LCLS) ... GSsiHi
Coastal Habitat Fisheries Assessment Research Mensuration [*National Oceanic and Atmospheric Administration*] ... CHARM
Coastal Harbor [*Telecommunications*] (TEL) ... CH
Coastal, Harbor, and Inland [*Waterways*] (MCD) ... CHI
Coastal Healthcare Group, Inc. [*NYSE symbol*] (SAG) ... DR
Coastal Helicopter Aircraft Carrier [*Ship symbol*] (NATG) ... CVHC
Coastal Management and Coordination Committee [*Victoria*] [*Australia*] ... CMCC
Coastal Management Programs [*Marine science*] (OSRA) ... CMP
Coastal Management Programs (USDC) ... CMP
Coastal Marine Automated Network [*National Weather Service*] (USDC) ... C-MAN
Coastal Marine Automated Network [*Marine science*] (OSRA) ... C-MAN
Coastal Marine Project (USDC) ... COMAR
Coastal Minelayer [*Navy symbol*] ... CMC
Coastal Motorboat [*Obsolete British*] ... CMB
Coastal Observation and Simulation with Topography [*Marine science*] (OSRA) ... COAST
Coastal Observations and Simulations with Topography (USDC) ... COAST
Coastal Ocean Dynamics Applications Radar (USDC) ... CODAR
Coastal Ocean Dynamics Applications RADAR [*Marine science*] (OSRA) ... CODAR
Coastal Ocean Dynamics Experiment [*National Oceanic and Atmospheric Administration*] ... CODE
Coastal Ocean Prediction Systems Program [*Marine science*] (OSRA) ... COPS
Coastal Ocean Probing Experiment [*Marine science*] (OSRA) ... COPE
Coastal Ocean Program [*National Oceanic and Atmospheric Administration*] (USDC) ... COP
Coastal Ocean Surface RADAR ... COSR
Coastal/Oceans Monitoring Satellite System (PDAA) ... COMSS
Coastal Patrol and Interdiction [*Navy*] (DOMA) ... CP & I
Coastal Patrol and Interdiction Craft [*Navy symbol*] ... CPIC
Coastal Patrol Boat [*Navy symbol*] ... CPC
Coastal Physican Grp [*NYSE symbol*] (TTSB) ... DR
Coastal Physician Group [*Associated Press*] (SAG) ... CstlPhys
Coastal Plains Commuter [*ICAO designator*] (AD) ... KA
Coastal Plains Experiment Station, Tifton, GA [*Library symbol Library of Congress*] (LCLS) ... GTiE
Coastal Plains Regional Library, Tifton, GA [*Library symbol Library of Congress*] (LCLS) ... GTi
Coastal Plains Sands ... CPS
Coastal RADAR Integration System (MCD) ... CRIS
Coastal Research Amphibious Buggy [*Army*] (MSC) ... CRAB
Coastal Research Center (GNE) ... CRC
Coastal Resources Management Council [*United Nations*] ... CRMC
Coastal Resources Management Programme [*Canada*] (EAIO) ... CRMP
Coastal River Squadron [*Navy*] (NVT) ... COSRIVRON
Coastal River Squadron Mobile Support Team [*Navy*] (DNAB) ... COSRIVRON MST
Coastal Security Zone (MCD) ... CSZ
Coastal Sentry Quebec ... CSQ
Coastal Shelf Oceanography Program [*Marine science*] (MSC) ... CSOP
[*The*] **Coastal Society** (EA) ... CS
[*The*] **Coastal Society** (EA) ... TCS
Coastal Squadron [*Navy*] (DNAB) ... COSRON
Coastal States Organization (EA) ... CSO
Coastal Structure Acoustic Raster Scanner (RDA) ... CSARS
Coastal Studies Institute [*Louisiana State University*] [*Research center*] ... CSI
Coastal Submarine [*Navy symbol*] ... SSC
Coastal Surveillance Center ... CSC
Coastal Surveillance RADAR (MCD) ... CSR
Coastal Survey Ship [*Marine science*] (MSC) ... CSS
Coastal Surveying Ship ... AGSC
Coastal Telegraph Station [*ITU designation*] (CET) ... CT
Coastal Transport Ltd. [*Steamship*] (MHDW) ... CTL
Coastal Upwelling Ecosystems Analysis [*Marine science*] (MSC) ... CUEA
Coastal Upwelling Experiment [*Marine science*] (MSC) ... CUE
Coastal Watching RADAR (NATG) ... CWR
Coastal Zone Act Reauthorization Amendments [*1990*] ... CZARA
Coastal Zone Color Scanner ... CZCS
Coastal Zone Information Center (GNE) ... CZIC
Coastal Zone Management ... CZM
Coastal Zone Management Act [*1972*] ... CZMA
Coastal Zone Management Advisory Committee [*Department of Commerce*] (MSC) ... CZMAC
Coastal Zone Management Program (GNE) ... CZMP
Coastal-Nonrigid Airship [*Royal Naval Air Service*] [*British*] ... C
Coastcast Corp. [*Associated Press*] (SAG) ... Coastcst
Coastcast Corp. [*NYSE symbol*] (SPSG) ... PAR
Coasting Flight ... CF
Coast-in-Point (NVT) ... CIP
Coastline Resources [*Vancouver Stock Exchange symbol*] ... CSY
Coastoro Resources [*Vancouver Stock Exchange symbol*] ... COQ
Coast-Out Point (NVT) ... COP
Coastwatchers' Association [*Australia*] ... CA
Coastwide Energy Services [*NASDAQ symbol*] (SAG) ... CNRG
Coastwide Energy Services [*Associated Press*] (SAG) ... CstEngy
Coastwise-Great Lakes and Inland Hull Association [*Defunct*] (EA) ... CGLIHA
Coat Cupboard [*Classified advertising*] (ADA) ... CC
Coat Hook ... CH
Coat of Arms (AABC) ... C/A
Coat Protein ... COP
Coat [*or Capsid*] **Protein** [*Cytology*] ... CP
Coated (KSC) ... CTD
Coated ... CTD
Coated Abrasive Manufacturers' Association [*British*] (BI) ... CAMA
Coated Abrasives Fabricators Association [*Defunct*] (EA) ... CAFA
Coated Abrasives Manufacturers Institute (EA) ... CAMI
Coated and Processed Paper Association [*Defunct*] ... CPPA
Coated Back [*Paper*] (WDMC) ... cb
Coated Cargo Tank (DNAB) ... CCT
Coated Cartridge [*Paper*] (DGA) ... C/CDGE
Coated Cartridge [*Paper*] (DGA) ... CC
Coated Compressed Tablet [*Pharmacy*] ... CCT
Coated Electrodes International [*British*] ... CEI
Coated Foam Tape ... CFT
Coated Front and Back [*Carbonless paper*] ... CFB
Coated Metal (AAG) ... CMET
Coated on the Back Side [*Carbonless paper*] ... CB
Coated on the Front Side [*Carbonless paper*] ... CF
Coated One Side [*Paper*] (WDMC) ... c1s
Coated One Size [*Paper*] ... C1S
Coated Paper Copier [*Reprography*] ... CPC
Coated Polycarbonate Visor ... CPV
Coated Powder Cathode ... CPC
Coated Solid-State Device [*Sensor*] ... CSSD
Coated Tablet [*Pharmacy*] ... CT
Coated Wire Electrode [*Sensor*] ... CWE
Coated-Front Paper (WDMC) ... cf
Coatepeque [*Guatemala*] [*ICAO location identifier*] (ICLI) ... MGCT
Coatesville, PA [*Location identifier FAA*] (FAAL) ... CVE
Coatesville, PA [*Location identifier FAA*] (FAAL) ... MQS
Coatesville, PA [*Location identifier FAA*] (FAAL) ... VZO
Coatesville, PA [*AM radio station call letters*] ... WCOJ
Coatesville Public Library, Coatesville, IN [*Library symbol Library of Congress*] (LCLS) ... InCoa
Coating (MSA) ... CTG
Coating Ageing-Resistant Aluminum Technology [*Materials science*] ... CARAT
Coating and Chemical Laboratory [*Aberdeen Proving Ground, MD*] [*Army*] (RDA) ... C & CL
Coating and Chemical Laboratory [*Aberdeen Proving Ground, MD*] [*Army*] ... CCL
Coatings, Adhesives, Sealants, and Elastomers [*Polyurethanes*] ... CASE
Coatings and Surfaces Technology [*National Centre for Tribology*] [*British*] ... CAST
Coats, NC [*Location identifier FAA*] (FAAL) ... HQT
Coaxial (AAG) ... CA
Coaxial (AAG) ... COAX
Coaxial Adapter Waveguide ... CAWG
Coaxial Cable Information System (NTCM) ... CCIS
Coaxial Cavity Resonator (IAA) ... CCR
Coaxial Diode Limiter ... CDL

Coaxial Directional Coupler ... CDC
Coaxial Injection Combustion (MCD) ... CIC
Coaxial Injection Combustion Model (MCD) ... CICM
Coaxial Line Attenuator ... CLA
Coaxial Output Printer (IAA) ... COP
Coaxial Power Divider ... CPD
Coaxial Single-Pole Relay ... CSR
Coaxial Slotted Line ... CSL
Coaxial Switch and Alternator Panel ... COSWAP
Coaxial Switching Matrix ... CSM
Coaxial Thermal Converter (IAA) ... CTC
Coaxial Thermal Voltmeter ... CTV
Coaxial to Twisted Pair Adapter (HGAA) ... ctpa
Coaxial Transceiver Interface ... CTI
Coaxial Triple-Stud Tuner ... CTST
Cobalamin [*Biochemistry*] ... Cbl
Cobalt [*Chemical symbol is Co*] ... C
Cobalt [*Chemical element*] ... Co
Cobalt [*Philately*] ... cob
Cobalt Base Alloy Foil ... CBAF
Cobalt Bomb [*Nuclear*] ... C (Bomb)
Cobalt Bomb [*Nuclear*] (AAG) ... CB
Cobalt Development Institute (EAIO) ... CDI
Cobalt Gray Equivalent [*Radiology*] ... CGE
Cobalt Information Center [*Battelle Memorial Institute*] [*Information service or system*] (IID) ... CIC
Cobalt Public Library, Cobalt, ON, Canada [*Library symbol*] [*Library of Congress*] (LCLS) ... CaOCob
Cobalt Public Library, Ontario [*Library symbol National Library of Canada*] (BIB) ... OCOB
Cobalt Thiocyanate Active Substance [*Organic analysis*] ... CTAS
Cobalt-60 ... Co-60
Cobalt-Chrome ... COBCRM
Cobaltiprotoporphyrin [*Medicine*] ... COPP
Cobamide [*Biochemistry*] ... Cba
Coban [*Guatemala*] [*ICAO location identifier*] (ICLI) ... MGCB
Cobancorp, Inc. [*Associated Press*] (SAG) ... Cobancp
Cobancorp, Inc. [*NASDAQ symbol*] (SAG) ... COBI
Cobar [*Australia Airport symbol*] (OAG) ... CAZ
Cobb [*New Zealand*] [*Seismograph station code, US Geological Survey*] (SEIS) ... COB
Cobb County-Marietta Public Library, Marietta, GA [*Library symbol Library of Congress*] (LCLS) ... GMarC
Cobb Elementary Library, Duluth, MN [*Library symbol*] [*Library of Congress*] (LCLS) ... MnDuCE
Cobb Memorial Library, North Truro,MA [*Library symbol*] [*Library of Congress*] (LCLS) ... MNot
Cobb on Slavery [*A publication*] (DLA) ... Cobb Slav
Cobbett on Pawns and Pledges [*A publication*] (DLA) ... Cobb P & Pl
Cobbett's Parliamentary History [*A publication*] (DLA) ... Cobb Parl Hist
Cobbett's Political Register [*A publication*] (DLA) ... Cobb Pol Reg
Cobbett's [*later, Howell's*] **State Trials** [*1163-1820*] [*England*] [*A publication*] (DLA) ... Cob St Tr
Cobbett's [*later, Howell's*] **State Trials** [*1163-1820*] [*England*] [*A publication*] (DLA) ... Cobb St Tr
Cobbey's Annotated Statutes [*Nebraska*] [*A publication*] (DLA) ... Cobbey's Ann St
Cobbey's Practical Treatise on the Law of Replevin [*A publication*] (DLA) ... Cobbey Repl
Cobbler ... COBB
Cobbler Shop ... CBSHP
Cobbly [*Agronomy*] ... C
Cobb's Digest of Statute Laws [*Georgia*] [*A publication*] (DLA) ... Cobb Dig
Cobb's New Digest, Laws of Georgia [*1851*] [*A publication*] (DLA) ... Cobb
Cobb's Reports [*121 Alabama*] [*A publication*] (DLA) ... Cobb
Cobb's Reports [*4-20 Georgia*] [*A publication*] (DLA) ... Cobb
Cobden Airways [*ICAO designator*] (AD) ... XF
Cobden Public Library, Cobden, ON, Canada [*Library symbol*] [*Library of Congress*] (LCLS) ... CaOCoBD
Cobden Public Library, Ontario [*Library symbol National Library of Canada*] (BIB) ... OCOBD
Cobe Laboratories, Denver, CO [*Library symbol Library of Congress*] (LCLS) ... CoDCo
Cobelda RADAR Automatic Preflight Analyzer (IEEE) ... CORAPRAN
Cobequid Resources Ltd. [*Vancouver Stock Exchange symbol*] ... KQR
Cobi Foods, Inc. [*Toronto Stock Exchange symbol*] ... CFJ
Cobija [*Bolivia*] [*Airport symbol*] (OAG) ... CIJ
Cobija [*Bolivia*] [*ICAO location identifier*] (ICLI) ... SLCO
Cobinamide [*Biochemistry*] ... Cbi
Coblentz Society (EA) ... CS
Cobleskill, NY [*AM radio station call letters*] (RBYB) ... WDCS
Cobleskill, NY [*AM radio station call letters*] (RBYB) ... WLAL-AM
Cobleskill, NY [*FM radio station call letters*] ... WQBJ
COBOL [*Common Business-Oriented Language*] [*Computer science*] (IAA) ... CO
COBOL [*Common Business-Oriented Language*] **Automatic Language Modifier** [*Computer science*] ... CALM
COBOL [*Common Business-Oriented Language*] **Communications Facility** (IAA) ... CCF
COBOL [*Common Business-Oriented Language*] **Compiler Validation System** [*Computer science*] ... CCVS
COBOL [*Common Business-Oriented Language*] **Conversion** [*Computer science*] (MCD) ... COCO
COBOL [*Common Business-Oriented Language*] **Element Subtype** [*Computer science*] ... COB
COBOL [*Common Business-Oriented Language*] **File Handler** (IAA) ... CFH
COBOL [*Common Business-Oriented Language*] **Information Bulletin** [*Air Force*] ... CIB
COBOL [*Common Business-Oriented Language*] **Instrumentation Package** [*Computer science*] ... CIP
COBOL [*Common Business-Oriented Language*] **Library** [*Computer science*] (MCD) ... COBLIB
COBOL [*Common Business-Oriented Language*] **Performance Monitor** [*Computer science*] (IAA) ... CPM
COBOL Program Generator (NITA) ... CPG
COBOL Sampler EDP Program [*DCAA*] [*Also DCAM*] (AAGC) ... COSAM
COBOL [*Common Business-Oriented Language*] **Shared Access Method** [*Pertec*] ... COSAM
COBOL Structured Facility [*IBM Corp.*] (NITA) ... COBOL/SF
COBOL [*Common Business-Oriented Language*]-to-COBOL Translator (IEEE) ... COTRAN
COBOL [*Common Business-Oriented Language*] **Tuner** ... COTUNE
COBOL [*Common Business-Oriented Language*] **Virtual Machine** ... CVM
Cobourg, ON [*FM radio station call letters*] ... CFMX
Cobourg, ON [*AM radio station call letters*] ... CHUC
Cobourg Public Library, Cobourg, ON, Canada [*Library symbol Library of Congress*] (LCLS) ... CaOCo
Cobourg Public Library, Ontario [*Library symbol National Library of Canada*] (NLC) ... OCO
Cobra Club [*Later, SAAC*] (EA) ... CC
Cobra Dane System Modernization (DWSG) ... CDSM
Cobra Electronics [*NASDAQ symbol*] (TTSB) ... COBR
Cobra Electronics Corp. [*NASDAQ symbol*] (SAG) ... COBR
Cobra Electronics Corp. [*Associated Press*] (SAG) ... CobraEl
Cobra Enterprises [*Vancouver Stock Exchange symbol*] ... CBB
Cobra Factor ... CoF
Cobra Fleet Life Extension Program [*Military*] ... C-FLEX
Cobra Golf, Inc. [*NASDAQ symbol*] (SAG) ... CBRA
Cobra Golf, Inc. [*Associated Press*] (SAG) ... CobraG
Cobra Jet [*Automotive engineering*] ... CJ
Cobra Night Fire Control System [*Military*] ... CONFICS
Cobra Owners Club of America (EA) ... COCOA
Cobra Toxin ... CTX
Cobra Venom Factor [*Immunochemistry*] ... CoVF
Cobra Venom Factor [*Immunochemistry*] ... CVF
Coburg/Brandensteinsebene [*Germany ICAO location identifier*] (ICLI) ... EDQC
Coburg/Steinrucken [*Germany ICAO location identifier*] (ICLI) ... EDQY
Cobyric Acid [*Biochemistry*] ... Cby
Coca [*Ecuador*] [*Airport symbol*] (OAG) ... OCC
Coca [*Ecuador*] [*ICAO location identifier*] (ICLI) ... SECO
Coca Cola Femsa SA de CV [*Commercial firm Associated Press*] (SAG) ... CCFem
Coca Cola Femsa SA de CV [*Associated Press*] (SAG) ... CCFemsa
Coca Cola South Pacific [*Commercial firm*] ... CCSP
Coca-Cola & Schweppes Beverages [*British*] ... CCSB
Coca-Cola Bott Consol [*NASDAQ symbol*] (TTSB) ... COKE
Coca-Cola Bottling Co. Consolidated [*Associated Press*] (SAG) ... CocaBtl
Coca-Cola Bottling Co. Consolidated [*NASDAQ symbol*] (NQ) ... COKE
Coca-Cola Collectors Club International (EA) ... CCCI
[*The*] **Coca-Cola Co.** [*Associated Press*] (SAG) ... CocaCl
[*The*] **Coca-Cola Co.** [*NYSE symbol*] (SPSG) ... KO
Coca-Cola Co., Business Information, Atlanta, GA [*OCLC symbol*] (OCLC) ... GCC
Coca-Cola Co., Law Library, Atlanta, GA [*OCLC symbol*] (OCLC) ... GCW
Coca-Cola Co., Marketing Information Center, Atlanta, GA [*Library symbol Library of Congress*] (LCLS) ... GACo
Coca-Cola Co., Technical Information Services, Atlanta, GA [*Library symbol Library of Congress*] (LCLS) ... GACCC
Coca-Cola Co., Technical Information Services, Atlanta, GA [*OCLC symbol*] (OCLC) ... GCT
Coca-Cola Enterprises [*NYSE symbol*] (TTSB) ... CCE
Coca-Cola Enterprises, Inc. [*NYSE symbol*] (SPSG) ... CCE
Coca-Cola Enterprises, Inc. [*Associated Press*] (SAG) ... CocaCE
Coca-Cola FEMSA [*NYSE symbol*] (SPSG) ... KOF
Coca-Cola FEMSA ADS [*NYSE symbol*] (TTSB) ... KOF
Cocaine [*Slang*] ... C
Cocaine (DAVI) ... COCAIN
Cocaine [*Slang*] (DSUE) ... COKE
Cocaine and Heroin ... C & H
Cocaine and Morphine (MAE) ... C & M
Cocaine Anonymous (EA) ... CA
Coccidioidomycosis [*Bacteriology*] (DAVI) ... cocci
Coccygeal [*Anatomy*] (DAVI) ... Cd
Coccygeal [*Anatomy*] ... COC
Cocensys, Inc. [*NASDAQ symbol*] (SAG) ... COCN
Cocesna [*ICAO designator*] (FAAC) ... COC
Cochabamba [*Bolivia*] [*Airport symbol*] (OAG) ... CBB
Cochabamba [*Bolivia*] [*Seismograph station code, US Geological Survey*] (SEIS) ... CCH
Cochabamba/Jorge Wilsterman [*Bolivia*] [*ICAO location identifier*] (ICLI) ... SLCB
Co-Chair of the Board (DD) ... cochr
Co-Channel Interface [*Telecommunications*] (NITA) ... CCI
Co-Channel Interference (NTCM) ... CCI
Cochin [*Region in India*] (ROG) ... COCH
Cochin [*India*] [*Airport symbol*] (OAG) ... COK
Cochin [*India*] [*ICAO location identifier*] (ICLI) ... VOCC
Cochin, India (ILCA) ... Coch Ind
Cochin Law Journal [*A publication*] (DLA) ... Co LJ
Cochin Law Journal [*A publication*] (DLA) ... Cochin LJ
Cochin Law Reports [*1909-48*] [*India*] [*A publication*] (DLA) ... Cochin
Cochin Law Reports [*1909-48*] [*India*] [*A publication*] (DLA) ... Cochin LR
Cochise Airlines [*ICAO designator*] (AD) ... DP

Cochise, AZ [*Location identifier FAA*] (FAAL) .... CIE
Cochise College, Douglas, AZ [*Library symbol Library of Congress*] (LCLS) .... AzDC
Cochise County Library District, Bisbee, AZ [*Library symbol*] [*Library of Congress*] (LCLS) .... AzBC
Cochiti [*New Mexico*] [*Seismograph station code, US Geological Survey*] (SEIS) .... COH
Cochlear Implant [*Otorhinolaryngology*] (DAVI) CI
Cochlear Implant Club International (EA) CICI
Cochlear Microphonics [*Response*] [*Auditory testing*] .... CM
Cochlear Nuclei [*Brain anatomy*] .... CN
Cochlear Potential [*Otolaryngology*] .... CP
Cochleare [*Spoonful*] [*Pharmacy*] .... COCH
Cochleare [*Spoonful*] [*Pharmacy*] .... COCHL
Cochleare Amplum [*A tablespoonful*] [*Pharmacy*] .... Coch Apm
Cochleare Amplum [*Heaping spoonful*] [*Pharmacy*] (MAH) .... COCHL AMP
Cochleare Amplum [*Tablespoonful*] [*Pharmacy*] (ROG) .... COCHL AMPL
Cochleare Infantum [*Teaspoonful*] [*Pharmacy*] .... COCH INFANT
Cochleare Infantum [*Teaspoonful*] [*Pharmacy*] .... COCHL INFANT
Cochleare Magnum [*Tablespoonful*] [*Pharmacy*] .... COCH MAG
Cochleare Magnum [*Tablespoonful*] [*Pharmacy*] (ROG) .... COCHL MAG
Cochleare Maximum [*Tablespoonful*] [*Pharmacy*] .... COCH MAX
Cochleare Medium [*Dessertspoonful*] [*Pharmacy*] .... COCH MED
Cochleare Medium [*Dessertspoonful*] [*Pharmacy*] (ROG) .... COCHL MED
Cochleare Minimum [*Teaspoonful*] [*Pharmacy*] .... COCH MIN
Cochleare Modicum [*Dessertspoonful*] [*Pharmacy*] .... COCH MOD
Cochleare Modicum [*Dessertspoonful*] [*Pharmacy*] (ROG) .... COCHL MOD
Cochleare Parvum [*Teaspoonful*] [*Pharmacy*] .... COCH PARV
Cochleare Parvum [*Teaspoonful*] [*Pharmacy*] (ROG) .... COCHL PARV
Cochleare Plenum [*Tablespoonful*] [*Pharmacy*] .... COCH PLEN
Cochleatim [*Spoonfuls*] [*Pharmacy*] (ROG) .... COCHLEAT
Cochran, GA [*FM radio station call letters*] .... WDCO
Cochran, GA [*Television station call letters*] .... WDCO-TV
Cochran, GA [*AM radio station call letters*] .... WVMG
Cochran, GA [*FM radio station call letters*] .... WVMG-FM
Cochrane [*Canada*] [*Airport symbol*] (OAG) .... YCN
Cochrane/Cochrane [*Chile*] [*ICAO location identifier*] (ICLI) .... SCHR
Cochrane Municipal Library, Alberta [*Library symbol National Library of Canada*] (NLC) .... ACOM
Cochrane Municipal Library, Cochrane, AB, Canada [*Library symbol Library of Congress*] (LCLS) .... CaACoM
Cochrane Public Library, Cochrane, ON, Canada [*Library symbol Library of Congress*] (LCLS) .... CaOCoc
Cochrane Public Library, Ontario [*Library symbol National Library of Canada*] (NLC) .... OCOC
Cochrane's Hindu Law [*A publication*] (DLA) .... Cochr Hind L
Cochran's Nova Scotia Reports [*1859*] [*A publication*] (DLA) .... Coch
Cochran's Nova Scotia Reports [*1859*] [*A publication*] (DLA) .... Coch N Sc
Cochran's Nova Scotia Reports [*1859*] [*A publication*] (DLA) .... Cochr
Cochran's Nova Scotia Reports [*1859*] [*A publication*] (DLA) .... NSR Coch
Cochran's Reports [*3-10 North Dakota*] [*A publication*] (DLA) .... Cochr
Cochran's Reports [*3-10 North Dakota*] [*A publication*] (DLA) .... Cochran
Cockayne's Syndrome [*Medicine*] .... CS
Cockburn and Rowe's English Election Cases [*1833*] [*A publication*] (DLA) .... C & R
Cockburn and Rowe's English Election Cases [*1833*] [*A publication*] (DLA) .... Cock & R
Cockburn and Rowe's English Election Cases [*1833*] [*A publication*] (DLA) .... Cock & Rowe
Cockburn and Rowe's English Election Cases [*1833*] [*A publication*] (DLA) .... Cockb & R
Cockburn and Rowe's English Election Cases [*1833*] [*A publication*] (DLA) .... Cockb & Rowe
Cockburn on Nationality [*A publication*] (DLA) .... Cock Nat
Cockburn Sound Conservation Council [*Western Australia*] .... CSCC
Cockburn Town, San Salvador Island [*Bahamas*] [*ICAO location identifier*] (ICLI) .... MYSM
Cockburn's Charge in the Tichborne Case [*A publication*] (DLA) .... Cock Tich Ca
Cockcroft-Walton Accelerator [*Physics*] .... CWA
Cockcroft-Walton Experiment [*Physics*] .... CWE
Cocke. Reports [*16-18 Alabama*] [*A publication*] (DLA) .... Cocke
Cocke. Reports [*14, 15 Florida*] [*A publication*] (DLA) .... Cocke
Cocke's Common and Civil Law Practice of the US Courts [*A publication*] (DLA) .... Cocke US Pr
Cocke's Constitutional History of the United States [*A publication*] (DLA) .... Cocke Const Hist
Cockfield Brown, Inc. [*Toronto Stock Exchange symbol*] .... CFD
Cockpit .... CCKPT
Cockpit .... CKPT
Cockpit Alerting and Warning System (MCD) .... CAWS
Cockpit Area Microphone (MCD) .... CAM
Cockpit Assessment of Reach [*Aviation*] (PDAA) .... CAR
Cockpit Automation Technology [*Air Force*] .... CAT
Cockpit Control System (DWSG) .... CCS
Cockpit Displayed Traffic Information .... CDTI
Cockpit Familiarization Trainer (MCD) .... CFT
Cockpit Geometry Evaluation [*Computer program*] [*Boeing Co.*] .... CGE
Cockpit Kill Indicator [*Military*] .... CKI
Cockpit Management System [*Aviation*] .... CMS
Cockpit Motor Yacht .... CMY
Cockpit Operating Manual (GAVI) .... COM
Cockpit Orientation Trainer [*Aviation*] (MCD) .... COT
Cockpit Orientation Trainer [*Aviation*] (NG) .... COTR
Cockpit Procedures Trainer [*Air Force*] (AFM) .... CPT
Cockpit Resource Management (MCD) .... CRM
Cockpit Systems Simulator [*Aviation*] .... CSS
Cockpit Television Sensor (MCD) .... CTV
Cockpit Television Sensor .... CTVS
Cockpit Voice Recorder .... CVR
Cockpit Weapons Emergency Procedural Trainer [*Military*] .... CWEPT
Cockpit-Display-of-Traffic Information [*NASA*] .... CDTI
Cockrell Hill, TX [*AM radio station call letters*] .... KRVA
Cockroach Antigen [*Immunology*] .... CR
Cocksfoot Mottle Virus [*Plant pathology*] .... COMV
Cocksfoot Streak Virus [*Plant pathology*] .... CSV
Coco Island [*Myanmar*] [*ICAO location identifier*] (ICLI) .... VBCI
Coco Solo, Canal Zone .... CS
Cocoa .... CCO
Cocoa Beach Apollo [*NASA*] (MCD) .... CBA
Cocoa Beach, FL [*FM radio station call letters*] .... WJRR
Cocoa Beach, FL [*FM radio station call letters*] .... WTKS
Cocoa Beach, FL [*AM radio station call letters*] .... WXXU
Cocoa Beach Public Library, Cocoa Beach, FL [*Library symbol Library of Congress*] (LCLS) .... FCb
Cocoa, Chocolate, and Confectionary Alliance [*British*] .... CCCA
Cocoa, FL [*Location identifier FAA*] (FAAL) .... COF
Cocoa, FL [*Location identifier FAA*] (FAAL) .... COI
Cocoa, FL [*Location identifier FAA*] (FAAL) .... IHR
Cocoa, FL [*Location identifier FAA*] (FAAL) .... PKC
Cocoa, FL [*Location identifier FAA*] (FAAL) .... PPU
Cocoa, FL [*Location identifier FAA*] (FAAL) .... RDX
Cocoa, FL [*Television station call letters*] .... WBCC
Cocoa, FL [*FM radio station call letters*] .... WLRQ
Cocoa, FL [*FM radio station call letters*] .... WMIE
Cocoa, FL [*AM radio station call letters*] .... WMYM
Cocoa, FL [*AM radio station call letters*] .... WRFB
Cocoa, FL [*Television station call letters*] .... WTGL
Cocoa, FL [*AM radio station call letters*] .... WWBC
Cocoa Merchants' Association of America (EA) .... CMAA
Cocoa/Patrick Air Force Base [*Florida*] [*ICAO location identifier*] (ICLI) .... KCOF
Cocoa Producers' Alliance .... COPAL
Cocoa Producers' Alliance (EAIO) .... CPA
Cocoa Public Library, Cocoa, FL [*Library symbol Library of Congress*] (LCLS) .... FCoa
Cocobeach [*Gabon*] [*ICAO location identifier*] (ICLI) .... FOOC
Coconut Cadang-Cadang Viroid [*Also, CCV*] CCCV
Coconut Cadang-Cadang Viroid [*Also, CCCV*] CCV
Coconut Fatty Alcohol [*Organic chemistry*] .... CFA
Coconut Grove [*Florida*] .... CG
Coconut Grove and Coral Gables [*Florida*] .... CG^2
Coconut Oil (PDAA) .... CCO
COCORP Extended Research Project [*Geology*] .... CERP
Cocos Island [*Keeling Islands, Australia*] [*Airport symbol*] (AD) .... CCK
Cocos Islands [*Australia ICAO location identifier*] (ICLI) .... APCC
Cocos Islands [*Australia ICAO location identifier*] (ICLI) .... APOS
Cocos [*Keeling*] **Islands** [*ANSI two-letter standard code*] (CNC) CC
Cocos [*Keeling*] **Islands** [*Seismograph station code, US Geological Survey Closed*] (SEIS) .... CCK
Cocos [*Keeling*] **Islands** [*ANSI three-letter standard code*] (CNC) .... CCK
Cocos [*Keeling*] **Islands** [*MARC geographic area code Library of Congress*] (LCCP) .... i-xb--
Cocos [*Keeling*] **Islands** [*MARC country of publication code Library of Congress*] (LCCP) .... xb
Cocos (Keeling) Islands Administration and Council [*Australia*] .... C(K)IAC
Co-Counsel, Inc. [*Associated Press*] (SAG) .... CoCou
Co-Counsel, Inc. [*Associated Press*] (SAG) .... CoCounsl
Co-Counsel, Inc. [*NASDAQ symbol*] (SAG) .... LEGL
Coctio [*Boiling*] .... COCT
Cod Liver Oil .... CLO
Coda Energy, Inc. [*NASDAQ symbol*] (NQ) .... CODA
Coda Energy, Inc. [*Associated Press*] (SAG) .... CodaEn
Coda Music Tech [*NASDAQ symbol*] (TTSB) .... COMT
Coda Music Technology, Inc. [*Associated Press*] (SAG) .... CodaMu
Coda Music Technology, Inc. [*NASDAQ symbol*] (SAG) .... COMT
CODAP [*Control Data Assembly Program*] **Language Block-Oriented Compiler** (MCD) .... COBLOC
Coddair Air East [*ICAO designator*] (AD) .... JJ
Coddington's Digest of the Law of Trade Marks [*A publication*] (DLA) .... Codd Tr M
Codd-Rennie [*Boundary condition*] [*Nuclear energy*] (NRCH) .... C-R
Code (DLA) C
Code (MCD) .... CD
Code .... CDE
Code Actuated Random Load Apparatus (MCD) .... CARLA
Code Address [*Telecommunications*] (ECII) .... CADD
Code Alarm [*NASDAQ symbol*] (TTSB) .... CODL
Code Amendments [*A publication*] (DLA) .... Code Am
Code Analysis Recording by Letters (PDAA) .... CARL
Code and Unit Test .... CUT
Code and Visual Entry Authorization Technique [*Closed-circuit TV*] (MCD) .... CAVEAT
Code Blue [*Emergency hospital code*] (DAVI) .... CB
Code Book (AFM) .... CB
Code Civil Annote, Dalloz [*A publication*] (ILCA) .... C Civ Ann
Code Clock Transfer Loop .... CCTL
Code Control (AFM) CC
Code Control Number Identifier [*Department of Health and Human Services*] (GFGA) .... CCNI
Code Converter CC
Code Converter (IAA) CCV

Code de Commerce [*Commercial Code*] [*French*] ... C COM
Code de Commerce [*Commercial Code*] (DLA) ... Code de Com
Code de Commerce Belge (DLA) ... CCB
Code de Justice Militaire [*A publication*] (DLA) ... Code de JM
Code Definition ... CD
Code des Faillites et Canqueroutes [*A publication*] (DLA) ... Code des F
Code d'Instruction Criminelle [*Code of Criminal Procedure*] [*A publication*] (ILCA) ... C Inst Crim
Code d'Instruction Criminelle [*Code of Criminal Procedure*] (DLA) ... C Instr Cr
Code d'Instruction Criminelle [*Code of Criminal Procedure*] [*A publication*] (ILCA) ... C Instr Crim
Code d'Instruction Criminelle [*Code of Criminal Procedure*] [*A publication*] (ILCA) ... CIC
Code Directing Character [*Computer science*] ... CDC
Code Division Multiple Access ... CDMA
Code du Travail [*Labor Code*] [*A publication*] (ILCA) ... C Trav
Code Excited Linear Prediction [*Computer science*] (ACRL) ... CELP
Code for Magnetic Characters (IEEE) ... CMC
Code for One-Dimensional Reactor Analysis (PDAA) ... CORA
Code Fragment Manager [*Computer science*] ... CFM
Code Francais Annote [*A publication*] (DLA) ... Code Fr An
Code Generator (IAA) ... CG
Code Identification Number (MSA) ... CIN
Code Impulse Modulation (IAA) ... CIM
Code Inserter Verifier [*Air Force*] ... CIV
Code Interface Module (CAAL) ... CIM
Code Language Telegram (IAA) ... CLT
Code Mark Inversion [*Telecommunications*] (TEL) ... CMI
Code Matching Technique ... CMT
Code Matrix Block (DNAB) ... CMB
Code Matrix Reader (PDAA) ... CMR
Code Municipal [*Quebec*] [*A publication*] (DLA) ... Code M
Code Names Dictionary [*A publication*] ... CND
Code Napoleon [*Napoleonic Code*] [*French Legal term*] ... CN
Code Not Allocated ... CNA
Code of Advertising Practices [*British*] ... CAP
Code of Alabama [*A publication*] (DLA) ... Ala Code
Code of Canon Law ... CC
Code of Civil and Commercial Procedure (DLA) ... CC Com Proc
Code of Civil Procedure [*A publication*] (DLA) ... CC Proc
Code of Civil Procedure [*A publication*] (DLA) ... CCP
Code of Civil Procedure [*A publication*] (DLA) ... Code Civ Pro
Code of Civil Procedure [*A publication*] (DLA) ... Code Civ Proc
Code of Civil Procedure [*A publication*] (DLA) ... Code of Civ Proc
Code of Civil Procedure [*Quebec*] [*A publication*] (DLA) ... CPC
Code of Civil Procedure [*India*] [*A publication*] (DLA) ... India Code Civ P
Code of Colorado Regulations [*A publication*] ... CCR
Code of Colorado Regulations [*A publication*] (DLA) ... Colo Admin Code
Code of Conduct [*Military*] (AFM) ... COC
Code of Criminal Procedure [*A publication*] (DLA) ... C Cr Pr
Code of Criminal Procedure [*A publication*] (DLA) ... C Crim Proc
Code of Criminal Procedure [*A publication*] (DLA) ... Code Cr Pro
Code of Criminal Procedure [*A publication*] (DLA) ... Code Cr Proc
Code of Criminal Procedure [*A publication*] (DLA) ... Code Crim Proc
Code of Criminal Procedure [*India*] [*A publication*] (DLA) ... India Code Crim P
Code of Fair Labor Practices (NOAA) ... CFLP
Code of Federal Regulation (DOMA) ... CFR
Code of Federal Regulations (ACII) ... CFR
Code of Federal Regulations Supplement [*A publication*] (GFGA) ... CFR Supp
Code of General Laws [*A publication*] (DLA) ... Code Gen Laws
Code of Georgia [*A publication*] (DLA) ... GA Code
Code of Iowa [*A publication*] (AAGC) ... Iowa Code
Code of Judicial Procedure [*A publication*] (DLA) ... C Jud Proc
Code of Justinian [*A publication*] (DSA) ... CJ
Code of Justinian [*A publication*] (DLA) ... Code
Code of Justinian [*A publication*] (DLA) ... Jus Code
Code of Laws of South Carolina [*A publication*] (DLA) ... SC Code
Code of Laws of South Carolina, Annotated [*A publication*] (DLA) ... SC Code Ann
Code of Maine Rules (AAGC) ... CMR
Code of Maine Rules [*Also CMR*] [*A publication*] (AAGC) ... Code Me R
Code of Maryland Regulations [*A publication*] ... COMAR
Code of Maryland Regulations [*A publication*] (DLA) ... MD Admin Code
Code of Massachusetts Regulations [*A publication*] ... CMR
Code of Massachusetts Regulations [*A publication*] (DLA) ... Mass Admin Code
Code of Military Justice ... CMJ
Code of Practice [*Legal term*] (DLA) ... Code Prac
Code of Practice [*Telecommunications*] (TEL) ... COP
Code of Practice [*Legal term*] ... CP
Code of Procedure [*Legal term*] (DLA) ... C Pr
Code of Procedure [*Legal term*] (DLA) ... Code Pro
Code of Procedure [*Legal term*] (DLA) ... Code Proc
Code of Procedure [*Legal term*] ... CP
Code of Professional Responsibility [*American Bar Association*] ... CPR
Code of Public General Laws [*A publication*] (DLA) ... Code Pub Gen Laws
Code of Public Local Laws [*A publication*] (DLA) ... Code Pub Loc Laws
Code of Rhode Island Rules [*A publication*] (AAGC) ... CRIR
Code of Theodosius [*Roman law*] [*A publication*] (DSA) ... C Th
Code of Theodosius [*Roman law*] [*A publication*] (DLA) ... Code Theod
Code Operations Coordinator (MUGU) ... COC
Code Penal [*Penal Code*] [*French*] (BARN) ... C Pen
Code Practice Oscillator ... CPO
Code Proficiency [*Amateur radio*] ... CP
Code Receiver [*Computer science*] (IAA) ... CR
Code Relations Index ... CRI
Code Reporter [*New York*] [*A publication*] (DLA) ... Co R
Code Reporter [*New York*] [*A publication*] (DLA) ... Co R (NY)
Code Reporter [*New York*] [*A publication*] (DLA) ... Co Rep
Code Reporter [*New York*] [*A publication*] (DLA) ... Code NY Rep
Code Reporter [*New York*] [*A publication*] (DLA) ... Code R
Code Reporter [*New York*] [*A publication*] (DLA) ... Code Rep
Code Reporter [*New York*] [*A publication*] (DLA) ... CR
Code Reports [*New York*] [*A publication*] (DLA) ... Code R (NY)
Code Reports, New Series [*New York*] [*A publication*] (DLA) ... Co R NS
Code Reports, New Series [*New York*] [*A publication*] (DLA) ... Code RNS
Code Reports, New Series [*New York*] [*A publication*] (DLA) ... Code RNS (NY)
Code Reports, New Series [*New York*] [*A publication*] (DLA) ... CRNS
Code Segment [*Computer science*] ... CS
Code Segment:Instruction Pointer [*Computer science*] ... CS:IP
Code Segment Table [*Computer science*] ... CST
Code Selection Language [*Computer science*] (BUR) ... CSL
Code Sequential Pulse Generator (IAA) ... CSPG
Code Ship Parametric Model (MCD) ... CSPM
Code Sort Optical Character Recognition [*Computer science*] ... CSOCR
Code Storage Unit ... CSU
Code Table (IAA) ... CT
Code Table Buffer ... CTB
Code Telegram ... CT
Code to Handle Angular Data (IEEE) ... CHAD
Code Tone Call Selective Signalling [*Telecommunications*] (PDAA) ... CTCSS
Code Transfer Logic ... CTL
Code Translation Data System [*Air Force*] ... CTDS
Code Universel de Produit [*Universal Product Code*] [*French*] ... CUP
Code Variante [*Codification*] (NATG) ... CV
Code Verification (IEEE) ... CODEVER
Code Wave (BARN) ... CW
Code Word (IAA) ... CW
Code-Alarm, Inc. [*Associated Press*] (SAG) ... CodeAl
Code-Alarm, Inc. [*NASDAQ symbol*] (NQ) ... CODL
Coded (IAA) ... CDD
Coded Acoustic Interrogator ... CAI
Coded Address [*NATO*] ... CODRESS
Coded Address Private Radio Intercommunication (MCD) ... CAPRI
Coded Analysis [*Navy*] ... CODAN
Coded Armaments System ... CAS
Coded Automatic Gain Control ... CAGC
Coded Automatic Reading Device ... CARD
Coded Biphase ... COBI
Coded Command ... CCMD
Coded Decimal Digit ... CDD
Coded Decimal Notation ... CDN
Coded Description Pattern (AFIT) ... CDP
Coded Discharge (DNAB) ... CODIS
Coded Division Multiplex ... CDM
Coded Doppler RADAR Command ... CODORAC
Coded Integrated Armament Control System (MCD) ... CIACS
Coded Modulator-Demodulator (PDAA) ... CODEM
Coded Optical Character [*Computer science*] (BUR) ... COC
Coded Pulse Anticlutter System (CET) ... CPACS
Coded Switch System [*To permit or deny the ability to arm nuclear weapons in strategic aircraft*] ... CSS
Coded Telemetry Processor ... CTP
Coded Time Sequence (MCD) ... CTS
Coded Voice System Digitization (NITA) ... CVSD
Coded Wire Tagging [*Pisciculture*] ... CWT
Coded-Access Teleconferencing System [*Telecommunications*] ... CATS
Coded-Bias Mosaic (MCD) ... COBM
Code-Division Multiple Access [*Navigation systems*] ... CDMA
Codeine (AAMN) ... Cod
Codeine [*Pharmacology*] (DAVI) ... CODEIN
Codeine Tablet [*Slang*] (DSUE) ... CODI
Coden [*Online database field identifier*] ... CD
Coden [*Online database field identifier*] ... CO
Co-Dependents Anonymous (EA) ... CoDA
Co-Dependents of Sexual Addicts [*Acronym is now organization's official name*] (EA) ... COSA
Coder and Random Access Switch (AAG) ... CRAS
Coder Sequential Pulse ... CSP
Coder-Decoder [*Telecommunications*] (MCD) ... CODEC
Coder-Decoder Group [*Army*] (AABC) ... CDG
Codes and Paging (NRCH) ... CAP
Code-View [*Computer software*] (PCM) ... CV
CodeView for Windows [*Program debugger*] [*Computer science*] (PCM) ... CVW
Codex ... C
Codex ... COD
Codex (VRA) ... cod
Codex Aleppensis (BJA) ... CA
Codex Alexandrinus (BJA) ... A
Codex Alimentarius Commission [*United Nations*] (PDAA) ... CAC
Codex Bezae (BJA) ... D
Codex Committee on Pesticide Residues [*Australia*] ... CCPR
Codex Committee on Residues of Veterinary Drugs in Food [*Australia*] ... CCRVDF
Codex Diplomaticus [*A publication*] (ILCA) ... Cod Dip
Codex Ephaemi [*Ephraem the Syrian*] [*A publication*] (ROG) ... C
Codex Hammurabi (BJA) ... CH
Codex Iuris Canonici [*Code of Canon Law*] [*Latin*] ... CIC
Codex Iustinianus [*Classical studies*] (OCD) ... Cod Iust
Codex Juris Civilis [*A publication*] (ILCA) ... C
Codex Juris Civilis [*Latin A publication*] (DLA) ... Cod Jur Civ
Codex Justinianus (BJA) ... CJ

Codex Justinianus [*Code of Justinian*] [*Latin A publication*] (DLA) .... Code
Codex Justinianus (BJA) .... CodJust
Codex Leningradensis (BJA) CL
Codex Marchalianus (BJA) .... Q
Codex Membranacius [*A book written on vellum or skins*] [*Latin*] (ROG) .... COD MEMB
Codex Petropolitanus (BJA) .... CP
Codex Prophetarum Cairensis (BJA) CC
Codex Reuchlinianus (BJA) .... CR
Codex Sinaiticus (BJA) .... S
Codex Theodosianus [*Theodosian Code*] [*438AD*] [*Latin*] [*A publication*] (DLA) .... C Theod
Codex Theodosianus [*Theodosian Code*] [*438AD*] [*Latin*] [*Legal term*] (OCD) .... Cod Theod
Codex Theodosianus [*Theodosian Code*] [*438AD*] [*Latin*] [*Legal term*] [*A publication*] (DLA) .... Cod Theodos
Codex Theodosianus [*Theodosian Code*] [*438AD*] [*Latin*] [*Legal term*] (DLA) .... Code Theodos
Codex Theodosianus [*Theodosian Code*] [*438AD*] [*Latin*] [*Legal term*] (BJA) .... CT
Codex Vaticanus (BJA) .... B
Codice Civile [*Civil Code*] [*Italian*] (ILCA) CC
Codice Commerciale [*Commercial Code*] [*A publication*] (ILCA) .... C Comm
Codices (VRA) .... cod
Codices (ROG) .... CODD
Codices Latini Antiquiores [*A publication*] (OCD) .... Codd Lat Ant
Codices Palatini (BJA) .... CPal
Codicil .... COD
Codicil .... CODL
Codification [*Legal term*] (ILCA) .... Cod
Codification File (MCD) .... CODFIL
Codified Statutes [*A publication*] (DLA) .... Cod St
Codifying Act of Sederunt (DLA) .... CAS
Coding (MSA) .... COD
Coding Board Officer .... CBO
Coding/Decoding Device .... CODEC
Coding Room Watch Officer [*Navy*] .... CRWO
Coding Specification .... CS
Coding Speed Test (DNAB) .... CST
Codling Moth Granulosis Virus .... CMGV
Codon Adaptation Index [*Genetics*] .... CAI
Codrington [*Barbuda Island*] [*ICAO location identifier*] (ICLI) .... TAPH
Codroy Valley Public Library, Upper Ferry, Newfoundland [*Library symbol National Library of Canada*] (NLC) .... NFUF
Codroy Valley Public Library, Upper Ferry, NF, Canada [*Library symbol Library of Congress*] (LCLS) .... CaNfUF
Cody [*Wyoming*] [*Airport symbol*] (OAG) .... COD
Cody, WY [*Location identifier FAA*] (FAAL) .... COD
Cody, WY [*AM radio station call letters*] .... KODI
Cody, WY [*FM radio station call letters*] .... KTAG
Cody, WY [*FM radio station call letters*] .... KYDZ
Coe College, Cedar Rapids, IA [*Library symbol Library of Congress*] (LCLS) .... IaCrC
Coe College, Cedar Rapids, IA [*OCLC symbol*] (OCLC) .... ION
Coe. Practice of the Judges' Chambers [*1876*] [*A publication*] (DLA) ..... Coe Ch Pr
Coe Ranch [*California*] [*Seismograph station code, US Geological Survey*] (SEIS) .... COE
Coe Township Library, Shepherd, MI [*Library symbol Library of Congress*] (LCLS) .... MiShep
COEA [*Cost and Operational Effectiveness Analysis*] **Cost Advisory Group** [*Military*] .... CCAG
Coeburn, VA [*FM radio station call letters*] .... WZQK
Co-Editor .... CO-ED
Coeducational .... COED
Co-Educational (AIE) .... CoEd
Coefficient C
Coefficient (KSC) .... COEF
Coefficient .... COEFF
Coefficient of Alienation [*Psychology*] .... k
Coefficient of Association [*Statistics*] .... Q
Coefficient of Beam Utilization [*Floodlighting*] .... CBU
Coefficient of Contingency [*Statistics*] CC
Coefficient of Correlation [*Statistics*] CC
Coefficient of Drag (MCD) .... CD
Coefficient of Drag-Area .... CDA
Coefficient of Fat Retention (AAMN) .... CR
Coefficient of Friction [*Physics*] (BARN) .... CF
Coefficient of Friction [*Physics*] .... COF
Coefficient of Haze [*Environment*] .... COH
Coefficient of Heat Transfer [*Symbol*] [*Thermodynamics*] .... h
Coefficient of Induced Drag [*Aviation*] (DA) .... C_{Di}
Coefficient of Intelligence CI
Coefficient of Lift CL
Coefficient of Linear Extensibility .... COLE
Coefficient of Linear Thermal Expansion .... CLTE
Coefficient of Linear Thermal Expansion .... CLTE
Coefficient of Luminous Intensity CLI
Coefficient of Merit [*Electronics*] (IAA) .... COM
Coefficient of Octanolwater Partition (GNE) .... Kow
Coefficient of Organic Carbon Partition (GNE) .... Koc
Coefficient of Overestimation .... CO
Coefficient of Oxygen Delivery .... COD
Coefficient of Performance .... COP
Coefficient of Performance (IEEE) .... CP
Coefficient of Physics [*Physics*] (DAVI) L
Coefficient of Profile Drag [*Aviation*] (DA) .... C_{Dp}
Coefficient of Protection [*Against insects*] .... CP
Coefficient of Retraction .... CR
Coefficient of Scleral Rigidity [*Ophthalmology*] (DAVI) .... K
Coefficient of Soil-Water Absorption (GNE) .... Kd
Coefficient of Temperature (DAVI) .... Q_{10}
Coefficient of Thermal Expansion .... CTE
Coefficient of Utilization .... CU
Coefficient of Variation [*Mathematics*] .... COV
Coefficient of Variation [*Mathematics*] CV
Coefficient of Variation [*Statistics*] (BARN) V
Coefficient Z-Axis [*Downforce on a racing car*] [*Aerodynamics*] .... CZ
Coeliac Axis (BABM) .... CA
Coeliac Society of Australia .... CSA
Coeliac Society of the United Kingdom (EAIO) .... CSUK
Coelieac [*or Celiac*] **Axis** [*Gastroenterology*] (DAVI) .... CA
Coelliptic Rendezvous Sequence [*Aerospace*] .... CRS
Coelliptic Sequence Initiation [*Aerospace*] .... CSI
Coen [*Australia Airport symbol*] (OAG) .... CUQ
Coenzyme [*Biochemistry*] .... Co
Coenzyme A [*Biochemistry*] .... CoA
Coenzyme A-Synthetizing Protein Complex [*Medicine*] (DMAA) .... CoA-SPC
Coenzyme M .... CoM
Coenzyme Q [*Ubiquinone*] [*Also, Q, U, UQ*] [*Biochemistry*] .... CoQ
Coenzyme Q [*Ubiquinone*] [*Also, CoQ, U, UQ*] [*Biochemistry*] .... Q
Coercion (MSA) .... CORCN
Coeroeni [*Surinam*] [*ICAO location identifier*] (ICLI) .... SMCI
Coeur D'Alene [*Idaho*] [*Airport symbol*] (OAG) .... COE
Coeur D'Alene, ID [*Location identifier FAA*] (FAAL) .... AUC
Coeur D'Alene, ID [*Location identifier FAA*] (FAAL) .... COE
Coeur D'Alene, ID [*Location identifier FAA*] (FAAL) .... HYD
Coeur D'Alene, ID [*FM radio station call letters*] .... KCDA
Coeur D'Alene, ID [*Television station call letters*] .... KCDT
Coeur D'Alene, ID [*AM radio station call letters*] .... KVNI
Coeur d'Alene Mines [*NYSE symbol*] (TTSB) .... CDE
Coeur D'Alene Mines Corp. [*NYSE symbol*] (SPSG) .... CDE
Coeur D'Alene Mines Corp. [*Associated Press*] (SAG) .... Coeur
Coeur d'Alene Mines 'MARCS' [*NYSE symbol*] (TTSB) .... CDEPr
Coeur D'Alene Public Library, Coeur D'Alene, ID [*Library symbol Library of Congress*] (LCLS) .... IdC
Coeur d'Alene Public Library, Coeur d'Alene, ID [*Library symbol*] [*Library of Congress*] (LCLS) .... IdCL
Coextrusion Welding .... CEW
Cofactor [*Laboratory*] (DAVI) .... CoF
Cofer's Kentucky Digest [*A publication*] (DLA) .... Cof Dig
Coffee .... COF
Coffee Association of Canada [*Association du Cafe du Canada*] (AC) .... CAC
Coffee Berry Disease .... CBD
Coffee Commission of the Inter-American Economic and Social Council [*United States*] .... CCIAESC
Coffee Development Group (EA) .... CDG
Coffee Growers' Association of El Salvador [*Defunct*] (EA) .... CGAES
Coffee House (ROG) .... CO HO
Coffee Mill .... COFML
Coffee People, Inc. [*Associated Press*] (SAG) .... CoffPeop
Coffee People, Inc. [*NASDAQ symbol*] (SAG) .... MOKA
Coffee Ringspot Virus [*Plant pathology*] .... CRV
Coffee, Sugar, and Cocoa Exchange (EA) .... CSCE
Coffee Table Book [*Large, extensively illustrated book designed for display and browsing*] .... CTB
Coffee Trade Federation [*British*] (DBA) .... CTF
Cofferdam [*Engineering*] .... COFF
Coffey's California Probate Decisions [*A publication*] (DLA) .... Cof
Coffey's California Probate Decisions [*A publication*] (DLA) .... Cof Pro
Coffey's California Probate Decisions [*A publication*] (DLA) .... Cof Prob
Coffey's California Probate Decisions [*A publication*] (DLA) .... Cof Prob Dec (Cal)
Coffey's California Probate Decisions [*A publication*] (DLA) .... Coff Prob
Coffey's California Probate Decisions [*A publication*] (DLA) .... Coffey
Coffey's California Probate Decisions [*A publication*] (DLA) .... Coffey Prob Dec
Coffey's California Probate Decisions [*A publication*] (DLA) ...... Coffey Probate Dec
Coffey's California Probate Decisions [*A publication*] (DLA) .... Coffey's Prob Dec
Coffeyville, KS [*Location identifier FAA*] (FAAL) .... CFV
Coffeyville, KS [*AM radio station call letters*] .... KGGF
Coffeyville, KS [*FM radio station call letters*] .... KUSN
Coffin [*Missile launch environment symbol*] C
Coffin Ground-Attack Missile .... CGM
Coffin Intercept Missile .... CIM
Coffin Strategic Missile .... CSM
Coffin Texts (BJA) .... CT
Coffin-Lowry Syndrome [*Medicine*] .... CLS
Coffman Cove, AK [*Location identifier FAA*] (FAAL) .... KCC
Coffs Harbour [*Australia ICAO location identifier*] (ICLI) .... ASCH
Coffs Harbour [*Australia Airport symbol*] (OAG) .... CFS
Cofield, NC [*Location identifier FAA*] (FAAL) CVI
Co-Fired, Multilayer Ceramic [*Materials science*] .... CMC
Coflexip [*NASDAQ symbol*] (SAG) .... CXIP
Coflexip ADS [*NASDAQ symbol*] (TTSB) .... CXIPY
Coflexip & Services, Inc. [*Associated Press*] (SAG) .... Coflexip
Coformycin [*Biochemistry*] .... CF
Cogdean [*England*] .... COGD
Cogeco, Inc. [*Toronto Stock Exchange symbol*] .... CGO
Cogeneration and Independent Power Coalition of America (EA) .... CIPCA
Cogeneration Coalition [*Later, CIPCA*] (EA) CIC
Cogeneration Coalition of America [*Later, CIPCA*] (EA) .... CICA
Cogeneration of Heat and Power .... CHP
Cogesco Mining Resources [*Toronto Stock Exchange symbol*] .... COJ

Coggan Monitor, Coggan, IA [*Library symbol Library of Congress*] (LCLS) ... IaCogM
Coggeshall [*England*] ... COGG
Coghlan Island, AK [*Location identifier FAA*] (FAAL) ... CGL
Coghlan's Epitome of Hindu Law Cases [*A publication*] (DLA) ... Cogh Epit
Cogitive Style (EDAC) ... CS
COGLA [*Canada Oil and Gas Lands Administration*] **Ocean Mining Resource Centre, APGTC , Ottawa, ON, Canada** [*Administration du Petrole et du Gaz des Terres du Canada*] [*Library symbol Library of Congress*] (LCLS) ... CaOOCOG
COGLA [*Canada Oil and Gas Lands Administration*] **Ocean Mining Resource Centre , Ottawa, Ontario** [*Centre de Ressources sur l'Extraction de Minerais Oceaniques, Administration du Petrole et du Gaz des Terres du Canada*] [*Library symbol National Library of Canada*] (NLC) ... OOCOG
Cognac (ADA) ... COG
Cognac/Chateau Bernard [*France ICAO location identifier*] (ICLI) ... LFBG
Cognac Information Bureau [*Commercial firm*] (EA) ... CIB
Cognac Information Centre [*British*] (CB) ... CIC
Cognate ... C
Cognate (ROG) ... COG
Cognate With (ROG) ... COGN W
Cognex Corp. [*NASDAQ symbol*] (NQ) ... CGNX
Cognex Corp. [*Associated Press*] (SAG) ... Cognex
Cognitive ... C
Cognitive [*Function tests*] [*Psychology*] (DAVI) ... COG
Cognitive Abilities Screening Instrument ... CASI
Cognitive Abilities Screening Instrument [*Medicine*] (DMAA) ... CASI
Cognitive Abilities Test [*Education*] ... CAT
Cognitive Abilities Test [*Academic achievement and aptitude test*] ... COGAT
Cognitive Acceleration through Science Education (AIE) ... CASE
Cognitive Acceleration through Science Education Project (AIE) ... CASEP
Cognitive and Affective Learning Model [*Psychology*] ... CALM
Cognitive Capacity Screening Examination [*Psychology*] ... CCSE
Cognitive Diagnostic Battery [*Test*] ... CDB
Cognitive Environmental Stimulation [*Medicine*] (DAVI) ... CES
Cognitive Failure Questionnaire [*Education*] (AIE) ... CFQ
Cognitive Hybrid Intelligent Learning Device ... CHILD
Cognitive Levels Matching [*Psychology*] (EDAC) ... CLM
Cognitive, Linguistic, and Social-Communicative Scales [*Speech evaluation test*] ... CLASS
Cognitive Operating System [*NASA*] ... COGNOSYS
Cognitive Research Trust [*British*] (DI) ... CORT
Cognitive Science Society (EA) ... CSS
Cognitive Skills Assessment Battery (EDAC) ... CSAB
Cognitive Stimulation [*Experimental psychology*] ... CS
Cognitive Style Mapping Inventory (EDAC) ... CSMI
Cognitive-Behavior Modification [*Psychology*] ... CBM
Cognitronics Corp. [*AMEX symbol*] (SPSG) ... CGN
Cognitronics Corp. [*Associated Press*] (SAG) ... Cognitr
Cognizance Symbol ... CS
Cognizant (NG) ... COG
Cognizant Development Engineer ... CDE
Cognizant Engineer ... CE
Cognizant Field Activity ... CFA
Cognizant Government Inspector (SAA) ... CGI
Cognizant Operating Authority (MUGU) ... COA
Cognizant Operations Engineer ... COE
Cognizant Operations Engineer's Parts List ... COEPL
Cognizant Quality Engineer (NRCH) ... CQE
Cognizant Security Authority [*Military*] ... CSA
Cognizant Security Office [*Controls industrial security at government facilities*] [*Military*] ... CSO
Cognizant Security Officer (AAGC) ... CSO
Cognizant Sustaining Engineer ... CSE
Cognizant Technical Manager ... CTM
Cognizant Transportation Office [*or Officer*] [*Air Force*] (AFM) ... CTO
Cognizant User Engineer [*Deep Space Network, NASA*] ... CUE
Cognos, Inc. [*NASDAQ symbol*] (NQ) ... COGN
Cognos Inc. [*NASDAQ symbol*] (TTSB) ... COGNE
Cognos, Inc. [*Associated Press*] (SAG) ... Cognos
Cognos, Inc. [*Toronto Stock Exchange symbol*] ... CSN
Cognos, Inc., Ottawa, Ontario [*Library symbol National Library of Canada*] (BIB) ... OOCOI
Cognos International Users' Group (AC) ... CIUG
Cogwheel [*Respiration*] [*Medicine*] (DAVI) ... sacc
Cohasset School, Cohasset, MN [*Library symbol*] [*Library of Congress*] (LCLS) ... MnCohS
Coheir [*Joint heir*] [*Genealogy*] ... COH
Cohen and Lee's Maryland Digest [*A publication*] (DLA) ... C & L Dig
Cohen & Steers Realty Income Fund [*Associated Press*] (SAG) ... CohenStr
Cohen & Steers Realty Income Fund [*Formerly, Real Estate Securities Income Fund, Inc.*] [*AMEX symbol*] (CTT) ... RIF
Cohen & Steers Rlty Inc. Fd [*AMEX symbol*] (TTSB) ... RIF
Cohen & Steers Total Return Realty Fund [*Associated Press*] (SAG) ... CohenST
Cohen & Steers Total Return Rt. Realty Fund [*NYSE symbol*] (SPSG) ... RFI
Cohen & Steers Total Rt Rty Fd [*NYSE symbol*] (TTSB) ... RFI
Cohen's Admiralty Jurisdiction, Law, and Practice [*A publication*] (DLA) ... Cohen Adm Law
Cohen's Criminal Appeals Reports [*England*] [*A publication*] (DLA) ... Crim App Rep
Cohen's Nova Scotia Reports [*A publication*] (DLA) ... NSR Coh
Coherence [*Statistics*] ... COH
Coherent (IAA) ... COH
Coherent Acceleration and Velocity Observations in Real Time ... CAVORT
Coherent Acoustic Torpedo System (MCD) ... CATS
Coherent Acquisition System (MCD) ... CAS
Coherent Anti-Stokes Raman Spectroscopy ... CARS
Coherent Anti-Stokes Resonance Raman Scattering [*Spectrometry*] ... CARRS
Coherent Array RADAR (MSA) ... COAR
Coherent Carrier Keying [*Computer science*] (IAA) ... CCK
Coherent Cloud Physics RADAR ... CCPR
Coherent Communic Sys [*NASDAQ symbol*] (TTSB) ... CCSC
Coherent Communications Systems Corp. [*NASDAQ symbol*] (SAG) ... CCSC
Coherent Communications Systems Corp. [*Associated Press*] (SAG) ... CoherC
Coherent Crystal Radiation (PDAA) ... CCR
Coherent Detector [*Electronics*] (OA) ... CD
Coherent Digital Phased Array System [*ARPA*] ... CODIPHASE
Coherent Doppler Measurement System ... CDMS
Coherent Echo Modulation and Detection (MCD) ... CEMAD
Coherent Electromagnetic Energy Transmission ... COMET
Coherent Emitter Location Testbed (IEEE) ... CELT
Coherent Event [*Trademark*] ... COHVENT
Coherent Forward Scattering [*Spectrometry*] ... CFS
Coherent Frequency Shift Keying ... CFSK
Coherent Frequency Synthesizer ... CFS
Coherent Frequency-Hopping Signal ... CFHS
Coherent Heterodyne Receiver (PDAA) ... CHR
Coherent Imaging RADAR ... CIR
Coherent, Inc. [*Associated Press*] (SAG) ... Cohernt
Coherent, Inc. [*NASDAQ symbol*] (NQ) ... COHR
Coherent Infrared Energy (AAG) ... CIE
Coherent Interpretation Time (MCD) ... CIT
Coherent LASER Illumination ... CLI
Coherent Light Detecting and Ranging [*RADAR*] [*Hughes Aircraft*] ... COLIDAR
Coherent Light Detector ... COLD
Coherent Light Detector System (MCD) ... COLIDS
Coherent Linear Frequency Modulated (IAA) ... CLFM
Coherent Master Oscillator (NG) ... COMO
Coherent Memory Filter ... CMF
Coherent Microwave Memory ... CMM
Coherent Monopulse Doppler RADAR ... CMDR
Coherent Multi-Channel (IAA) ... CMC
Coherent Multichannel Communication ... CMC
Coherent Optical Adaptive Techniques ... COAT
Coherent Optical Array ... COA
Coherent Optical Array Techniques ... COAT
Coherent Optical Device ... COD
Coherent Optical Fingerprint Identification System (MCD) ... COFIDS
Coherent Optical LASER ... COL
Coherent Optical Processing System ... COPS
Coherent Optical Processor ... COP
Coherent Optical RADAR Laboratory ... CORAL
Coherent Optical Receiver ... COR
Coherent Optical System of Modular Imaging Collectors ... COSMIC
Coherent Oscillator [*RADAR*] ... COHO
Coherent Phase Shift Keyed [*System*] [*Computer science*] ... CPSK
Coherent Phase Shift Keying (NITA) ... CPSK
Coherent Potential (OA) ... CP
Coherent Potential Approximation [*Physics*] ... CPA
Coherent Processing Interval [*Computer science*] ... CPI
Coherent RADAR Array ... CORA
Coherent RADAR Seeker Investigation (MCD) ... CORSI
Coherent Raman Spectroscopy (MCD) ... CRS
Coherent Side-Lobe Cancellation ... CSLC
Coherent Signal Processing System [*Army*] (AABC) ... CSPS
Coherent Signal Processor ... CSP
Coherent Space Mirror Complex ... COSMIC
Coherent Stokes Raman Spectroscopy ... CSRS
Coherent Synthetic Aperture RADAR (MCD) ... CSAR
Coherent Tilted Superlattice [*Solid state physics*] ... CTSL
Coherent Transient Spectroscopy (MCD) ... CTS
Coherent-on-Receive ... CORE
Coherent-on-Receive Doppler System [*RADAR*] ... CORDS
Cohesant Technologies [*NASDAQ symbol*] (TTSB) ... COHT
Cohesant Technologies, Inc. [*Associated Press*] (SAG) ... Cohes
Cohesant Technologies, Inc. [*Associated Press*] (SAG) ... Cohesant
Cohesant Technologies, Inc. [*NASDAQ symbol*] (SAG) ... COHT
Cohesant Technologies Wrrt [*NASDAQ symbol*] (TTSB) ... COHTW
Cohesion, Operational Readiness, and Training [*Army*] ... COHORT
Cohesion, Organization, Resourcefulness and Energy Model (EDAC) ... CORE
Cohesive Energy Density [*Solubility parameter*] ... CED
Cohesive Energy Ratio (MCD) ... CER
Cohesive Intermolecular Force ... CIF
Cohesive Unit Program [*Army*] ... CUP
Cohlmia Aviation [*ICAO designator*] (FAAC) ... CHL
Coho Energy [*NASDAQ symbol*] (TTSB) ... COHO
Coho Energy, Inc. [*NASDAQ symbol*] (SAG) ... COHO
Coho Energy, Inc. [*Associated Press*] (SAG) ... CohoEn
Cohort Production Intervals ... CPI
COHR, Inc. [*NASDAQ symbol*] (SAG) ... CHRI
COHR Inc. [*NASDAQ symbol*] (TTSB) ... CHRI
COHR, Inc. [*Associated Press*] (SAG) ... COHR
Cohu, Inc. [*NASDAQ symbol*] (SAG) ... COHU
Coiffeur ... CFFR
Coiffeuse ... CFFS
Coiffure ... COIFF
Coil [*Genetics*] ... C
Coil ... CL
Coil Finish (MSA) ... CF
Coil Power Programmer [*Nuclear energy*] (NRCH) ... CPP

Coil Predriver (IAA) ... CPD
Coil Sketch (MSA) ... CS
Coil Spring-loaded Beveled-edge Ring [*Automotive engineering*] ... CSBR
Coil Stock Cradle ... CSC
Coil Winding Equipment ... CWE
Coil Winding International Exhibition [*British*] (ITD) ... CWI
Coil Winding Machine ... CWM
Coiled [*Freight*] ... COIL
Coils [*Freight*] ... CLS
Coils per Slot [*Technical drawings*] ... CPS
Coimbatore [*India*] [*Airport symbol*] (OAG) ... CJB
Coimbatore [*India*] [*ICAO location identifier*] (ICLI) ... VOCB
Coimbra [*Portugal*] [*Seismograph station code, US Geological Survey*] (SEIS) ... COI
Coimbra [*Portugal ICAO location identifier*] (ICLI) ... LPCO
Coin and Fee Checking [*Telecommunications*] (TEL) ... CFC
Coin Bill Validator [*NASDAQ symbol*] (TTSB) ... CBVI
Coin Bill Validator, Inc. [*NASDAQ symbol*] (SAG) ... CBVI
Coin Bill Validator, Inc. [*Associated Press*] (SAG) ... CoinBill
Coin Box [*Telecommunications*] (TEL) ... CB
Coin Box Adapter [*Computer science*] (ECII) ... CBA
Coin Box Telephone [*Telecommunications*] ... CBT
[*The*] **Coin Coalition** (EA) ... TCC
Coin Collect [*Telecommunications*] (TEL) ... CC
Coin Collecting Box [*Telecommunications*] (TEL) ... CCB
Coin Collecting Box, Pay Station [*Telecommunications*] (TEL) ... CX
Coin Completing [*Telecommunications*] (TEL) ... CC
Coin Detection and Announcement [*Telecommunications*] (TEL) ... CDA
Coin Dimple ... CD
Coin Lake Gold Mines Ltd. [*Toronto Stock Exchange symbol*] ... COI
Coin Laundry Association (EA) ... CLA
Coin L-Band Ranging and Homing System [*Military*] ... COBRAH
Coin Level Indicator [*Telephone communications*] ... CLI
Coin Phone Operational and Information Network System [*Telecommunications*] (TEL) ... COIN
Coin Trunk [*Telecommunications*] (TEL) ... CN
Coin World [*A publication*] ... Coin W
[*The*] **Coinage of the Roman Republic** [*A publication*] (OCD) ... CRR
Coinbox Line [*Telecommunications*] (TEL) ... CO
Coinbox Set [*Telecommunications*] (TEL) ... CX
Coincidence Counts ... COINCNT
Coincidence Detection Program (SAA) ... CDT
Coincidence Gate ... CG
Coincidence Guidance ... C/G
Coincidence Moessbauer Spectroscopy (OA) ... CMS
Coincidence Site Lattice (MCD) ... CSL
Coincidence-Ledge-Dislocation (PDAA) ... CLD
Coincident Light Information Photographic Strips ... CLIPS
Coincident-Current (IAA) ... CC
Coincident-Current Magnetic Core ... CCMC
Coincident-Current Memory ... CCM
Coinmach Laundry Corp. [*Associated Press*] (SAG) ... Coinmch
Coinmach Laundry Corp. [*NASDAQ symbol*] (SAG) ... WDRY
Coin-Op Car Wash Association ... COCWA
Coin-Operated Amusement Device ... COAD
Coins on Stamps Unit [*American Topical Association*] (EA) ... COSSU
Coinsurance ... CO
Coinsurance ... COINS
COINTELPRO [*FBI Counterintelligence Program*] **Survivors** [*Defunct*] (EA) ... CS
Coinvestigator ... Co-I
Cokato Elementary School, Media Center, Cokato, MN [*Library symbol*] [*Library of Congress*] (LCLS) ... MnCoE
Cokato Museum, Cokato, MN [*Library symbol*] [*Library of Congress*] (LCLS) ... MnCoM
Cokato Public Library, Cokato, MN [*Library symbol*] [*Library of Congress*] (LCLS) ... MnCo
Coke on Courts [*or Fourth Institute*] [*England*] [*A publication*] (DLA) ... Co Cts
Coke on Courts [*or Fourth Institute*] [*England*] [*A publication*] (DLA) ... Co on Courts
Coke on Littleton [*England*] [*A publication*] (DLA) ... Co Lit
Coke on Littleton [*England*] [*A publication*] (DLA) ... Co Litt
Coke on Littleton [*England*] [*A publication*] (DLA) ... Co Litt (Eng)
Coke on Littleton [*England*] [*A publication*] (DLA) ... Coke Lit
Coke on Regenerated Catalyst [*Chemical engineering*] ... CRC
Coke Oven ... CO
Coke Oven Gas ... COG
Coke Oven Managers' Association [*British*] (BI) ... COMA
Coke Oven Production Technology ... COPT
Coker College, Hartsville, SC [*Library symbol Library of Congress*] (LCLS) ... ScHaC
Coker Gas Oil ... CGO
Coke's Bankrupt Law [*A publication*] (DLA) ... Co BL
Coke's Book of Entries [*1614*] [*England*] [*A publication*] (DLA) ... Co Ent
Coke's Book of Entries [*1614*] [*England*] [*A publication*] (DLA) ... Coke Ent
Coke's Book of Entries [*1614*] [*England*] [*A publication*] (DLA) ... Ent
Coke's Compleat Copyholder [*5 eds.*] [*1630-73 England*] [*A publication*] (DLA) ... Co Cop
Coke's English King's Bench Reports [*1572-1616*] [*A publication*] (DLA) ... Co
Coke's English King's Bench Reports [*1572-1616*] [*A publication*] (DLA) ... Co Rep
Coke's English King's Bench Reports [*1572-1616*] [*A publication*] (DLA) ... Coke
Coke's English King's Bench Reports [*1572-1616*] [*A publication*] (DLA) ... Coke (Eng)
Coke's English King's Bench Reports [*1572-1616*] [*A publication*] (DLA) ... Rep
Coke's English King's Bench Reports [*1572-1616*] [*A publication*] (DLA) ... Reports
Coke's Institutes [*England*] [*A publication*] (DLA) ... Co
Coke's Institutes [*England*] [*A publication*] (DLA) ... Co Inst
Coke's Institutes [*England*] [*A publication*] (DLA) ... Co Inst (Eng)
Coke's Institutes [*England*] [*A publication*] (DLA) ... Coke Inst
Coke's Institutes [*England*] [*A publication*] (DLA) ... Inst
Coke's Magna Charta [*or Second Institute*] [*A publication*] (DLA) ... Co MC
Coke's Pleadings [*Sometimes published separately*] [*A publication*] (DLA) ... Co Pl
Coke's Pleas of the Crown [*or Third Institute*] [*A publication*] (DLA) ... Co PC
Cokesbury Satellite Television Network [*United Methodist Publishing House*] [*Telecommunications service*] (TSSD) ... CSTN
Col [*With The*] [*Music*] ... C
Col Basso [*With the Bass*] [*Music*] ... CB
Col Canto [*With the Melody*] [*Music*] ... COL C
Col Legno [*With the Back of the Bow*] [*Music*] ... CL
Cola [*or Colatus*] [*Strain See also COLAT*] [*Pharmacy*] ... COL
[*The*] **Cola Clan** [*Later, Coca-Cola Collectors Club International*] (EA) ... TCC
Colatitude [*Navigation*] ... CO-L
Colatus [*Strained*] [*See also COL*] [*Pharmacy*] ... COLAT
Colborne Public Library, Ontario [*Library symbol National Library of Canada*] (BIB) ... OCOLB
Colbphon (BARN) ... col
Colby College, Waterville, ME [*OCLC symbol*] (OCLC) ... CBY
Colby College, Waterville, ME [*Library symbol Library of Congress*] (LCLS) ... MeWC
Colby Community College, Colby, KS [*Library symbol Library of Congress*] (LCLS) ... KColC
Colby Junior College for Women [*Later, CSC*] [*New Hampshire*] ... CJCW
Colby Junior College for Women [*Later, CSC*], New London, NH [*Inactive*] [*OCLC symbol*] (OCLC) ... CYC
Colby Junior College for Women [*Later, CSC*], New London, NH [*Library symbol Library of Congress*] (LCLS) ... NhNelC
Colby, KS [*Location identifier FAA*] (FAAL) ... CBK
Colby, KS [*Television station call letters*] ... KLBY
Colby, KS [*FM radio station call letters*] ... KQLS
Colby, KS [*FM radio station call letters*] ... KTCC
Colby, KS [*AM radio station call letters*] ... KXXX
Colby on Mortgage Foreclosures [*A publication*] (DLA) ... Col Mort
Colby Resources Corp. [*Vancouver Stock Exchange symbol*] ... CY
Colby's Criminal Law and Practice [*New York*] [*A publication*] (DLA) ... Col Crim Law
Colby's Massachusetts Practice [*A publication*] (DLA) ... Co Mass Pr
Colby's Massachusetts Practice [*A publication*] (DLA) ... Col Mass Pr
Colby's Practice [*A publication*] (DLA) ... Colb Pr
Colby-Sawyer College [*Formerly, CJCW*] [*New London, NH*] ... CSC
Colcemid [*Demecolcine*] [*Antineoplastic drug*] ... CMD
Colchester [*Municipal borough in England*] ... COLCH
Colchester [*Vermont*] [*Seismograph station code, US Geological Survey*] (SEIS) ... COV
Colchester - East Hants Regional Library, Truro, Nova Scotia [*Library symbol National Library of Canada*] (NLC) ... NSTC
Colchester Historical Society, Truro, Nova Scotia [*Library symbol National Library of Canada*] (BIB) ... NSTCH
Colchester, VT [*FM radio station call letters*] ... WWPV
Colchester-East Hants Regional Library, Truro, NS, Canada [*Library symbol Library of Congress*] (LCLS) ... CaNSTC
Colchicine [*Biochemistry*] ... CCH
Colchicine Binding Site on Tubulin [*Biochemistry*] ... CBST
Colchicine Sensitivity [*Medicine*] (DMAA) ... CLCS
Colchicine-Binding Protein [*Biochemistry*] ... CBP
Colchicine-Blocked Meiosis [*Biology*] (DOG) ... C-meiosis
Colchicine-Blocked Metaphase [*Biology*] (DOG) ... C-metaphase
Colchicine-Blocked Mitosis [*Biology*] (DOG) ... C-mitosis
Colchis Resources Ltd. [*Vancouver Stock Exchange symbol*] ... CLK
Cold ... C
Cold Acclimated [*Physiology*] ... CA
Cold Agglutination [*Test*] [*Clinical chemistry*] ... CA
Cold Agglutinin Disease [*Medicine*] (DMAA) ... CAD
Cold Agglutinin Syndrome [*Medicine*] (DMAA) ... CAS
Cold Air ... CA
Cold Air Mass [*Meteorology*] (BARN) ... k
Cold Air Turbine Drive (MCD) ... CATD
Cold and Hot Isostatic Pressing [*Materials science and technology*] ... CHIP
Cold and Hot Water ... CHW
Cold Bay [*Alaska*] [*Seismograph station code, US Geological Survey Closed*] (SEIS) ... CBA
Cold Bay [*Alaska*] [*Airport symbol*] (OAG) ... CDB
Cold Bay [*Alaska*] [*ICAO location identifier*] (ICLI) ... PACD
Cold Bay, AK [*Location identifier FAA*] (FAAL) ... CDB
Cold Brine Pump ... CBPMP
Cold Canvassing [*Business term*] ... CC
Cold Cathode Discharge ... CCD
Cold Cathode Electron Beam LASER (MCD) ... CCEBL
Cold Cathode Fluorescent Technology ... CCFT
Cold Cathode Fluorescent Tube ... CCFT
Cold Cathode Gauge Experiment [*Apollo*] [*NASA*] ... CCGE
Cold Cathode Ion Gauge ... CCIG
Cold Cathode Ion Source ... CCIS
Cold Cranking Ampere ... CCA
Cold Cranking Simulator Test [*for petroleum products*] ... CCS
Cold Dark Matter [*Astronomy*] ... CDM
Cold Filament Resistance ... CFR
Cold Filter Plugging Point ... CFPP
Cold Finished Steel Bar Institute (EA) ... CFSBI
Cold Flow Development Test System [*AEC*] ... CFDTS
Cold Flow Electric LASER (MCD) ... CFEL

Cold Flow Laboratory [*Martin Marietta Corp.*] .... CFL
Cold Flow Test .... CFT
Cold Fluctuating Temperature .... CFT
Cold Fluid (DICI) .... CF
Cold Fog Dissipation System .... CFD
Cold Front [*NWS*] (FAAC) .... CDFNT
Cold Front [*Meteorology*] .... CF
Cold Front Passage [*NWS*] (FAAC) .... CFP
Cold Fusion Markup Language [*Computer science*] (PCM) .... CFML
Cold Heading Wire .... CHW
Cold High Pressure Separator [*Chemical engineering*] .... CHPS
Cold, Hungry, and Dry [*Slang*] .... CH and D
Cold Intermediate Layer [*Oceanography*] CIL
Cold Isostatically Pressed [*Materials processing*] .... CIP
Cold Junction .... CJ
Cold Junction Box (MHDI) .... CJB
Cold Knife Conization [*Gynecology*] (DAVI) .... CKC
Cold Lake [*Canada*] [*Airport symbol*] (OAG) .... YOD
Cold Lake Canadian Forces Base, AB [*ICAO location identifier*] (ICLI) .... CYOD
Cold Lake Municipal Library, Alberta [*Library symbol National Library of Canada*] (NLC) .... ACLM
Cold Lake Municipal Library, Cold Lake, AB, Canada [*Library symbol Library of Congress*] (LCLS) .... CaACLM
Cold Leg [*Nuclear energy*] .... COLG
Cold Leg Check Valve [*Nuclear energy*] (NRCH) CLCV
Cold Leg Isolation Valve [*Nuclear energy*] (NRCH) CLIV
Cold Leg Temperature [*Nuclear energy*] (NRCH) .... TC
Cold Maritime Polar Air Mass [*Meteorology*] (BARN) .... mPK
Cold Metal Products [*NYSE symbol*] (SAG) .... CLQ
Cold Metals Products [*Associated Press*] (SAG) .... ColdMtl
Cold Molded Thermoforming [*Fiberglass production*] .... COMOFORM
Cold Molecular Weld .... CMW
Cold Month Mean Temperture [*Climatology*] .... CMMT
Cold Neutron Research Facility [*Physics*] .... CNRF
Cold Ocean-Warm Land [*Climatology*] .... COWL
Cold Pack [*Medicine*] .... CP
Cold Pipe [*Nuclear energy*] (NRCH) .... CP
Cold Plate Support Structure (MCD) .... CPSS
Cold Presors [*or Pressure*] Test [*Cardiology*] (DAVI) .... CPT
Cold Press [*Metallurgy*] (IAA) .... CP
Cold Press Molding .... PM
Cold Pressor Recovery Index (PDAA) .... CPRI
Cold Pressor Response Test [*Medicine*] .... CPR
Cold Pressor Response Test [*Medicine*] .... CPRT
Cold Protective Response [*Physiology*] .... CPR
Cold Regions Engineering Laboratory .... CREL
Cold Regions Research and Engineering Laboratory [*Hanover, NH*] [*Army Also, an information service or system*] (IID) .... CRREL
Cold Regions Research Co. (MCD) .... CRRC
Cold Regions Science and Technology Information Analysis Center [*DoD*] (MSC) .... CRSTIAC
Cold Regions Test Center [*Seattle, WA*] [*Army*] (RDA) .... CRTC
Cold Rocket Instrument Carrying Kit .... CRICKET
Cold Rolled Sections Association [*British*] (DBA) .... CRSA
Cold Running Intelligibility [*Test for hearing continuous speech*] (BABM) .... CRI
Cold Shutdown [*Nuclear energy*] (NRCH) .... CSD
Cold Side .... CSD
Cold Splice Miter-Joint .... CSM
Cold Spring Community Library, Cold Spring, MN [*Library symbol*] [*Library of Congress*] (LCLS) .... MnCls
Cold Spring Elementary/Rocori Junior School, Cold Spring, MN [*Library symbol*] [*Library of Congress*] (LCLS) .... MnClsE
Cold Spring Harbor Biological Laboratory, Cold Spring Harbor, NY [*Library symbol Library of Congress*] (LCLS) .... NCshB
Cold Spring Harbor Laboratory [*Cold Spring Harbor, NY*] .... CSH
Cold Spring Harbor Public Library, Cold Spring Harbor, NY [*Library symbol Library of Congress*] (LCLS) .... NCsh
Cold Spring Harbor Public Library, Cold Spring Harbor, NY [*Library symbol*] [*Library of Congress*] (LCLS) .... NCshL
Cold Spring, MN [*FM radio station call letters*] .... KMXK
Cold Stabilized [*Automotive engineering*] .... CS
Cold Start Entry [*Computer science*] .... CSE
Cold Start Injector [*Automotive engineering*] .... CSI
Cold Start Spark Advance [*Automotive engineering*] .... CSSA
Cold Start Spark Hold [*Automotive engineering*] .... CSSH
Cold Storage .... CS
Cold Storage and Ice Association of Victoria [*Australia*] .... CSIAV
Cold Storage Association of Queensland [*Australia*] .... CSAQ
Cold Storage Association of Tasmania [*Australia*] .... CSAT
Cold Storage Association of the Northern Territory [*Australia*] .... CSANT
Cold Storage Association of Western Australia .... CSAWA
Cold Temperature Carbon Monoxide Test Procedure [*Exhaust emissions testing*] [*Automotive engineering*] .... CTCOTP
Cold to the Opposite and Warm to the Same Side [*Audiometry*] .... COWS
Cold Transient [*Automotive engineering*] .... CT
Cold Type Composition [*Selection of Printing Industries of America*] .... CTC
Cold Vapor Atomic Absorption Spectrometry [*Also, CVAAS*] .... CVAA
Cold Vapor Atomic Absorption Spectrometry [*Also, CVAA*] .... CVAAS
Cold Wall .... CW
Cold War (CINC) .... CW
Cold War Activities Group [*Military*] (CINC) .... CWAG
Cold War Council .... CWC
Cold Water [*Technical drawings*] .... CW
Cold Water Reactor Test Assembly .... CWTA
Cold Water Tank .... CWT

Cold Water Temperature .... CWT
Cold Water Treatment [*Medicine*] .... CWT
Cold Weather Clothing and Individual Equipment [*Military*] .... CWCE
Cold Weather Exercise [*Military*] (NVT) .... COWEAEX
Cold Weather Injury [*Military*] .... CWINJ
Cold Weather Landing Exercise [*Military*] (NVT) .... COWLEX
Cold Weather Materiel Test Unit [*Military*] .... CWMTU
Cold Weather Modulator [*Automotive engineering*] .... CWM
Cold Weather Operations [*Military*] .... CWOP
Cold Weld [*Mechanics*] (BARN) .... CW
Cold Weld Evaluation Device (OA) .... CWED
Cold Welding .... CW
Cold-Cathode Fluorescent Lamp (PCM) .... CCFL
Cold-Cathode Fluorescent Lamp .... CFL
Cold-Drawn [*Metal*] .... CD
Cold-Drawn Copper (MSA) .... CDC
Cold-Drawn Steel .... CDS
Cold-Extractable Copper .... cxCu
Cold-Finished [*Metal*] (MSA) .... CF
Cold-Finished Steel (MSA) .... CFS
Cold-Finished Steel Bar .... CFSB
Coldfoot, AK [*Location identifier FAA*] (FAAL) .... CXF
Cold-Induced Vasodilation .... CIVD
Cold-Insoluble Fibrinogen [*Hematology*] .... CIF
Cold-Insoluble globulin [*Cytochemistry*] .... CIg
Cold-Iron Soldered Joint (IAA) CI
Coldplate (KSC) .... CP
Coldplate Clamp .... CPC
Cold-Punched [*Metal*] .... CP
Cold-Rolled [*Metal*] .... CR
Cold-Rolled and Tempered [*Metal*] .... CRT
Cold-Rolled Close-Annealed [*Metal*] .... CRCA
Cold-Rolled Half Hard [*Metal*] .... CRHH
Cold-Rolled Non-Oriented [*Metallurgy*] .... CRNO
Cold-Rolled Steel .... CRS
Cold-Rolled Steel (IAA) .... CRST
Coldset Offset [*Printing*] (DGA) .... CO
Cold-Shock Domain [*Genetics*] .... CSD
Cold-Shock Protein [*Biochemistry*] .... CSP
Coldspring Resources [*Vancouver Stock Exchange symbol*] .... CGB
Coldstream Guards [*British military*] .... CG
Coldstream Guards [*British military*] (DMA) .... Cm Gds
Coldstream's Scotch Court of Session Procedure [*A publication*] (DLA) .... Colds Pr
Cold-Temperature-Actuated Vacuum [*Automotive engineering*] .... CTAV
Cold-Water Detergent .... CWD
Coldwater Memorial Public Library, Ontario [*Library symbol National Library of Canada*] (BIB) .... OCOLD
Coldwater, MI [*FM radio station call letters*] .... WNWN
Coldwater, MI [*AM radio station call letters*] .... WTVB
Coldwater, MS [*FM radio station call letters*] .... WVIM
Coldwater Public Library, Coldwater, MI [*Library symbol Library of Congress*] (LCLS) .... MiCw
Cold-Water Soluble .... CWS
Coldwell's Reports [*41-47 Tennessee*] [*A publication*] (DLA) .... Col
Coldwell's Reports [*41-47 Tennessee*] [*A publication*] (DLA) .... Cold (Tenn)
Coldwell's Reports [*41-47 Tennessee*] [*A publication*] (DLA) .... Coldw
Coldwell's Reports [*41-47 Tennessee*] [*A publication*] (DLA) .... Coldw (Tenn)
Coldwell's Reports [*41-47 Tennessee*] [*A publication*] (DLA) .... Coldwell
Coldwell's Tennessee Supreme Court Reports [*1860-70*] [*A publication*] (DLA) .... Cold
Cold-Worked [*Nuclear energy*] (NRCH) .... CW
Cole Country Band Fan Club (EA) .... CCBFC
Cole. Criminal Informations [*1843*] [*A publication*] (DLA) .... Cole Cr Inf
Cole. Ejectment [*1857*] [*A publication*] (DLA) .... Cole Ejec
Cole. Ejectment [*1857*] [*A publication*] (DLA) .... Cole Eject
Cole National [*NYSE symbol*] (TTSB) .... CNJ
Cole National Corp. [*Associated Press*] (SAG) .... ColeNatl
Cole. Particulars and Conditions of Sale [*1879*] [*A publication*] (DLA) .... Cole Cond
Cole Taylor Financial Group, Inc. [*Associated Press*] (SAG) .... CTaylor
Cole Taylor Financial Group, Inc. [*NASDAQ symbol*] (SAG) .... CTFG
Cole Taylor Financial Grp [*NASDAQ symbol*] (TTSB) .... CTFG
Colebrooke's Digest of Hindu Law [*A publication*] (DLA) .... Cole Dig
Colectivo Latinoamericano de Trabajo Psico-Social [*Belgium*] .... COLAT
Colegio de Mexico, Mexico, Mexico City, Mexico [*Library symbol Library of Congress*] (LCLS) .... MxMCM
Colegio Ibero-Latino-Americano de Dermatologia [*Ibero Latin American College of Dermatology - ILACD*] (EA) .... CILAD
Colegio Universitario de Cayey, Cayey, PR [*Library symbol Library of Congress*] (LCLS) .... PrCaC
Colegio Universitario del Sagrado Corazon [*College of the Sacred Heart*], Santurce, PR [*Library symbol Library of Congress*] (LCLS) .... PrSaC
Colel Hibath Jerusalem [*Society of the Devotees of Jerusalem*] (EA) .... CHJ
Coleman [*Alberta*] [*Seismograph station code, US Geological Survey Closed*] (SEIS) .... CLM
Coleman [*Germany ICAO location identifier*] (ICLI) .... EDOR
Coleman and Caines' Cases [*New York*] [*A publication*] (DLA) .... C & C
Coleman and Caines' Cases [*New York*] [*A publication*] (DLA) .... Col & C Cas
Coleman and Caines' Cases [*New York*] [*A publication*] (DLA) .... Col & Cai
Coleman and Caines' Cases [*New York*] [*A publication*] (DLA) .... Col & Cai Cas
Coleman and Caines' Cases [*New York*] [*A publication*] (DLA) .... Col & Caines Cas (NY)
Coleman and Caines' Cases [*New York*] [*A publication*] (DLA) .... Cole & Cai Cas
Coleman and Caines' Cases [*New York*] [*A publication*] (DLA) .... Colem & C Cas

Coleman Area Library, Coleman, MI [Library symbol Library of Congress]
(LCLS) .... MiCole
Coleman Collieries [Vancouver Stock Exchange symbol] .... CMN
Coleman Co. [NYSE symbol] (TTSB) .... CLN
Coleman Co., Inc. [NYSE symbol] (SPSG) .... CLN
Coleman Co., Inc. [Associated Press] (SAG) .... Colemn
Coleman, MI [FM radio station call letters] .... WPRJ
Coleman, TX [Location identifier FAA] (FAAL) .... COM
Coleman, TX [AM radio station call letters] .... KSTA
Coleman, TX [FM radio station call letters] .... KSTA-FM
Coleman's Cases [New York] [A publication] (DLA) CC
Coleman's Cases [New York] [A publication] (DLA) .... Cole Cas
Coleman's Cases [New York] [A publication] (DLA) .... Cole Cas Pr
Coleman's Cases [New York] [A publication] (DLA) .... Cole Cases
Coleman's Cases [New York] [A publication] (DLA) .... Colem
Coleman's Cases [New York] [A publication] (DLA) .... Colem Cas
Coleman's Cases [New York] [A publication] (DLA) .... Coleman
Coleman's Cases of Practice [New York] [A publication] (DLA) .... Col Cas
Coleman's Cases of Practice [New York] [A publication] (DLA) .... Col Cas (NY)
Coleman's Reports [99, 101-106, 110-129 Alabama] [A publication] (DLA) .... Col
Coleman's Reports [99, 101-106, 110-129 Alabama] [A publication] (DLA) ...... Cole
Colentur [Let Them Be Strained] [Pharmacology] (DAVI) .... colen
Colentur [Let Them Be Strained] [Pharmacy] (ROG) .... COLENT
Coleoptera [Entomology] .... Col
Coleopterists' Society (EA) .... CS
Coleoptile Node-Tillers of Wheat [Plant pathology] .... CNT
Coleraine, MN [FM radio station call letters] .... KGPZ
Coleraine Public Library, Coleraine, MN [Library symbol] [Library of Congress] (LCLS) .... MnCol
Coleridge [England] .... COLER
Coler's Law of Municipal Bonds [A publication] (DLA) .... Col Mun B
Coles Associates Ltd., Charlottetown, PE, Canada [Library symbol] [Library of Congress] (LCLS) .... CaPCCOA
Coles Associates Ltd., Charlottetown, Prince Edward Island [Library symbol National Library of Canada] (NLC) .... PCCOA
Cole's Edition of Iowa Reports [A publication] (DLA) .... Cole
Coles Elementary School, Glen Cove, NY [Library symbol] [Library of Congress] .... NGlcCE
Coles Myer Ltd. [NYSE symbol] (CTT) .... CM
Coles Myer Ltd. [Australia] .... CML
Coles Myer Ltd. [Associated Press] (SAG) .... ColeMyr
Coles Myer Ltd ADR [NYSE symbol] (TTSB) .... CM
Coles Signal Laboratory [Army] (MCD) .... CSL
Colesburg [South Africa] [ICAO location identifier] (ICLI) .... FACB
Coletur [Let It Be Strained] [Pharmacy] .... COLET
Colfax Energy [Vancouver Stock Exchange symbol] .... CFX
Colfax Free Public Library, Colfax, IA [Library symbol Library of Congress] (LCLS) .... IaCol
Colfax, IL [FM radio station call letters] (RBYB) .... WAPU-FM
Colfax Public Library, Colfax, IN [Library symbol] [Library of Congress] (LCLS) .... InColf
Colfax, WA [AM radio station call letters] .... KCLX
Colfax, WA [FM radio station call letters] .... KRAO
Colgan Airways [ICAO designator] (AD) .... CJ
Colgate, SK [Television station call letters] CKCK-1
Colgate University (GAGS) .... Colgate U
Colgate University, Hamilton, NY [Library symbol Library of Congress] (LCLS) .... NHC
Colgate University, Hamilton, NY [OCLC symbol] (OCLC) VVC
Colgate-Palmolive [NYSE symbol] (TTSB) CL
Colgate-Palmolive Co. [NYSE symbol] (SPSG) CL
Colgate-Palmolive Co. [Associated Press] (SAG) .... ColgP
Colgate-Palmolive Co. [Associated Press] (SAG) .... ColgPal
Colgate-Palmolive Co., Technical Information Center, Piscataway, NJ [Library symbol Library of Congress] (LCLS) .... NjPwC
Colgate-Palmolive,$4.25 Pfd [NYSE symbol] (TTSB) .... CLPr
Colgate-Rochester Divinity School [Rochester, NY] .... CRDS
Colgate-Rochester Divinity School, Library, Rochester, NY [OCLC symbol] (OCLC) .... VQE
Colgate-Rochester Divinity School, Rochester, NY [Library symbol Library of Congress] (LCLS) .... NRCR
Coli Genetic Stock Center .... CGSC
Colicine Factor [Immunology] .... CF
Coliform Count [Microbiology] (OA) CC
Coliform Growth Response [Bioassay] .... CGR
Coligacao Democratico Social [Portugal] [Political party] (ECED) .... CDU
Colima [Mexico ICAO location identifier] (ICLI) .... MMIA
Colima Resources Ltd. [Vancouver Stock Exchange symbol] .... CJA
Colin Energy Corp. [Toronto Stock Exchange symbol] .... CN
Colistimethate-Nystatin-Vancomycin [Antibiotic mixture] .... CNV
Colistin [Also, CO] [Generic form] [An antibiotic] CL
Colistin [Also, CL] [Generic form An antibiotic] .... CO
Colistin [or Colimycin] - Nalidixic Acid [Antibacterial combination] [Clinical chemistry] .... CNA
Colla [With The] [Music] (ROG) C
Colla Destra [With the Right Hand] [Music] .... CD
Colla Parte [With the Solo Part] [Music] (ROG) .... COL P
Colla Parte [With the Solo Part] [Music] .... CP
Colla Sinistra [With the Left Hand] [Music] .... CS
Colla Voce [With the Voice] [Music] .... C VOC
Colla Voce [With the Voice] [Music] .... COL VO
Colla Voce [With the Voice] [Music] (ROG) .... COL VOCE
Colla Voce [With the Voice] [Music] CV
Collaborate [or Collaborator] (ROG) .... COLLAB
Collaboration (VRA) .... colab

Collaborative .... CLLBRTV
Collaborative Access Team .... CAT
Collaborative Atmospheric Boundary Layer Experiment (PDAA) .... CABLE
Collaborative Authoring Production and Transmission of Interactive Video for Education (AIE) .... CAPTIVE
Collaborative Clinical Research, Inc. [NASDAQ symbol] (SAG) .... CCLR
Collaborative Clinical Research, Inc. [Associated Press] (SAG) .... CollbClin
Collaborative Computational Projects [Daresbury Laboratory] [British] (IRUK) .... CCP
Collaborative Computing Environment .... CCE
Collaborative Corneal Transplantation Studies .... CCTS
Collaborative Forecasting and Replenishment [Computer science] .... CFAR
Collaborative International Pesticides Analytical Council Ltd. [See also CIMAP] [Wageningen, Netherlands] (EAIO) .... CIPAC
Collaborative Library System Development .... CLSD
Collaborative Ocular Melanoma Study [Medicine] .... COMS
Collaborative Perinatal Project .... CPP
Collaborative Pesticide Analytical Committee (DICI) .... CPAC
Collaborative Radiological Health Laboratory [Colorado State University] [Department of Health and Human Services Research center] (RCD) .... CRHL
Collaborative Research and Development Agreement .... CRADA
Collaborative Research Group [Of scientific institute] .... CRG
Collaborative Research, Inc. .... CR
Collaborative Research Support Program [Agency for International Development] .... CRSP
Collaborative UK Twin Location Auroral Sounding System [A radar interferometer with antennae in Finland and Iceland] .... CUTLASS
Collage (VRA) .... col
Collagen [Biochemistry] .... COL
Collagen [Biochemistry] .... COLL
Collagen Antigen [Immunology] (DAVI) .... CA
Collagen Corp. [NASDAQ symbol] (NQ) .... CGEN
Collagen Corp. [Associated Press] (SAG) .... Colagen
Collagen Matrix Support [Cell culture] .... CMS
Collagen Sponge Contraceptive .... CSC
Collagen Synthesis Inhibitory Factor [Biochemistry] .... CSIF
Collagen Vascular Disease [Medicine] .... CVD
Collagenase-Digestible Protein .... CDP
CollaGenex Pharmaceuticals, Inc. [NASDAQ symbol] (SAG) .... CGPI
CollaGenex Pharmaceuticals, Inc. [Associated Press] (SAG) .... ColGenx
Collagen-Glycosaminoglycan [Physiology] .... CG
Collagen-Induced Arthritis [Medicine] .... CIA
Collagen-Induced Autoimmune Ear Disease [Immunology and otorhinolaryngology] (DAVI) .... CIAED
Collapse .... COLPS
Collapsible Airborne Military Equipment Lifter .... CAMEL
Collapsible Maintenance Hangar (MCD) .... CMH
Collapsible Maintenance Shelter (MCD) .... CMS
Collapsible Mobile Hangar (MCD) .... CMH
Collapsible Mobile Shelter (MCD) .... CMS
Collapsible Rollup Antenna Mast .... CRAM
Collapsible Tube Manufacturers' Association [British] (BI) .... CTMA
Collar (MSA) .... CLR
Collar .... COL
Collar Pricing [Investment term] .... CP
Collar Tie .... CT
Coll'arco [With the Bow] [Music] .... CA
Collarette [Horticulture] .... Coll
Collate .... COL
Collate (WGA) .... COLL
Collated (ROG) .... COLD
Collated (ROG) .... COLLD
Collated and Perfect (ADA) .... C & P
Collateral C
Collateral .... CLLTRL
Collateral (WGA) .... COL
Collateral .... COLL
Collateral (WDMC) .... coll
Collateral [Finance] .... COLLAT
Collateral Action Officer [Army] (AABC) .... CAO
Collateral Branches [Genealogy] (ROG) .... COLLS
Collateral Damage Distance (AABC) .... CDD
Collateral Duty Alcoholism Counselor [Navy] (NVT) .... CODAC
Collateral Duty Inspector (MCD) .... CDI
Collateral Loan Brokers Association of New York (EA) .... CLBANY
Collateral Recurring Document Listing [Defense Intelligence Agency] (DNAB) .... CRDL
Collateral Trust [Bond] .... CLT
Collateral Trust (DLA) .... Coll Tr
Collateral Trust [Bond] .... CT
Collateral Trust Bond [Investment term] .... CTB
Collateralized Automobile Receivable Security .... CARS
Collateralized Bond Obligation [Investment term] (DFIT) .... CBO
Collateralized Depository Receipt [Finance] (EMRF) .... CDR
Collateralized Lease Equipment (TDOB) .... CLEO
Collateralized Loan Obligation (TDOB) .... CLO
Collateralized Mortgage Obligation [Federal Home Loan Mortgage Corp.] .... CMO
Collating and Binding .... CAB
Collatio [Novels of Justinian] [A publication] (DSA) .... Coll
Collation [Online database field identifier] .... CLLT
Collation [Online database field identifier] .... COL
Collation [Library science] (WDMC) .... COL
Collationes Brugenses (BJA) .... CBrug
Collationes Gandavenses (BJA) .... CGand

Collatis Pecuniis Poni Curaverunt [*They Collected the Money and Had Put in Position*] [*Latin*] .... CPPC
Collato [*Collated*] [*Latin*] .... COLL
Collator .... COLL
Collbran Public Library, Collbran, CO [*Library symbol Library of Congress*] (LCLS) .... CoCol
Colle Del Gigante [*Italy ICAO location identifier*] (ICLI) .... LIMI
Colleague (WGA) .... COL
Colleague .... COLL
Collect .... COL
Collect (WDMC) .... col
Collect (WDMC) .... coll
Collect [*or Collection*] (AFM) .... COLL
Collect Adapter .... CLAD
Collect and Transmit (DNAB) .... CAT
Collect Bill of Lading (AAGC) .... CBL
Collect Call [*Telecommunications*] (TEL) CC
Collect on Delivery (DFIT) .... COD
Collect On Delivery (WDMC) .... COD
Collectable .... CLLCTABL
Collectanea Alexandrina [*A publication*] (OCD) .... Coll Alex
Collectanea Juridica [*England*] [*A publication*] (DLA) .... Co Jurid
Collectanea Juridica [*A publication*] (DLA) .... Coll Jurid
Collecte Selective Quebec (AC) .... CSQ
Collected (ROG) .... COLLD
Collected Algorithm for Learning Machines [*Computer science*] .... CALM
Collected Alongside Ship [*Shipping*] .... CAS
Collected [*or Delivered*] by Barge [*Shipping*] .... C by B
Collected [*or Delivered*] by Truck [*Shipping*] .... C by T
Collected Least Squares [*Statistics*] .... CLS
Collected or Delivered by Truck or Barge [*Shipping*] .... C or D by T or B
Collected Original Resources in Education [*Carfax Publishing*] (NITA) .... CORE
Collectible .... CLLCTIBL
Collectif de Defense des Usagers de l'Acupuncture (AC) .... CODUA
Collectif de Recherche et d'Information Sociales [*Collective of Research and Social Information*] [*Canada*] .... CRIS
Collectif d'Information et de Travail Anti-Imperialiste [*Collective of Information and Anti-Imperialist Labour*] [*Canada*] .... CITA
Collectif d'Informations Sexuelles et Sexologiques [*Collective of Sexual Information and Sexology*] [*Canada*] .... CISS
Collecting (MSA) .... CLTG
Collecting Tubule (MAE) .... CT
Collection (WDAA) .... COL
Collection (VRA) .... coll
Collection .... COLLECT
Collection .... COLLN
Collection Activity Reports [*IRS*] .... CAR
Collection Advisory Center (MCD) .... CAC
Collection Agencies Association [*British*] (DBA) .... CAA
Collection Agency Practices .... CAP
Collection Agency Project [*Student legal action organization*] (EA) .... CAP
Collection Agent System for Hospitals [*Navy*] (GFGA) .... CASH
Collection Analysis Support Subsystem (MCD) .... CASS
Collection and Credit Agency (DLA) .... COLL & CR A
Collection and Delivery [*Shipping*] .... C & D
Collection and Distribution [*Transportation*] .... C & D
Collection and Jamming .... C & J
Collection Center [*FAA designator*] (FAAC) .... YPY
Collection/Classification/Cannibalization [*Military*] CCC
Collection, Classification, Cannibalization, and Field Expedients [*Military*] C3FE
Collection Control File [*Bureau of the Census*] (GFGA) .... CCF
Collection Coordination Facility (MCD) .... CCF
Collection Coordination Facility Support System (MCD) .... CCF-SS
Collection County Memorial Library, Walterboro, SC [*Library symbol*] [*Library of Congress*] (LCLS) .... ScW
Collection De Clercq. Catalogue Methodique et Raisonne: Antiquites Assyriens [*A publication*] (BJA) .... ColldeClercq
Collection des Tablettes Cuneiformes du Musee d'Art et d'Histoire de Geneve (BJA) .... MAH
Collection Development and Evaluation Section [*Reference and Adult Services Division*] [*American Library Association*] .... CODES
Collection Development Policy [*Libraries*] .... CDP
Collection Entry [*Banking*] CL
Collection, Holding, Transfer [*Shipboard waste disposal*] (MCD) .... CHT
Collection Intelligence Requirements (NVT) .... CIR
Collection Letter [*Business term*] (MHDB) .... Coll L
Collection Management [*A publication*] .... CM
Collection, Management, and Dissemination Section .... CMDS
Collection Management Authority (MCD) .... CMA
Collection Management Information System (MCD) .... COMIS
Collection Management System [*IRS*] .... CMS
Collection Nelson Rockefeller [*Identifying mark on art reproductions from the collection of Nelson Rockefeller*] .... CNR
Collection of Abstracts of Acts of Parliament [*A publication*] (DLA) .... Smee
[*A*] Collection of English Poems [*A publication*] .... CEP
Collection of Labor by Serial System (MCD) .... CLASS
Collection of the National Museum of Antiquities at Leiden (BJA) .... CNM
Collection on Wheels [*Shipping*] (DS) .... COW
Collection Operation Potential Yield System [*IRS*] .... COPYS
Collection Opportunity (MCD) .... COLOP
Collection Opportunity Requirements List (MCD) .... CORL
Collection, Repair, Evacuation (MCD) .... CRE
Collection/Requirements .... C/R
Collection Statute Expiration Date [*IRS*] .... COLSED

Collection Statute Expiration Date [*IRS*] .... CSED
Collection Voucher CV
Collective .... CLLCTV
Collective (MSA) .... CLTV
Collective Address Directory [*Navy*] (NVT) .... CAD
Collective address for NOTAM and SNOWTAM [*Switzerland ICAO location identifier*] (ICLI) .... LSZZ
Collective Address Group [*Navy*] (NVT) .... CAG
Collective Analysis Only (IAA) .... CAO
Collective Art Technology .... CAT
Collective Bancorp, Inc. [*NASDAQ symbol*] (NQ) .... COFD
Collective Bancorp, Inc. [*Associated Press*] (SAG) .... ColctBcp
Collective Bargaining (DCTA) .... CB
Collective Bargaining Institute [*New York, NY*] .... CBI
Collective Bargaining Negotiations and Contracts [*Bureau of National Affairs*] [*Information service or system*] .... CBNC
Collective Bargaining Organization .... CBO
Collective Bargaining Unit (MCD) .... CBU
Collective Black Artists (EA) .... CBA
Collective Call Sign [*Radio*] .... CCS
[*The*] Collective Catalogue of Belgium [*Database*] (IID) .... CCB
Collective Consciousness Society [*Vocal and instrumental group*] .... CCS
Collective Front-End Analysis (MCD) .... CFEA
Collective Investment Institution (MHDW) CII
Collective Measures Commission [*United Nations*] (DLA) .... CMC
Collective Negotiations .... CN
Collective of Self Help Groups [*Australia*] .... CSHG
Collective Pitch Lever .... CPL
Collective Protection [*from NBC contaminants*] [*Military*] (RDA) .... CP
Collective Protection Enclosure [*NBC contamination*] [*Military*] (RDA) .... CPE
Collective Protection Equipment .... CPE
Collective Protection Unit (IEEE) .... CPU
Collective Protective System [*Navy*] .... CPS
Collective Reserve Unit [*International finance*] .... CRU
Collective Security [*Army*] (MCD) .... COLSEC
Collective Stick Grip (MCD) .... CSG
Collective Television Reception (OA) .... CTR
Collective Trademark (MCD) .... CTM
Collective Training [*Army*] .... CT
Collective Training Facility [*Army*] (INF) .... CTF
Collective Training Plan [*Army*] .... CTP
Collective Training Range (MCD) .... CTR
Collective Volume [*Medicine*] (DAVI) .... coll vol
Collective-Bargaining Agreement .... CBA
Collective-Electronic Oscillator [*Physics*] .... CEO
Collective-Focusing Ion Accelerator (MCD) .... CFIA
Collectively (ROG) .... COLLECT
Collector [*Electronics*] C
Collector (IDOE) c
Collector [*Freight*] .... CLCT
Collector (DLA) .... Coll
Collector .... COLL
Collector [*Business term*] .... COLLR
Collector Capacitance (IDOE) .... C_c
Collector Car Appraisers Association (EA) .... CCAA
Collector Circle [*Defunct*] (EA) CC
Collector Coupled Structure (IAA) .... CCS
Collector Diffusion Isolation [*Electronics*] .... CDI
Collector, Diffusion, Isolation, Bipolar [*Electronics*] (NITA) .... CDIB
Collector Field Effect Register [*Electronics*] (OA) .... CFER
Collector of Public Moneys .... CPM
Collector Platemakers Guild (EA) .... CPG
Collector Ring [*Electricity*] .... CLRG
Collector Voltage (IDOE) .... V_c
Collector-Base (DNAB) .... CB
Collector-Region Width (IDOE) .... W_c
Collectors, Artists, and Dealers for Responsible Equity .... CADRE
Collector's Chronicle [*A publication*] CC
Collectors Club (EA) CC
Collectors Club, New York, NY [*Library symbol Library of Congress*] (LCLS) .... NNCo
Collectors Music Shop [*Record label*] .... CMS
Collectors of American Art (EA) .... CAA
Collectors of Numismatic Errors .... CONE
Collectors of Religion on Stamps (EA) .... COROS
Collectors of Unusual Data - International (EA) .... COUD-I
Collectors Record Club (EA) .... CRC
Collectors Record Society [*Record label*] .... CRS
Collectors Service Bureau (EA) .... CSB
Collectors Vehicle Specialists Association [*British*] (DBA) .... COVESA
Collector-Voltage Supply (IDOE) .... V_{cc}
Collects No Revenue [*Humorous interpretation for Canadian National Railways*] .... CNR
Colleen Casey Fan Club [*Defunct*] (EA) .... CCFC
College C
College (MCD) .... CLG
College (VRA) .... clg
College .... COL
College (WDMC) .... col
College .... COLG
College [*Army*] .... Colg
College [*or Collegiate*] .... COLL
College (WDMC) .... coll
College Ability Test .... CAT
College Admissions Assistance Center [*Defunct*] .... CAAC

College Admissions Center (EA) .... CAC
College Advanced Technology [*British technical colleges*] .... CAT
College, AK [*FM radio station call letters*] .... KSUA
College & Research Libraries [*A publication*] (BRI) .... CRL
College & Seminary Library, Inc., Naperville, IL [*Library symbol Library of Congress Obsolete*] (LCLS) .... INapC
College and University [*A publication*] (BRI) .... C & U
College and University [*A publication*] (DLA) .... Coll & U
College and University Booksellers' Group [*British*] .... CUBG
College and University Business Administration, Administrative Service [*National Association of College and University Business Officers*] [*A publication*] .... CUBA
College and University Computer Users Conference (EA) .... CUCUC
College and University Environment Scales [*Psychology*] .... CUES
College and University Machine Records Conference [*Later, CUCUC*] (EA) .... CUMREC
College and University Personnel Association (EA) .... CUPA
College and University Systems Exchange [*Acronym is now used as name of association*] .... CAUSE
College Andre Grasset, Montreal, PQ, Canada [*Library symbol Library of Congress*] (LCLS) .... CaQMCAG
College Andre Grasset, Montreal, Quebec [*Library symbol National Library of Canada*] (NLC) .... QMCAG
College Applicant Status Report [*Honeywell, Inc.*] [*Computer science*] ..... CASTOR
College Art Association (EA) .... CAA
College Art Association of America [*Later, CAA*] (EA) .... CAAA
College Assistance Migrant Program .... CAMP
College Athletic Business Management Association (EA) .... CABMA
College Band Directors National Association (EA) .... CBDNA
College Bibliocentre, Scarborough, Ontario [*Library symbol National Library of Canada*] (BIB) .... OSCB
[*The*] College Board (EA) .... TCB
College Board Admission Test (WDAA) .... CBAT
[*The*] College Board, New York, NY [*Library symbol*] [*Library of Congress*] (LCLS) .... NNCB
College Bois-De-Boulogne, Montreal, PQ, Canada [*Library symbol Library of Congress*] (LCLS) .... CaQMBB
College Bois-De-Boulogne, Montreal, Quebec [*Library symbol National Library of Canada*] (NLC) .... QMBB
[*The*] College Book of Verse [*A publication*] .... CBOV
College Bourgchemin (CEGEP) [*College d'Enseignement General et Professionnel*], Drummondville, PQ, Canada [*Library symbol Library of Congress*] (LCLS) .... CaQDCE
College Bourgchemin (CEGEP), Drummondville, Quebec [*Library symbol National Library of Canada*] (NLC) .... QDCE
College Bourget, Rigaud, PQ, Canada [*Library symbol Library of Congress*] (LCLS) .... CaQRCB
College Bourget, Rigaud, Quebec [*Library symbol National Library of Canada*] (NLC) .... QRCB
College Canadien des Enseignants [*Canadian College of Teachers - CCT*]..... CCE
College Cataloguing (ADA) .... COLCAT
College Caterers Association [*British*] (DBA) .... CCA
College Center of the Finger Lakes, Corning, NY [*Library symbol Library of Congress*] (LCLS) .... NCorniFL
College Certificate in Physical Education [*British*] .... CCPE
College Characteristics Analysis .... CCA
College Characteristics Index [*A questionnaire*] CCI
College Chemistry Consultants Service C3S
College Chips, Luther College, Decorah, IA [*Library symbol Library of Congress*] (LCLS) .... IaDCC
College Communautaire du New Brunswick, Bathurst, NB, Canada [*Library symbol Library of Congress*] (LCLS) .... CaNBBCC
College Communautaire du New Brunswick, Bathurst, New Brunswick [*Library symbol National Library of Canada*] (NLC) .... NBBCC
College Composition and Communication [*A publication*] (BRI) .... Col Comp
College Corner News, Liberty, IN [*Library symbol Library of Congress*] (LCLS) .... InLibCN
College Curriculum Support Project [*Bureau of the Census*] (GFGA) .... CCSP
College d'Alma, Lac St.-Jean, PQ, Canada [*Library symbol Library of Congress*] (LCLS) .... CaQALC
College d'Alma, Lac St.-Jean, Quebec [*Library symbol National Library of Canada*] (NLC) .... QALC
College de France, Paris, France [*Library symbol*] [*Library of Congress*] (LCLS) .... FrPCF
College de Joliette, Joliette, PQ, Canada [*Library symbol Library of Congress*] (LCLS) .... CaQJC
College de Joliette, Quebec [*Library symbol National Library of Canada*] (NLC) .... QJC
College de Jonquiere, Jonquiere, PQ, Canada [*Library symbol Library of Congress*] (LCLS) .... CaQJoC
College de Jonquiere, Quebec [*Library symbol National Library of Canada*] (NLC) .... QJOC
College de la Gaspesie, Gaspe, PQ, Canada [*Library symbol Library of Congress*] (LCLS) .... CaQGC
College de la Gaspesie, Gaspe, Quebec [*Library symbol National Library of Canada*] (NLC) .... QGC
College de la Prevention des Risques Technologiques [*College for the Prevention of Technological Risks*] [*France*] .... CPRT
College de la Region de l'Amiante (CEGEP), Thetford-Mines, Quebec [*Library symbol National Library of Canada*] (NLC) .... QTMC
College de l'Abitibi-Temiscamingue, Rouyn, Quebec [*Library symbol National Library of Canada*] (NLC) .... QRCN
College de l'Assomption, L'Assomption, PQ, Canada [*Library symbol Library of Congress*] (LCLS) .... CaQLASC

College de l'Assomption, Quebec [*Library symbol National Library of Canada*] (NLC) .... QLASC
College de Levis, Levis, PQ, Canada [*Library symbol Library of Congress*] (LCLS) .... CaQLeC
College de Levis, Quebec [*Library symbol National Library of Canada*] (NLC) .... QLC
College de Maisonneuve, Montreal, PQ, Canada [*Library symbol Library of Congress*] (LCLS) .... CaQMCDM
College de Maisonneuve, Montreal, Quebec [*Library symbol National Library of Canada*] (NLC) .... QMCDM
College de Matane, Quebec [*Library symbol National Library of Canada*] (NLC) .... QMATC
College de Montreal, Montreal, PQ, Canada [*Library symbol Library of Congress*] (LCLS) .... CaQMC
College de Montreal, Quebec [*Library symbol National Library of Canada*] (NLC) .... QMC
College de Rimouski, Rimouski, PQ, Canada [*Library symbol Library of Congress*] (LCLS) .... CaQRiC
College de Rouyn, Rouyn, PQ, Canada [*Library symbol Library of Congress Obsolete*] (LCLS) .... CaQRC
College de Ste.-Anne, La Pocatiere, Quebec [*Library symbol National Library of Canada*] (NLC) .... QPC
College de St.-Boniface, Manitoba [*Library symbol National Library of Canada*] (NLC) .... MSC
College de St. Boniface, St. Boniface, MB, Canada [*Library symbol Library of Congress*] (LCLS) .... CaMSC
College de Sainte-Anne, La Pocatiere, PQ, Canada [*Library symbol Library of Congress*] (LCLS) .... CaQPC
College de Shawinigan, Quebec [*Library symbol National Library of Canada*] (NLC) .... QSC
College de Sherbrooke (CEGEP) [*College d'Enseignement General et Professionnel*], Quebec [*Library symbol National Library of Canada*] (NLC) .... QSHERE
College de Sherbrooke (CEGEP) [*College d'Enseignement General et Professionnel*], Sherbrooke, PQ, Canada [*Library symbol Library of Congress*] (LCLS) .... CaQSherE
College de Victoriaville, Ecole du Meuble et du Bois Ouvre, Victoriaville, PQ, Canada [*Library symbol Library of Congress*] (LCLS) .... CaQVCEMBO
College de Victoriaville, Quebec [*Library symbol National Library of Canada*] (NLC) .... QVC
College de Victoriaville, Victoriaville, PQ, Canada [*Library symbol Library of Congress*] (LCLS) .... CaQVC
College d'Enseignement General et Professionnel [*College of General and Professional Instruction*] [*Canada*] .... CEGEP
College d'Enseignement General et Professionnel de l'Outaouais, Hull, PQ, Canada [*Library symbol Library of Congress*] (LCLS) .... CaQHC
College d'Enseignement General et Professionnel de Regional Cote Nord, Hauterive, PQ, Canada [*Library symbol Library of Congress*] (LCLS) .... CaQHaC
College d'Enseignement, Ste.-Foy, PQ, Canada [*Library symbol Library of Congress*] (LCLS) .... CaQSFC
College d'Enseignement, Ste.-Foy, Quebec [*Library symbol National Library of Canada*] (NLC) .... QSFC
College des Medecins de Famille du Canada (EAIO) .... CMFC
College Descriptive Index (EDAC) .... CDI
College Diploma in Agriculture [*British*] (DI) .... CDA
College Discovery [*Educational project for disadvantaged youngsters*] (EA) ...... CD
College Discovery and Development Program [*New York City*] (EDAC) .... CDDP
College Dominicain de Philosophie et de Theologie, Ottawa, ON, Canada [*Library symbol Library of Congress*] (LCLS) .... CaOOCDP
College Dominicain de Philosophie et de Theologie, Ottawa, Ontario [*Library symbol National Library of Canada*] (NLC) .... OOCDP
College du Nord Ouest, Rouyn, PQ, Canada [*Library symbol Library of Congress*] (LCLS) .... CaQRCN
College du Sacre-Coeur, Sherbrooke, PQ, Canada [*Library symbol Library of Congress*] (LCLS) .... CaQSherSC
College du Sacre-Coeur, Sherbrooke, Quebec [*Library symbol National Library of Canada*] (NLC) .... QSHERSC
College Edouard-Montpetit, Longueuil, PQ, Canada [*Library symbol Library of Congress*] (LCLS) .... CaQLoCE
College Edouard-Montpetit, Longueuil, Quebec [*Library symbol National Library of Canada*] (NLC) .... QLOCE
College Employers Links Project (AIE) .... CELP
College English Association (EA) .... CEA
College Entrance Examination Board [*Known as The College Board; acronym no longer used*] (EA) .... CEEB
College Eye Data Processing System [*Air Force*] (MCD) .... CEDPS
College - Fairbanks [*Alaska*] [*Seismograph station code, US Geological Survey Closed*] (SEIS) .... CMO
College Fiord [*Alaska*] [*Seismograph station code, US Geological Survey*] (SEIS) .... CFI
College Football Association (EA) .... CFA
College for Human Services [*Formerly, WTC*] .... CHS
College Fraternity Editors Association (EA) .... CFEA
College Fraternity Scholarship Officers Association .... CFSOA
College Fraternity Secretaries Association [*Later, FEA*] (EA) .... CFSA
College Heights Secondary School, Guelph, ON, Canada [*Library symbol*] [*Library of Congress*] (LCLS) .... CaOGCH
College Heights Secondary School, Guelph, Ontario [*Library symbol National Library of Canada*] (NLC) .... OGCH
College Institute Educators' Association of BC (AC) .... CIEA
College International de Podologie [*International College of Podology*] .... CIP
College International de Recherches Implantaires et Lariboisiere [*Rouen, France*] (EAIO) .... CIRIL
College International de Recherches pour la Production [*Later, CIESTPM*] (EAIO) .... CIRP

College International pour l'Etude Scientifique des Techniques de Production Mecanique [*International Institute for Production Engineering Research*] (EAIO) .... CIESTPM
College Inventory of Academic Adjustment [*Psychology*] .... CIAA
College Jean-De-Brebeuf, Montreal, PQ, Canada [*Library symbol Library of Congress*] (LCLS) .... CaQMDB
College Jean-De-Brebeuf, Montreal, Quebec [*Library symbol National Library of Canada*] (NLC) .... QMDB
College Jesus-Marie de Sillery, Quebec [*Library symbol National Library of Canada*] (NLC) .... QSILC
College Jesus-Marie de Sillery, Sillery, PQ, Canada [*Library symbol Library of Congress*] (LCLS) .... CaQSilC
College Lafleche, Trois-Rivieres, PQ, Canada [*Library symbol Library of Congress*] (LCLS) .... CaQTCL
College Lafleche, Trois-Rivieres, Quebec [*Library symbol National Library of Canada*] (NLC) .... QTCL
College Language Association (EA) .... CLA
College Law Bulletin [*A publication*] (DLA) .... Coll L Bull
College Law Digest [*A publication*] (DLA) .... Coll L Dig
College Letter [*British*] CL
College Level Academic Skills Project [*Florida*] (EDAC) .... CLASP
College Level Academic Skills Test .... CLAST
College Libraries Section [*Association of College and Research Libraries*] ...... CLS
College Lionel Groulx, Ste-Therese, Quebec [*Library symbol National Library of Canada*] (NLC) .... QMCLG
College Literature [*A publication*] (BRI) .... Col Lit
College Marguerite d'Youville, Ste.-Foy, PQ, Canada [*Library symbol Library of Congress*] (LCLS) .... CaQSFCM
College Marguerite d'Youville, Ste.-Foy, Quebec [*Library symbol National Library of Canada*] (NLC) .... QSFCM
College Mathieu, Gravelbourg, Saskatchewan [*Library symbol National Library of Canada*] (NLC) .... SGM
College Mathieu, Gravelbourg, SK, Canada [*Library symbol Library of Congress*] (LCLS) .... CaSGM
College Media Advisers (EA) .... CMA
College Media Journal [*A publication*] [*Alternative music*] (WDMC) .... CMJ
College Merici, Quebec, PQ, Canada [*Library symbol Library of Congress*] (LCLS) .... CaQQCM
College Merici, Quebec, Quebec [*Library symbol National Library of Canada*] (NLC) .... QQCM
College Militaire Royal [*Canada*] .... CMR
College Militaire Royal de Saint-Jean [*UTLAS symbol*] .... CMR
College Militaire Royal de Saint-Jean, Quebec [*Library symbol National Library of Canada*] (NLC) .... QSTJ
College Militaire Royal de Saint-Jean, Saint-Jean, PQ, Canada [*Library symbol Library of Congress*] (LCLS) .... CaQStJ
College Misericordia, Dallas, PA [*Library symbol Library of Congress*] (LCLS) .... PDalCM
College Music Society (EA) .... CMS
College of Aeronautics [*British*] .... COA
College of Agriculture and Forestry (AIE) .... CAF
College of Agriculture and Horticulture [*British*] (DI) .... CAH
College of American Pathologists (EA) .... CAP
College of Applied Arts and Technology .... CAAT
College of Art and Technology (AIE) .... CAT
College of Boca Raton, Boca Raton, FL [*Library symbol*] [*Library of Congress*] (LCLS) .... FBoC
College of Cape Breton, Archives and General Library, Sydney, NS, Canada [*Library symbol Library of Congress*] (LCLS) .... CaNSSXA
College of Cape Breton, Sydney, NS, Canada [*Library symbol Library of Congress*] (LCLS) .... CaNSSX
College of Chaplains [*of APHA*] (EA) .... COC-APHA
College of Charleston, Charleston, SC [*OCLC symbol*] (OCLC) .... SBM
College of Charleston, Charleston, SC [*Library symbol Library of Congress*] (LCLS) .... ScCC
College of Commerce (AIE) CC
College of Commerce and Technology (AIE) .... CCT
College of Creative Studies [*University of California, Santa Barbara*] .... CCS
College of Dieticians of Ontario [*L'Ordre des Dietetistes de l'Ontario*] (AC)..... CDO
College of Diplomates of the American Board of Orthodontics (EA) .... CDABO
College of Du Page, Glen Ellyn, IL [*OCLC symbol*] (OCLC) .... IBI
College of Du Page, Glen Ellyn, IL [*Library symbol Library of Congress*] (LCLS) .... IGleD
College of Eastern Utah, Price, UT [*Library symbol Library of Congress*] (LCLS) .... UPrE
College of Emmanuel and St. Chad, Saskatoon, Saskatchewan [*Library symbol National Library of Canada*] (NLC) .... SSESC
College of Emmanuel and St. Chad, Saskatoon, SK, Canada [*Library symbol Library of Congress*] (LCLS) .... CaSSESC
College of Emporia, Emporia, KS [*Library symbol Library of Congress*] (LCLS) .... KEmC
College of Engineers of Puerto Rico .... CEPR
College of Environmental Science and Forestry [*SUNY*] .... CESF
College of Estate Management [*British*] (BI) .... CEM
College of Family Physicians of Canada (EAIO) .... CFPC
College of Fisheries, St. John's, NF, Canada [*Library symbol Library of Congress*] (LCLS) .... CaNfSCF
College of Further and Higher Education (AIE) .... CFHE
College of Further Education (AIE) .... CFE
College of Future Education [*British*] .... F
College of General Practitioners [*British*] (BI) .... CGP
College of Great Falls [*Montana*] .... CGF
College of Great Falls, Great Falls, MT [*Library symbol Library of Congress*] (LCLS) .... MtGrCE
College of Health Sciences [*Iran*] .... CHS

College of Idaho, Caldwell, ID [*Library symbol Library of Congress*] (LCLS) .... IdCaC
College of Insurance (GAGS) .... C Insurance
College of Insurance, New York, NY [*Library symbol Library of Congress*] (LCLS) .... NNCI
College of Lake County, Grayslake, IL [*Library symbol Library of Congress*] (LCLS) .... IGralC
College of Law, University of Utah (DLA) .... CLUU
College of Librarianship Wales [*British*] (NITA) .... CLW
College of Marin, Kentfield, CA [*Library symbol Library of Congress*] (LCLS) .... CKenM
College of Marin, Kentfield, CA [*OCLC symbol*] (OCLC) .... CMK
College of Massage Therapists of Ontario (AC) .... CMTO
College of Medical Evangelists [*Los Angeles, CA*] .... CME
College of Medical Laboratory Technologists of Ontario (AC) .... CMLTO
College of Medicine and Dentistry of New Jersey [*Newark*] .... CMDNJ
College of Medicine and Dentistry of New Jersey, Newark, NJ [*OCLC symbol*] (OCLC) .... NJN
College of Mineral and Energy Resources [*West Virginia University*] (PDAA) .... COMER
College of Mount St. Joseph-On-The-Ohio, Mount St. Joseph, OH [*OCLC symbol*] (OCLC) .... CMJ
College of Mount St. Joseph-On-The-Ohio, Mount St. Joseph, OH [*Library symbol Library of Congress*] (LCLS) .... OMtsjC
College of Mount Saint Vincent, New York, NY [*Library symbol Library of Congress*] (LCLS) .... NNMtSV
College of Mount Saint Vincent, New York, NY [*OCLC symbol*] (OCLC) .... VZV
College of New Caledonia Library [*UTLAS symbol*] .... NCA
College of New Caledonia, Prince George, BC, Canada [*Library symbol Library of Congress*] (LCLS) .... CaBPGC
College of New Caledonia, Prince George, British Columbia [*Library symbol National Library of Canada*] (NLC) .... BPGC
College of New Rochelle (GAGS) .... C N Rochelle
College of New Rochelle [*New York*] .... CNR
College of New Rochelle, New Rochelle, NY [*Library symbol Library of Congress*] (LCLS) .... NNerC
College of New Rochelle, New Rochelle, NY [*OCLC symbol*] (OCLC) .... VZN
College of Notre Dame (GAGS) .... C Notre Dame
College of Notre Dame, Belmont, CA [*Library symbol Library of Congress*] (LCLS) .... CBelmN
College of Optometrists in Vision Development (EA) .... COVD
College of Optometry of Ontario .... COO
College of Osteopathic Healthcare Executives (EA) .... COHE
College of Osteopathic Medicine (DAVI) .... COM
College of Osteopathic Medicine and Surgery (OICC) .... COMS
College of Osteopathic Medicine and Surgery, Des Moines, IA [*Library symbol Library of Congress*] (LCLS) .... IaDmS
College of Osteopathic Physicians and Surgeons .... COPS
College of Our Lady of Mount Carmel, Washington, DC [*Library symbol Library of Congress*] (LCLS) .... DOLM
College of Our Lady of the Elms [*Chicopee, MA*] .... COLE
College of Our Lady of the Elms, Chicopee, MA [*Library symbol Library of Congress*] (LCLS) .... MChiL
College of Petroleum and Energy Studies [*British*] .... CPS
College of Petroleum and Minerals [*Dhahran, Saudi Arabia*] .... CPM
College of Phsicians & Surgeons of Saskatchewan (AC) .... CPSS
College of Physical Therapists of Alberta (AC) .... CPTA
College of Physicians and Surgeons, and School of Dentistry, San Francisco, CA [*Library symbol Library of Congress*] (LCLS) .... CSfCPS
College of Physicians of Philadelphia, Philadelphia, PA [*Library symbol Library of Congress OCLC symbol*] (LCLS) .... PPC
College of Physicians of Philadelphia, Philadelphia, PA [*Library symbol*] [*Library of Congress*] (LCLS) .... PPCP
College of Police Science, New York, NY [*Library symbol Library of Congress*] (LCLS) .... NNCPL
College of Preceptors [*British*] .... CP
College of Psychic Studies [*London*] .... CPS
College of St. Benedict [*St. Joseph, MN*] .... CSB
College of St. Benedict, St. Joseph, MN [*OCLC symbol*] (OCLC) .... MNF
College of St. Benedict, St. Joseph, MN [*Library symbol Library of Congress*] (LCLS) .... MnStjoS
College of St. Catherine [*St. Paul, MN*] .... CSC
College of St. Catherine, St. Paul, MN [*OCLC symbol*] (OCLC) .... MNE
College of St. Catherine, St. Paul, MN [*Library symbol Library of Congress*] (LCLS) .... MnSSC
College of Saint Elizabeth, Convent Station, NJ [*OCLC symbol*] (OCLC) .... CSE
College of Saint Elizabeth, Convent Station, NJ [*Library symbol Library of Congress*] (LCLS) .... NjConC
College of Saint Francis [*Joliet, IL*] .... CSF
College of Saint Francis, Joliet, IL [*OCLC symbol*] (OCLC) .... ICD
College of Saint Francis, Joliet, IL [*Library symbol Library of Congress*] (LCLS) .... IJolStF
College of Saint Gertrude, Library, Cottonwood, ID [*Library symbol*] [*Library of Congress*] (LCLS) .... IdCoStG
College of Saint Mary [*Omaha, NE*] .... CSM
College of Saint Mary of the Springs [*Ohio*] .... CSMS
College of Saint Mary-of-the-Wasatch, Salt Lake City, UT [*Library symbol Library of Congress Obsolete*] (LCLS) .... USIStM
[*The*] College of Saint Rose (GAGS) .... C St Rose
College of Saint Rose [*Albany, NY*] .... CSR
College of Saint Rose, Albany, NY [*Library symbol Library of Congress*] (LCLS) .... NAICSR
College of St. Scholastica (GAGS) .... C St Scholastica
College of Saint Scholastica [*Duluth, MN*] .... CSS

College of Saint Scholastica, Duluth, MN [*Library symbol Library of Congress*] (LCLS) .... MnDuStS
College of Saint Scholastica Library, Duluth, MN [*OCLC symbol*] (OCLC) .... MNS
College of Saint Teresa [*Winona, MN*] .... CST
College of Saint Teresa, Winona, MN [*Library symbol Library of Congress*] (LCLS) .... MnWinoCT
College of Saint Teresa, Winona, MN [*OCLC symbol*] (OCLC) .... MNZ
College of St. Thomas [*St. Paul, MN*] .... CST
College of St. Thomas, St. Paul, MN [*Library symbol Library of Congress*] (LCLS) .... MnSST
College of St. Thomas, St. Paul, MN [*OCLC symbol*] (OCLC) .... MNT
College of San Mateo [*California*] .... CSM
College of San Mateo Library, San Mateo, CA [*OCLC symbol*] (OCLC) .... CMT
College of San Mateo, San Mateo, CA [*Library symbol Library of Congress*] (LCLS) .... CSmatC
College of Santa Fe, Santa Fe, NM [*Library symbol Library of Congress*] (LCLS) .... NmSC
College of Santa Fe, Santa Fe, NM [*Library symbol*] [*Library of Congress*] (LCLS) .... NmSCS
College of Southern Idaho, Twin Falls, ID [*Library symbol*] [*Library of Congress*] (LCLS) .... IdTfSI
College of Speech Therapists [*British*] .... CST
College of Staten Island [*New York*] .... CSI
[*The*] **College of Staten Island of The City University of New York** (GAGS) .... C Staten Island (CUNY)
College of Staten Island, St. George Campus Library, Staten Island, NY [*OCLC symbol*] (OCLC) .... VSI
College of Staten Island, St. George Campus, Staten Island, NY [*Library symbol Library of Congress*] (LCLS) .... NSiCS
College of Steubenville, Steubenville, OH [*Library symbol Library of Congress*] (LCLS) .... OSteC
College of Technology and Art (AIE) .... CTA
College of the Albemarle, Dare County Center Library, Manteo, NC [*Library symbol*] [*Library of Congress*] (LCLS) .... NcManA
College of the Albemarle, Elizabeth City, NC [*Library symbol Library of Congress*] (LCLS) .... NcElcA
College of the Holy Cross [*Worcester, MA*] .... CHC
College of the Holy Cross, Worcester, MA [*OCLC symbol*] (OCLC) .... HCD
College of the Holy Cross, Worcester, MA [*Library symbol Library of Congress*] (LCLS) .... MWH
College of the Mainland, Texas City, TX [*Library symbol Library of Congress*] (LCLS) .... TxTCM
College of the Ozarks, Clarksville, AR [*Library symbol Library of Congress*] (LCLS) .... ArClC
College of the Sacred Heart [*Puerto Rico*] .... CSH
College of the Sequoias, Visalia, CA [*Library symbol Library of Congress*] (LCLS) .... CViCS
College of the Siskiyous Library, Weed, CA [*OCLC symbol*] (OCLC) .... CIS
College of the Siskoyous, Weed, CA [*Library symbol Library of Congress*] (LCLS) .... CWeeC
College of the Southwest, Hobbs, NM [*Library symbol Library of Congress*] (LCLS) .... NmHoSW
College of the Virgin Islands CVI
College of the Virgin Islands, St. Thomas, VI [*Library symbol Library of Congress*] (LCLS) .... VnStC
College of Trades and Technology [*St. John's, NF*] .... CTT
College of Trades and Technology, Medical Sciences Library, St. John's, NF, Canada [*Library symbol Library of Congress*] (LCLS) .... CaNfSCTM
College of Trades and Technology, St. John's, NF, Canada [*Library symbol Library of Congress*] (LCLS) .... CaNfSCT
College of Veterinarians of Ontario (AC) .... CVO
College of Veterinary Medicine [*University of Florida*] [*Research center*] (RCD) .... CVM
College of White Plains, White Plains, NY [*Library symbol Library of Congress*] (LCLS) .... NWhpG
College of White Plains, White Plains, NY [*OCLC symbol*] (OCLC) .... VZW
College of William and Mary (GAGS) .... C Wm & Mary
College of William and Mary, Law School, Williamsburg, VA [*Library symbol Library of Congress*] (LCLS) .... ViW-L
College of William and Mary, Law School, Williamsburg, VA [*OCLC symbol*] (OCLC) .... VWL
College of William and Mary, Williamsburg, VA [*Library symbol Library of Congress*] (LCLS) .... ViW
College of William and Mary, Williamsburg, VA [*OCLC symbol*] (OCLC) .... VWM
College of Wooster, Wooster, OH [*Library symbol Library of Congress*] (LCLS) .... OWoC
College of Wooster, Wooster, OH [*OCLC symbol*] (OCLC) .... WOO
College on Research and Development (HGAA) .... COLRAD
College on the Practice of Management Science .... CPMS
College Ouest Africaine des Chirurgiens [*West African College of Surgeons - WACS*] (EAIO) .... COAC
College Outpost [*Alaska*] [*Seismograph station code, US Geological Survey*] (SEIS) .... COL
College Park, MD [*Location identifier FAA*] (FAAL) .... CGS
College Park, MD [*FM radio station call letters*] .... WMUC
College Physical Education Association [*Later, NAPEHE*] .... CPEA
College Place, WA [*FM radio station call letters*] .... KGTS
College Placement Council (EA) .... CPC
College Placement Services [*Later, CCDM*] (EA) .... CPS
College Plaza Resource Centre, Alberta Public Works, Supply and Services, Edmonton, Alberta [*Library symbol National Library of Canada*] (NLC) .... AEPW
College Press Service (EA) .... CPS
College Proficiency Examination (WGA) .... CPE
College Publishers Group [*Defunct*] (EA) .... CPG
College Qualification Test (WGA) .... CQT
College Qualification Test .... CQU
College Reading and Study Skills Inventory (EDAC) .... CRSS
College Recruitment Database [*Executive Telecom System, Inc.*] [*Information service or system*] (CRD) .... CRD
College Republican National Committee (EA) .... CRNC
College Retirement Equities Fund [*New York, NY*] (EA) .... CREF
College Sainte-Croix, Montreal, PQ, Canada [*Library symbol Library of Congress*] (LCLS) .... CaQMStC
College Sainte-Marie, Montreal, PQ, Canada [*Library symbol Library of Congress*] (LCLS) .... CaQMSM
College Saint-Jean-Sur-Richelieu, Saint-Jean, PQ, Canada [*Library symbol Library of Congress*] (LCLS) .... CaQStJC
College Saint-Jean-Sur-Richelieu, Saint-Jean, Quebec [*Library symbol National Library of Canada*] (NLC) .... QSTJC
College Saint-Louis-Maillet, Edmundston, NB, Canada [*Library symbol Library of Congress*] (LCLS) .... CaNBESLM
College Scholarship Service [*Service mark of the College Entrance Examination Board*] .... CSS
College Science Improvement Program [*National Science Foundation Defunct*] .... COSIP
College Selection Service [*Peterson's Guides*] [*Information service or system*] (IID) .... CSS
College Self-Expression Scale .... CSES
College Senior Engineering Program [*Air Force*] .... CSEP
College Service Bureau (EA) .... CSB
College Sports Information Directors of America (EA) .... CoSIDA
College Station [*Texas*] [*Airport symbol*] (OAG) CLL
College Station/Easterwood Field [*Texas*] [*ICAO location identifier*] (ICLI) .... KCLL
College Station, TX [*Location identifier FAA*] (FAAL) CLL
College Station, TX [*FM radio station call letters*] .... KAMU
College Station, TX [*Television station call letters*] .... KAMU-TV
College Station, TX [*FM radio station call letters*] (RBYB) .... KEOS
College Station, TX [*FM radio station call letters*] .... KTSR
College Station, TX [*AM radio station call letters*] .... WTAW
College Stores Association .... CSA
College Stores of New England (SRA) .... CSNE
College Student Personnel Institute [*Defunct*] .... CSPI
College Student Questionnaires [*Psychology*] .... CSQ
College Swimming Coaches Association of America (EA) .... CSCAA
College Theology Society (EA) .... CTS
College Training Detachment .... CTD
College Universitaire de Hearst, Ontario [*Library symbol National Library of Canada*] (NLC) .... OHCU
College - University Resource Institute (EA) .... CURI
College Women's Assertion Sample (EDAC) .... CWAS
College Women's Volunteer Service [*World War II*] .... CWVS
College Work-Study [*Program*] .... CW-S
College Work-Study [*Financial aid*] (PAZ) .... CWS
College Work-Study Program .... CWSP
College Young Democrats of America (EA) .... CYD
Collegedale, TN [*FM radio station call letters*] .... WSMC
College-Level Examination Program [*Trademark/service mark of the College Entrance Examination Board*] .... CLEP
Colleges and Universitites, Ontario Ministry of Education, Toronto, Ontario [*Library symbol National Library of Canada*] (NLC) .... OTECU
Colleges, Institutes, and Schools in Education (AIE) .... CISE
Colleges of Education Learning Programme Project [*British*] .... CELPP
Colleges of Mid-America (EA) .... CMA
Collegeville, MN [*FM radio station call letters*] .... KNSR
Collegeville, MN [*FM radio station call letters*] .... KSJR
Collegial Association for the Development and Renewal of Educators (EDAC) .... CADRE
Collegiate .... COLGT
Collegiate (ROG) .... COLLEG
Collegiate Association for Research of Principle (EA) .... NCARP
Collegiate Association for the Research of Principles (DICI) .... CARP
Collegiate Basketball Officials Bureau [*Later, Eastern College Basketball Association*] (EA) .... CBOB
Collegiate Commissioners Association (EA) .... CCA
Collegiate Council for the United Nations (EA) .... CCUN
Collegiate Council of Women's Athletic Administrators (EA) .... CCWAA
Collegiate Soaring Association (EA) .... CSA
Collegium (ROG) .... COL
Collegium International Neuro-Psychopharmacologicum .... CINP
Collegium Internationale Activitatis Nervosae Superioris [*Milan, Italy*] (EAIO) .... CIANS
Collegium Internationale Activitatis Nervosae Superioris .... CINS
Collegium Internationale Allergologicum [*Berne, Switzerland*] (EA) .... CIA
Collegium Internationale Chirurgiae Digestivae [*Rome, Italy*] (EAIO) .... CICD
Collegium Internationale Neuro-Psychopharmacologicum (EA) .... CINP
Collegium Medicorum Theatri (EA) .... COMET
Colles' English Parliamentary Cases [*1697-1714*] [*A publication*] (DLA) .... Coll
Colles' English Parliamentary Cases [*1697-1714*] [*A publication*] (DLA) .... Coll PC
Colles' English Parliamentary Cases [*1697-1714*] [*A publication*] (DLA) .... Colles
Colles' English Parliamentary Cases [*1697-1714*] [*A publication*] (DLA) .... Colles (Eng)
Colles' English Parliamentary Cases [*1697-1714*] [*A publication*] (DLA) .... Colles PC
Collet on Torts and Measure of Damages [*A publication*] (DLA) .... Coll Tor
Collet-Sicard [*Syndrome*] [*Otorhinolaryngology and neurology*] (DAVI) .... CS
Collett Dickenson Pearce [*British advertising agency*] .... CDP
Collider Detector at Fermilab [*Particle physics*] .... CDF
Collidge Elementary School, Baldwin, NY [*Library symbol Library of Congress*] (LCLS) .... NBaldCE

Colliding Beam Accelerator [*High-energy physics*] ... CBA
Colliding Electron-Beam Storage Ring [*Nuclear energy*] (NRCH) ... CESR
Colliding-Pulse-Mode [*LASER*] ... CPM
Collie Club of America (EA) ... CCA
Collier [*Navy symbol Obsolete*] ... AC
Collier and Eaton's American Bankruptcy Reports [*A publication*] (DLA) ... Coll & E Bank
Collier and Eaton's American Bankruptcy Reports [*A publication*] (DLA) ... Collier & E Am Bankr
Collier and Eaton's American Bankruptcy Reports [*A publication*] (DLA) ... Collier Bank
Collier and Miller on Bills of Sale [*A publication*] (DLA) ... C & M Bills
Collier and Miller on Bills of Sale [*A publication*] (DLA) ... Coll & Mil BS
Collier County Free Public Library, Naples, FL [*Library symbol Library of Congress*] (LCLS) ... FNaC
Collier de Perles, Carre de Hermes [*Pearl Necklace, Silk Scarf from the boutique Hermes*] [*French Yuppie garb*] ... CPCH
Collier on Patents [*A publication*] (DLA) ... Coll Pat
Collier's Bankruptcy Cases [*A publication*] (DLA) ... CBC
Collier's Bankruptcy Cases [*A publication*] (DLA) ... Collier Bankr Cas
Collier's Law of Bankruptcy [*A publication*] (DLA) ... Coll Bank
Collier's Law of Contribution [*1875*] [*A publication*] (DLA) ... Coll Contr
Collier's Law of Mines [*A publication*] (DLA) ... Col Mines
Collier's Law of Mines [*A publication*] (DLA) ... Coll Min
Collierville, TN [*AM radio station call letters*] ... WCRV
Colliery ... COLL
Colliery (ROG) ... COLLY
Colliery Mazdoor Union [*India*] ... CMU
Colliery Screened (ROG) ... C/S
Collimated Holes Structure (PDAA) ... CHS
Collimated Monochromatic Light ... CML
Collimated Photon Scattering (MCD) ... CPS
Collimated Proportional Counter (PDAA) ... CPC
Collimated Slit Radiography (MCD) ... CSR
Collimation Test Module [*Nuclear energy*] (GFGA) ... CTM
Collimator (MSA) ... COLIM
Collimator Target (MCD) ... CT
Collin County Community College District, McKinney, TX [*Library symbol*] [*Library of Congress*] (LCLS) ... TxMckC
Collinear Exact Quantum Bend [*Kinetics*] ... CEQB
Collingswood Free Public Library, Collingswood, NJ [*Library symbol Library of Congress*] (LCLS) ... NjCo
Collingswood Publishing Co., Collingswood, NJ [*Library symbol Library of Congress*] (LCLS) ... NjCoC
Collingwood Air Services Ltd. [*Canada ICAO designator*] (FAAC) ... BLE
Collingwood & District Information Centre (AC) ... CDIC
Collingwood Energy [*Vancouver Stock Exchange symbol*] ... CIW
Collingwood, ON [*AM radio station call letters*] ... CKCB
Collingwood Public Library, Collingwood, ON, Canada [*Library symbol Library of Congress*] (LCLS) ... CaOCol
Collingwood Public Library, Ontario [*Library symbol National Library of Canada*] (NLC) ... OCOL
Collingwood Township Public Library, Brockville, ON, Canada [*Library symbol*] [*Library of Congress*] (LCLS) ... CaOCCT
Collingwood Township Public Library, Clarksburg, Ontario [*Library symbol National Library of Canada*] (NLC) ... OCCT
Collins & Aikman [*NYSE symbol*] (TTSB) ... CKC
Collins & Aikman Holdings Corp. [*NYSE symbol*] (SAG) ... CKC
Collins & Aikman Holdings Corp. [*Associated Press*] (SAG) ... CollAik
Collins Birmingham University International Language Database ... COBUILD
Collins Canada Division, Rockwell International, Toronto, Ontario [*Library symbol National Library of Canada*] (NLC) ... OTRIC
Collins English Dictionary [*A publication British*] ... CED
Collins Industries [*NASDAQ symbol*] (TTSB) ... COLI
Collins Industries, Inc. [*NASDAQ symbol*] (SAG) ... COLL
Collins Industries, Inc. [*Associated Press*] (SAG) ... Collins
Collins Motor Corp. [*Alternative engine technology*] ... CMC
Collins, MS [*FM radio station call letters*] ... WKNZ
Collins Public Library, Collins, IA [*Library symbol Library of Congress*] (LCLS) ... IaColn
Collins Radio Co. (KSC) ... CRC
Collins Radio Co., Dallas, TX [*Library symbol Library of Congress*] (LCLS) ... TxDaCR
Collins Resources Ltd. [*Vancouver Stock Exchange symbol*] ... CR
Collin's Solution (MAE) ... C_3
Collinson on the Law of Idiots and Lunatics [*A publication*] (DLA) ... Coll Id
Collinson on the Law of Idiots and Lunatics [*A publication*] (DLA) ... Coll Lun
Collinson on the Stamp Laws [*A publication*] (DLA) ... Coll St L
Collinsville [*Australia Airport symbol*] (OAG) ... KCE
Collinsville Community Unit 10, Collinsville, IL [*Library symbol Library of Congress*] (LCLS) ... IColCU
Collinsville Public Library, Collinsville, IL [*Library symbol Library of Congress*] (LCLS) ... ICol
Collinsville, VA [*AM radio station call letters*] ... WFIC
Collique [*Peru*] [*ICAO location identifier*] (ICLI) ... SPOL
Collision ... CLLSN
Collision (DS) ... Col
Collision [*Insurance*] ... COLL
Collision Alert [*Air traffic control*] ... CACA
Collision and Obstacle/Terrain Avoidance Warning System ... COTAWS
Collision Avoidance Aid ... CAA
Collision Avoidance, Proximity Warning, Station Keeping Equipment [*Military*] (NG) ... CAPWSK
Collision Avoidance RADAR and Navigation System [*Military*] ... CARNS
Collision Avoidance RADAR Simulator [*Maritime*] ... CARS
Collision Avoidance RADAR Trainer (PDAA) ... CART
Collision Avoidance System [*Aviation*] ... CAS
Collision Avoidance System / Pilot Warning Indicator [*Aviation*] (PDAA) ... CAS/PWI
Collision Avoidance System Proximity Warning Indicator [*Aviation*] (IAA) ... CASPWI
Collision Avoidance System Technical Evaluation [*Aviation*] (MCD) ... CASTE
Collision Avoidance System Using Baseband Reflectrometry [*Aviation*] (PDAA) ... CASBAR
Collision Damage Classification [*Insurance*] ... CDC
Collision Damage Waiver [*Insurance*] ... CDW
Collision Detect [*Computer science*] ... CD
Collision Detection [*Telecommunications*] (ACRL) ... CD
Collision Detector System (NASA) ... CDS
Collision Diameter of a Molecule [*Symbol*] [*IUPAC*] ... d
Collision Elimination [*Wiring hub*] [*Computer science*] (PCM) ... CE
Collision Number [*Symbol*] [*IUPAC*] ... Z
Collision Parts Journal [*A publication*] (EAAP) ... CPJ
Collision Prevention Advisory Group [*US*] ... COPAG
Collision Probability (OA) ... CP
Collision Risk Model [*Aviation*] (DA) ... CRM
Collision Threat Assessment ... CTA
Collision Warning System (MCD) ... CWS
Collision Warning System [*Automotive safety*] ... CWS
Collision-Activated Dissociation [*Spectrometry*] ... CAD
Collisional Mode (MCD) ... CMODE
Collisionally Activated Dissociation ... CAD
Collision-Dominated Quiescent Discharge ... CDQD
Collision-Force Method (PDAA) ... CFM
Collision-Imparted Velocity Method ... CIVM
Collision-Induced Absorption (MCD) ... CIA
Collision-Induced Decomposition [*or Dissociation*] [*Spectrometry*] ... CID
Collision-Induced Light Scattering (MCD) ... CILS
Collmberg [*German Democratic Republic*] [*Seismograph station code, US Geological Survey*] (SEIS) ... CLL
Collocated ... CL
Collocated Operating Bases (MCD) ... COB
Collocation [*Computer software package*] [*University of Birmingham*] [*British*] (NITA) ... CLOC
Collocation Flutter Analysis ... CFA
Collocation Flutter Analysis ... COFA
Collodion Glass Negative (VRA) ... CGNG
Collodion Print (VRA) ... CLPT
Colloid ... COLL
Colloid Antigen [*Immunology*] ... CA
Colloid Microthruster Experiment ... CME
Colloidal ... COL
Colloidal Array Filters [*for LASER applications*] ... CAF
Colloidal Bismuth Subcitrate [*Pharmacy*] ... CBS
Colloidal Gas Aphron [*Physical chemistry*] ... CGA
Colloidal Gold [*Chemistry*] ... CG
Colloidal Iron (OA) ... CI
Colloidal Iron Hydroxide ... CIH
Colloidal Organic Carbon [*Environmental chemistry*] ... COC
Colloidal Osmotic Pressure [*Analytical biochemistry*] ... COP
Colloidal System Test ... CST
Colloidal Thorium (OA) ... CT
Colloque International de Droit Compare [*A publication*] (DLA) ... Col Int'l Dr Comp
Colloque International de Marketing Gazier [*International Colloquium about Gas Marketing - ICGM*] (EA) ... CIMG
Colloque sur le Traitement Automatique des Textes [*Colloquium on the Computer Processing of Textual Data - CCPTD*] ... CTAT
Colloquia for Presidents and Academic Administrators [*Formerly, ICUA*] (EA) ... CPAA
Colloquial ... COLL
Colloquial (WDMC) ... coll
Colloquial ... COLLOQ
Colloquium Spectroscopicum Internationale ... CSI
Colloquium: The Australian and New Zealand Theological Review [*A publication*] (APTA) ... Coll
Colloredo [*Italy*] [*Seismograph station code, US Geological Survey*] (SEIS) ... COLI
Coll'Ottava [*With the Octave*] [*Music*] (ROG) ... C 8VA
Coll'Ottava [*With the Octave*] [*Music*] (ROG) ... COL OTTA
Coll'Ottava [*With the Octave*] [*Music*] ... Coll'Ott
Coll'Ottava [*With the Octave*] [*Music*] ... COLL'OTTA
Collotype (VRA) ... COLTY
Collpa [*Bolivia*] [*ICAO location identifier*] (ICLI) ... SLCY
Collpani [*Bolivia*] [*ICAO location identifier*] (ICLI) ... SLCL
Collunarium [*Nose Wash*] [*Pharmacy*] ... COLLUN
Collurania [*Italy*] [*Seismograph station code, US Geological Survey Closed*] (SEIS) ... CLR
Collutorium [*Mouthwash*] [*Pharmacy*] ... COLLUT
Collyer's Chancery Cases Tempore Bruce, V-C [*63 English Reprint*] [*1844-45*] [*A publication*] (ILCA) ... Coll CC
Collyer's Chancery Cases Tempore Bruce, V-C [*63 English Reprint*] [*1844-45*] [*A publication*] (DLA) ... Coll NC
Collyer's English Chancery Cases [*1845-47*] [*A publication*] (DLA) ... Col CC
Collyer's English Chancery Cases [*1845-47*] [*A publication*] (DLA) ... Coll
Collyer's English Chancery Cases [*1845-47*] [*A publication*] (DLA) ... Colly Ch Cas (Eng)
Collyer's English Chancery Reports [*A publication*] (DLA) ... Coll CR
Collyer's English Vice Chancellors' Reports [*1845-47*] [*A publication*] (DLA) ... Colly
Collyer's Law of Partnership [*A publication*] (DLA) ... Col Part
Collyer's Law of Partnership [*A publication*] (DLA) ... Coll Part

Collyer's Law of Partnership [*A publication*] (DLA) .... Colly Part
Collyrium [*Eye Wash*] [*Pharmacy*] (ROG) .... COLL
Collyrium [*Eye Wash*] [*Pharmacy*] .... COLLYR
Colmar [*France*] [*Airport symbol*] (OAG) .... CMR
Colmar/Houssen [*France ICAO location identifier*] (ICLI) .... LFGA
Colmar/Meyenheim [*France ICAO location identifier*] (ICLI) .... LFSC
Colmenar Viejo [*Spain ICAO location identifier*] (ICLI) .... LECV
Colocasia Bacilliform Virus [*Plant pathology*] .... COBV
Colocasia Bobone Disease Virus [*Plant pathology*] .... CBDV
Colocynthus [*Bitter Apples*] [*Pharmacy*] (ROG) .... COLOCYNTH
Coloforma, Heart Disease, Arrested Growth or Development, Genital Hypoplasia, and Ear Abnormalities [*Medicine*] .... CHARGE
Cologarithm [*Mathematics*] .... COLOG
Cologne [*West Germany*] [*Seismograph station code, US Geological Survey*] (SEIS) .... CLG
Cologne Air Transport [*Germany*] [*FAA designator*] (FAAC) .... GAG
Cologne/Bonn [*Germany Airport symbol*] (OAG) .... CGN
Cologne/Bonn-Main RR [*Germany Airport symbol*] (OAG) .... QKL
Coloma Public Library, Coloma, MI [*Library symbol Library of Congress*] (LCLS) .... MiCol
Colomb Bechar [*Algeria*] [*Airport symbol*] (AD) .... CBH
Colombia [*IYRU nationality code*] (IYR) .... CB
Colombia [*ucu (United States Miscellaneous Caribbean Islands) used in records cataloged before January 1978*] [*MARC country of publication code Library of Congress*] (LCCP) .... ck
Colombia [*ANSI two-letter standard code*] (CNC) .... CO
Colombia [*ANSI three-letter standard code*] (CNC) .... COL
Colombia .... Colom
Colombia [*MARC geographic area code Library of Congress*] (LCCP) .... s-ck--
Colombia Human Rights Information Committee (EA) .... CHIBCHA
Colombia, SC [*Location identifier FAA*] (FAAL) .... VYK
Colombian American Association (EA) .... CAA
Colombian Government Trade Bureau (EA) .... CGTB
Colombian-American Chamber of Commerce (EA) .... CACC
Colombian-American Chamber of Commerce (EA) .... COL-AMCHAM
Colombo [*Sri Lanka*] [*Airport symbol*] (OAG) .... CMB
Colombo [*Sri Lanka*] [*Seismograph station code, US Geological Survey*] (SEIS) .... COC
Colombo/Katunayake [*Sri Lanka*] [*ICAO location identifier*] (ICLI) .... VCBI
Colombo Law Journal [*A publication*] (DLA) .... Colombo LJ
Colombo/Ratmalana [*Sri Lanka*] [*ICAO location identifier*] (ICLI) VCCC
Colombus Air Force Base [*Mississippi*] [*ICAO location identifier*] (ICLI) .... KCBM
Colome Public Library, Colome, SD [*Library symbol Library of Congress*] (LCLS) .... SdCo
Colon [*Monetary unit*] [*Costa Rica, El Salvador*] C
Colon (AABC) .... CLN
Colon [*City in Panama*] (ROG) .... CO
Colon (WDAA) .... COL
Colon [*Panama*] [*ICAO location identifier*] (ICLI) .... MPCO
Colon [*Cuba ICAO location identifier*] (ICLI) .... MUCO
Colon [*Panama*] [*Airport symbol*] (OAG) .... ONX
Colon and Rectal [*or Colorectal*] **Surgery** [*Medicine*] .... CRS
Colon Classification [*Library science*] CC
Colon Mucoprotein Antigen [*Immunochemistry*] .... CMA
Colon Resection [*Medicine*] .... CR
Colon Township Library, Colon, MI [*Library symbol Library of Congress*] (LCLS) .... MiColo
Colonel (ROG) C
Colonel [*Military*] (AABC) .... COL
Colonel (DD) .... Col
Colonel .... COL
Colonel [*Air Force, Army, Marine Corps*] O6
Colonel By Campus, Algonquin College of Applied Arts and Technology, Ottawa, On tario [*Library symbol National Library of Canada*] (NLC) .... OOACC
Colonel By Secondary School, Ottawa, ON, Canada [*Library symbol Library of Congress*] (LCLS) .... CaOOCB
Colonel By Secondary School, Ottawa, Ontario [*Library symbol National Library of Canada*] (NLC) .... OOCB
Colonel Coon Collectors Club (EA) CCCC
Colonel Hill, Crooked Island [*Bahamas*] [*ICAO location identifier*] (ICLI) .... MYCI
Colonel, Royal Artillery Training [*British*] .... CRAT
Colonels International, Inc. (The) [*NASDAQ symbol*] (SAG) .... COLO
Colonels International, Inc. (The) [*Associated Press*] (SAG) .... Colonels
Colonel's Intl. [*NASDAQ symbol*] (TTSB) .... COLO
Colonel's Island [*AAR code*] .... COLI
Colonia [*Uruguay*] [*Airport symbol*] .... CYR
Colonia/Aeropuerto Deptal. [*Uruguay*] [*ICAO location identifier*] (ICLI) .... SUCA
Colonia Sabana [*Puerto Rico*] [*Seismograph station code, US Geological Survey*] (SEIS) .... CSB
Colonia Sarmiento [*Argentina*] [*Airport symbol*] (AD) .... OLN
Colonial .... CLNL
Colonial (ROG) .... COL
Colonial .... COLON
Colonial Air Lines .... CAL
Colonial Aircraft Co. .... CAC
Colonial Allowance [*British military*] (DMA) .... CA
Colonial [*or Commonwealth*] **and Continental Church Society** [*British*] .... CCCS
Colonial BancGroup [*NYSE symbol*] (TTSB) .... CNB
Colonial Bankgroup [*NYSE symbol*] (SAG) .... CNB
Colonial Bankgroup [*Associated Press*] (SAG) .... ColBgp
Colonial Beach, VA [*FM radio station call letters*] .... WGRQ
Colonial Bird Register [*Cornell University*] [*Information service or system*] (IID) .... CBR
Colonial Bishoprics' Fund [*British*] .... CBF
Colonial Coml [*NASDAQ symbol*] (TTSB) .... CCOM
Colonial Commercial Corp. [*NASDAQ symbol*] (NQ) .... CCOM
Colonial Commercial Corp. [*Associated Press*] (SAG) .... ColCm
Colonial Commercial Corp. [*Associated Press*] (SAG) .... ColCmc
Colonial Comml Cv Pfd [*NASDAQ symbol*] (TTSB) .... CCOMP
Colonial Dames [*An association*] (IIA) .... CD
Colonial Dames of America (EA) .... CDA
Colonial Data Tech [*NASDAQ symbol*] (TTSB) .... CDTX
Colonial Data Technologies Corp. [*AMEX symbol*] (SPSG) .... CDT
Colonial Data Technologies Corp. [*Associated Press*] (SAG) .... ColData
Colonial Development Corp. .... CDC
Colonial, Fish-Eating Water Bird .... CFEWB
Colonial Gas [*NASDAQ symbol*] (TTSB) .... CGES
Colonial Gas Co. [*NASDAQ symbol*] (NQ) .... CGES
Colonial Gas Co. [*Associated Press*] (SAG) .... ColnlGas
Colonial Heights, TN [*FM radio station call letters*] .... WLJQ
Colonial Heights, TN [*AM radio station call letters*] (RBYB) .... WPWT-AM
Colonial Heights, TN [*AM radio station call letters*] .... WZMC
Colonial Heights, VA [*FM radio station call letters*] .... WKHK
Colonial Heights, VA [*AM radio station call letters*] .... WSTK
Colonial High Income Muni [*NYSE symbol*] (TTSB) .... CXF
Colonial High Income Municipal Trust [*Associated Press*] (SAG) .... ColHIn
Colonial High Income Municipal Trust [*NYSE symbol*] (SPSG) .... CXE
Colonial Interim Hi Income [*NYSE symbol*] (TTSB) .... CIF
Colonial Intermarket Income Trust [*Associated Press*] (SAG) .... ColIntIn
Colonial Intermarket Income Trust I [*NYSE symbol*] (SPSG) .... CMK
Colonial Intermediate High Income Fund [*NYSE symbol*] (SPSG) .... CIF
Colonial Intermediate High Income Fund [*Associated Press*] (SAG) .... ColIHI
Colonial InterMkt Inc. Tr I [*NYSE symbol*] (TTSB) .... CMK
Colonial Inv Grade Muni [*NYSE symbol*] (TTSB) .... CXH
Colonial Investment Grade Municipal [*NYSE symbol*] (SPSG) .... CXH
Colonial Investment Grade Municipal Trust [*Associated Press*] (SAG) .... ColInvG
Colonial Law Journal [*A publication*] (DLA) .... Co LJ
Colonial Law Journal [*A publication*] (DLA) .... Col LJ
Colonial Law Journal (New Zealand) [*A publication*] (DLA) .... Col LJNZ
Colonial Law Journal Reports [*A publication*] (DLA) .... CLJ
Colonial Life Co. [*Trinidad*] .... CLICO
Colonial Medical Department [*British*] .... CMD
Colonial Military Forces [*British*] .... CMF
Colonial Monthly [*A publication*] .... Col Mon
Colonial Muni Inc. Tr [*NYSE symbol*] (TTSB) .... CMU
Colonial Municipal Income Trust [*NYSE symbol*] (SPSG) .... CMU
Colonial Municipal Income Trust [*Associated Press*] (SAG) .... ColMu
Colonial National Historic Park .... COLO
Colonial Office [*British*] .... CO
Colonial Oil & Gas Ltd. [*Toronto Stock Exchange symbol*] .... COO
Colonial Order of the Acorn (EA) .... COA
Colonial Penn Group, Inc., Marketing Research Library, Philadelphia, PA [*Library symbol Library of Congress*] (LCLS) .... PPColP
Colonial Police Medal [*British*] .... CPM
Colonial Properties Tr [*NYSE symbol*] (TTSB) .... CLP
Colonial Properties Trust [*NYSE symbol*] (SPSG) .... CLP
Colonial Properties Trust [*Associated Press*] (SAG) .... ColonPT
Colonial Secretary [*British*] (ADA) .... CS
Colonial Society of Massachusetts (EA) .... CSM
Colonial Society of Pennsylvania (EA) .... CSP
Colonial Treasure Hunters Association (EA) .... CTHA
Colonial Warriors United (EA) .... CWU
Colonial Waterbird Group [*Later, CWS*] (EA) .... CWG
Colonial Waterbird Society (EA) .... CWS
Colonial Williamsburg, Inc. (CDAI) .... CW
Colonial Williamsburg, Inc., Williamsburg, VA [*Library symbol Library of Congress*] (LCLS) .... ViWC
Colonialism and Indigenous Minorities Research and Action [*British*] (DI) .... CIMRA
Colonic Intestinal Metaplasia [*Oncology*] .... CIM
Colonie Interim Storage Site [*Colonie, NY*] (GAAI) .... CISS
Colonie Interim Storage Site [*Department of Energy*] .... CISS
Colonie Interim Storage Site (DOGT) .... CISS
Colonies per Milliliter [*Measurement*] (DAVI) .... col/ml
Colonist .... Col
Colonization Factor Antigen [*Analytical biochemistry*] .... CFA
Colonizing Efficiency Ratio [*Forestry*] .... CER
Colonnade (VRA) .... colnd
Colon-Specific Antigen [*Biochemistry*] (DAVI) .... CSA
Colon-Specific Antigen Protein [*Biochemistry*] (DAVI) .... CSAP
Colony .... CLNY
Colony [*or Colonies*] [*Bacteriology*] (DAVI) .... Col
Colony .... COL
Colony (VRA) .... colo
Colony Count and Culture [*Bacteriology*] (DAVI) .... CC & C
Colony Forming [*Cytology*] .... CF
Colony Forming Unit-Granulocyte [*Cytology*] .... CFU-G
Colony Overlay Test [*Microbiology*] .... COT
Colony Pacific Explorations Ltd. [*Toronto Stock Exchange symbol Vancouver Stock Exchange symbol*] .... CYX
Colony-Forming Ability [*Microbiology*] .... CFA
Colony-Forming Cell [*Cytology*] .... CFC
Colony-Forming Efficiency [*Cytology*] .... CFE
Colony-Forming Unit [*Cytology*] .... CFU
Colony-Forming Unit - Culture [*Cytology*] .... CFU-C
Colony-Forming Unit - Eosinophil [*Cytology*] .... CFU-Eo
Colony-Forming Unit Eosinophil [*Cytology*] (MAE) .... CFUeos
Colony-Forming Unit/Erythroid [*Cytology*] .... CFU-E
Colony-Forming Unit/Granulocyte Macrophage [*Cytology*] .... CFU-GM

Colony-Forming Unit - Granulocyte-Erythrocyte-Monocyte-Megakaryocyte [*Cytology*] .... CFU-GEMM
Colony-Forming Unit/Lymphoid [*Cytology*] .... CFU-L
Colony-Forming Unit/Megakaryocyte [*Cytology*] .... CFU-M
Colony-Forming Unit - Megakaryocyte [*Cytology*] (DAVI) .... CFU$_{MEG}$
Colony-Forming Unit Neutrophil-Monocyte [*Cytology*] (MAE) .... CFUnm
Colony-Forming Unit per Milliliter [*Cytology*] (DAVI) .... CFU$_{-mL}$
Colony-Forming Unit - Single Cell [*Cytology*] .... CFU-S
Colony-Forming Unit - Spleen [*Cytology*] .... CFUS
Colony-Stimulating Activity [*Genetics*] .... CSA
Colony-Stimulating Factor [*Hematology*] .... CSF
Colophon [*Publishing*] (WGA) .... COLO
Colophon [*Printing*] (DGA) .... COLOPH
Colophon Society [*Australia*] .... CS
Color C
Color (MSA) .... CLR
Color (VRA) .... clr
Color .... CLR
Color (WDMC) .... col
Color .... COL
Color Adjusted Transmission [*Optical coating to facilitate use of binoculars in low light*] [*Steiner-Optik of West Germany*] .... CAT
Color Allergy Screen Test .... CAST
Color Appearance Monitoring System [*Automotive quality control*] .... CAMS
Color Association of the United States .... CA
Color Association of the United States (EA) .... CAUS
Color Blindness, Blue Monocone-Monochromatic Type [*Medicine*] (DMAA) .... CBBM
Color Business Graphics (HGAA) .... CBG
Color Center LASER (PDAA) CCL
Color Changing Unit [*Medical technology*] .... CCU
Color Code [*as, for types of wire*] [*Technical drawings*] CC
Color Compensation [*Photography*] CC
Color Computer .... COCO
Color Contrast CC
Color Contrast Value CCV
Color Correction [*Color printing*] CC
Color Data Display .... CDD
Color Data System .... CDS
Color Detail [*Rorschach*] [*Psychology*] C
Color Developer System [*Canon, Inc.*] .... CD
Color Developing Unit (NITA) .... CDU
Color Diaposition Plate .... CDP
Color Difference Computer (MUGU) .... CODIC
Color Difference Meter .... CDM
Color Difference Signal .... CDS
Color Electronic Prepress Systems [*Printing technology*] .... CEPS
Color Evaluation Program .... CEP
Color Excess [*Astronomy*] .... E
Color Exterior Film (MCD) CX
Color Filter Array (IAA) .... CFA
Color Forming Ability [*Food technology*] .... CFA
Color Forming Units [*Food technology*] .... CFU
Color Graphics (MHDI) .... CG
Color/Graphics Adapter [*Computer technology*] .... CGA
Color Graphics Converter [*Computer science*] .... CGC
Color Graphics Indicator (HGAA) .... CGI
Color Graphics Printer .... CGP
Color Graphics Terminal (MCD) .... CGT
Color Guild Associates (EA) .... CGA
Color Image Assembly [*Graphic arts*] (DGA) .... CIA
Color Image Assembly and Manipulation System [*Graphic arts*] (DGA) .... CIAMS
Color Index C
Color Index CI
Color Infrared [*Image*] .... CIR
Color Interior Film (MCD) CI
Color Layout Programmer (DGA) .... CLP
Color Line [*Illustration*] (DGA) CL
Color Look-Up Table [*Computer graphics*] .... CLUT
Color Magnitude Diagrams .... CMD
Color Management System [*Computer science*] .... CMS
Color Marketing Group [*Washington, DC*] (EA) .... CMG
Color Mat Processor .... CMP
Color Mixture Curve .... CMC
Color Mixture Function .... CMF
Color Multifunction Display .... CMFD
Color Pack Camera .... CPC
Color Page [*Printing*] (DGA) .... COL P
Color Perception [*Medicine*] .... CP
Color Phase Alternation .... CPA
Color Photographic Association of Canada .... CPAC
Color Picture Signal .... CPS
Color Picture Tube [*Electronics*] (EECA) .... CPT
Color Pigments Manufacturing Association .... CPMA
Color Print [*Publishing*] .... C (Print)
Color Printing [*Filter*] [*Photography*] .... CP
Color Prints [*Not tinted*] (VRA) .... CLRP
Color Purple Educational Fund Foundation (EA) .... CPSF
Color Pyramid Test [*Psychology*] .... CPT
Color Rendition [*or Rendering*] Index [*Measure of Color distortion*] .... CRI
Color Response [*Psychology*] (BARN) .... CR
Color Reversal Intermediate [*Photography*] (NTCM) .... CRI
Color Sense (AAMN) C
Color Separation Overlay .... CSO
Color Shadow Mask [*Type of cathode ray tube*] (NITA) .... CSM

Color Specification .... CS
Color Strength [*Dye technology*] .... CS
Color Sync Signal .... CSS
Color Television (DEN) .... CTV
Color Temperature (NTCM) .... CT
Color Trace Tube (IAA) .... CTT
Color Transparency (WDMC) .... C/T
Color Uniformity Recognition Equipment [*Quality control*] .... CURE
Color Unit (MAE) .... CU
Color Video Tape (MCD) .... CVT
Color Vision [*Ophthalmology*] CV
Color Vision [*Ophthalmology*] VC
Color Vision Constant Speed [*Physiology*] (IAA) .... CCS
Color Vision Deviate [*Ophthalmology*] .... CVD
Color, Warmth, Movement Sensation [*Medicine*] (DMAA) .... CWMS
Color Word Test .... CWT
Color You See Is What You Get [*Computer science*] .... CYSIWIG
Color Your World, Inc. [*Toronto Stock Exchange symbol*] .... CYW
Colorado [*Dark-colored cigar*] C
Colorado [*Postal code*] .... CO
Colorado .... COL
Colorado (AFM) .... COLO
Colorado (ODBW) .... Colo
Colorado [*MARC country of publication code Library of Congress*] (LCCP) .... cou
Colorado [*MARC geographic area code Library of Congress*] (LCCP) .... n-us-co
Colorado Academy, Englewood, CO [*Library symbol Library of Congress*] (LCLS) .... CoEnCA
Colorado Academy of Family Physicians (SRA) .... CAFP
Colorado Academy of Physician Assistants (SRA) .... CAPA
Colorado Advanced Technology Institute .... CATI
Colorado Advanced Technology Institute .... CATT
Colorado Alliance of Research Libraries [*Denver, CO*] [*Library network*] .... CARL
[*The*] Colorado & Southern Railway Co. .... C & S
[*The*] Colorado & Southern Railway Co. [*AAR code*] .... CS
[*The*] Colorado & Wyoming Railway Co. [*AAR code*] .... CW
Colorado Appeals Reports [*A publication*] (DLA) .... Col App
Colorado Appellate Reports [*A publication*] (AAGC) .... Colo App
Colorado Asphalt Pavement Association (SRA) .... CAPA
Colorado Assessors' Association (SRA) .... CAA
Colorado Association of Campgrounds, Cabins, and Lodges (SRA) .... CACCL
Colorado Association of Commerce and Industry (SRA) .... CACI
Colorado Association of Community Centered Boards (SRA) .... CACCB
Colorado Association of D.A.R.E. [*Drug Abuse Resistance Education*] Officers (SRA) .... CADO
Colorado Association of Distributors (SRA) .... CAD
Colorado Association of Home Builders (SRA) .... CAHB
Colorado Association of Homes and Services for the Aging (SRA) .... CAHSA
Colorado Association of Life Underwriters (SRA) .... CALU
Colorado Association of Medical Equipment Services (SRA) .... CAMES
Colorado Association of Mortgage Brokers (SRA) .... CAMB
Colorado Association of Nonprofit Organizations (SRA) .... CANPO
Colorado Association of Public Employees (SRA) .... CAPE
Colorado Association of Realtors (SRA) .... CAR
Colorado Association of School Boards (SRA) .... CASB
Colorado Association of School Executives (SRA) .... CASE
Colorado Association of Soil Conservation Districts (SRA) .... CASCD
Colorado Association of Transit Agencies (SRA) .... CASTA
Colorado Association of Wheat Growers (SRA) .... CAWG
Colorado Automobile Dealers Association (SRA) .... CADA
Colorado Bankers Association (SRA) .... CBA
Colorado Bar Association (SRA) .... CBA
Colorado Beef Council (SRA) .... CBC
Colorado Casino Resorts [*NASDAQ symbol*] (TTSB) .... CCRI
Colorado Casino Resorts, Inc. [*NASDAQ symbol*] (SAG) .... CCRI
Colorado Casino Resorts, Inc. [*Associated Press*] (SAG) .... ColoCas
Colorado Cattle Feeders Association (SRA) .... CCFA
Colorado Cattlemen's Association (SRA) .... CCA
Colorado Center for Astrodynamics Research [*University of Colorado at Boulder*] [*Research center*] (RCD) .... CCAR
Colorado Center for Educational Assistance, Denver, CO [*Library symbol*] [*Library of Congress*] (LCLS) .... CoDEA
Colorado Chiropractic Association (SRA) .... CCA
Colorado City, AZ [*FM radio station call letters*] .... KCCA
Colorado City, TX [*FM radio station call letters*] .... KAUM
Colorado City, TX [*AM radio station call letters*] .... KVMC
Colorado College, Colorado Springs, CO [*OCLC symbol*] (OCLC) .... COC
Colorado College, Colorado Springs, CO [*Library symbol Library of Congress*] (LCLS) .... CoCC
Colorado College, Colorado Springs, CO [*Library symbol*] [*Library of Congress*] (LCLS) .... CoCCC
Colorado Community Health Network (SRA) .... CCHN
Colorado Congress of Foreign Language Teachers (EDAC) .... CCFLT
Colorado Constitution [*A publication*] (DLA) .... Colo Const
Colorado Contractors Association (SRA) .... CCA
Colorado Cooperative Council (SRA) CCC
Colorado Corn Growers Association (SRA) .... CCGA
Colorado Court of Appeals Reports [*A publication*] (DLA) .... CO A
Colorado Court of Appeals Reports [*A publication*] (DLA) .... Colo App
Colorado Court Reporters Association (SRA) .... CCRA
Colorado Credit Union League (SRA) .... CCUL
Colorado Creek, AK [*Location identifier FAA*] (FAAL) .... KCR
Colorado Decisions [*A publication*] (DLA) .... Colo Dec
Colorado Decisions, Federal [*A publication*] (DLA) .... Colo Dec Fed
Colorado Decisions Supplement [*A publication*] (DLA) .... Colo Dec Supp
Colorado Dental Association (SRA) .... CDA

Colorado Department of Education (EDAC) .... CDE
Colorado Department of Education, Resource Center, Denver, CO [*Library symbol*] [*Library of Congress*] (LCLS) .... CoDDE
Colorado Department of Public Health and Environment .... CDPHE
Colorado Department of Public Health and Environment (DOGT) .... CDPHE
Colorado Division of State Archives, Denver, CO [*Library symbol Library of Congress*] (LCLS) .... CoDAr
Colorado Dude/Guest Ranch Association (SRA) .... CDGRA
Colorado Education Association (SRA) .... CEA
Colorado Fuel & Iron Co., Pueblo, CO [*Library symbol Library of Congress*] (LCLS) .... CoPC
Colorado Genealogical Society (EA) .... CGS
Colorado General Hospital, Residents' Library, Denver, CO [*Library symbol Library of Congress*] (LCLS) .... CoDGH
Colorado Grain and Feed Association (SRA) .... CGFA
Colorado Greenhouse Growers Association (SRA) .... CGGA
Colorado Health Care Association (SRA) .... CHCA
Colorado High School Coaches Association (SRA) .... CHSCA
Colorado Hospital Association (SRA) .... CHA
Colorado Hotel and Lodging Association (SRA) .... CH&LA
Colorado Human Resource Association (SRA) .... CHRA
Colorado Industrial Commission Report [*A publication*] (DLA) .... Colo IC
Colorado Law Reporter [*A publication*] (DLA) .... Col L Rep
Colorado Law Reporter [*A publication*] (DLA) .... Col Law Rep
Colorado Law Reporter [*A publication*] (DLA) .... Colo L Rep
Colorado Law Reporter [*A publication*] (DLA) .... Colo LR
Colorado Library Network [*Colorado State Library*] [*Denver, CO*] [*Library network*] .... COLONET
Colorado Medtech [*NASDAQ symbol*] (TTSB) .... CMED
Colorado MEDtech, Inc. [*NASDAQ symbol*] (SAG) .... CMED
Colorado MEDtech, Inc. [*Associated Press*] (SAG) .... ColoMED
Colorado Midland .... CM
Colorado Migrant Education Resource Center (EDAC) .... CoMERC
Colorado Mining Association (EA) .... CMA
Colorado Motor Carriers' Association, Denver CO [*STAC*] .... COA
Colorado Motor Tariff Bureau, Inc., Denver CO [*STAC*] .... COB
Colorado Mountain College, Eastern Campus, Leadville, CO [*Library symbol Library of Congress*] (LCLS) .... CoLeC
Colorado Mountain College, Western Campus, Glenwood Springs, CO [*Library symbol Library of Congress*] (LCLS) .... CoGsC
Colorado National Monument .... COLM
Colorado Natural Areas Inventory [*Colorado State Department of Natural Resources*] [*Denver*] [*Information service or system*] (IID) .... CNAI
Colorado Natural Areas Program [*Colorado State Department of Natural Resources*] [*Information service or system*] (IID) .... CNAP
Colorado Nisi Prius Decisions [*A publication*] (DLA) .... Col NP
Colorado Nisi Prius Decisions [*A publication*] (DLA) .... Colo NP Dec
Colorado Northwestern Community College, Rangely, CO [*Library symbol Library of Congress*] (LCLS) .... CoRaC
Colorado Nursery Association (SRA) .... CNA
Colorado Nurses Association (SRA) .... CNA
Colorado Optometric Association (SRA) .... COA
Colorado Outfitters Association (SRA) .... COA
Colorado Podiatric Medical Association (SRA) .... CPMA
Colorado Potato Beetle .... CPB
Colorado Potato Beetle Spiroplasma [*Insect pathogen*] .... CPBS
Colorado Psychiatric Hospital, Residents' Library, Denver, CO [*Library symbol Library of Congress*] (LCLS) .... CoDPH
Colorado Psychiatric Society (SRA) .... CPS
Colorado Public Utilities Commission Decisions [*A publication*] (DLA) .... Colo PUC
Colorado Public Utilities Commission Report [*A publication*] (DLA) .... Colo PUC Rep
Colorado Ranger Horse Association (EA) .... CRHA
Colorado Register [*A publication*] (AAGC) .... CR
Colorado Reports [*A publication*] (DLA) .... CO
Colorado Reports [*A publication*] (DLA) .... Col
Colorado Reports [*A publication*] (DLA) .... Col Rep
Colorado Reports [*A publication*] (DLA) .... Colo
Colorado Research Corp. (AAG) .... CRC
Colorado Revised Statutes [*A publication*] (DLA) .... Col Rev Stat
Colorado Revised Statutes Annotated [*West*] [*A publication*] (AAGC) .... Colo Rev Stat Ann
Colorado River Association (EA) .... CRA
Colorado River Basin Project .... CRBP
Colorado River Board of California, Los Angeles, CA [*Library symbol Library of Congress*] (LCLS) .... CLCol
Colorado River Dam Fund [*Department of the Interior*] (GFGA) .... CRDF
Colorado River Indian Tribes Public Library, Parker, AZ [*Library symbol Library of Congress*] (LCLS) .... AzPa
Colorado River Municipal Water District .... CRMWD
Colorado River Storage Project [*Department of the Interior*] .... CRSP
Colorado School for the Deaf and Blind, Colorado Springs, CO [*Library symbol Library of Congress*] (LCLS) .... CoCD
Colorado School of Mines (GAGS) .... Colo Sch Mines
Colorado School of Mines [*Golden, CO*] .... CSM
Colorado School of Mines, Golden, CO [*Library symbol Library of Congress*] (LCLS) .... CoG
Colorado School of Mines, Golden, CO [*OCLC symbol*] (OCLC) .... COP
Colorado Society of Certified Public Accountants (SRA) .... CSCPA
Colorado Society of Osteopathic Medicine (SRA) .... CSOM
Colorado Speech-Language-Hearing Association (SRA) .... CSHA
Colorado Springs [*Colorado*] [*Airport symbol*] (OAG) .... COS
Colorado Springs, CO [*Location identifier FAA*] (FAAL) .... AFF
Colorado Springs, CO [*Location identifier FAA*] (FAAL) .... COS

Colorado Springs, CO [*AM radio station call letters*] .... KCMN
Colorado Springs, CO [*FM radio station call letters*] .... KEPC
Colorado Springs, CO [*FM radio station call letters*] .... KILO
Colorado Springs, CO [*AM radio station call letters*] .... KKCS
Colorado Springs, CO [*FM radio station call letters*] .... KKCS-FM
Colorado Springs, CO [*FM radio station call letters*] .... KKFM
Colorado Springs, CO [*Television station call letters*] .... KKTV
Colorado Springs, CO [*FM radio station call letters*] .... KRCC
Colorado Springs, CO [*AM radio station call letters*] .... KRDO
Colorado Springs, CO [*FM radio station call letters*] .... KRDO-FM
Colorado Springs, CO [*Television station call letters*] .... KRDO-TV
Colorado Springs, CO [*FM radio station call letters*] .... KSPZ
Colorado Springs, CO [*FM radio station call letters*] .... KTLF
Colorado Springs, CO [*AM radio station call letters*] .... KTWK
Colorado Springs, CO [*AM radio station call letters*] .... KVOR
Colorado Springs, CO [*AM radio station call letters*] .... KWYD
Colorado Springs, CO [*Television station call letters*] .... KXRM
Colorado Springs, CO [*Location identifier FAA*] (FAAL) .... LPI
Colorado Springs, CO [*Location identifier FAA*] (FAAL) .... SFC
Colorado Springs Fine Arts Center, Fine Arts and Anthropology of the Southwest, Library, Colorado Springs, CO [*Library symbol Library of Congress*] (LCLS) .... CoCF
Colorado Springs Maintenance and Operations System [*Space Defense Center*] .... COSMOS
Colorado Springs/Peterson Field [*Colorado*] [*ICAO location identifier*] (ICLI) .... KCOS
Colorado State Bar Association Report [*A publication*] (DLA) .... Colo St BA
Colorado State College [*Later, University of Northern Colorado*] .... CSC
Colorado State Department of Highways, Denver, CO [*Library symbol Library of Congress*] (LCLS) .... CoDCDH
Colorado State Department of Social Services, Denver, CO [*Library symbol Library of Congress*] (LCLS) .... CoDSS
Colorado State Historical Society, Denver, CO [*Library symbol Library of Congress*] (LCLS) .... CoHi
Colorado State Home and Training School, Grand Junction, CO [*Library symbol Library of Congress*] (LCLS) .... CoGjT
Colorado State Home and Training School, Medical Library, Wheatridge, CO [*Library symbol Library of Congress*] (LCLS) .... CoWeT-M
Colorado State Home and Training School, Residents' Library, Pueblo, CO [*Library symbol Library of Congress*] (LCLS) .... CoPT
Colorado State Home and Training School, Staff Library, Grand Junction, CO [*Library symbol Library of Congress*] (LCLS) .... CoGjTS
Colorado State Home and Training School, Staff Library, Pueblo, CO [*Library symbol Library of Congress*] (LCLS) .... CoPTS
Colorado State Home and Training School, Wheatridge, CO [*Library symbol Library of Congress*] (LCLS) .... CoWeT
Colorado State Home for the Aged, Trinidad, CO [*Library symbol Library of Congress*] (LCLS) .... CoTA
Colorado State Hospital, Children's Center, Pueblo, CO [*Library symbol Library of Congress*] (LCLS) .... CoPCS-C
Colorado State Hospital, Hospital Community Library, Pueblo, CO [*Library symbol Library of Congress*] (LCLS) .... CoPCS
Colorado State Hospital, Professional Library, Pueblo, CO [*Library symbol Library of Congress*] (LCLS) .... CoPCS-M
Colorado State Library, Denver, CO [*Library symbol Library of Congress*] (LCLS) .... Co
Colorado State Library, Denver, CO [*OCLC symbol*] (OCLC) .... COZ
Colorado State Library for the Blind and Physically Handicapped, Denver, CO [*Library symbol Library of Congress*] (LCLS) .... Co-B
Colorado State Library, Western Slope Clearinghouse, Grand Junction, CO [*Library symbol Library of Congress*] (LCLS) .... CoGjW
Colorado State Penitentiary, Canon City, CO [*Library symbol Library of Congress*] (LCLS) .... CoCcP
Colorado State Penitentiary, Colorado Women's Correctional Institution, Law Library, Canon City, CO [*Library symbol Library of Congress*] (LCLS) .... CoCcPWL
Colorado State Penitentiary, Colorado Women's Correctional Institution, Residents' Library, Canon City, CO [*Library symbol Library of Congress*] (LCLS) .... CoCcPW
Colorado State Penitentiary, Colorado Women's Correctional Institution, Staff Library, Canon City, CO [*Library symbol Library of Congress*] (LCLS) .... CoCcPWS
Colorado State Penitentiary, Law Library, Canon City, CO [*Library symbol Library of Congress*] (LCLS) .... CoCcPL
Colorado State Penitentiary, Medium Security Law Library, Canon City, CO [*Library symbol Library of Congress*] (LCLS) .... CoCcPML
Colorado State Penitentiary, Medium Security Residents' Library, Canon City, CO [*Library symbol Library of Congress*] (LCLS) .... CoCcPM
Colorado State Penitentiary, Medium Security Staff Library, Canon City, CO [*Library symbol Library of Congress*] (LCLS) .... CoCcPMS
Colorado State Penitentiary, Staff Library, Canon City, CO [*Library symbol Library of Congress*] (LCLS) .... CoCcPS
Colorado State Publications Depository and Distribution Center, Denver, CO [*OCLC symbol*] (OCLC) .... DDB
Colorado State Reformatory, Buena Vista, CO [*Library symbol Library of Congress*] (LCLS) .... CoBueR
Colorado State Reformatory, Law Library, Buena Vista, CO [*Library symbol Library of Congress*] (LCLS) .... CoBueRL
Colorado State Reformatory, Staff Library, Buena Vista, CO [*Library symbol Library of Congress*] (LCLS) .... CoBueRS
Colorado State University (GAGS) .... Colo St U
Colorado State University [*Fort Collins*] .... CSU
Colorado State University, Fort Collins, CO [*OCLC symbol*] (OCLC) .... COF
Colorado State University, Fort Collins, CO [*Library symbol Library of Congress*] (LCLS) .... CoFS

Colorado State University Research Foundation [*Research center*] (RCD) ... CSURF
Colorado State Veterans Center, Homelake, CO [*Library symbol Library of Congress*] (LCLS) ... CoHlV
Colorado State Veterans Nursing Home, Florence, CO [*Library symbol Library of Congress*] (LCLS) ... CoFloV
Colorado Supreme Court, Denver, CO [*Library symbol Library of Congress*] (LCLS) ... Co-SC
Colorado Supreme Court Library, Denver, CO [*OCLC symbol*] (OCLC) ... DVJ
Colorado Technical Reference Center [*University of Colorado - Boulder*] [*Information service or system*] (IID) ... CTRC
Colorado Tick Fever [*Hematology*] (DAVI) ... CTF
Colorado Union Catalog, Denver Public Library, Denver, CO [*OCLC symbol*] (OCLC) ... CLF
Colorado University (PDAA) ... CU
Colorado Video, Inc. ... CVI
Colorado Weights and Measures Laboratory [*National Institute of Standards and Technology*] ... CWML
Colorado Women's College [*Formerly, Temple Buell College*] ... CWC
Colorado Women's College, Denver, CO [*Library symbol Library of Congress*] (LCLS) ... CoDCW
Colorado Youth Center, Denver, CO [*Library symbol Library of Congress*] (LCLS) ... CoDYC
Colorado-Claro [*Medium-colored cigar*] ... CC
Colorado-Maduro [*Very dark-colored cigar*] ... CM
Colorado-Utah-Wyoming Committee, Chicago IL [*STAC*] ... CUW
Colorant Mixture Computer [*Du Pont trademark*] ... COMIC
Colorectal Cancer [*Oncology*] (DAVI) ... CRC
Colorectal Carcinoma [*Oncology*] ... CRC
Colo-Rectal Surgical Society ... CRSS
Colored ... CLD
Colored ... COL
Colored (ROG) ... COLD
Colored Digital Panel Meter (EECA) ... CDPM
Colored Electronic Attitude Director Indicator (MCD) ... CEADI
Colored Female ... C-F
Colored Methodist Episcopal Church (IIA) ... CME
Colored People's Time [*Slang*] ... CPT
Colored Plate [*Printing*] (DGA) ... COL PL
Colored-Bordered [*Paper*] (DGA) ... CB
Coloretur [*Let It Be Colored*] [*Pharmacy*] (ROG) ... COLOR
Color-Forming Units [*Biochemistry*] (DAVI) ... CFU
Colorimetric Solution ... CS
Colorimetry [*Biochemistry*] (MAE) ... color
Colorless [*Laboratory*] (DAVI) ... coll
Colortech Corp. [*Toronto Stock Exchange symbol*] ... CLR
Color-to-Color Register [*Graphic arts*] (DGA) ... CCR
Color-Word Interference Test ... CWIT
Colossal ... CLSSL
Colossal Energy, Inc. [*Vancouver Stock Exchange symbol*] ... COY
Colossal Magnetoresistance [*Physics*] ... CMR
Colossal Magnetoresistance [*Physics*] ... CMR
Colossal Resources [*NASDAQ symbol*] (TTSB) ... CLPZF
Colosseum [*Record label*] ... Csm
Colosseum of Motion Picture Salesmen (EA) ... CMPS
Colossians [*New Testament book*] ... Col
Colossians [*New Testament book*] (ROG) ... COLOSS
Colossus Resources [*Vancouver Stock Exchange symbol*] ... CZK
Colostomy and Ileostomy Association [*Medicine*] ... CIA
Colostomy Welfare Group [*British*] ... CWG
Colostrum-Free Bovine Serum ... CFBS
Colour Image Processor [*Computer science*] (NITA) ... CIP
Colour Index [*Used in the dye industry*] (DAVI) ... CI
Colour Printed Pottery Collectors Association (EA) ... CPPCA
Colour Sub Carrier [*Telecommunications*] (NITA) ... CSC
Colour Users' Association [*British*] (BI) ... CUA
Coloured Progressive Matrices ... CPM
Coloured Workers' Welfare Association [*British*] (BI) ... CWWA
Colour-Sergeant [*Army British*] (DMA) ... C/Sgt
Colour-Sergeant [*Army British*] ... COL-SERGT
Colour-Sergeant [*Army British*] (DMA) ... Col-Sgt
Colpocystourethropexy [*Medicine*] ... CCUP
Colposcopy [*Gynecology*] (DAVI) ... colpo
Colquechaca [*Bolivia*] [*ICAO location identifier*] (ICLI) ... SLHT
Colquhoun on Roman Civil Law [*A publication*] (DLA) ... Colq Civ Law
Colquhoun on Roman Civil Law [*A publication*] (DLA) ... Colq CL
Colquhoun on Roman Civil Law [*A publication*] (DLA) ... Colq Rom Civ Law
Colquhoun on Roman Civil Law [*A publication*] (DLA) ... Colq Rom Law
Colquhoun on the Judicature Acts [*A publication*] (DLA) ... Colq Jud A
Colquit's Reports [*1 Modern*] [*England*] [*A publication*] (DLA) ... Colq
Colquit's Reports [*1 Modern*] [*England*] [*A publication*] (DLA) ... Colquit
Colquitt-Thomas Regional Library, Moultrie, GA [*Library symbol Library of Congress*] (LCLS) ... GMoC
Colray Resources, Inc. [*Toronto Stock Exchange symbol*] ... CJR
Colson Canyon [*California*] [*Seismograph station code, US Geological Survey*] (SEIS) ... BCC
Colstrip Bicentennial Library, Colstrip, MT [*Library symbol*] [*Library of Congress*] (LCLS) ... MtCol
Colt [*Thoroughbred racing*] ... C
Colt Automatic Pistol Hammerless (DICI) ... CAPH
Colt Car Co. [*British ICAO designator*] (FAAC) ... CEA
Coltec Industries [*NYSE symbol*] (TTSB) ... COT
Coltec Industries, Inc. [*Associated Press*] (SAG) ... Coltec
Coltec Industries, Inc. [*NYSE symbol*] (SPSG) ... COT
Coltishall [*British ICAO location identifier*] (ICLI) ... EGYC
Coltman's Registration Appeal Cases [*1879-85*] [*England*] [*A publication*] (ILCA) ... Colt
Coltman's Registration Appeal Cases [*1879-85*] [*England*] [*A publication*] (DLA) ... Colt (Reg Ca)
Coltman's Registration Appeal Cases [*1879-85*] [*England*] [*A publication*] (DLA) ... Colt Reg Cas
Coltman's Registration Appeal Cases [*1879-85*] [*England*] [*A publication*] (DLA) ... Coltm
Colton High School, Colton, OR [*Library symbol Library of Congress*] (LCLS) ... OrColHS
Colton Public Library, Colton, CA [*Library symbol Library of Congress*] (LCLS) ... CCol
Colts Neck, NJ [*Location identifier FAA*] (FAAL) ... COL
Columba [*Constellation*] ... Col
Columba [*Constellation*] ... Colm
Columba House Fund [*Later, CIM*] (EA) ... CHF
Columbia [*Record Label*] [*Great Britain, Europe, Australia, etc.*] ... C
Columbia [*South Carolina*] [*Airport symbol*] ... CAE
Columbia [*Italy ICAO designator*] (FAAC) ... CLA
Columbia (ROG) ... COLUM
Columbia (ROG) ... COLUMB
Columbia [*Missouri*] [*Airport symbol*] (OAG) ... COU
Columbia [*South Carolina*] [*Seismograph station code, US Geological Survey Closed*] (SEIS) ... CSC
Columbia Airlines Ltd. [*Canada ICAO designator*] (FAAC) ... COL
Columbia & Cowlitz Railway Co. [*AAR code*] ... CLC
Columbia & Millstadt R. R. [*AAR code*] ... COML
Columbia Artists Management, Inc. ... CAMI
Columbia Bancorp [*NASDAQ symbol*] (SAG) ... CBMD
Columbia Bancorp [*Associated Press*] (SAG) ... ColumBc
Columbia Banking System [*NASDAQ symbol*] (TTSB) ... COLB
Columbia Banking Systems [*NASDAQ symbol*] (SAG) ... COLB
Columbia Banking Systems [*Associated Press*] (SAG) ... ColBnk
Columbia Basin Agricultural Research Center [*Oregon State University*] [*Research center*] (RCD) ... CBARC
Columbia Basin College, Pasco, WA [*Library symbol Library of Congress*] (LCLS) ... WaPaC
Columbia Basin Inter-Agency Committee [*Department of Commerce*] (NOAA) ... CBIAC
Columbia Bible College [*South Carolina*] ... CBC
Columbia Bible College, Clearbrook, British Columbia [*Library symbol National Library of Canada*] (BIB) ... BCCB
Columbia Bible College, Columbia, SC [*OCLC symbol*] (OCLC) ... SBI
Columbia Bible College, Columbia, SC [*Library symbol Library of Congress*] (LCLS) ... ScCoB
Columbia Bible College, Columbia, SC [*Library symbol*] [*Library of Congress*] (LCLS) ... ScCoBC
Columbia Broadcasting System [*Later, CBS, Inc.*] ... CBS
Columbia Broadcasting System, Inc., New York, NY [*Library symbol Library of Congress*] (LCLS) ... NNCBS
Columbia, CA [*Location identifier FAA*] (FAAL) ... CUF
Columbia, CA [*FM radio station call letters*] (RBYB) ... KTDO
Columbia Cellulose [*Company*] [*Canada*] ... COLCEL
Columbia Christian College, Portland, OR [*Library symbol Library of Congress*] (LCLS) ... OrPCol
Columbia City, IN [*FM radio station call letters*] ... WDJB
Columbia City, IN [*FM radio station call letters*] ... WJHS
Columbia College, Chicago, IL [*Inactive*] [*OCLC symbol*] (OCLC) ... IBZ
Columbia College, Chicago, IL [*Library symbol Library of Congress*] (LCLS) ... ICCC
Columbia College, Columbia, SC [*Library symbol Library of Congress*] (LCLS) ... ScCoC
Columbia College Library, Columbia, CA [*OCLC symbol*] (OCLC) ... CCY
Columbia Computing Services Ltd. [*Toronto Stock Exchange symbol*] ... CUP
Columbia County Historical Library, Valatie, NY [*Library symbol Library of Congress*] (LCLS) ... NValHi
Columbia County Historical Society, Bloomsburg, PA [*Library symbol Library of Congress*] (LCLS) ... PBbCHi
Columbia County, New York Official Historian, Hudson, NY [*Library symbol Library of Congress*] (LCLS) ... NHudHi
Columbia District Hospital, Medical Library, St. Helens, OR [*Library symbol Library of Congress*] (LCLS) ... OrSthDH
Columbia Encylopedia [*A publication*] ... CE
Columbia Falls, MT [*FM radio station call letters*] ... KCWX
Columbia First Federal Savings & Loan Association (MHDW) ... COAS
Columbia Gas System [*NYSE symbol*] (TTSB) ... CG
Columbia Gas System, Inc. [*NYSE symbol Toronto Stock Exchange symbol*] (SPSG) ... CG
Columbia Gas System Service Corp. [*of Columbia Gas System, Inc.*] ... CGSSC
Columbia Gay and Lesbian Alliance (EA) ... CGLA
Columbia Gulf Transmission Co., Houston, TX [*Library symbol Library of Congress*] (LCLS) ... TxHCG
Columbia HCA Healthcare Corp. [*NYSE symbol*] (SAG) ... COL
Columbia HCA Healthcare Corp. [*Formerly, Columbia Healthcare*] [*Associated Press*] (SAG) ... ColHCA
Columbia/HCA Hlthcare [*NYSE symbol*] (TTSB) ... COL
Columbia Healthcare [*NYSE symbol*] (SPSG) ... COL
Columbia Helicopters, Inc. [*ICAO designator*] (FAAC) ... WCO
Columbia Historical Society [*Later, HSWDC*] (EA) ... CHS
Columbia Historical Society, Washington, DC [*Library symbol Library of Congress*] (LCLS) ... DCHi
Columbia Homogenous Parallel Processor ... CHOPP
Columbia Hospital School of Nursing, Milwaukee, WI [*Library symbol Library of Congress*] (LCLS) ... WMCH
Columbia, IL [*FM radio station call letters*] ... WCBW

Columbia International Affairs Online [*Computer science*] ... Ciao
Columbia Journal of International Affairs [*A publication*] (DLA) ... Colum J Int'l Aff
Columbia Journalism Review [*A publication*] (BRI) ... CJR
Columbia Journalism Review [*A publication*] [*Columbia University*] [*New York, NY*] (WDMC) ... CJR
Columbia Junior College, Columbia, CA [*Library symbol Library of Congress*] (LCLS) ... CColumC
Columbia Jurist [*A publication*] (DLA) ... Colum Jr
Columbia Jurist [*A publication*] (DLA) ... Colum Jur
Columbia, KY [*AM radio station call letters*] ... WAIN
Columbia, KY [*FM radio station call letters*] ... WAIN-FM
Columbia, LA [*AM radio station call letters*] ... KCTO
Columbia, LA [*FM radio station call letters*] ... KCTO-FM
Columbia Laboratories [*AMEX symbol*] (TTSB) ... COB
Columbia Laboratories, Inc. [*AMEX symbol*] (SPSG) ... COB
Columbia Laboratories, Inc. [*Associated Press*] (SAG) ... COILB
Columbia Law Review [*A publication*] (BRI) ... CLR
Columbia Law Review [*A publication*] (ILCA) ... Col Law Rev
Columbia Law Times [*A publication*] (DLA) ... Colum LT
Columbia Leisure [*Vancouver Stock Exchange symbol*] ... COF
Columbia Mental Maturity Scale [*Psychology*] ... CMMS
Columbia Mental Maturity Test [*Psychology*] (DAVI) ... CMMT
Columbia, MO [*Location identifier FAA*] (FAAL) ... CBI
Columbia, MO [*Location identifier FAA*] (FAAL) ... COU
Columbia, MO [*FM radio station call letters*] ... KBIA
Columbia, MO [*FM radio station call letters*] ... KCMQ
Columbia, MO [*FM radio station call letters*] ... KCOU
Columbia, MO [*FM radio station call letters*] ... KFMZ
Columbia, MO [*AM radio station call letters*] ... KFRU
Columbia, MO [*Television station call letters*] ... KMIZ
Columbia, MO [*Television station call letters*] ... KOMU
Columbia, MO [*FM radio station call letters*] ... KOPN
Columbia, MO [*FM radio station call letters*] ... KOQL
Columbia, MO [*FM radio station call letters*] (RBYB) ... KPLA
Columbia, MO [*AM radio station call letters*] ... KTGR
Columbia, MO [*FM radio station call letters*] ... KWWC
Columbia/Mt. Pleasant, TN [*Location identifier FAA*] (FAAL) ... MRC
Columbia/Mt. Pleasant, TN [*Location identifier FAA*] (FAAL) ... PBC
Columbia, MS [*Location identifier FAA*] (FAAL) ... FOH
Columbia, MS [*AM radio station call letters*] ... WCJU
Columbia, MS [*AM radio station call letters*] ... WFFF
Columbia, MS [*FM radio station call letters*] ... WFFF-FM
Columbia National Fisheries Research Laboratory [*Later, NFCRC*] [*Department of the Interior Columbia, MO*] (GRD) ... CNFRL
Columbia National Fisheries Research Laboratory, Columbia, MO [*OCLC symbol*] (OCLC) ... FZX
Columbia, NC [*FM radio station call letters*] ... WRSF
Columbia, NC [*Television station call letters*] ... WUND
Columbia, Newberry & Laurens Railroad Co. [*AAR code*] ... CNL
Columbia, PA [*AM radio station call letters*] ... WNZT
Columbia Public Library, Columbia, IL [*Library symbol Library of Congress*] (LCLS) ... IColu
Columbia Research and Development Corp. (MCD) ... CRDC
Columbia River and Tributaries Study (NOAA) ... CR & T
Columbia River Basalt Group [*Geology*] ... CRBG
Columbia River Basalts [*Geology*] ... CRB
Columbia River Basin Treaty (NOAA) ... CRBT
Columbia River Conservation League (EA) ... CRCL
Columbia River Datum ... CRD
Columbia River Fisheries Development Program ... CRFDP
Columbia River Maritime Museum, Astoria, OR [*Library symbol Library of Congress*] (LCLS) ... OrAstM
Columbia River Operational Hydromet Management System (NOAA) ... CROHMS
Columbia River Salmon and Tuna Packers Association (EA) ... CRSTPA
Columbia, SC [*Location identifier FAA*] (FAAL) ... CUB
Columbia, SC [*Location identifier FAA*] (FAAL) ... EOV
Columbia, SC [*Location identifier FAA*] (FAAL) ... MMT
Columbia, SC [*Television station call letters*] ... WACH
Columbia, SC [*FM radio station call letters*] ... WARQ
Columbia, SC [*AM radio station call letters*] ... WCOS
Columbia, SC [*FM radio station call letters*] ... WCOS-FM
Columbia, SC [*AM radio station call letters*] ... WCTG
Columbia, SC [*Television station call letters*] ... WIS
Columbia, SC [*AM radio station call letters*] (RBYB) ... WISW
Columbia, SC [*FM radio station call letters*] ... WLTR
Columbia, SC [*Television station call letters*] ... WLTX
Columbia, SC [*FM radio station call letters*] ... WMHK
Columbia, SC [*FM radio station call letters*] ... WNOK
Columbia, SC [*AM radio station call letters*] ... WOIC
Columbia, SC [*Television station call letters*] ... WOLO
Columbia, SC [*FM radio station call letters*] ... WOMG-FM
Columbia, SC [*AM radio station call letters*] ... WQXL
Columbia, SC [*Television station call letters*] ... WRLK
Columbia, SC [*FM radio station call letters*] ... WUSC
Columbia, SC [*AM radio station call letters*] ... WVOC
Columbia Scholastic Press Advisers Association (EA) ... CSPAA
Columbia Scholastic Press Association (EA) ... CSPA
Columbia Sheep Breeders Association of America (EA) ... CSBA
Columbia Society of International Law. Bulletin [*A publication*] (DLA) ... Colum Soc'y Int'l L Bull
Columbia State Community College, Columbia, TN [*Library symbol*] [*Library of Congress*] (LCLS) ... TCoC
Columbia Survey of Human Rights Law [*A publication*] (DLA) ... Colum Surv Hum Rts L
Columbia Survey of Human Rights Law [*A publication*] (DLA) ... Colum Survey Human Rights L
Columbia Theological Seminary, Decatur, GA [*OCLC symbol*] (OCLC) ... GCL
Columbia Theological Seminary, Decatur, GA [*Library symbol Library of Congress*] (LCLS) ... GDC
Columbia, TN [*FM radio station call letters*] ... WAYM
Columbia, TN [*FM radio station call letters*] ... WKOM
Columbia, TN [*AM radio station call letters*] ... WKRM
Columbia, TN [*AM radio station call letters*] ... WMCP
Columbia, TN [*AM radio station call letters*] ... WMRB
Columbia Township Library, Unionville, MI [*Library symbol Library of Congress*] (LCLS) ... MiUnv
Columbia Union College, Takoma Park, MD [*OCLC symbol*] (OCLC) ... CUC
Columbia Union College, Takoma Park, MD [*Library symbol Library of Congress*] (LCLS) ... DColU
Columbia Unit District 4, Columbia, IL [*Library symbol Library of Congress*] (LCLS) ... IColuD
Columbia University (GAGS) ... Columbia U
Columbia University [*New York, NY*] ... CU
Columbia University, American Typefounders' Library, New York, NY [*Library symbol Library of Congress*] (LCLS) ... NNC-Typ
Columbia University, Avery Library of Architecture, New York, NY [*Library symbol Library of Congress*] (LCLS) ... NNC-A
Columbia University, Biological Sciences Library, New York, NY [*Library symbol Library of Congress*] (LCLS) ... NNC-B
Columbia University, Business-Economic Library, New York, NY [*Library symbol*] [*Library of Congress*] (LCLS) ... NNC-BE
Columbia University, College of Pharmacy, New York, NY [*Library symbol Library of Congress*] (LCLS) ... NNC-P
[*The*] **Columbia University College of Physicians and Surgeons Complete HomeMedical Guide** [*A publication*] ... CHMG
Columbia University, Division of War Research ... CUDWR
Columbia University, East Asiatic Library, New York, NY [*Library symbol Library of Congress*] (LCLS) ... NNC-EA
Columbia University Electronic Research Laboratory (SAA) ... CUERL
Columbia University Electronics Research Laboratories ... CUERL
Columbia University Hudson Laboratory ... CUHL
Columbia University, International Institute for the Study of Human Reproduction, Center for Population and Family Health, New York, NY [*Library symbol Library of Congress*] (LCLS) ... NNC-Pop
Columbia University, Lamont-Doherty Geological Observatory, Palisades, NY [*Library symbol Library of Congress*] (LCLS) ... NNC-G
Columbia University, Law Library, New York, NY [*Library symbol Library of Congress*] (LCLS) ... NNC-L
Columbia University, Medical Library, New York, NY [*Library symbol Library of Congress*] (LCLS) ... NNC-M
Columbia University, New York, NY [*Library symbol Library of Congress*] (LCLS) ... NNC
Columbia University Press ... CUP
Columbia University, Psychology Library, New York, NY [*Library symbol Library of Congress*] (LCLS) ... NNC-Ps
Columbia University, Teachers College, New York, NY [*Library symbol Library of Congress*] (LCLS) ... NNC-T
Columbia Valley Authority ... CVA
Columbia, Yale, Harvard [*Used to refer to a project involving the medical libraries of these universities*] ... COLYAHAR
Columbia-Greene Community College, Athens, NY [*Library symbol Library of Congress*] (LCLS) ... NAtC
Columbia-Greene Community College, Hudson, NY [*Library symbol Library of Congress*] (LCLS) ... NHudC
Columbia-Lafayette-Ouachita-Calhoun Regional Library, Magnolia, AR [*Library symbol*] [*Library of Congress*] (LCLS) ... ArMag
Columbian Squires (EA) ... CS
Columbiana County Court House, Lisbon, OH [*Library symbol Library of Congress*] (LCLS) ... OLiC
Columbiana Public Library, Columbiana, OH [*Library symbol Library of Congress*] (LCLS) ... OCoa
Columbia-Presbyterian Medical Center (DMAA) ... CPMC
Columbine Elementary School, Grand Junction, CO [*Library symbol Library of Congress*] (LCLS) ... CoGjCoE
Columbium [*A chemical element; modern name is niobium, see Nb*] ... Cb
Columbus [*Ohio*] [*Airport symbol*] (OAG) ... CMH
Columbus (ROG) ... COL
Columbus [*Georgia*] [*Airport symbol*] (OAG) ... CSG
Columbus [*Mississippi*] [*Airport symbol*] (OAG) ... GTR
Columbus [*Nebraska*] [*Airport symbol*] (OAG) ... OLU
Columbus [*Mississippi*] [*Airport symbol*] (AD) ... UBS
Columbus Air Transport, Inc. [*ICAO designator*] (FAAC) ... KLR
Columbus & Greenville Railway Co. ... C & G
Columbus & Greenville Railway Co. [*AAR code*] ... CAGY
Columbus Army Depot [*Ohio*] (AABC) ... COAD
Columbus Avia [*Ukraine*] [*FAA designator*] (FAAC) ... CBS
Columbus City School, Columbus, OH [*OCLC symbol*] (OCLC) ... CSS
Columbus College (GAGS) ... Columbus C
Columbus College, Columbus, GA [*Library symbol Library of Congress*] (LCLS) ... GColuC
Columbus College, Library, Columbus, GA [*OCLC symbol*] (OCLC) ... GCO
Columbus: Countdown 1992 [*An association*] (EA) ... CC 1992
Columbus County Public Library, Whiteville, NC [*Library symbol Library of Congress*] (LCLS) ... NcWhC
Columbus Elementary School, Freeport, NY [*Library symbol Library of Congress*] (LCLS) ... NFreeCE
Columbus Elementary School, Grand Junction, CO [*Library symbol Library of Congress*] (LCLS) ... CoGjCsE
Columbus Energy [*AMEX symbol*] (TTSB) ... EGY

Columbus Energy Corp. [*Associated Press*] (SAG) ... ColuEng
Columbus Energy Corp. [*AMEX symbol*] (SPSG) ... EGY
Columbus [*Georgia*] **Fort Benning** [*Airport symbol*] (OAG) ... QFE
Columbus, GA [*Location identifier FAA*] (FAAL) ... AWS
Columbus, GA [*FM radio station call letters*] ... WCGQ
Columbus, GA [*AM radio station call letters*] ... WDAK
Columbus, GA [*AM radio station call letters*] ... WEAM
Columbus, GA [*FM radio station call letters*] ... WFRC
Columbus, GA [*FM radio station call letters*] ... WFXE
Columbus, GA [*Television station call letters*] ... WJSP
Columbus, GA [*Television station call letters*] ... WLTZ
Columbus, GA [*AM radio station call letters*] ... WOKS
Columbus, GA [*Television station call letters*] ... WRBL
Columbus, GA [*AM radio station call letters*] ... WRCG
Columbus, GA [*FM radio station call letters*] ... WTJB
Columbus, GA [*AM radio station call letters*] ... WTMQ
Columbus, GA [*Television station call letters*] ... WTVM
Columbus, GA [*FM radio station call letters*] ... WVRK
Columbus, GA [*Television station call letters*] ... WXTX
Columbus, GA [*FM radio station call letters*] ... WYFK
Columbus, GA [*Location identifier FAA*] (FAAL) ... XLE
Columbus Gazette & Columbus Safeguard, Columbus Junction, IA [*Library symbol Library of Congress*] (LCLS) ... IaCjGS
Columbus High School, Columbus, MT [*Library symbol*] [*Library of Congress*] (LCLS) ... MtCoHS
Columbus Hospital, Health Sciences Library, Great Falls, MT [*Library symbol Library of Congress*] (LCLS) ... MtGrCH
Columbus, IN [*Location identifier FAA*] (FAAL) ... BAK
Columbus, IN [*AM radio station call letters*] ... WCSI
Columbus, IN [*FM radio station call letters*] ... WKKG
Columbus, IN [*FM radio station call letters*] ... WWWY
Columbus, KS [*FM radio station call letters*] ... KOCD
Columbus McKinnon [*NASDAQ symbol*] (TTSB) ... CMCO
Columbus, MS [*Location identifier FAA*] (FAAL) ... CBM
Columbus, MS [*Location identifier FAA*] (FAAL) ... IGB
Columbus, MS [*Location identifier FAA*] (FAAL) ... TBB
Columbus, MS [*Location identifier FAA*] (FAAL) ... UBS
Columbus, MS [*AM radio station call letters*] ... WACR
Columbus, MS [*FM radio station call letters*] ... WACR-FM
Columbus, MS [*Television station call letters*] ... WCBI
Columbus, MS [*AM radio station call letters*] ... WJWF
Columbus, MS [*FM radio station call letters*] ... WKOR
Columbus, MS [*FM radio station call letters*] ... WMBC
Columbus, MS [*FM radio station call letters*] ... WMUW
Columbus/Municipal [*New Mexico*] [*ICAO location identifier*] (ICLI) ... KCUS
Columbus, NE [*AM radio station call letters*] ... KJSK
Columbus, NE [*FM radio station call letters*] ... KKOT
Columbus, NE [*FM radio station call letters*] ... KLIR
Columbus, NE [*FM radio station call letters*] ... KTLX
Columbus, NE [*AM radio station call letters*] ... KTTT
Columbus, NE [*Location identifier FAA*] (FAAL) ... PLT
Columbus News Index [*Public Library of Columbus and Franklin County*] [*Information service or system*] (IID) ... CNI
Columbus, NM [*Location identifier FAA*] (FAAL) ... CUS
Columbus, OH [*Location identifier FAA*] (FAAL) ... BUZ
Columbus, OH [*Location identifier FAA*] (FAAL) ... CBP
Columbus, OH [*Location identifier FAA*] (FAAL) ... DDV
Columbus, OH [*Location identifier FAA*] (FAAL) ... DKG
Columbus, OH [*Location identifier FAA*] (FAAL) ... IVX
Columbus, OH [*Location identifier FAA*] (FAAL) ... LCK
Columbus, OH [*Location identifier FAA*] (FAAL) ... OSU
Columbus, OH [*Location identifier FAA*] (FAAL) ... OYY
Columbus, OH [*AM radio station call letters*] ... WBNS
Columbus, OH [*FM radio station call letters*] ... WBNS-FM
Columbus, OH [*Television station call letters*] ... WBNS-TV
Columbus, OH [*FM radio station call letters*] ... WBZX
Columbus, OH [*Television station call letters*] ... WCMH
Columbus, OH [*AM radio station call letters*] ... WCOL
Columbus, OH [*FM radio station call letters*] ... WCOL-FM
Columbus, OH [*FM radio station call letters*] ... WJZA
Columbus, OH [*FM radio station call letters*] ... WLVQ
Columbus, OH [*AM radio station call letters*] ... WMNI
Columbus, OH [*FM radio station call letters*] ... WNCI
Columbus, OH [*AM radio station call letters*] ... WOSU
Columbus, OH [*FM radio station call letters*] ... WOSU-FM
Columbus, OH [*Television station call letters*] ... WOSU-TV
Columbus, OH [*FM radio station call letters*] ... WSNY
Columbus, OH [*Television station call letters*] ... WSYX
Columbus, OH [*Television station call letters*] ... WTTE
Columbus, OH [*AM radio station call letters*] ... WTVN
Columbus, OH [*FM radio station call letters*] (RBYB) ... WUFM-FM
Columbus, OH [*AM radio station call letters*] ... WVKO
Columbus, Ohio Regional News Index [*Grandview Heights Public Library*] [*Information service or system*] (IID) ... CORNI
Columbus Orbital Facility [*Space technology*] ... COF
Columbus/Port Columbus International [*Ohio*] [*ICAO location identifier*] (ICLI) ... KCMH
Columbus Public Library, Columbus, NE [*Library symbol Library of Congress*] (LCLS) ... NbCo
Columbus Public Library, Columbus, OH [*Library symbol Library of Congress*] (LCLS) ... OCo
Columbus Realty Trust [*NYSE symbol*] (SPSG) ... CLB
Columbus Realty Trust [*Associated Press*] (SAG) ... ColumRT
Columbus Republic, Columbus, IN [*Library symbol*] [*Library of Congress*] (LCLS) ... InColuR
Columbus Research Tool [*Control Data Corp.*] ... CRT
Columbus SoPwr 8.375% Sub Db [*NYSE symbol*] (TTSB) ... CSJ
Columbus Southern Power Co. [*Associated Press*] (SAG) ... ColSP25
Columbus Southern Power Co. [*NYSE symbol*] (SAG) ... CSJ
Columbus Southern Power Co. [*NYSE symbol*] (SAG) ... CSU
Columbus State Hospital, Columbus, OH [*Library symbol Library of Congress*] (LCLS) ... OCoSH
Columbus Technical Institute, Columbus, OH [*OCLC symbol*] (OCLC) ... CTI
Columbus Technical Institute, Columbus, OH [*Library symbol Library of Congress*] (LCLS) ... OCoCT
Columbus, TX [*FM radio station call letters*] ... KULM
Columbus, WI [*FM radio station call letters*] ... WYKY
Columbus-Worthington, OH [*AM radio station call letters*] ... WRFD
Columellar Muscle ... CM
Column (IAA) ... CLM
Column (VRA) ... clm
Column [*Typesetting*] (WDMC) ... clm
Column (WDMC) ... col
Column (AAG) ... COL
Column (AFM) ... COLM
Column ... COLN
Column Base ... CB
Column Chromatography [*Analytical chemistry*] ... CC
Column Chromatography - High-Performance [*or Pressure*] **Liquid Chromatography** [*Analytical chemistry*] ... CC-HPLC
Column Code Suppression [*Computer science*] (IAA) ... CCS
Column Extractant [*Nuclear energy*] (NRCH) ... CX
Column Feed [*Nuclear energy*] (NRCH) ... CF
Column Gap [*Army*] (AABC) ... COLMGP
Column Liquid Chromatography ... CLC
Column Position Counter ... CPC
Column Product [*Nuclear energy*] (NRCH) ... CP
Column Research Council [*Later, SSRC*] (EA) ... CRC
Column Shock Protection [*Chromatography*] ... CSP
Column Split [*Computer science*] (IAA) ... CS
Column Valve Diaphragm ... CVD
Column Waste [*Nuclear energy*] (NRCH) ... CW
Column-Address Strobe (IEEE) ... CAS
Columnar-Lined Lower Esophagus [*Gastroenterology*] (DAVI) ... CLLE
Column-Digit Binary Network ... CDBN
Columnea Latent Viroid [*Plant pathology*] ... CLVd
Columns (ROG) ... COLS
Colusa, CA [*FM radio station call letters*] ... KKCY
Colusa, CA [*FM radio station call letters*] ... KPPL
Colusa County Free Library, Colusa, CA [*Library symbol Library of Congress*] (LCLS) ... CColu
Colusa County Genealogical Society, Colusa, CA [*Library symbol*] [*Library of Congress*] (LCLS) ... CColuGS
Colville [*Washington*] [*Seismograph station code, US Geological Survey Closed*] (SEIS) ... CLW
Colville River, AK [*Location identifier FAA*] (FAAL) ... CVL
Colville, WA [*FM radio station call letters*] ... KCRK
Colville, WA [*AM radio station call letters*] ... KCVL
Colvil's Manuscript Decisions, Scotch Court of Session [*A publication*] (DLA) ... Colvil
Colvin Aviation, Inc. [*ICAO designator*] (FAAC) ... NVE
Colyar on Guarantees [*A publication*] (DLA) ... Coly Guar (De)
Com Dev Ltd., Cambridge, Ontario [*Library symbol National Library of Canada*] (NLC) ... OCCD
Com/Tech Commun Tech [*NASDAQ symbol*] (TTSB) ... CMTK
Coma Berenices [*Berenice's Hair*] [*Constellation*] [*Latin*] (BARN) ... Com
Coma Level Greater than 400 Milligrams per Liter [*Medicine*] (DAVI) ... COM3
Coma Recovery Association (EA) ... CRA
Comac Condition Base Monitor Module [*Comac Systems Ltd.*] [*Software package*] (NCC) ... CCBMM
Comair [*ICAO designator*] (AD) ... OH
Comair Holdings [*NASDAQ symbol*] (TTSB) ... COMR
Comair, Inc. [*ICAO designator*] (FAAC) ... COM
Comair, Inc. [*Associated Press*] (SAG) ... Comair
Comair, Inc. [*NASDAQ symbol*] (SAG) ... COMR
Comanche Crew Support System [*Army*] (RDA) ... CCSS
Comanche, OK [*FM radio station call letters*] ... KDDQ
Comanche Petroleums [*Vancouver Stock Exchange symbol*] ... COA
Comanche, TX [*AM radio station call letters*] ... KCOM
Comando de Material - Fabrica Militar de Aviones [*Argentina ICAO aircraft manufacturer identifier*] (ICAO) ... IA
Comando de Operacoes do Continente [*Continental Operations Command*] [*Portugal*] ... COPCON
Comando de Resistencia Popular Javier Carrera [*Javier Carrera Popular Resistance Commando*] [*Chile*] (PD) ... CRP
Comando Geral do Ar [*Brazilian Air Force*] ... COMGAR
Comando Guerrilleros del Pueblo [*Guerrilla group*] [*Guatemala*] (EY) ... CGP
Comando Urbano Revolucionario [*Guatemala*] [*Political party*] (EY) ... CUR
Comandor Avia [*Ukraine*] [*FAA designator*] (FAAC) ... CMD
Comandos Armados de Liberacion [*Armed Liberation Commandos*] [*Puerto Rico*] (PD) ... CAL
Comandos Autonomos Anti-Capitalistas [*Spain Political party*] (EY) ... CAA
Comandos Revolucionarios del Pueblo [*Peru*] [*Political party*] (EY) ... CRP
Comaplex Resources International Ltd. [*Toronto Stock Exchange symbol*] ... CXR
Comarapa [*Bolivia*] [*ICAO location identifier*] (ICLI) ... SLCR
COMARC [*Cooperative Machine-Readable Cataloging Program*] [*Source file*] [*UTLAS symbol*] ... CMC
COMARCO, Inc. [*NASDAQ symbol*] (NQ) ... CMRO
Comarco, Inc. [*Associated Press*] (SAG) ... Comrco
Comayagua [*Honduras*] [*ICAO location identifier*] (ICLI) ... MHCG

Comb Filter [*Military*] (CAAL) ... CF
Combat [*In unit designations and symbols only*] ... C
Combat (AABC) ... CBT
Combat (AFM) ... CMBT
Combat (CINC) ... COMBT
Combat Action Ribbon [*Military decoration*] (VNW) ... CAR
Combat Active and Passive RADAR Identification System (MCD) ... CAPRIS
Combat Activity Report [*Navy*] ... COACT
Combat Air Crew ... CAC
Combat Air Delivery Division [*Air Force*] (AFM) ... CADD
Combat Air Operations Center (CINC) ... CAOC
Combat Air Patrol ... CAP
Combat Air Patrol Mission [*Air Force*] ... CPM
Combat Air Patrol Support [*Aircraft*] (PDAA) ... CAPS
Combat Air Traffic Controller [*Air Force*] (VNW) ... CATC
Combat Air Vehicle Navigation and Vision ... CAVNAV
Combat Aircraft Prototype (MCD) ... CAP
Combat Aircraft Recording and Data System ... CARDS
Combat Aircraft Service Unit [*Navy*] (MUGU) ... CASU
Combat Aircraft Service Unit (Fleet) [*Navy*] (DNAB) ... CASU(F)
Combat Aircraft Technology ... CAT
Combat Aircrew [*or Aircrewman*] ... CA
Combat Aircrew Recovery [*or Rescue*] **Aircraft** [*Later, ARRS, ARS*] ... CARA
Combat Aircrew Training Unit [*Navy*] ... CATU
Combat Airlift Support Unit [*Air Force*] ... CALSU
Combat Alert Aircrew [*Air Force*] ... CAAC
Combat Alert Center (SAA) ... CAC
Combat Analysis Capability (MCD) ... CAC
Combat Analysis Extended ... COMANEX
Combat Analysis Group [*Joint Chiefs of Staff*] ... CAG
Combat and Combat Support System (MCD) ... CCSS
Combat and Liaison (CINC) ... CL
Combat and Training Development Management Information System ... CTDMIS
Combat Applications Squadron [*Air Force*] ... CAS
Combat Aptitude Area (AABC) ... CO
Combat Area Surveillance System (PDAA) ... CASS
Combat Arms ... CA
Combat Arms Division (INF) ... CAD
Combat Arms Enlistment Bonus [*Military*] ... CAEB
Combat Arms Group [*Army*] (AABC) ... CAG
Combat Arms Regimental System [*Army*] ... CARS
Combat Artist Team ... CAT
Combat Assault ... CA
Combat Assessment of Readiness and Training (DOMA) ... CART
Combat Assistance Team [*US military advisory team, Vietnam*] (VNW) ... CAT
Combat Attrition and Intensity of War (MCD) ... CATIWAR
Combat Augmentation Subsystem (MCD) ... CBAS
Combat Aviation Battalion [*or Brigade*] ... CAB
Combat Aviation Group ... CAG
Combat Brigade Air Attack ... CBAA
Combat Brigade Air Cavalry ... CBAC
Combat Capabilities (MCD) ... COMCAP
[*Readiness status*] [*Fully*] **Combat Capable** [*Military*] (DOMA) ... C-1
Combat Cargo Command ... CCC
Combat Cargo Group (CINC) ... CCG
Combat Cargo Mission [*Air Force*] ... CCM
Combat Cargo Officer [*Military*] (NVT) ... CCO
Combat Cargo Task Force [*British military*] (DMA) ... CCTF
Combat Center [*Military*] ... CC
Combat Center Active [*Military*] (SAA) ... CCA
Combat Center and Crosstell (SAA) ... CC & T
Combat Center Director ... CCD
Combat Center Duty Officer [*Military*] (SAA) ... CCDO
Combat Center Function [*Military*] (SAA) ... CCF
Combat Center Group [*Military*] (SAA) ... CCG
Combat Center Programming Leader [*Military*] (SAA) ... CCPL
Combat Center Remoted [*Military*] ... CCR
Combat Center Simulation Generation System [*Military*] (SAA) ... CSGS
Combat Center Standby [*Military*] (SAA) ... CCS
Combat Center Status Indicator [*Military*] (SAA) ... CCSL
Combat Clothing [*NATO*] ... CC
Combat Clothing and Equipment Working Party [*NATO*] ... CCEWP
Combat Command [*Initialism may be followed by a number as, CC2, to indicate a specific, numbered command*] [*Army*] ... CC
Combat Command A ... CCA
Combat Command B ... CCB
Combat Command C ... CCC
Combat Command D ... CCD
Combat Command L ... CCL
Combat Command Reserve ... CCR
Combat Command V ... CCV
Combat Commandant [*Military*] ... CC
Combat Communications Equipment [*Military*] ... CCE
Combat Communications Flight ... CCFT
Combat Communications Group (AFIT) ... CCG
Combat Communications Group [*Air Force*] ... CCGP
Combat Communications Squadron [*Air Force*] (AFIT) ... CCS
Combat Configured Load [*Military*] (INF) ... CCL
Combat Consumption [*Military*] ... CC
Combat Consumption Support from D-Day to P-Day [*Military*] (AABC) ... DPSPT
Combat Control [*Army*] ... CC
Combat Control [*Army*] ... COMCON
Combat Control Elements [*Army*] ... CCE
Combat Control Group ... CCG
Combat Control Squadron ... CCS
Combat, Control, Support [*Army*] ... COMCONSUP
Combat Control System [*Military*] (CAAL) ... CCS
Combat Control System Mark 2 [*Navy*] ... CCS MK2
Combat Control Systems Improvement Program [*Military*] (CAAL) ... CCSIP
Combat Control Team [*Australia*] ... CCT
Combat Controller [*Air Force*] (VNW) ... CCT
Combat Correspondent ... CC
Combat Crew [*Air Force*] (AFM) ... CCr
Combat Crew Replacement Center [*World War II*] ... CCRC
Combat Crew Training [*Air Force*] (AFM) ... CCT
Combat Crew Training School [*Air Force*] (AFM) ... CCTS
Combat Crew Training School [*Air Force*] ... CCTSCH
Combat Crew Training Squadron (MCD) ... CCTS
Combat Crew Training Squadron [*Air Force*] ... CCTSq
Combat Crew Training Wing [*Air Force*] ... CCTW
Combat Crew Training Wing [*Air Force*] (AFM) ... CCTWg
Combat Cryptological Support Console (MCD) ... CCSC
Combat Damage/Assessment Model (MCD) ... CODAM
Combat Damage Information Center [*Military*] ... CDIC
Combat Data Director [*Military*] (SAA) ... CDD
Combat Data Information Center [*Army*] ... CDIC
Combat Days of Supply (MCD) ... CDOS
Combat Defense Force ... CDF
Combat Developer (AAGC) ... Cbt Dev
Combat Developer ... CBTDEV
Combat Developer Proponent (MCD) ... CDP
Combat Development ... CD
Combat Development Branch ... CDB
Combat Development Command [*Terminated, 1973*] [*Army*] (MCD) ... CDC
Combat Development Command Experimentation Center [*Terminated Army*] (MCD) ... CDCEC
Combat Development Command Infantry Agency [*Terminated Army*] ... CDCIA
Combat Development Command - Intelligence Agency [*Terminated Army*] (MCD) ... CDC-INTA
Combat Development Command Maintenance Agency [*Terminated Army*] ... CDCMA
Combat Development Command Transportation Agency [*Terminated Army*] ... CDCTA
Combat Development Experimentation Center [*Fort Ord, CA*] (MCD) ... CDEC
Combat Development Experimentation Center (AAGC) ... CDEC
Combat Development Objective Guide [*CDC*] ... CDOG
Combat Development Office ... CDO
Combat Development Phase (MCD) ... CDP
Combat Development Plan (MCD) ... CDP
Combat Development Process (MCD) ... CDP
Combat Development Project [*Army*] ... CDP
Combat Development Support Facility ... CDSF
Combat Development Support Manager [*Army*] ... CDSM
Combat Development Technical Evaluation Center ... CDTEC
Combat Development Test Center (CINC) ... CDTC
Combat Development Test Center - Vietnam ... CDTC-V
Combat Developments and Material Evaluation [*Program*] [*Army*] ... CD & ME
Combat Developments Evaluation Command (MCD) ... CDEC
Combat Developments Experimentation Command [*Army*] ... CDE
Combat Developments Experimentation Command [*Army*] (RDA) ... CDEC
Combat Developments Planning Group (MCD) ... CDPG
Combat Direction Center (NVT) ... CDC
Combat Direction Center Officer [*Navy*] (DOMA) ... CDCO
Combat Direction Systems (NVT) ... CDS
Combat Documentation (AFM) ... COMDOC
Combat Earthmover [*Army*] ... CEM
Combat Effective Training Management (MCD) ... CETRM
Combat Effectiveness Measure [*Military*] (CAAL) ... CEM
Combat Effectiveness Report (NATG) ... CER
Combat Effectiveness with Logistics Support (MCD) ... CELOGS
Combat Electronic Warfare and Intelligence O & S [*Operations and Support*] **Concept Development** ... CEWISCON
Combat Electronic Warfare Intelligence ... CEWI
Combat Element [*Marine Corps*] (DOMA) ... CE
Combat Elevation Launch ... CEL
Combat Emplacement Excavator ... CEE
Combat Engineer Battalion (DNAB) ... CBTENGRBN
Combat Engineer Mission Management Module [*Software*] ... CEM3
Combat Engineer Party [*Army*] (VNW) ... CEP
Combat Engineer Supply Vehicle (MCD) ... CESV
Combat Engineer Team [*Army*] (VNW) ... CET
Combat Engineer Tractor [*British*] (RDA) ... CET
Combat Engineer Vehicle [*Army*] ... CEV
Combat Equipment Battalion, North [*Military*] ... CEBN
Combat Equipment Group, Europe (MCD) ... CEGE
Combat Essential Items List [*Army*] ... CEIL
Combat Evaluation Group [*Strategic Air Command*] (SAA) ... CEG
Combat Evaluation Group [*Strategic Air Command*] ... CEVG
Combat Evaluation Model (MCD) ... CEM
Combat Evaluation Squadron [*Air Force*] ... CESq
Combat Excavator [*Military*] ... CEX
Combat Exercises [*Canadian Navy*] ... COMBATEX
Combat Field Feeding System [*Army*] (INF) ... CFFS
Combat Fitness Badge [*Army*] (INF) ... CFB
Combat Fitness Retraining Unit ... CFRU
Combat Gap Crosser [*Army*] ... CGC
Combat Group ... CG
Combat Gunnery Officers School [*Army Air Forces*] ... CGOS
Combat Identification [*Army*] (RDA) ... CID
Combat Identification Dismounted Soldier System [*Army*] (INF) ... CIDSS

Combat Identification System ... CIS
Combat Identification System Program Officer (MCD) ... CISPO
Combat Identification Systems Project Office [*Army*] ... CISPO
Combat Identification Tank Force [*Army*] ... CITF
Combat Identification Task Force [*Army*] (DOMA) ... CITF
Combat Illumination (MCD) ... COIL
Combat Indoctrination (MCD) ... CI
Combat Ineffective [*Military*] (NVT) ... CI
Combat Infantryman's Badge [*Military decoration*] ... CIB
Combat Information and Detection (NVT) ... CID
Combat Information Center [*Navy*] ... CIC
Combat Information Center Office [*or Officer*] [*Navy*] (MUGU) ... CICO
Combat Information Center Watch Officer [*Navy*] ... CICWO
Combat Information Net ... CIN
Combat Information Systems Flight [*Military*] ... CISF
Combat Intelligence ... CBTI
Combat Intelligence Center ... CIC
Combat Intelligence Officer [*Navy*] ... CIO
Combat Intelligence Operations Center (MCD) ... CIOC
Combat Intelligence Plot (NATG) ... CIP
Combat Intelligence Proficiency Course [*Military*] (INF) ... CIPC
Combat Intelligence System (MCD) ... CIS
Combat Intercept Control ... CIC
Combat Interviews ... CI
Combat Launch and Recovery Kit (AFM) ... CLARK
Combat Leader's Guide (INF) ... CLG
Combat Lessons Bulletin ... CLB
Combat Logistic Support System (AABC) ... CLSS
Combat Logistics Force [*Navy*] (GFGA) ... CLF
Combat Logistics Network [*DoD*] ... COMLOGNET
Combat Logistics Support Squadron [*Air Force*] ... CLSS
Combat Logistics System [*Air Force*] (GFGA) ... CLS
Combat Logistics Vehicle [*Army*] ... CLV
Combat Loss ... C/L
Combat Loss and Expenditure Data (MCD) ... COLED
Combat Loss and Expenditure Data - Vietnam ... COLED-V
Combat Maintenance Capability (MCD) ... CMC
Combat Maneuver Battalion [*Army*] ... CMB
Combat Maneuver Battalion [*Army*] ... COMANBAT
Combat Maneuver Training Center (INF) ... CMTC
Combat Maneuver Training Center - Instrumentation System [*Army*] ... CMTC-IS
Combat Maneuver Training Command ... CMTC
Combat Maneuver Training Complex [*Hohenfels Training Area*] [*Germany*] ... CMTC
Combat Material ... CM
Combat Material Research Laboratory [*Army*] ... CMRL
Combat Materiel Exploitation Center [*Military*] (VNW) ... CMEC
Combat Medical Badge [*Military decoration*] (AABC) ... CMB
Combat Merchant Mariners World War II (EA) ... CMMWWII
Combat Mission [*Military*] ... CM
Combat Mission Failure (AABC) ... CMF
Combat Mission Folder (AFM) ... CMF
Combat Mission Scenario [*Army*] ... CMS
Combat Mission Simulation (MCD) ... CMS
Combat Mission Trainer [*Air Force*] ... CMT
Combat Mobility System [*Army*] (RDA) ... CMSYS
Combat Mobility Vehicle [*Army*] (RDA) ... CMV
Combat Net Radio [*Military*] ... CNR
Combat Observation and Lasing Teams [*Army*] (INF) ... COLT
Combat Operation (INF) ... CO
Combat Operational Reserve Group (AAG) ... CORG
Combat Operational Support Aircraft (NVT) ... COSA
Combat Operations Center [*Air Force*] ... COC
Combat Operations Group (SAA) ... COG
Combat Operations Intelligence Center (MCD) ... COIC
Combat Operations, Naval Gunfire Activity ... CONGA
Combat Operations Report ... COR
Combat Operations Research Group [*Technical Operations, Inc.*] [*Fort Belvoir, VA*] ... CORG
Combat Operations Specialist Course [*Air Force*] (AFM) ... COSC
Combat Optimization and Analysis Program [*Air Force*] ... COAP
Combat Organization Potential [*DoD*] ... COP
Combat Outpost ... COP
Combat Outpost Line ... COPL
Combat Personnel Control System [*Air Force*] (GFGA) ... CPCS
Combat Photographer [*Military*] [*Slang*] (WDMC) ... 84 Charlie
Combat Potential Display [*SAGE*] [*Air Force*] ... CPD
Combat Power [*DoD*] ... CP
Combat Psychiatric Casualty [*Military*] (INF) ... CPC
Combat Radius Capability [*Military*] ... COMRAC
Combat Rated Thrust [*Navy*] (NG) ... CRT
Combat Rations [*Military*] (VNW) ... Cs
Combat Reaction ... CR
Combat Reaction Time ... CRT
Combat Readiness Air Group (DNAB) ... CRAG
Combat Readiness Air Wing ... CRAW
Combat Readiness Assessment Exercise [*Obsolete Navy*] (NG) ... CRAE
Combat Readiness by Electronic Service Testing [*Army*] (AABC) ... CREST
Combat Readiness Categories [*Navy*] (NG) ... CRCAT
Combat Readiness Electromagnetic Analysis and Measurement (MCD) ... CREAM
Combat Readiness Evaluation [*Army*] ... CRE
Combat Readiness Evaluation Criteria [*Navy*] (NG) ... CREC
Combat Readiness Medal [*Military decoration*] (AFM) ... CRM
Combat Readiness Rating System [*Air Force*] ... CRRS
Combat Readiness Requirements [*Canadian Navy*] ... CRR
Combat Readiness Trainer [*or Training*] ... CRT
Combat Ready (AFM) ... CR
Combat Ready Rate (MCD) ... CRR
Combat Ready Storage Program (DOMA) ... CRSP
Combat Reconnaissance Platoon ... CRP
Combat Reporting Center (AFM) ... CRC
Combat Reporting Post ... CRP
Combat Reporting System [*Air Force*] (MCD) ... CREST
Combat Required Operational Capability (AFIT) ... CROC
Combat Reserve [*Military*] ... CR
Combat Reserve Air Fleet [*Military*] ... CRAFT
Combat Resource Allocation Model (MCD) ... CRAM
Combat Rubber Raiding Craft (DOMA) ... CRRC
Combat Sample Generator [*Military*] ... COSAGE
Combat Search and Rescue [*Aviation*] ... CSAR
Combat Search and Rescue [*Aviation*] (MCD) ... CSR
Combat Security Police [*Air Force*] (VNW) ... CSP
Combat Service Group [*Army*] ... CSG
Combat Service Readiness (DWSG) ... CSR
Combat Service Support [*DoD*] (AABC) ... CSS
Combat Service Support Area [*Army*] ... CSSA
Combat Service Support Control System [*Army*] ... CSSCS
Combat Service Support Detachment [*Marine Corps*] (DOMA) ... CSSD
Combat Service Support Element [*Marine Corps*] (DOMA) ... CSSE
Combat Service Support Group [*Army*] ... CSSG
Combat Service Support Level [*Military*] (INF) ... CS^2
Combat Service Support Precommand Course ... CSS PCC
Combat Service Support System [*Army*] ... CS3
Combat Service Support System [*Army*] ... CSSS
Combat Service Support Training Simulator System [*Army*] ... CSSTSS
Combat Store Ship [*Navy symbol*] ... AFS
Combat Stress Reaction [*Army*] (ADDR) ... CSR
Combat Studies Institute [*Command and General Staff College, Fort Leavenworth*] [*Army*] (INF) ... CSI
Combat Supplies [*British*] ... CSUPS
Combat Support ... CS
Combat Support Air Traffic Management System (MCD) ... CSATMS
Combat Support Aviation Battalion [*Army*] ... CSAB
Combat Support Aviation Company [*Army*] ... CSAC
Combat Support Capability Management System (MCD) ... CSCMS
Combat Support Center [*Army*] ... CSC
Combat Support Company [*Army*] ... CSC
Combat Support Coordination Center ... CSCC
Combat Support Force ... CSF
Combat Support Group [*Army*] ... CSG
Combat Support Group [*Air Force*] (AFM) ... CSGp
Combat Support Hospital (AABC) ... CSH
Combat Support Liaison (CINC) ... CSL
Combat Support of the Army (AFIT) ... COSTAR
Combat Support Rearm and Refuel in Battalions [*Study*] [*Army Logistics Center*] ... COSRRIB
Combat Support Ship [*Military*] ... AFS
Combat Support Smoke Vehicle [*Army*] ... CSSV
Combat Support Squadron [*Air Force*] ... CMBTSPTSq
Combat Support Squadron [*Air Force*] ... CSS
Combat Support Training [*Military*] (AABC) ... CST
Combat Support Training System [*Military*] ... CSTS
Combat Support Units [*Army*] ... COMSUP
Combat Support Units [*Army*] ... CSU
Combat Support Vehicle (MCD) ... CSV
Combat Support Wing ... CSW
Combat Surveillance Agency [*Signal Corps*] ... CSA
Combat Surveillance and Target Acquisition [*Army*] ... CSTA
Combat Surveillance and Target Acquisition Equipment [*Army*] ... CS & TAE
Combat Surveillance and Target Acquisition Laboratory [*Army*] (RDA) ... CSTAL
Combat Surveillance and Target Acquisition Training Command [*Army*] ... CSTATC
Combat Surveillance Laboratory ... CSL
Combat Surveillance Night Vision and Target Acquisition Laboratories [*Army*] (RDA) ... CSNVTAL
Combat Surveillance RADAR ... CSR
Combat Surveillance Target Acquisition RADAR ... CSTAR
Combat Swimmer Mine Neutralization System (DOMA) ... CSMNS
Combat System [*Military*] (CAAL) ... CS
Combat System Alignment Document (NVT) ... CSAD
Combat System Alignment Test ... CSAT
Combat System Architecture [*Military*] ... CSA
Combat System Configuration Matrix [*Military*] (CAAL) ... CSCM
Combat System Coordinator [*Military*] (CAAL) ... CSC
Combat System Design Requirement [*Military*] (CAAL) ... CSDR
Combat System Detection [*Military*] (CAAL) ... CSD
Combat System Engineer [*Military*] (CAAL) ... CSE
Combat System Engineering Authorization ... CSEA
Combat System Engineering Development [*Military*] (CAAL) ... CSED
Combat System Engineering Development Site ... CSEDS
Combat System Exercise (MCD) ... CYSTEX
Combat System Initialization Procedure [*Military*] (CAAL) ... CSIP
Combat System Integration (MCD) ... CSI
Combat System Integration and Interface Control Group [*Military*] (CAAL) ... CSIICG
Combat System Integration Manager [*Military*] (CAAL) ... CSIM
Combat System Integration Test [*Military*] (CAAL) ... CSIT
Combat System Interface Test [*Military*] (CAAL) ... CSIT
Combat System Interface Test Tool (NVT) ... CSITT

Combat System Land-Based Test Site (CAAL) .... CSLBTS
Combat System Maintenance Central [*Navy*] (DOMA) .... CSMC
Combat System Management Plan [*Military*] (CAAL) .... CSMP
Combat System Manager [*Military*] (CAAL) .... CSM
Combat System Mission Demonstration [*Military*] (CAAL) .... CSMD
Combat System Operability Monitor [*Military*] (CAAL) .... CSOM
Combat System Operational Design [*Military*] (CAAL) .... CSOD
Combat System Operational Sequencing System [*Navy*] (DOMA) .... CSOSS
Combat System Ship Interface Criteria [*Navy*] (CAAL) .... COMSSIC
Combat System Ship Qualification Trial [*Military*] (CAAL) .... CSSQT
Combat System Steering Group [*Military*] (CAAL) .... CSSG
Combat System Support Equipment [*Military*] (CAAL) .... CSSE
Combat System Tactical Operation Manual [*Navy*] (NVT) .... CSTOM
Combat System Team Operational Trainer [*Military*] (CAAL) .... CSTOT
Combat System Test Implementation Plan [*Military*] (CAAL) .... CSTIP
Combat System Training Unit (NVT) .... CSTU
Combat System Working Group [*Military*] (CAAL) .... CSWG
Combat Systems Advisory Group [*NMC*] (DNAB) .... CSAG
Combat Systems Assessment [*Navy*] (DOMA) .... CSA
Combat Systems Assessment [*Navy*] (DOMA) .... CSAT
Combat Systems Certification Site [*Navy*] .... COMCERTS
Combat Systems Equipment Training (MCD) .... CSET
Combat Systems Improvement Program [*Navy*] (PDAA) .... CSIP
Combat Systems Mobile Training Team [*Navy*] (ANA) .... CSMTT
Combat Systems Operability Test (NVT) .... CSOT
Combat Systems Post-Overhaul Examination [*Navy*] (ANA) .... CSPOE
Combat Systems Readiness Review [*Navy*] (MCD) .... CSRR
Combat Systems Readiness Test (NVT) .... CSRT
Combat Systems Support [*Military*] (DNAB) .... CSS
Combat Systems Technical Aerospace Report .... CSTAR
Combat Systems Technical School Command .... CSTCS
Combat Systems Test Activity [*Aberdeen Proving Ground, MD*] [*Army*] (RDA) .... CSTA
Combat Systems Test and Support Facility [*Canadian Navy*] .... CSTSF
Combat Systems Test Development Director (DNAB) .... CSTDD
Combat Systems Text Agency [*Military*] .... CSTA
Combat Systems Training (NVT) .... CST
Combat Systems Training Exercise (DNAB) .... CSTEX
Combat Targeting Team [*Military*] .... CTT
Combat Team .... CT
Combat Terrain Information System [*Military*] .... CTIS
Combat Theater Communications Program [*Air Force*] (MCD) .... CTCP
Combat to Support Balance Study .... CSBS
Combat Tracking [*or Tracker*] **Team** .... CTT
Combat Training Center [*Army*] (INF) .... CTC
Combat Training Centers / Tactical Engagement Simulation .... CTC/TES
Combat Training Facilities [*DoD*] .... CTF
Combat Training Launch (AFM) .... CTL
Combat Training Launch Instrumentation [*Minuteman*] .... CTLI
Combat Training Theater .... CTT
Combat Training Unit .... CTU
Combat Trains Command Post [*Army*] (INF) .... CTCP
Combat Unit Training Center [*Army*] (MCD) .... CUTC
Combat Using Price Incentives Doctrine .... CUPID
Combat Vehicle [*Army*] CV
Combat Vehicle [*Army*] (AABC) .... CVEH
Combat Vehicle Armament System Technology [*Army*] .... CVAST
Combat Vehicle Command and Control [*Army*] (RDA) CVC2
Combat Vehicle Command and Control (RDA) CVCC
Combat Vehicle Crewman Uniform System [*Army*] (INF) .... CVCUS
Combat Vehicle Crewman's Protective Ensemble [*Army*] (RDA) .... CVCPE
Combat Vehicle Crewmen (MCD) CVC
Combat Vehicle - Heading Reference Unit .... CV-HRU
Combat Vehicle Kill Indicator (MCD) .... CVKI
Combat Vehicle Kill Indicator Pyrotechnic Device (MCD) .... CVKI-PD
Combat Vehicle LASER Detector Assembly (MCD) .... CVLD
Combat Vehicle Maintenance Policy Study .... CVMP
Combat Vehicle Night Sight .... CVNS
Combat Vehicle Program Review .... CVPR
Combat Vehicle Ram Simulation (MCD) .... COVERS
Combat Vehicle, Reconnaissance (Tracked) [*British military*] (MCD) .... CVR(T)
Combat Vehicle, Reconnaissance (Tracked) (Armoured Personnel Carrier) [*British military*] .... CVR(T)(APC)
Combat Vehicle, Reconnaissance (Tracked) (Recovery) [*British military*] .... CVR(T)(REC)
Combat Vehicle, Reconnaissance (Tracked)(Guided Weapon Carrier) [*British military*] .... CVR(T)(GW)
Combat Vehicle, Reconnaissance (Wheeled) [*British military*] (DMA) .... CVR(W)
Combat Vehicle Signature Management Plan [*Army*] (RDA) .... CVSMP
Combat Vehicle Simulator (MCD) .... CVS
Combat Vehicle Weapons System [*Army*] (AFIT) .... CBVWS
Combat Vehicle Weapons System [*Army*] .... CVWS
Combat Vehicle Weapons System (Long-Range) [*Army*] .... CVWS(LR)
Combat Visual Information Support Center [*DoD*] .... CVISC
Combat Water Survival Test [*Army*] (INF) .... CWST
Combat Wing Command Post .... CWCP
Combat Zone .... CZ
Combatant Command [*Military*] .... COCOM
Combatant Craft Passive Electronic Warfare [*Navy*] (CAAL) .... CCPEW
Combating Childhood Communicable Diseases Project [*Agency for International Development*] .... CCCD
Combat-Oriented General Support [*Army*] .... COGS
Combat-Oriented General Support Center (MCD) .... COGSC
Combat-Oriented Maintenance Organization [*Army*] .... COMO
Combat-Oriented Supply Organization (MCD) .... COSO
Combat-Service to the Army (KSC) .... CO-STAR
Combed Yarn Spinners Association [*Later, AYSA*] (EA) .... CYSA
Comberbach's English King's Bench Reports [*1685-99*] [*A publication*] (DLA) .... Com
Comberbach's English King's Bench Reports [*1685-99*] [*A publication*] (DLA) .... Comb
Combika [*Sao Paulo, Brazil*] [*Airport symbol*] (AD) .... CUK
Combinatio Nova [*New Combination*] [*Biology, taxonomy*] .... comb nov
Combination [*or Combine*] (AFM) .... COMB
Combination (VRA) .... comb
Combination (BARN) .... combi
Combination and Dissemination of Experiment Data System [*Army*] (RDA) .... CADEX
Combination Block [*Engraving*] (DGA) .... CB
Combination Companies [*Insurance*] CC
Combination Die (MCD) .... CD
Combination Die .... CNDI
Combination Drug .... CD
Combination Export Management [*Small Business Administration*] .... CEM
Combination Fabrication and Assembly (SAA) .... CFA
Combination Inventory [*LIMRA*] CI
Combination Network [*Graph theory*] .... CNW
Combination Neutron Source Rod [*Nuclear energy*] (NRCH) .... CNSR
Combination of Forward Combustion and Waterflooding [*Commercial oil production process*] .... COFCAW
Combination of Purpose [*JETDS nomenclature*] .... Q
Combination of Sequential Mutant Interaction Cycles [*Biochemistry*] .... COSMIC
Combination Product [*Medicine*] (MAE) .... CP
Combination Publication Authority .... CPA
Combination Type Oral Contraceptive [*Medicine*] .... COC
Combinatorial and Algebraic Machine-Aided Computation (WGA) .... CAMAC
Combinatorial Geometry .... COM-GEOM
Combinatory Categorical Grammar [*Artificial intelligence*] .... CCG
Combine Regency Network - Flaming Arrow Network [*Military*] .... CRN-FAN
Combined .... CMBD
Combined .... COMB
Combined Acceleration Vibration Climatic Test System .... CAVCTS
Combined Acceptance Trials .... CAT
Combined Accident Reduction Effort .... CARE
Combined Account Number File [*IRS*] .... CANF
Combined Acquisition and Tracking RADAR [*NASA*] (MCD) .... CATRADAR
Combined Action Company [*Formerly, Joint Action Co.*] [*Military*] .... CAC
Combined Action Forces [*Military*] (DNAB) .... CAF
Combined Action Group [*Senior command of all Combined Action Companies*] [*Military*] .... CAG
Combined Action Platoon .... CAP
Combined Active/Passive Emitter Rangings .... CAPER
Combined Active/Passive RADAR .... CAPAR
Combined Activities System [*Vietnam*] [*Air Force*] .... CAS
Combined Additional Coverage [*Insurance*] .... CAC
Combined Administrative Committee .... CADC
Combined Administrative Liquidating Agency [*Microfilmed SHAEF documents for each participating country after SHAEF was disbanded*] [*Post-World War II*] .... CALA
Combined Agencies Field Team [*US Military Government, Germany*] .... CAFT
Combined Agency for Middle East Supplies [*World War II*] .... CAMES
Combined Agricultural and Food Machinery Committee [*World War II*] .... CAFMC
Combined Air Documents Research Center .... CADRC
Combined Air Force Operating Base (CINC) .... CAFOB
Combined Air Operations [*Air Force*] (DOMA) .... COMAO
Combined Air Support [*Army*] (DOMA) .... CAS
Combined Air Transport Operations Room [*Allied office, World War II*] .... CATOR
Combined Airborne Surveillance and Control for Aerospace Defense .... CASCADE
Combined Aircraft Submarine Exercise [*NATO*] (NATG) .... CASEX
Combined Aircraft Transfer and Release Assembly (MCD) .... CATRA
Combined Air-Defense System [*Military*] (DOMA) .... CADS
Combined Allied Air Forces .... CAAF
Combined Allied Defense Experiment [*Military*] (SDI) .... CADE
Combined Allied Land Forces .... CALF
Combined Allied Naval Forces .... CANF
Combined Allied Naval Forces, Southwest Pacific Area .... CANFSWPA
Combined Allied Naval Forces, Southwest Pacific Ocean Area Operating Plan .... CANFSWPAOPPLAN
Combined Allowance for Logistics and Maintenance Support System [*Coast Guard*] (MCD) .... CALMS
Combined Allowance for Logistics Management .... CALM
Combined Altitude RADAR Altimeter [*Electronic defense system*] .... CARA
Combined Amphibious Task Force (NVT) .... CATF
Combined Amplitude Phase Shift Keying (MCD) .... CAPSK
Combined Analog-Digital Systems Simulator [*Computer science*] .... CADSS
Combined Annual Wage Reporting [*IRS*] .... CAWR
Combined Antenna System (CAAL) .... CAS
Combined Approach Control/International Station (FAAC) .... CAP/IS
Combined Approach System Investigation (SAA) .... CASI
Combined Arms (AABC) .... CA
Combined Arms and Service Staff School (DOMA) .... CAS^3
Combined Arms and Services Staff School [*Army*] (RDA) CAS3
Combined Arms and Support [*Army*] (AABC) .... CAAS
Combined Arms and Support Research Office [*Fort Leavenworth, KS*] .... CASRO
Combined Arms and Support Task Force Evaluation Model [*Army*] (RDA) .... CASTFOREM
Combined Arms and Tactics Department [*Military*] (INF) .... CATD
Combined Arms Army (MCD) .... CAA
Combined Arms Assessment Network [*DoD*] .... CAAN

Combined Arms Battalion (MCD) .... CAB
Combined Arms Battalions (Heavy) [*Army*] .... CAB(H)
Combined Arms Battalions (Light) [*Army*] .... CAB(L)
Combined Arms Center (AABC) .... CAC
Combined Arms Combat Development Activity [*Fort Leavenworth, KS*] [*Army*] (AABC) .... CACDA
Combined Arms Combat Development Activity C3I [*Command, Control, Communications, and Intelligence*] **Directorate** [*Fort Leavenworth, KS*] [*Army*] CACDA/C3I
Combined Arms Command and Control [*Army*] (RDA) CAC2
Combined Arms Command-Training [*Fort Leavenwoth, KS*] [*Army*] (INF) .... CAC-TNG
Combined Arms Exercise (MCD) .... CAX
Combined Arms Exercise [*Marine Corps*] (DOMA) .... CAX
Combined Arms Fighting Vehicle (MCD) .... CAFV
Combined Arms Group [*Army*] .... CAG
Combined Arms in a Nuclear/Chemical Environment [*Military*] (RDA) .... CANE
Combined Arms Initiative [*Army*] .... CAI
Combined Arms Live Fire Exercises (INF) .... CALFEX
Combined Arms Maneuver Battalion [*Experiment*] [*Army*] (INF) .... CAMB
Combined Arms Mission Area Analysis [*Army*] .... CAMAA
Combined Arms Modeling [*Military*] .... CAM
Combined Arms Multipurpose Missile System [*Army*] .... CAMMS
Combined Arms Operations Research Activity [*Fort Leavenworth, KS*] .... CAORA
Combined Arms Regiment [*Marine Corps*] (DOMA) .... CAR
Combined Arms Research Office .... CARO
Combined Arms Simulation Model (MCD) .... CASM
Combined Arms Studies and Analysis Activity [*Fort Leavenworth, KS*] .... CASAA
Combined Arms Support Command [*DoD*] (RDA) .... CASCOM
Combined Arms Support Command (DOMA) .... CASCOM
Combined Arms Systems Engineering .... CASE
Combined Arms Tactical Trainer [*Army*] (RDA) .... CATT
Combined Arms Tactical Training Simulator [*Army*] (MCD) .... CATTS
Combined Arms Team (MCD) .... CAT
Combined Arms Training [*Military*] (NVT) .... CMBARMTNG
Combined Arms Training Activity [*Fort Leavenworth, KS*] (INF) .... CATA
Combined Arms Training Board [*Military*] .... CATB
Combined Arms Training Center [*Army*] .... CATC
Combined Arms Training Developments Activity [*or Agency*] [*Army*] (RDA) .... CATRADA
Combined Arms Training Integrated Evaluation System [*Military*] .... CATIES
Combined Arms Training Strategy [*Army*] (DOMA) .... CATS
Combined Army Air Transport Organization [*World War II*] .... CAATO
Combined Army Tactical Training [*System*] (DOMA) .... CATT
Combined Artillery/Aviation Simulator (DWSG) .... CAAS
Combined Automated Resource System [*Department of Health and Human Services*] (GFGA) .... CARES
Combined Aviation Force .... CAF
Combined Black Publishers [*Defunct*] (EA) .... CBP
Combined Blood Count (WDAA) .... CBC
Combined Bomber Offensive [*World War II*] .... CBO
Combined Book Exhibit .... CBE
Combined Bureau, Middle East [*British military*] (DMA) .... CBME
Combined Cadet Force [*British equivalent of US ROTC*] .... CCF
Combined Cadet Force Association [*British military*] (DMA) .... CCFA
Combined Case Control [*IRS*] CCC
Combined Center Radar Approach Control [*FAA*] (TAG) .... CERAP
Combined Chiefs of Staff [*DoD*] .... CCOS
Combined Chiefs of Staff [*DoD*] .... CCS
Combined Cipher Machine .... CCM
Combined Civil Affairs Committee [*World War II*] .... CCAC
Combined Civil Affairs Committee, London Subcommittee [*World War II*] .... CCAC/L
Combined Civil Affairs Committee, Supply Subcommittee [*World War II*] .... CCAC/S
Combined Civil Affairs Liquidating Agency [*World War II*] .... CCALA
Combined Coding Machine .... CCM
Combined Combat Center, Direction Center [*Military*] (SAA) .... CC/DC
Combined Command for Reconnaissance Activities in Korea .... CCRAK
Combined Committee for North Africa [*World War II*] .... CCNA
Combined Committee on Air Training in North America .... CCATNA
Combined Communications Board [*World War II*] .... CCB
Combined Communications Board Publications .... CCBP
Combined Contaminants, Oxygen, and Humidity (MCD) .... CCOH
Combined Cooling Performance Factor .... CCPF
Combined Cortical Thickness (DNAB) .... CCT
Combined CUSUM [*Cumulative Sum*]/Stewart Method [*Laboratory analysis*] .... CCS
Combined Defense Improvement Projects .... CDIP
Combined Development Agency [*Anglo-American uranium procurement*] .... CDA
Combined Diesel and Gas [*Turbine*] .... CODAG
Combined Diesel or Gas Turbine Propulsion .... CODOG
Combined Diesel-Electric And Gas [*Turbine*] (DOMA) .... CODELAG
Combined Diptheria and Tetanus [*Vaccine*] [*Medicine*] .... CDT
Combined Displaced Persons Executive [*World War II*] .... CDPX
Combined Distribution Frame [*RADAR*] .... CDF
Combined Distribution Function (MCD) .... CDF
Combined Documents Exploitation Center [*Saigon, Vietnam*] (VNW) .... CDEC
Combined Double Tee [*Engineering*] (IAA) .... CDT
Combined Economic Warfare Agencies .... CEWA
Combined Edible Nut Trade Association [*British*] (DBA) .... CENTA
Combined Effects Bomb (MCD) .... CEB
Combined Effects Munition (MCD) .... CEM
Combined Effects Submissile (MCD) .... CES
Combined Electrolysis and Catalytic Exchange [*CANDU-reactor advantage*] .... CECE
Combined Elements and Integrated Systems (SSD) .... CE & IS
Combined Engineering Plant Exchange Record [*Telecommunications*] (TEL) .... CEPER
Combined English Stores [*Commercial firm British*] .... CES
Combined Environmental Reliability Testing [*Air Force*] (RDA) .... CERT
Combined Environmental, Vibration, Acceleration, Temperature [*Aerospace*] (AAG) .... CEVAT
Combined Exercise [*Military*] (NVT) .... COMBEX
Combined Exercise Planning Staff [*Military*] (MCD) .... CEPS
Combined Exports Market Committee [*World War II*] .... CEMC
Combined Federal Campaign [*Federal government*] (AABC) .... CFC
Combined Field Army (MCD) .... CFA
Combined Field Command (MCD) .... CFC
Combined Field Maintenance Shop [*Army*] (AABC) .... CFMS
Combined File Search [*IBM program*] [*Computer science*] .... CFS
Combined File Search Strategy [*Computer science*] .... CFSS
Combined Filter and Plot (NATG) .... CFP
Combined Food Board [*United States, United Kingdom, and Canada*] [*World War II*] .... CFB
Combined Forces Command [*Korea*] (MCD) .... CFC
Combined Function (OA) .... CF
Combined Gas and Gas (PDAA) .... COGAG
Combined Gas or Gas (PDAA) .... COGOG
Combined Gas Turbine or Gas Turbine Propulsion .... COGOG
Combined Ground Command Post (MCD) .... CGCP
Combined Health Appeal of America (EA) .... CHAA
Combined Health Information Database [*Public Health Service*] [*Information service or system*] (IID) .... CHID
Combined Heart and Power Association [*British*] (DBA) .... CHPA
Combined Heat and Power [*Generation*] .... CHP
Combined Heating Performance Factor .... CHPF
Combined Helicopter Outyear Procurement Package - Educational Requirement [*Army*] .... CHOPPER
Combined Helmholtz Integral Equation Formulation .... CHIEF
Combined High Frequency of Ventilation [*Medicine*] (DAVI) .... CHFV
Combined Higher Education Software Team (AIE) .... CHEST
Combined Immunodeficiency Disease [*Immunology*] .... CID
Combined Industry Committee [*Australia*] CIC
Combined In-Port Tactical Exercise [*Navy*] (NVT) .... CINTEX
Combined Instrument Panel .... CIP
Combined Intelligence Center (DOMA) CIC
Combined Intelligence Center, Iraq [*World War II*] CICI
Combined Intelligence Center, Vietnam CICV
Combined Intelligence Committee [*World War II*] CIC
Combined Intelligence Objectives Subcommittee [*World War II*] .... CIOS
Combined Intelligence Priorities Committee [*Later, CIU*] [*US and British London, World War II*] .... CIPC
Combined Intelligence Staff [*World War II*] .... CIS
Combined Intelligence Unit [*Formerly, CIPC*] [*RAF*] [*British*] .... CIU
Combined Intercept Valve [*Nuclear energy*] (NRCH) CIV
Combined Intermediate Valve [*Nuclear energy*] (NRCH) CIV
Combined Intermittent Therapy (DAVI) .... CIT
Combined Intracapsular Cataract Extraction [*Opthalmology*] (DAVI) .... CICE
Combined Jewish Philanthropies .... CJP
Combined Joint Task Forces [*NATO*] (ECON) .... CJTF
Combined Language Age [*of the hearing-impaired*] .... CLA
Combined LASER Instrumentation Package (NASA) .... CLIP
Combined Lease Plan .... CLP
Combined Liberated Areas Committee [*World War II*] .... CLAC
Combined Liberated Areas Committee, Supply Subcommittee [*World War II*] .... CLAC(S)
Combined Library Unions Committee [*Australia*] .... CLUC
Combined Limit [*Insurance*] .... C/L
Combined Line and Recording Trunk (IEEE) .... CLR
Combined Loads Orbiter Test (MCD) .... CLOT
Combined Logistics Stores Facility (DOMA) .... CLSF
Combined Mailing [*Postal Service*] [*United States*] (WDMC) .... comailing
Combined Maintenance Removal Interval (AFIT) .... CMRI
Combined [*Arms*] **Maneuver Training Center** [*Hohenfels, Germany*] [*Army*] (DOMA) .... CMTC
Combined Map and Electronic Display (MCD) .... COMED
Combined Master File [*Computer science*] .... CMF
Combined Meteorological Committee .... CMC
Combined Military Exploitation Center .... CMEC
Combined Military Interrogation Center .... CMIC
Combined Military Transportation [*British*] .... CMT
Combined Military Transportation Committee .... CMTC
Combined Miniature Deterrent Forces [*Organization in film "Fantastic Voyage"*] .... CMDF
Combined Mixer Settler [*Chemical engineering*] .... CMS
Combined Munitions Assignments Board [*World War II*] .... CMAB
Combined Name and Address File [*IRS*] .... CNAF
Combined National Veterans Association of America (EA) .... CNVAA
Combined Neutral and Earth (PDAA) .... CNE
Combined New Australia Party [*Political party*] .... CNA
Combined New Australia Party [*Political party*] .... CNAP
Combined Nomenclature [*EC*] (ECED) .... CN
Combined Nuclear and Steam [*Propulsion*] (DOMA) .... CONAS
Combined Nuclear Steam and Gas (PDAA) .... CONAG
Combined Nuclear Steam or Gas (PDAA) .... CONOG
Combined Office Material Procurement and Distribution .... COMPAD
Combined Officer of Merchant Navy Operations [*British*] .... COMNO
Combined Oil and Tanker Group (NATG) .... COT
Combined Operational Intelligence Center [*Navy*] .... COIC

Combined Operational Planning Committee [*Royal Air Force and US 8th Air Force*] [*World War II*] .... COPC
Combined Operational Service Command .... COSC
Combined Operations .... CO
Combined Operations Command [*British*] .... COC
Combined Operations Development Centre [*British military*] (DMA) .... CODC
Combined Operations Experimental Wing [*World War II*] .... COEW
Combined Operations Headquarters [*World War II*] .... COHQ
Combined Operations Headquarters, Zara [*Former Yugoslavia*] [*World War II*] .... COZA
Combined Operations Lasing Team [*Army*] (INF) .... COLT
Combined Operations Material Liaison Officer .... COMLO
Combined Operations Nuclear Medical Evaluation Team (MCD) .... CONMET
Combined Operations Personnel [*Navy British*] .... COP
Combined Operations Pilotage Party .... COPP
Combined Operations Repair Organization [*For invasion of France*] [*World War II*] .... COREP
Combined Operations Scout Unit .... COSU
Combined Operations Signal Maintenance Depot .... COSMD
Combined Operations Signal Maintenance Officer .... COSMO
Combined Operations Signal Officer .... COSO
Combined Operations Supply Depot .... COSD
Combined Operations Tug Organization [*For invasion of France*] [*World War II*] .... COTUG
Combined Opposition Parties [*Politics*] .... COP
Combined Opposition Party [*Pakistan*] [*Political party*] (FEA) .... COP
Combined Optical [*Photography*] .... COMOPT
Combined Orbital Maneuvering and Abort System [*NASA*] (NASA) .... COMAS
Combined Organic Movement for Education and Training [*British*] .... COMET
Combined Organizations of Numismatic Error Collectors of America (EA) .... CONECA
Combined Overload Repair Control (MCD) .... COREP
Combined Over-the-Beach Terminal Unit (NATG) .... COBTU
Combined Passenger Check List (ADA) .... CPCL
Combined Passive Active Detection [*RADAR*] .... COMPACT
Combined Pensioners' Association of Victoria. News [*A publication*] .... Combined Pension Ass Vic News
Combined Personnel Recovery Center (CINC) .... CPRC
Combined Photographic Interpretation Center .... CPIC
Combined Pituitary Hormone Deficiency [*Medicine*] .... CPHD
Combined Planning Staff [*Military British*] .... CPS
Combined Policy Committee [*NATO*] (NATG) .... CPC
Combined Principles Simulator [*Nuclear engine*] .... CPS
Combined Processor and RAM Module [*Computer science*] (NITA) .... CPR
Combined Procurement Processing Series (MCD) .... CPPS
Combined Production and Resources Board [*World War II*] .... CPRB
Combined Programming Language [*Computer science*] .... CPL
Combined Pulsed Neutron Experiment (MCD) .... CPNE
Combined Quarantine Force [*US/Venezuela/Dominican Republic/Argentina*] .... COMBQUARFOR
Combined Radiation Effects Test Chamber (OA) .... CRETC
Combined Radiation Test .... CRT
Combined Radiation Treatment [*Oncology*] .... CRT
Combined Raw Materials Board [*US and Britain*] [*World War II*] .... CRMB
Combined Readiness Air Exercise (MCD) .... CRAE
Combined Receiving and Transmitting Unit .... CRTU
Combined Reconnaissance and Intelligence Platoon [*Military*] (VNW) .... CRIP
Combined Reentry Effort in Small Systems .... CRESS
Combined Reference Frequency System .... CRFS
Combined Refining Process (PDAA) .... CRP
Combined Registered Publication Memoranda .... CRPM
Combined Release and Radiation Effects Satellite [*NASA*] .... CRRES
Combined Removal Interval [*Engine*] .... CMRI
Combined Resources Allocation Board [*World War II*] .... CRAB
Combined Retrospective Index Sets [*Information service or system*] (IID) .... CRIS
Combined Rocket Warhead (KSC) .... CROW
Combined Rotating Unit [*Nuclear energy*] .... CRU
Combined Rotation and Multiple-Pulse Spectroscopy [*Physics*] .... CRAMPS
Combined S-Band .... CSB
Combined Scottish Society of New South Wales [*Australia*] .... CSSNSW
Combined Sensor Tracking Exercise [*Military*] (NVT) .... COMSENEX
Combined Service Command (DOMA) .... CSC
Combined Service Territory [*Red Cross*] .... CST
Combined Services Detailed Interrogation Center [*World War II*] .... CSDIC
Combined Services Detailed Interrogation Center - Nonoperational Intelligence [*World War II*] .... CSDICNOI
Combined Services Entertainment [*British military*] (DMA) .... CSE
Combined Services Entertainment Unit [*British military*] (DMA) .... CSEU
Combined Services Support Program [*Navy*] (NG) .... CSSP
Combined Services Support Program School, Atlantic [*Navy*] (DNAB) .... COMBSVCSUPPSCOLANT
Combined Services Support Program School, Pacific [*Navy*] (DNAB) .... COMBSVCSUPPSCOLPAC
Combined Setter Clubs of America (EA) .... CSCA
Combined Sewer Overflow .... CSO
Combined Shaft Unit .... CSU
Combined Shipbuilding Committee [*World War II*] .... CSC
Combined Shipping Adjustment Board [*World War II*] .... CSAB
Combined Signal Board [*North Africa*] [*World War II*] .... CSB
Combined Single Limit [*Insurance*] .... CSL
Combined Special Forces Operational Detachment (CINC) .... CSFOD
Combined Special Operations Area [*Military*] (DOMA) .... CSOA
Combined Staff Planners .... CSP
Combined Station/Tower [*Aviation*] .... CS/T
Combined Steam and Gas [*Propulsion*] (MCD) .... COSAG

Combined Steam and Nuclear [*Propulsion*] (DOMA) .... COSAN
Combined Strategic Targets Committee [*World War II*] .... CSTC
Combined Stratospheric Measuring Program [*Army*] .... COSMEP
Combined Stress Reliability Test (MCD) .... CSRT
Combined Studies Group [*Central Intelligence Agency operation in Southeast Asia*] .... CSG
Combined Support Division [*Canadian Navy*] .... CSD
Combined Support Maintenance Shop [*USNG*] (MCD) .... CSMS
Combined Surveillance and Foliage Penetration RADAR (MCD) .... COMSFOR
Combined Symbol Matching [*Fax compression technology*] [*Compression Labs, Inc.*] (PCM) .... CSM
Combined System Test Stand (IEEE) .... CSTS
Combined Systems Acceptance Test (MCD) .... CSAT
Combined Systems Test .... CST
Combined Systems Test Unit (MCD) .... CSTU
Combined Target Area .... CTA
Combined Task Force [*NATO*] (NATG) .... CTF
Combined Task Group [*NATO*] (NATG) .... CTG
Combined Test Force [*Military*] .... CTF
Combined Test Team (MCD) .... CTT
Combined Thermomechanical Treatment .... CTMT
Combined Total Loan-to-Value Ratio [*Business term*] (EMRF) .... CTLVR
Combined Training Center .... CTC
Combined Training Exercise [*Military*] (ADDR) .... CTX
Combined Transport [*Shipping*] .... CT
Combined Transport Document [*Shipping*] .... CTD
Combined Transport Operator [*Shipping*] .... CTO
Combined Transportation Equipment Committee [*Combined Production and Resources Board*] [*World War II*] .... CTEC
Combined Travel Board [*Allied German Occupation Forces*] .... CTB
Combined Travel Security Board [*Allied German Occupation Forces*] .... CTSB
Combined Trials [*Shipbuilding*] .... CT
Combined Unconventional Warfare Task Force (CINC) .... CUWTF
Combined Union and Shop Committee [*Australia*] .... CUSC
Combined United Kingdom / Australian Long Range Weapons Committee .... CUKAC
Combined Universities Campaign for Nuclear Disarmament [*Canada*] .... CUCND
Combined Ventricular Hypertrophy (MAE) .... CVH
Combined VHF [*Very-High-Frequency*]-Band .... CVB
Combined Volume-Weighted Mean [*Statistics*] .... CVWM
Combined VOR and TACAN Navigational Facility [*FAA*] (TAG) .... VORTAC
Combined Wage Claim [*Unemployment insurance*] .... CWC
Combined Welfare Administration Fund .... CWAF
Combined Wheat Control Section [*Allied German Occupation Forces*] .... CWCS
Combined-Cycle Gas Turbines (ECON) .... CCGT
Combined-Heat-and-Power District Heating [*British*] (DI) .... CHPDH
Combined-Heat-and-Power Station [*Energy production*] .... CHP
Combining Power .... CP
Combining Power Test (AAMN) .... CPT
Comboni Missionaries of the Heart of Jesus (TOCD) .... mccj
Comboni Missionaries of the Heart of Jesus (Verona) (TOCD) .... MCCJ
Comboni Missionary Sisters (TOCD) .... CMS
Combustible (MSA) .... COMBL
Combustible Case Ammunition [*Weaponry*] [*Military*] (VNW) .... CBSS
Combustible Limit Relay (IAA) .... CLR
Combustible Metals [*Fire classification*] .... D
Combustible Storage Building (AAG) .... CSB
Combustion (AAG) .... COMB
Combustion .... COMBN
Combustion .... COMBSTN
Combustion and Explosives Research (AAG) .... C & ER
Combustion Chamber (KSC) CC
Combustion Chamber Deposits [*Fuels and lubricants testing*] .... CCD
Combustion Chemical Vapor Deposition .... CCVD
Combustion Control by Vortex Stratification [*Automotive engine design*] .... CCVS
Combustion Efficiency .... COMB EFF
Combustion Engineering [*Navy*] .... CE
Combustion Engineering Association [*British*] .... CEA
Combustion Engineering Nuclear Division [*AEC*] (MCD) .... CEND
Combustion Engineering Safety Analysis Report [*Nuclear energy*] (IAA) .... CESAR
Combustion Engineering Standard Safety Analysis Report [*Nuclear energy*] (NRCH) .... CESSAR
Combustion Engineering Superheater Ltd., Ottawa, ON, Canada [*Library symbol*] [*Library of Congress*] (LCLS) .... CaOOCES
Combustion Engineering Superheater Ltd., Ottawa, Ontario [*Library symbol National Library of Canada*] (NLC) .... OOCES
Combustion Equilibrium Calculation Computer Program (MCD) .... CECCP
Combustion Gas Analyzer Program [*Nuclear energy*] (NRCH) .... COGAP
Combustion Gas Control System [*Nuclear energy*] (NRCH) .... CGCS
Combustion, Heat, and Mass (PDAA) .... CHAM
Combustion Institute (EA) CI
Combustion Metamorphism [*Geology*] .... CM
Combustion Research Facility [*Department of Energy*] [*Livermore, CA*] .... CRF
Combustion Stability Monitor .... CSM
Combustion Turbine [*Type of cogenerator*] .... CT
Combustion Zone Temperature [*Fuel technology*] .... CZT
Combustor (MSA) .... CMBSTR
Combustor Exit Temperature (MCD) .... CET
Comcast Cl'A' [*NASDAQ symbol*] (TTSB) .... CMCSA
Comcast Cl'A'Spl(non-vtg) [*NASDAQ symbol*] (TTSB) .... CMCSK
Comcast Corp. [*NASDAQ symbol*] (NQ) .... CMCS
Comcast Corp. [*Associated Press*] (SAG) .... Comc
Comcast Corp. [*Associated Press*] (SAG) .... Comcast
Comcast UK Cable Partners Ltd. [*NASDAQ symbol*] (SAG) .... CMCA

Comcast UK Cable Partners Ltd. [*Associated Press*] (SAG) .... CmcstUK
Comcast UK Cable Partners'A' [*NASDAQ symbol*] (TTSB) .... CMCAF
Comdata Holding Corp. [*Associated Press*] (SAG) .... Comdata
Comdata Holdings Corp. [*NASDAQ symbol*] (NQ) .... CMDT
Comdial Corp. [*Associated Press*] (SAG) .... Cmdial
Comdial Corp. [*NASDAQ symbol*] (NQ) .... CMDL
Comdisco 8.75% cm Ser'A'Pfd [*NYSE symbol*] (TTSB) .... CDOPrA
Comdisco 8.75% cm Ser'B'Pfd [*NYSE symbol*] (TTSB) .... CDOPrB
Comdisco Disaster Recovery Services (HGAA) .... CDRS
Comdisco, Inc. [*NYSE symbol*] (SPSG) .... CDO
Comdisco, Inc. [*Associated Press*] (SAG) .... Comd
Comdisco, Inc. [*Associated Press*] (SAG) .... Comdis
Comdisco, Inc. [*Associated Press*] (SAG) .... Comdisco
Come [*Like, As*] [*Music*] (ROG) .... CO
Come Hither [*A publication*] .... CH
Come, Let Us Reason Together [*Labor mediators' slogan*] .... CLURT
Come Off Your Old Tired Ethics [*Prostitutes' lobbying group*] .... COYOTE
Come Primo [*As at First*] [*Music*] .... Co Imo
Come Quick - Danger [*International distress signal, used before SOS*] .... CQD
Come Sopra [*As Above*] [*Music*] (ROG) .... CO SA
Come Sopra [*As Above*] [*Music*] .... CO SO
Come Sopra [*As Above*] [*Music*] .... CS
Come-All-Ye [*A publication*] (BRI) .... CAY
Comed Aviation Ltd. [*British*] [*FAA designator*] (FAAC) .... CDE
Comed Financial I [*NYSE symbol*] (SAG) .... CWE
ComEd Financing 1 8.48% 'TOPrS' [*NYSE symbol*] (TTSB) .... CWEPrT
Comed Financing I [*Associated Press*] (SAG) .... Comed
Comedian [*or Comedy*] (ROG) .... COM
Comedian Society for Amateurs and Professionals [*Defunct*] (EA) .... CSAP
Comedy (WDMC) .... com
[*The*] **Comedy Channel** .... TCC
[*The*] **Comedy of Errors** [*Shakespearean work*] .... C of E
Comedy of Errors [*Shakespearean drama*] (BARN) .... Com Err
[*The*] **Comedy of Errors** [*Shakespearean work*] .... Err
Comedy Prescription [*An association*] (EA) .... CP
Comedy Store [*Nightclub in which inexperienced comedians appear free in return for exposure to an audience*] .... CS
Comedy Television [*Cable-television system*] .... CTV
Comedy Writers Association (EA) .... CWA
Comence (FAAC) .... CMNC
Comenius World Council (EA) .... CWC
Comercial Aerea SA de CV [*Mexico ICAO designator*] (FAAC) .... CRS
Comerica, Inc. [*NYSE symbol*] (SPSG) .... CMA
Comerica, Inc. [*Associated Press*] (SAG) .... Comeric
Comer's Forms of Writs [*A publication*] (DLA) .... Com Forms
Comerstone Natural Gas [*Formerly, Endevco, Inc.*] [*AMEX symbol*] (SPSG) .... CGA
Comet and Asteroid Rendezvous Docking (MCD) .... CARD
Comet Halley Active Monitoring Program .... CHAMP
Comet Halley American Southern-Hemisphere Expedition .... CHASE
Comet Industries [*Vancouver Stock Exchange symbol*] .... CMU
Comet Rendezvous and Asteroid Flyby [*Proposed NASA mission*] .... CRAF
Comet Rendezvous Mission .... CRM
Cometary Feasibility Study Group [*European Space Research Organization*] (IEEE) .... CFSG
Cometary Kilometric Radiation [*Astrophysics*] .... CKR
Cometary-Mass-to-Planets [*Astronomy*] .... CMTP
Comet-Like Object .... CLO
Come-Up .... C/U
Come-Up Time [*Time required for a retort to reach operating conditions*] .... CUT
Comforce Corp. [*AMEX symbol*] (SAG) .... CFS
Comforce Corp. [*AMEX symbol*] (TTSB) .... CFS
Comforce Corp. [*Associated Press*] (SAG) .... Comforce
Comfort .... CMFRT
Comfort Cooling Tower [*Air conditioning*] .... CCT
Comfort Index CI
Comfort Measures Only [*Medicine*] (DAVI) .... CMO
Comfort Public Library, Comfort, TX [*Library symbol Library of Congress*] (LCLS) .... TxComf
Comfort, TX [*FM radio station call letters*] .... KRNH
Comfortable Interpersonal Distance Scale (EDAC) .... CID
Comfortable Recreation Vehicle .... CRV
Comfortably Weird [*In the record business, refers to a successful performer who has retained his individuality*] .... CW
Comhairle Sabhailteacht Naisiunta [*National Safety Council*] [*Ireland*] (EAIO) .... CSN
Comhaltas Ceoltoiri Eireann [*Traditional Irish Singing and Dancing Society*] (EA) .... CCE
Comhaltas Peil Eitleoiga na Heireann [*Volleyball Association of Ireland*] [*See also VAI*] [*Ireland*] (EAIO) .... CPEH
Comhuriyet Halk Partisi [*Turkey*] .... CHP
Comic .... COM
Comic Book Retailers International [*An association*] (EA) .... CBRI
Comic Crusader [*A publication*] CC
Comicorum Atticorum Fragmenta [*A publication*] (OCD) .... CAF
Comicorum Graecorum Fragmenta [*A publication*] (OCD) .... CGF
Comicorum Romanum Fragmenta [*A publication*] (OCD) .... CRF
Comics Amateur Press Alliance .... CAPA
Comics Code Authority [*Regulatory body for comic book and comic magazine publishing industry*] .... CCA
Comics Magazine Association of America (EA) .... CMAA
Comilla [*Bangladesh*] [*Airport symbol*] (AD) .... CLA
Comilla [*Bangladesh*] [*ICAO location identifier*] (ICLI) .... VGCM
Cominco Ltd. [*AMEX symbol Toronto Stock Exchange symbol Vancouver Stock Exchange symbol*] (SPSG) .... CLT
Cominco Ltd. [*Associated Press*] (SAG) .... Cominc
Cominco Ltd., Toronto, ON, Canada [*Library symbol Library of Congress*] (LCLS) .... CaOTCom
Cominco Ltd., Toronto, Ontario [*Library symbol National Library of Canada*] (NLC) .... OTCOM
Cominco Ltd., Vancouver, BC, Canada [*Library symbol Library of Congress*] (LCLS) .... CaBVaCOM
Cominco Ltd., Vancouver, British Columbia [*Library symbol National Library of Canada*] (NLC) .... BVACOM
Cominco Resources International Ltd. [*Toronto Stock Exchange symbol Vancouver Stock Exchange symbol*] .... COR
Coming Off Pills Entirely .... COPE
COMINT [*Communications Intelligence*] **Receiver Test System** (MCD) .... CRTS
COMIREX [*Committee on Imagery Requirements and Exploitation*] **Advanced Exploitation System** (MCD) .... CADES
COMIREX [*Committee on Imagery Requirements and Exploitation*] **Automated Management System** (MCD) .... CAMS
Comision Andina de Juristas [*Andean Commission of Jurists - ACJ*] (EAIO) .... CAJ
Comision Asesora Regional de Pesca para el Atlantico Sudoccidental [*Regional Fisheries Advisory Commission for the South-West Atlantic*] [*Inactive*] (EAIO) .... CARPAS
Comision Centroamericana de Energia [*Central American Energy Commission*] (EAIO) .... COMENER
Comision Centroamericana de Transporte Maritimo [*Central American Commission of Maritime Transport*] [*Organization of Central American States*] [*San Salvador, El Salvador*] (EAIO) .... COCATRAM
Comision de Derechos Humanos de El Salvador [*Spain*] .... CDHES
Comision de Estudios de Historia de la Iglesia en Latinoamerica [*Commission of the Studies of History of the Church in Latin America*] [*Mexico*] .... CEHILA
Comision de Integracion Electrica Regional [*Commission of Regional Electrical Integration*] (EAIO) .... CIER
Comision de Pesca Continental para America Latina [*Commission for Inland Fisheries of Latin America*] [*FAO*] [*Italy*] (ASF) .... COPESCAL
Comision de Proteccion Fitosanitaria para el Caribe [*Caribbean Plant Protection Commission - CPPC*] (EAIO) .... CPFC
Comision de Solidaridad con las Familiares de Presos Politicos, Desaparecidos y Matados en Argentina .... COSOFAM
Comision Economica para America Latina y el Caribe [*Economic Commission for Latin America and the Caribbean - ECLAC*] [*Santiago, Chile*] [*United Nations*] (EAIO) .... CEPAL
Comision Economica y Social para Asia Occidental [*Economic and Social Commission for Western Asia*] [*Spanish United Nations*] (DUND) .... CESPAO
Comision Economica y Social para Asia y el Pacifico [*Economic and Social Commission for Asia and the Pacific*] [*Spanish United Nations*] (DUND) .... CESPAP
Comision Ejecutiva Permanente del Consejo Interamericano Economico y Social [*Permanent Executive Committee of the Inter-American Economic and Social Council*] (EA) .... CEPCIES
Comision Especial de Coordinacion Latinoamericana .... CECLA
Comision Especial de Expertos para el Estudio de las Necesidades Financieras quePlantea la Ejecucion de Planes de Reforma Agraria [*Consejo Interamericano Economico y Social*] [*Washington, DC*] .... CERA
Comision Femenil Mexicana Nacional (EA) .... CFM
Comision Interamericana del Atun Tropical [*Interamerican Tropical Tuna Commission - IATTC*] .... CIAT
Comision Latinoamericana de Aviacion Civil [*Latin American Civil Aviation Commission - LACAC*] (EAIO) .... CLAC
Comision Latinoamericana de Trabajadores de la Educacion [*Venezuela*] .... CLATEC
Comision Nacional Peruana de Cooperacion con la UNESCO [*Peruvian National Commission for the United Nations Educational, Scientific and Cultural Organization*] [*Peru*] (EAIO) .... CNPC
Comision Panamericana de Normas Tecnicas [*Pan American Standards Commission - PASC*] (EAIO) .... COPANT
Comision para la Defensa de los Derechos Humanos en Centroamerica [*Commission for the Defense of Human Rights in Central America - CDHRCA*] (EA) .... CODEHUCA
Comision Permanente del Pacifico Sur [*Permanent Commission for the South Pacific - PCSP*] (EAIO) .... CPPS
Comision Tecnica de la Red Andina Telecomunicaciones [*Technical Commission for the Andean Telecommunication Network*] (PDAA) .... COMTEC/RAT
Comiso [*Italy*] [*Airport symbol*] (AD) .... CIY
Comiso [*Italy ICAO location identifier*] (ICLI) .... LICB
Comissao Democratica Eleitoral [*Democratic Electoral Committee*] [*Portugal Political party*] (PPE) .... CDE
Comissao Eleitoral Monarquica [*Monarchy Electoral Committee*] [*Portugal*] (PPE) .... CEM
Comissao Eleitoral para a Unidade Democratico [*Electoral Committee for Democratic Unity*] [*Portugal Political party*] (PPE) .... CEUD
Comissao Nacional de Energia Nuclear [*National Commission for Nuclear Energy*] [*Brazil Information service or system*] (IID) .... CNEN
Comission Internationale de l'Organisation Scientifique du Travail [*International Committee of Work Study and Labour Management in Agriculture*] (EAIO) .... IOSTA
Comitan [*Mexico*] [*Seismograph station code, US Geological Survey*] (SEIS) .... COM
Comitatis Causa [*For the County's Sake*] [*Latin*] (ROG) .... COMIT CAUS
Comitato Italiano Atlantico [*Italian Atlantic Committee*] (EAIO) .... CIA
Comitato per la Difesa della Repubblica [*Committee for the Defense of the Republic*] [*San Marino*] [*Political party*] (PPW) .... CDR
Comitatus [*County*] [*Latin*] (ROG) .... COM
Comite Administratif de Coordination [*Administrative Committee on Coordination - ACC*] [*United Nations French*] (ASF) .... CAC

Comite Administrativo de Coordinacion [*Administrative Committee on Coordination - ACC*] [*United Nations Spanish*] (MSC) .... CAC
Comite Arctique International [*International Arctic Committee*] [*Monte Carlo, Monaco*] (EAIO) .... CAI
Comite Associe du Code National du Batiment [*Associate Committee of the National Building Code*] [*National Research Council of Canada*] .... CACNB
Comite Canadien de la Classification Ecologique du Territoire [*Canadian Committee on Ecological (Biophysical) Land Classification - CCELC*] .... CCCET
Comite Canadien d'Oceanographie [*Canadian Committee on Oceanography - CCO*] .... CCO
Comite Canadien pour le Programme Biologique International [*Canadian Committee for the International Biological Programme - CCIBP*] .... CCPBI
Comite Canadien sur le Financement de la Recherche dans les Universites [*Canadian Committee on Financing University Research - CCFUR*] .... CCFRU
Comite Canadien sur les Services Socio-Economiques [*Canada Committee on Socio-Economic Services - CCSES*] .... CCSSE
Comite Catholique Contre la Faim et pour le Developpement [*France*] .... CCFD
Comite Catholique International de Coordination Aupres de l'UNESCO CCIC
Comite Central de la Propriete Forestiere [*Central Committee for Forest Ownership in the EEC - CCFOE*] (EAIO) .... CCPF
Comite Chretien pour les Droits Humains en Amerique Latine [*Christian Committee for Human Rights in Latin America*] [*Canada*] (EAIO) .... CCDHAL
Comite Commun pour la Promotion de l'Aide aux Cooperatives [*Joint Committee for the Promotion of Aid to Cooperatives*] [*UN Food and Agriculture Organization*] .... COPAC
Comite Comunista Unificado Marxista-Leninista [*Peru*] [*Political party*] (EY) .... CCUML
Comite Consultatif de la Radioprotection [*Advisory Committee on Radiological Protection*] [*Canada*] .... CCRP
Comite Consultatif de la Surete Nucleaire [*Advisory Committee on Nuclear Safety*] [*Canada*] .... CCSN
Comite Consultatif International des Radiocommunications [*International Radio Consultative Committee*] [*of the International Telecommunications Union*] [*Switzerland*] .... CCIR
Comite Consultatif International du Coton [*International Cotton Advisory Committee*] CCIC
Comite Consultatif International Telegraphique et Telephonique [*Consultative Committee on International Telegraphy and Telephony*] [*of the International Telecommunications Union*] [*Switzerland*] .... CCITT
Comite Consultatif International Telephonique des Frequences [*International Telephone Consultative Committee*] (NATG) .... CCIF
Comite Consultatif Mondial de la Societe des Amis [*World Consultative Committee of the Society of Friends*] [*British*] (EAIO) .... CCMSA
Comite Consultatif National des Recherches sur les Ressources Hydrauliques [*National Advisory Committee on Water Resources Research*] [*Canada*] .... CCNRRH
Comite Consultatif pour les Standards des Mesurement Radiations Ionizant [*Consultative Committee for the Standards of Measurement of Ionizing Radiations*] [*International Standards Organization*] [*French*] (BARN) .... CCEMRI
Comite Contre la Torture [*Committee Against Torture - CAT*] [*Switzerland*] (EAIO) .... CCT
Comite d'Action de la Pomme de Terre [*Potato Action Committee*] [*Canadian Department of Agriculture*] .... CAP
Comite d'Action des Transports Publics des Communautes Europeennes [*Action Committee of Public Transport of the European Communities - ACPTEC*] (EAIO) .... CATPCE
Comite d'Action du Personnel Autochtone [*Native Employees Action Team*] [*Canada*] .... CAPA
Comite d'Action en France .... COMDAC
Comite d'Action et de Concertation du Conseil Democratique Revolutionnaire [*Chad*] [*Political party*] (EY) .... CAC-CDR
Comite d'Action Musulman [*Mauritian political party*] .... CAM
Comite d'Aide au Developpement [*OCDE*] .... CAD
Comite d'Appui au Peuple Espagnol [*Committee of Support for Spanish People*] [*Canada*] .... CAPE
Comite de Apoio de Reconstrucao do Partido Marxista-Leninista [*Support Committee for the Reconstruction of the Marxist-Leninist Party*] [*Portugal Political party*] (PPE) .... CARP M-L
Comite de Bourses de la Communaute Europeenne [*Committee of Stock Exchanges in the European Community - CSEE*] (EAIO) .... CBCE
Comite de Compradores de Material Aeronautico de America Latina (MCD) .... CCMA
Comite de Cooperacion Economica del Istmo Centroamericano [*Central American Economic Cooperation Committee*] .... CCE
Comite de Coordination de l'Assistance Technique [*ONU*] .... CCAT
Comite de Coordination des Associations de Constructeurs d'Appareillage [*Coordinating Committee for Common Market Associations of Manufacturers of Electrical Switchgear and Controlgear*] [*EC*] (ECED) .... CAPIEL
Comite de Coordination des Constructeurs des Machines Tournantes Electriques du Marche Commun [*Coordinating Committee for Common Market Associations of Manufacturers of Rotating Electric Machinery*] (EAIO) .... COMEL
Comite de Coordination des Experts Budgetaires Gouvernementaux [*Coordinating Committee of Government Budget Experts*] [*NATO*] (NATG) .... CCG
Comite de Coordination des Industries Textiles de la Communaute Economique Europeenne [*Coordination Committee for the Textile Industries in the European Economic Community*] [*Brussels, Belgium*] (EAIO) .... COMITEXTIL
Comite de Coordination des Plans Civils d'Urgence [*Civil Emergency Coordinating Committee*] [*NATO*] (NATG) .... CCPC
Comite de Coordination des Plans de Transport [*Coordinating Committee for Transport Planning*] [*NATO*] (NATG) .... CCPT
Comite de Coordination des Services Agricoles Canadiens [*Canadian Agricultural Services Coordinating Committee*] .... CCSAC
Comite de Coordination des Telecommunications [*Coordinating Committee for Communications*] [*NATO France*] (NATG) .... CCT
Comite de Coordination du Service Volontaire International [*Coordinating Committee for International Voluntary Service - CCIVS*] [*Paris, France*] (EA) .... CCSVI
Comite de Defense des Libertes Democratiques au Mali [*Committee for the Defense of Democratic Liberties in Mali*] (PD) .... CDLDM
Comite de Defense des Prisonniers en Indonesie [*France*] .... TAPOL
Comite de Defense du Peuple Canadien (Citoyens et Residents) [*Canadian People's (Citizens and Residents) Defence Committee*] .... CDPC
Comite de Fabricants Europeens d'Installations et de Distribution de Petrole [*Committee of European Manufacturers of Petroleum Measuring and Distributing Equipment*] [*EC*] (ECED) .... CECOD
Comite de Familiares de Presos Politicos Uruguayos [*Relatives' Committee for Uruguayan Political Prisoners*] [*Malmo, Sweden*] (EAIO) .... CFPPU
Comite de Formation et de Developpement Municipaux des Maritimes [*Maritime Municipal Training and Development Board*] [*Canada*] .... CFDMM
Comite de la Bibliographie et des Services d'Information en Sciences Humaines [*Committee on Bibliography and Information Services for the Social Sciences and Humanities - CBISSSH*] [*National Library of Canada*] .... CBSISH
Comite de la Science et de la Technologie dans les Pays en Voie de Developpement [*Committee on Science and Technology in Developing Countries*] .... COSTED
Comite de Liaison Commerce de Detail [*Liaison Committee of European Retail Trade Associations*] (EAIO) .... CLD
Comite de Liaison de la Construction Automobile [*Liaison Committee for the Motor Industry in the EEC Countries*] [*Brussels, Belgium*] (EAIO) .... CLCA
Comite de Liaison de la Construction de Carrosseries et de Remorques [*Liaison Committee of the Body- and Trailer-Building Industry*] (EAIO) .... CLCCR
Comite de Liaison de la Construction d'Equipements et de Pieces d'Automobiles [*Liaison Committee of Manufacturers of Motor Vehicle Parts and Equipment*] (EAIO) .... CLEPA
Comite de Liaison de l'Agrumiculture Mediterraneenne [*Liaison Committee for Mediterranean Citrus Fruit Culture - LCMCFC*] (EAIO) .... CLAM
Comite de Liaison de l'Industrie Europeenne des Tubes d'Acier [*Liaison Committee of the EEC Steel Tube Industry*] (EAIO) .... CLIETA
Comite de Liaison des Architectes de l'Europe Unie [*Liaison Committee of the Architects of United Europe*] [*EC*] (ECED) .... CLAEU
Comite de Liaison des Associations Europeennes de l'Industrie de la Parfumerie, des Produits Cosmetiques, et de Toilette [*European Federation of the Perfume, Cosmetics, and Toiletries Industry*] (EAIO) .... COLIPA
Comite de Liaison des Fabricants de Bicyclettes (EA) .... COLIBI
Comite de Liaison des Fabricants de Motocyclettes [*Liaison Committee of European Motorcycle Manufacturers*] [*Belgium*] (EAIO) .... COLIMO
Comite de Liaison des Fabricants de Pieces et Equipements de Deux Roues des Paysde la CEE [*Liaison Committee of Manufacturers of Parts and Equipment for Two-Wheeled Vehicles*] (EAIO) .... COLIPED
Comite de Liaison des Industries Cimentieres de la CEE [*Liaison Committee of the Cement Industries in the EEC*] (ECED) CLC
Comite de Liaison des Industries Metalliques Europeennes .... COLIME
Comite de Liaison des Organisations Non-Gouvernmentales de Developpement aupres des Communautes Europeennes [*Liaison Committee of Development Non-Governmental Organizations to the European Communities*] (EAIO) .... CLONG-CE
Comite de Liaison des Organisations Non-Gouvernmentales de Developpement aupres des Communautes Europeennes [*Liaison Committee of Development Non-Governmental Organizations to the European Communities*] (EAIO) .... NCOS
Comite de Liaison des Organismes Chretiens de Cooperation Internationale (EAIO) .... CLOCCI
Comite de Liaison des OrganizationSs Non-Gouvernmentales de Volontariat [*Committee for the Liaison of Non-Governmental Voluntary Organizations*] [*France*] (EAIO) .... CLONGV
Comite de Liaison des Petites et Moyennes Entreprises Industrielles des Pays de la CEE [*Liaison Committee for Small and Medium-Sized Industrial Enterprises in the EEC*] [*Brussels, Belgium*] (EAIO) .... EUROPMI
Comite de Liaison des Podologues de la CE [*Liaison Committee of Podologists of the Common Market*] (ECED) .... CLPCE
Comite de Liaison Entr'Aide et Action [*Help and Action Coordinating Committee*] (EAIO) .... CLEAA
Comite de Liaison Europeen de la Distribution Independante de Pieces de Rechangeet Equipements pour Automobiles [*European Liaison Committee for the Independent Distribution of Spare Parts and Equipment for Motor Cars*] [*EC*] (ECED) .... CLEDIPA
Comite de Liaison Europeen des Commissionnaires et Auxiliaires de Transport [*European Liaison Committee of Forwarders*] (EAIO) .... CLECAT
Comite de Liaison Europeen des Osteopathes [*European Liaison Committee for Osteopaths - ELCO*] (EA) .... CLEO
Comite de Liaison International des Broderies, Rideaux, et Dentelles [*International Liaison Committee for Embroideries, Curtains, and Laces*] .... CELIBRIDE
Comite de Liaison International des Cooperatives d'Epargne et de Credit [*International Liaison Committee on Co-Operative Thrift and Credit - ILCCTC*] [*Paris, France*] (EA) .... CLICEC
Comite de Problemas de Productos Basicos [*Committee on Commodity Problems*] [*Italy*] (ASF) .... CPPB
Comite de Solidaridad con el Pueblo Argentino [*Spain*] .... COSPA
Comite de Solidarite avec les Prisonniers Politiques Arabes et du Proche Orient [*Solidarity Committee for Arab and Near-Eastern Political Prisoners*] .... CSPPA
Comite de Solidarite Tiers-Monde/Trois-Rivieres [*Third World Solidarity Committee/Trois-Rivieres*] (AC) .... CSTM-TR

Comite de Surveillance Ecologique des Pulverisations Seriennes [*Canada*] ..... CSEPA
Comite de Travail des Malteries de la CEE [*Working Committee of European Economic Community Malters*] ..... EUROMALT
Comite de Unidad Campesina [*Committee of Peasant Unity*] [*Guatemala*] [*Political party*] (PD) ..... CUC
Comite des Amities Acadiennes [*Acadian Friendship Committee - AFC*] (EAIO) ..... CAA
Comite des Associations Europeennes de Cafe [*Committee of European Coffee Associations*] [*EC*] (ECED) ..... CAEC
Comite des Associations Europeennes de Fonderie [*Committee of European Foundry Associations*] (EA) ..... CAEF
Comite des Bibliotheques Publiques de la Region de Quebec (AC) ..... COBIPUQ
Comite des Constructeurs d'Automobiles du Marche Common [*Common Market Automobile Manufacturers Committee*] [*French*] ..... CCMC
Comite des Constructeurs de Materiel Frigorifique de la CEE [*Committee of Manufacturers of Refrigeration Equipment of the EEC*] ..... COMAF
Comite des Constructeurs Europeens de Materiel Alimentaire [*Committee of European Plant Manufacturers for the Food Industry*] [*Common Market*] ..... COCEMA
Comite des Demenageurs du Marche Commun ..... CODEMAC
Comite des Eglises Aupres des Migrants en Europe [*Churches' Committee on Migrants in Europe*] (EA) ..... CEME
Comite des Fabricants d'Acide Glutamique de la CEE [*Committee of Glutamic Acid Manufacturers of the European Economic Community*] (EAIO) ..... COFAG
Comite des Fabricants de Levure de Panification de la CEE [*Committee of Bread Yeast Manufacturers of the EEC*] ..... COFALEC
Comite des Forces Vives - Hery Velona [*Madagascar*] [*Political party*] (EY) .... CFV
Comite des Industries Cinematographiques des Communautes Europeennes [*Committee of the Cinematography Industries in the European Communities*] (EAIO) ..... CICCE
Comite des Industries de la Moutarde de la CEE [*EEC Committee for the Mustard Industries*] ..... CIMCEE
Comite des Industries des Mayonnaises et Sauces Condimentaires de la CEE [*Committee of the Industries of Mayonnaises and Table Sauces of the European Economic Community*] ..... CIMSCEE
Comite des Industries du Coton et des Fibres Connexes de la CEE [*Committee of the Cotton Industries of the European Economic Community*] (PDAA) ..... EUROCOTON
Comite des Industries Lainieres de la CEE [*Committee of the Wool Textile Industry in the EEC*] (EAIO) ..... INTERLAINE
Comite des Normes Gouvernementales en Informatique [*Government Electronic Data Processing Standards Committee*] [*Canada*] ..... CNGI
Comite des Organisations Commerciales des Pays de la CEE [*Committee of Commercial Organizations in the EEC Countries*] ..... COCCEE
Comite des Organisations de la Boucherie-Charcuterie de la CEE [*Committee of Butchery and Cooked Meats Organizations of the EEC*] ..... COBCCEE
Comite des Organisations Familiales aupres des Communautes Europeennes [*Committee of Family Organizations in the European Communities*] [*Common Market*] [*Belgium*] ..... COFACE
Comite des Organisations Professionnelles Agricoles de la CEE [*Committee of Professional Agricultural Organizations in the EEC*] ..... COPA
Comite des Paysans Africains [*African Farmers Committee - AFC*] (EAIO) ..... CPA
Comite des Peches pour l'Atlantique Centre-Est [*Committee for the Eastern Central Atlantic Fisheries - CECAF*] [*Senegal*] (MSC) ..... COPACE
Comite des Personnes Atteintes du VIH [*Committee of Persons Living with HIV*] (AC) ..... CPAVIH
Comite des Petites et Moyens Enterprises Commerciales [*Committee of Small and Medium Commercial Enterprises*] [*EEC*] (PDAA) ..... COPMEC
Comite des Semences du Marche Commun [*Seed Committee of the Common Market*] ..... COSEMCO
Comite des Services Bibliographiques pour le Canada [*Committee on Bibliographical Services for Canada*] ..... CSBC
Comite des Travaux Historiques et Scientifiques [*Ministere de l'Education Nationale*] [*Database*] ..... CTHS
Comite d'Etude de la Corrosion et de la Protection des Canalisations [*Committee for the Study of Pipe Corrosion and Protection*] (EAIO) ..... CEOCOR
Comite d'Etude des Droits des Autochtones [*Committee for Original Peoples' Entitlement*] [*Canada*] ..... CEDA
Comite d'Etude des Producteurs de Charbon d'Europe Occidentale [*Association of the Coal Producers of the European Community*] (EAIO) ..... CEPCEO
Comite d'Etude sur les Conditions du Logement [*Study Committee Study on Housing Conditions*] [*Canada*] ..... CECL
Comite d'Information sur la Lutte Solidarite [*Portugal*] ..... CILS
Comite d'Initiative pour le Congres du Peuple Europeen ..... CICPE
Comite d'Organisation du Congres Mondial d'Implantologie des Biomateriaux [*Organizing Committee of the World Congress on Implantology and Bio-Materials - OCWCIB*] [*Rouen, France*] (EAIO) ..... COCMIB
Comite du Commerce des Cereales et des Aliments du Betail de la Communaute Economique Europeenne [*Committee of the Cereals and Animal Feed Trade of the European Economic Community*] ..... COCERAL
Comite du Patrimoine Mondial [*World Heritage Committee - WHC*] (EAIO) ..... CPM
Comite Economique et Social [*Economic and Social Committee*] [*of CEE*] ..... CES
Comite Euro-International du Beton [*Euro-International Committee for Concrete*] ..... CEB
Comite Europe-Amerique Latine [*Belgium*] ..... CEAL
Comite European de Liaison du Commerce de Gros des Papiers et Cartons [*European Liaison Committee of Wholesalers of Paper and Cardboard*] (PDAA) ..... COMEPA
Comite European de Normalisation Electrotechnique [*European Committee for Electrotechnical Standardization*] (EAIO) ..... CENELEC
Comite Europeen de Controle Laitierbeurrier ..... CECLB
Comite Europeen de Cooperation des Industries de la Machine Outil [*European Committee for Cooperation of the Machine Tool Industries*] [*EC*] (ECED) ..... CECIMO
Comite Europeen de Cooperation Juridique [*French*] ..... CCJ
Comite Europeen de Coordination des Normes [*European Committee for Coordination of Standards*] ..... CEN
Comite Europeen de Coordination des Normes Electriques [*European Electrical Standards Coordinating Committee*] ..... CENEL
Comite Europeen de Droit Rural [*France*] ..... CEDR
Comite Europeen de la Chaudronnerie et de la Tolerie [*European Committee for Boilermaking and Kindred Steel Structures*] ..... CECT
Comite Europeen de la Culture du Houblon [*European Hop Growers Committee*] ..... CECH
Comite Europeen de l'Association Internationale de l'Ozone [*European Committee of the International Ozone Association*] (EAIO) ..... CEAIO
Comite Europeen de l'Hospitalisation Privee [*European Committee of Private Hospitalization*] [*EC*] [*Belgium*] (ECED) ..... CEHP
Comite Europeen de Liaison des Commerces Agro-Alimentaires [*European Liaison Committee for Agricultural and Food Trades*] (EAIO) ..... CELCAA
Comite Europeen de Liaison des Industries de la Machine a Coudre [*European Liaison Committee for the Sewing Machine Industries - ELCSMI*] [*Defunct*] (EAIO) ..... CELIMAC
Comite Europeen de Liaison des Negociants et Utilisateurs de Combustibles [*European Liaison Committee of Fuel Merchants and Users*] ..... CELNUCO
Comite Europeen de l'Industrie de la Robinetterie [*European Committee for the Valves and Fittings Industry*] [*EC*] [*Germany*] (ECED) ..... CEIR
Comite Europeen de l'Internationale du Personnel des Postes, Telegraphes et Telephones [*European Committee of the Postal, Telegraph and Telephone International*] [*EC*] (ECED) ..... EPTT
Comite Europeen de l'Outillage [*European Tool Committee - ETC*] (EA) ..... CEO
Comite Europeen de l'Outillage [*European Tool Committee*] [*France*] (EAIO) ..... COE
Comite Europeen de l'Outillage Agricole et Horticole [*European Committee for Agricultural and Horticultural Tools and Implements - ECAHTI*] (EA) ..... CEOAH
Comite Europeen de Normalisation [*European Committee for Standardization*] [*Belgium*] ..... CEN
Comite Europeen de Reflexion sur les Retraites [*European Pension Committee*] [*Paris, France*] (EAIO) ..... CERR
Comite Europeen de Rink Hockey [*European Committee for Rink Hockey*] (EAIO) ..... CERH
Comite Europeen des Associations des Fabricants de Peinture, d'Encres d'Imprimerie, et de Couleurs [*European Committee of Paint, Printing Ink, and Artists' Colours Manufacturers Associations*] (EAIO) ..... CEPE
Comite Europeen des Constructeurs de Broleurs [*European Committee of Manufacturers of Burners*] (EA) ..... CEB
Comite Europeen des Constructeurs de Machines a Bois [*European Committee of Woodworking Machinery Manufacturers*] (EAIO) ..... EUMABOIS
Comite Europeen des Constructeurs de Materiel Frigorifique [*European Committee of Manufacturers of Refrigeration Equipment*] (EAIO) ..... CECOMAF
Comite Europeen des Constructeurs de Materiel Textile [*European Committee of Textile Machinery Manufacturers*] (EAIO) ..... CEMATEX
Comite Europeen des Constructeurs de Materiels d'Incendie et de Secours [*European Committee of the Manufacturers of Fire Protection and Safety Equipment and Fire Fighting Vehicles*] (EAIO) ..... EUROFEU
Comite Europeen des Constructeurs de Pompes [*European Committee of Pump Manufacturers*] (EAIO) ..... EUROPUMP
Comite Europeen des Constructeurs d'Instruments de Pesage [*European Committee of Weighing Instrument Manufacturers - ECWIM*] (EAIO) ..... CECIP
Comite Europeen des Cooperatives de Production et de Travail Associe [*European Committee of Workers' Cooperatives*] [*EC*] (ECED) ..... CECOP
Comite Europeen des Equipements Techniques du Batiment [*European Committee for Building Technical Equipment - ECBTE*] (EAIO) ..... CEETB
Comite Europeen des Fabricants d'Appareils de Chauffage en Fonte (PDAA) ..... CEFACEF
Comite Europeen des Fabricants d'Appareils de Chauffage et de Cuisine Domestiques [*European Committee of Manufacturers of Domestic Heating and Cooking Appliances*] ..... CEFACD
Comite Europeen des Fabricants de Sucre [*European Committee of Sugar Manufacturers*] [*Common Market*] ..... CEFS
Comite Europeen des Federations Nationales de la Maroquinerie, Articles de Voyages, et Industries Connexes (EAIO) ..... CEDIM
Comite Europeen des Groupements de Constructeurs du Machinisme Agricole [*European Committee of Associations of Manufacturers of Agricultural Machinery*] (EAIO) ..... CEMA
Comite Europeen des Ingenieurs-Conseils [*European Committee of Consulting Engineers*] [*EC*] (ECED) ..... CEDIC
Comite Europeen des Materiels de Genie Civil [*Committee for European Construction Equipment - CECE*] (EAIO) ..... CEMGC
Comite Europeen des Materiels et Produits pour la Fonderie [*European Committee of Foundry Materials and Products*] (EAIO) ..... CEMAFON
Comite Europeen des Services des Conseillers [*European Committee for Consultant Services - ECCS*] (EAIO) ..... CESCE
Comite Europeen des Syndicats de l'Alimentation, du Tabac, et de l'Industrie Hoteliere [*European Trade Union Committee of Food and Allied Workers*] [*Common Market*] ..... CESA
Comite Europeen d'Etude du Sel [*European Committee for the Study of Salt - ECSS*] (EA) ..... CEES
Comite Europeen d'Etudes de Zoologie Agricole ..... CEZA
Comite Europeen du Beton [*European Committee for Concrete*] ..... CEB
Comite Europeen du Commerce des Produits Amylaces et Derives [*European Center for Trade in Starch Products and Derivatives*] [*Common Market*] ..... CECPA

Comite Europeen du Commerce et de la Reparation Automobiles [*European Committee for Motor Trades and Repairs*] [*EC*] (ECED) .... CECRA
Comite Europeen du The [*European Tea Committee*] [*EC*] (ECED) .... CEDT
Comite Europeen Permanent de Recherches sur la Protection des Populations contreles Risques de Toxicite a Long Terme [*Permanent European Research Committee for the Protection of the Population against the Hazards of Chronic Toxicity*] .... EUROTOX
Comite Europeen pour le Mini-Basketball [*European Committee for Mini-Basketball - ECMB*] [*Munich, Federal Republic of Germany*] (EAIO) .... CEMB
Comite Europeen pour le Progres Economique et Social [*European Committee for Economic and Social Progress*] .... CEPES
Comite Europeen pour l'Enseignement Catholique [*European Committee for Catholic Education*] (EAIO) .... CEEC
Comite Europeen pour les Problemes Criminels [*Council of Europe*] .... CEPC
Comite Europeen pour les Relations Economiques .... CERE
Comite Francais de Liberation Nationale [*Algeria*] .... CFLN
Comite General de la Cooperation Agricole de la CE [*General Committee of Agricultural Cooperation in the EC*] (EAIO) .... COGECA
Comite Generale de la Cooperation Agricole de la CEE [*General Committee of Agricultural Cooperation of the European Economic Community*] (PDAA) .... GOGECA
Comite Guatemalteco de Unidad Patriotica [*Guatemalan Committee of Patriotic Unity*] (PD) .... CGUP
Comite Illusionniste d'Expertise des Phenomenes Paranormaux [*International PSI Committee of Magicians - IPSICM*] (EAIO) .... CIEPP
Comite Interafricain d'Etudes Hydrauliques [*Inter-African Committee for Hydraulic Studies - ICHS*] [*Ouagadougou, Burkina Faso*] (EAIO) .... CIEH
Comite Interallie des Officiers Medecins de Reserve [*Interallied Committee of Medical Reserve Officers*] .... CIOMR
Comite Interamericano de Desarrollo Agricola [*Inter-American Committee for Agricultural Development*] .... CIDA
Comite Interamericano de la Alianza para el Progreso [*Inter-American Committee of the Alliance for Progress*] .... CIAP
Comite Interamericano de Proteccion Agricola [*Interamerican Committee for Crop Protection*] .... CIPA
Comite Interamericano Permanente Antiacridiana .... CIPA
Comite Inter-Eglises des Droits Humains en Amerique Latine [*Inter-Church Committee on Human Rights in Latin America*] [*Canada*] (EAIO) .... CIEDHAL
Comite Intergouvernemental de Recherches Urbaines et Regionales [*Intergovernmental Committee on Urban and Regional Research*] [*Canada*] .... CIRUR
Comite Intergouvernemental du Droit d'Auteur [*Intergovernmental Copyright Committee - IGC*] [*UNESCO*] (EAIO) .... CIDA
Comite Intergouvernemental pour les Migrations Europeennes [*Intergovernmental Committee for European Migration*] .... CIME
Comite Interministeriel de la Gestion du Personnel [*Personnel Administration Interdepartmental Committee*] [*Canada*] .... CIGP
Comite Interministeriel des Terres [*Interdepartmental Committee on Land*] [*Canada*] .... CIT
Comite Inter-Mouvement Aupres des Evacues [*France*] .... CIMADE
Comite Internacional de la Cruz Roja [*Switzerland*] .... CIRC
Comite International Catholique des Aveugles (EAIO) .... CICA
Comite International Catholique des Infirmieres et Assistantes Medico-Sociales [*International Committee of Catholic Nurses - ICCN*] [*Vatican City, Vatican City State*] (EAIO) .... CICIAMS
Comite International Contre la Repression [*International Committee Against Repression*] [*Paris, France*] (EAIO) .... CICR
Comite International d'Aide aux Intellectuels .... CIAI
Comite International d'Auschwitz [*International Auschwitz Committee*] .... CIA
Comite International de Cooperation dans les Recherches Nationales en Demographie [*Committee for International Cooperation in National Research in Demography*] (EAIO) .... CICRED
Comite International de Coordination et d'Action des Groupements de Techniciens des Industries de Revetements de Surface [*International Committee to Coordinate Activities of Technical Groups in Coatings Industry - ICCATCI*] (EAIO) .... CICATIRS
Comite International de Coordination pour l'Initiation a la Science et le Developpement des Activites Scientifiques Extra-Scolaires [*International Coordinating Committee for the Presentation of Science and the Development of Out-of-School Scientific Activities - ICC*] (EAIO) CIC
Comite International de Dachau .... CID
Comite International de Geophysique [*International Geophysical Committee*] .... CIG
Comite International de la Conserve CIC
Comite International de la Croix-Rouge [*International Committee of the Red Cross*] .... CICR
Comite International de La Croix-Rouge [*Switzerland ICAO designator*] (FAAC) .... RED
Comite International de la Culture du Houblon [*International Hop Growers Convention - IHGC*] (EAIO) .... CICH
Comite International de la Rayonne et des Fibres Synthetiques [*International Rayon and Synthetic Fibres Committee - IRSFC*] (EAIO) .... CIRFS
Comite International de la Teinture et du Nettoyage [*International Committee for Dyeing and Dry Cleaning*] .... CITEN
Comite International de Liaison des Associations Feminines [*International Liaison Committee of Women's Organizations*] [*French*] .... CILAF
Comite International de Liaison des Gynecologues et Obstetriciens .... CILOPGO
Comite International de Liaison pour la Navigation de Plaisance [*Pleasure Navigation International Joint Committee - PNIC*] [*The Hague, Netherlands*] (EAIO) .... CINP
Comite International de Liaison pour la Reunification et la Paix en Coree [*International Liaison Committee for Reunification and Peace in Korea*] (EAIO) .... CILRECO
Comite International de l'Inspection Technique Automobile [*International Motor Vehicle Inspection Committee*] [*Verviers, Belgium*] (EAIO) .... CITA
Comite International de Medecine d'Assurances sur la Vie [*International Committee for Life Assurance Medicine*] [*France*] (EAIO) .... CIMAV
Comite International de Medecine et de Pharmacie Militaires [*International Committee of Military Medicine and Pharmacy - ICMMP*] [*Liege, Belgium*] (EA) .... CIMPM
Comite International de Medecine Militaire [*International Committee of Military Medicine*] [*Belgium*] (EAIO) .... CIMM
Comite International de Photobiologie [*International Committee of Photobiology*] .... CIP
Comite International de Photogrammetrie Architecturale [*International Committee of Architectural Photogrammetry*] (EAIO) .... CIPA
Comite International de Plastiques en Agriculture [*International Committee of Plastics in Agriculture*] (EAIO) .... CIPA
Comite International de Prevention des Accidents du Travail de la Navigation Interieure/International Committee for the Prevention of Work Accidents in Inland Navigation (EAIO) .... CIPA/ICPA
Comite International de Recherche et d'Etude de Facteurs de l'Ambiance [*International Committee for Research and Study on Environmental Factors*] .... CIFA
Comite International de Sociologie Clinique [*International Committee on Clinical Sociology - ICCS*] (EA) .... CISC
Comite International de Solidarite avec la Jeuness Algerienne .... CISJA
Comite International de Soutien aux Antifascistes Iberiques .... CISAI
Comite International de Standardisation en Biologie Humaine [*International Committee for Standardization in Human Biology*] .... CISBH
Comite International de Standardisation en Hematologie [*International Committee for Standardization in Haematology*] (EAIO) .... CISH
Comite International de Television [*International Television Committee*] .... CIT
Comite International de Thermodynamique et de Cinetique Electro-Chimiques [*International Committee of Electro-Chemical Thermodynamics and Kinetics*] .... CITCE
Comite International d'Enregistrement des Frequences [*International Frequency Registration Board*] .... CIEF
Comite International des Associations Techniques de Fonderie [*International Committee of Foundry Technical Associations*] (EAIO) .... CIATF
Comite International des Cooperatives de Production et Artisanales [*International Committee of Producers' Cooperatives*] (EAIO) .... CICOPA
Comite International des Derives Tensio-Actifs [*International Committee of Tensio-Active Derivatives*] .... CID
Comite International des Echanges pres la Chambre de Commerce Internationale .... CIE
Comite International des Entreprises a Succursales [*International Associationof Chain Stores*] [*Later, International Center for Companies of the Food Trade and Industry*] (EAIO) .... CIES
Comite International des Federations Theatrales d'Amateurs de Langue Francaise .... CIFTA
Comite International des Jeux Mediterraneens [*Athens, Greece*] (EAIO) .... CIJM
Comite International des Mouvements d'Enfants et d'Adolescents [*International Committee of Children's and Adolescents' Movements*] [*Budapest, Hungary*] (EAIO) .... CIMEA
Comite International des Organisateurs de Festivals de Folklore [*International Committee of Folklore Festival Organizers*] [*Canada*] .... CIOFF
Comite International des Pharmaciens Homeopathiques [*International Committee of Homeopathic Pharmacists*] [*Karlsruhe, Federal Republic of Germany*] (EAIO) .... CIPH
Comite International des Poids et Mesures [*International Committee on Weights and Measures*] .... CIPM
Comite International des Sciences Historiques [*International Committee of Historical Sciences*] .... CISH
Comite International des Sciences Onomastiques [*International Committee of Onomastic Sciences*] .... CISO
Comite International des Sports des Sourds [*International Committee of Sports for the Deaf*] (EAIO) .... CISS
Comite International des Telecommunications de Presse (EAIO) .... CIPT
Comite International des Telecommunications de Presse [*International Press Telecommunications Council - IPTC*] (EAIO) .... CITP
Comite International des Transports Ferroviaires [*International Rail Transport Committee*] (EAIO) .... CIT
Comite International d'Esthetique et de Cosmetologie [*International Committee for Esthetics and Cosmetology*] .... CIDESCO
Comite International d'Histoire de l'Art (EAIO) .... CIHA
Comite International d'Historiens et Geographes de Langue Francaise [*International Committee of French-Speaking Historians and Geographers - ICFHG*] (EAIO) .... CIHGLF
Comite International du Film Ethnographique .... CIFE
Comite International du Mini-Basketball [*International Committee for Mini-Basketball*] [*Munich, Federal Republic of Germany*] (EAIO) .... CIM
Comite International Olympique [*International Olympic Committee*] .... CIO
Comite International Permanent de la Conserve [*International Permanent Committee on Canned Foods*] .... CIPC
Comite International Permanent des Linguistes [*Permanent International Committee of Linguists*] (EAIO) .... CIPL
Comite International pour la Diffusion des Arts et des Lettres par le Cinema [*International Committee for the Diffusion of Arts and Literature through the Cinema*] (EAIO) .... CIDALC
Comite International pour la Metrologie Historique [*International Committee for Historical Metrology*] (EAIO) .... CIMH
Comite International pour la Sauveguarde de la Langue Bretonne [*International Committee for the Defense of the Breton Language - ICDBL*] (EAIO) .... CISLB
Comite International pour la Securite et la Cooperation Europeennes [*International Committee for European Security and Co-Operation - ICESC*] (EAIO) .... CISCE

Comite International pour le Controle de la Productivite Laitiere du Betail [*International Committee for Recording the Productivity of Milk Animals - ICRPMA*] (EAIO) .... CICPLB

Comite International pour le Fair Play [*International Fair Play Committee*] [*Paris, France*] (EAIO) .... CIFP

Comite International pour les Etudes Myceniennes [*Standing International Committee for Mycenaean Studies*] (EAIO) .... CIPEM

Comite International pour l'Etude et le Developpement de la Construction Tubulaire [*International Committee for the Study and Development of Tubular Construction*] [*Canada*] .... CIDECT

Comite International pour l'Information et Documentation des Sciences Sociales [*International Committee for Social Sciences Documentation*] .... CIDSS

Comite International Radio Maritime [*International Maritime Radio Association*] (EAIO) .... CIRM

Comite International Radioaeronautique .... CIRA

Comite International Special des Perturbations Radioelectriques [*International Special Committee on Radio Interference*] (EAIO) .... CISPR

Comite International sur l'Alcool, les Drogues et la Securite Routiere [*International Committee on Alcohol, Drugs, and Traffic Safety*] (EAIO) .... CIADSR

Comite International Technique d'Experts Juridiques Aeriens [*International Technical Committee of Aerial Legal Experts*] .... CITEJA

Comite International Tzigane [*International Gypsy Committee*] .... CIT

Comite Interregional des Bibliotheques Publiques [*Interregional Committee of Public Libraries*] [*Canada*] .... CIBP

Comite Juridique International de l'Aviation .... CJIA

Comite Latinoamericano de Textos Teologicos .... CLATT

Comite Liquidant ou Detournant les Ordinateurs [*Committee to Liquidate or Neutralize Computers*] [*France*] (PD) .... CLODO

Comite Maritime International [*International Maritime Committee - IMC*] [*Antwerp, Belgium*] (EAIO) .... CMI

Comite Marxista-Leninista Portugues [*Portuguese Marxist-Leninist Committee*] (PPE) .... CM-LP

Comite Meteorologique International .... CMI

Comite Nacional de Turismo [*National Committee on Tourism*] [*El Salvador*] (EY) .... CONATUR

Comite National d'Action sur la Situation de la Femme du Canada [*National Action Committee on the Status of Women*] [*Canada*] .... CNA

Comite National de Jumelage [*National Committee for Town/City Twinning*] [*France*] (EAIO) .... CNJ

Comite National pour la Liberation de la Cote d'Ivoire [*National Committee for the Liberation of the Ivory Coast*] .... CNLCI

Comite Nationale de Lutte Contre le SIDA [*National Committee on the Fight Against AIDS*] [*Mauritania*] (EAIO) .... CNLS

Comite Nationale de Lutte Contre le SIDA [*National Committee on the Fight Against AIDS*] [*Burkina Faso*] (EAIO) .... CNL-SIDA

Comite Nordique des Commissions des Sciences Humaines [*Nordic Committee of the Research Councils for the Humanities - NCRCH*] (EAIO) .... CNCSH

Comite Oceanografico Nacional [*Chile*] [*Marine science*] (OSRA) .... CONA

Comite Olimpico Boliviano [*Bolivian Olympic Committee*] (EAIO) .... COB

Comite Olimpico Hondureno [*Honduran Olympic Committee*] (EAIO) .... COH

Comite Olympique Hongrois [*Hungarian Olympic Committee*] (EAIO) .... COH

Comite Organisateur de Jeux Olympiques [*Organizing Committee of the Olympic Games (1976)*] [*Canada*] .... COJO

Comite Permanent Canadien des Noms Geographiques [*Canadian Permanent Committee on Geographical Names - CPCGN*] .... CPCNG

Comite Permanent de Liaison des Kinesitherapeutes de la CEE [*Standing Liaison Committee of Physiotherapists within the EEC - SLCP*] [*Copenhagen, Denmark*] (EAIO) .... CPLK

Comite Permanent des Congres Internationaux de Zoologie [*Permanent Committee of International Zoological Congresses*] [*France*] .... CPCIZ

Comite Permanent des Congres Internationaux pour l'Apostolat des Laics [*Permanent Committee of International Congresses for the Lay Apostolate*] [*Italy*] .... COPECIAL

Comite Permanent des Industries du Verre de la CEE [*Brussels, Belgium*] (EAIO) .... CPIV

Comite Permanent des Secretaires Generaux [*Standing Committee of Secretaries General*] [*NATO*] (NATG) .... CSG

Comite Permanent des Sous-Ministres [*Continuing Committee of Deputy Ministers - CCDM*] [*Canada*] .... CPSM

Comite Permanent du CE de l'Association Internationale de la Savonnerie et de laDetergence [*Standing EEC Committee of the International Association of the Soap and Detergent Industry - SEECCIASDI*] [*Brussels, Belgium*] (EAIO) .... CPCEAISD

Comite Permanent Interetats de Lutte Contre la Secheresse dans le Sahel [*Permanent Interstate Committee for Drought Control in the Sahel*] (EAIO) .... CILSS

Comite Permanent International des Techniques et de l'Urbanisme Souterrains [*Permanent and International Committee of Underground Town Planning and Construction*] .... CPITUS

Comite Permanent International du Vinaigre [*Permanent International Committee on Vinegar*] [*Common Market*] .... CPIV

Comite Permanent International d'Urbanisme Souterrain .... CPIUS

Comite pour le Developpement des Alternatives a l'Incarceration [*Committee for the Development of Alternatives to Incarceration*] [*Canada*] .... CODAI

Comite pour l'Utilisation des Resultats de l'Annee Geophysique Internationale [*IGY completion committee*] .... CURAGI

Comite pro Maria [*An association Belgium*] (EAIO) .... CPM

Comite Regional d'Afrique Centrale pour la Conservation et l'Utilisation du Sol .... CRACCUS

Comite Regional d'Education pour le Developpement International de la Region de Lanaudiere (AC) .... CREDIL

Comite Regional Intersyndical de Montreal [*Montreal Regional Inter-Trade Union Committee*] [*Canada*] .... CRIM

Comite Regional Ouest-Africain pour la Conservation et l'Utilisation du Sol .... CROACUS

Comite Scientifique Consultatif des Peches Canadiennes dans l'Atlantique [*Canadian Atlantic Fisheries Scientific Advisory Committee - CAFSAC*] (ASF) .... CSCPCA

Comite Scientifique International de Recherches sur les Trypanosomiases .... CSIRT

Comite Scientifique pour les Recherches Antarctiques [*Scientific Committee on Antarctic Research*] (MSC) .... CSRA

Comite Scientifique pour les Recherches Oceaniques [*Scientific Committee on Oceanic Research - SCOR*] [*France*] (MSC) .... CSRO

Comite Sida Aide Montreal (AC) .... CSAM

Comite Special de l'Annee Geophysique Internationale [*Special Committee for the International Geophysical Year*] [*Superseded by CIG*] .... CSAGI

Comite Special du Programme Biologique International [*Special Committee for the International Biological Program*] .... CSPBI

Comite Sportif International du Travail [*International Workers Sport Committee*] [*Brussels, Belgium*] (EAIO) .... CSIT

Comite Syndical Europeen des Personnels de l'Education [*European Teachers Trade Union Committee*] [*EC*] (ECED) .... CSEE

Comite Syndical International du Tourisme Social et des Loisirs [*International Trade Unions Committee of Social Tourism and Leisure - ITUCSTL*] (EA) .... CSITSL

Comite Technique International de Prevention et d'Extinction du Feu [*International Technical Committee for the Prevention and Extinction of Fire*] (EAIO) .... CTIF

Comiteco [*Race of maize*] .... COM

Comitel, Bedarfsfluge, KG [*Austria*] [*FAA designator*] (FAAC) .... COE

Comites Communistes pour l'Autogestion [*Communist Committees for Self-Management*] [*France Political party*] (PPW) .... CCA

Comites Comunistas Revolucionarios, Marxistas-Leninistas [*Marxist-Leninist Revolutionary Communist Committees*] [*Portugal Political party*] (PPE) .... CCR M-L

Comites Reunis de l'Industrie de l'Ennoblissement Textile dans le CE [*EC*] (ECED) .... CRIET

COMLINE Business Analysis [*COMLINE International Corp.*] [*Japan Information service or system*] (CRD) .... CBA

COMLINE Industrial Monitor [*COMLINE International Corp.*] [*Japan Information service or system*] (CRD) .... CIM

Comma (FAAC) .... CMA

Comma (AABC) .... CMM

Comma (ROG) .... COM

Comma (WDMC) .... com

Comma Separated Values File [*Computer science*] .... CSV

Commack Public Library, Commack, NY [*Library symbol Library of Congress*] (LCLS) .... NCo

Commanche Peak Steam Electric Station (NRCH) .... CPSES

Command (ROG) C

Command .... CD

Command .... CM

Command (EY) .... CMD

Command (IBMDP) .... CMND

Command .... CMND

Command (AAG) .... COM

Command (AFM) .... COMD

Command (WGA) .... COMM

Command Access Keys .... CAK

Command Accountant [*Military British*] .... CA

Command Accounting and Finance Office (AFM) .... CAFO

Command Acknowledge (BUR) .... CAK

Command Acquisition Unit (NASA) .... CAU

Command Action (NATG) .... CA

Command Action Plan (NVT) .... CAP

Command Action Report [*Army*] .... CAR

Command Activation Unit (MCD) .... CAU

Command Active Multi-Beam Sonobuoy (PDAA) .... CAMBS

Command Active Sonobuoy System [*Navy*] .... CASS

Command Address [*Computer science*] (IAA) .... CAD

Command Advisory Board .... CAB

Command Aerospace Maintenance Manpower Information System .... CAMMIS

Command Airways [*South Africa ICAO designator*] (FAAC) .... CAH

Command Airways [*ICAO designator*] (AD) .... CT

Command Airways [*ICAO designator*] (AD) .... DD

Command Algorithmic Language [*Computer science*] (NITA) .... COMAL

Command Analysis [*Telecommunications*] (TEL) .... CANAL

Command Analysis Center .... CAC

Command Analysis of Office of Military Assistance Funding (MCD) .... CAOMAF

Command Analysis Pattern (KSC) .... CAP

Command and Administration .... C & A

Command and Administration System [*Army*] .... COADS

Command and Communications System [*or Subsystem*] [*NASA*] .... CCS

Command and Control .... C & C

Command and Control [*Pronounced "see-squared"*] .... C^2

Command and Control C2

Command and Control (AAGC) .... C^2

Command and Control (NVT) .... CAC

Command and Control Alert/Conferencing Network (CINC) .... CCACN

Command and Control Boat [*Navy symbol*] .... CCB

Command and Control Center .... C^3

Command and Control Center (AFM) CCC

Command and Control, Communications and Computers (PDAA) C4

Command and Control Defense Systems Office .... CCDSO

Command and Control Development Division [*Air Force*] .... CCDD

Command and Control Director [*Air Force*] .... CCD

Command and Control Division [*SHAPE Technical Center*] (NATG)	CCD
Command and Control - Division Air Defense (MCD)	CC-DAD
Command and Control Engineering Center [*Washington, DC*]	CCEC
Command and Control Exercise	C2X
Command and Control Information Processing [*Computer science*] (MHDI)	CCIP
Command and Control Information System [*Military*]	C²IS
Command and Control Information System [*Hughes Aircraft Co.*]	CCIS
Command and Control Micro-Computer Users Group [*Fort Leavenworth, KS*] [*Army*] (INF)	C²MUG
Command and Control Segment [*Air Force*] (DOMA)	CCS
Command and Control Set (MCD)	CCS
Command and Control Simulation System (MCD)	CCSS
Command and Control Standardization and Evaluation Team [*Military*]	CCSET
Command and Control Steering Committee	C2SC
Command and Control Subsystem (NASA)	CCS
Command and Control Switching System (DOMA)	CCSS
Command and Control System	C & CS
Command and Control System (DOMA)	C²S
Command and Control System	CCS
Command and Control System [*Army*] (RDA)	CCS
Command and Control System Interface Test [*Military*] (CAAL)	C & CSIT
Command and Control Systems Office [*Military*]	CCSO
Command and Control Systems Organization [*Defense Communications Agency*] [*Washington, DC*]	CCSO
Command and Control Technical Center [*DoD*]	CCTC
Command and Control Technical Center WWMCCS [*Worldwide Military Command and Control System*] ADP Directorate [*Automatic Data Processing*] [*DoD*]	CCTC-WAD
Command and Control Test Facility	CCTF
Command and Control Training Vehicles (MCD)	CCTV
Command and Control Vehicle [*Army*]	C²V
Command and Control Voice Communications System [*Defense Supply Agency*]	CCVCS
Command and Control Warfare [*Military*] (RDA)	C2W
Command and Control Zone (SSD)	CCZ
Command and Coordination Set	CCS
Command and Data Acquisition (NASA)	CDA
Command and Data Acquisition Station [*Aerospace*]	CDAS
Command and Data Handling (NASA)	C & DH
Command and Data Handling (DEN)	CDH
Command and Data Processing Area (MCD)	CDPA
Command and Data Simulator (NASA)	C & DS
Command and Data Simulator (NASA)	CADS
Command and Data-Handling Console	CDC
Command and Data-Handling Console (KSC)	CDHC
Command and Decision [*Military*] (CAAL)	C & D
Command and Decision Sensor Interface Data System (MCD)	CDSIDS
Command and Decision System (MCD)	CDS
Command and Edit Language (NITA)	CANDE
Command and Edit Program [*Burroughs Corp.*] [*Computer science*] (BUR)	CANDE
Command and Expenditure Report	CER
Command and General Staff [*Military*]	C & GS
Command and General Staff College [*Fort Leavenworth, KS*] [*Military*]	C & GSC
Command and General Staff College [*Fort Leavenworth, KS*] [*Military*]	CGSC
Command and General Staff Officer Course [*Military*] (INF)	CGSOC
Command and General Staff School [*Army*]	C & GS Sch
Command and General Staff School [*Army*]	C & GSS
Command and Launch Subsystem (MCD)	CLS
Command and Management Presentation [*Marine Corps*]	CAMP
Command and Response Unit	CRU
Command and Service Module [*NASA*] (IAA)	CASM
Command and Service Module [*NASA*] (MCD)	CSM
Command and Stability Augmentation System (MCD)	CSAS
Command and Staff	C & S
Command and Staff College [*Air Force*]	CSC
Command and Telemetry Data Handling (IEEE)	CTDH
Command and Telemetry System (AAG)	CTS
Command and Triangulation	CAT
Command Area Study and Mission Analysis Program [*Military*] (INF)	CASMAP
Command Arithmetic Unit	CAU
Command, Arming, Recording, and Timing (PDAA)	CART
Command Assessment Review [*Air Force*] (AAGC)	CAPCAR
Command Assessment Review (MCD)	CAR
Command Augmentation System	CAS
Command Authorization List	CAL
Command Automated Budget System [*Army*]	CABS
Command Automated Procurement System (MCD)	CAPS
Command Automated Support Network [*Marine Corps*] (DOMA)	CASN
Command Automated System for Procurement [*Army*]	CASPR
Command Automatic Card Tester	CACT
Command Aviation Net [*Military*] (INF)	CAN
Command Battle Simulation (MCD)	CBS
Command Budget Automated System [*Air Force*] (GFGA)	CBAS
Command Budget Estimates [*Military*] (AABC)	CBE
Command Cadet Team [*Military British*]	CCT
Command Car (SAA)	CC
Command Career Program Management (MCD)	CCPM
Command Center (AAG)	CC
Command Center Operations Chief (MCD)	CCOC
Command Center Processing and Display Systems [*Air Force*] (MCD)	CCPDS
Command Center Processing and Display Systems Replacement [*Military*] (GFGA)	CCPDS-R
Command Center Support System (MCD)	CCSS

Command Center Terminal System (MCD)	CCTS
Command Center Watch Officer (MCD)	CCWO
Command Chain [*Computer science*]	CC
Command Channel Interface Unit (MHDI)	CCIU
Command Chaplain [*AFSC*]	HC
Command Classified Control Register	CCCR
Command Code [*IRS*]	CC
Command Communications Boat	CCB
Command Communications Console	CCC
Command Communications Service Designator (CET)	CCSD
Command Comply Current Instructions	PLYINST
Command Computer (AAG)	CC
Command Computer Console	CMDCC
Command Computer Input Multiplexer (MCD)	CCIM
Command Conference [*Viking lander mission*] [*NASA*]	CC
Command Confirmation	CCN
Command Confirmation Buffer	COMB
Command Console (IAA)	CC
Command Contractor Data Management Review Board [*Air Force*] (AFIT)	CCDMRB
Command, Control, and Communications [*Pronounced "see-cubed"*]	C³
Command, Control, and Communications (AAGC)	C3
Command, Control, and Communications [*Air Force*]	CC & C
Command, Control, and Communications Agency Joint Test Organization [*Fort Huachuca, AZ*]	C3A-JTO
Command, Control, and Communications Battle Management [*Military*]	C³/BM
Command, Control, and Communications Countermeasures [*Warfare*]	C3CM
Command, Control, and Communications Countermeasures (AAGC)	C3CM
Command, Control, and Communications Counter-Measures (DOMA)	C³CM
Command, Control, and Communications Countermeasures (LAIN)	C3CM
Command, Control, and Communications Countermeasures Joint Test Force [*Kirtland Air Force Base, NM*]	C3CM-JTF
Command, Control, and Communications for Battle Management [*Military*] (DOMA)	C³BM
Command, Control, and Communications Master Plan (DOMA)	C³MP
Command Control and Communications Program [*Air Force*]	CC & CP
Command, Control, and Communications System (NATG)	CCCS
Command, Control, and Communications Systems (DOMA)	C³S
Command, Control, and Detection System [*Military*]	CCDS
Command, Control, and Intelligence [*Military*] (RDA)	C2I
Command, Control, and Intelligence [*Network*] [*Military*] (DOMA)	C²I
Command Control and Monitor System [*NASA*] (NASA)	CCMS
Command, Control, and Subordinate Systems [*Telecommunications*] (TEL)	CCS²
Command, Control, and Systems Integration Directorate [*Army and NASA joint operation*] (RDA)	C² SID
Command Control and Weather (SAA)	CCW
Command Control Block [*Computer science*] (BUR)	CCB
Command, Control Communication, and Computer Systems (USGC)	C4
Command, Control, Communications, and Combat Service Support [*Military*] (INF)	C⁴S²
Command, Control, Communications, and Computer Systems (NVT)	C⁴
Command, Control, Communications, and Computer Systems (DOMA)	C⁴S
Command, Control, Communications, and Intelligence (DOMA)	C³I
Command, Control, Communications, and Intelligence [*Pronounced "see-cubed eye"*]	C³I
Command, Control, Communications, and Intelligence (USGC)	C31
Command, Control, Communications, and Intelligence [*Telecommunications*] (TEL)	CCCI
Command, Control, Communications and Intelligence Acquisition Center [*Army*] (RDA)	C3IAC
Command, Control, Communications and Intelligence Systems (AAGC)	C31
Command, Control, Communications, Computer, and Intelligence [*Army*]	C4I
Command, Control, Communications Computer and Intelligence for the Warrior [*Army*]	C₄IFTW
Command, Control, Communications, Computers, and Intelligence (DOMA)	C⁴I
Command, Control, Communications, Computers and Intelligence	C4I
Command, Control, Communications, Computers, Intelligence, and Counter-Measures (DOMA)	C⁴ICM
Command, Control, Communications, Computers, Intelligence, and Interoperability [*Marine Corps*] (DOMA)	C⁴I²
Command, Control, Communications, Computing/Information and Intelligence	C⁴I²
Command, Control, Communications, Intelligence, and Interoperability	C³I²
Command Control Communications Laboratory Center (SAA)	CCCLC
Command, Control, Communications Systems Directorate (DOMA)	C³SYS DIR
Command Control Console (KSC)	CCC
Command Control/Destruct (MUGU)	CC/D
Command Control Destruct System (MUGU)	CCDS
Command Control Dial Panel	CCDP
Command Control Equipment (KSC)	CCE
Command Control Group [*Air Force*]	CCG
Command Control Handover and Keying (SAA)	CCH
Command Control Information Utility [*Military*]	CCIU
Command, Control, Intelligence Support Squadron [*Air Force*]	CCISS
Command Control Interactive Display Experimentation System [*Army*] (MCD)	CCIDES
Command Control Interface [*Army*] (AABC)	CCI
Command Control Number [*Air Force*] (AFM)	CCN
Command Control Operations Center [*Army*] (AABC)	CCOC
Command Control Order	CCO
Command Control Panel	CCP
Command Control Post	CCP
Command Control Receiver	CCR

Command Control Room .... CCR
Command, Control Simulation Integration Language [*ARPA*] .... CCSIL
Command, Control, Support [*Army*] .... CCS
Command Control Transmitter (MCD) .... CCT
Command Control Word (IAA) .... CCW
Command Cruiser-Destroyer Force, Pacific (DNAB) .... CDDP
Command Cruiser-Destroyer Force, Pacific (DNAB) .... COMCRUDESPAC
Command Data Buffer [*Air Force*] (MCD) .... CDB
Command Data Buffer [*Air Force*] (MCD) .... CDBFR
Command Data Format Control Handbook [*NASA*] (KSC) .... CDFCHB
Command Data Management Routine [*Computer science*] .... CDMR
Command Data Management System (NASA) .... CDMS
Command, Data Processing, and Instrumentation [*NASA*] .... CDPI
Command, Data Processing, and Instrumentation System [*NASA*] (NASA) .... CDPIS
Command Data Processing Interface Equipment .... CDPIE
Command Data Processor .... CDP
Command Data Word (MCD) .... CDW
Command Database (MCD) .... CDB
Command Database Interface Language (MCD) .... CDIL
Command Decision and Movement Control Charts .... COMDEC
Command Decision Echelon (MCD) .... CDE
Command Decision Subsystem [*Military*] (CAAL) .... CDSS
Command Decoder .... CD
Command Decoder (GFGA) .... CMD DCDR
Command Decoder Coaxial (MCD) .... CDC
Command Decoder Filter .... CDF
Command Definition Language [*Computer science*] (IAA) .... CDL
Command Delivering Orders Initiate Background Investigation [*Military*] (DNAB) .... DELCOMBI
Command Dental Service Report [*Air Force*] .... COMD DSR
Command Descriptor Table (NASA) .... CDT
Command Designated Position List (MCD) .... CDPL
Command Destruct (AAG) .... C/D
Command Destruct Control (AAG) .... CDC
Command Destruct Decoder .... CDD
Command Destruct Receiver (AFM) .... CDR
Command Destruct System (MCD) .... CDS
Command Destruct Transmitter (AFM) .... CDT
Command Destruct Unit (AABC) .... CDU
Command Detector Unit (MCD) .... CDU
Command Director of Administration (AAGC) .... CCTA
Command Disable System [*Air Force*] .... CDS
Command Display and Control Processor .... CDCP
Command Display Indicator (MCD) .... CDI
Command Display Unit (MCD) .... CDU
Command Distribution Rack .... CDR
Command Distribution Unit (IIA) .... CDU
Command Distributor Flip-Flop (SAA) .... CDFF
Command Document Capability List (IAA) .... CDCL
Command Document Control Number (AFIT) .... CDCN
Command Document Discard (IAA) .... CDD
Command Document End (IAA) .... CDE
Command Document Resynchronization (IAA) .... CDR
Command Document Start (IAA) .... CDS
Command Document User Information (IAA) .... CDUI
Command Duty Officer [*Navy*] .... CDO
Command Education Officer [*Military British*] .... CEO
Command Entertainments Officer [*Military British*] .... CEO
Command Equipment Management Office [*Military*] (AFM) .... CEMO
Command Equipment Management Program Review [*Military*] (MCD) .... CEMPR
Command Equipment Management Team [*Military*] .... CEMT
Command Evaluation and Training (SAA) .... COMENT
Command Evaluation Teams (MCD) .... COMET
Command Executive Procedure [*Computer science*] (OA) .... CEP
Command Field Exercise [*Military*] (INF) .... CFX
Command File (IAA) .... CMF
Command File (CDE) .... COM file
Command Forces .... CFOR
Command Generation Program [*Mariner*] [*NASA*] .... COMGEN
Command Generator Tracker (MCD) .... CGT
Command Ground Station [*Army*] (RDA) .... CGS
Command Group (MCD) .... CG
Command Group Training Support System (MCD) .... CGTSS
Command Guard List [*Navy*] (CAAL) .... CGL
Command Guidance [*Aerospace*] (AAG) .... CG
Command Guidance Computer (NASA) .... CGC
Command Guidance Test Vehicle .... CGTV
Command Guidance-Training Support System [*Military*] .... CGTSS
Command Guided Tactical Missile .... CGTM
Command Hardware/Software [*Army*] .... CHS
Command Hardware System [*Army*] .... CHS
Command Home All the Way [*Military*] (CAAL) .... CHAW
Command Indicator Performance Review (MCD) .... CIPR
Command Information (MCD) CI
Command Information (SAA) .... COIN
Command Information Bureau [*Military*] (CINC) .... CIB
Command Information Center [*Military*] CIC
Command Information Division (MCD) .... CID
Command Information Flow [*Military*] (CAAL) .... CIF
Command Information Program [*Military*] (AABC) .... CIP
Command Information Requirement Analysis (MCD) .... CIRA
Command Information Systems [*Army*] .... CIS
Command Input Block [*Computer science*] .... CIB
Command Input Buffer [*Computer science*] (IBMDP) .... CIB
Command Input Coupler (CET) CIC
Command Inspection [*Military*] (NVT) .... CMDINSP
Command Inspection Program [*Army*] (INF) .... CIP
Command Instrument System .... CIS
Command Instrument System Trainer [*Army*] .... CIST
Command Integrated Logistics Management Office .... CILSMO
Command Intelligence (MCD) CIC
Command Intelligence and Weather (SAA) .... CIW
Command Interface Control (MCD) CIC
Command Interface Test (KSC) .... CIT
Command Interface Unit (KSC) .... CIU
Command Interpreter (SSD) CI
Command Involvement Report [*Army*] .... CMD/INV
Command Issuing Office [*or Officer*] .... CIO
Command Job Language Interpreter [*Computer science*] [*Telecommunications*] .... CJLI
Command Language CL
[*The*] **Command Language** [*Computer science*] (PCM) .... TCL
Command Language for Interrogating Computers [*Royal RADAR Establishment*] [*British*] CLIC
Command Language Interpreter [*Computer science*] CLI
Command Language Processor .... CLP
Command Launch Computer (DWSG) .... CLCP
Command Launch Unit [*Military*] .... CLU
Command Liaison and Surveillance and Keying (SAA) .... CLS
Command Liaison Officer [*Military*] (DNAB) .... CLO
Command Line [*Military*] CL
Command Line Interface [*For Amiga computers*] CLI
Command Line Interpret [*Military*] (CAAL) CLI
Command Load Acceptance Message .... CLAM
Command Load Controller CLC
Command Logic Unit (MCD) .... CLU
Command Logistics Review Program [*DoD*] .... CLRP
Command Logistics Review Team (MCD) .... CLRT
Command Logistics Review Teams Expanded (MCD) .... CLRTX
Command Maintenance [*Military*] (AABC) .... COMAINT
Command Maintenance Inspection [*Army*] .... CMI
Command Maintenance Management Inspection [*Army*] .... CMMI
Command Maintenance Readiness Inspection [*Army*] (AABC) .... CMRI
Command Management Center [*Military*] .... CMC
Command Management Control List .... CMCL
Command Management Information System [*Air Force*] .... CMIS
Command Management Information System [*Air Force*] .... COMIS
Command Management Inventory Accounting [*Army*] .... CMIA
Command Management Review and Analysis [*Army*] .... CAMERA
Command Management System (MCD) .... CMS
Command Manpower Data System .... CMDS
Command Master Chief [*Navy*] (DOMA) .... CMC
Command Message .... CMDMSG
Command Message Formulator (SAA) .... CMF
Command Military Training .... CMT
Command Mode Rejection Ratio (HGAA) .... CMMRR
Command Model for Analysis and Design (MCD) .... COMMAND
Command Modular Operation Room Equipment (PDAA) .... COMMODORE
Command Modulator Assembly [*NASA*] .... CMA
Command Module [*NASA*] .... CM
Command Module Computer [*NASA*] (MCD) .... CMC
Command Module Electrical Power System [*NASA*] .... CEPS
Command Module Multiple Docking Assembly [*NASA*] (KSC) .... CMMDA
Command Module Pilot [*Apollo*] [*NASA*] .... CMP
Command Module Procedures Simulator [*NASA*] .... CMPS
Command Module - Service Module [*Combined*] [*NASA*] (MCD) .... CM-SM
Command Module Simulator [*NASA*] .... CMS
Command Money [*British military*] (DMA) .... CM
Command Monitor Panel (SSD) .... CMP
Command NODAL [*Network-Oriented Data Acquisition Language*] **Control Element** .... CNCE
Command Not Operationally Ready [*Navy*] (NVT) .... CNOR
Command Nuclear Target List (MCD) .... CNTL
Command Objective Plan [*Air Force*] .... COP
Command Observation Post (AABC) .... COP
Command of Camp [*Military*] (VNW) .... COC
Command of Quarters [*Army*] (VNW) .... CQ
Command Off the Line of Sight [*Military British*] .... COLOS
Command Operating Budget [*Army*] .... COB
Command Operating Budget Estimate/Execution (MCD) .... COBE
Command Operating Program [*Army*] (AABC) .... COP
Command Operating Program/Budget [*DoD*] (MCD) .... COP/B
Command Operationally Ready [*Navy*] (NVT) .... COR
Command Operations [*Army*] (AABC) .... CO
Command Operations Center [*Military*] (NVT) .... COC
Command Operations Priority Requirements List [*Air Force*] (AFM) .... COPRL
Command Operations Simulation Model with Interrogation Control (SAA) .... COSMIC
Command Orders .... CO
Command Output .... CO
Command Paper C
Command Papers [*A publication*] (DLA) .... Cd
Command Papers (DLA) .... Cmd
Command Papers [*A publication*] (DLA) .... Cmnd
Command Patrol Plane Replacement Squadrons Pacific .... COMPATPLANEREPRONSPAC
Command Paymaster [*British military*] (DMA) .... CP
Command Performance Indicator (MCD) .... CPI
Command Performance Indicator Review (MCD) .... CPIR

Command Performance Review	CPR
Command Personnel Management Inspections (AABC)	CPMI
Command Personnel Summary (AABC)	CPS
Command Pilot (AFM)	CP
Command Point (AFIT)	CP
Command Point of Contact [Navy] (AFIT)	CPC
Command Post [Military]	CP
Command Post Alerting Network [Military]	COPAN
Command Post Digital Display [SAGE] [Air Force]	CPDD
Command Post Duty Controller [Air Force]	CPDYCONTR
Command Post Exercise [Military]	CPEx
Command Post Exercise [Military]	CPX
Command Post Experience [Army British]	CPX
Command Post Officer [Military]	CPO
Command Post Record Capability [Military]	COPREC
Command Post Vehicle [British military] (DMA)	CPV
Command Pouch [Air Force] (AFM)	CP
Command Power Cruise Control [Diesel engines] [Automotive engineering]	CPCC
Command Processor [Computer science]	COMPROC
Command Processor [Computer science] (BUR)	CP
Command Processor Distributor (SAA)	CPD
Command Processor Distributor Control (MCD)	CPDC
Command Processor Module	CPM
Command Programmer Unit (DWSG)	CPU
Command Programming Language	CPL
Command Pulse (MSA)	CP
Command Pulse Output	CPO
Command Qualification Examination (MCD)	CQE
Command Quality Team (DOMA)	CQT
Command Radio Link	CORAL
Command Read Pulse (KSC)	CRP
Command Readiness Exercise System [Air Force] (GFGA)	CRES
Command Readout Station [Military]	CRS
Command Receiver (KSC)	C/R
Command Receiver Equipment (KSC)	CRE
Command Receiver Monitor (AAG)	CRM
Command Register	CR
Command Reject (IAA)	CMDR
Command Relationship Agreements [Army] (AABC)	CRA
Command Relationship Study	CRS
Command Relay Driver Unit (MCD)	CRDU
Command Reporting Center	CRC
Command Representative (CINC)	CR
Command/Response [Computer science] (ACRL)	C/R
Command/Response [Computer science]	CR
Command Retrieval Information System	CRIS
Command Retrieval System (DEN)	CRS
Command Review	CR
Command Review Board [Aerospace]	CRB
Command Scheduling Chain [Computer science] (IAA)	CSC
Command Scheduling Control Block [Computer science] (BUR)	CSCB
Command Security [NASDAQ symbol] (TTSB)	CMMD
Command Security Corp. [NASDAQ symbol] (SAG)	CMMD
Command Security Corp. [Associated Press] (SAG)	CmndSc
Command Security Service (MCD)	CSS
Command Selector	CS
Command Selector Control	CSC
Command Selector Panel (DNAB)	CSP
Command Selector Value (DNAB)	CSV
Command Senior Chief [Navy] (DOMA)	CSC
Command Sergeant Major [Army] (AABC)	COMDSGTMAJ
Command Sergeant Major [Army]	CSM
Command Sergeant Major [Army]	E9
Command Service Force, Pacific (MCD)	COMSERPAC
Command Session Abort [Computer science] (IAA)	CSA
Command Session Change Control (IAA)	CSCC
Command Session End [Computer science] (IAA)	CSE
Command Session Start [Computer science] (IAA)	CSS
Command Session User Information (IAA)	CSUI
Command Ship [Navy symbol Obsolete]	CC
Command Ship Data System [Navy] (MUGU)	CSDS
Command Signal Decoder	CSD
Command Signal Generator	CSG
Command Signal Limiter (MCD)	CSL
Command Software Subsystem [Space Flight Operations Facility, NASA]	CMDSW
Command Standard [Program, Commissary] (MCD)	COST
Command Start Point [Military]	CSPT
Command String Interpreter [Digital Equipment Corp.]	CSI
Command Study Advisory Committee [TRADOC] (MCD)	CSAC
Command Substitution System (NITA)	CSS
Command Subsystem Group (MCD)	CSG
Command Supply Depot [British military] (DMA)	COSD
Command Supply Discipline Program [Army]	CSDP
Command Supply Support (MCD)	CSS
Command Support Center (MCD)	CSC
Command Support Center Watch Officer (MCD)	CSCWO
Command Support Control Console	CSCC
Command Surgeon [AFSC]	SG
Command Surveillance and Weather	CSW
Command Synchronizer Slave (MCD)	CSS
Command System (NATG)	CS
Command System Operations Analysis Group Area [Space Flight Operations Facility, NASA]	CAG

Command Systems Support Activity	COSSACT
Command Tactical [Navy] (NVT)	COMTAC
Command Technical Inspection [Army] (AABC)	CTI
Command Telemetry Buoy	CTB
Command Test Vehicle (IAA)	CTV
Command to Line of Sight [Military British]	CLOS
Command Training Team (DNAB)	CTT
Command Translator and Programmer	CTP
Command Transmitter (KSC)	C/T
Command Trust Network (EA)	CTN
Command Uplink [NASA] (KSC)	CUL
Command Uplink Request [NASA] (KSC)	CUR
Command Vehicle	CV
Command Verification [NASA]	CV
Command Verification	CV
Command Verification/Drop	CVR/D
Command Verify/Transmit	CVT
Command Video Prelaunch Distribution System (IAA)	CVPDS
Command Voltage Regulator	CVR
Command Weapon Carrier (SAA)	COMD WC
Command Wire Improvised Explosive Device [Military] (LAIN)	CWIED
Command Word [Computer science] (MCD)	CW
Command Word Trap [Computer science] (IAA)	CWT
Command Works Office [British military] (DMA)	CWO
Commandable Acoustic Engine Ignition Detectors (MCD)	CAEDETS
Commandable Audio Engine Detector (MCD)	CAEDET
Commandant [Coast Guard]	C
Commandant (WGA)	CDT
Commandant	CMDT
Commandant [Military]	COM
Commandant [Air Force] (AFM)	COMDT
Commandant	COMDT
Commandant	COMMDT
Commandant	COMT
Commandant, Armed Forces Staff College (DNAB)	COMDTAFSC
Commandant Assistant [Coast Guard]	CA
Commandant, Civil Affairs Branch [British World War II]	CCAB
Commandant, Eleventh Naval District (MUGU)	COMELEVEN
Commandant, Fifth Naval District (MUGU)	COMFIVE
Commandant, First Naval District (MUGU)	COMONE
Commandant General [British military] (DMA)	CG
Commandant General [British military] (DMA)	Cmdt Gen
Commandant, Marine Corps Program Policy and Planning Guidance (MCD)	CMCPPG
Commandant, Marine Corps Schools [Quantico, VA]	CMCS
Commandant, Naval Base, San Diego	COMNAVBASEDIEGO
Commandant, Naval District, Washington, DC	COMNAVDIST WASHDC
Commandant, Naval District, Washington, DC	COMNDW
Commandant, Naval Operating Base	COMDTNOB
Commandant, Navy Yard	COMDTNY
Commandant, Ninth Naval District (MUGU)	COMNINE
Commandant, North Atlantic Treaty Organization Defense College (DNAB)	COMNATODEFCOL
Commandant Nucleus Department [Military British]	CND
Commandant of Cadets [Military]	COC
Commandant of the Coast Guard	CCG
Commandant of the Coast Guard (DNAB)	COMDTCOGARD
Commandant of the Marine Corps	CMC
Commandant of the Marine Corps	COMDTMARCORPS
Commandant of the Marine Corps Memorandum	CMCM
Commandant, Potomac River Naval Command (SAA)	COMPRNC
Commandant, Severn River Naval Command (SAA)	COMSRNC
Commandant, Third Naval District (MUGU)	COMTHREE
Commandant, Thirteenth Naval District (MUGU)	COMTHIRTEEN
Commandant, Twelfth Naval District (MUGU)	COMTWELVE
Commandant, United States Coast Guard	COMDTUSCG
Commandant, United States Marine Corps	COMDTUSMC
Commandant's Instruction	COMDTINST
Commandant's Training Strategy [Military]	CTS
Command-Destruct Epoxy [A plastic resin]	CDE
Commanded	CMDD
Commandement Aerien des Forces de Defense Aerienne [Air Defense Forces Air Command] (NATG)	CAFDA
Commandement Aerien Tactique [French Tactical Air Command]	CATAC
Commandement Allie des Approches de la Baltique [Baltic Approaches Allied Command] [NATO] (NATG)	CAAB
Commandement du Transport Aerien Militaire Francais [France ICAO designator] (FAAC)	CTM
Commander [Usually in combination, as: CNAB for Commander, Naval Air Bases]	C
Commander	CDR
Commander (EY)	CMDR
Commander	CMDR
Commander	COM
Commander (WGA)	COMD
Commander (AFM)	COMDR
Commander	COMM
Commander	COMMDR
Commander [Navy British]	Cr
Commander [Navy]	O5
Commander, Aegean Defense Sector (NATG)	COMAEGEANBASE
Commander Air Carter Ltd. [Canada ICAO designator] (FAAC)	CML
Commander Air Center	CAC
Commander, Air Defense Command	COMADC
Commander, Air Force, Atlantic Fleet	COMAIRLANT

Commander, Air Force Forces (AABC) .... COMAFFOR
Commander, Air Force, Pacific Fleet .... COMAIRPAC
Commander, Air Forces [Navy] .... COMAIR
Commander, Air Forces, Gulf [British military] (DMA) .... CAFG
Commander, Air Forces, Solomons .... COMAIRSOLS
Commander, Air Forces, South Pacific Force .... COMAIRSOPAC
Commander, Air Group [Navy] .... CAG
Commander, Air Transport .... COMAIRTRANS
Commander, Air Transport Squadron .... COMAIRTRANSRON
Commander, Airborne Early-Warning Wing (DNAB) ... COMAEWW
Commander Aircraft [NASDAQ symbol] (TTSB) .... CMDR
Commander Aircraft Co. [NASDAQ symbol] (SAG) ...... COMAIRSOLS
Commander Aircraft Co. [Associated Press] (SAG) .... ComndAr
Commander, Aircraft Support Control Unit [Navy] .... CASCU
Commander, Airship Group .... COMAIRSHIPGR
Commander, Alameda Group .... COMALAMGRU
Commander, Alaskan Air Command (MCD) .... COMAAC
Commander, Alaskan Sea Frontier (MUGU) .... COMALSEAFRON
Commander, Alaskan Sector .... COMALSEC
Commander, All Forces, Aruba-Curacao .... CAFAC
Commander, Allied Air Force Central Europe .... COMAAFACE
Commander, Allied Air Forces, Baltic Approaches (AABC) .... COMAIRBALTAP
Commander Allied Air Forces Central Europe [NATO] (PDAA) .... COMAAFCE
Commander, Allied Air Forces, Central Europe .... COMAIRCENT
Commander, Allied Air Forces, North Norway (NATG) .... COMAIRNON
Commander, Allied Air Forces, Northern Europe .... COMAIRNORTH
Commander, Allied Air Forces, Northern Europe .... GOVTLAIRNOREUR
Commander, Allied Air Forces, South Norway (NATG) .... COMAIRSONOR
Commander, Allied Air Forces, Southern Europe .... COMAIRSOUTH
Commander, Allied Forces, North Norway (NATG) .... COMNON
Commander, Allied Forces Southern Norway [Navy] (ANA) .... COMSONOR
Commander, Allied Land Forces, Central Europe .... COMLANDCENT
Commander, Allied Land Forces, Denmark (NATG) .... COMLANDENMARK
Commander, Allied Land Forces, Denmark (AFM) .... COMLANDMARK
Commander, Allied Land Forces, Norway .... COMLANDNORWAY
Commander, Allied Land Forces, Schleswig-Holstein .... COMLANDSCHLESWIG
Commander, Allied Land Forces, Schleswig-Holstein and Jutland
   (AABC) .... COMLANDJUT
Commander, Allied Land Forces, Southeastern Europe ...... COMLANDSOUTHEAST
Commander, Allied Land Forces, Southern Europe .... COMLANDSOUTH
Commander, Allied Land Forces, Zealand (AABC) .... COMLANDZEALAND
Commander, Allied Maritime Air Force Channel [NATO] .... COMMAIRCHAN
Commander, Allied Naval Forces, Baltic Approaches (AABC) ..... COMNAVBALTAP
Commander, Allied Naval Forces, Central Europe .... COMNAVCENT
Commander, Allied Naval Forces, North Norway (AABC) .... COMNAVNON
Commander, Allied Naval Forces, Northern Europe .... COMALNAVNOREUR
Commander, Allied Naval Forces, Northern Europe .... COMNAVNORTH
Commander, Allied Naval Forces, Scandinavian Approaches
   (AABC) .... COMNAVSCAP
Commander, Allied Naval Forces, South Norway (NATG) .... COMNAVSONOR
Commander, Allied Tactical Air Force, North Norway (AABC) .... COMTAFNORNOR
Commander, Allied Tactical Air Force, South Norway (AABC) ...... COMTAFSONOR
Commander, Allied Tactical Air Forces, Southern Norway .... COMATAFSONOR
Commander, Allied Task Forces, North Norway (AFM) .... COMTASKFORNON
Commander, Amphibious Force .... COMPHIB
Commander, Amphibious Force .... COMPHIBFOR
Commander, Amphibious Force, Atlantic Fleet .... CAFAF
Commander, Amphibious Force, Atlantic Fleet .... COMPHIBLANT
Commander, Amphibious Force, Europe .... COMPHIBEU
Commander, Amphibious Force, Northwest African Waters .... COMPHIBNAW
Commander, Amphibious Force, Pacific Fleet (DNAB) .... CAFPF
Commander, Amphibious Force, Pacific Fleet (MUGU) .... COMPHIBFORPAC
Commander, Amphibious Force, Pacific Fleet .... COMPHIBPAC
Commander, Amphibious Group (CINC) .... COMPHIBGRU
Commander, Amphibious Group Detachment (DNAB) .... COMPHIBGRUDET
Commander, Amphibious Group, Eastern Pacific
   (DNAB) .... COMPHIBGRUEASTPAC
Commander, Amphibious Ready Group [Navy] (NVT) .... CARG
Commander, Amphibious Squadron .... COMPHIBRON
Commander, Amphibious Task Force (NVT) .... CATF
Commander, Amphibious Task Force (AABC) .... COMATF
Commander, Amphibious Task Group (DNAB) .... CATG
Commander, Amphibious Training Command, Atlantic .... COMPHIBTRALANT
Commander, Amphibious Training Command, Pacific .... COMPHIBTRAPAC
Commander, Amphibious Training Command, United States Atlantic
   Fleet .... CATCUSAF
Commander, Amphibious Troops .... CAT
Commander and Staff Visualization Research Tool [Army] (RDA) .... CoVRT
Commander, Antarctic Support Activities [Military] (DNAB) .... CASA
Commander, Antarctic Support Activities .... COMANTARCTICSUPPACT
Commander, Antilles Defense Command (AABC) .... COMANTDEFCOM
Commander, Antisubmarine Warfare Force .... COMASWFOR
Commander, Antisubmarine Warfare Forces, Atlantic
   (MUGU) .... COMASWFORLANT
Commander, Antisubmarine Warfare Forces, Pacific (CINC) ...... COMASWFORPAC
Commander, Antisubmarine Warfare Group .... COMASWGRU
Commander, Antisubmarine Warfare Support Training Detachment
   (DNAB) .... COMASWSUPPTRADET
Commander, Area Antisubmarine Warfare Forces (DNAB) .... COMAREASWFOR
Commander, Army Forces .... COMARFOR
Commander at Arms [Navy British] .... CrAA
Commander, Atlantic Approaches Gibraltar (NATG) .... COMGIBLANT
Commander, Atlantic Fleet Bases, Antilles .... COMFLTBASTILLES
Commander, Atlantic Fleet Weapons Range (DNAB) .... COMLANTFLTWPNRAN
Commander, Atlantic Fleet Weapons Range .... COMLANTFLTWPNRNGE

Commander, Attack Carrier Air Wing .... COMATKCARAIRWING
Commander, Attack Carrier Striking Force .... COMATKCARSTRIKEFOR
Commander, Barrier Forces, Atlantic (NATG) .... COMBARFORCLANT
Commander, Barrier Pacific (CINC) .... COMBARPAC
Commander Base Area Command [Australia] .... CBAC
Commander, Battleship Division .... COMBATDIV
Commander, Battleships, Atlantic Fleet .... COMBATLANT
Commander, Battleships, Pacific Fleet .... COMBATPAC
Commander, Battleships-Cruisers, Atlantic Fleet (MUGU) .... COMBATCRULANT
Commander, Bay of Biscay Atlantic Subarea [NATO] .... COMBISLANT
Commander, BENELUX Subarea Channel .... COMBENECHAN
Commander, Black Sea Defense Sector (NATG) .... COMBLACKBASE
Commander Blue (Friendly) Force [Navy] (CAAL) .... COMBLUE
Commander, Bombing Squadron .... COMBOMRON
Commander, Bosphorus Fortifications (NATG) .... COMBOSFORT
Commander, Boston Group .... COMBSNGRU
Commander, Bremerhaven Naval Group (NATG) .... COMNAVBREM
Commander, Bremerton Group .... COMBREMGRU
Commander, Brest Subarea Channel .... COMBRESTCHAN
Commander, British Forces, Arabian Peninsula [British military] (DMA) ..... CBFAP
Commander, British Forces, Caribbean Area [NATO] (NATG) .... CBFCA
Commander, British Forces, Gulf [British military] (DMA) .... CBFG
Commander, British Naval Elbe Squadron (NATG) .... COMBRITELBE
Commander, British Naval Rhine Squadron (NATG) .... COMBRITRHIN
Commander, British Naval Staff .... CBNS
Commander, Canadian Atlantic Subarea [NATO] .... COMCANLANT
Commander, Canadian Destroyers, Atlantic .... CANCOMDESLANT
Commander, Canadian Destroyers, Far East .... CANCOMDESFE
Commander, Canadian Destroyers, Pacific .... CANCOMDESPAC
Commander, Caribbean Sea Frontier .... CCSF
Commander, Caribbean Sea Frontier (NATG) .... COMCARIBSEAFRON
Commander, Caribbean Sector Antisubmarine Warfare Group
   (DNAB) .... COMCARIBSECASWGRU
Commander, Carrier Air Wing [Navy] (NVT) .... COMCVW
Commander, Carrier Aircraft Service Unit .... COMCASU
Commander, Carrier Antisubmarine Air Group .... COMCARASWAIRGRU
Commander, Carrier Division .... COMCARDIV
Commander, Carrier Group (DNAB) .... COMCARGRU
Commander, Carrier Striking Force (AFM) .... COMCARSTRIKFOR
Commander, Carrier Striking Group .... COMCARSTRIKGRU
Commander, Carrier Striking Group One (AFM) .... COMCARSTRIKGRUONE
Commander, Carrier Striking Group Two (AFM) .... COMCARSTRIKGRUTWO
Commander, Carrier Training Squadron, Pacific Fleet .... COMTRAINCARRONPAC
Commander, Central Army Group, Central Europe .... COMCENTAG
Commander, Central Atlantic Subarea [NATO] .... COMCENTLANT
Commander, Central Mediterranean .... COMEDCENT
Commander, Central Pacific .... COMCENPAC
Commander, Central Region SEATO Field Forces (Designate) .... CCRSFF(D)
Commander, Central Region SEATO [Southeast Asia Treaty Organization]
   FieldForces (CINC) .... CCRSFF
Commander, Charleston Group .... COMCHASNGRU
Commander, Cherbourg Subarea Channel .... COMCHERCHAN
Commander, Coast Defenses .... CCD
Commander, Coast Guard Activities, Europe (DNAB) .... COMCOGARDACTEUR
Commander, Coast Guard District .... CCGD
Commander, Coast Guard District .... COMCOGARD
Commander, Coast Guard Force, Atlantic (DNAB) .... COMCOGARDLANT
Commander, Coast Guard Force, Europe (DNAB) .... COMCOGARDEUR
Commander, Coast Guard Group (DNAB) .... COMCOGARDGRU
Commander, Coast Guard, Maritime Section (DNAB) .... COMCOGARDMARSEC
Commander, Coast Guard Section Office, Far East Section
   (DNAB) .... COMCOGARDFESEC
Commander, Coast Guard Section Office, Guantanamo Section
   (DNAB) .... COMCOGARDGANTSEC
Commander, Coast Guard Southeast Squadron (DNAB) .... COMCOGARDSERON
Commander, Coast Guard Squadron (DNAB) .... COMCOGARDRON
Commander, Coast Guard World-Wide Military Command and Control
   System, Atlantic (DNAB) .... COMCOGARDLANTWWMCCS
Commander, Coastal Division (DNAB) .... COMCOSDIV
Commander, Coastal Squadron (DNAB) .... COMCOSRON
Commander, Coastal Surveillance Force (DNAB) .... COMCOSURVFOR
Commander, Columbia River Group .... COMCOLUMGRU
Commander, Combined Amphibious Task Force [Military] (NVT) .... CCATF
Commander, Composite Squadron .... COMCOMRON
Commander Corps Medium Artillery [British] .... CCMA
Commander Corps Royal Artillery [British] .... CCRA
Commander Corps Royal Corps of Transport [Military British] .... CCRCT
Commander Corps Royal Engineers [Military British] .... CCRE
Commander, Cruiser Division .... COMCRUDIV
Commander, Cruiser Forces, Atlantic Fleet (MCD) .... COMCRULANT
Commander, Cruiser Forces, Pacific Fleet .... COMCRUPAC
Commander, Cruiser Scouting Squadron .... COMCRUSCORON
Commander, Cruiser-Destroyer Flotilla [Acronym always followed by a
   number] [Navy] .... COMCRUDESFLOT
Commander, Cruiser-Destroyer Force [Navy] (DNAB) .... CCD
Commander, Cruiser-Destroyer Force .... COMCRUDES
Commander, Cruiser-Destroyer Forces, Atlantic (MCD) .... CCDL
Commander, Cruiser-Destroyer Forces, Atlantic [Navy]
   (DNAB) .... COMCRUDESLANT
Commander, Cruiser-Destroyer Forces, Atlantic Support Group [Navy]
   (DNAB) .... COMCRUDESLANTSUPPGRU
Commander, Cruiser-Destroyer Forces, Atlantic Support Group,
   Charleston [South Carolina] [Navy] (DNAB) .... COMCRUDESLANTSUPPGRUCHAR
Commander, Cruiser-Destroyer Forces, Atlantic Support Group, Mayport
   [Florida] [Navy] (DNAB) .... COMCRUDESLANTSUPPGRUMPT

Commander, Cruiser-Destroyer Forces, Atlantic Support Group, Norfolk, Virginia [Navy] (DNAB) .... COMCRUDESLANTSUPPGRUNORVA
Commander, Cruiser-Destroyer Forces, Pacific [Navy] (DNAB) .... CCDP
Commander, Cruiser-Destroyer Forces, Pacific [Navy] (MCD) .... COMCRUDESPAC
Commander, Cruiser-Destroyer Group [Navy] (DNAB) .... COMCRUDESGRU
Commander, Dardanelles Fortifications (NATG) .... COMDARFORT
Commander, Destroyer Development Group [Navy] .... COMDESDEVGRU
Commander, Destroyer Development Group, Pacific [Navy] (MCD) .... CDDGP
Commander, Destroyer Division .... COMDESDIV
Commander, Destroyer Flotilla .... COMDESFLOT
Commander, Destroyer Group .... COMDESGRU
Commander, Destroyer Squadron .... CDS
Commander, Destroyer Squadron .... COMDESRON
Commander, Destroyers .... COMDES
Commander, Destroyers, Atlantic Detachment (DNAB) .... COMDESLANTDET
Commander, Destroyers, Atlantic Fleet .... COMDESLANT
Commander, Destroyers, Pacific Detachment (DNAB) .... COMDESPACDET
Commander, Destroyers, Pacific Fleet .... COMDESPAC
Commander, Disaster Control Element .... CDCE
Commander, Disaster Control Force .... CDCF
Commander, Disaster Control Group .... CDCG
Commander, Disaster-Preparedness Group [Military] (DNAB) .... CDPG
Commander, Eastern Atlantic Forces .... COMEASTLANT
Commander, Eastern Mediterranean (AFM) .... COMEDEAST
Commander, Eastern Sea Frontier [Navy] .... CESF
Commander, Eastern Sea Frontier [Navy] (MUGU) .... COMEASTFRON
Commander, Eastern Sea Frontier [Navy] .... COMEASTSEAFRON
Commander, Emergency Recovery Force .... CERF
Commander, Emergency Recovery Group .... CERG
Commander, Emergency Recovery Section .... CERS
Commander, Emergency Recovery Unit .... CERU
Commander, Escort Division (DNAB) .... COMCORTDIV
Commander, Escort Squadron (DNAB) .... COMCORTRON
Commander, Experimental Division [Navy] .... COMEXDIV
Commander, Explosive Ordnance Disposal Group (DNAB) .... COMEODGRU
Commander, Field Command, Defense Atomic Support Agency (AABC) .... COMFLDCOMDASA
Commander, Fifth Allied Tactical Air Force (AFM) .... COMFIVEATAF
Commander Fighter Wing (MCD) .... COMFITWING
Commander, Fighting Squadron .... COMFIGHTRON
Commander, First Canadian Destroyer Flotilla .... CANCOMDESFLOT 1
Commander, [US] First Fleet .... COMFIRSTFLEET
Commander, [US] First Fleet (MUGU) .... COMFIRSTFLT
Commander, Fleet Activities (DNAB) .... COMFLEACT
Commander, Fleet Activities Detachment (DNAB) .... COMFLEACTDET
Commander, Fleet Air .... COMFAIR
Commander, Fleet Air, Adak, Alaska .... COMFAIRADAK
Commander, Fleet Air, Alameda .... COMFAIRALAMEDA
Commander, Fleet Air, Bermuda .... COMFAIRBERMUDA
Commander, Fleet Air, Brunswick .... COMFAIRBRUNSWICK
Commander, Fleet Air Defense (NATG) .... CFAD
Commander, Fleet Air Detachment .... CFAD
Commander, Fleet Air, Eastern Atlantic and Mediterranean (NATG) .... COMFAIRELM
Commander, Fleet Air, Hawaii (MUGU) .... COMFAIRHAWAII
Commander, Fleet Air, Jacksonville, Florida .... COMFAIRJAX
Commander, Fleet Air, Japan .... COMFAIRJAPAN
Commander, Fleet Air, Keflavik, Iceland .... COMFAIRKEFLAVIK
Commander, Fleet Air, Mediterranean .... COMFAIRMED
Commander, Fleet Air, Norfolk, Virginia .... COMFAIRNORFOLK
Commander, Fleet Air, Quonset Point, Rhode Island .... COMFAIRQUONSET
Commander, Fleet Air, San Diego, California .... COMFAIRSANDIEGO
Commander, Fleet Air, Southwest Pacific (MUGU) ..... COMFAIRSOWESTPAC
Commander, Fleet Air, Western Pacific .... COMFAIRWESTPAC
Commander, Fleet Air Wing .... CFAW
Commander, Fleet Air Wing .... COMFAIRWING
Commander, Fleet Air Wing, Atlantic .... CFAWL
Commander, Fleet Air Wing, Atlantic (NATG) .... COMFAIRWINGLANT
Commander, Fleet Air Wing, Northern Atlantic (AABC) ..... COMFAIRWINGNORLANT
Commander, Fleet Air Wing, Pacific .... CFAWP
Commander, Fleet Electronic Warfare Support Group (DNAB) .... COMFEWSG
Commander, Fleet Electronic Warfare Support Group Detachment (DNAB) .... COMFEWSGDET
Commander, Fleet Logistic Air Wing .... COMFLOGWING
Commander, Fleet Operational Training Command .... COTC
Commander, Fleet Operational Training Command, Atlantic Fleet ...... COTCLANT
Commander, Fleet Operational Training Command, Pacific Fleet ...... COTCPAC
Commander, Fleet Operational Training Command, Pacific Subordinate Command .... COTCPACSUBCOM
Commander, Fleet Train .... COFT
Commander, Fleet Training Group .... COMFLETRAGRU
Commander, Fleet Training Group and Underway Training Element (MUGU) .... COMFLETRAGRUWATE
Commander, Fleet Training Group, Atlantic (DNAB) ..... COMFLETRAGRULANT
Commander, Fleet Training Group, Pacific (DNAB) ...... COMFLETRAGRUPAC
Commander, Fleet Training Group, Western Pacific (DNAB) .... COMFLETRAGRUWESPAC
Commander, Florida Group .... COMFLAGRU
Commander, Flying [British military] (DMA) .... FLYCO
Commander, Fourth Allied Tactical Air Force, Central Europe ..... COMFOURATAF
Commander, French Rhine River Squadron [NATO] .... COMSUFRHIN
Commander, German Naval Forces, Baltic (NATG) ...... COMNAVGERBALT
Commander, German North Sea Subarea (NATG) ...... COMGERNORSEA
Commander, Gibraltar [Navy] (AABC) .... COMGIB
Commander, Gibraltar-Mediterranean Command (AFM) .... COMGIBMED

Commander, Greenland Patrol .... COMGREPAT
Commander, Guantanamo Bay, Cuba Sector, Antisubmarine Warfare Unit (DNAB) .... COMGTMOSECTASWU
Commander, Hawaiian Sea Frontier [Navy] .... COMHAWSEAFRON
Commander, Headquarters Squadron .... COMHEDRON
Commander, Hunter-Killer Force, Atlantic Fleet ..... COMHUKFORLAN
Commander, Iberian Atlantic Area (NATG) .... COMIBERLANT
Commander, Iceland Antisubmarine Warfare Group ..... COMICEASWGRU
Commander, Iceland Defense Force .... COMICEDEFOR
Commander, Iceland Defense Force (DNAB) .... COMIDF
Commander, Iceland Defense Force/Commander Iceland Antisubmarine Warfare Group (DNAB) .... COMICEDEFOR/COMICEASWGRU
Commander in Chief (AAGC) .... CinC
Commander in Chief (AAGC) .... CINC
Commander in Chief, Atlantic [Military] (DOMA) ...... CINCANT
Commander in Chief, Atlantic Forces (AAGC) .... CINCLANT
Commander in Chief, [US] Forces [Command] (DOMA) ..... CINCFOR
Commander in Chief, Southern Command (AAGC) ...... CINCSOUTH
Commander in Chief, [US] Space [Command] (DOMA) ..... CINCSPACE
Commander in Chief, [US] Special Operations [Command] (DOMA) ...... CINCSOC
Commander in Chief, [US] Strategic [Command] (DOMA) ...... CINCSTRAT
Commander in Chief, [US] Transportation [Command] (DOMA) ...... CINCTRANS
Commander in Chief, US Army Forces, Readiness [Command] (DOMA) .... CINCUSARRED
Commander in Chief, US European Command (DOMA) ...... CINCUSEUCOM
Commander in Chief, US Naval Forces Europe (DOMA) ...... CINCUSNAVEUR
Commander in Chief, USA Command [Established in 1993] (DOMA) .... CINCUSACOM
Commander, Inshore Fire Support Division (DNAB) ...... COMIFSDIV
Commander, Intelligence Center, Pacific (DNAB) ...... COMICPAC
Commander, International Ice Patrol [Coast Guard] .... CIIP
Commander, Joint Expeditionary Force .... COMJEF
Commander, Joint Military Postal Activity, Atlantic (DNAB) ..... CDRJPAA
Commander, Joint Military Postal Activity, Atlantic (DNAB) ..... CDRJPAALANT
Commander, Joint Task Element (DNAB) .... CDRJTE
Commander, Joint Task Force .... CJTF
Commander Joint Task Force (DOMA) .... CJTF
Commander Joint Task Force (AABC) .... COMJTF
Commander, Joint Task Group .... CJTG
Commander, Joint Unconventional Warfare Task Force (AABC) ..... COMJUWATF
Commander, Joint Unconventional Warfare Task Force (DNAB) ...... COMJUWTF
Commander, Land Forces [Army] (AABC) .... COMLANDFOR
Commander, Land Forces, North Norway (NATG) ...... COMLANDNON
Commander, Landing Force [Navy] (NVT) .... CLF
Commander, Landing Ship Tank Division (DNAB) ...... COMLSTDIV
Commander, Light Attack Wing - Pacific Fleet (MCD) ...... CLAWP
Commander, Logistics Support Force (DNAB) ...... COMLOGSUPPFOR
Commander, Long Beach Group .... COMLBEACHGRU
Commander, Mare Island Group .... COMAREGRU
Commander, Marianas .... COMMARIANAS
Commander, Marine Air Reserve Training .... COMART
Commander, Marine Forces .... COMMARFOR
Commander, Maritime Air Central Subarea [NATO] .... COMMAIRCENTLANT
Commander, Maritime Air Eastern Atlantic Area [NATO] ..... COMMAIREASTLANT
Commander, Maritime Air Gibraltar Subarea [NATO] (NATG) .... COMMAIRGIBLANT
Commander, Maritime Air Northeast Subarea Channel [NATO] .... COMMAIRNORECHAN
Commander, Maritime Air Northern Subarea [NATO] ...... COMMAIRNORLANT
Commander, Maritime Air Plymouth Subarea Channel [NATO] .... COMMAIRPLYMCHAN
Commander, Maritime Forces, Morocco .... COMOROCLANT
Commander, Maritime Prepositioned Force [Navy] (ANA) .... CMPF
Commander, Maritime Rhine (NATG) .... COMARRHIN
Commander, Maritime Surveillance and Reconnaissance Force (DNAB) .... COMARSURV
Commander, Maritime Surveillance and Reconnaissance Force Detachment (DNAB) .... COMARSURVRECFORDET
Commander, Maritime Surveillance and Reconnaissance Force, Passive ASRAP [Acoustic Sensor Range Prediction] Data (DNAB) .... COMARSURVRECFORPASRAP
Commander, Marshalls-Carolines Area .... COMARCARAREA
Commander, Mediterranean Defense Sector (NATG) ...... COMEDBASE
Commander, Mediterranean Operations Center .... COMEDOC
Commander Mexicana SA de CV [Mexico ICAO designator] (FAAC) ..... CRM
Commander, Middle East Force (DOMA) .... CMEF
Commander, Middle East Force (AABC) .... COMIDEASTFOR
Commander, Military Air Transport Service [Later, COMAC] ..... COMATS
Commander, Military Airlift Command [Formerly, COMATS] (AFM) .... COMAC
Commander, Military Assistance Group, Republic of China, Vietnam .... COMMAGROCV
Commander, Military Sea Transportation Service [Obsolete] ..... COMSTS
Commander, Military Sea Transportation Service, Atlantic Area .... COMSTSLANTAREA
Commander, Military Sea Transportation Service, Eastern Atlantic and Mediterranean Area .... COMSTSELMAREA
Commander, Military Sea Transportation Service, Far East (CINC) ..... COMSTSFE
Commander, Military Sea Transportation Service, Gulf Subarea .... COMSTSGULFSUBAREA
Commander, Military Sea Transportation Service, Management Information System .... COMSTS/MIS
Commander, Military Sea Transportation Service, Mid-Pacific Subarea .... COMSTSMIDPACSUBAREA
Commander, Military Sea Transportation Service, Northern Pacific Subarea .... COMSTSNORPACSUBAREA

Commander, Military Sea Transportation Service, Pacific Area .... COMSTSPACAREA
Commander, Military Sea Transportation Service, Southeast Asia (CINC) .... COMSTSSEA
Commander, Military Sea Transportation Service, West Pacific Area .... COMSTSWESTPACAREA
Commander, Military Sealift Command .... COMMSC
Commander, Military Sealift Command .... COMSC
Commander, Military Sealift Command, Atlantic .... COMSCLANT
Commander, Military Sealift Command, Eastern Atlantic and Mediterranean .... COMSCELM
Commander, Military Sealift Command, Europe (DNAB) .... COMSCEUR
Commander, Military Sealift Command, Far East .... COMSCFE
Commander, Military Sealift Command, Gulf Subarea .... COMSCGULF
Commander, Military Sealift Command, Mediterranean .... COMSCMED
Commander, Military Sealift Command, Pacific .... COMSCPAC
Commander, Military Sealift Command, Southeast Asia (DNAB) .... COMSCSEA
Commander, Mine Flotilla .... COMINFLOT
Commander, Mine Force, Atlantic Fleet [Navy] .... COMINELANT
Commander, Mine Force, Atlantic Fleet [Navy] .... COMINLANT
Commander, Mine Force, Pacific Fleet [Navy] .... COMINEPAC
Commander, Mine Group .... COMINGRP
Commander, Mine Group, Okinawa .... COMINGRPOK
Commander, Mine Squadron .... COMINRON
Commander, Mine Warfare Forces .... COMINEWARFOR
Commander, Minecraft [Navy] .... COMIN
Commander, Minecraft [Navy] (DNAB) .... COMINE
Commander, Minecraft Division [Navy] .... COMINDIV
Commander, Minecraft Division [Navy] (DNAB) .... COMINEDIV
Commander, Minecraft, Pacific Fleet [Navy] .... COMINPAC
Commander, Mobile Mine Assembly Group (DNAB) .... COMOMAG
Commander, Mobile Support Unit Detachment (DNAB) .... COMMOBSUPPUDET
Commander, Moroccan Sea Frontier Forces .... COMORSEAFRON
Commander, Motor Torpedo Boat Flotilla .... COMTBFLOT
Commander, Motor Torpedo Boat Squadron .... COMTBRON
Commander, Motor Torpedo Boat Squadron Training Center .... COMTBRONTRACENT
Commander, Naval Activities (DNAB) .... COMNAVACT
Commander, Naval Activities, Japan .... COMNAVJAP
Commander, Naval Activities, United Kingdom (DNAB) .... COMNAVACTUK
Commander, Naval Air Bases .... CNAB
Commander, Naval Air Bases .... COMNAB
Commander, Naval Air Force .... COMNAVAIR
Commander, Naval Air Force .... CNAL
Commander, Naval Air Force, Atlantic .... COMNAVAIRLANT
Commander, Naval Air Force, Atlantic Fleet (MCD) .... COMNAVAIRLANT
Commander, Naval Air Force, Pacific Fleet (MCD) .... COMNAVAIRPAC
Commander, Naval Air Reserve (DNAB) .... CNAR
Commander, Naval Air Reserve Force (DNAB) .... CNARF
Commander, Naval Air Systems Command (MCD) .... COMNAVAIRSYSCOM
Commander, Naval Air Technical Training (Lighter Than Air) .... CNATEC (LTA)
Commander, Naval Base .... CNB
Commander, Naval Base .... COMNAVBASE
Commander, Naval Base, Los Angeles .... CNBLA
Commander, Naval Communications (NVT) .... COMNAVCOMM
Commander, Naval Construction Battalions, Atlantic Detachment (DNAB) .... COMCBLANTDET
Commander, Naval Construction Battalions, Atlantic Fleet .... COMCBLANT
Commander, Naval Construction Battalions, Atlantic, Material Liaison Office (DNAB) .... COMCBLANT MLO
Commander, Naval Construction Battalions, Pacific Fleet .... COMCBPAC
Commander, Naval Data Automation Center (DNAB) .... COMNAVDAC
Commander, Naval Defense Forces, Eastern Pacific (MUGU) .... COMNAVDEFOREEASTPAC
Commander, Naval Education and Training Command, Representative Coordinator for Atlantic (DNAB) .... CNETLANTREP
Commander, Naval Education and Training Command, Representative Coordinator for Pacific (DNAB) .... CNETPACREP
Commander, Naval Electronic Systems Command (DNAB) .... COMNAVELEXSYSCOM
Commander, Naval Electronic Systems Command, Alternate Commander (DNAB) .... COMNAVELEXSYSCOM ALT
Commander, Naval Electronic Systems Command, Emergency Relocation Site Commander (DNAB) .... COMNAVELEXSYSCOM ERS
Commander, Naval Electronic Systems Command Headquarters (DNAB) .... COMNAVELEXSYSCOMHQ
Commander, Naval Facilities Engineering Command (DNAB) .... COMNAVFACENGCOM
Commander, Naval Facilities Engineering Command, Alternate Commander (DNAB) .... COMNAVFACENGCOM ALT
Commander, Naval Facilities Engineering Command Detachment (DNAB) .... COMNAVFACENGCOMDET
Commander, Naval Facilities Engineering Command, Emergency Relocation Site Commander (DNAB) .... COMNAVFACENGCOM ERS
Commander, Naval Facilities Engineering Command Headquarters (DNAB) .... COMNAVFACENGCOMHQ
Commander, [US] Naval Forces .... CNF
Commander, [US] Naval Forces .... COMNAVFOR
Commander, [US] Naval Forces, Azores .... COMNAVZOR
Commander, Naval Forces, Central Army Group Area and Bremerhaven (NATG) .... COMNAVCAG
Commander, [US] Naval Forces, Continental Air Defense Command (MUGU) .... COMNAVFORCONAD
Commander, [US] Naval Forces, Eastern Atlantic and Mediterranean .... COMNAVEASTLANTMED
Commander, [US] Naval Forces, Europe .... COMNAVEU

Commander, [US] Naval Forces, Far East .... COMNAVFE
Commander, [US] Naval Forces, Germany (MCD) .... COMNAVFORGER
Commander, [US] Naval Forces, Germany .... COMNAVGER
Commander, [US] Naval Forces, Iceland .... COMNAVFORICE
Commander, [US] Naval Forces, Iceland .... COMNAVICE
Commander, [US] Naval Forces, Japan (SAA) .... COMNAVFORJAP
Commander, [US] Naval Forces, Japan (AFM) .... COMNAVFORJAPAN
Commander, [US] Naval Forces, Korea .... COMNAVFORKOREA
Commander, [US] Naval Forces, Marianas .... COMNAVFMARIANAS
Commander, [US] Naval Forces, Marianas (CINC) .... COMNAVMARIANAS
Commander, [US] Naval Forces, Northwest African Waters .... COMNAVNAW
Commander, [US] Naval Forces, Philippines .... COMNAVFORPHIL
Commander, Naval Forces, Southern Europe (NATG) .... COMNAVSOUTH
Commander, [US] Naval Forces, Vietnam .... COMNAVFORV
Commander, Naval Inshore Warfare Command, Atlantic .... COMNAVINSWARLANT
Commander, Naval Intelligence Command (DNAB) .... CNIC
Commander, Naval Intelligence Command (DNAB) .... COMNAVINTCOM
Commander, Naval Legal Service Command (DNAB) .... COMNAVLEGSVCCOM
Commander, Naval Logistics Command, Pacific (DNAB) .... COMNAVLOGPAC
Commander, Naval Missile Center (MUGU) .... COMNMC
Commander, Naval Operating Base .... CNOB
Commander, Naval Operations Support Group (DNAB) .... COMNAVOPSUPPGRU
Commander, Naval Operations Support Group, Atlantic (DNAB) .... COMNAVOPSUPPGRULANT
Commander, Naval Operations Support Group, Pacific (DNAB) .... COMNAVOSUPPGRUPAC
Commander Naval Ordnance [Military systems command] .... COMNAVORD
Commander, Naval Ordnance Systems Command (MCD) .... COMNAVORDSYSCOM
Commander, Naval Reserve Construction Battalions, Pacific (DNAB) .... COMNRCBPAC
Commander, Naval Reserve Construction Force (DNAB) .... COMNRCF
Commander, Naval Reserve Construction Force Representative (DNAB) .... COMNRCFREP
Commander, Naval Reserve Inshore-Undersea Warfare Group (DNAB) .... COMNRIUWGRU
Commander, Naval Reserve Personnel Center (DNAB) .... COMNAVRESPERSCEN
Commander, Naval Reserve Personnel Center (DNAB) .... COMNRPC
Commander, Naval Reserve Security Group (DNAB) .... COMNAVRESSECGRU
Commander, Naval Reserves (NVT) .... CNAVRES
Commander, Naval Security Group (DNAB) .... COMNAVSECGRU
Commander, Naval Special Warfare Group (DNAB) .... COMNAVSPECWARGRU
Commander, Naval Special Warfare Group Detachment (DNAB) .... COMNAVSPECWARGRUDET
Commander, Naval Special Warfare Task Group (NVT) .... CNSWTG
Commander, Naval Supply Systems Command (DNAB) .... COMNAVSUPSYSCOM
Commander, Naval Supply Systems Command, Emergency Relocation Site Commander (DNAB) .... COMNAVSUPSYSCOM ERS
Commander, Naval Supply Systems Command Headquarters (DNAB) .... COMNAVSUPSYSCOMHQ
Commander, Naval Support Activity (AFM) .... COMNAVSUPPACT
Commander, Naval Support Force .... COMNAVSUPPFOR
Commander, Naval Support Force, Antarctic .... COMNAVSUPPFORANTARCTIC
Commander, Naval Surface Forces, Atlantic .... COMNAVSURFLA
Commander, Naval Surface Forces, Atlantic (DNAB) .... COMNAVSURFLANT
Commander, Naval Surface Forces, Atlantic Detachment (DNAB) .... COMNAVSURFLANTDET
Commander, Naval Surface Forces, Atlantic Representative (DNAB) .... COMNAVSURFLANTREP
Commander, Naval Surface Forces, Pacific (DNAB) .... COMNAVSURFPAC
Commander, Naval Surface Forces, Pacific Automatic Data Processing (DNAB) .... COMNAVSURFPAC ADP
Commander, Naval Surface Forces, Pacific Detachment (DNAB) .... COMNAVSURFPAC DET
Commander, Naval Surface Forces, Pacific Distributed Information System for CASREP/UNIT Status (DNAB) .... COMNAVSURFPAC DISCUS
Commander, Naval Surface Forces, Pacific, Emergency Relocation Site Commander (DNAB) .... COMNAVSURFPAC ERS
Commander, Naval Surface Forces, Pacific Representative (DNAB) .... COMNAVSURFPACREP
Commander, Naval Surface Group, Mediterranean (DNAB) .... COMNAVSURFGRUMED
Commander, Naval Surface Group, Mid-Pacific (DNAB) .... COMNAVSURFGRUMIDPAC
Commander, Naval Surface Group, Western Pacific (DNAB) .... COMNAVSURFGRUWESTPAC
Commander, Naval Surface Group, Western Pacific Detachment (DNAB) .... COMNAVSURFGRUWESTPACDET
Commander, Naval Surface Reserve Force (DNAB) .... COMNAVSURFRES
Commander, Naval Telecommunications Command (NVT) .... COMNAVTELCOM
Commander, Navy Military Personnel Command (NVT) .... COMNAVMILPERSCOM
Commander, Navy Recruiting Area (DNAB) .... CNRA
Commander, Navy Recruiting Command (DNAB) .... CNRC
Commander, Navy Recruiting Command (DNAB) .... COMNAVCRUITCOM
Commander, Navy Recruiting Command, Quality Assurance Team (DNAB) .... COMNAVCRUITCOM QAT
Commander, New London Group .... COMNEWLONGRU
Commander, New London [Connecticut] Test and Evaluation Detachment (DNAB) .... COMNLONTEVDET
Commander, New York Group .... COMNYKGRU
Commander, New Zealand Army Forces, Far East .... COMNZAFFE
Commander, New Zealand Assistance Detachment, Vietnam .... COMNEWZEDV
Commander, Norfolk Group .... COMNORVAGRU
Commander, Norfolk, Virginia Test and Evaluation Detachment (DNAB) .... COMNORVATEVDET

Commander, North American Antisubmarine Defense Force, Atlantic [*NATO*] ..... COMNORASDEFLANT
Commander, North American Defense Force, Atlantic [*NATO*] ..... COMNADEFLANT
Commander, North Pacific Force ..... COMNORPAC
Commander, North Sea Subarea, Central Europe (NATG) ..... COMNORSEACENT
Commander, Northeast Atlantic (NATG) ..... COMNEATLANT
Commander, Northeast Mediterranean (AABC) ..... COMEDNOREAST
Commander, Northeast Subarea Channel ..... COMNORECHAN
Commander, Northern Area Forces, Central Europe (NATG) ..... COMNAVNORCENT
Commander, Northern Army Group, Central Europe ..... COMNORTHAG
Commander, Northern Atlantic Subarea [*NATO*] ..... COMNORLANT
Commander, Northern Group ..... CNG
Commander, Northern Section (DNAB) ..... COMNORSECT
Commander, Northern Striking Force (DNAB) ..... COMNORSTRIKFOR
Commander, Nuclear Power Training Group, Atlantic (DNAB) ..... COMNUPWRTRAGRULANT
Commander, Nuclear Power Training Group, Pacific (DNAB) ..... COMNUPWRTRAGRUPAC
Commander, Nuclear Weapons Training Group, Atlantic (DNAB) ..... COMNUWPNTRAGRULANT
Commander, Nuclear Weapons Training Group, Pacific (DNAB) ..... COMNUWPNTRAGRUPAC
Commander, Ocean Atlantic Subarea [*NATO*] ..... COMOCEANLANT
Commander, Ocean Subarea ..... COMOCEANSUBAREA
Commander Ocean Systems, Atlantic (DOMA) ..... COSL
Commander Ocean Systems Pacific (DOMA) ..... COSP
Commander, Oceanographic Surveillance Systems, Atlantic (MUGU) ..... COMOCEANSYSLANT
Commander, Oceanographic Surveillance Systems, Pacific ..... COMOCEANSYSPAC
Commander of a Numbered Group ..... COMGRU
Commander of Airlift Forces [*Air Force*] (DOMA) ..... COMALF
Commander of Federal Republic of Nigeria ..... CFR
Commander of Service Cross [*British*] (ROG) ..... CSC
Commander of the [*Order of the*] **British Empire** [*Facetious translation: Can't Be Everywhere*] ..... CBE
Commander of the Dockyard at [*place*] ..... COMYARD
Commander of the Guard [*Military*] ..... COG
Commander of the Most Excellent Order of the Bath [*British*] ..... CB
Commander of the Order of Distinction [*Jamaica*] ..... CD
Commander of the Order of Leopold CL
Commander of the Order of Military Merit ..... CMM
Commander of the Order of Military Merit [*Canada*] (DD) ..... CMM
Commander of the Order of St. Lazarus of Jerusalem ..... CLJ
Commander of the Order of the Niger [*Nigeria*] ..... CON
Commander of the Royal Victorian Order [*British*] ..... CVO
Commander of Troops [*for a parade or review*] [*Military*] ..... COT
Commander, Operational Control Center ..... COMOPCONCEN
Commander, Operational Development Force [*Navy*] ..... COMOPDEVFOR
Commander, Operational Test and Evaluation Force [*Navy*] ..... COMOPTEVFOR
Commander Operational Test and Evaluation Force [*Navy*] (CAAL) ..... COTF
Commander, Operational Test and Evaluation Force, Atlantic [*Navy*] (DNAB) ..... COMOPTEVFORLANT
Commander, Operational Test and Evaluation Force, Pacific [*Navy*] (DNAB) ..... COMOPTEVFORPAC
Commander Orange (Aggressor) Force [*Navy*] (CAAL) ..... COMORANGE
Commander, Orange, Texas, Group; Inactive Reserve Fleet, Atlantic ..... COMORTEXGRU
Commander, Order of St. John of Jerusalem [*British*] ..... CStJ
Commander, Pacific Air Fleet ..... COMPAF
Commander, Pacific Electronic Intelligence Center (DNAB) ..... COMPACELINTCEN
Commander, Pacific Missile Range (MUGU) ..... COMPACMISRAN
Commander, Pacific Missile Range (AAG) ..... COMPMR
Commander, Pacific Missile Range Instruction (MUGU) ..... COMPMRINST
Commander, Pacific Missile Range Notice (MUGU) ..... COMPMRNOTE
Commander, Panama Sea Frontier ..... COMPASEAFRON
Commander, Panama Section (DNAB) ..... COMPASECT
Commander, Panama Section, Antisubmarine Warfare Group (DNAB) ..... COMPASECTASWGRU
Commander, Patrol Aircraft Service Unit ..... COMPASU
Commander, Patrol and Reconnaissance Force (DNAB) ..... COMPATRECONFOR
Commander, Patrol Antisubmarine Warfare Development Group (DNAB) ..... COMPATASWDEVGRU
Commander, Patrol Forces (NATG) ..... COMPATFOR
Commander, Patrol Forces, Northern Subarea, Atlantic (NATG) ..... COMPATFORNORLANT
Commander, Patrol Squadron ..... COMPATRON
Commander, Philadelphia Group ..... COMPHILAGRU
Commander, Philippine Military Assistance Group, Vietnam ..... COMPHILMAGV
Commander, Plymouth Subarea Channel ..... COMPLYMCHAN
Commander, [*US*] **Ports and Bases, France** ..... COMBASFRANCE
Commander, Puerto Rico Section Antisubmarine Warfare Unit (DNAB) ..... COMPRSECTASWU
Commander, Rapid Development Naval Force (DNAB) ..... COMRDNAVFOR
Commander, Republic of Korea Forces, Vietnam ..... COMROKFV
Commander, Republic of Korea Military Assistance Group, Vietnam ..... COMROKMAGV
Commander, Reserve Destroyer Squadron ..... COMRESDESRON
Commander, Reserve Naval Construction Battalions, Atlantic (DNAB) ..... COMRNCBLANT
Commander, Reserve Naval Construction Force (DNAB) ..... COMRNCF
Commander, River Division ..... COMRIVDIV
Commander, River Flotilla ..... COMRIVFLOT
Commander, River Flotilla One ..... COMRIVFLOTONE
Commander, River Patrol Force ..... COMRIVPATFOR
Commander, River Support Squadron ..... COMRIVSUPPRON
Commander, Riverine Division [*Navy*] ..... COMRNDN
Commander, Riverine Flotilla [*Navy*] ..... COMRNFLOT
Commander, Riverine Squadron [*Navy*] ..... COMRNRON
Commander, Royal Armoured Corps [*British military*] (DMA) ..... CRAC
Commander, Royal Army Ordnance Corps [*Military British*] ..... CRAOC
Commander, Royal Army Service Corps [*British*] ..... CRASC
Commander, Royal Artillery [*Division level*] [*British*] ..... CRA
Commander, Royal Corps of Transport [*Military British*] ..... CRCT
Commander, Royal Electrical and Mechanical Engineers [*Military British*] ..... CREME
Commander, Royal Engineers [*British*] ..... CRE
Commander, Royal Thai Military Assistance Group, Vietnam ..... COMRTMAGV
Commander, San Diego Group ..... COMDIEGOGRU
Commander, San Francisco Group ..... COMSANFRANGRU
Commander, Scouting Squadron ..... COMSCORON
Commander, Sea Frontier ..... COMSEAFRON
Commander Sea Training [*Canadian Navy*] ..... CST
Commander, Search and Rescue (DNAB) ..... COMSAR
Commander, SEATO [*Southeast Asia Treaty Organization*] **Field Forces** (CINC) ..... CSFF
Commander, Second Allied Tactical Air Force ..... COMTWOATAF
Commander, Second Fleet [*Atlantic*] (SAA) ..... COMSECFLT
Commander, Second Fleet (MUGU) ..... COMSECONDFLT
Commander, Second Fleet, Headquarters (MCD) ..... COMSECFLTHQ
Commander, Service Force ..... COMSERV
Commander, Service Force (DNAB) ..... COMSERVFOR
Commander, Service Force, Atlantic (DNAB) ..... COMSERFORLANT
Commander, Service Force, Atlantic (DNAB) ..... COMSERVLANT
Commander Service Force, Atlantic (MCD) ..... CSL
Commander, Service Force, Atlantic Fleet ..... COMSERVLANT
Commander, Service Force Group (DNAB) ..... COMSERVGRU
Commander, Service Force Group Detachment (DNAB) ..... COMSERVGRUDET
Commander Service Force, Pacific (MCD) ..... CSP
Commander, Service Force, Pacific Fleet ..... COMSERVPAC
Commander, Service Force, Pacific Petroleum School (DNAB) ..... COMSERVPACPETSCOL
Commander, Service Force, South Pacific Subordinate Command ..... COMSERFORSOPACSUBCOM
Commander, Service Force, Southwest Pacific ..... COMSERVSOWESPAC
Commander, Service Group Two [*Navy*] CSG2
Commander, Service Squadron ..... COMSERVRON
Commander, Seventh Fleet (MUGU) ..... COMSEVENTHFLT
Commander, Sixth Allied Tactical Air Force (AFM) ..... COMSIXATAF
Commander, Sixth Fleet (NATG) ..... COMSIXFLT
Commander, Sixth Fleet (NATG) ..... COMSIXTHFLT
Commander, South Atlantic Force ..... COMSOLANT
Commander, South Atlantic Maritime Area ..... CAMAS
Commander, South Pacific ..... COMSOPAC
Commander, Southeast Mediterranean (AFM) ..... COMEDSOUEAST
Commander, Southeast Pacific Force ..... COMSOEASTPAC
Commander, Southern Section (DNAB) ..... COMSOSECT
Commander, Southern Sector, Western Sea Frontier (MUGU) ..... COMSOSECWESTSEAFRON
Commander, Southwest Pacific Force ..... COMSOWESPAC
Commander, Special Operating Forces Central Command [*Navy*] (ANA) ..... COMSOCCENT
Commander, Stockton Group ..... COMSTOCKGRU
Commander, Straits and Marmara Defense Sector (NATG) ..... COMSAMAR
Commander, Strategic Reserve, Allied Land Forces, Central Europe (NATG) ..... COMSTRATRESCENT
Commander, Strategic Submarine Force (DNAB) ..... COMSTRATSUBFOR
Commander, Striking and Support Forces, Southern Europe ..... COMSTRIKFORSOUTH
Commander, Striking Fleet, Atlantic (MCD) ..... CMSTRKFLT
Commander Striking Fleet Atlantic [*Military*] ..... CMSTRKFLT-LANT
Commander, Striking Fleet, Atlantic (AABC) ..... COMSTRIKFLANT
Commander, Striking Fleet, Atlantic (AFM) ..... COMSTRIKFLTLANT
Commander, Striking Fleet, Atlantic Representative in Europe (NATG) ..... COMSTRIKFLANTREPEUR
Commander, Sub-Frontier Defense (DNAB) ..... COMSUBFRONDEF
Commander, Sub-Frontier Defense/Delaware Group (DNAB) ..... COMSUBFRONDEF/DELGRU
Commander, Sub-Frontier Defense/Southern Group (DNAB) ..... COMSUBFRONDEF/SOGRU
Commander, Submarine Allied Command, Atlantic (AABC) ..... COMSUBACLANT
Commander, Submarine Base ..... COMSUBASE
Commander, Submarine Development Group ..... COMSUBDEVGRU
Commander, Submarine Development Group Detachment (DNAB) ..... COMSUBDEVGRUDET
Commander, Submarine Development Group, Unmanned Vehicles (DNAB) ..... COMSUBDEVGRU UMV
Commander, Submarine Development Squadron (DNAB) ..... COMSUBDEVRON
Commander, Submarine Development Squadron Training Detachment (DNAB) ..... COMSUBDEVRONTRADET
Commander, Submarine Division ..... COMSUBDIV
Commander, Submarine Flotilla ..... COMSUBFLO
Commander, Submarine Flotilla (MUGU) ..... COMSUBFLOT
Commander, Submarine Force, Atlantic ..... COMSUBLANT
Commander, Submarine Force, Atlantic Representative (DNAB) ..... COMSUBLANTREP
Commander, Submarine Force, Eastern Atlantic ..... COMSUBEASTLANT
Commander, Submarine Force, Mediterranean (AABC) ..... COMSUBMED
Commander, Submarine Force, Northeast Mediterranean (AABC) ..... COMSUBMEDNOREAST
Commander, Submarine Force, Pacific ..... COMSUBPAC

Commander, Submarine Force, Pacific Command Center (DNAB) ... COMSUBPAC CC
Commander, Submarine Force, Pacific Emergency Command Center (DNAB) ... COMSUBPAC ECC
Commander, Submarine Force, Pacific, Over-the-Horizon Fleet Commander (DNAB) ... COMSUBPAC OTH
Commander, Submarine Force, Pacific Representative (DNAB) ... COMSUBPACREP
Commander, Submarine Force, Western Atlantic Area (AABC) ... COMSUBWESTLANT
Commander Submarine Group 8 ... COMSUBGRU 8
Commander, Submarine Group Detachment (DNAB) ... COMSUBGRUDET
Commander, Submarine Squadron ... COMSUBRON
Commander, Submarine Training Facilities ... COMSUBTRAFAC
Commander, Submarine Training Group (DNAB) ... COMSUBTRAGRU
Commander, Submarine Training Group, Northwest Area (DNAB) ... COMSUBTRAGRUNORWEST
Commander, Submarine Training Group, West Coast Area (DNAB) ... COMSUBTRAGRUWESCO
Commander, Submarines ... COMSUBS
Commander, Submarines, Northeast Mediterranean (NATG) ... COMSUBLEDNOREAST
Commander, Submarines, Southwest Pacific Force ... COMSUBSSOWESPAC
Commander, Subordinate Command, [*US*] Atlantic Fleet (NATG) ... COMSUCOMLANTFLT
Commander, Subordinate Command, [*US*] Naval Forces Eastern Atlantic and Mediterranean, Commander Headquarters Support Activities [*Said to be the longest English-language acronym*] ... COMSUBCOMNELMCOMHEDSUPPACT
Commander, Subordinate Command, [*US*] Naval Forces Eastern Atlantic and Mediterranean, Commander Headquarters Support Activities ... CSCN/CHSA
Commander, Subordinate Command, Service Force Pacific Fleet [*Navy*] ... CSFPSC
Commander, Support Operations Task Force, Europe (AFM) ... COMSOTFE
Commander, Surface Squadron (DNAB) ... COMSURFRON
Commander, Tactical Air Command (AFM) ... COMTAC
Commander, Tactical Air Control Group ... COMTACGRU
Commander, Tactical Air Control Squadron ... COMTACRON
Commander, Tactical Air Force, Denmark (NATG) ... COMTAFDEN
Commander, Taiwan Defense Command (MUGU) ... COMTAIWANDEFCOMD
Commander, Taiwan Patrol Force (CINC) ... COMTAIWANPATFOR
Commander, Task Element ... CTE
Commander, Task Force ... CTF
Commander, Task Group ... CTG
Commander, Task Unit ... CTU
Commander, Texas Group ... COMTEXGRU
Commander, Tongue Point Group, Inactive Reserve Fleet, Pacific ... COMTONGRU
Commander, Torpedo Squadron ... COMTORPRON
Commander, Training Command, Atlantic ... COMTRALANT
Commander, Training Command, Pacific ... COMTRAPAC
Commander, Transport Division ... COMTRANSDIV
Commander, Transport Group ... COMTRANSGR
Commander, Transport Group, South Pacific Force ... COMTRANSGRSOPAC
Commander, Transportation Division ... CTD
Commander, Transports, Amphibious Force ... COMTRANSPHIB
Commander, Transports, Amphibious Force, Atlantic Fleet ... COMTRANSPHIBLANT
Commander, Transports, Amphibious Force, Pacific Fleet ... COMTRANSPHIBPAC
Commander, United Kingdom Air Defense Region (AFM) ... COMUKADR
Commander, United States Air Force Forces ... COMUSAFFOR
Commander, United States Air Force Southern Command (AFM) ... COMUSAFSO
Commander, United States Air Force Task Force (AABC) ... COMUSAFTF
Commander, United States Army Forces ... COMUSARFOR
Commander, United States Army Forces Southern Command (AABC) ... COMUSARSO
Commander, United States Army, Japan (CINC) ... COMUSARJAPAN
Commander, United States Army Task Force ... COMUSARTF
Commander, United States Atlantic Subarea ... COMUSLANT
Commander, United States Facility (DNAB) ... COMUSFAC
Commander, United States Fleet Air Wing, Mediterranean (AABC) ... COMUSFAIRWINGMED
Commander, United States Force, Caribbean (DNAB) ... COMUSFORCARIB
Commander, United States Force, Caribbean Representative (DNAB) ... COMUSFORCARIBREP
Commander, United States Force, Iceland (DNAB) ... COMUSFORICE
Commander, United States Force, Marianas (DNAB) ... COMUSFORMAR
Commander, United States Forces (CINC) ... COMUS
Commander, United States Forces, Azores (AFM) ... COMUSFORAZ
Commander, United States Forces, Japan (MCD) ... COMUSJ
Commander, United States Forces, Japan (AFM) ... COMUSJAPAN
Commander, United States Forces, Korea (MCD) ... COMUSK
Commander, United States Forces, Korea (AFM) ... COMUSKOREA
Commander, United States Forces, Marianas ... COMUSMARIANAS
Commander, United States Forces, Southeast Asia (CINC) ... COMUSSEASIA
Commander, United States Joint Task Force (AABC) ... COMUSJTF
Commander, United States Joint Unconventional Warfare Task Force ... COMUSJUWTF
Commander, United States Land Forces ... COMUSLANDFOR
Commander, United States Marine Forces (AABC) ... COMUSMARFOR
Commander, United States Marine Task Force (AABC) ... COMUSMARTF
Commander, United States Military Assistance Command, Thailand (AFM) ... COMUSMACTHAI
Commander, United States Military Assistance Command, Vietnam ... COMUSMACV
Commander, United States Military Group (AFM) ... COMUSMILGP
Commander, United States Naval Advanced Base [*Weser River, West Germany*] ... COUSNAB
Commander, United States Naval Forces (AABC) ... COMUSNAVFOR
Commander, United States Naval Forces, Southern Command (MUGU) ... COMUSNAVSO
Commander, United States Naval Task Force (AABC) ... COMUSNAVTF
Commander, United States Ports and Bases, France ... COMUSBASFRANCE
Commander, United States Rhine River Patrol (NATG) ... COMUSRHIN
Commander, United States Special Advisory Group (AFM) ... COMUSSAG
Commander, United States Taiwan Defense Command (AFM) ... COMUSTDC
Commander, US Naval Forces, Azores (DNAB) ... CNFA
Commander, US Naval Forces, Caribbean (DNAB) ... COMNAVFORCARIB
Commander, US Naval Forces, Caribbean Detachment (DNAB) ... COMNAVFORCARIBDET
Commander, US Naval Forces Central Command (ANA) ... COMUSNAVCENT
Commander, US Naval Forces, Far East (DNAB) ... COMNAVFORFE
Commander, US Naval Forces, Marianas (DNAB) ... CNM
Commander, US Naval Forces, Marianas (DNAB) ... COMNAVMAR
Commander, Utility Squadron ... COMUTRON
Commander, Utility Wing ... COMUTWING
Commander, Utility Wing, Service Force, Atlantic ... COMUTWINGSERVLANT
Commander, Utility Wing, Service Force, Pacific ... COMUTWINGSERVPAC
Commander, Western Sea Frontier (MUGU) ... COMWESTSEAFRON
Commander, Western Sea Frontier ... CWSF
Commander, Western Transport Air Force [*Travis AFB*] (CINC) ... COMWESTAF
Commanderie de Bordeaux (EA) ... CB
Commanderie de Bordeaux (EA) ... CdB
Commanderie des Cordons Bleus de France (EA) ... CCBF
Commander-in-Chief [*Air Force*] ... CIC
Commander-in-Chief ... CINC
Commander-in-Chief (NATG) ... C-in-C
Commander-in-Chief [*US fleet*] ... COMINCH
Commander-in-Chief, Air Force Atlantic Command (AFM) ... CINCAFLANT
Commander-in-Chief, Air Force Strike Command (AFM) ... CINCAFSTRIKE
Commander-in-Chief, Air Forces, Europe (NATG) ... CINCAFE
Commander-in-Chief, Alaskan Command ... CINCAL
Commander-in-Chief, Allied Air Forces, Central Europe (MCD) ... CINCAIRCENT
Commander-in-Chief, Allied Air Forces, Central Europe ... CINCALAIRCENEUR
Commander-in-Chief, Allied Forces ... CINCAF
Commander-in-Chief, Allied Forces, Central Europe [*NATO*] ... CINCCENT
Commander-in-Chief, Allied Forces, Central Europe (MCD) ... CINCENT
Commander-in-Chief, Allied Forces, Mediterranean [*NATO*] ... CINCAFMED
Commander-in-Chief, Allied Forces, Northern Europe [*NATO*] ... CINCNORTH
Commander-in-Chief, Allied Forces, Southern Europe [*NATO*] ... CINCSOUTH
Commander-in-Chief, Allied Land Forces, Central Europe (MCD) ... CINCLANDCENT
Commander-in-Chief, America West Indies Station [*British*] ... CINCAWI
Commander-in-Chief, [*US*] Army Forces, Atlantic (AABC) ... CINCARLANT
Commander-in-Chief, [*US*] Army Forces in the Pacific ... CINCAFPAC
Commander-in-Chief, [*US*] Army Forces, Pacific (AFM) ... CINCARPAC
Commander-in-Chief, Army Strike Command (AFM) ... CINCARSTRIKE
Commander-in-Chief, [*US*] Asiatic Fleet ... CINCAF
Commander-in-Chief, Atlantic ... CINCATL
Commander-in-Chief, Atlantic ... CINCLANT
Commander-in-Chief, Atlantic Airborne Command Post (DNAB) ... CINCLANT ABNCP
Commander-in-Chief, Atlantic and Pacific (AFIT) ... CINCLANT/PAC
Commander-in-Chief, Atlantic and West Indies ... CINCA & WI
Commander-in-Chief, Atlantic Coordination of Atomic Operations (DNAB) ... CINCLANT CAO
Commander-in-Chief, Atlantic Fleet [*Navy*] ... CINCLANTFLT
Commander-in-Chief, Atlantic Representative (DNAB) ... CINCLANTREP
Commander-in-Chief, British Pacific Fleet ... CINCBPF
Commander-in-Chief, Canadian Northwest Atlantic [*World War II*] ... C in C CNA
Commander-in-Chief, Caribbean ... CINCARIB
Commander-in-Chief Channel and Southern North Sea ... CINCHAN
Commander-in-Chief, Continental Air Command (AFM) ... CINCAC
Commander-in-Chief, Continental Air Defense Command ... CINCONAD
Commander-in-Chief, [*US Fleet*], Convoy and Routing Section ... COMROUTE
Commander-in-Chief, East Indies Station [*British*] ... CINCEI
Commander-in-Chief, Eastern Atlantic Area [*NATO*] ... CINCEASTLANT
Commander-in-Chief, Europe ... CINCEUR
Commander-in-Chief, Far East ... CINCFE
Commander-in-Chief, Far East Station [*British*] ... CINCFES
Commander-in-Chief, Far East Station [*British*] ... CINCFESTA
Commander-in-Chief, Fleet [*British*] ... CINCFLT
Commander-in-Chief, Home Forces [*British*] ... C-in-CHF
Commander-in-Chief, Iberian Atlantic Area (NATG) ... CINCIBERLANT
Commander-in-Chief, Japan Area [*World War II*] ... CINCJAPA
Commander-in-Chief, Mediterranean ... CINCMED
Commander-in-Chief, Middle East Land Forces (NATG) ... CINCMELF
Commander-in-Chief, Middle East/Southern Asia and Africa South of the Sahara [*Military*] ... CINCMEAFSA
Commander-in-Chief, Military Airlift Command ... CINCMAC
Commander-in-Chief, Naval Forces, Eastern Atlantic and Mediterranean ... CINCNAVEASTLANTMED
Commander-in-Chief, Naval Forces, Eastern Atlantic and Mediterranean ... CINCNELM
Commander-in-Chief, Netherlands Forces in the East ... CINCNEDE
Commander-in-Chief, North American Air Defense ... CINCNORAD
Commander-in-Chief, [*US*] Northeast Command ... CINCNE
Commander-in-Chief, Northern Europe ... CINCNOREUR

Commander-in-Chief, Pacific ..... CINCPAC
Commander-in-Chief, Pacific Air Forces ..... CINCPACAF
Commander-in-Chief, Pacific Fleet [*Navy*] ..... CCPF
Commander-in-Chief, Pacific Fleet [*Navy*] ..... CINCPACFLT
Commander-in-Chief, Pacific Fleet [*Navy*] (VNW) ..... COMCINCPACFLT
Commander-in-Chief, Pacific Fleet, Alternate Command Element Commander (DNAB) ..... CINCPACFLT ACE
Commander-in-Chief, [*US*] **Pacific Fleet and Pacific Ocean Areas** ..... CINCPAC-CINCPOA
Commander-in-Chief, Pacific Fleet, Emergency Command Center Commander (DNAB) ..... CINCPACFLT ECC
Commander-in-Chief, Pacific Fleet, Emergency Relocation Site Commander (DNAB) ..... CINCPACFLT ERS
Commander-in-Chief, [*US*] **Pacific Fleet Headquarters, Pearl Harbor** ..... CINCPACHEDPEARL
Commander-in-Chief, Pacific Fleet, Oceanic Airspace Coordinator (DNAB) ..... CINCPACFLT OAC
Commander-in-Chief, Pacific Fleet Representative (DNAB) ..... CINCPACFLTREP
Commander-in-Chief, Pacific Ocean Areas ..... CINCPOA
Commander-in-Chief, Pacific Ocean Areas Headquarters, Pearl Harbor ..... CINCPOAHEDPEARL
Commander-in-Chief, Pacific Representative (AABC) ..... CINCPACREP
Commander-in-Chief, Pacific Representative, Philippines ..... CINCPACREPPHIL
Commander-in-Chief, Pacific Staff Instruction (CINC) ..... CINCPACSTAFFINSTR
Commander-in-Chief, Readiness Command ..... CINCRED
Commander-in-Chief, Readiness Command ..... CINCREDCOM
Commander-in-Chief, Royal Danish Air Force (NATG) ..... CINCRDAF
Commander-in-Chief, Royal Danish Navy (NATG) ..... CINCRDN
Commander-in-Chief, Royal Norwegian Air Force (NATG) ..... CINCRNAF
Commander-in-Chief, Royal Norwegian Navy (NATG) ..... CINCRNORN
Commander-in-Chief, South Atlantic Station [*British*] ..... CINCSA
Commander-in-Chief, Southern Command (AFM) ..... CINCSO
Commander-in-Chief, Southwest Pacific Area [*World War II*] ..... CINCSWPA
Commander-in-Chief, Specified Command, Middle East ..... CINCSPECOMME
Commander-in-Chief, Strategic Air Command ..... CINCSAC
Commander-in-Chief, Strike Command ..... CINCSTRIKE
Commander-in-Chief, Tactical Air Command ..... CINCTAC
Commander-in-Chief, United Kingdom Air Force (NATG) ..... CINCUKAIR
Commander-in-Chief, United Kingdom Home Fleet [*Also, CINCHOMEFLT*] (NATG) ..... CINCHF
Commander-in-Chief, United Kingdom Home Fleet [*Also, CINCHF*] (NATG) ..... CINCHOMEFLT
Commander-in-Chief, United Nations Command ..... CINCUNC
Commander-in-Chief, United Nations Command, Korea ..... CINCUNCKOREA
Commander-in-Chief, United Nations Forces in Korea (MCD) ..... CINCUNK
Commander-in-Chief, United States Air Force, Atlantic (AFM) ..... CINCUSAFLANT
Commander-in-Chief, United States Air Force Strike (AFM) ..... CINCUSAFSTRIKE
Commander-in-Chief, United States Air Forces in Europe ..... CINCUSAFE
Commander-in-Chief, United States Army, Europe ..... CINCUSAREUR
Commander-in-Chief, United States Army Forces, Naval Supply Center, Oakland [*California*] ..... CINCUSAFNSCO
Commander-in-Chief, United States Army, Pacific (AABC) ..... CINCUSARPAC
Commander-in-Chief, United States Atlantic Command ..... USCINCLANT
Commander-in-Chief, United States Central Command ..... USCINCCENT
Commander-in-Chief, United States Fleet [*Later, COMINCH*] ..... CINCUS
Commander-in-Chief, United States Naval Forces, Europe ..... CINCUSNAVEUR
Commander-in-Chief, United States Naval Forces, Europe, Emergency Relocation Site Commander (DNAB) ..... CINCUSNAVEUR ERS
Commander-in-Chief, United States Naval Forces, Europe, Intelligence Data-Handling System (DNAB) ..... CINCUSNAVEUR IDHS
Commander-in-Chief, United States Pacific Command ..... USCINCPAC
Commander-in-Chief, United States/Thai Forces ..... CINCUSTAF
Commander-in-Chief, US Readiness Command (MCD) ..... USCINCREDCOM
Commander-in-Chief, Vietnamese Navy ..... CINCVNN
Commander-in-Chief, Western Approaches [*British World War II*] ..... C in C WA
Commander-in-Chief, Western Atlantic Area [*NATO*] ..... CINCWESTLANT
Commander-in-Chief, Western Pacific [*World War II*] ..... CINCWESPAC
Commander-Instructor [*Navy British*] CI
Commanders Availability Report (CINC) ..... CAR
Commander's Control and Monitoring Unit (DNAB) ..... CCMU
Commander's Critical Information Requirement [*Army*] (INF) ..... CCIR
Commander's Critical Item List [*Army*] (AABC) CCIL
Commander's Distinguished Visitors [*Program*] [*Air Force*] ..... CDV
Commanders Evaluation Report [*Army*] ..... CER
Commander's Independent Thermal Viewer [*Military*] (RDA) ..... CITV
Commander's Independent Viewer [*Army*] (INF) CIV
Commander's Integrated Display [*Military*] (RDA) ..... CID
Commander's Intelligent Display [*Military*] (RDA) ..... CID
Commanders' Internal Management Conference [*Air Force*] ..... CIMC
Commanders' Internal Management Review [*Also known as Black Saturday*] [*Military*] (AAG) ..... CIMR
Commander's Manual [*Military*] ..... CM
Commander's Narrative Analysis [*Military*] ..... CNA
Commander's Office Writer [*British military*] (DMA) ..... CW
Commanders Operational Intelligence Requirements (MCD) ..... COIR
Commander's Operations Security Support System (MCD) ..... COSS
Commander's Organization Orientation Program [*Military*] (INF) ..... COOP
Commanders Research and Development Objective ..... CR & DO
Commander's Statement and Budget Summary (AFIT) ..... CSBS
Commander's Surveillance and Target Acquisition Information Needs (MCD) ..... CSTAIN
Commanders' Target Criteria [*Army*] (ADDR) ..... CTC
Commanders Training Management System [*DoD*] ..... CTMS
Commander's Weapons Station (MCD) ..... CWS
Commandery of Knights Templar [*Freemasonry*] (ROG) ..... CKT
Commanding (WGA) ..... CDG
Commanding ..... CMDG
Commanding (AFM) ..... COMDG
Commanding ..... COMDG
Commanding ..... COMMDG
Commanding Army Audit Agency - Midwestern District ..... CAAA-MWD
Commanding General ..... CG
Commanding General ..... COMDGEN
Commanding General ..... COMGEN
Commanding General, Air Defense Command (NATG) ..... CGADC
Commanding General, Aircraft Fleet Marine Force, Atlantic (NATG) ..... CGAIRFMLANT
Commanding General, Aircraft Fleet Marine Force, Pacific (MUGU) ..... CGAIRFMFPAC
Commanding General, Army Air Forces ..... CGAAF
Commanding General, Army Forces, Mid-Pacific [*World War II*] ..... COMGENAFMIDPAC
Commanding General, Continental Army Command (NATG) ..... CGCARC
Commanding General, Continental Army Command (NATG) ..... CGCONARC
Commanding General, European Command (NATG) ..... COMGENEUCOM
Commanding General, Fleet Marine Force (DNAB) ..... CGFMF
Commanding General, Fleet Marine Force, Atlantic (NATG) ..... CGFMFLANT
Commanding General, Fleet Marine Force, Pacific (MUGU) ..... CGFMFPAC
Commanding General, Ground Forces [*World War II*] ..... CCGN
Commanding General, India-Burma Theater [*World War II*] ..... CGIBT
Commanding General, Marine Aircraft Group ..... CGMAG
Commanding General, Marine Aircraft Wing ..... CGMAW
Commanding General, Marine Base ..... CGMB
Commanding General, Marine Brigade ..... CGMARBRIG
Commanding General, Mediterranean Theater of Operations [*World War II*] ..... CGMTO
Commanding General, Mediterranean Theater of Operations [*World War II*] ..... COMGENMED
Commanding General, Pacific Ocean Areas [*World War II*] ..... COMGENPOA
Commanding General, South Pacific Area [*World War II*] ..... COMGENSOPAC
Commanding General, Strategic Air Command (NATG) ..... CGSAC
Commanding General, Tactical Air Command (NATG) ..... CGTAC
Commanding General, Tenth Army ..... COMGENTEN
Commanding General, Third Air Division (NATG) ..... COMGENTHIRDAIR
Commanding General, Third Marine Air Wing (MUGU) ..... CGTHIRDMAW
Commanding General, United States Air Forces, Europe (NATG) ..... COMGENUSAFE
Commanding General, United States Army Air Defense Command (MUGU) ..... CGARADCOM
Commanding General, United States Army Air Defense Command ..... CGUSARADCOM
Commanding General, United States Army, Alaska (MUGU) ..... CGUSARAL
Commanding General, United States Army Combat Developments Command ..... CGUSADC
Commanding General, United States Army Combat Developments Command (MUGU) ..... CGUSARCDC
Commanding General, United States Army Communications Zone, Europe (NATG) ..... CGUSACOMZEUR
Commanding General, United States Army, Europe (NATG) ..... COMGENUSAREUR
Commanding General, United States Army Forces (CINC) ..... CGUSARF
Commanding General, United States Army Material Command ..... CGUSAMC
Commanding General, United States Army Material Command (CINC) ..... CGUSARMAC
Commanding General, United States Army Material Command (MUGU) ..... CGUSARMC
Commanding General, United States Army, Ryukyu Islands (CINC) ..... CGUSARYIS
Commanding General, United States Continental Army Command [*Obsolete*] ..... CGUSCONARC
Commanding General, United States Forces, European Theater [*World War II*] ..... CGUSFET
Commanding General's Management Information System [*Army*] ..... CGMIS
Commanding Officer C
Commanding Officer ..... CO
Commanding Officer [*Military British*] (ROG) ..... COMDG
Commanding Officer ..... COMDG OF
Commanding Officer [*Military slang*] ..... KO
Commanding Officer, Air Evacuation Squadron ..... COAIREVACRON
Commanding Officer, Atlantic Coast ..... COAC
Commanding Officer, Landing Force Air Support Control Unit ..... COLANFORASCU
Commanding Officer, Naval Advanced Base ..... CONAB
Commanding Officer, Naval Air Base ..... CONAB
Commanding Officer, Naval Air Station ..... CONAS
Commanding Officer, Naval Air Wing ..... CONAIR
Commanding Officer, Naval Divisions [*Canada*] ..... COND
Commanding Officer, Naval Supply Depot (MCD) ..... CONSD
Commanding Officer, Observation Squadron ..... COOBSRON
Commanding Officer, Pacific Coast [*Navy Canada*] ..... COPC
Commanding Officer, Port of Embarkation ..... COPOE
Commanding Officer, Research Operations Detachment (DNAB) ..... CORSCHOPSDET
Commanding Officer Reserve Divisions [*World War II Canada*] ..... CORD
Commanding Officer, Section Base [*Navy*] ..... COSECTBASE
Commanding Officer, Submarine Chaser Training Center ..... COSCTRACEN
Commanding Officer, United States Ship ..... COUSS
Commanding Officer, United States Special Forces (Provisional) (CINC) ..... COUSSF(P)
Commanding Officer's Leave Listing (DNAB) ..... COLL
Commanding Officer's Narrative Report ..... CONAR
Commanding Officer's Punishment (DNAB) ..... COP

Commanding Officer's Tactical Display System [*Navy*] (MCD) ... COTDS
Commanding Officer's Tactical Plan [*or Plot*] [*Navy*] (NG) ... COTP
Commanding Officer's Wife [*Slang*] (DNAB) ... COW
Commandment, Defense Intelligence School (DNAB) ... CDIS
Commando (NATG) ... CDO
Commando (CINC) ... CMDO
Commando (AFM) ... COMDO
Commando Anticomunista del Sur [*Southern Anticommunist Commando*] [*Guatemala*] (PD) ... CADS
Commando Association, Victoria [*Australia*] ... CAV
Commando Forces, Royal Marines [*British*] ... CdoFcsRM
Commando Logistics Regiment, Royal Marines [*British*] ... CdoLogRegtRM
Commando Shackle Relay [*Intelligence gathering*] [*Vietnam*] (MCD) ... CSR
Commando Training Centre [*British*] ... CTC
Commando Training Centre, Royal Marines [*British military*] (DMA) ... CTCRM
Commandos Rouges [*Military group*] [*Chad*] (EY) ... Codos
Commands Interested Have by Mail [*Military*] (DNAB) ... COINT
Commelina Virus X [*Plant pathology*] ... COMVX
Commemorate ... COMMEM
Commemorating ... COMMEMG
Commemoratio Professorum Burdigalensium [*of Ausonius*] [*Classical studies*] (OCD) ... Prof Burd
Commemoration (ADA) ... COM
Commemoration (DSUE) ... COMMEM
Commemorative Bucks of Michigan ... CBM
Commemorative Collectors Society [*Long Eaton, Nottinghamshire, England*] (EAIO) ... CCS
Commemorative Stamp Club [*US Postal Service*] ... CSC
Commemorative Stamp Posters ... CSP
Commence (ROG) ... COCE
Commence (ROG) ... COMMCE
Commence Exercise [*Military*] (NVT) ... COMEX
Commencement (ROG) ... COMM
Commencement ... COMMNCMNT
Commencement (ROG) ... COMMT
Commencement and Termination [*British railroad term*] ... C and T
Commencement of Rifling (NATG) ... CR
Commencing ... COM'G
Commencing at a Point ... CAP
Commendation (AABC) ... CMD
Commendation Ribbon [*Military decoration*] ... CR
Commendation Ribbon with Medal Pendant [*Military decoration*] ... CRWMP
Commendation Ribbon with Metal Pendant [*Military decoration*] ... CRMPT
Comment (MSA) ... CMNT
Comment (AABC) ... CMT
Comment [*Legal term*] (DLA) ... Com
Comment and Data Integration and Printing (IAA) ... CADIAP
Comment Issue ... CI
Comment Recevez-Vous [*French*] ... CRV
Commentaar op het Oude Testament [*Kampen*] [*A publication*] (BJA) ... ComOT
Commentaar op het Oude Testament [*A publication*] (BJA) ... COT
Commentaar op het Oude Testament [*Kampen*] [*A publication*] (BJA) ... COuT
Commentaire du Nouveau Testament [*Neuchatel*] [*A publication*] (BJA) ... CNT
Commentaries on Laws of Scotland [*7 eds.*] [*1800-70*] [*A publication*] (DLA) ... Bell's Comm Bell's
Commentaries upon Littleton, by Sir Edward Coke [*A publication*] (DLA) ... Co Litt
Commentario Biblico "San Jeronimo" [*A publication*] (BJA) ... ComBibSJeron
Commentarium pro Religionis et Missionariis [*Rome*] [*A publication*] (BJA) ... ComRelMiss
Commentary ... COM
Commentary (WDMC) ... com
Commentary (ROG) ... COME
Commentary ... COMM
Commentary [*A publication*] (BRI) ... Comt
Commentary [*or Pesher on Habakkuk*] **from Qumran. Cave One** (BJA) ... 1QpHab
Commentary on Hosea from Qumran. Cave One (BJA) ... 1QpHos
Commentary on the Mishnah [*Maimonides*] (BJA) ... CM
Commentationes Humanorum Litterarum [*A publication*] (BJA) ... CHL
Commentator [*MARC relator code*] [*Library of Congress*] (LCCP) ... cmm
Commenti Spirituali dell'Antico Testamento/del Nuovo Testamento [*Rome*] [*A publication*] (BJA) ... ComSpirAT/NT
Commerce [*Legal shorthand*] (LWAP) ... CMC
Commerce (ABBR) ... CMRC
Commerce ... COM
Commerce [*or Commercial*] ... COMM
Commerce (AAGC) ... Comm
Commerce (ROG) ... COMMCE
Commerce ... COMMRCE
Commerce Acquisition Regulation [*Department of Commerce*] ... CAR
Commerce Action Group for the Near East [*Terminated, 1981*] ... CAGNE
Commerce and Finance ... C & F
Commerce Bancorp [*NASDAQ symbol*] (TTSB) ... COBA
Commerce Bancorp New Jersey [*NYSE symbol*] (SAG) ... CBH
Commerce Bancorp New Jersey [*Associated Press*] (SAG) ... CmcBNJ
Commerce Bancorp New Jersey [*NASDAQ symbol*] (SAG) ... COBA
Commerce Bancshares [*NASDAQ symbol*] (TTSB) ... CBSH
Commerce Bancshares, Inc. [*NASDAQ symbol*] (NQ) ... CBSH
Commerce Bancshares, Inc. [*Associated Press*] (SAG) ... CmcBMO
Commerce Bank (Harrisburg) [*Associated Press*] (SAG) ... CmcBHb
Commerce Bank (Harrisburg) [*NASDAQ symbol*] (SAG) ... COBH
Commerce Bk Harrisburg PA [*NASDAQ symbol*] (TTSB) ... COBH
Commerce Building Daily (USDC) ... CBD
Commerce Building Daily [*Marine science*] (OSRA) ... CBD
Commerce Business Daily [*A publication*] (AAGC) ... CBD
Commerce City, CO [*AM radio station call letters*] (RBYB) ... KLDC
Commerce Clearing House (DFIT) ... CCH
Commerce Clearing House, Inc. [*Publisher*] [*Chicago, IL*] ... CCH
Commerce Clearing House, Washington, DC [*Library symbol Library of Congress*] (LCLS) ... DCCH
Commerce Control List (AAGC) ... CCL
Commerce Court (DLA) ... Comm Ct
Commerce Department ... C
Commerce Department ... CD
Commerce Department Procurement Regulations ... COMPR
Commerce, GA [*AM radio station call letters*] ... WJJC
Commerce Group [*NASDAQ symbol*] (TTSB) ... CGCO
Commerce Group Corp. [*NASDAQ symbol*] (NQ) ... CGCO
Commerce Group, Inc. [*NYSE symbol*] (SAG) ... CGI
Commerce Group, Inc. [*Associated Press*] (SAG) ... CmceG
Commerce Group, Inc. [*Associated Press*] (SAG) ... CmceGp
Commerce Laboratory [*NASA*] ... COMLAB
Commerce Procurement Data System [*Marine science*] (OSRA) ... CPDS
Commerce Procurement Data System (USDC) ... CPDS
Commerce Productivity Center ... CPC
Commerce, Science, and Transportation (DLA) ... CST
Commerce Technical Advisory Board [*Terminated, 1981*] [*Department of Commerce*] (EGAO) ... CTAB
Commerce Total Return Fund, Inc. (MHDW) ... CTO
Commerce, TX [*FM radio station call letters*] ... KEMM
Commerce, TX [*FM radio station call letters*] ... KETR
Commercial [*FCC*] (NTCM) ... C
Commercial [*Rate*] [*Value of the English pound*] ... CM
Commercial ... CML
Commercial (WDMC) ... cml
Commercial (ABBR) ... CMRCL
Commercial ... CO
Commercial (ROG) ... COM
Commercial (WDMC) ... com
Commercial (AFM) ... COML
Commercial (AAGC) ... Comm
Commercial (WDMC) ... comml
Commercial (ROG) ... COMML
Commercial ... COMRCL
Commercial Activities ... CA
Commercial Activities Management Information System (AAGC) ... CAMIS
Commercial Activities Program (AAGC) ... CAP
Commercial Activities Program Detachment [*Military*] (DNAB) ... CAPDET
Commercial Activities Program Detachment Regional Office [*Military*] (DNAB) ... CAPDETREGOFF
Commercial Advance Design [*Reports*] (MCD) ... CAD
Commercial Advanced Gas-Cooled Reactor (NUCP) ... CAGR
Commercial Agent ... CA
Commercial Air ... CA
Commercial Air (NOAA) ... COMAIR
Commercial Air Freight Movement ... CAFM
Commercial Air Movement ... CAM
Commercial Air Transport (DA) ... CAT
Commercial Airlift Review Board [*DOD*] (AAGC) ... CARB
Commercial and Allied Workers' Union [*Somali Republic*] ... CAWU
Commercial and Government Entity (MCD) ... CAGE
Commercial and Industrial (GFGA) ... C & I
Commercial and Industrial Bulletin [*Ghana*] [*A publication*] (DLA) ... CIB
Commercial and Industrial-Type Activity (AABC) ... CITA
Commercial and Industrial-Type Functions [*Army*] (MCD) ... CITF
Commercial and Legal Reporter [*A publication*] (DLA) ... Com & Leg Rep
Commercial and Municipal Law Reporter [*A publication*] (DLA) ... Com & Mun L Rep
Commercial Announcement (NTCM) ... CA
Commercial Arbitration Centre [*Northern Territory*] [*Australia*] ... CAC
Commercial Art Program [*Association of Independent Colleges and Schools specialization code*] ... CA
Commercial Artists' Guild ... CAG
Commercial Assets [*AMEX symbol*] (SPSG) ... CAX
Commercial Assets, Inc. [*Associated Press*] (SAG) ... CmclAst
Commercial Assets Mobilization [*Navy*] (DOMA) ... CAM
Commercial, Automatic Test System [*Military*] ... CATE
Commercial Aviation (IAA) ... CA
Commercial Bancshares [*NASDAQ symbol*] (TTSB) ... CLBK
Commercial Bancshares, Inc. [*AMEX symbol*] (SAG) ... CWV
Commercial Bank (ROG) ... C
Commercial Bank ... CB
Commercial Bank Address File [*IRS*] ... CBAF
Commercial Bank of Australia ... CBA
Commercial Bank of Ethiopia. Market Report [*A publication*] ... CBEMR
Commercial Bank of Korea ... CBK
Commercial Bank of New York [*NASDAQ symbol*] (SAG) ... CBNY
Commercial Bank of New York [*Associated Press*] (SAG) ... CmcBNY
Commercial Banking Co. of Sydney [*Australia*] ... CBC
Commercial Bankshares, Inc. [*NASDAQ symbol*] (SAG) ... CLBK
Commercial Bankshares, Inc. [*Associated Press*] (SAG) ... CmclBsh
Commercial BASIC ... C-BASIC
Commercial Best Practices Laboratory [*Army*] ... Comm BPL
Commercial Bill of Lading [*Shipping*] ... CBL
Commercial Bill of Lading [*Shipping*] (DNAB) ... CMBL
Commercial Blanket Bond [*Insurance*] ... CBB
Commercial Breeder Reactor ... CBR
Commercial Building Energy Efficiency Program [*Australia*] ... CBEEP
Commercial Cable Co. (MHDW) ... CC
Commercial Cable Co. ... COMCABCO

Commercial Cane Sugar ... CCS
Commercial Carrier ... CC
Commercial Cases [*1896-1941*] [*England*] [*A publication*] (DLA) ... Com Cas
Commercial Cases, Small Cause Court [*1851-60*] [*Bengal, India*] [*A publication*] (DLA) ... Com Cas SCC
Commercial Cases, Small Cause Court [*1851-60*] [*Bengal, India*] [*A publication*] (DLA) ... Rep Com Cas
Commercial Casualty Products [*Insurance*] ... CCP
Commercial Casualty Underwriting [*Insurance*] ... CCU
Commercial Change Proposal (MCD) ... CCP
Commercial Chemical Development Association [*Later, CDA*] (EA) ... CCDA
Commercial Code (DLA) ... Com C
Commercial Code (DLA) ... Comm C
Commercial Commodity Acquisition Program [*DoD*] (RDA) ... CCAP
Commercial Communications Satellite [*Japan*] ... CCS
Commercial Communications Work Order [*Air Force*] ... CCWO
Commercial Computer Documentation Set (MCD) ... CCDS
Commercial Computer Security Center [*British*] ... CCSC
Commercial COMSEC [*Communications Security*] **Endorsement Program** [*NASA*] ... CCEP
Commercial Construction and Selected Materials Handling Equipment (RDA) ... CCE/SMHE
Commercial Construction Equipment [*Plan*] [*Army*] ... CCE
Commercial Construction Equipment and Military Adaptation of Commercial Items (MCD) ... CCE/MACI
Commercial Consumables (CINC) ... CC
Commercial Continuity [*Broadcasting*] (NTCM) ... CC
Commercial Contract Change ... CCC
Commercial Contracting Officer ... CCO
Commercial Contractor-Furnished Equipment (AAG) ... CCFE
Commercial Credit Corp. (MHDW) ... CCC
Commercial Customer-Furnished Equipment ... CCFE
Commercial Cut Flower Growers' Association of New South Wales [*Australia*] ... CCFGANSW
Commercial Data Management System [*Computer science*] (PDAA) ... CDMS
Commercial Data Processing Center (IEEE) ... CDPC
Commercial Demonstration Fast Reactor ... CDFR
Commercial Dental Laboratories of Indiana (SRA) ... CDLI
Commercial Development Association (EA) ... CDA
Commercial Dock [*Shipping*] ... CD
Commercial Driver's License ... CDL
Commercial Driver's License Information System [*FHWA*] (TAG) ... CDLIS
Commercial Driver's License Information System ... CDLS
Commercial Earth Station ... CES
Commercial Egg Producers' Association [*Australia*] ... CEPA
Commercial Electronic Equipment [*Military*] ... CEE
Commercial Engineer ... CE
Commercial Enterprise ... CE
Commercial Equipment ... CE
Commercial Equipment Requirement List ... CERL
Commercial Equivalent Equipment ... CEE
Commercial Exchange of Philadelphia [*Defunct*] (EA) ... CEP
Commercial Experiment Transporter [*BTS*] (TAG) ... COMET
Commercial Fast Reactor [*British*] ... CFR
Commercial Federal [*NYSE symbol*] (TTSB) ... CFB
Commercial Federal Corp. [*NYSE symbol*] (SAG) ... CFB
Commercial Federal Corp. [*Associated Press*] (SAG) ... CmcFdl
Commercial Finance Company [*Generic term*] ... CFC
Commercial Financial Corp. Ltd. [*Toronto Stock Exchange symbol*] ... CMF
Commercial Financial Services Inc. ... CFS
Commercial Fisheries Research and Development Act ... CFRDA
Commercial Fishing [*Type of water project*] ... CMF
Commercial Food Equipment Service Association (EA) ... CFESA
Commercial Ground (IAA) ... CG
Commercial Ground High (IAA) ... CGH
Commercial High Level Waste [*Nuclear energy*] (NUCP) ... CHLW
Commercial Import Division [*Vietnam*] ... CID
Commercial Import Program ... CIP
Commercial Industrial Marine [*Automotive engineering*] ... CIM
Commercial Industrial Services Program [*Navy*] ... CIS
Commercial Information Management System [*Department of Commerce*] ... CIMS
Commercial Instruction Processor [*Honeywell, Inc.*] ... CIP
Commercial Instruction Set ... CIS
Commercial Instrument Landing ... CIL
Commercial Internet Exchange (PCM) ... CIX
Commercial Intertech [*NYSE symbol*] (SAG) ... TEC
Commercial Intertech Corp. [*Associated Press*] (SAG) ... CmlTek
Commercial Investment Real Estate Journal [*Commercial-Investment Real Estate Council*] [*A publication*] ... CIREJ
Commercial Invoice (DS) ... Com/I
Commercial Item Description ... CID
Commercial Item Drawing (MCD) ... CID
Commercial Item Support Program [*DoD*] (RDA) ... CISP
Commercial Language (HGAA) ... COML
Commercial Law [*Canada*] (DLA) ... Com L
Commercial Law (DLA) ... Com Law
Commercial Law Annual [*A publication*] (DLA) ... Com LA
Commercial Law Annual [*A publication*] (DLA) ... Com Law Ann
Commercial Law Association of Australia. Bulletin [*A publication*] ... CLAA Bulletin
Commercial Law Association of Australia. Bulletin [*A publication*] ... CLAAB
Commercial Law Bulletin [*Commercial Law League of America*] [*A publication*] ... CLB
Commercial Law Journal [*Commercial Law League of America*] [*A publication*] ... CLJ
Commercial Law League. Journal [*A publication*] (DLA) ... Com L League J
Commercial Law League of America [*Chicago, IL*] (EA) ... CLLA
Commercial Law Quarterly [*Australia A publication*] ... CLQ
Commercial Law Quarterly [*A publication*] ... Com LQ
Commercial Law Quarterly [*Australia A publication*] ... Comm LQ
Commercial Law Reports [*Canada*] [*A publication*] (DLA) ... Comm LR
Commercial Laws of the World [*A publication*] (DLA) ... CLW
Commercial Lending Newsletter [*Robert Morris Associates (National Association of Bank Loan and Credit Offices)*] [*A publication*] ... CLN
Commercial Liability Insurance [*International Risk Management Institute*] [*A publication*] ... CLI
Commercial Licensed Evaluation Facilities [*British*] ... CLEFS
Commercial Loan Insurance Corp. ... CLIC
Commercial Manager (DCTA) ... CM
Commercial Manual [*DoD*] ... CM
Commercial Mariculture Council of Queensland [*Australia*] ... CMCQ
Commercial Market Appraisal ... CMA
Commercial Marketing Representative (AAGC) ... CMR
Commercial Measuring Equipment (SAA) ... CME
Commercial Metals [*NYSE symbol*] (TTSB) ... CMC
Commercial Metals Co. [*NYSE symbol*] (SPSG) ... CMC
Commercial Metals Co. [*Associated Press*] (SAG) ... CmclMtl
Commercial/Military Spares Release (MCD) ... CMSR
Commercial Mission [*NASA*] ... COMM
Commercial Motor Vehicle (ADA) ... CMV
Commercial Motor Vehicle Safety Act [*1986*] ... CMVSA
Commercial Multi-Engine [*Aviation*] (AIA) ... CME
Commercial Multi-Peril [*Insurance*] ... CMP
Commercial Museum, Philadelphia, PA [*Library symbol Library of Congress Obsolete*] (LCLS) ... PPComm
Commercial Net Lease Realty, Inc. [*Associated Press*] (SAG) ... CmclNL
Commercial Net Lease Realty, Inc. [*NYSE symbol*] (SAG) ... NNN
Commercial Net Lease Rlty [*NYSE symbol*] (TTSB) ... NNN
Commercial Nondevelopment Items [*Military*] (AABC) ... CNDI
Commercial Nondevelopment Items of Law Enforcement Equipment (MCD) ... CNDI-LEE
Commercial Nuclear Fuel Plant (NRCH) ... CNFP
Commercial Office of Spain (EA) ... COS
Commercial Off-the-Shelf [*Software*] ... COTS
Commercial Oil & Gas Ltd. [*Toronto Stock Exchange symbol*] ... CMO
Commercial Operating System (IAA) ... COS
Commercial Operation and Maintenance Manual [*Military*] ... COMM
Commercial Operational Requirements Document [*Military*] ... CORD
Commercial or Industrial and Control Service Data System ... CICS
Commercial or Industrial-Type Activities (AAGC) ... CITA
Commercial Orchid Growers' and Exporters' Association [*Australia*] ... COGEAA
Commercial Paper [*Banking*] (MHDW) ... Com'l Ppr
Commercial Paper [*Banking*] ... CP
Commercial Paper Note [*Banking*] ... CPN
Commercial Passenger Fishing Vessel ... CPFV
Commercial Performance Index (MHDW) ... CPI
Commercial Pilot's Licence [*British*] (DBQ) ... CPL
Commercial Practices Program [*Air Force*] ... CPP
Commercial Printing Co., Trenton, NJ [*Library symbol Library of Congress*] (LCLS) ... NjTCP
Commercial Product Acquisition Team (EA) ... COMPACT
Commercial Product Acquisition Team [*Later, COMPACT*] [*An association Defunct*] (EA) ... CPAT
Commercial Product Development ... CPD
Commercial Production of Electronic Solid State Systems (MCD) ... COMPRESS
Commercial Products List (AFIT) ... CPL
Commercial Program Development ... CPD
Commercial Projected Window [*Technical drawings*] ... CPW
Commercial Property Coverage [*Insurance*] ... CPC
Commercial Property Products ... CPP
Commercial Property Underwriting [*Insurance*] ... CPU
Commercial Quality ... CQ
Commercial Rabbit Association [*British*] (BI) ... CRA
Commercial Radio ... CR
Commercial Receiver Test Program ... CRTP
Commercial Refrigerator Manufacturers Association (EA) ... CRMA
Commercial Relations and Exports (DS) ... CRE
Commercial Satellite Communications System ... COMSATCOM
Commercial Satellite Systems [*Berkeley, CA*] [*Telecommunications*] (TSSD) ... CSS
Commercial Service Area [*Military*] (AFM) ... CSA
Commercial Service Authorization [*Military*] ... CSA
Commercial Services Group, New South Wales [*Australia*] ... CSGNSW
Commercial Sex Worker [*Social science terminology for a prostitute*] ... CSW
Commercial Solvents Corp. ... CSC
Commercial Solvents Corp., Terre Haute, IN [*Library symbol Library of Congress Obsolete*] (LCLS) ... InTCS
Commercial Space Launch Act ... CSLA
Commercial Space Package ... CSP
Commercial Space Transportation Advisory Committee [*Department of Transportation*] [*Washington, DC*] (EGAO) ... COMSTAC
Commercial Spares Release ... CSR
Commercial Standard [*A publication*] ... CS
Commercial Steamship Company ... CSC
Commercial Subroutine Package [*IBM Corp.*] (BUR) ... CSP
Commercial Subsurface Transformer (IAA) ... CST
Commercial Synchronous Communication Satellite (NASA) ... CSCSAT
Commercial System [*Data General Corp.*] ... CS
Commercial Technology and Industrial Base (AAGC) ... CTIB
Commercial Telegraphers' Union [*Later, C/UBC*] (EA) ... CTU

Commercial Telegraphers Union (HGAA) ... CTUNA
Commercial Teleoperator Maneuvering System (SSD) ... CTMS
Commercial Television [*FCC*] (NTCM) ... CT
Commercial Television ... CTV
Commercial Test Equipment (MCD) ... CTE
Commercial Text-Books [*A publication*] ... CTB
Commercial Traffic Bulletin ... CTB
Commercial Trailer Association [*British*] ... CTA
Commercial Trailer-Mounted Generator Set Assembly ... CTMGSA
Commercial Training Device ... CTD
Commercial Training Device Requirement ... CTDR
Commercial Transaction System [*Business term*] (MHDB) ... CTS
Commercial Translator ... COMTRAN
Commercial Translator (IEEE) ... CT
Commercial Transport Navigation Display System ... CTNDS
Commercial Transportation Officer ... CTO
Commercial Traveler ... CT
Commercial Travelers Insurance Federation [*Defunct*] ... CTIF
Commercial Travellers and Sales Representatives' Guild of Western Australia ... CTSRGWA
Commercial Travellers' Association of Queensland [*Australia*] ... CTAQ
Commercial Travellers' Association of Western Australia ... CTAWA
Commercial Tribunal [*South Australia*] ... CT
Commercial Tribunal, New South Wales [*Australia*] ... CTNSW
Commercial Tribunal of Western Australia ... CTWA
Commercial Truck Maintenance Association (MHDB) ... CTMA
Commercial Type Property ... CTP
Commercial Union Assurance Co. Ltd. [*British*] (ECON) ... CU
Commercial Union Assurance Company of Australia Ltd. ... CUA
Commercial Users Program for Index Data (PDAA) ... CUPID
Commercial Utilisation Area ... CUA
Commercial Utility Cargo Vehicle [*Army*] (RDA) ... CUCV
Commercial Utility Vehicle ... CUV
Commercial Value ... CV
Commercial Value Movement Order (DCTA) ... CVMO
Commercial Vehicle [*Automotive engineering*] ... CV
Commercial Vehicle and Road Transport Club [*British*] (BI) ... CVRTC
Commercial Vehicle Industry Association of South Australia ... CVIASA
Commercial Vehicle Industry Association of Victoria [*Australia*] ... CVIAV
Commercial Vehicle Information System and Network ... CVISN
Commercial Vehicle Maintenance Implications (MCD) ... CVMI
Commercial Vehicle Manufacturers' Association [*Australia*] ... CVMA
Commercial Vehicle Operations [*Highway safety*] ... CVO
Commercial Vehicle Operations ... CVO
Commercial Vehicle Repair Parts (MCD) ... CVRP
Commercial Vehicle Safety Alliance [*FHWA*] [*RSPA*] (TAG) ... CVSA
Commercial Vehicle Substitute ... C/S
Commercial Warehouse Field Officer [*Military*] ... CWFO
Commercial Water Movement Number ... CWM
Commercial Weight ... CW
Commercial Wire Center Forecast Program [*Telecommunications*] (TEL) ... COMFOR
Commercial Zone (BARN) ... cmmz
Commercial-Accounts Receivable Management System (PDAA) ... C-ARMS
Commercial-Investment Real Estate Council (EA) ... CIREC
Commercialism (ABBR) ... CMRCLSM
Commercialist (ABBR) ... CMRCLST
Commercialistic (ABBR) ... CMRCLSTC
Commercialize (ABBR) ... CMRCLZ
Commercialized (ABBR) ... CMRCLZD
Commercializing (ABBR) ... CMRCLZG
Commercially Available (DNAB) ... CA
Commercially Available/Fabricated Training Device ... CAFTD
Commercially Available/Fabricated Training Device Requirement ... CAFTDR
Commercially Available/Fabricated Training Device Requirement ... CAFTR
Commercially Available Organic Chemicals Index [*Chemical Notation Association*] [*Databank*] [*British*] ... CAOCI
Commercially Developed Space Facility [*Proposed*] ... CDSF
Commercially Important Person ... CIP
Commercially Owned, Commercially Operated (AFIT) ... COCO
Commercially Owned, Government-Operated (AFIT) ... COGO
Commercial-Type Product (AAGC) ... CIP
Commerical Bank of Wales [*British*] ... CBW
Commerical Control (SAA) ... CC
Commericial Air Services (Pty) Ltd. [*South Africa ICAO designator*] (FAAC) ... CAW
Commingled Real Estate Funds (MHDW) ... CREF
Commiserate (ABBR) ... CMSRA
Commiserated (ABBR) ... CMSRAD
Commiserating (ABBR) ... CMSRAG
Commiseration (ABBR) ... CMSRAN
Commiserative (ABBR) ... CMSRAV
Commiseratively (ABBR) ... CMSRAVY
Commiserator (ABBR) ... CMSRAR
Commisioner of Metropolitan Police (BARN) ... CMP
Commissar (ABBR) ... CMSAR
Commissar (ABBR) ... CMSR
Commissar ... COMR
Commissariat ... COMRT
Commissariat a l'Energie Atomique [*Atomic Energy Commission - AEC*] [*France Research center*] ... CEA
Commissariat and Transport Corps [*British military*] (DMA) ... CTC
Commissariat for Montagnard Affairs ... CMA
Commissariat Staff Corps [*British military*] (DMA) ... CSC
Commissary [*Marine Corps*] ... C
Commissary (ABBR) ... CMSARY
Commissary (ABBR) ... CMSRY
Commissary ... COM
Commissary (ADA) ... COMM
Commissary ... COMMY
Commissary ... COMSRY
Commissary [*Air Force*] (AFM) ... COMSY
Commissary ... COMSY
Commissary Accounting and Reporting System [*Army*] ... CARP
Commissary Accounting and Reporting System [*Army*] ... CARS
Commissary Civilian Career Enhancement Program [*Air Force*] ... CCCEP
Commissary of Subsistence [*Military British*] (HGAA) ... Com Sub
Commissary of Subsistence [*Military British*] (ROG) ... CS
Commissary Operating Manual (AABC) ... COM
Commissary Operating Program [*Air Force*] (AFM) ... COP
Commissary Privilege Card [*DoD*] ... CPC
Commissary Resale Division of the Army Stock Fund (AABC) ... CORDASF
Commissary Store [*Military*] (DNAB) ... COMSYSTO
Commissary Store [*Army*] (AABC) ... COMSYSTR
Commissary Store [*Navy*] ... CS
Commissary Store Region [*Military*] (DNAB) ... COMSYSTOREG
Commissary Store Region Detachment [*Military*] (DNAB) ... COMSYSTOREGDET
Commissary Store Reserve Fund [*Military*] (DNAB) ... CSRF
Commissary Store Reserve Fund Grant [*Military*] (DNAB) ... CSRFG
Commissary Technician, Medical ... CMT
Commissary-General ... CG
Commissary-General [*British military*] (DMA) ... Com-Gen
Commissary-General of Subsistence [*Army British*] ... CGS
Commissaryman [*Navy rating*] ... CS
Commissaryman, First Class [*Navy rating*] ... CS1
Commissaryman, Master Chief [*Navy rating*] ... CSCM
Commissaryman, Second Class [*Navy rating*] ... CS2
Commissaryman, Third Class [*Navy rating*] ... CS3
Commissie voor Bibliografie en Documentatie [*Netherlands Bibliographical and Documentary Committee*] [*Information service or system*] (IID) ... COBIDOC
Commissie voor Internationaal Recht [*United Nations*] ... CIR
Commission [*Business term*] ... Cmm
Commission ... CMMN
Commission (DNAB) ... CMN
Commission (FAAC) ... CMSN
Commission (ABBR) ... CMSSN
Commission [*or Commissioner*] (AABC) ... COM
Commission (KSC) ... COMM
Commission (DD) ... comm
Commission (AAGC) ... Comm
Commission (DLA) ... Commiss
Commission ... COMMN
Commission ... COMMSN
Commission ... COMN
Commission (AFM) ... COMSN
Commission [*French Business term*] ... Con
Commission ... SOMM
Commission Africaine de l'Aviation Civile [*African Civil Aviation Commission - AFCAC*] (EAIO) ... CAFAC
Commission and Warrant [*British military*] (DMA) ... CW
Commission Canadienne de l'Annee Internationale de l'Enfant [*Canadian Commission for the International Year of the Child*] ... CCAIE
Commission Canadienne de Pedologie [*National Soil Survey Committee*] [*Canadian Department of Agriculture*] ... CCP
Commission Canadienne des Droits de la Personne [*Canadian Human Rights Commission - CHRC*] ... CCDP
Commission Canadienne des Grains [*Canadian Grain Commission*] ... CCG
Commission Canadienne du Ble [*Canadian Wheat Board - CWB*] ... CCB
Commission Canadienne du Lait [*Canadian Dairy Commission - CDC*] ... CCL
Commission Canadienne pour la Theorie des Machines et des Mecanismes [*Canadian Committee for the Theory of Machines & Mechanisms*] (AC) ... CCTMM
Commission Centrale pour la Navigation du Rhin [*Central Commission for the Navigation of the Rhine*] ... CCR
Commission Certified [*Bacteriology*] ... CC
Commission d'Appel de l'Immigration [*Immigration Appeal Board - IAB*] [*Canada*] ... CAI
Commission de Controle de l'Energie Atomique [*Atomic Energy Control Board - AECB*] ... CCEA
Commission de Cooperation Technique en Afrique [*Commission for Technical Cooperation in Africa*] ... CCTA
Commission de la Carte Geologique du Monde [*Commission for the Geological Map of the World - GMW*] (EAIO) ... CCGM
Commission de la Fonction Publique du Canada [*Public Service Commission - PSC*] [*Canada*] ... CFPC
Commission de la Sante et de la Securite du Travail du Quebec [*Quebec Workers Health and Security Commission*] [*Montreal*] [*Information service or system*] (IID) ... CSST
Commission de la Sante et de la Securite du Travail du Quebec, Montreal [*Library symbol National Library of Canada*] (NLC) ... QMCAT
Commission de la Sante et de la Securite du Travail du Quebec, Quebec, Quebec [*Library symbol National Library of Canada*] (NLC) ... QQCAT
Commission de l'Acces a l'Information, Centre de Documentation, Quebec, PQ, Canada [*Library symbol*] [*Library of Congress*] (LCLS) ... CaQQCAI
Commission de l'Enseignement Superieur des Provinces Maritimes [*Maritime Provinces Higher Education Commission*] [*Canada*] ... CESPM
Commission de Paris [*Paris Commission - PARCOM*] (EAIO) ... CP
Commission de Police du Quebec, Ste.-Foy, PQ, Canada [*Library symbol Library of Congress*] (LCLS) ... CaQSFCP

Commission de Police du Quebec, Ste.-Foy, Quebec [*Library symbol National Library of Canada*] (NLC) .... QSFCP

Commission de Representants Permanents [*Committee of Permanent Representatives*] [*EEC*] .... COREPER

Commission de Toponymie du Quebec, Quebec, Quebec [*Library symbol National Library of Canada*] (NLC) .... QQCT

Commission de Toponymie, Quebec, PQ, Canada [*Library symbol Library of Congress*] (LCLS) .... CaQQCT

Commission de Transport de la Communaute Urbaine de Montreal, Montreal, PQ, Canada [*Library symbol Library of Congress*] (LCLS) ..... CaQMCT

Commission de Transport de la Communaute Urbaine de Montreal, Quebec [*Library symbol National Library of Canada*] (NLC) .... QMCT

Commission d'Enquete pour le Crime Organise [*Organized Crime Investigating Commission*] [*Canada*] .... CECO

Commission des Accidents du Travail, Montreal, PQ, Canada [*Library symbol Library of Congress*] (LCLS) .... CaQMCAT

Commission des Champs de Bataille Nationaux [*National Battlefields Commission - NBC*] [*Canada*] .... CCBN

Commission des Communautes Europeennes [*Commission of the European Communities - CEC*] [*Belgium*] (EA) .... CCE

Commission des Droits de la Personne du Quebec, Montreal, Quebec [*Library symbol National Library of Canada*] (NLC) .... QMQDP

Commission des Droits de la Personne du Quebec, Quebec, Quebec [*Library symbol National Library of Canada*] (NLC) .... QQCDP

Commission des Episcopats de la Communaute Europeenne [*Association of Episcopacies of the European Community*] (EA) .... COMECE

Commission des Federations et Syndicats Nationaux des Entreprises de Recuperation de Ferrailles du Marche Commun [*Committee of the National Ferrous Scrap Federations and Associations of the Common Market - CNFSFACM*] (EAIO) .... COFENAF

Commission des Instruments et des Methodes d'Observation [*Commission for Instruments and Methods of Observation*] [*OMI*] .... CIMO

Commission des Nations Unies pour l'Inde et le Pakistan .... CNUIP

Commission des Nations Unies pour l'Unification et le Relevement de la Coree .... CNUURC

Commission des Operations de Bourse .... COB

Commission des Relations de Travail dans la Fonction Publique [*Public Service Staff Relations Board - PSSRB*] [*Canada*] .... CRTFP

Commission des Reparations [*Reparation Commission*] [*France*] .... CDR

Commission des Services Juridiques du Quebec, Montreal, Quebec [*Library symbol National Library of Canada*] (NLC) .... QMJSJ

Commission des Valeurs Mobilieres de Quebec, Quebec, PQ, Canada [*Library symbol Library of Congress*] (LCLS) .... CaQMCVM

Commission des Valeurs Mobilieres du Quebec, Montreal, Quebec [*Library symbol National Library of Canada*] (NLC) .... QMCVM

Commission d'Histoire de l'Historiographie [*Commission of the History of Historiography*] [*Ceret, France*] (EAIO) .... CHH

Commission du Codex Alimentarius [*Joint FAO-WHO Codex Alimentarius Commission*] (EA) .... CAC

Commission du Commerce International des Produits de Base [*United Nations*] .... CCIP

Commission du Danube [*Danube Commission - DC*] (EAIO) .... CD

Commission du Droit International [*United Nations*] .... CDI

Commission du Pacifique Sud [*South Pacific Commission - SPC*] (EAIO) .... CPS

Commission Dyers and Finishers' Association of Australia .... CDFAA

Commission Economique et Sociale pour l'Asie et le Pacifique [*Economic and Social Commission for Asia and the Pacific*] [*French United Nations*] (DUND) .... CESAP

Commission Economique et Sociale pour l'Asie Occidentale [*Economic and Social Commission for Western Asia - ESCWA*] (EAIO) .... CESAO

Commission Economique pour l'Afrique [*Economic Commission for Africa - ECA*] (EAIO) .... CEA

Commission Economique pour l'Europe [*Economic Commission for Europe - ECE*] [*French*] .... CEE

Commission Economique pour l'Europe/Organisation des Nations Unies [*Economic Commission for Europe/United Nations Organization*] (EAIO) .... CEE/ONU

Commission Electrotechnique Internationale [*International Electrotechnical Commission - IEC*] [*Switzerland*] (EAIO) .... CEI

Commission Episcopale de Cooperation Apostolique Canada-Amerique Latine .... CECAL

Commission Europeenne de Corrosion des Conduites Souterraines [*Brussels, Belgium*] (EAIO) .... CEOCOR

Commission Europeenne de la Corseterie [*European Corsetry Commission - ECC*] (EAIO) .... CEC

Commission Europeenne de l'Aviation Civile [*European Civil Aviation Conference - ECAC*] (EAIO) .... CEAC

Commission Europeenne de Marketing Industriel [*European Commission for Industrial Marketing*] [*Brixham, Devonshire, England*] (EAIO) .... CEMI

Commission Europeenne de Tourisme [*European Travel Commission - ETC*] [*Paris, France*] .... CET

Commission Europeenne des Constructeurs d'Appareillage Electrique d'Installations [*European Commission of Manufacturers of Electrical Installation Equipment*] (EAIO) .... CECAPI

Commission Europeenne des Droits de l'Homme [*European Commission of Human Rights - ECHR*] (EA) .... CEDH

Commission Europeenne des Forets .... CEF

Commission for Acceleration of Black Participation in Psychology .... CABPP

Commission for Accountability to the Public (EA) .... CAP

Commission for Aeronautical Meteorology [*WMO*] (MSC) .... CAeM

Commission for Agricultural Meteorology [*WMO*] (MSC) .... CAgM

Commission for Agricultural Meteorology [*WMO*] (ASF) .... CAM

Commission for Atmospheric Sciences [*WMO*] (MSC) .... CAS

Commission for Basic Systems [*WMO*] (MSC) .... CBS

Commission for Catholic Missions among the Colored People and the Indians (EA) .... CCMACPI

Commission for Climatology [*Marine science*] (OSRA) CCl

Commission for Climatology [*WMO*] CCl

Commission for Controlling the Desert Locust in North-West Africa [*United Nations*] (EA) .... CCDLNWA

Commission for Controlling the Desert Locust in the Near East [*United Nations*] (EA) .... CCDLNE

Commission for Development and Exchange [*International Council of Scientific Unions*] .... CDE

Commission for Educational Exchange between the United States of America and Afghanistan .... CEEUSA

Commission for Fisheries Research in the West Pacific .... WPFC

Commission for Geographical Education (EA) .... GCE

Commission for Historical Architectural Preservation .... CHAP

Commission for Hydrology [*World Meteorological Organization*] (GFGA) .... CHy

Commission for International Development (EA) .... CID

Commission for International Due Process of Law (EA) .... CIDPL

Commission for International Educational Reconstruction .... CIER

Commission for Local Administration [*British*] (BARN) .... CLA

Commission for Marine Geology [*of the International Union of Geological Sciences*] (EAIO) .... CMG

Commission for Marine Meteorology [*Marine science*] (OSRA) .... CMM

Commission for Maritime Meteorology [*World Meteorological Organization*] .... CMM

Commission for Organizing the Party of the Working People of Ethiopia (PD) .... COPWE

Commission for Racial Equality [*British*] .... CRE

Commission for Racial Justice (EA) .... CRJ

Commission for Social Justice (EA) .... CSJ

Commission for Special Applications of Meteorology and Climatology [*World Meteorological Organization*] .... CoSAMC

Commission for Synoptic Meteorology .... CSM

Commission for Teacher Preparation and Licensing .... CTPL

Commission for Technical Cooperation for Africa .... CTCA

Commission for the Accreditation of Public Libraries [*Proposed*] .... CAPL

Commission for the Advancement of Public Interest Organizations (EA) .... CAPIO

Commission for the Conservation of the Antarctic Marine Living Resources [*Australia*] (EAIO) .... CCAMLR

Commission for the Defense of Human Rights in Central America (EA) .... CDHRCA

Commission for the Exploration and Utilization of Space [*Former USSR*] .... CEUS

Commission for the Geological Map of the World [*Marine science*] (OSRA) .... CGMW

Commission for World Christian Action .... CWCA

Commission Gastronomique, Vinicole, et Touristique (EA) .... CGVT

Commission Generale de l'Assurance du Risque Atomique [*Paris, France*] (EAIO) .... CGARA

Commission Indo-Pacific des Peches [*Indo-Pacific Fishery Commission - IPFC*] (EAIO) .... CIPP

Commission Interamericaine d'Energie Nucleaire [*Inter-American Nuclear Energy Commission*] .... CIEN

Commission International d'Aeromodelisme [*International Aeromodelling Commission*] (PDAA) .... CIAM

Commission Internationale Catholique pour les Migrations [*International Catholic Migration Commission - ICMC*] [*Geneva, Switzerland*] (EAIO) ...... CICM

Commission Internationale Contre le Regime Concentrationnaire [*International Commission Against the Regime of Concentration Camps*] [*France*] .... CICRC

Commission Internationale d'Analyses .... CIA

Commission Internationale de Certification de Conformite de l'Equipement Electrique [*International Commission for Conformity Certification of Electrical Equipment*] [*French*] (EA) .... CEE

Commission Internationale de Juristes [*International Commission of Jurists - ICJ*] [*Switzerland*] .... CIJ

Commission Internationale de la Medecine du Travail [*International Commissionof Occupational Health - ICOH*] [*Information service or system*] (IID) .... CIMT

Commission Internationale de la Navigation Aerienne [*International Air Navigation Commission*] .... CINA

Commission Internationale de la Nomenclature Anatomique Veterinaire [*International Committee on Veterinary Anatomical Nomenclature - ICVAN*] [*Zurich, Switzerland*] (EAIO) .... CINAV

Commission Internationale de l'Eclairage [*International Commission on Illumination*] [*Vienna, Austria*] (EAIO) .... CIE

Commission Internationale de l'Enseignement de la Physique [*International Commission on Physics Education - ICPE*] (EAIO) .... CIEP

Commission Internationale de l'Etat Civil [*International Commission on Civil Status - ICCS*] (EAIO) .... CIEC

Commission Internationale de Lutte Biologique Contre les Ennemis des Cultures .... CILB

Commission Internationale de Marketing [*International Marketing Commission - IMC*] [*Brixham, Devonshire, England*] (EAIO) .... CIM

Commission Internationale de Meteorologie Aeronautique [*OMI*] .... CIMAe

Commission Internationale de Nomenclature Zoologique [*International Commission on Veterinary Anatomical Nomenclature*] [*British*] (EAIO) .... CINZ

Commission Internationale de Numismatique [*International Numismatic Commission*] [*Oslo, Norway*] (EA) .... CIN

Commission Internationale de Reglementation en veu de l'Approbation de l'Equipement Electrique [*International Commission on Rules for the Approval of Electrical Equipment*] (PDAA) .... CEE

Commission Internationale de Tourisme Aerien .... CITA

Commission Internationale des Activites Commerciales [*International Commission on Commercial Activities*] (EAIO) .... CAIC
Commission Internationale des Aumoniers Generaux des Prisons [*International Commission of Catholic Prison Chaplains - ICPC*] (EA) .... CIAGP
Commission Internationale des Examens de Conduite Automobile [*International Driving Tests Committee*] (EAIO) .... CIECA
Commission Internationale des Grands Barrages [*International Commission on Large Dams - ICOLD*] (EAIO) .... CIGB
Commission Internationale des Industries Agricoles et Alimentaires [*International Commission for Food Industries*] (EAIO) .... CIIA
Commission Internationale des Irrigations et du Drainage [*International Commission on Irrigation and Drainage - ICID*] (EAIO) .... CIID
Commission Internationale des Methodes d'Analyse des Pesticides [*Collaborative International Pesticides Analytic Council - CIPAC*] (EAIO) .... CIMAP
Commission Internationale des Peches de l'Atlantique Sud-Est [*International Commission for the Southeast Atlantic Fisheries - ICSEAF*] [*Madrid, Spain*] (EAIO) .... CIPASE
Commission Internationale des Professionals de la Sante (EAIO) .... CINPROS
Commission Internationale des Professionels de la Sante [*International Commission of Health Professionals for Health and Human Rights - ICHP*] (EA) .... CINPROS
Commission Internationale d'Etudes de la Police de Circulation [*International Study Commission for Traffic Police*] .... CIEPC
Commission Internationale d'Histoire Militaire [*International Commission of Military History*] (EAIO) .... CIHM
Commission Internationale d'Optique [*International Commission for Optics - ICO*] (EAIO) .... CIO
Commission Internationale du Chataignier CIC
Commission Internationale du Genie Rural [*International Commission of Agricultural Engineering*] [*ICSU*] (EAIO) .... CIGR
Commission Internationale du Peuplier [*International Poplar Commission*] .... CIP
Commission Internationale du Riz [*International Rice Commission - IRC*] [*United Nations*] (EAIO) .... CIR
Commission Internationale du Verre [*International Commission on Glass - ICG*] (EAIO) CIV
Commission Internationale Medico-Physiologique [*International Medico-Physiological Commission*] (PDAA) .... CIMP
Commission Internationale Permanente pour l'Epreuve des Armes a Feu [*Permanent International Commission for the Proof of Small-Arms - PICPSA*] (EAIO) .... CIP
Commission Internationale pour la Conservation des Thonides de l'Atlantique [*International Commission for the Conservation of Atlantic Tunas - ICCAT*] .... CICTA
Commission Internationale pour la Protection de la Moselle Contre la Pollution [*International Commission for the Protection of the Moselle Against Pollution - ICPMP*] (EA) .... CIPMP
Commission Internationale pour la Protection des Regions Alpines [*International Commission for the Protection of Alpine Regions*] (EAIO) .... CIPRA
Commission Internationale pour la Reglementation des Ascenseurs et Monte-Charge [*International Committee for Lift Regulations - ICLR*] (EAIO) .... CIRA
Commission Internationale pour la Sauvegarde du Patrimoine Culturel Islamique [*International Commission for the Preservation of Islamic Cultural Heritage - ICPICH*] (EA) .... CISPCI
Commission Internationale pour le Sauvetage Alpin [*International Commission for Alpine Rescue*] .... CISA
Commission Internationale pour l'Enseignement des Mathematiques [*International Commission on Mathematical Instruction - ICMI*] (EA) .... CIEM
Commission Internationale pour l'Etude Scientifique de la Famille [*International Scientific Commission on the Family*] .... COMIFA
Commission Internationale pour l'Exploration Scientifique de la Mer Mediterranee[*International Commission for the Scientific Exploration of the Mediterranea n Sea - ICSEM*] [*Monaco*] [*Research center*] (IRC) .... CIESM
Commission Internationale pour l'Organisation Scientifique du Travail en Agriculture [*International Committee of Scientific Management in Agriculture*] .... CIOSTA
Commission Internationale Technique de Sucrerie [*International Commission of Sugar Technology*] (EAIO) .... CITS
Commission Intersyndicale des Deshydrateurs Europeens [*European Dehydrators Association*] [*Common Market Paris, France*] .... CIDE
Commission Leaflets, American Telephone and Telegraph Cases [*A publication*] (DLA) CL
Commission Medicale Chretienne [*Christian Medical Commission*] [*Geneva, Switzerland*] (EA) .... CMC
Commission Mixte Internationale pour les Experiences Relatives a la Protection des Lignes de Telecommunication et des Canalisations Souterraines [*Joint International Commission for the Protection of Telecommunication Lines and Underground Ducts*] [*Switzerland*] .... CMI
Commission Mondiale d'Action Professionnelle [*World Committee for Trade Action - WCTA*] (EA) .... CMAP
Commission Oceanographique Intergouvernementale [*Intergovernmental Oceanographic Commission - IOC*] (EAIO) .... COI
Commission of Accredited Truck Driving Schools (EA) .... CATDS
Commission of Assembly of the Church of Scotland (DAS) .... CAC
Commission of Editors of Biochemical Journals .... CEBJ
Commission of Fine Arts [*Independent government agency*] .... CFA
Commission of International Union of Crystallography [*British*] .... CIUC
Commission of Professors of Adult Education (EA) .... CPAE
Commission of the Churches on International Affairs [*Switzerland*] (EAIO) .... CCIA
Commission of the Churches on International Affairs (of the World Council of Churches) (EA) .... CCIA/WCC
Commission of the European Communities [*See also CCE*] (EAIO) .... CEC
Commission of the Status and Role of Women (EA) .... CSRW
Commission of United States Latin American Relations (EA) .... CUSLAR
Commission on Accreditation for Law Enforcement Agencies (EA) .... CALEA
Commission on Accreditation of Rehabilitation Facilities (EA) .... CARF
Commission on Accreditation of Service Experiences [*Later, OECC*] .... CASE
Commission on Accreditations of Allied Health Education Programs (PGP) .... CAAHEP
Commission on Administrative Review [*House of Representatives*] .... CAR
Commission on Agricultural Workers (ECON) .... CAW
Commission on American Shipbuilding .... CAS
Commission on Archives and History of the United Methodist Church (EA) .... CAHUMC
Commission on Art and Antiquities .... CAA
Commission on Asian and Far Eastern Affairs of the International Chamber of Commerce .... CAFEA-ICC
Commission on Asian and Pacific Affairs [*International Chamber of Commerce*] .... CAPA
Commission on Atmospheric Chemistry and Global Pollution [*British*] .... CACGP
Commission on Biochemical Nomenclature [*IUPAC*] .... CBN
Commission on Chicago Historical and Architectural Landmarks .... CCHAL
Commission on Civil Rights .... CCR
Commission on College Geography (AEBS) .... CCG
Commission on College Physics .... CCP
Commission on Critical Choices for Americans .... CCCA
Commission on Crystallographic Apparatus [*International Council of Scientific Unions*] .... CCA
Commission on Education [*American Occupational Therapy Association*] .... COE
Commission on Education for Mission [*National Council of Churches*] (EA) .... CEM
Commission on Education in Agriculture and Natural Resources [*National Research Council*] [*Defunct*] .... CEANAR
Commission on Education of Teachers of Reading (EDAC) .... CETOR
Commission on Education of the World Leisure and Recreation Association (EAIO) .... CEWLRA
Commission on Elections [*Philippines*] .... COMELEC
Commission on Emergency Medical Services [*Defunct*] (EA) .... CEMS
Commission on Emotional and Learning Disorders in Children [*Canada*] .... CELDIC
Commission on English of the College Entrance Examination Board (EA) .... CECEEB
Commission on Epidemiological Survey [*Armed Forces Epidemiological Board*] (DNAB) .... CES
Commission on Family Ministries and Human Sexuality (EA) .... CFMHS
Commission on Federal Paperwork [*Terminated, 1978*] .... CFP
Commission on Financial Structure and Regulation [*White House*] .... CFSR
Commission on Folk Law and Legal Pluralism [*of the International Union of Anthropological and Ethnological Sciences*] (EAIO) .... CFLLP
Commission on Government Procurement [*Terminated, 1973*] .... CGP
Commission on Government Procurement [*Terminated, 1973*] .... COGP
Commission on Government Security [*Terminated, 1957*] .... CGS
Commission on Graduates of Foreign Nursing Schools (EA) .... CGFNS
Commission on Health and Healing [*Formerly, CCMW*] (EA) .... CHH
Commission on Highway Beautification .... CHB
Commission on Human Resources [*National Research Council*] .... CHR
Commission on Human Rights [*Geneva, Switzerland*] (EAIO) .... CHR
Commission on Increased Industrial Use of Agricultural Products .... CIIUAP
Commission on Independent Colleges and Universities [*Pennsylvania*] .... CICU
Commission on Industrial Relations [*Department of Employment*] [*British*] .... CIR
Commission on Instructional Technology (EA) .... CIT
Commission on Insurance Terminology of the American Risk and Insurance Association .... CIT
Commission on Intergovernmental Relations .... CIR
Commission on International Affairs (EA) .... CIA
Commission on International Commodity Trade .... CICT
Commission on Law and Public Affairs .... COLPA
Commission on Law Enforcement and Criminal Justice, Criminal Justice InformationSystem, Baton Rouge, LA [*Library symbol Library of Congress*] (LCLS) .... LBrCJIS
Commission on Marine and Coastal Resources [*California*] .... CMC
Commission on Marine Science, Engineering and Research [*Stratton Commission*] [*Inactive*] [*Marine science*] (OSRA) .... COMSER
Commission on Marine Science, Engineering, and Resources .... CMSER
Commission on Marine Science, Engineering and Resources [*Stratton Commission*] [*Defunct*] (USDC) .... COMSER
Commission on Marriage and Family Life [*of NCC*] [*Defunct*] .... CMFL
Commission on Ministries in Specialized Settings [*Federal government*] .... COMISS
Commission on Missionary Education [*Later, Department of Education for Missions*] (EA) .... CME
Commission on Molecular Structure and Spectroscopy .... CMSS
Commission on National Parks and Protected Areas [*of the International Union for Conservation of Nature and Natural Resources*] (EAIO) .... CNPPA
Commission on Natural Resources [*National Research Council*] .... CNR
Commission on Ore-Forming Fluid in Inclusions .... COFFI
Commission on Organization of the Executive Branch of the Government .... COEBG
Commission on Pastoral Research (EA) .... COMISS
Commission on Personnel Interchange [*Presidential*] .... CPI
Commission on Population Growth and the American Future [*Presidential commission*] .... CPGAF
Commission on Practice [*American Occupational Therapy Association*] .... COP
Commission on Preservation and Access .... CPA
Commission on Presidential Debates (EA) .... CPD
Commission on Private Philanthropy and Public Needs [*Defunct*] (EA) .... CPPPN
Commission on Professional and Hospital Activities (EA) .... CPHA

Commission on Professional Rights and Responsibilities of the NEA
[*Defunct*] (EA) .... CPRR-NEA
Commission on Professionals in Science and Technology (EA) .... CPST
Commission on Public Ethics [*Australia*] .... COPE
Commission on Quantities and Units in Clinical Chemistry (DAVI) .... CQUCC
Commission on Recent Crustal Movements [*Oceanography*] (MSC) .... CRCM
Commission on Reform Jewish Outreach (EA) .... CRJO
Commission on Reform of Undergraduate Education and Living [*University
of Illinois*] .... CRUEL
Commission on Rehabilitation Counselor Certification (EA) .... CRCC
Commission on Rehabilitation Education [*American Occupational Therapy
Association*] .... CORE
Commission on Religion in Appalachia (EA) .... CORA
Commission on Research Integrity [*Congressional group*] .... CRI
**Commission on Research of the World Leisure and Recreation
Association** (EA) .... CRWLRA
Commission on Rules and Missions of the Armed Services (AAGC) .... CORM
Commission on Rural Water [*Defunct*] (EA) .... CRW
Commission on Science Education .... CSE
Commission on Security and Cooperation in Europe [*Washington, DC*]
(EGAO) .... CSCE
Commission on Social Action of Reform Judaism (EA) .... CSARJ
Commission on Software Issues in the 80s [*Defunct*] (EA) .... COSIE
Commission on Soil Biology of the International Society of Soil Science
(EAIO) .... CSBISSS
Commission on Soil Biology of the International Society of Soil Science
[*Netherlands*] (EAIO) .... CSBUSSS
Commission on Soil Fertility and Plant Nutrition [*of the International Society
of Soil Science*] (EA) .... CSFPN
Commission on Soil Genesis, Classification, and Cartography [*of the
International Society of Soil Science*] (EA) .... CSGCC
Commission on Standards and Accreditation of Services for the Blind
[*Superseded by NAC*] .... COMSTAC
**Commission on Storage, Automatic Processing, and Retrieval of
Geological Data** (EAIO) .... COGEODATA
Commission on Sustainable Development .... CSD
Commission on the Aging (OICC) .... COA
Commission on the Isle Of Man Constitution. Report [*1959*] [*A publication*]
(DLA) .... MacDermott Commission
Commission on the Mentally Disabled [*Formerly, Mental and Physical
Disability Legal Research Services and Data Bases*] (EA) .... MPDLRSDB
Commission on the Nomenclature of Organic Chemistry [*IUPAC*] .... CON
Commission on the Patent System .... CPS
**Commission on the Status of Jewish War Orphans in Europe, American
Section** [*Defunct*] (EA) .... CSJWOE
Commission on the Status of Women [*Economic and Social Council of the
UN*] [*Vienna, Austria*] (EAIO) .... CSW
Commission on the Status of Women in Adult Education [*Later, WISE*]
(EA) .... CSWAE
Commission on the Study of Peace (EA) .... CSP
Commission on Transnational Corporations [*United Nations*] .... CTC
Commission on Transnational Corporations [*United Nations*] .... CTNC
Commission on Undergraduate Education in the Biological Sciences ..... CUEBS
Commission on US-African Relations (EA) .... CUSAR
Commission on US-Soviet Relations (EA) .... CUSSR
Commission on Voluntary Service and Action (EA) .... CVSA
Commission on World Mission and Evangelism (EAIO) .... CWME
**Commission on World Mission and Evangelism of the World Council of
Churches** [*Later, CWME*] (EA) .... CWMEWCC
Commission Permanente de la Convention Internationale des Peches
[*Permanent Commission of the International Fisheries Convention*] [*Political
party*] (MSC) .... CPCIP
Commission Permanente du Pacifique Sud [*Permanent Commission for the
South Pacific*] .... CPPS
**Commission Permanente Internationale de l'Acetylene, de la Soudure
Autogene, et des Industries qui S'y Rattachent** [*Permanent International
Committee on Acetylene, Oxy-Acetylene Welding, and Allied Industries*] ...... CPI
**Commission Permanente Internationale Europeenne des Gaz Industriels et
du Carbure de Calcium** [*Permanent International European Commission
on Industrial Gases and Calcium Carbide*] (EAIO) .... CPI
Commission Phytosanitaire Interafricaine .... CPI
**Commission pour le Marche Commun du Commerce International de
Bulbes a Fleurs etde Plantes** [*Common Market Commission for
International Trade in Flower Bulbs and Plants*] .... CIBEP
Commission pour l'Etude des Nuages [*OMI*] .... CEN
Commission Preparatoire Europeenne de Recherches Spatiales [*European
Preparatory Commission for Space Research*] .... COPERS
**Commission Regionale de l'Utilisation des Terres et des Eaux au Proche-
Orient** [*Regional Commission on Land and Water Use in the Near East -
RCLWUNE*] (EAIO) .... CRUTEPO
Commission Regionale Europeenne du Tourisme .... CRET
Commission Rochon, Centre de Documentation, Ste. Foy, PQ, Canada
[*Library symbol*] [*Library of Congress*] (LCLS) .... CaQSFCRO
Commission Scolaire de Sept-Iles, Quebec [*Library symbol National Library
of Canada*] (NLC) .... QSICS
**Commission Scolaire Regionale des Vieilles-Forges, Trois-Rivieres, PQ,
Canada** [*Library symbol Library of Congress*] (LCLS) .... CaQTCSRV
**Commission Scolaire Regionale des Vieilles-Forges, Trois-Rivieres,
Quebec** [*Library symbol National Library of Canada*] (NLC) .... QTCSRV
Commission Seismologique Europeenne [*European Seismological
Commission - ESC*] (EAIO) .... CSE
Commission Sericicole Internationale [*International Sericultural Commission -
ISC*] (EAIO) .... CSI
Commission Sportive Internationale [*Auto racing*] .... CSI

Commission Telephone Cases Leaflets [*New York*] [*A publication*]
(DLA) .... Comm Tel Cas
Commission to New Towns [*British*] .... CNT
Commission to Study the Organization of Peace (EA) .... CSOP
Commissional (ABBR) .... CMSNL
Commissionary (ABBR) .... CMSNY
Commissione Nazionale per le Societa e la Borsa .... CONSOB
Commissioned .... CD
Commissioned .... CMMND
Commissioned .... CMSND
Commissioned (WGA) .... COMD
Commissioned (DLA) .... commd
Commissioned .... COMMND
Commissioned .... COMND
Commissioned (DA) .... COMSND
Commissioned Corps Personnel Manual .... CCPM
Commissioned from the Ranks [*Canadian Navy*] .... CFR
Commissioned Loss to Enlisted Status [*Revocation of an officer's
appointment*] .... CLTE
Commissioned Officer [*Military*] .... Com Off
Commissioned Officer Corps [*National Oceanic and Atmospheric
Administration*] .... COC
Commissioned Officer Corps Advisory Group [*National Oceanic and
Atmospheric Administration*] (NOAA) .... COCAG
Commissioned Officer Residency Deferment [*Program of Public Health
Service*] .... CORD
Commissioned Officer Student Training and Extern Program [*Public Health
Service*] .... COSTEP
**Commissioned Officers Association of the United States Public Health
Service** (EA) .... COA
Commissioned Officers Mess [*Navy*] .... COM
Commissioned Officers' Mess Open [*Navy*] (DNAB) .... COMO
Commissioned Royal Marine Gunner [*British*] .... CdRMG
Commissioned Signals Boatswain [*British*] .... CdSB
Commissioned Supply Officer [*British*] .... CdSO
Commissioned Vessel Liaison Inquiry (DNAB) CVLI
Commissioned Warrant Officer .... CWO
Commissioned Warrant Officer Hospital Corps .... CWOHC
Commissioner .... CMMNR
Commissioner .... Cmmr
Commissioner .... CMSNR
Commissioner (ABBR) .... CMSSNR
Commissioner (WGA) .... COMM
Commissioner (ROG) .... COMMISR
Commissioner (EY) .... COMMR
Commissioner (DD) .... commr
Commissioner .... COMMR
Commissioner .... COMMSNR
Commissioner (ROG) .... COMMSR
Commissioner .... COMR
Commissioner .... COMS
Commissioner .... COMSNR
Commissioner, Chancery Court, County Palatine of Lancaster [*British*]
(ROG) .... CCHCOPALLANC
Commissioner for Affidavits for Colonies [*British*] (ROG) .... C AFFS for COLS
Commissioner for Enterprise Agreements [*New South Wales*] [*Australia*] ...... CEA
Commissioner for Oaths .... CO
Commissioner for Vocational Training [*New South Wales*] [*Australia*] .... CVT
Commissioner of Accounts .... CA
Commissioner of Appeals (DLA) .... COM APP
Commissioner of Crown Lands [*British*] CCL
Commissioner of Election Expenses [*Canada*] .... CEE
Commissioner of Official Languages [*Canada*] .... COL
Commissioner of Official Languages, Ottawa, ON, Canada [*Library symbol
Library of Congress*] (LCLS) .... CaOOCOL
Commissioner of Official Languages [*Commissaire aux Langues Officielles*]
Ottawa, Ontario [*Library symbol National Library of Canada*] (NLC) ...... OOCOL
Commissioner of Patents [*Legal term*] (DLA) .... COM PAT
Commissioner of Police for the Metropolis [*British*] (DI) .... CPM
Commissioner of Public Debt .... CPD
Commissioner of Soil Conservation [*Western Australia*] .... CSC
Commissioner of Taxation (ADA) .... C of T
Commissioner of Taxes [*Northern Territory*] [*Australia*] .... COT
Commissioner of the Great Seal [*British*] (ROG) .... COMGS
Commissioner's Adjusted Fair Market Value [*Business term*] (EMRF) .... CAFMV
Commissioner's Decisions [*US Patent and Trademark Office*] .... CD
Commissioners' Decisions [*US Patent and Trademark Office*] [*A publication*]
(DLA) .... Com Dec
Commissioner's Delegation Order (DLA) .... Comm Del Order
Commissioners Disability Table [*Insurance*] .... CDT
Commissioners Industrial Extended Mortality Table [*Insurance*] .... CIET
Commissioners of District of Columbia .... CDC
Commissioners of Inland Revenue [*British*] .... CIR
Commissioners of Sewers [*British*] (ROG) .... CS
Commissioner's Office [*Scotland Yard*] .... CO
Commissioners Standard Industrial Mortality Table [*Insurance*] .... CSI
Commissioners Standard Ordinary Table [*Insurance*] .... CSO
Commissioning (ABBR) .... CMSNG
Commissioning Accession Management System [*Military*] (DNAB) .... CAMS
Commissioning and Fitting Out .... CFO
Commissioning Detail .... COMMDET
Commissions Board of Trade .... CBOT
Commission's Yellowfin Regulatory Area [*Inter-American Tropical Tuna
Commission*] (MSC) .... CYRA
Commissural and Association [*Anatomy*] .... CA

Commissural Ganglion [*Neurology*] ..... COG
Commissural Gastric Driver [*Neurology*] ..... CGD
Commit (MSA) ..... CMT
Commit (AAG) ..... COMT
Commit Sequence Summary (AAG) ..... CSS
Commit Start (AAG) ..... CST
Commit Stop (AAG) ..... CS
Commited (ABBR) ..... CMTD
Commiting (ABBR) ..... CMTG
Commitment (ABBR) ..... CMTMT
Commitment (MCD) ..... COMM
Commitment Accounting and Management of Unit Supplies (MCD) ..... CAMUS
Commitment and Payment System (MCD) ..... CAPS
Commitment Authorization ..... CA
Commitment, Concurrency and Recovery [*Computer science*] (TNIG) ..... CCR
Commitment, Concurrency, and Recovery Element [*Computer science*] (TNIG) ..... CCRE
Commitment Control System (NRCH) ..... CCS
[*A*] **Commitment to Improve Our Nation** [*Canada*] ..... ACTION
Committal (ROG) ..... COML
Committed Change Incorporation Record (KSC) ..... CCIR
Committed Effective Dose Equivalent [*Radioactivity*] ..... CEDE
Committed Information Rate [*Telecommunications*] ..... CIR
Committed out of Engineering ..... COE
Committed Quitters ..... CQ
Committed Stem Cell [*Hematology*] ..... CSC
Committed to Ride (SAA) ..... CTR
Committed to Scheduled Programs [*Military*] (CINC) ..... CSP
Committee ..... CMMTE
Committee ..... CMTE
Committee ..... CMTTEE
Committee (AABC) ..... COM
Committee (WDMC) ..... com
Committee (ROG) ..... COME
Committee ..... COMM
Committee ..... COMTE
Committee ..... CTEE
Committee (EY) ..... CTTEE
Committee Against Government Waste (EA) ..... CAGW
Committee Against Registration and the Draft (EA) ..... CARD
Committee Against Repression in the Pacific and Asia [*Australia*] (EAIO) ..... CARPA
Committee Against Revising Staggers [*Group opposed to changes in the Staggers Act*] ..... CARS
Committee Against the Political Misuse of Psychiatry (EA) ..... CAPMP
Committee Against Torture [*See also CCT*] [*Geneva, Switzerland*] (EAIO) ..... CAT
Committee Charter (MCD) CC
Committee Code [*Database terminology*] (NITA) ..... COCO
Committee Draft [*Telecommunications*] (OSI) ..... CD
Committee for a Democratic Consensus (EA) ..... CDC
Committee for a Free Afghanistan (EA) ..... CFA
Committee for a Free China [*Defunct*] (EA) ..... CFC
Committee for a Free Estonia [*Defunct*] (EA) ..... CFE
Committee for a Free Gold Market (EA) ..... CFGM
Committee for a Free Latvia (EA) ..... CFL
Committee for a Free Lithuania [*Defunct*] (EA) ..... CFL
Committee for a Free Mozambique [*Defunct*] (EA) ..... CFM
Committee for a Free Namibia [*Defunct*] (EA) ..... CFN
Committee for a National Peace Academy [*Later, N-PAC*] (EA) ..... NPA
Committee for a National Trade Policy [*Defunct*] ..... CNTP
Committee for a New Ireland [*Defunct*] (EA) ..... CNI
Committee for a New Korea Policy (EA) ..... CNKP
Committee for a Progressive Congress (EA) ..... CPC
Committee for a Responsible Federal Budget (EA) ..... CRFB
Committee for a Strong Peaceful America [*Defunct*] (EA) ..... CSPA
Committee for a Voluntary Census (EA) CVC
Committee for Accuracy in Middle East Reporting in America (EA) ..... CAMERA
Committee for Action for Rural Indians (EA) ..... CARI
Committee for Agricultural Development [*Iowa State University*] [*Research center*] (RCD) ..... CAD
Committee for American Principles (EA) ..... CFAP
Committee for Ammunition Logistics Support [*Army*] (MCD) ..... CALS
Committee for an Extended Lifespan [*Defunct*] (EA) ..... CEL
Committee for an Independent Canada CIC
Committee for an International Program in Atmospheric Sciences and Hydrology [*United Nations*] ..... CIPASH
Committee for an Open Archives (EA) ..... COA
Committee for Anglophone Social Action [*Canada*] ..... CASA
Committee for Aquatic Microbiology [*United Nations*] (ASF) ..... CAM
Committee for Artistic and Intellectual Freedom in Iran (EA) ..... CAIFI
Committee for Automobile Reform ..... CAR
Committee for Better Transit (EA) ..... CBT
Committee for Children (EA) ..... CFC
Committee for Chilean Inquiry (EA) CCI
Committee for Collective Security [*Defunct*] (EA) ..... CCS
Committee for Common Security (EA) ..... CCS
Committee for Common Sense Speed Laws [*California*] [*Defunct*] (EA) ..... CCSSL
Committee for Competitive Television (NTCM) ..... CCT
Committee for Congested Production Areas [*1943-1944*] ..... CCPA
Committee for Conservation and Care of Chimpanzees (EA) CCCC
Committee for Constitutional Government (EA) ..... CCG
Committee for Consumers No-Fault (EA) ..... CCNF
Committee for Conventional Armaments ..... CCA
Committee for Coordination of Emergency Economic Planning [*US/Canada*] ..... CCEEP
Committee for Coordination of Joint Prospecting for Mineral Resources in Asian Offshore Areas, East Asia [*United Nations*] ..... CCOPEA
Committee for Co-Ordination of Joint Prospecting for Mineral Resources in South Pacific Offshore Areas (EAIO) ..... CCOP/SOPAC
Committee for Corporate Support of American Universities [*Later, Committee for Corporate Support of Private Universities*] (EA) ..... CCSAU
Committee for Corporate Support of Private Universities ..... CCSPU
Committee for Crescent Observation International (EA) ..... CCOI
Committee for Defense of Human Rights in Morocco (EA) ..... CDHRM
Committee for Defense of Soviet Political Prisoners (EA) ..... CDSPP
Committee for Do-It-Yourself Household Moving (EA) ..... DITY
Committee for Economic Development (EA) ..... CED
Committee for Education Funding (EA) ..... CEF
Committee for Effective Capital Recovery [*Defunct*] (EA) ..... CECR
Committee for Elimination of Death [*Later, CEL*] (EA) ..... CFED
Committee for Energy Awareness [*Later, USCEA*] (EA) ..... CEA
Committee for Energy Policy [*Organization for Economic Cooperation and Development*] (MCD) ..... CEP
Committee for Enlisted Classification Selection and Testing [*Navy*] (NVT) ..... CECSET
Committee for Environmental Information (IID) ..... CEI
Committee for Environmental Monitoring of Forest Insect Control Operations ..... EMOFICO
Committee for Environmentally Effective Packaging (EA) ..... CEEP
Committee for Equality of Citizens Before the Courts (EA) ..... CO-EQUAL
Committee for Equitable Access to Crude Oil (EA) ..... CEACO
Committee for Equitable Compensation [*Defunct*] (EA) ..... CEC
Committee for European Airspace Coordination [*NATO*] ..... CEAC
Committee for European Airspace Coordination [*NATO*] (NATG) ..... CEASC
Committee for European Construction Equipment [*British*] (EAIO) ..... CECE
Committee for European Economic Cooperation [*Marshall Plan*] [*Post-World War II*] ..... CEEC
Committee for Evaluating the Feasibility of Space Rocketry [*Navy Bureau of Aeronautics*] [*Obsolete*] ..... CEFSR
Committee for Exchange with Non-English Speaking Countries (AIE) ..... CENESC
Committee for Exploitation of the Oceans (BARN) ..... COMEXO
Committee for Food and Shelter [*Later, NAEH*] (EA) ..... CFS
Committee for Freedom of Choice in Cancer Therapy [*Later, CFCM*] (EA) ..... CFCCT
Committee for Freedom of Choice in Medicine (EA) ..... CFCM
Committee for Full Funding of Education Programs (EA) ..... CFFEP
Committee for Handgun Control (EA) ..... CHC
Committee for Handicapable Dancers (EA) ..... CHD
Committee for Hispanic Arts and Research (EA) ..... CHAR
Committee for Human Rights and Democracy in Turkey (EA) ..... CHRDT
Committee for Human Rights in Argentina [*British*] ..... CHRA
Committee for Human Rights in Rumania (EA) ..... CHRR
Committee for Human Rights in Syria (EA) ..... CHRS
Committee for Humane Legislation (EA) ..... CHL
Committee for Immediate Nuclear War (EA) ..... CINW
Committee for Imperial Defence [*British*] ..... CID
Committee for Independent Political Action ..... CIPA
Committee for Industrial Co-Operation [*European Economic Community/African, Caribbean, and Pacific States*] (DS) CIC
Committee for Industrial Development [*United Nations*] ..... CID
Committee for Information and Documentation on Science and Technology [*EEC*] (PDAA) ..... CIDST
Committee for Inland Fisheries of Africa [*UN Food and Agriculture Organization*] ..... CIFA
Committee for International Collaborative Activities [*An association*] ..... CICA
Committee for International Co-operation in Information Retrieval Among Examining Patent Offices ..... CICIREPATO
Committee for International Justice and Peace of the Episcopal Conference of England and Wales (EAIO) ..... CIJPECEW
Committee for International Municipal Cooperation ..... CIMC
Committee for Italic Handwriting [*Defunct*] (EA) ..... CIH
Committee for Justice and Liberty Foundation ..... CJL
Committee for Justice for Domingo and Viernes [*Defunct*] (EA) ..... CJDV
Committee for Leaving the Environment of America Natural ..... CLEAN
Committee for Liquidation of German War Potential [*Allied German Occupation Forces*] ..... CLWP
Committee for Medical Aid to Central America (EA) ..... COMACA
Committee for Modern Courts (EA) ..... CMC
Committee for Monetary Research and Education, Inc. [*Research center*] (RCD) ..... CMRE
Committee for Mother and Child Rights (EA) ..... CMCR
Committee for National Arbor Day (EA) ..... CNAD
Committee for National Health Insurance (EA) ..... CNHI
Committee for National Land Development Policy [*Defunct*] ..... CNLDP
Committee for National Security (EA) ..... CNS
Committee for National Theatre Week (EA) ..... CNTW
Committee for Nationalist Union [*British*] ..... CNU
Committee for Nonviolent Action [*Later, WRL*] (EA) ..... CNVA
Committee for Nordic Universities of Journalism [*See also RNJ*] (EAIO) ..... CNUJ
Committee for Nuclear Information [*Later, Committee for Environmental Information*] ..... CNI
Committee for Nuclear Responsibility (EA) ..... CNR
Committee for Oil Pipe Lines [*Later, AOPL*] ..... COPL
Committee for Oil Shale Development [*Defunct*] (EA) ..... COSHD
Committee for Open Debate on the Holocaust [*Defunct*] (EA) ..... CODH
Committee for Original People's Entitlement [*Eskimo claim to Canadian land*] ..... COPE
Committee for Overseas Science and Technology [*British*] (PDAA) ..... COST
Committee for Pedestrian Tolls [*Defunct*] (EA) ..... CPT
Committee for Positive Education [*Defunct*] (EA) ..... CPE

Committee for Presidents' Day [*Later, Presidents' Day National Committee*] (AEBS) ... CPD
Committee for Prisoner Humanity and Justice (EA) ... CPHJ
Committee for Private Offshore Rescue and Towing (EA) ... C-PORT
Committee for Privileges, House of Commons/Lords (DLA) ... C Priv
Committee for Production Sharing [*Defunct*] (EA) ... CPS
Committee for Proprietary Medicinal Products [*European Directorate*] ... CPMP
Committee for Public Education and Religious Liberty (EA) ... PEARL
Committee for Public Justice (EA) ... CPJ
Committee for Purchase of Products and Services of the Blind and Other Severely Handicapped [*Later, Committee for Purchase from the Blind and Other Severely Handicapped*] ... CPPSBOSH
Committee for Radiation Protection and Public Health [*EURATOM*] (NUCP) ... CRPPH
Committee for Real Ale (EA) ... CRA
Committee for Reciprocity Information [*A federal government body*] ... CRI
Committee for Rejection of Obnoxious Commercials ... CROC
Committee for Religious Freedom (EA) ... CRF
Committee for Research into Teacher Education (AIE) ... CRITE
Committee for Restoration of Democracy in Burma (EA) ... CRDB
Committee for Review of Our China Policy [*Defunct*] ... CROCP
Committee for Safe Bicycling [*Defunct*] (EA) ... CSB
Committee for Science, Engineering, and Public Policy ... COSEPP
Committee for Science, Engineering, and Public Policy [*Formerly, COSPUP*] [*National Academy of Sciences*] [*Washington, DC*] ... COSEPUP
Committee for Scientific and Technological Policy (DMAA) ... CSTP
Committee for Single Adoptive Parents (EA) ... CSAP
Committee for Single Six-Year Presidential Term (EA) ... CSSYPT
Committee for Small Business Exports (EA) ... COSBE
Committee for Small Business Exports (EA) ... CSBE
Committee for Solidarity with the Bolivian People [*Defunct*] (EA) ... CSBP
Committee for Stable Deterrence (EA) ... CSD
Committee for Sustainable Agriculture (EA) ... CSA
Committee for the Absorption of Soviet Emigres ... CASE
Committee for the Accreditation of Canadian Medical Schools [*Canada*] (PGP) ... CACMS
Committee for the Advancement of Role-Playing Games (EA) ... CARPG
Committee for the Aid to West Papuan Refugees [*Netherlands*] (EAIO) ... CAWPR
Committee for the Alliance for Progress [*Department of Commerce*] ... COMAP
Committee for the Application of the Behavioral Sciences to the Strategies of Peace (EA) ... ABSSOP
Committee for the Care of the Diabetic ... CCD
Committee for the Collegiate Education of Black Students ... CCEBS
Committee for the Coordination of National Bibliographic Control [*Defunct*] (EA) ... CCNBC
Committee for the Co-Ordination of Patriotic and Democracy-Loving Forces [*Thailand*] (PD) ... CCPDF
Committee for the Coordination of Services to Displaced Persons in Thailand [*Australia*] ... CCSDPT
Committee for the Defence of Human and National Rights in Ukraine [*Australia*] ... CDHNRU
Committee for the Defence of the Unjustly Prosecuted (EAIO) ... CDUP
Committee for the Defense National Interest (CINC) ... CDNI
Committee for the Defense of Human Rights in India (EA) ... CoDHRI
Committee for the Defense of Legitimate Rights [*Saudi Arabia*] (ECON) ... CDLR
Committee for the Defense of Persecuted Orthodox Christians [*Defunct*] (EA) ... CDPOC
Committee for the Defense of Persons Unjustly Persecuted [*Former Czechoslovakia*] [*Political party*] (PD) ... VONS
Committee for the Defense of Political Prisoners in Vietnam (EA) ... CDPPV
Committee for the Defense of the Revolution [*Cuba*] ... CDR
Committee for the Democratic Struggle [*Mexico*] ... COLUDE
Committee for the Development and Management of Fisheries in the South China Sea [*Thailand*] (EAIO) ... CDMSCS
Committee for the Development of Alternatives to Incarceration [*Canada*] ... CODAI
Committee for the Development of Art in Negro Colleges [*Later, CAA*] ... CDANC
Committee for the Economic Growth of Israel (EA) ... CEG-I
Committee for the Employment of Disabled People (AIE) ... CEDP
Committee for the Free World (EA) ... CFW
Committee for the Furtherance of Torah Observance (EA) ... CFTO
Committee for the Future of America (EA) ... CFA
Committee for the Game (EA) ... CG
Committee for the Global Atmospheric Research Program ... CGARP
Committee for the Implementation of Textile Agreements ... CITA
Committee for the Implementation of the Standardized Yiddish Orthography (EA) ... CISYO
Committee for the Jewish Idea (EA) ... CJI
Committee for the Maintenance of Jewish Standards (EA) ... CMJS
Committee for the Monument of Garibaldi (EA) ... CMG
Committee for the Mustard Industry of the European Communities [*Belgium*] (EAIO) ... CMI-EC
Committee for the National Institute for the Environment [*Lobby group*] ... CNIE
Committee for the Preservation of the Tule Elk (EA) ... CPTE
Committee for the Recovery of Archaeological Remains ... CRAR
Committee for the Reexamination of the History of the Second World War (EA) ... CRHSWW
Committee for the Reform of Animal Experimentation [*British*] ... CRAE
Committee for the Restoration of the Republic [*Defunct*] (EA) ... CRR
Committee for the Restructuring and Progress of Equity [*Actors' Trade Union*] [*British*] (DI) ... CRAPE
Committee for the Revision of the Criminal Code [*Allied German Occupation Forces*] ... CRICO
Committee for the Revolution in Oman and the Arabian Gulf [*Denmark*] ... KROAG
Committee for the Scientific Investigation of Claims of the Paranormal (EA) ... CSICOP
Committee for the Scientific Survey of Air Defence [*British World War II*] ... CSSAD
Committee for the Scientific Survey of Air Offence [*British World War II*] ... CSSAO
Committee for the Scientific Survey of Air Warfare [*British World War II*] ... CSSAW
Committee for the Status of Women in Philosophy (EA) ... CSWP
Committee for the Study of Environmental Manpower [*National Research Council*] ... CSEM
Committee for the Study of Handgun Misuse (EA) ... CSHM
Committee for the Study of the American Electorate (EA) ... CSAE
Committee for the Suit Against Government Misconduct (EA) ... CSAGM
Committee for the Survey of Chemistry [*National Academy of Sciences*] ... CSC
Committee for the Survival of a Free Congress ... CSFC
Committee for the Visual Arts [*Later, CVAAS*] (EA) ... CVA
Committee for the Visual Arts/Artists Space (EA) ... CVAAS
Committee for Thorough Agricultural Political Education [*Associated Milk Producers, Inc.*] ... C-TAPE
Committee for Time Uniformity [*Defunct*] ... CTU
Committee for Truth in Psychiatry (EA) ... CTIP
Committee for University Assistance [*Military British*] ... CUA
Committee for Veterinary Medicinal Products [*European Community*] ... CVMP
Committee for Western Civilization (EA) ... CWC
Committee for Wildlife on the Last Frontier ... WOLF
Committee for Women in Geophysics [*Defunct*] (EA) ... CWG
Committee for Women in Public Administration (EA) ... CWPA
Committee for World Development and World Disarmament [*Defunct*] (EA) ... CWDWD
Committee for Zero Automobile Growth (EA) ... CZAG
Committee in Defense of the Palestinian and Lebanese Peoples [*Defunct*] (EA) ... CDPLP
Committee in Solidarity with Latin American Nonviolent Movements (EA) ... CISLANM
Committee in Solidarity with the People of Guatemala (EA) ... CSPG
Committee in Solidarity with the People of Iran (EA) ... CSPI
Committee in Support of Solidarity (EA) ... CSS
Committee Insuring and Guaranteeing Anyone's Right to Smoke ... CIGARS
Committee Meeting Information System (MCD) ... COMIS
Committee of 200 [*An association*] ... C200
Committee of Agricultural Organizations in the European Communities (EAIO) ... CAO-EC
Committee of American Steamship Lines [*Later, AIMS*] (EA) ... CASL
Committee of Americans for Peace in the Middle East [*Defunct*] (EA) ... CAPME
Committee of Atomic Bomb Survivors in the US ... CABSUS
Committee of Black Americans for Truth about the Middle-East [*Defunct*] ... COBATAME
Committee of Black Gay Men (EA) ... CBGM
Committee of Butchery Organizations of the EEC (EAIO) ... CBOE
Committee of Catholics Who Care (EA) ... CCWC
Committee of Chinese Correspondence (EA) ... CCC
Committee of Combined Boards ... COB
Committee of Common Market Automobile Constructors [*EEC*] ... CCMAC
Committee of Concern ... COC
Committee of Concern for Central America (EA) ... CCCA
Committee of Concerned Africans [*Defunct*] (EA) ... CCA
Committee of Concerned Artists and Professionals (EA) ... CCAP
Committee of Concerned Catholics [*Defunct*] (EA) ... CCC
Committee of Concerned Scientists (EA) ... CCS
Committee of Control of the International Zone of Tangier ... CCIZT
Committee of Corporate Finance [*of the National Association of Securities Dealers*] ... CCF
Committee of Corporate Telecommunications Users [*An association*] (EA) ... CCTU
Committee of Direction of Fruit Marketing [*Queensland*] [*Australia*] ... CDFM
Committee of Directors of Polytechnics [*British*] ... CDP
Committee of Directors of Research Associations and Federation of Technology Centres [*British*] ... CDRA
Committee of Ecological Research for the Interoceanic Canal [*National Academy of Science*] (MSC) ... CERIC
Committee of EEC [*European Economic Community*] **Shipbuilders' Associations** (EAIO) ... CESA
Committee of Engineering Professors' Conference (ACII) ... CEPC
Committee of European Associations of Manufacturers of Electronic Components [*EC*] [*Italy*] (ECED) ... CEMEC
Committee of European Coffee Associations (EAIO) ... CECA
Committee of European Financial Executives Institutes [*EC*] (ECED) ... CEFEI
Committee of European Promotors of Exhibitions of Measurement and Automation (ACII) ... CEMA
Committee of Experts for the Transfer of Information between Community Languages [*EEC*] (PDAA) ... CETIL
Committee of Experts on the Transport of Dangerous Goods of the United Nations Economic and Social Council [*RSPA*] (TAG) ... ECOSOC
Committee of French American Wives [*Later, FAAC*] (EA) ... CFAW
Committee of French Speaking Societies (EA) ... CFSS
Committee of Glutamic Acid Manufacturers of the European Economic Community (EAIO) ... CGAMEEC
Committee of Heads of Administration [*NATO*] (NATG) ... CHA
Committee of Heads of Architecture Schools of Australasia [*Australia*] ... CHASA
Committee of Heads of Drama Departments in Scotland (AIE) ... CHDDS
Committee of International Development Institutions on the Environment (ECON) ... CIDIE
Committee of Interns and Residents (EA) ... CIR
Committee of Liberal Exiles [*British*] (EAIO) ... CLE

Committee of London and Scottish Bankers [British] ... CLSB
Committee of London Clearing Bankers [British] ... CLCB
Committee of Marketing Organizations [British] ... COMO
Committee of Middle East Trade [British Overseas Trade Board] (DS) ... COMET
Committee of National Institutes of Patent Agents [Winchester, Hampshire, England] (EA) ... CNIPA
Committee of National Security Companies [Memphis, TN] (EA) ... CONSCO
Committee of Presidents of Statistical Societies (EA) ... COPSS
Committee of Presidents of Statistical Societies (EA) ... CPSS
Committee of Professors in Operational Research (AIE) ... COPIOR
Committee of Publicly Owned Companies (EA) ... COPOC
Committee of Religion and Art of America [Later, FAAR] (EA) ... CRAA
Committee of Religious Concern for Peace (EA) ... CRCP
Committee of Responsibility ... COR
Committee of Returned Volunteers [Defunct] (EA) ... CRV
Committee of Scottish Higher Education Principals (AIE) ... COSHEP
Committee of Security Experts [Military] (CINC) ... CSE
Committee of Seismology [National Academy of Sciences] (USDC) ... CS
Committee of Singled-Out Taxpayers [Later, American Council of Taxpayers] (EA) ... COST
Committee of Small Magazine Editors and Publishers [In association name COSMEP, The International Association of Independent Publishers] (EA) ... COSMEP
Committee of Southern Churchmen (EA) ... CSC
Committee of Special Means [British military] (DMA) ... CSM
Committee of Stock Exchanges in the European Community [See also CBCE] (EAIO) ... CSEE
Committee of Ten Million (EA) ... COTM
Committee of the Acta Endocrinologica Countries ... CAEC
Committee of the Associated Trades [A union] [British] ... CAT
Committee of the Associations of Honey Importers and Packers of Europe (EAIO) ... CAHIPE
Committee of the House [British] (ROG) ... COMH
Committee of the National Ferrous Scrap Federations and Associations of the Common Market [See also COFENAF] (EAIO) ... CNFSFACM
Committee of the Regions [Belgium] (ECON) ... COR
Committee of the Whole [United Nations] ... COW
Committee of the Whole House, House of Lords [British] (DLA) ... CWH
Committee of Tin Mill Products Producers (EA) ... CTMPP
Committee of Transylvania (EA) ... CT
Committee of United States Citizens Living in Nicaragua (EA) ... CUSCLN
Committee of University Industrial Relations Librarians ... CUIRL
Committee of Urban Program Universities ... CUPU
Committee of Vice-Chancellors and Principals of the Universities of the United Kingdom [British] ... CVCP
Committee of Youth Hostel Organizations in the Nordic Countries (EA) ... CYHONC
Committee on a Multimedium Approach to Sludge Management [National Research Council] ... CMSM
Committee on Academic Science and Engineering [Federal Council for Science and Technology] ... CASE
Committee on Accounting Procedure (TDOB) ... CAP
Committee on Accreditation [American Library Association] ... COA
Committee on Administrative Services of Hospitals ... CASH
Committee on Advanced Television Transmission Systems [Australia] ... CATTS
Committee on Agriculture [Food and Agricultural Organization] [United Nations] ... COAG
Committee on Air and Water Conservation [Later, Committee for Environmental Affairs] [American Petroleum Institute] ... CAWC
Committee on Aircraft Engine Emissions [ICAO] (DA) ... CAEE
Committee on Aircraft Noise [ICAO] (DA) ... CAN
Committee on Allied Health Education and Accreditation (EA) ... CAHEA
Committee on American East Asian Relations [Defunct] (EA) ... AEAR
Committee on American Library Resources on South Asia [Later, CORMOSE A] (EA) ... CALROSA
Committee on American Library Resources on Southeast Asia [Later, CORMOSEA] (EA) ... CALROSEA
Committee on Amphibious Operations (SAA) ... CAO
Committee on Appeal for Human Rights ... COAHR
Committee on Application of Polarized Headlights [OECD] ... CAPH
Committee on Army and Navy Religious Activities [National Jewish Welfare Board] ... CANRA
Committee on Assessing the Progress of Education [Later, NAEP] (EA) ... CAPE
Committee on Atlantic Studies (EA) ... CAS
Committee on Atmospheric Problems of Aerospace Vehicles [American Meteorological Society] ... CAPAV
Committee on Atmospheric Sciences [Marine science] (OSRA) ... CAS
Committee on Autonomous Groups (EA) ... CAG
Committee on Aviation Medicine [NAS/NRC] ... CAM
Committee on Basic Research in Education ... COBRE
Committee on Bibliography and Information Services for the Social Sciences and Humanities [National Library of Canada] ... CBISSSH
Committee on Biological Information [British] (DIT) ... CBI
Committee on Biological Sciences Information [NAS/NRC] ... COBSI
Committee on Boarding Schools (EA) ... CBS
Committee on Canadian Labour History ... CCLH
Committee on Captured Enemy Electronics Equipment ... COCEEE
Committee on Carcinogenicity [British] ... COC
Committee on Cataloging: Description and Access [Association for Library Collections and Technical Services] ... CCDA
Committee on Changing International Realities (EA) ... CIR
Committee on Children's Television, Inc. (NTCM) ... CCTI
Committee on Christian Literature for Women and Children (EA) ... CCLWC
Committee on Christian Literature for Women and Children in Mission Fields [Later, CCLWC] (EA) ... CCLWCMF
Committee on Climatic Changes and the Ocean [Defunct Paris, France] (EAIO) ... CCCO
Committee on Codes and Standards [Defunct] (EA) ... CCS
Committee on Commodity Problems [Rome, Italy] [United Nations] (ASF) ... CCP
Committee on Comparative Urban Economics (EA) ... CCUE
Committee on Computer Science in Electrical Engineering Education [Military] ... COSINE
Committee on Constitutional and Legal Matters [UN Food and Agriculture Organization] ... CCLM
Committee on Consumer Policy [ISO] (DS) ... COPOLCO
Committee on Contamination of Extra-Terrestrial Exploration [NASA] ... CETEX
Committee on Continuing Education for School Personnel (EA) ... CCESP
Committee on Contracting Out [Defunct] (EA) ... COCO
Committee on Contributions for Elective State Officials ... CCESO
Committee on Cooperation in Latin America [of The National Council of Churches of Christ in the USA] (EA) ... CCLA
Committee on Cosmic Humanism (EA) ... CCH
Committee on Crime Prevention and Control [Economic and Social Council of the UN] [Vienna, Austria] (EAIO) ... CCPC
Committee on Data for Science and Technology (EA) ... CODATA
Committee on Data Interchange and Data Centers (MSC) ... CDIDC
Committee on Data Management and Computation [National Academy of Sciences] ... CODMAC
Committee on Decentralization of Controls after V-E Day [War Production Board] ... CODCAVE
Committee on Dental and Surgical Materials [British] (BABM) ... CDSM
Committee on Diagnostic Reading Tests [Defunct] (EA) ... CDRT
Committee on Domestic Technology Transfer [Federal Council for Science and Technology] ... CDTT
Committee on Donor Enlistment [Later, OR] (EA) ... CODE
Committee on Drugs and Alcohol ... CODA
Committee on Earth and Envionmental Sciences [Marine science] (OSRA) ... CEES
Committee on Earth and Environmental Sciences (USDC) ... CEES
Committee on Earth Observations Satellites [NASA] ... CEOS
Committee on Earth Sciences [President's Office of Science & Technology Policy] ... CES
Committee on East Asian Libraries ... CEAL
Committee on Economic Security [Terminated as formal agency, 1936, but continued informally for some time thereafter] ... CES
Committee on Education [American Library Association] ... COE
Committee on Education Needs for Teen-Age Unwed Mothers ... CENTAUM
Committee on Educational Policy in Agriculture [National Academy of Sciences] ... CEPA
Committee on Educational Reconstruction ... CER
Committee on Emergency Medical Identification (EA) ... CEMI
Committee on Energy and the Environment [National Research Council] ... CEE
Committee on Environment and Natural Resources (USDC) ... CENR
Committee on Environment and Natural Resources [National Science and Technology Council] ... CENR
Committee on Environmental Decision Making [National Research Council] ... CEDM
Committee on Environmental Protection [Marine science] (OSRA) ... CEP
Committee on Equal Opportunities in Science and Technology [National Science Foundation] ... CEOST
Committee on Evaluation and Information Systems (OICC) ... CEIS
Committee on Exchanges [Military] ... COMEX
Committee on Extension to the Standard Atmosphere ... COESA
Committee on Fair Employment Practices [World War II] ... CFEP
Committee on Fair Trade with China [Medina, WA] (EA) ... CFTC
Committee on Federal Laboratories [Federal Council for Science and Technology] [Terminated, 1976] ... CFL
Committee on Federal Laboratories [Federal Council for Science and Technology] [Terminated, 1976] (EGAO) ... COFL
Committee on Federalism and National Purpose [Defunct] (EA) ... CFNP
Committee on Fisheries [Food and Agriculture Organization] ... COFI
Committee on Food, Agriculture, and Forestry [Association of South East Asian Nations] [Jakarta, Indonesia] (EAIO) ... COFAF
Committee on Food from the Sea [National Council on Marine Resources and Engineering Development] (GFGA) ... CFFS
Committee on Foreign Correspondence [Freemasonry] ... CFC
Committee on Foreign Investment in the United States ... CFIUS
Committee on Foreign Resistance [War Cabinet] [British World War II] ... CFR
Committee on Foreign Resistance, Economic Policy [Ministry of Supply] [British World War II] ... CFR(EP)
Committee on Forestry [Food and Agricultural Organization] [United Nations] ... COFO
Committee on Free Press and Fair Trial [of the American Newspaper Publishers Association] (EA) ... CFPFT
Committee on Friendly Relations among Foreign Students [Later, ISS] (EA) ... CFR
Committee on Genetic Experimentation [ICSU] ... COGENE
Committee on Geological Sciences [Marine science] (OSRA) ... CGS
Committee on Geological Sciences [National Academy of Sciences] (USDC) ... CGS
Committee on Government Operations ... CGO
Committee on Health and Human Rights (EA) ... CHHR
Committee on Hearing and Bio-Acoustics ... CHABA
Committee on Human Artificial Insemination. Report [1960] [A publication] (ILCA) ... Feversham Cttee
Committee on Human Rights for Nicaragua [Later, CHRPN] (EA) ... CHRN
Committee on Human Rights for the People of Nicaragua (EA) ... CHRPN
Committee on Human Rights in Malaysia and Singapore (EA) ... COHRIMS
Committee on Human Rights of the US National Academy of Sciences (EA) ... CHRUSNAS

Committee on Imagery Requirements and Exploitation [*United States Intelligence Board*] .... COMIREX
Committee on Improvement of National Statistics [*Inter-American*] .... COINS
Committee on Indoor Air Quality [*Environmental Protection Agency*] (GFGA) .... CIAQ
Committee on Information and Cultural Relations (EAIO) .... CICR
Committee on Information Needs .... COIN
Committee on Institutional Cooperation (EA) CIC
[*The*] Committee on Institutional Cooperation Network [*Computer science*] (TNIG) .... CICNet
Committee on Instruction in the Use of Libraries [*Later, CUILL*] (EA) .... IULC
Committee on Integrity and Management Improvement [*Environmental Protection Agency*] (EPA) .... CIMI
Committee on Interagency Radiation Research and Policy Coordination .... CIRRPC
Committee on Interest and Dividends [*Terminated, 1974*] [*Federal Reserve Board*] .... CID
Committee on International Education in Agricultural Sciences [*See also SVLB*] [*Deventer, Netherlands*] (EAIO) .... CIEAS
Committee on International Environmental Affairs [*Department of State*] [*Washington, DC*] (EGAO) .... CIEA
Committee on International Exchange of Persons .... CIEP
Committee on International Exchange of Persons Conference Board of Associated Research Councils [*Later, Council for International Exchange of Scholars*] (EA) .... CIEPCBC
Committee on International Freedom to Publish (EA) .... CIFP
Committee on International Ocean Affairs (USDC) .... CIEA
Committee on International Ocean Affairs [*Department of State*] (NOAA) .... CIOA
Committee on International Policy in the Marine Environment [*National Council on Marine Resouces and Engineering Development*] (GFGA) .... CIPME
Committee on International Reference Atmosphere .... CIRA
Committee on International Relations [*National Education Association*] (AEBS) .... CIR
Committee on International Science, Engineering, and Technology [*US government interagency committee*] [*Washington, DC*] .... CISET
Committee on International Scientific and Technical Information Programs [*Commission on International Relations*] (PDAA) .... CISTIP
Committee on International Scientific and Technical Information Programs [*National Academy of Sciences - National Research Council*] .... CISTIP
Committee on International Security and Arms Control [*National Academy of Sciences*] .... CISAC
Committee on International Standardization [*National Researh Council*] (NUCP) .... COIS
Committee on Interpretation of the Nation-Wide Marine Definition [*Later, COI*] (EA) .... CINWMD
Committee on Invisible Exports [*British*] (DS) .... CIE
Committee on Invisible Exports [*British*] (DS) .... COIE
Committee on Invisibles and Financing Related to Trade [*United Nations Conference on Trade and Development*] .... CIFT
Committee on Israeli Censorship (EA) CIC
Committee on Jobs, Environment, and Technology [*Defunct*] (EA) .... CJET
Committee on Joint Support of Air Navigation Services [*International Civil Aviation Organization*] .... CJSANS
Committee on Justice and the Constitution (EA) .... COJAC
Committee on Latin American and Iberian Studies [*Harvard University*] [*Research center*] .... CLAIS
Committee on Legislation [*American Library Association*] .... COL
Committee on Library Automation [*American Library Association*] .... COLA
Committee on Life Sciences [*Federal interagency group*] .... CLS
Committee on Local Radio Audience Measurement [*National Association of Broadcasters*] (NTCM) .... COLRAM
Committee on Local Television Audience Measurement [*National Association of Broadcasters*] (NTCM) .... COLTAM
Committee on Man and Radiation [*National Research Council*] (NUCP) .... COMAR
Committee on Manpower Opportunities in Israel [*Later, IAC*] .... COMOI
Committee on Manpower Resources for Science and Technology .... CMR
Committee on Manpower Resources for Science and Technology [*British*] .... CMRST
Committee on Man's Underwater Activities (EA) .... CMU/WA
Committee on Marine Research, Education, and Facilities [*National Council on Marine Resources and Engineering Development*] (GFGA) .... CMREF
Committee on Marine Science and Engineering [*Federal Council for Science and Technology*] (NOAA) .... COMSE
Committee on Marine Technology [*British*] .... CMT
Committee on Materials [*Federal Council for Science and Technology*] .... COMAT
Committee on Medical Aspects of Food Policy [*British*] .... CMAFP
Committee on Medical Aspects of Food Policy [*British*] .... COMA
Committee on Medical Aspects of Radiation in the Environment [*British*] .... COMARE
Committee on Medical Journalism (DAVI) .... CMJ
Committee on Medical Research [*Subdivision of OSRD*] [*World War II*] .... CMR
Committee on Mediterranean Neogene Stratigraphy .... CMNS
Committee on Migration and Refugee Affairs (EA) .... CMRA
Committee on Migration and Resettlement [*Department of State*] [*World War II*] .... CMR
Committee on Migration, Refugees, and Demography (EA) .... CMRD
Committee on Militarism in Education [*Defunct*] (EA) .... CME
Committee on Military Nutrition Research .... CMNR
Committee on Mineral Resources and the Environment [*National Research Council*] .... COMRATE
Committee on Missionary Evangelism (EA) .... COME
Committee on Motor Vehicle Emissions [*National Academy of Sciences*] .... CMVE
Committee on Multiple Use of the Coastal Zone [*National Council on Marine Resources and Engineering Development*] (GFGA) .... CMUCZ
Committee on Mutagenicity [*British*] .... COM

Committee on National Library Information Systems .... CONLIS
Committee on National Statistics .... CNSTAT
Committee on National Student Citizenship in Every National Case of Emergency .... CONSCIENCE
Committee on Nationwide Television Audience Measurement (NTCM) .... CONTAM
Committee on New Alternatives in the Middle East [*Later, FOR*] (EA) .... CONAME
Committee on Nuclear and Alternative Energy Systems [*National Research Council*] [*Defunct*] .... CONAES
Committee on Ocean Exploration and Environmental Services [*National Council on Marine Resources and Engineering Development*] (GFGA) .... COEES
Committee on Office Systems and Technology [*Stanford University*] [*Stanford, CA*] (CSR) .... COST
Committee on Organization [*American Library Association*] .... COO
Committee on Overhead Reconnaissance [*Later, COMIREX*] .... COMOR
Committee on Paperless Entries [*Atlanta*] (MHDB) .... COPE
Committee on Parenthood Education [*Defunct*] (EA) .... COPE
Committee on Peaceful Uses of the Sea-Bed and Ocean Floor Beyond Limits of National Jurisdiction [*United Nations*] (EA) .... CPUSOFBLNJ
Committee on Period One [*US committee concerned with the period between the end of the German War and the end of the Japanese War*] [*World War II*] .... CPO
Committee on Persistent Pesticides (EA) .... CPP
Committee on Physics and Society [*of American Institute of Physics*] .... COMPAS
Committee on Planetary and Lunar Exploration [*National Research Council*] .... COMPLEX
Committee on Polar Research [*Later, PRB*] [*US*] .... CPR
Committee on Policy Implementation [*American Library Association*] .... COPI
Committee on Political Education [*AFL-CIO*] (EA) .... COPE
Committee on Political Parties .... CPP
Committee on Pollution Abatement and Control [*National Research Council*] (PDAA) .... COPAC
Committee on Power Plant Siting [*National Academy of Engineering*] .... COPPS
Committee on Principals and Directors of Central Institutions (AIE) .... COPADOCI
Committee on Procedure and Valuation of Reparations [*Allied German Occupation Forces*] .... CPVR
Committee on Professional Ethics, Rights, and Freedom (EA) .... CPERF
Committee on Program Evaluation and Support [*American Library Association*] .... COPES
Committee on Propagation (SAA) .... COP
Committee on Propagation [*National Defense Research Committee*] .... CP
Committee on Prosthetics Research and Development [*National Research Council*] .... CPRD
Committee on Public Doublespeak (EA) .... CPD
Committee on Public Engineering Policy [*National Academy of Engineering*] .... COPEP
Committee on Public Engineering Policy [*National Academy of Engineering*] .... CPEP
Committee on Publications and Communications [*International Council of Scientific Unions*] .... COPAC
Committee on Radiation Oncology Studies [*National Cancer Institute*] .... CROS
Committee on Radio Frequencies [*National Academy of Sciences*] .... CORF
Committee on Radioactive Waste Management [*Later, BRWM*] (EA) .... CRWM
Committee on Reactor Safety Technology .... CREST
Committee on Reciprocal Deliveries [*Allied German Occupation Forces*] .... CRD
Committee on Reference Materials [*ISO*] (DS) .... REMCO
Committee on Remote Sensing Programs for Earth Resource Survey [*Formerly, COSPEAR*] [*National Academy of Sciences*] .... CORSPERS
Committee on Renewable Energy Commerce and Trade (AAGC) .... CORECT
Committee on Research and Statistics [*American Library Association*] .... CORS
Committee on Research Evaluation [*US*] .... CORE
Committee on Research Materials on Southeast Asia (EA) .... CORMOSEA
Committee on Restrictions Against Disabled People (AIE) .... CORAD
Committee on Rhetoric, Administration, and Perspicacity [*Satirical bureaucracy term*] .... CRAP
Committee on Rural Economic and Social Trends .... CREST
Committee on Safety of Medicines [*British*] .... CSM
Committee on Sane Telephone Service .... COSTS
Committee on Scholarly Communications with the People's Republic of China .... CSCPRC
Committee on Scholarly Editions (EA) .... CSE
Committee on Science and Public Policy [*Later, COSEPUP*] [*National Academy of Sciences*] .... COSPUP
Committee on Scientific and Technical Information [*Federal Council for Science and Technology*] [*Defunct*] .... COSATI
Committee on Scientific and Technical Information (NITA) .... COST
Committee on Scientific and Technical Information [*Federal Council for Science and Technology*] [*Defunct*] (IEEE) .... CSTI
Committee on Scientific Information [*Federal Council for Science and Technology*] .... COSI
Committee on Seismology [*Marine science*] (OSRA) .... CS
Committee on Shipping Hydrography [*General Council of British Shipping*] (DS) .... COSH
Committee on Social Development and World Peace of the US Catholic Conference (EA) .... CSDWPUSCC
Committee on Societal Consequences of Transportation Noise Abatement [*National Research Council*] .... CTNA
Committee on Society, Development, and Peace [*of the Roman Catholic Church and the World Council of Churches*] [*Defunct*] (EA) .... SODEPAX
Committee on Solar Electromagnetic Radiation [*British*] (NUCP) .... CSER
Committee on Solar-Terrestrial Research [*National Academy of Sciences*] .... CSTR
Committee on SONAR Model Standards [*Navy*] .... COSMOS
Committee on South African War Resistance [*Defunct*] (EAIO) .... COSAWR

Committee on South Asian Women (EA) .... COSAW
Committee on Space Programs for Earth Observations (EGAO) .... COSPEAR
Committee on Space Research [*of the International Council of Scientific Unions*] [*French*] .... COSPAR
Committee on Special Educational Needs [*Scotland*] (AIE) .... COSPEN
Committee on Special Educational Projects [*Cornell University*] .... COSEP
Committee on State and Local Government Cooperation .... CSLGC
Committee on State Sovereignty [*Defunct*] (EA) .... CSS
Committee on Statistics of Drilling [*American Association of Petroleum Geologists*] (IID) .... CSD
Committee on Sugar Cane Diseases (EA) .... CSCD
Committee on Supply Questions in Liberated Areas (Official) [*World War II*] .... SLAO
Committee on Support of Research in the Mathematical Sciences [*National Academy of Sciences*] .... COSRIMS
Committee on Surface Mining and Reclamation (DICI) .... COSMAR
Committee on the Acquisition and Use of Scientific and Technical Information in Pesticide Regulatory Decision Making at the Federal and State Levels [*National Research Council*] .... CPRDM
Committee on the Administration of Justice [*British*] (DBA) .... CAJ
Committee on the Atlantic Salmon Emergency .... CASE
Committee on the Care of Children [*Defunct*] (EA) CCC
Committee on the Challenges of Modern Society [*Brussels, Belgium*] (EA) .... CCMS
Committee on the Constitutional System (EA) .... CCS
Committee on the Costs of Medical Care (DMAA) .... CCMC
Committee on the Development of Engineering Faculties .... CDEF
Committee on the Economic Impact of Defense and Disarmament (KSC) .... CEIDD
Committee on the Elimination of Discrimination Against Women [*United Nations*] .... CEDAW
Committee on the Exercise of the Inalienable Rights of the Palestinian People (EA) .... CEIRPP
Committee on the Health Services Industry [*Cost of Living Council*] [*Abolished, 1973*] .... CHSI
Committee on the Meteorological Effects of Stratospheric Aircraft .... COMESA
Committee on the Peaceful Uses of Outer Space [*United Nations*] (NITA) .... COPUOS
Committee on the Peaceful Uses of Outer Space [*United Nations*] (BARN) .... CPUOS
Committee on the Peaceful Uses of Outer Space [*United Nations*] (NTCM) .... CUPUOS
Committee on the Present Danger (EA) .... CPD
Committee on the Safety of Machines [*British*] .... CSM
Committee on the Safety of Nuclear Installation [*Nuclear Regulatory Commission*] (NRCH) .... CSNI
Committee on the Standardization of Hospital Graphics [*Defunct*] .... CSHG
Committee on the Status of Women in Anthropology (EA) .... COSWA
Committee on the Status of Women in Librarianship [*American Library Association*] .... COSWL
Committee on the Status of Women in Linguistics (EA) .... CSWL
Committee on the Status of Women in Microbiology (EA) .... CSWM
Committee on the Status of Women in Sociology (EA) .... CSWS
Committee on the Status of Women in the Archival Profession (EA) .... CSWAP
Committee on the Status of Women in the Economics Profession (EA) .... CSWEP
Committee on the Survey of Materials Science and Engineering [*National Academy of Sciences*] [*Obsolete*] .... COSMAT
Committee on the Teaching of Science [*ICSU*] (IRUK) .... CTS
Committee on the Teaching of Science of the International Council of Scientific Unions [*York, England*] (EAIO) .... ICSU-CTS
Committee on the Training of University Teachers (AIE) .... CTUT
Committee on the Unisex Military (EA) .... ComUnMil
Committee on the Unisex Military [*Defunct*] (EA) .... CUM
Committee on the World Food Crisis [*Defunct*] (EA) .... WFC
Committee on Thrombolytic Agents .... CTA
Committee on Tidal Hydraulics [*Army*] .... CTH
Committee on Toxicity [*British*] .... COT
Committee on Trade & the Environment [*World Trade Organization*] .... CTE
Committee on Tunneling and Underground Construction (EA) .... CTUC
Committee on Undersea Warfare .... CUW
Committee on Uniform Crime Records (EA) .... UCR
Committee on Uniform Securities Identification Procedures (MHDB) .... CUSIP
Committee on Uniform Traffic Accident Statistics [*Later, Traffic Records Committee*] (EA) .... CUTAS
Committee on Valuation of Securities .... CVS
Committee on Veterans Medical Problems [*US*] .... CVMP
Committee on Water [*National Academy of Science*] (MSC) .... COW
Committee on Water Resources Research [*US*] .... COWRR
Committee on Women in Asian Studies (EA) .... CWAS
Committee on Women in Public Relations (NTCM) .... CWPR
Committee on Women's Employment and Related Social Issues (EA).... CWERSI
Committee on Women's Employment and Related Social Issues (EA) ..... WERSI
Committee on World Food Security [*United Nations*] (EA) .... CFS
Committee on World Literacy and Christian Literature [*Later, Intermedia*] (EA) .... LIT-LIT
Committee Program Review Council (AAGC) .... CPRC
Committee to Abolish Sport Hunting (EA) .... CASH
Committee to Abolish the Fed (EA) .... CTAF
Committee to Aid Cold War Veterans (EA) .... CACWV
Committee to Aid Democratic Dissidents in Yugoslavia [*Defunct*] (EA).... CADDY
Committee to Assure the Availability of Casein [*Defunct*] (EA) .... CAAC
Committee to Award Miss Piggy the Oscar [*Defunct*] .... CAMPO
Committee to Bridge the Gap (EA) .... CBG
Committee to Cap the National Debt (EA) .... CCND

Committee to Combat Huntington's Disease [*Later, HDFA*] (EA) .... CCHD
Committee to Defend America by Aiding the Allies [*Active prior to US entry into World War II*] .... CDAAA
Committee to Defend Reproductive Rights (EA) .... CDRR
Committee to Defend the First Amendment [*Later, FARI*] (EA) .... CDFA
Committee to Defend the US Constitution [*Defunct*] (EA) .... CDUSC
Committee to Eliminate Legal-Size Files [*Defunct*] (EA) .... CELSF
Committee to Eliminate Premature Christmas Advertising and Display [*Defunct*] (EA) .... CEPCAD
Committee to End Pay Toilets in America [*Defunct*] .... CEPTIA
Committee to End the Marion Lockdown (EA) .... CEML
Committee to Eradicate Syphilis [*Defunct*] (EA) .... CES
Committee to Establish the Gold Standard (EA) .... CEGS
Committee to Expose, Oppose, and Depose Patriarchy (EA) .... CEODP
Committee to Form a US-Albania Friendship Association (EA) .... CFUSAFA
Committee to Halt Indoctrination and Demoralization in Education [*Group opposing sex education in schools*] .... CHIDE
Committee to Halt Useless College Killings [*Acronym is now organization's official name*] (EA) .... CHUCK
Committee to Investigate Assassinations .... CTIA
Committee to Investigate Copyright Problems .... CICP
Committee to Preserve American Color Television (EA) .... COMPACT
Committee to Promote Action [*Poverty program*] .... COMPACT
Committee to Promote Science and Technology .... CPST
Committee to Promote the Study of Austrian History (EA) .... CPSAH
Committee to Promote Uniformity in the Regulation of Motor Carriers .... CPURMC
Committee to Protect Journalists (EA) .... CPJ
Committee to Protect Our Children's Teeth [*Defunct*] (EA) .... CPCT
Committee to Re-Elect the President [*Also, CRP*] [*1972*] .... CREEP
Committee to Re-Elect the President [*Also, CREEP*] [*1972*] .... CRP
Committee to Remove Unnatural Deposits from the Environment [*Student legal action organization*] .... CRUDE
Committee to Rescue Italian Art .... CRIA
Committee to Resist Abortion (EA) .... CRA
Committee to Resist Acronym Proliferation .... CRAP
Committee to Resist the Efforts of the Ex-President [*Opposed Richard Nixon's visit to Oxford University, 1978*] .... CREEP
Committee to Restore the Constitution (EA) .... CRC
Committee to Retain Our Segregated Schools [*Group in Arkansas, organized to oppose STOP*] .... CROSS
Committee to Review Generic Requirements [*Nuclear Regulatory Commission*] .... CRGR
Committee to Save the Peace Symbol [*Student legal action organization*] .... CSPS
Committee to Stop Chemical Atrocities (EA) .... CSCA
Committee to Stop Children's Murder [*Defunct*] (EA) .... CSCM
Committee to Support Irish Political Prisoners (EA) .... CSIPP
Committee to Support Nicaragua [*Defunct*] (EA) .... CSN
Committee to Support the Antitrust Laws (EA) .... COSAT
[*The*] Committee to Unite America [*Defunct*] (EA) .... TCUA
Committee Urging Regulatory Reform for Efficient National Trucking [*Later, BCIPT*] (EA) .... CURRENT
Committees of Correspondence [*National Center for Science Education*] .... C/C
Committees of Correspondence (EA) .... COC
CommNet Cellular [*NASDAQ symbol*] (TTSB) .... CELS
CommNet Cellular, Inc. [*NASDAQ symbol*] (SAG) .... CELS
CommNet Cellular, Inc. [*Associated Press*] (SAG) .... Commnet
Commode [*Medicine*] .... COM
Commodities - Coal and Steel (NATG) .... C/CS
Commodities Data Information Service [*MJK Associates*] [*Santa Clara, CA*] [*Information service or system*] (IID) .... CDIS
Commodities Exchange Center [*New York, NY*] .... CEC
Commodities - Food and Agriculture (NATG) .... C/FA
Commodities Import Program [*Military*] .... CIP
Commodities Research Unit Ltd. [*Originator and Databank*] [*Information service or system*] (IID) .... CRU
Commodity (AABC) .... CMDTY
Commodity .... COM
Commodity .... COMMOD
Commodity Bookform Standard (MCD) .... CBS
Commodity Class Manager .... CCM
Commodity Classification Rates [*British*] (DS) .... CCR
Commodity Command Management Information System [*Army*] .... CCMIS
Commodity Command Standard System .... CCSS
Commodity Command Standard System - Modernization .... CCSS-MOD
Commodity Command Standard System Operating Instructions [*Army*] .... CCSSOI
Commodity Configuration Management System (AFIT) .... CCMS
Commodity Control List [*Office of Export Administration*] CCL
Commodity Coordinated Group Item (DNAB) .... CCGI
Commodity Coordination Groups .... CCG
Commodity Credit Corp. [*Department of Agriculture*] CCC
Commodity Credit Corporation (TDOB) .... CCO
Commodity Exchange [*Investment term*] .... CE
Commodity Exchange (EA) .... COMEX
Commodity Exchange Act .... CEA
Commodity Exchange Authority [*Later, CFTC*] [*Department of Agriculture*] .... CEA
Commodity Exchange Commission [*Functions transferred to CFTC*] .... CEC
Commodity Flow Survey [*BTS*] (TAG) .... CFS
Commodity Flow System .... CFS
Commodity Futures Law Reporter [*Commerce Clearing House*] [*A publication*] (DLA) .... Comm Fut L Rep
Commodity Futures Law Reporter [*Commerce Clearing House*] [*A publication*] (DLA) .... Commodity Futures L Rep

Commodity Futures Trading Commission [Formerly, CEA] [Independent government agency] ... CFTC
Commodity Futures Trading Commission, Washington, DC [Library symbol Library of Congress] (LCLS) ... DCFT
Commodity Information Services Co. (IID) ... CISCO
Commodity Integrated Materiel Manager ... CIMM
Commodity Letter of Credit ... CLOC
Commodity Management Master Plan (MCD) ... CMMP
Commodity Manager Code [Military] ... CMC
Commodity Manager Input Data (MCD) ... CMID
Commodity Master Plan [Army] ... CMP
Commodity Microanalysis, Inc. [Information service or system] (IID) ... CMI
Commodity News Services, Inc. [Information service or system] (IID) ... CNS
Commodity Options [I. P. Sharp Associates] [Database] ... COMOPTIONS
Commodity Oriented General Support ... COGS
Commodity Policy and Relief [British] ... CPR
Commodity Pool Operator ... CPO
Commodity Prices [A publication] ... CP
Commodity Production Statistics [United Nations Statistical Office] [Information service or system] (CRD) ... ICPDATA
Commodity Put and Call Trading Data [Database] [Chronometrics] [Information service or system] (CRD) ... COMPACT
Commodity Quotations, Inc. (IID) ... CQI
Commodity Rate ... CR
Commodity Research Bureau ... CRB
Commodity Stabilization Service [Name changed to Agricultural Stabilization and Conservation Service, 1961] ... CSS
Commodity Supplemental Food Program [Food and Nutrition Service] ... CSFP
Commodity Systems, Inc. [Information service or system] (IID) ... CSI
Commodity Trading Advisor ... CTA
Commodity Transportation Survey [Census Bureau] ... CTS
Commodity World News Network [Later, Futures World News] [Information service or system] (IID) ... CWN
Commodity-Embedded Insurance ... COIN
Commodity-Oriented Digital Label Input System ... CODILS
Commodo [In an Easy Style] [Music] ... COM
Commodo [In an Easy Style] [Music] (ROG) ... COMO
Commodore [Navy British] (ROG) ... C
Commodore ... CDRE
Commodore [British military] (DMA) ... Cmdre
Commodore ... COM
Commodore ... COMD
Commodore (ADA) ... COMDRE
Commodore ... COMM
Commodore ... COMMO
Commodore ... COMO
Commodore [Navy] ... O7
Commodore [ICAO designator] (AD) ... YJ
Commodore Air Train [Navy] ... COMAT
Commodore, Amphibious Forces [British military] (DMA) ... COMAF
Commodore Applied Technologies, Inc. [Associated Press] (SAG) ... CmdrA
Commodore Applied Technologies, Inc. [Associated Press] (SAG) ... CmdrAp
Commodore Applied Technologies, Inc. [AMEX symbol] (SAG) ... CXI
Commodore Aviation [Australia ICAO designator] (FAAC) ... GAR
Commodore Business Machines [Commercial firm] (NITA) ... CBM
Commodore Commanding Newfoundland Force [Navy Canada World War II] ... CCNF
Commodore, Contract-Built Ships [British military] (DMA) ... CCBS
Commodore, (Destroyers) Western Approaches [British] ... COM(D) WA
Commodore Dynamic Total Vision [Interactive TV] ... CDTV
Commodore Information Network [Commodore Business Machines, Inc.] [Information service or system] (TSSD) ... CIN
Commodore, Naval Air Stations, East Africa [British] ... COMNAS(EA)
Commodore, Royal Canadian Navy Barracks at [Place] ... COMBRAX
Commodore Superintendent Contract Built Ships [Navy British] ... CSCBS
Commodore Thomas ap Catesby Jones Society [Defunct] (EA) ... CTAPCJS
Commodore Training [Computer science] ... COMTRAIN
Commodus [of Scriptores Historiae Augustae] [Classical studies] (OCD) ... Comm
Common [Ecology] ... C
Common ... CMMN
Common ... Cmmn
Common ... CMN
Common ... CMN
Common ... COM
Common ... COMM
Common [Commonly used] (OPSA) ... COMMON
Common ... COMN
Common Access Method [Computer programming] (BYTE) ... CAM
Common Access Security Terminal ... CAST
Common Access Switching Equipment (AAG) ... CASE
Common Account Number [Environmental Protection Agency] (GFGA) ... CAN
Common Accounting Reporting System (ADA) ... CARS
Common Acute Lymphoblastic Leukemia Antigen [or Antiserum] [Immunochemistry] ... CALLA
Common Ada Interface Standard [British] ... CAIS
Common ADA Missile Packages (MCD) ... CAMP
Common Aerial Working [Telecommunications] (TEL) ... CAW
Common Agricultural Policy [Common Market] ... CAP
Common Air Interface [Telecommunications] ... CAI
Common Air Interference ... CAI
Common Algorithmic Language [Computer science] (HGAA) ... COMAL
Common and Bulk Items List ... CBIL
Common and Standard [Items] (AAG) ... CS
Common Antigen [Immunochemistry] ... CA
Common Anti-Tank Helicopter (MCD) ... CATH

Common Aperture Multifunction Array RADAR ... CAMAR
Common Aperture Multispectrum Seeker [Army] (MCD) ... CAMS
Common Aperture Technique for Imaging Electro-Optical Sensors (MCD) ... CATIES
Common Application Environment [Computer science] (BTTJ) ... CAE
Common Application Service Element [Computer science] (NITA) ... CASE
Common Application Service Element [Telecommunications] (OSI) ... CASE
Common Applications Environment [Computer science] (BARN) ... CAE
Common APSE [Ada Program Support Environment] Interface Set [Computer science] ... CAIS
Common Arterioventricular Canal [Cardiology] (DAVI) ... CAVC
Common Assembler Language [Computer science] (NITA) ... CAL
Common Assembly Language (MCD) ... CAL
Common Assembly Language for Electronic Warfare (MCD) ... CALEW
Common Assembly Language Scientific Subroutine Package [Computer science] (MHDI) ... CALSSR
Common Assessment Tasks ... CATS
Common Assessment Test [Education] ... CAT
Common Atrioventricular Orifice [Medicine] (DMAA) ... CAVO
Common Attitude Pointing System (MCD) ... CAPS
Common Base [Computer science] (MSA) ... CB
Common Basic Electronics Training (MCD) ... COBET
Common Batch Identification [Computer science] (EECA) ... CBI
Common Battery [Electronics; technical drawings] ... CB
Common Battery Signaling [Telecommunications] (TEL) ... CBS
Common Battery System (MCD) ... CBA
Common Battery System ... CBS
Common Beam Former ... CBF
Common Bench [Legal term] (DLA) ... B
Common Bench [Legal term] ... CB
Common Bench, New Series [A publication] ... CBNS
Common Bench Reports [A publication] ... CB
Common Bench Reports (Manning, Granger, and Scott) [1846-65] [England] [A publication] (DLA) ... Com B
Common Bench Reports (Manning, Granger, and Scott) [1846-65] [England] [A publication] (DLA) ... Comm B
Common Bias (IAA) ... CB
Common Bias, Common Control ... CBCC
Common Bias, Single Control ... CBSC
Common Bile Duct [Medicine] ... CBD
Common Bile Duct Exploration [Medicine] (DAVI) ... CBDE
Common Bile Duct Ligation [Medicine] ... CDL
Common Bile Duct Stenosis [Medicine] ... CBDS
Common Bill of Material (MCD) ... CBM
Common Brick [Construction] (BARN) ... cb
Common Bulkhead Joint ... CBJ
Common Business-Oriented Language [1959] [Computer science] ... COBOL
Common Carier Line Pool (HGAA) ... CCLP
Common Carotid Artery [Anatomy] ... CCA
Common Carotid Artery Blood Flow [Medicine] ... CCABF
Common Carrier [FCC] (NTCM) ... C
Common Carrier ... CC
Common Carrier Bureau [of FCC] ... CCB
Common Carrier Interface (MCD) ... CCI
Common Carrier Line (HGAA) ... CCL
Common Carrier Motor Freight Association, Dallas TX [STAC] ... CCA
Common Carrier Special Application ... CCSA
Common Cause (EA) ... CC
Common Cause Analysis (PDAA) ... COMCAN
Common Cause Failure [Nuclear energy] (NRCH) ... CCF
Common Cause Failure Analysis [Nuclear energy] (NRCH) ... CCFA
Common Channel Interoffice Signaling [Telecommunications] ... CCIS
Common Channel Network Controller [Telecommunications] ... CCNC
Common Channel Signaling [Telecommunications] (TEL) ... CCS
Common Channel Signaling Network Control [Telecommunications] (ACRL) ... CCNC
Common Channel Signaling System [Telecommunications] (TEL) ... SSCC
Common Channel Signalling Arrangement [Telecommunications] (NITA) ... CCSA
Common Channel Signalling System [Telecommunications] (NITA) ... CCSS
Common Chassis Advanced Technology Transition Demonstrator ... CCATTD
Common Claims File [Health insurance] (GHCT) ... CCF
Common Code (IAA) ... CC
Common Cold (HGAA) ... CC
Common Cold Foundation [Defunct] ... CCF
Common Cold Research Unit [British Medical Council] ... CCRU
Common Collector [Amplifier] ... CC
Common Command Language [Computer science] (IT) ... CCL
Common Command Set [Computer science] ... CCS
Common Communication Adapter [Computer science] ... CCA
Common Communications Format [International Standards Organization] (NITA) ... CCF
Common Communications Support [Computer science] (PCM) ... CCS
Common Control [Telecommunications] (TEL) ... CC
Common Control Circuit [Telecommunications] (IAA) ... CCC
Common Control Echo Suppressor [Telecommunications] (TEL) ... CCES
Common Control Interoffice Signaling ... CCIS
Common Control Language [Computer science] (NITA) ... CCL
Common Control Switching Arrangement [AT & T] [Telecommunications] ... CCSA
Common Control Unit [Army] (AABC) ... CCU
Common Core of Data [National Center for Educational Statistics] [Department of Education] (OICC) ... CCD
Common Council [or Councilman] ... CC
Common Cryptographic Architecture [IBM encryption software] (CDE) ... CCA
Common Customs Tariff [Common Market] ... CCT

Common Cycle CC
Common Damage Waiver .... CDW
Common Data Buffer (NASA) .... CDBFR
Common Data Bus [*Computer science*] .... CDB
Common Data Dictionary (MCD) .... CDD
Common Data Format [*Computer science*] .... CDF
Common Data Format .... CDF
Common Data Pool (MCD) .... COMPOOL
Common Data Translation Language .... CDTL
Common Database [*Computer science*] (CAAL) .... CDB
Common Database Design .... CDBD
Common Decking [*Lumber*] .... COMM DECK
Common Defense Installation (AFM) .... CDI
Common Denominator (AAG) .... CD
Common Depth Point [*Seismology*] .... CDP
Common Desktop Environment [*Graphical user interface*] (CDE) .... CDE
Common Destiny Alliance .... CoDA
Common Diagram System (IAA) .... CDS
Common Digitizer [*FAA*] .... CD
Common Display Logic [*Computer science*] .... CDL
Common Distributable Change (DNAB) .... CDC
Common Dollar Accounting (ADA) .... CDA
Common Doppler System (MCD) .... CDS
Common Duct [*Medicine*] .... CD
Common Duct Exploration [*Medicine*] (MAE) .... CDE
Common Effective Preferential Tariff .... CEPT
Common Electronic Parts .... CEP
Common Emitter .... CE
Common Entrance [*Examination for entry into public school*] [*British*] C
Common Entrance [*Examination for entry into public school*] [*British*] .... CE
Common Entrance Examination (BARN) .... CEE
Common Era .... CE
Common Error Analysis (MCD) .... CEA
Common European Demonstrator [*Automotive engineering*] ... CED
Common Experiments Monitoring and Test Equipment (MCD) ... CEMTE
Common External Tariff [*for EEC countries*] [*Also, CXT*] .... CET
Common External Tariff [*EEC*] [*Also, CET*] .... CXT
Common Facilities Test [*NASA*] (NASA) .... CFT
Common Femoral Artery [*Anatomy*] (DAVI) .... CFA
Common Field Effect Transistor [*Computer science*] (ADA) .... CFET
Common File System [*Computer science*] .... CFS
Common Fisheries Policy [*EEC*] .... CFP
Common Foreign and Security Policy [*European Union*] .... CFSP
Common Fund .... CF
Common Fund for Nonprofit Organizations [*Fairfield, CT*] (EA) .... CFNO
[*The*] Common Fund for Nonprofit Organizations [*Ford Foundation*] .... TCFNO
Common Gateway Interface [*Standard that extends the functionality of Web servers*] [*Computer science*] .... CGI
Common Graphics System (MCD) .... CGS
Common Ground Station [*Military*] (RDA) .... CGS
Common Ground Support Equipment (MCD) .... CGSE
Common Ground Support Equipment List (NVT) .... CGSEL
Common Ground - USA (EA) .... CGUSA
Common Hardware and Software [*Army*] .... CHS
Common Hardware Reference Platform [*Computer science*] .... CHRP
Common Hepatic Duct [*Gastroenterology*] (DAVI) .... CHD
Common Heritage Programme, Ottawa, Ontario [*Library symbol National Library of Canada*] (BIB) .... OOCHP
Common High Bandwidth Data Link - Shipboard Terminal (DWSG) .... CHBDL-ST
Common High-Order Language .... CHOL
Common ICAO [*International Civil Aviation Organization*] Data Interchange Network .... CIDIN
Common Input Processor .... CIP
Common Integrated Processor [*Hughes Air Corp.*] .... CIP
Common Interactive Graphics Application Routine [*Army*] .... CIGAR
Common Interest Network (EA) .... CIN
Common Intermediate Format (CDE) .... CIF
Common Internal Iliac Artery [*Medicine*] (DMAA) .... CIIA
Common Internet Scheme Syntax (DMAA) .... CISS
Common Intersection Point [*Graphical representation*] ..... CIP
Common Ion Effect .... CIE
Common Item Order (AFM) .... CIO
Common Language location Identifier [*Telecommunications*] (TSSD) CLLI
Common Language System [*Computer science*] (BUR) .... CLS
Common Law CL
Common Law and Equity Reports [*1853-55*] [*A publication*] (DLA) .... Eq R
Common Law and Equity Reports [*1853-55*] [*A publication*] (DLA) .... Equity Rep
Common Law and Equity Reports, Published by Spottiswoode [*A publication*] (DLA) .... Spottis CL & Eq Rep
Common Law Chamber Reports [*Ontario*] [*A publication*] (DLA) .... CL Ch
Common Law Chamber Reports [*Ontario*] [*A publication*] (DLA) .... CL Chamb
Common Law Chamber Reports [*Ontario*] [*A publication*] (DLA) .... CL Chamb Rep
Common Law Institute of Intellectual Property [*British*] (DBA) .... CLIP
Common Law Procedure [*England*] [*A publication*] (DLA) .... CLP
Common Law Procedure Acts (DLA) .... CLPA
Common Law Reports [*1853-85*] [*A publication*] (DLA) CL
Common Law Reports [*British*] .... CLR
Common Law Reports [*1835-50*] [*Canada*] [*A publication*] (DLA) .... CLR (Can)
Common Law Reports [*1853-85*] [*A publication*] (DLA) .... Com L Rep
Common Law Reports, Volume 3 [*England*] [*A publication*] (DLA) .... Das
Common Leaf Spot [*Plant pathology*] .... CLS
Common Leucocyte Antigen [*Immunology*] .... CLA
Common Line Receiver (IAA) .... CLR
Common LISP [*List Processing Language*] Interface Management [*Computer science*] .... CLIM

Common LISP Object System [*Computer science*] (BYTE) .... CLOS
Common Lodging House [*British*] (ROG) .... CLH
Common Lodging Houses Act [*1851*] [*British*] (ROG) .... CLHA
Common Log File [*Computer science*] .... CLF
Common Logistic Support Group [*Military*] .... CLSG
Common Machine Language [*Computer science*] .... CML
Common Main Objective [*Stereomicroscope optical element*] .... CMO
Common Maintenance Trainer (MCD) .... CMT
[*The*] Common Man in the Street [*The average man*] [*See also MITS*] .... T C MITS
Common Management Information Protocol (PCM) .... CMIP
Common Management Information Protocol Data Unit [*Telecommunications*] (OSI) .... CMIPDU
Common Management Information Service Element [*Telecommunications*] (OSI) .... CMISE
Common Manpower Standards (AFM) .... CMS
Common Manufacturing Information System (IAA) .... CMIS
Common Market (DLA) .... Comm Mkt
Common Market Group of International Rayon and Synthetic Fibres Committee (EAIO) .... CIFRS
Common Market Law Review [*A publication*] (DLA) ...... CML Rev
Common Market Law Review [*A publication*] (DLA) ...... CMLR
Common Market Law Review [*A publication*] (DLA) ...... Comm Market L Rev
Common Market Law Review [*A publication*] (DLA) ...... Common Mkt L Rev
Common Market Newspaper Publishers' Organization [*See also CAEJ*] [*Brussels, Belgium*] (EAIO) .... CMNPO
Common Market Reporter [*Commerce Clearing House*] [*A publication*] (DLA) .... CMR
Common Market Reporter [*Commerce Clearing House*] [*A publication*] (DLA) .... Comm Mkt Rep
Common Market Reporter (Commerce Clearing House) [*A publication*] (DLA) .... CCH Comm Mkt Rep
Common Market Travel Association (EAIO) .... CMT
Common Measure [*Music*] (IIA) .... CM
Common Memory Manager (NITA) .... CMM
Common Messaging Calls [*Computer science*] .... CMC
Common Meter [*Music*] C
Common Meter [*Music*] .... CM
Common Meter Double [*Music*] .... CMD
Common Migraine [*Neurology*] (DAVI) .... CM
Common Military Intelligence Skills (NVT) .... CMIS
Common Mode (IAA) .... CM
Common Mode [*NASA*] (GFGA) .... COM-M
Common Mode Error .... CME
Common Mode Failure [*Nuclear energy*] (NRCH) .... CMF
Common Mode Failure Analysis [*Nuclear energy*] (NRCH) .... CMFA
Common Mode Input Resistance .... CMIR
Common Mode Interface (IAA) .... CMI
Common Mode Logic .... CML
Common Mode Operation [*Telecommunications*] (TEL) .... CMO
Common Mode Processing System (CAAL) .... CMPS
Common Mode Rejection .... CMR
Common Mode Rejection Ratio .... CMRR
Common Mode Signal .... CMS
Common Mode Voltage .... CMV
Common Mode Voltage Range .... CMVR
Common Mode-to-Common Mode (IAA) .... CMTOCM
Common Mode-to-Differential Mode (IAA) .... CMTODM
Common Modular Multimode RADAR .... CMMR
Common Mounting System (PDAA) .... CMS
Common Nacelle System/Engine Build-Up (MCD) .... CNS/EBU
Common Name (ACRL) .... CN
Common Network Architecture (IAA) .... CNA
Common Network Management System [*Unisys Corp.*] .... CNMS
Common Network Representation [*Telecommunications*] (OSI) .... CNR
Common (Noun) [*Linguistics*] .... CN
Common Noun Keywords (PDAA) .... CNK
Common Nozzle Assembly (MCD) .... CNA
Common Null Cell Acute Lymphoblastic Leukemia [*Medicine*] .... CALL
Common Number System (AAG) .... CNS
Common Object Model [*Microsoft*] .... COM
Common Object Request Broken Architecture .... CORBA
Common Object Request Broker Architecture [*Computer science*] .... CORBA
Common Object Request Broker Architecture [*For computer databases*] .... CORBA
Common On-Line Package [*Fujitsu Ltd.*] [*Japan*] .... COP
Common Open Software Environment (PCM) .... COSE
Common Operating Environment .... COE
Common Operating System Control Language .... COSCL
Common Operational Research Equipment (NASA) .... CORE
[*A*] Common Operational Software (MCD) .... ACOS
Common Optoelectronics LASER Detection System ...... COLDS
Common Orders (DLA) .... CO
Common Ownership Design and Construct [*British*] ..... CODAC
Common Part Convergence Sublayer [*Electronics*] (ACRL) .... CPCS
Common Particular Meter [*Music*] .... CPM
Common Payload Support Equipment [*NASA*] (NASA) .... CPSE
Common Peak Developed Isovolumic Pressure [*Cardiology*] (DAVI) .... CPIP
Common Peripheral Channel (NITA) .... CPC
Common Personal Hygiene Equipment (KSC) .... CPHE
Common Pleas [*Legal term*] (DAS) .... Com Pl
Common Pleas [*Legal term*] .... CP
Common Pleas Division [*Legal term*] .... CPD
Common Pleas Division, English Law Reports [*1875-80*] [*A publication*] (DLA) .... Com P Div

Common Pleas Division, English Law Reports [*1875-80*] [*A publication*] (DLA) .... Com Pl
Common Pleas Division, English Law Reports [*1875-80*] [*A publication*] (DLA) .... Com Pl Div
Common Pleas Division, English Law Reports [*1875-80*] [*A publication*] (DLA) .... CP Div
Common Pleas Division, English Law Reports [*1875-80*] [*A publication*] (DLA) .... CP Div (Eng)
Common Pleas Division, English Law Reports [*1875-80*] [*A publication*] (DLA) .... CP (Eng)
Common Pleas Reporter [*Scranton, PA*] [*A publication*] (DLA) .... Com P Reptr
Common Pleas Reporter [*Scranton, PA*] [*A publication*] (DLA) .... Com Pl R (PA)
Common Pleas Reporter [*Scranton, PA*] [*A publication*] (DLA) .... Com Pl Reptr
Common Pleas Reporter [*Scranton, PA*] [*A publication*] (DLA) .... CP Rep
Common Pleas Reporter [*Scranton, PA*] [*A publication*] (DLA) .... CP Rept
Common Pleas Reports [*Upper Canada*] [*A publication*] (DLA) .... CPUC
Common Pleas Subpoena [*Legal*] [*British*] (ROG) .... CPSPA
Common Power Supply Group .... CPSG
Common Prayer .... CP
Common Price and Marketing Arrangement [*British*] .... CPMA
Common Procedural Terminology [*Human resources*] (WYGK) .... CPT
Common Process [*Telecommunications*] (TEL) .... CP
Common Professional Examination (DLA) .... CPE
Common Program Control Station [*Emergency Broadcast System*] .... CPCS
Common Program Interface [*Computer science*] .... CPI
Common Program Language [*Computer science*] (AABC) .... CPL
Common Program Support System .... CPSS
Common Programming Interface for Communication [*Telecommunications*] (ACRL) .... CPI/C
Common Programming Interface for Communications (CDE) .... CPI-C
Common Pulse Line .... CPL
Common Query System [*Navy*] (DNAB) .... CQS
Common RADAR Antenna Mount (DWSG) .... CRAM
Common Radio and Electronic Test Equipment [*Navy British*] (DEN) .... CRETE
Common Random Number [*Mathematics*] (IAA) .... CRN
Common Real-Time Operating System (CAAL) .... CROS
Common Reference Point [*Navigation*] (IAA) .... CRP
Common Register of Development Projects [*United Nations*] .... CORE
Common Return [*Electronics*] (IAA) .... CR
Common/See Individual Components List (MCD) .... COMSICL
Common Sense Algorithm (MCD) .... CSA
Common Serjeant [*British*] (ILCA) .... Com Serj
Common Serjeant [*British*] (ROG) .... CS
Common Service Area [*Computer science*] (BUR) .... CSA
Common Services Agency [*Scottish Health Service*] [*Research center*] .... CSA
Common Services Network [*Telecommunications*] (TEL) .... CSN
Common Services Rack [*Telecommunications*] (TEL) .... CSR
Common Services Subsystem [*Telecommunications*] (TEL) .... CSS
Common Services Unit [*Telecommunications*] (TEL) .... CSU
Common Set (MCD) .... CS
Common Signal Processor [*Military*] (DOMA) .... CSP
Common Signaling Channel (IEEE) .... CSC
Common Skills Shop [*Military*] (DNAB) .... CSS
Common Slavic [*Language, etc.*] .... CS
Common Source Noise Figure .... CSNF
Common Source Power Gain .... CSPG
Common Source Spot Noise .... CSSN
Common Source Spot Noise Figure .... CSSNF
Common Specialist Training .... CST
Common Specification Language (NATG) .... CSL
Common Specifications Statements Generator (KSC) .... COMGEN
Common Steel [*Projectile*] .... CS
Common Stock [*Investment term*] .... CS
Common Strategic Doppler (MCD) .... CSD
Common Strategic Rotary Launcher .... CSRL
Common Subnet Node [*Telecommunications*] (OSI) .... CSN
Common Supply Support [*Military*] (AABC) .... CSSPT
Common Supply Support Overseas [*Military*] .... COMSOS
Common Support Equipment (NASA) .... CSE
Common Support Module [*NASA*] (NASA) .... CSM
Common System Area (IAA) .... CSA
Common Systems Main Interconnecting [*Frame system*] [*Bell System*] .... COSMIC
Common Table of Allowances [*Army*] (AABC) .... CTA
Common Task Test [*Army*] (INF) .... CTT
Common Task Training [*Military*] (ADDR) .... CTT
Common Technical Interface Design Plan [*Joint technical document developed by the US, UK, and Germany*] [*Military*] (RDA) .... CTIDP
Common Terminal RADAR Approach Control [*Aviation*] (FAAC) .... CTRAC
Common Terminating System (MCD) .... CTS
Common Test Data Collection System (MCD) .... CTDCS
Common Test Facility .... CTF
Common Test Subroutine [*Computer science*] .... CTS
Common Test/Support Equipment (MCD) .... CTSE
Common Time C
Common Track Stores Indicator (CAAL) .... CTSI
Common Traffic Advisory Frequency [*FAA*] (TAG) .... CTAF
Common Traffic Advisory Frequency (FAAC) .... CTAF
Common Transmission Format (MCD) .... CTF
Common University Fund [*British*] .... CUF
Common Usage Equipment (NASA) .... CUE
Common Usage Item List (NASA) .... CUIL
Common Usage Radio Frequency Checkout Equipment (KSC) .... CURFCOE
Common Use (ROG) .... CU
Common Use Terminal Equipment [*Travel industry*] .... CUTE
Common User Access [*Computer science*] (BYTE) .... CUA
Common User Access Architecture [*Computer science*] (DOM) .... CUA Architecture
Common User Baseline for the Intelligence Community (MCD) .... CUBIC
Common User Data [*Telecommunications*] (TEL) .... CUDAT
Common User Data Network (ADA) .... CUDN
Common User Data Services (NITA) .... CUDS
Common User Data Terminal [*Military*] (AABC) .... CUDAT
Common User Digital Information Exchange [*Satellite communication*] (NVT) .... CUDIX
Common User Digital Information Exchange System [*or Subsystem*] [*Satellite communication*] (MCD) .... CUDIXS
Common User, Dynamic Allocation Multi-Media Network (MCD) .... CUDAMN
Common User Group [*SAGE*] .... CUG
Common User Interface [*Computer science*] .... CUI
Common User Interoffice Network [*Telecommunications*] (ECII) .... CUIN
Common User Land Transportation [*Military*] (NVT) .... CULT
Common User Radio Transmission System (IAA) .... CURTS
Common User System [*Telecommunications*] (TEL) .... CUS
Common Variable Hypogammaglobulinemia [*Medicine*] (MAE) .... CVH
Common Variable Immune Deficiency [*Immunology*] (DAVI) .... CVID
Common Variable Immunodeficiency [*Medicine*] CVI
Common Version [*Bible*] CV
Common Version of the Bible (BARN) .... Com Ver
Common Video System .... CVS
Common Weapon Control System [*Military*] .... CWCS
Common Weapon Control System Development Facility (MCD) .... CDF
Common X Interface [*Computer science*] CXI
Commonality and Standardization Effort (MCD) .... CASE
Commonality Candidate List [*NASA*] (NASA) CCL
Commonality Usage Board (NASA) .... CUB
Commonality Usage Proposal (NASA) .... CUP
Common-Channel Interface Signaling (IDOE) .... CCIS
Common-Equipment System (IAA) .... CES
Common-Impression Cylinder CIC
Commonly Used Acronym .... CUA
Commonly Used System Programs [*Digital Equipment Corp.*] .... CUSP
Common-Midpoint .... CMP
Common-Object Request Broker Architecture [*Computer science*] .... CORBA
Common-Object-File Format [*Computer science*] .... COFF
Commons Expenditure Committee [*British*] .... CEC
Commons, Open Spaces, and Footpaths Preservation Society [*British*] (BARN) .... COSFPS
Commons Registration Act [*Town planning*] [*British*] .... CRA
Commonweal [*A publication*] (BRI) .... Comw
Commonwealth .... CMNWLTH
Commonwealth .... COM
Commonwealth .... COMM
Commonwealth (DLA) .... Commonw
Commonwealth (DLA) .... Commw
Commonwealth (DLA) .... Com'w'th
Commonwealth (ADA) .... CTH
Commonwealth .... Cw
Commonwealth .... CWLTH
Commonwealth .... Cwth
Commonwealth Accreditation Agency [*Australia*] .... CAA
Commonwealth Act (DLA) .... Commonw Act
Commonwealth Acts (Australia) [*A publication*] (DLA) .... Austl C Acts
Commonwealth Advisory Aeronautical Research Council [*British*] (EAIO) .... CAARC
Commonwealth Agricultural Bureaux [*Database producer*] (EA) .... CAB
Commonwealth Agricultural Bureaux International [*Research center British*] (IRC) .... CABI
Commonwealth Air Force Telecommunications Network (IAA) .... CAFTN
Commonwealth Air Training Plan Museum, Inc., Brandon, Manitoba [*Library symbol National Library of Canada*] (NLC) .... MBCAM
Commonwealth Air Training Plan Museum, Inc., Brandon, MB, Canada [*Library symbol*] [*Library of Congress*] (LCLS) .... CaMBCAM
Commonwealth Air Transport Council [*British*] (EAIO) .... CATC
Commonwealth Aircraft Corp. Ltd. [*Australia ICAO aircraft manufacturer identifier*] (ICAO) CC
Commonwealth Aluminum [*NASDAQ symbol*] (TTSB) .... CALC
Commonwealth Aluminum Corp. [*NASDAQ symbol*] (SAG) .... CALC
Commonwealth Aluminum Corp. [*Associated Press*] (SAG) .... CmwAl
Commonwealth and Empire Radio for Civil Aviation [*British*] .... CERCA
Commonwealth Archivists Association [*Later, ACARM*] (EA) .... CAA
Commonwealth Arts Organization (EA) .... CAO
Commonwealth Association for Education and Training of Adults .... CAETA
[*The*] **Commonwealth Association for Education in Journalism & Communication** (AC) .... CAEJC
Commonwealth Association of Architects [*British*] (EAIO) .... CAA
Commonwealth Association of Legislative Counsel (AC) .... CALC
Commonwealth Association of Mental Handicap and Developmental Disabilities (EA) .... CAMHDD
Commonwealth Association of Museums [*Calgary, AB*] (EAIO) .... CAM
Commonwealth Association of Museums (AC) .... CAM
Commonwealth Association of Planners [*British*] (EAIO) .... CAP
Commonwealth Association of Polytechnics in Africa [*Nairobi, Kenya*] (EAIO) .... CAPA
Commonwealth Association of Science and Mathematics Educators [*British*] .... CASME
Commonwealth Association of Science, Technology, and Mathematics Educators [*London, England*] (EAIO) .... CASTME
Commonwealth Association of Scientific Agricultural Societies [*Canada*] .... CASAS
Commonwealth Association of Surveying and Land Economy [*British*] (EAIO) .... CASLE

Commonwealth Association of Tax Administrators [*British*] (EAIO) .... CATA
Commonwealth Banana Exporters Association [*Saint Lucia*] (EAIO) .... CBEA
Commonwealth Banking Corporation [*Australia*] .... CBC
Commonwealth Banking Corporation. Economic Newsletter [*A publication*] (ADA) .... CBEN
Commonwealth Board of Architectural Education [*British*] (EAIO) .... CBAE
Commonwealth Board of Surveying Education [*London, England*] (EAIO) .... CBSE
Commonwealth Broadcasting Association [*London, England*] (EAIO) .... CBA
Commonwealth Broadcasting Association. Handbook [*A publication*] .... CBA Handbook
Commonwealth Broadcasting Network [*British*] (NTCM) .... CBN
Commonwealth Bureau of Animal Health [*British*] .... CBAH
Commonwealth Bureau of Animal Nutrition [*British*] .... CBAN
Commonwealth Bureau of Dairy Science and Technology [*British*] .... CBDST
Commonwealth Bureau of Helminthology (BI) .... CBH
Commonwealth Bureau of Horticulture and Plantation Crops [*British*] .... CBHPC
Commonwealth Bureau of Pastures and Field Crops [*British*] .... CBPFC
Commonwealth Bureau of Soils [*British*] .... CAB
Commonwealth Bureau of Soils [*British*] .... CBS
Commonwealth Chess Association (EA) .... CCA
Commonwealth Club of California, San Francisco, CA [*Library symbol Library of Congress*] (LCLS) .... CSfCCL
Commonwealth Code, Commonwealth of the Northern Mariana Islands [*A publication*] .... CNMI
Commonwealth Committee for Defence (Operational Clothing and Combat Equipment) (ADA) .... CCD(OCCE)
Commonwealth Committee on Fuel Research [*British*] .... CCFR
Commonwealth Committee on Mineral Resources and Geology [*British*] .... CCMRG
Commonwealth Communications Council [*British World War II*] CCC
Commonwealth Copyright Office (DGA) .... CCO
Commonwealth Correspondents' Association (BI) .... CCA
Commonwealth Council for Educational Administration [*British*] (AIE) .... CCEA
Commonwealth Countries' League [*Middlesex, England*] (EAIO) CCL
Commonwealth Court (DLA) .... Commw Ct
Commonwealth Defence Conference - Operational Clothing and Combat Equipment (EA) .... CDC-OCCE
Commonwealth Defence Science Organisation [*British*] .... CDSO
Commonwealth Department of Employment, Education, and Training [*Australia*] .... CDEET
Commonwealth Development Bank of Australia .... CDBA
Commonwealth Development Corp. (ILCA) .... CDC
Commonwealth Development Finance Co. Ltd. [*Joint government and private agency in London established to aid businesses elsewhere in British Commonwealth*] .... CDFC
Commonwealth Dried Vine Fruits Grade Fixing Committee [*Australia*] .... CDVFGFC
Commonwealth Economic Committee [*British*] .... CEC
Commonwealth Economic Consultative Council [*British*] .... CECC
Commonwealth Ed, $1.90 Pref [*NYSE symbol*] (TTSB) .... CWEPrC
Commonwealth Ed, $2.00 Pref [*NYSE symbol*] (TTSB) .... CWEPrD
Commonwealth Ed $8.40 Pvet [*NYSE symbol*] (TTSB) .... CWEPrJ
Commonwealth Ed,$7.24 Pref [*NYSE symbol*] (TTSB) .... CWEPrE
Commonwealth Ed,$8.38 Pref [*NYSE symbol*] (TTSB) .... CWEPrI
Commonwealth Ed,$8.40 Pref [*NYSE symbol*] (TTSB) .... CWEPrF
Commonwealth Ed,$2.425 Pref [*NYSE symbol*] (TTSB) .... CWEPrK
Commonwealth Edison Co. (MHDB) .... CEC
Commonwealth Edison Co. [*Associated Press*] (SAG) .... CwE
Commonwealth Edison Co., Chicago, IL [*Library symbol Library of Congress*] (LCLS) .... ICComE
Commonwealth Education Conferences [*British*] .... CEC
Commonwealth Education Liaison Committee [*British*] .... CELC
Commonwealth Employment Service Advisory Committee [*Australia*] .... CESAC
Commonwealth Energy Management Program .... CEMP
Commonwealth Energy Sys [*NYSE symbol*] (TTSB) .... CES
Commonwealth Energy System [*NYSE symbol*] (SPSG) .... CES
Commonwealth Energy System [*Associated Press*] (SAG) .... ComES
Commonwealth Engineer [*A publication*] .... Commonwealth Eng
Commonwealth Engineering Conference (MCD) .... CEC
Commonwealth Engineers Council [*See also CAICB*] [*British*] (EAIO) .... CEC
Commonwealth Expedition [*British*] .... COMEX
Commonwealth Forestry Association [*Oxford, England*] (EAIO) .... CFA
Commonwealth Forestry Bureau [*Oxford, England*] .... CFB
Commonwealth Forestry Institute [*British*] .... CFI
Commonwealth Foundation (EAIO) .... CF
Commonwealth Fund for Technical Co-Operation [*British*] (EAIO) .... CFTC
Commonwealth Fund, New York, NY [*Library symbol Library of Congress*] (LCLS) .... NNCF
[*The*] **Commonwealth Games Association of Canada Inc.** [*Association Canadienne des Jeux du Commonwealth Inc.*] (AC) .... CGAC
Commonwealth Games Federation [*British*] (EAIO) .... CGF
Commonwealth Geographical Bureau (EA) .... CGB
Commonwealth Gold [*Vancouver Stock Exchange symbol*] .... CWC
Commonwealth Government Directory [*Australia A publication*] .... CGD
Commonwealth Hansard Editors Association (EAIO) .... CHEA
Commonwealth Heraldry Board [*Papatoetoe, New Zealand*] (EAIO) .... CHB
Commonwealth Holiday Inns of Canada .... CHIC
Commonwealth Human Ecology Council [*British*] .... CHE
Commonwealth Human Ecology Council [*British*] (EAIO) .... CHEC
Commonwealth Institute [*British*] (DI) CI
Commonwealth Institute of Biological Control [*Trinidad*] .... CIBC
Commonwealth Institute of Entomology [*British*] (MCD) .... CIE
Commonwealth Institute of Helminthology [*St. Albans, England*] .... CIH
Commonwealth International Law Cases [*A publication*] (DLA) CILC
Commonwealth International Philatelic Society [*Defunct*] (EA) .... CIPS
Commonwealth Internet Reference Group [*Information service or system*] .... CIRG
Commonwealth Investigation Branch [*Australia*] .... CIB
Commonwealth Jam Preserving and Condiment Manufacturers' Association [*Australia*] .... CJPCMA
Commonwealth Jet Services, Inc. [*ICAO designator*] (FAAC) .... CJS
Commonwealth Joint Communication Board [*British military*] (DMA) .... CJCB
Commonwealth Journalists Association [*British*] (EAIO) .... CJA
Commonwealth Judicial Journal [*A publication*] (DLA) .... Comm Jud J
Commonwealth Judicial Journal [*A publication*] (DLA) .... Commw Jud J
Commonwealth Land Party [*British*] (DAS) .... CLP
Commonwealth Law Enforcement Assistance Network [*Pennsylvania*] .... CLEAN
Commonwealth Law Review [*A publication*] .... Com LR
Commonwealth Law Review [*A publication*] (DLA) .... Commonw L Rev
Commonwealth Lawyers' Association [*British*] (EAIO) .... CLA
Commonwealth Legal Aid Commision [*Australia*] .... CLAC
Commonwealth Legal Education Association (EAIO) .... CLEA
Commonwealth Library Association .... CLA
Commonwealth Magistrates and Judges' Association (EAIO) .... CM & JA
Commonwealth Magistrates' Association [*British*] (EAIO) .... CMA
Commonwealth Medical Association [*British*] (EAIO) .... CMA
Commonwealth Medical Officers' Association [*Australia*] .... CMOA
Commonwealth Microfilm Library Ltd., Calgary, AB, Canada [*Library symbol Library of Congress*] (LCLS) .... CmL
Commonwealth Microfilm Library Ltd., Calgary, AB, Canada [*Library symbol*] [*Library of Congress*] (LCLS) .... CmLL
Commonwealth Military Forces [*British*] .... CMF
Commonwealth Minerals [*Vancouver Stock Exchange symbol*] .... CMY
Commonwealth Mycological Institute [*Research center British*] (IRC) .... CMI
Commonwealth Nation .... CN
Commonwealth National Library (DGA) .... CNL
Commonwealth National Library, Parliament House, Canberra, ACT, Australia [*Library symbol Library of Congress*] (LCLS) .... AuCNL
Commonwealth Nurses Federation (EA) .... CNF
Commonwealth of Australia .... COA
Commonwealth of Independent States [*Formerly, Soviet Union*] .... CIS
[*The*] **Commonwealth of Learning** (AC) .... COL
Commonwealth of Puerto Rico Rules and Regulations [*A publication*] (DLA) .... PRR & Regs
Commonwealth of World Citizens .... CWC
Commonwealth Office [*Formerly, CRO*] [*British*] .... CO
Commonwealth Office of Local Government [*Australia*] .... COLG
Commonwealth Ombudsman [*Australia*] .... CO
Commonwealth Parliamentary Association [*British*] (EAIO) .... CPA
Commonwealth Party [*Gibraltar*] [*Political party*] (PPE) .... CP
Commonwealth Pharmaceutical Association [*British*] (EAIO) .... CPA
Commonwealth Preference Area .... CPA
Commonwealth Preference Standstill Area (PDAA) .... CPSA
Commonwealth Press Union [*London, England*] (EAIO) .... CPU
Commonwealth Procurement Circular [*A publication*] .... CPC
Commonwealth Professional [*A publication*] .... Com Prof
Commonwealth Program for the Promotion of Excellence in Research [*Australia*] .... CPPER
Commonwealth Record [*Australia A publication*] .... Comm Rec
Commonwealth Record [*A publication*] .... Commonw Rec
Commonwealth Record [*Australia A publication*] .... CR
Commonwealth Refining Co. [*Puerto Rico*] .... CORCO
Commonwealth Regional Health Secretariat (EA) .... CRHS
Commonwealth Regional Renewable Energy Resources Information Service (IID) .... CRRERIS
Commonwealth Relations Office [*Later, CO*] [*British*] .... CRO
Commonwealth Research Centre .... CRC
Commonwealth Savings [*NASDAQ symbol*] (TTSB) .... CMSB
Commonwealth Savings Bank [*NASDAQ symbol*] (SAG) .... CMSB
Commonwealth Savings Bank [*Associated Press*] (SAG) .... CwltSav
Commonwealth Savings Bank of Australia .... CSBA
Commonwealth Scholarship Scheme [*Australia*] .... CSS
Commonwealth Science Council [*London, England*] (EAIO) .... CSC
Commonwealth Scientific and Industrial Research Automatic Computer [*British*] (IAA) .... CSIRAC
Commonwealth Scientific and Industrial Research Organisation [*Australia*] [*Information service or system*] (NITA) .... CSIRO
[*The*] **Commonwealth Scientific and Industrial Research Organization Network** [*Australia*] [*Computer science*] (TNIG) .... CSIRONET
Commonwealth Scientific and Research Organisation Network [*Australia*] [*Information service or system*] (NITA) .... CSIRONET
Commonwealth Scientific Committee [*British*] .... CSC
Commonwealth Secondary Scholarship Scheme [*Australia*] .... CSSS
Commonwealth Secretariat (DLA) .... Comm Sec
Commonwealth Secretariat (DLA) .... Commw Sec
Commonwealth Secretariat [*Australia*] .... CS
Commonwealth Secretariat [*British*] (EAIO) .... CS
Commonwealth Service Corps [*British*] .... CSC
Commonwealth Society for the Deaf [*British*] (ADA) .... CSD
Commonwealth Society of Teachers of Dancing [*Australia*] .... CSTD
Commonwealth/State Migration Committee [*Australia*] .... COSMIC
Commonwealth Steamship Owners' Association [*Australia*] .... CSOA
Commonwealth Steel Company Ltd. [*Australia*] .... COMSTEEL
Commonwealth Supply Council [*British World War II*] .... CSC
Commonwealth Taxation Board of Review [*Australia*] .... CTBR
Commonwealth Telecommunications Board [*Later, CTO*] [*British*] .... CTB
Commonwealth Telecommunications Organization [*England*] .... CTO
Commonwealth Trade Union Council [*British*] (EAIO) .... CTUC
Commonwealth Trading Bank of Australia .... CTBA
Commonwealth Trans-Antarctic Expedition [*1955-58*] .... CTAS

Commonwealth Transpacific [*Submarine cable in Pacific*]	COMPAC
Commonwealth Veterinary Association	CVA
Commonwealth War Graves Commission [*Maidenhead, Berkshire, England*] (EAIO)	CWGC
Commonwealth Weightlifting Federation [*Ammanford, Dyfed, Wales*] (EAIO)	CWF
Commonwealth Writers of Britain (BI)	CWB
Commonwealth Year Book [*A publication*]	CYB
Commonwealth Youth Exchange Council [*British*]	CYEC
Commonwealth Youth Programme [*British*]	CYP
Commonwealth-State Advisory Group [*Australia*]	CSAG
Commonwealth-State Housing Agreement (Service Personnel) [*Australia*]	CSHA(SP)
Communal	Comm
Communal Areas Management Program for Indigenous Resources	CAMPFIRE
Communal Studies Association (EA)	CSA
Communante des Associations d'Editeurs de Journaux [*Community of Associations of Newspaper Publishers*] [*EEC Belgium*] (PDAA)	CAEJ
Communaute de Travail des Brasseurs du Marche Commun [*Working Committee of Common Market Brewers*]	CBMC
Communaute de Travail des Regions Europeennes de Tradition Industrielle [*Association of Traditional Industrial Regions of Europe*] [*Lille, France*] (EAIO)	RETI
Communaute des Associations d'Editeurs de Journaux de la CEE [*Community of the Newspaper Publishing Associations of the EEC*] [*Belgium*]	CAEJ-CEE
Communaute des Chemins de Fer Europeens [*Belgium*] (EAIO)	CCFE
Communaute des Radios Publiques de Langue Francaise (EAIO)	CRPLF
Communaute Economique des Etats de l'Afrique Centrale [*Economic Community of Central African States - ECCAS*] [*Bangui, Central African Republic*] (EAIO)	CEEAC
Communaute Economique des Pays des Grands Lacs [*Economic Community of the Great Lakes Countries - ECGLC*] [*Gisenye, Rwanda*] (EAIO)	CEPGL
Communaute Economique du Betail et de la Viande [*Economic Community for Livestock and Meat - ECLM*] (EAIO)	CEBV
Communaute Economique Europeenne [*European Economic Community*]	CEE
Communaute EURAIL [*EURAIL Community*] [*An association Netherlands*] (EAIO)	CE
Communaute Europeenne [*European Community*]	CE
Communaute Europeenne de Credit Communal [*European Municipal Credit Community*]	CECC
Communaute Europeenne de Defense [*European Defense Community*]	CED
Communaute Europeenne de l'Energie Atomique	CEEA
Communaute Europeenne des Associations du Commerce de Gros de Biere des Pays Membres de la CEE [*European Community of Associations of the Wholesale Beer Trade of the EEC*]	CEGROB
Communaute Europeenne des Cooperatives de Consommateurs [*European Consumers' Cooperation Committee*] [*Common Market*]	EURO COOP
Communaute Europeenne des Organisations de Publicitaires [*European Community of Advertising Organizations*]	CEOP
Communaute Europeenne du Charbon et de l'Acier [*European Coal and Steel Community*]	CECA
Communaute Financiere Africaine [*Currency*] (ECON)	CFA
Communaute Internationale Baha'ie [*Baha'i International Community*]	CIB
Communaute Internationale des Associations de la Librairie [*International Community of Booksellers Associations*]	CIAL
Communaute Internationale des Obtenteurs de Plantes Ornementales et Fruitieres aReproduction Asexuee [*International Community of Breeders of Asexually Reproduced Fruit Trees and Ornamental Varieties*] [*Geneva, Switzerland*] (EAIO)	CIOPORA
Communaute Mondiale de Vie Chretienne [*World Christian Life Community*] [*Italy*] (EAIO)	CVX
Communaute Urbaine de Quebec [*Library symbol National Library of Canada*] (BIB)	QQCUQ
Commune (ABBR)	CMUN
Commune	COM
Commune	COMMN
Communed (ABBR)	CMUND
Communes Network [*British*] (EAIO)	CN
Communic Central [*NASDAQ symbol*] (TTSB)	CCIX
Communic Sys [*NASDAQ symbol*] (TTSB)	CSII
Communicability (ABBR)	CMUNCBT
Communicable (ABBR)	CMUNCB
Communicable [*Medicine*]	commun
Communicable Disease [*or a patient with such a disease*] [*Medicine*]	CD
Communicable Disease (DAVI)	commun dis
Communicable Disease Center	CDC
Communicable Disease Report [*A publication*]	CD
Communicable Disease Surveillance Centre [*British*]	CDSC
Communicableness (ABBR)	CMUNCBNS
Communicably (ABBR)	CMUNCBY
Communicant (ABBR)	CMUNCNT
Communicant [*Religion*] (ROG)	COM
Communicate (MDG)	CMCT
Communicate (ABBR)	CMUNC
Communicate [*or Communications*]	COM
Communicate	COMMUN
Communicated (ABBR)	CMUNCD
Communicating (ABBR)	CMUNCG
Communicating Alarm Response Equipment [*British Telecom*]	CARE
Communicating Applications Specifications	CAS
Communicating Magnetic Card (HGAA)	CMC
Communicating Magnetic Card Typewriter (AFIT)	CMCT
Communicating NATO Intentions (MCD)	CNI

Communicating Word Processing System	CWPS
Communicating Word Processor	CWP
Communication (ABBR)	CMUNCN
Communication (IAA)	CO
Communication (AFM)	COMM
Communication	COMMCTN
Communication	COMN
Communication Access Method (IAA)	CAM
Communication Access System (IAA)	CAS
Communication, Advertising, and Marketing Education Foundation [*British*]	CAM
Communication Advisors, Inc. [*Southfield, MI*] [*Telecommunications*] (TSSD)	CAI
Communication Analysis Section	CAS
Communication Analysis Tool for Space Station (MCD)	CATSS
Communication and Cognition (EA)	C & C
Communication and Cognition - Artificial Intelligence (EA)	CC-AI
Communication and Command Control Requirements (AAG)	CCCR
Communication and Control (IAA)	CAC
Communication and Data (IAA)	CAD
Communication and Data Management System (SSD)	CDMS
Communication and Data Subsystem	C & DSS
Communication and Information Systems [*Micro-Electronics Programme*] [*British*] (NITA)	CAIS
Communication and Instrumentation [*NASA*] (KSC)	C & I
Communication and Instrumentation [*NASA*] (KSC)	CI
Communication and Instrumentation Support Services [*NASA*] (KSC)	CISS
Communication and Instrumentation System [*CIS is preferred*] [*NASA*] (KSC)	C & IS
Communication and Instrumentation System [*Also, C & IS*] [*NASA*]	CIS
Communication and Navigation (MCD)	C & N
Communication and Navigation Research Laboratory (NASA)	CNRL
Communication and RADAR Assignment Coordinating Committee	CRACC
Communication and Social Science Information Service [*Canadian research collection network*]	CASSIS
Communication and Tracking [*NASA*] (NASA)	C & T
Communication and Tracking Subsystem [*Military*] (IAA)	CTS
Communication and Tracking Subsystem (MCD)	CTSS
Communication Application Platform [*Computer science*] (PCM)	CAP
Communication Association of the Pacific [*Later, WCA*] (EA)	CAP
Communication Automatic Processing Equipment	CAPE
Communication Cable, Inc. [*NASDAQ symbol*] (NQ)	CABL
Communication Cable, Inc. [*Associated Press*] (SAG)	CmCbINC
Communication Carrier Assembly [*Spaceship*]	CCA
Communication Center	CC
Communication Center Console	CCC
Communication Central Facility [*Air Force*]	CCF
Communication Check Point (DICI)	CCP
Communication Circuit Technical Control Facility (MCD)	CCTCF
Communication, Command, Control, Computer, and Intelligence (USGC)	C41
Communication Commission (EA)	CC
Communication Comptroller	CC
Communication Computer Programming Center (AFM)	CCPC
Communication Connect Time Monitor [*Computer science*]	CCTM
Communication Control Number (AAG)	CCN
Communication Control Program (BUR)	CCP
Communication Control System	CCS
Communication Control Unit	CCU
Communication Countermeasures	COMCM
Communication Countermeasures Evaluation Facility [*Air Force*] (MCD)	CCEF
Communication Deception System (DWSG)	CDS
Communication Desk (BUR)	CDK
Communication Disorders Specialist	CDS
Communication Effectiveness Centre [*Canada*]	CEC
Communication Electronic Equipment [*Military*]	CEE
Communication Electronic Instructions	CEI
Communication Electronics Element [*Army*] (AABC)	CEE
Communication Electronics Staff Officer (MCD)	CESO
Communication Engineering Standard	CES
Communication Exercise [*Military*] (INF)	COMEX
Communication Facilities Mediterranean and Middle East	COMMFACMEDME
Communication Identification Navigation	CIN
Communication Identifier [*Computer science*] (IBMDP)	CID
Communication Implementation Directive [*Air Force*]	CID
Communication Industrial Services	CIS
Communication Information	CI
Communication Information Bulletin (DNAB)	CIB
Communication Information System (IEEE)	CIS
Communication Installation Squadron [*Air Force*]	CISq
Communication Instructions for Reporting Enemy Sightings [*Navy*]	CIRES
Communication Intelligence Corp. (PCM)	CIC
Communication Intelligence Corp. [*NASDAQ symbol*] (SAG)	CICI
Communication Intelligence Corp. [*Associated Press*] (SAG)	CommIn
Communication Intelligence Security Regulation (MCD)	CISR
Communication Intercept and Direction Finding (MCD)	CIDF
Communication Interface Coordinator [*NASA*]	CIC
Communication Interface Monitor	CIM
Communication International [*Vancouver Stock Exchange symbol*]	CUA
Communication Interrupt Control Program [*Computer science*] (IBMDP)	CICP
Communication Jamming Processor (IEEE)	CJP
Communication Lieutenant [*British military*] (DMA)	CL
Communication Lieutenant-Commander [*British military*] (DMA)	CLCR
Communication Line Adapters	CLA
Communication Line Adapters for Teletype	CLAT
Communication Line Concentrator Module (MHDI)	CLCM

Communication Line Interface (MCD) CLI
Communication Line Interface Computer (MCD) CLIC
Communication Line Processor .... CLP
Communication Line Terminal [*Computer science*] .... CLT
Communication Line Terminator [*IBM Corp.*] .... COLT
Communication Linear Integrated Circuit (IAA) CLIC
Communication Link Analyzer (IEEE) .... CLA
Communication Link Subsystem .... CLSS
Communication Management System [*Computer science*] .... CMS
Communication Multiplexor Channel (DNAB) .... CMC
Communication Navigation (NFPA) .... CNI
Communication, Navigation, and Identification .... CNI
Communication Net Control Station [*Navy*] (NVT) .... NECOS
Communication Network .... CNET
Communication Network Management (HGAA) .... CNM
Communication Network System (IAA) .... CNS
Communication Online Test System (IAA) .... COLTS
Communication Operation Station .... COS
Communication Optimization Program Translator [*NASA*] .... COPTRAN
Communication Oriented Message System [*IBM Corp.*] .... CORMES
Communication Output Printer .... COP
Communication Personnel [*Marine Corps*] .... CP
Communication Physical Input/Output Control System (IAA) .... CPIOC
Communication Planning Corp. [*Jacksonville, FL*] [*Telecommunications*] (TSSD) .... CPC
Communication Prediction Program [*NASA*] (KSC) .... CPPM
Communication Radio and Teletype (Secure) System .... CRATTZ
Communication, Range, and Azimuth Unit [*Computer science*] .... COMRAZ
Communication Registered Publication Memoranda .... CRPM
Communication Representative .... CR
Communication Research and Development Satellite [*NASA*] (NASA) .... COMR & DSAT
Communication Research Center [*Florida State University*] [*Research center*] (RCD) .... CRC
Communication Research Center [*Boston University*] [*Research center*] (RCD) .... CRC
Communication Research Center [*University of Florida*] [*Research center*] (RCD) .... CRC
Communication Resources [*Haddonfield, NJ*] [*Telecommunications*] (TSSD) .... CR
Communication Satellite Planning Center [*Stanford University*] [*Research center*] (RCD) .... CSPC
Communication Scanner Base (IBMDP) .... CSB
Communication Science Research Center [*Battelle Memorial Institute*] (MCD) .... CSRC
Communication Sciences Laboratory [*University of Florida*] .... CSL
Communication Security Activity .... COMMSECACT
Communication Security Publication Memorandum [*Army*] .... CSPM
Communication Segment (MCD) .... CS
Communication Sequential Process [*Computer science*] .... CSP
Communication Service Facility (IAA) .... CSF
Communication Service Request .... CSR
Communication Services Ltd. [*Hong Kong*] [*Telecommunications*] .... CSL
Communication Services Manager [*Novell, Inc.*] .... CSM
Communication Signal Distribution System .... CSDS
Communication Skills Corp. [*British*] .... CSC
Communication Skills Self-Assessment Exam (DMAA) .... CSSAE
Communication Standing Order .... CSO
Communication Station [*Military*] (CAAL) .... COMSTA
Communication Station .... CS
Communication Studies (AIE) .... CS
Communication Subnet Processor (OSI) .... CSNP
Communication Subsystem (MCD) .... COMS
Communication Supplementary Activity .... COMMSUPACT
Communication Supplementary Detachment .... COMMSUPDET
Communication Support System (MCD) .... CSS
Communication System Control Element [*of TCCF*] (MCD) .... CSCE
Communication System Development (IAA) .... CSD
Communication System Discipline (IAA) .... COMSYSDISC
Communication, System, Results, Objectives, Exception, Participation, Motivation [*Business term*] (MHDB) .... CSROEPM
Communication System Simulation Language [*Computer science*] (IEEE) .... COMSL
Communication Systems Engineering Laboratory [*NASA*] (MCD) .... CSEL
Communication Systems Ltd. [*London, England*] [*Telecommunications*] (TSSD) .... COMSYS
Communication Systems Research Ltd. [*Ilkley, W. Yorkshire, England*] (TSSD) .... CSR
Communication Systems Sector [*or Segment*] **Replacement** [*Military*] .... CSSR
Communication Technical Evaluation Console (KSC) .... CTEC
Communication Training Consultants, Inc. [*New York, NY*] [*Telecommunications*] (TSSD) .... CTC
Communication Trench [*Military*] .... CT
Communication Valve Development [*British*] .... CVD
Communication Vector Table (BUR) .... CVT
Communication Watch Officer .... CWO
Communication with Extraterrestrial Intelligence [*Later, SETI*] [*Radioastronomy*] .... CETI
Communication Workers Alliance [*Philippines*] .... CWA
Communication Workers of Canada .... CWC
Communication Yeoman [*Navy rating British*] .... CY
Communication Zone [*British military*] (DMA) .... COMZONE
Communication-Electronic-Meteorological Board [*Air Force*] .... CEMB
Communication-Quebec, Trois-Rivieres, PQ, Canada [*Library symbol Library of Congress*] (LCLS) .... CaQTCO
Communication-Quebec, Trois-Rivieres, Quebec [*Library symbol National Library of Canada*] (NLC) .... QTCO
Communications C
Communications (DOMA) .... COM
Communications .... COMMS
Communications .... COMMUN
Communications (DD) .... commun
Communications (ROG) .... COMS
Communications Access Device (CET) .... CAD
Communications Access Manager (MHDB) .... CAM
Communications Acquisition Status and Assessment Report (MCD) .... CASAR
Communications Adapter .... CA
Communications Adaptor Board (NITA) .... CAB
Communications Advisory Team (OICC) .... CAT
Communications Afloat Program [*Military*] (DNAB) .... CAP
Communications / Air Traffic Service (SAA) .... COM/ATS
Communications Alert and Liaison System [*Office of Fisheries*] (MSC) .... CALL
Communications Allocation Order (CINC) .... CAO
Communications Analysis Corp. [*Framingham, MA*] [*Telecommunications*] (TSSD) .... CAC
Communications, Analysis, Simulation, and Evaluation [*Army*] (MCD) .... CASE
Communications and Configuration Console (MCD) .... CACC
Communications and Control Systems Laboratory .... CCSL
Communications and Data .... C & D
Communications and Data Centre (NITA) .... CDC
Communications and Data Handling (SSD) .... C & DH
Communications and Data Link (KSC) .... CADL
Communications and Data Processing Exposition .... COMDEX
Communications and Data Processing Operation .... CADPO
Communications and Data Subsystem (IAA) .... CADSS
Communications and Data Subsystems .... CDS
Communications and Data Systems Integration (NASA) .... CADSI
Communications and Distributed Resources Report [*International Dat a Corp.*] [*Defunct Information service or system*] (CRD) .... CDR
Communications and Distributed Systems [*British*] .... CDS
Communications and Electronics .... C & E
Communications and Electronics (IAA) .... CAE
Communications and Electronics [*SHAPE*] (MCD) .... CANDE
Communications and Electronics Command [*Formerly, ASC*] [*Army*] .... CEC
Communications and Electronics Engineering Library, Department of National Defence [*Bibliotheque du Genie Electronique et des Communications, Ministere de laDefense National*] **Ottawa, Ontario** [*Library symbol National Library of Canada*] (NLC) .... OONDC
Communications and Electronics Maintenance Squadron [*Air Force*] .... CEMS
Communications and Electronics Maintenance Squadron (AFM) .... CEMSq
Communications and Electronics Materiel Readiness Command [*Army*] .... CERCOM
Communications and Electronics Squadron (IAA) .... CAESQ
Communications & Entertainment Corp. [*NASDAQ symbol*] (SAG) .... CECO
Communications & Entertainment Corp. [*Associated Press*] (SAG) .... ComEnt
Communications and Information Handling Equipment and Services .... CO IN HES
Communications and Information Processing Group [*Rensselaer Polytechnic Institute*] [*Research center*] (RCD) .... CIPG
Communications and Information Services - Communications .... CIS-COMMS
Communications and Information Systems Committee [*NATO*] (EAIO) .... CCIS
Communications and Information Technology Research [*British*] .... CIT
Communications and Interface Group [*NASA*] (NASA) .... CIG
Communications and Media Law Association [*Australia*] .... CMLA
Communications and Navigation Airborne Radio Instrumentation [*Military*] (IAA) .... CANARI
Communications and Signal Processing [*British*] .... CSP
Communications and Systems Management [*Software module*] [*Stratus Computer, Inc.*] .... CASM
Communications and Tactical [*Publications*] [*Navy*] (NVT) .... COMTAC
Communications and Telemetry .... CMTM
Communications and Tracking System [*or Subsystem*] .... CATS
Communications and Tracking System [*or Subsystem*] .... CTS
Communications Antenna Sleeve .... CAS
Communications Area Local Station (NVT) .... CALS
Communications Area Master Station (NVT) .... CAMS
Communications Assist Team (NVT) .... CAT
Communications. Association for Computing Machinery .... CACM
Communications/Automatic Data Processing Center [*Fort Monmouth, NJ*] [*Army*] (GRD) .... COMM/ADP
Communications/Automatic Data Processing Laboratory [*Army Electronics Command*] [*Fort Monmouth, NJ*] .... CADPL
Communications Branch, National Research Council .... CBNRC
Communications Buffer [*Computer science*] .... CB
Communications Buffer [*Air Force*] .... COMB
Communications Buffer Memory [*Computer science*] .... CBM
Communications Bus .... CB
Communications Career Program [*Military*] .... CCP
Communications Carrier, Inc. [*Austin, TX*] [*Telecommunications*] (TSSD) CCI
Communications Center [*NATO*] (NATG) .... COMCEN
Communications Center .... COMMCEN
Communications Center (SAA) .... COMMCTR
Communications Center of Clarksburg [*Clarksburg, MD*] [*Telecommunications*] (TSSD) CCC
Communications Central [*Military*] CC
Communications Central [*NASDAQ symbol*] (SAG) CCIX
Communications Central [*Commercial firm Associated Press*] (SAG) .... ComCtrl
Communications Change Group (SAA) .... CCG
Communications Change Initiation Request (IAA) .... CCIR
Communications Change Log (IAA) CCL

Communications Change Request (IAA) .... CCR
Communications Channel (NITA) .... CMC
Communications Channel Adapter (IAA) .... CCA
Communications Circular Letter [*Navy*] CCL
Communications Collection Standard System (MCD) .... CCSS
Communications, Command, and Control CCC
Communications, Command, and Telemetry Systems (MCD) .... CCATS
Communications, Command, Control, and Intelligence (PDAA) C3I
Communications Command Group [*Air Force*] .... COMCG
Communications Command Technical Manual [*Army*] .... CCTM
Communications Computer (IAA) CC
Communications Concentrator Software Package [*Computer science*] .... CCSP
Communications Concepts, Inc. [*Newport Beach, CA*] [*Telecommunications*] (TSSD) CCI
Communications Consultants, Inc. [*Washington, NJ*] [*Telecommunications*] (TSSD) CCI
Communications Control (MCD) CC
Communications Control Applications Program .... CCAP
Communications Control Area (IAA) .... CCA
Communications Control Block [*Computer science*] .... CCB
Communications Control Console (MCD) CCC
Communications Control Equipment (MCD) .... CCE
Communications Control Facility [*Military*] .... CCF
Communications Control Field .... CCF
Communications Control Group Assembly [*Ground Communications Facility, NASA*] .... CCGA
Communications Control Interface (MCD) CCI
Communications Control Language CCL
Communications Control Link (DNAB) CCL
Communications Control Module [*Telecommunications*] (TEL) .... CCM
Communications Control Package .... CCP
Communications Control Panel .... CCP
Communications Control Processor .... CCP
Communications Control Program Initialization (MCD) .... CCPI
Communications Control Room (IAA) .... CCR
Communications Control Team [*Military*] .... CCT
Communications Controller (MCD) .... COMC
Communications Controller Multichannel [*Computer science*] .... CCM
Communications Coordination Committee for the United Nations (EA) .... CCCUN
Communications Council (EA) CC
Communications Countermeasures [*Military*] (NVT) .... COMMCM
Communications Coupling Unit (CET) .... CCU
Communications. CSIRO [*A publication*] .... COCO
Communications Data Base [*Canada*] [*Information service or system*] (IID) .... COMBASE
Communications Data Formatter (MCD) .... CDF
Communications/Data Manager (MCD) .... CDM
Communications Data Network Controller (MCD) .... CDNC
Communications Data Processing System (NVT) .... CDPS
Communications Data Processor [*Electronics*] .... CDP
Communications Data Terminal (MCD) .... CDT
Communications Decency Act .... CDA
Communications Decency Act .... CDA
Communications Design Center [*Carnegie-Mellon University*] [*Research center*] (RCD) .... CDC
Communications Desk Reference [*A publication*] (TSSD) .... CDR
Communications Detachment (MCD) .... COMMDET
Communications Digital Control Unit .... CDCU
Communications Direction and Coordination .... COMMDAC
Communications Display Terminal (IAA) .... CDT
Communications Distribution Amplifier (MCD) .... CDA
Communications, Distribution, and Switching Center [*NASA*] (KSC) .... CD & SC
Communications, Distribution, and Switching Center [*NASA*] (KSC) .... CDSC
Communications Duty Officer (FAAC) .... CDO
Communications Editing Unit (NOAA) .... COMED
Communications, Electronic, Technical, and Salaried Workers of Canada .... CWC
Communications - Electronics Deployment Report (MCD) .... CEDREP
Communications Electronics Evaluation and Test Agency (MCD) .... CEETA
Communications Electronics Management Center [*Air Force*] (AFIT) .... CEMC
Communications Electronics Management Systems .... CEMS
Communications Electronics Mission Order (MCD) .... CEMO
Communications Electronics Navigation [*Military*] .... CEN
Communications Electronics School [*Air Force*] .... CESCH
Communications, Energy & Paperworkers Union of Canada (AC) .... CEP
Communications Engineering and Installation Agency .... CEIA
Communications Engineering and Installation Department [*Army*] .... CEI
Communications Engineering Department [*Military*] (DNAB) .... CED
Communications Engineering Research Satellite (NITA) .... CERS
Communications Equipment .... CE
Communications Equipment Distributors Association (MHDI) .... CEDA
Communications Equipment Logistics (MCD) .... COMLOG
Communications Equipment Support Element (MCD) .... CESE
Communications Era Task Force [*Defunct*] (EA) .... CERATF
Communications Errors Statistics (CMD) .... CES
Communications Excellence to Black Audiences [*An award*] .... CEBA
Communications Exhibition [*Trade fair*] [*British*] .... COMEX
Communications Expansion Unit .... CEU
Communications Exploitation (MCD) .... COMMEX
Communications Facilities in Support of DA [*Department of the Army*] **Continuity of Operations Plan** (AABC) .... COOPCOMM
Communications Facility (IAA) .... CF
Communications Facility [*Control and Processing Co.*] .... COMFAX
Communications Factor (IAA) .... CF
Communications Field Exercise [*Military*] (NVT) .... COMMFEX
Communications for Online Systems [*Computer science*] (ODBW) .... COLS
Communications Fraud Control Association (EA) .... CFCA
Communications Frequency and Facility Information Systems [*ICAO databank*] (NITA) .... COFFI
Communications Front End (SSD) .... CFE
Communications Group [*Air Force*] .... CG
Communications Group, Inc. [*Concord, MA*] [*Telecommunications*] (TSSD) .... CGI
Communications Handler for Automatic Multiple Programs .... CHAMP
Communications High-Accuracy Airborne Location System [*Military*] .... CHAALS
Communications Identification Directory [*Air Force*] (CET) .... CID
Communications III, Inc. [*Columbus, OH*] (TSSD) .... COM III
Communications Improvement Memorandum [*Military*] .... CIM
Communications Industries Association of Japan [*Telecommunications*] .... CIAJ
Communications Industries Report [*A publication*] (EAAP) .... CIR
Communications Input and Output Control System (BUR) .... CIOCS
Communications Input/Output Multiplexer .... CIOM
Communications Input/Output Processor [*Computer science*] (NITA) .... CIOP
Communications Input-Output Control System [*Computer science*] (ECII) .... CIOCS
Communications Instructions [*Navy*] .... COMINST
Communications Instructions for Merchant Ships [*Navy*] .... CIMS
Communications Instructions for Reporting Vital Intelligence Sightings [*Military*] .... CIRVIS
Communications Instructor Console (MCD) CIC
Communications Integrated Control Engineering, Reporting, and Operations (MCD) .... CICERO
Communications Integration Test Site [*Military*] (CAAL) .... COMMITS
Communications Intelligence [*Military*] .... COMINT
Communications Intelligence Channel CIC
Communications Interface (MCD) CI
Communications Interface and Processing System (MCD) .... CIP
Communications Interface Assembly [*Computer science*] .... CIA
Communications Interface Equipment (MCD) .... CIE
Communications Interface Modules [*Computer science*] .... CIM
Communications Interface System (MCD) .... CIS
Communications Interface Table (MCD) .... CIT
Communications Interface Unit .... CIU
Communications Interrupt Analysis [*Sperry UNIVAC*] (IEEE) .... CIA
Communications Interrupt Program .... CIP
Communications Jamming [*Military*] .... COMJAM
Communications Jamming Operator [*Military*] .... CJO
Communications Junction Module Assembly [*Ground Control Facility, NASA*] .... CJMA
Communications Law Centre [*Australia*] CLC
Communications Line Adaptor (NITA) .... CLA
Communications Line Control CLC
Communications Line Expander [*Electrodata, Inc.*] [*Telecommunications*] .... CLE
Communications Line Multiplexer .... CLM
Communications Line Switch .... CLS
Communications Link Analysis and Simulation System (MCD) .... CLASS
Communications Link Analyzer System .... CLAS
Communications Link Characterization Experiment [*Communications Technology Satellite*] (MCD) .... CLCE
Communications Link Controller [*International Computers Ltd.*] [*Telecommunications*] CLC
Communications Load Exercise [*Military*] (CAAL) .... COMMLOADEX
Communications Logistics Network (IEEE) .... COMLOGNET
Communications [*Security*] **Logistics Support Unit** (DOMA) .... CLSU
Communications Maintenance and Storage (NASA) .... CM & S
Communications Maintenance Squadron [*Air Force*] .... CMSQ
Communications Management Agency .... CMA
Communications Management Configuration .... CMC
Communications Management Processor [*Information technology*] .... CMP
Communications Management Subsystem .... COMMS
Communications Management Systems [*Military*] (RDA) .... COMM MGT SYS
Communications Management Unit [*Aviation*] .... CMU
Communications Manager .... CM
Communications Manager/2 [*Software*] (CDE) CM/2
Communications Managers Association [*Bernardsville, NJ*] [*Telecommunications service*] (TSSD) .... CMA
Communications Market Association (EA) .... CMA
Communications Message Traffic Control Unit [*Air Force*] (AFM) .... CMTCU
Communications Mode Control .... CMC
Communications Mode Selection Control (MCD) .... CMSC
Communications Module [*AT&T*] (ACRL) .... CM
Communications Module Processor (ACRL) .... CMP
Communications Monitor (BTTJ) .... CM
Communications Monitoring and Control Subsystem (NVT) .... CMCS
Communications Monitoring Report .... CMR
Communications Moon Relay [*System*] [*NASA*] .... CMR
Communications Multiplexer [*Computer science*] .... CM
Communications Multiplexer (NITA) .... COMM MUX
Communications Multiplexer Module [*Computer science*] .... CMM
Communications, Navigation, and Positioning [*Military*] .... CNP
Communications, Navigation, and Surveillance .... CNS
Communications Need .... COMNEED
Communications Network .... CN
Communications Network (AFM) .... COMNET
Communications Network Architects, Inc. [*Washington, DC Telecommunications service*] (TSSD) .... CNA
Communications Network Architecture .... CNA
Communications Network Control Processor (IAA) .... CNCP
Communications Network Controller (IAA) .... CNC
Communications Network Design Program .... CNDP

Communications Network Emulator ... CNE
Communications Network for Manufacturing Application [*Computer science*] (TNIG) ... CNMA
Communications Network Management Interface ... CNMI
Communications Network Procedure [*Computer science*] (NITA) ... CNP
Communications Network Processor ... CNP
Communications Network Service [*Satellite Business Systems*] [*McLean, VA*] [*Telecommunications*] (TSSD) ... CNS
Communications Network Services [*Virginia Polytechnic Institute and State University*] [*Blacksburg*] (TSSD) ... CNS
Communications Network Simulation [*Computer science*] (NITA) ... CNS
Communications, Networks, and Information Processing Theory Group [*MIT*] (MCD) ... CNIPTG
Communications NODAL [*Network-Oriented Data Acquisition Language*] **Control Element** ... CNCE
Communications of the Association for Communicating Machinery (HGAA) ... CACAM
Communications Office Building (NASA) ... COB
Communications Officer [*Navy*] ... CO
Communications Officer ... COMMO
Communications Officer ... COMO
Communications Officer School [*Air Force*] ... COMMOSCH
Communications on Alternatives in Education [*Defunct*] (EA) ... KOA
Communications On-Line Processor ... COP
Communications Operating Directive (KSC) ... COD
Communications Operating System ... COS
Communications Operations Instructions [*Air Force*] ... COI
Communications Operations Officer [*Air Force*] ... COMMOPNSO
Communications Operations Report [*Air Force*] ... COR
Communications Operations Squadron [*Air Force*] ... COSQ
Communications Oriented Product Information and Control System (NITA) ... COPICS
Communications Oriented Software ... COS
Communications Outage Reporting System ... COORS
Communications Outage Restoral Section [*ADC*] ... COORS
Communications Patching Panel ... CPP
Communications Performance Monitoring and Assessment [*Military*] ... CPMAS
Communications Plan ... COMPLAN
Communications Planning and Development ... CPD
Communications Policy Branch, Saskatchewan Department of Justice, Regina, Saskatchewan [*Library symbol National Library of Canada*] (NLC) ... SRJC
Communications Port [*Computer science*] ... COM
Communications Procedure-Oriented Language [*Computer science*] ... CPOL
Communications Procedures Management System (MCD) ... CPMS
Communications Processing Center (CET) ... CPC
Communications Processing Interface (MCD) ... CPI
Communications Processing System ... CPS
Communications Processing Unit (CET) ... CPU
Communications Processor ... COM
Communications Processor ... CP
Communications Processor and Interface ... CPI
Communications Processor Assembly [*Ground Control Facility, NASA*] ... CPRA
Communications Processor Conversion Center ... CPCC
Communications Processor Utility [*Telecommunications*] (TEL) ... CPU
Communications Program Element ... CPE
Communications Programs [*NASA*] ... CP
Communications Project (EA) ... CP
Communications Publishing Group, Inc. [*Boston, MA*] [*Information service or system Telecommunications*] (TSSD) ... CPG
Communications Register ... CR
Communications Register Unit (IAA) ... CRU
Communications Regulatory Commission ... CRC
Communications Relay Center [*Air Force*] ... CRC
Communications Relay Group (MCD) ... CRG
Communications Relay Set (MCD) ... CRS
Communications Requirements Systems Configuration and Equipment List (NVT) ... CORESCEL
Communications Research Advisory Board [*Canada*] ... CRAB
Communications Research and Development Command [*Fort Monmouth, NJ*] [*Army*] ... CORADCOM
Communications Research Center [*University of Tennessee at Knoxville*] [*Research center*] (RCD) ... CRC
Communications Research Center (HGAA) ... CRS
Communications Research Centre [*Defunct Canada*] ... CRC
Communications Research Centre, Department of Communications [*Centre de Recherches sur les Communications, Ministere des Communications*] **Ottawa, Ontario** [*Library symbol National Library of Canada*] (NLC) ... OORPL
Communications Research Establishment (NATG) ... CRE
Communications Research Institute (MCD) ... CRI
Communications Research Laboratories [*Information service or system*] (IID) ... CRL
Communications Research Laboratory [*McMaster University*] [*Canada Research center*] (RCD) ... CRL
Communications/Research/Machines, Inc. [*Publisher*] ... CRM
Communications Resource Management System [*CHI/COR Information Management, Inc.*] ... CRMS
Communications Resources Data System [*Defense Communications Agency*] (MCD) ... CREDATA
Communications Routing Indicator ... COMRI
Communications Satellite (MUGU) ... COMMUNICAT
Communications Satellite (EECA) ... COMSAT
Communications Satellite (DOMA) ... COMSAT
Communications Satellite [*Japan*] ... CS
Communications Satellite Advanced Research [*AFSC*] ... CSAR
Communications Satellite Corp. (DFIT) ... COMSAT
Communications Satellite Corporation [*Washington, D.C.*] (WDMC) ... COMSAT
Communications Satellite Corp. [*See also COMSAT*] ... COMSATCORP
Communications Satellite Corp. [*See also COMSAT*] ... CSC
Communications Satellite for Experimental Purposes [*Japan Telecommunications*] ... CSE
Communications Satellite Program [*NASA*] ... CSP
Communications Satellite Project Office ... CSPO
Communications Satellite Relay (NG) ... CSR
Communications Security [*Military*] ... COMSEC
Communications Security Association (EA) ... COMSEC
Communications Security Control Group [*Navy*] (MCD) ... CSCG
Communications Security Control Terminal (MCD) ... CSCT
Communications Security Equipment Engineering Bulletin (MCD) ... CSEEB
Communications Security Equipment Systems Document [*National Security Agency*] (MCD) ... CSESD
Communications Security Establishment, Department of National Defence [*Centrede la Securite des Telecommunications, Ministere de la Defense Nationale*] **Ot tawa, Ontario** [*Library symbol National Library of Canada*] (NLC) ... OONDCS
Communications Security Interservice Depot Overhaul Standard (MCD) ... CIDOS
Communications Security Logistics (MCD) ... COMSECLOG
Communications Security Logistics Agency (MCD) ... CSLA
Communications Security Material Sub-Issuing Office [*Military*] (NVT) ... CMSIO
Communications Security Material System (MCD) ... CSMS
Communications Security Material Van-Issuing Office [*Military*] (NVT) ... CMVIO
Communications Security Mobile Issuing Office [*Military*] (NVT) ... CMMIO
Communications Security, Phase 1 [*Course*] [*Military*] (DNAB) ... COMSEC 1
Communications Security Publication ... CSP
Communications Security System (MCD) ... CSS
Communications Service Authorization [*Obsolete*] ... CSA
Communications Services (NITA) ... CS
Communications Services, Inc. [*Junction City, KS*] ... CSI
Communications Simulator [*Sperry UNIVAC*] ... CS
Communications Simulator Console (IAA) ... CSC
Communications Soft Hat [*NASA*] (KSC) ... CSH
Communications Solutions, Inc. [*San Jose, CA*] [*Information service or system Telecommunications*] (TSSD) ... CSI
Communications Spacecraft Operation Center [*NASA*] ... COMSOC
Communications Speaker ... COMSPK
Communications Squadron [*Air Force*] ... COMMSq
Communications Squadron [*Marine Corps*] ... COMSQN
Communications Squadron [*Air Force*] ... CS
Communications Station (MCD) ... COMMSTA
Communications Status and Restoration Coordination Office ... CSRCO
Communications Status Report (MCD) ... COMSTAT
Communications Status Report [*Military*] (NVT) ... COMSTATRPT
Communications Storage Unit ... COMM-STOR
Communications Strategic Rotary Launcher [*Military*] ... CSRL
Communications Subcommittee [*Allied German Occupation Forces*] ... CSC
Communications Subsystem ... CSS
Communications Supervisor (PDAA) ... COMSUP
Communications Supply Service Association (EA) ... CSSA
Communications Support ... COMS
Communications Support Area ... CSA
Communications Support Control Element (MCD) ... CSCE
Communications Support Element [*Military*] (AFM) ... CSE
Communications Support Requirements (MCD) ... COMSR
Communications Surveillance Transistor ... CST
Communications Switch Operating System (MCD) ... CSOS
Communications Switchboard Console ... CSC
Communications Switcher ... CS
Communications Switching System [*Army*] (RDA) ... CSW
Communications Switching Unit (CAAL) ... CSU
Communications/Symbiont Processor [*Sperry UNIVAC*] ... C/SP
Communications System ... CS
Communications System Category Code [*Air Force*] (AFIT) ... CSCC
Communications System Control Console ... CSCC
Communications System Control Equipment ... CSCE
Communications System Language (NITA) ... COMSYL
Communications System Planning Element ... CSPE
Communications System Replacement [*Military*] (GFGA) ... CSR
Communications System Status Display (KSC) ... CSSD
Communications Systems Agency [*Fort Monmouth, NJ*] [*Army*] (RDA) ... CSA
Communications Systems Center ... CSC
Communications Systems Developing Element ... CSDE
Communications Systems Engineer (KSC) ... CSE
Communications Systems Engineering Program [*Army*] (RDA) ... CSEP
Communications Systems, Inc. [*Associated Press*] (SAG) ... ComSys
Communications Systems, Inc. ... CSI
Communications Systems, Inc. [*NASDAQ symbol*] (NQ) ... CSII
Communications Systems Industrial Funds (MCD) ... CSIF
Communications Systems Management Association (MCD) ... CSMA
Communications Systems Technician (MCD) ... CST
Communications Tag Pool ... COMPOOL
Communications Task Group [*CODASYL*] ... CTG
Communications Technical Operations Center [*Air Force*] ... CTOC
Communications Technician (MCD) ... COMT
Communications Technician [*Navy rating*] ... CT
Communications Technician, Chief [*Navy rating*] ... CTC
Communications Technician, First Class [*Navy rating*] ... CT1
Communications Technician Intercept [*Navy rating*] (IAA) ... CTI
Communications Technician, Master Chief [*Navy rating*] ... CTCM
Communications Technician, Second Class [*Navy rating*] ... CT2

Communications Technician, Senior Chief [*Navy rating*] .... CTCS
Communications Technician, Third Class [*Navy rating*] CT3
Communications Technology .... CT
Communications Technology (NITA) .... CT
Communications Technology Management, Inc. [*McLean, VA*] [*Telecommunications*] (TSSD) .... CTM
Communications Technology Satellite .... CTS
Communications Technology Specialist [*International Communications Indust ries Association*] [*Designation awarded by*] (TSSD) .... CTS
Communications Terminal [*Computer science*] .... CT
Communications Terminal Module [*Computer science*] .... CTM
Communications Terminal Module Controller [*Computer science*] .... CTMC
Communications Terminal, Synchronous [*Computer science*] .... CTS
Communications Test Facility [*Fort Huachuca, AZ*] [*United States Army Electronic Proving Ground*] (GRD) .... CTF
Communications Test Lab (SSD) .... CTL
Communications Test Station [*NASA*] .... CTS
Communications Timing Procedure (NASA) .... CTP
Communications Trade Division (EA) .... CTD
Communications Union Canada .... CUC
Communications Unit Executor .... CUE
Communications Unlimited [*Charlotte, NC*] [*Telecommunications*] (TSSD) .... CU
Communications User Emulated System for Traffic Analysis (MHDI) .... CUESTA
Communications User Program [*Sperry UNIVAC*] .... CUP
Communications User Radio Transmission Sounding [*Navy*] .... CURTS
Communications Validating Office (CET) .... CVO
Communications Wing [*Air Force*] .... CW
Communications with and Service to the Public [*Army*] (AABC) .... CWSP
Communications Workers of America (EA) .... CWA
Communications World International, Inc. [*Associated Press*] (SAG) .... ComW
Communications World International, Inc. [*Associated Press*] (SAG) .... ComWld
Communications World International, Inc. [*NASDAQ symbol*] (NQ) .... CWII
Communications World Intl. [*NASDAQ symbol*] (TTSB) .... CWII
Communications Wrld Intl. Wrrt [*NASDAQ symbol*] (TTSB) .... CWIIW
Communications Yeoman [*Navy rating*] .... CYN
Communications Zone (MUGU) .... COMMZ
Communications Zone .... COMZ
Communications Zone (MCD) .... CZ
Communications Zone Indicator [*Air Force*] .... COZI
Communications-Data Field .... CDF
Communications-Electronics .... C-E
Communications-Electronics .... COMMEL
Communications-Electronics Agency [*Army*] .... C-EA
Communications-Electronics Board (NATG) .... CEB
Communications-Electronics Command [*Fort Monmouth, NJ*] [*Army*] (GRD) .... CECOM
Communications-Electronics Committee (AFM) .... CEC
Communications-Electronics Consolidated Mobilization Reserve List .... CECMRL
Communications-Electronics Coordinating Section [*NATO*] .... CECS
Communications-Electronics Directive .... CED
Communications-Electronics Doctrinal Projects Office [*Air Force*] .... CEDPO
Communications-Electronics Doctrine [*Series of Air Force manuals*] .... CED
Communications-Electronics Document .... CED
Communications-Electronics Engineering Installation Agency [*DoD*] .... CEEIA
Communications-Electronics Engineering Installation Agency-National Communications Command [*DoD*] (RDA) .... CEEIA-NCC
Communications-Electronics Facility Inoperative for Parts (MCD) .... CEFIP
Communications-Electronics Implementation Plan [*For major air command requirements within the communications-electronics area*] [*Air Force*] .... CEIP
Communications-Electronics Implementation Plan Amendment [*See CEIP*] [*Air Force*] (AFM) .... CEIPA
Communications-Electronics Officer [*Air Force*] .... CEO
Communications-Electronics Operating Instruction (CINC) .... CEOI
Communications-Electronics Policy Directives [*NATO*] (NATG) .... CEPD
Communications-Electronics Scheme Accounting and Control [*Air Force*] .... CESAC
Communications-Electronics Section [*of a joint military staff; also, the officer in charge of this section*] J-6
Communications-Electronics Security Group [*British*] .... CESG
Communications-Electronics Standing Instruction (AABC) .... CESI
Communications-Electronics Survivability and Vulnerability .... CESV
Communications-Electronics War Readiness Materiel (SAA) .... CEWRM
Communications-Electronics-Meteorological [*Equipment*] .... CEM
Communications-Electronics-Meteorological Program Aggregate Code [*Air Force*] (AFM) .... CEMPAC
Communications-Electronics-Meteorological Program Implementation Management System [*Air Force*] (CET) .... CEMPIMS
Communications-Failure Detecting and Switching Equipment (MDG) .... COMMSWITCH
Communications-Oriented Automatic Test (MCD) .... COATS
Communications-Oriented Language .... COL
Communications-Oriented Multiple Terminal Executive (MHDI) .... COMTEX
Communications-Oriented Peripheral [*or Processing*] **Equipment** .... COPE
Communications-Oriented Production Information and Control System [*IBM Corp.*] .... COPICS
Communications-Oriented Production Information and Control System Executive DataLink [*IBM Corp.*] .... COPICS EDL
Communications-Oriented Real-Time Executive .... CORTEX
Communications-Oriented User Programming Language .... COUPLE
Communicative (ABBR) .... CMUNCV
Communicative .... COMMUNV
Communicative Ability in Daily Living .... CADL
Communicative Disorders .... CD
Communicative Electronic Training System .... CETS
Communicative Technology Directorate [*Army Training Support Center*] [*Fort Eustis, VA*] .... CTD
Communicative Use of English as a Foreign Language (AIE) .... CUEFL
Communicatively (ABBR) .... CMUNCVY
Communicators for Nuclear Disarmament (EA) .... CFND
Communicatory (ABBR) .... CMUNCY
Communing (ABBR) .... CMUNG
Communio Viatorum [*Prague*] [*A publication*] (BJA) .... ComViat
Communion (ABBR) .... CMUNN
Communion [*Service*] (ROG) .... COMM
Communique (ABBR) .... CMUNG
Communique .... COMMNQ
Communiquer a Toutes Adresses [*To Be Circulated to All Addresses*] [*Telecommunications French*] .... CTA
Communis [*Common*] [*Latin*] .... CS
Communism (ABBR) .... CMUNSM
Communist (ABBR) .... CMUNST
Communist .... COM
Communist [*Slang*] .... commie
Communist Activities [*British*] .... CA
Communist Bloc Intelligence Service (NATG) .... CBIS
Communist Infiltration [*Name of 1960's FBI campaign against infiltrators*] .... COMINFIL
Communist Information .... COMINFORM
Communist International (PPE) .... Comintern
Communist Labor Party (EA) .... CLP
Communist League Proletarian Left [*Netherlands Political party*] (PPW) .... KBPL
Communist Party [*Political party*] .... COMM
Communist Party [*Political party*] .... CP
Communist Party [*Peru*] [*Political party*] (PD) .... PC
Communist Party (Bolsheviks) [*Political party*] .... CP (B)
Communist Party Marxist .... CPM
Communist Party of America [*Political party*] (CDAI) .... CPA
Communist Party of Arakan [*Myanmar*] [*Political party*] .... CPA
Communist Party of Argentina [*Political party*] .... CPA
Communist Party of Armenia [*Political party Defunct*] .... CPA
Communist Party of Australia [*Political party*] .... COM
Communist Party of Australia [*Political party*] (PPW) .... CPA
Communist Party of Azerbaidzhan [*Political party*] .... CPA
Communist Party of Belgium [*Political party*] .... CPB
Communist Party of Bohemia and Moravia [*Former Czechoslovakia*] [*Political party*] (EY) .... CPBM
Communist Party of Burma [*Political party*] (EY) .... CPB
Communist Party of Byelorussia [*Political party*] .... CPB
Communist Party of Canada [*Political party*] .... CPC
Communist Party of Canada (Marxist-Leninist) [*Political party*] .... CPC(M-L)
Communist Party of China [*Chung-Kuo Kung-Ch'an Tang*] [*Taiwan*] [*Political party*] (PPW) .... CPC
Communist Party of Colombia [*Political party*] (PPW) .... CPC
Communist Party of Czechoslovakia [*Political party*] (EY) .... CPCZ
Communist Party of Denmark [*Political party*] .... CPD
Communist Party of Ecuador [*Political party*] .... CPE
Communist Party of Estonia [*Political party*] .... CPE
Communist Party of Finland [*Political party*] .... CPF
Communist Party of Georgia [*Political party*] .... CPG
Communist Party of Germany [*Political party*] (EAIO) .... CPG
Communist Party of Great Britain [*Political party*] (DCTA) .... CPGB
Communist Party of India [*Political party*] (PPW) .... CPI
Communist Party of India (Marxist) [*Political party*] (PPW) .... CPI(M)
Communist Party of India - Marxist [*Political party*] (FEA) .... CPM
Communist Party of India (Marxist-Leninist) [*Political party*] (PD) .... CPI(ML)
Communist Party of Indo-China [*Political party*] (PPW) .... CPIC
Communist Party of Indonesia [*Political party*] (PD) .... CPI
Communist Party of Ireland [*Political party*] (PPW) .... CPI
Communist Party of Ireland (Marxist-Leninist) [*Political party*] (PPW) .... CPI M-L
Communist Party of Kampuchea [*Political party*] (PD) .... CPK
Communist Party of Kazakhstan [*Former USSR Political party*] .... CPK
Communist Party of Latvia [*Political party*] .... CPL
Communist Party of Lesotho [*Political party*] (PD) .... CPL
Communist Party of Lithuania [*Political party*] .... CPL
Communist Party of Luxembourg [*Political party*] .... CPL
Communist Party of Malaya [*Political party*] (PD) .... CPM
Communist Party of Malaya - Marxist-Leninist [*Political party*] (PD) .... CPM-ML
Communist Party of Malaya - Revolutionary Faction [*Malaysia*] [*Political party*] (PD) .... CPM-RF
Communist Party of Malta [*Political party*] .... CPM
Communist Party of Moldavia [*Political party*] .... CPM
Communist Party of Nepal [*Political party*] (FEA) .... CPN
Communist Party of New Zealand [*Political party*] .... CPNZ
Communist Party of Norway [*Political party*] .... CPN
Communist Party of Slovakia [*Political party*] .... CPS
Communist Party of Slovakia [*Former Czechoslovakia*] [*Political party*] (EY) .... CPSL
Communist Party of South Africa [*Political party*] (PD) .... CPSA
Communist Party of Sri Lanka [*Political party*] (FEA) .... CPSL
Communist Party of Syria and the Lebanon [*Political party*] (BJA) .... CPSL
Communist Party of Tadzhikistan [*Political party*] .... CPT
Communist Party of Thailand [*Political party*] (PD) .... CPT
Communist Party of the Philippines [*Political party*] .... CPP
Communist Party of the Philippines/Marxist-Leninist [*Political party*] .... CPP/ML
Communist Party of the Soviet Union [*Political party*] (PPW) .... CPSU
Communist Party of the United States of America [*Political party*] (EA) .... CPUSA
Communist Party of the USA/Marxist Leninist [*Political party*] (EA) .... CPUSA/ML
Communist Party of Turkey [*Political party*] (PD) .... CPT
Communist Party of Turkmenistan [*Political party*] .... CPT

Communist Party of Ukraine [*Political party*] .... CPU
Communist Party of Uzbekistan [*Political party*] .... CPUz
Communist Party of Venezuela [*Political party*] .... CPV
Communist Rebel Combat Captives (CINC) .... CRCC
Communist Suppression Operations Command [*Thailand*] .... CSOC
Communist Sympathizer .... COMSYMP
Communist Terrorist .... CT
Communist University of London [*England*] (AIE) .... CUL
Communist Workers' Movement [*British*] (PPW) .... CWM
Communist Workers Party [*Political party*] .... CWP
Communist Youth League .... CYL
Communist Youth League [*From the Russian*] .... KOMSOMOL
Communist Youth Union of Canada (Marxist-Leninist) .... CYUC (M-L)
Communistic (ABBR) .... CMUNSTC
Communistische Partij Holland [*Communist Party of Holland*] [*Netherlands*] (PPE) .... CPH
Communistische Partij van Nederland [*Communist Party of the Netherlands*] (PPE) .... CPN
Communitatis Europae Lex [*European Community Law*] [*Commission of the European Communities*] [*Information service or system*] (IID) .... CELEX
Communities Organization of People .... COOP
Communities Organized for Public Service (DICI) .... COPS
Community .... CMNTY
Community .... CMTY
Community (ABBR) .... CMUNT
Community (AABC) .... COM
Community (WGA) .... COMM
Community .... COMMUN
Community .... CTY
Community Access Television (WDAA) .... CATV
Community Action Agencies [*Community Services Administration*] .... CAA
Community Action Association of Pennsylvania (SRA) .... CAAP
Community Action on Latin America (EA) .... CALA
Community Action Party [*Thailand*] [*Political party*] (FEA) .... CAP
Community Action Program [*Community Services Administration*] .... CAP
Community Action Research Group (OICC) .... CARG
Community Action Team [*Department of Labor*] .... CAT
Community Action to Control High Blood Pressure [*HEW*] .... CATCH
Community Action to Reach the Elderly .... CARE
Community Activity Center (MCD) .... CAC
Community Adaptation Schedule [*Psychology*] .... CAS
Community Adjustment Profile System (DMAA) .... CAPS
Community Advisory Committee of the Murray-Darling Basin Ministerial Council [*Australia*] .... CACMDBMC
Community Aerodrome Radio Station (DA) .... CARS
Community Affairs (DLA) .... Com Affrs
Community Affairs and Regulatory Functions [*HUD*] (OICC) .... CARF
Community Affairs Officer .... CAO
Community AIDS Treatment Information Exchange [*Reseau Communautaire d'Infotraitement SIDA*] (AC) .... CATIE
Community/Airport Economic Development Model [*FAA*] .... CAEDM
Community Alert Patrol .... CAP
Community and Child Health Service [*Australia*] .... CCHS
Community and Economic Development Division (AAGC) .... CED
Community and Family Program Review Committee [*DoD*] .... CFRC
Community and Family Support Center [*Army*] .... CFSC
Community and Junior College Libraries Section [*Association of College and Research Libraries*] .... CJCLS
Community & Legal Aid Services Program (AC) .... CLASP
Community and Mental Handicap Educational Research [*British*] (DBA) .... CMHERA
Community and Organization Research Institute [*Research center*] (RCD) .... CORI
Community and Public Sector Union [*Australia*] .... CPSU
Community and Special Broadcasting Agency [*British*] .... CSBA
Community and Technical College Libraries .... CTCL
Community and Youth Service Association (AIE) .... CYSA
Community Antenna Relay [*Service*] [*FCC*] .... CAR
Community Antenna Relay Service [*FCC Telecommunications*] .... CARS
Community Antenna Television [*Later, CTV*] (IAA) .... CAT
Community Antenna Television [*Later, CTV*] .... CATV
Community Antenna Television [*Also, cable television*] (WDMC) .... CATV
Community Antenna Television Association (EA) .... CATA
Community Antenna Television System (IAA) .... CATVS
Community Anti-Drug Coalitions of America .... CADCA
Community Artists Residency Training (DICI) .... CART
Community Arts Council of Greater Victoria (AC) .... CACGV
Community Arts Councils, Inc. [*Later, American Council for the Arts*] (EA) .... CACI
Community Arts Network [*Australia*] .... CAN
Community Arts Teachers [*Australia*] .... CAT
Community Association for Riding for the Disabled (AC) .... CARD
Community Associations Institute (EA) .... CAI
Community Athenaeum Colleges of the Hellenic Advancement Council [*Australia*] .... CACHAC
Community Automatic Exchange [*Telephone*] (BUR) .... CAEX
Community Automatic Exchange [*Telephone*] .... CAX
Community Awareness and Emergency Response Program [*Environmental Protection Agency*] (GFGA) .... CAER
Community Bank League of New England (SRA) .... CBLNE
Community Bank Shares of Indiana, Inc. [*NASDAQ symbol*] (SAG) .... CBIN
Community Bank Shares of Indiana, Inc. [*Associated Press*] (SAG) .... CmBkIN
Community Bank Shares(Ind) [*NASDAQ symbol*] (TTSB) .... CBIN
Community Bank System, Inc. [*NASDAQ symbol*] (NQ) .... CBSI
Community Bank System, Inc. [*Associated Press*] (SAG) .... CmtyBS
Community Bank Systems [*NASDAQ symbol*] (TTSB) .... CBSI

Community Bankers Association of Georgia (SRA) .... CBA
Community Bankers Association of Illinois (SRA) .... CBAI
Community Bankers Association of Indiana (SRA) .... CBAI
Community Bankers Association of Kansas (SRA) .... CBA-KS
Community Bankers Association of New York State (SRA) .... CBANYS
Community Bankers Association of Ohio (SRA) .... CBAO
Community Bankers Association of Oklahoma (SRA) .... CBAO
Community Bankers of Florida (SRA) .... CBF
Community Bankers of Kentucky (SRA) .... CBK
Community Bankers of Wisconsin (SRA) .... CBW
Community Banks, Inc. [*NASDAQ symbol*] (NQ) .... CBKI
Community Banks, Inc. [*Associated Press*] (SAG) .... CmBkPa
Community Banks, Inc. [*AMEX symbol*] (SAG) .... CTY
Community Banks (PA) [*AMEX symbol*] (TTSB) .... CTY
Community Bankshares, Inc. [*NASDAQ symbol*] (NQ) .... CBNH
Community Bankshares, Inc. [*Associated Press*] (SAG) .... CmtyBn
Community Bankshares, Inc. [*Associated Press*] (SAG) .... CmtyBSC
Community Bankshares (NH) [*NASDAQ symbol*] (TTSB) .... CBNH
Community Based Corrections (OICC) .... CBC
Community Broadcasters Association [*Defunct*] (EA) .... CBA
Community Broadcasters of America [*Defunct*] (EA) .... CBA
Community Bulletin Board System .... CBBS
Community Business Lothian [*British*] .... CBL
Community Business Scotland News [*A publication*] .... CB NEWS
Community Cancer Care Evaluation [*Department of Health and Human Services*] (GFGA) .... CCCE
Community Care Network [*Medicine*] .... CCN
Community Care of Amer [*NASDAQ symbol*] (TTSB) .... CCAL
Community Care of America [*NASDAQ symbol*] (SAG) .... CCAI
Community Care of America [*Associated Press*] (SAG) .... ComCare
Community Care of America [*Associated Press*] (SAG) .... ComCre
Community Care Services, Inc. [*NASDAQ symbol*] (SAG) .... CCSE
Community Care Services, Inc. [*Associated Press*] (SAG) .... CmtyCr
Community Care Unit (MAE) .... CCU
Community Careers Resource Center (EA) .... CCRC
Community Case Management Services .... CCMS
Community Charge Registration Officer [*British*] .... CCRO
Community Child Care Cooperative [*Australia*] CCCC
Community Climate Model [*Meteorology*] .... CCM
Community Clinical Oncology Program [*Department of Health and Human Services*] (GFGA) .... CCOP
Community Code [*Database terminology*] (NITA) .... CM
Community Collaboration Office [*Veterans Administration*] (GFGA) .... CCO
Community College CC
Community College Activities Survey (EDAC) .... CCAS
Community College Assessment Program [*Academic achievement and aptitude test*] .... CCAP
Community College Association for Instruction and Technology (EA) .... CCAIT
Community College General Education Association (EDAC) .... CCGEA
Community College Goals Inventory [*Test*] .... CCGI
Community College Humanities Association (EA) .... CCHA
Community College Journalism Association (EA) .... CCJA
Community College League of California (SRA) CCLC
Community College of Allegheny County, Boyce Campus, Monroeville, PA [*Ina ctive*] [*OCLC symbol*] (OCLC) .... AIB
Community College of Allegheny County, Boyce Campus, Monroeville, PA [*Library symbol Library of Congress*] (LCLS) .... PMvAC
Community College of Allegheny County, Center North, Pittsburgh, PA [*OCLC symbol*] (OCLC) .... AIN
Community College of Allegheny County, Pittsburgh, PA [*OCLC symbol*] (OCLC) .... AIC
Community College of Allegheny County, Pittsburgh, PA [*Library symbol Library of Congress*] (LCLS) .... PPiAC
Community College of Allegheny County, South Campus, West Mifflin, PA [*OCLC symbol*] (OCLC) .... AIS
Community College of Allegheny County, South Campus, West Mifflin, PA [*Library symbol Library of Congress*] (LCLS) .... PWesAC
Community College of Baltimore, Baltimore, MD [*Library symbol Library of Congress*] (LCLS) .... MdBBJC
Community College of Denver [*Colorado*] .... CCD
Community College of Denver, Auraria Campus, Denver, CO [*Library symbol Library of Congress*] (LCLS) .... CoDCC-A
Community College of Denver, Aurora Educational Learning Center, North Campus, Denver, CO [*Library symbol Library of Congress*] (LCLS) .... CoDCC-E
Community College of Denver, Denver, CO [*Library symbol Library of Congress*] (LCLS) .... CoDCC
Community College of Denver, North AEC Project, Westminster, CO [*OCLC symbol*] (OCLC) .... DVE
Community College of Denver, North Campus, Denver, CO [*Library symbol Library of Congress*] (LCLS) .... CoDCC-N
Community College of Denver, North Campus, Westminster, CO [*OCLC symbol*] (OCLC) .... DVC
Community College of Denver, North Campus, Westminster, CO [*OCLC symbol*] (OCLC) .... DVN
Community College of Denver, Red Rocks Campus, Golden, CO [*OCLC symbol*] (OCLC) .... DVR
Community College of Denver, Red Rocks Campus, Lakewood, CO [*Library symbol Library of Congress*] (LCLS) .... CoDCC-R
Community College of Philadelphia, Philadelphia, PA [*OCLC symbol*] (OCLC) .... PDC
Community College of Philadelphia, Philadelphia, PA [*Library symbol Library of Congress*] (LCLS) .... PPCoC
Community College of Rhode Island [*Formerly, RIJC*] .... CCRI
Community College of the Air Force (AFM) .... CCAF

Community College of the Finger Lakes, Canandaigua, NY [Library symbol Library of Congress] (LCLS) .... NCanC
Community College of the Finger Lakes, Canandaigua, NY [OCLC symbol] (OCLC) .... ZFM
Community College Social Science Association (EA) .... CCSSA
Community College Unit [Office of Education] .... CCU
Community Colleges [Educational Resources Information Center (ERIC) Clearinghouse] [University of California at Los Angeles (UCLA)] (PAZ) .... JC
Community Colleges Data Base [Information service or system] (IID) .... COCO
Community Colleges for International Development (EA) .... CCID
Community Communications [Independent Local Radio] [British] CC
Community Concern for Senior Citizens [Defunct] (EA) .... CCSC
Community Conference Crew [World online service referees] CCC
Community/Corridor Traffic Safety Program .... C/CTSP
Community Council Against Violence [Australia] .... CCAV
Community Creativity, Inc. [Defunct] (EA) CCI
Community Data Information System [MJK Associates] (NITA) .... CDIS
Community Design Center Directors Association (EA) .... CDCDA
Community Design Group [North Carolina State University] [Research center] (RCD) .... CDG
Community Development .... CD
Community Development Administration [HUD] .... CDA
Community Development Bank .... CDB
Community Development Block Grant [HUD] .... CDBG
Community Development Corp. [Later, NCDC] .... CDC
Community Development - Data Information Analysis Laboratory (OICC) .... CD-DIAL
Community Development Foundation [SCF] [Absorbed by] (EA) .... CDF
Community Development Infrastructure Program [Australia] .... CDIP
Community Development Society (EA) .... CDS
Community Development Support [Australia] .... CDS
Community Development Trust (AIE) .... CDT
Community Development Work Study Program [Department of Housing and Urban Development] (GFGA) .... CDWSP
Community Dial Office [Small switching system] [Telecommunications] .... CDO
Community Dispute Services (EA) .... CDS
Community Dreamsharing Network (EA) .... CDN
Community Drying-Out Centre [British] (DI) .... CDOC
Community Economic Development Act of 1981 .... CEDA
Community Economic Stabilization Corporation [Member of FIRR] (CROSS) .... CESCO
Community Economics, Inc. (EA) .... CEI
Community Education Officer (ADA) .... CEO
Community Educational Radio Fixed Service (MSA) .... CERFS
Community Educational Resources .... CER
Community Educational Services Foundation (IID) .... CESF
Community Electoral Assistant [Australia] .... CEA
Community Electronic Teller System .... COMETS
Community Emergency Care Association [Defunct] (EA) .... CECA
Community Emergency Drought Relief Act of 1977 .... CEDRA
Community Employment Development [Department of Labor] .... CED
Community Energy Program [Office of Volunteer Liaison] [ACTION] .... CEP
Community Enhancement & Economic Development Society (AC) .... CEEDS
Community Enterprise Program [British] .... CEP
Community Enterprise Trust (AIE) .... CET
Community Environmental Council (EA) .... CEC
Community Equivalent Noise Level (PDAA) .... CENL
Community Facilities Administration [of HHFA] [Terminated] .... CFA
Community, Family, and Soldier [Support Command] [Korea] (DOMA) .... CFS
Community, Family, and Soldier Support Command - Korea [Army] ...... CFSSC-K
Community Federal Bancorp [NASDAQ symbol] (TTSB) .... CFTR
Community Federal Bancorp, Inc. [NASDAQ symbol] (SAG) .... CFTP
Community Federal Bancorp, Inc. [Associated Press] (SAG) .... ComFed
Community Fellows Program (EA) .... CFP
Community Financial Corp. [NASDAQ symbol] (SAG) .... CFFC
Community Financial Corp. [Associated Press] (SAG) .... ComtyFin
Community Financial Corp. (Illinois) [NASDAQ symbol] (SAG) .... CFIC
Community Financial Corp. (Illinois) [Associated Press] (SAG) .... CmFnIl
Community Financial Group [NASDAQ symbol] (SAG) .... CFGI
Community Financial Group [Associated Press] (SAG) .... CmtyF
Community Financial Group [Associated Press] (SAG) .... CmtyFncl
Community Financial Holding Corp. [NASDAQ symbol] (SAG) .... CMFH
Community Financial Holding Corp. [Associated Press] (SAG) .... CmtyFin
Community Financial (IL) [NQS] (TTSB) .... CFIC
Community Finl Group [NASDAQ symbol] (TTSB) .... CFGI
Community Finl Group Wrrt [NASDAQ symbol] (TTSB) .... CFGIW
Community Finl Hldg [NASDAQ symbol] (TTSB) .... CMFH
Community Finl VA [NASDAQ symbol] (TTSB) .... CFFC
Community First 7% Cv Dep Pfd [NASDAQ symbol] (TTSB) .... CFBXZ
Community First Bankshares [NASDAQ symbol] (SAG) .... CFBX
Community First Bankshares [Associated Press] (SAG) .... ComFB
Community First Bankshares [Associated Press] (SAG) .... ComFtBk
Community Fluorosis Index .... CFI
Community Food and Nutrition Programs [Community Services Administration] .... CFNP
Community for Creative Non-Violence (EA) .... CCNV
Community for Religious Research and Education (EA) .... CRRE
Community for Social Justice in the Middle East and North Africa (EA) .... CSJMENA
Community Free Library, Holley, NY [Library symbol Library of Congress] (LCLS) .... NHoll
Community General Hospital Library, Thomasville, NC [Library symbol] [Library of Congress] (LCLS) .... NcThCH
Community Guidance Service (EA) .... CGS
Community Health Action Planning Service .... CHAPS

Community Health Air Monitoring Program [Environmental Protection Agency] .... CHAMP
Community Health and Environmental Surveillance System [Environmental Protection Agency project] .... CHESS
Community Health Association .... CHA
Community Health Awareness Group .... C-HAG
Community Health Care Association of New York State (SRA) .... CHCANYS
Community Health Center .... CHC
Community Health Computing .... CHC
Community Health Council [British] .... CHC
Community Health Department, Lakeshore General Hospital [Departement de SanteCommunautaire, Hopital General du Lakeshore], Pointe-Claire, Quebec [Library symbol National Library of Canada] (NLC) .... QMLGC
Community Health Department, Montreal General Hospital [Departement de Sante Communautaire, Hopital General de Montreal], Quebec [Library symbol National Library of Canada] (NLC) .... QMGHC
Community Health Education Project .... CHEP
Community Health Information Network [Library network] .... CHIN
Community Health Network (DHSM) .... CHN
Community Health Nurses Association of Canada (AC) .... CHNAC
Community Health Program (MCD) .... CHP
Community Health Representative Program [Department of Health and Human Services] (GFGA) .... CHR
Community Health Service [HEW] .... CHS
Community Health Studies [A publication] .... Community Hlth Stud
Community Health Systems, Inc. [Associated Press] (SAG) .... ComHlSy
Community Health Systems, Inc. [NYSE symbol] (SAG) .... CYH
Community Help and Improvement Program .... CHIP
Community High School, Detroit Lakes, MN [Library symbol] [Library of Congress] (LCLS) .... MnDIH
Community Historical Society, Maxwell, IA [Library symbol Library of Congress] (LCLS) .... IaMaxHi
Community Hlth Sys [NYSE symbol] (TTSB) .... CYH
Community Homefinding, Relocation, and Referral Services [US Army Corps of Engineers] .... CHRRS
Community Hospital at Glen Cove, Glen Cove, NY [Library symbol Library of Congress] (LCLS) .... NGlcC
Community Hospital of Ottawa, Ottawa, IL [Library symbol Library of Congress] (LCLS) .... IOtCH
Community Hospital of Springfield, Springfield, OH [Library symbol Library of Congress] (LCLS) .... OSH
Community Housing and Infrastructure Program [Australia] .... CHIP
Community Housing Development Organization [Department of Housing and Urban Development] .... CHDO
Community Human and Industrial Development, Inc. [Office of Economic Opportunity] [Terminated] .... CHID
Community Hypertension Evaluation Clinic [New Jersey] .... CHEC
Community Improvement Program (EA) .... CIP
Community Improvement Scale [Psychology] .... CIS
Community Independent Living Service Delivery Systems (EDAC) .... CILSDS
Community, Industry, Accounting and Legal Consultants [Database] [Australia] .... CONSULT
Community Industry Scheme [Department of Employment] [British] .... CIS
Community Information CI
Community Information and Referral Service [Library science] .... CI & R
Community Information and Referral Service [United Way/Crusade of Mercy] [Information service or system] (IID) .... CIRS
Community Information Network [Cable TV programming service] .... CIN
Community Information Section [Public Library Association] .... CIS
Community Information Services .... CIS
Community Information Utility (BUR) .... CIU
Community Infrastructure Training Program .... CITP
Community Integrated Training and Education Program .... CITEP
Community Integrated Training Type Functions .... CITF
Community Intervention Trial for Smoking Cessation [Department of Health and Human Services] (GFGA) .... COMMIT
Community Investment Officer [Federal Home Loan Bank Board] .... CIO
Community Investors Bancorp [NASDAQ symbol] (TTSB) .... CIBI
Community Investors Bancorp, Inc. [NASDAQ symbol] (SAG) .... CIBI
Community Investors Bancorp, Inc. [Associated Press] (SAG) .... CmyIBc
Community Junior College .... CJC
Community Junior High School, Detroit Lakes, MN [Library symbol] [Library of Congress] (LCLS) .... MnDIJ
Community Land Trust [Agricultural economics] .... CLT
Community Land Use Game [Urban-planning game] .... CLUG
Community Language in the Secondary Curriculum [Project] (AIE) .... CLSC
Community Law Offices .... CLO
Community Leadership Workshop .... CLEW
Community Learning through America's Schools [National Education Association] .... CLASS
Community Legal Aid .... CLA
Community Legal Education Association (Manitoba) Inc. [Association d'Education Juridique Communautaire (Manitoba) Inc.] (AC) .... CLEA
Community Legal Education Ontario (AC) .... CLEO
Community Liaison Staff [Environmental Protection Agency] (GFGA) .... CLS
Community Library Association, Inc., Ketchem, ID [Library symbol] [Library of Congress] (LCLS) .... IdK
Community Library, Roundup, MT [Library symbol] [Library of Congress] (LCLS) .... MtRd
Community Living Arrangement [For the handicapped] .... CLA
Community Living Fund .... CLF
Community Living Oakville (AC) .... CLO
Community Living Stormont County [Integration Communautaire Comte de Stormont] (AC) .... CLSC
Community Management Training Scheme [Australia] .... CMT

Community Management Training Service [*Australia*] ... CMTS
Community Market Catalog ... CM
Community Med Trans [*NASDAQ symbol*] (TTSB) ... CMTI
Community Med Trans Wrrt [*NASDAQ symbol*] (TTSB) ... CMTIW
Community Medical Transport, Inc. [*NASDAQ symbol*] (SAG) ... CMTI
Community Medical Transport, Inc. [*Associated Press*] (SAG) ... CmtyMd T
Community Medical Transport, Inc. [*Associated Press*] (SAG) ... CtyMT
Community Memorial Hospital, Health Science Library, Menomonee Falls, WI [*Library symbol Library of Congress*] (LCLS) ... WMenofH
Community Memorial Museum of Sutter County, Yuba City, CA [*Library symbol*] [*Library of Congress*] (LCLS) ... CYcM
Community Mental Health Activities ... CMHA
Community Mental Health Center [*or Clinic*] ... CMHC
Community Mental Health Centers Act [*1975*] ... CMHCA
Community Mental Health Nurse (DAVI) ... CMHN
Community Mental Health Program ... CMHP
Community Modelling Effort [*Oceanography*] ... CME
Community Noise Equivalent Level ... CNEL
Community Noise Rating ... CNR
Community Nurse Practitioner ... CNP
Community Nursing Center (DMAA) ... CNC
Community Nursing Home ... CNH
Community Nursing Organization (DMAA) ... CNO
Community Nutrition Institute (EA) ... CNI
Community of All Hallows [*Anglican religious community*] ... CAH
Community of Interest [*Telecommunications*] (TEL) ... CI
Community of Interest [*DoD*] ... COI
Community of Jesus of Nazareth [*Anglican religious community*] ... CJN
Community of Reparation to Jesus in the Blessed Sacrament [*Anglican religious community*] ... CRJBS
Community of St. Clare [*Anglican religious community*] ... CSCl
Community of St. Denys [*Anglican religious community*] ... CSD
Community of St. Francis [*Anglican religious community*] ... CSF
Community of St. John the Baptist [*Anglican religious community*] ... CSJB
Community of St. John the Evangelist [*Anglican religious community*] ... CSJE
Community of St. Katharine of Egypt [*Anglican religious community*] ... CSK
Community of St. Laurence [*Anglican religious community*] ... CSL
Community of St. Mary the Virgin [*Anglican religious community*] ... CSMV
Community of St. Michael and All Angels [*Anglican religious community*] ... CSM and AA
Community of St. Peter [*Anglican religious community*] ... CSP
Community of St. Wilfrid [*Anglican religious community*] ... CSW
Community of the Blessed Virgin Mary [*Anglican religious community*] ... CBVM
Community of the Companions of Jesus the Good Shepherd [*Anglican religious community*] ... CJGS
Community of the Epiphany [*Anglican religious community*] ... CE
Community of the Glorious Ascension [*Anglican religious community*] ... CGA
Community of the Holy Cross [*Anglican religious community*] ... CHC
Community of the Holy Family [*Anglican religious community*] ... CHF
Community of the Holy Name of Jesus [*Anglican religious community*] ... CHN
Community of the Holy Rood [*Anglican religious community*] ... CHR
Community of the Holy Spirit (TOCD) ... CHS
Community of the Newspaper Publishing Associations of the European Economic Communities [*Belgium*] (EAIO) ... CNPA-EEC
Community of the Nursing Sisters of St. John the Divine [*Anglican religious community*] ... NSSJD
Community of the Presentation [*Anglican religious community*] ... CP
Community of the Resurrection [*Anglican religious community*] ... CR
Community of the Servants of the Cross [*Anglican religious community*] ... CSC
Community of the Sisters of the Church [*Anglican religious community*] ... CSC
Community of the Sisters of the Love of God [*Anglican religious community*] ... SLG
Community of the Whole Person (EA) ... CWP
Community of the Will of God [*Anglican religious community*] ... CWG
Community On-Line Intelligence Network System [*Computer network*] [*National Science Administration and Central Intelligence Agency*] ... COINS
Community Organization for Full Employment Economy ... COFFEE
Community Oriented Policing Services ... COPS
Community Outreach Information Network ... COIN
Community Patent Convention [*European Common Market*] ... CPC
Community Patrol Officer Program [*Police work*] ... CPOP
Community Placement ... CP
Community Planning and Design Center [*Information service or system*] (IID) ... CPDC
Community Planning and Development [*HUD*] (OICC) ... CPD
Community Planning and Management [*HUD*] ... CPM
Community Planning Association of Canada ... CPAC
Community Planning Association of Canada, Ottawa, ON, Canada [*Library symbol Library of Congress*] (LCLS) ... CaOOCP
Community Planning Association of Canada [*Association Canadienne d'Urbanisme*] **Ottawa, Ontario** [*Library symbol National Library of Canada*] (NLC) ... OOCP
Community Post Office ... CPO
Community Pre-School Employers' Association of Queensland [*Australia*] ... CPSEAQ
Community Pride Association (EA) ... CPA
Community Products, Inc. ... CPI
Community Program for Clinical Research on AIDS [*FDA*] ... CPCRA
Community Program for Education and Training in Technology [*EC*] (ECED) ... COMETT
Community Programme in Education and Training for Technology [*British*] ... COMETT
Community Programs Branch [*Australian Capital Territory*] ... CPB
Community Projects Foundation [*British*] ... CPF
Community Psych Ctrs [*NYSE symbol*] (TTSB) ... CMY
Community Psychiatric Centers [*NYSE symbol*] (SPSG) ... CMY
Community Psychiatric Centers [*Associated Press*] (SAG) ... CPsyc
Community Psychiatric Nursing Association [*British*] ... CPNA
Community Radio Association [*British*] ... CRA
Community Radio Watch ... CRW
Community Rating by Class ... CRC
Community Rating System [*National Flood Insurance Program*] ... CRS
Community Recreation and Skill Development Activities (AABC) ... CRSDA
Community Recreation Council [*Victoria*] [*Australia*] ... CRC
Community Redevelopment Agency ... CRA
Community Reference Bureau Databank [*European Atomic Energy Community*] (NITA) ... CRB
Community Refugee Settlement Scheme [*Australia*] ... CRSS
Community Regeneration [*Defunct*] (EA) ... CR
Community Reinvestment Act [*1977*] [*Requires banks to list credit facilities available to the communities they serve*] ... CRA
Community Relations [*Military*] (NVT) ... COMREL
Community Relations (AABC) ... CR
Community Relations Advisory Council [*Military*] ... CRAC
Community Relations Commission [*British*] ... CRC
Community Relations Director ... CRD
Community Relations Division [*Environmental Protection Agency*] (GFGA) ... CRD
Community Relations Plan ... CRP
Community Relations Service [*Department of Justice*] [*Terminated*] ... CRS
Community Release Program [*Australia*] ... CRP
Community Renewal Program ... CRP
Community Research Associates (EA) ... CRA
Community Research Bureau ... CRB
Community Research Center [*University of Illinois*] [*Research center*] (RCD) ... CRC
Community Research Initiative of Toronto [*Initiative de Recherche Communautaire de Toronto*] (AC) ... CRIT
Community Research Initiatives [*Community-based AIDS treatment organizations*] ... CRI's
Community Research Services [*Illinois State University*] [*Normal*] [*Information service or system*] (IID) ... CRS
Community Residential Care [*Veterans Administration*] (GFGA) ... CRC
Community Residential Facility [*For the handicapped*] ... CRF
Community Residential Unit [*Victoria*] [*Australia*] ... CRU
Community Resource and Research Center [*University of Nebraska - Lincoln*] [*Research center*] (RCD) ... CRRC
Community Resources Information Service, Inc. [*Information service or system*] (IID) ... CRIS
Community Resources Workshop Association [*Later, NAIEC*] (EA) ... CRWA
Community Rule, Rule of the Congregation [*or Manual of Discipline, Serekh ha-Yahad*] **from Qumran. Cave One** (BJA) ... 1QS
Community Savings FA [*NASDAQ symbol*] (SAG) ... CMSV
Community Savings FA [*Associated Press*] (SAG) ... CommSv
Community Security (NVT) ... COMSEC
Community Service [*An association*] (EA) ... CS
Community Service Activities [*AFL-CIO*] ... CSA
Community Service Announcement ... CSA
Community Service Council of Central Indiana [*United Way of Central Indiana*] [*Also, an information service or system*] (IID) ... CSC
Community Service Credit Union Council [*Defunct*] (EA) ... CSCUC
Community Service Employment for Older Americans [*Department of Labor*] ... CSEOA
Community Service Grant [*Corporation for Public Broadcasting*] ... CSG
Community Service Obligation ... CSO
Community Service Volunteers [*British*] ... CSV
Community Services Administration [*Superseded Office of Economic Opportunity*] [*HEW*] ... CSA
Community Services Block Grant ... CSBG
Community Services Grants Program [*Australia*] ... CSGP
Community Services Program [*Canada*] ... CSP
Community Shelter Plan [*Civil Defense*] ... CSP
Community Shelter Planning Officer, State [*Civil Defense*] ... CSPOS
Community Skills Unit (AIE) ... CSU
Community Standards Association [*British*] (DI) ... CSA
Community Support Framework [*EC*] (ECED) ... CSF
Community Support Program [*National Institute of Mental Health*] ... CSP
Community Systems Foundation (EA) ... CSF
Community Systems Foundation (Australia) ... CSF(A)
Community Task Force [*British*] ... CTF
Community Telecommunications Development Foundation [*Washington, DC*] (TSSD) ... CTDF
Community Telephone Plan (ADA) ... CTP
Community Television (NITA) ... CTV
Community Television Sydney [*Australia*] ... CTV
Community Trade Mark Office [*EC*] (ECED) ... CTMO
Community Training and Development [*An association*] (EA) ... CTD
Community Transit [*System*] [*Shipping EEC*] (DS) ... CT
Community Transportation Association of America [*ENO*] (TAG) ... CTAA
Community Transportation Coordinator [*MOCD*] (TAG) ... CTC
Community Trust Bancorp, Inc. [*Associated Press*] (SAG) ... CmtyTrBc
Community Trust Bancorp, Inc. [*NASDAQ symbol*] (SAG) ... CTBI
Community United Group Services [*British*] ... CUGS
Community Voice Mail [*Program providing the homeless with voice mail*] [*Telecommunications*] (ECON) ... CVM
Community Volunteer Services Commission of B'nai B'rith International (EAIO) ... CVS
Community Volunteer Services Commission of B'nai B'rith International (EA) ... CVSC
Community War Services [*of FSA*] [*World War II*] ... CWS
Community Water System [*Environmental Protection Agency*] ... CWS

Community Welfare Advisory Council [*New South Wales*] [*Australia*] .... CWAC
Community Welfare Planning Association, Social Research Library, Houston, TX [*Library symbol Library of Congress*] (LCLS) .... TxHCS
Community Work and Training Program [*Department of Labor*] .... CWTP
Community-Acquired Pneumonia .... CAP
Community-Based Clinical Trial [*Medicine*] .... CBCT
Community-Based Order (ADA) .... CBO
Community-Based Organization [*Organization which provides employment and training services*] [*CETA*] .... CBO
Community-Based Residential Facility .... CBRF
Community-General Hospital, Staff Library, Syracuse, NY [*OCLC symbol*] (OCLC) .... ZUG
Community-General Hospital, Syracuse, NY [*Library symbol Library of Congress*] (LCLS) .... NSyGH
Community-Oriented Police .... COP
Community-Oriented Police Enforcement .... COPE
Community-Oriented Primary Care [*Medicine*] .... COPC
Community-Oriented Programs Environment Scale [*Psychosocial assessment test*] .... COPES
Community-Supported Agriculture .... CSA
Communization (ABBR) .... CMUNZN
Communize (ABBR) .... CMUNZ
Communized (ABBR) .... CMUNZD
Communizing (ABBR) .... CMUNZG
Commutability (ABBR) .... CMUTABT
Commutable (ABBR) .... CMUTAB
Commutate (ABBR) .... CMUTA
Commutated (ABBR) .... CMUTAD
Commutated Aerial Direction .... CAD
Commutated Antenna Direction Finder (IEEE) .... CADF
Commutated Capacitor Filter (PDAA) .... CCF
Commutated Doppler Microwave Landing System (PDAA) .... CDMLS
Commutated Network (IAA) .... CN
Commutating (ABBR) .... CMUTAG
Commutating Detection System .... CODES
Commutation [*Army*] .... Comtn
Commutation Factor .... CF
Commutation of Rations and Quarters [*Military*] .... CRQ
Commutation Rate (MCD) .... C/R
Commutative (ABBR) .... CMUTAV
Commutative Principle for Addition [*Mathematics*] .... CPA
Commutative Principle for Multiplication [*Mathematics*] .... CPM
Commutator (ABBR) .... CMUTAR
Commutator [*Electromagnetism*] (IAA) .... COM
Commutator .... COMM
Commutator [*Automotive engineering*] .... COMTR
Commutator Assemblies [*SONAR*] (MCD) .... CA
Commutator End (MSA) .... CE
Commutatorless Motor (PDAA) .... CLM
Commute (ABBR) .... CMUT
Commuted (ABBR) .... CMUTD
Commuted Rations [*Acronym refers to married Marine living off base and receiving these special pay dispensations*] .... COMRAT
Commuted Rations, Proceed Time [*Marine Corps*] (DNAB) .... COMRATS PT
Commuter (ABBR) .... CMUTR
Commuter .... COM
Commuter Airline Association of America [*Later, RAA*] (EA) .... CAAA
Commuter Airlines [*Airline code*] .... CB
Commuter Services Corp. [*Formerly, ACSC*] .... CSC
Commuter Trip Reduction [*MOCD*] (TAG) .... CTR
Commuters Air Transport, Inc. .... CAT
Commuting (ABBR) .... CMUTG
Commuting Area Candidates [*Civil Service*] .... CAC
COMNET Corp. [*Formerly, Computer Network Corp.*] [*NASDAQ symbol*] (NQ) .... CNET
Comnet Corp. [*Associated Press*] (SAG) .... Comnet
Comodoro Rivadavia [*Argentina*] [*Airport symbol*] (OAG) .... CRD
Comodoro Rivadavia [*Argentina ICAO location identifier*] (ICLI) .... SAVF
Comodoro Rivadavia [*Argentina ICAO location identifier*] (ICLI) .... SAVU
Comodoro Rivadavia/Gral Mosconi [*Argentina ICAO location identifier*] (ICLI) .... SAVC
COMOPTEVFOR Acronym and Abbreviation List [*A publication*] (CAAL) .... CAAL
Comorian Franc [*Monetary unit*] (ODBW) .... CF
Comoro Islands [*MARC country of publication code Library of Congress*] (LCCP) .... cq
Comoro Islands [*MARC geographic area code Library of Congress*] (LCCP) .... i-cq--
Comoros [*ANSI three-letter standard code*] (CNC) .... COM
Comoros [*International civil aircraft marking*] (ODBW) D6
Comoros [*ANSI two-letter standard code*] (CNC) .... KM
Comox [*Canada*] [*Airport symbol*] (OAG) .... YQQ
Comox Canadian Forces Base, BC [*ICAO location identifier*] (ICLI) .... CYQQ
Comox Resources Ltd. [*Vancouver Stock Exchange symbol*] .... CXO
Comox Valley Multicultural & Immigrant Support Society (AC) .... CVMISS
Comp de Minas Buenaventura ADS [*NYSE symbol*] (TTSB) .... BVN
Compact [*Car size*] C
Compact (FAAC) .... CMPCT
Compact All-Purpose Range Instrument [*RADAR*] (MCD) .... CAPRI
Compact Automatic Retrieval Device [*Massachusetts Institute of Technology*] [*Computer science*] .... CARD
Compact Automatic Retrieval Display [*Computer science*] (IID) .... CARD
Compact Blazing Combustion Axiom [*Auto engineering*] .... COMBAX
Compact Buoy System .... CBS
Compact Cassette (IAA) CC
Compact Data Disk Association [*Defunct*] (EA) .... CDDA
Compact Design [*Automotive engineering*] .... CD
Compact Digital Audio Disk (ADA) .... CDAD
Compact Dimension 2-Stroke Engine [*Automotive engineering*] CDS2
Compact Disc and Cathode Ray Tube Applied Format [*Automotive navigation systems*] .... CDCRAFT
Compact Disc File Manager [*Computer science*] (NTCM) .... CD-FM
Compact Disc Group [*Defunct*] (EA) .... CDG
Compact Disc Plus Graphics .... CD + G
Compact Disc Read and Write .... CD-RAW
Compact Disc Read-Only Memory Extended Architecture [*Computer science*] (PCM) .... CD-ROM XA
Compact Disc Recordable .... CD-R
Compact Disc Recorder .... CD-R
Compact Disc Universal Disk Format .... CD-UDF
Compact Disc-Interactive [*Computer science*] .... CD-I
Compact Disc-Read Only Memory [*Computer science*] (ACRL) .... CD-ROM
Compact Disc-Write Once [*Computer science*] (DOM) .... CD-WO
Compact Disk [*Audio/video technology*] [*Philips*] .... CD
Compact Disk [*Audio/Video Technology*] [*Philips*] (ACRL) .... CD
Compact Disk Digital Audio [*Computer science*] .... CD-DA
Compact Disk File System [*Computer science*] (PCM) .... CDFS
Compact Disk - Interactive .... CD-I
Compact Disk Programmable Read-Only Memory [*Computer science*] .... CD-PROM
Compact Disk Read-Only Memory [*Computer science*] .... CD-ROM
Compact Disk Real-Time Operating System .... CD-RTOS
Compact Disk Television (BARN) .... CDTV
Compact Disk Video [*Audio/video technology*] .... CDV
Compact Disk Video Interactive [*Computer science*] .... CD-VI
Compact Edition [*Windows*] [*Computer science*] (PCM) .... CE
Compact Electronic Components Inspection Laboratory .... CECIL
Compact Floppy Disk [*Computer science*] (EECA) .... CFD
Compact Floppy Disk Drive [*Computer science*] (EECA) .... CFDD
Compact Fluorescent Lamp .... CFL
Compact Fluorescent Light .... CFL
Compact Gamma Ray Spectrometer .... CGRS
Compact Helicopter Approach Path Indicator (DA) .... CHAPI
Compact High-Energy Capacitor Module Advanced Technology Experiment [*For development of the rail gun*] .... CHECMATE
Compact High-Performance Aerial Gun (MCD) .... CHAG
Compact Ignition TOKAMAK [*Toroidal Kamera Magnetic*] [*Plasma physics*] .... CIT
Compact Indium Discharge (WDMC) .... CID
Compact Interactive Standard for Common Business-Oriented Language [*Computer science*] (HGAA) .... CIS-COBOL
Compact Iodide Daylight (WDMC) .... CID
Compact Molecular Cloud [*Chemistry*] (BARN) .... CMC
Compact Nuclear Brayton System .... CONUBS
Compact Operating System (IAA) .... COS
Compact Orbital Gears Ltd. .... COG
Compact Periscope (MCD) .... COP
Compact Personal Computer (HGAA) .... CPC
Compact Programmed Airline Reservation System [*Computer science*] (PDAA) .... CPARS
Compact Sounder .... CDS
Compact Source Iodide (WDMC) .... CSI
Compact Toroid (MCD) .... CT
Compact Transpiration Cooling .... CTC
Compact Very-Low-Frequency Equipment (DWSG) .... CVLFE
Compact Video CV
Compact Video Cassette Recorder CVC
Compact Video-Rate Optical Scanner [*Instrumentation*] .... CVROS
Compacted Earth (PDAA) .... CE
Compacted Earth Sodium Treated (PDAA) .... CEST
Compacted Graphite Iron [*Metallurgical engineering*] .... CGI
Compact-Flake-Graphite [*Type of Iron*] .... CFG
Compactor Co., Inc. CCI
Compagnia Aeronautica Italiana SPA [*Italy ICAO designator*] (FAAC) .... CAI
Compagnia Generale Ripreseaeree, SPA [*Italy*] [*FAA designator*] (FAAC) .... CGR
Compagnie [*Company*] [*French*] .... Cie
Compagnie Aerienne du Languedoc [*ICAO designator*] (AD) .... FQ
Compagnie Aerienne du Languedoc [*France ICAO designator*] (FAAC) .... LGD
Compagnie Aeronautique Europeene [*France ICAO designator*] (FAAC) .... FEU
Compagnie Africaine des Ingenieurs-Conseils .... CADIC
Compagnie Air Mediterrannee [*France ICAO designator*] (FAAC) .... MDT
Compagnie d'Assurance d'Hypotheques du Canada [*Mortgage Insurance Co. of Canada - MICC*] .... CAHC
Compagnie de Bauxites de Guinee [*Guinea*] [*ICAO designator*] (FAAC) .... GIC
Compagnie de Chemin de Fer Bas-Congo-Katanga [*Lower Congo-Katanga Railway*] [*Zaire*] .... BCK
Compagnie de Transport Aerien [*Switzerland ICAO designator*] (FAAC) .... CTA
Compagnie de Transports Aeriens [*Airline*] [*Switzerland*] .... CTA
Compagnie des Agents de Change [*French Stockbrokers Association*] [*Information Service or System*] (EAIO) .... CAC
Compagnie des Jeunes Canadiens [*Company of Young Canadians*] [*Federal crown corporation to employ young people, 1966-75*] .... CJC
Compagnie des Pretres de St. Sulpice [*Society of the Priests of St. Sulpice - SPSS*] [*France*] (EAIO) .... CPSS
Compagnie Europeenne d'Automatisme [*Became part of Compagnie Internationale d'Informatique*] .... CAE
Compagnie Europeenne de la Jeunesse .... CEJ
Compagnie Francaise pour l'Assurance du Commerce Exterieur .... COFACE
Compagnie Generale d'Electricite [*General Electric Company*] [*France*] .... CGE
Compagnie Generale des Eaux .... CGE
Compagnie Generale d'Industrie et de Participations .... CGIP

Compagnie Generale Electrique du Canada [*Canadian General Electric Co. Ltd.*] ..... CGE
Compagnie Industrielle de Telecommunication [*Computer manufacturer*] [*France*] ..... CIT
Compagnie Industrielle du Disque [*Record label*] [*France*] ..... CID
Compagnie Internationale de Papier du Canada [*Canadian International Paper Co.*] ..... CIP
Compagnie Internationale de Services en Informatique [*Information service or system*] [*France*] (NITA) ..... CISI-IAI
Compagnie Internationale de Services en Informatique-Electrical and Nuclear Energy [*France*] [*Information service or system*] (NITA) ..... CISI-ELECNUL
Compagnie Internationale de Services et Informatique [*International Information Services Company*] [*Information service or system France*] (IID) ..... CISI
Compagnie Internationale pour l'Informatique [*Formed by merger of SEA and CAE*] CII
Compagnie Maritime Camerounaise SA [*Shipping line*] (EY) ..... CMC
Compagnie Nationale Air Gabon [*ICAO designator*] (FAAC) ..... AGN
Compagnie Nationale Algerienne de Navigation [*Algerian National Shipping Company*] (AF) ..... CNAN
Compagnie Nationale Naganagani [*Burkina Faso*] [*ICAO designator*] (FAAC) ..... BFN
Compagnie Senegalaise de Transports Aeriens [*Senegal*] [*ICAO designator*] (ICDA) ..... DS
Companded Delta Modulation [*Telecommunications*] (TEL) ..... CDM
Companding and Frequency Modulation [*Telecommunications*] (TEL) ..... CFM
Companhia Brasileira de Trens Urbanos [*Railway system*] [*Brazil*] (EY) ..... CBTU
Companhia Danca Contemporanea [*Portugal*] ..... CDC
Companhia de Navegacao do Norte [*Shipping company*] [*Brazil*] (EY) ..... CONAN
Companhia Portuguesa Radio Marconi [*Portuguese Radio Marconi Co.*] [*Lisbon*] [*Information service or system*] (IID) ..... CPRM
Companhia Vale do Rio Doce ..... CVRD
Compania [*Company*] [*Spanish*] ..... CIA
Compania [*Company*] [*Spanish*] (DFIT) ..... Cia
Compania [*Company*] [*Spanish*] (BARN) ..... Compa
Compania Aerea de Servicios Tur Air [*Spain ICAO designator*] (FAAC) ..... TUU
Compania Aerea del Sur SA [*Uruguay*] [*ICAO designator*] (FAAC) ..... ASU
Compania Aero Transportes Panamenos SA [*Panama*] [*ICAO designator*] (FAAC) ..... AEP
Compania Aerotecnicas Fotograficas [*Spain ICAO designator*] (FAAC) ..... ATF
Compania Anonima Nacional Telefonos de Venezuela [*Associated Press*] (SAG) ..... CANTV
Compania Anonima Nacional Telefonos de Venezuela [*NYSE symbol*] (SAG) ..... VNT
Compania Boliviana De Energia [*NYSE symbol*] (TTSB) ..... BLP
Compania Boliviana de Energia Electrica [*Associated Press*] (SAG) ..... CoBolv
Compania Boliviana de Energia Electrica SA [*NYSE symbol*] (SPSG) ..... BLP
Compania Cervecerias ADS [*NASDAQ symbol*] (TTSB) ..... CCUUY
Compania Cervecerias Unides [*NASDAQ symbol*] (SAG) ..... CCUU
Compania Cervecerias Unides [*Associated Press*] (SAG) ..... Cervecer
Compania de Aviacion "Faucett" SA [*Peru*] [*ICAO designator*] (ICDA) ..... CF
Compania de Aviacion Faucett SA [*Peru*] [*ICAO designator*] (FAAC) ..... CFP
Compania de Aviacion Trans-Europa [*Spain ICAO designator*] (ICDA) ..... TR
Compania de Minas Buenaventura SA [*NYSE symbol*] (SAG) ..... BVN
Compania de Minas Buenaventura SA [*Associated Press*] (SAG) ..... CoMBuen
Compania de Servicios Aereos SA [*Spain ICAO designator*] (FAAC) ..... SAESA
Compania de Servicios Aereos SA [*Spain ICAO designator*] (FAAC) ..... SSS
Compania de Servicios Aereos, TAVISA [*Spain ICAO designator*] (FAAC) ..... TAV
Compania de Telecom Chile ADS [*NYSE symbol*] (TTSB) ..... CTC
Compania de Telecommunicaciones de Chile SA [*Associated Press*] (SAG) ..... ChileTel
Compania de Telecomunicaciones de Chile SA [*NYSE symbol*] (SAG) ..... CTC
Compania de Telefonos de Chile SA [*Associated Press*] (SAG) ..... ChileTel
Compania de Telefonos de Chile SA [*NYSE symbol*] (SAG) ..... CTC
Compania de Telefonos de Chile SA [*Santiago*] [*Telecommunications service*] ..... CTC
Compania Dominicana de Aviacion SA [*ICAO designator*] (OAG) ..... DO
Compania Dominicana de Aviacion SA [*Dominican Republic*] [*ICAO designator*] (FAAC) ..... DOA
Compania Helicopteros de Transporte SA [*Spain ICAO designator*] (FAAC) ..... HSO
Compania Helicopteros del Sureste SA [*Spain ICAO designator*] (FAAC) ..... HSE
Compania Hispano Irlandesa de Aviacion [*Spain ICAO designator*] (FAAC) ..... FUA
Compania Internacional Editora, Sociedad Anonima ..... CIESA
Compania Internada de Aviacion [*Colombia*] [*ICAO designator*] (FAAC) ..... IAN
Compania Mexicana de Aeroplanos SA [*Mexico ICAO designator*] (FAAC) ..... MDR
Compania Mexicana de Aviacion [*Mexican airline*] ..... CMA
Compania Mexicana de Aviacion [*ICAO designator*] (OAG) ..... MX
Compania Mexicana de Aviacion SA [*Mexico ICAO designator*] (FAAC) ..... MXA
Compania Mexicana de Taxis Aereos SA [*Mexico ICAO designator*] (FAAC) ..... CMX
Compania Nacional de Turismo Aereo [*Chilean airline*] ..... CINTA
Compania Panamena de Aviacion SA [*Panama*] [*ICAO designator*] (FAAC) ..... CMP
Compania Panamena de Aviacion, SA [*Panamanian airline*] ..... COPA
Compania Peruana de Vapores [*Peruvian airline*] ..... CPV
Compania Spantax [*Spain ICAO designator*] (FAAC) ..... BXS
Compania SPANTAX (Servicios y Transportes Aereos Air Charter) [*Spain ICAO designator*] (ICDA) ..... BX
Compania Sud America de Vapores [*Chilean airline*] ..... CSAV
Compania Telefonica Nacional de Espana [*National Telephone Co. of Spain*] [*Telecommunications*] ..... CTNE
Companies (ROG) ..... COS
Companies, Agencies, Markets, Positions (IIA) ..... CAMP
Companies and Their Brands [*Formerly, TND:CI*] [*A publication*] ..... CTB
Companies Registration Office [*British*] (DS) ..... CRO
Companies Update Bulletin [*National Companies and Securities Commission*] [*A publication*] ..... CUB
Companion C
Companion (MSA) ..... COMP
Companion Dog [*Dog show term*] ..... CD
Companion Dog [*Prefix*] ..... U-CD
Companion Dog, Excellent [*Dog show term*] ..... CDX
Companion Dog Excellent [*Prefix*] ..... U-CDX
Companion, Institute of Radio Engineers ..... CIRE
Companion Member of the Institution of Works and Highways Technician Engineers [*British*] (DBQ) ..... CMIWHTE
Companion of Honour [*British*] ..... CH
Companion of Literature [*Royal Society of Literature Award*] [*British*] (BARN) ..... C Litt
Companion of Literature [*Royal Society of Literature award*] [*British*] ..... CLit
Companion of the Association of Business Executives [*British*] (DBQ) ..... CABE
Companion of the [*Order of the*] **Bath** [*British*] ..... CB
Companion of the British Institute of Management (DBQ) ..... CBIM
Companion of the Distinguished Service Order [*British*] ..... CDS
Companion of the Distinguished Service Order [*British*] ..... CDSO
Companion of the Distinguished Service Order [*Canada*] (DD) ..... DSO
Companion of the [*Order of the*] **Indian Empire** [*British*] ..... CIE
Companion of the Institute of Marine Engineers [*British*] ..... CIMarE
Companion of the Institute of Personnel Management [*Formerly, FIPM*] [*British*] ..... CIPM
Companion of the Institute of Plumbing [*British*] (DBQ) ..... CompIP
Companion of the Institution of Agricultural Engineers [*British*] ..... CIAgrE
Companion of the Institution of Analysts and Programmers [*British*] (DBQ) ..... CmpnIAP
Companion of the Institution of Electrical Engineers [*British*] ..... CIEE
Companion of the Institution of Electrical Engineers [*British*] (EY) ..... CompIEE
Companion of the Institution of Electronic and Radio Engineers [*British*] ..... CompIERE
Companion of the Institution of Gas Engineers [*British*] (DBQ) ..... Companion IGasE
Companion of the Institution of Mechanical and General Technician Engineers [*British*] (DBQ) ..... CIMGTechE
Companion of the Institution of Mechanical Engineers [*British*] ..... CI Mech E
Companion of the Order of Canada CC
Companion of the Order of Canada (DD) CC
Companion of the Order of St. Michael and St. George [*Facetiously translated "Call Me God"*] [*British*] ..... CMG
Companion of the Order of the British Empire (ADA) ..... CBE
Companion of the Society of Certified Professionals [*British*] (DBQ) ..... CmpnSCP
Companion of the Society of Licensed Aircraft Engineers and Technologists [*British*] (DBQ) ..... CompSLEAT
Companion of the [*Order of the*] **Star of India** [*British*] ..... CSI
Companion of the Textile Institute [*British*] ..... CompTI
Companion to the Authorized Daily Prayer Book [*A publication*] (BJA) ..... CPB
Companion Trainer Aircraft ..... CTA
Companions ..... COM
Companions of Christ (TOCD) ..... COC
Companions of Doctor Who Fan Club [*Defunct*] (EA) ..... CODW
Companions of the Celtic Mission (EAIO) ..... CCM
Companions of the Forest of America (EA) ..... CFA
Companions of the Forest of America [*New York, NY*] (EA) ..... COFOA
Company [*Business term*] (AAG) ..... CO
Company (DD) ..... Co
Company ..... CO
Company ..... COMP
Company (ROG) ..... COMPY
Company ..... COY
Company and Securities Law Journal [*Australia A publication*] ..... C & SLJ
Company and Securities Law Journal [*Australia A publication*] ..... Co & Sec Law Journal
Company Average VOC [*Volatile Organic Compound*] **Emission** [*Environmental Protection Agency*] ..... CAVE
Company Buyer Study [*Life Insurance Management and Research Association*] ..... CBS
Company Cases [*India*] [*A publication*] (DLA) ..... Com Cas
Company Cases [*India*] [*A publication*] (DLA) ..... Comp Cas
Company Chemists' Association [*British*] ..... CCA
Company Collection Point [*Army*] (INF) ..... CCP
Company Commander CC
Co. Counsel Inc. Wrrt [*NASDAQ symbol*] (TTSB) ..... LEGIW
Company Credit Reports [*Teikoku DataBank Ltd.*] [*Japan Information service or system*] (CRD) ..... CCR
Company Data Coordinator ..... CDC
Company Distributing Point [*Army*] ..... CDP
Company Doctor [*NASDAQ symbol*] (TTSB) ..... CDOC
Company Doctor (The) [*NASDAQ symbol*] (SAG) ..... CDOC
Company Doctor (The) [*Associated Press*] (SAG) ..... CDoctr
Company Doctor (The) [*Associated Press*] (SAG) ..... CoDoctor
Company Doctor Wrrt [*NASDAQ symbol*] (TTSB) ..... CDOCW
Company Export Planning ..... CEP
Company Facts and Addresses [*EDIC*] [*Ringmer Near Lewes, East Sussex, England*] [*Information service or system*] (IID) ..... COAD
Company Fire Control [*Net*] (MCD) ..... CFC
Company First [*A mealtime whimsicality for use when guests are present*] ..... CF
Company Fiscal Year (NASA) ..... CFY
Company Form Instruction (MCD) ..... CFI
Company Headquarters [*British military*] (DMA) ..... CHQ
Company Law Journal [*A publication*] (DLA) ..... Comp LJ

Company Level Field Feeding Kitchen [*Army's Combat System Test Activity*] (INF) .... CLFFK
Company Lightweight Mortar System [*Army*] .... CLMS
Company Lightweight Mortar System [*Army*] (MCD) .... CLWM
Company Maintenance Team (INF) .... CMT
Company Midshipman Officer-of-the-Watch [*Navy*] (DNAB) .... CMOOW
Company Name [*Database terminology*] (NITA) .... CN
Company Nuclear Review and Audit Group (NRCH) .... CNRAG
Company of American Dance .... CAD
Company of Fifers and Drummers (EA) .... CFD
Company of Mary [*Roman Catholic women's religious order*] .... ODN
Company of Master Mariners of Australia .... CMMA
Company of Military Collectors and Historians [*Later, CMH*] (EA) .... CMCH
Company of Military Historians (EA) .... CMH
Company of Saint Paul (EA) .... CSP
Company of the Savior [*Roman Catholic women's religious order*] .... CS
Company of Young Canadians [*Federal crown corporation to employ young people, 1966-75*] .... CYC
Company Operating Facility .... COF
Company Organization Survey [*Bureau of the Census*] (GFGA) .... COS
Company Owned (NTCM) .... C-O
Company Pensions Information Centre [*British*] (CB) .... CPIC
Company Persistency Rater [*LIMRA*] .... CPR
Company Policy (MCD) .... CP
Company [*or Corporate*] Policy Statement .... CPS
Company Program Manager (MCD) .... CPM
Company Quartermaster-Sergeant .... CQMS
Company Route (GAVI) .... CO ROUTE
Company Secretary .... CS
Company Sergeant-Major [*Army British*] .... CSM
Company Sergeant-Major Instructor [*Army British*] .... CSMI
Company Source Inspection .... CSI
Company Standard Form Instruction .... CSFI
Company Standard Practice .... CSP
Company Team [*Combat Electronic Warfare Intelligence*] [*Army*] .... CT
Company Technical Document Center .... CTDC
Company Voluntary Arrangement [*Business term*] (ECON) .... CVA
Company's Risk [*Insurance*] .... CR
Company-to-Company Agreement (MCD) .... CCA
Compaq Computer [*NYSE symbol*] (TTSB) .... CPQ
Compaq Computer Corp. [*Associated Press*] (SAG) .... Compaq
Compaq Computer Corp. [*NYSE symbol*] (SPSG) .... CPQ
Compaq Computer Corp., Component Engineering Library, Houston, TX [*Library symbol*] [*Library of Congress*] (LCLS) .... TxHCCo
Compaq Extended Memory Manager [*Software*] .... CEMM
Compaq Telecommunications Corp. [*Dallas, TX*] .... CTC
Comparable Worth Project (EA) .... CWP
Comparably Efficient Interconnection [*Telecommunications*] .... CEI
Comparatio Aristophanis et Menandri [*of Plutarch*] [*Classical studies*] (OCD) .... Comp Ar et Men
Comparative .... COMP
Comparative (AAGC) .... Comp
Comparative .... COMPAR
Comparative .... COMPRTV
Comparative Administration Research Institute [*Kent State University, Ohio*] .... CARI
Comparative Administrative Science Quarterly [*A publication*] (DLA) .... Comp Admin Sci Q
Comparative and International Education Society (EA) .... CIES
Comparative and International Education Society of Canada .... CIESC
Comparative and International Law Journal of Southern Africa [*A publication*] (DLA) .... CILJSA
Comparative Animal Research Laboratory [*Department of Energy*] (GRD) .... CARL
Comparative Capital Cost (TEL) CCC
Comparative Distribution Analysis [*Marketing*] (WDMC) .... CDA
Comparative Drama [*A publication*] (BRI) .... Comp Dr
Comparative Education Review [*A publication*] .... Comp Ed Rev
Comparative Education Society [*Later, CIES*] (EA) .... CES
Comparative Education Society in Europe (EAIO) .... CESE
Comparative Estimating .... CE
Comparative Genomic Hybridization [*Biochemistry*] .... CGH
Comparative Guidance and Placement Program (EDAC) .... CGP
Comparative Guidance and Placement Program [*College Entrance Examination Board*] .... CGPP
Comparative Law Series. United States Bureau of Foreign and Domestic Commerce. General Legal Bulletin [*A publication*] (DLA) .... Comp LS
Comparative Law Yearbook [*A publication*] (DLA) .... Comp L Yb
Comparative Library Organization Committee [*American Library Association*] .... CLOC
Comparative Literature [*A publication*] (BRI) .... Comp L
Comparative Literature Association (EA) .... CLA
Comparative Literature Studies [*A publication*] (BRI) .... CLS
Comparative LOFAR Fixing [*Military*] (CAAL) .... CLF
Comparative Molecular Field Analysis [*Software*] .... CoMFA
Comparative Postwar Recovery Analysis (MCD) .... COPRA
Comparative Systems Laboratory .... CSL
Comparative Testing .... CT
Comparative Tracking Index [*Electronics*] (EECA) .... CTI
Comparative Wage Justice (ADA) .... CWJ
Comparator (CET) .... COMP
Comparator [*Computer science*] .... COMPTR
Comparator Buffer [*Computer science*] (MUGU) .... CB
Comparator Chart-Tooling (MCD) .... CCT
Comparator Sys [*NASDAQ symbol*] (TTSB) .... IDID

Comparator Systems Corp. [*Associated Press*] (SAG) .... Compartr
Comparator Systems Corp. [*NASDAQ symbol*] (SAG) .... IDID
Comparators [*JETDS nomenclature*] [*Military*] (CET) .... CM
Compare (DAVI) .... cf
Compare [*Computer science*] .... CMP
Compare (MSA) .... CMPR
Compare .... COMP
Compare (FAAC) .... COMPR
Compare .... CP
Compare Accumulator with Storage [*Computer science*] (IAA) .... CAS
Compare Alphabetic Equal [*Computer science*] (OA) .... CAE
Compare Alphabetic Unequal [*Computer science*] (OA) .... CAU
Compare and Difference Full Words (SAA) .... CDF
Compare and Difference Left Half Words (SAA) .... CDL
Compare and Difference of Masked BIT [*Binary Digit*] [*Computer science*] (SAA) .... CDM
Compare and Difference Right-Half Words (SAA) .... CDR
Compare Full Words (SAA) .... CMF
Compare Generiks [*NASDAQ symbol*] (TTSB) .... COGE
Compare Generiks, Inc [*Associated Press*] (SAG) .... CmpGen
Compare Generiks, Inc. [*NASDAQ symbol*] (SAG) .... COGE
Compare Generiks, Inc. [*Associated Press*] (SAG) .... CompG
Compare Generiks Unit [*NASDAQ symbol*] (TTSB) .... COGEU
Compare Generiks Wrrt'A' [*NASDAQ symbol*] (TTSB) .... COGEW
Compare Left Half Words (SAA) .... CML
Compare Mask (SAA) .... CMM
Compare Numeric Equal [*Computer science*] .... CNE
Compare Numeric Unequal [*Computer science*] .... CNU
Compare Right Half Words (SAA) .... CMR
Compare String with String [*Computer science*] (IAA) .... COMSS
Compare String with Word [*Computer science*] (IAA) .... COMSW
Compare Zone Equal [*Computer science*] .... CZE
Compare Zone Unequal [*Computer science*] .... CZU
Comparing Element (IAA) .... CE
Comparing Political Experiences [*National Science Foundation project*] .... CPE
Comparing Reading Approaches in First Grade Teaching .... CRAFT
Comparison .... COMP
Comparison (VRA) .... comp
Comparison Circuit [*Telecommunications*] (OA) CC
Comparison Group .... CG
Comparison Measuring Circuit (PDAA) .... CMC
Comparison of Annual Growth Rate .... CAGR
Comparison of Recognition Algorithms [*US Postal Service*] .... CORAL
Comparison Point Date [*Social Security Administration*] .... CPD
Comparison Test (MCD) .... CPT
Comparisons in Law and Monetary Comments [*A publication*] (DLA) .... Comparisons in L & Monet Com
Compartment (NASA) .... CMPRT
Compartment (MCD) .... COMP
Compartment (FAAC) .... COMPRT
Compartment (KSC) .... COMPT
Compartment (NITA) .... cpt
Compartment and Access [*Technical drawings*] .... C & A
Compartment Checkoff List (DNAB) CCL
Compartment Checkoff List [*Navy*] (NVT) .... CCOL
Compartment for Peptide Loading [*In antigen preventing cells*] [*Immunology*] .... CPL
Compartment of Uncoupling Receptor and Ligand [*Cytology*] .... CURL
Compartment Testing (NITA) .... CT
Compartmental (ABBR) .... CMPRTL
Compartmentalize (ABBR) .... CMPRTLZ
Compartmentalized (ABBR) .... CMPRTLZD
Compartmentalizing (ABBR) .... CMPRTLZG
Compartmented Consolidated Analysis Report Final (MCD) .... CARF
COMPAS [*Computer Acquisition System*] Online Interactive Language (PDAA) .... COIL
Compass C
Compass (MSA) .... CMPS
Compass .... COMP
Compass Airlines of Australia [*ICAO designator*] (FAAC) .... CYM
Compass Altitude Heading Reference System (DWSG) .... CAHRS
Compass Aviation [*British ICAO designator*] (FAAC) .... CPS
Compass Bancshares [*NASDAQ symbol*] (TTSB) .... CBSS
Compass Bancshares, Inc. [*NASDAQ symbol*] (SAG) .... CBSS
Compass Bancshares, Inc. [*Associated Press*] (SAG) .... CompBnc
Compass Bearing [*Navigation*] .... CB
Compass Control Alarm .... CCA
Compass Control System .... CCS
Compass Course CC
Compass Department [*British military*] (DMA) .... CD
Compass Direction Indicator (PDAA) .... CDI
Compass Equal Target Acquisition System .... CETAS
Compass Error [*Navigation*] .... CE
Compass Failure Annunciator .... CFA
Compass Heading .... CH
Compass Integrated System Compiler (IEEE) .... CISCO
Compass Locator .... COMLO
Compass Locator [*Aviation*] (DA) .... COMO
Compass Locator of Inner Marker Site .... LIM
Compass North .... CN
Compass Operation Alarm .... COA
Compass Resources Ltd. [*Vancouver Stock Exchange symbol*] .... CPE
Compass Re-Transmission Unit (PDAA) .... CRU
Compass System Controller (MCD) .... CSC
Compass System Extensively Altered (SAA) .... COSEAL

Compass Test Language ... CTL
Compass: Theology Review [*A publication*] (APTA) ... Com
Compass Tilt Signal ... CTS
Compass Vertical Angular Measurement (RDA) ... C/VAM
Compassion in World Farming [*British*] ... CIWF
Compassion International (EA) ... CI
Compassionate [*Army*] (AABC) ... COMPATE
Compassionate Case [*Airline notation*] ... CM
Compassionate Friends [*British*] [*An association*] (DBA) ... CF
[*The*] **Compassionate Friends** (EA) ... TCF
Compassionate Reassignment Not Favorably Considered [*Army*] (AABC) ... COMPATENFC
Compatibility (KSC) ... COMPAT
Compatibility ... CPT
Compatibility and Interoperability (RDA) ... C & I
Compatibility Engineering Change Proposal [*NASA*] (NASA) ... CECP
Compatibility Initialization Deck (IAA) ... CID
Compatibility Mock-Up (KSC) ... CMU
Compatibility of Materials (MCD) ... COMAT
Compatibility Operating System [*Computer science*] ... COS
Compatibility Test (MCD) ... CT
Compatibility Test Area [*NASA*] (KSC) ... CTA
Compatibility Test Capsule ... CTC
Compatibility Test Unit ... CTU
Compatibility Test Van [*Military*] ... CTV
Compatibility-Integration Mock-Up (MCD) ... CIMU
Compatible ... C
Compatible ... COMP
Compatible ... COMPTBL
Compatible ... COMPTBLE
Compatible Algebraic Compiler and Translator ... COMPACT
Compatible Communications Architecture [*Telecommunication protocol*] (CDE) ... CCA
Compatible Current-Sinking Logic (MSA) ... CCSL
Compatible Duplex System ... CDS
Compatible Expansion [*Noise-reduction system for manufacturing phonograph records*] [*CBS*] ... CX
Compatible Hardware and Milestone Program for Integrating Organizational Needs [*AFSC*] ... CHAMPION
Compatible High-Density Bipolar Code [*Telecommunications*] (TEL) ... CHDB
Compatible Independent Peripherals (IEEE) ... CIP
Compatible Instrument Landing System [*Aviation*] ... CILS
Compatible Land Use [*FAA*] (TAG) ... CLU
Compatible LASER System ... CLS
Compatible Materials List (NASA) ... CMAT
Compatible On-Board Ranging ... COBRA
Compatible Quadrature Amplitude Modulation [*Radio design*] [*Motorola, Inc.*] ... C-Quam
Compatible Sidelobe Suppression Technique (AAG) ... CSST
Compatible Single Sideband ... CSSB
Compatible Time-Shared System ... CTSS
Compatible Time-Sharing System [*Massachusetts Institute of Technology*] [*Computer science*] ... CTSS
Compatible With (DAVI) ... C/W
Compazine [*Tranquilizer*] [*Trademark of Smith, Kline, & French Co.*] ... CPZ
Comp-Data International, Inc. [*Vancouver Stock Exchange symbol*] ... CPN
CompDent Corp. [*Associated Press*] (SAG) ... CompDnt
CompDent Corp. [*NASDAQ symbol*] (SAG) ... CPDN
COMPENDEX [*Computerized Engineering Index, Inc.*] [*Bibliographic database*] (NITA) ... CMPX
Compendium of Copyright Office Practices [*A publication*] ... CCP
Compendium of Laws of Armed Forces [*United States*] [*A publication*] (DLA) ... Comp Armed Forces
Compendium of Pharmaceuticals and Specialities [*A publication*] ... CPS
Compendium of Plausible Materiel Options [*Army*] ... CPMO
Compensate [*or Compensating*] (KSC) ... COMP
Compensate [*or Compensator*] (AABC) ... COMPEN
Compensated Avalanche Diode ... CAD
Compensated Base [*Medicine*] (DAVI) ... CP
Compensated Gross Tons [*Measure of shipbuilding capacity*] ... CGT
Compensated Imaging System (MCD) ... CIS
Compensated Ion Chamber ... CIC
Compensated Linear Vector Dipole [*Seismology*] ... CLVD
Compensated Meatball Stabilization (PDAA) ... CMS
Compensated Pulsed Alternator (MCD) ... CPA
Compensated Work Therapy ... CWT
Compensating (MSA) ... COMPSG
Compensating Air Supply ... CAS
Compensation ... CMPNSTN
Compensation (ROG) ... COMPENSON
Compensation (ADA) ... COMPN
Compensation Act [*Forms*] ... CA
Compensation and Pension ... C & P
Compensation and Pension Service [*Veterans Administration*] ... CPS
Compensation Balance [*Watchmaking*] (ROG) ... COMPBAL
Compensation Court [*Australia*] ... CC
Compensation, Employment, and Performance Management Staff [*Department of Agriculture*] (GFGA) ... CEPMS
Compensation Factor ... CF
Compensation Fee ... CF
Compensation, Pension, and Education (MAE) ... CPE
Compensation System Analyst ... CSA
Compensation System Review ... CSR
Compensation Unit ... CU
Compensator Design [*Computer science*] ... COMPDES
Compensator Group Adapter [*Military*] (CAAL) ... CGA
Compensators [*JETDS nomenclature*] [*Military*] (CET) ... CN
Compensatory and Contingency Financing Facility [*International Monetary Fund*] ... CCFF
Compensatory Equipment Package (MCD) ... CEP
Compensatory Financing Facility [*International Monetary Fund*] ... CFF
Compensatory Ovarian Hypertrophy [*Endocrinology*] ... COH
Competence in Clearing Bacilli [*Test for leprosy bacilli*] ... CCB
Competence Level Unit [*Education*] ... CLU
Competence-Based Qualification [*Education*] (AIE) ... CBQ
Competency Based Education ... CBE
Competency Based Teaching (AIE) ... CBT
Competency Level ... CL
Competency Screening Test (EDAC) ... CST
Competency-Based Adult Education ... CBAE
Competency-Based Adult Vocational Education (EDAC) ... CBAVE
Competency-Based Career Education (OICC) ... CBCE
Competency-Based Education and Training ... CBET
Competency-Based Instruction ... CBI
Competency-Based Learning [*Education*] ... CBL
Competency-Based Teacher Education ... CBTE
Competency-Based Teacher Preparation ... CBTP
Competency-Based Teacher Training ... CBTT
Competent Authority ... CA
Competent Reliability History Survey [*Navy*] ... CRHS
Competent to Instruct [*British military*] (DMA) ... CTI
Competing Risks ... CR
Competition ... Comp
Competition [*or Competitive*] ... COMPET
Competition Advocate General [*Army*] ... CAG
Competition and Credit Control [*British*] ... CCC
Competition Engineering Program [*Air Force*] ... CEP
Competition Evaluation Exercise ... COMPEX
Competition Hot [*In "Harley-Davidson XLCH"*] ... CH
Competition in Contracting Act [*1984*] ... CICA
Competition Tribunal [*Tribunal de la Concurrence*], Ottawa, Ontario [*Library symbol National Library of Canada*] (BIB) ... OOCOT
Competition with Confidence (AFIT) ... CWC
Competition with Industrial Cooperation ... CWIC
Competition-Sensitive Information [*Military*] ... CSI
Competitive Access Provider [*Telecommunications*] ... CAP
Competitive Access Provider ... CAPS
Competitive Aircraft Data Summary Sheets (MCD) ... COMPASS
Competitive Business Operation Fund (AAGC) ... CBOF
Competitive Design ... CD
Competitive Development ... CD
Competitive Development Group [*Army*] (RDA) ... CDG
Competitive Development Phase ... CDP
Competitive Engineering Definition (PDAA) ... CED
Competitive Enzyme-Linked Immunosorbent Assay ... CELISA
Competitive Equality Banking Act [*1987*] ... CEBA
Competitive Equilibrium [*Mathematics*] ... CE
Competitive Events Guidelines [*A publication*] (EAAP) ... CEG
Competitive Health and Medical Plan [*Proposed*] ... CHAMP
Competitive in Situ Hybridization (DMAA) ... CISH
Competitive Industrial Concept Formulation ... CICF
Competitive Inhibition Enzyme Immunoassay [*Analytical biochemistry*] ... CIEIA
Competitive Intelligence [*Corporate libraries*] ... CI
Competitive Local Exchange Carrier ... CLEC
Competitive Market Analysis [*Real estate*] ... CMA
Competitive Media Reporting [*An association*] [*Broadcasting*] (WDMC) ... CMR
Competitive Medical Plans ... CMP
Competitive Operational Readiness Evaluation [*Air Force*] (AFM) ... CORE
Competitive Pipeline Price Index ... CPPI
Competitive Protein Binding [*Clinical chemistry*] ... CPB
Competitive Protein-Binding Analysis [*or Assay*] ... CPBA
Competitive Prototype Phase (MCD) ... CPP
Competitive Prototyping Strategy (DOMA) ... CPS
Competitive Research Grants Office [*for federal research in agriculture*] ... CRGO
Competitive Sensitive (MCD) ... CS
Competitive State Anxiety Inventory (EDAC) ... CSAI
Competitive Statistical Analysis (IAA) ... COMSTAT
Competitive Strategies [*NATO*] ... CS
Competitive Strategies Initiative [*Military*] (DOMA) ... CSI
Competitive Study Engineer ... CSE
Competitive Technologies [*AMEX symbol*] (TTSB) ... CTT
Competitive Technologies, Inc. [*Formerly, University Patents*] [*Associated Press*] (SAG) ... CompTch
Competitive Technologies, Inc. [*Formerly, University Patents*] [*AMEX symbol*] (SAG) ... CTT
Competitive Telecommunications Association (EA) ... COMPTEL
Competitive Voluntary Indefinite [*Status*] [*Army*] (INF) ... CVI
Competitive-Binding Assay ... CBA
Competitor (ADA) ... COMP
Compiegne/Margny [*France ICAO location identifier*] (ICLI) ... LFAD
Compilation (ROG) ... COMP
Compilation of the Federal Register ... CFR
Compile and Test (BUR) ... CAT
Compile, Load, and Go [*Computer science*] (BUR) ... CLG
Compile Online and Go [*Computer science*] ... COLINGO
Compiled Laws [*A publication*] (DLA) ... CL
Compiled Laws [*A publication*] (DLA) ... Comp Laws
Compiled Statutes [*A publication*] (DLA) ... Comp St
Compiled Statutes [*A publication*] (DLA) ... Comp Stat
Compiled Statutes [*A publication*] (DLA) ... CS

Compiler (IAA) ... COM
Compiler ... COMP
Compiler ... COMPLR
Compiler and Assembler by General Electric ... CAGE
Compiler and Generalized Translator [*Argonne National Laboratory*] [*List processor*] (IEEE) ... COGENT
Compiler, Executive Program, Assembler Routines ... CLEAR
Compiler for Automatic Machine Programming (BUR) ... CAMP
Compiler for Automatic Teaching Operation (IEEE) ... CATO
Compiler for Writing and Implementing Compilers ... CWIC
Compiler Generator and Translator [*Computer science*] (NITA) ... COGENT
Compiler Information File [*Computer science*] ... CIF
Compiler Language [*Computer science*] (DIT) ... CL
Compiler Language for Information Processing [*System Development Corp.*] [*Programming language*] ... CLIP
Compiler, Los Alamos Scientific Laboratories ... COLASL
Compiler/Massachusetts Institute of Technology (IEEE) ... COMIT
Compiler Monitor System (BUR) ... CMS
Compiler Object Code [*Telecommunications*] (TEL) ... COC
Compiler of Differentiable Expressions (PDAA) ... CODEX
Compiler Oriented for Multiprogramming and Multiprocessing Environments (IEEE) ... COMMEN
Compiler System ... COSY
Compiler Target Language [*Computer science*] (MHDB) ... CTL
Compiler Writer's Virtual Machine ... CWVM
Compiler Writing System (MCD) ... CWS
Compiler-Assembler ... COMPASS
Complainant (ROG) ... COMPLAINT
Complainant ... COMPLT
Complainant (ROG) ... COMPT
Complains Of [*Medicine*] ... C/O
Complaint ... COMP
Complaint (ROG) ... COMPLT
Complaint Administration System [*Office of Federal Contract Compliance*] (GFGA) ... CAS
Complaint Docket [*Legal term*] (DLA) ... CD
Complaint Type Investigation [*Army*] (AABC) ... CTI
Complaints Investigation Branch [*Scotland Yard*] ... CIB
Compleat Health Corp. [*Vancouver Stock Exchange symbol*] ... CLQ
Complement [*Immunochemistry*] ... C
Complement [*Linguistics*] ... C
Complement [*Immunochemistry*] (DAVI) ... Cb
Complement (IAA) ... CMPL
Complement (MSA) ... CMPLM
Complement (MUGU) ... COM
Complement (AFM) ... COMP
Complement ... COMPL
Complement ... CPL
Complement ... CPLMT
Complement 3 Degradation Product [*Immunology*] ... C3DP
Complement Accumulator ... CMA
Complement Carry ... CMC
Complement Component Three [*Hematology*] ... C3
Complement Factor H-Like [*Protein*] [*Medicine*] (DMAA) ... CFHL
Complement Fixation [*Immunochemistry*] (DAVI) ... CMP-FX
Complement Fixation [*Immunology*] (DAVI) ... com fix
Complement Fixation Inhibition [*Test*] [*Immunology*] ... CFI
Complement Hemolyzing 50 [*Immunology*] ... CH50
Complement Histolytica-Indirect Hemagglutination [*Hematology*] (DAVI) ... EH-IHA
Complement Lysis Inhibitor (DMAA) ... CLI
Complement Mediated Cell Lysis [*Immunology*] ... CML
Complement of Latitude ... Co-Lat
Complement Receptor [*Immunology*] ... CR
Complement Receptor Lymphocyte [*Immunology*] ... CRL
Complement Receptor Type 1 [*Medicine*] (DMAA) ... CR1
Complement Regulatory Protein [*Genetics*] ... CRP
Complement Requiring Neutralizing ... CRN
Complement Restriction Factors [*Biochemistry*] ... CRF
Complementarity-Determining Region [*Immunology*] ... CDR
Complementarity-Determining Residue [*Genetics*] ... CDR
Complementary/Alternative Medicine [*Medicine*] ... CAM
Complementary Analysis Team [*NASA*] (KSC) ... CAT
Complementary Bipolar Integrated Circuit [*Telecommunications*] (TEL) ... CBIC
Complementary Coded Decimal [*Computer science*] (HGAA) ... CCD
Complementary Color Removal [*Graphic arts*] (DGA) ... CCR
Complementary Constant Current Logic [*Computer science*] (MCD) ... C^3L
Complementary Constant Current Logic [*Computer science*] (BUR) ... CCCL
Complementary Cumulative Distribution Function [*Mathematics*] ... CCDF
Complementary Distribution [*Linguistics*] ... CD
Complementary Emitter Follower ... CEF
Complementary Enhanced Metal Oxide Semiconductor [*Electronics*] (NITA) ... CEMOS
Complementary Even Parity (PDAA) ... CEP
Complementary Expendable Launch Vehicle [*Space technology*] ... CELV
Complementary High-Performance Metal-Oxide Semiconductor ... CHMOS
Complementary Instruction Book [*Military*] ... CIB
Complementary Insulated-Gate Field-Effect Transistor (PDAA) ... CIGFET
Complementary Magnetic Oxide on Silicone [*Computer science*] ... CMOS
Complementary Manual [*Military*] ... CM
Complementary Metal-Oxide Semiconductor (PCM) ... CMOS
Complementary Metal-Oxide Semiconductor/Silicon-on-Sapphire [*Electronics*] ... CMOS/SOS
Complementary Metal-Oxide Semiconductor Transistor [*Electronics*] ... CMOS
Complementary Metal-Oxide Semiconductor Transistor [*Electronics*] ... CMOST
Complementary Metal-Oxide Silicon (NASA) ... CMOS
Complementary Offset Binary (HGAA) ... COB
Complementary Pair Switch Element ... CPSE
Complementary Semiconductor ... CSCR
Complementary Semiconductor Controlled Rectifier (MSA) ... CSCR
Complementary Silicon on Sapphire (MHDI) ... CSOS
Complementary Straight Binary [*Computer science*] (HGAA) ... CSB
Complementary Switching (IAA) ... COS
Complementary Symmetry (IAA) ... COS
Complementary Symmetry [*Electronics*] (ECII) ... CS
Complementary Symmetry/Metal Oxide Semiconductor ... COS/MOS
Complementary Technical Report [*Military*] (AFM) ... COMTECHREP
Complementary Transistor Logic [*Computer science*] ... CTL
Complementary Transistor Register [*Computer science*] (IAA) ... CTR
Complementary Transistor-Transistor Logic ... CTTL
Complementary Under-Color Removal [*Printing technology*] ... CUCR
Complementary Unijunction Transistor (IEEE) ... CUJT
Complement-Dependent Cytotoxicity [*Immunology*] ... CDC
Complement-Fixation [*Immunology*] ... CF
Complement-Fixation for Avian Leucosis Virus [*Immunology*] ... COFAL
Complement-Fixation for Murine Leukemia [*Test*] [*Immunology*] ... COMUL
Complement-Fixation Test [*Immunology*] ... CFT
Complement-Fixing Antibody [*Immunology*] ... CFA
Complement-Fixing Antibody Consumption [*Immunology*] (DAVI) ... CFAC
Complement-Fixing Islet Cell Antibodies [*Immunochemistry*] ... CF-ICA
Complement-Mediated Neutrophil Activation [*Medicine*] (DMAA) ... CMNA
Complete (NASA) ... C
Complete (MUGU) ... CMPL
Complete ... CMPLT
Complete (FAAC) ... CMPLT
Complete (ROG) ... COMP
Complete (AAG) ... COMPL
Complete ... CPL
Complete (ROG) ... CPLT
Complete Active Space Self Consistent Field (MCD) ... CASSCF
Complete Address Constant ... CAC
Complete ADR [*Applied Data Research, Inc.*] **Environment** (EA) ... CADRE
Complete Affinity Server Enclosure [*Computer science*] ... CASE
Complete Androgen Insensitivity Syndrome [*Medicine*] (DMAA) ... CAIS
Complete Answering Machine ... CAM
Complete Anthropomorphic Protective Enclosure (SAA) ... CAPE
Complete Assembly for Ferry [*Air Force*] ... CAF
Complete Assembly for Strike ... CAS
Complete Atmospheric Energetics Experiment [*Marine science*] (OSRA) ... CAENEX
Complete Atrioventricular Block [*Medicine*] (DMAA) ... CAVB
[*The*] **Complete Attorney** [*A publication*] (DLA) ... C Atty
Complete Attorney [*A publication*] (DLA) ... Com Att
Complete Automatic Reliable Testing ... CART
Complete Background Investigation ... CBI
Complete Band Shape (MCD) ... CBS
Complete Basis of Issue [*Military*] (AABC) ... CBOI
Complete Basis of Issue Plan [*Military*] (AABC) ... CBOIP
Complete Bed Rest [*Medicine*] ... CBR
[*The*] **Complete Bible, An American Translation** [*A publication*] (BJA) ... AmTrans
Complete Blood Count [*Medicine*] ... CBC
Complete Calls To [*Telecommunications*] (TEL) ... CCT
Complete Cell Analysis [*Medicine*] ... CCA
[*A*] **Complete Computerized Examination System** [*Anatomy and physiology*] ... ACCESS
Complete Controlled Quick Release ... CQR
Complete Correlation Matrix Memory [*Computer science*] (PDAA) ... CCMM
Complete Count Program [*Bureau of the Census*] (GFGA) ... CCP
Complete Crew ... CCRU
Complete Deal [*Coupon redemption*] ... C/D
Complete Depolarization ... DC
Complete Design Release [*Navy*] (NG) ... CDR
Complete Disk Checker [*Compact disks*] ... CDC
Complete Drawing [*Animation*] (NTCM) ... CD
Complete Element Matrix Analysis from Scatter [*Spectrometry*] ... CEMAS
Complete Engine Repair (NG) ... CER
Complete Engine Repair Requirements Card [*DoD*] ... CERRC
Complete Engineering Release ... CER
Complete Equipment Fighting Order [*British military*] (DMA) ... CEFO
Complete Fabrication ... CF
Complete Freund's Adjuvant [*Immunology*] ... CFA
Complete Games [*Baseball*] ... CG
Complete Heart Block [*Medicine*] ... CHB
Complete Iridectomy [*Ophthalmology*] ... CI
Complete Isaiah Scroll from Qumran. Cave One (BJA) ... 1QIalQIsa
Complete Left Bundle Branch Block [*Medicine*] (MAE) ... CLBBB
Complete Loss of Feedwater [*Nuclear energy*] (NRCH) ... CLOF
Complete Lower Motor Neuron [*Lesion*] [*Neurology*] (DAVI) ... CLMN
Complete Management [*AMEX symbol*] (TTSB) ... CMI
Complete Management, Inc. [*AMEX symbol*] (SAG) ... CMI
Complete Management, Inc. [*Associated Press*] (SAG) ... CmpMan
Complete Management Systems ... CMS
Complete Matched Set [*Philately*] ... CMS
Complete Medium [*Microbiology*] ... CM
Complete Meeting Package [*Meetings industry*] ... CMP
Complete Minimum Essential Medium ... CMEM
Complete Missile Container ... CMC
Complete Mixing Activated Sludge ... CMAS
Complete Neglect of Differential Overlap [*Quantum mechanics*] ... CNDO
Complete Operating Equipment ... COE

Complete Operating Information [*Computer science*] ... COIN
Complete Operational Capability ... COC
Complete Operational Software [*Telecommunications*] (TEL) ... OSC
Complete Operational System (MCD) ... COS
Complete Parallel Activity and Security System (IAA) ... COMPASS
Complete Physical [*Medicine*] (DAVI) ... CP
Complete Physical Examination [*Medicine*] (DAVI) ... CPX
Complete Power Failure [*Aviation*] ... CPF
Complete Provisions Only ... CPO
Complete Quadratic Combination [*Computer science*] ... CQC
Complete Reaction of Degeneration [*Physiology*] ... CRD
Complete Remission [*Medicine*] ... CR
Complete Remission Rate [*Oncology*] ... CRR
Complete Responders [*to medication*] ... CR's
Complete Response [*Medicine*] ... CR
Complete Right Bundle Branch Block [*Cardiology*] ... CRBBB
Complete Round [*Technical drawings*] ... CR
Complete Round Ammunition Shipment ... CRAMSHIP
Complete Round Chart ... CRC
Complete Sequence Number Packet [*Computer science*] (ACRL) ... CSNP
Complete Service Life ... CSL
Complete Service Supplier [*Vendor operations*] ... CSS
Complete Solicitor [*A publication*] (DLA) ... C Sol
Complete Solicitor [*A publication*] (DLA) ... Comp Sol
Complete Statistical System ... CSS
Complete Translation [*Telecommunications*] (TEL) ... CT
Complete Transposition of Great Arteries [*Medicine*] (DMAA) ... CTGA
Complete Treatment Module [*Telecommunications*] (TEL) ... CTM
Complete Utter Monumental Foul-Up [*Military slang*] [*Bowdlerized version*] ... CUMFU
Complete Utter Monumental Military Foul-Up [*Slang*] [*Bowdlerized version*] ... CUMMFU
Complete Vehicle Erector (SAA) ... CVE
Complete Verification Record (MCD) ... CVE
Complete With (MSA) ... C/W
Complete with Related Order [*Telecommunications*] (TEL) ... CRO
Completed ... CM
Completed (VRA) ... compl
Completed Active Duty Requirements, Enlisted [*Military*] ... CADRE
Completed as Ordered (ECII) ... CAO
Completed Contract Method (AAGC) ... CCM
Completed Discharge ... CODIS
Completed Loading [*Navy*] ... COLOD
Completed Procedure Turn [*Aviation*] (FAAC) ... COPT
Completed Stroke [*Neurology*] (DAVI) ... CS
Completed Suicide [*Psychiatry*] (DAVI) ... CS
Completely Automated Technique for Cataloguing and Acquisition of Literature forLibraries (NITA) ... CATCALL
Completely Automatic Operational System [*UNIVAC*] ... CAOS
Completely Built Up (ADA) ... CBU
Completely Built Up [*Automotive manufacturing*] ... CBU
Completely Denatured ... CD
Completely Denatured Alcohol ... CDA
Completely Finished Sets ... CFS
Completely Integrated Range Instrumentation System [*NASA*] ... CIRIS
Completely in-the-Canal [*Audiology*] ... CIC
Completely Knocked Down [*i.e., disassembled, as a toy or piece of furniture which must be assembled before use*] [*Freight*] ... CKD
Completely Knocked Down [*i.e., disassembled, as a toy or piece of furniture which must be assembled before use*] [*Freight*] ... COMKD
Completely Overlapped Subarray Antenna (MCD) ... COSA
Completely Reliable Source for Intelligence Information ... A
Completely Symmetric Function (PDAA) ... CSF
Completely Universal Processor and I/O [*Input/Output*] **Design** [*Computer science*] ... CUPID
Completion (ROG) ... COMPLON
Completion and Ready for Test (MCD) ... CART
Completion, Arithmetic, Vocabulary, Directions [*Psychology*] ... CAVD
Completion Code (ECII) ... CC
Completion Fitting-Out Period ... CFP
Completion Flag [*Computer science*] (IAA) ... CF
Completion Guarantor [*Motion picture financing*] (NTCM) ... CG
Completion of Bed Occupancy Care [*Veterans Administration*] ... CBOC
Completion of Calls Meeting Busy [*Telecommunications*] (NITA) ... CCMB
Completion of Calls to Busy Subscriber [*Telecommunications*] (DOM) ... CCBS
Completion of Overhaul (DNAB) ... COH
Completion of Post Overhaul Availability (DNAB) ... CPOA
Completion Tour of Duty ... CTD
Completions ... COM
Complex ... C
Complex ... CMPX
Complex ... COMPLX
Complex ... CPLX
Complex (KSC) ... CX
Complex Angle (PDAA) ... CA
Complex Arithmetic Vector Processor (RDA) ... CAVP
Complex Assessment Officer ... CAO
Complex Atmospheric Energetics Experiment [*National Science Foundation and USSR*] ... CAENEX
Complex Behavior Simulator ... CBS
Complex Carbohydrate Research Center [*Athens, GA*] ... CCRC
Complex Carbohydrate Structural Database [*University of Georgia*] ... CCSD
Complex Chemical Reaction ... CCR
Complex Coherence Function (PDAA) ... CCF
Complex Conjugate (MCD) ... CC
Complex Control Center (KSC) ... CCC
Complex Control Equipment [*NASA*] (IAA) ... CCE
Complex Control Room [*NASA*] (KSC) ... CCR
Complex Control Set (NASA) ... CCS
Complex Coordination Test (AAG) ... CCT
Complex Effluent Toxicity Information System [*Environmental Protection Agency*] ... CETIS
Complex Electromechanical Device ... CEM
Complex Empirical Orthogonal Function [*Mathematics*] ... CEOF
Complex Energetics Experiment ... CENEX
Complex Equipment Contract (MCD) ... CEC
Complex Facility Console [*Aerospace*] (AAG) ... CFC
Complex Facility Operator [*Aerospace*] (AAG) ... CFO
Complex Field Amplitude ... CFA
Complex Fourier Transform ... CFT
Complex Ginzburg-Landau Equation [*Physics*] [*For study of spatio temporal chaos*] ... CGLE
Complex Hazardous Air Release Model ... CHARM
Complex Hybrid Integrated Circuit [*Electronics*] (IAA) ... CHIC
Complex Impedance Spectroscopy ... CIS
Complex Information Processing (PDAA) ... CIP
Complex Inorganic Color Pigment [*Chemistry*] ... CICP
Complex Instruction Set Computer (MCD) ... CISC
Complex Integrated Circuit ... CIC
Complex Layered Oxide [*Physical chemistry*] ... CLO
Complex Maintenance Facility [*Deep Space Instrumentation Facility, NASA*] ... CMF
Complex Modulus Apparatus ... CMA
Complex Motor Unit [*Medicine*] (HGAA) ... CMU
Complex Notophyll Vine Forest ... CNVF
Complex Overhaul (NVT) ... COH
Complex Partial Seizures [*Medicine*] (DMAA) ... CPS
Complex Problem-Solving Environment ... CPSE
Complex Reaction Time [*or Timer*] [*Neurology*] (AAMN) ... CRT
Complex Reduced-Instruction-Set Architecture [*Intel Corp.*] ... CRISC
Complex Refraction Index ... CRI
Complex Repetitive Discharge [*Neurophysiology*] ... CRD
Complex Safety Officer [*Air Force*] (AFM) ... CSO
Complex Safety Technician [*Air Force*] (AFM) ... CST
Complex Spikes ... CS
Complex Support Controller [*NASA*] (KSC) ... CSC
Complex Support Office [*NASA*] (KSC) ... CSO
Complex Systems Research Center [*University of New Hampshire*] [*Research center*] (RCD) ... CSRC
Complex Targets Evaluation Model (MCD) ... CTEM
Complex Terrain Deposition [*Model*] [*Marine science*] (OSRA) ... COMPDEP
Complex Terrain Deposition [*Model*] (USDC) ... COMPDEP
Complex Terrain Screening [*Model*] (USDC) ... CTSCREEN
Complex Terrain Screening [*Model*] [*Marine science*] (OSRA) ... CTSCREEN
Complex Utility Routine ... CUR
Complex Variable Boundary Element Method (IAA) ... CVBEM
Complex Vehicle Erector (KSC) ... CVE
Complex Wiring System ... CWS
Complexity ... C
Complex-Valued Non-Linear Discriminant Function (PDAA) ... CNDF
Compliance [*Volume change per unit of applied pressure*] [*Medicine*] (DAVI) ... C
Compliance ... CMP
Compliance ... COMPL
Compliance (KSC) ... COMPLI
Compliance Advisory Panel [*Environmental Protection Agency*] ... CAP
Compliance Aid for Pharmaceuticals ... CAP
Compliance and Investigations Group [*U.S. Office of Personnel Management*] (BARN) ... CIG
Compliance and Program Staff to the Deputy Assistant Administrator [*Environmental Protection Agency*] (GFGA) ... CPSDAA
Compliance and Security (SAA) ... CS
Compliance Assurance Agreement [*Environmental Protection Agency*] (GFGA) ... CAA
Compliance Assurance Monitoring [*Environmental science*] [*Environmental Protection Agency*] ... CAM
Compliance Assurance Monitoring [*Environmental Protection Agency*] ... CAM
Compliance Audit Program [*Environmental technology*] ... CAP
Compliance Biomonitoring Inspection [*Environmental Protection Agency*] (GFGA) ... CBI
Compliance Data System [*Environmental Protection Agency*] (MCD) ... CDS
Compliance Division [*Environmental Protection Agency*] (GFGA) ... CD
Compliance Evaluation Inspection [*Environmental Protection Agency*] (GFGA) ... CEI
Compliance Level [*Automotive emissions standards*] ... CL
Compliance Management Information System [*FAA*] (TAG) ... CCMIS
Compliance Monitor Evaluation Log ... CMEL
Compliance Officer [*Department of Labor*] ... CO
Compliance Order Guide ... COG
Compliance Policy and Planning [*Environmental Protection Agency*] (GFGA) ... CPP
Compliance Policy Guide [*Food and Drug Administration*] ... CPG
Compliance Program and Schedule [*Environmental Protection Agency*] (GFGA) ... CPS
Compliance Registered Options Principal (MHDB) ... CROP
Compliance Review Information System [*Office of Federal Contract Compliance*] (GFGA) ... CRIS
Compliance Review Unit (OICC) ... CRU
Compliance Safety and Health Officer [*Occupational Safety and Health Administration*] ... CSHO

Compliance Sampling Inspection [*Environmental Protection Agency*] (GFGA)	CSI
Compliance Schedule Approval (DOMA)	CSA
Compliance Schedule for Existing Sources [*Environmental Protection Agency*]	CSEC
Compliance with Requirements (MCD)	CWR
Compliant Utilities and Applications [*Computer science*] (PCM)	CUA
Complicated Delivery [*Obstetrics*]	CD
Complicated Urinary Tract Infection [*Medicine*]	CUTI
Complication [*Medicine*] (DAVI)	CCX
Complication [*Medicine*] (AAMN)	CM
Complication [*Medicine*]	comp
Complication [*Medicine*]	COMPL
Complication [*Medicine*] (AAMN)	complic
Complied With (AFIT)	CW
Compliment (ROG)	COMP
Compliment	COMPL
Compliment (ROG)	COMPT
Complimentary (WDMC)	comp
Complimentary Copy	COMP
Complimentary Metal Oxide Semiconductor [*Electronics*] (ACRL)	CMOS
Complimentary Network Service [*Telecommunications*] (ACRL)	CNS
Complimentary Technical Manual	CTM
Compliments (ROG)	COMPTS
Compline	CP
Compline (WGA)	CPL
Complink Ltd. [*NASDAQ symbol*] (SAG)	CLNK
Complink Ltd. [*Associated Press*] (SAG)	Complnk
Complmentary Chromatic Adaptation [*Plant Biology*]	CCA
Component (DAVI)	C
Component (AFM)	CMPNT
Component (AAG)	CMPT
Component (AFM)	COMP
Component	COMPNNT
Component Acceptance Procedure (IAA)	CAP
Component Acceptance Test (IAA)	CAT
Component Acquisition Executive (DOMA)	CAE
Component Action List [*NASA*] (KSC)	CAL
Component Advanced Technology Test Bed [*US Army Tank-Automotive Command*] (RDA)	CATTB
Component Analog Video (NTCM)	CAV
Component and Material Engineering Request	CMER
Component and Material Evaluation Loop [*Nuclear energy*] (NRCH)	CAMEL
Component Automatic-Program Checkout Equipment [*Aerospace*] (AAG)	CAPCHE
Component Board (MSA)	CB
Component Board Assembly (MSA)	CBA
Component Catalog Review (IAA)	CCR
Component Change Control [*Navy*] (NG)	CCC
Component Change Control Board [*DoD*]	CCCB
Component Change Order (MCD)	CCO
Component Change Request (MCD)	CCR
Component Characteristic File (DNAB)	CCF
Component Characteristics Record	CCR
Component Check [*Nuclear energy*] (NRCH)	CC
Component Check Test [*Nuclear energy*] (NRCH)	CC (Test)
Component Checkout Area (AAG)	CCA
Component Commander [*Military*]	CC
Component Configuration Control Board (AFIT)	CCCB
Component Control Committee [*DoD*]	CCC
Component Control Index [*Navy*] (AFIT)	CCI
Component Control Issue Unit (DNAB)	CCIU
Component Control Section	CCS
Component Control Unit (DNAB)	CCU
Component Cooling [*Nuclear energy*] (NRCH)	CC
Component Cooling Heat Exchanger (IEEE)	CCHX
Component Cooling Service Water [*Nuclear energy*] (NRCH)	CCSW
Component Cooling System [*Nuclear energy*] (NRCH)	CCS
Component Cooling Water [*Nuclear energy*] (NRCH)	CCW
Component Cooling Water System [*Nuclear energy*] (NRCH)	CCWS
Component Cost Index	CCI
Component Design Augmented by Computer (PDAA)	COMDAC
Component Design Confirmation	CDC
Component Development and Integration Facility [*Butte, MT*] [*Department of Energy*]	CDIF
Component Disassembly Station [*Nuclear energy*] (NRCH)	CDS
Component Engineering Request	CER
Component/Equipment (MCD)	C/E
Component Error Propagation	CEP
Component Failure Impact Analysis [*IBM Corp.*]	CFIA
Component Failure Summary (KSC)	CFS
Component Flow Analysis [*Business term*] (MHDW)	CFA
Component Handling and Cleaning Facility [*Energy Research and Development Administration*]	CHCF
Component Identification	CID
Component Identification Designation (CAAL)	CID
Component Identification Sheet (MCD)	CIS
Component Improvement Program (DOMA)	CIP
Component Improvement Testing	CIP
Component Improvement Testing [*Military*]	CIT
Component Integration Labs [*Sunnyvale, CA*] (CDE)	CI Labs
Component Intergration Laboratories	CIL
Component Item Manager [*Air Force*] (AFIT)	CIM
Component List [*DoD*]	CL

Component Maintenance and Mock-Up Facility [*Nuclear energy*] (NRCH)	CMMF
Component Maintenance Manual (MCD)	CMM
Component Management Interface [*Computer science*]	CMI
Component Manufacturer [*Foundry Business Systems*] [*Software package*] (NCC)	CM
Component Meantime Between Removals (MCD)	CMBR
Component Metal Parts (MSA)	CMP
Component Modification Cards [*Nuclear energy*] (NRCH)	CMC
Component Object Model [*Computer science*]	COM
Component of End Items (MCD)	COEI
Component Open/Short Monitor	COSMON
Component Operational Data Notice [*NASA*] (KSC)	CODN
Component Overhaul/Repair Tracking Sheet (MCD)	CORTS
Component Parts (MCD)	CP
Component Parts Clause (AIA)	CPC
Component Parts manufacturer	CPM
Component Percentage Shipment Schedule (NG)	CPSS
Component Pilot Overhaul [*Navy*] (NG)	CPO
Component Pilot Rework [*Navy*] (NG)	CPR
Component Pilot Rework/Repair [*Navy*] (MCD)	CPR/R
Component Placement System [*Electronics*] (EECA)	COPS
Component Preparation Laboratory [*Oak Ridge*] [*Energy Research and Development Administration*]	CPL
Component Quality Assurance	CQA
Component Reclamation (AFIT)	COMREC
Component Record Intensive Management	CRIM
Component Reliability Prediction	CRP
Component Repair (MSA)	CR
Component Repair Data Sheets (NG)	CRDS
Component Repair Squadron (MCD)	CRS
Component Requiring Intensive Management	CRIM
Component Reword Analyst (MCD)	CRA
Component Save List [*Military*] (AFIT)	CSL
Component Scheduling Procedure	CSP
Component Selection Record	CSR
Component Sequencing and Insertion (PDAA)	COMSEQIN
Component Sequencing and Insertion [*Computer science*] (MHDB)	COMSEQUN
Component Source List (IAA)	CSL
Component Specification (AAG)	CS
Component Supports (NRCH)	CS
Component Test (KSC)	CT
Component Test Area	CTA
Component Test Equipment (KSC)	CTE
Component Test Laboratory (KSC)	CTL
Component Test Requirements Specifications (MCD)	CTRS
Component Test Set (MCD)	CTS
Component Test Stand [*Nuclear energy*] (NUCP)	CTS
Component Test System (IAA)	CTS
Component to Part Record	CPR
Component Transaction Service [*Computer science*]	CTS
Component Under Test (NITA)	CUT
Component Utilization Effectiveness	CUE
Components and Materials Laboratory	CML
Components Business Operations [*Chrysler campaign to increase sales*]	CBO
Components Evaluation Propulsion System (MCD)	CEPS
Components Hybrids and Manufacturing Technology (MCD)	CHMT
Components Life Evaluation and Reliability	CLEAR
Components of End Items [*Military*] (INF)	COEL
Components of End Items List (MCD)	COEIL
Components of Inventory Change Survey [*Bureau of the Census*] (GFGA)	CINCH
Components Only	CO
Components Response Information Center (MCD)	CRIC
Components Test Unit (AAG)	CTU
Compool Look-Up Memory Print	CLUMP
Compose [*Typesetting*] (WDMC)	comp
Compose	COMPS
Composed Document Printing Facility [*IBM Corp.*]	CDPF
Composed Document Viewing Utility [*IBM Corp.*]	CDVU
Composer [*MARC relator code*] [*Library of Congress*] (LCCP)	cmp
Composer (ROG)	COMP
Composer Recordings, Inc. [*Recording label*]	CRI
Composers and Lyricists Guild of America (EA)	CLGA
Composers, Authors, and Artists of America	CAAA
Composers, Authors, and Publishers Association of Canada	CAPAC
Composers' Autograph Publications [*Defunct*] (EA)	CAP
Composers Cooperative Society [*Later, Composers Theatre*]	CCS
Composers' Forum for Catholic Worship [*Defunct*] (EA)	CFCW
Composers' Guild of Great Britain (EAIO)	CGGB
Composers Theatre (EA)	CT
Composers-Authors Guild (EA)	CAG
Composing Reducing Camera [*Microfilm*] (NITA)	CRC
Composing Room Chapel [*Unions*] [*British*] (DGA)	CRC
Composite (ROG)	C
Composite (ABBR)	CMPSIT
Composite (MSA)	CMPST
Composite (AFM)	COMP
Composite	COMPST
Composite	CX
Composite Aeronautical Load List	CALL
Composite Air Strike Force [*Air Force*]	CASF
Composite Aircraft Program [*Military*] (RDA)	CAP
Composite Aircraft Squadron [*Navy symbol*]	VC
Composite Analog Video	CAV

Composite Armored Vehicle [*Army*] (RDA) .... CAV
Composite Armored Vehicle Advanced Technology Demonstrator (RDA) .... CAV ATD
Composite Army-Marine .... CAM
Composite Assessment of Leverage (EDAC) .... CAL
Composite Auxiliary Boiler [*of a ship*] (DS) .... CAXB
Composite Auxiliary Boiler Survey [*of a ship*] (DS) .... CAXBS
Composite Boson [*Physics*] .... CB
Composite Can and Tube Institute (EA) .... CCTI
Composite Cell Logic CCL
Composite Checkout [*Aerospace*] (AAG) .... CC/O
Composite Clinical and Laboratory Index [*Medicine*] (DMAA) CCLI
Composite Concept Vehicle CCV
Composite Correction Plan [*Environmental Protection Agency*] (GFGA) .... CCP
Composite Cost Effectiveness Index (PDAA) .... CCEI
Composite Cross [*Genetics*] CC
Composite Cutoff [*Aerospace*] (AAG) .... CC-O
Composite Cyclic Therapy (MAE) .... CCT
Composite Damage Risk .... CDR
Composite Double-Base [*Propellant*] .... CDB
Composite Educational Abilites Scale (AIE) .... CEAS
Composite Electrical Readiness Test (KSC) .... CERT
Composite Engineering Change Memo [*NASA*] (KSC) .... CECM
Composite External Symbol Dictionary (BUR) .... CESD
Composite Feed System .... CFS
Composite Flight Data Processing (FAAC) .... CFAD
Composite for the Lunar Excursion Module [*NASA*] (IEEE) .... CLEM
Composite Ganglioneuroblastoma [*Oncology*] .... CGNB
Composite Group [*Air Force*] .... COMPG
Composite Health Care System [*DoD*] .... CHCS
Composite High-Altitude Radiation Model (MCD) .... CHARM
Composite HTGR [*High-Temperature Gas-Cooled Reactor*] **Analysis Program** [*Nuclear energy*] (NRCH) .... CHAP
Composite Infantry Fighting Vehicle [*Army*] .... CIFV
Composite Interface Program (SAA) .... CIP
Composite Laminate Automated Sizing for Strength (MCD) .... CLASS
Composite Launch and Spacecraft Program System (MCD) .... CLASP
Composite Launch Sequence Plan (MCD) .... CLSP
Composite [*or Consolidated*] **Limit Order Book** [*Stock exchange term*] .... CLOB
Composite Main Rotor Blade (MCD) .... CMRB
Composite Maintenance Group [*Military British*] .... CMG
Composite Maneuver Augmentation (MCD) .... COMMA
Composite Mechanized Information and Document Retrieval System .... COMEINDORS
Composite Medical Facility (AFM) .... CMF
Composite Merge .... CM
Composite Military Police Strike Force (VNW) .... CMPSF
Composite Minimum Brightness (PDAA) .... CMB
Composite Mode Adjective Check List [*FAA*] .... CMACL
Composite Multiplex Signal (MCD) .... CMS
Composite Noise Rating [*Aviation*] .... CNR
Composite Operational Mission Profiles (MCD) .... COMP
Composite Operational Reporting System (CAAL) .... CORS
Composite Optical/X-Ray LASER Microscope .... COXRALM
Composite Primary Structures (MCD) .... CPS
Composite Professional Performance Score .... CPPS
Composite Quotation System (DICI) .... CQS
Composite RADAR Absorbing Structure (MCD) .... CRAS
Composite RADAR Data Processing (FAAC) .... CRAD
Composite Razor Blade (MCD) .... CRB
Composite Reactor Components Test Activity (NRCH) .... CRCTA
Composite Readiness Test .... CRT
Composite Rear Fuselage .... CRF
Composite Reentry Test Vehicle (MCD) .... CRTV
Composite Reporting System (MCD) .... COMPREP
Composite Research Aircraft .... CRA
Composite Resin Infusion Molding Process .... CRIMP
Composite Service [*Army*] (AABC) .... CS
Composite Signal Mixer .... CSM
Composite Signaling [*Telecommunications*] (TEL) CX
Composite Squadron .... COMPORON
Composite Squadron [*Air Force*] .... COMPS
Composite Standard Reference Section .... CSRS
Composite Standard Time Units .... CSTU
Composite Station Rate .... CSR
Composite Structures for Advanced Aircraft (MCD) .... CSAA
Composite Support Group [*Air Force*] .... COMPSG
Composite Tail Section [*Aviation*] (MCD) .... CTS
Composite Tape Lay-Up [*Engineering*] .... CTL
Composite Teacher Rating .... CTR
Composite Tool Kit [*Military*] (AFIT) .... CTK
Composite Training School [*British military*] (DMA) .... CTS
Composite Training Unit [*Military*] (NVT) .... COMPTU
Composite Training Unit Exercise [*Military*] (NVT) .... COMPTUEX
Composite Treatment Score [*Medicine*] (MEDA) .... CTS
Composite Utility .... CU
Composite Warfare Commander [*Military*] (NVT) .... CWC
Composite Warfare Oceanographic Support Module [*Navy*] (DOMA) .... CWOSM
Composite Wave (IEEE) .... CW
Composite Wave Filter .... CWF
Composite Weighted Work Unit (AFM) .... CWU
Composite Wing (MCD) .... COMPW
Compositech Ltd. [*Associated Press*] (SAG) .... Compt
Compositech Ltd. [*Associated Press*] (SAG) .... Comptch
Compositech Ltd. [*NASDAQ symbol*] (SAG) .... CTEK
Composite-Modified Double-Base [*Propellant*] .... CMDB
Composite-Rate Tax [*British*] .... CRT
Composites Institute (EA) CI
Composites Institute of Australia .... CIA
Composites Manufacturing Association of the Society of Manufacturing Engineers (EA) .... CMA/SME
Composition (MSA) .... CMPSN
Composition .... COMP
Composition .... COMP
Composition .... COMPN
Composition (ROG) .... COMPO
Composition .... COMPOS
Composition (VRA) .... comps
Composition .... COMPSN
Composition and Editing Display [*Later, MRTT*] (MCD) .... COED
Composition and Make-Up .... CAM
Composition and Markup [*Graphic arts*] (DGA) .... CAM
Composition Board (VRA) .... compbd
Composition Caster [*Monotype*] (DGA) CC
Composition Exploding (PDAA) .... CE
Composition Floor .... COMPF
Composition Information Services [*Commercial firm*] .... CIS
Composition Node Design Method [*For distillation*] .... CNDM
Composition of Ending Inventory .... COEI
Composition Reduction Printing .... CRP
Composition Roof .... COMPR
Composition Support System (DGA) .... CSSYS
Composition Technology, Inc. .... CTI
Composition with Creditors [*A publication*] (DLA) .... Comp Cred
Composition-4 [*Explosive*] C-4
Compositional Interdiffusion [*Chemistry*] (IAA) .... CID
Compositor [*MARC relator code*] [*Library of Congress*] (LCCP) .... cmt
Compositor [*Printers' term*] (DSUE) .... COMP
Compositor Hourly Rate (DGA) .... CHR
Compositus [*Compound*] [*Pharmacy*] C
Compositus [*Compound*] [*Pharmacy*] .... CO
Compositus [*Compound*] [*Pharmacy*] .... COMP
Compost (ABBR) .... CMPS
Compost (ABBR) .... CMPST
Composted (ABBR) .... CMPSTD
Composted Hardwood Barks .... CHB
Composting (ABBR) .... CMPSTG
Composure (ABBR) .... CMPSU
Compound [*Engines*] [*Lloyd's Register Shipping*] C
Compound [*Medicine*] (DHSM) .... CMP
Compound .... CMPD
Compound [*Medicine*] (AAMN) .... CO
Compound .... COMP
Compound .... COMPD
Compound (VRA) .... compd
Compound [*Medicine*] .... CP
Compound .... CPD
Compound Action Potential [*Biology*] .... APc
Compound Action Potential [*Biology*] .... CAP
Compound Animal Feeding Stuffs Manufacturers National Association [*British*] (BI) .... CAFSMNA
Compound Annual Growth Rate [*Business term*] .... CAGR
Compound Annual Return (ODBW) .... CAR
Compound Batch Identification [*Computer science*] .... CBI
Compound Carburetion [*Automotive engineering*] CC
Compound Card Terminal (CET) .... CCT
Compound Cathartic [*Pills*] CC
Compound Comminuted Fracture [*Medicine*] .... CCF
Compound Cycle Turbine Diesel Engine (MCD) .... CCTDE
Compound Cycle Turbofan Engine (PDAA) .... CCTE
Compound Cyclic Corrosion Test [*Materials science*] .... CCCT
Compound Department Architecture [*Digital Equipment Corp.*] [*Computer science*] .... CDA
Compound Diffraction Projector .... CDP
Compound Document Architecture .... CDA
Compound Document Interchange Format [*Computer science*] .... CDIF
Compound Document Processor [*Computer science*] .... CDP
Compound Elliptic Concentrator (PDAA) .... CEC
Compound Fracture [*Medicine*] .... FC
Compound Handling Machine .... CHM
Compound Hypermetropic Astigmatism [*Ophthalmology*] .... H + Hm
Compound Index File [*Computer science*] (PCM) .... CDX
Compound Induction Step Control (PDAA) .... CISC
Compound Inserting Machine .... CIM
Compound Interest Deposit [*Banking*] (DICI) .... CID
Compound Muscle Action Potential [*Neurophysiology*] .... CMAP
Compound Muscle Action Potential [*Medicine*] (DMAA) .... CMAP
Compound Myopic Astigmatism [*Ophthalmology*] .... M + Am
Compound Parabolic Concentrator [*Solar energy research*] .... CPC
Compound Pressure .... CPRESS
Compound Refractive Lens [*Optics*] .... CRL
Compound Sequential Probability Ratio Test .... CSPRT
Compound Series Test [*Intelligence test*] .... CST
Compound Spectral Array .... CSA
Compound Valve Hemispherical Head [*Engine*] .... CVH
Compound Vortex Combustion Chamber [*Auto engine*] CVCC
Compounded Annual Rate [*Finance*] (ODBW) .... car
Compounded Interest [*Business term*] CI
Compounding .... COMPNDNG
Compound-Specific Radiocarbon Analyses .... CSRA

Comprehending (ROG) .... COMPG
Comprehending Reflex Development, Attitude Formation, Memorizing, Procedural Learing (PDAA) .... CRAMP
Comprehensive .... CMPRHNSV
Comprehensive .... COMP
Comprehensive Ability Battery [Test] .... CAB
Comprehensive Agrarian Reform Programme [Philippines] (ECON) .... CARP
Comprehensive Agrimedia Measurement Study [Database] [Doane Marketing Research, Inc.] [Information service or system] (CRD) ...... CAMS
Comprehensive Aircraft Support Effectiveness Evaluation (MCD) .... CASEE
Comprehensive Airport Communications System (PDAA) .... CACS
Comprehensive Airship Sizing and Performance Computer Program .... CASCOMP
Comprehensive Analytical Method of Planning in the University Sphere [Cost simulation technique] .... CAMPUS
Comprehensive Analytical Methods of Planning .... CAMP
Comprehensive Analytical Test System .... CATS
Comprehensive Antijam Equipment (MCD) .... CAJE
Comprehensive Approach for Reusable Defense Systems [DoD] .... CARDS
Comprehensive Area Service Plan .... CASP
Comprehensive Areal Rainfall Program [British] .... CARP
Comprehensive Assembler System [Programming language] [1964 Control Data Corp.] .... COMPASS
Comprehensive Assessment and Referral Evaluation [Medicine] (DMAA).... CORE
Comprehensive Assessment Information Rule [Environmental Protection Agency] .... CAIR
Comprehensive Assessment of Treatment Outcome Research (BARN) .... CATOR
Comprehensive Assistance to Undergraduate Science Education [National Science Foundation] .... CAUSE
Comprehensive Automated Learning Resources System [Elgin Community College] [Information service or system] (IID) .... CALS
Comprehensive Automation of the Hydrometeorological Service .... CAHS
Comprehensive Automotive Release System [3M Corp.] [Computer software] .... CARS
Comprehensive Beacon RADAR .... CBR
Comprehensive Behavioral Services Model .... CBSM
Comprehensive Blast and Radiation Assessment System (MCD) .... COBRAS
Comprehensive Budget and Management Information System (MHDI) ..... CBMIS
Comprehensive Business Tax .... CBT
Comprehensive Cancer Center [Ohio State University] [Research center] (RCD) CCC
Comprehensive Cancer Center of Metropolitan Detroit [National Cancer Institute] [Research center] (RCD) .... CCCMD
Comprehensive Cancer Center Program [National Cancer Institute] .... CCCP
Comprehensive Cardiac Care Unit [Medicine] (DMAA) .... CCCU
Comprehensive Care [NYSE symbol] (SPSG) .... CMP
Comprehensive Care [Associated Press] (SAG) .... CompCre
Comprehensive Certificate of Origin [Department of Commerce] (BARN) ...... CCO
Comprehensive Clinical Evaluation Program [Army] .... CCEP
Comprehensive Clinical Evaluation Program [For Gulf War veterans] .... CCEP
Comprehensive Close Air Support [Military] .... CCAS
Comprehensive College Test .... CCT
Comprehensive Community Mental Health Centers Inventory [Department of Health and Human Services] (GFGA) .... CCMHC
Comprehensive Community Revitalization Project .... CCRP
Comprehensive Cooperative Agreement (MHDB) .... CCA
Comprehensive Core Medical Library [Database] [BRS Information Technologies] [Information service or system] (IID) .... CCML
Comprehensive Country Programming System [Department of State] .... CCPS
Comprehensive Crime Control Act [1984] (GFGA) .... CCCA
Comprehensive Data Handling System [Environmental Protection Agency] .... CDHS
Comprehensive Data Management (GFGA) .... CDM
Comprehensive Data Systems (OICC) .... CDS
Comprehensive Day Care Programs [An association] (EA) .... CDCP
Comprehensive Developmental Evaluation Chart [Child development test] [Psychology] .... CDEC
Comprehensive Dishonesty, Disappearance, and Destruction Policy [Insurance] .... CDDD
Comprehensive Dishonesty, Disappearance, and Destruction Policy [Insurance] .... DDD
Comprehensive Display System .... CDS
Comprehensive Dissertation Abstracts [University Microfilms International] [Information service or system] .... CDA
Comprehensive Dissertation Index [University Microfilms International] [Ann Arbor, MI Bibliographic database] [A publication] .... CDI
Comprehensive Drinker Profile [Test] [Psychology] .... CDP
Comprehensive Drug Abuse Prevention and Control Act (BARN) .... CDAPC
Comprehensive Dwelling Policies [Insurance] .... CDP
Comprehensive Electronic Office [Data General Corp.] .... CEO
Comprehensive Employment and Training Act [1973] [Formerly, MDTA Expired, 1982 Department of Labor] .... CETA
Comprehensive Employment and Training Plan [Department of Labor] .... CETP
Comprehensive Engine Management System .... CEMS
Comprehensive Envir'l Sys [NASDAQ symbol] (TTSB) .... COEV
Comprehensive Environmental Evaluation [British Antarctic Survey] .... CEE
Comprehensive Environmental Response, Compensation, and Liability Act [1980] .... CERCLA
Comprehensive Environmental Responsibility, Compensation, and Liability System .... CERCLIS
Comprehensive Environmental Systems, Inc. [Associated Press] (SAG) .... CmpEnv
Comprehensive Environmental Systems, Inc. [NASDAQ symbol] (SAG) ...... COEV
Comprehensive Evaluation of Basic Living Skills .... CEBLS
Comprehensive Export Schedule [US] .... CES

Comprehensive Extended Term Banker's Guarantee (DS) .... CXBG
Comprehensive External Trade Policy [Export Credits Guarantee Department] [British] .... CET
Comprehensive General and Automobile Liability [Insurance] .... CGAL
Comprehensive General Liability [Insurance] .... CGL
Comprehensive Geriatric Assessment [Medicine] (CPH) .... CGA
Comprehensive (Ground Water) Monitoring Evaluation [Environmental Protection Agency] (ERG) .... CME
Comprehensive (Ground Water) Monitoring Evaluation Log [Environmental Protection Agency] (ERG) .... CMEL
Comprehensive Health and Emergency Care [Medicine] .... CHEC
Comprehensive Health Assessments and Primary Care for Children [Proposed] .... CHAP
Comprehensive Health Center [Medicine] .... CHC
Comprehensive Health Education Foundation (EA) .... CHEF
Comprehensive Health Insurance Act .... CHIA
Comprehensive Health Insurance Plan [or Proposal] .... CHIP
Comprehensive Health Manpower Training Act [1971] .... CHMA
Comprehensive Health Planning [A requirement for HEW grants to local agencies] .... CHP
Comprehensive Health Planning Service [Federal government] .... CHPS
Comprehensive Homeless Assistance Plan [Homeless Assistance Act] (GFGA) .... CHAP
Comprehensive Housing Affordability Strategy .... CHAS
Comprehensive Human Resources Data System (MCD) .... CHRDS
Comprehensive Identification Process [Child development test] .... CIP
Comprehensive Improvement Assistance Program [HUD] .... CIAP
Comprehensive Incomes and Prices Policy (DICI) .... CIPP
Comprehensive Index to the Publications [A bibliographic publication] .... CIP
Comprehensive Industrywide Program of Communication [Defunct] (EA) .... CIPC
Comprehensive Information Service .... COMPIS
Comprehensive Information System and Database .... CIS & DB
Comprehensive Inorganic Chemistry [A publication] CIC
Comprehensive Land Use Plan .... CLUP
Comprehensive Language for Elegant Operating System and Translator Design (PDAA) .... CLEOPATRA
Comprehensive Language Program [Test] .... CLP
Comprehensive Mailing List System [Library of Congress] .... CMLS
Comprehensive Major Medical [Health insurance] (GHCT) .... CMM
Comprehensive Management Facility (IAA) .... CMF
Comprehensive Management Plan .... CMP
Comprehensive Manpower Planning (OICC) .... CMP
Comprehensive Manufacturing Control System .... CMCS
Comprehensive Medical Plan .... CMP
Comprehensive Medical Society [Defunct] (EA) .... CMS
Comprehensive Mental Health Assessment .... CMHA
Comprehensive Migrant Program [Department of Labor] .... CMP
Comprehensive Model .... COMO
Comprehensive Monitoring Evaluation .... CME
Comprehensive Occupational Data Analysis Program [Military] (AABC) .... CODAP
Comprehensive Occupational Therapy Evaluation [Scale] .... COTE
Comprehensive Ocean Atmosphere Data Set .... COADS
Comprehensive Offender Program Effort [Department of Labor] .... COPE
Comprehensive Omnibus Budget Reconciliation Act (GFGA) .... COBRA
Comprehensive Online Manufacturing and Engineering Tracking System (NITA) .... COMETS
Comprehensive Option Stiffness Method of Structural Analysis (PDAA) .... COSMOS
Comprehensive Organic Chemistry [A publication] .... COC
Comprehensive Organometallic Chemistry [A Publication] .... COMC
Comprehensive Outpatient Rehabilitation Facility (MEDA) .... COR
Comprehensive Outpatient Rehabilitation Facility [American Occupational Therapy Association] .... CORF
Comprehensive Payroll Accounting System (MHDB) .... CPACS
Comprehensive Personal Liability [Insurance] .... CPL
Comprehensive Plan, South Vietnam (CINC) .... CPSVN
Comprehensive Power Management System [Military] (CAAL) .... CPMS
Comprehensive Procurement Guidelines [EPA] (AAGC) .... CPG
Comprehensive Psychopathological Rating Scale .... CPRS
Comprehensive Radiance Profile Synthesizer .... CORPS
Comprehensive Renal Scintillation Procedure [Medicine] (DMAA) .... CRSP
Comprehensive Research Injury Scale (PDAA) .... CRIS
Comprehensive School [British] C
Comprehensive School Mathematics Program (EDAC) .... CSMP
Comprehensive Screening Tool for Determining Optimal Communication Mode [Speech evaluation test] .... CST
Comprehensive Self-Check [Computer] .... CSC
Comprehensive Sickle Cell Center [Terminated, 1977] [HEW] .... CSCC
Comprehensive State Ground Water Protection Program [Environmental science] .... CSGWPP
Comprehensive Support Software [Computer science] (NITA) .... CSS
Comprehensive System (SAA) .... CS
Comprehensive System of Personnel Development [Education] .... CSPD
Comprehensive System Readiness Tests (MCD) .... CSRT
Comprehensive Test Ban [Nuclear weapons] .... CTB
Comprehensive Test Ban Treaty .... CTBT
Comprehensive Testing Program [Academic achievement and aptitude test] .... CTP
Comprehensive Tests of Basic Skills [Education] .... CTBS
Comprehensive Transportation Information & Planning System [MTMC] (TAG) .... CTIPS
Comprehensive Treatment and Management Plan (DOGT) .... CTMP
Comprehensive Treatment and Management Plan [Department of Energy] .... CTMP

Comprehensive Treatment Plan [*Medicine*] (DAVI) .... CTP
Comprehensive Weight Control System .... COMPWCS
Comprehensive Work Training Program [*Employment and Training Administration*] [*Department of Labor*] .... CWTP
Comprenhensive Annual Financial Report .... CAFR
Compress (ABBR) .... CMPRS
Compress (MSA) .... CPRS
Compress .... SOMPRSS
Compressed (ABBR) .... CMPRSD
Compressed .... COMP
Compressed Air (AAG) .... CA
Compressed Air .... COMPA
Compressed Air Accumulator Rocket .... CAAR
Compressed Air and Gas Institute (EA) .... CAGI
Compressed Air Breathing Apparatus .... CABA
Compressed Air Circuit Breaker (MSA) .... CACB
Compressed Air Energy Storage (MCD) .... CAES
Compressed Air Equipment Distributors Association [*British*] (DBA) .... CAEDA
Compressed Air Institute (KSC) .... CAI
Compressed Air Loudspeaker .... CAL
Compressed Air Spraying .... CAS
Compressed Air System (NUCP) .... CARS
Compressed Air System (NRCH) .... CAS
Compressed Air Tunnel [*British*] .... CAT
Compressed Analog [*Sound processing strategies*] .... CA
Compressed Citation File .... CCF
Compressed Coherency Detection [*RADAR technique*] .... COCODE
Compressed Data Packet Data .... CDPD
Compressed Data Storage .... CDS
Compressed Data Storage System .... CDSS
Compressed Data Tape .... CDT
Compressed Digital Video [*Telecommunications*] .... CDV
Compressed Gas (DNAB) .... CG
Compressed Gas Association (EA) .... CGA
Compressed Gas Association, Inc. (AAGC) .... CGA
Compressed Index Sequential Access Method .... CISAM
Compressed International Trade Database [*United Nations*] .... COMTRADE
Compressed Limit Gauging Sampling (PDAA) .... CLGS
Compressed Medical Gas [*Food and Drug Administration*] .... CMG
Compressed Mortality File [*Medicine*] .... CMF
Compressed Mosiacked Image Data Record [*Geology*] .... CMIDR
Compressed Natural Gas .... CNG
Compressed Pulse Altimeter .... CPA
Compressed Pulse RADAR Altimeter .... CPRA
Compressed SLIP [*Serial Line Internet Protocol*] (CDE) .... CSLIP
Compressed Spectral Assay (MAE) .... CSA
Compressed Symbolic [*Programming language*] [*Control Data Corp.*] .... COSY
Compressed Tablet [*Pharmacy*] .... CP
Compressed Tablet [*Pharmacy*] .... CT
Compressed Tablet Triturate [*Pharmacology*] .... CTT
Compressed Volume File [*Computer science*] .... CVF
Compressed-Gas-Insulated Cable .... CGIC
Compressed-Gas-Insulated Transmission Line .... CGIT
Compressibility (ABBR) .... CMPRSBT
Compressible (ABBR) .... CMPRSB
Compressible Cell and Maker .... COMCAM
Compressible Flow Facility [*NASA*] .... CFF
Compressible Flow Wind Tunnel (MCD) .... CFWT
Compressibleness (ABBR) .... CMPRSBNS
Compressing (ABBR) .... CMPRSG
Compressing/Expanding [*Electronics*] (ACRL) .... Companding
Compression C
Compression (MUGU) .... CMP
Compression (ABBR) .... CMPRSN
Compression [*Automotive engineering*] .... COMP
Compression [*Automotive engineering*] .... COMPN
Compression (KSC) .... COMPR
Compression (MSA) .... CPRSN
Compression Bonding Encapsulation .... CBE
Compression/Decompression Standard [*Computer science*] .... codec
Compression Engine .... CE
Compression Factor [*Symbol*] [*Thermodynamics*] .... Z
Compression Hip Screw [*System*] [*Orthopedics*] (DAVI) .... CHS
Compression Ignition and Turbine Engine .... CITE
Compression Ignition Engine CI
Compression Ignition-Direct Injection .... CIDI
Compression in Transit .... CIT
Compression Labs [*NASDAQ symbol*] (TTSB) CLIX
Compression Labs, Inc. [*San Jose, CA*] [*Telecommunications*] (TSSD) CLI
Compression Labs, Inc. [*NASDAQ symbol*] (NQ) CLIX
Compression Labs, Inc. [*Associated Press*] (SAG) .... CmprsL
Compression Load Deflection (PDAA) .... CLD
Compression Mold Dies (MCD) .... CMD
Compression Ratio .... CR
Compression, Retrieval, and Maintenance [*of data*] (DNAB) .... CRAM
Compression Scanning Array RADAR [*Raytheon*] .... COSAR
Compression Switch .... CSW
Compression Yield Strength [*Engineering*] (BARN) .... CYS
Compressional Heating and Linear Injection Cusp Experiment .... CHALICE
Compression-Annealed Pyrolytic Boron Nitride (PDAA) .... CAPB
Compression-Annealed Pyrolytic Graphite (PDAA) .... CAPG
Compressive (ABBR) .... CMPRSV
Compressive Load Cell CLC
Compressive Safety Index [*Engineering design*] .... CSI
Compressively (ABBR) .... CMPRSVY

Compressor (ABBR) .... CMPRSR
Compressor (ABBR) .... CMPSR
Compressor .... CMPSR
Compressor [*Automotive engineering*] .... COMP
Compressor (MSA) .... COMPR
Compressor (MSA) .... CPRSR
Compressor Decompressor [*Computer science*] (PCM) .... CODEC
Compressor Discharge Pressure .... CDP
Compressor End Seal .... CES
Compressor Endurance Loops (MCD) .... CEL
Compressor Expander [*Telecommunications*] (IEEE) .... COMPANDER
Compressor Inlet Pressure (MSA) .... CIP
Compressor Inlet Temperature (NG) .... CIT
Compressor Inlet Variable Vane (MCD) CIVV
Compressor Research Facility (IAA) .... CRF
Comprised (ROG) .... COMPRD
Comprising (WGA) .... COMP
Compromise (ADA) .... CMP
Compromise (ROG) .... COM
Compromise Sales Agreement [*Business term*] (EMRF) .... CSA
Compromised Pulmonary Functions [*Medicine*] .... CPF
Compromising Emanations (AABC) .... CEM
Compromising Emanations Control (MCD) .... CEC
CompScript .... CPRX
CompScript, Inc. [*Associated Press*] (SAG) .... CmpScrpt
CompScript, Inc. [*NASDAQ symbol*] (SAG) .... CPRX
Compte [*Account*] [*French Business term*] (ROG) .... CTE
Compte Courant [*Current Account*] [*French Business term*] CC
Compte Ouvert [*Open Account*] [*French Business term*] .... c/o
Comptek Research, Inc. [*Associated Press*] (SAG) .... Comptek
Comptek Research, Inc. [*AMEX symbol*] (SPSG) .... CTK
Comptes Rendus. Academie des Inscriptions et Belles-Lettres [*A publication*] (OCD) .... CRAcad Inscr
Comptoir Commercial Franco-Africain [*Franco-African Trade Office*] [*Guinea*] (AF) .... CCFA
Comptoir du Livre [*Keren Hasefer*] [*A publication*] (BJA) .... CLKH
Compton Abbas [*British ICAO location identifier*] (ICLI) .... EGHA
Compton, CA [*Location identifier FAA*] (FAAL) .... CPM
Compton, CA [*FM radio station call letters*] .... KJLH
Compton College, Compton, CA [*Library symbol Library of Congress*] (LCLS) .... CComC
Compton County Historical and Museum Society [*Societe d'Histoire et du Musee du Comte de Compton*] Eaton Corner, Quebec [*Library symbol National Library of Canada*] (NLC) .... QECCH
Compton Gamma Ray Observatory [*Satellite*] .... CGRO
Compton, Meeson, and Roscoe's English Exchequer Reports [*1834-36*] [*A publication*] (DLA) .... CM & R
Compton Recoil Electron .... CRE
Compton Recoil Particle .... CRP
Compton Telescope [*NASA*] .... COMPTEL
Compton's Multimedia Encyclopedia [*A publication*] .... CMME
Comptroller C
Comptroller (ABBR) .... CMPTR
Comptroller (ABBR) .... CMTRLR
Comptroller .... COMP
Comptroller .... COMPT
Comptroller (DD) .... compt
Comptroller (AAGC) .... Compt
Comptroller .... COMPTLR
Comptroller and Auditor General .... CAG
Comptroller and Surveyor [*British*] (ROG) .... CS
Comptroller, Department of Defense (AAGC) .... CDOD
Comptroller General .... CG
Comptroller General .... COMPGEN
Comptroller General Decisions [*CCH*] [*A publication*] (AAGC) .... CGEN
Comptroller General Decisions [*Navy*] .... COMPGENDEC
[*The*] Comptroller General of the United States (AAGC) .... Comp Gen
Comptroller General Opinion .... CGO
Comptroller General Opinion [*A publication*] (DLA) .... Comp Gen Op
Comptroller General's Decision .... CGD
Comptroller General's Decision (AAGC) .... CGDN
Comptroller General's Opinion (AAGC) .... CGO
Comptroller General's Procurement Decisions [*A publication*] .... CPD
Comptroller of Accounts .... CA
Comptroller of the Army .... CA
Comptroller of the Army .... COA
Comptroller of the Army (Director of the Army Budget) .... COA(DAB)
Comptroller of the Army Directorate of Cost Analysis [*Washington, DC*] .... COMPT-CA
Comptroller of the Currency .... COC
Comptroller of the Navy .... COMPT
Comptroller Service Squadron [*Air Force*] .... CPTSq
Comptroller Service Squadron [*Air Force*] .... CPTSS
Comptroller Squadron [*Air Force*] .... CPTS
Comptroller Treasury Decisions [*A publication*] (DLA) .... Comptr Treas Dec
Comptroller-Director of Programs [*Army*] .... C-DP
Compu/Graphics Users Association [*Defunct*] (EA) .... CGUA
Compucats' Computer Club [*Defunct*] (EA) CCC
CompuCoin Systems [*NASDAQ symbol*] (TTSB) .... CMPC
Compucom Systems [*NASDAQ symbol*] (SAG) .... CMPC
Compucom Systems [*Associated Press*] (SAG) .... Cmpcm
Compucom Systems, Inc. [*NASDAQ symbol*] (SAG) .... CMPC
Compucom Systems [*Associated Press*] (SAG) .... Cmpcm
Compudata, Inc. [*Information service or system*] (IID) .... CDI
Compuflight Operation Service, Inc. [*ICAO designator*] (FAAC) .... XCO

Compugraphic United Kingdom Users' Association (DGA) ...... CUKUA
Compugraphics Users Association [Bend, OR] (EA) ...... CUA
Compu-Home Systems International, Inc. [Toronto Stock Exchange symbol] ...... CPH
Compulaw Digest [A publication] (ADA) ...... CLD
Compulsion (ABBR) ...... CMPUL
Compulsive (ABBR) ...... CMPULV
Compulsive Stutterers Anonymous (EA) ...... CSA
Compulsorily (ABBR) ...... CMPULRY
Compulsorily Preserved Superannuation Benefit ...... CPSB
Compulsory C
Compulsory (ABBR) ...... CMPULR
Compulsory (DSUE) ...... COMPUL
Compulsory Censorship [British World War II] CC
Compulsory Competitive Tendering [Australia] ...... CCT
Compulsory Insurance CI
Compulsory Purchase Act [Town planning] [British] ...... CPA
Compulsory Purchase Order [British] ...... CPO
Compulsory Third Party [Australia] ...... CTP
CompuMed, Inc. [NASDAQ symbol] (SAG) ...... CMPD
CompuMed, Inc. [Associated Press] (SAG) ...... CmpMd
CompuMed, Inc. [Associated Press] (SAG) ...... CmpuMed
CompuMed Inc. Wrrt [NASDAQ symbol] (TTSB) ...... CMPDW
Compunction (ABBR) ...... CMPUN
Compunctiously (ABBR) ...... CMPUNSY
CompuRAD, Inc. [Associated Press] (SAG) ...... CmpRD
CompuRAD, Inc. [NASDAQ symbol] (SAG) ...... COMD
Compurgation (ABBR) ...... CMPUR
CompUSA, Inc. [Associated Press] (SAG) ...... CompUSA
CompUSA, Inc. [NYSE symbol] (SPSG) ...... CPU
CompuServe Corp. [Associated Press] (SAG) ...... CmpuSrv
CompuServe Corp. [NASDAQ symbol] (SAG) ...... CSRV
CompuServe Corp. [NASDAQ symbol] (TTSB) ...... CSRV
CompuServe, Inc. [Commercial firm] ...... CSI
CompuServe, Inc. [ICAO designator] (FAAC) ...... XCS
CompuServe Information Manager [CompuServe, Inc.] (PCM) ...... CIM
CompuServe Information Service [CompuServe, Inc.] (IID) ...... CIS
CompuServe Information Service ...... CompuServe
CompuServe Information Service B [Communications protocol] (CDE) ...... CIS B
CompuServe Navigator [CompuServe, Inc.] [Telecommunications] (PCM) ...... CSNav
CompuServe Network Services [CompuServe, Inc.] [Columbus, OH] [Telecommunications] (TSSD) ...... CNS
COMPUSTAT Services, Inc. [Information service or system] (IID) ...... C/S
Computalog Gearhart Ltd. [Toronto Stock Exchange symbol] ...... CGH
Computalog Ltd. [NASDAQ symbol] (SAG) ...... CLTD
Computalog Ltd. [Associated Press] (SAG) ...... Computlg
Computalog Ltd [NASDAQ symbol] (TTSB) ...... CLTDF
Computation (ABBR) ...... CMPUTAN
Computation (ABBR) ...... CMPUTN
Computation (AFM) ...... COMP
Computation and Analysis Division [NASA] (MCD) ...... CAD
Computation and Communication Trade-Off Study [ARPA] ...... CACTOS
Computation and Data Flow Integrated Subsystem [Simulated flight tests] [NASA] ...... CADFISS
Computation and Data Processing Center (DIT) ...... CDPC
Computation and Data Reduction Center [Military] (DNAB) ...... CDRC
Computation Center CC
Computation Center-Advanced Graphics Laboratory [University of Texas at Austin] [Research center] (RCD) ...... AGL
Computation Fluid Dynamics ...... CFD
Computation of Manpower Programs Using Linear Programming (MCD) ...... COMPLIP
Computation of Miss Between Orbits [Air Force] (MCD) ...... COMBO
Computation of Vulnerable Area and Repair Time (MCD) ...... COVART
Computation Online of Network Chemical Engineering Process Technology (IAA) ...... CONCEPT
Computation Subsystem [Space Flight Operations Facility, NASA] ...... COMP
Computational (MDG) ...... CMP
Computational Aeroacoustics [Laser technology] ...... CAA
Computational Arithmetic Program ...... CAP
Computational Component (MCD) CC
Computational Element (NITA) ...... CE
Computational Engineering Research Institute, Inc. [Research center] (RCD) ...... CERI
Computational Fluid Dynamics [Chemical engineering] ...... CFD
Computational Fluid Mechanics Laboratory [University of Arizona] [Research center] (RCD) ...... CFML
Computational Fluids Dynamics [Organic chemistry] ...... CFD
Computational Linguistics (IEEE) CL
Computational Requirements for Engineering and Simulation, Training and Education [Time-sharing computer complex] [Air Force] ...... CREATE
Computational Science and Engineering Research Center (RDA) ...... ComSERC
Computational Systems [NASDAQ symbol] (TTSB) ...... CSIN
Computational Systems, Inc. [Associated Press] (SAG) ...... Cmputa
Computational Systems, Inc. [Associated Press] (SAG) ...... Computat
Computational Systems, Inc. [NASDAQ symbol] (SAG) ...... CSIN
Computational Transonic Aerodynamics (MCD) ...... CTA
Computations and Data Reduction Division [NASA] (KSC) ...... CDRD
Computations Life Office Administrations System (NITA) ...... CLOAS
Computation-Universal Cellular Space (PDAA) ...... CUCS
Compute [or Computer] (MDG) C
Compute [or Computer] (AABC) ...... CMPT
Compute (ABBR) ...... CMPU
Compute Air-Trans Systems, Inc. ...... CATS
Compute Element (IAA) ...... CE

Compute Parallel (IEEE) ...... COMPEL
Computed ...... CMPTD
Computed (ABBR) ...... CMPUTD
Computed Air-Release Point ...... CARP
Computed Body Tomography [Medicine] (CPH) ...... CBT
Computed Ephemeris Position ...... CEP
Computed Mission Coverage Index (MCD) ...... CMCI
Computed Point [Navigation] ...... CP
Computed Slant Detection Range ...... CSDR
Computed Thermography System [Computer science] ...... CTS
Computed Tomographic Metrizamide Myelography ...... CTMM
Computed Tomography [Also, CAAT, CAT] [Roentgenography] ...... CT
Computed Tomography with Multiplanar Reconstructions [Radiology] (DAVI) ...... CT/MPR
Computed Transaxial Tomography [Later, CT] ...... CTT
Computer (MUGU) ...... CMP
Computer (KSC) ...... CMPTR
Computer ...... CMPTR
Computer (ABBR) ...... CMPUTR
Computer ...... COM
Computer [or Computing] (AFM) ...... COMP
Computer (DD) ...... Comp
Computer (VRA) ...... compr
Computer (IAA) ...... CP
Computer [JETDS nomenclature] ...... K
Computer Access (IAA) ...... CA
Computer Access Corp. [Information service or system] (IID) ...... CAC
Computer Access Device ...... CAD
Computer Access Device Input (CET) ...... CADI
Computer Access Device Output (CET) ...... CADO
Computer Access Matrix (NITA) ...... CAM
Computer Access Security System (NITA) ...... CASS
Computer Access Technology Corp. (PCM) ...... CATC
Computer Accounting System [Boole & Babbage, Inc.] ...... CAS
Computer Accounting System / Computer Performance Analysis (MHDB) ...... CAS/CPA
Computer Accounting System for Office Expenditure (MHDB) ...... CASOE
Computer Achievement Monitoring (MCD) ...... CAM
Computer Acquisition System (PDAA) ...... COMPAS
Computer Adaptive Language for Development of Structural Analysis Programs [University of California at Berkeley] (NITA) ...... CAL/SAP
Computer Adaptive Testing ...... CAT
Computer Adaptor Display ...... CAD
Computer Address Decoder [Navy Navigation Satellite System] (DNAB) ...... CAD
Computer Address Matrix ...... CAM
Computer Address Panel (CAAL) ...... CAP
Computer Addressed Memory (NITA) ...... CAM
Computer Administrative Instruction (AABC) ...... CADMINI
Computer Advanced Software Products [Database producer] (IID) ...... CASPR
Computer Advisory Committee [Marine science] (OSRA) ...... CAC
Computer Advisory Committee (USDC) ...... CAC
Computer, Aerial Reconnaissance ...... COMAR
Computer Aid ...... CAID
Computer Aid System (NITA) ...... CAS
Computer Aided Art and Design (NITA) ...... CAAD
Computer Aided Batch Searching (NITA) ...... CABS
Computer Aided Design and Draughting (NITA) ...... CADD
Computer Aided Design and Graphics Laboratory [Purdue University] [Research center] (RCD) ...... CADLAB
Computer Aided Design and Numerical Analysis for Manufacture Group ...... CADNAM
Computer Aided Design Centre [Department of Trade and Industry] [British] (NITA) ...... CADC
Computer Aided Design for VLSI [Very Large Scale Integration] in Europe [British] ...... CAVE
Computer Aided Dispatch [Police communications] ...... CAD
Computer Aided Document Engineering [Computer software] (PCM) ...... CADE
Computer Aided Education (ECII) ...... CBE
Computer Aided Engineering Design System (NITA) ...... CAEDS
Computer Aided Engineering Graphics [FAA] (TAG) ...... CAEG
Computer Aided Engineering Support Office (NITA) ...... CAESO
Computer Aided Estimating and Planning System (NITA) ...... CAEPS
Computer Aided Instruction for Teacher Education (EDAC) ...... CAITE
Computer Aided Learning Centre [Victoria University] [Australia] ...... CALC
Computer Aided Learning in Mathematics (AIE) ...... CALM
Computer Aided Learning in Meteorology ...... CALMET
Computer Aided Linguistic Analysis ...... COALA
Computer Aided Management of Emergency Operations [Marine science] (OSRA) ...... CAMEO
Computer Aided Manufacturing International (EA) ...... CAM-I
Computer Aided Personal Reference Index System [Automic Energy Authority] [British] (NITA) ...... CAPRI
Computer Aided Problem Solving (NITA) ...... CAPS
Computer Aided Production for Current Awareness Services [Information service or system] (IID) ...... CAPCAS
Computer Aided Teaching of Applied Mathematics [Cambridge University, England] (EDAC) ...... CATAM
Computer Aided Three [Dimensional] Interactive Application ...... CATIE
Computer Aided Trading System ...... CATS
Computer Aided-Fraud (NITA) ...... CAF
Computer Aids for Chemical Engineering Education [National Academy of Engineering] ...... CACHE
Computer Aids for Human Translation [Carnegie-Mellon University] (NITA) ...... CAHT
Computer Air-Air Dispenser (MCD) ...... CAAD

Computer Algebra Information Network [*Computer science*] ... CAIN
Computer Algebra Systems (PDAA) ... CAS
Computer Amplifier Alarm ... CAA
Computer Analog Input ... CAI
Computer Analog Input/Output (DEN) ... CAI/O
Computer Analog Input/Output ... CAIOP
Computer Analysis and Design System (NITA) ... CADS
Computer Analysis and Simulation of Metaloxide Semiconductor Circuit (IAA) ... CASMOS
Computer Analysis of Maintenance Policies (MHDI) ... COAMP
Computer Analysis of Networks via Inversion of Network Equations (PDAA) ... CANINE
Computer Analysis of Networks with Design Orientation in the Frequency Domain (PDAA) ... CANDOFD
Computer Analysis of Thermochemical Data Tables [*University of Sussex*] [*Sussex, England*] ... CATCH
Computer Analysis of Transistors (IAA) ... CAT
Computer Analysis of Troubles on Trunk Circuits (PDAA) ... CANTOT
Computer Analysts & Programmers Ltd. [*British*] ... CAP
Computer Analyzed Newspaper Data On-Line [*Newspaper Advertising Bureau, Inc.*] [*Information service or system*] (IID) ... CAN DO
Computer & Aerospace Components Ltd. [*British*] ... CACL
Computer and Automated Systems Association [*Later, CASA/SME*] ... CASA
Computer and Automated Systems Association of Society of Manufacturing Engineers (EA) ... CASA/SME
Computer and Business Equipment Manufacturers Association [*Washington, DC*] (EA) ... CBEMA
Computer and Communications [*Database*] (IT) ... CMPCOM
Computer and Communications Access Device (AAGC) ... CCAD
Computer and Communications Industry Association (EA) ... CCIA
Computer and Communications Technology Corporation (AAGC) ... CCT
Computer and Human-Assisted Organization of a Technical Information Center [*National Institute of Standards and Technology*] ... CHAOTIC
Computer and Information Science Research Center [*Ohio State University*] [*Columbus, OH*] ... CISRC
Computer and Information Sciences ... COINS
Computer and Information Sciences Research Laboratory [*University of Alabama in Birmingham*] [*Research center*] (RCD) ... CIS
Computer and Language Independent Modules for Automatic Test Equipment (MHDI) ... CLIMATE
Computer and Management Show for Contractors (TSPED) ... CMC
Computer and Network Services Division [*Marine science*] (OSRA) ... CNSD
Computer and Network Services Division [*Formerly, Computer Support Group*] (USDC) ... CNSD
Computer and Peripherals Equipment Trade Association (MHDB) ... COMPETA
Computer and Photographic Assisted Learning ... CAPAL
Computer and System Engineering (IAA) ... CASE
Computer and Telecommunications Acronyms [*A publication*] ... CTA
Computer Animation Language ... CAL
Computer Annunciation Matrix (MCD) ... CAM
Computer Anxiety Index (EDAC) ... CAIN
Computer Application Control Code ... CACC
Computer Application Program (NASA) ... CAP
Computer Application Services, Inc. [*Los Alamitos, CA*] [*Telecommunications*] (TSSD) ... CASI
Computer Application Summary (IAA) ... CAS
Computer Applications for Ministry Network (EA) ... CAMNET
Computer Applications for the Graphic Arts ... CAFGA
Computer Applications Group [*Air Force*] ... CAG
Computer Applications Group [*Aslib*] (NITA) ... CAG
Computer Applications in the Biosciences [*A publication*] ... CABIOS
Computer Applications, Inc. (MCD) ... CAI
Computer Applications of Military Problems [*Computer users' group*] ... CAMP
Computer Applications Support and Development Office [*Navy*] ... CASDO
Computer Aptitude, Literacy, and Interest Profile [*Vocational guidance test*] ... CALIP
Computer Aptitude Quotient (EDAC) ... CAQ
Computer Architecture News [*A publication*] ... CAN
Computer Architecture Research Unit [*York University*] [*Canada Research center*] (RCD) ... CARU
Computer Architecture Specification Language (CSR) ... CASL
Computer Archive of Language Materials [*Stanford University*] (NITA) ... CALM
Computer Arts Society (EAIO) ... CAS
Computer Assembly ... CA
Computer Assistant to a Community Telephone Information Service (PDAA) ... CACTIS
Computer Assisted (IAA) ... COMPASS
Computer Assisted Careers Guidance System (AIE) ... CACGS
Computer Assisted Continuous Infusion [*Pharmacology*] (DAVI) ... CACI
Computer Assisted Depreciation and Life Analysis System [*BTS*] (TAG) ... CADLAS
Computer Assisted Diagnostic and Prescription Instruction (EDAC) ... CADPI
Computer Assisted Document Drafting ... CADD
Computer Assisted Drawing Management and Control [*Infodetics Co.*] (NITA) ... CADMAC
Computer Assisted Indexing Program (NITA) ... CAIP
Computer Assisted Information Retrieval System (NITA) ... CAIRS
Computer Assisted Instruction (AIE) ... CAI
Computer Assisted Instruction and Support for the Handicapped (EDAC) ... CAISH
Computer Assisted Language Learning and Instruction Consortium (EA) ... CALICO
Computer Assisted Language Teaching (AIE) ... CALT
Computer Assisted Learning (AIE) ... CAL
Computer Assisted Legal Retrieval (NITA) ... CALR
Computer Assisted Library Instruction Co., Inc. [*Information service or system*] (IID) ... CALICO
Computer Assisted Mechanistic Evaluation of Organic Reactions [*Data analysis*] ... CAMEO
Computer Assisted New Drug Application [*Medicine Australia*] ... CANDA
Computer Assisted PLA [*Product License Application*] **Review** [*FDA*] ... CAPLAR
Computer Assisted Referee Selection (NITA) ... CARS
Computer Assisted Simulation and Education System [*Simulation of doctor's decision making*] [*Netherlands*] (NITA) ... CASES
Computer Assisted Spanish English Transition Sequence (EDAC) ... CASETS
Computer Assisted Sperm Analyzer ... CASA
Computer Assisted Student Tutorial Learning Environment (EDAC) ... CASTLE
Computer Assisted Synthetic Analysis Group (NITA) ... CASAG
Computer Assisted Televideo [*Commercial firm*] [*Netherlands*] (NITA) ... CAT
Computer Assisted Virtual Environment ... CAVE
Computer Assoc Intl. [*NYSE symbol*] (TTSB) ... CA
Computer Associates [*A company*] [*Islandia, New York*] (WDMC) ... CA
Computer Associates Basic Language Extended [*Computer Associates International, Inc.*] (PCM) ... CABLE
Computer Associates International, Inc. [*NYSE symbol*] (SPSG) ... CA
Computer Associates International, Inc. [*Associated Press*] (SAG) ... CmpAsc
Computer Audio Interactive Video Manipulator [*Designed by Christopher Conley*] ... CAIVman
Computer Audio Research Laboratory [*Research center*] (RCD) ... CARL
Computer Audit Retrieval System [*Trade name for Sage Systems, Inc., computer software product*] ... CARS
Computer Audit Specialist [*IRS*] ... CAS
Computer Augmented Communication ... CAC
Computer Augmented Learning (CMD) ... CAL
Computer Augmented Video Education [*US Naval Academy*] (NITA) ... CAVE
Computer Automated Cargo Documentation (IAA) ... CACD
Computer Automated Diameter Control (PDAA) ... CADC
Computer Automatic Scheduling System ... CASS
Computer Automatic Virtual Environment [*Virtual reality system*] (CDE) ... CAVE
Computer Automation, Inc. [*Richardson, TX*] (TSSD) ... CA
Computer Automation, Inc. ... CAI
Computer Based English Language Testing (AIE) ... CBELT
Computer Book Review [*Comber Press*] [*Information service or system*] (CRD) ... CBR
Computer Brokers Exchange [*Information service or system*] (IID) ... CBE
[*The*] **Computer Bulletin** (IAA) ... TCB
Computer Bulletin Board System ... CBBS
Computer Burst Order (AABC) ... CBO
Computer Business Services, Inc. ... CBSI
Computer Calculator ... CC
Computer Call Network [*Telemarketing*] ... CCN
Computer Campaign Services [*Data processing firm in field of politics*] ... CCS
Computer Center [*Telecommunications*] (TEL) ... CC
Computer Center ... CMPCTR
Computer Center [*Haverford College*] [*Research center*] (RCD) ... HCCC
Computer Center [*Vanderbilt University*] [*Research center*] (RCD) ... VUCC
Computer Center [*Yale University*] [*Research center*] (RCD) ... YCC
Computer Center Management System (MHDB) ... CCMS
Computer Central Processing [*Telecommunications*] (TEL) ... CCP
Computer Character Recognition ... CCR
Computer Chemical System ... CCS
Computer Color Match Prediction ... CCMP
Computer Color Matching ... CCM
Computer Command Control [*General Motors Corp.*] ... CCC
Computer Command Engineer (MCD) ... CCE
Computer Command Ride [*Automotive engineering*] ... CCR
Computer Command Subsystem [*NASA*] ... CCS
Computer Communications Access Method (DNAB) ... CCAM
Computer Communications Console (AFM) ... CCC
Computer Communications Converter (MCD) ... CCC
Computer Communications Group [*Canada*] ... CCG
Computer Communications, Inc. ... CCI
Computer Communications Interface (IAA) ... CCI
Computer Communications Line Monitor (MCD) ... CCLM
Computer Communications Networks Group [*University of Waterloo*] [*Canada Information service or system Research center*] (IID) ... CCNG
Computer Community (IEEE) ... CC
[*The*] **Computer Co.** [*Information service or system*] (IID) ... TCC
[*The*] **Computer Co., Richmond, VA** [*Library symbol*] [*Library of Congress*] (LCLS) ... TcC
[*The*] **Computer Co., Richmond, VA** [*Library symbol Library of Congress*] (LCLS) ... ViRCC
Computer Complex ... CC
Computer Components and System Group [*Massachusetts Institute of Technology*] ... CCSG
Computer Composition Corp. [*Also, an information service or system*] (IID) ... CCC
Computer Composition International [*Telecommunications*] (NITA) ... CCI
Computer Concepts [*NASDAQ symbol*] (TTSB) ... CCEE
Computer Concepts Corp. [*NASDAQ symbol*] (SAG) ... CCEE
Computer Concepts Corp. [*Associated Press*] (SAG) ... CptConc
Computer Conference ... COMPCON
Computer Conferencing ... CC
Computer Consulting (IAA) ... CC
Computer Consulting Service (BUR) ... CCS
Computer Control and Display Panel (MCD) ... CCDP
Computer Control Communication (BUR) ... CCC
Computer Control Complex ... CCC
Computer Control Corp. ... CCC
Computer Control Group [*Military*] (CAAL) ... CCG
Computer Control Indicator (CAAL) ... CCI

Computer Control Loading ... CCL
Computer Control Panel ... CCP
Computer Control Station (IAA) ... CCS
Computer Control Unit ... CCU
Computer Controlled (IAA) ... CC
Computer Controlled Inking [*Graphic arts*] (DGA) ... CCI
Computer/Controlled Operating System [*Computer science*] (PDAA) ... C/COS
Computer Controller Multiplexer Unit ... CCMU
Computer Convention (IAA) ... COMPCON
Computer Core Segment (NASA) ... CCS
Computer Corp. of America ... CCA
Computer Cost Model ... COCOM
Computer Coupled Machines (NITA) ... CCM
Computer Coupling Unit (MCD) ... CCU
Computer Cross Select Unit ... CCSU
Computer Data Entry Keyboard ... CDEK
Computer Data Entry System (NITA) ... CDES
Computer Data Recording System (KSC) ... CDRS
Computer Data Switchboard ... CDS
Computer Data System ... CDS
Computer Data Systems [*NASDAQ symbol*] (SAG) ... CDSI
Computer Data Systems [*Associated Press*] (SAG) ... CmpData
Computer Data Systems, Inc. [*Information service or system*] (IID) ... CDSI
Computer Data Word (CET) ... CDW
Computer Dealers and Lessors Association (EA) ... CDLA
Computer Dealers Association [*Later, CDLA*] ... CDA
Computer Dealer's Exposition ... COMDEX
Computer Dealers Forum [*Acronym represents organization's former name*] [*Later, NCDF*] (EA) ... CRF
Computer Description Language (BUR) ... CDL
Computer Design and Education System ... CODES
Computer Design and Evaluation System (IEEE) ... CODES
Computer Design Language (CSR) ... CDL
Computer Design of Armoured Cables (PDAA) ... CODAC
Computer Detector Test Console (DNAB) ... CDTC
Computer Development Center (KSC) ... CDC
Computer Development Center (KSC) ... CDEVC
Computer Development Laboratory [*Fujitsu Ltd., Hitachi Ltd., and Mitsubishi Corp.*] [*Japan*] ... CDL
Computer Developments Limited Automatic Coding System (IEEE) ... CODEL
Computer Devices, Inc. ... CDI
Computer Digital Switching System (NITA) ... CDSS
Computer Direct Input [*Computer science*] (DCTA) ... CDI
Computer Direct to Telegraph ... CODIT
Computer Directions Advisors, Inc. [*Information service or system*] (IID) ... CDA
Computer Directions Corp. ... CDC
Computer Directions Group, Inc. [*Information service or system*] (IID) ... CDG
Computer Discount Warehouse (PCM) ... CDW
Computer Disk-Interactive ... CD-I
Computer Display and Exposition ... COMDEX
Computer Display Channel ... CDC
Computer Display Unit (MCD) ... CDU
Computer Distribution System [*FAA*] (TAG) ... CDS
Computer Dual Access Driver (MCD) ... CDAD
Computer Duplex System (BUR) ... CDS
Computer Economics Ltd. [*British*] (NITA) ... CEL
Computer Education and Applied Research Center ... CEARC
Computer Education for Management ... CEM
Computer Education Group [*British*] (BI) ... CEG
Computer Election Systems, Inc. ... CES
Computer Electrical System [*Davy Computing Ltd.*] [*Software package*] (NCC) ... COMPELS
Computer Electroencephalogram ... CEEG
Computer Electronics Telecommunications Instruments Automation (ADA) ... CETIA
Computer Emergency Response Team (PCM) ... CERT
Computer Emergency Response Team ... CERT
Computer Energy Distribution and Automated Control (MHDB) ... CEDAC
Computer Energy Time Unit (MCD) ... CETU
Computer Engineer ... CE
Computer Engineer Console ... CEC
Computer Engineering (DD) ... CompEng
Computer Engineering Service ... CES
Computer Enhanced Electronic Warfare Operations Centre [*Military Canada*] ... CEEWOC
Computer Enhanced Language Instruction Archive (AIE) ... CELIA
Computer Entry and Read-Out Control [*Computer science*] (PDAA) ... CERC
Computer Entry and Readout Equipment (KSC) ... CERE
Computer Entry Device [*Computer science*] (PDAA) ... CED
Computer Entry Keyboard ... CEK
Computer Entry Punch ... CEP
Computer Equipment Information Bureau [*Information service or system*] (IID) ... CEIB
Computer Equipment News [*A publication*] (APTA) ... CEN
Computer Equipment System for Surface-to-Air Missiles (MCD) ... CESSAM
Computer Evaluation of Scanning Electron Microscope Image ... CESEMI
Computer Execute Function (KSC) ... CEF
Computer Facilities Management (MCD) ... CFM
Computer Family Architecture ... CFA
Computer Fault Isolation (MCD) ... CFI
Computer Field Maintenance [*British*] ... CFM
Computer Flight Plan ... CFP
Computer Flight Testing (MCD) ... CFT
Computer for Advanced Spare Systems (IAA) ... COMPASS
Computer for Automatic Teaching Operations (DNAB) ... CATO
Computer for Automatic Teaching Operations-Compiler (DNAB) ... CATOCOMP
Computer for Automatic Teaching Operations-Resident (DNAB) ... CATORES
Computer for Special Small Tactical Application ... COSSTA
Computer for Uprange Point-of-Impact Determination [*NASA*] (KSC) ... CUPID
Computer Form, Fit, and Function (MCD) ... CF3
Computer Format Control Buffer ... CFCB
Computer Forms Printer (IAA) ... CFP
Computer Fraud [*A publication*] (NITA) ... CF
Computer Generated Forces [*Army*] ... CGF
Computer Generated Letter ... CGL
Computer Graphics (MCD) ... CG
Computer Graphics and Image Processing (MCD) ... CGIP
Computer Graphics Arrangement Program (PDAA) ... COGAP
Computer Graphics Display System [*Army*] (MCD) ... CGDS
Computer Graphics for Aerodynamic Analysis (MCD) ... CGAA
Computer Graphics Interface ... CGI
Computer Graphics Metafile ... CGM
Computer Graphics Processing (HGAA) ... CGP
Computer Graphics Research Group [*Ohio State University*] [*Research center*] (RCD) ... CGRG
Computer Graphics Structural Analysis ... CGSA
Computer Guidance Corp. ... CGC
Computer Guided Optical Registration [*VISCOM Optical Products, Inc.*] ... CGOR
Computer Hardware Acquisition and Modernization Program [*Department of Agriculture*] (GFGA) ... CHAMP
Computer Hardware, Advanced Mathematics, and Model Physics Initiative [*Department of Energy*] ... CHAMMP
Computer Hardware Description Language ... CHDL
Computer Horizons [*NASDAQ symbol*] (TTSB) ... CHRZ
Computer Horizons Corp. [*NASDAQ symbol*] (NQ) ... CHRZ
Computer Horizons Corp. [*Associated Press*] (SAG) ... CmptHz
Computer Hour ... CHR
Computer Identics Corp. [*NASDAQ symbol*] (NQ) ... CIDN
Computer Identics Corp. [*Associated Press*] (SAG) ... CmpIdn
Computer Image Generator [*or Generation*] (MCD) ... CIG
Computer in Control Logic (MCD) ... CICL
Computer Incident Advisory Capability [*Department of Energy*] ... CIAC
Computer Incident Advisory Capability [*Department of Energy*] [*Computer science*] ... CIAC
Computer Indentics [*NASDAQ symbol*] (TTSB) ... CIDN
Computer Independent Specification ... CIS
Computer Index for Neutron Data [*Information service or system*] (NITA) ... CINDA
Computer Index of Neutron Data [*Atomic Energy Authority*] [*Databank*] [*British*] ... CIND
Computer Index of Neutron Data [*Brookhaven National Laboratory*] [*Information service or system*] (CRD) ... CINDA
Computer Indicator (AFM) ... CI
Computer Indicator Test Console (DNAB) ... CITC
Computer Industry ... CI
Computer Industry Association [*Later, CCIA*] ... CIA
Computer Industry Coalition for Advanced Television Service ... CICATS
Computer Industry Council (EA) ... CIC
Computer Industry Daily [*Zif-Davis*] [*A publication*] (NITA) ... CID
Computer Industry Development Potential (IAA) ... CIDP
Computer Industry Software, Services, and Products [*Information service or system*] (IID) ... CISS
Computer Industry Training and Technology Corp., Inc. [*Commercial firm Australia*] ... CITTC
Computer Information Delivery Service (BARN) ... CIDS
Computer/Information/Library Sciences [*Abstracts*] ... C/I/L
Computer Information Network (SSD) ... CIN
Computer Information Processing (IAA) ... CIP
Computer Information Resources ... CIR
Computer Information Services [*Corp. for Public Broadcasting - CPB*] [*Information service or system*] (IID) ... CIS
Computer Innovations Distribution, Inc. [*Toronto Stock Exchange symbol*] ... CIC
Computer Input from Microfilm (ECII) ... CIM
Computer Input Matrix (KSC) ... CIM
Computer Input Microfilming (MCD) ... CIM
Computer Input Multiplexer (KSC) ... CIM
Computer Inquiries ... CI
Computer Inquiry III [*FCC*] ... CI-III
Computer Installation Management System (PDAA) ... CIMS
Computer Institute for Applications in Science and Engineering (MCD) ... CIASE
Computer Instruction and Training Assistance for the Blind ... CITAB
Computer Instruments Corp. ... CIC
Computer Integrated Command and Attack Systems (PDAA) ... CICAS
Computer Integrated Flexible Manufacturing (NITA) ... CIFM
Computer Integrated Manufacture/Data Collection System (NITA) ... CIM/DCS
Computer Integrated Manufacturing ... CIM
Computer Integrated Manufacturing/Mechanical Engineering System (NITA) ... CIM/ME
Computer Intelligence Corp. [*Information service or system*] (IID) ... CI
Computer Intelligence Corp. [*Information service or system*] (IID) ... CIC
Computer Interchange of Museum Information Committee ... CIMI
Computer Interconnect (ACRL) ... CI
Computer Interface Adapter ... CIA
Computer Interface Conditioning Unit (MCD) ... CICU
Computer Interface Control [*Part of digital television computer*] ... CIC
Computer Interface Control Unit (NASA) ... CICU
Computer Interface Device (NASA) ... CID
Computer Interface for Television (MCD) ... CINTEL
Computer Interface Module [*Computer science*] ... CIM
Computer Interface Technology (IEEE) ... CIT
Computer Interface Terminal (CET) ... CIT

Computer Interface Unit ... CIU
Computer Interpreter Language (MHDB) ... CIL
Computer Interrogator ... CI
Computer Interrupt Equipment (MHDB) ... CIE
Computer Investment Group, Inc. (NITA) ... CIG
Computer Investments Ltd. [*British*] (NITA) ... CIL
Computer Laboratory for Instruction in Psychological Research [*University of Colorado - Boulder*] [*Research center*] (RCD) ... CLIPR
Computer Laboratory of Harvard University ... CLHU
Computer Language (NITA) ... C
Computer Language (IAA) ... CL
Computer Language for Aeronautics and Space Programming [*NASA*] ... CLASP
Computer Language for Engineers and Technologists (MHDB) ... CLEAT
Computer Language for Information Processing (NITA) ... CLIP
Computer Language Magazine [*Miller Freeman Publications*] [*Information service or system*] (CRD) ... CLM
Computer Language Recorder ... CLR
Computer Language Research (IEEE) ... CLR
Computer Language Research, Inc. [*NASDAQ symbol*] (SAG) ... CLRI
Computer Language Research, Inc. [*Associated Press*] (SAG) ... CmpLR
Computer Language Rsch [*NASDAQ symbol*] (TTSB) ... CLRI
Computer Language to Aid and Stimulate Scientific, Mathematical, and Technical Education ... CLASSMATE
Computer Language Translator ... CLT
Computer Language Utility Extension (PDAA) ... CLUE
Computer Languages for the Processing of Text (DGA) ... CLPT
Computer/LASER Access Systems for Information Exchange ... CLASIX
Computer Launch and Separation Problem (MCD) ... CLASP
Computer Launch Interference Problems ... CLIP
Computer Law and Tax Report [*A publication*] (DLA) ... Computer L & T Rep
Computer Law and Tax Report [*A publication*] (DLA) ... Computer L & Tax
Computer Law Association (EA) ... CLA
Computer Law Service Reporter ... CLSR
Computer Law Service Reporter [*A publication*] (DLA) ... Computer L Serv Rep
Computer Layout Installation Planner (MHDB) ... CLIP
Computer Layout of Integrated Circuits (PDAA) ... CLIC
Computer League for Users in Education (EDAC) ... CLUE
Computer Learning Center (HGAA) ... CLC
Computer Learning Centers, Inc. [*NASDAQ symbol*] (SAG) ... CLCX
Computer Learning Centers, Inc. [*Associated Press*] (SAG) ... CptrLrn
Computer Learning Ctrs [*NASDAQ symbol*] (TTSB) ... CLCX
Computer Learning under Evaluation (IAA) ... CLUE
Computer Lessors Association [*Later, CDLA*] (EA) ... CLA
Computer Letter Service (HGAA) ... CLS
Computer Liaison Nurse (MEDA) ... CLN
Computer Library Services, Inc. [*Wellesley Hills, MA*] ... CLSI
Computer Line Terminal (HGAA) ... CLT
Computer Listing and Analysis of Maintenance Programs (MHDB) ... CLAMP
Computer Listing Service [*Computer Listing Service, Inc.*] [*Information service or system*] (IID) ... CLS
Computer Listings of Employment Opportunities [*The Copley Press, Inc.*] [*Database*] ... CLEO
Computer Literacy and Studies in Schools (AIE) ... CLASS
Computer Literacy Council (EA) ... CLC
Computer Load and Resource Analysis (MCD) ... CLARA
Computer Lock-On ... CLO
Computer Logging Unit and Editor (NITA) ... CLUE
Computer Logic Demonstrator ... CLD
Computer Logic Unit Tester (MCD) ... CLUT
Computer Machinery Corp. Ltd. [*Subsidiary of Microdata*] (MCD) ... CMC
Computer Main Memory [*Telecommunications*] (TEL) ... CMM
Computer Maintenance Test Set ... CMTS
Computer Management [*British A publication*] ... CM
Computer Management Association ... CMA
Computer Management/Computer-Assisted Instruction (MCD) ... CM/CAI
Computer Management Group [*British*] (NITA) ... CMG
Computer Management Sciences, Inc. [*NASDAQ symbol*] (SAG) ... CMSX
Computer Management Sciences, Inc. [*Associated Press*] (SAG) ... CompMS
Computer Management System [*Burroughs Corp.*] (BUR) ... CMS
Computer Marketing [*Standard & Poor's*] ... COMPMARK
Computer Marketing/Mailing (SAA) ... CM/M
Computer Marketing Services [*Anaheim, CA*] [*Information service or system*] (IID) ... CMS
Computer Marketplace [*NASDAQ symbol*] (TTSB) ... MKPL
Computer Marketplace, Inc. [*Associated Press*] (SAG) ... CptM
Computer Marketplace, Inc. [*Associated Press*] (SAG) ... CptMk
Computer Marketplace, Inc. [*Associated Press*] (SAG) ... CptrMkt
Computer Marketplace, Inc. [*NASDAQ symbol*] (SAG) ... MKPL
Computer Marketplace Wrrt'A' [*NASDAQ symbol*] (TTSB) ... MKPLW
Computer Marketplace Wrrt'B' [*NASDAQ symbol*] (TTSB) ... MKPLZ
Computer Measurement and Evaluation ... CME
Computer Measurement Group (EA) ... CMG
Computer Mediated Communication ... CMC
Computer Memories, Inc. (NITA) ... CMI
Computer Memory Element ... CME
Computer Memory Tester ... CMT
Computer Memory Unit ... CMU
Computer Message Transmission ... COMET
Computer Method of Sequencing Operations for Assembly Lines (MCD) ... COMSOAL
Computer Methods for Automatic Diagnosis (PDAA) ... COMAD
Computer Mgmt Sciences [*NASDAQ symbol*] (TTSB) ... CMSX
Computer Microfilm Corp. [*Information service or system*] (IID) ... CMC
Computer Microfilm International Corp. [*Information service or system*] (IID) ... CMIC
Computer Micrographics and Technology Group (NITA) ... COMTEC
Computer Micrographics Technology [*An association Defunct*] (EA) ... CMT
Computer Micrographics Technology (EA) ... COMtec
Computer Microtechnology (IAA) ... CM
Computer Model (MCD) ... COMO
Computer Model for Feasibility Analysis and Reporting [*United Nations*] (NITA) ... COMFAR
Computer Modelling Group [*Research center*] (RCD) ... CMG
Computer Module ... CM
Computer Monitor Adapter ... CMA
Computer Monitor and Control (MCD) ... CMAC
Computer Monitor and Control Console (CAAL) ... CMCC
Computer Multiple Listing Service [*Information service or system*] (IID) ... CMLS
Computer Musician Coalition (EA) ... CMC
Computer Network Corp. [*Information service or system*] (IID) ... COMNET
Computer Network Systems, Inc. (AAGC) ... CNSI
Computer Network Technology [*NASDAQ symbol*] (TTSB) ... CMNT
Computer Network Technology Corp. [*NASDAQ symbol*] (NQ) ... CMNT
Computer Network Technology Corp. [*Associated Press*] (SAG) ... CptNwk
Computer Networking and Communications Systems Program [*Georgia Institute of Technology, School of Information and Computer Science*] [*Atlanta*] [*Telecommunications service*] (TSSD) ... CNCS
Computer Networking Stand Alone Program ... COMPUNET
Computer Not Operational (IAA) ... CNO
Computer Numerical Control [*Computer science*] ... CNC
Computer Numerical Logic ... CNL
Computer Occupational Data Analysis Program ... CODAP
Computer of Average Transients [*Spectroscopy*] ... CAT
Computer On-Line Real-Time Applications Language [*Computer science*] (IEEE) ... CORAL
Computer Only Linofilm [*Graphic arts*] (DGA) ... COL
Computer Operated Branch Recording and Acquisition System (ADA) ... COBRA
Computer Operated Electronics Display [*Program*] [*Computer science*] (ECII) ... COED
Computer Operated Spectrophotometric Analysis of Cameras (NITA) ... COSAC
Computer Operated Spectrophotometric Analysis of Monitors (NITA) ... COSAM
Computer Operating and Programming Environment (DNAB) ... COPE
Computer Operating Instruction ... COI
Computer Operating Properly ... COP
Computer Operations Facility ... COF
Computer Operations Group ... COG
Computer Operations Management Association ... COMA
Computer Operations Procedures Manual ... COPM
Computer Operator Aptitude Battery [*Test*] ... COAB
Computer Operator Handbook ... COH
Computer Operator Proficiency Examination (SAA) ... COPE
Computer Operators' Course ... COC
Computer Optimal Media Planning and Selection System (PDAA) ... COMPASS
Computer Optimization Package [*or Program*] [*General Electric Co.*] ... COP
Computer Optimized Fabrication [*Sheet metal*] [*Raytheon Co.*] ... COF
Computer Optimized Sheetmetal Technology [*Raytheon Co.*] ... COST
Computer or Computerized Acquisition System (NITA) ... CAS
Computer Order Processing and Sales Accounting (IAA) ... COPSAC
Computer Orientated Reproducer Assembly (DGA) ... CORA
Computer Oriented Classicists (EA) ... COC
Computer Oriented Geological Society [*Database producer*] (IID) ... COGS
Computer Oriented Music Materials Processed for User Transformation or Exchange (NITA) ... COMMPUTE
Computer Oriented Record Keeping System (NITA) ... CORKS
Computer Output Microfilm [*or Microfiche or Microform*] (BUR) ... COM
Computer Output Microfilm Equipment ... COME
Computer Output Microfilm Package ... COMPAC
Computer Output Microform Catalog ... COMCAT
Computer Output to LASER Disk (PCM) ... COLD
Computer Outputer Microforms Program and Concept Study (MCD) ... COMPACS
Computer Outscoring Services [*NASDAQ symbol*] (SAG) ... COSI
Computer Outscoring Services [*Associated Press*] (SAG) ... CptOuts
Computer Outsourcing Svcs [*NASDAQ symbol*] (TTSB) ... COSI
Computer Owner Protection [*IDX Technologies, Inc.*] (PCM) ... COP
Computer Packages (MCD) ... COMPAC
Computer Paragraph ... CP
Computer Payroll (BUR) ... COMPAY
Computer Performance Analysis [*Boole & Babbage, Inc.*] ... CPA
Computer Performance Evaluation ... CPE
Computer Performance Evaluation Users Group [*Defunct*] (EA) ... CPEUG
Computer Performance Management ... CPM
Computer Performance Monitor (PDAA) ... CPM
Computer Peripheral Equipment (KSC) ... CPE
Computer Peripheral Manufacturers Association ... CPMA
Computer Peripheral Unit (IEEE) ... CPU
Computer Personnel Research Group [*Later, Special Interest Group for Computer Personnel Research*] ... CPRG
Computer Pete [*NASDAQ symbol*] (TTSB) ... CPCO
Computer Petroleum Corp. [*Information service or system*] (IID) ... CPC
Computer Petroleum Corp. [*NASDAQ symbol*] (SAG) ... CPCO
Computer Petroleum Corp. [*Associated Press*] (SAG) ... CptrPtl
Computer Planning and Control Technique (BUR) ... COMPACT
Computer Plotting Matrix System (PDAA) ... CPMS
Computer Pneumatic Input Panel ... CPIP
Computer Polarization Holography ... CPH
Computer Position Profile (PDAA) ... CPP
Computer Power Center ... CPC
Computer Power Supply ... CPS
Computer Power Support System ... CPSS

Computer Predicting and Automatic Course Tracking (PDAA) .... COMPACT
Computer Press Association (EA) .... CPA
Computer Print Console .... CPC
Computer Printer Unit (MCD) .... CPU
Computer Printout (ADA) .... CPO
Computer Printout Processing (PDAA) .... CPP
Computer Process Control .... CPC
Computer Processor Unit .... CPU
Computer Product News (MHDI) .... CPN
Computer Product Testing Service .... CPTS
Computer Products [*NASDAQ symbol*] (TTSB) .... CPRD
Computer Products Directory [*Information service or system*] (IID) .... CPD
Computer Products, Inc. [*Associated Press*] (SAG) .... CmpPr
Computer Products, Inc. [*NASDAQ symbol*] (NQ) .... CPRD
Computer Professionals for Social Responsibility (EA) .... CPSR
Computer Program (IEEE) .... COMPROG
Computer Program (MCD) .... CP
Computer Program Assistance Library (NITA) .... CPAL
Computer Program Associated Contractor .... CPAC
Computer Program Book .... CPB
Computer Program Change Instruction (NASA) .... CPCI
Computer Program Change Library (NASA) .... CPCL
Computer Program Change Request (NASA) .... CPCR
Computer Program Components (MCD) .... CPC
Computer Program Configuration Identification .... CPCI
Computer Program Configured Item (MCD) .... CPCI
Computer Program Contract End Item .... CPCEI
Computer Program Control Library (MCD) .... CPCL
Computer Program Design [*or Development*] **Specification** [*NASA*] (NASA) .... CPDS
Computer Program Detail Design Specification (MCD) .... CPDDS
Computer Program Development and Management System .... CPDAMS
Computer Program Development Center [*Air Force*] (MCD) .... CPDC
Computer Program Development Plan .... CPDP
Computer Program Deviation Request (MCD) .... CPDR
Computer Program End Item (NASA) .... CPEI
Computer Program for Automatic Control .... COMPAC
Computer Program Identification Numbers (MCD) .... CPIN
Computer Program Implementation Process .... CPIP
Computer Program Information Center (MCD) .... COPIC
Computer Program Integrated Document (OA) .... CPID
Computer Program Integration Contractor .... CPIC
Computer Program Library (BUR) .... CPL
Computer Program Module (NASA) .... CPM
Computer Program Operational Flight Program (MCD) .... CPOFP
Computer Program Package (CAAL) .... CPP
Computer Program Product Specification (MCD) .... CPPS
Computer Program Specification (AFM) .... CPS
Computer Program Submodule (MCD) .... CPSM
Computer Program System [*Boeing Co.*] .... CPS
Computer Program Tapes (MCD) .... CPT
Computer Program Test and Evaluation .... CPT & E
Computer Program Test Plan .... CPTP
Computer Program Test Plan (CAAL) .... CPTPL
Computer Program Test Procedure .... CPTP
Computer Program Test Procedures (CAAL) .... CPTPR
Computer Program Test Report (MCD) .... CPTR
Computer Program Update .... CPU
Computer Programmer Aptitude Battery [*Test*] .... CPAB
Computer Programmer's Manual (MCD) .... CPM
Computer Programming and Testing Activity (IEEE) .... CPTA
Computer Programming Concepts (BUR) .... CPC
Computer Programming Language [*for small computers*] (BARN) C
Computer Programming Performance Specification (MCD) .... CPPS
Computer Programming Service .... CPS
Computer Projects, Inc. [*Greensboro, NC*] [*Telecommunications*] (TSSD) .... CPI
Computer Projects Limited .... CPL
Computer Readability Editing System (MCD) .... CRES
Computer Readable Output [*Computer science*] (PCM) .... CRO
Computer Readable System .... CRS
Computer Reader Enquiry Service System [*Automated library system*] (NITA) .... CRESS
Computer Realtime Access Method (IAA) .... CREAM
Computer Recognition Systems [*Commercial firm*] [*British*] (NITA) .... CRS
Computer Recognition Systems Ltd. [*British*] .... CRSL
Computer Remote Terminal (MCD) .... CRT
Computer Repair, Parts, and Tools (SAA) .... CR
Computer Report on Importance (PDAA) .... CRIMP
Computer Research Group, Inc. [*Information service or system*] (IID) .... CRG
Computer Research, Systems, and Software (IEEE) .... COMPRESS
Computer Reservation System .... CRS
Computer Reset Pulse (KSC) .... CRP
Computer Resident Automatic Instruction (MCD) .... CRAI
Computer Resident Planning (MCD) .... CRP
Computer Resource .... CR
Computer Resource Management [*Army*] (IAA) .... CRM
Computer Resource Management Plan [*Army*] (RDA) .... CRMP
Computer Resource Unit .... CRU
Computer Resources Development Plan [*NASA*] (NASA) .... CRDP
Computer Resources Integrated Support Data (MCD) .... CRISD
Computer Resources Integrated Support Document [*Military*] .... CRISD
Computer Resources Integrated Support Plan [*Military*] (AFIT) .... CRISP
Computer Resources Life-Cycle Management Plan .... CRLCMP
Computer Resources Management Data (MCD) .... CRMD
Computer Resources Nucleus (AAGC) .... CORN
Computer Resources Nucleus [*FAA*] (TAG) .... CORN
Computer Resources Working Group [*Military*] (AFIT) .... CRWG
Computer Response Corp. .... CRC
Computer Results Corp. [*Information service or system*] (IID) .... CRC
Computer Retailers Association [*British*] (NITA) .... CRA
Computer Retrieval Editor [*Used to manage CORKIPER file family*] .... COREDITOR
Computer Retrieval of Information on Scientific Projects [*National Institutes of Health Information service or system*] (IID) .... CRISP
Computer Retrieval of Kinetic Parameters of Electrode Reactions .... CORKIPER
Computer Retrieval of Organic Structures Based on Wiswesser .... CROSSBOW
Computer Review and Orientation Course .... CROC
Computer Routine for Evaluation of Submarine Threats (MCD) .... CREST
Computer Run Report (NASA) .... CRR
Computer Scheduling System (IAA) .... CSS
Computer Science (DD) .... CompSc
Computer Science (BUR) .... CS
Computer Science and Engineering .... CSE
Computer Science Center [*University of Maryland*] [*Research center*] (RCD) .... CSC
Computer Science Center [*North Carolina A & T State University*] [*Research center*] (RCD) .... CSC
Computer Science Division .... CSD
Computer Science Laboratory [*Sony*] [*Japan*] (ECON) .... CSL
Computer Science Lecturers' Association [*British*] .... CSLA
Computer Science Network [*University Corp. for Atmospheric Research*] .... CSNET
Computer Science Teleprocessing System (IAA) .... CSTS
Computer Science Time-Sharing System (IAA) .... CSTS
Computer Sciences [*NYSE symbol*] (TTSB) .... CSC
Computer Sciences Corp. [*Database originator*] [*Associated Press*] (SAG) .... CompSci
Computer Sciences Corp. [*El Segunda, CA*] [*Database originator*] [*NYSE symbol*] (SPSG) .... CSC
Computer Sciences Corp., Technical Library, El Segundo, CA [*Library symbol Library of Congress*] (LCLS) .... CEsC
Computer Sciences Corp., Technical Library, El Segundo, CA [*Library symbol*] [*Library of Congress*] (LCLS) .... CEsCS
Computer Sciences Teleprocessing System (PDAA) .... CSTS
Computer Search Center [*Illinois Institute of Technology Research Center*] [*Chicago, IL*] [*Defunct*] .... CSC
Computer Search International Corp. [*Database producer*] .... CSI
Computer Search Services .... CSS
Computer Security (MSA) .... CMPSCTY
Computer Security Act [*1987*] .... CSA
Computer Security Evaluation Center .... CSEC
Computer Security Institute (EA) .... CSI
Computer Security Technical Vulnerability Reporting Program [*Army*] (ADDR) .... CSTVRP
Computer Select and Cross Connect Unit (MCD) .... CSCCU
Computer Sensitive Language [*Programming language*] .... CSL
Computer Sentry Software .... CSS
Computer Sequence Number .... CSN
Computer series [*Digital Scientific*] .... META
Computer Service and Bureaux Association [*British*] .... COSBA
Computer Service Center .... CSC
Computer Service Network (IAA) .... CSN
Computer Service Office (IAA) .... CSO
Computer Service Squadron [*Air Force*] .... COMPSERSq
Computer Services and Systems Division [*Environmental Protection Agency*] (GFGA) .... CSSD
Computer Services Association [*British*] .... CSA
Computer Services Co. [*British*] (NITA) .... CSC
Computer Services Division [*University of South Carolina at Columbia*] [*Research center*] (RCD) .... CSD
Computer Services for Motor-Freight Activities (PDAA) .... COSMA
Computer Services Industry Training Council [*British*] (NITA) .... COSIT
Computer Services - Long Beach (MCD) .... CSLB
Computer Services Procedures Manual .... CSPM
Computer Services Squadron [*Air Force*] .... CPUSS
Computer Services Support and Evaluation Agency .... CSSEA
Computer Set Control (CAAL) .... CSC
Computer Sharing Services, Inc. [*Information service or system*] (IID) .... CSS
Computer Simulated Design (DGA) .... CSD
Computer Simulation (RDA) .... CS
Computer Simulation Language (BUR) .... CSL
Computer Simulation Model (MCD) .... CSM
Computer Simulation Program .... CSP
Computer Slave [*Computer science*] (DGA) .... CS
Computer Society of Canada .... CSC
Computer Software (MCD) .... CS
Computer Software and Applications Conference .... COMPSAC
Computer Software and Peripheral Show (IEEE) .... COMPSO
Computer Software and Services Group (IAA) .... CSSG
Computer Software and Services Industry (HGAA) .... CSSI
Computer Software and Services Industry Association [*Formerly, ADAPSO*] (NITA) .... CSSIA
Computer Software Component (SSD) .... CSC
Computer Software Configuration Item [*Computer science*] .... CSCI
Computer Software Data Tapes (MCD) .... CSDT
Computer Software Diagnostic Manual .... CSDM
Computer Software Documentation .... CSD
Computer Software Management and Information Center [*University of Georgia*] [*NASA Research center*] (RCD) .... COSMIC
Computer Software Operator's Manual .... CSOM
Computer Software Trouble Report (MCD) .... CSTR
Computer Software Unit .... CSU

Computer Sports World [*Information service or system*] (IID) ...... CSW
Computer Status Lights (MCD) ...... CSL
Computer Status Matrix (MCD) ...... CSM
Computer Stock Inventory Control (MCD) ...... CSIC
Computer Stock Timing and Analysis Technique ...... COM-STAT
Computer Structure Language [*1974*] [*Computer science*] (CSR) ...... CSL
Computer Subprogram Design Document (MHDI) ...... CSDD
Computer Subsystem (NASA) ...... CSS
Computer Subsystem Controller ...... CSC
Computer Support Applications Manager [*Computer Support Corp.*] [*Computer science*] ...... CSAM
Computer Support Base (AFIT) ...... CSB
Computer Support Equipment (MCD) ...... CSE
Computer Support Group [*Marine science*] (OSRA) ...... CSG
Computer Support Group (USDC) ...... CSG
Computer Support in Military Psychiatry [*Project*] (RDA) ...... COMPSY
Computer Support Program [*NASA*] (NASA) ...... CSP
Computer Supported Purchasing ...... CSP
Computer Synthesized Imagery (MCD) ...... CSI
Computer System Acceptance Review ...... CSAR
Computer System Analyst (BUR) ...... CSA
Computer System Design (IAA) ...... CSD
Computer System Development Facility (MHDI) ...... CSDF
Computer System for Crop Response to Fertilizers [*United Nations*] (NITA) ...... CSCRF
Computer System for Main Frame Operations [*Bell System*] ...... COSMOS
Computer System for Medical Information Services (DIT) ...... COSMIS
Computer System Interface Circuits (IEEE) ...... CSIC
Computer System Language ...... CSL
Computer System Manual ...... CSM
Computer System Operators Manual ...... CSOM
Computer System Science Training [*IBM Corp.*] ...... CSST
Computer System Security Manager (DNAB) ...... CSSM
Computer System Security Officer (DNAB) ...... CSSO
Computer System Simulator [*Programming language*] [*1969*] ...... CSS
Computer Systems Analyst and Programmer [*Air Force*] .... COMPSYSANLSTPGMR
Computer Systems and Electronics Requirements Board [*British*] ...... CSERB
Computer Systems Association ...... CSA
Computer Systems Command [*Also, ACSC*] [*Army*] ...... CSC
Computer Systems Command Support Group, Fort Lee (MCD) ...... CSCSGL
Computer Systems Development Ltd. [*Software supplier*] [*London, England*] (NCC) ...... CSD
Computer Systems Director (KSC) ...... CSD
Computer Systems Engineer (PGP) ...... CSE
Computer Systems for Management Information and Control (PDAA) ...... COSMIC
Computer Systems Institute ...... CSI
Computer Systems Integration Review (NASA) ...... CSIR
Computer Systems International ...... CSI
Computer Systems Laboratory [*Bethesda, MD*] [*Department of Health and Human Services*] (GRD) ...... CSL
Computer Systems Officer (ADA) ...... CSO
Computer Systems Policy Project (BTTJ) ...... CSPP
Computer Systems Research Institute [*University of Toronto*] [*Research center*] (RCD) ...... CSRI
Computer Systems Selection and Acquisition Agency [*Army*] (MCD) ...... CSSAA
Computer Systems Squadron ...... CSSQ
Computer Systems Support and Evaluation Command ...... CSSEC
Computer Tape Recorder ...... CTR
Computer Task Group (HGAA) ...... CTG
Computer Task Group [*NYSE symbol*] (TTSB) ...... TSK
Computer Task Group, Inc. [*Associated Press*] (SAG) ...... CmpTsk
Computer Task Group, Inc. [*NYSE symbol*] (SPSG) ...... TSK
Computer Technology (IEEE) ...... CT
Computer Technology and Telecommunications Staff [*Department of Justice*] (GFGA) ...... CTTS
Computer Technology Associates [*Goddard Spaceflight Center - Greenbelt, MD*] [*NASA*] (NASA) ...... CTA
Computer Technology Center ...... CTC
Computer Technology Division (ACII) ...... COMPUTEC
Computer Technology Innovations (HGAA) ...... CTI
Computer Technology Limited [*British*] (NITA) ...... CTL
Computer Technology Research Corp. (IID) ...... CTR
Computer Telephone CI'1 [*NASDAQ symbol*] (TTSB) ...... CPTI
Computer Telephone Corp. [*Associated Press*] (SAG) ...... CmpTel
Computer Telephone Corp. [*NASDAQ symbol*] (NQ) ...... CPTL
Computer Telephony Integration [*Telecommunications*] ...... CTI
Computer Telewriter Systems (MCD) ...... CTS
Computer TELEX Exchange [*RCA Corp.*] ...... CTE
Computer Test Sequences Document (MCD) ...... CTSD
Computer Test Set ...... CTS
Computer Test Unit (MCD) ...... CTU
Computer Threat Research Association [*British*] (DBA) ...... CoTRA
Computer Time Bookers ...... CTB
Computer Time Sharing Service (MHDI) ...... CTSS
Computer Timing and Costing Model (MHDB) ...... CTCM
Computer to Communications Interface Unit ...... CCIU
Computer to PBX Interface [*Telecommunications*] (NITA) ...... CPI
Computer Town United Kingdom [*Computer literacy project*] (NITA) ...... CTUK
Computer Trade Video [*British*] [*A publication*] (NITA) ...... CTV
Computer Traders Association [*British*] (NITA) ...... CTA
Computer Training System ...... CTS
Computer Transceiver Systems, Inc. ...... CTSI
Computer Transformer ...... CT
Computer Translation, Inc. [*Information service or system*] (IID) ...... CTI
Computer Transponder (MCD) ...... CT

Computer Typing System ...... CTS
Computer Unit (EA) ...... CU
Computer Update Equipment ...... CUE
Computer Usage Control (NASA) ...... CUC
Computer Usage List Processor (IEEE) ...... CULP
Computer Usage's Business-Oriented Language [*Computer science*] ...... CUBOL
Computer Use in Social Services Network (EA) ...... CUSSN
Computer Use in the Health Service [*British*] ...... CUHS
Computer User Education [*An association*] ...... CUE
Computer User Terminal Equipment [*Airport computer system*] ...... CUTE
Computer Users Association ...... CUA
Computer Users Associations Group (MHDB) ...... CUAG
Computer Users for Social Responsibility (EA) ...... CUSR
Computer Users in Speech and Hearing (EA) ...... CUSH
Computer Users Survival Electronic Magazine [*Information service or system*] (IID) ...... CUSEM
Computer Users' Tape System (ODBW) ...... CUTS
Computer Utility Educational System (MCD) ...... CUES
Computer Utilization Accounting System (IEEE) ...... CUAS
Computer Utilization Efficiency (IAA) ...... CUE
Computer Utilization Monitor (IAA) ...... CUM
Computer Utilization Reporting System (IEEE) ...... CURES
Computer Utilized Turning System [*Warner & Swasey*] ...... CUTS
Computer Validation Program (DNAB) ...... CVP
Computer Video Instrument (NITA) CVI
Computer Virus as a Weapon [*DoD*] ...... CVW
Computer Virus Industry Association (EA) ...... CVIA
Computer Vision CV
Computer Vision and Image Processing ...... CVIP
Computer Vision and Understanding ...... CVIU
Computer Vision Graphics and Image Processing [*A publication*] ...... CVGIP
Computer Vision Laboratory [*University of Maryland*] [*Research center*] (RCD) CVL
Computer Vision Syndrome ...... CVS
Computer Voice Response ...... CVR
Computer Weekly [*British*] [*A publication*] (NITA) ...... CW
Computer with On-Line Remote Devices [*National Institute of Standards and Technology*] ...... CORD
Computer Wizard [*Information service or system*] (IID) ...... CW
Computer Word Processing (IAA) ...... CWP
Computer World Trade Group [*British*] ...... CWTG
Computer-Accessed [*or-Aided*] Telemetry System ...... CATS
Computer-Adjusted Spectrometry System ...... COMPASS
Computer-Administered [*or Assisted*] Instruction (RDA) ...... CAI
Computer-Administered Programmed Instruction (OA) ...... CAPI
Computer-Aided [*or Assisted*] (HGAA) ...... CA
Computer-Aided Abrasive Machining Oscillation Studies (PDAA) ...... CAMOS
Computer-Aided Acquisition and Logistic Support/Concurrent Engineer (USGC) ...... CALS/CE
Computer-Aided Acquisition and Logistics Support (MCD) ...... CALS
Computer-Aided Acquisition and Logistics System (AAGC) ...... CALS
Computer-Aided Adult Learning (HGAA) ...... CAAL
Computer-Aided Alerting Subsystem (CAAL) ...... CAAS
Computer-Aided Analysis (SSD) ...... CAA
Computer-Aided Analysis and Information Recovery Systems (MCD) ...... CAIRS
Computer-Aided Analytical Solution for Engineers ...... CAASE
Computer-Aided Approach Spacing [*Aviation*] ...... CAAS
Computer-Aided Architectural Design (MCD) ...... CAAD
Computer-Aided Batch Scheduling ...... CABS
Computer-Aided Building (PDAA) ...... CAB
Computer-Aided Building Design (PDAA) ...... CABD
Computer-Aided Building-Design System [*Computer science*] ...... CABDS
Computer-Aided Calibration (ACII) ...... CAC
Computer-Aided Chartroom ...... COACH
Computer-Aided Circuit Analysis [*Electronics*] ...... CACA
Computer-Aided Circuit Design ...... CACD
Computer-Aided Classification ...... CAC
Computer-Aided [*or -Assisted*] Communication System ...... CACS
Computer-Aided Control System Design (PDAA) ...... CACSD
Computer-Aided Cost Estimating (BTTJ) ...... CACE
Computer-Aided [*or Assisted*] Data Entry (IAA) ...... CADE
Computer-Aided Data Management Procedure (MCD) ...... CADMP
Computer-Aided Design ...... CAD
Computer-Aided Design, Analysis, and Reliability (IEEE) ...... CADAR
Computer-Aided Design and Analysis ...... CADA
Computer-Aided Design and Construction System (PDAA) ...... CADACS
Computer-Aided Design and Design Automation ...... CADDA
Computer-Aided Design and Drafting [*Software package*] (MCD) ...... CADD
Computer-Aided Design and Drafting ...... CADD
Computer-Aided Design and Electrical Test ...... CADET
Computer-Aided Design and Engineering (MHDI) ...... CADAE
Computer-Aided Design and Evaluation (MCD) ...... CADE
Computer-Aided Design and Evaluation Technology (MCD) ...... CADET
Computer-Aided Design and Fabrication (MCD) ...... CADF
Computer-Aided Design and Manufacturing (MCD) ...... CADAM
Computer-Aided Design and Numerical Control (DNAB) ...... CADNC
Computer-Aided Design and Numerical Control Effort ...... CADANCE
Computer-Aided Design and System Analysis Tool (MCD) ...... CADSAT
Computer-Aided Design and Test [*System*] ...... CADAT
Computer-Aided Design and Test (MHDB) ...... CADTES
Computer-Aided Design Centre [*British*] (EECA) ...... CADC
Computer-Aided Design/Computer-Aided Manufacturing ...... CAD/CAM
Computer-Aided Design Development ...... CADD
Computer-Aided Design Drafting via Tektronix (MCD) ...... CADD/TEK
Computer-Aided Design Engineering (RDA) ...... CADE

Computer-Aided Design Engineering and Manufacturing (IAA) .... CADEM
Computer-Aided Design Environment [*Software system*] (IEEE) .... COMRADE
Computer-Aided Design Experiment Translator .... CADET
Computer-Aided Design for Communications (PDAA) .... CADCOM
Computer-Aided Design Interactive System (IAA) .... CADIS
Computer-Aided Design Laboratory [*Pennsylvania State University*] [*Research center*] (RCD) .... CAD-LAB
Computer-Aided Design, Manufacture, and Test (MCD) .... CADMAT
Computer-Aided Design/Manufacturing [*Army*] (RDA) .... CAD/M
Computer-Aided Design/Numerical Control (AABC) .... CD/NC
Computer-Aided Design of Electronic Products (IEEE) .... CADEP
Computer-Aided Design of Fire Escapes [*Micro Core Ltd.*] [*Software package*] (NCC) .... CAFE
Computer-Aided Design of Industrial Cabling Systems (PDAA) .... CADICS
Computer-Aided Design of Information System (IAA) .... CADIS
Computer-Aided Design of Integrated Circuits (MCD) .... CADIC
Computer-Aided Design of Linear Integrated Circuits (MHDB) .... CADLIC
Computer-Aided Design of Optical Character Recognition (MHDI) .... CADOCR
Computer-Aided Design of Optical Systems [*Energy Soft Computer Systems Ltd.*] [*Software package*] (NCC) .... CADOS
Computer-Aided Design of Printed Circuit Artwork (PDAA) .... CADOPCART
Computer-Aided Design Reliability .... CADR
Computer-Aided Design System .... CADS
Computer-Aided Detection .... CAD
Computer-Aided Development and Evaluation System (MHDI) .... CADES
Computer-Aided Dispatching [*Vehicle fleet management*] .... CAD
Computer-Aided Document Management and Control System (HGAA) .... CADMAC
Computer-Aided Document Origination (MHDI) .... CADO
Computer-Aided Drafting [*or Drawing*] .... CAD
Computer-Aided Education (BUR) .... CAE
Computer-Aided Electronic Warfare Information Systems [*Air Force*] (GFGA) .... CAEWIS
Computer-Aided Embarkation Management System [*Navy*] .... CAEMS
Computer-Aided Emulation Design System .... CAEDS
Computer-Aided Engineering .... CAE
Computer-Aided Engineering and Architectural Design System (RDA) .... CAEDS
Computer-Aided Engineering Center [*University of Wisconsin - Madison*] [*Research center*] (RCD) .... CAE
Computer-Aided Engineering Centre [*Heriot-Watt University*] [*British*] (CB) .... CAE
Computer-Aided Engineering Laboratory [*Lawrence Institute of Technology*] [*Research center*] (RCD) .... CAE LAB
Computer-Aided Environmental Control System (MCD) .... CAECS
Computer-Aided Environmental Design Analysis and Realization (MHDB) .... CEDAR
Computer-Aided Exercise Facility (MCD) .... CAEF
Computer-Aided Exploration (BTTJ) .... CAEX
Computer-Aided Facility Management .... CAFM
Computer-Aided Fault Finding (PDAA) .... CAFF
Computer-Aided Film Editor .... CAFE
Computer-Aided Flight Operations Center .... CAFOC
Computer-Aided Function Allocation and Evaluation System .... CAFES
Computer-Aided Gear Changing [*Automotive engineering*] .... CAG
Computer-Aided Genetic Engineering .... CAGE
Computer-Aided Geometric Design (MCD) .... CAGD
Computer-Aided Industrial Design (BTTJ) .... CAID
Computer-Aided Industry (IAA) .... CAI
Computer-Aided Information Logistics (IAA) .... CAIL
Computer-Aided Inspection (BTTJ) .... CAI
Computer-Aided [*or -Assisted*] **Instruction** .... CAI
Computer-Aided Instruction (IEEE) .... CAIS
Computer-Aided Instruction System (MHDB) .... CAINS
Computer-Aided Instruction System [*Programming language*] [*1971*] (CSR) .... CAISYS
Computer-Aided Interactive Testing System (EDAC) .... CAITS
Computer-Aided Laboratory Automation System (IAA) .... CALAS
Computer-Aided Layout and Fabrication (MCD) .... CALFAB
Computer-Aided Layout of Masks (PDAA) .... CALM
Computer-Aided [*or -Assisted*] **Learning** (BUR) .... CAL
Computer-Aided Lighting [*Automotive engineering*] .... CAL
Computer-Aided Line Balance .... CALB
Computer-Aided Livestock Marketing .... CALM
Computer-Aided Loads Analysis (MCD) .... CALA
Computer-Aided LOFT Lines (MCD) .... CALL
Computer-Aided Logistics [*Army*] .... CAL
Computer-Aided Logistics Support [*Army*] .... CALS
Computer-Aided Logistics System [*Air Force*] (DOMA) .... CALS
Computer-Aided Logistics/Technical Information Management System [*Military*] (GFGA) .... CAL/TIMS
Computer-Aided Machine Loading (MHDB) .... CAMECEC
Computer-Aided Maintenance Management .... CAMM
Computer-Aided Makeup [*Graphic arts*] .... CAM
Computer-Aided Maneuver Evaluation, Reconstruction, and Analysis [*British*] .... CAMERA
Computer-Aided Manufacturing .... CAM
Computer-Aided Mask Preparation (DNAB) .... CAMP
Computer-Aided Materials Management System [*Canadian provincial governments*] .... CAMMS
Computer-Aided Mathematics .... CAM
Computer-Aided Measurement and Control [*NASA*] .... CAMAC
Computer-Aided Mechanical Drafting .... CAMD
Computer-Aided Message Processing (LAIN) .... CAMP
Computer-Aided Milestone Schedule .... CAMS
Computer-Aided Missile Synthesis [*Army*] (MCD) .... CAMS
Computer-Aided Navigation Equipment (MCD) .... CANE
Computer-Aided Office (IAA) .... CAO
Computer-Aided Operations Research Facility [*Kings Point, NY*] [*National Maritime Research Center Department of Transportation*] (MCD) .... CAORF
Computer-Aided Optimization .... CAO
Computer-Aided Parameter Design .... CAPD
Computer-Aided Passive Ranging Indicator [*Military*] (CAAL) .... CAPRI
Computer-Aided Patient Management .... CAPM
Computer-Aided Pattern Evaluation and Recognition (KSC) .... CAPER
Computer-Aided Personnel Scheduling .... CAPS
Computer-Aided Pipe Sketching [*System*] [*Du Pont*] .... CAPS
Computer-Aided Piping Design and Construction (MCD) .... CAPDAC
Computer-Aided Placement and Routing System (PDAA) .... CAPARS
Computer-Aided Planning .... CAP
Computer-Aided Planning and Estimating [*Marlow Microplan National Engineering Laboratory*] [*Software package*] (NCC) .... CAPE
Computer-Aided Plant Management .... CAPM
Computer-Aided Polymer Data System (IID) .... CAPDAS
Computer-Aided Preparation of Electrical Routing (MCD) .... CAPER
Computer-Aided Presentation (IAA) .... CAP
Computer-Aided Process Design (MCD) .... CAPD
Computer-Aided Process Engineering .... CAPE
Computer-Aided Process Planning (MCD) .... CAPP
Computer-Aided Process Synthesis .... CAPS
Computer-Aided Processing and Terminal Access Information Network [*Rutgers University*] [*New Brunswick, NJ Library computer network*] ..... CAPTAIN
Computer-Aided Processing of Industrial Cabling Systems (PDAA) .... CAPICS
Computer-Aided Product Launch Application .... CAPLA
Computer-Aided [*or Assisted*] **Production** .... CAP
Computer-Aided Production Control (MHDB) .... CAPC
Computer-Aided Production Management (IAA) .... CAPM
Computer-Aided Production Planning and Control [*John Yates & Associates*] [*Software package*] (NCC) .... CAPPAC
Computer-Aided Program Simulator .... CAPS
Computer-Aided Programming .... CAP
Computer-Aided Programming System .... CAPS
Computer-Aided [*or Assisted*] **Publishing** .... CAP
Computer-Aided Pulse Plating [*Electrochemistry*] .... CAPP
Computer-Aided Purchasing (HGAA) .... CAP
Computer-Aided [*or Assisted*] **Quality** .... CAQ
Computer-Aided Quality Assurance .... CAQA
Computer-Aided Question Answering [*Computer science*] (MHDB) .... CQA
Computer-Aided RADAR Design (KSC) .... CARD
Computer-Aided Railway Engineering System (MCD) .... CARES
Computer-Aided Rapid Prototyping .... CARP
Computer-Aided Real Time Transcription [*Medical records*] (DAVI) .... CART
Computer-Aided Redundant System Reliability Analysis (MCD) .... CARSRA
Computer-Aided Reference Service [*University of Arizona Library, University of Utah*] [*Information service or system*] .... CARS
Computer-Aided Release Point (MCD) .... CARP
Computer-Aided Reliability and Design (MHDB) .... CARAD
Computer-Aided Reliability Data Analysis (MHDB) .... CARDA
Computer-Aided Reliability Data Systems [*Bell System*] .... CARDS
Computer-Aided Reliability Estimation .... CARE
Computer-Aided Reliability Model (MCD) .... CARM
Computer-Aided Remote Driving [*for robotic command vehicles*] (RDA) .... CARD
Computer-Aided Reorder Trap Analysis [*Bell Laboratories*] .... CARTA
Computer-Aided Repair (IAA) .... CAR
Computer-Aided Requirements Analysis (MCD) .... CARA
Computer-Aided Requirements Definition Software .... CARDS
Computer-Aided Research into Stock Market Applications .... CARISMA
Computer-Aided Risk Evaluation (ODBW) .... CARE
Computer-Aided Routing System .... CARS
Computer-Aided Scantling Determination (PDAA) .... CASCADE
Computer-Aided Scheduling .... CAS
Computer-Aided Selling (IAA) .... CAS
Computer-Aided Ship Design and Construction .... CASDAC
Computer-Aided Ship Design and Construction .... CASDC
Computer-Aided Software Development [*Computer science*] .... CASD
Computer-Aided Software Engineering .... CASE
Computer-Aided Software Testing (MCD) .... CAST
Computer-Aided Stock Holdings (PDAA) .... CASH
Computer-Aided Structural Design (MCD) .... CASD
Computer-Aided Structural Detailing of Ships (DNAB) .... CASDS
Computer-Aided Structural Technology (MCD) .... CAST
Computer-Aided Styling .... CAS
Computer-Aided System Design [*Programming language*] (BUR) .... CASD
Computer-Aided System Engineering (MCD) .... CASE
Computer-Aided System Evaluation .... CASE
Computer-Aided System for the Development of Aircrew Training (MCD) .... CASDAT
Computer-Aided System Hardware (MHDI) .... CASH
Computer-Aided Systems Analysis (MCD) .... CASA
Computer-Aided Tactical Information System (IEEE) .... CATIS
Computer-Aided Teaching .... CAT
Computer-Aided Teaching System (IEEE) .... CATS
Computer-Aided Technical Illustration (MCD) .... CATI
Computer-Aided Technical Management (DOMA) .... CATM
Computer-Aided Technology (MCD) .... CAT
Computer-Aided Telephony Performance Assessment (PDAA) .... CATPASS
Computer-Aided Test [*Telecommunications*] (TEL) .... CAT
Computer-Aided Test Equipment (MSA) .... CATE
Computer-Aided Test Generator (PDAA) .... CATGEN
Computer-Aided Testing [*Hoskyns Group Ltd.*] [*Software package*] (NCC) ...... CAT
Computer-Aided Text Processing (IAA) .... CATP
Computer-Aided Time Standard (PDAA) .... CATS

Computer-Aided Tomography (ACRL) .... CAT
Computer-Aided Trade (DS) .... COMPAT
Computer-Aided Training (RDA) .... CAT
Computer-Aided Training Evaluation and Scheduling (MCD) .... CATES
Computer-Aided Training System .... CATS
Computer-Aided Transceiver .... CAT
Computer-Aided Transcription .... CAT
Computer-Aided Translation (IEEE) .... CAT
Computer-Aided Travel Assistant .... CATA
Computer-Aided Tree (PDAA) .... CAT
Computer-Aided Troubleshooting .... CATS
Computer-Aided Typesetting (OA) .... CAT
Computer-Aided Typesetting Process .... CATP
Computer-Aided Victim Identification [*Computer software*] .... CAV-ID
Computer-Aided Work Sampling .... CAWS
Computer-Aided Writing .... CAW
Computer-Aided Written Communication .... CAWC
Computer-Animated Photographic Terrain View (MCD) .... CAPTV
Computer-Assisted Accounting (BUR) .... CAA
Computer-Assisted Acquisition System [*for libraries*] .... CAAS
Computer-Assisted Action Information System [*NATO*] .... CAIS
Computer-Assisted Area Source Emissions [*Environmental Protection Agency*] .... CAASE
Computer-Assisted Audit Techniques .... CAAT
Computer-Assisted Axial Tomography [*Also, CAT, CT*] [*Roentgenography*] .... CAAT
Computer-Assisted Bibliographic Service [*University of South Dakota*] (OLDSS) .... CABS
Computer-Assisted Classification and Assignment System (IEEE) .... COMPASS
Computer-Assisted Computer Language (SSD) .... CACL
Computer-Assisted Counseling [*Proposed for Air Force*] .... CAC
Computer-Assisted Data Entry (GFGA) .... CADE
Computer-Assisted Data Evaluation (ODBW) .... CADE
Computer-Assisted Decision Making System .... CDM
Computer-Assisted Densitometric Image Analysis [*Microbiology*] .... CADIA
Computer-Assisted Description of Patterns (PDAA) .... CADEP
Computer-Assisted Design .... CAD
Computer-Assisted Detailing of Ships .... CASDOS
Computer-Assisted Development Aids .... CADA
Computer-Assisted Diabetic Instruction [*System*] [*Endocrinology*] (DAVI) .... CADI
Computer-Assisted Diagnosis .... CAD
Computer-Assisted Dial Access Video Retrieval System (MHDI) .... CADAVRS
Computer-Assisted Dialog .... CAD
Computer-Assisted Dispatching/Mapping .... CADMAP
Computer-Assisted Dispatching System [*IBM Corp.*] .... CADS
Computer-Assisted Display Systems (MCD) .... CADS
Computer-Assisted Disposal Simulation [*Game*] .... CADISIM
Computer-Assisted Distribution and Assignment (NVT) .... CADA
Computer-Assisted Drug Design .... CADD
Computer-Assisted Dynamic Data Monitoring and Analysis System .... CADDMAS
Computer-Assisted Electron Microscope .... CEM
Computer-Assisted Enrollment [*IBM Corp.*] (IEEE) .... CAE
Computer-Assisted Entry .... CAE
Computer-Assisted Estimating .... CAE
Computer-Assisted Estimating and Management Information Systems .... CAE/MIS
Computer-Assisted Fault Isolation Test .... CAFIT
Computer-Assisted Force Management System [*Air Force*] (PDAA) .... CAFMS
Computer-Assisted Image .... CAI
Computer-Assisted Indexing and Categorizing [*or Classification*] .... CAIC
Computer-Assisted Industrial Simulation [*Army*] .... CAISIM
Computer-Assisted Information Retrieval Service [*Mississippi State University*] (OLDSS) .... CAIRS
Computer-Assisted Instruction Center .... CAIC
Computer-Assisted Instruction Project [*Army-Signal Center and School*] [*Fort Monmouth, NJ*] .... CAI
Computer-Assisted Instruction Study Management System (MCD) .... CAISMS
Computer-Assisted Instruction with Voice Response (MHDI) .... CAIVR
Computer-Assisted Interactive Resources Scheduling System .... CAIRS
Computer-Assisted Interactive Video .... CAIV
Computer-Assisted Interrogation (IAA) .... CAINT
Computer-Assisted Interviewing (GFGA) .... CAI
Computer-Assisted Introduction System (SSD) .... CAIS
Computer-Assisted Job Evaluation [*Human resources*] (WYGK) .... CAJE
Computer-Assisted Language Analysis System (PDAA) .... CALAS
Computer-Assisted Language Learning (ADA) .... CALL
Computer-Assisted Learning Network .... CALN
Computer-Assisted Legal Research (DLA) .... CALR
Computer-Assisted Legislative Liaison; On-Line Political Evaluation .... CALLIOPE
Computer-Assisted Library Mechanization .... CALM
Computer-Assisted Logic Design (PDAA) .... CALD
Computer-Assisted Logistics Simulation [*Navy*] .... CALOGSIM
Computer-Assisted Logistics Simulation [*Navy*] (MCD) .... CALS
Computer-Assisted Mailing (IAA) .... CAM
Computer-Assisted Maintenance .... CAM
Computer-Assisted Maintenance Planning and Control System .... CAMCOS
Computer-Assisted Maintenance Simulation [*Army*] .... CAMSIM
Computer-Assisted Makeup [*Graphic arts*] .... CAM
Computer-Assisted Makeup and Imaging Systems .... CAMIS
Computer-Assisted/Managed Instructional Language (CSR) .... CAMIL
Computer-Assisted Management for Emergency Operations [*Database*] .... CAMEO
Computer-Assisted Management of Learning (PDAA) .... CAMOL
Computer-Assisted Management of Portfolios .... CAMP
Computer-Assisted Manpower Analysis System (MCD) .... CAMAS
Computer-Assisted Manufacturing (PCM) .... CAM
Computer-Assisted Map Maneuver Simulation (MCD) .... CAMMS
Computer-Assisted Map Maneuver System [*Military*] (INF) .... CAMMS
Computer-Assisted Mapping and Records Activities System (IEEE) .... CAMRAS
Computer-Assisted Match Program [*Military*] .... CAMP
Computer-Assisted Mathematics Program [*Scott, Foresman, 1968-1969*] [*Textbook series*] (BUR) .... CAMP
Computer-Assisted Menu Planning .... CAMP
Computer-Assisted Message Preparation Relay and Distribution (PDAA) .... CAMPRAD
Computer-Assisted Message Processing System (MCD) .... CAMPS
Computer-Assisted Messaging Services [*Electronic mail*] [*Computer science*] .... CAMS
Computer-Assisted Metabolic Prediction [*Biochemistry*] .... CAMP
Computer-Assisted Method Assembly [*Analytical method writing*] .... CAMA
Computer-Assisted Micrographic Retrieval (PDAA) .... CAMR
Computer-Assisted Mission Planner System (MCD) .... CAMPS
Computer-Assisted Molecular Design .... CAMD
Computer-Assisted Molecular Modeling [*Chemistry*] .... CAMM
Computer-Assisted Movie Production (IEEE) .... CAMP
Computer-Assisted Network Scheduling System (IEEE) .... CANS
Computer-Assisted Order Routing and Execution System [*Tokyo Stock Exchange*] [*Japan*] (ODBW) .... CORES
Computer-Assisted Paperless Automated Support System [*USPS*] (AAGC) .... COMPASS
Computer-Assisted Pathology Encoding and Reporting System [*Medicine*] (DHSM) .... CAPER
Computer-Assisted Pericardiac Surgery [*Cardiology*] (DMAA) .... CASPER
Computer-Assisted Personal Interviewing (GFGA) .... CAPI
Computer-Assisted Photo-Interpretation Research (MCD) .... CAPIR
Computer-Assisted Picking System (WDMC) .... CAPS
Computer-Assisted Placement Service [*British*] .... CAPS
Computer-Assisted Policy Evaluation (MCD) .... CAPE
Computer-Assisted Post Mortem Identification (RDA) .... CAPMI
Computer-Assisted Power System Engineering (MCD) .... CAPSE
Computer-Assisted Pricing Proposal System (MCD) .... CAPPS
Computer-Assisted Printing .... CAP
Computer-Assisted Prisoner Transportation Index Service [*National Sheriffs' Association*] .... CAPTIS
Computer-Assisted Problem Solving (IEEE) .... CAPS
Computer-Assisted Product Search [*Information service or system*] (IID) .... CAPS
Computer-Assisted Program Evaluation Review-Technique Simulation [*Army*] .... CAPERTSIM
Computer-Assisted Prosthesis Selection [*Orthopedic surgery*] .... CAPS
Computer-Assisted Psychiatric Evaluation and Review System [*Medicine*] (DMAA) .... CAPERS
Computer-Assisted Psychosocial Evaluation .... CAPE
Computer-Assisted Radiotherapy [*Medicine*] (DMAA) .... CART
Computer-Assisted Records Retrieval (ADA) .... CARR
Computer-Assisted Reference Center [*Information service or system*] (IID) .... CARC
Computer-Assisted Reference Service [*Indiana University Libraries*] (OLDSS) .... CARS
Computer-Assisted Reliability and Maintainability Simulation [*Game*] .... CARMSIM
Computer-Assisted Repair Simulation [*Game*] .... CARESIM
Computer-Assisted Reporting [*Journalism*] (WDMC) .... CAR
Computer-Assisted Research (BUR) .... CAR
Computer-Assisted Research On-Line [*Information service or system*] (IID) .... CAROL
Computer-Assisted Research Services [*Brigham Young University*] [*Information service or system*] (IID) .... CARS
Computer-Assisted Retrieval .... CAR
Computer-Assisted Route Development (IAA) .... CARD
Computer-Assisted Scanning Techniques .... CAST
Computer-Assisted Search (CAAL) .... CAS
Computer-Assisted Search Planning (MCD) .... CASP
Computer-Assisted Self Assessment [*Medicine*] (DMAA) .... CASA
Computer-Assisted Sensory Examination .... CASE
Computer-Assisted Simulation of Supply and Related Systems .... CASSARS
Computer-Assisted Study Skills Improvement Program (EDAC) .... CASSIP
Computer-Assisted Surveillance Subsystem (MCD) .... COMPASS
Computer-Assisted System for Theater Level Engineering [*Army*] (AABC) .... CASTLE
Computer-Assisted System Operation (PDAA) .... CASO
Computer-Assisted Tactical Intelligence System (MCD) .... CATIS
Computer-Assisted Teaching and Learning System (PDAA) .... CATALYST
Computer-Assisted Technique for Numerical Indexing Purposes .... CATNIP
Computer-Assisted Telephone Inquiry .... CATI
Computer-Assisted Telephone Interviewing .... CATI
Computer-Assisted Terrain Mobility Analysis Techniques (MCD) .... CATMAT
Computer-Assisted Test Assembly [*Microcomputer program*] .... CATA
Computer-Assisted Test Construction (EDAC) .... CATC
Computer-Assisted Test Shop .... CATS
Computer-Assisted Testing (BUR) .... CAT
Computer-Assisted Three-Dimensional Interactive Application (ACRL) .... CATIA
Computer-Assisted Tomography .... CAT
Computer-Assisted Tomography Scanner [*Radiology*] (DAVI) .... CATSCAN
Computer-Assisted Total Value Assessment [*Army*] (MCD) .... CATVA
Computer-Assisted Trading System [*American Meat Exchange, Inc.*] [*Information service or system*] .... CATS
Computer-Assisted Training .... CAT
Computer-Assisted Training (IEEE) .... COMAT
Computer-Assisted Training System [*IRS*] .... CATS

Computer-Assisted Unit Data Acquisition/Reduction (PDAA) .... CAUDAR
Computer-Assisted Utility System Evaluation (MCD) .... CAUSE
Computer-Assisted War [*Slang*] (DNAB) .... CAW
Computer-Assisted Yeast Identification System [*AFRC Institute of Food Research*] [*Information service or system*] (IID) .... COMPASS
Computer-Associated [*or -Assisted*] **Device** .... CAD
Computer-Associated Diagnostic and Evaluation Tests (CAAL) .... CADET
Computer-Associated [*or Assisted*] **Self-Assessment** [*British*] .... CASA
Computer-Augmented Block System (MHDB) .... CABS
Computer-Augmented Design and Manufacturing [*Trademark of Cadam, Inc.*] [*Aviation*] .... CADAM
Computer-Augmented Loft Lines [*Graphic arts*] (MCD) .... CALL
Computer-Augmented Oscilloscope System (PDAA) .... CAOS
Computer-Automated Frequency Control (MHDB) .... CAFC
Computer-Automated Laboratory System .... CALS
Computer-Automated Measurement and Control (MSA) .... CAMAC
Computer-Automated Real-Time Betting Information Network (IEEE).... CARBINE
Computer-Automated Social Simulation .... CASS
Computer-Automated Speech Perception System (PDAA) .... CASPERS
Computer-Automated Structure Evaluator [*Database*] .... CASE
Computer-Automated Support Equipment .... CASE
Computer-Automated Test System [*AT & T*] .... CATS
Computer-Automated Transit Systems .... CATS
Computer-Automated Ultrasonic Inspecting Systems (MCD) .... CAUIS
Computer-Automated Ultrasonic System (MCD) .... CAUS
Computer-Based Accounting .... CBA
Computer-Based Analytical Chemistry [*Conference*] [*Munich, 1982*] .... COBAC
Computer-Based Automation .... CBA
Computer-Based Behavioral Studies (MCD) .... CBBS
Computer-Based Bibliographic Search Services .... CBBS
Computer-Based Bibliographic Search Services [*Washington State University Libraries*] (OLDSS) .... COBBS
Computer-Based Case Tracing [*Medicine*] .... COMTRAC
Computer-Based Conferencing (PDAA) .... CBC
Computer-Based Consultant (MCD) .... CBC
Computer-Based Education [*Project*] .... C-BE
Computer-Based Education and Training .... CBET
Computer-Based Education Research Laboratory [*University of Illinois*] [*Research center*] .... CERL
Computer-Based Electronic Mail (MCD) .... CBEM
Computer-Based Estimating Technique for Contractors .... COBESTCO
Computer-Based Examination .... CBX
Computer-Based Financial Management System [*Harper & Shuman, Inc.*] [*Cambridge, MA*] [*Information service or system*] (IID) .... CFMS
Computer-Based Information Center [*Free Library of Philadelphia*] (OLDSS) .... CBIC
Computer-Based Information Services [*Information service or system*] (IID).... CIS
Computer-Based Instruction [*Education*] .... CBI
Computer-Based Instruction System (IEEE) .... CBIS
Computer-Based Instruction System (IEEE) .... COBIS
Computer-Based Laboratory for Automated School Systems [*System Development Corp. project*] .... CLASS
Computer-Based Learning .... CBL
Computer-Based Loans System (MHDI) .... COBLOS
Computer-Based Maintenance Aid Presentation System (MCD) .... CMAS
Computer-Based Management Information System (MHDB) .... CBMIS
Computer-Based Management System (IAA) .... CBMS
Computer-Based Medical System .... CBMS
Computer-Based Message System [*Electronic mail*] .... CBMS
Computer-Based Operations Management System (MHDI) .... COMS
Computer-Based Optimization Routines and Techniques for Effective X (DIT) .... CORTEX
Computer-Based Patient Record Institute [*Medicine*] .... CPRI
Computer-Based Recruit Assignment (MCD) .... COBRA
Computer-Based Reference (CDE) .... CBR
Computer-Based Reference Assistance [*University of Northern Colorado*] (OLDSS) .... COBRA
Computer-Based Reference Service [*Information service or system*] .... CBRS
Computer-Based Resource Units [*Education*] .... CBRU
Computer-Based Terminal .... CBT
Computer-Based Training .... CBT
Computer-Based Training System (MCD) .... CBTS
Computer-Calculated (DAVI) CC
Computer-Chemistry-System [*Yokogawa Hewlett Packard Ltd.*] [*Japan*] .... CCS
Computer-Compatible Tape .... CCT
Computer-Compatible Terminal (MCD) .... CCT
Computer-Controlled Action Entry Panel (DNAB) .... CCAEP
Computer-Controlled Area Sterilization Multisensor System .... CASMS
Computer-Controlled Automated Cargo Handling Envelope .... CACHE
Computer-Controlled Automatic Test Equipment .... CATE
Computer-Controlled Catalytic Converter [*Automotive engineering*] C-4
Computer-Controlled Catalytic Converter [*Automotive engineering*] CCCC
Computer-Controlled Coil Ignition [*Automotive engineering*] .... C^3I
Computer-Controlled Coil Ignition [*Automotive engineering*] CCCI
Computer-Controlled Dampers [*Automotive suspension feature*] .... CD
Computer-Controlled Display .... CCD
Computer-Controlled Information Readout .... CCIR
Computer-Controlled Interconnect System (MCD) .... CCIS
Computer-Controlled Launch Set [*NASA*] (KSC) .... CCLS
Computer-Controlled Machine Tool (MHDB) .... CCMT
Computer-Controlled Microfilm Search System (MCD) .... CCMSS
Computer-Controlled Monitor [*Philips Consumer Electronics Co.*] (PCM) .... CCM
Computer-Controlled Multiplexer (MCD) .... CCM
Computer-Controlled Polisher [*Instrumentation*] .... CCP
Computer-Controlled Radiation Therapy [*Medicine*] (DMAA) .... CCRT
Computer-Controlled Receiving System (DNAB) .... CCRS
Computer-Controlled Scanning Electron Microscope .... CCSEM
Computer-Controlled Suspension [*Volvo*] [*Automotive engineering*] .... CCS
Computer-Controlled Teletext .... CCT
Computer-Controlled Test Management System [*Environmental science*].... CTMS
Computer-Controlled Vehicle [*Public transit systems*] CCV
Computer-Controlled Vehicle System (IAA) .... CVS
Computer-Controlled X-Ray Diffractometer .... CCXD
Computer-Developed Instruction .... CDI
Computer-Directed Communication .... CODIC
Computer-Directed Drawing .... CDD
Computer-Directed Drawing Instrument .... CDDI
Computer-Directed Instrument .... CDI
Computer-Directed Training Lesson Building System .... CDTLBS
Computer-Directed Training System .... CDTS
Computer-Driven Simulation Environment [*FAA*] .... CDSE
Computer-Driven Tactical System (MCD) .... CDTS
Computer-Enhanced Instruction .... CEI
Computer-Enhanced Radio Emission Surveillance [*British*] .... CERES
Computer-Extended Instruction (IEEE) .... CEI
Computer-Generate Volume Hologram (PDAA) .... CGVH
Computer-Generated Acquisition Documents System (AAGC) .... CGADS
Computer-Generated Hologram .... CGH
Computer-Generated Hologram .... CGH
Computer-Generated Holographic Scanner [*Instrumentation*] .... CGHS
Computer-Generated Image Visual System (MCD) .... CGIVS
Computer-Generated Imagery .... CGI
Computer-Generated Purchase Request .... CGPR
Computer-Generated/Synthesized Imagery (MCD) .... CGSI
Computer-Generated Volume Hologram .... CGVH
Computer-Graphics Aided Three-Dimensional Interactive Application System [*IBM Corp.*] .... CATIA
Computer-Graphics Language for Your Design Equations (PDAA) .... CLYDE
Computer-Graphics-Augmented Design and Manufacturing (MCD) .... CADAM
Computer-Graphics-Augmented Design and Manufacturing (IAA) .... CODEM
Computer-Guided Instruction (IAA) .... CGI
Computer-Guided Teaching (EDAC) .... CGT
Computer-Harmonized, Application-Tailored (MCD) .... CHAT
Computer-Human Interaction (BUR) .... CHI
Computer-Human Interface .... CHI
Computer-Informationsdienst Graz [*Graz Computer-Information Service*] [*Austria*] (IID) .... CIG
Computer-Integrated Design .... CID
Computer-Integrated Design - Computer-Integrated Manufacturing (ADA) .... CIDCIM
Computer-Integrated Design - Manufacturing and Automation Center .... CID-MAC
Computer-Integrated Draughting [*Terminal Display Systems Ltd.*] [*Software package*] (NCC) .... CID
Computer-Integrated Environment (IAA) .... CIE
Computer-Integrated Factory .... CIF
Computer-Integrated Instruction (NVT) CII
Computer-Integrated Manufacturing System .... CIMS
Computer-Integrated Processing (ECON) .... CIP
Computer-Integrated Research .... CIR
Computer-Integrated Telephony [*Computer science*] .... CIT
Computer-Integrated Test Equipment .... CITE
Computerised AIDS [*Acquired Immune Deficiency Syndrome*] **Network** [*Medicine Australia*] .... CAIN
Computerised Information Retrieval in Schools [*Project*] (AIE) .... CIRIS
Computerised Instrumented Residential Audit [*Energy auditing*] .... CIRA
Computerised Legal Information Retrieval System [*CLIRS Ltd.*] [*Information service or system*] (IID) .... CLIRS
Computerised Personnel Information System [*British*] .... CPIS
Computerised Retrieval Information Service on Precision Engineering [*Cranfield Institute of Technology*] [*A database*] [*British*] (NITA) .... CRISPE
Computerization and Mechanization of Local Office Tasks (MHDB) .... CAMELOT
Computerization of Army Movement Schedules (CINC) .... COAMS
Computerization of PAYE [*Pay as You Earn*] **Taxation** [*Inland Revenue*] [*British*] .... COP
Computerization of World Facts [*Stanford Research Institute*] [*Databank*] .... COMPACT
Computerize (ABBR) .... CMPUTRZ
Computerized (ABBR) .... CMPUTRZD
Computerized .... COMPTRZD
Computerized Adaptive Screening Test (MCD) .... CAST
Computerized Administration of Patent Documents Reclassified According to the IPC [*International Patent Classification*] [*INPADOC*] [*Information service or system*] (ADA) .... CAPRI
Computerized Advance Personnel Requirements Information [*or Inventory*] [*Navy*] .... CAPRI
Computerized Aerospace Ground Equipment (MCD) .... CAGE
Computerized Agency Processing System (IAA) .... CAPS
Computerized Agricultural Research Information System (NITA) .... CARIS
Computerized AIDS [*Acquired Immune Deficiency Syndrome*] **Information Network** [*Los Angeles Gay and Lesbian Community Services Center*] [*Database*] .... CAIN
Computerized Aircraft Maintenance Program .... CAMP
Computerized Aircraft Performance System (MCD) .... CAPS
Computerized Air-Launched Missile Management System (MCD) .... CALMMS
Computerized Alert Monitor (LAIN) .... CAM
Computerized Algorithmic Satellite Scheduler [*NASA*] .... CASS
Computerized Analysis for Programming Investments (MHDI) .... CAPRI
Computerized Anatomical Man [*NASA*] .... CAM

Computerized Annotated Bibliography System [*Alberta University*] [*Canada*] .... CABS

Computerized Applicant Search, Evaluation, and Selection (SAA) .... CASES

Computerized Application and Reference System .... CARS

Computerized Area Pricing [*Telecommunications*] (TEL) .... CAPRI

Computerized Arrythmia Monitoring System [*Medicine*] (CPH) .... CAMS

Computerized Assignment of Personnel [*Military*] .... CAP

Computerized Attack/Defense System [*Title of a science fiction novel by John Sievert*] .... CADS

Computerized Audio Report Information and Status (IAA) .... CARIS

Computerized Audit and Record Evaluation System [*Medical records*] (DHSM) .... CARE

Computerized, Automated, Bus Spacing and Dispatching System .... CABSADS

Computerized Automated Psychophysiological Device .... CAP

Computerized Automatic Inertial Test Set (MCD) .... CAITS

Computerized Automatic Rating Technique (DEN) .... CART

Computerized Automatic Systems Tester (MCD) .... CAST

Computerized Automation and Robotics Information Center [*Society of Manufacturing Engineers*] [*Information service or system*] (IID) .... CARIC

Computerized Automotive Maintenance System [*Buick's factory to dealership communication system*] .... CAMS

Computerized Automotive Replacement Scheduling [*Bell System*] .... CARS

Computerized Automotive Reporting Service (BUR) .... CARS

Computerized Axial Tomography [*Also, CAAT, CT*] [*Usually used in combination, as CATscan*] [*Roentgenography*] .... CAT

Computerized Axial Tomography Scanner [*Roentgenography*] .... CATscan

Computerized Battle Simulation .... COMBAT-SIM

Computerized Bibliographic Retrieval [*Hope College*] (OLDSS) .... CBR

Computerized Biology Data and Program Bank at the University of Notre Dame [*Information service or system Defunct*] (IID) .... BIOBUND

Computerized Biomechanical Man-Model [*Air Force*] .... COMBIMAN

Computerized Boolean Reliability Analysis [*Boeing*] .... COBRA

Computerized [*or Computer-Controlled*] Branch Exchange [*Telecommunications*] .... CBX

Computerized Bulletin Board .... CBB

Computerized Cable Upkeep Administrative Program [*Bell System*] .... CCUAP

Computerized Clinical Information System [*Micromedex, Inc.*] [*Database*] .... CCIS

Computerized Conferencing and Communications Center [*New Jersey Institute of Technology*] [*Research center*] (RCD) CCCC

Computerized Criminal History [*FBI*] .... CCH

Computerized Deployment Execution System .... CODES

Computerized Design from Engineering Models (PDAA) .... CODEM

Computerized Dispersive Spectroscopy .... CDS

Computerized Distribution and Control of Microfilm [*American Motors Corp.*] .... CODICOM

Computerized Documentation Service/Integrated Set of Information Systems [*UNESCO*] (IID) .... CDS/ISIS

Computerized Documentation System [*UNESCO*] (IID) .... CDS

Computerized Drawing Electrical Information (NG) .... CODEIN

Computerized Electro Neuro-Ophthalmograph .... CENOG

Computerized Emission Tomogram (WGA) .... CET

Computerized Engineering Index [*Engineering Index, Inc.*] [*New York, NY Bibliographic database*] .... COMPENDEX

Computerized Environmental Legislative Data System [*Army*] .... CELDS

Computerized Equipment Pricing System [*Council of Petroleum Accountants Societies*] [*Information service or system*] (CRD) .... CEPS

Computerized Evaluation of the Logistics System [*Army*] .... COMPELS

Computerized Exercise Machine .... CEM

Computerized Exploration and Technical Underwater Surveyor (PDAA) .... CETUS

Computerized Facial Recognition .... CFR

Computerized Facilities Design (PDAA) .... COFAD

Computerized Fleet Analysis, Inc. .... CFA

Computerized Flight Test System (PDAA) .... CFTS

Computerized Forwarding System [*US Postal Service*] .... CFS

Computerized Freight Remittance System [*Pronounced "coffers"*] .... COFRS

Computerized Fuel Gauge (DWSG) .... CFG

Computerized Gas Chromatography .... CGC

Computerized Head-End Access Information Network (HGAA) .... CHAIN

Computerized Heuristic Occupational Information and Career Exploration System (EDAC) .... CHOICES

Computerized Hierarchy and Relationship Table .... CHART

Computerized Homes Underwriting Management Systems [*Department of Housing and Urban Development*] (GFGA) .... CHUMS

Computerized Hospital Information System (MCD) .... CHICS

Computerized Hospital Information System .... CHIS

Computerized Industrial Environmental Legislation [*UNEP*] [*United Nations*] (DUND) .... CIEL

Computerized Industrial Tomography [*Nondestructive testing method*] .... CIT

Computerized Information Research (IAA) .... CIR

Computerized Information Retrieval and Contract Entry [*Computer science*] .... CIRCE

Computerized Information Retrieval and Current Awareness (MHDI) .... CIRCA

Computerized Information Retrieval Service [*University of Houston Libraries*] (OLDSS) .... CIRES

Computerized Information Retrieval Service [*California State University, Fullerton*] (OLDSS) .... CIRS

Computerized Information Service [*Public Library of Columbus and Franklin County*] (OLDSS) .... CIS

Computerized Information System of Organic Chemistry [*Developed in China*] [*Computer science*] .... CISOC

Computerized Integrated and Automated Manufacturing (IAA) .... CIAM

Computerized Interactive Graphics (MCD) .... CIG

Computerized Issue of Results and Certificates for Entries (PDAA) .... CIRCE

Computerized Laboratory Notebook .... CLN

Computerized Laser-Assisted Sight System [*Military*] (INF) .... CLASS

Computerized Legal Information Retrieval System (ADA) .... CLIRS

Computerized Lesson-Authoring System (EDAC) .... CLAS

Computerized Librarian-Assisted Search Service [*Nicholls State University*] (OLDSS) .... CLASS

Computerized Library Acquisitions System [*Lukac Data Systems*] [*Lewis and Clark College Discontinued*] [*Information service or system*] (IID) .... CLAS

Computerized Link Analysis System .... CLANS

Computerized Literature Access Search Service [*Colorado State University Libraries*] [*Information service or system*] .... CLASS

Computerized Literature Searching Service .... CLSS

Computerized Litigation Support (HGAA) .... CLS

Computerized Loan Origination [*for mortgages*] .... CLO

Computerized Logic-Oriented Design System [*Air Force*] .... CLODS

Computerized Lubrication Control [*Sun Oil Co.*] CLC

Computerized Maintenance and Administration Support III [*Telecommunications*] (TEL) .... COMASIII

Computerized Maintenance Management System .... CMMS

Computerized Management Network [*For Agricultural Cooperative Extension Service Education*] [*Virginia Polytechnic Institute Database*] .... CMN

Computerized Manufacturing System (MCD) .... CMS

Computerized Materials Retrieval System [*Computer science*] (ECII) .... CMRS

Computerized Measurements for Safeguards and Accountability (PDAA) .... COMSAC

Computerized Medical Imaging Society (EA) .... CMIS

Computerized Medical Information Support System [*Veterans Administration*] .... COMISS

Computerized Microscopic Imaging System [*Genetics*] .... CMIS

Computerized Modular Monitoring (OA) .... CMM

Computerized Moment Stability System [*Navy*] .... CMSS

Computerized Movement Planning and Status System [*Military*] (AABC) .... COMPASS

Computerized Muscle Exerciser and Trainer [*Bodylog, Inc.*] .... COMET

Computerized National Range Documentation .... CONRAD

Computerized Notation System (MEDA) .... CNS

Computerized Numerical Control [*Computer science*] .... CNC

Computerized Office Layout (PDAA) .... COL

Computerized Officer Planning System [*Navy*] (NVT) .... COPS

Computerized Online System for the Management of Spares [*Army*] .... COSMOS

Computerized Online Testing .... COLT

Computerized Operating Room Information System .... CORIS

Computerized Operational Audit Routine .... COPAR

Computerized Optimization of Elastic Booster Autopilot .... COEBRA

Computerized Optimization Procedure for Stabilators (PDAA) .... COPS

Computerized Outside Plant Records [*Telecommunications*] (TEL) .... COPR

Computerized Parcel Shipping System .... CPSS

Computerized Patient Record .... CPR

Computerized Performance and Analysis Response Evaluator (IEEE) .... COMPARE

Computerized Performance Monitoring System (DNAB) .... CPMS

Computerized Performance Rating [*of a horse*] .... CPR

Computerized Principles of Structures (ADA) .... COMPOST

Computerized Private Branch Exchange [*Telecommunications*] .... CPBX

Computerized Production Operating System Extension (NITA) .... COMPOSE

Computerized Production Process Planning (MCD) .... CPPP

Computerized Radiology Society [*Later, CMIS*] (EA) .... CRS

Computerized Reader Enquiry Service System (IEEE) .... CRESS

Computerized Real Estate Assessment and Land Records (MCD) .... CREALR

Computerized Rearrangements of Special Subjects [*or Subject Specialties*] .... CROSS

Computerized Recall Identification System [*Automobile industry*] .... CRIS

Computerized Reference and Bibliographic Services [*University of Maryland at Baltimore*] (OLDSS) .... CRABS

Computerized Reference Service [*William Paterson College of New Jersey*] (OLDSS) .... CRS

Computerized Register of Voice Research [*No longer maintained*] [*Southern Illinois University at Carbondale*] [*Information service or system*] (IID) .... CRVR

Computerized Registry Information System [*UNIDO*] [*United Nations*] (DUND) .... CORIS

Computerized Relationship Layout Planning .... CORELAP

Computerized Relative Allocation of Facilities Technique [*IBM Corp.*] .... CRAFT

Computerized Reliability Analysis Method .... CRAM

Computerized Reliability Organization System .... CROS

Computerized Research Information Service [*Colorado School of Mines*] (OLDSS) .... CRIS

Computerized Reservation Systems (BTTJ) .... CRS

Computerized Resources Information Bank [*United States Geological Survey*] [*Later, MRDS*] (IID) .... CRIB

Computerized Retrieval Service .... CRS

Computerized Safety and Facility Design (PDAA) .... COSFAD

Computerized Scientific Management Planning System (AAG) .... CSMPS

Computerized Specifications Management System (DNAB) .... CSMS

Computerized Spot Television Evaluation and Processing [*Advertising*] .... COM-STEP

Computerized Static Automatic Restoring Equipment for Power System (PDAA) .... COMPSAP

Computerized Status Accounting System (MCD) .... CSAS

Computerized Stress Inventory [*Personality development test*] [*Psychology*] .... CSI

Computerized Telephone Number File [*FBI listing, begun in 1970, of political activists' telephone numbers*] [*Obsolete*] .... CTNF

Computerized Test of Spelling Errors (EDAC) .... CTSE

Computerized Tomoangiography [*Radiology*] (DAVI) .... CTA

Computerized Tomography (ECON) .... CT

Computerized Tomography [*Also, CATSCAN*] [*Medical test*] (PAZ) .... CT scan

Computerized Tomography Society [*Later, Computerized Radiology Society - CRS*] (EA) .... CTS

Computerized Topographic Scanner [*Medicine*] .... CTS
Computerized Training System [*Army Signal Center and School*] [*Fort Monmouth, NJ*] (RDA) .... CTS
Computerized Training Systems Directorate [*Army Training Support Activity*] [*Fort Gordon, GA*] .... CTSD
Computerized Transaxial Tomography .... CTAT
Computerized Travel Aid [*Mobility device for the blind*] .... CTA
Computerized Ultrasonic Scan System (MCD) .... CUSS
Computerized Understanding of Morphology-Language Acquisition Under Development in Education (PDAA) .... CUM LAUDE
Computerized Uniterm Search System (NITA) .... CUSS
Computerized Vocational Information System [*Guidance program*] .... CVIS
Computerizing (ABBR) .... CMPUTRZG
Computerizing Medical Examination [*IBM Corp.*] .... CME
Computerland Corp. (MHDW) .... CLD
Computer-Linked Information for Container Shipping (IAA) .... CLIS
Computer-Managed Instruction .... CMI
Computer-Managed Laboratory .... CML
Computer-Managed Learning (ADA) .... CML
Computer-Managed Parts Manufacture .... CMPM
Computer-Managed Process Planning (MCD) .... CMPP
Computer-Managed Training (MHDI) .... CMT
Computer-Management Distributed Information Software (MHDI) .... CMDIS
Computer-Marked Assignment [*Education*] [*British*] .... CMA
Computer-Matching Privacy and Protection Act .... CMPPA
Computer-Mediated Conferencing (IT) .... CMC
Computer-Mediated Interaction (PDAA) .... CMI
Computer-Mediated Teleconferencing (MHDB) .... CMT
Computer-Modelling System [*Computer Modelling International Ltd.*] [*Software package*] (NCC) .... CMS
Computer-Operated [*or -Oriented*] **Electronic Display** .... COED
Computer-Operated Machine Evaluation Technique [*Air Force*] (MCD) .... COMET
Computer-Operated Management Evaluation Technique [*AEC-Army*] .... COMET
Computer-Operated Marketing, Mailing and News Distribution System [*Computer science*] (MHDB) .... COMMANDS
Computer-Operated Micro-Program Automatic Commissioning Technique (PDAA) .... COMPACT
Computer-Operated Multifunction Electronic Test System (MCD) .... COMETS
Computer-Operated Transmission Measuring Set (PDAA) .... COTMS
Computer-Operated Universal Test .... COUNT
Computer-Operated Universal Test System (IAA) .... COUTS
Computer-Oriented Bearing Response Analysis [*Computer science*] (PDAA) .... COBRA
Computer-Oriented Design of Electronic Devices .... CODED
Computer-Oriented Language [*Programming language*] [*Computer science*] .... COL
Computer-Oriented Language Translator (IEEE) .... COLT
Computer-Oriented Managed Inventory Control System (MHDB) .... COMICS
Computer-Oriented Management Information System (IAA) .... CMIS
Computer-Oriented Manufacturing Production and Control System (IAA) .... COMPACS
Computer-Oriented Mechanical Design (MCD) .... COMMEND
Computer-Oriented Metering Planning and Advisory System [*Aviation*] (DA) .... COMPAS
Computer-Oriented Method of Program Analysis, Review, and Evaluation [*Computer science*] (MHDB) .... COMPARE
Computer-Oriented Microwaves Practices (PDAA) .... COMP
Computer-Oriented Modal Control and Appraisal System .... COMCAS
Computer-Oriented Notation Concerning Infrared Spectral Evaluation [*Programming language*] [*Analytical chemistry*] .... CONCISE
Computer-Oriented Partial Sum (NVT) .... COPS
Computer-Oriented Photo-Unit [*Linofilm*] (DGA) .... COPHU
Computer-Oriented Programmed Instruction (IEEE) .... COPI
Computer-Oriented Purchasing and Engineering System (MHDB) .... COPES
Computer-Oriented Reference System for Automatic Information Retrieval [*Forsvarets Forskningsamsalt*] [*Sweden*] .... CORSAIR
Computer-Oriented Reporting Efficiency (AFM) .... CORE
Computer-Oriented Retrieval of Auto Larcenists .... CORRAL
Computer-Oriented System for Management Order Synthesis [*IBM Corp.*] (BUR) .... COSMOS
Computer-Oriented System - Newly Organized Storage-to-Retrieval Apparatus (KSC) .... COSNOSTRA
Computer-Output-Typesetting (PDAA) .... COT
Computer-Planning and Aircraft-Weighing Scales .... CPAWS
Computer-Prescribed Instruction (IEEE) .... CPI
Computer-Produced Drawing (IAA) .... CPD
Computer-Programmed Automatic Checkout and Test System .... COMPACT
Computer-Readable Databases [*A publication*] .... CRD
Computer-Readable Databases: a Directory and Data Sourcebook [*A publication*] .... CRDB
Computer-Reinforced Design (PDAA) .... CORD
Computer-Related Equipment (IAA) .... CORE
Computer-Related Systems Validation [*Engineering*] .... CRSV
Computers [*JETDS nomenclature*] [*Military*] (CET) .... CP
Computers and Adult Basic Education [*Liverpool Institute of Higher Education*] [*British*] (AIE) .... CABE
Computers and Automation (BUR) .... CA
Computers and Automation Universal Mailing List (IEEE) .... CAUML
Computers and Communications .... C & C
Computers and Communications (WDMC) .... c&c
Computers and Communications .... COMPUNICATIONS
Computers and Computing Information Resources Directory [*A publication*] .... CCIRD
Computers and Law [*Australia A publication*] .... Comp & L
Computers and Law [*A publication*] (DLA) .... Comp & Law
Computers and Law [*A publication*] (DLA) .... Comput & Law
Computers and Medieval Data Processing [*Canada*] [*A publication*] (NITA) .... CAMDAP
Computers and Software Review Panel [*NASA*] (NASA) .... CSRP
Computers and Systems (IEEE) .... C & S
Computers and Systems (IAA) .... CAS
Computers and Systems (MCD) .... CS
Computers and the Humanities [*A publication*] (BRI) .... Compt & H
Computers at Oregon State University, North Carolina Educational Computing Service, Dartmouth College, and the Universities of Iowa and Texas at Austin [*An educational consortium*] .... CONDUIT
Computers, Electronics and Control Symposium (MHDI) .... CEC
Computers for Advanced Space Transportation System (MCD) .... CASTS
Computers for the Advancement of Medicine & Science [*Information service or system*] (IID) .... CAMS
[*The*] **Computers in Manufacturing Show** [*British*] (ITD) .... CIM
Computers in Mechanical Engineering [*American Society of Mechanical Engineers*] [*A publication*] (NITA) .... CIME
Computers in Nursing (MEDA) .... CIN
Computers in Teaching Initiative (AIE) .... CTI
Computers in Teaching Initiative Support Service (AIE) .... CTISS
Computers in the City Exhibition [*British*] (ITD) CIC
Computers in the Curriculum [*Education*] (AIE) CIC
Computers in Training as a Resource (AIE) .... CITAR
Computers, Information Processing, and Office Machines .... CIPOM
Computers Lawyers Association (EA) .... CLA
Computers, Learners, Users, Educators Association [*New Jersey*] (EDAC) .... CLUES
Computers Users' Committee [*United Nations Development Program*] .... CUC
Computer-Stored Ambulatory Record (MCD) .... COSTAR
Computer-Supported Cooperative Work [*Computer science*] .... CSCW
Computer-Supported Telecommunications Applications .... CSTA
Computer-to-Computer (NASA) .... C-to-C
Computer-to-Computer .... C-to-C
Computer-to-Computer Transfer Channel (ECII) .... CCTC
Computer-to-Plate [*Printing*] (DGA) .... CTP
ComputerTown, United States of America [*Defunct*] (EA) .... CTUSA
Computer-Using Educators of Kentucky (EDAC) .... CUE-KY
Computervision [*Commercial firm British*] CV
Computervision Corp. [*Associated Press*] (SAG) .... Cmptvsn
Computervision Corp. [*NYSE symbol*] (SPSG) .... CVN
Computervision Graphics Operating System (MHDI) .... CGOS
Computing .... CMPTG
Computing .... CMPTG
Computing (ABBR) .... CMPUG
Computing (ABBR) .... CMPUTG
Computing Across America [*From book title, "Computing Across America: The Bicycle Odyssey of a High-Tech Nomad" by Steven K. Roberts*] .... CAA
Computing and Communications Services Office [*Telecommunications*] .... CCSO
Computing and Data Processing Services [*University of Maine*] [*Research center*] (RCD) .... CAPS
Computing and Data Processing Society (HGAA) .... CDPS
Computing and Information Services [*McMaster University*] [*Canada*] (IRC) .... CIS
Computing & Information Systems [*East Carolina University*] [*Research center*] (RCD) .... CIS
Computing and Information Technology [*Princeton University*] [*Research center*] (RCD) .... CIT
Computing Assistance Program [*Taylor University*] [*Information service or system*] (IID) .... CAP
Computing Australia Recruiting Directory [*A publication*] .... CARD
Computing Center [*Emory University*] [*Research center*] (RCD) .... EUCC
Computing Center [*University of Rochester*] [*Research center*] (RCD) .... UCC
Computing Center [*University of Cincinnati*] [*Research center*] (RCD) .... UCCC
Computing Centre [*University of East Anglia*] [*British*] (IRUK) .... CPC
Computing Department, Loeb's MIS, Ottawa, Ontario [*Library symbol National Library of Canada*] (BIB) .... OOLM
Computing Devices of Canada, Ottawa, ON, Canada [*Library symbol Library of Congress*] (LCLS) .... CaOOCDC
Computing Devices of Canada, Ottawa, Ontario [*Library symbol National Library of Canada*] (NLC) .... OOCDC
Computing Index [*Computer analysis*] CI
Computing Information Center [*University of Washington*] [*Seattle*] [*Information service or system*] (IID) CIC
Computing Media .... CM
Computing Power Index [*Computer science*] (PDAA) .... CPI
Computing Research Laboratory [*New Mexico State University*] [*Research center*] (RCD) .... CRL
Computing Services Association [*British*] .... CSA
Computing Services Center [*Texas A & M University*] [*Research center*] (RCD) .... CSC
Computing Services Division [*Seton Hall University*] [*Research center*] (RCD) .... CSD
Computing Services Office [*Telecommunications*] .... CSO
Computing Support Services [*California Institute of Technology*] [*Research center*] (RCD) .... CSS
Computing System for Air Cargo (DA) .... COSAC
Computing Technology Industry Association [*Lombard, IL*] [*An association*] (CDE) .... CompTIA
Computone Corp. [*NASDAQ symbol*] (SAG) .... CMPT
Computone Corp. [*Associated Press*] (SAG) .... Computne
Computrac, Inc. [*Associated Press*] (SAG) .... Cmptrc
Computrac, Inc. [*AMEX symbol*] (SPSG) .... LLB
Computrex Centres [*Vancouver Stock Exchange symbol*] CXC
Computron Software [*NASDAQ symbol*] (TTSB) .... CTRN

Computron Software, Inc. [*Associated Press*] (SAG) .... Cmputrn
Computron Software, Inc. [*NASDAQ symbol*] (SAG) .... CTRN
Compuware Corp. [*Associated Press*] (SAG) .... Compuwr
Compuware Corp. [*NASDAQ symbol*] (SAG) .... CPWR
Comrade (ABBR) .... CMRD
COMRADE [*Computer-Aided Design Environment*] **Data Management System** .... CDMS
COMRADE [*Computer-Aided Design Environment*] **Data Storage Facility** .... CDSF
COMRADE [*Computer-Aided Design Environment*] **Permanent File Management System** .... CPFMS
Comradeship (ABBR) .... CMRDSP
Comrey Personality Scale .... CPS
COMSAT Capital 1 8.125%'MIPS' [*NYSE symbol*] (TTSB) .... CQPrA
Comsat Corp. [*Associated Press*] (SAG) .... Comsat
Comsat Corp. [*See also COMSAT*] [*NYSE symbol*] (SPSG) .... CQ
Comsat Corp. Capital [*Associated Press*] (SAG) .... CsatCap
COMSAT [*Communications Satellite Corp.*] **General Integrated System** (NITA) .... CGIS
COMSAT [*Communications Satellite Corp.*] **International Communications, Inc.** (TSSD) CICI
COMSAT [*Communications Satellite Corp.*] **Maritime Communications Satellite** (MCD) .... CMCS
COMSAT [*Communications Satellite Corp.*] **Nonreflecting** [*Solar cell*] .... CNR
COMSAT [*Communications Satellite Corp.*] **Video Enterprises** [*Washington, DC*] (TSSD) .... CVE
COMSAT [*Communications Satellite Corp.*], Washington, DC [*OCLC symbol*] (OCLC) .... CLD
COMSAT [*Communications Satellite Corp.*], Washington, DC [*OCLC symbol*] (OCLC) .... CMD
COMSEC [*Communications Security*] **Equipment Asset Reporting System** (MCD) .... CEARS
COMSEC [*Communications Security*] **Equipment Modification Application and Reporting System** [*Army*] (MCD) .... CEMARS
COMSEC [*Communications Security*] **Field Office of Record** [*Army*] (AABC) .... CFOR
COMSEC [*Communications Security*] **Logistic Support Center** [*Army*] (AABC) .... CLSC
COMSEC [*Communications Security*] **Logistic Support Unit** [*Army*] (AABC) .... CLSU
COMSEC [*Communications Security*] **Logistics Data Center** (AABC) .... CLDC
COMSEC [*Communications Security*] **Material Issuing Office** [*Military*] (NVT) .... CMIO
COMSEC [*Communications Security*] **Material Management Center** (MCD) .... CMMC
COMSEC [*Communications Security*] **Mode Control Device** [*Army*] (DWSG) .... CMCD
COMSEC [*Communications Security*] **Priorities Field Evaluation** (MCD) .... CPFE
COMSEC [*Communications Security*] **Regional Issuing Office** [*or Officer*] [*Army*] (AABC) .... CRIO
COMSEC [*Communications Security*] **Repair Center** [*Army*] (NG) .... CRC
COMSEC [*Communications Security*] **Research and Engineering Coordinating Group** [*Army*] (AABC) .... CREC
COMSEC [*Communications Security*] **Resources Program** [*Army*] (AABC) .... CRP
COMSEC [*Communications Security*] **Wargaming** [*Simulation*] (MCD) .... CSWG
Comshare Communications Interface (IAA) CCI
Comshare, Inc. [*Associated Press*] (SAG) .... Comshr
Comshare, Inc. [*NASDAQ symbol*] (NQ) .... CSRE
ComSouth Bankshares [*AMEX symbol*] (TTSB) .... CSB
Comsouth Bankshares, Inc. [*Associated Press*] (SAG) .... ComsthB
Comsouth Bankshares, Inc. [*AMEX symbol*] (SAG) .... CSB
Comstate Resources Ltd. [*Toronto Stock Exchange symbol*] .... CSR
Comstock Bank [*Associated Press*] (SAG) .... ComstBk
Comstock Bank [*NASDAQ symbol*] (SAG) .... LODE
Comstock Mealybug [*Plant pest*] .... CMB
Comstock on Executors [*A publication*] (DLA) .... Comp Ex
Comstock on Guardian and Ward [*A publication*] (DLA) .... Com G & W
Comstock Resources [*NASDAQ symbol*] (TTSB) .... CMRE
Comstock Resources [*Associated Press*] (SAG) .... ComstkRs
Comstock Resources [*NYSE symbol*] (SAG) .... CRK
Comstock Resources, Inc. [*NASDAQ symbol*] (NQ) .... CMRE
Comstock Resources, Inc. [*Associated Press*] (SAG) .... CmstRs
Comstock Township Library, Comstock, MI [*Library symbol Library of Congress*] (LCLS) .... MiCom
Comstock's Digest of the Law of Dower [*A publication*] (DLA) .... Com Dow
Comstock's Reports [*1-4 New York Court of Appeals*] [*A publication*] (DLA) .... Com
Comstock's Reports [*1-4 New York Court of Appeals*] [*A publication*] (DLA) .... Coms
Comstock's Reports [*1-4 New York Court of Appeals*] [*A publication*] (DLA) .... Comst
Comtec Cable Accessories Ltd. [*British*] (NITA) .... CCA
Com-Tech Communication Technologies, Inc. [*NASDAQ symbol*] (SAG) .... CMTK
Com-Tech Communication Technologies, Inc. [*Associated Press*] (SAG) .... ComTch
Com-Tech Communication Technologies, Inc. [*Associated Press*] (SAG) .... ComYch
Comtech Group International Ltd. [*Toronto Stock Exchange symbol*] .... CTG
Comtech Telecommns [*NASDAQ symbol*] (TTSB) .... CMIL
Comtech Telecommunications Corp. [*NASDAQ symbol*] (NQ) .... CMTL
Comtech Telecommunications Corp. [*Associated Press*] (SAG) .... Comtch
Comten Network Gateway [*NCR Corp.*] [*Computer science*] (NITA) .... CNG
Comterm, Inc. [*Toronto Stock Exchange symbol*] .... CMT
Comtrex Systems [*NASDAQ symbol*] (TTSB) .... COMX
Comtrex Systems Corp. [*Associated Press*] (SAG) .... Comtrx
Comtrex Systems Corp. [*NASDAQ symbol*] (NQ) .... COMX
Comunicacion, Intercambio, y Desarrollo Humano en America Latina .... CIDHAL
Comunidad Democratica Centroamericana [*Central American Democratic Community*] (EAIO) .... CDC
Comunidades Eclesiales de Base [*Spanish*] .... CEB
Comunity Care Plan [*Medicine*] .... CCP
Comunn na Clarsaich [*Clarsach Society*] (EAIO) CC
Comverse Technology [*NASDAQ symbol*] (TTSB) .... CMVT
Comverse Technology [*Associated Press*] (SAG) .... Comvers
Comverse Technology, Inc. [*NASDAQ symbol*] (NQ) .... CMVT
Comyn on Landlord and Tenant [*A publication*] (DLA) .... Com L & T
Comyn on the Law of Usury [*A publication*] (DLA) .... Com Us
Comyn's Digest of the Laws of England [*1762-1882*] [*A publication*] (ILCA) .... CD
Comyn's Digest of the Laws of England [*1762-1882*] [*A publication*] (DLA) .... Com Dig
Comyn's Digest of the Laws of England [*1762-1882*] [*A publication*] (DLA) .... Comyn's Dig
Comyn's English King's Bench Reports [*1695-1741*] [*A publication*] (DLA) .... Com
Comyn's English King's Bench Reports [*1695-1741*] [*A publication*] (DLA) .... Com Rep
Comyn's English King's Bench Reports [*1695-1741*] [*A publication*] (DLA) .... Comyn
Comyn's English King's Bench Reports [*1695-1741*] [*A publication*] (DLA) .... Comyns
Comyn's Law of Contracts [*A publication*] (DLA) .... Com Con
Con [*With*] [*Music*] (ROG) C
Con Anima [*With a Soulful Feeling*] [*Music*] (ROG) .... CON AN
Con Devotione [*With Devotion*] [*Music*] (ROG) .... CON DEVE
Con Dolore [*With Sadness*] [*Music*] (ROG) .... CON DOL
Con Espressione [*With Expression*] [*Music*] (ROG) .... C ESPR
Con Espressione [*With Expression*] [*Music*] .... CON ESP
Con Espressione [*With Expression*] [*Music*] .... CON ESPR
Con Fuoco [*With Force*] [*Music*] (ROG) .... CON FUO
Con Furia [*With Fury*] [*Music*] (ROG) .... CON FUR
Con Grazia [*With Grace*] [*Music*] (ROG) .... CON GRA
Con Gustoso [*With Taste*] [*Music*] (ROG) .... CON GUST
Con Moto [*With the Movement*] [*Music*] (ROG) .... CON MO
Con Ottava [*With the Octave*] [*Music*] (ROG) .... CON 8VA
Con Sordino [*With Mute*] [*Music*] .... CS
Con Tenerezza [*With Tenderness*] [*Music*] (ROG) .... CON TENA
CONAD [*Continental Air Defense Command*] **Operational Employment Concept** (AABC) .... COEC
CONAF [*Conceptual Design for the Army in the Field*] **Evaluation Model** .... CEM
ConAgra Cap L.C. 9% Pfd [*NYSE symbol*] (TTSB) .... CAGPrA
ConAgra Cap L.C.9.35% Pfd [*NYSE symbol*] (TTSB) .... CAGPrC
ConAgra Cap L.C.Adj Pfd'B' [*NYSE symbol*] (TTSB) .... CAGPrB
Conagra Capital [*NYSE symbol*] (SAG) .... CAG
ConAgra Capital [*Associated Press*] (SAG) .... CnCap
ConAgra, Inc. [*NYSE symbol*] (SPSG) .... CAG
ConAgra, Inc. [*Associated Press*] (SAG) .... ConAg
ConAgra, Inc. [*Associated Press*] (SAG) .... ConAgr
Conair AS [*Denmark ICAO designator*] (FAAC) .... OYC
Conair Aviation Ltd. [*Canada ICAO designator*] (FAAC) .... CRC
Conakry [*Guinea*] [*Airport symbol*] (OAG) .... CKY
Conakry/Gbessia [*Guinea*] [*ICAO location identifier*] (ICLI) .... GUCY
CONARC [*Continental Army Command*] **Alternate Headquarters Plan** [*Obsolete*] .... CONALT
CONARC [*Continental Army Command*] **Automated System Support Agency** [*Obsolete*] (AABC) .... CASSA
CONARC [*Continental Army Command*] **Class One Automated System** [*Later, BASOPS*] (MCD) .... COCOAS
CONARC [*Continental Army Command*] **Education Data System** [*Obsolete*] (AABC) .... CONEDS
CONARC [*Continental Army Command*] **Emergency Relocation Plan** [*Obsolete*] .... CONREP
CONARC [*Continental Army Command*] **Intelligence Center** [*Obsolete*] (AABC) .... CONTIC
CONARC [*Continental Army Command*] **Logistics Operations - Streamline** [*Obsolete*] .... CONLOS
CONARC [*Continental Army Command*] **Operating Program** [*Obsolete*] (AABC) .... CONOPPR
Conard [*Henry S.*] **Environmental Research Area** [*Grinnell College*] [*Research center*] (RCD) .... CERA
Conative Negative Variation (MAE) .... CNV
Concanavalin [*Biochemistry*] .... CON
Concanavalin A [*Biochemistry*] .... Con A
Concanavalin A (DMAA) .... Con A
Concanavalin A [*Biology*] (DOG) .... conA
Concanavilin A-Horse-Radish Peroxidas [*Medicine*] (DMAA) .... Con A-HRP
Concatenate (CDE) .... cat
Concave Cc
Concave (MSA) .... CNCV
Conceal (ABBR) .... CNCEL
Concealable (ABBR) .... CNCELB
Conceal-Control-Command-Instruction [*NATO*] CCCI
Concealed [*Ecology*] C
Concealed (ABBR) .... CNCELD
Concealed (MSA) .... CNCL
Concealed Figures Test (EDAC) .... CFT
Concealed Original Optical Locating System (PDAA) .... COOLS
Concealed Product Identification Number [*Automotive*] .... CPIN
Concealed Target Detection (MCD) .... CONTAD
Concealed Weapon Detector .... CWD
Concealed Weapons .... CW
Concealer (ABBR) .... CNCELR

Concealing (ABBR) .... CNCELG
Concealment (ABBR) .... CNCELT
Concealment Device [*Criminology*] (LAIN) .... CD
Concede (ABBR) .... CNCED
Conceded (ABBR) .... CNCEDD
Concededly (ABBR) .... CNCEDDY
Conceder (ABBR) .... CNCEDR
Conceding (ABBR) .... CNCEDG
Conceicao Do Araguaia [*Brazil*] [*Airport symbol*] (OAG) .... CDJ
Conceicao Do Araguaia [*Brazil ICAO location identifier*] (ICLI) .... SBAA
Conceit (ABBR) .... CNCET
Conceited (ABBR) .... CNCETD
Conceitedly (ABBR) .... CNCETDY
Conceiting (ABBR) .... CNCETG
Conceivability (ABBR) .... CNCEVBT
Conceivable (ABBR) .... CNCEVB
Conceivably (ABBR) .... CNCEVBY
Conceive (ABBR) .... CNCEV
Conceived (ABBR) .... CNCEVD
Conceiver (ABBR) .... CNCEVR
Conceiving (ABBR) .... CNCEVG
Concensys, Inc. [*Associated Press*] (SAG) .... Cocensys
Concentra Corp. [*Associated Press*] (SAG) .... Concntr
Concentra Corp. [*NASDAQ symbol*] (SAG) .... CTRA
Concentracion de Fuerzas Populares [*Concentration of Popular Forces*] [*Ecuador*] [*Political party*] (PPW) .... CFP
Concentrate (ABBR) .... CNCEN
Concentrate (ABBR) .... CNCNTRA
Concentrate [*or Concentration*] (AFM) .... CONC
Concentrate .... CONCNTRT
Concentrate Transfer System [*Nuclear energy*] (NRCH) .... CTS
Concentrated (ABBR) .... CNCED
Concentrated .... CONCD
Concentrated (DAVI) .... concentr
Concentrated .... CONCTD
Concentrated (BABM) .... Cond
Concentrated Area Review [*US Postal Service*] .... CAR
Concentrated Boric Acid Storage Tank [*Nuclear energy*] (NRCH) .... CBAST
Concentrated Complete Fertilizer [*Imperial Chemical Industries*] [*British*] .... CCF
Concentrated Employment Program [*Also known as CIEP*] [*Department of Labor*] .... CEP
Concentrated Impact Employment Program [*Also known as CEP*] [*Department of Labor*] .... CIEP
Concentrated Liquor Discharge (DICI) .... CLD
Concentrated Liquor Outlet (DICI) .... CLO
Concentrated Oil of Vitriol .... COV
Concentrated Orange Juice for Manufacturing .... COJM
Concentrated Phosphate Export Association .... CPEA
Concentrated Range Extension with Gain [*Telecommunications*] (TEL) .... CREG
Concentrated Rust-Inhibiting [*or Inhibitor*] [*Chemistry*] .... CRI
Concentrated Sea Water .... CSW
Concentrated Solar Energy Imitator (PDAA) .... CSEI
Concentrated Strength [*of solutions*] [*Pharmacy*] .... CS
Concentrated Super-Phosphate (OA) .... CSP
Concentrated Urban Enforcement [*Bureau of Alcohol, Tobacco, and Firearms*] .... CUE
Concentrated Urban Placement Service [*Department of Labor*] .... CUPS
Concentrated Volume [*of solutions*] (AAMN) CV
Concentrating (ABBR) .... CNCEG
Concentrating (ABBR) .... CNCNTRAG
Concentrating .... CONCTG
Concentration [*in the blood phase*] [*Medicine*] (DAVI) C
Concentration (ABBR) .... CNCENN
Concentration (ABBR) .... CNCNTRN
Concentration .... CON
Concentration .... CONCN
Concentration .... CONTRTN
Concentration by Volume [*Chemistry*] c
Concentration Camp CC
Concentration Camp Syndrome [*Psychiatry*] .... CCS
Concentration - Dependent Regulation of Oxygen .... CDRO
Concentration/Exposure Time [*Herbicides*] .... CET
Concentration Factor [*Nuclear energy*] (NUCP) .... CF
Concentration Length CL
Concentration, minimal [*Medicine*] (DMAA) .... Cm
Concentration Module Extension [*Telecommunications*] (TEL) .... CMX
Concentration Module Main [*Telecommunications*] (TEL) .... CMM
Concentration of Adenosine Monophosphate [*Medicine*] (DMAA) .... CAMP
Concentration of Total Carbon Dioxide [*Medicine*] (DAVI) .... $ctCO_2$
Concentration on Engineering Design (AAG) .... COED
Concentration Stress Test [*Psychical stress*] .... CST
Concentration-Based Exemption Criteria [*Environmental science*] .... CBEC
Concentration-Modulated Absorption Spectrometry .... COMAS
Concentrative (ABBR) .... CNCENV
Concentratively (ABBR) .... CNCENVY
Concentrator (ABBR) .... CNCENR
Concentrator Isolation Working Subsystem [*Telecommunications*] (TEL) .... CIWS
Concentrator Terminal Buffer [*Computer science*] (IBMDP) .... CTB
Concentratus [*Concentrated*] [*Pharmacy*] (ROG) .... CONC
Concentric (ABBR) .... CNCENC
Concentric (ABBR) .... CNCNTRC
Concentric (MSA) .... CNCTRC
Concentric .... CONC
Concentric Flight Plan (KSC) .... CFP
Concentric Hemispherical Analyzer [*Surface analysis*] .... CHA
Concentric Line Oscillator .... CLO
Concentric Research Information Service (IID) .... CRIS
Concentric Rings [*Botany*] .... CR
Concentric Sequence Initiation [*Aerospace*] .... CSI
Concentrically (ABBR) .... CNCENCY
Concentricity (ABBR) .... CNCENCT
Concentric-Orbit Rendezvous [*NASA*] .... COR
Concepcion [*Chile*] [*Airport symbol*] (OAG) .... CCP
Concepcion [*Bolivia*] [*Airport symbol*] (OAG) .... CEP
Concepcion [*Chile*] [*Seismograph station code, US Geological Survey*] (SEIS) .... CON
Concepcion [*Paraguay*] [*ICAO location identifier*] (ICLI) .... SGCO
Concepcion [*Bolivia*] [*ICAO location identifier*] (ICLI) .... SLCP
Concepcion/Carriel Sur [*Chile*] [*ICAO location identifier*] (ICLI) .... SCIE
Concept (ABBR) .... CNCPT
Concept .... CNCPT
Concept Alternative Selection [*Automotive project management*] .... CAS
Concept Analysis (MCD) .... CAA
Concept Approval [*Automotive project management*] .... CA
Concept Assessment Kit [*Child development test*] .... CAK
Concept Chart (AFIT) CC
Concept Code [*Database terminology*] (NITA) CC
Concept Definition (MCD) .... CD
Concept Definition Proposal (MCD) .... CDP
Concept Demonstration Model .... CDM
Concept Demonstration/Validation Phase (AAGC) .... CD/V
Concept Development .... CD
Concept Development Associates, Inc. [*Information service or system*] (IID) .... CDA
Concept Development Investigation .... CDI
Concept Development Phase (MCD) .... CDP
Concept Development Plan .... CDP
Concept Development Process (MCD) .... CDP
Concept Developments Talks .... CDT
Concept Developments Tasks (MCD) .... CDT
Concept Evaluation Program [*Army*] .... CEP
Concept Evaluation Technique [*Psychometrics*] .... CET
Concept Evaluation Test (MCD) .... CET
Concept Exploration .... CE
Concept Exploration and Definition [*Military*] .... CED
Concept Exploration Development Phase [*DoD*] .... CED
Concept Feasibility (AABC) .... CF
Concept Feasibility Analysis .... CFA
Concept Feasibility Report .... CFR
Concept for a Radiological Detection System (CINC) .... CCRDES
Concept for Low-Cost Air-to-Air Weapon (MCD) .... CLAW
Concept Formation Test [*Psychology*] .... CFT
Concept Formulation [*DoD*] .... CF
Concept Formulation/Contract Definition [*Procurement procedure*] .... CF/CD
Concept Formulation Data Bank (DNAB) .... CFDB
Concept Formulation Package [*Military*] .... CFP
Concept Formulation Package - Technical Development Plan [*Air Force*] .... CFP/TDP
Concept Formulation Studies .... CFS
Concept Game [*A war game*] .... CONGA
Concept Identification [*Psychology*] CI
Concept Initiation [*Automotive project management*] CI
Concept/International Programs Definitions [*Military*] .... C/IPD
Concept Learning System [*Computer science*] (BUR) .... CLS
Concept Memory Test (EDAC) .... CMT
Concept of a Family of Army Divisions (AABC) .... CONFAD
Concept of Operations (DOMA) .... CONOP
Concept of Operations (DOMA) .... CONOPS
Concept of Operations (MCD) .... COO
Concept Outline Plan (DOMA) .... COP
Concept Plan (NVT) .... CONPLAN
Concept Requirement [*Automotive project management*] .... CR
Concept Tech Group [*Associated Press*] (SAG) .... ConcpT
Concept Tech Group [*Associated Press*] (SAG) .... ConcT
Concept Tech Group [*NASDAQ symbol*] (SAG) .... TGSI
Concept to Customer .... CTC
Concept to Division [*Automotive project management*] .... CD
Concept Verification Test (NASA) .... CVT
Conception (ABBR) .... CNCPN
Conception Abbey and Seminary, Conception, MO [*Library symbol Library of Congress*] (LCLS) .... MoConA
Conception Assistee par Ordinateur [*Computer-Assisted Design - CAD*] [*French*] .... CAO
Conception Bay South Public Library, Manuels, Newfoundland [*Library symbol National Library of Canada*] (NLC) .... NFM
Conception Bay South Public Library, Manuels, NF, Canada [*Library symbol Library of Congress*] (LCLS) .... CaNfM
Conceptive (ABBR) .... CNCPTV
Conceptronic, Inc. [*NASDAQ symbol*] (SAG) .... CNCP
Conceptronic, Inc. [*Associated Press*] (SAG) .... Concept
Concepts About Print Test (EDAC) .... CAP
Concepts Analysis Agency [*Bethesda, MD*] [*Army*] (AABC) .... CAA
Concepts Analysis Agency, Bethesda, MD [*Library symbol Library of Congress*] (LCLS) .... MdBeCA
Concepts Analysis Group [*Army*] .... CAG
Concepts and Analysis Division [*US Army Engineer Topographic Laboratories*] .... CAD
Concepts Direct [*NASDAQ symbol*] (TTSB) .... CDIR
Concepts Direct, Inc. [*NASDAQ symbol*] (SAG) .... CDIR
Concepts Direct, Inc. [*Associated Press*] (SAG) .... ConcptD

Concepts, Doctrine, and Force [*Design*] ... CODAF
Concepts Evaluation Model [*Military*] ... CEM
Concepts of Postal Economics [*A series of newsletters of Mail Advertising Corp.*] ... COPE
Concepts, Trends, Relationships, Issues, Problems, Solutions ... CTRIPS
Concepts-Based Requirements System ... CBRS
Conceptual (ABBR) ... CNCPTL
Conceptual (VRA) ... concep
Conceptual Armored Cavalry (MCD) ... CARCAV
Conceptual Communications Area [*Computer science*] (TNIG) ... CCA
Conceptual Data Store [*Telecommunications*] (OSI) ... CDS
Conceptual Design and Rendering System [*Computer engineering*] ... CDRS
Conceptual Design for the Army in the Field ... CONAF
Conceptual Design Requirement (NRCH) ... CDR
Conceptual Design Study ... CDS
Conceptual Flight Profile (MCD) ... CFP
Conceptual Level (EDAC) ... CL
Conceptual Network-Based Language [*NEC Corp.*] ... CL
Conceptual Operational System ... COS
Conceptual Organization [*Psychometrics*] ... CO
Conceptual Project Design Description (NRCH) ... CPDD
Conceptual Quotient [*Psychology*] ... CQ
Conceptual Recoilless Weapons (MCD) ... CRW
Conceptual Reference Mission [*NASA*] ... CRM
Conceptual Satellite Surveillance System ... CS^3
Conceptual Satellite Surveillance System ... CSSS
Conceptual Schema Definition Language [*Computer science*] (MHDI) ... CSDL
Conceptual Signaling and Status Store [*Telecommunications*] (OSI) ... CSS
Conceptual Site Treatment Plan [*Department of Energy*] ... CSTP
Conceptual Site Treatment Plan (DOGT) ... CSTP
Conceptual System Design Description ... CSDD
Conceptual Systems Test ... CST
Conceptual Thought, Random Net Simulation (MUGU) ... CONTRANS
Conceptual Understanding through Blind Evaluation [*Educational test*] ... CUBE
Conceptualism (ABBR) ... CNCPTSM
Conceptualist (ABBR) ... CNCPTST
Conceptualize (ABBR) ... CNCPTLZ
Conceptualized (ABBR) ... CNCPTLZD
Conceptualizing (ABBR) ... CNCPTLZG
Conceptually (ABBR) ... CNCPTLY
Conceptually-Oriented Program in Elementary Science [*New York University*] (AEBS) ... COPES
Conceptus, Inc. [*Associated Press*] (SAG) ... Concepts
Conceptus, Inc. [*NASDAQ symbol*] (SAG) ... CPTS
Conceptus Inc. [*NASDAQ symbol*] (TTSB) ... CPTS
Concern (ABBR) ... CNCR
Concern (ABBR) ... CNCRN
Concern Against Nuclear Technology Organisations [*British*] (DI) ... CANTO
CONCERN/America (EA) ... CA
Concern for Dying (EA) ... CFD
Concern for Health Options: Information, Care and Education [*An association*] (EA) ... CHOICE
Concern for Helping Animals in Israel (EA) ... CHAI
Concern for the Health of Our Kids and the Environment [*Adelaide*] [*Australia*] ... CHOKE
Concern, Inc. [*An association*] (EA) ... CI
Concerned (ABBR) ... CNCRND
Concerned about Trident [*Ecology group*] ... CAT
Concerned Agoraphobics Learning to Live [*An association*] (PAZ) ... CALI
Concerned American Indian Parents (EA) ... CAIP
Concerned Americans for Individual Rights (EA) ... CAIR
Concerned Americans for Military Improvements (EA) ... CAMI
Concerned Broadcasters Using Inter-City Video Transmission Facilities (EA) ... CBUIVTF
Concerned Broadcasters Using Inter-City Video Transmission Facilities (EA) ... CON-VID
Concerned Citizens for Charity (DICI) ... CCC
Concerned Citizens for Nuclear Safety [*Advocacy group, New Mexico*] ... CCNS
Concerned Citizens for the Nuclear Breeder (EA) ... CCNB
Concerned Citizens for Universal Service [*Defunct*] (EA) ... CCUS
Concerned Citizens Information Council [*Group opposing sex education in schools*] ... CCIC
Concerned Citizens' Movement [*St. Christopher and Nevis*] [*Political party*] (EY) ... CCM
Concerned Citizens of America [*Defunct*] (EA) ... CCA
Concerned Educators Against Forced Unionism (EA) ... CEAFU
Concerned Educators Allied for a Safe Environment (EA) ... CEASE
Concerned Friends of Ontario Citizens in Care Facilities (AC) ... CFOCCF
Concerned Guatemala Scholars [*Defunct*] (EA) ... CGS
Concerned Neighbors in Action (EA) ... CNA
Concerned Persons for Adoption (EA) ... CPFA
Concerned Pet Owners' Association (EA) ... CPOA
Concerned Relatives of Nursing Home Patients (EA) ... CRNHP
Concerned Senators for the Arts (EA) ... CSA
Concerned Seniors for Better Government (EA) ... CSBG
Concerned South Africans Group (ECON) ... COSAG
Concerned United Birthparents (EA) ... CUB
Concerned Women for America (EA) ... CWA
Concerning (ABBR) ... CNCRG
Concerning (ABBR) ... CNCRNG
Concerning (ADA) ... CON
Concerning (ROG) ... CONC
Concerning [*Legal term*] (ROG) ... CONCG
Concerns of Motherhood (EA) ... CM
Concerns of Police Survivors [*An association*] ... COPS
Concerns-Based Adoption Model (EDAC) ... CBAM
Concert Artist [*Record label*] [*Great Britain*] ... CA
Concert Artists Association [*British*] (BI) ... CAA
Concert Artists Guild (EA) ... CAG
Concert Dance Company ... CDC
Concert Hall Society [*Record label*] ... CHS
Concert Industry Ltd. [*Vancouver Stock Exchange symbol*] ... CNG
Concert Music Broadcasters Association (EA) ... CMBA
Concert Name [*Database terminology*] (NITA) ... CN
Concert Productions International [*Canada*] ... CPI
Concert Resources, Inc. [*Vancouver Stock Exchange symbol*] ... CCJ
Concertacion de los Partidos de la Democracia [*Chile*] [*Political party*] (EY) ... CPD
Concertacion Democratica Cubana [*Political party*] (EY) ... CDC
Concertation Unit for Biotechnology in Europe ... CUBE
Concerteum [*Record label*] [*France*] ... Cum
Concerto [*Music*] ... CON
Concerto [*Music*] ... CONC
Concerto [*Music*] ... CTO
Concerts and Recitals of Serious Music (Annual Licence) [*Public-performance tariff class*] [*British*] ... LA
Concerts and Recitals of Serious Music (Permits) [*Public-performance tariff class*] [*British*] ... L
Concession (MSA) ... CON
Concession (DD) ... Conc
Concession ... CONCSSN
Concession ... CSN
Concessional Finance Facility ... CFF
Conchologists of America (EA) ... CA
Conchology ... CONCH
Conchology (WGA) ... CONCHOL
Conciencia de Patria [*Bolivia*] [*Political party*] (EY) ... Condepa
Conciertos Mexicanos [*Record label*] [*Mexico*] ... CM
Conciliable (ABBR) ... CNCLAB
Conciliate (ABBR) ... CNCLA
Conciliated (ABBR) ... CNCLAD
Conciliating (ABBR) ... CNCLAG
Conciliation (ABBR) ... CNCLAN
Conciliation (ROG) ... CONCIL
Conciliation Commission for Palestine [*of the UN*] ... CCP
Conciliation Committees [*Australia*] ... CC
Conciliation Officer (Tribunal) [*British*] ... COT
Conciliator (ABBR) ... CNCLAR
Conciliatory (ABBR) ... CNCLARTRY
Conciliatory (ABBR) ... CNCLARY
Concilium [*Council*] [*Latin*] (WGA) ... CONC
Concise (ABBR) ... CNCIS
Concise (ROG) ... CONC
Concise Australian Reference Book [*A publication*] (ADA) ... ARB
Concise Command Language [*Computer science*] (MHDI) ... CCL
Concise Dictionary of American Literary Biography [*A publication*] ... CDALB
Concise Handbooks of Art [*A publication*] ... CHA
Concise Oxford Dictionary [*A publication*] ... COD
Concise Oxford English Dictionary [*A publication*] ... COED
Concise Scots Dictionary [*Aberdeen University Press*] [*A publication*] ... CSD
Concise Tax Service [*Australia A publication*] ... CTS
Concisely (ABBR) ... CNCISY
Concision (ABBR) ... CNCISN
Concisus [*Cut*] [*Medicine*] ... C
Concisus [*Cut*] [*Medicine*] (ROG) ... CON
Concisus [*Cut*] [*Medicine*] ... CONCIS
Conclave (ABBR) ... CNCLAV
Conclave (ABBR) ... CNCLV
Conclave of Mystical Masons [*Freemasonry*] (ROG) ... CMM
Conclude (ABBR) ... CNCLD
Conclude (ABBR) ... CNCLU
Concluded (ABBR) ... CNCLUD
Concluder (ABBR) ... CNCLUR
Concluding (ABBR) ... CNCDG
Concluding (ABBR) ... CNCLUG
Conclusion (WGA) ... C
Conclusion [*Broadcasting*] (WDMC) ... CC
Conclusion (ABBR) ... CNCLSN
Conclusion (ABBR) ... CNCLUN
Conclusion ... CON
Conclusion ... conc
Conclusion (MSA) ... CONCL
Conclusion (ROG) ... CONCLON
Conclusions, Recommendations, and Lessons Learned ... CRLL
Conclusive (ABBR) ... CNCLSV
Conclusive (ABBR) ... CNCLUV
Conclusively (ABBR) ... CNCLUVY
Concoct (ABBR) ... CNCOC
Concocted (ABBR) ... CNCOCD
Concocting (ABBR) ... CNCOCG
Concoction (ABBR) ... CNCOCN
Concoctive (ABBR) ... CNCOCV
Concoctor (ABBR) ... CNCOCR
Concomitance (ABBR) ... CNCOM
Concomitant (ABBR) ... CNCMTNT
Concomitant (ABBR) ... CNCOMT
Concora Medium Test ... CMT
Concord (ABBR) ... CNCRD
Concord [*City in California, Massachusetts, New Hampshire, and North Carolina*] (ROG) ... CON

Concord [*New Hampshire*] [*Airport symbol*] (AD) ... CON
Concord Airlines Nigeria Ltd. [*ICAO designator*] (FAAC) ... CND
Concord, CA [*Location identifier FAA*] (FAAL) ... CCR
Concord, CA [*Television station call letters*] ... KFCB
Concord, CA [*AM radio station call letters*] ... KKIS
Concord, CA [*AM radio station call letters*] (RBYB) ... KRHT-AM
Concord, CA [*TV station call letters*] (RBYB) ... KTNC-TV
Concord, CA [*FM radio station call letters*] ... KVHS
Concord Camera [*NASDAQ symbol*] (TTSB) ... LENS
Concord Camera Corp. [*Associated Press*] (SAG) ... CcdCam
Concord Camera Corp. [*NASDAQ symbol*] (NQ) ... LENS
Concord College, Athens, WV [*Library symbol Library of Congress*] (LCLS) ... WvAC
Concord Council [*Defunct*] (EA) ... CC
Concord - Diablo Valley College [*California*] [*Seismograph station code, US Geological Survey Closed*] (SEIS) ... CNC
Concord EFS [*NASDAQ symbol*] (TTSB) ... CEFT
Concord EFS, Inc. [*NASDAQ symbol*] (NQ) ... CEFT
Concord EFS, Inc. [*Associated Press*] (SAG) ... CncEFS
Concord Energy [*Vancouver Stock Exchange symbol*] ... CCD
Concord Energy [*NASDAQ symbol*] (TTSB) ... CODE
Concord Energy, Inc. [*NASDAQ symbol*] (SAG) ... CODE
Concord Energy, Inc. [*Associated Press*] (SAG) ... ConcEgy
Concord Fabrics Cl'A' [*AMEX symbol*] (TTSB) ... CIS
Concord Fabrics, Inc. [*AMEX symbol*] (SPSG) ... CIS
Concord Fabrics, Inc. [*Associated Press*] (SAG) ... ConcdF
Concord Fabrics, Inc. [*Associated Press*] (SAG) ... ConcF
Concord Free Public Library, Concord, MA [*Library symbol Library of Congress*] (LCLS) ... MCo
Concord Grape Association (EA) ... CGA
Concord Health Group, Inc. [*NASDAQ symbol*] (SAG) ... CHGR
Concord Health Group, Inc. [*Associated Press*] (SAG) ... ConcH
Concord, MA [*AM radio station call letters*] ... WADN
Concord, MA [*FM radio station call letters*] ... WIQH
Concord, NC [*AM radio station call letters*] ... WEGO
Concord, NC [*FM radio station call letters*] ... WPEG
Concord, NC [*Television station call letters*] ... WUNG
Concord, NH [*Location identifier FAA*] (FAAL) ... CON
Concord, NH [*Location identifier FAA*] (FAAL) ... EPP
Concord, NH [*FM radio station call letters*] ... WEVO
Concord, NH [*FM radio station call letters*] ... WJYY
Concord, NH [*AM radio station call letters*] ... WKXL
Concord, NH [*FM radio station call letters*] ... WKXL-FM
Concord, NH [*Television station call letters*] (RBYB) ... WNBU
Concord, NH [*AM radio station call letters*] ... WNHA
Concord, NH [*FM radio station call letters*] ... WSPS
Concord, NH [*FM radio station call letters*] ... WVNH
Concord Public Library, Concord, NC [*Library symbol Library of Congress*] (LCLS) ... NcCo
Concord Scientific Corp., Downsview, Ontario [*Library symbol National Library of Canada*] (NLC) ... OTCOS
Concord Video and Film Council (EAIO) ... CVFC
Concordance (ABBR) ... CNCRDNC
Concordance (ROG) ... CONC
Concordance [*Computer software*] (NITA) ... CONCORD
Concordance Generation System [*A text editing system*] [*University of Toronto*] [*Canada*] (NITA) ... COGS
Concordance Words in Titles [*Indexing*] ... CWIT
Concordant (ABBR) ... CNCRDT
Concordantly (ABBR) ... CNCRDTY
Concorde out, Concorde Home ... COCH
Concorde out, Tourist Class Home ... COTCH
Concordia [*Brazil*] [*Airport symbol Obsolete*] (OAG) ... CCI
Concordia [*Record label*] ... Cdia
Concordia [*Argentina*] [*Airport symbol*] (OAG) ... COC
Concordia [*Brazil ICAO location identifier*] (ICLI) ... SBCE
Concordia College, Bronxville, NY [*Library symbol Library of Congress*] (LCLS) ... NBronC
Concordia College, Conover, NC [*Library symbol Library of Congress Obsolete*] (LCLS) ... NcConC
Concordia College, Edmonton, AB, Canada [*Library symbol Library of Congress*] (LCLS) ... CaAEC
Concordia College, Edmonton, Alberta [*Library symbol National Library of Canada*] (NLC) ... AEC
Concordia College (Illinois) (GAGS) ... Concordia C (Ill)
Concordia College, Milwaukee, WI [*Library symbol Library of Congress*] (LCLS) ... WMC
Concordia College, Milwaukee, WI [*Library symbol*] [*Library of Congress*] (LCLS) ... WMCC
Concordia College, Moorhead, MN [*Library symbol Library of Congress*] (LCLS) ... MnMohC
Concordia College, Portland, OR [*Library symbol Library of Congress*] (LCLS) ... OrPCC
Concordia College, St. Paul, MN [*OCLC symbol*] (OCLC) ... MNC
Concordia College, St. Paul, MN [*Library symbol Library of Congress*] (LCLS) ... MnSCC
Concordia College, Seward, NE [*OCLC symbol*] (OCLC) ... NBC
Concordia Collegiate Institute [*New York*] ... CCI
Concordia/Commodoro Pierrest Egui [*Argentina ICAO location identifier*] (ICLI) ... SAAC
Concordia Historical Institute (EA) ... CHI
Concordia Historical Institute, St. Louis, MO [*Library symbol Library of Congress*] (LCLS) ... MoSCH
Concordia Hospital, Winnipeg, Manitoba [*Library symbol National Library of Canada*] (NLC) ... MWCH
Concordia Hospital, Winnipeg, MB, Canada [*Library symbol Library of Congress*] (LCLS) ... CaMWCH
Concordia, KS [*Location identifier FAA*] (FAAL) ... CNK
Concordia, KS [*FM radio station call letters*] ... KCKS
Concordia, KS [*AM radio station call letters*] ... KNCK
Concordia, KS [*FM radio station call letters*] ... KVCO
Concordia Lutheran College, Ann Arbor, MI [*Library symbol Library of Congress*] (LCLS) ... MiAaC
Concordia Lutheran College, Austin, TX [*Library symbol Library of Congress*] (LCLS) ... TxAuC
Concordia Lutheran Seminary, Edmonton, Alberta [*Library symbol National Library of Canada*] (BIB) ... AECO
Concordia Mutual Life Association (EA) ... CML
Concordia Paper Holding ADS [*NASDAQ symbol*] (TTSB) ... CPLNY
Concordia Paper Holding Ltd. [*Associated Press*] (SAG) ... ConcPap
Concordia Paper Holding Ltd. [*NASDAQ symbol*] (SAG) ... CPLN
Concordia Parish Library, Ferriday, LA [*Library symbol Library of Congress*] (LCLS) ... LFC
Concordia Seminary, St. Louis, MO [*Library symbol Library of Congress*] (LCLS) ... MoSCS
Concordia Senior College, Fort Wayne, IN [*Library symbol Library of Congress*] (LCLS) ... InFwC
Concordia Teachers College [*Illinois, Nebraska*] ... CTC
Concordia Teachers College (Nebraska) (GAGS) ... Concordia Teachers C (Nebr)
Concordia Teachers College, River Forest, IL [*OCLC symbol*] (OCLC) ... ICE
Concordia Teachers College, River Forest, IL [*Library symbol Library of Congress*] (LCLS) ... IRivfT
Concordia Teachers College, Seward, NE [*Library symbol Library of Congress*] (LCLS) ... NbSeT
Concordia Theological Seminary [*Later, Concordia Seminary*] [*Missouri*] ... CTS
Concordia Theological Seminary, Fort Wayne, IN [*Library symbol Library of Congress*] (LCLS) ... InFwCT
Concordia Theological Seminary, Fort Wayne, IN [*OCLC symbol*] (OCLC) ... ITC
Concordia Theological Seminary, Springfield, IL [*Library symbol Library of Congress Obsolete*] (LCLS) ... ISC
Concordia Tract Mission (EA) ... CTM
Concordia University Faculty Association [*Association des Professeurs de l'Universite Concordia*] (AC) ... CUFA
Concordia University Library [*UTLAS symbol*] ... CNC
Concordia University, Librry Studies Program, Montreal, PQ, Canada [*Library symbol*] [*Library of Congress*] (LCLS) ... CaQMGLS
Concordia University, Loyola Campus, Montreal, PQ, Canada [*Library symbol Library of Congress*] (LCLS) ... CaQML
Concordia University, Sir George Williams Campus, Department of Geography, Montreal, PQ, Canada [*Library symbol Library of Congress*] (LCLS) ... CaQMGG
Concordia University, Sir George Williams Campus, Department of Geography, University Map Collection, Montreal, PQ, Canada [*Library symbol Library of Congress*] (LCLS) ... CaQMGGM
Concordia University, Sir George Williams Campus, Montreal, PQ, Canada [*Library symbol Library of Congress*] (LCLS) ... CaQMG
Concordia - Youth Service Volunteers (EAIO) ... CYSV
Concore Health Group, Inc. [*Associated Press*] (SAG) ... ConcHlth
Concors Latvian Air Service [*FAA designator*] (FAAC) ... COS
Concours International de Musique de Montreal [*Montreal International Music Competition*] (AC) ... CIMM
Concourse (ABBR) ... CNCOR
Concourse ... CONCRS
Concrete ... CON
Concrete ... CONC
Concrete ... CONCR
Concrete (VRA) ... concr
Concrete ... CONCRT
Concrete Arch [*Bridges*] ... KA
Concrete Articulated Production Tower (PDAA) ... CONAPT
Concrete Block ... CB
Concrete Block ... CCB
Concrete Block Association (MHDB) ... CBA
Concrete Brick Manufacturers Association [*British*] (DBA) ... CBMA
Concrete Cancer [*Refers to disintegration caused by weathering and pollutants*] ... CC
Concrete Ceiling ... CC
Concrete Ceiling ... CCC
Concrete Deep Water Structure [*Oil platform*] ... CONDEEP
Concrete Floor ... CCF
Concrete Floor [*Technical drawings*] ... CF
Concrete Forming Association of Ontario (AC) ... CFAO
Concrete Industries Council (EA) ... CIC
Concrete Industry Board ... CIB
Concrete Island Drilling System [*Offshore oil exploration*] ... CIDS
Concrete Joint Institute [*Defunct*] (EA) ... CJI
Concrete Lintel Association [*British*] (DBA) ... CLASS
Concrete Masonry Association of Australia Cooperative ... CMAAC
Concrete Masonry Unit [*Technical drawings*] ... CMU
Concrete Median Barrier (OA) ... CMB
Concrete Missile Entry Warning System (MCD) ... CMEWS
Concrete Mixer Manufacturers' Association [*British*] (BI) ... CMMA
Concrete Paviors' Association of New South Wales [*Australia*] ... CPANSW
Concrete Piercing ... CP
Concrete Pipe Association of Australia ... CPAA
Concrete Pipe Association of South Carolina (SRA) ... CPASC
Concrete Pipe Associations (EA) ... CPA
Concrete Plant Manufacturers Bureau (EA) ... CPMB
Concrete Pressure Vehicle (PDAA) ... CPV
Concrete Reinforcing Steel Institute (EA) ... CRSI

Concrete Repair Association [*British*] (DBA) .... CRA
Concrete Sawing and Drilling Association (EA) .... CSDA
Concrete Slab (OA) .... CS
Concrete Society [*British*] (EAIO) .... CS
Concrete Splash Block [*Technical drawings*] .... CSB
Concrete Technology Information Analysis Center [*Army Corps of Engineers*] [*Vicksburg, MS*] (IID) .... CTIAC
Concurrency Control Bus [*Computer science*] (NITA) .... C & B
Concurrency Control Unit (NITA) .... CCU
Concurrency Controller [*Computer science*] CC
Concurrency Update Group .... CUG
Concurrent C
Concurrent (AFM) .... CNCR
Concurrent Admission Program [*DoD*] .... CONAP
Concurrent Algorithmic Programming Language [*Computer science*] (CSR) .... CAP
Concurrent Budget Resolution (AAGC) .... CBR
Concurrent Care Concern [*Medicine*] CCC
Concurrent Computer [*NASDAQ symbol*] (TTSB) .... CCUR
Concurrent Computer [*Associated Press*] (SAG) .... ConcCm
Concurrent Computer Corp. [*NASDAQ symbol*] (NQ) .... CCUR
Concurrent Concession (MDG) CC
Concurrent Engineering .... CE
Concurrent Engineering for Composites Materials Program [*University of Delaware, Center for Composite Materials*] (RDA) .... CECM
Concurrent High-Level Language [*Computer science*] (MCD) .... CHLL
Concurrent Input/Output System [*Computer science*] (PCM) .... CIOSYS
Concurrent Language [*Computer science*] .... CLANG
Concurrent Machine Environment [*International Computers Ltd.*] [*British*] (NITA) .... CME
Concurrent Media Conversion (IAA) .... CMC
Concurrent Operating System [*Sperry UNIVAC*] [*Computer science*] (IEEE) .... COS
Concurrent Peripheral Operations (BUR) .... CPO
Concurrent Photon Amplification [*Air Force*] .... CPA
Concurrent Planometric [*A discrimination task*] .... CP
Concurrent Processor Architecture Control (MCD) .... CPAC
Concurrent Spare Parts (AFM) .... CSP
Concurrent Stereometric [*A discrimination task*] .... CS
Concurrent With .... C/W
Concurrent with Aircraft Delivery (MCD) .... CWAD
Concurrent with Design Release (MCD) .... CWDR
Concurrently (FAAC) .... CNCNT
Concurring (ABBR) .... CNCRG
Concursos y Certamenes Culturales [*Database*] [*Ministerio de Cultura*] [*Spanish*] [*Information service or system*] (CRD) .... CECU
Concussion (DSUE) .... CONCUSS
Condaka Metals Corp. [*Vancouver Stock Exchange symbol*] .... CKA
Condamine [*Queensland*] [*Airport symbol*] (AD) .... ONM
Condat-Sur-Vezere [*France ICAO location identifier*] (ICLI) .... LFDZ
Condemn (MSA) .... CDM
Condemnation [*Legal term*] (DLA) c
Condemnation [*Legal shorthand*] (LWAP) .... COMDN
Condemnation [*Legal term*] (DLA) .... Condem
Condemnation Rate .... CR
Condemned C
Condemned (WGA) .... CD
Condemned (AABC) .... CND
Condemned [*Prisoners'*] **Cell** (IIA) CC
Condemned or Suppressed .... COS
Condemno [*I Condemn*] [*Used by Romans in criminal trials*] [*Latin*] C
Condensate (KSC) .... CNDS
Condensate and Feedwater [*Nuclear energy*] (NRCH) .... CFW
Condensate and Feedwater Chemistry Control System [*Nuclear energy*] (NRCH) .... CFCCS
Condensate and Feedwater System [*Nuclear energy*] (NRCH) .... CFS
Condensate and Feedwater System [*Nuclear energy*] (NRCH) .... CFWS
Condensate and Refueling Water Storage System [*Nuclear energy*] (NRCH) .... CRWSS
Condensate Booster Pump [*Nuclear energy*] (NRCH) .... CBP
Condensate Cleanup System [*Nuclear energy*] (NRCH) .... CCS
Condensate Cooling System [*Nuclear energy*] (NRCH) .... CCS
Condensate Demineralization Effluent [*Nuclear energy*] (NRCH) .... CDE
Condensate Demineralization Subsystem [*Nuclear energy*] (NRCH) .... CDS
Condensate Extraction Pump [*Chemical engineering*] .... CEP
Condensate Filter Demineralizer [*Nuclear energy*] (NRCH) .... CFR
Condensate Heat Exchanger (MCD) .... CH-X
Condensate Polishing System [*Nuclear energy*] (NRCH) .... CPS
Condensate Storage and Transfer System [*Nuclear energy*] (NRCH) .... CSTS
Condensate Storage Facility [*Nuclear energy*] (NRCH) .... CSF
Condensate Storage System [*Nuclear energy*] (NRCH) .... CSS
Condensate Storage Tank [*Nuclear energy*] (NRCH) .... CST
Condensate Transfer and Storage [*Nuclear energy*] (NRCH) .... CTS
Condensate Water Servicing Unit .... CWSU
Condensation [*Physics*] (BARN) .... S
Condensation Figure [*Surface physical chemistry*] .... CF
Condensation Nuclei .... CN
Condensation Nuclei Counter .... CNC
Condensation Nuclei Detector (MCD) .... CND
Condensation Nucleus [*Marine science*] (OSRA) .... CN
Condensation Particle Counter [*Marine science*] (OSRA) .... CPC
Condensation Pressure Spread .... CPS
Condensation Trail [*in the air*] .... CONTRAIL
Condensed .... COND
Condensed Chemical Dictionary [*A publication*] .... CCD
Condensed Ecclesiastical Reports [*A publication*] (DLA) .... Cond Ecc R
Condensed Ecclesiastical Reports [*A publication*] (DLA) .... Cond Eccl
Condensed English Chancery Reports [*A publication*] (DLA) .... Cond Ch R
Condensed English Chancery Reports [*A publication*] (DLA) .... Cond Eng Ch
Condensed Exchequer Reports [*A publication*] (DLA) .... Cond Ex R
Condensed Exchequer Reports [*A publication*] (DLA) .... Cond Exch R
Condensed Logic Diagram [*Electronics*] (IAA) .... CLD
Condensed Nearest Neighbor [*Mathematics*] .... CNN
Condensed Negative Binomial Distribution [*Statistics*] .... CNBD
Condensed or Dried .... COD
Condensed Strike Data Transmission System (MCD) .... CONTRAST
Condensed Tannin [*Botany*] .... CT
Condensed Tannin Leucoanthocyanin .... CTL
Condensed Tannin Proanthocyanidin .... CTP
Condenser c
Condenser [*Automotive engineering*] .... COND
Condenser .... CONDR
Condenser Absolute Pressure .... CAP
Condenser Air Removal [*Nuclear energy*] (NRCH) .... CAR
Condenser Circulating Water [*Nuclear energy*] (NRCH) .... CCW
Condenser Cooling Water [*Nuclear energy*] (NRCH) .... CCW
Condenser Discharge Unit .... CDU
Condenser Heat Rejection (IAA) .... CHR
Condenser Load Compensation [*Portable electric generators*] CLC
Condenser Vacuum Pump Effluent Treatment System [*Nuclear energy*] (NRCH) .... CVPETS
Condenser-Radiator Fan Module [*Automotive cooling systems*] .... CRFM
Condensing .... CONDG
Condensing Vacuole (OA) CV
Conders. Highway Cases [*A publication*] (DLA) .... Cond HC
Conde-Sur-Noireau [*France ICAO location identifier*] (ICLI) .... LFAN
Condition [*Automotive advertising*] .... CD
Condition (MDG) .... CND
Condition (AFM) .... COND
Condition [*Legal term*] (ROG) .... CONDON
Condition (MSA) .... CONDTN
Condition and Recommendation (AABC) .... CAR
Condition BIT [*Binary Digit*] [*Computer science*] .... CB
Condition Code CC
Condition Code Register .... CCR
Condition Education Division [*Department of Education*] (GFGA) .... CED
Condition Identification Work Authorization [*Business term*] (NRCH) .... CIWA
Condition Monitored Maintenance (NASA) .... CMM
Condition Monitoring (DS) .... CM
Condition Monitoring (MCD) .... COM
Condition Monitoring System (CAAL) .... CMS
Condition of Detail .... CD
Condition on Admission [*Medicine*] (ADA) .... COA
Condition on Discharge [*Medicine*] (DAVI) .... COD
Condition Precedent [*Legal term*] .... CP
Condition Reservation Code [*Army*] (AABC) .... CRC
Condition Status [*Computer science*] .... CS
Condition Subsequent [*Legal term*] .... CS
Conditional (ROG) .... CONDL
Conditional Amount of Sample Information [*Statistics*] .... CASI
Conditional Analysis for Random Networks [*Electronics*] (OA) .... CARN
Conditional Antimicrobial Reporting [*Microbiology*] .... CAR
Conditional Authorization [*Environmental science*] .... CA
Conditional Branch .... CB
Conditional Breakpoint Instruction .... CBI
Conditional Breakpoint Instruction .... CBPI
Conditional Command Processor [*Computer science*] (MHDI) .... CCP
Conditional Exemption [*Environmental science*] .... CE
Conditional Freedom (ADA) .... CF
Conditional Grant .... CG
Conditional Instability of the Second Kind .... CISK
Conditional Lease (ADA) CL
Conditional Mean Square Error [*Statistics*] .... CMSE
Conditional Nonoperation [*Computer science*] .... CNOP
Conditional Open Probability Analysis [*Mathematics*] .... COPA
Conditional Pardon (ADA) .... CP
Conditional Peak Flow [*Biology*] .... CPF
Conditional Prepayment Rate [*for mortgages*] .... CPR
Conditional Proof [*Method in logic*] .... CP
Conditional Purchase [*Business term*] (ADA) .... CP
Conditional Relaxation Analysis Method .... CRAM
Conditional Release [*Nuclear energy*] (NRCH) .... CR
Conditional Release Authorization (SAA) .... CRA
Conditional Release Violator [*FBI standardized term*] .... CRV
Conditional Response Analog Machine .... CORA
Conditional Sale [*Legal shorthand*] (LWAP) .... CS
Conditional Sale - Chattel Mortgage Reporter [*Commerce Clearing House*] [*A publication*] (DLA) .... Condit Sale - Chat Mort Rep
Conditional Select Multiplexer .... CSM
Conditional Symmetric Instability [*Marine science*] (OSRA) .... CSI
Conditional Symmetric Instability (USDC) .... CSI
Conditional (Tense) [*Linguistics*] .... COND
Conditional Transfer of Control .... CTC
Conditional Use Permit (GNE) .... CUP
Conditional Value of Sample Information [*Statistics*] .... CVSI
Conditional Variable Incremental Computer (IEEE) CVIC
Conditional Voluntary Indefinite [*Status*] [*Army*] (INF) CVI
Conditionally Accepted Tag (NRCH) .... CAT
Conditionally Exempt Small Quantity Generator .... CESQG
Conditionally Exempt Specified Wastestream [*Environmental science*] .... CESW

Conditionally Qualified (AFM) ... CQ
Conditionally Streptomycin Dependent [*Pharmacology*] (DAVI) ... CSD
Condition-Based Maintenance [*Army*] ... CBM
Conditioned Abstinence (AAMN) ... CA
Conditioned Avoidance Response [*Psychometrics*] ... CAR
Conditioned Bald Eagle Total Value ... CBETV
Conditioned Emotional Response [*Psychology*] ... CER
Conditioned Medium [*For growing microorganisms*] ... CM
Conditioned Medium Reconstituting Factor [*Immunochemistry*] ... CMRF
Conditioned Nausea and Vomiting [*Medicine*] ... CNV
Conditioned Orientation Reflex ... COR
Conditioned Orientation Reflex Audiometry [*Medicine*] (MAE) ... CORA
Conditioned Orienting Response [*Neurology*] (DAVI) ... COR
Conditioned Place Preference [*Psychophysiology*] ... CPP
Conditioned Reflex (WGA) ... COND REF
Conditioned Reflex [*Machine*] (IEEE) ... CONFLEX
Conditioned Reflex [*or Response*] [*Psychometrics*] ... CR
Conditioned Reflex Analog (IEEE) ... CORA
Conditioned Response (WGA) ... COND RESP
Conditioned Stimulus [*Psychometrics*] ... CS
Conditioned Wrinkle Recovery Angle [*Textile technology*] ... CWRA
Conditioner (NASA) ... CONDR
Conditioner ... CONDTR
Conditioning [*Neurophysiology*] ... C
Conditioning ... COND
Conditioning [*Automotive engineering*] ... CONDTG
Conditioning Container (AAG) ... CC
Conditioning Thio Emulsion [*Roux Laboratories, Inc.*] ... CTE
Conditions and Performance [*Report to Congress*] [*FHWA*] (TAG) ... C&P
Conditions, Covenants, and Restrictions [*On condominiums*] ... CC & R
Conditions of Assembly and Release Transfer ... CART
Conditions of Execution (MCD) ... COFE
Conditions of Participation [*Department of Health and Human Services*] (GFGA) ... COP
Conditions of Service [*Engineering*] ... COS
Condobolin [*Australia Airport symbol*] (OAG) ... CBX
Condom Catheter Collecting System [*Medicine*] (DMAA) ... CCCS
Condominio ... COND
Condominium ... CONDO
Condominium (VRA) ... condo
Condominium [*Real estate*] (DLA) ... CONDOMIN
Condominium/Cooperative [*Real estate*] ... CONDOP
Condominium Research and Education Society ... CRES
Condom-Valence-Sur-Baise [*France ICAO location identifier*] (ICLI) ... LFID
Condon, Kinzua & Southern Railroad Co. [*AAR code*] ... CKSO
Condon Public Library, Condon, OR [*Library symbol Library of Congress*] (LCLS) ... OrCon
Condor Aero Services, Inc. [*ICAO designator*] (FAAC) ... CNR
Condor Data Link ... CDL
Condor Data Link System ... CDLS
Condor Flugdienst GmbH [*Germany ICAO designator*] (FAAC) ... CFG
Condor Minerals and Energy Ltd. [*Australia*] ... CME
Condor Missile System ... CMS
Condor Services, Inc. [*NASDAQ symbol*] (NQ) ... COND
Condor Services, Inc. [*Associated Press*] (SAG) ... Condor
Condorcocha [*Ecuador*] [*ICAO location identifier*] (ICLI) ... SECC
Condoto [*Colombia*] [*Airport symbol*] (OAG) ... COG
Condoto/Mandinga [*Colorado ICAO location identifier*] (ICLI) ... SKCD
Conduct (AABC) ... CDT
Conduct (MSA) ... CNDCT
Conduct [*or Conductivity*] (ROG) ... COND
Conduct and Utilization of Research in Nursing ... CURN
Conduct of Fire Trainer [*Army*] ... COFT
Conduct of Fire Trainer - Improved [*Army*] (MCD) ... COFTI
Conductance ... cd
Conductance [*Symbol*] [*IUPAC*] ... G
Conductance Increase Mechanism ... CIM
Conductance of Upstream Segment [*Physics*] (DAVI) ... Gus
Conducted Emission (IEEE) ... CE
Conducted Susceptibility (IEEE) ... CS
Conduction Analysis Program Using Eigenvalues [*NASA*] ... CAPE
Conduction Analysis via Eigenvalues [*NASA*] (MCD) ... CAVE
Conduction Band [*Electronics*] ... CB
Conduction Band Minimum [*Electronics*] ... CBM
Conduction Electron Polarization ... CEP
Conduction Electron Spin Resonance ... CESR
Conduction Nerve Velocity [*Neurology*] (CPH) ... CNV
Conduction Velocity [*Neurology*] ... CV
Conduction Velocity of Slower Fibers (PDAA) ... CVSF
Conductive Channel (IAA) ... CC
Conductive Coating ... CC
Conductive Education Association (AIE) ... CEA
Conductive Hearing Impairment Language Development Program (EDAC) ... CHILD
Conductive Plastic ... CP
Conductive Plastic Potentiometer ... CPP
Conductivity ... C
Conductivity (MAE) ... cond
Conductivity Cell Volume [*Hematology*] ... CCV
Conductivity Detector ... CD
Conductivity Element [*Nuclear energy*] (NRCH) ... CE
Conductivity Indicator Transmitter [*Nuclear energy*] (NRCH) ... CIT
Conductivity Modulated Bipolar [*Computer science*] ... CMB
Conductivity Recording Switch [*Nuclear energy*] (NRCH) ... CRS
Conductivity (Salinity)-Temperature-Depth [*Oceanography*] ... C/STD
Conductivity, Temperature, and Depth [*Oceanography*] ... CTD
Conductivity Temperature Depth Transmissometer [*Oceanography*] ... CTDT
Conductivity Transmitter (IAA) ... CT
Conductivity-Connected Charge-Coupled Device [*Electronics*] (EECA) ... C_4D
Conductivity-Connected Charge-Coupled Device [*Electronics*] (EECA) ... CCCCD
Conductivity-Modulated Field Effect Transistor (PDAA) ... COMFET
Conductivity-Recording Controller (IAA) ... CDRC
Conductivity-Temperature-Depth Probe [*Marine science*] (OSRA) ... CTD
Conductivity-Temperature-Depth Profiler [*Marine science*] (OSRA) ... CTD
Conductometric ... Cond
Conductor ... C
Conductor (ADA) ... CDR
Conductor [*MARC relator code*] [*Library of Congress*] (LCCP) ... cnd
Conductor (KSC) ... COND
Conductor (AAG) ... CONDR
Conductor Generalis (DLA) ... COND GEN
Conductor Head (KSC) ... CH
Conductor, Insulator, Semiconductor (IAA) ... CIS
Conductus, Inc. [*NASDAQ symbol*] (SAG) ... CDTS
Conductus, Inc. [*Associated Press*] (SAG) ... Conductu
Conduit ... CDT
Conduit (KSC) ... CND
Conduit [*Automotive engineering*] ... CONDT
Conduit [*Electronics*] (IAA) ... CT
Condylocephalic [*Medicine*] (DAVI) ... cc
Condylomata Acuminata [*Medicine*] ... CA
Condy's Edition of Marshall on Insurance [*A publication*] (DLA) ... Cond Marsh
Cone ... CE
Cone ... CO
Cone Angle [*NASA*] (NASA) ... CA
Cone Length [*Botany*] ... COLGTH
Cone Mills [*NYSE symbol*] (TTSB) ... COE
Cone Mills Corp. [*NYSE symbol*] (SPSG) ... COE
Cone Mills Corp. [*Associated Press*] (SAG) ... ConeMl
Cone Mills Corp., Greensboro, NC [*Library symbol Library of Congress*] (LCLS) ... NcGCM
Cone Peak [*Hawaii*] [*Seismograph station code, US Geological Survey*] (SEIS) ... CPK
Cone Penetrometer Tests [*Computer science*] ... CPT
Cone Point (MSA) ... CP
Cone Resistance Value [*Civil engineering*] (IAA) ... CRV
Conejos County Public Library, La Jara, CO [*Library symbol*] [*Library of Congress*] (LCLS) ... CoLja
Conemaugh & Black Lick Railroad Co. [*AAR code*] ... CBL
Conesco Industries, Ltd. [*NASDAQ symbol*] (NQ) ... CNSC
Conestoga Bancorp [*NASDAQ symbol*] (TTSB) ... CONE
Conestoga Bancorp, Inc. [*NASDAQ symbol*] (SAG) ... CONE
Conestoga Bancorp, Inc. [*Associated Press*] (SAG) ... Conestga
Conestoga College of Applied Arts & Technology, Learning Resource Centre, Kitchener, ON, Canada [*Library symbol*] [*Library of Congress*] (LCLS) ... CaOKITC
Conestoga Enterprises [*NASDAQ symbol*] (TTSB) ... CENI
Conestoga Enterprises, Inc. [*NASDAQ symbol*] (SAG) ... CENI
Conestoga Enterprises, Inc. [*Associated Press*] (SAG) ... ConestEn
Conestoga Society (EA) ... CS
Confabulate [*An informal meeting*] [*Slang*] (WDMC) ... confab
Confectio [*Confection*] [*Pharmacy*] ... CONF
Confectionary ... CONFCTY
Confectioner (ROG) ... CONFEC
Confectioner, Tobacconist, and Newsagent [*British*] (DI) ... CTN
Confectioners Benevolent Fund [*British*] (BI) ... CBF
Confectionery ... CONF
Confectionery and Allied Trades Sports Association [*British*] (BI) ... CATSA
Confectionery and Mixed Business Association of Australia ... CMBA
Confectionery and Mixed Business Association of Australia and New Zealand ... CMBANZ
Confectionery Manufacturers Association of Canada [*Association Canadienne des Fabricants de Confiseries*] (AC) ... CMAC
Confectionery, Tobacco, and Newsagent [*British*] ... CTN
Confectionery Workers' Union of Australia ... CWUA
Confederacion de Organizaciones Turisticas de l' America Latina [*Confederation of Latin American Travel Organizations*] [*Spanish*] (BARN) ... COTAL
Confederacion Democratica [*Democratic Confederation*] [*Chile*] [*Political party*] ... CODE
Confederacion Espanola de Derechas Autonomas [*Spanish Confederation of Autonomous Rightist Forces*] [*Political party*] (PPE) ... CEDA
Confederacion Evangelica Mundial [*World Evangelical Fellowship*] ... CEM
Confederacion Interamericana de Ganaderos ... CIAGA
Confederacion Internacional de Organizaciones Sindicales Libres [*International Confederation of Free Trade Unions*] ... CIOSL
Confederacion Latinoamericana de Asociaciones Cristianas de Jovenes [*Latin American Confederation of YMCAs - LACYMCA*] (EAIO) ... CLACJ
Confederacion Latinoamericana de Bioquimica Clinica [*Latin American Confederation of Clinical Biochemistry - LACCB*] (EAIO) ... CLBC
Confederacion Latinoamericana de Cooperativas de Ahorro y Credito [*Latin American Confederation of Savings and Loan Cooperatives*] (EAIO) ... COLAC
Confederacion Latinoamericana de Prensa Turistica [*Latin American Confederation of Touristic Press*] [*Medellin, Colombia*] (EAIO) ... CLAPTUR
Confederacion Norte, Centroamericana, y del Caribe de Futbol [*North and Central American and Caribbean Football Confederation*] (EAIO) ... CONCACAF
Confederacion Panamericana de Badminton [*Panamerican Badminton Conferation - PBC*] (EAIO) ... CPB
Confederacion Panamericana de Basketball [*Pan American Basketball Confederation - PABC*] (EAIO) ... CPB

Confederacion Sudamericana de Atletismo [*South American Athletic Confederation - SAAC*] (EAIO) .... CSA

Confederacion Universitaria Centroamericana [*Confederation of Central American Universities*] (EAIO) .... CSUCA

Confederate Action Party of Australia [*Political party*] .... CAP

Confederate Air Force (EA) .... CAF

Confederate Army .... CA

Confederate High Command, International [*Later, AT*] [*An association*] (EA) .... CHC

Confederate Historical Society [*British*] .... CHS

Confederate Memorial Association .... CMA

Confederate Memorial Library, Hillsboro, NC [*Library symbol Library of Congress*] (LCLS) .... NcHil

Confederate Memorial Literary Society (EA) .... CMLS

Confederate National Congress (EA) .... CNC

Confederate Stamp Alliance (EA) .... CSA

Confederate States (HGAA) .... CS

Confederate States Army .... CSA

Confederate States Navy .... CSN

Confederate States of America .... CSA

Confederate States Ship .... CSS

Confederated .... CNFDRTD

Confederated Spanish Societies [*Defunct*] (EA) .... CSS

Confederated Unions of America [*Later, NFIU*] .... CUA

Confederation (WGA) .... CONF

Confederation (ADA) .... CONFD

Confederation (EY) .... CONFED

Confederation .... CONGDRTN

Confederation Africaine de Football [*African Football Confederation - AFC*] (EAIO) .... CAF

Confederation Arabe d'Athletisme [*Arab Amateur Athletic Federation - AAAF*] (EAIO) .... CAA

Confederation Art Gallery and Museum, Charlottetown, PE, Canada [*Library symbol Library of Congress*] (LCLS) .... CaPCCA

Confederation Art Gallery and Museum, Charlottetown, Prince Edward Island [*Library symbol National Library of Canada*] (NLC) .... PCCA

Confederation Centre Library, Charlottetown, PE, Canada [*Library symbol Library of Congress*] (LCLS) .... CaPCL

Confederation Centre Library, Charlottetown, Prince Edward Island [*Library symbol National Library of Canada*] (NLC) .... PCL

Confederation College of Applied Arts and Technology [*UTLAS symbol*] ..... TBC

Confederation College, Thunder Bay, ON, Canada [*Library symbol Library of Congress*] (LCLS) .... CaOTBCC

Confederation College, Thunder Bay, Ontario [*Library symbol National Library of Canada*] (NLC) .... OTBCC

Confederation des Associations des Etudiants de l'Universite Laval (AC) .... CADEUL

Confederation des Associations et Societes Medicales d'Afrique [*Confederation of African Medical Associations and Societies - CAMAS*] [*Nigeria*] (EAIO) .... CASMA

Confederation des Associations Latino-Americaines (AC) .... CASA

Confederation des Associations Linguistiques et Culturelles du Quebec (AC) .... CALCQ

Confederation des Brasseurs du Marche Commun [*Belgium*] (EAIO) .... CBMC

Confederation des Caisses Populaires et d'Economie Desjardins du Quebec (AC) .... CCPEDQ

Confederation des Caisses Populaires et d'Economie Desjardins du Quebec, Levis, PQ, Canada [*Library symbol*] [*Library of Congress*] (LCLS) .... CaQLeCCP

Confederation des Compagnonnages Europeens [*European Companions - EC*] [*France*] (EAIO) .... CCE

Confederation des Educateurs Americains [*Confederation of American Educators*] .... CEA

Confederation des Educateurs Physiques du Qubec (AC) .... CEEP

Confederation des Industries Agro-Alimentaires de la CEE [*Confederation of the Food and Drink Industries of the ECC*] (EAIO) .... CIAA

Confederation des Industries Agro-Alimentaires de l'Union des Industries de la Communaute Europeenne [*Commission of the Agricultural and Food Industries of the Union of Industries of the European Community*] (EAIO) .... CIAA de l'UNICE

Confederation des Organismes Familiaux du Quebec Inc. (AC) .... COFAQ

Confederation des Organismes Provinciaux de Personnes Handicapees du Quebec (AC) .... COPHAN

Confederation des Sourds et des Malentendants du Canada (AC) .... CSMC

Confederation des Syndicats Canadiens [*Confederation of Canadian Unions - CCU*] .... CSC

Confederation des Syndicats Nationaux [*Confederation of National Trade Unions - CNTU*] [*Canada*] .... CSN

Confederation des Travailleurs Catholiques du Canada [*Catholic Federation of Labour, 1922-1960*] .... CTCC

Confederation Europeene des Taxis [*Belgium*] (EAIO) .... CET

Confederation Europeenne de Baseball Amateur [*European Amateur Baseball Confederation - EABC*] (EA) .... CEBA

Confederation Europeenne de Billard .... CEB

Confederation Europeenne de l'Agriculture [*European Confederation of Agriculture*] (EAIO) .... CEA

Confederation Europeenne de l'Industrie de la Chaussure [*European Confederation of the Footwear Industry*] (ECED) .... CEC

Confederation Europeenne de l'Industrie de Pates, Papiers, et Cartons [*European Confederation of Pulp, Paper, and Board Industries*] (EAIO) ..... CEPAC

Confederation Europeenne de Scoutisme [*European Confederation of Scouts - ECS*] (EAIO) .... CES

Confederation Europeenne des Cadres [*European Confederation of Managers*] [*EC*] (ECED) .... CEC

Confederation Europeenne des Categories Auxiliaires des Activites Viti-Vinicole [*European Confederation of Auxiliary Occupations in the Wine Trade*] [*Common Market*] .... CECAVI

Confederation Europeenne des Detaillants en Tabac [*European Federation of Tobacco Retail Organizations*] (EAIO) .... CEDT

Confederation Europeenne des Independants [*European Confederation of the Self Employed*] [*EC Germany*] (ECED) .... CEDI

Confederation Europeenne des Industries du Bois [*European Confederation of Woodworking Industries*] .... CEIB

Confederation Europeenne des Industries du Bois [*European Confederation of Woodworking Industries*] (EAIO) .... CEI-BOIS

Confederation Europeenne des Relations Publiques [*European Confederation of Public Relations*] .... CERP

Confederation Europeenne d'Etudes Phytosanitaires [*European Confederation for Plant Protection Research*] .... CEP

Confederation Europeenne d'Organismes de Controle (EAIO) .... CEOC

Confederation Europeenne du Commerce de Detail [*European Federation for Retail Trade*] (EAIO) .... CECD

Confederation Europeenne du Jouet [*France*] (EAIO) .... CEJ

Confederation Europeenne Therapeutique Physique [*European Confederation for Physical Therapy*] (EAIO) .... CETP

Confederation Fiscale Europeenne [*European Fiscal Confederation*] (EAIO) .... CFE

Confederation for an Independent Poland (PD) .... KPN

Confederation for the Advancement of State Education .... CASE

Confederation Francaise de la Cooperation Agricole .... CFCA

Confederation Francaise Democratique du Travail [*French Democratic Confederation of Labor*] (BARN) .... CFDL

Confederation Generale de la Publicite (AC) .... COGEP

Confederation Generale Kamerounaise du Travail [*Cameroonian General Confederation of Workers*] .... CGKT

Confederation High School, Nepean, Ontario [*Library symbol National Library of Canada*] (NLC) .... ONC

Confederation Interalliee des Officiers de Reserve [*Interallied Confederation of Reserve Officers*] (EAIO) .... CIOR

Confederation Interamericaine d'Education Catholique [*Inter-American Confederation of Catholic Education*] .... CIEC

Confederation Internationale Catholique des Institutions Hospitalieres [*International Catholic Confederation of Hospitals*] .... CICIH

Confederation Internationale de Genealogie et d'Heraldique [*International Confederation of Genealogy and Heraldry - ICGH*] [*Paris, France*] (EAIO) .... CIGH

Confederation Internationale de la Boucherie et de la Charcuterie [*International Federation of Meat Traders' Associations*] .... CIBC

Confederation Internationale de la Coiffure [*International Conference of the Hairdressing Trade*] CIC

Confederation Internationale de la Representation Commerciale de la Communaute Europeenne [*International Confederation of Commercial Representation in the European Community*] .... CIRCCE

Confederation Internationale de Musique Electroacoustique [*International Confederation for Electroacoustic Music - ICEM*] (EAIO) .... CIME

Confederation Internationale des Accordeonistes [*International Confederation of Accordionists*] .... CIA

Confederation Internationale des Anciens Prisonniers de Guerre [*International Confederation of Former Prisoners of War*] [*Paris, France*] (EAIO) .... CIAPG

Confederation Internationale des Associations de Diplomes en Sciences Economiques et Commerciales [*International Confederation of Associations of Graduates in Economic and Commercial Sciences*] .... CIADEC

Confederation Internationale des Associations d'Experts et de Conseils [*International Confederation of Associations of Experts and Consultants*] .... CIDADEC

Confederation Internationale des Betteraviers Europeens [*International Confederation of European Sugar-Beet Growers*] (EAIO) .... CIBE

Confederation Internationale des Cadres [*International Confederation of Executive Staffs*] [*Paris, France*] (EAIO) CIC

Confederation Internationale des Cinemas d'Art et d'Essai [*International Experimental and Art Film Theatres Confederation*] [*France*] .... CICAE

Confederation Internationale des Corps de Fonctionnaires [*International Confederation of Public Service Officers*] .... CICF

Confederation Internationale des Fabricants de Tapis et de Tissus d'Ameublement [*International Confederation of Manufacturers of Carpets and Furnishing Fabrics*] (EAIO) .... CITTA

Confederation Internationale des Fonctionnaires [*International Confederation of Public Service Officers*] .... CIF

Confederation Internationale des Industries Techniques du Cinema .... CIITC

Confederation Internationale des Ingenieurs Agronomes [*International Confederation of Technical Agricultural Engineers*] .... CITA

Confederation Internationale des Ingenieurs et Techniciens de l'Agriculture [*International Confederation of Agricultural Engineers and Technicians*] [*Switzerland*] .... CITA

Confederation Internationale des Instituts Catholiques d'Education des Adultes Ruraux [*International Confederation of Catholic Rural People's Schools*] .... CIEPRC

Confederation Internationale des Negociants en Oeuvres d'Art [*International Confederation of Art Dealers*] (EAIO) .... CINOA

Confederation Internationale des Sages Femmes .... CISF

Confederation Internationale des Societes d'Auteurs et Compositeurs [*International Confederation of Societies of Authors and Composers*] .... CISAC

Confederation Internationale des Societes Musicales [*International Confederation of Societies of Music - ICSM*] (EA) .... CISM

Confederation Internationale des Societes Populaires de Musique .... CISPM

Confederation Internationale des Syndicats Chretiens [*International Federation of Christian Trade Unions*] .... CISC

Confederation Internationale des Syndicats Libres [*International Confederation of Free Trade Unions*] .... CISL

Confederation Internationale des Travailleurs Intellectuels [*International Confederation of Professional and Intellectual Workers*] .... CITI

Confederation Internationale du Commerce des Pailles, Fourrages, Tourbes et Derives [*International Straw, Fodder and Peat Trade Confederation*] [*EC*] (ECED) .... CIPF

Confederation Internationale du Commerce et des Industries des Legumes Secs [*International Pulse Trade and Industry Confederation*] [*EC*] (ECED) .... CICILS

Confederation Internationale du Credit Agricole [*International Confederation of Agricultural Credit*] [*Zurich, Switzerland*] (EAIO) .... CICA

Confederation Internationale du Credit Populaire [*International Confederation of Popular Credit - ICPC*] [*Paris, France*] (EAIO) .... CICP

Confederation Internationale du Lin et du Chanvre [*International Linen and Hemp Confederation*] (EAIO) CILC

Confederation Internationale pour la Chirurgie Plastique et Reconstructive [*International Confederation for Plastic and Reconstructive Surgery*] (EAIO) .... CICPR

Confederation Internationale pour le Desarmement et la Paix [*International Confederation for Disarmament and Peace - ICDP*] [*London, England*] (EA) .... CIDP

Confederation Life Association, Toronto, ON, Canada [*Library symbol Library of Congress*] (LCLS) .... CaOTCLA

Confederation Life Association, Toronto, Ontario [*Library symbol National Library of Canada*] (NLC) .... OTCLA

Confederation Mondiale de Centres Communautaires Juifs [*World Confederation of Jewish Community Centers*] (EAIO) .... CMCCJ

Confederation Mondiale des Activites Subaquatiques [*World Underwater Federation - WUF*] [*ICSU Paris, France*] (EAIO) .... CMAS

Confederation Mondiale des Organisations de la Profession Enseignante [*World Confederation of Organizations of the Teaching Profession - WCOTP*] (EAIO) .... CMOPE

Confederation Mondiale du Travail [*World Confederation of Labour - WCL*] [*Brussels, Belgium*] (EAIO) .... CMT

Confederation Nationale de la Construction [*Civil Engineering, Road and Building Contractors, and Auxiliary Trades Confederation*] [*Brussels, Belgium*] (EY) .... CNC

Confederation Nationale des Cadres du Quebec (AC) .... CNCQ

Confederation Nordique des Cadres, Techniciens, et Autres Responsables [*Nordic Confederation of Supervisors, Technicians, and Other Managers*] (EAIO) .... NAU

Confederation of Aerial Industries [*British*] (DBA) .... CAI

Confederation of African Medical Associations and Societies [*Nigeria*] (EAIO) .... CAMAS

Confederation of All Type Canaries [*Defunct*] (EA) .... CATC

Confederation of American Educators .... CAE

Confederation of American Indians (EA) .... CAI

Confederation of Arab Trade Unions .... CATU

Confederation of Ariel Industries (NITA) .... CAI

Confederation of Art and Design Associations (AIE) .... CADA

Confederation of Asian-Pacific Chambers of Commerce and Industry [*Taipei, Taiwan*] (EAIO) .... CACCI

Confederation of Associations of Specialist Engineering Contractors (DBA) .... CASEC

Confederation of Australasian Performing Arts Presenters [*Australia*] ...... CAPAP

Confederation of Brewers in the Common Market [*Belgium*] (EAIO) .... CBCM

Confederation of British Associations (DBA) .... CBA

Confederation of British Industry .... CBI

Confederation of British Road Passenger Transport (ILCA) .... CBRPT

Confederation of Building Contractors [*British*] (DBA) .... CBC

Confederation of Canadian Unions .... CCU

Confederation of Construction Professions [*British*] (DBA) .... CCP

Confederation of Construction Specialists [*British*] (DBA) .... CCS

Confederation of Design and Technology Associations [*British*] .... CDTA

Confederation of Entertainment Unions [*British*] .... CEU

Confederation of Entertainment Unions [*British*] (DCTA) .... COEU

Confederation of European Bath Manufacturers (EAIO) .... COFEB

Confederation of European Computer Users Associations (EAIO) .... CECUA

Confederation of European Specialists in Pediatrics (EAIO) .... CESP

Confederation of Free Trade Unions [*India*] .... CFTU

Confederation of Health Service Employees [*Pronounced "cozy"*] [*A union*] [*British*] (DCTA) .... COHSE

Confederation of Health Service Employees [*British*] (ODBW) .... Cohse

Confederation of Importers and Marketing Organizations in Europe of Fresh Fruit and Vegetables [*Brussels, Belgium*] (EAIO) .... CIMO

Confederation of Independent Orders, Ku Klux Klan (EA) .... CIOKKK

Confederation of Independent Trade Unions (EAIO) .... CITU

Confederation of Indian Organizations [*British*] (DBA) .... CIO

Confederation of Information Communication Industries [*British*] CICI

Confederation of Institute Directors (AIE) .... CID

Confederation of Insurance Trade Unions [*British*] (DCTA) .... COITU

Confederation of International Contractors' Associations [*Paris, France*] (EAIO) .... CICA

Confederation of International Scientific and Technological Organizations for Development [*ICSU*] [*Paris, France*] [*Defunct*] (EAIO) .... CISTOD

Confederation of International Trading Houses Associations [*The Hague, Netherlands*] (EAIO) .... CITHA

Confederation of Iranian Students [*Germany*] (PD) .... CISNU

Confederation of Irish Industry (EAIO) CII

Confederation of Khmer Nationalists [*Cambodia*] (PD) .... CNK

Confederation of National Educational Associations .... CONEA

Confederation of National Trade Unions [*Canada*] .... CNTU

Confederation of Non-Governmental Organizations for Overseas Development .... CONGOOD

Confederation of Photographic Industries [*British*] (DBA) .... CPI

Confederation of Regions [*Canada Political party*] .... COR

Confederation of Registered Gas Installers [*British*] (DI) .... CORGI

Confederation of Resident & Ratepayer Associations (AC) .... CORRA

Confederation of Roofing Contractors [*British*] (DBA) .... CRC

Confederation of Shipbuilding and Engineering Unions [*British*] .... CSEU

Confederation of Socialist Parties of the European Community [*Belgium Political party*] (EAIO) .... CSPEC

Confederation of Tanners' Associations in the European Community [*Brussels, Belgium*] (EAIO) .... COTANCE

Confederation of the Canons Regular of Saint Augustine [*Italy*] (EAIO) .... CCRSA

Confederation of the National Hotel and Restaurant Associations in the EC (ECED) .... HOTREC

Confederation of University Faculty/Associations of British Columbia (AC) .... CUFA/BC

Confederation of Western Australian Industry, Inc. [*Australia*] .... CWAI

Confederation Quebecoise des Centres d'Hebergement et de Readaptation (AC) .... CQCHR

Confederation Quebecoise des Cooperatives d'Habitation (AC) .... CQCH

Confederation Syndicale Mondiale des Enseignants [*World Confederation of Teachers - WCT*] [*Brussels, Belgium*] (EAIO) .... CSME

Confer [*Compare, Consult*] [*Latin*] .... CF

Confer [*Compare*] [*Latin*] .... CNFR

Confer [*Compare*] [*Latin*] .... CONF

Conference .... CNFRNC

Conference (AFM) .... CONF

Conference (ROG) .... CONFCE

Conference Administrative des Postes et Telecommunications des Etats de l'Afrique de l'Ouest [*Conference of Posts and Telecommunications Administrations of the States of West Africa*] .... CAPTEAO

Conference Administrative Regionale de Radiodiffusion a Ondes Hectometriques [*Regional Administrative FM Broadcasting Conference*] [*Canada*] .... CARR

Conference Aeronautique Internationale [*International Aeronautical Conference*] .... CAI

[*The*] Conference Board [*Formerly, National Industrial Conference Board*] .... CB

[*The*] Conference Board (EA) .... TCB

[*The*] Conference Board Abstract Database [*The Conference Board, Inc.*] [*Information service or system*] (CRD) .... CBABS

[*The*] Conference Board Data Base [*The Conference Board, Inc.*] [*Information service or system*] (CRD) .... CBDB

Conference Board in Canada, Ottawa, ON, Canada [*Library symbol Library of Congress*] (LCLS) .... CaOOCBC

Conference Board of Associated Research Councils (EA) .... CBARC

Conference Board of Canada .... CBC

Conference Board of Canada, Ottawa, Ontario [*Library symbol National Library of Canada*] (NLC) .... OOCBC

Conference Board of Major Printers [*Defunct*] (EA) .... CBMP

Conference Board of the Mathematical Sciences (EA) .... CBMS

Conference Canadienne des Administrateurs en Transport Motorise [*Canadian Conference of Transport Administrators*] .... CCATM

Conference Canadienne des Arts [*Canadian Conference of the Arts - CCA*] .... CCA

Conference Chretienne pour la Paix [*Christian Peace Conference - CPC*] [*Prague, Czechoslovakia*] (EAIO) .... CCP

Conference Committee for Refugee Rabbis (EA) .... CCRR

Conference de la Haye de Droit International Prive [*Hague Conference on Private International Law*] (EA) .... CODIP

Conference de Solidarite des Pays Afro-Asiatiques .... CSPAA

Conference des Administrations des Postes et Telecommunications de l'Afrique Centrale [*Conference of Posts and Telecommunications Administrations of Central Africa*] (PDAA) .... CAPTAC

Conference des Communautes Ethniques de Langue Francaise [*Standing Committee of French-Speaking Ethnical Communities - SCFSEC*] (EA) .... CCELF

Conference des Cooperatives Forestieres du Quebec (AC) .... CCFQ

Conference des Directeurs des Bibliotheques Publiques de l'Ile de Montreal [*Conference of Public Library Directors of the Island of Montreal*] (AC) .... CDPIM

Conference des Eglises de Toute l'Afrique [*All Africa Conference of Churches - AACC*] (EAIO) .... CETA

Conference des Eveques de la Region Nord de l'Afrique [*North African Episcopal Conference*] (EAIO) .... CERNA

Conference des Juges du Quebec (AC) .... CJQ

Conference des Ministres de l'Education des Pays d'Expression Francaise .... CONFEMEN

Conference des Ministres Europeens du Travail [*Conference of European Ministers of Labour*] (EAIO) .... MTV

Conference des Nations Unies pour le Commerce et le Developpement [*United Nations Conference on Trade and Development - UNCTAD*] [*French*] .... CNUCD

Conference des Organismes Regionaux de Loisirs du Quebec (AC) .... CORLQ

Conference des Recteurs et des Principaux des Universites du Quebec [*Conference of Rectors & Principals of Quebec Universities*] (AC) .... CREPUQ

Conference des Recteurs et des Principaux des Universites du Quebec .... CREPUQ

Conference des Recteurs et des Principaux des Universites du Quebec, Montreal, PQ, Canada [*Library symbol Library of Congress*] (LCLS) .... CaQMCRP

Conference des Recteurs et des Principaux des Universites du Quebec, Montreal, Quebec [*Library symbol National Library of Canada*] (NLC) .... QMCRP

Conference des Societes d'Ingenieurs de l'Europe Occidental et des Etats-Unis d'Amerique [*Conference of Engineering Societies of Western Europe and the United States of America*] .... EU?

Conference Euorpeenne des Horaires et des Services Directs [*European Conference of Time-tables and Direct Services*] (PDAA) ....

Conference Europeenne des Administrations des Postes et des
Telecommunications [*Conference of European Postal and
Telecommunications Administrations*] [*Telecommunications*] (EAIO) .... CEPT
Conference Europeenne des Experts Meteorologistes de
l'Aeronautique .... CEEMA
Conference Europeenne des Experts Radiotelegraphistes de
l'Aeronautique .... CEERA
Conference Europeenne des Horaires des Trains de Marchandises
[*European Freight Timetable Conference*] .... CEM
Conference Europeenne des Horaires des Trains de Voyageurs [*European
Passenger Timetable Conference*] [*Switzerland*] .... CEH
Conference Europeenne des Ministres des Transports [*European
Conference of Ministers of Transport - ECMT*] [*France*] .... CEMT
Conference Europeenne des Pouvoirs Locaux .... CEPL
Conference Europeenne des Telecommunications par Satellite [*European
Conference on Satellite Communications*] .... CETS
Conference Europeenne des Telecommunications par Satellites
[*Benelux*] .... CETS
Conference for Basic Human Rights in the ASEAN [*Associaton of South
East Asian Nations*] Countries [*British*] .... COBRA
Conference for Catholic Lesbians (EA) CCL
Conference for Chinese Oral and Performing Literature (EA) .... CHINOPERL
Conference for Health Council Work [*Later, Conference on Community Health
Planning*] .... CHCW
Conference for Higher Education in Art and Design [*British*] .... CHEAD
Conference for Independent Further Education [*British*] .... CIFE
Conference for Progressive Labor Action .... CPLA
Conference for Progressive Political Action .... CPPA
Conference for Reconciliation, Restitution Fund (EA) .... CONREC
Conference for Secondary School English Department Chairpersons
(EA) .... CSSEDC
Conference for the Advancement of Private Practice [*in social work*] .... CAPP
Conference for the Study of Political Thought (EA) .... CSPT
Conference for Universal Reason and Ethics [*Founded by motion picture
actor Lew Ayres*] .... CURE
Conference for World Mission [*British Council of Churches*] .... CWM
Conference Group on French Politics and Society (EA) .... CGFPS
Conference Group on German Politics (EA) .... CGGP
Conference Group on Italian Politics (EDAC) .... CGIP
Conference Group on Italian Politics and Society (EA) .... CONGRIPS
Conference Internationale Administrative des Radiocommunications
Aeronautiques .... CIARA
Conference Internationale Catholique du Guidisme [*International Catholic
Conference of Guiding*] (EAIO) .... CICG
Conference Internationale de la Mutualite et des Assurances Sociales ..... CIMAS
Conference Internationale de Liaison entre Producteurs d'Energie
Electrique [*International Conference of Producers of Electrical Energy*] ..... CILPE
Conference Internationale de Service Social [*International Conference of
Social Service*] .... CISS
Conference Internationale de Sociologie Religieuse [*International
Conference of Sociology of Religion*] .... CISR
Conference Internationale des Africanistes de l'Ouest .... CIAO
Conference Internationale des Associations d'Ingenieurs [*International
Federatiio of Engineering Associations*] (PDAA) .... CIAI
Conference Internationale des Charites Catholiques [*International
Conference of Catholic Charities*] CICC
Conference Internationale des Controles d'Assurances des Etats Africains
[*International Conference of African States on Insurance Supervision*]
(EAIO) .... CICA
Conference Internationale des Grands Reseaux Electriques a Haute
Tension [*International Conference on Large High Voltage Electric
Systems*] (EAIO) .... CIGRE
Conference Internationale des Trains Speciaux d'Agences de Voyages
[*International Conference on Special Trains for Travel Agencies*] (EAIO) ..... CITA
Conference Internationale du Goudron [*International Tar Conference - ITC*]
(EAIO) .... CIG
Conference Internationale du Scoutisme Catholique [*International
Conference of Catholic Scouting*] .... CISC
Conference Internationale Permanente de Directeurs d'Instituts
Universitaires pour la Formation de Traducteurs et d'Interpretes
[*Standing International Conference of the Directors of University Institutes
for the Training of Translators and Interpreters*] (EAIO) .... CIUTI
Conference Internationale pour l'Enseignement Universitaire des Relations
Publiques [*International Conference on University Education for Public
Relations*] .... CIEURP
Conference Internationale pour l'Unite Technique des Chemins de Fer .... UT
Conference Internationale sur l'Assistance aux Refugies en Afrique
[*International Conference on Assistance for Refugees in Africa - ICARA*]
[*United Nations Geneva, Switzerland*] (EAIO) .... CIARA
Conference Letter Report (SAA) .... CLR
Conference Location (NITA) CL
Conference Lodges [*Freemasonry*] (ROG) CL
Conference Ministerielle des Etats d'Afrique de l'Ouest et du Centre sur
les Transports Maritimes [*Ministerial Conference of West and Central
African States on Maritime Transportation - MCWCS*] [*Abidjan, Ivory
Coast*] (EAIO) .... CMEAOC
Conference Mondiale de l'Energie [*World Energy Conference - WEC*]
(EAIO) .... CME
Conference Mondiale des Experts Radiotelegraphistes de
l'Aeronautique .... CMERA
Conference of Actuaries in Public Practice [*Itasca, IL*] (EA) .... CAPP
Conference of Administrators of College and University Counseling
Services (EA) .... CACUCS
Conference of American Renting and Leasing Associations (EA) .... CARALA

Conference of American Small Business Organizations [*AFSB*] [*Absorbed
by*] (EA) .... CASBO
Conference of Americans of Central and Eastern European Descent
[*Defunct*] (EA) .... CACEED
Conference of Association Society Executives (EA) .... CASE
Conference of Baltic Oceanographers [*Germany*] (EAIO) .... CBO
Conference of Business Economists (EA) .... CBE
Conference of California Historical Societies .... CCHS
Conference of Casualty Insurance Companies [*Indianapolis, IN*] (EA) CCIC
Conference of Catholic Schools of Nursing (EA) .... CCSN
Conference of Central and East African States .... CCEAFS
Conference of Chaplains-General [*Australia*] .... CCHAPG
Conference of Chief Executive Officers of Bulk Handling Authorities
[*Australia*] .... CCEOBHA
Conference of Chief Justices (EA) .... CCJ
Conference of Church Workers Among the Deaf [*Later, ECD*] (EA) .... CCWAD
Conference of Churches of Western Australia [*Australia*] .... CCWA
Conference of Commissioners on Uniformity of Legislation in Canada
(DLA) .... Conf Comm Uniformity Legis
Conference of Consumer Organizations (EA) .... COCO
Conference of Defence Associations Institute [*Institut du Congres des
Associations de la Defense*] (AC) .... CDA
Conference of Diocesan Executives [*Episcopalian*] .... CODE
Conference of Directors of Danube Lines [*Budapest, Hungary*] (EAIO) .... CDDL
Conference of Directors of National Libraries in Asia and Oceania
[*Australia*] .... CDNLAO
Conference of Directors of State University Librarians of Illinois [*Library
network*] .... CODSULI
Conference of Drama Schools [*British*] .... CDS
Conference of Eastern College Librarians .... CECL
Conference of Educational Administrators Serving the Deaf (EA) .... CEASD
Conference of European Churches (EA) .... CEC
Conference of Executives of State Associations of Counties [*Later, National
Council of County Association Executives*] (EA) .... CESAC
Conference of Funeral Service Examining Boards of the United States
(EA) .... CFSEB
Conference of Independent African States (NATG) .... CIAS
Conference of Industrial Research Associations (DGA) .... CIRA
Conference of Insurance Legislators [*Later, NCOIL*] (EA) .... COIL
Conference of International Catholic Organizations [*Geneva, Switzerland*]
(EAIO) .... CICO
Conference of Internationally-Minded Schools .... CIS
Conference of Jesuit Student Personnel Administrators [*Later, JASPA*]
(EA) .... CJSPA
Conference of Jewish Communal Service (EA) .... CJCS
Conference of Jewish Organizations (BARN) .... COJO
Conference of LASER Engineering and Applications (EA) .... CLEA
Conference of Latin Americanist Geographers .... CLAG
Conference of Latin Bishops of Arab Regions [*Jersalem, Israel*] (EAIO) ..... CELRA
Conference of Liberal Arts Colleges for Women (EA) .... CLACW
Conference of Local Environmental Health Administrators [*Later,
NCLEHA*] (EA) .... CLEHA
Conference of Major Religious Superiors of Women's Institutes of the
United States of America [*Later, LCWR*] .... CMSW
Conference of Major Superiors of Men (EA) .... CMSM
Conference of Major Superiors of Religious Brothers of Australia .... CMSRBA
Conference of Major Superiors of Women's Religious Institutes of
Australia .... CMSWA
Conference of Mennonites in Canada (AC) .... CMC
Conference of Minister for Immigration and Ethnic Affairs [*Australia*] .... CMIEA
Conference of Ministers of Education [*World War II*] .... CME
Conference of Minority Public Administrators (EA) .... COMPA
Conference of Municipal Public Health Engineers [*Later, NCLEHA*]
(EA) .... CMPHE
Conference of Mutual Casualty Companies [*Later, CCIC*] (EA) .... CMCC
Conference of National Armaments Directors [*NATO*] .... CNAD
Conference of National Park Concessioners (EA) .... CNPC
Conference of National Social Science Councils and Analogous
Bodies .... CNSSC
Conference of New Emerging Forces [*Indonesia*] (CINC) .... CONEFO
Conference of New Law Librarians .... CONELL
Conference of Officers of Affiliated States and Territorial
Associations .... COASTA
Conference of Peripheral Maritime Regions of the EEC (EAIO) .... CPMR
Conference of Pharmaceutical Ingredients .... CPhI
Conference of Philosophical Societies (EA) .... CPS
Conference of Podiatry Executives (EA) .... COPE
Conference of Presidents and Officers of State Medical Associations
[*Later, FMA*] (EA) .... CPOSMA
Conference of Presidents of Major American Jewish Organizations
(EA) .... CPMAJO
Conference of Prince Hall Grand Masters (EA) .... CPHGM
Conference of Private Organizations (EA) .... CONPOR
Conference of Private Organizations [*Defunct*] (EA) .... CPO
Conference of Public Health Laboratorians .... COPHL
Conference of Public Health Laboratory Directors [*Later, COPHL*] (EA).... CPHLD
Conference of Public Health Veterinarians (EA) .... CPHV
Conference of Radiation Control Program Directors (EA) .... CRCPD
Conference of Research Workers in Animal Diseases (EA) .... CRWAD
Conference of Scottish Centrally Funded Colleges (AIE) .... CSCFC
Conference of Small Private Colleges [*Defunct Defunct*] (EA) .... CSPC
Conference of Societies for the History of Pharmacy [*Madrid, Spain*]
(EAIO) .... CSHP
Conference of Speakers and Presiding Officers of Commonwealth
Parliaments [*Canada*] (EAIO) .... CSPOCP

Conference of State and Provincial Health Authorities of North America [*Defunct*] (EA) .... CSPHA
Conference of State and Provincial Public Health Laboratory Directors (EA) .... CSPPHLD
Conference of State and Territorial Directors of Public Health Education (EA) .... CSTDPHE
Conference of State and Territorial Health Officers with Public Health Service (EA) .... CSTHOPHS
Conference of State Bank Supervisors [*Washington, DC*] (EA) .... CSBS
Conference of State Cable Agencies (EA) .... CSCA
Conference of State Cemetery Association Secretaries (EA) .... CSCAS
Conference of State Court Administrators (EA) .... COSCA
Conference of State Health and Environmental Managers [*Conference of Stat e Sanitary Engineers*] [*Acronym is based on former name, Defunct*] (EA) .... CSSE
Conference of State Sanitary Engineers .... CSSE
Conference of State Societies [*Later, National Conference of State Societies*] (EA) .... CSS
Conference of State Utility Commission Engineers [*Later, NCRUCE*] (EA) .... CSUCE
Conference of the American Armies .... CAA
Conference of the Committee on Disarmament [*Formerly, ENDC*] [*NATO*] .... CCD
Conference of the Electronics Industry [*British*] (BI) .... CEI
Conference of the Labour Party [*British*] .... CLP
Conference of the Methodist Church in the Caribbean and the Americas (EAIO) .... CMCCA
Conference of the Methodist Church in the Caribbean and the Americas (EAIO) .... MCCA
Conference of the Parties [*Governments which have ratified UN climate change convention of 1992*] .... COP
Conference of UN Representatives, UNA [*United Nations Association*]-USA (EA) .... CUNR
Conference of University Administrators [*British*] [*An association*] (DBA) .... CUA
Conference on Alternative State and Local Policies [*Later, CPA*] (EA) .... CASLP
Conference on Alternative State and Local Public Policies [*Later, CPA*] (EA) .... CASLPP
Conference on Application Development Systems (MHDI) .... COADS
Conference on Asian Affairs [*Later, AS*] (MCD) .... CAA
Conference on Asian History (EA) .... CAH
Conference on British Studies (EA) .... CBS
Conference on Charitable Foundations. Proceedings. New York University [*A publication*] (DLA) .... Conf on Char Found NYU Proc
Conference on Charitable Foundations. Proceedings. New York University [*A publication*] (DLA) .... NYU Conf on Char Found Proc
Conference on Christian Politics, Economics, and Citizenship (IIA) .... COPEC
Conference on Christianity and Literature (EA) CCL
Conference on College Composition and Communication (EA) CCCC
Conference on Computers in Undergraduate Science Education .... COMUSE
Conference on Conceptual and Terminological Analysis in the Social Sciences [*1981*] .... CONTA
Conference on Confidence and Security-Building Measures and Disarmament in Europe .... CDE
Conference on Consumer Finance Law (EA) .... CCFL
Conference on Critical Legal Studies (EA) .... CCLS
Conference on Data Systems Languages [*Defunct*] (EA) .... CODASYL
Conference on Disarmament .... CD
Conference on Dual Distribution .... CDD
Conference on Early American History (EA) .... CEAH
Conference on Economic Progress [*Defunct*] (EA) .... CEP
Conference on Electrical Insulation and Dielectric Phenomena [*National Academy of Sciences*] .... CEIDP
Conference on English Education (EA) .... CEE
Conference on European Security and Cooperation .... CESC
Conference on Fair Use .... CONFU
Conference on Faith and History (EA) .... CFH
Conference on Forces in Europe .... CFE
Conference on Industrial Robot Technology .... CIRT
Conference on Inter-American Telecommunications [*Organization of American States*] [*Telecommunications*] .... CITEL
Conference on Interlibrary Communications and Information Networks [*September 28 - October 2, 1970*] .... CICIN
Conference on International Economic Cooperation .... CIEC
Conference on Jewish Material Claims Against Germany (EA) .... CJMCAG
Conference on Jewish Social Studies (EA) .... CJSS
Conference on LASER and Electro-Optical Systems .... CLEOS
Conference on LASERs and Electro-Optics (MCD) .... CLEO
Conference on Latin American History (EA) .... CLAH
Conference on Non-Governmental Organizations in Consultative Status with the United Nations Economic and Social Council (EAIO) .... CONGO
Conference on Optical Fiber Communication [*Optical Society of America*] [*Washington, DC*] (TSSD) .... OFC
Conference on Oriental-Western Literary Relations [*Later, ALD*] (EA) .... COWLR
Conference on Personal Finance Law [*Later, CCFL*] (EA) .... CPFL
Conference on Precision Electromagnetic Measurements (EA) .... CPEM
Conference on Psychoanalytic Education and Research .... COPER
Conference on Research in Peace History (EA) .... CRPH
Conference on Safe Transportation of Hazardous Articles (EA) .... COSTHA
Conference on Science and Religion [*Later, UDC*] (EA) .... CSR
Conference on Science and World Affairs .... COSWA
Conference on Science, Philosophy, and Religion (EA) .... CSPR
Conference on Scientific Ocean Drilling [*JOIDES*] .... COSOD
Conference on Security and Cooperation in Europe (PD) .... CSCE
Conference on Security, Stability, Development, and Cooperation in Africa .... CSSDCA
Conference on Self-Operating Systems [*Computer science*] .... COSOS
Conference on the Application of Science and Technology to the Development of Africa .... CASTAFRICA
Conference on the Application of Science and Technology to the Development of Latin America .... CASTALA
Conference on the Atlantic Community (EA) .... CONTAC
Conference on the Public Service .... CPS
Conference on the Sociology of the Languages of American Women [*1976*] .... SLAW
Conference on Training Architects in Conservation [*London, England*] .... COTAC
Conference on Transportation Unity [*Defunct*] (EA) .... CTU
Conference on University Purchasing (AIE) .... COUP
Conference Paper .... CP
Conference Papers Index [*A database*] (NITA) .... CONF
Conference Permanente de l'Europe de la Federation Internationale de Basketball [*Standing Conference for Europe of the International Basketball Federation*] (EAIO) .... CPEFIBA
Conference Permanente de l'Industrie Europeenne de Produits Emailles .... EUREMAIL
Conference Permanente des Recteurs, Presidents, et Vice Chanceliers des Universites Europeennes (EAIO) .... CRE
Conference Permanente des Recteurs, Presidents et Vice Chancellors (AIE) .... CRE
Conference Permanente d'Etudes sur les Civilisations du Monde Mediterraneen [*Standing Conference of Studies on the Civilisations of the Mediterranean World*] (EAIO) .... CPM
Conference Permanente Mediterraneenne pour la Cooperation Internationale [*Standing Mediterranean Conference for International Cooperation*] (EA) .... COPEMCI
Conference Permanente Mediterraneenne pour la Cooperation Internationale [*Standing Mediterranean Conference for International Cooperation - COPEMCI*] (EAIO) .... CPM
Conference Preparatory Meeting [*ITU/WARC*] .... CPM
Conference Proceedings (ADA) .... CP
Conference Proceedings Index [*Database*] [*British Library*] [*Information service or system*] (CRD) .... CPI
Conference Proceedings. Inter-American Bar Association [*A publication*] (DLA) .... Conf Proc Inter-Amer Bar Assoc
Conference Regionale du Service Volontaire International [*Regional Conference on International Voluntary Service*] (EAIO) .... CRSVI
Conference Reguliere sur les Problemes Universitaires [*Standing Conference on University Problems*] [*Council of Europe*] [*Strasbourg, France*] (EAIO) .... CC-PU
Conference Report (DLA) .... Conf Rept
Conference Report .... CR
Conference Reports [*North Carolina*] [*A publication*] (DLA) .... Conference (NC)
Conference Reports, by Cameron and Norwood [*North Carolina*] [*A publication*] (DLA) .... Conf
Conference Room (DNAB) .... CR
Conference Services Office [*American Library Association*] .... CSO
Conference Society of Alberta (AC) .... CSA
Conference Spatiale Europeenne [*European Space Conference*] .... CSE
Conference sur la Securite Europeene [*Conference on Security in Europe*] (NATG) .... CSE
Conference Terms (DS) .... CT
Conference Title [*Database terminology*] (NITA) .... CT
Conference to Explore Machine Readable Bibliographic Interchange .... CEMBI
Conference Upon Research and Education in World Government (EA) .... CURE
Conference Year [*Database terminology*] (NITA) .... CY
Conferences in Energy, Physics, and Mathematics [*Fachinformationszentrum Karlsruhe GmbH*] [*Germany Information service or system*] (CRD) .... CONF
Conferences on Research on International Peace and Security [*Founded International Peace Research Association*] .... COROIPAS
Conferencia Interamericana de Bienestar Social [*Interamerican Social Welfare Conference*] .... CIBS
Conferencia Interamericana de Seguridad Social [*Inter-American Conference on Social Security - IACSS*] (EAIO) .... CISS
Conferentia Episcopalis Pacifici [*Episcopal Conference of the Pacific*] (EAIO) .... CEPAC
Conferentia Episcopalis Scandiae [*Scandinavian Episcopal Conference - SEC*] (EAIO) .... CES
Conferred (ROG) .... CONFD
Conferring (ROG) .... CONFG
Confessing Synod Ministries (EA) .... CSM
Confessions .... CF
Confessor C
Confessor (ROG) .... CONF
Confessor, Doctor [*Ecclesiastical*] (ROG) .... CD
Confessor Pontifex [*Confessor and Bishop*] [*Latin*] (ADA) .... CONFPONT
Confidence (ADA) .... CON
Confidence (FAAC) .... CONFDC
Confidence and Security-Building Measures .... CSBM
Confidence Development Plan .... CDP
Confidence Firing Kit .... CFK
Confidence Interval [*Statistics*] CI
Confidence Level [*Statistical mathematics*] CL
Confidence Limits CL
Confidence Probability [*Mathematics*] .... CP
Confidence Range [*Statistics*] .... CR
Confidence Test Program [*NASA*] (KSC) .... CTP
Confidence Training Launch .... CTL
Confidence-Building Measure .... CBM
Confidence-Building Measure [*for European military security*] .... CBM's
Confidential C
Confidential (AFM) .... CONF
Confidential [*Security classification*] [*Military*] .... CONFD

Confidential (DSUE) ... CONFI
Confidential (ADA) ... CONFID
Confidential Admiralty Fleet Order [*British military*] (DMA) ... CAFO
Confidential Admiralty Merchant Shipping Instructions ... CAMSI
Confidential Air Force Order [*British military*] (DMA) ... CAFO
Confidential and Secret Weekly Orders [*Naval Air Stations*] ... CASWO
Confidential Book [*Navy British*] ... CB
Confidential Bulletin ... CB
Confidential Bulletin [*Navy*] ... CONFBUL
Confidential Business Information [*Environmental Protection Agency*] ... CBI
Confidential Business Information [*Government regulations*] ... CBI
Confidential Chemicals Identification System (GNE) ... CCID
Confidential Cover Sheet (AAG) ... CCS
Confidential Damage Level (SAA) ... CDL
Confidential Document [*Navy*] ... CD
Confidential Employment Listing [*American Chemical Society*] ... CELACS
Confidential, Formerly Restricted Data ... CFRD
Confidential Hydrographic Office [*later, Naval Oceanographic Office*] **Reports - Atlantic** [*Navy*] ... CONHYDROLANT
Confidential Informant [*Department of Justice*] ... CI
Confidential Material Control Officer (DNAB) ... CMCO
Confidential Measurement-Based Self-Evaluation [*Project*] (AIE) ... COMBSE
Confidential Memorandum ... CM
Confidential - Modified Handling [*Army*] ... CONF-MH
Confidential - Modified Handling Authorized [*Army*] (AFM) ... C-MHA
Confidential - Modified Handling Authorized [*Army*] ... CONFMOD
Confidential Restricted Data ... CRD
Configurable Network Computing [*J.D. Edwards*] ... CNC
Configurable Network Computing [*Software*] [*JD Edwards*] ... CNC
Configurable Unified Search Engine [*Internet*] (DAVI) ... CUSI
Configuration ... CONF
Configuration (KSC) ... CONFIG
Configuration (FAAC) ... CONFIGN
Configuration Acceptance Inspection ... CAI
Configuration Accountability Systems, Aerospace ... CASA
Configuration Accountability Transmittal ... CAT
Configuration Accounting and Management Report (MCD) ... CAMR
Configuration Accounting Number ... CAN
Configuration Advisor (IAA) ... CONAD
Configuration Alternative (MCD) ... CA
Configuration Analysis and Performance (MCD) ... CAPER
Configuration Analysis Tool (MCD) ... CAT
Configuration and Acceptance Review (MCD) ... CAR
Configuration and Administration ... C & A
Configuration and Data Management (DNAB) ... CADM
Configuration and Data Management Support System ... CADMSS
Configuration and Switching Equipment Subsystem (MCD) ... CSES
Configuration and Trace System [*Military*] ... CTS
Configuration and Traceability (KSC) ... CAT
Configuration and Tuning Module [*Computer science*] ... CTM
Configuration Audit Inspection [*Army*] (AABC) ... CAI
Configuration Audit Plan ... CAP
Configuration Audit Review ... CAR
Configuration Baseline ... CB
Configuration Block Diagram [*Telecommunications*] (TEL) ... CBD
Configuration Breakdown List ... CBL
Configuration Change Board [*NASA*] (MCD) ... CCB
Configuration Change Control Board [*NASA*] (KSC) ... CCCB
Configuration Change Directive (KSC) ... CCD
Configuration Change Notice (DOMA) ... CCN
Configuration Change Order ... CCO
Configuration Change Plan (KSC) ... CCP
Configuration Change Point (NASA) ... CCP
Configuration Change Proposal (MCD) ... CCP
Configuration Change Request ... CCR
Configuration Control (AAG) ... CC
Configuration Control Action (KSC) ... CCA
Configuration Control and Management (MCD) ... CC/M
Configuration Control and Sensing Unit (CET) ... CCSU
Configuration Control Board [*DoD*] ... CCB
Configuration Control Board Data [*or Directive*] [*DoD*] ... CCBD
Configuration Control Function [*Telecommunications*] (TEL) ... CCF
Configuration Control Logic (NASA) ... CCL
Configuration Control Number (AAG) ... CCN
Configuration Control Panel ... CCP
Configuration Control Phase (MCD) ... CCP
Configuration Control Reporting System [*Navy*] (MCD) ... CCRS
Configuration Control Review (SSD) ... CCR
Configuration Control Room [*Social Security Administration*] ... CCR
Configuration Control Secretariat (KSC) ... CCS
Configuration Control Unit (MCD) ... CCU
Configuration Control Verification List (MCD) ... CCVL
Configuration Data Control (AAG) ... CDC
Configuration Data Management ... CDM
Configuration Data Package (DNAB) ... CDP
Configuration Data Requirement (DNAB) ... CDR
Configuration Data Table (MCD) ... CDT
Configuration Definition ... CD
Configuration Design Audit (MCD) ... CDA
Configuration Development of Advanced Fighters [*Military*] (MCD) ... CDAF
Configuration Development System (MCD) ... CDS
Configuration Deviation List (MCD) ... CDL
Configuration Element (AFIT) ... CE
Configuration End Item (AFIT) ... CEI
Configuration Enhanced Radiation Rejection [*Space technology*] ... CERR
Configuration File (CDE) ... CFG file
Configuration Identification (MCD) ... CI
Configuration Identification Control and Accounting ... CICA
Configuration Identification Documentation ... CID
Configuration Identification Index ... CII
Configuration Identification Number [*Military*] ... CIN
Configuration Identification Package (SAA) ... CIP
Configuration Identification Tables (AABC) ... CIT
Configuration Index ... CI
Configuration Index and Status Report (KSC) ... CISR
Configuration Index Document (MCD) ... CID
Configuration Information System ... CIS
Configuration Inspection (NASA) ... CI
Configuration [*or Contract*] **Inspection Log** ... CIL
Configuration Inspection Report (MCD) ... CIR
Configuration, Installation, and Distribution Architecture [*Computer science*] (PCM) ... CID
Configuration Interaction [*Quantum mechanics*] ... CI
Configuration Item ... CI
Configuration Item Data List (NASA) ... CIDL
Configuration Item Development Specifications (MCD) ... CIDS
Configuration Item Product Fabrication Specification (MCD) ... CIPFS
Configuration Item Specification ... CIS
Configuration Item Specification (MCD) ... CISPEC
Configuration Item Validation [*or Verification*] **Review** ... CIVR
Configuration Management ... CM
Configuration Management Accounting (NASA) ... CMA
Configuration Management and Change Control System [*Social Security Administration*] ... CMCCS
Configuration Management and Project Control Staff [*Social Security Administration*] ... CMPCS
Configuration Management Branch [*NASA*] (KSC) ... CMB
Configuration Management Integrated Support Tool [*Marine science*] (OSRA) ... CMIST
Configuration Management Integrated Support Tool (USDC) ... CMIST
Configuration Management Manual (DNAB) ... CMM
Configuration Management Office [*NASA*] (DNAB) ... CMO
Configuration Management Operating Systems Manual (MCD) ... CMOSM
Configuration Management Plan [*or Program*] ... CMP
Configuration Management Program Plan [*DoD*] ... CMPP
Configuration Management Review (AABC) ... CMR
Configuration Management Staff [*Social Security Administration*] ... CMS
Configuration Management System ... CMS
Configuration Management Tool (SSD) ... CMT
Configuration Management Version Control [*Computer science*] (PCM) ... CMVC
Configuration Process [*Telecommunications*] (TEL) ... CONFG
Configuration Report and Accounting Program [*Military*] ... CORAP
Configuration Report Server (ACRL) ... CRS
Configuration Requirements Processing (MCD) ... CRP
Configuration Review (MCD) ... CR
Configuration Review Board Directive [*Military*] ... CRBD
Configuration Selection Register ... CSR
Configuration Standardization Document [*Deep Space Instrumentation Facility, NASA*] ... CSD
Configuration State Function (MCD) ... CSF
Configuration Status Accounting ... CSA
Configuration Status Accounting Data List (MCD) ... COSADL
Configuration Status Accounting Data Requirements (MCD) ... CSADR
Configuration Status Accounting Document (MCD) ... CSAD
Configuration Status Accounting Report (KSC) ... CSAR
Configuration Status Accounting System ... CSAS
Configuration Switch Controller (CET) ... CSC
Configuration Switching Equipment (MCD) ... CSE
Configuration Usage Evaluator / Data Set Optimizer (PDAA) ... CUE/DSO
Configuration Utilization Efficiency (BUR) ... CUE
Configuration Utilization Evaluator (IAA) ... CUE
Configuration Verification and Accounting System ... CVAS
Configuration Verification Index ... CVI
Configuration Verification List (MCD) ... CVL
Configuration Verification Review (MCD) ... CVR
Configuration Verification Test ... CVT
Configuration Work Package Item [*Army*] (AABC) ... CWPI
Configured Article ... CA
Configured Article Identifier ... CAI
Confine (FAAC) ... CFN
Confine (AABC) ... CNF
Confine [*or Confinement*] (AFM) ... CONF
Confined Area Landing ... CAL
Confined Detonating Cord (MCD) ... CDC
Confined Detonating Fuze ... CDF
Confined Disposal Facilities ... CDF
Confined to Camp [*Military*] ... CC
Confined to Post ... C to P
Confinement at Hard Labor [*Army*] (AABC) ... CHL
Confinement Factor [*Nuclear energy*] (NRCH) ... CF
Confinement Physics Research Facility ... CPRF
Confinement to Barracks [*A military punishment*] ... CB
Confirm (AAG) ... CFM
Confirmatio Chartarum [*Confirmation of the Charters*] [*Latin Legal term*] (DLA) ... Conf Chart
Confirmation [*Purchasing*] ... CONF
Confirmation of Balance [*Banking*] ... C of B
Confirmation of Broadcast Order (WDMC) ... CBO
Confirmation of Number of Order [*Purchasing*] (IAA) ... CONO
Confirmation Rolls (ROG) ... CONF R

Confirmation to Receive [*Computer science*] .... CFR
Confirmatory Test [*Army*] (AABC) .... CT
Confirmed (DAVI) .... conf
Confirmed and Compatible (MEDA) .... C & C
Confirmed and Made a Matter of Record [*Army*] (AABC) .... CMMR
Confirmed Exposure but Unconscious [*Advertising*] .... CEBUS
Confirming Design Layout Report Date [*Bell System*] (TEL) .... CDLRD
Confirming Engineering Information Report Date [*Bell System*] (TEL) .... CEIRD
Confirming Informal Order [*Telecommunications*] (TEL) .... CIO
Confirming Requisition Follows (FAAC) .... COREQ
Confirming Telephone [*or message*] Authority Of .... COTA
Conflagration Control (DNAB) .... CONFLAG
Conflict (MSA) .... CFL
Conflict Alert [*Aviation*] .... CA
Conflict Alert/Minimum Safe Altitude Warning [*FAA*] (TAG) .... CA/MSAW
Conflict Alert System [*Aviation*] .... CAS
Conflict and Peace Data Bank .... COPDAB
Conflict Management Group [*An association*] .... CMG
Conflict Management Survey [*Interpersonal skills and attitudes test*] .... CMS
Conflict of Interest [*Legal term*] .... COI
Conflict of Laws [*Legal term*] (DLA) .... CONF L
Conflict Resolution .... CR
Conflict Resolution Advisory [*FAA*] (TAG) .... CRA
Conflict Resolution/Alternatives to Violence Training Center (EA) .... CR/AVTC
Conflict Resolution Center (EA) .... CRC
Conflict Resolution Inventory [*Psychology*] .... CRI
Conflict Tactics Scale (EDAC) .... CTS
Confluence (ROG) .... CON
Confluent Education Development and Research Center [*Defunct*] (EA) .... CEDARC
Confocal Flourescence Imaging Microscopy [*Medicine*] .... CFIM
Confocal LASER Scanning Microscope [*or Microscopy*] .... CLSM
Confocal Scanning LASER Microscope [*or Microscopy*] .... CSLM
Confoederatio Internationalis ad Qualitates Plantarum Edulium Perquirendas [*International Association for Quality Research on Food Plants*] .... CIQ
Conformal Array (CAAL) .... CFA
Conformal Fuel Tank (MCD) .... CFT
Conformal Solution Theory (MCD) .... CST
Conformal Tactical Array (MCD) .... CONTACT
Conformal Wire Grating .... CWG
Conformal-Array Antenna (PDAA) .... CAA
Conformance .... CONF
Conformance Inspection Record (SAA) .... CIR
Conformance Testing Service [*Computer science*] (TNIG) .... CTS
Conformational Analysis of Molecules in Solution by Empirical and Quantum Techniques .... CAMSEQ
Conforms to Copyright Guidelines .... CCG
Conforms to Copyright Law CCL
Confortair, Inc. [*Canada ICAO designator*] (FAAC) .... COF
Confraternidad Evangelica Latinoamericana [*Confraternity of Evangelicals in Latin America*] [*Argentina*] (EAIO) .... CONELA
Confraternity (ROG) .... CFR
Confraternity New Testament [*A publication*] (BJA) .... CNT
Confraternity of Christian Doctrine .... CCD
Confraternity of the Blessed Sacrament (EA) .... CBS
Confraternity Version (BJA) CV
Confrerie de la Chaine des Rotisseurs [*France*] (EAIO) .... CCR
Confrerie des Chevaliers du Goute Boudin [*Brotherhood of Knights of the Black Pudding Tasters - BKBPT*] (EA) .... CCGB
Confrerie des Chevaliers du Tastevin (EA) .... CCT
Confuse (MSA) .... CFS
Confused and Disabled Elderly Patient .... CADE
Confused Artificial Insemination .... CAI
Confusion (MSA) .... CFSN
Confusion Reflector Material .... CRM
Congdon Park Elementary School, Duluth, MN [*Library symbol*] [*Library of Congress*] (LCLS) .... MnDuCOE
Congdon's Digest [*Canada*] [*A publication*] (DLA) .... Cong Dig
Congdon's Mining Laws of California [*A publication*] (DLA) .... Cong Min L
Congenital [*Medicine*] (WGA) .... CONG
Congenital [*Medicine*] .... CONGEN
Congenital [*Medicine*] (DMAA) .... congen
Congenital Absence of Left Pericardium [*Medicine*] (DMAA) .... CALP
Congenital Absence of Vagina [*Medicine*] .... CAV
Congenital Adrenal Hyperplasia [*Medicine*] .... CAH
Congenital Adrenal Virilism [*Medicine*] .... CAV
Congenital Alcoholic Syndrome [*Medicine*] (DMAA) .... CAS
Congenital Atonic Sclerotic Muscular Dystrophy [*Medicine*] (DMAA) .... CASMD
Congenital Bilateral Absence of the Vas Deferens [*Medicine*] .... CBAVD
Congenital Central Hypoventilation Syndrome [*Medicine*] .... CCHS
Congenital Contracture Arachnodactyly [*Medicine*] .... CCA
Congenital Cytomegalovirus [*Medicine*] .... CMV
Congenital Diaphragmatic Hernia [*Medicine*] .... CDH
Congenital Dislocation [*or Dysplasia*] of the Hip [*Medicine*] .... CDH
Congenital Disorders of Neuromuscular Transmission (PAZ) .... CDNT
Congenital Dyserythropoietic Anemia [*Hematology*] .... CDA
Congenital Ectropion Uveae [*Medicine*] (DMAA) .... CEU
Congenital Erythropoietic Porphyria [*Medicine*] .... CEP
Congenital Eyelid Tetrad [*Medicine*] (DMAA) .... CET
Congenital Generalized Hypertrichosis [*Werewolf syndrome*] [*Medicine*] .... CGH
Congenital Generalized Hypertrichosis [*Medicine*] .... CGH
Congenital Heart Block [*Medicine*] (DMAA) .... CHB
Congenital Heart Disease [*Medicine*] .... CHD
Congenital Heinz Body Hemolytic Anemia [*Medicine*] .... CHBA

Congenital Heinz Body Hemolytic Anemia [*Medicine*] (DMAA) .... CHBHA
Congenital Hemidysplasia with Ichthyosiform Erythroderma and Limb Defects Syndr ome [*Medicine*] (DMAA) .... CHILD
Congenital Hepatic Fibrosis [*Medicine*] (DMAA) .... CHF
Congenital Hereditary Retinoschisis [*Ophthalmology*] (DAVI) .... CHRS
Congenital Hypertrophy of the Retinal Pigment Epithelium [*Medicine*] (DMAA) .... CHRPE
Congenital Hypomyelination [*Medicine*] .... CH
Congenital Hypoplastic Anemia [*Hematology*] .... CHA
Congenital Hypothyroidism [*Medicine*] .... CHT
Congenital Inclusion Body Hemolytic Anemia [*Medicine*] (AAMN) .... CIB HA
Congenital Lipoid Adrenal Hyperplasia [*Medicine*] (DMAA) .... CLAH
Congenital Lobar Overinflation [*Medicine*] .... CLO
Congenital Localized Absence of Skin [*Medicine*] (MAE) .... CLAS
Congenital Malformation [*Medicine*] .... CM
Congenital Malformation of Heart [*Medicine*] .... CMH
Congenital Multicystic Kidney [*Nephrology*] (DAVI) .... CMK
Congenital Muscular Dystrophy [*Medicine*] .... CMD
Congenital Myocardial Sympathetic Dysinnervation [*Medicine*] (DMAA) .... CMSD
Congenital Myotonic Dystrophy [*Medicine*] .... CMD
Congenital Nephrogenic Diabetes Insipidus [*Medicine*] .... CNDI
Congenital Nevomelanocytic Nevi [*Medicine*] .... CNN
Congenital Nonspherocytic Hemolytic Anemia [*Medicine*] .... CNSHA
Congenital Nonspherocytic Hemolytic Disease [*Medicine*] (MAE) .... CNHD
Congenital Nystagmus [*Ophthalmology*] (AAMN) .... CN
Congenital Polyvalvular Disease [*Medicine*] (DMAA) .... CPVD
Congenital Portocaval Shunt [*Medicine*] .... C-PCS
Congenital Pulmonary Cystic Lymphangiectasis [*Medicine*] .... CPCL
Congenital Pulmonary Lymphangiectasia [*Medicine*] (DMAA) .... CPL
Congenital Rubella Syndrome [*Medicine*] .... CRS
Congenital Self-Healing Histiocytosis [*Medicine*] (DMAA) .... CSHH
Congenital Stationary Night Blindness [*Medicine*] .... CSNB
Congenital Syphilis [*Medicine*] .... CS
Congenital Thymic Dysplasia [*Medicine*] (MAE) .... CTD
Congenital Urinary Tract Deformity [*Medicine*] (AAMN) .... CUD
Congenitally Corrected Transposition [*Of the great vessels*] [*Cardiology*] (DAVI) .... CCT
Congenitally Corrected Transposition of the Great Arteries [*Cardiology*] (DAVI) .... CCTGA
Congested Freeway Driving Schedule [*For vehicle emission measurements*] .... CFDS
Congestion (FAAC) .... CGSTN
Congestion [*Telecommunications*] (TEL) .... CONG
Congestion Avoidance and Reduction for Automobiles and Trucks [*FHWA*] (TAG) .... CARAT
Congestion/Demand Management [*TXDOT*] (TAG) .... CDM
Congestion Management Systems [*VDOT*] (TAG) .... CMS
Congestion Mitigation and Air Quality [*Improvement program*] [*VDOT*] (TAG) .... CMAQ
Congestion Mitigation & Air Quality [*An association*] .... CMAQ
Congestive Cardiac Failure [*Medicine*] .... CCF
Congestive Cardiomyopathy [*Medicine*] (CPH) .... CCM
Congestive Heart Disease [*Cardiology*] (DAVI) .... CHD
Congestive Heart Failure [*Medicine*] .... CHF
Congestive Myocardiopathy [*Medicine*] .... CM
Congestive Right Ventricular Failure [*Medicine*] (DMAA) .... CRVF
Congius [*Gallon*] [*Pharmacy*] C
Congius [*Gallon*] [*Pharmacy*] .... CONG
Conglomerate [*Lithology*] .... CGL
Conglomerate .... CONGL
Conglutinating Complement Absorption Test [*Immunochemistry*] .... CCAT
Conglutinating Complement Fixation (PDAA) .... CCF
Congo [*MARC country of publication code Library of Congress*] (LCCP) .... cf
Congo [*ANSI two-letter standard code*] (CNC) .... CG
Congo [*ANSI three-letter standard code*] (CNC) .... COG
Congo (WDAA) .... CON
Congo [*MARC geographic area code Library of Congress*] (LCCP) .... f-cf--
Congo (Kinshasa) [*Zaire*] [*MARC country of publication code Library of Congress*] (LCCP) .... cg
Congo (Kinshasa) [*Zaire*] [*MARC geographic area code Library of Congress*] (LCCP) .... f-cg--
Congo Military Mission - United States .... COMISH-US
Congo Protestant Relief Agency [*Defunct*] .... CPRA
Congo Red [*A dye*] .... CoR
Congo River and Basin [*MARC geographic area code Library of Congress*] (LCCP) .... fg----
Congo Town, Andros Island [*Bahamas*] [*ICAO location identifier*] (ICLI) .... MYAK
Congolese .... Cong
Congolese Progressive Students [*Zaire*] (PD) .... ECP
Congolese Socialist Party [*Zaire*] [*Political party*] (PD) .... PSC
Congoleum Corp. [*NYSE symbol*] (SAG) .... CGM
Congoleum Corp. [*Associated Press*] (SAG) .... Conglm
Congoleum Corp.'A' [*NYSE symbol*] (TTSB) .... CGM
Congo-Red Millipore Filter .... CRMF
Congou [*Tea trade*] (ROG) .... CONO
Congratulations (DSUE) .... CONGRATS
Congregate Housing Services Program [*HUD*] .... CHSP
Congregatie Broeders van Huybergen [*Brothers of the Immaculate Conception of the Mother of God - BICMG*] [*Huybergen, Netherlands*] (EAIO) .... CBH
Congregatio a Sacro Corde Jesu [*Congregation of the Priests of the Sacred Heart*] [*Roman Catholic religious order*] CCV
Congregatio a Sancta Cruce [*Congregation of Holy Cross*] [*Roman Catholic religious order*] .... CSC

Congregatio Caritatis Verbi Incarnati [*Congregation of the Sisters of Charity of the Incarnate Word*] [*Roman Catholic religious order*] ... CCVI
Congregatio Clericorum Regularium Marianorum sub titulo Immaculatae ConceptionisBeatae Mariae Virginis [*Marian Fathers*] [*Roman Catholic religious order*] ... MIC
Congregatio Filiarum Minimarum Mariae [*Minim Daughters of Mary Immaculate*] [*Roman Catholic religious order*] ... CFMM
Congregatio Filiorum Sacratissimi Cordis Jesu [*Sons of the Sacred Heart*] [*Verona Fathers Roman Catholic religious order*] ... FSCJ
Congregatio Fratrum Caritate [*Brothers of Charity*] [*Roman Catholic religious order*] ... FC
Congregatio Fratrum Cellitarum seu Alexianorum [*Alexian Brothers*] [*Roman Catholic religious order*] ... CFA
Congregatio Fratrum Immaculatae Conceptionis Beatae Mariae Virginis [*Brothers of the Immaculate Conception of the Blessed Virgin Mary*] (EAIO) ... FIC
Congregatio Fratrum Pauperum [*Brothers of the Poor of St. Francis*] [*Roman Catholic religious order*] ... CFP
Congregatio Fratrum Sancti Francisci Xaverii [*Brothers of St. Francis Xavier*] [*Xaverian Brothers*] [*Roman Catholic religious order*] ... CFX
Congregatio Immaculati Cordis Mariae [*Congregation of the Immaculate Heart of Mary*] [*Roman Catholic men's religious order*] ... CICM
Congregatio Iosephitarum [*Josephite Fathers*] [*Roman Catholic religious order*] ... CJ
Congregatio Jesu et Mariae [*Congregation of Jesus and Mary*] [*Eudist Fathers*] [*Roman Catholic religious order*] ... CJM
Congregatio Mariae [*Fathers of the Company of Mary*] [*Roman Catholic religious order*] ... CM
Congregatio Missionariorum a Sancta Familia [*Congregation of the Missionaries of the Holy Family*] [*Roman Catholic men's religious order*] ... MSF
Congregatio Missionariorum a Sancto Carlo [*Congregation of the Missionary Fathers of St. Charles*] [*Formerly, PSSC*] [*Roman Catholic religious order*] ... CS
Congregatio Missionariorum de Mariannhill [*Congregation of Mariannhill Missionaries*] [*Mariannhill Fathers*] [*Roman Catholic religious order*] [*Italy*] ... CMM
Congregatio Missionariorum Filiorum Immaculati Cordis Beatae Maria Virginia [*Congregation of Missionary Sons of the Immaculate Heart of the Blessed Virgin Mary*] [*Claretians*] [*Roman Catholic religious order*] ... CMF
Congregatio Missionis Sancti Vicentii a Paulo [*Congregation of the Mission of St. Vincent de Paul*] [*Vincentians*] [*Roman Catholic men's religious order*] ... CM
Congregatio Passionis [*Congregation of the Passion*] [*Passionists*] [*Roman Catholic religious order*] ... CP
Congregatio Pretiosissimi Sanguinis [*Society of the Most Precious Blood*] [*Roman Catholic religious order*] ... CPPS
Congregatio Reformatorium Praemonstratensium [*Premonstratensians*] [*Roman Catholic men's religious order*] ... CRP
Congregatio Resurrectionis [*Congregation of the Resurrection*] [*Roman Catholic religious order*] ... CR
Congregatio Sacerdotum a Corde Jesu [*Congregation of the Priests of the Sacred Heart of Jesus*] [*Roman Catholic religious order*] ... SCJ
Congregatio Sacratissimorum Cordium [*Missionaries of the Sacred Hearts of Jesus and Mary*] [*Roman Catholic religious order*] ... CSSCC
Congregatio Sancti Basilii [*Congregation of the Priests of St. Basil*] [*Basilians*] [*Roman Catholic men's religious order*] ... CSB
Congregatio Sancti Joseph [*Congregation of St. Joseph*] [*Roman Catholic religious order*] ... CSJ
Congregatio Sancti Pauli [*Paulists*] [*Roman Catholic men's religious order*] ... CSP
Congregatio Sancti Spiritus [*Congregation of the Holy Ghost*] [*Holy Ghost Fathers*] [*Roman Catholic religious order*] ... CSSP
Congregatio Sanctissimi Redemptoris [*Congregation of the Most Holy Redeemer*] [*Redemptionists*] [*Roman Catholic men's religious order*] ... CSSR
Congregatio Sororum Apostolatus Catholici [*Pallottine Sisters of the Catholic Apostolate*] [*Roman Catholic religious order*] ... CSAC
Congregatio Sororum Sacrae Familiae de Nazareth [*Sisters of the Holy Family of Nazareth*] [*Roman Catholic religious order*] ... CSFN
Congregation ... C
Congregation (BJA) ... Cngrn
Congregation (BJA) ... Cong
Congregation (ROG) ... CONGN
Congregation ... CONREG
Congregation de Hermanas Guadalupanas de la Salle (TOCD) ... HGS
Congregation de la Fraternite Sacerdotale [*Congregation of the Sacerdotal Fraternity*] [*Canada*] (EAIO) ... CFS
Congregation de la Mere du Carmel [*Congregation of Mother of Carmel*] [*Alwaye Kerala, India*] (EAIO) ... CMC
Congregation de Notre Dame de la Retraite au Cenacle [*Congregation of Our Lady of the Retreat in the Cenacle*] (EAIO) ... RC
Congregation des Soeurs Servantes du Coeur Immaculae de Marie [*Servants of the Immaculate Heart of Mary*] [*Good Shepherd Sisters*] [*Roman Catholic religious order*] ... SCIM
Congregation for the Doctrine of the Faith ... CDF
Congregation of Augustinian Sisters Servants of Jesus and Mary (TOCD) ... OSA
Congregation of Bon Secours (TOCD) ... CBS
Congregation of Charity of the Most Sacred Heart of Jesus [*Roman Catholic religious order*] ... CCJ
Congregation of Christian Brothers [*Formerly, Christian Brothers of Ireland*] [*Roman Catholic religious order*] ... CFC
Congregation of Clerics Regular [*Theatine Fathers*] [*Roman Catholic religious order*] ... CR
Congregation of Daughters of Jesus [*Roman Catholic religious order*] ... FJ
Congregation of Humility of Mary [*Roman Catholic women's religious order*] ... CHM
Congregation of Incarnate Word and Blessed Sacrament (TOCD) ... CVI
Congregation of Jesus and Mary (TOCD) ... CJM
Congregation of Jesus and Mary, Eudist Fathers (TOCD) ... cjm
Congregation of Jesus Crucified (TOCD) ... OSB
Congregation of Marianhill Missionaries Marianhill Fathers & Brothers (TOCD) ... CMM
Congregation of Mariannhill Missionaries, Mariannhill Fathers and Brothers (TOCD) ... cmm
Congregation of Marians of the Immaculate Conception (TOCD) ... mic
Congregation of Marians of the Immaculate Conception (TOCD) ... MIC
[*The*] **Congregation of Maronite Lebanese Missionaries** (TOCD) ... CMLM
Congregation of Maronite Monks (TOCD) ... omar
Congregation of Maronite Monks (TOCD) ... OMar
Congregation of Mary Queen (TOCD) ... CMR
Congregation of Missionary Catechists of the Sacred Heart of Jesus and Mary (TOCD) ... MCSJM
Congregation of Mother Coredemptrix (TOCD) ... CMC
Congregation of Mother Coredemptrix (TOCD) ... cmc
Congregation of Notre Dame (TOCD) ... CND
Congregation of Notre Dame de Sion [*Roman Catholic women's religious order*] ... NDS
Congregation of Oblates of Bethany [*Roman Catholic women's religious order*] ... COB
Congregation of Our Lady, Help of the Clergy [*Roman Catholic women's religious order*] ... CLHC
Congregation of Our Lady of Mount Carmel (TOCD) ... OCarm
Congregation of Our Lady of the Holy Rosary [*Roman Catholic women's religious order*] ... RSR
Congregation of Our Lady of the Retreat in the Cenacle [*Roman Catholic women's religious order Italy*] ... RC
Congregation of Priests of Mercy [*Fathers of Mercy*] [*Roman Catholic religious order*] ... CPM
Congregation of St. Brigid [*Roman Catholic women's religious order*] ... CSB
Congregation of St. John (TOCD) ... FJ
Congregation of St. John (TOCD) ... fj
Congregation of St. John the Baptist (TOCD) ... CSJB
Congregation of St. Joseph (TOCD) ... CSJ
Congregation of St. Joseph (TOCD) ... csj
Congregation of Salesians [*Australia*] ... CS
Congregation of Sisters of Nazareth (TOCD) ... CSN
Congregation of Sisters of St. Thomas of Villanova [*Roman Catholic religious order*] ... SSTV
Congregation of the Benedictine Sisters of Perpetual Adoration of Pontifical Jurisdiction (TOCD) ... OSB
Congregation of the Benedictine Sisters of the Sacred Heart (TOCD) ... OSB
Congregation of the Blessed Sacrament (TOCD) ... SSS
Congregation of the Blessed Sacrament (TOCD) ... sss
Congregation of the Divine Spirit [*Roman Catholic women's religious order*] ... CDS
Congregation of the Fathers of Mercy (TOCD) ... CPM
Congregation of the Fathers of Mercy (TOCD) ... cpm
Congregation of the Incarnate Word and the Blessed Sacrament [*Roman Catholic women's religious order*] ... IWBS
Congregation of the Incarnate Word and the Blessed Sacrament [*Roman Catholic women's religious order*] ... SIW
Congregation of the Incarnate Word and the Blessed Sacrament [*Roman Catholic women's religious order*] ... VI
Congregation of the Marianites of the Holy Cross (TOCD) ... MSC
Congregation of the Mission [*Vincentians*] (DAS) ... CM
Congregation of the Mission, Vincentian Fathers (TOCD) ... cm
Congregation of the Missionaries of the Holy Family (TOCD) ... msf
Congregation of the Missionaries of the Holy Family (TOCD) ... MSF
Congregation of the Oblates of the Virgin Mary [*Rome, Italy*] (EAIO) ... OVM
Congregation of the Oratory [*Oratorians*] [*Roman Catholic men's religious order*] ... CO
Congregation of the Oratory [*Oratorians*] [*Roman Catholic men's religious order*] ... CongOrat
Congregation of the Passion (TOCD) ... CP
Congregation of the Passion, Passionist Fathers (TOCD) ... cp
Congregation of the Priests of the Sacred Heart of Jesus (TOCD) ... scj
Congregation of the Religious Brothers of the Third Order Regular of St. Francis (TOCD) ... OSF
Congregation of the Resurrection, Resurrectionist Fathers (TOCD) ... cr
Congregation of the Resurrection Theatine Fathers (TOCD) ... CR
Congregation of the Sacerdotal Fraternity [*Canada*] (EAIO) ... CSF
Congregation of the Sacred Hearts and of Perpetual Adoration (TOCD) ... SSCC
Congregation of the Sacred Hearts of Jesus and Mary (TOCD) ... sscc
Congregation of the Sacred Hearts of Jesus and Mary [*Rome, Italy*] (EAIO) ... SSCC
Congregation of the Sacred Stigmata [*Stigmatine Fathers and Brothers*] [*Roman Catholic religious order*] ... CSS
Congregation of the Servants of Christ [*Anglican religious community*] ... SC
Congregation of the Sisters Marianites of Holy Cross [*Roman Catholic religious order*] ... MSC
Congregation of the Sisters of St. Felix [*Felician Sisters*] [*Roman Catholic religious order*] ... CSSF
Congregation of the Sisters of St. Louis, Juilly-Monaghan (TOCD) ... SSL
Congregation of the Sisters of the Adoration of the Blessed Sacrament [*Kerala, India*] (EAIO) ... SABS
Congregation of the Sisters of the Family [*Roman Catholic religious order*] ... SSF
Congregation of the Sisters of the Holy Faith [*Australia*] ... CHF
Congregation of the Sisters of the Holy Family (TOCD) ... SSF
Congregation of the Sisters of the Holy Family of Nazareth [*Australia*] ... CSFN
Congregation of the Sisters of the Third Order of St. Francis Oldenburg, IN (TOCD) ... OSF

Congregation of the Third Order of St. Francis of Mary Immaculate, Joliet IL (TOCD) .... OSF
Congregation Organized by United Genial Hackers .... COUGH
Congregation Shaar Hashomayim Library-Museum, Westmount, PQ, Canad [*Library symbol*] [*Library of Congress*] (LCLS) .... CaQWsmSH
Congregation Shaar Hashomayim Library-Museum, Westmount, Quebec [*Library symbol National Library of Canada*] (NLC) .... QWSH
Congregation Sons of Israel and David, Temple Beth-El, Providence, RI [*Library symbol Library of Congress*] (LCLS) .... RPT
Congregational .... CONG
Congregational .... CONGL
Congregational .... CONGR
Congregational .... CONGREGTNL
Congregational Christian Churches National Association (EA) .... CCCNA
Congregational Christian Historical Society (EA) .... CCHS
Congregational Christian Service Committee [*Superseded by UCBWM*] (EA) .... CCSC
Congregational Church in England and Wales (BI) .... CCEW
Congregational Churches Fellowship [*Australia*] .... CCF
Congregational Libraries Association of British Columbia (AC) .... CLABC
Congregational Publishing Society .... CPS
Congregational Union .... CU
Congregational Union of England and Wales (BARN) .... CUEW
Congregationalist [*Slang*] (DSUE) .... CONGO
Congregationalist Witchcraft Association Corporation (AC) .... CWA
Congregationis Missionum [*The Congregation of Lazarists*] (ROG) .... CM
Congregazione della Passione [*Congregation of the Passion*] .... CP
Congres Canadien pour la Promotion des Etudes chez la Femme [*Canadian Congress for Learning Opportunities for Women*] .... CCPEF
Congres des Psychanalystes de Langue Francaise [*Congress of Romance Language Psychoanalysts*] (EAIO) .... CPLF
Congres du Peuple Europeen .... CPE
Congres du Travail du Canada [*Canadian Labour Congress - CLC*] .... CTC
Congres Haitien Canada-Quebec (AC) .... CHCQ
Congres International des Editeurs [*International Congress of Publishers*] .... CIE
Congres International des Fabrications Mecaniques [*International Mechanical Engineering Congress*] .... CIM
Congres International des Sciences de l'Activite Physique [*International Congress of Physical Activity Sciences*] [*Canada*] .... CISAP
Congres International des Techniques de Vide en Recherche Spatiale [*International Congress for Vacuum Techniques in Space Research*] (PDAA) .... CIVRES
Congres Internationaux de Medecine Tropicale et de Paludisme [*International Congresses on Tropical Medicine and Malaria*] .... CIMTP
Congres Islamique Mondial .... CIM
Congres Juif Canadien [*Canadian Jewish Congress*] .... CJC
Congres Juif Mondial [*World Jewish Congress*] .... CJM
Congres Mondial Acadien (AC) .... CMA
Congres National d'Initiative Democratique [*Mali*] [*Political party*] (EY) .... CNID
Congres Panafricain du Cameroun [*Political party*] (EY) .... CPC
Congreso Nacional de Canarias [*Spain Political party*] (EY) .... CNC
Congress C
Congress .... CNGRS
Congress [*or Congressman*] .... CON
Congress (AFM) .... CONG
Congress (AAGC) .... Cong
Congress and Session Number (NITA) .... CS
Congress for Automotive Repair and Service .... CARS
Congress for Cultural Freedom [*British*] .... CCF
Congress for Democracy [*India*] .... CFD
Congress for Jewish Culture (EA) .... CJC
Congress for the Education of the Partially Seeing (AEBS) .... CEPS
Congress for the Unity of Black Students .... CUBS
Congress Liberation Party [*Nyasaland*] [*Political party*] .... CLP
Congress of African Peoples .... CAP
Congress of American Unions .... CAU
Congress of Arabic and Islamic Studies [*Madrid, Spain*] (EA) .... CAIS
Congress of Astrological Organizations [*Defunct*] (EA) .... CAO
Congress of County Medical Societies (EA) .... CCMS
Congress of Democratic Unions (AC) .... CDU
Congress of Independent Unions (EA) .... CIU
Congress of Independent Unions .... COIU
Congress of Industrial Organizations [*Later, AFL-CIO*] (GPO) .... CIO
Congress of Industrial Organizations, Political Action Committee [*Later, COPE*] .... CIOPAC
Congress of Irish Unions .... CIU
Congress of Italian-American Organizations .... CIAO
Congress of Joke-Abused Cities .... COJAC
Congress of Lung Association Staff (EA) .... CLAS
Congress of National Black Churches (EA) .... CNBC
Congress of Neurological Surgeons .... CNS
Congress of Organizations of the Physically Handicapped (EA) .... COPH
Congress of Racial Equality (EA) .... CORE
Congress of Russian Americans (EA) .... CRA
Congress of Scientists on Survival [*Inactive*] .... SOS
Congress of South African Trade Unions .... COSATU
Congress of Southeast Asian Librarians (EAIO) .... CONSAL
Congress of the International Theater Institute .... CITI
Congress of the People [*South Africa*] [*Political party*] (PPW) .... Cope
Congress of Unions of Employees in the Public and Civil Services [*Malaya*] .... CUEPACS
Congress of Unions of South Africa .... CUSA
Congress of Unrepresented People .... COUP
Congress of World Unity (EA) .... CWU
Congress on Research in Dance (EA) .... CORD

Congress Party [*India*] [*Political party*] .... CP
Congress Task Force (EA) .... CTF
Congress Watch (EA) .... CW
Congressional (ROG) C
Congressional .... CNGRSNL
Congressional (AAGC) .... Cong
Congressional (ROG) .... CONG
Congressional .... CONGL
Congressional Action Fund (EA) .... CAF
Congressional Agenda: 80's [*Later, CA: 90's*] (EA) .... CA: 80's
Congressional Agenda: 90's (EA) .... CA: 90's
Congressional Air Ltd. [*ICAO designator*] (FAAC) .... CGA
Congressional Alcohol Fuels Caucus (EA) .... CAFC
Congressional Arts Caucus (EA) .... CAC
Congressional Arts Caucus Education Program (EA) .... CACEP
Congressional Automotive Caucus (EA) .... CAC
Congressional Black Associates [*An association*] (EA) .... CBA
Congressional Black Caucus (EA) .... CBC
Congressional Border Caucus [*An association*] (EA) .... CBC
Congressional Budget Office [*Washington, DC*] .... CBO
Congressional Caucus for Women's Issues (EA) CC
Congressional Caucus on National Security (EA) .... CCNS
Congressional Clearinghouse on the Future (EA) .... CCF
Congressional Club (EA) CC
Congressional Coal Group (EA) .... CCG
Congressional Coalition for Soviet Jews (EA) .... CCSJ
Congressional Committee Prints [*A publication*] (DLA) .... Comm Print
Congressional Competitiveness Caucus (EA) CCC
Congressional Crime Caucus [*Defunct*] (EA) CCC
Congressional Data Sheet (MCD) .... CDS
Congressional Debates [*United States*] [*A publication*] (DLA) .... Cong Deb
Congressional Delegate [*or Delegation*] (CINC) .... CODEL
Congressional Descriptive Summaries (RDA) .... CDS
Congressional Digest [*A publication*] (AAGC) .... Cong Dig
Congressional Digest, Washington, DC [*Library symbol Library of Congress*] (LCLS) .... DCD
Congressional District .... CD
Congressional District Data [*Bureau of the Census*] .... CDD
Congressional Economic Leadership Institute (EA) .... CELI
Congressional Education Associates [*Private, nonpartisan consulting group*] .... CEA
Congressional Election Cases [*United States*] [*A publication*] (DLA) ..... Cong El Cas
Congressional Fact Paper [*Army*] .... CFP
Congressional Flying Service (SAA) .... CFS
Congressional Friends of Human Rights Monitors (EA) .... CFHRM
Congressional Globe [*A publication*] (DLA) .... Cong Gl
Congressional Globe [*A publication*] (DLA) .... Cong Globe
Congressional Hispanic Caucus (EA) .... CHC
Congressional Human Rights Caucus (EA) .... CHRC
Congressional Index (Commerce Clearing House) [*A publication*] (DLA) .... Cong Index (CCH)
Congressional Information Service [*Publisher*] (AAGC) .... CIS
Congressional Information Service, Bethesda, MD [*Library symbol Library of Congress*] (LCLS) .... MdBeCl
Congressional Information Service, Inc. [*Bethesda, MD*] [*Database producer*] [*Information service or system*] .... CIS
Congressional Information Sources, Inventories, and Directories (MCD) .... CISID
Congressional Institute for the Future (EA) .... CIF
Congressional Interference CI
Congressional Liaison CL
Congressional Liaison Office .... CLO
Congressional Library (ROG) .... CONG LIB
Congressional Management Foundation (EA) .... CMF
Congressional Medal of Honor .... CMH
Congressional Medal of Honor Society (EA) .... CMHS
Congressional Monitoring Group on Southern Africa (EA) .... CMGSA
Congressional Office of Science and Technology .... COST
Congressional Office of the Budget .... COB
Congressional Presentation Document .... CPD
Congressional Quarterly (AAGC) .... CQ
Congressional Quarterly, Inc. [*Washington, DC*] .... CQ
Congressional Quarterly Service [*A publisher*] [*Washington, D.C.*] (WDMC) ..... CQ
Congressional Record [*A publication*] (AAGC) .... Cong Rec
Congressional Record On-Line [*Capitol Services, Inc.*] [*Washington, DC Bibliographic database*] .... CRECORD
Congressional Report on Communications [*Arlington, VA*] [*A publication*] (TSSD) .... CRC
Congressional Reports Elimination Act .... CREA
Congressional Research Service [*Formerly, Legislative Reference Service*] [*Washington, DC*] [*Library of Congress OCLC symbol*] .... CRS
Congressional Rural Caucus (EA) .... CRC
Congressional Session [*Online database field identifier*] .... CS
Congressional Space Caucus (EA) .... CSC
Congressional Staff Club (EA) .... CSC
Congressional Steel Caucus (EA) .... CSC
Congressional Textile Caucus (EA) .... CSC
Congressional Travel and Tourism Caucus (EA) .... CTTC
Congressional Underwater Explorers Club (EA) .... CUEC
Congressional Union (EA) .... CU
Congressional Wives for Soviet Jewry (EA) .... CWSJ
Congressionally Mandated Mobility Study [*DoD*] .... CMMS
Congressman .... Cong
Congressman .... CONGRSMAN

Congressus Internationalis Ornithologicus [*International Ornithological Congress - IOC*] (EA) ... CIO
Congruent (MSA) ... CONGR
Congruent Melting Point ... CMP
Conhairle Natsiunta Spoirt [*National Sports Council*] (EAIO) ... COSPOIR
Coniagas Mines Ltd. [*Toronto Stock Exchange symbol*] ... CO
Conic (ADA) ... CON
Conic Section (BARN) ... con sec
Conical (MSA) ... CONL
Conical Alignment Kit ... CAK
Conical Fin ... COF
Conical Flow Field ... CFF
Conical Monopole Antenna ... CMA
Conical Monopole Antenna Kit ... CMAK
Conical Scan (NG) ... CONSCAN
Conical Scan Antenna ... CSA
Conical Scanning Optical Microscope ... CSOM
Conical Scan-on-Receive Only (NG) ... COSRO
Conical Scan-on-Receive Only (CET) ... CSORO
Conical Shaped Charge (NASA) ... CSC
Conical Shell Vibration ... CSV
Conical Shock Tube ... CST
Conical Tank [*Liquid gas carriers*] ... co
Conico [*Race of maize*] ... CON
Conico Norteno [*Race of maize*] ... C-N
Coniectanea Biblica [*Lund*] [*A publication*] (BJA) ... ConBib
Coniectanea Neotestamentica [*Uppsala*] [*A publication*] (BJA) ... CnNT
Coniectanea Neotestamentica [*Uppsala*] [*A publication*] (BJA) ... ConiNT
Coniectanea Neotestamentica [*Uppsala*] [*A publication*] (BJA) ... ConNeot
Coniectanea Neotestamentica [*Uppsala*] [*A publication*] (BJA) ... ConNT
Conifair Aviation, Inc. [*Canada ICAO designator*] (FAAC) ... ROY
Coniferous Forest Biome [*Ecological biogeographic study*] ... CFB
Coningsby [*British ICAO location identifier*] (ICLI) ... EGXC
Coningsby FTU [*British ICAO designator*] (FAAC) ... CBY
Coniston Branch, Nickel Centre Public Library, Ontario [*Library symbol National Library of Canada*] (NLC) ... OCNC
Coniunx [*Wife*] [*Latin*] (GPO) ... Con
Conization [*Of the cervix*] [*Gynecology*] (DAVI) ... cone
Conization [*Gynecology*] (DAVI) ... coniz
Conjectanea Neotestamentica [*A publication*] (BJA) ... CN
Conjectural (ADA) ... CJ
Conjoint Society of Massage and Medical Gymnastics [*British*] ... CSMMG
Conjugable Oxidation Product [*Fuel technology*] ... COP
Conjugata Diagonalis [*Pelvic measurement*] [*Anatomy*] ... CD
Conjugata Vera [*Conjugate diameter of pelvic inlet*] [*Anatomy*] ... CV
Conjugata Vera Obstetrica [*Conjugate diameter of pelvic inlet*] [*Anatomy*] ... CVO
Conjugate Acid-Base Pair [*Chemistry*] ... CABP
Conjugate (Counter) Base [*Chemistry*] ... CB
Conjugate Filter Data Link ... CONFIDAL
Conjugate Gradient (IAA) ... CG
Conjugate Gradient Method of Approximate Programming ... CGMAP
Conjugate Gradient Optimization Algorithm Program [*Lighting system design*] ... CGOAP
Conjugated Bilirubin [*Chemistry*] ... Bc
Conjugated Bilirubin [*Gastroenterology and neonatology*] (DAVI) ... BILI-C
Conjugated Equine Estrogen [*Endocrinology*] ... CEE
Conjugated Estrogens [*Endocrinology*] ... CE
Conjugated Linoleic Acid [*Antineoplastic drug*] ... CLA
Conjugation (WGA) ... C
Conjugation ... CONJ
Conjugation (ADA) ... CONJUG
Conjugation Factor [*Plant genetics*] ... CF
Conjugation-Parity [*Physics*] ... CP
Conjugation-Parity Asymmetry [*Physics*] ... CPA
Conjugi [*To My Spouse*] [*Latin*] ... COI
Conjugi Optimo [*To My Most Excellent Spouse*] [*Latin*] ... CO
Conjunction ... CJ
Conjunction [*Grammar*] (ROG) ... CON
Conjunction ... CONJ
Conjunction (VRA) ... conj
Conjunctiva [*Ophthalmology*] (DAVI) ... conj
Conjunctiva [*Ophthalmology*] (DAVI) ... conjunc
Conjunctiva and Sclera [*Ophthalmology*] ... C & S
Conjunctival Secretion [*Ophthalmology*] (DAVI) ... CS
Conjunctival Secretions [*Medicine*] (MEDA) ... CS
Conjunctive Alteration File ... CAF
Conjunctive Alteration Indicator ... CAI
Conjunctive Normal Formula ... CNF
Conjunctivitis [*Medicine*] (DMAA) ... CJ
Conjunctivitis [*Medicine*] ... CONJ
Conjux [*Consort, Spouse*] [*Genealogy*] ... CON
Conklin Community School, Alberta [*Library symbol National Library of Canada*] (BIB) ... ACONS
Conklin Elementary School, Rockford, IL [*Library symbol*] [*Library of Congress*] (LCLS) ... IRoCoE
Conklin, NY [*FM radio station call letters*] (RBYB) ... WMTT
Conkling's Admiralty [*A publication*] (DLA) ... Conk Adm
Conkling's Executive Powers [*A publication*] (DLA) ... Conk Ex Pow
Conkling's Iowa Justice of the Peace [*A publication*] (DLA) ... Conk JP
Conkling's Treatise on Jurisdiction and Practice of the United States Courts [*A publication*] (DLA) ... Conk Treat
Conkling's Treatise on Jurisdiction and Practice of the United States Courts [*A publication*] (DLA) ... Conk US Pr
CONMED Corp. [*NASDAQ symbol*] (NQ) ... CNMD
Conmed Corp. [*Associated Press*] (SAG) ... Conmed
Connair [*ICAO designator*] (AD) ... CK
Connaissement [*Bill of Lading*] [*Legal term French*] ... CONNT
Connaitre la Bible [*Bruges*] [*A publication*] (BJA) ... CIB
Connaught Biosciences, Inc. [*Toronto Stock Exchange symbol*] ... CSE
Connaught Laboratories, Inc. ... CLI
Connaught Laboratories Ltd., Willowdale, Ontario [*Library symbol National Library of Canada*] (NLC) ... OTCL
Connaught Medical Research Laboratories, Toronto, ON, Canada [*Library symbol Library of Congress*] (LCLS) ... CaOTCL
Connaught Rangers [*Military British*] (DAS) ... Conn R
Connaught Rangers [*Military British*] (ROG) ... CONN RANG
Connaught Rangers [*Military British*] ... CR
Connaught Regional Airport [*Ireland*] [*ICAO location identifier*] (ICLI) ... EIKN
Conneaut Elementary School, Bowling Green, OH [*Library symbol*] [*Library of Congress*] (LCLS) ... OBgCE
Conneaut, OH [*FM radio station call letters*] ... WGOJ
Conneaut, OH [*AM radio station call letters*] ... WWOW
Connect (FAAC) ... CNCT
Connect Confirmation (ACRL) ... CC
Connect Data Set to Line [*Computer science*] (IAA) ... CDSL
Connect, Inc. [*NASDAQ symbol*] (SAG) ... CNKT
Connect, Inc. [*Associated Press*] (SAG) ... Connct
Connect Request (ACRL) ... CR
Connectair [*ICAO designator*] (AD) ... AX
Connectair Charters Ltd. [*Canada ICAO designator*] (FAAC) ... BSN
Connected (ROG) ... CONN
Connected Case [*Different case from case cited but arising out of same subject matter or intimately connected therewith*] [*Used in Shepard's Citations*] [*Legal term*] (DLA) ... cc
Connected Network of Adaptive Processors System ... CNAPS
Connected Replenishment [*Military*] (NVT) ... CONREP
Connected Speech Recognition (MCD) ... CSR
Connected Two-Color Simulated Photon Echo [*Spectroscopy*] ... C2CSE
Connected With (IAA) ... CW
Connecticut (ROG) ... CON
Connecticut ... CONN
Connecticut (ODBW) ... Conn
Connecticut [*Postal code*] ... CT
Connecticut [*MARC country of publication code Library of Congress*] (LCCP) ... ctu
Connecticut [*MARC geographic area code Library of Congress*] (LCCP) ... n-us-ct
Connecticut Academy of Family Physicians (SRA) ... CAFP
Connecticut Academy of Science and Engineering (SRA) ... CASE
Connecticut Advanced Nuclear Engineering Laboratory ... CANEL
Connecticut Agricultural Experiment Station ... CAES
Connecticut Agricultural Experiment Station, New Haven, CT [*Library symbol Library of Congress*] (LCLS) ... CtNhAS
Connecticut Aircraft Nuclear Experiment (NRCH) ... CANE
Connecticut Ambulance Association (SRA) ... CAA
Connecticut Art Directors Club (SRA) ... CADC
Connecticut Assessment of Educational Progress (EDAC) ... CAEP
Connecticut Association for Home Care (SRA) ... CAHC
Connecticut Association for Human Services (SRA) ... CAHS
Connecticut Association of Boards of Education (SRA) ... CABE
Connecticut Association of Child Caring Agencies (SRA) ... CACCA
Connecticut Association of Health Sciences Libraries [*Library network*] ... CAHSL
Connecticut Association of Land Surveyors (SRA) ... CALS
Connecticut Association of Metal Finishers (SRA) ... CAMF
Connecticut Association of Not-for-Profit Providers for the Aging (SRA) ... CANPFA
Connecticut Association of Optometrists (SRA) ... CAO
Connecticut Association of Professional Accountants (SRA) ... CAPA
Connecticut Association of Public School Superintendents (SRA) ... CAPSS
Connecticut Association of Purchasing Management (SRA) ... CAPM
Connecticut Association of Realtors (SRA) ... CAR
Connecticut Association of Residential Facilities (SRA) ... CARF
Connecticut Association of Schools (SRA) ... CAS
Connecticut Association of Third Party Administrators (SRA) ... CATPA
Connecticut Automotive Trades Association (SRA) ... CATA
Connecticut Ballet Theatre ... CBT
Connecticut Bank & Trust Co. (MHDW) ... CBT
Connecticut Bankers Association (SRA) ... CBA
Connecticut Bar Association (SRA) ... CBA
Connecticut Broadcasters Association (SRA) ... CBA
Connecticut Building Congress (SRA) ... CBC
Connecticut Business and Industry Association (SRA) ... CBIA
Connecticut Campground Owners Association (SRA) ... CCOA
Connecticut Catholic Hospital Council (SRA) ... CCHC
Connecticut Census Data Center [*Connecticut State Office of Policy and Management*] [*Information service or system*] (IID) ... CCDC
Connecticut Chemosensory Clinical Research Center [*University of Connecticut*] [*Research center*] (RCD) ... CCCRC
Connecticut Christmas Tree Growers (SRA) ... CCTGA
Connecticut Circuit Court Reports [*A publication*] (DLA) ... Cir
Connecticut Circuit Court Reports [*A publication*] (DLA) ... Conn Cir
Connecticut Circuit Court Reports [*A publication*] (DLA) ... Conn Cir Ct
Connecticut College (GAGS) ... Conn C
Connecticut College, New London, CT [*OCLC symbol*] (OCLC) ... CTL
Connecticut College, New London, CT [*Library symbol Library of Congress*] (LCLS) ... CtNlC
Connecticut College of Emergency Physicians (SRA) ... CCEP
Connecticut Community Providers Association (SRA) ... CCPA
Connecticut Compensation Commissioners, Compendium of Awards [*A publication*] (DLA) ... Conn Comp Com
Connecticut Conference of Municipalities (SRA) ... CCM
Connecticut Constitution [*A publication*] (DLA) ... Conn Const

Connecticut Construction Exposition [*Key Productions, Inc.*] (TSPED) ... CONEX
Connecticut Construction Industries Association (SRA) ... CCIA
Connecticut Credit Union League (SRA) ... CCUL
Connecticut Decisions [*A publication*] (DLA) ... Conn Dec
Connecticut Department of Environmental Protection ... CTDEP
Connecticut Department of Environmental Protection (DOGT) ... CTDEP
Connecticut Education Association (SRA) ... CEA
Connecticut Electric Association (SRA) ... CEA
Connecticut Energy [*NYSE symbol*] (TTSB) ... CNE
Connecticut Energy Corp. [*NYSE symbol*] (SPSG) ... CNE
Connecticut Energy Corp. [*Associated Press*] (SAG) ... ConnEn
Connecticut Farm Bureau Association (SRA) ... CFBA
Connecticut Film Circuit [*Library network*] ... CFC
Connecticut Florists Association (SRA) ... CFA
Connecticut Food Association (SRA) ... CFA
Connecticut General Statutes, Annotated [*A publication*] (DLA) ... CGSA
Connecticut General Statutes, Annotated [*A publication*] (DLA) ... Conn Gen Stat Ann
Connecticut Guild of Craftsmen (SRA) ... CGC
Connecticut Heating and Cooling Contractors Association (SRA) ... CHCC
Connecticut Historical Society, Hartford, CT [*Library symbol Library of Congress*] (LCLS) ... CtHi
Connecticut Hospital Association (SRA) ... CHA
Connecticut Industrial Arts Association (EDAC) ... CIAA
Connecticut Institute of Water Resources [*Storrs, CT*] [*Department of the Interior*] (GRD) ... IWR
Connecticut Irrigation Contractors (SRA) ... CICA
Connecticut Law Journal [*Administrative Rules*] (AAGC) ... Conn L J
Connecticut League for Nursing (SRA) ... CLN
Connecticut Leather Co. [*Original name of Coleco Industries*] ... COLECO
Connecticut Legislative Service (West) [*A publication*] (DLA) ... Conn Legis Serv
Connecticut Light & Power Co. ... CL & P
Connecticut Mental Health Center, New Haven, CT [*Library symbol Library of Congress*] (LCLS) ... CtNhMH
Connecticut Mutual Life Insurance Co. ... CM
Connecticut Nat Gas [*NYSE symbol*] (TTSB) ... CTG
Connecticut Natural Gas Corp. ... CNG
Connecticut Natural Gas Corp. [*Associated Press*] (SAG) ... ConnNG
Connecticut Natural Gas Corp. [*NYSE symbol*] (SPSG) ... CTG
Connecticut Nurserymen's Association (SRA) ... CNA
Connecticut Nurses Association (SRA) ... CNA
Connecticut On-Line Law-Enforcement Communications and Teleprocessing [*Computer law-enforcement system*] ... COLLECT
Connecticut Opticians Association (SRA) ... COA
Connecticut Podiatric Medical Association (SRA) ... CPMA
Connecticut Primary Care Association (SRA) ... CPCA
Connecticut Psychiatric Society (SRA) ... CPS
Connecticut Public Acts [*A publication*] (DLA) ... Conn Pub Acts
Connecticut Public and Special Acts (DLA) ... Conn Acts
Connecticut Reports [*A publication*] (DLA) ... Conn R
Connecticut Reports [*A publication*] (DLA) ... Conn Rep
Connecticut Reports [*A publication*] (DLA) ... Conn Reports
Connecticut Reports [*A publication*] (DLA) ... Connect Rep
Connecticut Reports [*A publication*] (DLA) ... Connecticut R
Connecticut Reports [*A publication*] (DLA) ... Connecticut Rep
Connecticut Reports [*A publication*] (DLA) ... CT
Connecticut Reports, by Day [*1802-13*] [*A publication*] (DLA) ... Day(Conn)
Connecticut River Watershed Council (EA) ... CRWC
Connecticut Society of Certified Public Accountants (SRA) ... CSCPA
Connecticut Society of Eye Physicians (SRA) ... CSEP
Connecticut Society of Oral Surgeons (SRA) ... CSOS
Connecticut Society of Professional Engineers (SRA) ... CSPE
Connecticut Special Acts [*A publication*] (DLA) ... Conn Spec Acts
Connecticut State Association of Life Underwriters (SRA) ... CSALU
Connecticut State Dental Association (SRA) ... CSDA
Connecticut State Department of Health, Hartford, CT [*Library symbol Library of Congress*] (LCLS) ... Ct-H
Connecticut State Library, Hartford, CT [*Library symbol Library of Congress*] (LCLS) ... Ct
Connecticut State Library, Hartford, CT [*OCLC symbol*] (OCLC) ... CZL
Connecticut Supplement [*A publication*] (DLA) ... Conn S
Connecticut Supplement [*A publication*] (DLA) ... Conn Sup
Connecticut Supplement [*A publication*] (DLA) ... Conn Supp
Connecticut Supplement [*A publication*] (DLA) ... CS
Connecticut Valley Historical Museum, Springfield, MA [*Library symbol Library of Congress*] (LCLS) ... MSCV
Connecticut Water Service, Inc. [*Associated Press*] (SAG) ... ConnWt
Connecticut Water Service, Inc. [*NASDAQ symbol*] (NQ) ... CTWS
Connecticut Workmen's Compensation Decisions [*A publication*] (DLA) ... Conn Comp Dec
Connecticut Wtr Svc [*NASDAQ symbol*] (TTSB) ... CTWS
Connecticut Yankee Station [*Nuclear energy*] (NUCP) ... CY
Connecticutensis Academiae Socius [*Fellow of the Connecticut Academy of Arts and Sciences*] ... CAS
Connecting (ECII) ... CCTG
Connecting Arrangement [*Telecommunications*] ... CA
Connecting Block [*Telecommunications*] (TEL) ... CB
Connecting Carrier ... CC
Connecting Circuit [*Electronics*] (IAA) ... CCT
Connecting Device (IAA) ... CD
Connecting Line ... CL
Connecting Line Freight ... CLF
Connecting Link for Application and Source Peripherals [*Computer science*] ... CLASP
Connecting Machine (IAA) ... CM
Connecting-Rod ... CONNROD
Connecting-Rod ... CONROD
Connection (NFPA) ... C
Connection ... CON
Connection (AABC) ... CONEC
Connection ... CONNECT
Connection [*Technical drawings*] ... CX
Connection Admission Control [*Telecommunications*] (ACRL) ... CAC
Connection Control Language [*Computer science*] ... CCL
Connection Conversion ... CONVERS
Connection Co-Processor Application Manager [*Computer science*] ... CCAM
Connection Endpoint Identifier [*Telecommunications*] (ACRL) ... CEI
Connection Establishment (MCD) ... CONESTAB
Connection Fitting Out [*Navy*] ... CFO
Connection Machine [*Naval Research Laboratory*] (PS) ... CM
Connection Manager (ACRL) ... CM
Connection Naval Air Reserve Training Program ... CONARESTRAPROG
Connection Pending [*Telecommunications*] (TEL) ... CP
Connection Point [*Computer science*] (IBMDP) ... CP
Connection Reactivation ... CONVATE
Connection Request [*Computer science*] (TNIG) ... CR
Connection Table to Coordinates [*Data analysis*] ... CONCORD
Connectionless Acknowledged Information ... CAI
Connectionless Broadband Data Service [*Telecommunications*] ... CBDS
Connectionless Data Transmission [*Telecommunications*] (OSI) ... CDT
Connectionless Mode Network Protocol [*Telecommunications*] (OSI) ... CLNP
Connectionless Mode Network Service [*Telecommunications*] (OSI) ... CLNS
Connectionless Network Protocol ... CLNP
Connectionless Network Protocol (DOMA) ... CLNP
Connectionless Network Service [*Telecommunications*] (ACRL) ... CLNS
Connectionless Transport Service [*Computer science*] (TNIG) ... CLTS
Connectionless-Mode Transport Service [*Telecommunications*] (ACRL) ... CLTS
Connection-Oriented (ACRL) ... CO
Connection-Oriented Network Protocol [*Computer science*] ... CONP
Connection-Oriented Network Service [*Telecommunications*] (OSI) ... CONS
Connection-Related Function [*Telecommunications*] ... CRF
Connections per Circuit per Hour [*Telecommunications*] (TEL) ... CCH
Connective Therapeutics [*NASDAQ symbol*] (TTSB) ... CNCT
Connective Therapeutics, Inc. [*NASDAQ symbol*] (SAG) ... CNCT
Connective Therapeutics, Inc. [*Associated Press*] (SAG) ... Connect
Connective Tissue ... CT
Connective Tissue Activating Peptide [*Medicine*] (DMAA) ... CTAP
Connective Tissue Massage [*Medicine*] ... CTM
Connective-Tissue Disease [*Medicine*] ... CTD
Connective-Tissue Growth Factor [*Biochemistry*] ... CTGF
Connective-Tissue-Type Mast Cell [*Cytology*] ... CTMC
Connectivity Language/1 [*Apple*] (CDE) ... CL/1
Connectivity Table [*Computer science*] ... CT
Connector (KSC) ... CONN
Connector Backing Shell ... CBS
Connector Bracket Experiment (MCD) ... CBE
Connector Bracket (Power) (MCD) ... CBP
Connector Bracket Signal (MCD) ... CBS
Connector Circuit ... CC
Connector Data Base [*Aviation*] ... CDB
Connector for Networked Information Transfer [*Massachusetts Institute of Technology*] [*Information service or system*] (IID) ... CONIT
Connector Panel ... CP
Connector Position Assurance [*Automotive electronics*] ... CPA
Connector Replacement (MCD) ... CR
Connectorized Exchange Cable Splicing [*Telecommunications*] (TEL) ... CONECS
Connects [*Macintosh*] [*Computer science*] ... Ke:nx
Connel [*Washington*] [*Seismograph station code, US Geological Survey*] (SEIS) ... CNL
Connell on Parishes [*A publication*] (DLA) ... Con Par
Connellan Airways Ltd. ... CONN
Connellsville, PA [*Location identifier FAA*] (FAAL) ... COV
Connellsville, PA [*Location identifier FAA*] (FAAL) ... VVS
Connellsville, PA [*AM radio station call letters*] ... WCVI
Conner and Lawson's Irish Chancery Reports [*1841-43*] [*A publication*] (DLA) ... C & L
Conner Peripherals, Inc. (MHDW) ... CNNR
Conner Peripherals, Inc. [*NYSE symbol*] (SPSG) ... CNR
Conner Peripherals, Inc. [*Associated Press*] (SAG) ... ConrPr
Conners Teaching Rating Scale ... CTRS
Connersville, IN [*Location identifier FAA*] (FAAL) ... CV
Connersville, IN [*AM radio station call letters*] ... WCNB
Connersville, IN [*AM radio station call letters*] ... WIFE
Connersville News-Examiner, Connersville, IN [*Library symbol Library of Congress*] (LCLS) ... InCoNE
Connersville Public Library, Connersville, IN [*Library symbol Library of Congress*] (LCLS) ... InCo
Connetquot High School, Bohemia, NY [*Library symbol Library of Congress*] (LCLS) ... NBohCH
Connetquot Public Library, Bohemia, NY [*Library symbol Library of Congress*] (LCLS) ... NBoh
Connie Causey Fan Club (EA) ... CCFC
Connie Francis Fan Club [*Defunct*] (EA) ... CFFC
Connie Stevens Fan Club (EA) ... CSFC
Conning Director [*Navy*] ... CD
Conning Tower [*Naval architecture*] ... CONTWR
Connolly Elementary School, Glen Cove, NY [*Library symbol*] [*Library of Congress*] (LCLS) ... NGlcCoE
Connoly's New York Surrogate Reports [*A publication*] (DLA) ... Con
Connoly's New York Surrogate Reports [*A publication*] (DLA) ... Con Sur

Connoly's New York Surrogate Reports [*A publication*] (DLA) .... Conn
Connoly's New York Surrogate Reports [*A publication*] (DLA) .... Conn Surr
Connoly's New York Surrogate Reports [*A publication*] (DLA) .... Conn Surr Rep
Connoly's New York Surrogate Reports [*A publication*] (DLA) .... Connoly
Connoly's New York Surrogate Reports [*A publication*] (DLA) .... Connoly Sur Rep
Connoly's New York Surrogate Reports [*A publication*] (DLA) .... Connoly Surr Rep
Connoly's New York Surrogate Reports [*A publication*] (DLA) .... Cy
Connor and Lawson's Irish Chancery Reports [*1841-43*] [*A publication*] (DLA) .... Con & L
Connor and Lawson's Irish Chancery Reports [*1841-43*] [*A publication*] (DLA) .... Con & Law
Connor and Lawson's Irish Chancery Reports [*1841-43*] [*A publication*] (DLA) .... Connor & L
Connor and Simonton's South Carolina Digest [*A publication*] (DLA).......... C & S Dig
Connor and Simonton's South Carolina Equity Digest [*A publication*] (DLA) .... Con & Sim
Connor-Jasper Middle School, Bovey, MN [*Library symbol*] [*Library of Congress*] (LCLS) .... MnBovM
Connor's Irish Digest [*A publication*] (DLA) .... Con Dig
Connors State Agricultural College [*Oklahoma*] .... CSAC
Connotation .... CONN
Connradh na Gaedhilge [*The Gaelic League, founded in 1893*] .... CG
Conoco, Inc., Law Library, Houston, TX [*Library symbol*] [*Library of Congress*] (LCLS) .... TxHCC-L
Conoco, Inc., North American Exploration Headquarters, Houston, TX [*Library symbol*] [*Library of Congress*] (LCLS) .... TxHCC-N
Conococheague District Library, Chambersburg, PA [*Library symbol Library of Congress*] (LCLS) .... PChCo
Conococheague District Library, Chambersburg, PA [*OCLC symbol*] (OCLC) .... PCO
Conolog Corp. [*NASDAQ symbol*] (SAG) .... CNLG
Conolog Corp. [*Associated Press*] (SAG) .... Conolg
Conolog Corp. [*Associated Press*] (SAG) .... Conolog
Conolog Corp. Unit [*NASDAQ symbol*] (TTSB) .... CNLGU
Conolog Corp. Wrrt'A' [*NASDAQ symbol*] (TTSB) .... CNLGW
Conoseal Pipe Joint .... CPJ
Conover's Digested Index [*Ohio, Indiana, and Illinois*] [*A publication*] (DLA) .... Con Dig Ind
Conover's Reports [*Wisconsin*] [*A publication*] (DLA) .... Con
Conover's Reports [*Wisconsin*] [*A publication*] (DLA) .... Conover
Conpac Resources Ltd. [*Vancouver Stock Exchange symbol*] .... CPQ
Conpak Seafoods, Inc. [*Toronto Stock Exchange symbol*] .... CPQ
Conquer [*or Conqueror*] (WDAA) .... CONQ
Conquering Hero [*British, for returning soldiers*] .... CH
Conquest (ROG) .... CONQ
Conquest Airlines Corp. [*ICAO designator*] (FAAC) .... CAC
Conquest Inds Wrrt [*NASDAQ symbol*] (TTSB) .... CAIRW
Conquest Industries Corp. [*NASDAQ symbol*] (SAG) .... CAIR
Conquest Industries Corp. [*Associated Press*] (SAG) .... Cngln
Conquest Industries Corp. [*Associated Press*] (SAG) .... Cnqln
Conquest Industries Corp. [*Associated Press*] (SAG) .... Conqlnd
Conquest of Hunger Program [*Rockefeller Foundation*] (EA) .... CHP
Conqueyrac [*France ICAO location identifier*] (ICLI) .... LFNI
Conquista [*Brazil*] [*Airport symbol*] (OAG) .... COQ
Conquistador .... CONQUISDR
Conrad, MT [*Location identifier FAA*] (FAAL) .... CRD
Conrad Public Library, Conrad, IA [*Library symbol*] [*Library of Congress*] (LCLS) .... IaCon
Conrad Public Library, Conrad, MT [*Library symbol*] [*Library of Congress*] (LCLS) .... MtCon
Conrad Record, Conrad, IA [*Library symbol Library of Congress*] (LCLS) .... IaConR
Conrad Technologies, Inc. .... CTI
Conradson Carbon Residue Test [*for petroleum products*] .... CCR
CONRAIL [*Consolidated Rail Corp.*] **Analysis Model** [*Computer science*] .... CRAM
Conrail, Inc. [*Associated Press*] (SAG) .... Conrail
Conrail, Inc. [*NYSE symbol*] (SPSG) .... CRR
Conroe Aviation Services, Inc. [*ICAO designator*] (FAAC) .... CXO
Conroe, TX [*Location identifier FAA*] (FAAL) .... CXO
Conroe, TX [*FM radio station call letters*] (RBYB) .... KCHC-FM
Conroe, TX [*TV station call letters*] (RBYB) .... KHIM-TV
Conroe, TX [*AM radio station call letters*] .... KJOJ
Conroe, TX [*FM radio station call letters*] (RBYB) .... KKHT
Conroe, TX [*AM radio station call letters*] .... KSSQ
Conroe, TX [*Television station call letters*] .... KTFH
Conrotatory [*Chemistry*] .... CON
Conroy's Custodian Reports [*1652-1788*] [*Ireland*] [*A publication*] (DLA) .... Con Cus
Conroy's Custodian Reports [*1652-1788*] [*Ireland*] [*A publication*] (DLA) .... Conr
Cons Westn & Pac Res [*NASDAQ symbol*] (TTSB) .... CWNPF
Consanguineous Donor [*Medicine*] .... CD
Conscience [*A publication*] .... Cons
Conscience and Military Tax Campaign - US (EA) .... CMTC
Conscientious Objector .... CO
Conscientious Objector .... CONOBJTR
Conscientious Objectors' News [*British*] .... CON
Consciousness .... CON
Consciousness [*Neurology and psychiatry*] (DAVI) .... CS
Consciousness Research and Training Project (EA) .... CRTP
Consciousness-Raising .... CR
Conscot Resources Ltd. [*Vancouver Stock Exchange symbol*] .... CNU
Conseco, Inc. [*NYSE symbol*] (SPSG) .... CNC
Conseco, Inc. [*Associated Press*] (SAG) .... Consc
Conseco, Inc. [*Associated Press*] (SAG) .... Conseco
Conseco Inc. 7%'PRIDES' [*NYSE symbol*] (TTSB) .... CNCPrE
Conseco Inc. Series'D'Cv Pfd [*NYSE symbol*] (TTSB) .... CNCPrD
Conseco Industries Ltd. [*Associated Press*] (SAG) .... Conesco
Consecrated (ROG) .... CON
Consecrated .... CONS
Consecrated (VRA) .... consr
Consecratione [*Decretum Gratiani*] [*A publication*] (DSA) .... Cons
Consecutive (ADA) .... CONS
Consecutive (MSA) .... CONSEC
Consecutive Case Conference (MAE) CCC
Consecutive Duty Tour [*Air Force*] .... CDT
Consecutive Number Control (IAA) .... CNC
Consecutive Number Printer .... CNP
Consecutive Oversea Tour [*Military*] (AFM) .... COT
Consecutive Voyage Charter (DNAB) CVC
Consecutive-Valve Actuation [*Nuclear energy*] (NRCH) .... CVA
Consecutive-Weeks Discount [*Marketng*] (DOAD) .... CWD
Conseil [*Council*] [*French*] (DLA) .... Cons
Conseil Acadien de Cooperation Culturelle en Atlantique [*Acadian Council of Cultural Cooperation in Atlantic Canada*] .... CACC
Conseil Africain de l'Arachide [*African Groundnut Council*] (EAIO) .... CAA
Conseil Africain-Canadien (AC) .... CAC
Conseil Asiatique d'Analystes Financiers [*Asian Council of Securities Analysts - ASAC*] [*Tokyo, Japan*] (EAIO) .... CAAF
Conseil Canadien de Coordination de la Deficience Auditive [*Canadian Co-Ordinating Council on Deafness - CCCD*] .... CCCDA
Conseil Canadien de Developpement Social [*Canadian Council on Social Development*] (EAIO) .... CCDS
Conseil Canadien de la Documentation Juridique [*Canadian Law Information Council*] .... CCDJ
Conseil Canadien de la Main-d'Oeuvre en Genie [*Canadian Engineering Manpower Council*] .... CCMG
Conseil Canadien de la Medecine Sportive [*Canadian Academy of Sport Medicine - CASM*] .... CCMS
Conseil Canadien de la Musique [*Canadian Music Council*] (EAIO) .... CCM
Conseil Canadien de la Securite (AC) .... CCS
Conseil Canadien de Protection des Animaux [*Canadian Council on Animal Care*] .... CCPA
Conseil Canadien de Recherche en Sciences Sociales [*Social Sciences Research Council of Canada - SSRCC*] .... CCRSS
Conseil Canadien de Recherches sur les Humanites [*Humanities Research Council of Canada - HRCC*] .... CCRH
Conseil Canadien des Arpenteurs-Geometres [*Canadian Council of Land Surveyors - CLS*] .... CCAG
Conseil Canadien des Aveugles [*Canadian Council of the Blind*] (EAIO) .... CCA
Conseil Canadien des Droits des Personnes Handicapees (AC) .... CCDPH
Conseil Canadien des Eglises [*Canadian Council of Churches*] (EAIO) .... CCE
Conseil Canadien des Fabricants des Produits du Tabac [*Canadian Tobacco Manufacturers' Council*] .... CCFPT
Conseil Canadien des Ingenieurs [*Canadian Council of Engineers*] CCI
Conseil Canadien des Metiers d'Art (AC) .... CCMA
Conseil Canadien des Ministres des Ressources [*Canadian Council of Resource Ministers*] .... CCMR
Conseil Canadien des Ministres des Ressources et de l'Environnement [*Canadian Council of Resource and Environment Ministers - CCREM*] .... CCMRE
Conseil Canadien des Producteurs d'Oeufs [*Canadian Egg Producers Council*] .... CCPO
Conseil Canadien des Transformateurs d'Oeufs et de Volailles [*Formerly, Canadian Produce Council*] (AC) .... CCTOV
Conseil Canadien d'Experimentation des Jouets [*Canadian Toy Testing Council*] .... CCEJ
Conseil Canadien du Bois (AC) .... CCB
Conseil Canadien du Multiculturalisme [*Canadian Multicultural Council*] .... CCM
Conseil Canadien du Porc [*Formerly, Canadian Swine Council*] (AC) .... CCP
Conseil Canadien pour la Cooperation Internationale [*Canadian Council for International Cooperation - CCIC*] CCCI
Conseil Canadien pour la Readaptation des Handicapes [*Canadian Rehabilitation for the Disabled*] (EAIO) .... CCRH
Conseil Canadien pour la Recherche en Education [*Canadian Council for Research in Education*] .... CCRE
Conseil Canadien pour l'Education Multiculturelle et Interculturelle (AC) .... CCEMI
Conseil Canadien sur le Tabagisme et la Sante [*Canadian Council on Smoking and Health*] .... CCTS
Conseil Constitutionnel [*Constitutional Council*] [*French*] (DLA) .... Cons Const
Conseil Consultatif Canadien sur la Situation de la Femme (AC) .... CCSSF
Conseil Consultatif de la Politique du Personnel [*Advisory Council on Personnel Policy*] [*Canada Public Service Commission and Treasury Board*] .... CCPP
Conseil Consultatif de la Situation de la Femme [*Advisory Council on the Status of Women*] [*Canada*] .... CCSF
Conseil Consultatif des Athletes [*Athletes' Advisory Council*] [*Canada*] .... CCA
Conseil Cooperatif Acadien de la Nouvelle-Ecosse (AC) .... CCANE
Conseil d'Assistance Economique Mutuelle [*Council for Mutual Economic Assistance - CMEA*] [*French*] (AF) .... CAEM
Conseil de Commerce Canada-Arabe (AC) .... CCCA
Conseil de Cooperation Douaniere [*Customs Co-Operation Council - CCC*] (EAIO) .... CCD
Conseil de Developpement du Loisir Scientifique (AC) .... CDLS
Conseil de la Boulangerie du Quebec [*Quebec Bakery Council*] (AC) .... CBQ
Conseil de la Cooperation Culturelle du Conseil de l'Europe [*Council for Cultural Cooperation of the Council of Europe*] (EAIO) .... CCCCE
Conseil de la Cooperation d'Ontario (AC) .... CCO
Conseil de la Cooperation du Quebec (AC) .... CCQ
Conseil de la Culture des Laurentides (AC) CCL
Conseil de la Gravure du Quebec [*1978, founded 1971 as AGQ, CQE from 1984*] [*Canada*] (NGC) .... CGQ

Conseil de la Jeunesse d'Afrique [*African Youth Council*] [*Senegal*] .... CJA
Conseil de la Jeunesse de Cote d'Ivoire [*Ivory Coast Youth Council*] .... CJCI
Conseil de la Langue Francaise, Quebec, PQ, Canada [*Library symbol Library of Congress*] (LCLS) .... CaQQCLF
Conseil de la Langue Francaise, Quebec, Quebec [*Library symbol National Library of Canada*] (NLC) .... QQCLF
Conseil de la Peinture du Quebec [*1978, founded 1966 as SAPQ, SAVVQ from 1980, CAPQ from 1982*] [*Canada*] (NGC) .... CPQ
Conseil de la Peinture du Quebec (AC) .... CPQ
Conseil de la Politique Scientifique du Quebec, Quebec, PQ, Canada [*Library symbol Library of Congress*] (LCLS) .... CaQQCPS
Conseil de la Reine [*Canada*] (DD) .... CR
Conseil de la Sante et des Services Sociaux de la Region de Montreal Metropolitain, Service de Reference, Montreal, PQ, Canada [*Library symbol*] [*Library of Congress*] (LCLS) .... CaQMCSSS
Conseil de la Sculpture du Quebec [*1978, founded 1961 as ASQ*] [*Canada*] (NGC) .... CSQ
Conseil de la Sculpture du Quebec (AC) .... CSQ
Conseil de la Vie Francaise en Amerique (AC) .... CVFA
Conseil de l'Entente [*Entente Council - EC*] (EAIO) .... CE
Conseil de l'Enveloppe du Batiment du Quebec (AC) .... CEBQ
Conseil de l'Europe [*Council of Europe*] (EAIO) .... CE
Conseil de l'Industrie Electronique du Quebec (AC) .... CIEQ
Conseil de l'Industrie Laitiere du Quebec Inc. [*Quebec Dairy Council Inc.*] (AC) .... CILQ
Conseil de Presse du Quebec (AC) .... CPQ
Conseil de Recherche Agricole du Canada [*Canadian Agricultural Research Council*] .... CRAC
Conseil de Recherches en Sciences Humaines du Canada [*Social Sciences and Humanities Research Council of Canada - SSHRCC*] .... CRSHC
Conseil de Recherches Medicales [*Medical Research Council*] [*Canada*] ...... CRM
Conseil de Securite [*United Nations*] .... CS
Conseil Democratique Revolutionnaire [*Democratic Revolutionary Council*] [*Chad*] (PD) .... CDR
Conseil des Affaires Sociales et de la Famille, Quebec, PQ, Canada [*Library symbol Library of Congress*] (LCLS) .... CaQQASF
Conseil des Affaires Sociales et de la Famille, Quebec, Quebec [*Library symbol National Library of Canada*] (NLC) .... QQASF
Conseil des Agences de Securite et d'Investigation du Quebec Inc. (AC) .... CASIQ
Conseil des Artistes Peintres du Quebec [*1982, founded 1966 as SAPQ*] [*Canada*] (NGC) .... CAPQ
Conseil des Arts du Canada [*Canada Council*] (EAIO) .... CAC
Conseil des Arts Textiles du Quebec (AC) .... CATQ
Conseil des Associations d'Ingenieurs du Commonwealth Britannique [*Commonwealth Engineers Council*] (EAIO) .... CAICB
Conseil des Assurances de Dommages (AC) .... CAD
Conseil des Barreaux de la Communaute Europeenne [*Council of the Bars and Law Societies of the European Community*] (EAIO) .... CCBE
Conseil des Bibliotheques du Gouvernement Federal (AC) .... CBGF
Conseil des Bourses de Valeurs [*French*] (ECON) .... CBV
Conseil des Communautes Musulmanes du Canada [*Council of Muslim Communities of Canada*] (EAIO) .... CCMC
Conseil des Communes d'Europe [*Council of European Municipalities*] .... CCE
Conseil des Directeurs Medias du Quebec (AC) .... CDMQ
Conseil des Ecoles Francaises de la Communaute Urbaine de Toronto [*Metro Toronto French-Language School Council*] (AC) .... CEFCUT
Conseil des Federations Commerciales d'Europe [*Council of European Commercial Federations*] .... CFCE
Conseil des Federations Industrielles d'Europe [*Council of European Industrial Federations*] .... CFIE
Conseil des Metiers d'Art du Quebec (AC) .... SOMART
Conseil des Ministres Arabes de la Justice [*Council of Arab Ministers of Justice - CAMJ*] [*Rabat, Morocco*] (EAIO) .... CMAJ
Conseil des Operations de Bourse [*French*] (ECON) .... COB
Conseil des Organisations Internationales Directement Interessees a l'Enfance eta l'Adolescence [*Council of International Organizations Directly Interested in Children and Youth*] [*Geneva, Switzerland*] (EAIO) .... COIDIEA
Conseil des Organismes Francophones du Toronto Metropolitain (AC) .... COFTM
Conseil des Premiers Ministres des Maritimes [*Council of Maritime Premiers - CMP*] [*Canada*] .... CPMM
Conseil des Provinces Atlantiques pour les Sciences (AC) .... CPAS
Conseil des Regions d'Europe [*Council of European Regions - CER*] (EAIO) .... CRE
Conseil des Syndicats Hospitaliers de Montreal Inc. [*Montreal Council of Hospital Syndicates Inc.*] (AC) .... CSHM
Conseil des Travailleurs et Travailleuses de l'Estrie (AC) .... CTTE
Conseil des Travailleurs et Travailleuses de l'Outaouais Quebecois (AC) .... CTOQ
Conseil des Travailleurs et Travailleuses de Quebec (AC) .... CTQ
Conseil des Travailleurs et Travailleuses des Laurentides-Lanaudiere (AC) .... CTLL
Conseil des Travailleurs et Travailleuses du Montreal Metropolitain (AC) .... CTM
Conseil des Universites du Quebec, Quebec, PQ, Canada [*Library symbol Library of Congress*] (LCLS) .... CaQQCU
Conseil des Universites du Quebec, Ste.-Foy, Quebec [*Library symbol National Library of Canada*] (NLC) .... QQCU
Conseil d'Etat [*Council of State*] [*French*] (ILCA) .... CE
Conseil d'Expansion Economique [*Economic Expansion Council*] [*Canada*].... CEE
Conseil d'Intervention pour l'Acces des Femmes au Travail (AC) .... CIAFT
Conseil du Patronat du Quebec (AC) .... CPQ
Conseil du Salut du Peuple [*People's Salvation Council*] [*Burkina Faso*] (PD) .... CSP
Conseil du Statut de la Femme, Quebec, PQ, Canada [*Library symbol Library of Congress*] (LCLS) .... CaQQCSF
Conseil du Travails de l'Abitibi-Temiscaminque (AC) .... CTAT
Conseil Economique et Social [*United Nations*] .... CE et S
Conseil Economique et Social des Nations-Unies [*United Nations Economic and Social Council*] .... CESNU
Conseil Europeen de Coordination pour le Developpement des Essais de Performancedes Combustibles et des Lubrifiants pour Moteurs [*Coordinating European Council for the Development of Performance Tests for Lubricants and Engine Fuels - CEC*] (EAIO) .... CEC
Conseil Europeen de la Construction Electrodomestique [*European Committee of Manufacturers of Electrical Domestic Equipment*] (EA) ...... CECED
Conseil Europeen des Federations de l'Industrie Chimique [*European Council of Chemical Manufacturers Federations - ECCMF*] [*Belgium*] (EAIO) .... CEFIC
Conseil Europeen des Jeunes Agriculteurs [*European Committee of Young Farmers*] [*Common Market*] .... CEJA
Conseil Europeen du "Codex Alimentarius" .... CODEXAL
Conseil Europeen du Comite International de l'Organisation Scientifique [*European Council of International Committee of Scientific Management*] .... CECIOS
Conseil Europeen du Cuir Brut [*European Untanned Leather Council*] .... CECB
Conseil Europeen pour la Construction de Lanceures d'Engins Spatiaux [*European Council for the Construction of Spacecraft Launching Areas*] [*France*] .... CECLES
Conseil Europeen pour la Protection des Animaux [*European Council for Animal Welfare - ECAW*] (EA) .... CEPA
Conseil General des Peches pour la Mediterranee [*General Fisheries Council for the Mediterranean*] .... CGPM
Conseil Inter-Americain de Securite [*Inter-American Safety Council*] .... CIAS
Conseil Interamericain du Commerce et de la Production .... CICEP
Conseil Intergouvernemental des Pays Exportateurs de Cuivre [*Intergovernmental Council of Copper Exporting Countries - ICCEC*] (EAIO) .... CIPEC
Conseil International de la Chasse et de la Conservation du Gibier [*International Council for Game and Wildlife Conservation*] (EAIO) CIC
Conseil International de la Langue Francaise [*International Council of the French Language - ICFL*] (EAIO) .... CILF
Conseil International de la Musique [*International Music Council*] .... CIM
Conseil International de la Musique Populaire [*International Folk Music Council*] .... CIMP
Conseil International de la Philosophie et des Sciences Humaines [*International Council for Philosophy and Humanistic Studies*] (EAIO) .... CIPSH
Conseil International de la Preparation a l'Enseignement [*International Council on Education for Teaching*] .... CIPE
Conseil International de l'Action Sociale [*International Council on Social Welfare - ICSW*] [*Vienna, Austria*] (EA) .... CIAS
Conseil International de l'Education Physique et Sportive [*International Council of Sport and Physical Education*] .... CIEPS
Conseil International de l'Etain [*International Tin Council - ITC*] [*Defunct*] (EAIO) .... CIE
Conseil International de Musique [*UNESCO*] [*Record label*] .... CIDM
Conseil International d'Education des Adultes [*International Council for Adult Education*] [*Canada*] .... CIEA
Conseil International d'Education Mesologique des Pays de Langue Francaise [*Established 1977*] [*Canada*] .... CIEM
Conseil International des Agences Benevoles [*International Council of Voluntary Agencies - ICVA*] (EA) .... CIAB
Conseil International des Archives [*International Council on Archives*] .... CIA
Conseil International des Compositeurs [*International Council of Composers*] CIC
Conseil International des Economies Regionales [*International Council for Local Development*] (EAIO) .... CIER
Conseil International des Employeurs du Commerce [*International Council of Commerce Employers*] .... CIEC
Conseil International des Femmes [*International Council of Women - ICW*] [*Paris, France*] (EA) .... CIF
Conseil International des Infirmieres [*International Council of Nurses - ICN*] [*Geneva, Switzerland*] (EA) CII
Conseil International des Machines a Combustion [*International Council on Combustion Engines*] [*Paris, France*] (EAIO) .... CIMAC
Conseil International des Organisations de Festivals de Folklore et d'Arts Traditionnels [*International Council of Folklore Festival Organizations and Folk Art - ICFFO*] (EAIO) .... CIOFF
Conseil International des Organismes de Travailleuses Familiales [*International Council of Home-Help Services*] .... CIOTF
Conseil International des Praticiens du Plan Comptable International [*International Council of Practitioners of the International Plan of Accounts*] .... CIPCI
Conseil International des Radios-Televisions d'Expression Francaise [*International Association of Broadcasting Manufacturers - IABM*] (EAIO) .... CIRTEF
Conseil International des Ressources Phytogenetiques [*International Board for Plant Genetic Resources - IBPGR*] (EAIO) .... CIRP
Conseil International des Sciences Sociales [*International Social Science Council - ISSC*] (EAIO) .... CISS
Conseil International des Services d'Aide Familiale [*International Council of Homehelp Services - ICHS*] [*Driebergen-Rijsenburg, Netherlands*] (EAIO) .... CISAF
Conseil International des Tanneurs [*International Council of Tanners - ICT*] (EAIO) .... CIT
Conseil International des Unions Scientifiques [*International Council of Scientific Unions*] .... CIUS

Conseil International d'Etudes Canadiennes [*International Council for Canadian Studies - ICCS*] .... CIEC

Conseil International du Batiment pour la Recherche, l'Etude, et la Documentation [*International Council for Building Research, Studies, and Documentation*] (EAIO)

Conseil International du Ble [*International Wheat Council - IWC*] (EAIO) .... CIB

Conseil International du Cinema et de la Television [*International Film and Television Council*] .... CICT

Conseil International du Film d'Enseignement [*International Council for Educational Films*] .... CIFE

Conseil International du Sport Militaire [*International Military Sports Council*] [*Belgium*] .... CISM

Conseil International Formule 40 [*International F-40 Council*] [*Paris, France*] (EAIO) CIF40

Conseil International pour la Recherche en Agroforesterie [*International Council for Research in Agroforestry*] (EAIO) .... CIRAF

Conseil International pour le Developpement du Cuivre [*International Copper Development Council*] (AF) .... CIDEC

Conseil International pour le Recherche en Linguistique Fondamentale et Appliquee [*International Research Council on Pure and Applied Linguistics - IRCPAL*] (EA) .... CIRELFA

Conseil International pour l'Education des Handicapes de la Vue [*International Council for Education of the Visually Handicapped - ICEVH*] (EAIO) .... CIEHV

Conseil International pour l'Education Physique et la Science du Sport [*International Council of Sport Science and Physical Education - ICSSPE*] (EAIO) .... CIEPSS

Conseil International pour l'Exploration de la Mer [*International Council for the Exploration of the Sea*] .... CIEM

Conseil International pour l'Organization Scientifique [*World Management Council*] (EA) .... CIOS

Conseil Jeunesse Francophone de la Colombie-Britannique (AC) .... CJFCB

Conseil Jeunesse Provincial [*Manitoba*] (AC) .... CJP

Conseil Jeunesse Provincial [*Nouvelle-Ecosse*] (AC) .... CJP

Conseil Mondial de la Paix [*World Peace Council - WPC*] (EAIO) .... CMP

Conseil Mondial de l'Alimentation [*World Food Council*] [*French United Nations*] (DUND) .... CMA

Conseil Mondial d'Education [*World Council for Curriculum and Instruction*] .... CME

Conseil Mondial des Associations d'Education Comparee [*World Council of Comparative Education Societies - WCCES*] (EA) .... CMAEC

Conseil Mondial pour l'Assemblee Constituante des Peuples [*World Council for the Peoples World Convention*] .... CMACP

Conseil National Canadien du Travail [*National Council of Canadian Labour - NCCL*] .... CNCT

Conseil National de la Resistance Guadeloupeenne [*Political party*] (EY) .... CNRG

Conseil National de l'Industrie Laitiere du Canada [*National Dairy Council of Canada*] .... CNIL

Conseil National de l'Ordre des Medecins [*France*] .... CNOM

Conseil National de Recherche Scientifique [*International Council of Scientific Unions*] .... CNRS

Conseil National de Recherches Canada [*National Research Council Canada*] .... CNRC

Conseil Oecumenique de Jeunesse en Europe [*Ecumenical Youth Council in Europe*] [*Northern Ireland*] (EAIO) .... COJE

Conseil Oecumenique des Eglises [*World Council of Churches*] .... COE

Conseil Oleicole International [*International Olive Oil Council - IOOC*] (EAIO) .... COI

Conseil Parlementaire du Mouvement Europeen .... CPME

Conseil Pationa de Recherches [*Canada*] [*Marine science*] (OSRA) .... CNR

Conseil Pedagogique Interdisciplinaire du Quebec (AC) .... CPIQ

Conseil Permanent de la Convention Internationale de Stresa sur les Fromages (EAIO) .... CPCISF

Conseil pour la Liberation du Congo-Kinshasa [*Council for the Liberation of the Congo-Kinshasa*] [*Zaire*] (PD) CLC

Conseil pour l'Homologation des Etablissements Theologiques en Afrique [*Accrediting Council for Theological Education in Africa - ACTEA*] (EAIO) .... COHETA

[*Le*] **Conseil pour l'Unite Canadienne** [*The Council for Canadian Unity*] (AC) .... CUC

Conseil Provincial du Quebec des Metiers de la Construction (AC) .... CPQMC

Conseil Quebecois de l'Estampe [*1984, founded 1971 as AGQ, CGQ from 1978*] [*Canada*] (NGC) .... CQE

Conseil Quebecois de l'Estampe Inc. (AC) .... CQE

Conseil Quebecois des professionnels et Cadres (AC) .... CQPC

Conseil Quebecois du Commerce de Detail (AC) .... CQCD

Conseil Quebecois du Theatre (AC) .... CQT

Conseil Regional de Developpement, Trois-Rivieres, PQ, Canada [*Library symbol Library of Congress*] (LCLS) .... CaQTCRD

Conseil Regional de Developpement, Trois-Rivieres, Quebec [*Library symbol National Library of Canada*] (NLC) .... QTCRD

Conseil Regional de la Sante et des Services Sociaux, Chicoutimi, PQ, Canada [*Library symbol Library of Congress*] (LCLS) .... CaQCCRS

Conseil Regional de la Sante et des Services Sociaux, Chicoutimi, Quebec [*Library symbol National Library of Canada*] (NLC) .... QCCRS

Conseil Regional de la Sante et des Services Sociaux de la Region Cote-Nord, Hauterive, PQ, Canada [*Library symbol Library of Congress*] (LCLS) .... CaQHaCR

Conseil Regional de la Sante et des Services Sociaux de la Region Cote-Nord, Hauterive, Quebec [*Library symbol National Library of Canada*] (NLC) .... QHACR

Conseil Regional de la Sante et des Services Sociaux de la Region Outaouais-Hull, Hull, PQ, Canada [*Library symbol Library of Congress*] (LCLS) .... CaQHCRS

Conseil Regional de la Sante et des Services Sociaux de la Region Outaouais-Hull, Hull, Quebec [*Library symbol National Library of Canada*] (NLC) .... QHCRS

Conseil Regional de la Sante et des Services Sociaux des Cantons de l'Est, Sherbrooke, PQ, Canada [*Library symbol Library of Congress*] (LCLS) .... CaQSherCR

Conseil Regional de la Sante et des Services Sociaux des Cantons de l'Est, Sherbrooke, Quebec [*Library symbol National Library of Canada*] (NLC) .... QSHERCR

Conseil Regional de la Sante et des Services Sociaux Laurentides Lanaudiere, Saint-Jerome, ON, Canada [*Library symbol Library of Congress*] (LCLS) .... CaOStJeCR

Conseil Regional de la Sante et des Services Sociaux Laurentides-Lanaudiere, Saint-Jerome, Quebec [*Library symbol National Library of Canada*] (NLC) .... QSTJECR

Conseil Regional de la Sante et des Services Sociaux, Longueuil, PQ, Canada [*Library symbol Library of Congress*] (LCLS) .... CaQLoCRS

Conseil Regional de la Sante et des Services Sociaux, Longueuil, Quebec [*Library symbol National Library of Canada*] (NLC) .... QLCRS

Conseil Regional de la Sante et des Services Sociaux, Quebec, Quebec [*Library symbol National Library of Canada*] (NLC) .... QQCRS

Conseil Regional de la Sante et des Services Sociaux, Rimouski, PQ, Canada [*Library symbol Library of Congress*] (LCLS) .... CaQRCRS

Conseil Regional de la Sante et des Services Sociaux, Rimouski, Quebec [*Library symbol National Library of Canada*] (NLC) .... QRCRS

Conseil Regional de la Sante et des Services Sociaux Rouyn-Noranda, Noranda, PQ,Canada [*Library symbol Library of Congress*] (LCLS) .... CaQNCRS

Conseil Regional de la Sante et des Services Sociaux Rouyn-Noranda, Noranda, Quebec [*Library symbol National Library of Canada*] (NLC) .... QNCRS

Conseil Regional de la Sante et des Services Sociaux, Trois-Rivieres, PQ, Canada [*Library symbol Library of Congress*] (LCLS) .... CaQTCRS

Conseil Regional de la Sante et des Services Sociaux, Trois-Rivieres, Quebec [*Library symbol National Library of Canada*] (NLC) .... QTCRS

Conseil Regional des Travailleurs et Travailleuses Centre du Quebec (AC) .... CRTCQ

Conseil Scientifique pour l'Afrique au Sud de Sahara [*Scientific Council for Africa South of the Sahara*] .... CSA

Conseil Superieur de l'Audioviseul [*France*] (EY) .... CSA

Conseil Superieur de Livre [*Canada*] .... CSL

Conseil Superieur du Sport en Afrique [*Supreme Council for Sport in Africa - SCSA*] [*Yaounde, Cameroon*] (EAIO) .... CSSA

Conseil Universitaire des Directeurs de Biologie du Canada (AC) .... CUDBC

Conseiller [*Councillor, Judge*] [*French*] (ILCA) .... Cons

Conseiller de la Reine [*Queen's Counsel*] [*Canada*] .... CR

Conseillers en Gestion et Informatique [*Montreal, PQ*] [*Telecommunications service*] (TSSD) .... CGI

Conseillers en Gestion et Informatique CGI, Inc., Centre de Documentation, Quebec, PQ, Canada [*Library symbol*] [*Library of Congress*] (LCLS) .... CaQQCGI

Consejo de Defensa Centroamericana [*Central American Defense Council*] [*Guatemala, Guatemala*] (EAIO) .... CONDECA

Consejo de Educacion de Adultos de America Latina [*Santiago, Chile*] (EAIO) .... CEAAL

Consejo Empresarial Mexicano para Asuntos Internacionales [*The Mexican Business Council for International Affairs*] (CROSS) .... CEMAL

Consejo Episcopal Latinoamericano [*Latin American Episcopal Council*] (EAIO) .... CELAM

Consejo Interamericano de Comercio y Produccion [*Interamerican Council of Commerce and Production*] .... CICYP

Consejo Interamericano de Musica [*Inter-American Music Council*] (EA) .... CIDEM

Consejo Interamericano do Escultismo [*Inter-American Scout Committee - IASC*] [*San Jose, Costa Rica*] (EAIO) .... CIE

Consejo Interamericano Economico-Social [*Inter-American Economic and Social Council*] (EA) .... CIES

Consejo Interamericano para la Educacion, la Ciencia, y la Cultura [*Inter-American Council for Education, Science, and Culture*] (EA) .... CIECC

Consejo Internacional de Buena Vecindad, AC [*International Good Neighbor Council - IGNC*] [*Monterrey, Mexico*] (EAIO) .... CIBV

Consejo Internacional de la Pelicula de Ensenanza [*International Council for Educational Films*] .... CIPE

Consejo Internacional de Mujeres [*International Council of Women*] .... CIM

Consejo Internacional del Trigo [*International Wheat Council - IWC*] (EAIO) ..... CIT

Consejo Latinoamericano de Ciencias Sociales [*Latin American Social Sciences Council - LASSC*] (EAIO) .... CLACSO

Consejo Latinoamericano de Iglesias [*Latin American Council of Churches*] (EAIO) .... CLAI

Consejo Latinoamericano de Mujeres Catolicas [*Latin American Council of Catholic Women*] (EAIO) .... CLAMUC

Consejo Latino-Americano de Radiacon Cosmica [*Latin-American Council on Cosmic Radiation*] [*Bolivia*] (PDAA) .... CLARC

Consejo Mundial de Artes y Oficios [*World Crafts Council*] .... CMAO

Consejo Mundial de Iglesias [*Switzerland*] .... CMI

Consejo Mundial de la Alimentacion [*World Food Council*] [*Spanish United Nations*] (DUND) .... CMA

Consejo Nacional de la Industria Maquiladora [*National Council of the Maquiladora Industry*] [*Mexican/US business organization*] (CROSS) .... CNIM

Consejo Universitario Inter-Americana para el Desarrollo Economico y Social [*Inter-American University Council for Economic and Social Development - IUCESD*] (EA) .... CUIDES

Consensus .... Con

Consensus Voluntary Reference Compound [*Environmental science*] .... CVRC

Consent (ROG) .... CONST

Consent Agreement/Final Order (GFGA) .... CAFO

Consent to Medical Treatment [*British Medical Association computer program*] .... COMET

Consep, Inc. [*Associated Press*] (SAG) .... Consep
Consep, Inc. [*NASDAQ symbol*] (SAG) .... CSEP
Consequence .... CONS
Consequence (ROG) .... CONSCE
Consequence [*Legal*] [*British*] (ROG) .... CONSEQCE
Consequence Limiting Control System [*Nuclear energy*] (NRCH) .... CLCS
Consequent [*Legal*] [*British*] (ROG) .... CONSEQT
Consequential Arc Back .... CAB
Conserva [*Conserve*] [*Pharmacy*] .... CONS
Conservation (AABC) .... CON
Conservation .... CONSERV
Conservation .... CONSERVE
Conservation Administration News [*A publication*] .... CAN
Conservation Analytical Laboratory [*Smithsonian Institution*] .... CAL
Conservation and Environment Library Information System .... CELIS
[*Department of*] Conservation and Environment, Victoria [*State*] (EERA) ..... VDCE
Conservation and Protection-Western and Northern Region, Environment Canada [*Conservation et Protection-Region de l'Ouest et du Nord, Environnement Canada*], Edmonton, Alberta [*Library symbol National Library of Canada*] (NLC) .... AEECW
Conservation and Renewable Energy .... CRE
Conservation and Renewable Energy Inquiry and Referral Service [*Department of Energy*] [*Information service or system*] (IID) .... CAREIRS
Conservation and Renewable Energy Inquiry and Referral Service [*Database*] .... CEIRS
Conservation and Renewable Energy Office [*Canada*] .... CREO
Conservation and Renewable Energy Office, Energy, Mines, and Resources Canada [*Bureau de la Conservation de l'Energie et de l'Energie Renouvelable, Energie, Mines, et Ressources Canada*] Toronto, Ontario [*Library symbol National Library of Canada*] (NLC) .... OTEMR
Conservation and Renewable Energy Program [*Department of Energy*]..... C & RE
Conservation and Research Foundation (EA) .... CRF
Conservation Association of Botanical Societies (DBA) .... CABS
Conservation Commission of the Northern Territory [*Australia*] .... CCNT
Conservation Committee of California Oil and Gas Producers (SRA) ..... CCCOGP
Conservation Council for the South East Region and Canberra [*Australia*] .... CCSERC
Conservation Council of New Brunswick [*Conseil de la Conservation du Nouveu-Brunswick*] (AC) .... CCNB
Conservation Council of Ontario [*Le Conseil de Conservation de l'Ontario*] (AC) .... CCO
Conservation Data Centers (GNE) .... CDC
Conservation Division, Environment Canada [*Division de la Conservation, Environnement Canada*] Ottawa, Ontario [*Library symbol National Library of Canada*] (NLC) .... OOEOB
Conservation Education and Research Program (GNE) .... CERP
Conservation Education Association (EA) .... CEA
Conservation Education Diving Archeology Museums .... CEDAM
Conservation Environment and Historic Preservation [*Commercial firm*] .... CEHP
Conservation, Exploration, Diving, Archeology, Museums [*Acronym is used as name of an international organization interested in these five subjects*] (EA) .... CEDAM
[*Department of*] Conservation, Forests and Lands of Victoria [*State*] (EERA) .... VCF&L
Conservation Foundation (EA) .... CF
Conservation Fund [*An association*] (EA) .... CF
Conservation International (EA) CI
Conservation Law Foundation (ECON) .... CLF
Conservation Law Society of America [*Defunct*] .... CLSA
Conservation League (EA) CL
Conservation Materials and Services .... CMS
Conservation Monitoring Centre [*World trade of endangered species products*] .... CMC
Conservation of Antarctic Marine Living Resources [*International agreement signed in 1982*] .... CAMLR
Conservation OnLine [*Database collection*] [*Internet*] .... COOL
Conservation Program Improvements Act .... CPIA
Conservation Reporting and Evaluation System [*Department of Agriculture*] .... CRES
Conservation Research Report [*A publication*] .... CRR
Conservation Reserve Program [*Department of Agriculture Department of Energy*] .... CRP
Conservation Society [*British*] (DCTA) .... CS
Conservation Tillage Information Center .... CTIC
Conservation Treaty Support Fund [*An association*] (EA) .... CTSF
Conservation Trust [*British*] (EAIO) .... CT
Conservation Voltage Reduction [*Public Utilities Commission*] .... CVR
Conservation Zone Advisory Committee [*Australia*] .... COZAC
Conservatism-Radicalism Opinionaire [*Student attitude test*] .... C-R
Conservative [*Politics*] C
Conservative .... CONS
Conservative Action for Electoral Reform [*British*] .... CAER
Conservative Action Foundation (EA) .... CAF
Conservative Action Foundation/Coalition Against Nuclear Annihilation [*Research center*] (RCD) .... CAF/CANA
Conservative Alliance (EA) .... CALL
Conservative and National Liberal Party [*British*] .... CNL
Conservative and Unionist Central Office [*British*] (DAS) .... CUCO
Conservative and Unionist Party [*British Political party*] .... CONS
Conservative Baptist Association of America (EA) .... CBAA
Conservative Baptist Foreign Mission Society (EA) .... CBFMS
Conservative Baptist Home Mission Society (EA) .... CBHMS
Conservative Baptist Theological Seminary, Denver, CO [*Library symbol Library of Congress*] (LCLS) .... CoDCB

Conservative Baptist Theological Seminary, Englewood, CO [*OCLC symbol*] (OCLC) .... CBS
Conservative Book Club .... CBC
[*The*] Conservative Caucus (EA) .... TCC
[*The*] Conservative Caucus Research, Analysis, and Education Foundation (EA) .... TCCRAEF
Conservative Central Council [*British*] CCC
Conservative Clubs of America (EA) .... CCA
Conservative Collegiate Forum (AIE) .... CCF
Conservative Democratic Forum (EA) .... CDF
Conservative Democratic Political Action Committee (EA) .... CDPAC
Conservative Leadership Political Action Committee (EA) .... CLPAC
Conservative Library Association [*Defunct*] .... CLA
Conservative Majority for Citizen's Rights (EA) .... CMCR
Conservative Mennonite Board of Missions and Charities [*Later, RMM*] (EA) .... CMBMC
Conservative Nationalist Party [*British*] .... CN
Conservative Nationalist Party [*Australia Political party*] .... ConsNP
Conservative Network (EA) .... CN
Conservative Opportunity Society (EA) .... COS
Conservative Orthopedics International Association (EA) .... COIA
Conservative Orthopedics International Association (EA) .... IACO
Conservative Party [*South Africa*] [*Political party*] .... CP
Conservative Party of Australia [*Political party*] .... CPA
Conservative Party of Australia [*Political party*] .... CVP
Conservative Party of South Africa [*Konserwatiewe Party van Suid-Afrika*] [*Political party*] (PPW) .... CPSA
Conservative Party's Defense Committee [*British*] .... CPDC
Conservative Political Action Conference .... CPAC
Conservative Political Centre [*British*] .... CPC
Conservative Savings Corp. [*NASDAQ symbol*] (NQ) .... CONS
Conservative Savings Corp. [*Associated Press*] (SAG) .... ConsSv
Conservative Savings Corp. [*Associated Press*] (SAG) .... ConsvSv
Conservative Society [*British*] (DI) .... CONSOC
Conservative Society of America .... CSA
Conservative Trade Unionists [*British*] .... CTU
Conservative Victory Committee [*An association*] (EA) CVC
Conservative Way Forward [*British Political party*] .... CWF
Conservative Youth Federation [*Defunct*] (EA) .... CYF
Conservatives for a Constitutional Convention (EA) CCC
Conservatoire [*Conservatory*] [*French*] .... Cons
Conservatoire d'Art Dramatique de Montreal, Quebec [*Library symbol National Library of Canada*] (NLC) .... QMCADQ
Conservatoire d'Art Dramatique de Quebec, Montreal, PQ, Canada [*Library symbol Library of Congress*] (LCLS) .... CaQMCADQ
Conservatoire d'Art Dramatique de Quebec, Quebec, PQ, Canada [*Library symbol Library of Congress*] (LCLS) .... CaQQCAD
Conservatoire d'Art Dramatique du Quebec, Quebec [*Library symbol National Library of Canada*] (NLC) .... QQCAD
Conservatoire de Musique de Montreal, Montreal, PQ, Canada [*Library symbol Library of Congress*] (LCLS) .... CaQMCOM
Conservatoire de Musique de Montreal, Quebec [*Library symbol National Library of Canada*] (NLC) .... QMCOM
Conservatoire de Musique du Quebec, Quebec, PQ, Canada [*Library symbol Library of Congress*] (LCLS) .... CaQQCMQ
Conservator (DLA) .... Cons
Conservatorium (ADA) .... CON
Conservatorship (DLA) .... Consv
Conservatory .... CONSERV
conservatory .... CONSRVTRY
Conservatory .... CONSV
Conserve (AABC) .... CONSV
Conserve, Preserve, and Restore (GNE) .... CPR
Conserved ATPase [*Adenosine Triphosphatase*] Domain [*Biochemistry*] .... CAD
Conserved DNA [*Deoxyribose Nucleic Acid*] Element [*Genetics*] .... CDE
Conserved Vector Current CVC
Conservez Taxe Payee [*Retain Charge Paid*] [*French Business term*] .... CTP
Consider (AABC) .... CONS
Consider (ROG) .... CONSID
Consider (FAAC) .... CSDR
Consider All Factors (BARN) .... caf
Consider Yourself Kissed [*Correspondence*] .... CYK
Considerable (FAAC) .... CSDRBL
Considerable Conduct Disorder .... CCD
Considerant [*Whereas, In View*] [*French*] (ILCA) .... Cons
Consideration .... CON
Consideration .... CONSON
Considered [*Legal*] [*British*] (ROG) .... CONSD
Consiel du Statut de la Femme, Quebec, Quebec [*Library symbol National Library of Canada*] (NLC) .... QQCSF
Consiglio Nazionale delle Ricerche [*National Research Council*] [*Italy*] [*Information service or system*] (IID) .... CNR
Consiglio Nazionale delle Ricerche, Rome, Italy [*Library symbol Library of Congress*] (LCLS) .... ItRC
Consiglio Nazionale Scienza Tecnologia [*Italy*] .... CNST
Consign .... CONS
Consignee [*Business term*] (DS) .... cnee
Consignee [*Business term*] (ROG) .... CONSGEE
Consignment [*Business term*] (DS) .... cnmt
Consignment [*Business term*] .... CONS
Consignment [*Business term*] .... CONSGT
Consignment [*Business term*] (ROG) .... CONST
Consignment Item Request (MCD) .... CIR
Consignment Note [*Shipping*] .... CN
Consignment Note Control Label Number (DS) .... CCLN

Consilio et Prudentia [*By Counsel and Prudence*] [*Latin*] (ADA) .... CONS et PRUD
Consilium Conferentiarum Episcopalium Europae [*Council of European Bishops' Conferences*] (EAIO) .... CCEE
Consilium, Inc. [*Associated Press*] (SAG) .... Consilm
Consilium, Inc. [*NASDAQ symbol*] (NQ) .... CSIM
Consist (AABC) .... CONS
Consist Of (MSA) .... C/O
Consistency .... CNSISTY
Consistency and Correction Software [*Bureau of the Census*] (GFGA) .... CONCOR
Consistency Index [*Botany*] CI
Consistency Recording Controller .... CRC
Consistent .... CNSIST
Consistent (FAAC) .... CNSTNT
Consistent Payment Rate [*Finance*] (EMRF) .... CPR
Consistent With (DAVI) .... C/W
Consisting Of [*Freight*] .... CON OF
Consistorial Decisions, Scotland, by George Ferguson, Lord Hermand [*A publication*] (DLA) .... Ferg
Consistory of Masonic Magic [*Freemasonry*] (ROG) .... CMM
Conso Products [*NASDAQ symbol*] (TTSB) .... CNSO
Conso Products Co. [*NASDAQ symbol*] (SAG) .... CNSO
Conso Products Co. [*Associated Press*] (SAG) .... ConsoPd
Consociatio Internationalis Musicae Sacrae [*Rome, Italy*] (EAIO) .... CIMS
Consoer, Townsend & Associates, Chicago, IL [*Library symbol Library of Congress*] (LCLS) .... ICCT
Consol [*Navigation*] (AIA) .... CON
Consol Delivery & Logistics [*NASDAQ symbol*] (TTSB) .... CDLI
Consol Ed NY,$5 Pfd [*NYSE symbol*] (TTSB) .... EDPrA
Consol Ed NY,6% Cv B Pref [*NYSE symbol*] (TTSB) .... EDPPrB
Consol Ed NY,4.65% C Pfd [*NYSE symbol*] (TTSB) .... EDPrC
Consol Synthetic Fuel [*Coal liquefaction process*] .... CSF
Consolan Facility [*Aviation*] .... CONSO
Consolata Missionaries (TOCD) .... imc
Consolata Missionaries (TOCD) .... IMC
Consolata Missionary Sisters [*Roman Catholic religious order*] .... MC
Consolation .... CONSLTN
Console (KSC) .... CNSL
Console [*Computer science*] (IAA) .... CON
Console [*Computer science*] .... CONS
Console (AAG) .... CSL
Console Action Processor .... CAP
Console Command Processor [*Digital Research*] .... CCP
Console Communication System (MCD) .... CCS
Console Communications Equipment (MCD) .... CCE
Console Computer Interface Adapter .... CCIA
Console Control Circuit CCC
Console Control Package .... CCP
Console Digital Display Programmer (MUGU) .... CDDP
Console for Optical Measurement and Precise Analysis of Radiation from Electronics .... COMPARE
Console Input (BTTJ) .... CONIN
Console Input/Output .... CONIO
Console Intelligence Unit (MCD) .... CIU
Console Internally Generated and Refreshed Symbols (CAAL) .... CIGARS
Console Keyset (MCD) .... CK
Console Lighting Panel (MCD) .... CLP
Console Local Equipment (MCD) .... CLE
Console Message Processor [*Computer science*] .... CMP
Console Operating System (NASA) .... COS
Console Operator Proficiency Examination [*Computer Usage Co.*] .... COPE
Console Output (BTTJ) .... CONOUT
Console Processor (NASA) .... CP
Console Programming System (IAA) .... CPS
Console Remote Equipment (MCD) .... CRE
Console Reply Queuing .... CRQ
Console Send/Receive [*Computer science*] (IAA) .... CSR
Console Set Group .... CSG
Console Simulator [*Computer science*] .... CONSIM
Console to Computer Buffer (MUGU) .... CCB
Console Typewriter (IAA) .... CT
Console Typewriter (IAA) .... CTW
Console-Oriented Model Building [*Computer science*] .... COMB
Console-Oriented Statistical Matrix Operator System [*Computer science*] .... COSMOS
Consolidate (MSA) .... CNSLD
Consolidate .... CONS
Consolidate (AFM) .... CONSOL
Consolidate (FAAC) .... CSLDT
Consolidate Acquisition Directive [*DoD*] .... CAD
Consolidate Air Defense Order of Battle (MCD) .... CADOB
Consolidate Time Rate .... CTR
Consolidate-Cargo Container Service (DS) .... CCS
Consolidated [*Accounting*] .... CN
Consolidated .... CON
Consolidated .... CONS
Consolidated (DD) .... consol
Consolidated (ADA) .... CONSOLTD
Consolidated Accelerated Navy Documentation Organization .... CAN DO
Consolidated Acquistion Reporting System [*Army*] .... CARS
Consolidated Actuarial Data System [*Health insurance*] (GHCT) .... CADS
Consolidated Administrative Management Organization [*AID*] .... CAMO
Consolidated Advance Field Team [*Navy*] .... CAFT
Consolidated Aerospace Equipment List (MCD) .... CAEL
Consolidated Aerospace Ground Equipment List .... CAGEL
Consolidated Aerospace Supplier Evaluation (NRCH) .... CASE
Consolidated Afloat Requisitioning Guide (DNAB) .... CARGO
Consolidated AGE Ground Equipment List (MCD) .... CAGEL
Consolidated Air Mission Results Analysis (CINC) .... CAMRA
Consolidated Air Target Material Notices [*NOO*] .... CATMN
Consolidated Air Tour Manual [*Air travel term*] .... CATM
Consolidated Aircraft Corp. [*Later, General Dynamics Corp.*] (AAG) .... CAC
Consolidated Aircraft Maintenance .... CAM
Consolidated Aircraft Maintenance Group [*Air Force*] .... CAMG
Consolidated Aircraft Maintenance Squadron [*Air Force*] .... CAMS
Consolidated Aircraft Maintenance Squadron [*Air Force*] .... CAMSq
Consolidated Aircraft Maintenance Training .... CAMT
Consolidated Aircraft Maintenance Wing [*Air Force*] .... CAMW
Consolidated Amhawk Enterprise [*Vancouver Stock Exchange symbol*] .... CVK
Consolidated Ammunition Bulk Shippers (MCD) .... CABS
Consolidated Analysis Centers, Inc. .... CACI
Consolidated Andex Resources Ltd. [*Vancouver Stock Exchange symbol*] .... CON
Consolidated Annuities [*Insurance*] (DSUE) .... CONSOLS
Consolidated Anti-Jam Equipment (MCD) .... CAJE
Consolidated Aquanauts Vital Equipment .... CAVE
Consolidated Army System for Processing Entitlements to Reservists .... CASPER
Consolidated Ascot Petroleum [*Toronto Stock Exchange symbol Vancouver Stock Exchange symbol*] .... CSP
Consolidated Assistance and Relocation Efforts (MCD) .... CARE
Consolidated Athletic Commission (EA) .... CAC
Consolidated Atomic Time .... CAT
Consolidated Audio-Visual Coordinating Office [*Military*] (DNAB) .... CAVCO
Consolidated Automated Support Station (MCD) .... CASS
Consolidated Balance Sheet [*Accounting*] .... CBS
Consolidated Base Personnel Office [*Air Force*] .... CBPO
Consolidated Base Personnel Office Letter [*Air Force*] .... CBPOL
Consolidated Bel-Air [*Vancouver Stock Exchange symbol*] .... CBT
Consolidated Boulder Mountain [*Vancouver Stock Exchange symbol*] .... CBM
Consolidated Boundary Explorations [*Vancouver Stock Exchange symbol*] .... CBX
Consolidated Brinco Ltd. [*Toronto Stock Exchange symbol*] .... CBW
Consolidated BRX Mining & Petroleum Ltd. [*Vancouver Stock Exchange symbol*] CIX
Consolidated Business System (IAA) .... CBS
Consolidated Callinan Flin Flon Mines Ltd. [*Vancouver Stock Exchange symbol*] .... CFF
Consolidated Canarctic Industries Ltd. [*Vancouver Stock Exchange symbol*] .... CCA
Consolidated Carma Corp. [*Toronto Stock Exchange symbol*] .... CVP
Consolidated Carriers Tariff Bureau .... CCTB
Consolidated Change Table (MCD) .... CCT
Consolidated Churchill Enterprises, Inc. [*Vancouver Stock Exchange symbol*] .... CHH
Consolidated Cigar Holdings, Inc. [*NYSE symbol*] (SAG) .... CIG
Consolidated Cigar Holdings, Inc. [*Associated Press*] (SAG) .... CnCigar
Consolidated Cima Resources [*Vancouver Stock Exchange symbol*] .... CNA
Consolidated Cisco Resources [*Vancouver Stock Exchange symbol*] .... CSU
Consolidated Civilian Personnel Office [*Air Force*] .... CCPO
Consolidated Civilian Personnel Office Field Division [*Air Force*] (DNAB) .... CCPOFD
Consolidated Command, Control, and Communications Program (MCD) .... CCCP
Consolidated Command Post [*Military*] .... CCP
Consolidated Communications Recording Facility (MCD) .... CCRF
Consolidated Computer (IAA) CC
Consolidated Computer and Control Center CCCC
Consolidated Computer Security Program [*Military*] (GFGA) .... CCSP
Consolidated Container Processing System (MCD) .... CCPS
Consolidated Cryptologic Program [*DoD*] (AABC) .... CCP
Consolidated CSA Minerals, Inc. [*Vancouver Stock Exchange symbol*] .... CNV
Consolidated Customer Order Processing (IAA) .... CCOP
Consolidated Cyll Industry [*Vancouver Stock Exchange symbol*] .... CIY
Consolidated Data Base (PDAA) .... CDB
Consolidated Decision Package Set [*Military*] .... CDPS
Consolidated Defense Intelligence Program .... CDIP
Consolidated Defense Supply Material .... CDSM
Consolidated Deficiency and Improvement Data Systems .... CDIDS
Consolidated Delivery & Logistis, Inc. [*NASDAQ symbol*] (SAG) .... CDLI
Consolidated Delivery & Logistis, Inc. [*Associated Press*] (SAG) .... ConslDel
Consolidated Delivery Status Report (MCD) .... CDSR
Consolidated Delivery Status Report System (MCD) .... CDSRS
Consolidated Development Increment Package .... CDIP
Consolidated Diesel Electric Co. .... CONDEC
Consolidated Ed 7.75%'QUICS' [*NYSE symbol*] (TTSB) .... EDL
Consolidated Edison (MHDW) .... Con Ed
Consolidated Edison [*NYSE symbol*] (TTSB) .... ED
Consolidated Edison Co. (MHDB) .... CEC
Consolidated Edison Co., Inc., New York, NY [*Library symbol Library of Congress*] (LCLS) .... NNConE
Consolidated Edison Co. of New York, Inc. [*Associated Press*] (SAG) .... ConE
Consolidated Edison Co. of New York, Inc. [*Associated Press*] (SAG) .... ConEd
Consolidated Edison Co. of New York, Inc. [*NYSE symbol*] (SPSG) .... ED
Consolidated Edison Thorium Reactor .... CETR
Consolidated Edison Uranium (GAAI) .... CEU
Consolidated Edison Uranium Solidification Program [*Oak Ridge National Laboratory*] .... CEUSP
Consolidated Eglin Real-Time System (MCD) .... CERTS
Consolidated Electric Power Asia (ECON) .... CEPA
Consolidated Electrodynamics Corp. .... CEC
Consolidated Electronics Corp. .... CEC
Consolidated Engineering Technology Corp. (MCD) .... CETEC

Consolidated Entry Level Training (MCD) .... CELT
Consolidated Environmental Technologies [*Commercial firm British*] (ECON) .... CET
Consolidated Explorer Petroleum Corp. [*Vancouver Stock Exchange symbol*] .... CEP
Consolidated Facilities Corp. [*Railroads*] .... CONFAC
Consolidated Federal Fund Report [*Bureau of the Census*] (GFGA) .... CFFR
Consolidated Federal Law Enforcement Training Center [*Later, FLETC*] [*Department of the Treasury*] .... CFLETC
Consolidated Film Industries [*Commercial firm*] .... CFI
Consolidated Financial Statement (HGAA) .... CFS
Consolidated First Fund [*Vancouver Stock Exchange symbol*] .... FFP
Consolidated Five Star Resources [*Vancouver Stock Exchange symbol*] .... CFR
Consolidated Flight Record Custodian [*Air Force*] (AFM) .... CFRC
Consolidated Fredonia Resources Ltd. [*Vancouver Stock Exchange symbol*] .... CFN
Consolidated Free Library District, Athol Branch, Athol, ID [*Library symbol*] [*Library of Congress*] (LCLS) .... IdCC-A
Consolidated Free Library District, Coeur d'Alene, ID [*Library symbol*] [*Library of Congress*] (LCLS) .... IdCC
Consolidated Free Library District, Rathdrum Branch, Rathdrum, ID [*Library symbol*] [*Library of Congress*] (LCLS) .... IdCC-R
Consolidated Free Library District, Service Center, Couer d'Alene, ID [*Library symbol*] [*Library of Congress*] (LCLS) .... IdCC-SC
Consolidated Free Library District, Spirit Lake Branch, Spirit Lake, ID [*Library symbol*] [*Library of Congress*] (LCLS) .... IdCC-SL
Consolidated Freight Classification .... CFC
Consolidated Freightways [*NASDAQ symbol*] (SAG) .... CFWY
Consolidated Freightways [*NYSE symbol*] (TTSB) .... CNF
Consolidated Freightways [*Associated Press*] (SAG) .... CnsFrtC
Consolidated Freightways, Inc. .... CF
Consolidated Freightways, Inc. [*NYSE symbol*] (SPSG) .... CNF
Consolidated Freightways, Inc. [*Associated Press*] (SAG) .... CnsFrt
Consolidated Fuel Reprocessing Program [*Oak Ridge National Laboratory*] .... CFRP
Consolidated Function Ordinary [*IBM Corp.*] .... CFO
Consolidated Funds Ordinary [*Insurance*] .... CFO
Consolidated Gas Supply Corp., Chelyan, WV [*Library symbol Library of Congress*] (LCLS) .... WvCheC
Consolidated Gas Supply Corp., Clarksburg, WV [*Library symbol Library of Congress*] (LCLS) .... WvClC
Consolidated General Orders in Chancery [*A publication*] (DLA) .... Cons Ord in Ch
Consolidated General Orders in Chancery [*A publication*] (DLA) .... Consolid Ord
Consolidated General Western Industries Ltd. [*Vancouver Stock Exchange symbol Toronto Stock Exchange symbol*] .... CVW
Consolidated Gold Fields [*British*] .... CGF
Consolidated Gold Fields [*British*] .... CONSGOLD
Consolidated Gold Standard Resources, Inc. [*Vancouver Stock Exchange symbol*] .... CGQ
Consolidated Goldwest [*Vancouver Stock Exchange symbol*] .... KGG
Consolidated Graphics [*NASDAQ symbol*] (TTSB) .... COGI
Consolidated Graphics, Inc. [*NASDAQ symbol*] (SAG) .... COGI
Consolidated Graphics, Inc. [*Associated Press*] (SAG) .... ConsGph
Consolidated Group of Tribes and Organizations .... CGTO
Consolidated Guidance (RDA) .... CG
Consolidated Hazardous Item List (MCD) .... CHIL
Consolidated HCI Holdings Corp. [*Toronto Stock Exchange symbol*] .... CXA
Consolidated Headquarters Squadron [*Military*] .... CHS
Consolidated Health Care Associates, Inc. [*NASDAQ symbol*] (SAG) .... CHCA
Consolidated Health Care Associates, Inc. [*Associated Press*] (SAG) .... ConHCre
Consolidated Heron Resources [*Vancouver Stock Exchange symbol*] .... CNS
Consolidated Hlth Care Assoc [*NASDAQ symbol*] (TTSB) .... CHCA
Consolidated Indescor Corp. [*Formerly, Indescor Hydrodynamics, Inc.*] [*Vancouver Stock Exchange symbol*] .... CIF
Consolidated Index of Translations into English .... CITE
Consolidated Industrial Relations Office (MUGU) .... CIRO
Consolidated Inland Recovery [*Vancouver Stock Exchange symbol*] .... ILG
Consolidated Instrument Package [*Atmospheric research*] .... CIP
Consolidated Intelligence Communication Center (MCD) CICC
Consolidated Intelligence Periodic Summary .... CIPR
Consolidated Intelligence Program [*Military*] (AFM) .... CIP
Consolidated Intelligence Resource Information System [*Air Force*] (MCD) .... CIRIS
Consolidated Interchangeable and Substitute Item List .... CISIL
Consolidated Intermediate Repair Facility .... CIRF
Consolidated Knobby Lake Mines Ltd. [*Vancouver Stock Exchange symbol*] .... CKO
Consolidated Labor Union of the Philippines .... CLUP
Consolidated Link Layer Management [*Telecommunications*] (ACRL) .... CLLM
Consolidated Listing (AFM) CL
Consolidated Load List (DNAB) CLL
Consolidated Logistics Information Planning and Programming Requirements .... CLIPPR
Consolidated Lone Star Resource Corp. [*Vancouver Stock Exchange symbol*] .... CQL
Consolidated Louanna Gold Mines Ltd. [*Toronto Stock Exchange symbol*] .... CLU
Consolidated Mail Room [*Air Force*] (AFM) .... CMR
Consolidated Maintenance Center (MCD) .... CMC
Consolidated Maintenance Squadron [*Air Force*] .... CMS
Consolidated Management Office [*Military*] .... CMO
Consolidated Manitou Resources [*Vancouver Stock Exchange symbol*] .... CSM
Consolidated Marbenor Mines Ltd. [*Toronto Stock Exchange symbol*] .... CBN
Consolidated Master Cross-Reference List [*Defense Supply Agency*] .... CMCRL
Consolidated Master Cross-Reference List [*Defense Supply Agency*] .... CMRL
Consolidated Material Distribution Objectives [*Air Force*] .... CMDO
Consolidated Material List (MCD) .... CML
Consolidated McKinney Resources, Inc. [*Vancouver Stock Exchange symbol*] .... CKY
Consolidated Mercantile [*NASDAQ symbol*] (TTSB) .... CSLMF
Consolidated Mercantile Corp. [*Toronto Stock Exchange symbol*] .... CMC
Consolidated Mercantile Corp. [*NASDAQ symbol*] (NQ) .... CSLM
Consolidated Mercatile Corp. [*Associated Press*] (SAG) .... CnsMerc
Consolidated Metropolitan Area [*Later, CMSA*] [*Census Bureau*] (WDMC) .... CMA
Consolidated Metropolitan Statistical Area [*Census Bureau*] .... CMSA
Consolidated Midland Corp. (DAVI) .... CMC
Consolidated Mining & Smelting Co., Central Technical Library, Trail, BC, Canada [*Library symbol Library of Congress*] (LCLS) .... CaBTC
Consolidated Nat Gas [*NYSE symbol*] (TTSB) .... CNG
Consolidated National Interveners [*An association*] (EA) .... CNI
Consolidated Natural Gas Co. [*NYSE symbol*] (SPSG) .... CNG
Consolidated Natural Gas Co. [*Associated Press*] (SAG) .... ConsNG
Consolidated Naval Telecommunications Program System (DNAB) .... CNTPS
Consolidated Navy Electronic Warfare School (PDAA) .... CNEWS
Consolidated Navy Electronic Warfare Test Plan (CAAL) .... CNEWTP
Consolidated Nev Goldfields [*NASDAQ symbol*] (TTSB) .... KNVCF
Consolidated Nevada Goldfields Corp. [*Associated Press*] (SAG) .... ConsNev
Consolidated Nevada Goldfields Corp. [*NASDAQ symbol*] (SAG) .... KNVC
Consolidated New Equipment Training Plan (MCD) .... CNETP
Consolidated Nord Resources Ltd. [*Vancouver Stock Exchange symbol*] .... CKN
Consolidated Norex Resources Corp. [*Toronto Stock Exchange symbol Vancouver Stock Exchange symbol*] .... CXK
Consolidated Nuclear Steam Generator .... CNSG
Consolidated Omab Enterprises Ltd. [*Vancouver Stock Exchange symbol*] .... CEB
Consolidated Omnibus Budget Reconciliation Act of 1985 [*Health insurance law*] .... COBRA
Consolidated Operability Test [*or Trial*] (NG) .... COT
Consolidated Operations and Delay Analysis System [*FAA*] (TAG) .... CODAS
Consolidated Ordnance Allowance List [*Navy*] .... COAL
Consolidated Pace II Industries Ltd. [*Vancouver Stock Exchange symbol*] .... CKP
Consolidated Package Store [*Military*] (DNAB) .... CPS
Consolidated Papers [*NYSE symbol*] (TTSB) .... CDP
Consolidated Papers, Inc. [*NYSE symbol*] (SAG) .... CDP
Consolidated Papers, Inc. [*Associated Press*] (SAG) .... ConPap
Consolidated Paymaster [*Vancouver Stock Exchange symbol*] .... CPY
Consolidated PCR Industries Ltd. [*Vancouver Stock Exchange symbol*] .... CTQ
Consolidated Personal Property Shipping Office [*Military*] (DNAB) .... CPPSO
Consolidated Personnel Management Information System [*OST*] (TAG) .... CPMIS
Consolidated Petroquin [*Vancouver Stock Exchange symbol*] .... PQN
Consolidated Pilot Training Program [*Air Force*] .... CPT
Consolidated Pipe Lines Co. [*Toronto Stock Exchange symbol*] .... CPP
Consolidated Products [*NASDAQ symbol*] (TTSB) .... COPI
Consolidated Products, Inc. [*Associated Press*] (SAG) .... ConPd
Consolidated Products, Inc. [*Associated Press*] (SAG) .... ConsPdts
Consolidated Products, Inc. [*NYSE symbol*] (SAG) .... COP
Consolidated Products, Inc. [*NASDAQ symbol*] (NQ) .... COPI
Consolidated Professor Mines Ltd. [*Toronto Stock Exchange symbol*] .... CPF
Consolidated Programming Document .... CPD
Consolidated Progress Report .... CPR
Consolidated Property Account (MCD) .... CPA
Consolidated Rail Corp. [*Also, CR, CRC*] .... CONRAIL
Consolidated Rail Corporation (USGC) .... Conrail
Consolidated Rail Corp. [*Also, CONRAIL, CRC*] [*AAR code*] .... CR
Consolidated Rail Corp. [*Also, CR, CONRAIL*] .... CRC
Consolidated Rail Corp. (Eastern District) [*AAR code*] .... CRE
Consolidated Rambler Mines Ltd. [*Toronto Stock Exchange symbol*] .... CRR
Consolidated Ramrod Gold Corp. [*Associated Press*] (SAG) .... ConRam
Consolidated Ramrod Gold Corp. [*Vancouver Stock Exchange symbol*] .... CYN
Consolidated Ramrod Gold Corp. [*NASDAQ symbol*] (SAG) .... CYNX
Consolidated Reactor Uranium [*Vancouver Stock Exchange symbol*] .... CRC
Consolidated Record Communications Center [*Army*] (AABC) .... CRCC
Consolidated Record of Uncontrolled Naval Calamitious Happenings .... CRUNCH
Consolidated Recreation (DNAB) .... CONSOLREC
Consolidated Regal Resources Ltd. [*Vancouver Stock Exchange symbol*] .... KRE
Consolidated Remain-in-Place List (MCD) .... CRIPL
Consolidated Repair Parts List (MCD) .... CRPL
Consolidated Repairable Item List .... CRIL
Consolidated Report .... CR
Consolidated Reporting and Evaluating System, Tactical [*Computer program*] [*Air Force*] .... CREST
Consolidated Reserve Components Reporting System (MCD) .... CORCAPS
Consolidated Reserve Personnel Office [*Air Force*] (AFM) .... CRPO
Consolidated Residual Undeleted Subordinated Tranches [*Finance*] .... CRUST
Consolidated Revenue .... CR
Consolidated Rexspar Minerals & Chemicals Ltd. [*Toronto Stock Exchange symbol*] .... CRM
Consolidated Rio Plata Resources [*Vancouver Stock Exchange symbol*] .... COP
Consolidated Rules of Practice [*Environmental Protection Agency*] (GFGA) .... CROP
Consolidated RVNAF [*Republic of Vietnam Armed Forces*] **Improvement and Modernization Program** (AABC) .... CRIMP
Consolidated Schedule Technique .... CST
Consolidated Scientific Computing System [*Marine science*] (OSRA) .... CSCS
Consolidated Scientific Computing System (USDC) .... CSCS
Consolidated Sea Gold Corp. [*Vancouver Stock Exchange symbol*] .... CDE
Consolidated Security Operations Center [*Military*] .... CSOC
Consolidated Ships Allowance List .... COSAL
Consolidated Ships Electronic Design [*Navy*] (NG) .... CSED
Consolidated Shorebase Material Allowance List (AAGC) .... COSMAL

Consolidated Shore-Based Allowance List (MCD) .... COSBAL
Consolidated Short-Term Demand Simulation System [*Department of Energy*] (GFGA) .... CSTDSS
Consolidated Silver Butte Mines [*Vancouver Stock Exchange symbol*] .... CSB
Consolidated Silver Standard Mines Ltd. [*Vancouver Stock Exchange symbol*] .... CDS
Consolidated Site Base Loading .... CSBL
Consolidated Space Operations Center [*Colorado Springs, CO*] [*Military*] .... CSOC
Consolidated Special Information Dissemination Office [*Proposed for military intelligence gathering, late 1940's, but never activated*] .... CONSIDO
Consolidated Spot Buying [*Radio and TV advertising*] .... CSB
Consolidated Stainless [*NASDAQ symbol*] (TTSB) .... PIPE
Consolidated Stainless, Inc. [*Associated Press*] (SAG) .... CnStain
Consolidated Stainless, Inc. [*NASDAQ symbol*] (SAG) .... PIPE
Consolidated Standing Route Order [*Army*] (AABC) .... CSRO
Consolidated State Maintenance Shop [*USNB*] (MCD) .... CSMS
Consolidated States Racing Association [*Auto racing sanctioning organization*] .... CSRA
Consolidated Statutes [*A publication*] (DLA) .... Con St
Consolidated Statutes [*A publication*] (DLA) .... Con Stat
Consolidated Statutes [*A publication*] (DLA) .... CS
Consolidated Statutes of British Columbia [*A publication*] (DLA) .... CSBC
Consolidated Statutes of Canada [*A publication*] (DLA) .... CSC
Consolidated Statutes of Lower Canada [*A publication*] (DLA) .... CSLC
Consolidated Statutes of Manitoba [*A publication*] (DLA) .... CSM
Consolidated Statutes of New Brunswick [*A publication*] (DLA) .... CSNB
Consolidated Statutes of Upper Canada [*A publication*] (DLA) .... CSUC
Consolidated Steam Generator (PDAA) .... CSG
Consolidated Stikine Silver Ltd. [*Vancouver Stock Exchange symbol*] .... CKI
Consolidated Stock Status Report .... CSSR
Consolidated Stores [*NYSE symbol*] (TTSB) .... CNS
Consolidated Stores Corp. [*NYSE symbol*] (SPSG) .... CNS
Consolidated Stores Corp. [*Associated Press*] (SAG) .... CnStor
Consolidated Suntec Ventures [*Vancouver Stock Exchange symbol*] .... CQV
Consolidated Supply Contract [*Department of Housing and Urban Development*] (GFGA) .... CSC
Consolidated Supply Program [*Department of Housing and Urban Development*] (GFGA) .... CSP
Consolidated Supply Support Activity (MCD) .... CSS
Consolidated Support Equipment List (MCD) .... CSEL
Consolidated Support Model (MCD) .... CSM
Consolidated Support System .... CSS
Consolidated Surplus Sales Office [*Military - Merged with Defense Supply Agency*] .... CSSO
Consolidated Talcorp Ltd. [*Toronto Stock Exchange symbol*] .... CZZ
Consolidated Tape Association (EA) .... CTA
Consolidated Tape System [*Preferred name is Consolidated Transaction Reporting System*] [*Investment term*] .... CTS
Consolidated Technology [*Commercial firm Associated Press*] (SAG) .... ConTech
Consolidated Technology [*NASDAQ symbol*] (SAG) .... COTG
Consolidated Technology Grp [*NASDAQ symbol*] (TTSB) .... COTG
Consolidated Telecommunications Center System (MCD) .... CTCS
Consolidated Telecommunications Program [*Military*] (GFGA) .... CTP
Consolidated Telemetry Checkout System [*Air Force*] .... CTCS
Consolidated Tenants League (EA) .... CTL
Consolidated Test Data System [*Military*] .... CTDS
Consolidated Thompson-Lundmark Gold Mines Ltd. [*Toronto Stock Exchange symbol*] .... TLG
Consolidated TOE Update [*DoD*] .... CTU
Consolidated Tomoka Land [*AMEX symbol*] (SPSG) .... CTO
Consolidated Tomoka Land Co. [*Associated Press*] (SAG) .... CnsTom
Consolidated Training Facility [*Army*] .... CTF
Consolidated Training Request [*Military*] .... CTR
Consolidated Training Support Work Group [*DoD*] .... CTSWG
Consolidated Translation Survey [*CIA*] .... CTS
Consolidated Treaty Series [*A publication*] (DLA) .... CTS
Consolidated TVX Mining Corp. [*Toronto Stock Exchange symbol*] CVX
Consolidated Undrained Shear with Pore Pressure Measurement [*Nuclear energy*] (NUCP) .... CAU
Consolidated Undrained Triaxial Test with Pore Pressure Measurements [*Nuclear energy*] (NUCP) .... CIU
Consolidated Unit Personnel Section .... CUPS
Consolidated Vacuum Corp., Rochester, NY [*Library symbol Library of Congress*] (LCLS) .... NRCV
Consolidated Wellington Resources [*Vancouver Stock Exchange symbol*] .... CWG
Consolidated Western & Pacific Resources [*Associated Press*] (SAG) .... ConWPac
Consolidated Western & Pacific Resources [*NASDAQ symbol*] (SAG) .... CWNP
Consolidated Western Steel (AAG) .... CWS
Consolidated Westrex Development [*Vancouver Stock Exchange symbol*] .... KWD
Consolidated Working Fund (OICC) .... CWF
Consolidated WWMCCS [*Worldwide Military Command and Control System*] **Program** [*DoD*] .... CWP
Consolidated-Bathurst, Inc. [*Toronto Stock Exchange symbol*] .... CB
Consolidated-Vultee Aircraft Corp. [*Later, General Dynamics Corp.*] .... CONVAIR
Consolidated-Vultee Aircraft Corp. [*Later, General Dynamics Corp.*] .... CVAC
Consolidating Station .... CSTA
Consolidation .... CONSLDTN
Consolidation above Battalion Level [*Army*] (RDA) .... CABL
Consolidation Aerial Port System [*or Subsystem*] [*Air Force*] (MCD) .... CAPS
Consolidation and Management of Supply Consumption Rates (MCD) .... COMSCOR
Consolidation Coal - Bethlehem Steel - National Steel - Republic Steel [*Coke pellet process developed by four-company group of steel and coke producers*] .... CONSOL-BNR
Consolidation/Containerization Point .... CCP
Consolidation Exercise [*Military*] (NVT) .... CONSOLEX
Consolidation Incineration Facility .... CIF
Consolidation Loan Program [*Department of Education*] (GFGA) .... CLP
Consolidation Lodges [*Freemasonry*] (ROG) CL
Consolidation of Administration at Battalion Level [*Army*] .... CABLE
Consolidation of [*Telecommunications*] **Center** (MCD) CC
Consolidation of Functions and Facilities Cutoff (MCD) .... COFF
Consolidation of Military Pay Services [*Strategic Air Command proposal*] .... COMPS
Consolidation of Military Personnel Activities at Fixed Installations (AABC) .... COMPACT
Consolidation of Pay and Personnel Functions [*Military*] .... COPPER
Consolidation of Supply and Maintenance Regulations [*Military*] (AABC) .... COSAMREG
Consolidation of Telecommunications Center on Oahu (MCD) .... COTCO
Consolidator .... CONSLDTR
Consols [*Consolidateds*] .... CN
Consoltex Canada, Inc. [*Toronto Stock Exchange symbol*] .... CTX
Consommation et Corporations Canada [*Consumer and Corporate Affairs Canada-CCA*] CCC
Conson [*Viet Nam*] [*ICAO location identifier*] (ICLI) .... VVCS
Consonans [*Tinkling*] (DAVI) .... cons
Consonant [*Linguistics*] C
Consonant .... CONS
Consonantal [*Linguistics*] .... K
Consonant-Vowel CV
Consonant-Vowel-Consonant [*Cuneiform sign*] (BJA) CVC
Consórcio G. Grupo Dina [*NYSE symbol*] (SPSG) .... DIN
Consorcio G Grupo Dina ADS [*NYSE symbol*] (TTSB) .... DIN
Consorcio G Grupo Dina SA de CV [*Commercial firm Associated Press*] (SAG) .... CGDina
Consorcio G Grupo Dina'L'ADS [*NYSE symbol*] (TTSB) .... DIN.L
Consort Art Graphics [*British*] .... CAG
Consort Aviation [*British ICAO designator*] (FAAC) .... CFL
Consort Coarse Servo .... CCS
Consort Energy Corp. [*Vancouver Stock Exchange symbol*] .... CEW
Consort Municipal Library, Alberta [*Library symbol National Library of Canada*] (NLC) .... ACONM
Consort Municipal Library, Consort, AB, Canada [*Library symbol Library of Congress*] (LCLS) .... CaAConM
Consort Observation Time .... COT
Consort Parallax Servo .... CXS
Consort Speed Servo .... CSS
Consortia of London Boroughs [*British*] .... CLB
Consortium C
Consortium .... CNSRTM
Consortium Communications International, Inc. [*New York, NY*] [*Telecommunications*] (TSSD) CCI
Consortium Data Network [*University of Michigan*] [*Ann Arbor*] [*Information service or system*] (IID) .... CDNET
Consortium Europeen de Transports Maritimes [*Shipping company*] [*France*] (EY) .... CETRAMAR
Consortium for Advanced Residential Buildings .... CARB
Consortium for an Advanced Silent Transport (MCD) .... CAST
Consortium for Assessment and Testing in Schools (AIE) .... CATS
Consortium for Atlantic Studies [*Arizona State University*] [*Research center*] .... CAS
Consortium for Continental Reflection Profiling [*Cornell University*] [*Ithaca, NY*] .... COCORP
Consortium for Continuing Higher Education - Librarians' Networking Committee [*Library network*] .... CCHENV-LNC
Consortium for Graduate Study in Business for Negroes [*Later, CGSM*] .... CGSBN
Consortium for Graduate Study in Management [*St. Louis, MO*] (EA) .... CGSM
Consortium for Health Information and Library Sciences [*Library network*] .... CHI
Consortium for Information Resources, Framingham, MA [*OCLC symbol*] (OCLC) .... CIR
Consortium for International Cooperation in Higher Education [*Defunct*] (EA) .... CICHE
Consortium for International Earth Science Information Network [*Information service or system*] (IID) .... CIESIN
Consortium for International Studies Education (EA) .... CISE
[*The*] **Consortium for Oceanographic Research and Education** [*A lobby group*] .... CORE
Consortium for Peaceful Coexistence (EA) .... CPC
Consortium for School Networking [*Internet*] .... CoSN
Consortium for Sharing Instructional Materials [*Library network*] .... CSIM
Consortium for Superconducting Electronics .... CSE
Consortium for the Advancement of Building Sciences [*Pennsylvania State University*] [*Research center*] (RCD) .... CABS
Consortium for the Advancement of Physics Education .... CAPE
Consortium for the Advancement of Private Higher Education (EA) .... CAPHE
Consortium for the Education of Non-Traditional Students (BARN) .... CENTS
Consortium for the Study of Intelligence (EA) .... CSI
Consortium of Academic and Special Libraries in Montana [*Library network*] .... CASLIM
Consortium of Academic Libraries in Manchester [*British*] (AIE) .... CALIM
Consortium of Central Massachusetts Health Related Libraries [*Library network*] .... CCMHRL
Consortium of Doctors (EA) .... COD
Consortium of Evangelical Relief and Development Organizations (DICI) .... CERDO
Consortium of Fire Brigade Uniform Supplies [*British*] .... CFBUS
Consortium of Graduate Liberal Studies Programs (EA) .... CGLSP
Consortium of Jazz Organizations and Artists [*Later, AJA*] (EA) .... CJOA

Consortium of Latin American Studies Programs ... CLASP
Consortium of Local Authorities in Wales ... CLAW
Consortium of Local Authorities Special Programme [*British*] ... CLASP
Consortium of Local Education Authorities for the Provision of Science Equipment [*British*] ... CLEAPSE
Consortium of National Hispanic Organizations [*Defunct*] (EA) ... CNHO
Consortium of Professional Associations to Supervise Studies of Special Programsfor the Improvement of Instruction in American Education ... CONPASS
Consortium of Publishers for Employment ... COPE
Consortium of Regional Environmental Education Councils ... CREEC
Consortium of Registered Nurses for Eye Acquisition [*Later, ANET*] (EA) ... CORNEA
Consortium of Rhode Island Academic and Research Libraries [*Library network*] ... CRIARL
Consortium of Social Science Associations (EA) ... COSSA
Consortium of Universities of the Metropolitan Washington Area ... CUMWA
Consortium of University Film Centers [*Library network*] (EA) ... CUFC
Consortium of University Research Libraries [*British*] (IID) ... CURL
Consortium on Advanced Biosensors (EA) ... CAB
Consortium on Automated Analytical Laboratory Systems [*National Institute of Standards & Technology*] ... CAALS
Consortium on Chemical Information [*British*] ... COCI
Consortium on Financing Higher Education (EA) ... COFHE
Consortium on International Development ... CID
Consortium on Peace Research, Education, and Development (EA) ... COPRED
Consortium on Soils of the Tropics ... CST
Consortium Perfectae Caritatis [*Association of Perfect Love*] (EA) ... CPC
Consortium Research Development [*Office of Education*] ... CORD
Consortium to Develop an Online Catalog [*European Community*] (MHDB) ... CONDOC
Consortium to Establish a Registry for Alzheimer's Disease ... CERAD
Consorzio Interuniversitario Lombardo per l'Elaborazione Automatica [*Lombard Interuniversity Consortium for Data Processing*] [*Information service or system*] (IID) ... CILEA
Consorzio per il Sistema Informativo Piemonte [*Piedmont Consortium for Information Systems*] [*Information service or system*] (IID) ... CSI
Conspecific Sperm Precedence [*Entomology*] ... CSP
Conspectus of Workers' Compensation Legislation [*Australia A publication*] ... CWCL
Conspergere [*Dust or Sprinkle*] [*Pharmacy*] ... CONSPERG
Conspicuity Enhancement [*Aviation*] ... CE
Conspicuous ... conspic
Conspicuous Gallantry Medal [*British*] ... CGM
Conspicuous Service Cross [*Later, DSC*] [*British*] ... CSC
Conspicuously ... CNSP
Conspiracy (ILCA) ... Consp
Constable ... C
Constable ... CONS
Constable ... CONST
Constable on Patrol ... COP
Constable Point [*Greenland*] [*ICAO location identifier*] (ICLI) ... BGCO
Constabulary (AABC) ... CONSTAB
Constance-Lethbridge Rehabilitation Centre [*Centre de Readaptation Constance-Lethbridge*] **Montreal, Quebec** [*Library symbol National Library of Canada*] (NLC) ... QMLR
Constant ... C
Constant (DNAB) ... CON
Constant ... CONST
Constant [*Medicine*] (DMAA) ... const
Constant ... K
Constant Absolute Vorticity Trajectory ... CAVT
Constant Air Monitor [*Nuclear energy*] (NRCH) ... CAM
Constant Alert Cycle ... CAC
Constant Altitude Glide ... CAG
Constant Amplitude ... CA
Constant Angular Velocity [*Videodisk format*] ... CAV
Constant Area Quantization (MCD) ... CAQ
Constant Axial Offset Control (NRCH) ... CAOC
Constant Bandwidth (MCD) ... CB
Constant Bandwidth (MCD) ... CBW
Constant Bandwidth Frequency Modulation (MHDB) ... CBFM
Constant BIT [*Binary Digit*] **Density** [*Control feature of magnetic tape recorders*] [*Computer science*] ... CBD
Constant Bit Rate [*Telecommunications*] (CDE) ... CBR
Constant Blow Energy [*Teledyne Roxon 400*] [*Hydraulics*] ... CBE
Constant Boiling Mixture ... CBM
Constant Boiling Point ... CBP
Constant Capacitance - Deep Level Transient Spectroscopy (PDAA) ... CC-DLTS
Constant Conditions ... CC
Constant Control Oil (IAA) ... CCO
Constant Cost Integer Code [*Computer science*] (IAA) ... CCIC
Constant Current [*Electronics*] (IAA) ... CC
Constant Current Flux Reset ... CCFR
Constant Current Fringes ... CDF
Constant Current Generator ... CCG
Constant Current Light Emitting Diode (DICI) ... CCLED
Constant Current Modulation ... CCM
Constant Current Operation (IAA) ... CCO
Constant Current Transformer ... CCT
Constant Delay Line ... CDL
Constant Delta Height [*Aerospace*] ... CDH
Constant Denaturing Gradient Electrophoresis [*Analytical biochemistry*] ... CDGE
Constant Density Recording ... CDR
Constant Depression [*Automotive engineering*] ... CD
Constant Deviation Prism ... CDP
Constant Differential Height [*Aerospace*] (MCD) ... CDH
Constant [*or Continuous*] **Distending Pressure** (AAMN) ... CDP
Constant Dollar Accounting (ADA) ... CDA
Constant Dose Range [*Radiation in atmosphere*] ... CDR
Constant Drainage (WGA) ... CD
Constant Elasticity of Substitution [*Industrial production*] ... CES
Constant Electric Contact (IAA) ... CEC
Constant Electric Field [*Medicine*] (DMAA) ... CEF
Constant Energy Differences ... CED
Constant Energy Synchronous Luminescence Spectroscopy ... CESLS
Constant Error [*Psychology*] ... CE
Constant Extension Rate Tensile Test ... CERT
Constant Extinction Angle (IAA) ... CEA
Constant False Alarm Probability [*Military*] ... CFAP
Constant False Alarm Rate [*or Ratio*] [*Military*] ... CFAR
Constant Feed Lubricator ... CFL
Constant Final State Spectroscopy (MCD) ... CFS
Constant Flow Rate ... CFR
Constant Fraction Discriminator [*Electronics*] (OA) ... CFD
Constant Fraction Trigger (OA) ... CFT
Constant Frequency [*Electronics*] ... CF
Constant Frequency Generator (MCD) ... CFG
Constant Frequency Variable Dot ... CFVD
Constant Funding (MCD) ... CF
Constant Gradient Gel Electrophoresis [*Medicine*] (DMAA) ... CGGE
Constant Hazard Ratio ... CHR
Constant Heat Summation ... CHS
Constant Hot Water [*British*] ... CHW
Constant Human Immunoglobulin ... Ch
Constant Impedance Mechanical Modulation (AAG) ... CIMM
Constant Infusion Excretory Urogram [*Medicine*] (DMAA) ... CIXA
Constant Infusion Excretory Urogram [*Medicine*] (MAE) ... CIXU
Constant Initial State Spectroscopy (MCD) ... CIS
Constant Injection System [*Automotive engineering*] ... CIS
Constant Level Balloon ... CLB
Constant Level Discriminator [*Electronics*] (OA) ... CLD
Constant Level Speech ... CLS
Constant Light Compensating (OA) ... CLC
Constant Linear Velocity [*Videodisk format*] ... CLV
Constant Load Rupture (OA) ... CLR
Constant Load Tensile Test ... CLT
Constant Magnetic Field (MHDB) ... CMF
Constant Maturity Treasury (TDOB) ... CMT
Constant Mean Curvature [*Mathematics*] ... CMC
Constant Misery [*Slang*] ... CM
Constant Miss Proportional Guidance ... CMPG
Constant Momentum Transfer Average (MCD) ... CMTA
Constant Net Loss [*Telecommunications*] (TEL) ... CNL
Constant Offset Profile [*Seismology*] ... COP
Constant Optimal Performance Theorem [*Physics*] ... COPT
Constant Optimum Separation Lane [*Aviation*] (DA) ... COS
Constant Parity [*Physics*] ... CP
Constant Pattern Generator ... CPG
Constant Phase Angle [*Electronics*] (BARN) ... CPA
Constant Position Mounting System (PDAA) ... CPMS
Constant Positive Airway Pressure [*Medicine*] ... CPAP
Constant [*or Continuous*] **Positive-Pressure Breathing** [*Medicine*] (DAVI) ... CPPB
Constant Potential (DEN) ... CP
Constant Potential Accelerator ... CPA
Constant Power (DA) ... CP
Constant Prepayment Rate [*Mortgage-backed securities*] ... CPR
Constant Pressure (MSA) ... CP
Constant Pressure Date (DNAB) ... CPD
Constant Problem Size ... CPS
Constant Product Curve [*Economics*] ... CPC
Constant Property ... CP
Constant Purchasing Power ... CPP
Constant Rate (OA) ... CR
Constant Rate Injector [*Instrumentation*] ... CRI
Constant Rate of Heating ... CRH
Constant Rate of Penetration (OA) ... CRP
Constant Ratio Elasticity of Substitution (PDAA) ... CRES
Constant Ratio Rule (PDAA) ... CRR
Constant Ratios of Elasticities of Substitution-Homothetic [*Statistics*] ... CRESH
Constant Reflector Voltage (IAA) ... CRV
Constant Region [*Immunochemistry*] ... C
Constant Returns to Scale [*Econometrics*] ... CRTS
Constant Ringing Drop [*Alarm system*] ... CRD
Constant Ringing Relay [*Alarm system*] ... CRR
Constant Routine ... CR
Constant Scattering Length (OA) ... CSL
Constant Security Surveillance [*Shipping*] ... CSS
[*The*] **Constant Society** (EA) ... TCS
Constant Speed Unit [*Aviation*] (ADA) ... CSU
Constant Stimulus Difference [*Pair comparison*] [*Aircraft noise*] ... CSD
Constant Stress Rate (IAA) ... CSR
Constant Tangential Velocity ... CTV
Constant Temperature Anemometer System ... CTAS
Constant Temperature Circulator [*Instrumentation*] ... CTC
Constant Temperature Sampling [*Automotive engineering*] ... CTS
Constant Tension Band [*Mechanical clamping device*] ... CTB
Constant Time Loci ... CTL
Constant Torque Compensation ... CTC
Constant Vacuum Control [*Automotive emissions*] ... CVC

Constant Value ... CV
Constant Velocity (SAA) ... CONVEL
Constant Velocity ... CV
Constant Velocity Alignment [*Drive system coupling*] ... CVA
Constant Velocity Recording ... CVR
Constant Velocity Transmission ... CVT
Constant Voltage (IAA) ... CV
Constant Voltage and Constant Frequency (BUR) ... CVCF
Constant Voltage/Constant Current (IEEE) ... CV/CC
Constant Voltage Current Limiting (IAA) ... CVCL
Constant Voltage Reference ... CVR
Constant Voltage Source ... CVS
Constant Voltage Transformer ... CVT
Constant Voltage Unit ... CVU
Constant Volume ... CV
Constant Volume Drop Time ... CVDT
Constant Volume Sampling [*ACF Industries*] ... CVS
Constant Wall Temperature [*Engineering*] ... CWT
Constant Wear (KSC) ... CW
Constanta [*Romania*] [*Airport symbol*] (OAG) ... CND
Constanta/M. Kogalniceau [*Romania*] [*ICAO location identifier*] (ICLI) ... LRCK
Constant-Adjustment Matrix, Flexible-Accelerator Path [*Economic theory*] ... CFAP
Constant-Angle Mie Scattering [*Optics*] ... CAMS
Constant-Angle Reflection Interference Spectroscopy ... CARIS
Constant-Choice Perceptual Maze Test ... CCPM
Constant-Control Oil Pressure (MSA) ... CCOP
Constant-Depth Temperature Sensor [*Oceanography*] ... CDTS
Constant-Flow/High Pressure [*Oxygen system*] ... CF/HP
Constantian Society (EA) ... CS
Constantine [*Roman emperor, 272-337AD*] (ROG) ... CONST
Constantine [*Algeria*] [*Airport symbol*] (OAG) ... CZL
Constantine/Ain El Bey [*Algeria*] [*ICAO location identifier*] (ICLI) ... DABC
Constantine Order [*Freemasonry*] (ROG) ... CO
Constantinople [*Later, Istanbul*] [*Turkey*] (ROG) ... CON
Constantinople [*Later, Istanbul*] [*Turkey*] (ROG) ... CONST
Constantinople [*Later, Istanbul*] [*Turkey*] (DSUE) ... CONSTANT
Constantinople [*Later, Istanbul*] [*Province in Turkey*] ... CPLE
Constantinople Pentateuch (BJA) ... CP
Constantinopolitana (ROG) ... CPA
Constantinus Coptius [*Flourished, 16th century*] [*Authority cited in pre-1607 legal work*] (DSA) ... Constan Copti
Constantius Rogerius [*Flourished, 16th century*] [*Authority cited in pre-1607 legal work*] (DSA) ... Constan Roger
Constantly Operating ... CO
Constant-Output Amplifier (MUGU) ... COA
Constant-Output Level Adapter ... COLA
Constants Board Assembly ... CBA
Constants Change Display (MCD) ... CCD
Constant-Speed Drive ... CSD
Constant-Speed Drive/Starter (NG) ... CSDS
Constant-Switch-Pace Symmetric Random Signal (PDAA) ... CSRS
Constant-Viscosity [*Rubber*] ... CV
Constant-Volume Feeder [*Nuclear energy*] (NUCP) ... CVF
Constant-Wear Garment [*Apollo*] [*NASA*] ... CWG
Constanza [*Dominican Republic*] [*ICAO location identifier*] (ICLI) ... MDCZ
Constatine Township Library, Constatine, MI [*Library symbol Library of Congress*] (LCLS) ... MiCon
Constellate Consultants (P) Ltd. [*Information service or system*] (IID) ... CONCON
Constipated (DSUE) ... CONSTI
Constituency ... CONST
Constituency ... CONSTIT
Constituency Labour Party [*British*] (BARN) ... CLP
Constituency Proportion Distribution ... CPD
Constituent (DAVI) ... constit
Constituent Assembly [*Vietnam*] ... CA
Constituent Concentration in a Waste Extract ... CCWE
Constituent Concentrations in the Waste [*Environmental Protection Agency*] ... CCW
Constituted Soil Columns [*Agronomy*] ... CSS
Constitutio [*Point at Issue, Regulation, Settlement*] [*Latin*] (OCD) ... CONST
Constitutio Carolina Criminalis [*A publication*] (DSA) ... CCC
Constitution ... CONS
Constitution [*or Constitutional*] ... CONST
Constitution [*or Constitutional*] [*Medicine*] (DAVI) ... constit
Constitution ... CONSTN
Constitution (ROG) ... CONSTON
Constitution and Ancient Charges [*Freemasonry*] (ROG) ... CAC
Constitution Bancorp of New England, Inc. (MHDW) ... CBNEV
Constitution General Grand Chapter [*Freemasonry*] (ROG) ... CGGC
Constitution of the United States [*A publication*] (DLA) ... Const US
Constitution of Virginia [*A publication*] (DLA) ... CV
Constitution Parties of the United States [*An association*] (EA) ... CPUS
Constitutional (AAGC) ... Const
Constitutional [*Legal shorthand*] (LWAP) ... CONSTAL
Constitutional ... CONSTL
Constitutional Acts of Canada [*Database*] [*Federal Department of Justice*] [*Information service or system*] (CRD) ... CAC
Constitutional and Parliamentary Information [*A publication*] (DLA) ... Const & Parliam Inf
Constitutional Aplastic Anemia [*Medicine*] ... CAA
Constitutional Commentary [*A publication*] (DLA) ... Const Commentary
Constitutional Commission [*An association*] (EA) ... CC
Constitutional Consultative Committee on the Political Future of Nigeria [*Political party*] ... CCC
Constitutional Convention ... CON-CON
Constitutional Educational League ... CEL
Constitutional Officer (DNAB) ... CNO
Constitutional Psychopathic Inferior [*or Inferiority*] ... CPI
Constitutional Psychopathic State ... CPS
Constitutional Pure Red Cell Aplasia [*Medicine*] (DMAA) ... CPRCA
Constitutional Reform Centre [*British*] (CB) ... CRC
Constitutional Repeating Unit [*Organic chemistry*] ... CRU
Constitutional Reports [*South Carolina*] [*A publication*] (DLA) ... Const Rep
Constitutional Reports, New Series, Printed by Mills [*South Carolina*] [*A publication*] (DLA) ... Const NS
Constitutional Reports, New Series, Printed by Mills [*South Carolina*] [*A publication*] (DLA) ... Const SCNS
Constitutional Reports, Printed by Harper [*1 South Carolina*] [*A publication*] (DLA) ... Const
Constitutional Reports, Printed by Mills [*South Carolina*] [*A publication*] (DLA) ... Const
Constitutional Reports, Printed by Treadway [*South Carolina*] [*A publication*] (DLA) ... Const
Constitutional Reports, Printed by Treadway [*South Carolina*] [*A publication*] (DLA) ... Const RSC
Constitutional Reports, Printed by Treadway [*South Carolina*] [*A publication*] (DLA) ... Const SC
Constitutional Review [*A publication*] (DLA) ... Const Rev
Constitutional Revival (EA) ... CR
Constitutional Rights Foundation (EA) ... CRF
Constitutionalist Party [*Malta*] [*Political party*] (PPE) ... CP
Constitutionally Delayed Short Stature [*Medicine*] ... CDSS
Constitutiones Othoni [*At the end of Lyndewood's Provinciale*] [*A publication*] (DLA) ... Const Oth
Constitutiones Tiberii [*A publication*] (DLA) ... CT
Constitutions and Laws of the American Indian Tribes [*A publication*] (DLA) ... CLAIT
Constitutions of African States [*A publication*] (DLA) ... Const Afr States
Constitutions of Dependencies and Special Sovereignties [*A publication*] (DLA) ... Const Dep & Sp Sov
Constitutions of Nations [*A publication*] (DLA) ... Const Nations
Constitutive Transcript [*Genetics*] ... CT
Constitutive Transcription Unit [*Genetics*] ... CTU
Constitutive Transport Element [*Biochemistry*] ... CTE
Constrado Structural Analysis System [*Structures & Computers Ltd.*] [*Software package*] (NCC) ... CONSAS
Constrained Deconvolution Technique [*Computer science*] ... CD
Constrained Force Model (PDAA) ... CONFORM
Constrained Least Squares (PDAA) ... CLS
Constrained Optimal Design [*Computer science*] (RDA) ... COD
Constrained Optimization Procedure (MCD) ... COP
Constrained Procedure (AAG) ... CP
Constrained Structure Generation ... CONGEN
Constraint (KSC) ... CONSTR
Constraint Control ... C/C
Constraint Handling in Prolog [*A programming language*] [*Computer science*] ... CHIP
Constraint Logic Programming ... CLP
Constraint Qualification (DNAB) ... CQ
Constraint Satisfaction Problem [*Computer science*] ... CSP
Constricted Double Heterojunction (MCD) ... CDH
Constricted Double Heterostructure [*Electronics*] (NITA) ... CDH
Constriction, Sclerosis, Hemorrhage, Exudate, Papilledema [*Ophthalmology*] ... CSHEP
Construcciones Aeronauticas SA [*Spain ICAO aircraft manufacturer identifier*] (ICAO) ... CS
Construct [*or Construction*] (AFM) ... CONST
Construct State (BJA) ... Constr
Constructeurs Europeens de Locomotives Thermiques et Electriques [*European Manufacturers of Thermal and Electric Locomotives*] (EAIO) ... CELTE
Constructing ... CONSTRCT
Constructing Contractor (AAG) ... CC
Constructing Quartermaster [*Army*] ... CQM
Construction ... CONS
Construction (DD) ... const
Construction (VRA) ... constr
Construction ... CONSTR
Construction (AAGC) ... Constr
Construction ... CONSTRCTN
Construction ... CONSTRN
Construction (ROG) ... CONSTRON
Construction Acquisition Improvement Implementation Team (AAGC) ... CAITT
Construction Acquisition Work Group (AAGC) ... CAWG
Construction Advanced Planning and Sequencing [*Nuclear energy*] (NRCH) ... CAPS
Construction and Development ... C & D
Construction and Equipment ... C & E
Construction and Machinery ... C & M
Construction and Machinery ... CM
Construction and Management of Distributed Office Systems [*ESPRIT*] (NITA) ... COMANDOS
Construction and Mining Equipment Association of Australia ... CMEAA
Construction and Operating License ... COL
Construction and Overhaul Testing ... COT
Construction and Repair [*Coast Guard*] ... C and R
Construction and Repair [*Military*] ... CANDR
Construction and Repair, Alteration [*Coast Guard*] ... CONALT
Construction and Road Transport (ADA) ... CART

Construction and Startup/Turnover Surveillance Group [*Nuclear energy*] (NRCH) .... CSTS
Construction and Use (DCTA) .... C & U
Construction Appraisal Team (NRCH) .... CAT
Construction Apprentice (MUGU) .... CP
Construction Assistance Vehicle [*Navy*] (MCD) .... CAV
Construction Association of Michigan (SRA) .... CAM
Construction Association of New Brunswick Inc. (AC) .... CANB
Construction Authorization (NRCH) .... CA
Construction Battalion [*SEABEE*] [*Navy*] .... CB
Construction Battalion [*Navy*] .... CBN
Construction Battalion [*CB*] [*Acronym is a phonetic reference to a member of this Naval unit*] .... SEABEE
Construction Battalion [*USNR classification*] .... VCB
Construction Battalion Base Unit [*Obsolete Navy*] ...... CBBU
Construction Battalion Center [*Navy*] (MCD) .... CBC
Construction Battalion Center Management Information System [*Navy*]
(DNAB) .... CBCMIS
Construction Battalion Detachment [*Navy*] .... CBD
Construction Battalion Detachment [*Navy*] (DNAB) ..... CBNDET
Construction Battalion Maintenance Unit [*Navy*] .... CBMU
Construction Battalion Maintenance Unit Detachment [*Navy*]
(DNAB) .... CBMUDET
Construction Battalion Replacement Depot [*Navy*] ...... CBRD
Construction Battalion Unit [*Navy*] .... CBU
Construction Battalions, Atlantic [*Navy*] .... CBLANT
Construction Battalions, Pacific [*Navy*] .... CBPAC
[*The*] Construction Briefing Collection [*A publication*] (AAGC) ...... CBC
Construction Briefing Paper [*A publication*] (AAGC) ..... CB
Construction Briefing Paper [*A publication*] (AAGC) ..... CBP
Construction Briefings [*A publication*] (AAGC) ...... Constr Briefings
Construction Change Request .... CCR
Construction, Civil Engineering, Mining [*A publication*] ...... CCEM
Construction Claims Monthly [*Business Publishers, Inc.*] [*A publication*]
(AAGC) .... CCM
Construction Completion Date (AFM) .... CCD
Construction Computer Applications Newsletter [*Database*] [*Construction Industry Press*] [*Information service or system*] (CRD) ...... CCAN
[*The*] Construction Contractor [*A publication*] (AAGC) CC
Construction Contractor Appraisal Support System (AAGC) ...... CCASS
Construction Coordination Group [*NASA*] (KSC) .... CCG
Construction Corp. [*Myanmar*] (DS) .... CONCORP
Construction Corps CC
Construction Corps of the Philippines [*World War II*] ...... CONCOR
Construction Cost Index CCI
Construction Criteria Base [*Information service or system*] (IID) ...... CCB
Construction Defect .... CD
Construction Design Criteria [*Telecommunications*] (TEL) ...... CDC
Construction Discrepancy Report .... CDR
Construction Dollar Control System [*AT & T*] .... CDCS
Construction Dollar Spreading [*System*] [*AT & T*] ..... CDS
Construction Economics European Committee (EAIO) ...... CEEC
Construction Electrician [*Navy rating*] .... CE
Construction Electrician [*Navy rating*] (DNAB) ...... CONSTELEC
Construction Electrician, Chief [*Navy rating*] .... CEC
Construction Electrician, First Class [*Navy rating*] CE1
Construction Electrician, Master Chief [*Navy rating*] .... CECM
Construction Electrician, Power [*Navy rating*] .... CEP
Construction Electrician, Power, Construction Apprentice [*Navy rating*]
(DNAB) .... CEPCA
Construction Electrician, Power, Constructionman [*Navy rating*]
(DNAB) .... CEPCN
Construction Electrician, Power, First Class [*Navy rating*] (DNAB) CEP1
Construction Electrician, Power, Second Class [*Navy rating*] (DNAB) CEP2
Construction Electrician, Power, Third Class [*Navy rating*] (DNAB) CEP3
Construction Electrician, Second Class [*Navy rating*] CE2
Construction Electrician, Senior Chief [*Navy rating*] ...... CECS
Construction Electrician, Shop [*Navy rating*] .... CES
Construction Electrician, Shop, Construction Apprentice [*Navy rating*]
(DNAB) .... CESCA
Construction Electrician, Shop, Constructionman [*Navy rating*] (DNAB) ...... CESCN
Construction Electrician, Shop, First Class [*Navy rating*] (DNAB) CES1
Construction Electrician, Shop, Second Class [*Navy rating*] (DNAB) CES2
Construction Electrician, Shop, Third Class [*Navy rating*] (DNAB) CES3
Construction Electrician, Telephone [*Navy rating*] .... CET
Construction Electrician, Telephone, Construction Apprentice [*Navy rating*] (DNAB) ...... CETCA
Construction Electrician, Telephone, Constructionman [*Navy rating*]
(DNAB) .... CETCN
Construction Electrician, Telephone, First Class [*Navy rating*] (DNAB) CET1
Construction Electrician, Telephone, Second Class [*Navy rating*] (DNAB) CET2
Construction Electrician, Telephone, Third Class [*Navy rating*] (DNAB) CET3
Construction Electrician, Third Class [*Navy rating*] CE3
Construction Electrician, Wiring [*Navy rating*] .... CEW
Construction Electrician, Wiring, Construction Apprentice [*Navy rating*]
(DNAB) .... CEWCA
Construction Electrician, Wiring, Constructionman [*Navy rating*]
(DNAB) .... CEWCN
Construction Electrician, Wiring, First Class [*Navy rating*] (DNAB) CEW1
Construction Electrician, Wiring, Second Class [*Navy rating*] (DNAB) CEW2
Construction Electrician, Wiring, Third Class [*Navy rating*] (DNAB) CEW3
Construction Engineer .... CONSTENGR
Construction Engineering (DD) .... ConstEng
Construction Engineering Research Laboratory [*Champaign, IL*] [*Army*] ...... CERL
Construction Equipment Advertisers [*Later, CEA PRC*] (EA) ...... CEA

Construction Equipment Advertisers and Public Relations Council [*Milwaukee, WI*] (EA) .... CEA PRC
Construction Equipment and Materials Handling Equipment [*Military*]
(RDA) .... CE/MHE
Construction Equipment Management System .... CEMS
Construction Financial Management Association (EA) ...... CFMA
Construction Industries of Rhode Island (SRA) .... CIRI
Construction Industry Collective Bargaining Commission [*Terminated, 1978*] [*Department of Labor*] (EGAO) ...... CICBC
Construction Industry Commission [*Canada*] CIC
Construction Industry Computing Association (EAIO) ...... CICA
Construction Industry Development Council [*Canada*] ...... CIDC
Construction Industry Foundation [*Defunct*] (EA) ...... CIF
Construction Industry Institute [*Australia*] CII
Construction Industry Joint Conference (EA) .... CIJC
Construction Industry Management Board [*Defunct*] (EA) ...... CIMB
Construction Industry Manufacturers Association (EA) ...... CIMA
Construction Industry Press [*Information service or system*] (IID) ...... CIP
Construction Industry Reform Strategy .... CIRS
Construction Industry Research and Information Association [*Research center British*] (IRC) ...... CIRIA
Construction Industry Stabilization Committee [*Abolished, 1974*] ...... CISC
Construction Industry Training Board (MCD) .... CITB
Construction Industry Training Center (MCD) .... CITC
Construction Industry Translation and Information Services [*Dublin, Ireland*] ...... CITIS
Construction Information Center Co. Ltd. [*Information service or system*]
(IID) CIC
Construction Information Online Retrieval Network [*Information service or system*] (IID) ...... CORNET
Construction Injury Liability Monthly [*Business Publishers, Inc.*]
[*A publication*] (AAGC) .... CILM
Construction/Inspection Procedure (NRCH) .... C/IP
Construction Interface Surveillance Control Section (SAA) ...... CISCS
Construction Joint [*Technical drawings*] .... CJ
Construction Keyed Lock (ADA) .... CK
Construction Labor Report (AAGC) .... CLR
Construction Labour Relations - An Alberta Association (AC) ...... CLRA
Construction Law Reports (AAGC) .... CLR
Construction Lawyer [*ABA*] [*A publication*] (AAGC) ...... Constr Law
Construction Litigation Reporter (AAGC) .... CLR
Construction Management .... CM
Construction Management (DD) .... ConstMgmt
Construction Management Accounting System (MHDI) ...... CMAS
Construction Management Association of America (EA) ...... CMAA
Construction Management Control System [*General Services Administration*] ...... CMCS
Construction Materials Testing (MHDI) .... CMT
Construction Mechanic [*Navy rating*] .... CM
Construction Mechanic, Automotive [*Navy rating*] ...... CMA
Construction Mechanic, Chief [*Navy rating*] .... CMC
Construction Mechanic, Construction [*Navy rating*] ...... CMH
Construction Mechanic, Construction Apprentice [*Navy rating*] (DNAB) ...... CMCA
Construction Mechanic, First Class [*Navy rating*] CM1
Construction Mechanic, Master Chief [*Navy rating*] ...... CMCM
Construction Mechanic, Second Class [*Navy rating*] CM2
Construction Mechanic, Senior Chief [*Navy rating*] ...... CMCS
Construction Mechanic, Third Class [*Navy rating*] CM3
Construction Number (LAIN) .... C/N
Construction of Aircraft and Related Procurement .... CARP
Construction of Embedded Dedicated Real-Time System [*Computer science*] ...... CEDAR
Construction of Facilities .... C of F
Construction of Facilities [*NASA*] (KSC) .... COF
Construction Period Recapture [*Nuclear power plant licensing*] ...... CPR
Construction Permit [*FCC*] .... CP
Construction Permit Containment Support Fixture (NRCH) ...... CPCSF
Construction Permit Power Reactor (NRCH) .... CPPR
Construction Permit Research Reactor (NRCH) .... CPRR
Construction Plant-Hire Association [*British*] (DBA) ...... CPA
Construction Procedures [*Nuclear energy*] (NRCH) ...... CP
Construction Productivity Advancement Research [*Military*] (RDA) ...... CPAR
Construction Products Manufacturers Council [*Defunct*] (EA) ...... CPMC
Construction Program Administration System [*Telecommunications*]
(TEL) .... CPAS
Construction Progress Reporting Survey [*Bureau of the Census*]
(GFGA) .... CPRS
Construction Project Alternative Selection Program [*Bell System*] ...... CONPASP
Construction Project Control (IAA) .... CPC
Construction Quality Assurance [*Environmental science*] ...... CQA
Construction Quality Control [*Environmental science*] ...... CQC
Construction Recruit [*Navy*] .... CR
Construction Report, Building Permits [*A publication*] ...... CRBP
Construction Report, Construction Activity [*A publication*] ...... CRCA
Construction Report, Housing Starts [*A publication*] ...... CRHS
Construction Requirements Review Committee [*Military*] (AABC) ...... CRRC
Construction Risk Management [*International Risk Management Institute*]
[*A publication*] .... CRM
Construction Safety Association of Ontario, Toronto, Ontario [*Library symbol National Library of Canada*] (NLC) ...... OTCSAO
Construction Scheduling and Coordination [*AT & T*] ...... CSC
Construction Special Operations Center .... CSOC
Construction Specification (DAC) .... Con Spec
Construction Specifications Canada [*Toronto, ON*] ...... CSC
Construction Specifications Institute (EA) .... CSI

Construction Statistics Division [*Washington, DC Department of Commerce*] (OICC) ... CSD
Construction Surveyors Institute [*Later, Architects and Surveyors Institute*] (EA) ... CSI
Construction Tender [*Coast Guard symbol*] (DNAB) ... WLIC
Construction Test Procedure (NRCH) ... CTP
Construction Training Unit ... CTU
Construction Unit [*Computer science*] ... CU
Construction Unit Value (DCTA) ... CUV
Construction Verification Notification [*Nuclear energy*] (NRCH) ... CVN
Construction Work in Progress ... CWIP
Construction Workers Federation [*San Marino*] (EAIO) ... CWF
Construction Writers Association (EA) ... CWA
Constructional Engineering Union [*British*] ... CEU
Construction-Differential Subsidy [*Authorized by Merchant Marine Act of 1936*] ... CDS
Constructionman [*Nonrated enlisted man*] [*Navy*] ... CN
Constructionman, Apprentice [*Navy*] ... CA
Constructionman Apprentice, Builder, Striker [*Navy rating*] ... BUCA
Constructionman Apprentice, Construction Electrician, Striker [*Navy rating*] ... CECA
Constructionman Apprentice, Engineering Aid, Striker [*Navy rating*] ... EACA
Constructionman Apprentice, Equipment Operator, Striker [*Navy rating*] ... EOCA
Constructionman Apprentice, Steelworker, Striker [*Navy rating*] ... SWCA
Constructionman Apprentice, Utilitiesman, Striker [*Navy rating*] ... UTCA
Constructionman, Construction Electrician, Striker [*Navy rating*] ... CECN
Constructionman, Construction Mechanic, Striker [*Navy rating*] ... CMCN
Constructionman, Engineering Aid, Striker [*Navy rating*] ... EACN
Constructionman, Equipment Operator, Striker [*Navy rating*] ... EOCN
Constructionman Recruit [*Navy*] ... CR
Constructionman, Steelworker, Striker [*Navy rating*] ... SWCN
Constructionman, Utilitiesman, Striker [*Navy rating*] ... UTCN
Constructive Action, Inc. [*Whittier, CA*] (EA) ... CAI
Constructive Availability (CAAL) ... CA
Constructive Cost Model ... COCOMO
Constructive Dilemma [*Rule of inference*] [*Logic*] ... CD
Constructive Error Score (EDAC) ... CES
Constructive Placement [*Railcar*] ... CP
Constructive Republican Alternative Programs [*Position papers on legislative issues prepared for Republican House leaders during Lyndon Johnson administration*] ... CRAP
Constructive Solid Geometry ... CSG
Constructive Total Loss [*Insurance*] ... CTL
Constructive Total Loss Only [*Insurance*] ... CTLO
Constructive Variational Geometry [*Computer science*] ... CVG
Constructor [*Freemasonry*] (ROG) ... C
Constructor (ADA) ... CON
Constructor ... CONSTR
Constructor Syntax (MHDI) ... CS
Construe (ROG) ... CONSTR
Const's Edition of Bott's Poor Law Cases [*A publication*] (DLA) ... Bott PL Const
Const's Edition of Bott's Poor Law Cases [*A publication*] (DSA) ... Const
Const's Edition of Bott's Poor Law Cases [*A publication*] (DLA) ... Const Bott
Consuelo, San Pedro De Macoris [*Dominican Republic*] [*ICAO location identifier*] (ICLI) ... MDCO
Consuetudines Feudorum [*The Book of Feuds*] [*Latin A publication*] (DLA) ... Consuet Feud
Consuetudines Feudorum [*The Book of Feuds*] [*Latin A publication*] (DLA) ... F
Consul [*License plate code assigned to foreign diplomats in the US*] ... C
Consul [*or Consulate*] ... C
Consul [*or Consulate*] (AABC) ... CON
Consul ... CONS
Consul [*Latin*] (OCD) ... COS
Consul ... CS
Consul General ... CG
Consul General ... CGEN
Consul General ... CONGEN
Consul General (EY) ... CONSGEN
Consul Suffectus [*Latin*] (OCD) ... COS SUFF
Consular Agent ... CA
Consular Clerk [*British*] (ROG) ... CC
Consular Corps ... CC
Consular Corps College and International Consular Academy (EA) ... CONSUL
Consular Declaration ... CD
Consular Invoice ... CI
Consular Invoice (ODBW) ... con inv
Consular Law Society (EA) ... CLS
Consular Liaison Officer ... CLO
Consular Security Officer ... CSO
Consular Shipping Adviser ... CONSA
Consular Shipping Adviser ... CSA
Consules [*Consuls*] [*Latin*] ... CC
Consules [*Consuls*] [*Latin*] ... COSS
Consulier Engineering [*Associated Press*] (SAG) ... Consulier
Consulier Engineering, Inc. [*Associated Press*] (SAG) ... Consul
Consulier Engineering, Inc. [*NASDAQ symbol*] (NQ) ... CSLR
Consulier Engr [*NASDAQ symbol*] (TTSB) ... CSLR
Consult ... CON
Consult [*or Consultation, Consultant*] [*Medicine*] ... CONS
Consulta di i Cumitati Nationalisti [*Corsica*] (PD) ... CCN
Consultancy and Research Unit [*Department of Information Studies, University of Sheffield*] [*British*] (AIE) ... CRU
[*The*] Consultancy and Research Unit, University of Sheffield [*England*] [*Information service or system*] (IID) ... CRUS
Consultant (DAVI) ... Cons

Consultant ... CONSLNT
Consultant (AABC) ... CONSLTNT
Consultant ... CONSULT
Consultant [*Medicine*] (DMAA) ... consult
Consultant Agreement (MCD) ... CA
Consultant in Dental Surgery [*Medical Officer designation*] [*British*] ... C
Consultant Orthodontists Group [*British*] (DBA) ... COG
Consultant Report (NATG) ... CR
Consultant-Adviser ... CA
Consultant-Initiated Activity [*LIMRA*] ... CIA
Consultants and Consulting Organizations Directory [*A publication*] ... CCO
Consultants and Consulting Organizations Directory [*Gale Research Co.*] [*Detroit, MI*] [*Information service or system*] [*A publication*] ... CCOD
Consultants Association for the Natural Industry ... CANI
Consultants (Computer & Financial) [*Commercial firm*] [*British*] ... CCF
Consultants Directory for Business and Industry [*A publication*] ... CDBI
Consultants' Network (EA) ... CN
Consultation [*Medicine*] ... C
Consultation ... CNSLTN
Consultation (DSUE) ... CON
Consultation [*Legal*] [*British*] (ROG) ... CONSN
Consultation ... CONSULTN
Consultation and Education ... C & E
Consultation on Church Union (EA) ... COCU
Consultation Paper (DCTA) ... C/P
Consultative Committee for Local Ecumenical Projects in England [*Church of England*] ... CCLEPE
Consultative Committee for Nuclear Research [*EEC*] (PDAA) ... CCNR
Consultative Committee for Photometry and Radiometry [*International Committee on Weights and Measures*] ... CCPR
Consultative Committee for Public Information [*United Nations*] ... CCPI
Consultative Committee for Space Data Systems (SSD) ... CCSDS
Consultative Committee for the Definition of the Second ... CCDS
Consultative Committee for the Standards of Measurement of Ionizing Radiations [*International Bureau of Weights and Measures*] ... CCEDMRI
Consultative Committee for Units [*International Bureau of Weights and Measures*] ... CCU
Consultative Committee International Telephony and Telegraphy ... CCITT
Consultative Committee of Accountancy Bodies [*United Kingdom and Ireland*] ... CCAB
Consultative Committee of the Bars and Law Societies of the European Community (ILCA) ... CCBE
Consultative Committee on Administrative Questions [*United Nations*] ... CCAQ
Consultative Committee on Electricity [*International Bureau of Weights and Measures*] ... CCE
Consultative Committee on Exotic Animal Diseases [*Australia*] ... CCEAD
Consultative Committee on International Radio [*Australia*] ... CCIR
Consultative Committee on International Telephony [*Later, CCITT*] [*ITU*] ... CCIT
Consultative Committee on Safety in the Offshore Petroleum Industry [*Australia*] ... CCOSOP
Consultative Committee on Substantive Questions [*United Nations*] ... CCSQ
Consultative Committee on the Curriculum [*British*] ... CCC
Consultative Committee on the Definition of the Meter [*International Bureau of Weights and Measures*] ... CCDM
Consultative Committee on Thermometry [*International Bureau of Weights and Measures*] ... CCT
Consultative Council for Postal Studies [*Universal Postal Union*] (EY) ... CCPS
Consultative Council of Jewish Organizations (EA) ... CCJO
Consultative Council of Professional Management Organizations [*British*] (DBA) ... CCPMO
Consultative Council on Local Government Finance [*British*] ... CCLGF
Consultative Environmental Review [*Australia*] ... CER
Consultative Examination [*Social Security Administration*] (OICC) ... CE
Consultative Group [*NATO*] ... CG
Consultative Group on Food Production and Investment in Developing Countries [*United Nations*] ... CGFPI
Consultative Group on International Agricultural Research (EA) ... CGIAR
Consultative Group on Potentially Harmful Effects of Space Experiments ... CGOPHEOSE
Consultative Political Council [*Laos*] ... CPC
Consultec Canada Ltd. [*Vancouver, BC*] [*Telecommunications*] (TSSD) ... CCL
Consulting ... CNSLTNG
Consulting (DD) ... cons
Consulting Chemists and Chemical Engineers ... CCCE
Consulting Committee on Educational Matters (AIE) ... CCEM
Consulting Communications Engineers, Inc. [*Villanova, PA*] (TSSD) ... CCE
Consulting Engineer ... CE
Consulting Engineers Council [*Later, ACEC*] (EA) ... CEC
Consulting Engineers of British Columbia (AC) ... CEBC
Consulting Engineers of New Brunswick (AC) ... CENB
Consulting Engineers of NWT (AC) ... CENT
Consulting Physician (ROG) ... CP
Consulting Surgeon [*British*] (ROG) ... CS
Consulting Teacher ... CT
Consulting Traffic Bureau ... CTB
Consulting Traffic Manager ... CTM
Consumable Case Rocket ... CCR
Consumable Electrode Vacuum Melting ... CEVM
Consumable Maintenance and Overhaul List (MCD) ... CMOL
Consumable Maintenance and Overhaul Material List [*Navy*] (MCD) ... CMOML
Consumable Toroidal Igniter (MCD) ... CTI
Consumable Vacuum Melt [*Steel*] ... CVM
Consumable-Anode, Radial, One-Side, Electrolytic [*Automotive engineering*] ... CAROSEL
Consumable-Electrode Vacuum-Arc Remelt [*Nuclear energy*] (NRCH) ... CEVAR

Consumables Management (NASA) .... CM
Consumables Status (MCD) .... CS
Consumatum Est [*It Is Finished*] [*Freemasonry*] [*Latin*] (ROG) .... CE
Consumer .... CNSMR
Consumer .... CNSR
Consumer .... CONSMR
Consumer .... CONSUM
Consumer Action for Energy Conservation [*British*] .... CAFEC
Consumer Action Now (EA) .... CAN
Consumer Aerosol Products Council .... CAPCO
Consumer Affairs Advisory Committee of the Australian Capital Territory .... CAACACT
Consumer Affairs Clearinghouse .... CACH
Consumer Affairs Council, Northern Territory [*Australia*] .... CACNT
Consumer Affairs Office [*Federal Energy Administration*] .... CAO
Consumer Aid Series [*National Highway Traffic Safety Administration*] .... CAS
Consumer Alert (EA) .... CA
Consumer and Commercial Credit (Prentice-Hall) [*A publication*] (DLA) .... Cons & Com Cred (P-H)
Consumer and Corporate Affairs Canada [*UTLAS symbol*] .... CCA
Consumer and Environmental Health Services Administration [*HEW*] .... CEHSA
Consumer and Marketing Service [*Later, AMS*] [*Department of Agriculture*] .... C & MS
Consumer and Marketing Service [*Later, AMS*] [*Department of Agriculture*] (IAA) .... CAMS
Consumer and Marketing Service [*Later, AMS*] [*Department of Agriculture*] .... CMS
Consumer and Marketing Service, Service and Regulatory Announcements [*Later, AMS*] [*Department of Agriculture*] .... C & MSSRA
Consumer and Producer Price Indexes [*Department of Labor*] [*Database*] .... CPI/PPI
Consumer and Professional Relations Division [*of HIAA*] [*Washington, DC*] (EA) .... CPRD
Consumer Attorneys of California (SRA) .... CAC
Consumer Bankers Association [*Arlington, VA*] (EA) .... CBA
Consumer Buying Expectations Survey [*Formerly, Quarterly Survey of Intentions*] [*Bureau of the Census*] .... CBE
Consumer Choice Health Plan .... CCHP
Consumer Coalition for Health [*Inactive*] (EA) .... CCH
Consumer Commission on the Accreditation of Health Services [*Defunct*] (EA) .... CCAHS
Consumer Complaint Guide .... CCG
Consumer Computing Device (PCM) .... CCD
Consumer Confidence Index [*Conference Board*] CCI
Consumer Consultative Committee [*British*] CCC
Consumer Council [*American National Standards Institute*] CC
Consumer Credit Association [*British*] (EAIO) .... CCA
Consumer Credit Counseling Services [*Banking*] .... CCCS
Consumer Credit Counselors [*Banking*] CCC
Consumer Credit Education Foundation (EA) .... CCEF
Consumer Credit Guide [*Commerce Clearing House*] [*A publication*] (DLA) .... Cons Cred Guide
Consumer Credit Guide (Commerce Clearing House) [*A publication*] (DLA) .... Consumer Cred Guide (CCH)
Consumer Credit Insurance CCI
Consumer Credit Insurance Association [*Chicago, IL*] (EA) .... CCIA
Consumer Credit Letter [*Business Publishers, Inc.*] [*Information service or system*] (CRD) CCL
Consumer Credit Project [*Defunct*] (EA) .... CCP
Consumer Credit Protection Act [*1969*] .... CCPA
Consumer Demographics, Inc. [*Information service or system*] (IID) .... CDI
Consumer Digital Subscriber Line [*Telecommunications*] .... CDSL
Consumer Discount Network .... CDN
Consumer Distribution Marketing .... CDM
Consumer Drug Information [*American Society of Hospital Pharmacists*] [*Database*] [*Information service or system*] (IID) .... CDIF
Consumer Drug Information Fulltext [*American Society of Hospital Pharmacists*] [*Database*] [*Information service or system*] .... CDIF
Consumer Drug Information Service [*Australia*] .... CDIS
Consumer Economic Study Report [*Department of Agriculture*] .... CESR
Consumer Education and Information Liaison [*Federal interagency group*] .... CEIL
Consumer Education Research Center (EA) .... CERC
Consumer Education Research Group [*Later, CERC*] (EA) .... CERG
Consumer Education Resource Network .... CERN
Consumer Electronics Bus [*Residential wiring standard*] .... CEBus
Consumer Electronics Group [*Education Industries Association*] (NTCM) .... CEG
Consumer Electronics Show [*Computer industry*] .... CES
Consumer Energy Council of America (EA) .... CECA
Consumer Energy Council of America Research Foundation (EA) .... CECA/RF
Consumer Expenditure Survey [*Bureau of Labor Statistics*] (GFGA) .... CES
Consumer Federation of America (EA) .... CFA
Consumer Goods System [*Computer science*] .... COGS
Consumer Hazards Analytical Information Service [*Laboratory of the Government Chemist*] [*British*] (NITA) .... CHAIS
Consumer Health Information Program and Services [*LSCA*] .... CHIPS
Consumer Health Organization of Canada (AC) .... CHOC
Consumer Help on the Individual's Conservation of Energy [*Student legal action organization*] .... CHOICE
Consumer Housing Assistance Grants .... CHAG
Consumer Information CI
Consumer Information Association .... CIA
Consumer Information Center (EA) CIC
Consumer Information Regulation [*National Highway Traffic Safety Administration*] .... CIR
Consumer Information Series [*National Institute of Standards and Technology*] .... CIS
Consumer Information Service [*Electronic mail*] .... CIS
Consumer Information System .... CIS
Consumer Interests Foundation .... CIF
Consumer Interpol (EA) CI
Consumer Level Quality Audit Program [*Military*] .... COLQUAP
Consumer News and Business Channel [*A cable division of NBC*] .... CNBC
Consumer Organization of Diabled People of Newfoundland & Labrador (AC) .... COD
Consumer Pesticide Project (EA) .... CPP
Consumer Portfolio Services [*Associated Press*] (SAG) .... ConPort
Consumer Portfolio Services [*NASDAQ symbol*] (SAG) .... CPSS
Consumer Portfolio Svcs [*NASDAQ symbol*] (TTSB) .... CPSS
Consumer Premise Equipment (DOMA) .... CPE
Consumer Price Index [*Department of Labor*] [*Database*] .... CPI
Consumer Price Index for All Urban Consumers (OICC) .... CPI-U
Consumer Price Index for Services .... CPIS
Consumer Price Index for Urban Wage Earners and Clerical Workers (OICC) .... CPI-W
Consumer Product and Manufacturer Ratings [*A publication*] .... CPR
Consumer Product Information Center .... CPIC
Consumer Product Safety Act [*1972*] (DLA) .... CPS Act
Consumer Product Safety Act [*1972*] .... CPSA
Consumer Product Safety Commission [*Federal agency*] .... CPSC
Consumer Product Safety Commission, Washington, DC [*OCLC symbol*] (OCLC) .... CPR
Consumer Product Safety Guide (Commerce Clearing House) [*A publication*] (DLA) .... Consumer Prod Safety Guide (CCH)
Consumer Products Information Index [*National Institute of Standards and Technology*] .... CPII
Consumer Protection Act .... CPA
Consumer Protection Advisory Committee (ODBW) .... CPAC
Consumer Protection Agency .... CPA
Consumer Protection and Environmental Health Service [*Later, Environmental Health Service*] [*US government*] .... CPEHS
Consumer Protection Center (EA) .... CPC
Consumer Purchasing Service .... CPS
Consumer Pwr $2.08'A'Pfd [*NYSE symbol*] (TTSB) .... CMSPrI
Consumer Safety Committee [*Queensland*] [*Australia*] .... CSC
Consumer Safety Glazing Committee .... CSGC
Consumer Satisfaction Index .... CSI
Consumer Savings Alliance (EA) .... CSA
Consumer Services Organization (EA) .... CSO
Consumer Sounding-Board (IEEE) .... CSB
Consumer Sourcebook [*A publication*] .... CS
Consumer Sourcebook [*A publication*] .... CSB
Consumer Survival Kit [*Program on public TV*] .... CSK
Consumer Technology Index [*Computer Intelligence InfoCorp*] (PCM) .... CTI
Consumer Value Stores .... CVS
Consumer Video (NITA) CV
Consumers' Advisory Board .... CAB
Consumer's Advisory Council .... CAC
Consumers and Taxpayers .... CONTAX
Consumers' Association (EAIO) .... CA
Consumers' Association of Canada .... CAC
Consumer's Association of Canada, Ottawa, Ontario [*Library symbol National Library of Canada*] (BIB) .... OOCOAC
Consumers' Association of Jamaica .... CAJ
Consumers' Association of Trinidad and Tobago .... CATT
Consumers' Association of Western Australia .... CAWA
Consumers' Consultative Committee [*EC*] (ECED) CCC
Consumers Cooperative Association [*Later, Farmland Industries*] (EA) .... CCA
Consumers Distributing Co. Ltd. [*Toronto Stock Exchange symbol*] .... CDG
Consumers Education and Protective Association International (EA) .... CEPA
Consumers Financial Corp. [*NASDAQ symbol*] (NQ) .... CFIN
Consumers Financial Corp. [*Associated Press*] (SAG) .... CnsFn
Consumers Financial Corp. [*Associated Press*] (SAG) .... ConsFn
Consumers Finl [*NASDAQ symbol*] (TTSB) .... CFIN
Consumers Finl 8.50% Cv Pfd [*NASDAQ symbol*] (TTSB) .... CFINP
Consumers for the Free Market [*Pittsburgh, PA*] (EA) .... CFM
Consumers for World Trade (EA) .... CWT
Consumers' Gas Co. Ltd. [*Toronto Stock Exchange symbol*] .... CGT
Consumers in the European Community Group .... CECG
Consumers' Law Reform Association [*Australia*] .... CLRA
Consumers' Law Reform Association, Queensland [*Australia*] .... CLRAQ
Consumers Opposed to Inflation in the Necessities (EA) .... COIN
Consumers Organization for the Hearing Impaired [*Defunct*] (EA) .... COHI
Consumers Packaging, Inc. [*Toronto Stock Exchange symbol*] .... CGC
Consumers Power Co. [*NYSE symbol*] (SAG) .... CMS
Consumers Power Co. [*Associated Press*] (SAG) .... CnP
Consumers Power Co. Financing I [*NYSE symbol*] (SAG) .... CMS
Consumers Power Co. Financing I [*Associated Press*] (SAG) .... CnPF
Consumers Power Co., Parnall Technical Library, Jackson, MI [*Library symbol*] [*Library of Congress*] (LCLS) .... MiJaCP
Consumers Public Power District .... CPPD
Consumers Pwr $4.16 Pfd [*NYSE symbol*] (TTSB) .... CMPSPrA
Consumers Pwr $4.50 Pfd [*NYSE symbol*] (TTSB) .... CMSPrB
Consumers Pwr $7.45cmPfd [*NYSE symbol*] (TTSB) .... CMSPrD
Consumers Pwr $7.68 Pfd [*NYSE symbol*] (TTSB) .... CMSPrH
Consumers Pwr $7.72 Pfd [*NYSE symbol*] (TTSB) .... CMSPrE
Consumers Pwr $7.76 Pfd [*NYSE symbol*] (TTSB) .... CMSPrG
Consumers Pwr Fin 1 8.36%'TOPrS' [*NYSE symbol*] (TTSB) .... CMSPrJ
Consumer's Reliability Risk .... CRR
Consumers' Research (EA) .... CR

Consumers Union of United States (EA) .... CU
Consumers United for Rail Equity (EA) .... CURE
Consumers United to Stop Food Irradiation (AC) .... CUSFI
Consumers Water [*NASDAQ symbol*] (TTSB) .... CONW
Consumers Water Co. [*NASDAQ symbol*] (SAG) .... CONW
Consumers Water Co. [*Associated Press*] (SAG) .... ConWat
Consuming Interest [*A publication*] (ADA) CI
Consumnes River College, Sacramento, CA [*Library symbol Library of Congress*] (LCLS) .... CSCR
Consumption C
Consumption (ROG) .... CONSUMP
Consumption Data Exchange .... CDE
Consumption Entry [*Economics*] .... CE
Consumption Function [*Economics*] .... CF
Consumption Levels Enquiry [*British*] .... CLE
Consumption Variation (MCD) .... COVAR
Contact C
Contact (AABC) .... CNTC
Contact (KSC) .... CONT
Contact .... CONT
Contact .... CTC
Contact [*Amateur Radio*] (BARN) .... QSO
Contact a Family Computer Assisted Learning (AIE) .... CAFCAL
Contact Adhesive .... CA
Contact Analog [*Submarine instrumentation*] (MCD) .... CONALOG
Contact Analog Flight Display .... CAFD
Contact and Repair Test Equipment (MCD) .... CARTE
Contact Approach [*Aviation*] (DA) .... CAP
Contact Approach [*Aviation*] (IAA) .... CTAP
Contact Approach Control (FAAC) .... CAC
Contact Area, Articular [*Medicine*] .... CA
Contact Area Commander .... CAC
Contact Area Summary Position Estimate Report [*Military*] (NVT) .... CASPER
Contact Back-Up (DNAB) .... CBU
Contact Breaker .... CB
Contact Center (EA) CC
Contact Center (FAAC) .... CTCEN
Contact Center Control (FAAC) .... CTCC
Contact Charge Transfer (MCD) .... CCT
Contact Children's Services [*Australia*] .... CCS
Contact Clock (IAA) CCL
Contact Closure (KSC) CC
Contact Conversion Exercise [*Military*] (NVT) .... CONVERSIONEX
Contact Dermatitis [*Medicine*] .... CD
Contact End Resistance [*Photovoltaic energy systems*] .... CER
Contact Equipment Handling Area [*Nuclear energy*] (NRCH) .... CEHA
Contact Evaluation Plot (NVT) .... CEP
Contact Flight Rules [*Same as VFR*] [*Meteorology*] .... CFR
Contact Glow Discharge Electrolysis .... CGDE
Contact Handled .... CH
Contact Image Sensing [*Reprography*] .... CIS
Contact Ion Thruster .... CIT
Contact Ion-Pair [*Physical chemistry*] .... CIP
Contact Karate .... C-K
Contact Lens [*Ophthalmology*] CL
Contact Lens [*Ophthalmology*] (DAVI) .... ctl
Contact Lens Association for Optometry (EA) .... CLAO
Contact Lens Association of Ophthalmologists (EA) .... CLAO
Contact Lens Manufacturers Association (EA) .... CLMA
Contact Lens Practitioners (PDAA) .... CLP
Contact Lens Registry Examination [*National Contact Lens Examiners*] .... CLRE
Contact Lens Society of America (EA) .... CLSA
Contact Limit Line [*Technical drawings*] CLL
Contact Literacy Center (EA) CLC
Contact Load Resistor (IAA) .... CLR
Contact Lost [*RADAR*] CL
Contact Maker .... CM
Contact Microradiography (DICI) .... CMR
Contact Motion Analysis (CAAL) .... CMA
Contact Party [*Army*] .... CONPY
Contact Party [*Army*] .... CP
Contact Personality Factor Test [*Psychology*] .... CPFT
Contact Potential Difference .... CPD
Contact Preclude (DNAB) .... CP
Contact Print (VRA) .... CONPR
Contact Process Cell [*Nuclear energy*] (GFGA) .... CPC
Contact Publishers [*Holland*] C
Contact Resistance [*Electricity*] (IAA) .... CR
Contact Resistance Variation [*Telecommunications*] (TEL) .... CRV
Contact Sensitivity [*Allergy and dermatology*] (DAVI) .... CS
Contact Soil Sampling Device [*Aerospace*] .... CSSD
Contact Team .... CT
Contact Teleministries USA (EA) .... CTUSA
Contact Tension .... CT
Contact Test Set [*Military*] .... CTS
Contact Test Set - Electro Optical Augmentation [*Military*] (DWSG) .... CTS-EOA
Contact Ventures [*Vancouver Stock Exchange symbol*] .... CVU
Contactair Flugdienst & Co. [*Germany ICAO designator*] (FAAC) .... KIS
Contact-Bend-Stretch (PDAA) .... C-B-S
Contact-Lens-Induced Keratoconjunctivitis [*Ophthalmology*] .... CLK
Contactless Vacuum Controller CVC
Contact-Making Ammeter (KSC) .... CMA
Contact-Making Clock .... CMC
Contact-Making Voltmeter .... CMV
Contact-Making Voltmeter .... CMVM
Contactor (MSA) .... CNTOR
Contactor Control Relay (MCD) .... CCR
Contactor, Running .... COR
Contactor, Starting .... COS
Contacts, Activities, Time [*Computer science*] .... CAT
Contadora [*Panama*] [*Airport symbol*] (OAG) .... OTD
Contagion [*Medicine*] (DMAA) .... contag
Contagious .... CONTAG
Contagious Bovine Pleuropneumonia [*Veterinary medicine*] .... CBPP
Contagious Diseases .... CD
Contagious Diseases Act [*British*] .... CDA
Contagious Equine Metritis .... CEM
Contagious Pustular Dermatitis [*Dermatology*] .... CPD
Contain (AABC) .... CNTN
Contain .... CNTN
Contain (ROG) .... CONTN
Contained (MSA) .... CNTD
Contained .... CONTD
Contained Disposal Facility .... CDF
Contained-Liquid Membranes [*Chemical engineering*] .... CLM
Container (DCTA) C
Container [*Shipping*] (DS) .... CNT
Container (MSA) .... CNTNR
Container (KSC) .... CNTR
Container .... CO
Container (MCD) .... CONT
Container (KSC) .... CONTNR
Container .... CONTNR
Container (KSC) .... CONTR
Container Agreement (DNAB) .... CA
Container Anchorage Terminal (NVT) .... CAT
Container and Chassis Identification and Reporting System [*Military*] (MCD) .... CCIRS
Container and Chassis Identification Reporting and Recording System [*DoD*] (PDAA) .... CCIRRS
Container Automated Marking Systems .... CAMS
Container Base (DS) .... CB
Container Control (DCTA) CC
Container Corp. of America [*Later, Marcor, Inc.*] .... CCA
Container Cost Data Reporting .... CCDR
Container Delivery System [*Military*] .... CDS
Container Deposit Legislation .... CDL
Container Design Retrieval System (MCD) .... CDRS
Container Distribution System (MCD) .... CDS
Container Express [*Army*] (AABC) .... CONEX
Container for Export (NATG) .... CONEX
Container Freight Station [*Shipping*] .... CFS
Container Fumigated (ADA) .... CF
Container Handling Equipment .... CHE
Container Handling in Terminal Operations [*Army study*] (RDA) .... CHITO
Container Inspection Training and Assistance Team [*RSPA*] (TAG) .... CITAT
Container Lift Adapter for Helicopter (MCD) .... CLAH
Container Offloading and Transfer System (MCD) .... COTS
Container on Flatcar [*Shipping*] .... COFC
Container Operating Control System (PDAA) .... COCS
Container Over-the-Shore .... COTS
Container Repair Building .... CRB
Container, Restrainer, Environment, Energy Absorption, Post-Crash Failure [*Aviation*] (PDAA) .... CREEP
Container Safety Convention [*ISO*] (DS) .... CSC
Container Service Tariff [*Shipping*] (DS) .... CST
Container Systems Standardization/Coordination Group .... CSS/CG
Container Tariff .... CT
Container Terminal [*Shipping*] .... CT
Container Terminal Operator [*Shipping*] (DS) .... CTO
Container, Weapon, Individual Equipment [*Army*] (ADDR) .... CWIE
Container Weapon System (MCD) .... CWS
Container Yard [*Shipping*] (DCTA) .... CY
Containerboard and Kraft Paper Group (EA) .... CKPG
Containerization and Intermodal Institute (EA) CII
Containerization Institute [*Later, CII*] CI
Containerized Ammunition Distribution System .... CADS
Containerized Ammunition Distribution System Van (DOMA) .... CADSVAN
Containerized Avionics Maintenance System (NG) .... CAMS
Containerized Hospital Emergency Mobile (PDAA) .... CHEM
Containerized Lighter Aboard Ship System (IAA) .... CLASS
Containerized Liquid Waste Sampler .... COLIWASA
Containerized Shipment and Storage of Ammunition (MCD) .... COSSA
Containerless Processing (SSD) .... CP
Containers in Barrels or Boxes [*Freight*] .... CNTRS BB
Containing .... CONT
Containing (WDMC) .... cont
Containing .... CONTG
Containing .... CTG
Containment (IEEE) .... CTMT
Containment Air Removal [*Recirculation fan*] (IEEE) .... CAR
Containment and Meteorology for Radiation Exposure [*Nuclear energy*] (NRCH) .... COMRADEX
Containment and Reactor Vessel Isolation Control System (NRCH) .... CRVICS
Containment Atmosphere Control [*Monitor, or System*] [*Nuclear energy*] (IEEE) .... CAC
Containment Atmosphere Dilution [*Nuclear energy*] (NRCH) .... CAD
Containment Atmosphere Dilution System [*Nuclear energy*] (IEEE) .... CADS
Containment Atmosphere Recirculation System [*Nuclear energy*] (NRCH) .... CARS

Containment Atmospheric Monitoring [*Nuclear energy*] (NRCH) ..... CAM
Containment Building [*Nuclear energy*] (NRCH) ..... CB
Containment Building Ventilation [*Nuclear energy*] (NRCH) ..... CBV
Containment Combustion Gas Control System [*Nuclear energy*] (IEEE) ..... CCGCS
Containment Cooling Actuation Signal [*Nuclear energy*] (NRCH) ..... CCAS
Containment Cooling System [*Nuclear energy*] (NRCH) ..... CCS
Containment Cooling Unit [*Nuclear energy*] (NRCH) ..... CCU
Containment Depressurization Actuation [*Nuclear energy*] (NRCH) ..... CDA
Containment Depressurization Alarm [*Nuclear energy*] (IEEE) ..... CDA
Containment Design Basis Accident [*Nuclear energy*] (NRCH) ..... CDBA
Containment Environmental Control System [*Nuclear energy*] (NRCH) ..... CECS
Containment Failure Mode [*Nuclear energy*] (NRCH) ..... CFM
Containment Gaseous Radiation Monitor [*Nuclear energy*] (IEEE) ..... CGRM
Containment Heat Removal System [*Nuclear energy*] (NRCH) ..... CHRS
Containment Integrated Leak Rate Test [*Nuclear energy*] (NRCH) ..... CILRT
Containment Integrity [*Nuclear energy*] (NRCH) CI
Containment Iodine Removal System [*Nuclear energy*] (NRCH) ..... CIRS
Containment Isolation [*Nuclear energy*] (NRCH) CI
Containment Isolation A [*Nuclear energy*] (NRCH) ..... CIA
Containment Isolation Actuation Signal [*Nuclear energy*] (NRCH) ..... CIAS
Containment Isolation B [*Nuclear energy*] (NRCH) ..... CIB
Containment Isolation Signal [*Nuclear energy*] (NRCH) ..... CIS
Containment Isolation System [*Nuclear energy*] (NRCH) ..... CIS
Containment Isolation Valve [*Nuclear energy*] (IEEE) CIV
Containment Leakage [*Nuclear energy*] (NRCH) CL
Containment Leakage Control [*Nuclear energy*] (IEEE) CLC
Containment Leakage System [*Nuclear energy*] (IEEE) ..... CLS
Containment Person Air Lock [*Nuclear energy*] (IEEE) ..... CPAL
Containment Pressure High Signal [*Nuclear energy*] (IEEE) ..... CPHS
Containment Pressure Protection [*Nuclear energy*] (IEEE) ..... CPP
Containment Purge [*Nuclear energy*] (NRCH) ..... CP
Containment Purge System [*Nuclear energy*] (NRCH) ..... CPS
Containment Radiation Monitor [*Nuclear energy*] (IEEE) ..... CRM
Containment Recirculation Spray System [*Nuclear energy*] (NRCH) ..... CRS
Containment Rupture [*Nuclear energy*] (NRCH) ..... CR
Containment Rupture Signal [*Nuclear energy*] (IEEE) ..... CRS
Containment Safety [*Nuclear energy*] (NRCH) ..... CS
Containment Spray [*Nuclear energy*] (NRCH) ..... CS
Containment Spray Actuating Signal [*Nuclear energy*] (NRCH) ..... CSAS
Containment Spray Cooling [*Nuclear energy*] (NRCH) ..... CSC
Containment Spray Heat Exchange [*Nuclear energy*] (NRCH) ..... CSHX
Containment Spray Injection System [*Nuclear energy*] (NRCH) ..... CSIS
Containment Spray Pump [*Nuclear energy*] (NRCH) ..... CSP
Containment Spray Recirculation System [*Nuclear energy*] (NRCH) ..... CSRS
Containment Spray System [*Nuclear energy*] (NRCH) ..... CSS
Containment Steam Explosion [*Nuclear energy*] (IEEE) ..... CSE
Containment Support Fixture [*Nuclear energy*] (NRCH) ..... CSF
Containment Systems Experiment [*Nuclear energy*] ..... CSE
Containment Vacuum Pump [*Nuclear energy*] (IEEE) ..... CVP
Containment Vacuum Pump Valve [*Nuclear energy*] (NRCH) ..... CVPV
Containment Vent Header [*Nuclear energy*] (NRCH) ..... CVH
Containment Ventilation Isolation [*Nuclear energy*] (NRCH) CVI
Contains (ROG) ..... CONTS
Contamana [*Peru*] [*ICAO location identifier*] (ICLI) ..... SPCM
Contaminant Analysis Automation ..... CAA
Contaminant Collection Unit (OA) ..... CCU
Contaminant Control Cartridge (MCD) CCC
Contaminated (KSC) ..... CONTAM
Contaminated Normal [*Statistics*] ..... CN
Contaminated Oil Settling (PDAA) ..... COS
Contaminated Oil Settling Tank (AAG) ..... COST
Contaminated Small Bowel [*Medicine*] (DMAA) ..... CSB
Contaminated Small Bowel Syndrome [*Medicine*] (DMAA) ..... CSBS
Contamination Control Area [*Army*] (ADDR) ..... CCA
Contamination Control Station (MCD) ..... CCS
Contamination Control System (NASA) ..... CCS
Contamination Free Manufacturing [*Semiconductor manufacturing*] ..... CFM
Contamination Index [*Medicine*] CI
Contamination Mode [*NASA*] (KSC) ..... CM
Contamination/Overpressure (MCD) ..... C/O
Contamination Technology (SSD) ..... CONT
Contamination-Decontamination Experiment [*Nuclear energy*] ..... CDE
[*Hyperbolic*] **Contangent** [*Mathematics*] (BARN) ..... ctnh
Contango [*Premium or interest paid*] [*London Stock Exchange*] ..... CGO
Contano [*Parts so marked to rest*] [*Music*] ..... CONT
Conte (VRA) ..... cnte
Conte Corrente [*Running Account*] ..... C/C
Conte Crayon (VRA) ..... cnte
Contecs Intl Ltd ADS [*NASDAQ symbol*] (TTSB) ..... DLVRY
Contel ASC [*ICAO designator*] (FAAC) XCL
CONTEL [*Continental Telecom Corp.*] **Customer Support** [*Telecommunications service*] (TSSD) ..... CCS
Contel Service Corp., Atlanta, GA [*Library symbol*] [*Library of Congress*] (LCLS) ..... GACSC
Contemplate (AABC) ..... CONTEM
Contemplative Sisters of St. Benedict (TOCD) ..... OSB
Contemplatives of Good Shepherd (TOCD) ..... CGS
Contemporaneous Reserve Accounting [*Banking*] ..... CRA
Contemporaneous Reserve Requirements [*Banking*] ..... CRR
Contemporary (ADA) ..... CONT
Contemporary (VRA) ..... cont
Contemporary ..... CONTEMP
Contemporary ..... CONTEMP
Contemporary Acapella Society of America (EA) ..... CASA
Contemporary American Business Leaders [*A publication*] ..... CABL
Contemporary American Patriot Club (EA) ..... CAP
Contemporary Archive on Latin America [*Defunct British*] ..... CALA
Contemporary Art Centre of South Australia ..... CACSA
Contemporary Art Society ..... CAS
Contemporary Authors [*A publication*] ..... CA
Contemporary Authors Autobiography Series [*A publication*] ..... CAAS
Contemporary Authors Bibliographical Series [*A publication*] ..... CABS
Contemporary Authors First Revision Series [*A publication*] ..... CAR
Contemporary Authors New Revision Series [*A publication*] ..... CANR
Contemporary Authors: Permanent Series [*A publication*] ..... CAP
Contemporary Books [*Publisher's imprint*] ..... CB
Contemporary Christian [*Music*] (WDMC) CC
Contemporary Civilization [*University course*] CC
Contemporary Deep Rack Interior (MCD) ..... CDRI
Contemporary Digital Services, Inc. [*New Rochelle, NY*] [*Telecommunications*] (TSSD) ..... CDSI
Contemporary Education [*A publication*] (BRI) ..... Cont Ed
Contemporary English Version [*Of the Bible*] ..... CEV
Contemporary Entertainment Services [*Air carrier designation symbol*] ..... CESX
Contemporary Evaluation Form [*Army*] ..... CEF
Contemporary Force (OA) ..... cf
Contemporary Games [*A publication*] ..... CG
Contemporary Graphic Artists [*A publication*] ..... CGA
Contemporary Heroes and Heroines [*A publication*] ..... CHH
Contemporary Historical Examination Current Operations [*Air Force*] (AFM) ..... CHECO
Contemporary Historical Vehicle Association (EA) ..... CHVA
Contemporary Hit Radio ..... CHR
Contemporary Issues Clearinghouse [*Defunct*] (EA) CIC
Contemporary Issues Criticism [*A publication*] CIC
Contemporary Issues in Science Program (EDAC) ..... CIIS
Contemporary Jewish Learning Materials [*A publication*] (BJA) ..... CJLM
Contemporary Law Review [*India*] [*A publication*] (DLA) ..... Cont L Rev
Contemporary Literary Criticism [*Reference publication; often pronounced "click"*] CLC
Contemporary Men of Letters [*A publication*] ..... CML
Contemporary Music Project [*Defunct*] (EA) ..... CMP
Contemporary Music Society (EA) ..... CMS
Contemporary Musicians [*A publication*] ..... CM
Contemporary Newsmakers [*Later, Newsmakers*] [*A publication*] ..... CN
Contemporary Pacific [*A publication*] (BRI) ..... Cont Pac
Contemporary Psychology [*A publication*] (BRI) ..... CP
Contemporary Records [*Los Angeles*] [*Record label*] ..... Cty
Contemporary Records (New York) [*Record label*] ..... CtyNY
Contemporary Review [*A publication*] (BRI) ..... CR
Contemporary Rock (LAIN) ..... CR
Contemporary Science Series [*A publication*] ..... CSS
Contemporary Sociology [*A publication*] (BRI) ..... CS
Contemporary Specialty Services [*Merchandiser*] [*Chicago, IL*] ..... CSS
Contemporary Theatre [*A publication*] ..... CT
Contemporary Theatre, Film, and Television [*A publication*] ..... CTFT
Contemporary World Writers [*A publication*] ..... CWW
Contempt [*FBI standardized term*] ..... CMPT
Contempt of Court ..... COC
Content [*of gas in blood phase*] (AAMN) C
Content Addressable Computing System ..... CACS
Content Addressable File Store [*Computer science*] (PDAA) ..... CADS
Content Addressable File Store [*Computer science*] (NITA) ..... CAFS
Content and Source of Cataloging Data for Local Use (PDAA) ..... CASCADE
Content Dependent Information Language ..... CODIL
Content Indication Codes (NG) CIC
Content of Thought [*Medicine*] (DMAA) ..... COT
Content Replication Service [*Microsoft Corp.*] [*Computer science*] ..... CRS
Content Scramble System [*Computer science*] ..... CSS
Content Vectoring Protocol [*Computer science*] ..... CVP
Content Vectoring Protocol [*Computer science*] ..... CVP
Content-Addressable Array Parallel Processor [*Computer science*] ..... CAAPP
Content-Addressable Data Manager ..... CADM
Content-Addressable File Store [*Computer science*] (IEEE) ..... CAFS
Content-Addressable Memory [*Computer science*] (IAA) ..... CA
Content-Addressable Memory [*Computer science*] ..... CAM
Content-Addressable Parallel Processor [*Computer science*] ..... CAPP
Content-Addressable Random Access Memory [*Computer science*] (HGAA) ..... CARAM
Content-Addressed Film System [*Computer science*] (PDAA) ..... CAFS
Contention Priority Oriented Demand Assignment [*Protocol*] [*Computer science*] ..... CPODA
Contents ..... CONT
Contents (ODBW) ..... cont
Contents (WDMC) ..... cont
Contents, Abstracts, and Photocopies Services [*India*] [*Information service or system*] ..... CAPS
Contents Directory Entry [*Computer science*] (MHDI) ..... CDE
Contents of Decrement Part of Register [*Computer science*] (NHD) ..... CDR
Contere [*Rub Together*] [*Pharmacy*] ..... CONTER
Conterminous United States Mineral Resource Assessment Program [*Department of the Interior*] ..... CUSMAP
Contest ..... CNTST
Contested ..... CONT
Contested Election Cases [*United States*] [*A publication*] (DLA) ..... Cont Elect Case
Context Addressed Segment Sequential Memory [*Computer science*] ..... CASSM
Context Control Object [*Telecommunications*] (OSI) ..... CCO
Context Free (BUR) ..... CF
Context Free Transduction Grammar (MHDI) ..... CFTG
Context, Input, Process, Product [*Computer science*] ..... CIPP

Context Sensitive Grammar [*Computer science*] (IAA) .... CSG
Context-Free Grammar [*Computer science*] .... CFG
Context-Free Language [*Computer science*] .... CFL
Context-Free Phrase Structure Grammar [*Computer science*] (PDAA) .... CFPSG
Context-Free Programmed Grammar (PDAA) .... CFPG
Context-Free Syntactical Translator .... CFST
Context-Sensitive Language [*Computer science*] (IAA) .... CSL
Contextual Indexing and Faceted Taxonomic Access System [*Computer science*] (BARN) .... CIFT
Contextual Indexing and Faceted Taxonomic System [*Modern Language Association of America*] [*A database*] (NITA) .... CIFT
ContiCurrency Foreign Exchange and Money Market Database [*No longer available online*] .... CCFX
Contifinancial Corp. [*NYSE symbol*] (SAG) .... CFN
ContiFinancial Corp. [*NYSE symbol*] (TTSB) .... CFN
Contifinancial Corp. [*Associated Press*] (SAG) .... Contifin
Conti-Flug Koln/Bonn [*Germany ICAO designator*] (FAAC) .... EPC
Contigency Movement After-Effect (PDAA) .... CMAE
Contiguous (NASA) .... CONTIG
Contiguous Fisheries Zone [*Offshore*] .... CFZ
Contiguous Node Group Restoral Supervision and Switching .... CONGRESS
Contiguous United States .... CONUS
Contiguous-Disk File [*Computer science*] (PDAA) .... CDF
Continence Aids Assistance Scheme [*Australia*] .... CAAS
Continence Restored (EA) .... CR
Continent .... CONT
Continent, Antwerp-Hamburg Range [*Shipping*] (DS) .... CONT (AH)
Continent between Bordeaux and Hamburg [*Business term*] .... CB & H
Continent between Havre and Hamburg [*Business term*] .... CH & H
Continent, Bordeaux-Hamburg Range [*Shipping*] (DS) .... CONT (BH)
Continent, Britain & Asia [*Commercial firm*] (DS) .... COBRA
Continent, Havre-Hamburg Range [*Shipping*] (DS) .... CONT (HH)
Continental [*Air mass*] C
Continental (AFM) .... CON
Continental .... Cont
Continental (ROG) .... CONTIN
Continental (AABC) .... CONTL
Continental .... CONTNTL
Continental Advance Section [*Originally called Coastal Base Section*] [*World War II*] .... CONAD
Continental Advertising Agency Network [*Later, Advertising and Marketing International Network*] (EA) .... CAAN
Continental Africa Chamber of Commerce (EA) .... CACC
Continental Africa Project [*National Academy of Sciences*] .... CAP
Continental Air Command .... CAC
Continental Air Command .... CONAC
Continental Air Command (MCD) .... CONARC
Continental Air Defense Command [*Discontinued, 1975*] .... CADC
Continental Air Defense Command [*Discontinued, 1975*] .... CONAD
Continental Air Defense Integration, North .... CADIN
Continental Air Defense Objectives Plan (AABC) .... CADOP
Continental Air Defense System .... CADS
Continental Air Forces .... CAF
Continental Air Services .... CAS
Continental Aircraft Control and Warning (MUGU) .... CAC & W
Continental Airlines [*ICAO designator*] (AD) .... CO
Continental Airlines (MHDB) .... CONT
Continental Airlines, Inc. [*NYSE symbol*] (SPSG) .... CAI
Continental Airlines, Inc. (MCD) .... CAL
Continental Airlines, Inc. [*CAB official abbreviation*] .... CO
Continental Airlines, Inc. [*ICAO designator*] (FAAC) .... COA
Continental Airlines, Inc. [*Associated Press*] (SAG) .... CtlAir
Continental Airways (AAG) .... CA
Continental Airways and Communications Service [*Air Force*] .... CACS
Continental Army .... CONAR
Continental Army and Major Overseas Commands Systems [*Later, ASMIS*] .... CARMOCS
Continental Army Command [*See CONARC*] .... CAC
Continental Army Command [*Responsible for induction, processing, training of active duty personnel*] [*Superseded by FORSCOM*] .... CONARC
Continental Army Management Information System (RDA) .... CAMIS
Continental Association of CPA [*Certified Public Accountant*] **Firms** (EA) .... CACPAF
Continental Association of Funeral and Memorial Societies .... CAFMS
Continental Association of Resolute Employers [*Washington, DC*] (EA) .... CARE
Continental Assurance Co. .... CA
Continental Aviation & Engineering Corp. .... CAE
Continental Aviation Ltd. [*Ghana*] [*ICAO designator*] (FAAC) CCL
Continental Ballistic Missile .... CBM
Continental Bank of Canada [*Toronto Stock Exchange symbol*] .... CTL
Continental Baptist Mission (EA) .... CBM
Continental Base Section .... CBS
Continental Basketball Association (EA) .... CBA
Continental Breakfast .... CB
Continental Can [*Formerly, Viatech, Inc.*] [*NYSE symbol*] (SPSG) .... CAN
Continental Can Co., Inc. [*Associated Press*] (SAG) .... ContCan
Continental Car Ferry Centre [*British*] .... CCFC
Continental Carbon Co., Houston, TX [*Library symbol Library of Congress*] (LCLS) .... TxHCC
Continental Choice Care, Inc. [*NASDAQ symbol*] (SAG) CCCI
Continental Choice Care, Inc. [*Associated Press*] (SAG) .... CtlCC
Continental Choice Care, Inc. [*Associated Press*] (SAG) .... CtlCCare
Continental Choice Care Wrrt [*NASDAQ symbol*] (TTSB) .... CCCIW
Continental Circuits Corp. [*NASDAQ symbol*] (SAG) .... CCIR
Continental Circuits Corp. [*Associated Press*] (SAG) .... CntlCir
[*Tropical*] **Continental Cold Air Mass** (BARN) .... cTk
Continental Communications Division [*Military*] .... CCD
Continental Confederation of Adopted Indians (EA) .... CCAI
Continental Control Area [*FAA*] .... CCA
Continental Datanet, Inc. [*Vancouver Stock Exchange symbol*] .... CDJ
Continental Depositary Receipt [*Banking*] (MHDW) .... CDR
Continental Divide (FAAC) .... CONTDVD
Continental Divide Trail Society (EA) .... CDTS
Continental Division, Transport Control Center [*Military*] .... CTCC
Continental Dorset Club (EA) .... CDC
Continental Electronic Security Division [*Military*] .... CESD
Continental Electronics Manufacturing Co. (AAG) .... CEMCO
Continental Entry Charts [*Air Force*] .... CEC
Continental Exercise [*Military*] .... CONEX
Continental Flood Basalt [*Geology*] .... CFB
Continental Flood Basalt Province [*Geology*] .... CFBP
Continental Football League .... CFL
Continental Gold Corp. [*Vancouver Stock Exchange symbol*] .... CUG
Continental Group Co., Inc., Chicago, IL [*Library symbol Library of Congress*] (LCLS) .... ICCon
Continental Group, Inc. [*Toronto Stock Exchange symbol*] .... CH
Continental Homes Holding Corp. [*NYSE symbol*] (SPSG) .... CON
Continental Homes Holding Corp. [*Associated Press*] (SAG) .... CtlHme
Continental Horsepower (IAA) .... CONTHP
Continental Illinois National Bank and Trust Co., Research and Information Services, Chicago, IL [*Library symbol*] [*Library of Congress*] (LCLS) .... ICConB
Continental Info Sys [*NASDAQ symbol*] (TTSB) .... CISC
Continental Information Systems Corp. [*NASDAQ symbol*] (SAG) .... CISC
Continental Information Systems Corp. [*Associated Press*] (SAG) .... CntlInfo
Continental Intelligence Data Processing System (MCD) .... CIDPS
Continental Land Masses Air Traffic Control [*NASA*] (MCD) .... COLM/ATC
Continental Limits, United States .... CLUS
Continental Limits, United States of America [*Navy*] .... CLUSA
Continental Lithospheric Mantle [*Geology*] .... CLM
Continental Margin Sedimentology [*Oceanography*] (MSC) .... COMSED
Continental Margins Program [*Australia*] .... CMP
Continental Marines .... CM
Continental Mark II Owner's Association (EA) .... CMOA
Continental Materials Corp. [*Associated Press*] (SAG) .... ContMtl
Continental Materials Corp. [*AMEX symbol*] (SPSG) .... CUO
Continental Medical Systems [*NYSE symbol*] (SPSG) .... CNM
Continental Merchant Bank [*Nigeria*] .... CMB
Continental [*United States*] **Meteorological Teletype System** [*Navy*] .... COMET
Continental Micronesia, Inc. [*Guam*] [*ICAO designator*] (FAAC) .... CMI
Continental Mortgage & Equity Trust [*NASDAQ symbol*] (NQ) .... CMET
Continental Mortgage & Equity Trust [*Associated Press*] (SAG) .... CtlMtg
Continental Motosport Club (EA) .... CMC
Continental National America [*Insurance group*] .... CNA
Continental NORAD Region [*Aviation*] (FAAC) .... CONR
Continental Offshore Stratigraphic Test [*Offshore oil technology*] .... COST
Continental Oil, Atlantic Refining, Tidewater Oil, and Cities Service [*Group of companies joined together for mutual drilling ventures*] .... CATC
Continental Oil Co. [*ICAO designator*] (FAAC) .... CON
Continental Oil Co. .... CONOCO
Continental Oil Co., R and D Technical Information Service, Ponca City, OK [*Library symbol Library of Congress*] (LCLS) .... OkPoC
Continental Operations Range (MCD) .... COR
Continental Organization of Distributor Enterprises, Inc. .... CODE
Continental Pacific [*Vancouver Stock Exchange symbol*] .... CXF
Continental Pharma [*Belgium*] [*Research code symbol*] .... CP
Continental Pharma Cryosan, Inc. [*Toronto Stock Exchange symbol*] .... CPM
Continental Plan [*Hotel rate*] .... CP
Continental Polar Air Mass .... CP
Continental Polar Air Mass (MSA) .... CPAM
Continental Polar Cold Air Mass (BARN) .... cPk
Continental Quilting Congress (EA) .... CQC
Continental Scientific Drilling Committee [*National Academy of Science*] .... CSDC
Continental Scientific Drilling Program [*National Science Foundation, USGS, and Department of Energy*] .... CSDP
Continental Sediment [*Geology*] .... CS
Continental Service Corps (EA) .... CSC
Continental Shelf .... CONSHELF
Continental Shelf Crawler .... CSC
Continental Shelf Discus [*Buoy system*] (MSC) .... CSD
Continental Shelf Mining .... CSM
Continental Shelf Sedimentology [*Oceanography*] (MSC) .... CONSED
Continental Shelf Submersible [*Undersea exploration vehicle*] (MCD) .... CONSUB
Continental Shelf Wave .... CSW
Continental Silver [*Vancouver Stock Exchange symbol*] .... CVR
Continental Tire System .... CTS
Continental Transportation Association [*Defunct*] (EA) .... CTA
Continental Tropical Air [*Meteorology*] (DA) .... CT
Continental Tropical Air Mass (MSA) .... CTAM
Continental Tyre Ltd. [*Vancouver Stock Exchange symbol*] .... CYH
Continental, Union, Shell, and Superior [*In CUSS I, ocean drilling barge named after oil companies that financed its development*] .... CUSS
Continental United States .... CONUS
Continental U.S. [*Television news company*] [*St. Paul, MN*] (WDMC) .... Conus
Continental United States .... CUS
Continental United States and the Military District of Washington [*Refers to the numbered armies in that area*] (AABC) .... CONUSAMDW
Continental United States Intelligence [*Domestic intelligence project*] [*Army*] .... CONUS INTEL
Continental United States Operations [*Army*] .... CONOPS
Continental United States Over-the-Horizon [*RADAR system*] .... CONUS OTH

Continental United States Over-the-Horizon-Backscatter [*RADAR system*] ... CONUS OTH-B
Continental Wage Schedule [*Military*] (AABC) ... CWS
[*Tropical*] **Continental Warm Air Mass** (BARN) ... cTw
Continental Waste Industries [*NASDAQ symbol*] (SAG) ... CONT
Continental Waste Industries [*Associated Press*] (SAG) ... ContW
Continental Waste Industries [*Associated Press*] (SAG) ... ContWst
Continental-Oceanic [*Crust*] **Boundary** [*Geology*] ... COB
Continent-Ocean Boundary [*Geology*] ... COB
Contingencies of the Army ... CA
Contingency (AABC) ... CNTGCY
Contingency [*Type classification*] (MCD) ... CON
Contingency (MCD) ... CONT
Contingency (KSC) ... CONTG
Contingency Abort [*NASA*] (NASA) ... CA
Contingency Action/Limited Objective Warfare (DOMA) ... CALOW
Contingency Airfield Logistic System (DWSG) ... CALS
Contingency Amphibious Plan [*NATO*] (NATG) ... CAP
Contingency Analysis Model (KSC) ... CAM
Contingency and Confidential Intelligence (CINC) ... C & CI
Contingency and Training [*Army*] (AABC) ... C & T
Contingency Contracting Officers [*Military*] (RDA) ... CCO
Contingency Extravehicular Transfer [*NASA*] (KSC) ... CEVT
Contingency Financing Mechanism [*International Monetary Fund*] ... CFM
Contingency for Movement [*Army*] ... CFM
Contingency Force Pool ... CFP
Contingency Intermediate-Level Maintenance Center (DOMA) ... CILMC
Contingency Landing Area [*NASA*] ... CLA
Contingency Landing Site [*NASA*] (NASA) ... CLS
Contingency Landing Support Officer (MCD) ... CLSO
Contingency Lines of Communication, Europe [*Military*] (AABC) ... CLOCE
Contingency MAGTF [*Marine Air Ground Task Force*] (DOMA) ... CMAGTF
Contingency Maintenance Allocation Chart (MCD) ... CMAC
Contingency of Operations Planning (MCD) ... COOP
Contingency Operation Mobility Planning and Execution System [*Military*] ... COMPES
Contingency Operational Contracting Support Program [*Air Force*] (AAGC) ... COCSP
Contingency Operations Plan (MCD) ... COP
Contingency Operations Plans Report (NVT) ... COPS
Contingency Operations Selection Techniques (MCD) ... COST
Contingency Operations Space [*Army*] ... COPS
Contingency Orbit Insertion [*NASA*] (KSC) ... COI
Contingency Plan [*Military*] ... CONPLAN
Contingency Planning (MCD) ... CP
Contingency Planning Aid (NASA) ... CPA
Contingency Planning Facilities Lists (CINC) ... CPFL
Contingency Planning Guidance (DOMA) ... CPG
Contingency Planning Support Capability (AFM) ... CPSC
Contingency Planning System (MHDB) ... CPS
Contingency Reference Book (MCD) ... CRB
Contingency Relief Force [*Military*] ... CRF
Contingency Remoting System [*Military*] (RDA) ... CRS
Contingency Rerouting of Communications [*NATO*] (NATG) ... CRDCS
Contingency Reserve (MCD) ... CR
Contingency Response Program [*DoD*] ... CORE
Contingency Retention Stock [*Military*] (AFIT) ... CRS
Contingency Sample [*NASA*] (KSC) ... CS
Contingency Special Airlift Mission [*Air Force*] ... C-SAM
Contingency Support Center (MCD) ... CSC
Contingency Support Force [*Air Force*] (DOMA) ... CSF
Contingency Support Package (MCD) ... CSP
Contingency Support Staff (MCD) ... CSS
Contingency Support Stocks [*Military*] (AABC) ... CONSSTOCS
Contingency Support Stocks [*Military*] (NVT) ... CONSTOCS
Contingency TAC Automated Planning System (MCD) ... CTAPS
Contingency Transfer System [*Aerospace*] ... CTS
Contingency Transportation Requirements System (MCD) ... CONTREQS
Contingent ... COT
Contingent Aftereffects [*Visual*] ... CAE
Contingent Employee Liability Insurance ... CELI
Contingent Liability Ledger [*DoD*] ... CLL
Contingent Negative Variation [*Electrocortical measurement*] ... CNV
Contingent Valuation [*Environmental medicine*] ... CV
Contingent Value Method [*Pisciculture*] ... CVM
Contingent Value Right [*Finance*] ... CVR
Continuance ... CONTCE
Continuance [*Legal term*] (DLA) ... CONTIN
Continuation ... CONTN
Continuation Clause ... CC
Continuation Incentive Pay [*Proposed*] [*Army*] ... COIN
Continuation of Message (ACRL) ... COM
Continuation of Pay (DNAB) ... COP
Continuation of Rolle's Reports [*2 Rolle*] [*A publication*] (DLA) ... Con
Continuation-in-Part [*Patent application*] ... CIP
Continucare [*AMEX symbol*] (SAG) ... CNU
Continucare [*Associated Press*] (SAG) ... Continucre
Continue[*d*] (WDMC) ... cont
Continue [*or Continuing*] (AFM) ... CONT
Continue (DAVI) ... contin
Continue Calling Until (FAAC) ... CONCA
Continue Present Duty [*Military*] ... CONPRESDU
Continue Present Management [*Medicine*] (DAVI) ... CPM
Continue Same [*Treatment*] [*Medicine*] (DAVI) ... CS
Continue to Hold [*Aviation*] (FAAC) ... CONTH
Continue Treatment [*Medicine*] ... CT
Continue Treatment at Naval Hospital or Medical Facility Indicated ... CONTREAT
Continue-Any [*Mode*] [*Computer science*] (IBMDP) ... CA
Continued ... CON
Continued (ODBW) ... cont
Continued (WDMC) ... contd
Continued ... CONTD
Continued (ROG) ... CONTIND
Continued Automated Multi-Baseline (MCD) ... CAMB
Continued Development ... CD
Continued Fraction Expansion (IAA) ... CFE
Continued Health Care Benefit Program [*DoD*] ... CHCBP
Continued Lymphocyte Culture [*Immunology*] ... CLC
Continued on Active Duty (AABC) ... COAD
Continued Skin Peeling Syndrome [*Dermatology*] ... CSPS
Continuentur [*Continue*] [*Pharmacy*] (ROG) ... CONT
Continuentur Remedia [*Continue the Medicines*] [*Pharmacy*] ... CONT REM
Continue-Specific [*Mode*] [*Computer science*] (IBMDP) ... CS
Continuetur [*Let It Be Continued*] [*Pharmacy*] ... CONTIN
Continuetur Remedium [*Let the Medicine Be Continued*] [*Pharmacy*] (ROG) ... CONTIN REM
Continuing ... CONTNG
Continuing Action Maintenance Instruction ... CAMI
Continuing Airworthiness Panel [*ICAO*] (DA) ... CAP
Continuing Balance System [*Army*] (MCD) ... CBS
Continuing Balance System - Expanded [*Army*] (AABC) ... CBS-X
Continuing Calibration ... CC
Continuing Calibration Blank [*Laboratory analysis*] ... CCB
Continuing Calibration Verification [*Laboratory analysis*] ... CCV
Continuing Care [*Medicine*] (DAVI) ... CC
Continuing Care Accreditation Commission [*American Association of Homes for Aging*] ... CCAC
Continuing Committee of Deputy Ministers [*Canada*] ... CCDM
Continuing Committee of the National Women's Conference [*Later, NW*] (EA) ... CCNWC
Continuing Committee on Muslim-Christian Cooperation (EA) ... CCMCC
Continuing Community Care [*Psychology*] (DAVI) ... CCC
Continuing Criminal Enterprise ... CCE
Continuing Dental Education ... CDE
Continuing Disability Investigation [*Social Security Administration*] (OICC) ... CDI
Continuing Education ... CE
Continuing Education Achievement Unit (IEEE) ... CEAU
Continuing Education and Training (ACII) ... CET
Continuing Education Approval and Recognition Program (DMAA) ... CEARP
Continuing Education Center [*Veterans Administration*] (GFGA) ... CEC
Continuing Education Council [*Later, CNCE*] (EA) ... CEC
Continuing Education Credit (DAVI) ... CEC
Continuing Education Delivery Systems ... CEDS
Continuing Education Field Unit [*Veterans Administration*] (GFGA) ... CEFU
Continuing Education for Laboratory Technicians [*Union Carbide Co.*] ... CELT
Continuing Education for Senior Citizens ... CESC
Continuing Education for Young Women ... CEYW
Continuing Education in Mental Retardation Program [*American Associaton on Mental Deficiency*] (EDAC) ... CEMR
Continuing Education Learning Laboratory (EA) ... CELL
Continuing Education Program [*State University of New York at Albany*] [*Research center*] ... CEP
Continuing Education Recognition Program [*For nurses*] ... CERP
Continuing Education Re-Education Program (DAVI) ... CERP
Continuing Education Service for State and Local Government Officials ... CESSLGO
Continuing Education Standing Committee (AIE) ... CESC
Continuing Education Unit [*American Management Association*] ... CEU
Continuing Health Education (MCD) ... CHE
Continuing Intelligence Requirement (MCD) ... CIR
Continuing Legal Education ... CLE
Continuing Legal Education of the Bar, University of California Extension (DLA) ... CCEB
Continuing Legal Education, University of Kentucky College of Law (DLA) ... KCLE
Continuing Legal Education, University of Montana (DLA) ... CLEM
Continuing Legal Education, University of Oklahoma Law Center (DLA) ... OCLE
Continuing Library Education Network and Exchange [*American Library Association Information service or system*] (EA) ... CLENE
Continuing Library Education Network and Exchange Round Table (EA) ... CLENERT
Continuing Library Education Planning and Advisory Project ... COLEPAC
Continuing Medical Education ... CME
Continuing Numerical Data Projects ... CNDP
Continuing Professional Development (PDAA) ... CPD
Continuing Professional Education ... CPE
Continuing Property Records ... CPR
Continuing Property Records ... CPR
Continuing Resolution ... CR
Continuing Resolution Authority [*Military*] (AFM) ... CRA
Continuing Revolution ... CR
Continuing Smoker (DAVI) ... CS
Continuing Survey of Food Intakes by Individuals [*Department of Agriculture*] (GFGA) ... CSFII
Continuing-Care Retirement Communities ... CCRC
Continuing-Care Retirement Community ... CCRC
Continuity [*Telecommunications*] (TEL) ... COT
Continuity Accept Limit ... CAL
Continuity and Logic Unit ... CONALOG
Continuity Check ... CCHK

Continuity Message [*Telecommunications*] (TEL) .... CM
Continuity of Government .... COG
Continuity of Operations (MCD) .... CONOPS
Continuity of Operations, Alaskan Air Command .... COPAAC
Continuity of Operations Plan [*Army*] .... COOP
Continuity of Operations Plan [*Navy*] .... COOPLAN
Continuity of Operations Plan [*Military*] .... COP
Continuity of Operations Plan, Department of the Air Force (AFM) .... COPDAF
Continuity of Operations Plan of the Joint Chiefs of Staff .... COOP-JCS
Continuity of Service Set (MCD) .... CSS
Continuity Signal [*Telecommunications*] (NITA) .... COT
Continuity Test Current .... CTC
Continuity Tone Detector [*Telecommunications*] (TEL) .... CTD
Continuity Transceiver [*Telecommunications*] (TEL) .... CT
Continuity Transceiver Module [*Telecommunications*] (TEL) .... CTM
Continuo [*Thorough Bass*] [*Music*] .... CONT
Continuous [*Botany*] C
Continuous [*Aviation code*] .... CNS
Continuous (GAVI) .... CON
Continuous [*or Continuously*] (DAVI) .... CONT
Continuous .... CONTNS
Continuous Acceleration Device .... CAD
Continuous Accumulation of Coriolis Acceleration [*Bioscience*] .... CACA
Continuous Acquisition and Life-Cycle Support [*Military*] (RDA) .... CALS
Continuous Acquisition and Life-Cycle Support (AAGC) .... CALS
Continuous Action [*Acronym is brand of decongestant capsule*] .... CONTAC
Continuous Affinity Recycle Extraction [*Chemical engineering*] .... CARE
Continuous Aim Correction [*Military*] (CAAL) .... CAC
Continuous Air Circulation (IIA) .... CAC
Continuous Air Monitor [*Nuclear energy*] (NRCH) .... CAM
Continuous Air Monitoring Program [*or Project*] [*Environmental Protection Agency*] .... CAMP
Continuous Air Patrol [*Proposed defense for missiles*] [*Military*] .... CAP
Continuous Aircraft Reliability Evaluation (PDAA) .... CARE
Continuous Airworthiness Visit .... CAV
Continuous Alarm Reporting Service [*Telecommunications*] (TEL) .... CARS
Continuous Ambulatory Peritoneal Dialysis [*Medicine*] .... CAPD
Continuous Annealing and Processing Line [*Steel manufacture*] .... CAPL
Continuous Annealing Line (PDAA) .... CAL
Continuous Annular Chromatograph .... CAC
Continuous Arteriovenous Hemodialysis [*Medicine*] (DMAA) .... CAVHD
Continuous Arteriovenous Hemofiltration [*Medicine*] .... CAVH
Continuous Arteriovenous Ultrafiltration [*Medicine*] (DMAA) .... CAVU
Continuous Atrial Fibrillation [*or Flutter*] [*Cardiology*] (DAVI) .... CAF
Continuous Audit Program [*Finance*] [*Computer science*] (IEEE) .... CAP
Continuous Automated Placement Survey [*Department of Labor*] .... CAPS
Continuous Automated Single Base Line [*Automated control system*] .... CASBL
Continuous Automatic Line Monitoring System .... CALMS
Continuous Automatic Multi-Base Propellant Line (MCD) .... CAMBL
Continuous Beam [*Camutek*] [*Software package*] (NCC) .... CONTB
Continuous Belt Xanthator [*Rayon technology*] .... CBX
Continuous Bladder Irrigation [*Urology*] .... CBI
Continuous Blowdown (AAG) .... CB
Continuous Boat Track [*Navy*] (CAAL) .... CBT
Continuous Boresight Correction (MCD) .... CBC
Continuous Breakdown (WDAA) .... CB
Continuous Business Forms Manufacturers (DGA) .... CBFM
Continuous Butt-Weld [*Metal industry*] .... CBW
Continuous Care Manikin [*Medical training*] [*Navy*] .... CCM
Continuous Casting [*Metalworking*] CC
Continuous Casting Machine [*Metalworking*] .... CCM
Continuous Catalyst Regeneration [*Chemical engineering*] .... CCR
Continuous Coding Transformation (MCD) .... CCT
Continuous Color Sequence [*Telecommunications*] .... CCS
Continuous Commercial Service [*Equipment specifications*] .... CCS
Continuous Complete Remission [*Oncology*] (DAVI) .... CCR
Continuous Composite Servo [*Optical disc recording format*] (BYTE) .... CCS
Continuous Composite Write (CDE) .... CCW
Continuous Comprehensive Evaluation [*Army*] (RDA) .... C²E
Continuous Contractor Field Service .... CCFS
Continuous Cooling Transformation .... CCT
Continuous Correlation Processing .... CCP
Continuous Countercurrent Ion-Exchange [*Chemistry*] CCIX
Continuous Current CC
Continuous Current-Monitoring Device .... CCMD
Continuous Cyclic Peritoneal Dialysis [*Medicine*] .... CCPD
Continuous Deformation Monitoring System [*US Army Engineer Topographic Laboratories*] (RDA) .... CDMS
Continuous Deionization .... CDI
Continuous Disability History Sample [*Social Security Administration*] (GFGA) .... CDHS
Continuous Distending Airway Pressure [*Medicine*] (DMAA) .... CDAP
Continuous Distending Pressure [*Medicine*] (DAVI) .... CDP
Continuous Dress Creep Feed (PDAA) .... CDCE
Continuous Duty (IAA) .... CD
Continuous Duty (MSA) .... CDTY
Continuous Duty Target .... CDT
Continuous Duty Target Source .... CDTS
Continuous Dynamical System .... CDS
Continuous Dynode Electron Multiplier [*Instrumentation*] .... CDEM
Continuous Edge Graphics [*Edson Laboratories*] [*Computer science*] .... CEG
Continuous Edge Graphics-Digital Signal Processor [*Edson Laboratories*] [*Computer science*] (PCM) .... CEG-DSP
Continuous Election Beam [*Accelerator facility*] .... CEB
Continuous Electrical Stimulation .... CES

Continuous Electrocardiogram in Ambulatory Patients [*Medicine*] .... CELIA
Continuous Electrocardiographic Monitoring [*Medicine*] (CPH) .... CEM
Continuous Electron Beam Accelerator Facility [*Physics*] .... CEBAF
Continuous Electro-Slag Melting (PDAA) .... CESM
Continuous Emission Monitoring [*Environmental Protection Agency*] (GFGA) .... CEM
Continuous Emission Rate Monitoring System [*Environmental science*].... CERMS
Continuous Emissions Monitor [*Environmental Protection Agency*] .... CEM
Continuous Emissions Monitoring System .... CEMS
Continuous Estimation Program .... CEP
Continuous Estrus [*Endocrinology*] .... CE
Continuous Evaluation [*DoD*] .... CE
Continuous Explosion-Puffing System [*Food technology*] .... CEPS
Continuous Extravascular Infusion [*Medicine*] .... CEI
Continuous Fiber Reinforcing Mat [*Fiberglass*] .... CFRM
Continuous Filament Mat .... CFM
Continuous Flow [*Chemical engineering*] [*Nuclear energy*] (NRCH) .... CF
Continuous Flow Analysis .... CFA
Continuous Flow Diffusion (SSD) .... CFD
Continuous Flow Electrophoresis [*Physical chemistry*] .... CFE
Continuous Flow Electrophoresis [*Physical chemistry*] (SSD) .... CFEP
Continuous Flow Electrophoresis in Space [*Physical chemistry*] .... CFES
Continuous Flow Electrophoresis System [*Chemical separation*] .... CFES
Continuous Flow Hypersonic Tunnel [*NASA*] .... CFHT
Continuous Flow Intersection [*Automated traffic management*] .... CFI
Continuous Flow Isoelectric Focusing [*Materials processing*] .... CFIF
Continuous Flow Manufacturing [*Automotive engineering*] .... CFM
Continuous Flow Ventilation [*Medicine*] (DMAA) .... CFV
Continuous Forest Inventory (DICI) .... CFI
Continuous Fourier Transport .... CFT
Continuous Fuel Injection .... CFI
Continuous Functional Monitoring .... CFM
Continuous Gas LASER .... CGL
Continuous Gradient Ray Tracing System .... CONGRATS
Continuous Grinding Gauge .... CGG
Continuous Heating Transformation [*Chemical engineering*] .... CHT
Continuous Hepatic Artery Infusion [*Medicine*] (DAVI) .... CHAI
Continuous High-Amplitude EEG [*Electroencephalogram*] **Rhythmical Synchronous Slowing** [*Medicine*] (DMAA) .... CHERSS
Continuous Hormones as Replacement Therapy [*Medicine*] .... CHART
Continuous Ideally Stirred Tank Reactor [*Chemical engineering*] .... CISTR
Continuous Image Microfilm (IEEE) .... CIM
Continuous Imprint Marking [*of medical linen*] (MCD) .... CIM
Continuous Improvement Process .... CIP
Continuous Inflating Pressure .... CIP
Continuous In-Flight Performance Recorder [*Aviation*] (PDAA) .... CIPR
Continuous Infrared (MCD) .... CIR
Continuous Injection [*Automotive engineering*] CI
Continuous Injection System [*Automotive engineering*] .... CIS
Continuous Insulin Delivery System [*Endocrinology and pharmacology*] (DAVI) .... CIDS
Continuous Interleaved Sampling .... CIS
Continuous Interlock (MCD) CI
Continuous Intramuscular Insulin Infusion .... CIMII
Continuous Intrathecal Baclofen Infusion [*Medicine*] .... CIBI
Continuous Intravenous Infusion of Propranolol [*Medicine*] .... CIP
Continuous Isoelectric Focusing [*Materials processing*] .... CIEF
Continuous LASER Argon-Age Microprobe .... CLAAMP
Continuous Level of Production Plan .... CLOPP
Continuous Lightweight Exterior CLX
Continuous Line Bucket [*Deep mining system*] .... CLB
Continuous Line Plotter .... CLP
Continuous Liner [*Fitting for a propeller shaft*] CL
Continuous Log of Ongoing Events (PDAA) .... CLOOGE
Continuous Longitudinal Manpower Survey [*Department of Labor*] .... CLMS
Continuous Loop Tubular Reactor [*Chemical engineering*] .... CLTR
Continuous Maximum Rating [*of equipment*] (DEN) .... CMR
Continuous Measurement Survey [*US Census Bureau*] .... CMS
Continuous Mechanical Ventilation [*Medicine*] (DAVI) .... CMV
Continuous Melting, Casting and Rolling (MHDB) .... CMCR
Continuous Membrane Column [*Chemical engineering*] .... CMC
Continuous Monitor .... CM
Continuous Motion Assembly Machine .... COMAM
Continuous Motor Unit Activity [*Medicine*] (DMAA) .... CMUA
Continuous Multibay Frames [*Jacys Computing Services*] [*Software package*] (NCC) .... CMF
Continuous Multiple Access Collator [*Proposed by Mortimer Taube, 1957*] [*Computer science*] .... COMAC
Continuous Murmur [*Cardiology*] (DAVI) .... CM
Continuous National Survey [*National Opinion Research Center*] .... CNS
Continuous Negative Pressure [*Medicine*] .... CNP
Continuous Negative Pressure Breathing [*Physiology*] .... CNPB
Continuous Negative Pressure Ventilation [*Medicine*] (DMAA) .... CNPV
Continuous Net Settlement .... CNS
Continuous Noise .... CN
Continuous Observation [*Nursing order*] (CPH) .... CO
Continuous Officer Professional Education (DNAB) .... COPE
Continuous Oil Analysis Treatment [*Automotive maintenance*] .... COAT
Continuous Online Trading System [*London Stock Exchange*] (NITA) .... COLT
Continuous Opacity Monitor [*Environmental Protection Agency*] (GFGA) .... COM
Continuous Operation during Hours Shown [*Broadcasting*] C
Continuous Operation Production Allocation and Control [*Computer science*] .... COPAC
Continuous Operation Program [*Computer science*] (MDG) .... COP
Continuous Orbital Guidance System .... COGS

Continuous Page Facsimile Recorder .... CPFR
Continuous Particle Electrophoresis .... CPE
Continuous Particle Electrophoresis Device (OA) .... CPED
Continuous Particle Monitor [*Environmental Protection Agency*] (GFGA) .... CPM
Continuous Passive Motion [*Medicine*] .... CPM
Continuous Path [*Robotics*] .... CP
Continuous Patrol Aircraft .... CPA
Continuous Performance Measure (MCD) .... CPM
Continuous Performance Test [*Psychology*] .... CPT
Continuous Phase (OA) .... CP
Continuous Phase Frequency Shift Keying .... CPFSK
Continuous Phase Shift Modulation [*Army*] .... CPSM
Continuous Plankton Recorder [*Oceanography*] (MSC) .... CPR
Continuous Plug Flow Reactor [*Chemical engineering*] .... CPFR
Continuous Positive Airway Pressure [*Resuscitation system*] [*Medicine*] .... CPAP
Continuous Positive Pressure Breathing [*Physiology*] .... CPPB
Continuous Positive Pressure Ventilation [*Medicine*] .... CPPV
Continuous Primary Test [*Psychiatry*] (DAVI) .... CPT
Continuous Process Control [*Design Software Ltd.*] [*Software package*] (NCC) .... CPC
Continuous Process Improvement [*Chemical engineering*] .... CPI
Continuous Processing Machine (PDAA) .... CPM
Continuous Production Operation Sheet .... CPOS
Continuous Progress Indicator [*Telecommunications*] (TEL) .... CPR
Continuous Quality Improvement [*Quality control*] .... CQI
Continuous Random Analog to Frequency Transmission .... CRAFT
Continuous Rating Permitting Over-Load .... CRPO
Continuous Ream Discharge [*Papermaking*] .... CRD
Continuous Receiver On [*Electronic device*] .... CRO
Continuous Record of Personnel (ADA) .... CRP
Continuous Reflectometry for Radius Versus Time Experiment [*Nuclear testing verification*] .... CORRTEX
Continuous Reinforcement [*Psychometrics*] .... CRF
Continuous, Remote, Unobstructive Monitoring of Biobehavioral Systems .... CRUMBS
Continuous Ring Tone [*Telecommunications*] (TEL) .... CRT
Continuous Rod (NG) .... CR
Continuous Rod Warhead (MCD) .... CRW
Continuous Sampler Monitor [*Radioactivity*] .... CSM
Continuous Sampling Plan (IEEE) .... CSP
Continuous Sampling Run (DNAB) .... CSR
Continuous Scan [*Computer science*] (IAA) .... CS
Continuous Seam Diffusion Bonding .... CSDB
Continuous Segregated Stirred Tank Reactor [*Chemical engineering*] .... CSSTR
Continuous Seismic Profiling (NUCP) .... CSP
Continuous Seismic Wave [*Radio transmission*] (IAA) .... CSW
Continuous Self Mode Locking [*Electronics*] (OA) .... CSML
Continuous Service [*British military*] (DMA) .... CS
Continuous Service Certificate [*Navy*] .... CSC
Continuous Service Rating [*Engine technology*] .... CSR
Continuous Sheet Memory [*Computer science*] (BUR) .... CSM
Continuous Sheet Music (MCD) .... CSM
Continuous Slope Delta Modulation [*Telecommunications*] .... CSDM
Continuous Slow Ultrafiltration [*Medicine*] (DMAA) .... CSUF
Continuous Slowing Down Models [*Physics*] .... CSM
Continuous Space-Discrete Time (PDAA) .... CSDT
Continuous Speech Recognizer [*ITT Corp.*] (NITA) .... CSR
Continuous Stationery [*Commercial firm*] [*British*] (DGA) .... CONT/S
Continuous Stationery [*Commercial firm British*] .... CS
Continuous Stirred Tank Biological Reactor [*Chemical engineering*] .... CSTBR
Continuous Stirred Tank Fermentator (OA) .... CSTF
Continuous Stirred Tank Membrane Reactor [*Chemical engineering*] .... CSTMR
Continuous Stirred Tank Reactor [*Chemical engineering*] .... CSTR
Continuous Stirred Tank Reactor with an Ultrafiltration Membrane [*Chemical en gineering*] .... CSTR/UF
Continuous Stratification Profiler .... CSP
Continuous Strip Film (DNAB) .... CS
Continuous Stripping [*Surgery*] (DAVI) .... CS
Continuous Subcarrier Barrage (MCD) .... CSB
Continuous Subcutaneous Insulin Infusion [*Medicine*] .... CSII
Continuous Subcutaneous Insulin Infusion Pump [*Medicine*] (DMAA) .... CSIIP
Continuous Submarine Duty Incentive Pay (DNAB) .... CONSUB
Continuous Surveillance Service (MCD) .... CSS
Continuous Survey (DS) .... CS
Continuous Survey of Machinery .... CSM
Continuous Symmetry Measure [*Physical chemistry*] .... CSM
Continuous System Modeling Program [*Computer science*] .... CSMP
Continuous Systems Simulation Language [*Computer science*] .... CSSL
Continuous Thymus-Cell [*Cell line*] .... CTC
Continuous Tone [*Color printing*] .... CT
Continuous Tone-Coded Squelch System [*Telecommunications*] (PDAA) .... CTCSS
Continuous Tubular Reactor [*Chemical engineering*] .... CTR
Continuous until Cancelled [*Insurance*] .... CUC
Continuous Update Memory Display .... CUMD
Continuous Variable Damper [*Automotive suspensions*] .... CVD
Continuous Velocity Joint [*Automotive engineering*] .... CVJ
Continuous Venous Infusion [*Chemotherapy*] (DAVI) CVI
Continuous Vent System (KSC) .... CVS
Continuous Vertical Retort [*Metallurgy*] [*Fuel technology*] .... CVR
Continuous Video Recorder (IAA) .... CVR
Continuous Vulcanization CV
Continuous Wage and Benefit History [*Unemployment insurance*] .... CWBH
Continuous Water Movement (SAA) .... CWM
Continuous Wave [*A form of radio transmission*] .... CW
Continuous Wave Acquisition and Track (MCD) .... CWAT
Continuous Wave Acquisition RADAR [*Military*] .... CWAR
Continuous Wave Detector (IAA) .... CWD
Continuous Wave Deuterium Fluoride .... CWDF
Continuous Wave Fixed Frequency Electromechanical Modulation (IAA) .... CWFFEMM
Continuous Wave Frequency-Modulated (MSA) .... CWFM
Continuous Wave Gas .... CWG
Continuous Wave Illuminator (NG) .... CWI
Continuous Wave Illuminator RADAR [*Military*] .... CWIR
Continuous Wave Indicator (DWSG) .... CWI
Continuous Wave Intermediate Frequency .... CWIF
Continuous Wave Jammer (MCD) .... CWJ
Continuous Wave LASER .... CWL
Continuous Wave Nuclear Magnetic Resonance .... CWNMR
Continuous Wave Oscillator .... CWO
Continuous Wave Signal Generator (IAA) .... CWSIGGEN
Continuous Wave Space Duplexed .... CWSD
Continuous Wave Surface-to-Air Missile (MCD) .... CWSAM
Continuous Wave Tactical Detection Console (NATG) .... CWTDC
Continuous Wave Target Detection (NATG) .... CWTD
Continuous Wave Transmitter (CAAL) .... CWX
Continuous Wave Traveling Wave Tube (MCD) .... CWTWT
Continuous Wave Tunable (IAA) .... CWT
Continuous Wave Video .... CWV
Continuous Weather Watch (MCD) .... CWW
Continuous Window .... CONTW
Continuous Work History Sample [*Department of Labor*] .... CWHS
Continuous Working Level Monitor (GNE) .... CWLM
Continuous-Access Guided Communication [*Computer science*] (PDAA) .... CAGC
Continuous-Action [*Pharmacy*] .... CA
Continuous-Beam Analysis [*Jacys Computing Services*] [*Software package*] (NCC) .... CBA
Continuous-Descent Approach (PDAA) .... CDA
Continuous-Filament Ceramic Composite [*Materials science*] .... CFCC
Continuous-Flow Centrifuging [*Clinical chemistry*] .... CFC
Continuous-Flow Fast Atom Bombardment [*Spectroscopy*] .... CF-FAB
Continuous-Flow Stirred Tank Reactor [*Chemical engineering*] .... CFSTR
Continuous-Flow Tank Reactor [*Chemical engineering*] .... CTR
Continuous-Flow Tub .... CT
Continuous-Grain Silicon .... CGS
Continuously Advertised Nutritionally Deficient Yummies [*In cookbook title, "The Taming of the CANDY Monster"*] .... CANDY
Continuously Charge-Coupled Random Access Memory [*Computer science*] (PDAA) C3RAM
Continuously Charge-Coupled Random Access Memory [*Computer science*] (IAA) .... CCCRAM
Continuously Computed Impact Point [*Type of bombing sighting system*] [*Air Force*] .... CCIP
Continuously Computed Release Point (MCD) .... CCRP
Continuously Contemporary Accounting (ADA) .... CCA
Continuously Contemporary Accounting (ADA) .... COCOA
Continuously Displayed Impact Point (MCD) .... CDIP
Continuously Expecting Transfer Interface [*IBM Corp.*] .... CETI
Continuously Fed Batch Reactor [*Chemical engineering*] .... CFBR
Continuously Habitable Zone (DICI) .... CHZ
Continuously Offered Long-Term Securities [*Merrill Lynch & Co.*] [*Finance*] .... COLTS
Continuously Reinforced Concrete Pavement (OA) .... CRCP
Continuously Stirred Tank .... CST
Continuously Stirred Tank Reactor [*Chemical engineering*] .... CSTR
Continuously Updated Dynamic Optimizing Systems (IEEE) .... CUDOS
Continuously Variable CV
Continuously Variable Accessory Drive .... CVAD
Continuously Variable Filter [*Spectrometry*] .... CVF
Continuously Variable, for Emergency .... CVE
Continuously Variable Gearbox (PDAA) .... CVG
Continuously Variable Hydromechanical Transmission [*Engineering*] .... CVHT
Continuously Variable Mechanical Advantage Shifter .... CVMAS
Continuously Variable Slope Delta Modulation [*Telecommunications*] .... CVSD
Continuously Variable Slope Delta Modulation [*Telecommunications*] (TEL) .... CVSDM
Continuously Variable Stroke [*Automotive engineering*] .... CVS
Continuously Variable Transaxle [*Automotive engineering*] .... CTX
Continuously Variable Transmission [*Of engines*] .... CVT
Continuously Varying Cell Constant [*Electrochemical instrumentation*] CVCC
Continuously Welded Rail (ADA) .... CWR
Continuously-Advancing Longwall Mining (PDAA) .... CALM
Continuously-Computed Optimum Release (PDAA) .... CCOR
Continuous-Moment Sum Rules (PDAA) .... CMSR
Continuous-Random-Network [*Noncrystalline structure*] .... CRN
Continuous-Reading Meter Relay .... CRMR
Continuous-Release [*Pharmacy*] .... CR
Continuous-Transmission Frequency-Modulated [*SONAR*] .... CTFM
Continuous-Wave Doppler [*Radiology*] (DAVI) .... CWD
Continuous-Wound (DEN) .... CW
Continuum [*A publication*] .... Cont
Continuum Co. [*NYSE symbol*] (SPSG) .... CNU
Continuum Co. [*Associated Press*] (SAG) .... Contin
ContiTire System [*German*] .... CTS
Contl Can [*NYSE symbol*] (TTSB) .... CAN
Contl Choice Care [*NASDAQ symbol*] (TTSB) CCCI
Contl Circuits [*NASDAQ symbol*] (TTSB) .... CCIR
Contl Homes Hldg [*NYSE symbol*] (TTSB) .... CON
Contl Materials [*AMEX symbol*] (TTSB) .... CUO
Contl Mtg & Eg Tr SBI [*NASDAQ symbol*] (TTSB) .... CMETS

Contol Unit Group [*Computer science*] .... CUG
Contolled Substance, Class Two [*Department of Health and Human Services*] (DAVI) CII
Contour (MSA) .... CTR
Contour Analysis by Random Triangulation Algorithm (IAA) .... CARTA
Contour Blind & Shade (Canada) Ltd. [*Toronto Stock Exchange symbol*] ...... CBM
Contour Check Template (MCD) .... CCT
Contour Check Template Set (MCD) .... CCTS
Contour Control System (IAA) .... CCS
Contour Mapping On-Boresight (MCD) .... CMO
Contour Mapping RADAR System (MCD) .... COMAR
Contour Medical [*NASDAQ symbol*] (TTSB) .... CTMI
Contour Medical, Inc. [*Associated Press*] (SAG) .... ContMed
Contour Medical, Inc. [*NASDAQ symbol*] (SAG) .... CTMI
Contour Plotting System .... CPS
Contour RADAR Data (PDAA) .... CONRAD
Contour Rolls (AAG) .... CRRL
Contour Template .... CT
Contour-Clamped Homogeneous Electric Field [*Instrumentation*] .... CHEF
Contoured Femoral Stem [*Total hip prosthesis*] [*Orthopedics*] (DAVI) .... CFS
Contra [*Against*] [*Latin*] C
Contra [*Against*] [*Latin*] .... CON
Contra [*Against*] [*Latin*] .... CONT
Contra [*Against*] [*Latin*] (ROG) .... CONTR
Contra Apionem [*Against Apion*] [*Josephus*] (BJA) .... Ap
Contra Apionem [*Against Apion*] [*Josephus*] (BJA) .... CAp
Contra Bonos Mores [*Contrary to Good Manners*] [*Latin*] .... CONT BON MOR
Contra Bonos Mores [*Contrary to Good Manners*] [*Latin*]
(ROG) .... CONTR BON MOR
Contra Costa College, San Pablo, CA [*Library symbol Library of Congress*]
(LCLS) .... CSpaW
Contra Costa County Library, Pleasant Hill, CA [*Library symbol Library of Congress*] (LCLS) .... CPlhC
Contra Costa Historical Society, Martinez, CA [*Library symbol Library of Congress*] (LCLS) .... CMartCH
Contra Credit [*Banking*] CC
Contra Credit [*Banking*] (MHDW) .... Con Cr
Contra Credit [*Bookkeeping*] (ODBW) .... con cr
Contraband .... CONTBD
Contraband Control [*Navy*] .... CBC
Contraband Control Base [*Navy*] .... CCB
Contrabass [*Music*] .... CB
Contrabass [*Music*] .... CBs
Contraceptive Commodity Management Information System [*United Nations*] (ECON) .... CCMIS
Contraceptive Research and Development Program [*Research center*]
(RCD) .... CONRAD
Contraceptive Technique [*Gynecology*] .... CT
Contraceptive Vaginal Ring [*Gynecology*] .... CVR
Contract .... CNTRCT
Contract (ROG) .... CON
Contract .... CONT
Contract (ODBW) .... cont
Contract (AAGC) .... Cont
Contract (WDMC) .... cont
Contract [*or Contractor*] (AFM) .... CONTR
Contract [*Legal term*] .... CONTT
Contract [*Legal shorthand*] (LWAP) .... K
Contract [*Navy*] .... KT
Contract Acceptance and Purchase Order .... CAPO
Contract Accounting Standard .... CAS
Contract Acquisition Cost Report (MCD) .... CACR
Contract Action Directive (MCD) .... CAD
Contract Adjustment Board (AAGC) .... CAB
Contract Administration [*or Administrator*] [*DoD*] .... CA
Contract Administration Advisory Board [*DoD*] .... CAAB
Contract Administration Automated Records Retrieval System
(MCD) .... CAARRS
Contract Administration Control (DNAB) .... CAC
Contract Administration Data [*DoD*] .... CAD
Contract Administration Data File [*DoD*] (AFM) .... CADF
Contract Administration Function (DNAB) .... CAF
Contract Administration Office [*or Officer*] [*Navy*] .... CAO
Contract Administration Panel [*Military*] .... CAP
Contract Administration Plan .... CAP
Contract Administration Report [*DoD*] .... CAR
Contract Administration Services [*DoD*] .... CAS
Contract Administration Southeast Area (Office of Naval Research) .... CASEAREA(ONR)
Contract Administration Subservice .... CASS
Contract Air (TAG) .... CA
Contract Air Cargo, Inc. [*FAA designator*] (FAAC) .... TSU
Contract Air Mail .... CAM
Contract Amendment Proposal .... CAP
Contract and Material .... C & M
Contract and Purchase Department [*British military*] (DMA) .... CPD
Contract Appeals [*Department of the Interior pre-1954*] (AAGC) .... CA
Contract Appeals Board [*Veterans Administration*] .... CAB
Contract Appeals Decision Reporter [*CCH*] [*A publication*] (AAGC) .... CADR
Contract Appeals Decisions [*CCH*] [*A publication*] (AAGC) .... Contr App Dec
Contract Appeals Decisions (Commerce Clearing House) [*A publication*]
(DLA) .... Cont App Dec (CCH)
Contract Appraisal Report .... CAR
Contract Audit Closing Statements (AAGC) .... CACS
Contract Audit Manual .... CAM

Contract Auditor Coordinator .... CAC
Contract Authorization .... CA
Contract Authorization Request (AAG) .... CAR
Contract Award .... CA
Contract Award Date (AAG) .... CAD
Contract Award Rates Delivery Study [*Army*] .... CARDS
Contract Baseline Report (MCD) .... CBR
Contract Brief .... CB
Contract Budget Baseline (MCD) .... CBB
Contract Budget Estimate (MCD) .... CBE
Contract Bulk Inclusive Tour [*Airline fare*] .... CBIT
Contract Carrier Conference [*Later, ICC*] (EA) CCC
Contract Cases, Federal (AFIT) .... CCF
Contract Cases, Federal [*A publication*] (DLA) .... Cont Cas Fed
Contract Change Authorization (KSC) .... CCA
Contract Change Board (MCD) .... CCB
Contract Change Board Directive (SAA) .... CCBD
Contract Change Directive (DNAB) .... CCD
Contract Change Estimate .... CCE
Contract Change Identification (MCD) CCI
Contract Change Mass Estimate (NASA) .... CCME
Contract Change Negotiation (NASA) .... CCN
Contract Change Notice (MCD) .... CCN
Contract Change Order .... CCO
Contract Change Release .... CCR
Contract Change Request .... CCR
Contract Change System (DNAB) .... CCS
Contract Cleaning and Maintenance Association [*British*] .... CCMA
Contract Clearance Approval Authority (AAGC) .... CCAA
Contract Closeout Extension (AFIT) .... CCE
Contract Completion Date [*Telecommunications*] (TEL) .... CCD
Contract Completion Notices [*DoD*] .... CCN
Contract Completion Studies (MCD) .... CCS
Contract Configuration Process [*Telecommunications*] (TEL) .... CCP
Contract Cost Analysis Organization [*Navy*] (AFIT) .... CCAO
Contract Cost Data Reports (AAGC) .... CCDR
Contract Data Change Notice (MCD) .... CDCN
Contract Data Coordinator (NG) .... CDC
Contract Data List .... CDL
Contract Data Management Officer (MCD) .... CDMO
Contract Data Package (AAGC) .... CDP
Contract Data Requirement (MCD) .... CDR
Contract [*or Contractor*] Data Requirements List .... CDRL
Contract Data Requirements Management System [*Computer science*] ..... CDRMS
Contract Deficiency Listing (AFM) .... CDL
Contract Definition [*Military*] .... CD
Contract Definition .... CONDEF
Contract Definition Concept (DNAB) .... CDC
Contract Definition Phase [*DoD*] .... CDP
Contract Definition Test .... CDT
Contract Demonstration [*Army*] (AFIT) .... CD
Contract Design .... CD
Contract Design Exposition [*Atlanta Market Center*] (TSPED) .... CONEXION
Contract Design Package (MCD) .... CDP
Contract Dispute Resolution Board [*States*] (AAGC) .... CDRB
Contract Disputes Act of 1978 (AAGC) .... CDA
Contract Document Change Notice (MCD) .... CDCN
Contract Documentation Requirements Records [*NASA*] (NASA) .... CDRR
Contract End Item (MCD) .... CEI
Contract End Item Number .... CEIN
Contract Energy Managers [*British*] .... CEM
Contract Engineering and Technical Services Personnel [*Air Force*]
(AFIT) .... CETSP
Contract Engineers (MCD) .... CE
Contract Estimating and Pricing (MCD) .... CEP
Contract Exploration (MCD) .... CE
Contract [*or Contractor*] Field Service (AFM) .... CFS
Contract Field Support .... CFS
Contract Field Technician .... CFT
Contract Finance Committee [*Military*] .... CFC
Contract Financial Reporting Manual .... CFRM
Contract Financial Requirements Estimate [*NASA*] (KSC) .... CFRE
Contract Financial Status (AFM) .... CFS
Contract Financing Office (AAGC) .... CFO
Contract Flooring Association [*British*] (DBA) .... CFA
Contract Formulation .... CF
Contract Formulation .... CONFORM
Contract Fund Status Report [*Army*] (AABC) .... CFSR
Contract Furnished (MCD) .... CF
Contract Furnishings Council (EA) .... CFC
Contract Furnishings Forum (EA) .... CFF
Contract/Grant Number [*Database terminology*] (NITA) .... CN
Contract/Grant Numbers [*Database terminology*] (NITA) .... CG
Contract Heat Treatment Association [*British*] (DBA) .... CHTA
Contract History File [*Military*] (AFIT) .... CHF
Contract Implementation Plan (MCD) .... CIP
Contract Information Processor .... CIP
Contract Information Reporting Groups [*Navy*] (AFIT) .... CIRG
Contract Information Subsystem .... CISS
Contract Information System [*Environmental Protection Agency*] (GFGA) .... CIS
Contract Item Material List .... CIML
Contract Item Number (MCD) .... CIN
Contract Items CI
Contract Items Specification (MCD) .... CIS
Contract Items Specification and Schedule (MCD) .... CISS

Contract Laboratory Program [*Environmental Protection Agency*] .... CLP
Contract Labour Branch [*Admiralty*] [*British*] .... CLB
Contract Law CL
Contract Letter [*DLA*] (AAGC) .... CONTRLTR
Contract Liaison and Master Planning Office [*Military*] .... CLIMPO
Contract Line Item Number [*Army*] (AABC) .... CLIN
Contract Line Item Status (MCD) .... CLIS
Contract Lineage Equivalent [*Formula used by certain publications for
   calculating number of lines of advertising copy*] .... CLE
Contract Logistic Support Plan (MCD) .... CLSP
Contract Machine Accessory (MCD) .... CMA
Contract Maintenance Activity (AFM) .... CMA
Contract Maintenance Data .... CMD
Contract Maintenance Plan .... CMP
Contract Maintenance Team (MCD) .... CMT
Contract Management .... CM
Contract Management [*NCMA*] [*A publication*] (AAGC) ...... Cont Mgmt
Contract Management Assistance Officer [*NASA*] (NASA) .... CMAO
Contract Management District .... CMD
Contract Management Information System (MCD) .... CMIS
Contract Management Network (MCD) .... CMN
Contract Management Office [*Jet Propulsion Laboratory, NASA*] ...... CMO
Contract Management Plan [*Military*] .... CMP
Contract Management Region .... CMR
Contract Management Review [*DoD*] .... CMR
Contract Managers' Association [*A union*] [*British*] .... CMA
Contract Manufacturers Association (EA) .... CMA
Contract Modification .... CM
Contract Monitor of Progress [*Air Force*] (AFIT) .... CMP
Contract Monitoring Point (AFM) .... CMP
Contract Motor Vehicle Service .... CMVS
Contract Note [*Banking*] .... CN
Contract Number [*Computer science*] .... CN
Contract Number Prefix [*Database terminology*] (NITA) .... CP
Contract Nursing Home (DAVI) .... CNH
Contract of Affreightment [*Shipping*] .... COA
Contract on Order (AFIT) .... COO
Contract Operations Data [*DoD*] .... COD
Contract Packager and/or Manufacturer [*Pharmaceutical distribution*] ...... CPM
Contract Parts Material Order .... CPMO
Contract Pilot School .... CPS
Contract [*or Contractor*] Plant Services (NG) .... CPS
Contract Potential Difference (MCD) .... CPD
Contract Price .... C/P
Contract Price of Items Terminated [*Business term*] .... CPIT
Contract Pricing Proposal (MCD) .... CPP
Contract Pricing Report .... CPR
Contract Procurement Request (MUGU) .... CPR
Contract Program Manager (MCD) .... CPM
Contract Progress Control (MCD) .... CPC
Contract Provider Organization [*Information service or system*] (HCT) ...... CPO
Contract Purchasing System Review (DOMA) .... CPSR
Contract Regarding an Interim Supplement to Tanker Liability for Oil
   Pollution [*Oil industry*] .... CRISTAL
Contract Regulation Tribunal [*New South Wales*] [*Australia*] ...... CRT
Contract Repair Initial Support List (AFIT) .... CRISL
Contract Repair Service (MCD) .... CRS
Contract [*or Contractor*] Report .... CR
Contract Required Detection Limits .... CRDL
Contract Requirement .... C/R
Contract Requirement Card .... CRC
Contract Requirements Master Record [*Military*] .... CRMR
Contract Research and Development (SSD) .... CR & D
Contract Research and Development .... CRAD
Contract Review and Selection Criteria [*DoD*] .... CRSC
Contract Revision Number (NASA) .... CRN
Contract Serial Number (AFM) .... CSN
Contract Service Rework Orders (NG) .... CSRO
Contract Services Association (AAGC) .... CSA
Contract Services Association of America (EA) .... CSA
Contract Services Program [*General Services Administration*] (GFGA) ...... CSP
Contract Settlement Appeal Board [*United States*] (DLA) .... CSAB
Contract Settlement Board [*Canada*] (AAGC) .... CSB
Contract Specialist (GFGA) .... CS
Contract Start Date (SSD) .... CSD
Contract Stationers Forum (EA) .... CSF
Contract Status File [*Military*] (AFIT) .... CSF
Contract Status Report .... CSR
Contract Strategy Paper .... CSP
Contract Student Numbers (AIE) .... CSN
Contract Subline Item Number (MCD) .... CSLIN
Contract Supplemental Tooling (NASA) .... CST
Contract Supply Facility .... CSF
Contract Support Detachment .... CSD
Contract Surgeon [*Military*] .... CS
Contract Surgeon [*Military*] (AABC) .... CSN
Contract Target Cost (MCD) .... CTC
Contract Task Change Proposal (AAG) .... CTCP
Contract Task Charge (DNAB) .... CTC
Contract Technical Compliance (MUGU) .... CTC
Contract Technical Compliance Inspection .... CTCI
Contract Technical Data File (AAGC) .... CTDF
Contract Technical Instructor [*Army*] (AABC) .... CTI
Contract Technical Manager .... CTM
Contract Technical Representative (NASA) .... CTR

Contract [*or Contractor*] Technical Services [*Air Force*] .... CTS
Contract Technical Services Personnel (AFM) .... CTSP
Contract Termination and Completion (MCD) .... CTC
Contract Termination Inventory [*DoD*] .... CTI
Contract Termination Manual (AAG) .... CTM
Contract Termination Settlement .... CTS
Contract Trainer End Item (SAA) .... CTEI
Contract War Service .... CWS
Contract Work Breakdown Structure .... CWBS
Contract Work Hours and Safety Standards Act .... CWHSSA
Contract Work Notification (KSC) .... CWN
Contract Work Statement (MCD) .... CWS
Contract Work Study Association (MHDB) .... CWSA
Contracted Advisory and Assistance Services [*DoD*] .... CAAS
Contracted Gaussian-Type Orbital [*Atomic physics*] .... CGTO
Contracted Ground [*Personnel*] (OSRA) .... CG
Contracted Out Money-Purchase Schemes [*Pension plan*] [*British*] ...... COMPS
Contractile Element [*of skeletal muscle*] .... CE
Contractile Force [*Medicine*] .... CF
Contractile Pulse (PDAA) .... CP
Contracting .... CNTRCTNG
Contracting (WDMC) .... cont
Contracting Activity .... CA
Contracting and Acquisition Newsletter [*A publication*] .... CAAN
Contracting Data Management System [*Military*] (MCD) .... CDMS
Contracting Lead Time (AAGC) .... CALT
Contracting Officer [*Also, CONTRO, KO*] .... CO
Contracting Officer [*Also, CO, KO*] (KSC) .... CONTRO
Contracting Officer [*Also, CO, CONTRO*] .... KO
Contracting Officer .... KOR
Contracting Officer's Representative (TEL) .... COR
Contracting Officer's Technical Representative (DOMA) .... COTAR
Contracting Officers' Technical Representative [*Army*] .... COTR
Contracting Officer's Warrant Program (AAGC) .... COWP
Contracting Officer's Warrant System (AAGC) .... COWS
Contracting Operator Fast Fourier Transform Identification (PDAA) ...... COFFTI
Contracting Plasterers' and Lathers' International Association [*Later,
   IAWCC*] (EA) .... CPLIA
Contracting Squadron [*Air Force*] .... CONS
Contraction C
Contraction (WGA) .... CONTR
Contraction (MEDA) .... CONTRX
Contraction [*Obstetrics and orthopedics*] (DAVI) .... CTXN
Contraction [*Medicine*] .... Z
Contraction Augmenting Factor [*Medicine*] .... CAF
Contraction Peak Force [*Medicine*] (DMAA) .... CPF
Contraction Stress Test [*Obstetrics*] .... CST
Contraction Time (MAE) .... CT
Contractions Handbook .... CTH
Contractor .... CONTR
Contractor (ROG) .... CONTROR
Contractor .... COR
Contractor [*Navy*] .... KR
Contractor .... KTR
Contractor Acceptance Test (AABC) .... CAT
Contractor Alert List (AAGC) .... CAL
Contractor All Risk (AIA) .... CAR
Contractor All-Risk Incentive Contract [*Air Force*] .... CARIC
Contractor Attention List .... CAL
Contractor Bonding Tape [*3M Co.*] .... CBT
Contractor Change Evaluation (AAG) .... CCE
Contractor Change Proposal (MCD) .... CCP
Contractor Change Request (NASA) .... CCR
Contractor Claims Settlement Program [*Military*] (DNAB) .... CCSP
Contractor Company Code [*Database terminology*] (NITA) CC
Contractor Cost Data Reporting (MCD) .... CCDR
Contractor Cost Reduction .... CCR
Contractor Critical Design Review (MCD) .... CCDR
Contractor Data Management Program [*Air Force*] (AFIT) .... CDMP
Contractor Deficiency Report (AAGC) .... CDR
Contractor Design Freeze Baseline (MCD) .... CDFB
Contractor Design Review (DOMA) .... CDR
Contractor Developed Material .... CDM
Contractor Developed Specifications (MCD) .... CDS
Contractor Development Test and Evaluation .... CDT & E
Contractor Employee Compensation System Review [*DoD*] ...... CECSR
Contractor Employee Protection Program [*DOE*] (AAGC) .... CEPP
Contractor End Item (MCD) .... CEI
Contractor Engineer - Furnish and Install (AABC) .... CEFI
Contractor Engineering and Technical Services (AFM) .... CETS
Contractor Engineering and Technical Support .... CETS
Contractor Establishment Code (AAGC) .... CEC
Contractor Estimating Methods Review [*DoD*] .... CEMR
Contractor Evidence Audit Team [*Environmental Protection Agency*]
   (ERG) .... CEAT
Contractor Experience List [*DoD*] .... CEL
Contractor Facilities and Capital Cost of Money .... CFCCOM
Contractor Field Maintenance Service [*Army*] .... CFMS
Contractor Field Services Personnel .... CFSP
Contractor Field Services Support .... CFSS
Contractor Field Team (MCD) .... CFT
Contractor Fin Opener Crank (NG) .... CFOC
Contractor Final Inspection (MCD) .... CFI
Contractor Financial Management (DOMA) .... CFM
Contractor Fiscal Year (AAGC) .... CFY

Contractor/Foreign Testing [*Air Force*] ... CFT
Contractor Functional Demonstration (KSC) ... CFD
Contractor Furnish and Install (MSA) ... CF & I
Contractor Furnished Equipment Notice [*Military*] (DOMA) ... CFEN
Contractor Furnished Requirements ... CFR
Contractor Identification Data System (AAGC) ... CIDS
Contractor Improvement Program (AAGC) ... CIP
Contractor Independent Technical Effort [*DoD*] ... CITE
Contractor Independent Technical Effort (IEEE) ... CITEC
Contractor Input to Total Performance [*DoD*] ... CITP
Contractor Installation Make or Buy Authorization (AAG) ... CIMBA
Contractor Insurance and Pension Review [*DoD*] ... CIPR
Contractor Integrated Technical Information Systems [*Military*] ... CITIS
Contractor Interface Guide ... CIG
Contractor Inventory ... CI
Contractor Inventory Redistribution System (MCD) ... CIRS
Contractor Inventory Utilization Group (MCD) ... CIUG
Contractor Involved in Litigation (AAGC) ... CIL
Contractor Line Item (MCD) ... CLI
Contractor Logistics Support [*DoD*] ... CLS
Contractor Logistics Support Services (MCD) ... CLSS
Contractor Logistics Support Services Management Information System (MCD) ... CLSS MIS
Contractor Maintenance and Supply Services [*DoD*] ... CMSS
Contractor Maintenance Data Reporting System [*Department of State*] ... CMDRS
Contractor Maintenance Engineering Support (MCD) ... CMES
Contractor Maintenance Personnel (MCD) ... CMP
Contractor Maintenance Service [*or Support*] (MCD) ... CMS
Contractor Maintenance Supply and Support [*DoD*] ... CMSS
Contractor Maintenance Trainer [*Military*] ... CMT
[*A*] **Contractor Managed Account** (AAG) ... ACMA
Contractor Management Reserve (MCD) ... CMR
Contractor Material Review Board [*NASA*] (NASA) ... CMRB
Contractor Missile Installation ... CMI
Contractor Non-SECOMO [*Software Engineering Cost Model*] **Activity Factor** ... CNSAF
Contractor Obligation and Liquidation Tracking System [*Army*] ... COLTS
Contractor Operated and Maintained Base Supply (MCD) ... COMBS
Contractor Overhaul Facility ... COF
Contractor Packaging Capability Review [*DoD*] ... CPCR
Contractor Parts List ... CPL
Contractor Performance Assessment Reporting System (AAGC) ... CPARS
Contractor Performance Certification Program [*Army*] (RDA) ... CP2
Contractor Performance Evaluation ... CPE
Contractor Performance Evaluation Group ... CPEG
Contractor Performance Evaluation Plan [*or Program*] [*Military*] (AABC) ... CPEP
Contractor Performance Evaluation Review Group (AAGC) ... CPERG
Contractor Performance Evaluation System ... CPES
Contractor Performance Factor [*DoD*] ... CPF
Contractor Performance Measurement (MCD) ... CPM
Contractor Performance Measurement Course [*DSMC*] (AAGC) ... CPMC
Contractor Performance Record [*DoD*] ... CPR
Contractor Performance Report ... CPR
Contractor Performance Review System (AAGC) ... CPRS
Contractor Performance Summary (AAGC) ... CPS
Contractor Personnel Employment Report (NG) ... CPER
Contractor Preliminary Inspection ... CPI
Contractor Procurement List (NATG) ... CPL
Contractor Procurement System Review [*DoD*] ... CPSR
Contractor Property Management System ... CPMS
Contractor Provided Training ... CPT
Contractor Quality Control (DNAB) ... CQC
Contractor Recommend Support Plan [*Military*] ... CRSP
Contractor Registration System (AAGC) ... CRS
Contractor Relations Specialist [*DoD*] ... CRS
Contractor Reports Register ... CRR
Contractor Required Shipment Date ... CRSD
Contractor Resident Office (AAG) ... CRO
Contractor Responsible Action (MCD) ... KRA
Contractor Review Board (AAGC) ... CRB
Contractor Risk Assessment Guide [*Military*] ... CRAG
Contractor Risk Assessment Guide (DOMA) ... CRSG
Contractor Sensitization (DNAB) ... CS
Contractor Source Inspection [*Military*] ... CSI
Contractor Standard Item (AAG) ... CSI
Contractor Standard Parts ... CSP
Contractor State Code [*Database terminology*] (NITA) ... CS
Contractor Storage Site (AFM) ... CSS
Contractor Supply Center [*Army*] ... CSC
Contractor Supply Center List ... CSCL
Contractor Support ... CS
Contractor Support Area (KSC) ... CSA
Contractor Support Equipment Recommendation Data (MCD) ... CSERD
Contractor Support Facility (MCD) ... CSF
Contractor Support Material List (MCD) ... CSML
Contractor Support Milestone (DNAB) ... CSM
Contractor Support Plan ... CSP
Contractor Support Service (MCD) ... CSS
Contractor Technical Assistance (MCD) ... CTA
Contractor Technical Evaluation (CAAL) ... CTE
Contractor Technical Manual Plan [*DoD*] ... CTMP
Contractor Technical Meeting (AAG) ... CTM
Contractor Technical Support (MCD) ... CTS
Contractor Test and Evaluation (MCD) ... CTE
Contractor Training Equipment (SAA) ... CTE
Contractor Training Instruction (DNAB) ... CTI
Contractor Transition Plan ... CTP
Contractor Turnaround Time ... CTAT
Contractor Using Price Incentive Doctrine (SAA) ... CUPID
Contractor Weighted Average Share (AAGC) ... CWAS
Contractor Weighted Average Share-Not Applicable (AAGC) ... CWAS-NA
Contractor Work Authorization (KSC) ... CWA
Contractor Work Plan (NRCH) ... CWP
Contractor-Acquired Materiel (AFM) ... CAM
Contractor-Acquired Operational Equipment ... CAOE
Contractor-Acquired Property (AFM) ... CAP
Contractor-Assisted ... CA
Contractor-Furnished Accessories (AFIT) ... CFA
Contractor-Furnished Aircraft Equipment (AFM) ... CFAE
Contractor-Furnished and Equipped ... CFAE
Contractor-Furnished Engineers (MCD) ... CFE
Contractor-Furnished Equipment ... CFE
Contractor-Furnished Equipment / Contractor-Furnished Aircraft Equipment (SAA) ... CFE/CFAE
Contractor-Furnished Equipment - Repairable Items Support System (MCD) ... CFE-RISS
Contractor-Furnished Information (MCD) ... CFI
Contractor-Furnished Material ... CFM
Contractor-Furnished Product (AAGC) ... CFP
Contractor-Furnished Property [*Air Force*] ... CFP
Contractor-Furnished Special Support Equipment (AFIT) ... CFSSE
Contractor-Furnished Technicians (MCD) ... CFT
Contractor-Held Air Force Property (AFM) ... CHAP
Contractor-Managed Base Supply [*Facility*] (MCD) ... COMBS
Contractor-Operated Civil Engineer Supply Store ... COCESS
Contractor-Operated Parts Stores [*Military*] ... COPARS
Contractor-Operated Storage Site (MCD) ... COSS
Contractor-Oriented Data Abstract Modules [*Air Force*] ... CODAM
Contractor-Owned, Contractor-Operated (AABC) ... COCO
Contractor-Prepared, Government-Approved ... CP/GA
Contractor-Recommended Change List ... CRCL
Contractor-Recommended Coding (MCD) ... CRC
Contractors Accounting System (PDAA) ... CONACS
Contractor's Advisory Board (SAA) ... CAB
Contractors Association of West Virginia (SRA) ... CAWV
Contractor's Control Data Bank (DNAB) ... CCDB
Contractor's Demonstration Inspection ... CDI
Contractor's Development Testing (MUGU) ... CDT
Contractor's Early Warning System (MCD) ... CEWS
Contractor's Identification Number ... CIDNO
Contractor's Information Submittal [*or Submitted*] (MCD) ... CIS
Contractor's Manual Prepared after Negotiated Authorization for Contract ... CMA
Contractors' Mechanical Plant Engineers [*British*] (BI) ... CMPE
Contractors Mutual Association [*Defunct*] (EA) ... CMA
Contractors' Operational Representative ... COR
Contractors Panel [*Aerospace*] (AAG) ... CN/PNL
Contractor's Preliminary Design Review (MCD) ... CPDR
Contractor's Profile System [*Department of Health and Human Services*] (GFGA) ... CPS
Contractors Pump Bureau (EA) ... CPB
Contractor's Summary Cost Breakdown (MCD) ... CSCB
Contractor's Training (MCD) ... CT
Contractor's Weighted Average Share in Cost Risk [*Accounting*] ... CWAS
Contractor's Work Estimate [*Military*] ... CWE
Contract-Relax, Antagonistic-Contract Method [*Medicine*] ... CRAC
Contract-Relax Method [*Medicine*] ... CR
Contract-Research Organization (ECON) ... CRO
Contracts Compliance Regional Office [*DoD*] ... CCO
Contracts Equal Employment Opportunity Program (AAGC) ... CEEOP
Contracts Group Office ... CGO
Contracts Maintenance Log (MCD) ... CML
Contracts Management Division [*Environmental Protection Agency*] (GFGA) ... CMD
Contracts Processing System (MCD) ... CPS
Contracts Station (AAG) ... CS
Contractual Data Status Reporting System (MCD) ... CDSR
Contractual Engineering Project (AFIT) ... CEP
Contractual Nontechnical Report (AAG) ... CNR
Contractual Requirements, Recording, Analysis, and Management [*Air Force*] ... CRAM
Contractual Research and Development (MCD) ... CR & D
Contractual Technical Report (AAG) ... CTR
Contracture [*or Contraction*] [*Orthopedics*] (DAVI) ... C
Contradiction (ADA) ... CONTR
Contraindicated [*Medicine*] ... CONTRA
Contralateral [*Anatomy*] ... C
Contralateral [*Anatomy*] ... CL
Contralateral [*Anatomy*] (MAE) ... contralat
Contralateral Axillary Metastasis [*Medicine*] (MAE) ... CAM
Contralateral Local Anesthesia [*Medicine*] (DMAA) ... CLA
Contralateral Optic Tectum [*Medicine*] ... COT
Contralateral Pyramidal Tract (PDAA) ... CPT
Contralateral Routing of Signal [*Audiometry*] ... CROS
Contralateral Threshold Shift (OA) ... CTS
Contralto [*Music*] ... C
Contralto [*Music*] ... CON
Contralto [*Music*] ... CONTR
Contrans Corp. [*Toronto Stock Exchange symbol*] ... CSS
Contrapposto (VRA) ... cntrps

Contrappunto [*Counterpoint*] [*Music*] (ROG) ... CP
Contrapuntist [*Music*] ... CPTST
Contrario [*Opponent or Enemy*] [*Spanish*] ... CONTRA
Contrary (WGA) ... CONT
Contrary ... CONTR
Contrary (ROG) ... CONTRY
Contrast (ADA) ... C
Contrast ... CONTR
Contrast ... CT
Contrast (MSA) ... CTRS
Contrast Baths [*Physical therapy*] (DAVI) ... CB
Contrast Contour Seeker ... CCS
Contrast Density/Appearance Time [*of images on a film*] ... CD/AT
Contrast Echocardiology [*Cardiology*] (DAVI) ... CE
Contrast Enhanced Lithography ... CEL
Contrast Enhancement Computed Tomography [*Radiology*] (DAVI) ... CECT
Contrast Enhancement Material [*Photoprocessing*] ... CEM
Contrast Gate (MCD) ... CG
Contrast Gate Amplifier ... CGA
Contrast Index [*Photography*] ... CI
Contrast Light Compensation (IAA) ... CLC
Contrast Media [*Radiology*] ... CM
Contrast Media Appearance Picture [*Also known as coronary arteriography*] [*Radiology*] ... CMAP
Contrast Media-Induced Acute Renal Insufficiency [*Medicine*] ... CM-ARI
Contrast Optical LASER Tracking Subsystem [*Missile guidance*] ... COLTS
Contrast Rendering Factor (PDAA) ... CRF
Contrast Sensitivity Function [*of the retina*] ... CSF
Contrast Spatial Frequency [*Vision research*] ... CSF
Contrast Transfer Function [*Video technology*] ... CTF
Contrast Value ... CV
Contrast-Enhancement Layer [*Photoprocessing*] ... CEL
Contraterrene [*Anti-matter in science fiction*] (BARN) ... CT
Contraves/Raytheon Air Defense System ... CRADS
Contre Complications Bronchiques [*Vaccine for "bronchial complaints"*] [*Medicine*] ... CCB
Contrepoint [*Record label*] [*France*] ... Cpt
Contre-Reforme Catholique [*In association name CRC Canada*] [*Catholic Counter-Reform Canada*] ... CRC
Contrexeville [*France ICAO location identifier*] (ICLI) ... LFXC
Contribute (AABC) ... CNTR
Contributing (ADA) ... CONTBG
Contributing (ADA) ... CTG
Contributing to Delinquency of Minor [*FBI standardized term*] ... C to D of M
Contributing Value [*Shipping*] ... CV
Contribution (WGA) ... CONTBN
Contribution ... CONTR
Contribution ... CONTRBTN
Contribution (WDMC) ... contrib
Contribution (MSA) ... CONTRIB
Contribution a l'Histoire Juridique de la Ire Dynastie Babylonienne [*A publication*] (BJA) ... CHJB
Contribution Margin [*Accounting*] ... CM
Contributions Greater Than [*Database terminology*] (NITA) ... CG
Contributions in Aid of Construction [*IRS*] ... CIAC
Contributions Less Than [*Database terminology*] (NITA) ... CL
Contributions of Infantry to the Battle Test [*Combat Develolpments Experimentation Center*] [*Army*] (INF) ... CIBT
Contributions Record [*Database terminology*] (NITA) ... CR
Contributor (WGA) ... CONTBR
Contributor [*Publishing*] (WDMC) ... contrib
Contributor (ROG) ... CONTRIBOR
Contributor ... CTR
Contributory Employee Stock Ownership Plan ... CESOP
Contributory Negligence [*Legal shorthand*] (LWAP) ... CNEGL
Contributory Place (ROG) ... CP
Contritus [*Broken, ground*] [*Pharmacy*] (DAVI) ... contrit
[*A*] **Contrived Reduction of Nomenclature Yielding Mnemonics** [*Humorous interpretation of the term*] ... ACRONYM
Contro-Clusive Magnetism [*Pest control concept*] ... CCM
Control [*Referring to a group in an experiment*] (DAVI) ... C
Control [*Officer's rating*] [*British Royal Navy*] ... C
Control (IAA) ... CNL
Control (KSC) ... CNTL
Control ... CNTRL
Control ... CNTRL
Control (AFM) ... CON
Control ... CONL
Control (MSA) ... CONT
Control (WDMC) ... cont
Control ... CONTL
Control ... CONTR
Control (KSC) ... CONTRL
Control (AAG) ... CTL
Control (WGA) ... CTRL
Control Accelerometer (IAA) ... CA
Control Access Manager (BUR) ... CAM
Control Accumulator ... C/A
Control Actuation System ... CAS
Control Adjustment Strap ... CAS
Control Advisory Release (NRCH) ... CAR
Control Air Data System (MCD) ... CADS
Control Air Force Specialty Code ... CAFSC
Control Alarm Indicator (MCD) ... CAI
Control and Acquisition Interface (KSC) ... CAI
Control and Analysis Centers [*ERADCOM*] (RDA) ... CAC
Control and Assessment Team [*Military*] (GFGA) ... CAT
Control and Authorization Process (KSC) ... CAP
Control and Auxiliary Power Supply System ... CAPS
Control and Command Systems Support Agency [*NATO*] (NATG) ... CCSSA
Control and Computation System [*or Subsystem*] [*Navy*] (MCD) ... CCS
Control and Coordination [*Army*] ... CAC
Control and Data Acquisition System (MCD) ... CODAS
Control and Data Retrieval System [*Formerly, DCDRS*] [*Air Force*] (MCD) ... CDRS
Control and Diagnostic Unit [*Computer science*] ... CDU
Control and Display (GFGA) ... C & D
Control and Display (IAA) ... CAD
Control and Display Panel (MCD) ... CDP
Control and Display Subsystem (MCD) ... CDS
Control and Display Unit (NASA) ... CADU
Control and Display Unit (NASA) ... CDU
Control and Evaluation ... C & E
Control and Guidance (MCD) ... C & G
Control and Indicating Equipment ... CIE
Control and Indication (MCD) ... C & I
Control and Information Center (NASA) ... CIC
Control and Instrumentation (NRCH) ... C & I
Control and Line (AABC) ... C & L
Control and Monitor Panel ... CAMP
Control and Monitoring (NASA) ... C & M
Control and Monitoring Processor (IEEE) ... CAMP
Control and Processing [*Company*] [*INSCOM*] ... C & P
Control and Processing Center (MCD) ... CPC
Control and Protection of Transoceanic Air Lanes of Communication ... CAPTALC
Control and Protection Panel ... CPP
Control and Reporting (NATG) ... C and R
Control and Reporting Center [*Air Force*] ... CRC
Control and Reporting Center/Post [*Air Force*] (MCD) ... CRC/P
Control and Reporting Post [*RADAR*] [*Air Force*] ... CRP
Control and Reporting System (NATG) ... CRS
Control and Reporting Unit ... CRU
Control and Reproducibility Monitor (IEEE) ... CRM
Control and Simulation Facility (MCD) ... CSF
Control and Simulation Language [*Computer science*] ... CSL
Control and Status Logic (KSC) ... CSL
Control and Status System [*NASCOM*] (MCD) ... CSS
Control and Surveillance of Friendly Forces (MCD) ... CASOFF
Control and Switching Equipment [*RADAR*] ... CSE
Control and Timing Unit [*Computer science*] ... CTU
Control and Traffic Center ... CTC
Control Anticipation Parameter (PDAA) ... CAP
Control Area [*Computer science*] ... CA
Control Area [*ICAO International Civil Aviation Organization=>> Term*] (GAVI) ... CTA
Control Area (FAAC) ... CTLA
Control Armourer [*British military*] (DMA) ... CA
Control Assembly ... CA
Control Assembly ... CONTA
Control Assembly Program (BUR) ... CAP
Control Assembly Set (MCD) ... CAS
Control Attenuator Timer (KSC) ... CAT
Control Augmentation ... CA
Control Augmentation System ... CAS
Control Automation System [*IBM Corp.*] ... CAS
Control Automation System Manufacturing Interface Tape (IAA) ... CASMIT
Control Block Data Base (ECII) ... CBB
Control Blocks Configuration [*Computer science*] (ECII) ... CBC
Control Board ... CB
Control Board Operator [*Lighting*] (NTCM) ... CBO
Control Booth ... CB
Control Boundary (FAAC) ... CTLB
Control Branch [*Military*] ... CB
Control Break ... CB
Control Buffer [*Computer science*] (IAA) ... CB
Control Building [*Nuclear energy*] (NRCH) ... CB
Control Building Environmental Control System [*Nuclear energy*] (NRCH) ... CBECS
Control Button ... CB
Control by Ship (NATG) ... CONSHIP
Control by Wire (MCD) ... CBW
Control Cabin ... CC
Control Card Listing [*Computer science*] ... CCL
Control Center ... CC
Control Center Mock-Up ... CCMU
Control Center Programming Center [*NASA*] (KSC) ... CCPC
Control Center Rack (MCD) ... CCR
Control Chamber [*Diving apparatus*] ... CC
Control Channel Information Demodulator ... CCID
Control Character [*Keyboard*] (CINC) ... CTRL
Control Chief Hldgs [*NASDAQ symbol*] (TTSB) ... DIEM
Control Chief Holdings [*Associated Press*] (SAG) ... ContrCh
Control Chief Holdings [*NASDAQ symbol*] (SAG) ... DIGM
Control Circuit ... CC
Control Circuit Resistance ... CCR
Control Circuits Design Section ... CCDS
Control Civil and Military [*British*] (AIA) ... CCM
Control Code (IAA) ... CC
Control Command Processor (IAA) ... CCP

Control Commission for Germany [*World War II*] .... CCG
Control Commission Military Section [*British World War II*] ..... CCMS
Control Commission Shipping Bureau [*Allied German Occupation Forces*] .... CCSB
Control, Communication, and Display Subsystem (MCD) .... CCDS
Control Communications Module [*Telecommunications*] (ECII) ...... CCM
Control Communications Unit [*Telecommunications*] (ECII) .... CCU
Control Computer (KSC) CC
Control Computer System [*or Subsystem*] (IAA) .... CCS
Control Configured Propulsion (MCD) .... CCP
Control Configured Vehicle [*Air Force*] CCV
Control Connector (IAA) CC
Control Console CC
Control Contactor (IEEE) .... CCR
Control Converter (MCD) CC
Control Core Cell (PDAA) CCC
Control Counter [*Computer science*] CC
Control Creation Edition [*Microsoft Corp.*] [*Computer science*] (PCM) .... CCE
Control Current Impedance CCI
Control Data .... CD
Control Data Assembly Program [*Control Data Corp.*] .... CODAP
Control Data Communications Control Procedure [*Telecommunications*] (TEL) .... CDCCP
Control Data Corp. [*Information service or system*] (IID) .... CDC
Control Data Corp. [*Toronto Stock Exchange symbol*] .... CTD
Control Data Corporation Distributed Communications Network [*Telecommunications*] .... CDCNET
Control Data Education Institutes .... CDEI
Control Data Institute .... CDI
Control Data Mathematic Program (IAA) .... CDM
Control Data Panel .... CDP
Control Data Structural System (DNAB) .... CONSTRUCTS
Control Data System (NASA) .... CDS
Control Data Systems [*NASDAQ symbol*] (SAG) .... CDAT
Control Data Systems, Inc. [*Associated Press*] (SAG) .... CtrlDt
Control Data Terminal .... CDT
Control Data Unit .... CDU
Control Detonating Fuses (KSC) .... CDF
Control Development Kit [*Microsoft Corp.*] (PCM) .... CDK
Control Devices, Inc. [*Associated Press*] (SAG) .... ContDev
Control Devices, Inc. [*NASDAQ symbol*] (SAG) .... SNSR
Control Diagram Language [*Computer science*] (IEEE) .... CODIL
Control Diastolic Pressure [*Cardiology*] .... CDP
Control Diet .... CD
Control Differential Transformer .... CDT
Control Differential Transmitter .... CDX
Control Direction Indicator (MCD) .... CDI
Control Director Intercept (CINC) .... CDI
Control/Display Ratio [*Quality control*] .... C/D
Control Distribution Center (AAG) .... CDC
Control Distribution System .... CDS
Control Drawing Change Request (AAG) .... CDCR
Control Electrical Artificer [*Navy rating British*] .... CEA
Control Electrical Mechanic [*British military*] (DMA) .... CEM
Control Electrical Mechanician [*Navy rating British*] .... CEMN
Control Electrician [*British military*] (DMA) .... CE
Control Electronics Assembly [*Aerospace*] .... CEA
Control Electronics Section [*Apollo*] [*NASA*] .... CES
Control Electronics System (MCD) .... CES
Control Electronics Unit (MCD) .... CEU
Control Element (MCD) .... CE
Control Element Assembly [*Nuclear energy*] (NRCH) .... CEA
Control Element Assembly Calculator [*Nuclear energy*] (NRCH) ..... CEAC
Control Element Drive Mechanism [*Nuclear energy*] (NRCH) ..... CEDM
Control Element Drive Mechanism Control System [*Nuclear energy*] (NRCH) .... CEDMCS
Control Element Drive System [*Nuclear energy*] (NRCH) .... CEDS
Control Element Test Stand [*Nuclear energy*] (NRCH) .... CETS
Control Encoder Coupler (NASA) .... CEC
Control Energy [*Vancouver Stock Exchange symbol*] .... CTY
Control Engineering .... CE
Control Equipment (IAA) .... CE
Control Error (IAA) .... CE
Control Escort Vessel [*Navy symbol*] .... DEC
Control Filter Post (NATG) .... CFP
Control Flag [*Computer science*] (IAA) .... CF
Control Flight Test Bed .... CFTB
Control Flow Diagram (MCD) .... CFD
Control Flow Jet .... CFJ
Control Footing .... CF
Control for Submarine Discharge Torpedo (MCD) .... CSDT
Control for Surface-Launched Torpedoes (MCD) .... CSLT
Control [*or Controlled*] Fragmentation Munitions (CINC) ...... COFRAM
Control from Shore (NATG) .... CONSHORE
Control Function [*Computer science*] (IAA) .... CF
Control Functional Diagram .... CFD
Control Functional Unit [*Data link*] (NG) .... CFU
Control Funds Status Report (SSD) .... CFSR
Control Grid .... CG
Control Group .... CG
Control Group Adapter (MCD) .... CGA
Control Guidance Subsystem (OA) .... CGS
Control Heading (BUR) .... CH
Control Hole (BUR) .... CH
Control in Information Systems .... COINS

Control Indicator CI
Control Indicator Assembly (MCD) .... CIA
Control Indicator Power Distribution Unit [*Military*] (CAAL) .... CIPDU
Control Indicator Set (MCD) .... CIS
Control Indicator Unit (OA) .... CIU
Control Inlet Panel [*Aerospace*] (AAG) .... CIP
Control Inquiry Card [*Computer science*] (IAA) CIC
Control Installation Code [*Air Force*] (AFIT) CIC
Control Instrument Co. (MCD) CIC
Control Interface Assembly (MCD) .... CIA
Control Interface Document .... CID
Control Interface Module [*Chemistry*] .... CIM
Control Interval Definition Field [*Computer science*] (BUR) .... CIDF
Control Joint (MCD) .... CJ
Control Joint [*Technical drawings*] .... CJT
Control Joint (AAG) .... CLJ
Control Key [*Electronics*] .... CNTRL
Control Language [*Computer science*] (BUR) CL
Control Language Services [*Computer science*] (IAA) .... CLS
Control Language Translator [*Computer science*] (IEEE) ..... COLT
Control Launch Center (MUGU) CLC
Control Launch Subsystem (OA) .... CLS
Control Leader [*Computer science*] CL
Control Level Item CLI
Control Line Register .... CLR
Control Logic CL
Control Logic and Drive Assembly .... CLDA
Control Logic Array .... CLA
Control Logic Read Index [*Computer science*] (ECII) .... CLRNDX
Control Magnetization Curve .... CMC
Control Maintenance & Management Systems (ACII) .... CMMS
Control Maintenance Unit .... CMU
Control Mark (DEN) .... CM
Control Memory [*Telecommunications*] (TEL) .... CM
Control Memory Access Register [*Computer science*] (NITA) ..... CMAR
Control Memory Address Register [*Computer science*] ..... CMAR
Control Message Automation [*Aviation*] .... CMA
Control Mode (MCD) .... CM
Control Module .... CM
Control Moment Gyro Assembly [*Aerospace*] .... CMGA
Control Moment Gyro Electrical Assembly [*Aerospace*] ..... CMGEA
Control Moment Gyro Inverter Assembly [*Aerospace*] (MCD) ..... CMGIA
Control Moment Gyro System [*or Subsystem*] [*Aerospace*] (KSC) ..... CMGS
Control Moment Gyroscope [*Aerospace*] .... CMG
Control Monitor (MCD) .... CM
Control Monitor and Isolation Subsystem (MCD) .... CMIS
Control Network System [*Chiefly British*] .... CNS
Control Number .... CN
Control of Advertisements Regulations [*Town planning*] [*British*] ..... CAR
Control of Aircraft Maintenance and Servicing .... CAMS
Control of Banking (Prentice-Hall) [*A publication*] (DLA) .... Cont of Banking (P-H)
Control of Destination of Ships .... CDS
Control of Electromagnetic Radiations [*Purpose is to deny the enemy aircraft the use of electromagnetic radiations for navigation, while still providing essential services*] ...... CONELRAD
Control of Engineering Material, Acquisition, Storage and Transport (IAA) .... CEMAST
Control of Industrial Major Accident Hazards [*British*] .... CIMAH
Control of Intensive Farming [*British*] .... COIF
Control of Logistics Expense [*USAREUR*] (MCD) .... COLEX
Control of Material Planning Activities (PDAA) .... COMPACE
Control of Materials Planning and Isometric Drawings .... COMPAID
Control of Official Histories [*British*] .... COH
Control of Operation Programs .... COP
Control of Panel Emulator .... CPE
Control of Pesticides Regulations [*British*] .... COPR
Control of Pollution Act [*1974*] [*British*] (DCTA) .... COPA
Control of Pollution Act [*1974*] [*British*] .... CPA
Control of Radio Transmission [*British World War II*] .... CRT
Control of Recombination [*Genetics*] .... CRE
Control of Rents and Furnished Lets [*British*] .... FRC
Control of Sea Ice Information (NATG) .... ICECON
Control of Substances Hazardous to Health [*British*] .... COSHH
Control of Unwanted Radiated Energy .... CURE
Control Officers' Console .... COC
Control Orbitron Gauge .... COG
Control Order (MCD) .... CO
Control Ordered SONAR Hardware (PDAA) .... COSH
Control Panel .... CP
Control Panel [*Electronics*] (ECII) .... CTLPL
Control Panel Device [*Computer science*] (DOM) .... CDEV
Control Panel Subassembly .... CPS
Control Parameter Assembly Program .... CPAP
Control Pascal [*Compiler*] [*Computer science*] .... CP
Control Pattern Generator .... CPG
Control Phasing Unit [*for aircraft*] (RDA) .... CPU
Control Point .... CP
Control Point Custodian [*Military*] (AFIT) .... CPC
Control Position Indicator (IAA) .... CPI
Control Post [*RADAR*] .... CP
Control Power Supply .... CPS
Control Power Transformer (MSA) .... CPT
Control Pressure System (AAG) .... CPS
Control Procedures (MCD) .... CP
Control Processes in Multicellular Organisms .... CPMO

Control Processing Unit (MCD) ... CPU
Control Processor (IEEE) ... CP
Control Program [*Computer science*] ... CP
Control Program Assist [*IBM Corp.*] ... CPA
Control Program Facility (MCD) ... CPF
Control Program for Microcomputers [*Operating system*] ... CP/M
Control Program for Microcomputers (DOM) ... CP/M
Control Program for Microprocessors [*Computer science*] ... CP/M
Control Program/Monitor [*Computer science*] ... CP/M
Control Program - Real-Time [*Xerox Corp.*] ... CP-R
Control Program Services (IAA) ... CPS
Control Program-Five [*Operating system*] [*Xerox Corp.*] ... CP-V
Control Programs Development Division [*Environmental Protection Agency*] (GFGA) ... CPDD
Control Programs Support (IEEE) ... CPS
Control Purchasing Authority (NVT) ... CPA
Control Quality Monitor ... CQM
Control Question Test [*For lie detectors*] ... CQT
Control Rate Gyro [*Aerospace*] (KSC) ... CRG
Control Rating [*British military*] (DMA) ... CR
Control Read/Write (MCD) ... CRW
Control Read-Only Memory [*Computer science*] ... CROM
Control Recognition Character [*Computer science*] (ECII) ... CRC
Control Reconfiguration Strategy (MCD) ... CRS
Control Record Listing [*IRS*] ... CRL
Control Red Bank Demand Indicator (IEEE) ... CBDI
Control Register [*Computer science*] (IAA) ... CR
Control Register Zero [*Computer science*] (PCM) ... CR0
Control Relay ... CR
Control Relay Automatic ... CRA
Control Relay Forward ... CRF
Control Relay Hand ... CRH
Control Relay Latch ... CRL
Control Relay Master ... CRM
Control Relay Translator (IAA) ... CRT
Control Relay Unlatch ... CRU
Control Repeater Amplifier ... CRA
Control Restrictive Instruction for Structural Programming (MCD) ... CRISP
Control Risks Information Services [*British Information service or system*] (IID) ... CRIS
Control Rod [*Nuclear energy*] (NRCH) ... CR
Control Rod Absorber [*Nuclear energy*] (NUCP) ... CRA
Control Rod Analysis [*Nuclear energy*] ... CORONA
Control Rod Assembly [*Nuclear energy*] (NRCH) ... CRA
Control Rod Disconnect Driveline [*Nuclear energy*] (NRCH) ... CRDD
Control Rod Drive [*Nuclear energy*] (IEEE) ... CD
Control Rod Drive [*or Driveline*] [*Nuclear energy*] (NRCH) ... CRD
Control Rod Drive Assembly [*Nuclear energy*] (IEEE) ... CRDA
Control Rod Drive Control System [*Nuclear energy*] (NRCH) ... CRDCS
Control Rod Drive Hydraulic System [*Nuclear energy*] (NRCH) ... CRDHS
Control Rod Drive Mechanism [*Nuclear energy*] (GFGA) ... CRDM
Control Rod Drive Mechanism Shroud [*Nuclear energy*] (NRCH) ... CRDMS
Control Rod Drive Motor [*Nuclear energy*] (IEEE) ... CRDM
Control Rod Drive System [*Nuclear energy*] (NRCH) ... CRDS
Control Rod Drive Ventilating Fan [*Nuclear energy*] (NRCH) ... CRDVF
Control Rod Guide Tube [*Nuclear energy*] (NRCH) ... CRGT
Control Rod Mechanism [*Nuclear energy*] (NUCP) ... CRM
Control Rod Position Indication [*Nuclear energy*] (NRCH) ... CRPI
Control Rod Scram Accumulator [*Nuclear energy*] (IEEE) ... CRSA
Control ROM [*Read-Only Memory*] **Address Register** [*Computer science*] ... CRAR
Control Room (MSA) ... CR
Control Room [*Nuclear energy*] (NRCH) ... CTRM
Control Room Air Conditioning System [*Nuclear energy*] (NRCH) ... CRACS
Control Room Area Ventilation System [*Nuclear energy*] (NRCH) ... CRAVS
Control Room Design Review/Audit [*Nuclear energy*] (NRCH) ... CRDR/A
Control Room Emergency Ventilation System (IEEE) ... CREVS
Control Room Isolation [*Nuclear energy*] (NRCH) ... CRI
Control Room Operator [*Nuclear energy*] (NRCH) ... CRO
Control Room Patching and Labeling ... CORPAL
Control Route Tag (MCD) ... CRT
Control Routine ... CR
Control Scanner ... CS
Control Science [*Vancouver Stock Exchange symbol*] ... CLD
Control Section (IAA) ... CS
Control Section (MCD) ... CSECT
Control Section Report [*NATO*] ... CSR
Control Segment (MCD) ... CS
Control Servo Input (NASA) ... CSI
Control Set ... CS
Control Setting Panel (IAA) ... CSP
Control Shift Register (CET) ... CSR
Control Signal ... CS
Control Signal Processor [*for spacecraft*] ... CSP
Control Signaling Subsystem [*Telecommunications*] (TEL) ... CSS
Control Slip (CINC) ... CS
Control Software, Inc. ... CSI
Control Staff Instructions [*Army*] (MCD) ... COSIN
Control Station (MCD) ... CS
Control Station Manual Operating Level (AAG) ... CSMOL
Control Status Register ... CSR
Control Stick Assembly (MCD) ... CSA
Control Stick Boost and Pitch Compensator (MCD) ... CSBPC
Control Stick Maneuver (MCD) ... CSM
Control Stick Sensor Assembly (MCD) ... CSSA
Control Stick Steering [*Aviation*] (NG) ... CSS
Control Stick Tie-In [*Aviation*] (MUGU) ... CSTI
Control Store ... CS
Control Store Address Register ... CSAR
Control Store Data Register ... CSDR
Control Submarine Chaser [*136 feet*] [*Navy symbol Obsolete*] ... PCSC
Control Subroutine Language [*Computer science*] (IEEE) ... CONSUL
Control Subsystem ... CSS
Control Switch (MSA) ... CS
Control Switch (MSA) ... CSW
Control Switching Assembly ... CSA
Control Switching Module [*Electronics*] (ECII) ... CSM
Control Switching Point (BUR) ... CSP
Control Symbol Number (AFM) ... CSN
Control Synthetic Gas [*Process*] ... CSG
Control System Design Program ... CSDP
Control System Development (MCD) ... CSD
Control System Jet ... CSJ
Control System Program [*Manufacturing engineering*] [*Computer science*] ... CSP
Control System Simulation Equipment (MCD) ... CSSE
Control System Test (AAG) ... CST
Control System Test Vehicle (DNAB) ... CSTV
Control Systems (MCD) ... CS
Control Systems Analysis Program (MCD) ... CSAP
Control Systems Development Division [*NASA*] (NASA) ... CSDD
Control Systems Engineering ... CSE
Control Systems Integration Group (SAA) ... CSIG
Control Systems Laboratory [*University of Illinois*] (MCD) ... CSL
Control Systems Procurement Office (SAA) ... CSPO
Control Systems Society (EA) ... CSS
Control Tag (MCD) ... CT
Control Techniques Guidelines [*Environmental Protection Agency*] ... CTG
Control Technology and Application Training Series (ACII) ... CTA
Control Technology Document [*Environmental Protection Agency*] (GFGA) ... CTD
Control Technology Office [*Environmental Protection Agency*] (GFGA) ... CTO
Control Test Bed ... CTB
Control Test Vehicles ... CTV
Control Tower [*For chart use only*] [*Aviation*] ... CT
Control Tower Operator [*Army*] (AABC) ... CTO
Control Track Direction Computer (AABC) ... CTDC
Control Transformer ... CT
Control Translator [*Honeywell, Inc.*] [*Computer science*] ... CONTRAN
Control Transmitter (MUGU) ... CX
Control Unit [*Computer science*] ... CU
Control Unit Busy (CMD) ... CUB
Control Unit / Control Block [*Computer science*] (IAA) ... CUCB
Control Unit End (CMD) ... CUE
Control Unit Group Input/Output Control Unit [*Computer science*] ... CUG IOC
Control Unit Interface [*Computer science*] (IAA) ... CUI
Control Unit Terminal [*Computer science*] ... CUT
Control Unit Terminal Mode (CDE) ... CUT mode
Control Unit Tester [*Sperry UNIVAC*] (BUR) ... CUT
Control Users Handbook ... CUH
Control, Utility, and Support (IAA) ... CUS
Control Valve [*Automotive engineering*] ... C/VAL
Control Valve ... CV
Control Valve [*Computer science*] (ECII) ... CV
Control Valve Module (NASA) ... CVM
Control Valve Primary Coolant (MCD) ... CVPC
Control Valve Secondary Coolant (MCD) ... CVSC
Control Van [*Diving apparatus*] ... CV
Control Van Connecting Room (NATG) ... CVCR
Control Variable Valve ... CVV
Control Vision Unit [*Automotive engineering*] ... CVU
Control Wheel Steering (NG) ... CWS
Control Withdrawal Prohibit [*Nuclear energy*] (NRCH) ... CWP
Control Word (MCD) ... CW
Control Word Address ... CWA
Control Zone [*Aviation*] ... CTLZ
Control Zone [*Aviation*] ... CTR
Control Zone [*Aviation*] ... CTZ
Control Zone [*For chart use only*] [*Aviation*] ... CZ
Controladora Comercial Mexicana SA de CV [*Associated Press*] (SAG) ... ConCMx
Controladora Comercial Mexicana SA de CV [*NYSE symbol*] (SAG) ... MCM
Control-Device Resource [*Computer science*] (BYTE) ... cdev
Controles Nucleares del Norte, SA [*Spain*] ... NUCLENOR
Controllability and Observability ... C & O
Controllability, Observability, and Maintenance Engineering Technique (PDAA) ... COMET
Controllable and Reversible Pitch Propeller [*For ships*] (MCD) ... CRP
Controllable Pitch Propeller [*For ships*] (MCD) ... CPP
Controllable RADAR Target Simulator ... CRTS
Controllable Twist Rotor [*Aviation*] ... CTR
Controllable-Displacement-Factor Frequency Changer (DICI) ... CDFFC
Controlled [*Currency exchange rate*] [*British*] ... C
Controlled ... CONTRLLD
Controlled (IAA) ... CTLD
Controlled Acceleration Propulsion (SSD) ... CAP
Controlled Access Area (MCD) ... CAA
Controlled Access System (IAA) ... CAS
Controlled Access Unit [*Computer science*] ... CAU
Controlled Airspace ... CAS
Controlled Airspace (IAA) ... CTA
Controlled Airspace [*ICAO designator*] (FAAC) ... CTAS
Controlled Alternating Parachute Exit System (PDAA) ... CAPES

Controlled American Source [Military] (CINC) .... CAS
Controlled Amortization Bond .... CAB
Controlled Approach (IAA) .... CA
Controlled Area Network [Communication engineering] .... CAN
Controlled Assembly Parts List [Aerospace] (AAG) ...... CAPL
Controlled Atmosphere .... CA
Controlled Atmosphere Brazing [Metallurgy] .... CAB
Controlled Atmosphere Electron Microscopy .... CAEM
Controlled Atmosphere Packaging .... CAP
Controlled Atmosphere Protected [Army] (MCD) ...... CONAP
Controlled Avalanche Transistor (IAA) .... CAT
Controlled Avalanche Transit Time [Electronics] ...... CATT
Controlled Barrier System .... CBS
Controlled Blip Scan (CET) .... CBS
Controlled Canister Purge [Automotive engineering] ...... CCP
Controlled Carrier Modulation (KSC) .... CCM
Controlled Circulation [Newspaper and magazine distribution] (NTCM) CC
Controlled Circulation Audit [Name changed to Business Publications Audit of Circulation] .... CCA
Controlled Collection Objective (MCD) .... CCO
Controlled Combustion System [Antipollution device for automobiles] .... CCS
Controlled Commodity .... COCOM
Controlled Communications Systems [Chicago, IL] [Telecommunications] (TSSD) .... CCS
Controlled COMSEC [Communications Security] **Items** CCI
Controlled Configuration Explosive [Military] .... CCE
Controlled Cord Traction [Medicine] .... CCT
Controlled Current Distribution [Telecommunications] (OA) ...... CCD
Controlled Current Feedback Transformer (MSA) ...... CCFT
Controlled Data Analysis Workshops [Magnetospheric physics] ...... CDAW
Controlled Date of Separation [Military] (AFM) ...... CDOS
Controlled Delivery System .... CDS
Controlled Departure Time [FAA] (TAG) .... CDT
Controlled Deployment Specular Reflector [Army] (AABC) ...... CDSR
Controlled Depth/Rapid Deployment Moored Sweep [Navy] (CAAL) ...... CD/RDMS
Controlled Digital Simulator .... CODIS
Controlled Direct Injection [Automotive engineering] ...... CDI
Controlled Dissemination (MCD) .... CD
Controlled Drinker-Control [Medicine] (DMAA) ...... CD-C
Controlled Drinker-Experimental [Chemical dependency] (DAVI) ...... CD-E
Controlled Droplet Application (PDAA) .... CDA
Controlled Drug .... CD
Controlled Dynamic Range .... CDR
Controlled Ecosystem Pollution Experiment [National Science Foundation project] .... CEPEX
Controlled Element Computer .... CEC
Controlled Energy Flow Forming .... CEFF
Controlled Energy Relief Valve (MCD) .... CERV
Controlled Environment .... CE
Controlled Environment Agriculture .... CEA
Controlled Environment Facilities .... CEF
Controlled Environment Gravity Tube System (PDAA) ...... CEGTS
Controlled Environment Room [Agricultural science] (OA) ...... CER
Controlled Environment Testing .... CET
Controlled Environmental Forestry .... CEF
Controlled Environmental System [NASA] .... CES
Controlled Environmental Vault (ACRL) .... CEV
Controlled Environments Ltd., Winnipeg, Manitoba [Library symbol National Library of Canada] (NLC) .... MWCE
Controlled Experimental Ecosystem [Study technique] ...... CEE
Controlled Facility [Aerospace] (AAG) .... CF
Controlled Field Actuator [Computer science] (NITA) ...... CFA
Controlled Firing Area [Aviation] (FAAC) .... CFA
Controlled Flash Evaporation .... CFE
Controlled Flight into Terrain .... CFIT
Controlled Flight Toward Terrain (PDAA) .... CFTT
Controlled Flow .... CONFLOW
Controlled Foods International Ltd. [Toronto Stock Exchange symbol] ...... CFS
Controlled Force Circulation [Boilers] .... CFC
Controlled Foreign Company [or Corporation] .... CFC
Controlled Fragmentation (SAA) .... CF
Controlled Fuel Injection [Engineering] .... CFI
Controlled Fusion Atomic Data Center [Department of Energy] (IID) ...... CFADC
Controlled Ground Landing (AAG) .... CGL
Controlled Handling of Internal Executive Functions [UNIVAC] ...... CHIEF
Controlled Hardening [Ferrous metallurgy] .... CH
Controlled Helium Atmosphere Plant (PDAA) .... CHAP
Controlled High Flux Dialysis [Medicine] (DMAA) ...... CHFD
Controlled Humidity (MCD) .... CH
Controlled Hypertension [Medicine] .... CH
Controlled Impact Demonstration [FAA, NASA] ...... CID
Controlled Impact Reentry (MCD) .... CIR
Controlled Impulse (MCD) .... CIMP
Controlled Intact Reentry (IAA) .... CIR
Controlled Interceptor Trainer [Aerospace] (AAG) ...... CIT
Controlled Internal Extension (MCD) .... CIE
Controlled Interval Inspection (MCD) CII
Controlled Ionization CI
Controlled Item CI
Controlled Item Code [Air Force] (AFIT) CIC
Controlled Items List CIL
Controlled Large Aperture Wavefront Sampling (MCD) ...... CLAWS
Controlled Leakage System (SAA) .... CLS
Controlled Letter Contract Reduction (IEEE) .... CLCR
Controlled Low-Strength Material .... CLSM

Controlled Materials Officer .... CMO
Controlled Materials Plan [of War Production Board] [World War II] ...... CMP
Controlled Materials Plan Regulation (National Production) [of War Production Board] [World War II] (DLA) ...... CMP Reg
Controlled Materials Production [Nuclear energy] ...... CMP
Controlled Mechanical Ventilation .... CMV
Controlled Minefield [Navy] .... CM
Controlled Mission Equipment (MCD) .... CME
Controlled Monitor Interface Calibrator (PDAA) ...... CMIC
Controlled Multiple Address Letter (AFM) .... CMAL
Controlled Multivibrator .... CMV
Controlled Nucleation Thermochemical Deposition (MCD) ...... CNTD
Controlled Object Deck Exploitation (PDAA) .... CODE
Controlled Oral Word Association Test [Speech and language pathology] (DAVI) ...... COWAT
Controlled Orbital Decay and Input System (DNAB) ...... CODIS
Controlled Overhead Management Performance and Standard System .... COMPASS
Controlled Oxygen Fugacity [Apparatus] .... COF
Controlled Path System [Computer science] .... CPS
Controlled Plasma Glassification [Of solid waste] ...... CPG
Controlled Precision Oscillator .... CPO
Controlled Process Serum Replacements [Cell culture] ...... CPSR
Controlled Production Planning Officer .... CPPO
Controlled Production Unit [Project sponsored by the Elder Craftsmen] ...... CPU
Controlled Products Area .... CPA
Controlled Quick Release .... CQR
Controlled Radial Steering (PDAA) .... CRS
Controlled Radiation [or Reception] Pattern Antenna ...... CRPA
Controlled Range Air Burst Fuze (RDA) .... CRAB
Controlled Range Network (MCD) .... CORN
Controlled Recirculation Boiling Water Reactor .... CRBR
Controlled Rectifier .... CR
Controlled Referral Plan .... CRP
Controlled Reflex [Neurology and psychiatry] (DAVI) ...... CR
Controlled Release [Neurology and psychiatry] (DAVI) ...... CR
Controlled Release Device (KSC) .... CRD
Controlled Release Society (EA) .... CRS
Controlled Reluctance Eddy Current Generator (PDAA) ...... CREG
Controlled Residual Element [Nuclear energy] .... CRE
Controlled Response [Neurology and psychiatry] (DAVI) ...... CR
Controlled Response in Maitland Emergencies .... CRIME
Controlled Retracting Injection Port [System for underground coal burning] ...... CRIP
Controlled Rheology [Plastics technology] .... CR
Controlled Rotary Vane [Compressor] [Automotive engineering] ...... CRV
Controlled Rupture Accuracy (MUGU) .... CRA
Controlled Saturation Logic (IAA) .... CSL
Controlled Short Takeoff and Landing [Acronym used for a type of aircraft] ...... C-STOL
Controlled Silicon Rectifier [Electronics] (IAA) .... CSR
Controlled Solid Rocket Motors (KSC) .... CSRM
Controlled Stock (SAA) .... CS
Controlled Stress [Physiology] .... CS
Controlled Substance Sensing Device (AAGC) .... CSSD
Controlled Substances Act [1970] (GFGA) .... CSA
Controlled Supply Rate (AABC) .... CSR
Controlled Surface Porosity .... CSP
Controlled Surface Process .... CSP
Controlled Swirl Scavenging [Automotive engine design] ...... CSS
Controlled Takeoff and Landing (MCD) .... CTOL
Controlled Temperature .... CT
Controlled Temperature Bath .... CTB
Controlled Temperature Furnace .... CTF
Controlled Temperature Profile [Vapor trap] [Nuclear energy] (NRCH) ...... CTP
Controlled Term [Online database field identifier] ...... CT
Controlled Thermal Severity (OA) .... CTS
Controlled Thermolytic Dissociation .... CTD
Controlled Thermonuclear Fusion .... CTF
Controlled Thermonuclear Fusion .... CTNF
Controlled Thermonuclear Reaction [or Reactor] [National Institute of Standards and Technology] ...... CTR
Controlled Thermonuclear Research .... CTR
Controlled Thrust Assembly (NASA) .... CTA
Controlled Time of Arrival [FAA] (TAG) .... CTA
Controlled Tornado Research (MCD) .... CTR
Controlled Tuning Fork Oscillator .... CTFO
Controlled Variable [Psychology] (BARN) CV
Controlled Variable Time [Fuze] (NVT) .... CVT
Controlled Ventilation [Automotive engineering] CV
Controlled Ventilation CV
Controlled Visual Flight .... CVF
Controlled Visual Flight Rules [Military] .... CVFR
Controlled Visual Rules [FAA] .... CVR
Controlled Work Area (MCD) .... CWA
Controlled Yeast Lysate .... CYL
Controlled-Circulation [Boiler] .... C/C
Controlled-Pore Ceramic [Organic chemistry] .... CPC
Controlled-Pore Glass [Corning] .... CPG
Controlled-Potential Coulometer [Nuclear energy] (NRCH) ...... CPC
Controlled-Potential Electrolysis .... CPE
Controlled-Release Hydrocodone [An analgesic] [Pennwalt Corp.] ...... CRHC
Controlled-Slip Differentials (IEEE) .... CSD
Controlled-Source Audiofrequency Megnetotellurics [Geophysics] ...... CSAMT
Controlled-Time of Arrival (GAVI) .... CTA

Controller (ECII) C
Controller .... CNTLR
Controller (NASA) .... CNTRL
Controller .... CNTRLLR
Controller (AFM) .... CON
Controller (KSC) .... CONT
Controller (DD) .... cont
Controller [*Computer hardware*] (NITA) .... CONTROL
Controller Active State (IAA) .... CACS
Controller Adaptor Unit [*Computer science*] (NITA) .... CAU
Controller Administration Service, Europe [*Air Force*] .... CASEUR
Controller/Attitude-Direct Electronics (NASA) .... CADE
Controller Automated Spacing Aid [*FAA*] (TAG) .... CASA
Controller Central Operating Authority (NATG) .... CCOA
Controller Checkout Console (NASA) CCC
Controller Decision Evaluation .... CODE
Controller Defence Communications Network [*Navy British*] .... CDCN
Controller/Director Information File (AFM) .... CDIF
Controller Error (AFM) .... CONE
Controller General of Civil Aviation [*British*] .... CGCA
Controller General of Economy [*Military British*] .... CGE
Controller General of Machine Tools [*Ministry of Supply*] [*British*] .... CGMT
Controller General of Munitions Production [*Ministry of Supply*] [*British*] .... CGMP
Controller Input Test Equipment .... CITE
Controller Interface Unit (MCD) .... CIU
Controller Military Accounts [*British military*] (DMA) .... CMA
Controller of Accounts .... CA
Controller of American Supplies and Repair [*Ministry of Aircraft Production*] [*British World War II*] .... CASR
Controller of Chemical Defence Department [*Ministry of Supply*] [*British*] .... CCDD
Controller of Chemical Research and Development [*Ministry of Supply*] [*British*] .... CCRD
Controller of Communications [*RAF*] [*British*] .... C of C
Controller of Communications Equipment Overseas [*British*] .... CCEO
Controller of Merchant Shipbuilding and Repairs [*Navy British*] .... CMSR
Controller of Physical Research and Signals Development [*Ministry of Supply*] [*British*] .... CPRSD
Controller of Projectile Development [*Ministry of Supply*] [*British World War II*] .... CPD
Controller of Research and Development [*Ministry of Aircraft Production*] [*British*] .... CRD
Controller of Research and Development Establishments and Research [*British*] (RDA) .... CER
Controller of the Navy [*British*] .... C of N
Controller Oriented Processor Series [*Computer science*] (PDAA) .... COPS
Controller Overload Prediction Technique (PDAA) .... COPTEC
Controller Pilot Datalink Communications (GAVI) .... CPDLC
Controller Processor Signal (CAAL) .... CPS
Controller Supply Rate (DOMA) .... CSR
Controllerate Royal Ordnance Factories (PDAA) .... CROF
Controllers Council (EA) CC
Controllers Institute of America [*Later, FEI*] .... CIA
Controllers' Operations and Procedures Committee (FAAC) .... COPCOM
Control-Oriented Computer (MCD) .... CORC
Control-Oriented Language [*Computer science*] .... COL
Control-Oriented Language [*Computer science*] (IEEE) .... COOL
Control-Oriented Processor [*Computer science*] (PDAA) .... COP
Controls [*JETDS nomenclature*] [*Military*] (CET) C
Controls and Displays System [*or Subsystem*] [*Aerospace*] .... C & DS
Controls and Panel Arrangement by Logical Evaluation (PDAA) .... CAPABLE
Controls Assembly Set .... CAS
Controls Mock-Up .... CMU
Controversiae [*of Seneca the Elder*] [*Classical studies*] (OCD) .... Controv
Controversiarum Excerpta [*of Seneca the Elder*] [*Classical studies*] (OCD) .... Con Ex
Controversy (ROG) .... CONTROV
Controverted Elections Judges [*England*] (DLA) .... Cont El
Contundere [*To Be Bruised, Pounded*] [*Pharmacy*] (ROG) .... CONTUND
Contusus [*Bruised*] [*Medicine*] C
Contusus [*Bruised*] [*Medicine*] .... CONT
Contusus [*Bruised*] [*Medicine*] .... CONTUS
Conurbation Transport Authority .... CTA
CONUS [*Continental United States*] **Air Defense Effectiveness Model** (MCD) .... CADEM
CONUS [*Continental United States*] **Air Defense Engagement Simulation** .... CADENS
CONUS [*Continental United States*] **Air Defense Modernization** .... CADM
CONUS [*Continental United States*] **Airborne Reconnaissance for Damage Assessment** (MCD) .... CARDA
CONUS [*Continental United States*] **and Overseas Microfilm User Tests** .... COMUT
CONUS [*Continental United States*] **Army** (MCD) .... CONUSA
CONUS [*Continental United States*] **Army Installation Management Study** .... CAIMS
Conus Branch [*Anatomy*] .... CB
CONUS [*Continental United States*] **Depot Equipment** [*Military*] .... CDE
CONUS [*Continental United States*] **Freight Management System** [*DoD*] .... CFM
CONUS [*Continental United States*] **Ground Station** (MCD) .... CGS
CONUS [*Continental United States*] **Installation Logistics Support** (MCD) .... COILS
CONUS [*Continental United States*] **Installation Maintenance Support** (MCD) .... COIMS
CONUS [*Continental United States*] **Installation Supply Support** (MCD) .... COISS
CONUS [*Continental United States*] **Installation Transportation System** (MCD) .... COITS
CONUS [*Continental United States*] **Meteorological Data System** [*or Distribution*] (MCD) .... COMEDS
CONUS [*Continental United States*] **Net Depot Method** .... CND
CONUS [*Continental United States*] **Replacement Center** [*Military*] (GFGA) .... CRC
CONUS [*Continental United States*] **Sustaining Increment** [*Army*] (AABC) .... CSI
CONUS [*Continental United States*] **Telephone Modernization Program** .... CTMP
CONVAIR [*Consolidated-Vultee Aircraft Corp.*] **Astronautics Corp.** [*Later, Gener al Dynamics Corp.*] (AAG) .... CAC
CONVAIR [*Consolidated-Vultee Aircraft Corp.*] **Astronautics Corp. Astronautics Corp.** [*Later, General Dynamics Corp.*] (AAG) .... CVA
CONVAIR [*Consolidated-Vultee Aircraft Corp.*] **Daingerfield** [*Later, General Dynamics/Daingerfield*] (AAG) .... C-D
CONVAIR [*Consolidated-Vultee Aircraft Corp.*] **Fort Worth** [*Later, General Dynamics/Fort Worth*] (AAG) .... CFW
CONVAIR [*Consolidated-Vultee Aircraft Corp.; later, General Dynamics Corp.*] **Government-Owned Facilities and Equipment** (AAG) .... CGOFE
Convalescence [*Medicine*] (DAVI) .... conv
Convalescent [*Medicine*] (AFM) .... CONV
Convalescent [*Medicine*] (ROG) .... CONVAL
Convalescent .... CONVAL
Convalescent [*Medicine*] (ROG) .... CONVALESC
Convalescent and Rehabilitation [*Military*] .... C & R
Convalescent Antidote for Nerve Agent (DOMA) .... CANA
Convalescent Camp [*Military*] CVC
Convalescent Growing Nursery (MEDA) .... CGN
Convalescent Hospital (DAVI) .... CH
Convalescent Hospital (DAVI) .... Conv Hosp
Convalescent Hospital for Children, Library, Rochester, NY [*OCLC symbol*] (OCLC) .... VQF
Convalescent Status [*Medicine*] .... CS
Convalescent Training Depot (NATG) .... CTD
Convalescent Unit [*of a hospital*] .... CU
Convection (ADA) C
Convection .... CNV
Convection (MSA) .... CONVN
Convection Loss Cone (MCD) CLC
Convection Microthermal Oven .... CMT
Convection Suppression Device [*for energy collectors*] .... CSD
Convective (FAAC) .... CNVTV
Convective and Precipitation/Electrification [*Experiment*] (USDC) .... CaPE
Convective and Precipitation/Electrification [*Experiment*] [*Marine science*] (OSRA) .... CaPE
Convective Available Potential Energy .... CAPE
Convective Boundary Layer [*Marine science*] (OSRA) .... CBL
Convective Boundary Layer (USDC) .... CBL
Convective Combustion (MCD) CC
Convective Condensation Level [*Meteorology*] CCL
Convective Heat Transfer .... CHT
Convective Heating and Ablative Program [*Army*] .... CHAP
Convective Instability Base (PDAA) .... CIB
Convective Instability Top (PDAA) .... CIT
Convective Internal Boundary Layer (GFGA) .... CIBL
Convective Storms Division [*National Center for Atmospheric Research*] .... CSD
Convector (DAC) .... Conv
Convector (MSA) .... CONVR
Convectron-Microsyn Erection Circuit (SAA) .... CMEC
Convenant, Condition, and Restriction [*Business term*] (EMRF) .... CC & R
Convene (AABC) .... CVN
Convenience (MSA) .... CNVC
Convenience (ADA) .... CON
Convenience .... CONV
Convenience .... CONVEN
Convenience of the Government .... C of G
Convenience of the Government .... COG
Convenience Store .... C-STORE
Convenience Store (WDMC) .... c-store
Convenience Store Association of Michigan (SRA) .... CSAM
Convenience, Value, Service .... CVS
Convenient .... CONV
Convenient (AABC) .... CONVN
Convenient .... CONVNT
Convenient (ROG) .... CONVT
Convenient Automotive Services Institute (EA) .... CASI
Convening Authority .... CA
Convenor .... Cvnr
Convent .... CNVNT
Convent .... CONV
Convent General of the Knights York Cross of Honour (EA) .... KYCH
Convent of Immaculate Conception Sisters of St. Benedict, Ferdinand, IN [*OCLC symbol*] (OCLC) XIC
Convent of the Holy Rood [*British*] (BI) .... CHR
Convention .... CNVNTN
Convention [*or Conventional*] .... CONV
Convention Africaine [*African Covenant*] .... CA
Convention and Visitors Bureau .... C & VB
Convention Democratic Party [*Liberia*] [*Political party*] (EY) .... CDP
Convention des Institutions Republicaines [*Convention of Republican Institutions*] [*France Political party*] (PPE) .... CIR
Convention Europeenne de la Construction Metallique [*EC*] (ECED) .... CECM
Convention for Safe Containers (MCD) .... CSC
Convention for the Conservation of Antarctic Seals [*Australia*] .... CCAS
Convention II (EA) CII
Convention Information System (IAA) .... CIS
Convention Internationale Concernant le Transport des Marchandises par Chemins de Fer [*International Convention Concerning the Carriage of Goods by Rail*] .... CIM

Convention Internationale Concernant le Transport des Voyageurs et des Bagages par Chemins de Fer [*International Convention Concerning the Carriage of Passengers and Luggage by Rail*] CIV
Convention Liaison Council (EA) CLC
Convention Liberale [*Cameroon*] [*Political party*] (EY) CL
Convention Magazine [*Generic term for a publication covering science-fiction fans' conventions*] .... CONZINE
Convention Nationale des Patriotes Progressistes-Parti Social-Democrate [*Burkina Faso*] [*Political party*] (EY) .... CNPP-PSD
Convention of American Instructors of the Deaf (EA) .... CAID
Convention of Dublin [*Freemasonry*] (ROG) .... C of D
Convention of Edinburgh [*Freemasonry*] (ROG) .... C of E
Convention of London [*Freemasonry*] (ROG) .... C of L
Convention of National Societies of Electrical Engineers of Western Europe (EAIO) .... EUREL
Convention of Scottish Local Authorities (EAIO) .... COSLA
Convention of the Conservation of Antarctic Marine Living Resources (USDC) .... CCAMLR
Convention of the Estates of Scotland [*A publication*] (DLA) .... Conv Est
Convention of York [*Freemasonry*] (ROG) .... CY
Convention on Biological Diversity [*1992*] [*United Nations*] [*Marine science*] (OSRA) .... CBD
Convention on Civil Liability for Oil Pollution Damage (DS) CLC
Convention on International Trade in Endangered Species [*Of wild fauna and flora*] .... CITES
Convention on the Conservation of Migratory Species of Wild Animals (ASF) .... CMSWA
Convention on the Continental Shelf (NOAA) .... CCS
Convention on the Contract for the International Carriage of Goods by Road [*Geneva*] [*19 May 1956*] (DLA) .... CMR
Convention on the Regulation of Antarctic Mineral Resource Activities (GNE) .... CRAMRA
Convention People's Party [*1949-1966*] [*Ghana*] .... CPP
Convention Relative au Contrat de Transport de Marchandises en Navigation Interieure [*Convention on the Carriage of Goods by Inland Waterways*] .... CMN
Convention Services Manager .... CSM
Conventional (AFM) .... CONVL
Conventional CV
Conventional (MSA) .... CVNTL
Conventional Air Warfare Exercise (DNAB) .... CAWEX
Conventional Airfield Attack Missile (MCD) .... CAAM
Conventional Airfield Attack Munitions [*Army*] .... CAM
Conventional Airfield Attack System [*Army*] .... CAAS
Conventional Alloy (OA) .... CA
Conventional Ammunition Integrated Management System .... CAIMS
Conventional Ammunition Integrated Management System (DNAB) .... CLAIMS
Conventional Ammunition Maintenance, Preservation, and Packaging Set (MCD) .... CAMPPS
Conventional Ammunition Working Capital Fund [*DoD*] .... CAWCF
Conventional and Alternative Transportation Systems Laboratory [*University of Florida*] [*Research center*] (RCD) .... CATS
Conventional Armaments Planning System (DOMA) .... CAPS
Conventional Armed Forces and Conventional Armaments .... CAFCA
Conventional Armed Forces in Europe (ECON) .... CAFE
Conventional Arms Transfers .... CAT
Conventional Boom Sprayer .... CBS
Conventional Buoy Mooring (DS) .... CBM
Conventional Catamaran (PDAA) .... CONCAT
Conventional Circuit Analysis Program (DNAB) .... CCAP
Conventional Color (OA) CC
Conventional Combustion Environmental Assessment [*Environmental Protection Agency*] (GFGA) .... CCEA
Conventional Defense Improvements (DOMA) .... CDI
Conventional Defense Initiative [*Military*] (SDI) .... CDI
Conventional District [*Church of England*] .... CD
Conventional Engine Anti-Pollution System [*Automotive engineering*] .... CEAPS
Conventional Force Data Base [*Model*] .... CFDB
Conventional Forces in Europe [*Military*] .... CFE
Conventional Friend Virus .... CFV
Conventional Geometry Smart Projectile .... CGSP
Conventional Grain-Oriented Product (MCD) .... CGO
Conventional Instruction (RDA) CI
Conventional Insulin Treatment [*Medicine*] .... CIT
Conventional International Origin .... CIO
Conventional Land Attack Tomahawk Missile (MCD) .... CLAT
Conventional Landing (MCD) CL
Conventional Mechanical Ventilation .... CMV
Conventional Military Fuels (RDA) .... CMF
Conventional Mortgage-Backed Security .... CMBS
Conventional Munition Disposal (PDAA) .... CMD
Conventional Munitions Master Plan (DOMA) .... CMMP
Conventional Munitions System [*Military*] .... CMS
Conventional Old Oil Prices .... COOP
Conventional Ordnance Release Computer (NG) .... CORC
Conventional Ordnance Status System (MCD) .... COSS
Conventional Oxidation Catalysis [*of gasoline engine exhausts*] .... COC
Conventional Polyethylene .... CPE
Conventional Solvent Extraction [*Separation science and technology*] .... CSX
Conventional Spin Hamiltonian (PDAA) .... CSH
Conventional Stability Talks [*Arms control*] .... CST
Conventional Standoff Weapon .... CSW
Conventional System [*Indexing*] (NITA) .... CS
Conventional Systems Committee [*DoD*] (DOMA) .... CSC
Conventional Tactical Air Model (MCD) .... CONTACA

Conventional Takeoff [*Aviation*] (NATG) .... CTO
Conventional Take-off and Landing [*Aircraft*] .... CTOL
Conventional Therapy [*Medicine*] .... CT
Conventional Tillage [*Agroecosystem*] .... CT
Conventional Vehicle [*Environmental science*] CV
Conventional Ventilation [*Medicine*] CV
Conventional [*Non-Nuclear*] War Capability (AAG) .... CWC
Conventional Weapon Index (MCD) .... CWI
Conventional Weapon Technical Proficiency Inspection [*Military*] (CAAL) .... CTPI
Conventional Weapons Loading Exercise [*Navy*] (ANA) .... CONVWEPS LOADEX
Conventional Weapons Tactical Proficiency Inspection [*Navy*] (DOMA) .... CWTPI
Conventional Weapons Technology (MCD) .... CWT
Conventional Weighted Least Square .... CWLS
Conventional Wisdom [*Professional political opinion*] .... CW
Conventional Wisdom Watch [*Newsweek Magazine*] .... CW
Conventionally Fueled Vehicle [*Automotive engineering*] .... CFV
Conventionally Refined Carrageenan [*Food grade*] .... CRC
Conventional-Transmission Electron Microscope .... CEM
Conventional-Transmission Electron Microscope .... CTEM
Conventions, Meetings, Incentive Travel [*Of CMI World, a publication aimed at those markets*] .... CMI
Convention-Seminar Cassettes [*Commercial firm*] .... CSC
Conventual (TOCD) .... conu
Conventual Franciscans (TOCD) .... OFMConv
Conventual Franciscans, Friars Minor (TOCD) .... ofm
Conventures Ltd. [*Toronto Stock Exchange symbol*] .... CVY
Converge (FAAC) .... CNVG
Convergence (IAA) .... CONV
Convergence [*Medicine*] (DMAA) .... converg
Convergence (MSA) .... CONVG
Convergence Source-Image Distortion [*Crystal*] .... CSID
Convergence Sublayer [*Electronics*] (ACRL) .... CS
Convergence Zone [*Military*] (NVT) .... CZ
Convergence Zone Propagation [*Military*] .... CZP
Convergence Zone Range [*Military*] (CAAL) .... CZR
Convergence Zone Resolution Pattern [*Military*] (CAAL) .... CZRP
Convergence Zone Width [*Military*] (CAAL) .... CZW
Convergencia Democratica [*Democratic Convergence*] [*El Salvador*] [*Political party*] (EY) .... CD
Convergencia Democratica de Catalunya [*Democratic Convergence of Catalonia*] [*Spain Political party*] (PPE) .... CDC
Convergencia Democratica en Uruguay [*Democratic Convergence in Uruguay*] (PD) .... CDU
Convergencia i Unio [*Convergence and Union*] [*Spain Political party*] (PPE) .... CiU
Convergent Beam Diffraction .... CBD
Convergent Beam Electron Diffraction [*Analytical technique*] .... CBED
Convergent Exhaust Nozzle Control (MCD) .... CENC
Convergent Force Field [*Neuromechanics*] .... CFF
Convergent Stereoscopic [*Photography*] .... CS
Convergent Strabismus [*Ophthalmology*] (DAVI) .... conv strab
Convergent Technologies Expo [*Publications and Communications, Inc.*] (TSPED) .... CT
Convergent Technologies Operating System [*Computer science*] .... CTOS
Convergent-Divergent Nozzle .... CDN
Converging Approach Standards Technical Working Group [*FAA*] (TAG) .... CASTWG
Converging Guide Accelerator (MCD) .... CGA
Converging Runway Display Aid [*FAA*] (TAG) .... CRDA
Converging-Diverging (MCD) .... CD
Conversation (AABC) .... CON
Conversation .... CONV
Conversation (ROG) .... CONVERS
Conversation Factor [*Computer science*] .... CF
Conversation Specifications and Work Requirements (DNAB) .... CSWR
Conversational Algebraic Language [*Adaptation of JOSS language*] [*Computer science*] .... CAL
Conversational Analyzer and Drafting System (PDAA) .... CADS
Conversational and Interactive Project Evaluation and Control System [*IBM Corp.*] .... CIPREC
Conversational Circuit Analysis Program [*Computer science*] (PDAA) .... CONCAP
Conversational Communication Access Method .... CCAM
Conversational Compiling System [*Xerox Corp.*] (IEEE) .... CCS
Conversational Computer Statistical System (PDAA) .... CCSS
Conversational English .... CE
Conversational Extensible Language [*Computer science*] (CSR) .... CEL
Conversational File Information Retrieval and Management System [*Computer science*] (MCD) .... CONFIRM
Conversational Graphical Programming Language (PDAA) .... CGPL
Conversational Interactive Digital/Analog Simulator [*IBM Corp.*] (IEEE) .... CIDAS
Conversational Language for Input/Output [*Computer science*] .... CLIO
Conversational Language for Interactive Computing CLIC
Conversational Macro Package (PDAA) .... COMAP
Conversational Mode Terminal [*Friden, Inc.*] (IEEE) .... CMT
Conversational Modeling Language [*Computer science*] .... CML
Conversational Monitor System [*IBM Corp.*] [*Computer science*] .... CMS
Conversational On-Line Real-Time Algorithm Definition [*Computer science*] (MHDB) .... CONRAD
Conversational On-Line Storage and Retrieval [*Computer science*] (MHDB) .... COSTAR
Conversational Parts Programming Language [*Computer science*] (IEEE) .... CAPT
Conversational Problem Solver (PDAA) .... COPS
Conversational Program Module [*Fujitsu Ltd.*] [*Japan*] .... CPM
Conversational Programming Language [*High-level language*] [*Digital Equipment Corp.*] [*Computer science*] .... CPL

Conversational Programming System [*Computer science*] .... CPS
Conversational Remote Batch Entry [*Computer science*] .... CRBE
Conversational Remote Job Entry [*Computer science*] .... CRJE
Conversational Software System [*National CSS, Inc.*] .... CSS
Conversational Statistical Analysis (MCD) .... COSAN
Conversational System with On-Line Remote Terminals [*Computer science*] (IEEE) .... CONSORT
Conversational Terminal System [*Computer science*] (BUR) .... CTS
Conversational Time-Sharing [*Computer science*] (IEEE) .... CTS
Conversational Traffic Analysis (MCD) .... COTRAN
Conversational Utility Program for Information Display (PDAA) .... CUPID
Conversational Voice [*Medicine*] CV
Conversazione [*Conversation*] [*Italian*] (ROG) .... CONVERS
Converse .... CNV
Converse .... CONVRS
Converse College (GAGS) .... Converse C
Converse College, Spartanburg, SC [*OCLC symbol*] (OCLC) .... SCO
Converse College, Spartanburg, SC [*Library symbol Library of Congress*] (LCLS) .... ScSpC
Converse County Library, Douglas, WY [*Library symbol Library of Congress*] (LCLS) .... WyDo
Converse, Inc. [*Associated Press*] (SAG) .... Converse
Converse, Inc. [*NYSE symbol*] (SAG) .... CVE
Converse Jackson Township Public Library, Converse, IN [*Library symbol Library of Congress*] (LCLS) .... InCon
Conversion .... CNVRSN
Conversion (FAAC) .... CNVSN
Conversion .... CONV
Conversion (ROG) .... CONVERSN
Conversion (MSA) .... CVRSN
Conversion [*Legal shorthand*] (LWAP) .... CVSN
Conversion Adjustment Factor .... CAF
Conversion, Alteration, and Repair [*Navy*] .... CAR
Conversion and Check Limit (IAA) CCL
Conversion and Recording Equipment (MCD) .... CARE
Conversion Complete (IAA) .... CCMP
Conversion Computer Unit .... CCU
Conversion Control Officer [*Army*] .... CCO
Conversion Electron Mossbauer Spectroscopy .... CEMS
Conversion Factor (MCD) .... CF
Conversion Factor .... CvF
Conversion for Reclaiming Earth in the Americas [*An association*] .... CREA
Conversion in Lieu of Procurement [*Military*] .... CILOP
Conversion in Place [*Aerospace*] (AAG) .... CIP
Conversion Industries, Inc. [*AMEX symbol*] (SPSG) .... CVD
Conversion Industries, Inc. [*Vancouver Stock Exchange symbol*] .... CVE
Conversion Kit (MCD) .... CK
Conversion Loss CL
Conversion Master Plan (CAAL) .... CMP
Conversion, Memory, and Fault Indication [*Telecommunications*] (TEL) .... C/MFI
Conversion of Production System [*Engineering Index, Inc.*] .... COPS
Conversion of Range Telemetry Systems (MCD) .... CORTS
Conversion of Serials (MCD) .... CONSER
Conversion of Serials Project [*Database project*] (NITA) .... CONSER
Conversion Process Controller System .... CPCS
Conversion Program System (NRCH) .... CPS
Conversion Programmer's Guide .... CPG
Conversion Ratio [*Endocrinology*] (DAVI) .... CR
Conversion Result Register (IAA) .... CRR
Conversion Tech Intl. [*NASDAQ symbol*] (TTSB) .... CTIX
Conversion Tech Intl.Wrrt'A' [*NASDAQ symbol*] (TTSB) .... CTIXW
Conversion Tech Intl.Wrrt'B' [*NASDAQ symbol*] (TTSB) .... CTIXZ
Conversion Technologies International, Inc. [*Associated Press*] (SAG) .... ConvT
Conversion Technologies International, Inc. [*Associated Press*] (SAG) .... ConvTch
Conversion Technologies International, Inc. [*NASDAQ symbol*] (SAG) .... CTIX
Conversion to Full-Time Manning .... CFTM
Conversion Unit [*British military*] (DMA) .... CU
Conversional FORTRAN [*Formula Translating System*] (IAA) .... CFOR
Convert (FAAC) .... CNVRT
Convert (BARN) .... Cnvt
Convert (ECII) .... CNVT
Convert (AABC) .... CONVT
Convert .... CVT
Convert Character Code (OA) CCC
Convert Clock Input [*Computer science*] (IAA) CCI
Convert Gray to Binary .... CGB
Convert Makers of America [*Later, CMOA*] (EA) .... CMA
Convert Movement Our Apostolate (EA) .... CMOA
Convert to Binary (IAA) .... CVB
Convert to Decimal (IAA) .... CVD
Converted (DCTA) .... CONV
Converted Aerial Targets (NG) .... CAT
Converted Battalion Anti-Tank [*Military*] (PDAA) .... CONBAT
Converted Destroyer .... CONVDD
Converted Prelease (ADA) .... CPL
Converter [*Electronics*] (ECII) .... CNVT
Converter (IAA) .... CON
Converter (KSC) .... CONV
Converter .... CONVRTR
Converter Amplifier Unit (MCD) .... CAU
Converter Clutch Override [*Automotive engineering*] .... CCO
Converter Compressor Facility (KSC) .... CCF
Converter Display Group .... CDG
Converter Enhanced, Electronically Managed Automatic Transmission .... CEEMAT
Converter, Frequency to DC [*Direct Current*] **Voltage** (MCD) .... CFD
Converter Multiplexer (CAAL) .... CMUX
Converter/Programmer (MCD) .... C/P
Converter, Pulse to DC [*Direct Current*] **Voltage** (NASA) .... CPD
Converter Regulator Unit (MCD) .... CRU
Converter Simulator Signal Unit (MCD) .... CSSU
Converter, Variable Resistance, to DC [*Direct Current*] **Voltage** (NASA) .... CVRD
Converter, Voltage, AC [*Alternating Current*] **to DC** [*Direct Current*] (MCD) .... CVAD
Converter, Voltage Discrete, AC [*Alternating Current*] (NASA) .... CVDA
Converters [*Electronic*] [*JETDS nomenclature*] [*Military*] (CET) CV
Convertible [*Rate*] [*Value of the English pound*] .... CN
Convertible .... CONV
Convertible .... CONVRTBL
Convertible [*Automotive engineering*] CV
Convertible [*Stock exchange term*] (SPSG) CV
Convertible [*Stock exchange term*] .... CVT
Convertible Adjustable Preferred Stock [*Investment term*] (DFIT) .... CAPS
Convertible Adjustable Rate Preferred Stock (MHDB) .... CAP
Convertible Bond Option [*Finance*] (EMRF) .... CBO
Convertible Circuit Breaker .... CCB
Convertible Hldgs [*NYSE symbol*] (TTSB) .... CNV
Convertible Hldgs Inc Shrs [*NYSE symbol*] (TTSB) .... CNVPr
Convertible Holdings [*NYSE symbol*] (SPSG) .... CNV
Convertible Holdings [*Associated Press*] (SAG) .... ConvHld
Convertible Holdings [*Associated Press*] (SAG) .... CvHd
Convertible Lens [*Photography*] CL
Convertible Money Market Preferred Stock [*Investment term*] .... CMMP
Convertible Note .... CN
Convertible Note .... CVNT
Convertible Preferred Stock [*Investment term*] .... CPS
Convertible Report (PDAA) .... CR
Convertible Security [*Investment term*] (DFIT) CV
Convertible Security [*Business term*] (MHDW) CVC
Convertible Unsecured Loan Stock [*Finance*] .... CULS
Convertible Wraparound Mortgage [*Banking*] .... CWM
Converting Enzyme .... CE
Converting Equipment Manufacturers Association (EA) .... CEMA
Converting Machinery and Materials (DGA) .... CMM
Converting-Enzyme Inhibitor [*Biochemistry*] .... CEI
ConVest Energy Corp. [*Associated Press*] (SAG) .... CnvstE
ConVest Energy Corp. [*AMEX symbol*] (SPSG) .... COV
ConVest Energy Partners Ltd. (MHDW) .... CEP
Convex (MSA) CVX
Convex CX
Convex Computer [*Associated Press*] (SAG) .... Convex
Convex Computer Corp. (MHDW) .... CNVX
Convex Computer Corp. [*NYSE symbol*] (SPSG) .... CNX
Convex Set Stochastic Dominance [*Statistics*] .... CSD
Convexity, Symmetry, Maximum [*Statistics*] .... CSM
Convexo-Concave [*Replacement heart valves*] [*Cardiology*] .... C-C
Convey [*Legal shorthand*] (LWAP) .... COVY
Conveyance [*Transportation*] (DCTA) .... CONV
Conveyance .... CONVCE
Conveyance [*Legal shorthand*] (LWAP) .... COVCE
Conveyancer [*or Conveyancing*] [*Legal term*] (DLA) .... Conv
Conveyancer [*Legal term*] (DLA) .... Convey
Conveyancers' Year Book [*1940-51*] [*A publication*] (DLA) .... Conv YB
Conveyancing [*Legal shorthand*] (LWAP) .... COVNG
Conveyancing Review [*1957-63*] [*Scotland*] [*A publication*] (DLA) .... Conv Rev
Conveyancing Review [*1957-63*] [*Scotland*] [*A publication*] (DLA) .... CR
Conveyed (ROG) .... CONVD
Conveying .... CNVYG
Conveyor (KSC) .... CNVR
Conveyor .... CNVYR
Conveyor .... CONVYR
Conveyor Control System .... CCS
Conveyor Equipment Manufacturers Association (EA) .... CEMA
Conveyor Equipment Manufacturers Association .... ConEMA
Conveyor Section of the Material Handling Institute (EA) .... CS
Conveyorized Automatic Tube Tester [*Computer science*] .... CATT
Convict (ADA) C
Convict (AABC) .... CNVT
Convict (ADA) .... CON
Convict .... CONV
Convicted Poacher [*Legal*] [*British*] (ROG) .... CP
Conviction by Civil Court .... CBCC
Convicts' Association for a Good Environment [*Defunct*] .... CAGE
Convivium Septem Sapientium [*of Plutarch*] [*Classical studies*] (OCD) .... Conv Sept Sap
Convocation .... CONV
Convocation .... CONVOC
Convolutional Coding Unit .... CCU
Convolutional Decoder Assembly .... CDA
Convolvulus Jalapa [*Jalap Plant*] [*Pharmacology*] (ROG) .... CONVOLV JAP
Convoy (NVT) .... CONV
Convoy and Routing [*Section*] [*US Fleet*] .... C & R
Convoy and Routing [*Section*] [*US Fleet*] .... CANDR
Convoy and Routing [*Section*] [*US Fleet*] .... CONROUTE
Convoy Commodore [*Navy*] (NVT) CC
Convoy Commodore [*Navy*] .... CONCOMO
Convoy Control Officer [*Navy*] .... CCO
Convoy Escort Vessel [*Navy*] .... CEV
Convoy Exercise [*Navy*] (NVT) .... CONVEX
Convoy, Routing, and Scheduling System [*USAREUR*] .... CRASS
Convulsive Disorder [*Medicine*] .... CD

Convulsive Dose [Medicine] ..... CD
Convulsive Shock Therapy [Medicine] ..... CST
Conway, AR [Location identifier FAA] (FAAL) ..... CWS
Conway, AR [AM radio station call letters] ..... KCON
Conway, AR [AM radio station call letters] ..... KFCA
Conway, AR [FM radio station call letters] ..... KHDX
Conway, AR [FM radio station call letters] ..... KMJX
Conway, AR [FM radio station call letters] ..... KTOD
Conway, AR [AM radio station call letters] ..... KUCA
Conway, NH [AM radio station call letters] ..... WBNC
Conway, NH [FM radio station call letters] (RBYB) ..... WBNC-FM
Conway, NH [FM radio station call letters] ..... WMWV
Conway, SC [Location identifier FAA] (FAAL) ..... HYW
Conway, SC [FM radio station call letters] ..... WHMC
Conway, SC [Television station call letters] ..... WHMC-TV
Conway, SC [AM radio station call letters] ..... WJXY
Conway, SC [FM radio station call letters] ..... WJXY-FM
Conway, SC [AM radio station call letters] ..... WPJS
Conway, SC [FM radio station call letters] ..... WYAV
Conway Twitty Fan Club [Defunct] (EA) ..... CTFC
Conwest Exploration Co. Ltd. [Toronto Stock Exchange symbol] ..... CEX
Conwest Exploration Company Ltd. [NASDAQ symbol] (SAG) ..... CEXC
Conwest Exploration Company Ltd. [Associated Press] (SAG) ..... Conwst
Conyers, GA [AM radio station call letters] ..... WPBS
Coober Pedy [Australia Airport symbol] (OAG) ..... CPD
Cooch Behar [India] [Airport symbol] (AD) ..... COH
Cooch-Behar [India] [ICAO location identifier] (ICLI) ..... VECO
Coode on the Written Law [A publication] (DLA) ..... Coode Wr L
Cooder Brown Band Fan Club (EA) ..... CBBFC
Coode's Legislative Expression [A publication] (DLA) ..... Coode Leg Exp
Cook [Ranking title] [British Women's Royal Naval Service] C
Cook [Navy British] ..... CK
Cook [N. B.] Corp. Ltd. [Toronto Stock Exchange symbol Vancouver Stock Exchange symbol] ..... NBC
Cook County Clerk's Office, Chicago, IL [Library symbol] [Library of Congress] (LCLS) ICC
Cook County High School, Grand Marais, MN [Library symbol] [Library of Congress] (LCLS) ..... MnGmH
Cook County Hospital, Dr. Frederick Tice Memorial Library, Chicago, IL [Library symbol Library of Congress] (LCLS) ..... ICCH
Cook County Law Library, Chicago, IL [Library symbol Library of Congress] (LCLS) ICCL
Cook County School of Nursing, Chicago, IL [Library symbol Library of Congress] (LCLS) ..... ICCN
Cook Inlet Aviation, Inc. [ICAO designator] (FAAC) ..... CKA
Cook Inlet Native Association [Defunct] (EA) ..... CINA
Cook Island [MARC geographic area code Library of Congress] (LCCP) ..... pocw--
Cook Islandair [ICAO designator] (AD) ..... KH
Cook Islands [ANSI two-letter standard code] (CNC) ..... CK
Cook Islands [ANSI three-letter standard code] (CNC) ..... COK
Cook Islands [MARC country of publication code Library of Congress] (LCCP) ..... cw
Cook Islands International [New Zealand] [ICAO designator] (FAAC) CII
Cook Islands International [ICAO designator] (AD) ..... KC
Cook Islands Party [Political party] (PPW) ..... CIP
Cook Memorial Public Library District, Libertyville, IL [Library symbol Library of Congress] (LCLS) ..... ILib
Cook on Corporations [A publication] (DLA) ..... Cook Corp
Cook on Stock, Stockholders, and General Corporation Law [A publication] (DLA) ..... Cook Stock Stockh & Corp Law
Cook Public Library, Cook, MN [Library symbol] [Library of Congress] (LCLS) ..... MnCoo
Cook Public School, Cook, MN [Library symbol] [Library of Congress] (LCLS) ..... MnCooS
Cook Transit R. R. [AAR code] ..... COOK
Cooke. Act Book of the Ecclesiastical Court of Whalley [A publication] (DLA) ..... Cooke
Cooke. Agricultural Tenancies [3rd ed.] [1882] [A publication] (DLA) ..... Coo Agr T
Cooke. Agricultural Tenancies [3rd ed.] [A publication] (DLA) ..... Cooke Agr T
Cooke Air Force Base [Later, VAFB] (AAG) ..... CAFB
Cooke and Alcock's Great Britain Reports [Ireland] [A publication] (DLA) ..... Co & Al
Cooke and Alcock's Irish King's Bench Reports [1833-34] [A publication] (DLA) ..... C & A
Cooke and Alcock's Irish King's Bench Reports [1833-34] [A publication] (DLA) ..... Coo & Al
Cooke and Alcock's Irish King's Bench Reports [1833-34] [A publication] (DLA) ..... Cooke & Al (Ir)
Cooke and Alcock's Reports [Ireland] [A publication] (DLA) ..... Cooke & A
Cooke and Alcock's Reports [Ireland] [A publication] (DLA) ..... Cooke & Al
Cooke and Alcock's Reports [Ireland] [A publication] (DLA) ..... Cooke & Alc
Cooke and Harwood's Charitable Trusts [2nd ed.] [1867] [A publication] (DLA) ..... C & H Char Tr
Cooke and Harwood's Charitable Trusts Acts [A publication] (DLA) ..... Coo & H Tr
Cooke and Harwood's Charitable Trusts Acts [A publication] (DLA) ..... Cooke & H Ch Tr
Cooke County Junior College, Gainsville, TX [Library symbol Library of Congress] (LCLS) ..... TxGaiC
Cooke on Life Insurance [A publication] (DLA) ..... Cooke Ins
Cooke on the Agricultural Holdings Act [A publication] (DLA) ..... Cooke Agr Hold
Cooked ..... CKD
Cooked ..... CKD
Cooked Cured-Meat Pigment [Food technology] ..... CCMP
Cooked Potato Weight [Food technology] (OA) ..... CPW
Cooked Therapeutic Inflight Meal (DNAB) ..... CTIM

Cooker C
Cooker Control Unit ..... CCU
Cooker Restaurant [NYSE symbol] (TTSB) ..... CGR
Cooker Restaurant, Inc. [NYSE symbol] (SAG) ..... CGR
Cooker Restaurant, Inc. [Associated Press] (SAG) ..... Cooker
Cookery and Food Association [British] (BI) ..... CFA
Cookery Officer [Navy British] ..... CK
Cooke's Admiralty Cases [Quebec] [A publication] (DLA) ..... Cook Adm
Cooke's Bankrupt Laws [A publication] (DLA) ..... Coo Bankr
Cooke's Bankrupt Laws [A publication] (DLA) ..... Cooke BL
Cooke's Cases of Practice [125 English Reprint] [A publication] (DLA) ..... Cooke (Eng)
Cooke's Cases of Practice, English Common Pleas [A publication] (DLA) ..... Cooke
Cooke's Enfranchisement of Copyholds [2nd ed.] [1853] [A publication] (DLA) ..... Coo Cop
Cooke's Enfranchisement of Copyholds [2nd ed.] [1853] [A publication] (DLA) ..... Cooke Cop
Cooke's English Common Pleas Reports [1706-47] [A publication] (DLA) ..... Cooke CP
Cooke's Inclosure Acts [A publication] (DLA) ..... Coo IA
Cooke's Inclosure Acts [A publication] (DLA) ..... Cooke IA
Cooke's Inclosure Acts [A publication] (DLA) ..... Cooke Incl Acts
Cooke's Law of Defamation [A publication] (DLA) ..... Coo Def
Cooke's Law of Defamation [A publication] (DLA) ..... Cooke Def
Cooke's New York Highway Laws [A publication] (DLA) ..... Cooke High
Cooke's Practical Register of the Common Pleas [A publication] (DLA) ..... Cooke Pr Reg
Cooke's Practice Cases [1706-47] [England] [A publication] (DLA) ..... Ca Prac CP
Cooke's Practice Cases [1706-47] [England] [A publication] (DLA) ..... Rep Cas Pr
Cooke's Practice Reports, English Common Pleas [A publication] (DLA) ..... Cooke Pr Cas
Cooke's Tennessee Reports [A publication] (DLA) ..... Cooke
Cooke's Tennessee Reports [A publication] (DLA) ..... Cooke (Tenn)
Cooke's Tennessee Reports [A publication] (DLA) ..... Cooke's Rep
Cookeville General Hospital, Stephen Farr Health Sciences Library, Cookeville, TN [Library symbol Library of Congress] (LCLS) ..... TCooH
Cookeville, TN [Location identifier FAA] (FAAL) ..... CJE
Cookeville, TN [Television station call letters] ..... WCTE
Cookeville, TN [FM radio station call letters] ..... WGSQ
Cookeville, TN [FM radio station call letters] (RBYB) ..... WHRS-FM
Cookeville, TN [AM radio station call letters] ..... WHUB
Cookeville, TN [FM radio station call letters] ..... WHUB-FM
Cookeville, TN [Television station call letters] ..... WKZX
Cookeville, TN [AM radio station call letters] ..... WPTN
Cookeville, TN [FM radio station call letters] ..... WTTU
Cookeville, TN [FM radio station call letters] ..... WWOG
Cookham [England] ..... COOK
Cookhouse [South Africa] [ICAO location identifier] (ICLI) ..... FACH
Cookie ..... CK
Cookie and Snack Bakers Association (EA) ..... CSBA
Cookie Cutter Collectors Club (EA) CCCC
Cooking Advancement Research and Education Foundation (EA) ..... CAREF
Cooking for Survival Consciousness (EA) ..... CSC
Cook's Lower Canada Admiralty Court Cases [A publication] (DLA) ..... Co A
Cook's Penal Code [New York] [A publication] (DLA) ..... Cook's Pen Code
Cook's Vice-Admiralty Reports [Canada] [A publication] (DLA) ..... Cook Adm
Cook's Vice-Admiralty Reports [Canada A publication] (DLA) ..... Cook V Adm
Cook's Vice-Admiralty Reports [Canada A publication] (DLA) ..... Cook Vice-Adm
Cookstown Public Library, Ontario [Library symbol National Library of Canada] (BIB) ..... OCOO
Cooktown [Australia Airport symbol] (OAG) ..... CTN
Cookware Manufacturers Association (EA) ..... CMA
Cool Dehumidified Air (PDAA) ..... CDA
Cool Down (AAG) ..... CLDWN
Cool Mist Vaporizer [Medicine] (DMAA) ..... CMV
Cool Room ..... CLRM
Cool Thermal Energy Storage [Air-conditioning] (PS) ..... CTES
Cool Water Coal Gasification [Fuel technology] ..... CWCG
Cool White (DAC) ..... CW
Cool White Deluxe (DAC) ..... CWX
Coolah [New South Wales] [Airport symbol] (AD) ..... CLH
Coolangatta [Australia ICAO location identifier] (ICLI) ..... ABCG
Coolangatta [Queensland] [Airport symbol] (AD) ..... OOL
Coolant (AAG) ..... CLNT
Coolant (MSA) ..... COOL
Coolant Boiling and Rod Arrays [Nuclear energy] (NRCH) ..... COBRA
Coolant Control Assembly (NASA) ..... CCA
Coolant Control Engine Vacuum Switch [Automotive engineering] ..... CCEVS
Coolant Control Valve CCV
Coolant Distribution Unit [Computer science] ..... CDU
Coolant Fan Control [Automotive engineering] ..... CFC
Coolant Level Sensor [Automotive engineering] ..... COLS
Coolant Override Valve [Automotive engineering] ..... COV
Coolant Pump [Nuclear energy] (NRCH) ..... CP
Coolant Pump Power Inverters (MCD) ..... CPPI
Coolant Recovery System [Automotive engineering] ..... CRS
Coolant Reserve System [Automotive engineering] ..... CRS
Coolant Sampling (DNAB) ..... CS
Coolant Spark Control [Automotive engineering] ..... CSC
Coolant Temperature Override [Automotive engineering] ..... CTO
Coolant Temperature Sensor [Automotive engineering] ..... CTS
Coolant Vacuum Switch Cold Closed [Automotive engineering] ..... CVSCC
Coolant-Controlled Exhaust Gas Recirculation [Automotive engineering] ..... CCEGR

Cooldown [*Nuclear energy*] (NRCH) .... C/D
Cool-Down Facility (NASA) .... CDF
Cooled (MSA) .... CLD
Cooled High-Energy Firing Unit .... CHEFU
Cooled Infrared Radiometer (PDAA) .... CIR
Cooled-Anode Transmitting (DEN) .... CAT
Cooled-Anode Transmitting Tube .... CATT
Cooled-Anode Transmitting Valve (IAA) .... CATV
Cooled-Grating Array Spectrometer [*Instrumentation*] .... CGAS
Cooler (MSA) .... CLR
Cooler Flusher Tank Cell [*Nuclear energy*] (NRCH) .... CFTC
Cooler Flusher Tank Equipment [*Nuclear energy*] (NRCH) .... CFTE
Cooler Liquid Electron Tube .... CLET
Coolest Ultra Tiny Individuals on Earth [*Toy figures*] [*Mattel, Inc.*] .... CUTIE
Cooley Electronics Laboratory [*University of Michigan*] [*Research center*] (RCD) .... CEL
Cooley Family Association of America (EA) .... CFA
Cooley Law Review [*A publication*] (DLA) .... Cooley L Rev
Cooley on Constitutional Limitations [*A publication*] (DLA) .... Cooley Const Lim
Cooley on Constitutional Limitations [*A publication*] (DLA) .... Cooley Const Limit
Cooley on Taxation [*A publication*] (DLA) .... Cool Tax
Cooley on Taxation [*A publication*] (DLA) .... Cooley Tax
Cooley on Taxation [*A publication*] (DLA) .... Cooley Tax'n
Cooley on Torts [*A publication*] (DLA) .... Cool Torts
Cooley's Anemia Foundation (EA) .... CAF
Cooley's Constitutional Law [*A publication*] (DLA) .... Cool Con Law
Cooley's Constitutional Law [*A publication*] (DLA) .... Cooley Const Law
Cooley's Constitutional Limitations [*A publication*] (DLA) .... Cool Con Lim
Cooley's Edition of Blackstone's Commentaries [*A publication*] (DLA) .... Cool Black
Cooley's Edition of Blackstone's Commentaries [*A publication*] (DLA) .... Cooley Bl Comm
Cooley's Michigan Digest [*A publication*] (DLA) .... Cool Mich Dig
Cooley's Reports [*5-12 Michigan*] [*A publication*] (DLA) .... Cooley
Coolidge, AZ [*FM radio station call letters*] (RBYB) .... KBZR
Coolidge, AZ [*AM radio station call letters*] .... KCKY
Coolidge Center for Environmental Leadership (EA) .... CCEL
Coolidge High School Library, Sioux Falls, SD [*Library symbol Library of Congress*] (LCLS) .... SdSifH
Coolidge Public Library, Coolidge, AZ [*Library symbol Library of Congress*] (LCLS) .... AzCo
Coolimation Test Module [*Nuclear energy*] (NRCH) .... CTM
Cooling (PS) C
Cooling (MSA) .... CLG
Cooling .... COOL
Cooling .... COOLG
Cooling Coil (AAG) CC
Cooling Effect Detection and Control .... CEDAC
Cooling Fan (MSA) .... CF
Cooling Tower [*Nuclear energy*] (NRCH) .... CT
Cooling Tower Institute (EA) .... CTI
Cooling Water [*Nuclear energy*] (NRCH) .... CW
Cooling Water/Hot Water Return [*Nuclear energy*] (NRCH) .... CHR
Cooling Water/Hot Water Return [*Nuclear energy*] (NRCH) .... CHWR
Cooling Water Return [*Nuclear energy*] (NRCH) .... CWR
Cooling Water System [*Nuclear energy*] (NRCH) .... CWS
Cooling-Induced Luminescence [*In glass containing rare earth salts*] CIL
Coolullah [*Australia*] [*Airport symbol*] (AD) .... WCO
Cooma [*Australia ICAO location identifier*] (ICLI) .... ASCM
Cooma [*Australia Airport symbol*] (OAG) .... OOM
Coomassie Brilliant Blue [*A stain*] .... CBB
Coomb [*Combe*] [*British*] (ROG) .... CB
Coombs' Test [*for the presence of globulin on the surface of red cells*] [*Hematology*] .... CT
Coon Peak [*Utah*] [*Seismograph station code, US Geological Survey*] (SEIS) .... CPU
Coon Rapids Enterprise, Coon Rapids, IA [*Library symbol Library of Congress*] (LCLS) .... IaCoon
Coonabarabran [*Australia Airport symbol*] (OAG) .... COJ
Coonamble [*Australia Airport symbol*] (OAG) .... CNB
Cooney Tunnel [*Armidale*] [*Australia Seismograph station code, US Geological Survey*] (SEIS) .... COO
Co-op Action Action Plan [*Advertising*] (WDMC) .... CAP Rate
Cooper Aerial Surveys Ltd. [*British*] [*FAA designator*] (FAAC) .... SVY
Cooper & Chyan Technology [*NASDAQ symbol*] (TTSB) .... CCTI
Cooper & Chyan Technology, Inc. [*NASDAQ symbol*] (SAG) .... CCTI
Cooper & Chyan Technology, Inc. [*Associated Press*] (SAG) .... CoopChy
Cooper Cameron [*NYSE symbol*] (TTSB) .... RON
Cooper Cameron Corp. [*Associated Press*] (SAG) .... Coop Ca
Cooper Cameron Corp. [*NYSE symbol*] (SAG) .... RON
Cooper Canada Ltd. [*Toronto Stock Exchange symbol*] .... CPC
[*The*] **Cooper Companies, Inc.** [*NYSE symbol*] (SPSG) .... COO
[*The*] **Cooper Companies, Inc.** [*Associated Press*] (SAG) .... CoopCo
Cooper Cos. [*NYSE symbol*] (TTSB) .... COLL
Cooper Development Co. [*NASDAQ symbol*] (NQ) .... COOL
Cooper Development Co. [*Associated Press*] (SAG) .... CooprD
Cooper Ind 6.00%'DECS'1998 [*NYSE symbol*] (TTSB) .... CXW
Cooper Indus [*NYSE symbol*] (TTSB) .... CBE
Cooper Industries [*NYSE symbol*] (SAG) .... CXW
Cooper Industries, Inc. [*Formerly, Cooper-Bessemer Corp.*] [*NYSE symbol*] (SPSG) .... CBE
Cooper Industries, Inc. [*Formerly, Cooper-Bessemer Corp.*] [*Associated Press*] (SAG) .... Cooper
Cooper Landing, AK [*Location identifier FAA*] (FAAL) .... JLA
Cooper Life Sciences [*NASDAQ symbol*] (TTSB) .... ZAPS
Cooper Life Sciences, Inc. [*Associated Press*] (SAG) .... CooprL
Cooper Life Sciences, Inc. [*NASDAQ symbol*] (NQ) .... ZAPS
Cooper Medical Center, Camden, NJ [*Library symbol Library of Congress*] (LCLS) .... NjCaC
Cooper Nuclear Station (NRCH) .... CNS
Cooper Ornithological Society (EA) .... COS
Cooper Skybird Air Charters Ltd. [*Kenya*] [*ICAO designator*] (FAAC) .... SKY
Cooper Tire & Rubber [*NYSE symbol*] (TTSB) .... CTB
Cooper Tire & Rubber Co. [*Associated Press*] (SAG) .... CooprTr
Cooper Tire & Rubber Co. [*NYSE symbol*] (SPSG) .... CTB
Cooper Union for the Advancement of Science and Art, New York, NY [*Library symbol Library of Congress*] (LCLS) .... NNCoo
Cooperage [*Freight*] .... COOPG
Cooperate .... COOp
Cooperating Administrator [*Education*] (AEE) .... CA
Cooperating Agency Method for Event Reporting and Analysis (IAA) .... CAMERA
Cooperating Individual [*FBI*] CI
Cooperating Libraries in Consortium [*St. Paul, MN*] [*Library network*] CLIC
Cooperating Libraries of Greater Springfield [*Library network*] .... CLGS
Cooperating Teachers' Attitude Questionnaire .... CTAQ
Cooperating Users' Exchange .... CUE
Cooperating Users of Burroughs Equipment (EA) .... CUBE
Cooperation and Coordination .... CAC
Cooperation Canada Mozambique (AC) .... COCAMO
Cooperation Europeene dans la Domaine de la Recherche Scientifique et Technique [*European Cooperation in the Field of Scientific and Technical Research*] (MSC) .... COST
Cooperation for Development [*British*] (EAIO) .... CD
Cooperation for Open Systems Interconnection Networking in Europe (OSI) .... COSINE
Cooperation in Automation of Data and Documentation for Imports/Exports and Agriculture [*EC*] (ECED) .... CADDIA
Cooperation in Documentation and Communication [*An association*] .... CODOC
Cooperation in Library Automation (NITA) .... COLA
Cooperation in Space [*Former USSR*] .... COSPAS
Cooperation Internationale en Matiere de Documentation sur l'Economie des Transports [*International Cooperation in the Field of Transport Economics Documentation*] [*France*] [*Information service or system*] (IID) .... CIDET
Cooperation Internationale pour le Developpement et la Solidarite [*International Cooperation for Development and Solidarity*] [*Formerly, Cooperation Internationale pour le Developpement Socio-Economique*] (EAIO) .... CIDSE
Cooperation via Televised Instruction in Education [*Colorado State University*] .... CO-TIE
Cooperativa .... COOP
Cooperative (AABC) .... COOP
Cooperative .... COOPRTV
Co-Operative Action Programme [*UNESCO*] (EA) .... CO-ACTION
Cooperative Advanced Digital Research Experiment (MCD) .... CADRE
Cooperative Advertising (WDMC) .... co-op
Cooperative Africana Microform Project, Archives-Libraries Committee, African Studies Association, Center for Research Libraries, Chicago, IL [*Library symbol Library of Congress*] (LCLS) .... ICRL(CAMP)
Cooperative Agreement .... CA
Cooperative Agreement Officer [*Department of Housing and Urban Development*] (GFGA) .... CAO
Cooperative Agricole des Producteurs de Cereales de la Region d'Arras .... CAPCRA
Cooperative Agricultural Pest Survey Program [*Information service or system*] (IID) .... CAPS
Cooperative Agricultural Research Program [*Tennessee State University*] [*Research center*] (RCD) .... CARP
Cooperative Air Defense System (MCD) .... CADS
Cooperative Alliance for Refuge Enhancement .... CARE
Cooperative Alumni Association (EA) .... CAA
Cooperative Analysis of Broadcasting [*Term used in TV rating*] .... CAB
Co-Operative and Commerce Bank [*Nigeria*] .... CCB
Cooperative Applications Satellite [*France*] [*NASA*] .... CAS
Cooperative Area Manpower Planning System [*Environmental Protection Agency*] .... CAMPS
Cooperative Arid Lands Agriculture Research Program [*Established by Egypt, Israel, and the US at the University of San Diego in 1981*] .... CALAR
Cooperative Assessment of Experiential Learning Project (EDAC) .... CAEL
Cooperative Assistance Fund (EA) .... CAF
Cooperative Association of Professional Salespeople [*Defunct*] (EA) .... CAPS
Cooperative Association of Tractor Dealers (EA) .... CATD
Cooperative Atomic Migration .... CAM
Cooperative Auto Research Program [*Department of Transportation*] .... CARP
Cooperative Automation Group [*British Library*] [*Information service or system Defunct*] (IID) .... CAG
Cooperative Average Fuel Economy (BARN) .... CAFE
Cooperative Awards in Pure Science [*British*] .... CAPS
Cooperative Awards in Science and Engineering [*British*] .... CASE
[*The*] **Co-Operative Bank of Concord** [*NASDAQ symbol*] (NQ) .... COBK
Co-Operative Bank of Concord [*Associated Press*] (SAG) .... CoOpBk
Cooperative Bankshares [*NASDAQ symbol*] (SAG) .... COOP
Cooperative Bankshares [*Associated Press*] (SAG) .... CoopBk
Cooperative Bibliographic Center for Indiana Libraries .... COBICIL
Cooperative Bureau for Teachers [*Superseded by IES*] (EA) .... CBT
Cooperative Business International [*Washington, DC*] (EA) .... CBI
Cooperative Cardiovascular Project .... CCP
Co-Operative, Career & Work Education Association of Canada [*Association Canadienne pour l'Alternance Travail-Etudes*] [*Also, National Co-Operative Education Centre*] (AC) .... CCWEAC

Co-Operative Central Bank [*Malaysia*] ... CCB
Cooperative College Ability Test (WGA) ... CCAT
Cooperative College Development Program ... CCDP
Cooperative College Library Center [*Atlanta, GA*] [*Library network*] ... CCLC
Cooperative College Library Center, Atlanta, GA [*OCLC symbol*] (OCLC) ... CCL
Cooperative College Library Center, Inc., Atlanta, GA [*Library symbol Library of Congress*] (LCLS) ... GACCLC
Co-Operative College of Canada, Saskatoon, Saskatchewan [*Library symbol National Library of Canada*] (NLC) ... SSC
Cooperative College of Canada, Saskatoon, SK, Canada [*Library symbol Library of Congress*] (LCLS) ... CaSSC
Cooperative College Registry [*Defunct*] ... CCR
Cooperative College - School Service (OICC) ... CCSS
Cooperative College-School Science [*Program*] [*Defunct National Science Foundation*] ... CCSS
Cooperative Commonwealth Federation [*Later, New Democratic Party - NDP*] [*Political party Canada*] ... CCF
Co-Operative Commonwealth Federation [*Later, NDP*] [*Canadian*] (PPW) ... CCF
Cooperative Communicators Association (EA) ... CCA
Cooperative Computing System [*Echo detection*] ... CCS
Cooperative Contracts and Agreements [*Business term*] ... COCA
Cooperative Convection Precipitation Experiment [*Meteorology*] ... CCOPE
Cooperative Core Laboratories and Clinical Nutrition Research Unit [*Research center*] (RCD) ... CNRU
Cooperative Corporations (DLA) ... Coop Corp
Cooperative Council for Oklahoma School Administration (SRA) ... CCOSA
Cooperative Council of North Carolina (SRA) ... CCNC
Cooperative Credit Purchasing Co. [*Company that buys banks' bad debts*] [*Japan*] (ECON) ... CCPC
Cooperative Defense Efforts (MCD) ... CDE
Cooperative Degree Program [*Army*] (INF) ... COOP
Cooperative Development Environment [*Computer science*] (PCM) ... CDE
Cooperative Development Services [*British*] ... CDS
Co-Operative Digest, United States Reports [*A publication*] (DLA) ... Co-Op Dig
Cooperative d'Information et de Recherche Ecologiste du Quebec [*Environmental Information & Research Group*] (AC) ... CIREQ
Cooperative Distributed Interactive Atmospheric Catalog [*Marine science*] (OSRA) ... CODIAC
Cooperative Distributed Interactive Atmospheric Catolog (USDC) ... CODIAC
Cooperative Documents Network Project [*University of Guelph Library*] [*Information service or system*] ... CODOC
Cooperative Documents Project [*Ontario Universities Library Cooperative System*] [*Canada*] (NITA) ... CODOC
Cooperative Economic Insect Report [*Department of Agriculture*] [*A publication*] ... CEIR
Cooperative Education Association (EA) ... CEA
Cooperative Educational Enterprises ... CEE
Cooperative Educational Research Laboratory, Inc. ... CERLI
Cooperative Educational Service Agency [*National Science Foundation*] ... CESA
Cooperative Educational Services ... CES
Cooperative Energy Development Corp. [*Toronto Stock Exchange symbol*] ... COE
Cooperative Enforcement Agreement [*Environmental Protection Agency*] (GFGA) ... CEA
Cooperative Engagement Capability [*Navy*] (DOMA) ... CEC
Cooperative Engineering Program [*Automotive industry*] ... CEP
Cooperative English Test ... CET
Cooperative Expendable Jammer ... CEJ
Cooperative Export Financing Corp. (MHDW) ... CEFCO
Cooperative Extension Service [*Department of Agriculture*] ... CES
Cooperative Extension Service Telephone Network [*University of Illinois at Champaign-Urbana*] [*Telecommunications service*] (TSSD) ... TELENET
Cooperative Federee du Quebec (AC) ... CFQ
Cooperative Finance Association of America (EA) ... CFAA
Cooperative Finance Corp. [*of National Rural Utilities*] ... CFC
Cooperative Financing Facility [*Export-Import Bank*] ... CFF
Cooperative Food Distributors of America [*Later, NGA*] (EA) ... CFDA
Cooperative for American Relief Everywhere [*Formerly, Cooperative for American Remittances Everywhere*] (AEBS) ... CARE
Cooperative for American Remittances Everywhere [*Former name*] ... CARE
Cooperative Forest Fire Prevention [*Forest Service, Department of Agriculture*] ... CFFP
Cooperative Fuels Research [*Committee*] ... CFR
Cooperative Generic Technology [*Centers for cooperative government and industry work*] ... COGENT
Cooperative Hazardous Materials Enforcement Development Program [*RSPA*] (TAG) ... COHMED
Cooperative Health Manpower Education Program [*Veterans Administration*] (GFGA) ... CHMEP
Cooperative Health Statistics System [*Medicine*] ... CHSS
Cooperative High-Performance Sequential Inference Machine [*NEC Corp.*] ... CHI
Cooperative Holocene Mapping Project [*Geology*] ... COHMAP
Cooperative Home Care Associates ... CHOA
Cooperative Housing Association of Ontario Inc. [*L'Association de l'Habitation Co-Operative de l'Ontario*] [*Formerly, Ontario Co-Op Housing Committee*] (AC) ... CHAO
Cooperative Housing Bulletin [*A publication*] (EAAP) ... CHB
Cooperative Housing Federation of Nova Scotia (AC) ... CHFNS
Cooperative Housing Foundation (EA) ... CHF
Cooperative Housing Journal [*A publication*] (EAAP) ... CHJ
Cooperative Housing Societies Association of New South Wales [*Australia*] ... CHSANSW
Cooperative Human Linkage Center [*Genetics research*] ... CHLC
Cooperative Human Linkage Center ... CHLC
Cooperative Human Tissue Network ... CHTN
Cooperative Hurricane Upper Air Station [*National Weather Service*] (NOAA) ... CHUAS
Cooperative Immunoassay ... CIA
Cooperative Independent Surveillance (DA) ... CIS
Cooperative Industrial and Commercial Reference and Information Service ... CICRIS
Cooperative Information Network [*Library network*] ... CIN
Cooperative Information Network, Coeur d'Alene, ID [*Library symbol*] [*Library of Congress*] (LCLS) ... IdCCIN
Cooperative Institute fo Climate Studies [*Marine science*] (OSRA) ... CICS
Cooperative Institute for Aerospace Science and Terrestrial Applications [*University of Nevada*] [*Research center*] (RCD) ... CIASTA
Cooperative Institute for Arctic Research [*Marine science*] (OSRA) ... CIFAR
Cooperative Institute for Arctic Research (USDC) ... CIFAR
Cooperative Institute for Climate Studies (USDC) ... CICS
Cooperative Institute for Limnology and Ecosystems Research (USDC) ... CILER
Cooperative Institute for Limnology and Ecosystems Research [*Marine science*] (OSRA) ... CILER
Cooperative Institute for Marine and Atmospheric Studies [*Coral Gables, FL*] [*NOAA, Rosenstiel School of Marine and Atmospheric Science of the University of Miami*] (GRD) ... CIMAS
Cooperative Institute for Marine Resources Studies [*Marine science*] (OSRA) ... CIMRS
Cooperative Institute for Marine Resources Studies (USDC) ... CIMRS
Cooperative Institute for Mesoscale Meteorological Studies [*University of Oklahoma, NOAA*] [*Research center*] (RCD) ... CIMMS
Cooperative Institute for Research in Environmental Sciences ... CIRES
Cooperative Institute for Research in the Atmosphere [*Colorado State University, NOAA*] [*Research center*] (RCD) ... CIRA
Cooperative Institute of Meteorology Satellite Studies [*Marine science*] (OSRA) ... CIMSS
Cooperative Institute of Meteorology Satellite Studies (USDC) ... CIMSS
Cooperative Institutional Research Program [*UCLA*] ... CIRP
Co-Operative Insurance Development Bureau [*Canada*] (EAIO) ... CIDB
Cooperative Insurance Society [*British*] ... CIS
Cooperative Intelligence Network System [*Proposed*] [*Navy*] ... COINS
Cooperative International Pupil-to-Pupil Program (EA) ... CIPPP
Cooperative International Pupil-to-Pupil Program (EA) ... CIPTPP
Cooperative Internationale de Recherche et d'Action en Matiere de Communication (EAIO) ... CIRCOM
Cooperative Investigation of the Caribbean and Adjacent Regions [*UNESCO*] ... CICAR
Cooperative Investigation of the Mediterranean ... CIM
Cooperative Investigation of the Northern Part of the Eastern Central Atlantic ... CINECA
Cooperative Investigations of Tropical Reef Ecosystems [*Smithsonian Institution*] (MSC) ... CITRE
Cooperative League of the United States of America (EA) ... CLUSA
Co-Operative Legislation [*ILO*] [*United Nations Information service or system*] (DUND) ... COOPLEG
Cooperative Libraries in Central Connecticut [*Library network*] ... CLICC
Cooperative Library Agency for Systems and Services [*San Jose, CA*] [*Telecommunications*] (TSSD) ... CLASS
Cooperative Library Agency for Systems and Services, San Jose, CA [*Library symbol Library of Congress*] (LCLS) ... CSjCLA
Cooperative Library Network of Clackamas County, Oak Grove, OR [*Library symbol*] [*Library of Congress*] (LCLS) ... OrOgCL
Cooperative Logistic Supply Support Arrangement [*Military*] (AFIT) ... CLSSA
Cooperative Logistic Support Arrangement [*Military*] (AFM) ... CLSA
Cooperative Logistics ... CL
Cooperative [*or Coordinated*] **Logistics Support Program** [*Air Force*] (MCD) ... CLSP
Cooperative Machine-Readable Cataloging Program [*Library of Congress*] ... COMARC
Cooperative Management Housing Insurance Fund [*Federal Housing Administration*] ... CMHIF
Cooperative Merchandising Agreement (DOAD) ... CMA
Cooperative Meteorological Rocket Network [*NASA*] ... CMRN
Cooperative National Park Resource Studies Unit, University of Hawaii [*Research center*] (RCD) ... CPSU/UH
Cooperative National Park Resources Studies Unit [*Research center*] (RCD) ... CPSU
Cooperative National Plant Pest Survey and Detection Program [*Department of Agriculture*] [*Hyattsville, MD Database*] ... CNPPSDP
Cooperative Network of In-Service Resources (OICC) ... CNIR
Cooperative North Scandinavian Enalapril Survival Study [*Medicine*] ... CONSENSUS
Cooperative Observational Week (MUGU) ... COW
Cooperative Office Distributive Education (AEBS) ... CODE
Cooperative Oklahoma Profiler Studies-1991 [*Marine science*] (OSRA) ... COPS-91
Cooperative Oklahoma Profiler Studies-1991 (USDC) ... COPS-91
Cooperative Oncology Group [*National Cancer Institute*] ... COG
Cooperative Online Serials [*Library of Congress*] ... CONSER
Cooperative Online Serials Acquisition Project (NITA) ... COSAP
Cooperative Operating System Environment [*Computer science*] ... COSE
Cooperative Opportunities Document (AAGC) ... COD
Cooperative Phantom Jamming (MCD) ... CPJ
Cooperative Planting Program (GNE) ... CPP
Cooperative Power [*Later, SPG*] (EA) ... CP
Cooperative Power Association [*Nuclear energy*] (NRCH) ... CPA
Cooperative Preservation of Architectural Records [*Defunct*] (EA) ... COPAR
Cooperative Program (WDMC) ... co-op
Cooperative Program for Educational Opportunity (EA) ... CPEO
Cooperative Program for Monitoring and Evaluation of Long Range Transmission (EERA) ... EMEP

Cooperative Program for Operational Meteorology, Education and Training [*Marine science*] (OSRA) .... COMET
Cooperative Program for Operational Meteorology, Education and Training [*National Center for Atmospheric Research*] (USDC) .... COMET
Cooperative Program in Educational Administration .... CPEA
Cooperative Program of Research on Aquaculture [*UN Food and Agriculture Organization*] .... COPRAQ
Cooperative Project for Educational Development [*Office of Education*] .... COPED
Cooperative Projects with Industry [*National Research Council, Canada*] .... COPI
Cooperative Publication Association (EA) .... CPA
Cooperative Radiation Effects Simulation Program [*Military*] (DNAB) .... CORES
Cooperative Recreation Service [*Later, World Around Songs*] (EA) .... CRS
Cooperative Research [*in agriculture*] .... COR
Cooperative Research Act .... CRA
Cooperative Research Action for Technology .... CRAFT
Cooperative Research and Development Agreement [*Department of Energy National Laboratories*] .... CRADA
Cooperative Research and Development Agreement [*Government-industry programs*] .... CRADA
Cooperative Research and Development Agreement [*Department of Energy National Laboratories*] .... CRDA
Cooperative Research Centre for Viticulture [*Australia*] .... CRCV
Cooperative Research Centres Committee [*Australia*] .... CRCC
Cooperative Research Council .... CRC
Cooperative Research Institute [*Defunct*] (EA) .... CORE
Cooperative Research Program [*Military and Office of Education*] .... CRP
Cooperative Research Service [*Kentucky State University*] [*Research center*] (RCD) .... CRS
Co-Operative Retail Services [*British*] .... CRS
Cooperative Retail Society (ODBW) .... CRS
Cooperative School Program [*US Employment Service*] [*Department of Labor*] .... CSP
Cooperative Society .... CS
Cooperative State Research, Education, and Extension Service [*US Department of Agriculture*] .... CSREES
Cooperative State Research Service [*Department of Agriculture Washington, DC*] .... CSRS
Cooperative Statistical Program [*For IUD data*] .... CSP
Cooperative Study in the Mediterranean (OSRA) .... CSM
Cooperative Study in the Mediterranean [*Intergovernmental Oceanographic Commission Coordination Group*] (USDC) .... CSM
Cooperative Study of the Kuroshio [*UNESCO*] .... CSK
Cooperative Study of the Kuroshio and Adjacent Regions [*Marine science*] (OSRA) .... CSK
Cooperative Study of the Kuroshio and Adjacent Regions [*Intergovernmental Oceanographic Commission Coordination Group*] (USDC) .... CSK
Cooperative Survey of the Eastern Tropical Pacific (MSC) .... EASTROPIC
Cooperative Threat Reduction [*Military*] (RDA) .... CTR
Cooperative Tracking System (MCD) .... CTS
Cooperative Union of Canada .... CUC
Cooperative Union Serials System .... CUSS
Cooperative Upper-Air Station [*National Weather Service*] (NOAA) .... CUAS
Cooperative Upper-Air Unit [*National Weather Service*] .... CUA
Cooperative Users of Equimatics Financial Systems (CSR) .... CUEFS
Cooperative Users of FICS and MARS [*Atlanta, GA*] (CSR) .... CUFAM
Cooperative Weapon Delivery (MCD) .... CWD
Cooperative Weapons Data Indexing Committee [*AEC and DoD*] .... CWDIC
Cooperative Whole Grain Education Association (EA) .... CWGEA
Cooperative Wholesale Society [*British*] .... CWS
Co-Operative Wholesale Society [*British*] .... CWS
Cooperative Wildlife Research Laboratory [*Southern Illinois University at Carbondale*] [*Research center*] (RCD) .... CWRL
Cooperative Wind Tunnel .... CWT
Cooperative Work Experience Education Association (EA) .... CWEEA
Cooperative Youth Initiative [*British*] .... CYI
Cooperatively Assembled Virginia Low Intensity Educational Reactor (NRCH) .... CAVALIER
Cooperatives Research Unit [*British*] .... CRU
Cooper-Harper Rating [*NASA*] (NASA) .... CHR
Cooper-Johnson, Yellowknife, Northwest Territories [*Library symbol National Library of Canada*] (BIB) .... NWYCJ
Coopers' and Allied Workers' Federation of Great Britain [*A union*] .... CAWFGB
Coopers & Lybrand Accounting and Distributive Inventory System (MHDB) .... CLAUDIUS
Coopers & Lybrand Consulting Group, Ottawa, Ontario [*Library symbol National Library of Canada*] (BIB) .... OOCLCG
Coopers & Lybrand USA [*New York, NY Telecommunications*] (TSSD) .... C & L
Coopers Appreciation [*An association*] (EA) .... CA
Cooper's Chancery and Practice Reporter [*Upper Canada*] [*A publication*] (DLA) .... Coop C & PR
Cooper's Equity Digest [*A publication*] (DLA) .... Coop Eq Dig
Cooper's Equity Pleading [*A publication*] (DLA) .... Coop Eq Pl
Coopers' Federation of Great Britain and Ireland [*A union*] .... CFGBI
Cooper's Florida Reports [*21-24 Florida*] [*A publication*] (DLA) .... Cooper
Cooper's Institutes of Justinian [*A publication*] (DLA) .... Coop Inst
Cooper's Institutes of Justinian [*A publication*] (DLA) .... Cooper Just Inst
Coopers' International Union of North America .... CIU
Coopers' International Union of North America (EA) .... CIUNA
Cooper's Judgment [*A publication*] (DLA) .... Coop Judg
Coopers Lake [*Montana*] [*Seismograph station code, US Geological Survey Closed*] (SEIS) .... CKM
Cooper's Law of Libel [*A publication*] (DLA) .... Coop Lib
Cooper's Medical Jurisprudence [*A publication*] (DLA) .... Coop Med Jur
Cooper's Public Records of Great Britain [*A publication*] (DLA) .... Coop Rec
Cooper's Reports [*21-24 Florida*] [*A publication*] (DLA) .... Coop
Cooper's Select Early Cases [*Scotland*] [*A publication*] (DLA) .... Coop Sel EC
Cooper's Tennessee Chancery Reports [*A publication*] (DLA) .... Coop
Cooper's Tennessee Chancery Reports [*A publication*] (DLA) .... Coop Ch
Cooper's Tennessee Chancery Reports [*A publication*] (DLA) .... Coop Ten Chy
Cooper's Tennessee Chancery Reports [*A publication*] (DLA) .... Coop Tenn Ch
Cooper's Tennessee Chancery Reports [*A publication*] (DLA) .... Cooper
Cooper's Tennessee Chancery Reports [*A publication*] (DLA) .... Cooper Ch
Cooper's Tennessee Chancery Reports [*A publication*] (DLA) .... Tenn Ch
Coopersmith Self-Esteem Inventory [*Psychometrics*] .... CSEI
Cooperstown & Charlotte Valley Railway Corp. [*AAR code*] .... CACV
Cooperstown, ND [*Location identifier FAA*] (FAAL) .... TOW
Cooperstown Public Library, Cooperstown, ND [*Library symbol Library of Congress*] (LCLS) .... NdCo
Coopersville District Library, Coopersville, MI [*Library symbol Library of Congress*] (LCLS) .... MiCoop
Coopworth Sheep Society of Australia .... CSAA
Co-Orbit Support System (SSD) .... COSS
Coorbital Interceptor Scoring Technique .... CIST
Co-Orbiting Platform (SSD) .... COP
Coordinacion de Organismos Empresariales de Comercio Exterior [*Mexican Business Coordinating Council for NAFTA*] (CROSS) .... COECE
Coordinacion Democratica [*Democratic Coordination*] [*Spain Political party*] (PPE) .... CD
Coordinacion Revolucionaria de las Masas [*Revolutionary Coordination of the Masses*] [*El Salvador*] (PD) .... CRM
Coordinador Nacional de Bases [*National Coordination of Bases*] [*Colorado*] (PD) .... CNB
Coordinadora Civilista Nacional [*Panama*] [*Political party*] (EY) .... COCINA
Coordinadora de Organizaciones Feministas [*Coordination of Feminist Organizations*] [*Puerto Rico*] (EAIO) .... COF
Coordinadora Democratica [*Democratic Coordinating Board*] [*Nicaragua*] (PPW) .... CD
Coordinadora Democratica Nicaraguense Ramiro Sacasa [*Nicaragua*] [*Political party*] (EY) .... CDN
Coordinadora Guerrillera Nacional [*Colorado*] (EY) .... CGN
Coordinadora Guerrillera Simon Bolivar [*Colorado Political party*] (EY) .... CGSB
Coordinadora Nacional de Organizaciones Cafetaleras [*National network of small coffee producers*] [*Mexico*] (CROSS) .... CNOC
Coordinamento delle Industrie Radiologiche ed Elettromedicali [*Coordination Committee of the Radiological and Electromedical Industries*] [*EC*] (ECED) .... COCIR
Coordinamento Uruguaiano di Solidarieta in Italia .... CUSI
Coordinant .... COORD
Coordinate .... COOR
Coordinate [*or Coordination*] (AFM) .... COORD
Coordinate Adder (SAA) .... COAD
Coordinate, Anticipate, and Verify (MCD) .... CAV
Coordinate Conversion Computer (MCD) CCC
Coordinate Conversion Routine .... COCO
Coordinate Converter (AAG) CC
Coordinate Data Set .... CORDAT
Coordinate Data Terminal (MCD) .... CDT
Coordinate Data Transmission .... CDT
Coordinate Index CI
Coordinate Indexing Group [*ASLIB*] (DIT) .... CIG
Coordinate Measuring Machine .... CMM
Coordinate Rotation Digital Computer .... CORDIC
Coordinate Transformation System (MCD) .... CTS
Coordinated Activity Allowance List [*Military*] (NVT) .... COAAL
Coordinated Activity List [*Navy*] (NVT) .... COOAL
Coordinated Agency-Wide Research Activities [*National Science Foundation*] .... CARA
Coordinated Aircraft/Stores Program [*Obsolete Navy*] (NG) .... COASP
Coordinated Air-Sea Experiment [*Marine science*] (OSRA) .... CASE
Coordinated Air-Sea Experiment (USDC) .... CASE
Coordinated ASW [*Antisubmarine Warfare*] **Services and Training** [*Navy*] (NVT) .... CAST
Coordinated Atomic Operations (CINC) .... CAO
Coordinated Bargaining Committee (DICI) .... CBC
Coordinated Building Communication (PDAA) .... CBC
Coordinated Care Program [*Medicine*] .... CCP
Coordinated Caribbean Transport [*US shipping line*] (IMH) .... CCT
Coordinated Cockpit Display (MCD) .... CCD
Coordinated Command, Control, Communications and Computing for Integrated Information and Intelligence [*Military*] C5I3
Coordinated Commentary Programming [*Computer science*] .... CCP
Coordinated Containerization Point .... CCP
Coordinated Design Data Required .... CDDR
Coordinated Eastern Arctic Experiment [*Marine science*] (OSRA) .... CEAREX
Coordinated Eastern Arctic Experiment (USDC) .... CEAREX
Coordinated Ecosystem Research (USDC) .... CER
Coordinated Ecosystem Research [*Marine science*] (OSRA) .... CER
Coordinated Electronic Countermeasures Exercise [*Military*] (NVT) .... COREX
Coordinated Evaluation System [*National Institute of Standards and Technology*] .... CES
Coordinated Examination Program [*Internal Revenue Service*] .... CEP
Coordinated Experimental Research [*Program*] [*National Science Foundation*] .... CER
Coordinated Federal Lands Highways Technial Information Program [*MTMC*] (TAG) .... CTIP
Coordinated Federal Wage System (MCD) .... CFWS
Coordinated Financial Planning .... CFP
Coordinated Fire Line (AABC) .... CFL
Coordinated Geometry [*Programming language*] [*1957*] (CSR) .... COGO

Coordinated Helps in Language Development (ADA) .... CHILD
Coordinated Human Resource Technology (MCD) .... CHRT
Coordinated Hungarian Relief [*Defunct*] (EA) .... CHR
Coordinated Information Transfer for Education (AEBS) .... CITE
Coordinated Joint Outline Emergency Plan [*Military*] (CINC) .... CJOEP
Coordinated Keysort Index (ADA) .... COOKI
Coordinated Management of Meaning [*Communications theory*] .... CMM
Coordinated Manual Control .... CMC
Coordinated Navy Total Acquisition Control [*System*] .... CONTAC
Coordinated Occupational Information Network [*COIN Educational Products*] [*Information service or system*] (IID) .... COIN
Coordinated Operability Test .... COT
Coordinated Procurement Program Appraisal [*DoD*] .... COPPA
Coordinated Program of Research in Distributed Computing [*British*] (NITA) .... CPRDC
Coordinated Reconnaissance Plan (CINC) .... CRP
Coordinated Regional Allowance List (AFIT) .... CORAL
Coordinated Resources Plan .... CRP
Coordinated Science Laboratory [*University of Illinois*] [*Research center*] .... CSL
Coordinated Ship Development Plan [*Navy*] .... CSDP
Coordinated Ship Electronics Device [*Navy*] .... CSED
Coordinated Shipboard [*or Shorebased*] **Allowance List** [*Navy*] .... COSAL
Coordinated Shipboard [*or Shorebased*] **Allowance List** [*Navy*] .... COSBAL
Coordinated Shore Maintenance Allowance List [*Navy*] (CAAL) .... COSMAL
Coordinated Shorebased Material Allowance List [*Air Force*] (AFIT) .... COSMAL
Coordinated Situation System .... CSS
Coordinated Test Plan [*Obsolete*] .... CTP
Coordinated Test Program [*Military*] (AABC) .... CTP
Coordinated Transfer Application System [*For medical students*] .... COTRANS
Coordinated Universal Time (NASA) .... CUT
Coordinated Universal Time (USDC) .... UTC
Coordinated Vocational-Academic Education .... CVAE
Coordinates Computed (MUGU) CC
Coordinateur Automatique de Traffic .... CAUTRA
Coordinating Agency for Supplier Evaluation .... CASE
Co-Ordinating Animal Welfare [*British*] .... CAW
Coordinating Area Production Urgency Committee .... CAPUC
Coordinating Authority (NATG) .... COORAUTH
Coordinating Board of Jewish Organizations (EA) .... CBJO
Coordinating Board of Tobacco Trade Associations [*Later, NATD*] (EA) .... CBTTA
Co-Ordinating Body on the Seas of East Asia .... COBSEA
Coordinating Committee (MCD) .... CDCOM
Coordinating Committee .... COCOM
Coordinating Committee for Ellis Island (EA) .... CCEI
Coordinating Committee for International Voluntary Service [*France*] (EAIO) .... CCIVS
Coordinating Committee for Satellite Communication [*Switzerland*] (NITA) .... CCSC
Coordinating Committee for Slavic and East European Library Resources .... COCOSEERS
Coordinating Committee for the World Climate Program [*Marine science*] (OSRA) .... CCWCP
Co-ordinating Committee of Democratic Forces [*Ghana*] [*Political party*] (EY) .... CCDF
Coordinating Committee of Independent Trade Unions .... CCITU
Coordinating Committee of Overseas Students Organization [*British*] .... CCOSO
Coordinating Committee of Technical Assistance .... CCTA
Coordinating Committee of Trade Union Organizations [*Ceylon*] .... CCTUO
Coordinating Committee on Export Controls [*From Western to Eastern bloc nations*] .... COCOM
Coordinating Committee on Export Controls (ACRL) .... CoCOM
Coordinating Committee on Materials Research and Development [*Executive Office of the President*] .... CCMRD
Coordinating Committee on Multilateral Export Controls (AAGC) .... COCOM
Coordinating Committee on Oceanography .... CCO
Coordinating Committee on Science and Technology [*Australia*] .... CCST
Coordinating Committee on the Ozone Layer [*United Nations*] (OSRA) .... CCOL
Coordinating Committee on Toxics and Drugs (EA) .... CCTD
Coordinating Committee on Women in the Historical Profession [*Later, CCWHP/CGWH*] (EA) .... CCWHP
Coordinating Committee on Women in the Historical Profession/ Conference Group onWomen's History (EA) .... CCWHP/CGWH
Coordinating Council for Computers in Construction (EA) CCCC
Coordinating Council for Higher Education .... CCHE
Coordinating Council of Literary Magazines [*Later, CLMP*] (EA) .... CCLM
Coordinating Council of National Archaeological Societies (EA) .... CCONAS
Coordinating Council of National Court Organizations [*Defunct*] (EA) .... CCNCO
Coordinating Council of Private Educational Associations .... COCOPEA
Coordinating Council of South African Trade Unions .... CCSATU
Coordinating Council on Manufactured Housing Finance [*Defunct*] (EA) .... CCMHF
Coordinating Council on Medical Education [*Superseded by CFMA*] (EA) .... CCME
Coordinating Draft [*of field manuals*] [*Military*] (INF) .... CD
Coordinating Equipment Research Committee .... CER
Coordinating European Council for the Development of Performance Tests for Lubricants and Engine Fuels (EA) .... CEC
Coordinating Fuel Research (MCD) .... CFR
Coordinating Information for Texas Educators [*Texas State Education Agency*] [*No longer available*] [*Information service or system*] (IID) .... CITE
Coordinating Installations (MCD) CI
Coordinating Justice for Cyprus Committee [*Australia*] .... CJCC
Coordinating Lubricant and Equipment Research Committee [*Coordinating Research Council*] .... CLR
Coordinating of Research and Development [*Navy*] .... CORD
Coordinating Office for Regional Resource Centers .... CORRC
Coordinating Organization Director (SAA) .... COD
Coordinating Organization of Book Associations [*Defunct*] .... COBA
Coordinating Panel [*NATO*] .... CP
Coordinating Research Council (EA) .... CRC
Coordinating Research Council of the Petroleum Industry .... CRCPI
Coordinating Secretariat of National Unions of Students [*in Africa*] .... COSEC
Coordinating Working Party on Atlantic Fishery Statistics .... CWP
Coordination [*ICAO designator*] (FAAC) .... CDN
Coordination [*Channel*] [*Electronics*] (ECII) .... CO-ORD
Coordination .... COORDN
Coordination and Contract Summary Sheet .... CCSS
Coordination and Control of Personnel Surveys [*Military*] (DNAB) .... CCOPS
Coordination and Equipment .... C & E
Coordination and Information Center [*Department of Energy*] [*Information service or system*] (IID) CIC
Coordination and Training Team [*Special Operations Force*] [*Military*] (DOMA) .... CTT
Coordination Committee for Transport Planning [*NATO*] (NATG) .... CCTP
Coordination Control Board (MCD) .... CCB
Coordination Council for North American Affairs .... CCNAA
Coordination Council on Control of Liquor Abuse .... CCCLA
Co-ordination de l'Opposition Democratique [*Gabon*] [*Political party*] (EY) .... COD
Coordination Document .... CD
Coordination Drawing .... CD
Coordination in Development (EA) .... CODEL
Coordination in Direct Support (NVT) .... CIDS
Coordination Letter Report (SAA) .... CLR
Coordination Line (NVT) CL
Coordination Message [*Aviation code*] .... CDN
Coordination Number [*Chemistry*] .... CN
Coordination Number Invariance [*Chemistry*] .... CNI
Coordination of Allied Supplies [*World War II*] .... CAS
Coordination of Atomic Operations Communications Net .... CAOCOMNET
Coordination of Atomic Operations - Standard Operating Procedures .... CAO-SOP
Coordination of Benefits [*Insurance*] .... COB
Coordination of Geostationary Meteorological Satellites [*National Oceanic and Atmospheric Administration*] .... CGMS
Coordination of Hybrid and Integrated Circuit Operations (IAA) .... CHICO
Coordination of Operating Data by Automatic Computer .... CODAC
Coordination of Recent and Projected System Efforts [*DoD*] .... CORPSE
Coordination of Record and Data Base System [*Telecommunications*] (TEL) .... CORDS
Coordination of Systems, Integrated Goals, and Networks [*DoD*] .... COSIGN
Coordination Processor [*Telecommunications*] .... CP
Coordinative Retrieval of Selectively Sorted Permuted Analogue-Title Entries [*Computer science*] .... CROSSPATE
Coordinator .... COORDNTR
Coordinator (DNAB) .... CORD
Coordinator ASW [*Antisubmarine Warfare*] **Services and Training** (DOMA) .... CASTEX
Coordinator, Department of the Navy Studies and Analyses (DNAB) .... CDONSA
Coordinator for Industrial Cooperation [*Functions ceased, 1937*] CIC
Coordinator for International Relations [*Australia*] .... CIR
Coordinator for Narcotics Affairs [*Department of State*] .... CNA
Coordinator General (ADA) .... COG
Coordinator of Army Studies (AABC) .... CAS
Coordinator of Chain Operations [*Coast Guard*] (DNAB) .... COCO
Coordinator of Commercial and Cultural Relations [*New Deal*] .... CCCR
Coordinator of Information .... COI
Coordinator of Inter-American Affairs .... CIAA
Coordinators of Data Processing Education (HGAA) .... CODE
Coors (Adolph)Cl'B' [*NASDAQ symbol*] (TTSB) .... ACCOB
Coors [*Adolph*] **Co.** [*NASDAQ symbol*] (NQ) .... ACCO
Coors [*Adolph*] **Co.** [*Associated Press*] (SAG) .... Coors
Coos Bay, OR [*Television station call letters*] .... KCBY
Coos Bay, OR [*FM radio station call letters*] (RBYB) .... KDCQ
Coos Bay, OR [*AM radio station call letters*] .... KHSN
Coos Bay, OR [*Television station call letters*] .... KMTZ
Coos Bay, OR [*AM radio station call letters*] .... KRSR
Coos Bay, OR [*FM radio station call letters*] .... KSBA
Coos Bay, OR [*FM radio station call letters*] (RBYB) .... KYSG
Coos Bay, OR [*FM radio station call letters*] .... KYTT
Coos Bay Public Library, Coos Bay, OR [*OCLC symbol*] (OCLC) .... BAY
Coos Bay Public Library, Coos Bay, OR [*Library symbol Library of Congress*] (LCLS) .... OrCb
Coos Bay Wagon Road [*Lands*] [*Department of the Interior*] .... CBWR
Coos County Library Association [*Library network*] .... CCLA
Coosa, GA [*FM radio station call letters*] .... WSRM
Coosa Valley Librarians Association [*Library network*] .... CVLA
Cootamundra [*Australia Airport symbol*] (OAG) .... CMO
Coote on Mortgages [*A publication*] (DLA) .... Coo Mort
Coote on Mortgages [*A publication*] (DLA) .... Coote
Coote on Mortgages [*A publication*] (DLA) .... Coote Mor
Coote. Practice of the Court of Probate [*9th ed.*] [*1883*] [*A publication*] (DLA) .... Coote Pro Pr
Coote. Practice of the Court of Probate, Edited by Tristram [*A publication*] (DLA) .... Coote & Tr Pr Pr
Coote's Admiralty Practice [*A publication*] (DLA) .... Coote Adm
Coote's Ecclesiastical Court Practice [*A publication*] (DLA) .... Coote Ecc Pr
Coote's Law of Landlord and Tenant [*A publication*] (DLA) .... Coote L & T
Copa Girls Alumnae Association (EA) .... CGAA

Copacabana [Record label] [Brazil] .... Cop
Copacabana [Record label] [Brazil] .... Copa
Copacabana [Bolivia] [ICAO location identifier] (ICLI) .... SLCC
Copaipo [Chile] [Airport symbol] (AD) .... CPO
Copaquilla [Bolivia] [ICAO location identifier] (ICLI) .... SLCQ
Copart, Inc. [Associated Press] (SAG) .... Copart
Copart, Inc. [NASDAQ symbol] (SAG) .... CPRT
Co-Partner (ROG) .... CO-PTR
Co-Payment Requirement Rider [Health insurance] (GHCT) .... CRI
Copconda-York [Vancouver Stock Exchange symbol] .... CYK
Copeland, KS [FM radio station call letters] .... KJIL
Copeland, KS [FM radio station call letters] .... KYBD
Copeland Resources [Vancouver Stock Exchange symbol] .... KPL
Copeland/Sewell Family Organization (EA) .... CSFO
Copenhagen [Denmark] [Later, RSV] [Geomagnetic observatory code] .... COP
Copenhagen [Denmark] [Airport symbol] (OAG) .... CPH
Copenhagen (BARN) .... Cpn
Copenhagen Airtaxi [Denmark ICAO designator] (FAAC) .... CAT
Copenhagen, Brussels, and Amsterdam [Refers to a group of expressionist artists based in these three cities] .... COBRA
Copenhagen Business School [Denmark] (ECON) .... CBS
Copenhagen, NY [FM radio station call letters] .... WWLF
Copernicus (ROG) .... COP
Copernicus Common (DOMA) .... COPCOM
Cope's Reports [63-72 California] [A publication] (DLA) .... Cope
Coplague High School, Copiague, NY [Library symbol] [Library of Congress] (LCLS) .... NCopHS
Copiague Memorial Public Library, Copiague, NY [Library symbol Library of Congress] (LCLS) .... NCop
Copiah-Jefferson Regional Library, Hazelhurst, MS [Library symbol Library of Congress] (LCLS) .... MsHz
Copiah-Lincoln Junior College [Wesson, MS] .... CLJC
Copiapo [Chile] [Seismograph station code, US Geological Survey] (SEIS) .... CPP
Copiapo/Chamonate [Chile] [ICAO location identifier] (ICLI) .... SCHA
Copi-Elgot-Wright [Electronics] .... CEW
Copier .... COPR
Copier Dealers Association (EA) .... CDA
Copilot .... CP
Copilot .... CPLT
Copilot/Gunner (MCD) .... CPG
Copilot/Gunner Panel (MCD) .... CPGP
Copilot/Gunner Stabilized Sight (MCD) .... CGSS
Copilot/Tactical Coordinator [In S-3 Viking] [Navy] (DOMA) .... COTAC
Copilot Time (DNAB) .... CPT
Coping in Tough Times (AC) .... CITT
Coping Operations Preference Enquiry [Personality development test] [Psychology] .... COPE
Copinger. Copyright [11th ed.] [1971] [A publication] (DLA) .... Cop Cop
Copinger on Title Deeds [A publication] (DLA) .... Cop Tit D
Copinger's Index to Precedents [A publication] (DLA) .... Cop Ind Pr
Coplanar Waveguide .... CPW
Copley News Service .... CNS
Copley Newspapers, Inc., James S. Copley Library, La Jolla, CA [Library symbol Library of Congress] (LCLS) .... CLjC
Copley Pharmaceutical [NASDAQ symbol] (TTSB) .... CPLY
Copley Pharmaceutical, Inc. [Associated Press] (SAG) .... CopleyPh
Copley Pharmaceutical, Inc. [NASDAQ symbol] (SAG) .... CPLY
Copley Properties [AMEX symbol] (TTSB) .... COP
Copley Properties, Inc. [AMEX symbol] (SPSG) .... COP
Copley Properties, Inc. [Associated Press] (SAG) .... Copley
Copolar Attenuation [Telecommunications] (TEL) .... CPA
Copolyester Elastomer [Plastics technology] .... COPE
Copolymer Composition Distribution (PDAA) .... CCD
Copolymerized With [Organic chemistry] .... co
Copper [Chemical symbol is Cu] C
Copper [Chemical symbol is Cu] (MSA) .... COP
Copper .... COP
Copper [Chemical symbol is Cu] .... COPR
Copper [Chemical symbol is Cu] .... CPR
Copper (VRA) .... cu
Copper (GNE) .... Cu
Copper Alloy Tubing .... CAT
Copper Amine Oxidase [An enzyme] .... CAO
Copper and Brass Fabricators Council (EA) .... CBFC
Copper and Brass Fabricators Foreign Trade Association [Later, CBFC] (EA) .... CBFFTA
Copper and Brass Research Association [Later, CDA] .... CABRA
Copper and Brass Research Association [Later, CDA] .... CBRA
Copper and Brass Servicenter Association (EA) .... CBSA
Copper and Brass Warehouse Association (PDAA) .... CABWA
Copper and Brass Warehouse Association [Later, CBSA] (EA) .... CBWA
Copper Band [Dentistry] .... CuB
Copper Cable Steel-Reinforced (IAA) .... CCSR
Copper Center, AK [Location identifier FAA] (FAAL) .... CZC
Copper Chromite CC
Copper Concentric Neutral (PDAA) .... CCN
Copper Cylinder and Boiler Manufacturers' Association [British] (BI) .... CCBM
Copper Data Center [Inactive] [Battelle Memorial Institute] [Information service or system] .... CDC
Copper Development Association (EA) .... CDA
Copper Distributed Data Interface [Computer science] (TNIG) .... CDDI
Copper Distributed Digital Interface [Computer science] .... CDDI
Copper Ethanolamine .... CEN
Copper Fastened .... CF
Copper, Indium, Gallium, and Selenium [Photovoltaics] .... CIGS

Copper Jacketed Steel .... CJS
Copper Lake Explorations Ltd. [Vancouver Stock Exchange symbol] .... CKX
Copper, Lead, or Zinc [Freight] .... CLZ
Copper Mine [Northwest Territories] [Seismograph station code, US Geological Survey Closed] (SEIS) .... CMC
Copper Nickel Alloy (MSA) .... CNA
Copper Nickel Jacket (IAA) .... CNJ
Copper or Steel [Freight] .... CS
Copper Oxidation Corrosion Test (PDAA) .... COCT
Copper Oxide (KSC) .... CUO
Copper Oxide Modulator .... COM
Copper Oxide Rectifier .... COR
Copper Pair [Telecommunications] .... CP
Copper Phthalocyanine [Colored pigment] .... CPC
Copper Products Development Association [Later, INCRA] .... CPDA
Copper Queen Library, Bisbee, AZ [Library symbol Library of Congress] (LCLS) .... AzB
Copper Range R. R. [AAR code] .... COPR
Copper Range Railroad (IIA) .... CR
Copper Recovery Corp. .... CRC
Copper Reduction Test [Chemistry] (DAVI) .... CRT
Copper Refineries Ltd. [Australia] .... CRL
Copper Reverbatory Furnace Slag (PDAA) .... CRFS
Copper Shielding Braid .... CSB
Copper Smelters and Refiners Association [British] (DBA) .... CSRA
Copper Stack Resources Ltd. [Vancouver Stock Exchange symbol] .... CTK
Copper State Air Service, Inc. [FAA designator] (FAAC) .... COP
Copper, Steel, or Zinc [Freight] .... CSZ
Copper Sulfate Treated Sorbeads .... CSTS
Copper Sulfide Rectifier .... CSR
Copper T [An intrauterine contraceptive device] (DAVI) .... TCu
Copper Technical Data Centre [Australia] .... CTDC
Copper Trade Association .... CTA
[The] Copper Treasure Inventory Scroll from Qumran. Cave Three (BJA) 3QInv
Copper Unit of Pressure (WGA) .... CUP
Copper Weld .... CW
Copper Weld Steel [Telecommunications] (TEL) .... CWS
Copper-7 [A contraceptive device] [Gynecology] (DAVI) Cu-7
Copperas Cove, TX [FM radio station call letters] .... KOOV
Copper-Brazed Crosley [Engine] [Automotive engineering] .... COBRA
Copper-Chrome Arsenate [Wood preservative] (ADA) .... CCA
Copper-Clad Steel Wire (IAA) .... CCSW
Copper-Cored Ground Electrode [Automotive engineering] .... CCGE
Coppered C
Coppered .... COPD
Copperhill, TN [AM radio station call letters] .... WLSB
Copper-Indium-Diselenide [Inorganic chemistry] .... CIS
Coppermine [Canada] [Airport symbol] (OAG) .... YCO
Coppermine, NT [ICAO location identifier] (ICLI) .... CYCO
Copperopolis, CA [FM radio station call letters] (RBYB) .... KRVR
Copperplate (VRA) .... cuplt
Coppersmith [British] .... CS
Coppersmith (KSC) .... CSMITH
Coppersmiths Society [A union] [British] .... CS
Copperton [South Africa] [ICAO location identifier] (ICLI) .... FACO
Coppin State College, Baltimore, MD [Library symbol Library of Congress] (LCLS) .... MdBCS
Coppin State College, Parlett L. Moore Library, Baltimore, MD [OCLC symbol] (OCLC) .... MDP
Copp's Land Office Decisions [A publication] (DLA) .... Copp Land
Copp's Manual for Courts-Martial [A publication] (DLA) .... Copp Ct Mar
Copp's Public Land Laws [A publication] (DLA) .... Copp LL
Copp's Public Land Laws [A publication] (DLA) .... Copp Pub Land Laws
Copp's Public Land Laws [A publication] (DLA) .... Copp Pub LL
Copp's United States Mining Decision [A publication] (DLA) .... Copp Min Dec
Coprecipitation .... CO-PPT
Coprecipitation X-Ray Fluorescence Spectroscopy .... COPREX
COPRED Students Peace Network [Later, COPRED-SPWG] (EA) .... COPRED-SPN
COPRED [Consortium on Peace Research, Education, and Development] StudentsPeace Working Group (EA) .... COPRED-SPWG
Coprinus Ianiger [A fungus] Cl
Coprinus Micaceous [A fungus] .... Cm
Co-Production .... COPRO
Coproduction for Security Program [US and Italy] .... CSP
Coproporphyrin [Also, CP] [Clinical chemistry] .... COPRO
Coproporphyrin [Also, COPRO] [Clinical chemistry] .... CP
Coproporphyrinogen Oxidase (DMAA) .... CPO
Coptic [MARC language code Library of Congress] (LCCP) .... cop
Coptic .... COP
Coptic .... COPT
Coptic (VRA) .... Copt
Copula Pyramidna [Neuroanatomy] .... CP
Copulative .... COP
Copulative (ROG) .... COPUL
Copulatory Mechanism [Medicine] .... CM
Copy C
Copy (ROG) .... CO
Copy (WGA) .... COP
Copy (MCD) .... CP
Copy (BUR) .... CPY
Copy (AABC) .... CY
Copy and Add Logical Word (CET) .... CAL
Copy Control Character [Computer science] (IAA) CCC
Copy Editor (WDMC) .... CE

Copy Editor (WDMC) .... ce
Copy Furnished [*Army*] (AABC) .... CF
Copy Libraries .... COPYLIB
Copy of Reply Be Furnished This Office [*Army*] (AABC) .... CORBFUS
Copy Payments Center [*for copyrighted material*] .... CPC
Copy Processing System [*Photocomposition*] .... CPS
Copy Research Council (EA) .... CRC
Copy to Go (NTCM) .... CTG
Copyhold [*British Legal term*] (ROG) C
Copyhold [*British Legal term*] (ROG) .... CO HO
Copying of Parts (ADA) .... COP
Copying Products and Inked Ribbon Association (EA) .... CPIRA
Copyright C
Copyright (WDMC) .... cop
Copyright (WDMC) .... copr
Copyright (TEL) .... COPR
Copyright .... COPT
Copyright (DLA) .... COPY
Copyright (WDMC) .... copy
Copyright [*Deltiology*] .... CPY
Copyright and Literary Property [*Legal term*] (DLA) .... COPY & LIT P
Copyright Bulletin [*A publication*] (DLA) .... Copy Bull
Copyright Clearance Center (EA) CCC
Copyright Collective of Canada (AC) CCC
Copyright Convergence Group [*Australia*] .... CCG
Copyright Copying Guidelines (EDAC) .... CCG
Copyright Decisions [*A publication*] (DLA) .... Copy Dec
Copyright Holder [*MARC relator code*] [*Library of Congress*] (LCCP) .... cph
Copyright in Transmitted Electronic Documents .... CITED
Copyright Law Reporter (Commerce Clearing House) [*A publication*] (DLA) .... Copyright L Rep (CCH)
Copyright Law Symposium. American Society of Composers, Authors, and Publishers (DLA) .... ASCAP Sympos
Copyright Law Symposium. American Society of Composers, Authors, and Publishers [*A publication*] (DLA) .... Copyright L Symp(ASCAP)
Copyright Licensing Agency [*Government body*] [*British*] .... CLA
Copyright Licensing Organisation [*British*] (AIE) .... CLO
Copyright Office [*US*] .... CO
Copyright Office Publication and Interactive Cataloging System [*Library of Congress Washington, DC*] .... COPICS
Copyright Receipt Office [*British Library Automated Information Service*] (NITA) .... CRO
Copyright Royalty Tribunal [*Library of Congress*] .... CRT
Copyright Society of the USA (EA) .... CSUSA
Copyrighted .... COP
Copytele, Inc. [*NASDAQ symbol*] (NQ) .... COPY
CopyTele, Inc. [*Associated Press*] (SAG) .... Copytel
Copywriter's Council of America (EA) .... CCA
Copywriting .... CW
Coqualeetza Archives, Sardis, British Columbia [*Library symbol National Library of Canada*] (NLC) .... BSC
Coque [*Boil*] [*Pharmacy*] .... COQ
Coque ad Medietatis Consumptionem [*Boil to the Consumption of Half*] [*Pharmacy*] (ROG) .... COQ ad MED CONSUMPT
Coque in Sufficiente Aquae [*Boil in Sufficient Water*] [*Pharmacy*] (ROG) .... COQ in SA
Coque Secundum Artem [*Boil According to Rule*] [*Pharmacy*] .... Coq SA
Coque Simul [*Boil at the Same Time*] [*Pharmacy*] (DAVI) .... coq simul
Coquille, OR [*FM radio station call letters*] .... KSHR
Coquille, OR [*AM radio station call letters*] .... KWRO
Coquille Public Library, Coquille, OR [*Library symbol Library of Congress*] (LCLS) .... OrCo
Coquitlam Public Library, British Columbia [*Library symbol National Library of Canada*] (NLC) .... BC
Cor Anglais [*English Horn*] .... CA
Cor Pulmonale [*Medicine*] .... CP
Cor Therapeutics [*NASDAQ symbol*] (TTSB) .... CORR
Cor Therapeutics, Inc. [*NASDAQ symbol*] (SAG) .... CORR
Cor Therapeutics, Inc. [*Associated Press*] (SAG) .... CorTher
Coracoacromial [*Anatomy*] .... CA
Coracoclavicular [*Anatomy*] (MAE) CC
Coracoid Process [*Anatomy*] .... CP
Corair [*France ICAO designator*] (FAAC) .... COZ
Coral [*Quality of the bottom*] [*Nautical charts*] .... Co
Coral (ROG) .... COR
Coral [*Record label*] [*USA, Europe*] .... Crl
Coral Air [*ICAO designator*] (AD) .... VY
Coral Cove, FL [*FM radio station call letters*] .... WYNF
Coral Energy Corp. [*Vancouver Stock Exchange symbol*] .... CGL
Coral Gables [*Florida*] .... CG
Coral Gables, FL [*FM radio station call letters*] .... WHQT
Coral Gables, FL [*AM radio station call letters*] .... WRHC
Coral Gables, FL [*AM radio station call letters*] .... WVCG
Coral Gables, FL [*FM radio station call letters*] .... WVUM
Coral Gold Corp. [*Vancouver Stock Exchange symbol*] .... CLH
Coral Harbour [*Canada*] [*Airport symbol*] (OAG) .... YZS
Coral Harbour, NT [*ICAO location identifier*] (ICLI) .... CYZS
Coral Head [*Quality of the bottom*] [*Nautical charts*] .... Co Hd
Coralline Lethal Orange Disease .... CLOD
Coralta Resources [*Vancouver Stock Exchange symbol*] .... COU
Coralville Courier, Coralville, IA [*Library symbol Library of Congress*] (LCLS) .... IaCorvC
Coralville Public Library, Coralville, IA [*Library symbol Library of Congress*] (LCLS) .... IaCorv
Coram [*Before*] [*Latin*] (ROG) .... COR
Coram Healthcare [*NYSE symbol*] (TTSB) .... CRH
Coram Healthcare Corp. [*Associated Press*] (SAG) .... CoramH
Coram Healthcare Corp. [*NYSE symbol*] (SAG) .... CRH
Coran Nobis and Allied Statutory Remedies [*A publication*] (DLA) .... Coran N
Coras Iompair Eireann [*Irish Transport Co.*] .... CIE
Corazon De Jesus [*Panama*] [*Airport symbol*] (OAG) .... CZJ
Corbeil Branch, East Ferris Township Public Library, Ontario [*Library symbol National Library of Canada*] (NLC) .... OCEFT
Corben Club (EA) CC
Corbett and Daniell's English Election Cases [*1819*] [*A publication*] (DLA) .... C & D
Corbett and Daniell's English Election Cases [*1819*] [*A publication*] (DLA) .... Corb & D
Corbett and Daniell's English Election Cases [*1819*] [*A publication*] (DLA) .... Corb & Dan
Corbin [*Virginia*] [*Seismograph station code, US Geological Survey*] (SEIS) .... CBN
Corbin, KY [*AM radio station call letters*] .... WCTT
Corbin, KY [*FM radio station call letters*] .... WCTT-FM
Corbin, KY [*AM radio station call letters*] .... WKDP
Corbin, KY [*FM radio station call letters*] .... WKDP-FM
Corbin Research [*An association*] (EA) .... CR
Corbit-Calloway Memorial Library, Odessa, DE [*OCLC symbol*] (OCLC) .... CRB
Corby Distilleries Ltd. [*Toronto Stock Exchange symbol Vancouver Stock Exchange symbol*] .... CDL
Corcom, Inc. [*NASDAQ symbol*] (NQ) .... CORC
Corcom, Inc. [*Associated Press*] (SAG) .... Corcom
Corcoran Art Gallery, Washington, DC [*Library symbol Library of Congress*] (LCLS) .... DCA
Corcoran, CA [*Location identifier FAA*] (FAAL) .... COR
Corcoran, CA [*Location identifier FAA*] (FAAL) .... CRO
Corcoran, CA [*FM radio station call letters*] .... KLCZ
Corcoran School of Art, Washington, DC [*Library symbol Library of Congress*] (LCLS) .... DCAS
Cord C
Cord .... CD
Cord Around Neck [*Neonatology and obstetrics*] (DAVI) .... CAN
Cord [*Umbilical*] **Blood Leukocytes** [*Hematology*] .... CBL
Cord Compression [*Medicine*] CC
Cord on Legal and Equitable Rights of Married Women [*A publication*] (DLA) .... Cord Mar Wom
Cord Welt .... CDWT
Cordage Institute (EA) CI
Cordage Manufacturers Institute [*British*] (DBA) .... CMI
Cordele, GA [*FM radio station call letters*] .... WKKN
Cordele, GA [*Television station call letters*] .... WSST
Cordele, GA [*AM radio station call letters*] .... WUWU
Cordell Hull Dam [*TVA*] .... CHD
Cordell Hull Foundation for International Education (EA) .... CHFIE
Cordell, OK [*FM radio station call letters*] .... KCDL
Cordery. Solicitors [*6th ed.*] [*1968*] [*A publication*] (DLA) .... Cord Sol
Cordi Marian Sisters (TOCD) .... MCM
Cordiale Resources, Inc. [*Vancouver Stock Exchange symbol*] .... COD
Cordiant ADS [*NYSE symbol*] (TTSB) .... CDA
Cordiant PLC [*NYSE symbol*] (SAG) .... CDA
Cordiant PLC [*Associated Press*] (SAG) .... Cordiant
Cordic Arithmetic Processor (IAA) .... CAP
Cordierite [*A mineral*] .... Crd
Cordillera [*A mountain chain*] (BARN) .... Cord
Cordillera People's Liberation Army [*Philippines*] [*Political party*] (EY) .... CPLA
Cordillo Downs [*South Australia*] [*Airport symbol*] (AD) .... ODL
Cordi-Marian Missionary Sisters [*Roman Catholic religious order*] .... MCM
Cordis Corp. [*NASDAQ symbol*] (NQ) .... CORD
Cordis Corp. [*Associated Press*] (SAG) .... Cordis
Cordis Corp. Library, Miami, FL [*Library symbol*] [*Library of Congress*] (LCLS) .... FMCC
Cordless Switchboard Section [*Telecommunications*] (NITA) .... CSS
Cordless Switchboard System .... CSS
Cordless Telephone .... CT
Cordoba [*Monetary unit*] [*Nicaragua*] C
Cordoba [*Argentina*] [*Airport symbol*] (OAG) .... COR
Cordoba [*Spain ICAO location identifier*] (ICLI) .... LEBA
Cordoba [*Spain*] [*Airport symbol*] (OAG) .... ODB
Cordoba [*Argentina ICAO location identifier*] (ICLI) .... SACE
Cordoba [*Argentina ICAO location identifier*] (ICLI) .... SACF
Cordoba [*Argentina ICAO location identifier*] (ICLI) .... SACG
Cordoba [*Argentina ICAO location identifier*] (ICLI) .... SACO
Cordoba [*Argentina ICAO location identifier*] (ICLI) .... SACU
Cordoba/Area de Material [*Argentina ICAO location identifier*] (ICLI) .... SACA
Cordoba Durchmusterung [*Star chart*] .... CD
Cordon and Search [*Military*] .... C & S
Cordova [*Alaska*] [*Airport symbol*] (OAG) .... CDV
Cordova [*Alaska*] [*Seismograph station code, US Geological Survey*] (SEIS) .... CVA
Cordova [*Alaska*] [*ICAO location identifier*] (ICLI) .... PACV
Cordova Airlines, Inc. .... COA
Cordova, AK [*Location identifier FAA*] (FAAL) .... CKU
Cordova, AK [*AM radio station call letters*] .... KLAM
Cordova, AL [*FM radio station call letters*] .... WFFN
Cordova, KS [*FM radio station call letters*] (RBYB) .... KCDV-FM
Cordova Public Library, Cordova, AK [*Library symbol Library of Congress*] (LCLS) .... AkC
Corduroy Council of America [*Defunct*] (EA) .... CCA
Corduroy Trousers [*Slang*] (DSUE) .... CORDS
Core (IAA) C
Core .... CR
Core and Drum Corrector .... CADCO

Core and Random Access Manager [*General Automation, Inc.*] .... CRAM
Core Australian Specification for Management and Administrative Computing .... CASMAC
Core Automated Maintenance System (MCD) .... CAMS
Core Auxiliary Cooling System [*Nuclear energy*] (NRCH) .... CACS
Core Auxiliary Cooling Water [*Nuclear energy*] (NRCH) .... CACW
Core Auxiliary Cooling Water System [*Nuclear energy*] (NRCH) .... CACWS
Core Auxiliary Heat Exchanger [*Nuclear energy*] (NRCH) .... CAHE
Core Binding Factor Beta [*Genetics*] .... CBFB
Core Block Table [*Computer science*] (OA) .... CBT
Core College Curriculm (EDAC) CCC
Core Component Cleaning System [*Nuclear energy*] (NRCH) .... CCCS
Core Component Conditioning Station [*Nuclear energy*] (NRCH) .... CCCS
Core Component Pot [*Nuclear energy*] (NRCH) .... CCP
Core Component Receiving Container [*Nuclear energy*] (NRCH) .... CCRC
Core Component Test Loop [*Nuclear energy*] (NRCH) .... CCTL
Core Conflictional Relationships Theme [*Psychology*] .... CCRT
Core Current Driver .... CCD
Core Current Layer (OA) CCL
Core Damage Frequency [*Nuclear energy*] (NRCH) .... CDF
Core Diode Logic .... CDL
Core Disruptive Accident [*Nuclear energy*] (NRCH) .... CDA
Core Division Multiplexing (IAA) .... CDM
Core Element Assembly Motion Inhibit [*Nuclear energy*] (IEEE) .... CMI
Core File (IEEE) .... COFIL
Core Flood Alarm [*Nuclear energy*] (IEEE) .... CFA
Core Flood Isolation Valve Assembly [*Nuclear energy*] (IEEE) .... CFIA
Core Flood Tank [*Nuclear energy*] (NRCH) .... CFT
Core Flooding System [*Nuclear energy*] (NRCH) .... CF
Core Flooding System Isolation Valve Interlock [*Nuclear energy*] (NRCH) .... CFI
Core Former Structure [*Nuclear energy*] (NRCH) .... CFS
Core Image Converter [*Computer science*] CIC
Core Image Dictionary [*Computer science*] (IAA) .... CID
Core Image Library (CMD) CIL
Core, Inc. [*NASDAQ symbol*] (SAG) .... CORE
CORE Inc. [*NASDAQ symbol*] (TTSB) .... CORE
Core, Inc. [*Associated Press*] (SAG) .... Core Inc
Core Indus [*NYSE symbol*] (TTSB) .... CRI
Core Industries, Inc. [*Associated Press*] (SAG) .... CoreIn
Core Industries, Inc. [*NYSE symbol*] (SPSG) .... CRI
Core Instrumentation Facility [*Army*] .... CIF
Core Instrumentation Subsystem (MCD) .... CIS
Core Insulation [*Nuclear energy*] CI
Core Laboratories, Inc., Dallas, TX [*Library symbol Library of Congress*] (LCLS) .... TxDaCL
Core Laboratories NV [*Associated Press*] (SAG) .... CoreLab
Core Laboratories NV [*NASDAQ symbol*] (SAG) .... CRLB
Core Laboratories N.V. [*NASDAQ symbol*] (TTSB) .... CRLBF
Core Load Overlay Builder [*General Automation, Inc.*] .... CLOB
Core Local Area Network (SSD) .... CLAN
Core Logic Intervalometer CLI
Core Logic Intervalometer CLIV
Core Materials Corp. [*AMEX symbol*] (SAG) .... CME
Core Materials Corp. [*Associated Press*] (SAG) .... CoreMatl
Core Maximum Fraction of Limiting Power Density [*Nuclear energy*] (NRCH) .... CMFLPD
Core Maximum Power Fraction [*Nuclear energy*] (IEEE) .... CMPF
Core Measurement Table (IAA) .... CMT
Core Mechanical Mock-Up [*Nuclear energy*] (NRCH) .... CMM
Core Melt Review Group [*Nuclear energy*] (NRCH) .... CMRG
Core Melt Technology [*Metal casting*] .... CMT
Core Melt Through [*Nuclear energy*] (IEEE) .... MT
Core Memory .... CM
Core Memory Driver .... CMD
Core Memory Unit (MCD) .... CMU
Core Monitoring Computer [*Nuclear energy*] (NRCH) .... CMC
Core Nodal Switching Subsystems [*Electronics*] (ACRL) .... CNSS
Core Operating Limit Supervisory System [*Nuclear energy*] (NRCH) .... COLSS
Core Operating Limit Support System [*Nuclear energy*] (NRCH) .... COLSS
Core Operating System [*Computer science*] (NITA) .... COS
Core Performance Log [*Nuclear energy*] (IEEE) .... CPL
Core Prime (SAA) .... CP
Core Protection Calculator [*or Computer*] [*Nuclear energy*] (NRCH) .... CPC
Core Removal Coding (DNAB) .... CRC
Core Research for Evolutional Science and Technology [*Japan*] .... CREST
Core Restraint Mechanism [*Nuclear energy*] (NRCH) .... CRM
Core Restraint Test Facility [*Nuclear energy*] (NRCH) .... CRTF
Core Sample Vacuum Container [*NASA*] .... CSVC
Core Segment (NASA) .... CS
Core Segment Development Facility [*Nuclear energy*] (NRCH) .... CSDF
Core Segment Interface Unit (NASA) .... CSIU
Core Segment Processing Unit (NASA) .... CSPU
Core Segment Simulator (NASA) .... CSS
Core Sharing [*Computer science*] (IAA) .... CS
Core Shift .... CS
Core Shift Driver (CET) .... CSD
Core Special Assembly [*Nuclear energy*] (NRCH) .... CSA
Core Spray [*Nuclear energy*] (NRCH) .... CS
Core Spray Injection System [*Nuclear energy*] (IAA) .... CSIS
Core Standby Cooling [*Nuclear energy*] (IEEE) .... CSC
Core Standby Cooling System [*Nuclear energy*] (NRCH) .... CSCS
Core States Financial [*NYSE symbol*] (SAG) .... CFL
Core States Financial [*Associated Press*] (SAG) .... CoreStF
Core Storage Element .... CSE
Core Storage Terminal Table [*Computer science*] .... CSTT
Core Structure Accident [*Nuclear energy*] (NRCH) .... CSA
Core Support Barrel [*Nuclear energy*] (NRCH) .... CSB
Core Support Cylinder [*Nuclear energy*] (NRCH) .... CSC
Core Support Structure [*Nuclear energy*] (NRCH) .... CSS
Core Technologies [*NASDAQ symbol*] (TTSB) .... CTXR
Core Temperature [*Medicine*] .... Tc
Core Test Facility .... CTF
Core Transistor Logic [*Computer science*] .... CTL
Core Transistor Register .... CTR
Core Ventures [*Vancouver Stock Exchange symbol*] .... CYR
Coreceptor Skewed [*Immunology*] .... CRS
Core-Dominated Quasar [*Astronomy*] .... CDQ
Corel Corp. [*Associated Press*] (SAG) .... CorelCp
Corel Corp. [*NASDAQ symbol*] (SAG) .... COSF
Corel Corp. [*NASDAQ symbol*] (TTSB) .... COSFF
Corel Photopaint [*Computer science*] .... cpt
Core-Mantle Boundary [*Geology*] .... CMB
Core-Mark International, Inc. [*Toronto Stock Exchange symbol Vancouver Stock Exchange symbol*] .... CMK
Corepressor Binding Domain [*Genetics*] .... CBD
Co-Respondent (DSUE) .... CO-RE
Co-Responsibility Levy [*Cereal production tax*] [*British*] .... CR
CoreStaff, Inc. [*Associated Press*] (SAG) .... CreStaff
CoreStaff, Inc. [*NASDAQ symbol*] (SAG) .... CSTF
CoreStates Financial [*NYSE symbol*] (TTSB) .... CFL
CoreStates Financial Corp. [*NYSE symbol*] (SPSG) .... CFL
Corey-Pauling-Koltun [*Molecular models*] .... CPK
CorFile on Disc, Corporate and Industry Research Reports (IID) .... CIRR
Corfu [*Greece*] [*Airport symbol*] (OAG) .... CFU
Corfu [*Washington*] [*Seismograph station code, US Geological Survey*] (SEIS) .... CRF
Corfu Free Library, Corfu, NY [*Library symbol Library of Congress*] (LCLS) .... NCorf
Corimon ADS [*NYSE symbol*] (TTSB) .... CRM
Corimon CA [*NYSE symbol*] (SPSG) .... CRM
Corimon CA SACA [*Associated Press*] (SAG) .... Corimon
Corinaldo [*Italy*] [*Seismograph station code, US Geological Survey*] (SEIS) .... CRN
[*The*] **Corinth & Counce Railroad Co.** [*AAR code*] .... CCR
Corinth, MS [*Location identifier FAA*] (FAAL) .... CRX
Corinth, MS [*FM radio station call letters*] .... WADI
Corinth, MS [*AM radio station call letters*] .... WCMA
Corinth, MS [*AM radio station call letters*] .... WKCU
Corinth, MS [*FM radio station call letters*] .... WXRZ
Corinth Resources Ltd. [*Vancouver Stock Exchange symbol*] .... CTH
Corinthian (VRA) .... Corin
Corinthians [*New Testament book*] (BJA) C
Corinthians [*New Testament book*] .... Cor
Coriolanus [*Shakespearean work*] .... Cor
Coriolis Absorber .... CA
Coriolis Acceleration Platform .... CAP
Coriolis Correction .... Z
Coriolis Sickness Susceptibility Index [*Orientation*] .... CSSI
Cork (MSA) .... CK
Cork .... CRK
Cork [*Ireland*] [*ICAO location identifier*] (ICLI) .... EICK
Cork [*Ireland*] [*Airport symbol*] (OAG) .... ORK
Cork Base .... CKB
Cork Board (AAG) .... CKBD
Cork Floor (AAG) .... CKF
Cork Institute of America [*Defunct*] (EA) .... CIA
Cork Insulation Material .... CIM
Cork Leather and Celastic [*Orthotic*] [*Orthopedics*] (DAVI) CLC
Cormack Public Library, Cormack, NF, Canada [*Library symbol Library of Congress*] (LCLS) .... CaNfCo
Cormack Public Library, Newfoundland [*Library symbol National Library of Canada*] (NLC) .... NFCO
Corn, Beans, Miami [*Tongue-in-cheek description of a crop rotation system, allowing farmers to spend winter in Florida*] .... CBM
Corn Belt Library System [*Library network*] .... CBLS
Corn Belt Library System, Bloomington, IL [*Library symbol Library of Congress*] (LCLS) .... IBloC
Corn Belt Library System, Normal, IL [*OCLC symbol*] (OCLC) .... JAF
Corn Belt Livestock Feeders Association [*Later, NCA*] .... CBLFA
Corn, Corn, Oats, Meadow, Meadow [*Crop rotation*] .... CCOMM
Corn Flour (OA) .... CF
Corn Gluten Meal .... CGM
Corn Growers Association of North Carolina (SRA) .... CGANC
Corn Industries Research Foundation [*Later, CRA*] (EA) .... CIRF
Corn Island [*Nicaragua*] [*ICAO location identifier*] (ICLI) .... MNCI
Corn Items Collectors Association (EA) CIC
Corn Meal Agar [*Growth medium*] .... CMA
Corn Oil .... CO
Corn Refiners Association (EA) .... CRA
Corn, Soybean, and Milk Products [*Main ingredients of a formulated food*] .... CSM
Corn Stunt [*Plant pathology*] .... CS
Corn Stunt Organism [*Plant pathology*] .... CSO
Corn Stunt Spiroplasma [*Plant pathology*] .... CSS
Corn Syrup Solids .... CSS
Corn Trade Clauses [*Shipping*] .... CTC
Cornea, Conjunctiva, and Sclera [*Ophthalmology*] (DAVI) .... CC & S
Cornea, Sclera, Conjuctiva [*Ophthalmology*] (DAVI) .... CSC
Corneal Dystrophy [*Medicine*] (DMAA) .... CD
Corneal Endothelial Cell [*Medicine*] (CPH) .... CEC
Corneal Opacity [*Medicine*] (MAE) .... CO
Corneal Thickness [*Ophthalmology*] (DAVI) .... CT

Corneal Transplant [*Medicine*] ..... CT
Corned Beef [*Restaurant slang*] ..... CB
Cornelia de Lange Parents Group [*Later, Cornelia de Lange Syndrome Foundation*] (EA) ..... CLPG
Cornelia De Lange Syndrome [*Medicine*] ..... CdLS
Cornelia De Lange Syndrome Foundation (EA) ..... CdLSF
Cornelia, GA [*AM radio station call letters*] ..... WCON
Cornelia, GA [*FM radio station call letters*] ..... WCON-FM
Cornelio Procopio [*Brazil*] [*Airport symbol*] (OAG) ..... CKO
Cornelius Court Elementary School, Uniondale, NY [*Library symbol*] [*Library of Congress*] (LCLS) ..... NUnCCE
Cornelius Nepos [*Historian, 31-14BC*] (ROG) ..... CORN NEP
Cornelius Public Library, Cornelius, OR [*Library symbol Library of Congress*] (LCLS) ..... OrCor
Cornell (ROG) ..... CORN
Cornell Aeronautical Laboratory (KSC) ..... CAL
Cornell Aeronautical Laboratory, Buffalo, NY [*Library symbol Library of Congress*] (LCLS) ..... NBuCA
Cornell Aeronautical Laboratory, Inc. (SAA) ..... CALI
Cornell Aeronautical Laboratory Shock Tunnel (SAA) ..... CALST
Cornell College, Mount Vernon, IA [*Library symbol Library of Congress*] (LCLS) ..... IaMvC
Cornell College, Mount Vernon, IA [*OCLC symbol*] (OCLC) ..... IMV
Cornell Computer Services [*Cornell University*] [*Information service or system*] (IID) ..... CCS
Cornell Computing Language [*Computer science*] ..... CORC
Cornell Corrections, Inc. [*Associated Press*] (SAG) ..... CornCor
Cornell Corrections, Inc. [*AMEX symbol*] (SAG) ..... CRN
Cornell Dubilier Electronics (MUGU) ..... CDE
Cornell Electron Storage Ring [*Atomic physics*] ..... CESR
Cornell Feline Health Center [*Cornell University*] [*Research center*] (RCD) ..... CFHC
Cornell High-Energy Synchrotron Source Laboratory [*Cornell University*] [*Research center*] ..... CHESS
Cornell Hotel Administration Simulation Exercise [*Computer-programmed management game*] ..... CHASE
Cornell Index [*Psychology*] CI
Cornell Information Technologies [*Information service or system*] (IID) ..... CIT
Cornell Institute for Social and Economic Research [*Cornell University*] [*Research center*] (RCD) ..... CISER
Cornell Laboratory for Environmental Applications of Remote Sensing [*Cornell University*] [*Information service or system*] (IID) ..... CLEARS
Cornell Law Journal [*A publication*] (DLA) ..... Cornell LJ
Cornell Law Review [*A publication*] (ILCA) ..... CLR
Cornell Law School (DLA) ..... CLS
Cornell Learning and Recognizing Automaton ..... CLARA
Cornell List Processor [*Computer science*] ..... CLP
Cornell Local Roads Program [*Cornell University*] [*Research center*] (RCD) ..... CLRP
Cornell Manufacturing Engineering and Productivity Program [*Cornell University*] [*Research center*] (RCD) ..... COMEPP
Cornell Maritime Press (DGA) ..... CMP
Cornell Medical Index [*Psychology*] ..... CMI
Cornell National Supercomputer Facility [*Cornell University*] [*Research center*] (RCD) ..... CNSF
Cornell Parent Behavior Description (EDAC) ..... CPBD
Cornell Parent Behavior Inventory (EDAC) ..... CPBI
Cornell Reconstruction of Accident Speeds on the Highway ..... CRASH
Cornell University [*Record label*] ..... Corn
Cornell University (GAGS) ..... Cornell U
Cornell University [*Ithaca, NY*] ..... CU
Cornell University, Ithaca, NY [*OCLC symbol*] (OCLC) ..... COO
Cornell University, Ithaca, NY [*Library symbol Library of Congress*] (LCLS) ..... NIC
Cornell University Laboratory of Ornithology (EA) ..... CULO
Cornell University, Medical College, New York, NY [*Library symbol Library of Congress*] (LCLS) ..... NNCorM
Cornell University, Medical College, New York, NY [*OCLC symbol*] (OCLC) ..... VYC
Cornell University, Medical College, Oskar Diethelm Historical Library, New York, NY [*Library symbol*] [*Library of Congress*] (LCLS) ..... NNCorM-D
Cornell University, Medical College, Oskar Diethelm Historical Library, New York, NY [*Library symbol Library of Congress*] (LCLS) ..... NNCorM-D
Cornell University, New York State School of Industrial and Labor Relations, Sanford V. Lenz Library, New York, NY [*Library symbol*] [*Library of Congress*] (LCLS) ..... NNCorl
Cornell University Research Laboratory ..... CRL
Cornell University Research Laboratory for Diseases of Dogs ..... CRLDD
Cornell Word Form 2 [*Psychology*] CWF2
Cornell-Guggenheim Aviation Safety Center (SAA) ..... CGASC
Cornellian, Mount Vernon, IA [*Library symbol Library of Congress*] (LCLS) ..... IaMvCor
Corn-Equivalent Feed Unit ..... CFU
Corner (ADA) ..... CNR
Corner (KSC) ..... COR
Corner ..... COR
Corner (WDMC) ..... cor
Corner [*Commonly used*] (OPSA) ..... CORNER
Corner (VRA) ..... crnr
Corner Bead [*Technical drawings*] (DAC) ..... COR BD
Corner Brook City Library, Corner Brook, NF, Canada [*Library symbol Library of Congress*] (LCLS) ..... CaNfCB
Corner Brook City Public Library, Newfoundland [*Library symbol National Library of Canada*] (NLC) ..... NFCB
Corner Brook, NF [*AM radio station call letters*] ..... CBY
Corner Brook, NF [*Television station call letters*] ..... CBYT
Corner Brook, NF [*AM radio station call letters*] ..... CFCB
Corner Brook, NF [*Television station call letters*] ..... CJWN
Corner Brook, NF [*FM radio station call letters*] ..... CKOZ
Corner Brook, NF [*AM radio station call letters*] ..... CKXX
Corner Guard [*Technical drawings*] ..... CG
Corner Wear [*Deltiology*] ..... COR/WR
Cornerback [*Football*] ..... CB
Corners [*Commonly used*] (OPSA) ..... CORNERS
Corners [*Postal Service standard*] (OPSA) ..... CORS
Corners ..... CORS
Corner's Forms of Writs on the Crown Side [*A publication*] (DLA) ..... Corn Wr
Corner's Queen's Bench Practice [*A publication*] (DLA) ..... Corn Pr
Cornerstone Bank [*AMEX symbol*] (SAG) ..... CBN
Cornerstone Bank [*Associated Press*] (SAG) ..... CornerBk
Cornerstone Bank [*Associated Press*] (SAG) ..... CrnrB
Cornerstone Christian School Library, Grand Junction, CO [*Library symbol*] [*Library of Congress*] (LCLS) ..... CoGjCS
Cornerstone Financial Corp. [*Associated Press*] (SAG) ..... CrnrFn
Cornerstone Financial Corp. [*NASDAQ symbol*] (NQ) ..... CSTN
Cornerstone Imaging [*NASDAQ symbol*] (TTSB) ..... CRNR
Cornerstone Imaging, Inc. [*Associated Press*] (SAG) ..... CorImag
Cornerstone Imaging, Inc. [*NASDAQ symbol*] (SAG) ..... CRNR
Cornerstone Natural Gas [*Associated Press*] (SAG) ..... CornNG
Cornerstone Propane Partners LP [*NYSE symbol*] (SAG) ..... CNO
Cornerstone Propane Partners LP [*Associated Press*] (SAG) ..... CornPrp
Cornet ..... COR
Cornet ..... CORT
Cornette Library Online Information Service [*West Texas State University*] (OLDSS) ..... CLOIS
Cornhusker Army Ammunition Plant (AABC) ..... CAAP
Cornhusks (VRA) ..... crnhs
Cornice (DAC) ..... Corn
Corning, AR [*FM radio station call letters*] ..... KBKG
Corning, AR [*AM radio station call letters*] ..... KCCB
Corning, CA [*FM radio station call letters*] ..... KCEZ
Corning Community College, Corning, NY [*Library symbol Library of Congress*] (LCLS) ..... NCorniCC
Corning Community College, Corning, NY [*OCLC symbol*] (OCLC) ..... ZDG
Corning Del L.P. 6% 'MIPS' [*NYSE symbol*] (TTSB) ..... GLWPrM
Corning Delaware Ltd. [*Associated Press*] (SAG) ..... CornD
Corning Delaware LP [*NYSE symbol*] (SAG) ..... GLW
Corning Free Public Library, Corning, IA [*Library symbol Library of Congress*] (LCLS) ..... IaCorn
Corning Glass Works ..... CGW
Corning Glass Works, Corning, NY [*Library symbol Library of Congress*] (LCLS) ..... NCorniC
Corning, IA [*Location identifier FAA*] (FAAL) ..... CRZ
Corning, Inc. [*Associated Press*] (SAG) ..... CorningIn
Corning, Inc. [*Wall Street slang name: "Glow Worm"*] [*NYSE symbol*] (SPSG) ..... GLW
Corning Museum of Glass, Corning, NY [*Library symbol Library of Congress*] (LCLS) ..... NCorniM
Corning Museum of Glass, Corning, NY [*OCLC symbol*] (OCLC) ..... YKM
Corning, NY [*AM radio station call letters*] ..... WCBA
Corning, NY [*FM radio station call letters*] ..... WCBA-FM
Corning, NY [*FM radio station call letters*] ..... WCEB
Corning, NY [*AM radio station call letters*] ..... WCLI
Corning, NY [*FM radio station call letters*] ..... WNKI
Corning, NY [*FM radio station call letters*] ..... WSQE
Corning, NY [*Television station call letters*] ..... WYDC
Corning Public Library, Corning, NY [*Library symbol Library of Congress*] (LCLS) ..... NCorni
Corning Resources [*Vancouver Stock Exchange symbol*] ..... CGU
Corning Uniformity Limit Level ..... CULL
Corning-Elmira [*New York*] [*Airport symbol*] (AD) ..... ELM
Cornish [*MARC language code Library of Congress*] (LCCP) ..... cor
Cornish (ROG) ..... CORN
Cornish Association of South Australia ..... CASA
Cornish on Purchase Deeds [*A publication*] (DLA) ..... Corn Deeds
Cornish on Purchase Deeds [*A publication*] (DLA) ..... Corn Pur D
Cornish on Purchase Deeds [*A publication*] (DLA) ..... Cornish Purch Deeds
Cornish on Remainders [*A publication*] (DLA) ..... Corn Rem
Cornish on Uses [*A publication*] (DLA) ..... Corn Us
Cornish Scottish Australia [*Mine*] ..... CSA
Cornmeal ..... CM
Corno [*Cornet or Horn*] [*Music*] (ROG) ..... COR
Corn-Soybeans-Corn-Soybeans-Corn [*Crop rotation*] ..... CBCBC
Cornstock Bk Carson City Nev [*NASDAQ symbol*] (TTSB) ..... LODE
Cornu Ammonis [*Anatomy*] ..... CA
Cornu Cervi [*Hartshorn*] [*Pharmacy*] (ROG) CC
Cornu Cervi Ustum [*Burnt Hartshorn*] [*Pharmacy*] (ROG) ..... CCU
Cornu Double Prism ..... CDP
Cornucopia of Disability Information [*Internet*] (PAZ) ..... CODI
Cornucopia Resources Ltd. [*Toronto Stock Exchange symbol Vancouver Stock Exchange symbol*] ..... CNP
Cornucopia Resources Ltd. [*NASDAQ symbol*] (NQ) ..... CNPG
Cornucopia Resources Ltd. [*Associated Press*] (SAG) ..... Cornucp
Cornucopia Resources Ltd [*NASDAQ symbol*] (TTSB) ..... CNPGF
Cornu-Jellet Prism ..... CJP
Cornwall [*County in England*] ..... CORN
Cornwall [*County in England*] (ROG) ..... CORNW
Cornwall [*County in England*] ..... CRNWL
Cornwall and Devon Miners Royal Garrison Artillery [*British military*] (DMA) ..... C & DM RGA
Cornwall General Hospital, Cornwall, ON, Canada [*Library symbol Library of Congress*] (LCLS) ..... CaOCGH

Cornwall General Hospital, Ontario [Library symbol National Library of Canada] (NLC) .... OCGH
Cornwall Light Infantry [British military] (DMA) CLI
Cornwall, NY [AM radio station call letters] .... WRWD
Cornwall, ON [FM radio station call letters] .... CFLG
Cornwall, ON [FM radio station call letters] (RBYB) .... CHOD
Cornwall, ON [Television station call letters] CJOH-8
Cornwall, ON [AM radio station call letters] .... CJSS
Cornwall Petroleum [Vancouver Stock Exchange symbol] .... COW
Cornwall Public Library, Cornwall, NY [Library symbol Library of Congress] (LCLS) .... NCorn
Cornwall Public Library, Cornwall, ON, Canada [Library symbol Library of Congress] (LCLS) .... CaOC
Cornwall Public Library, Ontario [Library symbol National Library of Canada] (NLC) .... OC
Cornwall R. R. [AAR code] .... CWL
Cornwall's Table of Precedents [A publication] (DLA) .... Cornw Tab
Cornwell Avenue School, West Hempstead, NY [Library symbol] [Library of Congress] (LCLS) .... NWhCE
Cornwell's Digest [A publication] (DLA) .... Corn Dig
Cornwell-Weisskopf Formula .... CWF
Coro [Venezuela] [Airport symbol] (OAG) .... CZE
Coro Foundation (EA) .... CF
Coro/Internacional, Falcon [Venezuela ICAO location identifier] (ICLI) .... SVCR
Coroico [Bolivia] [ICAO location identifier] (ICLI) .... SLIC
Corolla C
Corolla Resources Ltd. [Vancouver Stock Exchange symbol] .... CRA
Corollary .... COROL
Corollary (ADA) .... COROLL
Corollary Discharge Interneuron [Neurology] .... CDI
Corollary Discharge Neuron [Neurophysiology] .... CD
Corona [A publication] .... COR
Corona Australis [Constellation] .... CorA
Corona Australis [Constellation] .... CrA
Corona Borealis [Constellation] .... CorB
Corona Borealis [Constellation] .... CrB
Corona, CA [Television station call letters] .... KVEA
Corona, CA [AM radio station call letters] .... KWRM
Corona Current Detector .... CCD
Corona Diagnostic Mission (SSD) .... CDM
Corona, Eddy Current, Beta Ray, Microwave .... CEBM
Corona Extinction Voltage (IEEE) .... CEV
Corona Inception Voltage (PDAA) CIV
Corona, NM [Location identifier FAA] (FAAL) .... CNX
Corona Onset Voltage .... COV
Corona Public Library, Corona, CA [Library symbol Library of Congress] (LCLS) .... CCoro
Corona Starting Voltage .... CSV
Coronado 15 Class Racing Association (EA) .... CFCRA
Coronado Aerolineas Ltda. [Colombia] [ICAO designator] (FAAC) .... CRA
Coronado National Memorial .... CORO
Coronado Public Library, Coronado, CA [Library symbol Library of Congress] (LCLS) .... CCoron
Coronado Resources, Inc. [Vancouver Stock Exchange symbol] .... CRD
Coronae Borealis [Astronomy] .... CrB
Coronagraph Polarimeter .... CP
Coronal Mass Ejection [Astrophysics] .... CME
Coronal Mass Ejection [Cosmology] .... CME
Corona-Penetrating Enzyme (MAE) .... CPE
Coronary [Cardiology] (DAVI) .... cor
Coronary Angiography [Cardiology] (DMAA) .... CAG
Coronary Angioplasty Versus Excisional Atherectomy Trial [Cardiology study] .... CAVEAT
Coronary Arrhythmia Monitoring Unit [Cardiology] (DAVI) .... CAMU
Coronary Arteriosclerotic Heart Disease .... CASHD
Coronary Arteriovenous Fistula [Cardiology] .... CAVF
Coronary Artery [Medicine] .... CA
Coronary Artery Aneurysm [Cardiology] .... CAA
Coronary Artery Bypass [Medicine] .... CAB
Coronary Artery Bypass Graft [Medicine] .... CABG
Coronary Artery Bypass Graft [Cardiology] (DMAA) .... CARB
Coronary Artery Bypass Graft Surgery [Medicine] .... CABGS
Coronary Artery Bypass Surgery [Medicine] .... CABS
Coronary Artery Disease [Medicine] .... CAD
Coronary Artery Graft Bypass [Cardiology] (DAVI) .... CAGB
Coronary Artery Heart Disease [Cardiology] (DAVI) .... CAHD
Coronary Artery Obstruction [Cardiology] (DMAA) .... CAO
Coronary Artery Occlusive Disease [Medicine] (DMAA) .... CAOD
Coronary Artery Risk Development in Young Adults [Epidemiologic study] .... CARDIA
Coronary Artery Risk Evaluation Program [Air Force] .... CARE
Coronary Artery Surgery Study [Medicine] .... CASS
Coronary Artery Surgery Trial [Medicine] .... CAST
Coronary Artery Vein Graft [Medicine] (DMAA) .... CAVG
Coronary Atherosclerotic Heart Disease [Medicine] (MAE) .... CAHD
Coronary Blood Flow [Medicine] .... CBF
Coronary Care Nursing [Medicine] (MAE) .... CCN
Coronary Care Team [Medicine] .... CCT
Coronary Care Training Project [Cardiology] (DAVI) .... CCTP
Coronary Care Unit [of a hospital] .... CCU
Coronary Club (EA) CC
Coronary Collateral [Medicine] (AAMN) CC
Coronary Drug Project .... CDP
Coronary Drug Project Group [Medicine] (BABM) .... CDPG
Coronary Flow [Medicine] .... CF

Coronary Heart Disease [Medicine] .... CHD
Coronary Insufficiency [Medicine] CI
Coronary Intensive Care Unit [of a hospital] .... CICU
Coronary Perfusion Pressure [Cardiology] .... CPP
Coronary Prevention Group [British] .... CPG
Coronary Primary Prevention Trial [National Heart, Lung, and Blood Institute] .... CPPT
Coronary Prognostic Index [Medicine] (AAMN) .... CPI
Coronary Reserve [Cardiology] .... CR
Coronary Sclerosis [Medicine] .... CS
Coronary Sinus [Cardiology] .... CS
Coronary Sinus Blood Flow [Cardiology] .... CSBF
Coronary Status [Cardiology] .... CS
Coronary Thrombosis [Medicine] .... CT
Coronary Unit (IIA) .... CU
Coronary Vascular Resistance [Medicine] .... CVR
Coronary Vascular Resistance Index [Cardiology] (DAVI) .... CVRI
Coronary Vein Graft [Medicine] .... CVG
Coronation (ROG) .... CR
Coronation, AB [Television station call letters] CKRD-1
Coronation, AB [ICAO location identifier] (ICLI) .... CYCT
Coronation Public Library, Alberta [Library symbol National Library of Canada] (NLC) .... ACOR
Coronavirus CV
Coronel Fontana [Argentina] [Seismograph station code, US Geological Survey] (SEIS) .... CFA
Coronel Olmedo [Argentina ICAO location identifier] (ICLI) .... SACD
Coroner (ROG) .... COR
Coroner (DLA) .... CORON
Coroners' Rolls [British] .... COR
Coroner's Society Cases [England] [A publication] (DLA) .... Cor Soc Cas
Coronet (ADA) .... COR
Coronet Carpets, Inc. [Toronto Stock Exchange symbol] .... RUG
Coronie [Surinam] [ICAO location identifier] (ICLI) .... SMCO
Corotating Interaction Region [Planetary science] .... CIR
Corotation Eccentricity Resonance [Planetary science] .... CER
Corotation Inclination Resonance [Planetary science] .... CIR
Corotation Resonance [Planetary science] .... CR
Corowa [New South Wales] [Airport symbol] (AD) .... COW
Corozal [Belize] [Airport symbol] (OAG) .... CZH
Corozal [Colombia] [Airport symbol] (AD) .... CZU
Corozal [Colombia ICAO location identifier] (ICLI) .... SKCZ
Corozal, PR [FM radio station call letters] .... WORO
Corpo de Tropas Paraquedistas [Paratroopers Corps] [Air Force Portugal] ..... CTP
Corpora Alata [Insect anatomy] .... CA
Corpora Amylacea [Neurology] .... CA
Corpora Cardiaca [Endocrinology] CC
Corporacion Aereo Cencor SA de CV [Mexico ICAO designator] (FAAC) .... CNC
Corporacion Aereo Internacional SA de CV [Mexico ICAO designator] (FAAC) .... CAI
Corporacion Andina de Fomento [Commercial firm Colorado] (ECON) .... CAF
Corporacion Area Ejecutiva SA de CV [Mexico ICAO designator] (FAAC) .... CEJ
Corporacion Bancaria de Espana [NYSE symbol] (SAG) .... AGR
Corporacion Bancaria de Espana [Associated Press] (SAG) .... Argentar
Corporacion Bancaria de Espana [Spain] (ECON) .... CBE
Corporacion Centroamericana de Dervicios de Navagacion Aerea [Mexico] [FAA designator] (FAAC) .... YGD
Corporacion de Investigaciones Economicas para Latinoamerica .... CIEPLAN
Corporacion Dominicana de Aviacion [Dominican Aviation Corporation] [Airline Dominican Republic] .... CDA
Corporal .... CORP
Corporal .... CORPL
Corporal .... CORPL
Corporal [Military] (AABC) .... CPL
Corporal [Army, Marine Corps] E4
Corporal of Horse [British military] (DMA) .... COH
Corporal-Major of Horse [British] .... CMH
Corporate (ROG) .... CORP
Corporate (VRA) .... corp
Corporate .... CORPRT
Corporate Accountability Research Group [Formed by consumer-advocate Ralph Nader] .... CARG
Corporate Action Project [Defunct] (EA) .... CAP
Corporate Administrative Contracting Officer [DoD] .... CACO
Corporate Affairs Processing System .... CAPS
Corporate Agents, Inc. [Information service or system] (IID) .... CAI
Corporate Air [ICAO designator] (FAAC) .... CPT
Corporate Air, Inc. [ICAO designator] (FAAC) .... CPO
Corporate Aircraft Co. [ICAO designator] (FAAC) .... CPO
Corporate Airlink [Canada] [FAA designator] (FAAC) .... COO
Corporate and Foundation Givers [A publication] .... CFG
Corporate and Industry Research Reports Index [JA Micropublishing, Inc.] [Database] .... CIRR
Corporate and Staff Development .... C & SD
Corporate Angel Network (EA) .... CAN
Corporate Author Authority List .... CAAL
Corporate Average Fuel Economy [Automobile industry] .... CAFE
Corporate Average Fuel Efficiency [Automobile Industry] .... CAFE
Corporate Aviation Services, Inc. [ICAO designator] (FAAC) .... CKE
Corporate Business Law Journal [A publication] .... CBLJ
Corporate Capital Charge (MCD) CCC
Corporate Committee of Telecommunications Users (EA) .... CCTU
Corporate Communication (WDMC) CC
Corporate Communications System [Bell-Northern Research Ltd.] [Computer science] .... COCOS

Corporate Conservation Council (EA) ... CCC
Corporate Consolidated Data Network [*IBM Corp.*] [*Telecommunications*] ... CCDN
Corporate Contract Officer ... CCO
Corporate Control Procedure (MCD) ... CCP
Corporate Conversions [*Information service or system*] (IID) ... CC
Corporate Council for the Liberal Arts [*Defunct*] (EA) ... CCLA
Corporate Counsel Review [*A publication*] (DLA) ... Corp Counsel Rev
Corporate Customer Order Control Program (IAA) ... CCOCP
Corporate Customer Satisfaction Monitor ... CCSM
Corporate Data Exchange (EA) ... CDE
Corporate Data Sciences [*Commercial firm*] (NITA) ... CDS
Corporate Database [*Computer science*] ... CDB
Corporate Depositary (DLA) ... Corp Dep
Corporate Electronic Publishing (HGAA) ... CEP
Corporate Electronic Publishing Systems Exhibition [*or Exposition*] (ITD) ... CEPS
Corporate Emergency Response Center [*Nuclear emergency planning*] ... CERC
Corporate Engineering and Sales Directive ... CEASD
Corporate Engineering Standard (IAA) ... CES
Corporate Engineering Transfer and Obsoletion System (IAA) ... CETOS
Corporate Equity-Reducing Transaction ... CERT
Corporate Experimental Research Vehicle [*General Motors Corp.*] [*Automotive engineering*] ... CERV
Corporate Express [*NASDAQ symbol*] (TTSB) ... CEXP
Corporate Express, Inc. [*NASDAQ symbol*] (SAG) ... CEXP
Corporate Express, Inc. [*Associated Press*] (SAG) ... CorpEx
Corporate Express, Inc. [*Associated Press*] (SAG) ... CorpExp
Corporate Finance Director ... CFD
Corporate Finance Partner ... CFP
Corporate Foods Ltd. [*Toronto Stock Exchange symbol*] ... CFL
Corporate Fund for Dance ... CFD
Corporate High Yield Fd II [*NYSE symbol*] (TTSB) ... KYT
Corporate High Yield Fund [*NYSE symbol*] (TTSB) ... COY
Corporate High Yield Fund, Inc. [*Associated Press*] (SAG) ... CorpHY
Corporate High Yield Fund, Inc. [*NYSE symbol*] (SAG) ... COY
Corporate High Yield II [*Associated Press*] (SAG) ... CpHYII
Corporate High Yield II [*NYSE symbol*] (SAG) ... KYT
Corporate Home Office Administrative Contracting Officer (AAGC) ... CACO
Corporate Home Office Auditor (AAGC) ... CHOA
Corporate Income Fund ... CIF
Corporate Income Tax [*Economics*] ... CIT
Corporate Industrial Preparedness Representative [*Military*] ... CIPR
Corporate Information, BC Rail, Vancouver, British Columbia [*Library symbol National Library of Canada*] (NLC) ... BVABCR
Corporate Information Center [*Later, ICCR*] ... CIC
Corporate Information Centre, Royal Trust, Toronto, Ontario [*Library symbol National Library of Canada*] (BIB) ... OTROT
Corporate Information Management [*DoD*] (RDA) ... CIM
Corporate Information Officer ... CIO
Corporate Information Processing Standards (MCD) ... CIPS
Corporate Information System (MCD) ... CIS
Corporate Information Technology ... CIT
Corporate Information Technology Plan ... CITP
Corporate Information Technology Strategy ... CITS
Corporate Integrated Information System [*Consumer and Corporate Affairs Canada*] [*Information service or system*] (IID) ... CIIS
Corporate Jobs Outlook [*Information service or system*] (IID) ... CJO
Corporate Lawyers' Association of New South Wales [*Australia*] ... CLANSW
Corporate Library, Domglas, Inc., Mississauga, Ontario [*Library symbol National Library of Canada*] (NLC) ... OMDO
Corporate Library, Mutual Life of Canada, Waterloo, Ontario [*Library symbol National Library of Canada*] (BIB) ... OWTML
Corporate Library Update [*A publication*] ... CLU
Corporate Management Committee [*Australia*] ... CMC
Corporate Manufacturing Practice (IAA) ... CMP
Corporate Manufacturing Transfer System (IAA) ... COMATS
Corporate Member of the Institution of Electrical and Electronics Incorporated Engineers [*British*] (DBQ) ... MIElecIE
Corporate Memory Systems, Inc. [*Computer science*] (PCM) ... CMSI
Corporate Minimum Tax ... CMT
Corporate Mountaineers Cult ... CMC
Corporate Office (AAG) ... CO
Corporate Oil & Gas [*Vancouver Stock Exchange symbol*] ... CPA
Corporate Ombudsman Association (EA) ... COA
Corporate Organization and Procedures Economy (SAA) ... COPE
Corporate Payment System ... CPS
Corporate Planning Office [*AFSC*] ... CCX
Corporate Planning System (IAA) ... CPS
Corporate Practice Review [*A publication*] (DLA) ... Corp Prac Rev
Corporate Practice Review [*A publication*] (DLA) ... Corp Pract Rev
Corporate Purchasing Agreements (MCD) ... COPA
Corporate Quality Assurance Regulations (MCD) ... CQAR
Corporate Renaissance Group [*NASDAQ symbol*] (TTSB) ... CREN
Corporate Renaissance Group, Inc. [*Associated Press*] (SAG) ... CorpRen
Corporate Renaissance Group, Inc. [*NASDAQ symbol*] (SAG) ... CREN
Corporate Reorganization and American Bankruptcy Review [*A publication*] (DLA) ... Corp Reorg & Am Bank Rev
Corporate Reorganizations [*A publication*] (DLA) ... Corp Reorg
Corporate Research and Development ... CRD
Corporate Research and Information Centre, Nova Scotia Power Corp., Halifax, Nova Scotia [*Library symbol National Library of Canada*] (NLC) ... NSHPC
Corporate Research Information Service [*Frederick Research*] ... CRIS
Corporate Resource and Allocation (MHDB) ... CORPORAL
Corporate Responsibility Task Force of the Business Roundtable (EA) ... CRTF
Corporate Security Regulation Appendices ... CSRA
Corporate Services Administration Department [*Medicine*] (DMAA) ... CSAD
Corporate Shareholder System (IAA) ... CSS
Corporate Source [*Online database field identifier*] ... COR
Corporate Source [*Online database field identifier*] ... CS
Corporate Source Name [*Database terminology*] (NITA) ... CN
Corporate Tax Administration, Alberta Treasury, Edmonton, Alberta [*Library symbol National Library of Canada*] (NLC) ... AETCT
Corporate Tax Association [*Australia*] ... CTA
Corporate Tax Association of Australia ... CTAA
Corporate Technical Information Center (DIT) ... CTIC
Corporate Technology Database [*Corporate Technology Information Services, Inc.*] (CRD) ... CTD
Corporate Technology Group [*British*] ... CTG
Corporate Technology Information Services, Inc. [*Information service or system*] (IID) ... CorpTech
Corporate Trade Exchange [*Automated Clearing House*] ... CTX
Corporate Trade Payment [*Automated Clearing House*] ... CTP
Corporate Transfer Agents Association [*New York, NY*] (EA) ... CTAA
Corporate Travel Index [*A publication*] ... CTI
Corporate Trust [*Legal term*] (DLA) ... C Tr
Corporate Trustee (DLA) ... Corp Tr
Corporate Value Associates [*Commercial firm British*] ... CVA
Corporate Word [*Database terminology*] (NITA) ... CW
Corporate-Higher Education Forum [*Forum Entreprises-Universites*] (AC) ... C-HEF
Corporate-Owned Life Insurance (WYGK) ... COLI
Corporation (DD) ... Corp
Corporation (AFM) ... CORP
Corporation ... CORP
Corporation ... CORPN
Corporation (ROG) ... CPN
Corporation [*Prentice-Hall, Inc.*] [*A publication*] (DLA) ... P-H Corp
Corporation Commission ... CC
Corporation Consulting Group [*British*] ... CCG
Corp. de Developpement du Canada [*Canada Development Corp. - CDC*] ... CDC
Corporation des Bibliothecaires Professionnels du Quebec [*Corporation of Professsional Librarians of Quebec*] (AC) ... CBPQ
Corporation des Concessionnaires d'Automobiles du Quebec Inc. (AC) ... CCAQ
Corporation des Entrepreneurs en Maconnerie du Quebec (AC) ... CEMQ
Corporation des Entrepreneurs Specialises du Grand Montreal (AC) ... CESGM
Corporation des Maitres Electriciens du Quebec [*Corporation of Master Electricians of Quebec*] (AC) ... CMEQ
Corporation des Maitres Entrepreneurs en Refrigeration du Quebec [*Corporation of Air Treatment & Cold Processing Entreprises*] (AC) ... CETAF
Corporation des Maitres Mecaniciens en Tuyauterie du Quebec [*Corporation of Master Pipe Mechanics of Quebec*] (AC) ... CMMTQ
Corporation des Officiers Municipaux Agrees du Quebec [*Corporation of Chartered Municipal Officers of Quebec*] (AC) ... COMAQ
Corporation des Proprietaires Immobiliers du Quebec (AC) ... CORPIQ
Corporation des Secretaires Municipaux du Quebec Inc. (AC) ... CSMQ
Corporation des Services aux Etablissements Touristiques Quebecois (AC) ... CSETQ
Corporation des Thanatologues du Quebec (AC) ... CTQ
Corporation des Traducteurs, Traductrices, Terminologues et Interpretes du Nouveau-Brunswick [*Corporation of Translators, Terminologists & Interpreters of New Brunswick*] (AC) ... CTINB
Corporation for Economics and Industrial Research [*Subsidiary of Control Data Corporation*] ... CEIR
Corporation for Enterprise Development (EA) ... CFED
Corporation for Information Systems Research and Development (MCD) ... CIRAD
Corporation for Jefferson's Poplar Forest (EA) ... CJPF
Corporation for Laser Optics Research ... COLOR
Corporation for Maintaining Editorial Diversity in America (EA) ... C/MEDIA
Corporation for Menke's Disease (EA) ... CMD
Corporation for Open Systems [*Telecommunications*] (EA) ... COS
Corporation for Public Broadcasting (EA) ... CPB
Corporation for Research and Educational Networking [*Internet*] ... CREN
Corporation for Research and Educational Networking [*Computer science*] (TNIG) ... CREN/BITNET
Corporation Guide [*Prentice-Hall, Inc.*] [*A publication*] (DLA) ... Corp Guide
Corporation Index System [*Securities and Exchange Commission*] (GFGA) ... CIN
Corporation Network [*Telephone communications*] ... CORNET
Corporation of Certified Secretaries (AIE) ... CCS
Corporation of Insurance and Financial Advisers [*British*] ... CIFA
Corporation of Land Surveyors of the Province of British Columbia [*Also, BC Land Surveyors*] [*Formerly, Provincial Land Surveyors*] (AC) ... BCLS
Corporation of Lloyds [*Also, Lloyd's of London*] [*Insurance*] (DS) ... CL
Corporation of London [*The City of London as opposed to Greater London*] ... C of L
Corporation Pierre Boucher, Trois-Rivieres, Quebec [*Library symbol National Library of Canada*] (NLC) ... QTCPB
Corporation Pierre-Boucher, Trois-Rivieres, PQ, Canada [*Library symbol Library of Congress*] (LCLS) ... CaQTCPB
[*La*] **Corporation Professionnelle des Administrateurs Agrees du Quebec** [*The Order of Chartered Administrators of Quebec*] (AC) ... CPAAQ
Corporation Professionnelle des Conseillers en Relations Industrielles du Quebec (AC) ... CPCRIQ
Corporation Professionnelle des Conseilliers et Conseillieres d'Orientation du Quebec (AC) ... CPCCOQ
Corporation Professionnelle des Ergotherapeutes du Quebec (AC) ... CPEQ
Corporation Professionnelle des Medecins du Quebec [*Professional Corporation of Physicians of Quebec*] (AC) ... CPMQ
Corporation Professionnelle des Medecins Veterinaires du Quebec (AC) ... CPMVQ

Corporation Professionnelle des Orthophonistes et Audiologistes du Quebec (AC) .... CPOAQ
Corporation Professionnelle des Physiotherapeutes du Quebec (AC) .... CPPQ
Corporation Professionnelle des Psychologues du Quebec (AC) .... CPPQ
Corporation Professionnelle des Technologistes Medicaux du Quebec (AC) .... CPTMQ
Corporation Professionnelle des Technologues Professionnelles du Quebec (AC) .... CPTPQ
Corporation Professionnelle des Travailleurs Sociaux du Quebec (AC) .... CPTSQ
Corporation Professionnelle des Urbanistes du Quebec (AC) .... CPUQ
Corporation Standard Practice (AAG) .... CSP
Corporation Tax [British] .... CT
Corporation-Management Edition (Prentice-Hall, Inc.) [A publication] (DLA) .... Corp-Mgmt Ed (P-H)
Corporations and Associations [A publication] (DLA) ...... Corp & Ass'ns
Corporations and Labor Union Returns Act .... CALURA
Corporations Code [A publication] (DLA) .... Corp C
Corporeal Pin [Method of tuberculin and histoplasmin testing] [Medicine] .... CORPPIN
Corpori [To the Body] [Pharmacy] .... CORP
Corps C
Corps [Army] .... COR
Corps Adjutant [British military] (DMA) .... CA
Corps Advisory Detachment .... CAD
Corps Airborne Stand-Off RADAR (MCD) .... CASTOR
Corps Airspace Management Element (MCD) .... CAME
Corps and Division Training Coordination Program [DoD] .... CORTRAIN
Corps Area [Army] .... CA
Corps Area Communications Center [Army] .... CACC
Corps Area Communications System [Vietnam] (MCD) .... CACS
Corps Area Signal Center (MCD) .... CASC
Corps Artillery Intelligence Officer [British] .... CAIO
Corps Automation Requirements [Army] .... CAR
Corps Aviation Company [Army] (VNW) .... CAC
Corps Battle Simulation [Army] .... CBS
Corps Battle Simulation .... CORSIM
Corps Brandenburgia (EA) .... CB
Corps Commander [British military] (DMA) CC
Corps Commander Coast Artillery [British] .... CCCA
Corps Communications (MCD) .... CORCOM
Corps Communications Support Requirement Simulations (MCD) ...... CCOMSRS
Corps Contingency Force [Army] (AABC) .... CCF
Corps d'Afrique .... C d'A
Corps Diplomatique [Diplomatic Corps] .... CD
Corps Division Evaluation Model [Army] (RDA) .... CORDIVEM
Corps Eligible [Army] (RDA) .... CE
Corps Epidemiological Reference Office [Military] .... CERO
Corps Expeditionaire Francais .... CEF
Corps Front Luxembourgeois [Resistance organization in Luxembourg] [World War II] .... CFL
Corps Headquarters [Army] .... CHQ
Corps Interim Upgrade System (MCD) .... CIUS
Corps Maintenance Area .... CMA
Corps Material Direct Support Activity (MCD) .... CMDSA
Corps Material Management Center (MCD) .... CMMC
Corps Material Management System (MCD) .... CMMS
Corps Movement Control Organization [Royal Corps of Transport] [British] .... CMCO
Corps Observation .... CO
Corps of Armourers [British military] (DMA) .... C of A
Corps of Cadets .... COC
Corps of Drivers Royal Artillery [British military] (DMA) .... CDRA
Corps of Engineers [Army] .... C of E
Corps of Engineers [Army] .... CE
Corps of Engineers [Army] (AAG) .... COE
Corps of Engineers [Army] (MUGU) .... COREN
Corps of Engineers [Army] (SAA) .... CORENG
Corps of Engineers Automation Plan [DoD] (GFGA) .... CEAP
Corps of Engineers Ballistic Missile Construction Agency [Army] .... CEBMCA
Corps of Engineers Ballistic Missile Construction Office [Army] .... CEBMCO
Corps of Engineers Board of Contract Appeals [Army] .... ENGBCA
Corps of Engineers (Civil Works) [Army] .... COE(CW)
Corps of Engineers Command [Army] (AAGC) .... CE
Corps of Engineers Guide Specifications for Emergency Type Construction [Army] .... CE-E
Corps of Engineers, Lower Mississippi Valley Division, New Orleans Planning Division [Louisiana] .... COELMN/PD
Corps of Engineers Management Information System [DoD] (GFGA) ...... COEMIS
Corps of Engineers Manual for Military Construction [Army] .... EMMC
Corps of Engineers Office of Appalachian Studies [Army] (AABC) .... CEOAS
Corps of Engineers Reserve Fleet .... CERF
Corps of Engineers Technical Committee [Army] .... CETC
Corps of Engineers Waterborne Commerce Statistics Center [Army] (AABC) .... CEWCSC
Corps of Indian Electrical and Mechanical Engineers [British military] (DMA) .... IEME
Corps of Intelligence Police [Army] (DOMA) .... CIP
Corps of Military Accountants [British military] (DMA) .... CMA
Corps of Military Mounted Police [British military] (DMA) .... CMMP
Corps of Military Police [British] .... CMP
Corps of Military Police (India) [British military] (DMA) .... CMP(I)
Corps of Ordnance Artificers [British military] (DMA) .... COA
Corps of Permanent Instructors [British military] (DMA) .... CPI
Corps of Signals [British] (DAS) .... CS

Corps of Transportation [Army] .... CT
Corps of Volunteers Artillery Regiment [British military] (DMA) .... VAR
Corps Personnel Operations Center [Army] .... CPOC
Corps Phase Line .... CPL
Corps Reinforcement Unit [British military] (DMA) .... CRU
Corps Service Area [Army] (AABC) .... COSA
Corps Service Area .... CSA
Corps Specifications Revision (AAG) .... CSR
Corps Storage Area [Military] (AABC) .... CSA
Corps Support Brigade .... CSB
Corps Support Command [Army] (AABC) .... COSCOM
Corps Support Missile System (MCD) .... CSMS
Corps Support Services [Military] .... CSS
Corps Support Weapon System .... CSWS
Corps Surface-to-Air Missile [Army] (DOMA) .... CORPSAM
Corps Surface-to-Air Missile/Medium Extended Air Defense System [Military] (RDA) .... CSAM/MEADS
Corps Tactical Operations Center .... CTOC
Corps Tactical Operations System (MCD) .... CTOS
Corps Tactical Zone [Military] .... CTZ
Corps/Theater Automatic Data Processing Service Center [Military] .... CTASC
Corpse [DSUE] .... CORP
Corptech Industry, Inc. [Vancouver Stock Exchange symbol] .... CH
Corpus [Body] [Latin] (DLA) C
Corpus [Referring to the uterus] [Gynecology] (DAVI) .... CO
Corpus [Body] [Latin] .... COR
Corpus Allatum .... CA
Corpus Callosum [Brain anatomy] CC
Corpus Cardiacum (PDAA) CC
Corpus Christi (ROG) CC
Corpus Christi [Texas] [Airport symbol] (OAG) .... CRP
Corpus Christi Army Depot (AABC) .... CCAD
Corpus Christi Bancshares [Associated Press] (SAG) .... CCBncsh
Corpus Christi Bancshares [AMEX symbol] (SPSG) .... CTZ
Corpus Christi Campaign (EA) CCC
Corpus Christi College [Cambridge and Oxford] CCC
Corpus Christi/Corpus Christi Naval Air Station [Texas] [ICAO location identifier] (ICLI) .... KNGP
Corpus Christi/International [Texas] [ICAO location identifier] (ICLI) .... KCRP
Corpus Christi Public Library, Corpus Christi, TX [OCLC symbol] (OCLC)..... CCA
Corpus Christi State University, Corpus Christi, TX [OCLC symbol] (OCLC) .... TXF
Corpus Christi, TX [Location identifier FAA] (FAAL) .... CUX
Corpus Christi, TX [Location identifier FAA] (FAAL) .... EKI
Corpus Christi, TX [FM radio station call letters] .... KBNJ
Corpus Christi, TX [FM radio station call letters] .... KBSO
Corpus Christi, TX [AM radio station call letters] .... KCCT
Corpus Christi, TX [AM radio station call letters] .... KCTA
Corpus Christi, TX [FM radio station call letters] .... KEDT
Corpus Christi, TX [Television station call letters] .... KEDT-TV
Corpus Christi, TX [AM radio station call letters] .... KEYS
Corpus Christi, TX [FM radio station call letters] .... KFGG
Corpus Christi, TX [Television station call letters] .... KIII
Corpus Christi, TX [FM radio station call letters] .... KLTG
Corpus Christi, TX [FM radio station call letters] .... KMXR
Corpus Christi, TX [Television station call letters] .... KORO
Corpus Christi, TX [Television station call letters] .... KRIS
Corpus Christi, TX [AM radio station call letters] .... KRYS
Corpus Christi, TX [FM radio station call letters] .... KRYS-FM
Corpus Christi, TX [AM radio station call letters] .... KSIX
Corpus Christi, TX [AM radio station call letters] .... KUNO
Corpus Christi, TX [FM radio station call letters] .... KZFM
Corpus Christi, TX [Television station call letters] .... KZTV
Corpus Christi, TX [Location identifier FAA] (FAAL) .... NCX
Corpus Christi, TX [Location identifier FAA] (FAAL) .... NGP
Corpus Christi, TX [Location identifier FAA] (FAAL) .... NGW
Corpus Christi, TX [Location identifier FAA] (FAAL) .... NHT
Corpus Christi, TX [Location identifier FAA] (FAAL) .... NPJ
Corpus Christi, TX [Location identifier FAA] (FAAL) .... OYC
Corpus Christianorum [Turnhout] [BJA] .... CChr
Corpus Cultus Deae Syriae (BJA) .... CCDS
Corpus des Tablettes en Cuneiformes Alphabetiques Decouvertes a Ras Shamra-Ugarit de 1929 a 1939 (BJA) .... CTA
Corpus des Tablettes en Cuneiformes Alphabetiques Decouvertes a Ras Shamra-Ugarit de 1929 a 1939 (BJA) .... CTCA
Corpus Glossariorum Biblicorum (BJA) .... CGB
Corpus Glossariorum Latinorum (BJA) .... CGL
Corpus Inscriptionum Chaldaicarum (BJA) .... CICh
Corpus Inscriptionum Elamicarum [A publication] (BJA) .... CIE
Corpus Inscriptionum et Monumentorum Religionis Mithriacae [A publication] (BJA) .... CIMRM
Corpus Inscriptionum Himjariticarum (BJA) .... CIH
Corpus Inscriptionum Judaicarum [A publication] (BJA) .... CIJ
Corpus Inscriptionum Regni Bosporani (BJA) .... CIRB
Corpus Inscriptionum Semiticarum [A publication] (OCD) .... CISem
Corpus Juris [Body of Law] [Latin] .... CJ
Corpus Juris [Body of Law] [Latin] (ROG) .... CORP JUR
Corpus Juris Annotations [A publication] .... CJ Ann
Corpus Juris Canonici [The Body of the Canon Law] [Latin] (DLA) .... CJ Can
Corpus Juris Canonici [The Body of the Canon Law] [Latin A publication] (DLA) .... Corp Jur Can
Corpus Juris Canonici [The Body of the Canon Law] [Latin A publication] (DLA) .... Corp Jus Canon
Corpus Juris Civilis [The Body of the Civil Law] [Latin] (DLA) .... CJ Civ
Corpus Juris Civilis [The Body of the Civil Law] [Latin] (DLA) .... CJC

Corpus Juris Civilis [*The Body of the Civil Law*] [*Latin A publication*] (DLA) .... Corp Jur Civ
Corpus Juris Secundum [*A publication*] .... CJS
Corpus Juris Secundum Supplement [*West*] [*A publication*] (AAGC) .... CJS Supp
Corpus Luteum [*Endocrinology*] CL
Corpus Luteum Insufficiency [*Medicine*] (DMAA) CLI
Corpus Luteum Stimulating Hormone (BARN) .... CLSH
Corpus Medicorum Graecorum [*A publication*] (OCD) .... CMG
Corpus Medicorum Latinorum [*A publication*] (OCD) .... CML
CORPUS [*Corps of Reserve Priests United for Service*] **- National Association Resigned/Married Priests** (EA) .... CORPUS
Corpus of Ancient Near Eastern Seals in North American Collections [*Washington, DC*] (BJA) .... CANES
Corpus of Dated Palestinian Pottery (BJA) .... CPP
Corpus of Palestinian Pottery (BJA) .... CPP
Corpus Papyrorum Judaicarum (BJA) .... CPJ
Corpus Poetarum Latinorum [*A publication*] (OCD) .... CPL
Corpus Reformatorum (BJA) .... CR
Corpus Scriptorum Christianorum Orientalium [*Louvain*] (BJA) .... CsChrO
Corpus Striatum (MAE) .... CS
Corpus Tannaiticum (BJA) .... CorpTann
Corpuscular Volume [*Hematology*] CV
Corrales, NM [*AM radio station call letters*] .... KIVA
Corrales, NM [*FM radio station call letters*] .... KSVA
Correct [*or Correction*] C
Correct [*In marking school papers*] (BARN) C
Correct (ROG) .... COR
Correct [*or Corrected or Correction*] (AFM) .... CORR
Correct (ECII) .... COT
Correct .... CQ
Correct [*Computer science British*] .... CQT
Correct (MUGU) .... CRT
Correct Age Stocking and Height [*Inventory*] [*Forestry*] .... CASH
Correct Calling Station Identifier [*Telecommunications*] (PCM) .... CSID
Correct Code (MCD) CC
Correct Copy [*A printing direction*] CX
Correct End Item (KSC) .... CEI
Correct Operation Factor [*Telecommunications*] (OA) .... COF
Correct [*an error*] **or Amplify** [*information*] [*US Copyright Office form*] .... CA
Correct, Pause, Recovery [*Automobile driving*] .... CPR
Correct Report [*Laboratory*] (DAVI) .... CORR
Correct Seating Institute .... CSI
Correct Selection [*Statistics*] .... CS
Correct Time (IAA) .... CT
Correct Words per Minute [*Typewriting, etc.*] .... CWPM
Correctable Gate [*Computer science*] (MDG) .... CORREGATE
Corrected (MSA) .... CRCTD
Corrected Adjusted Sinus Node Recovery Time [*Medicine*] (DMAA) .... CASRT
Corrected Blood Volume [*Medicine*] .... CBV
Corrected Copy CC
Corrected Copy (DNAB) .... CORCY
Corrected Count Increment [*Hematology*] CCI
Corrected Count Increment [*Hematology*] CI
Corrected Effective Temperature (IEEE) .... CET
Corrected Geomagnetic Latitude .... CGL
Corrected Geomagnetic Latitude and Geomagnetic Local Time (DICI) .... CGL/GLT
Corrected Geomagnetic Time .... CGM
Corrected Geomagnetic Time .... CGT
Corrected Head Count .... CHC
Corrected Infection Efficiency [*of plant pathogens*] .... CIE
Corrected Mean Temperature .... CMT
Corrected Outside Air Temperature .... COAT
Corrected Relative Net Protein Ratio [*Nutrition*] .... CRNPR
Corrected Retention Time [*Medicine*] (DAVI) .... CRT
Corrected Sedimentation Rate [*Medicine*] .... CSR
Corrected Sinus Node Recovery Time [*Medicine*] (DMAA) .... CNRT
Corrected Sinus Node Recovery Time [*Medicine*] .... CSNRT
Corrected Transposition (MAE) .... CT
Corrected Unpostable [*IRS*] .... CU
CorRecTerm [*Mergenthaler typesetting*] .... CRT
Correcting Computer (MCD) .... CORCOM
Correctio Romana [*Edition of the Decretals*] [*A publication*] (DSA) .... Corr Rom
Correction .... CO
Correction .... COR
Correction (WDMC) .... cor
Correction (WDMC) .... corr
Correction .... CRRCT
Correction (MUGU) .... CRTN
Correction Action Committee .... CAC
Correction Action Reporting System .... CARS
Correction and Rehabilitation Group [*Air Force*] .... CRG
Correction and Rehabilitation Squadron [*Air Force*] .... CRS
Correction Control Number [*Army*] .... CORCN
Correction/Discrepancy (DNAB) .... C/D
Correction Education Demonstration Project Act of 1978 .... CEDPA
Correction Factor .... CF
Correction Field (MCD) .... CF
Correction Memo (MCD) .... CM
Correction Notice (MCD) .... CN
Correction of Deficiency (MCD) .... COD
Correction Processor .... CP
Correction System .... COSY
Correction to Follow .... CTF
Correction Tracking and Ranging Station .... COTAR
Correction, Update, and Extension Software Program [*Department of Commerce*] (GFGA) .... CUE
Correction with Glasses [*Optometry*] (MAE) .... cgl
Correctional .... CRRCTNL
Correctional Administrators Association of America [*Later, ASCA*] (EA) .... CAA
Correctional Association of New York State (SRA) .... CANYS
Correctional Custody Facility [*Military*] (AABC) .... CCF
Correctional Custody Unit [*Navy*] .... CCU
Correctional Education Association (EA) .... CEA
Correctional Facilities Association [*Defunct*] (EA) .... CFA
Correctional Health Care Program .... CHCP
Correctional Holding Detachment [*Military*] (AABC) .... CHD
Correctional Industries Association (EA) .... CIA
Correctional Institutions Environment Scale [*Personality development test*] [*Psychology*] .... CIES
Correctional Officer .... CO
Correctional Officers' Interest Blank [*Screening and placement test*] .... COIB
Correctional Reporting System [*Army*] .... CRS
Correctional Service Associates .... CSA
Correctional Service Federation - USA (EA) .... CSF/USA
Correctional Services Advisory Council [*South Australia*] .... CSAC
Correctional Services Corp. [*Associated Press*] (SAG) .... CorrecSv
Correctional Services Corp. [*Associated Press*] (SAG) .... CrrcS
Correctional Services Corp. [*NASDAQ symbol*] (SAG) .... CSCQ
Correctional Services of Ontario, Toronto, ON, Canada [*Library symbol Library of Congress*] (LCLS) .... CaOTCS
Correctional Training Facility [*Army*] (AABC) .... CTF
Corrections Corp. Amer [*NYSE symbol*] (TTSB) CXC
Corrections Corp. of America .... CCA
Corrections Corp. of America [*Associated Press*] (SAG) .... CorCp
Corrections Corp. of America [*Associated Press*] (SAG) .... CorctCp
Corrections Corp. of America [*NYSE symbol*] (SAG) CXC
Corrections Cp Amer Wrrt [*NYSE symbol*] (TTSB) .... CXC.WS
Corrections to Applied Research Laboratories Ion-Sputtering Mass Analyzers [*Computer science*] .... CARISMA
Correctionville News, Correctionville, IA [*Library symbol Library of Congress*] (LCLS) .... IaCorrN
Corrective .... CORREC
Corrective Action (MCD) .... CA
Corrective Action Board .... CAB
Corrective Action Directive [*or Disposition*] .... CAD
Corrective Action Effectiveness (MCD) .... CAE
Corrective Action Management Unit [*Environmental science*] .... CAMU
Corrective Action Order [*Environmental Protection Agency*] (ERG) .... CAO
Corrective Action Plan [*Department of Health and Human Services*] (GFGA) .... CAP
Corrective Action Reply .... CAR
Corrective Action Report .... CAR
Corrective Action Request .... CAR
Corrective Action Tracking System [*Environmental Protection Agency*] (GFGA) .... CATS
Corrective Eye Care Foundation [*Later, CLMA*] (EA) .... CECF
Corrective Lens [*Freight*] .... C LN
Corrective Maintenance .... CM
Corrective Maintenance Action [*Military*] (CAAL) .... CMA
Corrective Maintenance Burden .... CMB
Corrective Maintenance Card (MCD) .... CMC
Corrective Maintenance Downtime (MCD) .... CMDT
Corrective Maintenance System (NVT) .... CMS
Corrective Management (MCD) .... CM
Corrective Measure Study [*Environmental science*] .... CMS
Corrective Measures Implementation .... CMI
Corrective Optics Space Telescope Axial Replacement [*NASA*] .... COSTAR
Corrective Septorhinoplasty [*Otorhinolaryngology*] (DAVI) .... CSR
Corrective Therapist [*or Therapy*] .... CT
Corrective Therapy Department [*Medical rehabilitation*] (DAVI) .... CTD
Corrector [*MARC relator code*] [*Library of Congress*] (LCCP) .... crr
Corregidor, Cavite [*Philippines*] [*ICAO location identifier*] (ICLI) .... RPXR
Corregidor-Bataan Memorial Commission [*Government agency*] [*Terminated, 1967*] .... CBMC
Correlate (MSA) .... CORRE
Correlated Color Temperature (IEEE) .... CCT
Correlated Data Processor .... CDP
Correlated Double Sampling .... CDS
Correlated Orientation Tracking and Ranging (MSA) .... COTAR
Correlated RADAR Data Printout [*Electronics*] (SAA) .... CORDP
Correlated RADAR Data Printout [*Electronics*] .... CORDPO
Correlated RADAR Data Printout - Separation of RADAR Data [*Electronics*] .... CORDPO-SORD
Correlated Spectroscopy .... COSY
Correlating Users Exchange (SAA) .... CUE
Correlation (KSC) .... CORR
Correlation Air Navigation .... CAN
Correlation Bombing System [*Air Force*] (MCD) .... CBS
Correlation Cancellation System .... CCS
Correlation Coefficient (MCD) CC
Correlation Coefficient [*Statistics*] (BARN) .... R
Correlation Coefficient (DAVI) .... r
Correlation Data Analyzer Recorder (CAAL) .... CODAR
Correlation Detection and Ranging (MCD) .... CODAR
Correlation Display Analyzing and Recording .... CODAR
Correlation Echo Sound Processor [*Oceanography*] .... CESP
Correlation Factor (AABC) .... CF
Correlation Metric Construction [*Analysis of chemical reaction*] .... CMC

Correlation of the Recognition of Degradation with Intelligibility Measurements [*Telecommunications*] (TEL) ...... CORODIM
Correlation Processor ...... CP
Correlation RADAR ...... CORAD
Correlation Radio Link (MUGU) ...... CORAL
Correlation Radiometer (MCD) ...... CR
Correlation Spectrometer ...... COSPEC
Correlation Track ...... CT
Correlation Tracking and Ranging [*System*] [*Satellite and missile tracking term RADAR*] ...... COTAR
Correlation Tracking and Ranging Angle Measuring Equipment [*RADAR*] ...... COTAR-AME
Correlation Tracking and Ranging Data Acquisition System [*RADAR*] ...... COTAR-DAS
Correlation Tracking and Ranging Data Measuring Equipment [*RADAR*] ...... COTAR-DME
Correlation Tracking and Triangulation ...... COTAT
Correlation-Protected Instrument Landing System ...... CP-ILS
Correlative ...... COR
Correlative ...... CORR
Correlative ...... CORREL
Correlator Acquisition [*Military*] ...... CA
Correspond (ROG) ...... COR
Correspond (DLA) ...... corr
Correspond (MSA) ...... CORRES
Correspondances Judiciaires [*Canada*] [*A publication*] (DLA) ...... Cor Jud
Correspondances Judiciaires [*Canada*] [*A publication*] (DLA) ...... Correspondances Jud
Correspondence ...... COR
Correspondence (WDMC) ...... cor
Correspondence (WDMC) ...... corr
Correspondence ...... CORR
Correspondence (AFM) ...... CORR
Correspondence (WDMC) ...... corres
Correspondence [*or Corresponding*] ...... CORRESP
Correspondence Aid [*A publication*] ...... CA
Correspondence Analysis [*Statistical analysis*] ...... CA
Correspondence and Service Branch [*BUPERS*] ...... C & SB
Correspondence Chess League of America (EA) ...... CCLA
Correspondence Control Unit [*Environmental Protection Agency*] (GFGA) ...... CCU
Correspondence Course CC
Correspondence Factor Analysis ...... CFA
Correspondence Printer (MHDI) ...... CP
Correspondence Quality (IAA) ...... CQ
Correspondence Quality Control Program (MCD) ...... CQCP
Correspondence Review Group [*NASA*] (NASA) ...... CRG
Correspondence Routing Form (NRCH) ...... CRF
Correspondence Survey Officer (MCD) ...... CSO
Correspondent (WDMC) ...... cor
Correspondent (DLA) ...... corr
Correspondent [*Journalism*] (WDMC) ...... corres
Correspondent ...... CORRSPNDNT
Correspondent Committee [*Defunct*] (EA) CC
Correspondent Validity File [*IRS*] ...... CVF
Corresponding ...... CORR
Corresponding (VRA) ...... corr
Corresponding Fellow ...... CF
Corresponding Fellow (WGA) ...... Corr Fell
Corresponding Member ...... CM
Corresponding Member (BARN) ...... Corr Mem
Corresponding Member of the International Institute of Arts and Letters .... CIAL
Corresponding Member of the Zoological Society [*British*] ...... CMZS
Corresponding Objects Grid [*Computer science*] ...... COG
Corresponding Secretary (WDAA) ...... COR SEC
Corresponding Secretary (BARN) ...... Corr Sec
Corresponding Secretary (IIA) ...... CS
Corresponding States Equation [*Physics*] ...... CSE
Corresponding States Liquid Density [*Chemical engineering*] ...... COSTALD
Corresponding Studies Course [*DoD*] ...... CSC
Corrida Oils Ltd. [*Toronto Stock Exchange symbol*] ...... COL
Corridor (AABC) ...... COR
Corridor (DA) ...... CORR
Corridor [*Board on Geographic Names*] ...... CRDR
Corridor Aerogeophysics of the Southeastern Ross Transect Zone [*Geology*] ...... CASERTZ
Corridor Assignment [*Aviation*] (FAAC) ...... CORAS
Corrie Resources [*Vancouver Stock Exchange symbol*] (CIE) ...... CIE
Corriente Batllista Independiente [*Uruguay*] [*Political party*] (EY) ...... CBI
Corriente Critica [*Mexico Political party*] (EY) CC
Corriente Nacionalista de Unidad y Reconciliacion [*Nicaragua*] [*Political party*] (EY) ...... CNUR
Corrientes [*Argentina*] [*Airport symbol*] (OAG) ...... CNQ
Corrientes [*Argentina ICAO location identifier*] (ICLI) ...... SARC
Corrigenda (BJA) ...... corr
Corrigendum [*Publishing*] (WGA) ...... COR
Corrin [*Biochemistry*] ...... Crn
Corris, Machynlleth & River Dovey Tramway [*Wales*] ...... CM & RDT
Corris Railway [*Wales*] ...... COR R
Corrosion (KSC) ...... CORR
Corrosion (MSA) ...... CRSN
Corrosion Advice Bureau [*British Steel Corp.*] (PDAA) ...... CAB
Corrosion and Cathodic Protection (IAA) ...... CACP
Corrosion and Protection Association ...... CAPA
Corrosion Center of Excellence [*US Army Materials Technology Laboratory*] ...... CTX

Corrosion Control [*Lloyds Register*] (DS) CC
Corrosion Control Unit (DNAB) ...... CORCONU
Corrosion Evaluation and Test Area [*NASA*] ...... CETA
Corrosion Fatigue (PDAA) ...... CF
Corrosion Fatigue Crack Propagation (PDAA) ...... CFCP
Corrosion Interception Sleeve ...... CIS
Corrosion of Reinforcing Steel in Concrete [*Rilem Technical Committee*] [*British*] ...... CRC
Corrosion Prevention/Deterioration Control ...... CP/DC
Corrosion Prevention Panel ...... CPP
Corrosion Protection [*Telecommunications*] (TEL) ...... CP
Corrosion Resistant [*Material*] [*Manufacturing*] (DCTA) ...... CR
Corrosion Resistant (AAG) ...... CRE
Corrosion Resistant (MCD) ...... CRES
Corrosion Resistant Alloy [*Metallurgy*] ...... CRA
Corrosion Status Index [*Military*] (RDA) ...... CSI
Corrosion-Fatigue Crack Growth Rate (PDAA) ...... CFCGR
Corrosion-Resistant Cladding [*Nuclear energy equipment*] ...... CRC
Corrosion-Resistant Nebulizer ...... CRN
Corrosion-Resistant Steel [*Manufacturing*] ...... CRES
Corrosive (MSA) ...... COR
Corrosive (MSA) ...... CRSV
Corrosive Contaminants, Oxygen, and Humidity (MCD) ...... CCOH
Corrpro Companies [*Associated Press*] (SAG) ...... Corrpro
Corrpro Co. [*NYSE symbol*] (TTSB) ...... CO
Corrugated (WGA) ...... COR
Corrugated ...... CORR
Corrugated ...... CORRGTD
Corrugated ...... CORU
Corrugated Asbestos Cement (ADA) ...... CAC
Corrugated Case Materials Association [*British*] (DBA) ...... CCMA
Corrugated Container Institute [*Defunct*] (EA) CCI
Corrugated, Cupped, or Indented [*Freight*] CCI
Corrugated Furnace (DS) ...... CF
Corrugated Galvanized Iron ...... CGI
Corrugated Metal Pipe [*Technical drawings*] ...... CMP
Corrugated or Cupped [*Freight*] CC
Corrugated Plate Inteceptor (PDAA) ...... CPI
Corrugated Stainless-Steel Tubing ...... CSST
Corrugated Steel Pipe (DICI) ...... CSP
Corrugated TEFLON Tubing ...... CTT
Corrugated Wire Glass [*Technical drawings*] ...... CWG
Corrugated-Laminated Coaxial [*Cable*] ...... CLOAX
Corrugating Medium Test [*For containerboard*] ...... CMT
Corrupt ...... COR
Corrupt ...... CORR
Corrupt Commissioners [*Federal operation investigating illegal practices by Oklahoma's county commissioners*] ...... CORCOM
Corrupted [*or Corruption*] ...... CORRUP
Corruption (ROG) ...... CORR
Corry, PA [*Location identifier FAA*] (FAAL) ...... ORJ
Corry, PA [*AM radio station call letters*] ...... WWCB
Corse Aero Service [*France ICAO designator*] (FAAC) ...... CSS
Corse Air International [*France ICAO designator*] (FAAC) ...... CRL
Corse Air International [*France ICAO designator*] (ICDA) ...... CS
Corse-Mediterranee Compagnie [*France ICAO designator*] (FAAC) ...... CCM
Corset and Brassiere Association of America [*Later, AAMA*] (EA) ...... CBAA
Corset and Brassiere Council [*Defunct*] (EA) ...... CBC
Corset and Brassiere Women's Club [*Later, UC*] (EA) ...... CBWC
Corsica (ROG) ...... COR
Corsica ...... CORS
Corsica (VRA) ...... Cors
Corsica/Sardinia/Calabria Microplate [*Geology*] ...... CSC
Corsicana, TX [*Location identifier FAA*] (FAAL) ...... CGQ
Corsicana, TX [*Location identifier FAA*] (FAAL) ...... CRS
Corsicana, TX [*AM radio station call letters*] ...... KAND
Corsicana, TX [*FM radio station call letters*] (RBYB) ...... KICI
Corson Family History Association (EA) ...... CCFHA
[*A*] Corsortium on Restorative Dentistry Education [*Medicine*] (DMAA) ...... ACORDE
Cort Business Services [*NYSE symbol*] (TTSB) ...... CBS
Cort Business Services Corp. [*NASDAQ symbol*] (SAG) ...... CORT
Cort Business Services Corp. [*Associated Press*] (SAG) ...... CortBus
Cort Business Svcs Wrrt [*NASDAQ symbol*] (TTSB) ...... CORTW
CORTA (Orly Ouest) [*France ICAO location identifier*] (ICLI) ...... LFFA
Cortaro, AZ [*AM radio station call letters*] ...... KEVT
Corte [*France ICAO location identifier*] (ICLI) ...... LFKT
Corte Costituzionale [*Constitutional Court*] [*Italian*] (DLA) ...... C Cost
Corte di Cassazione [*Court of Appeal*] [*Italian*] (DLA) ...... Cass
Corte Internacional de Justicia [*International Court of Justice*] [*Spanish United Nations*] (DUND) ...... CIJ
Cortech, Inc. [*Associated Press*] (SAG) ...... Cortech
Cortech, Inc. [*NASDAQ symbol*] (SAG) ...... CRTQ
Cortecs International Ltd. [*Associated Press*] (SAG) ...... Cortecs
Cortecs International Ltd. [*NASDAQ symbol*] (SAG) ...... DLVR
Corten Steel (VRA) ...... crtnstl
Cortex [*Anatomy*] C
Cortex [*Bark*] [*Pharmacy*] ...... CORT
Cortex Cinchonae [*Bark of Cinchona or Peruvian Bark*] [*Pharmacy*] (ROG) ...... CORT CINCHON
Cortex Pharmaceuticals [*NASDAQ symbol*] (TTSB) ...... CORX
Cortex Pharmaceuticals, Inc. [*Associated Press*] (SAG) ...... Cortex
Cortex Pharmaceuticals, Inc. [*Associated Press*] (SAG) ...... Cortx
Cortex Pharmaceuticals, Inc. [*NASDAQ symbol*] (NQ) ...... CORX
Cortez [*Colorado*] [*Airport symbol*] (OAG) ...... CEZ

Cortez, CO [*FM radio station call letters*] ... KISZ
Cortez, CO [*FM radio station call letters*] ... KRTZ
Cortez, CO [*FM radio station call letters*] ... KSJD
Cortez, CO [*AM radio station call letters*] ... KVFC
Cortez Public Library, Cortez, CO [*Library symbol Library of Congress*] (LCLS) ... CoCo
Cortical ... cort
Cortical Area/Total Area (Ratio) ... CA/TA
Cortical Auditory Evoked Potential [*Medicine*] (DMAA) ... CAEP
Cortical Blood Flow [*Urology*] ... CBF
Cortical Collecting Tubule [*Anatomy*] ... CCT
Cortical Evoked Potential [*Neurophysiology*] ... CEP
Cortical Granule Exocytosis [*Cytology*] ... CGE
Cortical Magnification Factor ... CMF
Cortical Necrosis of Kidneys [*Medicine*] (DMAA) ... CNK
Cortical Plate [*Neuroanatomy*] ... CP
Cortical Plate Thickness [*Anatomy*] ... CT
Cortical Segment of Middle Cerebral Artery [*Cardiology*] (DAVI) ... M_4
Cortical Spoking [*Ophthalmology*] (DAVI) ... CS
Cortical Spreading Depression [*Medicine*] ... CSD
Cortical Stromal Hyperplasia [*Medicine*] (MAE) ... CSH
Cortically Induced Movement [*Medicine*] ... CIM
Cortically Originating Extra-Pyramidal System [*Physiology*] ... COEPS
Cortically Orignating Extrapyramidal Symptoms [*Neurology*] (DAVI) ... COEPS
Cortico-Cortical Connection [*Neurology*] ... CC
Corticoid Sensitive [*Laboratory*] (DAVI) ... CS
Corticoliberin-Like Immunoreactivity ... CLI
Corticosomatosensory Evoked Potential [*Electrophysiology*] ... CSEP
Cortico-Spinal Tract [*Anatomy*] ... CST
Corticosteroid [*Endocrinology*] ... CS
Corticosteroid-Binding Globulin [*Transcortin*] [*Endocrinology*] ... CBG
Corticosteroid-Binding Globulin Variant [*Medicine*] (DMAA) ... CBGv
Corticosterone [*A hormone*] ... CORT
Corticosterone [*A hormone*] ... CT
Corticosterone Methyl Oxidase [*An enzyme*] ... CMO
Corticosterone Side-Chain Isomerase (DMAA) ... CSCI
Corticotrophin-Like Intermediate-Lobe Peptide [*Endocrinology*] ... CLIP
Corticotrophin-Releasing Factor [*Also, CRH*] [*Endocrinology*] ... CRF
Corticotrophin-Releasing Hormone [*Also, CRF*] [*Endocrinology*] ... CRH
Corticotropin Releasing Factor [*Neurochemistry*] ... CRF
Corticotropin-Releaseing Factor Receptor [*Medicine*] (DMAA) ... CRFR
Corticotropin-Releasing Factor-Like Immunoreactivity [*Medicine*] ... CRF-LI
Cortina d'Ampezzo [*Italy*] [*Airport symbol*] (AD) ... CDF
Cortisol [*Pharmacology*] (DAVI) ... CORTIS
Cortisol Glucose Tolerance Test [*Medicine*] (DAVI) ... CGTT
Cortisol Production Rate [*Medicine*] (MAE) ... CPR
Cortisol [*or Cortical*] **Secretion Rate** [*Medicine*] (MAE) ... CSR
Cortisone [*Endocrinology*] ... COR
Cortisone [*Endocrinology*] ... cort
Cortisone Acetate [*Endocrinology*] ... CA
Cortisone Glucose Tolerance Test [*Medicine*] ... CGTT
Cortisone [*Primed*] **Oral Glucose Tolerance Test** [*Medicine*] ... COGTT
Cortisone-Resistant Thymocyte [*Biochemistry*] ... CRT
Cortland County Historical Society, Cortland, NY [*Library symbol Library of Congress*] (LCLS) ... NCortHi
Cortland Free Library, Cortland, NY [*Library symbol Library of Congress*] (LCLS) ... NCort
Cortland, NY [*FM radio station call letters*] ... WIII
Cortland, NY [*AM radio station call letters*] ... WKRT
Cortland, NY [*FM radio station call letters*] ... WSUC
Cortland, OH [*AM radio station call letters*] ... WKTX
Corumba/Internacional [*Brazil ICAO location identifier*] (ICLI) ... SBCR
Corumba Mato Grosso [*Brazil*] [*Airport symbol*] (OAG) ... CMG
Corundum [*CIPW classification*] [*Geology*] ... C
Corus Bankshares, Inc. [*NASDAQ symbol*] (SAG) ... CORS
Corus Bankshares, Inc. [*Associated Press*] (SAG) ... CorusBk
Corvair Model Group (EA) ... CMG
Corvair Society of America (EA) ... CORSA
Corvallis [*Oregon*] [*Seismograph station code, US Geological Survey*] (SEIS) ... COR
Corvallis Clinic, Corvallis, OR [*Library symbol Library of Congress*] (LCLS) ... OrCC
Corvallis Environmental Research Laboratory [*Oregon*] [*Environmental Protection Agency*] ... CERL
Corvallis Environmental Research Laboratory [*Corvallis, OR*] [*Environmental Protection Agency*] (GRD) ... ERL/COR
Corvallis, OR [*Location identifier FAA*] (FAAL) ... CVO
Corvallis, OR [*FM radio station call letters*] ... KBVR
Corvallis, OR [*FM radio station call letters*] ... KEJO
Corvallis, OR [*FM radio station call letters*] ... KFAT
Corvallis, OR [*FM radio station call letters*] ... KFLY
Corvallis, OR [*AM radio station call letters*] ... KLOO
Corvallis, OR [*AM radio station call letters*] ... KOAC
Corvallis, OR [*Television station call letters*] ... KOAC-TV
Corvallis, OR [*Location identifier FAA*] (FAAL) ... LWG
Corvallis Public Library, Corvallis, OR [*Library symbol Library of Congress*] (LCLS) ... OrC
Corvallis Workstation Operation (HGAA) ... CWO
Corvas International [*NASDAQ symbol*] (TTSB) ... CVAS
Corvas International, Inc. [*Associated Press*] (SAG) ... Corvas
Corvas International, Inc. [*NASDAQ symbol*] (SAG) ... CVAS
Corvel Corp. [*Associated Press*] (SAG) ... Corvel
CorVel Corp. [*NASDAQ symbol*] (SPSG) ... CRVL
Corvette [*Navy symbol Obsolete*] ... DDC
Corvette Petroleum Corp. [*Vancouver Stock Exchange symbol*] ... CRV
, Corvettes [*Zwillenberg*] [*Department store chain name derived from the owner's name, a business parter, and a Canadian warship*] ... EJ Korvette
Corvinus. Elementa Juris Civilis [*A publication*] (DLA) ... Corvin El
Corvinus' Jus Feodale [*A publication*] (DLA) ... Corv Jus
Corvita Corp. [*Associated Press*] (SAG) ... Corvita
Corvita Corp. [*NASDAQ symbol*] (SAG) ... CVTA
Corvita Corp. [*NASDAQ symbol*] (TTSB) ... CVTAC
Corvus [*Constellation*] ... Corv
Corvus [*Constellation*] ... Crv
Corwith Herald, Corwith, IA [*Library symbol Library of Congress*] (LCLS) ... IaCorwH
Cory on Accounts [*A publication*] (DLA) ... Cory Acc
Corydon Democrat, Corydon, IN [*Library symbol Library of Congress*] (LCLS) ... InCorD
Corydon, IN [*FM radio station call letters*] ... WGZB
Corydon, IN [*FM radio station call letters*] ... WHKW
Corydon, IN [*AM radio station call letters*] ... WOCC
Corydon, IN [*FM radio station call letters*] (RBYB) ... WSFR-FM
Corydon Public Library, Corydon, IN [*Library symbol Library of Congress*] (LCLS) ... InCor
Corydon Times-Republican, Corydon, IA [*Library symbol Library of Congress*] (LCLS) ... IaCoryTR
Corynebacteria, Mycobacteria, Nocardiae [*Trehalose containing genera*] ... CMN
Corynebacterium [*Genus of microorganisms*] (MAH) ... C
Corynebacterium Pseudotuberculosis Phospholipase D [*An enzyme*] ... Cor-PLD
Coryton on Copyrights [*A publication*] (DLA) ... Cory Cop
Coryton on Patents [*A publication*] (DLA) ... Cor Pat
Coryton on Patents [*A publication*] (DLA) ... Cory Pat
Coryton on Stage Rights [*A publication*] (DLA) ... Cory St R
Coryton's Reports [*Bengal*] [*A publication*] (DLA) ... Cor
Coryton's Reports [*Calcutta*] [*A publication*] (DLA) ... Cory
Coryton's Reports, Calcutta High Court [*A publication*] (DLA) ... Coryton
Coryza [*Medicine*] ... CZ
COSAL [*Coordinated Shipboard Allowance List*] **Processing Point** ... COPP
Cosanti Foundation [*Later, Arcosanti*] (EA) ... CF
Cosby, Mason, and Martland Public Library, Noelville, Ontario [*Library symbol National Library of Canada*] (NLC) ... ONCMM
Coscan Development Corp. [*Toronto Stock Exchange symbol*] ... COT
Cosecant ... COSEC
Cosecant [*Mathematics*] (GPO) ... CSC
Cosecant, Hyperbolic [*Mathematics*] (ROG) ... COSECH
Cosecant, Hyperbolic [*Mathematics*] (GPO) ... CSCH
Coseka Resources Ltd. [*Toronto Stock Exchange symbol*] ... CKS
Cosford [*British ICAO location identifier*] (ICLI) ... EGWC
Coshocton, OH [*FM radio station call letters*] (RBYB) ... WOSE-FM
Coshocton, OH [*AM radio station call letters*] ... WTNS
Coshocton, OH [*FM radio station call letters*] ... WTNS-FM
Cosiguina [*Nicaragua*] [*Seismograph station code, US Geological Survey*] (SEIS) ... COS
Cosine ... CN
Cosine [*Mathematics*] (MCD) ... COS
Cosine Emission Law [*Optics*] ... CEL
Cosine, Hyperbolic [*Mathematics*] ... COSH
Cosine Integral ... Ci
Cosine Tracking and Triangulation (SAA) ... COTAT
Cosine Trajectory Angle and Range (IAA) ... COTAR
Cosite Analysis Model [*Computer science*] ... COSAM
Cosmetic ... CSMTC
Cosmetic & Fragrance Concepts, Inc. (MHDW) ... COSF
Cosmetic and Perfumery Retail Association [*British*] ... COPRA
Cosmetic Career Women [*Later, CEW*] ... CCW
Cosmetic Center [*Formerly, Cosmetic & Fragrance Concept*] [*NASDAQ symbol*] (SPSG) ... COSC
Cosmetic Center Cl'A' [*NASDAQ symbol*] (TTSB) ... COSCA
Cosmetic Center Cl'B'(vtg) [*NASDAQ symbol*] (TTSB) ... COSCB
Cosmetic Center, Inc. [*Associated Press*] (SAG) ... CosCtr
Cosmetic Executive Women (EA) ... CEW
Cosmetic Group USA [*NASDAQ symbol*] (TTSB) ... CUSA
Cosmetic Group USA, Inc. [*Associated Press*] (SAG) ... Cosmetic
Cosmetic Group USA, Inc. [*Associated Press*] (SAG) ... Cosmtc
Cosmetic Group USA, Inc. [*NASDAQ symbol*] (SAG) ... CUSA
Cosmetic Group USA Wrrt [*NASDAQ symbol*] (TTSB) ... CUSAW
Cosmetic Industry Buyers and Suppliers (EA) ... CIBS
Cosmetic Ingredient Review (EA) ... CIR
Cosmetic Pharmaceutical ... Cosmoceutical
Cosmetic, Toiletry, and Fragrance Association (EA) ... CTFA
Cosmetic, Toiletry, and Perfumery Association [*British*] (DBA) ... CTPA
Cosmetics for the Community of Tomorrow [*Acronym used as brand name*] ... KOSCOT
Cosmetologist ... CSMTLGST
Cosmetology Accrediting Commission [*Later, NACCAS*] (EA) ... CAC
Cosmetology Program [*Association of Independent Colleges and Schools specialization code*] ... CS
Cosmic and Solar Particle Investigation [*Astronomy*] ... COSPIN
Cosmic Anisotropy Telescope ... CAT
Cosmic Background Explorer [*NASA*] ... COBE
Cosmic Background Radiation ... CBR
Cosmic Background Radiation Anisotropy [*Astronomy*] (ECON) ... COBRA
Cosmic Black-Body Radiation [*Astrophysics*] ... CBR
Cosmic Dust Collection Facility (SSD) ... CDCF
Cosmic Dust Detector ... CDD
Cosmic Far-Infrared Background ... CFIRB
Cosmic Infrared Background Radiation ... CIB
Cosmic Microwave Background [*Of radiation*] ... CMB
Cosmic Microwave Background Radiation ... CMBR

Cosmic Noise Absorption ... CNA
Cosmic Ray ... CR
Cosmic Ray Albedo Neutron Decay [*Geophysics*] ... CRAND
Cosmic Ray Altimeter ... CRA
Cosmic Ray Anti-Matter Detector (PDAA) ... CRAMD
Cosmic Ray Detector [*NASA*] ... CRD
Cosmic Ray Emulsion Plastic Equipment [*NASA*] (MCD) ... CREPE
Cosmic Ray Exposure [*Geophysics*] ... CRE
Cosmic Ray Flux ... CRF
Cosmic Ray Gas ... CRG
Cosmic Ray Ionization Program [*NASA*] ... CRISP
Cosmic Ray Isotope Experiment (MCD) ... CRIE
Cosmic Ray Logic Box (IAA) ... CRLB
Cosmic Ray Nuclear [*or Nuclei*] **Experiment** (MCD) ... CRANE
Cosmic Ray Nuclei [*or Nuclear*] **Experiment** (SSD) ... CRNE
Cosmic Ray Observatory ... CRO
Cosmic Ray Particle ... CRP
Cosmic Ray Physics Laboratory (NASA) ... CRPL
Cosmic Ray Satellite [*Japan*] ... CORSA
Cosmic Ray Shower ... CRS
Cosmic Ray Telescope ... CRT
Cosmic Top Secret (NATG) ... CTS
Cosmic X-Ray Background ... CXB
Cosmic-Ray Subsystem [*Astrophysics*] ... CRS
Cosmis Rays ... CR
Cosmo Communications Corp. [*NASDAQ symbol*] (NQ) ... CSMO
Cosmo Communictions [*Associated Press*] (SAG) ... CosmoCm
Cosmo Dog ... CD
Cosmogenic (IAA) ... CP
Cosmography ... COSMOG
Cosmopolitan Area Network [*Telecommunications*] (ACRL) ... CAN
Cosmopolitan Associates [*Later, OC*] ... CA
Cosmopolitan International (EA) ... CI
Cosmopolitan Soccer League (EA) ... CSL
Cosmos Club, Washington, DC [*Library symbol Library of Congress*] (LCLS) ... DCos
Cosmos Public School, Cosmos, MN [*Library symbol*] [*Library of Congress*] (LCLS) ... MnCosPS
Cosmos Resources, Inc. [*Vancouver Stock Exchange symbol*] ... CES
Cosne-Sur-Loire [*France ICAO location identifier*] (ICLI) ... LFGH
Coso Basin North [*California*] [*Seismograph station code, US Geological Survey*] (SEIS) ... CBHM
Coso Springs South [*California*] [*Seismograph station code, US Geological Survey*] (SEIS) ... CSSM
COSPAR [*Committee on Space Research*] **International R eference Atmosphere** ... CIRA
Cosponsor ... COSP
Cossack National Press Association [*Defunct*] (EA) ... CNPA
Cossack-American Citizens' Committee (EA) ... CACC
Cost ... C
Cost About ... ca
Cost Account [*Accounting*] ... CA
Cost Account Code [*Accounting*] ... CAC
Cost Account Manager (MCD) ... CAM
Cost Account Number [*Accounting*] (NG) ... CAN
Cost Account Package [*Accounting*] (NASA) ... CAP
Cost Account Performance Measurement and Analysis Report (MCD) ... CAPMAR
Cost Account Performance Status Report [*Accounting*] (MCD) ... CAPSR
Cost Account Plan ... CAP
Cost Accountant [*Accounting*] (AABC) ... CA
Cost Accounting Code [*NASA*] (NASA) ... COSTA
Cost Accounting Schedule (MCD) ... CAS
Cost Accounting Standards [*Accounting*] (MCD) ... CAS
Cost Accounting Standards Board [*US*] [*Terminated*] ... CASB
Cost Accounting Standards Board's Cost of Money Factors [*Form*] (AAGC) ... CASB-CMF
Cost Accounting Standards Guide [*CCH*] [*A publication*] (AAGC) ... CASG
Cost Accounting Standards Guide [*Commerce Clearing House*] [*A publication*] (DLA) ... Cost Acc'g Stand Guide
Cost Accumulation System ... CAS
Cost Adjustment Factor ... CAF
Cost Advisory Group [*Army*] ... CAG
Cost Allocation Procedure [*Environmental Protection Agency*] (GFGA) ... CAP
Cost Allocation Report [*DoD*] ... CAR
Cost Allocation Review ... CAR
Cost Analysis Brief (MCD) ... CAB
Cost Analysis Improvement Group [*DoD*] (DOMA) ... CAIG
Cost Analysis Information Report [*Air Force*] (MCD) ... CAIR
Cost Analysis Monthly Exchange [*Army*] ... CAME
Cost Analysis of LASER Investment, Production, Engineering, and Research Cost Mode (MCD) ... CALIPER
Cost Analysis of Maintenance Policy ... COAMP
Cost Analysis Office [*Army*] (RDA) ... CAO
Cost Analysis Organization (SAA) ... CAOS
Cost Analysis Plan ... CAP
Cost Analysis Task Force [*NASA*] (KSC) ... CATF
Cost Analysis Technical Manual ... CATEM
Cost and Economic Analysis Center (DOMA) ... CEAC
Cost and Economic Information System [*DoD*] (MCD) ... CEIS
Cost and Freight [*Shipping*] ... C & F
Cost and Freight [*Shipping*] ... CAF
Cost and Freight (DFIT) ... C&F
Cost and Freight [*Shipping*] ... CF
Cost and Freight [*"INCOTERM," International Chamber of Commerce official code*] [*Business term*] ... CFR
Cost and Insurance [*Shipping*] ... C & I
Cost and Insurance [*Shipping*] ... CI
Cost and Material Position System (MCD) ... CAMPS
Cost and Operational Effectiveness Analysis [*Military*] (AABC) ... COEA
Cost and Performance ... CP
Cost and Performance Analysis [*Air Force*] (AFIT) ... CPA
Cost and Performance Effectiveness Ratios ... CAPERS
Cost and Performance Summary Report [*Army*] ... CPSR
Cost and Schedule Planning and Control ... CSPC
Cost and Training Effectiveness Analysis ... COTA
Cost and Training Effectiveness Analysis ... CTEA
Cost as an Independent Variable (AAGC) ... CAIV
Cost Assignment to Telecommunication Services [*Telecommunications*] ... CATS
Cost Audit Board (NASA) ... CAB
Cost/Benefit [*Accounting*] ... C/B
Cost Breakdown Structure (MCD) ... CBS
Cost Bulletin [*A publication*] ... Cost Bull
Cost/Burden Reduction ... C/BR
Cost Category Code (MCD) ... CCC
Cost Category Input (SAA) ... CCI
Cost Category Input Form (SAA) ... CCIF
Cost Category Reporting System (MCD) ... CCRS
Cost Center (AFM) ... CC
Cost Center Determination (AAG) ... CCD
Cost Center Performance Measurement System (AFM) ... CCPMS
Cost Change Commitment Notice ... CCCN
Cost Charge Number (MCD) ... CCN
Cost Code (MCD) ... CC
Cost Committee Advisory Group ... CCAG
Cost Comparison Handbook [*A publication*] (MCD) ... CCH
Cost Contract Fee Appendix (SAA) ... CCFA
Cost Control and Action Group ... CCAG
Cost Control Item (MCD) ... CCI
Cost Control Program (NASA) ... CCP
Cost Control System ... CCS
Cost Data Bank Index ... CDBI
Cost Data Bank System (AFIT) ... CDBS
Cost Data Base Management System [*Air Force*] ... CDBMS
Cost Data Plan ... CDP
Cost Data Sheet (MCD) ... CDS
Cost Differential (MCD) ... COSDIF
Cost Document Library System [*Air Force*] (AFIT) ... CDLS
Cost Driver Attribute ... CDA
Cost Effective Surface Torpedo (MCD) ... CEST
Cost Effectiveness [*Accounting*] ... CE
Cost Effectiveness Analysis of Bonuses and Reenlistment Policies ... CEABREP
Cost Effectiveness Analysis of the Tactical Operations System [*Military*] (MCD) ... CEATOS
Cost Effectiveness and Reliability Technology for the Automotive Industry ... CERTAIN
Cost Effectiveness Index [*Economics*] ... CEI
Cost Effectiveness Study [*Economics*] ... CES
Cost Element (MCD) ... CE
Cost Element Monitor [*Air Force*] ... CEM
Cost Estimate and Updating Form (MCD) ... CEUF
Cost Estimate Change Order (NRCH) ... CECO
Cost Estimate Control Data Center (AABC) ... CECDC
Cost Estimate Dispersion (KSC) ... CED
Cost Estimate Error Report ... CEER
Cost Estimate Input Sheet [*Jet Propulsion Laboratory, NASA*] ... CEIS
Cost Estimate Request ... CER
Cost Estimating Data Center ... CEDC
Cost Estimating Relation [*or Relationship*] (AFM) ... CER
Cost Estimating Techniques for System Acquisition [*Army*] ... CETSA
Cost Evaluation Plan (AAGC) ... CEP
Cost, Freight, and Exchange [*Shipping*] ... CF and E
Cost, Freight, and Insurance [*Shipping*] ... CF & I
Cost, Freight, and Insurance [*Shipping*] ... CFI
Cost, Freight, Assurance [*Shipping*] ... CFA
Cost Growth (DNAB) ... CG
Cost Improvement Program ... CIP
Cost Improvement Proposal (MCD) ... CIP
Cost Index (GAVI) ... CI
Cost Indicator Code [*Army*] (AFIT) ... CIC
Cost Information Reports [*DoD*] ... CIR
Cost Information System ... CIS
Cost Inspection Service [*Navy*] ... CIS
Cost Inspector ... CI
Cost, Insurance, and Freight [*Shipping*] [*"INCOTERM," International Chamber of Commerce official code*] ... CIF
Cost, Insurance, Freight, and Commission [*Shipping*] ... CIF & C
Cost, Insurance, Freight, and Commission [*Shipping*] ... CIFC
Cost, Insurance, Freight, and Exchange [*Shipping*] ... CIF & E
Cost, Insurance, Freight, and Exchange [*Shipping*] ... CIFE
Cost, Insurance, Freight, and Interest [*Shipping*] ... CIF & I
Cost, Insurance, Freight, and Interest [*Shipping*] ... CIFI
Cost, Insurance, Freight, Commission, and Exchange [*Shipping*] ... CIFCE
Cost, Insurance, Freight, Commission, and Interest [*Shipping*] ... CIFC & I
Cost, Insurance, Freight, Commission, and Interest [*Shipping*] ... CIFCI
Cost, Insurance, Freight, Commission, Exchange, and Interest [*Shipping*] ... CIFCE & I
Cost, Insurance, Freight, Free Out [*Shipping*] ... CIFFO
Cost, Insurance, Freight, Interest, and Exchange [*Shipping*] ... CIFI & E

Cost, Insurance, Freight, London Terms [*Shipping*] ... CIFLT
Cost Laid Down ... CLD
Cost, Lawsuits, On-Air Requirements, and Time Available ... CLOT
Cost, Life, Interchangeability, Function, and Safety [*Navy*] (NG) ... CLIFS
Cost Limit Review Board ... CLRB
Cost Management Group [*An association*] (EA) ... CMG
Cost Management Improvement Program ... CMIP
Cost Management System ... CMS
Cost Measurement Technique (AAG) ... COMET
Cost of Alternative Military Programs (SAA) ... CAMP
Cost of Analysis Organization [*Navy*] (NG) ... CAO
Cost of Arms [*Army*] (AABC) ... C/A
Cost of Attaining Personnel Requirement ... CAPER
Cost of Compliance [*Automotive emissions standards*] ... COC
Cost of Electricity (MCD) ... COE
Cost of Facilities (NASA) ... C of F
Cost of Facilities Capital (AAGC) ... CFC
Cost of Funds [*Business term*] (EMRF) ... COF
Cost of Funds Index [*Banking*] ... COFI
Cost of Goods Sold (AAGC) ... CGS
Cost of Goods Sold ... COGS
Cost of Illness [*Environmental medicine*] ... COI
Cost of Knowing ... CoK
Cost of Living [*Economics*] (AAG) ... C of L
Cost of Living [*Economics*] (AAG) ... CL
Cost of Living [*Economics*] ... COL
Cost of Living Adjustment ... COLA
Cost of Living Allowance [*Economics*] ... COLA
Cost of Living Award (PDAA) ... COLA
Cost of Living Bonus (DGA) ... COLB
Cost of Living Council [*Also, COLC*] [*Terminated, 1974 Pronounced "click"*] ... CLC
Cost of Living Council [*Also, CLC*] [*Terminated, 1974*] ... COLC
Cost of Money [*DoD*] ... COM
Cost of Money Factor (SSD) ... CMF
Cost of Quality [*Engineering*] ... COQ
Cost of Sale [*Accounting*] ... C/S
Cost of Sales Adjustment [*Economics*] (DCTA) ... COSA
Cost of Service Indexing ... COSI
Cost of Social Security [*International Labor Organization*] [*Information service or system United Nations*] (DUND) ... COSS
Cost on Delivery (MCD) ... COD
Cost Operating Budget (NOAA) ... COB
Cost Operating Profits [*Accounting*] ... COP
Cost Optimization Utilizing Reference Technique (PDAA) ... COURT
Cost Optimizing System to Evaluate Reliability (MHDB) ... COSTER
Cost per Average Pound Saved ... CAPS
Cost per Click [*Computer science*] ... CPC
Cost per Entered Employment [*Job Training and Partnership Act*] (OICC) ... CEE
Cost per Flight [*NASA*] ... CPF
Cost per Gross Rating Point [*Advertising*] (NTCM) ... CPGRP
Cost per Hand Stitch [*Tailoring*] ... CPHS
Cost per Inquiry ... CPI
Cost Per Inquiry (WDMC) ... cpi
Cost per Instruction [*Computer science*] ... CPI
Cost per Interview [*Marketing*] (WDMC) ... CPI
Cost Per Interview (WDMC) ... cpi
Cost per Man-Hour (MCD) ... C/MH
Cost per Order [*Advertising*] (WDMC) ... CPO
Cost per Point [*Advertising*] (WDMC) ... CPP
Cost per Positive Termination [*Job Training and Partnership Act*] (OICC) ... CPPT
Cost per Region [*Agricultural economics*] ... CR
Cost per Reportable Result ... CPRR
Cost per Thousand [*Advertising*] ... CPM
Cost per Thousand (ODBW) ... CPT
Cost per Unit ... CPU
Cost per Unit Requirement (MCD) ... CUR
Cost Performance Index (MCD) ... CPI
Cost Performance Management (MCD) ... CPM
Cost Performance Report (MCD) ... CPR
Cost Planning and Appraisal [*Air Force Systems Command, Aeronautical Systems Division*] ... CPA
Cost Planning and Control System (MCD) ... CPCS
Cost Planning and Evaluations System ... COPES
Cost Plus [*Insurance*] ... CP
Cost Plus [*NASDAQ symbol*] (TTSB) ... CPWM
Cost Plus a Percentage of Cost ... CPPC
Cost Plus Award [*Military*] ... CPA
Cost Plus Award Fee [*Business term*] ... CPAF
Cost Plus Fixed Fee [*Business term*] ... CPFF
Cost Plus Fixed Fee [*Investment term*] (DFIT) ... CPFF
Cost Plus Incentive [*Business term*] (MSA) ... CPI
Cost Plus, Inc. [*Associated Press*] (SAG) ... CostPlus
Cost Plus, Inc. [*NASDAQ symbol*] (SAG) ... CPWM
Cost Plus No Fee [*Business term*] (MCD) ... CPNF
Cost Price [*Business term*] (ADA) ... CP
Cost Price of the Items Canceled [*Business term*] ... CPIC
Cost/Pricing Data [*Military*] (DOMA) ... C/PD
Cost Principles for Educational Institutions [*OMB Circular*] (AAGC) ... A-21
Cost Principles for State and Local Governments (AAGC) ... A-87
Cost Progress Evaluation (MCD) ... COPE
Cost Proposal ... CP
Cost Proposal Outline (AAG) ... CPO
Cost Proposal Requirement (MCD) ... CPR
Cost Quality Management System [*for hospitals*] ... CQMS
Cost Quote Request ... CQR
Cost Realism Committee (AAGC) ... CRC
Cost Reduction Alternative Study [*Economics*] (NASA) ... CRAS
Cost Reduction Curve [*Economics*] (NASA) ... CRC
Cost Reduction Early Decision Information Techniques [*Hughes Aircraft Co.*] ... CREDIT
Cost Reduction Journal ... CRJO
Cost Reduction Program [*Economics*] (AFM) ... CRP
Cost Reduction Report [*Economics*] ... CRR
Cost Reimbursement [*Type of contract*] (AAGC) ... Cost
Cost Reimbursement ... CR
Cost Reimbursement Contract [*Government contracting*] ... CRC
Cost Reimbursement Incentive Contracting [*Government contracting*] ... CRIC
Cost Reporting Requirements ... CRR
Cost Savings Model (MCD) ... CSM
Cost/Schedule ... C/S
Cost/Schedule Control (MCD) ... C/SC
Cost Schedule Control System (MCD) ... CS2
Cost/Schedule Control System (MCD) ... CSCS
Cost/Schedule Control System Criteria ... C/SC2
Cost/Schedule Control System Criteria ... C/SCSC
Cost Schedule, Logistics, and NATO Standardization (MCD) ... CSLS
Cost/Schedule Planning and Control Specification [*Air Force*] ... C/SPCS
Cost/Schedule Reporting System (SSD) ... C/SRS
Cost Schedule Status Report [*Military*] ... CSSR
Cost Schedule Technical Control System ... CSTCS
Cost, Scheduling, Reporting ... CSR
Cost Sensitivity Factor (NASA) ... CSF
Cost Sharing ... CS
Cost System Indicator (AFIT) ... CSI
Cost to Manuacture ... CTM
Cost Travel Chargeable ... TRAVCHAR
Cost Variance (MCD) ... CV
Costa [*Rib*] [*Anatomy*] ... C
Costa [*Entomology*] ... Co
Costa I [*First rib*] [*Costa II, second rib is C_2, etc., through C12 Orthopedics*] (DAVI) ... C_1
Costa Mesa, CA [*AM radio station call letters*] (RBYB) ... KNNZ
Costa Mesa Historical Society, Costa Mesa, CA [*Library symbol*] [*Library of Congress*] (LCLS) ... CCmHi
Costa Rica (VRA) ... C Rica
Costa Rica [*ANSI two-letter standard code*] (CNC) ... CR
Costa Rica [*MARC country of publication code Library of Congress*] (LCCP) ... cr
Costa Rica [*ANSI three-letter standard code*] (CNC) ... CRI
Costa Rica [*MARC geographic area code Library of Congress*] (LCCP) ... nccr--
Costa Rica International, Inc. [*Associated Press*] (SAG) ... CostaRica
Costa Rica International, Inc. [*NASDAQ symbol*] (SAG) ... RICA
Costal Margin [*Medicine*] ... CM
Costal Ocean Program [*Marine science*] (OSRA) ... COP
Cost-Benefit Analysis [*Accounting*] ... CBA
Co-Steel, Inc. [*Toronto Stock Exchange symbol*] ... CEI
Cost-Effective Ratio [*Economics*] ... CER
Cost-Effective Shape Technology (MCD) ... CEST
Cost-Effectiveness Analysis [*Economics*] ... CEA
Cost-Effectiveness Analysis Methodology [*Economics*] (MCD) ... CEAM
Costermonger [*Fruit or vegetable seller*] [*British*] (DSUE) ... COSTER
Cost-Estimating System (ODBW) ... CES
Cost-Exchange Ratio [*DoD*] ... CER
Cost-Factoring System for Force Readiness Projection (MCD) ... COFACTS
Cost-Free Evaluation ... CFE
Costilla County Library, San Luis, CO [*Library symbol Library of Congress*] (LCLS) ... CoSl
Costilla Energy, Inc. [*NASDAQ symbol*] (SAG) ... COSE
Costilla Energy, Inc. [*Associated Press*] (SAG) ... CostEner
Costing and Assessing via Substantival History ... CASH
Costing and Data Management System ... CADMS
Costing Out Policy Systems (PDAA) ... COPS
Costing System (DGA) ... CS
Cost-No Fee [*Type of contract*] (AAGC) ... C-NF
Costo y Flete [*Cost and Freight*] [*Shipping*] [*Spanish*] ... C & F
Costochondral [*Anatomy*] ... CC
Costochondral Junction [*Medicine*] (DAVI) ... CCJ
Cost-of-Living Index [*Economics*] ... CLI
Cost-of-Living Index [*Economics*] ... COLI
Cost-of-Ownership ... COO
Cost-of-Ownership Reduction Investment (MCD) ... COORI
Costophrenic Angle [*Medicine*] (DMAA) ... CPA
Cost-Oriented Models Built to Analyze Tradeoffs (MCD) ... COMBAT
Cost-Oriented Production and Inventory Loading Operations Technique Works (MHDB) ... COPILOT
Cost-Oriented Resource Estimating Model [*Air Force*] (GFGA) ... CORE
Cost-Oriented Systems Technique ... COST
Costovertebral [*Angle*] [*Anatomy*] (DAVI) ... CV
Costovertebral Angle [*Medicine*] ... CVA
Costovertebral Angle Tenderness [*Medicine*] (MAE) ... CVAT
Cost-Plus-Incentive Fee [*Business term*] ... CIF
Cost-Plus-Incentive Fee [*Business term*] (AFM) ... CPIF
Cost-Plus-Incentive-Award Fee [*Business term*] (MCD) ... CPIAF
Cost-Reimbursement Contracting (AAGC) ... CRC
Cost-Reimbursement Facilities Contract (AAGC) ... CRFC
Costs, Budgeting, and Economics ... CBE
Costs Chargeable to Fund Authorization [*Army*] ... CHGFA
Costs Chargeable to Purchase Authorization Advice ... CHGPAA
Costs of Hard Rock Tunnelling (PDAA) ... COHART
Costs of the Soviet Empire [*International economics*] ... CSE
Cost-Schedule-Milestone [*Chart*] ... CSM
Cost-Stirling [*Antibodies*] [*Immunology*] (DAVI) ... C/S

Costume (ROG) .... COST
Costume (VRA) .... cstu
Costume Designers Guild (EA) .... CDG
Costume Jewelry Board of Trade of New York [Inactive] .... CJBT
Costume Jewelry Salesmen's Association (EA) .... CJSA
Costume Jewelry Trade Association [Defunct] .... CJTA
Costume Society of America (EA) .... CSA
Cost-Volume-Power .... CVP
Cost-Volume-Profit [Analysis] (MCD) .... CVP
Cost-Volume-Profit (AAGC) .... C-V-P
Cosumnes River College, Sacramento, CA [OCLC symbol] (OCLC) .... CCR
Cosworth Vega Owner's Association [Defunct] (EA) .... CVOA
Cotabato [Philippines] [Airport symbol] (OAG) .... CBO
Cotabato, North Cotabato [Philippines] [ICAO location identifier] (ICLI) .... RPWC
Cotacachi [Ecuador] [ICAO location identifier] (ICLI) .... SEHI
Cotangent [Mathematics] .... COT
Cotangent [Mathematics] (IAA) .... CTG
Cotangent [Mathematics] .... CTN
Cotangent, Hyperbolic [Mathematics] .... COTH
Cotangent, Hyperbolic [Mathematics] .... CTGH
Cotati, CA [Television station call letters] .... KRCB-TV
Cote St. Luc Public Library, Quebec [Library symbol National Library of Canada] (NLC) .... QCSTL
Cotelligent Group [NASDAQ symbol] (TTSB) .... COTL
Cotelligent Group, Inc. [Associated Press] (SAG) .... CotellG
Cotelligent Group, Inc. [NASDAQ symbol] (SAG) .... COTL
Cotenancy and Joint Ownership [Legal term] (DLA) .... COTEN & JT O
Cotgrave's Dictionary [A publication] (ROG) .... Cotg
Cotgrave's Dictionary [A publication] .... Cotr
Cothran's Annotated Statutes of Illinois [A publication] (DLA) .... Coth Stat
Coto 47 [Costa Rica] [ICAO location identifier] (ICLI) .... MRCC
Coto 47 [Costa Rica] [Airport symbol] (OAG) .... OTR
Cotonou [Benin] [Airport symbol] (OAG) .... COO
Cotonou [Dahomey] [Airport symbol] (AD) .... COO
Cotonou [Benin] [ICAO location identifier] (ICLI) .... DBBV
Cotonou/Cadjehoun [Benin] [ICAO location identifier] (ICLI) .... DBBB
Cotquean (DSUE) .... COT
Co-Transfer Agent (DLA) .... Co-T/Agt
Co-Trustee (DLA) .... Co-Tr
Cotswold [England] .... COTSW
Cotswold Executive Aviation [British ICAO designator] (FAAC) .... CWD
Cotswold Personality Assessment [Psychology] .... CPA
Cott Beverages Ltd. [Toronto Stock Exchange symbol] .... BCB
Cott Corp. [NASDAQ symbol] (SAG) .... COTT
Cott Corp. [Associated Press] (SAG) .... CottCp
Cott Corp. [NASDAQ symbol] (TTSB) .... COTTF
Cottage (ADA) .... COTT
Cottage .... CTG
Cottage (ADA) .... CTGE
Cottage and Rural Enterprises [British] (DI) .... CARE
Cottage Garden Society [British] (DBA) .... CGS
Cottage Grove, OR [FM radio station call letters] .... KCGR
Cottage Grove, OR [AM radio station call letters] .... KNND
Cottage Industry Miniaturists Trade Association (EA) .... CIMTA
Cottage Program International (EA) .... CPI
Cottages .... COTTS
Cottbus [Germany ICAO location identifier] (ICLI) .... ETCO
Cottenham. Reports, Chancery [1846-48] [England] [A publication] (DLA) .... Cott
Cotter .... COT
Cottesloe [England] .... COTT
Cottesmore [British ICAO location identifier] (ICLI) .... EGXJ
Cottesmore TTTE [British ICAO designator] (FAAC) .... COT
Cottey College, Nevada, MO [Library symbol Library of Congress] (LCLS) .... MoNvC
Cottica [Surinam] [ICAO location identifier] (ICLI) .... SMCT
Cotton (AAG) C
Cotton (MSA) .... COT
Cotton (VRA) .... cot
Cotton (ROG) .... COTT
Cotton .... CTN
Cotton and Rayon Merchants Association [British] (BI) .... CRMA
Cotton Canvas Manufacturers Association [British] (BI) .... CCMA
Cotton, Climate, Cattle, and Citrus [Traditional elements of Arizona's economy] .... 4C's
Cotton Council International (EA) CCI
Cotton Covered [Wire insulation] (IAA) CC
Cotton Double Silk [Wire insulation] (IAA) .... CDS
Cotton Effect .... CE
Cotton Elastic Bandage (DAVI) .... CEB
Cotton Equalization Program .... CEP
[New York] Cotton Exchange (BARN) .... CTN
Cotton Export Market Acreage Program .... CEMAP
Cotton Fire and Marine Underwriters Association .... CFMUA
Cotton Importers Association (EA) .... CIA
Cotton Inc. [An association] (EA) CI
Cotton Insurance Association [Defunct] (EA) .... CIA
Cotton, Jute, or Sisal [Freight] .... CJS
Cotton Leaf Crumple [Plant pathology] CLC
Cotton Management Expert [Computer program to improve crop production] .... COMAX
Cotton Marketing Board [Australia] .... CMB
Cotton Mather [Initials used as pseudonym] .... CM
Cotton or Wool [Freight] .... CW
Cotton Piece Goods .... CPG
Cotton Plant - Fargo Railway Co. [AAR code] .... CPF

Cotton Public School, Cotton, MN [Library symbol] [Library of Congress] (LCLS) .... MnCotS
Cotton Research Corp. .... CRC
Cotton Seed .... CS
Cotton Silk [Wire insulation] (IAA) .... CS
Cotton Stabilization Corp. [New Deal] .... CSC
Cotton States Life Ins [NASDAQ symbol] (TTSB) .... CSLI
Cotton States Life Insurance [NASDAQ symbol] (SAG) .... CSLI
Cotton States Life Insurance [Associated Press] (SAG) .... CtnSLf
[The] Cotton Textiles Export Promotion Council of India (ECON) .... TEXPROCIL
Cotton Valley [Vancouver Stock Exchange symbol] .... CLY
Cotton Warehouse Association of America (EA) .... CWAA
Cotton Warehouse Inspection Service [Defunct] (EA) .... CWIS
Cottonian Manuscripts [British Museum] [A publication] (DLA) .... Cott Mss
Cotton's Abridgment of the Records [A publication] (DLA) .... Cot Abr
Cottonseed [Freight] .... COTNSD
Cottonseed Flour .... CF
Cottonseed Meal .... CSM
Cottonseed Oil (OA) .... CSO
Cottonseed Oil Assistance Program [Department of Agriculture] .... COAP
Cottonseed Protein Isolate CI
Cottontail Rabbit Papillomavirus .... CRPV
Cottonwood [California] [Seismograph station code, US Geological Survey] (SEIS) .... CWC
Cottonwood, AZ [AM radio station call letters] .... KVRD
Cottonwood, AZ [FM radio station call letters] .... KVRD-FM
Cottonwood, AZ [AM radio station call letters] (RBYB) .... KYBC-AM
Cottonwood, AZ [FM radio station call letters] .... KZGL
Cottonwood, ID [FM radio station call letters] .... KNWO
Cottonwood Mountains [California] [Seismograph station code, US Geological Survey] (SEIS) .... CTW
Cottonwood Public Library, Cottonwood, AZ [Library symbol Library of Congress] (LCLS) .... AzCot
Cottonwood Public School, Cottonwood, MN [Library symbol] [Library of Congress] (LCLS) .... MnCtwPS
Cotton-Wool Exudate [Ophthalmology] (DAVI) .... CWE
Cotton-Wool Spot [Ophthalomology] (DAVI) .... CWS
Cottony Blight [of turf grass] .... CB
Cotuit Library, Cotuit, MA [Library symbol] [Library of Congress] (LCLS) .... MCot
Cotulla/Municipal [Texas] [ICAO location identifier] (ICLI) .... KCOT
Cotulla, TX [Location identifier FAA] (FAAL) .... COT
Cotyledon [Botany] C
Cotyledon [Botany] .... Ct
Couch .... COU
Couch Potatoes [Defunct] (EA) .... CP
Couchant [Heraldry] (ADA) .... COUCH
Couchiching Institue on Public Affairs (AC) .... CIPA
Coudersport & Port Allegany [AAR code] .... CPA
Coudersport, PA [AM radio station call letters] .... WFRM
Coudersport, PA [FM radio station call letters] .... WFRM-FM
Couer d'Alene High School, Couer d'Alene, ID [Library symbol] [Library of Congress] (LCLS) .... IdCHS
Cougar Air, Inc. [Canada ICAO designator] (FAAC) .... CAJ
Cougar Club of America (EA) .... CCA
Cougar Helicopter, Inc. [Canada ICAO designator] (FAAC) .... CHI
Cough [Medicine] C
Cough [Medicine] .... CGH
Cough and Deep-Breathe [Medicine] .... C & DB
Cough, Turn, and Deep Breathe [Medicine] .... CT & DB
Couhe/Verac [France ICAO location identifier] (ICLI) .... LFDV
Could .... CD
Could (ADA) .... CLD
Could Not Test [Laboratory] (DAVI) .... CNT
Couldn't Be Cuter [Slang] .... CBC
Coulee Dam National Recreation Area .... CODA
Coulomb [Symbol] [SI unit of electric charge] C
Coulomb [Unit of electric charge] .... CB
Coulomb [Unit of electric charge] .... COUL
Coulomb [Unit of quality] [Electronics] (WDAA) .... Q
Coulomb Blockade [Physics] .... CB
Coulomb Excitation [Nuclear physics] (OA) .... CE
Coulomb Explosion Imaging [Nuclear physics] .... CEI
Coulombs per Cubic Meter .... C/M³
Coulombs per Kilogram .... C/KG
Coulombs per Volt .... C/V
Coulometric .... Coul
Coulommiers/Voisins [France ICAO location identifier] (ICLI) .... LFPK
Coulsdon Library, Croydon, United Kingdom [Library symbol Library of Congress] (LCLS) .... UkCrC
Coulston and Forbes on Waters [6th ed.] [1952] [A publication] (DLA) .... Coul & F Wat
Coulter Counter [Medicine] (DMAA) CC
Coulter Diagnostics, Inc., Hialeah, FL [Library symbol Library of Congress] (LCLS) .... FHiaC
Council [Australia] C
Council (ADA) CL
Council .... CNCL
Council .... CNCL
Council .... COUN
Council (ROG) .... COUNC
Council Accepted [Medicine] .... CA
Council Against Communist Aggression [Later, CDF] (EA) .... CACA
Council Against Poverty (IIA) .... CAP
Council, AK [Location identifier FAA] (FAAL) CIL

Council Bluffs Free Public Library, Council Bluffs, IA [*Library symbol Library of Congress*] (LCLS) .... IaCb
Council Bluffs Free Public Library, Council Bluffs, IA [*OCLC symbol*] (OCLC) .... IWB
Council Bluffs, IA [*Location identifier FAA*] (FAAL) .... CBF
Council Bluffs, IA [*Television station call letters*] .... KBIN
Council Bluffs, IA [*FM radio station call letters*] .... KIWR
Council Bluffs, IA [*AM radio station call letters*] .... KLNG
Council Bluffs, IA [*FM radio station call letters*] .... KQKQ
Council Chambers [*Freemasonry*] (ROG) .... CO CH
Council Deputies (NATG) .... CD
Council District Library, Council, ID [*Library symbol*] [*Library of Congress*] (LCLS) .... IdCnL
Council for a Beautiful Israel (EA) .... CBI
Council for a Black Economic Agenda (EA) .... CBEA
Council for a Competitive Economy (EA) .... CCE
Council for a Department of Peace (EA) .... CODEP
Council for a Livable World (EA) .... CLW
Council for a Livable World Education Fund (EA) .... CLWEF
Council for a Nuclear Weapons Freeze [*Later, IFLN*] (EA) .... CNWF
Council for a Secure America (EA) .... CSA
Council for a Tobacco-Free Ontario (AC) .... CTFO
Council for a Volunteer Military [*Defunct*] (EA) .... CVM
Council for Academic Freedom and Democracy [*British*] .... CAFD
Council for Accreditation in Occupational Hearing Conservation (EA) .... CAOHC
Council for Accreditation of Counseling and Related Educational Programs (AEE) .... CACREP
Council for Acupuncture [*British*] (DBA) .... CFA
Council for Adult and Experiential Learning (EA) .... CAEL
Council for Advancement and Support of Education (EA) .... CASE
Council for Advancement of Secondary Education [*Defunct*] (EA) .... CASE
Council for Agricultural and Chemurgic Research (EA) .... CACR
Council for Agricultural Science and Technology (EA) .... CAST
Council for Aid to Education [*Formerly the Council for Financial Aid to Education*] (NFD) .... CAE
Council for Alternatives to Stereotyping in Entertainment [*Defunct*] (EA) .... CASE
Council for American Private Education (EA) .... CAPE
Council for Arms Control [*British*] (DBA) .... CAC
Council for Basic Education (EA) .... CBE
Council for Better Hearing and Speech Month (EA) .... CBHSM
Council for Biology in Human Affairs .... CBHA
Council for British Archaeology .... CBA
Council for Business and the Arts in Canada .... CBAC
Council for Cable Information [*Defunct*] (EA) CCI
Council for Career Planning [*Defunct*] (EA) .... CCP
Council for Chemical Research (EA) .... CCR
Council for Children with Behavioral Disorders (EA) .... CCBD
Council for Children's Television and Media (EA) .... CCTM
Council for Christian Education in Schools [*Australia*] .... CCES
Council for Christian Medical Work [*Later, CHH*] (EA) .... CCMW
Council for Christian Social Action [*Later, OCIS*] [*United Church of Christ*] .... CCSA
Council for Civil Liberties in Western Australia .... CCLWA
Council for Clinical Training [*Later, ACPE*] (EA) .... CCT
Council for Complementary Alternative Medicine [*British*] .... CCAM
Council for Computer Development [*British*] (NITA) .... CCD
Council for Computerized Library Networks (IID) .... CCLN
Council for Continuous Improvement CCI
Council for Court Excellence (EA) .... CCE
Council for Cultural Co-Operation [*Council of Europe*] (EY) CCC
Council for Dance Education and Training [*British*] .... CDET
Council for Democracy in Korea [*Defunct*] (EA) .... CDK
Council for Democracy in the Americas [*Defunct*] (EA) .... CDA
Council for Democratic and Secular Humanism (EA) .... CODESH
Council for Democratic Government [*Japan*] (ECON) .... CDG
Council for Disabled Children (AIE) .... CDC
Council for Distributive Teacher Education .... CDTE
Council for Economic Advisors (AAGC) .... CEO
Council for Economic and Environmental Development (BARN) .... CEED
Council for Economic Growth and Security [*Defunct*] .... CEGS
Council for Economic Mutual Assistance [*Also known as CMEA, COMECON*] [*Communist-bloc nations: Poland, Russia, East Germany, Czechoslovakia, Romania, Bulgaria, Hungary Dissolved 1991*] .... CEMA
Council for Education and Training in Youth and Community Work (AIE) .... CETYCW
Council for Education in the Commonwealth (EAIO) .... CEC
Council for Education in World Citizenship [*British*] .... CEWC
Council for Education on Electronic Media (NTCM) .... CEEM
Council for Educational Advance [*British*] .... CEA
Council for Educational Development and Research (EA) .... CEDaR
Council for Educational Diagnostic Services [*Council for Exceptional Children*] .... CEDS
Council for Educational Freedom in America (EA) .... CEFA
Council for Educational Technology [*London, England*] [*Telecommunications Information service or system*] (TSSD) .... CET
Council for Elementary Science International (EA) .... CESI
Council for Environmental Conservation (EAIO) .... CoEnCo
Council for Environmental Education [*British*] .... CEE
Council for Equal Rights in Adoption .... CERA
Council for European Studies (EA) .... CES
Council for Excellence in Government (EA) .... CEG
Council for Exceptional Children (EA) .... CEC
Council for Export Trading Companies [*Washington, DC*] (EA) .... CETC
Council for Financial Aid to Education (EA) .... CFAE
Council for Fishing Vessel Safety (EA) .... CFVS
Council for Health and Human Services Ministries (EA) .... CHHSM
Council for Health and Welfare Services, United Church of Christ [*Later, CHHSM*] (EA) .... CHWS
Council for Higher Education [*US and Israel*] .... CHE
Council for Holocaust Survivors with Disabilities (EA) .... CHSD
Council for Independent Distribution [*Later, CPDA*] .... CID
Council for Independent School Aid (EA) .... CISA
Council for Indian Education (EA) .... CIE
Council for Industry and Higher Education (AIE) .... CIHE
Council for Inter-American Cooperation [*Later, NFTC*] .... CIAC
Council for Inter-American Security (EA) .... CIS
Council for Intercultural Studies and Programs [*Defunct*] (EA) .... CISP
Council for Interdisciplinary Communication in Medicine .... CIDCOMED
Council for Interinstitutional Leadership (EA) CIL
Council for International Business Risk Management (EA) .... CIBRM
Council for International Congresses of Entomology [*London, England*] (EA) .... CICE
Council for International Exchange of Scholars (EA) .... CIES
Council for International Organizations on Medical Sciences [*Geneva, Switzerland*] (EA) .... CIOMS
Council for International Progress in Management (EA) .... CIPM
Council for International Understanding (EA) .... CIU
Council for International Urban Liaison (EA) .... CIUL
Council for Intersocietal Studies (EA) .... CIS
Council for Jewish Education (EA) .... CJE
Council for Languages and Other International Studies [*Later, NCLIS*] (EA) .... CLOIS
Council for Latin America [*Later, COA*] .... CLA
Council for Lay Life and Work .... CLLW
Council for Learning Disabilities (EA) .... CLD
Council for Learning Resources in Colleges [*British*] .... COLRIC
Council for Liberal Learning [*Defunct*] (EA) CLL
Council for Livestock Protection [*Defunct*] (EA) .... CLP
Council for Management Education and Development (AIE) .... CMED
Council for Medical Affairs (EA) .... CFMA
Council for Microphotography and Document Reproduction [*British*] (DIT) .... CMDR
Council for Microphotography and Document Reproduction [*British*] .... MICRODOC
Council for Middle Eastern Affairs [*Defunct*] (EA) .... CMEA
Council for Military Aircraft Propulsion Standards .... CMAPS
Council for Military Aircraft Standards .... CMAS
Council for Museum Anthropology (EA) .... CMA
Council for Mutual Economic Assistance [*Also known as CEMA, COMECON*] [*Communist-bloc nations: Poland, Russia, East Germany, Czechoslovakia, Romania, Bulgaria, Hungary Dissolved 1991*] [*Former USSR*] .... CMEA
Council for Mutual Economic Assistance [*Also known as CEMA, CMEA*] [*Communist-bloc nations: Poland, Russia, East Germany, Czechoslovakia, Romania, Bulgaria, Hungary Dissolved 1991*] .... COMECON
Council for National Academic Awards [*British*] .... CNAA
Council for National Cooperation in Aquatics (EA) .... CNCA
Council for National Parks [*British*] .... CNP
Council for Native American Indian Progress (EA) .... CNAIP
Council for Noncollegiate Continuing Education (EA) .... CNCE
Council for Noncollegiate Continuing Education Units .... CN-CEU
Council for Old World Archaeology [*Defunct*] (EA) .... COWA
Council for Opportunity in Graduate Management Education [*Defunct*] (EA) .... COGME
Council for Overseas Colleges of Arts, Sciences, and TETOC [*British*] .... COCAST
Council for Partnership on Rice Research in Asia [*A consortium of agricultural research institutes*] .... CORRA
Council for Periodical Distributors Associations (EA) .... CPDA
Council for Philosophical Studies (EA) .... CPS
Council for Postgraduate Medical Education [*British*] (DI) .... CPME
Council for Professional Education for Business [*Later, AACSB*] .... CPEB
Council for Religion in Independent Schools (EA) .... CRIS
Council for Research in Music Education (EA) .... CRME
Council for Research on Turkish History [*Defunct*] (EA) .... CRTH
Council for Responsible Genetics (EA) .... CRG
Council for Responsible Nutrition (EA) .... CRN
Council for Rural Housing and Development (EA) .... CRHD
Council for Science and Society [*British*] .... CSS
Council for Science and Technological Information (HGAA) .... COSHTI
Council for Scientific and Industrial Research. Bulletin [*A publication*] .... CSIR Bull
Council for Scientific Policy .... CSP
Council for Sex Information and Education (EA) .... CSIE
Council for Small Industries in Rural Areas [*British*] .... COSIRA
Council for Social and Economic Studies (EA) .... CSES
Council for Standards in Human Service Education .... CSHSE
Council for Technical Education and Training for Overseas Countries (BARN) .... CTETOC
Council for Technical Education and Training for Overseas Countries [*British*] .... TETOC
Council for Technological Advancement (EA) .... CTA
Council for Technology Education Associations (EA) .... CTEA
Council for Television Development [*Defunct*] .... CTD
Council for Tertiary Education in Scotland (AIE) .... CTES
Council for Textile Recycling (EA) .... CTR
Council for the Accreditation of Correspondence Colleges [*British*] .... CACC
Council for the Accreditation of Teacher Education (AIE) .... CATE
Council for the Advancement and Support of Education .... CASE

Council for the Advancement of Arab-British Understanding [London, England] .... CAABU
Council for the Advancement of Citizenship (EA) .... CAC
Council for the Advancement of Consumer Policy (EA) .... CACP
Council for the Advancement of Hospital Recreation [Defunct] (EA) .... CAHR
Council for the Advancement of Science Writing (EA) .... CASW
Council for the Advancement of Small Colleges [Later, CIC] (EA) .... CASC
Council for the Advancement of Standards for Student Services/ Development Programs (EA) .... CAS
Council for the Advancement of the African People [British] .... CAAP
Council for the Advancement of the Psychological Professions and Sciences [Later, AAP] .... CAPPS
Council for the British Societies for Relief Abroad (DAS) .... COBSRA
Council for the Care of Churches [British] CCC
Council for the Defense of Freedom (EA) .... CDF
Council for the Development of Economic and Social Research in Africa [Dakar, Senegal] (EAIO) .... CODESRIA
Council for the Education of the Partially Seeing [Later, Division for the Visually Handicapped] (EA) .... CEPS
Council for the Encouragement of Music and the Arts [Later, Arts Council] .... CEMA
Council for the Investigation of Fertility Control [Obstetrics] (DAVI) .... CIFC
Council for the National Interest [Australia] .... CNI
Council for the National Register of Health Service Providers in Psychology (EA) .... CNRHSPP
Council for the Principality [British] .... CP
Council for the Protection of Rural England (EAIO) .... CPRE
Council for the Protection of Rural Wales (EAIO) .... CPRW
Council for the Securities Industry [Stock exchange] [London, England] .... CSI
Council for the Securities Industry [Levy] [British] .... SCI
Council for the Single Mother and Her Child [Australia] .... CSMHC
Council for the Study of Mankind [Defunct] (EA) .... CSM
Council for Tobacco Research .... CTR
Council for Tobacco Research - USA (EA) .... CTR-USA
Council for UHF Broadcasting (EA) .... CUB
Council for Understanding Mental Illness [Defunct Defunct] (EA) .... CUMI
Council for Unified Research and Education [Defunct] (EA) .... CURE
Council for University Classics Departments (AIE) .... CUCD
Council for Urban Affairs [Terminated, 1970] .... CUA
Council for Voluntary Youth Service (AIE) .... CVYS
Council for Women in Independent Schools (EA) .... CWIS
Council, ID [Location identifier FAA] (FAAL) .... CQI
Council Moslem League [Pakistan] [Political party] .... CML
Council of 1890 College Presidents (EA) .... CCP
Council of Academic Societies (DAVI) .... CAS
Council of Academies of Engineering and Technological Sciences [National Academyof Engineers] .... CAETS
Council of Active Independent Oil and Gas Producers (EA) .... CAIOGP
Council of Administrators of Large Urban Public Libraries [Canada] .... CALUPL
Council of Administrators of Special Education (EA) .... CASE
Council of Adult Stutterers [Later, NCS] (EA) .... CAS
Council of Affiliated Associations of Jewelers of America (EA) .... CAAJA
Council of Affiliated Marriage Enrichment Organizations [Defunct] (EA) .... CAMEO
Council of AFL-CIO Unions for Scientific, Professional, and Cultural Employees [Later, Department for Professional Employees, AFL-CIO] .... SPACE
Council of African Affairs (IIA) .... CAA
Council of Agriculture [Queensland] [Australia] .... COA
Council of Agriculture, Queensland [Australia] .... CA(Q)
Council of Air-Conditioning and Refrigeration Industry (EA) .... CARI
Council of American Artist Societies (EA) .... CAAS
Council of American Building Officials (EA) .... CABO
Council of American Chambers of Commerce in Europe [Later, European Council of American Chambers of Commerce] (EA) .... CACCE
Council of American Embroiderers (EA) .... CAE
Council of American Flag-Ship Operators (EA) .... CASO
Council of American Forensic Entomologists .... CAFE
Council of American Homeowners (EA) .... CAH
Council of American Indian Artists (EA) .... CAIA
Council of American Jewish Museums (EA) .... CAJM
Council of American Maritime Museums (EA) .... CAMM
Council of American Master Mariners (EA) .... CAMM
Council of American Official Poultry Tests (EA) .... CAOPT
Council of American Overseas Research Centers (EA) .... CAORC
Council of American Survey Research Organizations (EA) .... CASRO
Council of Arab Ministers of Justice [See also CMAJ] [Rabat, Morocco] (EAIO) .... CAMJ
Council of Archives and Research Libraries in Jewish Studies (EA) .... CARLJS
Council of Archives New Brunswick [Conseil des Archives du Nouveau-Brunswick] (AC) .... CANB
Council of Association Attorneys (EA) .... CAA
Council of Australian Humanist Societies .... CAHS
Council of Australian Machine Tool and Robotics Manufacturers .... CAMTRON
Council of Australian Power Lifting Associations .... CAPLO
Council of Australian Public Abattoir Authorities .... CAPAA
Council of Australian Public Library Associations .... CAPLA
Council of Better Business Bureaus [Arlington, VA] (EA) .... CBBB
Council of Bible Believing Churches (EA) .... CBBC
Council of Biology Editors (EA) .... CBE
Council of Black Architectural Schools [Defunct] (EA) .... COBAS
Council of Black Federal Employees (EA) .... COBFE
Council of British Ceramic Sanitaryware Manufacturers .... CBCSM
Council of British Cotton Textiles (DBA) .... CBCT
Council of British Manufacturers of Petroleum Equipment .... CBMPE
Council of Canadian Filmmakers .... CCFM

Council of Canadian Studies Programme Administrators .... CCSPA
Council of Canadians [An association] .... COC
Council of Canning Association Executives [Later, CFPAE] (EA) .... CCAE
Council of Car Care Centers (EA) CCCC
Council of Chemical Associations [Defunct] (EA) .... CCA
Council of Chief State School Officers (EA) .... CCSSO
Council of Churches CC
Council of Churches for Britain and Ireland (EAIO) .... CCBI
Council of Churches, South Australia .... CCSA
Council of Citizens with Low Vision (EA) CCLV
Council of City Research and Information Libraries [British] (NITA) .... COCRIL
Council of Civil Service Unions [British] .... CCSU
Council of Colleges of Arts and Sciences (EA) .... CCAS
Council of Communication Management (EA) .... CCM
Council of Communication Societies [Defunct] (EA) .... CCS
Council of Community Blood Centers (EA) .... CCBC
Council of Community Churches [Later, National Council of Community Churches] (EA) CCC
Council of Community Services of New York State (SRA) .... CCSNYS
Council of Conservationists (EA) CC
Council of Conservative Citizens (EA) CCC
Council of Construction Employers [Defunct] (EA) .... CCE
Council of Consulting Organizations (EA) .... CCO
Council of Consumer Advisers (EA) .... CCA
Council of Container Carriers CCC
Council of County Territorial Associations [British military] (DMA) .... CCTA
Council of Cultural Ministers [Australia] .... CCM
Council of Dance Administrators (EA) .... CODA
Council of Deans (DAVI) .... COD
Council of Defence .... COD
Council of Defense and Space Industry Associations (EA) .... CODSIA
Council of Deliberation [Freemasonry] (ROG) .... CD
Council of Development Finance Agencies .... CDFA
Council of Disabled Persons, Victoria [Australia] .... CDV
Council of Drama in Education (AC) .... CODE
Council of Eastern Orthodox Youth Leaders of the Americas [Defunct] (EA) .... CEOYLA
Council of Economic Advisers [to the President] .... CEA
Council of Education of the Deaf [Australia] .... CED
Council of Educational Facility Planners (EA) .... CEFP
Council of Educational Facility Planners, International (EA) .... CEFPI
Council of Emperor of East and West [Freemasonry] (ROG) .... C of EE & W
Council of Energy Resource Tribes (EA) .... CERT
Council of Engineering and Scientific Society Executives (EA) .... CESSE
Council of Engineering Institutions [British] .... CEI
Council of Engineering Society Secretaries [Later, CESSE] (EA) .... CESS
Council of Engineers and Scientists Organizations .... CESO
Council of Estonian Societies in Australia .... CESA
Council of Europe (NUCP) .... CE
Council of Europe .... COE
Council of Europe, Debates of the Consultative Assembly [A publication] (DLA) .... Eur Conslt Ass Deb
Council of Europe Resettlement Fund .... CERF
Council of European and Japanese National Shipowners Associations [England] (EAIO) .... CENSA
Council of European Industrial Federations .... CEIF
Council of European Municipalities .... CEM
Council of European Municipalities and Regions .... CEMR
Council of European National Youth Committees (EA) .... CENYC
Council of European Regions (EAIO) .... CER
Council of European-American Associations [Later, FEAO] .... CEAA
Council of Families with Visual Impairment (EA) .... CFVI
Council of Fashion Designers of America (EA) .... CFDA
Council of Federal Libraries (AC) .... CFL
Council of Federated Jewish Organizations [Defunct] (EA) .... CFJO
Council of Federated Organizations [Also, CFO] [Defunct] .... COFO
Council of Film Organizations (EA) .... CFO
Council of Fleet Specialists (EA) .... CFS
Council of Food Processors Association Executives (EA) .... CFPAE
Council of Foreign Ministers .... CFM
Council of Forest Industries (AC) .... COFI
Council of Forest Industries of British Columbia, Vancouver, BC, Canada [Library symbol Library of Congress] (LCLS) .... CaBVaCF
Council of Forest Industries of British Columbia, Vancouver, British Columbia [Library symbol National Library of Canada] (NLC) .... BVACF
Council of Free Czechoslovakia (EA) .... CFC
Council of General Motors Credit Unions [Warren, MI] (EA) .... CGMCU
Council of Georgist Organizations (EA) .... CGO
Council of Governing Bodies of Australian Zoos .... COBAZ
Council of Governments [Voluntary organizations of municipalities and counties] .... COG
Council of Governors Policy Advisors (EA) .... CGPA
Council of Graduate Schools (EA) .... CGS
Council of Graduate Schools in the United States (EA) .... CGSUS
Council of Graphological Societies (EA) .... COGS
Council of Health Organizations .... COHO
Council of Home Health Agencies and Community Health Services [Later, NAHC] .... CHHA/CHS
Council of Hotel and Restaurant Trainers (EA) .... CHART
Council of Housing Producers [Defunct] (EA) .... CHP
Council of Hungarian Associations in South Australia .... CHASA
Council of Hungarian Associations in Western Australia .... CHAWA
Council of Independent Black Institutions (EA) .... CIBI
Council of Independent Colleges (EA) CIC
Council of Independent Managers [Milwaukee, WI] (EA) .... CIM

Council of Indian Nations ..... CIN
Council of Indian Nations [*An association*] ..... CIN
Council of Industrial Boiler Owners (EA) ..... CIBO
Council of Industrial Design [*British*] ..... CID
Council of Industrial Design [*British*] ..... COID
Council of Institute of Telecommunication Engineers ..... CITE
Council of Institutional Investors [*Washington, DC*] (EA) CII
Council of Intellectual Disability Agencies [*Victoria*] [*Australia*] ..... CIDA
Council of Intergovernmental Coordinators (EA) CIC
Council of International Civil Aviation ..... CICA
Council of International Fellowship (EA) ..... CIF
Council of International Investigators (EA) CII
Council of International Lay Associations [*Defunct*] (EA) ..... CILA
Council of International Programs (EA) ..... CIP
Council of International Trade Union Cooperation [*Sweden*] (EAIO) ..... CITUC
Council of Iron Foundry Associations ..... CFA
Council of Iron Producers [*British*] (BI) ..... CIP
Council of Jewish Federations (EA) ..... CJF
Council of Jewish Federations and Welfare Funds [*Later, CJF*] (EA) ..... CJFWF
Council of Jewish Organizations in Civil Service ..... CJO
Council of Jewish Organizations in Civil Service (EA) ..... CJOCS
Council of Jews from Germany [*British*] (EAIO) ..... CJG
Council of Justice to Animals and Humane Slaughter Association (EAIO) ..... CJA & HSA
Council of Landscape Architectural Registration Boards (EA) ..... CLARB
Council of Large Public Housing Authorities (EA) ..... CLPHA
Council of Law Reporting [*Australia*] ..... CLR
Council of Law Reporting of New South Wales [*Australia*] ..... CLRNSW
Council of Lebanese American Organizations (EA) ..... CLAO
Council of Legal Education [*British*] ..... CLE
Council of Library Association Executives (EA) ..... CLAE
Council of Life Insurance Consultants (EA) CLIC
Council of Literary Magazines and Presses (EA) ..... CLMP
Council of Local Education Authorities/School Teacher Committee (AIE) ..... CLEA/ST
Council of Logistics Management ..... CLM
Council of Lutheran Church Men [*Defunct*] (EA) ..... CLCM
Council of Maritime Premiers [*See also CPMM*] [*Canada*] ..... CMP
Council of Masajid of United States (EA) ..... CMUS
Council of Mechanical Specialty Contracting Industries [*Later, ASC*] (EA) ..... CMSCI
Council of Medical Specialty Societies (EA) ..... CMSS
Council of Medical Staffs (MEDA) ..... CMS
Council of Mennonite Colleges (EA) ..... CMC
Council of Michigan Foundations (SRA) ..... CMF
Council of Military Organization ..... COMO
Council of Mining and Metallurgical Institutions [*British*] (EAIO) ..... CMMI
Council of Ministers [*European Economic Commission*] (DLA) ..... COM
Council of Mortgage Lenders [*British*] (DBA) ..... CML
Council of Motion Picture Organizations [*Defunct*] (EA) ..... COMPO
Council of Motorcycle Clubs ..... CMC
Council of Music and Drama [*Queensland*] [*Australia*] ..... CMD
Council of Muslim Communities of Canada (EAIO) ..... CMMC
Council of Mutual Savings Institutions [*New York, NY*] (EA) ..... CMSI
Council of Name Studies [*British*] (DBA) ..... CNS
Council of National Library and Information Associations (EA) ..... CNLIA
Council of National Library Associations [*Later, CNLIA*] (EA) ..... CNLA
Council of National Organizations for Adult Education (EA) ..... CNO-AE
Council of National Organizations for Children and Youth [*Later, NCOCY*] (EA) ..... CNOCY
Council of National Representatives [*Of the International Council of Nurses*] (DAVI) ..... CNR
Council of Nature Conservation Ministers [*Australia*] ..... CNCM
Council of Nordic Master-Craftsmen [*Oslo, Norway*] (EAIO) ..... CNMC
Council of Nordic Teachers' Associations [*Copenhagen, Denmark*] (EAIO) ..... CNTA
Council of North Atlantic Shipping Associations [*Also, CONASA*] ..... CNASA
Council of North Atlantic Shipping Associations [*Also, CNASA*] ..... CONASA
Council of Nova Scotia Archives (AC) ..... CNSA
Council of Oil-Importing Nations ..... COIN
Council of Ontario Construction Associations (AC) ..... COCA
Council of Ontario Universities (EDAC) ..... COU
Council of Ontario Universities, Toronto, ON, Canada [*Library symbol Library of Congress*] (LCLS) ..... CaOTCOU
Council of Ontario Universities, Toronto, Ontario [*Library symbol National Library of Canada*] (NLC) ..... OTCOU
Council of Organizations Serving the Deaf [*Defunct*] (EA) ..... COSD
Council of Oriental Organizations ..... COO
Council of Outdoor Educators of Ontario (AC) ..... COEO
Council of Pennsylvania State College and University Library Directors [*Library network*] ..... COPSCAULD
Council of Petroleum Accountants Societies (EA) ..... COPAS
Council of Philatelic Organizations (EA) ..... COPO
Council of Planning Librarians (EA) ..... CPL
Council of Pollution Control Financing Agencies [*Defunct*] (EA) ..... CPCFA
Council of Polytechnic Librarians [*British*] (NITA) ..... COPOL
Council of Prairie & Pacific University Libraries [*Formerly, Council of Prairie University Libraries*] (AC) ..... COPPUL
Council of Presidents (EA) ..... CP
Council of Principals (AIE) ..... CP
Council of Professional Associations on Federal Statistics (EA) ..... COPAFS
Council of Professions, New South Wales [*Australia*] ..... CPNSW
Council of Profit Sharing Industries [*Later, PSCA*] (EA) ..... COPSI
Council of Progress Associations of Victoria [*Australia*] ..... CPAV
Council of Protestant Colleges and Universities [*Defunct*] (EA) ..... CPCU
Council of Protocol Executives (EA) ..... COPE
Council of Psychoanalytic Psychotherapists (EA) ..... CPP
Council of Public Education [*Victoria*] [*Australia*] ..... CPE
Council of Regional Groups [*Association for Library Collections and Technical Services*] ..... CRG
Council of Regional School Accrediting Commissions (EA) ..... CORSAC
Council of Registrars [*Internet group*] ..... CORE
Council of Rehabilitation Specialists (EA) ..... CRS
Council of Relief Agencies Licensed for Operation in Germany [*Post-World War II*] ..... CRALOG
Council of Religious Jewish Workers of America [*Defunct*] (EA) ..... CRJWA
Council of Repertory Theatres [*British*] ..... CORT
Council of Reprographics Executives [*Defunct*] (EA) ..... CORE
Council of Research and Academic Libraries [*Library network*] ..... CORAL
Council of Resident Summer Theatres [*Defunct*] (EA) ..... CORST
Council of Review Board [*Army*] ..... CRB
Council of Sales Promotion Agencies [*New York, NY*] (EA) ..... CSPA
Council of Savings and Loan Financial Corporations (EA) ..... CSLFC
Council of Scientific and Industrial Research [*Information service or system South Africa*] (IID) ..... CSIR
Council of Scientific Society Presidents (EA) ..... CSSP
Council of Scottish Clan Associations [*Later, COSCA*] (EA) ..... CSCA
Council Of Smaller Enterprises ..... COSE
Council of Social Science Data Archives [*Defunct*] ..... CSSDA
Council of Social Service [*British*] ..... CSS
Council of Social Service, Tasmania [*Australia*] ..... COSST
Council of Social Welfare Ministers, National Secretariat [*Australia*] ..... CSWMNS
Council of Societies for the Study of Religion (EA) ..... CSSR
Council of Societies in Dental Hypnosis [*Defunct*] (EA) ..... CSDH
Council of Specialized Accrediting Agencies [*Defunct*] (EA) ..... CSAA
Council of Spokane Area Libraries [*Library network*] ..... COSAL
Council of State Administrators of Vocational Rehabilitation (EA) ..... CSAVR
Council of State and Territorial Epidemiologists (EA) ..... CSTE
Council of State Chambers of Commerce (EA) ..... CSCC
Council of State Community Affairs Agencies (EA) ..... COSCAA
Council of State Governments (EA) ..... CSG
Council of State Governments, Lexington, KY [*OCLC symbol*] (OCLC) ..... KSC
Council of State Governments, State Information Center, Lexington, KY [*Library symbol Library of Congress*] (LCLS) ..... KyLxCS
Council of State Housing Agencies (EA) ..... CSHA
Council of State Policy and Planning Agencies [*Later, CGPA*] (EA) ..... CSPA
Council of State Science Supervisors (EA) ..... CSSS
Council of States [*An association*] ..... COS
Council of Stock Theatres ..... COST
Council of Student Personnel Associations in Higher Education [*Defunct*] ..... COSPA
Council of Subject Teaching Associations (AIE) ..... COSTA
Council of Subject Teaching Associations (AIE) ..... CSTA
Council of Teaching Hospitals (EA) ..... COTH
Council of Teaching Hospitals and Health Systems (DMAA) ..... COTH
Council of Technical Examining Bodies [*British*] ..... CTEB
Council of the Alleghenies (EA) ..... CA
Council of the Americas (EA) ..... CoA
Council of the Americas/Fund for Multinational Management Education ..... CoA/FMME
Council of the Brass and Bronze Ingot Industry (EA) ..... CBBII
Council of the City of Sydney ..... CCS
Council of the European Communities ..... CEC
Council of the Great City Schools (EA) ..... CGCS
Council of the Haida Nation (AC) ..... CHN
Council of the Knights of the Red Cross [*Freemasonry*] (ROG) ..... CKRC
Council of the Living Theatre [*Defunct*] (EA) ..... CLT
Council of the Museum of Victoria [*Australia*] ..... CMV
Council of the Organization of American States [*OAS*] ..... COAS
Council of the Printing Industries of Canada (HGAA) ..... CPI
Council of the Southern Mountains [*Defunct*] (EA) ..... CSM
Council of the State Library of Victoria [*Australia*] ..... CSLV
Council of the Thirteen Original States (EA) ..... CTOS
Council of the World Poultry [*British*] ..... CWP
Council of Tourism Associations of British Columbia [*Formerly, Tourism Industry Association of BC*] (AC) ..... COTA
Council of Travel and Tourism [*British*] (DBA) ..... CTT
Council of Tree and Landscape Appraisers (EA) ..... CTLA
Council of Underground Machinery Manufacturers [*British*] ..... CUMM
Council of United States Universities for Rural Development in India ..... CUSURDI
Council of United States Universities for Soil and Water Development in Arid andSub-Humid Areas ..... CUSUSWASH
Council of University Institutes for Urban Affairs [*Later, UAA*] (EA) ..... CUIUA
Council of University Teaching Hospitals [*Defunct*] (EA) ..... CUTH
Council of Urban Health Providers [*Defunct*] (EA) ..... CUHP
Council of Urban Rebuilding Enterprises ..... CURE
Council of Veteran, Vintage and Thoroughbred Motor Clubs [*Australia*] ..... CVVTMC
Council of Western European Union (IIA) ..... CWEU
Council of Wisconsin Libraries [*Information service or system*] (IID) ..... COWL
Council of Women Chiropractors [*Defunct*] (EA) ..... CWC
Council of Women Citizens ..... CWC
Council of World Organizations Interested in the Handicapped [*Later, ICOD*] (EA) ..... CWOIH
Council of Writers Organizations (EA) ..... CWO
Council of Young Israel Rabbis (EA) ..... CYIR
Council Officer [*British*] (ROG) ..... CO
Council on Accreditation of Nurse Anesthetists Educational Programs (PGP) ..... CANAEP

Council on Accreditation of Services for Families and Children (EA) .... COA
Council on Adoptable Children (EA) .... COAC
Council on Advanced Programming .... CAP
Council on Aging .... COA
Council on Alcohol Policy (EA) .... CAP
Council on Alternate Fuels (EA) .... CAF
Council on American-Islamic Relations .... CAIR
Council on America's Military Past (EA) .... CAMP
Council on Anthropology and Education (EA) .... CAE
Council on Anxiety Disorders (EA) .... CAD
Council on Arteriosclerosis of the American Heart Association (EA) .... CAAHA
Council on Atmospheric Sciences .... COAS
Council on Atmospheric Studies .... CAS
Council on Biological Sciences Information (DIT) .... CBSI
Council on Botanical and Horticultural Libraries (EA) .... CBHL
Council on Broadcast Education [*Later, CEEM*] (NTCM) .... COBE
Council on Career Development for Minorities (EA) .... CCDM
Council on Certification of Nurse Anesthetists (EA) .... CCNA
Council on Children, Media, and Merchandising (NTCM) .... CCMM
Council on Chiropractic Education (EA) .... CCE
Council on Chiropractic Orthopedics (EA) .... CCO
Council on Chiropractic Physiological Therapeutics (EA) .... CCPT
Council on Christian Unity (EA) .... CCU
Council on Clinical Classifications (HCT) CCC
Council on Clinical Optometric Care (EA) .... CCOC
Council on Competitiveness (EA) CC
Council on Competitiveness (EA) .... CoC
Council on Compulsive Gambling of New Jersey (EA) .... CCGNJ
Council on Consumer Information [*Later, ACCI*] (EA) CCI
Council on Cooperation in Teacher Education [*Defunct*] .... CCTE
Council on Cooperative College Projects [*Later, CCP*] (EA) .... CCCP
Council on Documentation Research [*Defunct*] .... CDR
Council on Drug Abuse [*Canada*] .... CODA
Council on Drug Abuse (AC) .... CODA
Council on Economic and Cultural Affairs [*Later, ADC*] [*Rockefeller Brothers Fund, Ford Foundation activity*] .... CECA
Council on Economic Policy [*Inactive*] .... CEP
Council on Economic Priorities (EA) .... CEP
Council on Economics and National Security [*Defunct*] (EA) .... CENS
Council on Education for Foreign Medical Graduates (BABM) .... CEFMG
Council on Education for Public Health (EA) .... CEPH
Council on Education in Professional Responsibility [*Later, CLEPR*] (EA) .... CEPR
Council on Education in the Geological Sciences .... CEGS
Council on Education of the American Medical Record Association (DAVI) .... COEAMRA
Council on Education of the Deaf (EA) .... CED
Council on Educational Finance [*National Education Association*] (AEBS) .... CEF
Council on Electrolysis Education (EA) .... CEE
Council on Employee Benefits (EA) .... CEB
Council on Energy Policy [*Proposed Presidential council*] .... CEP
Council on Engineering Laws [*Defunct*] (EA) .... CEL
Council on Environmental Alternatives (EA) .... CEA
Council on Environmental Pollutants .... CEP
Council on Environmental Quality [*of Federal Council on Science and Technology*] [*Washington, DC*] .... CEQ
Council on Environmental Remediation (AAGC) .... CER
Council on Family Health (EA) .... CFH
Council on Federal Health Programs (DMAA) .... CFHP
Council on Fertilizer Application [*Defunct*] .... CFA
Council on Fine Art Photography (EA) .... CFAP
Council on Foreign Economic Policy [*Functions transferred to Secretary of State, 1961*] .... CFEP
Council on Foreign Relations (EA) .... CFR
Council on Foreign Relations and Royal Institute of International Affairs [*British*] .... CFRRIIA
Council on Foreign Relations, New York, NY [*Library symbol Library of Congress*] (LCLS) .... NNCFR
Council on Forest Engineering (EA) .... COFE
Council on Foundations (EA) .... CF
Council on Foundations [*Formerly the National Committee on Foundations and Trusts for Community Welfare*] (NFD) .... COF
Council on Foundations, New York, NY [*Library symbol Library of Congress*] (LCLS) .... NNCFo
Council on Gift Annuities [*Informal name for the American Council on Gift Annuities*] (NFD) .... CGA
Council on Governmental Ethics Laws (EA) .... COGEL
Council on Governmental Relations (EA) .... COGR
Council on Graduate Medical Education [*Department of Health and Human Services*] .... COGME
Council on Graduate Medical Education .... COGME
Council on Health Information and Education (EA) .... CHIE
Council on Health Research for Development [*Switzerland*] (ECON) .... COHRED
Council on Hemispheric Affairs (EA) .... COHA
Council on Higher Education in the American Republics [*Later, ICHE*] .... CHEAR
Council on Homosexuality & Religion [*Conseil de l'Homosexualite et la Region*] (AC) .... CHR
Council on Hotel, Restaurant, and Institutional Education (EA) .... CHRIE
Council on International and Public Affairs Program (EA) .... CIPA
Council on International Cooperation in the Study and Utilization of Outer Spac e .... INTERCOSMOS
Council on International Economic Policy [*Terminated, 1977*] .... CIEP
Council on International Educational Exchange (EA) .... CIEE
Council on International Nontheatrical Events (EA) .... CINE
Council on International Scientific and Technological Cooperation .... CISTC
Council on Interracial Books for Children (EA) .... CIBC
Council on Islamic Affairs (EA) .... CIA
Council on Law Enforcement Education and Training [*An association*] .... CLEET
Council on Legal Education for Professional Responsibility (EA) .... CLEPR
Council on Legal Education Opportunity (EA) .... CLEO
Council on Library Resources (EA) .... CLR
Council on Library Technology (NITA) .... COLT
Council on Library-Media Technical-Assistants (EA) .... COLT
Council on Marine Resources and Engineering Development .... CMRED
Council on Medical Education - of the American Medical Association (EA) .... CME-AMA
Council on Medical Television [*Later, HESCA*] (EA) .... CMT
Council on Mind Abuse [*Canada*] .... COMA
Council on Multiemployer Pension Security [*Defunct*] (EA) .... COMPS
Council on Municipal Performance .... CMP
Council on Municipal Performance [*Defunct*] (EA) .... COMP
Council on National Literatures (EA) .... CNL
Council on Naturopathic Medicine (PGP) .... CNME
Council on Nutritional Anthropology (EA) .... CNA
Council on Occupational Licensing [*Later, NCOL*] (EA) .... COL
Council on Ocean Law (EA) .... COL
Council on Oceanograhic Laboratory Directors [*Marine science*] (OSRA) .... COLD
Council on Oceanographic Laboratory Directors (USDC) .... COLD
Council on Optical Radiation Measurement .... CORM
Council on Optometric Education (EA) .... COE
Council on Peace Research in History (EA) .... CPRH
Council on Plastics and Packaging in the Environment (EA) .... COPPE
Council on Podiatric Medical Education (EA) .... CPME
Council on Podiatry Education [*Later, CPME*] (EA) .... CPE
Council on Population and Environment (EA) .... COPE
Council on Postal Suppression .... COPS
Council on Postsecondary Accreditation (EA) .... COPA
Council on Postsecondary Accreditation (DAVI) .... CPA
Council on Professional Certification (EA) .... CPC
Council on Professional Standards in Speech-Language Pathology and Audiology (EA) .... COPS
Council on Rehabilitation Education (PGP) .... CORE
Council on Rehabilitation Education (EA) .... CRE
Council on Religion and International Affairs [*Later, CCEIA*] (EA) .... CRIA
Council on Religion and Law [*Defunct*] (EA) .... CORAL
Council on Religion and the Homosexual [*Defunct*] (EA) .... CRH
Council on Research and Technology (EA) .... CORETECH
Council on Research in Bibliography, Inc. (DIT) .... CRB
Council on Resident Education in Obstetrics and Gynecology (EA) .... CREOG
Council on Roentgenology of the American Chiropractic Association (EA) .... CRACA
Council on School Administration [*Canada*] (AEBS) .... CSA
Council on Size and Weight Discrimination (EA) .... CSWD
Council on Social Work Education (EA) .... CSWE
Council on Soil Testing and Plant Analysis (EA) .... CSTPA
Council on Southern Africa (EA) .... CSA
Council on Standards for International Educational Travel (EA) .... CSIET
Council on Student Travel [*Later, CIEE*] (EA) .... CST
Council on Superconductivity for American Competitiveness .... CSAC
Council on Synthetic Fuels (EA) .... CSF
Council on Tall Buildings and Urban Habitat (EA) .... CTBUH
Council on Technology Teacher Education (EA) .... CTTE
Council on Thai Studies .... COTS
Council on the Aging, New South Wales [*Australia*] .... COTANSW
Council on the Continuing Education Unit [*Later, IACET*] (EA) .... CCEU
Council on the Study of Religion (EA) .... CSR
Council on Undergraduate Research (EA) .... CUR
Council on Wage and Price Stability [*Also, CWPS*] [*Abolished, 1981*] .... COWPS
Council on Wage and Price Stability [*Also, COWPS*] [*Abolished, 1981*] .... CWPS
Council on Women and the Church [*Later, JFW*] (EA) .... COWAC
Council on World Tensions [*Later, Institute on Man and Science*] (EA) .... CWT
Council on Youth Opportunity [*Disbanded 1971; functions taken over by Domestic Council and OMB*] .... CYO
Council Operations and Exercise Committee [*NATO*] .... COEC
Council Recycling Debate [*Australia*] .... CRR
Council Rock High School, Newtown, PA [*Library symbol Library of Congress*] (LCLS) .... PNtC
Council Situation Room [*NATO*] (NATG) .... CSR
Council to Save the Postcard [*Defunct*] (EA) .... CSP
Counciling .... CNCLNG
Councillor (ROG) C
Councillor .... CLLR
Councillor (ODBW) .... Cllr
Councillor (ADA) .... CLR
Councillor .... CNCLR
Councillor (ROG) .... COR
Councillor (ADA) .... CR
Councilor (ABBR) .... CNCLR
Counsel [*or Counseling or Counselor*] (AFM) .... CNSL
Counsel .... CNSL
Counsel .... COL
Counsel .... COUN
Counsel (ROG) .... CSL
Counsel and Care for the Elderly [*British*] .... CCE
Counsel Corp. [*Associated Press*] (SAG) .... Counsl
Counsel Corp. [*Toronto Stock Exchange symbol*] .... CXS
Counsel Corp. [*NASDAQ symbol*] (SAG) .... CXSN
Counsel Corp. [*NASDAQ symbol*] (TTSB) .... CXSNF
Counsel for Procurement Reform (AAGC) .... CPR
Counseling .... CNSLNG

Counseling and Assistance Center [*Military*] (NVT) ... CAAC
Counseling and Assistance Director [*Military*] (DNAB) ... CAAD
Counseling and Human Services Specialist (PGP) ... CHSS
Counseling and Personnel Services [*Educational Resources Information Center*] [*Information retrieval*] (AEBS) ... CAPS
Counseling and Student Services [*Educational Resources Information Center (ERIC) Clearinghouse*] [*University of North Carolina at Greensboro*] (PAZ) ... CG
Counseling and Testing Site ... CTS
Counseling at the Local Level [*Small Business Administration*] ... CALL
Counseling Effectiveness Rating Scale (EDAC) ... CERS
Counseling Practice Beliefs Inventory (EDAC) ... CPBI
Counseling Satisfaction Inventory [*Education*] ... CSI
Counseling Services Assessment Blank [*Test for counseling centers*] ... CSAB
Counseling-Orientation Preference Scale (EDAC) ... COS
Counselling and Career Development Organisation [*British*] (AIE) ... CCDO
Counselling Assistance to Small Enterprises [*Canada*] ... CASE
Counsellor ... Cnsllr
Counsellor ... CNSLLR
Counsellor of the Incorporated Society of Organ Builders [*British*] (DI) ... CISOB
Counsellors' Magazine [*1796-98*] [*A publication*] (DLA) ... Couns Mag
Counsellors Tandem [*NYSE symbol*] (SPSG) ... CTF
Counsellors Tandem [*NYSE symbol*] (TTSB) ... CTF
Counsellors Tandem Securities Fund [*Associated Press*] (SAG) ... CTF
Counselor ... CNSLNR
Counselor ... COUNS
Counselor Activity Inventory [*Guidance*] ... CAI
Counselor Advisor University Summer Education [*Department of Labor program*] ... CAUSE
Counselor Association (EA) ... CA
Counselor Behavior Evaluation Form (EDAC) ... CBE
Counselor Interview Competence Scale (EDAC) ... CICS
Counselor Structured ... CS
Counselor-in-Training [*for summer camps*] ... CIT
Count ... C
Count ... CNT
Count ... CT
Count Back Order and Sample Select [*Computer science*] ... CBOSS
Count Clock [*NASA*] (KSC) ... CTCL
Count - Double Count (MUGU) ... CDC
Count Down ... C/D
Count Dracula Fan Club (EA) ... CDFC
Count Dracula Society (EA) ... CDS
Count Forward [*Computer science*] ... CF
Count Median Diameter (MAE) ... CMD
Count on Losing this Sunday [*Humorous interpretation of NFL team name*] ... COLTS
Count per Minute (MSA) ... CT/M
Count per Second (MSA) ... CT/S
Count Rate Meter ... CRM
Count Reduction Technique [*Food bacteriology*] ... CRT
Count Register [*Computer science*] ... CX
Count Reverse [*Computer science*] ... CR
Count Routine Applied to Zero Input [*Computer program*] ... CRAZI
Count Strength Product ... CSP
Count/Time Data System (IEEE) ... C/TDS
Countdown [*Aerospace*] (AAG) ... CD
Countdown [*Credit card*] [*British*] ... CD
Countdown [*NASA*] (KSC) ... CTDN
Countdown and Status Receiving Station [*or System*] [*NASA*] (KSC) ... CASRS
Countdown and Status Transmission System [*NASA*] (KSC) ... CASTS
Countdown Clock [*Aerospace*] ... CDC
Countdown Demonstration Test [*NASA*] ... CDDT
Countdown Demonstration Test [*NASA*] ... CDT
Countdown Deviation Request [*Aerospace*] (AAG) ... CDR
Countdown Modification Request [*Aerospace*] (AAG) ... CMR
Countdown Sequence Timer [*Aerospace*] (IAA) ... CST
Countdown Time [*Aerospace*] ... CDT
Countdown Working Group [*NASA*] (KSC) ... CDWG
Counted Thread Society of America (EA) ... CTSA
Counter ... C
Counter (MDG) ... CNT
Counter (MSA) ... CNTR
Counter ... CNTR
Counter ... CT
Counter (KSC) ... CTR
Counter (WDMC) ... ctr
Counter Accelerometer Unit (MCD) ... CAU
Counter Air (MCD) ... CA
Counter Air Operations Center (DNAB) ... CAOC
Counter Angle Deception Jammer [*Military*] (CAAL) ... CADJ
Counter Anti-Submarine Warfare (PDAA) ... CASW
Counter Artillery and Mortar RADAR Acquisition Simulation (MCD) ... CAMRAS
Counter Battery ... CB
Counter Battery Staff Officer [*World War I*] [*Canada*] ... CBSO
Counter Bombardment [*British military*] (DMA) ... CB
Counter Control [*Military*] ... CNCT
Counter/Counter-Countermeasure [*Military*] ... C/CCM
Counter Current Flow Limit [*Nuclear energy*] ... CCFL
Counter Display Unit (MCD) ... CDU
Counter Electromotive Cell ... CEM
Counter Electromotive Cell (MCD) ... CEMC
Counter Electromotive Force (MCD) ... CEMF
Counter Filling System ... CFS
Counter Flip-Flop [*Computer science*] ... CFF
Counter Force (MCD) ... CF
Counter Improvised Nuclear Device Emergency Response [*British*] ... CINDER
Counter Infiltration - Counter Guerilla Concept and Requirement Plan (CINC) ... CIGCOREP
Counter Information Services [*British*] ... CIS
Counter Intelligence Center Corps School, Fort Holabird, Baltimore, MD [*Library symbol Library of Congress*] (LCLS) ... MdBCIC
Counter Intelligence, Combat [*World War II*] ... CIC
Counter Logic (IAA) ... CL
Counter, n Stages [*Electronics*] (DEN) ... CT/N
Counter Position Exit (IAA) ... CPE
Counter Recoil-Operated Weapon Launcher [*Military*] (VNW) ... CROW
Counter Recovery Time ... CRT
Counter Register ... CR
Counter Rotation (PDAA) ... CR
Counter Shift Register [*Computer science*] (IAA) ... CSR
Counter Technical Intelligence Activities (MCD) ... CTIA
Counter Tenor [*Music*] ... CTEN
Counter Timer ... CT
Counter/Timer Circuit [*Computer science*] ... CTC
Counter Tube [*Electronics*] (IAA) ... CT
Counter Voltage ... CV
Counteracting Chromatographic Electrophoresis ... CACE
Counter-Agency for Sabotage and Espionage [*Military*] (DNAB) ... CASE
Counter-Air and Interdiction ... CAINT
Counter-Assault Tactical [*In television movie "C.A.T. Squad"*] ... CAT
Counterattack ... C/A
Counterattack (AABC) ... CATK
Counterbalance (KSC) ... CBAL
Counterbattery ... CBTRY
Counter-Battery Fire ... CBF
Counterbattery Intelligence Officer [*Army*] (AABC) ... CBIO
Counter-Battery Officer ... CBO
Counterbattery RADAR [*Military*] ... COBRA
Counterbore (KSC) ... CBORE
Counterbore Arbor [*Tool*] ... CBAR
Counterbore Cutter [*Tool*] (AAG) ... CBCU
Counterbore Other Side ... CBOREO
Counter-C^3 [*Command, Control, and Communications*] [*Pronounced "see-see-cubed"*] ... CC^3
Counterclaim [*Legal shorthand*] (LWAP) ... C/CL
Counterclaim [*Legal term*] (ROG) ... COCLM
Counterclaim [*Legal term*] (DLA) ... COUNTCL
Counterclaim [*Legal term*] (ROG) ... CTRCLM
Counterclockwise ... CC
Counterclockwise (WGA) ... CCKW
Counterclockwise (FAAC) ... CCLKWS
Counterclockwise ... CCW
Counterclockwise (IDOE) ... ccw
Counterclockwise ... CNTCLKWS
Counterclockwise (AFM) ... CNTCLKWZ
Counterclockwise Bottom Angular Down (OA) ... CCWBAD
Counterclockwise Bottom Angular Up (OA) ... CCWBAU
Counterclockwise Bottom Horizontal (OA) ... CCWBH
Counterclockwise Down Blast (OA) ... CCWDB
Counterclockwise Orbit [*Aviation*] (FAAC) ... CCLKOB
Counterclockwise Top Angular Down (OA) ... CCWTAD
Counterclockwise Top Angular Up (OA) ... CCWTAU
Counterclockwise Top Horizontal (OA) ... CCWTH
Counterclockwise Up Blast (OA) ... CCWUB
Counter-Countermeasures [*Military*] ... CCM
Countercurrent ... CC
Countercurrent Chromatography ... CCC
Countercurrent Cooling Crystallization [*Tsukishima Kikai Co., Tokyo*] [*Chemical engineering*] ... CCCC
Countercurrent Decantation [*Engineering*] ... CCD
Countercurrent Digestion [*Ore leach process*] ... CCD
Countercurrent Distribution [*Analytical chemistry*] ... CCD
Countercurrent Electrophoresis [*Also, CE*] [*Analytical chemistry*] ... CCE
Countercurrent Electrophoresis [*Also, CCE*] [*Analytical chemistry*] ... CE
Countercurrent Electrophoresis [*Analytical chemistry*] (DAVI) ... CEP
Countercurrent Immunoelectrophoresis (PDAA) ... CCIE
Countercurrent Immunoelectrophoresis [*Immunology*] (DAVI) ... CIE
Counter-Double-Current Distribution [*Analytical chemistry*] ... CDCD
Counterdrill ... CDRILL
Counterdrill Other Side ... CDRILLO
Counterelectrophoresis [*Analytical chemistry*] ... CEP
Counterespionage ... CE
Counterfeit [*FBI standardized term*] ... CTFT
Counterfeiting (DLA) ... COUNTERF
Counterfeiting [*FBI standardized term*] ... CTFG
Counterfeiting Intelligence Bureau [*International Chamber of Commerce*] [*British*] (CB) ... CIB
Counterfire [*Military*] (AFM) ... CF
Counterfire and Air Defense (MCD) ... CF & AD
Counterfire Reference Grid (AABC) ... CRG
Counterflashing [*Technical drawings*] ... CFL
Counterflashing (MSA) ... CFLG
Counterflow Centrifugal Elutriation [*Analytical biochemistry*] ... CCE
Counterflow Film Cooling ... CFFC
Counterflow Reactor [*Chemical engineering*] ... CFR
Counterflow Virtual Impactor [*Instrumentation*] ... CVI
Counterimmunoelectrophoresis [*Also, CIEP*] [*Analytical biochemistry*] ... CIE
Counterimmunoelectrophoresis [*Also, CIE*] [*Analytical biochemistry*] ... CIEP
Countering Attack Helicopter (MCD) ... CATCH
Counterinsurgency (CINC) ... CI

Counterinsurgency (AABC)	CINSGCY
Counterinsurgency	COIN
Counterinsurgency Operations	COINOPS
Counterinsurgency Plan (CINC)	CIP
Counterinsurgency Research and Development System (MCD)	CIRADS
Counterinsurgency Support Office [Army] (VNW)	CSO
Counterinsurgency/Survival, Evasion, Resistance, and Escape (DNAB)	CI/SERE
Counterintelligence (MCD)	CI
Counterintelligence Analysis Division [DoD]	CIAD
Counterintelligence and Investigative Activities [Military]	C & IA
Counterintelligence Corps [Military]	CIC
Counterintelligence Group [Military]	CIG
Counterintelligence Interrogation Center [Military]	CIIC
Counterintelligence Periodic Summary (MCD)	CIPS
Counterintelligence Program [FBI program carried out against political activists from 1956 to 1971]	COINTELPRO
Counterintelligence Records Information System [Army]	CRIS
Counterintelligence Team (NVT)	CIT
Counterintelligence Working Party [US Military Government, Germany]	CIWP
Counter-Lock-Cord [Tennis shoe technology] [Autry Industries, Inc.]	CLC
Countermarked	CM
Countermeasure	CM
Countermeasure Office [of Harry Diamond Laboratories] [Military] (RDA)	CMO
Countermeasures (AABC)	CTMS
Countermeasures [JETDS nomenclature]	L
Countermeasures, Airborne Infrared	CAIR
Countermeasures and Deception [RADAR]	CM & D
Countermeasures and Test Directorate [Army] (RDA)	CMTD
Countermeasures/Counter Countermeasures [Army] (RDA)	CM/CCM
Countermeasures Dispenser (MCD)	CMD
Countermeasures Dispenser Set (MCD)	CDS
Countermeasures Dispenser Set (MCD)	CMDS
Countermeasures Evaluation (CAAL)	CME
Countermeasures Evaluation - Infrared and Optical	CERFIRO
Countermeasures Homing (CET)	CMH
Countermeasures Internal Management System (PDAA)	CIMS
Countermeasures Launcher Modular System [Navy] (CAAL)	CLAMS
Countermeasures Penetrating Antiarmor Munitions (MCD)	CPAM
Countermeasures Receiving Set	CRS
Countermeasures Receiving System	CMRS
Countermeasures Set (MCD)	CMS
Countermeasures Set, Acoustic (NVT)	CSA
Countermeasures Subsystem (DWSG)	CMS
Countermilitary Potential	CMP
Countermine/Counterintrusion Department [Army] (RDA)	CCID
Countermission Analysis (MCD)	CMA
Countermortar	CM
Countermortar Fire	CMF
Countermortar RADAR	CMR
Counternarcotics [Military] (DOMA)	CN
Counternarcotics Command Management System [Army] (RDA)	CN/CMS
Counternarcotics Command Management System [Army] (RDA)	CN/CMS
Counter-Obstacle Team [Army] (INF)	COT
Counter-Obstacle Vehicle [Military] (RDA)	COV
Counteroffer [Legal shorthand] (LWAP)	C/OFF
Counter-Operating Voltage	COV
Counterpart	COPART
Counterpart (ROG)	COPT
Counterpart [Legal term] (ROG)	CTRPT
Counterpoint [Music] (ROG)	COPT
Counterpoint [Music]	CP
Counterpoint [Music]	CPT
Counterpoise [Electricity] (IAA)	CP
Counterpoise (MSA)	CPSE
Counterpoise Antenna (IAA)	CA
Counter-Propaganda Directorate [British]	CPD
Counterpunch (KSC)	CPUNCH
Counter-Racism, Equal Opportunity [Military] (NVT)	CREO
CounterRADAR Measures	CRM
CounterRADAR Missile	CRM
Counterreconnaissance [Army] (IAA)	CRCN
Counterreconnaissance [Army]	CRECON
Counter-Revolutionary Warfare [British military] (DMA)	CRW
Counter-Revolutionary Wing [Special Air Service] [Military British]	CRW
Counter-Rotating Optical Wedge	CROW
Counter-Rotation [or Rotating] Platform (MHDB)	CRP
Counter-Sabotage (AABC)	CS
Countershaft [Automotive engineering]	CO/SHFT
Countershaft (MSA)	CTSHFT
Countershocks	CS
Countersink (WGA)	CK
Countersink [Technical drawings]	CS
Countersink [Engineering] (IAA)	CSINK
Countersink (KSC)	CSK
Countersink Cutter	CSCU
Countersink Other Side	CSKO
Countersink Other Side	Csk-OS
Countersniper Team [Army] (INF)	CST
Counterstamped [Numismatics]	CS
Countersunk	CTSK
Countersunk Head	CSKH
Countersurge Missile Mortar System (MCD)	COSMMOS
Countersurge Mortar System (MCD)	COSMOS
Counter-Target-Acquisition (MCD)	CTA

Counter-Targeting [Navy] (DOMA)	CTTG
Counter-Tenor [Music]	C
Countertenor [Music]	CT
Counterterrorist (ADA)	CT
Counterterrorist Joint Task Force [Military]	CTJTF
Counter-Terrorist Warfare (LAIN)	CTW
Counter-Timer Control	CTC
Countertrade [Economics] (IMH)	CT
Countervailing Duty [Customs] (FEA)	CVD
Counterweight (AAG)	C/W
Counterweight [Automotive engineering]	C/WT
Counterweight	CNTRWT
Counterweight (AAG)	CTW
Counterweight (KSC)	CTWT
Countess	CTS
Countess	CTSS
Counties (Wales)	CW
Counting (KSC)	CTG
Counting Device	CD
Counting Fingers [Also, FC]	CF
Counting Switch	CS
Count-Key-Data Device [Computer science]	CKD
Countries and Peoples [A publication]	CP
Countries of the World [A publication]	CW
Countries of the World and Their Leaders Yearbook [A publication]	COW
Country	C
Country	CNTRY
Country	CO
Country (ROG)	COU
Country (VRA)	ctry
Country [Online database field identifier]	CY
Country Analysis Strategy Paper [Bureau of Inter-American Affairs] [Department of State]	CASP
Country and New Town Properties [British]	CNTP
Country and Regional Specialist [Navy] (MCD)	CARS
Country and Western [Music]	C & W
Country, Area, or Regional Staff Officer [Military] (DNAB)	CARSO
Country Assistance Strategy Statement [Military] (CINC)	CASS
Country Bill [Banking]	CB
Country, Bluegrass, Blues [New York nightclub] [Later, CMGB & OMFUG]	CBGB
Country, Bluegrass, Blues, and Other Music for Uplifting Gourmandizers [Formerly, CBGB] [New York nightclub] (EA)	CNGB & OMFUG
Country Bound Connection [An association] (EA)	CBC
Country Bread Manufacturers' Association [Western Australia] [Australia]	CBMA
Country Bread Manufacturers of Western Australia	CBMWA
Country Centres Project [Australia]	CCP
Country Cheque [Banking] [British]	CC
Country Clearing	CC
Country Clearing Office	CCO
Country Club	CC
Country Club Hills Public Library District, Country Club Hills, IL [Library symbol Library of Congress] (LCLS)	ICch
Country Club Hills Public Library District, Country Club Hills, IL [Library symbol] [Library of Congress] (LCLS)	ICchP
Country Club Hotels [British]	CCH
Country Code (AFM)	CC
Country Connection [Airline code] [Australia]	XL
Country Dance and Song Society of America (EA)	CDSSA
Country Dance Society of America [Later, CDSSA] (EA)	CDSA
Country Day School Headmasters Association of the US (EA)	CDSHA
Country Development Strategy Statement [Agency for International Development]	CDSS
Country Economic Profiles [I. P. Sharp Association Pty. Ltd.] [Australia Information service or system] (CRD)	CEP
Country Edition Fan Club [Defunct] (EA)	CEFC
Country Fire Fan Club (EA)	CFFC
Country Gentlemen's Association [British]	CGA
Country Grammar School [British]	CGS
Country Handbooks [A publication]	CH
Country Indicator Code [Computer science] (ACRL)	CIC
Country Information Package (MCD)	CIP
Country Intelligence Study (MCD)	CIS
Country Joe and His All Star Band [Pop music group]	CJASB
Country Joe and the Fish [Pop music group]	CJF
Country Landowners' Association [British]	CLA
Country Liberal Party [Australia] (ADA)	CLP
Country Life Library of Sport [A publication]	CLLS
Country Living [A publication]	CL
Country Logistics Improvement Program [Air Force]	CLIP
Country Mayors' Association [New South Wales] [Australia]	CMA
Country Meatworks Association of New South Wales [Australia]	CMANSW
Country Music [Radio station format] (WDMC)	c
Country Music Association (EA)	CMA
Country Music Disk Jockeys Association [Defunct] (EA)	CMDJA
Country Music Fan Club [Defunct] (EA)	CMFC
Country Music Foundation (EA)	CMF
Country Music Foundation Library and Media Center, Nashville, TN [Library symbol Library of Congress] (LCLS)	TNC
Country Music Guild of Australasia [Australia]	CMGA
Country Music Showcase International (EA)	CMSI
Country Music Television [Cable-television system] (WDMC)	CMT
Country Music Television [Cable-television system]	CMTV
Country Name [Database terminology] (NITA)	CN

Country National Party [*Political party Australia*] ... CN
Country Nationalist Party [*Australia Political party*] ... CNP
Country of Destination [*International trade*] (DCTA) ... COD
Country of Origin [*International trade*] (DCTA) ... COO
Country Party [*Political party*] [*Australia*] (BARN) ... CP
Country Policy Programme [*Foreign trade*] [*British*] ... CPP
Country Press Association (DGA) ... CPA
Country Press Association of New South Wales [*Australia*] ... CPANSW
Country Press Association of South Australia ... CPASA
Country Press Association of Western Australia ... CPAWA
Country Profile (ADA) ... CP
Country Progressive National Party [*Australia Political party*] ... CPN
Country Public Libraries Association, New South Wales [*Australia*] ... CPLANSW
Country Radio Broadcasters (EA) ... CRB
Country Regional Councils' Association of Western Australia ... CRCAWA
Country Representative ... CR
Country Representative/Freight Forwarder (AAGC) ... CR/FF
Country Shires Association of Western Australia ... CSAWA
Country Standard Technical Order (MCD) ... CSTO
Country Star Rest Cv'A' Pfd [*NASDAQ symbol*] (TTSB) ... CAFEP
Country Star Restaurants [*NASDAQ symbol*] (TTSB) ... CAFE
Country Star Restaurants, Inc. [*NASDAQ symbol*] (SAG) ... CAFE
Country Star Restaurants, Inc. [*Associated Press*] (SAG) ... CtryStr
Country Support Team [*United Nations*] ... CST
Country Team [*Military*] (CINC) ... CT
Country Whence Consigned [*Shipping*] (DS) ... CWC
Country Wide Trans Svcs [*NASDAQ symbol*] (TTSB) ... CWTS
Country Wide Transport Services, Inc. [*Associated Press*] (SAG) ... CtryWTr
Country Wide Transport Services, Inc. [*NASDAQ symbol*] (SAG) ... CWTS
Country Women's Association ... CWA
Country Women's Council USA (EA) ... CWC
Country Wool Merchants Association [*British*] (BI) ... CWMA
Country Workshops, Inc. [*An association*] (EA) ... CWI
CountryBaskets [*Associated Press*] (SAG) ... CB
CountryBaskets [*NYSE symbol*] (SAG) ... GXA
CountryBaskets [*NYSE symbol*] (SAG) ... GXF
CountryBaskets [*NYSE symbol*] (SAG) ... GXG
CountryBaskets [*NYSE symbol*] (SAG) ... GXH
CountryBaskets [*NYSE symbol*] (SAG) ... GXI
CountryBaskets [*NYSE symbol*] (SAG) ... GXJ
CountryBaskets [*NYSE symbol*] (SAG) ... GXK
CountryBaskets [*NYSE symbol*] (SAG) ... GXR
CountryBaskets [*NYSE symbol*] (SAG) ... GXU
Countrybkts Australia Index Fd [*NYSE symbol*] (TTSB) ... GXA
Countrybkts France Index Fd [*NYSE symbol*] (TTSB) ... GXF
Countrybkts Germany Index Fd [*NYSE symbol*] (TTSB) ... GXG
Countrybkts Hong Kong Index Fd [*NYSE symbol*] (TTSB) ... GXH
Countrybkts Italy Index Fd [*NYSE symbol*] (TTSB) ... GXI
Countrybkts Japan Index Fd [*NYSE symbol*] (TTSB) ... GXJ
Countrybkts S.Africa Index Fd [*NYSE symbol*] (TTSB) ... GXR
Countrybkts UK Index Fd [*NYSE symbol*] (TTSB) ... GXK
Countrybkts US Index Fd [*NYSE symbol*] (TTSB) ... GXU
[*The*] **Country's Best Yogurt** [*Store franchise*] ... TCBY
Countryside ... CNTRYSD
Countryside Act [*Town planning*] [*British*] ... CA
Countryside Commission [*British*] ... CC
Countryside Commission for Scotland ... CCS
Countryside Recreation Research Advisory Group [*British*] ... CRRAG
Countrywide [*ICAO designator*] (AD) ... MB
Countrywide Credit Indus [*NYSE symbol*] (TTSB) ... CCR
Countrywide Credit Industries, Inc. [*NYSE symbol*] (SPSG) ... CCR
Countrywide Credit Industries, Inc. [*Associated Press*] (SAG) ... CntCrd
Countrywide Holidays Association [*British*] (DBA) ... CHA
Countrywood Elementary School, Huntington Station, NY [*Library symbol*] [*Library of Congress*] (LCLS) ... NHsCE
Counts Palatine [*Rulers of historical region now part of Germany*] ... CO PAL
Counts per Hour ... CPH
Counts Per Inch (CDE) ... cpi
Counts per Minute ... C/M
Counts per Minute ... C/MIN
Counts per Minute ... CPM
Counts per Minute (IDOE) ... NPM
Counts per Second (NASA) ... C/S
Counts per Second (DEN) ... CPS
Counts per Second (IDOE) ... NPS
Countway Library of Medicine, Boston, MA [*Library symbol Library of Congress*] (LCLS) ... MBCo
County ... C
County (WDMC) ... c/o
County ... CNTY
County (EY) ... CO
County (VRA) ... co
County ... CT
County [*Board on Geographic Names*] ... CTY
County ... CY
County Agricultural Committee (BARN) ... CAC
County Air Services Ltd. [*British ICAO designator*] (FAAC) ... CAK
County Alderman [*British*] ... CA
County and City Data Book [*Bureau of the Census*] (GFGA) ... CCDB
County & Regional Municipality Librarians of Ontario (AC) ... CARML
County Architect [*British*] ... CA
County Architects Society [*British*] (BI) ... CAS
County Attorney ... CA
County Bank of Chesterfield [*Associated Press*] (SAG) ... CBChest
County Bank of Chesterfield [*NASDAQ symbol*] (SAG) ... CBDC
County Bank of Chesterfield [*NASDAQ symbol*] (TTSB) ... CBOC
County Borough ... CB
County Borough Council [*British*] (ROG) ... CBC
County Borough of Wigan Public Libraries, Central Library, Wigan, United Kingdom [*Library symbol Library of Congress*] (LCLS) ... UkWg
County Boundary File [*Bureau of the Census*] (GFGA) ... CBF
County Business Patterns [*Bureau of the Census*] [*Information service or system A publication*] ... CBP
County Chasers of America (EA) ... CCA
County Circuit [*As in "CC Rider," i.e., a traveling preacher*] ... CC
County Clerk [*British*] (ROG) ... CC
County College of Morris, Dover, NJ [*Library symbol*] [*Library of Congress*] (LCLS) ... NjDC
County Commissioner ... CC
County Commissioners Association of Ohio (SRA) ... CCAO
County Commissioners Association of Pennsylvania (SRA) ... CCAP
County Constituency [*British*] ... CC
County Council [*or Councillor*] [*British*] ... CC
County Council [*British*] (ROG) ... CO COUNC
County Council Cases [*Scotland*] [*A publication*] (DLA) ... County Cc Cas
County Council Cases [*Scotland*] [*A publication*] (DLA) ... County Co Cas
County Councils Association [*British*] (BI) ... CCA
County Counseling Center [*Psychology*] (DAVI) ... CCC
County Court ... CC
County Court Appeals [*A publication*] (DLA) ... CCA
County Court Cases [*England*] [*A publication*] (DLA) ... Co Ct Cas
County Court Judge (DLA) ... CCJ
County Court Practice (ILCA) ... CCP
County Court Reports [*Pennsylvania*] [*A publication*] (DLA) ... Co Ct Rep (PA)
County Court Rules (ILCA) ... CCR
County Courts [*Legal*] [*British*] ... COCTS
County Courts and Bankruptcy Cases [*A publication*] (DLA) ... County Cts & Bankr Cas
County Courts Chronicle [*1847-1920*] [*England*] [*A publication*] (DLA) ... C Cts Chr
County Courts Chronicle [*1847-1920*] [*England*] ... CCCHRON
County Courts Chronicle [*1847-1920*] [*England*] [*A publication*] (DLA) ... Co Ct Ch
County Courts Chronicle [*1847-1920*] [*England*] [*A publication*] (DLA) ... Co Ct Chr
County Courts Chronicle [*1847-1920*] [*England*] [*A publication*] (DLA) ... Count Cts Ch
County Courts Chronicle [*1847-1920*] [*England*] [*A publication*] (DLA) ... Count Cts Chron
County Courts Chronicle [*1847-1920*] [*England*] [*A publication*] (DLA) ... County Cts Chron
County Courts Chronicle [*1847-1920*] [*England*] [*A publication*] (DLA) ... Cty Ct Chron
County Courts Reporter [*in Law Journal*] [*London*] [*A publication*] (DLA) ... CC Rep
County Courts Reports [*1860-1920*] [*England*] [*A publication*] (DLA) ... CCR
County Courts Reports [*1860-1920*] [*England*] [*A publication*] (DLA) ... Co Ct R
County Courts Reports [*1860-1920*] [*England*] [*A publication*] (DLA) ... Co Ct Rep
County Courts Reports [*1860-1920*] [*England*] [*A publication*] (DLA) ... County Cts Rep
County Courts Reports [*1860-1920*] [*England*] [*A publication*] (DLA) ... Cty Ct R
County/Coverage Service [*ISI audience data*] (NTCM) ... C/CS
County Education District ... CED
County Education Officers' Society [*British*] ... CEOS
County Emergency Planning Officers Society [*British*] ... CEPO
County Engineers Association of Ohio (SRA) ... CEAO
County Extension Service [*Agriculture*] ... CES
County Intermediate Unit Superintendents [*of NEA*] [*Later, AASA*] (EA) ... CIUS
County Law Enforcement Applied Regionally ... CLEAR
County Links Access to Information about Resources and Expertise [*Education*] (AIE) ... CLAIRE
County Londonderry [*Northern Ireland*] ... CO DERRY
County of Carleton Law Library, Ottawa, Ontario [*Library symbol National Library of Canada*] (NLC) ... OOCCL
County of Henrico Public Library, Richmond, VA [*OCLC symbol*] (OCLC) ... VHP
County of London Regiment (Volunteers) [*British military*] (DMA) ... CLRV
County of Los Angeles Public Library ... CoLAPL
County of Strathcona Library, Sherwood Park, AB, Canada [*Library symbol Library of Congress*] (LCLS) ... CaASpS
County of Strathcona Library, Sherwood Park, Alberta [*Library symbol National Library of Canada*] (NLC) ... ASPS
County Office Manager ... COM
County Placita [*British*] (ROG) ... CO PLAC
County Registrars Office (BARN) ... CRO
County Reports [*A publication*] (DLA) ... County R
County Road Safety Officers' Association [*British*] (DBA) ... CRSOA
County Statistics [*Bureau of the Census*] (GFGA) ... CO-STAT
County Surveyors Society [*British*] (DCTA) ... CSS
Couny ... CNT
Coup sur Coup [*In Small Doses at Short Intervals*] [*French*] ... CSC
Coupe [*Automotive*] ... CP
Coupe ... CP
Coupe [*Automotive*] (WGA) ... CPE
Coupe Automatic [*Model designation of an automobile*] ... CA
Coupe Concept Vehicle [*Austin Rover*] ... CCV
Coupe Einspritz [*Coupe Fuel-Injection*] [*German*] ... CE
Coupe Sport [*Automotive*] ... CS
Coupe Sport Injection [*Automobile designation*] ... CSI
Coupe Sport Injection Automatic [*Automobile designation*] ... CSIA
Coupe Sport Leicht [*Automobile model designation*] [*German*] ... CSL
Couper's Judiciary Cases [*1868-85*] [*Scotland*] [*A publication*] (DLA) ... CJC
Couper's Justiciary Reports [*1868-85*] [*Scotland*] [*A publication*] (DLA) ... Cou
Couper's Justiciary Reports [*1868-85*] [*Scotland*] [*A publication*] (DLA) ... Coup

Couper's Justiciary Reports [*1868-85*] [*Scotland*] [*A publication*] (DLA) ... Coup Just
Couper's Justiciary Reports [*1868-85*] [*Scotland*] [*A publication*] (DLA) ... Couper
Coupeville, WA [*Location identifier FAA*] (FAAL) ... NRA
Couple (KSC) ... CPL
Couple to Couple League (EA) ... CCL
Coupled (MSA) ... CPLD
Coupled Biquad [*Electronics*] (OA) ... CB
Coupled Breeding Superheating Reactor ... CBSR
Coupled Cavity Travelling Wave Tube (PDAA) ... CCTWT
Coupled Channel [*Electronics*] ... CC
Coupled Chermosphere-Ionosphere-Plasmasphere [*Model*] (USDC) ... CTIP
Coupled Cluster [*Physical chemistry*] ... CC
Coupled Cluster Approach (MCD) ... CCA
Coupled Cluster Singles Doubles and Triples [*Physical chemistry*] ... CCSDT
Coupled Diffusion Control (MCD) ... CDC
Coupled Electron Pair Approximation [*Physics*] ... CEPA
Coupled Fast Reactivity Measurement Facility [*Idaho Falls, ID*] [*Department of Energy*] (NRCH) ... CFRMF
Coupled Fuselage-Aiming Mode (MCD) ... CFAM
Coupled General Circulation Model ... CGCM
Coupled Global Climate Model ... CGCM
Coupled Hartree-Fock [*Quantum mechanics*] ... CHF
Coupled Hydrosphere Atmosphere Research Model [*Marine science*] (OSRA) ... CHARM
Coupled Hydrosphere-Atmosphere Research Model (USDC) ... CHARM
Coupled Impedance Synthesis ... CIS
Coupled Microwave Plasma [*Spectrometry*] ... CMP
Coupled Mode Theory (PDAA) ... CMT
Coupled Model Intercomparison Project [*Marine science*] (OSRA) ... CMIP
Coupled Monostable Trigger Circuit [*Electronics*] (OA) ... CMTC
Coupled Ocean Atmosphere Mesoscale Prediction System [*Marine science*] (OSRA) ... COAMPS
Coupled Ocean-Atmosphere Response Experiment [*Marine science*] (OSRA) ... COARE
Coupled Ocean-Atmosphere Response Experiment [*Tropical Ocean-Global Atmosphere*] (USDC) ... COARE
Coupled Ocean-Land-Atmosphere 1-Dimensional [*Model*] (USDC) ... COLA1D
Coupled Ocean-Land-Atmosphere One-Dimensional [*Model*] [*Marine science*] (OSRA) ... COCAID
Coupled Optics and Flow Field Integration (MCD) ... COFFI
Coupled Oscillator (DEN) ... CO
Coupled Range-Finders ... CR
Coupled States [*Physics*] ... CS
Coupled Vibration Dissociation (IEEE) ... CVD
Coupled Vibration Dissociation Process ... CVDP
Coupled Vibration Dissociation Vibration (IEEE) ... CVDV
Coupled-Cluster Singles and Doubles [*Quantum chemistry*] ... CCSD
Coupled-Pair Functional (MCD) ... CPF
Coupler (AAG) ... CPLR
Coupler Cut-Through ... CCT
Coupler Electronics Unit ... CEU
Coupler Interface Unit (MCD) ... CIU
Couplers [*JETDS nomenclature*] [*Military*] (CET) ... CU
Couples, Inc. [*An association*] (EA) ... CI
Coupling ... CP
Coupling (KSC) ... CPLG
Coupling Capacitor Potential Device (IEEE) ... CCPD
Coupling Capacitor Voltage Transformer ... CCVT
Coupling Control Unit ... CCU
Coupling Data Unit (MCD) ... CDU
Coupling Display Manual Control-Optics (SAA) ... CDCO
Coupling Display Optical Hand Controller (KSC) ... CDOH
Coupling Display Scanning Telescope Manual Control (IAA) ... CDSC
Coupling Display Unit ... CDU
Coupling Display Unit - IMU [*Inertial Measurement Unit*] (SAA) ... CDUM
Coupling Display Unit Optic (IAA) ... CDUO
Coupling Factor [*Cytology*] ... CF
Coupon ... C
Coupon (ROG) ... COUP
Coupon ... CP
Coupon (ADA) ... CPN
[*With*] **Coupon** [*Commerce*] (BARN) ... cum cp
Coupon Bond [*Investment term*] ... CB
Coupon Exchange Club [*Commercial firm*] (EA) ... CEC
Coupon Preparation Requirement (MCD) ... CPR
Coupon Reading and Marking Machine (MHDI) ... CRAMM
Coupons Attached [*Business term*] ... CA
Cour Canadienne de l'Impot [*Tax Review Board - TRB*] ... CCI
Cour de Cassation [*Court of Appeal*] [*French*] ... C de CASS
Cour de Cassation [*Court of Appeal*] [*French*] (DLA) ... Cass
Cour de Cassation, Assemblee Pleniere [*France*] ... Cass Ass Plen
Cour de Cassation, Chambres Reunies [*France*] (ILCA) ... Cass Ch Reun
Cour de Cassation, Commerciale [*French*] (ILCA) ... Cass Civ Com
Cour de Cassation, Commerciale [*French*] (ILCA) ... Cass Com
Cour de Cassation, Deuxieme Section Civile [*French*] (ILCA) ... Cass Cive 2e
Cour de Cassation, Premiere Section Civile [*French*] (ILCA) ... Cass Civ 1re
Cour de Cassation, Sociale [*French*] (ILCA) ... Cass Civ Soc
Cour de Cassation, Troisieme Section Civile [*French*] (ILCA) ... Cass Civ 3e
Cour du Banc de la Reine [*Court of Queen's Bench*] [*Quebec*] [*Canada*] (ILCA) ... CBR
Cour Internationale de Justice [*International Court of Justice*] ... CIJ
Cour Permanente d'Arbitrage [*Permanent Court of Arbitration - PCA*] [*Hague, Netherlands*] (EAIO) ... CPA
Cour Permanente de Justice Internationale [*Permanent Court of International Justice*] [*Later, CIJ*] ... CPJI
Cour Supreme du Canada [*Supreme Court of Canada*] (DLA) ... Can CS
Courage Stroke Network (EA) ... CSN
Courant [*Of the Current Month*] [*French*] ... CT
Courant Alternatif [*Alternating Current*] [*French*] ... CA
Courant Continu [*Direct Current*] [*French*] ... CC
Courant Institute of Mathematical Sciences [*New York University*] [*Research center*] (RCD) ... CIMS
Courant-Isaacson-Rees [*Method*] ... CIR
Courchevel [*France*] [*Airport symbol*] (OAG) ... CVF
Courchevel [*France ICAO location identifier*] (ICLI) ... LFLJ
Courier ... COUR
Courier ... COUR
[*The*] **Courier** [*Code name for Robert W. Owen, participant in the Iran-Contra affair during the Reagan Administration*] ... TC
Courier Air Service ... CAS
Courier and Periodicals Division [*Later, UNESCO Publications and Periodicals*] ... CPD
Courier and Transport Service Ltd. [*British*] ... CATS
Courier Corp. [*Associated Press*] (SAG) ... Courer
Courier Corp. [*NASDAQ symbol*] (NQ) ... CRRC
Courier, Digby, Nova Scotia [*Library symbol National Library of Canada*] (NLC) ... NSDC
Courier, Digby, NS, Canada [*Library symbol*] [*Library of Congress*] (LCLS) ... CaNSDiC
Courier Mail [*Brisbane*] [*A publication*] ... C Mail
Courier, Middletown, NJ [*Library symbol Library of Congress*] (LCLS) ... NjMiC
Courier Post, Cherry Hill, NJ [*Library symbol Library of Congress*] (LCLS) ... NjChCP
Courier Services, Inc. [*ICAO designator*] (FAAC) ... CSD
Courier Transfer Office [*or Officer*] ... CTO
Courier Transfer Station ... CTS
Courier-Journal & Louisville Times Co., Inc., Louisville, KY [*Library symbol Library of Congress*] (LCLS) ... KyLoC
Courier-Mail (Brisbane) [*A publication*] ... BCM
Courma-Rharous [*Mali*] [*ICAO location identifier*] (ICLI) ... GAGR
Courrier de la Nouvelle-Ecosse, Yarmouth, Nova Scotia [*Library symbol National Library of Canada*] (NLC) ... NSYC
Courrier de la Nouvelle-Ecosse, Yarmouth, NS, Canada [*Library symbol*] [*Library of Congress*] (LCLS) ... CaNSYC
Course ... C
Course ... CO
Course [*Commonly used*] (OPSA) ... COURSE
Course ... CRS
Course (AABC) ... CRS
Course ... CRSE
Course ... CRSE
Course [*Postal Service standard*] (OPSA) ... CRSE
Course ... CSE
Course [*Ships*] (CINC) ... CUS
Course Administrative Data [*DoD*] ... CAD
Course Alignment ... CA
Course Alignment Servo ... CAS
Course Alignment Subsystem ... CASS
Course Alignment Unit ... CAU
Course and Distance Calculator [*or Computer*] ... CDC
Course and Speed Calculator [*or Computer*] ... CSC
Course and Speed Made Good over the Ground [*Military*] (NATG) ... CSG
Course and Speed Made Good through the Water [*Military*] (NATG) ... CSW
Course Angle [*Navigation*] ... C
Course Approval and Monitoring Form [*Inner London Education Authority*] [*British*] (AIE) ... CAMF
Course Author Language [*Computer science*] ... CAL
Course Content Improvement ... CCI
Course Deviation Indicator [*Aviation*] ... CDI
Course Generator ... CG
Course Indicator (IEEE) ... CI
Course Made Good [*Navy*] ... CMG
Course Made Good over the Ground [*Military*] (NVT) ... COG
Course Made Good through the Water [*Military*] (NATG) ... CTW
Course Monitoring Tire [*Tire testing*] ... CMT
Course of Construction ... C of C
Course of Instruction [*Military*] ... COI
Course Ordered Transmitter ... COT
Course Pennant [*Navy British*] ... CO
Course per Gyro Compass [*Navigation*] ... CPGC
Course Record Book [*Education*] (AIE) ... CRB
Course Setting Bombsight ... CSBS
Course Severity Adjustment Factor [*Tire testing*] ... CSAF
Course Status Report ... CSR
Course Technology, Inc. [*Publishing*] ... CTI
Course Training Standard [*Air Force*] (AFM) ... CTS
Course Winner [*Horse racing*] ... C
Course-Line Computer [*Aviation*] (MCD) ... CLC
Course-of-Action [*Military*] ... COA
Courses by Newspaper (EDAC) ... CbN
Courseware Authoring Language Generator [*Computer science*] (MCD) ... CALGEN
Courseware Authoring Tools [*Stanford University computer software project*] ... CAT
Coursewriter [*IBM Corp. programming language*] ... CW
Court ... C
Court (DLA) ... COT
Court [*Commonly used*] (OPSA) ... COURT

Court ... CRT
Court (DD) ... Crt
Court (VRA) ... ct
Court ... CT
Court ... CT
Court Appointed Special Advocates [*In association name National CASA Association*] ... CASA
Court Decisions, National Labor Relations Act [*A publication*] (DLA) ... Ct D
Court Decisions, National Labor Relations Act [*A publication*] (DLA) ... Ct Dec NLRA
Court Druggist [*Foresters*] [*British*] (ROG) ... CD
Court Employment Project (EA) ... CEP
Court House ... CH
Court House [*British*] (ROG) ... CO HO
Court House Library, West Point, MS [*Library symbol Library of Congress*] (LCLS) ... MsWpCt
Court Information Service [*South Australia*] ... CIS
Court Interpreters and Translators Association (EA) ... CITA
Court Journal and District Court Record [*A publication*] (DLA) ... Court J & Dist Ct Rec
Court Library, Department of Justice, Yellowknife, Northwest Territories [*Library symbol National Library of Canada*] (BIB) ... NWYC
Court Management Journal [*A publication*] (DLA) ... Ct Mgmt J
Court Martial Reports, Air Force Cases [*A publication*] (DLA) ... ACM
Court Martial Reports, Army Cases [*United States*] [*A publication*] (DLA) ... CM
Court Martial Reports, Citators and Indexes [*A publication*] (DLA) ... CMR Cit & Ind
Court Martial Reports, Coast Guard Cases [*New York*] [*A publication*] (DLA) ... CGCM
Court Martial Reports, Judge Advocate General of the Air Force [*A publication*] (DLA) ... CMR JAG AF
Court Martial Reports, Judge Advocate General of the Armed Forces and United States Court of Military Appeals [*A publication*] (DLA) ... CMR JAG & US Ct of Mil App
Court Martial Reports, Navy Cases [*A publication*] (DLA) ... NCM
Court of Appeal ... CA
Court of Appeal in Chancery [*England*] (DLA) ... Ch App
Court of Appeal Reports [*New Zealand*] [*A publication*] (DLA) ... Rep in CA
Court of Appeals for the District of Columbia Circuit (AAGC) ... CADC
Court of Appeals for the Federal Circuit [*Highest US patent court*] ... CAFC
Court of Appeals for the Federal Circuit (AAGC) ... Fed Cir
Court of Appeals Reports [*New Zealand*] [*A publication*] (DLA) ... CA
Court of Appeals Reports [*New Zealand*] [*A publication*] (DLA) ... Ct App NZ
Court of Appeals Reports [*New Zealand*] [*A publication*] (DLA) ... Ct Rep NZ
Court of Arbitration of Sport [*See also TAS*] [*Lausanne, Switzerland*] (EAIO) ... CAS
Court of Arches [*England*] (DLA) ... Arch
Court of Arches [*England*] (DLA) ... CA
Court of Bankruptcy, Undischarged [*British*] ... CBU
Court of Chancery [*New Jersey*] (DLA) ... Ch
Court of Civil Appeals, Dallas, TX [*Library symbol Library of Congress*] (LCLS) ... TxDaCiA
Court of Claims ... CCLS
Court of Claims [*Renamed CAFC in 1992*] (AAGC) ... Ct Cl
Court of Claims ... CTCLS
Court of Claims Act (DLA) ... Ct Cl Act
Court of Claims Reports [*United States*] [*A publication*] (DLA) ... C Cl
Court of Claims Reports ... CCLSR
Court of Claims Reports [*New York*] [*A publication*] (DLA) ... Ct Cl NY
Court of Claims Rules [*A publication*] (DLA) ... Ct Cl R
Court of Claims Trial Division [*Defunct*] (AAGC) ... Ct Cl Trial Div
Court of Claims Trial Judge Opinion (AAGC) ... Ct Cl TJ Op
Court of Common Pleas ... CCP
Court of Common Pleas (DLA) ... CP
Court of Common Pleas (DLA) ... Ct Com Pl
Court of Criminal Appeals [*England*] (DLA) ... Crim App
Court of Crown Cases Reserved [*England*] (DLA) ... CCR
Court of Customs and Patent Appeals ... CCPA
Court of Customs and Patent Appeals (DLA) ... Ct Cust & Pat App
Court of Customs and Patent Appeals Reports [*A publication*] (DLA) ... CA
Court of Customs Appeals (DLA) ... Ct Cust App
Court of Customs Appeals Reports [*1919-29*] [*A publication*] (DLA) ... CA
Court of Customs Appeals Reports [*1919-29*] [*A publication*] (DLA) ... Ct Cust App
Court of Divorce and Matrimonial Causes [*England*] (DLA) ... D
Court of Error [*Legal term*] (DLA) ... CT ERR
Court of Errors and Appeals [*New Jersey*] (DLA) ... Ct Err & App
Court of Errors and Appeals [*New Jersey*] (DLA) ... Ct Errors and App
Court of Errors and Appeals [*New Jersey*] (DLA) ... Ct of Er and Appeals
Court of Exchequer [*Scotland*] (DLA) ... CES
Court of Exchequer [*England*] [*Legal term*] (DLA) ... Ex
Court of Exchequer [*England*] [*Legal term*] (DLA) ... Exch
Court of Federal Claims (AAGC) ... CFC
Court of Federal Claims [*Formerly Claims Court*] (AAGC) ... COFC
Court of First Instance (BARN) ... CFI
Court of Industrial Relations [*Philippines*] ... CIR
Court of International Trade. Reports [*A publication*] (DLA) ... CIT
Court of International Trade. Rules [*A publication*] (DLA) ... CITR
Court of Justice ... COJ
Court of Justice of the European Communities ... CJ
Court of Justice of the European Communities (DLA) ... CJEC
Court of Justice of the European Communities (DLA) ... ECJ
Court of Justiciary (DLA) ... Ct Just
Court of Military Appeals ... CMA
Court of Military Appeals ... COMA
Court of Military Appeals Reports [*A publication*] (DLA) ... CMA
Court of Military Review (AFM) ... CMR
Court of Military Review (AFM) ... COMR
Court of Petty Sessions [*Australia*] ... CPS
Court of Probate ... CP
Court of Quarter Sessions [*Legal*] [*British*] (ROG) ... CQS
Court of Session [*Scotland*] [*A publication*] (DLA) ... C Sess
Court of Session [*Scotland*] ... CS
Court of Session Cases [*Scotland*] [*A publication*] (DLA) ... C of S Ca
Court of Session Cases [*Scotland*] [*A publication*] (DLA) ... Court Sess Ca
Court of Session Cases [*Scotland*] [*A publication*] (DLA) ... CSC
Court of Session Cases [*Scotland*] [*A publication*] (DLA) ... Ct Sess Cas
Court of Session Cases [*Scotland*] [*A publication*] (DLA) ... SC
Court of Session Cases, Fifth Series [*Scotland*] [*A publication*] (DLA) ... C of S Ca 5th Series
Court of Session Cases, First Series, by Shaw, Dunlop, and Bell [*Scotland*] [*A publication*] (DLA) ... C of S Ca 1st Series
Court of Session Cases, Fourth Series, by Rettie, Crawford, and Melville [*Scotland*] [*A publication*] (DLA) ... C of S Ca 4th Series
Court of Session Cases, House of Lords [*Scotland*] [*A publication*] (DLA) ... HHL
Court of Session Cases, House of Lords [*Scotland*] [*A publication*] (DLA) ... SCHL
Court of Session Cases, Second Series, by Dunlop, Bell, and Murray [*Scotland*] [*A publication*] (DLA) ... C of S Ca 2d Series
Court of Session Cases, Third Series, by Macpherson, Lee, and Bell [*Scotland*] [*A publication*] (DLA) ... C of S Ca 3rd Series
Court of Special Sessions [*Legal term*] (DLA) ... CT SPEC SESS
Court of Summary Jurisdiction [*British*] (ROG) ... CSJ
Court Order (DLA) ... Ct/O
Court Physician (ROG) ... CP
Court Reporter (AABC) ... CTREPTR
Court Reporting Program [*Association of Independent Colleges and Schools specialization code*] ... CR
Court Reporting Typist ... CRT
Court Rolls [*British*] ... CT
Court Rolls [*British*] (ROG) ... CT R
Court Rolls of Ramsey Abbey [*1928*] [*England*] [*A publication*] (DLA) ... Ault
Court Services Department [*South Australia*] ... CSD
Court Trust [*Includes executor, administrator, guardian*] [*Legal term*] (DLA) ... CT
Courtauld's All-Purpose Simulator (IEEE) ... CAPS
Courtaulds Ltd. [*AMEX symbol*] (SPSG) ... COU
Courtaulds Ltd. [*Associated Press*] (SAG) ... Courtld
Courtaulds Ltd., Cornwall, ON, Canada [*Library symbol Library of Congress Obsolete*] (LCLS) ... CaOCC
Courtaulds, plc ADR [*AMEX symbol*] (TTSB) ... COU
Courtauld's Rapid Extract, Sort, and Tabulate System (IEEE) ... CRESTS
Courtelary [*Switzerland ICAO location identifier*] (ICLI) ... LSZJ
Courtenay and District Museum, Courtenay, BC, Canada [*Library symbol Library of Congress*] (LCLS) ... CaBCoM
Courtenay and District Museum, Courtenay, British Columbia [*Library symbol National Library of Canada*] (NLC) ... BCOM
Courtenay, BC [*AM radio station call letters*] ... CFCP
Courtenay, BC [*Television station call letters*] ... CHAN-4
Courtesy ... CRTSY
Courtesy Announcement (NTCM) ... CA
Courtesy Lamp [*Automotive engineering*] ... C/LP
Courtesy Motorboat Examination [*Coast Guard*] (IIA) ... CME
Courtesy Return Envelope (NFD) ... CRE
Courthouse ... Ct Ho
Courthouse (VRA) ... cths
Courtier ... CRTR
Court-Martial ... CM
Court-Martial Appeal Court of Canada ... CMAC
Court-Martial Appointing Order ... CMAO
Court-Martial, European Theater of Operations [*United States*] (DLA) ... CM-ETO
Court-Martial Forfeiture ... CMF
Court-Martial Index and Summary (DNAB) ... CMIS
Court-Martial Officer ... CMO
Court-Martial Orders [*Navy*] ... CMO
Court-Martial Report (AFM) ... CMR
Courtnay and Maclean's Scotch Appeals [*6, 7 Wilson and Shaw*] [*A publication*] (DLA) ... Cour & Macl
Courtnay and Maclean's Scotch Appeals [*6, 7 Wilson and Shaw*] [*A publication*] (DLA) ... Court & Macl
Courtney Foundation for the Welfare of Mother and Babies [*British*] ... WOMB
Courts [*Commonly used*] (OPSA) ... COURTS
Courts [*Postal Service standard*] (OPSA) ... CTS
Courts ... CTS
Courts of London Sessions [*British*] (BARN) ... CLS
Courtship Analysis [*Psychology*] ... CA
Courts-Martial Appeal Rules [*British military*] (DMA) ... CMAR
Courts-Martial (Appeals) Act [*British military*] (DMA) ... CMAA
Courtyard (VRA) ... ctyd
Courvan Mining Co. Ltd. [*Toronto Stock Exchange symbol*] ... CVN
Cous Creek Copper Mines [*Vancouver Stock Exchange symbol*] ... COK
Coushatta, LA [*AM radio station call letters*] ... KRRP
Coushatta, LA [*FM radio station call letters*] ... KSBH
Cousin ... C
Cousin ... COUS
Cousin (ROG) ... COZ
Cousin [*Genealogy*] ... CSN
Cousins Properties [*NYSE symbol*] (TTSB) ... CUZ
Cousins Properties, Inc. [*Associated Press*] (SAG) ... CousPr
Cousins Properties, Inc. [*NYSE symbol*] (SPSG) ... CUZ
Cousteau Society [*Established to Fund Marine Research*] (GNE) ... CS
[*The*] **Cousteau Society** (EA) ... TCS
Cout, Assurance, Fret [*Cost, Insurance, Freight - CIF*] [*Shipping*] [*French*] ... CAF

Cout et Fret [*Cost and Freight*] [*Shipping*] [*French*] ... C & F
Couterpoise Procedure [*Physical chemistry*] ... CP
Coutlee's Digest, Canada Supreme Court [*A publication*] (DLA) ... Cout Dig
Coutlee's Unreported Cases [*1875-1907*] [*Canada*] [*A publication*] (DLA) ... Cout
Coutlee's Unreported Cases [*1875-1907*] [*Canada*] [*A publication*] (DLA) ... Coutlee
Coutlee's Unreported Cases [*1875-1907*] [*Canada*] [*A publication*] (DLA) ... Coutlee Unrep (Can)
Coutts Public Library, Alberta [*Library symbol National Library of Canada*] (NLC) ... ACOU
Couvent des Ursulines, Quebec, PQ, Canada [*Library symbol Library of Congress*] (LCLS) ... CaQQU
Couvent des Ursulines, Quebec, Quebec [*Library symbol National Library of Canada*] (NLC) ... QQU
Coval Air Ltd. [*Canada ICAO designator*] (FAAC) ... CVL
Covalently Closed Circular [*Configuration of DNA*] [*Microbiology*] ... CCC
Covalently Closed Circular DNA [*Deoxyribonucleic Acid*] [*Genetics*] (DOG) ... cccDNA
Covariance (DMAA) ... COV
Covariance Analysis Program for the Study of Augmented Inertial Navigators (MCD) ... CAPTAIN
Cove [*Maps and charts*] ... C
Cove ... CV
Cove ... CV
Cove Resources [*Vancouver Stock Exchange symbol*] ... COV
Covefort [*Utah*] [*Seismograph station code, US Geological Survey*] (SEIS) ... CFU
Covenant ... COV
Covenant (ROG) ... COVT
Covenant ... CVNNT
Covenant Bank for Savings [*NASDAQ symbol*] (SAG) ... CNSK
Covenant Bank for Savings [*Associated Press*] (SAG) ... CoventBk
Covenant Bank for Savings [*Associated Press*] (SAG) ... CovnB
Covenant Fellowship of Presbyterians (EA) ... CFP
Covenant House [*An association*] (EA) ... CH
Covenant of the Goddess (EA) ... COG
Covenant Theological Seminary, St. Louis, MO [*Library symbol Library of Congress*] (LCLS) ... MoSCT
Covenant Transport, Inc. [*Associated Press*] (SAG) ... Covenant
Covenant Transport, Inc. [*NASDAQ symbol*] (SAG) ... CVTI
Covenant Transport'A' [*NASDAQ symbol*] (TTSB) ... CVTI
Covenant Young Adults [*Defunct*] (EA) ... CYA
Covenanted [*Legal term*] (ROG) ... COVTD
Covenantee [*Legal term*] (ROG) ... COVTEE
Covenantor [*Legal term*] (ROG) ... COVTOR
Covenants, Conditions, Restrictions, and Reservations (MHDB) ... CCR & R
Covendo [*Bolivia*] [*ICAO location identifier*] (ICLI) ... SLVD
Covent Garden [*Royal Opera or Royal Ballet*] [*British*] ... CG
Coventry [*City in England*] ... COV
Coventry [*England*] [*Airport symbol*] (OAG) ... CVT
Coventry [*British ICAO location identifier*] (ICLI) ... EGBE
Coventry and District Archaeological Society [*British*] (DBA) ... CADAS
Coventry and Hughes' Digest of the Common Law Reports [*A publication*] (DLA) ... C & H Dig
Coventry and Hughes' Digest of the Common Law Reports [*A publication*] (DLA) ... Cov & H Dig
Coventry Climax [*Auto racing engine manufacturer*] [*British*] ... CC
Coventry. Common Recoveries [*1820*] [*A publication*] (DLA) ... Cov Rec
Coventry. Conveyancers' Evidence [*1832*] [*A publication*] (DLA) ... Cov Conv Ev
Coventry Corp. [*Associated Press*] (SAG) ... Coventry
Coventry Corp. [*NASDAQ symbol*] (SPSG) ... CVTY
Coventry Corp., Coventry, United Kingdom [*Library symbol Library of Congress*] (LCLS) ... UkCov
Coventry. Mortgage Precedents [*1827*] [*A publication*] (DLA) ... Cov Mort
Coventry Ordnance Works [*British military*] (DMA) ... COW
Coventry, RI [*FM radio station call letters*] ... WCVY
Coventry Ventures [*Vancouver Stock Exchange symbol*] ... CVQ
Cover (VRA) ... bv
Cover [*of a magazine*] ... C
Cover (MSA) ... COV
Cover ... CVR
Cover Aft ... CA
Cover and Deception (CINC) ... C & D
Cover and Deception, Direction, and Coordination ... C & DDAC
Cover and Deception, Direction, and Coordination (MCD) ... CDDAC
Cover, Artillery Protection [*Military*] (PDAA) ... CAP
Cover Collectors Circuit Club (EA) ... CCCC
Cover Collectors Club (EA) ... CoCo
Cover Forward ... CF
Cover Gas Clean-Up System [*Nuclear energy*] (NUCP) ... CGCS
Cover Gas Evaluation Loop [*Nuclear energy*] (NRCH) ... CGEL
Cover Gas Monitoring Subsystem [*Nuclear energy*] (NRCH) ... CGMS
Cover Layer Assembly (KSC) ... CLA
Cover Layer Automated Design (MHDI) ... CLAD
Cover Note [*Insurance*] ... CN
Cover Paper and Board [*Printing*] (DGA) ... CP & B
Cover Point [*Cricket*] (ROG) ... COV PT
Cover Point [*Lacrosse position*] ... CP
Cover Screen [*Medicine*] (DAVI) ... CS
Cover Test [*Ophthalmology*] ... CT
Cover Your Anatomy [*Military, government slang*] [*Bowdlerized version*] ... CYA
Cover Your Anatomy with Paper [*Military, government slang*] [*Bowdlerized version*] ... CYAWP
Coverage ... CVGE
Coverage Exercise (MUGU) ... COVEX
Cover-All Technologies [*Associated Press*] (SAG) ... CoverAll
Cover-All Technologies [*NASDAQ symbol*] (SAG) ... COVR
Covered (VRA) ... bv
Covered ... COVD
Covered Button Association of New York (EA) ... CBANY
Covered Carriage Trucks [*British railroad term*] ... CCT
Covered Conductors Association [*British*] (BI) ... CCA
Covered Hopper [*Freight*] ... CVRD HPR
Covered Lighter [*Self-propelled*] [*Navy symbol*] ... YF
Covered Lighter [*Non-self-propelled*] [*Navy symbol*] ... YFN
Covered Lighter (Range Tender) [*Self-propelled*] [*Navy symbol*] ... YFRT
Covered Lighter (Repair) [*Navy symbol Obsolete*] ... YRL
Covered Lighter (Special Purpose) [*Later, YFNX*] [*Navy symbol*] ... YFNG
Covered Option [*Investment term*] ... CO
Covered Option Securities (TDOB) ... COPS
Covered Pedestrian Space ... CPS
Covered Radio Teletype (NVT) ... CRATT
Covered Threads Association [*Defunct*] (EA) ... CTA
Covering ... COVER
Covering Fire Mine (MCD) ... CFM
Covering Force (MCD) ... CF
Covering Force Area (AABC) ... CFA
Coverings, Facing, or Floor [*Freight*] ... COVFF
Covers [*JETDS nomenclature*] [*Military*] (CET) ... CW
Coversed Sine [*Mathematics*] ... Covers
Covert Active Modular Electro-Optical System (MCD) ... CAMEO
Covert All-Weather Gun System ... CAWGS
Covert Camera Spy [*System*] ... CCS
Covert Communications ... COCO
Covert Elementary School, Elmont, NY [*Library symbol Library of Congress*] (LCLS) ... NElmoCE
Covert Entrepreneurial Organization [*Term used by Carl S. Taylor in his book on street gangs, Dangerous Society*] ... CEO
Covert Family Association (EA) ... CFA
Covert Investigation [*Police term*] ... CI
Covert Local Area Sensor System for Intrusion Classification (LAIN) ... CLASSIC
Covert Submarine Transmitter and Receiver (MCD) ... CO-STAR
Covert Survivable in Weather Reconnaissance and Strike [*Military*] (DOMA) ... COSIRS
Covert Viewing System ... CVS
Coves [*Commonly used*] (OPSA) ... COVES
Coves ... CVS
Covilha [*Portugal ICAO location identifier*] (ICLI) ... LPCV
Covina Public Library, Covina, CA [*Library symbol Library of Congress*] (LCLS) ... CCov
Covina Public Library, Covina, CA [*OCLC symbol*] (OCLC) ... CVP
Covington [*Diocesan abbreviation*] [*Kentucky*] (TOCD) ... COV
Covington & Burling, Washington, DC [*OCLC symbol*] (OCLC) ... DCO
Covington & Burling, Washington, DC [*Library symbol Library of Congress*] (LCLS) ... DCov
Covington/Cincinnati, OH [*Location identifier FAA*] (FAAL) ... JDP
Covington/Cincinnati, OH [*Location identifier FAA*] (FAAL) ... SIC
Covington/Cincinnati, OH [*Location identifier FAA*] (FAAL) ... URN
Covington Friend, Attica, IN [*Library symbol Library of Congress*] (LCLS) ... InAttCF
Covington, GA [*Location identifier FAA*] (FAAL) ... VOF
Covington, GA [*AM radio station call letters*] ... WGFS
Covington, IN [*FM radio station call letters*] ... WCDV
Covington, IN [*FM radio station call letters*] ... WFOF
Covington, KY [*AM radio station call letters*] ... WCVG
Covington, KY [*Television station call letters*] ... WCVN
Covington, KY/Cincinnati, OH [*Location identifier FAA*] (FAAL) ... CVG
Covington, LA [*AM radio station call letters*] ... WASO
Covington, PA [*FM radio station call letters*] ... WDKC
Covington Public Library, Covington, IN [*Library symbol Library of Congress*] (LCLS) ... InCov
Covington, TN [*Location identifier FAA*] (FAAL) ... COO
Covington, TN [*AM radio station call letters*] ... WKBL
Covington, TN [*FM radio station call letters*] ... WKBL-FM
Covington, VA [*FM radio station call letters*] ... WIQO
Covington, VA [*AM radio station call letters*] ... WKEY
Cow Castle Creek [*South Carolina*] [*Seismograph station code, US Geological Survey*] (SEIS) ... COW
Cow Head Public Library, Cow Head, NF, Canada [*Library symbol Library of Congress*] (LCLS) ... CaNfCH
Cow Head Public Library, Newfoundland [*Library symbol National Library of Canada*] (NLC) ... NFCH
Cow Observers Worldwide [*An association*] (EA) ... COW
Cow Parsnip Mosaic Virus [*Plant pathology*] ... COPMV
Cowan. Land Rights in Scotland [*A publication*] (ILCA) ... Cow LR
Cowan, TN [*AM radio station call letters*] ... WZYX
Cowater International, Inc., Ottawa, Ontario [*Library symbol National Library of Canada*] (BIB) ... OOCOW
Cowboy ... CWBY
Cowboy Artists of America (EA) ... CAA
Cowboy Artists of America Museum Foundation (EA) ... CAAMF
Cowboy Television Network ... CTN
Cowboys for Christ (EA) ... CFC
Cowdery's Law Encyclopaedia [*California*] [*A publication*] (DLA) ... Cowd L Enc
Cowell's East India Digest [*A publication*] (DLA) ... Cow Dig
Cowell's Institutiones Juris Anglicani [*A publication*] (DLA) ... Cow Inst
Cowell's Interpreter [*A publication*] (DLA) ... Cow Int
Cowell's Interpreter [*A publication*] (DLA) ... Cowell
Cowell's Law Dictionary [*A publication*] (DLA) ... Cow Dic
Cowell's Law Dictionary [*A publication*] (DLA) ... Cow Dict
Cowell's Law Dictionary [*A publication*] (DLA) ... Cowell
Cowen on Warrants of Attachment [*A publication*] (DLA) ... Cow Att

Cowen's Criminal Digest [*A publication*] (DLA) .... Cow Cr Dig
Cowen's Criminal Law [*New York*] [*A publication*] (DLA) .... Cow Cr L
Cowen's Criminal Reports [*New York*] [*A publication*] (DLA) .... Cow Cr
Cowen's Criminal Reports [*New York*] [*A publication*] (DLA) .... Cow Cr R
Cowen's Criminal Reports [*New York*] [*A publication*] (DLA) .... Cow Cr Rep
Cowen's Criminal Reports [*New York*] [*A publication*] (DLA) .... Cow Crim (NY)
Cowen's New York Reports [*A publication*] (DLA) .... Cow
Cowen's New York Reports [*A publication*] (DLA) .... Cow NY
Cowen's New York Reports [*A publication*] (DLA) .... Cow R
Cowen's New York Treatise on Justices of the Peace [*A publication*] (DLA) .... Cow JP
Cowen's New York Treatise on Justices of the Peace [*A publication*] (DLA) .... Cow Just
Cowen's New York Treatise on Justices of the Peace [*A publication*] (DLA) .... Cow Tr
Cowichan Valley Association for Community Living [*Formerly, Duncan & District Association for the Mentally Handicapped*] (AC) .... CVACL
Cowichan Valley Intercultural & Immigrant Society (AC) .... CVIIAS
Cowichan Valley Museum, Duncan, BC, Canada [*Library symbol*] [*Library of Congress*] (LCLS) .... CaBDUCVM
Cowichan Valley Museum, Duncan, British Columbia [*Library symbol National Library of Canada*] (NLC) .... BDUCVM
Cowles Communications, Inc., New York, NY [*Library symbol Library of Congress*] (LCLS) CcI
Cowley/Lovell/Byron, WY [*Location identifier FAA*] (FAAL) .... HCY
Cowl-Flap Angle [*Air Force*] .... CFA
Cowling Number [*IUPAC*] .... Co
Cowlitz, Chehalis & Cascade Railroad (IIA) .... CC & C
Cowpea .... CP
Cowpea Aphid-Borne Mosaic Virus [*Plant pathology*] .... CABMV
Cowpea Aphid-Borne Mosaic Virus .... CAMV
Cowpea Chloretic Mottle Virus .... CCMV
Cowpea Mild Mottle Virus [*Plant pathology*] .... CPMMV
Cowpea Mosaic Virus [*Plant pathology*] .... CPMV
Cowpea Mottle Virus [*Plant pathology*] .... CPMOV
Cowpea Ringspot Virus [*Plant pathology*] .... CPRSV
Cowpea Severe Mosaic Virus [*Plant pathology*] .... CPSMV
Cowpea Trypsin Inhibitor [*Biochemistry*] .... CpTI
Cowpens National Battlefield Site .... COWP
Cowper Greens [*Political party Australia*] .... CG
Cowper's Cases [*Third volume of Reports in Chancery*] [*A publication*] (DLA) .... Cowp Cas
Cowper's English King's Bench Reports [*1774-78*] [*A publication*] (DLA) .... Cow
Cowper's English King's Bench Reports [*1774-78*] [*A publication*] (DLA) .... Cowp
Cowper's English King's Bench Reports [*1774-78*] [*A publication*] (DLA) .... Cowp (Eng)
Cowra [*Australia Airport symbol*] (OAG) .... CWT
Cow's Milk .... CM
Cow's Milk Allergy [*Medicine*] (DMAA) .... CMA
Cow's Milk Base Formula .... CMBF
Cowsills Fan Club (EA) .... CFC
Cox. Advocate [*1852*] [*A publication*] (DLA) .... Cox Adv
Cox and Atkinson's Registration Appeal Cases [*1843-46*] [*England*] [*A publication*] (DLA) .... Cox & Atk
Cox and Saunders' Criminal Law Consolidation Acts [*3rd ed.*] [*1870*] [*A publication*] (DLA) .... Cox & S Cr L
Cox Communications, Inc. [*NYSE symbol*] (SAG) .... COX
Cox Communications, Inc. [*Associated Press*] (SAG) .... CoxCm
Cox Communications'A' [*NYSE symbol*] (TTSB) .... COX
Cox Coronary Heart Institute, Dayton, OH [*Library symbol Library of Congress*] (LCLS) .... ODaCox
Cox. Law and Science of Ancient Lights [*1871*] [*A publication*] (ILCA) .... Cox Anc L
Cox, Macrae, and Hertslet's English County Court Cases [*1847-58*] [*A publication*] (DLA) .... Cox & M'C
Cox, Macrae, and Hertslet's English County Court Reports [*1847-58*] [*A publication*] (DLA) .... CM & H
Cox, Macrae, and Hertslet's English County Court Reports [*1847-58*] [*A publication*] (DLA) .... Cox M & H
Cox, Macrae, and Hertslet's English County Court Reports [*1847-58*] [*A publication*] (DLA) .... Cox Mc & H
Cox, Macrae, and Hertslet's Reports, Crown Cases [*1847-58*] [*England*] [*A publication*] (DLA) .... Mac & H
Cox Radio, Inc. [*Associated Press*] (SAG) .... CoxRad
Cox Radio, Inc. [*NYSE symbol*] (SAG) .... CXR
Coxe's Reports [*1 New Jersey Law*] [*A publication*] (DLA) .... Coxe
Coxe's Translation of Guterbach's Bracton [*A publication*] (DLA) .... Coxe Bract
Coxheath Gold Holdings Ltd. [*Toronto Stock Exchange symbol*] .... CXG
Cox's American Trade-Mark Cases [*A publication*] (DLA) .... Am Tr M Cas
Cox's American Trade-Mark Cases [*A publication*] (DLA) .... Cox Am T Cas
Cox's American Trade-Mark Cases [*A publication*] (DLA) .... Cox Am TM Cas
Cox's American Trade-Mark Cases [*A publication*] (DLA) .... Cox Tr M Ca
Cox's American Trade-Mark Cases [*A publication*] (DLA) .... Cox Tr M Cas
Cox's Bazar [*Bangladesh*] [*Airport symbol*] (OAG) .... CXB
Cox's Bazar [*Bangladesh*] [*ICAO location identifier*] (ICLI) .... VGCB
Cox's Chancery Practice [*A publication*] (DLA) .... Cox Ch Pr
Cox's Common Law Practice [*A publication*] (DLA) .... Cox CL Pr
Cox's County Court Cases [*1860-1919*] [*England*] [*A publication*] (DLA) .... Cox CC
Cox's County Court Cases [*1860-1919*] [*England*] [*A publication*] (DLA) .... Cox Cty Ct Ca
Cox's County Court Cases [*1860-1919*] [*England*] [*A publication*] (DLA) .... Cox Cty Ct Cas.
Cox's Criminal Law Digest [*A publication*] (DLA) .... Cox Cr Dig
Cox's Crown Cases [*A publication*] (DLA) .... Cox CC
Cox's Edition of Peere Williams' Reports [*England*] [*A publication*] (DLA) .... Cox PW
Cox's English Chancery Cases [*A publication*] (DLA) .... Cox Ch
Cox's English Chancery Cases [*A publication*] (DLA) .... Cox Ch Cas (Eng)
Cox's English Chancery Reports [*1783-96*] [*A publication*] (DLA) .... Cox
Cox's English Criminal Cases [*A publication*] (DLA) CCC
Cox's English Criminal Cases [*A publication*] (DLA) .... Cox
Cox's English Criminal Cases [*A publication*] (DLA) .... Cox CC
Cox's English Criminal Cases [*A publication*] (DLA) .... Cox Cr Ca
Cox's English Criminal Cases [*A publication*] (DLA) .... Cox Cr Cas
Cox's English Criminal Cases [*A publication*] (DLA) .... Cox Crim Cas
Cox's Equity Cases [*England*] [*A publication*] (DLA) .... Cox Eq
Cox's Equity Cases [*England*] [*A publication*] (DLA) .... Cox Eq Cas
Cox's Institutions of the English Government [*A publication*] (DLA) .... Cox Gov
Cox's Institutions of the English Government [*A publication*] (DLA) .... Cox Inst
Cox's Joint Stock Company Cases [*1864-72*] [*England*] [*A publication*] (DLA) .... Cox JS Cas
Cox's Joint Stock Company Cases [*1864-72*] [*England*] [*A publication*] (DLA) .... Cox JS Comp
Cox's Joint Stock Company Cases [*1864-72*] [*England*] [*A publication*] (DLA) .... Cox Jt Stk
Cox's Magistrates' Cases [*1859-1919*] [*England*] [*A publication*] (DLA) .... Cox Mag Ca
Cox's Magistrates' Cases [*1859-1919*] [*England*] [*A publication*] (ILCA) .... Cox Mag Cas
Cox's Magistrates' Cases [*1859-1919*] [*England*] [*A publication*] (DLA) .... Cox MC
Cox's Manual of Trade-Mark Cases [*A publication*] (DLA) .... Cox Man Tr M
Cox's Manual of Trade-Mark Cases [*A publication*] (DLA) .... Cox Tr M
Cox's Principles of Punishment [*1877*] [*A publication*] (DLA) .... Cox Pun
Cox's Questions for the Use of Students [*A publication*] (DLA) .... Cox Ques
Cox's Registration and Elections [*14th ed.*] [*1885*] [*A publication*] (DLA) .... Cox Elect
Cox's Registration and Elections [*14th ed.*] [*1885*] [*A publication*] (DLA) .... Cox Reg
Cox's Reports [*25-27 Arkansas*] [*A publication*] (DLA) .... Cox
Coxsackie [*Virus*] (MAE) C
Coxswain .... COX
Coxswain [*British military*] (DMA) .... Coxn
Coxswain, Construction Battalion, Stevedore .... COXCBS
Coxswain, Ship Repair, Canvasman .... COXSRS
Coxswain, Ship Repair, Rigger .... COXSRR
Coyhaique [*Chile*] [*Airport symbol*] .... GXQ
Coyhaique [*Chile*] [*Airport symbol*] (AD) .... GXQ
Coyhaique/Teniente Vidal [*Chile*] [*ICAO location identifier*] (ICLI) .... SCCY
Coyle, NJ [*Location identifier FAA*] (FAAL) .... CYN
Coyote Hills [*California*] [*Seismograph station code, US Geological Survey*] (SEIS) .... CYH
Coyotepe [*Nicaragua*] [*Seismograph station code, US Geological Survey*] (SEIS) .... CYN
Cozad, NE [*Location identifier FAA*] (FAAL) .... CZD
Cozad, NE [*AM radio station call letters*] .... KAMI
Cozad, NE [*FM radio station call letters*] .... KAMI-FM
Cozumel [*Mexico*] [*Airport symbol*] (OAG) .... CZM
Cozumel/Internacional [*Mexico ICAO location identifier*] (ICLI) .... MMCZ
Cozzo Spadaro [*Italy ICAO location identifier*] (ICLI) .... LICO
C.P. Clare [*NASDAQ symbol*] (TTSB) .... CPCL
CP National Network Services [*Concord, CA*] [*Telecommunications*] (TSSD) .... CPNS
CP1 [*Nevada*] [*Seismograph station code, US Geological Survey*] (SEIS) .... CPX
CP-17 [*Nevada*] [*Seismograph station code, US Geological Survey Closed*] (SEIS) .... CPN
CPA [*Certified Public Accountant*] **Associates** (EA) .... CPAA
CPA Cesar Augusto de la Cruze Lepe [*Mexico ICAO designator*] (FAAC) .... AUG
CPA [*Canadian Psychological Association*] **Interest Group on Women and Psychology** .... IGWAP
CPAC, Inc. [*Associated Press*] (SAG) .... CPAC
CPAC, Inc. [*NASDAQ symbol*] (SAG) .... CPAK
CPB, Inc. [*Associated Press*] (SAG) .... CPB
CPB, Inc. [*NASDAQ symbol*] (NQ) .... CPBI
CPC International, Inc. [*Formerly, Corn Products Co.*] [*NYSE symbol*] (SPSG) .... CPC
CPC International, Inc., Argo, IL [*Library symbol Library of Congress*] (LCLS) .... IArgoC
CPC Intl. [*NYSE symbol*] (TTSB) .... CPC
CPG Cyclic Stick Trigger (MCD) .... CCST
CPG Missile Control Panel (MCD) .... CMCP
CPG Missile Selection (MCD) .... CMSL
CPG Rocket Selection (MCD) .... CRKT
CPI Aerostructures [*NASDAQ symbol*] (TTSB) .... CPIA
CPI Aerostructures, Inc. [*Associated Press*] (SAG) .... CPI Aero
CPI Aerostructures, Inc. [*NASDAQ symbol*] (SAG) .... CPIA
CPI Corp. [*Associated Press*] (SAG) .... CPI
CPI Corp. [*NYSE symbol*] (SPSG) .... CPY
C-Polysaccharide [*Clinical chemistry*] .... CPS
CPS [*Itek Copy Processing System*] **User Group** [*Defunct*] (EA) .... CPSUG
CPU Power Calibration Instrument .... CPCI
CR [*Christian Rovsing*] **Computer Systems, Inc.** [*Los Angeles, CA*] [*Telecommunications*] (TSSD) .... CRCS
CRA [*Conzinc Riotinto of Australia*] **Exploration Ltd.** .... CRAE
CRA Managed Care [*NASDAQ symbol*] (TTSB) .... CRAA
CRA Managed Care, Inc. [*Associated Press*] (SAG) .... CRA
CRA Managed Care, Inc. [*NASDAQ symbol*] (SAG) .... CRAA
Crab Angle Sensing System (MCD) .... CASS
Crab Apple [*Defunct*] (EA) .... CA
Crab Orchard & Egyptian Railroad [*American Rail Heritage Ltd.*] .... CO & E

Crab Orchard & Egyptian Railroad [*American Rail Heritage Ltd.*] [*AAR code*] .... COER
Crabb on the Common Law [*A publication*] (DLA) .... Crabb CL
Crabb on the Common Law [*A publication*] (DLA) .... Crabb Com Law
Crabb on the Law of Real Property [*A publication*] (DLA) .... Crabb Real Prop
Crabb on the Law of Real Property [*A publication*] (DLA) .... Crabb RP
Crabbe's United States District Court Reports [*A publication*] (DLA) .... Crab
Crabbe's United States District Court Reports [*A publication*] (DLA) .... Crabbe
Crabb's Digest of Statutes [*A publication*] (DLA) .... Crabb Dig Stat
Crabb's English Synonyms [*A publication*] (DLA) .... Crabb Eng
Crabb's History of the English Law [*A publication*] (DLA) .... Crabb Eng L
Crabb's History of the English Law [*A publication*] (ILCA) .... Crabb Eng Law
Crabb's History of the English Law [*A publication*] (DLA) .... Crabb Hist Eng Law
Crabb's Precedents in Conveyancing [*A publication*] (DLA) .... Crabb Prec
Crabb's Technological Dictionary [*A publication*] (DLA) .... Crabb Technol Dict
Crabb's Technological Dictionary [*A publication*] (DLA) .... Techn Dict
Crabb's Treatise on Conveyancing [*A publication*] (DLA) .... Crabb Conv
Crab-Oriented Gyro (SAA) .... COG
Crabtree-Horsham Affective Trait Scale (EDAC) .... CHATS
Crack Arrest Temperature [*Nuclear energy*] (NRCH) .... CAT
Crack Initiation Temperature (PDAA) .... CIT
Crack Opening Displacement .... COD
Crack Opening Displacement Application (PDAA) .... CODA
Crack Propagation (AAG) .... CP
Crack Resources Ltd. [*Vancouver Stock Exchange symbol*] .... CCR
Crack Surface Displacement (PDAA) .... CSD
Crack Surface Opening Displacement .... CSOD
Crack Tip-Opening Angle (MCD) .... CTOA
Crack Tip-Opening Displacement (MCD) .... CTOD
Cracker Barrel Old Country Store [*NASDAQ symbol*] (SAG) .... CBRL
Cracker Barrel Old Country Store, Inc. [*Associated Press*] (SAG) .... CrkrBrl
Cracker Brl Old Ctry [*NASDAQ symbol*] (TTSB) .... CBRL
Crackle (VRA) .... ckcl
Crack-Opening Angle (MCD) .... COA
Craddock [*City in South Africa*] (ROG) .... CRA
Cradle (MSA) .... CRDL
Cradock [*South Africa*] [*ICAO location identifier*] (ICLI) .... FACD
Craft (AABC) .... CFT
Craft (DNAB) .... CRA
Craft .... CRFT
Craft and Amphibious Material Department [*British military*] (DMA) .... CAMD
Craft Council of Victoria [*Australia*] CCV
Craft Design and Technology .... CDT
Craft Digital Assistant [*Computer science*] .... CDA
Craft Inclination [*Aerospace*] (AAG) CI
Craft Landing Zone [*Military*] (DOMA) .... CLZ
Craft Loss [*Shipping*] .... C/L
Craft Masonry [*Freemasonry*] (ROG) .... CM
Craft Member of the British Horological Institute (DBQ) .... CMBHI
Craft of Opportunity Program [*Minesweeper*] (DOMA) .... COOP
Craft Union Department [*AFL-CIO*] .... CUD
Craft Yarn Council of America (EA) .... CYCA
Craft-Access Terminal [*Computer science*] .... CAT
Craftech Manufacturing, Inc. [*Toronto Stock Exchange symbol*] .... CTH
Crafted with Pride in USA Council (EA) .... CPUSAC
Crafter .... CFTR
Craftmade International, Inc. [*NASDAQ symbol*] (SAG) .... CRFT
Craftmade International, Inc. [*Associated Press*] (SAG) .... Crftmde
Craftmade Intl. [*NASDAQ symbol*] (TTSB) .... CRFT
Crafts, Protective and Custodial [*Military*] (DNAB) .... CPC
Craftsman [*Military British*] .... CFN
Craftsman .... CFT
Craftsman (MUGU) .... CFTMN
Craftsman [*Military British*] (DMA) .... Cftn
Craftsman Homeowner Club (EA) .... CHC
Craftsman of the Incorporated British Institute of Certified Carpenters (DI) .... CIBICC
Craftsman of the Institute of Carpenters [*British*] (DBQ) .... CIOC
Craftsmen .... CFTMN
Craftsmen Potters Association [*British*] (DBA) .... CPA
Cragar Industries, Inc. [*Associated Press*] (SAG) .... CragrInd
Cragar Industries, Inc. [*NASDAQ symbol*] (SAG) .... CRGR
Cragar Industries, Inc. [*Associated Press*] (SAG) .... CrgrInd
Craig [*Alaska*] [*Airport symbol*] (OAG) .... CGA
Craig [*Colorado*] [*Seismograph station code, US Geological Survey Closed*] (SEIS) .... CGC
Craig and Phillips' English Chancery Reports [*1840-41*] [*A publication*] (DLA) .... C & P
Craig and Phillips' English Chancery Reports [*1840-41*] [*A publication*] (DLA) .... Cr & Ph
Craig and Phillips' English Chancery Reports [*1840-41*] [*A publication*] (DLA) .... Craig & P
Craig and Phillips' English Chancery Reports [*1840-41*] [*A publication*] (DLA) .... Craig & Ph
Craig and Phillips' English Chancery Reports [*1840-41*] [*A publication*] (DLA) .... Craig & Ph (Eng)
Craig, CO [*Location identifier FAA*] (FAAL) .... CAG
Craig, CO [*AM radio station call letters*] .... KRAI
Craig, CO [*FM radio station call letters*] .... KRAI-FM
Craig Consumer Electronics [*Associated Press*] (SAG) .... CraigCE
Craig Consumer Electronics [*NASDAQ symbol*] (SAG) .... CREG
Craig Consumers Electronics [*NASDAQ symbol*] (TTSB) .... CREG
Craig Corp. [*Associated Press*] (SAG) .... Craig
Craig Corp. [*NYSE symbol*] (SAG) .... CRG
Craig Corp. CI'A' [*NYSE symbol*] (TTSB) .... CRGPr

Craig Cove [*Vanuatu*] [*Airport symbol*] (OAG) CCV
Craig Heritage Park, Parksville, British Columbia [*Library symbol National Library of Canada*] (NLC) .... BPCH
Craig House Technoma Workshop, Pittsburgh, PA [*OCLC symbol*] (OCLC) .... PIC
Craig Mountain Railway [*AAR code*] .... CMT
Craigie, Stewart, and Paton's House of Lords Appeals from Scotland [*1726-1857*] [*A publication*] (DLA) .... Pat App
Craigie, Stewart, and Paton's Scotch Appeal Cases [*1726-1821*] [*A publication*] (DLA) .... Cr & St
Craigie, Stewart, and Paton's Scotch Appeal Cases [*1726-1821*] [*A publication*] (DLA) .... Cr S & P
Craigie, Stewart, and Paton's Scotch Appeal Cases [*1726-1821*] [*A publication*] (DLA) .... Craig & St
Craigie, Stewart, and Paton's Scotch Appeal Cases [*1726-1821*] [*A publication*] (DLA) .... Craig S & P
Craigie, Stewart, and Paton's Scotch Appeal Cases [*1726-1821*] [*A publication*] (DLA) .... Craig St & Pat
Craigie, Stewart, and Paton's Scotch Appeal Cases [*1726-1821*] [*A publication*] (DLA) .... CS & P
Craigie, Stewart, and Paton's Scotch Appeal Cases [*1726-1821*] [*A publication*] (DLA) .... Paton
Craigius Jus Feudale [*A publication*] (DLA) .... Craig Jus Feud
Craigius Jus Feudale [*A publication*] (DLA) .... Craigius Jus Feud
Craig-Moffat County Public Library, Craig, CO [*Library symbol Library of Congress*] (LCLS) .... CoCra
Craigmont Mines [*Toronto Stock Exchange symbol Vancouver Stock Exchange symbol*] .... CRI
Craig's Etymological, Technological, and Pronouncing Dictionary [*A publication*] (DLA) .... Craig Dict
Craig's Practice [*A publication*] (DLA) .... Craig Pr
Craik-Leibovich [*Physics*] CL
Craik's English Causes Celebres [*A publication*] (DLA) .... Craik CC
Crailsheim [*Germany ICAO location identifier*] (ICLI) .... EDER
Crain, Inc. [*Toronto Stock Exchange symbol*] .... CRL
Crainfield Institute of Technology [*British ICAO designator*] (FAAC) .... CFD
Craiova [*Romania*] [*Airport symbol*] (OAG) .... CRA
Craiova [*Romania*] [*ICAO location identifier*] (ICLI) .... LRCV
Cramahe Township Public Library, Castleton, Ontario [*Library symbol National Library of Canada*] (BIB) .... OCCR
Cramer - von Mises Test [*Statistics*] .... CVM
Cranberry .... CRNBRRY
Cranberry Institute (EA) CI
Cranborne [*England*] .... CRANB
Cranbrook [*Canada*] [*Airport symbol*] (OAG) .... YXC
Cranbrook Academy of Art (GAGS) .... Cranbrook Acad Art
Cranbrook Academy of Art, Bloomfield Hills, MI [*Library symbol Library of Congress*] (LCLS) .... MiBloA
Cranbrook, BC [*Television station call letters*] CBUBT-7
Cranbrook, BC [*AM radio station call letters*] .... CKEK
Cranbrook, BC [*FM radio station call letters*] (RBYB) .... CKKR
Cranbrook, BC [*ICAO location identifier*] (ICLI) .... CYXC
Cranbrook Eductional Community, Archives and Historical Collections, Bloomfield Hills, MI [*Library symbol*] [*Library of Congress*] (LCLS) .... MiBloCAr
Cranbrook Institute of Science, Bloomfield Hills, MI [*Library symbol Library of Congress*] (LCLS) .... MiBloC
Cranbrook Public Library, British Columbia [*Library symbol National Library of Canada*] (NLC) .... BCR
Cranbury Press, Cranbury, NJ [*Library symbol Library of Congress*] (LCLS) .... NjCrbP
Cranch. Circuit Court Reports [*United States*] [*A publication*] (DLA) .... Cr
Cranch. Circuit Court Reports [*United States*] [*A publication*] (DLA) .... Cr CC
Cranch. Circuit Court Reports [*United States*] [*A publication*] (DLA) .... Cra
Cranch. Circuit Court Reports [*United States*] [*A publication*] (DLA) .... Cra CC
Cranch. Circuit Court Reports [*United States*] [*A publication*] (DLA) .... Cranch CC
Cranch's Decisions on Patent Appeals [*A publication*] (DLA) .... Cr Pat Dec
Cranch's District of Columbia Reports [*1-5 District of Columbia*] [*1801-40*] [*A publication*] (DLA) .... Cranch
Cranch's Patent Decisions [*United States*] [*A publication*] (DLA) .... Cranch Pat Dec
Crandall Library, Glens Falls, NY [*Library symbol Library of Congress*] (LCLS) .... NGlf
Crandell Feline Kidney [*Cytology*] .... CRFK
Crane [*Shipping*] (DS) .... CR
Crane (MSA) .... CRN
Crane .... CRN
Crane, Aircraft Maintenance (MCD) .... CAM
Crane Army Ammunition Activity (AABC) .... CAAA
Crane Attachment Lorry Mounted (PDAA) .... CALM
Crane Co. [*NYSE symbol*] (TTSB) .... CR
Crane Co. [*Associated Press*] (SAG) .... Crane
Crane Co., Chicago, IL [*Library symbol Library of Congress*] (LCLS) .... ICCra
Crane Engines [*Trains*] [*British*] C
Crane Load CL
Crane Manufacturers Association of America (EA) .... CMAA
Crane on Deck (MCD) .... COD
Crane Oral Dominance Test [*English and Spanish test*] .... CODT
Crane Ship [*Navy symbol Obsolete*] .... AB
Crane, TX [*AM radio station call letters*] .... KXOI
Crane, TX [*FM radio station call letters*] .... KXXL
Crane-Load Moment-Indicator (PDAA) .... CLM
Cranenburgh's Criminal Cases [*India*] [*A publication*] (DLA) .... Crane CC
Crane's Reports [*22-29 Montana*] [*A publication*] (DLA) .... Crane
Cranfield [*British ICAO location identifier*] (ICLI) .... EGTC
Cranfield Institute of Technology [*British*] (ARC) .... CIT
Cranfield Institute of Technology [*California*] .... CIT

Cranfield Institute of Technology, Cranfield, Bedfordshire, United Kingdom [*Library symbol Library of Congress*] (LCLS) .... UkCraT
Cranfield Product Engineering Centre [*Cranfield Institute of Technology*] [*Research center British*] (CB) .... CPEC
Cranfield Robotics and Automation Group [*British*] .... CRAG
Cranfield Unit for Precision Engineering [*British*] .... CUPE
Cranford Citizen & Chronicle, Cranford, NJ [*Library symbol Library of Congress*] (LCLS) .... NjCrC
Cranford Historical Society, Cranford, NJ [*Library symbol Library of Congress*] (LCLS) .... NjCrHi
Cranford Public Library, Cranford, NJ [*Library symbol Library of Congress*] (LCLS) .... NjCr
Cranial [*Anatomy*] .... CR
Cranial [*Anatomy*] .... cran
Cranial Academy (EA) .... CA
Cranial Computed Tomography [*Medicine*] (DMAA) .... CCT
Cranial Nerve [*Anatomy*] .... CN
[*First*] **Cranial Nerve** [*Second cranial nerve is NII, etc., through NVIII*] [*Medicine*] (DAVI) .... NI
Cranial Nerves [*Neurology*] (DAVI) .... cr nn
Cranial Nerves [*Anatomy*] (MAE) .... cr ns
Cranial Nerves [*Neurology*] (DAVI) .... CrN
Cranial Radiotherapy .... CRT
Craniocaudal [*Anatomy*] CC
Craniocerebral Trauma [*Medicine*] .... CCT
Craniocervical [*Anatomy*] (HGAA) CC
Craniofacial Biology Group of the International Association for Dental Research (EA) .... CBG
Craniofacial Dyssynostosis [*Medicine*] (DMAA) .... CFDS
Craniofacial Microsomia [*Medicine*] (DMAA) .... CFM
Craniofacial Pattern Profile [*Medicine*] (DMAA) .... CFPP
Craniofrontonasal Dysostosis [*Medicine*] (DMAA) .... CFND
Craniology .... CRAN
Craniology (ROG) .... CRANIOL
Craniomandibular Joint [*Anatomy*] .... CMJ
Craniomandibular Orthepedic Repositioning Device [*Dentistry and oral surgery*] (DAVI) .... CMOR
Craniometry (ROG) .... CRANIOM
Craniospinal [*Anatomy*] (AAMN) .... CrSp
Craniosynostosis, Boston Type [*Medicine*] (DMAA) .... CSB
Craniotomy (ROG) .... CRANIOT
Crank (KSC) .... CRK
Crank Angle (MCD) .... CA
Crankcase [*Automotive engineering*] .... C/C
Crankcase .... CRK
Crankcase (KSC) .... CRKC
Crankcase Depression Regulator [*AC Spark Plug Co.*] [*Automotive engineering*] .... CDR
Crankcase Depression Regulator Valve [*Emissions*] [*Automotive engineering*] .... CDRV
Cranking Amperes [*Battery*] [*Automotive engineering*] .... CA
Crankpin (MSA) .... CPIN
Crankshaft [*Automotive engineering*] .... C/S
Crankshaft .... CRKSFT
Crankshaft .... CRNKSHFT
Crankshaft .... CSHAFT
Crankshaft Position [*Automotive engineering*] .... CP
Crankshaft Position Sensor [*Automotive engineering*] .... CPS
Crankshaft Rate (NVT) .... CSR
Cranksheave (MSA) .... CRKSHV
Cranwell [*British ICAO location identifier*] (ICLI) .... EGYD
Cranwell FTU [*British ICAO designator*] (FAAC) .... CWL
Crary's New York Practice, Special Pleading [*A publication*] (DLA) .... Cra NY Pr
Crary's New York Practice, Special Pleading [*A publication*] (DLA) .... Crar Pr
Cras [*Tomorrow*] [*Pharmacy*] .... CR
Cras Mane [*Tomorrow Morning*] [*Pharmacy*] .... CM
Cras Mane Sumendus [*To Be Taken Tomorrow Morning*] [*Pharmacy*] .... CMS
Cras Nocte [*Tomorrow Night*] [*Pharmacy*] .... CN
Cras Nocte Sumendus [*To Be Taken Tomorrow Night*] [*Pharmacy*] .... CNS
Cras Vespere [*Tomorrow Evening*] [*Pharmacy*] .... CR VESP
Cras Vespere [*Tomorrow Evening*] [*Pharmacy*] CV
Crash Avoidance Research Data File [*NHTSA*] (TAG) .... CARD
Crash Boat .... CB
Crash Damage (MCD) .... CD
Crash Damage Material List (MCD) .... CDML
Crash Damage Overhaul (MCD) .... CDOVHL
Crash Damage Rate (MCD) .... CDR
Crash Data Position Indication Recorder (MCD) .... CDPIR
Crash Data Position Indicator Recorder Subsystem (PDAA) .... CDPIRS
Crash Finish [*of paper*] [*Graphic arts*] (DGA) .... CF
Crash Impact Absorbing Structure [*Automotive safety*] .... CIAS
Crash Injury Research and Engineering Network [*Medicine*] (DMAA) .... CIREN
Crash Injury Research Organization [*Cornell University*] .... CIRO
Crash Injury Scale Intermediate Level Investigation (PDAA) .... CISILI
Crash Locator Beacon [*Aviation*] (AFM) .... CLB
Crash Locator Beacon [*Aviation*] (FAAC) .... CLBN
Crash Outcome Data Evaluation System [*BTS*] (TAG) .... CODES
Crash Phone Activated [*Aviation*] (FAAC) .... CPA
Crash Position Indicator [*Aviation*] (AFM) .... CPI
Crash Position Indicator/Flight Data Recorder [*Aviation*] (MCD) .... CPI/FDR
Crash Vehicle Simulator .... CVS
Crash-Resistant Fuel System (RDA) .... CRFS
Crash-Survivable Flight Data Recorder (MCD) .... CSFDR
Crashworthiness Data System [*NHTSA*] (TAG) .... CDS
Crashworthy Fuel Systems [*Aviation*] .... CWFS
Crassulacean Acid Metabolism [*Biochemistry*] .... CAM
Crassus [*of Plutarch*] [*Classical studies*] (OCD) .... Crass
Crastinus [*Of Tomorrow*] [*Pharmacy*] .... CRAST
Crate .... CR
Crate .... CRT
Crateaudun [*France ICAO location identifier*] (ICLI) .... LFOC
Crated - Rocket Unit [*Military*] .... CRU
Crater [*Costa Rica*] [*Seismograph station code, US Geological Survey*] (SEIS) A10
Crater (ROG) .... CRA
Crater [*Constellation*] .... Crat
Crater [*Constellation*] .... Crt
Crater Lake National Park .... CRLA
Crater Production Rate [*Geology*] .... CPR
Cratering Demolition Device .... CDD
Crater-Lamp Recorder .... CLR
Craters of the Moon National Monument .... CRMO
Crates .... CTS
Crateus [*Brazil*] [*Airport symbol*] (AD) .... CTH
Crating (MSA) .... CTG
C-Rating Overall [*Military*] (CAAL) .... CROVL
Crating, Packaging Instructions .... CPI
Crato [*Brazil*] [*Airport symbol*] (AD) .... CQQ
Craton, Lodge and Knight [*British*] .... CLK
Cratylus [*of Plato*] [*Classical studies*] (OCD) .... Cra
Cravath, Swaine & Moore, New York, NY [*Library symbol*] [*Library of Congress*] (LCLS) .... NNCAM
Craven Community College, Havelock Learning Center, Havelock, NC [*Library symbol*] [*Library of Congress*] (LCLS) .... NcHavCr
Craven Resources Ltd. [*Vancouver Stock Exchange symbol*] .... CNI
Craven Technical Institute, New Bern, NC [*Library symbol Library of Congress*] (LCLS) .... NcNbC
Craven-Pamlico-Carteret Regional Library [*Library network*] .... C-P-C
Craven-Pamlico-Carteret Regional Library, New Bern, NC [*Library symbol Library of Congress*] (LCLS) .... NcNbCP
Cravo Norte [*Colombia*] [*Airport symbol*] (OAG) .... RAV
Crawford & Co. (MHDW) .... CRAW
Crawford & Co. [*Associated Press*] (SAG) .... Crwfd
Crawford & Co. Cl'B' [*NYSE symbol*] (TTSB) .... CRD.B
Crawford and Dix's Irish Abridged Cases [*A publication*] (DLA) .... Ab Ca
Crawford and Dix's Irish Abridged Cases [*A publication*] (DLA) .... Abr Cas
Crawford and Dix's Irish Abridged Cases [*A publication*] (DLA) .... C & DAC
Crawford and Dix's Irish Abridged Cases [*A publication*] (DLA) .... Cr & Dix Ab Ca
Crawford and Dix's Irish Abridged Cases [*A publication*] (DLA) .... Cr & Dix Ab Cas
Crawford and Dix's Irish Abridged Cases [*A publication*] (DLA) .... Craw & D Ab Cas
Crawford and Dix's Irish Abridged Cases [*A publication*] (DLA) .... Craw & D Abr Cas
Crawford and Dix's Irish Abridged Cases [*A publication*] (DLA) .... Craw & D (Ir)
Crawford and Dix's Irish Abridged Cases [*A publication*] (DLA) .... Crawf & D Abr Cas
Crawford and Dix's Irish Circuit Court Cases [*A publication*] (DLA) .... C & D
Crawford and Dix's Irish Circuit Court Cases [*A publication*] (DLA) .... C & DCC
Crawford and Dix's Irish Circuit Court Cases [*A publication*] (DLA) .... Cr & Dix
Crawford and Dix's Irish Circuit Court Cases [*A publication*] (DLA) .... Cr & Dix CC
Crawford and Dix's Irish Circuit Court Cases [*A publication*] (DLA) .... Craw & D
Crawford and Dix's Irish Circuit Court Cases [*A publication*] (DLA) .... Craw & DCC (Ir)
Crawford and Dix's Irish Circuit Court Cases [*A publication*] (DLA) .... Craw & Dix
Crawford and Dix's Irish Circuit Court Cases [*A publication*] (DLA) .... Crawf & D
Crawford and Dix's Irish Circuit Court Cases [*A publication*] (DLA) .... Crawf & Dix
Crawford and Dix's Irish Circuit Court Cases [*A publication*] (DLA) .... Ir Cir Cas
Crawford and Dix's Irish Criminal Cases [*A publication*] (DLA) .... Crawf & Dix
Crawford Bay, BC [*FM radio station call letters*] .... CBTE
Crawford Bay, BC [*FM radio station call letters*] .... CKKC-FM
Crawford Community Library, Crawford, CO [*Library symbol Library of Congress*] (LCLS) .... CoCfC
Crawford Community Library, Crawford, CO [*Library symbol*] [*Library of Congress*] (LCLS) .... CoCfCL
Crawford County Democrat, English, IN [*Library symbol Library of Congress*] (LCLS) .... InEngD
Crawford County Historical Society, Meadville, PA [*Library symbol Library of Congress*] (LCLS) .... PMCHi
Crawford County Legal Journal [*Pennsylvania*] [*A publication*] (DLA) .... Craw Co Leg J (PA)
Crawford County Legal Journal [*Pennsylvania*] [*A publication*] (DLA) .... Crawford Co Leg Jour
Crawford County Library, Grayling, MI [*Library symbol Library of Congress*] (LCLS) .... MiGray
Crawford County Public Library, English, IN [*Library symbol Library of Congress*] (LCLS) .... InEng
Crawford, GA [*FM radio station call letters*] .... WGMG
Crawford Small Parts Dexterity Test [*Education*] .... CSPDT
Crawford W. Long Memorial Hospital, Atlanta, GA [*Library symbol Library of Congress*] (LCLS) .... GACL
Crawford&Co. Cl'A'non-vtg [*NYSE symbol*] (TTSB) .... CRD.A
Crawford's Reports [*53-69, 72-101 Arkansas*] [*A publication*] (DLA) .... Craw
Crawford's Reports [*53-69, 72-101 Arkansas*] [*A publication*] (DLA) .... Craw (Ark)
Crawfordsville District Public Library, Crawfordsville, IN [*Library symbol Library of Congress*] (LCLS) .... InC
Crawfordsville, IN [*Location identifier FAA*] (FAAL) .... CFJ
Crawfordsville, IN [*AM radio station call letters*] .... WCVL
Crawfordsville, IN [*FM radio station call letters*] .... WIMC
Crawfordsville, IN [*FM radio station call letters*] .... WNDY

Crawfordsville Journal and Review, Crawfordsville, IN [*Library symbol Library of Congress*] (LCLS) .... InCJR
Crawfordville, FL [*FM radio station call letters*] .... WAKU
Crawler/Transporter [*Aerospace*] (KSC) .... C/T
Crawler/Transporter Intercom System [*Aerospace*] (KSC) .... CTIS
Crawler/Transporter/Mobile Service Structure [*Aerospace*] (KSC) .... CT/MSS
Crawlerway [*NASA*] (KSC) .... CW
Cray Fortran [*Programming language*] (NITA) .... CFT
Cray Operating System [*Computer science*] .... COS
Cray Research [*NYSE symbol*] (TTSB) .... CYR
Cray Research, Inc. [*Associated Press*] (SAG) .... CrayRs
Cray Research, Inc. .... CRI
Cray Research, Inc. [*NYSE symbol*] (SPSG) .... CYR
Crayfish (DSUE) .... CRAY
Crayon (VRA) .... cray
Crayon, Water Color, and Craft Institute (EA) .... CWCCI
Crazy .... CRZY
Crazy Horse Memorial Foundation (EA) .... CHMF
Crazy Woman Creek Bancorp, Inc. [*Associated Press*] (SAG) .... CrazyW
Crazy Woman Creek Bancorp, Inc. [*NASDAQ symbol*] (SAG) .... CRZY
Crazy Woman Creek Bncp [*NASDAQ symbol*] (TTSB) .... CRZY
Crazy Woman, WY [*Location identifier FAA*] (FAAL) .... CZI
CRC Press [*Boca Raton, FL*] .... CRC
C-Reactive Protein [*Clinical chemistry*] .... CRP
C-Reactive Protein Antiserum [*Clinical chemistry*] .... CRPA
Cream [*Pharmacy*] (DAVI) .... CR
Cream [*Philately*] .... cr
Cream (ADA) .... CRM
Cream .... CRM
Cream Laid [*Paper*] (DGA) CL
Cream of Tartar Substitute .... CTS
Cream Received in Separating Cottonseed Oil .... CRISCO
Cream Ridge Fruit Research Center [*Rutgers University*] [*Research center*] (RCD) .... CRRC
Cream Shade [*Paper*] .... CS
Cream Silver Mines Ltd. [*Vancouver Stock Exchange symbol*] .... CEM
Cream Wove [*Paper*] (DGA) .... CW
Cream Wove Large Post [*Paper*] (DGA) .... CWP
Creamery .... CRMRY
Creamware (VRA) .... crmwr
Crease [*Deltiology*] .... CR
Crease Clinic Library, Essondale, BC, Canada [*Library symbol Library of Congress*] (LCLS) .... CaBEC
Crease Recovery Angle [*Textile technology*] .... CRA
Creasy on International Law [*A publication*] (DLA) .... Creas Int L
Creasy's Ceylon Reports [*A publication*] (DLA) .... Creasy
Creasy's Colonial Constitutions [*A publication*] (DLA) .... Creas Col Const
Creasy's Rise and Progress of the English Constitution [*A publication*] (DLA) .... Creas Eng Cons
Create Occurrence Table [*University of Minnesota*] (NITA) .... COT
Create Test File (IAA) .... CRTF
Create, Update, Interrogate, and Display [*Computer science*] (MHDI) .... CUPID
Created C
Created [*or Creation*] .... CR
Creatine [*Biochemistry*] .... creat
Creatine Kinase [*Also, CPK*] [*An enzyme*] .... CK
Creatine Kinase B [*An enzyme*] .... CKB
Creatine Kinase, Muscle Type (DMAA) .... CKM
Creatine Phosphate [*Phosphocreatine; see PC*] [*Biochemistry*] .... CP
Creatine Phosphate [*or Phosphocreatine*] [*Biochemistry*] (DAVI) .... CrP
Creatine Phosphokinase [*Biochemistry*] (DAVI) .... CP
Creatine Phosphokinase [*Preferred form is CK*] [*An enzyme*] .... CPK
Creatine Phosphokinase Depleted [*Medicine*] .... CPKD
Creatine Phosphokinase Isoenzyme [*Biochemistry*] (DAVI) .... CPKI
Creatine Phosphokinase Isoenzyme [*Biochemistry*] (DAVI) .... CPKISO
Creating an Automatic Design .... CAD
Creatinine [*Biochemistry*] .... Cr
Creatinine [*Biochemistry*] (DAVI) .... CREA
Creatinine [*Biochemistry*] .... creat
Creatinine Clearance [*Clinical chemistry*] CC
Creatinine Clearance [*Clinical chemistry*] (MAE) .... Ccr
Creatinine Clearance [*Biochemistry*] (DAVI) .... CrCl
Creatinine Height Index [*Biochemistry*] (DAVI) .... CHI
Creatinine Phosphate [*Biochemistry*] (AAMN) .... Cr P
Creatinine Urine [*Test*] [*Biochemistry*] (DAVI) .... CREA-U
Creatinine Urine Spot [*Test*] [*Biochemistry*] (DAVI) .... CREA-S
Creation .... CREAT
Creation Facilities Program [*Computer science*] (IBMDP) .... CFP
Creation Health Foundation (EA) .... CHF
Creation of New Enterprises [*British*] (DI) .... CONE
Creation Research .... CR
Creation Research Society (EA) .... CRS
Creation Science Legal Defense Fund (EA) .... CSLDF
Creation Science Movement [*British*] .... CSM
Creation Sheet (SAA) .... CS
Creation Social Science and Humanities Society (EA) .... CSSHS
Creation-Evolution .... CREVO
Creative .... CREATV
Creative and Performing Arts .... CAPA
[*The*] Creative and Supportive Trust [*British*] (DI) .... CAST
Creative Art Group [*Australia*] .... CAG
Creative Artists Agency .... CAA
Creative Artists Public Service Program (EA) .... CAPS
Creative Audio and Music Electronics Organization (EA) .... CAMEO
Creative BioMolecules [*NASDAQ symbol*] (TTSB) .... CBMI

Creative BioMolecules, Inc. [*NASDAQ symbol*] (SAG) .... CBMI
Creative BioMolecules, Inc. [*Associated Press*] (SAG) .... CrBioMol
[*The*] Creative Coalition .... TCC
Creative Computer Applications, Inc. [*AMEX symbol*] (SAG) .... CAP
Creative Computer Applications, Inc. [*Associated Press*] (SAG) .... CreatC
Creative Computers [*NASDAQ symbol*] (TTSB) .... MALL
Creative Computers, Inc. [*Associated Press*] (SAG) .... CreaCpt
Creative Computers, Inc. [*NASDAQ symbol*] (SAG) .... MALL
Creative Computing Services [*Information service or system*] (IID) .... CCS
Creative Development Unit [*Australian Film Commission*] .... CDU
Creative Director (DOAD) .... CD
Creative Education Foundation (EA) .... CEF
Creative Electronic Systems .... CES
Creative Imagination Scale [*Psychology*] (EDAC) .... CIS
Creative Incentive Coalition CIC
Creative Industries Group, Inc. [*Auburn Hills, MI*] (TSSD) .... CIG
Creative Industries of Detroit, Inc. [*Warren, MI*] [*Telecommunications*] (TSSD) .... CID
Creative Initiative [*Later, BWF*] (EA) CI
Creative Learning Products [*NASDAQ symbol*] (TTSB) .... CLPI
Creative Learning Products, Inc. [*NASDAQ symbol*] (NQ) .... CLPI
Creative Learnings Products [*Associated Press*] (SAG) .... CreatLrn
Creative List Services, Inc. [*Information service or system*] (IID) .... CLS
Creative Management Technologies (AAGC) .... CMT
Creative Med Dev [*NASDAQ symbol*] (TTSB) .... CMDI
Creative Modern Design .... CMD
Creative Multimedia Corp. [*Database producer*] (IID) .... CMC
Creative Music Foundation (EA) .... CMF
Creative Playthings Foundation [*Defunct*] .... CPF
Creative Printers of America .... CPA
Creative Problem-Solving (PDAA) .... CPS
Creative Problem-Solving Institute (EDAC) .... CPSI
Creative Progm Tech Venture [*NASDAQ symbol*] (TTSB) .... CPTV
Creative Programing & Technology [*Associated Press*] (SAG) .... CrePrg
Creative Programming & Technology [*NASDAQ symbol*] (SAG) .... CPTV
Creative Research Systems [*Information service or system*] (IID) .... CRS
Creative Resources Guild (EA) .... CRG
Creative Services Association [*British*] (DBA) .... CSA
Creative Strategies International (HGAA) .... CSI
Creative Strategies Research International [*Information service or system*] (IID) .... CSRI
Creative Technologies [*NASDAQ symbol*] (TTSB) .... CRTV
Creative Technologies Corp. [*Associated Press*] (SAG) .... CreTch
Creative Technologies Corp. [*NASDAQ symbol*] (SAG) .... CRTV
Creative Technology [*NASDAQ symbol*] (TTSB) .... CREAF
Creative Technology Ltd. [*NASDAQ symbol*] (SAG) .... CREA
Creative Technology Ltd. [*Associated Press*] (SAG) .... CreTcLtd
Creative Time (EA) .... CT
Creative Times Project [*Later, CT*] (EA) .... CTP
Creative Tour Operators Association .... CTOA
Creative Tourist Agents' Conference [*British*] (BI) .... CTAC
Creative Use of Leisure Time under Restrictive Environments [*Federally funded prison program*] .... CULTURE
Creative Visual Dynamics (OA) .... CVD
Creativity Attitude Survey [*Educational test*] .... CAS
Creativity Checklist [*Educational test*] .... CCH
Creativity Quotient [*Testing term*] .... CQ
Creativity Tests for Children [*Child development test series*] .... CT
Creche and Kindergarten Association of Queensland [*Australia*] .... CKAQ
Credence Systems [*NASDAQ symbol*] (TTSB) .... CMOS
Credence Systems Corp. [*NASDAQ symbol*] (SAG) .... CMOS
Credence Systems Corp. [*Associated Press*] (SAG) .... CredSys
Credentialing Commission (EA) .... CR
Credicorp Ltd. [*Associated Press*] (SAG) .... Credicp
Credit (AFM) .... CR
Credit .... CRDT
Credit (AABC) .... CRED
Credit [*or Creditor*] (ROG) .... CT
Credit Acceptance [*NASDAQ symbol*] (TTSB) .... CACC
Credit Acceptance Corp. [*NASDAQ symbol*] (SAG) .... CACC
Credit Acceptance Corp. [*Associated Press*] (SAG) .... CrdAcp
Credit Account [*Business term*] .... CA
Credit Account Voucher (DCTA) .... CAV
Credit Agricole [*France*] .... CA
Credit and Load Management System [*Software*] [*British*] .... CALMS
Credit Associate [*Society of Certified Consumer Credit Executives*] [*Designation awarded by*] .... CA
Credit Authorization Terminal .... CAT
Credit Balance .... CB
Credit Card [*Business term*] (ADA) CC
Credit Card Authorisation and Fund Transfer System [*British*] .... CRAFTS
Credit Card Purchase (AFM) .... CCP
Credit Card Reader .... CCR
Credit Card Service Bureau .... CCSB
Credit Card Service Bureau of America [*Later, CCSB*] .... CCSBA
Credit Card Users of America [*Beverly Hills, CA*] (EA) .... CCUA
Credit Clearing Outward (DCTA) .... CCO
Credit Code (DNAB) .... CDC
Credit Control Act [*1969*] .... CCA
Credit de la Cote-D'Ivoire [*Credit Bank of the Ivory Coast*] CCI
Credit Depot [*NASDAQ symbol*] (TTSB) .... LEND
Credit Depot Corp. [*Associated Press*] (SAG) .... CrdDept
Credit Depot Corp. [*NASDAQ symbol*] (SAG) .... LEND
Credit Factoring International [*Commercial firm British*] .... CFI
Credit for Exports [*Bank*] [*British*] .... CFX

Credit Insurance Logistics Automated (PDAA) .... CRILA
Credit Licensing Authority [*Victoria*] [*Australia*] .... CLA
Credit Limit (DCTA) CL
Credit Lyonnais Bank Nederland [*Credit Lyonnais' Dutch subsidiary*] (ECON) .... CLBN
Credit Memo .... CM
Credit Note [*Business term*] .... CN
Credit Officers Group (EA) .... COG
Credit Populaire d'Algerie [*People's Credit Bank of Algeria*] (IMH) .... CPA
Credit Professionals International (EA) .... CPI
Credit Protection Association [*British*] (DBA) .... CPA
Credit Rating [*Business term*] (ADA) .... CR
Credit Reference Association of Australia .... CRAA
Credit Report [*Business term*] .... CR
Credit Requisition (MCD) .... CR
Credit Research Center [*Purdue University*] [*Research center*] (RCD) .... CRC
Credit Research Foundation [*Lake Success, NY*] (EA) .... CRF
Credit Suisse [*Bank*] .... CS
Credit Suisse Financial Products [*British*] (ECON) .... CSFP
Credit Suisse First Boston [*Banking*] (ECON) .... CSFB
Credit Systems Inc. .... CSI
Credit Transfer .... CT
Credit Transfer Fee [*Business term*] .... CTF
Credit Tribunal [*Victoria*] [*Australia*] .... CT
Credit Union .... CRU
Credit Union .... CU
Credit Union Australia Ltd. .... CUA
Credit Union Central of Manitoba, Winnipeg, Manitoba [*Library symbol National Library of Canada*] (NLC) .... MWCU
Credit Union Central of Manitoba, Winnipeg, MB, Canada [*Library symbol Library of Congress*] (LCLS) .... CaMWCU
Credit Union Central, Regina, Saskatchewan [*Library symbol National Library of Canada*] (NLC) .... SRCU
Credit Union Central, Regina, SK, Canada [*Library symbol Library of Congress*] (LCLS) .... CaSRCU
Credit Union Executives Society .... CUES
Credit Union League of Great Britain (DI) .... CULGB
Credit Union National Association (EA) .... CUNA
Credit Union Office (DNAB) .... CUO
Credit Union Share Draft .... CUSD
Credit Union Stabilisation Board [*South Australia*] .... CUSB
Credit Valley Hospital, Mississauga, Ontario [*Library symbol National Library of Canada*] (NLC) .... OMCVH
Credit Women - International [*Later, CPI*] (EA) .... CW-I
Credit Women's Breakfast Clubs of North America [*Later, CPI*] (EA) .... CWBCNA
Creditable Record .... CR
Crediton [*England*] .... CRED
Creditor (ROG) .... CR
Creditor [*Legal shorthand*] (LWAP) .... CROR
Creditors' Bill [*Legal term*] (DLA) .... CRED B
Creditreform Databank [*Verband der Vereine Creditreform eV*] [*Information service or system*] (IID) VC
Credo [*Creed*] [*Latin*] .... CR
Credo Pete [*NASDAQ symbol*] (TTSB) .... CRED
Credo Petroleum Corp. [*NASDAQ symbol*] (NQ) .... CRED
Credo Petroleum Corp. [*Associated Press*] (SAG) .... CredoPt
Cree [*MARC language code Library of Congress*] (LCCP) .... cre
Cree Airways Corp. [*Canada ICAO designator*] (FAAC) .... CRE
Cree Questionnaire [*Psychology*] .... CQ
Cree Regional Authority, Grand Council of the Crees (of Quebec) [*Administration Regionale Crie, Grand Conseil des Cris (du Quebec)*] **Val D'Or, Quebec** [*Library symbol National Library of Canada*] (NLC) .... QVGCCQ
Cree Research [*NASDAQ symbol*] (TTSB) .... CREE
Cree Research, Inc. [*NASDAQ symbol*] (SAG) .... CREE
Cree Research, Inc. [*Associated Press*] (SAG) .... CreeRsh
Cree School Board, Chisasibi, James Bay, Quebec [*Library symbol National Library of Canada*] (BIB) .... QCCS
Creed Taylor, Inc. [*Recording label*] .... CTI
Creede Public Library, Creede, CO [*Library symbol Library of Congress*] (LCLS) .... CoCre
Creedence Clearwater Revival [*Rock music group*] .... CCR
Creedmore Psychiatric Center, Queens Village, New York, NY [*Library symbol Library of Congress*] (LCLS) .... NNCre
Creek (ADA) .... CK
Creek [*Maps and charts*] .... CR
Creek [*Commonly used*] (OPSA) .... CR
Creek [*Commonly used*] (OPSA) .... CREEK
Creek .... CRK
Creek (MCD) .... CRK
Creek Chub [*Ichthyology*] Cc
Creek Indian Memorial Association (EA) .... CIMA
Creel Associates, Inc. [*Oak Brook, IL*] (TSSD) .... CA
Creemore Public Library, Ontario [*Library symbol National Library of Canada*] (BIB) .... OCR
Creep Form Block (MCD) .... CFB
Creep Form Block Template (MCD) .... CFBT
Creep in Axisymmetric Shells .... CRASH
Creep Isostatic Pressing .... CRISP
Creeping [*Horticulture*] .... CR
[*The*] **Creighton University** (GAGS) .... Creighton U
Creighton University, Alumni Library, Omaha, NE [*Library symbol Library of Congress*] (LCLS) .... NbOC-A
Creighton University, Alumni Library, Omaha, NE [*OCLC symbol*] (OCLC) .... OCA
Creighton University, Health Sciences Library, Omaha, NE [*Library symbol Library of Congress*] (LCLS) .... NbOC-H
Creighton University, Health Sciences Library, Omaha, NE [*OCLC symbol*] (OCLC) .... OCM
Creighton University, Law Library, Omaha, NE [*OCLC symbol*] (OCLC) CLL
Creighton University, Omaha, NE [*Library symbol Library of Congress*] (LCLS) .... NbOC
Creighton University, School of Dentistry, Omaha, NE [*Library symbol Library of Congress*] (LCLS) .... NbOC-D
Creighton University, School of Law, Omaha, NE [*Library symbol Library of Congress*] (LCLS) .... NbOC-L
Creighton University, School of Medicine and School of Pharmacy, Omaha, NE [*Library symbol Library of Congress*] (LCLS) .... NbOC-M
Creil [*France ICAO location identifier*] (ICLI) .... LFPC
Cremate [*or Crematorium*] (DSUE) .... CREM
Cremation Association of America [*Later, CANA*] (EA) .... CAA
Cremation Association of North America (EA) .... CANA
Cremation Society of Great Britain .... CSGB
Crematory .... CRMTRY
Cremona Public Library, Alberta [*Library symbol National Library of Canada*] (NLC) .... ACRE
Crenated [*Red blood cells*] [*Hematology*] (DAVI) .... CREN
Crendon [*England*] .... CREN
Crenellation (VRA) .... crnltn
Creo Society [*Defunct*] (EA) .... CS
Creoles and Pidgins [*MARC language code Library of Congress*] (LCCP) .... crp
Creosote [*Telecommunications*] (TEL) C
Creosote .... CRE
Creosote Bushes [*Ecology*] .... C/B
Creosoted Wood Duct [*Telecommunications*] (TEL) .... CWD
Crepe .... CRP
Crepitus [*Crepitation*] [*Medicine*] .... CREP
Crescendo [*Music*] (ROG) .... CR
Crescendo [*Music*] .... CRES
Crescendo [*Music*] .... CRESC
Crescendo [*Music*] (ODBW) .... cresc
Crescendo [*Music*] .... CRESO
Crescent [*Commonly used*] (OPSA) .... CRECENT
Crescent [*Commonly used*] (OPSA) .... CRES
Crescent (ODBW) .... Cres
Crescent .... CRES
Crescent (MCD) .... CRES
Crescent (DD) .... Cres
Crescent .... CRESC
Crescent [*Commonly used*] (OPSA) .... CRESCENT
Crescent [*Commonly used*] (OPSA) .... CRESENT
Crescent (ADA) .... CRS
Crescent [*Commonly used*] (OPSA) .... CRSCNT
Crescent (ROG) .... CRSCT
Crescent [*Commonly used*] (OPSA) .... CRSENT
Crescent [*Commonly used*] (OPSA) .... CRSNT
Crescent City [*California*] [*Airport symbol*] (OAG) .... CEC
Crescent City, CA [*FM radio station call letters*] .... KCRE
Crescent City, CA [*AM radio station call letters*] .... KFVR
Crescent City, CA [*AM radio station call letters*] .... KPOD
Crescent City Public Library, Crescent City, CA [*Library symbol Library of Congress*] (LCLS) CCc
Crescent City Public Library, Crescent City, CA [*Library symbol*] [*Library of Congress*] (LCLS) CCcL
Crescent Heights High School, Medicine Hat, AB, Canada [*Library symbol Library of Congress*] (LCLS) .... CaAMCH
Crescent Heights High School, Medicine Hat, Alberta [*Library symbol National Library of Canada*] (NLC) .... AMCH
Crescent Mines Ltd. [*Vancouver Stock Exchange symbol*] .... CRS
Crescent North, CA [*FM radio station call letters*] .... KPOD-FM
Crescent Real Estate Eq [*NYSE symbol*] (TTSB) .... CEI
Crescent Real Estate Equities [*Associated Press*] (SAG) .... CresRE
Crescentic .... CR
Crescit sub Pondere Virtus [*Virtue Increases under a Burden*] [*Latin*] .... Cres sub Pond Virt
Cresco, IA [*Location identifier FAA*] (FAAL) .... CJJ
Cresco, IA [*FM radio station call letters*] .... KCZQ
Cresco Public Library, Cresco, IA [*Library symbol*] [*Library of Congress*] (LCLS) .... IaCre
Cresco Public Library, Cresco, IA [*Library symbol Library of Congress*] (LCLS) .... IaCresco
Cresco Times-Plain Dealer, Cresco, IA [*Library symbol Library of Congress*] (LCLS) .... IaCrescoTP
Cresco Times-Plain Dealer, Cresco, IA [*Library symbol*] [*Library of Congress*] (LCLS) .... IaCreTP
Crescomm Transmission Services, Inc. [*Fairfield, NJ*] [*Telecommunications*] (TSSD) .... CTS
Cresol Formaldehyde .... CF
Cresol Red [*Acid-base indicator*] (AAMN) .... CR
Cresolphthalein Complexone [*Analytical chemistry*] .... CPC
Cressent [*A publication*] (BRI) .... Cres
Cresson, PA [*FM radio station call letters*] .... WBXQ
Cresswell's Insolvency Cases [*1827-29*] [*England*] [*A publication*] (DLA) .... Cress
Cresswell's Insolvency Cases [*1827-29*] [*England*] [*A publication*] (ILCA) .... Cress Ins Ca
Cresswell's Insolvency Cases [*1827-29*] [*England*] [*A publication*] (DLA) .... Cress Ins Cas
Cresswell's Insolvency Cases [*1827-29*] [*England*] [*A publication*] (DLA) .... Cress Insolv Cas
Crest [*Commonly used*] (OPSA) .... CREST
Crest [*Postal Service standard*] (OPSA) .... CRST
Crest .... CRST

Crest Factor [*Physics*] (IAA) ..... CF
Crest Hill, IL [*FM radio station call letters*] ..... WCCQ
Crest Resources Ltd. [*Vancouver Stock Exchange symbol*] ..... CQR
Crest Time (MAE) ..... CT
Crest Working Voltage [*Electronics*] (IAA) ..... CWV
Crestar Financial [*NYSE symbol*] (TTSB) ..... CF
Crestar Financial Corp. [*Associated Press*] (SAG) ..... Crestar
Crestbrook Forest Industries Ltd. [*Toronto Stock Exchange symbol Vancouver Stock Exchange symbol*] ..... CFI
Crested Butte, CO [*FM radio station call letters*] ..... KBUT
Crested Corp. [*NASDAQ symbol*] (SAG) ..... CBAG
Crested Corp. [*Associated Press*] (SAG) ..... CrstCp
Crested Fowl Club of America [*Later, CFFA*] (EA) ..... CFCA
Crested Fowl Fanciers' Association (EA) ..... CFFA
Crestline, OH [*FM radio station call letters*] ..... WAPQ
Crestline, OH [*FM radio station call letters*] (RBYB) ..... WYXZ-FM
Creston, BC [*AM radio station call letters*] ..... CFKC
Creston, IA [*Location identifier FAA*] (FAAL) ..... CSQ
Creston, IA [*FM radio station call letters*] ..... KITR
Creston, IA [*AM radio station call letters*] ..... KSIB
Creston News-Advertiser, Creston, IA [*Library symbol Library of Congress*] (LCLS) ..... IaCresNA
Creston Public Library, British Columbia [*Library symbol National Library of Canada*] (NLC) ..... BCRE
Creston Valley Museum, Creston, British Columbia [*Library symbol National Library of Canada*] (NLC) ..... BCVM
Crestview/Bob Sikes [*Florida*] [*ICAO location identifier*] (ICLI) ..... KCEW
Crestview, FL [*Location identifier FAA*] (FAAL) ..... CEW
Crestview, FL [*FM radio station call letters*] ..... WAAZ
Crestview, FL [*AM radio station call letters*] ..... WCNU
Crestview, FL [*AM radio station call letters*] ..... WJSB
Crestwood Elementary School, East Grand Forks, MN [*Library symbol*] [*Library of Congress*] (LCLS) ..... MnEgfCE
Crestwood Library District, Crestwood, IL [*Library symbol Library of Congress*] (LCLS) ..... ICw
Crestwood Library District, Crestwood, IL [*Library symbol*] [*Library of Congress*] (LCLS) ..... ICwL
Crestwood, MO [*FM radio station call letters*] ..... KSHE
Creswell, OR [*FM radio station call letters*] (RBYB) ..... KNRQ-FM
Cresyl Diphenylphosphate ..... CDP
Cresyl Glycidyl Ether [*Organic chemistry*] ..... CGE
Cresyl Red [*Chemistry*] (DAVI) ..... CR
Cresyl Violet [*Biological stain*] CV
Creta Praeparata [*Prepared Chalk*] [*Pharmacy*] (ROG) ..... CRET PP
Cretaceous [*Geology*] ..... CRET
Cretaceous [*Period, era, or system*] [*Geology*] ..... K
Cretaceous and Tertiary [*Geology*] ..... C-T
Cretaceous Normal Superchron [*Geology*] ..... CNS
Cretaceous-Tertiary [*Geology*] ..... KT
Cretan Airlines SA [*Greece*] [*ICAO designator*] (FAAC) ..... KRT
Cretans' Association "Omonoia" (EA) ..... CAO
Crete, IL [*FM radio station call letters*] ..... WEMG
Crete, NE [*FM radio station call letters*] ..... KDNE
Crete, NE [*FM radio station call letters*] ..... KKNB
Crete Public Library, Crete, IL [*Library symbol Library of Congress*] (LCLS) ..... ICre
Crete Public Library, Crete, NE [*Library symbol Library of Congress*] (LCLS) ..... NbCr
Creutzfeldt-Jakob Disease [*Neurological disorder*] ..... CJ
Creutzfeldt-Jakob Disease [*Neurological disorder*] ..... CJD
Crew (MSA) ..... CR
Crew Accommodations and Support Equipment (SSD) ..... CASE
Crew Activities Scheduling Program [*NASA*] (KSC) ..... CASP
Crew Activity Plan (MCD) ..... CAP
Crew Activity Planning System (SSD) ..... CAPS
Crew and Equipment Translation Aids [*NASA*] ..... CETA
Crew and Passenger Support Equipment [*Military*] (AFIT) ..... CPSE
Crew Augmented Stability Factor [*Boating*] ..... CASF
Crew Ballistic Shelter (MCD) ..... CBS
Crew Boat ..... CB
Crew Cargo Module [*NASA*] (KSC) ..... CCM
Crew Certified (MCD) CC
Crew Chief (MCD) CC
Crew Chief ..... CRC
Crew Chief ..... CRCH
Crew Chief (FAAC) ..... CRCHF
Crew Command Input Device ..... CCID
Crew [*or Crewman*] Communications Umbilical [*Apollo*] [*NASA*] ..... CCU
Crew Compartment (MCD) CC
Crew Compartment Cooling Unit [*NASA*] (KSC) ..... CCCU
Crew Compartment Fit and Function [*NASA*] (KSC) C2F2
Crew Compartment Fit and Function [*NASA*] ..... CCFF
Crew Correctable Maintenance Action (MCD) ..... CCMA
Crew Emergency Vehicle (MCD) ..... CERV
Crew Environment Requirements (SAA) ..... CER
Crew Equipment Compartment (MCD) ..... CEC
Crew Equipment Integration [*or Interface*] Test (MCD) ..... CEIT
Crew Escape System (MCD) ..... CES
Crew Escape Technologies [*Air Force*] ..... CREST
Crew Evaluation Launcher (SAA) ..... CEL
Crew Evaluator [*Military*] (INF) ..... CE
Crew Factor (SSD) ..... CFT
Crew Gunnery Simulator (PDAA) ..... CGS
Crew Habitability and Protection [*NASA*] (KSC) ..... CH & P
Crew Interface (MCD) CI
Crew Life-Support Monitor [*NASA*] (KSC) ..... CLSM

Crew Loose Equipment [*Aerospace*] (MCD) ..... CLE
Crew Loose Equipment Nomenclature [*Aerospace*] (MCD) ..... CLENOM
Crew Member ..... CR/M
Crew Member Identification ..... CM-ID
Crew Member Trainee (DNAB) ..... CMT
Crew Module [*NASA*] (NASA) ..... CM
Crew Module Computer (MCD) ..... CMC
Crew Natural Resources [*Vancouver Stock Exchange symbol*] ..... CWT
Crew [*or Crewman*] Optical Alignment Sight [*or Subsystem*] [*NASA*] ..... COAS
Crew Passive Dosimeter [*NASA*] (KSC) ..... CPD
Crew Personal Equipment ..... CPE
Crew Personal Hygiene Equipment ..... CPHE
Crew Procedures Change Request (MCD) ..... CPCR
Crew Procedures Control Board [*NASA*] (NASA) ..... CPCB
Crew Procedures Division [*NASA*] (NASA) ..... CPD
Crew Procedures Documentation System (MCD) ..... CPDS
Crew Procedures Evaluation Simulator (MCD) ..... CPES
Crew Procedures Management Plan [*NASA*] (NASA) ..... CPMP
Crew Procedures Simulator ..... CPS
Crew Procedures Trainer ..... CPT
Crew Procedures Trainer / Combat Training Launch (SAA) ..... CPT/CTL
Crew Provisioning Report ..... CPR
Crew Public Library, Salem, IA [*Library symbol Library of Congress*] (LCLS) ..... IaSal
Crew Quarters (KSC) ..... CQ
Crew Reception Area [*Apollo*] [*NASA*] ..... CRA
Crew Research Laboratory [*Randolph Air Force Base, TX*] ..... CRL
Crew Research Management (GAVI) ..... CRM
Crew Reserve Status [*Military*] (AFM) ..... CRS
Crew Resource Management [*FAA*] (TAG) ..... CRM
Crew Rest [*Military*] (AFM) ..... CR
Crew Safety System ..... CSS
Crew Scheduling and Training Plan (NVT) ..... CSTP
Crew Software Interface (MCD) ..... CSI
Crew Software Training Aid (MCD) ..... CSTA
Crew Station [*NASA*] (KSC) ..... CS
Crew Station Design Facility (MCD) ..... CSDF
Crew Station Maintenance Manual [*Navy*] (CAAL) ..... CSMM
Crew Station Research and Development Facility [*Ames Research Center*] ..... CSRDF
Crew Station Review [*NASA*] (NASA) ..... CSR
Crew Station Trainer [*NASA*] ..... CST
Crew System Ergonomics Information Analysis Center [*DoD*] (IID) ..... CSERIAC
Crew Systems (SSD) ..... CS
Crew Systems Division [*NASA*] ..... CSD
Crew Systems Laboratory [*NASA*] (NASA) ..... CSL
Crew Systems Operating Procedures (MCD) ..... CSOP
Crew Systems Trainer [*NASA*] (NASA) ..... CST
Crew Task Demand ..... CTD
Crew Task Detail ..... CTD
Crew Training Air Force ..... CREWTAF
Crew Training Air Force ..... CTAF
Crew Training and Procedures Division [*Johnson Space Center*] [*NASA*] (NASA) ..... CTPD
Crew Training Officer (SAA) ..... CTO
Crew Transfer Tunnel [*NASA*] ..... CTT
Crew Weapons Sight ..... CWS
Crewcuts Fan Club (EA) ..... CFC
Crewe, VA [*FM radio station call letters*] (RBYB) ..... WBZU
Crewe, VA [*AM radio station call letters*] ..... WSVS
Crew-Initiated Automatic Test ..... CIAT
Crew-in-the-Loop ..... CITL
Crew-Loading Analysis (DNAB) ..... CLA
Crewman (KSC) ..... CM
Crewman (NASA) ..... CMN
Crewman ..... CMN
Crewman (AABC) ..... CRMN
Crew-Operated (SAA) ..... C-O
Crew-Served Weapon ..... C/S
Crew-Served Weapon Sight ..... CSWS
Crew-Served Weapon Thermal Sight [*Army*] (INF) ..... CSWTS
Crew-Served Weapons Captured ..... CSWC
Crewstation Evaluation Facility [*Warminster, PA*] [*Naval Air Development Center*] (GRD) ..... CREST
Crew-Vehicle Simulation Research Facility [*National Aeronautics and Space Administration Ames*] (GAVI) ..... CVSRF
CRH, Ltd. [*NASDAQ symbol*] (NQ) ..... CRHC
CRH PLC [*Associated Press*] (SAG) ..... CRH
CRH plc [*NASDAQ symbol*] (TTSB) ..... CRHCY
CRI IMI MAE [*Formerly, Insured Mortgage Association*] [*NYSE symbol*] (SPSG) ..... CMM
CRI Liquidating Real Estate Investment Trust [*NYSE symbol*] (SPSG) ..... CFR
CRI Liquidating Real Estate Investment Trust [*Associated Press*] (SAG) ..... CRI Liq
CRI Liquidating REIT [*NYSE symbol*] (TTSB) ..... CFR
Criciuma [*Brazil ICAO location identifier*] (ICLI) ..... SBCM
Cricket Association ..... CA
Cricket Club CC
Cricket Union of Victoria [*Australia*] ..... CUV
Crigler-Najjar Syndrome [*Medicine*] ..... CNS
Criimi Mae, Inc. [*NYSE symbol*] (SAG) ..... CMM
Criimi Mae, Inc. [*Associated Press*] (SAG) ..... Criimi
Criimi Mae, Inc. [*Associated Press*] (SAG) ..... CriimiMa
Crikey [*An exclamation*] [*British*] (DSUE) ..... CRI

Crim Elementary School, Bowling Green, OH [*Library symbol*] [*Library of Congress*] (LCLS) .... OBgCrE
Crime .... CRI
Crime Aboard Aircraft .... CAA
Crime and Delinquency [*A publication*] (DLA) .... Crime & Del
Crime and Delinquency Abstracts [*A publication*] .... CDAB
Crime and Delinquency Abstracts [*A publication*] (DLA) .... Crime & Delin'cy Abst
Crime and Delinquency Literature [*A publication*] (DLA) .... Crime & Delin'cy Lit
Crime and Justice Bulletin [*A publication*] .... C & J
Crime and Social Justice [*Australia A publication*] .... CSJ
Crime Intelligence [*British*] (DI) CI
Crime on Government Reservation .... CGR
Crime on High Seas .... CHS
Crime on Indian Reservation .... CIR
Crime Prevention Unit [*British*] .... CPU
Crime Report Information System [*Metropolitan Police database*] [*British*] .... CRIS
Crime Reporters Association [*British*] (DBA) .... CRA
Crime Reporting Information System [*British*] (NITA) .... CRIS
Crime Scene Unit (LAIN) .... CSU
Crime Stoppers International (EA) .... CSI
Crime Stoppers USA [*Later, CSI*] (EA) .... CS
Crime Victims Research and Treatment Center [*Medical University of South Carolina*] [*Research center*] (RCD) CVC
Crime Writers' Association (EAIO) .... CWA
Crimea Air [*Ukraine*] [*FAA designator*] (FAAC) .... CRF
Crimean .... CRI
Crimean Astrophysical Observatory .... CAO
Crimean Hemorrhagic Fever [*Medicine*] (PDAA) .... CHF
Crimean-Congo Hemorrhagic Fever [*Medicine*] .... CCHF
Crimes Compensation Tribunal [*Victoria*] [*Australia*] .... CCT
Criminal (DLA) .... Cr
Criminal (AFM) .... CRIM
Criminal (ROG) .... CRIML
Criminal .... CRMNL
Criminal Act (DLA) .... Cr Act
Criminal Appeal Reports [*England*] [*A publication*] (DLA) .... C App R
Criminal Appeal Reports [*England*] [*A publication*] (DLA) .... CAR
Criminal Appeal Reports [*England*] [*A publication*] (DLA) .... Cr App R
Criminal Appeal Reports [*England*] [*A publication*] (DLA) .... Cr App Rep
Criminal Appeal Reports [*England*] [*A publication*] (DLA) .... Crim App
Criminal Appeal Reports [*England*] [*A publication*] (DLA) .... Crim App (Eng)
Criminal Appeal Reports [*England*] [*A publication*] (DLA) .... Crim App R
Criminal Appeal Reports (Sentencing) [*England*] [*A publication*] (DLA) .... Cr App R(S)
Criminal Appeals (DLA) .... Cr App
Criminal Bar Association [*British*] (DBA) .... CBA
Criminal Case and Comment [*A publication*] (DLA) .... Crim Case & Com
Criminal Code [*A publication*] (DLA) .... Cr Code
Criminal Code [*A publication*] (DLA) .... Crim Code
Criminal Code and Code of Criminal Procedure [*Kansas*] [*A publication*] (DLA) .... Kan Crim Code & Code of Crim Proc
Criminal Code of Practice [*A publication*] (DLA) .... Cr Code Prac
Criminal Conversation [*Adultery*] [*Slang*] (DSUE) .... CRIM CON
Criminal Deportee (ADA) .... CD
Criminal Enforcement Division [*Office of Enforcement and Compliance Monitoring*] [*Environmental Protection Agency*] (EPA) .... CED
Criminal Evidence (LAIN) .... CE
Criminal Headquarters for Underworld Master Plan [*Organization in TV series "Lancelot Link"*] .... CHUMP
Criminal Identification and Investigation CII
Criminal, Immoral, and Narcotic .... CIN
Criminal Informant CI
Criminal Injuries Compensation Board [*British*] .... CICB
Criminal Injuries Compensation Board [*British*] (DLA) .... Crim Inj Comp Bd
Criminal Intelligence [*Branch of the Metropolitan Police, London*] CI
Criminal Intelligence Bureau .... CIB
Criminal Investigation [*or Investigator*] [*Military*] CI
Criminal Investigation Command (MCD) CIC
Criminal Investigation Command [*Army*] (DOMA) .... CIDC
Criminal Investigation Department [*Often loosely referred to as Scotland Yard*] [*Facetious translation: Copper in Disguise*] [*British*] .... CID
Criminal Investigation Detachment .... CID
Criminal Investigation Division [*Army*] .... CID
Criminal Investigation Field Office [*Military*] .... CIFO
Criminal Investigations Policy and Oversight (AAGC) .... CIPO
Criminal Justice and Behavior [*A publication*] (BRI) .... Crim J & B
Criminal Justice Archive and Information Network [*Department of Justice*] (GFGA) .... CJAIN
Criminal Justice Information System .... CJIS
Criminal Justice Institute (BARN) .... CJI
Criminal Justice Journal [*A publication*] (DLA) .... Crim JJ
Criminal Justice Legal Foundation .... CJLF
Criminal Justice Quarterly [*A publication*] (DLA) .... Crim Just Q
Criminal Justice Reference Library [*University of Texas*] .... CJRL
Criminal Justice Review [*A publication*] (DLA) .... Crim Just Rev
Criminal Justice Statistics Association (EA) .... CJSA
Criminal Justice System .... CJS
Criminal Law (DLA) .... Crim Law
Criminal Law and Procedure .... CLP
Criminal Law Journal [*A publication*] .... Crim Law J
Criminal Law Journal Reports [*India*] [*A publication*] (DLA) .... India Crim LJR
Criminal Law Magazine [*A publication*] (DLA) .... Cr L Mag
Criminal Law Magazine [*A publication*] (DLA) .... Cr Law Mag
Criminal Law Magazine [*A publication*] (DLA) .... Crim L Mag
Criminal Law Magazine and Reporter [*A publication*] (DLA) .... Criminal L Mag & Rep
Criminal Law Recorder [*A publication*] (DLA) .... Cr Law Rec
Criminal Law Recorder [*A publication*] (DLA) .... Crim L Rec
Criminal Law Reports [*A publication*] .... CRIM LR
Criminal Law Reports, by Green [*United States*] [*A publication*] (DLA) .... Crim Law Reps (Green)
Criminal Law Reports, by Green [*United States*] [*A publication*] (DLA) .... Green Cr Rep
Criminal Law Reports, by Green [*United States*] [*A publication*] (DLA) .... Green Crim Reports
Criminal Law Review Division [*New South Wales*] [*Australia*] .... CLRD
Criminal Lawyer [*India*] [*A publication*] (DLA) .... Cr L
Criminal Matters .... CM
Criminal Offence [*British*] .... CO
Criminal Office .... CO
Criminal Procedure [*Legal term*] (DLA) .... Cr P
Criminal Procedure [*Legal term*] (DLA) .... Crim Pro
Criminal Procedure [*Legal term*] (DLA) .... Crim Proc
Criminal Procedure Law [*New York, NY A publication*] .... CPL
Criminal Record Office [*Scotland Yard*] .... CRO
Criminal Recorder [*A publication*] (DLA) .... Crim Rec
Criminal Records Directorate [*Army*] (ADDR) .... CRD
Criminal Rulings [*Bombay, India*] [*A publication*] (DLA) .... Cr Rg
Criminal Sexual Conduct .... CSC
Criminal Sexual Psychopath .... CSP
Criminalistic Laboratory Information Systems [*FBI*] .... CLIS
Criminally Receiving Stolen Property .... CRSP
Criminally Uttering and Publishing False [*or Forged*] **Check** [*Legal term*] .... CU & PFC
Criminologica [*A publication*] (DLA) .... Criminol
Criminologie [*Criminology*] [*French*] (DLA) .... Criminol
Criminologist (WDAA) .... CRIM
Criminologist (DLA) .... Criminol
Criminology (ADA) .... CRIMINOL
Criminology Research Council [*Australia*] .... CRC
Criminology Research Unit [*Australia*] .... CRU
Criminology Series [*A publication*] .... CSA
Crimp [*Engineering*] .... CRP
Crimping Tool Kit .... CTK
Crimp-On Snap-In Contacts (MUGU) .... COSI-KON
Crimson (ROG) .... CR
Crimson (ROG) .... CRIM
Crimson Clover Latent Virus [*Plant pathology*] CCLV
[*The*] **Crimson Group** [*Cambridge, MA*] [*Telecommunications*] (TSSD) .... TCG
Crimsonstar Resources [*Vancouver Stock Exchange symbol*] .... KRQ
Crinkled Single Aluminized Mylar (NASA) .... CSAM
Crip Flow Management Facility [*NASA*] (GFGA) .... CFMF
Crip Flow Management Facility [*NASA*] .... CFMS
Cripple Creek Public Library, Cripple Creek, CO [*Library symbol Library of Congress*] (LCLS) .... CoCri
Crippled and Other Health Impaired [*Obsolete*] .... COHI
Crippled Children's Seaside Home Society [*Australia*] .... CCSHS
Crippled Children's Services .... CCS
Crippled Children's Society (DAVI) .... CCS
Cripples' Help Society [*British*] (BI) .... CHS
Cripp's Church and Clergy Cases [*1847-50*] [*England*] [*A publication*] (DLA) .... Ch & Cl Cas
Cripp's Church and Clergy Cases [*1847-50*] [*England*] [*A publication*] (DLA) .... Cripp Ch Cas
Cripp's Church and Clergy Cases [*1847-50*] [*England*] [*A publication*] (DLA) .... Cripps
Cripp's Church and Clergy Cases [*1847-50*] [*England*] [*A publication*] (DLA) .... Cripps Cas
Cripp's Church and Clergy Cases [*1847-50*] [*England*] [*A publication*] (DLA) .... Cripp's Ch Cas
Cripp's Church and Clergy Cases [*1847-50*] [*England*] [*A publication*] (DLA) .... Cripps Church Cas
Cripp's Compulsory Acquisition of Land [*11th ed.*] [*1962*] [*A publication*] (DLA) .... Cripp Comp
Cripp's Law Relating to Church and Clergy [*8th ed.*] [*1937*] [*A publication*] (DLA) .... Cripp Ch L
Crisan Resources Ltd. [*Vancouver Stock Exchange symbol*] .... CRU
Crisciuma [*Brazil*] [*Airport symbol*] (OAG) .... CCM
Crisfield, MD [*FM radio station call letters*] (RBYB) .... WBEY
Crisis Action Management System .... CAMS
Crisis Action Package (AAGC) .... CAP
Crisis Action System (MCD) .... CAS
Crisis Action Team (MCD) .... CAT
Crisis Action Weather Support System (MCD) .... CAWSS
Crisis Assessment Group [*NATO*] (NATG) .... CAG
Crisis Basic Imagery File (MCD) .... CRBIF
Crisis Condition (MCD) .... CRISCON
Crisis Confrontation .... CRICON
Crisis Home Alert Technique .... CHAT
Crisis Intervention Clinic (HGAA) CIC
Crisis Management Information Report .... CRIMREP
Crisis Management INTERCOM System (MCD) .... CMIS
Crisis Management Organization [*DoD*] .... CMO
Crisis Management Plan (MCD) .... CRIMP
Crisis Management System .... CMS
Crisis Management Team [*Army*] (INF) .... CMT
Crisis on Location [*Psychological test*] .... COL
Crisis Relocation (MCD) .... CR
Crisis Relocation Plans [*Federal Emergency Management Agency*] .... CRP

Crisis Resolution Center [*Psychiatry*] (DAVI) ... CRC
Crisis Resolution Center [*Psychiatry*] (DAVI) ... CRU
Crisis Response [*A publication*] ... CR
Crisis Staffing Procedures (MCD) ... CSP
Crisis Task Force (MCD) ... CTF
Crisis-Oriented Program ... COP
CRISTA Ministries [*Later, CRISTA*] (EA) ... CM
Crista Terminalis [*Cardiology*] ... CT
Cristalandia [*Brazil*] [*Airport symbol*] (AD) ... CLZ
Cristalandia/Santa Isabel do Morro [*Brazil ICAO location identifier*] (ICLI) ... SBSY
Cristalerias de Chile ADS [*NYSE symbol*] (SPSG) ... CGW
Cristalerias de Chile SA [*Associated Press*] (SAG) ... CristChile
Cristalerias de Chile SA [*Associated Press*] (SAG) ... CristChle
[*The*] **Cristian & Missionary Alliance in Canada** [*Alliance Chretienne et Missionaire au Canada*] [*Also, The Alliance Church*] (AC) ... C&MA
Cristo Redentor [*Argentina ICAO location identifier*] (ICLI) ... SAMC
Cristobalite [*A mineral*] ... CR
Cristobalite-Tridymite [*A form of silica*] ... CT
Criswell Bible College, Dallas, TX [*Library symbol*] [*Library of Congress*] (LCLS) ... TxDaCB
Critchfield's Reports [*5-21 Ohio State*] [*A publication*] (DLA) ... Critch
Critchfield's Reports [*5-21 Ohio State*] [*A publication*] (DLA) ... Critch (Ohio St)
Criteria Air Pollutant [*Environmental Protection Agency*] (GFGA) ... CAP
Criteria and Standards Division [*Environmental Protection Agency*] (GFGA) ... CSD
Criteria of Teacher Selection [*Project*] (AIE) ... CATS
Criterion [*Theatre and restaurant at Piccadilly Circus*] [*London*] (DSUE) ... CRI
Criterion (AABC) ... CRIT
Criterion Action Element [*Army*] (ADDR) ... CAE
Criterion-Referenced English Syntax Test (EDAC) ... CREST
Criterion-Referenced Instruction ... CRI
Criterion-Referenced Measurement [*Education*] ... CRM
Criterion-Referenced Test [*or Testing*] [*Education*] ... CRT
Critias [*of Plato*] [*Classical studies*] (OCD) ... Criti
Critical [*Telecommunications*] (TEL) ... CRIT
Critical Acquisition Position [*Military*] (RDA) ... CAP
Critical Aeronautical Material and Equipment List ... CAMEL
Critical Aggregation Concentration [*Electrolyte induced aggregation of dispersed species*] ... CAC
Critical Agricultural Materials Act [*1984*] ... CAMA
Critical Air Blast [*Test*] ... CAB
Critical Angle Prism Sensor (KSC) ... CAPS
Critical Aquifer Protection Area [*Environmental Protection Agency*] (FFDE) ... CAPA
Critical Area Flag ... CAF
Critical Assembly [*Nuclear energy*] (NRCH) ... CA
Critical Assembly Fuel Element Exchange [*Nuclear energy*] ... CAFEE
Critical Bandwidth [*of noise*] ... CBW
Critical Bibliography to Religion in America [*A publication*] (BJA) ... CBRA
Critical Carbohydrate Level [*Nutrition*] ... CCL
Critical Care [*Medicine*] ... CC
Critical Care Manual ... CCM
Critical Care Medical Unit (DMAA) ... CCMU
Critical Care Recovery Unit [*Medicine*] (DAVI) ... CCRU
Critical Care Registered Nurse ... CCRN
Critical Care Unit [*Medicine*] ... CCU
Critical Care Workstation [*Medicine*] (DMAA) ... CCW
Critical Coagulation Concentration [*Colloidal chemistry*] ... CCC
Critical Collection Problems Committee [*United States Intelligence Board*] [*Obsolete*] ... CCPC
Critical Color Flicker Frequency (PDAA) ... CCFF
Critical Commodities List [*Department of Commerce*] ... CCL
Critical Communications System [*Military*] (AABC) ... CRITCOM
Critical Components List ... CCL
Critical Compression Pressure ... CCP
Critical Compression Ratio ... CCR
Critical Condition [*Medicine*] ... CC
Critical Control Circuit ... CCC
Critical Control Point [*Food technology*] ... CCP
Critical Crevice Solution (PDAA) ... CCS
Critical Damping Resistance External ... CDRX
Critical Decision Point ... CDP
Critical Demulsification Temperature (PDAA) ... CDF
Critical Design and Qualification Review (NASA) ... CDQR
Critical Design Audit (MCD) ... CDA
Critical Design Review (AFM) ... CDR
Critical Design Review Commercial (MCD) ... CDRC
Critical Design Review Meeting (SAA) ... CDRM
Critical Dimension Scanning Electron Microscopes ... CD-SEM
Critical Dissolution Time [*Chemistry*] ... CDT
Critical Emulsification Temperature (PDAA) ... CET
Critical Engine Inoperative (MCD) ... CEI
Critical Error Detection (MCD) ... CED
Critical Examination (CAAL) ... CE
Critical Experiment Laboratory ... CEL
Critical Experiment Pulsed Fast Reactor ... CEPFR
Critical Experiment Reactor (NRCH) ... CER
Critical Experiment Station [*Nuclear energy*] (GFGA) ... CES
Critical Experiment Tank ... CET
Critical Experiments Facility [*Nuclear energy*] (OA) ... CEF
Critical Field Length (MCD) ... CFL
Critical Field Strength (AAG) ... CFS
Critical Flashover [*Voltage*] (IEEE) ... CFO
Critical Flicker Frequency [*Optics*] (AAMN) ... CFF
Critical Flicker Fusion [*Ophthalmology*] ... CFF
Critical Flicker Fusion Threshold [*Ophthalmology*] (PDAA) ... CFFT
Critical Flocculation Concentration [*Electrolyte induced flocculation of dispersed species*] ... CFC
Critical Flow Model (MCD) ... CFM
Critical Flow Orifice [*Engineering*] ... CFO
Critical Flow Venture-Constant Volume Sampler (ERG) ... CFV-CVS
Critical Flow Venturi [*Engineering*] ... CFV
Critical Frequency (MSA) ... CRITF
Critical Frequency (CET) ... FC
Critical Friendly Zone [*Army*] (ADDR) ... CFZ
Critical Fusion Frequency [*Optics*] (IAA) ... CF
Critical Fusion Frequency [*Optics*] ... CFF
Critical Grid Current ... CGC
Critical Grid Voltage ... CGV
Critical Health Manpower Shortage Areas ... CHMSA
Critical Heat Flux [*Nuclear energy*] ... CHF
Critical Heat Flux Ratio [*Nuclear energy*] (NRCH) ... CHFR
Critical Height (DA) ... CH
Critical Height [*Aviation*] (DA) ... HC
Critical Hours [*Broadcasting term*] ... CH
Critical Housing Shortage At [*named place*] [*Army*] ... CRITHOUS
Critical Human Performance and Evaluation (IEEE) ... CHPAE
Critical Impact Velocity (MCD) ... CIV
Critical Incident Stress Debriefing ... CISD
Critical Incident Technique [*Department of Health and Human Services*] (GFGA) ... CIT
Critical Index Management (HGAA) ... CIM
Critical Influence ... CI
[*A*] **Critical Insight into Israel's Dilemmas** [*Jewish student newspaper*] ... ACIID
Critical Inspection of Bearings for Life Extension (MCD) ... CIBLE
Critical Intelligence ... CI
Critical Intelligence Communication ... CRITICOMM
Critical Intelligence Communications System [*DIN/DSSCS*] ... CRITICOM
Critical Intelligence Parameter (CAAL) ... CIP
Critical Intelligence Report (CINC) ... CRITIC
Critical Intermediate Design Review (NASA) ... CIDR
Critical Isotope Reactor, General Atomics ... CIRGA
Critical Issues Council [*Defunct*] (EA) ... CIC
Critical Issues Demonstration (MCD) ... CID
Critical Issues Fund [*National Trust for Historic Preservation*] ... CIF
Critical Item ... CI
Critical Item Code ... CIC
Critical Item Development Specification (CAAL) ... CIDS
Critical Item Inspection [*California Highway Patrol's accident inspection program*] ... CII
Critical Item List (MCD) ... CIL
Critical Item Review Committee [*Air Force*] (AFIT) ... CIRC
Critical Item Tag (MCD) ... CIT
Critical Items and Residual Hazards List (MCD) ... CIRHS
Critical Job Element (GFGA) ... CJE
Critical Labor Level (ADA) ... CLL
Critical Laboratory Evaluation Roast [*Food technology*] ... CLER
Critical Legal Studies Philosophy ... CLS
Critical Link Factor ... CLF
Critical List [*Medicine*] ... CL
Critical Load Level ... CLL
Critical Mass [*Later, CMEP*] [*An association*] (EA) ... CM
Critical Mass Energy Project (EA) ... CMEP
Critical Mass Laboratory ... CML
Critical Materials Parts List (MCD) ... CMPL
Critical Micelle Concentration ... CMC
Critical Military Target ... CMT
Critical Mission Function [*Army*] (RDA) ... CMF
Critical Nuclear Material ... CNM
Critical Nuclear Weapons Design Information (MCD) ... CNWDI
Critical Occupational Specialty [*Military*] (INF) ... COS
Critical Officer Personnel Requirement [*Air Force*] ... COPR
Critical Off-Time [*Medicine*] (MAE) ... COT
Critical Operational Issues Testing [*DoD*] ... COI
Critical Outcome Data Evaluation System [*Auto safety research*] ... CODES
Critical Outcomes Data Evaluation System [*Automobile accident reporting*] ... CODES
Critical Path ... CP
Critical Path Analysis ... CPA
Critical Path Bar (PDAA) ... CPB
Critical Path Length ... CPL
Critical Path Method [*Graph theory*] [*Telecommunications*] (TEL) ... CPM
Critical Path Network ... CPN
Critical Path Planning ... CPP
Critical Path Planning and Scheduling ... CPPS
Critical Path Scheduling [*or System*] ... CPS
Critical Path Scheduling Method [*Management*] ... CPSM
Critical Path Technique ... CPT
Critical Performance Weight (SAA) ... CPW
Critical Period ... CP
Critical Phase System Software [*NASA*] (NASA) ... CPSS
Critical Pigment Volume Concentration [*Paint technology*] ... CPVC
Critical Pitting Temperature [*Metallurgy*] ... CPT
Critical Power [*Nuclear energy*] (NRCH) ... CP
Critical Power Ratio [*Nuclear energy*] (NRCH) ... CPR
Critical Problem Report [*NASA*] (NASA) ... CPR
Critical Process Team (AAGC) ... CPT
Critical Processing Unit ... CPU
Critical Qualification Design Review (NASA) ... CQDR
Critical Quality Element (NRCH) ... CQE

Critical Quarterly [*A publication*] (BRI) .... Crit Q
Critical Ratio .... CR
Critical Ratio of the Difference .... CRD
Critical Reactor Component (NRCH) .... CRC
Critical Reasoning Test Battery .... CRTB
Critical Reflection Activation Analysis .... CRAA
Critical Relative Humidity .... CRH
Critical Reliability Action Report (AAG) .... CRAR
Critical Requirements Review (NASA) .... CRR
Critical Resolved Shear Stress .... CRSS
Critical Resource Allocation Method (PDAA) .... CRAM
Critical Review [*A publication*] (BRI) .... Crit R
Critical Rule Curve (NOAA) .... CRC
Critical Safety Item [*Military*] .... CSI
Critical Safety Item Program [*Army*] .... CSIP
Critical Sector Detector [*FAA*] (TAG) .... CSD
Critical Sensitive .... CS
Critical Serum Chemistry Value (DMAA) .... CSCV
Critical Shear Stress .... CSS
Critical Shortage Report (AAG) .... CSR
Critical Sliding Velocity [*Automotive safety, vehicle rollover*] .... CSV
Critical Solution Temperature .... CST
Critical Solvent De-Ashing [*Coal processing*] .... CSD
Critical Specifications Element (DNAB) .... CSE
Critical Speed Formula .... CSF
Critical Subsystems Development (MCD) .... CSD
Critical Success Factor [*Management tool*] .... CSF
Critical Surface Tension [*Physical chemistry*] .... CST
Critical Technical Parameters (RDA) .... CTP
Critical Technologies Institute [*Federally funded research and development center*] .... CTI
Critical Temperature .... CT
Critical Temperature Threshold [*Chemical technology*] .... CTT
Critical Terrain; Obstacles; Cover and Concealment; Observation and Fields of Fire; Avenues of Approach [*Military*] .... COCOA
Critical Thermal Maximum .... CTM
Critical Tolerance Factor (MCD) .... CTF
Critical Tool Service .... CTS
Critical Tracking Task [*System for preventing drunken driver from starting car*] .... CTT
Critical Transportation Item (MCD) .... CTI
Critical Trauma Care [*Medicine*] (BARN) .... CTC
Critical Turning Distance Add (SAA) .... CTDA
Critical Water Temperature (OA) .... CWT
Criticality .... CRTL
Criticality Analysis (KSC) .... CA
Criticality Experiment [*Nuclear energy*] (NRCH) CX
Criticallity Data Center .... CDC
Critically Sensitive Level 3 [*Information*] CS3
Critically Sensitive Level 4 [*Information*] CS4
Critical-Path Management .... CPM
Critical-Size Defect [*Medicine*] .... CSD
Criticare Systems [*NASDAQ symbol*] (TTSB) .... CXIM
Criticare Systems, Inc. [*Associated Press*] (SAG) .... Criticre
Criticare Systems, Inc. [*NASDAQ symbol*] (NQ) .... CXIM
Criticised [*Soundness of decision or reasoning in cited case criticised for reasons given*] [*Used in Shephard's Citations*] [*Legal term*] (DLA) c
Criticism .... CRIT
Criticism [*A publication*] (BRI) .... Critm
Critique [*A publication*] (BRI) .... Critiq
Crito [*of Plato*] [*Classical studies*] (OCD) .... Cri
Croatia (ECON) .... CRO
Croatia .... Croat
Croatia Airlines [*ICAO designator*] (FAAC) .... CTN
Croatian Academy of America (EA) .... CAA
Croatian Australian Association .... CAA
Croatian Catholic Union of the USA and Canada (EA) .... CCU
Croatian Christian Democratic Party [*Political party*] (EY) .... CCDP
Croatian Christian Democratic Party [*Political party*] .... HKDS
Croatian Defense Association [*Political party*] .... HOS
Croatian Democratic Community [*Political party*] .... CDC
Croatian Democratic Party [*Political party*] (EY) .... CDP
Croatian Democratic Union [*Political party*] (EY) .... CDU
Croatian Democratic Union of Bosnia-Herzegovina [*Political party*] (EY) .... CDU-BH
Croatian Ethnic School [*Australia*] .... CES
Croatian Fraternal Union of America (EA) .... CFU
Croatian Liberation Movement [*Australia*] .... CLM
Croatian Male Choir, Melbourne [*Australia*] .... CMCM
Croatian National Congress (EA) .... CNC
Croatian Party of Law [*Political party*] .... CPL
Croatian Party of Rights [*Political party*] .... CPR
Croatian Peasant Party (EA) .... CPP
Croatian Peasants Party [*Political party*] (EY) .... CPP
Croatian Philatelic Society .... CPS
Croatian Revolutionary Brotherhood [*Former Yugoslavia*] (PD) .... HRB
Croatian Serbian Slovene Genealogical Society (EA) .... CSSGS
Croatian Social-Liberal Party [*Political party*] .... CSLP
Croatian Workers Association of America (EA) .... CWAA
Croce Rossa Italiana [*Italian Red Cross*] .... CRI
Crochet .... CR
Crochet Association International (EA) .... CAI
Crocker National Bank, San Francisco, CA [*Library symbol Library of Congress*] (LCLS) .... CSfCAB
Crocker on Sheriffs and Constables [*A publication*] (DLA) .... Crock Sh

Crocker on the Duties of Coroners in New York [*A publication*] (DLA) .... Crock Cor
Crocker Realty Investors, Inc. [*AMEX symbol*] (SAG) .... CKT
Crocker Realty Investors, Inc. [*Associated Press*] (SAG) .... Crockr
Crocker Realty Trust [*AMEX symbol*] (TTSB) .... CKT
Crocker Realty Trust, Inc. [*Associated Press*] (SAG) .... CrckrRT
Crocker's Notes on Common Forms [*Massachusetts*] [*A publication*] (DLA) .... Crock Forms
Crocker's Notes on the Public Statutes of Massachusetts [*A publication*] (DLA) .... Crock Notes
Crockery .... CKRY
Crockery Township Library, Nunica, MI [*Library symbol Library of Congress*] (LCLS) .... MiNun
Crockett Public Library, Crockett, TX [*Library symbol Library of Congress*] (LCLS) .... TxCr
Crockett, TX [*Location identifier FAA*] (FAAL) .... CCP
Crockett, TX [*FM radio station call letters*] .... KBHT
Crockett, TX [*AM radio station call letters*] .... KIVY
Crockett, TX [*FM radio station call letters*] .... KIVY-FM
Crocodile (DSUE) .... CROC
Crocus Saffron [*Pharmacy*] (ROG) .... CROC
Croes Newydd [*Welsh depot code*] .... CNYD
Croesus Resources, Inc. [*Vancouver Stock Exchange symbol*] .... CWV
Croft Readiness Assessment in Comprehension Kit [*Child development test*] .... CRAC-KIT
Croghan [*New York*] [*Seismograph station code, US Geological Survey*] (SEIS) .... CROG
Crohn's and Colitis Foundation of America, Inc. (PAZ) .... CCFA
Crohn's Disease [*Gastroenterology*] (DAVI) .... CD
Crohn's Disease Activity Index [*Medicine*] .... CDAI
Croissant (DD) .... crois
Croix de Guerre [*French military decoration*] .... C de G
Croke's English King's Bench Reports [*1582-1641*] [*A publication*] (DLA) .... Cro
Croke's English King's Bench Reports [*1582-1641*] [*A publication*] (DLA) .... Croke
Croke's English King's Bench Reports Tempore Charles I [*1625-41*] [*A publication*] (DLA) .... Cro Car
Croke's English King's Bench Reports Tempore Charles I [*1625-41*] [*A publication*] (DLA) .... Cro Car (Eng)
Croke's English King's Bench Reports Tempore Charles I [*1625-41*] [*A publication*] (DLA) .... Cro Cas
Croke's English King's Bench Reports Tempore Charles I [*1625-41*] [*A publication*] (DLA) .... R3 Cro
Croke's English King's Bench Reports Tempore Elizabeth [*1582-1603*] [*A publication*] (DLA) .... Cro Eliz
Croke's English King's Bench Reports Tempore Elizabeth [*1582-1603*] [*A publication*] (DLA) .... Cro Eliz (Eng)
Croke's English King's Bench Reports Tempore Elizabeth [*1582-1603*] [*A publication*] (DLA) .... R1 Cro
Croke's English King's Bench Reports Tempore James [*Jacobus*] I [*A publication*] (DLA) .... R2 Cro
Croke's English King's Bench Reports Tempore James (Jacobus) I [*A publication*] (DLA) .... Cro Jac
Croke's English King's Bench Reports Tempore James (Jacobus) I [*A publication*] (DLA) .... Cro Jac (Eng)
Cro-Magnon (VRA) .... CrMg
Cromaine Library, Hartland, MI [*Library symbol Library of Congress*] (LCLS) .... MiHal
Cromemco Local Area Network [*Cromemco, Inc.*] [*Mountain View, CA*] [*Telecommunications*] (TSSD) .... C-NET
Cromolyn Sodium [*Pharmacology*] .... CS
Crompton and Jervis' English Exchequer Reports [*1830-32*] [*A publication*] (DLA) .... C & J
Crompton and Jervis' English Exchequer Reports [*1830-32*] [*A publication*] (DLA) .... Cromp & J
Crompton and Jervis' English Exchequer Reports [*1830-32*] [*A publication*] (DLA) .... Cromp & J (Eng)
Crompton and Jervis' English Exchequer Reports [*1830-32*] [*A publication*] (DLA) .... Cromp & Jer
Crompton and Jervis' English Exchequer Reports [*1830-32*] [*A publication*] (DLA) .... Cromp & Jerv
Crompton & Knowles [*NYSE symbol*] (TTSB) .... CNK
Crompton & Knowles Corp. [*NYSE symbol*] (SPSG) .... CNK
Crompton & Knowles Corp. [*Associated Press*] (SAG) .... CrmpKnl
Crompton and Meeson's English Exchequer Reports [*1832-34*] [*A publication*] (DLA) .... C & M
Crompton and Meeson's English Exchequer Reports [*1832-34*] [*A publication*] (DLA) .... Cr & M
Crompton and Meeson's English Exchequer Reports [*1832-34*] [*A publication*] (DLA) .... Cromp & M
Crompton and Meeson's English Exchequer Reports [*1832-34*] [*A publication*] (DLA) .... Cromp & M (Eng)
Crompton and Meeson's English Exchequer Reports [*1832-34*] [*A publication*] (DLA) .... Cromp & Mees
Crompton, Meeson, and Roscoe's English Exchequer Reports [*1834-36*] [*A publication*] (DLA) .... Cr M & R
Crompton, Meeson, and Roscoe's English Exchequer Reports [*1834-36*] [*A publication*] (DLA) .... Cromp M & R
Crompton, Meeson, and Roscoe's English Exchequer Reports [*1834-36*] [*A publication*] (DLA) .... Cromp M & R (Eng)
Crompton's English Exchequer Reports [*A publication*] (DLA) .... Cromp Ex R
Crompton's English Exchequer Reports [*A publication*] (DLA) .... Cromp Exch R
Crompton's Jurisdiction of Courts [*A publication*] (DLA) .... Cromp Cts
Crompton's Jurisdiction of Courts [*A publication*] (DLA) .... Cromp JC
Crompton's Jurisdiction of Courts [*A publication*] (DLA) .... Cromp Jur
Crompton's Office of a Justice of the Peace [*1637*] [*A publication*] (DLA) .... Crom

Crompton's Office of a Justice of the Peace [*1637*] [*A publication*] (DLA) ... Cromp Just
Crompton's Rules and Cases of Practice [*A publication*] (DLA) ... Cromp R & C Pr
Cromwell [*New Zealand*] [*Airport symbol*] (AD) ... CWE
Cromwell Association (EA) ... CA
Cromwell High School, Cromwell, MN [*Library symbol*] [*Library of Congress*] (LCLS) ... MnCrwHS
Cronar Dot Litho [*Du Pont*] ... CDL
Cronar Halftone Litho [*Du Pont*] ... CHL
Cronholm-Ottosson Rating Scale [*Psychopathology*] ... CORS
Cronos Group [*NASDAQ symbol*] (TTSB) ... CRNSF
Cronos Group [*Associated Press*] (SAG) ... CronosG
Cronus Airlines [*Greece*] [*FAA designator*] (FAAC) ... CUS
Cronus Industries, Inc. (MHDW) ... CRNS
Crook Community Library, Crook, CO [*Library symbol Library of Congress*] (LCLS) ... CoCroo
Crook County Library, Prineville, OR [*Library symbol Library of Congress*] (LCLS) ... OrPr
Crook County Library, Prineville, OR [*Library symbol*] [*Library of Congress*] (LCLS) ... OrPrC
Crooked Creek [*Alaska*] [*Airport symbol*] (OAG) ... CKD
Crooked Creek, AK [*Location identifier FAA*] (FAAL) ... CKD
Crooked Creek Colony School, Alberta [*Library symbol National Library of Canada*] (BIB) ... ACCCS
Crooked Island [*Bahamas*] [*Airport symbol*] (OAG) ... CRI
Crookston [*Diocesan abbreviation*] [*Minnesota*] (TOCD) ... CR
Crookston, MN [*Location identifier FAA*] (FAAL) ... CKN
Crookston, MN [*FM radio station call letters*] ... KQHT
Crookston, MN [*AM radio station call letters*] ... KROX
Crookston, MN [*FM radio station call letters*] ... KYCK
Crookston, NE [*FM radio station call letters*] ... KINI
Crookston Public Library, Crookston, MN [*Library symbol*] [*Library of Congress*] (LCLS) ... MnCr
Crooksville, OH [*FM radio station call letters*] ... WYBZ
Crop Condition Assessment ... CCA
Crop Development Centre [*University of Saskatchewan*] [*Canada*] (IRC) ... CDC
Crop Dryer Manufacturers Council (EA) ... CDMC
Crop Evolution Laboratory [*University of Illinois*] ... CEL
Crop Growers [*NASDAQ symbol*] (TTSB) ... CGRO
Crop Growers Corp. [*NASDAQ symbol*] (SAG) ... CGRO
Crop Growers Corp. [*Associated Press*] (SAG) ... CropGrw
Crop Growth Rate (OA) ... CGR
Crop Husbandry Adviser [*Ministry of Agriculture, Fisheries, and Food*] [*British*] ... CHA
Crop Identification Technology Assessment for Remote Sensing [*NASA*] ... CITARS
Crop Insurance Research Bureau [*Indianapolis, IN*] (EA) ... CIRB
Crop Protection Chemical ... CPC
Crop Protection Chemicals Reference ... CPCR
Crop Protection Institute (EA) ... CPI
Crop Quality Council (EA) ... CQC
Crop Reporting Board ... CRB
Crop Science Society of America (EA) ... CSSA
Crop Science Society of South Australia ... CSSSA
Crop Water Stress Index [*Agronomy*] ... CWSI
Crop-Hail Insurance Actuarial Association [*Later, NCIS*] (EA) ... CHIAA
Cropland Adjustment Program ... CAP
Cropland Conversion Program ... CCP
Cropper and Burgess [*Bank in "He Knew He Was Right" by Anthony Trollope*] ... C and B
Cropping Index ... CI
Crops Estimating Memorandum [*Department of Agriculture*] (GFGA) ... CEM
Crops Research Division [*of ARS, Department of Agriculture*] ... CR
Crops Research Division Agricultural Research Service [*Washington, DC*] [*Department of Agriculture*] ... CR-ARS
Croquet Association [*British*] ... CA
Croquet Association of Ireland (EAIO) ... CAI
Croquet Club [*British*] ... CC
Croquet Foundation of America (EA) ... CFA
Croquet Players' Association of New South Wales [*Australia*] ... CPANSW
Crosby Memorial Library, Picayune, MS [*Library symbol Library of Congress*] (LCLS) ... MsPi
Crosby, MN [*FM radio station call letters*] ... KTCF
Crosby, Stills, and Nash [*Rock music group*] [*Later, CSN & Y*] ... CSN
Crosby, Stills, Nash, and Young [*Rock music group*] [*Formerly, CSN*] ... CSN & Y
Crosby-Ironton Elementary School, Crosby, MN [*Library symbol*] [*Library of Congress*] (LCLS) ... MnCroE
Crosby-Ironton High School, Crosby, MN [*Library symbol*] [*Library of Congress*] (LCLS) ... MnCroH
Crosfield Users Group (EA) ... CUG
Crosier Fathers' Library, Hastings, NE [*Library symbol Library of Congress*] (LCLS) ... NbHCro
Crosier Heritage Association [*Defunct*] (EA) ... CHA
Crosier Missions (EA) ... CM
Crosier Seminary Library, Onamia, MN [*Library symbol*] [*Library of Congress*] (LCLS) ... MnOnC
Crosier Theological Seminary [*Onamia, MN*] ... CTS
Crosley Automobile Club (EA) ... CAC
Crosley on Wills [*1828*] [*A publication*] (DLA) ... Cros Wills
Cross (ADA) ... C
Cross (DAC) ... Cr
Cross ... CR
Cross (ADA) ... CRS
Cross [*Referring to sections*] [*Pathology*] (DAVI) ... X
Cross [*As in X-roads*] ... X
Cross Air AG [*Switzerland ICAO designator*] (FAAC) ... CRX
Cross Angle ... CR
Cross Arm (AAG) ... XARM
Cross Assembler [*Computer science*] (MHDI) ... XASM
Cross Bar [*Automotive engineering*] ... C/BAR
Cross Border Humanitarian Assistance (DOMA) ... CBHA
Cross Bracing (MSA) ... XBRA
Cross Branch Data Link (MCD) ... CBDL
Cross Cancer Institute [*Alberta Cancer Board*] [*Canada*] (IRC) ... CCI
Cross Cancer Institute, Edmonton, AB, Canada [*Library symbol Library of Congress*] (LCLS) ... CaAECCI
Cross Cancer Institute, Edmonton, Alberta [*Library symbol National Library of Canada*] (NLC) ... AECCI
Cross Channel ... CC
Cross City, FL [*Location identifier FAA*] (FAAL) ... CTY
Cross City, FL [*AM radio station call letters*] ... WDFL
Cross City, FL [*FM radio station call letters*] ... WDFL-FM
Cross Claim [*Legal shorthand*] (LWAP) ... XCL
Cross [*A. T.*] **Co.** [*AMEX symbol*] (SPSG) ... ATX
Cross, [*A. T.*] **Co.** [*Associated Press*] (SAG) ... Cross
Cross Connection ... XCO
Cross Connection ... XCONN
Cross Connection Point [*Telecommunications*] (TEL) ... CCP
Cross Correlation ... CC
Cross Corsen [*France ICAO location identifier*] (ICLI) ... LFIC
Cross Country [*Also, XCY*] ... XC
Cross Country [*Also, XC*] ... XCY
Cross Country Ski Areas Association (EA) ... CCSAA
Cross Couple ... CC
Cross Cultural Communication Centre, Toronto, ON, Canada [*Library symbol*] [*Library of Congress*] (LCLS) ... CaOTCCC
Cross Cultural Communication Centre, Toronto, Ontario [*Library symbol National Library of Canada*] (NLC) ... OTCCC
Cross Cultural Medicine ... CCM
Cross Deck Pendant (MCD) ... CDP
Cross Direction ... CD
Cross Etel [*France ICAO location identifier*] (ICLI) ... LFIE
Cross Fade ... CF
Cross Feed ... CRSFD
Cross File Search Database [*Information service or system*] (IID) ... CROS
Cross Front [*Photography*] ... CF
Cross Grain [*Technical drawings*] ... CRG
Cross Gris-Nez [*France ICAO location identifier*] (ICLI) ... LFIN
Cross Hair (IEEE) ... XHAIR
Cross Head Speed (MCD) ... CHS
Cross, Iddings, Pirsson, and Washington [*Norms*] [*Geology*] ... CIPW
Cross in Front of Left Foot [*Dance terminology*] ... XfL
Cross Industry Standard ... CIS
Cross Industry Working Team ... XIWT
Cross Information Co. [*Boulder, CO*] [*Telecommunications*] (TSSD) ... CIC
Cross Jobourg [*France ICAO location identifier*] (ICLI) ... LFIJ
Cross La Garde [*France ICAO location identifier*] (ICLI) ... LFJG
Cross Lake [*Canada*] [*Airport symbol*] (OAG) ... YCR
Cross Lake, MB [*AM radio station call letters*] ... CFNC
Cross Lake Minerals [*Vancouver Stock Exchange symbol*] ... CRN
Cross Launcher Assign [*Navy*] (CAAL) ... CLA
Cross. Lien and Stoppage in Transitu [*1840*] [*A publication*] (DLA) ... Cross Lien
Cross Linked Enzyme Crystal ... CLEC
Cross Linking by Activated Species of Inert Gases (MCD) ... CASING
Cross Member [*Automotive engineering*] ... C/MBR
Cross Member [*Automotive engineering*] ... X/MBR
Cross Metal Oxide Semiconductor (NITA) ... XMOS
Cross Modulation [*Telecommunications*] (OA) ... CM
Cross of Honour [*British military*] (DMA) ... HC
Cross of the Order of the Niger ... CON
Cross of Valour [*Military award*] [*Canada*] ... CV
Cross Pointer Indicator (MCD) ... CPI
Cross Polarization [*Atomic physics*] ... CP
Cross Pollinated [*Genetics*] ... CP
Cross Products [*Statistics*] ... CP
Cross Program Auditor [*Applied Data Research, Inc.*] ... CPA
Cross Reference (AFM) ... CREF
Cross Reference ... CRREF
Cross Reference (MCD) ... XR
Cross Reference (NG) ... X-REF
Cross Reference Listing ... CRL
Cross Section ... CS
Cross Section ... XS
Cross Section ... XSECT
Cross Section (VRA) ... xsect
Cross Section (IDOE) ... X-section
Cross Section Information Storage and Retrieval System [*National Neutron Cross Section Center*] (NITA) ... CSISAS
Cross Sectional Area ... CSA
Cross Shaft [*Automotive engineering*] ... C/SHFT
Cross Spectral Density [*Physics*] (IAA) ... CDS
Cross System Product (BTTJ) ... CSP
Cross Tabulation of Frequencies ... CTAB
Cross Talk (IEEE) ... XT
Cross Tell (IEEE) ... XTEL
Cross Timbers Oil [*NYSE symbol*] (TTSB) ... XTO
Cross Timbers Oil Co. [*Associated Press*] (SAG) ... CrosTmb
Cross Timbers Oil Co. [*NYSE symbol*] (SPSG) ... XTO
Cross Timbers Royalty Tr [*NYSE symbol*] (TTSB) ... CRT
Cross Timbers Royalty Trust [*Associated Press*] (SAG) ... CrosTim

Cross Timbers Royalty Trust [NYSE symbol] (SAG) .... CRT
Cross Utilization File (MCD) .... CUF
Cross Utilization Training .... CUT
Crossability Indices [Botany] .... CI's
Crossair [ICAO designator] (AD) LX
Crossbar [Bell System] .... XB
Crossbar .... XBAR
Crossbar Switch (NITA) .... XB
Crossbar Tandem [Telecommunications] (TEL) .... XBT
Crossbow Archery Development Association (EAIO) .... CADA
CROSSBOW [Computer Retrieval of Organic Structures Based on Wiswesser]
 Subcommittee Working Group .... CSWG
Cross-Chain LORAN [Long-Range Navigation] Atmospheric Sounding
 System (USDC) .... CLASS
Cross-Channel Coordination Center [NATO] (NATG) CCCC
Cross-Channel Data Link (MCD) .... CCDL
Cross-Channel Rejection .... CCR
Cross-Charm LORAN [Longe-Range Navigation] Atmospheric Sounding
 System [Marine science] (OSRA) .... CLASS
Cross-Check Procedure (NG) .... CCP
Cross-Clamp [of carotid artery] XC
CrossCom Corp. [Associated Press] (SAG) .... CrosCom
CrossCom Corp. [NASDAQ symbol] (SAG) .... XCOM
CrossComm Corp. [NASDAQ symbol] (TTSB) .... XCOM
Cross-Continent Auto Retailers, Inc. [Associated Press] (SAG) .... CrosCAu
Cross-Continent Auto Retailers, Inc. [NYSE symbol] (SAG) .... CCF
Cross-Correlation Function .... CCF
Cross-Correlation Histogram [Statistics] .... CCH
Cross-Country Movement [Maps] .... CCM
Cross-Country Skiing .... XCS
Cross-Cultural Cognitive Examination (DMAA) .... CCCE
Cross-Cultural Dance Resources (EA) .... CCDR
Cross-Cultural Shamanism Network (EA) .... CCSN
Crosscurrents International Institute (EAIO) CII
Crosscurrents International Institute (EA) CII
Crossed [Stereo images] C
Crossed [Telecommunications] (TEL) .... XD
Crossed Diagonal [Medicine] (DMAA) .... CD
Crossed Electroimmunodiffusion [Analytical biochemistry] .... CEID
Crossed Electrophoresis (MCD) .... CEP
Crossed Field Closing Switch .... CFCS
Crossed Immunoaffinoelectrophoresis [Analytical biochemistry] .... CIAE
Crossed Immunoelectrophoresis [Analytical biochemistry] .... CIE
Crossed Molecular Beam [Instrumentation] .... CMB
Crossed Olivocochlear Bundles [Audiology] .... COCB
Crossed Olivocochlear Potential [Audiology] .... COCP
Crossed Radioimmunoelectrophoresis [Analytical biochemistry] .... CRIE
Crossed Straight Leg Raising [Sign] [Neurology] (DAVI) .... XSLR
Crossed With (DAVI) X
Crossed-Field Amplifier [Air Force] .... CFA
Crossed-Field Output Tube .... CFOT
Crossed-Field Photomultiplier (IAA) .... CFPM
Crossed-Field Plasma Sheath .... CFPS
Crossed-Field Tube .... CFT
Crossed-Film Cryotron .... CFC
Crossett, AR [Location identifier FAA] (FAAL) .... CRT
Crossett, AR [AM radio station call letters] .... KAGH
Crossett, AR [FM radio station call letters] .... KAGH-FM
Cross-Examination Debate Association (EA) .... CEDA
Crossfeed (NASA) .... XFD
Cross-Field Acceleration .... XFA
Cross-Field Jammer .... CFJ
Crossfield Municipal Library, Alberta [Library symbol National Library of
 Canada] (NLC) .... ACRM
Crossfield Municipal Library, Crossfield, AB, Canada [Library symbol Library
 of Congress] (LCLS) .... CaACrM
Crossfire (MSA) .... CFR
Crossfire Injection [Automotive engineering] .... CFI
Crossflow Engine [Automotive engineering] .... XFLO
Crossflow Filtration [Process engineering] .... CFF
Cross-Functional Analysis (ADA) .... CFA
Cross-Guide Coupler .... CGC
Crosshatch Generator .... CHG
Crosshead (MSA) .... CRSHD
Crossing [Commonly used] (OPSA) .... CROSSING
Crossing (VRA) .... crsg
Crossing [Commonly used] (OPSA) .... CRSSING
Crossing [Commonly used] (OPSA) .... CRSSNG
Crossing .... XG
Crossing (MCD) .... XING
Crossing .... XING
Crossing [Aviation] (FAAC) .... XNG
Crossing Protective Device .... CPD
Cross-Interleaved Reed-Solomon Code [Computer science] .... CIRC
Crossland Industries Corp. [Vancouver Stock Exchange symbol] .... CD
Cross-Leveling, Redistribution, Replenishment, and Excessing (MCD) ...... CRRE
Cross-Lines Alternative School .... CLAS
Cross-Linked Biotinylated Microtubule [Biochemistry] .... CBMT
Cross-Linked Dextran Polymer [Organic chemistry] .... CDP
Cross-Linked Enzyme Crystal .... CLEC
Cross-Linked Polyethylene [Organic chemistry] .... CLP
Cross-Linked Polyethylene [Organic chemistry] (MCD) .... CLPE
Cross-Linked Polyethylene [Organic chemistry] (NRCH) .... XLPE
Cross-Linked Smectites [Inorganic chemistry] .... CLS
Cross-Linking Agent .... CLA

Cross-linking Electron Resist (PDAA) .... CER
Crossman Communities, Inc. [NASDAQ symbol] (SAG) .... CROS
Crossman Communities, Inc. [Associated Press] (SAG) .... Crossman
Crossmann Communities [NASDAQ symbol] (TTSB) .... CROS
Crossmatch [Hematology] (DAVI) X
Crossmatch (MAE) .... XM
Crossmatch [Hematology] (DAVI) .... X-mat
Crossmatch: Transfusion .... CT
Cross-Modulation Factor (DEN) .... CMF
Cross-Office Highway [Telecommunications] (TEL) .... XON
Cross-Office Slot [Telecommunications] (TEL) .... XOS
Cross-Organizational Program Analysis [Department of Commerce]
 (GFGA) .... COPA
Crossover [Genetics] .... CO
Crossover [Technical drawings] (MSA) .... CRSVR
Crossover (IDOE) .... xover
Cross-Over Electrophoresis (PDAA) .... COE
Crossover Value [Genetics] .... COV
Crosspoint [Switching element] (MSA) .... XPT
Crosspoint Control Unit (NITA) .... XCU
Crosspoint Switching Matrix (IAA) .... CSM
Cross-Pointer Course Indicator (MCD) .... CPCI
Cross-Polarization Discrimination [Telecommunications] .... XPD
Cross-Polarization Evaluation Radio Echo System (PDAA) .... CERES
Cross-Polarization Interference [in radio transmission] .... XPI
Cross-Polarization Magic Angle Spinning [Spectroscopy] .... CPMAS
Cross-Polarization Nuclear Magnetic Resonance [Physics] .... CPNMR
Cross-Power Spectral Density .... CPSD
Cross-Question [Transcripts] .... XQ
Cross-Range Error .... CRE
Cross-Range Error Function .... CEF
Cross-Range Velocity Correlator (MUGU) .... CRVC
Cross-Reacting Determinant [Immunochemistry] .... CRD
Cross-Reacting Material [Immunology] .... CRM
Cross-Reactive Idiotype [Genetics] .... CRI
Cross-Reference (WDMC) .... cf
Cross-Reference File .... CRF
Cross-Reference List XL
Cross-Reference Project .... CRP
Cross-Reference Utility [Computer science] .... CULL
Crossroad [Commonly used] (OPSA) .... CROSSROAD
Crossroad [Postal Service standard] (OPSA) .... XRD
Crossroad .... XRD
Crossroad .... XROAD
Crossroads [Maps and charts] .... CR
Crossroads .... XRDS
Crossroads Center, Mount Airy, NC [Library symbol] [Library of Congress]
 (LCLS) .... NcMtaC
Crossroads Joint Task Force [Atomic weapons testing] .... CJTF
Crossroads Technical Instrumentation [Atomic weapons testing] .... CTI
Cross-Scan Ground Map Pencil (DNAB) .... CSGMP
Cross-Scan Terrain Avoidance (DNAB) .... CSTA
Cross-Scan Terrain-Avoidance Displays .... CRAN
Cross-Section .... CRS
Cross-Section Data Reduction .... CSDR
Cross-Section Echocardiography (DAVI) .... CSE
Cross-Section Information Storage and Retrieval System [Brookhaven
 National Laboratory] [Information service or system] .... CSISRS
Cross-Section Measurement System .... CMS
Cross-Sectional and Special Studies Branch [Department of Education]
 (GFGA) .... CSSB
Cross-Sectional Area .... CSA
Cross-Sectional Area [Cardiology] .... XSA
Cross-Service Agreement [Obsolete Military] .... CSA
Cross-Service Order [Military] (AFM) .... CSO
Cross-Species Mapping [Zoology] .... CSM
Cross-Spin Stabilization Systems .... CSSS
Cross-Strike Discontinuity [Tectonics] .... CSD
Crosstalk (IDOE) .... xtalk
Crosstalk [Telecommunications] (MSA) .... XTALK
Crosstalk Application Script Language [Programming language] [1987]
 [Computer science] .... CASL
Crosstalk Communicator [Computer software] [Digital Communications
 Associates] (PCM) .... CCM
Cross-Talk Unit .... CU
Crosstell Input CXI
Crosstell Output .... CXO
Cross-Tell Simulator (IEEE) .... XTS
Crosstelling Technician (SAA) .... CTT
Crosstrack [Cross track error] (GAVI) .... XTK
Cross-Track Contiguous .... CTC
Cross-Track Distance [Aerospace] .... CTD
Cross-Track Error .... CTE
Cross-Track Noncontiguous .... CTNC
Crosstrail [Military] .... CT
Crossville, TN [Location identifier FAA] (FAAL) .... CSV
Crossville, TN [Location identifier FAA] (FAAL) .... HCH
Crossville, TN [AM radio station call letters] .... WAEW
Crossville, TN [AM radio station call letters] .... WCSV
Crossville, TN [FM radio station call letters] .... WEGE
Crossville, TN [Television station call letters] .... WINT
Crossville, TN [FM radio station call letters] (RBYB) .... WMKW-FM
Crossville, TN [FM radio station call letters] .... WXVL
Crosswind [Aviation] (FAAC) .... XW
Crosswind Force .... CWF

Crossword Association [*British*] (DBA) ... CA
Crossword Club [*Romsey, Hampshire, England*] (EAIO) ... CC
Croswell's Collection of Patent Cases [*United States*] [*A publication*] (DLA) ... Crosw Pat Ca
Croswell's Collection of Patent Cases [*United States*] [*A publication*] (DLA) ... Crosw Pat Cas
Crosyton, TX [*Location identifier FAA*] (FAAL) ... CZX
Crotalus Adamanteus Venom ... CAV
Croton Free Library, Croton-On-Hudson, NY [*Library symbol Library of Congress*] (LCLS) ... NCroh
Croton Public Library, Newaygo, MI [*Library symbol Library of Congress*] (LCLS) ... MiNew-C
Crotonaldehyde (PDAA) ... CA
Crotone [*Italy*] [*Airport symbol*] (AD) ... CTW
Crotone [*Italy ICAO location identifier*] (ICLI) ... LIBC
Crotonylidene Diurea [*Fertilizer*] ... CDU
Crotonyloxymethyl(trihydroxy)cyclohexene [*Antineoplastic drug*] ... CROTCE
Crounse's Reports [*3 Nebraska*] [*A publication*] (DLA) ... Crounse
Croup-Associated [*Virus*] ... CA
Crouse-Hinds Co. ... CHC
Crouse-Irving Hospital, School of Nursing, Library, Syracuse, NY [*OCLC symbol*] (OCLC) ... ZUZ
Crouse-Irving Hospital, Syracuse, NY [*Library symbol Library of Congress*] (LCLS) ... NSyCH
Crow Canyon [*California*] [*Seismograph station code, US Geological Survey*] (SEIS) ... CYC
Crow Executive Air, Inc. [*FAA designator*] (FAAC) ... CCG
Crow River Regional Library, Willmar, MN [*Library symbol Library of Congress*] (LCLS) ... MnWilRL
Crowd, Lift, Actuate, Swing [*Backhoe controls for tractors*] ... CLAS
Crowder Communications Corp. [*Vancouver Stock Exchange symbol*] ... CWD
Crowding Effect LASER (IAA) ... CEL
Crowell-Collier & Macmillan, Inc. [*Later, Macmillan, Inc.*] [*Publishers*] ... CCM
Crowfoot (MSA) ... CRFT
Crowley, LA [*FM radio station call letters*] ... KAJN
Crowley, LA [*AM radio station call letters*] ... KPWS
Crowley, LA [*AM radio station call letters*] ... KSIG
Crowley, Milner & Co. [*AMEX symbol*] (SPSG) ... COM
Crowley, Milner & Co. [*Associated Press*] (SAG) ... CrowlMil
Crowley Ridge Regional Library, Jonesboro, AR [*Library symbol*] [*Library of Congress*] (LCLS) ... ArJCR
Crown [*Paper size*] ... CR
Crown [*Dentistry*] (DAVI) ... CR
Crown (MSA) ... CRN
Crown ... CRWN
Crown Agent ... CA
Crown Agents for Overseas Governments [*British*] ... CAOG
Crown Agents for the Colonies [*British*] ... CAC
Crown Air Systems [*ICAO designator*] (FAAC) ... CKR
Crown Airways, Inc. [*ICAO designator*] (FAAC) ... CRO
Crown Amer Realty Tr [*NYSE symbol*] (TTSB) ... CWN
Crown American Realty Trust [*Associated Press*] (SAG) ... CrwnAm
Crown American Realty Trust [*NYSE symbol*] (SPSG) ... CWN
Crown and Bridge [*Dentistry*] (DAVI) ... C & B
Crown and Bridge [*Dentistry*] (DAVI) ... Cr & Br
Crown and Sleeve Coping Prosthesis [*Dentistry*] ... CSC
Crown Andersen, Inc. [*NASDAQ symbol*] (NQ) ... CRAN
Crown Andersen, Inc. [*Associated Press*] (SAG) ... CrwnAn
Crown Asset Disposal Corp. [*Canada*] ... CADC
Crown Aviation [*ICAO designator*] (AD) ... CC
Crown Books [*NASDAQ symbol*] (TTSB) ... CRWN
Crown Books Corp. [*NASDAQ symbol*] (NQ) ... CRWN
Crown Books Corp. [*Associated Press*] (SAG) ... CwnBk
Crown Bute Resources Ltd. [*Vancouver Stock Exchange symbol*] ... CBL
Crown Cases ... CC
Crown Cases Reserved ... CCR
Crown Cases Reserved (DLA) ... Cr Cas Res
Crown Casino [*NASDAQ symbol*] (TTSB) ... DICE
Crown Casino Corp. [*Associated Press*] (SAG) ... CwnCas
Crown Casino Corp. [*NASDAQ symbol*] (SAG) ... DICE
Crown Cat Fanciers Federation [*Defunct*] (EA) ... CCFF
Crown Centl Pet'A' [*AMEX symbol*] (TTSB) ... CNP.A
Crown Central Cl'B' [*AMEX symbol*] (TTSB) ... CNP.B
Crown Central Petroleum Corp. [*AMEX symbol*] (SPSG) ... CNP
Crown Central Petroleum Corp. [*Associated Press*] (SAG) ... CrnCP
Crown Circuit Assistant [*Legal term*] (DLA) ... CRCA
Crown Circuit Companion [*Ireland*] [*A publication*] (DLA) ... Cr Cir Comp
Crown Clerk [*British*] (ROG) ... CC
Crown Colony ... CC
Crown Competition Factor (PDAA) ... CCF
Crown Cork & Seal [*NYSE symbol*] (TTSB) ... CCK
Crown Cork & Seal Co., Inc. [*NYSE symbol*] (SPSG) ... CCK
Crown Cork & Seal Co., Inc. [*Associated Press*] (SAG) ... CwnCork
Crown Cork & Seal Co., Inc. [*Associated Press*] (SAG) ... CwnCrk
Crown Cork Manufacturers' Technical Council [*British*] (BI) ... CCMTS
Crown Cork&Seal 4.50% Cv Pfd [*NYSE symbol*] (TTSB) ... CCKPr
Crown Court (ILCA) ... CC
Crown Crafts [*NYSE symbol*] (TTSB) ... CRW
Crown Crafts, Inc. [*NYSE symbol*] (SAG) ... CRW
Crown Crafts, Inc. [*Associated Press*] (SAG) ... CwnCr
Crown Estate Commissioner [*British*] ... CEC
Crown Estate Commissioner [*British*] ... CREST
Crown Forest Industries Ltd. [*Toronto Stock Exchange symbol Vancouver Stock Exchange symbol*] ... CRF
Crown International Airlines [*ICAO designator*] (AD) ... RL
Crown Laboratories [*ECM, exchange symbol*] (TTSB) ... CLLEC
Crown Laboratories, Inc. [*AMEX symbol*] (SAG) ... CLL
Crown Laboratories, Inc. [*Associated Press*] (SAG) ... CrwnL
Crown Land Reports, Queensland [*A publication*] (DLA) ... CLQ
Crown Law Department [*Western Australia*] ... CLD
Crown Life Insurance Co. [*Toronto Stock Exchange symbol*] ... CLA
Crown Life Properties, Inc. [*Toronto Stock Exchange symbol*] ... CFM
Crown Mine [*Nevada*] [*Seismograph station code, US Geological Survey Closed*] (SEIS) ... CMN
Crown Octavo [*Book size*] ... Cr 8vo
Crown Office [*British*] ... CO
Crown Office Rules [*A publication*] (DLA) ... COR
Crown Pac Partners L.P. [*NYSE symbol*] (TTSB) ... CRO
Crown Pacific Partners Ltd. [*NYSE symbol*] (SAG) ... CRO
Crown Pacific Partners Ltd. [*Associated Press*] (SAG) ... CwnPac
Crown Pleas [*Legal term*] (DLA) ... CP
Crown Point Center Public Library, Crown Point, IN [*Library symbol Library of Congress*] (LCLS) ... InCrp
Crown Point Community Schools, Crown Point, IN [*Library symbol Library of Congress*] (LCLS) ... InCrpCS
Crown Point Community Schools, Crown Point, IN [*OCLC symbol*] (OCLC) ... IPO
Crown Point, IN [*FM radio station call letters*] ... WWJY
Crown Point, IN [*FM radio station call letters*] (RBYB) ... WZCO-FM
Crown Prosecution Service [*British*] (ECON) ... CPS
Crown Research Institute [*New Zealand*] ... CRI
Crown Resource Corp. [*Associated Press*] (SAG) ... CrwnRs
Crown Resources Corp. [*NASDAQ symbol*] (NQ) ... CRRS
Crown Side [*Records*] [*British*] (ROG) ... CS
Crown Solicitor [*Australia*] ... CS
Crown Solicitor's Office [*British*] (ADA) ... CSO
Crown Television Productions [*Commercial firm*] [*British*] ... CTV
Crown Theological Library [*A publication*] ... CTL
Crown/Treasury of Relevant Quotations [*A publication*] ... CTRQ
Crown Trust Co. [*Toronto Stock Exchange symbol*] ... CRT
Crown Vantage [*NASDAQ symbol*] (TTSB) ... CVAN
Crown Vantage, Inc. [*Associated Press*] (SAG) ... CrwnVn
Crown Vantage, Inc. [*NASDAQ symbol*] (SAG) ... CVAN
Crown Victoria Association (EA) ... CVA
Crown Zellerbach Corp. ... CZ
Crown Zellerbach Corp., San Francisco, CA [*Library symbol Library of Congress*] (LCLS) ... CSfCZ
Crownair [*Canada ICAO designator*] (FAAC) ... CRW
Crown-Andersen [*NASDAQ symbol*] (TTSB) ... CRAN
Crowncap Collectors Society International (EA) ... CCSI
Crown-Crisp Experimental Index [*Personality development test*] [*Psychology*] ... CCEI
Crowned ... C
Crown-Heel [*Length of fetus*] [*Medicine*] ... CH
Crown-Rump Distance [*Of fetus*] [*Medicine*] (DAVI) ... CRD
Crown-Rump Length [*of fetus*] [*Medicine*] ... CR
Crown-Rump Length [*of fetus*] [*Medicine*] ... CRL
Crownsville State Hospital, Crownsville, MD [*Library symbol Library of Congress*] (LCLS) ... MdCvH
Crownx, Inc. [*Toronto Stock Exchange symbol*] ... CRX
Crows Landing, CA [*Location identifier FAA*] (FAAL) ... NRC
Crowsnest Public Library, Coleman, Alberta [*Library symbol National Library of Canada*] (NLC) ... ACOL
Crowther's Ceylon Reports [*A publication*] (DLA) ... Crow
Crowther's Ceylon Reports [*A publication*] (DLA) ... Crowth
Crowther's Ceylon Reports [*A publication*] (DLA) ... Crowther
Crowthorne and Minety [*England*] ... CROWT & MIN
Croydon [*Australia Airport symbol Obsolete*] (OAG) ... CDQ
Croydon [*Borough of London*] ... CROYD
Croydon Advertiser, Croydon, United Kingdom [*Library symbol Library of Congress*] (LCLS) ... UkCrA
Croydon Library, Croydon, United Kingdom [*Library symbol Library of Congress*] (LCLS) ... UkCr
Crozet, VA [*FM radio station call letters*] ... WCYK
Crozet, VA [*FM radio station call letters*] (RBYB) ... WCYK-FM
Crozet, VA [*FM radio station call letters*] (RBYB) ... WMRY
CRREL [*Cross-Leveling, Redistribution, Replenishment, and Excessing*] **Instrumented Vehicle** [*Automobile traction testing*] ... CIV
CRT [*Cathode-Ray Tube*] **Display Unit** (MCD) ... CDU
CRT [*Cathode-Ray Tube*] **Readout** (CAAL) ... CRO
Crucible and Tool Steel Association [*British*] (BI) ... CTSA
Crucible Institute [*Formerly, CMA*] (EA) ... CI
Crucible Manufacturers Association [*Later, CI*] ... CMA
Crucible Materials Research Center (MCD) ... CMRC
Crucible Melt Extraction [*Metal fiber technology*] ... CME
Cruciform Monument (BJA) ... CM
Cruciform Wing Module (MCD) ... CWM
Cruciform Wing Weapon (MCD) ... CWW
Crude (BARN) ... crd
Crude Barrel Equivalent [*Oil*] ... CBE
Crude Birth Rate [*Medicine*] ... CBR
Crude Coal Tar [*Medicine*] (CPH) ... CCT
Crude Coal Tar in Petroleum [*Pharmacology*] (DAVI) ... CCT in PET
Crude Death Rate [*Medicine*] ... CDR
Crude Distillation Unit [*Petroleum technology*] ... CDU
Crude Fiber ... CF
Crude Magazine [*Generic term for a one-person science-fiction fan magazine, produced by an inexperienced publisher*] ... CRUDZINE
Crude Marijuana Extract ... CME
Crude Marriage Rate ... CMR

Crude Mortality Ratio (MAE) .... CMR
Crude Myosin [*Food technology*] .... CM
Crude Oil Analyses File [*Petroleum Information Corp.*] [*Information service or system*] (CRD) .... COIL
Crude Oil Analysis System [*National Institute for Petroleum and Energy Research*] (CRD) .... COASYS
Crude Oil Equalization Tax [*Proposed, 1978*] .... COET
Crude Oil Equivalent (PDAA) .... COE
Crude Oil Processing Plant .... COPP
Crude Oil Production [*Database*] [*Petroleum Intelligence Weekly*] [*Information service or system*] (CRD) .... COP
Crude Oil Washing [*of cargo tank*] .... COW
Crude Palm Kernel Oil .... CPKO
Crude Protein .... CP
Crude Sulfate Turpentine .... CST
Crude Tall Oil [*Industrial chemistry*] .... CTO
Cruise (WDAA) .... CR
Cruise .... CRUS
Cruise [*Automotive advertising*] .... CRUZ
Cruise (GAVI) .... CRZ
Cruise [*ICAO*] (FAAC) .... CRZ
Cruise .... CSE
Cruise Altitude [*Aviation*] .... CA
Cruise America [*AMEX symbol*] (TTSB) .... RVR
Cruise America, Inc. [*Associated Press*] (SAG) .... CruisAm
Cruise America, Inc. [*AMEX symbol*] (SPSG) .... RVR
Cruise and Maintain [*Aviation*] .... CAM
Cruise and Maintain [*Aviation*] (FAAC) .... CRZAM
Cruise Ballistic Missile (MCD) .... CBM
Cruise/Entry Data Acquisition Unit [*NASA*] .... CEDAU
Cruise Guidance Control [*Aviation*] .... CGC
Cruise Guide Indicator [*Aviation*] .... CGI
Cruise Lines International Association (EA) .... CLIA
Cruise Missile (MCD) .... CM
Cruise Missile (BARN) .... CRM
Cruise Missile Alarm System (MCD) .... CMAS
Cruise Missile Carrier Aircraft .... CMC
Cruise Missile Carrier Aircraft (MCD) .... CMCA
Cruise Missile Guidance Set (MCD) .... CMGS
Cruise Missile Guidance System (MCD) .... CMGS
Cruise Missile Integration .... CMI
Cruise Missile Mission Control Aircraft (MCD) .... CMMCA
Cruise Missile Planning (MCD) .... CMP
Cruise Missile Project Office (AAGC) .... CMPO
Cruise Missile Support Activity (DOMA) .... CMSA
Cruise Missile-Advanced Guidance (MCD) .... CMAG
Cruise on Dignities [*A publication*] (DLA) .... Cru Dign
Cruise on Titles of Honor [*A publication*] (DLA) .... Cru Titl
Cruise on Uses [*A publication*] (DLA) .... Cru Us
Cruise Passengers Club International (EA) .... CPCI
Cruise Speed [*Aviation*] VC
Cruise, Transition, Hover, Bob-Up (MCD) .... CTHB
Cruise Vehicle [*Military*] (AFM) CV
Cruise Well to Right [*Aviation*] (FAAC) .... CRZWTR
Cruiser C
Cruiser .... CR
Cruiser [*Navy*] .... CRU
Cruiser Division [*Navy*] .... CRUDIV
Cruiser Flag [*Navy British*] .... CR
Cruiser, Guided Missile [*NATO*] .... CG
Cruiser, Guided Missile and Command [*NATO*] .... CGC
Cruiser, Light [*British military*] (DMA) CL
Cruiser Minelayer .... CM
Cruiser Minerals [*Vancouver Stock Exchange symbol*] .... CUE
Cruiser Olympia Association (EA) .... COA
Cruiser, Scout .... CS
Cruiser Squadron [*Navy*] .... CS
Cruiser Submarine [*Navy symbol Obsolete*] .... SC
Cruiser Submarine [*Navy symbol Obsolete*] .... SSC
Cruiser-Destroyer Flotilla [*Navy symbol*] .... CRUDESFLOT
Cruiser-Destroyer Force, Atlantic Fleet [*Navy symbol*] .... CRUDESLANT
Cruiser-Destroyer Force, Pacific Fleet [*Navy symbol*] .... CRUDESPAC
Cruiser-Destroyerman [*A publication*] (DNAB) .... CDDMAN
Cruisermen's Association (EA) .... CA
Cruisers (NATG) CC
Cruisers, Atlantic Fleet [*Navy*] .... CRULANT
Cruisers, Atlantic Fleet [*Navy*] .... CRULANTFLT
Cruisers, Battle Force [*Navy*] .... CRUBATFOR
Cruisers, Pacific Fleet [*Navy*] .... CRUPAC
Cruisers, Pacific Fleet [*Navy*] .... CRUPACFLT
Cruiser-Scouting Aircraft Squadron [*Navy symbol*] .... VCS
Cruiser-Scouting Force [*Navy*] .... CRUSCOFOR
Cruiser-Scouting Squadron [*Navy*] .... CRUSCORON
Cruise's Digest of the Law of Real Property [*1804-35*] [*England*] [*A publication*] (DLA) .... Cru
Cruise's Digest of the Law of Real Property [*1804-35*] [*England*] [*A publication*] (DLA) .... Cru Dig
Cruise's Digest of the Law of Real Property [*1804-35*] [*England*] [*A publication*] (DLA) .... Cruise Dig
Cruise's Digest of the Law of Real Property [*1804-35*] [*England*] [*A publication*] (DLA) .... Cruise's Dig
Cruise's Fines and Recoveries [*A publication*] (DLA) .... Cru Fin
Cruising (KSC) .... CRUIS
Cruising Association [*British*] (EAIO) .... CA
Cruising Club [*British*] CC
Cruising Club of America (EA) .... CCA
Cruising Speed .... CSPD
Cruising Speed [*Aviation code*] (AIA) .... VNO
Crump on Marine Insurance [*A publication*] (DLA) .... Crump Ins
Crump on Marine Insurance [*A publication*] (DLA) .... Crump Mar Ins
Crump. Practice under the Judicature Acts [*A publication*] (DLA) .... Crump Jud Pr
Crump. Sale and Pledge [*A publication*] (DLA) .... Crump S & Pl
Crumrine's Reports [*116-146 Pennsylvania*] [*A publication*] (DLA) .... Crumrine
Crus Cerebri [*Medicine*] (DMAA) CC
Crusade .... CRSD
Crusade Against Corruption (EA) .... CAC
Crusade for a Cleaner Environment [*Defunct*] (EA) .... CCE
Crusade for Decency (EA) .... CD
Crusade to Abolish War and Armaments by World Law (EA) .... CAWAWL
Crusader .... CRSDR
Crusader (ROG) .... XDR
Crusader Armaments [*Army*] (RDA) .... CR ARM
Crusader Mobility [*Army*] (RDA) .... CR MOB
Crusader Munitions/Resupply [*Army*] (RDA) .... CR MUN/RES
Crusaders for Christ (EA) CC
Crush, Tear, Curl [*Tea processing*] .... CTC
Crushed or Ground .... CG
Crushed Stone (BARN) .... crst
Crushed Stone Producers' Association of Queensland [*Australia*] .... CSPAQ
Crusher and Portable Plant Association [*Defunct*] (EA) .... CAPPA
Crusher and Portable Plant Association .... CPPA
Crustacean Cardioactive Peptide [*Biochemistry*] .... CCAP
Crustacean Society (EA) .... CS
[*The*] **Crustacean Society** (EA) .... TCS
Crustal Accretion-Differentiation Supervent [*Geology*] .... CADS
Crustal Dynamics Project [*NASA*] .... CDP
Crustal Evolution Education Project [*National Association of Geology Teachers*] (EDAC) .... CEEP
Crutch Training [*Orthopedics*] (DAVI) .... CrTr
Crutch Walking [*Medicine*] .... CW
Crutchfield [*Kentucky*] [*Seismograph station code, US Geological Survey*] (SEIS) .... CRU
Crux [*Constellation*] .... Cru
Cruz Alta [*Brazil*] [*Airport symbol*] (OAG) .... CZB
Cruz Alta/Carlos Ruhl [*Brazil ICAO location identifier*] (ICLI) .... SBCL
Cruz Bay, VI [*FM radio station call letters*] .... WDCM
Cruz Bay, VI [*FM radio station call letters*] (RBYB) .... WWKS-FM
Cruzada Civica Nacionalista [*Nationalist Civic Crusade*] [*Venezuela Political party*] (PPW) .... CCN
Cruzada Civilista Nacional [*Panama*] [*Political party*] (EY) .... CCN
Cruzeiro [*Monetary unit*] [*Brazil*] .... CR
Cruzeiro [*Monetary unit*] [*Brazil*] .... Cruz
Cruzeiro Do Sul [*Brazil*] [*Airport symbol*] (OAG) .... CZS
Cruzeiro do Sul [*ICAO designator*] (AD) .... SC
Cruzeiro Do Sul/Internacional [*Brazil ICAO location identifier*] (ICLI) .... SBCZ
CRW Financial [*NASDAQ symbol*] (TTSB) .... CRWF
CRW Financial, Inc. [*Associated Press*] (SAG) .... CRW Fn
CRW Financial, Inc. [*NASDAQ symbol*] (SAG) .... CRWF
Cryderman Air Service [*Air carrier designation symbol*] .... CASX
Cryderman Air Service [*ICAO designator*] (FAAC) .... CTY
Cryderman Gold, Inc. [*Vancouver Stock Exchange symbol*] .... KGI
Cryenco Sciences [*NASDAQ symbol*] (TTSB) .... CSCI
Cryenco Sciences, Inc. [*Associated Press*] (SAG) .... Cryenco
Cryenco Sciences, Inc. [*NASDAQ symbol*] (SAG) .... CSCI
Crying Vital Capacity [*Medicine*] (AAMN) CVC
Cryofixation [*Electron microscopy*] .... CF
Cryogenic .... CRYGNC
Cryogenic .... CRYO
Cryogenic (KSC) .... CRYOG
Cryogenic Acoustic Microscopy (MCD) .... CAM
Cryogenic Continuous Film Memory [*Computer science*] (DIT) .... CCFM
Cryogenic Dark Matter Search [*Astrophysics*] .... CDMS
Cryogenic Data Center [*National Institute of Standards and Technology*] .... CDC
Cryogenic Distillation (MCD) .... CD
Cryogenic Electrically Suspended Gyroscope .... CESG
Cryogenic Engineering Conference (EA) .... CEC
Cryogenic Engineering Laboratory [*National Institute of Standards and Technology*] .... CEL
Cryogenic Explosive Valve .... CEV
Cryogenic Expulsive Bladder .... CEB
Cryogenic Fluid Management Experiment (MCD) .... CFME
Cryogenic Fluid Management Facility (MCD) .... CFMF
Cryogenic Fluid Storage .... CFS
Cryogenic Fluid Storage Container .... CFSC
Cryogenic Focusing [*Instrumentation*] .... CF
Cryogenic Gas Chromatography .... CGC
Cryogenic Gas Storage System (MCD) .... CGSS
Cryogenic Inertial Navigating System .... CINS
Cryogenic In-Ground (OA) .... CIG
Cryogenic Instrumentation System .... CIS
Cryogenic Interferometer Spectrometer (MCD) .... CIS
Cryogenic Limb Array Etalon Spectrometer (MCD) .... CLAES
Cryogenic Limb Scanning Interferometer Radiometer (MCD) .... CLSIR
Cryogenic Positive Expulsion Bladder .... CPEB
Cryogenic Pressure Transducer .... CPT
Cryogenic Quartz Crystal Microbalance .... CQCM
Cryogenic Rare Event Search with Superconducting Thermometers [*Astrophysics*] .... CRESST
Cryogenic Society of America (EA) .... CSA
Cryogenic Storage and Transfer System (MCD) .... CSTS

Cryogenic Storage Container ... CSC
Cryogenic Storage System [*Apollo project*] [*NASA*] ... CSS
Cryogenic Temperature Sensor [*or Source*] ... CTS
Cryogenic Transmission Electron Microscopy ... CTEM
Cryogenic Upper Atmosphere Limb Emission Radiometer (MCD) ... CULER
Cryogenic Vacuum Calorimeter ... CVC
Cryogenic Whole Air Sampler [*Instrumentation*] ... CWAS
Cryogenics (SSD) ... CRY
Cryoglobulin [*Clinical medicine*] ... CG
Cryoglobulin [*Biochemistry*] (DAVI) ... CRYO
Cryolife, Inc. [*NASDAQ symbol*] (SAG) ... CRYL
Cryolife, Inc. [*Associated Press*] (SAG) ... Cryolife
Cryomedical Sciences [*NASDAQ symbol*] (TTSB) ... CMSI
Cryomedical Sciences, Inc. [*NASDAQ symbol*] (NQ) ... CMSI
Cryomedical Sciences, Inc. [*Associated Press*] (SAG) ... Cryomed
Cryonics Association of Australia ... CAA
Cryoprecipitate [*Laboratory*] (DAVI) ... CPP
Cryostatic Switching-Avalanche and Recombination (MCD) ... CRYOSAR
Cryosurgery [*Medicine*] (DAVI) ... cryo
Cryotherapy [*Medicine*] (DAVI) ... cryo
Cryotron Associative Processor (IEEE) ... CAP
Crypt Cell Production Rate [*Medicine*] ... CCPR
Cryptanalysis [*Air Force*] (AFM) ... CRYPTA
Cryptic Masonry [*Freemasonry*] (ROG) ... CM
Crypto Access Authorization [*Military*] (AABC) ... CAA
Crypto Radio Service ... CRS
Cryptoancillary Unit (AABC) ... CAU
Cryptocenter Watch Officer ... CCWO
Cryptococcal Antibody [*Immunology*] (DAVI) ... CRY-AB
Cryptococcal Antigen [*Immunology*] (DAVI) ... CRY-AG
Cryptococcus [*Genus of microorganism*] (CPH) ... C
Cryptococcus [*Immunology*] (DAVI) ... CRYPTO
Crypto-Communication Network (MDG) ... CRYPTONET
Cryptofacility Security Questionnaire [*Army*] ... CSQ
Cryptograph (MSA) ... CTGH
Cryptographer [*Navy rating*] ... CR
Cryptographic [*or Cryptography*] (AFM) ... CRYPTO
Cryptographic Aid, General Publication (CET) ... KAG
Cryptographic Equipment Facility (MCD) ... CEF
Cryptographic Repair Facilities ... CRF
Cryptographic Supplement to the Industrial Security Manual [*DoD*] ... CSISM
Cryptologic Program [*Military*] (GFGA) ... CCP
Cryptologic Readiness Group [*Military*] (DOMA) ... CRG
Cryptologic Support Center [*Military*] ... CSC
Cryptologic Support Group [*Military*] (NVT) ... CSG
Cryptologic Technician, Administrative, Chief [*Navy rating*] (DNAB) ... CTAC
Cryptologic Technician, Administrative, First Class [*Navy rating*] (DNAB) ... CTA1
Cryptologic Technician, Administrative, Master Chief [*Navy rating*] (DNAB) ... CTACM
Cryptologic Technician, Administrative, Second Class [*Navy rating*] (DNAB) ... CTA2
Cryptologic Technician, Administrative, Senior Chief [*Navy rating*] (DNAB) ... CTACS
Cryptologic Technician, Administrative, Third Class [*Navy rating*] (DNAB) ... CTA3
Cryptologic Technician, Interpretative, Chief [*Navy rating*] (DNAB) ... CTIC
Cryptologic Technician, Interpretative, First Class [*Navy rating*] (DNAB) ... CTI1
Cryptologic Technician, Interpretative, Master Chief [*Navy rating*] (DNAB) ... CTICM
Cryptologic Technician, Interpretative, Second Class [*Navy rating*] (DNAB) ... CTI2
Cryptologic Technician, Interpretative, Senior Chief [*Navy rating*] (DNAB) ... CTICS
Cryptologic Technician, Interpretative, Third Class [*Navy rating*] (DNAB) ... CTI3
Cryptologic Technician, Maintenance, Chief [*Navy rating*] (DNAB) ... CTMC
Cryptologic Technician, Maintenance, First Class [*Navy rating*] (DNAB) ... CTM1
Cryptologic Technician, Maintenance, Master Chief [*Navy rating*] (DNAB) ... CTMCM
Cryptologic Technician, Maintenance, Second Class [*Navy rating*] (DNAB) ... CTM2
Cryptologic Technician, Maintenance, Senior Chief [*Navy rating*] (DNAB) ... CTMCS
Cryptologic Technician, Maintenance, Third Class [*Navy rating*] (DNAB) ... CTM3
Cryptologic Technician O (Communications), Chief [*Navy rating*] (DNAB) ... CTOC
Cryptologic Technician O (Communications), First Class [*Navy rating*] (DNAB) ... CTO1
Cryptologic Technician O (Communications), Master Chief [*Navy rating*] (DNAB) ... CTOCM
Cryptologic Technician O (Communications), Second Class [*Navy rating*] (DNAB) ... CTO2
Cryptologic Technician O (Communications), Senior Chief [*Navy rating*] (DNAB) ... CTOCS
Cryptologic Technician O (Communications), Third Class [*Navy rating*] (DNAB) ... CTO3
Cryptologic Technician R (Collection), Chief [*Navy rating*] (DNAB) ... CTRC
Cryptologic Technician R (Collection), First Class [*Navy rating*] (DNAB) ... CTR1
Cryptologic Technician R (Collection), Master Chief [*Navy rating*] (DNAB) ... CTRCM
Cryptologic Technician R (Collection), Second Class [*Navy rating*] (DNAB) ... CTR2
Cryptologic Technician R (Collection), Senior Chief [*Navy rating*] (DNAB) ... CTRCS
Cryptologic Technician R (Collection), Third Class [*Navy rating*] (DNAB) ... CTR3
Cryptologic Technician, Seaman Apprentice [*Navy*] (DNAB) ... CTSA
Cryptologic Technician, Technical, Chief [*Navy rating*] (DNAB) ... CTTC
Cryptologic Technician, Technical, First Class [*Navy rating*] (DNAB) ... CTT1
Cryptologic Technician, Technical, Master Chief [*Navy rating*] (DNAB) ... CTTCM
Cryptologic Technician, Technical, Second Class [*Navy rating*] (DNAB) ... CTT2
Cryptologic Technician, Technical, Senior Chief [*Navy rating*] (DNAB) ... CTTCS
Cryptologic Technician, Technical, Third Class [*Navy rating*] (DNAB) ... CTT3
Cryptologic Van Junction Box [*Navy*] (ANA) ... CVJB
Cryptopathic Effect ... CPE
Crysler Branch, Stormont, Dundas, and Glengarry County Library, Ontario [*Library symbol National Library of Canada*] (BIB) ... OCRSDG
Crystal [*or Crystallize*] (IAA) ... CR
Crystal [*or Crystallography*] ... CRY
Crystal ... CRYS
Crystal (VRA) ... crys
Crystal [*or Crystalline or Crystallize or Crystallography*] ... CRYST
Crystal ... CRYSTL
Crystal ... CTAL
Crystal ... XL
Crystal ... XTAL
Crystal (IDOE) ... xtal
Crystal Beach, TX [*FM radio station call letters*] (RBYB) ... KSTB-FM
Crystal Beach, TX [*FM radio station call letters*] ... KTKX
Crystal Can Relay ... CCR
Crystal City, TX [*FM radio station call letters*] ... KHER
Crystal Colloidal Array [*Chemistry*] ... CCA
Crystal Control ... CC
Crystal Current ... CC
Crystal Cut [*Symbol*] (DEN) ... X
Crystal Data Center [*National Institute of Standards and Technology*] ... CDC
Crystal Diffraction Spectrometer (MCD) ... CDS
Crystal Diffusion Reflection ... CDR
Crystal Diode ... CD
Crystal Document Management System [*Printer technology*] ... CDMS
Crystal Driver ... CD
Crystal Examination Screen [*Medicine*] (DAVI) ... CRYST
Crystal Falls Community Library, Crystal Falls, MI [*Library symbol Library of Congress*] (LCLS) ... MiCf
Crystal Field [*Ionic Model*] ... CF
Crystal Field Stabilization Energy ... CFSE
Crystal Field Surface Orbital-Bond Energy Bond Order [*Model for chemisorption*] ... CFSO-BEBO
Crystal Field Theory [*Chemistry*] ... CFT
Crystal Filter (IAA) ... CF
Crystal Frequency Indicator ... CFI
Crystal Frequency Multiplier ... CFM
Crystal Gayle Fan Club [*Defunct*] (EA) ... CGFC
Crystal Holder [*JETDS nomenclature*] [*Military*] (CET) ... HC
Crystal Impedance ... CI
Crystal Impedance Meter ... CIM
Crystal Kit ... CK
Crystal Lake [*New York*] [*Seismograph station code, US Geological Survey*] (SEIS) ... CLY
Crystal Lake, IL [*AM radio station call letters*] ... WAIT
Crystal Lattice Dislocation (PDAA) ... CLD
Crystal Marker Oscillator ... CMO
Crystal Mountain [*Vancouver Stock Exchange symbol*] ... CYM
Crystal Number [*On urinalysis*] [*Biochemistry*] (DAVI) ... CRY N
Crystal Oil [*AMEX symbol*] (TTSB) ... COR
Crystal Oil Co. [*Associated Press*] (SAG) ... CrystOil
Crystal Oil Corp. [*AMEX symbol*] (SPSG) ... COR
Crystal Oscillator ... CO
Crystal Oscillator (IEEE) ... XO
Crystal Oscillator ... XTLO
Crystal Palace National Sports Centre [*British*] ... CPNSC
Crystal Palace, Sydenham [*British*] ... CP
Crystal Pressure Transducer ... CPT
Crystal Quartz Modern ... CQM
Crystal Rectifier (AAG) ... CR
Crystal River, FL [*FM radio station call letters*] ... WKTK
Crystal River, FL [*FM radio station call letters*] ... WXJC
Crystal River Plant (NRCH) ... CRP
Crystal Shamrock [*ICAO designator*] (FAAC) ... CYT
Crystal Size Distribution ... CSD
Crystal Springs Library, Crystal Springs, MS [*Library symbol Library of Congress*] (LCLS) ... MsCs
Crystal Unit [*Piezoelectricity*] ... CU
Crystal Unit Cell ... CUC
Crystal Video Receiver ... CVR
Crystal Violet [*An indicator*] [*Chemistry*] ... CV
Crystal Violet Lactone [*Organic chemistry*] ... CVL
Crystal Violet Tetrazolium (OA) ... CVT
Crystal Violet-Pectate [*Microbiological medium*] ... CVP
Crystal-Controlled Oscillator ... CCO
Crystal-Controlled Transmitter ... CCT
Crystal-Induced Chemotactic Factor [*Immunology*] ... CCF
Crystalline ... C
Crystalline Amino Acid [*Biochemistry*] (DAVI) ... CAA
Crystalline Colloidal Array [*Chemistry*] ... CCA
Crystalline Egg Albumin (MAE) ... CEA
Crystalline Insulin ... CI
Crystalline or Powdered ... CP
Crystalline Overthrust Structures on the Platform Localizing Unconventional Me thane ... COSPLUM
Crystalline Style ... CST
Crystalline Sucrose Unit [*i.e., sugar cube*] [*Slang*] ... CSU

Crystalline Transitional Material (NASA) .... CTM
Crystalline Zinc Insulin [Medicine] .... CZI
Crystallite Orientation Distribution Function (MCD) .... CODF
Crystallization .... CRYSTN
Crystallized .... CRYSTD
Crystallized Polyethylene Terephthalate [Plastics technology] ..... CPET
Crystallographic [Origin] [Of precious stones] .... CRST
Crystallographic Computing Network [AEC] (IID) .... CRYSNET
Crystallographic Laboratory [MIT] (MCD) CL
Crystallographic Shear [Crystallography] .... CS
Crystallographic Shear Plane .... CSP
Crystallographic Structural Database [University of Cambridge] [British
Information service or system] (CRD) .... CSD
Crystallography (IAA) .... CR
Crystallography (ROG) .... CRYSTAL
Crystallography (ROG) .... CRYSTALLOG
Crystallume Inc. [NASDAQ symbol] (TTSB) .... CRYS
Crystals [JETDS nomenclature] [Military] (CET) .... CR
CS Owner's Association (EA) .... CSOA
CSA Air, Inc. [ICAO designator] (FAAC) .... IRO
CSA Fraternal Life [Acronym represents organization's former name] (EA) ...... CSA
CSA Management Ltd. [Toronto Stock Exchange symbol] .... CSA
CSAID Binding Protein [Biochemistry] .... CSBP
CSB [Chemical Species Balance] Existing Chemicals Assessment Tracking
System [Environmental Protection Agency] (EPA) .... CECATS
CSB Financial [NASDAQ symbol] (TTSB) .... CSBF
CSB Financial Corp. [NASDAQ symbol] (SAG) .... COSB
CSB Financial Corp. [Associated Press] (SAG) .... CSB Fn
CSB Financial Group, Inc. [NASDAQ symbol] (SAG) .... CSBF
CSB Financial Group, Inc. [Associated Press] (SAG) .... CSBFin
CSC Clearing Corp. (EA) .... CSCCC
CSE Aviation Ltd. [British] [FAA designator] (FAAC) .... CSE
CSF Holdings, Inc. [Associated Press] (SAG) .... CSF Hd
CSF Holdings, Inc. [NASDAQ symbol] (SAG) .... CSFC
CSG Systems International, Inc. [NASDAQ symbol] (SAG) ...... CSGS
CSG Systems International, Inc. [Associated Press] (SAG) ..... CSGSys
CSG Systems Intl. [NASDAQ symbol] (TTSB) .... CSGS
CSI Computer Specialists [Associated Press] (SAG) .... CSI
CSI Computer Specialists [NASDAQ symbol] (SAG) .... CSIS
CSI Computer Specialists Wrrt'A' [NASDAQ symbol] (TTSB) ... CSISW
CSIRO [Commonwealth Scientific and Industrial Research Organisation]
Activities Archive [Database] .... ACTC
CSIRO [Commonwealth Scientific and Industrial Research Organisation]
Activities File [Database] .... ACTF
CSIRO [Commonwealth Scientific and Industrial Research Organisation] Films
[Database] .... FILM
CSIRO [Commonwealth Scientific and Industrial Research Organization]
Infolink News [Database] .... CINS
C.S.I.S. [Canadian Security Intelligence Service], Information Centre , Montreal,
PQ, Canada [Library symbol Library of Congress] (LCLS) ... CaQMRS
CSIS [Canadian Security Intelligence Service] Open Information Centre
Ontario [Bibliotheque du SCRS (Service Canadien du Renseignement de
Securite), Ottawa] [Library symbol National Library of Canada] (NLC) ... OORSS
CSK Corp. [Associated Press] (SAG) .... CSK
CSK Corp. [NASDAQ symbol] (NQ) .... CSKK
CSK Corp. ADS [NASDAQ symbol] (TTSB) .... CSKKY
CSL Lighting Manufacturing [Associated Press] (SAG) .... CSL Lgt
CSL Lighting Manufacturing [NASDAQ symbol] (SAG) .... CSLX
CSL Lighting Mfg [NASDAQ symbol] (TTSB) .... CSLX
CSM [Command and Service Module] and ATM Communications Specialist
[Apollo Telescope Mount] [NASA] .... CATCO
CSM [Command and Service Module] Environmental and Electrical Systems
Engineer [NASA] .... EECOM
CSM [Command and Service Module] Navigation Update [NASA] ... CNU
CSP, Inc. [Associated Press] (SAG) .... CSP
CSP Inc. [NASDAQ symbol] (NQ) .... CSPI
CSS Industries [Associated Press] (SAG) .... CSS
CSS Industries [NYSE symbol] (TTSB) .... CSS
CSS Industries [Associated Press] (SAG) .... CSS Inds
CSS Industries, Inc. [NYSE symbol] (SPSG) .... CSS
C.S.S.M.M. [Centre de Services Sociaux du Montreal Metropolitan], Mon treal,
PQ, Canada [Library symbol] [Library of Congress] (LCLS) ...... CaQMCSSMM
CSSMM [Centre de Services Sociaux du Montreal Metropolitain], Montreal,
Quebec [Library symbol National Library of Canada] (NLC) ...... QMCSSMM
CST Entertainment [AMEX symbol] (TTSB) .... CLR
CST Entertainment Imaging [Formerly, Color Systems Technology, Inc.]
[AMEX symbol] (SPSG) .... CLR
CST Entertainment Imaging, Inc. [Associated Press] (SAG) ..... CSTEnt
CSU Regional Atmospheric Modeling System (USDC) ...... CSU-RAMS
CSX Corp. [Formed by merger of Chessie System, Inc. and Seaboard Coast
Line Railroad] [Formerly, CO] [NYSE symbol] (SPSG) .... CSX
CT Financial Services [Formerly, Canada Trustco Mortgage Co.] [Vancouver
Stock Exchange symbol] .... CT
CT Financial Services, Inc. [Toronto Stock Exchange symbol] ...... CFS
CT Fini Services [TS Symbol] (TTSB) .... CFS
CTC Air, SA [Spain] [FAA designator] (FAAC) .... CTC
CTEC Corp. [Associated Press] (SAG) .... CTEC
C-TEC Corp. [NASDAQ symbol] (NQ) .... CTEX
C-TEC Corp.'B' [NASDAQ symbol] (TTSB) .... CTEXB
Ctenidial Analog [Biology] .... CA
Ctenidial Nerve [Biology] .... CTN
Ctenidial Sinus [Biology] .... CS
Ctenocephalides [A genus of fleas] [Entomology] (DAVI) .... Ct
C-Terminal Parathyroid Hormone [Endocrinology] (DAVI) ...... CPTH

CTG Compression Technology Group, Inc. [Vancouver Stock Exchange
symbol] .... CGN
CTI Technologies Corp. [Vancouver Stock Exchange symbol] ...... CJT
CTL Credit [NASDAQ symbol] (TTSB) .... CTLI
CTL Credit, Inc. [Associated Press] (SAG) .... CTL Cr
CTL Credit, Inc. [NASDAQ symbol] (SAG) .... CTLI
CTS Corp. [NYSE symbol] (SPSG) .... CTS
CTS Information Resource Centre, Ontario Ministry of Government
Services, Toronto [Library symbol National Library of Canada] (BIB) ...... OTGSI
CTV News Research Library, CTV Television Network, Toronto, Ontario
[Library symbol National Library of Canada] (NLC) .... OTCTVN
CTV Television Network, CTV News Research Library, Toronto, ON,
Canada [Library symbol] [Library of Congress] (LCLS) ...... CaOTCTVN
CU Bancorp. [Associated Press] (SAG) .... CU Bnc
CU Bancorp [NASDAQ symbol] (SPSG) .... CUBN
Cuadra Associates, Inc. [Information service or system] (IID) ...... CA
Cuajimalpa [Mexico] [Later, TEO] [Geomagnetic observatory code] ...... CUA
Cuamba [Mozambique] [ICAO location identifier] (ICLI) .... FQCB
Cub Koda Fan Club [Defunct] (EA) .... CKFC
Cub Master [Scouting] .... CM
Cuba C
Cuba [ANSI two-letter standard code] (CNC) .... CU
Cuba [MARC country of publication code Library of Congress] (LCCP) ... cu
Cuba [ANSI three-letter standard code] (CNC) .... CUB
Cuba [License plate code assigned to foreign diplomats in the US] ...... DC
Cuba [MARC geographic area code Library of Congress] (LCCP) ...... nwcu
Cuba [IYRU nationality code] (IYR) .... RC
Cuba Hill Elementary School, Huntington, NY [Library symbol Library of
Congress] (LCLS) .... NHuCE
Cuba Library, Cuba, NY [Library symbol Library of Congress] (LCLS) ...... NCu
Cuba Library, Cuba, NY [Library symbol] [Library of Congress] (LCLS) ...... NCuL
Cuba, MO [AM radio station call letters] .... KFXE
Cuba, MO [AM radio station call letters] .... KGNN
Cuba, MO [FM radio station call letters] (RBYB) .... KGNN-FM
Cuba, MO [Location identifier FAA] (FAAL) .... UBX
Cuba Resource Center [Defunct] (EA) .... CRC
Cuban American Foundation (EA) .... CAF
Cuban American Legal Defense and Education Fund (EA) ...... CALDEF
Cuban American National Council (EA) .... CANC
Cuban American National Foundation (EA) .... CANF
Cuban Association for the United Nations (EAIO) .... CAUN
Cuban Communist Party [Political party] .... CCP
Cuban Communist Party [Political party] .... KKP
Cuban/Haitian Entrant Program [Department of Health and Human Services]
(GFGA) .... CHEP
Cuban National Planning Council [Later, CANC] (EA) .... CNPC
Cuban Nationalist Movement .... CNM
Cuban Navy .... CN
Cuban Peso [Monetary unit] (ODBW) .... CUP
Cuban Philatelic Society of America (EA) .... CPSA
Cuban Refugee Program [HEW] .... CRP
Cuban Refugee Program Staff [HEW] .... CRPS
Cuban Representation of Exiles [Also known as Representacion Cubana del
Exilio] (EA) .... RECE
Cuban Victor [Record label] .... CubV
Cuban Women's Club (EA) .... CWC
Cubana Airlines [ICAO designator] (AD) .... CU
Cubana Airways (DS) .... CU
Cuban-American Committee for Normalization of Relations with Cuba
(EA) .... CACNRWC
Cube .... CU
Cube Alignment Kit .... CAK
Cube Corner Holder .... CCH
Cube Corner Reflector .... CCR
Cube Order Index Rule .... COI
Cube Resources [Vancouver Stock Exchange symbol] .... CUB
Cube-Connected Cycle (MCD) CCC
Cube-On-Edge [Metal grain structure] .... COE
Cubi Naval Air Station, Bataan [Philippines] [ICAO location identifier]
(ICLI) .... RPMB
Cubic C
Cubic (IAA) .... CB
Cubic (EY) .... CU
Cubic .... CUB
Cubic Boron Nitride [Cutting tool edges] .... CBN
Cubic Capacity (DS) CC
Cubic Capacity of Bunkers [British] (ADA) .... CCB
Cubic Capacity of Holds [British] (ADA) .... CCH
Cubic Centimeter cc
Cubic Centimeter (ROG) .... CCM
Cubic Centimeter (AAMN) .... cm³
Cubic Centimeter (ROG) .... CMR₃
Cubic Centimeter .... CUCM
Cubic Centimeter per Liter [Measurement] (DAVI) .... cc/l
Cubic Centimeter Per Minute (IAA) .... CCPM
Cubic Centimeters at Standard Temperature and Pressure [Also,
CSTP] .... CCSTP
Cubic Centimeters at Standard Temperature and Pressure [Also,
CCSTP] .... CSTP
Cubic Chain-of-Rotators [Equation of state] .... CCOR
Cubic Close Packing [Crystallography] .... CCP
Cubic Contents CC
Cubic Corp. [AMEX symbol] (SPSG) .... CUB
Cubic Corp. [Associated Press] (SAG) .... Cubic
Cubic Corp., San Diego, CA [Library symbol Library of Congress] (LCLS)... CSdCu

Cubic Decameters per Day ... DAM^3/D
Cubic Decimeter (IAA) ... CUDM
Cubic Decimeter (ROG) ... Dm^3
Cubic Dekameter ... DAM^3
Cubic Dekameter ... Dkm^3
Cubic Feet (AFM) ... CF
Cubic Feet (IDOE) ... cu ft
Cubic Feet [*or Foot*] (MSA) ... CUFT
Cubic Feet (EG) ... FT^3
Cubic Feet ... ft3
Cubic Feet per Day ... CFD
Cubic Feet per Foot Day ... $FT^3/(FT D)$
Cubic Feet per Hour ... CFH
Cubic Feet per Minute ... CFM
Cubic Feet per Minute/Second (DEN) ... CFM/S
Cubic Feet per Second ... CFS
Cubic Feet per Second ... CUSEC
Cubic Feet per Second ... FT^3/S
Cubic Foot (DAS) ... CFT
Cubic Foot (IDOE) ... cu ft
Cubic Foot per Minute (WDAA) ... FT^3/MIN
Cubic Foot per Second [*Marine science*] (OSRA) ... cfs
Cubic Hectometer (WDAA) ... HM^3
Cubic Inch (MCD) ... CI
Cubic Inch (IDOE) ... cu in
Cubic Inch ... CUIN
Cubic Inch ... IN^3
Cubic Inch Displacement [*in engines*] ... CID
Cubic Inches (IDOE) ... cu in
Cubic Inches per Minute (IAA) ... CIM
Cubic Inches per Revolution (MCD) ... CIPR
Cubic Kilometer ... KM^3
Cubic Meter (ROG) ... CBM
Cubic Meter ... CUM
Cubic Meter ... M^3
Cubic Meter ... m3
Cubic Meter (IDOE) ... m^3
Cubic Meters per Day ... M^3/D
Cubic Meters per Joule ... M^3/J
Cubic Meters per Kilogram ... M^3/KG
Cubic Meters per Meter Day ... $M^3/(M D)$
Cubic Meters per Meter Year ... $M^3/(M A)$
Cubic Meters per Minute ... M^3/MIN
Cubic Meters per Second ... CUMECS
Cubic Meters per Second ... M^3/S
Cubic Micrometer (WDAA) ... MU M^3
Cubic Micron (IAA) ... CUMN
Cubic Micron ... CUMU
Cubic Mile (HGAA) ... CUMI
Cubic Millimeter ... CMM
Cubic Millimeter ... CUMM
Cubic Millimeter ... MM^3
Cubic Millimeters per Second [*Measurement*] (DAVI) ... cmm/s
Cubic Root (IAA) ... CURT
Cubic Spline Regression [*Statistics*] ... CRS
Cubic Stabilized Zirconia ... CSZ
Cubic Tonnage [*Shipping*] ... CT
Cubic Weight ... CW
Cubic Yard ... CUYD
Cubic Yard (KSC) ... CY
Cubic Yard (ADA) ... CYD
Cubic Yard ... YD^3
Cubic Yard Bank Measurement (DAC) ... Cybm
Cubic Yard Compacted Measurement (DAC) ... CYCM
Cubic Zirconia [*Simulated diamonds*] ... CZ
Cubicle (MSA) ... CUB
Cubicle (VRA) ... cub
Cubicle ... CUBE
Cubist Pharmaceuticals, Inc. [*NASDAQ symbol*] (SAG) ... CBST
Cubist Pharmaceuticals, Inc. [*Associated Press*] (SAG) ... CubistPh
Cubitainer (MCD) ... CU
Cubital Tunnel Syndrome [*Medicine*] (DMAA) ... CuTS
CUC International [*Associated Press*] (SAG) ... CUC Intl
CUC International, Inc. [*Formerly, Comp-U-Card International*] [*NYSE symbol*] (SPSG) ... CU
CUC Intl. [*NYSE symbol*] (TTSB) ... CU
Cucos, Inc. [*NASDAQ symbol*] (NQ) ... CUCO
Cucos, Inc. [*Associated Press*] (SAG) ... Cucos
Cucui [*Brazil*] [*Airport symbol*] (AD) ... CBZ
Cucui [*Brazil ICAO location identifier*] (ICLI) ... SBKU
Cucumber [*Slang*] (DSUE) ... CU
Cucumber [*Slang*] (DSUE) ... CUE
Cucumber [*Slang*] (DSUE) ... CUKE
Cucumber Green Mottle Mosaic Virus [*Plant pathology*] ... CGMMV
Cucumber Mosaic Virus ... CMV
Cucumber Pale Fruit Viroid ... CPFV
Cucumber Soilborne Virus ... CSBV
Cucumber Virus 4 [*Plant pathology*] ... CV4
Cucumber Yellows Virus [*Plant pathology*] ... CUYV
Cucurbita Cruenta [*Cupping Glass*] [*Pharmacy*] ... CC
Cucurbitula Cruenta [*Cupping Glass with Scarificator*] [*Pharmacy*] (ROG) ... CUCURB CRUENT
Cucuta [*Colombia*] [*Airport symbol*] (OAG) ... CUC
Cucuta/Camilo Daza [*Colorado ICAO location identifier*] (ICLI) ... SKCC
Cudahy Public Library, Cudahy, WI [*Library symbol Library of Congress*] (LCLS) ... WC
Cuddapah [*India*] [*ICAO location identifier*] (ICLI) ... VOCP
Cuddapan [*Queensland*] [*Airport symbol*] (AD) ... UDD
Cuddesdon Theological College [*Later, Rippon College, Cuddesdon*] [*Oxford*] [*British*] (ROG) ... CUDD
Cuddon. Copyhold Acts [*1865*] [*A publication*] (ILCA) ... Cudd Copyh
Cue Indexing System (IEEE) ... CIS
CUEA Synthesis and Publication Segment [*Marine science*] (MSC) ... SYNAPSE
Cued Speech Center (EA) ... CSC
Cuenca [*Ecuador*] [*Airport symbol*] (OAG) ... CUE
Cuenca [*Ecuador*] [*ICAO location identifier*] (ICLI) ... SECU
Cuenta Abierta [*Open Account*] [*Spanish Business term*] ... CA
Cuenta y Riesgo [*For Account and Risk Of*] [*Spanish Business term*] ... C/R
Cuernavaca [*Mexico ICAO location identifier*] (ICLI) ... MMCB
Cuero, TX [*AM radio station call letters*] (RBYB) ... KTXC
Cuero, TX [*FM radio station call letters*] (RBYB) ... KVCQ
Cuers/Pierrefeu [*France ICAO location identifier*] (ICLI) ... LFTF
Cuesta College, San Luis Obispo, CA [*Library symbol Library of Congress*] (LCLS) ... CSluCu
Cufar [*Guinea-Bissau*] [*ICAO location identifier*] (ICLI) ... GGCF
CUG [*Control Unit Group*] **Interrupt Inhibit** ... CII
Cuglieri [*Italy*] [*Seismograph station code, US Geological Survey*] (SEIS) ... CUG
Cuiaba [*Brazil*] [*Airport symbol*] (OAG) ... CGB
Cuiaba/Marechal Rondon [*Brazil ICAO location identifier*] (ICLI) ... SBCY
Cuirassed [*Numismatics*] ... CUIR
Cuisine ... CSN
Cuito Cuanavale [*Angola*] [*ICAO location identifier*] (ICLI) ... FNCV
Cujus [*Of Which*] [*Latin*] ... CUJ
Cujus Libet [*Of Any You Please*] [*Pharmacy*] ... CUJ LIB
Cujus Libet [*Of Any You Please*] [*Pharmacy*] (ROG) ... CUJUSL
Culbro Corp. [*NYSE symbol*] (SPSG) ... CUC
Culbro Corp. [*Associated Press*] (SAG) ... Culbro
Cul-de-Sac [*Medicine*] (MAE) ... CDS
Culdrose [*British ICAO location identifier*] (ICLI) ... EGDR
Culebra [*Puerto Rico*] [*Airport symbol*] (OAG) ... CPX
Culebra [*Puerto Rico*] [*Seismograph station code, US Geological Survey*] (SEIS) ... CUP
Culebra [*Puerto Rico*] [*ICAO location identifier*] (ICLI) ... TJCP
Culebra, PR [*FM radio station call letters*] (RBYB) ... WJVP-FM
Culebra, PR [*FM radio station call letters*] (RBYB) ... WXZX-FM
Culex [*Genus of microorganisms*] (MAH) ... C
Culex [*Classical studies*] (OCD) ... Cul
Culham Conceptual Tokamak Reactor [*Nuclear energy British*] (NUCP) ... CCTR
Culham Laboratory Reports [*United Kingdom Atomic Energy Authority*] ... CLM
Culham On-Line Single Experimental Console [*Computer science*] (OA) ... COSEC
Culiacan [*Mexico*] [*Airport symbol*] (OAG) ... CUL
Culiacan [*Mexico*] [*Seismograph station code, US Geological Survey Closed*] (SEIS) ... CUL
Culiacan [*Mexico ICAO location identifier*] (ICLI) ... MMCL
Culinary (ADA) ... CUL
Culinary and Fine Arts Club [*Later, Culinary Arts Club*] (EA) ... C & FA
Culinary Arts Program [*Association of Independent Colleges and Schools specialization code*] ... CU
Culinary Institute of America [*Hyde Park, NY*] ... CIA
Cullen Frost Bankers [*NASDAQ symbol*] (TTSB) ... CFBI
Cullen/Frost Bankers, Inc. [*NASDAQ symbol*] (NQ) ... CFBI
Cullen-Frost Bankers, Inc. [*Associated Press*] (SAG) ... CullnFr
Cullen's Bankrupt Law [*A publication*] (DLA) ... Cull BL
Culligan Water Tech [*NYSE symbol*] (TTSB) ... CUL
Cullman, AL [*Location identifier FAA*] (FAAL) ... CPP
Cullman, AL [*AM radio station call letters*] ... WFMH
Cullman, AL [*FM radio station call letters*] ... WFMH-FM
Cullman, AL [*FM radio station call letters*] ... WKUL
Cullman, AL [*AM radio station call letters*] ... WXXR
Cullman County Library [*Library network*] ... CCPL
Cullompton [*England*] ... CULL
Cullowhee, NC [*Location identifier FAA*] (FAAL) ... HQL
Cullowhee, NC [*FM radio station call letters*] ... WWCU
Culp, Inc. [*NASDAQ symbol*] (NQ) ... CULP
Culp, Inc. [*Associated Press*] (SAG) ... Culp Inc
Culpeper, VA [*FM radio station call letters*] ... WCUL
Culpeper, VA [*AM radio station call letters*] ... WCVA
Culpeper, VA [*FM radio station call letters*] ... WPVB
Cult Awareness Network (EA) ... CAN
Cult of the Virgin (EA) ... CV
Cultists Anonymous [*British*] (DBA) ... CA
Cultivar [*Cultural Variety*] [*Biology*] ... cv
Cultivated [*Botany*] ... cult
Cultivated Mushroom Institute of America ... CMIA
Cultivation (ROG) ... CULTIVON
Cultivator ... CULTVR
Cultural ... CLTRL
Cultural ... CULT
Cultural Action Committee ... CAC
Cultural Affairs Library, Nova Scotia Department of Tourism and Culture, Halifa x, Nova Scotia [*Library symbol National Library of Canada*] (NLC) ... NSHDR
Cultural Affairs Officer [*United States Information Service*] ... CAO
Cultural and Recreational Education Achieved through Investigations Ordinarily Neglected [*University course*] ... CREATION
Cultural Association of Bengal (EA) ... CAB
Cultural Attitudes Repertory Technique (EDAC) ... CART

Cultural Auction of Many Extraordinary Lots of Treasure [*St. Louis, Missouri*] ... CAMELOT
Cultural Awareness Program ... CAP
Cultural Centre [*Centre Culturel*] **Verdun, Quebec** [*Library symbol National Library of Canada*] (NLC) ... QVEC
Cultural Council [*Australia*] ... CC
Cultural Deprivation [*Psychology*] (AEBS) ... CD
Cultural Disadvantage ... CD
Cultural / Ethnic Diversity (MEDA) ... CED
Cultural Exchange Officer [*United States Information Service*] ... CEO
Cultural Exchange Society of America (EA) ... CESA
Cultural Expression in the Navy Workshop (DNAB) ... CEN
Cultural Information Analysis Center (SAA) ... CIAC
Cultural [*formerly, Counterinsurgency*] **Information Analysis Center** [*Discontinued*] (MCD) ... CINFAC
Cultural Information Service (EA) ... CIS
Cultural Integration Fellowship (EA) ... CIF
Cultural Pollution Index ... CPI
Cultural Resource Management [*Archaeology*] ... CRM
Cultural Resources Protection on the Outer Continental Shelf [*Oceanography*] (MSC) ... CRPOCS
Cultural Survival (EA) ... CS
Cultural Tourism Advisory Group [*Australia*] ... CTAG
Cultural Travel Organizations International (EA) ... CTOI
Cultural Work, Inc. [*An association*] (EA) ... CWI
Culture [*Microbiology*] ... CULT
Culture [*Biochemistry*] (DAVI) ... Cx
Culture and Life [*A publication*] ... C & L
Culture and Sensitivity ... C & S
Culture and Susceptibility [*Medicine*] (MEDA) ... C & S
Culture Centre of Algae and Protozoa [*Freshwater Biological Association*] [*British*] (CB) ... CCAP
Culture Filtrate [*Analytical biochemistry*] ... CF
Culture Media [*Bacteriology*] (DAVI) ... CM
Culture Shock Inventory [*Interpersonal skills and attitudes test*] ... CSI
Culture Supernatant [*Microbiology*] ... CS
Culture Supply Room [*Microbiology*] ... CSR
Cultured Marble Institute (EA) ... CMI
Cultured Pearl Association of America (EA) ... CPAA
Cultured Thymic Epithelium [*Immunochemistry*] ... CTE
Culture-Negative Neutrocytic Ascite [*Bacteriology*] ... CNNA
Culture-Positive Toxin-Positive [*Medicine*] (DMAA) ... CPTP
Culture-Postive Toxin-Negative [*Medicine*] (DMAA) ... CPTN
Cultuur-en Ontspanningscentrum [*Center for Culture and Recreation*] [*Netherlands*] ... COC
Cultwatch Response [*An association*] (EA) ... CR
Culver City, CA [*Location identifier FAA*] (FAAL) ... CVR
Culver Club (EA) ... CC
Culver, IN [*Location identifier FAA*] (FAAL) ... CPB
Culver Public Library, Culver, IN [*Library symbol Library of Congress*] (LCLS) ... InCu
Culver Senior High School, Culver, OR [*Library symbol*] [*Library of Congress*] (LCLS) ... OrCuHS
Culver-Stockton College [*Canton, MO*] ... CSC
Culver-Stockton College, Canton, MO [*Library symbol Library of Congress*] (LCLS) ... MoCanC
Culvert ... CULV
Culvert Analysis and Design (MHDB) ... CANDE
Cum [*With*] [*Latin*] ... C
Cum Correction [*With lenses*] [*Ophthalmology*] ... cc
Cum Dividend [*With Dividend*] [*Latin Stock exchange term*] ... Cum Div
Cum Dividendo [*With Dividend*] [*Latin Stock exchange term*] ... CD
Cum Dividendo [*With Dividend*] [*Stock exchange term*] (ADA) ... CDIV
Cum Entitlement [*With Entitlement*] [*Latin Legal term*] (ADA) ... CE
Cum Laude Approbatur [*Latin*] ... cl
Cum Laude Society (EA) ... CLS
Cum Omnibus Bonis Quiescat [*May He, or She, Repose with All Good Souls*] [*Latin*] ... COBQ
Cum Rights [*With Rights*] (ADA) ... CR
Cum Tanto [*With the Same Amount Of*] [*Pharmacy*] ... C TANT
Cum Testamento Annexo [*With the Will Annexed*] [*Latin*] ... CTA
Cumana [*Venezuela*] [*Airport symbol*] (OAG) ... CUM
Cumana [*Venezuela*] [*Seismograph station code, US Geological Survey*] (SEIS) ... CUM
Cumana, Sucre [*Venezuela ICAO location identifier*] (ICLI) ... SVCU
Cumann Cheol Tire Eireann [*Folk Music Society of Ireland*] (EAIO) ... CCTE
Cumann Cluiche Corr na hEireann [*Rounders Association of Ireland*] (EAIO) ... CCCE
Cumann Innealtoiri Comhairle na hEirann [*Association of Consulting Engineers of Ireland*] (EAIO) ... CICE
Cumann Leabharann na hEireann [*Library Association of Ireland*] (EAIO) ... CLNh
Cumann Luthchleas Gael [*Gaelic Athletic Association*] (EAIO) ... CLG
Cumann Muinteoiri Eireann [*Irish National Teachers' Organization*] (EAIO) ... CME
Cumann Peile na Heireann [*Football Association of Ireland*] [*Ireland*] (EAIO) ... CPE
Cumberland [*Maryland*] [*Airport symbol*] (OAG) ... CBE
Cumberland [*County in England*] ... CUMB
Cumberland [*England*] (BARN) ... Cumbld
Cumberland Airlines [*ICAO designator*] (AD) ... NQ
Cumberland & Pennsylvania Railroad (IIA) ... C & P
Cumberland College of Tennessee, Lebanon, TN [*Library symbol Library of Congress*] (LCLS) ... TLebC
Cumberland College, Williamsburg, KY [*Library symbol Library of Congress*] (LCLS) ... KyWilC
Cumberland County Advertiser-Press, Inc., Bridgeton, NJ [*Library symbol Library of Congress*] (LCLS) ... NjBAP
Cumberland County Clerk, Bridgeton, NJ [*Library symbol Library of Congress*] (LCLS) ... NjBCoC
Cumberland County College, Vineland, NJ [*Library symbol Library of Congress*] (LCLS) ... NjVC
Cumberland County Historical Society and Hamilton Library Association, Carlisle,PA [*Library symbol Library of Congress*] (LCLS) ... PCarlH
Cumberland County Historical Society, Greenwich, NJ [*Library symbol Library of Congress*] (LCLS) ... NjGrHi
Cumberland County Museum, Amherst, Nova Scotia [*Library symbol National Library of Canada*] (NLC) ... NSCCM
Cumberland County Museum, Amherst, NS, Canada [*Library symbol*] [*Library of Congress*] (LCLS) ... CaNSCCM
Cumberland County Public Library, Fayetteville, NC [*Library symbol Library of Congress*] (LCLS) ... NcFayC
Cumberland County Public Library, North Carolina Foreign Language Center, Fayetteville, NC [*Library symbol Library of Congress*] (LCLS) ... NcFayC-F
Cumberland Gap National Historical Park [*National Park Service designation*] ... CUGA
Cumberland Holdings, Inc. [*Associated Press*] (SAG) ... CmbHld
Cumberland Holdings, Inc. [*NASDAQ symbol*] (SAG) ... CUMB
Cumberland House, SK [*FM radio station call letters*] (RBYB) ... CJCF
Cumberland, KY [*AM radio station call letters*] ... WCPM
Cumberland, KY [*FM radio station call letters*] ... WSEH
Cumberland Law Journal [*Pennsylvania*] [*A publication*] (DLA) ... Cumb
Cumberland Law Journal [*Pennsylvania*] [*A publication*] (DLA) ... Cumb Law Jrnl
Cumberland Law Journal [*Pennsylvania*] [*A publication*] (DLA) ... Cumberland LJ (PA)
Cumberland, MD [*Location identifier FAA*] (FAAL) ... RYP
Cumberland, MD [*AM radio station call letters*] ... WCBC
Cumberland, MD [*FM radio station call letters*] ... WKGO
Cumberland, MD [*AM radio station call letters*] ... WNTR
Cumberland, MD [*FM radio station call letters*] ... WROG
Cumberland, MD [*AM radio station call letters*] ... WTBO
Cumberland Museum, British Columbia [*Library symbol National Library of Canada*] (NLC) ... BCUM
Cumberland Plateau [*Tennessee*] [*Seismograph station code, US Geological Survey*] (SEIS) ... CPO
Cumberland Plateau Seismological Observatory ... CPSO
Cumberland Presbyterian Theological Seminary, Bethel College, McKenzie, TN [*Library symbol Library of Congress*] (LCLS) ... TMckB-C
Cumberland Public Library, Cumberland, WI [*Library symbol Library of Congress*] (LCLS) ... WCu
Cumberland Railway & Coal (MHDB) ... CC
Cumberland Railway & Coal Co. [*AAR code*] ... CDC
Cumberland Regional Library, Amherst, Nova Scotia [*Library symbol National Library of Canada*] (NLC) ... NSAMC
Cumberland Regional Library, Amherst, NS, Canada [*Library symbol Library of Congress*] (LCLS) ... CaNSAMC
Cumberland Resources Ltd. [*Vancouver Stock Exchange symbol*] ... CBD
Cumberland Township Library, Navan, ON, Canada [*Library symbol*] [*Library of Congress*] (LCLS) ... CaONCU
Cumberland Township Library, Navan, Ontario [*Library symbol National Library of Canada*] (BIB) ... ONCU
Cumberland Trail Library System [*Library network*] ... CTLS
Cumberland Trail Library System, Flora, IL [*OCLC symbol*] (OCLC) ... IEZ
Cumberland Trail Library System, Flora, IL [*Library symbol Library of Congress*] (LCLS) ... IFlCL
Cumberland's Law of Nature [*A publication*] (DLA) ... Cumb Nat
Cumberland-Samford Law Review [*A publication*] (DLA) ... Cum Sam L Rev
Cumberland-Samford Law Review [*A publication*] (DLA) ... Cumb-Sam L Rev
Cumbria [*County in England*] (WGA) ... CUMB
Cumene Hydroperoxide [*Organic chemistry*] ... CHP
Cumhuriyetci Turk Partisi [*Republican Turkish Party*] [*Turkish Cyprus*] [*Political party*] (PPE) ... CTP
Cumming, GA [*AM radio station call letters*] ... WMLB
Cumming, GA [*FM radio station call letters*] ... WWEV
Cummins and Dunphy's Remarkable Trials [*A publication*] (DLA) ... Cum & Dun Rem Tr
Cummins and Dunphy's Remarkable Trials [*A publication*] (DLA) ... Rem Tr
Cummins Engine [*NYSE symbol*] (TTSB) ... CUM
Cummins Engine Co., Inc. [*NYSE symbol*] (SPSG) ... CUM
Cummins Engine Co., Inc. [*Associated Press*] (SAG) ... CumEng
Cummins' Manual of Civil Law [*A publication*] (DLA) ... Cum Civ L
Cummins Natural Gas Engines [*Cummins Engine Co., Inc.*] ... CNGE
Cummins' Reports [*1866-67*] [*Idaho*] [*A publication*] (DLA) ... Cummins
Cumulate (ABBR) ... CMULA
Cumulated (ABBR) ... CMULAD
Cumulated Index Medicus [*A publication*] ... CIM
Cumulated Machine-Readable Cataloging [*Computer science*] ... CUMARC
Cumulated Summaries ... CUMS
Cumulating (ABBR) ... CMULAG
Cumulation (ABBR) ... CMULAN
Cumulative (WGA) ... CM
Cumulative (ABBR) ... CMULAV
Cumulative (KSC) ... CUM
Cumulative Abbreviated Trouble File [*Telecommunications*] (TEL) ... CAT
Cumulative Amount (DNAB) ... CA
Cumulative Annual Growth Rate [*Business term*] ... CAGR
Cumulative Annual Regular Military Compensation (MCD) ... CARMC
Cumulative Auction-Market Preferred Stock [*Investment term*] ... CAMPS
Cumulative Audience [*Telecommunications*] ... CUME
Cumulative Average Unit Cost ... CAUC
Cumulative Bulletin [*US Internal Revenue Service*] [*A publication*] (AAGC) ... CB
Cumulative Changes (NATG) ... CC

Cumulative Damage Function [*Nuclear energy*] (NRCH) .... CDF
Cumulative Data Report (MCD) .... CDR
Cumulative Data Statistics (NASA) .... CUDS
Cumulative Detection Probability (CAAL) .... CDP
Cumulative Distribution Function [*Statistics*] .... CDF
Cumulative Elapsed Time .... CET
Cumulative Failure Rate .... CFR
Cumulative Financial Requirements (MCD) .... CFR
Cumulative Form Inception (MCD) .... CFI
Cumulative Frequency .... CF
Cumulative Frequency Distribution (KSC) .... CFD
Cumulative Index (DLA) CI
Cumulative Index to Nursing and Allied Health Literature [*Database*] .... CINAHL
Cumulative List [*Internal Revenue code with names of exempt organizations*] CL
Cumulative List Indicator [*IRS*] .... CU
Cumulative Monthly Issue [*Material*] (AAG) .... CMI
Cumulative Mortality [*Radiology*] .... CM
Cumulative Paperback Index 1939-1959 [*A publication*] .... CPI
Cumulative Percentage Frequency .... CPF
Cumulative Pocket Parts (DLA) .... Cum PP
Cumulative Population Doubling .... CPD
Cumulative Population Doubling Level .... CPDL
Cumulative Preference [*Commerce*] (BARN) .... cum pref
Cumulative Preferred [*A class of stock*] [*Investment term*] .... CMPF
Cumulative Preferred Stock [*Investment term*] .... CPS
Cumulative Probability Distribution (IEEE) .... CPD
Cumulative Probability of Success (MAE) .... CPS
Cumulative Pulmonary Toxicity Dose [*Deep-sea diving*] .... CPTD
Cumulative Quality Point Ratio .... CQPR
Cumulative Radiation Effect .... CRE
Cumulative Radio Audience Method (NTCM) .... CRAM
Cumulative Results Criterion (IEEE) .... CRC
Cumulative Sporulation [*of fungal colonies*] .... CSP
Cumulative Sum .... CUSUM
Cumulative Sum Control Charts [*Statistics*] .... CSCC
Cumulative Sum Diagram [*Statistics*] .... CSD
Cumulative Sum Techniques (MHDB) .... CST
Cumulative Supplement (DLA) .... Cum Supp
Cumulative Techniques and Procedures in Clinical Microbiology [*Medicine*] (DMAA) .... CUMITECH
Cumulative Trauma Disorder [*Medicine*] .... CTD
Cumulative Volcano Amplitude [*Volcanology*] .... CVA
Cumulative Weight Percent .... CWP
Cumulative Working Level Months [*Radon exposure measure*] (ERG) .... CWLM
Cumulatively (ABBR) .... CMULAVY
Cumulonimbus [*Cloud*] [*Meteorology*] .... CB
Cumulonimbus (ABBR) .... CMULNBMS
Cumulonimbus [*Cloud*] [*Meteorology*] .... CN
Cumulonimbus [*Cloud*] [*Meteorology*] (AIA) .... Cu Nim
Cumulonimbus [*Cloud*] [*Meteorology*] .... CUN
Cumulonimbus Mamma [*NWS*] (FAAC) .... CBMAM
Cumulonimbus Mammatus [*Cloud*] [*Meteorology*] .... CM
Cumulus [*Cloud*] [*Meteorology*] C
Cumulus (ABBR) .... CMUL
Cumulus (ABBR) .... CMULS
Cumulus (ABBR) .... CMULU
Cumulus [*Cloud*] [*Meteorology*] .... CU
Cumulus [*Cloud*] [*Meteorology*] .... K
Cumulus and Cumulonimbus [*Clouds*] [*Meteorology*] .... CUCB
Cumulus Fractus [*Type of cloud*] [*Meteorology*] (DNAB) .... CF
Cumulus Fractus [*NWS*] (FAAC) .... CUFRA
Cumulus Technology Ltd. [*Vancouver Stock Exchange symbol Toronto Stock Exchange symbol*] .... CUH
CUNA [*Credit Union National Association*] **Retirement Savings Fund** .... CRSF
Cunagua [*Cuba ICAO location identifier*] (ICLI) .... MUCC
Cunard Steamship Co. (MHDB) .... CSSCO
Cuneate Nucleus [*Neuroanatomy*] .... CN
Cuneiform (VRA) .... cunif
Cuneiform Inscriptions and the Old Testament (BJA) .... COT
[*The*] **Cuneiform Inscriptions of Western Asia** [*A publication*] (BJA) .... CIWA
Cuneiform Texts from Babylonian Tablets in the British Museum (BJA) .... CT
Cuneiform Texts from Cappadocian Tablets in the British Museum (BJA) .... CCT
Cunnamulla [*Australia Airport symbol*] (OAG) .... CMA
Cunningham & Walsh [*Advertising agency*] .... C & W
Cunningham on Hindu Law [*A publication*] (DLA) .... Cun Hind L
Cunningham on Simony [*A publication*] (DLA) .... Cun Sim
Cunningham's Bills, Notes, and Insurances [*A publication*] (DLA) .... Cun Bills
Cunningham's Dictionary [*A publication*] (DLA) .... Cun Dict
Cunningham's English King's Bench Reports [*A publication*] (DLA) .... Ann
Cunningham's English King's Bench Reports [*A publication*] (DLA) .... Cun
Cunningham's English King's Bench Reports [*A publication*] (DLA) .... Cunn
Cunningham's English King's Bench Reports [*A publication*] (DLA) .... Cunningham
Cunningham's English King's Bench Reports [*A publication*] (DLA) .... Cunningham (Eng)
Cunningham's Law Dictionary [*A publication*] (DLA) .... Cun LD
Cunningham's Law of Notes and Bills of Exchange [*A publication*] (DLA) .... Cun Bill Exch
Cunningham's Maxims and Rules of Pleading [*A publication*] (DLA) .... Cun Pl
CUNY [*City University of New York*] **Data Service** [*Information service or system*] (IID) .... CDS
Cup C
Cup to Disk [*Ratio*] [*Opthalmology*] (DAVI) .... C/D
Cupboard .... CPBRD
Cupboard .... CPD
Cupboard .... CUP
Cupertino, CA [*FM radio station call letters*] .... KKUP
Cupertino National Bank [*NASDAQ symbol*] (SAG) .... CUNB
Cupertino National Bank [*Associated Press*] (SAG) .... CupNBk
Cupertino Natl Bancorp [*NASDAQ symbol*] (TTSB) .... CUNB
Cupol [*Record label*] [*Sweden*] .... Cup
Cupola .... CUP
Cupro Nickel .... CN
Cuprum [*Copper*] [*Chemical element*] .... Cu
Curacao [*Netherlands Antilles*] .... CU
Curacao [*Netherlands Antilles*] [*Airport symbol*] (OAG) .... CUR
Curacao [*Netherlands Antilles*] [*ICAO location identifier*] (ICLI) .... TNCF
Curacao Group [*MARC geographic area code Library of Congress*] (LCCP) .... nwco--
Curacao Tourist Board (EA) .... CTB
Curacy [*or Curate*] C
Curaray [*Ecuador*] [*ICAO location identifier*] (ICLI) .... SECR
Curate (ROG) .... CUR
Curate in Charge [*Church of England*] CIC
Curate-in-Charge [*Church of England*] .... C-in-C
Curate-in-Charge [*Church of England*] (ROG) .... CUR-in-CH
Curates' Alliance [*British*] .... CA
Curates' Augmentation Fund [*British*] .... CAF
Curatio [*A Dressing*] [*Pharmacy*] .... CURAT
Curative [*Medicine*] .... CUR
Curative Dose [*Medicine*] .... CD
Curative Health Services, Inc. [*NASDAQ symbol*] (SAG) .... CURE
Curative Health Services, Inc. [*Associated Press*] (SAG) .... CurHlth
Curative Technologies [*NASDAQ symbol*] (SPSG) .... CURE
Curative Technologies, Inc. [*Associated Press*] (SAG) .... CurTch
Curative Technology [*NASDAQ symbol*] (TTSB) .... CURE
Curator .... CUR
Curator Resources [*Vancouver Stock Exchange symbol*] .... CUR
Curb Weight [*Automotive engineering*] .... CW
Curbside (MSA) .... CRBSD
Curculio [*of Plautus*] [*Classical studies*] (OCD) .... Curc
Curd Firmness Tester [*For milk products*] .... CFT
Cure AIDS [*Acquired Immune Deficiency Syndrome*] **Now** [*An association*] (EA) .... CAN
CURE [*Citizens United to Reduce Emmissions*] **Formaldehyde Poisoning Association** (EA) .... CURE
Cure Rate Index [*Rubber technology*] .... CRI
Cure to Handling .... CTH
Curecanti Recreation Area [*National Park Service designation*] .... CURE
Cured in Place [*Gaskets and seals*] .... CIP
Cured-In- Place Pipe [*Civil Engineering*] .... CIPP
Cure-In-Place Gasket .... CIPG
Curettage and Desiccation [*Gynecology*] (DAVI) .... C & D
Curettage and Electrodesiccation [*Fulguration*] [*Medicine*] (DAVI) .... C & F
Curia [*Court*] [*Latin*] (DLA) .... CUR
Curia Advisari Vult [*The Court Wishes to Consider*] [*Latin Legal term*] .... CAV
Curia Advisari Vult [*The Court Wishes to Consider*] [*Latin Legal term*] (ROG) .... CUR ADV VULT
Curia Phillippica [*Latin*] (DLA) .... CUR PHIL
Curia Regis [*King's Court*] [*Latin Legal term*] (DLA) .... CR
Curia Regis [*King's Court*] [*Latin Legal term*] (ROG) .... CUR REG
Curia Regis Rolls [*British Legal term*] (DLA) .... Cr R
Curia Regis Rolls [*British*] .... CUR
Curia Regis Rolls [*British Legal term*] (DLA) .... Cur Reg R
Curichi [*Bolivia*] [*ICAO location identifier*] (ICLI) .... SLQY
Curico/General Freire [*Chile*] [*ICAO location identifier*] (ICLI) .... SCIC
Curie [*Unit of radioactivity*] [*See Ci*] C
Curie (IDOE) c
Curie [*Unit of radioactivity*] [*Preferred unit is Bq, Becquerel*] Ci
Curie [*Unit of radioactivity*] [*See Ci*] (AAMN) .... Cu
Curie Hour (MAE) .... Cihr
Curie Point Pyrolysis (PDAA) .... CPP
Curie-Hour [*Measurement*] (DAVI) .... c-hr
Curing Agent .... CA
Curing, Extrusion, Plasticity, and Recovery (PDAA) .... CEPAR
Curiosity (DSUE) .... CURIO
Curious (ROG) .... CUR
Curious to Know [*An inquisitive customer*] [*Merchandising slang*] .... C to K
Curitiba [*Brazil*] [*Airport symbol*] (OAG) .... CWB
Curitiba [*Brazil ICAO location identifier*] (ICLI) .... SBCW
Curitiba/Afonso Pena [*Brazil ICAO location identifier*] (ICLI) .... SBCT
Curitiba/Bacacheri [*Brazil ICAO location identifier*] (ICLI) .... SBBI
Curium [*Chemical element*] .... Cm
Curlew Lake [*Vancouver Stock Exchange symbol*] .... CWQ
Curling Club CC
Curl's Algorithm for Logic Compression .... CALC
Curly Top Virus .... CTV
Curly-Coated Retriever Club of America (EA) .... CCRCA
Curran Memorial Library, Port Au Port East, Newfoundland [*Library symbol National Library of Canada*] (NLC) .... NFPEC
Curran Memorial Library, Port Au Port East, NF, Canada [*Library symbol Library of Congress*] (LCLS) .... CaNfPeC
Currant [*Nevada*] [*Seismograph station code, US Geological Survey*] (SEIS) .... CND
Currency C
Currency .... CUR
Currency (AFM) .... CURR
Currency .... CY
Currency Adjustment and Bunkering Adjustment Factors [*British*] (DCTA) .... CABAF
Currency Adjustment Charge [*Business term*] .... CAC

Currency Adjustment Factor [*Business term*] .... CAF
Currency Bond .... CB
Currency Clearinghouse .... CCH
Currency Exchange Database [*GE Information Services*] [*Information service or system*] (CRD) .... CEDB
Currency Exploitation .... CE
Currency Market Analysis [*MMS International*] [*Information service or system*] (CRD) .... CMA
Currency Market Service [*Database*] [*Money Market Services, Inc.*] [*Information service or system*] (CRD) .... CMS
Currency Overprinting and Processing Equipment [*Bureau of Printing and Engraving*] .... COPE
Currency Regulation .... CR
Currency Sign [*Telecommunications*] (TEL) .... CS
Currency Transaction Report [*IRS*] .... CTR
Current C
Current .... CT
Current (AAG) .... CUR
Current (IDOE) .... cur
Current (EY) .... CURR
Current (ROG) .... CURRT
Current .... CURT
Current Account [*Business term*] .... CA
Current Account [*Business term*] (IAA) .... CAC
Current Account Deficit [*Economics*] .... CAD
Current Actions Center .... CAC
Current Actions Duty Officer [*Air Force*] .... CADO
Current Address (DNAB) .... CA
Current Adjusting Type .... CAT
Current Advances in Plant Science [*A database*] [*Pergamon*] (NITA) .... CAPS
Current Aerospace Research Activities (KSC) .... CARA
Current Agricultural Research Information System [*Food and Agriculture Organization*] [*United Nations Information service or system*] (IID) .... CARIS
Current Analysis [*Program*] [*Department of State*] .... CA
Current and Past Psychopathology Scales [*Psychology*] .... CAPPS
Current Annotated Bibliography of Irrigation [*Bet Dagan, Israel*] [*A publication*] .... IRRICAB
Current Annual Increment (DICI) .... CAI
Current Approval Plan [*Army*] .... CAP
Current ARDC [*Air Research and Development Command*] **Technical Efforts** [*DoD program*] .... CATE
Current Assessment Plan .... CAP
Current Asset [*Business term*] .... CA
Current Australian Reference Books [*A publication*] .... CARB
Current Awareness and Document Retrieval for Engineers (DIT) .... CADRE
Current Awareness Bibliographies [*DTIC*] .... CAB
Current Awareness Bulletin for Librarians and Information Scientists [*British*] [*A publication*] (NITA) .... CABLIS
Current Awareness in Biological Sciences [*Pergamon Press*] [*Information service or system*] (IID) .... CABS
Current Awareness Literature Service [*Department of Agriculture*] [*Beltsville, MD*] .... CALS
Current Awareness Service [*Cryogenic literature bibliography*] [*Cryogenic Data Center*] .... CAS
Current Awareness System in Coordination Chemistry .... CASCC
Current Background .... CB
Current Balance Earth Leakage (PDAA) .... CBEL
Current Balance Record [*Banking*] (IAA) .... CBR
Current Bibliographic Directory of the Arts and Sciences [*A publication*] .... CBD
Current Biography [*A publication*] .... CB
Current Biotechnology Abstracts [*Royal Society of Chemistry*] [*Information service or system*] (IID) .... CBA
Current BIT [*Binary Digit*] [*Computer science*] (IAA) .... CB
Current BIT [*Binary Digit*] **Monitor Unit** [*Computer science*] .... CBMU
Current Break-Off and Memory (OA) .... CBOM
Current Cancer Research Project Analysis Center [*Database producer*] .... CCRESPAC
Current Cases [*1965-71*] [*Ghana*] [*A publication*] (DLA) CC
Current Cash [*or Cost*] **Equivalent** (ADA) .... CCE
Current Challengers CC
Current Chemical Reactions [*A publication*] .... CCR
Current Clinical Trials [*A publication*] .... CCT
Current Comment and Legal Miscellany [*A publication*] (DLA) .... Cur Com
Current Comment and Legal Miscellany [*A publication*] (DLA) .... Current Com & Leg Mis
Current Complaints [*Medicine*] CC
Current Contents/Chemical Sciences [*A publication*] .... CC/CS
Current Control Relay (DNAB) .... CCR
Current Controlled Negative Resistance [*Electronics*] (IAA) .... CCNR
Current Cost CC
Current Cost Accounting .... CCA
Current Cost Operating Profits [*Accounting*] .... CCOP
Current Data BIT [*Binary Digit*] [*Computer science*] .... CDB
Current Density .... CD
Current Depth Measurement Subsystem [*National Ocean Survey*] (MSC) .... CDMS
Current Design Expendable [*Refers to payload type*] [*NASA*] .... CDE
Current Design Reusable [*Refers to payload type*] [*NASA*] .... CDR
Current Device Register .... CDR
Current Difference Logic (DGA) .... CDI
Current Digest [*A publication*] .... CD
Current Directional Relay .... CDR
Current Directory Structure [*Computer science*] (PCM) .... CDS
Current Discharge (IAA) .... CD
Current Discharge Line (IAA) .... CDL
Current Discontinuity Device (IAA) .... CDD
Current Domestic Value [*of goods in the country of origin*] .... CDV
Current Driver .... CD
Current Economic Reporting Program [*Department of State*] .... CERP
Current Efficiency [*Electrochemistry*] .... CE
Current Employment Statistics [*Bureau of Labor Statistics*] (OICC) .... CES
Current Employment Status .... CES
Current Energy Patents [*A publication*] .... CEP
Current Engineering and Manufacturing Services Staff [*Automotive industry*] .... CEMSS
Current Enlistment Date [*Military*] .... CED
Current Estimate (AFIT) .... CE
Current Evangelism Ministries (EA) .... CEM
Current Expendable (NASA) .... CE
Current Expenditure [*Economics*] C
Current Exploitation (MCD) .... CE
Current Fault File [*Telecommunications*] (TEL) .... CFF
Current Feedback (IAA) .... CF
Current File User [*Computer science*] (OA) .... CFU
Current Files Area .... CFA
Current Fiscal Year (AFM) .... CFY
Current Flight Plan [*FAA*] (TAG) .... CPL
Current Flight Plan Message [*Aviation code*] .... CPL
Current Force (IAA) .... CF
Current Gain .... CG
Current Gate Tube .... CGT
Current Good Manufacturing Practice [*Food and Drug Administration*] .... CGMP
Current History [*A publication*] (BRI) .... Cu H
Current Image Diffraction (MCD) .... CID
Current Imaging Tunneling Spectroscopy .... CITS
Current Income Shares, Inc. [*NYSE symbol*] (SPSG) .... CUR
Current Income Shares, Inc. [*Associated Press*] (SAG) .... CurInc
Current Inc. Shares [*NYSE symbol*] (TTSB) .... CUR
Current Index to Legal Periodicals [*University of Washington*] [*Information service or system*] (CRD) .... CILP
Current Index to Statistics [*MathSci database subfile*] (IT) .... CIS
Current Indian Cases [*1912-15*] [*A publication*] (DLA) .... Cur IC
Current Indian Cases [*1912-15*] [*A publication*] (DLA) .... Cur Ind Cas
Current Indian Cases, Old Series [*India*] [*A publication*] (DLA) CIC
Current Indicator and Integrator CII
Current Industrial Reports [*Census Bureau*] .... CIR
Current Information Database .... CID
Current Information Section (ADA) .... CIS
Current Information Selection [*IBM Technical Information Retrieval Center*] [*White Plains, NY*] .... CIS
Current Information Service [*Australia*] .... CIS
Current Information Tapes for Engineering .... CITE
Current Information Transfer in English .... CITE
Current Injection Equivalent Circuit Approach (MCD) .... CIECA
Current Injection Logic [*Computer science*] CIL
Current Injection Probe .... CIP
Current Input Differential Amplifier [*Electronics*] (OA) .... CIDA
Current Instruction Register .... CIR
Current Intelligence Bulletin [*A publication*] .... CIB
Current Intelligence, Group (NATG) .... CIG
Current Intelligence Indication Center (CINC) CIIC
Current Intelligence Operations Center (MCD) .... CIOC
Current Intelligence Requirement List (MCD) .... CIRL
Current Intelligence Targets Groups [*Military*] .... CITG
Current Intelligence Traffic Exploitation System (PDAA) .... CITES
Current Interrupter [*Electronics*] (IAA) CI
Current Laboratory Practice [*A publication*] .... CLP
Current Law Consolidation [*England*] [*A publication*] (DLA) CLC
Current Law Monthly [*A publication*] (DLA) .... CLM
Current Law Reports [*Palestine*] [*A publication*] (DLA) .... CLR
Current Law Reports [*Ceylon*] [*A publication*] (DLA) .... Cur LR
Current Law Statutes, Annotated [*A publication*] (DLA) .... CL Stats
Current Law Year Book [*A publication*] (ILCA) .... CLY
Current Law Year Book [*A publication*] (DLA) .... Current LY
Current Layer (OA) CL
Current Leading Component (PDAA) CLC
Current Legal Forms with Tax Analysis [*A publication*] (DLA) .... CLF
Current Legal Problems [*A publication*] (DLA) .... Curr Legal Prob
Current Liabilities [*Insurance*] CL
Current Line Pointer [*Computer science*] (IBMDP) .... CLP
Current List of Medical Literature .... CLML
Current Literature Alerting Search Service [*Biological Abstracts*] (NITA) .... CLASS
Current Literature Awareness Search Service [*BIOSIS*] [*Database*] .... CLASS
Current Literature on Water [*Database*] [*South African Water Information Centre*] [*Information service or system*] (CRD) .... CLOW
Current Logic [*Electronics*] (IAA) CL
Current Logical Byte Address (IAA) .... CLBA
Current Loop: Interface Standard (NITA) CL
Current Market Appraisal .... CMA
Current Market Value [*Business term*] (ADA) .... CMV
Current Medical Information and Technology (DAVI) .... CMIT
Current Medical Information and Terminology .... CMIT
Current Medical Terminology .... CMT
Current Medicine for Attorneys [*A publication*] (DLA) .... Current Med for Att'ys
Current Meter [*Marine science*] (OSRA) .... CM
Current Meter Data Base [*National Ocean Survey*] (MSC) .... CMD
Current Meter Intercomparison Experiment [*National Ocean Survey*] (MSC) .... CMICE
Current Meter Speed and Detection .... CUMSAD
Current Monitor [*Instrumentation*] .... CM
Current Months Total Program Forecast (MCD) .... CMTPF

Current Mortality Sample [Department of Health and Human Services] (GFGA) .... CMS
Current New York Time (DOAD) .... CNYT
Current Notes on International Affairs [A publication] .... Curr No Int Aff
Current Oil in Place [Petroleum technology] .... COIP
Current on Board (DNAB) .... COB
Current Operating Allowances .... COA
Current Operating Budget Year .... COBY
Current Operating Procedure (MCD) .... COP
Current Operating Time .... COT
Current Operation Expenditure [Business term] .... COE
Current Operational Data System .... CODAS
Current Operational Group [NATO] (NATG) .... COG
Current Operations .... COPS
Current Operations Division [Tactical Air Command] .... COD
Current Operator - Next Operator [Computer science] (MDG) .... CO/NO
Current or Voltage .... CURTAGE
Current Paper .... CP
Current Period .... CP
Current Perpendicular to Plane Magnetoresistance [Physics] .... CPP-MR
Current Physics Bibliographies [A publication] (MCD) .... CPB
Current Physics Information [American Institute of Physics] [New York, NY Information service or system] .... CPI
Current Physics Selected Articles [A publication] (MCD) .... CPSA
Current Physics Titles [A publication] .... CPT
Current/Pneumatic [Nuclear energy] (NRCH) .... C/P
Current/Pneumatic [Nuclear energy] (NRCH) .... I/P
Current Population Survey [Census Bureau] .... CPS
Current Population Survey Processing Branch [Bureau of the Census] (GFGA) .... CPSPB
Current Practices .... CP
Current Priority Indicator .... CPI
Current Privilege Level [Computer programs] (BYTE) .... CPL
Current Procedural Technology [Department of Health and Human Services] (GFGA) .... CPT
Current Procedural Terminology [American Medical Association] .... CPT
Current Processor Mode .... CPM
Current Product Engineering .... CPE
Current Property Law [British] .... CPL
Current Property Law [British A publication] (DLA) .... Cur Prop L
Current Property Law [British A publication] (DLA) .... Current Prop L
Current Property Lawyer [1852-53] [England] [A publication] (DLA) .... CPL
Current Protocols in Immunology [A publication] .... CPI
Current Protocols in Molecular Biology [A publication] .... CPMB
Current Pulse Generator [Electronics] (IAA) .... CPG
Current Purchasing Power .... CPP
Current Rate [Business term] .... CR
Current Relay (MSA) .... CR
Current Replacement Cost [Accounting] .... CRC
Current Requirements .... CRQ
Current Requisition File [DoD] .... CRF
Current Research and Development in Scientific Documentation [A publication] .... CRDSD
Current Research File [NIOSH] [Database] .... CRF
Current Research in Britain [A publication] .... CRB
Current Research Information System [Department of Agriculture Information service or system] .... CRIS
Current Retail Trade Reports [A publication] .... CRTR
Current Sensitive Relay (DNAB) .... CSR
Current Sensor Unit [American Solenoid Co.] [Somerset, NJ] .... CSU
Current Series [Army] .... CS
Current Ship's Maintenance Project .... CSMP
Current SIGINT [Signal Intelligence] Operations Center [National Security Agency] (MCD) .... CSOC
Current Sink Logic (IAA) .... CSL
Current Situation Room (MCD) .... CSR
Current Sleep Walker [Medicine] (DMAA) .... CSW
Current Smoker (DAVI) .... CS
Current Source .... CS
Current Source (MSA) .... IGEN
Current Source Amplifier .... CSA
Current Source Logic (IAA) .... CSL
Current Source-Density [Neuroelectricity] .... CSD
Current Steering Switch (KSC) .... CSS
Current Strength .... CS
Current Summary of Threat (MCD) .... CST
Current Switch (IAA) .... CS
Current Switch Emitter/Follower (OA) .... CSEF
Current Switch Logic (IEEE) .... CSL
Current Switching Diode Logic (IAA) .... CSDL
Current Switching Mode (IAA) .... CSM
Current System Description (SSD) .... CSD
Current Tech [Vancouver Stock Exchange symbol] .... ONE
Current Technology [VS, exchange symbol] (TTSB) .... ONE
Current, Temperature, Density .... CTD
Current Time Sensing (CAAL) .... CTS
Current to Current [Converter] (NRCH) .... I/I
Current to Pressure [Electropneumatic] (ACII) .... I/P
Current Transactions (NATG) .... CT
Current Transfer Ratio [Bell System] .... CTR
Current Transformer .... CRT
Current Transformer .... CT
Current Transformer [Instrumentation] .... CT
Current Use Value (MHDB) .... CUV
Current Value Accounting .... CVA

Current Value/Constant Purchasing Power [Accounting] .... CV/CPP
Current Values Table .... CVT
Current Variable Attenuator .... CVA
Current Variable Inductor CVI
Current Viewing Resistor .... CVR
Current Vital Signs [Medicine] .... CVS
Current Voltage Characteristic (OA) CVC
Current Voltage Converter (IAA) CVC
Current Voltage Regulator (IAA) .... CVR
Current Wage Developments [A publication] .... CWD
Current Word Pointer .... CWP
Current Working Estimate [Military] .... CWE
Current Year (DOMA) .... CY
Current Yield [Banking] .... CY
Current-Controlled Amplifier [Electronics] (ECII) .... CCA
Current-Controlled Inductor [Electronics] (IAA) CCI
Current-Controlled Oscillator (IEEE) .... CCO
Current-Controlled Voltage Source (IEEE) .... CCVS
Current-Hogging Injection Logic [Electronics] (IEEE) .... CHIL
Current-Hogging Injection Logic (IDOE) .... CHIL
Current-Hogging Logic [Electronics] .... CHL
Currentis [Of the Current Month or Year] [Latin] C
Currentis [Of the Current Month or Year] [Latin] .... CUR
Current-Limiting Device [Short-circuit limiter] .... CLD
Current-Limiting Resistor (MSA) .... CLR
Current-Logic-Current-Switching [Electronics] .... CLCS
Current-Mode Complementary Transistor Logic [Computer science] (IEEE) .... CMCTL
Current-Mode Digital-to-Analog Converter [Computer science] .... CMDAC
Current-Mode Logic [Computer science] .... CML
Current-Mode Switching [Computer science] (MSA) .... CMS
Current-Voltage Diagram .... CVD
Curriculum .... CURR
Curriculum .... CURR
Curriculum .... CURRIC
Curriculum Adaptation Network for Bilingual, Bicultural Education .... CANBBE
Curriculum Advisory Committee [American Occupational Therapy Association] .... CAC
Curriculum Analysis Taxonomy [Education] (AIE) .... CAT
Curriculum and Accreditation Secretariat [Victoria] [Australia] .... CAS
Curriculum and Instruction Development [Program] [National Science Foundation] .... CID
Curriculum and Instructional Standards [Military] (DNAB) .... CIS
Curriculum and Research (ADA) .... C & R
Curriculum and Resource Information Service (AIE) .... CRIS
Curriculum Assessment and Teacher/Trainer Training .... CATTT
Curriculum Association (AIE) .... CA
Curriculum Coordinating Committees (EDAC) CCC
Curriculum Corporation [Commercial firm Australia] CC
Curriculum Council for Wales (AIE) .... CCW
Curriculum Development Manager (MCD) .... CDM
Curriculum Evaluation and Management Centre [University of Newcastle upon Tyne] [British] (CB) .... CEMC
Curriculum Improvement Resulting from Creative Utilization of Instructional Two-Way Television Project [Wisconsin] (EDAC) .... CIRCUIT
Curriculum Led Institutional Development (AIE) .... CLID
Curriculum Materials Centre, Education Library, Memorial University, St. John's, Newfoundland [Library symbol National Library of Canada] (NLC) .... NFSMEC
Curriculum Perspective [A publication] .... Curric P
Curriculum Research and Development Group [University of Hawaii] [Research center] (RCD) .... CRDG
Curriculum Resource Materials .... CRM
Curriculum Resources Centre, Niagara South Board of Education, Allanburg, Ontario [Library symbol National Library of Canada] (BIB) .... OAN
Curriculum Review [A publication] (BRI) .... Cur R
Curriculum Review Board of the American Association of Medical Assistants (DAVI) .... CRB
Curriculum Review Integrated Product Team [Army] .... CRIPT
Curriculum Vitae [Job applications] CV
Curriculum-Based Assessment [Education] .... CBA
Currie, Coopers & Lybrand Ltd., Montreal, PQ, Canada [Library symbol Library of Congress] (LCLS) .... CaQMCCL
Currie, Coopers & Lybrand Ltd., Montreal, Quebec [Library symbol National Library of Canada] (NLC) .... QMCCL
Currie, Coopers & Lybrand Ltd., Toronto, ON, Canada [Library symbol Library of Congress] (LCLS) .... CaOTCCL
Currie, Coopers & Lybrand Ltd., Toronto, Ontario [Library symbol National Library of Canada] (NLC) .... OTCCL
Currie Rose Resources, Inc. [Vancouver Stock Exchange symbol] .... CUI
Currituck County Public Library, Coinjock, NC [Library symbol Library of Congress] (LCLS) .... NcCoi
Curry College, Milton, MA [OCLC symbol] (OCLC) .... CUM
Curry College, Milton, MA [Library symbol Library of Congress] (LCLS) .... MMiltC
Curry Public Library, Gold Beach, OR [Library symbol Library of Congress] (LCLS) .... OrGb
Curry's Abridgment of Blackstone [A publication] (DLA) .... Cur Bl
Curry's Reports [6-19 Louisiana] [A publication] (DLA) .... Curry
Curschmann-Steinert [Syndrome] [Medicine] (DAVI) .... CS
Curse of Agade (BJA) .... CA
Cursitor Baron of the Exchequer [British] (ROG) .... CURS BE
Cursive (BJA) .... curs
Cursor Centered [Automotive engineering] CC
Cursor Control [Computer science] (BUR) CC
Cursor Position (MCD) .... CPOS

Cursus Cancellariae [*Latin*] (DLA) ... CURS CAN
Cursus Sacrae Scripturae [*Paris*] (BJA) ... CSS
Cursus Scaccarii [*Latin*] (DLA) ... CUR SCACC
Curtain ... CRTN
Curtain (MSA) ... CURT
Curtain Sided Trailer [*Shipping*] (DCTA) ... CS
Curteis' English Ecclesiastical Reports [*A publication*] (DLA) ... Curt
Curteis' English Ecclesiastical Reports [*A publication*] (DLA) ... Curt Ecc
Curteis' English Ecclesiastical Reports [*A publication*] (DLA) ... Curt Eccl
Curteis' English Ecclesiastical Reports [*A publication*] (DLA) ... Curt Eccl (Eng)
Curtin University Environmental Studies Group [*Australia*] ... CUESG
Curtis' Admiralty Digest [*A publication*] (DLA) ... Curt Adm Dig
Curtis' American Conveyancer [*A publication*] (DLA) ... Curt Conv
Curtis Bay Railroad Co. [*AAR code*] ... CURB
Curtis' Circuit Court Reports [*United States*] [*A publication*] (DLA) ... Curt
Curtis' Circuit Court Reports [*United States*] [*A publication*] (DLA) ... Curtis
Curtis' Commentaries on the United States Courts [*A publication*] (DLA) ... Curt US Courts
Curtis Completion Form [*Psychology*] ... CCF
Curtis' Copyright [*1847*] [*A publication*] (DLA) ... Curt Cop
Curtis' Decisions of the United States Supreme Court [*A publication*] (DLA) ... Cur Dec
Curtis' Decisions of the United States Supreme Court [*A publication*] (DLA) ... Curt Cond Rep
Curtis' Decisions of the United States Supreme Court [*A publication*] (DLA) ... Curt Dec
Curtis' Decisions of the United States Supreme Court [*A publication*] (DLA) ... Curtis SC Reports
Curtis' Decisions of the United States Supreme Court [*A publication*] (DLA) ... Curtis US Sup Ct R
Curtis' Digest [*United States*] [*A publication*] (DLA) ... Curt Dig
Curtis' Edition, United States Supreme Court Reports [*A publication*] (DLA) ... Curt
Curtis' Edition, United States Supreme Court Reports [*A publication*] (DLA) ... Curt Cond
Curtis' Edition, United States Supreme Court Reports [*A publication*] (DLA) ... Curtis
Curtis' Equity Precedents [*A publication*] (DLA) ... Curt Eq Pr
Curtis' History of the Constitution of the United States Courts [*A publication*] (DLA) ... Curt US Const
Curtis Institute of Music [*Pennsylvania*] ... CIM
Curtis Institute of Music, Philadelphia, PA [*Library symbol Library of Congress*] (LCLS) ... PPCI
Curtis Mathes Hldg [*NASDAQ symbol*] (TTSB) ... CRTM
Curtis Mathes Holding Corp. [*Associated Press*] (SAG) ... CMathes
Curtis Mathes Holding Corp. [*NASDAQ symbol*] (SAG) ... CRTM
Curtis Memorial Public Library, Meriden, CT [*Library symbol Library of Congress*] (LCLS) ... CtMer
Curtis, Milburn & Eastern Railroad Co. [*AAR code*] ... CMER
Curtis on Patents [*A publication*] (DLA) ... Curt Pat
Curtis on the Jurisdiction of United States Courts [*A publication*] (DLA) ... Curt Jur
Curtis Publishing Co., Research Library, Philadelphia, PA [*Library symbol Library of Congress Obsolete*] (LCLS) ... PPCuP
Curtis' United States Circuit Court Decisions [*A publication*] (DLA) ... Curt CC
Curtis' United States Circuit Court Reports [*A publication*] (DLA) ... Cur
Curtis' United States Circuit Court Reports [*A publication*] (DLA) ... Curtis CC
Curtiss-Wright [*NYSE symbol*] (TTSB) ... CW
Curtiss-Wright Corp. [*Associated Press*] (SAG) ... CurtWr
Curtiss-Wright Corp. [*ICAO aircraft manufacturer identifier*] (ICAO) ... CW
Curtiss-Wright Corp. [*NYSE symbol*] (SPSG) ... CW
Curtiss-Wright Corp. ... CWC
Curtiss-Wright of Canada [*Toronto Stock Exchange symbol*] ... CWA
Curtiss-Wright Research Reactor ... CWRR
Curuzu Cuatia [*Argentina ICAO location identifier*] (ICLI) ... SATU
Curuzu Cuatia [*Argentina*] [*Airport symbol*] (OAG) ... UZU
Curve (MSA) ... CRV
Curve ... CURV
Curve [*Postal Service standards*] (OPSA) ... CURV
Curve [*Commonly used*] (OPSA) ... CURVE
Curve Interpreter for Microprocessor (MCD) ... CIMP
Curve Lake Indian Band Library, Ontario [*Library symbol National Library of Canada*] (BIB) ... OCLI
Curve of Merit [*Electronics*] (IAA) ... COM
Curved ... cvd
Curved Dash Olds Owners Club (EA) ... CDOOC
Curved End-to-End Anastomosis [*Stapler*] [*Medicine*] (DMAA) ... CEEA
Curved Motion Cutter ... CMC
Curved Orthotropic Bridge Analysis (PDAA) ... COBRA
Curvilinear Body [*in Batten disease*] ... CLB
Curwen's Abstract of Titles [*A publication*] (DLA) ... Cur Ab Tit
Curwen's Laws of Ohio [*1 vol.*] [*1854*] [*A publication*] (DLA) ... Curw LO
Curwen's Overruled Cases [*Ohio*] [*A publication*] (DLA) ... Cur Ov Ca
Curwen's Overruled Cases [*Ohio*] [*A publication*] (DLA) ... Curw
Curwen's Overruled Cases [*Ohio*] [*A publication*] (DLA) ... Curw Ov Cas
Curwen's Revised Statutes of Ohio [*A publication*] (DLA) ... Curw RS
Curwen's Statutes of Ohio [*A publication*] (DLA) ... Cur Stat
Curwen's Statutes of Ohio [*A publication*] (DLA) ... Curw
Curwensville, PA [*FM radio station call letters*] ... WOKW
[*The*] **Curwood Collector** [*A publication*] (EA) ... TCC
Cusac Gold Mines [*NASDAQ symbol*] (TTSB) ... CUSIF
Cusac Gold Mines Ltd. [*Associated Press*] (SAG) ... Cusac
Cusac Gold Mines Ltd. [*NASDAQ symbol*] (SAG) ... CUSI
Cusac Gold Mines Ltd. [*NASDAQ symbol*] (SAG) ... CUSW
Cusac Inds Ltd Wrrt [*NASDAQ symbol*] (TTSB) ... CUSWF
Cusac Industries Ltd. [*Toronto Stock Exchange symbol Vancouver Stock Exchange symbol*] ... CQC
Cusac Industries Ltd. [*Associated Press*] (SAG) ... Cusac
Cusco [*Peru*] [*Seismograph station code, US Geological Survey*] (SEIS) ... CUS
Cushing, OK [*Location identifier FAA*] (FAAL) ... CUH
Cushing, OK [*AM radio station call letters*] ... KUSH
Cushing on Trustee Process [*A publication*] (DLA) ... Cush Trust Pr
Cushing, Storey, and Joselyn's Election Cases [*Massachusetts*] [*A publication*] (DLA) ... CS & J
Cushing's Election Cases in Massachusetts [*A publication*] (DLA) ... Cush Elec Cas
Cushing's Law and Practice of Legislative Assemblies [*A publication*] (DLA) ... Cush Law & Prac Leg Assem
Cushing's Law and Practice of Legislative Assemblies [*A publication*] (DLA) ... Cush Leg Ass
Cushing's Law and Practice of Legislative Assemblies [*A publication*] (DLA) ... Cush Parl Law
Cushing's Manual of Parliamentary Law [*A publication*] (DLA) ... Cush Man
Cushing's Massachusetts Supreme Judicial Court Reports [*1848-53*] [*A publication*] (DLA) ... Cush
Cushing's Reports [*1848-53*] [*A publication*] (DLA) ... Cush (Mass)
Cushing's Reports [*1848-53*] [*A publication*] (DLA) ... Cushing
Cushing's Study of the Roman Law [*A publication*] (DLA) ... Cush Rom Law
Cushing's Syndrome [*Endocrinology*] (DAVI) ... CS
Cushion ... CSHN
Cushion (MSA) ... CUSH
Cushion Air System Parametric Assessment Rig (PDAA) ... CASPAR
Cushion Air Tread Articulate [*Vehicle*] [*Army*] ... CATA
Cushion Control Point [*Navy*] (ANA) ... CCP
Cushion Craft ... CC
Cushion Landing Zone [*Navy*] (ANA) ... CLZ
Cushion Lift (AAG) ... C
Cushioning Pads ... CP
Cushitic [*MARC language code Library of Congress*] (LCCP) ... cus
Cushman Club of America (EA) ... CCA
Cushman Foundation for Foraminiferal Research (EA) ... CFFR
Cushman's Reports [*23-29 Mississippi*] [*A publication*] (DLA) ... Cush
Cushman's Reports [*23-29 Mississippi*] [*A publication*] (DLA) ... Cushm
CUSO [*Canadian University Service Overseas*], Ottawa, Ontario [*Library symbol National Library of Canada*] (NLC) ... OOCUS
Cusp Creek [*British Columbia*] [*Seismograph station code, US Geological Survey Closed*] (SEIS) ... CCC
Cusp Injection Experiment [*Nuclear energy British*] (NUCP) ... CUSIE
Cusparia [*Angustura Bark*] [*Pharmacology*] (ROG) ... CUSPAR
Cuspid [*Dentistry*] (DAVI) ... cusp
Cuspidore Hitters Association Worldwide [*Defunct*] (EA) ... CHAW
Custer Battlefield Historical and Museum Association (EA) ... CBHMA
Custer Battlefield National Monument [*National Park Service designation*] ... CUST
Custer County Junior College [*Montana*] ... CCJC
Custer County Library, Custer, SD [*Library symbol Library of Congress*] (LCLS) ... SdCu
Custer County Public Library, Westcliffe, CO [*Library symbol Library of Congress*] (LCLS) ... CoWc
Custer, SD [*FM radio station call letters*] ... KACP
Custer, SD [*FM radio station call letters*] (RBYB) ... KAWK-FM
Custer, SD [*AM radio station call letters*] ... KFCR
Custer's Ecclesiastical Reports [*A publication*] (DLA) ... Cust Rep
Custodial Parent ... CP
Custodial, Protective, and Crafts [*US government workers*] ... CPC
Custodian [*Banking*] (AFM) ... CUST
Custodian ... CUSTDN
Custodian (ADA) ... CUSTOD
Custodian Account [*Banking*] ... CA
Custodian Contractor ... CC
Custodian of Allied and Enemy Property [*British World War II*] ... CAEP
Custodian of Fund ... C of F
Custodian of Postal Effects [*Military*] (AFM) ... COPE
Custodian of Records (HGAA) ... COR
Custody (AFM) ... CUST
Custody Action for Lesbian Mothers (EA) ... CALM
Custody Authorization/Custody Receipt Listing ... CA/CRL
Custody Pending Completion of Use ... CPCU
Custom ... CSTM
Custom [*Automotive engineering*] ... CUST
Custom and Port [*International trade*] ... C/P
Custom Asynchronous Receiver/Transmitter [*Automotive engineering*] ... CART
Custom Chip [*Personal computers*] ... CC
Custom Chrome [*NASDAQ symbol*] (TTSB) ... CSTM
Custom Chrome, Inc. [*NASDAQ symbol*] (SPSG) ... CSTM
Custom Chrome, Inc. [*Associated Press*] (SAG) ... CustCh
Custom Clothing Guild of America [*Defunct*] (EA) ... CCGA
Custom Computer System (IEEE) ... CCS
Custom Contract Service [*IBM Corp.*] ... CCS
Custom Control Factory [*Desaware Co.*] ... CCF
Custom Defined Function [*Computer science*] (PCM) ... CDF
Custom Electronic Design Installation Association (EA) ... CEDIA
Custom House [*Business term*] ... CH
Custom Input/Output Unit [*Computer science*] (IEEE) ... CIOU
Custom Integrated Circuit (PDAA) ... CIC
Custom Integrated System [*Computer science*] (PDAA) ... CIS
Custom Interest Profile ... CIP
Custom Local Area Signaling Services [*Telecommunications*] (ACRL) ... CLASS
Custom Local Area Signaling Services ... Class
Custom Logic and Array Simulation Systems for Integrated Circuits (PDAA) ... CLASSIC

Custom Logic Array [*Electronics*] (IAA) ... CLA
Custom Metallized Multigate Array [*NASA*] ... CMMA
Custom Microfilm Systems, Inc., Riverside, CA [*Library symbol Library of Congress*] (LCLS) ... CusM
Custom Network Broadcasting, Inc. (TSSD) ... CNB-TV
Custom of the Port [*Shipping*] ... COP
Custom Packages for Automation [*3D Digital Design & Development Ltd.*] [*Software package*] (NCC) ... CPFA
Custom Patrol Officer [*British*] ... CPO
Custom Petroleum [*Vancouver Stock Exchange symbol*] ... CUT
Custom Quality Studio [*Photography*] ... CQS
Custom Refresh Controller ... CRC
Custom Roll Forming Institute (EA) ... CRFI
Custom Spherical Resins ... CSR
Custom Tailors and Designers Association of America (EA) ... CTDA
Custom, Tradition, and Usage (MCD) ... CTU
Custom Work Order [*Telecommunications*] (TEL) ... CWO
Custom Xpress Delivery ... CXD
Customary (ROG) ... CUSTMY
Customary Behavior [*Psychology*] ... CUB
Customary, Prevailing, and Reasonable Charges [*Department of Health and Human Services*] (GFGA) ... CPR
Customary Quick Dispatch ... CQD
Custom-Built Installation Process Offering [*Computer science*] (HGAA) ... CBIPO
Customedix Corp. [*AMEX symbol*] (SPSG) ... CUS
Customedix Corp. [*Associated Press*] (SAG) ... Custmd
Customer (MSA) ... CUST
Customer ... CUST
Customer ... CUSTR
Customer Acceptance Readiness Review [*Apollo*] [*NASA*] ... CARR
Customer Acceptance Review Item Disposition (NASA) ... CARID
Customer Access Facilities [*Telecommunications*] ... CAF
Customer Access Line Charge [*Telecommunications*] ... CALC
Customer Access Network ... CAN
Customer Account Representative (AFM) ... CAR
Customer Acquisition Unit (NASA) ... CAU
Customer Activated Terminal ... CAT
Customer Applicability Code (MCD) ... CAC
Customer Application Summary (IAA) ... CAS
Customer Assistance Office ... CAO
Customer Assistance Program (PCM) ... CAP
Customer Authorization for Additional Work ... CAAW
Customer Code [*Telecommunications*] (TEL) ... CUS
Customer Communications Exchange [*Bell System*] ... CCX
Customer Controlled Reconfiguration [*Telecommunications*] (TSSD) ... CCR
Customer Coordination Center (SSD) ... CCC
Customer Cost Analysis [*Business term*] (MHDW) ... CCA
Customer Data and Operations Language (SSD) ... CDOL
Customer Data and Operations System (SSD) ... CDOS
Customer Data Requirements List (MCD) ... CDRL
Customer Data Services Facility (SSD) ... CDSF
Customer Depot Complaint System (MCD) ... CDCS
Customer Dial Pulse Receiver [*Telecommunications*] (TEL) ... CDPR
Customer Digital Switching System [*Telecommunications*] (MHDI) ... CDSS
Customer Engineer [*Computer science*] ... CE
Customer Engineering Letter (MCD) ... CEL
Customer Engineering Monitor [*IBM Corp.*] ... CEMON
Customer/Field Support Elements (RDA) ... C/FSE
Customer File (MCD) ... CF
Customer Furnished (MCD) ... CF
Customer Identification Code ... CIC
Customer Information Control System [*Pronounced "kicks"*] [*IBM Corp.*] [*Computer science*] ... CICS
Customer Information Control System Virtual Storage [*IBM Corp.*] [*Computer science*] ... CICS/VS
Customer Information File [*Computer science*] (BUR) ... CIF
Customer Information Squawk Sheet ... CIS
Customer Information System [*IBM Corp.*] ... CIS
Customer Initiated Entry [*Banking*] ... CIE
Customer Inspection Record ... CIR
Customer Integrated And/Or Reference File System (IAA) ... CIRF
Customer Integration (SSD) ... CI
Customer Integration Office (SSD) ... CIO
Customer Integration Panel (SSD) ... CIP
Customer Interface Control System (GFGA) ... CICS
Customer Item ... CI
Customer Item Squawks ... CIS
Customer Local Area Signal Service (HGAA) ... CLASS
Customer Master File ... CMF
Customer Material Return ... CMR
Customer Memory Update [*Telecommunications*] ... CMU
Customer Network Control Center [*Telecommunications*] (TEL) ... CNCC
Customer Network Management [*Telecommunications*] (ACRL) ... CNM
Customer Network Management Agent [*Telecommunications*] (ACRL) ... CNMA
Customer Networks Control Centre [*Telecommunications*] ... CNCC
Customer On-Line Order Processing System ... COOP
Customer Order Control Automated System (IAA) ... COCAS
Customer Order Processing (BUR) ... COP
Customer Order Processing System ... COPS
Customer Order Set (IAA) ... CO
Customer Oriented Manufacturing Management Systems (ACII) ... COMMS
Customer Owned and Maintained (OA) ... COAM
Customer Owned and Telephone Company Maintained [*Telecommunications*] (TEL) ... COTM
Customer Premise (NRCH) ... CU
Customer Premises Equipment [*Telecommunications*] ... CPE
Customer Premises Equipment (ACRL) ... CPE
Customer Premises System [*Bell System*] ... CPS
Customer Proven [*GMC truck marketing*] ... CP
Customer Provided Equipment [*Telecommunications*] ... CPE
Customer Provided Terminal [*Telecommunications*] (IAA) ... CPT
Customer Reaction Survey ... CRS
Customer Records and Billing [*Bell System*] ... CRB
Customer Relations Manager (DCTA) ... CRM
Customer Replaceable Unit (IAA) ... CRU
Customer Requirements Data Set (SSD) ... CRDS
Customer Requirements List (MCD) ... CRL
Customer Reservations System [*Airlines*] ... CRS
Customer Satisfaction ... CUSAT
Customer Satisfaction Index [*Automotive retailing*] ... CSI
Customer Satisfaction Research Institute [*Lenexa, KS*] [*Telecommunications*] (TSSD) ... CSRI
Customer Service (BUR) ... CS
Customer Service Administration Control Center System [*Telecommunications*] (TEL) ... CSACCS
Customer Service Center ... CSC
Customer Service Department Procedure ... CSDP
Customer Service Officer ... CSO
Customer Service Representative ... CSR
Customer Service System [*Computer surveillance*] [*British*] ... CSS
Customer Service Unit (IAA) ... CSU
Customer Set-Up [*Computer science*] ... CSU
Customer Signature Required (MSA) ... CSR
Customer Specific Integrated Circuit [*Electronics*] ... CSIC
Customer Subscriber Identification [*Telecommunications*] (PCM) ... CSID
Customer Supply Assistance [*Military*] ... CSA
Customer Supply Assistance Office [*Military*] ... CSAO
Customer Support (BUR) ... CS
Customer Support Branch (AFIT) ... CSB
Customer Support Operation ... CSO
Customer Support Unit (AFIT) ... CSU
Customer Switching System [*Telecommunications*] (TEL) ... CSS
Customer Technical Assistance ... CTA
Customer Test [*Army*] ... CT
Customer Trouble Report Analysis Plan [*Telecommunications*] (TEL) ... CTRAP
Customer Utilization (SSD) ... CU
Customer within Country (AAGC) ... cc
Customer Work Authorization (AAG) ... CWA
Customer Work Order File (MCD) ... CWORF
Customer-Bank Communication Terminal [*Computerized banking*] ... CBCT
Customer-Furnished Material (NASA) ... CFM
Customer-Initiated Call [*Marketing*] (IAA) ... CIC
Customer-Integrated Automated Procurement System (AFM) ... CIAPS
Customer-Operated Terminal [*Computer science*] ... COT
Customer-Oriented Data System (DIT) ... CODAS
Customer-Oriented Terminal [*Computer science*] ... COT
Customer-Orienting Program [*Computer science*] ... COP
Customer-Originated Change (AAG) ... COC
Customer-Owned Coin-Operated Telephone (WDMC) ... COCOT
Customer-Owned Goods ... COG
Customer-Owned Property ... COP
Customer-Premises Facility Terminal [*Telecommunications*] (TEL) ... CPFT
Customer-Requested Earlier Due Date [*Business term*] (MHDB) ... CREDD
Customers Having Abundant Product Possibilities [*Term coined by William F. Doescher, publisher of "D & B Reports"*] [*Lifestyle classification*] ... Chapp
Customer's Other Service [*Telecommunications*] (TEL) ... COS
Customer's Own Goods (WDMC) ... COG
Customer's Own Material (WGA) ... COM
Customer's Own Merchandise (WDMC) ... COM
Customers Own Transport (DCTA) ... COT
Customer's Report [*Telecommunications*] (TEL) ... CR
Customer's Request (SAA) ... CR
Customer's Terminal Equipment [*Telecommunications British*] ... CTE
Customer-Vended Equipment (AAG) ... CVE
Customhouse ... Cus Ho
Customized ... CUST
Customized Assurance Plans [*Automotive engineering*] ... CAP
Customized Health Information Project [*Computer science*] ... CHIP
Customized Multimedia Connection ... CMC
Customized Networking Platform ... CNP
Customized Processor [*IBM Corp.*] (IEEE) ... CP
Customized-Information-Delivery System [*Bell Communications Research Laboratory*] ... CID
Customs ... CSTMS
Customs ... CUST
Customs Accelerated Passenger Inspection System [*US Customs Service*] ... CAPIS
Customs Act [*Canada*] ... CA
Customs Acts Legislation Service [*Australia A publication*] ... CALS
Customs Additional Code (DS) ... CAC
Customs Agents' Association of Queensland [*Australia*] ... CAAQ
Customs and Economic Union of Central Africa ... CEUCA
Customs and Excise ... CE
Customs and Excise Departmental Reference and Information Computer (PDAA) ... CEDRIC
Customs and Excise Division, Department of National Revenue [*Division des Douanes et de l'Accise, Ministere du Revenu National*] **Ottawa, Ontario** [*Library symbol National Library of Canada*] (NLC) ... OONR
Customs and Excise Institutions List [*Database*] (IID) ... INST
Customs and Excise Laboratory [*Canada*] ... CEL

Customs and Excise Management Act (DS) ... CEMA
Customs and International Trade Bar Association (EA) ... CITBA
Customs and Patent Appeals Reports (Customs) [*A publication*] (DLA) ... Cust & Pat App (Cust) (F)
Customs and Patent Appeals Reports (Patents) [*A publication*] (DLA) ... Cust & Pat App (Pat) (F)
Customs and Usages (DLA) ... CUS & US
Customs Appeals Decisions [*A publication*] (DLA) ... CAD
Customs Assigned Number [*Shipping*] [*British*] ... CAN
Customs Automatic Data Processing Intelligence Network [*US Customs Service*] ... CADPIN
Customs Available [*Aviation*] (DA) ... CUS
Customs Brokers' Council of Australia ... CBCA
Customs Bulletin [*A publication*] (DLA) ... Cust Bull
Customs Bulletin and Decisions [*A publication*] (DLA) ... Cust B & Dec
Customs Bureau ... CB
Customs Clearance (DS) ... CCL
Customs Clearance Status [*British*] (DS) ... CCS
Customs Consolidation Act [*British*] ... CCA
Customs Co-Operation Council [*See also CCD*] [*Brussels, Belgium*] (EAIO) ... CCC
Customs Co-Operation Council Nomenclature [*See also BTN*] ... CCCN
Customs Court ... CUSTCT
Customs Court Decisions [*A publication*] (DLA) ... CD
Customs Court Reports [*A publication*] (DLA) ... Cu Ct
Customs Court Reports [*United States*] [*A publication*] (DLA) ... Cust Ct
Customs Court Rules [*A publication*] (DLA) ... Cust Ct R
Customs Decisions [*Department of the Treasury*] [*A publication*] (DLA) ... CD
Customs Declaration ... C/D
Customs Duties and Import Regulations [*A publication*] (DLA) ... Cust D
Customs Enforcement Officer [*US Customs Service*] ... CEO
Customs Entry Charge (DCTA) ... CEC
Customs Entry Processing and Cargo System (PDAA) ... CEPACS
Customs Form ... CF
Customs Handling of Import and Export Freight [*EC*] (ECED) ... CHIEF
Customs Has Been Notified [*Aviation*] (FAAC) ... CUSNO
Customs, Immigration, and Quarantine ... CIQ
Customs Information Exchange [*An arm of US Customs Service*] ... CIE
Customs Officers' Association of Australia ... COAA
Customs Optical Reader Passport Systems [*A scanning device capable of reading the latest US passports*] ... CORPS
Customs Penalty Decisions [*A publication*] (DLA) ... Cust Pen Dec
Customs Port Investigator [*US Customs Service*] ... CPI
Customs Registered Number [*British*] (DS) ... CRN
Customs Regulations of the United States ... CRUS
Customs Rules Decisions [*A publication*] (DLA) ... CRD
Customs Tariff Act [*Canada*] ... CTA
Customs Transaction Code (DS) ... CTC
Customs Union [*British*] (DAS) ... CU
Customs Value per Gross Kilogram (DS) ... CVGK
Customs Value per Gross Pound (DS) ... CVGP
Custos Privati Sigilli [*Keeper of the Privy Seal*] [*Latin*] ... CPS
Custos Rotulorum [*Keeper of the Rolls*] [*Latin*] ... CR
Custos Sigilli [*Keeper of the Seal*] [*Latin*] ... CS
Cut and Paste ... C & P
Cut Bank [*Montana*] [*ICAO location identifier*] (ICLI) ... KCTB
Cut Bank, MT [*Location identifier FAA*] (FAAL) ... CTB
Cut, Carat, Clarity, Color [*Factors in determining the value of a diamond*] ... 4C's
Cut, Carat, Clarity, Color [*Factors in determining the value of a diamond*] ... CCCC
Cut Down, Annoyed, Guilty, Eye-Opener [*Clinical questions asked to detect alcoholism*] ... CAGE
Cut Film [*Photography*] ... CF
Cut Holes and Sink 'Em [*Navy ammunition disposal project*] ... CHASE
Cut Image [*Computer science*] (PCM) ... CIMG
Cut In ... CI
Cut Length (ADA) ... CL
Cut Length (MSA) ... CLTH
Cut Off [*Military*] (AABC) ... COFF
Cut Out ... CO
Cut Out Background [*Printing*] ... COB
Cut Paraboloidal Reflector ... CPR
Cut Sizes [*Paper*] (DGA) ... CS
Cut Stone ... CUTS
Cut, Tear, and Curl [*Tea*] ... CTC
Cut to Length ... CTL
Cut to Length and Notch ... CTLN
Cutaneous Basophil Hypersensitivity [*Immunology*] ... CBH
Cutaneous Discrimination [*Psychometric test*] ... CD
Cutaneous Genuine Histiocytic Lymphoma ... CGHL
Cutaneous Germinal Center Cell-Derived Lymphomas ... CGCCL
Cutaneous Lymphocyte-Associated Antigen [*Immunology*] ... CLA
Cutaneous Lymphoid Infiltrates ... CLI
Cutaneous Malignant Lymphomas ... CML
Cutaneous Malignant Melanoma [*Medicine*] (MAE) ... CMM
Cutaneous Non-Epidermotropic Lymphoma (PDAA) ... CNEL
Cutaneous Peripheral T-Cell-Derived Lymphomas ... CPTL
Cutaneous Squamous Cell Carcinoma [*Medicine*] (DMAA) ... CSCC
Cutaneous Stimulation [*Psychometric test*] ... CS
Cutaneous T-Cell Lymphoma [*Medicine*] ... CTCL
Cutaneous Trunci Muscle [*Anatomy*] ... CTM
Cutaneous Water Loss ... CWL
CutCo Indus [*NASDAQ symbol*] (TTSB) ... CUTC
Cutco Industries, Inc. [*NASDAQ symbol*] (NQ) ... CUTC
Cutco Industries, Inc. [*Associated Press*] (SAG) ... Cutco
Cutdown [*Cardiovascular and surgery*] (DAVI) ... CD
Cuthbert College (ROG) ... CUTHB
Cuthbert Cudgel [*Pseudonym used by T. Houston*] ... CC
Cuthbert, GA [*AM radio station call letters*] ... WCUG
Cuticle ... C
Cuticular Plate [*Biology*] ... CP
Cutis Marmorata Telangiectatica Congenita [*Medicine*] (DMAA) ... CMTC
Cutlass Bay, Cat Island [*Bahamas*] [*ICAO location identifier*] (ICLI) ... MYCX
Cutlass Industries Corp. [*Vancouver Stock Exchange symbol*] ... CUC
Cutler on Naturalization Laws [*A publication*] (DLA) ... Cut Nat
Cutler's Insolvent Laws of Massachusetts [*A publication*] (DLA) ... Cut Ins L
Cutler's Legal System of the English, the Hindoos, Etc. [*A publication*] (DLA) ... Cut Leg Sys
Cutler's Trademark and Patent Cases [*A publication*] (DLA) ... Cut Pat Cas
Cutlery (MSA) ... CTLRY
Cutlery ... CUTLY
Cutlery and Allied Trades Research Association [*British*] (IRUK) ... CATRA
Cutoff (MSA) ... CO
Cutoff [*Telecommunications*] (TEL) ... CTO
Cutoff Frequency ... COF
Cutoff Frequency (IDOE) ... f_{co}
Cutoff Shear [*Tool*] (AAG) ... COSR
Cutoff Signal (KSC) ... COS
Cutoff Valve ... COV
Cutoff Velocity and Range ... COVER
Cutoff Voltage ... COV
Cut-Out Halftone [*Graphic arts*] (DGA) ... COHT
Cutout Valve ... COV
Cutral-Co [*Argentina*] [*Airport symbol*] (OAG) ... CUT
Cutral-Co [*Argentina ICAO location identifier*] (ICLI) ... SAZW
Cuttack Law Times [*India*] [*A publication*] (ILCA) ... CLT
Cuttack Law Times [*India*] [*A publication*] (DLA) ... Cut LT
Cuttack Law Times [*India*] [*A publication*] (DLA) ... Cutt LT
Cutter [*Ship*] (ROG) ... CR
Cutter (MSA) ... CTR
Cutter [*Ship*] ... CUT
Cutter & Buck [*NASDAQ symbol*] (TTSB) ... CBUK
Cutter & Buck, Inc. [*NASDAQ symbol*] (SAG) ... CBUK
Cutter & Buck, Inc. [*Associated Press*] (SAG) ... CutterB
Cutter Laboratories [*Research code symbol*] ... CL
Cutter Laboratories, Berkeley, CA [*Library symbol Library of Congress*] (LCLS) ... CBCL
Cutter Location File ... CL
Cutter Protein Hydrolysate Five Percent in Water [*Pharmacology*] (DAVI) ... CPH 5
Cut-Through Operate (IAA) ... CTO
Cutting (MSA) ... CTG
Cutting ... CUT
Cutting ... CUTG
Cutting and Welding Permit ... CWP
Cutting Die Institute (EA) ... CDI
Cutting Disposal System [*Oil well drilling*] ... CDS
Cutting Fluid [*Metallurgy*] ... CF
Cutting Fluid Manufacturers Association [*Defunct*] (EA) ... CFMA
Cutting Needle Biopsy [*Medicine*] ... CNB
Cutting or Molding Machine ... CMM
Cutting Specification (AAG) ... CS
Cutting Tool Manufacturers Association [*Later, Cutting Tool Manufacturers of America*] (EA) ... CTMA
Cutting Tool Manufacturers of America (EA) ... CTMA
Cutting with Intent to Kill ... CWIK
Cutty Resources, Inc. [*Vancouver Stock Exchange symbol*] ... CUY
Cuvee Extra ... CE
Cuvier Mines, Inc. [*Toronto Stock Exchange symbol*] ... CUV
Cuyahoga Community College, Cleveland, OH [*Library symbol Library of Congress*] (LCLS) ... OCICC
Cuyahoga Community College, Learning Resource Center, Cleveland, OH [*OCLC symbol*] (OCLC) ... CUL
Cuyahoga County Public Library (IID) ... CCPL
Cuyahoga County Public Library, Cleveland, OH [*OCLC symbol*] (OCLC) ... CXP
Cuyahoga County Public Library, Cleveland, OH [*Library symbol Library of Congress*] (LCLS) ... OCICo
Cuyahoga Falls, OH [*AM radio station call letters*] ... WCUE
[*The*] **Cuyahoga Valley Railway Co.** [*AAR code*] ... CUVA
Cuyos Pies Beso [*Very Respectfully*] [*Formal correspondence*] [*Spanish*] ... CPB
Cuzco [*Peru*] [*Airport symbol*] (OAG) ... CUZ
Cuzco/Velazco Astete [*Peru*] [*ICAO location identifier*] (ICLI) ... SPZO
CV REIT [*Real Estate Investment Trust*], Inc. [*Associated Press*] (SAG) ... CV REI
CV REIT, Inc. [*NYSE symbol*] (SPSG) ... CVI
CV Sportsmark International, Inc. [*Vancouver Stock Exchange symbol*] ... SML
CV Therapeutics, Inc. [*Associated Press*] (SAG) ... CV Ther
CV Therapeutics, Inc. [*NASDAQ symbol*] (SAG) ... CVTX
CVB Financial [*AMEX symbol*] (TTSB) ... CVB
CVB Financial Corp. [*AMEX symbol*] (SPSG) ... CVB
CVB Financial Corp. [*Associated Press*] (SAG) ... CVB Fn
CVS Corp. [*NYSE symbol*] (SAG) ... CVS
CVS Corp. [*Associated Press*] (SAG) ... CVS Corp
CW Communications, Inc. [*Publisher*] ... CWCI
CW Conference Management Group [*Framingham, MA*] [*Telecommunications service*] (TSSD) ... CW/CMG
CWA/UTW Bargaining Council (EA) ... C/UBC
Cwaliton [*Qualiton*], Swansea [*Record label*] [*Wales*] ... Cwal
CWE, Inc. [*Associated Press*] (SAG) ... CWE
CWE, Inc. [*NASDAQ symbol*] (SAG) ... CWEX
CWM Mortgage Hldgs [*NYSE symbol*] (TTSB) ... CWM
CWM Mortgage Holdings, Inc. [*NYSE symbol*] (SAG) ... CWM

CWM Mortgage Holdings, Inc. [*Associated Press*] (SAG) ... CWM Mt
Cwmni Cyfngedig Cyhoeddus [*Public Limited Company*] [*Welsh*] (ODBW) ... ccc
Cyan (WDMC) ... C
Cyan, Magenta, and Yellow [*Color model*] (BYTE) ... CMY
Cyan, Magenta, Yellow, Black [*Color model*] (PCM) ... CMYK
Cyan, Yellow, Magenta, Black [*Color model*] (PCM) ... CYMK
Cyanacetic Acid Hydrazine [*Organic chemistry*] (DAVI) ... CAH
Cyana-Mexique (MSC) ... CYAMEX
Cyanamid, Niagara Falls, ON, Canada [*Library symbol Library of Congress*] (LCLS) ... CaONfCy
Cyanamid, Niagara Falls, Ontario [*Library symbol National Library of Canada*] (NLC) ... ONFCY
Cyanide [*Organic chemistry*] (DAVI) ... Cn
Cyanide (WDAA) ... CY
Cyanide (KSC) ... CYN
Cyanide Amenable to Chlorination (EG) ... CNA
Cyanide Amenable to Chlorination ... CN-ATC
Cyanide Anion [*Organic chemistry*] (DAVI) ... CN
Cyanide Total (EG) ... CNT
Cyanmethemoglobin [*Immunology*] (DAVI) ... HiCN
Cyanoacrylate Adhesive ... CA
Cyanoacrylate Adhesive ... CAA
Cyanoacrylate Tissue Adhesive [*Medicine*] ... CTA
Cyanocethydrazide [*Antihelminthic*] (ADA) ... CAH
Cyanocobalamin [*Pharmacology*] (DAVI) ... B_{12}
Cyanocobalamin [*Biochemistry*] ... CNCbl
Cyano(dihydroxy)pyridine [*Biochemistry*] ... CNDP
Cyanoethyl [*Organic chemistry*] ... CE
Cyanoethyl Ethyl-M-Toluidine [*Organic chemistry*] ... CEEMT
Cyanoethyl Methylaniline [*Organic chemistry*] ... CEMA
Cyanoethylethylamine [*Organic chemistry*] ... CEEA
Cyanoethylsucrose ... CES
Cyanoethylurea [*Immunochemistry*] ... CEU
Cyanogen [*Toxic compound*] (AAMN) ... CN
Cyanogen [*Toxic compound*] ... CY
Cyanogen Bromide (PDAA) ... CNbr
Cyanogen Chloride [*Poison gas*] [*Army symbol*] ... CK
Cyanogen Radical [*Organic chemistry*] (DAVI) ... CN
Cyanohydroxybutene [*Organic chemistry*] ... CHB
Cyanonaphthalene [*Organic chemistry*] ... CN
Cyano(nitro)quinoxalinedione [*Organic chemistry*] ... CNQX
Cyanopindolol [*Organic chemistry*] ... CYP
Cyanosis [*Medicine*] (DAVI) ... C
Cyanosis [*Medicine*] ... CYAN
Cyanosis, Clubbing, or Edema [*Medicine*] (MAE) ... CCE
Cyanotech Corp. [*NASDAQ symbol*] (NQ) ... CYAN
Cyanotech Corp. [*Associated Press*] (SAG) ... Cyanotc
Cyanotic Congenital Heart Disease (DAVI) ... CCHD
Cyanotoluene [*Organic chemistry*] ... CNT
Cyanotrimethyl-Androsterone [*Endocrinology*] (DAVI) ... CTA
Cyanotype (VRA) ... CTYP
Cyatho Theae [*In a Cup of Tea*] [*Pharmacy*] (ROG) ... CYATH THEAE
Cyathus [*Glassful*] [*Pharmacy*] ... CYATH
Cyathus Amplus [*Tumblerful*] [*Pharmacy*] ... CYATH AMP
Cyathus Vinarius [*Wineglassful*] [*Pharmacy*] (ROG) ... C VINAR
Cyathus Vinosus [*Wineglassful*] [*Pharmacy*] ... CYATH VIN
Cyathus Vinosus [*Wineglassful*] [*Pharmacy*] (ROG) ... CYATH VINOS
[*The*] **Cybele Society** (EA) ... TCS
Cyber Cash Inc. [*NASDAQ symbol*] (TTSB) ... CYCH
Cyber Optics Corp. [*Associated Press*] (SAG) ... CybrOpt
Cyber Optics Corp. [*Associated Press*] (SAG) ... CybrOpt
Cyber Record Manager [*Computer science*] ... CRM
CYBER Record Manager Basic Access Method [*Computer science*] (NITA) ... CRM/BAM
CyberCash, Inc. [*Associated Press*] (SAG) ... CybrCsh
CyberCash, Inc. [*NASDAQ symbol*] (SAG) ... CYCH
CyberGuard Corp. [*NASDAQ symbol*] (SAG) ... CYBG
CyberGuard Corp. [*Associated Press*] (SAG) ... CybGrd
CyberMedia, Inc. [*Associated Press*] (SAG) ... CyberMd
CyberMedia, Inc. [*NASDAQ symbol*] (SAG) ... CYBR
Cybermedix, Inc. [*Toronto Stock Exchange symbol*] ... CYB
Cybernetic ... CYBRNTC
Cybernetic Anthropomorphous Machine [*Robot*] [*Army*] ... CAM
Cybernetic Anthropomorphous Machine System [*Robot*] [*Army*] ... CAMS
Cybernetic Data Products Corp. [*Telecommunications service*] (TSSD) ... CDP
Cybernetic Logistics Planning, Control, and Management Information System [*Military*] (AABC) ... CYBERLOG
Cybernetic Organism [*Concept of machine to alter man's bodily functions for space environment*] ... CYBORG
Cybernetics (IAA) ... CY
Cybernetics (ADA) ... CYBER
Cybernetics Products, Inc. [*NASDAQ symbol*] (NQ) ... CYBR
Cybernetics Products, Inc. [*Associated Press*] (SAG) ... Cybrnet
Cybernetics Research Consultants [*British*] (NITA) ... CRC
Cybernetics Research Institute ... CRI
Cyberonics, Inc. [*Associated Press*] (SAG) ... Cyberonic
Cyberonics, Inc. [*NASDAQ symbol*] (SAG) ... CYBX
CyberOptics Corp. [*NASDAQ symbol*] (NQ) ... CYBE
Cybex Computer Products [*NASDAQ symbol*] (TTSB) ... CBXC
Cybex Corp. [*NASDAQ symbol*] (SAG) ... CBXC
Cybex Corp. [*Associated Press*] (SAG) ... Cybex
Cybex International [*AMEX symbol*] (SAG) ... CYB
Cybex International [*Associated Press*] (SAG) ... CybexIntl
Cycad Society (EA) ... CS
CyCare Systems [*NYSE symbol*] (TTSB) ... CYS
CyCare Systems, Inc. [*Associated Press*] (SAG) ... Cycare
CyCare Systems, Inc. [*NYSE symbol*] (SPSG) ... CYS
Cyclazocine [*Morphine antagonist*] ... Cyc
Cyclc3PSS Corp. [*Associated Press*] (SAG) ... Cyclc3pss
Cyclc3PSS Corp. [*NASDAQ symbol*] (SAG) ... OZON
Cycle [*Electricity*] ... C
Cycle (AAG) ... CY
Cycle ... CYC
Cycle ... CYCL
Cycle ... CYCL
Cycle ... CYL
Cycle Control Unit [*IRS*] ... CCU
Cycle Count (MCD) ... CC
Cycle Engineers' Institute ... CEI
Cycle Log Reduction [*Time required for a given amount of bacteriological kill*] ... CLR
Cycle Parts and Accessories Association (EA) ... CPA
Cycle Parts and Accessories Association (EA) ... CPAA
Cycle Pressure Ratio (MCD) ... CPR
Cycle Program Control (MCD) ... CPC
Cycle Program Counter (IEEE) ... CPC
Cycle Proof Listing [*IRS*] ... CPL
Cycle Sequence ... CS
Cycle Shift ... CS
Cycle Stealing [*Computer science*] (IAA) ... CS
Cycle Stealing Unit [*Computer science*] (IAA) ... CSU
Cycle Test Hours ... CTH
Cycle Time (NVT) ... CT
Cycle Time and Inventory Reduction (MCD) ... CIR
Cycles between Overhaul (MCD) ... CBO
Cycles between Scheduled Visits (MCD) ... CBSV
Cycles per Day ... CPD
Cycles per Hour ... C/H
Cycles per Minute (ADA) ... C/M
Cycles per Minute ... C/MIN
Cycles per Minute ... CPM
Cycles Per Minute (WDMC) ... cpm
Cycles per Second [*See also HZ*] (IAA) ... C
Cycles per Second [*See also Hz*] ... C/S
Cycles per Second [*See also Hz*] ... CC/S
Cycles per Second [*See also Hz*] ... CPS
Cycles Per Second [*Telecommunications*] (WDMC) ... cps
Cycles per Second [*See also Hz*] ... CY/SEC
Cycles per Second Alternating Current (AAG) ... CPSAC
Cycle-Significant Items (MCD) ... CSI
Cycle-Speedway Council [*British*] (DBA) ... CSC
Cyclic [*Biochemistry*] ... c
Cyclic Adenosine Diphosphoribose [*Biochemistry*] ... CADPR
Cyclic Adenosine Monophosphate [*Also, cAMP*] [*Biochemistry*] ... CAMP
Cyclic Adenosine Monophosphate Phosphodiesterase (PDAA) ... CAMP-PDE
Cyclic Air Sampling Monitor ... CASM
Cyclic AMP [*Adenosine Monaphorphate*] **-Dependent Protein Kinase** [*Biochemistry*] ... cAPK
Cyclic AMP [*Adenosine Monophosphate*] **Response Element Binding Proteins** [*Genetics*] (DOG) ... CREBs
Cyclic AMP [*Adenosine Monophosphate*] **Responsive Element Modulator** [*Genetics*] ... CREM
Cyclic AMP [*Adenasine Monophosphate*] **Responsive Element-Binding Protein** [*Biochemistry*] ... CREB
Cyclic Catalytic Reforming [*Chemical engineering*] (IAA) ... CCR
Cyclic Check [*Computer science*] (IAA) ... CC
Cyclic Check BIT [*Binary Digit*] [*Computer science*] (IAA) ... CCB
Cyclic Check Character [*Computer science*] ... CCC
Cyclic Code (BUR) ... CC
Cyclic Control Time (MCD) ... CCT
Cyclic Corrosion Test ... CCT
Cyclic Cytidine Monophosphate [*Biochemistry*] ... cCMP
Cyclic Data Management Routine [*Computer science*] ... CDMR
Cyclic Error Detection Code (MCD) ... CEDC
Cyclic Fatty Acid [*Organic chemistry*] ... CFA
Cyclic Guanosine Monophosphate [*Biochemistry*] ... cGMP
Cyclic Instrumental Neutron Activation Analysis ... CINAA
Cyclic Lysine Anhydride [*Medicine*] (DMAA) ... CLA
Cyclic Multilayered Alloy [*Electroplating technology*] ... CMA
Cyclic Nucelotide-Gated [*Neurobiology*] ... CNG
Cyclic Nucleotide Gated Channel (DMAA) ... CNGC
Cyclic Nucleotide-Gated [*Ion channels*] [*Neurobiology*] ... CNG
Cyclic Permutation Code ... CPC
Cyclic Permuted ... CP
Cyclic Pitch Control Stick ... CPCS
Cyclic Redundancy Character (PDAA) ... CRC
Cyclic Redundancy Check [*Computer science*] ... CRC
Cyclic Redundancy Check Character [*Computer science*] (IEEE) ... CRCC
Cyclic Redundancy Check Generator/Checker [*Microprocessing*] (NITA) ... CRCGR
Cyclic Redundancy Code (PDAA) ... CRC
Cyclic Strain Attenuator (NASA) ... CSA
Cyclic Time Processor (MCD) ... CTP
Cyclic Voltametric Stripping [*Electrochemistry*] ... CVS
Cyclic Voltammetry [*Analytical electrochemistry*] ... CV
Cyclic Vomiting Syndrome Association ... CVSA
Cyclic-Adenosine Monophosphate-Responsive Element Modulator [*Genetics*] ... CREM
Cyclical Stress Sensitivity Limit ... CSSL
Cyclically Harvested Earth-Orbit Production System ... CHEOPS

Cyclic-AMP [*Adenosine Monophosphate*] **Receptor Protein** [*Also, CRP*] [*Genetics*] ... CAP
Cyclic-AMP [*Adenosine Monophosphate*] **Receptor Protein** [*Also, CAP*] [*Genetics*] ... CRP
Cyclic-AMP [*Adenosine Monophosphate*] **Response Element** [*Genetics*] ... CRE
Cyclic-AMP [*Adenosine Monophosphate*]-Responsive Transcriptional Enhancer [*Genetics*] ... CRE
Cyclic-Nucleotide-Binding [*Neurobiology*] ... CNB
Cyclin Kinase Inhibitor [*Biochemistry*] ... CKI
Cyclin-Dependent Kinase [*An enzyme*] ... CDK
Cyclin-Dependent Kinases [*Genetics*] (DOG) ... cdks
Cycling [*Chemical engineering*] (IAA) ... CY
Cycling Club ... CC
Cycling Clutch-Orifice Tube [*Automobile air-conditioning system*] ... CCOT
Cycling Fibroblast [*Cytology*] ... CF
Cycling Oiler [*Navy*] (MCD) ... CO
Cycling Strength Test ... CST
Cyclists' Rights Action Group [*Australia*] ... CRAG
Cyclists' Touring Club ... CTC
Cyclobutane Pyrimidine Dimer [*Organic chemistry*] ... CPD
Cyclocytidine Hydrochloric Acid [*Organic chemistry*] (DAVI) ... Cyclo C
Cyclodextrin [*Organic chemistry*] ... CD
Cyclodextrin Glucanotransferase (DMAA) ... CGT
Cyclodextrin Glycosyltransferase [*An enzyme*] ... CGTase
Cyclodextrin Transglycosylase [*An enzyme*] ... CTG
Cyclododecatriene [*Organic chemistry*] ... CDDT
Cyclododecatriene [*Organic chemistry*] ... CDT
Cyclogenesis [*NWS*] (FAAC) ... CYCLGN
Cycloheptatriene [*Organic chemistry*] ... CHT
Cyclohexadiene [*Organic chemistry*] ... CHD
Cyclohexane [*Organic chemistry*] ... C
Cyclohexanedimethanol [*Organic chemistry*] ... CHDM
Cyclohexanone [*Organic chemistry*] ... CH
Cyclohexenedicarboxylic Acid [*Organic chemistry*] ... CA
Cyclohexenedicarboxylic Acid [*Organic chemistry*] ... CHDC
(Cyclohexenyl)cyclohexanone [*Organic chemistry*] ... CHCH
Cycloheximide [*Also, CHX, CXM, Cyh*] [*Fungicide*] ... CH
Cycloheximide [*Also, CH, CXM, Cyh*] [*Fungicide*] ... CHX
Cycloheximide [*Also, CH, CHX, Cyh*] [*Fungicide*] ... CXM
Cycloheximide [*Also, CH, CHX, CXM*] [*Fungicide*] ... Cyh
Cyclohexyl Isocyanate [*Organic chemistry*] ... CHI
Cyclohexyl Methacrylate [*Organic chemistry*] ... CHMA
Cyclohexyladenosine [*Biochemistry*] ... CHA
Cyclohexylamine [*Organic chemistry*] ... CHA
Cyclohexylamine Carbonate [*Corrosion prevention*] ... CHC
Cyclohexylaminoethanesulfonic Acid [*A buffer*] ... CHES
Cyclohexylaminopropanesulfonic Acid [*A buffer*] ... CAPS
Cyclohexylbenzothiazole Sulfenamide [*Organic chemistry*] ... CBS
Cyclohexylbenzothiazyl Sulphenamide (PDAA) ... CBTS
Cyclohexyldithiobenzothiazole [*Organic chemistry*] ... CDB
Cyclohexylene Diisocyanate [*Organic chemistry*] ... CHDI
(Cyclohexylenedinitrilo)tetraacetic Acid [*Organic chemistry*] ... CDTA
Cyclohexylidenecyclohexane [*Organic chemistry*] ... CCH
Cyclohexyllinoleic Acid [*Organic chemistry*] ... CHLA
Cyclohexylphenyl(piperidinylethyl)silanol [*Organic chemistry*] ... CPPS
Cyclohexylpyrrolidone [*Organic chemistry*] ... CHP
Cyclohexylthiophthalimide [*Organic chemistry*] ... CTP
Cycloidal Propeller [*on a ship*] (DS) ... CYCLD
Cyclone ... CYC
Cyclone Melting System [*Coal technology*] ... CMS
Cyclonic Extratropical Storms [*National Oceanic and Atmospheric Administration*] ... CYCLES
Cyclonium (MAE) ... Cy
Cyclooctadiene [*Organic chemistry*] ... COD
Cyclooctatetraene [*or Cyclooctatetraenyl*] [*Organic chemistry*] ... COT
Cyclooctylamino-nitropyridine [*Organic chemistry*] ... COANP
Cycloolefin Copolymer ... COC
Cyclooxygenase [*An enzyme*] ... COX
Cyclopaedia of Freemasonry [*A publication*] (ROG) ... C of F
Cyclopedia ... CYC
Cyclopedia ... CYCL
Cyclopedia ... CYCLO
Cyclopedia Law Dictionary [*A publication*] (DLA) ... Cyc Dict
Cyclopedia of Law and Procedure [*New York*] [*A publication*] (DLA) ... CYC
Cyclopedia of Law and Procedure [*A publication*] (DLA) ... Cyc Law & Proc
Cyclopedia of Law and Procedure Annotations [*A publication*] (DLA) ... Cyc Ann
Cyclopedia of Portraits ... CYP
Cyclopenta(alpha)phenanthrene [*Organic chemistry*] ... CPAP
Cyclopentadiene [*Organic chemistry*] ... CPD
Cyclopentadienyl [*Also, cp*] [*Organic radical*] ... Cp
Cyclopentenophenanthrene [*Organic chemistry*] (AAMN) ... CPP
Cyclopentenylcytosine [*Biochemistry*] ... CPEC
Cyclopentyltheophylline [*Organic chemistry*] ... CPT
Cyclophilin [*Biochemistry*] ... CYP
Cyclophosphamide [*Cytoxan*] [*Antineoplastic drug*] ... C
Cyclophosphamide [*Cytoxan*] [*Antineoplastic drug*] ... CP
Cyclophosphamide [*Cytoxan*] [*Antineoplastic drug*] ... CPA
Cyclophosphamide [*Cytoxan*] [*Antineoplastic drug*] ... CPM
Cyclophosphamide [*or Cytoxan*] [*Antineoplastic drug*] (DAVI) ... CX
Cyclophosphamide [*Cytoxan*] [*Antineoplastic drug*] ... CY
Cyclophosphamide [*Cytoxan*] [*Antineoplastic drug*] ... CYC
Cyclophosphamide [*Cytoxan*] [*Antineoplastic drug*] (MAE) ... Cyclo
Cyclophosphamide [*Cytoxan*] [*Antineoplastic drug*] ... CYP
Cyclophosphamide [*Antineoplastic drug*] (DAVI) ... CYT
Cyclophosphamide, Adriamycin, Bleomycin, Oncovin [*Vincristine*], Prednisone [*Antineoplastic drug regimen*] ... CABOP
Cyclophosphamide, Adriamycin, Cisplatin [*Antineoplastic drug regimen*] (DAVI) ... CAP-I
Cyclophosphamide, Adriamycin, Cisplatin Hexamethylmelamire [*Antineoplastic drug regimen*] (DAVI) ... CHAD
Cyclophosphamide, Adriamycin, Dacarbazine [*Antineoplastic drug regimen*] ... CAD
Cyclophosphamide, Adriamycin, Dacarbazine [*DTIC*] [*Antineoplastic drug regimen*] (DAVI) ... CADIC
Cyclophosphamide, Adriamycin, DIC [*Dacarbazine*] [*Antineoplastic drug regimen*] ... CyADIC
Cyclophosphamide, Adriamycin, Fluorouracil [*Antineoplastic drug regimen*] ... CAF
Cyclophosphamide, Adriamycin [*Doxorubicin*], Fluorouracil by Continuous Infusion [*Antineoplastic drug regimen*] (DAVI) ... CAFFI
Cyclophosphamide, Adriamycin, Fluorouracil, Prednisone [*Antineoplastic drug regimen*] ... CAFP
Cyclophosphamide, Adriamycin, Fluorouracil, Vincristine, Prednisone [*Antineoplastic drug regimen*] ... CAFVP
Cyclophosphamide, Adriamycin, High-dose Cisplatin [*Antineoplastic drug regimen*] (DAVI) ... CAP-II
Cyclophosphamide, Adriamycin, High-Dose Platinol [*Cisplatin*] [*Antineoplastic drug regimen*] ... CAP-II
Cyclophosphamide, Adriamycin, Methotrexate [*Antineoplastic drug regimen*] ... CAM
Cyclophosphamide, Adriamycin, Methotrexate, Bleomycin [*Antineoplastic drug regimen*] ... CAMB
Cyclophosphamide, Adriamycin, Methotrexate, Etoposide, Oncovin [*Vincristine*] [*Antineoplastic drug regimen*] ... CAMEO
Cyclophosphamide, Adriamycin, Methotrexate, Fluorouracil [*Antineoplastic drug regimen*] (DAVI) ... CAMF
Cyclophosphamide, Adriamycin, Methotrexate, Folinic acid-SF [*Antineoplastic drug regimen*] ... CAMF
Cyclophosphamide, Adriamycin, Methotrexate, Procarbazine [*Antineoplastic drug regimen*] ... CAMP
Cyclophosphamide, Adriamycin, Oncovin [*Vincristine*] [*Antineoplastic drug regimen*] ... CAO
Cyclophosphamide, Adriamycin, Platinol [*Cisplatin*] [*Antineoplastic drug regimen*] ... CAP
, Cyclophosphamide, Adriamycin, Platinol [*Vincristine*] [*Cisplatin*] [*Antineoplastic drug regimen*] ... VOCAP
Cyclophosphamide, Adriamycin, Prednisone [*Antineoplastic drug regimen*] ... CAP
Cyclophosphamide, Adriamycin, Procarbazine, Bleomycin, Oncovin [*Vincristine*], Prednisone [*Antineoplastic drug regimen*] ... CAP-BOP
Cyclophosphamide, Adriamycin [*Doxorubicin*], Vincristine [*Antineoplastic drug regimen*] ... CAV
Cyclophosphamide, Adriamycin, Vincristine, Prednisone [*Antineoplastic drug regimen*] (DAVI) ... CAVP-I
Cyclophosphamide, Adriamycin, VM-26, Prednisone [*Antineoplastic drug regimen*] (DAVI) ... CAVP
Cyclophosphamide, Adriamycin, VP-16, Prednisone, Methotrexate [*Antineoplastic drug regimen*] (DAVI) ... CAVPM
, Cyclophosphamide, Alkeran [*Lomustine*] [*Melphalan*] [*Antineoplastic drug regimen*] ... MOCCA
Cyclophosphamide and VP-16 [*Antineoplastic drug*] (DAVI) ... CV
Cyclophosphamide, CCNU [*Lomustine*], Methotrexate [*Antineoplastic drug regimen*] ... CCM
Cyclophosphamide, CCNU [*Lomustine*] **VP-16, Vincristine** [*Antineoplastic drug regimen*] (DAVI) ... CCVV
Cyclophosphamide, CCNU [*Lomustine*], VP-16, Vincristine, Cisplatin [*Antineoplastic drug regimen*] (DAVI) ... CCVVP
Cyclophosphamide, Cisplatin, Fluorouracil, and Extramustine [*Medicine*] (DMAA) ... CCFE
Cyclophosphamide, Fluorouracil, Prednisone [*Antineoplastic drug regimen*] ... CFP
Cyclophosphamide, Hexamethylmelamine, Adriamycin, Cisplatin [*Antineoplastic drug regimen*] (DAVI) ... CHAP-S
Cyclophosphamide, Hexamethylmelamine, Adriamycin, Diamminedichloroplatinum [*Cisplatin*] [*Antineoplastic drug regimen*] ... CHAD
Cyclophosphamide, Hexamethylmelamine, Cisplatin [*Antineoplastic drug regimen*] (DAVI) ... CHD
Cyclophosphamide, Hexamethylmelamine, Cisplatin plus Radiotherapy [*Antineoplastic drug regimen*] (DAVI) ... CHD-R
Cyclophosphamide, Hexamethylmelamine, Fluorouracil [*Antineoplastic drug regimen*] ... CHF
Cyclophosphamide, Hexamethylmelamine, Fluorouracil, Platinol [*Cisplatin*] [*Antineoplastic drug regimen*] ... CHEX-UP
Cyclophosphamide, Hydroxydaunomycin [*Adriamycin*], Oncovin [*Vincristine*] [*Antineoplastic drug regimen*] ... CHO
Cyclophosphamide, Hydroxydaunomycin [*Adriamycin*], Oncovin , Bleomycin [*Vincristine*] [*Antineoplastic drug regimen*] ... CHOB
Cyclophosphamide, Hydroxydaunomycin [*Adriamycin*], Oncovin , Prednisone [*Vincristine*] [*Antineoplastic drug regimen*] ... CHOP
Cyclophosphamide, Hydroxydaunomycin [*Adriamycin*], Oncovin , Prednisone, Bleomycin [*Vincristine*] [*Antineoplastic drug regimen*] ... CHOP-Bleo
Cyclophosphamide, Hydroxydaunomycin [*Adriamycin*], Oncovin , Procarbazine, Prednisone [*Vincristine*] [*Antineoplastic drug regimen*] ... CHOPP
Cyclophosphamide, Hydroxydaunomycin [*Adriamycin*], Oncovin , Radiation therapy [*Vincristine*] [*Antineoplastic drug regimen*] ... CHOR
Cyclophosphamide, Hydroxydaunomycin [*Adriamycin*], VM-26 , Prednisone [*Teniposide*] [*Antineoplastic drug regimen*] ... CHVP
Cyclophosphamide, Hydroxyurea, Dactinomycin Oncovin [*Vincristine*], Methotrexate, Adriamycin [*Antineoplastic drug regimen*] ... CHAMOMA

Cyclophosphamide, Mechlorethamine [*Mustargen*], Oncovin , Procarbazine, Prednisone [*Vincristine*] [*Antineoplastic drug regimen*] .... C-MOPP

Cyclophosphamide [*Cytoxan*], Methotrexate, 5-Fluorouracil, Bleomycin [*Antineoplastic drug regimen*]   (DAVI) .... CMF-BLEO

Cyclophosphamide [*Cytoxan*], Methotrexate, 5-Fluorouracil, Fluoxymesterone [*Antineoplastic drug regimen*]   (DAVI) .... CMF-FLU

Cyclophosphamide [*Cytoxan*], Methotrexate, 5-Fluorouracil, Hydroxyurea [*Antineoplastic drug regimen*]   (DAVI) .... CMFH

Cyclophosphamide, Methotrexate, 5-Fluorouracil, Prednisone, Vincristine, Adriamycin [*Antineoplastic drug regimen*]   (DAVI) .... CMFP-VA

Cyclophosphamide [*Cytoxan*], Methotrexate, 5-Fluorouracil, Tamoxifen [*Antineoplastic drug regimen*]   (DAVI) .... CMF-TAM

Cyclophosphamide [*Cytoxan*] Methotrexate, 5-Fluorouracil, Vincristine [*Antineoplastic drug regimen*]   (DAVI) .... CMFV

Cyclophosphamide, Methotrexate, CCNU [*Lomustine*] [*Antineoplastic drug regimen*] .... CMC

Cyclophosphamide, Methotrexate, CCNU [*Lomustine*], Vincristine, Adriamycin,Procarbazine [*Antineoplastic drug regimen*] .... CMC-VAP

Cyclophosphamide, Methotrexate, Fluorouracil [*Antineoplastic drug regimen*] .... CMF

Cyclophosphamide, Methotrexate, Fluorouracil, Adriamycin, Oncovin (Vincristine) [*Antineoplastic drug regimen*] .... CMF/AV

Cyclophosphamide, Methotrexate, Fluorouracil, Adriamycin, Vincristine, Prednisone [*Antineoplastic drug regimen*] .... CMFAVP

Cyclophosphamide, Methotrexate, Fluorouracil, Prednisone [*Antineoplastic drug regimen*] .... CMFP

Cyclophosphamide, Methotrexate, Fluorouracil, Tamoxifen [*Antineoplastic drug regimen*] .... CMFT

Cyclophosphamide, Methotrexate, Fluorouracil, Vincristine, Adriamycin, Testosterone [*Antineoplastic drug regimen*] .... CMFVAT

Cyclophosphamide, Methotrexate, Fluorouracil, Vincristine, Prednisone [*Antineoplastic drug regimen*] .... CMFVP

Cyclophosphamide, Methotrexate, Prednisone, 5-Fluorouracil [*Antineoplastic drug regimen*]   (DAVI) .... CMPF

Cyclophosphamide, Mitoxantrone, Fluorouracil [*Antineoplastic drug regimen*]   (DAVI) .... CNF

Cyclophosphamide, Oncovin [*Vincristine*] [*Antineoplastic drug regimen*] .... CO

Cyclophosphamide, Oncovin [*Vincristine*], ara-C, Prednisone [*Antineoplastic drug regimen*] .... COAP

Cyclophosphamide, Oncovin [*Vincristine*], ara-C , Prednisone, Bleomycin [*Cytarabine*] [*Antineoplastic drug regimen*] .... COAP-BLEO

Cyclophosphamide, Oncovin [*Vincristine*], L-PAM , Adriamycin [*Melphalan*] [*Antineoplastic drug regimen*] .... CONPADRI

Cyclophosphamide, Oncovin [*Vincristine*], MeCCNU [*Semustine*] [*Antineoplastic drug regimen*] .... COM

Cyclophosphamide, Oncovin [*Vincristine*], MeCCNU , Bleomycin [*Semustine*] [*Antineoplastic drug regimen*] .... COMB

Cyclophosphamide, Oncovin [*Vincristine*], Methotrexate [*Antineoplastic drug regimen*] .... COM

Cyclophosphamide, Oncovin [*Vincristine*], Methotrexate [*Antineoplastic drug regimen*] .... COMe

Cyclophosphamide, Oncovin [*Vincristine*], Methotrexate, ara-C [*Antineoplastic drug regimen*] .... COMA

Cyclophosphamide, Oncovin [*Vincristine*], Methotrexate, Bleomycin [*Antineoplastic drug regimen*] .... COMB

Cyclophosphamide, Oncovin [*Vincristine*], Methotrexate/citrovorum factor, Adriamycin, ara-C [*Cytarabine*] [*Antineoplastic drug regimen*] .... COMA-A

Cyclophosphamide, Oncovin [*Vincristine*], Methotrexate, Fluorouracil [*Antineoplastic drug regimen*] .... COMF

Cyclophosphamide, Oncovin [*Vincristine*], Methotrexate, Prednisone [*Antineoplastic drug regimen*] .... COMP

Cyclophosphamide, Oncovin [*Vincristine*], Methotrexate with Leucovorin, araC [*Antineoplastic drug regimen*] .... COMLA

Cyclophosphamide, Oncovin [*Vincristine*], Prednisone [*Also, CVP*] [*Antineoplastic drug regimen*] .... COP

Cyclophosphamide, Oncovin [*Vincristine*], Prednisone, Adriamycin [*Antineoplastic drug regimen*] .... COPA

Cyclophosphamide, Oncovin [*Vincristine*], Prednisone, Adriamycin, Bleomycin [*Antineoplastic drug regimen*] .... COPA-BLEO

Cyclophosphamide, Oncovin [*Vincristine*], Prednisone, Bleomycin [*Antineoplastic drug regimen*] .... COPB

Cyclophosphamide [*or Chlorambucil*], Oncovin , Prednisone, Bleomycin [*Vincristine*] [*Antineoplastic drug regimen*] .... COP-BLEO

Cyclophosphamide, Oncovin [*Vincristine*], Prednisone, Bleomycin, Adriamycin, Matulane [*Procarbazine*] [*Antineoplastic drug regimen*] .... COP-BLAM

Cyclophosphamide, Oncovin [*Vincristine*], Prednisone, Doxorubicin [*Adriamycin*] [*Antineoplastic drug regimen*] .... COPAD

Cyclophosphamide, Oncovin [*Vincristine*], Procarbazine, Prednisone [*Antineoplastic drug regimen*] .... COPP

Cyclophosphamide, Platinol [*Cisplatin*] [*Antineoplastic drug regimen*] ..... CTX-PLAT

Cyclophosphamide, Prednisone [*Antineoplastic drug regimen*] .... CP

Cyclophosphamide, Prednisone, Oncovin [*Vincristine*], Bleomycin [*Antineoplastic drug regimen*] .... CPOB

Cyclophosphamide, Rubidazone [*Zorubicin*], Oncovin , Prednisone [*Vincristine*] [*Antineoplastic drug regimen*] .... CROP

Cyclophosphamide, Rubidazone, Oncovin [*Vincristine*], Prednisone, L-Asparaginase, Methotrexate [*Antineoplastic drug regimen*]   (DAVI) .... CROPAM

Cyclophosphamide, Vinblastine, Procarbazine, Prednisone [*Antineoplastic drug regimen*] .... CVPP

Cyclophosphamide, Vinblastine, Procarbazine, Prednisone, CCNU [*Lomustine*] [*Antineoplastic drug regimen*] .... CVPP-CCNU

Cyclophosphamide, Vincristine, Adriamycin [*Antineoplastic drug regimen*] ..... CVA

Cyclophosphamide, Vincristine, Adriamycin, BCNU [*Carmustine*], Methotrexate, Procarbazine [*Antineoplastic drug regimen*] .... CVA-BMP

Cyclophosphamide, Vincristine, Adriamycin, Dacarbazine [*Antineoplastic drug regimen*] .... CYVADIC

Cyclophosphamide, Vincristine, Adriamycin, Dactinomycin [*Actinomycin D*] [*Antineoplastic drug regimen*] .... CYVADACT

Cyclophosphamide, Vincristine, Fluorouracil, Methotrexate [*Antineoplastic drug regimen*] .... CVFM

Cyclophosphamide, Vincristine, Methotrexate [*Antineoplastic drug regimen*] .... CVM

Cyclophosphamide, Vincristine, Methotrexate, Adriamycin, Dacarbazine [*Antineoplastic drug regimen*] .... CYVMAD

Cyclophosphamide, Vincristine, Methotrexate, Daunomycin, and Predinisone Consolidation and Maintenance [*Antineoplastic drug regimen*]   (DAVI) SLA-212

Cyclophosphamide [*Cytoxan*], Vincristine, Prednisone, Bleomycin [*Antineoplastic drug regimen*]   (DAVI) .... CVP + Bleo

Cyclophosphamide, Vincristine, Prednisone [*Also, COP*] [*Antineoplastic drug regimen*] .... CVP

Cyclophosphamide, Vincristine, Triflurothymidine, Papaverine [*Antineoplastic drug regimen*] N3

Cyclophosphamide, VM-26 Prednisolone [*Antineoplastic drug regimen*]   (DAVI) .... PEP

Cyclopropane (Anesthetic) [*Organic chemistry*] .... cyclo

Cyclopropanecarboxylic Acid [*Organic chemistry*] .... CPCA

Cyclopropenoid Fatty Acid [*Biochemistry*] .... CPFA

Cyclops [*of Euripides*] [*Classical studies*]   (OCD) .... Cyc

Cyclopss Corp. [*NASDAQ symbol*]   (TTSB) .... OZON

Cyclopyrophosphoglycerate [*Biochemistry*] .... CPP

Cyclorama [*Staging and scenery*] .... CYC

Cycloserine [*Antibacterial*]   (AAMN) .... CS

Cyclosporin A [*See CYA*] [*An immunosuppressant drug*] .... CSA

Cyclosporin A [*See CSA*] [*An immunosuppressant drug*] .... CYA

Cyclosporin A, Azathioprine, Prednisone [*Antineoplastic drug regimen*] .... CSA-AZA-P

Cyclosporin C [*An immunosuppressant drug*] .... CSC

Cyclosporin D [*An immunosuppressant drug*] .... CSD

Cyclosporine [*An immunosuppressant drug*] .... CY

Cyclotron [*Physics*]   (DAVI) .... cyc

Cyclotron   (IAA) .... CYCLO

Cyclotron Laboratory CL

Cyclotron Wave Device .... CWD

Cycocel   (BARN) CCC

Cycomm International, Inc. [*Associated Press*]   (SAG) .... Cycom

Cycomm International, Inc. [*Associated Press*]   (SAG) .... Cycomm

Cycomm International, Inc. [*AMEX symbol*]   (SPSG) .... CYI

Cycomm Int(New) [*AMEX symbol*]   (TTSB) .... CYI

Cydia Pomenella Granulosis Virus .... CpGV

Cyfeillion Cymru [*Friends of Wales*] [*Australia*] CC

Cygne Designes [*NASDAQ symbol*]   (TTSB) .... CYDS

Cygne Designs, Inc. [*NASDAQ symbol*]   (SAG) .... CYDS

Cygne Designs, Inc. [*Associated Press*]   (SAG) .... CygneD

Cygnus [*Constellation*] .... Cyg

Cygnus [*Constellation*] .... Cygn

Cygnus Therapeutic Systems [*NASDAQ symbol*]   (SPSG) .... CYGN

Cygnus Therapeutic Systems [*Associated Press*]   (SAG) .... Cygnus

Cygrus Inc. [*NASDAQ symbol*]   (TTSB) .... CYGN

Cylinder C

Cylinder   (MCD) CL

Cylinder .... CY

Cylinder   (AAG) .... CYL

Cylinder Axis [*Optometry*] CX

Cylinder Escape Probability   (PDAA) .... CEP

Cylinder Gas Audit .... CGA

Cylinder, Head, and Sector [*Computer science*] .... CHS

Cylinder Identification [*Automotive engineering*] .... CID

Cylinder Lock .... CYLL

Cylinder Manufacturers Association [*Defunct*]   (EA) .... CMA

Cylinder or Drum [*Freight*] .... CYL DRM

Cylinder Rate   (NVT) .... CR

Cylinder Stroke Control .... CSC

Cylinder-Cylinder-Head-Sector [*Computer science*]   (IBMDP) .... CCHS

Cylinder-Head Temperature .... CHT

Cylinder-Pressure Monitoring and Conditioning Detection System .... CYLDET

Cylindric Lens   (ROG) .... CYLL

Cylindrical [*Leaf characteristic*] [*Botany*] C

Cylindrical   (VRA) .... cyl

Cylindrical   (ROG) .... CYLL

Cylindrical .... CYLNDL

Cylindrical Electrostatic Probe [*NASA*]   (MCD) .... CEP

Cylindrical Electrostatic Probe Experiment [*NASA*] .... CEPE

Cylindrical Fire Tube Boiler [*of a ship*]   (DS) .... CFTB

Cylindrical Fire Tube Boiler Survey [*of a ship*]   (DS) .... CFTBS

Cylindrical Horizontal Tank [*Liquid gas carriers*] .... ch

Cylindrical Internal Reflectance - Infrared Spectroscopy .... CIR-IR

Cylindrical Internal Reflection [*Spectroscopy*] .... CIR

Cylindrical LASER Plasma .... CLASP

Cylindrical Lens [*Ophthalmology*] .... CYL

Cylindrical Magnetic Film .... CMF

Cylindrical Mirror Analyzer [*Analytical instrumentation*] .... CMA

Cylindrical Perforated .... CP

Cylindrical Surface   (MSA) .... CYLS

Cylindrical Vertical Tank [*Liquid gas carriers*] cv

Cylindrical Vibration Mount .... CVM

Cylindrical Water Tube Boiler [*of a ship*]   (DS) .... CWTB

Cylindrical Water Tube Boiler Survey [*of a ship*]   (DS) .... CWTBS

Cylindrical with Adaxial Channel [*Leaf characteristics*] [*Botany*] cc

Cylindrically Guided Wave Technique [*Nuclear energy equipment*] .... CGWT
Cylindrically Symmetrical Field .... CSF
Cylink Corp. [*NASDAQ symbol*] (TTSB) .... CYLK
Cymbeline [*Shakespearean work*] .... Cym
Cymbidium Mosaic Virus [*Plant pathology*] .... CYBMV
Cymbidium Ringspot Virus [*Plant pathology*] .... CYRSV
Cymbidium Society of America (EA) .... CSA
Cymdeithas Diogelu Cymru Wledig [*Council for the Protection of Rural Wales*] (EAIO) .... CDCW
Cymdeithas Swyddogion Addysg Bellach a Gwasanaeth Leuctid Cymru [*Welsh Association of Further Education and Youth Service Offices*] ..... CSABGC
Cymdeithas y Cymmrodorion [*Honorable Society of Cymmrodorion*] [*British*] CC
Cymdeithas yr Laith Gymraeg [*Welsh Language Society*] (EAIO) .... CLG
Cymomotive Force [*Telecommunications*] (TEL) .... CMF
Cymric [*Language, etc.*] (ROG) .... CYM
Cymric Resources Ltd. [*Toronto Stock Exchange symbol*] .... CYI
Cynara Virus [*Plant pathology*] CV
Cynegeticus [*of Xenophon*] [*Classical studies*] (OCD) .... Cyn
Cynipidae [*Entomology*] .... Cyn
Cynomolgus Monkey Kidney [*Medicine*] .... CMK
Cynosurus Mottle Virus [*Plant pathology*] .... CYMOV
Cynthiana Argus, Cynthiana, IN [*Library symbol Library of Congress*] (LCLS) .... InCyA
Cynthiana, KY [*AM radio station call letters*] .... WCYN
Cynthiana, KY [*FM radio station call letters*] .... WCYN-FM
Cypair Tours Ltd. [*Cyprus*] [*ICAO designator*] (FAAC) .... CYC
Cypher Policy Board [*British World War II*] .... CPB
Cypher Security Committee [*British World War II*] .... CSC
Cypher Writing [*Freemasonry*] (ROG) .... CW
Cyphernetics Text Processing Language [*1970*] [*Computer science*] (CSR) .... CYPHERTEXT
Cypress [*Botany*] (ROG) .... CYP
Cypress (VRA) .... cyp
Cypress Bioscience [*NASDAQ symbol*] (TTSB) .... CYPB
Cypress Bioscience, Inc. [*NASDAQ symbol*] (SAG) .... CYPB
Cypress Bioscience, Inc. [*Associated Press*] (SAG) .... CypBio
Cypress Bioscience, Inc. [*Associated Press*] (SAG) .... CyprB
Cypress Bioscience, Inc. [*Associated Press*] (SAG) .... CyprBio
Cypress Bioscience Wrrt [*NASDAQ symbol*] (TTSB) .... CYPBW
Cypress Gardens, FL [*AM radio station call letters*] .... WHNR
Cypress Hills, SK [*Television station call letters*] CBCP-2
Cypress Junior College, Cypress, CA [*Library symbol Library of Congress*] (LCLS) .... CCyC
Cypress Semiconductor [*NYSE symbol*] (TTSB) .... CY
Cypress Semiconductor [*Associated Press*] (SAG) .... CypSem
Cypress Semiconductor Corp. [*NYSE symbol*] (SPSG) .... CY
Cypress Semiconductor Corp. (MHDW) .... CYPR
Cypress, TX [*AM radio station call letters*] .... KYND
Cyprianus Florentinus [*Flourished, 12th century*] [*Authority cited in pre-1607 legal work*] (DSA) .... Cy
Cyprianus Florentinus [*Flourished, 12th century*] [*Authority cited in pre-1607 legal work*] (DSA) .... Cyp
Cypriot Classical (BJA) CC
Cypriot Communist Party [*Political party*] .... KKP
Cypriot Liberation Army .... CLA
Cypriote (BJA) .... Cy
Cypriote Archaic (BJA) .... CA
Cypriote Geometric (BJA) .... CG
Cyproheptadine [*Antihistaminic and antipruritic*] .... CYP
Cypros Pharmaceutical [*NASDAQ symbol*] (TTSB) .... CYPR
Cypros Pharmaceutical Corp. [*NASDAQ symbol*] (SAG) .... CYPR
Cypros Pharmaceutical Corp. [*Associated Press*] (SAG) .... Cypros
Cypros Pharmaceutical Wrrt'B' [*NASDAQ symbol*] (TTSB) .... CYPRZ
Cyproterone Acetate [*Endocrinology*] .... CA
Cyproterone Acetate [*Endocrinology*] .... CPA
Cyproterone Acetate [*Endocrinology*] (MAE) .... CTA
Cyprus [*MARC geographic area code Library of Congress*] (LCCP) .... a-cy--
Cyprus (BARN) C
Cyprus [*IYRU nationality code*] (IYR) .... CP
Cyprus [*ANSI two-letter standard code*] (CNC) .... CY
Cyprus [*MARC country of publication code Library of Congress*] (LCCP) .... cy
Cyprus [*ANSI three-letter standard code*] (CNC) .... CYP
Cyprus (VRA) .... Cyp
Cyprus .... CYPR
Cyprus Airways [*ICAO designator*] (AD) .... CY
Cyprus Airways Ltd. (IMH) .... CA
Cyprus Airways Ltd. [*ICAO designator*] (FAAC) .... CYP
Cyprus Amax Minerals [*NYSE symbol*] (SPSG) .... CYM
Cyprus Amax Minerals Co. [*Associated Press*] (SAG) .... Cyprus
Cyprus American Archaeological Research Institute [*Research center*] (IRC) .... CAARI
Cyprus Broadcasting Corp. (IMH) .... CBC
Cyprus Broadcasting Corp. .... CyBC
Cyprus Federation of America .... CFA
Cyprus International Institute of Management (ECON) .... CIIM
Cyprus Law Reports [*A publication*] (DLA) .... CLR
Cyprus Law Reports [*A publication*] (DLA) .... Cyprus LR
Cyprus Minerals Co. (MHDW) .... CYPM
Cyprus National Committee of the International Association on Water Pollution Research and Control (EAIO) .... CNCIAWPRC
Cyprus News Agency .... CNA
Cyprus Olympic Committee (EAIO) .... COC
Cyprus Tourism Organization (EA) .... CTO
Cyprus Turkish Airways [*ICAO designator*] (AD) .... YK
Cyprus Turkish Tourist Enterprises Ltd. (EY) .... CTTE
Cyrano Resources, Inc. [*Vancouver Stock Exchange symbol*] .... CYO
Cyrenaica Defence Force [*British military*] (DMA) .... CYDEF
Cyril E. King Airport [*FAA*] (TAG) .... STT
Cyril Hayes Press, Inc. [*Publisher*] .... CHP
Cyrillic Union Catalog [*Library of Congress*] .... CUC
Cyrix Corp. [*Associated Press*] (SAG) .... Cyrix Cp
Cyrix Corp. [*NASDAQ symbol*] (SAG) .... CYRX
Cyrk, Inc. [*NASDAQ symbol*] (SAG) .... CYRK
Cyropaedia [*of Xenophon*] [*Classical studies*] (OCD) .... Cyr
Cyrus [*Persian emperor, d. 529BC*] (ROG) .... CYR
Cyrus Public School, Cyrus, MN [*Library symbol*] [*Library of Congress*] (LCLS) .... MnCyS
Cyrus the King [*Freemasonry*] (ROG) .... C the K
Cyst Fluid [*Biochemistry*] (DAVI) .... CYFL
Cysteamine-S-Phosphate [*Biochemical analysis*] .... CASP
Cysteic Acid [*An amino acid*] .... Cya
Cysteine [*One-letter symbol*] [*Also, Cys, CySH*] C
Cysteine [*Also, C, CySH*] [*An amino acid*] .... Cys
Cysteine [*Also, C*] [*An amino acid*] (DOG) .... cys
Cysteine [*Also, C, Cys*] [*An amino acid*] .... CySH
Cysteine Proteinase Inhibitor [*Biochemistry*] .... CPI
Cysteine Rich Neurotrophic Factor [*Neurochemistry*] .... CRNF
Cysteine String Protein [*Biochemistry*] .... CSP
Cysteine Sulphinic Acid (PDAA) .... CSA
Cysteine-Peptone-Liver Infusion Media [*Medicine*] (MAE) .... CPLM
Cysteine-Rich Domain [*Genetics*] .... CRD
Cysteine-Rich Intestinal Protein [*Medicine*] (DMAA) .... CRIP
Cystic Adenomatoid Malformation .... CAM
Cystic Adventitial Degeneration of the Popliteal Artery [*Medicine*] .... CADPA
Cystic Duct [*Medicine*] .... CD
Cystic Fibrosis [*Medicine*] .... CF
Cystic Fibrosis Antigen [*Medicine*] (DMAA) .... CFAG
Cystic Fibrosis Factor Activity [*Medicine*] (AAMN) .... CFFA
Cystic Fibrosis Foundation (EA) .... CFF
Cystic Fibrosis of the Pancreas [*Medicine*] .... CFP
Cystic Fibrosis Pancreatic Insufficiency [*Medicine*] .... CFPI
Cystic Fibrosis Pancreatic Sufficiency [*Medicine*] .... CFPS
Cystic Fibrosis Protein [*Biochemistry*] (DAVI) .... CFP
Cystic Fibrosis Research Trust [*British*] .... CFRT
Cystic Fibrosis Society .... CFS
Cystic Fibrosis Transmembrane-Conductance Regulator [*Genetics*] .... CFTR
Cystic Medial Necrosis [*of aorta*] [*Medicine*] .... CMN
Cystic Medial Necrosis of Ascending Aorta [*Medicine*] (MAE) .... CMN-AA
Cystidine-Uridine-Guanidine [*Organic chemistry*] (DAVI) .... CUG
Cystine [*Also, CyS*] [*An amino acid*] .... Cys
Cystine [*An amino acid*] [*Also, CYS, CYSTIN*] (DAVI) .... Cys-Cys
Cystine Guanine [*Medicine*] (DMAA) .... CG
Cystine Trypticase Agar [*Microbiology*] .... CTA
Cystine-Lactose-Electrolyte Deficient [*Clinical chemistry*] .... CLED
Cystine-Tellurite [*Medium*] [*Microbiology*] .... CT
Cystinosis Foundation (EA) .... CF
Cystogram [*Urology*] (DAVI) .... CYSTO
Cystoid Macular Edema [*Ophthalmology*] .... CME
Cystometrogram [*or Cystometrography*] [*Urology*] .... CMG
Cystoscopic Examination [*Medicine*] (MAE) .... cysto
Cystoscopy [*Medicine*] .... CYS
Cystoscopy [*Medicine*] .... Cysto
Cystoscopy and Dilatation [*Medicine*] .... C & D
Cystoscopy and Panendoscopy [*Medicine*] .... C & P
Cystoscopy and Pyelogram [*Medicine*] .... C & P
Cystoscopy and Voiding Urethrogram [*Radiology and urology*] (DAVI) .... CVUG
Cystourethrogram [*Medicine*] .... CUG
Cystylaminopeptidase [*An enzyme*] .... CAP
Cytarabine [*Cytosine arabinoside*] [*Also, ara-C, CAR*] [*Antineoplastic drug*] .... CA
Cytarabine [*Cytosine arabinoside*] [*Also, ara-C, CA*] [*Antineoplastic drug*] .... CAR
Cytarabine [*ara C*], Bleomycin, Oncovin , Methotrexate with Leucovorin [*Vincristine*] [*Antineoplastic drug regimen*] .... CytaBOM
Cytarabine, Daunorubicin [*Antineoplastic drug regimen*] .... CAD
Cytarabine, Methotrexate, Leucovorin [*Folinic acid-SF*], Oncovin [*Vincristine*] [*Antineoplastic drug regimen*] .... CAMELEON
Cytarabine, Thioguanine [*Antineoplastic drug*] (CDI) .... CT
Cytec Industries [*NYSE symbol*] (TTSB) .... CYT
Cytec Industries, Inc. [*NYSE symbol*] (SPSG) .... CYT
Cytec Industries, Inc. [*Associated Press*] (SAG) .... Cytec
Cytel Corp. [*Associated Press*] (SAG) .... Cytel
Cytel Corp. [*NASDAQ symbol*] (SAG) .... CYTL
Cytidine [*One-letter symbol; see Cyd*] C
Cytidine [*Also, C*] [*A nucleoside*] .... Cyd
Cytidine Cyclic Phosphate [*Medicine*] (DMAA) .... CCP
Cytidine Diphosphate [*Biochemistry*] .... CDP
Cytidine Diphosphate Choline [*Biochemistry*] (MAE) .... CDPC
Cytidine Diphosphoabequose [*Biochemistry*] .... CDPAbe
Cytidine Monophosphate [*Biochemistry*] .... CMP
Cytidine Monophosphate-N-Acetylneuraminic Acid (PDAA) .... CMPNAN
Cytidine Triphosphate [*Biochemistry*] .... CTP
Cytidine Triphosphate Tritium-Labeled [*Chemistry*] (DAVI) .... CTP H
Cytidyl-Cytidyl-Adenyl [*Biochemistry*] (BABM) .... C-C-A
Cytocare, Inc. [*Associated Press*] (SAG) .... Cytocre
Cytochalasin B [*Biochemistry*] .... CB
Cytochalasin D [*Biochemistry*] .... CD
Cytochalasin D [*Biochemistry*] .... CYTD
Cytochemical Bioassay .... CBA
Cytochrome [*Biochemistry*] (MAE) C
Cytochrome [*Biochemistry*] .... Cyt
Cytochrome C Oxidase (DMAA) .... CCO

Cytochrome C Oxidase (DMAA) ... COX
Cytochrome Oxidase [*An enzyme*] ... CO
Cytochrome Oxidase [*An enzyme*] ... COXI
Cytochrome Oxidase I [*An enzyme*] ... COI
Cytochrome System [*Laboratory*] (DAVI) ... Cyt Sys
Cytochrome-c Peroxidase [*An enzyme*] ... CCP
Cytoclonal Pharm Wrrt'C' [*NASDAQ symbol*] (TTSB) ... CYPHW
Cytoclonal Pharm Wrrt'D' [*NASDAQ symbol*] (TTSB) ... CYPHZ
Cytoclonal Pharmaceuticals [*NASDAQ symbol*] (TTSB) ... CYPH
Cytoclonal Pharmaceuticals, Inc. [*NASDAQ symbol*] (SAG) ... CYPH
Cytoclonal Pharmaceuticals, Inc. [*Associated Press*] (SAG) ... CytoPh
Cytogen Corp. [*NASDAQ symbol*] (NQ) ... CYTO
Cytogen Corp. [*Associated Press*] (SAG) ... Cytogn
Cytogen Corp. Wrrt [*NASDAQ symbol*] (TTSB) ... CYTOW
Cytogenetics ... CYTOGENET
Cytokeratin [*Cytology*] ... CK
Cytokine Synthesis Inhibitory Factor [*Immunology*] ... CSIF
Cytokine-Suppressive Antiinflammatory Drug [*Biochemistry*] ... CSAID
Cytokinin [*Biochemistry*] ... CK
Cytologic Thymus-Dependent Lymphocyte [*Endocrinology*] (DAVI) ... CTL
Cytology ... CYT
Cytology ... CYTOL
Cytolytic Thymus-Dependent Lymphocyte [*Cell biology*] ... CTL
Cytolytic T-Lymphocyte Line [*Cell line*] ... CTLL
Cytolytic T-Lymphocyte Precursor [*Immunochemistry*] ... CTLP
Cytomegalic Inclusion Bodies [*Cytology*] (DAVI) ... CIB
Cytomegalic Inclusion Disease [*Ophthalmology*] ... CID
Cytomegalic Inclusion Disease [*Ophthalmology*] ... CMI
Cytomegalic Inclusion Disease [*Ophthalmology*] (MAE) ... CMID
Cytomegalic Inclusion Disease [*Medicine*] (DMAA) ... CMID
Cytomegalovirus [*A virus*] ... CMV
Cytomegalovirus [*Immunology*] (DAVI) ... CYTOMG
Cytomegalovirus Immune Globulin [*Biochemistry*] ... CMVIG
Cytomegalovirus Immune Globulin Intravenous [*Immunology*] ... CMV-IGIV
Cytomegalovirus Infection ... CMV
Cytopathic Effect [*Medicine*] ... CE
Cytopathogenic [*or Cytopathic*] **Effect** [*Microbiology*] ... CPE
Cytophotometric Data Converter [*Instrumentation*] ... CYDAC
Cytoplasm Average Optical Density [*Microscopy*] ... CYAD
Cytoplasm Sum Optical Density [*Microscopy*] ... CYSD
Cytoplasmic Androgen Binder [*Endocrinology*] ... CAB
Cytoplasmic Hypovirulence [*Pathology*] ... CH
Cytoplasmic Immunoglobulin [*Immunology*] ... C-Ig
Cytoplasmic Immunoglobulin M [*Immunology*] (DAVI) ... cIgM
Cytoplasmic Incompatibility [*Entomology*] ... CI
Cytoplasmic Male Sterility [*Botany*] ... CMS
Cytoplasmic Membrane [*Botany*] ... CM
Cytoplasmic Metabolic Factor (PDAA) ... CMF
Cytoplasmic Microtubule Network [*Cytology*] ... CMTN
Cytoplasmic Polyhedrosis Virus [*Medicine*] (PDAA) ... CPV
Cytoplasmic Retinoic Acid-Binding Protein [*Biochemistry*] ... CRABP
Cytoplasmic Shape [*Microscopy*] ... CYSH
Cytoplasmic Size [*Microscopy*] ... CYSZ
Cytoproct [*Protozoology*] ... CYP
Cytosine [*Also, Cyt*] [*Biochemistry*] ... C
Cytosine [*Also, C*] [*Biochemistry*] ... Cyt
Cytosine Arabinoside [*Antineoplastic drug*] (MAE) ... ara-C
Cytosine Arabinoside [*Medicine*] (DMAA) ... CA
Cytosine Arabinoside [*ara-C*], Adriamycin, Thioguanine [*Antineoplastic drug regimen*] ... CAT
Cytosine Arabinoside and Thioguanine [*Antineoplastic drug regimen*] (DAVI) ... AT
Cytosine Arabinoside and Thioguanine [*Antineoplastic drug regimen*] (DAVI) ... CAT
Cytosine Arabinoside, Azacytidine, Prednisone, Vincristine, Daunomycin [*Antineoplastic drug regimen*] (DAVI) ... DZAPO
Cytosine Arabinoside Daunomycin [*Also, DA*] [*Antineoplastic drug regimen*] (DAVI) ... AD
Cytosine Arabinoside [*ara-C*], L-Asparaginase, Rubidomycin , Thioguanine [*Daunorubicin*] [*Antineoplastic drug regimen*] ... CART
Cytosine Arabinoside Monophosphate [*Biochemistry*] ... ara-CMP
Cytosine Arabinoside Triphosphate [*Biochemistry*] ... ara-CTP
Cytosine Arabinoside, Vincristine, L-Asparaginase, Prednisone [*Antineoplastic drug regimen*] (DAVI) ... calasp
Cytosine Diphosphate [*Biochemistry*] ... CDP
Cytosine Monophosphate [*Biochemistry*] ... CMP
Cytosine Triphosphate [*Biochemistry*] ... CTP
Cytoskeleton [*Cytology*] ... CSK
Cytosolic Androgen Receptor [*Endocrinology*] ... CAR
Cytostatic Factor [*Cytology*] ... CSF
Cytotactin-Binding Proteoglycan ... CTBP
Cytotechnologist ... CT
Cytotechnologist (HCT) ... CYTO
Cytotechnologist (American Society of Clinical Pathologists) (DAVI) ... CT(ASCP)
Cytotechnology ... CYTECH
Cytotechnology Programs Review Committee of the American Society of Cytology (DAVI) ... CPRCASC
Cytotherapeutics, Inc. [*NASDAQ symbol*] (SAG) ... CTII
Cytotherapeutics, Inc. [*Associated Press*] (SAG) ... Cytothr
Cytotoxic Activated Macrophage [*Biochemistry*] ... CAM
Cytotoxic Assay (MAE) ... CTA
Cytotoxic Dose [*Toxicology*] ... CD
Cytotoxic Factor ... CTF
Cytotoxic Index [*Cytochemistry*] ... CI
Cytotoxic Necrotizing Factor [*Immunology*] ... CNF
Cytotoxic T Lymphocyte [*Hematology*] ... CTL
Cytotoxic T Lymphocyte Antigen [*Immuno chemistry*] ... CTLA
Cytotoxicity Negative - Absorption Positive [*Immunology*] ... CYNAP
Cytoxan [*Cyclophosphamide*] [*Also, C, CP, CPA, CPM, CY, CYC, CYP, CYT*] [*Antineoplastic drug*] ... CTX
Cytoxan [*Cyclophosphamide*] [*Antineoplastic drug*] ... CYT
Cytoxan, Bleomycin, Procarbazine Prednisone, Adriamycin [*Antineoplastic drug regimen*] (DAVI) ... CBPPA
Cytoxan, Fluorouracil, Methotrexate [*Antineoplastic drug*] (CDI) ... CFM
Cytoxan, Flurouracil, Predinose, Methotrexate [*Antineoplastic drug*] (CDI) ... CFPT
Cytoxan [*Cyclophosphamide*], Oncovin , Methotrexate, Bleomycin, Adriamycin,Prednisone [*Vincristine*] [*Antineoplastic drug regimen*] (DAVI) ... COMBAP
Cytoxan, Oncovin, Platinol, Etoposide [*Antineoplastic drug*] (CDI) ... COPE
Cytrax Corp. [*NASDAQ symbol*] (SAG) ... CYTR
Cytrax Corp. [*Associated Press*] (SAG) ... CytRx
CytRx Corp. [*NASDAQ symbol*] (TTSB) ... CYTR
Cytyc Corp. [*NASDAQ symbol*] (TTSB) ... CYTC
CZ [*Convergence Zone*] **Area Reduction Tactic** [*Military*] (CAAL) ... CZARTAC
CZ [*Convergence Zone*] **Confirmation Pattern** [*Military*] (CAAL) ... CZCP
CZ [*Convergence Zone*] **Investigation** [*Military*] (CAAL) ... CZINVEST
CZ [*Convergence Zone*] **Investigation Pattern** [*Military*] (CAAL) ... CZIP
Czar Public Library, Alberta [*Library symbol National Library of Canada*] (NLC) ... ACZ
Czar Resources Ltd. [*Toronto Stock Exchange symbol*] ... CZR
Czech [*Language, etc.*] ... CZE
Czech [*MARC language code Library of Congress*] (LCCP) ... cze
Czech Air Force [*ICAO designator*] (FAAC) ... CEF
Czech Air Handling [*Czechoslovakia*] [*ICAO designator*] (FAAC) ... AHD
Czech Airlines JSC [*FAA designator*] (FAAC) ... CSA
Czech American National Alliance (EA) ... CANA
Czech and Slovak Federal Republic (RDA) ... CSFR
Czech Catholic Union (EA) ... CCU
Czech Government Flying Service [*ICAO designator*] (FAAC) ... CGF
Czech Government Flying Service [*FAA designator*] (FAAC) ... CIE
Czech Heritage Foundation (EA) ... CHF
Czech Inds Wrrt'A' [*NASDAQ symbol*] (TTSB) ... CZCHW
Czech Industries [*NASDAQ symbol*] (TTSB) ... CZCH
Czech Industries, Inc. [*NASDAQ symbol*] (SAG) ... CZCH
Czech Industries, Inc. [*Associated Press*] (SAG) ... Czech
Czech Republic Fund [*NYSE symbol*] (TTSB) ... CRF
[*The*] **Czech Republic Fund, Inc.** [*NYSE symbol*] (SAG) ... CRF
[*The*] **Czech Republic Fund, Inc.** [*Associated Press*] (SAG) ... CzechFd
Czech World Union (EA) ... CWU
Czechoslovak Airlines [*ICAO designator*] (AD) ... OK
Czechoslovak Association of Canada (EAIO) ... CAC
Czechoslovak Association of Victoria [*Australia*] ... CAV
Czechoslovak Christian Democracy (EA) ... CCD
Czechoslovak Ex-servicemen's Association [*Australia*] ... CESA
Czechoslovak Genealogical Society (EA) ... CGS
Czechoslovak Journal of International Law [*A publication*] (DLA) ... Czech J Int'l L
Czechoslovak National Committee of the International Association on Water Pollution Research and Control (EAIO) ... CNCIAWPRC
Czechoslovak National Council of America (EA) ... CNCA
Czechoslovak National Group of International Association of Penal Law (EAIO) ... CNGIAPL
Czechoslovak Neurological Society (EAIO) ... CNS
Czechoslovak Philatelic Society [*Later, SCP*] ... CZPS
Czechoslovak Rationalist Federation of America (EA) ... CRFA
Czechoslovak Red Cross ... CRC
Czechoslovak Socialist Republic ... CSSR
Czechoslovak Society of America [*Later, CSA Fraternal Life*] ... CSA
Czechoslovak Society of Arts and Sciences (EA) ... CSAS
Czechoslovak Society of Arts and Sciences in America [*Later, CSAS*] (EA) ... CSASA
Czechoslovak Yearbook of International Law [*A publication*] (DLA) ... Czech YB Int'l L
Czechoslovakia [*MARC country of publication code Library of Congress*] (LCCP) ... cs
Czechoslovakia [*ANSI two-letter standard code*] (CNC) ... CS
Czechoslovakia [*ANSI three-letter standard code*] (CNC) ... CSK
Czechoslovakia [*IYRU nationality code*] ... CZ
Czechoslovakia ... CZECH
Czechoslovakia ... CZS
Czechoslovakia ... CZ-SLOV
Czechoslovakia [*MARC geographic area code Library of Congress*] (LCCP) ... e-cs--
Czechoslovakia [*License plate code assigned to foreign diplomats in the US*] ... PH
Czechoslovakian Kronen [*Monetary unit*] ... CZKR
Czechoslovak-US Economic Council (EA) ... CUSEC
Czochralski Crystal Growth [*Crystallization process*] ... CZ

D
By Meaning

D & B Computing Services [*Information service or system*] (IID) .... D & BCS
D & E Communications [*Associated Press*] (SAG) .... D & E Cm
D & E Communications [*NASDAQ symbol*] (SAG) .... DECC
D & K Wholesale Drug [*NASDAQ symbol*] (SAG) .... DKWD
D & K Wholesale Drug, Inc. [*Associated Press*] (SAG) .... D & K Whl
D & N Financial Corp. [*Associated Press*] (SAG) .... D & N Fn
D & N Financial Corp. [*Associated Press*] (SAG) .... D & NF
D & N Financial Corp. [*NASDAQ symbol*] (SPSG) .... DNFC
D. B. Communications, Inc. [*Bethesda, MD*] [*Telecommunications service*]
(TSSD) .... DBC
D. R. Moon Memorial Library, Stanley, WI [*Library symbol Library of
Congress*] (LCLS) .... WSt
D T Industries [*NASDAQ symbol*] (TTSB) .... DTII
D. T. Watson Home for Crippled Children, Leetsdale, PA [*OCLC symbol*]
(OCLC) .... PID
Da [*Give*] [*Pharmacy*] .... D
Da Capo [*Return to Beginning*] [*Music*] .... DC
Da Capo Senza Replica [*From the Beginning, Playing Only Once the Parts
Marked with Repeats*] [*Music*] .... DCSR
Da Nang [*Vietnam*] (VNW) .... DNG
Da Nang East Yard [*Vietnam*] [*Navy*] .... DNEY
DA System Coordination (MCD) .... DASC
Daallo Airlines [*Djibouti*] [*FAA designator*] (FAAC) .... DAO
Dabajuro [*Venezuela*] [*Airport symbol*] (AD) .... DJV
Dabou [*Ivory Coast*] [*ICAO location identifier*] (ICLI) .... DIDB
Dabrowa Gornicza [*Poland*] [*Seismograph station code, US Geological
Survey*] (SEIS) .... DGP
Dac Cong [*North Vietnamese combat engineers*] (VNW) .... DACON
DAC Maintainability Representative (MCD) .... DMR
Dacarbazine, CCNU [*Lomustine*], Vincristine [*Antineoplastic drug regimen*] ...... DCV
Dacca [*Bangladesh*] [*Airport symbol*] .... DAC
Dacca Reports [*India*] [*A publication*] (DLA) .... DR
Dacca Stock Exchange [*Bangladesh*] .... DSE
Dachiardite [*A zeolite*] .... DAC
Dachshund Club of America (EA) .... DCA
DACOM-Net Service [*A packet-switching public data network*] .... DNS
Dacono-Air [*Former USSR*] [*FAA designator*] (FAAC) .... DCA
Dacro-Cysto-Rhinostomy [*Medicine*] .... DCR
Dacron and Nylon .... DACRYLON
Dacron Braid Lacquered (MDG) .... DL
Dacryocystography [*Ophthalmology*] (CPH) .... DCG
Dactinomycin (Actinomycin-D) [*Also, act-D, AMD*] [*Antineoplastic drug*] ...... DACT
Dactinomycin, Methotrexate, Cytoxan [*Antineoplastic drug*] (CDI) .... DMC
Dada-Surrealism .... D-S
Daddy's Little Girl .... DLG
Dade City, FL [*AM radio station call letters*] .... WDCF
Dade City, FL [*FM radio station call letters*] (RBYB) .... WGUL-FM
Dadeville, AL [*AM radio station call letters*] .... WDLK
Dadeville, AL [*FM radio station call letters*] .... WDVI
Dadeville, AL [*FM radio station call letters*] .... WZLM
Dadri [*India*] [*ICAO location identifier*] (ICLI) .... VIDR
Dads Advising Dads .... DADS
Dads Against Discrimination [*An association*] (EA) .... DAD
Dadu [*Pakistan*] [*Airport symbol*] (AD) .... DDU
Dadu [*Pakistan*] [*ICAO location identifier*] (ICLI) .... OPDD
Dadyburjar. Small Court Appeals [*India*] [*A publication*] (DLA) .... Dady
Daedalian Foundation (EA) .... DF
Daemen College, Buffalo, NY [*Library symbol Library of Congress*]
(LCLS) .... NBuDa
Daemen College, Buffalo, NY [*OCLC symbol*] (OCLC) .... VVH
Daet, Camarines Norte [*Philippines*] [*ICAO location identifier*] (ICLI) .... RPUD
Daf Yomi (BJA) .... DY
Dafare [*Djibouti*] [*Seismograph station code, US Geological Survey*] (SEIS) ...... DAF
Daffodil (DSUE) .... DAFF
Dafrey Resources, Inc. [*Vancouver Stock Exchange symbol*] .... DFY
Dag Hammarskjold Foundation [*Sweden*] (EAIO) .... DHF
Dag Hammarskjold Library [*United Nations*] (DUND) .... DHL
Dagabour [*Ethiopia*] [*ICAO location identifier*] (ICLI) .... HADB
Dagali [*Norway ICAO location identifier*] (ICLI) .... ENDI
Dagge's Criminal Law [*A publication*] (DLA) .... Dag Cr L
Daggett, CA [*Location identifier FAA*] (FAAL) .... DAG
Daguerreotype (VRA) .... DTYP
Daguerrotype [*Photography*] (ROG) .... DAGUERR
D'Aguesseau. Oeuvres [*A publication*] (DLA) .... D'Agu Oeuv
D'Aguilar on Courts-Martial [*A publication*] (DLA) .... Dag Ct M
Daharki [*Pakistan*] [*ICAO location identifier*] (ICLI) .... OPDK

Dahl Creek, AK [*Location identifier FAA*] (FAAL) .... DCK
Dahlemer Binz [*Germany ICAO location identifier*] (ICLI) .... EDKV
Dahlen [*Saxony*] (ROG) .... DAHL
Dahlgren Rifle .... DR
Dahlgren Smoothbore .... DSB
Dahlgren, VA [*Location identifier FAA*] (FAAL) .... NDY
Dahlgren's Maritime International Law [*A publication*] (DLA) .... Dahl Mar Int L
Dahlia Mosaic Virus [*Plant pathology*] .... DMV
Dahl-Kirkam Telescope .... DKT
Dahlonega [*Georgia*] [*Mint mark, when appearing on US coins*] .... D
Dahlonega, GA [*AM radio station call letters*] .... WDGR
Dahlonega, GA [*FM radio station call letters*] (RBYB) .... WKHC-FM
Dahl-Wade-Till Valve [*Medicine*] .... DWT
Dahomey (ROG) .... DAH
Dahomey [*Benin*] [*MARC country of publication code Library of Congress*]
(LCCP) .... dm
Dahomey [*Benin*] [*MARC geographic area code Library of Congress*]
(LCCP) .... f-dm--
Dahomy (VRA) .... Dah
Dahra/Warehouse 32 [*Libya*] [*ICAO location identifier*] (ICLI) .... HLRA
Dai Nippon Printing Co. Ltd. [*Publisher*] [*Japan*] .... DNP
Dai'ei, Inc. [*Associated Press*] (SAG) .... Dai Ei
Dai'ei, Inc. [*NASDAQ symbol*] (NQ) .... DAIE
Daiei Inc.ADS [*NASDAQ symbol*] (TTSB) .... DAIEY
Daig Corp. [*NASDAQ symbol*] (SAG) .... DAIG
Daig Corp. [*Associated Press*] (SAG) .... DaigCp
Daigo Proving Ground and Research Centre [*Japan*] .... D-PARC
Dai-Ichi Kangyo Bank [*Japan*] .... DKB
Daiichi Seiyaku Co. Ltd. [*Japan*] [*Research code symbol*] .... DJ
Dail Eireann [*House of Representatives*] [*Ireland*] (ILCA) .... DE
Daily .... D
Daily (WDMC) .... d
Daily (AFIT) .... DA
Daily .... DLY
Daily .... DLY
Daily (ROG) .... DY
Daily Abstract [*Tea trade*] (ROG) .... DA
Daily Activity Report [*Military*] .... DAR
Daily Adjustable Progressive Resistance Exercise .... DAPRE
Daily Advance, Dover, NJ [*Library symbol Library of Congress*] (LCLS) .... NjDA
Daily Aerial Reconnaissance and Surveillance [*Military*] (DOMA) .... DARS
Daily Air Activity Report (CINC) .... DAAR
Daily Allowance .... DA
Daily Ambient Photophase [*Biochronometry*] .... DAPP
Daily and Weekly till Forbidden [*Advertising*] .... D & WTF
Daily and Weekly till Forbidden [*Advertising*] .... DWTF
Daily Audience Barometer [*British*] (ADA) .... DAB
Daily Automatic Rescheduling Technique [*Computer science*] .... DART
Daily Average Occupied Beds [*Medicine*] .... DAOB
Daily Bulletin [*Military*] (AABC) .... DB
Daily Cadweld Inspection Report [*Nuclear energy*] (NRCH) .... DCIR
Daily Call-In .... DCI
Daily Census [*Medicine*] .... DC
Daily Child Behavior Checklist [*Psychology*] (EDAC) .... DCBC
Daily Clintonian, Clinton, IN [*Library symbol Library of Congress*] (LCLS) .... InCliC
Daily Communication Report .... DCR
Daily Consumer News [*Consumers' Association*] [*Information service or
system*] (IID) .... DCN
Daily Courier, Waterloo, IA [*Library symbol Library of Congress*] (LCLS) .... IaWC
Daily Cumulative Persistence [*Environmental science*] .... DCP
Daily Delinquency Penalty [*IRS*] .... DDP
Daily Demand Rate .... DDR
Daily Docket [*Costing*] (DGA) .... DD
Daily Double [*Horse racing*] .... DD
Daily Effective Circulation [*Advertising*] (WDMC) .... DEC
Daily Effective Circulation [*Advertising*] (WDMC) .... DEC
Daily Effective Repair Rate (MCD) .... DERR
Daily Effective Supply Rate (MCD) .... DESR
Daily Electronic Feed [*ABC news service*] (WDMC) .... DEF
Daily Encephalic Photophase [*Biochronometry*] .... DEPP
Daily Equipment Status Report [*Army*] (AABC) .... DESPORT
Daily Estimated Position Location [*Navy*] (NVT) .... DEPLOC
Daily Estimated Position Summary [*Navy*] .... DEPSUM
Daily European Naval Activity Summary (MCD) .... DENAS
Daily Express Film Award [*British*] .... DEFA
Daily Fetal Movement Count [*Obstetrics*] (DAVI) .... DFMC

Daily Fetal Movements Record .... DFMR
Daily Field Activity Report .... DFAR
Daily Flight Log [*Aviation*] (FAAC) .... DFL
Daily Guardian [*A publication*] .... DG
Daily Indicator Status Report (MCD) .... DISR
Daily Industrial Index Analyzer [*News-a-tron Corp.*] [*Information service or system*] (CRD) .... DIIA
Daily Inspection [*Military*] (MCD) .... DI
Daily Inspection Call Record (MCD) .... DICR
Daily Intelligence Bulletin [*British*] [*A publication*] (NITA) .... DIB
Daily Intelligence Digest .... DID
Daily Intelligence Summary [*Air Force*] .... DISUM
Daily Intelligence Summary Cable (MCD) .... DISC
Daily Iowan, Iowa City, IA [*Library symbol Library of Congress*] (LCLS) .... IaIaI
Daily Issue Store [*British military*] (DMA) .... DIS
Daily Journal [*NASDAQ symbol*] (TTSB) .... DJCO
Daily Journal Corp. [*Associated Press*] (SAG) .... DlyJour
Daily Journal Corp. South Carolina [*NASDAQ symbol*] (NQ) .... DJCO
Daily Journal, Elizabeth, NJ [*Library symbol Library of Congress*] (LCLS) .... NjEliJ
Daily Journal of the Supreme Court .... DJSC
Daily JUMPS [*Joint Uniform Military Pay System*] **Update Output Listing** (AABC) .... DJUOL
Daily Law and Bank Bulletin [*Ohio*] [*A publication*] (DLA) .... L & B Bull
Daily Legal News [*Pennsylvania*] [*A publication*] (DLA) .... Daily L N
Daily Legal News [*Pennsylvania*] [*A publication*] (DLA) .... DLN
Daily Legal News (Pennsylvania) [*A publication*] (DLA) .... Daily Leg News (PA)
Daily Legal Record [*Pennsylvania*] [*A publication*] (DLA) .... Daily L R
Daily Legal Record [*Pennsylvania*] [*A publication*] (DLA) .... Daily Leg (PA)
Daily Letter Telegram (IAA) .... DLT
Daily List of Mail (IAA) .... DLM
Daily Mail National Film Award [*British*] .... DMNFA
Daily Market Report [*Coffee, Sugar, and Cocoa Exchange*] [*A publication*] .... DMR
Daily Maximum Benefit [*Insurance*] .... DMB
Daily Mechanical Report .... DMR
Daily Mercury, Mackay, QLD, Australia [*Library symbol Library of Congress*] (LCLS) .... AuMacD
Daily Metabolic Turnover (SAA) .... DMT
Daily Mirror [*A publication*] .... DM
Daily News, Amherst, Nova Scotia [*Library symbol National Library of Canada*] (NLC) .... NSADN
Daily News, Amherst, NS, Canada [*Library symbol*] [*Library of Congress*] (LCLS) .... CaNSADN
Daily News Record [*A publication*] [*New York, NY*] (WDMC) .... DNR
Daily News, Truro, Nova Scotia [*Library symbol National Library of Canada*] (NLC) .... NSTDN
Daily News, Truro, NS, Canada [*Library symbol*] [*Library of Congress*] (LCLS) .... CaNSTDN
Daily Observer, Beachwood, NJ [*Library symbol Library of Congress*] (LCLS) .... NjBeacO
Daily Official List [*London Stock Exchange prices*] .... DOL
Daily Operability Test [*Military*] (CAAL) .... DOT
Daily Operating Log .... DOL
Daily Operational Report .... DOR
Daily Outage Report (SSD) .... DOR
Daily Penalty (ROG) .... DP
Daily Princetonian, Princeton, NJ [*Library symbol Library of Congress*] (LCLS) .... NjPD
Daily Problem Status Report .... DPSR
Daily Production Report .... DPR
Daily Readiness [*Testing*] (MCD) .... DRED
Daily Receipt of Obligation [*Military*] .... DRO
Daily Record [*Penny newspaper in "He Knew He Was Right" by Anthony Trollope*] .... DR
Daily Record, Des Moines, IA [*Library symbol Library of Congress*] (LCLS) .... IaDmR
Daily Register [*New York City*] [*A publication*] (DLA) .... Reg
Daily Register, Oelwein, IA [*Library symbol Library of Congress*] (LCLS) .... IaOeR
Daily Register, Red Bank, NJ [*Library symbol Library of Congress*] (LCLS) .... NjRbR
Daily Regulatory Reporter .... DRR
Daily Replacement Factor [*Of lymphocytes*] [*Medicine*] .... DRF
Daily Report .... DR
Daily Report of Obligation [*Navy*] (NG) .... DRO
Daily Reports Notice [*Air Force*] (AFM) .... DRN
Daily Review .... DR
Daily River Stages (NOAA) .... DRS
Daily Routine Order .... DRO
Daily Sentinel, Le Mars, IA [*Library symbol Library of Congress*] (LCLS) .... IaLemS
Daily Sentinel, Lellars, IA [*Library symbol*] [*Library of Congress*] (LCLS) .... IaLelS
Daily Service Report .... DSR
Daily Staff Digest (SAA) .... DSD
Daily Status Report (AAG) .... DSR
Daily Subsistance Allowance Rates [*Business travel*] (BARN) .... DSAR
Daily Summary (MCD) .... DAISY
Daily Summary of Enemy Intelligence [*World War II*] .... DSEI
Daily Systems Operability Test [*for surface-to-air missiles*] .... DSOT
[*The*] **Daily Times of Nigeria** [*A publication*] .... DTN
Daily Times-Herald, Carroll, IA [*Library symbol Library of Congress*] (LCLS) .... IaCarTH
Daily Traffic Assignment Model [*Aviation*] .... DTAM
Daily Transaction File .... DTF
Daily Transaction Register File [*Computer science*] .... DTRF
Daily Transaction Registering [*or Reporting*] [*Computer science*] .... DTR
Daily Travel Allowance [*Business term*] (WDAA) .... DTA
Daily Turn On Procedures [*Computer science*] (MCD) .... DTOP
Daily Value [*Nutrition*] .... DV
Daily Vehilce-Miles of Travel [*FHWA*] (TAG) .... DVMT
Daily Water Flow (IAA) .... DWF
Daily Wear Contact Lenses .... DW
Daily Weighted Average [*Data sampling*] .... DWA
Daily Wireless Bulletin (IAA) .... DWB
Daimler and Lanchester Owners' Club (EA) .... DLOC
Daimler and Lanchester Owners Club of North America (EA) .... DLOC of NA
Daimler-Benz [*Name of German engine factory*] [*World War II*] .... DB
Daimler-Benz AG [*NYSE symbol*] (SPSG) .... DAI
Daimler-Benz AG [*Manufacturer of Mercedes-Benz cars and trucks*] [*German*] .... DBAG
Daimler-Benz AG [*Associated Press*] (SAG) .... DBenz
Daimler-Benz Aktieng ADS [*NYSE symbol*] (TTSB) .... DAI
Daingerfield, TX [*AM radio station call letters*] .... KEGG
Daingerfield, TX [*FM radio station call letters*] (RBYB) .... KWSK-FM
Daini Denden Kikaku .... DDK
Dainippon Pharmaceutical Co. [*Japan*] [*Research code symbol*] .... AB
Dainippon Pharmaceutical Co. [*Japan*] [*Research code symbol*] .... P
Dairen [*Republic of China*] [*Seismograph station code, US Geological Survey Closed*] (SEIS) .... DAI
Dairo Air Services Ltd. [*Uganda*] [*ICAO designator*] (FAAC) .... DSR
Dairy .... DRY
Dairy and Food Industries Supply Association (EA) .... DFISA
Dairy Appliance Manufacturers' and Distributors' Association Ltd. (BI) .... DAMDA
Dairy Breeding Research Center [*Pennsylvania State University*] [*Research center*] (RCD) .... DBRC
Dairy Council of California (SRA) .... DCC
Dairy, Cowshed, and Milk Shop Order [*1885-1886*] [*Legal*] [*British*] (ROG) .... DCMO
Dairy Division, Alberta Agriculture, Wetaskiwin, Alberta [*Library symbol National Library of Canada*] (NLC) .... AWAD
Dairy Engineers' Association [*British*] (BI) .... DEA
Dairy Export Enhancement Program [*Department of Agriculture*] .... DEEP
Dairy Export Incentive Program .... DEIP
Dairy Farmers for Responsible Dairy Policy (EA) .... DFRDP
Dairy Forage Research Center [*Department of Agriculture*] [*Madison, WI*] (GRD) .... DFRC
Dairy Goat Society of Australia .... DGSA
Dairy Herd Improvement (OA) .... DHI
Dairy Herd Improvement Association [*Later, AIPL*] (EA) .... DHIA
Dairy Herd Improvement Registry .... DHIR
Dairy Husbandry Adviser [*Ministry of Agriculture, Fisheries, and Food*] [*British*] .... DHA
Dairy Indemnity Payment Program [*Department of Agriculture*] .... DIPP
Dairy Industries Supply Association [*Later, DFISA*] .... DISA
Dairy Industry Advisory Committee [*Australia*] .... DIAC
Dairy Industry Appeals Tribunal [*Queensland*] [*Australia*] .... DIAT
Dairy Industry Association of Australia .... DIAA
Dairy Industry Authority of Western Australia .... DIAWA
Dairy Industry Committee (EA) .... DIC
Dairy Information System [*British*] (NITA) .... DAISY
Dairy Institute of California (SRA) .... DIC
Dairy Mart Conven Str'A' [*NASDAQ symbol*] (TTSB) .... DMCVA
Dairy Mart Conven Str'B' [*NASDAQ symbol*] (TTSB) .... DMCVB
Dairy Mart Convenience Stores [*NASDAQ symbol*] (SAG) .... DMCV
Dairy Mart Convenience Stores, Inc. [*Associated Press*] (SAG) .... Dairy
Dairy Produce Packers Ltd. [*British*] .... DPP
Dairy Products Improvement Institute (EA) .... DPII
Dairy Products Manufacturers' Association of Western Australia .... DPMAWA
Dairy Products Quality Checked Association (EA) .... DPQCA
Dairy Queen [*Commercial firm*] .... DQ
Dairy Remembrance Fund (EA) .... DRF
Dairy Research and Development Corp. [*Australia*] .... DRDC
Dairy Research, Inc. (EA) .... DRINC
Dairy Science Abstracts [*Database*] [*Commonwealth Bureau of Dairy Science and Technology*] [*Information service or system*] (CRD) .... DSA
Dairy Shorthorn Association of Australia .... DSAA
Dairy Shrine (EA) .... DS
Dairy Society International [*Australia*] .... DSI
Dairy Suppliers Foundation [*Defunct*] (EA) .... DSF
Dairy Termination Program [*Department of Agriculture*] .... DTP
Dairy Trade Federation [*British*] (ECON) .... DTF
Dairy Training and Merchandising Institute [*Later, MTI*] (EA) .... DTMI
Dairy Yield (OA) .... DY
Dairylea Cooperative (EA) .... DC
Dairymen's League Cooperative Association [*Later, DC*] (EA) .... DLCA
Daisetta, TX [*Location identifier FAA*] (FAAL) .... DAS
Daisy Behavioural Language [*Computer science*] (NITA) .... DABL
Daisy Chains [*Oil industry term*] .... DC
"Daisy Cutter" [*A type of World War II bomb*] .... DC
Daisy Fault Simulator [*On Daisy CAD work station*] (NITA) .... DFS
Daisy Mentor Valid (NITA) .... DMV
Daisy Testability Analyser (NITA) .... DTA
Daisy Wheel [*Printer*] .... DW
Daisytek International Corp. [*Associated Press*] (SAG) .... Daisytk
Daisytek International Corp. [*NASDAQ symbol*] (SAG) .... DZTK
Daisytek Intl. [*NASDAQ symbol*] (TTSB) .... DZTK
Daiwa Institute of Research Ltd. [*Database producer*] (IID) .... DIR
Dajabon [*Dominican Republic*] [*ICAO location identifier*] (ICLI) .... MDDJ
Dajarra [*Queensland*] [*Airport symbol*] (AD) .... DJR
Dajnavna Sigurnost [*Bulgarian Secret Police affiliated with the KGB*] .... DS
Daka [*Kazakhstan*] [*ICAO designator*] (FAAC) .... DKA
Daka International, Inc. [*Associated Press*] (SAG) .... Daka

Daka International, Inc. [*NASDAQ symbol*] (CTT) .... DKAI
DAKA Intl. [*NASDAQ symbol*] (TTSB) .... DKAI
Dakair [*France ICAO designator*] (FAAC) .... DAK
Dakar [*Senegal*] [*Seismograph station code, US Geological Survey Closed*] (SEIS) .... DAK
Dakar [*Senegal*] [*Airport symbol*] (OAG) .... DKR
Dakar [*Senegal*] [*ICAO location identifier*] (ICLI) .... GOOO
Dakar [*Senegal*] [*ICAO location identifier*] (ICLI) .... GOOV
Dakar/Yoff [*Senegal*] [*ICAO location identifier*] (ICLI) .... GOOY
Dakhla [*Mauritania*] [*Airport symbol*] (OAG) VIL
Dakka Tourist Agency [*Israel*] .... DTA
Dakomat [*Poland ICAO designator*] (FAAC) .... DKM
Dakon Metals, Inc. [*Vancouver Stock Exchange symbol*] .... DKN
Dakota [*MARC language code Library of Congress*] (LCCP) .... dak
Dakota (ODBW) .... Dak
Dakota City, NE [*AM radio station call letters*] .... KTFJ
Dakota Clinic, Fargo, ND [*Library symbol Library of Congress*] (LCLS) .... NdFD
Dakota County Library, West St. Paul, MN [*Library symbol Library of Congress*] (LCLS) .... MnWspD
Dakota Energy Corp. [*Vancouver Stock Exchange symbol*] .... DKT
Dakota Indian Foundation .... DIF
Dakota Information Service to the Community (IID) .... DISC
Dakota Microfilm Service, Inc., Denver, CO [*Library symbol Library of Congress*] (LCLS) .... DmS
Dakota Microfilm Service, Inc., Orlando, FL [*Library symbol Library of Congress*] (LCLS) .... DmS-O
Dakota Microfilm Service, Inc., Saint Paul, MN [*Library symbol Library of Congress*] (LCLS) .... DmS-SP
Dakota Mining [*Formerly, MinVen Gold Corp.*] [*AMEX symbol*] (SPSG) .... DKT
Dakota Mining Corp. [*Associated Press*] (SAG) .... DakotaM
Dakota, Minnesota & Eastern Railroad .... DM & E
Dakota Reports [*A publication*] (DLA) .... Dakota
Dakota State College, Madison, SD [*Library symbol Library of Congress*] (LCLS) .... SdMadT
Dakota Territory (ROG) .... DT
Dakota Territory Reports [*A publication*] (DLA) .... Da
Dakota Territory Reports [*A publication*] (DLA) .... Dak
Dakota Wesleyan University [*South Dakota*] .... DWU
Dakota Wesleyan University, Layne Library, Mitchell, SD [*OCLC symbol*] (OCLC) .... SDW
Dakota Wesleyan University, Mitchell, SD [*Library symbol Library of Congress*] (LCLS) .... SdMW
Dakota Women of All Red Nations (EA) .... DWARN
Dakota Wowapipahi Library, Marty, SD [*Library symbol Library of Congress*] (LCLS) .... SdMar
Dakotah, Inc. [*Associated Press*] (SAG) .... Dakotah
Dakotah, Inc. [*NASDAQ symbol*] (SAG) .... DKTH
Dakotas (FAAC) .... DKTS
Daktronics, Inc. [*NASDAQ symbol*] (SAG) .... DAKT
Daktronics, Inc. [*Associated Press*] (SAG) .... Daktron
Dal Segno [*Repeat from the Sign*] [*Music*] .... DAL S
Dal Segno [*Repeat from the Sign*] [*Music*] .... DAL SEG
Dal Segno [*Repeat from the Sign*] [*Music*] .... DS
(D-Ala, D-Leu) Enkephalin [*Biochemistry*] .... DADL
(D-Ala, D-Leu) Enkephalin [*Biochemistry*] .... DADLE
(D-Ala^2)-Met-enkephalinamide [*Analgesic peptide*] .... DALA
Dala-Jarna [*Sweden ICAO location identifier*] (ICLI) .... ESKD
Dalaman [*Turkey*] [*Airport symbol*] (OAG) .... DLM
Dalaman [*Turkey ICAO location identifier*] (ICLI) .... LTBS
Dalat [*South Vietnam*] [*Airport symbol*] (AD) .... DLI
Dalat/Lienkhuong [*Viet Nam*] [*ICAO location identifier*] (ICLI) .... VVDL
Dalbandin [*Pakistan*] [*Airport symbol*] (AD) .... DWP
Dalbandin [*Pakistan*] [*ICAO location identifier*] (ICLI) .... OPDB
d'Albertis [*Australia*] [*Airport symbol*] (AD) .... DLB
Dalby [*Australia Airport symbol*] (OAG) .... DBY
Dalby Agricultural College [*Australia*] .... DAC
Dalcho Historical Society of the Episcopal Diocese of South Carolina, Charleston, SC [*Library symbol Library of Congress*] (LCLS) .... ScCDHHi
Dalcho Historical Society of the Episcopal Diocese of South Carolina, Charleston, SC [*Library symbol*] [*Library of Congress*] (LCLS) .... ScCDHi
Dalcroze Society of America (EA) .... DSA
Dale [*Commonly used*] (OPSA) .... DALE
Dale .... DL
Dale .... DL
Dale Carnegie Course .... DCC
Dale Chapp Fan Club [*Defunct*] (EA) .... DCFC
Dale News, Dale, IN [*Library symbol*] [*Library of Congress*] (LCLS) .... InDaDN
Dale News, Dale, IN [*Library symbol Library of Congress*] (LCLS) .... InDaN
Daleco Res [*NASDAQ symbol*] (TTSB) .... DLOVF
Daleco Resources Corp. [*Associated Press*] (SAG) .... Daleco
Daleco Resources Corp. [*Vancouver Stock Exchange symbol*] .... DLO
Daleco Resources Corp. [*NASDAQ symbol*] (NQ) .... DLOV
Dale-Parizeau, Inc. [*Toronto Stock Exchange symbol*] .... DPZ
Daler [*Numismatics*] .... D
Dale's Clergyman's Legal Handbook [*A publication*] (DLA) .... Dale Cl HB
Dale's Ecclesiastical Reports [*England*] [*A publication*] (DLA) .... Dale Ecc
Dale's Ecclesiastical Reports [*England*] [*A publication*] (DLA) .... Dale Eccl
Dale's Judgments [*1868-71*] [*England*] [*A publication*] (DLA) .... Dale
Dale's Law of the Parish Church [*5th ed.*] [*1975*] [*A publication*] (DLA) .... Dale Par Ch
Dale's Legal Ritual [*Ecclesiastical Reports*] [*1868-71 England*] [*A publication*] (DLA) .... Dale Leg Rit
Dales Pony Society [*British*] (BI) .... DPS
Dale's Reports [*2-4 Oklahoma*] [*A publication*] (DLA) .... Dale
Daleville, AL [*AM radio station call letters*] .... WTKN
Dalhart [*Texas*] [*ICAO location identifier*] (ICLI) .... KDHT
Dalhart, TX [*Location identifier FAA*] (FAAL) .... DHT
Dalhart, TX [*AM radio station call letters*] .... KXIT
Dalhart, TX [*FM radio station call letters*] .... KXIT-FM
Dalhousie [*India*] [*Seismograph station code, US Geological Survey Closed*] (SEIS) .... DLH
Dalhousie Ocean Studies Programme [*Dalhousie University*] [*Canada Research center*] (RCD) .... DOSP
Dalhousie Ocean Studies Programme, Dalhousie University, Halifax, Nova Scotia [*Library symbol National Library of Canada*] (NLC) .... NSHDOS
Dalhousie Review [*A publication*] (BRI) .... Dal R
Dalhousie University, Archives, Halifax, NS, Canada [*Library symbol*] [*Library of Congress*] (LCLS) .... CaNSHDA
Dalhousie University, Halifax, Nova Scotia [*Library symbol National Library of Canada*] (NLC) .... NSHD
Dalhousie University, Halifax, NS, Canada [*Library symbol Library of Congress*] (LCLS) .... CaNSHD
Dalhousie University Health Sciences Library [*UTLAS symbol*] .... DLM
Dalhousie University, Institute of Public Affairs, Halifax, NS, Canada [*Library symbol Library of Congress*] (LCLS) .... CaNSHDIP
Dalhousie University Law Library [*UTLAS symbol*] .... DLL
Dalhousie University, Law School, Halifax, NS, Canada [*Library symbol Library of Congress*] (LCLS) .... CaNSHDL
Dalhousie University Library [*UTLAS symbol*] .... DAL
Dalhousie University, Map Library, Halifax, NS, Canada [*Library symbol Library of Congress*] (LCLS) .... CaNSHDMA
Dalhousie University, W. K. Kellog Health Sciences Library, Halifax, NS, Canada [*Library symbol Library of Congress*] (LCLS) .... CaNSHDM
Dali Management [*Gestion Dali*], Ottawa, Ontario [*Library symbol National Library of Canada*] (BIB) .... OODM
Dalian [*China*] [*ICAO location identifier*] (ICLI) .... ZYTL
Dalien [*China*] [*Airport symbol*] (OAG) .... DLC
Dalison's English Common Pleas Reports [*A publication*] (DLA) .... Dal
Dalison's English Common Pleas Reports [*A publication*] (DLA) .... Dal C P
Dalison's English Common Pleas Reports [*Bound with Benloe*] [*123 English Reprint*] [*A publication*] (DLA) .... Dalison
Dalison's Reports in Keilway [*1533-64*] [*England*] [*A publication*] (DLA) .... Dal in Keil
Dalkeith Branch, Stormont, Dundas, and Glengarry County Library, Ontario [*Library symbol National Library of Canada*] (BIB) .... ODSDG
Dallam County Free Library, Dalhart, TX [*Library symbol*] [*Library of Congress*] (LCLS) .... TxDah
Dallam's Digest [*Texas*] [*A publication*] (DLA) .... Dallam Dig (Tex)
Dallam's Digest and Opinions [*Texas*] [*A publication*] (DLA) .... Dall Dig
Dallam's Texas Decisions, from Dallam's Digest [*A publication*] (DLA) .... Dall Dec
Dallam's Texas Supreme Court Decisions [*A publication*] (DLA) .... Dall
Dallas [*Texas*] [*Seismograph station code, US Geological Survey*] (SEIS) .... DAL
Dallas [*Texas*] [*Seismograph station code, US Geological Survey Closed*] (SEIS) .... DLS
Dallas [*Branch in the Federal Reserve regional banking system*] (BARN) .... K
Dallas Area Media Project [*Library network*] .... DAMP
Dallas Area Rapid Transit [*FHWA*] (TAG) .... DART
Dallas Baptist College, Dallas, TX [*OCLC symbol*] (OCLC) .... IDA
Dallas Baptist College, Dallas, TX [*Library symbol Library of Congress*] (LCLS) .... TxDaB
Dallas Center Public Library, Dallas Center, IA [*Library symbol Library of Congress*] (LCLS) .... IaDc
Dallas Christian College, Dallas, TX [*OCLC symbol*] (OCLC) .... TDC
Dallas Christian College, Dallas, TX [*Library symbol Library of Congress*] (LCLS) .... TxDaDC
Dallas Cotton Exchange (EA) .... DCE
Dallas County Community College District, Dallas, TX [*OCLC symbol*] (OCLC) .... TDJ
Dallas County Community College System, Dallas, TX [*Library symbol Library of Congress*] (LCLS) .... TxDaCS
Dallas County Courthouse, Adel, IA [*Library symbol Library of Congress*] (LCLS) .... IaAdeCoC
Dallas County Law Library, Dallas, TX [*Library symbol Library of Congress*] (LCLS) .... TxDaDL
Dallas County News, Adel, IA [*Library symbol Library of Congress*] (LCLS) .... IaAdeN
Dallas Cowboys Cheerleaders .... DCC
Dallas/Dallas-Love Field [*Texas*] [*ICAO location identifier*] (ICLI) .... KDAL
Dallas Encephalopathic and Abortifactive Disease [*Acronym used as title of novel*] .... DEAD
Dallas Enviro-Health Systems Ltd. [*Vancouver Stock Exchange symbol*] .... DEH
Dallas Express Airlines, Inc. [*FAA designator*] (FAAC) .... DXP
Dallas/Fort Worth [*Texas*] [*Airport symbol*] .... DFW
Dallas Fort Worth Teleport Ltd. [*Irving, TX*] [*Telecommunications*] (TSSD) .... DFWT
Dallas, GA [*AM radio station call letters*] (RBYB) .... WDPC-AM
Dallas Gold & Silver Exchange, Inc. [*Associated Press*] (SAG) .... DallG
Dallas Gold & Silver Exchange, Inc. [*AMEX symbol*] (SAG) .... DLS
Dallas/Hensley Field Naval Air Station [*Texas*] [*ICAO location identifier*] (ICLI) .... KNBE
Dallas Historical Society, Dallas, TX [*Library symbol Library of Congress*] (LCLS) .... TxDaHi
Dallas' Laws of Pennsylvania [*A publication*] (DLA) .... Dall
Dallas' Laws of Pennsylvania [*A publication*] (DLA) .... Dall L
Dallas' Laws of Pennsylvania [*A publication*] (DLA) .... Dall Laws
Dallas [*Texas*] **Love Field** [*Airport symbol*] .... DAL
Dallas Morning News, Dallas, TX [*Library symbol*] [*Library of Congress*] (LCLS) .... TxDaMN
Dallas Museum of Fine Arts, Dallas, TX [*Library symbol Library of Congress*] (LCLS) .... TxDaMF
Dallas, NC [*AM radio station call letters*] .... WAAK

Dallas, NC [*FM radio station call letters*] .... WSGE
Dallas, OR [*AM radio station call letters*] .... KWIP
Dallas, PA [*FM radio station call letters*] .... WDLS
Dallas' Pennsylvania and United States Reports [*A publication*] (DLA) .... D
Dallas' Pennsylvania and United States Reports [*A publication*] (DLA) .... Dall
Dallas' Pennsylvania and United States Reports [*A publication*] (DLA) .... Dallas
Dallas' Pennsylvania Reports [*A publication*] (DLA) .... Dal
Dallas' Pennsylvania Reports [*4*] [*A publication*] (DLA) .... Dall (PA)
Dallas Power & Light Co. .... DP & L
Dallas Power & Light Co., Dallas, TX [*Library symbol Library of Congress*] (LCLS) .... TxDaP
Dallas Public Library, Dallas, OR [*Library symbol Library of Congress*] (LCLS) .... OrDal
Dallas Public Library, Dallas, TX [*OCLC symbol*] (OCLC) .... IGA
Dallas Public Library, Dallas, TX [*Library symbol Library of Congress*] (LCLS) .... TxDa
Dallas' Report of Cooper's Opinion on the Sentence of a Foreign Court of Admiralty [*A publication*] (DLA) .... Dal Coop
Dallas' Report of Cooper's Opinion on the Sentence of a Foreign Court of Admiralty [*A publication*] (DLA) .... Dall Coop
Dallas Semiconductor [*Associated Press*] (SAG) .... DalSem
Dallas Semiconductor [*NYSE symbol*] (TTSB) .... DS
Dallas' Styles of Writs [*Scotland*] [*A publication*] (DLA) .... Dall
Dallas' Styles of Writs [*Scotland*] [*A publication*] (DLA) .... Dall Sty
Dallas' Supreme Court Decisions [*Texas*] [*A publication*] (DLA) .... Dall Tex
Dallas Symphony Orchestra (BARN) .... DSO
Dallas Theological Seminary and Graduate School, Dallas, TX [*Library symbol Library of Congress*] (LCLS) .... TxDaTS
Dallas, TX [*Location identifier FAA*] (FAAL) .... ADS
Dallas, TX [*Location identifier FAA*] (FAAL) .... DDA
Dallas, TX [*FM radio station call letters*] .... KCBI
Dallas, TX [*Television station call letters*] .... KDAF
Dallas, TX [*Television station call letters*] .... KDFI
Dallas, TX [*Television station call letters*] .... KDFW
Dallas, TX [*AM radio station call letters*] (RBYB) .... KDFX
Dallas, TX [*FM radio station call letters*] .... KDMX
Dallas, TX [*Television station call letters*] .... KDTX
Dallas, TX [*FM radio station call letters*] .... KERA
Dallas, TX [*Television station call letters*] .... KERA-TV
Dallas, TX [*AM radio station call letters*] .... KGGR
Dallas, TX [*FM radio station call letters*] .... KKDA
Dallas, TX [*AM radio station call letters*] .... KLIF
Dallas, TX [*FM radio station call letters*] .... KLUV
Dallas, TX [*AM radio station call letters*] .... KMRT
Dallas, TX [*AM radio station call letters*] .... KNON
Dallas, TX [*FM radio station call letters*] (RBYB) .... KRBV
Dallas, TX [*AM radio station call letters*] .... KRLD
Dallas, TX [*FM radio station call letters*] .... KRRW
Dallas, TX [*FM radio station call letters*] .... KRSM
Dallas, TX [*AM radio station call letters*] .... KTCK
Dallas, TX [*FM radio station call letters*] .... KVTT
Dallas, TX [*Television station call letters*] .... KXTX
Dallas, TX [*FM radio station call letters*] .... KYNG
Dallas, TX [*FM radio station call letters*] .... KZPS
Dallas, TX [*Location identifier FAA*] (FAAL) .... LUE
Dallas, TX [*Location identifier FAA*] (FAAL) .... LVF
Dallas, TX [*Location identifier FAA*] (FAAL) .... NBE
Dallas, TX [*Location identifier FAA*] (FAAL) .... RBD
Dallas, TX [*Television station call letters*] .... WFAA
Dallas, TX [*FM radio station call letters*] .... WRR
Dallas Union Terminal [*AAR code*] .... DUTC
Dallas' United States Reports [*A publication*] (DLA) .... Dal
Dallas' United States Supreme Court Reports [*A publication*] (DLA) .... D
Dallas' United States Supreme Court Reports [*A publication*] (DLA) .... Dall S C
Dallas-Fort Worth/Regional Airport [*Texas*] [*ICAO location identifier*] (ICLI) .... KDFW
Dallas-Fort Worth, TX [*Location identifier FAA*] (FAAL) .... BXN
Dallas-Fort Worth, TX [*Location identifier FAA*] (FAAL) .... FLQ
Dallas-Fort Worth, TX [*Location identifier FAA*] (FAAL) .... PKQ
Dallas-Fort Worth, TX [*Location identifier FAA*] (FAAL) .... RRA
Dallas-Fort Worth, TX [*Location identifier FAA*] (FAAL) .... VYN
[*The*] **Dalles** [*Oregon*] [*Airport symbol*] (AD) .... DLS
Dallison [*or Dalison*] **in Keilway's Reports, English King's Bench** [*A publication*] (DLA) .... Dall in Keil
Dallol [*Ethiopia*] [*ICAO location identifier*] (ICLI) .... HADL
Dalmatian Club of America (EA) .... DCA
Dalmatian Resources Ltd. [*Vancouver Stock Exchange symbol*] .... DTN
Dalmys (Canada) Ltd. [*Toronto Stock Exchange symbol*] .... DYC
Daloa [*Ivory Coast*] [*ICAO location identifier*] (ICLI) .... DIDL
Daloa [*Ivory Coast*] [*Airport symbol*] (OAG) .... DJO
Dalrymple. Decisions of the Scotch Court of Session [*A publication*] (DLA) .... Dalr
Dalrymple. Decisions of the Scotch Court of Session [*A publication*] (DLA) .... Dalr Dec
Dalrymple (Lord Hailes). Decisions of the Scotch Court of Session [*1776-91*] [*A publication*] (DLA) .... Hailes
(Dalrymple of) Stair's Decisions of the Scotch Court of Session [*A publication*] (DLA) .... Dalr
Dalrymple on Feudal Property [*A publication*] (DLA) .... Dalr Feu Pr
Dalrymple on Feudal Property [*A publication*] (DLA) .... Dalr Feud Prop
Dalrymple on Tenures [*A publication*] (DLA) .... Dalr Ten
Dalrymple on the Polity of Entails [*A publication*] (DLA) .... Dalr Ent
Dalrymple. Scotch Court of Session Cases [*A publication*] (DLA) .... Dal
Dalton [*Physics*] [*Chemistry*] (DOG) .... Da
Dalton [*Australia Seismograph station code, US Geological Survey Closed*] (SEIS) .... DLN
Dalton [*California*] [*Seismograph station code, US Geological Survey Closed*] (SEIS) .... DLT
Dalton College, Dalton, GA [*Library symbol*] [*Library of Congress*] (LCLS) .... GDalC
Dalton Computer Services, Inc. [*Information service or system*] (IID) .... DCS
Dalton, GA [*Location identifier FAA*] (FAAL) .... DNN
Dalton, GA [*Location identifier FAA*] (FAAL) .... UWI
Dalton, GA [*AM radio station call letters*] .... WBLJ
Dalton, GA [*AM radio station call letters*] (RBYB) .... WDAL
Dalton, GA [*Television station call letters*] .... WELF
Dalton, GA [*AM radio station call letters*] .... WTTI
Dalton, GA [*FM radio station call letters*] (RBYB) .... WYYU
Dalton, MA [*Location identifier FAA*] (FAAL) .... DXT
Dalton on Sheriffs [*A publication*] (DLA) .... Dal Sh
Dalton on Sheriffs [*A publication*] (DLA) .... DS
Dalton Regional Library, Dalton, GA [*Library symbol Library of Congress*] (LCLS) .... GDal
Dalton-Dalton-Newport, Cleveland, OH [*OCLC symbol*] (OCLC) .... ODN
Dalton's Justices of the Peace [*Many eds.*] [*1618-1746*] [*A publication*] (DLA) .... Dalt
Dalton's Justices of the Peace [*Many eds.*] [*1618-1746*] [*A publication*] (DLA) .... Dalt Just
Dalton's Sheriff [*A publication*] (DLA) .... Dalt Sh
Daly City Public Library, Daly City, CA [*Library symbol Library of Congress*] (LCLS) .... CDc
Daly Elementary School, Port Washington, NY [*Library symbol Library of Congress*] (LCLS) .... NptwDE
Daly Waters [*Northern Territory, Australia*] [*Airport symbol*] (AD) .... DYW
Daly's Hand-Book on Practice in the Lord Mayor's Court [*A publication*] (DLA) .... Daly May Ct
Daly's Nature of Surrogate's Courts [*New York*] [*A publication*] (DLA) .... Daly Sur
Daly's New York Common Pleas Reports [*A publication*] (DLA) .... Dal
Daly's New York Common Pleas Reports [*A publication*] (DLA) .... Daly
Daly's New York Common Pleas Reports [*A publication*] (DLA) .... Daly's R
Dam .... D
Dam [*Commonly used*] (OPSA) .... DAM
Dam .... DM
Dam .... DM
Damage (AABC) .... DAM
Damage (AFM) .... DMG
Damage Analysis and Fundamental Studies (MCD) .... DAFS
Damage Analysis in Rapid Time (MCD) .... DART
Damage and Vulnerability (MCD) .... DV
Damage Assessment and Casualty Report [*Military*] .... DACAR
Damage Assessment and Casualty Report [*Military*] (AFM) .... DACAS
Damage Assessment Computer Program [*Military*] .... DACOMP
Damage Assessment Department (SAA) .... DAD
Damage Assessment Reduction and Evaluation (SAA) .... DARE
Damage Assessment Routines (MDG) .... DAR
Damage before Launch (CINC) .... DBL
Damage Control [*or Controlman*] [*Navy*] .... DC
Damage Control Assessment (MCD) .... DCA
Damage Control Assistant [*Military*] (NVT) .... DCA
Damage Control Booklet (DNAB) .... DCB
Damage Control Breathing Apparatus (PDAA) .... DCBA
Damage Control Center (NATG) .... DCC
Damage Control Diagrams [*Naval Ship Systems Command*] .... DCD
Damage Control Group [*Military*] (DNAB) .... DCG
Damage Control Headquarters [*Military British*] .... DCHQ
Damage Control Hulk (DNAB) .... DCH
Damage Control In-Port Training (NVT) .... DCIPT
Damage Control Instructor [*Navy*] (DNAB) .... DCI
Damage Control Petty Officer [*Navy*] (DNAB) .... DCPO
Damage Control School [*Navy*] .... DCS
Damage Control Suit [*Navy*] .... DCS
Damage Control Suit System [*Navy*] .... DCSS
Damage Control System (KSC) .... DCS
Damage Control Texts [*Naval Ship Systems Command*] .... DCT
Damage Control Training Center [*Military*] (DNAB) .... DAMCONTRACEN
Damage Controlman, Chief [*Navy*] (DNAB) .... DCC
Damage Controlman, Fireman [*Navy*] .... DCFN
Damage Controlman, Fireman Apprentice [*Navy*] .... DCFA
Damage Controlman, First Class [*Navy*] (DNAB) DC1
Damage Controlman, Second Class [*Navy*] (DNAB) DC2
Damage Controlman, Third Class [*Navy*] (DNAB) DC3
Damage Done [*Insurance*] (ODBW) .... DD
Damage Equivalent .... DE
Damage Equivalent of Normally Incident (IAA) .... DENI
Damage Evaluation Team (SAA) .... DET
Damage Expectancy (NATG) .... DE
Damage Free [*Business term*] .... DF
Damage Information Reporting System [*Military*] (MCD) .... DIRS
Damage Limitation [*Strategy*] [*Military*] .... DL
Damage Limiting Program .... DLP
Damage Modes and Effects Analysis (MCD) .... DMEA
Damage Risk Contours .... DRC
Damage Tolerant/Easy Repair Structures (MCD) .... DETERS
Damage Waiver [*Insurance*] .... DW
Damaged (CINC) .... DA
Damaged Disc Syndrome [*Medicine*] (DMAA) .... DDS
Damaged DNA [*Deoxyribonucleic Acid*] **Binding Factor** [*Biochemistry*] .... DDBF
Damaged Goods .... DG
Damaged Lyman-Alpha [*Galaxy*] .... DLA
Damaged Weapons Control (DNAB) .... DWC

Damage-Risk Criteria [Tolerable limits for noise exposure]	DRC
Damages [Legal term] (DLA)	DAMG
Damaging Winds Algorithm [Marine science] (OSRA)	DWA
Damaging Winds Algorithm (USDC)	DWA
Damark International, Inc. [Associated Press] (SAG)	Damark
Damark International, Inc. [NASDAQ symbol] (SAG)	DMRK
Damark International'A' [NASDAQ symbol] (TTSB)	DMRK
Damascus [Syria] [Airport symbol] (OAG)	DAM
Damascus [Syria] [ICAO location identifier] (ICLI)	OSBF
Damascus [Syria] [ICAO location identifier] (ICLI)	OSDT
Damascus [Syria] [ICAO location identifier] (ICLI)	OSSS
Damascus [Syria] [ICAO location identifier] (ICLI)	OSTT
Damascus Document [or Sefer Berit Damesek] from Qumran. Cave Six (BJA)	6QD
Damascus/International [Syria] [ICAO location identifier] (ICLI)	OSDI
Damask (VRA)	dmsk
Damasus [Flourished, 13th century] [Authority cited in pre-1607 legal work] (DSA)	D
Damasus [Flourished, 13th century] [Authority cited in pre-1607 legal work] (DSA)	Da
Damasus [Flourished, 13th century] [Authority cited in pre-1607 legal work] (DSA)	Damas
Damazin [Sudan] [ICAO location identifier] (ICLI)	HSDZ
Damba [Angola] [ICAO location identifier] (ICLI)	FNDB
Damblain [France ICAO location identifier] (ICLI)	LFYD
Dame	D
Dame	DM
Dame Commander of the [Order of the] British Empire	DBE
Dame Commander of the Order of St. Michael and St. George [British]	DCMG
Dame Commander of the Order of the Bath [British] (ADA)	DCB
Dame Commander of the Royal Victorian Order [British]	DCVO
Dame Grand Cross of [the Order of] Saint John of Jerusalem [British] (ADA)	GCStJ
Dame Grand Cross of the Order of Saint John of Jerusalem [British] (ADA)	DGCStJ
Dame Grand Cross of the Order of Saint Michael and Saint George [British] (ADA)	GCMG
Dame Grand Cross of the Order of the Bath [British] (ADA)	GCB
Dame Grand Cross of the Order of the British Empire (ADA)	GBE
Dame Grand Cross of the Royal Victorian Order [British] (ADA)	GCVO
Dame of Grace, Order of St. John of Jerusalem [Later, D St J] [British]	DGStJ
Dame of Justice/Grace of the Order of St. John of Jerusalem [British]	D St J
Dame of Justice of St. John of Jerusalem [Later, D St J] [British]	DJStJ
Damen Financial [NASDAQ symbol] (TTSB)	DFIN
Damen Financial Corp. [Associated Press] (SAG)	Damen
Damen Financial Corp. [NASDAQ symbol] (SAG)	DFIN
Dames and Moore Chicago Branch Library, Park Ridge, IL [Library symbol Library of Congress] (LCLS)	IParkD
Dames & Moore, Inc. [Associated Press] (SAG)	DameMr
Dames & Moore, Inc. [NYSE symbol] (SPSG)	DM
Dames of Malta (EA)	D of M
Dames of the Loyal Legion of the United States of America (EA)	DLL
Damghan [Iran] [ICAO location identifier] (ICLI)	OIIU
Damianus Gulianus [Authority cited in pre-1607 legal work] (DSA)	DG
Damien Dutton Society for Leprosy Aid (EA)	DDS
Damien Dutton Society for Leprosy Aid (EA)	DDSLA
Damien Ministries (EA)	DM
Damietta-Latakia Line [Nile river delta] [Geology]	DLL
D-Amino Acid Oxidase [An enzyme]	DAAO
D-Amino Phosphonovaleric Acid	D-APV
Damme [Germany ICAO location identifier] (ICLI)	EDWC
Damn	D
Damn Fool Ground Officer [Military slang] (DNAB)	DFGO
Damn Your Lame Excuses [Facetious translation for the name of a Toronto-based specialty store chain]	DYLEX
Damned Average Raiser [A diligent student] [Slang]	DAR
Damned Bad	DB
Damned Good Airplane	DGA
Damned Old Fool About Books [Acronym created by Eugene Field]	DOFAB
Damned Young Fools [Officers under the age of thirty] [British naval slang]	DYF
Damocles [Greek courtier, c.300BC] (ROG)	DAM
Damon and Pythias [Fourth-century BC Greek philosophers renowned for their loyalty to one another]	D & P
Damon Runyon Memorial Fund for Cancer Research [Later, DRWWCF] (EA)	DRMF
Damon Runyon-Walter Winchell Cancer Fund (EA)	DRWWCF
Damp Rag [Decontamination method] [Nuclear energy] (NRCH)	D-R
Damped Aerodynamic Righting Attitude Control	DARAC
Damped Aerodynamic Righting Attitude Control System	DARACS
Damped Least Square [Mathematics]	DLS
Damped Lyman-Alpha System [Galactic science]	DLAS
Damper (KSC)	DMPR
Dampf-Kraft-Wagen [Steam-Powered Vehicle] [German]	DKW
Dampier and Maxwell's British Guiana Reports [A publication] (DLA)	Alves
Dampier Port Authority [Australia]	DPA
Dampier's Paper Book, Lincoln's Inn Library [A publication] (DLA)	Dampier MSS
Dampier's Paper Book, Lincoln's Inn Library [A publication] (DLA)	DPB
Damping (MSA)	DPG
Damping Factor	DF
Damping Ratio (IAA)	DR
Damping Structural Vibrations	DSV
Damp-Proof Course [Civil engineering] (IAA)	DPC
Dampproof Membrane (DAC)	Dpm
Damp-Proofing (AAG)	DP
Dan' Air [Benin] [FAA designator] (FAAC)	DAI
Dan Korona [Danish Crown] [Monetary unit]	Dkr
Dan River Mills Co., Danville, VA [Library symbol Library of Congress] (LCLS)	ViDR
Dana College, Blair, NE [Library symbol Library of Congress] (LCLS)	NbBlaD
Dana College, C. A. Dana-Life Library, Blair, NE [OCLC symbol] (OCLC)	DAN
Dana Corp. [Associated Press] (SAG)	DanaCp
Dana Corp. [NYSE symbol] (SAG)	DCN
Dana Hall School Library, Wellesley, MA [Library symbol Library of Congress] (LCLS)	MWelD
Dana-Farber Cancer Institute [Harvard Medical School] [Research center] (RCD)	DFCI
Danaher Corp. [Associated Press] (SAG)	Danher
Danaher Corp. [NYSE symbol] (SPSG)	DHR
Danair [ICAO designator] (AD)	DX
Danair AS [Denmark ICAO designator] (FAAC)	DAN
Dan-Air Services [ICAO designator] (AD)	DA
Danang [South Vietnam] [Airport symbol] (AD)	DAD
Danang [Vietnam] [Airport symbol] (OAG)	DAD
Danang [Viet Nam] [ICAO location identifier] (ICLI)	VVDN
Dana's Edition of Wheaton's International Law [A publication] (DLA)	Dana Wh
Dana's Kentucky Supreme Court Reports [1833-40] [A publication] (DLA)	Dana
Dana's Reports [31-39 Kentucky] [A publication] (DLA)	Dana
Dana's Reports [31-39 Kentucky] [A publication] (DLA)	Dana (KY)
Danbury [England]	DANB
Danbury [Connecticut] [Airport symbol Obsolete] (OAG)	DXR
Danbury Airways, Inc. [ICAO designator] (FAAC)	DSA
Danbury, CT [FM radio station call letters]	WDAQ
Danbury, CT [FM radio station call letters]	WFAR
Danbury, CT [AM radio station call letters]	WLAD
Danbury, CT [FM radio station call letters]	WXCI
Danbury Public Library, Danbury, CT [Library symbol Library of Congress] (LCLS)	CtDab
Danbus Resources, Inc. [Vancouver Stock Exchange symbol]	DBS
Dance	DNC
Dance Artists' Nationwide Space Emergency [In association name, DANSE Coalition] (EA)	DANSE
Dance Critics Association (EA)	DCA
Dance Data Bank Project [University of California] [Los Angeles] [Information service or system] (IID)	DDBP
Dance Educators of America (EA)	DEA
Dance Films Association (EA)	DFA
Dance Halls (Commercial) [Public-performance tariff class] [British]	D
Dance History Scholars (EA)	DHS
Dance in Canada Association	DICA
Dance Kaleidoscope [Indiana]	DK
Dance Magazine [A publication] (BRI)	Dance
Dance Magazine Foundation (EA)	DMF
Dance Masters of America (EA)	DMA
Dance/Movement Therapy	D/M
Dance Network Australia	DNA
Dance Notation Bureau (EA)	DNB
Dance Research Foundation (EA)	DRF
Dance Research Journal [A publication] (BRI)	Dance RJ
Dance Services Network	DSN
Dance Teachers' Association (AIE)	DTA
Dance Theater of Harlem	DTH
Dance Theater Workshop (EA)	DTW
Dance Touring Program [National Endowment for the Arts]	DTP
Dance Tuition Schools [Public-performance tariff class] [British]	DS
Danceable Jazz [In music group name Dazz Band]	DAZZ
Dance-Oriented Rock [Music] (BARN)	DOR
Dancer-Fitzgerald-Sample [Advertising agency]	DFS
Dancers for Disarmament [Defunct] (EA)	DFD
Dancers Responding to AIDS [An association]	DRA
Dancing (ADA)	DCG
Dancing in the Streets	DITS
Dancing Room Only	DRO
Dandelion Latent Virus [Plant pathology]	DLV
Dandenong and District Aborigines Cooperative Society [Australia]	DDACS
Dandie Dinmont Terrier Club of America (EA)	DDTCA
D&N Financial Wrrt [NASDAQ symbol] (TTSB)	DNFCW
D&N Finl Corp. [NASDAQ symbol] (TTSB)	DNFC
Dandus [To Be Given] [Pharmacy]	DAND
Dandy [Ship's rigging] (ROG)	DY
Dane [Ontario] [Seismograph station code, US Geological Survey Closed] (SEIS)	DAN
Dane County Hospital, Verona, WI [Library symbol Library of Congress] (LCLS)	WVD
Dane County Regional-Truax Field [FAA] (TAG)	MSN
Daneborg [Greenland] [ICAO location identifier] (ICLI)	BGDB
Dane's Abridgment of American Law [A publication] (DLA)	Dan Abr
Dane's Abridgment of American Law [A publication] (DLA)	Dane Abr
Dane's Abridgment of American Law [A publication] (DLA)	Dane's Abr
Dang [Nepal] [Airport symbol] (OAG)	DNP
Dang [Nepal] [ICAO location identifier] (ICLI)	VNDG
Danger	DGR
Danger	DNG
Danger Area [ICAO] (FAAC)	D
Danger Area (DA)	DA
Danger Areas in the Pacific	DAPAC
Danger List [Medicine]	DL
Dangerous [FBI standardized term]	DANG
Dangerous and Hazardous [MARAD] (TAG)	D&H
Dangerous and Suspicious	D & S

Dangerous Articles Tariff .... DAT
Dangerous Cargo (FAAC) .... DGCGO
Dangerous Cargo Manifest [*RSPA*] (TAG) .... DCM
Dangerous Defective [*British*] .... DD
Dangerous Drug .... DD
Dangerous Drug Cabinet [*Lockable auxiliary to bathroom medicine chest*] .... DDC
Dangerous Drugs Act [*British*] .... DDA
Dangerous Goods [*Shipping*] .... DG
Dangerous Goods Advisory Service [*British*] (NITA) .... DAGAS
Dangerous Goods Board [*IATA*] (DS) .... DGB
Dangerous Goods Note [*Shipping*] (DCTA) .... DGN
Dangerous Goods Panel [*ICAO*] (DA) .... DGP
Dangerous Infectious Disease [*British*] (ROG) .... DID
Dangerous Weapon .... DW
Danghila [*Ethiopia*] [*Airport symbol*] (AD) .... DNG
Dangling, at Bedside [*Medicine*] .... d
Dangling Construction [*Used in correcting manuscripts, etc.*] .... DGL
Dangriga [*Belize*] [*Airport symbol*] (OAG) .... DGA
Danguilla [*Ethiopia*] [*ICAO location identifier*] (ICLI) .... HADN
Dania Kommunista Partja [*Communist Party of Denmark*] [*Political party*] .... DKP
Daniel [*Old Testament book*] .... Dan
Daniel [*Old Testament book*] (DSA) .... Dani
Daniel [*Old Testament book*] .... Danl
Daniel [*Old Testament book*] .... Dn
Daniel Arbour & Associes, Montreal, Quebec [*Library symbol National Library of Canada*] (NLC) .... QMDA
Daniel Hudson Burnham [*Architect and urban planner, 1846-1912*] .... DHB
Daniel Indus [*NYSE symbol*] (TTSB) .... DAN
Daniel Industries, Inc. [*NYSE symbol*] (SPSG) .... DAN
Daniel Industries, Inc. [*Associated Press*] (SAG) .... Daniel
Daniel K. Inouye [*US Senator from Hawaii*] .... DKI
Daniel Library, Sir Sandford Fleming College, Peterborough, Ontario [*Library symbol National Library of Canada*] (BIB) .... OPETSFD
Daniel, Mann, Johnson, & Mendenhall [*A major contributor to architecture in Jakarta, Sidney, Manila, and Seoul*] .... DMJM
Daniel McVicar Fan Club (EA) .... DMFC
Daniel Moller [*Deceased, 1600*] [*Authority cited in pre-1607 legal work*] (DSA) .... Dan Moll
Daniel. Trade Marks [*1876*] [*A publication*] (DLA) .... Dan T M
Daniell. Forms and Precedents in Chancery [*7th ed.*] [*1932*] [*A publication*] (DLA) .... Dan Forms
Daniell. Forms and Precedents in Chancery [*7th ed.*] [*1932*] [*A publication*] (ILCA) .... DCF
Daniell's Chancery Pleading and Practice [*A publication*] (DLA) .... Daniell Ch Pl & Prac
Daniell's Chancery Pleading and Practice [*A publication*] (DLA) .... Daniell Ch Pr
Daniell's Chancery Pleading and Practice [*A publication*] (DLA) .... Daniell Ch Prac
Daniell's Chancery Practice [*A publication*] (DLA) .... Dan Ch
Daniell's Chancery Practice [*A publication*] (DLA) .... Dan Ch Pr
Daniell's Chancery Practice [*A publication*] (DLA) .... DCP
Daniell's Exchequer and Equity Reports [*159 English Reprint*] [*1817-23*] [*A publication*] (DLA) .... Dan
Daniell's Exchequer and Equity Reports [*159 English Reprint*] [*1817-23*] [*A publication*] (DLA) .... Dan Exch
Daniell's Exchequer and Equity Reports [*159 English Reprint*] [*1817-23*] [*A publication*] (DLA) .... Dan Exch (Eng)
Daniels Canyon [*Utah*] [*Seismograph station code, US Geological Survey*] (SEIS) .... DAU
Daniels' Compendium Compensation Cases [*England*] [*A publication*] (DLA) .... Dan
Daniels County Free Library, Scobey, MT [*Library symbol*] [*Library of Congress*] (LCLS) .... MtSc
Daniels Harbour Public Library, Daniels Harbour, NF, Canada [*Library symbol Library of Congress*] (LCLS) .... CaNfDH
Daniels Harbour Public Library, Newfoundland [*Library symbol National Library of Canada*] (NLC) .... NFDH
Daniel's Law of Attachment [*A publication*] (DLA) .... Dan Att
Daniel's Negotiable Instruments [*A publication*] (DLA) .... Dan Neg Ins
Daniel's Negotiable Instruments [*A publication*] (DLA) .... Daniel Neg Inst
Daniels Primary Center, Roosevelt, NY [*Library symbol*] [*Library of Congress*] (LCLS) .... NRoosDP
Danielson Holding [*AMEX symbol*] (TTSB) .... DHC
Danielson Holding Corp. [*Associated Press*] (SAG) .... DanlHd
Danielson Holding Corp. [*AMEX symbol*] (SPSG) .... DHC
Danish .... DA
Danish .... DAN
Danish [*MARC language code Library of Congress*] (LCCP) .... dan
Danish Agricultural Organizations (ECON) .... DANAGRO
Danish Air Force [*ICAO designator*] (FAAC) .... DAE
Danish Air Force [*Denmark*] [*FAA designator*] (FAAC) .... DAF
Danish Air Transport [*ICAO designator*] (FAAC) .... DTR
Danish American Chamber of Commerce (EA) .... DACC
Danish American Heritage Society (EA) .... DAHS
Danish American Women's Association [*Defunct*] (EA) .... DAWA
Danish Army (NATG) .... DA
Danish Army [*ICAO designator*] (FAAC) .... DAR
Danish Atomic Energy Commission .... DAEC
Danish Brotherhood in America (EA) .... DBA
Danish Brotherhood in America (EA) .... DBIA
Danish Building Research Institute .... DBRI
Danish Committee for Scientific and Technical Information and Documentation [*Information service or system*] (IID) .... DANDOK
Danish Consultate General, Reference Library, New York, NY [*Library symbol*] [*Library of Congress*] (LCLS) .... NNDCG
Danish Defense Research Board .... DDRB
Danish Defense Research Establishment (NATG) .... DDRE
[*The*] **Danish Ethernet Network** [*Computer science*] (TNIG) .... DENet
Danish International Development Agency .... DANIDA
Danish Krone [*Monetary unit*] .... D KR
Danish Krone [*Monetary unit*] (NATG) .... DK
Danish Machine-Readable Catalogue (NITA) .... DANMARC
Danish Meteorological Institute .... DMI
Danish Meteorological Institute [*Denmark ICAO location identifier*] (ICLI) .... EKMI
Danish National Committee of the International Association on Water Pollution Research and Control (EAIO) .... DNCIAWPRC
Danish Navy [*ICAO designator*] (FAAC) .... DNY
Danish Ordinances [*A publication*] (DLA) .... Dan Ord
Danish Reactor (NRCH) .... DR
Danish Sailors' and Firemen's Union (EA) .... DSFU
Danish Social-Liberal Party [*Political party*] (EAIO) .... DSLP
Danish Space Research Institute .... DSRI
Danish Tourist Board (EAIO) .... DTB
Danish West Indies .... DWI
Danka Business Systems [*NASDAQ symbol*] (SAG) .... DANK
Danka Business Systems [*Associated Press*] (SAG) .... Danka
Danka Business Systems ADR [*NASDAQ symbol*] (TTSB) .... DANKY
Dankoe Mines Ltd. [*Vancouver Stock Exchange symbol*] .... DKO
Danmarks Kommunistiske Parti [*Communist Party of Denmark*] [*Political Party*] (PPW) .... DKP
Danmarks Laererhojskole [*Royal Danish School of Educational Studies*], Kobenhavn, Denmark [*Library symbol Library of Congress*] (LCLS) .... DnKL
Danmarks Nationalsocialistisk Arbejdersparti [*National Socialist Worker's Party of Denmark (or Danish NAZI Party)*] (PPE) .... DNSAP
Danmarks Paedagogiske Bibliotek [*Danish National Library of Education*], Kobenhavn, Denmark [*Library symbol Library of Congress*] (LCLS) .... DnKP
Danmarks Radio (EY) .... DSR
Danmarks Retsforbund [*Justice Party of Denmark*] (PPE) .... DR
Danmarks Statistik [*Denmark*] .... DS
Danmarks Statistiks TidsseriedataBank [*Denmark Information service or system*] (CRD) .... DSTB
Danmarks Tekniske Bibliotek [*National Technological Library of Denmark*] [*Information service or system*] (IID) .... DTB
Danmarks Veterinaer- og Jordbrugsbase [*Danish Veterinary and Agricultural Library Catalogue*] [*Information service or system*] .... DVJB
Danmarkshavn [*Greenland*] [*ICAO location identifier*] (ICLI) .... BGDH
Danmarkshavn [*Greenland*] [*Seismograph station code, US Geological Survey*] (SEIS) .... DAG
Dannemiller, Lawrence B., Columbus OH [*STAC*] .... DLB
Dannemiller Memorial Educational Foundation (EA) .... DMEF
Dannemora [*New York*] [*Seismograph station code, US Geological Survey*] (SEIS) .... DANY
Danner's Reports [*42 Alabama*] [*A publication*] (DLA) .... Dan
Danner's Reports [*42 Alabama*] [*A publication*] (DLA) .... Dann
Danner's Reports [*42 Alabama*] [*A publication*] (DLA) .... Danner
Dannevirke [*New Zealand*] [*Seismograph station code, US Geological Survey Closed*] (SEIS) .... DNN
Danninger Med Tech [*NASDAQ symbol*] (TTSB) .... DANN
Danninger Medical Technology [*NASDAQ symbol*] (SAG) .... DANN
Danninger Medical Technology, Inc. [*Associated Press*] (SAG) .... Danngr
Dann's Reports [*1 Arizona*] [*A publication*] (DLA) .... Dann
Dann's Reports [*22 California*] [*2nd ed. 1871*] [*A publication*] (DLA) .... Dann
Danny Boy Breeders Association (EA) .... DBBA
Danny Cooksey Fan Club (EA) .... DCFC
Danny Foundation (EA) .... DF
Danny Vann Fan Club (EA) .... DVFC
Dano [*Burkina Faso*] [*ICAO location identifier*] (ICLI) .... DHOA
Danquah. Akan Laws and Customs [*Ghana*] [*A publication*] (DLA) .... DALC
Danquah. Cases in Akan Law [*Ghana*] [*A publication*] (DLA) .... DCAL
Danra Resources Ltd. [*Vancouver Stock Exchange symbol*] .... DND
DANSE Coalition (EA) .... DC
Dansgaard-Oeschger [*Climatic cycles*] .... D-O
Dansk Fiskeriteknologisk Institut [*Danish Fisheries Technology Institute*] [*Also, an information service or system*] (IID) .... DFTI
Dansk Fiskeriteknologisk Institut [*Danish Institute of Fisheries Technology*] [*Information service or system*] (IID) .... FTI
Dansk Industri Syndikat A/S [*Danish manufacturer of a machine gun mount being tested by US Army*] (RDA) .... DISA
Dansk Normal Nul [*Oceanography*] .... DNN
Dansk Samling [*Danish Union*] (PPE) .... DS
Danske Lov [*Laws in Force*] [*Denmark*] (ILCA) .... DL
Danske Statsbaner [*Danish State Railways*] .... DSB
Danskin, Inc. [*NASDAQ symbol*] (SAG) .... DANS
Danskin, Inc. [*Associated Press*] (SAG) .... Danskin
Danson and Lloyd's English Mercantile Cases [*A publication*] (DLA) .... Dan & L
Danson and Lloyd's English Mercantile Cases [*A publication*] (DLA) .... Dan & Ll
Danson and Lloyd's English Mercantile Cases [*A publication*] (DLA) .... Dan & Lld
Danson and Lloyd's English Mercantile Cases [*A publication*] (DLA) .... Dans & L
Danson and Lloyd's English Mercantile Cases [*A publication*] (DLA) .... Dans & LL
Danstar Resources Ltd. [*Vancouver Stock Exchange symbol*] .... DST
[*The*] **Dansville & Mount Morris Railroad Co.** [*AAR code*] .... DMM
Dansville, NY [*Location identifier FAA*] (FAAL) .... DSV
Dansville, NY [*AM radio station call letters*] .... WDNY
Dansville, NY [*FM radio station call letters*] .... WDNY-FM
Dansville Senior High School Library, Dansville, NY [*OCLC symbol*] (OCLC) .... RVZ
Dansyl [*As substituent on nucleoside*] [*Biochemistry*] .... dns
Dansyl Derivative of Oligothymidilate [*Biochemistry*] .... DDO
Dansyl Glutamate [*Biochemistry*] .... DG
Dansylaspartate [*Biochemistry*] .... DA
Dansylcadaverine [*Biochemistry*] .... DACAD

Dante Alighieri Society [*Australia*] ... DAS
Dante Alighieri Society of Southern California [*Defunct*] (EA) ... DASSC
Dante Society of America (EA) ... DSA
Dantiscum [*Dantzig*] (ROG) ... DANTISC
Dantrolene Blood Level [*Clinical chemistry*] ... DBL
Dantrolene Sodium [*Muscle relaxant*] ... DS
Danube [*River in central Europe*] ... DAN
Danube Commission (BARN) ... DANCOM
Danube Commission (EA) ... DC
Danube River and Basin [*MARC geographic area code Library of Congress*] (LCCP) ... eo----
Danube River Field Organization [*Allied German Occupation Forces*] ... DRFO
Danube Tourist Commission [*Formerly, Working Group for the Promotion of Tourism inthe Danube Region*] [*Austria*] (EAIO) ... WGPTDR
Danube-Air Ltd. [*Hungary ICAO designator*] (FAAC) ... DBE
Danvers Archival Center, Peabody Institute, Danvers, MA [*Library symbol Library of Congress*] (LCLS) ... MDaAr
D'Anvers' General Abridgment of the Common Law [*A publication*] (DLA) ... D Abr
D'Anvers' General Abridgment of the Common Law [*A publication*] (DLA) ... D'An
D'Anvers' General Abridgment of the Common Law [*A publication*] (DLA) ... Danv
D'Anvers' General Abridgment of the Common Law [*A publication*] (DLA) ... Danv Abr
Danvers State Hospital, Hathorne, MA [*Library symbol Library of Congress*] (LCLS) ... MHathD
Danville [*Virginia*] [*Airport symbol*] (OAG) ... DAN
Danville [*Illinois*] [*Airport symbol*] (OAG) ... DNV
Danville & Western Railroad (IIA) ... D & W
Danville Community College, Danville, VA [*Library symbol Library of Congress*] (LCLS) ... ViDC
Danville Community Unit School District, Danville, IL [*Library symbol*] [*Library of Congress*] (LCLS) ... IDanviSD
Danville, IL [*FM radio station call letters*] (RBYB) ... WBOM
Danville, IL [*AM radio station call letters*] ... WDAN
Danville, IL [*FM radio station call letters*] ... WDNL
Danville, IL [*FM radio station call letters*] ... WIAI
Danville, IL [*AM radio station call letters*] ... WITY
Danville, IL [*FM radio station call letters*] ... WWDZ
Danville, IN [*FM radio station call letters*] ... WSYW-FM
Danville Junior College [*Illinois*] ... DJC
Danville Junior College, Danville, IL [*Library symbol Library of Congress*] (LCLS) ... IDanviC
Danville, KY [*Location identifier FAA*] (FAAL) ... DVK
Danville, KY [*FM radio station call letters*] ... WDFB
Danville, KY [*Television station call letters*] ... WDKY
Danville, KY [*AM radio station call letters*] ... WHIR
Danville, KY [*FM radio station call letters*] (RBYB) ... WHIR-FM
Danville, PA [*AM radio station call letters*] ... WPGM
Danville, PA [*FM radio station call letters*] ... WPGM-FM
Danville Public Library, Danville, IL [*Library symbol Library of Congress*] (LCLS) ... IDanvi
Danville Public Library, Danville, IN [*Library symbol Library of Congress*] (LCLS) ... InDan
Danville Public Library, Danville, VA [*Library symbol Library of Congress*] (LCLS) ... ViD
Danville Republican, Danville, IN [*Library symbol Library of Congress*] (LCLS) ... InDanR
Danville State Hospital, Danville, PA [*Library symbol Library of Congress*] (LCLS) ... PDanSH
Danville State Hospital, Danville, PA [*OCLC symbol*] (OCLC) ... PHJ
Danville, VA [*Location identifier FAA*] (FAAL) ... DAN
Danville, VA [*FM radio station call letters*] ... WAKG
Danville, VA [*AM radio station call letters*] ... WBTM
Danville, VA [*Television station call letters*] ... WDRG
Danville, VA [*AM radio station call letters*] ... WDVA
Danville, VA [*AM radio station call letters*] ... WILA
Danville, VA [*AM radio station call letters*] ... WVOV
Danville, VT [*FM radio station call letters*] ... WSHX
Danville, WV [*FM radio station call letters*] ... WZAC
Danygraig [*Welsh depot code*] ... DG
Danzig Study Group [*German Philatelic Society*] (EA) ... DSG
Danziger Statistische Mitteilungen [*Danzig*] [*A publication*] ... DSM
Daoist Sanctuary (EA) ... DS
Daon Centre Ltd. [*Partnership units*] [*Vancouver Stock Exchange symbol*] ... DNC
Dapango [*Togo*] [*ICAO location identifier*] (ICLI) ... DXDP
Daphne Virus X [*Plant pathology*] ... DVX
Dapsone [*Antimalarial medication*] (VNW) ... DDS
Daptazole (MAE) ... Dapt
Dar Es Salaam [*Tanzania*] [*Airport symbol*] (OAG) ... DAR
Dar Es Salaam [*Tanzania*] [*Geomagnetic observatory code*] ... DRS
Dar Es Salaam Law Journal [*A publication*] (DLA) ... D Es S LJ
Dar Es Salaam University. Law Journal [*A publication*] (DLA) ... D Es S ULJ
Dar Es-Salaam [*Tanzania*] [*ICAO location identifier*] (ICLI) ... HTDC
Dar Es-Salaam [*Tanzania*] [*ICAO location identifier*] (ICLI) ... HTDQ
Dar Es-Salaam/Dar Es-Salaam [*Tanzania*] [*ICAO location identifier*] (ICLI) ... HTDA
Darab [*Iran*] [*ICAO location identifier*] (ICLI) ... OISD
Darband [*Pakistan*] [*Seismograph station code, US Geological Survey*] (SEIS) ... DBP
Darband/Ravar [*Iran*] [*ICAO location identifier*] (ICLI) ... OIKD
Darby and Bosanquet's Statutes of Limitation [*2nd ed.*] [*1893*] [*A publication*] (DLA) ... Da & Bos
Darby and Bosanquet's Statutes of Limitations [*2nd ed.*] [*1893*] [*A publication*] (DLA) ... Darb & B Lim
DARC [*Description, Acquisition, Retrieval, and Conception*] **Pluridata System** [*Association for Research and Development of Chemical Informatics*] [*Information service or system*] (IID) ... DPDS
DARCOM [*Development and Readiness Command, Army*] **Announcement DistributionSystem** (RDA) ... DADS
DARCOM [*Development and Readiness Command, Army*] **Career/Control Inventory** (MCD) ... DCI
DARCOM [*Development and Readiness Command, Army*] **Logistics Assistance Activity** (MCD) ... DLAA
DARCOM [*Development and Readiness Command, Army*] **Modification Application Plan** (MCD) ... DMAP
DARCOM [*Development and Readiness Command, Army*] **Operations Center** (MCD) ... DOC
DARCOM [*Development and Readiness Command, Army*] **Readiness Evaluation System** (MCD) ... DRES
DARCOM [*Development and Readiness Command, Army*] **Technical Steering Committee** (MCD) ... DTSC
Darcy [*Physics*] ... D
D'Arcy-MacManus & Masius [*Advertising agency*] ... DM & M
Dardanelle & Russellville Railroad Co. [*AAR code*] ... DR
Dardanelle, AR [*AM radio station call letters*] ... KCAB
Dardanelle, AR [*FM radio station call letters*] (RBYB) ... KCJC
Dardanelle, AR [*FM radio station call letters*] ... KWKK
Dardanelle, AR [*AM radio station call letters*] ... KWXT
Darden Restaurants [*NYSE symbol*] (TTSB) ... DRI
Darden Restaurants, Inc. [*Associated Press*] (SAG) ... Darden
Darden Restaurants, Inc. [*NYSE symbol*] (SAG) ... DRI
Dare [*To Give*] [*Latin*] (MAE) ... d
Dare County Library, Manteo, NC [*Library symbol Library of Congress*] (LCLS) ... NcMan
Darien Airlines [*ICAO designator*] (AD) ... DG
Darien, GA [*FM radio station call letters*] ... WYNR
Darien Library [*UTLAS symbol*] ... DAR
Darien Library, Darien, CT [*Library symbol Library of Congress*] (LCLS) ... CtD
Darien Public Library, Darien, WI [*Library symbol Library of Congress*] (LCLS) ... WDar
Dark ... DK
Dark (VRA) ... dk
Dark ... DRK
Dark Agouti [*Rat strain*] ... DA
Dark Avenger Mutation Engine [*A polymorphic encryption engine*] (PCM) ... DAME
Dark Blend [*Philately*] ... DrBl
Dark Cove Public Library, Dark Cove, NF, Canada [*Library symbol Library of Congress*] (LCLS) ... CaNfDC
Dark Cove Public Library, Newfoundland [*Library symbol National Library of Canada*] (NLC) ... NFDC
Dark Field Illumination ... DFI
Dark Green ... DG
Dark Green Leafy Vegetable (DI) ... DGLF
Dark Ignition ... DI
Dark Line Defect (PDAA) ... DLD
Dark Mantle Deposit [*Lunar surface*] ... DMD
Dark Mantling Material [*Lunar surface*] ... DMM
Dark Matter [*Astrophysics*] ... DM
Dark on Light ... DL
Dark Red [*Philately*] ... DR
Dark Shadows [*Television program*] ... DS
Dark Shadows Fan Club (EA) ... DSFC
Dark Skies for Comet Halley [*Defunct*] (EA) ... DSCH
Dark Trace ... DT
Dark-Eyed Junco [*Ornithology*] ... DJ
Darkness [*or Darktime*] [*Endocrinology*] ... D
Darkroom [*Photography*] ... DR
Darling [*Correspondence*] (DSUE) ... DARL
Darling Downs Health Services Foundation [*Australia*] ... DDHSF
Darling Downs Institute Press (DGA) ... DDIP
Darling International [*NASDAQ symbol*] (TTSB) ... DARL
Darling International, Inc. [*NASDAQ symbol*] (SAG) ... DARL
Darling International, Inc. [*Associated Press*] (SAG) ... Darling
Darling. Practice of the Scotch Court of Session [*A publication*] (DLA) ... D Pr
Darling. Practice of the Scotch Court of Session [*A publication*] (DLA) ... Darl Pr Ct Sess
Darlington County Library, Darlington, SC [*OCLC symbol*] (OCLC) ... SCD
Darlington County Library, Darlington, SC [*Library symbol Library of Congress*] (LCLS) ... ScDa
Darlington International Raceway [*Auto racing*] ... DIR
Darlington Public Library, Darlington, IN [*Library symbol Library of Congress*] (LCLS) ... InDar
Darlington, SC [*FM radio station call letters*] ... WDAR-FM
Darlington, SC [*AM radio station call letters*] (RBYB) ... WDZS
Darmstadt [*Germany ICAO location identifier*] (ICLI) ... EDES
Darned Insulting, Rotten, Terrible Yarns [*Book title*] ... DIRTY
Darnell Army Hospital, Medical Library, Fort Hood, TX [*Library symbol Library of Congress*] (LCLS) ... TxFhH
DARPA [*Defense Advanced Research Projects Agency*] **Initiatives in Concurrent Engineering** [*DoD*] ... DICE
Darra-I-Soof [*Afghanistan*] [*ICAO location identifier*] (ICLI) ... OADF
Darrell Waltrip [*Race car driver*] ... DW
Darrow's Solution [*For antidiarrhea potassium therapy*] (DAVI) ... KNL
Darryl McDaniels [*A rap recording artist whose initials appear in the album title, "Run-D.M.C."*] ... DMC
Dart & Kraft, Inc. [*Toronto Stock Exchange symbol*] (SPSG) ... DKI
Dart & Kraft, Inc., Northbrook, IL [*Library symbol*] [*Library of Congress*] (LCLS) ... INbD
Dart Drug Corp. [*NASDAQ symbol*] (SAG) ... DART

Dart Drug Corp. [*Associated Press*] (SAG) ... DartGp
Dart Group Cl'A' [*NASDAQ symbol*] (TTSB) ... DARTA
Dart on Vendors and Purchasers [*A publication*] (DLA) ... Dart
Dart on Vendors and Purchasers [*A publication*] (DLA) ... Dart Vend
Darta [*France ICAO designator*] (FAAC) ... DRT
Dartford International Freight Terminal [*British*] (DS) ... DIFT
Dartmoor Pony Society of America (EA) ... DPSA
Dartmoor Prison [*Devon, England*] (AD) ... Moor
Dartmouth [*Municipal borough in England*] ... DARTM
Dartmouth (BARN) ... Drt
Dartmouth College [*Hanover, NH*] ... Dart Coll
Dartmouth College (GAGS) ... Dartmouth C
Dartmouth College, Business Administration and Engineering Library, Hanover, NH [*Library symbol Library of Congress*] (LCLS) ... NhD-BE
Dartmouth College Case [*A publication*] (DLA) ... Dart Col Ca
Dartmouth College, Dana Biomedical Library, Hanover, NH [*Library symbol Library of Congress*] (LCLS) ... NhD-D
Dartmouth College, Hanover, NH [*OCLC symbol*] (OCLC) ... DRB
Dartmouth College, Hanover, NH [*Library symbol Library of Congress*] (LCLS) ... NhD
Dartmouth College, Hood Museum, Hanover, NH [*Library symbol*] [*Library of Congress*] (LCLS) ... NhD-H
Dartmouth College Information System [*Library network*] (IT) ... DCIS
Dartmouth College, Kresge Physical Sciences Library, Hanover, NH [*Library symbol Library of Congress*] (LCLS) ... NhD-K
Dartmouth College, Paddock Music Library, Hanover, NH [*Library symbol*] [*Library of Congress*] (LCLS) ... NhD-P
Dartmouth Computing Services ... DCS
Dartmouth District School Board, Nova Scotia [*Library symbol National Library of Canada*] (NLC) ... NSDDS
Dartmouth General Hospital, Dartmouth, NS, Canada [*Library symbol Library of Congress*] (LCLS) ... CaNSDGH
Dartmouth General Hospital, Nova Scotia [*Library symbol National Library of Canada*] (NLC) ... NSDGH
Dartmouth Intensive Language Model (EDAC) ... DILM
Dartmouth, NS [*AM radio station call letters*] ... CFDR
Dartmouth, NS [*FM radio station call letters*] ... CFRQ
Dartmouth Public Library, Darmouth, MA [*Library symbol*] [*Library of Congress*] (LCLS) ... MDar 1
Dartmouth Regional Library, Dartmouth, Nova Scotia [*Library symbol National Library of Canada*] (NLC) ... NSD
Dartmouth Regional Library, Dartmouth, NS, Canada [*Library symbol Library of Congress*] (LCLS) ... CaNSD
Dartmouth Regional Vocational School, Dartmouth, Nova Scotia [*Library symbol National Library of Canada*] (NLC) ... NSDRV
Dartmouth Time-Sharing System [*Computer science*] ... DTSS
Darton College, Albany, GA [*Library symbol*] [*Library of Congress*] (LCLS) ... GAIDC
Darton, Longman & Todd [*Publisher*] [*British*] ... DLT
Daru [*Papua New Guinea*] [*Airport symbol*] (OAG) ... DAU
Daru [*Papua New Guinea*] [*Seismograph station code, US Geological Survey Closed*] (SEIS) ... DNG
Daru [*Sierra Leone*] [*Airport symbol*] (AD) ... DSL
Darvon Compound 63 [*Eli Lilly & Co.*] (DAVI) ... DC63
Darwaz [*Afghanistan*] [*ICAO location identifier*] (ICLI) ... OADZ
Darwell Public Library, Alberta [*Library symbol National Library of Canada*] (NLC) ... ADAR
Darwin [*Australia ICAO location identifier*] (ICLI) ... ADDA
Darwin [*Australia ICAO location identifier*] (ICLI) ... ADDD
Darwin [*Australia ICAO location identifier*] (ICLI) ... ADDN
Darwin [*Australia ICAO location identifier*] (ICLI) ... ADDX
Darwin [*Australia ICAO location identifier*] (ICLI) ... ADRM
Darwin [*California*] [*Seismograph station code, US Geological Survey*] (SEIS) ... DAC
Darwin [*Australia Seismograph station code, US Geological Survey Closed*] (SEIS) ... DAR
Darwin [*Australia Airport symbol*] (OAG) ... DRW
Darwin Bushwalking Club [*Australia*] ... DBC
Darwin, MN [*Location identifier FAA*] (FAAL) ... DWN
Darwin Office of Equal Opportunity [*Australia*] ... DOEO
Darwin Pensioners and Senior Citizens' Association [*Australia*] ... DPSCA
Darwin Port Authority [*Australia*] ... DPA
Darwin R. Barker Library Association, Fredonia, NY [*Library symbol Library of Congress*] (LCLS) ... NFred
Darwin Region Tourism Association [*Australia*] ... DRTA
Darwin Turf Club [*Australia*] ... DTC
Darwin's Criminal Law [*A publication*] (DLA) ... Darw Cr L
Das Akkadische Syllabar [*A publication*] (BJA) ... AS
Das Alexanderreich aus Prosopographischer Grundlage [*A publication*] (OCD) ... Alexanderreich
Das Alte Testament im Lichte des Alten Orients [*A publication*] (BJA) ... ATAO
Das Heilige Land (BJA) ... HL
Das Heilige Land in Vergangenheit und Gegenwart [*A publication*] (BJA) ... HLVG
Das Heisst [*That Is*] [*German*] ... DH
Das Island [*United Arab Emirates*] [*ICAO location identifier*] (ICLI) ... OMAS
Das Ist [*That Is*] [*German*] ... DI
Das Kleine Wunder [*The Little Wonder*] [*Initialism used as name of German automobile, manufactured by Auto Union*] ... DKW
Das Land der Bibel (BJA) ... LdB
Das Neue Israel [*A publication*] (BJA) ... NI
Das Neue Testament Deutsch. Neues Goettinger Bibelwerk [*A publication*] (BJA) ... NTD
Das Nordhebraeische Sagenbuch [*A publication*] (BJA) ... NHS
DASD [*Direct Access Storage Device*] **Dump Restore** [*Computer science*] (IBMDP) ... DDR
Dasent's Bankruptcy and Insolvency Reports [*1853-55*] [*England*] [*A publication*] (DLA) ... Das
Dasent's Bankruptcy and Insolvency Reports [*1853-55*] [*England*] [*A publication*] (DLA) ... Dasent
Dash Automatic Test Equipment ... DATE
Dash Lake Resources [*Vancouver Stock Exchange symbol*] ... DAL
Dash Pot [*Relay*] ... DP
Dashboard ... DBD
Dasheen Mosaic Virus [*Plant pathology*] ... DAMV
Dasher Owners of America (EA) ... DOA
Dasher Resources [*Vancouver Stock Exchange symbol*] ... DSR
Dashpot (IDOE) ... pot
Dashpot Cup Retention Nut [*Nuclear energy*] (NRCH) ... DCRN
Dasht-E-Naz [*Iran*] [*ICAO location identifier*] (ICLI) ... OINZ
Dashtyari [*Iran*] [*ICAO location identifier*] (ICLI) ... OIZD
Dassault Systemes ... DASTY
Dassault-Breguet [*Avions Marcel Dassault*] [*France ICAO aircraft manufacturer identifier*] (ICAO) ... DA
Dassel Elementary School, Media Center, Dassel, MN [*Library symbol*] [*Library of Congress*] (LCLS) ... MnDES
Dassel-Cokato Jr./Sr. High School, Cakoto, MN [*Library symbol*] [*Library of Congress*] (LCLS) ... MnCoD
Dassen Gold Resources Ltd. [*Vancouver Stock Exchange symbol*] ... DAS
Dassler's Edition, Kansas Reports [*A publication*] (DLA) ... Dass Ed
Dassler's Edition, Kansas Reports [*A publication*] (DLA) ... Dass Ed (Kan)
Dassler's Kansas Digest [*A publication*] (DLA) ... Dass Dig
Dassler's Kansas Statutes [*A publication*] (DLA) ... Dass Stat
Dastascope Corp. [*Associated Press*] (SAG) ... Datascpe
Dat, Dicat, Dedicat [*He Gives, Devotes, and Dedicates*] [*Latin*] ... DDD
Data ... D
Data (WDMC) ... d
Data Above Video System (NITA) ... DAVID
Data above Voice [*Telecommunications*] (TEL) ... DAV
Data Abstract Tape [*Computer science*] ... DAT
Data Acceptance Check [*Bureau of the Census*] (GFGA) ... DAC
Data Acceptance Tests ... DAT
Data Access and Dissemination System (AAGC) ... DADS
Data Access Arrangement [*Telecommunications Obsolete*] ... DAA
Data Access Language [*Apple, Inc.*] (PCM) ... DAL
Data Access Line ... DAL
Data Access Objects [*Microsoft Corp.*] (PCM) ... DAO
Data Access Protocol [*Telecommunications*] ... DAP
Data Access Register [*Computer science*] (MDG) ... DAR
Data Access Security ... DAS
Data Access Security System (IAA) ... DASS
Data Access System Language ... DASL
Data Accession List (NASA) ... DAL
Data Accountability System ... DAS
Data Accounting Flow Assessment (MHDB) ... DAFA
Data Accumulating and Reporting Sheet ... DARS
Data Accumulation and Distribution Units [*Navy*] (MCD) ... DADU
Data Accumulation and Transfer Sheet ... DATS
Data Acquisition (MDG) ... DA
Data Acquisition (IAA) ... DACQ
Data Acquisition ... DAQ
Data Acquisition and Analysis (NOAA) ... DACAN
Data Acquisition and Control (NASA) ... DAC
Data Acquisition and Control ... DAC
Data Acquisition and Control ... DAX
Data Acquisition and Control Buffer (MCD) ... DACB
Data Acquisition and Control Buffer Unit (NASA) ... DACBU
Data Acquisition and Control Executive [*Hewlett-Packard Co.*] ... DACE
Data Acquisition and Control Processor [*Computer science*] (NITA) ... DA/CP
Data Acquisition and Control Unit ... DACU
Data Acquisition and Data Management ... DADM
Data Acquisition and Decommutation Equipment ... DADE
Data Acquisition and Digital Signal Processing ... DADiSP
Data Acquisition and Display System [*or Subsystem*] ... DADS
Data Acquisition and Distribution ... DA & D
Data Acquisition and Information System [*Telecommunications*] (NITA) ... DAIS
Data Acquisition and Interpretation System ... DAISY
Data Acquisition and Monitoring Equipment [*Electronics*] ... DAME
Data Acquisition and Processing ... DA & P
Data Acquisition and Processing Program [*Later, DMSP*] [*Air Force*] ... DAPP
Data Acquisition and Processing System ... DAPS
Data Acquisition and Processing Unit [*Viking orbiter system*] [*NASA*] ... DAPU
Data Acquisition and Reduction Center (IAA) ... DARC
Data Acquisition and Reduction System ... DARS
Data Acquisition and Reporting System [*Data processing*] ... DARS
Data Acquisition and Reports Control [*Army*] (AABC) ... DARC
Data Acquisition and Transmission System (MCD) ... DATS
Data Acquisition and Visual Display System (NRCH) ... DAVDS
Data Acquisition Bus (NASA) ... DAB
Data Acquisition Camera ... DAC
Data Acquisition Center (KSC) ... DAQC
Data Acquisition Chassis (AAG) ... DAC
Data Acquisition Computer ... DAC
Data Acquisition, Control, and Simulation Centre [*University of Alberta*] [*Research center*] (RCD) ... DACS
Data Acquisition Control System (IEEE) ... DACS
Data Acquisition Controller ... DAC
Data Acquisition Division [*National Weather Service*] ... DATAC
Data Acquisition Equipment (KSC) ... DAE
Data Acquisition Facility [*of STADAN*] ... DAF
Data Acquisition Frequency Table (MCD) ... DAFT

Data Acquisition Language [*Computer science*] (CSR) .... DAL
Data Acquisition List (MCD) .... DAL
Data Acquisition Logging System .... DALS
Data Acquisition Multiprogramming System [*IBM Corp.*] [*Computer science*] .... DAMPS
Data Acquisition Package (IAA) .... DAP
Data Acquisition Package (IAA) .... DP
Data Acquisition Plan (MCD) .... DAP
Data Acquisition Recorder .... DAR
Data Acquisition Recording System .... DARS
Data Acquisition Requirements Document (KSC) .... DARD
Data Acquisition Signal Analysis [*Computer science*] (NITA) .... DASA
Data Acquisition Station .... DAS
Data Acquisition Statistical Recorder .... DASR
Data Acquisition Support Document (KSC) .... DASD
Data Acquisition System .... DAS
Data Acquisition System, Correlation Tracking and Ranging [*Air Force*] .... DASCOTAR
Data Acquisition System for Crash Avoidance Research [*NHTSA*] (TAG) .... DASCAR
Data Acquisition Test [*Later, DST*] .... DAT
Data Acquisition/Transmittal Sheet .... DA/TS
Data Acquisition Unit .... DAU
Data Adapter (MCD) .... DA
Data Adapter Unit .... DAU
Data Adaptive Evaluator and Monitor .... DAEMON
Data Adaptive Signal Estimator (MCD) .... DASE
Data Addition, Verification, and Editing [*Lotus 1-2-3*] .... DAVE
Data Address Line .... DAL
Data Addressed Memory [*Computer science*] .... DAM
Data Administration Center Equipment [*Telecommunications*] (TEL) .... DACE
Data Administration Management Association International (EA) .... DAMA
Data Administration Section (MCD) .... DAS
Data Administrative Services .... DAS
Data Administrator .... DA
Data Aids for Training, Operations, and Maintenance .... DATOM
Data Amplification Sheet (KSC) .... DAS
Data Analog Computer .... DATAC
Data Analysing Robot Youth Lifeform [*From the movie entitled "D.A.R.Y.L."*] .... DARYL
Data Analysis (AFM) .... DA
Data Analysis (IEEE) .... DATAN
Data Analysis and Display [*Computer science*] .... DADISP
Data Analysis and Processing (SAA) .... DA & P
Data Analysis and Processing Facility .... DAPF
Data Analysis and Reduction System .... DARES
Data Analysis and Statistical Experimental Language [*Computer science*] (MHDI) .... DASEL
Data Analysis and Technique Development Center .... DATDC
Data Analysis and Technique Development Center [*Alexandria, VA*] .... DATICO
Data Analysis Computer .... DAC
Data Analysis Console (AFM) .... DAC
Data Analysis Control (MCD) .... DAC
Data Analysis Database .... DADB
Data Analysis Facility .... DAF
Data Analysis Group [*Military*] .... DAG
Data Analysis Information Memorandum .... DAIM
Data Analysis Laboratory [*Temple University*] [*Research center*] .... DAL
Data Analysis [*Program*] **of Massachusetts Institute of Technology** .... DAMIT
Data Analysis of the Interpreter System (IAA) .... DAISY
Data Analysis Program .... DAP
Data Analysis Real-Time [*Southwest Research Institute*] .... DART
Data Analysis Recording Tape .... DART
Data Analysis, Recovery, and Training Systems (MCD) .... DARTS
Data Analysis Reduction Tape (SAA) .... DART
Data Analysis Software [*Telecommunications*] (TEL) .... DAS
Data Analysis Station (NASA) .... DAS
Data Analysis System [*Computer science*] (NITA) .... DAS
Data Analysis System .... DASY
Data and Analysis Center for Software [*Air Force Information service or system*] (IID) .... DACS
Data and Computation Center [*University of Wisconsin, Madison*] [*Research center*] (RCD) .... DAC
Data and Control Signal Interface (NASA) .... DCSI
Data and Dimensions Interface .... DDI
Data and Information Management System [*Computer science*] (ODBW) .... DIMS
Data and Information Resource Directory [*Navy*] (GFGA) .... DIRD
Data and Information System [*Marine science*] (OSRA) .... IGBP-DIS
Data and Information Systems Division [*IT & T*] .... DISD
Data and Instruction Management Machine (NITA) .... DIM
Data and Structure Definition Language [*Computer science*] (BUR) .... DASDL
Data and Telecommunications .... DATEC
Data Archive on Adolescent Pregnancy and Pregnancy Prevention [*Sociometrics Corp.*] [*Information service or system*] (IID) .... DAAPPP
Data Area Initializer and Verifier [*Telecommunications*] (TEL) .... DAIV
Data Arithmetic Unit [*Computer science*] .... DAU
Data Article Requirements (AAG) .... DAR
Data Assembler .... DA
Data Assembly Centers [*Marine science*] (OSRA) .... DAC
Data Association Message .... DAM
Data Authentication Algorithm (HGAA) .... DAA
Data Authentication Code [*Telecommunications*] (OSI) .... DAC
Data Automated Tower Simulator [*Army, Air Force*] .... DATS
Data Automatic Reduction Equipment (CET) .... DARE
Data Automation (AFM) .... DA
Data Automation Activity (AFM) .... DAA
Data Automation Design Office [*Air Force*] .... ADO
Data Automation Design Office [*Air Force*] (AFM) .... DADO
Data Automation Equipment .... DAE
Data Automation Officer [*Air Force*] .... DAO
Data Automation Panel (MCD) .... DAP
Data Automation Proposal (AFM) .... DAP
Data Automation Requirement .... DAR
Data Automation Research and Experimentation (CET) .... DARE
Data Automation System [*or Subsystem*] [*NASA*] .... DAS
Data Auxiliary Set [*Telecommunications*] (TEL) .... DAS
Data Available .... DA
Data Available (MCD) .... DAV
Data Available - Low (MCD) .... DAVL
Data Avionics Information System (MCD) .... DAIS
Data Bank .... D (Bank)
Data Bank .... DB
Data Bank (AABC) .... DBK
Data Bank .... DBNK
Data Bank Release Notice (NASA) .... DBRN
Data Base Administrator/Manager [*Army*] .... DBA/M
Data Base and Transaction Management System [*IBM Corp.*] .... DTMS
Data Base Configuration [*Computer science*] (ECII) .... DBC
Data Base Directory Service [*Formerly, Data Base User Service*] [*Knowledge Industry Publications, Inc. Database*] .... DBDS
Data Base File [*Military*] (AABC) .... DBF
Data Base Index [*SDC Information Services*] .... DBI
Data Base Management Element (SSD) .... DBME
Data Base Management Software Package (MHDI) .... XBASE
Data Base Supplier (NITA) .... DBS
Data Bibliography Card .... DBC
Data Block Reader [*Computer science*] (SAA) .... DBR
Data Broadcasting [*NASDAQ symbol*] (TTSB) .... DBCC
Data Broadcasting Corp. [*NASDAQ symbol*] (SAG) .... DBCC
Data Broadcasting Corp. [*Associated Press*] (SAG) .... DtBdcst
Data Buffer Module (IEEE) .... DBM
Data Buoy Cooperation Council [*Marine science*] (OSRA) .... DBCP
Data Buoy Office [*National Oceanic and Atmospheric Administration*] (DNAB) .... DBO
Data Buoy Project [*Navy Coast Guard*] (DNAB) .... DBP
Data Buoy Project Office [*Later, NDBC*] [*National Oceanic and Atmospheric Administration*] .... DBPO
Data Bus [*Computer science*] (MCD) .... DB
Data Bus Control [*Computer science*] (MCD) .... DBC
Data Bus Control Unit [*Computer science*] (KSC) .... DBCU
Data Bus Coupler [*Computer science*] (MCD) .... DBC
Data Bus Element [*Computer science*] .... DBE
Data Bus Enable [*Computer science*] .... DBE
Data Bus File Number (NASA) .... DBFN
Data Bus Generation and Maintenance Package [*Computer science*] (MCD) .... DBGMP
Data Bus Group [*Computer science*] (MCD) .... DBG
Data Bus In [*Computer science*] .... DBIN
Data Bus Interface Adapter [*Computer science*] (MCD) .... DBIA
Data Bus Interface Unit [*Computer science*] (MCD) .... DBIU
Data Bus Interface Unit-Launch [*Computer science*] (MCD) .... DBI
Data Bus Isolation Amplifier [*Computer science*] (MCD) .... DBIA
Data Bus Monitor [*Computer science*] .... DBM
Data Bus Network [*Computer science*] (MCD) .... DBN
Data Bus Wire [*Computer science*] (MCD) .... DBW
Data Call .... DC
Data Camera .... DC
Data Capture and Management System (IAA) .... DCMS
Data Capture Subsystem (MCD) .... DCS
Data Capture Unit (AIE) .... DCU
Data Carrier Detect [*or Detector*] [*Data communication signal*] [*Telecommunications*] (TEL) .... DCD
Data Carrier System [*Teltone Corp.*] [*Kirkland, WA*] (TSSD) .... DCS
Data Cartridge .... DC
Data Cassette (CDE) .... D/CAS
Data Cell [*Computer science*] .... DC
Data Center (EA) .... DC
Data Center for Atomic and Molecular Ionization Processes .... DCAMIP
Data Center Operations [*Social Security Administration*] .... DCO
Data Center Operations Management Plan [*Social Security Administration*] .... DCOMP
Data Change Notice (KSC) .... DCN
Data Change Proposal .... DCP
Data Channel [*Computer science*] .... DC
Data Channel [*Computer science*] .... DCH
Data Channel (PCM) .... D-channel
Data Channel Converter (NITA) .... DCC
Data Channel Filter [*Computer science*] .... DCF
Data Channel Module [*Computer science*] (NOAA) .... DCM
Data Check (BUR) .... DC
Data Checklist .... DCL
Data Chief .... DCH
Data Circuit Concentration .... DCC
Data Circuit-Terminating Equipment [*Computer science*] (BUR) .... DCE
Data Circuit-Terminating Equipment Ready [*Computer science*] (ACRL) .... DCER
Data Classification System (IAA) .... DCS
Data Classifier (IEEE) .... DC
Data Code .... DC
Data Code and Speed Conversion Subsystem [*Computer science*] (NITA) .... DCSCS

Data Collecting Device (IAA) ... DCD
Data Collection ... DATACOL
Data Collection (IAA) ... DATCOL
Data Collection ... DC
Data Collection Access Method ... DCAM
Data Collection, Analysis, and Corrective Action (CAAL) ... DCACA
Data Collection and Analysis System [*NASA*] ... DCAS
Data Collection and Data Relay [*Telecommunications*] (TEL) ... DCDR
Data Collection and Distribution Units [*Military*] (AABC) ... DCDU
Data Collection and Evaluation System (NVT) ... DCES
Data Collection and Location System [*Telecommunications*] ... DCLS
Data Collection and Platform Location System [*National Weather Service*] [*Weather satellite system*] (NOAA) ... DCPLS
Data Collection and Processing System (IAA) ... DACAPS
Data Collection and Reduction System ... DCRS
Data Collection Center [*Army Infantry Board*] (RDA) ... DCC
Data Collection Form [*Civil Defense*] ... DCF
Data Collection Module, High Speed ... DCMH
Data Collection Module, Low Speed ... DCML
Data Collection Operating System ... DCOS
Data Collection Order (MCD) ... DCO
Data Collection Plan (MCD) ... DCP
Data Collection Platform [*National Weather Service*] [*Weather satellite system*] ... DCP
Data Collection Platform Radio Sets [*National Weather Service*] [*Weather satellite system*] (NOAA) ... DCPRS
Data Collection/Relay (MCD) ... DC/R
Data Collection System [*or Subsystem*] [*Computer science*] ... DCS
Data Collection Unit ... DCU
Data Command Unit (MCD) ... DCU
Data Communication [*Computer science*] (BUR) ... DC
Data Communication Access Method (IAA) ... DCAM
Data Communication Channel (DOM) ... DCC
Data Communication Control Character (IEEE) ... DCCC
Data Communication Dealers Association (EA) ... DCDA
Data Communication Equipment ... DCE
Data Communication Input Buffer ... DCIB
Data Communication Interrogate (OA) ... DCI
Data Communication Network Architecture (BUR) ... DCNA
Data Communication Operating System ... DACOS
Data Communication Output Selector (KSC) ... DCOS
Data Communication Preprocessor ... DCPP
Data Communication Processing System ... DCPS
Data Communication Processor [*Computer science*] (BUR) ... DCP
Data Communication Read (OA) ... DCR
Data Communication Service (NITA) ... DATACOM
Data Communication Services [*Regie des Telegraphes et des Telephones*] [*Brussels, Belgium*] ... DCS
Data Communication System [*or Subsystem*] ... DCS
Data Communication Terminal System [*Computer science*] (DA) ... DCTS
Data Communication to Disk Control ... DC/DC
Data Communication Write [*Computer science*] (HGAA) ... DCW
Data Communications ... DATACOM
Data Communications Administrator ... DCA
Data Communications Channel ... DCC
Data Communications Control Unit (DEN) ... DCCU
Data Communications Controller [*Computer science*] ... DCC
Data Communications Corp. [*Information service or system*] (IID) ... DCC
Data Communications Corp. of Korea [*Seoul, South Korea*] [*Telecommunications service*] (TSSD) ... DACOM
Data Communications Equipment (DOM) ... DCE
Data Communications Equipment Monitoring and Switching (MCD) ... DACEMS
Data Communications Formatter (IAA) ... DCF
Data Communications Handler (DNAB) ... DCH
Data Communications, Inc. [*Information service or system*] (IID) ... Da-Com
Data Communications, Inc. ... DCI
Data Communications Interface ... DCI
Data Communications Interrogate (HGAA) ... DCI
Data Communications Multiplexer ... DCM
Data Communications Network [*Air Force*] (NITA) ... DATACOM
Data Communications Network [*Computer science*] (ACRL) ... DCN
Data Communications Terminal ... DCT
Data Communications Testing Branch [*Social Security Administration*] ... DCTB
Data Communications Unit ... DCU
Data Communications Utility [*Social Security Administration*] ... DCU
Data Compendium (MCD) ... DATCOM
Data Composition, Inc. [*Information service or system*] (IID) ... DCI
Data Compression Library (CDE) ... DCL
Data Compressor (MCD) ... DACOMP
Data Computation Complex [*NASA*] (NASA) ... DCC
Data Computation Subsystem Group ... DCSG
Data Concentrating Equipment [*Computer science*] (DGA) ... DCE
Data Concentrator [*Computer science*] (BUR) ... DC
Data Condition Code ... DCC
Data Conditioning System [*NASA*] ... DCS
Data Consistency Orbit ... DACO
Data Consultants of Europe (NITA) ... DCE
Data Control (AFM) ... DC
Data Control Block [*Computer science*] ... DCB
Data Control Bus [*Computer science*] (NITA) ... DCB
Data Control Characters (CMD) ... DCC
Data Control Equipment (IAA) ... DCE
Data Control Facility (MCD) ... DCF
Data Control Group (MCD) ... DCG
Data Control Language [*NCR Corp.*] ... DCL
Data Control List (IAA) ... DCL
Data Control Multiplex System ... DCMS
Data Control Office (AAG) ... DCO
Data Control Panel Submodule ... DCPS
Data Control Processor (IAA) ... DCP
Data Control Services (BUR) ... DCS
Data Control System [*Burroughs Corp.*] (AAG) ... DCS
Data Control Unit ... DCU
Data Control Unit-Receiver (MCD) ... DCU-R
Data Control Word (CMD) ... DCW
Data Controller ... DACON
Data Controller ... DC
Data Conversion [*Computer science*] (KSC) ... D/C
Data Conversion and Limit Check Submodule [*Computer science*] (IAA) ... DCLCS
Data Conversion Equipment [*Computer science*] ... DCE
Data Conversion File [*Bureau of the Census*] (GFGA) ... DCF
Data Conversion Machine (MCD) ... DCM
Data Conversion Receiver [*Computer science*] ... DCR
Data Conversion System [*Computer science*] ... DCS
Data Conversion Transmitter [*Computer science*] ... DCT
Data Converter-Control Indicator (DNAB) ... DCCI
Data Coordinator (MCD) ... DC
Data Coordinator and Retriever [*Computer science*] ... DCR
Data Correction [*IBM Corp.*] ... DACOR
Data Correction Amplifier ... DCA
Data Correction Indicator Panel (MUGU) ... DCIP
Data Correlation and Documentation System (IAA) ... DCD
Data Correlation and Transfer System ... DATACORTS
Data Correlation Control Unit ... DCCU
Data Correlation Facility ... DCF
Data Correlator ... DACOR
Data Count Field [*Computer science*] (ACRL) ... DCF
Data Count Printout [*Computer science*] ... DACPO
Data Counter [*Computer science*] (IAA) ... DC
Data Country Code [*Telecommunications*] (OSI) ... DCC
Data Courier, Inc. (IID) ... DCI
Data Debugging Tool ... DDT
Data Definition [*Computer science*] (BUR) ... DD
Data Definition Control System ... DDCS
Data Definition Language [*NCR Corp.*] ... DDL
Data Definition Name (ECII) ... DDNAME
Data Definition Statement (NITA) ... DD
Data Demand ... DD
Data Demand Module (IEEE) ... DDM
Data Depository (MCD) ... DD
Data Description (MCD) ... DD
Data Description Facility (PDAA) ... DDF
Data Description Language [*Computer science*] ... DAD
Data Description Language [*Computer science*] ... DDL
Data Description Language Committee [*CODASYL*] ... DDLC
Data Description Language Computer (IAA) ... DDLC
Data Description Table (BUR) ... DDT
Data Development, Inc. [*Database producer*] (IID) ... DDI
Data Dialog ... DDL
Data Dialog System (MCD) ... DDS
Data Dictionary [*Computer science*] ... DADIC
Data Dictionary [*Computer science*] ... DD
Data Dictionary/Directory [*Computer science*] ... DD/D
Data Dictionary/Directory System [*Computer science*] ... DD/DS
Data Dictionary File [*Computer science*] (PCM) ... DDF
Data Dictionary System [*Computer science*] ... DDS
Data Differential Analyzer (OA) ... DDA
Data Diffusion Machine [*Computer science*] ... DDM
Data Digital Audio Tape (CDE) ... DATA/DAT
Data Dimensions [*NASDAQ symbol*] (TTSB) ... DDIM
Data Dimensions, Inc. [*NASDAQ symbol*] (SAG) ... DDIM
Data Dimensions, Inc. [*Associated Press*] (SAG) ... DtaDimn
Data Directed Programming System [*British*] (DIT) ... DDPS
Data Direction Register [*Microcomputer*] ... DDR
Data Directory [*Computer science*] (IAA) ... DD
Data Discrepancy Report (MCD) ... DDR
Data Display (NASA) ... DD
Data Display ... DDIS
Data Display Board ... DDB
Data Display Buffer ... DDB
Data Display Central ... DDC
Data Display Controller ... DDC
Data Display Generator ... DDG
Data Display Indicator ... DDI
Data Display Module (MCD) ... DDM
Data Display Monitoring (MCD) ... DDM
Data Display Parameter ... DDP
Data Display Set (MCD) ... DDS
Data Display System [*or Subsystem*] ... DDS
Data Display System ... DDS
Data Display Unit (NASA) ... DDU
Data Dissemination System [*European Space Agency - Information Retrieval Service*] [*Rome, Italy*] ... DDS
Data Distribution Center ... DDC
Data Distribution List ... DDL
Data Distribution Panel (KSC) ... DDP
Data Distribution Point [*NATO*] (NATG) ... DDP
Data Distribution System [*or Subsystem*] ... DDS
Data Division [*Computer science*] ... DD

Data, Document, and Records Management (SSD)	DDRM
Data Documentation Costs	DDC
Data Documents [*NASDAQ symbol*] (TTSB)	DDII
Data Documents, Inc. [*NASDAQ symbol*] (SAG)	DDII
Data Documents, Inc. [*Associated Press*] (SAG)	DtaDoc
Data Down Link [*Computer science*] (MCD)	DDL
Data Drawing and Parts List	DDPL
Data Drawing List	DDL
Data Element [*Computer science*]	DE
Data Element Definition [*DoD*]	DED
Data Element Description List [*Computer science*]	DEDL
Data Element Descriptor [*Computer science*] (IAA)	DED
Data Element Dictionary [*A publication Army*]	DED
Data Element Dictionary/Directory [*A publication*]	DED/D
Data Element Dictionary Number	DE-NUM
Data Element Management Accounting and Reporting	DELMAR
Data Element Management Accounting and Reporting (MCD)	DEMAR
Data Element Number (MCD)	DEN
Data Elements Standardization Requirements (MCD)	DES
Data Encoder	DE
Data Encoder Unit	DEU
Data Encoder Unit Transmitter	DEUT
Data Encryption Algorithm	DEA
Data Encryption Equipment [*Telecommunications*] (OSI)	DEE
Data Encryption Standard [*National Institute of Standards and Technology*]	DES
Data Encryption Unit	DEU
Data Engineering Section	DES
Data Entry	DE
Data Entry Aboard Ship [*Navy*] (NVT)	DEAS
Data Entry and Display Assembly [*Apollo*] [*NASA*]	DEDA
Data Entry and Display Panel (MCD)	DEDP
Data Entry and Display Subsystem	DEDS
Data Entry Application Language	DEAL
Data Entry Control System	DECS
Data Entry Facility	DEF
Data Entry Keyboard [*Computer science*] (MCD)	DEK
Data Entry Language	DEL
Data Entry Management Association (EA)	DEMA
Data Entry Mode (MCD)	DEM
Data Entry Panel (MCD)	DEP
Data Entry Reporting System	DERS
Data Entry/Separation (MCD)	DE/S
Data Entry System	DES
Data Entry System Controller	DESC
Data Entry Unit	DEU
Data Event Block [*Computer science*] (EECA)	DEB
Data Event Control Block [*Computer science*] (BUR)	DECB
Data Exception Error Protection	DEEP
Data Exchange (IAA)	DATEX
Data Exchange	DAX
Data Exchange	DEX
Data Exchange Agreement	DEA
Data Exchange Annex (AABC)	DEA
Data Exchange Auxiliary Console (CAAL)	DEAC
Data Exchange Control	DXC
Data Exchange Control Unit (NASA)	DECU
Data Exchange File [*Computer science*]	DXF
Data Exchange Format (PCM)	DXF
Data Exchange Interface [*Computer science*]	DXI
Data Exchange Optimization Study [*DoD*] (MCD)	DEOS
Data Exchange Program	DEP
Data Exchange Service (IAA)	DATE
Data Exchange System (NASA)	DES
Data Exchange System [*Texas Instruments, Inc.*]	DXS
Data Exchange System/Operating System (NITA)	DXS/OS
Data Exchange System Statement Translator [*Texas Instruments, Inc.*]	DXSST
Data Exchange System/Transaction Language (NITA)	DXS/TL
Data Exchange Test Facility (DA)	DETF
Data Exchange Unit	DEU
Data Extension Frame [*Computer science*] (NITA)	DEF
Data Extent Block (MCD)	DEB
Data Extraction (CAAL)	DX
Data Facility Data Set Services	DFDSS
Data Facility Extended	DFE
Data Facility Hierarchical Storage Manager [*IBM Corp.*] (NITA)	DFHSM
Data Facility Product	DFP
Data Field [*Computer science*]	DF
Data File [*Computer science*]	DAT
Data File [*Computer science*]	DTA
Data File Generator (MCD)	DATAGEN
Data File/Media Management System	DFMMS
Data File Number	DFN
Data File Utility [*Computer science*] (IBMDP)	DFU
Data Flag Branch [*Computer science*] (NITA)	DFB
Data Flag Branch Manager [*Computer science*] (NITA)	DFBM
Data Flag Branch Register [*Computer science*] (NITA)	DFBR
Data Flow Control [*Computer science Telecommunications*] (IBMDP)	DFC
Data Flow Diagram	DFD
Data Flow Engineer (MCD)	DFE
Data Flow Graph	DFG
Data Flow Programming Language	DFPL
Data Flow Signal Processor (MCD)	DFSP
Data Folder	DF
Data for Allotments Transmitted Electronically (MCD)	DATE

Data for Development International Association [*See also DD*] [*Marseille, France*] (EAIO)	DFD
Data Format Converter	DFC
Data from Aeromechanics' Test and Analytics-Management and Analysis Package (RDA)	DATAMAP
Data Function Information Book	DFIB
Data Functional Diagram (MCD)	DFD
Data Gathering Monitoring [*System*]	DGM
Data Gathering System (MCD)	DGS
Data General [*NYSE symbol*] (TTSB)	DGN
Data General/Communications System [*Data General Corp.*] (NITA)	DG/CS
Data General Corp. [*Associated Press*] (SAG)	DataGn
Data General Corp. [*Computer manufacturer*]	DG
Data General Corp. [*Computer manufacturer*]	DGC
Data General Corp. [*NYSE symbol*] (SPSG)	DGN
Data General Corp., Westboro, MA [*OCLC symbol*] (OCLC)	DAT
Data General/Data Base Management System [*Data General Corp.*] (NITA)	DG/DBMS
Data General/Transaction Processing Management System [*Data General Corp.*] (NITA)	DG/TPMS
Data General UNIX (CDE)	DG/UX
Data General's Standard Applications and Graphics Environment [*Engineering software*]	DG/STAGE
Data General's System Programming Language	DG/L
Data Generating Program	DGP
Data Generation	DGEN
Data Generator (MCD)	DG
Data Graphics Corp.	DGC
Data Ground Station [*NASA*] (KSC)	DGS
Data groupie [*Person who likes to spend time in the company of programmers and data processing professionals.*] (CDE)	droupie
Data Handbook (MCD)	DH
Data Handling and Control Unit	DHCU
Data Handling and Display Subsystem	DHDS
Data Handling Center (KSC)	DHC
Data Handling Equipment	DHE
Data Handling Function (SSD)	DHF
Data Handling Recording System [*Computer science*] (PDAA)	DHRS
Data Handling Subsystem (NATG)	DHSS
Data Handling System	DHS
Data Hardware Project Engineer [*NASA*]	DHPE
Data I/O [*NASDAQ symbol*] (TTSB)	DAIO
Data I/O Corp. [*NASDAQ symbol*] (NQ)	DAIO
Data Identification [*or Identifier*]	DID
Data Identification Number (AFM)	DIN
Data Identification Table (MCD)	DIT
Data, Images, and Text [*European Patent Office*]	DATIMTEX
Data Immediate Access Diagram	DIAD
Data in Associative Storage [*Computer science*] (MHDB)	DATAS
Data in Real Time	DIRT
Data in Voice [*Telecommunications*]	DIV
Data Independent Analysis Library (CAAL)	DIAL
Data Independent Architecture Model	DIAM
Data Index for Software Configuration (MCD)	DISC
Data Index for Software Control (MCD)	DISC
Data Information Access Link [*Computer science*]	DIAL
Data Information Accession List (MCD)	DIAL
Data Information and Manufacturing System (PDAA)	DIMS
Data, Information, and System Control	DISC
Data Information Requirements System [*Military*]	DIRS
Data Information System for Management Control [*Military*]	DISC
Data Information Test Material Checkout	DITMCO
Data Information Unit [*Marine science*] (OSRA)	DIU
Data In-Line [*Computer science*] (IAA)	DIL
Data Input [*Computer science*] (IEEE)	DI
Data Input Bus [*Computer science*] (MDG)	DIB
Data Input Check (HGAA)	DIC
Data Input Clerk [*Computer science*]	DIC
Data Input Consoles [*Computer science*] (NVT)	DIC
Data Input/Data Output [*Computer science*]	DI/DO
Data Input Display [*Computer science*]	DID
Data Input Display Console [*Computer science*]	DIDC
Data Input Ensemble (NITA)	DIEN
Data Input/Output [*Computer science*]	DIO
Data Input Processor [*Computer science*]	DIP
Data Input Register [*Computer science*]	DIR
Data Input Strobe (NITA)	DIST
Data Input Subsystem [*Computer science*] (SAA)	DISS
Data Input Supervisor [*Computer science*] (IAA)	DIS
Data Input System [*Computer science*]	DIS
Data Input Voice Output Telephone System	DIVOTS
Data Input-Voice Answerback [*Telecommunications*] (EECA)	DIVA
Data Inquiry Terminal	DIT
Data Inserter	DATIN
Data Insertion Converter	DIC
Data Inspection Station	DIS
Data Integrator (MCD)	DI
Data Interchange	DI
Data Interchange Code (IAA)	DIC
Data Interchange Format	DIF
Data Interchange in the Shipping Industry	DISH
Data Interchange Standards Association	DISA
Data Interchange Standards Association (AAGC)	DISA
Data Interchange Utility (IAA)	DIU
Data Interface	DI

Data Interface Facility (SSD) ... DIF
Data Interface Unit ... DIU
Data Interfile Transfer, Testing, and Operations Utility [*IBM program product*] ... DITTO
Data Interpretation and Analysis Center [*Canadian Navy*] ... DIAC
Data Interpretation Module ... DIM
Data Interpretation System (BTTJ) ... DIS
Data Inventory Control System (MCD) ... DAICS
Data Inventory Control System ... DATICS
Data I-O [*Associated Press*] (SAG) ... Data IO
Data I-O Corp. [*Associated Press*] (SAG) ... Dta IO
Data Item ... DI
Data Item Catalog (IAA) ... DIC
Data Item Category ... DIC
Data Item Description ... DID
Data Item Description System (MCD) ... DIDS
Data Item Requirement ... DIR
Data Key Idle ... DKI
Data Language ... DL
Data Language Version 1 [*Computer science*] ... DL/1
Data Length (IAA) ... DL
Data Librarian System (PDAA) ... DLS
Data Line Flight Direction Unit (MCD) ... DLFDU
Data Line Monitor ... DLM
Data Line Terminal (IAA) ... DLT
Data Line Terminal Module [*Military*] (RDA) ... DLTM
Data Line Translator (IAA) ... DLT
Data Line Unit ... DLU
Data Link ... DL
Data Link (KSC) ... DLK
Data Link (FAAC) ... DOLLY
Data Link Acquisition (MCD) ... DLA
Data Link Adapter ... DLA
Data Link Address ... DLA
Data Link and Transponder Analysis System (DA) ... DATAS
Data Link Connection Identifier [*Computer science*] ... DLCI
Data Link Connector [*Electronics*] ... DLC
Data Link Control [*Computer science*] (BUR) ... DLC
Data Link Control Chip [*Computer science*] (HGAA) ... DLCC
Data Link Control Field [*Computer science*] ... DLCF
Data Link Control Panel [*Computer science*] (MCD) ... DLCP
Data Link Controller [*Computer science*] (NITA) ... DALK
Data Link Controller Series [*or Serial*] [*Electronics*] ... DLCS
Data Link Controller-Processor [*Automotive engineering Electronics*] ... DLCP
Data Link Decoder (MCD) ... DLD
Data Link Equipment ... DLE
Data Link Escape [*Computer science*] (NITA) ... DLE
Data Link Escape Character [*Keyboard*] (CMD) ... DLE
Data Link Escape Character [*Computer science*] (EECA) ... DLEC
Data Link Hardware (IAA) ... DLH
Data Link Layer Header [*Telecommunications*] (ACRL) ... DLH
Data Link Layer Trailer [*Telecommunications*] (ACRL) ... DLT
Data Link Occupied [*Computer science*] (HGAA) ... DLO
Data Link Pre-Processor [*Ferranti Ltd.*] ... DLPP
Data Link Processor [*Burroughs Corp.*] [*Computer science*] (BUR) ... DLP
Data Link Processor Unit (DA) ... DLPU
Data Link Programs (MCD) ... DLP
Data Link Receiver [*Computer science*] (MCD) ... DLR
Data Link Reference Point (NVT) ... DLRP
Data Link Service Access Point (TNIG) ... DLSAP
Data Link Set ... DLS
Data Link Simulator ... DLS
Data Link Software (IAA) ... DLS
Data Link Splitter (DA) ... DLS
Data Link Summary Message (MCD) ... DLSM
Data Link Support ... DLS
Data Link Switching [*Computer science*] (PCM) ... DLS
Data Link Switching [*IBM Co.*] (ACRL) ... DLSw
Data Link Terminal ... DLT
Data Link Terminal Repeater (NASA) ... DLTR
Data Link Test Message ... DLTM
Data Link Test Set ... DALTS
Data Link Translator ... DLT
Data Link Transmission Repeater (NASA) ... DLTR
Data Link Vulnerability Analysis [*DoD*] (RDA) ... DVAL
Data List [*DoD*] ... DL
Data List File ... DLF
Data Listing Programs (IEEE) ... DLP
Data Logging and Transmission System (MCD) ... DALATS
Data Logging System ... DLS
Data Logic Canada, Library Education Services, Ottawa, ON, Canada [*Library symbol Library of Congress*] (LCLS) ... CaOODLC
Data Loop Transceiver [*Computer science*] ... DLT
Data Lower Half Byte (IAA) ... DLH
Data Maintenance Diagnostic Program ... DMDP
Data Management (KSC) ... DM
Data Management (MSA) ... DMGT
Data Management Agent (MCD) ... DMA
Data Management Analysis ... DMA
Data Management and Operations (SSD) ... DM & O
Data Management and Research Liaison Staff [*Environmental Protection Agency*] (GFGA) ... DMRLS
Data Management and Retrieval System ... DMRS
Data Management and User Services System [*National Oceanic and Atmospheric Administration*] (GFGA) ... DAMUS
Data Management Block ... DMB
Data Management Center (CAAL) ... DMC
Data Management Channel ... DMC
Data Management Computer (KSC) ... DMC
Data Management Facility ... DMF
Data Management Group (MCD) ... DMG
Data Management Information System [*DoD*] ... DMIS
Data Management Language [*Digital Equipment Corp.*] ... DML
Data Management Module [*Aviation*] ... DMM
Data Management Office [*or Officer*] [*Air Force*] (AFM) ... DMO
Data Management Operating System ... DMOS
Data Management Plan [*Jet Propulsion Laboratory, NASA*] ... DMP
Data Management Policy Office [*Army*] ... DMPO
Data Management Program ... DMP
Data Management Routine ... DMR
Data Management Service (IEEE) ... DMS
Data Management Summary Processor (KSC) ... DMSP
Data Management System [*Computer science*] (MCD) ... DATAMAN
Data Management System [*Computer science*] ... DMS
Data Management System/Computer Subsystem [*Computer science*] ... DMS/CS
Data Management System Problem Specification Model [*Air Force*] ... DMSPSM
Data Management System Simulator [*NASA*] (NASA) ... DMSS
Data Management Unit [*Computer science*] ... DMU
Data Management Utility System ... DMUS
Data Manager ... DM
Data Manager (KSC) ... DMAN
Data Manipulation Language [*Digital Equipment Corp.*] [*Computer science*] ... DML
Data Manipulation Mode ... DMM
Data Master ... DM
Data Material Required, Increasing Urgency [*Navy*] (NG) ... DMRI
Data Measurement Corp. [*NASDAQ symbol*] (NQ) ... DMCB
Data Measurement Corp. [*Associated Press*] (SAG) ... DtaMea
Data Measurement Unit (SAA) ... DMU
Data Measuring System ... DMS
Data Memory ... DM
Data Memory Access ... DMA
Data Microfilming Corp., Whittier, CA [*Library symbol Library of Congress*] (LCLS) ... DmC
Data Migration Facility [*Computer science*] ... DMF
Data Model Diagramer [*Computer science*] ... DMD
Data Model Normalizer [*Computer science*] ... DMN
Data Monitoring System ... DMS
Data Moving System (PDAA) ... DAMOS
Data Multiplex [*Computer*] ... DMX
Data Multiplex Subsystem [*Computer science*] ... DMSS
Data Multiplex System [*Computer science*] ... DMS
Data Multiplexer (NITA) ... DMX
Data Multiplexing Network [*FAA*] (TAG) ... DMN
Data Name ... DN
Data Name Card ... DNC
Data Net (MCD) ... DN
Data Net Control Unit (NVT) ... DNCU
Data Net Identification Code (NITA) ... DNIC
Data Network (CET) ... DATANET
Data Network Access Method ... DNAM
Data Network Architecture (IAA) ... DNA
Data Network Control Centre (NITA) ... DNCC
Data Network Identification Code [*Telecommunications*] (TEL) ... DNIC
Data Network Modified Emulator Program [*Telecommunications*] (TEL) ... DMEP
Data Network on Environmentally Significant Chemicals (DCTA) ... DESCNET
Data Network Service Centre (NITA) ... DNSC
Data Number ... DN
Data Observing Testing Console ... DOTC
Data of Establishment (WDAA) ... D/E
Data on Occupations Retrieval System [*Great Britain Manpower Services Commission*] [*Information service or system*] (CRD) ... DOORS
Data on Vocational Education [*Department of Education*] (GFGA) ... DOVE
Data Operating Control ... DOC
Data Operation Center (IAA) ... DOC
Data Operational Requirements Board [*NATO Military Committee*] (NATG) ... DATOR
Data, Operations, and Control ... DOC
Data Optimizing Computer ... DOC
Data Organization Service (IAA) ... DOS
Data Output [*Computer science*] (IEEE) ... DO
Data Output Bus [*Computer science*] ... DOB
Data Output Channel (MSA) ... DOC
Data Output Multiplexer [*Computer science*] (KSC) ... DOM
Data Output Register [*Computer science*] ... DOR
Data Output Strobe (NITA) ... DOST
Data over Circuit-Switched Voice [*Computer science*] (PCM) ... DOCSV
Data over Voice [*Telecommunications*] (TEL) ... DOV
Data over Voice Multiplexer [*Telecommunications*] (ACRL) ... DVM
Data Package (SSD) ... DP
Data Package Set (CAAL) ... DPS
Data Packet (Subsystem) [*Telecommunications*] (TEL) ... DP(S)
Data Path ... DP
Data Path Bus ... DPB
Data Path Control [*Computer science*] (IAA) ... DPC
Data Path Unit [*Computer science*] ... DPU
Data [*or Digital*] **Phone Line Formatter** ... DPLF
Data Plotting Board ... DPB
Data Pointer [*Computer memory*] ... DP
Data Pointer [*Computer memory*] (BYTE) ... DPTR
Data Preparation and Maintenance (CAAL) ... DPM

Data Present Signal	DPS
Data Presentation System (IAA)	DPS
Data Printer	DP
Data Printout Program	DROP
Data Process Work Request (AAG)	DPWR
Data Processing	DP
Data Processing Activities	DPA
Data Processing Agency	DPA
Data Processing Algorithm	DPA
Data Processing, Analysis, and Archiving (NOAA)	DPAA
Data Processing and Control (Unit) (CAAL)	DPAC
Data Processing and Information Retrieval (DIT)	DPIR
Data Processing and Information Science Contents [BRS Information Technologies] [Online database Discontinued]	DISC
Data Processing and/or Computer Programming Programs [Association of Independent Colleges and Schools specialization code]	DP
Data Processing and Services Subsystem (NOAA)	DPSS
Data Processing and Software (NASA)	DP & S
Data Processing and Software	DP & S
Data Processing and Software (NASA)	DPS
Data Processing and Software Subsystem (NASA)	DP & SS
Data Processing Area	DPA
Data Processing Assembly (MCD)	DPA
Data Processing Automatic Equipment	DPAE
Data Processing Automatic Publication Service	DAPS
Data Processing Automatic Record Standardization	DPARS
Data Processing Branch (IEEE)	DPB
Data Processing Center	DPC
Data Processing Central	DPC
Data Processing Computer (CAAL)	DPC
Data Processing Control (AFM)	DPC
Data Processing Control Area [Space Flight Operations Facility, NASA]	DPCA
Data Processing Control Center [or Console] [Space Flight Operations Facility, NASA]	DPCC
Data Processing Customer Engineering (ADA)	DPCE
Data Processing Department	DPD
Data Processing Detachment	DPD
Data Processing Directive (ODBW)	DPD
Data Processing Division [IBM Corp.]	DPD
Data Processing Equipment	DPE
Data Processing Facility	DPF
Data Processing Federation [France] (NITA)	DPF
Data Processing Field Office (MCD)	DPFO
Data Processing, Financial and General (IAA)	DPFAG
Data Processing Group [Army] (AABC)	DPG
Data Processing Group [Air Force] (AFM)	DPGp
Data Processing Installation	DPI
Data Processing Language	DPL
Data Processing Machine (AAG)	DPM
[Society of] Data Processing Machine Operators and Programmers (NITA)	DPMOAP
Data Processing Management Association (EA)	DPMA
Data Processing Manager	DPM
Data Processing Network [Trademark of Northern Telecom Ltd.] (IAA)	DPN
Data Processing Officer (AIE)	DPO
Data Processing Operation	DPO
Data Processing Products Contract	DPPC
Data Processing Programming Support Office [Military]	DPPSO
Data Processing Project Engineer	DPPE
Data Processing Request	DPR
Data Processing Requirements Summary	DPRS
Data Processing Resources [NASDAQ symbol] (TTSB)	DPRC
Data Processing Resources Corp. [NASDAQ symbol] (SAG)	DPRC
Data Processing Resurces Corp. [Associated Press] (SAG)	DtaProc
Data Processing Service (IAA)	DPS
Data Processing Service Center	DPSC
Data Processing Service Center, Pacific (DNAB)	DPSCPAC
Data Processing Service Request (NVT)	DPSR
Data Processing Services Co. [Information service or system] (IID)	DPS
Data Processing Software System (NASA)	DPS
Data Processing Standards [NASA] (KSC)	DPS
Data Processing Subsystem	DPSS
Data Processing Supplies Association [Later, IOSA] (MCD)	DPSA
Data Processing Switching System [Space Flight Operations Facility, NASA]	DPSS
Data Processing System [or Subsystem]	DPS
Data Processing System Requirements	DPSR
Data Processing System Simulator (IEEE)	DPSS
Data Processing Systems Office [Picatinny Arsenal, NJ]	DPSO
Data Processing Technician [Navy rating]	DP
Data Processing Technician, First Class [Navy rating]	DP1
Data Processing Technician, Second Class [Navy rating]	DP2
Data Processing Technician, Third Class [Navy rating]	DP3
Data Processing Unit	DPU
Data Processor and Computer Test Equipment	DPCTE
Data Procurement Document (SSD)	DPD
Data Project Directive (AFM)	DPD
Data Project Management System (IEEE)	DPMS
Data Project Plan (AFIT)	DPP
Data Protection Act [1980's] [British]	DP
Data Protection Act [British] (NITA)	DPA
Data Protection Agency [British]	DPA
Data Protection Register (NITA)	DPR
Data Protection Registrar [British]	DPR

Data Publishing International [Netherlands] [Information service or system] (IID)	DPI
Data Pulse (IAA)	DP
Data Quality Control	DQC
Data Quality Control Monitor	DQCM
Data Quality Monitors (MDG)	DQM
Data Quality Objective	DQO
Data Race [NASDAQ symbol] (TTSB)	RACE
Data Radio Channel	DARC
Data Rate [Telecommunications] (TEL)	DR
Data Rate Changer	DRC
Data Rate Indicator (NASA)	DRI
Data Rate Selector	DRS
Data Reaction System (AAG)	DRS
Data Readout [Navy] (NVT)	DRO
Data Ready Queue [IBM Corp.] (IBMDP)	DRQ
Data Receiver [or Recorder]	DR
Data Receiving Station (KSC)	DRS
Data Reception Process [Telecommunications] (TEL)	DRP
Data Reception, Recording, and Transmission (MCD)	DRRT
Data Reckoning Tracer (MSA)	DRT
Data Record Number (MCD)	DRN
Data Recorder (MCD)	DR
Data Recorder/Reproducer (MCD)	DRR
Data Recording (CET)	DATREC
Data Recording (MSA)	DRCDG
Data Recording and Processing Equipment	DRAPE
Data Recording Camera	DRC
Data Recording Control (NITA)	DRC
Data Recording Controller [Computer science] (BUR)	DRC
Data Recording Device [Computer science] (BUR)	DRD
Data Recording Equipment (OA)	DRE
Data Recording Instrument (IAA)	DRI
Data Recording Interface (MCD)	DRI
Data Recording Set	DRS
Data Recording System (MUGU)	DRS
Data Recording System Analyst (MUGU)	DRSA
Data Records Management (MCD)	DRM
Data Recovery [Computer science] (ECII)	DR
Data Recovery Tester [Computer science] (HGAA)	DRT
Data Recovery Vehicle	DRV
Data Reduction (KSC)	DR
Data Reduction (MSA)	DRDCN
Data Reduction (MCD)	DRON
Data Reduction Analysis Tape	DRAT
Data Reduction and Analysis	DR & A
Data Reduction and Analysis System	DRANS
Data Reduction and Computing Group [Range Commanders Council] [NASA]	DR-CG
Data Reduction and Computing Working Group [Range Commanders Council] [NASA]	DR-CWG
Data Reduction and Processing Facility (IAA)	DRAPF
Data Reduction Center [or Complex]	DRC
Data Reduction Compiler [or Computer] (MCD)	DRC
Data Reduction Equipment	DRE
Data Reduction Input Program [Computer science]	DRIP
Data Reduction Interpreter	DRI
Data Reduction Laboratory	DRL
Data Reduction Procedure [or Program]	DRP
Data Reduction Software (IAA)	DRS
Data Reduction System [Computer science]	DRS
Data Reduction Translator	DART
Data Reduction Working Group (SAA)	DRWG
Data Redundancy Reduction [or Removal] (KSC)	DRR
Data Reference [Environment Canada] [Information service or system Information service or system] (CRD)	D-REF
Data Reference Number	DRN
Data Reference Unit	DRU
Data Reformatter Assembly	DRA
Data Register	DR
Data Regulations (KSC)	DREG
Data Relay Satellite [NASA]	DRS
Data Relay Satellite System [NASA]	DRSS
Data Relay Station (NASA)	DRS
Data Relay System (CAAL)	DRS
Data Release Notice (DNAB)	DRN
Data Reorganization Utility [Computer science]	DRU
Data Reorganizer (IAA)	DR
Data Report	DR
Data Reporting and Accounting (AFM)	DR & A
Data Reporting Form	DRF
Data Reporting Guideline [Environmental Protection Agency]	DRG
Data Repository for Addressing Combat Unified Logistics Analysis	DRACULA
Data Request	DR
Data Request	DRQ
Data Request Form [NASA] (NASA)	DRF
Data Request Keyboard	DRK
Data Requirement Description [NASA] (MCD)	DRD
Data Requirement Form (KSC)	DRF
Data Requirement List (KSC)	DRL
Data Requirements [NASA]	DR
Data Requirements and Analysis (MCD)	DR & A
Data Requirements and Distribution List [Navy]	DRDL
Data Requirements/Change Request (MCD)	DR/CR
Data Requirements Document [NASA] (NASA)	DRD

Data Requirements Justification [*Military*] .... DRJ
Data Requirements Language .... DRL
Data Requirements List Item (SSD) .... DRLI
Data Requirements List/Schedule .... DRL/S
Data Requirements Review Board [*DoD*] .... DRRB
Data Requirements Specification (KSC) .... DRS
Data Research Associates [*NASDAQ symbol*] (TTSB) .... DRAI
Data Research Associates, Inc. [*Information service or system*] (IID) .... DRA
Data Research Associates, Inc. [*NASDAQ symbol*] (SAG) .... DRAI
Data Research Associates, Inc. [*Associated Press*] (SAG) .... DtaRsh
Data Resource Administrator .... DRA
Data Resource Center [*Bureau of the Census*] (GFGA) .... DRC
Data Resource Management (NITA) .... DRM
Data Resources Directory Publications Subsystem [*Department of Energy*] [*Database*] .... DRD
Data Resources, Inc. [*Database originator and operator*] [*Information service or system*] (IID) .... DRI
Data Resources Management System .... DRMS
Data Retrieval and Storage .... DRS
Data Retrieval Area (MCD) .... DARE
Data Retrieval, Entry, and Management .... DREAM
Data Retrieval, Entry, and Management Systems (DGA) .... DREAMS
Data Retrieval Language [*National Institute of Standards and Technology*] .... DRL
Data Retrieval Mode .... DRM
Data Retrieval Program (CAAL) .... DRP
Data Retrieval System [*Computer science*] (BUR) .... DRS
Data Retrival Unit (GAVI) .... DRU
Data Return Capsule [*or Container*] .... DRC
Data Review Board [*Military*] (AFIT) .... DRB
Data Review Technician .... DRT
Data Routing and Error Detecting .... DRED
Data Routing Indicator .... DRI
Data Routing Patch Panel (MCD) .... DRPP
Data Safety Monitoring Board [*Generic term*] .... DSMB
Data Scanning (BUR) .... DS
Data Scanning and Formatting .... DSF
Data Scanning and Routing .... DSR
Data Security (IAA) .... DS
Data Security Officer (HGAA) .... DSO
Data Segment .... DS
Data Segment Table (IAA) .... DST
Data Selection and Storage Buffer (IAA) .... DSSB
Data Selector and Tagger (MUGU) .... DASAT
Data Selector Unit (OA) .... DSU
Data Self-Auditing Program [*Environmental Protection Agency*] (EPA) .... DSAP
Data Self-Test Program .... DSTP
Data Separator Card (MCD) .... DSC
Data Series (IAA) .... DS
Data Server System .... DSS
Data Service Unit [*Telecommunications*] .... DSU
Data Services Center [*International City Management Association*] [*Information service or system*] (IID) .... DSC
Data Services Division [*Census*] (OICC) .... DUSD
Data Services Educational Profile .... DSEP
Data Services Operations [*Informatics, Inc.*] (IID) .... DSO
Data Services Planning Form .... DSPF
Data Servicing Unit / Channel Servicing Unit (HGAA) .... DSU/CSU
Data Set [*Computer science*] .... DS
Data Set Adapter [*Computer science*] .... DSA
Data Set Analysis System [*Computer science*] (HGAA) .... DSAS
Data Set Block .... DSB
Data Set by Key [*Computer science*] (IAA) .... DSBK
Data Set Catalog [*Computer science*] (IAA) .... DSCAT
Data Set Control Block [*Computer science*] .... DSCB
Data Set Controller .... DSC
Data Set Definition [*Computer science*] (IBMDP) .... DSD
Data Set Extension [*IBM Corp.*] [*Computer science*] (BUR) .... DSE
Data Set Identification [*Computer science*] (IBMDP) .... DSID
Data Set Identifier .... DSI
Data Set Label [*Computer science*] .... DSL
Data Set Manager (MCD) .... DSM
Data Set Name .... DSN
Data Set Optimizer [*Boole & Babbage, Inc.*] .... DSO
Data Set Organization (IAA) .... DSORG
Data Set Ready [*Model signal*] .... DSR
Data Set Ready (NITA) .... DSR
Data Sheet (NATG) .... DS
Data Signalling Rate Select (IAA) .... DSRS
Data Simulation Language .... DSL
Data Smoothing Network [*Telecommunications*] .... DSN
Data Source Name [*Computer science*] .... DSN
Data Source Panel (MCD) .... DSP
Data Source Terminal (MCD) .... DST
Data Spanning (IAA) .... DASPAN
Data Specification Request .... DSR
Data Standardization Project [*DoD*] .... DSP
Data Station [*Spectroscopy*] .... DS
Data Statistics Comparison Software [*Computer science*] .... DSC
Data Status Display .... DSD
Data Status Messages (KSC) .... DSM
Data Status Word .... DSW
Data Storage [*Computer science*] (NASA) .... DS
Data Storage and Retrieval (MSA) .... DS & R
Data Storage and Retrieval (MCD) .... DSR
Data Storage Description Language .... DSDL
Data Storage Device .... DSD
Data Storage Distribution Unit (MCD) .... DSDU
Data Storage Electronics Assembly [*Apollo*] [*NASA*] .... DSEA
Data Storage Equipment .... DSE
Data Storage Memory .... DSM
Data Storage Set (MCD) .... DSS
Data Storage System .... DSS
Data Storage Terminal .... DST
Data Storage Unit .... DSU
Data Storage Unit Receptacle (MCD) .... DSUR
Data Stream Compatability (IAA) .... DSC
Data Stream Direct [*Computer science*] .... DSD
Data Structure and System Development (SSD) .... DSSD
Data Structure Diagram .... DSD
Data Structures Language [*Computer science*] (BUR) .... DSL
Data Submitted Information (KSC) .... DSI
Data Subscriber Line Carrier [*Computer science*] (HGAA) .... DSLC
Data Subscriber Terminal Equipment [*Telecommunications*] (IAA) .... DSTE
Data Summary Sheets (MCD) .... DSS
Data Summary Tape (OA) .... DST
Data Support Command [*Army*] .... DATCOM
Data Support Element (MCD) .... DSE
Data Survey Report (AAG) .... DSR
Data Switch Operating System .... DSOS
Data Switch Wrrt [*NASDAQ symbol*] (TTSB) .... DASWZ
Data Switching and Data Handling (AFM) .... DS & DH
Data Switching Equipment [*Computer science*] (ACRL) .... DSE
Data Switching Exchange [*Telecommunications*] .... DSE
Data Switching System .... DSS
Data Synchronization (DEN) .... DS
Data Synchronization [*or Synchronizer*] **Unit** .... DSU
Data Synchronizer Channel .... DSC
Data Sys Network Corp. [*NASDAQ symbol*] (TTSB) .... DSYS
Data Sys Network Wrrt [*NASDAQ symbol*] (TTSB) .... DSYSW
Data System .... DS
Data System Console (CAAL) .... DSC
Data System Development Plan .... DSDP
Data System Integration [*NASA*] .... DSI
Data Systems Administration (NVT) .... DSA
Data Systems and Analysis Directorate (MCD) .... DSAD
Data Systems and Mathematics Staff [*Bureau of Radiological Health*] (IID) .... DSMS
Data Systems & Software [*NASDAQ symbol*] (TTSB) .... DSSI
Data Systems & Software, Inc. [*Associated Press*] (SAG) .... DataSyst
Data Systems & Software, Inc. [*NASDAQ symbol*] (SAG) .... DSSI
Data Systems and Statistics (AFM) .... DS & S
Data Systems and Statistics Officer [*Air Force*] .... DS & SO
Data Systems Application Division [*Agricultural Research Service*] .... DSAD
Data Systems Architecture (SSD) .... DSA
Data Systems Authorization Directory (AFIT) .... DSAD
Data Systems Automation Office [*Columbus, Ohio*] [*Military*] .... DSAO
Data Systems Automation Program .... DSAP
Data Systems Controller (MCD) .... DSC
Data Systems Coordinating Activity [*DoD*] (DNAB) .... DSCA
Data Systems Design Center [*Air Force*] .... DSDC
Data Systems Designator (AFM) .... DSD
Data Systems Engineer .... DSENGR
Data Systems Engineering .... DSE
Data Systems Engineering Group (MCD) .... DSEG
Data Systems Environment Functions and Application Design [*Course*] [*Computer science*] .... DSE/FAD
Data Systems Group [*Computer science*] (ACRL) .... DSG
Data Systems Inquiry (AABC) .... DSI
Data Systems Modernization .... DSM
Data Systems Network Corp. [*Associated Press*] (SAG) .... DataSysN
Data Systems Network Corp. [*Associated Press*] (SAG) .... DatSN
Data Systems Network Corp. [*NASDAQ symbol*] (SAG) .... DSYS
Data Systems Office .... DSO
Data Systems Participating Agency (DNAB) .... DSPA
Data Systems Research and Development [*Oak Ridge National Laboratory*] .... DSRD
Data Systems Specification .... DSS
Data Systems Supervisor (MCD) .... DSS
Data Systems Support Office (MCD) .... DASSO
Data Systems Technician [*Navy rating*] .... DS
Data Systems Technician, Chief [*Navy rating*] .... DSC
Data Systems Technician, First Class [*Navy rating*] DS1
Data Systems Technician, Master Chief [*Navy rating*] .... DSCM
Data Systems Technician, Second Class [*Navy rating*] DS2
Data Systems Technician, Senior Chief [*Navy rating*] .... DSCS
Data Systems Technician, Third Class [*Navy rating*] DS3
Data Systems Test [*Formerly, DAT*] .... DST
Data Tabulation (OICC) .... DT
Data Tabulation and Editing Program Language (IAA) .... DATEPLAN
Data Tags [*National Library of Medicine*] [*Searchable field*] (NITA) .... DT
Data Takeoff [*Air Force*] .... DTO
Data Tape Punch (IAA) .... DTP
Data Tape Recorder (IAA) .... DTR
Data Technical Control .... DTC
Data Technical Support Group [*Telecommunications*] (TEL) .... DATEC
Data Technology Corp. .... DTC
Data Telecommunications [*RCA Global Communications Data Transmission Service over Telephone Circuits*] [*Telecommunications*] (TEL) .... DATEL
Data Telemetering Register .... DTR
Data Telemetry Exploitation Aid (MCD) .... DTEA

Data Ten to Eleven (PDAA)	DTE
Data Terminal	DT
Data Terminal Display	DTD
Data Terminal Equipment [Computer science]	DTE
Data Terminal Operator [Computer science]	DTO
Data Terminal Reader	DTR
Data Terminal Ready [Computer science Telecommunications]	DTR
Data Terminal Set (NVT)	DTS
Data Terminal System (IAA)	DTS
Data Terminal Unit [Telecommunications]	DTU
Data Terminals & Communications, Inc.	DTC
Data Terminating Unit (TEL)	DTU
Data Test Center [Telecommunications] (TEL)	DTC
Data Test Station	DTS
Data Training Ltd. [British] (NITA)	DTL
Data Transcriber	DT
Data Transfer [Computer science]	DX
Data Transfer Acknowledge [Computer memory management]	DTACK
Data Transfer and Certification Record (KSC)	DTCR
Data Transfer Area [Computer science]	DTA
Data Transfer Command Word (NASA)	DTCW
Data Transfer Done	DTD
Data Transfer Protocol [Telecommunications] (OSI)	DTP
Data Transfer Rate	DTR
Data Transfer Register	DTR
Data Transfer Sequence (IAA)	DTS
Data Transfer System [Army] (AABC)	DTS
Data Transfer Timing	DTT
Data Transfer Unit	DTU
Data Transformation Corp. [ICAO designator] (FAAC)	XDT
Data Transition Tracking	DTT
Data Transition Tracking Loop	DTTL
Data Translation [NASDAQ symbol] (TTSB)	DATX
Data Translation Corp. [Associated Press] (SAG)	DtaTrn
Data Translation II, Inc. [Associated Press] (SAG)	DtTrns
Data Translation, Inc. [NASDAQ symbol] (NQ)	DATX
Data Translator (IEEE)	DT
Data Translator (MCD)	DTR
Data Transmission	DT
Data Transmission and Control System (AAG)	DTCS
Data Transmission and Processing (NATG)	DATAP
Data Transmission and Switching	DTAS
Data Transmission Center (KSC)	DTC
Data Transmission Channel (CMD)	DTC
Data Transmission Control Unit [Burroughs Corp.]	DTCU
Data Transmission Factor	DTF
Data Transmission Feature	DTF
Data Transmission Function	DTF
Data Transmission Generator (MCD)	DTG
Data Transmission Network Corp. [NASDAQ symbol] (NQ)	DTLN
Data Transmission Network Corp. [Associated Press] (SAG)	DtTrNw
Data Transmission Ntwk [NASDAQ symbol] (TTSB)	DTLN
Data Transmission/Recording Subsystem	DT/RSS
Data Transmission Service (IAA)	DTS
Data Transmission Study Group [Military]	DTSG
Data Transmission System	DATS
Data Transmission System [Air Force]	DTS
Data Transmission Terminal (NITA)	DTT
Data Transmission Terminal Unit [Burroughs Corp.]	DTTU
Data Transmission Unit	DTU
Data Transmittal and Routing Form (NRCH)	DTRF
Data Transmittal Form (MCD)	DTF
Data Transmitting Equipment	DTE
Data Transmitting Equipment (MSA)	DXE
Data Transport Computer	DTC
Data Transporting Network	DTN
Data Under Voice [Bell System]	DUV
Data Universal Numbering System [Dun's number] [Business term]	DUNS
Data Update Edit Language [Computer science]	DUEL
Data Upper Half Byte (IAA)	DUH
Data Use Access Laboratories Inc. (NITA)	DUALABS
Data Use and Access Laboratories - Communications, Inc. [Information service or system] (IID)	DUAL-COMM
Data Use Identifier (AFM)	DUI
Data User Part [Integrated Services Digital Network] [Telecommunications] (OSI)	DUP
Data Users' Note [NASA] (MCD)	DUN
Data Utility Complex (IAA)	DUX
Data Utilization Center [Navy] (NVT)	DUC
Data Utilization Console	DUC
Data Utilization Station	DUS
Data Valid (IEEE)	DAV
Data Validation Program [NASA]	DVP
Data Value-Added Reseller	DVAR
Data Vetting	DV
Data/Voice Communications System (SSD)	DVCS
Data/Voice Data (MCD)	D/VD
Data Voice Exchange (MCD)	DVX
Data Word (NASA)	DW
Data Word Buffer [Computer science] (MDG)	DW
Data Word In (MCD)	DWI
Data-Aided Loop [NASA]	DAL
Data-Aided Receiver [NASA]	DAR
Databank of Atomic and Molecular Physics [Queen's University Belfast] [British] (NITA)	DAMP

Databank of Program Evaluations [University of California, Los Angeles] (IID)	DOPE
Databank Update Request (NASA)	DBUR
Database [Computer science]	DB
Database	DB
Database Access Facility	DBAF
Database Access Manager [Computer science] (BTTJ)	DAM
Database Access Method	DBAM
Database Access Module (NITA)	DBAM
Database Access Service [Eastern Telecommunications Philippines, Inc.] [Information service or system] (IID)	DBS
Database Acquisition for Student Health	DASH
Database Action Diagram (CDE)	DAD
Database Administration [or Administrator] [Computer science] (BUR)	DBA
Database Administration Working Group [CODASYL]	DBAWG
Database Administrator Control System	DBACS
Database Command Language	DBCL
Database Computer (MCD)	DBC
Database Control Block	DBCB
Database Control System	DBCS
Database/Data Communications [IBM Corp.]	DB/DC
Database Definition (BYTE)	DBD
Database Definition File (NITA)	DDF
Database Definition Language	DBDL
Database Definition Language Processor (BYTE)	DDLP
Database Description [Computer science] (BUR)	DBD
Database Description (ACRL)	DD
Database Design Aid [Computer science] (BUR)	DBDA
Database Design Document	DBD
Database Design Document (MCD)	DBDD
Database Diagnostics (NITA)	DBD
Database Directory (IAA)	DBD
Database File Numbers (MCD)	DBFN
Database Generation [Computer science]	DBGEN
Database Generation System (MCD)	DBGS
Database Generator	DBG
Database Graphics Toolkit [Blackhawk Data Corp.]	DGT
Database Guide to German Host Operators [Database]	INFOHOST
Database Handling System	DBHS
Database Imagery Derived Information (MCD)	DBIDI
Database Information Science and Practice [Database]	INFODATA
Database Information Services (NITA)	DIS
Database Information System	DIS
Database Input Languages [Computer science]	DBIL
Database Input/Output Control	DBIOC
Database Language [Computer science]	DBL
Database Language Task Group [CODASYL]	DBLTG
Database List (CINC)	DBL
Database Load [Computer science]	DBL
Database Machines (AAGC)	DBM
Database Management [or Manager] [Computer science] (NVT)	DBM
Database Management and Control System (MCD)	DBMCS
Database Management Software [Computer science]	DBMS
Database Management System [or Subsystem] [Computer science] (BUR)	DBMS
Database Management System [Computer science]	DMS
Database Management System Problem Specification Model	DBMSPSM
Database Network	DBN
Database of Antiviral and Immunomodulatory Therapies for AIDS [Acquired Immune Deficiency Syndrome]	DAITA
Database of Expressed Sequence Tags [Genetics]	dBEST
Database of Off-Site Waste Management [Public Data Access, Inc.] [No longer available online] [Information service or system]	DOWM
Database Operating System (IAA)	DBOS
Database Options Menu	DOM
Database Organization and Maintenance [or Management] Processor	DBOMP
Database Oriented Interrogation Technique [Comserv Corp.]	DOIT
Database Processor	DBP
Database Program Conversion Task Group [CODASYL]	DPCTG
Database Promotion Center, Japan [Information service or system] (IID)	DPC
Database Query (MCD)	DBQ
Database Recovery Control [Computer science] (HGAA)	DBRC
Database Reference [A publication]	D/R
Database Retrieval	DBR
Database Size/Program Size	D/P
Database Software (IAA)	DBS
Database System (MCD)	DBS
Database System Relational/Structured Query Language [NCR Corp.]	DBSR/SQL
Database Task Group [CODASYL]	DBTG
Database Two [Computer science] (HGAA)	DB2
Database Update Time	DBUT
Data-Cache Unit [Computer science]	DCU
DataCenter/OSx (CDE)	DC/OSx
DataEase Query Language [Search method] [Computer science] (PCM)	DQL
Data-Entry Virtual Terminal [Computer science]	DEVT
Dataflex Corp. [Associated Press] (SAG)	Datflx
Dataflex Corp. [NASDAQ symbol] (NQ)	DFLX
Dataflow Systems, Inc. [Information service or system] (IID)	DfS
Datagram [Telecommunications]	DG
Datagram Delivery Protocol	DDP
Datakey, Inc. [Associated Press] (SAG)	Datkey
Datakey, Inc. [NASDAQ symbol] (NQ)	DKEY
Data-Line Concentration System [Bell System]	DLCS
Datalogix International, Inc. [Associated Press] (SAG)	Datalgx

Datalogix International, Inc. [*NASDAQ symbol*] (SAG) .... DLGX
Datalogix Intl. [*NASDAQ symbol*] (TTSB) .... DLGX
Datamac Computer Users Group (HGAA) .... DCUG
Datamarine International, Inc. [*Associated Press*] (SAG) .... Datmar
Datamarine International, Inc. [*NASDAQ symbol*] (NQ) .... DMAR
Datamarine Int'l [*NASDAQ symbol*] (TTSB) .... DMAR
Data-Matching Agency .... DMA
Datamation Industry Directory (MCD) .... DID
Datametrics Corp. [*Associated Press*] (SAG) .... Datamet
Datametrics Corp. [*AMEX symbol*] (SPSG) .... DC
Data-Net [*Data-Net, Inc.*] [*Rochester, NY*] [*Telecom:nunications*] (TSSD) .... DNET
Data-Phone Digital Service [*Trademark of the American Telephone & Telegraph Co.*] .... DDS
Dataphone Digital System [*AT&T*] (NITA) .... DDS
Dataphone Switched Digital Service [*AT & T*] .... DSDS
Datapint $1 cm Pfd [*NYSE symbol*] (TTSB) .... DPTPrA
Datapoint Corp. [*Associated Press*] (SAG) .... Datapt
Datapoint Corp. [*Associated Press*] (SAG) .... Datpt
Datapoint Corp. [*NYSE symbol*] (SPSG) .... DPT
Dataport Network Information System [*California*] [*Bulletin board system*] .... DNIS
Data-Processing Station .... DPS
Dataram Corp. [*Associated Press*] (SAG) .... Dataram
Dataram Corp. [*AMEX symbol*] (SPSG) .... DTM
Dataroute Serving Area [*TransCanada Telephone System/Computer Communications Group*] .... DSA
Data-Sampling Automatic Receiver (MCD) .... DSAR
Data-Scanner Distributor .... DSD
Datascope Computer Output Microfilmer [*Eastman Kodak Co.*] .... DACOM
Datascope Corp. [*Associated Press*] (SAG) .... Datscp
Datascope Corp. [*NASDAQ symbol*] (NQ) .... DSCP
Data-Set Definition Table [*Computer science*] .... DSDT
Dataset Generator (SAA) .... DSG
Dataset Printer (SAA) .... DSP
Dataskil Integrated Library System [*International Computers Ltd.*] [*British*] (NITA) .... DILS
Datastream Systems [*NASDAQ symbol*] (TTSB) .... DSTM
Datastream Systems, Inc. [*Associated Press*] (SAG) .... Datastr
Datastream Systems, Inc. [*NASDAQ symbol*] (TTSB) .... DSTM
Datasystem Interactive Communications Access Method [*Digital Equipment Corp.*] .... DICAM
Data-Tech Institute [*Clifton, NJ*] (TSSD) .... DTI
Datatech Systems Ltd. [*Toronto Stock Exchange symbol*] .... DTK
Datatracker International [*Vancouver Stock Exchange symbol*] .... DTE
Datatrend Services [*NASDAQ symbol*] (TTSB) .... DATA
Datatrend Svcs Wrrt [*NASDAQ symbol*] (TTSB) .... DATAW
Datatron Assembly System [*Burroughs Corp.*] .... DAS
Datatron Users' Organization .... DUO
Data-VHS (CDE) .... D-VHS
Dataware Technologies [*NASDAQ symbol*] (TTSB) .... DWTI
Dataware Technologies, Inc. [*Associated Press*] (SAG) .... Dataware
Dataware Technologies, Inc. [*NASDAQ symbol*] (SAG) .... DWTI
Datawatch Corp. [*Associated Press*] (SAG) .... Dtawtc
Datawatch Corp. [*Associated Press*] (SAG) .... Dtawtch
Datawatch Corp. [*NASDAQ symbol*] (SAG) .... DWCH
DataWorks Corp. [*Associated Press*] (SAG) .... DtaWks
DataWorks Corp. [*NASDAQ symbol*] (SAG) .... DWRX
Date .... D
Date [*Online database field identifier*] .... DA
Date (AFM) .... DT
Date (WDMC) .... dt
Date and Place of Birth .... DPOB
Date Arrived Station [*Military*] (AFM) .... DAS
Date Deficiency [*or Discrepancy*] Discovered (MCD) .... DDD
Date Departed Continental United States [*Military*] (AFM) .... DDCONUS
Date Departed Last Duty Station [*Military*] (AFM) .... DDLDS
Date Departed United States [*Military*] .... DDUS
Date Due Calibration [*Military*] (AFIT) .... DDC
Date Eligible for Return from Overseas [*Military*] .... DEROS
Date Expected Delivery [*Medicine*] .... DED
Date Filed [*IRS*] .... DF
Date Growers' Institute [*Defunct*] (EA) .... DGI
Date Material Required .... DMR
Date Number .... DN
Date of Admission [*Medicine*] (AAMN) .... D/A
Date of Admission [*Medicine*] .... DOA
Date of Availability [*Military*] (AFM) .... DOA
Date of Birth .... DB
Date of Birth .... DOB
Date of Change .... DOC
Date of Change of Accountability [*Military*] .... DOCA
Date of Commencement .... DOC
Date of Contract Award (DNAB) .... DOA
Date of Current Appointment [*Military*] .... DOCA
Date of Current Enlistment [*Military*] .... DOCE
Date of Death .... DOD
Date of Departure [*Military*] (AABC) .... DODPRT
Date of Departure [*Army*] .... DOPRT
Date of Draft [*Business term*] .... D/D
Date of Enlistment [*Military*] .... DOE
Date of Entering Office .... EOD
Date of Entry [*Military*] .... DE
Date of Estimated Closing (AAGC) .... DEC
Date of Estimated Return from Overseas [*Military*] .... DEROS
Date of Examination [*Medicine*] (DAVI) .... DOE
Date of Extension [*Military*] .... DE

Date of First Demand [*Military*] (AFIT) .... DOFD
Date of Full Availability .... DOFA
Date of Information (MCD) .... DOI
Date of Initial Appointment .... DIA
Date of Injury [*Medicine*] (HGAA) .... DI
Date of Injury [*Medicine*] .... DOI
Date of Introduction (ADDR) .... DOI
Date of Last Adjustment/Date of Last Demand [*Military*] (AFIT) .... DOLA/DOLD
Date of Last Follow-Up (AFIT) .... DOLF
Date of Last Inventory (AFIT) .... DOLI
Date of Last Menstrual Period [*Medicine*] (DMAA) .... DLMP
Date of Last Normal Menstrual Period [*Medicine*] (DMAA) .... DLNMP
Date of Last Payment [*Insurance*] .... DLP
Date of Last Transaction (AFIT) .... DOLT
Date of Permanent Grade .... DPG
Date of Prescribed Period [*Social Security Administration*] (OICC) .... DPP
Date of Publication [*Online database field identifier*] .... DP
Date of Rank [*Air Force*] .... DOR
Date of Rank [*Air Force*] .... DR
Date of Rank, Current Grade [*Air Force*] (AFM) .... DORCG
Date of Rank, Permanent Grade [*Air Force*] (AFM) .... DORPG
Date of Request (AFM) .... DOR
Date of Separation [*Military*] .... DOS
Date of Service .... DOS
Date of Service [*Military*] .... DS
Date of Surgery (DAVI) .... DOS
Date of Trade [*Investment term*] .... DOT
Date of Treatment [*Medicine*] (DAVI) .... DORx
Date Physically Completed (AAGC) .... DPC
Date Race, Inc. [*Associated Press*] (SAG) .... DataRce
Date Race, Inc. [*NASDAQ symbol*] (SAG) .... RACE
Date Required to Load (AABC) .... DRL
Date Returned from Overseas [*Military*] .... DROS
Date to Be Agreed (AIA) .... dtba
Date to Follow [*Telecommunications*] (TEL) .... DTF
Datebook (WDMC) .... DB
Dated .... D/D
Dated (AFM) .... DTD
Dated Drawing List (MCD) .... DDL
Dated Forecast Authorization Equipment Data (MCD) .... DFAED
Datel Industries Ltd. [*Toronto Stock Exchange symbol Vancouver Stock Exchange symbol*] .... DTL
Datenbank fuer Forderungsvorhaben [*Ongoing Research Project Data Bank*] [*Ministry for Research and Technology*] [*Information service or system*] (IID) .... DAVOR
Datenbank fuer Wassergefahrdende Stoffe [*Data Bank on Substances Harmful to Water*] [*Information service or system Germany*] (IID) .... DABAWAS
Datenbank ueber Gifte und Vergiftungen [*Databank for Poisons and Poisoning*] [*German*] .... GIFTPOOL
Datennachweis Informationssystem [*Arbeitsgemeinschaft Sozialwissenschaftlicher Institut*] [*Germany Information service or system Defunct*] (CRD) .... DANIS
Date-Time Group [*Group of figures at head of radio or Teletype message indicating filing time*] .... DTG
Date-Time-Next Meeting (DI) .... DTNM
Dathina [*Yemen*] [*Airport symbol*] (AD) .... DAH
DATICO [*Digital Automatic Tape Intelligence Checkout*] Acceptance Test Evaluation (MCD) .... DATE
DATICO [*Digital Automatic Tape Intelligence Checkout*] Missile Interface Simulator .... DMIS
Dating Problems Checklist [*Psychology*] .... DPC
Dative (ROG) .... D
Dative .... DAT
Datron Systems [*NASDAQ symbol*] (TTSB) .... DTSI
Datron Systems, Inc. [*Associated Press*] (SAG) .... Datron
Datron Systems, Inc. [*NASDAQ symbol*] (NQ) .... DTSI
Datsun Owners Club [*Defunct*] (EA) .... DOC
Datum .... D
Datum (MSA) .... DAT
Datum, Inc. [*NASDAQ symbol*] (NQ) .... DATM
Datum, Inc. [*Associated Press*] (SAG) .... Datum
Datum Level .... DL
Datum Point .... DP
Datum Position [*Arbitrary*] [*Navy British*] .... ZZ
Datumone Petroleum [*Vancouver Stock Exchange symbol*] .... DAT
Datur Omnibus Mori [*It Is Allotted unto All to Die*] [*Latin*] .... DOM
Datur Talis Dosis [*Give Of Such A Dose*] [*Pharmacology*] (DAVI) .... dtd
Datura stramonium [*Jimsonweed*] .... DATST
Daughter .... D
Daughter .... DA
Daughter .... DAU
Daughter .... DAUGR
Daughter .... DGHTR
Daughter (WGA) .... DGT
Daughter (ROG) .... DR
Daughter .... DT
Daughter [*Citizens band radio slang*] .... XYD
Daughter and Co-Heir [*Genealogy*] (ROG) .... DAU & COH
Daughter and Co-Heiress [*Genealogy*] .... D & COH
Daughter and Heir [*Genealogy*] (ROG) .... DAU & H
Daughter and Heiress [*Genealogy*] .... D & H
Daughter Of [*Genealogy*] .... D/O
Daughters (ROG) .... DAUHS
Daughters and Sons United (EA) .... D & SU
Daughters of Bilitis [*Superseded by United Sisters*] (EA) .... DOB

Daughters of Bosses ... DOB
Daughters of Charity [*Australia*] ... DC
Daughters of Charity of Most Precious Blood (TOCD) ... DCPB
Daughters of Charity of St. Vincent de Paul [*Roman Catholic religious order*] ... DC
Daughters of Divine Charity (TOCD) ... FDC
Daughters of Divine Providence (TOCD) ... FDP
Daughters of Divine Zeal (TOCD) ... FDZ
Daughters of Evrytania (EA) ... DE
Daughters of Hirsutism Association of America (EA) ... DOHA
Daughters of Isabella, International Circle (EA) ... DIIC
Daughters of Jesus [*Roman Catholic religious order*] ... FI
Daughters of Jesus of Kermaria [*See also FJ*] [*Paris, France*] (EAIO) ... DJK
Daughters of Mary and Joseph [*Roman Catholic religious order*] ... DMJ
Daughters of Mary, Help of Christians [*Salesian Sisters of St. John Bosco*] [*Roman Catholic religious order*] ... FMA
Daughters of Mary Immaculate [*Marianist Sisters*] [*Roman Catholic religious order*] ... FMI
Daughters of Mary Immaculate (Chaldean) (TOCD) ... DMI
Daughters of Mary of the Immaculate Conception [*Roman Catholic religious order*] ... DM
Daughters of Mercy (Croatian) (TOCD) ... DOM
Daughters of Our Lady of Fatima (TOCD) ... DLF
Daughters of Our Lady of Holy Rosary (TOCD) ... FMSR
Daughters of Our Lady of Mercy [*Roman Catholic religious order*] ... DM
Daughters of Our Lady of the Sacred Heart (TOCD) ... FDNSC
Daughters of Our Mother of Peace (TOCD) ... SMP
Daughters of Penelope (EA) ... DP
Daughters of Providence (TOCD) ... FDLP
Daughters of St. Francis of Assisi [*Roman Catholic religious order*] ... DSF
Daughters of St. Mary of Providence [*Roman Catholic religious order*] ... DSMP
Daughters of St. Paul, Missionary Sisters of the Catholic Editions [*Roman Catholic religious order*] ... DSP
Daughters of St. Rita of the Immaculate Heart [*Roman Catholic religious order*] ... DSR
Daughters of Scotia [*Bayonne, NJ*] ... D of S
Daughters of Scotia (EA) ... DS
Daughters of the American Revolution, Hendrick Hudson Chapter, Hudson, NY [*Library symbol Library of Congress*] (LCLS) ... NHudDAR
Daughters of the American Revolution, Washington, DC [*Library symbol Library of Congress*] (LCLS) ... DNDAR
Daughters of the Cincinnati (EA) ... DC
Daughters of the Confederacy ... D of C
Daughters of the Cross [*Roman Catholic religious order*] ... DC
Daughters of the Cross of Liege [*Roman Catholic religious order*] ... FC
Daughters of the Defenders of the Republic, USA (EA) ... DDR
Daughters of the Divine Redeemer [*Roman Catholic religious order*] ... DDR
Daughters of the Elderly Bridging the Unknown Together (EA) ... DEBUT
Daughters of the Heart of Mary [*Roman Catholic religious order*] ... DHM
Daughters of the Holy Spirit [*Roman Catholic religious order*] ... DHS
Daughters of the Holy Spirit Nazareth of the Good Shepherd (TOCD) ... HSpS
Daughters of the Immaculate Heart of Mary [*Roman Catholic religious order*] ... IHM
Daughters of the King (EA) ... DK
Daughters of the Most Holy Redeemer [*Roman Catholic religious order*] ... DMHR
Daughters of the Nile, Supreme Temple (EA) ... DNST
Daughters of the Republic of Texas (EA) ... DRT
Daughters of the Republic of Texas Museum, Austin, TX [*Library symbol Library of Congress*] (LCLS) ... TxAuDR
Daughters of the Revolution ... DR
Daughters of the Sacred Heart of Jesus [*Bethlehemite Sisters*] [*Roman Catholic religious order*] ... SCIF
Daughters of Union Veterans of the Civil War, 1861-1865 (EA) ... DUV
Daughters of Utah Pioneers Museum Library, Salt Lake City, UT [*Library symbol Library of Congress*] (LCLS) ... USlD
Daughters of Wisdom [*Montfort Sisters*] [*Roman Catholic religious order*] ... DW
Daunomycin [*Antineoplastic drug*] ... DM
Daunomycin and Cytosine Arabinoside [*Antineoplastic drug regimen*] (DAVI) ... DA
Daunomycin, ara-C [*Cytarabine*], Thioguanine [*Antineoplastic drug regimen*] ... DAT
Daunomycin, Cytarabine [*Antineoplastic drug*] (CDI) ... DC
Daunomycin Cytarabine, Prednisolone, Mercaptopurine [*Antineoplastic drug*] (CDI) ... DCPM
Daunomycin Cytarabine, Thioguanine [*Antineoplastic drug*] (CDI) ... DCT
Daunomycin, Vincristine, L-Asparaginase, Prednisone [*Antineoplastic drug regimen*] (DAVI) ... DVLP
Daunorubicin [*Daunomycin, Rubidomycin*] [*Also, DNR, DRB, R*] [*Antineoplastic drug*] ... D
Daunorubicin [*Antineoplastic drug*] (DAVI) ... Daun
Daunorubicin [*Daunomycin*] [*Also, D, DRB, R*] [*Antineoplastic drug*] ... DNR
Daunorubicin [*Antineoplastic drug*] (DAVI) ... DR
Daunorubicin [*Daunomycin*] [*Also, D, DNR, R*] [*Antineoplastic drug*] ... DRB
Daunorubicin, ara-C [*Cytarabine*] [*Antineoplastic drug regimen*] ... DA
Daunorubicin, Cyclocytidine [*Ancitabine*], Mercaptopurine, Prednisone [*Antineoplastic drug regimen*] ... DCCMP
Daunorubicin, Cytarabine, Mercaptopurine, Prednisone [*Antineoplastic drug regimen*] ... DCMP
Daunorubicin, Oncovin [*Vincristine*], ara-C, Prednisone [*Antineoplastic drug regimen*] ... DOAP
Daunorubicin, Vincristine, Prednisone [*Antineoplastic drug*] (CDI) ... DVP
Daunorubicin, Vincristine, Prednisone, L-Asparaginase [*Antineoplastic drug regimen*] ... DVPL-ASP
Dauphin [*Canada*] [*Airport symbol*] (OAG) ... YDN
Dauphin County Library System, Harrisburg, PA [*OCLC symbol*] (OCLC) ... HBP
Dauphin County Library System, Harrisburg, PA [*Library symbol Library of Congress*] (LCLS) ... PHarD
Dauphin County Reporter [*Pennsylvania*] [*A publication*] (DLA) ... Dauph
Dauphin County Reporter [*Pennsylvania*] [*A publication*] (DLA) ... Dauph Co Rep
Dauphin County Reports [*Pennsylvania*] [*A publication*] (DLA) ... Dau Co Rep
Dauphin Deposit [*NASDAQ symbol*] (TTSB) ... DAPN
Dauphin Deposit Corp. [*NASDAQ symbol*] (NQ) ... DAPN
Dauphin Deposit Corp. [*Associated Press*] (SAG) ... Dauphn
Dauphin, MB [*AM radio station call letters*] ... CKDM
Dauphin, MB [*ICAO location identifier*] (ICLI) ... CYDN
Dauphin Public Library, Dauphin, MB, Canada [*Library symbol Library of Congress Obsolete*] (LCLS) ... CaMDa
Davao [*Philippines*] [*Seismograph station code, US Geological Survey*] (SEIS) ... DAV
Davao [*Philippines*] [*Airport symbol*] (OAG) ... DVO
Davao/Francisco Bangoy International [*Philippines*] [*ICAO location identifier*] (ICLI) ... RPWD
DavCo Restaurants [*NASDAQ symbol*] (TTSB) ... DVCO
Davco Restaurants, Inc. [*Associated Press*] (SAG) ... Davco
Davco Restaurants, Inc. [*NASDAQ symbol*] (SAG) ... DVCO
Dave & Buster's [*NASDAQ symbol*] (TTSB) ... DANB
Dave & Busters, Inc. [*NASDAQ symbol*] (SAG) ... DANB
Dave & Busters, Inc. [*Associated Press*] (SAG) ... Dave&B
Dave Durham and the Bull Durham Band Fan Club (EA) ... DDBDBFC
Davel Communications Corp. [*Associated Press*] (SAG) ... Davel
Davel Communications Corp. [*NASDAQ symbol*] (SAG) ... DAVL
Davel Communications Grp [*NASDAQ symbol*] (TTSB) ... DAVL
Davenport [*Diocesan abbreviation*] [*Iowa*] (TOCD) ... DAV
Davenport [*Washington*] [*Seismograph station code, US Geological Survey*] (SEIS) ... DVW
Davenport Downs [*Queensland*] [*Airport symbol*] (AD) ... DVP
Davenport, IA [*Location identifier FAA*] (FAAL) ... BBC
Davenport, IA [*Location identifier FAA*] (FAAL) ... CVA
Davenport, IA [*Location identifier FAA*] (FAAL) ... DVN
Davenport, IA [*FM radio station call letters*] ... KALA
Davenport, IA [*FM radio station call letters*] (RBYB) ... KCQQ
Davenport, IA [*AM radio station call letters*] ... KFQC
Davenport, IA [*AM radio station call letters*] ... KJOC
Davenport, IA [*Television station call letters*] ... KLJB
Davenport, IA [*Television station call letters*] ... KQCT
Davenport, IA [*FM radio station call letters*] ... KUUL
Davenport, IA [*Television station call letters*] ... KWQC
Davenport, IA [*AM radio station call letters*] ... WOC
Davenport Industries Ltd. [*Vancouver Stock Exchange symbol*] ... DVO
Davenport Library, Bath, NY [*Library symbol Library of Congress*] (LCLS) ... NBa
Davenport Public Library, Davenport, IA [*Library symbol Library of Congress*] (LCLS) ... IaDa
Davenport Public Library, Davenport, IA [*OCLC symbol*] (OCLC) ... IOS
Davenport Public Museum, Davenport, IA [*Library symbol Library of Congress*] (LCLS) ... IaDaM
Davenport, Rock Island & North Western Railway Co. [*AAR code*] ... DRI
Davic Enterprise, Inc. [*Vancouver Stock Exchange symbol*] ... DVT
David [*Panama*] [*Airport symbol*] (OAG) ... DAV
David A. Howe Public Library, Wellsville, NY [*Library symbol Library of Congress*] (LCLS) ... NWel
David Allan Coe Fan Club (EA) ... DACFC
David & Charles [*Commercial firm British*] ... D & C
David Ben-Gurion (BJA) ... DBG
David Birney Fan Club (EA) ... DBFC
David Brown [*Prefix designation on Aston-Martin cars*] [*British*] ... DB
David Brown Racing [*Prefix designation on Aston-Martin racing cars*] [*British*] ... DBR
David Cassidy Support Group (EA) ... DCSG
David Copperfield Fan Club (EA) ... DCFC
David Davies Memorial Institute of International Studies (MSC) ... DDMIIS
David Dunlap Observatory, University of Toronto, Ontario [*Library symbol National Library of Canada*] (NLC) ... OTUD
David/Enrique Malek [*Panama*] [*ICAO location identifier*] (ICLI) ... MPDA
David Ezekiel Joshua [*Shanghai*] (BJA) ... DEJ
David Frizzell Fan Club (EA) ... DFFC
David Hasselhoff Fan Club (EA) ... DHFC
David Heavener Fan Club (EA) ... DHFC
David Hedison Fan Club [*Defunct*] (EA) ... DHFC
David Herbert Lawrence [*British novelist, 1885-1930*] ... DHL
David Jones Society [*British England*] (EAIO) ... DJS
David Kaufmann Collection. Hungarian Academy of Sciences [*Budapest*] (BJA) ... DK
David Kirchner Fan Club [*Defunct*] (EA) ... DKFC
David Library of the American Revolution, Washington Crossing, PA [*Library symbol Library of Congress*] (LCLS) ... PWacD
David Lipscomb College [*Tennessee*] ... DLC
David Lipscomb College, Nashville, TN [*OCLC symbol*] (OCLC) ... TDL
David Lipscomb College, Nashville, TN [*Library symbol Library of Congress*] (LCLS) ... TNL
David Minerals Ltd. [*Vancouver Stock Exchange symbol*] ... DAV
David on Building Societies [*A publication*] (DLA) ... Dav Bdg Soc
David Rappaport Fan Club (EA) ... DRFC
David Sarnoff Research Center [*RCA*] (MCD) ... DSRC
David See Flying Services [*British*] [*FAA designator*] (FAAC) ... DSF
David Selby Official Fan Club (EA) ... DSOFC
David Syme & Co. Ltd., Melbourne, V, Australia [*Library symbol Library of Congress*] (LCLS) ... AuMDS
David Syme Faculty of Business [*Chisholm Institute of Technology*] [*Australia*] ... DSFB
David Taylor Dance Theatre ... DTDT

David Thompson University Centre [Nelson, BC] [Pronounced "dee-tuck"] [Canada] .... DTUC
David Thompson University Centre [Formerly, Notre Dame University of Nelson], Nelson, BC, Canada [Library symbol Library of Congress] (LCLS) .... CaBNND
David W. Taylor Model Basin [Also, DTMB, TMB] [Later, DTNSRDC, NSRDC] (MUGU) .... DATMOBAS
David W. Taylor Model Basin [Also, DATMOBAS, TMB] [Later, DTNSRDC, NSRDC] [Washington, DC] .... DTMB
David W. Taylor Model Basin [Also, DATMOBAS, DTMB] [Later, DTNSRDC, NSRDC] .... TMB
David W. Taylor Naval Ship Research and Development Center [Later, DTRC] [Bethesda, MD] .... DTNSRDC
David W. Taylor Naval Ship Research and Development Center Aviation and Surface Effects Department [Bethesda, MD] .... DTNSRDC/ASED
David W. Taylor Naval Ship Research and Development Center Central Instrumentation Department [Bethesda, MD] .... DTNSRDC/CID
David W. Taylor Naval Ship Research and Development Center Computation Mathematics/Logistics Department [Bethesda, MD] .... DTNSRDC/CMLD
David W. Taylor Naval Ship Research and Development Center Detachment (DNAB) .... DTNSRDCDET
David W. Taylor Naval Ship Research and Development Center Financial Management Department [Bethesda, MD] .... DTNSRDC/FMD
David W. Taylor Naval Ship Research and Development Center Materials Department [Annapolis, MD] .... DTNSRDC/MAT
David W. Taylor Naval Ship Research and Development Center Naval Laboratories History Program [Bethesda, MD] .... DTNSRDC-NLHP
David W. Taylor Naval Ship Research and Development Center Propulsion and Auxiliary Systems Department [Annapolis, MD] .... DTNSRDC/PAS
David W. Taylor Naval Ship Research and Development Center Propulsion and Auxiliary Systems Department [Annapolis, MD] .... DTNSRDC-PASD
David W. Taylor Naval Ship Research and Development Center Ship Acoustics Department [Bethesda, MD] .... DTNSRDC/SAD
David W. Taylor Naval Ship Research and Development Center Ship Hydromechanics Department [Bethesda, MD] .... DTNSRDC/SHD
David W. Taylor Naval Ship Research and Development Center Ship Materials Engineering Department [Annapolis, MD] .... DTNSRDC/SME
David W. Taylor Naval Ship Research and Development Center Ship Performance Department [Bethesda, MD] .... DTNSRDC/SPD
David W. Taylor Naval Ship Research and Development Center Ship Systems Integration Department [Bethesda, MD] .... DTNSRDC/SSID
David W. Taylor Naval Ship Research and Development Center Systems Development Department [Bethesda, MD] .... DTNSRDC/SDD
David W. Taylor Research Center [Bethesda, MD] [United States Space and Naval Warfare Systems Command] (GRD) .... DTRC
David W. Taylor Research Center Computation Mathematics/Logistics Department [Bethesda, MD] .... DTRC/CMLD
David W. Taylor Research Center Propulsion and Auxiliary Systems Department [Bethesda, MD] .... DTRC/PAS
David W. Taylor Research Center Ship Hydromechanics Department [Bethesda, MD] .... DTRC/SHD
David W. Taylor Research Center Ship Materials Engineering Department [Bethesda, MD] .... DTRC/SME
David W. Taylor Research Center Ship Systems Integration Department [Bethesda, MD] .... DTRC/SSID
David White, Inc. [Associated Press] (SAG) .... DavWht
Davidge and Kimball's Internal Revenue Laws [A publication] (DLA) .... D & K Int Rev
Davidge and Kimball's Internal Revenue Laws [A publication] (DLA) .... Dav & Kim IRL
Davidon-Fletcher-Powell [Method] .... DFP
Davidson & Associates, Inc. [NASDAQ symbol] (SAG) .... DAVD
Davidson & Associates, Inc. [Associated Press] (SAG) .... Davdsn
Davidson and Dicey's Concise Precedents in Conveyancing [A publication] (DLA) .... Dav & Dic Pr
Davidson Area Mental Health Center, Thomasville, NC [Library symbol] [Library of Congress] (LCLS) .... NcThDM
Davidson Avenue Elementary School, Lynbrook, NY [Library symbol] [Library of Congress] (LCLS) .... NLynDE
Davidson College, Davidson, NC [Library symbol Library of Congress] (LCLS) .... NcDaD
Davidson College, Davidson, NC [OCLC symbol] (OCLC) .... NNM
Davidson County Community College, Lexington, NC [Library symbol Library of Congress] (LCLS) .... NcLxDC
Davidson County Public Library, Lexington, NC [Library symbol Library of Congress] (LCLS) .... NcLxD
Davidson Laboratory [Stevens Institute of Technology] .... DL
Davidson, NC [FM radio station call letters] .... WDAV
Davidson on Banks and Banking [Canada A publication] (DLA) .... Dav B & B
Davidson Tisdale Mines Ltd. [Toronto Stock Exchange symbol] .... DDT
Davidson's Conveyancing [A publication] (DLA) .... Dav Conv
Davidson's Precedents in Conveyancing [A publication] (DLA) .... Dav Prec Conv
Davidson's Reports [92-111 North Carolina] [A publication] (DLA) .... Davidson
Davie County Public Library, Mocksville, NC [Library symbol Library of Congress] (LCLS) .... NcMoc
Davie, FL [AM radio station call letters] .... WAVS
Davies' District Court Reports [2 Ware] [United States] [A publication] (DLA) .... Dav (US)
Davies' District Court Reports [2 Ware] [United States] [A publication] (DLA) .... Davies (US)
Davies' English Patent Cases [1785-1816] [A publication] (DLA) .... Dav
Davies' English Patent Cases [1785-1816] [A publication] (DLA) .... Dav P C
Davies' English Patent Cases [1785-1816] [A publication] (DLA) .... Dav Pat Cas
Davies' English Patent Cases [1785-1816] [A publication] (DLA) .... Davies (Eng)

Davies Herbarium, University of Louisville [Kentucky] .... DHL
Davies' Irish King's Bench and Exchequer Reports [1604-12] [A publication] (DLA) .... Dav
Davies on Annuities [A publication] (DLA) .... Dav Ann
Davies on French Mercantile Law [A publication] (DLA) .... Dav Fr Merc Law
Davies' Patent Cases [1785-1816] [A publication] (DLA) .... Davies
Davies' United States District Court Reports [Republished as 2 Ware] [A publication] (DLA) .... Dav
Davies' United States District Court Reports [Republished as 2 Ware] [A publication] (DLA) .... Davies
Davis [Australia Geomagnetic observatory code] .... DVS
Davis 3-Wheel Club of America (EA) D3WCA
Davis' Abridgment of Coke's Reports [A publication] (DLA) .... Dav Coke
Davis' Administrative Law Treatise [A publication] (DLA) .... Davis Admin Law
Davis and Elkins College [West Virginia] .... DEC
Davis and Elkins College, Elkins, WV [OCLC symbol] (OCLC) .... WVD
Davis and Elkins College, Elkins, WV [Library symbol Library of Congress] (LCLS) .... WvED
Davis, CA [FM radio station call letters] .... KDVS
Davis, CA [FM radio station call letters] .... KQBR
Davis Computer Systems, Inc. .... DCS
Davis County Genealogical Society, Bloomfield, IA [Library symbol Library of Congress] (LCLS) .... IaBlGen
Davis County Library, Farmington, UT [Library symbol Library of Congress] (LCLS) .... UFD
Davis County Republican, Bloomfield, IA [Library symbol Library of Congress] (LCLS) .... IaBlDR
Davis' Criminal Law [A publication] (DLA) .... Dav Cr Law
Davis' Criminal Law [A publication] (DLA) .... Davis Cr Law
Davis' Criminal Law Consolidation Acts [A publication] (DLA) .... Dav Cr Cons
Davis Distributing Ltd. [Toronto Stock Exchange symbol] .... DAD
Davis' English Church Canons [A publication] (DLA) .... Dav Can
Davis' English Church Canons [A publication] (DLA) .... Dav Eng Ch Can
Davis Escape Apparatus [British military] (DMA) .... DEA
Davis' Hawaiian Reports [A publication] (DLA) .... Dav
Davis' Hawaiian Reports [A publication] (DLA) .... Davis
Davis' Hawaiian Reports [A publication] (DLA) .... Davis Rep
Davis' Indiana Digest [A publication] (DLA) .... Dav Dig
Davis' Indiana Digest [A publication] (DLA) .... Dav Ind Dig
Davis' Justice of the Peace [A publication] (DLA) .... Dav Jus
Davis' Land Court Decisions [1898-1908] [A publication] (DLA) .... Dav Land Ct Cas
Davis' Land Court Decisions [1898-1908] [A publication] (DLA) .... Davis L Ct Cas
Davis' Land Court Decisions (Massachusetts) [1898-1908] [A publication] (ILCA) .... Davis Land Ct Dec (Mass)
Davis' Law of Building Societies [A publication] (DLA) .... Davis Bdg
Davis' Law of Building Societies [A publication] (DLA) .... Davis Bldg Soc
Davis' Law of Master and Servant [A publication] (DLA) .... Dav M & S
Davis' Law of Registration and Election [A publication] (DLA) .... Dav Elec
Davis' Massachusetts Conveyancer's Handbook [A publication] (DLA) .... Davis Mass Convey Hdbk
Davis Medical Group [Commercial firm] .... DMG
Davis on Friendly Societies and Trade Unions [A publication] (DLA) .... Dav Fr Soc
Davis on Industrial and Provident Societies [A publication] (DLA) ...... Dav Ind Soc
Davis on the Labor Laws [A publication] (DLA) .... Dav Lab L
Davis Online Reference Services [University of California, Davis] (OLDSS) .... DORS
Davis, Polk & Wardwell, Law Library, New York, NY [Library symbol Library of Congress] (LCLS) .... NNDPW
Davis Polk & Wardwell, Library, New York, NY [OCLC symbol] (OCLC) .... DPW
Davis' Precedents of Indictment [A publication] (DLA) .... Dav Prec Ind
Davis' Reports [Abridgment of Sir Edward Coke's Reports] [A publication] (DLA) .... Dav
Davis Submerged Escape Apparatus [British military] (DMA) .... DSEA
Davis' Trade Unions [A publication] (DLA) .... Dav Tr Un
Davis' United States Supreme Court Reports [A publication] (DLA) .... Dav
Davis' United States Supreme Court Reports [A publication] (DLA) .... Davis
Davis' United States Supreme Court Reports [A publication] (DLA) .... Davis (JCB)
Davis Water & Waste [NYSE symbol] (TTSB) .... DWW
Davis Water & Waste Industries, Inc. [Associated Press] (SAG) .... DavWtr
Davis Water & Waste Industries, Inc. [NYSE symbol] (SPSG) .... DWW
Davis-Bacon Act [1921] .... DBA
Davis-Bacon Act Decision [DOL] (AAGC) .... DB
Davis-Besse Nuclear Power Station (NRCH) .... DBNPS
Davis-Keays Mining [Vancouver Stock Exchange symbol] .... DVK
Davison and Merivale's English Queen's Bench Reports [A publication] (DLA) .... D & M
Davison and Merivale's English Queen's Bench Reports [A publication] (DLA) .... D & Mer
Davison and Merivale's English Queen's Bench Reports [A publication] (DLA) .... Dav & M
Davison and Merivale's English Queen's Bench Reports [A publication] (DLA) .... Dav & M (Eng)
Davison and Merivale's English Queen's Bench Reports [A publication] (DLA) .... Dav & Mer
Davison and Merivale's King's Bench Reports [64 RR] [1843-44] [A publication] (DLA) .... DM
Davison Elementary School, Malverne, NY [Library symbol Library of Congress] (LCLS) .... NMalvDE
Davison on Registration and Elections [A publication] (DLA) .... Dav Reg
Davison United States Army Airfield (AABC) .... DUSAA
Davisson-Germer Experiment [Physics] .... DGE
Davox Corp. [Associated Press] (SAG) .... Davox
Davox Corp. [NASDAQ symbol] (NQ) .... DAVX
Davy Crockett [A tactical atomic weapon] [Army] .... DC
Davy McKee Research & Development [British] (IRUK) .... DMRD

Davys' English King's Bench Reports [*A publication*] (DLA) .... Davys
Davys' English King's Bench Reports [*A publication*] (DLA) .... Davys (Eng)
Daw [*New Britain*] [*Seismograph station code, US Geological Survey Closed*] (SEIS) .... DAW
Daw Technologies [*NASDAQ symbol*] (TTSB) .... DAWK
Daw Technologies, Inc. [*Associated Press*] (SAG) .... Daw Tch
Daw Technologies, Inc. [*NASDAQ symbol*] (SAG) .... DAWK
Dawe on Arrest in Civil Cases [*A publication*] (DLA) .... Daw Ar
Dawe on Crimes and Punishments [*A publication*] (DLA) .... Daw Cr & Pun
Dawe's Epitome of the Law of Landed Property [*A publication*] (DLA) .... Daw Land Pr
Dawe's Real Estate Law [*A publication*] (DLA) .... Daw Real Pr
Dawlatabad [*Afghanistan*] [*ICAO location identifier*] (ICLI) .... OADD
Dawn Air, Inc. [*ICAO designator*] (FAAC) .... DWN
Dawn and Dusk Combat Air Patrol .... DADCAP
Dawn Battle Order [*British military*] (DMA) .... DBO
Dawn Bible Students Association (EA) .... DBSA
Dawson City [*Yukon*] [*Airport symbol*] (AD) .... YDA
Dawson College, Glendive, MT [*Library symbol Library of Congress*] (LCLS) .... MtGD
Dawson College Library [*UTLAS symbol*] .... DAW
Dawson College, Montreal, Quebec [*Library symbol National Library of Canada*] (NLC) .... QMDC
Dawson County High School, Glendive, MT [*Library symbol*] [*Library of Congress*] (LCLS) .... MtGDH
Dawson County Junior College [*Montana*] .... DCJC
Dawson Creek [*Canada*] [*Airport symbol*] (OAG) .... YDQ
Dawson Creek, BC [*AM radio station call letters*] .... CJDC
Dawson Creek, BC [*FM radio station call letters*] .... CJDC-FM
Dawson Creek, BC [*Television station call letters*] .... CJDC-TV
Dawson Creek, BC [*ICAO location identifier*] (ICLI) .... CYDQ
Dawson Creek Public Library, British Columbia [*Library symbol National Library of Canada*] (NLC) .... BDC
Dawson Creek Public Library, Dawson Creek, BC, Canada [*Library symbol Library of Congress*] (LCLS) .... CaBDC
Dawson Eldorado Gold [*Vancouver Stock Exchange symbol*] .... DEG
Dawson, GA [*Television station call letters*] .... WACS
Dawson Geophysical [*NASDAQ symbol*] (TTSB) .... DWSN
Dawson Geophysical Co. [*Associated Press*] (SAG) .... Dawson
Dawson Geophysical Co. [*NASDAQ symbol*] (NQ) .... DWSN
Dawson Production Services, Inc. [*Associated Press*] (SAG) .... DawsnP
Dawson Production Services, Inc. [*NASDAQ symbol*] (SAG) .... DPSI
Dawson Production Svcs [*NASDAQ symbol*] (TTSB) .... DPSI
Dawson Public Library, Dawson, YT, Canada [*Library symbol Library of Congress*] (LCLS) .... CaYDaw
Dawson Public Library, Yukon [*Library symbol National Library of Canada*] (NLC) .... YDAW
Dawson, YT [*ICAO location identifier*] (ICLI) .... CYDA
Dawson-Boyd Public Library, Dawson, MN [*Library symbol*] [*Library of Congress*] (LCLS) .... MnDawPS
Dawson's Attorney's [*A publication*] (DLA) .... Daw Att
Dawson's Code of Civil Procedure [*Colorado*] [*A publication*] (DLA) .... Dawson's Code
Dawson's Origo Legum [*A publication*] (DLA) .... Daw Or Leg
Dax/Seyresse [*France ICAO location identifier*] (ICLI) .... LFBY
Daxor Corp. [*Associated Press*] (SAG) .... Daxor
Daxor Corp. [*AMEX symbol*] (SPSG) .... DXR
Dax's Exchequer Precedents [*A publication*] (DLA) .... Dax Exch Pr
Dax's Practice in the Offices of the Masters [*A publication*] (DLA) .... Dax Mast Pr
Day [*Broadcasting term*] .... D
Day [*SI symbol*] .... d
Day [*Approach and landing charts*] [*Aviation*] .... D
Day (WDMC) .... d
Day .... DA
Day (MSA) .... DY
Day Activity Center .... DAC
Day and Night [*Approach and landing charts*] [*Aviation*] .... DN
Day and Night Average Sound Levels .... DNL
Day and Night Television System [*Army*] (MCD) .... DANTS
Day Beacon [*USCG*] (TAG) .... DBN
Day Book [*Accounting*] .... DB
Day Care Center .... DCC
Day Care Mother (ADA) .... DCM
Day Fighter/Ground Attack [*British military*] (DMA) .... DF/GA
Day Fighter Leaders School [*British military*] (DMA) .... DFLS
Day Frequency (IAA) .... DF
Day Hospital .... DH
Day/Hour:Minute:Second (NASA) .... DD/HH:MM:SS
[*A*] **Day in the Life** [*Series*] [*Photojournalism project*] .... DITL
[*A*] **Day in the Life of America** [*Photojournalism project*] .... DITLA
[*A*] **Day in the Life of Hawaii** [*Photojournalism project*] .... DITLOHA
Day Letter [*Telegraphy*] .... DL
Day/Night Approach Computer Image Generator [*Aviation*] .... D/NCIG
Day/Night Camera System (MCD) .... DNCS
Day/Night Reflex Sight [*Military*] (INF) .... DNRS
Day Night Switching Equipment [*Telecommunications*] .... DNSW
Day Number (SSD) .... DN
Day of Admission [*Medicine*] (DAVI) .... d/A
Day of Ammunition .... DOA
Day of Discharge (DAVI) .... d/D
Day of Sale [*Business term*] (ADA) .... DOS
Day of Supply [*Military*] .... D of S
Day of Supply [*Military*] .... DOFS
Day of Surgery (DAVI) .... D/S
Day of Year .... DOY
Day Order [*Investment term*] .... DO
Day Plane Guard [*Military*] (NVT) .... DPLG
Day Press Rate [*Telegraph rate*] (NTCM) .... DPR
Day Return [*Round trip fare within one calendar day*] [*British*] .... D
Day Room Orderly [*Army*] .... DRO
Day Runner [*NASDAQ symbol*] (TTSB) .... DAYR
Day Runner, Inc. [*NASDAQ symbol*] (SAG) .... DAYR
Day Runner, Inc. [*Associated Press*] (SAG) .... DayRun
Day Sailer Association (EA) .... DSA
Day Television [*Sensing equipment*] .... DTV
Day Television Tracking System [*Military*] .... DTTS
Day Treatment Center [*Medicine*] (DAVI) .... DTC
Day Visual Flight Rules [*FAA*] (TAG) .... DVFR
Day-After Recall [*Advertising*] .... DAR
Daybreak .... DABRK
Daydream Island [*Australia Airport symbol*] (OAG) .... DDI
Daydream Island [*Queensland*] [*Airport symbol*] (AD) .... DEQ
Day-for-Night (WDMC) .... D/N
Daylight (FAAC) .... DALGT
Daylight (NTCM) .... DAY
Daylight (MSA) .... DL
Daylight (WDMC) .... dlt
Daylight Factor (DAC) .... DF
Daylight Impression [*Psychical research*] .... DI
Daylight Opening .... DLO
Daylight Rapid Contacting (DGA) .... DRC
Daylight Saving Time .... DST
Daylight Saving Time Coalition [*Inactive*] (EA) .... DSTC
Daylight Time .... DT
Daylight View Plan Position Indicator (CET) .... DVPPI
Daylight Visual Observation (MCD) .... DAVO
Day-Month-Year (DNAB) .... DA-MON-YR
Day-Night Capability [*Aerospace*] (AAG) .... DNC
Day-Night Indirect Attack Seeker (DNAB) .... DNIAS
Day-Old .... DO
Days a Week [*Classified advertising*] .... DAW
Days after Acceptance [*Business term*] .... DA
Days after Anthesis [*Botany*] .... DAA
Days after Contact .... DAC
Days after Contract [*Business term*] (MCD) .... DAC
Days after Contract Award [*Business term*] (MCD) .... DACA
Days after Date [*Business term*] .... DD
Days after Delivery .... DD
Days after Deployment .... DAD
Days after Emergence [*Botany*] .... DAE
Days after Flowering [*Botany*] .... DAF
Days after Pollination [*Botany*] .... DAP
Days after Receipt of Order (MCD) .... DARO
Days after Sight [*Business term*] .... DS
Days after Transplanting [*Botany*] .... DT
Days after Treatment [*Agriculture*] .... DAT
Days At Sea [*Marine science*] (OSRA) .... DAS
Days at Sea (USDC) .... DAS
Days before Anthesis [*Botany*] .... DBA
Days before Launch [*Usually followed by a number*] [*NASA*] (KSC) L
Days before Move Operation [*Usually followed by a number*] [*NASA*] (KSC) .... M
Day's Connecticut Reports [*A publication*] (DLA) .... Day
Day's Connecticut Reports [*A publication*] (DLA) .... Day's Ca
Day's Connecticut Reports [*A publication*] (DLA) .... Day's Ca Er
Day's Connecticut Reports [*A publication*] (DLA) .... Day's Cases
Day's Connecticut Reports [*A publication*] (DLA) .... Day's Conn Rep
Day's Date .... DD
Days Delay at Address within CONUS [*Continental United States*] **Authorized Chargeable as Leave** [*Military*] .... DDALVAHP
Days Delay Enroute Authorized Chargeable as Leave [*Military*] .... DDALV
Day's Election Cases [*1892-93*] [*England*] [*A publication*] (DLA) .... Day
Day's Election Cases [*1892-93*] [*England*] [*A publication*] (DLA) .... Day Elect Cas
Days in Culture [*of cells*] .... DIC
Days in Vitro [*Cell culture*] .... DIV
Days Lost [*Military*] .... DL
Days of Grace [*for payment*] [*Business term*] .... DOG
Days of Our Lives [*NBC-TV daytime serial*] .... DOOL
Days of Supply [*Rations*] .... DOS
Days per Thousand .... DPT
Days Post Inoculation [*Medicine*] (DMAA) .... DPI
Days Postpollination [*Botany*] .... DPP
Days' Purposes [*Shipping*] .... DP
Days Sales Outstanding [*Business term*] (MHDB) .... DSO
Days since Planting [*Botany*] .... DSP
Day-Second-Foot [*Measurement*] .... DSF
Daysland Public Library, Alberta [*Library symbol National Library of Canada*] (NLC) .... ADA
Daystrom Analog-to-Digital Integrating Translator .... DADIT
Daytime (NTCM) .... D
Daytime Broadcasters Association [*Defunct*] (EA) .... DBA
Daytime Multiple Sleep Latency Test [*Neurology*] (DAVI) .... DMSLT
Daytime Running Lights [*Automotive engineering*] .... DRL
Day-Timer Pen Scheduler .... DTPS
Dayton [*Ohio*] [*Airport symbol*] (OAG) .... DAY
Dayton Air Force Depot .... DAFD
Dayton and Montgomery County Public Library, Dayton, OH [*OCLC symbol*] (OCLC) .... DMM
Dayton and Montgomery County Public Library, Dayton, OH [*Library symbol Library of Congress*] (LCLS) .... ODa
Dayton Area Office [*Energy Research and Development Administration*] .... DAO

Dayton Art Institute, Dayton, OH [*Library symbol Library of Congress*] (LCLS) ... ODaA
Dayton Development Corp. [*Vancouver Stock Exchange symbol*] ... DD
Dayton Engineering Laboratories Co. ... DELCO
Dayton Hudson [*NYSE symbol*] (TTSB) ... DH
Dayton Hudson Corp. [*NYSE symbol*] (SAG) ... DH
Dayton Hudson Department Store Co. [*Division of Dayton-Hudson Corp.*] ... DHDSC
Dayton/James M. Coxdayton Municipal [*Ohio*] [*ICAO location identifier*] (ICLI) ... KDAY
Dayton Mining [*AMEX symbol*] (TTSB) ... DAY
Dayton Mining Corp. [*AMEX symbol*] (SAG) ... DAY
Dayton Mining Corp. [*Associated Press*] (SAG) ... DaytonMn
Dayton Mining Group [*Associated Press*] (SAG) ... DaytMn
Dayton Museum of Natural History, Dayton, OH [*Library symbol Library of Congress*] (LCLS) ... ODaMNH
Dayton, OH [*Location identifier FAA*] (FAAL) ... ATD
Dayton, OH [*Location identifier FAA*] (FAAL) ... DAY
Dayton, OH [*Location identifier FAA*] (FAAL) ... EGK
Dayton, OH [*Location identifier FAA*] (FAAL) ... FAE
Dayton, OH [*Location identifier FAA*] (FAAL) ... FFO
Dayton, OH [*Location identifier FAA*] (FAAL) ... JQC
Dayton, OH [*Location identifier FAA*] (FAAL) ... MGY
Dayton, OH [*Location identifier FAA*] (FAAL) ... VUQ
Dayton, OH [*AM radio station call letters*] ... WDAO
Dayton, OH [*FM radio station call letters*] ... WDPR
Dayton, OH [*FM radio station call letters*] ... WDPS
Dayton, OH [*Television station call letters*] ... WDTN
Dayton, OH [*FM radio station call letters*] ... WGXM
Dayton, OH [*AM radio station call letters*] ... WHIO
Dayton, OH [*Television station call letters*] ... WHIO-TV
Dayton, OH [*FM radio station call letters*] ... WHKO
Dayton, OH [*AM radio station call letters*] ... WING
Dayton, OH [*Television station call letters*] ... WKEF
Dayton, OH [*FM radio station call letters*] ... WMMX
Dayton, OH [*AM radio station call letters*] ... WONE
Dayton, OH [*Television station call letters*] ... WPTD
Dayton, OH [*Television station call letters*] ... WRGT
Dayton, OH [*FM radio station call letters*] ... WTUE
Dayton, OH [*FM radio station call letters*] ... WWSU
Dayton Reports [*Ohio*] [*A publication*] (DLA) ... Dayton Rep
Dayton Reports (Ohio) [*A publication*] (DLA) ... Dayton (Ohio)
Dayton Review, Dayton, IA [*Library symbol Library of Congress*] (LCLS) ... IaDayR
Dayton Superior and Common Pleas Reports [*Ohio*] [*A publication*] (DLA) ... Dayton
Dayton Term Reports [*Ohio*] [*A publication*] (DLA) ... Dayt Term Rep
Dayton, TN [*Location identifier FAA*] (FAAL) ... DTE
Dayton, TN [*AM radio station call letters*] ... WDNT
Dayton, TN [*FM radio station call letters*] ... WDNT-FM
Dayton, TN [*AM radio station call letters*] ... WREA
Dayton, WA [*FM radio station call letters*] ... KZHR
Dayton/Wright-Patterson Air Force Base [*Ohio*] [*ICAO location identifier*] (ICLI) ... KFFO
Daytona Beach [*Florida*] [*Airport symbol*] (OAG) ... DAB
Daytona Beach Community College, Daytona Beach, FL [*Library symbol*] [*Library of Congress*] (LCLS) ... FDbCC
Daytona Beach, FL [*Television station call letters*] ... WAYQ
Daytona Beach, FL [*FM radio station call letters*] ... WCFB
Daytona Beach, FL [*Television station call letters*] ... WESH
Daytona Beach, FL [*FM radio station call letters*] ... WJHM
Daytona Beach, FL [*AM radio station call letters*] ... WMFJ
Daytona Beach, FL [*AM radio station call letters*] ... WNDB
Daytona Beach, FL [*TV station call letters*] (RBYB) ... WNTO-TV
Daytona Beach, FL [*AM radio station call letters*] ... WROD
Daytona International Speedway [*Auto racing*] ... DIS
Dayton-Hudson Corp. [*Associated Press*] (SAG) ... DaytHd
Dayton-Miami Valley Library Consortium - Library Division [*Library network*] ... DMVC
Dayton's Law of Surrogates [*A publication*] (DLA) ... Day Sur
Dayton's Law of Surrogates [*A publication*] (DLA) ... Dayt Sur
Day-Wilson-Campbell, Toronto, Ontario [*Library symbol National Library of Canada*] (BIB) ... OTDW
DB - Panhard Registry (EA) ... DBPR
DB with Respect to a Circular Polarized Antenna (GFGA) ... DBCI
DBA Systems [*NASDAQ symbol*] (TTSB) ... DBAS
DBA Systems, Inc. [*Associated Press*] (SAG) ... DBA
DBA Systems, Inc. [*NASDAQ symbol*] (NQ) ... DBAS
DBH [*Dopamine Beta-Hydroxylase*] **Index** ... DBHI
DBMO and Psophometrically Weighted for Sound Programme Transmission [*Telecommunications*] (NITA) ... DBMOPS
DBMO and Psophometrically Weighted for Telephony [*Telecommunications*] (NITA) ... DBMOP
DBT Online, Inc. [*Associated Press*] (SAG) ... DBT Onl
DBT Online, Inc. [*NASDAQ symbol*] (SAG) ... DBTO
DC Noise Margin (MCD) ... DCM
DC Resistance (IDOE) ... R_{dc}
DC Technology Missile (MCD) ... DCTM
DC Voltage (IDOE) ... dcv
DC [*Direct Current*] **Voltage** (ACII) ... VDC
DC Volts (IDOE) ... dcv
DC Working Voltage (IDOE) ... WVdc
DC Working Voltage (IDOE) ... ydcw
DCAA [*Defense Contract Audit Agency*] **Integrated Information System** [*DoD*] (GFGA) ... DIIS
DCAS [*Defense Contract Administration Services*] **Quality Assurance Staff Development Office** ... DQADO
DCASR [*Defense Contract Administration Services Region*], Atlanta ... DCRA
DCASR [*Defense Contract Administration Services Region*], Boston ... DCRB
DCASR [*Defense Contract Administration Services Region*], Chicago ... DCRI
DCASR [*Defense Contract Administration Services Region*], Cleveland ... DCRO
DCASR [*Defense Contract Administration Services Region*], Dallas ... DCRT
DCASR [*Defense Contract Administration Services Region*], Detroit ... DCRD
DCASR [*Defense Contract Administration Services Region*], Los Angeles ... DCRL
DCASR [*Defense Contract Administration Services Region*], New York ... DCRN
DCASR [*Defense Contract Administration Services Region*], Philadelphia ... DCRP
DCASR [*Defense Contract Administration Services Region*], St. Louis ... DCRS
DCASR [*Defense Contract Administration Services Region*], San Francisco ... DCRC
DCH Consultants, Inc., Ottawa, ON, Canada [*Library symbol*] [*Library of Congress*] (LCLS) ... CaOODCH
DCH Consultants, Inc., Ottawa, Ontario [*Library symbol National Library of Canada*] (NLC) ... OODCH
DC-Induced Second Harmonic Generation (MCD) ... DCSHG
DCSLOG [*Deputy Chief of Staff for Logistics*] **Data Processing Center** [*Military*] (AABC) ... DDPC
DCSOPS [*Deputy Chief of Staff for Operations and Plans*]/ACSI Computer System [*Assistant Chief of Staff for Intelligence*] [*Army*] ... DACS
DCX, Inc. [*Associated Press*] (SAG) ... DCX
DCX, Inc. [*NASDAQ symbol*] (NQ) ... DCXI
DDB Needham Worldwide, Inc. Information Center, Chicago, IL [*Library symbol*] [*Library of Congress*] (LCLS) ... ICDDB
DDL Electronics [*Formerly, Data-Design Laboratories*] [*NYSE symbol*] (SPSG) ... DDL
DDL Electronics [*Associated Press*] (SAG) ... DDL Elc
DDL Foodshow [*Food emporium which derives its name from its creator, movie producer Dino DeLaurentiis*] ... DDL
De Aar [*South Africa*] [*ICAO location identifier*] (ICLI) ... FADA
De Abrahamo [*Philo*] (BJA) ... Abr
De Abstinentia [*of Porphyry*] [*Classical studies*] (OCD) ... Abst
De Aedificiis [*of Procopius*] [*Classical studies*] (OCD) ... Aed
De Aeternitate Mundi [*Philo*] (BJA) ... Aet
De Agricultura [*Philo*] (BJA) ... Agr
De Agricultura or De Re Rustica Origines [*of Cato*] [*Classical studies*] (OCD) ... Agr Rust Orig
De Amicitia [*of Cicero*] [*Classical studies*] (OCD) ... Amic
De Andreis Seminary, Lemont, IL [*Library symbol Library of Congress*] (LCLS) ... ILeD
De Anima [*of Aristotle*] [*Classical studies*] (OCD) ... De An
De Antro Nympharum [*of Porphyry*] [*Classical studies*] (OCD) ... De Antr Nymph
De Aquae Ductu Urbis Romae [*of Frontinus*] [*Classical studies*] (OCD) ... Aq
De Architectura [*of Vitruvius*] [*Classical studies*] (OCD) ... De Arch
De Baca Resources, Inc. [*Vancouver Stock Exchange symbol*] ... DEB
De Badande Vannerna [*Sweden*] ... DBV
De Baptismo [*of Tertullian*] [*Classical studies*] (OCD) ... De Bapt
De Beers Consolidated Mines [*NASDAQ symbol*] (NQ) ... DBRS
De Bello Gothico [*of Procopius*] [*Classical studies*] (OCD) ... Goth
De Bello Judaico [*Josephus*] (BJA) ... BellJud
De Bello Vandalico [*of Procopius*] [*Classical studies*] (OCD) ... Vand
De Bene Esse [*Conditionally*] [*Latin Legal term*] (DLA) ... DBE
De Beneficiis [*of Seneca the Younger*] [*Classical studies*] (OCD) ... Ben
De Bilt [*Netherlands*] [*Later, WIT*] [*Geomagnetic observatory code*] ... DBN
De Bilt [*Netherlands ICAO location identifier*] (ICLI) ... EHDB
De Boeken van het Oude Testament [*Roermond/Maaseik*] [*A publication*] (BJA) ... BOT
De Boeken van het Oude Testament [*Roermond/Maaseik*] [*A publication*] (BJA) ... BOuT
De Bonis Asportatis [*Trespass to Personalty*] [*Latin Legal term*] (DLA) ... DBA
De Bonis Non [*Of the Goods Not Yet Administered*] ... DBN
De Caelo [*of Aristotle*] [*Classical studies*] (OCD) ... Cael
De Candolle [*Botanist, 1778-1841*] (ROG) ... DC
De Causis Plantarum [*of Theophrastus*] [*Classical studies*] (OCD) ... Caus Pl
De Cherubim [*Philo*] (BJA) ... Cher
De Civitate Dei [*of Augustine*] [*Classical studies*] (OCD) ... De Civ D
De Clementia [*of Seneca the Younger*] [*Classical studies*] (OCD) ... Clem
De Coloribus [*of Aristotle*] [*Classical studies*] (OCD) ... Col
De Colyar's English County Court Cases [*1867-82*] [*A publication*] (DLA) ... De Col
De Colyar's English County Court Cases [*1867-82*] [*A publication*] (DLA) ... De Coly
De Colyar's Law of Guaranty [*A publication*] (DLA) ... De Col Guar
De Compositione Verborum [*of Dionysius Halicarnassensis*] [*Classical studies*] (OCD) ... Comp
De Confusione Linguarum [*Philo*] (BJA) ... Conf
De Constantia Sapientis [*of Seneca the Younger*] [*Classical studies*] (OCD) ... Constant
De Consulatu Honorii [*of Claudianus*] [*Classical studies*] (OCD) ... Cons Hon
De Consulatu Stilichonis [*of Claudianus*] [*Classical studies*] (OCD) ... Cons Stil
De Corona [*of Demosthenes*] [*Classical studies*] (OCD) ... De Cor
De Dato [*Of Today's Date*] [*Latin*] ... DD
De Decalogo [*Philo*] (BJA) ... Decal
De Defectu Oraculorum [*of Plutarch*] [*Classical studies*] (OCD) ... De Def Or
De Demosthene [*of Dionysius Halicarnassensis*] [*Classical studies*] (OCD) ... Dem
De Deo [*Philo*] (BJA) ... Deo
De Deo Socratico [*of Apuleius*] [*Classical studies*] (OCD) ... De Deo Soc
De Die [*Daily*] [*Pharmacy*] ... DD
De Die in Diem [*From Day to Day*] [*Latin*] ... DD in D
De Die in Diem [*From Day to Day*] [*Latin*] ... DE D in D
De Dion-Bouton [*Automobile*] [*French*] ... DDB
De Divinatione [*of Cicero*] [*Classical studies*] (OCD) ... Div
De Divinatione per Somnia [*of Aristotle*] [*Classical studies*] (OCD) ... Div Somn

De Dogmate Platonis [*of Apuleius*] [*Classical studies*] (OCD) .... De Dog Plat
De Domo Sua [*of Cicero*] [*Classical studies*] (OCD) .... Dom
De Ea Re Ita Censuere [*Concerning That Matter Have So Decreed*] [*Latin Legal term*] (DLA) .... DERIC
De Ebrietate [*Philo*] (BJA) .... Ebr
De Exilio [*of Plutarch*] [*Classical studies*] (OCD) .... De Exil
De Exsecrationibus [*Philo*] (BJA) .... Exs
De Facie in Orbe Lunae [*of Plutarch*] [*Classical studies*] (OCD) .... De Fac
De Facto Cases [*Australia A publication*] .... DFC
De Fato [*of Cicero*] [*Classical studies*] (OCD) .... Fat
De Finibus [*of Cicero*] [*Classical studies*] (OCD) .... Fin
De Fooz on Mines [*A publication*] (DLA) .... DeF Min
De Fortuna Alexandri [*of Plutarch*] [*Classical studies*] (OCD) .... De Alex Fort
De Fortuna Romanorum [*of Plutarch*] [*Classical studies*] (OCD) .... De Fort Rom
De Fraterno Amore [*of Plutarch*] [*Classical studies*] (OCD) .... De Frat Amor
De Fuga et Inventione [*Philo*] (BJA) .... Fug
De Funiak Springs, FL [*FM radio station call letters*] .... WMXZ
De Funiak Springs, FL [*AM radio station call letters*] .... WZEP
De Garrulitate [*of Plutarch*] [*Classical studies*] (OCD) .... De Garr
De Generatione Animalium [*of Aristotle*] [*Classical studies*] (OCD) .... Gen An
De Generatione et Corruptione [*of Aristotle*] [*Classical studies*] (OCD) .... Gen Corr
De Genio Socratis [*of Plutarch*] [*Classical studies*] (OCD) .... De Gen
De Gex and Jones' English Bankruptcy Appeals [*1857-59*] [*A publication*] (ILCA) .... De G & J By
De Gex and Jones' English Bankruptcy Appeals [*1857-59*] [*A publication*] (DLA) .... De G & JB
De Gex and Jones' English Bankruptcy Reports [*1857-59*] [*A publication*] (DLA) .... D & JB
De Gex and Jones' English Bankruptcy Reports [*1857-59*] [*A publication*] (DLA) .... DG & JB
De Gex and Jones' English Chancery Reports [*A publication*] (DLA) .... D & J
De Gex and Jones' English Chancery Reports [*A publication*] (ILCA) .... De G & J
De Gex and Jones' English Chancery Reports [*A publication*] (DLA) .... DG & J
De Gex and Smale's English Chancery Reports [*63-64 English Reprint*] [*1846-52*] [*A publication*] (DLA) .... D & S
De Gex and Smale's English Chancery Reports [*63-64 English Reprint*] [*1846-52*] [*A publication*] (DLA) .... De G & S
De Gex and Smale's English Chancery Reports [*63-64 English Reprint*] [*1846-52*] [*A publication*] (ILCA) .... De G & Sm
De Gex and Smale's Reports Tempore Knight-Bruce and Parker, Vice-Chancellor's Court [*1846-52*] [*England*] [*A publication*] (DLA) .... D & Sm
De Gex, Fisher, and Jones' English Bankruptcy Reports [*A publication*] (DLA) .... DF & JB
De Gex, Fisher, and Jones' English Bankruptcy Reports [*A publication*] (DLA) .... DG F & JB
De Gex, Fisher, and Jones' English Bankruptcy Reports [*A publication*] (DLA) .... F & J Bank
De Gex, Fisher, and Jones' English Chancery Reports [*A publication*] (DLA) .... De G F & J
De Gex, Fisher, and Jones' English Chancery Reports [*A publication*] (DLA) .... De Gex F & J
De Gex, Fisher, and Jones' English Chancery Reports [*A publication*] (DLA) .... DF & J
De Gex, Fisher, and Jones' English Chancery Reports [*A publication*] (DLA) .... DG F & J
De Gex, Jones, and Smith's English Bankruptcy Appeals [*1862-65*] [*A publication*] (DLA) .... De G J & S By
De Gex, Jones, and Smith's English Bankruptcy Reports [*A publication*] (DLA) .... DG J & SB
De Gex, Jones, and Smith's English Bankruptcy Reports [*A publication*] (DLA) .... DJ & SB
De Gex, Jones, and Smith's English Chancery Reports [*A publication*] (DLA) .... De G J & S
De Gex, Jones, and Smith's English Chancery Reports [*A publication*] (DLA) .... De G J & S (Eng)
De Gex, Jones, and Smith's English Chancery Reports [*A publication*] (DLA) .... De G J & Sm
De Gex, Jones, and Smith's English Chancery Reports [*A publication*] (DLA) .... De Gex J & S
De Gex, Jones, and Smith's English Chancery Reports [*A publication*] (DLA) .... DG J & S
De Gex, Jones, and Smith's English Chancery Reports [*A publication*] (DLA) .... DJ & S
De Gex, Macnaghten, and Gordon's English Bankruptcy Appeals [*1837-55*] [*A publication*] (DLA) .... De G M & G By
De Gex, Macnaghten, and Gordon's English Bankruptcy Reports [*A publication*] (DLA) .... D M & GB
De Gex, Macnaghten, and Gordon's English Bankruptcy Reports [*A publication*] (DLA) .... De G M & G
De Gex, Macnaghten, and Gordon's English Bankruptcy Reports [*A publication*] (DLA) .... De Gex M & GB
De Gex, Macnaghten, and Gordon's English Bankruptcy Reports [*A publication*] (DLA) .... DG M & GB
De Gex, Macnaghten, and Gordon's English Chancery Reports [*A publication*] (DLA) .... D M & G
De Gex, Macnaghten, and Gordon's English Chancery Reports [*A publication*] (DLA) .... De G M & G
De Gex, Macnaghten, and Gordon's English Chancery Reports [*A publication*] (DLA) .... DG M & G
De Gex, Macnaghten, and Gordon's English Reports [*A publication*] (DLA) .... De Gex M & G
De Gex's English Bankruptcy Reports [*A publication*] (DLA) .... De G
De Gex's English Bankruptcy Reports [*A publication*] (DLA) .... De G Bankr
De Gex's English Bankruptcy Reports [*A publication*] (DLA) .... De G Bankr (Eng)
De Gex's English Bankruptcy Reports [*A publication*] (DLA) .... De Gex
De Gex's English Bankruptcy Reports [*A publication*] (DLA) .... DG
De Gigantibus [*Philo*] (BJA) .... Gig
De Gloria Atheniensium [*of Plutarch*] [*Classical studies*] (OCD) .... De Glor Ath
De Graff, OH [*FM radio station call letters*] .... WDEQ
De Grammaticis [*of Suetonius*] [*Classical studies*] (OCD) .... Gram
De Haas-van Alphen [*Effect*] .... DHVA
De Handschriften van de Dode Zee in Nederlandse Vertaling [*Amsterdam*] [*A publication*] (BJA) .... HDZNV
De Haruspicum Responso [*of Cicero*] [*Classical studies*] (OCD) .... Har Resp
De Havilland Aircraft Co. .... DH
De Havilland Aircraft Co., Canada .... DACC
De Havilland Aircraft of Canada Ltd. [*ICAO aircraft manufacturer identifier*] (ICAO) .... DH
De Havilland Aircraft of Canada Ltd., Downsview, Ontario [*Library symbol National Library of Canada*] (NLC) .... OTDHA
De Havilland Aircraft of Canada Ltd., Downsview, Toronto, ON, Canada [*Library symbol Library of Congress*] (LCLS) .... CaOTDHA
De Havilland, Inc. [*Canada*] [*FAA designator*] (FAAC) .... DHC
De Imitatione [*of Dionysius Halicarnassensis*] [*Classical studies*] (OCD) .... De Imit
De Interpretatione [*of Aristotle*] [*Classical studies*] (OCD) .... Int
De Inventione Rhetorica [*of Cicero*] [*Classical studies*] (OCD) .... Inv Rhet
De Iona [*Philo*] (BJA) .... Iona
De Iosepho [*Philo*] (BJA) .... Ios
De Iside et Osiride [*of Plutarch*] [*Classical studies*] (OCD) .... De Is et Os
De Isocrate [*of Dionysius Halicarnassensis*] [*Classical studies*] (OCD) .... Isoc
De Kalb & Western Transportation R. R. [*AAR code*] .... DKWT
De Kalb, IL [*FM radio station call letters*] .... WDEK
De Kalb, IL [*FM radio station call letters*] .... WDKB
De Kalb, IL [*AM radio station call letters*] .... WLBK
De Kalb, IL [*FM radio station call letters*] .... WNIU
De Kooy (Den Helder) [*Netherlands ICAO location identifier*] (ICLI) .... EHKD
De La Rue Automatic Cash System [*Banknote-disbursing equipment*] [*British*] .... DACS
De Lagatione ad Caium [*Philo*] (BJA) .... Legat
De Land, FL [*FM radio station call letters*] .... WOCL
De Land, FL [*AM radio station call letters*] .... WXVQ
De Land, FL [*AM radio station call letters*] .... WYND
De Latenter Vivendo [*of Plutarch*] [*Classical studies*] (OCD) .... De Lat Viv
De Lege Agraria [*of Cicero*] [*Classical studies*] (OCD) .... Leg Agr
De Legibus [*of Cicero*] [*Classical studies*] (OCD) .... Leg
De Lineis Insecabilibus [*of Aristotle*] [*Classical studies*] (OCD) .... Lin Ins
De Lingua Latina [*of Varro*] [*Classical studies*] (OCD) .... Ling
De Lolme on the English Constitution [*A publication*] (DLA) .... De Lolme Eng Const
De Lysia [*of Dionysius Halicarnassensis*] [*Classical studies*] (OCD) .... Lys
De Mello's Extradition Cases [*1877-1913*] [*Malaya*] [*A publication*] (DLA) .... De M
De Memoria [*of Aristotle*] [*Classical studies*] (OCD) .... Mem
De Migratione Abrahami [*Philo*] (BJA) .... Mig
De Monogamia [*of Tertullian*] [*Classical studies*] (OCD) .... De Monog
De Mortibus Persecutorum (BJA) .... DMP
De Mulierum Virtutibus [*of Plutarch*] [*Classical studies*] (OCD) .... De Mul Vir
De Mundo [*of Aristotle*] [*Classical studies*] (OCD) .... Mund
De Musica [*of Plutarch*] [*Classical studies*] (OCD) .... De Mus
De Mutatione Nominum [*Philo*] (BJA) .... Mut
De Natura Animalium [*of Aelianus*] [*Classical studies*] (OCD) .... NA
De Natura Deorum [*of Cicero*] [*Classical studies*] (OCD) .... Nat D
De Novo Corp. [*NASDAQ symbol*] (TTSB) .... DNVOF
De Novo Thymidylate [*Synthesis*] [*Biochemistry*] (DAVI) .... dTMP
De Odeon Kring [*The Odeon Club, for homosexuals*] [*Holland*] .... DOK
De Officiis [*of Cicero*] [*Classical studies*] (OCD) .... Off
De Olympiade Onder Dectatuur [*The Olympics Under Dictatorship*] [*An exhibition in 1936 by 150 artists protesting Nazi repression*] [*Reconstructed in 1996 by the Amsterdam Municipal Archives*] .... DOOD
De Opficio Mundi [*Philo*] (BJA) .... Op
De Oratore [*of Cicero*] [*Classical studies*] (OCD) .... De Or
De Partibus Animalium [*of Aristotle*] [*Classical studies*] (OCD) .... Part An
De Paul University [*Chicago, IL*] .... DEPU
De Paul University, Chicago, IL [*OCLC symbol*] (OCLC) .... IAC
De Paul University, Chicago, IL [*Library symbol Library of Congress*] (LCLS) .... ICD
De Paul University, Law Library, Chicago, IL [*OCLC symbol*] (OCLC) .... IBC
De Paul University, Law Library, Chicago, IL [*Library symbol Library of Congress*] (LCLS) .... ICD-L
De Pauw University, Archives, Greencastle, IN [*Library symbol Library of Congress*] (LCLS) .... InGrD-Ar
De Pauw University, Greencastle, IN [*OCLC symbol*] (OCLC) .... IDU
De Pauw University, Greencastle, IN [*Library symbol Library of Congress*] (LCLS) .... InGrD
De Pere, WI [*FM radio station call letters*] (RBYB) .... WKSZ
De Plantatione [*Philo*] (BJA) .... Plant
De Poetis [*of Suetonius*] [*Classical studies*] (OCD) .... Poet
De Posteritate Caini [*of Philo*] (BJA) .... Post
De Praemiis et Poenis [*of Philo*] (BJA) .... Praem
De Praescriptione Haereticorum [*of Tertullian*] [*Classical studies*] (OCD) .... De Praescr Haeret
De Profectu in Virtute [*of Plutarch*] [*Classical studies*] (OCD) .... De Prof Virt
De Profundis .... DP
De Providentia [*of Seneca the Younger*] [*Classical studies*] (OCD) .... Prov
De Providentia [*of Philo*] (BJA) .... Provid
De Provinciis Consularibus [*of Cicero*] [*Classical studies*] (OCD) .... Prov Cons
De Pythiae Oraculis [*of Plutarch*] [*Classical studies*] (OCD) .... De Pyth Or
De Queen & Eastern Railroad Co. [*AAR code*] .... DQE
De Queen, AR [*AM radio station call letters*] .... KDQN
De Queen, AR [*FM radio station call letters*] .... KDQN-FM
De Re Rustica [*of Varro*] [*Classical studies*] (OCD) .... Rust
De Republica [*of Cicero*] [*Classical studies*] (OCD) .... Rep

De Respiratione [*of Aristotle*] [*Classical studies*] (OCD) .... Resp
De Rhetoribus [*of Suetonius*] [*Classical studies*] (OCD) .... Rhet
De Ridder, LA [*Location identifier FAA*] (FAAL) .... DRI
De Ridder, LA [*Location identifier FAA*] (FAAL) .... DSR
De Ridder, LA [*AM radio station call letters*] .... KDLA
De Ridder, LA [*FM radio station call letters*] .... KEAZ
De Ridder, LA [*FM radio station call letters*] .... KROK
De Rigo ADS [*NYSE symbol*] (TTSB) .... DER
De Sacrificiis Abelis et Caini [*Philo*] (BJA) .... Sac
De Sales Hall School of Theology, Hyattsville, MD [*Library symbol Library of Congress*] (LCLS) .... MdHyD
De Saltatione [*of Lucian*] [*Classical studies*] (OCD) .... Salt
De Sanctis, Storia dei Romani [*1907-1966*] [*A publication*] (OCD) .... De Sanctis Stor Rom
De Scriptoribus Ecclesiasticis Prolegomena [*of St. Jerome*] [*Classical studies*] (OCD) .... De Script Eccles Proleg
De Senectute [*of Cicero*] [*Classical studies*] (OCD) .... Sen
De Sensu [*of Aristotle*] [*Classical studies*] (OCD) .... Sens
De Sera Numinis Vindicta [*of Plutarch*] [*Classical studies*] (OCD) .... De Sera
De Smet Public Library, De Smet, SD [*Library symbol Library of Congress*] (LCLS) .... SdDs
De Sobrietate [*of Philo*] (BJA) .... Sob
De Sollertia Animalium [*of Plutarch*] [*Classical studies*] (OCD) .... De Soll An
De Somniis [*of Philo*] (BJA) .... Som
De Soto, Inc. [*NYSE symbol*] (SPSG) .... DSO
De Soto, Inc., Des Plaines, IL [*Library symbol Library of Congress*] (LCLS) .... IDesD
De Soto, MO [*FM radio station call letters*] .... KDJR
De Soto, MO [*AM radio station call letters*] .... KHAD
De Soto National Memorial .... DESO
De Specialibus Legibus [*of Philo*] (BJA) .... Spec
De Spectaculis [*of Tertullian*] [*Classical studies*] (OCD) .... De Spect
De Superstitione [*of Plutarch*] [*Classical studies*] (OCD) .... De Superst
De Syria Dea [*of Lucian*] [*Classical studies*] (OCD) .... Syr D
De Testimonio Animae [*of Tertullian*] [*Classical studies*] (OCD) .... De Anim
De Thucydide [*of Dionysius Halicarnassensis*] [*Classical studies*] (OCD) .... Thuc
De Tomaso Industries, Inc. [*NASDAQ symbol*] (SAG) .... DTOM
De Tomaso Industries, Inc. [*Associated Press*] (SAG) .... DTomaso
De Tour Area School and Public Library, De Tour Village, MI [*Library symbol Library of Congress*] (LCLS) .... MiDet
De Tranquillitate Animi [*of Plutarch*] [*Classical studies*] (OCD) .... De Tranq Anim
De Tranquillitate Animi [*of Seneca the Younger*] [*Classical studies*] (OCD).... Tranq
De Vectigalibus [*of Xenophon*] [*Classical studies*] (OCD) .... Vect
De Verborum Obligationibus [*A publication*] (DLA) .... VO
De Veterum Censura [*of Dionysius Halicarnassensis*] [*Classical studies*] (OCD) .... Vett Cens
De Viris Illustribus [*of St. Jerome*] [*Classical studies*] (OCD) .... De Vir Ill
De Virtutibus [*of Philo*] (BJA) .... Virt
De Vita Contemplativa [*Philo*] (BJA) .... Cont
De Vita Mosis [*Philo*] (BJA) .... Mos
De Witt and Weeresinghe's Appeal Court Reports [*Ceylon*] [*A publication*] (DLA) .... W & W
De Witt, AR [*AM radio station call letters*] (RBYB) .... KDEW
De Witt, AR [*FM radio station call letters*] (RBYB) .... KDEW-FM
De Witt Public Library, De Witt, MI [*Library symbol Library of Congress*] (LCLS) .... MiDew
De Xenophane [*of Aristotle*] [*Classical studies*] (OCD) .... Xen
Deaccentuator (IDOE) .... deac
Deacon .... D
Deacon .... DCN
Deacon .... DEA
Deacon .... DEAC
Deacon (ROG) .... DN
Deacon Air Ballistic (MUGU) .... DAB
Deacon and Chitty's English Bankruptcy Cases [*A publication*] (DLA) .... Deacon & C Bankr Cas (Eng)
Deacon and Chitty's English Bankruptcy Records [*1832-35*] [*A publication*] (DLA) .... Deacon & C Bankr Cas
Deacon and Chitty's English Bankruptcy Reports [*1832-35*] [*A publication*] (DLA) .... D & C
Deacon and Chitty's English Bankruptcy Reports [*1832-35*] [*A publication*] (DLA) .... D & Ch
Deacon and Chitty's English Bankruptcy Reports [*1832-35*] [*A publication*] (DLA) .... D & Chit
Deacon and Chitty's English Bankruptcy Reports [*1832-35*] [*A publication*] (DLA) .... Dea & Ch
Deacon and Chitty's English Bankruptcy Reports [*1832-35*] [*A publication*] (DLA) .... Dea & Chit
Deacon and Chitty's English Bankruptcy Reports [*1832-35*] [*A publication*] (DLA) .... Deac & C
Deacon and Chitty's English Bankruptcy Reports [*1832-35*] [*A publication*] (DLA) .... Deac & Ch
Deacon and Chitty's English Bankruptcy Reports [*1832-35*] [*A publication*] (DLA) .... Deac & Chit
Deacon and Chitty's English Bankruptcy Reports [*1832-35*] [*A publication*] (DLA) .... Deacon & C
Deacon and Martyr [*Church calendars*] .... DM
Deacon and Nike [*Research rocket*] .... DAN
Deacon on Criminal Law of England [*A publication*] (DLA) .... Deac Cr Law
Deacon-Arrow (SAA) .... DA
Deaconess Community of St. Andrew [*Anglican religious community*] .... DssCSA
Deaconess Hospital, Medical Library, Cleveland, OH [*Library symbol Library of Congress*] (LCLS) .... OClDe
Deaconess Hospital, Milwaukee, WI [*Library symbol Library of Congress*] (LCLS) .... WMDe
Deaconess Hospital, Oklahoma City, OK [*Library symbol Library of Congress*] (LCLS) .... OkOkD
Deaconess Hospital, School of Nursing, Spokane, WA [*Library symbol Library of Congress*] (LCLS) .... WaSpD
Deaconess Medical Center, Billings, MT [*Library symbol*] [*Library of Congress*] (LCLS) .... MtBilD
Deacon's Bankruptcy Law and Practice [*3rd ed.*] [*1864*] [*A publication*] (DLA) .... Deac Bank Pr
Deacon's Digest of the Criminal Law [*A publication*] (DLA) .... Deac Dig
Deacon's English Bankruptcy Cases [*A publication*] (DLA) .... Deacon Bankr Cas
Deacon's English Bankruptcy Cases [*A publication*] (DLA) .... Deacon Bankr (Eng)
Deacon's English Bankruptcy Reports [*1835-40*] [*A publication*] (DLA) .... Deac
Deactivate (KSC) .... DACT
Deactivated Shutdown Hours [*Electronics*] (IEEE) .... DSH
Deactivated War Trophy (DICI) .... DEWAT
Deactivation (KSC) .... DEACT
Dead [*or Deceased*] .... D
Dead Air Space .... D
Dead Air Space [*Physiology*] .... DS
Dead Band .... DB
Dead Band Setting [*Electronics*] (ECII) .... DDB
Dead before Arrival [*Term used by some members of Congress to describe 1986 federal budget proposals*] .... DBA
Dead Blackout (IIA) .... DBO
Dead Body (IIA) .... DB
Dead Cat Lying in the Road [*Traffic report*] .... DCLIR
Dead Center .... DC
Dead Despite Resuscitation Attempt [*Medicine*] (CPH) .... DDRA
Dead, Dying, Diseased, Disabled [*Food processors' classification of animals unfit for use*] 4-D
Dead Fetus in Uterus .... DFU
Dead Freight [*Shipping*] .... DF
Dead Heat .... DH
Dead in the Water [*Navy*] (NVT) .... DIW
Dead Indian [*Careless man*] [*Army slang*] .... DI
Dead Item Purge [*Military*] (AFIT) .... DIP
Dead Letter Box (BARN) .... DLB
Dead Letter Office [*US Postal Service*] .... DLO
Dead Light (AAG) .... DL
Dead Load .... DL
Dead Man Controls (SAA) .... DMC
Dead [*or Died*] **of Disease** (DAVI) .... DOD
Dead of Injuries [*Medicine*] (BARN) .... DOI
Dead of Intercurrent Disease [*Medicine*] (MAE) .... DID
Dead Old Martian Bacterium [*Humorous biology terminology*] .... DOMB
Dead on Arrival [*Medicine*] .... DOA
Dead on Arrival [*Rock music group*] .... DOA
Dead On Arrival Despite Resuscitative Attempts [*Emergency medicine*] (DAVI) .... DOA-DRA
Dead Point .... DP
Dead Reckoning [*Navigation*] .... DR
Dead Reckoning [*Plot*] [*Navy*] (DOMA) .... DR
Dead Reckoning Analog [*or Analyzer*] **Indicator** .... DRAI
Dead Reckoning Analyzer .... DRA
Dead Reckoning Automatic Computer [*Obsolete*] .... DRACO
Dead Reckoning Equipment (MSA) .... DRE
Dead Reckoning Indicator (MSA) .... DRI
Dead Reckoning Module .... DRM
Dead Reckoning Own Ship .... DROS
Dead Reckoning Plotter .... DRP
Dead Reckoning Tracer [*RADAR*] .... DRT
Dead Reckoning Trainer .... DRT
Dead Reckoning Trainer .... DRTR
Dead Reprint (DGA) .... D RPT
Dead Rise (DS) .... DR
Dead Sea Isaiah Scroll (BJA) .... DSI
Dead Sea Scrolls (BJA) .... DSS
Dead Sea Scrolls: Manual of Discipline (BJA) .... DSD
Dead Space [*Medicine*] (DAVI) .... D
Dead Space [*Medicine*] (DAVI) V
Dead Time .... DT
Dead Time Correction .... DTC
Dead Time Log .... DTL
Dead White European Males [*Derogatory appellation for Western culture*].... DWEM
Dead White Male .... DWM
Dead-End Shaft .... DES
Deadhead [*Freight*] .... DH
Deadhorse [*Alaska*] [*ICAO location identifier*] (ICLI) .... PASC
Deadhorse [*Alaska*] [*Airport symbol*] (OAG) .... SCC
Deadhorse, AK [*Location identifier FAA*] (FAAL) .... PVQ
Deadhorse, AK [*Location identifier FAA*] (FAAL) .... SCC
Deadhorse, AK [*Location identifier FAA*] (FAAL) .... SKO
Dead-Letter Box (LAIN) .... DLB
Deadline (AABC) .... DL
Deadline Data [*Computer science*] [*Database terminology*] (NITA) .... DD
Deadline Date .... DD
Deadline Date [*Air Force*] (AFM) .... DLD
Deadline Delivery Date .... DDD
Deadly Serious Party of Australia [*Political party*] .... DSA
Deadly Weapon Act .... DWA
Deadman's Cay [*Bahamas*] [*Airport symbol*] (OAG) .... LGI
Deadman's Cay, Long Island [*Bahamas*] [*ICAO location identifier*] (ICLI) .... MYLD
Deadweight .... DW
Deadweight .... DWT
Deadweight All Told [*Shipping*] .... DWAT

Deadweight Capacity ... DWC
Deadweight Cargo Capacity [*Shipping*] ... DWCC
Deadweight Gauge ... DWG
Deadweight Loss [*of grain*] [*Agriculture*] ... DL
Deadweight Tester ... DWT
Deadweight Tons [*Shipping*] ... DWT
Deadwood School, Alberta [*Library symbol National Library of Canada*] (BIB) ... ADWS
Deadwood, SD [*AM radio station call letters*] ... KDSJ
Deadwood, SD [*FM radio station call letters*] ... KSQY
Deady and Lane's Oregon General Laws [*A publication*] (DLA) ... Dead Or Laws
Deady's United States Circuit and District Court Reports [*A publication*] (DLA) ... Dea
Deady's United States Circuit and District Court Reports [*A publication*] (DLA) ... Deady
Deaerating ... DEARTG
Deaerating Cold Weather Oil System ... DCWOS
Deaerating Feed Tank ... DFT
Deaerator (NRCH) ... DA
Deaf and Dumb (IIA) ... DD
Deaf and Hard of Hearing ... DHH
Deaf and Hard of Hearing Entrepreneurs Council (EA) ... DHHEC
Deaf Artists of America (EA) ... DAA
Deaf/Blind ... DB
Deaf Broadcasting Campaign [*British*] ... DBC
Deaf Broadcasting Campaign [*England*] ... DEC
Deaf Communicating Terminal [*Telephone for the deaf*] ... DCT
Deaf Communications Institute [*Defunct*] (EA) ... DCI
Deaf Missions (EA) ... DM
Deaf Society of New South Wales [*Australia*] ... DSNSW
Deaf Society, Queensland [*Australia*] ... DSQ
Deaf Sons of Master Masons ... DESOMS
Deaf-Blind Care Association [*Australia*] ... DBCA
Deafen (ABBR) ... DEFN
Deafened (ABBR) ... DEFND
Deafening (ABBR) ... DEFNG
Deafeningly (ABBR) ... DEFNGY
Deafer (ABBR) ... DEFR
Deafest (ABBR) ... DEFST
Deafly (ABBR) ... DEFY
Deafmute (ABBR) ... DEFMT
Deafness (ABBR) ... DEFNS
Deafness Foundation [*Victoria*] [*Australia*] ... DF(V)
Deafness, Onycho-Osteodystrophy, Mental Retardation Syndrome [*Medicine*] (DMAA) ... DOOR
Deafness Research Foundation (EA) ... DRF
Deafness, Speech, & Hearing Publications, Inc. (AEBS) ... DSH
Deaggregated Human Gammaglobulin [*Medicine*] (DMAA) ... DHGG
Deak International Resources Corp. [*Toronto Stock Exchange symbol*] ... DEA
Deal Proneness Index [*Marketing*] ... DPI
Deal-Cased Frame [*Carpentry*] ... DCF
Dealer (ABBR) ... DELR
Dealer (MSA) ... DLR
Dealer [*Automotive sales*] ... DR
Dealer ... LR
Dealer Association Information Service [*Association of Free Newspapers*] [*British*] ... DAIS
Dealer Bank Association [*Washington, DC*] (EA) ... DBA
Dealer Election Action Committee [*Campaign funding*] ... DEAC
Dealer Information System for Customer Satisfaction [*Automotive retailing*] ... DISCUS
Dealer Management Association [*Exeter, NH*] [*Commercial firm*] (EA) ... DMA
Dealer Operations Manager [*Automotive retailing*] ... DOM
Dealer Operations Manager [*Automobile sales*] ... DOM
Dealer Proceeds Withheld [*Automobile sales*] ... DPW
Dealer Tankwagon [*Gasoline*] ... DTW
Dealer-Authorized Value-Added Retailer (HGAA) ... DAVAR
Dealers Alliance (EA) ... DA
Dealers Art Exchange (EA) ... DAE
Dealers' Office Realtime Information System [*London Stock Exchange*] (NITA) ... DORIS
Dealers Repurchase Agreement (TDOB) ... REPOS
Dealers Safety and Mobility Council (EA) ... DSMC
Dealing (ABBR) ... DELG
Dealing ... DLG
Deals and Battens [*Business term*] ... DB
Deals and Boards [*Business term*] (ROG) ... D & B
Deals, Battens, and Boards [*Business term*] ... DBB
Dealt in Flat [*Investment term*] (DFIT) ... F
Dealy Clearance [*Aviation*] (FAAC) ... DLC
Deaminated-O-Methyl Metabolite [*Biochemistry*] (MAE) ... DOM
Deamino [*As substituent on nucleoside*] [*Biochemistry*] ... o
Deamino-Agrinine Vasopressin [*Medicine*] (DMAA) ... DAVP
Deamino-D-arginine Vasopressin [*Antidiuretic*] ... DDAVP
Deaminophenylalaninedehydroproline [*Biochemistry*] ... DPD
Dean ... D
Dean (ROG) ... DEA
Dean and Chapter [*Anglican Church*] ... D & C
Dean and Chapter of Canterbury [*Anglican Church*] (ROG) ... DCC
Dean and Chapter of St. Paul's [*Anglican Church*] (ROG) ... DCP
Dean and Chapter of Westminster [*Anglican Church*] (ROG) ... DCW
Dean Foods [*NYSE symbol*] (TTSB) ... DF
Dean Foods Co. [*Associated Press*] (SAG) ... DeanFd
Dean Foods Co. [*NYSE symbol*] (SPSG) ... DF
Dean Martin Association (EAIO) ... DMA
Dean Martin Collector's Club [*Defunct*] (EA) ... DMCC
Dean of Arts, Social Sciences and Humanities ... DASSH
Dean of the Faculty ... DF
Dean of the Faculty, Aeronautics [*Air Force Academy*] ... DFAN
Dean Witter, Discover & Co. [*NYSE symbol*] (SPSG) ... DWD
Dean Witter Discover & Co. [*Associated Press*] (SAG) ... DWDisc
Dean Witter Discover & Co. [*Associated Press*] (SAG) ... DWDsc
Dean Witter Government Income Trust [*Associated Press*] (SAG) ... DWGI
Dean Witter Government Income Trust SBI [*NYSE symbol*] (SPSG) ... GVT
Dean Witter Gvt Income SBI [*NYSE symbol*] (TTSB) ... GVT
Deane and Swabey's English Ecclesiastical Reports [*A publication*] (DLA) ... D & S
Deane and Swabey's English Ecclesiastical Reports [*A publication*] (DLA) ... D & Sw
Deane and Swabey's English Ecclesiastical Reports [*A publication*] (DLA) ... Dea & Sw
Deane and Swabey's English Ecclesiastical Reports [*A publication*] (DLA) ... Deane
Deane and Swabey's English Ecclesiastical Reports [*A publication*] (DLA) ... Deane & S Eccl
Deane and Swabey's English Ecclesiastical Reports [*A publication*] (DLA) ... Deane & S Eccl (Eng)
Deane and Swabey's English Ecclesiastical Reports [*A publication*] (DLA) ... Deane & S Eccl Rep
Deane and Swabey's English Ecclesiastical Reports [*A publication*] (DLA) ... Deane & Sw
Deane and Swabey's English Ecclesiastical Reports [*A publication*] (DLA) ... Deane Ecc
Deane and Swabey's English Ecclesiastical Reports [*A publication*] (DLA) ... Deane Ecc Rep
Deane and Swabey's English Ecclesiastical Reports [*A publication*] (DLA) ... Deane Ecc Rep B
Deane and Swabey's English Probate and Divorce Reports [*A publication*] (DLA) ... Deane
Deane on the Effect of War as to Neutrals [*A publication*] (DLA) ... Deane Neut
Deane's English Blockade Cases [*A publication*] (DLA) ... Deane
Deane's English Blockade Cases [*A publication*] (DLA) ... Deane Bl
Deane's Reports [*24-26 Vermont*] [*A publication*] (DLA) ... Deane
Dean's Grant Project (EDAC) ... DGP
Dean's Medical Jurisprudence [*A publication*] (DLA) ... Dean Med Jur
Deanship (ABBR) ... DENSP
Dear (ROG) ... D
Dear (ROG) ... DR
Dear and Anderson's Scotch Session Cases [*1829-32*] [*A publication*] (DLA) ... D & A
Dear Old Dad (DICI) ... DOD
Dearborn Chemical Co. Ltd., Mississauga, Ontario [*Library symbol National Library of Canada*] (NLC) ... OMDEAC
Dearborn County Recorder's Office, Lawrenceburg, IN [*Library symbol Library of Congress*] (LCLS) ... InLawCR
Dearborn Heights, MI [*AM radio station call letters*] ... WNZK
Dearborn Historical Museum, Dearborn, MI [*Library symbol Library of Congress*] (LCLS) ... MiDbHi
Dearborn, MI [*AM radio station call letters*] ... WDOZ
Dearborn, MI [*FM radio station call letters*] ... WHFR
Dearborn, MI [*FM radio station call letters*] ... WNIC
Dearborn Public [*Henry Ford Centennial*] **Library, Dearborn, MI** [*Library symbol Library of Congress*] (LCLS) ... MiDb
Deargentur Pilulae [*Let The Pills Be Silverized*] [*Pharmacy*] ... DEARG PIL
Dearness (ABBR) ... DERNS
Dearsley and Bell's English Crown Cases [*1856-58*] [*A publication*] (DLA) ... D & B
Dearsley and Bell's English Crown Cases [*1856-58*] [*A publication*] (DLA) ... D & B CC
Dearsley and Bell's English Crown Cases [*1856-58*] [*A publication*] (DLA) ... Dears & B
Dearsley and Bell's English Crown Cases [*1856-58*] [*A publication*] (DLA) ... Dears & B Crown Cas
Dearsley and Bell's English Crown Cases [*1856-58*] [*A publication*] (DLA) ... Dears & BCC
Dearsley's Criminal Process [*1853*] [*A publication*] (DLA) ... Dears Cr Pr
Dearsley's Criminal Process [*1853*] [*A publication*] (ILCA) ... Dearsl Cr Pr
Dearsley's English Crown Cases [*1852-56*] [*A publication*] (DLA) ... Dears C C
Dearsley's English Crown Cases Reserved [*169 English Reprint*] [*1852-56*] [*A publication*] (DLA) ... Dears
Deas and Anderson's Decisions [*1829-33*] [*Scotland*] [*A publication*] (DLA) ... Deas & A
Deas and Anderson's Decisions [*1829-33*] [*Scotland*] [*A publication*] (DLA) ... Deas & And
Deas on the Law of Railways in Scotland [*A publication*] (DLA) ... Deas Ry
Dease Lake, BC [*ICAO location identifier*] (ICLI) ... CYDL
Deasphalted Oil [*Petroleum refining*] ... DAO
Deasy Elementary School, Glen Cove, NY [*Library symbol*] [*Library of Congress*] (LCLS) ... NGlcDE
Death ... D
Death and Dying [*Medical course*] ... D & D
Death and Indemnity Compensation [*Veterans Administration*] (GFGA) ... DIC
Death Anxiety Scale ... DAS
Death Attitude Indicator ... DAI
Death Certificate ... DC
Death from Accidental Injuries [*Military*] ... DAI
Death from Disease [*Military*] ... DD
Death Gratuity Payment [*Army*] (AABC) ... DGRTP
Death of Ur-Nammu (BJA) ... DUN
Death on the High Seas Act ... DOHSA

Death Penalty Information Center (EA) .... DPIC
Death Rate .... DR
Death Row .... DR
Death Row Support Project (EA) .... DRSP
Death Under Anaesthesia .... DUA
Death Valley [California] [Airport symbol] (OAG) .... DTH
Death Valley National Monument .... DEVA
Death Valley Resources [Vancouver Stock Exchange symbol] .... DV
Deaths Total Ratio [Measurement] [Medicine] (DAVI) .... D/T
Deaurentur Pilulae [Let the Pills Be Gilded] [Pharmacology] (DAVI) .... Deaug Pil
Deaurentur Pilulae [Let The Pills Be Gilded] [Pharmacy] .... DEAUR PIL
Deauretur [Let It Be Gilded] [Pharmacy] .... DEAUR
Deauville [France] [Airport symbol] (AD) .... DOL
Deauville/Saint-Gatien [France ICAO location identifier] (ICLI) .... LFRG
Deaza [As substituent on nucleoside] [Biochemistry] c
Deb Shops [NASDAQ symbol] (TTSB) .... DEBS
Deb Shops, Inc. [NASDAQ symbol] (NQ) .... DEBS
Deb Shops, Inc. [Associated Press] (SAG) .... DebShp
Deballasted Test Vehicle .... DBT
Debark (AABC) .... DEBK
Debarkation Control Center [Navy] (CAAL) .... DCC
Debarred Bidder's List .... DBL
Debarred Bidders List System [GSA bulletin board] [Now EPL] (AAGC) .... DBLS
DeBartolo Realty [NYSE symbol] (TTSB) .... EJD
DeBartolo Realty Co. [NYSE symbol] (SAG) .... EJD
Debate [Legal shorthand] (LWAP) .... DEB
Debates on the Judiciary [A publication] (DLA) .... Deb Jud
Debba [Sudan] [ICAO location identifier] (ICLI) .... HSDB
Debbie Fox Foundation [Later, NACH] (EA) .... DFF
Debbie Harry Collector's Society (EA) .... DHCS
Debbie Myers Fan Club (EA) .... DMFC
Debby Boone Fan Club [Defunct] (EA) .... DBFC
Debden, SK [Television station call letters] CBKFT-3
DeBeers Cons Mns ADR [NASDAQ symbol] (TTSB) .... DBRSY
DeBeers Consolidated Mines [Associated Press] (SAG) .... DBeer
DeBeers Consolidated Mines Ltd. [Associated Press] (SAG) .... DBeer
Debendox Action Group [British] (DBA) .... DAG
Debenture [Type of bond] [Investment term] .... D
Debenture [Type of bond] [Investment term] .... DB
Debenture [Type of bond] [Investment term] .... DEB
Debenture [Investment term] (ODBW) .... deb
Debenture [Investment term] (ROG) .... DEBRE
Debenture Rights [Investment term] (MHDW) .... DB RTS
Debenture Stock [Investment term] (ADA) .... DS
Deberny and Peignot (DGA) .... D & P
Debevoise & Plimpton, New York, NY [Library symbol] [Library of Congress] (LCLS) .... NNDP
Debility (AAMN) .... Debil
Debility, Dependency, and Dread [Factors producing compliance in hostages, prisoners, etc.] .... DDD
Debit .... DB
Debit (ROG) .... DBT
Debit .... DEB
Debit .... DR
Debit Accounting Information Retrieval .... DAIR
Debit Collection .... DC
Debit Memorandum (MCD) .... DM
Debit Note [Business term] .... DN
Debit Note Only .... DNO
Debit Request .... DR
Debit sans Brene [Charge without Abatement] [French Business term] .... DSB
Debit sans Brevet [Debt without Writ] [French Legal term] (DLA) .... DSB
Debita Spissitudo [Proper Consistency] [Pharmacy] (MAH) .... DEB SPIS
Debita Spissitudo [Proper Consistence] [Pharmacy] .... DEB SPISS
Debits Tax (ADA) .... DT
Debitum Sine Brevi [Debt without Writ] [Latin Legal term] (DLA) .... DSB
Debolt Community Library, Alberta [Library symbol National Library of Canada] (NLC) .... ADC
Debolt Community Library, Debolt, AB, Canada [Library symbol] [Library of Congress] (LCLS) .... CaADeC
Deborah Harry Appreciation Society (EA) .... DHAS
Deboyne [Louisiade Archipelago, Papua] [Airport symbol] (AD) .... DOY
Debra Markos [Ethiopia] [Airport symbol] (AD) .... DBM
Debra Tabor [Ethiopia] [Airport symbol] (AD) .... DBT
Debre Marcos [Ethiopia] [ICAO location identifier] (ICLI) .... HADM
Debre Tabor [Ethiopia] [ICAO location identifier] (ICLI) .... HADT
Debre Zeit/Harar Meda [Ethiopia] [ICAO location identifier] (ICLI) .... HAHM
Debrecen [Hungary] [Seismograph station code, US Geological Survey Closed] (SEIS) .... DEB
Debrecen [Hungary ICAO location identifier] (ICLI) .... LHDC
Debreceni Agrartudomanyi Egyetem, Debrecen, Hungary [Library symbol Library of Congress] (LCLS) .... HuDeAgE
Debreceni Orvostudomanyi Egyetem, Debrecen, Hungary [Library symbol Library of Congress] (LCLS) .... HuDeOE
Debreceni Reformatus Kollegium Nagykonyvtara, Debrecen, Hungary [Library symbol Library of Congress] (LCLS) .... HuDeK
Debrett Ancestry Research [British] .... DAR
Debrett's Business History Research [British] .... DBHR
Debridement [Medicine] (DAVI) .... deb
Debriefing Display Program (SAA) .... DDP
Debris (VRA) .... dbrs
Debrisoquin [Pharmacology] (DAVI) .... DBQ
Debt and Correspondence Branch [BUPERS] .... D & CB
Debt Collection Agency (DCTA) .... DCA

Debt Collection and Management Assistance Service [Department of Education] (GFGA) .... DCMAS
Debt Collection Order (DCTA) .... DCO
Debt Crisis Network [Defunct] (EA) .... DCN
Debt Liquidation Schedule .... DLS
Debt Market Analysis [MMS International] [Information service or system] (CRD) .... DMA
Debt Service Ratio (ODBW) .... DSR
Debt Service Reserve Fund [Information service or system] (HCT) .... DSRF
Debt Service Reserve/Letter of Credit Program [Investment term] .... DSR/LOC
Debt to Asset Ratio [Economics] .... D/A
Debtor .... DR
Debtor and Creditor (DLA) .... Debt & Cred
Debtor Reporting System [World Bank] .... DRS
Debtor-in-Possession (TDOB) .... DIP
Debtors Anonymous (EA) .... DA
Debug Syntax Analysis [Telecommunications] (TEL) .... DSAN
Debugging Mode .... DM
Debugging System .... DS
DeBurgh's Maritime International Laws [A publication] (DLA) .... DeB Mar Int L
Debut (WDAA) .... DEB
Debutanized Pyrolysis Gasoline .... DPG
Debutante .... DEB
Debye [Unit of electric moment or movement] .... D
Debye Dipole Theory [Physics] .... DDT
Debye-Falkenhagen Effect [Physics] .... DFE
Debye-Huckel-Manning [Theory] [Physical chemistry] .... DHM
Debye-Hueckel Equation [Physics] .... DHE
Debye-Sears Cell [Physics] .... DSC
Debye-Sears Effect [Physics] .... DSE
DEC [Digital Equipment Corp.] Automatic Design (NITA) .... DECADE
DEC-[Digital Equipment Corp.] Intel-Xerox Standard (CDE) .... DIX standard
DEC [Digital Equipment Corporation] Managment Control Center (CDE) .... DECmcc
DEC [Digital Equipment Corp.] Network (NITA) .... DECNET
Deca [A prefix meaning multiplied by 10] [SI symbol] .... da
Deca [or Deka] [A prefix meaning multiplied by 10] (KSC) .... DK
Decabromodiphenyl Oxide [Flame retardant] [Organic chemistry] .... DBDPO
Decadal-to-Centennial [Marine science] (OSRA) .... DecCen
Decade (WGA) .... DEC
Decade Counter .... DC
Decade Counting Assembly (IEEE) .... DCA
Decade Counting Unit .... DCU
Decade Frequency Oscillator (IAA) .... DFO
Decade of North American Geology [Geological Society of America] .... DNAG
[A] Decade of Study of the Constitution [Defunct] (EA) .... DSC
Decade Ratio Transformer .... DRT
Decade Resolver Bridge .... DRB
Decade Scaler (MSA) .... DS
Decade Synchronic Bridge .... DSB
Decaffeinated (WDAA) .... DECAF
Decaflucrotriphenylphosphine .... DFTPP
Decagram [Unit of issue] [Military] (DNAB) .... DC
Decal .... DEC
Decalcomania [An adhesive paper] (WDMC) .... decal
Decalcomania .... DECAL
Decalin [A trademark] .... D
Decaliter (AAMN) .... dl
Decalitre .... DCL
Decalogue Society of Lawyers (EA) .... DSL
Decameter .... DCM
Decameter .... DM
Decamethonium [Organic chemistry] (DAVI) C10
Decametric Radio Emission .... DAM
Decamired .... DM
Decanediylbis(phosphonic acid) [Organic chemistry] .... DBPA
Decanediylbis-phosphonic Acid [Organic chemistry] .... DBPA
Decani [Of the Dean] [Music] .... DEC
Decanning Scuttle .... DS
Decanta [Pour Off] [Pharmacy] .... DEC
Decanter Oil [Petroleum technology] .... DO
Decanus [Dean] [Latin] (ILCA) .... Dec
Decanus Ruralis [Rural Dean] .... DR
Decapacitation Factor [with reference to sperm] [Medicine] .... DF
Decapitation, Disembowelment, and Dismemberment [Types of movies] 3-D
Decarboxylase Base Moeller [Biochemistry] (DAVI) .... DBK
Decarboxylase Base Moeller [Medium] [Microbiology] .... DBM
Decarburization (MSA) .... DECARB
Decathalon Association [Acronym is used as name of association] (EA) .... DECA
Decatur [Illinois] [Airport symbol] (OAG) .... DEC
Decatur [ICAO designator] (AD) .... DK
Decatur, AL [Location identifier FAA] (FAAL) .... DCU
Decatur, AL [AM radio station call letters] .... WAJF
Decatur, AL [AM radio station call letters] .... WAVD
Decatur, AL [FM radio station call letters] .... WDRM
Decatur, AL [AM radio station call letters] .... WHOS
Decatur, AL [AM radio station call letters] .... WRSA
Decatur, AL [FM radio station call letters] .... WYFD
Decatur Aviation, Inc. [ICAO designator] (FAAC) .... DAA
Decatur Baptist College [Iowa] .... DBC
Decatur County Historical Society, Greensburg, IN [Library symbol Library of Congress] (LCLS) .... InGrebDHi
Decatur County Historical Society, Greensburg, IN [Library symbol] [Library of Congress] (LCLS) .... InGrebHi
Decatur County Recorder's Office, Greensburg, IN [Library symbol Library of Congress] (LCLS) .... InGrebCR

Decatur Daily, Decatur, AL [Library symbol Library of Congress] (LCLS) ...... ADeD
Decatur Daily Democrat, Decatur, IN [Library symbol] [Library of Congress] (LCLS) ...... InDecD
Decatur, GA [AM radio station call letters] (RBYB) ...... WATB
Decatur, GA [AM radio station call letters] ...... WXLL
Decatur, IL [Television station call letters] ...... WAND
Decatur, IL [AM radio station call letters] ...... WDZ
Decatur, IL [FM radio station call letters] ...... WDZQ
Decatur, IL [Television station call letters] ...... WFHL
Decatur, IL [FM radio station call letters] ...... WJMU
Decatur, IL [FM radio station call letters] ...... WSOY
Decatur, IL [FM radio station call letters] ...... WSOY-FM
Decatur, IL [FM radio station call letters] ...... WYDS
Decatur, IN [Location identifier FAA] (FAAL) ...... DCR
Decatur, IN [AM radio station call letters] ...... WADM
Decatur, IN [FM radio station call letters] ...... WQHK
Decatur Memorial Hospital, Medical Staff and Nursing School Library, Decatur, IL [Library symbol Library of Congress] (LCLS) ...... IDecH
Decatur Public Library, Decatur, IL [Library symbol Library of Congress] (LCLS) ...... IDec
Decatur Public Library, Decatur, IN [Library symbol Library of Congress] (LCLS) ...... InDec
Decatur Township Library, Webster Memorial Library Building, Decatur, MI [Library symbol Library of Congress] (LCLS) ...... MiDecD
Decatur, TX [FM radio station call letters] (RBYB) ...... KDKR-FM
Decatur, TX [Television station call letters] ...... KMPX
Decatur, TX [FM radio station call letters] (RBYB) ...... KRNB
Decay (MAE) ...... DK
Decay Heat [Nuclear energy] (NRCH) ...... DH
Decay Heat Closed Cooling [Nuclear energy] (IEEE) ...... DHCC
Decay Heat Removal [Nuclear energy] (NRCH) ...... DHR
Decay Heat Removal Service [or System] [Nuclear energy] (NRCH) ...... DHRS
Decay in Flight [Nuclear physics] ...... DIF
Decay Rate Meter ...... DRM
Decay Time (MSA) ...... DT
Decay-Accelerating Factor [Biochemistry] ...... DAF
Decayed [Quality of the bottom] [Nautical charts] ...... dec
Decayed and Filled [Dentistry] (DAVI) ...... DF
Decayed, Extracted, or Filled [Dentistry] ...... DEF
Decayed, Missing, and Filled Teeth [Dentistry] ...... DMFT
Decayed, Missing, Filled [Dentistry] ...... DMF
Decayed, Missing, or Filled Surfaces [Dentistry] ...... DMFS
Decaying Extrastellar Body [Astronomy] ...... DEB
Decays per Minute [Radiochemistry] ...... DPM
Decca [Record label] [Great Britain, Europe, Australia, etc.] ...... D
Decca ...... DEC
DECCA Integrated Airborne Navigator ...... DIAN
DECCA Long-Range Area Coverage (MCD) ...... DELRAC
Decca Tracking and Ranging (MCD) ...... DECTRA
Deccan Horse [British military] (DMA) ...... DH
Deccan Trap [Geology] ...... DT
Decceleration Time ...... DCT
Decease (ROG) ...... DECE
Deceased ...... D
Deceased (ADA) ...... DCD
Deceased ...... DEC
Deceased (WDMC) ...... dec
Deceased (AFM) ...... DECD
Deceased (ROG) ...... DECED
Deceased (DAVI) ...... DECS
Deceased Confirmed Dead at Scene [Criminology] (LAIN) ...... DCDS
Decedent [Legal shorthand] (LWAP) ...... DCDT
Decelerate (MSA) ...... DCLR
Decelerate [Aviation] (FAAC) ...... DCLRT
Deceleration (NVT) ...... DECEL
Deceleration Enleanment [Automotive fuel systems] ...... DE
Deceleration Spark Advance Control [Automotive engineering] ...... DSAC
Deceleration Throttle Modulator [Automotive engineering] ...... DTM
Deceleration Units of Gravity versus Time (KSC) ...... G vs T
Deceleration Units of Gravity Versus Velocity (KSC) ...... G vs V
Decelerator and Aileron [NASA] ...... DECELERON
Decem [Ten] [Latin] X
December ...... D
December (CDAI) ...... Dcb
December (ADA) ...... DE
December (EY) ...... DEC
December (ODBW) ...... Dec
December (ROG) ...... DECR
December (BARN) ...... Xbre
December and June [Denotes semiannual payment of interest or dividends in these months] [Business term] ...... D & J
December, March, June, September [Denotes quarterly payments of interest or dividends in these months] [Business term] ...... DMJS
December-January-February [Marine science] (OSRA) ...... DJF
Decency in Broadcasting (NTCM) ...... DIB
Decennial Census Division [Census] (OICC) ...... DCD
Decennie Internationale d'Exploration des Oceans [International Decade of Ocean Exploration] (MSC) ...... DIEO
Decent Old Buffer [British Slang] ...... DOB
Decent Suit of Civvies [British slang military decoration] [World War I] ...... DSC
Decentralize ADP [Automatic Data Processing] Service Support System DAS3
Decentralized Advanced Replenishment Technique (AFIT) ...... DART
Decentralized Automated Service Support System [Army] (RDA) DAS3
Decentralized Data Entry (IEEE) ...... DDE
Decentralized Data Processing Network System (BUR) ...... DNS

Decentralized Hospital Computer Program [Veterans Administration] ...... DHCP
Decentralized Open Network Architecture (BUR) ...... DONA
Decentralized Pharmacy (DAVI) ...... DCP
Decentralized Printing Program [Army] ...... DPP
Decentralized Toll Office [Telecommunications] (TEL) ...... DTO
Decentralized Warehouse (AFIT) ...... DW
Deception Battalion [Army] (ADDR) ...... BAT-D
Deception Island [Antarctica] [Seismograph station code, US Geological Survey Closed] (SEIS) ...... DEC
Deception Jamming System ...... DJS
Deception, PQ [ICAO location identifier] (ICLI) ...... CYGY
Deceptive Deployment Basing [Military] D2B
Deceptive Electronic Countermeasure [Military] (CAAL) ...... DECM
Deceptive Maneuver (MCD) ...... DECPT MAN
Deceptive Self-Screening Jammer (MCD) ...... DSSJ
Decertify ...... DC
Decessit [Died] [Latin] ...... D
Decessit sine Prole [Died without Issue] [Latin] ...... DSP
Decessit sine Prole Legitima [Died without Legitimate Issue] [Latin] ...... DSPL
Decessit sine Prole Mascula [Died without Male Issue] [Latin] ...... DSPM
Decessit sine Prole Mascula Superstita [Died without Surviving Male Issue] [Latin] ...... DSPMS
Decessit sine Prole Superstita [Died without Surviving Issue] [Latin] ...... DSPS
Decessit sine Prole Virile [Died without Male Issue] (ADA) ...... DSPV
Decessit Vita Matris [Died during the Lifetime of the Mother] [Latin] ...... DVM
Decessit Vita Patris [Died during the Lifetime of the Father] [Latin] ...... DVP
DECHEMA [Deutsche Gesellschaft fuer Chemisches Apparatewesen, Chemische Technik, und Biotechnologie eV] Corrosion Data Base [Germany Information service or system] (CRD) ...... DECOR
DECHEMA [Deutsche Gesellschaft fuer Chemisches Apparatewesen, Chemische Technik, und Biotechnologie eV] Environmental Technology Equipment Databank [Information service or system Germany] (IID) ...... DETEQ
DECHEMA [Deutsche Gesellschaft fuer Chemisches Apparatewesen, Chemische Technik, und Biotechnologie eV] Equipment Suppliers Databank [Database] ...... DEQUIP
DECHEMA [Deutsche Gesellschaft fuer Chemisches Apparatewesen, Chemische Technik, und Biotechnologie eV] Research and Education Databank [Frankfurt Am Main, Federal Republic of Germany] [Information service or system] (IID) ...... DERES
DECHEMA [Deutsche Gesellschaft fuer Chemisches Appartewesen, Chemische Technik, und Biotechnologie eV] Stoffdaten Dienst [DECHEMA Physical Property Data Service] [Information service or system] (IID) ...... DSD
DECHEMA [Deutsche Gesellschaft fuer Chemisches Apparatewesen, Chemische Technik, und Biotechnologie eV] Thermophysical Property Data Bank [Germany Information service or system] (CRD) ...... DETHERM
DECHEMA [Deutsche Gesellschaft fuer Chemisches Apparatewesen, Chemische Technik, und Biotechnologie eV] Thermophysical Property Data Bank - Data Evaluation System [Database] ...... DETHERM-SDC
DECHEMA [Deutsche Gesellschaft fuer Chemisches Apparatewesen, Chemische Technik, und Biotechnologie eV] Thermophysical Property Data Bank - Data RetrievalSystem [Database] ...... DETHERM-SDR
Deci [A prefix meaning divided by ten] [SI symbol] ...... d
Decibel [Symbol] [SI unit of sound level] ...... dB
Decibel (WDMC) ...... db
Decibel Above the Reference Coupling (MCD) ...... DBX
Decibel A-Weighted ...... dB(A)
Decibel A-Weighted ...... dBA
Decibel Meter (KSC) ...... DBM
Decibel Unit ...... dBU
Decibels above Milliwatt per Square Meter (MCD) ...... DB/M²
Decibels above One Carrier ...... dBc
Decibels above One Kilowatt (DEN) ...... dBK
Decibels above One Milliwatt ...... dBM
Decibels above One Milliwatt (IAA) ...... DBMW
Decibels above One Milliwatt, Referred to or Measured at a Point of Zero Transmission Level, Psophometrically Weighted dBm0p
Decibels above One Picowatt (DEN) ...... dBP
Decibels above One Picowatt (IAA) ...... DBPW
Decibels above One Volt ...... dBV
Decibels above One Watt ...... dBW
Decibels above Reference Acoustic Power (DEN) ...... dBRAP
Decibels above Reference Noise ...... dBRN
Decibels above Reference Noise, C-Message Weighted (IEEE) ...... dBRNC
Decibels, Adjusted ...... dBA
Decibels below One Milliwatt ...... DBM
Decibels Expanded [Initialism is name of electronics company and brand name of its products] ...... dbx
Decibels (Isotropic) (MCD) ...... DBI
Decibels on the A Scale ...... dba
Decibels per Square Meter ...... DBSM
Decibels Referred to Carrier (IDOE) ...... dBc
Decibels to One Milliwatt [Unit of signal strength] [Telecommunications] (NITA) ...... DBM
Decidual Proclactin (BABM) ...... dhPRL
Decidual Prolactin [Medicine] (DAVI) ...... dhPRL
Deciduous ...... D
Deciduous (MAE) ...... dec
Deciduous ...... DECID
Deciduous (Primary) Molar [Dentistry] ...... DM
Deciduous Tree Fruit Disease Workers [An association] (EA) ...... DTFDW
Decigram [Unit of measure] ...... DCG
Decigram [Unit of measure] (GPO) ...... DG
Decigram (IDOE) ...... DG
Decigram [Unit of measure] ...... dgm
Decile [Statistics] (BARN) ...... Dec

Deciliter [*NHTSA*] (TAG) .... DI
Deciliter [*Unit of measure*] (GPO) .... DL
Decimal (BUR) .... D
Decimal (KSC) .... DEC
Decimal Add .... DA
Decimal Adjust Accumulator .... DAA
Decimal Classification .... DC
Decimal Code Binaire [*Binary Coded Decimal*] [*French Computer science*] .... DCB
Decimal Code Translator .... DCT
Decimal Counting Unit .... DCU
Decimal Counting Unit (IDOE) .... dcu
Decimal Device (ECII) .... DD
Decimal Digit (DIT) .... DECIT
Decimal Digital Differential Analyzer .... DDDA
Decimal Display .... DD
Decimal Divide .... DD
Decimal Equivalent Chart .... DEC
Decimal Factor (MCD) .... DF
Decimal Fraction (MDG) .... DF
Decimal Index of Art in the Lowlands [*A publication*] .... DIAL
Decimal Keyboard [*Computer science*] .... DKB
Decimal Multiply .... DM
Decimal Number .... DN
Decimal Number System (AAG) .... DNS
Decimal Place [*Mathematics*] (IAA) .... DP
Decimal Rate Multiplier (IAA) .... DRM
Decimal Reduction Time (DAVI) .... D
Decimal Register Binary .... DRB
Decimal Subtract .... DS
Decimal to Binary [*Computer science*] (KSC) .... D/B
Decimal to Binary [*Computer science*] (BUR) .... DTB
Decimal to Binary Conversion [*Computer science*] (IAA) .... DBC
Decimal to Hexadecimal (IEEE) .... D-H
Decimal to Octal [*Computer science*] (IEEE) .... D-O
Decimal to Octal Conversion .... DOC
Decimal Voltage Output .... DVO
Decimalisation Day [*February 15, 1971, day English money was decimalized*] .... D (Day)
Decimal-to-Analog (CET) .... DA
Decimate (ROG) .... DEC
Decimeter [*Unit of measure*] .... DE
Decimeter [*Unit of measure*] (ROG) .... DEC
Decimeter [*Unit of measure*] .... DECIM
Decimeter [*Unit of measure*] .... DM
Decimeter Height-Finder [*RADAR*] .... DMH
Decimetric Wave [*Electromagnetism*] (IAA) .... DMW
Decimomannu [*Italy ICAO location identifier*] (ICLI) .... LIED
Decimp Data Line Switch [*Computer science*] .... DDHS
DeciNEM [*One-tenth of a NEM*] [*See NEM*] .... dn
Decineper [*Physics*] (DEN) .... dN
Decineper [*Reference unit*] (NITA) .... DN
Decision (ADA) .... D
Decision .... DCSN
Decision .... DEC
Decision .... DECIS
Decision (AFM) .... DECN
Decision Acknowledge (BUR) .... DAK
Decision Aiding Information System .... DAISY
Decision Aids for Resource Expenditure (MCD) .... DARE
Decision Aids for Target Aggregation (MCD) .... DATA
Decision Altitude [*Aviation*] (DA) .... DA
Decision Analysis [*Military*] (DOMA) .... DA
Decision and Simulation System [*Computer science*] .... DSS
Decision and Switching .... DS
Decision Area (MCD) .... DA
Decision Assist System (SAA) .... DAS
Decision Authority, Decision Memorandum [*Military*] (MCD) .... DADM
Decision Box, Event Box, Logic Box, Time Arrow, and Activity Box (PDAA) .... DELTA
Decision Circuit Reception .... DCR
Decision Coordinating Paper .... DCP
Decision Critical Path Method .... DCPM
Decision Data [*Computer science*] (NITA) .... DD
Decision, Design, and the Computer [*Symposium*] .... DDC
Decision Direct Measurement (IAA) .... DDM
Decision Element .... DE
Decision Error .... DE
Decision Evaluation and Logic .... DEAL
Decision Expediting [*Graphic Sciences, Inc., copying machine*] .... DEX
Decision Feedback Equalizer (IAA) .... DFE
Decision Graphics, Inc. .... DGI
Decision Height [*Aviation*] .... DH
Decision Information Distribution System - Civil Defense [*Military*] (AABC) .... DIDS-CD
Decision Information Screening Center (MCD) .... DISC
Decision Information Services Ltd. [*Information service or system*] (IID) .... DIS
Decision Leaflets [*US Patent Office*] .... DL
Decision Logic Table [*DoD*] .... DLT
Decision Logic Translator .... DLT
Decision Maker .... DM
Decision/Making/Information [*Information service or system*] (IID) .... D/M/I
Decision Making Organizer [*Test*] .... DMO
Decision Making System .... DMS
Decision Mapping via Optimum Go-No Networks .... DEMON
Decision Module Compiler (DNAB) .... DMC
Decision of Sergeant Arabin [*A publication*] (DLA) .... Arabin
Decision Outstanding [*Computer science*] (BUR) .... DOS
Decision Package [*Military*] .... DP
Decision Package Sets .... DPS
Decision Point (CAAL) .... DP
Decision Process Pattern (RDA) .... DPP
Decision Program Set .... DPS
Decision Response Time .... DRT
Decision Risk Analysis [*Army*] .... DRA
Decision Sciences Corp. (IID) .... DSC
Decision Sciences Institute (EA) .... DSI
Decision Sheet (NATG) .... DS
Decision Support Graphics [*Hewlett-Packard Co.*] .... DSG
Decision Support Software (NITA) .... DSS
Decision Support System .... DSS
Decision Support Template [*Military*] (INF) .... DST
Decision Table [*Computer science*] .... DETAB
Decision Table [*Computer science*] .... DT
Decision Table, Experimental [*Computer science*] .... DETAB-X
Decision Table General Translator [*Computer science*] (IAA) .... DETABGT
Decision Table Information Bulletin (HGAA) .... DTIB
Decision Table Language [*Ace Microsystems*] [*A programming language*] (NITA) .... D
Decision Table Processor [*IBM Corp.*] .... DETAP
Decision Table Processor [*IBM Corp.*] .... DTABL
Decision Table to COBOL [*Common Business-Oriented Language*] **Processor** [*Computer science*] .... DETOC
Decision Table Translator [*Computer science*] .... DETRAN
Decision Threshold Computer .... DTC
Decision Translator (NITA) .... DETRAN
Decision Unit [*Management*] (RDA) .... DU
Decision Unit Tracking System [*Nuclear energy*] (NRCH) .... DUTS
Decision-Making Ability Test [*Psychology*] (BARN) .... DMAT
Decision-Making Unit (WDMC) .... DMU
DecisionOne Holdings [*NASDAQ symbol*] (TTSB) .... DOCI
Decision-Oriented Evaluation System .... DOES
Decision-Oriented Scheduling System (MCD) .... DOSS
Decision-Oriented Templating Techniques .... DOTT
Decisions de l'Orateur (NITA) .... DLO
Decisions from the Chair (Parliamentary) [*England*] [*A publication*] (DLA) .... Dec Ch
Decisions Given by the Office of the Umpire (Unemployment Insurance) Respecting Claims to Out-of-Work Donation [*England*] (DLA) .... OUUI
Decisions in Review and Appeal Cases (Basutoland, Bechuanaland, and Swaziland) [*A publication*] (ILCA) .... DRA (BB & S)
Decisions Lost [*Boxing*] .... LD
Decisions of General Appraisers [*United States*] [*A publication*] (DLA) .... GA
Decisions of Joint Commission [*A publication*] (DLA) .... Dec Jt Com
Decisions of the California Public Utilities Commission [*A publication*] (DLA) .... Cal PUC
Decisions of the Commissioner of Patents [*A publication*] (DLA) .... Dec Com Pat
Decisions of the Commissioner of Patents [*A publication*] (DLA) .... Pat Dec
Decisions of the Commissioners under the National Insurance (Industrial Injuries) Acts Relating to Scotland [*A publication*] (DLA) .... CSI
Decisions of the Commissioners under the National Insurance (Industrial Injuries) Acts Relating to Wales [*A publication*] (DLA) .... CWI
Decisions of the Comptroller General [*A publication*] (DLA) .... Comp Gen
Decisions of the Comptroller General [*A publication*] (AAGC) .... Comp Gen Dec
Decisions of the Comptroller General .... DCG
Decisions of the Comptroller General of the United States [*A publication*] (DLA) .... Dec US Comp Gen
Decisions of the Comptroller of the Treasury [*A publication*] (AAGC) .... Comp Dec
Decisions of the Comptroller of the United States Treasury [*A publication*] (DLA) .... Comp Dec
Decisions of the Department of the Interior [*A publication*] (DLA) .... Interior Dec
Decisions of the Department of the Interior, Pension and Retirement Claims [*United States*] [*A publication*] (DLA) .... P and RD
Decisions of the Employees' Compensation Appeals Board [*Department of Labor*] (DLA) .... Empl Comp App Bd
Decisions of the Federal Maritime Commission [*United States*] [*A publication*] (DLA) .... Dec Fed Mar Comm'n
Decisions of the Federal Maritime Commission [*United States*] [*A publication*] (DLA) .... FMC
Decisions of the First Comptroller of the United States Treasury [*A publication*] (DLA) .... Bowler's First Comp Dec
Decisions of the Industrial Accident Commission of California [*A publication*] (DLA) .... Cal IAC
Decisions of the Industrial Accident Commission of California [*A publication*] (DLA) .... Cal Ind Acc Com
Decisions of the Industrial Accident Commission of California [*A publication*] (DLA) .... Cal Ind Acc Com Dec
Decisions of the Industrial Accident Commission of California [*A publication*] (DLA) .... Cal Ind Com
Decisions of the Industrial Accident Commission of California [*A publication*] (DLA) .... Calif Ind Accdt Com Dec
Decisions of the Industrial Accident Commission of California [*A publication*] (DLA) .... Dec of Ind Acc Com
Decisions of the Industrial Accident Commission of California [*A publication*] (DLA) .... IAC Dec
Decisions of the Industrial Accident Commission of California [*A publication*] (DLA) .... IAC of Cal
Decisions of the Industrial Accident Commission of California [*A publication*] (DLA) .... Ind Acc Com
Decisions of the Industrial Accident Commission of California [*A publication*] (DLA) .... Indust Acc Com

Decisions of the Judicial Committee of the Privy Council re the British North American Act, 1867, and the Canadian Constitution [*A publication*] (DLA) .... Olms
Decisions of the Lands Tribunal (Rating) [*A publication*] (DLA) LVC
Decisions of the Native Appeal and Divorce Court (Transvaal and Natal) [*South Africa*] [*A publication*] (ILCA) .... NAC (N & T)
Decisions of the Native Appeal Court (North Eastern Division) [*South Africa*] [*A publication*] (ILCA) .... NAC (NE)
Decisions of the Sadr Court [*1845-62*] [*Bengal, India*] [*A publication*] (DLA) ..... SD
Decisions of the United States Comptroller General [*A publication*] (DLA) .... Dec US Compt Gen
Decisions of the United States Maritime Commission [*A publication*] (DLA) .... Dec US Mar Comm'n
Decisions of the United States Railroad Labor Board [*A publication*] (DLA) .... USRR Lab Bd Dec
Decisions of the Water Courts [*1913-36*] [*South Africa*] [*A publication*] (DLA) .... Hall
Decisions of the Water Courts [*1913-36*] [*South Africa*] [*A publication*] (DLA) .... Krummeck
Decisions of the Zillah Courts, Lower Provinces [*India*] [*A publication*] (DLA) .... Beng Zillah
Decisions Won [*Boxing*] .... WD
Decistere [*Unit of measure*] (ROG) .... DS
Deck (NASA) .... D
Deck .... DK
Deck and Engineering Duties, General Service [*USNR officer designation*] ..... DE
Deck Board Tie Connector [*Simpson Strong-Tie*] [*Construction*] .... DBT
Deck Cargo .... DC
Deck Compression Chamber (PDAA) .... DCC
Deck Cooling System (MCD) .... DCS
Deck Count .... DC
Deck Court .... DC
Deck Decompression Chamber [*Undersea technology*] .... DDC
Deck Drain Valve .... DDV
Deck Edge .... DKE
Deck Edge Light (AAG) .... DELT
Deck Edge Outlet [*Navy*] .... DEO
Deck Hand Uncertified [*Shipping*] (DS) .... DHU
Deck Landing Control Officer [*British*] .... DLCO
Deck Landing Projector Sight [*British military*] (DMA) .... DLPS
Deck Landing Qualification [*Navy*] (DOMA) .... DLQ
Deck Landing Training .... DLT
Deck Landing Training School .... DLTS
Deck Motion Compensator (MCD) .... DMC
Deck of Cards (MCD) .... DOC
Deck Piercing .... DP
Deck Stowage Only [*Shipping*] .... DSO
Deck Surface Light (AAG) .... DSLT
Deck Watch [*A small chronometer*] [*Navy*] .... DW
Deck Watch Time [*Navigation*] .... DWT
Deck Working Space .... DWS
Decker Resources Ltd. [*Vancouver Stock Exchange symbol*] .... DKR
Deckers Outdoor [*NASDAQ symbol*] (TTSB) .... DECK
Deckers Outdoor Corp. [*NASDAQ symbol*] (SAG) .... DECK
Deckers Outdoor Corp. [*Associated Press*] (SAG) .... DeckOut
Deckerville, MI [*Location identifier FAA*] (FAAL) .... DQV
Deckerville Public Library, Deckerville, MI [*Library symbol Library of Congress*] (LCLS) .... MiDeck
Decking (DAC) .... Dkg
Deck-Landing Training/Practice [*Navy British*] .... DLT/P
Deck-Launched Intercept (MCD) .... DLI
Deckle-Edged [*Paper*] .... DE
Deck-Operated Remote Inspection Submersible .... DORIS
Declaration (ADA) .... DCL
Declaration .... DEC
Declaration (ROG) .... DECL
Declaration (ROG) .... DECLAN
Declaration [*Legal shorthand*] (LWAP) .... DECLN
Declaration (ROG) .... DECLON
Declaration (ADA) .... DECN
Declaration Date [*of dividend payment*] [*Investment term*] .... DD
Declaration de Guerre [*Declaration of War*] [*French*] (ILCA) .... DG
Declaration of Atlantic Unity [*Defunct*] .... DAU
Declaration of Design Performance [*British*] .... DDP
Declaration of Independence House and Library [*An association*] (EA) .... DIHL
Declaration of Independence Second Centennial Commemorative National Committee (EA) .... DISCCNC
Declarative Alvey Compiler Target Language [*Computer science*] (NITA) .... DACTL
Declaratory Judgements [*A publication*] (DLA) .... Decl J
Declare .... DECL
Declared [*Cricket*] (ROG) .... DEC
Declared .... DECD
Declared (ROG) .... DELCD
Declared Dead [*Military*] .... DED
Declared Excess [*Military*] .... DE
Declared Excess Personal Property Catalog [*Military*] .... DEPPC
Declared Management Zone .... DMZ
Declared National Program [*to share oceanographic data with other nations*] .... DNP
Declared or Paid after Stock Dividend or Split-Up [*Investment term*] (DFIT) ..... H
Declared or Paid in the Preceding 12 Months [*Investment term*] (DFIT) .... E
Declared or Paid in the Preceding 12 Months Plus Stock Dividend [*Investment term*] (DFIT) .... R

Declared or Paid This Year on a Cumulative Issue with Dividends in Arrears [*Investment term*] (DFIT) .... K
Declared Value (WDAA) .... D/V
Declassified Documents Reference System [*Research Publications, Inc.*] [*Woodbridge, CT*] .... DDRS
Declassify [*Military*] (NVT) .... DECL
Declension (ROG) .... DEC
Declension .... DECL
Declension .... DECN
Declination .... D
Declination .... DEC
Declination .... DEC
Declination of Launch Asymptote [*NASA*] (KSC) .... DLA
Decline (WDAA) .... DCL
Decline .... DECL
Decline Transfer (NOAA) .... DCLTR
Declines Appointment (NOAA) .... DAP
Declining Error Rate .... DER
Declutch .... DCLU
Deco Plantminder [*Vancouver Stock Exchange symbol*] .... DCO
Decoctum [*Decoction*] [*Pharmacy*] .... DECOCT
Decode (MSA) .... DCD
Decoder (AAG) .... DCDR
Decoder .... DEC
Decoder (NITA) .... DECDR
Decoder Connector .... DC
Decoder Driver (MCD) .... DD
Decoder Read-Only Memory .... DROM
Decoder Simulator (IAA) .... DS
Decoder Switching Unit .... DSU
Decoding Memory Drive [*Computer science*] (MDG) .... DE-ME-DRIVE
Decoding Part (IAA) .... DCT
Decommission (FAAC) .... DCMSN
Decommission (DNAB) .... DECMSN
Decommissioned .... DCMSND
Decommissioned (DNAB) .... DECMSND
Decommissioned (AFM) .... DECOM
Decommissioned (DNAB) .... DECOMD
Decommissioning [*Date*] [*Navy*] (NVT) .... DECOMG
Decommissioning [*Date*] [*Navy*] (NVT) .... DECOMM
Decommutation .... DECOMM
Decommutation and Readout System [*Computer science*] .... DARS
Decommutator .... DECOM
Decommutator Conditioning Unit (KSC) .... DCCU
Decommutator Control Memory (MCD) .... DCM
Decommutator Distribution Unit (MCD) .... DDU
Decommutator Interface Controller (MCD) .... DIFC
Decompensation [*Cardiology*] .... decomp
Decomposable Plant Material [*Soil science*] .... DPM
Decompose .... DEC
Decompose [*or Decomposition*] .... DECOMP
Decomposed Ammonia Radioisotope Thruster [*Aerospace*] .... DART
Decomposed Block Code (IAA) .... DBC
Decomposition Diagramer [*Computer science*] .... DCD
Decomposition Mathematical Programming System .... DECOMP
Decomposition Sintering (RDA) .... DS
Decompression (MSA) .... DECOMPN
Decompression .... DECOMPR
Decompression Computation and Analysis Program .... DCAP
Decompression Illness .... DCI
Decompression Sickness [*Deep-sea diving*] .... DCS
Decontaminate (AABC) .... DECON
Decontaminate and Decommission [*Nuclear energy*] .... D & D
Decontaminating Agent, Multipurpose [*Military*] (DOMA) .... DAM
Decontaminating Agent, Noncorrosive .... DANC
Decontaminating Solution Number Two [*Chemical defense*] [*Army*] (RDA) ... DS-2
Decontamination .... DC
Decontamination .... DECN
Decontamination .... DECON
Decontamination (KSC) .... DECONTN
Decontamination and Decommissioning (DOGT) .... D&D
Decontamination and Waste Treatment Facility .... DWTF
Decontamination Apparatus, Portable .... DAP
Decontamination as Precursor to Decommissioning [*Nuclear energy*] (NRCH) .... DPD
Decontamination Capabilities - Chemical Units and Teams (MCD) .... DECAP-CHUTE
Decontamination Facility .... DF
Decontamination Factor .... DF
Decontamination Hot Shop [*Nuclear energy*] (NRCH) .... DHS
Decontamination Kit Individual Equipment [*Army*] (DOMA) .... DKIE
Decontamination Shop [*Nuclear energy*] (NRCH) .... DS
Decontrolled Defense Supply Material .... DDSM
Deconvoluted Total Ion Current [*Spectrometry*] .... DTIC
Deconvolution [*Computer program*] (MCD) .... DCR
Decor .... DCR
Decora Industries [*NASDAQ symbol*] (TTSB) .... DECO
Decora Industries, Inc. [*NASDAQ symbol*] (SAG) .... DECO
Decora Industries, Inc. [*Associated Press*] (SAG) .... Decora
Decorah, IA [*Location identifier FAA*] (FAAL) .... DEH
Decorah, IA [*AM radio station call letters*] .... KDEC
Decorah, IA [*FM radio station call letters*] .... KDEC-FM
Decorah, IA [*FM radio station call letters*] .... KLCD
Decorah, IA [*FM radio station call letters*] .... KLNI
Decorah, IA [*FM radio station call letters*] (RBYB) .... KVIK

Decorah, IA [*AM radio station call letters*] ... KWLC
Decorah Journal, Decorah, IA [*Library symbol Library of Congress*] (LCLS) ... IaDJ
Decorah Public Opinion, Decorah, IA [*Library symbol Library of Congress*] (LCLS) ... IaDPO
Decorated [*or Decoration*] (ROG) ... DEC
Decorated End-Papers [*Publishing*] ... DEP
Decorating ... DECOR
Decoration (AABC) ... DCR
Decoration ... DCTN
Decoration ... DECRTN
Decoration and Design [*Building*] [*New York City*] ... D & D
Decoration for Exceptional Civilian Service [*Army civilian employee award*] ... DECS
Decorative ... DEC
Decorative (VRA) ... dec
Decorative (ROG) ... DECOR
Decorative Arts Trust (EA) ... DAT
Decorative Fabrics Institute [*Defunct*] (EA) ... DFI
Decorative Furniture Manufacturers Association [*Defunct*] (EA) ... DFM
Decorative Laminate Products Association (EA) ... DLPA
Decorative Lighting Association [*British*] (DBA) ... DLA
Decorator ... DCRTR
Decorator and Painter for Australia and New Zealand [*A publication*] ... DPANZ
Decorator Indus [*AMEX symbol*] (TTSB) ... DII
Decorator Industries, Inc. [*Associated Press*] (SAG) ... Decorat
Decorator Industries, Inc. [*AMEX symbol*] (SPSG) ... DII
Decorator Remodeling [*A publication*] ... DR
Decorators Club (EA) ... DC
Decorstone Industry [*Vancouver Stock Exchange symbol*] ... DSS
Decoupled Gun (MCD) ... DCG
Decoustics/ACS Centre for Acoustical Research [*York University*] [*Research center*] (RCD) ... DACARY
Decoy [*Missile mission symbol*] ... D
Decoy Discrimination Group (AAG) ... DDG
Decoy Discrimination RADAR ... DDR
Decoy Dispensing Set (MCD) ... DDS
Decoy Ejection Mechanism ... DEM
Decoy Launching System [*Navy*] (CAAL) ... DLS
Decoy Low-Level Electronics ... DLLE
Decrease ... DC
Decrease (KSC) ... DCR
Decrease (AAG) ... DEC
Decrease (WDMC) ... dec
Decrease [*or Decrement*] (MSA) ... DECR
Decrease Feedback ... Dec-FB
Decrease, Relative (DAVI) ... dec (R)
Decreased (MUGU) ... DECD
Decreased Fuel Ingestion ... DFI
Decreasing Consumption of Oxygen [*Endocrinology*] ... DECO
Decreasing Failure Rate ... DFR
Decreasing Failure Rate Average ... DFRA
Decreasing Mean Residual Life ... DMRL
Decree (ADA) ... D
Decree [*Legal shorthand*] (LWAP) ... DCRE
Decrees and Judgments in Federal Anti-Trust Cases [*United States*] [*A publication*] (DLA) ... Shale
Decrement (EECA) ... DCMT
Decrement ... DEC
Decrement (GAVI) ... DECR
Decrement (MSA) ... DECRT
Decrement Accumulator ... DAC
Decrement, Test, Branch if Condition True [*Computer science*] ... DBCC
Decrescendo [*Decreasing in Loudness*] [*Music*] (ROG) ... DEC
Decrescendo [*Decreasing in Loudness*] [*Music*] ... DECRES
Decrescendo [*Decreasing in Loudness*] [*Music*] ... DECRESC
Decret [*Decree*] [*French*] (ILCA) ... D
Decretales Gregorii IX [*A publication*] (DSA) ... Decret Greg IX
Decretalia of the Canon Law [*A publication*] (DLA) ... Decretal
Decret-Loi [*Decree-Law*] [*French*] (ILCA) ... DL
Decreto [*Decree*] [*Italian*] (ILCA) ... D
Decreto Governatoriale [*Governor's Decree*] [*Italian*] (ILCA) ... DG
Decreto Legge [*Decree-Law*] [*Italian*] (ILCA) ... DL
Decreto Legislativo [*Legislative Decree*] [*Italian*] (ILCA) ... D Lg
Decreto Ministeriale [*Ministerial Decree*] [*Italian*] (ILCA) ... DM
Decretum [*Decree*] [*Latin*] ... D
Decubitus [*Lying Down*] [*By extension, the medical term for bedsores*] ... DECUB
Decubitus Angina [*Cardiology*] (DAVI) ... DA
Decubitus Ulcer [*Dermatology*] (DAVI) ... DU
Decylidenimino(octyl)guanidine [*Organic chemistry*] ... DIOG
Dedendum [*Design engineering*] ... DED
Dederunt [*They Gave*] [*Latin*] ... DD
Dedham Historical Society, Dedham, MA [*Library symbol Library of Congress*] (LCLS) ... MDedHi
Dedham, MA [*AM radio station call letters*] (RBYB) ... WBPS
Dedicated [*or Dedication*] (ROG) ... DED
Dedicated (VRA) ... ded
Dedicated Access Facility [*Library science*] ... DAF
Dedicated and Switched Digital Access [*Tylink Corp.*] ... DSDA
Dedicated Communications Network (MCD) ... DECOMNET
Dedicated Computer Message Switching ... DCMS
Dedicated Control Unit (SSD) ... DCU
Dedicated Data Calibration System ... DDCS
Dedicated Demand Assignment Signaling (MCD) ... DDAS
Dedicated Display and Control Subsystem (NASA) ... DD & CS
Dedicated Display Device (MCD) ... DDD
Dedicated Display Indicator (NASA) ... DDI
Dedicated Display Processing Function (NASA) ... DDPF
Dedicated Displays (MCD) ... DD
Dedicated Experiment Processor [*Spacelab mission*] ... DEP
Dedicated Function Pushbutton ... DFP
Dedicated Intelligence Network (MCD) ... DIN
Dedicated Interface Unit ... DIU
Dedicated Landline ... DL
Dedicated Man/Months [*Jet Propulsion Laboratory, NASA*] ... DMM
Dedicated Natural Gas Vehicle [*Automotive engineering*] ... DNGV
Dedicated Packet Group ... DPG
Dedicated Planning Terminal (CAAL) ... DPT
Dedicated Printer Share [*AC DataLink*] [*Computer science*] ... DPS
Dedicated Road Infrastructure for Vehicle Safety in Europe [*British*] ... DRIVE
Dedicated Road Infrastructure for Vehicle safety in Europe [*Automotive navigation systems*] ... DRIVE
Dedicated Road Infrastructure of Vehicle Safety [*European Community*] (MHDB) ... DRIVE
Dedicated Short-Range Communications ... DSRC
Dedicated Signal Conditioner (MCD) ... DSC
Dedicated Solar Sortie Mission [*Aerospace*] (MCD) ... DSSM
Dedicated Terminal Facility [*Telecommunications*] (TSSD) ... DTF
Dedicated Terminal Facility [*Telecommunications*] (TSSD) ... DTX
Dedicated Test Training Detachment (MCD) ... DTTD
Dedicated Theater Planning Terminal [*Military*] (MCD) ... DTPT
Dedicated to Eliminating Acronymic Designations [*An association*] ... DEAD
Dedicated Total Buried Plant [*Telecommunications*] (TEL) ... DTBP
Dedicated User Port [*Telecommunications*] (ACRL) ... DUP
Dedicated Wooden Money Collectors (EA) ... DWMC
Dedicatee [*MARC relator code*] [*Library of Congress*] (LCCP) ... dte
Dedication ... DEDIC
Dedication and Everlasting Love to Animals [*An association*] ... DELTA
Dedication & Everlasting Love to Animals [*Rescue*] ... DELTA
Dedicator [*MARC relator code*] [*Library of Congress*] (LCCP) ... dto
Dedit [*or Dedicavit*] [*Gave, Dedicated*] [*Latin*] ... DD
Dedougou [*Burkina Faso*] [*ICAO location identifier*] (ICLI) ... DHOD
Dedougu [*Upper Volta*] [*Airport symbol*] (AD) ... DGU
Deduced Reckoning [*Navigation*] (OA) ... DR
Deduct ... DDT
Deduct [*or Deductible*] (AABC) ... DED
Deductible Average [*Business term*] ... D/A
Deductible Average Clause [*Insurance*] ... DAC
Deductible Employee Contribution [*IRS*] ... DEC
Deductible Requirement Rider [*Health insurance*] (GHCT) ... DRI
Deduction Theorem [*Logic*] ... DT
Deductive Analysis of Missile Systems (MCD) ... DAMS
Deductive Communicator (IEEE) ... DEDUCOM
Deductive Estimation of Risk from Existing Knowledge [*Data analysis*] ... DEREK
Deductively Augmented Data Management [*Computer science*] ... DADM
Dedza [*Malawi*] [*Airport symbol*] (AD) ... DDZ
Dedza [*Malawi*] [*ICAO location identifier*] (ICLI) ... FWDZ
Dee Scofield Awareness Program [*Defunct*] (EA) ... DSAP
Deed (ROG) ... D
Deed of Grant in Trust ... DOGIT
Deed Poll ... DP
Deelen [*Netherlands ICAO location identifier*] (ICLI) ... EHDL
Deemphasis ... DE
Deep (MSA) ... D
Deep (FAAC) ... DP
Deep Airborne Expendable Bathythermograph [*Naval Oceanographic Office*] ... DAXBT
Deep and Meaningful ... D & M
Deep Attack Programs Office [*Army*] ... DAPO
Deep Basing [*Underground placement of missiles*] ... DB
Deep Battle Area (INF) ... DBA
Deep Bed Farming Society (EA) ... DBFS
Deep Brain Stimulation [*Neurology*] (DAVI) ... DBS
Deep Breath [*or Breathe*] [*Medicine*] ... DB
Deep Breathing and Coughing [*Medicine*] (DAVI) ... DB & C
Deep Breathing Exercise [*Medicine*] (DAVI) ... DBE
Deep Case Hardened ... DCH
Deep Catalytic Crack [*Chemical engineering*] ... DCC
Deep Cerebellar Nuclei [*Brain anatomy*] ... DCN
Deep Chest Therapy [*Medicine*] (DAVI) ... DCT
Deep Chlorophyll Maximum [*Oceanography*] ... DCM
Deep Discount Issue [*In bond listings of newspapers*] [*Investment term*] ... DC
Deep Draft Navigation [*Type of water project*] ... DDN
Deep Earth Penetrating Projectile (MCD) ... DEPP
Deep Electric Research Investigation [*Navy*] ... DERI
Deep Etch [*Lithography term*] ... DE
Deep Experimental Torpedo [*Also, DSWS*] [*Later, EXTOR*] (MCD) ... DEXTOR
Deep External Pudendal Artery [*Anatomy*] ... DEP
Deep Foundations Institute (EA) ... DFI
Deep Hypothermia and Circulatory Arrest [*Medicine*] (DMAA) ... DHCA
Deep Inelastic Scattering [*Particle physics*] ... DIS
Deep Interdiction ... DI
Deep Knee Bends (DAVI) ... DKB
Deep Knowledge Based Systems [*Computer science*] ... DKBS
Deep Level Transient Spectroscopy ... DLTS
Deep Look Surveillance (MCD) ... DLS
Deep Mobile Target ... DMT
Deep Observation and Sampling of the Earth's Continental Crust [*National Science Foundation*] ... DOSECC
Deep Ocean Cable Burial ... DOCB
Deep Ocean Environment ... DOE

Deep Ocean Floor .... DOF
Deep Ocean Installation .... DOI
Deep Ocean Instrumented Station (SAA) .... DOMAINS
Deep Ocean Long Path Hydrographic Instrument (ECON) .... DOLPHIN
Deep Ocean Manned Instrumented Station [*National Oceanic and Atmospheric Administration*] (PDAA) .... DOMAINS
Deep Ocean Mining Environmental Study [*National Oceanic and Atmospheric Administration*] .... DOMES
Deep Ocean Mining Operations [*Marine science*] (MSC) .... DOMO
Deep Ocean Moored Buoy [*Marine science*] (MSC) .... DOMB
Deep Ocean Object Location and Recovery [*Navy*] .... DOOLAR
Deep Ocean Optical Measurement .... DOOM
Deep Ocean Ordnance .... DOO
Deep Ocean Research Vehicle (IEEE) .... DORV
Deep Ocean Search System [*Marine science*] .... DOSS
Deep Ocean Sediment Probe [*Marine science*] (MSC) .... DOSP
Deep Ocean Simulation Facility (SAA) .... DOSF
Deep Ocean Technology .... DOT
Deep Ocean Technology Project .... DOTP
Deep Ocean Test-in-Place and Observation System [*Navy*] .... DOTIPOS
Deep Ocean Tracer Experiment [*Marine science*] (OSRA) .... DOTREX
Deep Ocean Transponder .... DOT
Deep Ocean Untended Digital Data Acquisition System [*Marine science*] (MSC) .... DOUDDAS
Deep Ocean Work Boat [*Marine science*] (MSC) .... DOWB
Deep Oceanic Turbulence .... DOT
Deep Oceanographic Survey Vehicle [*Naval Oceanographic Office*] .... DOSV
Deep Operating Work Board (IEEE) .... DOWB
Deep Passive Sensors (MCD) .... DPS
Deep Passive Sonobuoy System (MCD) .... DPSS
Deep Penetration [*Air Force*] .... DP
Deep Penetration Strike Aircraft .... DPSA
Deep Pressure Touch .... DPT
Deep Pseudopupil [*Optical effect*] .... DPP
Deep Pulse [*Medicine*] .... DP
Deep Quest .... DQ
Deep Reconnaissance Zone [*Army*] (AABC) .... DRZ
Deep Reflections from the Upper Mantle [*Geology*] .... DRUM
Deep Research Vehicle [*or Vessel*] [*NOO*] .... DRV
Deep River Public Library, Ontario [*Library symbol National Library of Canada*] (NLC) .... ODRI
Deep Scattering Layer [*Undersea populations*] .... DSL
Deep Seabed Hard Mineral Resources Act .... DSHMRA
Deep Seismic Sounding [*Geophysics*] .... DSS
Deep Seismic Sounding Program [*Former USSR*] .... DSS
Deep Shipboard Expendable Bathythermograph [*Oceanography*] .... DSXBT
Deep Shock Insulin [*Endocrinology*] (DAVI) .... DSI
Deep Sleep Therapy .... DST
Deep South Petroleum [*Vancouver Stock Exchange symbol*] .... DSP
Deep Space Antenna [*Aerospace*] (IAA) .... DSA
Deep Space Communications Complex (MCD) .... DSCC
Deep Space Instrumentation Facility .... DSIF
Deep Space Measurement (KSC) .... DSM
Deep Space Network [*NASA*] .... DSN
Deep Space Probe .... DSP
Deep Space Station [*NASA*] .... DSS
Deep Space Surveillance RADAR (MCD) .... DSSR
Deep Space Surveillance Satellite [*Military*] .... DSSS
Deep Springs College, Deep Springs, CA [*Library symbol Library of Congress*] (LCLS) .... CDs
Deep Submergence Device (NVT) .... DSD
Deep Submergence Group .... DSG
Deep Submergence Program (MCD) .... DSP
Deep Submergence Rescue System [*Navy*] (NVT) .... DSRS
Deep Submergence Rescue Vehicle [*Navy*] .... DSRV
Deep Submergence Research Vessel .... DSRV
Deep Submergence Search Vehicle [*Research submarine*] [*Navy*] .... DSSV
Deep Submergence Systems [*Navy*] .... DEEPSUBSYS
Deep Submergence Systems [*Navy*] .... DSS
Deep Submergence Systems Project Office [*Navy*] .... DEEPSUBSYSPROJO
Deep Submergence Systems Project Office [*Arlington, VA*] [*Navy*] .... DSSP
Deep Submergence Systems Project Office [*Navy*] .... DSSPO
Deep Submergence Systems Project Technical Office [*San Diego, CA*] [*Navy*] .... DSSPTO
Deep Submergence Systems Review Group [*Navy*] .... DSSRG
Deep Submergence Vehicle [*Navy symbol*] .... DSV
Deep Submergence Weapon System [*Also, DEXTOR*] (MCD) .... DSWS
Deep Suspended DIFAR [*Military*] (CAAL) .... DSD
Deep Tank (MSA) .... DT
Deep Tank Aft (DS) .... DTa
Deep Tank Forward [*Shipping*] (DS) .... DTf
Deep Tank Midship [*Shipping*] (DS) .... DTm
Deep Tank Midship Aft [*Shipping*] (DS) .... DTma
Deep Tank Midship Forward [*Shipping*] (DS) .... DTmf
Deep Tech International [*NASDAQ symbol*] (TTSB) .... DEEP
Deep Tendon Reflex [*Physiology*] .... DTR
Deep Transverse Arrest [*Obstetrics*] .... DTA
Deep Trench Latrine [*British military*] (DMA) .... DTL
Deep Ultraviolet [*Lithography*] .... DUV
Deep Underground Command Center (MCD) .... DUCC
Deep Underground Communications System (AFM) .... DUCS
Deep Underground Missile Basing .... DUMB
Deep Underground Sanguine System [*Navy*] (MCD) .... DUSS
Deep Underground Support Center [*Air Force*] (DNAB) .... DUNS
Deep Underground Support Center [*Air Force*] .... DUSC
Deep Underwater Measuring Device .... DUMD
Deep Underwater Muon and Neutrino Detection [*Astrophysics*] .... DUMAND
Deep Underwater Nuclear Counting .... DUNC
Deep Unmanned Submersibles .... DUMS
Deep Venous [*or Vein*] **Thrombosis** [*Medicine*] .... DVT
Deep Water [*Nautical charts*] .... DW
Deep Water Cay, Grand Bahama Island [*Bahamas*] [*ICAO location identifier*] (ICLI) .... MYGD
Deep Water Dump .... DWD
Deep Water Environmental Survival Training [*Navy*] .... DWEST
Deep Water Fording Kit [*Army*] .... DWF
Deep Water Isotopic Current Analyzer [*TVA*] (MSC) .... DWICA
Deep Water Port [*Marine science*] (MSC) .... DWP
Deep Water Ports Act [*1974*] [*Environmental Protection Agency*] (EPA) .... DPA
Deep Water Ports Act [*1974*] (MSC) .... DWPA
Deep Western Boundary Current [*Oceanography*] .... DWBC
Deep X-Ray .... DXR
Deep X-Ray Therapy .... DXRT
Deep X-Ray Therapy .... DXT
Deep-Bed Filter and Blower Building [*Nuclear energy*] (NRCH) .... DBFB
Deep-Diving Research Vehicles (KSC) .... DRV
Deep-Diving Submarines, General Overhaul Specifications (DNAB) .... DDGOS
Deep-Diving System .... DDS
Deep-Diving Vehicle [*Navy*] .... DDV
Deep-Drawn [*Metals*] .... DD
Deep-Drawn Metal Part .... DDMP
Deepening (FAAC) .... DPNG
Deepest Working Depth .... DWD
Deep-Etched Halftone [*Engraving*] (DGA) .... DEHT
Deep-Operating Torpedo (MCD) .... DOT
Deep-Sea Drilling Project [*Later, IPOD*] [*National Science Foundation*] .... DSDP
Deep-Sea Particles .... DSP
Deep-Sea System for Evaluating Acoustic Transducers [*Navy*] (MCD) .... DEEPSEAT
Deep-Sea Test Facilities Study Group (SAA) .... DSTFSG
Deepsea Ventures, Inc., Gloucester Point, VA [*Library symbol Library of Congress*] (LCLS) .... ViGpD
Deep-Sea Winch .... DSW
Deepstar [*A manned, self-propelled submersible vehicle built by Western Electric Corp.*] .... DS
DeepTech International, Inc. [*NASDAQ symbol*] (SAG) .... DEEP
DeepTech International, Inc. [*Associated Press*] (SAG) .... DeepTech
Deep-Towed Explosive Source [*Seismology*] .... DETES
Deepwater Escort Hydrofoil [*Also, DBH*] (MCD) .... DEH
Deepwater Motion Picture System .... DMPS
Deepwater Ports Act (GNE) .... DPA
Deepwater Ports Project Office [*Marine science*] (MSC) .... DPPO
Deepwell Pump [*Liquid gas carriers*] .... d
Deer Breeders' Co-operative Association [*Australia*] .... DCBA
Deer Creek Reservoir [*Utah*] [*Seismograph station code, US Geological Survey*] (SEIS) .... DCU
Deer Environment Ecology and Resources [*An association*] .... DEER
Deer Kidney Virus .... DKV
Deer Lake [*Canada*] [*Airport symbol*] (OAG) .... YDF
Deer Lake Elementary School, Bemidji, MN [*Library symbol*] [*Library of Congress*] (LCLS) .... MnBemDE
Deer Lake, NF [*FM radio station call letters*] .... CFDL
Deer Lake, NF [*ICAO location identifier*] (ICLI) .... CYDF
Deer Lake Public Library, Deer Lake, NF, Canada [*Library symbol Library of Congress*] (LCLS) .... CaNfDL
Deer Lake Public Library, Newfoundland [*Library symbol National Library of Canada*] (NLC) .... NFDL
Deer Lodge Hospital, Winnipeg, Manitoba [*Library symbol National Library of Canada*] (NLC) .... MWDL
Deer Lodge Hospital, Winnipeg, MB, Canada [*Library symbol Library of Congress*] (LCLS) .... CaMWDL
Deer Lodge, MT [*Location identifier FAA*] (FAAL) .... DDG
Deer Lodge, MT [*AM radio station call letters*] .... KDRG
Deer Park Consolidated Community School District 82, Ottawa, IL [*Library symbol Library of Congress*] (LCLS) .... IOtDSD
Deer Park High School, Deer Park, NY [*Library symbol*] [*Library of Congress*] (LCLS) .... NDpHS
Deer Park, NY [*Location identifier FAA*] (FAAL) .... DPK
Deer Park Public Library, Deer Park, NY [*Library symbol Library of Congress*] (LCLS) .... NDp
Deer Park, WA [*FM radio station call letters*] .... KAZZ
Deer River High School, Deer River, MN [*Library symbol*] [*Library of Congress*] (LCLS) .... MnDerH
Deer Trail, CO [*AM radio station call letters*] .... KTMG
Deer Unlimited of America (EA) .... DUA
Deere & Co. [*NYSE symbol*] (SPSG) .... DE
Deere & Co. [*Associated Press*] (SAG) .... Deere
Deere & Co. [*ICAO designator*] (FAAC) .... JDC
Deere & Co., Moline, IL [*OCLC symbol*] (OCLC) .... IEJ
Deere & Co., Moline, IL [*Library symbol Library of Congress*] (LCLS) .... IMolD
Deere Funk [*Automotive industry supplier*] .... DF
Deerfield Academy, Deerfield, MA [*Library symbol Library of Congress*] (LCLS) .... MDeeD
Deerfield, MA [*FM radio station call letters*] .... WGAJ
Deerfield Public Library, Deerfield, IL [*Library symbol Library of Congress*] (LCLS) .... IDf
Deering [*Alaska*] [*Airport symbol*] (OAG) .... DRG
Deering's Annotated California Code [*A publication*] (DLA) .... Cal Code
Deering's Annotated California Code [*A publication*] (DLA) .... Cal (subject) Code (Deering)

Deering's Annotated California Code [*A publication*] (DLA) .... Deering's Cal Code Ann
Deering's California Advance Legislative Service [*A publication*] (DLA) .... Deering's Cal Adv Legis Serv
Deering's California General Laws, Annotated [*A publication*] (DLA) .... Cal Gen Laws Ann (Deering)
Deering's California General Laws, Annotated [*A publication*] (DLA) .... Deering's Cal Gen Laws Ann
Dees on the Law of Insolvent Debtors [*A publication*] (DLA) .... Dees Ins
Deescalate (ABBR) .... DEESC
Deescalated (ABBR) .... DEESCD
Deescalating (ABBR) .... DEESCG
Deescalation (ABBR) .... DEESCN
De-Evolution [*Acronym is name of musical group*] .... DEVO
Deex Resources Corp. [*Vancouver Stock Exchange symbol*] .... DXR
Defamation, Identification, and Publication .... DIP
Defatted Peanut Flour [*Food industry*] .... DPF
Defatted Soy Flour (OA) .... DSF
Default [*Business term*] .... DEF
Default Transfer Area [*Computer science*] (PCM) .... DTA
Defeasance (ROG) .... DEFSCE
Defeat Armor Road Target Mine .... DARTM
Defeat Opiate Addiction [*An association*] .... DOA
Defeated .... D
Defeated .... DEF
Defecation .... DEF
Defecation Motor Program [*Physiology*] .... DMP
Defecation-Collection Device [*Apollo*] [*NASA*] .... DCD
Defect Action Level [*FDA*] .... DAL
Defect Action Sheet [*A publication*] .... DAC
Defect Control System [*The Software Edge, Inc.*] [*Computer science*] (PCM) .... DCS
Defect Information and Servicing Control [*Aviation*] .... DISC
Defect Introduction Rate .... DIR
Defect Prevention Reports .... DPR
Defection [*or Defector*] (ABBR) .... DEF
Defection, Intercept-Passive Submarine (MCD) .... DIPS
Defective (MSA) .... DEF
Defective (IAA) .... DEFEC
Defective Equipment Repair Program [*Telephone company*] .... DERP
Defective Equipment Review (MCD) .... DER
Defective Leukemia Virus [*Medicine*] (DMAA) .... DLV
Defective Material Notice (KSC) .... DMN
Defective Materiel Report [*Air Force*] .... DMR
Defective Parts and Components Control Program .... DPCCP
Defective Verb [*Grammar*] (ROG) .... DEFECT
Defective Vision (ADA) .... DV
Defective-Interfering [*Virology*] .... DI
Defence (ROG) .... DEFCE
Defence .... DEFNC
Defence Act (DLA) .... DA
Defence Adviser [*British*] .... DA
Defence Aid Supply Committee [*Later, ISC*] [*World War II*] .... DASC
Defence Analysts Ltd. [*British*] .... DAL
Defence and Civil Institute of Environmental Medicine [*Canada*] .... DCIEM
Defence and Ex-Services Party of Australia [*Political party*] .... DEP
Defence Arrangements for Indian Ocean [*British World War II*] .... DIO
Defence Attache [*British*] (DS) .... DA
Defence Automatic Data Processing Training Centre [*British military*] (DMA) .... DADPTC
Defence Chemical, Biological, and Radiation Establishment [*Canada*] .... DCBRE
Defence Chemical, Biological, and Radiation Laboratories [*Canada*] .... DCBRL
Defence Communication Network [*British*] (NATG) .... DCN
Defence Communications Automatic Relay Station .... DEFCOMARS
Defence Components and Equipment Exhibition [*British*] (ITD) .... DCEE
Defence Construction Canada .... DCC
Defence Construction [*1951*] **Ltd.** [*Canada*] .... DCL
Defence Council Instructions [*Military British*] .... DCI
Defence Counter-Proliferation Initiative (ECON) .... DCI
Defence Electric Light [*British military*] (DMA) .... DEL
Defence Equipment Policy Committee [*British*] (RDA) .... DEPC
Defence Equipment Procurement Council [*British*] .... DEPC
Defence Fellowship [*British*] .... DF
Defence for Children International Movement [*See also DEI*] [*Database producer*] (EAIO) .... DCI
Defence Force Communications Network [*Australia*] .... DEFCOMMNET
Defence Force Development Committee [*Australia*] .... DFDC
Defence Force Discipline Appeal Tribunal [*Australia*] .... DFDAT
Defence Force Reserves [*Australia*] .... DFR
Defence Force Retirement and Death Benefits Scheme [*Australia*] .... DFRDBS
Defence Forces Charter [*Australia*] .... DEFFC
Defence Housing Committee [*Australia*] .... DHC
Defence Industries Council of Western Australia .... DICWA
Defence Industry Productivity Program [*Canada*] .... DIPP
Defence Information Bulletin [*A publication*] .... DIB
Defence Institute of Physiology and Allied Sciences [*New Delhi, India*] .... DIPAS
Defence Intelligence [*British*] .... DI
Defence Intelligence Staff [*British*] .... DIS
Defence Light [*British military*] (DMA) .... DL
Defence Light Section [*British military*] (DMA) .... DLS
Defence Manufacturers Association [*British*] (DS) .... DMA
Defence Material Standardization Committee [*British military*] (DMA) .... DMSC
Defence Movement Coordination Committee [*Australia*] .... DMC
Defence National Storage and Distribution Centre [*Australia*] .... DNSDC
Defence Oceanology International Exhibition [*British*] (ITD) .... DOI
Defence of Airfields [*British World War II*] .... DA
Defence of the Realm Act [*World War I*] [*British*] .... DORA
Defence Operational Analysis Establishment [*British*] .... DOAE
Defence Operational Analysis Organisation [*Far East*] .... DOAO(FE)
Defence Operational Requirements [*British military*] (DMA) .... DORS
Defence Operations [*British World War II*] .... DO
Defence Operations and Intelligence Centre [*Australia*] .... DOIC
Defence Planning Committee [*NATO*] (NATG) .... DPC
Defence Planning Working Group [*of Defense Ministers*] [*NATO*] (NATG) .... DPWG
Defence Policy and Requirements Committee [*British military*] (DMA) .... DPRC
Defence Policy Staff [*British*] .... DPS
Defence Production Board [*NATO*] (NATG) .... DPB
Defence Production Chief [*British*] .... DPC
Defence Production Committee [*NATO*] (NATG) .... DPC
Defence Production Supply Board [*NATO*] (NATG) .... DPSB
Defence Products Ltd. [*British ICAO designator*] (FAAC) .... RAN
Defence Quality Assurance .... DQA
Defence Quality Assurance Board [*British*] (RDA) .... DQAB
Defence Regulation (DAS) .... DR
Defence Required Strategic Capability .... DRSC
Defence Requirements Committee [*British military*] (DMA) .... DRC
Defence Research Agency [*British*] .... DRA
Defence Research Analysis Establishment [*Canada*] .... DRAE
Defence Research Board [*Canada*] .... DRB
Defence Research Chemical Laboratories [*Canada*] .... DRCL
Defence Research Committee [*British*] .... DRC
Defence Research Directors [*NATO*] (NATG) .... DRD
Defence Research Establishment [*Atlantic Canada*] [*UTLAS symbol*] .... DRE
Defence Research Establishment, Atlantic [*Canada*] .... DREA
Defence Research Establishment Atlantic, Canada Department of National Defence [*Centre de Recherches pour la Defense Atlantique, Ministere de la Defense Nationale*] **Dartmouth, Nova Scotia** [*Library symbol National Library of Canada*] (NLC) .... NSHN
Defence Research Establishment, Atlantic Defence Research Board, Halifax, NS, Canada [*Library symbol Library of Congress*] (LCLS) .... CaNSHN
Defence Research Establishment, Ottawa [*Canada*] .... DREO
Defence Research Establishment Ottawa, Department of National Defence [*Centrede Recherches pour la Defense Ottawa, Ministere de la Defense Nationale*] **Ont ario** [*Library symbol National Library of Canada*] (NLC) .... OODRC
Defence Research Establishment, Pacific [*Canada*] .... DREP
Defence Research Establishment Pacific, Canada Department of National Defence [*Centre de Recherches pour la Defense Pacifique, Ministere de la Defense Nationale*] **Esquimalt, British Columbia** [*Library symbol National Library of Canada*] (NLC) .... BEPN
Defence Research Establishment, Suffield [*Canada*] (MCD) .... DRES
Defence Research Establishment Suffield, Canada Department of National Defence [*Centre de Recherches pour la Defense Suffield, Ministere de la Defense Nationale*] **Ralston, Alberta** [*Library symbol National Library of Canada*] (NLC) .... ARS
Defence Research Establishment, Suffield, Test Centre [*British*] (NATG) .... DRESTC
Defence Research Establishment, Toronto [*Canada*] .... DRET
Defence Research Establishment, Valcartier [*Canada*] .... DREV
Defence Research Establishment Valcartier, Canada Department of National Defence[*Centre de Recherches pour la Defense Valcartier, Ministere de la Defense Na tionale*] **Courcelette, Quebec** [*Library symbol National Library of Canada*] (NLC) .... QQC
Defence Research Establishment, Valcartier, Canada Department of National Defence, Quebec, PQ, Canada [*Library symbol Library of Congress*] (LCLS) .... CaQQC
Defence Research Information Centre [*Research center British*] .... DRIC
Defence Research Kingston Laboratory [*Canada*] (MCD) .... DRKL
Defence Research Medical Laboratory [*Canada*] .... DRML
Defence Research Northern Laboratory [*Canada*] .... DRNL
Defence Research Policy Committee [*British*] .... DRPC
Defence Research Telecommunication Establishment [*Canada*] .... DRTE
Defence Review Committee [*NATO*] (NATG) .... DRC
Defence Sales Organisation [*Ministry of Defence*] [*British*] .... DSO
Defence Scientific Information Service [*Canada Information service or system*] (IID) .... DSIS
Defence Secretariat [*Ministry of Defence*] [*British*] .... DS
Defence Signal Board [*British*] .... DSB
Defence Standards Laboratories [*British*] .... DSL
Defence Stock Number .... DSN
Defence Studies Methodology [*British*] .... DSM
Defence Systems Analysis Group [*Canada*] .... DSAG
Defence Technology Enterprises Ltd. [*British*] (IRUK) .... DTE
Defence Telecommunications Network [*British military*] (DMA) .... DTN
Defence Telecommunications Research Establishment [*British*] .... DTRE
Defence-Protected Build-Down [*Nuclear arms reduction strategy*] [*British*] .... DPB
Defencively Armed Merchant Ship [*World War I*] [*British*] .... DAMS
Defendant .... D
Defendant [*Legal shorthand*] (LWAP) .... D
Defendant .... DEF
Defendant .... DEFT
Defendant .... DFT
Defended Area Model [*Army*] (AABC) .... DAM
Defended Area Model II Engagement Evaluation [*Army*] (AABC) .... DAM II-EE
Defended Area Model II Engagement Planning [*Army*] (AABC) .... DAM II-EP
Defended Modular Array Basing [*Military*] .... DMAB
Defender Australia Ltd. .... DAL
Defender Tank Antimissile System [*British*] [*Military*] (INF) .... TAMS
Defenders of Furbearers [*Later, Defenders of Wildlife*] .... DOF

Defenders of Nature Foundation [*Guatemala*] (EAIO) .... DNF
Defenders of the American Constitution (EA) .... DAC
Defenders of the Christian Faith [*Later, CCI*] (EA) .... DCF
Defenders of Wildlife .... DOW
Defense [*Basketball; lacrosse*] .... D
Defense (AFM) .... DEF
Defense .... DEFNS
Defense Acquisition and Display System (AAGC) .... DADS
Defense Acquisition Board [*DoD*] .... DAB
Defense Acquisition Circular [*DoD*] (RDA) .... DAC
Defense Acquisition Data System (AAGC) .... DADS
Defense Acquisition Executive (AAGC) .... DAE
Defense Acquisition Executive (MCD) .... DAE
Defense Acquisition Executive/Procurement Executive (AAGC) .... DAE/PE
Defense Acquisition Executive Summary .... DAES
Defense Acquisition Improvement Program [*DoD*] .... DAIP
Defense Acquisition Package [*DoD*] .... DAP
Defense Acquisition Pilot Program [*Army*] (RDA) .... DAPP
Defense Acquisition Program .... DAP
Defense Acquisition RADAR .... DAR
Defense Acquisition Regulation [*or Requirement*] .... DAR
Defense Acquisition Regulatory Council [*Also DARC*] (AAGC) .... DAR Council
Defense Acquisition Regulatory Council (MCD) .... DARC
Defense Acquisition Regulatory System [*DoD*] (RDA) .... DARS
Defense Acquisition Scholarship Program [*DoD*] (RDA) .... DASP
Defense Acquisition University [*DoD*] (RDA) .... DAU
Defense Acquisition Workforce Improvement Act (RDA) .... DAWIA
Defense Activity Address System (MCD) .... DAAS
Defense Activity for Nontraditional Education Support [*Military*] (MCD) .... DANE
Defense Activity for Nontraditional Education Support [*Military*] .... DANTES
Defense Activity North Carolina (MCD) .... DAN
Defense ADPE [*Automatic Data Processing Equipment*] **Reutilization Office** .... DARO
Defense Advanced Disposal Management Course [*Army*] .... DADMC
Defense Advanced Inventory Management Course [*Army*] .... DAIMC
Defense Advanced Procurement Management Course [*Army*] .... DAPMC
Defense Advanced Research Projects Agency [*Arlington, VA*] [*DoD*] .... DARPA
Defense Advisory Committee on Women in the Services [*DoD Washington, DC*] .... DACOWITS
Defense Advisory Panel on Government Industry Relations [*DoD*] .... DAPGIR
Defense Aerial Gunner .... DAG
Defense Against Methods of Entry [*Military intelligence*] .... DAME
Defense Against Missiles Systems .... DAMS
Defense against Rocket and Mortar Attack Fires [*Military*] (VNW) .... DARMA
Defense Against Self-Defense [*Suggested program against falling missiles*] .... DAS
Defense Against Sound Equipment [*Military intelligence*] .... DASE
Defense Against Underwater Swimmers [*Military*] (MCD) .... DAUS
Defense Aid [*Lend-Lease*] [*World War II*] .... DA
Defense Aid [*Lend-Lease*] **Administration Expenses** [*World War II*] .... DAAE
Defense Aid [*Lend-Lease*] **Agricultural, Industrial, and Other Commodities** [*World War II*] .... DAAI & OC
Defense Aid [*Lend-Lease*] **Aircraft and Aeronautical Material** [*World War II*] .... DAA & AM
Defense Aid [*Lend-Lease*] **Facilities and Equipment** [*World War II*] .... DAF & E
Defense Aid [*Lend-Lease*] **Ordnance and Ordnance Stores** [*World War II*] .... DAO & OS
Defense Aid Report (IIA) .... DAR
Defense Aid [*Lend-Lease*] **Services and Expenses** [*World War II*] .... DAS & E
Defense Aid [*Lend-Lease*] **Special Fund** [*World War II*] .... DASF
Defense Aid [*Lend-Lease*] **Tanks and Other Vehicles** [*World War II*] .... DAT & OV
Defense Aid [*Lend-Lease*] **Testing, Reconditioning, etc., of Defense Articles** [*World War II*] .... DATRDA
Defense Aid [*Lend-Lease*] **Vessels and Other Watercraft** [*World War II*] .... DAV & OW
Defense Air (MCD) .... DEFAIR
Defense Air Transportation Administration [*Abolished 1962, functions transferred to Office of the Under Secretary of Commerce for Transportation*] .... DATA
Defense Airborne Reconnaissance Office .... DARO
Defense Analysis Seminar [*Military*] .... DAS
Defense Analysis Special Report (MCD) .... DASR
Defense and Tactical Armament Control .... DATAC
Defense Area Communications Control Center .... DACCC
Defense Area Communications Control Center, Alaska .... DACCC-AL
Defense Area Communications Control Center, CONUS .... DACCC-CON
Defense Area Communications Control Center, Europe (NATG) .... DACCEUR
Defense Atomic Research Facility (MCD) .... DARF
Defense Atomic Support Agency [*Later, DNA*] .... DASA
Defense Atomic Support Agency Data Center .... DASA-DC
Defense Atomic Support Agency Data Division (SAA) .... DASADD
Defense Atomic Support Agency Technical Letters .... DASTL
Defense Atomic Support Agency Technical Publications .... DASA-TP
Defense Attache .... DAT
Defense Attache (AFM) .... DATT
Defense Attache Liaison Officer (AFM) .... DALO
Defense Attache Office (AFM) .... DAO
Defense Attache System [*Department of State*] .... DAS
Defense Attache System Property Accounting (MCD) .... DASPA
Defense Attache System Vehicle Accounting (MCD) .... DASVA
Defense Audiovisual Agency [*DoD*] .... DAVA
Defense Audiovisual Booking and Distribution System .... DAVBADS
Defense Audiovisual Depository System .... DADS
Defense Audiovisual Information System [*DoD*] .... DAVIS
Defense Audiovisual Support Activity .... DAVSA
Defense Audit Service [*Abolished 1982, functions transferred to Office of the Inspector General (DoD)*] .... DAS
Defense Audit Service, Pacific (DNAB) .... DASPAC
Defense Automated Addressing System (AAGC) .... DAAS
Defense Automated Depot System (MCD) .... DADS
Defense Automated Document Management System (MCD) .... DADMS
Defense Automated Visual Information System [*Database*] (IID) .... DAVIS
Defense Automatic Addressing System (AFIT) .... DAAS
Defense Automatic Addressing System Office (NATG) .... DAASO
Defense Automatic Integrated Switching [*Army communications system*] .... DAIS
Defense Automotive Supply Center .... DASC
Defense Base Act .... DBA
Defense Basic Logistics Support Analysis [*DoD*] (RDA) .... DBLSA
Defense Budget Project (EA) .... DBP
Defense Business Operating Fund [*Military*] (DOMA) .... DBOF
Defense Capability Under Fallout (SAA) .... DECUF
Defense Case Control System (DNAB) .... DCCS
Defense Center Control Building [*Army*] (AABC) .... DCCB
Defense Center Data Processing [*Army*] (AABC) .... DCDP
Defense Central Index of Investigations (AFM) .... DCII
Defense Ceramic Information Center [*Later, MCIC*] [*Battelle Memorial Institute*] (MCD) .... DCIC
Defense Civil Disturbance Facility List .... DCDFL
Defense Civil Preparedness Agency [*FEMA*] [*Washington, DC*] .... DCPA
Defense Clothing and Textile Supply Center [*Later, Defense Personnel Support Center*] [*DoD*] .... DC & TSC
Defense Clothing and Textile Supply Center [*Later, Defense Personnel Support Center*] [*DoD*] .... DCTSC
Defense Clothing and Textile Supply Center [*Later, Defense Personnel Support Center*] [*DoD*] .... DEFCLOTH & TEXSUPCEN
Defense Combat Evaluation (AABC) .... DCE
Defense Command .... DEFCOM
Defense Commercial Communications Activity [*Military*] .... DECCA
Defense Commercial Communications Center [*Military*] .... DECCC
Defense Commercial Communications Office [*Military*] .... DECCO
Defense Commercial Contracting Office (DOMA) .... DECCO
Defense Commercial Telecommunications Network (DOMA) .... DCTN
Defense Commissary Agency [*DoD*] .... DeCA
Defense Committee (NATG) .... DC
Defense Committee on Research [*Air Force*] .... DCOR
Defense Common Market (MCD) .... DCM
Defense Communication Engineering Agency (AABC) .... DECEA
Defense Communications Agency [*Arlington, VA*] [*DoD*] .... DCA
Defense Communications Agency Center for Command, Control, and Communications Systems [*Arlington, VA*] .... DCA/CCCCS
Defense Communications Agency Circular .... DCAC
Defense Communications Agency Command and Control Systems Organization [*Washington, DC*] .... DCA/CCSO
Defense Communications Agency, Europe (NATG) .... DCAEUR
Defense Communications Agency Instruction .... DCAI
Defense Communications Agency Joint Data Systems Support Center [*Washington, DC*] .... DCA/JDSSC
Defense Communications Agency/MILSATCOM [*Military Satellite Communications*] **Systems Office** [*Arlington, VA*] .... DCA/MSO
Defense Communications Agency Note [*or Notice*] .... DCAN
Defense Communications Agency Operations Center .... DCAOC
Defense Communications Agency Operations Center Complex .... DOCC
Defense Communications Agency Systems Engineering Facility [*Reston, VA*] .... DCASEF
Defense Communications Agency, Technical Library, Washington, DC [*Library symbol Library of Congress*] (LCLS) .... DDCA
Defense Communications and Army Switched System (RDA) .... DCASS
Defense Communications and Army Transmissions System [*DoD*] .... DCATS
Defense Communications Board .... DCB
Defense Communications Control Center .... DCCC
Defense Communications Control Complex (IAA) .... DCCC
Defense Communications Control System [*Air Force*] .... DCCS
Defense Communications Department (IAA) .... DCD
Defense Communications Engineering Center [*Reston, VA*] [*DoD*] (GRD) .... DCEC
Defense Communications Engineering Office [*Army*] .... DCEO
Defense Communications Engineering Office [*Army*] (AABC) .... DECEO
Defense Communications Planning Group (KSC) .... DCPG
Defense Communications Satellite Project [*or Program*] .... DCSP
Defense Communications Satellite System [*Telecommunications*] (TEL) .... DCSS
Defense Communications Station Technical Control (DNAB) .... DCSTC
Defense Communications System [*DoD*] .... DCS
Defense Communications System [*DoD*] (DNAB) .... DEFCOMMSYS
Defense Communications System Air Operational Network (AFM) .... DCSAIROPNET
Defense Communications System Automatic Digital Information Network [*DoD*] .... DCS/AUTODIN
Defense Communications System Automatic Digital Network [*DoD*] .... DCSADN
Defense Communications System Data Network (NG) .... DCSDATANET
Defense Communications System Operations Center (RDA) .... DCSOC
Defense Communications System Organization .... DCSO
Defense Communications System - Personnel Emergency Actions Book .... DCS/PEAB
Defense Communications System SCF [*Satellite Control Facility*] **Interface System** (MCD) .... DSIS
Defense Communications System Teletype Network (AFM) .... DCSTTYNET
Defense Communications Systems Configuration Items (MCD) .... DCSCI
Defense Components and Equipment Exposition .... DCEE
Defense Computer Institute .... DCI
Defense Concept Paper [*Military*] (RDA) .... DCP

Defense Concessions Committee ... DCC
Defense Condition [*The higher number indicates a higher state of military readiness*] [*Numbered from 1 through 5*] [*Military*] (DOMA) ... DEFCON
Defense Construction Service (NATG) ... DCS
Defense Construction Supply Center [*Defense Supply Agency*] ... DCSC
Defense Construction Supply Center [*Defense Supply Agency*] ... DEFCONTRSUPCEN
Defense Contract Action Data System (AAGC) ... DCADS
Defense Contract Adjustment Board (AAGC) ... DCAB
Defense Contract Administration Services [*DoD*] ... DCAS
Defense Contract Administration Services Agency (AAGC) ... DCASA
Defense Contract Administration Services District [*DoD*] (AABC) ... DCASD
Defense Contract Administration Services Management Area [*DoD*] (MCD) ... DCASMA
Defense Contract Administration Services Management Area Regional Office (AAGC) ... DCASMARO
Defense Contract Administration Services Office [*DoD*] (AABC) ... DCASO
Defense Contract Administration Services Plant Office [*DoD*] (DNAB) ... DCASPO
Defense Contract Administration Services Plant Representative Office [*DoD*] (AABC) ... DCASPRO
Defense Contract Administration Services Region [*DoD*] ... DCASR
Defense Contract Administration Services Region (USGC) ... DCASR
Defense Contract Administrator (MCD) ... DCA
Defense Contract Audit Agency [*DoD*] ... DCAA
Defense Contract Audit Agency Contract Audit Manual [*A publication*] (AAGC) ... DCAA CAM
Defense Contract Audit Agency Instruction (AAGC) ... DCAAI
Defense Contract Audit Agency Manual [*A publication*] (AAGC) ... DCAAM
Defense Contract Audit Agency Manual [*A publication*] (AAGC) ... DCAM
Defense Contract Audit Agency Pamphlets [*DoD*] ... DCAAP
Defense Contract Audit Agency Regulation [*A publication*] (AAGC) ... DCAAR
Defense Contract Audit Institute (AAGC) ... DCAI
Defense Contract Litigation Reporter [*Shepard's McGraw-Hill*] [*A publication*] (AAGC) ... DCLR
Defense Contract Management Agency ... DCMA
Defense Contract Management Area Operation (DOMA) ... DCMAO
Defense Contract Management Area Operations (RDA) ... DCMAO
Defense Contract Management Command [*DoD*] ... DCMC
Defense Contract Management District [*Replaced DCASR*] (AAGC) ... DCMD
Defense Contract Management Regions (DOMA) ... DCMR
Defense Contract Property Disposition [*DoD*] (RDA) ... DCPD
Defense Contract Services Administration Region ... DCSAR
Defense Contracting for Information Resources Course [*DoD*] (RDA) ... DCIRC
Defense Contractor Planning Report ... DCPR
Defense Contre Aeronefs [*Antiaircraft Defense*] [*French*] ... DCA
Defense Control Administration ... DCA
Defense Control Center (AABC) ... DCC
Defense Cooperation Agreement (MCD) ... DCA
Defense Council of Integrity in Management and Improvement [*DoD*] ... DCIMI
Defense Counsel ... DC
Defense Counterintelligence Board (MCD) ... DCIB
Defense Courier Service [*DoD*] ... DCS
Defense Credit Union Council (EA) ... DCUC
Defense Criminal Investigation Service ... DCIS
Defense Customer Supply Assistance Office [*DoD*] ... DCSAO
Defense Data Network ... DDN
Defense Data Repository System [*DoD*] ... DDRS
Defense Department [*US government*] ... D
Defense Department [*US government*] (MCD) ... DD
Defense Department Form (AAG) ... DDF
Defense Depot [*DoD*] ... DD
Defense Depot - Mechanicsburg, Pennsylvania [*DoD*] ... DDMP
Defense Depot - Memphis, Tennessee [*DoD*] ... DDMT
Defense Depot - Ogden, Utah [*DoD*] ... DDOU
Defense Depot Operations Management Course [*DoD*] ... DDOMC
Defense Depot - Tracy, California [*DoD*] ... DDTC
Defense des Enfants - International [*Defence for Children International Movement - DCI*] (EAIO) ... DEI
Defense Development and Engineering Laboratories [*Military*] ... DDEL
Defense Development Data Exchange Program (MCD) ... DDDEP
Defense Development Data Exchange Program (AAGC) ... DDEP
Defense Development Exchange Program (AFM) ... DDEP
Defense Development Research and Engineering (MCD) ... DDR & E
Defense Development Sharing Program [*US and Canada*] (RDA) ... DDSP
Defense Development Sharing Program [*US and Canada*] (RDA) ... DSP
Defense Disposal Executive Development Seminar [*DoD*] ... DDEDS
Defense Disposal Manual [*DoD*] (AFIT) ... DDM
Defense Dissemination Program (MCD) ... DDP
Defense Dissemination System (MCD) ... DDS
Defense Distinguished Service Medal [*Military decoration*] ... DDSM
Defense Documentation Center [*for Scientific and Technical Information*] [*Later, DTIC Alexandria, VA*] ... DDC
Defense Documentation Center for Scientific and Technical Information [*DoD*] (DNAB) ... DDCSTI
Defense Eastern Regional Audit Office [*DoD*] ... DERA
Defense Economic Analysis Council (MCD) ... DEAC
Defense Economic Impact Modeling System ... DEIMS
Defense Electric Power Administration [*Terminated, 1977*] [*Department of the Interior*] ... DEPA
Defense Electric Supply Center ... DEFELECSUPCEN
Defense Electronic Countermeasure ... DECM
Defense Electronic Products ... DEP
Defense Electronics [*A publication*] (DOMA) ... DE
Defense Electronics Division (SAA) ... DED
Defense Electronics, Inc. ... DEI
Defense Electronics Management Center (DNAB) ... DEMC
Defense Electronics Products Integrated Control Technique (PDAA) ... DEPICT
Defense Electronics Supply [*or Support*] **Center** [*DSA*] ... DESC
Defense Emergency (AABC) ... DE
Defense Employment Cost Index [*DoD*] ... DECI
Defense Energy Information System [*DoD Washington, DC*] (AFM) ... DEIS
Defense Energy Task Group (DNAB) ... DETG
Defense Engineering Data Office ... DEDO
Defense Enrollment Eligibility Reporting System [*DoD*] ... DEERS
Defense Enterprise Program [*DoD*] ... DEP
Defense Entry and Departure Act [*1918*] ... DEPA
Defense Environmental Corporate Information Management [*DoD*] ... DECIM
Defense Environmental Management Information System [*Navy*] ... DEMIS
Defense Environmental Restoration Account [*DoD*] ... DERA
Defense Environmental Restoration Program [*DoD*] ... DERP
Defense Equal Opportunity Management Institute ... DEOMI
Defense Estimate for Production (MCD) ... DEP
Defense Estimates Analytical Computer On-Line Network (MCD) ... DEACON
Defense Estimative Brief (MCD) ... DEB
Defense European and Pacific Redistribution Activity [*DoD*] (AFIT) ... DEPRA
Defense European Redistribution Activity [*DoD*] (MCD) ... DERA
Defense Exchange Agreement (MCD) ... DEA
Defense Experimental Program to Stimulate Competitive Research (RDA) ... DEPSCoR
Defense Facsimile System (MCD) ... DFS
Defense Family Housing [*Army*] (AABC) ... DFH
Defense Family-Housing Management Account (DNAB) ... DFHMA
Defense Federal Acquisition Regulation Supplement (RDA) ... DFARS
Defense Field Operations Department (SAA) ... DFOD
Defense Finance and Accounting Service [*DoD*] ... DFAS
Defense Finance Economic Committee (NATG) ... DFEC
Defense Financial and Investment Review [*Pronounced "dee-fair"*] [*DoD*] ... DFAIR
Defense Fisheries Administration [*Abolished, 1953*] ... DFA
Defense Food Order [*Production and Marketing Administration*] [*Department of Agriculture*] (DLA) ... DFO
Defense for Children International - United States of America (EA) ... DCI-USA
Defense Force Section Base [*Navy*] ... DFSB
Defense Foreign Counterintelligence [*Program*] [*DoD*] ... FCI
Defense Foreign Disclosure Coordinating Office ... FDCO
Defense Freight Railway Interchange Fleet [*Army*] (AABC) ... DFRIF
Defense Freight Railway Interchange Fleet [*Army*] (DNAB) ... DRIF
Defense Fuel Quality Assurance Office [*DoD*] ... DFQAO
Defense Fuel Quality Assurance Residency [*DoD*] (DNAB) ... DFQAR
Defense Fuel Region [*DoD*] ... DFR
Defense Fuel Region/Europe [*Military*] (DOMA) ... DFR/E
Defense Fuel Region/Middle East [*Military*] (DOMA) ... DFR/ME
Defense Fuel Supply Center [*Alexandria, VA*] (MCD) ... DFSC
Defense Fuel Support [*DoD*] (DNAB) ... DFS
Defense Fuel Support Point [*DoD*] ... DFSP
Defense Fuels Automated Management System [*DoD*] ... DFAMS
Defense General Supply Center ... DEFGENSUPCEN
Defense General Supply Center ... DGSC
Defense Grouping (DNAB) ... DG
Defense Guidance ... DG
Defense Guidance Memorandum ... DGM
Defense High-Level Radioactive Waste [*Nuclear energy*] ... DHLW
Defense Homes Corp. [*World War II*] ... DHC
Defense Identification Code (NATG) ... DIC
Defense Identification Zone ... DIZ
Defense Improved Management Engineering System [*Military*] ... DIMES
Defense Inactive Item Program (NG) ... DIIP
Defense In-Depth Simulation ... DIDSIM
Defense Indications Status Report (MCD) ... DISR
Defense Industrial and Management Engineering Office [*DoD*] ... DIMEO
Defense Industrial Base [*DoD*] ... DIB
Defense Industrial Facilities Protection Program [*DoD*] ... DIFPP
Defense Industrial Fund ... DIF
Defense Industrial Network [*DoD*] ... DINET
Defense Industrial Plant (USGC) ... DIPEC
Defense Industrial Plant Equipment Center [*DoD*] ... DEFINDPLANTEQUIPCEN
Defense Industrial Plant Equipment Center [*DoD*] (AFM) ... DIPEC
Defense Industrial Plant Equipment Facility [*DoD*] ... DIPEF
Defense Industrial Procurement Program [*Canada*] ... DIPP
Defense Industrial Production Equipment Center ... DIPEC
Defense Industrial Reserve [*DoD*] ... DIR
Defense Industrial Security Clearance Office ... DISCO
Defense Industrial Security Education and Training Office (AABC) ... DISTO
Defense Industrial Security Institute [*DoD*] ... DISI
Defense Industrial Security Program [*DoD*] ... DISP
Defense Industrial Supply Center ... DEFINDSUPCEN
Defense Industrial Supply Center ... DISC
Defense Industrial Supply Depot ... DEFINDSUPDEP
Defense Industrial Supply Depot ... DISD
Defense Industrial Support Center (MCD) ... DISC
Defense Industry ... DI
Defense Industry Advisory Council [*Later, IAC*] (AFM) ... DIAC
Defense Industry Advisory Group Europe [*Terminated, 1977*] ... DIAGE
Defense Industry Cooperation Agreement [*Military*] ... DICA
Defense Industry Development and Support Administration [*Turkey*] ... DIDA
Defense Industry Export Advisory Group ... DIEAG
Defense Industry Initiative (AAGC) ... DII
Defense Industry Studies Program (NG) ... DISP
Defense Information (AFM) ... DI
Defense Information Analysis Center [*DoD*] ... DIAC
Defense Information Automated Locator System (AABC) ... DIALS

Defense Information Distribution System [*Proposed in-home disaster warning system*] .... DIDS
Defense Information Guidance Series [*A publication*] (DNAB) .... DIGS
Defense Information Infrastructure [*Military*] .... DII
Defense Information Memorandum (NATG) .... DIM
Defense Information Network [*DoD*] .... DINET
Defense Information School .... DINFOS
Defense Information Services Activity (USGC) .... DISA
Defense Information Services Agency (DOMA) .... DISA
Defense Information System Network .... DISN
Defense Information Systems Agency [*Formerly, DSA*] [*DoD*] .... DISA
Defense Information Systems Agency [*Formerly, DCA*] (DOMA) .... DISA
Defense Information Systems Security Program [*Military*] (DOMA) .... DISSP
Defense Infrared Test (MCD) .... DIRT
Defense Institute of Security Assistance (MCD) .... DISA
Defense Institute of Security Assistance Management [*Air Force*] .... DISAM
Defense Institute of Security Assistance Management, Wright-Patterson AFB, OH [*OCLC symbol*] (OCLC) .... DIS
Defense Instruction (ADA) .... DI
Defense Integrated Data System (AFM) .... DIDS
Defense Integrated Data System Program Management Office [*DoD*] .... DIDSO
Defense Integrated Financial System (AAGC) .... DIFS
Defense Integrated Management Engineering System [*Military*] (AFM) ...... DIMES
Defense Integrated Material Management (MCD) .... DIMM
Defense Integrated Secure Network (DOMA) .... DISNET
Defense Intelligence Acquisition Manual (MCD) .... DIAM
Defense Intelligence Agency [*Formerly, JJ-2*] .... DEFINTELAGCY
Defense Intelligence Agency [*Formerly, JJ-2*] [*DoD Washington, DC*] .... DIA
Defense Intelligence Agency Dissemination Center (DNAB) .... DIDAC
Defense Intelligence Agency Guidance Letter (MCD) .... DIAGL
Defense Intelligence Agency Instruction (MCD) .... DIAI
Defense Intelligence Agency Manual (MCD) .... DIAM
Defense Intelligence Agency Memorandum (MCD) .... DIAM
Defense Intelligence Agency On-Line Information System (MCD) .... DIAOLS
Defense Intelligence Agency Regulation .... DIAR
Defense Intelligence Agency, Washington, DC [*OCLC symbol*] (OCLC) .... DIA
Defense Intelligence Air Order of Battle (MCD) .... DIAOB
Defense Intelligence Analytical Memorandum (MCD) .... DIANM
Defense Intelligence Board (MCD) .... DIB
Defense Intelligence Commentary (MCD) .... DIC
Defense Intelligence Dissemination, Storage, and Retrieval System (MCD) .... DIDSRS
Defense Intelligence Electronic Order of Battle (MCD) .... DIEOB
Defense Intelligence Estimate (MCD) .... DIE
Defense Intelligence Interoperability Panel .... DIIP
Defense Intelligence Missile Order of Battle (MCD) .... DIMOB
Defense Intelligence Naval Order of Battle (MCD) .... DINOB
Defense Intelligence Notice (MCD) .... DIN
Defense Intelligence Objectives and Priorities (MCD) .... DIOP
Defense Intelligence Officer [*Defense Intelligence Agency*] (MCD) .... DIO
Defense Intelligence Order of Battle Systems (MCD) .... DIOBS
Defense Intelligence Photoreconnaissance On-Line Exploitation System (MCD) .... DIPOLES
Defense Intelligence Plan (MCD) .... DIP
Defense Intelligence Production Schedule (MCD) .... DIPS
Defense Intelligence Projection for Planning (MCD) .... DIPP
Defense Intelligence Relay Center (MCD) .... DIRC
Defense Intelligence Report (MCD) .... DIR
Defense Intelligence Requirement Manual (AFM) .... DIRM
Defense Intelligence School .... DIS
Defense Intelligence School [*Air Force*] .... DISCH
Defense Intelligence School, Washington, DC [*Library symbol Library of Congress*] (LCLS) .... DN-IS
Defense Intelligence Space Exploitation and Correlation System (MCD) .... DISECS
Defense Intelligence Special Career Automated System (MCD) .... DISCAS
Defense Intelligence Staff (MCD) .... DIS
Defense Intelligence Summary (MCD) .... DIS
Defense Intelligence Thesaurus (MCD) .... DIT
Defense Intelligence Videocassettes (MCD) .... DIV
Defense Intercontinental Ballistic Missile .... DICBM
Defense International Logistics Management Course [*DoD*] .... DILMC
Defense Intransit Item Visibility System (MCD) .... DIIVS
Defense Inventory Management Course [*DoD*] .... DIMC
Defense Investigative Review Council .... DIRC
Defense Investigative Service [*DoD*] .... DIS
Defense Item Data Utilization .... DIDU
Defense Item Entry Control (AFIT) .... DIEC
Defense Item Entry Control Office [*Military*] .... DIECO
Defense Item Entry Control Program [*Military*] (AABC) .... DIECP
Defense Item Management Coding Program [*DoD*] (AFIT) .... DIMPC
Defense Land Fallout Interpretive Code (MCD) .... DELFIC
Defense Language Aptitude Battery [*Army*] (INF) .... DLAB
Defense Language Aptitude Test [*Army*] (AABC) .... DLAT
Defense Language Institute [*DoD Washington, DC*] .... DLI
Defense Language Institute, East Coast Center (AABC) .... DLIEC
Defense Language Institute, English Language Center (AABC) .... DLIEL
Defense Language Institute, English Language Center [*Military*] .... DLIELC
Defense Language Institute, Foreign Language Center (AABC) .... DLIFLC
Defense Language Institute, Southwest Branch (AABC) .... DLISW
Defense Language Institute, Support Command - El Paso (AABC) ...... DLISC-EP
Defense Language Institute, Systems Development Agency (AABC) .... DLISDA
Defense Language Institute, West Coast Branch (AABC) .... DLIWC
Defense Language Institute, West Coast Branch, Presidio of Monterey, CA [*Library symbol Library of Congress*] (LCLS) .... CPmD

Defense Language Proficiency Tests [*Military*] .... DLPT
Defense Language Program (AFM) .... DLP
Defense Legal Services Agency [*DoD*] .... DLS
Defense Legal Services Agency [*DoD*] .... DLSA
Defense Liaison Group (CINC) .... DLG
Defense Liaison Office (MCD) .... DLO
Defense Liaison Officer to the White House (AABC) .... DEFLOWH
Defense Logistics Acquisition Regulation (AAGC) .... DLAR
Defense Logistics Agency [*Alexandria, VA*] .... DLA
Defense Logistics Agency, Alexandria, VA [*OCLC symbol*] (OCLC) .... DLO
Defense Logistics Agency, Cameron Station, Alexandria, VA [*Library symbol Library of Congress*] (LCLS) .... VIAIDL
Defense Logistics Agency Handbook [*A publication*] (AAGC) .... DLAH
Defense Logistics Agency Manual [*A publication*] (AAGC) .... DLAM
Defense Logistics Agency Pamphlet (AAGC) .... DLAP
Defense Logistics Agency Publishing System [*CD-ROM*] (AAGC) .... DLAPS
Defense Logistics Agency Regulation [*DoD*] (GFGA) .... DLAR
Defense Logistics Agency-Headquarters Staff Instructor (AAGC) .... DLA-HSI
Defense Logistics Analysis Office (MCD) .... DLAO
Defense Logistics Area (MCD) .... DLA
Defense Logistics Instructor Development Course [*Army*] .... DLIDC
Defense Logistics Management Training Board (AFM) .... DLMTB
Defense Logistics Procurement Regulation (MCD) .... DLPR
Defense Logistics Service Center [*Military*] (AFIT) .... DLSC
Defense Logistics Standards Systems Office .... DLSSO
Defense Logistics Studies Information Exchange [*Army*] .... DLSIE
Defense Logistics Support Center [*Military*] .... DLSC
Defense Logistics System Center .... DLSC
Defense Management Educating and Training [*DoD*] (AFM) .... DMET
Defense Management Education and Training Board [*DoD*] .... DMETB
Defense Management Journal Office [*DoD*] .... DMJO
Defense Management Report [*DoD*] .... DMR
Defense Management Review [*Army*] (RDA) .... DMR
Defense Management Review Decision [*Army*] (RDA) .... DMRD
Defense Management Review Directive (AAGC) .... DMRD
Defense Management Simulation (OA) .... DMS
Defense Management System (NATG) .... DMS
Defense Manpower Administration [*Superseded by Office of Manpower Administration, 1953*] [*Department of Labor*] .... DMA
Defense Manpower Commission .... DMC
Defense Manpower Data Center [*Alexandria, VA*] .... DMDC
Defense Manpower Data Center Management [*or Market*] Research Branch [*Arlington, VA*] .... DMDC/MRB
Defense Manpower Data Center Survey and Market Analysis Division [*Arlington, VA*] .... DMDC/SMAD
Defense Manpower Policy .... DMP
Defense Manpower Requirements Report (DNAB) .... DMRR
Defense Manpower Static Model .... DMSM
Defense Manufacturers and Supplies Association of America (AAGC) ...... DMAS
Defense Manufacturing Board [*DoD*] .... DMB
Defense Manufacturing Board [*DoD*] (EGAO) .... DMD
Defense Mapping Agency [*Washington, DC*] .... DMA
Defense Mapping Agency Aerospace Center [*Formerly, ACIC*] .... DMAAC
Defense Mapping Agency Aerospace Center Directorate of Systems and Techniques .... DMAAC-ST
Defense Mapping Agency Aerospace Center Technical Library/Translation Section .... DMAAC-TC
Defense Mapping Agency Automated Distribution Management System (DNAB) .... DADMS
Defense Mapping Agency Branch Office (DNAB) .... DMABO
Defense Mapping Agency Branch Office Detachment (DNAB) .... DMABODET
Defense Mapping Agency Distribution Center (DNAB) .... DMADISTRCEN
Defense Mapping Agency Federal Acquisition Regulation Supplement [*A publication*] (AAGC) .... MFARS
Defense Mapping Agency Hydrographic Center [*Later, DMAHTC*] .... DMAHC
Defense Mapping Agency Hydrographic/Topographic Center [*Washington, DC Also, an information service or system*] (IID) .... DMAHTC
Defense Mapping Agency Liaison Office (DNAB) .... DMALO
Defense Mapping Agency Office of Distribution Services (DNAB) .... DMAODS
Defense Mapping Agency Topographic Center [*Later, DMAHTC*] .... DMATC
Defense Mapping Agency Vertical Obstruction File (DNAB) .... D-VOF
Defense Mapping School [*Army*] (AABC) .... DMS
Defense Market Measures [*Database on Department of Defense contracts*] (NITA) .... DMM
Defense Marketing Group [*AMA*] .... DMG
Defense Marketing Survey (MCD) .... DMS
Defense Markets & Technology [*Predicasts, Inc.*] [*Database*] .... DM & T
Defense Master Priority Requirements List .... DMPRL
Defense Material Allotment System (AFIT) .... DMAS
Defense Material Billing System (AFIT) .... DMBS
Defense Material Item .... DMI
Defense Material Specifications and Standards Board (DNAB) .... DMSSB
Defense Materials Procurement Agency [*Abolished 1953, functions transferred to General Services Administration*] (DLA) .... DMP
Defense Materials Procurement Agency [*Abolished 1953, functions transferred to General Services Administration*] .... DMPA
Defense Materials Service [*of GSA*] .... DMS
Defense Materials System .... DMS
Defense Materials Systems Office .... DMSO
Defense Materiel Council [*DoD*] .... DMC
Defense Materiel Interservicing Program [*DoD*] .... DMIP
Defense Materiel Utilization Program [*DoD*] .... DMUP
Defense Mechanism Test [*Psychometrics*] .... DMT
Defense Mechanisms Inventory [*Psychology*] .... DMI
Defense Medical Activity SL (USGC) .... DMSA

Defense Medical Facilities Office [*DoD*] (GFGA) .... DMFO
Defense Medical Information System (DOMA) .... DMIS
Defense Medical Material Board (AFM) .... DMMB
Defense Medical Purchase Description [*Defense Supply Agency*] .... DMPD
Defense Medical Regulating Information System (DOMA) .... DMRIS
Defense Medical Supply Center [*Later, Defense Personnel Support Center*] .... DMSC
Defense Medical Support Activity (DOMA) .... DMSA
Defense Medical Systems Support Center [*DoD*] (GFGA) .... DMSSC
Defense Meritorious Service Medal [*Military decoration*] .... DMSM
Defense Messaging System (DOMA) .... DMS
Defense Metals Equipment Center (DNAB) .... DMEC
Defense Metals Information Center [*Later, MCIC*] [*Battelle Memorial Institute*] (MCD) .... DMIC
Defense Meteorological Satellite Program [*Formerly, DAPP*] [*Air Force*] .... DMSP
Defense Meteorological Satellite System [*Air Force*] .... DMSS
Defense Metropolitan Area Telephone Service [*or System*] (MCD) .... DMATS
Defense Microelectronics (IIA) .... DME
Defense Minerals Exploration Administration [*Department of the Interior*] .... DMEA
Defense Missile Systems (KSC) .... DMS
Defense Mobilization Board [*Terminated, 1958*] .... DMB
Defense Mobilization Order .... DMO
Defense Modeling and Simulation Office [*Military*] .... DMSO
Defense National Agency Check Center [*DoD*] .... DNACC
Defense National Communications Control Center .... DNCCC
Defense National Communications Control Center System (IAA) .... DNCCCS
Defense Navigation Planning Group [*DoD*] .... DNPG
Defense Navigation Satellite Development Program (MCD) .... DNSDP
Defense Navigation Satellite System [*Formerly, SSPN*] (MCD) .... DNSS
Defense Notice [*Classification given to British news items which are considered harmful to national security and which are voluntarily censored by the press*] .... D
Defense Nuclear Agency [*DoD Washington, DC*] .... DNA
Defense Nuclear Agency Technical Publications [*DoD*] .... DNA-TP
Defense Nuclear Agency-Atomic Energy Commission (DNAB) .... DNA-AEC
Defense Nuclear Facilities Safety Board [*Military*] (DOMA) .... DNFSB
Defense Occupational Specialties [*Army*] .... DOS
Defense of Airborne Vehicles in Depth .... DAVID
Defense Office Building [*Pentagon*] (DNAB) .... DOB
Defense Officer Personnel Management Act [*1980*] (MCD) .... DOPMA
Defense Officer Personnel Management Study (NVT) .... DOPMS
Defense Operations Center .... DOC
Defense Order .... DO
Defense Order Priority Rating [*DoD*] (GFGA) .... DOPR
Defense Organization Entity Standards [*DoD*] .... DOES
Defense Organization Entity System [*DoD*] (MCD) .... DOES
Defense Orientation Conference Association (EA) .... DOCA
Defense Orthopedic Footwear Clinic [*Military*] (AABC) .... DOFC
Defense Outplacement Referral System [*DoD*] .... DORS
Defense Personnel Support Center .... DEFPERSUPPCEN
Defense Personnel Support Center (AFM) .... DPSC
Defense Personnel Support Center, Directorate of Medical Material Library, Philadelphia, PA [*Library symbol*] [*Library of Congress*] (LCLS) .... PPDef-M
Defense Personnel Support Center, Directorate of Medical Material Library, Philadelphia, PA [*Library symbol Library of Congress*] (LCLS) .... PPDef-M
Defense Pest Management Information Analysis Center [*Database*] [*DoD Washington, DC*] .... DPMIAC
Defense Petroleum Supply Center .... DPSC
Defense Planning and Programming Catalog (MCD) .... DPPC
Defense Planning and Programming Guidance .... DPPG
Defense Planning and Resources Board [*Formerly, Defense Resources Board*] (DOMA) .... DPRB
Defense Planning Council .... DPC
Defense Planning Guidance [*Formerly, Defense Guidance*] (DOMA) .... DPG
Defense Planning Programming Category .... DPPC
Defense Planning Questionnaire (MCD) .... DPQ
Defense Planning Staff [*Military*] (AABC) .... DPS
Defense Plant Corp. [*Subsidiary of Reconstruction Finance Corp.*] [*Obsolete*] .... DPC
Defense Plant Installation .... DPI
Defense Plant Representative Office (RDA) .... DPRO
Defense Plant Representative Offices [*or Officers*] (RDA) .... DPRO
Defense Plant Representatives Office (DOMA) .... DPRO
Defense Point .... DP
Defense Policy Advisory Committee [*DoD*] .... DPAC
Defense Policy Advisory Committee on Trade [*DoD*] .... DPACT
Defense Policy Guidance [*Military*] .... DPG
Defense Policy Planning Guidance (NVT) .... DPPG
Defense Position Questionnaire (MCD) .... DPQ
Defense Printing Service .... DPS
Defense Priorities and Allocations System [*DoD*] (GFGA) .... DPAS
Defense Priorities System [*DoD*] .... DPS
Defense Procurement Circular [*DoD*] .... DPC
Defense Procurement Management Course [*DoD*] .... DPMC
Defense Procurement Program [*DoD*] .... DPP
Defense Production Act [*Obsolete*] (NG) .... DPA
Defense Production Administration [*Functions transferred to Office of Defense Mobilization*] .... DPA
Defense Production Guarantees, Army .... DPG
Defense Program Management Office [*DoD*] .... DPMO
Defense Program Memorandum (AABC) .... DPM
Defense Program Operation (AAG) .... DPO
Defense Program Review Committee [*Military*] (CAAL) .... DPRC
Defense Projects Support Office [*NASA*] .... DPSO
Defense Property Disposal Detachment (AFIT) .... DPDD
Defense Property Disposal Office [*DoD*] .... DPDO
Defense Property Disposal Precious Metals Recovery [*DoD*] (AFIT) .... DPDM-R
Defense Property Disposal Precious Metals Recovery Office - Earle [*New Jersey*] [*DoD*] .... DPDPMRO-E
Defense Property Disposal Program [*DoD*] (DNAB) .... DPDP
Defense Property Disposal Region [*DoD*] .... DPDR
Defense Property Disposal Region [*DoD*] (DNAB) .... DPDREG
Defense Property Disposal Region, Pacific Detachment [*DoD*] (DNAB) .... DPDRPACDET
Defense Property Disposal Region, Pacific Sales Office [*DoD*] (DNAB) .... DPDRPACSO
Defense Property Disposal Service [*DoD*] .... DPDS
Defense Protective Service (DOMA) .... DPS
Defense Race Relations Institute [*Air Force*] .... DRRI
Defense RDT & E [*Research, Development, Test, and Evaluation*] **Online System** [*DTIC*] (MCD) .... DROL
Defense RDT & E [*Research, Development, Test, and Evaluation*] **Online System** [*DTIC*] .... DROLS
Defense RDT&E On-Line System (AAGC) .... DROLLS
Defense [*or Disaster*] **Readiness** (OICC) .... DR
Defense Readiness Condition [*Army*] .... DEFCON
Defense Readiness Posture [*Army*] (AABC) .... DEFREP
Defense Reconnaissance Support Program .... DRSP
Defense Reconnaissance Tactical Support Activity (MCD) .... DRTSA
Defense Regional Communications Control Center .... DRCCC
Defense Regional Communications Control Center, Far East (CINC) .... DRCCC-FE
Defense Regional Communications Control Center, Southeast Asia (CINC) .... DRCCC-SEA
Defense [*or Disaster*] **Relief Act** (OICC) .... DRA
Defense Reorganization Act .... DRA
Defense Representative, North Atlantic and Mediterranean Area .... DEFREPNAMA
Defense Representative North Atlantic and Mediterranean Areas / United States Regional Office (SAA) .... DEFREPNAMA/USRO
Defense Research Advisory Committee (NATG) .... DRAC
Defense Research and Development Laboratory [*India*] .... DRDL
Defense Research and Engineering [*DoD*] .... DR & E
Defense Research and Engineering Network [*DoD*] .... DREN
Defense Research and Engineering Office [*DoD*] .... DREO
Defense Research Establishment [*Israel*] .... DRE
Defense Research Group [*NATO*] .... DRG
Defense Research Institute [*Later, DRI - Defense Research and Trial Lawyers Association*] (EA) .... DRI
Defense Research Laboratory .... DRL
Defense Research Laboratory/University of Texas (MUGU) .... DRL/UT
Defense Research Member (AAGC) .... DRM
Defense Research Office, Latin America [*Army*] (AABC) .... DRO-LA
Defense Research Sciences .... DRS
Defense Resource Management (AAGC) .... DRM
Defense Resources Board .... DRB
Defense Resources Model [*Congressional Budget Office*] (GFGA) .... DRM
Defense Resources Planning Operation (AAG) .... DRPO
Defense Retail Interservice Logistic Support [*Military*] .... DRILS
Defense Retail Interservice Support [*Military*] (MCD) .... DRIS
Defense Retiree and Annuitant Pay System [*DoD*] .... DRAS
Defense Reutilization and Marketing Office [*DoD*] .... DRMO
Defense Reutilization and Marketing Service [*DoD*] .... DRMS
Defense Reutilization and Materials Organization (DOMA) .... DRMO
Defense Review Board [*Aerospace*] .... DRB
Defense SAAMS [*Special Airlift Assignment Missions*] **Program Management Office** [*DoD*] .... DSPMO
Defense Satellite Communication Systems Installation (RDA) .... DCSI
Defense Satellite Communications Program (MCD) .... DSCP
Defense Satellite Communications Support Training Device .... DSCS-TD
Defense Satellite Communications System [*Military*] .... DEFSATCOM
Defense Satellite Communications System [*DoD*] .... DSCS
Defense Satellite Communications System Network Control Facility (MCD) .... DSCS NCF
Defense Satellite Communications System Operations Control Element (MCD) .... DSCS OCE
Defense Satellite Communications System Program Office (MCD) .... DSCS PO
Defense Satellite Communications Systems Operations Center (DOMA) .... DSCSOC
Defense Satellite Meteorological Program (LAIN) .... DSMP
Defense Satellite Platform [*Strategic Defense Initiative*] .... DSP
Defense Satellite Platform-East [*Strategic Defense Initiative*] .... DSP-E
Defense Satellite Platform-West [*Strategic Defense Initiative*] .... DSP-W
Defense Satellite Program (MCD) .... DSP
Defense Science and Engineering Program (MCD) .... DSEP
Defense Science Board [*DoD*] .... DSB
Defense Science Board Subcommittee [*DoD*] .... DSBS
Defense Science Program .... DSP
Defense Sciences Office [*Arlington, VA*] [*DoD*] (GRD) .... DSO
Defense Scientists Immigration Program (AFM) .... DEFSIP
Defense Sector [*Navy*] .... DEFSEC
Defense Secure Network [*Military*] .... DSN
Defense Secure Network [*Computer science*] (RDA) .... DSNET
Defense Secure Network (DOMA) .... DSNET
Defense Security Assistance Agency .... DSAA
Defense Security Assistance Program (NVT) .... DSAP
Defense Security Officer [*Military*] .... DSO
Defense Sensor Interpretation and Application Training Program (AFM) .... DSIATP
Defense Shipping Authority .... DSA

Defense Shipping Council [*NATO*] ... DSC
Defense Shipping Executive Board [*NATO*] ... DSEB
Defense Signals Staff (NATG) ... DSS
Defense Simulation Internet [*Computer science*] (RDA) ... DSI
Defense Simulation Internet [*Army*] (RDA) ... DSI
Defense Small Business Advanced Technology Program ... DESAT
Defense Small Purchase Course [*DoD*] (RDA) ... DSPC
Defense Solid Fuels Administration [*Terminated, 1954*] ... DSFA
Defense Solid Fuels Order [*United States*] [*A publication*] (DLA) ... SFO
Defense Source Register (MCD) ... DSR
Defense Space Communications Squadron ... DSCS
Defense Special Assessment [*Defense Intelligence Agency*] (DOMA) ... DSA
Defense Special Missile and Astronautics Center [*Pronounced "deff-smack"*] [*National Security Agency*] ... DEFSMAC
Defense Special Projects Group (MCD) ... DSPG
Defense Special Security Communications System [*Pronounced "discus"*] ... DSSCS
Defense Special Security Communications System Address Group (MCD) ... DAG
Defense Special Security System (MCD) ... DSSS
Defense Specification Management Course [*Army*] ... DSMC
Defense Standard Ammunition Computer System [*DoD*] (GFGA) ... DSACS
Defense Standard Contract Administration Procedure ... DEFSCAP
Defense Standardization and Specification Program [*DoD*] (RDA) ... DSSP
Defense Standardization Manual [*DoD*] ... DSM
Defense Standardization Program [*DoD*] ... DSP
Defense Steering Group [*Military*] ... DSG
Defense Stock Fund [*DoD*] ... DSF
Defense Subcontract Model (AAGC) ... DSM
Defense Subsistence Office [*DoD*] ... DSO
Defense Subsistence Region [*DoD*] ... DSR
Defense Subsistence Region - Europe (AABC) ... DSRE
Defense Subsistence Region, Pacific [*DoD*] (DNAB) ... DSRPAC
Defense Subsistence Supply Center [*Later, Defense Personnel Support Center*] ... DEFSUBSUPCEN
Defense Subsistence Supply Center [*Later, Defense Personnel Support Center*] ... DSSC
Defense Subsystem Development and Demonstration (MCD) ... DSDD
Defense Superior Service Medal [*Military decoration*] ... DSSM
Defense Supply Advisor (DOMA) ... DSA
Defense Supply Agency [*Later, Defense Logistics Agency*] [*Alexandria, VA*] ... DSA
Defense Supply Agency Administrative Support Center [*DoD*] ... DSASC
Defense Supply Agency Contract Administration Services [*DoD*] ... DSACAS
Defense Supply Agency Contractor Experience List [*DoD*] ... DSACEL
Defense Supply Agency Handbook [*DoD*] ... DSAH
Defense Supply Agency Handbook [*DoD*] ... DSAHBK
Defense Supply Agency Industrial Equipment Reserve [*DoD*] ... DSAIER
Defense Supply Agency Manual [*DoD*] ... DSAM
Defense Supply Agency Poster [*DoD*] (MCD) ... DSAP
Defense Supply Agency Regulation [*DoD*] ... DSAR
Defense Supply Agency - Western Regional Audit Office [*DoD*] ... DSA-WRAO
Defense Supply Association [*Later, ALA*] (EA) ... DSA
Defense Supply Center (AABC) ... DSC
Defense Supply Center Indication List (DNAB) ... DSCIL
Defense Supply Corp. [*World War II*] ... DSC
Defense Supply Management Agency ... DSMA
Defense Supply Procurement Regulation [*Military*] ... DSPR
Defense Supply Service [*DoD*] ... DSS
Defense Supply Service - Washington [*DoD*] ... DSS-W
Defense Support (CINC) ... DS
Defense Support Agency ... DSA
Defense Support Program ... DSP
Defense Suppression ... DS
Defense Suppression Concept Plan (MCD) ... DSCP
Defense Suppression Expendable Drone (MCD) ... DSED
Defense Suppression Group [*DoD*] (MCD) ... DSG
Defense Suppression Integration Analysis (MCD) ... DSIA
Defense Suppression Missile ... DSM
Defense Suppression Rocket ... DSR
Defense Surplus Bidders Control Office ... DSBCO
Defense Surplus Sales Office ... DSSO
Defense Switched [*or Switchboard*] **Network** ... DSN
Defense System Evaluation Squadron [*Air Force*] ... DSESq
Defense System Operator [*ECM operator*] ... DSO
Defense System Simulator ... DESSIM
Defense System Terminal Equipment (MCD) ... DSTE
Defense Systems Acquisition Management [*DoD*] ... DSAM
Defense Systems Acquisition Review Council [*Pentagon board*] (MCD) ... DSARC
Defense Systems Analysis [*DoD*] ... DSA
Defense Systems Application Program [*DoD*] ... DSAP
Defense Systems Evaluation Group [*Air Force*] ... DSEG
Defense Systems Evaluation Squadron [*Air Force*] (AFM) ... DSES
Defense Systems Group ... DSG
Defense Systems Management College [*Fort Belvoir, VA*] [*Army*] (RDA) ... DSMC
Defense Systems Management College - Program Management Course [*DoD*] ... DSMC-PMC
Defense Systems Management Course [*Air Force*] ... DSMC
Defense Systems Management School [*Fort Belvoir, VA*] (AABC) ... DSMS
Defense Technical Center ... DTC
Defense Technical Information Center [*Formerly, DDC*] [*Alexandria, VA*] [*DoD Information service or system*] ... DTIC
Defense Technical Information Center, Alexandria, VA [*OCLC symbol*] (OCLC) ... DTI
Defense Technical Information Center, Cameron Station, Alexandria, VA [*Library symbol Library of Congress*] (LCLS) ... ViAlD
Defense Technical Intelligence Report (MCD) ... DTIR
Defense Technical Review Activity [*or Agency*] [*Military*] (AABC) ... DTRA
Defense Technology and Industrial Base ... DTIB
Defense Technology Area Plan [*Defense Technical Information Center*] ... DTAP
Defense Technology Information Repository (MCD) ... DETIR
Defense Technology Security Administration ... DTSA
Defense Technology Study Team ... DTST
Defense Telecommunication System Center (LAIN) ... DTSC
Defense Telecommunications Command and Control System (MCD) ... DTCCS
Defense Telephone Service [*DoD*] ... DTS
Defense Telephone Service - Washington [*DoD*] ... DTS-W
Defense Teleprinter Network (NATG) ... DTN
Defense Test Range (MCD) ... DTR
Defense Trade Advisory Group (AAGC) ... DTAG
Defense Trade Policy [*Office of*] (DOMA) ... DTP
Defense Traffic Management Branch (DNAB) ... DTMB
Defense Traffic Management Regulations (AAGC) ... DTMR
Defense Traffic Management Service ... DTMS
Defense Transport Administration [*Terminated, functions transferred to Interstate Commerce Commission*] ... DTA
Defense Transportation Order [*Department of Commerce*] ... DTO
Defense Transportation Policy Council [*MTMC*] (TAG) ... DTPC
Defense Transportation System [*DoD*] ... DTS
Defense Unit [*Military*] ... DU
Defense Unit Classification System ... DUCS
Defense Unit Platform ... DUP
Defense Unit Platform Interceptor [*Strategic Defense Initiative*] ... DUPI
Defense Unit Platform Subsystem [*Strategic Defense Initiative*] ... DUPS
Defense Value Engineering Services Officer ... DVEO
Defense Visual Flight Rule [*Military*] (DA) ... DFVR
Defense Visual Flight Rules ... DVFR
Defense Vocational Aptitude Battery [*Military*] (NVT) ... DVAB
Defense Warehousing and Shipping Program [*Military*] ... DWASP
Defense Waste Management Plan (GAAI) ... DWMP
Defense Waste Processing Facility [*Department of Energy*] ... DWPF
Defense Weapons System ... DWS
Defense Weapons System Management Center ... DEFWEAPSYSMGTCEN
Defense Weapons System Management Center ... DWSMC
Defense Western Regional Audit Office [*DoD*] ... DWRA
Defense Western Regional Telecommunications Office [*DoD*] ... DWRTO
Defense Work Measurement Standard Time Data Program [*Air Force*] (AFM) ... DWMSTDP
Defense-Wide Intelligence Plan [*DoD*] ... D-WIP
Defensive Air Combat Maneuvering [*Military*] ... DACM
Defensive Back [*Football*] ... DB
Defensive Concentration ... DEFCON
Defensive Contact [*Artillery fire*] [*Military*] (VNW) ... DEFCON
Defensive Counterair [*Army*] (ADDR) ... DCA
Defensive Countermaneuvering ... DCM
Defensive Driving Course [*National Safety Council*] ... DDC
Defensive End [*Football*] ... DE
Defensive Fire ... DF
Defensive Guard [*Football*] ... DG
Defensive Missile Order of Battle (MCD) ... DMOB
Defensive Radio Warfare (NATG) ... DRW
Defensive Response [*Psychology*] ... DR
Defensive Satellite (MCD) ... DSAT
Defensive Tackle [*Football*] ... DT
Defensive Target [*Military*] ... DT
Defensive Technology Study [*Military*] (SDI) ... DTS
Defensively-Equipped Merchant Ship ... DEMS
Defensively-Equipped Merchant Ship School ... DEMSS
Defensiveness Scale for Children [*Psychology*] ... DSC
Defensor [*Defender*] [*Coin inscription*] [*Latin*] (ROG) ... DEF
Defensor Fidei [*Defender of the Faith*] [*Latin*] ... DF
Defer (AABC) ... DFR
Deferoxamine [*Also, Desferrioxamine*] [*Chelating agent*] ... DF
Deferoxamine [*Pharmacology*] (DAVI) ... DFO
Deferoxamine [*Also, Desferrioxamine*] [*Chelating agent*] ... DFOA
Deferoxamine Methanesulfonate [*or Desferrioxamine Mesylate*] [*Pharmacology*] ... DFOM
Deferred [*Finance*] ... D
Deferred ... DEF
Deferred Adverse Tax Consequences Implementation Group [*IRS*] ... DATCIG
Deferred Annuity [*Insurance*] (ADA) ... DA
Deferred Annuity Fund ... DAF
Deferred Commercial Annuity [*Insurance*] ... DCA
Deferred Compensation Administrator ... DCA
Deferred Delivery [*Especially, of securities*] ... DD
Deferred Delivery ... DEFEL
Deferred Delivery ... DFDEL
Deferred Development ... DD
Deferred Development Program [*Military*] ... DDP
Deferred Exchange-Rate Guarantee [*Investment term*] (ECON) ... DERG
Deferred Execution ... DEX
Deferred Maintenance and Repair [*DoD*] ... DMAR
Deferred Nesting Program (MCD) ... DNP
Deferred Ordinary (ADA) ... DO
Deferred Organic Supply (MCD) ... DOS
Deferred Pay Fund ... DPF
Deferred Payment [*Business term*] (ADA) ... D/P
Deferred Payment Account [*Business term*] (WDAA) ... DPA
Deferred Payment Plan [*Banking, finance*] ... DPP
Deferred Premium Payment Plan [*Business term*] (IIA) ... DPPP
Deferred Specification Compliance Change (MCD) ... DSCC

Deferred Telegram ... DT
Defiance College, Defiance, OH [*OCLC symbol*] (OCLC) ... DEF
Defiance College, Defiance, OH [*Library symbol Library of Congress*] (LCLS) ... ODefC
Defiance Inc. [*NASDAQ symbol*] (TTSB) ... DEFI
Defiance, OH [*Location identifier FAA*] (FAAL) ... DFI
Defiance, OH [*FM radio station call letters*] ... WDFM
Defiance, OH [*AM radio station call letters*] ... WONW
Defiance, OH [*FM radio station call letters*] ... WZOM
Defiance Precision Products [*NASDAQ symbol*] (NQ) ... DEFI
Defiance Precision Products [*Associated Press*] (SAG) ... DefnInc
Defiance Public Library, Defiance, OH [*Library symbol Library of Congress*] (LCLS) ... ODef
Defiant Minerals [*Vancouver Stock Exchange symbol*] ... DFM
Defibrillate [*Cardiology*] ... DEFIB
Deficiencies in Allowance List [*Military*] (NVT) ... DIAL
Deficiency [*or Deficient*] ... def
Deficiency (ABBR) ... DEFI
Deficiency (ROG) ... DEFIC
Deficiency (AABC) ... DEFN
Deficiency Abatement Program/Management Information System [*Navy*] ... DAP/MIS
Deficiency Action Report (NATG) ... DAR
Deficiency Analysis Data System (DNAB) ... DADS
Deficiency Analysis Summary ... DAS
Deficiency and Disposition Report [*Nuclear energy*] (NRCH) ... DDR
Deficiency and Replacement ... DFRP
Deficiency Corrective Action Program [*Surface missile systems*] ... DCAP
Deficiency Factor (MAE) ... DF
Deficiency in Allowance [*Military*] (MSA) ... DIA
Deficiency Notice [*Government contracting*] ... DN
Deficiency Report [*Air Force*] (AFM) ... DR
Deficiency Reporting System [*Military*] ... DRS
Deficiency Review Board (AFIT) ... DRB
Deficient Equippage Reporting Procedures ... DERP
Deficit ... DEF
Deficit (CPH) ... defic
Deficit Budget ... DB
Deficit Reduction Act [*1984*] ... DEFRA
Deficit Reduction Coalition [*Defunct*] (EA) ... DRC
Define [*or Definite*] (KSC) ... DEF
Define Area ... DA
Define Byte [*Computer science*] (PCM) ... DB
Define Constant (MDG) ... DC
Define Constant with Wordmark ... DCW
Define Control Block [*Computer science*] (OA) ... DCB
Define Control Block Dummy [*Computer science*] (OA) ... DCBD
Define Device Table (MCD) ... DDT
Define Double-Word [*Computer science*] (PCM) ... DD
Define File Processor [*Computer science*] ... DFP
Define Storage ... DS
Define Symbol ... DS
Define Symbol Address [*Computer science*] (IAA) ... DSA
Define the File [*Computer science*] (BUR) ... DTF
Define Word (PCM) ... DW
Defined Antigen Substrate Sphere [*Medicine*] (PDAA) ... DASS
Defined Benefit Plan [*Human resources*] (WYGK) ... DBP
Defined Context Set [*Telecommunications*] (OSI) ... DCS
Defined Contribution Plan [*Insurance*] (WYGK) ... DCP
Defined Culture Medium [*For blastoderms*] ... DCM
Defined Flora Animal [*Medicine*] (DMAA) ... DF
Defined Formula Diets [*Dietetics*] (DAVI) ... DFD
Defined Readout [*Telecommunications*] (OA) ... DR
Defined Substrate [*Medicine*] (MAE) ... DS
Defined User Command (IAA) ... DUC
Defining Advertising Goals for Measured Advertising Results [*Title of book written by Russell Colley and published by the Association of National Advertisers*] ... DAGMAR
Defining Issues Test (EDAC) ... DIT
Definite (FAAC) ... DFNT
Definite Article (WDAA) ... DEF ART
Definite Clause Grammar [*Computer programming*] (BYTE) ... DCG
Definite Decoding ... DD
Definite Quantity (AFM) ... DQ
Definite Quantity Control ... DQC
Definite Tape File [*Computer science*] (OA) ... DTF
Definitely Dull [*Medicine*] ... DD
Definite-Quantity Price List [*Type of contract*] (AAGC) ... DQ/PL
Definite-Time [*Relay*] ... DEFT
Definite-Time Relay (MSA) ... DTR
Definition ... DEF
Definition ... DF
Definition ... DFNTN
Definition, Analysis, and Mechanization ... DAM
Definition and Preliminary Design (SSD) ... D & PD
Definition of Control, Display, and Communications Requirement (DNAB) ... DCDCR
Definition Phase Review (NASA) ... DPR
Definitions Abbreviations and Conventions [*Handbook*] ... DEACON
Definitive (ROG) ... DEF
Definitive Contract ... DC
Definitive Election Results Evaluation Computer (DI) ... DEREC
Definitive Observation Unit [*Medicine*] (MEDA) ... DOU
Definitive Orbit Determination System [*NASA*] ... DODS
Definitive Zone ... DZ
Definitized Spare Parts List (AAG) ... DSPL
Deflagrate (ABBR) ... DEF
Deflagration to Detonation Transition (IEEE) ... DDT
Deflate (ABBR) ... DEFL
Deflating (MSA) ... DFL
Deflect (ABBR) ... DEF
Deflect [*or Deflection*] (MSA) ... DEFL
Deflect (AAG) ... DEFLT
Deflect (KSC) ... DFL
Deflect Amplifier Circuit Card (DWSG) ... DACCA
Deflecta Shield Corp. [*Associated Press*] (SAG) ... DeflcShd
Deflecta Shield Corp. [*NASDAQ symbol*] (SAG) ... TRUX
Deflectable Photomultiplier ... DPM
Deflecta-Shield Corp. [*NASDAQ symbol*] (TTSB) ... TRUX
Deflected Jet Exhaust ... DJE
Deflected Lamine Electrophoresis ... DLE
Deflected Nasal Septum [*Medicine*] ... DNS
Deflection (IAA) ... D
Deflection (AAG) ... DEFLTN
Deflection (ADA) ... DEFT
Deflection (DAC) ... Dflct
Deflection Coil Amplifier ... DCA
Deflection Coil Drive ... DCD
Deflection Coil Set ... DCS
Deflection Error [*Military*] ... DE
Deflection Error Average [*Military*] (MUGU) ... DEA
Deflection Error Probable [*Military*] (AFM) ... DEP
Deflection Factor (IEEE) ... DF
Deflection Modulation (IAA) ... DM
Deflection of the Vertical ... V
Deflection Plate [*Technical drawings*] ... DP
Deflection Probable Errors (MCD) ... DFPE
Deflection Refractive Index Detector ... DRID
Deflection Sensitivity (IDOE) ... S
Deflection Temperature under Load [*Plastics technology*] ... DTUL
Deflection Yoke ... DY
Deflection Yoke Amplifier ... DYA
Deflector [*Automotive engineering*] ... DEFL
Deflector (AAG) ... DEFLTR
Deflector (MSA) ... DFTR
Defloration (ABBR) ... DEFLOR
Defogger [*Automotive engineering*] ... DEFGR
Defogging (AAG) ... DF
Defoliation ... DEF
Defoliation (CINC) ... DEFOL
Deformability Index ... DI
Deformable Device [*Texas Instruments, Inc.*] [*Computer science*] ... DMD
Deformation of Aligned Phase (MCD) ... DAP
Deformity ... deform
Deformographic Storage Display Tube [*IBM Corp.*] ... DSDT
Defraction Limited Thermograph System (MCD) ... DLTS
Defrauding [*FBI standardized term*] ... DEFR
Defrost ... DEF
Defrost (MSA) ... DFR
Defroster [*Automotive engineering*] ... DEFR
Deftness (ABBR) ... DEFTNS
Defueling Water Cleanup System (GAAI) ... DWCS
Defunctus [*Deceased*] [*Latin*] (ADA) ... DEF
DeFuniak Springs, FL [*FM radio station call letters*] (RBYB) ... WAKJ
Deganawidah-Quetzalcoatl University [*Initials preferred to spelled-out name*] [*California*] ... DQU
Degasifier ... DGSFR
Degaussing ... DEGUSG
Degaussing ... DG
Degaussing and Deperming [*Navy*] ... D & D
Degaussing and Deperming [*Navy*] ... DEG & DEP
Degaussing Calibration (NVT) ... DEG
Degaussing Calibration (NVT) ... DEGCALB
Degaussing Compass ... DCMPS
Degaussing Computer ... DCMPTR
Degaussing Officer [*Navy*] ... DGO
Degaussing Range Officer [*Navy*] ... DGRO
Degaussing Services [*Navy*] (NVT) ... DEGSVC
Degaussing Ship [*Navy symbol*] ... ADG
Degaussing System ... DGS
Degaussing Technical Officer [*Navy*] ... DGTO
Degaussing Vessel [*British military*] (DMA) ... DGV
Degaussing Wiping Officer [*Navy*] ... DGWO
Degelis, PQ [*FM radio station call letters*] ... CFVD
Degenerate Electron Gas ... DEG
Degenerate Four-Wave Mixing [*Optical reflection*] ... DFWM
Degenerate Oscillating System ... DOS
Degeneration ... DEG
Degeneration ... degen
Degeneration Reaction ... DR
Degenerative Arthritis ... DA
Degenerative Disc Disease [*Medicine*] ... DDD
Degenerative Disease (DAVI) ... DD
Degenerative Diseases Research Foundation (EA) ... DDRF
Degenerative Joint Disease ... DJD
DeGeorge Financial Corp. [*NASDAQ symbol*] (SAG) ... DEGE
DeGeorge Financial Corp. [*Associated Press*] (SAG) ... DeGrgeFnl
Deggendorf/Steinkirchen [*Germany ICAO location identifier*] (ICLI) ... EDMW
Degge's Parson's Counsellor and Law of Tithes [*A publication*] (DLA) ... Degge
Deglutiatur [*Swallow*] [*Pharmacy*] ... DEGLUT

Deglutiendus [*To be Taken or Swallowed*] [*Pharmacy*] (ROG) .... DEGLUTIEND
DeGoyler and MacNaughton Library, Dallas, TX [*Library symbol Library of Congress*] (LCLS) .... TxDaDM
DeGoyler Foundation, Dallas, TX [*Library symbol Library of Congress*] (LCLS) .... TxDaDF
Degradable (ABBR) .... DEGRAD
Degradation (DSUE) .... DEGRA
Degradation Conversion Factor (MCD) .... DCF
Degradation Failure Rate .... DFR
Degradation of RADAR Defense System .... DRADS
Degradation of RADAR Defense System .... DRDS
Degradation Products [*Hematology*] .... DP
Degrade .... DEG
Degraded Amyloid [*Medicine*] .... DAM
Degraded Mission Assessment .... DMA
Degraded Mission Capability .... DMC
Degraduation Effects Program .... DEP
DeGraff Memorial Hospital, North Tonawanda, NY [*Library symbol Library of Congress*] (LCLS) .... NNotD
Degrease .... DGR
Degree .... D
Degree (IDOE) .... d
Degree (IDOE) .... deg
Degree (AFM) .... DEG
Degree (IAA) .... DG
Degree Celsius [*British Standards Institution*] .... degC
Degree Centigrade (IAA) .... DEGCENT
Degree Completion Program [*Army*] (INF) .... DCP
Degree Days .... DD
Degree Fahrenheit [*British Standards Institution*] .... degF
Degree Kelvin [*British Standards Institution*] .... degK
Degree Of Anoxicity [*Biology*] .... DOA
Degree of Cell Rupture .... DCR
Degree of Conjugation [*Analytical biochemistry*] .... DC
Degree of Control (MCD) .... DOC
Degree of Cooperation [*Military*] (NVT) .... DOC
Degree of Difficulty [*Diving*] .... DD
Degree of Disorder [*Coatings*] .... DOD
Degree of Elasticity (IAA) .... DE
Degree of Financial Leverage .... DFL
Degree of Freedom .... DOF
Degree of Honor Protective Association [*St. Paul, MN*] (EA) .... DHPA
Degree of Operating Leverage [*Finance*] .... DOL
Degree of Pocahontas .... D of P
Degree of Polymerization .... DP
Degree of Protection .... DOP
Degree of Pyritization [*Geology*] .... DOP
Degree of Reading Power [*Test*] .... DRP
Degree of Substitution .... DS
Degree of Total Leverage [*Finance*] .... DTL
Degree Rankine [*British Standards Institution*] .... degR
Degree Year [*Database terminology*] (NITA) .... DG
Degrees (IDOE) .... deg
Degrees Baume .... B
Degrees Celsius C
Degrees Celsius (KSC) .... DC
Degrees Celsius .... OC
Degrees Fahrenheit (KSC) .... DF
Degrees Fahrenheit (AAG) .... DGF
Degrees Fahrenheit (MCD) .... F
Degrees Fahrenheit .... OF
Degrees Kelvin (KSC) .... DK
Degrees Kelvin .... K
Degrees of Freedom (DOG) .... D/F
Degrees of Freedom [*of movement*] .... DF
Degrees per Revolution .... DPR
Degrees per Second .... DEG/SEC
Degrees per Second .... DPS
Degrees Rankine (KSC) .... DR
DeGroot, Dr. A. T., Texas Christian University, Fort Worth, TX [*Library symbol Library of Congress*] (LCLS) .... Deg
DeHart on Military Law [*A publication*] (DLA) .... De Hart Mil Law
DeHart on Military Law [*A publication*] (DLA) .... DeH ML
Dehbid [*Iran*] [*ICAO location identifier*] (ICLI) .... OISI
Dehloran [*Iran*] [*ICAO location identifier*] (ICLI) .... OICR
Dehra Dun [*India*] [*Later, SAB*] [*Geomagnetic observatory code*] .... DDI
Dehra Dun [*India*] [*ICAO location identifier*] (ICLI) .... VIDN
Dehshir [*Iran*] [*ICAO location identifier*] (ICLI) .... OIYD
Dehumidify (MSA) .... DHMY
Dehydratase [*An enzyme*] .... DH
Dehydrated .... DEHYD
Dehydrated and Convenience Foods Council [*Defunct*] (EA) .... DCFC
Dehydrated Castor Oil [*Organic chemistry*] .... DCO
Dehydrated Foods Industry Council [*Later, DCFC*] .... DFIC
Dehydrated Humulinic Acid (OA) .... DHA
Dehydrator (MSA) .... DYHR
Dehydroabietic Acid [*Organic chemistry*] .... DHAA
Dehydroacetic Acid [*Pharmacology*] .... DHA
Dehydroascorbic Acid [*Also, DHA*] [*Oxidized form of Vitamin C*] [*Biochemistry*] .... DAA
Dehydroascorbic Acid [*Also, DAA*] [*Oxidized form of Vitamin C*] [*Biochemistry*] .... DHA
Dehydrocholesterol [*Organic chemistry*] .... DHC
Dehydrocholic Acid [*Organic chemistry*] (MAE) .... DH
Dehydrocholic Acid [*Organic chemistry*] .... DHC
Dehydroepiandrosterone [*Also, DHA, DHEA, DHIA*] [*Endocrinology*] (AAMN) .... DEA
Dehydroepiandrosterone [*Also, DEA, DHEA, DHIA*] [*Endocrinology*] .... DHA
Dehydroepiandrosterone [*Also, DEA, DHA, DHIA*] [*Endocrinology*] .... DHEA
Dehydroepiandrosterone Sulfate [*Biochemistry*] .... DHAS
Dehydroepiandrosterone Sulfate [*Biochemistry*] .... DHEAS
Dehydroepiandrosterone Sulfate [*Biochemistry*] (AAMN) .... DS
Dehydrogenase [*An enzyme*] .... DH
Dehydrogenative Polymerization [*Biology*] .... DHP
Dehydroisoandrosterone [*Also, DEA, DHA, DHEA*] [*Endocrinology*] .... DHIA
Dehydroproline [*Biochemistry*] .... DHP
Dehydrotestosterone [*A banned performance-enhancng drug*] (ECON) .... DHT
Dehydroxyphenylglycol [*Also, DOPEG*] [*Organic chemistry*] .... DHPG
Dei Gratia [*By the Grace of God*] [*Latin*] (GPO) .... DG
Dei Gratia Britanniarum Regina, Fidei Defensor [*By the Grace of God, Queen of England, Defender of the Faith*] [*Latin*] (ROG) .... DG BRIT REG FD
Dei Verbum [*Dogmatic Constitution on Divine Revelation*] [*Vatican II document*] .... DV
Deicing .... DI
Deictic [*Linguistics*] .... d
Deidre Hall Fan Club (EA) .... DHFC
Deification (ABBR) .... DEIFCN
Deified (ABBR) .... DEIFD
Deifier (ABBR) .... DEIFR
Deifying (ABBR) .... DEIFG
De-Inking Pulp [*Process*] [*Paper recycling*] .... DIP
Deionization .... DI
Deionization Reverse Osmosis [*Water treatment*] .... DIRO
Deionization-Filtration .... DF
Deionized Water [*Pharmacology*] (DAVI) .... DW
Deionized-Distilled Water .... DDW
Deir Ez Zor [*Syria*] [*Airport symbol*] (OAG) .... DEZ
Deir Ez Zor [*Syria*] [*ICAO location identifier*] (ICLI) .... OSDZ
Deiters' Cell [*Anatomy*] .... DC
Deja Vu Research Group (EAIO) .... DVRG
Dejectiones Alvi [*Discharge from the Bowels*] [*Pharmacy*] (ROG) .... DEJ ALVI
Dejerine Sottas Syndrome [*Medicine*] .... DSS
Dejerine-Sottas Syndrome [*Medicine*] .... DSS
Dejour Mines Ltd. [*Toronto Stock Exchange symbol*] .... DEJ
Deka (IDOE) .... da
Dekagram [*Unit of measure*] .... DAG
Dekagram [*Unit of measure*] .... DEKAG
Dekagram [*Unit of measure*] (ROG) .... DG
Dekagram [*Unit of measure*] (GPO) .... DKG
Dekagram [*Unit of measure*] (ROG) .... DKGM
DeKalb Community College, Clarkston, GA [*OCLC symbol*] (OCLC) .... GCD
DeKalb County Library System, Regional Service-Rockdale and Newton Counties, Decatur, GA [*Library symbol Library of Congress*] (LCLS) .... GD
DeKalb County School System, Decatur, GA [*Library symbol*] [*Library of Congress*] (LCLS) .... GDDS
DeKalb General Hospital, Decatur, GA [*Library symbol Library of Congress*] (LCLS) .... GDH
DeKalb Genetics [*Associated Press*] (SAG) .... DklbGn
DeKalb Genetics [*Associated Press*] (SAG) .... DklbGn
DeKalb Genetics [*NASDAQ symbol*] (SAG) .... SEED
DeKalb Genetics [*NASDAQ symbol*] (SAG) .... SEED
DEKALB Genetics'B' [*NASDAQ symbol*] (TTSB) .... SEEDB
DeKalb Historical Society, Decatur, GA [*Library symbol Library of Congress*] (LCLS) .... GDD
DeKalb, IL [*Location identifier FAA*] (FAAL) .... DKB
Dekaliter [*Unit of measure*] .... DAL
Dekaliter [*Unit of measure*] (ROG) .... DEKAL
Dekaliter [*Unit of measure*] (GPO) .... DKL
Dekaliter [*Unit of measure*] (ROG) .... DL
Dekameter .... DAM
Dekameter [*Unit of measure*] (ROG) .... DEKAM
Dekameter [*Unit of measure*] (GPO) .... DKM
Dekameter [*Unit of measure*] .... DM
DekaNEM [*Ten NEM*] [*See NEM*] .... DN
Dekanewton [*Unit of force*] .... daN
Dekastere [*Unit of measure*] .... DKS
Dekastere [*Unit of measure*] (ROG) .... DS
Dekeleia [*Greece*] [*Later, PEN*] [*Geomagnetic observatory code*] .... DEK
Dekeleia/Tatoi [*Greece*] [*ICAO location identifier*] (ICLI) .... LGTT
Dekese [*Zaire*] [*ICAO location identifier*] (ICLI) .... FZVT
Dekker & Nordemann [*Publisher*] .... D & N
Dekoratie voor Trouwe Dienst [*Decoration for Devoted Service*] [*South Africa*] .... DTD
DeKoven Foundation for Church Work, Racine, WI [*Library symbol Library of Congress*] (LCLS) .... WRacD
DeKretser's Matara Appeals [*Ceylon*] [*A publication*] (DLA) .... De Krets
Del Electronics Corp. [*AMEX symbol*] (SPSG) .... DEL
Del Electronics Corp. [*Associated Press*] (SAG) .... DelElc
Del Global Technologies [*AMEX symbol*] (TTSB) .... DEL
Del Global Technologies Corp. [*Associated Press*] (SAG) .... DelGlobal
Del Global Technologies Corp. [*NASDAQ symbol*] (SAG) .... DGTC
Del Gray Fan Club (EA) .... DGFC
Del Greco Assertive Behavior Inventory [*Psychology*] (EDAC) .... DABI
Del Laboratories [*AMEX symbol*] (TTSB) .... DLI
Del Laboratories, Inc. [*Associated Press*] (SAG) .... DelLabs
Del Laboratories, Inc. [*AMEX symbol*] (SPSG) .... DLI
Del Mar College, Corpus Christi, TX [*Library symbol Library of Congress*] (LCLS) .... TxCcD
Del Monte, Bukidnon [*Philippines*] [*ICAO location identifier*] (ICLI) .... RPWT
Del Norske Arbeiderparti [*Norwegian Labor Party*] (BARN) .... DNA

Del Norte Chrome [*Vancouver Stock Exchange symbol*] ... DEE
Del Reeves Fan Club (EA) ... DRFC
Del Rio [*Texas*] [*Airport symbol Obsolete*] (OAG) ... DRT
Del Rio/International [*Texas*] [*ICAO location identifier*] (ICLI) ... KDRT
Del Rio Language Screening [*Speech and language therapy*] (DAVI) ... DRLS
Del Rio/Laughlin Air Force Base [*Texas*] [*ICAO location identifier*] (ICLI) ... KDLF
Del Rio, TX [*Location identifier FAA*] (FAAL) ... DLF
Del Rio, TX [*Location identifier FAA*] (FAAL) ... ILH
Del Rio, TX [*AM radio station call letters*] (RBYB) ... KDLK
Del Rio, TX [*FM radio station call letters*] ... KDLK-FM
Del Rio, TX [*FM radio station call letters*] ... KTDR
Del Rio, TX [*Television station call letters*] ... KTRG
Del Rio, TX [*AM radio station call letters*] ... KWMC
Del Shannon Appreciation Society (EAIO) ... DSAS
Del Valle, TX [*AM radio station call letters*] ... KIXL
Delacorte Press [*Publisher*] ... DP
Delactonized Ascorbate [*Biochemistry*] ... DELA
Delafield on Post Mortem Examinations [*A publication*] (DLA) ... Del PM Ex
Delafield, WI [*FM radio station call letters*] ... WHAD
Delafon on Naval Courts Martial [*A publication*] (DLA) ... Del Ct M
Delahaye Club of America (EA) ... DCA
Delalande [*France*] [*Research code symbol*] ... MD
Delamination, Bond, Crack [*Plastics technology*] ... DBC
DeLancey Divinity School, Buffalo, NY [*Library symbol Library of Congress Obsolete*] (LCLS) ... NBuDD
Delancey, NY [*Location identifier FAA*] (FAAL) ... DNY
Delancey Street Foundation (EA) ... DSF
Deland, FL [*Location identifier FAA*] (FAAL) ... DED
Delane's Election Revision Cases [*England*] [*A publication*] (DLA) ... Del El Cas
Delane's English Revision Cases [*1832-35*] [*A publication*] (DLA) ... Del
Delane's Revision Courts Decisions [*England*] [*A publication*] (DLA) ... Delane
Delano, CA [*Location identifier FAA*] (FAAL) ... DLO
Delano, CA [*AM radio station call letters*] ... KCHJ
Delano, CA [*FM radio station call letters*] ... KDNO
Delano, CA [*FM radio station call letters*] ... KKXX
Delano Elementary School, Delano, MN [*Library symbol*] [*Library of Congress*] (LCLS) ... MnDeE
Delano High School, Delano, MN [*Library symbol*] [*Library of Congress*] (LCLS) ... MnDeH
Delano Middle School, Delano, MN [*Library symbol*] [*Library of Congress*] (LCLS) ... MnDeM
Delano Public Libbrary, Delano, MN [*Library symbol*] [*Library of Congress*] (LCLS) ... MnDe
Delareyville [*South Africa*] [*ICAO location identifier*] (ICLI) ... FADL
Delary [*Sweden*] [*Seismograph station code, US Geological Survey*] (SEIS) ... DEL
Delavan, WI [*Location identifier FAA*] (FAAL) ... LVV
Delaware [*Postal code*] ... DE
Delaware (AFM) ... DEL
Delaware [*MARC language code Library of Congress*] (LCCP) ... del
Delaware (ODBW) ... Del
Delaware [*MARC country of publication code Library of Congress*] (LCCP) ... deu
Delaware [*Ontario*] [*Seismograph station code, US Geological Survey*] (SEIS) ... DLA
Delaware [*MARC geographic area code Library of Congress*] (LCCP) ... n-us-de
Delaware Academy of Medicine, Wilmington, DE [*OCLC symbol*] (OCLC) ... DLF
Delaware & Hudson Railway Co. [*Nickname: Delay and Hesitate*] ... D & H
Delaware Association of Conservation Districts (SRA) ... DACD
Delaware Association of Nonprofit Agencies (SRA) ... DANA
Delaware Association of Realtors (SRA) ... DAR
Delaware Association of Rehabilitation Facilities (SRA) ... DELARF
Delaware Association of School Administrators (SRA) ... DASA
Delaware Business Connection ... DBC
Delaware Cases [*1792-1830*] [*A publication*] (DLA) ... Del Cas
Delaware Chancery Reports [*A publication*] (DLA) ... D Ch
Delaware Chancery Reports [*A publication*] (DLA) ... DE CH
Delaware Chancery Reports [*A publication*] (DLA) ... Del Ch
Delaware Chancery Reports [*A publication*] (DLA) ... Del Civ Dec
Delaware Code (DLA) ... Del Code
Delaware Code, Annotated [*A publication*] (DLA) ... DE C Ann
Delaware Code, Annotated [*A publication*] (ILCA) ... Del C Ann
Delaware Code, Annotated [*A publication*] (DLA) ... Del Code Ann
Delaware Constitution [*A publication*] (DLA) ... Del Const
Delaware County District Library, Delaware, OH [*Library symbol Library of Congress*] (LCLS) ... OD
Delaware County Historical Society, Chester, PA [*Library symbol Library of Congress*] (LCLS) ... PCDHi
Delaware County Historical Society, Hopkinton, IA [*Library symbol Library of Congress*] (LCLS) ... IaHoDHi
Delaware County Institute of Science, Media, PA [*Library symbol Library of Congress*] (LCLS) ... PMedS
Delaware County Law Journal [*Pennsylvania*] [*A publication*] (DLA) ... Del Co L J (PA)
Delaware County Leader, Hopkinton, IA [*Library symbol Library of Congress*] (LCLS) ... IaHoDL
Delaware County Reports [*Pennsylvania*] [*A publication*] (DLA) ... Bliss
Delaware County Reports [*Pennsylvania*] [*A publication*] (DLA) ... Del
Delaware County Reports [*Pennsylvania*] [*A publication*] (DLA) ... Del Co
Delaware County Reports [*Pennsylvania*] [*A publication*] (DLA) ... Del Co (PA)
Delaware County Reports [*Pennsylvania*] [*A publication*] (DLA) ... Del Co R
Delaware County Reports [*Pennsylvania*] [*A publication*] (DLA) ... Del Co Reps
Delaware County Reports [*Pennsylvania*] [*A publication*] (DLA) ... Del County
Delaware County Reports [*Pennsylvania*] [*A publication*] (DLA) ... Del County Rep
Delaware County Reports [*Pennsylvania*] [*A publication*] (DLA) ... Delaware Co Reps
Delaware Credit Union League (SRA) ... DCUL
Delaware Criminal Cases [*A publication*] (DLA) ... Del Cr Cas
Delaware Criminal Cases [*A publication*] (DLA) ... Houst Cr Rep
Delaware Criminal Cases [*A publication*] (DLA) ... Houst Crim Cas
Delaware Criminal Cases [*A publication*] (DLA) ... Houst Crim Cases
Delaware Criminal Cases [*A publication*] (DLA) ... Houst Crim Rep
Delaware. Department of Community Affairs and Economic Development, Division of Libraries, Dover, DE [*Library symbol Library of Congress*] (LCLS) ... De
Delaware Department of State, Division of Historical and Cultural Affairs, Hall of Records, Dover, DE [*Library symbol Library of Congress*] (LCLS) ... De-Ar
Delaware Division of Libraries, Dover, DE [*OCLC symbol*] (OCLC) ... DWA
Delaware Education Accountability System (EDAC) ... DEAS
Delaware General Corporation Law [*A publication*] (DLA) ... Del GCL
Delaware Group Dividend & Income Fund [*Associated Press*] (SAG) ... DelaGP
Delaware Group Dividend Income [*NYSE symbol*] (SPSG) ... DDF
Delaware Group Global Dividend Fund [*Associated Press*] (SAG) ... DEGpGl
Delaware Group Global Dividend Fund [*Associated Press*] (SAG) ... DEGpGlb
Delaware Group Global Dividend Fund [*NYSE symbol*] (SAG) ... DGF
Delaware Grp Dividend Income [*NYSE symbol*] (TTSB) ... DDF
Delaware Grp Global Div & Inc. [*NYSE symbol*] (TTSB) ... DGF
Delaware Journal of Corporate Law [*A publication*] (DLA) ... Delaware J Corp L
Delaware, Lackawanna & Western Railroad [*Nicknames: Delay, Linger & Wait; Darn Long & Winding; Dirty, Long & Weary*] ... DL & W
Delaware, Lackawanna & Western Railroad ... DL & WRR
Delaware, Lackawanna & Western Railroad [*AAR code*] ... DLW
Delaware Law School of Widener College, Wilmington, DE [*OCLC symbol*] (OCLC) ... DLA
Delaware Lawyer [*A publication*] (DLA) ... Del Law
Delaware, Maryland & Virginia Railroad ... DM & V
Delaware, Maryland, Virginia [*Peninsula*] ... DELMARVA
Delaware, OH [*Location identifier FAA*] (FAAL) ... DLZ
Delaware, OH [*FM radio station call letters*] ... WCEZ
Delaware, OH [*AM radio station call letters*] ... WDLR
Delaware, OH [*FM radio station call letters*] ... WSLN
Delaware Ostego Corp. [*Associated Press*] (SAG) ... DelaOts
Delaware Otsego Corp. [*NASDAQ symbol*] (NQ) ... DOCP
Delaware Rapid Interlibrary Loan Project [*Library network*] ... DRILL
Delaware Register of Regulations [*A publication*] (DLA) ... Del Reg of Regs
Delaware Reports [*A publication*] (DLA) ... D
Delaware Reports [*A publication*] (DLA) ... Del
Delaware Resources Corp. [*Vancouver Stock Exchange symbol*] ... DLW
Delaware River Basin Commission [*Successor to INCODEL*] ... DELRIBACO
Delaware River Basin Commission [*Successor to INCODEL*] ... DRBC
Delaware River Port Authority ... DRPA
Delaware State College [*Dover*] ... DSC
Delaware State College, Dover, DE [*Library symbol Library of Congress*] (LCLS) ... DeDS
Delaware State Hospital, New Castle, DE [*Library symbol Library of Congress*] (LCLS) ... DeNcD
Delaware Supreme Court Reports [*1832-*] [*A publication*] (ILCA) ... Del
Delaware Technical and Community College, Dover, DE [*Library symbol Library of Congress*] (LCLS) ... DeDT
Delaware Technical and Community College, Northern Campus, Wilmington, DE [*Library symbol Library of Congress*] (LCLS) ... DeWT
Delaware Technical and Community College, Southern Campus, Georgetown, DE [*Library symbol Library of Congress*] (LCLS) ... DeGeT
Delaware Technical and Community College, Southern Campus, Georgetown, DE [*OCLC symbol*] (OCLC) ... DTS
Delaware Technical and Community College, Stanton Campus, Newark, DE [*Library symbol Library of Congress*] (LCLS) ... DeST
Delaware Technical and Community College, Stanton Campus, Newark, DE [*OCLC symbol*] (OCLC) ... DLE
Delaware Technical and Community College, Wilmington, DE [*OCLC symbol*] (OCLC) ... DLD
Delaware Term Reports [*A publication*] (DLA) ... Del Term R
Delaware Township, NJ [*FM radio station call letters*] ... WDVR
Delaware Valley College of Science and Agriculture, Doylestown, PA [*Library symbol Library of Congress*] (LCLS) ... PDoN
Delaware Valley News, Frenchtown, NJ [*Library symbol Library of Congress*] (LCLS) ... NjFrtD
Delaware Water Gap National Recreation Area ... DEWA
Delay [*Electronics*] ... D
Delay ... DEL
Delay (WDMC) ... del
Delay (KSC) ... DLY
Delay Account Of (FAAC) ... DLAC
Delay Amplification Factor (IAA) ... DAF
Delay Amplifier [*Electronics*] (OA) ... DA
Delay and Retransmit ... DART
Delay Asymptotic Relative Efficiency (IAA) ... DARE
Delay/Capacity [*Airport terminal*] [*FAA*] ... DELCAP
Delay Code ... DC
Delay Computer Tomographic Myelography [*Radiology*] (DAVI) ... DCTM
Delay Cost Model ... DECOM
Delay Driver (MCD) ... DD
Delay Enroute Authorized as Ordinary Leave Provided It Does Not Interfere with Reporting Date [*Military*] ... DALVP
Delay Equalizer, Fixed Set (IAA) ... DEF
Delay Equalizer, Variable (IAA) ... DEV
Delay Flip-Flop [*Computer science*] (IAA) ... DFF
Delay Fuse ... DF
Delay Ignition [*or Igniting*] **Tracer** [*Military*] (MCD) ... DIT
Delay in Arriving at Port of Embarkation [*Navy*] ... DELRIVEPOE
Delay in Returning to Duty Station [*Military*] (DNAB) ... DELURN
Delay in Separation Code [*Military*] (AABC) ... DISC

Delay Indefinite (FAAC)	DI
Delay Indefinite (DA)	DLI
Delay Key On	DKO
Delay Line	DL
Delay Line Assembly	DLA
Delay Line Case	DLC
Delay Line Memory	DLM
Delay Line Register	DLR
Delay Line Synthesizer	DLS
Delay Line Time Compression	DELTIC
Delay Locked Loop [Computer science] (IAA)	DLL
Delay Message [Aviation code]	DLA
Delay Modulation (NITA)	DM
Delay Multivibrator	DMV
Delay Shift Keying (IAA)	DSK
Delay Study Analysis	DSA
Delay Time [Aviation] (FAAC)	DLAT
Delay Timer Multiplier (IEEE)	DTM
Delay Unit [Telecommunications] (TEL)	D/U
Delay Valve Two-Way [Automotive engineering]	DVTW
Delayed Accessory Bus [Automotive engineering]	DAB
Delayed Action [Pharmacy]	DA
Delayed Action Bomb	DAB
Delayed Action Fuse	DAF
Delayed Action Incendiary Device	DAID
Delayed Action Tablet [Pharmacy]	DAT
Delayed Allergic Response [Medicine] (BARN)	DAR
Delayed Alpha Particle	DAP
Delayed Anovulatory Syndrome [Medicine] (DMAA)	DAS
Delayed Arming [of explosive device]	DA
Delayed Atomization Cuvette [Laboratory analysis]	DAC
Delayed Auditory Feedback [Audiology]	DAF
Delayed Automatic Gain Control (MSA)	DAGC
Delayed Automatic Reclose (IAA)	DAR
Delayed Automatic Volume (IAA)	DAV
Delayed Automatic Volume Control	DAVC
Delayed Auto-Reclose (PDAA)	DAR
Delayed Breeder or Alternative [Nuclear energy] (NRCH)	DBOA
Delayed Broadcast [Television]	DB
Delayed Call Limited [Telecommunications] (TEL)	DCL
Delayed Coincidence Spectroscopy	DCS
Delayed Coker [Chemical engineering]	DC
Delayed Compliance Order [Compliance Assurance Agreement] [Environmental Protection Agency] (EPA)	DCO
Delayed Conditional Necrosis (MAE)	DCN
Delayed Contact Closure	DCC
Delayed Cutaneous Hypersensitivity [Medicine] (AAMN)	DCH
Delayed Cutaneous Reaction [Dermatology] (DAVI)	DCR
Delayed Delivery [Especially, of Securities]	DD
Delayed Dialing Tone [Telecommunications] (TEL)	DDT
Delayed Disposition Record (MCD)	DDR
Delayed Double Diffusion [Test] (DAVI)	3D
Delayed Echo RADAR Marker	DERM
Delayed Enlistment [or Entry] Program [Military] (AFM)	DEP
Delayed Erythema Dose [Medicine] (DMAA)	DED
Delayed Free Recall	DFR
Delayed Hemolytic Transfusion Reaction [Medicine]	DHTR
Delayed Hypersensitivity [Immunology]	DH
Delayed Hypersensitivity Reaction [Medicine]	DHR
Delayed Hypersensitivity to Tuberculin [Medicine]	DHT
Delayed Impact Space Missile (IAA)	DISM
Delayed Ischemic Deficit [Medicine]	DID
Delayed Jam on Target	DJOT
Delayed Light Emission [Green plant phenomenon]	DLE
Delayed Matching to Sample [Psychology]	DMTS
Delayed Matching-to-Sample [Psychology]	DMS
Delayed Merge Package (MCD)	DMP
Delayed Muscle Soreness	DMS
Delayed Neutron	DN
Delayed Neutron Activation Analysis (PDAA)	DNAA
Delayed Neutron Counting	DNC
Delayed Neutron Monitor [Nuclear energy] (NRCH)	DNM
Delayed Neutron Monitoring Subsystem [Nuclear energy] (NRCH)	DNMS
Delayed Nonmatch to Sample [Test design]	DNMS
Delayed on Target	DOT
Delayed Opening	OPD
Delayed Opening Chaff	DOC
Delayed Opening Leaflet System [Military propaganda]	DOLLS
Delayed Order Notice [Telecommunications] (TEL)	DON
Delayed Output [Computer science]	DLO
Delayed Pressure Urticaria [Dermatology] (DAVI)	DPU
Delayed Primary Closure [Medicine]	DPC
Delayed Printer Simulator	DPS
Delayed Procurement (NASA)	DP
Delayed Procurement Item	DPI
Delayed Procurement Program	DPP
Delayed Pulse Oscillator	DPO
Delayed Quick Cure (MCD)	DQC
Delayed Range on Target [Air Force]	DROT
Delayed Readout Detector [Satellite instrument]	DROD
Delayed Reenlistment Program [Air Force]	DRP
Delayed Sensitivity [Medicine] (DMAA)	DS
Delayed Sleep Phase Syndrome	DSPS
Delayed Sound Reinforcement	DSR
Delayed Time (KSC)	DT

Delayed Time Base (IAA)	DTB
Delayed Time/Telemetry (KSC)	DT/TM
Delayed Weather	DW
Delayed-Fluorescence Optically Detected Magnetic Resonance [Physics]	DF-ODMR
Delayed-Onset Muscle Soreness	DOMS
Delayed-Type Hypersensitivity [Immunology]	DTH
Delay-On-Pull-In	DPOI
Delbancor Industry [Vancouver Stock Exchange symbol]	DLB
Delburne Public Library, Alberta [Library symbol National Library of Canada] (NLC)	ADE
Delcan, Don Mills, ON, Canada [Library symbol] [Library of Congress] (LCLS)	CaODmD
Delcan, Don Mills, Ontario [Library symbol National Library of Canada] (NLC)	ODMD
Delchamps, Inc. [Associated Press] (SAG)	Delchm
Delchamps, Inc. [NASDAQ symbol] (NQ)	DLCH
Delco Chassis Division [General Motors Corp.]	DCD
Delco Electronics Division, General Motors Corp., Technical Library, Kokomo, IN [OCLC symbol] (OCLC)	IKN
Delco Remy America	DRA
Delcommune [Zaire] [Seismograph station code, US Geological Survey] (SEIS)	DCC
Delcorp Resources, Inc. [Vancouver Stock Exchange symbol]	DLP
D'Eldona Resources Ltd. [Toronto Stock Exchange symbol]	DL
Deleatur [Delete] [Latin] (DLA)	Dele
Delegacion del Parlamento Europeo para las Relaciones con los Paises de Latinoamerica [Europe-Latin America Interparliamentary Assembly - ELAIA] [Luxembourg, Luxembourg] (EAIO)	DPERPLA
Delegacy (ROG)	DEL
Delegate [or Delegation] (ADA)	DEL
Delegate	DELEG
Delegate Production Policy (MCD)	DPP
Delegate Production System (MCD)	DPS
Delegate [or Delegation] to Western Union [NATO] (NATG)	DELWU
Delegated Engineering Representative	DER
Delegated Procurement System [Science]	DELPRO
Delegation (ROG)	DELEG
Delegation	Delgn
Delegation Catholique pour la Cooperation (EA)	DCC
Delegation for Afro-American and Caribbean Cultural Affairs	DAACA
Delegation for Assistance to Jewish Emigrants [World War II organization]	DELASEM
Delegation for Friendship among Women (EA)	DFW
Delegation for Scientific and Technical Information (IID)	DIST
Delegation for Scientific and Technical Information, Communication, and Culture [Information service or system] (IID)	DIXIT
Delegation General pour l'Armament [General Armaments Delegation] [France]	DGA
Delegation of Authority (MCD)	DOA
Delegation of Disclosure Authority Letters [Military] (AFIT)	DDL
Delegation of Procurement Authority	DPA
Delegation of the Commission of the European Communities [Delegation de la C ommission des Communautes Europeennes], Ottawa, Ontario [Library symbol National Library of Canada] (BIB)	OOCEEC
Delegation Order (DLA)	Del Order
Delegation Order [Legal term] (DLA)	DO
Delegationen for Vetenskaplig och Teknisk Informationsforsorjning [Swedish Delegation for Scientific and Technical Information] [Information service or system Defunct] (IID)	DFI
Delete (OSI)	DEL
Delete (WDMC)	del
Delete [Computer science] (ECII)	DEL
Delete (WDMC)	dele
Delete (ABBR)	DELE
Delete (AAG)	DELT
Delete (FAAC)	DLT
Delete Character [Keyboard] (CMD)	DEL
Delete in Its Entirety (AAG)	DELENT
Delete Key (CDE)	DEL key
Deleted	D
Deleted in Azoospermia [Genetics]	DAZ
Deleted in Colon Cancer [Gene]	DCC
Deleted in Colorectal Carcinomas [A gene]	DCC
Deleted Quality Review Transaction [IRS]	DQ
Deleted Unpostable [IRS]	DU
Deleted Unpostable from Cards [IRS]	DC
Deleting Important Program Files [Computer science]	DLLs
Deletion Mutant [Genetics]	DM
Deletion Reason/Supply History Code	DRSHC
Deletions/Deferments [Military]	D/D
Delft Atmospheric Research RADAR (MCD)	DARR
Delftware (VRA)	delfwr
Delgado Community College, New Orleans, LA [Library symbol Library of Congress] (LCLS)	LNDC
Delgratia Mining [NASDAQ symbol] (TTSB)	DELGF
Delgratia Mining Corp. [NASDAQ symbol] (SAG)	DELG
Delgratia Mining Corp. [Associated Press] (SAG)	Delgrt
Delhi [India] [Airport symbol] (OAG)	DEL
Delhi [India] [Airport symbol] (AD)	NDH
Delhi [India] [ICAO location identifier] (ICLI)	VIDF
Delhi Civil Decisions [India] [A publication] (DLA)	Del Civ Dec
Delhi Hills, OH [FM radio station call letters]	WJYC
Delhi/Indira Gandhi International [India] [ICAO location identifier] (ICLI)	VIDP
Delhi, LA [FM radio station call letters] (RBYB)	KGGM

Delhi, NY [*FM radio station call letters*] ... WDHI
Delhi Pacific Resources Ltd. [*Toronto Stock Exchange symbol*] ... DPM
Delhi Public Library, Delhi, ON, Canada [*Library symbol Library of Congress*] (LCLS) ... CaODe
Delhi Public Library, Ontario [*Library symbol National Library of Canada*] (NLC) ... ODE
Delhi/Safdarjung [*India*] [*ICAO location identifier*] (ICLI) ... VIDD
Deli/Prepared Meats Committee (EA) ... DPMC
Delia Municipal Library, Alberta [*Library symbol National Library of Canada*] (NLC) ... ADM
Delia Municipal Library, Delia, AB, Canada [*Library symbol Library of Congress*] (LCLS) ... CaADM
Deliberate (ABBR) ... DEL
Deliberate Self-Harm Syndrome ... DSH
Deliberation (ROG) ... DELIB
Delicatamente [*Delicately*] [*Music*] ... DELIC
Delicatamente [*Delicately*] [*Music*] (ROG) ... DELICAT
Delicatessen ... DELI
Delicatessen ... DELI
Delicatessen and Fine Food Association [*British*] (DBA) ... DAFFA
Delicatissimo [*Very Delicately*] [*Music*] (ROG) ... DELICATISS
Delicato [*Delicately*] [*Music*] (ROG) ... DELO
Delight ... DLGHT
Delijan [*Iran*] [*ICAO location identifier*] (ICLI) ... OIIN
Delineated (ROG) ... DELIND
Delineation (MSA) ... DEL
Delineavit [*He (or She) Drew It*] [*Latin*] (ROG) ... DEL
Delineavit [*He (or She) Drew It*] [*Latin*] (WGA) ... DELIN
Delineavit [*He (or She) Drew It*] [*Latin*] ... DELT
Delinquency (ABBR) ... DELCY
Delinquency (ABBR) ... DELIN
Delinquency ... DELNQY
Delinquency Delivery Report (MCD) ... DDR
Delinquency Investigation Inventory Profile [*IRS*] ... DIIP
Delinquency Item Summary and Forecast (MCD) ... DISAF
Delinquent ... DEL
Delinquent (MUGU) ... DELINQ
Delinquent ... DELQ
Delinquent Account ... DELACCT
Delinquent Accounts and Returns [*IRS*] ... DAR
Delinquent Investigation Research File [*IRS*] ... DIRF
Delinquent Supplier Data Transmittal (MCD) ... DSDTR
Delinquent Year [*IRS*] ... DY
Deliquency Account Inventory Profile [*IRS*] ... DAIP
Deliquency Report [*Military*] (VNW) ... DR
Deliquescence Humidity ... DH
Deliquescent ... DELIQ
Delirium Tremens [*Also, DT's*] [*Hallucinatory condition of advanced alcoholism*] ... DT
Delirium Tremens [*Also, DT*] [*Hallucinatory condition of advanced alcoholism*] ... DT's
Delitzsch (BJA) ... Del
Delius Society (EA) ... DS
Deliver [*or Delivery*] (KSC) ... DEL
Deliver (ROG) ... DELR
Deliver (ADA) ... DELV
Deliver (AABC) ... DLVR
Deliver by Telephone [*Message handling*] ... DELPHO
Deliverable Contract Item (KSC) ... DCI
Deliverable Data Package (SSD) ... DDP
Deliverable, Executable Machine Instructions ... DEMI
Deliverable Items List (NASA) ... DIL
Deliverance ... DELVRNC
Delivered (WDMC) ... dd
Delivered ... DD
Delivered ... DELD
Delivered (DLA) ... Delv
Delivered ... DELV'D
Delivered ... DLD
Delivered (NATG) ... DLVD
Delivered Alongside Ship ... DAS
Delivered at Docks ... DD
Delivered at Frontier [*Seller's responsibility is fulfilled when goods have arrived at frontier, but before "customs border," of country named*] [*"INCOTERM," International Chamber of Commerce official code*] ... DAF
Delivered Capacity ... DC
Delivered Duty Paid [*"INCOTERM," International Chamber of Commerce official code*] ... DDP
Delivered Duty Unpaid ... DDU
Delivered Energy ... DE
Delivered Horsepower to Propeller (IAA) ... DHP
Delivered in Room [*Obstetrics*] (CPH) ... DIR
Delivered Sound [*Shipping*] ... DD/S
Delivered Source Instructions ... DSI
Delivered Source Lines [*of Code*] ... DSL
Delivered System Capability ... DSC
Delivered Weight [*Business term*] (ADA) ... DW
Delivered with Standard Wiring ... DSW
Deliverer of Services (OICC) ... DOS
Delivering Information Solutions to Customers [*British*] ... DISC
Delivery [*or Delivered*] ... D
Delivery ... DELY
Delivery ... DLVRY
Delivery (MSA) ... DLVY
Delivery (ROG) ... DLY
Delivery ... DY
Delivery (ODBW) ... dy
Delivery Against Cost [*Business term*] ... DAC
Delivery Against Payment [*Business term*] (ADA) ... D/P
Delivery and Impact Analysis System (MCD) ... DIAS
Delivery and Transport Management System [*Software package*] [*British*] ... DTMS
Delivery Distribution Indicator (MCD) ... DDI
Delivery Distribution Point (MCD) ... DDP
Delivery Ex Option [*Shares*] ... DELXO
Delivery History Report (AFIT) ... DHR
Delivery Indicator Group (NATG) ... DIG
Delivery Issue Team (MCD) ... DIT
Delivery Lead Time [*Army*] ... DLT
Delivery Note (ADA) ... D/N
Delivery of Advanced Network Technology for Europe (ECON) ... DANTE
Delivery on Field ... DOF
Delivery on Wheels [*Shipping*] (DS) ... DOW
Delivery Order [*Business term*] ... D/O
Delivery Order (DFIT) ... D/O
Delivery Order Initiating Meeting Procurement ... DOIM
Delivery Order Manager [*Army*] ... DOM
Delivery Point ... DP
Delivery Rate [*DoD*] ... DR
Delivery Room [*Medicine*] ... DR
Delivery Schedule ... DS
Delivery System-Light [*Army*] (INF) ... GPADS-L
Delivery Term [*Military*] ... DLT
Delivery Time ... DT
Delivery to Surgery Interval [*Gynecology*] ... DSI
Delivery Versus Payment ... DVP
Delivery with Equipment (MCD) ... DWE
Delkin (Lusiwasi) [*Zambia*] [*ICAO location identifier*] (ICLI) ... FLDE
Dell Computer Corp. [*NASDAQ symbol*] (NQ) ... DELL
Dell Computer Corp. [*Associated Press*] (SAG) ... DellCpt
Dell Drive Array [*Computer science*] ... DDA
Dell Embedded Diagnostics [*Computer science*] (PCM) ... DED
Dell Rapids Carnegie Public Library, Dell Rapids, SD [*Library symbol Library of Congress*] (LCLS) ... SdDel
Dell SCSI Array [*Computer science*] ... DSA
Dellaterra Resources Ltd. [*Vancouver Stock Exchange symbol*] ... DEL
Delle-Ile [*France ICAO location identifier*] (ICLI) ... LFEA
Dells, WI [*Location identifier FAA*] (FAAL) ... DLL
Delmar Chemicals, La Salle, Quebec [*Library symbol National Library of Canada*] (NLC) ... QLDC
Delmarva Power & Light Co. [*Associated Press*] (SAG) ... DelmPL
Delmarva Power & Light Co. [*NYSE symbol*] (SPSG) ... DEW
Delmarva Power Financing I [*Associated Press*] (SAG) ... Delmrv
Delmarva Power Financing I [*NYSE symbol*] (SAG) ... DEW
Delmarva Pwr & Lt [*NYSE symbol*] (TTSB) ... DEW
Deloitte, Haskins & Sells, Calgary, Alberta [*Library symbol National Library of Canada*] (BIB) ... ACDH
DeLorean Club International (EA) ... DCI
DeLorean Motor Club of America [*Defunct*] (EA) ... DMCA
DeLorean Motor Co. [*Initials used as name of its cars*] ... DMC
Deloro Stellite Co., Belleville, Ontario [*Library symbol National Library of Canada*] (BIB) ... OBEDS
Delphax Systems, Mississauga, ON, Canada [*Library symbol Library of Congress*] (LCLS) ... CaOMDS
Delphax Systems, Mississauga, Ontario [*Library symbol National Library of Canada*] (NLC) ... OMDS
Delphi Financial Group, Inc. [*Associated Press*] (SAG) ... DelpFin
Delphi Financial Group, Inc. [*NASDAQ symbol*] (SAG) ... DLFI
Delphi Fin'l Group'A' [*NASDAQ symbol*] (TTSB) ... DLFI
Delphi, IN [*FM radio station call letters*] ... WNJY
Delphi Information Sys [*NASDAQ symbol*] (TTSB) ... DLPH
Delphi Information Systems [*Associated Press*] (SAG) ... DelpInf
Delphi Information Systems, Inc. [*NASDAQ symbol*] (NQ) ... DLPH
Delphi International Group (EA) ... DIG
Delphi Public Library, Delphi, IN [*Library symbol Library of Congress*] (LCLS) ... InDel
Delphian Society ... DS
Delphinium Society (EA) ... DS
Delphinus [*Constellation*] ... Del
Delphinus [*Constellation*] ... Delph
Delphos Citizens Bancorp, Inc. [*NASDAQ symbol*] (SAG) ... DCBI
Delphos Citizens Bancorp, Inc. [*Associated Press*] (SAG) ... DelphCt
Delphos, OH [*FM radio station call letters*] ... WDOH
Delphos Public Library, Delphos, OH [*Library symbol Library of Congress*] (LCLS) ... ODelp
Delray Beach, FL [*AM radio station call letters*] ... WDBF
Delray Beach Library, Delray Beach, FL [*Library symbol Library of Congress*] (LCLS) ... FDlb
Delray Connecting Railroad (MHDB) ... DCR
Delray Connecting Railroad Co. [*AAR code*] ... DC
Delrina Corp. [*Associated Press*] (SAG) ... Delrina
Delrina Corp. [*NASDAQ symbol*] (SAG) ... DENA
Delta [*Phonetic alphabet*] [*International*] (DSUE) ... D
Delta ... DLT
Delta Aerotaxi [*Italy ICAO designator*] (FAAC) ... DEA
Delta Air [*ICAO designator*] (AD) ... DI
Delta Air Charter Ltd. [*Canada ICAO designator*] (FAAC) ... SNO
Delta Air Lines [*NYSE symbol*] (TTSB) ... DAL
Delta Air Lines Cv Dep Pfd [*NYSE symbol*] (TTSB) ... DALPrC
Delta Air Lines, Inc. (AAG) ... DA

Delta Air Lines, Inc. [*NYSE symbol Air carrier designation symbol*] (SPSG) ..... DAL
Delta Air Lines, Inc. [*Associated Press*] (SAG) ..... DeltaA
Delta Air Lines, Inc. [*Associated Press*] (SAG) ..... DeltaAir
Delta Air Lines, Inc. [*ICAO designator*] ..... DL
Delta Air Lines, Inc. (MCD) ..... DLT
Delta Air Transport [*Belgium ICAO designator*] (FAAC) ..... DAT
Delta Amplitude (AAG) ..... DA
Delta and Pine Land [*NYSE symbol*] (TTSB) ..... DLP
Delta & Pine Land Co. [*NASDAQ symbol*] (SAG) ..... COTN
Delta & Pine Land Co. [*Associated Press*] (SAG) ..... DeltPine
Delta Aviation SA [*Spain ICAO designator*] (FAAC) ..... DET
Delta Branch, Rideau Lakes Union Library, Ontario [*Library symbol National Library of Canada*] (BIB) ..... ODRL
Delta Channel [*Used for communicating between the phone company switch and an ISDN adapter*] [*Computer science*] ..... D-channel
Delta Clipper Experimental Advanced [*Rocket*] [*An experimental rocket that takes off and lands on its tail*] [*NASA*] ..... DC-XA
Delta, CO [*AM radio station call letters*] ..... KDTA
Delta, CO [*FM radio station call letters*] (RBYB) ..... KKNN
Delta College, University Center, MI [*Library symbol Library of Congress*] (LCLS) ..... MiUcD
Delta Community Library, Delta Junction, AK [*Library symbol Library of Congress*] (LCLS) ..... AkDj
Delta Computec [*NASDAQ symbol*] (TTSB) ..... DCIS
Delta Dental Plan ..... DDP
Delta Dental Plans Association (EA) ..... DDPA
Delta Downs [*Australia Airport symbol Obsolete*] (OAG) ..... DDN
Delta Honor Camp, Delta, CO [*Library symbol Library of Congress*] (LCLS) ..... CoDelC
Delta Houseboat Rental Association (EA) ..... DHRA
Delta [*or Digital*] **Inertial Guidance System** [*NASA*] ..... DIGS
Delta Jet SA [*Spain ICAO designator*] (FAAC) ..... DEJ
Delta Junction, AK [*Location identifier FAA*] (FAAL) ..... DJN
Delta Junction/Allen Army Air Field [*Alaska*] [*ICAO location identifier*] (ICLI) ..... PABI
Delta Junction/Fort Greely, AK [*Location identifier FAA*] (FAAL) ..... BIG
Delta Kappa Epsilon [*Society*] ..... DKE
Delta Kappa Gamma Society, International (AEBS) ..... DKG
Delta Milliohm Sensor ..... DMS
Delta Ministry [*Later, DMM*] (EA) ..... DM
Delta Ministry of Mississippi [*Defunct*] (EA) ..... DMM
Delta Modulation [*Telecommunications*] (TEL) ..... DEM
Delta Modulation ..... DM
Delta Modulation (NITA) ..... DMOD
Delta Modulation System ..... DMS
Delta Multivibrator ..... DMV
Delta Museum and Archives, British Columbia [*Library symbol National Library of Canada*] (NLC) ..... BDEM
Delta Natural Gas [*NASDAQ symbol*] (TTSB) ..... DGAS
Delta Natural Gas Co. [*Associated Press*] (SAG) ..... DeltNG
Delta Natural Gas Co., Inc. [*NASDAQ symbol*] (NQ) ..... DGAS
Delta Nu Alpha Transportation Fraternity (EA) ..... DNA
Delta, OH [*FM radio station call letters*] ..... WBUZ
Delta Petroleum [*NASDAQ symbol*] (SAG) ..... DPTR
Delta Petroleum Corp. [*Associated Press*] (SAG) ..... DltaPtr
Delta Pi Epsilon [*Fraternity*] (AEE) ..... DPE
Delta Pressure/Delta Time (MCD) ..... DP/DT
Delta Psi Kappa [*Society*] ..... DPK
Delta Public Library, Delta, CO [*Library symbol Library of Congress*] (LCLS) ..... CoDel
Delta Pulse Code Modulation [*Electronics*] (IAA) ..... DPCM
Delta Region Aviation Command [*Military*] (VNW) ..... DRAC
Delta Regional Primate Research Center, Science Information Service, Covington, LA [*Library symbol Library of Congress*] (LCLS) ..... LCovD
Delta Sigma Modulator (IAA) ..... DSM
Delta Sigma Rho-Tau Kappa Alpha (EA) ..... DSR-TKA
Delta Society (EA) ..... DS
Delta Spin Test Facility (MCD) ..... DSTF
Delta State College, Cleveland, MS [*Library symbol Library of Congress*] (LCLS) ..... MsCleD
Delta State University (GAGS) ..... Delta St U
Delta Teen-Lift (EA) ..... DTL
Delta, UT [*Location identifier FAA*] (FAAL) ..... DTA
Delta, UT [*FM radio station call letters*] ..... KFMD
Delta, UT [*AM radio station call letters*] ..... KNAK
Delta Valley & Southern Railway Co. [*AAR code*] ..... DVS
Delta Velocity (KSC) ..... DV
Delta Velocity Display ..... DVD
Delta Velocity Launch ..... DVL
Delta Velocity On/Off ..... DVO
Delta Velocity Planet ..... DVP
Delta Velocity Ullage ..... DVU
Delta Vocational Technical Center, Delta, CO [*Library symbol*] [*Library of Congress*] (LCLS) ..... CoDelV
Delta Waterfowl Research Station, Delta, MB, Canada [*Library symbol Library of Congress*] (LCLS) ..... CaMDW
Delta Waterfowl Research Station, Manitoba [*Library symbol National Library of Canada*] (NLC) ..... MDW
Delta Wing Orbiter (KSC) ..... DWO
Delta Woodside Ind. [*NYSE symbol*] (TTSB) ..... DLW
Delta Woodside Industries, Inc. [*Associated Press*] (SAG) ..... DeltaW
Delta Woodside Industries, Inc. [*NYSE symbol*] (CTT) ..... DLW
Delta Woodside Industries, Inc. (MHDW) ..... DLWD
Delta-Amino Levulinic Acid [*Biochemistry*] (DAVI) ..... ALA
Delta-Aminolevulinate Dehydratase (DMAA) ..... ALADH
Delta-Aminolevulinate Synthase (DMAA) ..... ALAS
Delta-Aminolevulinic Acid [*Biochemistry*] ..... DALA
Delta-Aminovaleric Acid [*Organic chemistry*] ..... DAV
Delta-Guanidinovaleric Acid [*Biochemistry*] ..... DGVA
DeltaPoint, Inc. [*Associated Press*] (SAG) ..... DeltPnt
DeltaPoint, Inc. [*NASDAQ symbol*] (SAG) ..... DTPT
DeltaPoint Inc. [*NASDAQ symbol*] (TTSB) ..... DTPT
Delta-Sleep-Inducing Peptide ..... DSIP
Deltec Resources Ltd. [*Vancouver Stock Exchange symbol*] ..... DEC
Deltex [*Slovakia*] [*ICAO designator*] (FAAC) ..... DTX
Deltiologists of America (EA) ..... D of A
Delton District Library, Delton, MI [*Library symbol Library of Congress*] (LCLS) ..... MiDelD
Deltopectoral [*Anatomy*] (DAVI) ..... DP
Deltorphin [*Biochemistry*] ..... DT
Deluge Valve (DAC) ..... DEL V
Delusion ..... DEL
Delusion (ABBR) ..... DELU
Deluxe (MSA) ..... DLX
Deluxe Corp. [*Associated Press*] (SAG) ..... Deluxe
DeLuxe Corp. [*NYSE symbol*] (SPSG) ..... DLX
Deluxe Paint Animation [*Electronic art*] ..... DA
Delyn Cooperative Development Agency [*British*] ..... DCDA
Delyse [*Record label*] [*Great Britain*] ..... Dely
DEM Inc. [*NASDAQ symbol*] (TTSB) ..... DEMI
Demagnetize ..... DMGZ
Demagnetizer ..... DMTZR
Demagogue (ROG) ..... DEM
Dema'i (BJA) ..... Dem
Demand ..... DEM
Demand Actuated Road Transit ..... DART
Demand and Resource Evaluation (ODBW) ..... DARE
Demand and Supply (WDAA) ..... D & S
Demand Assigned/Time Division Multiple Access ..... DA/TDMA
Demand Assignment [*Telecommunications*] (TEL) ..... DA
Demand Assignment Controller ..... DAC
Demand Assignment Multiple Access [*Telecommunications*] ..... DAMA
Demand Base (DNAB) ..... DB
Demand Curve [*Economics*] ..... D
Demand Deposit Account (TDOB) ..... DDA
Demand Deposit Accounting [*Banking*] (MDG) ..... DDA
Demand Deposit Program Library [*Computer science*] (OA) ..... DDPL
Demand Deposits ..... DD
Demand Development Interval (MCD) ..... DDI
Demand Development Period (MCD) ..... DDP
Demand Draft [*Business term*] ..... DD
Demand Forecasting Program (BUR) ..... DFP
Demand History File [*DoD*] ..... DHF
Demand Indicator (KSC) ..... DI
Demand Loan ..... D/L
Demand Meter ..... DM
Demand Meter, Printing ..... DP
Demand Mode Integral Rocket Ramjet (MCD) ..... DMIRR
Demand Note [*Banking*] ..... D/N
Demand Order Number [*Army*] (AABC) ..... DON
Demand Processing Unit [*Military*] ..... DPU
Demand Protocol Architecture [*Computer science*] (PCM) ..... DPA
Demand Return Disposal ..... DRD
Demand Return Disposal Average Monthly Demand ..... DRAMD
Demand Scheduled Bus (OA) ..... DSB
Demand Totalizing Relay (KSC) ..... DTR
Demand Valve ..... DV
Demand-Assignment Signaling (MCD) ..... DAS
Demand-Assignment Signaling and Switching Subsystem [*Telecommunications*] (IAA) ..... DASSS
Demand-Assignment Signaling and Switching Unit ..... DASS
Demand-Increasing Costs [*Economics*] ..... DIC
Demanding Equal Access to Facts and Warnings Aired on TV for Citizens Who are Hearing-Impaired [*Student legal action organization*] (EA) ..... DEAFWATCH
Demand-Page Virtual Memory [*Computer science*] (PDAA) ..... DPVM
Demand-Side Management ..... DSM
Demarcation Membrane System [*Medicine*] (DMAA) ..... DMS
Demarcation Unit (MCD) ..... DU
Demarest's New York Surrogate's Court Reports [*A publication*] (DLA) ..... Dem
Demarest's New York Surrogate's Court Reports [*A publication*] (DLA) ..... Dem (NY)
Demarest's New York Surrogate's Court Reports [*A publication*] (DLA) ..... Dem Surr
Demarest's New York Surrogate's Court Reports [*A publication*] (DLA) ..... Demarest
DeMary Memorial Public Library, Rupert, ID [*Library symbol*] [*Library of Congress*] (LCLS) ..... IdRu
Dembidollo [*Ethiopia*] [*Airport symbol*] (OAG) ..... DEM
Dembidollo [*Ethiopia*] [*ICAO location identifier*] (ICLI) ..... HADD
Demeclocycline [*Also, DMCT*] [*Antimicrobial compound*] ..... DMC
Dementia Alzheimer Type [*Medicine*] ..... DAT
Dementia Praecox [*or a patient with this condition*] [*Medical slang*] ..... DP
Dementia Rating Scale [*Psychometric testing*] ..... DRS
Dementia with Lewy Bodies [*Nerve cell pathology*] ..... DLB
Demerol [*Meperidine hydrochloride*] [*Analgesic compound Trademark*] ..... Dem
Demerol [*Trademark of Winthrop Pharmaceuticals*] [*Analgesic compound*] (DAVI) ..... DEMERIL
Demerol-Phenergan-Thorazine [*Drug regime*] ..... DPT
(Demethoxy)daunorubicin [*Antineoplastic drug*] ..... DMDR

Demethylchlortetracycline [*Obsolete name*] [*Antimicrobial compound See DMC*] ..... DMCT
Demetrius [*of Plutarch*] [*Classical studies*] (OCD) ..... Demetr
Demeure Historique [*An association France*] (EAIO) ..... DH
Demi Official [*Military British*] ..... DO
Demijohn [*Freight*] ..... DEM
Demijohn [*Freight*] (WGA) ..... DEMJ
Demijohn [*Freight*] ..... DJN
Demilitarization ..... DMIL
Demilitarization / Explosive Ordnance Demolition ..... DMIL/EOD
Demilitarization Protective Ensemble (RDA) ..... DPE
Demilitarize (AABC) ..... DEMIL
Demilitarized Zone ..... DMZ
Demineralized [*Water*] (NRCH) ..... DM
Demineralized Bone [*Medicine*] ..... DMB
Demineralized Bone Matrix [*Substance which, when surgically implanted, stimulates development of new bone*] ..... DBM
Demineralized Bone Powder [*Medicine*] ..... DBP
Demineralized Makeup Water [*Nuclear energy*] (NRCH) ..... DMW
Demineralized Oil [*Petroleum Refining*] ..... DMO
Demineralized Water ..... DMW
Demineralized Water (NRCH) ..... DW
Demineralized Water Makeup System [*Nuclear energy*] (NRCH) ..... DWMS
Demineralized Water Storage Tank [*Nuclear energy*] (NRCH) ..... DWST
Demineralizer ..... DMNRLZR
Deming, NM [*Location identifier FAA*] (FAAL) ..... DMN
Deming, NM [*FM radio station call letters*] ..... KDEM
Deming, NM [*AM radio station call letters*] ..... KOTS
Deming, NM [*FM radio station call letters*] (RBYB) ..... KZPI-FM
Deming Public Library, Deming, NM [*Library symbol Library of Congress*] (LCLS) ..... NmD
Demi-Pension [*Hotel rate*] ..... DP
Demirkoy [*Turkey*] [*Seismograph station code, US Geological Survey*] (SEIS) ..... DMK
Demised (ROG) ..... DEMD
Demisit-Sene-Prole [*Died without issue*] [*Latin*] ..... DSP
Demobilize (AABC) ..... DEMOB
Demobilized (ABBR) ..... DEMOBED
Democracia Cristiana [*Christian Democratic Party*] [*Colorado Political party*] (PPW) ..... DC
Democracia Cristiana [*Christian Democratic Party*] [*Paraguay*] [*Political party*] (PD) ..... DC
Democracia Popular - Union Democrata Cristiana [*People's Democracy - Christian Democratic Union*] [*Ecuador*] [*Political party*] (PPW) ..... DP-UDC
Democracia Socialista [*Spain Political party*] (EY) ..... DS
Democracy (ABBR) ..... DEMOC
Democracy and Peace (Iterim) League [*Myanmar*] [*Political party*] ..... DPIL
Democracy Fund [*Defunct*] (EA) ..... DF
[*The*] **Democracy International** (EA) ..... DI
[*The*] **Democracy International** (EA) ..... TDI
Democracy Now in Ulster [*Northern Ireland*] [*An association*] ..... DNU
Democracy Project (EA) ..... DP
Democrat [*or Democratic*] ..... D
Democrat [*or Democratic*] (EY) ..... DEM
Democrat, Orange City, IA [*Library symbol Library of Congress*] (LCLS) ..... IaOcD
Democrat Youth Community of Europe [*Formerly, Conservative and Christian Democrat Youth Community of Europe*] (EA) ..... DEMYC
Democraten '66 [*Democrats '66*] [*Netherlands*] (PPW) D-66
Democrat-Farmer-Labor [*Party*] [*Minnesota*] ..... DFL
Democratiaid Rhyddfrydol Cymru [*Welsh Liberal Democrats*] [*Political party Wales*] (EAIO) ..... DRC
Democratic ..... DEM
Democratic Action Committee [*Pakistan*] [*Political party*] ..... DAC
Democratic Action Congress [*Trinidad and Tobago*] [*Political party*] (PPW) ..... DAC
Democratic Action Party [*Malaysia*] [*Political party*] (PPW) ..... DAP
Democratic Action Party [*Malta*] [*Political party*] (PPE) ..... DAP
Democratic Agenda (EA) ..... DA
Democratic Alliance [*Philippines*] [*Political party*] (FEA) ..... DA
Democratic Alliance of Burma [*Myanmar*] [*Political party*] (EY) ..... DAB
Democratic and Social Republican Party [*Mauritania*] [*Political party*] (EY) ..... DSRP
Democratic and Social Union [*Mauritania*] [*Political party*] (EY) ..... DSU
Democratic Business Council (EA) ..... DBC
Democratic Candidate Fund (EA) ..... DCF
Democratic Community of Vojvodina Hungarians [*Former Yugoslavia*] [*Political party*] ..... DCVH
Democratic Community of Vojvodina Hungarians [*Former Yugoslavia*] [*Political party*] ..... VDMK
Democratic Confederate Republic of Koryo [*Reunified Korean state*] [*Proposed*] ..... DCRK
Democratic Congress Alliance [*Gambia*] ..... DCA
Democratic Congressional Campaign Committee (EA) ..... DCCC
Democratic Conservative Party [*Nicaragua*] [*Political party*] (PD) ..... PCD
Democratic Constitutional Rally [*Tunisia*] [*Political party*] (BARN) ..... DCR
Democratic Council on Ethnic Americans [*Defunct*] (EA) ..... DCEA
Democratic Front for the Liberation of Palestine (PD) ..... DFLP
Democratic Front for the Salvation of Somalia (PD) ..... DFSS
Democratic Governors Association (EA) ..... DGA
Democratic Governors Conference (EA) ..... DGC
Democratic Justice Party [*Mauritania*] [*Political party*] (EY) ..... DJP
Democratic Justice Party [*South Korea Political party*] (PPW) ..... DJP
Democratic Kampuchea [*Pol Pot's regime in Cambodia*] ..... DK
Democratic Korea Party [*South Korea Political party*] (PPW) ..... DKP
Democratic Labor Association [*Philippines*] ..... DLA
Democratic Labor Party [*Trinidad and Tobago*] [*Political party*] (PPW) ..... DLP
Democratic Labor Party [*Australia Political party*] ..... DLP
Democratic Labor Party [*Barbados*] [*Political party*] (PPW) ..... DLP
Democratic Labour Movement [*Guyana*] [*Political party*] (PPW) ..... DLM
Democratic Leadership Council (EA) ..... DLC
Democratic League of Kosovo [*Albania*] [*Political party*] (ECON) ..... DLK
Democratic Left Party [*Turkey Political party*] (MENA) ..... DLP
Democratic Liberal Party [*Taiwan*] [*Political party*] (EY) ..... DLP
Democratic Liberal Party [*South Korea Political party*] ..... DLP
Democratic Malaysia Indian Party [*Political party*] (FEA) ..... DMIP
Democratic Movement for Change [*Political party*] [*Israel*] ..... DMC
Democratic National Committee (EA) ..... DNC
Democratic National Committee - Department of Constituent Coordination [*Defunct*] (EA) ..... DNCDCC
Democratic National Committee - Women's Affairs Division [*Later, DNCWD*] (EA) ..... DNCWAD
Democratic National Committee - Women's Division [*Formerly, DNCWAD*] (EA) ..... DNCWD
Democratic National Salvation Front [*Romania*] [*Political party*] (ECON) ..... DNSF
Democratic National Strategy Council (EA) ..... DNSC
Democratic Nationalist Party [*1959-1966*] [*Malta*] [*Political party*] (PPE) ..... DNP
Democratic Non-Party Nationalist Party [*British*] ..... DemNPN
Democratic Opposition of Slovenia [*Political party*] (EY) ..... DEMOS
Democratic Party [*Slang*] ..... DEMP
Democratic Party [*Kenya*] [*Political party*] (EY) ..... DP
Democratic Party [*Lithuania*] [*Political party*] (EAIO) ..... DP
Democratic Party [*Thailand*] [*Political party*] (PPW) ..... DP
Democratic Party [*Poland Political party*] (PPW) ..... DP
Democratic Party [*Cook Island*] [*Political party*] (PPW) ..... DP
Democratic Party [*Uganda*] [*Political party*] (PD) ..... DP
Democratic Party [*Ecuador*] [*Political party*] (PD) ..... PD
Democratic Party for British Gibraltar (PPW) ..... DPBG
Democratic Party of Albania [*Political party*] (EY) ..... DPA
Democratic Party of Kurdistan [*Iraq*] [*Political party*] (PPW) ..... DPK
Democratic Party of Nigeria and the Cameroons ..... DPNC
Democratic Party of Tadzhikistan [*Political party*] ..... DPT
Democratic Party - St. Maarten [*Netherlands Antilles*] [*Political party*] (EY) ..... DP-StM
Democratic Party - Statia [*Netherlands Antilles*] [*Political party*] (EY) ..... DP-StE
Democratic People's Party [*Taiwan*] [*Political party*] (ECON) ..... DPP
Democratic People's Republic of Korea [*IYRU nationality code*] (IYR) ..... DK
Democratic People's Republic of Korea [*Also known as North Korea*] ..... DPRK
Democratic People's Republic of Korea ..... DRK
Democratic People's Republic of Korea [*ANSI two-letter standard code*] (CNC) ..... KP
Democratic People's Republic of Korea [*Aircraft nationality and registration mark*] (FAAC) ..... P
Democratic People's Republic of Korea [*ANSI three-letter standard code*] (CNC) ..... PRK
Democratic Policy Commission [*Defunct*] (EA) ..... DPC
Democratic Popular Front for the Liberation of Palestine (BJA) ..... DPFLP
Democratic Progressive Party [*Transkei*] [*Political party*] (PPW) ..... DPP
Democratic Progressive Party [*Taiwan*] [*Political party*] ..... DPP
Democratic Reform Party [*South Africa Political party*] (EY) ..... DRP
Democratic Republic of China (CINC) ..... DRC
Democratic Republic of the Congo [*Later, Zaire*] ..... DRC
Democratic Republic of Vietnam [*North Vietnam*] ..... DRV
Democratic Republic of Vietnam [*North Vietnam*] ..... DRVN
Democratic Republican Independent Voter Education Committee [*Political Action Committee*] ..... DRIVE
Democratic Republican Party [*South Korea Political party*] (PPW) ..... DRP
Democratic Rural Union [*Brazil*] ..... UDR
Democratic Senatorial Campaign Committee [*Commercial firm*] (EA) ..... DSCC
Democratic Socialist Organizing Committee [*Later, DSA*] (EA) ..... DSOC
Democratic Socialist Party [*Japan Political party*] (PPW) ..... DSP
Democratic Socialist Party [*South Korea Political party*] (PPW) ..... DSP
Democratic Socialist Party [*Ireland*] [*Political party*] (PPW) ..... DSP
Democratic Socialist Party [*Australia Political party*] ..... DSP
Democratic Socialist Party [*India*] [*Political party*] (PPW) ..... DSP
Democratic Socialists of America [*Political party*] (EA) ..... DSA
Democratic Study Group (EA) ..... DSG
Democratic Tradition Education Project [*Australia*] ..... DTEP
Democratic Turnhalle Alliance [*Namibia*] [*Political party*] (EY) ..... DTA
Democratic Unification Party [*South Korea Political party*] (PPW) ..... DUP
Democratic Unionist Party [*Sudan*] [*Political party*] (PD) ..... DUP
Democratic Unionist Party [*Northern Ireland*] [*Political party*] ..... DUP
Democratic United National Front [*Sri Lanka*] [*Political party*] (ECON) ..... DUNF
Democratic Women's Union of Canada ..... DWUC
Democratic Workers' Congress [*Ceylon*] ..... DWC
Democratic Yemen Airlines (ALYEMDA) [*People's Democratic Republic of Yemen*] [*ICAO designator*] (ICDA) ..... DY
Democratie Chretienne Francaise [*French Christian Democracy*] [*Political party*] (PPE) ..... DCF
Democratie Integrale au Cameroun [*Political party*] (EY) ..... DIC
Democratisch Alternatief 1991 [*Democratic Alternative 1991*] [*Suriname*] [*Political party*] (EY) ..... DA '91
Democratische Partij - Bonaire [*Democratic Party - Bonaire*] [*Netherlands Antilles*] [*Political party*] (EY) ..... DP-B
Democratische Partij - Bovenwinden [*Democratic Party - Windward Islands*] [*Netherlands Antilles*] [*Political party*] (PPW) ..... DP
Democratische Partij - Curacao [*Democratic Party - Curacao*] [*Netherlands Antilles*] [*Political party*] (EY) ..... DP-C
Democratische Partij van Curacao [*Democratic Party - Curacao*] [*Netherlands Antilles*] [*Political party*] (PPW) ..... DP
Democrats Abroad (EA) ..... DA

Democrazia Nazionale - Constituente di Destra [*National Democracy - Right Constituent*] [*Italy Political party*] (PPE) .... DN
Democrazia Proletaria [*Proletarian Democracy*] [*Italy Political party*] (PPE) .... DP
Democritus [*Fifth century BC*] [*Classical studies*] (OCD) .... Democr
Democritus Nuclear Research Center [*Greece*] .... DNRC
Demodulate/Modulate .... D/M
Demodulated Noise (CAAL) .... DEMON
Demodulation/Remodulation (IAA) .... DR
Demodulator [*Telecommunications*] (KSC) .... DEM
Demodulator [*Telecommunications*] (AAG) .... DEMOD
Demodulator Band Filter (MSA) .... DBF
Demodulator BIT [*Binary Digit*] Synchronizer (MCD) .... DBS
Demodulator Neon Driver .... DND
Demographic Adjustment Factor (NTCM) .... DAF
Demographic and Health Survey [*Agency for International Development*] .... DHS
Demographic Data for Development, International Statistical Program Center [*Bureau of the Census*] (GFGA) .... DDI
Demographic Data Retrieval System [*Census Bureau*] [*Information service or system*] (IID) .... DDRS
Demographic Online Retrieval Information System [*CACI, Inc.*] .... DORIS
Demographic Research Co., Inc. [*Information service or system*] (IID) .... DRC
Demographic Surveys Division [*Census*] (OICC) .... DSD
Demographics [*The external characteristics of a population*] (WDMC) .... demos
Demographics Laboratory [*Information service or system*] (IID) .... DEM/LAB
Demography .... DEMOG
Demokratesch Partei [*Democratic Party*] [*Luxembourg*] [*Political party*] (PPE) .... DP
Demokraticheska Partiia [*Democratic Party*] [*Bulgaria*] [*Political party*] (PPE) .... DP
Demokraticheska Sgovor [*Democratic Alliance*] [*Bulgaria*] [*Political party*] (PPE) .... DS
Demokraticka Strana [*Democratic Party*] [*Former Czechoslovakia*] [*Political party*] (PPE) .... DS
Demokratik Halk Partisi [*Democratic People's Party*] [*Turkish Cyprus*] [*Political party*] (PPE) .... DHP
Demokratik Merkez Partisi [*Democratic Centre Party*] [*Turkey Political party*] (EY) .... DMP
Demokratik Mucadele Partisi [*Democratic Struggle Party*] [*Turkish Cyprus*] [*Political party*] (EY) .... DMP
Demokratiki Enosis [*Democratic Union*] [*Greek*] (PPE) .... DE
Demokratiki Enosis Kyprou [*Democratic Union of Cyprus*] [*Political party*] (PPE) .... DEK
Demokratiki Parataksis [*Democratic Front*] [*Greek*] (PPE) .... DP
Demokratiko Komma [*Democratic Party*] [*Greek Cyprus*] [*Political party*] (PPE) .... DEKO
Demokratiko Komma [*Democratic Party*] [*Cyprus*] [*Political party*] (EY) .... DIKO
Demokratikon Komma Ergazomenou Laou [*Democratic Party of Working People*] [*Greek*] (PPE) .... DKEL
Demokratikon Sosialistikon Komma [*Democratic Socialist Party*] [*Greece*] [*Political party*] (PPE) .... DSK
Demokratikos Sinaspismos [*Democratic Coalition*] [*Greece*] [*Political party*] (PPE) .... DS
Demokratikos Synagermos [*Democratic Rally*] [*Greek Cyprus*] [*Political party*] (PPE) .... DS
Demokratische Bauernpartei Deutschlands [*Democratic Farmers' Party of Germany*] (PPW) .... DBD
Demokratische Fortschrittliche Partei [*Democratic Progressive Party*] [*Austria*] (PPE) .... DFP
Demokratische Partei Oesterreichs [*Democratic Party of Austria*] (PPE) .... DPO
Demokratische Partei Saar [*Democratic Party of the Saar*] [*Germany Political party*] (PPE) .... DPS
Demokratische Volkspartei [*Democratic People's Party*] [*Germany*] (PPE) ...... DVP
Demokratischer Aufbruch [*Democratic Awakening*] [*Later, Christian Democratic Union*] [*Germany*] (EAIO) .... DA
Demokratischer Jugendverband Europas [*Democrat Youth Community of Europe*] [*Political party*] (EAIO) .... DJE
Demokratiska Foerbundet av Finlands Folk [*Finnish People's Democratic League*] (PPE) .... DFFF
Demokratiske Sosialister - Arbeidernes Informasjon Kommitte [*Democratic Socialists - Workers' Information Committee*] [*Norway Political party*] (PPE) .... DS-AIK
Demokratska Partija Socijalista [*Democratic Party of Socialists*] [*Montenegro*] [*Political party*] (EY) .... DPS
Demokratski Savez Kosovo [*Democratic Alliance of Kosovo*] [*Serbia*] [*Political party*] (EY) .... DSK
Demolish [*Technical drawings*] .... DEM
Demolition .... DEMLTN
Demolition .... DEMO
Demolition .... DEMOL
Demolition .... DML
Demolition Bomb .... DEMBOMB
Demolition Duty (DNAB) .... DML DY
Demolition Firing Device .... DFD
Demolition Order (ROG) .... DO
Demolition Research Unit .... DRU
Demolition Rocket (NATG) .... DR
Demolombe's Code Napoleon [*A publication*] (DLA) .... Demol
Demolombe's Code Napoleon [*A publication*] (DLA) .... Demol C N
Demonax [*of Lucian*] [*Classical studies*] (OCD) .... Demon
Demonologic (ABBR) .... DEMONOL
Demonology (ABBR) .... DEMON
Demonstrate (AFM) .... DMST
Demonstrated Compliance Parameter Limits [*Environmental science*] [*Environmental Protection Agency*] .... DCPL
Demonstration .... DEM
Demonstration (WDAA) .... DEMO

Demonstration (AFM) .... DMSTN
Demonstration Account [*For messages to and from UTLAS*] .... DEM
Demonstration Advanced Avionics System (MCD) .... DAAS
Demonstration Air Force .... DAF
Demonstration and Evaluation Report (MCD) .... DER
Demonstration and Research Center for Early Education [*George Peabody College, Nashville*] .... DARCEE
Demonstration and Shakedown Operation Piggyback [*Kit*] [*Military*] .... DASOP
Demonstration and Shakedown Operations [*Military*] (AFM) .... DASO
Demonstration and Training .... D & T
Demonstration and Validation (MCD) .... DV
Demonstration and Validation (MCD) .... DVAL
Demonstration and Validation In-Process Review .... DEVA IPR
Demonstration Cities and Metropolitan Development Act .... DCMDA
Demonstration Detail Test Objectives (AAG) .... DDTO
Demonstration Division [*Marine science*] (OSRA) .... DD
Demonstration Division [*Forecast Systems Laboratory*] (USDC) .... DD
Demonstration Flight Rating Test (MCD) .... DFRT
Demonstration Flight Satellite (MCD) .... DFS
Demonstration of Operational Feasibility .... DOF
Demonstration of Site Remediation Technology [*Environmental science*] .... DESRT
Demonstration Power Reactor (NRCH) .... DPR
Demonstration Programs Administration [*HUD*] .... DPA
Demonstration Reliability Acceptance Test .... DRAT
Demonstration Reprocessing Plant [*Nuclear energy*] (NUCP) .... DRP
Demonstration Site Operational Test Series .... DSOTS
Demonstration Test Motor (MCD) .... DTM
Demonstration/Validation (MCD) .... DEM/VAL
Demonstration/Validation Phase (AAGC) .... DEM/VAL
Demonstrative (BJA) .... Dem
Demonstrative .... DEMON
Demonstrative (ROG) .... DEMONS
Demonstrative (Pronoun) [*Linguistics*] .... DEMONSTR
Demonstrator (KSC) .... DEMO
Demonstrator .... DEMONST
Demonstrator (IAA) .... DMNSTR
Demonstrators Association of Illinois (EA) .... DAI
Demopolis, AL [*Location identifier FAA*] (FAAL) .... RZO
Demopolis, AL [*Television station call letters*] .... WIIQ
Demopolis, AL [*AM radio station call letters*] .... WXAL
Demopolis, AL [*FM radio station call letters*] .... WZNJ
Demorest, GA [*FM radio station call letters*] (RBYB) .... WPPR-FM
DeMorgans Theorems [*Rules of replacement*] [*Logic*] .... DeM
Demos D Scale [*Psychology*] .... DDS
Demosthenes [*of Plutarch*] [*Classical studies*] (OCD) .... Dem
Demosthenes [*Greek orator, 384-322BC*] [*Classical studies*] (OCD) .... Dem
Demote (AABC) .... DEM
Demountable [*Technical drawings*] .... DMT
Demountable Cathode Lamp .... DCL
Demountable Externally Anchored Low-Stress Magnet (MCD) .... DEALS
Demountable, Rack, Off-Loading, and Pick-Up System [*British Army*] ...... DROPS
Demulcent [*Softening, Lubricating*] [*Pharmacy*] (ROG) .... DEM
Demultiplexer [*Computer science*] .... DEMUX
Demultiplexer [*Computer science*] .... DMUX
Demultiplexing/Mixing/Remultiplexing [*Device*] [*Telecommunications*] (TEL) .... DMR
Demur (ABBR) .... DEM
Demurrage [*Shipping*] .... DEM
Demurrer (ROG) .... DEMUR
Demy [*Half*] [*Size of paper*] (ADA) .... D
Demy [*Half*] [*Size of paper*] .... DEM
Demy [*Half*] [*Size of paper*] (ROG) .... DY
Demycinosyltylosin [*Antibacterial*] .... DMT
Demystify the Established Standardized Tests [*Project*] .... DETEST
Den, Aoyama, and Takemake [*Early investors in automobile manufacturer Nissan*] [*Initials used in creating automobile name DATSUN*] [*Japan*] .... DAT
Den Sivile Flyskole [*Norway ICAO designator*] (FAAC) .... TTX
Dena Kaye Fan Club (EA) .... DKFC
Denali Fault System [*Geology*] .... DFS
DenAmerica Corp. [*AMEX symbol*] (SAG) .... DEN
DenAmerica Corp. [*AMEX symbol*] (TTSB) .... DEN
DenAmerica Corp. [*Associated Press*] (SAG) .... DenAmer
Denar Mines Ltd. [*Vancouver Stock Exchange symbol*] .... DER
Denarii [*Pence*] [*Monetary unit*] [*British*] .... D
Denarius [*or Denarii*] [*Silver coin in Ancient Rome; gold coin in Roman Empire*] .... D
Denarius Weight [*Pennyweight*] [*Latin*] .... DWT
Denatured .... DENAT
Denatured .... DNTRD
Denatured Uranium [*Nuclear reactor technology*] .... DU
Denaturing Gradient-Gel Electrophoresis [*Analytical Biochemistry*] .... DGGE
Denazification, Demilitarization, Deindustrialization [*Allied policy for Germany after World War II*] .... 3D's
Denbighshire [*County in Wales*] (ROG) .... DEN
Denbighshire [*County in Wales*] .... DENB
Denbighshire [*County in Wales*] .... DENBIGHS
Denbighshire [*County in Wales*] .... DENBS
Denbury Resources [*NASDAQ symbol*] (TTSB) .... DENRF
Dendrite Arm Spacing (RDA) .... DAS
Dendrite International [*NASDAQ symbol*] (TTSB) .... DRTE
Dendrite International, Inc. [*Associated Press*] (SAG) .... Dendrte
Dendrite International, Inc. [*NASDAQ symbol*] (SAG) .... DRTE
Dendritic Algorithm [*Organic molecules*] .... DENDRAL
Dendritic Cell [*Cytology*] .... DC

Dendritic Epidermal Cell [*Cytology*] ... DEC
Dendritic Epidermal T Cell [*Biochemistry*] ... DETC
Dendrobium Vein Necrosis Virus [*Plant pathology*] ... DVNV
Dendrodendritic Synaptosome [*Medicine*] (DMAA) ... DDS
Dendrology (ABBR) ... DEND
Dendrology (ABBR) ... DENDROL
Dendrometer (ABBR) ... DENDRO
Dendrotoxin [*Biochemistry*] ... DTX
Dene Nation, Yellowknife, Northwest Territories [*Library symbol National Library of Canada*] (BIB) ... NWYD
Denfeld High School, Duluth, MN [*Library symbol*] [*Library of Congress*] (LCLS) ... MnDuDH
Dengue [*Virus*] ... DEN
Dengue Hemorrhagic Fever [*Medicine*] ... DHF
Dengue Hemorrhagic Fever Syndrome [*Medicine*] ... DHFS
Dengue Shock Syndrome [*Medicine*] ... DSS
Denham [*Australia Airport symbol*] (OAG) ... DNM
Denham [*British ICAO location identifier*] (ICLI) ... EGLD
Denham Springs, LA [*AM radio station call letters*] ... WBIU
Denial [*Psychology*] ... Dn
Denied [*Legal term*] (DLA) ... D
Denied [*Legal term*] (DLA) ... Den
Denied (AAGC) ... den
Denied Usage Channel Evaluator [*Telecommunications*] (TEL) ... DUCE
Denied-Boarding Compensation [*Airlines*] ... DBC
Denier [*Later, tex*] ... den
Denier per Filament [*Textile technology*] ... DPF
Deniliquin [*Australia Airport symbol*] (OAG) ... DNQ
Denio's New York Reports [*A publication*] (DLA) ... D
Denio's New York Reports [*A publication*] (DLA) ... Den
Denio's New York Reports [*A publication*] (DLA) ... Denio R
Denio's New York Supreme Court Reports [*1845-48*] [*A publication*] (DLA) ... Denio
Denis Browne Splint [*Orthopedics*] (DAVI) ... DBS
Denis Island [*Seychelles Islands*] [*Airport symbol*] (OAG) ... DEI
Denis' Reports [*32-46 Louisiana*] [*A publication*] (DLA) ... Den
Denis' Reports [*32-46 Louisiana*] [*A publication*] (DLA) ... Denis
Denison & Pacific Suburban Railway Co. [*AAR code*] ... DPS
Denison and Pearce's English Crown Cases [*1844-52*] [*A publication*] (DLA) ... D & P
Denison and Pearce's English Crown Cases [*1844-52*] [*A publication*] (DLA) ... Den & P
Denison and Pearce's English Crown Cases [*1844-52*] [*A publication*] (DLA) ... Den & PCC
Denison and Pearce's English Crown Cases Reserved [*169 English Reprint*] [*1844-52*] [*A publication*] (DLA) ... Den
Denison and Scott's House of Lords Appeal Practice [*A publication*] (DLA) ... Den & Sc Pr
Denison Bulletin, Denison, IA [*Library symbol Library of Congress*] (LCLS) ... IaDenB
Denison Carnegie Library, Denison, IA [*Library symbol Library of Congress*] (LCLS) ... IaDen
Denison, IA [*Location identifier FAA*] (FAAL) ... DNS
Denison, IA [*AM radio station call letters*] ... KDSN
Denison, IA [*FM radio station call letters*] ... KDSN-FM
Denison Mines Ltd. [*Toronto Stock Exchange symbol Vancouver Stock Exchange symbol*] ... DEN
Denison Public Library, Denison, TX [*Library symbol Library of Congress*] (LCLS) ... TxDeni
Denison Review, Denison, IA [*Library symbol Library of Congress*] (LCLS) ... IaDenR
Denison, TX [*FM radio station call letters*] ... KTCY
Denison University, Granville, OH [*OCLC symbol*] (OCLC) ... DNU
Denison University, Granville, OH [*Library symbol Library of Congress*] (LCLS) ... OGraD
Denison's English Crown Cases [*1844-52*] [*A publication*] (DLA) ... D
Denison's English Crown Cases [*1844-52*] [*A publication*] (DLA) ... Den C C
Denison's English Crown Cases [*1844-52*] [*A publication*] (DLA) ... Denison Cr Cas
Denison-Sherman, TX [*AM radio station call letters*] ... KDSX
Denison-Sherman, TX [*FM radio station call letters*] (RBYB) ... KDVE-FM
Denmark [*IYRU nationality code*] ... D
Denmark [*Message traffic*] [*Military*] (DNAB) ... DA
Denmark (NATG) ... DE
Denmark ... DEN
Denmark (VRA) ... Den
Denmark (ODBW) ... Den
Denmark ... DENM
Denmark [*ANSI two-letter standard code*] (CNC) ... DK
Denmark [*MARC country of publication code Library of Congress*] (LCCP) ... dk
Denmark [*ANSI three-letter standard code*] (CNC) ... DNK
Denmark [*MARC geographic area code Library of Congress*] (LCCP) ... e-dk--
Denmark [*International civil aircraft marking*] (ODBW) ... OY
Denmark Cheese Association [*Defunct*] (EA) ... DCA
Denmark Strait Overflow Water [*Oceanography*] ... DSOW
Denmark Technical College, Denmark, SC [*Library symbol*] [*Library of Congress*] (LCLS) ... ScDeTC
Denmark-America Foundation (EA) ... DAF
Dennis Brutus Defense Committee (EA) ... DBDC
Dennis Elementary School, Rockford, IL [*Library symbol*] [*Library of Congress*] (LCLS) ... IRoDE
Dennis Memorial Library, Newton, NJ [*Library symbol Library of Congress*] (LCLS) ... NjNet
Dennis R. Williams [*Designer's mark on US bicentennial dollar*] ... DRW
Denniston [*New Zealand*] [*Seismograph station code, US Geological Survey Closed*] (SEIS) ... DNS
Dennysville, ME [*FM radio station call letters*] (RBYB) ... WHRR-FM
Dennysville, ME [*FM radio station call letters*] ... WVZD
Denomination (ROG) ... DENN
Denomination ... DENOM
Denominational Executives of Christian Education (EA) ... DECE
Denominational Ministry Strategy [*Later, CSM*] (EA) ... DMS
Denominative [*or Denominator*] (BJA) ... denom
Denominator [*In formulas for life annuities and life insurance premiums*] ... D
Denominator (ROG) ... DENR
Denominazione di Origine Controllata [*Italian wine designation*] ... DOC
Denominazione di Origine Controllata e Garantita [*Italian wine designation*] ... DOCG
Denotation (ABBR) ... DENOT
Denote (MSA) ... DEN
Denote Chassis ... DCH
Denouement (ROG) ... DEN
DeNovo [*Associated Press*] (SAG) ... DeNvo
DeNovo [*NASDAQ symbol*] (SAG) ... DNVO
Denpasar [*Indonesia*] [*Seismograph station code, US Geological Survey*] (SEIS) ... DNP
Denpasar [*Indonesia*] [*Airport symbol*] (OAG) ... DPS
Dense (FAAC) ... DNS
Dense Blasting Agent (MCD) ... DBA
Dense Canalicular System [*Medicine*] (DMAA) ... DCS
Dense Deposit Disease (MAE) ... DDD
Dense Electronic Population ... DEP
Dense Flint (AAG) ... DF
Dense Gas Dispersion [*Computer model*] ... DEGADIS
Dense Grade Aggregate ... DGA
Dense Hydrous Magnesium Silicate [*Geochemistry*] ... DHMS
Dense Intramembranous Deposit Disease [*Medicine*] (DMAA) ... DIDD
Dense Ionized Medium [*Astrophysics*] ... DIM
Dense Media Separation (PDAA) ... DMS
Dense Medium Separating [*Chemical engineering*] ... DMS
Dense Non-Aqueous Phase Liquid [*Chemical engineering*] ... DNAPL
Dense Pac Microsystems, Inc. [*Associated Press*] (SAG) ... DnsePc
Dense Parenchyma [*Medicine*] (DMAA) ... DY
Dense Plasma Focus ... DPF
Dense Random Packing of Hard Spheres (MCD) ... DRPHS
Dense Tar Surfacing ... DTS
Dense Tubular System ... DTS
Dense Upper Cloud [*ICAO*] (FAAC) ... DUC
Dense Vortex Plasma ... DVP
Dense Wave Division Multiplexing [*Lucent*] ... DWDM
Dense-Branching Morphology [*Physical chemistry*] ... DBM
Dense-Cored Vesicles [*Anatomy*] ... DCV
Densely Packaged Encased Standard Element (AAG) ... DPESE
Dense-Pac Microsystems [*NASDAQ symbol*] (TTSB) ... DPAC
Dense-Pac Microsystems, Inc. [*NASDAQ symbol*] (NQ) ... DPAC
Densest Random Packing [*Solid state physics*] ... DRP
Dense-Staining Material [*Cytology*] ... DSM
Densified Refuse-Derived Fuel (RDA) ... DRDF
Densimeter (DNAB) ... DE
Densities of States [*Photovoltaic energy systems*] ... DOS
Density ... D
Density (IDOE) ... d
Density ... DEN
Density (AFM) ... DENS
Density (IDOE) ... dens
Density ... DY
Density [*Heat transmission symbol*] ... p
Density Altitude [*Navigation*] ... DA
Density Altitude [*Computer*] ... DENALT
Density Controller ... DC
Density Dependent (OA) ... DD
Density Dependent [*Biology*] ... Dep
Density Dependent Inhibition [*of cell growth*] ... DDI
Density Dependent Recruitment [*Pisciculture*] ... DDR
Density Functional Theory [*Quantum chemistry*] ... DFT
Density Gradient ... DG
Density Gradient Electrophoresis ... DGE
Density Gradient Sedimentation [*Analytical biochemistry*] ... DGS
Density Indicator ... DI
Density Manipulation Subsystem (MCD) ... DMS
Density Meter [*Instrumentation*] ... DM
Density of States [*Physics*] ... DOS
Density of Water ... DOW
Density Phenomena [*Japan*] ... DENPA
Density Probe (MUGU) ... DENPRE
Density Report [*Army*] ... DR
Density Standard [*Medicine*] (MAE) ... DS
Density Unknown [*Medicine*] (MAE) ... DU
Density-Dependent Phosphoprotein [*Medicine*] (DMAA) ... DDP
Density-Depth ... DEDE
Denslow's Notes to Second Edition [*1-3 Michigan*] [*A publication*] (DLA) ... Dens
Dent [*Idaho*] [*Seismograph station code, US Geological Survey Closed*] (SEIS) ... DEI
Dental ... D
Dental (AABC) ... DEN
Dental (ROG) ... DENT
Dental ... DENTL
Dental (MSA) ... DNTL
Dental ... DNTL
Dental Activity (AABC) ... DENTAC
Dental Admission Test [*Education*] ... DAT

Dental Amalgamator	DAMLG
Dental Anesthetic [Medicine]	DA
Dental Apprentice	DA
Dental Aptitude Test [Education] (AEE)	DAT
Dental Aptitude Test (GAGS)	DAT
Dental Assistant	DA
Dental Assistants' Association of Western Australia	DAAWA
Dental Assisting National Board (EA)	DANB
Dental Auxiliary Teacher Education [Medicine] (DMAA)	DATE
Dental Auxiliary Utilization	DAU
Dental Battalion (DNAB)	DENBN
Dental Board of New South Wales [Australia]	DBNSW
Dental Board of Queensland [Australia]	DBQ
Dental Board of South Australia	DBSA
Dental Board of the Australian Capital Territory	DBACT
Dental Board of Victoria [Australia]	DBV
Dental Branch [British military] (DMA)	DB
Dental Capitation Plan [Insurance] (WYGK)	DCP
Dental Care Network [Blue Cross and Blue Shield] [Insurance]	DCN
Dental Care Plan [Insurance] (WYGK)	DCP
Dental Civic Action Program [Vietnam]	DENTCAP
Dental Co. [Marine Corps]	DENCO
Dental Continuation Pay [Military] (AABC)	DCP
Dental Corps [Navy]	DC
Dental Corps [Air Force]	DENTCORPS
Dental Corps, General Service [USNR officer designation]	DCR
Dental Cosmos Library, Philadelphia, PA [Library symbol Library of Congress Obsolete] (LCLS)	PPDC
Dental Dealers of America (EA)	DDA
Dental Distress Syndrome [Medicine] (DMAA)	DDS
Dental Documentary Foundation	DDF
Dental Education Center [Veterans Administration] (GFGA)	DEC
Dental Estimates Board [British] (DI)	DEB
Dental Examining Board	DEB
Dental Explanation of Benefits [Army]	DEOB
Dental Exposure Normalization Technique [Medicine] (DMAA)	DENT
Dental Fear Syndrome	DFS
Dental Gold Institute (EA)	DGI
Dental Group Management Association (EA)	DGMA
Dental Guidance Council for Cerebral Palsy (EA)	DGCCP
Dental Health Education and Research Foundation [Australia]	DHERF
Dental Health International (EA)	DHI
Dental Hygiene Aptitude Test (EDAC)	DHAT
Dental Hygienist [British military] (DMA)	DH
Dental Information (EA)	DI
Dental Laboratories and Dental Prosthetists' Association of New South Wales [Australia]	DLDPANSW
Dental Laboratories Association [British] (DBA)	DLA
Dental Laboratory Conference [Defunct] (EA)	DLC
Dental Library, University of Manitoba, Winnipeg, Manitoba [Library symbol National Library of Canada] (NLC)	MWUD
Dental Maintenance Organization	DMO
Dental Manufacturers of America (EA)	DMA
Dental Mechanic [Ranking title] [British Royal Navy]	DM
Dental Officer	DO
Dental Officer Training Plan [Canada]	DOTP
Dental Pay	DENPAY
Dental Practice Board of England and Wales [British]	DPB
Dental Practitioner's Formulary	DPF
Dental Preferred Provider Organization [Insurance] (WYGK)	DPPO
Dental Prosthetic Technician	DP
Dental Prosthetics [Dentistry] (DAVI)	DP
Dental Recruit	DR
Dental Repair Technician [Navy]	DRM
Dental Research Information Center (DIT)	DRIC
Dental Research Institute [University of California, Los Angeles] [Research center] (RCD)	DRI
Dental Suction Apparatus	DSCAPRS
Dental Surgery [or Surgeon] [Medical Officer designation] [British]	DS
Dental Surgery Assistant [British]	DSA
Dental Surgery Attendant [Ranking title] [British Royal Navy]	D
Dental Technician [Navy rating]	DT
Dental Technician, Chief [Navy rating]	DTC
Dental Technician, First Class [Navy rating]	DT1
Dental Technician, Master Chief [Navy rating]	DTCM
Dental Technician, Second Class [Navy rating]	DT2
Dental Technician, Senior Chief [Navy rating]	DTCS
Dental Technician, Third Class [Navy rating]	DT3
Dental Therapy Assistant (RDA)	DTA
Dental, Visual, and Hearing Insurance	DVH
Dental X-Ray Teaching and Training Replica	DEXTER
Dentalman [Nonrated enlisted man] [Navy]	DN
Dentate Granule Cell	DG
Dentate Gyrus [Neuroanatomy]	DG
Dentate Line [Anatomy]	DL
Dentatorubral Pallidoluysian Atrophy [Medicine]	DRPLA
Dentes [Applied to Teeth] (ROG)	D
Dentinger Library, Falher, AB, Canada [Library symbol] [Library of Congress] (LCLS)	CaAFalD
Dentinogenesis Imperfecta [Medicine] (DMAA)	DI
Dentist	DDS
Dentist (WDAA)	DEN
Dentistry (DAVI)	DE
Dentistry	DENT
Dentistry	DNTSTRY

Dentition [Medicine]	DENT
Dento-Enamel Junction [Dentistry]	DEJ
Denton [Texas] [Seismograph station code, US Geological Survey Closed] (SEIS)	DNT
Denton Avenue Elementary School, New Hyde Park, NY [Library symbol] [Library of Congress]	NNhpDE
Denton, MD [AM radio station call letters]	WKDI
Denton Public Library, Denton, NC [Library symbol Library of Congress] (LCLS)	NcDe
Denton, TX [Location identifier FAA] (FAAL)	DTO
Denton, TX [Television station call letters]	KDTN
Denton, TX [FM radio station call letters] (RBYB)	KHCK
Denton, TX [FM radio station call letters]	KHKS
Denton, TX [AM radio station call letters] (RBYB)	KICI
Denton, TX [AM radio station call letters] (RBYB)	KINF-AM
Denton, TX [FM radio station call letters]	KNTU
Dentonia Resources Ltd. [Vancouver Stock Exchange symbol]	DTA
Dentsply International [Associated Press] (SAG)	Dentsply
Dentsply International [NASDAQ symbol] (SAG)	XRAY
Dentur [Give] [Pharmacy]	D
Dentur [Give] [Pharmacy]	DENT
Dentur Tales Doses [Give in Such Doses] [Pharmacy]	DENT TAL DOS
Dentur Tales Doses [Give in Such Doses] [Pharmacy]	DTD
Denture (ABBR)	DENT
Denture	DENTR
Denver [Colorado] [Mint mark, when appearing on US coins]	D
Denver [Colorado] [Seismograph station code, US Geological Survey] (SEIS)	DEN
Denver [Colorado] [Airport symbol]	DEN
Denver [Colorado] (ROG)	DENV
Denver [Colorado] [ICAO location identifier] (ICLI)	KRDE
Denver & Rio Grande Railroad	D & RG
[The] Denver & Rio Grande Western Railroad Co.	D & RGW
[The] Denver & Rio Grande Western Railroad Co. [AAR code]	DRGW
Denver & Salt Lake Railroad	D & SL
Denver & Salt Lake Railroad [AAR code]	DSL
Denver & Santa Fe Railway	D & SF
Denver Area Project, Denver, CO [OCLC symbol] (OCLC)	DVX
Denver Art Museum, Denver, CO [Library symbol Library of Congress] (LCLS)	CoDA
Denver Articulation Screening Exam [Speech evaluation test]	DASE
Denver Audiometric Screening Test	DAST
Denver Auditory Phoneme Sequencing Test [Speech and language therapy] (DAVI)	DAPST
Denver AWIPS [Advanced Weather Interactive Processing System] Risk Reduction and Requirements Evaluation [Workstation] [Marine science] (OSRA)	DARE
Denver AWIPS Risk Reduction and Requirements Evaluation [Workstation] (USDC)	DARE
Denver Bar Association. Record [A publication] (DLA)	Den BA Rec
Denver Botanic Gardens, Inc., Denver, CO [Library symbol Library of Congress] (LCLS)	CoDDB
Denver, CO [Location identifier FAA] (FAAL)	APA
Denver, CO [Location identifier FAA] (FAAL)	BJC
Denver, CO [Location identifier FAA] (FAAL)	BKF
Denver, CO [Location identifier FAA] (FAAL)	CHY
Denver, CO [Location identifier FAA] (FAAL)	GQW
Denver, CO [Location identifier FAA] (FAAL)	HMX
Denver, CO [FM radio station call letters]	KALC
Denver, CO [AM radio station call letters]	KBNO
Denver, CO [FM radio station call letters]	KBPI
Denver, CO [Television station call letters]	KCEC
Denver, CO [FM radio station call letters]	KCFR
Denver, CO [Television station call letters]	KCNC
Denver, CO [Television station call letters]	KDVR
Denver, CO [FM radio station call letters] (RBYB)	KHIH-FM
Denver, CO [AM radio station call letters]	KHOW
Denver, CO [AM radio station call letters]	KJME
Denver, CO [AM radio station call letters]	KKFN
Denver, CO [FM radio station call letters] (RBYB)	KKHK-FM
Denver, CO [AM radio station call letters]	KKYD
Denver, CO [AM radio station call letters]	KLZ
Denver, CO [Television station call letters]	KMGH
Denver, CO [AM radio station call letters]	KNUS
Denver, CO [AM radio station call letters]	KOA
Denver, CO [FM radio station call letters]	KOSI
Denver, CO [AM radio station call letters]	KPOF
Denver, CO [AM radio station call letters]	KRFX
Denver, CO [AM radio station call letters]	KRKS
Denver, CO [Television station call letters]	KRMA
Denver, CO [Television station call letters] (RBYB)	KRMT
Denver, CO [AM radio station call letters] (RBYB)	KRRF-AM
Denver, CO [Television station call letters]	KTVD
Denver, CO [Television station call letters]	KUBD
Denver, CO [Television station call letters]	KUSA
Denver, CO [FM radio station call letters]	KUVO
Denver, CO [Television station call letters]	KWGN
Denver, CO [AM radio station call letters]	KXKL
Denver, CO [FM radio station call letters]	KXKL-FM
Denver, CO [FM radio station call letters]	KYGO-FM
Denver, CO [Location identifier FAA] (FAAL)	RRV
Denver, CO [Location identifier FAA] (FAAL)	SPO
Denver, CO [Location identifier FAA] (FAAL)	TOT
Denver, CO [Location identifier FAA] (FAAL)	ZDV

Denver Developmental Screening Test [*For mental development of infants*] ... DDST
Denver Express, Inc. [*ICAO designator*] (FAAC) ... FEC
Denver Eye Screening Test ... DEST
Denver Federal Records Center, Denver, CO [*Library symbol Library of Congress*] (LCLS) ... CoDFR
Denver Handwriting Analysis [*Educational test*] ... DHA
Denver International Airport [*Facetious translation: Delay It Again*] (ECON) ... DIA
Denver Jet, Inc. [*ICAO designator*] (FAAC) ... DJT
Denver Journal of International Law [*A publication*] (DLA) ... Denver J Int'l L
Denver Journal of International Law and Policy [*A publication*] (DLA) ... Denver J Int L & Policy
Denver Laboratories [*Great Britain*] [*Research code symbol*] ... R
Denver Law Librarians Group, Denver, CO [*OCLC symbol*] (OCLC) ... COY
Denver Law Libraries, Denver, CO [*Library symbol*] [*Library of Congress*] (LCLS) ... CoDLL
Denver Legal News [*A publication*] (DLA) ... Den L N
Denver Legal News [*A publication*] (DLA) ... Denver L N
Denver, Longmont [*Colorado*] [*ICAO location identifier*] (ICLI) ... KZDV
Denver Museum of Natural History, Denver, CO [*Library symbol Library of Congress*] (LCLS) ... CoDMNH
Denver Post, Inc., Denver, CO [*Library symbol Library of Congress*] (LCLS) ... CoDDP
Denver Public Library, Denver, CO [*Library symbol Library of Congress*] (LCLS) ... CoD
Denver Public Library, Denver, CO [*OCLC symbol*] (OCLC) ... DPL
Denver Public Library, Denver General Hospital Library, Denver, CO [*Library symbol Library of Congress*] (LCLS) ... CoD-H
Denver Public Library, Denver, IA [*Library symbol Library of Congress*] (LCLS) ... IaDv
Denver Public Schools, Professional Library, Denver, CO [*Library symbol Library of Congress*] (LCLS) ... CoDPS
Denver Research Institute [*University of Denver*] [*Research center*] ... DRI
Denver Silver [*Vancouver Stock Exchange symbol*] ... DEV
Denver Special Librarians, Denver, CO [*OCLC symbol*] (OCLC) ... DVS
Denver/Stapleton International [*Colorado*] [*ICAO location identifier*] (ICLI) ... KDEN
Denver Wildlife Research Center [*Colorado*] [*Department of Agriculture*] (GRD) ... DWRC
Denville Free Public Library, Denville, NJ [*Library symbol Library of Congress*] (LCLS) ... NjDe
Deny All Knowledge [*Telecommunications*] (TEL) ... DAK
Denying ... DENYG
Denying Appeal (DLA) ... Den App
Denying Reargument [*Legal term*] (DLA) ... Den Rearg
Denying Rehearing [*Legal term*] (DLA) ... Den Reh
Deny's Tuberculin [*Medicine*] (DAVI) ... BF
Denys-Drash Syndrome [*Medicine*] ... DDS
Deo Dedit [*He Gave to God*] [*Latin*] ... DD
Deo Gratias [*Thanks Be to God*] [*Latin*] (GPO) ... DG
Deo Optimo Maximo [*To God, Most Good, Most Great*] [*Latin*] ... DOM
Deo Volente [*God Willing*] [*Latin*] ... DV
Deobstruent [*Removing Obstructions*] [*Pharmacy*] (ROG) ... DEO
Deodorant (ABBR) ... DEOD
Deodorization (ABBR) ... DEODZN
Deodorize (ABBR) ... DEODZ
Deodorized (ABBR) ... DEODZD
Deodorized Tincture of Opium [*Pharmacy*] ... DTO
Deodorizer (ABBR) ... DEODZR
Deodorizing (ABBR) ... DEODZG
Deorbit (NASA) ... DEORB
Deorbit, Entry, and Landing [*Aerospace*] (MCD) ... DEL
Deorbit/Landing [*Aerospace*] (MCD) ... D/L
Deoxidized High-Residual Phosphorus [*Copper*] ... DHP
Deoxidized Low-Residual Phosphorus [*Copper*] ... DLP
Deoxophylloerythroetioporphyrin [*Biochemistry*] ... DPEP
Deoxy [*or Desoxy*] [*Biochemistry*] ... d
Deoxyaconitine [*Biochemistry*] ... DAT
Deoxyadenosine Diphosphate [*Biochemistry*] ... dADP
Deoxyadenosine Monophosphate [*Biochemistry*] ... dAMP
Deoxyadenosine Triphosphate [*Biochemistry*] ... dATP
Deoxycholate [*Biochemistry*] (MAE) ... DC
Deoxycholate [*Biochemistry*] ... DOC
Deoxycholate-Citrate Agar [*Microbiology*] ... DCA
Deoxycholate-Citrate-Lactose-Sucrose [*Agar*] [*Microbiology*] ... DCLS
Deoxycholic Acid [*Biochemistry*] ... DCA
Deoxycoformycin [*Also, dCF*] [*Antileukemia drug*] ... DCF
Deoxycorticoid (MAE) ... DOC
Deoxycorticosterone [*Endocrinology*] ... DOC
Deoxycorticosterone [*or Desoxycorticosterone*] **Acetate** [*Also, DOCA*] [*Endocrinology*] ... DCA
Deoxycorticosterone [*or Desoxycorticosterone*] **Acetate** [*Also, DCA*] [*Endocrinology*] ... DOCA
Deoxycorticosterone Glucoside [*Also, DOCG*] [*Endocrinology*] ... DCG
Deoxycorticosterone Glucoside [*Also, DCG*] [*Endocrinology*] ... DOCG
Deoxycytidine Diphosphate [*Biochemistry*] ... dCDP
Deoxycytidine Monophosphate [*Biochemistry*] ... dCMP
Deoxycytidine-Phosphate [*Biochemistry*] (DAVI) ... dCMP
Deoxycytidinetriphosphatase [*An enzyme*] ... dCTPase
Deoxycytidinetriphosphate [*Organic chemistry*] ... DCTP
Deoxycytidylate [*Biochemistry*] ... dC
Deoxy-D-Glucose [*Also, DG, DOG*] [*Biochemistry*] ... DDG
Deoxy-D-glucose [*Also, DDG, DOG*] [*Biochemistry*] ... DG
Deoxy-D-glucose [*Also, DDG, DG*] [*Biochemistry*] ... DOG
Deoxydifluorocytidine [*Antineoplastic drug*] ... DDFC
Deoxyephedrine [*or Desoxyephedrine*] [*Pharmacology*] ... D-O-E
Deoxyerythronolide B Synthase [*An enzyme*] ... DEBS
Deoxyfructoserotonin [*Antibacterial*] ... DFS
Deoxyglucose [*Biochemistry*] (DAVI) ... DG
Deoxyglucose Imaging [*Medicine*] (CPH) ... DGI
Deoxyglucose-Phosphate [*Biochemistry*] ... DGP
Deoxyguanosine [*Biochemistry*] ... DG
Deoxyguanosine Diphosphate [*Biochemistry*] ... dGDP
Deoxyguanosine Monophosphate [*Biochemistry*] ... dGMP
Deoxyguanosine Triphosphate [*Biochemistry*] ... DGTP
Deoxyguanylate [*Biochemistry*] ... dG
Deoxyheptulosonic Acid [*Biochemistry*] ... dHpuA
Deoxyiauridine Triphosphatase [*An enzyme*] ... DUTPase
Deoxyinosine Diphosphate [*Biochemistry*] ... dIDP
Deoxyinosine Monophosphate [*Biochemistry*] ... dIMP
Deoxyinosine Triphosphate [*Biochemistry*] ... dITP
Deoxyketosteroids (MEDA) ... DKS
Deoxymannojirimycin [*Biochemistry*] ... dMM
Deoxymorpholinofructose [*Biochemistry*] ... DMF
Deoxynivalenol [*A mycotoxin*] ... DON
Deoxynojirimycin [*Biochemistry*] ... dNM
Deoxynorlaudanosolinecarboxylic Acid [*Biochemistry*] ... DNLCA
Deoxynucleoside Monophosphate [*Biochemistry*] ... DNMP
Deoxynucleoside Triphosphate [*Biochemistry*] ... DNTP
Deoxyribonuclease [*Preferred form, DNase*] [*An enzyme*] ... DNAase
Deoxyribonuclease [*An enzyme*] ... DNase
Deoxyribonucleic Acid [*Biochemistry, genetics*] ... DNA
Deoxyribonucleic Acid - Chloroplast [*Biochemistry, genetics*] [*Also, cpDNA, ctDNA*] ... Chl-DNA
Deoxyribonucleic Acid, Chloroplast [*Biochemistry, genetics*] [*Also, Chl-DNA, ctDNA*] ... cpDNA
Deoxyribonucleic Acid, Chloroplast [*Biochemistry, genetics*] [*Also, Chl-DNA, cpDNA*] ... ctDNA
Deoxyribonucleic Acid, Cloned [*Biochemistry, genetics*] ... cDNA
Deoxyribonucleic Acid, Complementary [*Biochemistry, genetics*] ... cDNA
Deoxyribonucleic Acid, Double-Stranded [*Genetics*] [*Biochemistry*] ... dsDNA
Deoxyribonucleic Acid, heteroduplex [*Biochemistry, genetics*] ... hDNA
Deoxyribonucleic Acid, Histone [*Biochemistry, genetics*] ... hDNA
Deoxyribonucleic Acid - Kinetoplast [*Biochemistry, genetics*] ... K-DNA
Deoxyribonucleic Acid, Mitochondrial [*Biochemistry, genetics*] ... mtDNA
Deoxyribonucleic Acid, Nuclear [*Biochemistry, genetics*] ... nDNA
Deoxyribonucleic Acid Polymerase [*An enzyme*] ... DNAp
Deoxyribonucleic Acid, Recombinant [*Biochemistry, genetics*] ... rDNA
Deoxyribonucleic Acid, Ribosomal [*Biochemistry, genetics*] ... rDNA
Deoxyribonucleic Acid, Ribosomal - Chloroplast [*Biochemistry, genetics*] ... Chl-rDNA
Deoxyribonucleic Acid, Single Copy Nuclear [*Biochemistry, genetics*] ... scnDNA
Deoxyribonucleic Acid, Single-Stranded [*Biochemistry, genetics*] ... ssDNA
Deoxyribonucleic Acid, Traditional Form [*DNA with right-handed helix*] [*Biochemistry, genetics*] ... B DNA
Deoxyribonucleic Acid, Zigzag [*DNA with left-handed helix*] [*Biochemistry, genetics*] ... Z DNA
Deoxyribonucleic Acid-Phosphorus [*Biochemistry*] (DAVI) ... DNA-P
Deoxyribonucleoprotamine [*Biochemistry*] ... DNP
Deoxyribonucleoprotein [*Biochemistry*] ... DNP
Deoxyribose [*Biochemistry*] (MAE) ... d
Deoxyribose [*Genetics*] **and Laboratory** (DAVI) ... dRib
Deoxyribosylthymine Diphosphate [*Biochemistry*] ... dTDP
Deoxyribosylthymine Monophosphate [*Biochemistry*] ... dTMP
Deoxyribosylthymine Triphosphate [*Biochemistry*] ... dTTP
Deoxyspergualin [*Antineoplastic drug*] ... DSG
Deoxystreptamine [*Organic chemistry*] ... DOS
Deoxythymidine [*Organic chemistry*] ... DT
Deoxythymidine Diphosphate [*Biochemistry*] ... DTDP
Deoxythymidine Monophosphate [*Biochemistry*] ... DTMP
Deoxythymidine Triphosphate [*Biochemistry*] ... DTTP
Deoxyuridine [*Biochemistry*] (MAE) ... dU
Deoxyuridine Diphosphate [*Biochemistry*] ... dUDP
Deoxyuridine Monophosphate [*Biochemistry*] ... dUMP
Deoxyuridine Triphosphate [*Biochemistry*] ... dUTP
Deoxyuridylate [*Biochemistry*] (DAVI) ... dUMP
Deoxyxanthosine Diphosphate [*Biochemistry*] ... dXDP
Deoxyxanthosine Monophosphate [*Biochemistry*] ... dXMP
Deoxyxanthosine Triphosphate [*Biochemistry*] ... dXTP
DEP Corp. [*Associated Press*] (SAG) ... DEP
DEP Corp. [*NASDAQ symbol*] (NQ) ... DEPC
DEP Corp. 'A' [*NASDAQ symbol*] (TTSB) ... DPCAQ
DEP Corp.'B' [*NASDAQ symbol*] (TTSB) ... DPCBQ
Deparizo [*India*] [*ICAO location identifier*] (ICLI) ... VEDZ
Depart ... D
Depart (AFM) ... DEP
Depart ... DEPT
Depart (DA) ... DP
Depart (AABC) ... DPRT
Depart ... DPT
Departamento de Agricultura de la Generalitat de Cataluna [*Spain ICAO designator*] (FAAC) ... FGC
Departamento de Inteligencia Nacional [*National Intelligence Department*] [*Chilean secret police Superseded by CNI*] ... DINA
Departed (ABBR) ... DEPD
Departed Station (SAA) ... DS
Departement de Demographie, Universite de Montreal, Quebec [*Library symbol National Library of Canada*] (NLC) ... QMUDD
Departement de Geographie, Universite de Sherbrooke, Quebec [*Library symbol National Library of Canada*] (NLC) ... QSHERUG

Departement de Geographie, Universite du Quebec, Chicoutimi, Quebec [*Library symbol National Library of Canada*] (NLC) ..... QCUG

Departement de Geologie et de Mineralogie, Universite Laval, Quebec, Quebec [*Library symbol National Library of Canada*] (NLC) ..... QQLAGM

Departement de Sante Communautaire, Centre Hospitalier Regional de la Mauricie, Shawinigan, Quebec [*Library symbol National Library of Canada*] (BIB) ..... QSHCHS

Departement de Sante Communautaire, Hopital Charles Lemoyne, Greenfield Park, Quebec [*Library symbol National Library of Canada*] (NLC) ..... QMHCLC

Departement de Sante Communautaire, Hopital Sainte-Justine, Montreal, Quebec [*Library symbol National Library of Canada*] (NLC) ..... QMSTJS

Departement de Sante Communautaire, Hopital Saint-Luc, Montreal, Quebec [*Library symbol National Library of Canada*] (NLC) ..... QMHSLC

Departement des Archives et Statistiques de la Ville de Quebec, Quebec, PQ, Canada [*Library symbol Library of Congress*] (LCLS) ..... CaQQCH

Departement des Archives et Statistiques de la Ville de Quebec, Quebec, Quebec [*Library symbol National Library of Canada*] (NLC) ..... QQCH

Departement Documentation et Information Geologique [*Geological Information and Documentation Department*] [*Bureau of Geological and Mining Research*] [*Information service or system*] (IID) ..... DIG

Departing (ABBR) ..... DEPG

Departing Roster (DNAB) ..... DEROS

Department ..... D

Department ..... DEP

Department [*Also dept or dpt*] (WDMC) ..... dep

Department ..... DEPART

Department (EY) ..... DEPT

Department (DD) ..... dept

Department ..... DEPT

Department (ODBW) ..... Dept

Department (IAA) ..... DP

Department ..... DPT

Department 56 [*NYSE symbol*] (TTSB) ..... DFS

Department 56, Inc. [*Associated Press*] (SAG) Dept56

Department 56, Inc. [*NYSE symbol*] (SPSG) ..... DFS

Department 9911, Northern Telecom Ltd., Belleville, Ontario [*Library symbol National Library of Canada Obsolete*] (NLC) ..... OBNE

Department Administrative Order [*Department of Commerce*] (NOAA) ..... DAO

Department Approved Training (OICC) ..... DAT

Department for Education [*British*] ..... DFE

Department for Professional Employees [*AFL-CIO*] ..... DPE

Department for the Arts [*Western Australia*] [*Australia*] ..... DFA

Department Head Instruction (NRCH) ..... DHI

Department Head Procedures (NRCH) ..... DHP

Department Information Bulletin ..... DIB

Department Instrument Equipment Reserve ..... DIER

Department of Aboriginal Affairs, Darwin, NT, Australia [*Library symbol Library of Congress*] (LCLS) ..... AuDDa

Department of Aboriginal Sites [*Australia*] ..... DAS

Department of Administrative Services - Purchasing and Sales Group [*Australia*] ..... DAS-PSG

Department of Aeronautics and Astronautics [*MIT*] (MCD) ..... DAA

Department of Agricultural Engineering, University of Alberta, Edmonton, Alberta [*Library symbol National Library of Canada*] (NLC) ..... AEUAG

Department of Agriculture ..... D of A

Department of Agriculture ..... DA

Department of Agriculture ..... DOA

Department of Agriculture Acquisition Regulation [*Superseded AGPR in 1984*] (AAGC) ..... AGAR

Department of Agriculture and Fisheries [*New South Wales*] [*Australia*] ..... DAF

Department of Agriculture and Fisheries [*Scotland*] ..... DAF

Department of Agriculture and Fisheries for Scotland ..... DAFS

Department of Agriculture, Animal Disease Research Institute, Ottawa, ON, Canada [*Library symbol Library of Congress*] (LCLS) ..... CaOOAgA

Department of Agriculture, Animal Research Institute, Ottawa, ON, Canada [*Library symbol Library of Congress*] (LCLS) ..... CaOOAgAR

Department of Agriculture, Central Experimental Farm Reference Library, Ottawa, ON, Canada [*Library symbol Library of Congress Obsolete*] (LCLS) ..... CaOOAgC

Department of Agriculture, Chemistry Division, Ottawa, ON, Canada [*Library symbol Library of Congress Obsolete*] (LCLS) ..... CaOOAgCh

Department of Agriculture, Engineering Research Service, Ottawa, ON, Canada [*Library symbol Library of Congress*] (LCLS) ..... CaOOAgER

Department of Agriculture, Entomology Research Institute, Ottawa, ON, Canada [*Library symbol Library of Congress*] (LCLS) ..... CaOOAgE

Department of Agriculture, Food Production and Marketing Branch, Laboratory Services Section, Ottawa, ON, Canada [*Library symbol Library of Congress*] (LCLS) ..... CaOOAgFP

Department of Agriculture for Northern Ireland [*British*] (IRUK) ..... DANI

Department of Agriculture, Horticultural Division, Ottawa, ON, Canada [*Library symbol Library of Congress Obsolete*] (LCLS) ..... CaOOAgH

Department of Agriculture, Legal Library, Ottawa, ON, Canada [*Library symbol Library of Congress Obsolete*] (LCLS) ..... CaOOAgL

Department of Agriculture, Neatby Library, Ottawa, ON, Canada [*Library symbol Library of Congress*] (LCLS) ..... CaOOAGCH

Department of Agriculture, Plant Research Institute, Ottawa, ON, Canada [*Library symbol Library of Congress*] (LCLS) ..... CaOOAgB

Department of Agriculture Procurement Regulation [*A publication*] (AAGC) ..... AGPR

Department of Agriculture, Research Station, Ottawa, ON, Canada [*Library symbol Library of Congress*] (LCLS) ..... CaOOAgO

Department of Agriculture, Soil Research Institute, Ottawa, ON, Canada [*Library symbol Library of Congress*] (LCLS) ..... CaOOAgSR

Department of Allied Health Education and Accreditation [*AMA*] (DAVI) ..... DAHEA

Department of Allied Health Evaluation [*AMA*] ..... DAHE

Department of Anatomy, University of Toronto, Ontario [*Library symbol National Library of Canada*] (NLC) ..... OTUAN

Department of Applied Physics, University of Toronto, Ontario [*Library symbol National Library of Canada*] (NLC) ..... OTUAP

Department of Army Directed Effort ..... DADE

Department of Army Financial Information System ..... DARFIS

Department of Army Logistics Support Officer ..... DALSO

Department of Army Productivity (Improvement) Program ..... DAPP

Department of Art and Art History, McMaster University, Hamilton, Ontario [*Library symbol National Library of Canada*] (NLC) ..... OHMAH

Department of Art History, Carleton University, Ottawa, Ontario [*Library symbol Obsolete National Library of Canada*] (NLC) ..... OOCCAH

Department of Arts and Cultural Heritage [*Australia*] ..... DACH

Department of Arts, Culture, Science, and Technology [*South Africa*] [*Research center*] ..... DACST

Department of Atomic Energy [*India*] ..... DAE

Department of Audiovisual Instruction [*of NEA*] [*Later, AECT*] (EA) ..... DAVI

Department of Bantu Administration and Development [*An agency of South African government*] ..... BAD

Department of Biochemistry, University of Toronto, Ontario [*Library symbol National Library of Canada*] (NLC) ..... OTUB

Department of Biotechnology [*Medicine*] ..... DBT

Department of Botany, University of Toronto, Ontario [*Library symbol National Library of Canada*] (NLC) ..... OTUDB

Department of Bush Fire Services [*New South Wales*] [*Australia*] ..... DBFS

Department of Business and Regional Development [*New South Wales, Australia*] ..... B & RD

Department of Business, Industry, and Regional Development [*Queensland*] [*Australia*] ..... DBIRD

Department of Business, Technology, and Communications [*Northern Territory*] [*Australia*] ..... DBTC

Department of Central Index [*Computer center*] [*Department of Health and Social Security*] [*British*] ..... DCI

Department of Central Intelligence [*Thailand*] (CINC) ..... DCI

Department of Chemical Engineering and Applied Chemistry, University of Toronto,Ontario [*Library symbol National Library of Canada*] (NLC) ..... OTUCE

Department of Chemistry, University of Toronto, Ontario [*Library symbol National Library of Canada*] (NLC) ..... OTUC

Department of City and Regional Planning [*MIT*] (MCD) ..... DCRP

Department of Civil Engineering, University of Toronto, Ontario [*Library symbol National Library of Canada*] (NLC) ..... OTUCI

Department of Classroom Teachers [*of NEA*] (EA) ..... DCT

Department of Command, Leadership, and Management [*DoD*] ..... DCLM

Department of Commerce ..... COMM

Department of Commerce ..... DC

Department of Commerce ..... DOC

Department of Commerce and Community Affairs ..... DCCA

Department of Commerce Appeals Board (AAGC) ..... DCAB

Department of Commerce Board of Contract Appeals ..... COMMBCA

Department of Commerce Library (IID) ..... DOCL

Department of Commerce/National Technical Information Service, Department of Energy/Office of Scientific and Technical Information, National Aeronautics and Space Administration Scientific and Technical Information Branch, and Department ofDefense/Defense Technical Information Center ..... CENDI

Department of Commerce Procurement Regulation [*A publication*] (AAGC) ..... DOCPR

Department of Communications [*Canada*] ..... DOC

Department of Communications and the Arts [*Australia*] ..... DoCA

Department of Communications [*Ministere des Communications*] Ottawa, Ontario [*Library symbol National Library of Canada*] (NLC) ..... OOCO

Department of Community Development [*Proposed government department*] ..... DCD

Department of Community Health [*Australia*] ..... DCH

Department of Computer Science [*University of Illinois*] [*Research center*] (RCD) ..... DCS

Department of Computing Service [*University of Waterloo*] [*Research center*] (RCD) ..... DCS

Department of Conservation and Environment [*Proposed name for US Department of the Interior*] ..... DCE

Department of Conservation and Natural Resources [*Victoria*] [*Australia*] ..... DCNR

Department of Conservation, Forests, and Lands [*Victoria*] [*Australia*] ..... DCFL

Department of Consumer and Corporate Affairs [*Ministere de la Consommation etdes Corporations*] Ottawa, Ontario [*Library symbol National Library of Canada*] (NLC) ..... OOCI

Department of Continuing Education (AIE) ..... DCE

Department of Correctional Services [*Northern Territory, South Australia*] ..... DCS

Department of Corrective Services [*New South Wales, Western Australia*] ..... DCS

Department of Courts Administration [*New South Wales*] [*Australia*] ..... DCA

Department of Criminology, University of Ottawa [*Departement de Criminologie,Universite d'Ottawa*] Ontario [*Library symbol National Library of Canada*] (NLC) ..... OOUC

Department of Data Management [*Veterans Administration*] ..... DDM

Department of Defence, Army [*Australia*] ..... DEFAR

Department of Defence, Australia ..... DODA

Department of Defence, Navy [*Australia*] ..... DEFNAV

Department of Defense ..... DD

Department of Defense [*Washington, DC*] ..... DoD

Department of Defense (AAGC) ..... DOD

Department of Defense (USGC) ..... DOD

Department of Defense (USDC) ..... DOD

Department of Defense Acquisition Quality Assurance Course (RDA) ... DODAQAC
Department of Defense Acquisition Quality Assurance Management Course (RDA) ... DODAQAMC
Department of Defense Activity Address Code (AABC) ... DODAAC
Department of Defense Activity Address Designer (MCD) ... DODAAD
Department of Defense Activity Address Directory (AFM) ... DODAAD
Department of Defense Activity Address File ... DODAAF
Department of Defense Aircraft Ground Fire Suppression and Rescue Office ... DOD-AGFSRS
Department of Defense Ammunition Code (AFM) ... DODAC
Department of Defense Authorized Data List ... DODADL
Department of Defense Automatic Address System (MCD) ... DODAAS
Department of Defense Central Automated Personnel System (AFM) ... DODCAPS
Department of Defense Central Control Point (AAGC) ... DODCCP
Department of Defense Civilian Personnel Manual (MCD) ... DODCPM
Department of Defense Claimant Program ... DDCP
Department of Defense Clothing and Textile Board (EGAO) ... DOD C & T
Department of Defense Computer Institute ... DODCI
Department of Defense Computer Security Center (GFGA) ... DODCSC
Department of Defense Consolidated List of Principal Military Items ... DODCLIPMI
Department of Defense Consolidated List of Principal Military Items ... DODCLPMI
Department of Defense Damage Assessment Center ... DODDAC
Department of Defense Dependents Schools ... DODDS
Department of Defense Dependents Schools, Atlantic (DNAB) ... DODDSLANT
Department of Defense Directive ... DODD
Department of Defense Disease and Injury Codes (DNAB) ... DDIC
Department of Defense Education Education Activity [*DoD*] ... DODEA
Department of Defense Emergency Plans (AABC) ... DODEP
Department of Defense Exercise Planning (AFM) ... DODEP
Department of Defense Explosives Safety Board [*Alexandria, VA*] ... DDESB
Department of Defense FAR Supplement [*A publication*] (AAGC) ... DFARS
Department of Defense for Health Affairs ... DoD/HA
Department of Defense Foreign Counterintelligence Program ... DODFCI
Department of Defense Foreign Disclosure Coordinating Office (AABC) ... DODFDCO
Department of Defense Grant and Agreement Regulation [*A publication*] (AAGC) ... DODGAR
Department of Defense Gravity Experiment [*Satellite*] ... DODGE
Department of Defense Gravity Experiment, Multipurpose [*Satellite*] ... DODGE-M
Department of Defense Handbook ... DODH
Department of Defense Handbook ... DODHBK
Department of Defense High School Newspaper Service ... DODHSNS
Department of Defense Household Goods Commercial Storage Office ... DODHGCSO
Department of Defense Household Goods Field Office ... DODHGFO
Department of Defense Identification Badge ... DODIDENTBAD
Department of Defense Identification Code (AFM) ... DODIC
Department of Defense Index of Specifications and Standards ... DIS
Department of Defense Index of Specifications and Standards ... DODISS
Department of Defense Industrial Equipment Reserve (AABC) ... DODIER
Department of Defense Industrial Security Bulletin ... DODISB
Department of Defense Industrial Security Letter ... DODISL
Department of Defense Industrial Security Manual ... DODISM
Department of Defense Industrial Security Regulation ... DODISR
Department of Defense Information Security Program Regulation (MCD) ... DODISPR
Department of Defense Inspector General ... DODIG
Department of Defense Inspector General Audit Report Tracking System (AAGC) ... DOD IGARTS
Department of Defense Instruction ... DODI
Department of Defense Instruction ... DODINST
Department of Defense Intelligence Information System (MCD) ... DODIIS
Department of Defense Intelligence Production Program [*CIA terminology*] ... DODIPP
Department of Defense Intelligence Reports (DNAB) ... DOD-IR
Department of Defense Inventory Manager ... DODIM
Department of Defense Item Code ... DODIC
Department of Defense Item Entry Control ... DODIEC
Department of Defense Item Standardization Code ... DODISC
Department of Defense Logistics Systems Plan (MCD) ... DODLOGPLAN
Department of Defense Management Information System ... DOD/MIS
Department of Defense Manned Space Flight ... DDMS
Department of Defense Manual ... DODM
Department of Defense Manual ... DODMNL
Department of Defense Master Urgency List (AFM) ... DODMUL
Department of Defense Material Distribution System (MCD) ... DODMDS
Department of Defense Medical Examination Review Board ... DODMERB
Department of Defense Military Assistance Manual ... DODMAM
Department of Defense Military Pay and Allowance Committee ... DODMPAC
Department of Defense Military Pay and Allowance Entitlements Manual (AABC) ... DODPM
Department of Defense Military Personnel Records Center ... DODMPRC
Department of Defense Military Traffic Management Agency (AAG) ... DDMTMA
Department of Defense National Agency Check Center (AABC) ... DODNACC
Department of Defense Oversized Flatcar (INF) ... DODX
Department of Defense, Pacific Research Office (CINC) ... DODPRO
Department of Defense Performance-Oriented Packaging of Hazardous Materials [*Washington, DC*] ... DOD/POPHM
Department of Defense Poster ... DODPSTR
Department of Defense Precious Metals Recovery Program ... DODPMRP
Department of Defense Product Engineering Services Office (MCD) ... DPESO
Department of Defense Production ... DDP
Department of Defense Program Element Code (AFIT) ... DOD-PEC
Department of Defense Project Specification (MCD) ... DDPS
Department of Defense Regulation ... DODR
Department of Defense Research and Engineering ... DODRE
Department of Defense Resource Management System (NG) ... DRMS
Department of Defense Single Stock Point (MCD) ... DOD-SSP
Department of Defense Small Arms Serialization Program ... DODSASP
Department of Defense Surplus Property Bidders List ... DODSPBL
Department of Defense Systems Management Center (MCD) ... DESMC
Department of Defense-Owned Rail Cars [*MTMC*] (TAG) ... DODX
Department of Disarmament and Arms Regulation [*United Nations*] ... DDAR
Department of Economic, Administrative, and Policy Studies (AIE) ... DEAPSIE
Department of Economic Affairs [*Department of Agriculture*] ... DEA
Department of Economic Affairs of the United Nations ... ECA
Department of Economic and Social Affairs of the United Nations [*Later, Depart ment of Social Affairs*] ... ESA (UN)
Department of Economic Development: Mines and Small Business, Government of the Yukon, Whitehorse, Yukon [*Library symbol National Library of Canada*] (NLC) ... YWED
Department of Economics and Social Science [*MIT*] (MCD) ... DESS
Department of Education [*Generic*] ... DE
Department of Education [*Cabinet department*] (CDAI) ... DOE
Department of Education ... DoEd
Department of Education [*Cabinet department*] ... Ed
Department of Education and Science [*British*] ... DES
Department of Education Financial Management Information System (GFGA) ... EDFMIS
Department of Education of Northern Ireland [*British*] ... DENI
Department of Education Organization Act (GFGA) ... DEOA
Department of Education Procurement Regulations [*A publication*] (AAGC) ... EDPR
Department of Electrical Engineering, University of Toronto, Ontario [*Library symbol National Library of Canada*] (NLC) ... OTUEE
Department of Elementary, Kindergarten, and Nursery Education [*of NEA*] [*Later, American Association of Elementary, Kindergarten, Nursery Educators*] ... EKNE
Department of Elementary School Principals [*of NEA*] (EA) ... DESP
Department of Emergency Medicine (MEDA) ... DEM
Department of Employment [*Formerly, DEP, MOL*] [*British*] ... DE
Department of Employment and Productivity [*Later, DE*] [*British*] ... DEP
Department of Employment and Training [*Victoria*] [*Australia*] ... DET
Department of Employment, Small Firms and Tourism Division [*British*] ... DESFTD
Department of Employment / Training Agency [*British*] ... DE/TA
Department of Energy (ILCA) ... DE
Department of Energy [*British*] ... DEn
Department of Energy [*Washington, DC*] ... DOE
Department of Energy ... DoE
Department of Energy (WDAA) ... DOEN
Department of Energy Acquisition Regulation [*A publication*] (AAGC) ... DEAR
Department of Energy and Natural Resources ... DENR
Department of Energy/Assistant Secretary for Energy Technology [*Washington, DC*] ... DOE/ET
Department of Energy, Bartlesville Energy Technology Center, Bartlesville, OK [*OCLC symbol*] (OCLC) ... DOB
Department of Energy Board of Contract Appeals (AAGC) ... DOEBCA
Department of Energy Board of Contract Appeals (AAGC) ... EBCA
Department of Energy Contract Adjustment Board (AAGC) ... ECAB
Department of Energy, Mines, and Resources [*Canada*] ... DEMR
Department of Energy, Mines, and Resources, Canada Center for Mineral and EnergyTechnology, Ottawa, ON, Canada [*Library symbol Library of Congress*] (LCLS) ... CaOOM
Department of Energy, Mines, and Resources, Petroleum Incentives Program, Ottawa, ON, Canada [*Library symbol Library of Congress*] (LCLS) ... CaOOPI
Department of Energy Nevada Operations Office [*Marine science*] (OSRA) ... DOE/NV
Department of Energy, Office of Energy Research [*Washington, DC*] ... DOE/ER
Department of Energy Procurement Regulation [*A publication*] (AAGC) ... DOE-PR
Department of Energy Property Management Regulations [*A publication*] (AAGC) ... DOE-PMR
Department of Energy Technical Information Center [*Oak Ridge, TN*] [*Database producer*] ... DOE-TIC
Department of Energy's Remote Console Information System [*Department of Energy*] [*Database*] ... DOE/RECON
Department of Environment and Heritage [*Queensland*] ... DEH
Department of Environment, Lands, and Planning [*Australian Capital Territory*] ... DELP
Department of Environment Quality ... DEQ
Department of Environmental and Drug-Induced Pathology [*Later, DETP*] (EA) ... DEDIP
Department of Environmental and Toxicologic Pathology [*An association*] (EA) ... DETP
Department of Executive Officer ... DEO
Department of External Affairs [*Ministere des Affaires Exerieures*] **Ottawa,Ontario** [*Library symbol National Library of Canada*] (NLC) ... OOE
Department of Family and Community Services [*South Australia*] ... DFCS
Department of Family Life [*Later, Commission on Marriage and Family Life*] [*of NCC*] (EA) ... DFL
Department of Family Services and Housing Welfare [*Queensland*] [*Australia*] ... DFSHW
Department of Finance (ADA) ... D of F
Department of Finance [*Ministere des Finances*] **Ottawa, Ontario** [*Library symbol National Library of Canada*] (NLC) ... OOF

Department of Fine Art, University of Toronto, Ontario [*Library symbol National Library of Canada*] (NLC) ... OTUFA
Department of Fisheries [*South Australia*] ... DOF
Department of Fisheries and Oceans [*Canada*] (OSRA) ... DFO
Department of Food and Agriculture [*Victoria*] [*Australia*] ... DFA
Department of Foreign Affairs (CINC) ... DFA
Department of Foreign Affairs and Information [*South Africa*] ... DFAI
Department of Foreign Languages [*National Education Association*] (AEBS) ... DFL
Department of Forestry [*Queensland*] [*Australia*] ... DOF
Department of Geography, Acadia University, Wolfville, Nova Scotia [*Library symbol Obsolete National Library of Canada*] (NLC) ... NSWAG
Department of Geography, Bishop's University, Lennoxville, Quebec [*Library symbol National Library of Canada*] (NLC) ... QLBG
Department of Geography, Brandon University, Manitoba [*Library symbol National Library of Canada*] (NLC) ... MBCG
Department of Geography, Brock University, St. Catharines, Ontario [*Library symbol National Library of Canada*] (NLC) ... OSTCBG
Department of Geography, Lakehead University, Thunder Bay, Ontario [*Library symbol National Library of Canada*] (NLC) ... OPALG
Department of Geography, Memorial University, St. John's, Newfoundland [*Library symbol National Library of Canada*] (NLC) ... NFSMG
Department of Geography, Queen's University, Kingston, Ontario [*Library symbol National Library of Canada*] (NLC) ... OKQG
Department of Geography, Sir George Williams Campus, Concordia University, Montreal, Quebec [*Library symbol National Library of Canada*] (NLC) ... QMGG
Department of Geography, University of British Columbia, Vancouver, British Columbia [*Library symbol National Library of Canada*] (NLC) ... BVAUG
Department of Geography, University of Lethbridge, Alberta [*Library symbol National Library of Canada*] (NLC) ... ALUG
Department of Geography, University of Manitoba, Winnipeg, Manitoba [*Library symbol National Library of Canada*] (NLC) ... MWUG
Department of Geography, University of Regina, Saskatchewan [*Library symbol National Library of Canada*] (NLC) ... SRUG
Department of Geography, University of Western Ontario, London, Ontario [*Library symbol National Library of Canada*] (NLC) ... OLUG
Department of Geological Sciences, McGill University, Montreal, Quebec [*Library symbol National Library of Canada*] (NLC) ... QMMGS
Department of Geological Sciences, Queen's University, Kingston, Ontario [*Library symbol National Library of Canada*] (NLC) ... OKQGS
Department of Geological Sciences, University of Toronto, Ontario [*Library symbol National Library of Canada*] (NLC) ... OTUG
Department of Geology and Geophysics [*MIT*] (MCD) ... DGG
Department of Health [*British*] (ECON) ... DOH
Department of Health (AIE) ... DoH
Department of Health and Human Resources, Government of the Yukon, Whitehorse, Yukon [*Library symbol National Library of Canada*] (NLC) ... YWHHR
Department of Health and Human Services ... DHHS
Department of Health and Human Services [*Formerly, HEW*] ... HHS
Department of Health and Human Services Acquisition Regulations (GFGA) ... HHSAR
Department of Health and Human Services Grant Appeals Board (AAGC) ... HHSGAB
Department of Health and Social Security [*British*] ... DHSS
Department of Health, Education, and Welfare [*Later, DHHS*] ... DHEW
Department of Health, Education, and Welfare [*Sometimes facetiously translated "Halls of Eternal Warfare"*] [*Later, HHS*] ... HEW
Department of Health, Education and Welfare Grant Appeals Board (AAGC) ... HEWGAR
Department of Health, Education, and Welfare [*Later, HHS*] **Procurement Regulations** ... HEWPR
Department of Health, Education, and Welfare, Washington, DC [*OCLC symbol*] (OCLC) ... HEW
Department of Health, Safety, and Welfare [*Western Australia*] ... DOHSW
Department of Health Services (DOGT) ... DHS
Department of History in Art, University of Victoria, British Columbia [*Library symbol National Library of Canada*] (NLC) ... BVIVA
Department of Home Economics [*of NEA*] [*Later, HEEA*] (EA) ... DHE
Department of Housing and Community Development (OICC) ... DHCD
Department of Housing and Local Government [*Queensland*] [*Australia*] ... DHLG
Department of Housing and Urban Development ... DHUD
Department of Housing and Urban Development ... HUD
Department of Housing and Urban Development Board of Contract Appeals (AAGC) ... HUD BCA
Department of Human Resources (IAA) ... DHR
Department of Human Services and Health [*Australia*] ... DHSH
Department of Humanitarian Affairs [*United Nations*] ... DHA
Department of Indian Affairs and Northern Development [*Canada*] ... DIAND
Department of Indian and Northern Affairs Library [*UTLAS symbol*] ... INA
Department of Industrial and Economic Development ... DIED
Department of Industrial Cooperation [*University of Maine*] [*Research center*] (RCD) ... DIC
Department of Industries and Development [*Northern Territory*] [*Australia*] ... DID
Department of Industry [*British*] (DCTA) ... DI
Department of Industry [*British*] (DS) ... DOI
Department of Industry and Economic Planning ... DIEP
Department of Industry, Science, and Technology [*Australia*] ... DIST
Department of Industry, Trade and Technology [*South Australia*] ... DITT
Department of Information and Broadcasting ... DIB
Department of Information Technology [*Commonwealth of Virginia*] [*Telecommunications service*] (TSSD) ... DIT
Department of Infrastructure and Government Assets [*Western Australia*] ... DIGA
[*Official Decisions of the*] **Department of Interior** (AAGC) ... ID
Department of Internal Security ... DIS
Department of International Economic and Social Affairs [*United Nations Information service or system*] (IID) ... DIESA
Department of Justice ... D of J
Department of Justice (AABC) ... DOJ
Department of Justice [*Queensland, Tasmania*] [*Australia*] ... DOJ
Department of Justice Library [*UTLAS symbol*] ... JUS
Department of Justice [*Ministere de la Justice*] **Ottawa, Ontario** [*Library symbol National Library of Canada*] (NLC) ... OOJ
Department of Labor ... D of L
Department of Labor ... DL
Department of Labor ... DOL
Department of Labor Acquisition Regulation [*A publication*] (AAGC) ... DOLAR
Department of Labor International Technical Assistance Corps ... DOLITAC
Department of Labor, Manpower Administration ... DLMA
Department of Labor Procurement Regulation [*A publication*] (AAGC) ... DOLPR
Department of Labor Recreation Association ... DLRA
Department of Labour [*South Australia, Victoria*] ... DOL
Department of Labour and Administrative Services [*Northern Territory*] [*Australia*] ... DLAS
Department of Labour, Women's Bureau, Ottawa, ON, Canada [*Library symbol Library of Congress*] (LCLS) ... CaOOLWB
Department of Land Administration [*Western Australia*] ... DLA
Department of Lands [*Queensland*] [*Australia*] ... DOL
Department of Lands and Housing [*Northern Territory*] [*Australia*] ... DLH
Department of Law [*Northern Territory*] [*Australia*] ... DOL
Department of Legal Affairs of the United Nations ... LEG (UN)
Department of Manufacturing and Industry Development [*Victoria*] [*Australia*] ... DMID
Department of Marine and Harbours [*South Australia, Western Australia*] ... DMH
Department of Mathematics, University of Toronto, Ontario [*Library symbol National Library of Canada*] (NLC) ... OTUDM
Department of Mechanical Engineering, University of Toronto, Ontario [*Library symbol National Library of Canada*] (NLC) ... OTUM
Department of Mechanics [*JHU*] ... DME
Department of Medicare and Surgery [*Veterans Administration*] (GFGA) ... DM & S
Department of Medicine ... DOM
Department of Memorial Affairs [*Veterans Administration*] ... DMA
Department of Mental Health [*or Hygiene*] ... DMH
Department of Metallurgical Engineering, University of Toronto, Ontario [*Library symbol National Library of Canada*] (NLC) ... OTUME
Department of Mineral Resources [*New South Wales*] [*Australia*] ... DMR
Department of Mines [*Tasmania*] [*Australia*] ... DOM
Department of Mines and Technical Survey [*Canada*] (DNAB) ... DM & TS
Department of Mines and Technical Survey [*Canada*] ... DMTS
Department of Mining Engineering, University of Toronto, Ontario [*Library symbol National Library of Canada*] (NLC) ... OTUMI
Department of Motor Vehicles ... DMV
Department of National Defence [*Canada*] ... DND
Department of National Defence, Air Technical Library, Ottawa, ON, Canada [*Library symbol*] [*Library of Congress*] (LCLS) ... CaOONDAT
Department of National Defence, Chief Computer Services, Ottawa, ON, Cana da [*Library symbol Library of Congress*] (LCLS) ... CaOONDC
Department of National Defence, Chief Construction and Properties, Ottawa, ON, Canada [*Library symbol Library of Congress*] (LCLS) ... CaOONDCP
Department of National Defence, Chief Engineering and Maintenance, Ottawa, ON, Canada [*Library symbol Library of Congress*] (LCLS) ... CaOONDEM
Department of National Defence, Defence and Civil Institute of Environmental Medicine, Toronto, ON, Canada [*Library symbol Library of Congress*] (LCLS) ... CaOTDR
Department of National Defence, Directorate of Information Services, Ottawa, ON,Canada [*Library symbol Library of Congress*] (LCLS) ... CaOONDIS
Department of National Defence, General Engineering and Maintenance, Dire ctorate of Clothing, Ottawa, ON, Canada [*Library symbol Library of Congress*] (LCLS) ... CaOONDCG
Department of National Defence, Historical Section, Ottawa, ON, Canada [*Library symbol Library of Congress*] (LCLS) ... CaOONDH
Department of National Defence, Judge Advocate General's Library, Ottawa, ON, Canada [*Library symbol Library of Congress*] (LCLS) ... CaOONDJ
Department of National Defence, Land Technical Library, Ottawa, ON, Canada [*Library symbol Library of Congress*] (LCLS) ... CaOONDLT
Department of National Defence, Mapping and Charting Establishment, Ottawa, ON, Canada [*Library symbol Library of Congress*] (LCLS) ... CaOONDMC
Department of National Defence, Marine Technical Library, Ottawa, ON, Canada [*Library symbol Library of Congress*] (LCLS) ... CaOONDMT
Department of National Defence, Medical Library, Ottawa, ON, Canada [*Library symbol Library of Congress*] (LCLS) ... CaOONDM
Department of National Defence, Operational Research and Analysis Establishment,Ottawa, ON, Canada [*Library symbol Library of Congress*] (LCLS) ... CaOONDORAE
Department of National Defence, Ottawa, ON, Canada [*Library symbol Library of Congress*] (LCLS) ... CaOOND
Department of National Defence [*Ministere de la Defense Nationale*] **Ottawa,Ontario** [*Library symbol National Library of Canada*] (NLC) ... OOND
Department of National Defence, Translation Bureau, Ottawa, ON, Canada [*Library symbol*] [*Library of Congress*] (LCLS) ... CaOONDT
Department of National Health and Welfare, Banting Research Centre, Ottawa, ON, Canada [*Library symbol Library of Congress*] (LCLS) ... CaOONHBR
Department of National Health and Welfare, Health Protection Board, Place Vanier, Vanier Reading Room, Ottawa, ON, Canada [*Library symbol*] [*Library of Congress*] (LCLS) ... CaOONHP
Department of National Health and Welfare, Health Services and Promotion Branch,Ottawa, ON, Canada [*Library symbol Library of Congress*] (LCLS) ... CaOONHHS

Department of National Health and Welfare [*Ministere de la Sante Nationale etdu Bien-Etre Social*] **Ottawa, Ontario** [*Library symbol Obsolete National Library of Canada*] (NLC) .... OONH

Department of National Savings [*British*] .... DNS

Department of Natural Resources [*Department of Agriculture*] [*Sometimes facetiously referred to as Department of Nuts with Rifles*] .... DNR

Department of Naval Architecture and Marine Engineering [*MIT*] (MCD) .... DNAME

Department of Naval Instruction (DNAB) .... DEPTNAVINSTR

Department of Naval Science (DNAB) .... DEPNAVSCI

Department of Naval Science (DNAB) .... DPTNAVSCI

Department of Northern Saskatchewan, La Ronge, Saskatchewan [*Library symbol National Library of Canada*] (NLC) .... SLNS

Department of Nuclear Engineering [*MIT*] (MCD) .... DNE

Department of Nutrition, Food Science, and Technology [*MIT*] (MCD) .... DNFST

Department of Organization and Field Services, AFL-CIO (EA) .... DOFS

Department of Overseas Trade [*British*] .... DOT

Department of Parks, Wildlife, and Heritage [*Tasmania*] [*Australia*] .... DPWH

Department of Pathology, Banting-Best Institute, University of Toronto, Ontario [*Library symbol National Library of Canada*] (NLC) .... OTUPA

Department of Physical Research [*British*] .... DPR

Department of Physics, University of Toronto, Ontario [*Library symbol National Library of Canada*] (NLC) .... OTUP

Department of Planning and Housing [*Victoria*] [*Australia*] .... DPH

Department of Planning and Urban Development [*Western Australia*] [*Australia*] .... DPUD

Department of Plant Biology [*Carnegie Institution of Washington*] [*Research center*] (RCD) .... DPB

Department of Prices and Consumer Protection [*British*] .... DPCP

Department of Primary Industry, Fisheries, and Energy .... DPIFE

Department of Productivity [*Government Aircraft Factory*] [*Australia ICAO aircraft manufacturer identifier*] (ICAO) .... CD

Department of Productivity and Labour Relations [*Western Australia*] .... DPLR

Department of Public and Consumer Affairs .... DPCA

Department of Public Health .... DPH

Department of Public Information [*United Nations*] .... DPI

Department of Public Instruction, Division for Library Services, Cooperative Children's Book Center, Madison, WI [*Library symbol Library of Congress*] (LCLS) .... WMaPI-CC

Department of Public Instruction, Division for Library Services, Professional Library, Madison, WI [*Library symbol Library of Congress*] (LCLS) .... WMaPI

Department of Public Instruction, Division for Library Services, Public Library Services, Madison, WI [*Library symbol Library of Congress*] (LCLS) .... WMaPI-PL

Department of Public Instruction, Division for Library Services, Reference and Loan Library, Madison, WI [*Library symbol Library of Congress*] (LCLS) .... WMaPI-RL

Department of Public Libraries and Information, City of Virginia Beach, Reference Department, Virginia Beach, VA [*Library symbol Library of Congress*] (LCLS) .... ViVb

Department of Public Social Services .... DPSS

Department of Public Welfare .... DPW

Department of Public Works .... DPW

Department of Rapid Transit Systems [*Taipei*] (ECON) .... DORTS

Department of Rare Books and Special Collections, McGill University, Montreal, Quebec [*Library symbol National Library of Canada*] (NLC) .... QMMRB

Department of Regional Economic Expansion [*Canada*] .... DREE

Department of Regional Industrial Expansion [*Canada*] .... DRIE

Department of Regional Industrial Expansion [*Ministere de l'Expansion Industrielle Regionale*] **Ottawa, Ontario** [*Library symbol National Library of Canada*] (NLC) .... OOTC

Department of Renewable Resources, Government of the Yukon, Whitehorse, Yukon [*Library symbol National Library of Canada*] (NLC) .... YWRR

Department of Resource Industries [*Queensland*] [*Australia*] .... DRI

Department of Road Transport [*South Australia*] [*Australia*] .... DRT

Department of Roads and Transport [*Tasmania*] [*Australia*] .... DRT

Department of Rural Education [*of NEA*] [*Later, REA*] (EA) .... DRE

Department of School Education [*New South Wales, Victoria*] [*Australia*] .... DSE

Department of Science and Technology [*Science and Technology Information Institute*] [*Philippines*] (IID) .... DOST

Department of Science, Technology, Energy, and Materials [*Proposed Cabinet department*] .... STEAM

Department of Scientific and Industrial Research [*of the Privy Council for Scientific and Industrial Research*] [*Later, SRC*] [*British*] .... DSIR

Department of Secretary of State, Translation Bureau, Terminology and Documentation Branch, Ottawa, ON, Canada [*Library symbol*] [*Library of Congress*] (LCLS) .... CaOOSSTE

Department of Security Council Affairs of the United Nations .... SCA(UN)

Department of Small Business [*Australia*] .... DSB

Department of Social Security [*British*] .... DSS

Department of Social Services [*in various governmental agencies*] .... DSS

Department of State .... D of S

Department of State .... DOS

Department of State .... DS

Department of State Acquisition Regulation [*A publication*] (AAGC) .... DOSAR

Department of State. Bulletin [*A publication*] .... DSB

Department of State Contract Appeals Board (AAGC) .... DSCAB

Department of State Correspondents Association (EA) .... DOSCA

Department of State Correspondents Association (EA) .... DSCA

Department of State. Newsletter [*A publication*] .... SNL

Department of State Procurement Regulations .... DOSPR

Department of State Services [*Western Australia*] [*Australia*] .... DSS

Department of State, Washington, DC [*OCLC symbol*] (OCLC) .... DOS

Department of Supply and Service [*Canada*] (IMH) .... DSS

Department of Supply and Services, Canadian Government Expositions Centre, Ottawa, ON, Canada [*Library symbol Library of Congress*] (LCLS) .... CaOOGE

Department of Supply and Services [*Ministere des Approvisionnements et Services*] **Ottawa, Ontario** [*Library symbol National Library of Canada*] (NLC) .... OODP

Department of Surgery .... DOS

Department of Tank Design [*British*] (MCD) .... DTD

Department of Technical and Further Education [*Australia*] .... DTAFE

Department of Technical Cooperation [*British*] .... DTC

Department of Technical Cooperation for Development [*United Nations*] .... TCD

Department of Technology and Society (EA) .... DTS

Department of Territorial Affairs, Government of the Yukon, Whitehorse, Yukon [*Library symbol Obsolete National Library of Canada*] (NLC) .... YWTA

Department of the Air Force .... DAF

Department of the Air Force Command and Control System .... DAFCCS

Department of the Air Force Integrated Command and Control Systems (MCD) .... DAFICCS

Department of the Air Force Special Order (AFM) .... DAFSO

Department of the Air Member for Personnel [*British*] .... DAMP

Department of the Air Member for Supply and Organization [*British*] .... DAMSO

Department of the Air Member for Training [*British*] .... DAMT

Department of the Army .... DA

Department of the Army .... DEPTAR

Department of the Army .... DOA

Department of the Army Acquisition Management Review Agency (MCD) .... DAAMRA

Department of the Army Active Duty Board .... DAADB

Department of the Army Administrative Area .... DAAA

Department of the Army Air Traffic Coordinating Officer .... DAATCO

Department of the Army Allocation Committee, Ammunition (AABC) .... DAACA

Department of the Army Alternate Command and Control Element (AABC) .... DAACCE

Department of the Army Alternate Command and Control Element (AABC) .... DACE

Department of the Army Audiovisual Media Production Program .... DAAVMPP

Department of the Army Audiovisual Production Program (MCD) .... DAAPP

Department of the Army Audiovisual Program .... DAAP

Department of the Army Avionics Master Plan (AABC) .... DAAMP

Department of the Army Certificate of Achievement .... DACA

Department of the Army Civilian .... DAC

Department of the Army Classification Review Committee (MCD) .... DACRS

Department of the Army Command and Control Reporting System (AABC) .... DAXREP

Department of the Army Command and Control System (AABC) .... DACCS

Department of the Army Communication Resources Plan (AABC) .... DACRP

Department of the Army Communications Center (AABC) .... DACC

Department of the Army Compassionate Review Board .... DACRB

Department of the Army Corps of Engineers [*Military Project*] (AAGC) .... DACA

Department of the Army Corps of Engineers (Civil Works Project) (AAGC) .... DACW

Department of the Army Critical Items List .... DACIL

Department of the Army Data Elements Management System (MCD) .... DADEMS

Department of the Army Decoration for Meritorious Civilian Service .... DADMCS

Department of the Army, Deputy Chief of Staff for Logistics .... DADCSLOG

Department of the Army Distribution/Allocation Committee (AABC) .... DADAC

Department of the Army Equipment Data Review Committee (AABC) .... DAEDARC

Department of the Army Equipment Publication .... DAEP

Department of the Army Field Manuals .... DAFM

Department of the Army Forward Depot (AABC) .... DAFD

Department of the Army Forward-Floating Depot (AABC) .... DAFFD

Department of the Army Historical Advisory Committee [*Washington, DC*] (EGAO) .... DAHAC

Department of the Army in Process Review (MCD) .... DAIPR

Department of the Army Inspector General .... DAIG

Department of the Army Integrated Materiel Support .... DAIMS

Department of the Army Integrated Technical Document Manual (MCD) .... DAITDM

Department of the Army Intelligence Plan .... DAIP

Department of the Army International Rationalization Office (RDA) .... DAIRO

Department of the Army Liaison Team (AABC) .... DALT

Department of the Army Logistics Readiness Liaison Visits (AABC) .... DALRLV

Department of the Army Long-Range Technological Forecast .... DALRTF

Department of the Army/Main (AABC) .... DEPTAR/MAIN

Department of the Army Management Information System (AABC) .... DAMIS

Department of the Army Management Review and Improvement Program (AABC) .... DAMRIP

Department of the Army Master Priority List (AABC) .... DAMPL

Department of the Army Material Priority List .... DAMPL

Department of the Army Material Readiness Command (MCD) .... DAMRC

Department of the Army Materiel Annex (AABC) .... DAMA

Department of the Army Materiel Program .... DAMP

Department of the Army Military Personnel Management Team (AABC) .... DAMPMT

Department of the Army Mobilization Command and Control System (MCD) .... DA MOB C2S

Department of the Army Modification Work Order .... DAMWO

Department of the Army Motion Picture/Television Production Board (AABC) .... DAMP/TVPB

Department of the Army Motion Picture/Television Production Program .... DAMP/TVPP

Department of the Army Movements Management System (MCD) .... DAMMS

Department of the Army Movements Management System-Redesign (GFGA) ... DAMMS-R
Department of the Army, Office of the Chief, Army Reserve ... DAAR
Department of the Army Pamphlet ... DA PAM
Department of the Army Pamphlet ... DAP
Department of the Army Panel on Environmental Physiology ... DAPEP
Department of the Army Physical Security Review Board (MCD) ... DAPSRB
Department of the Army Plan for Assistance in Department of Health, Education, and Welfare (AABC) ... DA-AHEW
Department of the Army Plan for [*Possession, Control, and*] **Operation of Railroads** (AABC) ... DA-OPRR
Department of the Army Policy for Disclosure of Classified Military Information [*to foreign government*] (AABC) ... DADCMI
Department of the Army Productivity Improvement Program ... DAMPIP
Department of the Army Program Report ... DAPR
Department of the Army Program Review (RDA) ... DAPR
Department of the Army Programming Priority List ... DAPPL
Department of the Army Property Accountability Task Force (MCD) ... DAPATF
Department of the Army Publication (DOMA) ... DAP
Department of the Army Regional Representative (AABC) ... DARR
Department of the Army Relocation Sites (AABC) ... DARS
Department of the Army Requisitioning, Receipt, and Issue System ... DARRIS
Department of the Army Secure Facsimile (AABC) ... DARFAX
Department of the Army Security Agency (MCD) ... DASA
Department of the Army Shipping Document ... DASD
Department of the Army Special Order ... DASO
Department of the Army Special Photographic Office (AABC) ... DASPO
Department of the Army Standard Port System ... DASPS
Department of the Army Standard Port System - Enhanced (MCD) ... DASPS-E
Department of the Army Standard Port System - Enhanced - System Development Group (MCD) ... DASPS-E-SDG
Department of the Army Strategic Logistics [*Study*] ... DASL
Department of the Army Suitability Evaluation Board (AABC) ... DASEB
Department of the Army System Coordinator (RDA) ... DASC
Department of the Army Systems Staff Officer (AABC) ... DASSO
Department of the Army Technical Bulletin (MCD) ... DATB
Department of the Army Technical Manual (NATG) ... DATM
Department of the Army Technical Manual Repair Parts Special Tool List ... DATMRPSTL
Department of the Army Telecommunications Plan (MCD) ... DATEP
Department of the Army Training and Support Committee (AABC) ... DATSC
Department of the Army Visual Information Production Program ... DAVIPP
Department of the Army Vocabulary of Information Elements (AABC) ... DAVIE
Department of the Attorney General and of Justice, Sydney, NSW, Australia [*Library symbol Library of Congress*] (LCLS) ... AuSAJ
Department of the Attorney-General [*Commonwealth, Queensland*] [*Australia*] ... DAG
Department of the Chief Minister [*Northern Territory*] [*Australia*] ... DCM
Department of the Chief of Naval Information [*British military*] (DMA) ... DCNI
Department of the Commandant-General, Royal Marines [*British*] ... CGRM
Department of the Director, Women's Royal Naval Service [*British*] ... DWRNS
Department of the Environment [*Formerly, MPBW, MT*] [*British*] ... DOE
Department of the Environment, Parks Canada, Ste.-Foy, PQ, Canada [*Library symbol Library of Congress*] (LCLS) ... CaQQEPC
Department of the Financial Secretary of the War Office [*British*] ... DFSWO
Department of the Interior ... D of I
Department of the Interior (MCD) ... DI
Department of the Interior (AABC) ... DOI
Department of the Interior ... DoI
Department of the Interior Acquisition Regulation [*A publication*] (AAGC) ... DIAR
Department of the Interior Board of Contract Appeals ... IBCA
Department of the Interior, Decisions Relating to Public Lands [*A publication*] (DLA) ... Pub Lands Dec
Department of the Interior Energy Board [*Marine science*] (OSRA) ... DIEB
Department of the Interior Energy Board (USDC) ... DIEB
Department of the Legislative Assembly of the Northern Territory [*Australia*] ... DLANT
Department of the Master General of the Ordnance [*British*] ... DMGO
Department of the Medical Director-General [*Navy British*] ... DMDG
Department of the Navy ... DN
Department of the Navy ... DON
Department of the Navy Automatic Data Processing Management (DNAB) ... DONADPM
Department of the Navy Civilian (DNAB) ... DNC
Department of the Navy Declassification Team (DNAB) ... DNDT
Department of the Navy Federal Equal Opportunity Recruitment Program (DNAB) ... DON FEORP
Department of the Navy Five-Year Program ... DNFYP
Department of the Navy Management Information Control System ... DONMICS
Department of the Navy Occupational Level (DNAB) ... DONAL
Department of the Navy Office Automation and Communication Systems (GFGA) ... DONOACS
Department of the Navy Policy and Planning Guidance (MCD) ... DNPPG
Department of the Navy Program Information Center ... DONPIC
Department of the Navy System Acquisition Review Council (MCD) ... DNSARC
Department of the Pacific [*Marine Corps*] ... DP
Department of the Premier and Cabinet [*South Australia, Tasmania, Victoria*] [*Australia*] ... DPC
Department of the Premier, Economic and Trade Development [*Queensland*] [*Australia*] ... DPETD
Department of the Prime Minister and Cabinet [*Australia*] ... DPMC
Department of the Secretary of State [*Secretariat d'Etat*] **Ottawa, Ontario** [*Library symbol National Library of Canada*] (NLC) ... OOSS
Department of the Secretary of State, Translation Bureau, Multilingual Services, Ottawa, ON, Canada [*Library symbol*] [*Library of Congress*] (LCLS) ... CaOOSSTM
Department of the Secretary of State, Translation Bureau, Translation Services, Ottawa, ON, Canada [*Library symbol*] [*Library of Congress*] (LCLS) ... CaOOSSTR
Department of the Treasury [*Commonly TD, Treasury Department*] ... D of T
Department of the Treasury (AFM) ... DOT
Department of the Treasury ... TREAS DEPT
Department of the Treasury, Internal Revenue Service, Washington, DC [*Library symbol Library of Congress*] (LCLS) ... DTI
Department of Tourism, Recreation, and Cultural Affairs, Public Library Services, Winnipeg, MB, Canada [*Library symbol Library of Congress*] (LCLS) ... CaMWPL
Department of Tourism, Sport, and Racing [*Queensland*] [*Australia*] ... DTSR
Department of Tourism, Sport, and Recreation [*Tasmania*] [*Australia*] ... DTSR
Department of Toxic Substances Control ... DTSC
Department of Toxic Substances Control (DOGT) ... DTSC
Department of Trade [*British*] ... DoT
Department of Trade [*British*] (DS) ... DT
Department of Trade [*British*] (ADA) ... DTR
Department of Trade and Industry [*British*] (NITA) ... DOTI
Department of Trade and Industry [*British*] ... DTI
Department of Transport [*Canada*] ... DOT
Department of Transport [*British*] (DA) ... DOTp
Department of Transport [*British*] (DS) ... DTp
Department of Transport and Works [*Northern Territory*] [*Australia*] ... DTW
Department of Transportation ... DOT
Department of Transportation and Development, Aviation Office, Baton Rouge, LA [*Library symbol Library of Congress*] (LCLS) ... LBrTD-Av
Department of Transportation and Development, Office of Highways, Research and Development Library, Baton Rouge, LA [*Library symbol Library of Congress*] (LCLS) ... LBrTD-H
Department of Transportation and Development, Office of Public Works, Baton Rouge, LA [*Library symbol Library of Congress*] (LCLS) ... LBrTD-Pw
Department of Transportation Board of Contract Appeals (AAGC) ... DOT BCA
Department of Transportation/Climatic Impact Assessment Program (NASA) ... DOT/CIAP
Department of Transportation Coast Guard Office of Navigation [*Washington, DC*] ... DOT-CG-N
Department of Transportation Continuity of Operations Plan [*Federal emergency plan*] ... DOTCOOP
Department of Transportation Contract Adjustment Board (AAGC) ... DOTCAB
Department of Transportation Contract Appeals Board ... DOTCAB
Department of Transportation Contract Assistance Program (AAGC) ... DOTCAP
Department of Transportation Federal Aviation Administration Air Traffic Service [*Washington, DC*] ... DOT/FAA/AT
Department of Transportation Federal Aviation Administration Airport Capacity Program Office [*Washington, DC*] ... DOT/FAA/CP
Department of Transportation Federal Aviation Administration Office of Airport Planning and Programming [*Washington, DC*] ... DOT/FAA/PP
Department of Transportation Federal Aviation Administration Office of Airports Programs [*Washington, DC*] ... DOT/FAA/AP
Department of Transportation Federal Aviation Administration Office of Aviation Medicine [*Washington, DC*] ... DOT/FAA/AM
Department of Transportation Federal Aviation Administration Office of Aviation Safety [*Washington, DC*] ... DOT/FAA/ASF
Department of Transportation Federal Aviation Administration Office of Environment and Energy [*Washington, DC*] ... DOT/FAA/EE
Department of Transportation Federal Aviation Administration Office of Systems Engineering Management [*Washington, DC*] ... DOT/FAA/EM
Department of Transportation Federal Aviation Administration Program Engineeringand Maintenance Service [*Washington, DC*] ... DOT/FAA/PM
Department of Transportation Federal Aviation Administration Program EngineeringService [*Washington, DC*] ... DOT/FAA/PS
Department of Transportation Federal Aviation Administration Systems EngineeringService [*Washington, DC*] ... DOT/FAA/ES
Department of Transportation Federal Aviation Administration Systems Research and Development Service [*Washington, DC*] ... DOT/FAA/RD
Department of Transportation Financial Assistance Program (AAGC) ... DOTFAP
Department of Transportation Inspector General ... DOTIG
Department of Transportation National Highway Traffic Safety Administration [*Washington, DC*] ... DOT-HS
Department of Transportation Office of Assistant Secretary for Systems Development and Technology [*Washington, DC*] ... DOT-OS
Department of Transportation Office of Supersonic Transportation [*Washington, DC*] ... DOT-SST
Department of Transportation Procurement Regulations (AAGC) ... DOTPR
Department of Transportation's Emergency Organization ... DOTEO
Department of Treasury [*Victoria*] [*Australia*] ... DOT
Department of Treasury and Finance [*Australia*] ... DTF
Department of Trusteeship and Information from Non-Self-Governing Territories ofthe United Nations ... TRIUN
Department of University Computer Systems [*University of Connecticut*] [*Research center*] (RCD) ... DUCS
Department of Urban and Community Affairs, Office of Planning and Technical Assistance, Baton Rouge, LA [*Library symbol Library of Congress*] (LCLS) ... LBrUC
Department of Veterans Affairs [*Formerly, Veterans Administration*] ... DVA
Department of Veterans Affairs [*Canada*] ... DVA
Department of Veterans Affairs [*Pre-1989, Veterans Administration*] (AAGC) ... VA
Department of Veterans Affairs Board of Contract Appeals (AAGC) ... VABCA
Department of Veterans Benefits [*Veterans Administration*] ... DVB
Department [*or Division*] **of Vocational Rehabilitation** [*Later, DTVE*] [*Department of Education*] (OICC) ... DVR

Department of Wildlife (GNE) .... DOW
Department of Wildlife and Fisheries, Louisiana Stream Control Commission, BatonRouge, LA [*Library symbol Library of Congress*] (LCLS) .... LBrWF-S
Department of Works [*Military British*] .... D of W
Department of Works, Municipality of Metropolitan Toronto, Ontario [*Library symbol National Library of Canada*] (BIB) .... OTMW
Department of Zoology, University of Toronto, Ontario [*Library symbol National Library of Canada*] (NLC) .... OTUZ
Department Operating Instruction .... DOI
Department Organization Order [*Department of Commerce*] (NOAA) .... DOO
Department Performance Rating .... DPR
Department Personnel Manual .... DPM
Department Reports, State Department [*New York*] [*A publication*] (DLA) .... Dept R
Department Standardization Office [*Navy*] .... DEPSO
Department Summary Schedule [*NASA*] (NASA) .... DSS
Department Supply Storage Point/Stock Storage Depot [*DoD*] .... DSSP/SSD
Department Training .... DT
Department Work Order (MCD) .... DWO
Departmental (ABBR) .... DEPTL
Departmental Circulars .... DC
Departmental Civilian Personnel Branch .... DCPB
Departmental Computing .... DC
Departmental Coordinating Committee on Ocean Minings [*Canada*] .... DCOM
Departmental Data Coordinator (MCD) .... DDC
Departmental Data Processing Center [*Department of Labor*] .... DDPC
Departmental Entry Processing Systems [*Customs processing for sea and airports*] [*October, 1981*] [*British*] (DCTA) .... DEPS
Departmental Estimate (AAG) .... DE
Departmental Industrial Equipment Reserve (AAGC) .... DIER
Departmental Industrial Plant Reserve [*DoD*] (AFIT) .... DIPR
Departmental Industrial Reserve System .... DIRS
Departmental Information Locator System [*Department of Agriculture*] (GFGA) .... DILS
Departmental Instruction (AAG) .... DI
Departmental Letter [*Air Force*] (AAGC) .... DL
Departmental Library, Environment Canada [*Bibliotheque du Ministere, Environnemet Canada*] **Ottawa, Ontario** [*Library symbol National Library of Canada*] (NLC) .... OOFF
Departmental Management System [*Department of Labor*] .... DMS
Departmental Materiel Requisition .... DMR
Departmental Notice (AAG) .... DN
Departmental On-Line Reporting System [*Military*] .... DOLARS
Departmental Organization Order [*Marine science*] (OSRA) .... DOO
Departmental Personnel Instruction .... DPI
Departmental Property Management System .... DPMS
Departmental Records Branch [*Military*] .... DRB
[*A*] **Departmental Reporting System** [*IBM Corp.*] .... ADRS
Departmental Science Development [*National Science Foundation*] .... DSD
Departmental Square Feet (MCD) .... DSF
Departmental Staff Records (AIE) .... DSR
Departmentalized Billing .... DB
Departmentally-Initiated Review .... DIR
Departure (ABBR) .... DEPT
Departure (ABBR) .... DEPU
Departure .... P
Departure Airfield (AABC) .... DAF
Departure Airfield Control (AABC) .... DAFC
Departure Airfield Control Group [*Military*] (AABC) .... DACG
Departure Airfield Control Group [*Military*] (AABC) .... DAFCG
Departure Airfield Group [*Army*] (ADDR) .... DACO
Departure Approval Request [*Aviation*] (DNAB) .... DAR
Departure Approved [*Aviation*] (FAAC) .... DA
Departure Control .... DEPCON
Departure Control (DA) .... DPC
Departure Control (MUGU) .... DPT
Departure Control System [*IATA*] (DS) .... DCS
Departure Date .... DD
Departure End of Runway [*Aviation*] (DA) .... DER
Departure from Nucleate Boiling (NRCH) .... DNB
Departure from Nucleate Boiling Ratio (NRCH) .... DNBR
Departure from Specifications (DNAB) .... DFS
Departure Locator .... DL
Departure Message [*Aviation code*] .... DEP
Departure Point (AFM) .... DP
Departure Procedure [*Aviation*] (FAAC) .... DPCR
Departure Sequencing Engineering Development Model [*FAA*] (TAG) .... DSEDM
Departure Sequencing Program [*FAA*] (TAG) .... DSP
DePaul Rehabilitation Hospital Medical Library, Milwaukee, WI [*Library symbol Library of Congress*] (LCLS) .... WMDR
DePaul University (GAGS) .... DePaul U
Dependable .... DPNDBL
Depended Variable (IAA) .... DV
Dependencies (ROG) .... DEP
Dependency (ABBR) .... DEPEND
Dependency [*Psychology*] .... Dy
Dependency and Indemnity Compensation [*Military*] (AFM) .... D & IC
Dependency and Indemnity Compensation [*Military*] .... DIC
Dependency Certificate Filed .... DCF
Dependency Graph and Control [*Computer science*] .... DG
Dependent .... DEP
Dependent (AFM) .... DEPN
Dependent Care Assistance Plan [*Insurance*] (WYGK) .... DCAP
Dependent Care Program [*Insurance*] (WYGK) .... DCP
Dependent Care Tax Credit .... DCTC
Dependent Charge Group [*Telecommunications*] (TEL) .... DCG
Dependent Coverage Rider [*Health insurance*] (GHCT) .... DC
Dependent Coverage Waiver [*Insurance*] (WYGK) .... DCW
Dependent Drainage [*Medicine*] .... DD
Dependent Housing Area [*Army*] (AABC) .... DHA
Dependent Lu [*Logical Unit*] **Requester/Server** (CDE) .... DLUR/DLUS
Dependent Meteorological Office .... DMO
Dependent Overseas Territory .... DOT
Dependent Political Entity [*Board on Geographic Names*] .... PCLD
Dependent Relative Allowance (DLA) .... DRA
Dependent Variable (AAMN) .... DV
Dependent Vehicle .... DV
Dependent-Care Reimbursement [*Insurance*] (WYGK) .... DCR
Dependents Assistance Act .... DAA
Dependents Assistance Team [*Military*] (DNAB) .... DAT
Dependents' Daylight Cruise [*Navy*] (NVT) .... DEPCRU
Dependents' Dental Plan [*DoD*] .... DDP
Dependents' Education Office (Atlantic) (DNAB) .... DEO(A)
Dependents' Education Office (Pacific) (DNAB) .... DEO(P)
Dependents' Evacuation Pay [*Military*] .... DEPEVACPAY
Dependents' Medical Care Act [*HEW*] .... DMCA
Dependents Not Authorized Overseas Duty Station [*Military*] .... DEPNOTAUTH
Dependents Overseas [*Military*] .... DOS
Dependents Rate [*Air Force*] (AFM) .... DR
Dependents Schooling Office [*Military*] .... DSO
Depends on Experience [*Employment*] (ODBW) .... DOE
Depends on Experience [*Employment*] (ODBW) .... doe
Deperming [*Navy*] (ANA) .... DEPERM
Deperming and Flashing Station [*Navy*] .... DEPERMSTA
Depew, NY [*FM radio station call letters*] .... WBLK
Depicting (VRA) .... depict
Depilate (ABBR) .... DEP
Depilation (ABBR) .... DEPL
Depilatorium [*Depilatory*] [*Pharmacy*] .... DEPILAT
Depilatory (ABBR) .... DEP
Depleted Base Transistor (IAA) .... DBT
Depleted MORB [*Mid-Ocean Ridge Basalt*] **Mantle** [*Geology*] .... DMM
Depleted Uranium .... DU
Depletion (KSC) .... DEPL
Depletion (NITA) .... D-FET
Depletion Allowance [*Business term*] .... DA
Depletion Etch Method (IAA) .... DEMOD
Depletion Metal-Oxide Semiconductor (BUR) .... DMOS
Depletion Perturbation Theory (PDAA) .... DPT
Depletion-Approximation Replacement (MCD) .... DAR
Depletion-Layer Transistor (IEEE) .... DLT
Depletion-Mode Metal Semiconductor Field Effect Transistor (IAA) .... DMESFET
Deploy (KSC) .... DEPL
Deploy (AABC) .... DPL
Deploy (KSC) .... DPLY
Deploy (NASA) .... DPY
Deployable Acoustic Readiness Training System (MCD) .... DARTS
Deployable Array Working Group (DWSG) .... DAWG
Deployable Automatic Relay Terminal [*Air Force*] .... DART
Deployable Defense System (IEEE) .... DDS
Deployable Field Headquarters .... DFH
Deployable Maintenance Platform (MCD) .... DMP
Deployable Medical [*Equipment*] [*Military*] .... DEPMED
Deployable Medical System [*Military*] .... DEPMEDS
Deployable Payloads Projects Office [*Kennedy Space Center*] [*NASA*] (NASA) .... DPO
Deployable Receive Segment Engineering Model (MCD) .... DRSEM
Deployable Solar Array .... DSA
Deployable Solar Panel .... DSP
Deployable Universal Combat Earthmover (RDA) .... DEUCE
Deployed Electronics Assembly (MCD) .... DEA
Deployed Mechanical Assembly (MCD) .... DMA
Deployed Operating Base (MCD) .... DOB
Deployment .... DEP
Deployment Action Team [*Army*] (DOMA) .... DAT
Deployment Adjustment Notification [*Military*] (CINC) .... DAN
Deployment Adjustment Request [*Military*] (CINC) .... DAR
Deployment and Support [*Military*] .... D & S
Deployment Area Location Code [*Army*] (AABC) .... DALC
Deployment Assembly [*Skylab*] [*NASA*] .... DA
Deployment Control Unit [*Army*] (DOMA) .... DCU
Deployment Data File .... DEPDA
Deployment/Employment/Mobilization Status System [*MTMC*] (TAG) .... DEMSTAT
Deployment Exercise [*Military*] (ADDR) .... DEPEX
Deployment for Training .... DFT
Deployment Indicator Code .... DEPID
Deployment Manifest [*Army*] .... DEPL-MAN
Deployment Manning Document (MCD) .... DMD
Deployment Mobilization Troop Basis (AABC) .... DMTB
Deployment Model [*Army*] (AABC) .... DEMOD
Deployment on NIKE/X Study [*Military*] .... DEPEX
Deployment Operations Team .... DOT
Deployment Payload (MCD) .... DP
Deployment Pennant [*Navy British*] .... DP
Deployment Pointing Panels (NASA) .... DPP
Deployment Position RADAR (MCD) .... DPR
Deployment Readiness Assistance Program [*Military*] .... DRAP
Deployment Readiness Condition [*Army*] (AABC) .... DRC
Deployment Readiness Review [*Aviation*] (FAAC) .... DRR

Deployment Reporting System .... DEPREP
Deployment Staff Exercise (MCD) .... DESEX
Deployment Status of Army Units (AABC) .... DEPSTAR
Deployment Summary Report [*Air Force*] .... DEPSUM
Depo Tech Inc. [*NASDAQ symbol*] (TTSB) .... DEPO
Depoe Bay, OR [*FM radio station call letters*] (RBYB) .... KDEP-FM
Depolarization .... DEPOL
Depolarization Shift [*Electrophysiology*] .... DS
Depolarized Light Intensity .... DLI
Depolarized Light Mixing (PDAA) .... DLM
Depolarizing After-Potential [*Neurochemistry*] .... DAP
Depolarizing Bipolar Cell [*In the retina*] .... DPBC
Depolymerized Rubber .... DPR
Depolymerized Scrap Rubber [*Waste recycling*] .... DSR
Depomedroxyprogesterone Acetate [*Contraceptive*] .... DMPA
Deponent .... DEP
Deponent (ABBR) .... DEPON
Deponent [*Legal term*] (ROG) .... DEPT
Deponent .... DPT
Depo-Provera [*Contraceptive*] [*The Upjohn Co.*] .... D-P
Deport (ROG) .... DEP
Deportation [*FBI standardized term*] .... DEP
Deposed .... DEP
Deposit [*or Depositor*] (EY) .... DEP
Deposit (WDMC) .... dep
Deposit .... depo
Deposit (ROG) .... DEPT
Deposit .... DP
Deposit .... DPST
Deposit .... DPST
Deposit (ADA) .... DPT
Deposit Account [*Banking*] .... DA
Deposit Account Number (NG) .... DAN
Deposit Administration .... DA
Deposit Administration Arrangement (WYGK) .... DAA
Deposit and Difference [*Tea trade*] (ROG) .... D & D
Deposit Book .... D/B
Deposit Byte [*Computer science*] (NHD) .... DPB
Deposit Certificate [*Banking*] (MHDW) .... Dep Ctf
Deposit Fund Account .... DFA
Deposit Guaranty [*NASDAQ symbol*] (TTSB) .... DEPS
Deposit Guaranty Corp. [*NYSE symbol*] (SAG) .... DEP
Deposit Guaranty Corp. [*Associated Press*] (SAG) .... DepGty
Deposit Guaranty Corp. [*NASDAQ symbol*] (NQ) .... DEPS
Deposit Insurance Flexibility Act [*1982*] .... DIFA
Deposit Insurance Fund [*Pronounced "diff"*] .... DIF
Deposit Interest Retention Tax [*Ireland*] .... DIRT
Deposit Liquidation Board .... DLB
Deposit, NY [*FM radio station call letters*] .... WIYN
Deposit Passbook [*Banking*] .... DPB
Deposit Receipt [*Banking*] .... DR
Deposit Ticket/Debit Voucher [*Computer science*] .... DT/DV
Depositary [*Banking*] .... DEP
Depositary [*Banking*] (EY) .... DEPOS
Deposited Carbon .... DC
Deposited Plan (ADA) .... DP
Deposition (ADA) .... DEP
Deposition [*Legal shorthand*] (LWAP) .... DEPO
Deposition .... DEPOSN
Deposition and Discovery [*Legal term*] (DLA) .... DEPOS & D
Deposition Form [*Army*] (ADDR) .... DF
Deposition Rate [*Electrochemistry*] .... DR
Deposition Thickness Controller (IAA) .... DTC
Depositional Remanent Magnetization (IAA) .... DRM
Depository .... DEP
Depository Institution Management Interlocks Act [*1978*] .... DIMIA
Depository Institutions Deregulation and Monetary Control Act of 1980 .... DIDA
Depository Institutions Deregulation and Monetary Decontrol Act [*1980*] .... DIDMCA
Depository Institutions Deregulation Committee [*Department of the Treasury*] [*Terminated, 1986*] .... DIDC
Depository Library Council to the Public Printer (EA) .... DLCPP
Depository Transfer Check [*Banking*] .... DTC
Depository Trust Co. .... DTC
Deposits in Court [*Legal term*] (DLA) .... DEP in CT
Deposit-Taking Company [*Generic term that originated in Hong Kong*] .... DTC
Deposit-Taking Institution (ADA) .... DTI
Depositus [*Laid to Rest*] [*Latin*] .... D
Depot [*DoD*] .... D
Depot (AFM) .... DEP
Depot (MCD) .... DPO
Depot .... DPT
Depot Acceptance Procedures .... DAP
Depot Activity .... DEPACTV
Depot Automatic Rescheduling Technique .... DART
Depot Automatic Test System for Avionics (DWSG) .... DATSA
Depot Command Management System .... DCMS
Depot Component/Equipment Rework Report [*Navy*] (NG) .... DCERR
Depot Condemnation Percent (NASA) .... DCP
Depot Control Number .... DCN
Depot Fixed (AAG) .... DF
Depot Inspection and Repair .... DIR
Depot Installation Management Information System [*Army*] .... DIMIS
Depot Installed (SAA) .... DEP INST
Depot Integrated Maintenance Support Agreement [*Air Force*] .... DIMSA
Depot Level Activity (NATG) .... DLA
Depot Level Inspection Auto Repair (MCD) .... DLIR
Depot Level Maintenance [*Air Force*] (AFM) .... DLM
Depot Level Maintenance Facility (MCD) .... DLMF
Depot Level Maintenance Plant .... DLMP
Depot Level Maintenance Requirement Review (AFIT) .... DLMRR
Depot Level of Maintenance (AAGC) .... D Level
Depot Level Repairable (NVT) .... DLR
Depot Logistics Report (MCD) .... DLR
Depot Maintenance (AAGC) .... DM
Depot Maintenance Activity (MCD) .... DMA
Depot Maintenance Control [*or Coordinator*] **Center** [*Army*] (AABC) .... DMCC
Depot Maintenance Data Bank [*DARCOM*] (MCD) .... DMDB
Depot Maintenance Equipment (SAA) .... DME
Depot Maintenance Facility (SAA) .... DMF
Depot Maintenance Facility - Recycle (SAA) .... DMF-R
Depot Maintenance Industrial Fund (MCD) .... DMIF
Depot Maintenance Industrial Funding Customer (MCD) .... DMIFCUS
Depot Maintenance Interservice .... DMI
Depot Maintenance Interservice Support Agreement [*Military*] .... DMISA
Depot Maintenance Level .... DML
Depot Maintenance Literature (MCD) .... DML
Depot Maintenance Management Information System [*Air Force*] (GFGA) .... DMMIS
Depot Maintenance Management Subsystem (DNAB) .... DMMS
Depot Maintenance Plant Equipment (MCD) .... DMPE
Depot Maintenance Production Report .... DMPR
Depot Maintenance Service (AFIT) .... DMS
Depot Maintenance Service Air Force Industrial Fund (AFIT) .... DMSAFIF
Depot Maintenance Study [*Army*] .... DMS
Depot Maintenance Support (AAG) .... DMS
Depot Maintenance Support Plan [*Air Force*] (AFM) .... DMSP
Depot Maintenance Work Request [*or Requirement*] [*Army*] (AABC) .... DMWR
Depot Maintenance Workload Plan (MCD) .... DMWP
Depot Management Data Collection System (MCD) .... DMDCS
Depot Management Information System [*Army*] .... DEPMIS
Depot Manufacture (MCD) .... DM
Depot Master Item Data File [*Army*] .... DMIDF
Depot Materiel Maintenance and Support Activities [*Army*] .... DMM & SA
Depot Museum, Aitken, MN [*Library symbol*] [*Library of Congress*] (LCLS) .... MnADM
Depot of Supplies [*Marine Corps*] .... D of S
Depot of Supplies [*Marine Corps*] .... DOFS
Depot Operation Management System [*Army*] .... DOMS
Depot Overhaul (MCD) .... D/O
Depot Overhaul Factor .... DOF
Depot Paymaster [*Military British*] (ROG) .... DPM
Depot Plant Modernization Plan [*Army*] .... DPMP
Depot Property Officer .... DPO
Depot Purchased Equipment Management [*DoD*] .... DPEM
Depot Quartermaster [*Marine Corps*] .... DQM
Depot Quartermaster, Norfolk, Virginia [*Marine Corps*] .... DQN
Depot Quartermaster, Pearl Harbor, Hawaii [*Marine Corps*] .... DQPH
Depot Quartermaster, Philadelphia, Pennsylvania [*Marine Corps*] .... DQP
Depot Quartermaster, Quantico, Virginia [*Marine Corps*] .... DQQ
Depot Quartermaster, Richmond, Virginia [*Marine Corps*] .... DQR
Depot Quartermaster, San Francisco, California [*Marine Corps*] .... DQSF
Depot Recovery Factor (MCD) .... DRF
Depot Repair Cycle (MCD) .... DRC
Depot Repair Cycle Time .... DRCT
Depot Stockage List [*Army*] .... DSL
Depot Supply Center .... DSC
Depot Supply System [*Army*] .... DSS
Depot Support Supply Plan (AFIT) .... DSSP
Depot System Support Activity Far East [*US Army Materiel Command*] .... D-SAFE
Depot Systems Command [*Army*] (RDA) .... DESCOM
Depot Tooling Equipment .... DTE
Depot Training Center .... DTC
Depot Turn-Around Time (MCD) .... DTAT
Depot Vehicle Automatic Tester .... DEVAT
Depot Working Standards .... DWS
DepoTech Corp. [*NASDAQ symbol*] (SAG) .... DEPO
DepoTech Corp. [*Associated Press*] (SAG) .... DpoTch
Depot-Installed Maintenance Automatic Test Equipment .... DIMATE
Depreciation .... D
Depreciation [*Accounting, Economics*] .... DEPR
Depreciation .... DEPREC
Depreciation, Depletion, and Amortization .... DD & A
Depreciation Factor (IAA) .... DF
Depreciation Percentage [*Finance*] (WDAA) .... DP
Depressed [*Technical drawings*] .... DEP
Depressed [*Psychiatry*] (DAVI) .... depr
Depressed .... DPRSD
Depressed DNA Synthesis [*Medicine*] (DMAA) .... DDS
Depressed Reticle Dive [*Military*] .... DRD
Depressed Sight Line (MCD) .... DSL
Depressed Water Leg [*Nuclear energy*] (NRCH) .... DWL
Depressed-Trajectory Intercontinental Ballistic Missile (MCD) .... DICBM
Depression .... D
Depression [*Board on Geographic Names*] (MSA) .... DEPR
Depression Adjective Check Lists [*Psychology*] .... DACL
Depression after Delivery (EA) .... DAD
Depression and Related Affective Disorders Association (EA) .... DRADA
Depression: Awareness, Recognition, and Treatment [*National Institute of Mental Health program*] .... DART

Depression Deviation Indicator .... DDI
Depression/Elevation (CAAL) .... D/E
Depression Obvious [*Psychology*] .... DO
Depression Position-Finder .... DPF
Depression Pure Disease [*Medicine*] (DMAA) .... DPD
Depression Range Finder [*British military*] (DMA) .... DRF
Depression Sine Depression [*Psychology*] .... DSD
Depression Subtle [*Psychology*] .... DS
Depressive Neurosis [*Psychiatry*] (DAVI) .... depr neur
Depressives Anonymous: Recovery from Depression (EA) .... DARD
Depressives Anonymous: Recovery from Depression (EA) .... DARFD
Depressurize (NASA) .... DEPRESS
Deprived Eye [*Optics*] .... DE
Deproteinized Natural Rubber .... DPNR
Deptford [*Region of London*] .... DPFD
Depth .... D
Depth .... DEP
Depth (MSA) .... DP
Depth (VRA) .... dp
Depth .... DPT
Depth (FAAC) .... DPTH
Depth Appearing [*Typography*] (DGA) .... DA
Depth Bomb [*Military*] .... DB
Depth Charge [*Aerial*] [*Navy*] .... DC
Depth Control Tank .... DCT
Depth Cut Out [*Navy*] (NG) .... DCO
Depth Deviation Indicator .... DDI
Depth Dose [*Radiation therapy*] (DAVI) .... E_d
Depth Electroencephalogram [*or Electroencephalography*] [*Neurology*] (DAVI) .... DEEG
Depth Electrography [*Neurology*] (DAVI) .... DEEG
Depth Gauge .... DEGA
Depth, Height, or Altitude [*Physics*] (BARN) .... Y
Depth Keeping .... DKPG
Depth Molded (DS) .... Dm/d
Depth of Burial [*of explosives*] .... DOB
Depth of Burst (NATG) .... DOB
Depth of Cut Line (MCD) .... DCL
Depth of Discharge .... DOD
Depth of Discharge [*Electric vehicles*] .... DOD
Depth of Field [*or Focus*] [*Photography*] .... DF
Depth of Field (MCD) .... DOF
Depth of Flash Optical Landing System [*Navy*] .... DFOLS
Depth of Focus [*Optics*] .... DOF
Depth of Hold .... DPH
Depth of Modulation .... DOM
Depth of Ship .... D
Depth Perception (PAZ) .... DP
Depth Resolved Surface Coil Spectroscopy .... DRESS
Depth Sounder .... DS
Depth Telemetering Pinger .... DTP
Depth Under Notch (PDAA) .... DUN
Depth-Charge Projector .... DCP
Depth-Charge Thrower .... DCT
Depth-Charges Track .... DCT
Depth-Duration-Area .... DDA
Depth-First Search .... DFS
Depth-Selective Conversion Electron Mossbauer Spectroscopy .... DSCEMS
DePue Public Library, DePue, IL [*Library symbol Library of Congress*] (LCLS) .... IDep
DePue Unit, School District 103, DePue, IL [*Library symbol Library of Congress*] (LCLS) .... IDepSD
Depuratus [*Purified*] [*Pharmacy*] .... DEP
Deputation .... DEPUTN
Deputy .... D
Deputy (AFM) .... DEP
Deputy (WDMC) .... dep
Deputy .... DEPT
Deputy .... DEPY
Deputy .... DPTY
Deputy .... DPTY
Deputy .... DY
Deputy Adjutant and Quartermaster General [*British*] .... DA & QMG
Deputy Adjutant-General [*Military*] .... DAG
Deputy Adjutant-General, Royal Artillery [*British military*] (DMA) .... DAGRA
Deputy Administrator [*NASA*] .... AD
Deputy Advocate [*Legal term*] (DLA) .... DA
Deputy Advocate-General [*Military British*] (ROG) .... DAG
Deputy Air Officer Commanding [*British military*] (DMA) .... DAOC
Deputy Air Officer Commanding-in-Chief [*British military*] (DMA) .... DAOC-in-C
Deputy Air Wing Commander [*No longer used*] [*Navy*] (DOMA) .... DCAG
Deputy and Scientific Director of Army Research .... DSDAR
Deputy Assistant (DAS) .... DA
Deputy Assistant Adjutant [*Military British*] (ROG) .... DAA
Deputy Assistant Adjutant-General [*British*] .... DAAG
Deputy Assistant Administrator (GFGA) .... DAA
Deputy Assistant Chaplain-General [*British*] .... DACG
Deputy Assistant Chief of Staff (NATG) .... DACOS
Deputy Assistant Commissary-General [*Military British*] (ROG) .... DACG
Deputy Assistant Director .... DAD
Deputy Assistant Director, Army Veterinary Services .... DADAVS
Deputy Assistant Director for Management Support Division [*Vietnam*] .... DAD/MSD
Deputy Assistant Director for Plans and Evaluation [*Vietnam*] .... DAD/PE
Deputy Assistant Director for the Psychological Operations Division [*Vietnam*] .... DAD/POD
Deputy Assistant Director of Army Dental Services [*British*] .... DADADS
Deputy Assistant Director of Army Health [*British*] .... DADAH
Deputy Assistant Director of Artillery [*British*] .... DADA
Deputy Assistant Director of Inland Water Transport [*British military*] (DMA) .... DADIWT
Deputy Assistant Director of Labor [*Allied Control Commission*] [*World War II*] .... DADL
Deputy Assistant Director of Mechanical Engineering [*British military*] (DMA) .... DADME
Deputy Assistant Director of Medical Services [*Military*] .... DADMS
Deputy Assistant Director of Ordnance Services (Engineering) [*British*] .... DADOS(E)
Deputy Assistant Director of Ordnance Stores [*Military*] .... DADOS
Deputy Assistant Director of Public Relations [*British military*] (DMA) .... DADPR
Deputy Assistant Director of Quartering [*British*] .... DADQ
Deputy Assistant Director of Railway Transport [*British military*] (DMA) .... DADRT
Deputy Assistant Director of Remounts [*British*] .... DADR
Deputy Assistant Director of Supplies and Transport [*British*] .... DADST
Deputy Assistant Director of Transportation [*British*] .... DADT
Deputy Assistant Director of Veterinary and Remount Services [*British military*] (DMA) .... DADVRS
Deputy Assistant Director of Veterinary Services (DMA) .... DADVS
Deputy Assistant Director-General of Medical Services [*British*] (ADA) .... DADGMS
Deputy Assistant Inspector General (GFGA) .... DAIG
Deputy Assistant Judge Advocate General [*Legal term*] (DLA) .... DAJAG
Deputy Assistant Master-General of Ordnance [*British*] .... DAMGO
Deputy Assistant Military Secretary [*British*] .... DAMS
Deputy Assistant Provost-Marshall [*British*] .... DAPM
Deputy Assistant Quartermaster General .... DAQMG
Deputy Assistant Secretary, Army (Procurement) (AAGC) .... DASA(P)
Deputy Assistant Secretary for Employment and Training [*Department of Labor*] .... DASET
Deputy Assistant Secretary of Defense .... DASD
Deputy Assistant Secretary of Defense (Civilian Personnel) (DNAB) .... DASD(CP)
Deputy Assistant Secretary of Defense (Equal Opportunity) (DNAB) .... DASD(EO)
Deputy Assistant Secretary of Defense (Military Personnel Policy) (DNAB) .... DASD(MP)
Deputy Assistant-Adjutant and Quartermaster-General [*British*] .... DAA & QMG
Deputy Associate Administrator [*NASA*] .... AAD
Deputy Associate Regional Administrator .... DARA
Deputy Base Manager (MUGU) .... DBM
Deputy Brigade Commander [*Army*] .... DBC
Deputy Captain [*Military British*] (ROG) .... DC
Deputy Censorship Office [*London*] [*World War II*] .... DCO
Deputy Chaplain-General [*British*] .... DCG
Deputy Chief .... DC
Deputy Chief (CINC) .... DEPCH
Deputy Chief Architect [*British*] .... DCA
Deputy Chief, Chemical Warfare Service [*Army*] .... DCCWS
Deputy Chief Civil Affairs Officer [*US and Britain*] .... DCCAO
Deputy Chief Constable .... DCC
Deputy Chief for Intelligence (AAG) .... DCI
Deputy Chief Naval Adviser [*British*] .... DCNA
Deputy Chief Naval Engineering Officer [*British*] .... DCNEO
Deputy Chief of Defence Staff [*British*] .... DCDS
Deputy Chief of Defence Staff (Operational Requirements) [*British*] .... DCDS(OR)
Deputy Chief of Maintenance (MCD) .... DCM
Deputy Chief of Mission [*Diplomatic corps*] .... DCM
Deputy Chief of Naval Material .... DCNM
Deputy Chief of Naval Material (DNAB) .... DEPCHNAVMAT
Deputy Chief of Naval Material (Acquisition) (MCD) .... DCNM(A)
Deputy Chief of Naval Material, Development .... DCNM(D)
Deputy Chief of Naval Material (Logistics) (MCD) .... DCNM(L)
Deputy Chief of Naval Material, Management and Organization .... DCNM(M & O)
Deputy Chief of Naval Material, Material and Facilities .... DCNM(M & F)
Deputy Chief of Naval Material (Material and Facilities) (DNAB) .... DEPCHNAVMAT(MAT & FAC)
Deputy Chief of Naval Material, Programs and Financial Management .... DCNM(P & FM)
Deputy Chief of Naval Operations .... DCNO
Deputy Chief of Naval Operations, Administration .... DCNOA
Deputy Chief of Naval Operations (Air) .... DCNO(AIR)
Deputy Chief of Naval Operations (Development) .... DCNO(D)
Deputy Chief of Naval Operations, Fleet Operations and Readiness .... DCNOFOR
Deputy Chief of Naval Operations (Logistics) .... DCNO(L)
Deputy Chief of Naval Operations (Manpower and Naval Reserve) .... DCNO(M & NR)
Deputy Chief of Naval Operations (Manpower, Personnel, and Training) (DNAB) .... DCNO(MPT)
Deputy Chief of Naval Operations (Personnel and Naval Reserve) .... DCNO(P & R)
Deputy Chief of Naval Operations (Plans and Policies) .... DCNO(P & P)
Deputy Chief of Naval Operations (Readiness) [*British*] .... DCNO(R)
Deputy Chief of Naval Operations (Submarine Warfare) (DNAB) .... DCNO(SW)
Deputy Chief of Naval Staff [*Marine Corps; also, British Navy*] .... DCNS
Deputy Chief of Personnel Operations (AABC) .... DCOPO
Deputy Chief of Staff .... DC of S
Deputy Chief of Staff .... DCOFS
Deputy Chief of Staff (NATG) .... DCOS
Deputy Chief of Staff .... DCS
Deputy Chief of Staff [*Military*] (CAAL) .... DEPCOS
Deputy Chief of Staff, Air Force .... DC/SAF

Deputy Chief of Staff, Army ... DC of SA
Deputy Chief of Staff, Communications-Electronics [Army] (AABC) ... DCSC-E
Deputy Chief of Staff, Comptroller ... DCS/C
Deputy Chief of Staff, Comptroller (AABC) ... DCSCOMPT
Deputy Chief of Staff, Development ... DCS/D
Deputy Chief of Staff, Development, Air Force ... AFDDC
Deputy Chief of Staff / Flight Facilities (SAA) ... DCS/FF
Deputy Chief of Staff for Administration ... DCA
Deputy Chief of Staff for Combat Developments (AABC) ... DCSCD
Deputy Chief of Staff for Doctrine ... DCSDOC
Deputy Chief of Staff for Information Management [Army] ... DCSIM
Deputy Chief of Staff for Intelligence [Army] (AABC) ... DCSI
Deputy Chief of Staff for Logistics and Engineering [See also AF/LE] [Air Force] (DOMA) ... DCS/LE
Deputy Chief of Staff (for Manpower and Reserve Affairs) (RDA) ... DCS(M & RA)
Deputy Chief of Staff for Military Government [World War II] ... DCSMG
Deputy Chief of Staff for Operations [Army] ... DCSOPS
Deputy Chief of Staff for Operations, Air Force ... AFODC
Deputy Chief of Staff for Operations and Intelligence (AABC) ... DCSOI
Deputy Chief of Staff for Operations and Intelligence [Army] ... DCSOT
Deputy Chief of Staff for Operations and Plans [Army] ... DCSOPS
Deputy Chief of Staff for Operations - Force Development [Army] ... DCSOPS-FD
Deputy Chief of Staff for Personnel, Administration, and Logistics ... DCSPAL
Deputy Chief of Staff for Plans and Operations (AFM) ... DCS/P & O
Deputy Chief of Staff for Plans and Programs ... DCS/P & P
Deputy Chief of Staff for Plans and Research ... DCPR
Deputy Chief of Staff for Plans and Research [Army] ... DCSPR
Deputy Chief of Staff for Programs and Resources (AFM) ... DCS/P & R
Deputy Chief of Staff for Research, Development, and Acquisition [Army] ... DCSRDA
Deputy Chief of Staff for Research, Development, and Studies [Marine Corps] (DOMA) ... DCS RD & S
Deputy Chief of Staff for Reserve Officers' Training Corps (AABC) ... DCSROTC
Deputy Chief of Staff for Resource Management (AABC) ... DCSRM
Deputy Chief of Staff for Test and Evaluation [Army] ... DCSTE
Deputy Chief of Staff for Training [Army] ... DCST
Deputy Chief of Staff for Training and Schools (AABC) ... DCSTS
Deputy Chief of Staff, Force Development (AABC) ... DCSFOR
Deputy Chief of Staff, Installations and Logistics [Marine Corps] (DOMA) ... DC/S(I & L)
Deputy Chief of Staff, Intelligence [Air Force] (MCD) ... DCS/INT
Deputy Chief of Staff, Logistics [Army] (KSC) ... DCSL
Deputy Chief of Staff, Logistics [Army] ... DCSLOG
Deputy Chief of Staff, Logistics and Administration [NATO] (NATG) ... DCLA
Deputy Chief of Staff, Management Information Systems (AABC) ... DCSMIS
Deputy Chief of Staff, Materiel ... DCSM
Deputy Chief of Staff, Military Operations [Army] ... DC/SMO
Deputy Chief of Staff, Operations [NATO] (NATG) ... DCO
Deputy Chief of Staff, Operations ... DCSO
Deputy Chief of Staff, Operations and Administration ... DCSOA
Deputy Chief of Staff, Operations and Training (AABC) ... DCSO & T
Deputy Chief of Staff, Personnel [Air Force] ... AFPDC
Deputy Chief of Staff, Personnel ... DCS/P
Deputy Chief of Staff, Personnel [Army] ... DCSPER
Deputy Chief of Staff, Personnel and Administration (AABC) ... DCSPA
Deputy Chief of Staff, Personnel and Organization [NATO] (NATG) ... DCPO
Deputy Chief of Staff, Plans and Operations (MCD) ... DCPO
Deputy Chief of Staff, Plans and Policy [NATO] (NATG) ... DCPANDP
Deputy Chief of Staff, Research and Development [Army] ... DCSR & D
Deputy Chief of Staff, Research and Technology ... DCS/R & T
Deputy Chief of Staff, Reserve Components [Army] ... DCS/RC
Deputy Chief of Staff, Systems and Logistics ... DCS/S & L
Deputy Chief of the Air Staff [British] ... DCAS
Deputy Chief of the General Staff in the Field [Military British] ... DCGS
Deputy Chief of the Imperial General Staff [Military British] ... DCIGS
Deputy Chief of the Military Planning Office ... DCMPO
Deputy Chief Patrol Inspector [Immigration and Naturalization Service] ... DCPI
Deputy Chief Political Officer [British Military Administration] ... DCPO
Deputy Chief Quartermaster ... DCQM
Deputy Chief Scientific Officer [British] ... DCSO
Deputy Chief Signal Officer [British military] (DMA) ... DCSO
Deputy Chief Veterinary Officer (DAVI) ... DCVO
Deputy Chief Veterinary Officr (BABM) ... DCVO
Deputy Chief-of-Staff Operational Requirements [Army] ... DCSOR
Deputy Chief-of-Staff (Research Development and Logistics) [Air Force] ... DCS(RDL)
Deputy Clerk of Session [British] ... DCS
Deputy Commandant ... DC
Deputy Commandant Royal Engineers [British] ... DCRE
Deputy Commander (DNAB) ... D-CDR
Deputy Commander (DNAB) ... DEPCOM
Deputy Commander, Atlantic Naval Facilities Engineering Command (DNAB) ... DEPCOMLANTNAVFACENGCOM
Deputy Commander, Fleet Electronic Warfare Support Group [Navy] (DNAB) ... DEPCOMFEWSG
Deputy Commander for Logistics (MCD) ... DCL
Deputy Commander for Research and Development [Navy] ... DEPCDR(R & D)
Deputy Commander for Resources [Air Force] (DOMA) ... DCR
Deputy Commander for Ship Acquisitions [Navy] ... DEPCDR(SA)
Deputy Commander, Military Sea Transport Service [Obsolete Navy] ... DEPCOMSTS
Deputy Commander, Naval Striking and Support Forces, Southern Europe (NATG) ... DEPCOMSTRIKFORSOUTH
Deputy Commander of Aerospace Systems [Inglewood, CA] [Air Force] ... DCAS
Deputy Commander of Operations ... DCO
Deputy Commander, Operational Test and Evaluation Force, Atlantic [Navy] (DNAB) ... DEPCOMOPTEVFORLANT
Deputy Commander, Operational Test and Evaluation Force, Pacific [Navy] ... DCOTFP
Deputy Commander, Operational Test and Evaluation Force, Pacific [Navy] ... DEPCOMOPTEVFORPAC
Deputy Commander, Pacific Naval Facilities Engineering Command (DNAB) ... DEPCOMPACNAVFACENGCOM
Deputy Commander, United States Military Assistance Command, Thailand ... DEPCOMUSMACTHAI
Deputy Commander, United States Military Assistance Command, Vietnam ... DEPCOMUSMACV
Deputy Commanding General ... DCG
Deputy Commanding General, Continental Army Command [Later, DCG/T] [Army] ... DCG/CONARC
Deputy Commanding General for International Cooperative Programs [Army] ... DCGICP
Deputy Commanding General for Materiel Development [Army] ... DCGMD
Deputy Commanding General for Materiel Readiness [Army] ... DCGMR
Deputy Commanding General for Research, Development, and Acquisition [Army] ... DCGRDA
Deputy Commanding General, Training [Formerly, DCG/CONARC] [Army] ... DCG/T
Deputy Commanding Officer ... DCO
Deputy Commissary-General ... DCG
Deputy Commissioner [British] (ADA) ... DC
Deputy [Police] Commissioner (LAIN) ... DC
Deputy Commissioner Medical Services [British] (DAS) ... DCMS
Deputy Comptroller (DNAB) ... DEPCOMPT
Deputy Consul ... DC
Deputy Controller of Property [World War II] ... DCP
Deputy Controller (Polaris) [Navy British] ... DC(P)
Deputy Controller (Polaris) [Navy British] ... DCPolaris
Deputy Counsel [British] (ADA) ... DC
Deputy County Architect [British] ... DCA
Deputy Crown Solicitor (ADA) ... DCS
Deputy Director ... DD
Deputy Director ... DEPDIR
Deputy Director [KSC Directorate] (MCD) ... DY
Deputy Director (Attaches and Human Resources) [Defense Intelligence Agency] (DNAB) ... DD(A & HR)
Deputy Director, Auxiliary Territorial Service [British military] (DMA) ... DDATS
Deputy Director, Contract Administration Services [DoD] ... DDCAS
Deputy Director, Contract Administration Services Memorandum [DoD] ... DDCASM
Deputy Director, Defense Research and Engineering [Army] ... DDDRE
Deputy Director, Defense Research and Engineering [OSD] (AAGC) ... DDR&E
Deputy Director, Defense Research and Engineering (Test and Evaluation) [DoD] (DOMA) ... 'DDDR & E (T & E)
Deputy Director for Acquisition Career Management [Army] (RDA) ... DDACM
Deputy Director for Administration [National Security Agency] ... DDA
Deputy Director for Collection [Defense Intelligence Agency] (DNAB) ... DD(C)
Deputy Director for Field Management and Evaluation [National Security Agency] ... DDF
Deputy Director for Intelligence [CIA] (DOMA) ... DDI
Deputy Director for Plans and Policy [National Security Agency] ... DDPP
Deputy Director for Programs and Resources [National Security Agency] ... DDPR
Deputy Director for Support [Defense Intelligence Agency] (DNAB) ... DD(S)
Deputy Director for Test and Evaluation [NASA] ... DD-T & E
Deputy Director, Home Guard [British military] (DMA) ... DDHG
Deputy Director (Information Systems) [Defense Intelligence Agency] (DNAB) ... DD(IS)
Deputy Director, National Security Agency ... D/DIRNSA
Deputy Director of Armament Supply (Eastern Theater) ... DDAS (ET)
Deputy Director of Armaments [British] ... DDA
Deputy Director of Army Nursing Services [British military] (DMA) ... DDANS
Deputy Director of Bomber Operations [Air Ministry] [British World War II] ... DDBOps
Deputy Director of Central Intelligence [CIA] (ECON) ... DDCI
Deputy Director of Civil Affairs [War Office] [British World War II] ... DDCA
Deputy Director of Combined Operations (India) ... DDCO (I)
Deputy Director of Dental Services [Military British] ... DDDS
Deputy Director of Design [British] ... DDD
Deputy Director of Equipment [Air Force British] ... DDE
Deputy Director of Home Operations [Air Ministry] [British World War II] ... DDHO
Deputy Director of Hygiene and Pathology [Military British] ... DDHP
Deputy Director of Inland Water Transport [British military] (DMA) ... DDIWT
Deputy Director of Intelligence [Air Ministry] [British World War II] ... DDI
Deputy Director of Labour [British] ... DDL
Deputy Director of Manpower Planning [Military British] ... DDMP
Deputy Director of Mechanical Engineering [British] ... DDME
Deputy Director of Medical Organization for War [Military British] ... DDMOW
Deputy Director of Medical Services [Military British] ... DDMS
Deputy Director of Military Intelligence [British] ... DDMI
Deputy Director of Military Operations and Intelligence [British] ... DDMOI
Deputy Director of Military Training [British] ... DDMT
Deputy Director of Movements and Quartering [Military British] ... DDMQ
Deputy Director of Naval Construction [British] ... DDNC
Deputy Director of Naval Intelligence [British] ... DDNI
Deputy Director of Operations [Air Force] ... DDO
Deputy Director of Operations and Administration (DNAB) ... DDOA
Deputy Director of Operations and Intelligence [Air Ministry] [British] ... DDOI
Deputy Director of Operations Division [Air Ministry] [British] ... DDOD

Deputy Director of Ordnance Factories, Explosives Factories [*Ministry of Supply*] [*British World War II*] .... DDOF(X)
Deputy Director of Ordnance Services [*British*] .... DDOS
Deputy Director of Organisation [*Air Ministry*] [*British*] .... DDO
Deputy Director of Organisation, Auxiliary Territorial Service [*British military*] (DMA) .... DDOATS
Deputy Director of Personal Services [*Navy British*] .... DDPS
Deputy Director of Plans [*CIA*] .... DDP
Deputy Director of Post-Hostilities Plans [*Military British*] .... DDPHP
Deputy Director of Prisoners of War [*British*] .... DDPOW
Deputy Director of Public Relations [*Military British*] .... DDPR
Deputy Director of Quartering [*Military British*] .... DDQ
Deputy Director of Recruiting and Demobilization [*Military British*] .... DDRD
Deputy Director of Royal Artillery [*Military British*] .... DDRA
Deputy Director of Science [*Military British*] .... DDS
Deputy Director of Selection of Personnel [*Military British*] .... DDSP
Deputy Director of Staff Duties [*Military British*] .... DDSD
Deputy Director of Supply and Transport [*British*] .... DDST
Deputy Director of Tactical Investigation [*Military British*] .... DDTI
Deputy Director of Technical Administration [*Ministry of Supply*] [*British*] .... DDTA
Deputy Director of Veterinary Services [*British military*] (DMA) .... DDVS
Deputy Director of Works, Electrical and Mechanical [*British*] .... DDWE & M
Deputy Director Pacific Division, Bureau of Yards and Docks [*Later, NFEC*] [*Navy*] .... DEPDIRPACDOCKS
Deputy Director (Personnel, Career Development, and Training) [*Defense Intelligence Agency*] (DNAB) .... DD(PCD & T)
Deputy Director, Veterinary Remount Service [*British military*] (DMA) .... DDVRS
Deputy Directorate of Weapons, Polaris [*Navy British*] .... DDWP
Deputy Director-General [*British*] .... DDG
Deputy Director-General of Military Railways [*British military*] (DMA) .... DDGMR
Deputy Director-General of Ordnance Factories [*Ministry of Supply*] [*British World War II*] .... DDGOF
Deputy Director-General of Ordnance Factories, Engineering Factories [*Ministry of Supply*] [*British World War II*] .... DDGOF(E)
Deputy Director-General of Ordnance Factories, Filling Factories [*Ministry of Supply*] [*British World War II*] .... DDGOF(F)
Deputy Director-General of Production [*Ministry of Aircraft Production*] [*British World War II*] .... DDGP
Deputy Director-General of Transportation [*British military*] (DMA) .... DDGT
Deputy Disbursing Officer (DNAB) .... DDO
Deputy Educators Against Narcotics [*Defunct*] .... DEAN
Deputy for Contract Financing [*Air Force*] .... DCF
Deputy for Flight Operations [*NASA*] (KSC) .... DFO
Deputy for Intelligence .... DI
Deputy for Launch Operations [*NASA*] (KSC) .... DLO
Deputy for Materiel .... DM
Deputy for Nuclear Affairs (NATG) .... DNA
Deputy for Operations .... DO
Deputy General Grand High Priest [*Freemasonry*] .... DGGHP
Deputy General Manager [*AEC*] .... DGM
Deputy General Purchasing Agent [*Military*] .... DGPA
Deputy General Secretary (DCTA) .... DGS
Deputy Grand Director of Ceremonies [*Freemasonry*] .... DGDC
Deputy Grand High Priest [*Freemasonry*] .... DGHP
Deputy Grand Marshal (ROG) .... DGM
Deputy Grand Master [*Freemasonry*] .... DGM
Deputy Inspector [*British*] (ROG) .... DI
Deputy Inspector of Naval Ordnance .... DINO
Deputy Inspector-General .... DIG
Deputy Inspector-General for Safety [*Air Force*] .... DIGS
Deputy Inspector-General of Hospitals and Fleet [*Navy British*] (ROG) .... DIH
Deputy Judge Advocate General .... DJAG
Deputy Justice of Peace Clerk [*British*] (ROG) .... DJPC
Deputy Keeper of the Signet (DLA) .... DKS
Deputy Lieutenant [*British*] .... DL
Deputy Local Naval Commander .... DLNC
Deputy Lord Mayor [*British*] (ADA) .... DLM
Deputy Managing Director .... DMD
Deputy Marshal of Ceremonies (ROG) .... DMC
Deputy Master [*Freemasonry*] (ROG) .... DM
Deputy Master-General [*Military British*] .... DMG
Deputy Military Governor [*US Military Government, Germany*] .... DMG
Deputy Military Secretary [*British*] .... DMS
Deputy Missile Combat Crew Commander .... DMCCC
Deputy, Naval Education Development (MCD) .... DNED
Deputy of Space Systems [*Air Force*] .... DSS
Deputy of the Air Member for Supply and Organization [*British*] .... DAMSO
Deputy Operations Deputy [*In JCS system*] [*Military*] .... DEPOPSDEP
Deputy Paymaster in Chief .... DPIC
Deputy Police Commissioner for Public Information (LAIN) .... DCPI
Deputy Prime Minister [*British*] .... DPM
Deputy Principal Officer [*Foreign Service*] .... DPO
Deputy Program Management [*DoD*] .... DPM
Deputy Program Manager (DOMA) .... DPM
Deputy Program Manager for Logistics (AFIT) .... DPML
Deputy Project Manager .... DPM
Deputy Provincial Grand Master [*Freemasonry*] (ROG) .... D PROV GM
Deputy Provincial Grand Master [*Freemasonry*] (ROG) .... DPGM
Deputy Provincial Grand Master [*Freemasonry*] .... DProGM
Deputy Provost Marshal [*British*] .... DPM
Deputy Public Affairs Officer [*United States Information Service*] .... DPAO
Deputy Quartermaster General .... DQMG
Deputy Quartermaster-Sergeant [*British*] .... DQMS
Deputy Regional Administrator .... DRA
Deputy Regional Commander .... DRC
Deputy Regional Counsel (GFGA) .... DRC
Deputy Registrar-General [*British*] .... DR-G
Deputy Remembrancer [*A publication*] (DLA) .... DR
Deputy Safeguard [*Missile defense*] **System Manager** (AABC) .... DSAFSM
Deputy Scientific Adviser [*British*] .... DSA
Deputy Seal Keeper [*British*] (ROG) .... DSK
Deputy Secretary (ADA) .... DEPSEC
Deputy Secretary General (NATG) .... DSG
Deputy Secretary General (NATG) .... DSYG
Deputy Secretary of Defense (AABC) .... DEPSECDEF
Deputy Secretary of Defense .... DSD
Deputy Secretary of the General Staff (Coordination and Reports) [*Army*] (AABC) .... DSGS(CAR)
Deputy Sector Advisor .... DSA
Deputy Senior Advisor .... DSA
Deputy Senior Air Staff Officer [*British military*] (DMA) .... DSASO
Deputy Senior Officer, Assault Group [*British military*] (DMA) .... DSOAG
Deputy Sheriff (DLA) .... DS
Deputy Sheriff Clerk (ROG) .... DSC
Deputy Supreme Allied Commander (AABC) .... DSAC
Deputy Supreme Allied Commander, Atlantic (NATG) .... DEPSACLANT
Deputy Supreme Allied Commander, Europe (NATG) .... DSACEUR
Deputy Supreme Commander, Allied Expeditionary Force .... DSCAEF
Deputy System Manager [*Army*] (AABC) .... DSAFSM
Deputy Under Secretary of Defense (RDA) .... DUSD
Deputy Under Secretary of Defense (Acquisitions) (AAGC) .... DUSD (A)
Deputy Under Secretary of Defense (for Advanced Technology) (RDA) .... DUSD(AT)
Deputy Under Secretary of Defense for Policy .... DUSDP
Deputy Under Secretary of Defense for Research and Engineering (Communications, Command, Control, and Intelligence) [*Military*] .... DUSDRE(C^3I)
Deputy Under Secretary of Defense for Research and Engineering (Test and Evaluation) [*Military*] .... DUSDRE (T & E)
Deputy Under Secretary of Defense-Policy (AAGC) .... DUSD (P)
Deputy Under Secretary of Defense-Test and Evaluation (AAGC) .... DUSD (T&E)
Deputy Under Secretary of the Army (AABC) .... DUSA
Deputy Undersecretary for Field Coordination [*HUD*] .... DUSFC
Deputy Under-Secretary of Defense (Acquisition Policy) (DNAB) .... DUSD(AP)
Deputy Under-Secretary of Defense (Communications, Command, Control, and Intelligence) (DNAB) .... DUSD(C_3I)
Deputy Under-Secretary of Defense (Policy Review) (DNAB) .... DUSD(PR)
Deputy Under-Secretary of the Navy (DNAB) .... DUSN
Deputy Worshipful Master [*Freemasonry*] (ROG) .... DWM
Deputy-Secretary [*British*] .... DS
Deputy-Secretary to the Admiralty [*British*] .... DSA
Depuy, Inc. [*Associated Press*] (SAG) .... Depuy
Depuy, Inc. [*NYSE symbol*] (SAG) .... DPU
DeQueen, AR [*Location identifier FAA*] (FAAL) .... DEQ
Dequeue [*Computer science*] .... DEQ
Dequincy, LA [*Location identifier FAA*] (FAAL) .... DQU
Der Babylonische Talmud [*Goldschmidt*] [*A publication*] (BJA) .... GBT
Der Betrieb-Data Bank [*Handelsblatt GmbH*] [*Germany Information service or system*] (IID) .... DB
Der Bote aus Zion [*Berlin*] [*A publication*] (BJA) .... BZion
Der Deutsche Pionier [*A publication*] (BJA) .... DP
Der Grosse Baumeister aller Welten [*The Grand Architect of the Universe*] [*Freemasonry*] [*German*] .... DGBAW
Der Grosse Brockhaus [*A publication*] .... GB
Der Kleine Pauly [*A publication*] (OCD) .... Kl Pauly
Der Treue Zionswaechter [*Altona*] [*A publication*] (BJA) .... TZ
Dera Ghazi Khan [*Pakistan*] [*ICAO location identifier*] (ICLI) .... OPDG
Dera Ismail Khan [*Pakistan*] [*Airport symbol*] (OAG) .... DSK
Dera Ismail Khan [*Pakistan*] [*ICAO location identifier*] (ICLI) .... OPDI
Derated (GAVI) .... D
Derated Takeoff Engine Pressure Ratio (GAVI) .... DE-TO PR
De-Rating and Rating Appeals [*England and Scotland*] [*A publication*] (DLA) .... DR
De-Rating Appeals [*England*] [*A publication*] (DLA) .... DRA
Derating Factor .... DF
Deraya Air Taxi PT [*Indonesia*] [*ICAO designator*] (FAAC) .... DRY
Derby [*Australia ICAO location identifier*] (ICLI) .... APDB
Derby [*Colorado*] [*Seismograph station code, US Geological Survey Closed*] (SEIS) .... DER
Derby (ROG) .... DERB
Derby [*Australia Airport symbol*] (OAG) .... DRB
Derby [*England*] [*Airport symbol*] (AD) .... DXY
Derby Center, VT [*FM radio station call letters*] .... WMOO
Derby, KS [*FM radio station call letters*] .... KRZZ
Derby Public Library, Derby, CT [*Library symbol Library of Congress*] (LCLS) .... CtDe
Derby Public Library, Derby, KS [*Library symbol Library of Congress*] (LCLS) .... KDe
Derbyshire [*County in England*] .... DERB
Derbyshire [*County in England*] (DAS) .... Derbs
Derbyshire [*County in England*] (ROG) .... DERBSH
Derbyshire [*County in England*] .... DERBY
Derbyshire [*County in England*] (ODBW) .... Derby
Derbyshire [*County in England*] .... DERBYS
Derbyshire England Red Cap Club of America (EA) .... DERCCA
Derbyshire Imperial Yeomanry [*British military*] (DMA) .... DIY
Derbyshire Yeomanry [*British military*] (DMA) .... DY
Derecha Democratica Espanola [*Spanish Right-Wing Democratic Party*] (PPW) .... DDP
Derecha Emergente de Venezuela [*Political party*] (EY) .... DEV

Derecho de Importacion Centroamericano [*Central American Import Right*] [*Central American Common Market*] (EY) .... DICA
Derekh Erets Rabbah [*or Derek Erez Rabbah*] (BJA) .... DER
Derekh 'Erets Zuta [*or Derek Erez Zuta*] (BJA) .... DEZ
Derigidize (NASA) .... DERIGID
DeRigo SPA [*NYSE symbol*] (SAG) .... DER
DeRigo SPA [*Associated Press*] (SAG) .... DeRigo
Derim [*Papua New Guinea*] [*Airport symbol*] (OAG) .... DER
Deringer Duell Head Process .... DDHP
Derivable (ABBR) .... DERIVB
Derivation [*or Derivative*] (IAA) .... D
Derivation [*or Derivative*] .... DER
Derivation [*or Derivative*] .... DERIV
Derivation (ABBR) .... DERIVN
Derivation & Tabulation Associates, Inc. [*Information service or system*] (IID) .... DATA
Derivation of Frequency with Respect to Time (IAA) .... DF
Derivative (WGA) .... D
Derivative (ABBR) .... DERIVV
Derivative Activation Analysis [*Analytical chemistry*] .... DAA
Derivative Cyclic Voltammetry [*Analytical electrochemistry*] .... DCV
Derivative Differential Thermal Analysis (PDAA) .... DDTA
Derivative Fighter Engine .... DFE
Derivative of Chromosome [*Genetics*] (DAVI) .... der
Derivative Program (MCD) .... DERIVP
Derivative Thermogravimetry .... DTG
Derivative Ultraviolet Absorption Spectrometer [*Instrumentation*] .... DUVAS
Derived (ROG) .... DER
Derived (ROG) .... DERIV
Derived (ABBR) .... DERIVD
Derived Air Concentration (MCD) .... DAC
Derived Attainable Performance [*Industrial engineering*] .... DAP
Derived Concentration Guide .... DCG
Derived Delta Modulation .... DDM
Derived Emergency Reference Level [*of radiation*] .... DERL
Derived File Access Method [*Computer science*] (PDAA) .... DFAM
Derived Limit (PDAA) .... DL
Derived Operand (MCD) .... DO
Derived Services Network [*Telecommunications*] (NITA) .... DSN
Derived Services Switching Centre (NITA) .... DSSC
Derived Working Limit (NUCP) .... DWL
Deriving (ABBR) .... DERIVG
Derjaguin-Landau-Verwey-Overbeek [*Colloid science*] .... DLVO
Derjaguin-Landau-Verwey-Overbeek Theory [*Stability of colloidal dispersions*] .... DLVO Theory
Derlan Industries Ltd. [*Toronto Stock Exchange symbol*] .... DRL
Derma [*Skin*] [*Medicine*] (ROG) .... DERM
Derma Sciences [*NASDAQ symbol*] (TTSB) .... DSCI
Derma Sciences, Inc. [*Associated Press*] (SAG) .... DermaSci
Derma Sciences, Inc. [*NASDAQ symbol*] (SAG) .... DSCI
Dermal Clinical Evaluation Society .... DCES
Derma-Lock Medical Corp. [*Norway*] (NQ) .... DERM
Dermatan Sulfate [*Biochemistry*] .... DS
Dermatine .... DER
Dermatitis [*Medicine*] .... DERM
Dermatitis Herpetiformis [*Medicine*] .... DH
Dermatofibrosarcoma Protuberans [*Oncology*] .... DFSP
Dermatologist [*or Dermatology*] .... D
Dermatologist .... DERMTLGST
Dermatology (DAVI) .... DER
Dermatology [*or Dermatologist*] .... DERM
Dermatology (ABBR) .... DERMAT
Dermatology .... DERMATOL
Dermatology .... DERN
Dermatology and Syphilology [*Medicine*] (MAE) .... D & S
Dermatology and Syphilology Technician [*Navy*] .... DST
Dermatology Foundation (EA) .... DF
Dermatology Nurses' Association (EA) .... DNA
Dermatomyositis [*Medicine*] .... DM
Dermatomyositis [*Medicine*] .... DMS
Dermatopathology [*Medical specialty*] (DHSM) .... DMP
Dermatophagoides pteronyssinus [*House dust*] .... Dp
Dermatophagoides pteronyssinus [*House dust*] .... Dpt
Dermatophyte (ABBR) .... DERM
Dermatophyte Test Medium (AAMN) .... DTM
Dermoepidermal Junction [*Anatomy*] .... DEJ
Dermonecrotic Toxin [*Immunology*] .... DNT
Dermo-Optical Perception [*Parapsychology*] .... DOP
Dermorphin [*Biochemistry*] .... DM
Dermott, AR [*AM radio station call letters*] .... KGPL
Dermott, AR [*FM radio station call letters*] .... KXSA-FM
Derogatis Sexual Functioning Inventory [*Psychology*] .... DSFI
Derogatis Stress Profile [*Personality development test*] [*Psychology*] .... DSP
Derogatory (DCTA) .... DEROG
Derotational Varus Osteotomy [*Orthopedics*] (DAVI) .... DVR
Derrick (DS) .... DR
Derrick (MSA) .... DRK
Derricks (DS) .... DER
Derry, NH [*AM radio station call letters*] .... WDER
Derry, NH [*Television station call letters*] .... WNDS
Dersam [*New York*] [*Seismograph station code, US Geological Survey*] (SEIS) .... DNY
DeRuyter, NY [*FM radio station call letters*] .... WVOA
Derwent Classes [*Database terminology*] (NITA) CL
Derwent Classification [*Database terminology*] (NITA) CL

Derwent Public Library, Alberta [*Library symbol National Library of Canada*] (NLC) .... ADER
Derwent Public Library, Derwent, AB, Canada [*Library symbol*] [*Library of Congress*] (LCLS) .... CaADer
Derwent Valley Environment Group [*Australia*] .... DVEG
Des Laufenden Monats [*Of the Current Month*] [*German*] .... DLM
Des Moines [*Diocesan abbreviation*] [*Iowa*] (TOCD) .... DM
Des Moines [*Iowa*] [*Seismograph station code, US Geological Survey Closed*] (SEIS) .... DMI
Des Moines [*Iowa*] [*Airport symbol*] (OAG) .... DSM
Des Moines [*Iowa*] [*ICAO location identifier*] (ICLI) .... KDSM
Des Moines & Central Iowa Railway Co. [*AAR code*] .... DCI
Des Moines Area Community College, Ankeny, IA [*Library symbol Library of Congress*] (LCLS) .... IaAnkD
Des Moines County Historical Society, Burlington, IA [*Library symbol Library of Congress*] (LCLS) .... IaBDHi
Des Moines County News, West Burlington, IA [*Library symbol Library of Congress*] (LCLS) .... IaWbuN
Des Moines, IA [*Television station call letters*] .... KCCI
Des Moines, IA [*FM radio station call letters*] .... KDFR
Des Moines, IA [*Television station call letters*] .... KDIN
Des Moines, IA [*FM radio station call letters*] .... KDMI
Des Moines, IA [*AM radio station call letters*] (RBYB) .... KDMI-AM
Des Moines, IA [*Television station call letters*] .... KDPS
Des Moines, IA [*Television station call letters*] .... KDSM
Des Moines, IA [*FM radio station call letters*] .... KGGO
Des Moines, IA [*FM radio station call letters*] .... KHKI
Des Moines, IA [*AM radio station call letters*] .... KIOA
Des Moines, IA [*FM radio station call letters*] .... KIOA-FM
Des Moines, IA [*AM radio station call letters*] .... KKDM
Des Moines, IA [*AM radio station call letters*] .... KKSO
Des Moines, IA [*FM radio station call letters*] .... KLYF
Des Moines, IA [*FM radio station call letters*] .... KRNT
Des Moines, IA [*FM radio station call letters*] .... KSTZ
Des Moines, IA [*FM radio station call letters*] .... KUCB
Des Moines, IA [*AM radio station call letters*] .... KWKY
Des Moines, IA [*AM radio station call letters*] (RBYB) .... KXTK-AM
Des Moines, IA [*Location identifier FAA*] (FAAL) .... VGU
Des Moines, IA [*AM radio station call letters*] .... WHO
Des Moines, IA [*Television station call letters*] .... WHO-TV
Des Moines Metropolitan Service Area Library Cooperative, Des Moines, IA [*Library symbol Library of Congress*] (LCLS) .... IaDmMet
Des Moines Public Library, Des Moines, IA [*Library symbol Library of Congress*] (LCLS) .... IaDm
Des Moines Register-Tribune, Des Moines, IA [*Library symbol Library of Congress*] (LCLS) .... IaDmRT
Des Moines Union Railway Co. [*AAR code*] .... DMU
Des Plaines, IL [*FM radio station call letters*] .... WYLL
Desacetylvincaleukoblastine .... DAVLB
Desaguadero [*Bolivia*] [*Seismograph station code, US Geological Survey Closed*] (SEIS) .... DSG
DeSales Secular Institute (EA) .... DSI
Desalinization (ABBR) .... DESAL
Desalkylflurazepam [*Sedative*] .... DAF
Desalter (MSA) .... DSLTR
Desaparagine Insulin [*Pharmacology*] .... DAA
Desarrollo Quimico Industrial, SA [*Spain*] .... DEQUISA
Desaturated (NASA) .... DESAT
Desaturated Phosphatidylcholine [*Biochemistry*] .... DPC
Desaussure. South Carolina Equity Reports [*1784-1816*] [*A publication*] (DLA) .... Des
Desaussure. South Carolina Equity Reports [*A publication*] (DLA) .... Desaus
Desaussure. South Carolina Equity Reports [*A publication*] (DLA) .... Desaus Eq
Desborough [*England*] .... DESB
DesBrisay Museum and National Exhibit Centre, Bridgewater, Nova Scotia [*Library symbol National Library of Canada*] (NLC) .... NSBDM
DesBrisay Museum and National Exhibit Centre, Bridgewater, NS, Canada [*Library symbol*] [*Library of Congress*] (LCLS) .... CaNSBDM
Desbromoleptophos [*Insecticide*] .... DBL
Desc S.A. ADS [*NYSE symbol*] (TTSB) .... DES
Desc SA de CV [*NYSE symbol*] (SAG) .... DES
Desc SA de CV [*Associated Press*] (SAG) .... DescSA
Descend .... DESC
Descend [*Aviation*] (FAAC) .... DSND
Descend at Pilot's Discretion [*Aviation*] (FAAC) .... DAPD
Descend Immediately [*Aviation*] (FAAC) .... DSNDI
Descend on Course [*Aviation*] .... DOC
Descend So as to Cross [*Aviation*] (FAAC) .... DSATX
Descend So as to Reach [*Aviation*] (FAAC) .... DSATR
Descend To [*Aviation*] .... DES
Descend to and Cross [*Aviation*] (FAAC) .... DTAX
Descend to and Cruise [*Aviation*] (FAAC) .... DCRZ
Descend to and Maintain [*Aviation*] (FAAC) .... DTAM
Descend Well to Right [*Aviation*] (FAAC) .... DWTR
Descend Well to Right of Course [*Aviation*] (FAAC) .... DWRC
Descendant (WDAA) .... DESC
Descendant .... DESCDT
Descendants of Black African Natives in the American North [*Proposed appellation*] .... DOBANIAN
Descendants of Founders of New Jersey (EA) .... DFNJ
Descendants of Mexican War Veterans [*An association*] (EA) .... DMWV
Descendants of the Illegitimate Sons and Daughters of the Kings of Britain (EA) .... DISDKB
Descendants of the New Jersey Settlers (EA) .... DNJS
Descendants of the Signers of the Declaration of Independence (EA) .... DSDI

Descending Aorta [*Anatomy*] ... DA
Descending Medial Longitudinal Fasciculus ... DMLF
Descending Neuron [*Neurology*] ... DN
Descending Node Orbit (MCD) ... DNO
Descent (KSC) ... DES
Descent (NASA) ... DESC
Descent [*Aviation*] (FAAC) ... DSCNT
Descent (KSC) ... DSNT
Descent Advisor [*FAA*] (TAG) ... DA
Descent Advisor (GAVI) ... DA
Descent and Distribution [*Legal term*] (DLA) ... DESC & D
Descent Battery Pack (KSC) ... DBP
Descent Engine [*NASA*] (KSC) ... DE
Descent Engine Control Assembly [*Apollo*] [*NASA*] ... DECA
Descent Orbit Insertion [*Aerospace*] ... DOI
Descent Performance Test ... DPT
Descent Power System [*NASA*] ... DPS
Descent Propulsion System ... DPS
Descent Rate Indicator [*Aviation*] ... DRI
Descent Rate RADAR ... DRR
Descent Stage [*NASA*] (KSC) ... DS
Descent State [*NASA*] (KSC) ... D/S
Descent System ... DS
Deschutes County Library, Bend, OR [*Library symbol Library of Congress*] (LCLS) ... OrBe
Describe (KSC) ... DESCR
Describe Each Element in the Procedure (PDAA) ... DEEP
Describe Macro Language [*Computer science*] ... DML
Described (ROG) ... DESCRD
Describing Function ... DF
Describing Function Analyzer [*NASA*] ... DFA
Descripcion del Patrimonio Historico-Artistico Espanol [*Database*] [*Ministerio de Cultura*] [*Spanish*] [*Information service or system*] (CRD) ... DPHA
Description (MCD) ... DESC
Description (MSA) ... DESCP
Description ... DESCRON
Description (ABBR) ... DESCRPN
Description and Instructions ... DI
Description and Operations (NASA) ... D & O
Description and Operations ... D & O
Description, Installation, and Maintenance ... DIM
Description of Leaf (ROG) ... DL
Description of Proposed Actions and Alternatives [*Military*] ... DOPAA
Description, Operation, and Maintenance ... DOM
Description Pattern ... DP
Descriptive Cataloging of Rare Books [*American Library Association*] ... DCRB
Descriptive Intermediate Attributed Notation for ADA [*Computer science*] (NITA) ... DIANA
Descriptive Item File ... DIF
Descriptive Language Implemented by Macroprocessors ... DLIMP
Descriptive Macro Code Generation System [*Computer science*] ... DMACS
Descriptive Macro Simulation Language [*Computer science*] (PDAA) ... DMSL
Descriptive Macro-Code Generation System (DNAB) ... DMCGS
Descriptive Method ... DM
Descriptive Method Item Identification [*DoD*] ... DMII
Descriptive Test of Mathematics Skills (EDAC) ... DTMS
Descriptive Tests of Language Skills (EDAC) ... DTLS
Descriptive Video Services [*for the sight-impaired*] [*Public Broadcasting Service*] ... DVS
Descriptor [*Online database field identifier*] ... DE
Descriptor (NITA) ... DES
Descriptor [*Computer science*] ... DSCRP
Descriptor Attribute Matrix ... DAM
Descriptor Base Register [*Computer science*] (IAA) ... DBR
Descriptor Code [*Database terminology*] (NITA) ... DC
Descriptor Database System ... DDBS
Descriptor Entry Version [*Database terminology*] (NITA) ... DE
Descriptor Justification Form [*ERIC*] ... DJF
Descriptor Privilege Level [*Computer science*] (BYTE) ... DPL
Descriptor Queue Element [*Computer science*] (IAA) ... DQE
Descriptor Word Index ... DWI
Desen Computer Industries, Inc. [*Vancouver Stock Exchange symbol*] ... DCP
Desensitization Test [*Allergy*] ... DST
Desensitize (MSA) ... DSNTZ
Desensitized Fertilizer-Grade Ammonium Nitrate [*Nonexplosive*] ... DEFGAN
Deseret Medical, Inc., Sandy, UT [*Library symbol*] [*Library of Congress*] (LCLS) ... USaD
Deseronto, ON [*Television station call letters*] ... CJOH-6
Deseronto Public Library, Ontario [*Library symbol National Library of Canada*] (NLC) ... ODES
Desert [*Hawaii*] [*Seismograph station code, US Geological Survey*] (SEIS) ... DES
Desert [*Board on Geographic Names*] ... DSRT
Desert ... DSRT
Desert Air Force [*British*] ... DAF
Desert Battle Dress Uniform [*Military*] (INF) ... DBDU
Desert Bighorn Council (EA) ... DBC
Desert Biome [*Ecological biogeographic study*] ... DB
Desert Botanical Garden [*An association*] (EA) ... DBG
Desert Botanical Garden [*An association*] (EA) ... DES
Desert Camouflage Uniform [*Military*] ... DCU
Desert Center, CA [*FM radio station call letters*] ... KZAL
Desert Community Bank [*NASDAQ symbol*] (SAG) ... DCBK
Desert Community Bank [*Associated Press*] (SAG) ... Desert
Desert Field Exercise [*Military*] (NVT) ... DESFEX
Desert Firing Exercise [*Military*] (NVT) ... DESFIREX
Desert Fishes Council (EA) ... DFC
Desert Hot Springs [*California*] [*Seismograph station code, US Geological Survey Closed*] (SEIS) ... DHS
Desert Locust Control Committee [*Food and Agriculture Organization*] [*United Nations*] (EA) ... DLCC
Desert Mobility Vehicle System [*Army*] ... DMVS
Desert National Wildlife Range ... DNWR
Desert Pacific [*ICAO designator*] (AD) ... NP
Desert Protective Council (EA) ... DPC
Desert Research Institute [*University of Nevada*] [*Research center*] ... DRI
Desert Rose Resources [*Vancouver Stock Exchange symbol*] ... DRO
Desert Test Center [*Fort Douglas, UT*] [*Army*] (AABC) ... DTC
Desert Tortoise Council (EA) ... DTC
Desert Tortoise Preserve Committee (EA) ... DTPC
Desert Training Center [*Army*] ... DTC
Deserted Medieval Village [*British*] ... DMV
Deserter [*Military*] ... D
Deserter [*Military*] (AABC) ... DSTR
Deserter's Effects [*Military*] ... DESEFF
Desertification Information System [*UNEP*] [*United Nations*] (DUND) ... DESIS
Desertification Library [*Database*] [*UNEP*] [*United Nations*] (DUND) ... DELI
Desertion ... DES
Deservicing, Maintenance, and Checkout Facility [*NASA*] (NASA) ... DMCF
Deserving Airman Commissioning Program [*Military*] ... DACP
Desethylamiodarone [*Biochemistry*] ... DEA
Desferrioxamine [*Also, Deferoxamine*] [*A chelating agent*] ... DES
Desferrioxamine [*Deferoxamine*] [*Pharmacology*] (DAVI) ... DF
Desferrioxamine [*Also, Deferoxamine*] [*A chelating agent*] (AAMN) ... DFO
Desglycinamide-Arginine-Vasopressin [*Antidiuretic*] ... DGAVP
Deshapremi Janatha Viyaparaya [*Patriotic People's Organisation*] [*Sri Lanka*] [*Political party*] ... DJV
Deshoo [*Afghanistan*] [*ICAO location identifier*] (ICLI) ... OAOO
Desialylated Ovine Submaxillary Mucin [*Biochemistry*] ... DOSM
Desiccant [*Chemistry*] ... DSCC
Desiccant-Enhanced Radiative Cooling [*Solar-cooling concept*] ... DESRAD
Desiderata (ABBR) ... DESID
Desiderative (ABBR) ... DESIDER
Desideratum [*Wanted*] [*Latin*] (ADA) ... DESID
Desiderius Pastor [*Pseudonym used by Gerard Moultree*] ... DP
Design (AAG) ... D
Design (NASA) ... DES
Design (VRA) ... des
Design ... DGN
Design (AFM) ... DSGN
Design ... DSGN
Design Acceptance [*or Approval*] **Test** ... DAT
Design Acceptance [*or Approval*] **Test Report** ... DATR
Design Accreditation and Certification Advisers (AIE) ... DACA
Design Action Request (MCD) ... DAR
Design Action to Follow ... DAF
Design Advisory Group (IAA) ... DAG
Design Agent (CAAL) ... DA
Design Aid for Post-Processors [*IBM Corp.*] ... DAPP
Design Aids for Real-Time Systems [*Computer science*] (MCD) ... DARTS
Design Analysis Language [*Programming language*] ... DAL
Design Analysis System (MCD) ... DAS
Design and Art Technician Education Council (AIE) ... DATEC
Design and Artists Copyright Society Ltd. [*British*] ... DACS
Design and Computational Experiments ... DACE
Design and Demonstration Electronic Computer (MHDB) ... DADEC
Design and Development (SSD) ... D & D
Design and Development (ADA) ... DAD
Design and Drafting Management Council [*Defunct*] (EA) ... DDMC
Design and Drafting Techniques ... DDT
Design and Industries Association [*British*] ... DIA
Design and Performance Specification (MCD) ... D & PS
Design and Procedure Standard [*NASA*] ... DPS
Design and Production ... D & P
Design and Programming Language (IAA) ... DPL
Design and Technology Association (AIE) ... DATA
Design and Technology in Education (AIE) ... DESTECH
Design and Test Alliance [*Technology research group*] ... DTA
Design and Verification Routine [*Sperry Univac*] (NITA) ... DVR
Design Approval Data ... DAD
Design Approval Layout (SAA) ... DAL
Design Approval Primary Inspection Agency [*Department of Housing and Urban Development*] (GFGA) ... DAPIA
Design Approval Test (DNAB) ... DAT
Design, Architecture, Software, and Testing (MCD) ... DAST
Design Assessment Report [*Nuclear energy*] (NRCH) ... DAR
Design Augmented by Computer [*General Motors Corp.*] ... DAC
Design Authorization ... DA
Design Automation (BUR) ... DA
Design Automation Routing Tool (IAA) ... DART
Design Bandwidth ... DBW
Design Baseline (NASA) ... DB
Design Baseline Program (MCD) ... DBP
Design Basis Accident [*Nuclear energy*] ... DBA
Design Basis Depressurization Accident [*Nuclear energy*] (NRCH) ... DBDA
Design Basis Earthquake [*Nuclear energy*] (NRCH) ... DBE
Design Basis Event [*Nuclear energy*] (NRCH) ... DBE
Design Basis Fault [*Nuclear energy*] (NRCH) ... DBF
Design Basis Flooding Level [*Nuclear energy*] (NRCH) ... DBFL
Design Basis Incident [*Nuclear energy*] (NRCH) ... DBI
Design Basis Pipe Break [*Nuclear energy*] (NRCH) ... DBPB

Design Basis Tornado [*Nuclear energy*] (NRCH)	DBT
Design, Build, Operate, Maintain	DBOM
Design Burst (KSC)	DB
Design Business Group [*British*] (DBA)	DBG
Design Capability Line [*Army*] (AABC)	DCL
Design Center of Connecticut Technology	DCCT
Design Certificate Board	DCB
Design Certification Review [*NASA*] (KSC)	DCR
Design Change (AAG)	DC
Design Change Approval Committee (SAA)	DCAC
Design Change Authorization (KSC)	DCA
Design Change Clearance Sheet (MCD)	DCCS
Design Change Control	DCC
Design Change Control Program	DCCP
Design Change Coordination Committee (SAA)	DCCC
Design Change Cost Analysis (PDAA)	DCCA
Design Change Document	DCD
Design Change Information (SAA)	DCI
Design Change Listing	DCL
Design Change Notice	DCN
Design Change Package (IEEE)	DCP
Design Change Proposal	DCP
Design Change Recommendation [*or Request*]	DCR
Design Change Request Engineering Order	DCREO
Design Change Request Serial Engineering Order (MCD)	DCRSEO
Design Change Review Board	DCRB
Design Change Schedule	DCS
Design Change Summary (AAG)	DCS
Design Change Verification	DCV
Design Change Work Order	DCWO
Design Characteristic Review (AAG)	DCR
Design Communication Algorithm (MCD)	DECAL
Design Communication System (MCD)	DCS
Design Competition Phase (AAGC)	DCP
Design Concept	DC
Design Concept Change (AAG)	DCC
Design Concern Report (NASA)	DCR
Design Contractor (NRCH)	DC
Design Control Drawing	DCD
Design Control Specification (KSC)	DCS
Design Controlled Repair Parts (MCD)	DCRP
Design Cooperative [*British*]	DC
Design Corrective Action Form	DCAF
Design Corrective Action Report (NASA)	DCAR
Design Council [*British*] (DI)	DC
Design Criteria Plan (IEEE)	DCP
Design Criteria Specification (NASA)	DCS
Design Data Book	DDB
Design Data Package	DDP
Design Data Sheet [*Naval Ship Engineering Center*]	DDS
Design Data Transmittal (NRCH)	DDT
Design Decision Memo (MCD)	DDM
Design Decision Notice (MCD)	DDN
Design Definition Document [*NASA*] (NASA)	DDD
Design, Development, Fabrication, Testing	DDFT
Design Development Plan (NASA)	DDP
Design Development Record (MCD)	DDR
Design Development Test	DDT
Design, Development, Test, and Evaluation	DDT & E
Design Deviation [*Aerospace*] (AAG)	DD
Design Direction Approval [*Automotive project management*]	DDA
Design Discharge Format	DDF
Design Disclosure Data	DDD
Design Disclosure for Systems and Equipment	DDSE
Design Disclosure Formats [*Naval Applied Science Laboratory*]	DDF
Design Disclosure Standard	DDS
Design Drafting Reference Information	DDRI
Design Effect [*Ratio used in statistics*]	DEFT
Design Electrical Rating [*Nuclear energy*] (NRCH)	DER
Design Engine Inspection (AFM)	DEI
Design Engineer	DGE
Design Engineering (KSC)	DE
Design Engineering Analysis [*Army*]	DEA
Design Engineering Directorate (KSC)	DED
Design Engineering Identification (NASA)	DEI
Design Engineering Inspection Simulation (NASA)	DEIS
Design Engineering Program [*Military*]	DEP
Design Engineering Show and Conference (ITD)	DES
Design Engineering Support (MCD)	DES
Design Engineers Field Experience with Soldiers [*Army*] (RDA)	DEFEWS
Design Evaluation	DE
Design Evaluation Inspection Simulator (NASA)	DEIS
Design Evaluation/Qualification (KSC)	DE/Q
Design Evaluation Test	DET
Design Evaluation Vehicle	DEV
Design Expansion System	DES
Design External Pressure (NRCH)	DEP
Design Eye Point [*Cockpit visibility*]	DEP
Design Fabrication Assembly	DFA
Design Failure-Mode Analysis	DFMA
Design Failure-Mode Effects Analysis [*Automotive engineering*]	DFMEA
Design Feasibility Test	DFT
Design Field Change (NRCH)	DFC
Design for Assembly [*Automotive engineering*]	DFA
Design for Automation [*Manufacturing technology*]	DFA

Design for Maintainability (RDA)	DFM
Design for Manufacture and Assembly (RDA)	DFMA
Design for Manufacturing	DFM
Design for Manufacturing and Assembly	DFMA
Design for Reliability (RDA)	DFR
Design for Testability [*Military*]	DFT
Design Formula	DF
Design Guidance Package [*Military*] (CAAL)	DGP
Design Guide [*Army Corps of Engineers*] (AAGC)	DG
Design Handbook	DH
Design Hazard Analysis (MCD)	DHA
Design History Society [*British*] (DBA)	DHS
Design Hourly Volume [*Transportation*]	DHV
Design Implementation Guide [*Telecommunications*] (TEL)	DIG
Design Improvement Program	DIP
Design Improvement Study	DIS
Design Industries Foundation for AIDS [*Acquired Immune Deficiency Syndrome*] (EA)	DIFFA
Design Information Bulletin	DIB
Design Information Manual (KSC)	DIM
Design Information Release	DIR
Design Information Worksheet	DIW
Design Institute for Physical Property Data [*AIChE*]	DIPPR
Design Institute of Australia	DIA
Design Institute of Australia Federal Secretariat	DIA-FS
Design Integration (DNAB)	DI
Design Integration Sheet (MCD)	DIS
Design Integration Subsystem	DIS
Design Interface Meeting (NASA)	DIM
Design Internal Pressure [*Nuclear energy*] (NRCH)	DIP
Design International (EA)	DI
[*A*] Design Language for Indicating Behavior [*1967*] [*Computer science*] (CSR)	ADLIB
Design Layout Report Date [*Telecommunications*] (TEL)	DLRD
Design Limit and Endurance	DL & E
Design Limit Load Factor	DLIF
Design Limit Load Factor (MCD)	DLLF
Design Load Limit (MSA)	DLL
Design, Manage, Construct	DMC
Design Management Award [*Financial Times and London Business School*] [*British*]	DMA
Design Management Institute (EA)	DMI
Design Manual	DM
Design Margin Evaluation (NG)	DME
Design Memorandum	DM
Design Mission Effect	DME
Design Mission Evaluation	DME
Design Modified	DM
Design Objective (IEEE)	DO
Design Objective Reliability	DOR
Design of Advanced Fossil Fuel System	DAFFS
Design of Aircraft Wing Structures [*Computer program*]	DAWNS
Design of Data Acquisition Subsystem (NOAA)	DDAS
Design of Experiments [*Army*] (RDA)	DOE
Design Office Language [*Computer science*]	DOLAN
Design Operation Capability (MCD)	DOC
Design Optimization Codes for Structures (MCD)	DOCS
Design Option Decision Tree	DODT
Design Organization, Record, Analyze, Charge, Estimate (MHDB)	DORACE
Design Performance Optimization (NASA)	DESPOT
Design Point Vehicle	DPV
Design Professions Technical Specialty Index [*National Society of Professional Engineers*] [*Information service or system*] (IID)	DPTSI
Design Proof (NASA)	DP
Design Proof Tests	DPT
Design Proof Unit (KSC)	DPU
Design Proposal	DP
Design Qualification (MCD)	DQ
Design Qualification Requirement	DQR
Design Qualification Test Plan (MCD)	DQTP
Design Quality Assurance [*Telecommunications*] (TEL)	DQA
Design, Quality, Reliabilty	DQR
Design Realization, Evaluation, and Modelling (MHDI)	DREAM
Design Reference Mission [*NASA*]	DRM
Design Reference Mission Profile [*DoD*]	DRMP
Design Reference Model (KSC)	DRM
Design Reference Timeline (MCD)	DRT
Design Release Engineering Change Proposal (MCD)	DRECP
Design Release [*or Request*] Review	DRR
Design Requirement	DR
Design Requirement Drawing (MCD)	DRD
Design Requirement Sheet [*Military*]	DRS
Design Requirements Baseline (NASA)	DRB
Design Requirements Baseline	DRBL
Design Requirements Review [*NASA*] (NASA)	DRR
Design Research Center [*Carnegie-Mellon University*] [*Research center*] (RCD)	DRC
Design Review (AAG)	DR
Design Review Agreement (MCD)	DRA
Design Review and Acceptance Group [*Reviews nuclear weapon designs for DoD*]	DRAAG
Design Review Board	DRB
Design Review List (MCD)	DRL
Design Rock-Mass Strength [*Mining technology*]	DRMS
Design Rule Checker [*For integrated circuitry*]	DRC

Design Safety Criteria [*Nuclear energy*] (NRCH) ... DSC
Design Safety Factor ... DSF
Design Schedule Analysis ... DSA
Design Science Institute ... DSI
Design Section Drawing Record (MCD) ... DSDR
Design Selection Specification Engineer ... DSSE
Design Services Allocation (DNAB) ... DSA
Design Sheet ... DS
Design Simulator ... DESSIM
Design Specification (MCD) ... DS
Design Specification ... DSPEC
Design Specification ... DSS
Design Speed for Maximum Gust Intensity (GAVI) ... VS
Design Standards ... DS
Design Standards Manual (AAG) ... DSM
Design Stop Order ... DSO
Design Studies Evaluation Group [*NATO*] ... DSEG
Design Support Test (MCD) ... DST
Design Systems Group (HGAA) ... DSG
Design Technical Information [*or Instruction*] (KSC) ... DTI
Design [*or Development*], Test, and Mission Operations [*NASA*] ... DTMO
Design/Test Contractor (KSC) ... DTC
Design Test Model ... DTM
Design Thermal Transient [*Nuclear energy*] (NRCH) ... DTT
Design to Cost (MCD) ... DTC
Design to Cost / Life Cycle Cost (SSD) ... DTC/LCC
Design to Cut (MHDB) ... DTC
Design to Life-Cycle Cost ... DTLCC
Design to Operations and Support Cost ... DTOSC
Design to Price (NVT) ... DTP
Design to Unit Production Cost [*Army*] ... DTUPC
Design Transition Temperature (NRCH) ... DTT
Design under Design ... DUD
Design Verification Demonstration ... DVD
Design Verification Period (MCD) ... DVP
Design Verification Plan and Report ... DVPR
Design Verification Program [*or Plan*] (MCD) ... DVP
Design Verification Rig (MCD) ... DVR
Design Verification Specification (NASA) ... DVS
Design Verification Test ... DVT
Design Work Study ... DWS
Design Year [*DoD*] ... DY
Design-and-Build (ECON) ... D & B
Designate (AFM) ... DESG
Designate [*or Designation*] (KSC) ... DESIG
Designate (AABC) ... DSG
Designate (AFM) ... DSGN
Designate Command Line [*Computer science*] ... DCL
Designate Senior Official (AAGC) ... DSO
Designated (FAAC) ... DSGND
Designated Acquisition Program ... DAP
Designated Adult [*Most serious person in a group of flippant people*] ... DA
Designated Agency Ethics Official (AAGC) ... DAEO
Designated Aircraft Maintenance Inspector ... DAMI
Designated Alert Detachment [*Military*] (MCD) ... DAD
Designated Approval Authority (MCD) ... DAA
Designated as Naval Aviation Pilot [*Marine Corps*] ... DESIGNAP
Designated Deployment Area ... DDA
Designated Development Agency (MCD) ... DDA
Designated Disabled Persons Liaison Officer (AIE) ... DDPLO
Designated Engineer Representative [*FAA title*] (AFM) ... DER
Designated Field Activity [*DoD*] ... DFA
Designated for Prompt Mobilization ... DPM
Designated Force Potential [*Military*] ... DFP
Designated Ground Zero (MSA) ... DGZ
Designated Hitter [*Formerly, DPH*] [*Also, DH Baseball*] ... DESI
Designated Hitter [*Formerly, DPH*] [*Also, DESI Baseball*] ... DH
Designated Independent Senior Acquisition Official (AAGC) ... DISAO
Designated Industry Group (AAGC) ... DIG
Designated Inspection Points (MCD) ... DIP
Designated Maintenance Activity (MCD) ... DMA
Designated Manufacturing Inspection Representative (MCD) ... DMIR
Designated Market Area [*Advertising*] ... DMA
Designated Mechanic Examiners ... DME
Designated National Agency [*for exchange of oceanographic data*] (MSC) ... DNA
Designated Official (NRCH) ... DO
Designated Official for Environmental Matters (GNE) ... DOEM
Designated Operational Coverage (DA) ... DOC
Designated Order Turnaround [*NYSE term*] ... DOT
Designated Overhaul Point ... DOP
Designated Pinch Hitter [*Later, DH*] [*Baseball*] ... DPH
Designated Processing Agency (MCD) ... DPA
Designated Procuring Activity (MCD) ... DPA
Designated Project Manager ... DPM
Designated Qualified Person [*Department of Agriculture*] ... DQP
Designated Repair [*or Rework*] **Point** [*Military*] (CAAL) ... DRP
Designated Responsible Activity (MCD) ... DRA
Designated Security Agency (NATG) ... DSA
Designated Security-Assessed Position ... DSAP
Designated Self-Regulatory Organization (MHDB) ... DSRO
Designated Special Disbursing Agent ... DESIGDISBAGENT
Designated Special Emphasis Engineering (KSC) ... DSEE
Designated Spouse Equivalent ... DSE
Designated Stock Point ... DSP
Designated Student and Naval Flight Surgeon (DNAB) ... DESFLTSURG
Designated Student Naval Aviator ... DESNAVAV
Designated Subsystems Project Manager [*NASA*] (NASA) ... DSPM
Designated Systems Management Group [*Military*] ... DSMG
Designated Systems Management Group [*Military*] ... DSMGP
Designated Work Group ... DWG
Designating Optical Tracker [*Telescope*] ... DOT
Designation Accuracy Test Equipment ... DATE
Designation Acquisition Track (IAA) ... DAT
Designation Equipment ... DE
Designation Indicator ... DI
Designator (KSC) ... DES
Designator ... dsgnr
Designator Detection System (MCD) ... DDS
Designator Detector (MCD) ... DD
Designator Register [*Computer science*] ... DR
Designatus [*Named*] [*Latin*] ... DES
Designavit [*He, or She, Drew It*] [*Latin*] (ROG) ... DES
Design-Build-Operate (AAGC) ... DBO
Design-Build-Operate-Transfer (AAGC) ... DBOT
Design-Build-Own-Operate (AAGC) ... DBOO
Design-Drafting-Numerical Control [*Automotive engineering*] ... DDN
Designed Agency Safety and Health Official (ERG) ... DASHO
Designed Data [*Vancouver Stock Exchange symbol*] ... DDC
Designed for Disassembly [*Product design*] ... DFD
Designed for Victory [*Auto racing engine designation*] ... DFV
Designed Horsepower (IAA) ... DHP
Designed Load Waterline [*Technical drawings*] (IAA) ... DLWL
Designed, Verified, and Assigned Date [*Telecommunications*] (TEL) ... DVA
Designed Water Line [*Technical drawings*] ... DWL
Designee for Verification [*NASA*] (NASA) ... DV
Designer (WDAA) ... DES
Designer (ABBR) ... DESIG
Designer (WDAA) ... DSGN
Designer ... DSGNR
Designer Choice Logic ... DCL
Designer Finance Trust [*Associated Press*] (SAG) ... DesgnF
Designer Finance Trust [*NYSE symbol*] (SAG) ... DSH
Designer Holdings [*NYSE symbol*] (TTSB) ... DSH
Designer Holdings Ltd. [*Associated Press*] (SAG) ... DesignH
Designer Holdings Ltd. [*NYSE symbol*] (SAG) ... DSH
[*The*] **Designer Menswear Show** [*British*] (ITD) ... DMS
Designer Shoe Guild (EA) ... DSG
Designer Software [*Computer science*] ... DS
Designers and Art Directors Association [*British*] (BI) ... DADA
Designers d'Interieur du Canada [*Interior Designers of Canada - IDC*] ... DIC
Designers Lighting Forum ... DLF
Designers' Workbench (TEL) ... DWB
Design-for-Discard [*Engineering*] ... DFD
Designing ... DSGNG
Designing Out Labour Electronically (NITA) ... DOLE
Designing Out Maintenance ... DOM
Design-Rated Full Power (DNAB) ... DRFP
Designs Coordination Group [*Telecommunications*] (TEL) ... DCG
Designs for Change [*An association*] (EA) ... DC
Designs for Change (EA) ... DFC
Designs for Information ... DFI
Designs, Inc. [*NASDAQ symbol*] (NQ) ... DESI
Designs, Inc. [*Associated Press*] (SAG) ... Designs
Design-Specified Transformer (IAA) ... DST
Design-to-Price Electronic Warfare [*Military*] (CAAL) ... DTPEW
Design-to-Price Electronic Warfare Suite [*Navy*] (MCD) ... DTPEWS
Design-to-Price Electronics Warfare System [*Military*] ... DPEWS
Desi-Lucille Arnaz Co. ... DESILU
Desipramine [*Antidepressant*] (DAVI) ... DMI
Desirability Function ... DEFUNCT
Desirable Body Weight [*Medicine*] ... DBW
Desirable Objective (KSC) ... DO
Desirade/Grande-Anse, Guadeloupe [*French Antilles*] [*ICAO location identifier*] (ICLI) ... TFFA
Desire (AABC) ... DES
Desire (FAAC) ... DSR
Desired (ABBR) ... DESID
Desired Delivery Date (AFM) ... DDD
Desired Deposit of Dividends [*Investment term*] (MHDW) ... DDD
Desired Ground Zero [*Bombing*] ... DGZ
Desired Ground Zero Program [*Military*] (IAA) ... DGZPRO
Desired Ground Zero Tape Prepare Program [*Bombing*] (SAA) ... DGZPRO
Desired Image Distribution Using Orthogonal Constraints [*Illinois Institute of Technology*] ... DIDOC
Desired Intermediate Vertex (IAA) ... DIV
Desired Learner Outcomes [*Education*] ... DLO
Desired Mean Point of Impact [*Military*] ... DMPI
Desired Point of Impact [*Military*] ... DPI
Desired Work Load ... DWL
Desiree Coleman Fan Club (EA) ... DCFC
Desires to Transfer (NOAA) ... DESTR
Desk Accessory [*Computer science*] (BYTE) ... DA
Desk and Derrick [*Oil industry*] ... D & D
Desk Assistant [*Broadcasting*] (WDMC) ... da
Desk Calculator (IAA) ... DECAL
Desk Checking (IAA) ... DC
Desk, Combination Flat Top and Typewriter ... FT & TW
Desk, Double-Pedestal Flat-Top ... DPFT
Desk, Double-Pedestal Typewriter ... DPTW
Desk Side Computer System [*General Electric Co.*] ... DSCS

Desk Side Time Shared [General Electric Co.] [Computer science]	DSTS
Desk Stand (IAA)	DS
Desk Top	DT
Desk Top Computer	DTC
Desk Top Server (CDE)	DTS
Desktalk Systems, Inc.	DSI
Desktop Analysis Tool [A publication]	DAT
Desktop and Electronic Publishing Online Terminal	DEPOT
Desktop Application Director [Computer science] (PCM)	DAD
Desktop Color Separation [Quark, Inc.] (PCM)	DCS
DeskTop Conferencing [Fujitsu Networks Industry, Inc.] [Computer science] (PCM)	DTC
Desktop Data [NASDAQ symbol] (TTSB)	DTOP
Desktop Data, Inc. [Associated Press] (SAG)	DeskTopDt
Desktop Data, Inc. [Associated Press] (SAG)	DskDt
Desktop Data, Inc. [NASDAQ symbol] (SAG)	DTOP
Desktop Engineering	DE
Desktop Functional Equivalent [Computer science]	DFE
Desktop Management Interface [Computer science] (PCM)	DMI
Desktop Management Suite [Computer science]	DMS
Desktop Management Task Force (PCM)	DMTF
Desktop Manufacturing	DTM
Desktop Mapping System	DMS
Desktop Marketing System [CD-ROM] [Computer science]	DTMS
Desktop Network Interface [Cabletron Systems, Inc.] [Computer science]	DNI
Desktop Page Composition System [Vision Research]	DPCS
Desktop Publishing [Computer science]	DP
Desktop Publishing [Computer science]	DTP
Desktop Publishing Applications Association (EA)	DPAA
Desktop Publishing Association (EA)	DPA
Desktop Publishing Editor [Computer program]	DPE
Desktop Replacement [Computer science]	DTR
Desktop Security Suite [McAfee Associates, Inc.] [Computer science]	DSS
Desktop Systems Group [Novell, Inc.] (PCM)	DSG
Desktop Video [Telecommunications] (PCM)	DTV
Desktop Videoconferencing	DTVC
Desmethyldiazepam [Biochemistry]	DD
Desmethylimipramine [Antidepressant]	DMI
Desmethylmetoxuron [Organic chemistry]	DMM
Desmodium Yellow Mottle Virus [Plant pathology]	DYMV
Desoctapeptide Insulin [Medicine]	DOP
Desolventizer-Toaster-Dryer-Cooler [Oil technology]	DTDC
Desorption Chemical Ionization	DCI
Desorption Induced by Electronic Transition [Physics]	DIET
Desorption Ionization	DI
Desorption Ionization Fourier Transform Mass Spectrometry	DI-FTMS
DeSoto Club of America (EA)	DCA
DeSoto, Inc. [Associated Press] (SAG)	DeSoto
DeSoto, Inc. [NYSE symbol] (SAG)	DSO
DeSoto Parish Library, Mansfield, LA [Library symbol Library of Congress] (LCLS)	LMaD
Desoxycorticosterone Acetate [Endocrinology] (MAH)	DCA
Desoxycorticosterone Secretion Rate [Endocrinology] (MAE)	DOC-SR
Desoxycorticosterone Trimethylacetate [Endocrinology]	DCTMA
Desoxycorticosterone Trimethylacetate [Pharmacology] (DAVI)	DTMA
Desoxycorticosterone Triphenylacetate [Endocrinology] (AAMN)	DCTPA
Desoxyephedrine Hydrochloride [Pharmacy] (AAMN)	DOE
Desoxypyridoxine [or Deoxypyridoxine] Hydrochloride [Pharmacology] (DAVI)	DPD
Despatch	DESP
Despatch Rider [Military British]	DR
Despatch-Rider Letter-Service [Military British]	DRLS
Despeciated Bovine Serum	DBS
Despin Control Electronics [Aerospace]	DCE
Despin Control Subsystem [Aerospace]	DCS
Despite Resuscitation Attempts [Medicine] (MEDA)	DRA
Despues de Jesucristo [After Jesus Christ] [Spanish] (GPO)	d de JC
Despun Antenna Test Satellite [Air Force]	DATS
Despun Heat Shield	DHS
Desquamative Interstitial Pneumonia [Medicine]	DIP
Dessaussure's Equity [South Carolina] [A publication] (DLA)	Dess
Dessaussure's Equity [South Carolina] [A publication] (DLA)	Dessaus
Dessert (WDAA)	DES
Dessertspoon (ADA)	Dsp
Dessertspoon (WGA)	DSTSPN
Dessie [Ethiopia] [Airport symbol] (OAG)	DSE
Dessie/Combolcha [Ethiopia] [ICAO location identifier] (ICLI)	HADC
Destainer Power Supply [Electrophoresis]	DPS
Destec Energy [Associated Press] (SAG)	Destec
Destec Energy [NYSE symbol] (SPSG)	ENG
Destilla [Distill] [Pharmacy] (ROG)	DESTIL
Destillata [Distilled] [Pharmacy]	DEST
Destin, FL [AM radio station call letters]	WBZR
Destin, FL [FM radio station call letters]	WMMK
Destination	D
Destination (AABC)	DEST
Destination (DNAB)	DESTIN
Destination	DESTN
Destination (KSC)	DSTN
Destination Access Register [Computer science] (NITA)	DAR
Destination Address	DA
Destination Address Field [Computer science] (IBMDP)	DAF
Destination Change [Military] (NVT)	DESCHA
Destination Code Base	DCB
Destination Control Table [Computer science] (IAA)	DCT

Destination/Destination [Inspection/Acceptance point] (MCD)	DD
Destination Digital Media Computers [Computer science]	DMC
Destination Digital Media Computers	DMC
Destination Field	DF
Destination Final Acceptance Test (LAIN)	DFAT
Destination Hospital [Aeromedical evacuation]	DH
Destination Index [Computer science]	DI
Destination Load Model (SAA)	DLM
Destination Management Company [Generic term]	DMC
Destination Point Code [Telecommunications] (TEL)	DPC
Destination Queues [Computer science] (MDG)	DQ
Destination Rail Station [MARAD] (TAG)	DRFS
Destination Service Access Point	DSAP
Destination Warning Marker	DWM
Destination Word Marker (CMD)	DWM
Destined (FAAC)	DSTND
Destiny Research Foundation (EA)	DRF
Destiny Resources Ltd. [Vancouver Stock Exchange symbol]	DNY
Destor-Porcupine Deformation Zone [Geology]	DPDZ
Destour Socialist Party [Tunisia] [Political party] (PD)	PSD
Destra [Right] [Italian]	D
Destra [Right] [Italian]	DEST
Destra Mano [Right Hand] [Music] [Italian]	DM
Destra Nazionale [National Right] [Italy Political party] (PPE)	DN
Destratification Impeller Unit	DIU
Destratification Motor Impeller	DMI
Destratification Motor Impeller Unit	DMIU
Destratification Motor Unit	DMU
Destron Fearing [NASDAQ symbol] (TTSB)	DFCO
Destron Fearing Corp. [NASDAQ symbol] (SAG)	DFCO
Destron Fearing Corp. [Associated Press] (SAG)	DstFear
Destron/Idi, Inc. [Vancouver Stock Exchange symbol]	DID
Destroy (AABC)	DEST
Destroyed	D
Destroyed [or Destructor] (AAG)	DESTR
Destroyed (VRA)	destr
Destroyer [Navy British]	D
Destroyer [Navy symbol]	DD
Destroyer [Navy]	DES
Destroyer [Navy British]	DEST
Destroyer Advisory Board [Navy]	DAB
Destroyer, Antisubmarine Helicopter	DASH
Destroyer, Antisubmarine Helicopter [NATO]	DDH
Destroyer Antisubmarine Transportable Array Detector	DASTARD
Destroyer Battle Force [Navy]	DESBATFOR
Destroyer Development Division [Navy] (DNAB)	DESDEVDIV
Destroyer Development Group [Navy]	DESDEVGRU
Destroyer Development Squadron [Navy] (DNAB)	DESDEVRON
Destroyer Division [Navy]	DESDIV
Destroyer Engineered Operating Cycle (MCD)	DDEOC
Destroyer Escort [Navy symbol]	DE
Destroyer Escort Experimental (MCD)	DEX
Destroyer Escort, Guided Missile [British military] (DMA)	DEG
Destroyer Escort RADAR (IAA)	DER
Destroyer Experimental (MCD)	DX
Destroyer Flag [Navy British]	DF
Destroyer Flotilla [Navy]	DESFLOT
Destroyer Flotilla [Navy]	DF
Destroyer Force, Atlantic Fleet [Navy symbol]	DESLANT
Destroyer Force, Pacific Fleet [Navy symbol]	DESPAC
Destroyer, Guided Missile [Surface-to-air] [NATO]	DG
Destroyer, Guided Missile [Surface-to-air/Surface-to-surface] [NATO]	DGM
Destroyer, Guided Missile (Surface-to-Surface) [NATO]	DGS
Destroyer Helicopter System (MCD)	DHS
Destroyer Leader [Navy]	DL
Destroyer Leader, Guided Missile (MCD)	DLG
Destroyer Life Extension [Canadian Navy program]	DELEX
Destroyer Minelayer [Navy symbol] (MCD)	DM
Destroyer Minesweeper [Navy symbol Obsolete]	DMS
Destroyer Repair [Navy]	DESREP
Destroyer Representative [Navy]	DESREP
Destroyer Rocket	DESROC
Destroyer Schoolship [Navy] (NVT)	DESS
Destroyer Scouting Force [Navy]	DESCOFOR
Destroyer SONAR Analysis Center [Navy] (NVT)	DESAC
Destroyer Squadron [Navy]	DESRON
Destroyer/Submarine Antisubmarine Warfare Exercise [Military] (NVT)	DESUBEX
Destroyer Surface-Effect Ship (MCD)	DS
Destroyer Tactical Bulletin [Navy]	DTB
Destroyer Tender [Navy symbol]	AD
Destroyer Variant [Surface warfare study] [Navy] (DOMA)	DDV
Destroyers, Asiatic Fleet [Navy]	DESAF
Destroyers/Cruisers, Pacific Fleet [Navy]	DESCRUPAC
Destroyers, Disbursing Office [Navy]	DDO
Destroyers, Southwest Pacific Fleet [Navy]	DESSOWESPAC
Destruct (KSC)	DEST
Destruct Charge	DC
Destruct Command Receiver (KSC)	DCR
Destruct Command System (MUGU)	DCS
Destruct Logic Decoder	DLD
Destruct Package Building (SAA)	DPB
Destruct Package Installation Facility (SAA)	DPIF
Destruct Safe Arm Device	DSAD
Destruct System Test Set	DSTS

Destruction and Removal Efficiency [*Of waste incinerators*] .... DRE
Destruction Initiation Unit (CAAL) .... DIU
Destruction of Aircraft or Motor Vehicles .... DAMV
Destruction of Government Property .... DGP
Destruction of Interstate Property .... DIP
Destructive Action Link (ECON) .... DAL
Destructive Dilemma [*Rule of inference*] [*Logic*] .... DD
Destructive Firing (SAA) .... DESTR FIR
Destructive Lot Acceptance Testing (NASA) .... DLAT
Destructive Part Analysis .... DPA
Destructive Physical Analysis .... DPA
Destructive Readout .... DRO
Destructive Readout Memory (DNAB) .... DRM
Destructively Distilled .... DEST-DIST
Destructor [*Military*] .... DST
Destructor [*Military*] .... DSTR
Desty on Commerce and Navigation [*A publication*] (DLA) .... Dest Com & Nav
Desty on Shipping and Admiralty [*A publication*] (DLA) .... Dest Sh & Adm
Desty on Taxation [*A publication*] (DLA) .... Desty Tax'n
Desty on the Federal Constitution [*A publication*] (DLA) .... Dest Fed Cons
Desty's California Digest [*A publication*] (DLA) .... Dest Cal Dig
Desty's Federal Citations [*A publication*] (DLA) .... Dest Fed Cit
Desty's Federal Procedure [*A publication*] (DLA) .... Dest Fed Proc
Desulfurize Pyrolysis Gasoline [*Petroleum refining*] .... DPG
Desuperheater .... DSUPHTR
Deswell Inds Wrrt [*NASDAQ symbol*] (TTSB) .... DSWWF
Deswell Industries [*NASDAQ symbol*] (TTSB) .... DSWLF
Deswell Industries, Inc. [*Associated Press*] (SAG) .... Deswell
Deswell Industries, Inc. [*Associated Press*] (SAG) .... Deswll
Deswell Industries, Inc. [*NASDAQ symbol*] (SAG) .... DSWL
Deswell Industries, Inc. [*NASDAQ symbol*] (SAG) .... DSWW
Desynchronized Sleep [*Medicine*] (MEDA) .... DS
Det Gamle Testament [*S. Michelet, S.Mowinckel, og N. Mersel*] [*Oslo*]
   [*A publication*] (BJA) .... GTMMM
Det Norske Arbeiderparti [*Norwegian Labor Party*] (PPE) .... DNA
Det Norske Luftfartselskap AS [*Norwegian Airlines Ltd.*] (EY) .... DNL
Det Nye Folkepartiet [*New People's Party*] [*Norway*] (PPE) .... DNF
Detach .... DET
Detachable (DLA) .... Det
Detachable Container Association [*Defunct*] (EA) .... DCA
Detached (VRA) .... detch
Detached .... DTCH
Detached Duty (DNAB) .... DETD
Detached Enlisted Men's List [*Army*] .... DEML
Detached Experiment Carrier (MCD) .... DEC
Detached from Duty Indicated and from All Other Duty Assigned .... DETALL
Detached Officer's List [*Army*] .... DOL
Detached Service [*Army*] .... DS
Detached Youth Worker (AIE) .... DYW
Detachment .... DET
Detachment [*British military*] (DMA) .... Detmt
Detachment Equipment Authorization List [*Military*] .... DEAL
Detachment of Patients .... DOP
Detachment Support Package (MCD) .... DSP
Detachments Left in Contact [*Military*] .... DLIC
Detail (AAG) .... D
Detail .... DET
Detail (VRA) .... det
Detail (AABC) .... DTL
Detail .... DTL
Detail Assembly Panel .... DAP
Detail Assembly Template .... DAT
Detail Checkout Specifications (MCD) .... DCS
Detail Condition (MDG) .... DC
Detail Condition Register .... DCR
Detail Design Review (MCD) .... DDR
Detail Finish Specification (MCD) .... DFS
Detail Matching Figures Test [*Psychology*] (EDAC) .... DMF
Detail Networks (MCD) .... DN
Detail Process Standard (MCD) .... DPS
Detail Program Interrelationships (NASA) .... DPI
Detail Specification (MCD) .... DS
Detail Velocity Display (IEEE) .... DVD
Detailed Acceptance Test Procedure (KSC) .... DATP
Detailed Acceptance Test Specification (KSC) .... DATS
Detailed Budget Decision (AFM) .... DBD
Detailed Checklist .... DCL
Detailed Checkout .... DCO
Detailed Checkout Procedures (MCD) .... DCOP
Detailed Configuration List (MCD) .... DCL
Detailed Control Room Design Review [*Nuclear energy*] (NRCH) .... DCRDR
Detailed Data Display .... DDD
Detailed Data List (MCD) .... DDL
Detailed Design [*Phase*] .... DD
Detailed Design Review and Evaluation (MCD) .... DDR & E
Detailed Design Specification (MCD) .... DDS
Detailed Elementary Wiring Diagrams .... DEWD
Detailed European Evaluation (MCD) .... DEEVAL
Detailed Experiment Plan (MCD) .... DEP
Detailed Experimental Computer-Assisted Language .... DECAL
Detailed Forecast (MCD) .... DF
Detailed Function System Requirement .... DFSR
Detailed Functional Requirements Review (SSD) .... DFRR
Detailed Functional Specification (DA) .... DFS
Detailed Human Engineering Plan .... DHEP

Detailed Individual Test Plan (MCD) .... DITP
Detailed In-Process Review (MCD) .... DIPR
Detailed Inspection Procedure (MCD) .... DIP
Detailed Interrogation Center [*Navy*] .... DIC
Detailed Issue Depot [*Military supply organization for Allied armies in Europe*]
   [*World War II*] .... DID
Detailed Labor and Time Analysis [*PERT*] .... DELTA
Detailed Labor Estimate (MCD) .... DLE
Detailed Maneuver Table .... DMT
Detailed Monthly Trade Monitor [*Database*] [*Data Resources, Inc.*]
   [*Information service or system*] (CRD) .... DMTM
Detailed Operating Procedure .... DOP
Detailed Pass Plan (SAA) .... DPP
Detailed Performance Analysis [*Bell System*] .... DPA
Detailed Photo Interpretation Report (DNAB) .... DPIR
Detailed Plan Execution (MCD) .... DPE
Detailed Project Plan .... DPP
Detailed Report .... DR
Detailed Requirements Document (MCD) .... DRD
Detailed Routing Instructions (NATG) .... DETRINS
Detailed Secondary Objective (MCD) .... DSO
Detailed Ship Loading .... DSL
Detailed Supplementary Objective (MCD) .... DSO
Detailed System Design [*Computer science*] .... DSD
Detailed System Functional Requirements .... DSFR
Detailed System Test .... DST
Detailed Test Description (MCD) .... DTD
Detailed Test Objective [*NASA*] .... DTO
Detailed Test Plan [*or Procedure*] .... DTP
Detailed Test Procedures (NASA) .... DTPR
Detailed Test Specification .... DTS
Detailed to Duty in a Flying Status Not Involving Flying Effective upon
   Reporting [*Military*] (DNAB) .... DIFDENREPT
Detailed Traffic Analysis [*Telecommunications*] (TEL) .... DTA
Detailed Troop Decontamination [*Military*] (INF) .... DTD
Detailed Type Specification (MCD) .... DTS
Detailed Work Statement (MCD) .... DWS
Details of Agreement [*NATO*] (NATG) .... DOFA
Detain (AABC) .... DTN
Detained on Board [*Referring to seamen*] .... DOB
Detained Pay .... D/P
Detainee .... DET
Detect, Recognize, Identify, and Locate [*Military*] .... DRIL
Detectability of Yes-No .... DYN
Detectable Least Signal Increment [*Instrumentation*] .... DLSI
Detected Pulse Interference (CET) .... DPI
Detected Radiant Power .... DRP
Detected Safety Violation .... DSV
Detecting [*JETDS nomenclature*] .... S
Detecting Heads [*JETDS nomenclature*] [*Military*] (CET) .... DT
Detecting Magnetometer (IAA) .... DM
Detecting Mechanism (IAA) .... DM
Detecting, Ranging, and Tracking System (MCD) .... DRTS
Detecting Ulcers caused by NSAIDS [*Nonsteroidal Anti-Inflammatory Drugs*]
   Early with Sucrose .... DUNES
Detection [*or Detector*] (AFM) .... DET
Detection (KSC) .... DETEC
Detection (NASA) .... DETN
Detection (IAA) .... DTN
Detection, Action, and Response Technique .... DART
Detection and Classification of Acoustic Lens (IAA) .... DECAL
Detection and Control Unit (MCD) .... DCU
Detection and Discrimination .... D & D
Detection and Mapping [*Package*] [*NASA*] .... DAM
Detection and Range [*Early name for RADAR*] .... DERAX
Detection and Ranging Set (CAAL) .... DRS
Detection and Tracking of Satellites (CINC) .... DATOS
Detection and Warning .... D & W
Detection, Classification, and Targeting [*or Tracking*] .... DC & T
Detection, Classification, and Targeting [*or Tracking*] (MCD) .... DCT
Detection Coil [*Magneto-encephalography*] .... DC
Detection, Discrimination, and Designation .... D^3
Detection, Discrimination, and Tracking .... DD & T
Detection Limit [*Analytical chemistry*] .... DL
Detection of Intercontinental Ballistic Missile (IAA) .... DICBM
Detection of Unauthorized Equipment [*Bell Laboratories*] .... DUE
Detection Operational Program [*Military*] (CAAL) .... DOP
Detection RADAR .... DR
Detection RADAR Automatic Monitoring (CET) .... DRAM
Detection RADAR Data Processing (CET) .... DRDP
Detection RADAR Data Takeoff [*Air Force*] .... DRDTO
Detection RADAR Electronic Component .... DREC
Detection RADAR Environmental Display [*Air Force*] .... DRED
Detection Scheme with Fixed Thresholds [*Communication signal*] .... DSFT
Detection Scheme with Learning of Thresholds [*Communication signal*] .... DSLT
Detection Systems [*NASDAQ symbol*] (TTSB) .... DETC
Detection Systems, Inc. [*NASDAQ symbol*] (NQ) .... DETC
Detection Systems, Inc. [*Associated Press*] (SAG) .... DetSys
Detection Threshold (CAAL) .... DT
Detection Threshold Computer [*Telecommunications*] (TEL) .... DTC
Detection Track Evaluation and Assignment Systems [*Navy*] (NG) .... DTEAS
Detection/Tracker (NVT) .... D/T
Detective .... D
Detective .... DET
Detective .... DET

Detective - Agents - Science Fiction - Thriller [Acronym used as title of magazine] .... DAST
Detective Constable [Scotland Yard] .... DC
Detective Constable [Scotland Yard] [British] (ADA) .... DET CON
Detective, Enigma, and Mystery [Publisher] [Former USSR] (ECON) .... DEM
Detective Inspector [Scotland Yard] [British] (ADA) .... DET INSP
Detective Inspector [Scotland Yard] .... DI
Detective Quantum Efficiency [Photon device] .... DQE
Detective Sergeant [Scotland Yard] [British] (ADA) .... DET SGT
Detective Sergeant [Scotland Yard] .... DS
Detective Superintendent .... D-SUPT
Detector (NFPA) .... D
Detector (NFPA) .... DE
Detector .... DETR
Detector Amplifier (IAA) .... DA
Detector Angular Subtense [Instrumentation] .... DAS
Detector Assembly .... DA
Detector Back Bias .... DBB
Detector Balanced Bias .... DBB
Detector Dependent Response [Measurement] .... DDR
Detector Mosaic .... DM
Detector, Selector, and Effector [Social science] .... DSE
Detector Tracker Switch .... DTS
Detector Transfer Function (MAE) .... DTF
Detent [Mechanical Engineering] (NASA) .... DET
Detent [Mechanical engineering] .... DTT
Detention (DSUE) .... DETEN
Detention (MSA) .... DETN
Detention Clause [Insurance] .... D/C
Detention of Pay (DNAB) .... DP
Detention of Pay (DNAB) .... DTNTN
Detention Quarters [British] .... DQ
Detergent (ROG) .... DET
Detergent Aid .... DA
Detergent Inhibitor [Lubricants] .... DI
Deteriorate .... DTRT
Deterioration Control .... DC
Deterioration Factor [Automotive engineering] .... DF
Deterioration Index [Index of intellectual impairment on intelligence test] .... DI
Deterioration Quotient [Medicine] .... DQ
Determination [or Determine] (KSC) .... DET
Determination (KSC) .... DETER
Determination .... determin
Determination [Legal term] (ROG) .... DETERMN
Determination .... DETN
Determination and Findings .... D & F
Determination Effective Levels of Task Automation [Computer science] .... DELTA
Determination of Air-Launched Missile Environment (MCD) .... DAME
Determination of Dependency .... DD
Determination of Direction and Range (IAA) .... DODAR
Determinative (ROG) .... DET
Determine (ROG) .... DETERME
Determine (AABC) .... DETM
Determine (FAAC) .... DTRM
Determined .... DETD
Determined (ROG) .... DETED
Determined (ROG) .... DETERMD
Determined (NVT) .... DTMD
Determined Involved Supermodels Helping to End Suffering [An association] .... DISHES
Determiner [Linguistics] .... DET
Determining Economic Quantities of Maintenance Resources (PDAA) .... DEQMAR
Deterministic (IAA) .... D
Deterministic Bounded Cellular Space (PDAA) .... DBCS
Deterministic Complete Sequential Machine (PDAA) .... DCSM
Deterministic Context Sensitive Language [Computer science] (MHDI) .... DCSL
Deterministic Equivalent (PDAA) .... DE
Deterministic Finite Automation (MCD) .... DFA
Deterministic Finite-State Machine (PDAA) .... DFSM
Deterministic Microgrinding [Optics manufacturing] (RDA) .... DMG
Deterministic Mix Evaluation Worldwide (MCD) .... DMEW
Deterministic Pushdown Automata (PDAA) .... DPDA
Deterministic Time Division Multiplexing [FAA] (TAG) .... DTDM
Detmold [Germany ICAO location identifier] (ICLI) .... EDUD
Detonation Fragmentation and Air Blast (SAA) .... DFA
Detonation Sensing Module [Automotive electronics] .... DSM
Detonator (MSA) .... DET
Detonator Inspection Gauge .... DIG
Detoxification (DSUE) .... DETOX
Detoxification (AAMN) .... DTX
Detrahatur [Let It, or Them, Be Drawn] [Pharmacy] (ROG) .... DETRAH
Detrahatur [Let It, or Them, Be Drawn] [Pharmacy] (ROG) .... DETRAHAT
Detrended Correspondence Analysis [Mathematics] .... DCA
Detrex Corp. [Associated Press] (SAG) .... DetrxC
Detrex Corp. [NASDAQ symbol] (NQ) .... DTRX
Detrex Corporation [NASDAQ symbol] (TTSB) .... DTRX
Detrimental (AABC) .... DETR
Detrital Remanent Magnetization [Geophysics] .... DRM
Detritiation Factor .... DTF
Detroit [City in Michigan] (ROG) .... DET
Detroit [Michigan] [Airport symbol] (OAG) .... DTT
Detroit [Michigan] [Airport symbol] (AD) .... DTT
Detroit [Michigan] [Airport symbol] .... DTW
Detroit Adjustment Inventory [Psychology] .... DAI

Detroit Air Defense Sector [ADS] .... DEADS
Detroit & Canada Tunnel Corp. [Associated Press] (SAG) .... DetCan
Detroit & Canada Tunnel Corp. [NASDAQ symbol] (NQ) .... DTUN
Detroit & Cda Tunl [NASDAQ symbol] (TTSB) .... DTUN
Detroit & Mackinac Railway Co. .... D & M
Detroit & Mackinac Railway Co. .... D & MRR
Detroit & Mackinac Railway Co. [AAR code] .... DM
[The] Detroit & Toledo Shore Line Railroad Co. .... D & TSL
[The] Detroit & Toledo Shore Line Railroad Co. [AAR code] .... DTS
Detroit & Western [Later, DW] [AAR code] .... DETW
Detroit & Western [AAR code] .... DW
Detroit Area Consortium of Catholic Colleges [Library network] .... DACCC
Detroit Arsenal [Michigan] [Army] (MCD) .... DA
Detroit Arsenal [Michigan] [Army] (NATG) .... DAR
Detroit Arsenal Tank Plant [Army] .... DATP
Detroit Art Registration Information System [Detroit Institute of Arts] [Information service or system] (IID) .... DARIS
Detroit Baptist Divinity School, Allen Park, MI [Library symbol Library of Congress] (LCLS) .... MiApDB
Detroit Bar Association, Detroit, MI [Library symbol Library of Congress] (LCLS) .... MiDB
Detroit Bar Association, Detroit, MI [Library symbol] [Library of Congress] (LCLS) .... MiDBA
Detroit Bar Journal [A publication] (DLA) .... Det BJ
Detroit Bar Quarterly [A publication] (DLA) .... Detroit BQ
Detroit, Caro & Sandusky Railroad (IIA) .... DC & S
Detroit Chancery [Catholic Church] Archives, Detroit, MI [Library symbol Library of Congress] (LCLS) .... MiDC
Detroit [Michigan] City Airport [Airport symbol] (OAG) .... DET
Detroit College of Law [Michigan] .... DCL
Detroit College of Law (GAGS) .... Detroit C Law
Detroit College of Law [Michigan] (DLA) .... Detroit Coll L
Detroit College of Law, Detroit, ME [Library symbol] [Library of Congress] (LCLS) .... MiDCL
Detroit Cooperative Cataloging Center, Detroit, MI [OCLC symbol] (OCLC) .... EYQ
Detroit Data Center [IRS] .... DDC
Detroit Deere Corp. [Proposed trademark] .... DEDEC
Detroit/Detroit City [Michigan] [ICAO location identifier] (ICLI) .... KDET
Detroit Diesel [NYSE symbol] (SPSG) .... DDC
Detroit Diesel Allison Division [of General Motors Corp.] .... DDA
Detroit Diesel Allison Division [of General Motors Corp.] .... DDAD
Detroit Diesel Allison Division, General Motors Corp., Indianapolis, IN [OCLC symbol] (OCLC) .... IDD
Detroit Diesel Corp. [Automotive industry supplier] .... DDC
Detroit Diesel Corp. [Associated Press] (SAG) .... DetDiesl
Detroit Diesel Electronic [or Engine] Control [Automotive engineering] .... DDEC
Detroit Edison 7.74% Dep Pfd [NYSE symbol] (TTSB) .... DTEPrF
Detroit Edison 7.75% Dep Pfd [NYSE symbol] (TTSB) .... DTEPrI
Detroit Edison 8.50% 'QUIDS' [NYSE symbol] (TTSB) .... DTD
Detroit Edison 7.625% 'QUIDS' [NYSE symbol] (TTSB) .... DTA
Detroit Edison Co. [Associated Press] (SAG) .... DetE
Detroit Edison Co. [Associated Press] (SAG) DetE25
Detroit Edison Co. [Associated Press] (SAG) DetE26
Detroit Edison Co. [Associated Press] (SAG) .... DetEd
Detroit Edison Co. [NYSE symbol] (SAG) .... DTA
Detroit Edison Co. [NYSE symbol] (SAG) .... DTD
Detroit Edison Co. [NYSE symbol] (SPSG) .... DTE
Detroit Edison Co., Detroit, MI [Library symbol Library of Congress] (LCLS) .... MiDEd
Detroit Edison Co., Information Services, Detroit, MI [OCLC symbol] (OCLC) .... EEE
Detroit Fast Food Workers' Union [Defunct] (EA) .... DFWU
Detroit Free Press [A publication] .... DFP
Detroit General Hospital, Medical Library, Detroit, MI [Library symbol Library of Congress] (LCLS) .... MiDGH
Detroit Historical Society, Detroit, MI [Library symbol Library of Congress] (LCLS) .... MiDHi
Detroit Institute for Children .... DIC
Detroit Institute of Arts, Detroit, MI [Library symbol Library of Congress] (LCLS) .... MiDA
Detroit Institute of Arts, Research Library, Detroit, MI [OCLC symbol] (OCLC) .... EYT
Detroit Institute of Technology .... DIT
Detroit Institute of Technology, Detroit, MI [Library symbol Library of Congress] (LCLS) .... MiDIT
Detroit Jazz Center [Defunct] (EA) .... DJC
Detroit Jazz Center/Jazz Research Institute [Later, DJC] (EA) .... DJC/JRI
Detroit Lakes [Minnesota] [Airport symbol Obsolete] (OAG) .... DTL
Detroit Lakes, MN [AM radio station call letters] .... KDLM
Detroit Lakes, MN [FM radio station call letters] (RBYB) .... KFGX-FM
Detroit Lakes, MN [FM radio station call letters] .... KKDL
Detroit Lakes, MN [FM radio station call letters] (RBYB) .... KRCQ
Detroit Lakes Public Library, Detroit Lakes, MN [Library symbol] [Library of Congress] (LCLS) .... MnDl
Detroit Lakes Technical Institute, Detroit Lakes, MN [Library symbol] [Library of Congress] (LCLS) .... MnDITI
Detroit Law Journal [A publication] (DLA) .... Det LJ
Detroit Law Journal [A publication] (DLA) .... Detroit L J
Detroit Law Review [A publication] (DLA) .... Det L Rev
Detroit Law Review [A publication] (DLA) .... Detroit L Rev
Detroit Lawyer [A publication] (DLA) .... Detroit L
Detroit Legal News [A publication] (DLA) .... Det Leg N
Detroit Legal News [A publication] (DLA) .... Detroit Leg N
Detroit Medical Center .... DMC

Detroit/Metropolitan Wayne County [*Michigan*] [*ICAO location identifier*] (ICLI) .... KDTW
Detroit, MI [*Location identifier FAA*] (FAAL) .... DMI
Detroit, MI [*Location identifier FAA*] (FAAL) .... DWC
Detroit, MI [*Location identifier FAA*] (FAAL) .... DXP
Detroit, MI [*Location identifier FAA*] (FAAL) .... EJR
Detroit, MI [*Location identifier FAA*] (FAAL) .... HUU
Detroit, MI [*Location identifier FAA*] (FAAL) .... LSW
Detroit, MI [*Location identifier FAA*] (FAAL) .... NOI
Detroit, MI [*Location identifier FAA*] (FAAL) .... VQM
Detroit, MI [*FM radio station call letters*] (RBYB) .... WCHB-FM
Detroit, MI [*FM radio station call letters*] .... WDET
Detroit, MI [*AM radio station call letters*] .... WDFN
Detroit, MI [*Television station call letters*] .... WDIV
Detroit, MI [*FM radio station call letters*] (RBYB) .... WDRQ-FM
Detroit, MI [*FM radio station call letters*] .... WDTR
Detroit, MI [*FM radio station call letters*] .... WGPR
Detroit, MI [*Television station call letters*] .... WGPR-TV
Detroit, MI [*FM radio station call letters*] .... WHYT
Detroit, MI [*Television station call letters*] .... WJBK
Detroit, MI [*FM radio station call letters*] .... WJLB
Detroit, MI [*AM radio station call letters*] .... WJR
Detroit, MI [*FM radio station call letters*] .... WJZZ
Detroit, MI [*Television station call letters*] .... WKBD
Detroit, MI [*FM radio station call letters*] .... WKQI
Detroit, MI [*FM radio station call letters*] .... WLLZ
Detroit, MI [*AM radio station call letters*] .... WLQV
Detroit, MI [*AM radio station call letters*] .... WLTI
Detroit, MI [*FM radio station call letters*] .... WMUZ
Detroit, MI [*FM radio station call letters*] .... WMXD
Detroit, MI [*FM radio station call letters*] .... WOMC
Detroit, MI [*AM radio station call letters*] .... WQBH
Detroit, MI [*FM radio station call letters*] .... WQRS
Detroit, MI [*FM radio station call letters*] .... WRIF
Detroit, MI [*Television station call letters*] .... WTVS
Detroit, MI [*AM radio station call letters*] .... WWJ
Detroit, MI [*Television station call letters*] (RBYB) .... WWJ-TV
Detroit, MI [*FM radio station call letters*] .... WWWW
Detroit, MI [*Television station call letters*] .... WXON
Detroit, MI [*AM radio station call letters*] .... WXYT
Detroit, MI [*Television station call letters*] .... WXYZ
Detroit, MI [*FM radio station call letters*] .... WYCD
Detroit, MI [*FM radio station call letters*] .... WYST
Detroit Ordnance District [*Army*] .... DOD
Detroit Osteopathic Hospital, Highland Park, MI [*Library symbol Library of Congress*] (LCLS) .... MiHpDH
Detroit Public Library .... DPL
Detroit Public Library, Burton Historical Collection, Detroit, MI [*Library symbol Library of Congress*] (LCLS) .... MiD-B
Detroit Public Library, Detroit, MI [*OCLC symbol*] (OCLC) .... EYP
Detroit Public Library, Detroit, MI [*Library symbol Library of Congress*] (LCLS) .... MiD
Detroit Signal Laboratory [*Army*] .... DSL
Detroit Stock Exchange (MHDB) .... DSC
Detroit Suburban Network [*Radio*] .... DSN
Detroit Terminal Railroad Co. [*AAR code*] .... DT
Detroit Tests of Learning Aptitude [*Education*] .... DTLA
Detroit, Toledo & Ironton Railroad Co. [*Nickname: Damned Tough and Independent*] .... DT & I
Detroit, Toledo & Ironton Railroad Co. [*AAR code*] .... DTI
Detroit Tooling Association (EA) .... DTA
Detroit Waldhorn Society (EA) .... DWS
Detroit/Willow Run [*Michigan*] [*ICAO location identifier*] (ICLI) .... KYIP
Detrucking Point .... DP
Detrusor Instability [*Urology*] (DAVI) .... DI
Detur [*Give*] [*Pharmacy*] (MAE) .... d
Detur [*Give*] [*Pharmacy*] .... DET
Detur Ad [*Let It Be Given To*] [*Pharmacy*] .... DD
Detur et Signatur [*Let It Be Given and Labeled*] [*Pharmacy*] .... D et S
Detur et Signatur [*Let It Be Given and Labeled*] [*Pharmacy*] (DAVI) .... D et S
Detur in Duplo [*Let Twice as Much Be Given*] [*Pharmacy*] (ROG) .... D in 2PLO
Detur in Duplo [*Let Twice as Much Be Given*] [*Pharmacy*] .... D in DUP
Detur in Duplo [*Let Twice as Much Be Given*] [*Pharmacy*] (DAVI) .... Det in 2 Plo
Detur in Duplo [*Let Twice as Much Be Given*] [*Pharmacy*] (DAVI) .... Det in Dup
DEU [*Display Electronics Unit*] **Control Program** [*NASA*] (NASA) .... DCP
DEU [*Display Electronics Unit*] **Control Program** [*End Item*] .... DCPA
DEU [*Display Electronics Unit*] **Control Program End Item** [*NASA*] (NASA) .... DCPEI
DEU [*Display Electronics Unit*] **Message Processor** (NASA) .... DMP
Deumba [*Fiji*] [*ICAO location identifier*] (ICLI) .... NFND
Deus [*God*] [*Latin*] (GPO) .... D
Deus Meumque Jus [*God and My Right*] [*Freemasonry*] [*Latin*] .... DMJ
Deus Misereatur [*67th Psalm*] [*Music*] .... DeM
Deuterated Hydrogen Y [*Type of zeolite*] .... DHY
Deuterated Polyethylene [*Organic chemistry*] .... DPE
Deuterated Potassium Dihydrogen Phosphate [*Electronics*] (BARN) .... DKDP
Deuterated Triglycine Sulfate [*Organic chemistry*] .... DTGS
Deutereium Fluoride (IEEE) .... DF
Deuterium [*Also, H^2*] [*Radioisotope of hydrogen*] .... D
Deuterium [*Also, D*] [*Radioisotope of hydrogen*] .... H^2
Deuterium [*Radioisotope of hydrogen*] (DAVI) .... H$_B$
Deuterium Hydrogen [*Protium*] **Oxide** [*Organic chemistry*] (DAVI) .... DHO
Deuterium/Hydrogen Ratio .... D/H
Deuterium Isotope Effect (MCD) .... DIE
Deuterium Moderated Pile Low Energy [*Reactor*] .... DIMPLE

Deuterium-Deuterium Reaction [*Nuclear energy*] (NRCH) .... D-D
Deuterium-Tritium Reaction [*Fusion program*] .... D-T
Deuterocanonicals .... DC
Deutero-Isaiah (BJA) .... DtIs
Deuteron [*Nuclear physics*] (WGA) .... D
Deuteronomist Source of the Pentateuch (BJA) .... D
Deuteronomy [*Old Testament book*] .... Deut
Deuteronomy [*Old Testament book*] .... Dt
Deuteronomy Rabba (BJA) .... DeutR
Deuteronomy Rabba (BJA) .... DR
Deuteronomy Rabba (BJA) .... Dtr
Deutsch-Albanische Freundschaftsgesellschaft EV [*German Albanian Friendship Society*] [*Germany*] (EAIO) .... DAFG
Deutsch-Amerikanische Petroleum Gesellschaft [*German-American Petroleum Society*] .... DAPG
Deutsch-Amerikanischer National-Kongress [*German-American National Congress*] (EA) .... DANK
Deutsche Adels-Gesellschaft in Nord Amerika [*Association of the German Nobility in North America*] (EA) .... DAGNA
Deutsche Aerospace (ECON) .... DASA
Deutsche Allgemeine Nachrichten Agentur [*German general news agency, sponsored by US newspapermen as a successor to the NAZI-controlled DNB*] [*Post-World War II*] .... DANA
Deutsche Arbeitsfront [*German Workers Front*] [*Post-World War II*] .... DAF
Deutsche Arbeitsgemeinschaft fuer Rechen-Anlagen [*German Working Committee for Computing Machines*] .... DARA
Deutsche Ba Luftfahrtgesellschaft MBH [*Germany ICAO designator*] (FAAC) .... BAG
Deutsche Bibliothek [*Database producer*] .... DB
Deutsche Bibliothek, Zeppelinallee, Frankfurt am Main, Germany [*Library symbol Library of Congress*] (LCLS) .... GyFmDB
Deutsche Biologische Literatur [*German Biological Literature*] [*Also, DT BIOL Database Forschungsinstitut Senckenberg*] [*Information service or system*] (CRD) .... DBL
Deutsche Biologische Literatur [*German Biological Literature*] [*Also, DBL Database Forschungsinstitut Senckenberg*] [*Information service or system*] .... DT BIOL
Deutsche Bundesbahn [*German Federal Railway*] [*Since 1949*] [*Germany*] .... DB
Deutsche Bundesbahn [*German Federal Railway*] [*Since 1949*] [*Germany*] .... DBB
Deutsche Demokratische Arbeiterpartei [*German Democratic Workers' Party*] [*Germany Political party*] (PPW) .... DDAP
Deutsche Demokratische Partei [*German Democratic Party*] [*Political party*] (PPE) .... DDP
Deutsche Demokratische Republik [*German Democratic Republic (East Germany)*] .... DDR
Deutsche Dermatologische Gesellschaft [*German Dermatological Society*] (EAIO) .... DDG
Deutsche Forschungs und Versuchsanstalt fuer Luft und Raumfahrt [*German Research Institute for Air and Space Travel*] [*An association*] .... DFVLR
Deutsche Forschungs-and Versuchsanstalt fur Luft EV [*Germany ICAO designator*] (FAAC) .... AOT
Deutsche Forschungsanstalt fuer Luft-und Raumfahrt [*Germany*] .... DLR
Deutsche Frauenbewegung [*German Women's Movement*] [*Germany*] (PPW) .... DFB
Deutsche Genossenschaftsbank [*Germany*] .... DG
Deutsche Gesellschaft fuer Amerikastudien [*German Association for American Studies*] (EA) .... DGA
Deutsche Gesellschaft fuer Chemisches Apparatewesen, Chemische Technik, und Biotechnologie eV [*Database producer*] (IID) .... DECHEMA
Deutsche Gesellschaft fuer Dokumentation [*German Society for Documentation*] [*Information service or system*] (IID) .... DGD
Deutsche Gesellschaft fuer Operations Research [*German Society for Operational Research*] [*Germany*] .... DGOR
Deutsche Girozentrale - Deutsche Kommunalbank [*West German bank*] .... DGZ
Deutsche Grammophon Gesellschaft [*Phonograph recording company*] .... DGG
Deutsche Hannover Partei [*German Hanover Party*] (PPE) .... DHP
Deutsche Kommunistische Partei [*German Communist Party*] [*Political party*] (PPE) .... DKP
Deutsche Lufthansa AG [*German Lufthansa*] [*Airline*] (EG) .... DLH
Deutsche Lufthansa AG [*Germany*] [*ICAO designator*] (OAG) .... LH
Deutsche Mark [*Monetary unit*] [*Germany*] .... DM
Deutsche Mittelstandspartei [*German Middle Class Party*] (PPW) .... DMP
Deutsche Morgan Grenfell [*Germany*] .... DMG
Deutsche Morgan Grenfell [*Germany*] [*Banking*] .... DMG
Deutsche Motorrad Register [*German Motorcycle Register*] [*Defunct*] (EA) .... DMR
Deutsche Nachrichtenburo [*German News Bureau*] .... DNB
Deutsche Partei [*German Party*] [*Political party*] (PPE) .... DP
Deutsche Patent Datenbank [*German Patent Database*] [*German Patent Office*] [*Information service or system*] (IID) .... PATDPA
Deutsche Presse Agentur [*German Press Agency*] .... DPA
Deutsche Rechtspartei [*German Party of the Right*] [*Political party*] (PPE) .... DRP
Deutsche Reichsbahn [*German Democratic Republic Railway*] (DCTA) .... DR
Deutsche Reichsbahn [*German State Railways*] [*Pre-1945*] .... DRB
Deutsche Reichspartei [*German National Party*] [*Political party*] (PPE) .... DR
Deutsche Rettungsflugwacht EV [*Germany ICAO designator*] (FAAC) .... AMB
Deutsche Schiffs Revision und Klassifikation [*German ship classification society*] (DS) .... DSRK
Deutsche Sex Partei [*German Political party*] .... DSP
Deutsche Soziale Union [*German Social Union*] (PPW) .... DSU
Deutsche Stiftung fur Internationale Entwicklung [*German Foundation for International Development*] (EAIO) .... DSIE
Deutsche Telecom eV [*Germany Telecommunications*] .... DT
Deutsche Telekom AG [*Associated Press*] (SAG) .... Deut Tel
Deutsche Telekom AG [*NYSE symbol*] (SAG) .... DT
Deutsche Terminboerse [*Derivatives market*] [*Germany*] .... DTB

Deutsche Theologie [*A publication*] (BJA) .... DT
Deutsche Tourenwagen Meisterschaft [*German Touring Car Championship*] .... DTM
Deutsche Umsiedlungstreuhandgesellschaft [*A publication*] (BJA) .... DUT
Deutsche Vereinigung fuer Datenschutz [*German Data Protection Organization*] .... DVD
Deutsche Vereinigung gegen Politischen Missbrauch der Psychiatrie [*Germany*] .... DVPMP
Deutsche Verlags-Anstalt [*Publishing company*] .... DVA
Deutsche Volkspartei [*German People's Party (1919-1933)*] (PPE) .... DVP
Deutsche Volksunion [*German People's Union*] [*Political party*] (PD) .... DVU
Deutsche Waffen Stillstandkommission [*German Armistice Commission, in France*] [*World War II*] .... DWStK
Deutsche Waffen- und Munitionsfabriken [*German Weapons and Munitions Factory*] [*World War II*] .... DWM
Deutsche Welle [*Radio network*] [*Germany*] .... DW
Deutscher Akademischer Austauschdienst [*German Academic Exchange Service*] (EA) .... DAAD
Deutscher Aktien Index [*German Index of Stock Prices*] [*A publication*] (BARN) .... DAX
Deutscher Bundestag, Abteilung Wissenschaftliche Dokumentation, Bonn, Germany [*Library symbol Library of Congress*] (LCLS) .... GyBoDB
Deutscher Depeschen-Dienst [*Press agency*] [*Germany*] .... DDD
Deutscher Gewerkschaftsbund [*Confederation of German Trade Unions*] [*Germany*] (DCTA) .... DGB
Deutscher Koordinierungsausshuss [*Coordinating European Council*] .... DKA
Deutscher Kulturbund [*German Cultural Federation*] [*Germany*] (PPE) .... DK
Deutscher Nachrichten Dienst [*German News Service*] (BARN) .... DND
Deutscher Normenausschuss [*German Standards Committee*] [*Later, DIN*] (EG) .... DNA
Deutscher Orden der Harugari [*German Order of Harugari*] (EA) .... DOH
Deutscher Taschenbuch Verlag [*Publisher*] .... DTV
Deutscher Verein zur Erforschung Palaestinas [*A publication*] (BJA) .... DPV
Deutsches Afrika Korps [*World War II*] .... DAK
Deutsches Arzneibuch [*German Medical Book*] [*Medicine*] .... DAB
Deutsches Bibliotheksinstitut [*German Library Institute*] [*Information service or system*] (IID) .... DBI
Deutsches Bucherverzeichnis [*A bibliographic publication*] [*German*] .... DBV
Deutsches Foerschungsnetz [*German*] [*Computer science*] (TNIG) .... DFN
Deutsches Informationszentrum fuer Technische Regeln [*German Information Center for Technical Rules*] [*German Institute for Standardization*] [*Information service or system*] (IID) .... DITR
Deutsches Institut fuer Medizinische Dokumentation und Information [*German Institute for Medical Documentation and Information*] [*Ministry for Youth, Family, and Health Affairs Database producer*] [*Information service or system*] (IID) .... DIMDI
Deutsches Institut fuer Normung [*German Institute for Standardization*] (IID) .... DIN
Deutsches Institut fuer Urbanistik [*Vereins fuer Kommunalwissenschaften eV*] [*Database producer*] .... DIFU
Deutsches Institut fuer Wirtschaftsforschung [*Data Resources, Inc.*] [*Database*] .... DIW
Deutsches Kunststoff-Institut, Darmstadt, Germany [*Library symbol Library of Congress*] (LCLS) .... GyDaD
Deutsches Recht [*German Law*] (ILCA) .... DR
Deutsches Reich [*German Empire*] .... DR
Deutsches Reichspatent [*German State Patent*] .... DRP
Deutsches Teppich-Forschungsinstitut [*German Carpet Research Institute - GCRI*] (EAIO) .... TFI
Deutschland [*Germany*] [*German*] .... D
Deutschlandfunk [*Radio network*] [*Germany*] .... DLF
Deutschnationale Volkspartei [*German National People's Party*] .... DNVP
Deutsch-Sowjetische-Freundschaft [*German-Soviet Friendship*] [*Common street name in East Germany*] .... DSF
Deutz Magnetic Valve System [*Diesel engines*] .... DMVS
Deva [*Romania*] [*Seismograph station code, US Geological Survey*] (SEIS) .... DEV
Devant [*Front*] (BARN) .... dev
Devar [*Afghanistan*] [*ICAO location identifier*] (ICLI) .... OADV
Devco Railway [*Cape Breton Development Corp. - Coal Div.*] [*AAR code*] .... DVR
Devcon International [*NASDAQ symbol*] (TTSB) .... DEVC
Devcon International Corp. [*NASDAQ symbol*] (NQ) .... DEVC
Devcon International Corp. [*Associated Press*] (SAG) .... Devcon
Develcon Electronics Ltd. [*Toronto Stock Exchange symbol*] .... DLC
Develet Hava Yollari [*Airline*] .... DHY
Develop [*or Development*] (AFM) .... DEV
Develop (MSA) .... DVL
Develop and Qualify .... DAQ
Developed [*Medicine*] (DAVI) .... D
Developed Area Ratio [*Propellers*] (DNAB) .... DAR
Developed Armament Probable Error (SAA) .... DAPE
Developed Country .... DC
Developed Height (MSA) .... DEV HGT
Developed Horsepower .... DHP
Developed Layout Template (MCD) .... DLT
Developed Length (AAG) .... DL
Developed Pressure [*Cardiology*] .... DP
Developed Technology Resource [*NASDAQ symbol*] (TTSB) .... DEVT
Developed Template (MCD) .... DT
Developed Width (MSA) .... DEV WD
Developed Width (AAG) .... DW
Developer [*Photography*] (DGA) .... D
Developer .... DVLPR
Developer Demonstrator .... DD
Developer Evaluation .... DE
Developer Oxidation Product [*Photography*] .... DOP
Developer Technical Support (CDE) .... DTS
Developer's Digest [*Australia A publication*] .... DD
Developers Div Rlty 9.44% Pfd [*NYSE symbol*] (TTSB) .... DDRPrB
Developers Div Rlty 9.50% Pfd [*NYSE symbol*] (TTSB) .... DDRPrA
Developers Diversified Realty [*NYSE symbol*] (SPSG) .... DDR
Developers Diversified Realty Corp. [*Associated Press*] (SAG) .... DevD
Developers Diversified Realty Corp. [*Associated Press*] (SAG) .... DevlDv
Developers Diversified Rlty [*NYSE symbol*] (TTSB) .... DDR
Developing Activity [*Military*] (DOMA) .... DA
Developing Agency (CAAL) .... DA
Developing and Printing .... D & P
Developing Anti-Sexist Innovations (AIE) .... DASI
Developing Cognitive Abilities Test [*Canadian Comprehensive Assessment Program*] .... DCAT
Developing Countries Farm Radio Network (EAIO) .... DCFRN
Developing Countries Foundation of 1962 [*Denmark*] (EAIO) .... DCF
Developing Country .... DC
Developing Economies [*A publication*] .... DEC
Developing Education [*A publication*] .... Developing Ed
Developing European Learning through Technological Advance [*EC*] (ECED) .... DELTA
Developing Improved Sizing Procedures Over Sanitary Area Landfills .... DISPOSAL
Developing Learning Readiness .... DLR
Developing Nations Tractor [*Ford Motor Co.*] .... DNT
Developing Proboscis .... DP
Developing Systems Training and Devices Directorate [*Army*] .... DST & DD
Developing Understanding of Self and Others [*Educational tool*] .... DUSO
Developing-Out Paper .... DOP
Development .... D
Development .... DEV
Development (AAGC) .... Dev
Development .... DEVEL
Development (DD) .... devel
Development .... DEVLPMT
Development .... Devpt
Development .... DEVT
Development .... DVLP
Development .... Dvlpmt
Development Acceptance (AABC) .... DEVA
Development Acceptance in Process Review (RDA) .... DEVAIPR
Development Acceptance Test [*Army*] .... DAT
Development Advisory Service (ODBW) .... DAS
Development Aid from People to People (EAIO) .... DAPP
Development Alternatives, Inc. .... DAI
Development & Commercial Bank [*Malaysia*] .... D & C
Development and Configuration Management Information System (MCD) .... DACMIS
Development and Education Command .... DEC
Development and Engineering Directorate [*Army*] (RDA) .... DRCDE
Development and Evaluation of a Firearms Training Facility .... DEFT
Development and Procurement Costs of Aircraft (MCD) .... DAPCA
Development and Production Costs for Aircraft (SAA) .... DAPCA
Development and Project Planning Centre [*University of Bradford*] [*British*] (IRC) .... DPPC
Development and Proof Services [*Aberdeen Proving Ground, MD*] (MCD) .... DPS
Development and Readiness Command [*Formerly, AMC*] [*See also MDRC Alexandria, VA*] [*Army*] .... DARCOM
Development and Readiness Command Automated Logistics Management Systems Agency [*Army*] (AABC) .... DARCOMALMSA
Development and Readiness Command Circular [*Army*] .... DARCOM-C
Development and Readiness Command Facilities and Services Center [*Army*] (AABC) .... DARCOMFASC
Development and Readiness Command Field Safety Agency [*Army*] (AABC) .... DARCOMFSA
Development and Readiness Command Installation Management Course [*Military*] .... DARCIMC
Development and Readiness Command Installations and Service Agency [*Army*] (AABC) .... DARCOMI & SA
Development and Readiness Command Logistics Data Center [*Army*] (AABC) .... DARCOMLDC
Development and Readiness Command Logistics Systems Support Agency [*Army*] (AABC) .... DARCOMLSSA
Development and Readiness Command Procurement Instruction [*Army*] (MCD) .... DARCOMPI
Development and Reproductive Toxicology [*Database*] [*Environmental Protection Agency*] .... DART
Development and Technical Assistance .... DATA
Development and Technology .... D & T
Development and Test Support .... DTS
Development and Training Center [*Navy*] (NVT) .... DATC
Development Assessment and Instruction for Success in the Early Years [*Education*] (AIE) .... DAISEY
Development Assist Test .... DAT
Development Assistance .... DA
Development Assistance Committee [*Organization for Economic Cooperation and Development*] [*Paris, France*] (EAIO) .... DAC
Development Assistance Group .... DAG
Development Association. Bulletin [*A publication*] .... Devt Assoc Bull
Development at Birth Index [*Medicine*] .... DBI
Development Bank of the Great Lake States [*Zaire*] (EAIO) .... DBGLS
Development Big Hydrofoil [*Also, DEH*] (MCD) .... DBH
Development Capital Corp. [*British*] .... DCC
Development Center (MCD) .... DC
Development Center (MCD) .... DEVCTR

Development Change [*Aerospace*] (AAG) .... DEVC
Development Change Notice [*Aerospace*] .... DCN
Development Characteristic .... DC
Development Commission [*British*] .... DC
Development Committee .... DC
Development Committee [*ISO*] (DS) .... DEVCO
Development Concept Paper (MCD) .... DCP
Development Configuration Management Board (MCD) .... DCMB
Development Contract Officer (MUGU) .... DCO
Development Control Center .... DCC
Development Control Program (SAA) .... DCP
Development Cost Plan (NASA) .... DCP
Development Costs .... DC
Development Council for Research (MUGU) .... DCR
Development Data Sheet (MCD) .... DDS
Development Decade [*Ten-year plan designed to bring about self-sufficiency in developing countries*] [*United Nations*] .... DD
Development Directive .... DD
Development Discrepancy Report .... DDR
Development Display Assembly .... DDA
Development Economics Group .... DEG
Development Economics Research Centre [*University of Warwick*] [*British*] (CB) .... DERC
Development Education Exchange Papers [*FAO*] [*Information service or system United Nations*] (DUND) .... DEEP
Development Engineering .... DE
Development, Engineering, and Acquisition [*Directorate*] [*Army*] (RDA) .... DEA
Development Engineering Division (SAA) .... DED
Development Engineering Inspection (MCD) .... DEI
Development Engineering Management System [*Air Force*] .... DEMS
Development Engineering Review (AAG) .... DER
Development Environment for Pronunciation Expert Systems [*Computer science*] .... DEPES
Development Ephemeris .... DE
Development Estimate .... DE
Development Evaluation Facility (LAIN) .... DEF
Development Field Office [*Air Force*] .... AFDFO
Development Finance Company [*Generic term*] [*Banking*] .... DFC
Development Fixture (MCD) .... DF
Development Flight (NASA) .... DF
Development Flight Test [*Military*] (CAAL) .... DFT
Development Fund .... DF
Development Group for Alternative Policies (EA) .... DGAP
Development Import Finance Facility [*Australia*] [*Defunct*] .... DIFF
Development in Science Education [*National Science Foundation*] (GRD) .... DISE
Development Information Network [*United Nations*] (NITA) .... DEVNET
Development Information Processing System .... DIPS
Development Information System [*United Nations Information service or system*] (IID) .... DIS
Development Integrated (MCD) .... DI
Development Interim Control Equipment (IAA) .... DICE
Development International [*Defunct*] (EA) .... DI
Development Investigations in Military Orbiting Systems .... DEIMOS
Development Job Outline Engineering Order [*DAC*] .... DJOEO
Development Laboratory Unit (MCD) .... DLU
Development Land Tax [*British*] .... DLT
Development Loan Committee [*Department of State*] .... DLC
Development Loan Fund [*Abolished 1961, functions redelegated to Agency for International Development*] .... DLF
Development Management System [*IBM Corp.*] .... DMS
Development Manager .... DM
Development Manmouths Nominal .... DMMnom
Development Milestone [*Aerospace*] (AAG) .... DM
Development Motor (MCD) .... DM
Development Needs Analysis .... DNS
Development of a Corps Logistics Analysis Methodology .... DCSLAM
Development of Advanced Rate Techniques .... DART
Development of European Learning through Technological Advance [*British*] .... DELTA
Development of Improved Management Engineering Systems [*Military*] (AABC) .... DIMES
Development of Integrated Logistics (NATG) .... DEVIL
Development of Integrated Management Engineering Systems [*Military*] .... DIMES
Development of Integrated Monetary Electronics [*EC*] (ECED) .... DIME
Development of Learning and Teaching in the Arts (AIE) .... DELTA
Development of Learning through Technological Advance [*European Community*] (MHDB) .... DELTA
Development of Minicomputers in an Environment of Scientific and Technological Information Centers [*Computer science*] .... DOMESTIC
Development of Operational Reasoning Skills .... DOORS
Development of Opportunities through Meaningful Education [*Project*] .... DOME
Development of Reasoning in Science .... DORIS
Development of Regional Impact [*Land use*] .... DRI
Development of Substitute Materials .... DSM
Development Operations Division [*NASA*] (KSC) .... DOD
Development Optical Diagnostic Equipment [*Military*] .... DODE
Development Phase (NASA) .... DP
Development Plan .... DP
Development Planning Memo (MCD) .... DPM
Development Planning Objective .... DPO
Development Planning Officer [*Military*] .... DPO
Development Planning Reports (MCD) .... DPR
Development Play (EDAC) .... DP
Development Production Prove Out [*Army*] (RDA) .... DPPO

Development Program [*Military*] .... DP
Development Program Grant (MHDB) .... DPG
Development Program Manuals (AFIT) .... DPM
Development Program Plan .... DPP
Development Project Engineer (NRCH) .... DPE
Development Project Office for Selected Ammunition [*Army*] (RDA) .... DPO-SA
Development Project Officer (MCD) .... DPO
Development Project Team (MCD) .... DPT
Development Proposal (NVT) .... DP
Development Proposal Manager (MCD) .... DPM
Development Prototype .... DP
Development Prototype (NG) .... DPT
Development Prototype Launcher .... DPL
Development Quotient .... DQ
Development Reactor Mock-Up .... DRM
Development Readiness Command Program Manager - Nuclear [*Army*] .... DRCPM-NUC
Development Reentry Vehicle [*Aerospace*] (IAA) .... DRV
Development Reference Service [*Society for International Development*] (IID) .... DRS
Development Rehabilitation of the Environment through Arts and Media [*Philippines Earth Savers movement*] .... DREAM
Development Release Order .... DRO
Development Report .... DR
Development Requirements Specification [*Nuclear energy*] (NRCH) .... DRS
Development Research Associates, Inc., Institute for New Enterprise Development .... DRA/INED
Development Resources Panel [*United Nations Development Program*] .... DRP
Development Revision Record (KSC) .... DRR
Development Sciences Information System [*Information service or system Canada*] (IID) .... DEVSIS
Development Signature Approval .... DSA
Development Signature Approval - Advanced Assembly Outline .... DSA/AAO
Development Signature Approval - Fabrication Order .... DSA/FO
Development Site System Training Program (SAA) .... DSSTP
Development Society of Southern Africa (EAIO) .... DSSA
Development Specification (AAGC) .... B SPEC
Development Stimulating Factor [*Biochemistry*] .... DSF
Development Student Engineer (MCD) .... DSE
Development Suitability Test (MCD) .... DST
Development Support Equipment .... DSE
Development Support Library (IAA) .... DSL
Development System .... DS
Development Telemetry Equipment (MCD) .... DTM
Development Test [*or Testing*] (MCD) .... DT
Development, Test, and Evaluation (AFM) .... DT & E
Development, Test, and Evaluation (DOMA) .... DT & E
Development, Test, and Experimentation .... DT & E
Development, Test, and Mission Support (MCD) .... DTMS
Development Test Article .... DTA
Development Test Facility (SSD) .... DTF
Development Test Instrumentation (NASA) .... DTI
Development Test/Operational Test .... DT/OT
Development Test Requirement Specification (NRCH) .... DTRS
Development Test Requirements Assessment [*Military*] .... DTRA
Development Test Requirements Document [*NASA*] (NASA) .... DTRD
Development Test Satellite .... DTS
Development Test Supportability Demonstration [*Army*] .... DTSD
Development Threat Package .... DTP
Development through Industry .... DTI
Development Training Group .... DTG
Development Trouble Report .... DTR
Development Trust for the Young Disabled [*British*] (IRUK) .... DTYD
Development Type (AABC) .... DT
Development Unit Executive Group [*Scotland*] (AIE) .... DUEG
Development Validation Acceptance .... DEVA
Development Verification Testing (RDA) .... DVT
Development Work Order .... DWO
Development Work Request .... DWR
Development Work Statement (NRCH) .... DWS
Development-Accelerator-Releasing Couplers [*Photography*] .... DAR
Developmental .... DEVLPMNTL
Developmental .... DEVPMTL
Developmental Activities Screening Inventory [*Psychology*] .... DASI
Developmental Activity Center .... DAC
Developmental Age .... DA
Developmental Army Mobilization System (DOMA) .... DARMS
Developmental Articulation Profile [*Speech evaluation test*] .... DAP
Developmental Assessment for the Severely Handicapped [*Test*] .... DASH
Developmental Assessment of Life Experiences [*Test*] .... DALE
Developmental Assessment of Spanish Grammar (EDAC) .... DASG
Developmental Basis of Issue [*Military*] (AABC) .... DBOI
Developmental Biology Center [*Case Western Reserve University*] [*Research center*] (RCD) .... DBC
Developmental Bulletin (MCD) .... DB
Developmental Cycle Research Plan .... DCRP
Developmental Disabilities Office [*Department of Health and Human Services*] .... DDO
Developmental Disabilities Service .... DDS
Developmental Disabilities Special Interest Section [*American Occupational Therapy Association*] .... DDSS
Developmental Disability [*Medicine*] .... DD
Developmental Disability Center [*Columbia University*] [*Research center*] (RCD) .... DDC

Developmental Disability Center for Children [*Louisiana State University*] [*Research center*] (RCD) .... DDCC
Developmental Economic Education Program .... DEEP
Developmental Engineering Inspection Board (AAG) .... DEIB
Developmental Fast Hydrofoil (MCD) .... DFH
Developmental Flight Instrumentation [*NASA*] .... DFI
Developmental Ground Support Equipment (DNAB) .... DGSE
Developmental Hand Function Test .... DEHFT
Developmental History [*Medicine*] (DMAA) .... DH
Developmental Independent Evaluator [*Army*] .... DIE
Developmental Indicators for the Assessment of Learning [*Education*] .... DIAL
Developmental Indicators for the Assessment of Learning - Revised [*Child development test*] .... DIAL-R
Developmental Instrumentation Medium-Left .... DML
Developmental Instrumentation Medium-Right (NASA) .... DMR
Developmental [*Instrumentation*] MDM [*Manipulator Deployment Mechanism*] Left .... DML
Developmental Optical Correlator (PDAA) .... DOC
Developmental Potential of Preschool Children [*Psychology*] .... DPPC
Developmental Sentence Analysis [*Education*] .... DSA
Developmental Sentence Scoring [*for the hearing-impaired*] .... DSS
Developmental Software Support Environment [*Army*] .... DSSE
Developmental Software Support Environment Plan [*Army*] .... DSSEP
Developmental Tactical Operations Systems (MCD) .... DEVTOS
Developmental Tasks for Kindergarten Readiness [*Child development test*] .... DTKR
Developmental Technician Team (MCD) .... DTT
Developmental Test Model .... DTM
Developmental Test of Visual Perception [*Frostig*] .... DTVP
Developmental Test of Visual-Motor Integration [*Beery & Buktenica*] .... VMI
Developmental Therapeutics Program [*National Cancer Institute*] .... DTP
Developmental Training Center [*Indiana University*] [*Research center*] (RCD) .... DTC
Developmental Training Effectiveness Analysis [*Military*] .... DTEA
Developmentally Delayed .... DD
Development-Forward (MCD) .... DF
Development-Inhibitor Anchimeric Releasing [*Photography*] .... DIAR
Development-Inhibitor-Releasing [*Photography*] .... DIR
Development-Left (MCD) .... DL
Development-Right (MCD) .... DR
Developments in Manufacturing Industry [*A publication*] .... Devts Mfuring Ind
Deventer/Teuge [*Netherlands ICAO location identifier*] (ICLI) .... EHTE
Devereux Adolescent Behavior [*Rating scale*] [*Also, ABRS*] [*Psychology*] .... DAB
Devereux and Battle's North Carolina Equity Reports [*A publication*] (DLA) .... D & B
Devereux and Battle's North Carolina Equity Reports [*A publication*] (DLA) .... Dev & B
Devereux and Battle's North Carolina Equity Reports [*A publication*] (DLA) .... Dev & B Eq
Devereux and Battle's North Carolina Equity Reports [*A publication*] (DLA) .... Dev & Bat Eq
Devereux and Battle's North Carolina Law Reports [*A publication*] (DLA) .... D & B
Devereux and Battle's North Carolina Law Reports [*A publication*] (DLA) .... Dev & B
Devereux and Battle's North Carolina Law Reports [*A publication*] (DLA) .... Dev & Bat
Devereux and Battle's North Carolina Law Reports [*A publication*] (DLA) .... Dev & BL (NC)
Devereux Child Behavior [*Rating scale*] [*Psychology*] .... DCB
Devereux Elementary School Behavior [*Rating scale*] [*Psychology*] .... DESB
Devereux's Kinne's Blackstone [*A publication*] (DLA) .... Dev Kin Bl
Devereux's Kinne's Kent [*A publication*] (DLA) .... Dev Kin Kent
Devereux's North Carolina Equity Reports [*A publication*] (DLA) .... Dev Eq
Devereux's North Carolina Law Reports [*A publication*] (DLA) .... Dev
Devereux's North Carolina Law Reports [*A publication*] (DLA) .... Dev L
Devereux's Reports, United States Court of Claims [*A publication*] (DLA) .... Dev
Devereux's Reports, United States Court of Claims [*A publication*] (DLA) .... Dev CC
Devereux's Reports, United States Court of Claims [*A publication*] (DLA) .... Dev Ct Cl
Devet Elementary School, Valley Stream, NY [*Library symbol Library of Congress*] (LCLS) .... NVsDE
Deviant Flight Plan .... DFP
Deviated Nasal Septum [*Otorhinolaryngology*] (DAVI) .... DNS
Deviating Oscillator .... DO
Deviation .... D
Deviation (AAG) .... DEV
Deviation (MSA) .... DEVN
Deviation Approval Request [*NASA*] (KSC) .... DAR
Deviation Approved as Requested [*Aviation*] (FAAC) .... DAAR
Deviation Authorization .... DA
Deviation Clause [*Business term*] .... DC
Deviation Dependent Sensitivity [*Navigation*] (IAA) .... DDS
Deviation Difficulty [*Aerospace*] (AAG) .... DD
Deviation Drawing (MCD) .... DD
Deviation for Failure Location .... DFL
Deviation for Replacement Time .... DRT
Deviation from Mean Standard (MUGU) .... DMS
Deviation Indicating Controller (IAA) .... DIC
Deviation Indicator .... DI
Deviation Intelligence Quotient [*Education*] .... DIQ
Deviation of Temperature and Salinity .... DOTS
Deviation Range .... DR
Deviation Ratio .... DR

Deviation Report .... DR
Deviation Request Number (DNAB) .... DEVNO
Deviation Test Bridge .... DTB
Device (KSC) .... DEV
Device .... DV
Device (MSA) .... DVC
Device .... DVC
Device Adapter (IAA) .... DA
Device Address (ACRL) .... DA
Device Assembly Facility .... DAF
Device Assignment Table .... DAST
Device Assignment Table (MCD) .... DAT
Device Attachment Control Unit [*IBM Corp.*] .... DACU
Device Base Control Block [*Computer science*] (IBMDP) .... DVB
Device Characteristics Table [*Computer science*] (IBMDP) .... DCT
Device Cluster Controller .... DCC
Device Communications [*Computer science*] .... DEVCOM
Device Context (PCM) .... DC
Device Control .... DC
Device Control Area (IAA) .... DCA
Device Control Block [*Computer science*] (PCM) .... DCB
Device Control Character [*Computer science*] (IEEE) .... DCC
Device Control Character [*Computer science*] (CMD) .... DCX
Device Control Entry [*Computer science*] .... DCE
Device Control Unit .... DCU
Device Coordinate .... DC
Device Dependent Routine .... DDR
Device Description (ACII) .... DD
Device Description Language (ACII) .... DDL
Device Development Kit [*Microsoft Corp.*] .... DDK
Device Driver Kit [*Computer science*] (PCM) .... DDK
Device End .... DE
Device Error Tabulation [*Computer science*] (IAA) .... DET
Device Evaluation Network [*FDA*] [*Information service or system*] .... DEN
Device Flag [*Computer science*] .... DF
Device for Automatic Remote Data Collection [*Marine science*] (OSRA) .... DARC
Device for Automatic Remote Data Collection (USDC) .... DARC
Device for Automatic Remote Data Collection [*National Weather Service*] .... DARDC
Device for Automatic Word Identification and Discrimination [*Computer science*] .... DAWID
Device Function [*Computer science*] (IAA) .... DF
Device Handler .... DH
Device Identifier .... DID
Device Independence .... DI
Device Independent Access Level [*Telecommunications*] (OSI) .... DIAL
Device Independent Bitmap (CDE) .... DIB
Device Independent Disk Operation [*Computer science*] (IAA) .... DIDO
Device Independent Typesetting Run Off [*Typography*] (DGA) .... DITROFF
Device Initialize [*Computer science*] (IAA) .... DIN
Device Input Format .... DIF
Device Interface [*Electronics*] (ECII) .... DI
Device Interface Module .... DIM
Device Media Control Language [*CODASYL/Honeywell, Inc.*] .... DMCL
Device Message Handler [*IBM Corp.*] (NITA) .... DMH
Device Mount Unit (MCD) .... DMU
Device Multiplexing Nonsynchronized Inputs [*Computer science*] .... DMNI
Device Multiplexing Nonsynchronized Outputs [*Computer science*] (CET) .... DMNO
Device Name Table (IAA) .... DNT
Device Output Format .... DOF
Device Programmer Interface [*Computer science*] (EECA) .... DPI
Device Reference Table .... DRT
Device Rise Time [*Photomultipliers for scintillation counting*] (IEEE) .... DRT
Device Selector .... DS
Device, Simulator, and Simulation [*Army*] (RDA) .... DSS
Device State Register (NITA) .... DSR
Device Status Byte [*Computer science*] (BUR) .... DSB
Device Status Word (CMD) .... DSW
Device Strategy Module (IAA) .... DSM
Device under Test .... DUT
Device-Dependent Bitmap [*Computer science*] (PCM) .... DDB
Device-Driver Interface [*Computer science*] .... DDI
Device-Independent Bitmap [*Microsoft, Inc.*] (PCM) .... DIB
Device-Independent Display Operator Console Support (BUR) .... DIDOCS
Device-Independent Format [*Computer science*] .... DVI
Device-Oriented Electronic (IAA) .... DOE
Devices .... DVCS
Devices Management Directorate [*Army*] .... DMD
Device-Switching Unit .... DSU
Devil Mountain [*Alaska*] [*Seismograph station code, US Geological Survey*] (SEIS) .... DMA
Devil Pups (EA) .... DP
Devilled [*Culinary*] (ROG) .... DEVD
Devil's Advocate .... DA
Devils Lake [*North Dakota*] [*Airport symbol*] (OAG) .... DVL
Devils Lake Carnegie Library, Devils Lake, ND [*Library symbol Library of Congress*] (LCLS) .... NdDe
Devils Lake, ND [*FM radio station call letters*] (RBYB) .... KAOB
Devils Lake, ND [*AM radio station call letters*] .... KDLR
Devils Lake, ND [*FM radio station call letters*] .... KDVL
Devils Lake, ND [*FM radio station call letters*] (RBYB) .... KQZZ-FM
Devils Lake, ND [*FM radio station call letters*] .... KZZY
Devils Lake, ND [*Television station call letters*] .... WDAZ
Devils Postpile National Monument .... DEPO

Devils Tower National Monument .... DETO
Devin Register [*An association*] (EA) .... DR
Devine, TX [*Location identifier FAA*] (FAAL) .... HHH
Devine, TX [*FM radio station call letters*] .... KTXX
Devis de Construction Canada [*Construction Specifications Canada*] [*Formerly, Association des Redacteurs de Devis du Canada - ARDC*] .... DCC
Devis Directeurs Nationaux [*Canada*] (DD) .... DDN
Devisavit Vel Non [*Issue of fact as to whether a will in question was made by the testator*] [*Latin Legal term*] (DLA) .... DVN
Devise (ROG) .... DEVE
devise [*Legal shorthand*] (LWAP) .... DVS
Devised (ROG) .... DEVD
Devisengesetz [*Law on Exchange Control*] [*German*] (DLA) .... DevG
Devjo Industries, Inc. [*Toronto Stock Exchange symbol*] .... DEV
DeVlieg Bullard, Inc. [*Associated Press*] (SAG) .... DeVBul
DeVlieg Bullard, Inc. [*Associated Press*] (SAG) .... DeVBul
DeVlieg Bullard, Inc. [*NASDAQ symbol*] (SAG) .... DVLG
DeVlieg Bullard, Inc. [*NASDAQ symbol*] (SAG) .... DVLG
Devlin on Deeds [*A publication*] (DLA) .... Devl Deeds
Devlin on Deeds and Real Estate [*A publication*] (DLA) .... Dev Deeds
Devnic Energy, Inc. [*Toronto Stock Exchange symbol*] .... DVE
Devo Fan Club (EA) .... DFC
Devon [*South Africa*] [*ICAO location identifier*] (ICLI) .... FADV
Devon Cattle Association (EA) .... DCA
Devon Coal Research Centre, Alberta [*Library symbol National Library of Canada*] (NLC) .... ADCR
Devon Energy [*AMEX symbol*] (TTSB) .... DVN
Devon Energy Corp. [*Associated Press*] (SAG) .... DevnE
Devon Energy Corp. [*AMEX symbol*] (CTT) .... DVN
Devon Group [*NASDAQ symbol*] (TTSB) .... DEVN
Devon Group, Inc. [*NASDAQ symbol*] (NQ) .... DEVN
Devon Group, Inc. [*Associated Press*] (SAG) .... Devon
Devon Industries [*Vancouver Stock Exchange symbol*] .... DIV
Devon Militia [*British military*] (DMA) .... DM
Devon Public Library, Alberta [*Library symbol National Library of Canada*] (NLC) .... AD
Devonian [*Geology*] .... DEV
Devonian Group of Charitable Foundations, Calgary, AB, Canada [*Library symbol Library of Congress*] (LCLS) .... CaACDG
Devonian Group of Charitable Foundations, Calgary, Alberta [*Library symbol National Library of Canada*] (NLC) .... ACDG
Devonian Period [*Geology*] .... D
Devonion Resources [*Vancouver Stock Exchange symbol*] .... DVN
Devonport [*Australia ICAO location identifier*] (ICLI) .... AMDV
Devonport [*Tasmania*] [*Australia Airport symbol*] (OAG) .... DPO
Devonshire [*County in England*] .... DEVON
Devonshire [*County in England*] .... Devons
Devonshire and Dorset Regiment [*British military*] (DMA) .... D & D
Devonshire County [*England*] (BARN) .... Dev
Devonshire Hussar Imperial Yeomanry [*Military British*] (ROG) .... DHIY
Devotional and Practical Commentary [*A publication*] .... DPC
Devotions .... DEVS
Devran Petroleum Ltd. [*Vancouver Stock Exchange symbol*] .... DVP
DeVry, Inc. [*Associated Press*] (SAG) .... DeVry
DeVry, Inc. [*NYSE symbol*] (SAG) .... DV
Devtek Corp. [*Toronto Stock Exchange symbol*] .... DEK
Devteron [*A nuclear particle*] .... d
Dew [*Meteorology*] (BARN) .... W
DEW [*Distant Early Warning*] **East Military Identification Zone** .... DEMIZ
Dew Point .... DP
Dew Point [*NWS*] (FAAC) .... DWPNT
Dew Point Moisture Monitors [*Nuclear energy*] (NRCH) .... DPMM
Dew Point Sensing Device .... DPSD
Dew Point Tester .... DPT
Dewan Bahasa Dan Pustaka, Kuala Lumpur, Malaysia [*Library symbol Library of Congress*] (LCLS) .... DbP
Dewan Pengurus Sementara [*Provisional Management Board Section*] [*Indonesia*] .... DPS
Dewar Cryogenic Refrigerator .... DCR
Dewatering (MSA) .... DEWTRG
D'Ewes' Journal and Parliamentary Collection [*A publication*] (DLA) .... D'Ewes J
Dewey Decimal Classification [*Also, DDC*] .... DC
Dewey Decimal Classification [*Also, DC*] .... DDC
Dewey Decimal Number [*Online database field identifier*] .... DD
Dewey on Divorce Law [*A publication*] (DLA) .... Dew Div
Dewey's Compiled Statutes of Michigan [*A publication*] (DLA) .... Dew St
Dewey's Kansas Court of Appeals Reports [*A publication*] (DLA) .... Dew
Dewey's Reports [*60-70 Kansas*] [*A publication*] (DLA) .... Dew
DeWitt Historical Society of Tompkins County, Ithaca, NY [*Library symbol Library of Congress*] (LCLS) .... NIHi
Dewitt, MI [*FM radio station call letters*] .... WQHH
DeWitt State Hospital, Auburn, CA [*Library symbol Library of Congress*] (LCLS) .... CAuD
DeWitt's Reports [*24-42 Ohio State*] [*A publication*] (DLA) .... DeWitt
Dewoitine [*French aircraft type*] [*World War II*] .... D
DeWolfe Cos. [*AMEX symbol*] (TTSB) .... DWL
[*The*] **DeWolfe Cos., Inc.** [*Associated Press*] (SAG) .... DeWolfe
[*The*] **DeWolfe Cos., Inc.** [*AMEX symbol*] (SAG) .... DWL
Dew-Point Temperature [*Measure of humidity*] .... DPT
Dewsbury Central Library, Dewsbury, United Kingdom [*Library symbol Library of Congress*] (LCLS) .... UkDw
Dexamethasone [*Also, DEX, DXM*] [*Antineoplastic drug*] .... D
Dexamethasone [*Also, D, DXM*] [*Antineoplastic drug*] .... DEX
Dexamethasone [*Also, D, DEX*] [*Antineoplastic drug*] .... DXM
Dexamethasone Suppression Test [*Clinical chemistry*] .... DST
Dexamethasonyl Galactoside [*Biochemistry*] .... DEXGAL
Dexamphetamine Sulfate Tablet [*Slang*] (DSUE) .... DEX
Dexamthasonyl Glucopyranoside [*Biochemistry*] .... DEXGLU
Dexedrine .... DEX
Dexedrine .... DEXIE
Dexfield Review Sentinel, Redfield, IA [*Library symbol Library of Congress*] (LCLS) .... IaRedfRS
Dexleigh Corp. [*Toronto Stock Exchange symbol*] .... DXH
Dexter [*Right*] [*Latin*] .... D
Dexter [*Right*] [*Latin*] (ROG) .... DEX
Dexter [*Right*] [*Latin*] .... DEXT
[*The*] **Dexter Corp.** [*NYSE symbol*] (SPSG) .... DEX
[*The*] **Dexter Corp.** [*Associated Press*] (SAG) .... Dexter
Dexter District Library, Dexter, MI [*Library symbol Library of Congress*] (LCLS) .... MiDex
Dexter Free Library, Dexter, NY [*Library symbol Library of Congress*] (LCLS) .... NDex
Dexter, ME [*FM radio station call letters*] .... WGUY
Dexter, MO [*Location identifier FAA*] (FAAL) .... DXE
Dexter, MO [*AM radio station call letters*] .... KDEX
Dexter, MO [*FM radio station call letters*] .... KDEX-FM
Dexter Museum, Dexter, IA [*Library symbol Library of Congress*] (LCLS) .... IaDexM
Dexterous Hand Master [*Robotics*] .... DHM
Dextran [*Organic chemistry*] .... DEX
Dextran (MAE) .... DX
Dextran Blue [*Organic chemistry*] (MAE) .... DB
Dextran Sulfate [*Organic chemistry*] .... DXS
Dextran Sulphate Precipitable (OA) .... DSP
Dextran-Coated Charcoal .... DCC
Dextran-Coated Charcoal Analysis [*Analytical biochemistry*] .... DCCA
Dextro [*Configuration in chemical structure*] .... D
Dextroamphetamine Sulfate [*CNS stimulant*] .... DAS
Dextro-Levo(rotary) [*Also, r, rac*] [*Chemistry*] .... dl
Dextromethorphan [*Antitussive*] [*Pharmacy*] .... DM
Dextromethorphan [*Pharmacology*] (DAVI) .... DME
Dextromethorphan [*Antitussive*] [*Pharmacy*] .... DMH
Dextroposition of Aorta [*Cardiology*] (DAVI) .... DPA
Dextro(rotatory) [*Chemistry*] .... d
Dextrorotatory (DOG) .... dex
Dextrose [*Medicine*] (MAE) .... D
Dextrose [*Pharmacology*] (DAVI) .... dex
Dextrose [*Pharmacology*] .... DXT
Dextrose (5%) in Hartman's Solution [*Medicine*] D/5HS
Dextrose (5%) in Lactated Ringer's Solution [*Medicine*] D5LR
Dextrose 5% in Normal Saline [*Pharmacology*] (DAVI) D5/NS
Dextrose (5%) in Normal Saline Solution [*Medicine*] D5/NSS
Dextrose (5%) in Saline [*Medicine*] D5/S
Dextrose (5%) in Water [*Medicine*] D5/W
Dextrose Agar [*Microbiology*] .... DA
Dextrose and Saline [*Medicine*] .... D/S
Dextrose and Sodium Chloride [*Injection*] [*Pharmacology*] (DAVI) .... D/S
Dextrose Equivalent [*Food technology*] .... DE
Dextrose Five Percent [*Pharmacology*] (DAVI) D5
Dextrose in Normal Saline [*Pharmacology*] (DAVI) .... D/NS
Dextrose in Water [*Medicine*] .... D/W
Dextrose:Nitrogen Ratio .... D:N
Dextrose Solution Mixture [*Medicine*] (MAE) .... DSM
Dextrose Stick (DAVI) .... DS
Dextrose to Nitrogen Ratio (AAMN) .... D/NR
Dextrose-Gelatin-Veronal [*Solution*] [*Microbiology*] .... DGV
Dextrose-Gelatin-Veronal Buffer [*Microbiology*] (MAE) .... DGVB
Dextro-Stix [*Pharmacology*] (DAVI) .... dex
Dextrotransposition of the Great Arteries [*Cardiology*] (DAVI) .... D-TGA
Dextro-Tubocurarine [*Organic chemistry*] .... DTC
Dezful [*Iran*] [*ICAO location identifier*] (ICLI) .... OIAD
Dezimal Klassifikation [*Netherlands*] .... DK
D-Glutamylgycine [*Biochemistry*] .... DGG
DH Technology [*NASDAQ symbol*] (TTSB) .... DHTK
DH Technology, Inc. [*Associated Press*] (SAG) .... DH Tch
DH Technology, Inc. [*NASDAQ symbol*] (NQ) .... DHTK
Dhahran [*Saudi Arabia*] [*Airport symbol*] (OAG) .... DHA
Dhahran/International [*Saudi Arabia*] [*ICAO location identifier*] (ICLI) .... OEDR
Dhaka [*Bangladesh*] [*ICAO location identifier*] (ICLI) .... VGFR
Dhaka [*Bangladesh*] [*ICAO location identifier*] (ICLI) .... VGHQ
Dhaka/Tejgaon [*Bangladesh*] [*ICAO location identifier*] (ICLI) .... VGTJ
Dhaka/Zia International [*Bangladesh*] [*ICAO location identifier*] (ICLI) .... VGZR
Dhala [*Aden*] [*Airport symbol*] (AD) .... DHL
Dhanbad [*India*] [*ICAO location identifier*] (ICLI) .... VEDB
Dhangarhi [*Nepal*] [*Airport symbol*] (OAG) .... DHI
Dhangarhi [*Nepal*] [*ICAO location identifier*] (ICLI) .... VNDH
Dharma Realm Buddhist Association (EA) .... DRBA
DHL Airways, Inc. [*FAA designator*] (FAAC) .... DHL
Dhoney [*Ship's rigging*] (ROG) .... DHY
Dhorpatan [*Nepal*] [*ICAO location identifier*] (ICLI) .... VNDR
Dhoxaton [*Greece*] [*Airport symbol*] (AD) .... DXT
DI Industries [*Associated Press*] (SAG) .... DI Ind
DI Industries [*Formerly, Drillers, Inc.*] [*AMEX symbol*] (SPSG) .... DRL
Di-(2-Ethylhexyl) Hydrogen Phosphate [*Organic chemistry*] (DAVI) .... EHP
DIA [*Defense Intelligence Agency*] **Integrated Intelligence System** .... DIIS
Dia Met Minerals Ltd. [*Associated Press*] (SAG) .... DiaMet
Dia Met Minerals Ltd. [*Vancouver Stock Exchange symbol*] .... DMM
Dia Met Minerals Ltd. [*AMEX symbol*] (SAG) .... DMM
DIA [*Defense Intelligence Agency*] **Outline Plotting System** .... DOPS
Diabetes [*Medicine*] (DHSM) .... DIA
Diabetes [*or Diabetic*] .... DIAB

Diabetes and Your Eyes [National Eye Institute] [A publication] ... D & YE
Diabetes Association of Queensland [Medicine Australia] ... DAQ
Diabetes Association of the Australian Capital Territory ... DAACT
Diabetes Association of Western Australia ... DAWA
Diabetes Australia ... DA
Diabetes Australia - New South Wales [Medicine Australia] ... DANSW
Diabetes Center of Eastern Virginia [Eastern Virginia Medical School] ... DCEV
Diabetes Control and Complications [Medicine] ... DC & C
Diabetes Control and Complications Trial ... DCCT
Diabetes Foundation, Inc. [Later, JDC] ... DFI
Diabetes in Early Pregnancy [Medicine] ... DIEP
Diabetes Insipidus ... DI
Diabetes Insipidus, Diabetes Mellitus, Optic Atrophy, and Deafness [Medicine] ... DIMOAD
Diabetes Insipidus, Diabetes Mellitus, Optic Atrophy, Deafness Syndrome [Medicine] (DMAA) ... DIDMOAD
Diabetes Mellitus [Medicine] ... DM
Diabetes Mellitus Ketoacidosis [Endocrinology] (DAVI) ... DMKA
Diabetes Mellitus Out of Control [Medicine] (MEDA) ... DMOC
Diabetes Mellitus Out of Control [Medicine] (DMAA) ... DMOOC
Diabetes Opinion Survey [Child development test] [Psychology] ... DOS
Diabetes Out of Control [Endocrinology] (DAVI) ... DOC
Diabetes Out of Control [Medicine] (MEDA) ... DOOC
Diabetes Personalized Alerting Service ... DIAPAS
Diabetes Research and Training Center [Washington University] [Research center] (RCD) ... DRTC
Diabetes Research and Training Center [Yeshiva University] [Research center] (RCD) ... DRTC
Diabetes Research and Training Center [University of Chicago] [Research center] (RCD) ... DRTC
Diabetes Research and Training Center [University of Michigan] [Research center] (RCD) ... MDRTC
Diabetes Research Institute [University of Miami] [Research center] (RCD) ... DRI
Diabetes Research Institute Fund ... DRIF
Diabetes Retrieval Element Generator and Executor ... DREGE
Diabetes-Associated Peptide [Biochemistry] ... DAP
Diabetes-Prone [Medicine] ... DP
Diabetes-Resistant [Medicine] ... DR
Diabetic [Medicine] (DAVI) ... Db
Diabetic Father [Medicine] ... DF
Diabetic Floor Routine [Medicine] (DMAA) ... DFR
Diabetic Glomerulosclerosis [Endocrinology] (DAVI) ... DGS
Diabetic Ketoacidosis [Medicine] ... DKA
Diabetic Management [Medicine] (DAVI) ... DBK
Diabetic Management [Medicine] ... DBM
Diabetic Mother [Medicine] ... DM
Diabetic Polyneuropathy [Medicine] (DMAA) ... DPN
Diabetic Retinopathic Study [National Eye Institute] ... DRS
Diabetic Retinopathy [Medicine] ... DR
Diabetic Retinopathy Vitrectomy Study [National Eye Institute] ... DRVS
Diabetic Ulcer Meal [Airline notation] ... DUML
Diabetic Urine [Endocrinology] (DAVI) ... DU
Diablo Application Compiler Language [Computer science] (MHDI) ... DACL
Diablo Canyon Nuclear Power Plant (NRCH) ... DCNPP
Diablo Valley College, Concord, CA [Library symbol Library of Congress] (LCLS) ... CConE
Diabrasive International Ltd. [Toronto Stock Exchange symbol] ... DAB
Diacetone Acrylamide [Organic chemistry] ... DAA
Diacetone Alcohol [Organic chemistry] ... DAA
Diacetoxydiphenylmethylpyridine [Pharmacology] ... DAMP
Diacetoxyscirpenol [Fungal toxin] ... DAS
Diacetyl Monooxine [Organic chemistry] ... DAM
Diacetyldiaminodiphenylsulfone [Antibacterial compound] ... DADDS
Diacetyldianhydrogalacitol [Antineoplastic drug] ... DADAG
Diacetyldihydrofluorescein [Organic chemistry] ... DADF
Diacetyldioxohexahydrotriazine [Laundry bleach activator] ... DADHT
Diacetylferrocene [Organic chemistry] ... DAF
Diacetylfluorescein [Organic chemistry] ... DAF
Diacetyl(glucarodilactone) [Biochemistry] ... DAGDL
Diacetylmorphine [Pharmacology] ... DAM
Diack Newsletter [Database] [Diack, Inc.] [Information service or system] (CRD) ... DNL
Diacrin Inc. Unit [NASDAQ symbol] (TTSB) ... DCRNZ
Diacylglycerol [Organic chemistry] ... DAG
Diacylglycerol Kinase [An enzyme] ... DGK
Diademed [Numismatics] ... DIAD
Diagnose (NASA) ... DIAGN
Diagnosis ... D
Diagnosis (AABC) ... DG
Diagnosis ... DIAG
Diagnosis ... Dx
Diagnosis and Recommended Integrated System [Plant pathology] ... DRIS
Diagnosis and Remediation of Handwriting Problems [Educational test] ... DRHP
Diagnosis Code ... DX
Diagnosis, Objectives, Method, Evaluation [Formula] [LIMRA] ... DOME
Diagnosis Undetermined [or Unknown] [Medicine] ... DU
Diagnosis-Related Group (ECON) ... DRG
Diagnosis-Related Group [Insurance] (WYGK) ... DRG
Diagnosis-Rework Action (AAG) ... DRA
Diagnostic ... DGNSTC
Diagnostic ... DGNSTC
Diagnostic (BJA) ... diagn
Diagnostic (MSA) ... DIGN
Diagnostic Abilities in Math [Educational test] ... DAM
Diagnostic Acceptability Measure (PDAA) ... DAM
Diagnostic Achievement Battery ... DAB
Diagnostic Aid ... DA
Diagnostic Analysis of Reading Errors [Educational test] ... DARE
Diagnostic Analyzer ... DA
[A] Diagnostic and Prescriptive Technique [Teaching process] ... ADAPT
Diagnostic and Repair Expert [Computer-aided tank maintenance program] [Army] (RDA) ... DARE
Diagnostic and Statistical Manual [of Mental Disorders, Third Edition] ... DSM-III
Diagnostic and Statistical Manual of Mental Disorders [A publication] ... DSM
Diagnostic and Statistical Manual of Mental Disorders [A publication] ... DSM-III-R
Diagnostic and Therapeutic Technology Assessment [Medicine] ... DATTA
Diagnostic Center ... DC
Diagnostic Chemicals Ltd. ... DCL
Diagnostic Chemicals Ltd., Charlottetown, Prince Edward Island [Library symbol National Library of Canada] (NLC) ... PCDC
Diagnostic Code [Medicine] ... DC
Diagnostic Connector Assembly (RDA) ... DCA
Diagnostic Control Program (IAA) ... DCP
Diagnostic Control Software ... DCS
Diagnostic Control Store ... DCS
Diagnostic Controlled MODEM [Computer science] (BUR) ... DCM
Diagnostic Cost Group ... DCG
Diagnostic Decision Logic Table [Computer science] ... DDLT
Diagnostic Decision Table [Computer science] ... DDT
Diagnostic Development Branch [National Institutes of Health] ... DDB
Diagnostic Display Unit (MCD) ... DDU
Diagnostic Educational Grouping ... DEG
Diagnostic Energy Reserve Module [Airbags and safety systems] ... DERM
Diagnostic Execution Program (NOAA) ... DEP
Diagnostic Executive Program (NITA) ... DEP
Diagnostic Expert-Final Test [IBM Corp.] ... DEFT
Diagnostic Flow Chart [Computer science] (IEEE) ... DFC
Diagnostic FORTRAN [Formula Translating System] (IAA) ... DISTRAN
Diagnostic FORTRAN [Computer science] (IEEE) ... DITRAN
Diagnostic Function Test [Computer science] ... DFT
Diagnostic Health Services, Inc. [NASDAQ symbol] (SAG) ... DHSM
Diagnostic Health Services, Inc. [Associated Press] (SAG) ... DiagH
Diagnostic Health Services, Inc. [Associated Press] (SAG) ... DiagHlt
Diagnostic Health Svcs [NASDAQ symbol] (TTSB) ... DHSM
Diagnostic Imaging [Radiology] (DAVI) ... DI
Diagnostic Inspection [Clean Water Act] [Environmental Protection Agency] (EPA) ... DI
Diagnostic Interview for Children and Adolescents ... DICA
Diagnostic Interview for Genetic Studies ... DIGS
Diagnostic Interview Schedule [Psychology] ... DIS
Diagnostic Interview Schedule for Children [Psychology] ... DISC
Diagnostic Interview Schedule for Children - Parents Form [Psychology] ... DISC-P
Diagnostic Inventory of Personality and Symptoms [Personality development test] [Psychology] ... DIPS
Diagnostic Laparoscopy [or Laparotomy] (DAVI) ... DL
Diagnostic Machine Aids/Digital [Raytheon Co.] [Programming language] (CSR) ... DMAD
Diagnostic Mathematics Inventory ... DMI
Diagnostic Medical Instruments [Commercial firm] (DAVI) ... DMI
Diagnostic Medical Sonographer (DAVI) ... DMS
Diagnostic Methodology Section [National Institute of Dental Research] ... DMS
Diagnostic Monitor [Computer science] ... DIAMON
Diagnostic Monitor [Computer science] (IAA) ... DM
Diagnostic Monitor Executive [Computer science] ... DME
Diagnostic Prescriptive Arithmetic (EDAC) ... DPA
Diagnostic Prescriptive Teacher [or Teaching] ... DPT
Diagnostic Problem Solver [Computer science] ... DPS
Diagnostic Problem-Knowledge Coupler ... DPKC
Diagnostic Products [NYSE symbol] (TTSB) ... DP
Diagnostic Products Corp. [Associated Press] (SAG) ... DiagPd
Diagnostic Products Corp. [NYSE symbol] (SPSG) ... DP
Diagnostic Products Corp. ... DPC
Diagnostic Radiology [Medicine] ... DR
Diagnostic Reading Scales [Diagnostic assessment test] (PAZ) ... DMR
Diagnostic Reading Scales [Education] ... DRS
Diagnostic Related Group [Medicine] ... DRG
Diagnostic/Retrieval Sys [AMEX symbol] (TTSB) ... DRS
Diagnostic Retrieval Systems [Associated Press] (SAG) ... DiagRet
Diagnostic/Retrieval Systems, Inc. [Associated Press] (SAG) ... Diag
Diagnostic/Retrieval Systems, Inc. [AMEX symbol] (SPSG) ... DRS
Diagnostic Rework Sheets (AAG) ... DRS
Diagnostic Rhyme Test ... DRT
Diagnostic Rifle Marksmanship Simulator (MCD) ... DRIMS
Diagnostic Roentgenology [Radiology] (DAVI) ... DRnt
Diagnostic Screening Test: Achievement [Educational test] ... DSTA
Diagnostic Screening Test: Language [Educational test] ... DSTL
Diagnostic Screening Test: Math [Educational test] ... DSTM
Diagnostic Screening Test: Reading [Educational test] ... DSTR
Diagnostic Screening Test: Spelling [Educational test] ... DSTS
Diagnostic Simulation System ... DSS
Diagnostic Skills Battery [Educational test] ... DSB
Diagnostic Spelling Potential Test [Educational test] ... DSPT
Diagnostic Test Equipment (WDAA) ... DTE
Diagnostic Test Flow Diagram (MCD) ... DTFD
Diagnostic Test Mode [Automotive engineering] ... DTM
Diagnostic Test of Arithmetic Strategies ... DTAS
Diagnostic Test Set (IAA) ... DTS
Diagnostic Time [Computer science] (DNAB) ... DT

Diagnostic Trouble Code [*Automotive engineering*] ..... DTC
Diagnostic Turbulent Flux [*Marine science*] (OSRA) ..... DTF
Diagnostic Turbulent Flux (USDC) ..... DTF
Diagnostic Utility System ..... DUS
Diagnostically Optimizable Recursive Keyword [*Program generator*] (NITA) ..... DORK
Diagnostic-Assistance Reference Tool ..... DART
Diagnostics ..... Diags
Diagonal (FAAC) ..... DGNL
Diagonal ..... DIAG
Diagonal (WDMC) ..... diag
Diagonal Bands [*Navigation markers*] ..... Diag
Diagonal Braked Vehicle [*FAA*] ..... DBV
Diagonal Conducting Wall (MCD) ..... DCW
Diagonal Conjugate [*Medicine*] ..... DC
Diagonal Engines (DS) ..... D
Diagonal European Airways Link [*France*] [*FAA designator*] (FAAC) ..... DGL
Diagonal Polarization [*Physics*] (ECON) ..... D
Diagonal Proof Line [*Technical drawings*] ..... DPL
Diagonal Reporter, Diagonal, IA [*Library symbol Library of Congress*] (LCLS) ..... IaDiaR
Diagonostic Cost Group [*Medicine*] (HCT) ..... DCG
Diagonostic Medical Sonographer (HCT) ..... DMS
Diagram ..... D
Diagram (ADA) ..... DIA
Diagram (KSC) ..... DIAG
Diagram (VRA) ..... diag
Diagram (WDMC) ..... diag
Diagrammatic ..... DIAGR
Diahydrogalacititol, Adriamycin, Cisplatin [*Antineoplastic drug regimen*] (DAVI) ..... DAP I
Diakonia of the Americas (EA) ..... DOTA
Dial a Teacher Assistance [*Telephone service*] ..... DATA
Dial Access Information Retrieval System [*Shippensburg State College, Shippensburg, PA*] ..... DAIRS
Dial Access Technical Education [*Telecommunications*] (PDAA) ..... DATE
Dial Assist Operator (CET) ..... DAO
Dial Assistance Switchboard (CET) ..... DAS
Dial Central Office (MCD) ..... DCO
Dial Corp. [*Associated Press*] (SAG) ..... DialCp
Dial Corp. [*NYSE symbol*] (SPSG) ..... DL
Dial Corp. $4.75cmPfd [*NYSE symbol*] (TTSB) ..... DLPr
Dial Depth Gauge ..... DDG
Dial Dictation Relay Panel (HGAA) ..... DDRP
Dial Drive Belt ..... DDB
Dial Illumination ..... DLILMN
Dial Indicating ..... DLINDG
Dial Line Service Observing [*Telecommunications*] (TEL) ..... DLSO
Dial Lock ..... DLOCK
Dial Long Line [*Bell System*] ..... DLL
Dial Marking Kit ..... DMK
Dial Network Management System [*Telecommunications*] ..... DNMS
Dial Page, Inc. [*Associated Press*] (SAG) ..... DialPge
Dial Page, Inc. [*NASDAQ symbol*] (SAG) ..... DPGE
Dial Pulse [*Telecommunications*] ..... DP
Dial Pulse Access [*Telecommunications*] (TEL) ..... DPA
Dial Pulse Originating [*Telecommunications*] (TEL) ..... DPO
Dial Pulse Originating Incoming Register [*Telecommunications*] ..... DPOIR
Dial Pulse Receiver [*Telecommunications*] (PDAA) ..... DPR
Dial Pulse Repeater [*Telecommunications*] (IAA) ..... DPR
Dial Pulse Sender [*Telecommunications*] (PDAA) ..... DPS
Dial Pulse Terminating [*Telecommunications*] (TEL) ..... DPT
Dial Service Analysis [*Telecommunications*] (TEL) ..... DSA
Dial Service Assistance [*Telecommunications*] (CET) ..... DSA
Dial Service Assistance Switchboard [*Telecommunications*] (CET) ..... DSAS
Dial Service Auxiliary [*Telecommunications*] (IAA) ..... DSA
Dial System ..... DS
Dial Telephone Exchange (DNAB) ..... DTE
Dial Teletypewriter Exchange ..... DTWX
Dial Teletypewriter Service (IAA) ..... DTWS
Dial Terminal Unit (CAAL) ..... DTU
Dial Test Indicator ..... DTI
Dial Tone [*Telecommunications*] (TEL) ..... DT
Dial Tone First [*Telecommunications*] (TEL) ..... DTF
Dial Unit (MAE) ..... du
Dial-a-Bus [*TRB*] (TAG) ..... DAB
Dial-a-Design [*Computer-based design service*] ..... DAD
Dial-a-Ride [*TRB*] (TAG) ..... DAR
Dial-a-Ride Transportation ..... DART
Dialdehyde Starch [*Wet-strength agent*] ..... DAS
Dialect (ADA) ..... DIA
Dialect [*or Dialectal*] ..... DIAL
Dialect (WDMC) ..... dial
Dialect Notes [*A publication*] ..... DN
Dialect of Algorithmic Language ..... DIALGOL
Dialectic (WDAA) ..... DIA
Dialectic Information System (PDAA) ..... DIS
Dialectic Problem Solver ..... DPS
Dialed Digit Receiver [*Telecommunications*] (TEL) ..... DDR
Dialed Number Identification Service [*Telecommunications*] (ACRL) ..... DNIS
Dialektischer Materialismus ..... DIAMAT
Dialing Code Information [*Telecommunications British*] ..... DCI
Dialkyl Dihexadecylmalonate [*Organic chemistry*] ..... DDM
Dialkylglycine Decarboxylase [*An enzyme*] ..... DGD
Diallyl Chlorendate [*Fire retardant*] ..... DAC
Diallyl Isophthalate [*Organic chemistry*] ..... DAIP
Diallyl Maleate [*Organic chemistry*] ..... DAM
Diallyl Phthalate [*Organic chemistry*] ..... DAP
Diallyl Sulfide ..... DAS
Diallyl Tetrabromophthalate [*Organic chemistry*] ..... DATBP
Diallyldiethylammonium Chloride [*Organic chemistry*] ..... DADEAC
Diallyldimethylammonium Chloride [*Organic chemistry*] ..... DADMAC
Diallylmelamine [*Organic chemistry*] ..... DAM
Diallylpentobarbital [*Sedative*] ..... DAPB
Diallyltartardiamide [*Also, DATDA*] [*Organic chemistry*] ..... DATD
Diallyltartardiamide [*Also, DATD*] [*Organic chemistry*] ..... DATDA
Dialog Terminal System (IAA) ..... DIS
Dialog Terminal System (IAA) ..... DTS
Dialogi [*of Seneca the Younger*] [*Classical studies*] (OCD) ..... Dial
Dialogi Deorum [*of Lucian*] [*Classical studies*] (OCD) ..... Dial D
Dialogi Meretricii [*of Lucian*] [*Classical studies*] (OCD) ..... Dial Meret
Dialogi Mortuorum [*of Lucian*] [*Classical studies*] (OCD) ..... Dial Mort
Dialogic Corp. [*Associated Press*] (SAG) ..... Dialogic
Dialogic Corp. [*NASDAQ symbol*] (SAG) ..... DLGC
Dialogue (NTCM) ..... DIA
Dialogue ..... DIAL
Dialogue (WDMC) ..... dial
Dialogue: Canadian Philosophical Review [*A publication*] (BRI) ..... Dialogue
Dialogue Foundation (EA) ..... DF
Dialogue, Music, and Effects [*Film*] (WDMC) ..... D-M-E
Dialogue with People of Living Faith and Ideologies [*A publication*] (BJA) ..... DFI
Dialogus de Oratoribus [*of Tacitus*] [*Classical studies*] (OCD) ..... Dial
Dial-on-Demand Routing [*Telecommunications*] (PCM) ..... DDR
Dial-Up Networking [*Microsoft Windows 95*] [*Computer science*] ..... DUN
Dial-Up Networking [*Computer science*] ..... DUN
Dial-Up Wide Area Network Gaming Operation [*Computer science*] ..... Dwango
Dialysate of Hydroponic Plasma [*Hematology*] (DAVI) ..... HPD
Dialysis and You [*of the DAY Association*] [*Defunct*] (EA) ..... DAY
Dialysis Corp. Amer [*NASDAQ symbol*] (TTSB) ..... DCAI
Dialysis Corp. Amer Unit [*NASDAQ symbol*] (TTSB) ..... DCAIU
Dialysis Corp. Amer Wrrt [*NASDAQ symbol*] (TTSB) ..... DCAIW
Dialysis Corp. of America [*NASDAQ symbol*] (SAG) ..... DCAI
Dialysis Corp. of America [*Associated Press*] (SAG) ..... DialCp
Dialysis Corp. of America [*Associated Press*] (SAG) ..... DialCpA
Dialysis Disequilibrium Syndrome ..... DDS
Dialysis Encephalopathy Syndrome [*Medicine*] (DMAA) ..... DES
Dialysis Fluid [*Physiology*] ..... DF
Dialysis-Related Muscle Cramps [*Medicine*] ..... DMC's
Dialyzable Fraction ..... DF
Dialyzable Leukocyte Extract [*Hematology*] ..... DLE
Dialyzed Fetal Calf Serum ..... dFCS
Diamant [*France*] [*Research code symbol*] ..... SD
Diamantina [*Brazil*] [*Airport symbol*] (AD) ..... DMT
Diamantina Lakes [*Queensland*] [*Airport symbol*] (AD) ..... DYM
Diameter ..... D
Diameter [*Symbol*] [*IUPAC*] ..... d
Diameter ..... DI
Diameter ..... DIA
Diameter (VRA) ..... dia
Diameter (IDOE) ..... dia
Diameter (IDOE) ..... diam
Diameter ..... DIAM
Diameter at Breast Height [*Of trees*] ..... DBH
Diameter at Ground Height [*Botany*] ..... DGH
Diameter Bolt Circle [*Technical drawings*] ..... DBC
Diameter of Driving-Wheel in Inches [*Railroad term*] ..... W
Diametral Tensile Strength [*Material science*] ..... DTS
Diametrical Pitch ..... DP
Diametrics Medical [*NASDAQ symbol*] (TTSB) ..... DMED
Diametrics Medical, Inc. [*Associated Press*] (SAG) ..... Diametrc
Diametrics Medical, Inc. [*NASDAQ symbol*] (SAG) ..... DMED
Diamidinoindole [*Organic chemistry*] ..... DAI
Diamidinophenylindole [*A dye*] [*Organic chemistry*] ..... DAPI
Diamine Oxidase [*Also, DO*] [*An enzyme*] ..... DAO
Diamine Oxidase [*Also, DAO*] [*An enzyme*] ..... DO
Diamineanisole Sulfate [*Organic chemistry*] ..... DAAS
Diaminoacetanilide [*Organic chemistry*] ..... DAA
Diamino(adamantyl)ethylpyrimidine [*Biochemistry*] ..... DAEP
Diaminoanisole [*A dye*] [*Organic chemistry*] ..... DAA
Diaminobenzanilide [*Organic chemistry*] ..... DABA
Diaminobenzene [*Organic chemistry*] ..... DAB
Diaminobenzidine [*Organic chemistry*] ..... DAB
Diaminobenzoic Acid [*Organic chemistry*] ..... DABA
Diaminobutanoic Acid [*An amino acid*] ..... DAB
Diaminochlorobenzene [*Organic chemistry*] ..... DACB
Diaminocyclohexane [*Organic chemistry*] ..... DACH
Diaminocyclohexane(carboxyphthalato)platinum [*Antineoplastic drug*] ..... DACCP
Diaminocyclohexanetetraacetic Acid [*Also, OCTA*] [*Organic chemistry*] ..... DCTA
Diamino(diethoxyphosphinyl)triazine [*Organic chemistry*] ..... DAPT
Diaminodiphenyl Ether [*Organic chemistry*] ..... DADPE
Diaminodiphenyl Sulfone [*Also, DAPSONE, DDS*] [*Pharmacology*] ..... DADPS
Diaminodiphenyl Sulfone [*Also, DADPS, DDS*] [*Pharmacology*] ..... DAPSONE
Diaminodiphenyl Sulfone [*Also, DADPS, DAPSONE*] [*Pharmacology*] ..... DDS
Diaminodiphenyl Sulfoxide [*Pharmacology*] (MAE) ..... DDSO
Diaminodiphenylmethane [*Organic chemistry*] ..... DADPM
Diaminodiphenylmethane [*Organic chemistry*] ..... DAPM
Diaminodiphenylmethane [*Organic chemistry*] ..... DDM
Diaminoguanidine Nitrate [*Organic chemistry*] ..... DAGN
Diaminohydroxypropanetetraacetic Acid [*Also, DTA, DPTA*] [*Organic chemistry*] ..... DHPTA

Diaminomaleonitrile [*Organic chemistry*] .... DAMN
Diaminophenylthiazole [*Pharmacology*] .... DAPT
Diaminopimelic Acid [*Also, DAPA, DPM*] [*An amino acid*] .... DAP
Diaminopimelic Acid [*Also, DAP, DPM*] [*An amino acid*] .... DAPA
Diaminopimelic Acid [*Also, DAP, DAPA*] [*An amino acid*] .... DPM
Diaminopropanoic Acid [*An amino acid*] .... DPR
Diaminopropanoltetraacetic Acid [*Also, DTA, DHPTA*] [*Organic chemistry*] .... DPTA
Diaminopropanoltetraacetic Acid [*Also, DPTA, DHPTA*] [*Organic chemistry*] .... DTA
Diaminopurine [*Biochemistry*] .... DAP
Diaminopyridine [*Organic chemistry*] .... DAP
Diaminostilbenedisulfonic Acid [*Also, DASD, DASDS*] [*Organic chemistry*] .... DAS
Diaminostilbenedisulfonic Acid [*Also, DAS, DASDS*] [*Organic chemistry*] .... DASD
Diaminostilbenedisulfonic Acid [*Also, DAS, DASD*] [*Organic chemistry*] .... DASDS
Diaminotriazine Xanthene Biphenyl Imide [*Biochemistry*] .... DIXBI
Diaminotriazine Xanthene Thymine [*Biochemistry*] .... DIXT
Diamino(tribromopropyl)triazine [*Flame retardant*] [*Organic chemistry*] .... DABT
Diaminotrinitrobenzene [*An explosive*] .... DATB
Diaminotropolone [*Biochemistry*] .... DAT
Diaminovaleric Acid [*Biochemistry*] .... DAV
Diaminovaleric Acid .... DAVA
Diamminedichloroplatinum [*Cisplatin*], Vindesine, Bleomycin [*Antineoplastic drug regimen*] .... DVB
Diamminodichloroplatinum [*Cisplatin*] [*Also, CDDP, cis-DDP, CPDD, CPT, P*] [*Antineoplastic drug*] .... DDP
Diammonium Phosphate [*Inorganic chemistry*] .... DAP
Diamon .... DMND
Diamond (ADA) .... D
Diamond .... DIA
Diamond (MSA) .... DMD
Diamond (VRA) .... dmd
Diamond and Gemstone Remarketing Association [*Defunct*] (EA) .... DGRA
Diamond Anvil Cell [*Spectrometry*] .... DAC
Diamond Aviation, Inc. [*ICAO designator*] (FAAC) .... SPK
Diamond Core Drill Manufacturers Association (EA) .... DCDMA
Diamond Council of America (EA) .... DCA
Diamond Cut Lug (DICI) .... DCL
Diamond Dealers Club (EA) .... DDC
Diamond Depositions: Science and Technology [*A publication*] .... DD:S & T
Diamond Flap [*Envelopes*] .... DF
Diamond Grain Configuration .... DGC
Diamond Industrial Products Association [*British*] (DBA) .... DIPA
Diamond Locking Knurl .... DLK
Diamond Manufacturers and Importers Association of America .... DMI
Diamond Manufacturers and Importers Association of America (EA) .... DMIAA
Diamond Multimedia Systems [*NASDAQ symbol*] (TTSB) .... DIMD
Diamond Multimedia Systems, Inc. [*Associated Press*] (SAG) .... DiamM
Diamond Multimedia Systems, Inc. [*NASDAQ symbol*] (SAG) .... DIMD
Diamond Offshore Drilling [*NYSE symbol*] (TTSB) .... DO
Diamond Offshore Drilling, Inc. [*Associated Press*] (SAG) .... DiaOff
Diamond Offshore Drillings, Inc. [*NYSE symbol*] (SAG) .... DO
Diamond Ordnance Fuze Laboratory [*Later, Harry Diamond Laboratories*] [*AMC Washington, DC*] .... DOFL
Diamond Ordnance Radiation Facility [*Nuclear reactor*] .... DORF
Diamond Penetrator Hardness .... DPH
Diamond Pyramid Hardness (MSA) .... DPH
Diamond Pyramid Hardness Number .... DPN
Diamond Radiation Facility .... DRF
Diamond Ranch [*California*] [*Seismograph station code, US Geological Survey*] (SEIS) .... DIR
Diamond Resources [*Vancouver Stock Exchange symbol*] .... DMD
Diamond Roads, Long Island [*Bahamas*] [*ICAO location identifier*] (ICLI) .... MYLR
Diamond Sakha Airlines [*Former USSR*] [*FAA designator*] (FAAC) .... DSL
Diamond Setters Fraternal Guild [*Defunct*] (EA) .... DSFG
Diamond Shamrock [*NYSE symbol*] (TTSB) .... DRM
Diamond Shamrock Co. [*NYSE symbol*] (SPSG) .... DRM
Diamond Shamrock Corp., Harrison, NJ [*Library symbol Library of Congress*] (LCLS) .... NjHarN
Diamond Shamrock Corp., Research Library, Painesville, OH [*Library symbol Library of Congress*] (LCLS) .... OPaD
Diamond Shamrock R & M, Inc. [*Associated Press*] (SAG) .... DiaShm
Diamond T Register (EA) .... DTR
Diamond Thin-Film [*Coating technology*] .... DTF
Diamond Tool Engineering Co. .... DTE
Diamond Trade and Precious Stone Association of America (EA) .... DTPSAA
Diamond Trade Association of America [*Later, DTPSAA*] (EA) .... DTAA
Diamond Walnut Growers (EA) .... DWG
Diamond Wheel Manufacturers Institute (EA) .... DWMI
Diamondlike Carbon [*Materials science*] .... DLC
Diamondlike Hydrocarbon [*Coating material*] .... DLHC
Diamonds, Emeralds, Amethysts, and Rubies .... DEAR
Diamonds Fields Artillery [*British military*] (DMA) .... DFA
Diamond-Square-Diamond [*Lipscomb polyhedral rearrangement in borane anion and carborane series*] .... dsd
Diamondville, WY [*FM radio station call letters*] .... KBCK
Diana Corp. [*Associated Press*] (SAG) .... DianaCp
Diana Corp. [*NYSE symbol*] (SPSG) .... DNA
Diana Resources Ltd. [*Vancouver Stock Exchange symbol*] .... DNR
Diana Vreeland [*Fashion editor, 1903-1989*] .... DV
Diane Von Furstenberg [*Couturiere*] .... DVF
Dianhydrogalacitol [*Antineoplastic drug*] (DAVI) .... DAG
Dianhydrogalactitol, Adriamycin, Platinol [*Cisplatin*] [*Antineoplastic drug regimen*] .... DAP-II
Dianhydrogalactitol and VP-16 [*Antineoplastic drug regimen*] (DAVI) .... DV
Dianilinogossypol [*Organic chemistry*] .... DAG
Dianisidine Diisocyanate (DICI) .... DADI
Di'anno Fan Club (EA) .... DFC
Dianon Systems [*NASDAQ symbol*] (TTSB) .... DIAN
Dianon Systems, Inc. [*NASDAQ symbol*] (SPSG) .... DIAN
Dianon Systems, Inc. [*Associated Press*] (SAG) .... Dianon
Diapaga [*Burkina Faso*] [*ICAO location identifier*] (ICLI) .... DHED
Diapaga [*Burkina Faso*] [*Airport symbol*] (OAG) .... DIP
Diapaga [*Upper Volta*] [*Airport symbol*] (AD) .... DIP
Diapason [*Octave*] [*Music*] .... DIAP
Diapause Hormone [*In insects*] [*Endocrinology*] .... DH
Diaper .... DPR
Diaper Service Accreditation Council (EA) .... DSAC
Diaper Service Industry Association [*Later, NADS*] (EA) .... DSIA
Diaphon [*Record label*] [*Australia*] .... Dia
Diaphone [*Fog signal*] .... DIA
Diaphoretic [*Inducing Perspiration*] [*Pharmacy*] (ROG) .... DIA
Diaphosgene [*A choking agent*] (ADDR) .... DP
Diaphragm .... D
Diaphragm (NTCM) .... DIA
Diaphragm (MSA) .... DIAPH
Diaphragm (IAA) .... DP
Diaphragm (IAA) .... DPHGM
Diaphragm Gland .... DGLD
Diaphragm Nerve Stimulation .... DNS
Diaphragm Operated Valve .... DOV
Diaphragmatic (MAE) .... diaph
Diaphragmatic Electrical Activity .... Edi
Diaphragmatic Hernia [*Gastroenterology*] (DAVI) .... DH
Diaphragmatic Myocardial Infarct [*Cardiology*] (MAE) .... DMI
Diarachidoylphosphatidylcholine [*Biochemistry*] .... DAPC
Diarios y Noticias [*News agency*] [*Argentina*] (EY) .... DYN
Diarrhea [*Medicine*] .... D
Diarrhea and Dehydration [*Gastroenterology*] (DAVI) .... D & D
Diarrhea and Vomiting [*Medicine*] .... D & V
Diarrhea/Constipation (MEDA) .... D/C
Diarrhea with Fever and Vomiting [*Medicine*] (DMAA) .... DFV
Diarrhetic Shellfish Poisoning [*Medicine*] .... DSP
Diary of Social Legislation and Policy [*Australia A publication*] .... DSLP
Diary Publishers' Association [*British*] (BI) .... DPA
Diastatic Power .... DP
Diastematic Club of America [*Later, IDC*] (EA) .... DCA
Diastolic [*Medicine*] .... DIAS
Diastolic [*Medicine*] (WDAA) .... DIAST
Diastolic Blood Pressure [*Medicine*] .... DBP
Diastolic Control Team [*Cardiology*] (DAVI) .... DCT
Diastolic Filling Period [*Medicine*] .... DFP
Diastolic Gallop [*Medicine*] .... DG
Diastolic Murmur [*Medicine*] .... DM
Diastolic Pressure [*Medicine*] .... DP
Diastolic Pressure Time Index (AAMN) .... DPTI
Diastolic/Systolic [*Ratio*] [*Cardiology*] .... D/S
Diastolic Time [*Cardiology*] .... DT
Diastolic Transmembrane Voltage, Maximum [*Cardiology*] (DAVI) .... $DTMV_{max}$
Diastrophic Dysplasia [*Medicine*] .... DTD
DiaSys Corp. [*Associated Press*] (SAG) .... DiaSys
DiaSys Corp. [*NASDAQ symbol*] (SAG) .... DIYS
DiaSys Corp. Wrrt [*NASDAQ symbol*] (TTSB) .... DIYSW
Diatec Resources Ltd. [*Vancouver Stock Exchange symbol*] .... DTR
Diathermy [*Medicine*] .... D
Diathermy [*Medicine*] .... DIA
Diathermy [*Medicine*] .... DIATH
Diathermy, Massage, and Exercise [*Physical therapy*] (DAVI) .... DMX
Diathermy Short Wave [*Physical therapy*] (DAVI) .... Diath SW
Diatomaceous Earth (PDAA) .... DE
Diatomic Molecule Spectra and Energy Levels Center .... DMSELC
Diatoms [*Quality of the bottom*] [*Nautical charts*] .... Di
Diatrizoate (MAE) .... DTZ
Diazaanthracenedione [*Organic chemistry*] .... DAAD
Diazabicycloheptene [*Organic chemistry*] .... DBH
Diazabicyclooctane [*Organic chemistry*] .... DABCO
Diazabicycloundecene [*Biochemistry*] .... DBU
Diazabutadiene [*Organic chemistry*] .... DAB
Diazafluorenone [*Organic chemistry*] .... DFO
Diazepam [*Also, DAP, DZ*] [*A sedative*] .... D
Diazepam [*Also, D, DZ*] [*A sedative*] .... DAP
Diazepam [*Also, D, DAP*] [*A sedative*] .... DZ
Diazepam [*Also, D, DAP, DZ*] [*Antiepileptic drug*] .... DZP
Diazepam Binding Inhibitor [*Biochemistry*] .... DBI
Diaziquone [*Antineoplastic drug*] (DAVI) .... AZQ
Diazo Print .... DPR
Diazobenzyloxymethol [*Organic chemistry*] .... DBM
Diazobenzyloxymethyl Paper [*Genetics*] (DOG) .... DBM paper
Diazobicyclononene [*Organic chemistry*] .... DBN
Diazobicycloundecane [*Organic chemistry*] .... DBU
Diazodicyanoimidazole [*Organic chemistry*] .... DDI
Diazodinitrophenol [*Organic chemistry*] .... DDNP
Diazonaphthoquinone [*Organic chemistry*] .... DNQ
Diazonaphthoquinone-Sensitized Novolac [*Photoresist resin system*] .... DQN
Diazooxo-L-norleucine [*Antineoplastic drug*] .... DON
Diazouracil [*Pharmacology*] .... DU
Diazyme Unit [*Of hydrolytic enzyme activity*] .... DU
Dibasic Acid [*Waste from adipic acid production*] .... DBA
Dibasic Ester [*DuPont organic solvent*] .... DBE
Dibenzamine [*Pharmacology*] (DAVI) .... DBZ

Dibenzanthracene [*Carcinogen*] ...... DBA
Dibenzothiophene [*Organic chemistry*] ...... DBT
Di(benzotriazolyl)oxalate [*Organic chemistry*] ...... DBTO
Dibenzoylacetylene [*Organic chemistry*] ...... DBA
Dibenzoylbenzene [*Organic chemistry*] ...... DBB
Dibenzyl Ether [*Organic chemistry*] ...... DBE
Dibenzylamine [*Organic chemistry*] ...... DBA
Dibenzylethylenediamine [*Organic chemistry*] ...... DBED
Dibenzylmethylamine [*Organic chemistry*] ...... DBMA
Dibenzylphosphoryl Chloride [*Organic chemistry*] ...... DBPCI
Dibi Resources, Inc. [*Vancouver Stock Exchange symbol*] ...... DBI
Di-Binary Digit [*Two consecutive binary digits*] (TEL) ...... DIBIT
DIBOL Debugging Technique [*Digital Equipment Corp.*] ...... DDT
Diboll, TX [*FM radio station call letters*] ...... KAFX-FM
Diboll, TX [*AM radio station call letters*] (RBYB) ...... KSML
Dibrell Brothers, Inc. [*NASDAQ symbol*] (NQ) ...... DBRL
Dibromochloropropane [*Pesticide*] ...... DBCP
Dibromodifluoromethane [*Fire extinguishing agent*] [*Organic chemistry*]
   (ADA) ...... DB
Dibromodinitrofluorescein [*A dye*] [*Biochemistry*] (DAVI) ...... eosin B
Dibromodulcitol [*Mitolactol*] [*Antineoplastic drug*] ...... DBD
Dibromodulcitol, Adriamycin, Vincristine, Halotestin [*Fluoxymesterone*]
   [*Antineoplastic drug regimen*] ...... DAVH
Dibromoethane [*Same as EB, EDB*] [*Organic chemistry*] ...... DBE
Dibromohydroxymercurifluorescein [*Antiseptic*] ...... DOMF
Dibromomannitol [*or Mitobronitol*] [*Antineoplastic drug*] (DAVI) ...... DBK
Dibromomannitol [*Mitobronitol*] [*Antineoplastic drug*] ...... DBM
Dibromomethyl(isopropyl)benzoquinone [*Organic chemistry*] ...... DBMIB
Dibromoneopentyl Glycol [*Flame retardant*] [*Organic chemistry*] ...... DBNPG
Dibromonitrilopropionamide [*Organic chemistry*] ...... DBNPA
Dibromophenol [*Organic chemistry*] ...... DBP
Dibromoquinonechlorimide [*Solution*] [*Organic chemistry*] (DAVI) ...... BCQ
Dibromoquinonechlorimide Solution [*Organic chemistry*] (DAVI) ...... BQC Sol
Dibromosalicil [*Germicide*] ...... DBS
Dibromostyrene [*Organic chemistry*] ...... DBS
Dibrugarh [*India*] [*Airport symbol*] (OAG) ...... DIB
Dibucaine Number [*Organic chemistry*] (DAVI) ...... BUCAIN
Dibucaine Number [*Anesthesiology*] ...... DN
Dibutanoylmorphine [*An analgesic*] ...... DMB
Di(butoxyethyl) Phthalate [*Organic chemistry*] ...... DBOEP
Dibutyl Butylphosphonate [*Organic chemistry*] ...... DBBP
Dibutyl Hyponitrite [*Organic chemistry*] ...... DBHN
Dibutyl Maleate [*Organic chemistry*] ...... DBM
Dibutyl Phosphate [*Organic chemistry*] (NUCP) ...... DBP
Dibutyl Phosphate [*Organic chemistry*] (NUCP) ...... DPB
Dibutyl Phthalate [*Also, DBPh*] [*Organic chemistry*] ...... DBP
Dibutyl Phthalate [*Also, DBP*] [*Organic chemistry*] ...... DBPh
Dibutyl Sebacate [*Organic chemistry*] ...... DBS
Dibutyl Sulfate [*Organic chemistry*] ...... DBS
(Dibutylaminosulfenyl)methylcarbamate [*Insecticide*] ...... DBSC
Dibutylindolocarbazole [*Organic chemistry*] ...... DBIC
Dibutylmagnesium [*Organic chemistry*] ...... DBM
Dibutylmalonic Acid [*Organic chemistry*] ...... DBMA
Dibutylnitrosamine [*Also, DBNA*] [*Organic chemistry*] ...... DBN
Dibutylnitrosamine [*Also, DBN*] [*Organic chemistry*] ...... DBNA
Dibutylphosphoric Acid [*Organic chemistry*] ...... DBP
Dibutyltin [*Organic chemistry*] ...... DBT
Dibutyltin Dilaurate [*Organic chemistry*] ...... DBTDL
Dibutyltin Dilaurate [*Organic chemistry*] ...... DBTL
Dibutyryl CAMP [*Cyclic Adenosine Monophosphate*] [*Biochemistry*] ...... DAMP
Dibutyryl Cyclic Adenosine Monophosphate [*Organic chemistry*]
   (DAVI) ...... DCAMP
Dicalcium Phosphate [*Inorganic chemistry*] ...... DCP
Dicalcium Phosphate Dihydrate [*Inorganic chemistry*] ...... DCPD
Dicapryl Phthalate [*Organic chemistry*] ...... DCP
Dicarbethoxydihydrocollidine [*Biochemistry*] ...... DDC
Dicarbethoxy(dimethyl)(ethyl)dihydropyridine [*Biochemistry*] ...... DDEP
Dicarbethoxythiamine [*Pharmacology*] ...... DCET
Dicarboxyfluorescein [*A biological stain*] ...... DCF
Dicarboxylic Aciduria [*Medicine*] ...... DCA
Diccionario de Citas [*A publication*] ...... DDC
Diccionario Enciclopedico Salvat [*A publication*] ...... DES
Dice Fanual Similarity and Index [*Ecology*] ...... DFSI
Dicentric (MAE) ...... dic
Dice's Reports [*79-91 Indiana*] [*A publication*] (DLA) ...... Dice
Dicetyl Phosphate [*Organic chemistry*] ...... DCP
Dicey. Conflict of Laws [*A publication*] (DLA) ...... Dicey & Morris
Dicey. Conflict of Laws [*A publication*] (DLA) ...... Dicey Confl Laws
Dicey. Law of Domicil [*A publication*] (DLA) ...... Dic Dom
Dicey. Law of Domicil [*A publication*] (DLA) ...... Dicey Dom
Dicey. Law of Domicil [*A publication*] (DLA) ...... Dicey Domicil
Dicey on Parties to Actions [*A publication*] (DLA) ...... Dic Par
Dicey's Lectures Introductory to the Study of the Law of the English
   Constitution [*A publication*] (DLA) ...... Dicey Const
Dichloral Urea [*Medicine*] (MAE) ...... DCU
Dichloro Analog of Zomepirac [*Biochemistry*] ...... DCZ
Dichloro (Methyl) Benzhydrol [*Organic chemistry*] ...... DMB
Dichloroacetate [*Organic chemistry*] ...... DCA
Dichloroacetic Acid [*Pharmacology*] (DAVI) ...... DCA
Dichloroacetic Acid [*Organic chemistry*] ...... DCAA
Dichloroacetyl Chloride [*Organic chemistry*] ...... DCAC
Dichloroallyl Diisopropylthiocarbamate [*Di-allate*] [*Herbicide*] ...... DATC
Dichloroaniline [*Dye intermediate*] ...... DCA
Dichlorobenzidine [*Organic chemistry*] ...... DCB
Dichlorobenzoate [*Organic chemistry*] ...... DCB

Dichlorobenzophenone [*Also, DCBP*] [*Organic chemistry*] ...... DBP
Dichlorobenzophenone [*Also, DBP*] [*Organic chemistry*] ...... DCBP
Dichlorobenzotrifluoride [*Organic chemistry*] ...... DCBTF
Dichlorobenzyl Chloride [*Organic chemistry*] ...... DCBC
Dichlorobiphenyl [*Organic chemistry*] ...... DCB
Dichloro-bis(trifluoromethyl)diphenylurea [*Insectproofing agent for wool*] ...... DTDU
Dichlorodiammineplatinum [*Organic chemistry*] ...... DDP
Dichlorodibenzodioxin [*Also, DDD*] [*Organic chemistry*] ...... DCDD
Dichlorodibenzodioxin [*Also, DCDD*] [*Organic chemistry*] ...... DDD
Dichlorodicyanobenzoquinone [*Organic chemistry*] ...... DDQ
Dichlorodimethylhydantoin [*Organic chemistry*] ...... DDH
Dichlorodiphenyl Disulfide [*Insecticide*] ...... DDDS
Dichlorodiphenyldichloroethane [*Also, TDE*] [*Insecticide*] ...... DDD
Dichlorodiphenyldichloroethylene [*Pesticide residue*] ...... DDE
Dichlorodiphenylmethane [*Organic chemistry*] ...... DDM
Dichlorodiphenylmethylcarbinol [*Also, DMC*] [*Insecticide*] ...... DCPC
Dichlorodiphenylmethylcarbinol [*Also, DCPC*] [*Insecticide*] ...... DMC
Dichlorodiphenylsulfone [*Organic chemistry*] ...... DCDPS
Dichlorodiphenyltrichloroethane [*Insecticide*] ...... DDT
Dichloroethane [*Organic chemistry*] ...... DCE
Dichloroethyl Ether [*Organic chemistry*] ...... DCEE
Dichlorohexafluorobutane [*Organic chemistry*] (MAE) ...... DCHFB
Dichloroisocoumarin [*Organic chemistry*] ...... DCI
Dichloroisocyanuric Acid [*Organic chemistry*] ...... DCCA
Dichloroisoprenaline [*Organic chemistry*] ...... DCI
Dichloroisoproterenol [*Pharmacology*] ...... DCI
Dichloromaleic Acid [*Organic chemistry*] ...... DCM
Dichloromaleic Acid [*Organic chemistry*] ...... DCMA
Dichloro-meta-Xylenol [*Organic chemistry*] ...... DCMX
Dichloromethane [*Anesthetic*] [*Organic chemistry*] ...... DCM
Dichloromethotrexate [*Also, DCMTX*] [*Antineoplastic drug*] ...... DCM
Dichloromethotrexate [*Also, DCM*] [*Antineoplastic drug*] ...... DCMTX
Dichloromethotrexate [*Antineoplastic drug*] (DAVI) ...... DCMXT
Dichloromethotrexate [*Antineoplastic drug*] (CDI) ...... DMC
Dichloromethyl Methyl Ether [*Organic chemistry*] ...... DCME
Dichloronitroaniline [*Also, DICHLORAN*] [*Fungicide*] ...... DCNA
Dichloronitroaniline [*Also, DCNA*] [*Fungicide*] ...... DICHLORAN
Dichloronitrosalicylanilide [*Economic poison*] [*Organic chemistry*] ...... DCN
Dichlorophenol [*Organic chemistry*] ...... DCP
Dichlorophenolindophenol [*Also, DCPI, DCPIP, DPIP*] [*Analytical reagent*] ...... DCIP
Dichlorophenolindophenol [*Also, DCIP, DCPIP, DPIP*] [*Analytical reagent*] ...... DCPI
Dichlorophenolindophenol [*Also, DCIP, DCPI, DPIP*] [*Analytical reagent*] ...... DCPIP
Dichlorophenolindophenol [*Also, DCIP, DCPI, DCPIP*] [*Analytical reagent*] ...... DPIP
Di(chlorophenoxy)methane (IIA) ...... DCPM
(Dichlorophenoxy)triethylamine [*Herbicide*] ...... DCPTA
(Dichlorophenyl) Methyl Isopropylphosphoramidothioate [*Herbicide*] ...... DMPA
(Dichlorophenyl)dimethylurea [*Herbicide*] ...... DCMU
(Dichlorophenyl)methylurea [*Organic chemistry*] ...... DCPMU
Dichloropropane [*Pesticide*] ...... DCP
Dichloropropene-Dichloropropane [*Pesticide*] ...... DD
Dichloropropionanilide [*Also, DPA*] [*Herbicide*] ...... DCPA
Dichloropropionanilide [*Also, DCPA*] [*Herbicide*] ...... DPA
Dichloropropyl Acrylate [*Organic chemistry*] ...... DCOPA
Dichlororibofuranosylbenzimidazole [*Biochemistry*] ...... DRB
Dichlorosilane [*Photovoltaic energy systems*] ...... DCS
Dichlorotetrafluorobenzene [*Organic chemistry*] ...... DCFB
Dichlorotoluene [*Organic chemistry*] ...... DCT
(Dichlorotriazinyl)aminofluorescein [*Also, DTAF*] [*Analytical biochemistry*] ...... DCTAF
(Dichlorotriazinyl)aminofluorescein [*Also, DCTAF*] [*Analytical biochemistry*] ...... DTAF
Dichlorovinylcysteine [*Biochemistry*] ...... DCVC
Dichlorovinylglutathione [*Biochemistry*] ...... DCVG
Dichlorvos (GNE) ...... DDVP
Dichotic Environmental Sounds Test [*Medicine*] (DMAA) ...... DEST
Dichotic Pitch Discrimination Test [*Medicine*] (DMAA) ...... DPT
Dichroic Microspectrophotometer ...... DMSP
Dichroic Mirror ...... DM
Dichroic Parametric Mirror ...... DPM
Dichromated Gelatin ...... DCG
Dicionario Bibliografico Portugues [*A bibliographic publication*] [*Portugal*] ...... DBP
Dick Clark Companies ...... DCC
dick clark productions [*NASDAQ symbol*] (TTSB) ...... DCPI
Dick Clark Productions, Inc. [*Associated Press*] (SAG) ...... DClark
Dick Clark Productions, Inc. [*NASDAQ symbol*] (NQ) ...... DCPI
Dick Curless Fan Club (EA) ...... DCFC
Dick Damron International Fan Club [*Defunct Defunct*] (EA) ...... DDIFC
Dick Family Association (EA) ...... DFA
Dicke-Fix [*Electronics*] ...... DF
Dicke-Fix [*Electronics*] (CET) ...... DFX
Dickens' English Chancery Reports [*A publication*] (DLA) ...... Dick
Dickens' English Chancery Reports [*A publication*] (DLA) ...... Dick Ch
Dickens' English Chancery Reports [*A publication*] (DLA) ...... Dick Ch (Eng)
Dickens' English Chancery Reports [*A publication*] (DLA) ...... Dickens
Dickens' English Chancery Reports, by Wyatt [*A publication*] (DLA) ...... Wy Dick
Dickens Society (EA) ...... DS
Dickey [*Maine*] [*Seismograph station code, US Geological Survey*] (SEIS) D1A
Dickey [*Maine*] [*Seismograph station code, US Geological Survey*] (SEIS) D2A
Dickey [*Maine*] [*Seismograph station code, US Geological Survey*] (SEIS) D3A
Dickinson [*North Dakota*] [*Airport symbol Obsolete*] (OAG) ...... DIK
Dickinson College, Carlisle, PA [*OCLC symbol*] (OCLC) ...... DKC
Dickinson College, Carlisle, PA [*Library symbol Library of Congress*]
   (LCLS) ...... PCarlD
Dickinson County Courthouse, Spirit Lake, IA [*Library symbol*] [*Library of Congress*] (LCLS) ...... IaSplCoC

Dickinson County Library, Iron Mountain, MI [*Library symbol Library of Congress*] (LCLS) ..... MilrmD

Dickinson County Library, Norway Branch, Norway, MI [*Library symbol Library of Congress*] (LCLS) ..... MilrmD-N

Dickinson Law Review [*A publication*] (DLA) ..... Dk LR

Dickinson Law Review [*A publication*] (DLA) ..... DLR

Dickinson Library, Deerfield, MA [*Library symbol Library of Congress*] (LCLS) ..... MDee

Dickinson Memorial Library, Orange City, FL [*Library symbol Library of Congress*] (LCLS) ..... FOrD

Dickinson, ND [*FM radio station call letters*] (RBYB) ..... KCAD-FM

Dickinson, ND [*AM radio station call letters*] ..... KDIX

Dickinson, ND [*FM radio station call letters*] ..... KDPR

Dickinson, ND [*Television station call letters*] ..... KDSE

Dickinson, ND [*AM radio station call letters*] ..... KLTC

Dickinson, ND [*Television station call letters*] ..... KQCD

Dickinson, ND [*FM radio station call letters*] ..... KRRB

Dickinson, ND [*FM radio station call letters*] ..... KRRD

Dickinson, ND [*Television station call letters*] ..... KXMA

Dickinson Public Library, Dickinson, ND [*Library symbol Library of Congress*] (LCLS) ..... NdDi

Dickinson Robinson Group Ltd. [*British*] ..... DRG

[*The*] Dickinson School of Law (GAGS) ..... Dickinson Sch Law

Dickinson School of Law [*Pennsylvania*] ..... DSL

Dickinson School of Law, Sheeley-Lee Law Library, Carlisle, PA [*OCLC symbol*] (OCLC) ..... DKL

Dickinson School of Law, Sheeley-Lee Law Library, Carlisle, PA [*Library symbol Library of Congress*] (LCLS) ..... PCarlD-L

Dickinson State College, Dickinson, ND [*Library symbol Library of Congress*] (LCLS) ..... NdDiS

Dickinson State College, Dickinson, ND [*OCLC symbol*] (OCLC) ..... NDI

Dickinson's International Law Annual [*A publication*] (DLA) ..... Dick Int'l L Ann

Dickinson's Justice [*A publication*] (DLA) ..... Dick Just

Dickinson's New Jersey Equity Precedents [*A publication*] (DLA) ..... Dick

Dickinson's New Jersey Equity Precedents [*A publication*] (DLA) ..... Dick Eq Pr

Dickinson's New Jersey Equity Precedents [*A publication*] (DLA) ..... Dick (NJ)

Dickinson's Practical Guide to the Quarter Sessions [*A publication*] (DLA) ..... Dick Quar Ses

Dicks of America [*An association*] (EA) ..... DOA

Dickson, TN [*AM radio station call letters*] ..... WDKN

Dickson, TN [*FM radio station call letters*] (RBYB) ..... WNRZ-FM

Dickson, TN [*FM radio station call letters*] ..... WQZQ

Dickson, TN [*FM radio station call letters*] ..... WYYB

Dickson's Analysis of Blackstone's Commentaries [*A publication*] (DLA) ..... Dick Black

Dickson's Analysis of Kent's Commentaries [*A publication*] (DLA) ..... Dick Kent

Dickson's Law of Evidence in Scotland [*A publication*] (DLA) ..... Dick Ev

Dicon Systems Ltd. [*Toronto Stock Exchange symbol*] ..... DCY

Diconjugate Bilirubin [*Biochemistry*] ..... DB

Dicrotic Notch [*Cardiology*] ..... DN

Dicta (DLA) ..... D

Dicta (DLA) ..... Dic

Dicta of Denver Bar Association [*A publication*] (DLA) ..... Dicta

Dictaphone ..... DICT

Dictaphone (IAA) ..... DICTA

Dictaphone Machine Transcriber ..... DMT

Dictation ..... DICT

Dictation Equipment ..... DE

Dictator ..... DICT

Dictator ..... DICT

Dictatorships and Double Standards [*Title of an article written by Jeane Kirkpatrick in 1979 that became basis of conservative foreign policy*] ..... D & DS

Dicti Anni [*Of the Said Year*] [*Latin*] ..... DA

Diction (WDMC) ..... dict

Dictionaries, Encyclopedias, and Other Word-Related Books [*A publication*] ..... DEOWRB

Dictionary ..... DIC

Dictionary ..... DICT

Dictionary (WDMC) ..... dict

Dictionary of Abbreviations in Medicine [*A publication*] ..... DAM

Dictionary of American English [*A publication*] ..... DAME

Dictionary of American History [*A publication*] ..... DAH

Dictionary of American Hymnology [*Database*] [*Hymn Society of America, Inc.*] [*Information service or system*] (IID) ..... DAH

Dictionary of American Literary Biography [*A publication*] ..... DALB

Dictionary of American Naval Fighting Ships [*A publication*] ..... DANFS

Dictionary of American Regional English [*A publication*] ..... DARE

Dictionary of American Regional English Project [*University of Wisconsin - Madison*] [*Research center*] (RCD) ..... DARE

Dictionary of American Slang [*A publication*] ..... DAS

Dictionary of Americanisms [*A publication*] ..... DA

Dictionary of Assyrian Botany [*A publication*] (BJA) ..... DAB

Dictionary of Biblical Theology [*A publication*] (BJA) ..... DBT

[*The*] Dictionary of Biographical Quotation [*A publication*] ..... DBQ

Dictionary of Canadian Biography [*A publication*] ..... DCB

Dictionary of Canadian Biography, Toronto, Ontario [*Library symbol National Library of Canada*] (BIB) ..... OTDCB

Dictionary of Carribean English Usage [*A publication*] ..... DCEU

Dictionary of Christ and the Gospels [*A publication*] (BJA) ..... DCG

Dictionary of Christ and the Gospels [*James Hasting*] [*A publication*] (BJA) ..... HDCG

Dictionary of Christian Antiquities [*A publication*] (BJA) ..... DCA

Dictionary of Christian Biography and Literature [*A publication*] (OCD) ..... DCB

Dictionary of Computer and Control Systems Abbreviations, Signs, and Symbols [*New York: Odyssey Press, 1965*] [*A publication*] ..... DCCSA

Dictionary of Electrical Abbreviations, Signs, and Symbols [*A publication*] ..... DEIA

Dictionary of Electronics Abbreviations, Signs, and Symbols [*A publication*] ..... DEA

Dictionary of Folklore, Mythology, and Legend [*A publication*] ..... DFML

[*A*] Dictionary of Forces' Slang [*A publication*] ..... DFS

Dictionary of Industrial Engineering Abbreviations [*A publication*] (KSC) ..... DIEA

Dictionary of Initials - What They Mean [*A publication*] ..... DIWTM

Dictionary of International Biography [*A publication*] ..... DIB

Dictionary of Jamaican English [*A publication*] ..... DJE

Dictionary of Literary Biography [*A publication*] ..... DLB

Dictionary of Naval Abbreviations [*A publication*] ..... DICNAVAB

Dictionary of Occupational Titles [*Department of Labor*] [*A publication*] ..... DOT

Dictionary of Old English [*University of Toronto*] [*Canada Information service or system*] (IID) ..... DOE

Dictionary of Organic Compounds [*A publication*] ..... DOCS

Dictionary of Physics and Mathematics Abbreviations, Signs, and Symbols [*A publication*] ..... DPMA

Dictionary of Scientific Biography [*A publication*] ..... DSB

[*A*] Dictionary of Slang and Unconventional English [*A publication*] ..... DSUE

Dictionary of South African Biography [*A publication*] ..... DSAB

Dictionary of the Apostolic Church [*A publication*] (BJA) ..... DAC

Dictionary of the Apostolic Church [*James Hasting*] [*A publication*] (BJA) ..... HDAC

Dictionary of the Bible [*A publication*] (BJA) ..... DB

Dictionary of the Bible [*A publication*] (BJA) ..... DBi

[*A*] Dictionary of the Bible [*James Hasting*] [*A publication*] (BJA) ..... HDB

Dictionary of the History of Ideas [*A publication*] ..... DHI

Dictionary of the Older Scottish Tongue [*A publication*] ..... DOST

[*A*] Dictionary of the Underworld [*A publication*] ..... DU

Dictionary Operation and Control for Thesaurus Organization (PDAA) ..... DOCTOR

Dictionary Research Centre [*University of Exeter*] [*British*] (IRC) ..... DRC

Dictionary Research Centre [*Macquarie University*] [*Australia*] ..... DRC

Dictionary Society of North America (EA) ..... DSNA

Dictionnaire Apologetique de la Foi Catholique [*A publication*] (BJA) ..... DAFC

Dictionnaire Biographique du Canada [*A publication*] ..... DBC

Dictionnaire de la Bible [*A publication*] (BJA) ..... DB

Dictionnaire de la Bible. Supplement [*A publication*] (BJA) ..... DBS

Dictionnaire de Spiritualite Ascetique et Mystique, Doctrine et Histoire [*Paris*] [*A publication*] (BJA) ..... DS

Dictionnaire des Antiquites Grecques et Romaines d'Appres les Textes et les Monuments [*A publication*] (BJA) ..... DAGR

Dictionnaire des Inscriptions Semitiques de l'Ouest [*A publication*] (BJA) ..... DISO

Dictionnaire d'Histoire et de Geographie Ecclesiastique [*A publication*] (BJA) ..... DHGE

Dictum (DLA) ..... D

Dictum [*As Before*] [*Latin*] (DAVI) ..... do

Dicumyl Peroxide [*Organic chemistry*] ..... DCP

Dicyandiamide [*or Dicyanodiamide*] [*Also, DICY*] [*Organic chemistry*] ..... DCD

Dicyanoanthracene [*Organic chemistry*] ..... DCA

Dicyanobenzene [*Also, DCNB*] [*Organic chemistry*] ..... DCB

Dicyanobenzene [*Also, DCB*] [*Organic chemistry*] ..... DCNB

Dicyanodiamide [*Also, DCD*] [*Organic chemistry*] ..... DICY

Dicyanoethylene [*Organic chemistry*] ..... DCE

Dicyanomethylenetrinitrofluorene [*Organic chemistry*] ..... DTF

Dicyanonaphthalene [*Organic chemistry*] ..... DCN

Dicyclohexyl [*Organic chemistry*] ..... DCH

Dicyclohexyl Phthalate [*Organic chemistry*] ..... DCHP

Dicyclohexylamine [*Organic chemistry*] ..... DCHA

Dicyclohexylamine Nitrite [*Organic chemistry*] (MAE) ..... DCHN

Dicyclohexylborane [*Organic chemistry*] ..... DCHBH

Dicyclohexylcarbodiimide [*Also, DCCD, DCCI*] [*Organic chemistry*] ..... DCC

Dicyclohexylcarbodiimide [*Also, DCC, DCCI*] [*Organic chemistry*] ..... DCCD

Dicyclohexylcarbodiimide [*Also, DCC, DCCD*] [*Organic chemistry*] ..... DCCI

Dicyclopentadiene [*Also, DCPD*] [*Organic chemistry*] ..... DCP

Dicyclopentadiene [*Also, DCP*] [*Organic chemistry*] ..... DCPD

Dicyclopentadine ..... DCPCD

Did Not Answer (IIA) ..... DA

Did Not Arrive [*For no-show hotel reservation*] ..... DNA

Did Not Attend ..... DNA

Did Not Bat [*Cricket*] ..... DNB

Did Not Come ..... DNC

Did Not Compete [*Yacht racing*] (IYR) ..... DNC

Did Not Finish ..... DNF

Did Not Keep Appointment [*Medicine*] (CPH) ..... DNK

Did Not Keep Appointment [*Medicine*] ..... DNKA

Did Not Play ..... DNP

Did Not Qualify [*Automobile racing*] ..... DNQ

Did Not Receive Questionnaire ..... DNRQ

Did Not Report (OICC) ..... DNR

Did Not Respond ..... DNR

Did Not Show [*Medicine*] ..... DNS

Did Not Start [*Racing*] (IYR) ..... DNS

Did Not Suit ..... DNS

Did Not Test [*Medicine*] ..... DNT

Didache (BJA) ..... Did

Didactic ..... DID

Didactic (VRA) ..... did

Didacus de Segura [*Flourished, 16th century*] [*Authority cited in pre-1607 legal work*] (DSA) ..... Dida de Segu

Didanosine [*Drug used in the treatment of AIDS*] ..... DDI

Didcot [*British depot code*] ..... D

Dideazatetrahydrofolic Acid [*Antineoplastic drug*] ..... DATHF

Didecyl Glutarate [*Organic chemistry*] ..... DDG

Didecyl Phthalate [*Organic chemistry*] ... DDP
Didehydrodideoxycytidine [*Antiviral*] ... DDDC
Didehydrodideoxythymidine [*Antiviral*] ... DDDT
Didehydroretinoic Acid [*Biochemistry*] ... DDRA
Didemethylchlordimeform [*A pesticide*] ... DDCDM
Dideoxyadenosine [*Biochemistry Medicine*] ... ddA
Dideoxyadenosine Monophosphate [*Biochemistry*] ... DDAMP
Dideoxycytidine [*Biochemistry*] ... DDC
Dideoxycytidine Triphosphate [*Biochemistry*] ... ddCTP
Dideoxyfluorouridine [*Medicine*] (DMAA) ... DFU
Dideoxyguanosine [*Antiviral*] ... DDG
Dideoxyguanosine Triphosphate [*Biochemistry*] ... DDGTP
Dideoxyinosine [*Medicine*] ... ddI
Dideoxyinosine Monophosphate [*Biochemistry*] ... DDIMP
Dideoxyinosine Videx [*An AIDS treatment drug*] (CDI) ... DDI
Dideoxyribonucleotide Triphosphate [*Organic chemistry*] ... ddNTP
Dideoxythymidine [*Biochemistry*] ... DDT
Dideoxythymidine Triphosphate [*Biochemistry*] ... ddTTP
Didi [*Guinea*] [*ICAO location identifier*] (ICLI) ... GUDD
Didicyclohexylammonium Naphthylthiolphosphate [*Organic chemistry*] ... DDNTP
Didius Iulianus [*of Scriptores Historiae Augustae*] [*Classical studies*] (OCD) ... Did Iul
Dido and Pluto Handmaiden for Nuclear Experiments [*Nuclear reactor at Harwell, England*] ... DAPHNE
Didodecyldimethyl Ammonium Bromide [*Inorganic chemistry*] ... DDAB
Didodecyldimethyl Ammonium Bromide [*Organic chemistry*] ... DDAB
Didsbury Public Library, Alberta [*Library symbol National Library of Canada*] (NLC) ... ADI
Didymium [*Mixture of rare-earth elements*] [*Chemistry*] (ROG) ... D
Didymium [*Mixture of rare-earth elements*] [*Chemistry*] (ROG) ... DI
Didyr [*Burkina Faso*] [*ICAO location identifier*] (ICLI) ... DHCD
Die Aegyptischen Personnennamen [*A publication*] (BJA) ... APn
Die Agada der Tannaiten (BJA) ... AdT
Die Akkadische Namengebung [*A publication*] (BJA) ... AN
Die Akkadische Namengebung [*A publication*] (BJA) ... ANg
Die Antike Kunstprosa [*A publication*] (OCD) ... Ant Kunstpr
Die Aramaeische Sprache unter den Achaimeniden [*A publication*] (BJA) ... ASA
Die Attische Beredsamkeit [*A publication*] (OCD) ... Att Ber
Die Bahn [*Tourist card for rail travel*] [*Germany*] ... DB
Die Boghazkoi-Texte im Umschrift [*A publication*] (BJA) ... BoTU
Die Cast Zinc ... DCZ
Die Casting Federation [*Defunct*] (EA) ... DCF
Die Casting Mold (MCD) ... DCM
Die Casting Research Foundation (EA) ... DCRF
Die Christliche Welt [*A publication*] (BJA) ... ChrW
Die Deborah (BJA) ... DE
Die Deutsche Kirche im Orient [*Cairo*] [*A publication*] (BJA) ... DKO
Die Entstehung des Judentums [*A publication*] (BJA) ... EJ
Die Entwicklung der Glyptik Waehrend der Akkad-Zeit [*A publication*] (BJA) ... EGA
Die Evangelischen Missionen (BJA) ... EM
Die Forged Aluminum ... DFA
Die Furcht des Herrn Ist der Weisheit Anfang [*Fear of the Lord Is the Beginning of Wisdom*] [*(Ps., CXI. 10) Motto of Dorothee Hedwig, Princess of Anhalt (1587-1608); Johann Sigismund, Elector of Brandenburg (1572-1619)*] ... DFDHIDWA
Die Griechische Christliche Schriftsteller der Ersten Drei Jahrhunderten (BJA) ... GRCHRSCHR
Die Heilige Schrift des Alten Testaments [*Bonn*] [*A publication*] (BJA) ... HS
Die Heilige Schrift des Alten Testaments [*Bonner Bibel*] [*A publication*] (BJA) ... HSAT
Die Heilige Schrift des Alten Testaments [*Bonner Bibel*] [*A publication*] (BJA) ... HSATes
Die Heilige Schrift in Deutscher Uebersetzung. Echter-Bibel [*Wuerzburg*] [*A publication*] (BJA) ... EB
Die Hethitischen Gesetze. Documenta et Monumenta Orientis Antiqui 7 [*Leiden*] [*A publication*] (BJA) ... HG
Die Inschriften von Cyros, Koenig von Babylon [*A publication*] (BJA) ... Cyr
Die Israelitischen Eigennamen [*A publication*] (BJA) ... IEN
Die Juedische Presse [*The Jewish Press*] [*German*] (BJA) ... JP
Die Katholischen Missionen (BJA) ... KathM
Die Keilinschriften der Achaemeniden [*A publication*] (BJA) ... KiA
Die Keilinschriften und das Alte Testament [*A publication*] (BJA) ... KAT
Die Lexikalischen Tafelserien der Babylonier und Assyrer in den Berliner Museen [*A publication*] (BJA) ... LTBA
Die Lock ... DLX
Die Musik [*A publication*] ... DM
Die Provinzeinteilung des Assyrischen Reiches [*A publication*] (BJA) ... PeAR
Die Religion der Griechen [*A publication*] (OCD) ... Rel d Griech
Die Religionen der Menschheit [*A publication*] (BJA) ... RdM
Die Republikaner [*Republican Party*] [*Germany Political party*] (PPW) ... REP
Die Set Manufacturers Service Bureau (EA) ... DSMSB
Die Sprache der Palmyrenischen Inschriften [*Leipzig*] [*A publication*] (BJA) ... SPI
Die Sumerischen und Akkadischen Koeningsinschriften [*A publication*] (BJA) ... SAK
Die Tempel von Babylon und Borsippa [*A publication*] (BJA) ... TBB
Die Template (MSA) ... DT
Die Transkriptionen des Hieronymus in Seinem Kommentarwerken [*A publication*] (BJA) ... TrKH
Die Welt der Bibel. Kleinkommentare zur Heiligen Schrift [*Duesseldorf*] [*A publication*] (BJA) ... KK
Die Zoologie des Talmuds [*L. Lewysohn*] [*A publication*] (BJA) ... Zdt
Diebold Generator for Statistical Tabulation (MUGU) ... DIGEST
Diebold, Inc. [*NYSE symbol*] (SPSG) ... DBD
Diebold, Inc. [*Associated Press*] (SAG) ... Diebold
Diebougou [*Burkina Faso*] [*ICAO location identifier*] (ICLI) ... DHOU
Diebus Alternis [*Every Other Day*] [*Pharmacy*] ... DIEB ALT
Diebus Secundis [*Every Second Day*] [*Pharmacy*] ... DIEB SECUND
Diebus Tertiis [*Every Third Day*] [*Pharmacy*] ... DIEB TERT
Diecast Exchange Club (EA) ... DEC
Diecasting Development Council (EA) ... DDC
Diecasting Society [*British*] (DBA) ... DCS
Dieciocho [*Costa Rica*] [*ICAO location identifier*] (ICLI) ... MRDO
Died ... D
Died (VRA) ... d
Died a Natural Death ... DND
Died in Emergency Room (MAE) ... DIE
Died Of (DAVI) ... d/o
Died of Disease (MAE) ... DD
Died of Disease ... DOD
Died of Injuries [*Military*] (AABC) ... DOI
Died of Other Causes [*Medicine*] ... DOC
Died of Wounds [*Military*] ... DOW
Died of Wounds Resulting from Action with Enemy [*Military*] ... DWA
Died on [*Operating*] **Table** [*Medicine*] (DAVI) ... DOT
Died Unmarried (WDAA) ... DU
Died Unmarried [*Genealogy*] ... DUM
Died with Disease [*Medicine*] ... DWD
Died without Issue (DLA) ... DWI
Diego [*Blood group*] ... Di
Diego Garcia [*British Indian Ocean Territory*] [*ICAO location identifier*] (ICLI) ... FJDG
Diego Suarez [*Madagascar*] [*Airport symbol*] (OAG) ... DIE
Diehl Graphsoft [*NASDAQ symbol*] (TTSB) ... DIEG
Diehl Graphsoft, Inc. [*NASDAQ symbol*] (SAG) ... DIEG
Diehl Graphsoft, Inc. [*Associated Press*] (SAG) ... Diehl
Diehl Graphsoft, Inc. [*Associated Press*] (SAG) ... DiehlG
Diel Vertical Migration [*Zooplankton*] ... DVM
Dielectric ... D
Dielectric (IAA) ... DIEL
Dielectric ... DIELEC
Dielectric ... DLCTRC
Dielectric Analyzer ... DEA
Dielectric Breakdown Model [*Physics*] ... DBM
Dielectric Constant ... DC
Dielectric Constant ... K
Dielectric Constant Change [*Analytical chemistry*] ... DCC
Dielectric Constant Indicator ... DCI
Dielectric Dissipation Factor ... DDF
Dielectric Foil (IAA) ... DEF
Dielectric Heating Equipment ... DHE
Dielectric Infrared Beamsplitter ... DIB
Dielectric Isolation ... DI
Dielectric Loading Factor [*Electronics*] (MDG) ... DL
Dielectric Loading Factor [*Electronics*] (IAA) ... DLF
Dielectric, Magnetic and Capacitor (IAA) ... DMC
Dielectric Outer Diameter (IAA) ... DOD
Dielectric Relaxation Current (PDAA) ... DRC
Dielectric Rod Antenna ... DRA
Dielectric Spectroscopy ... DS
Dielectric Stimulated Arcing (PDAA) ... DSA
Dielectric Strength Test ... DST
Dielectric Thermal Analysis ... DETA
Dielectric Waveguide (MCD) ... DIELGUIDE
Dielectric Withstand Voltage (MCD) ... DWV
Dielectrically Isolated Arrays of Monolithic Devices (MCD) ... DIAMOND
Dielectrically Isolated Integration Circuit ... DIIC
Dielectro-Kinetic Laboratories, LLC ... DKL
Dielectrophoresis ... DEP
Diemakers and Diecutters Association [*Later, NADD*] (EA) ... DDA
Dienbienphu [*Viet Nam*] [*ICAO location identifier*] (ICLI) ... VVDB
Dienst Grondwaterverkenning [*TNO Institute of Applied Geoscience*] [*Information service or system Netherlands*] (IID) ... DGV
Dienstanweisung [*Service regulations*] [*German military - World War II*] ... DAW
Diepdaume Mines [*Vancouver Stock Exchange symbol*] ... DPP
Diepholz [*Germany ICAO location identifier*] (ICLI) ... EDND
Dieppe [*France*] [*Airport symbol Obsolete*] (OAG) ... DPE
Dieppe/Saint-Aubin [*France ICAO location identifier*] (ICLI) ... LFAB
Dierdorf/Wienau [*Germany ICAO location identifier*] (ICLI) ... EDKE
Dierkundige Vereniging van Suidelike Afrika [*Zoological Society of Southern Africa - ZSSA*] (EAIO) ... DVSA
Dies [*Day*] [*Latin*] ... D
Diesel [*British Waterways Board sign*] ... D
Diesel (ABBR) ... DESL
Diesel ... DIES
Diesel (MSA) ... DSL
Diesel ... DSL
Diesel Air Start System (IEEE) ... DASS
Diesel Automobile Association [*Defunct*] (EA) ... DAA
Diesel Belt Drive (MSA) ... DBD
Diesel Direct (MSA) ... DD
Diesel Direct Drive ... DDD
Diesel Electric ... DE
Diesel Electric ... DIEL
Diesel Electric Multiple Unit (ADA) ... DEMU
Diesel Electric Reduction Drive ... DERD
Diesel Electric Ship (IAA) ... DES
Diesel Electric Tandem Motor Drive ... DET
Diesel Electric Trawler (IAA) ... DET
Diesel Electronic Submarine (MCD) ... DES

Diesel Engine Driven (NATG) .... DED
Diesel Engine Intelligent Monitoring System [*Automotive engineering*] .... DEIMOS
Diesel Engine Manufacturers Association [*Defunct*] (EA) .... DEMA
Diesel Engine Monitoring and Control [*ASMAP Electronics Ltd.*] [*Software package*] (NCC) .... DEMAC
Diesel Engine Oil .... DEO
Diesel Engine, Reduction Drive .... DER
Diesel Engined Road Vehicle .... DERV
Diesel Fire Pump [*Nuclear energy*] (NRCH) .... DFP
Diesel Fuel [*or Fueled*] (CINC) .... DF
Diesel Fuel and Coolant [*Nuclear energy*] .... DFC
Diesel Fuel, Marine (NVT) .... DFM
Diesel Fuel Oil System [*Nuclear energy*] (NRCH) .... DFOS
Diesel Fuel Waiver (DNAB) .... DFW
Diesel Fuel with an Antarctic Additive .... DFA
Diesel Geared Drive .... DGD
Diesel Geared - Motor Geared .... DG-MG
Diesel General [*Service*] [*Automotive engineering*] .... DG
Diesel Generator (NRCH) .... DG
Diesel Generator Auxiliary System [*Nuclear energy*] (NRCH) .... DGAS
Diesel Generator Building [*Nuclear energy*] (NRCH) .... DGB
Diesel Generator Combustion Air Intake and Exhaust System [*Nuclear energy*] (NRCH) .... DGCAIES
Diesel Generator Cooling Water System [*Nuclear energy*] (NRCH) .... DGCWS
Diesel Generator Fuel Oil Storage and Transfer System [*Nuclear energy*] (NRCH) .... DGFOSTS
Diesel Generator Lubrication System [*Nuclear energy*] (NRCH) .... DGLS
Diesel Generator Starting System [*Nuclear energy*] (NRCH) .... DGSS
Diesel Mechanic [*or Mechanical*] .... DM
Diesel Moderate [*Service*] [*Automotive engineering*] .... DM
Diesel Multiple Unit .... DMU
Diesel Odor Analysis System .... DOAS
Diesel Oil .... D
Diesel Oil .... DESOIL
Diesel Oil .... DO
Diesel Oil, Bentonite, Cement [*Oil well drilling technology*] .... DOBC
Diesel Particulate .... DP
Diesel Particulate Filter [*Automotive emissions*] .... DPF
Diesel Particulate Filter .... DPF
Diesel Particulate Matter [*Environmental chemistry*] .... DPM
Diesel Particulate Trap [*Automotive engineering*] .... DPT
Diesel Radial [*Aircraft engine*] .... DR
Diesel Reduction Drive .... DRD
Diesel Run Control Solenoid Valve (IEEE) .... RSV
Diesel Sea Water (DNAB) .... DSW
Diesel Severe [*Service*] [*Automotive engineering*] .... DS
Diesel Tank Vessel .... DITA
Diesel V-Belt Drive .... DVBD
Diesel-Driven Auxiliary Feed Water Pump (IEEE) .... DDAFP
Diesel-Electric Direct Drive .... DEDD
Dieses Jahres [*Of This Year*] [*German*] (ROG) .... DJ
Dieses Monats [*Of This Month*] [*German*] (ROG) .... DM
Diet and Elimination [*Gastroenterology*] (DAVI) .... D & E
Diet and Excretion [*Gastroenterology*] (DAVI) .... D & E
Diet as Tolerated [*Medicine*] .... DAT
Diet Beverage .... DB
Diet for Age [*Medicine*] (DAVI) .... DFA
Diet/Health Knowledge Survey [*Department of Agriculture*] (GFGA) .... DHK
Diet Kitchen .... DK
Dietary (WDAA) .... DIET
Dietary .... DTRY
Dietary Fiber [*Nutrition*] .... DF
Dietary Food Management .... DFM
Dietary Information Processing System (SAA) .... DIPS
Dietary Managers Association (EA) .... DMA
Dietary Reference Intakes .... DRI
Dietary Restriction [*Medicine*] .... DR
Dietary Supplement Health and Education Act of 1994 .... DSHEA
Dietetic .... DIETC
Dietetic Technician (DAVI) .... Diet Tech
Dietetic Technician (HCT) .... DT
Dietetics .... DIET
Diethanol Cocoamide [*Surfactants*] .... DEC
Diethanolamine [*Also, DIOLAMINE*] [*Organic chemistry*] .... DEA
Diethanolamine [*Also, DEA*] [*USAN*] [*Organic chemistry*] .... DIOLAMINE
Diethoxyacetophenone [*Organic chemistry*] .... DEAP
Diethoxyanthracene [*Organic chemistry*] .... DEA
Diethoxyethylene [*Organic chemistry*] .... DEE
Diethyl Azodicarboxylate [*Organic chemistry*] .... DEAD
Diethyl Diazomalonate [*Organic chemistry*] .... DEDM
Diethyl Dicarbocyanine Iodide [*Organic chemistry*] .... DDI
Diethyl Dicarbonate [*Fungistatic agent*] .... DEDC
Diethyl Ether (PDAA) .... DEE
Diethyl Hydrogen Phosphite [*Organic chemistry*] .... DEHP
Diethyl Ketone [*Organic chemistry*] .... DEK
Diethyl Maleate [*Biochemistry*] .... DEM
Diethyl Malonate [*Organic chemistry*] .... DEM
Diethyl Nitrophenyl Phosphorothioate [*Insecticide*] .... DNTP
Diethyl Phthalate [*Organic chemistry*] .... DEP
Diethyl Pyrocarbonate [*Chemical preservative*] [*Also, DEPC*] [*Organic chemistry*] .... DEP
Diethyl Pyrocarbonate [*Chemical preservative*] [*Also, DEP*] [*Organic chemistry*] .... DEPC
Diethyl Succinate [*Organic chemistry*] .... DES
Diethyl Sulfate [*Organic chemistry*] .... DES
Diethyl Zinc [*Used for deacidification of paper to arrest book decay*] .... DEZ
Diethylacetoacetamide [*Organic chemistry*] .... DEAA
Diethylaluminum Chloride [*Organic chemistry*] .... DEAC
Diethylaluminum Hydride [*Organic chemistry*] .... DEAH
Diethylaluminum Iodide [*Organic chemistry*] .... DEAI
Diethylaluminum Tetramethylpiperidide [*Organic chemistry*] .... DATMP
Diethylamine [*Organic chemistry*] .... DEA
Diethylamine Analog of Ethmozine [*Biochemistry*] .... DAAE
Diethylaminoethanol [*Organic chemistry*] .... DEAE
Diethylaminoethyl [*Organic radical*] .... DEAE
Diethylaminoethyl Cellulose [*Organic chemistry*] (MAE) .... DEAE
Diethylaminoethyl Chloride [*Organic chemistry*] .... DEC
Diethylaminoethyl Dextran [*Organic chemistry*] .... DEAE-D
Diethylaminoethyl Mercaptan [*Organic chemistry*] .... DEAEM
Diethylaminoethyl Methacrylate [*Organic chemistry*] .... DEAEMA
Diethylaminoethyl-Cellulose (DOG) .... DEAE-cellulose
Diethylaminopropylamine [*Organic chemistry*] .... DEAPA
Diethylaminosulfur Trifluoride [*Organic chemistry*] .... DAST
Diethylammonium Diethyldithiocarbamate [*Organic chemistry*] .... DADDTC
Diethylanilinesulfonic Acid [*Organic chemistry*] .... DEASA
Diethylbarbituric Acid (MAE) .... DEBA
Diethylbutanediol [*Organic chemistry*] (AAMN) .... DEB
Diethylcarbamazine [*Anthelmintic drug*] .... DEC
Diethylcarbamazine Citrate [*Biochemistry*] .... DECC
Diethylcarbamoyl Chloride [*Organic chemistry*] .... DECC
Diethylcarbamoyl Chloride (GNE) .... DECC
Diethylchlorothiophosphate [*Ethyl Chemical Co.*] [*Organic chemistry*] .... DECTP
Diethylcyclohexane [*Organic chemistry*] .... DECH
Diethyldithio Carbamic Acid [*Organic chemistry*] .... DDCA
Diethyldithiocarbamate [*Also, DDTC, DEDC*] [*Organic chemistry*] .... DDC
Diethyldithiocarbamate [*Also, DDC, DEDC*] [*Organic chemistry*] .... DDTC
Diethyldithiocarbamate [*Also, DDC, DDTC*] [*Organic chemistry*] .... DEDC
Diethyldithiocarbamic Acid [*Organic chemistry*] (AAMN) .... DDC
Diethyldithiocarbonate [*Analytical chemistry*] .... DIECA
Diethyldithiophosphate [*Organic chemistry*] .... dtp
Diethylene Glycol [*Organic chemistry*] .... DEG
Diethylene Glycol Adipate [*Organic chemistry*] .... DEGA
Diethylene Glycol Butyl Acetate [*Organic chemistry*] .... DGBA
Diethylene Glycol Butyl Ether [*Organic chemistry*] .... DGBE
Diethylene Glycol Dimethyl Ether [*Organic chemistry*] .... DIGLYME
Diethylene Glycol Dinitrate [*Explosive*] .... DEGN
Diethylene Glycol Succinate [*Organic chemistry*] .... DEGS
Diethylene Glycolamine [*Organic chemistry*] .... DEGA
Diethylene Phosphoramide [*Organic chemistry*] (BABM) .... DEPA
Diethylenediamine [*Organic chemistry*] .... dien
Diethylenetriamine [*Also, DTA*] [*Organic chemistry*] .... DETA
Diethylenetriamine [*Also, DETA*] [*Organic chemistry*] .... DTA
Diethylenetriamine Penta-Acetic Acid [*Organic chemistry*] (DAVI) .... DPTA
Diethylenetriamine Producers Importers Alliance (EA) .... DPIA
Diethylenetriaminepentaacetic Acid [*Also, DETPA, DTPA*] [*Chelating agent*] .... DETP
Diethylenetriaminepentaacetic Acid [*Also, DETP, DTPA*] [*Chelating agent*] .... DETPA
Diethylenetriaminepentaacetic Acid [*Also, DETP, DETPA*] [*Chelating agent*] .... DTPA
Diethylglycine [*Biochemistry*] .... DEG
Di(ethylhexyl) Adipate [*Also, DOA*] [*Organic chemistry*] .... DEHA
Di(ethylhexyl)phosphoric Acid [*Organic chemistry*] .... DEHPA
Di(ethylhexyl)phthalate [*Also, DOP, DHP*] [*Organic chemistry*] .... DEHP
Diethylhydroxylamine [*Also, DEHA*] [*Organic chemistry*] .... DEH
Diethylhydroxylamine [*Also, DEH*] [*Organic chemistry*] .... DEHA
Diethyl-Iminodiacetic Acid [*Biochemistry*] (DAVI) .... DIEDA
Diethylmandelamide [*Organic chemistry*] .... DEM
Diethyl-m-toluamide [*Insect repellent*] .... DEET
Diethylnitrosamine [*Also, DENA*] [*Carcinogen*] .... DEN
Diethylnitrosamine [*Also, DEN*] [*Carcinogen*] .... DENA
Diethyloxadicarbocyanine Iodide [*A dye*] .... DODCI
(Diethyl)phenylenediamine [*Organic chemistry*] .... DPD
Diethyl(phenyl)xanthine [*Organic chemistry*] .... DPX
Diethylpropanediol [*Biochemistry*] .... DEP
Diethyl(ribityl)isoalloxazine [*Biochemistry*] .... DERI
Diethylstilbestrol [*Endocrinology*] .... DES
Diethylstilbestrol Adenosis [*Oncology*] .... DESAD
Diethyltartarate [*Organic chemistry*] .... DET
Diethyltelluride .... DETe
Diethylthiacarbocyanine [*Organic chemistry*] .... DETC
Diethylthiatricarbocyanine [*Organic chemistry*] .... DTTC
Diethylthiourea [*Organic chemistry*] .... DETU
Diethyltoluamide [*Also, DETA*] [*Insect repellant*] [*Organic chemistry*] .... DET
Diethyltoluamide [*Also, DET*] [*Insect repellant*] [*Organic chemistry*] .... DETA
Dietician (WDAA) .... DIET
Dieticians' Board of Victoria [*Australia*] .... DBV
Diet-Induced Obese [*Mice*] .... DIO
Dietitian .... D
Dietrich, AK [*Location identifier FAA*] (FAAL) .... DTK
Dieuze-Gueblange [*France ICAO location identifier*] (ICLI) .... LFQZ
DIFAR [*Directional Frequency Analyzing and Recording*] **Pointing Tactic** [*Military*] (CAAL) .... DIPTAC
DIFAR [*Directional Frequency Analyzing and Recording*] **Tactic** [*Military*] (CAAL) .... DITAC
DIFAR Triangular Tactic (NVT) .... TRITAC
Difference .... D
Difference (AFM) .... DIF
Difference .... DIFCE
Difference (KSC) .... DIFF

Difference (ROG) .... DIFFCE
Difference (DSUE) .... DIFFER
Difference, Center .... DC
Difference Channel (MSA) .... DCHAN
Difference Figure of Merit (MCD) .... DFOM
Difference Frequency Generator (MCD) .... DFG
Difference in Conditions .... DIC
Difference in Depth of Modulation (IEEE) .... DDM
Difference in Height .... DH
Difference in Pressure .... DP
Difference Index [*Protein calculation*] [*Biochemistry*] .... DI
Difference Limen [*Physiology, psychology*] .... DL
Difference of Gaussians [*Image processing*] .... DOG
Difference of Latitude [*Navigation*] (MUGU) .... DL
Difference of Latitude [*Navigation*] .... DLAT
Difference of Latitude [*Navigation*] L
Difference of Longitude [*Navigation*] .... DLO
Difference of Longitude [*Navigation*] .... DLONG
Difference of Messing Subscription [*British military*] (DMA) .... DMS
Difference of Potential .... DP
Difference of Rate .... DRATE
Difference, Port [*Navigation*] .... DP
Difference Pressure Control Switch .... DPCS
Difference Pressure Indicating [*Engineering*] .... dPI
Difference Sensation [*Psychology*] .... DS
Difference Spectroscopy .... DS
Difference, Starboard [*Navigation*] .... DS
Difference Threshold [*Psychology*] (IAA) .... DT
Differenced-Range Doppler .... DRD
Differenced-Range Versus Integrated Doppler [*Charged particle measurement*] .... DRVID
Different (VRA) .... dif
Different .... DIFF
Different .... DIFT
Different Coupling [*Music*] .... DC
Different Orbitals for Different Spins [*Atomic physics*] .... DODS
Different Premises Address [*Telecommunications*] (TEL) .... DPA
Different Premises Information [*Telecommunications*] (TEL) .... DPI
Different Premises Subscriber [*Telecommunications*] (TEL) .... DPS
Different Premises Telephone Number [*Telecommunications*] (TEL) .... DPT
Different Version .... DV
Differential (IDOE) .... d
Differential .... DFRN
Differential (AFM) .... DIF
Differential (AABC) .... DIFF
Differential Absorption Ratio (IAA) .... DAR
Differential Agglutination Titer [*Hematology*] .... DAT
Differential Air-Speed Hold (PDAA) .... DASH
Differential Amplifier .... DA
Differential Amplifier (MSA) .... DIFA
Differential Amplifier (IAA) .... DIFFAMP
Differential Amplitude Discriminator (PDAA) .... DAD
Differential Analyzer (IEEE) .... DA
Differential Analyzer Replacement [*Programming language*] [*1967*] (CSR) .... DARE
Differential and Alignment Unit and Total Error Corrector (PDAA) .... DATEC
Differential and Full Wave Rectifier (IAA) .... DIFFFWR
Differential Anodic Stripping Voltammetry [*Electronics*] .... DASV
Differential Antibody Titer [*Immunology*] (DAVI) .... DAT
Differential Aptitude Test [*Psychology*] .... DAT
Differential Aptitude Test-Verbal Reasoning [*Psychology*] (EDAC) .... DAT-VR
Differential Area Force Law (MCD) .... DAFL
Differential Ballistic Wind .... DBW
Differential Ballistic Wind Computer .... DBWC
Differential Ballistic Wind Offset .... DBWO
Differential Base Current Drift .... DBCD
Differential Bearing Indicator .... DBI
Differential Blood Count .... DIFF
Differential Calculus (AAG) .... DC
Differential Calculus (IAA) .... DIFFCALC
Differential Coefficient .... D
Differential [*or Differentially*] **Coherent Phase Shift Keyed** [*or Keying*] [*System*] [*Computer science*] .... DCPSK
Differential Compound Engine (PDAA) .... DCE
Differential Computing Potentiometer .... DCP
Differential Corrected Spectral Unit [*Spectrometry*] .... DCSU
Differential Correction .... DC
Differential Correlation Radiometer (MCD) .... DCR
Differential Cross Section [*Chemistry*] .... DCS
Differential Cross Talk (IAA) .... DC
Differential Current Density .... DCD
Differential Current Integrator (IAA) .... DCI
Differential Current Mode Logic [*Computer science*] (NITA) .... DCML
Differential Diagnosis [*Medicine*] .... DD
Differential Diagnosis [*Medicine*] (CPH) .... DDx
Differential Diagnosis (AAMN) .... Diff Diag
Differential Difference Equation [*Mathematics*] (IAA) .... DDE
Differential Distribution Law [*Meteorology*] .... DDL
Differential Doppler .... DD
Differential Dynamic Programming (MCD) .... DDP
Differential Electrochemistry/Mass Spectrometry .... DEMS
Differential Electronically-Locking Test Accessory .... DELTA
Differential Encoding Phase Shift Keying (MCD) .... DEPSK
Differential Energy Spectrum .... DES
Differential Equation .... DE
Differential Equation Analyzer Program (MCD) .... DEAP
Differential Equation Solver .... DES
Differential Equations Pseudocode Interpreter [*Jet Propulsion Laboratory, NASA*] .... DEPI
Differential Fluorescence Induction [*Analytic biochemistry*] .... DFI
Differential Frequency (IAA) .... DF
Differential Gain .... DG
Differential Generator .... DG
Differential Global Positioning System .... DGPS
Differential In-Depth Analysis (PDAA) .... DIDA
Differential Input Operational Amplifier [*Electronics*] .... DIOA
Differential Interface Velocity [*Engineering*] .... DIV
Differential Interference Contrast [*Microscope*] .... DIC
Differential Interference Contrast Microscope .... DICM
Differential Interference Microscopy (PDAA) .... DIM
Differential LASER Doppler Velocimeter (PDAA) .... DLDV
Differential LASER Gyro (MCD) .... DILAG
Differential Leukocyte Count [*Hematology*] .... DLC
Differential Light Scattering .... DLS
Differential Line Driver Receiver (IAA) .... DLDR
Differential Load Sensing [*Hydraulics*] .... DLS
Differential Logistics Services Center [*AEC*] .... DLSC
Differential Long-Baseline Interferometer [*Radio interferometry*] .... DLBI
Differential Lung Ventilation .... DLV
Differential Maneuvering Simulator [*Aviation*] .... DMS
Differential Mechanism (IAA) .... DM
Differential Microwave Radiometer [*Cosmic Background Explorer*] [*NASA*] .... DMR
Differential Mobility Analyzer [*Marine science*] (OSRA) .... DMA
Differential Mode [*Electronics*] (OA) .... DM
Differential Multi-Junction Thermal Converter (PDAA) .... DMJTC
Differential Multiple Simulator (MCD) .... DMS
Differential Non-Linearity (OA) .... DNL
Differential (of) .... D
Differential of Time (IDOE) .... dt
Differential of Velocity (IDOE) .... dv
Differential Oil Temperature [*Automotive engineering*] .... DOT
Differential Operational Amplifier [*Electronics*] (OA) .... DOA
Differential Optical Absorption Spectrometer .... DOAS
Differential, Oral, Visual, Aural, Computerized Kinesthetic .... DOVACK
Differential Orbit Improvement .... DOI
Differential Paramagnetic Effect [*Low-temperature physics*] .... DPE
Differential Phase [*Telecommunications*] .... DP
Differential Phase Exchange Keying (IEEE) .... DPEK
Differential Phase Shift (PDAA) .... DPS
Differential Phase Shift Keying [*Telecommunications*] .... DPSK
Differential Photocalorimetry [*Analytical technique*] .... DPC
Differential Power Switch .... DPS
Differential Pressure .... DP
Differential Pressure Control .... DPC
Differential Pressure Feedback (KSC) .... DPF
Differential Pressure Indicator [*Automotive engineering*] .... DPI
Differential Pressure Isolation Switch (IEEE) .... DPIS
Differential Pressure Seawater .... DPSW
Differential Pressure Transducer .... DPT
Differential Pressure Unit (DNAB) .... DPU
Differential Procedure Feedback [*Military*] .... DPF
Differential Protection Current Transformer .... DPCT
Differential Pulse .... DP
Differential Pulse Anodic Stripping Voltametry [*Electrochemistry*] .... DPASV
Differential Pulse Code Modulation [*Transmission technique*] .... DPCM
Differential Pulse Polarography [*Analytical chemistry*] .... DPP
Differential Pulse Voltammetry [*Analytical chemistry*] .... DPV
Differential Range Delay Time .... DRDT
Differential Rate .... DR
Differential Reactive Current Project Relay .... DRCPR
Differential Read Data Enhancement [*Computer science*] .... DRDE
Differential Refractive Index Detector (MCD) .... DRI
Differential Reinforced Clostridial Medium (PDAA) .... DRCM
Differential Reinforcement [*Psychometrics*] .... DRF
Differential Reinforcement of Low Rate [*Psychometrics*] .... DRL
Differential Reinforcement of Other Behavior [*Psychometrics*] .... DRO
Differential Relay (KSC) .... DFRL
Differential Relay .... DR
Differential Rheumatoid Agglutination Test [*Medicine*] (DMAA) .... DRAT
Differential Scanning Calorimeter [*or Calorimetry*] [*Instrumentation*] .... DSC
Differential Scatter [*Remote sensing technique*] .... DISC
Differential Sense [*Computer science*] .... DIFF SENS
Differential Shunt Winding [*Wiring*] (DNAB) .... DSW
Differential Signal Control .... DSC
Differential Skin Surface Temperature .... DST
Differential Spacing [*Typography*] .... DS
Differential Spacing Justifying [*Typography*] (SAA) .... DSJ
Differential Survey Treatment (NTCM) .... DST
Differential Temperature Measuring Device .... DTMD
Differential Temperature Switch (NRCH) .... DTS
Differential Thermal [*or Thermogravimetric*] **Analysis** [*or Analyzer*] .... DTA
Differential Thermocouple Voltmeter .... DTVM
Differential ThermoGravimetry (DICI) .... DTG
Differential Throttle Control .... DTC
Differential Time (IEEE) .... DT
Differential Time Relay (IEEE) .... DIFFTR
Differential Transmission Spectrum .... DTS
Differential Vacuum Delay Valve [*Automotive engineering*] .... DVDV
Differential Value Profile [*Psychology*] .... DVP
Differential Vector Equation .... DVE
Differential Velocity (NASA) .... DFRN

Differential Velocity (KSC) ... DV
Differential Very Long Baseline Interferometry (MCD) ... DVLBI
Differential Voltage (IEEE) ... DV
Differential Voltage Amplifier ... DVA
Differential Voltage-Controlled Current Source (IEEE) ... DVCCS
Differential Wave Impedance (DEN) ... DWI
Differential-Absorption and Scattering [*Remote sensing technique*] ... DAS
Differential-Absorption Carbon Monoxide Monitor (MCD) ... DACOM
Differential-Absorption LIDAR [*Spectroscopy*] ... DIAL
Differential-Absorption Remote Sensing [*LASER*] ... DARS
Differential-Algebraic Equations [*Mathematics*] ... DAE
Differentially Coherent Pulse Code Modulation ... DCPCM
Differentially Encoded Coherent Phase Shift Keying [*Telecommunications*] (TEL) ... DECPSK
Differentially (Expressed) Gastrula [*Genetics*] ... DG
Differential-Mode Noise [*Electronics*] (IAA) ... DMN
Differentiated Infiltrating Tumor [*Oncology*] ... DI
Differentiated Staffing [*Education*] (AEE) ... DS
Differentiation ... D
Differentiation Factor [*Biochemistry*] ... DF
Differentiation Inducting Factor [*Immunology*] ... DIF
Differentiation Inhibitory Activity [*Cytology*] ... DIA
Differentiation Retarding Factor [*Cytology*] ... DRF
Differentiation with Asymmetrical Reinforcement ... DAR
Differentiation with Symmetrical Reinforcement ... DSR
Differs (FAAC) ... DFRS
Difficult (FAAC) ... DFCLT
Difficult ... DIFCLT
Difficult (ROG) ... DIFCT
Difficult (DAVI) ... diff
Difficult Communication ... DC
Difficult to Deliver [*US Postal Service*] ... DTD
Difficult to Monitor (ACII) ... DTM
Difficult to Test [*Audiology*] ... DTT
Difficulty ... DIFCLTY
Difficulty (ROG) ... DIFCTY
Difficulty [*of a test item*] [*Psychology*] ... p
Difficulty Index (AEE) ... DI
Difficulty Report (AFIT) ... DIREP
Difficulty-Importance-Frequency ... DIF
Diffraction (MSA) ... DIFFR
Diffraction Limited (MCD) ... DL
Diffraction Limited Focusing ... DLF
Diffraction Limited Modulation Transfer Function (MCD) ... DMTF
Diffraction Limited Raman LASER ... DLRL
Diffues Axonal Injury [*Neurology*] (DAVI) ... DAi
Diffuse [*Immunology*] ... D
Diffuse (FAAC) ... DFUS
Diffuse ... DIF
Diffuse Alveolar Damage [*Medicine*] ... DAD
Diffuse and Perivascular [*Medicine*] ... DPV
Diffuse Cortical Sclerosis [*Medicine*] (DMAA) ... DCS
Diffuse [*or Disseminated*] **Cutaneous Leishmaniasis** [*Medicine*] (DMAA) ... DCL
Diffuse Elastic Neutron Scattering (MCD) ... DENS
Diffuse Esophageal Spasm [*Medicine*] ... DES
Diffuse Galactic Light ... DGL
Diffuse Histiocytic [*Lymphoma*] [*Oncology*] (DAVI) ... DH
Diffuse Histiocytic Lyphoma [*Medicine*] ... DHL
Diffuse Idiopathic Skeletal Hyperostosis [*Medicine*] ... DISH
Diffuse Infiltrative Lung Disease [*Medicine*] ... DILD
Diffuse Infrared Background Experiment [*Spectral instrumentation*] ... DIRBE
Diffuse Interstellar Band [*Astrophysics*] ... DIB
Diffuse Interstitial Fibrosis [*Medicine*] (AAMN) ... DIF
Diffuse Interstitial Pulmonary Calcification [*Medicine*] (AAMN) ... DIPC
Diffuse Intravascular Coagulation [*or Coagulopathy*] [*Hematology*] ... DIC
Diffuse Ionized Gas [*Astrophysics*] ... DIG
Diffuse Large-Cell Lymphoma [*Oncology*] ... DLCL
Diffuse Leiomyomatosis [*Medicine*] ... DL
Diffuse Low-Energy Electron Diffraction [*Microscopy*] ... DLEED
Diffuse Lymphoma [*Oncology*] (DAVI) ... DL
Diffuse Mixed [*Lymphoma*] [*Oncology*] (DAVI) ... DM
Diffuse Mixed Lymphoma [*Oncology*] ... DML
Diffuse Neuroendocrine System [*Also, DNS*] ... DNE
Diffuse Neuroendocrine System [*Also, DNE*] ... DNS
Diffuse Noxious Inhibitory Control (PDAA) ... DNIC
Diffuse Obstructive Pulmonary Syndrome [*Medicine*] (MAE) ... DOPS
Diffuse Poorly Differentiated Lymphocytic (Lymphoma) [*Oncology*] ... DPDL
Diffuse, Poorly Differentiated, Lymphocytic Lymphoma [*Oncology*] (DAVI) ... DPDLL
Diffuse Process Such as Pericarditis [*Cardiology*] ... DPSP
Diffuse Proliferative Glomerulonephritis [*Medicine*] ... DPGN
Diffuse Proliferative Lupus Nephritis [*Medicine*] ... DPLN
Diffuse Pulmonary Disease [*Medicine*] ... DPD
Diffuse Reflectance Infrared Fourier Transform [*Spectrometry*] ... DRIFT
Diffuse Reflectance Infrared Fourier Transform Spectroscopy ... DRIFTS
Diffuse Reflectance Infrared Spectroscopy [*Physics*] ... DRIS
Diffuse Reflectance Using Infrared Dispersive Spectrophotometry ... DRUIDS
Diffuse Reflection Attachment [*Spectroscopy*] ... DRA
Diffuse Reflection Spectroscopy ... DRS
Diffuse Undifferentiated Lymphoma [*Oncology*] ... DUL
Diffuse Unilateral Subacute Neuroretinitis [*Ophthalmology*] ... DUSN
Diffuse Well-Differentiated Lymphocytic [*Oncology*] ... DWDL
Diffuse, Well-Differentiated, Lymphocytic Lymphoma [*Oncology*] (DAVI) ... DWDLL
Diffuse, Well-Differentiated, Lymphoma [*Oncology*] (DAVI) ... DWDL
Diffused Alloy Power ... DAP
Diffused Base ... DB
Diffused Base Alloy (IAA) ... DA
Diffused Eutectic Aluminum Process (IEEE) ... DEAP
Diffused Junction ... DJ
Diffused Junction (IDOE) ... dj
Diffused Mesa ... DM
Diffused Planar ... DP
Diffused-Alloy Transistor [*Electronics*] (ECII) ... DAT
Diffuser (AAG) ... DFSR
Diffuser [*Freight*] [*Microbiology*] ... DIF
Diffuse-Reflectance Ultraviolet-Visible [*Spectra*] ... DRUV
Diffusing ... DIFFUS
Diffusing Capacity ... D
Diffusing Capacity for Carbon Dioxide [*Medicine*] (DAVI) ... DC_{CO}
Diffusing Capacity for Carbon Monoxide (MAE) ... Dco
Diffusing Capacity for Lung Carbon Dioxide [*Medicine*] (DAVI) ... $DLCO_2$
Diffusing Capacity of the Alveolar Capillary Membrane [*Medicine*] (DAVI) ... Dm
Diffusing Capacity of the Lung (AAMN) ... DL
Diffusing Capacity of the Lung Expressed as Volume [*Medicine*] (DAVI) ... Dx
Diffusing Capacity of the Lungs for Carbon Monoxide ... DLCO
Diffusing Capacity of the Lungs for Carbon Monoxide per Square Meter of Body Su rface [*Medicine*] (DAVI) ... D_LCO/M^2
Diffusing Capacity of the Lungs for Oxygen [*Medicine*] (DAVI) ... D_{LO2}
Diffusing Wave Spectroscopy ... DWS
Diffusion ... DIFFSN
Diffusion (WDAA) ... DIFFU
Diffusion Bonding ... DB
Diffusion Brazing ... DFB
Diffusion Coefficient [*Symbol*] [*IUPAC*] ... D
Diffusion Coefficient [*or Permeability constant as described by Krogh*] [*Medicine*] (DAVI) ... Dk
Diffusion Constant [*Medicine*] (DAVI) ... D
Diffusion Destainer [*Electrophoresis*] ... DD
Diffusion Formed Coating ... DFC
Diffusion in Metals and Alloys Data Center [*National Institute of Standards and Technology*] ... DIMADC
Diffusion in Metals and Alloys Data Center [*National Institute of Standards and Technology*] (IID) ... DMDC
Diffusion Index [*Economics*] ... DI
Diffusion Metal-Oxide Semiconductor [*Telecommunications*] (TEL) ... DMOS
Diffusion Monte Carlo [*Mathematics*] ... DMC
Diffusion of Arsenic in Silicon (PDAA) ... DASI
Diffusion of Exemplary Educational Practices (EDAC) ... DEEP
Diffusion per Unit of Alveolar Volume [*Medicine*] (DAVI) ... D/V_A
Diffusion per Unit Volume [*Measurement*] (DAVI) ... D/V
Diffusion Pressure ... DP
Diffusion Pressure Deficit ... DPD
Diffusion Pump ... DP
Diffusion Self-Aligned Metal-Oxide Semiconductor (BUR) ... DSAMOS
Diffusion Self-Aligned Metal-Oxide Semiconductor Field Effect Transistor [*Electronics*] (IAA) ... DSAMOSFET
Diffusion Self-Aligned Metal-Oxide Semiconductor Transistor [*Electronics*] (IAA) ... DSAMOST
Diffusion Self-Alignment ... DSA
Diffusion Transfer [*Reprography*] ... DTR
Diffusion Transfer Processing System [*Reprography*] ... DTPS
Diffusion Transfer Reversal [*Reprography*] ... DTR
Diffusion under [*Epitaxial*] **Film** (IEEE) ... DUF
Diffusion Welding ... DFW
Diffusion-Limited Aggregation [*Physical chemistry*] ... DLA
Diffusion-Limited Cluster Aggregation [*Physical chemistry*] ... DLCA
Diffusive Boundary Layer [*Physical chemistry*] ... DBL
Diffusive Equilibration in a Thin-Film [*Physical chemistry*] ... DET
Diffusive Mixing of Organic Solutions [*Materials processing*] ... DMOS
Difluorodeoxycytidine [*Biochemistry*] ... DFDC
Difluoro(dinitro)benzene [*Organic chemistry*] ... DFDNB
Difluoro-Diphenyl-Dichloroethane [*Organic chemistry*] (DAVI) ... DFDD
Difluorodiphenyltrichloroethane [*Insecticide*] ... DFDT
Difluoromethylarginine [*Organic chemistry*] ... DFMA
Difluoromethylornithine [*Organic chemistry*] ... DFMO
Difluorophosphate [*Inorganic chemistry*] ... DFP
Difluorourea [*Organic chemistry*] ... DFU
Difurfurylideneacetone [*Organic chemistry*] ... DIFA
Digalactosyl Diacyl Glycerol [*Organic chemistry*] ... DGDG
Digalactosyl Diglycerideafta [*Organic chemistry*] ... DIS
Diganglioside [*Chemistry*] ... GD
Digby General Hospital, Nova Scotia [*Library symbol National Library of Canada*] (NLC) ... NSDG
Digby, NS [*FM radio station call letters*] ... CJLS-2
Digby, NS [*AM radio station call letters*] ... CKDY
Digby's History of the Law of Real Property [*A publication*] (DLA) ... Digby RP
Digby's Introduction to the History of Real Property [*A publication*] (DLA) ... Dig R Pr
Digby's Sales and Transfer of Shares [*A publication*] (DLA) ... Dig Shares
Digene Corp. [*NASDAQ symbol*] (TTSB) ... DIGE
DiGeorge Syndrome [*Medicine*] ... DGS
Digeratur [*Let It Be Digested*] [*Pharmacy*] ... Dig
Digest ... D
Digest ... DGST
Digest [*1901-06*] [*Lahore, India*] [*A publication*] (DLA) ... Dig
Digest ... DIG
Digest Law of Libels [*A publication*] (DLA) ... Dig LL
Digest of Commercial Law of the World [*A publication*] (DLA) ... Dig CLW

Digest of Decisions, Pennsylvania Workmen's Compensation Board [*A publication*] (DLA) ... PA WC Bd Dec Dig
Digest of Intelligence and Security Services (MCD) ... DISS
Digest of International Law (Hackworth) [*A publication*] (DLA) ... DIL (Hack)
Digest of International Law (Moore) [*A publication*] (DLA) ... DIL (Moore)
Digest of International Law (Whiteman) [*A publication*] (DLA) ... DIL (White)
Digest of Justinian [*A publication*] (DLA) ... D
Digest of Justinian [*A publication*] (DLA) ... Dig
Digest of Justinian [*A publication*] (DLA) ... Digest
Digest of Justinian [*A publication*] (DLA) ... Just Dig
Digest of Justinian, Proem [*A publication*] (DLA) ... Dig Proem
Digest of Manx Cases [*1925-47*] [*A publication*] (DLA) ... Farrant
Digest of Maxims, by James S. Bracton [*A publication*] (DLA) ... Bract
Digest of Middle East Studies [*A publication*] (BRI) ... DOMES
Digest of Ontario Case Law [*A publication*] (DLA) ... Ont Dig
Digest of Operations (DNAB) ... DIGOPS
Digest of Opinions of Judge Advocate General, United States [*A publication*] (DLA) ... Dig Ops JAG
Digest of Opinions of the Attorney General of Texas [*A publication*] (DLA) ... Tex Dig Op Att'y Gen
Digest of Public General Bills [*Library of Congress A publication*] ... D
Digest of Reports of the Average Adjusters Association [*1895*] [*A publication*] (DLA) ... Av Adj Assoc Dig
Digest of Writs [*A publication*] (DLA) ... Dig
Digest to Cowen's New York Reports [*A publication*] (DLA) ... Cow Dig
Digesta [*Latin*] (OCD) ... Dig
Digestibility Coefficient (OA) ... DC
Digestible Energy (OA) ... DE
Digestible Organic Matter in Dry (OA) ... DOMD
Digestible Protein [*Medicine*] (MAE) ... DP
Digestive ... GSTV
Digestive Anlage ... DA
Digestive Disease National Coalition (EA) ... DDNC
Digestive Energy [*Medicine*] (MAE) ... DE
Digestive Gland ... DG
Digestum Novum [*A publication Authority cited in pre-1607 legal work*] (DSA) ... N
Digestum Vetus [*A publication*] (DSA) ... Dig Vet
Digestum Vetus [*A publication*] (DSA) ... V
Digex Incorp. [*Associated Press*] (SAG) ... Digex
Digex Incorp. [*NASDAQ symbol*] (SAG) ... DIGX
Diggings [*i.e., Lodgings*] [*British*] (ROG) ... DIGS
Digi International [*NASDAQ symbol*] (TTSB) ... DGII
Digi International, Inc. [*NASDAQ symbol*] (NQ) ... DGII
Digi International, Inc. [*Associated Press*] (SAG) ... DigiIntl
Digico Automated Radio-Immunoassay Analytical System (PDAA) ... DARIAS
Digicon, Inc. [*AMEX symbol*] (SPSG) ... DGC
Digicon, Inc. [*Associated Press*] (SAG) ... Digic
Digicon, Inc. [*Associated Press*] (SAG) ... Digicon
Digicon Inc. Wrrt [*AMEX symbol*] (TTSB) ... DGCWS
Digimetrics, Inc. [*Associated Press*] (SAG) ... Digimet
Digimetrics, Inc. [*NASDAQ symbol*] (NQ) ... DIGM
Dig-In Angle ... DIA
Digioxigenin(dibromoacetate) [*Biochemistry*] ... DDBA
Digiset Oriented Setting System [*Siemens-Hell*] (NITA) ... DOSY
Digit [*or Digital*] (MDG) ... D
Digit ... DGT
Digit Copying [*Psychiatry*] ... DC
Digit Plane Driver [*Computer science*] (IEEE) ... DPD
Digit Present ... DP
Digit Receiver ... DR
Digit/Record Mark [*Computer science*] (MDG) ... DIGRM
Digit/Record Mark Group/Mark [*Computer science*] (MDG) ... DIGRMGM
Digit Select (BUR) ... DS
Digit Storage Relay ... DSR
Digit Symbol [*Psychometrics*] ... DS
Digit Tube (IEEE) ... DT
Digit Zero Trigger (IAA) ... DZT
Digital (MSA) ... DGTL
Digital ... DGTL
Digital (AFM) ... DIG
Digital ... DIGI
Digital (KSC) ... DIGTL
Digital Access and Crossconnect System [*Telecommunications*] (TEL) ... DACS
Digital Access Cross-Current System [*Telecommunications*] (NITA) ... DACS
Digital Access Line (IAA) ... DAL
Digital Access Signaling System [*Telecommunications*] (OSI) ... DASS
Digital Access Signalling System ... DASS
Digital Access Signalling System (NITA) ... DASS
Digital Access Timeslot Selector (MCD) ... DATS
Digital Access to Wide Area Network [*Telemax Corp.*] ... DAWN
Digital Acoustic Emission Monitor (PDAA) ... DAEM
Digital Acoustic Sensor Simulation (MCD) ... DASS
Digital Acoustic Simulation System (MCD) ... DASS
Digital Acoustic Target ... DAT
Digital Acquisition and Control System (MCD) ... DACS
Digital Acquisition and Documentation Equipment (KSC) ... DADE
Digital Adapter for Subscriber Loops [*Telecommunications*] (NITA) ... DASL
Digital Adapter Unit (MCD) ... DAU
Digital Adaptive Area Correlation ... DAAC
Digital Adaptive Recording System ... DARS
Digital Adaptive Technique for Efficient Communications ... DATEC
Digital Address ... DAD
Digital Address System (MCD) ... DAS
Digital Advance Production Order [*Telecommunications*] (TEL) ... DAPO
Digital Advanced Lead-Computing Optical Signature (MCD) ... DALCOS
Digital Air Data Computer ... DADC
Digital Air Data Computer Status ... DADCOK
Digital Air Data Computer Test Set ... DADCTS
Digital Air Data System ... DADS
Digital Airborne Computer (IEEE) ... DIGITAR
Digital Aircraft Simulator (MCD) ... DAS
Digital Alphanumeric Video Insertion Equipment [*Aviation*] (OA) ... DAVIE
Digital Alternate Representation of Musical Symbols ... DARMS
Digital Alternator ... DA
Digital Altimeter Scanner ... DAS
Digital Altimeter Setting Indicator [*FAA*] (TAG) ... DASI
Digital Altimeter Setting Indicator [*Aviation*] (FAAC) ... DASI
Digital Amplifier Unit (DWSG) ... DAU
Digital Analog [*Computer science*] (IEEE) ... DIAN
Digital Analog Convertera (NITA) ... DACVR
Digital/Analog Daily System Operability Tests (MCD) ... DADSOT
Digital Analog Data System (CAAL) ... DADS
Digital Analog Simulator [*Computer science*] ... DAS
Digital Analog Simulator (NITA) ... DIAN
Digital Analog System [*Computer science*] (IAA) ... DAS
Digital Analogic Function Table [*Electronics*] (ECII) ... DAFT
Digital Analysis Converter (NITA) ... DAC
Digital Analysis Library [*Computer Design*] [*Software package*] (NCC) ... DAL
Digital Analyzing Voltmeter [*Electricity*] (NITA) ... DAV
Digital and Video Interactive Device (EDAC) ... DAVID
Digital Angle Data ... DAD
Digital Angle Data Recorder ... DADR
Digital Angle Recorder ... DAR
Digital Angular Readout by LASER Interferometry (MCD) ... DARI
Digital Angular Readout by LASER Interferometry (MCD) ... DARLI
Digital Angular Torquing Equipment ... DATE
Digital Animated Control System ... DACS
Digital Antijam Radio Teletype System (MCD) ... DARTS
Digital Applications International [*Commercial firm*] [*British*] (NITA) ... DAI
Digital Applique Unit (MCD) ... DAU
Digital Approach and Landing System [*Aviation*] (IAA) ... DALS
Digital Area Correlator ... DAC
Digital Arithmetic Center ... DAC
Digital Assembly Program (MCD) ... DAP
Digital Attenuator System ... DAS
Digital Attitude and Rate System (IEEE) ... DARS
Digital Attitude Reference System ... DARS
Digital Audio Broadcast [*or Broadcasting*] (IAA) ... DAB
Digital Audio Disc [*Audio/video technology*] ... DAD
Digital Audio Disc Corp. [*Sony Corp.*] ... DADC
Digital Audio Distribution System ... DADS
Digital Audio for Television [*System to improve sound*] [*Public Broadcasting Service*] ... DATE
Digital Audio Radio Service ... DARS
Digital Audio Stationary Head [*Recording*] (NTCM) ... DASH
Digital Audio Tape [*Also facetiously translated as Damn the Artist and Talent*] ... DAT
Digital Audio/Video Interactive Decoder [*Computer science*] ... DAVID
Digital Audio Visual Council (DOM) ... DAVIC
Digital Automanual Switching Unit [*Telecommunications*] (TEL) ... DAMSU
Digital Automated RADAR Tracking System (MCD) ... DARTS
Digital Automatic Acquisition (MCD) ... DAA
Digital Automatic Flight Control System ... DAFCS
Digital Automatic Frequency Control ... DAFC
Digital Automatic Gain Control (MCD) ... DAGC
Digital Automatic Measuring Equipment (MHDB) ... DAME
Digital Automatic Multiple Pressure Recorder [*Lewis Research Center*] ... DAMPR
Digital Automatic Pattern Recognition (IEEE) ... DAPR
Digital Automatic Readout Tracker [*Computer science*] (IAA) ... DART
Digital Automatic Stabilization Equipment (MCD) ... DASE
Digital Automatic Stabilization Equipment Computer (MCD) ... DASEC
Digital Automatic Stabilization Equipment System [*or Subsystem*] (MCD) ... DASES
Digital Automatic Tape Intelligence Checkout ... DATICO
Digital Automatic Tester and Classifier ... DATAC
Digital Automatic Tracking and Ranging [*or Remoting*] [*Air Force*] ... DATAR
Digital Automatic Weather Network ... DAWN
Digital Autonomous Terminal Access Communication [*Data Bus*] ... DATAC
Digital Autopilot (MCD) ... DAP
Digital Autopilot Flight Director System (MCD) ... DAFDS
Digital Autopilot Requirements (NASA) ... DAR
Digital Autotransducer and Recorder (IEEE) ... DATAR
Digital Auxiliary Information Code [*Computer science*] ... DAXI
Digital Avionic Transmission System (IAA) ... DATS
Digital Avionics Control ... DIGAC
Digital Avionics Control System (MCD) ... DACS
Digital Avionics Information System [*Air Force*] ... DAIS
Digital Avionics Integration System ... DAIS
Digital Avionics Processor [*Northrop Corp.*] ... DAP
Digital Avionics Research System (MCD) ... DARE
Digital Avionics System (MCD) ... DAS
Digital Azimuth Control ... DAC
Digital Azimuth Control / Environmental Control ... DACEC
Digital Azimuth Control Unit ... DACU
Digital Azimuth Range Tracking System ... DARTS
Digital Bar and Altitude Setting Indicator (DWSG) ... DBASI
Digital Bargraph Display ... DBD
Digital Bargraph Display Unit ... DBDU
Digital Barometer Altimeter Setting Indicator [*Aviation*] (FAAC) ... DBASI
Digital Beacon Simulator (MCD) ... DBS

Digital Beam-Forming (PDAA) ... DBF
Digital Biometrics [*NASDAQ symbol*] (TTSB) ... DBII
Digital Biometrics, Inc. [*NASDAQ symbol*] (SAG) ... DBII
Digital Biometrics, Inc. [*Associated Press*] (SAG) ... DigitBio
Digital Block [*Computer science*] ... DB
Digital Block And-Or Gate [*Computer science*] (IEEE) ... DBAO
Digital Block Clock Oscillator [*Computer science*] ... DBCO
Digital Block Flip-Flop [*Computer science*] ... DBFF
Digital Block Flop [*Computer science*] (IAA) ... DBF
Digital Block Inverter Amplifier [*Computer science*] ... DBIA
Digital Block Multivibrator [*Computer science*] ... DBMV
Digital Block Noninverting Amplifier [*Computer science*] ... DBNA
Digital Block Schmitt Trigger [*Computer science*] ... DBST
Digital Block Slave Clock [*Computer science*] ... DBSC
Digital Bombing-Navigation System ... DBNS
Digital Bright RADAR Indicator Tower Equipment [*Air traffic control*] ... DBRITE
Digital Buffer Unit ... DBU
Digital Business Oriented Language [*Digital Equipment Corp.*] (NITA) ... DIBOL
Digital Camera Control System ... DCCS
Digital Camera System [*Eastman Kodak Co.*] ... DCS
Digital Capacitance Measuring System (MCD) ... DCMS
Digital Capacitance Meter (IDOE) ... DCM
Digital Card and-or Gate [*Computer science*] ... DCAO
Digital Card Clock Oscillator [*Computer science*] ... DCCO
Digital Card Flip-Flop [*Computer science*] ... DCFF
Digital Card Inverting Amplifier [*Computer science*] ... DCIA
Digital Card Multivibrator [*Computer science*] ... DCMV
Digital Card Noninverting Amplifier [*Computer science*] ... DCNA
Digital Card Schmitt Trigger [*Computer science*] ... DCST
Digital Card Slave Clock [*Computer science*] ... DCSC
Digital Cartographic Database [*Computer science*] ... DCDB
Digital Cassette Recorder ... DCR
Digital Central Office [*Trademark of the Stromberg-Carlson Corp.*] [*Telecommunications*] ... DCO
Digital Centroid Terminal Correlation ... DCTC
Digital Channel Link ... DCL
Digital Channel Selection (IAA) ... DICS
Digital Charge-Coupled Logic (MCD) ... DCCL
Digital Chart of the World [*Database*] [*Army*] ... DCW
Digital Check Character Generator (PDAA) ... DCCG
Digital Circuit Engineer (IAA) ... DIGCIRENGR
Digital Circuit Module [*Computer science*] ... DCM
Digital Circuit Multiplication [*Computer science*] (ACRL) ... DCM
Digital Circuit Multiplication Equipment [*Telecommunications*] ... DCME
Digital Circuit Quality Monitor [*Computer science*] ... DCQM
Digital Classified Software (NITA) ... DCS
Digital Clock ... DC
Digital Clock Distribution - Local Primary Reference [*Navigation systems*] ... DCD-LPR
Digital Clock Indicator ... DCI
Digital Clock Pulse ... DCP
Digital Clock Pulse Generator ... DCPG
Digital Cockpit Simulation Facility (MCD) ... DCSF
Digital Code (AAG) ... DC
Digital Coded RADAR ... DCR
Digital Coded Voice (IAA) ... DCV
Digital Coefficient Unit [*Computer science*] (RDA) ... DCU
Digital Coherent Detector (OA) ... DCD
Digital Color Television ... DCTV
Digital Comm Tech [*AMEX symbol*] (TTSB) ... DCT
Digital Command and Control Unit (NASA) ... DCCU
Digital Command Assembly [*NASA*] (KSC) ... DCA
Digital Command Communications System (MCD) ... DCCS
Digital Command Language [*Digital Equipment Corp.*] (NITA) ... DCL
Digital Command Signal [*Telecommunications*] (OSI) ... DCS
Digital Command System [*or Subsystem*] ... DCS
Digital Communication Console (IAA) ... DCC
Digital Communication System [*Computer science*] ... DCS
Digital Communication through Orbiting Needle (IAA) ... DICON
Digital Communications ... DIGICOM
Digital Communications and Control Unit (MCD) ... DCCU
Digital Communications Associates, Inc. [*Alpharetta, GA*] (CDE) ... DCA
Digital Communications Experimental Facility [*Air Force*] ... DICEF
Digital Communications Management System [*Navy*] ... DCMS
Digital Communications Protocol [*Computer science*] (NITA) ... DCP
Digital Communications Satellite Subsystem (MCD) ... DCSS
Digital Communications System (NITA) ... DIGICOM
Digital Communications System Evaluator (MCD) ... DICOS
Digital Communications System Evaluator (MCD) ... DICOSE
Digital Communications Technology Corp. [*AMEX symbol*] (SAG) ... DCT
Digital Communications Technology Corp. [*Associated Press*] (SAG) ... DigitCT
Digital Communications Terminal (MCD) ... DCT
Digital Compact Cassette [*Audio technology*] ... DCC
Digital Compact Disk ... DCD
Digital Comparator ... DC
Digital Computer ... DC
Digital Computer (IEEE) ... DIGCOM
Digital Computer (IAA) ... DIGCOMP
Digital Computer Association (MUGU) ... DCA
Digital Computer Control Panel ... DCCP
Digital Computer Interface System (MCD) ... DCIS
Digital Computer Laboratory [*Massachusetts Institute of Technology*] (MCD) ... DCL
Digital Computer Newsletter [*A publication*] (DNAB) ... DCN
Digital Computer / Power Supply ... DC/PS
Digital Computer Processor (IEEE) ... DCP
Digital Computer Programming [*Computer science*] (BUR) ... DCP
Digital Computer Switching Unit (MCD) ... DCSU
Digital Computer System [*Vancouver Stock Exchange symbol*] ... DCS
Digital Computer Trainer (IAA) ... DCT
Digital Computer Unit (MCD) ... DCU
Digital Concentration Readout [*Computer science*] ... DCR
Digital Condition Register (NITA) ... DCR
Digital Conference Module [*Telecommunications*] (NITA) ... DCM
Digital Consulting Associates, Inc. [*Andover, MA*] [*Later, DCI*] [*Telecommunications*] (TSSD) ... DCAI
Digital Consulting, Inc. [*Andover, MA*] (TSSD) ... DCI
Digital Control (IAA) ... DC
Digital Control and Automation System (NITA) ... DCAS
Digital Control and Interface Unit (MCD) ... DCIU
Digital Control and Vector Generator ... DCVG
Digital Control Computer ... DCC
Digital Control Design Language [*1968*] [*Computer science*] (CSR) ... DCDL
Digital Control Design System (IEEE) ... DCDS
Digital Control Element (NITA) ... DCE
Digital Control Interface [*Computer science*] (PCM) ... DCI
Digital Control Loading [*System*] (MCD) ... DCL
Digital Control Signal Processor (NASA) ... DCSP
Digital Control Station [*Computer science*] ... DCS
Digital Control System ... DCS
Digital Control Unit (KSC) ... DCU
Digital Control Variable Gain Linear Amplifier (IAA) ... DCVGLA
Digital Conversion Receiver ... DCR
Digital Coordinate Transformation System ... DCTS
Digital Cordless Standard [*Telecommunications*] (ACRL) ... DCS
Digital Correlation Demonstrator ... DICODE
Digital Countdown Display [*Computer science*] ... DCD
Digital Countdown Display System [*Computer science*] ... DCDS
Digital Countdown System [*Computer science*] ... DCS
Digital Counter/Locator [*Medical dictation and transcription equipment*] (DAVI) ... DCL
Digital Counting Unit ... DCU
Digital Cross Current ... DCC
Digital Cross-Connect System [*Telecommunications*] ... DCS
Digital Curve Tracer (IAA) ... DCT
Digital Daily System Operability Test ... DDSOT
Digital Data (CET) ... DD
Digital Data Acquisition and Processing System ... DDAPS
Digital Data Acquisition and Reduction System (MCD) ... DDARS
Digital Data Acquisition System ... DDAS
Digital Data Archives System ... DDAS
Digital Data, Auxiliary Storage, Track Display, Outputs, and RADAR Display ... DATOR
Digital Data Base [*Computer science*] (PDAA) ... D2B
Digital Data Buffer ... DDB
Digital Data Calibration System (KSC) ... DDCS
Digital Data Cell (NASA) ... DDC
Digital Data Communication (IAA) ... DIDAC
Digital Data Communications Message Protocol [*Digital Equipment Corp.*] ... DDCMP
Digital Data Communications System (MCD) ... DIDACS
Digital Data Computer ... DIDAC
Digital Data Conversion [*Computer science*] (NITA) ... DDC
Digital Data Conversion Equipment ... DDCE
Digital Data Converter ... DDC
Digital Data Display ... DIDAD
Digital Data Display System ... DDDS
Digital Data Distributor (CET) ... DDD
Digital Data Down Link [*Computer science*] (MCD) ... DDDL
Digital Data Exchange [*Telecommunications*] (TEL) ... DDX
Digital Data Exchange Standards [*Telecommunications*] (DGA) ... DDES
Digital Data Exchange-Packet [*Telecommunications*] (TSSD) ... DDX-P
Digital Data Generator (IEEE) ... DDG
Digital Data Group ... DDG
Digital Data Handling ... DDH
Digital Data Handling and Display System (NRCH) ... DDH & DS
Digital Data Handling Assembly (MCD) ... DDHA
Digital Data Handling System (NOAA) ... DDHS
Digital Data Indicator (MCD) ... DDI
Digital Data Link ... DDL
Digital Data Link Monitor ... DDLM
Digital Data Logger ... DDL
Digital Data Measuring System ... DDMS
Digital Data Multiplexer [*Telecommunications*] (ACRL) ... DDM
Digital Data Network ... DDN
Digital Data Network [*NASDAQ symbol*] (TTSB) ... DIDA
Digital Data Network Wrrt [*NASDAQ symbol*] (TTSB) ... DIDAW
Digital Data Output Conversion Element [*or Equipment*] ... DDOCE
Digital Data Processing Center [*or Complex*] (MCD) ... DDPC
Digital Data Processing Equipment ... DDPE
Digital Data Processing System ... DDPS
Digital Data Processing Unit (IEEE) ... DDPU
Digital Data Processor ... DDP
Digital Data Processor ... DIDAP
Digital Data Receiver ... DDR
Digital Data Recorder (MCD) ... DDR
Digital Data Recorder Reproducer (DWSG) ... DDRR
Digital Data Recording Head ... DDRH
Digital Data Recording System ... DDRS
Digital Data Regenerative Repeater (DNAB) ... DDRR

Digital Data Satellite Service [*Communications Satellite Corp.*] ..... DIGISAT
Digital Data Secure (DWSG) ..... DDS
Digital Data Service [*Telecommunications*] (ADA) ..... DDS
Digital Data Service (CDE) ..... DDS
Digital Data Servo ..... DDS
Digital Data Storage [*Computer science*] ..... DDS
Digital Data Storage Unit ..... DDSU
Digital Data Switching Group (CAAL) ..... DDSG
Digital Data Switching Matrix ..... DDSM
Digital Data System ..... DDS
Digital Data System (IAA) ..... DIDAS
Digital Data Terminal (MCD) ..... DDT
Digital Data Terminal Equipment ..... DDTE
Digital Data Terminal Equipment Service Module ..... DDTESM
Digital Data Terminal Equipment Service Submodule (IAA) ..... DDTESS
Digital Data Test Set (MCD) ..... DDTS
Digital Data Transceiver ..... DDT
Digital Data Transmission System (KSC) ..... DDTS
Digital Data Transmitter ..... DDT
Digital Data Unit (MUGU) ..... DDU
Digital Database (MCD) ..... DDB
Digital Database Maps (MCD) ..... DDM
Digital Database Transformation Program (MCD) ..... DDBTP
Digital Dataphone Service [*Telecommunications*] (DOM) ..... DDS
Digital Dealers Association (EA) ..... DDA
Digital Debugging Tape ..... DDT
Digital Decoder Driver Unit (MCD) ..... DDDU
Digital Delay Line [*Electronic musical instruments*] ..... DDL
Digital Demand Recorder (IAA) ..... DDR
Digital Demodulation Technique ..... DDT
Digital Depth Detector (DNAB) ..... DDD
Digital Descriptor Sys Unit [*NASDAQ symbol*] (TTSB) ..... DDSIU
Digital Descriptor Sys Wrrt'A' [*NASDAQ symbol*] (TTSB) ..... DDSIW
Digital Descriptor Sys Wrrt'B' [*NASDAQ symbol*] (TTSB) ..... DDSIZ
Digital Descriptor Systems [*NASDAQ symbol*] (SAG) ..... DDSI
Digital Descriptor Systems [*Associated Press*] (SAG) ..... DigDs
Digital Descriptor Systems [*Associated Press*] (SAG) ..... DigDsc
Digital Design Language [*Air Force Computer science*] ..... DDL
Digital Design Language-PASCAL (MCD) ..... DDL-P
Digital Diagnostic Diskette [*Computer science*] (NITA) ..... DDD
Digital Diagnostic Tool [*Automotive engineering*] ..... DDT
Digital Differencing Junction ..... DDJ
Digital Differential Analyzer [*Algorithm*] [*Computer science*] (IAA) ..... DD
Digital Differential Analyzer [*Algorithm*] [*Computer science*] ..... DDA
Digital Differential Analyzer [*Computer science*] (BARN) ..... DDA
Digital Directory Assistance, Inc. [*Information service or system*] (IID) ..... DDA
Digital Disk Recorder (DOM) ..... DDR
Digital Display ..... DD
Digital Display Alarm ..... DDA
Digital Display and Control Set (MCD) ..... DDCS
Digital Display Conversion [*Computer science*] (NITA) ..... DDC
Digital Display Converter (BUR) ..... DDC
Digital Display Driver (KSC) ..... DDD
Digital Display Generator ..... DDG
Digital Display Generator Element ..... DDGE
Digital Display Indicator (MCD) ..... DDI
Digital Display Machine ..... DDM
Digital Display Makeup ..... DDM
Digital Display Processor (CMD) ..... DDP
Digital Display Scope ..... DDS
Digital Display Unit ..... DDU
Digital Distributing Unit ..... DDU
Digital Distribution Frame [*Telecommunications*] (TEL) ..... DDF
Digital Document Interchange Format ..... DDIF
Digital Doppler System (MCD) ..... DIGIDOPS
Digital Drafting System ..... DDS
Digital Drive Amplifier (AABC) ..... DDA
Digital Dynamics Simulator (IEEE) ..... DDS
Digital Echo Suppressor (NITA) ..... DES
Digital Electric Monitor ..... DEMON
Digital Electrohydraulic (NRCH) ..... DEH
Digital Electron Beam Scanner ..... DEBS
Digital Electronic Continuous Ranging ..... DECOR
Digital Electronic Countermeasure (LAIN) ..... DECM
Digital Electronic Countermeasures Analyzer (MCD) ..... DECA
Digital Electronic Engine Control (MCD) ..... DEEC
Digital Electronic Flight Control System (MCD) ..... DEFCS
Digital Electronic Fuel Injection [*Automotive engineering*] ..... DEFI
Digital Electronic Image Stabilization (PS) ..... DEIS
Digital Electronic Mapping of European Territory ..... DEMETER
Digital Electronic Message Systems ..... DEMS
Digital Electronic Universal Calculating [*or Computing*] **Engine** ..... DEUCE
Digital Electrophysiological Data Acquisition and Analysis System [*Neurometrics*] ..... DEDAAS
Digital Element (IEEE) ..... DE
Digital Element Test Set ..... DETS
Digital Element Tester Console (MCD) ..... DETC
Digital Elevation Database (RDA) ..... DEDB
Digital Elevation Model [*For study of topography*] ..... DEM
Digital Elevation Model ..... DEM
Digital Encoder (MSA) ..... DE
Digital Encoder Handbook ..... DEH
Digital Encoder Handbook ..... DEHB
Digital Encryption Standard [*Computer science*] (PCM) ..... DES
Digital Encyclopedia Workstation [*Medinfo 86*] ..... DEW
Digital End Office [*Telecommunications*] ..... DEO
Digital Engine Control Unit (MCD) ..... DECU
Digital Engine Monitor Display (PDAA) ..... DEMD
Digital Equation-Solving Computer (IEEE) ..... DESC
Digital Equip 8.875% Dep'A'Pfd [*NYSE symbol*] (TTSB) ..... DECPrA
Digital Equipment [*Electronics*] (IAA) ..... DE
Digital Equipment [*NYSE symbol*] (TTSB) ..... DEC
Digital Equipment Computer Users Society (EA) ..... DECUS
Digital Equipment Corp. [*Maynard, MA*] [*NYSE symbol*] (SPSG) ..... DEC
Digital Equipment Corp. [*ICAO designator*] (FAAC) ..... DGT
Digital Equipment Corp. [*Associated Press*] (SAG) ..... Digital
Digital Equipment Corp. Australia Proprietary Ltd. ..... DEC
Digital Equipment Corporation Author Language [*Computer science*] (CSR) ..... DECAL
Digital Equipment Corp., Colorado Springs, Colorado Springs, CO [*OCLC symbol*] (OCLC) ..... DCX
Digital Equipment Corp., Corporate Library, Maynard, MA [*OCLC symbol*] (OCLC) ..... DEC
Digital Equipment Corp., Hudson, Westboro, MA [*OCLC symbol*] (OCLC) ..... DHL
Digital Equipment Corp. Laboratory ..... DECLAB
Digital Equipment Corp., Marlboro, Marlboro, MA [*OCLC symbol*] (OCLC) ..... DMR
Digital Equipment Corp., Merrimack, Merrimack, NH [*OCLC symbol*] (OCLC) ..... DMK
Digital Equipment Corp., Salem, Salem, NH [*OCLC symbol*] (OCLC) ..... DNI
Digital Equipment Corp., Spit Brook, Nashua, NH [*OCLC symbol*] (OCLC) ..... DTN
Digital Equipment Corporation Telecommunications Network ..... DECNET
Digital Equipment Corp., Tewkesbury, Tewkesbury, MA [*OCLC symbol*] (OCLC) ..... DTW
Digital Equipment Corp., Westminster, Westminster, MA [*OCLC symbol*] (OCLC) ..... WMD
Digital Equipment of Canada Ltd., Kanata, Ontario [*Library symbol National Library of Canada*] (NLC) ..... OKMD
Digital Equipment Technology Analysis Center (MCD) ..... DETAC
Digital Equipment's Business-Oriented Language [*Computer science*] ..... DIBOL
Digital Error Detection Subsystem [*Computer science*] (AABC) ..... DEDS
Digital Error Monitoring System (MCD) ..... DEMS
Digital Ethernet Personal Computer Adapter ..... DEPCA
Digital European Backbone [*System*] (MCD) ..... DEB
Digital European Cordless Telecommunications [*or Telephone*] ..... DECT
Digital European Cordless Telephone (ACRL) ..... DECT
Digital Evaluation Computer ..... DEC
Digital Evaluation Equipment ..... DEE
Digital Evaluation Unit ..... DEU
Digital Event Timer (KSC) ..... DET
Digital Events Evaluator (MCD) ..... DEE
Digital Exchange System (MCD) ..... DES
Digital Expansion System ..... DES
Digital Experimental Airborne Navigator ..... DEXAN
Digital Facility Terminal [*Telecommunications*] (TEL) ..... DFT
Digital Facsimile Interface System ..... DFIS
Digital Fascimile System (MCD) ..... DFS
Digital Fast Fourier Transform Processor (PDAA) ..... DIFFTRAP
Digital Fault Analysis ..... DFA
Digital Feature Analysis Data [*Military*] ..... DFAD
Digital Ferrite Phase Shifter ..... DFPS
Digital Field System ..... DFS
Digital Filtering Technique ..... DFT
Digital Fire Control [*Military*] (CAAL) ..... DFC
Digital Fire Control Computer [*Military*] (MCD) ..... DFCC
Digital Fire Control System [*Military*] (CAAL) ..... DFCS
Digital Flight Control and Landing System ..... DFCLS
Digital Flight Control Operational Flight Program (MCD) ..... DFCOFP
Digital Flight Control Software [*NASA*] (NASA) ..... DFCS
Digital Flight Control System ..... DFCS
Digital Flight Controller (AAG) ..... DFC
Digital Flight Data Acquisition Unit [*Aviation*] ..... DFDAU
Digital Flight Data Recording System (MCD) ..... DFDRS
Digital Flight Display ..... DFD
Digital Flight Guidance System (IEEE) ..... DFGS
Digital Flight Guidance System/Computer (GAVI) ..... DFGS/C
Digital Flight-Data Recorder (MCD) ..... DFDR
Digital Fly by Wire [*Aviation*] ..... DFBW
Digital Force Balance Pressure Transducer ..... DFBPT
Digital Fourier Transform [*or Transformation*] [*Computer science*] ..... DFT
Digital Frequency Analyzer ..... DFA
Digital Frequency Discrimination [*Military*] (CAAL) ..... DFD
Digital Frequency Display ..... DFD
Digital Frequency Meter [*or Monitor*] ..... DFM
Digital Frequency Synthesizer ..... DFS
Digital Function Generator ..... DFG
Digital Future Coalition ..... DFC
Digital Gas Turbine Engine Control (MCD) ..... DIGATEC
Digital Generation Systems [*NASDAQ symbol*] (TTSB) ..... DGIT
Digital Generator Video (DNAB) ..... DGV
Digital Geoballistic Computer ..... DGBC
Digital Geoballistic Computer ..... DGC
Digital Geoballistic Computer System (NITA) ..... DGBC
Digital Ground Bus ..... DGBUS
Digital Ground System ..... DGS
Digital Group (NITA) ..... DG
Digital Group Multiplexer (MCD) ..... DGM
Digital Guidance and Control Computer ..... DIGACC
Digital Guidance and Control Equipment (IAA) ..... DIGACE
Digital Guided Weapon Technology (MCD) ..... DGWT

Digital Hardware Voter Monitor (MCD) ... DHVM
Digital High-Definition Display (KSC) ... DHDD
Digital High-Speed Standard Eastern Automatic Computer ... DYSEAC
Digital Identification Signal [*Computer science*] ... DIS
Digital Ignorant Mechanism [*Pocket calculator facetiously described by T. R. Reid in his book, "The Chip"*] ... DIM
Digital Image Analysis and Display [*Computer science*] (NITA) ... DIAD
Digital Image Analysis and Display System [*Computer science*] ... DIADS
Digital Image Analysis Laboratory [*University of Arizona*] [*Research center*] (RCD) ... DIAL
Digital Image Complex for Image Feature Extraction and Recognition System (MCD) ... DICIFER
Digital Image Enhancement [*Microscopy*] ... DIE
Digital Image Manipulation and Enhancement Systems ... DIMES
Digital Image Processing (LAIN) ... DIP
Digital Image Rectification System (MCD) ... DIRS
Digital Imagery Processing System (MCD) ... DIPS
Digital Imagery Test Bed (MCD) ... DITB
Digital Imaging and Communications in Medicine ... DICOM
Digital Imaging Medical System ... DIMS
Digital Imaging Microscope ... DIM
Digital Imaging Spectrophotometer [*or Spectroscopy*] ... DIS
Digital Impact Predictor ... DIP
Digital Incremental Plotter ... DIP
Digital Index [*Photography*] ... DX
Digital Inertial Guidance System ... DIGS
Digital Infared Image Reformatter ... DIIR
Digital Information Detection [*Computer science*] (IAA) ... DID
Digital Information Display [*Computer science*] ... DID
Digital Information Display System [*Computer science*] ... DIDS
Digital Information Transfer Set (CAAL) ... DITS
Digital Information Transfer System ... DITS
Digital Input [*Computer science*] ... DI
Digital Input [*Computer science*] (KSC) ... DIN
Digital Input Adaptor [*Computer science*] (NITA) ... DIA
Digital Input [*or Integrating*] **Computer** [*Computer science*] ... DIC
Digital Input Control [*Computer science*] (IAA) ... DIC
Digital Input/Digital Output [*Computer science*] ... DIDO
Digital Input Gate ... DIG
Digital Input Group Voltage (IAA) ... DIV
Digital Input Module [*Computer science*] ... DIM
Digital Input Multiplexer (CAAL) ... DIM
Digital Input/Output [*Computer science*] ... DIO
Digital Input/Output Buffer [*Computer science*] ... DIOB
Digital Input/Output Control [*Computer science*] ... DIOC
Digital Input/Output Display Equipment ... DIODE
Digital Input/Output Interface [*Computer science*] (KSC) ... DIOI
Digital Input/Output Package [*Computer science*] ... DIOP
Digital Input Simulator [*Computer science*] ... DISIM
Digital Input Unit [*Computer science*] ... DIU
Digital Input Voice Answerback [*Telecommunications*] (NITA) ... DIVA
Digital Inquiry - Voice Answerback [*Touch-tone*] [*Bell System*] [*Telecommunications*] ... DIVA
Digital Insertion Unit [*Computer science*] ... DIU
Digital Instrumentation Programmer ... DIP
Digital Instrumentation RADAR ... DIR
Digital Instrumentation Subsystem ... DIS
Digital Instrumentation Technology, Inc. (PCM) ... DIT
Digital Integral Ballistic Analyzer (NG) ... DIBA
Digital Integrated Attack and Navigation Equipment ... DIANE
Digital Integrated Automatic Landing System [*Aviation*] ... DIALS
Digital Integrated Avionics System (MCD) ... DIAS
Digital Integrated Business System [*Digital Equipment Corp.*] ... DIBS
Digital Integrated Circuit [*Computer science*] ... DIC
Digital Integrated Circuit Element [*Computer science*] ... DICE
Digital Integrated Circuit Training Aid [*Computer science*] (IAA) ... DICTA
Digital Integrated Design Language [*Computer science*] (CSR) ... DIDL
Digital Integrated Solid-State Controller for Low-Cost Automation (PDAA) ... DISCOLA
Digital Integration System (IEEE) ... DIS
Digital, Intel, and Xerox [*Telecommunications*] (ACRL) ... DIX
Digital Interactive Complex for Image Feature Extraction and Recognition [*Air Force*] ... DICIFER
Digital Interchange Code (NITA) ... DIC
Digital Interchange Utility (NITA) ... DIU
Digital Interconnecting Box (DWSG) ... DIB
Digital Intercontinental Conversion Equipment (MCD) ... DICE
Digital Interface Adapter [*Computer science*] (MCD) ... DIA
Digital Interface and Control Unit ... DICU
Digital Interface Code Converter [*Computer science*] ... DICC
Digital Interface Component (MCD) ... DIC
Digital Interface Countermeasures Equipment [*Air Force*] ... DICE
Digital Interface Switching System ... DISS
Digital Interface Test Unit [*Computer science*] (KSC) ... DITU
Digital Interface Unit [*Computer science*] (KSC) ... DIU
Digital Interface Weapon Aiming Computer (MCD) ... DIWAC
Digital Interferometric Analyzer and Display (MCD) ... DIAD
Digital International Switching Center [*Telecommunications*] (TEL) ... DISC
Digital International Switching Unit [*Telecommunications*] (TEL) ... DISU
Digital Intravenous Angiography [*Cardiology*] (DAVI) ... DIVA
Digital Isolation Amplifier ... DIA
Digital Junction [*Telecommunications*] (TEL) ... DJ
Digital Junction Switching Unit (IAA) ... DJSU
Digital Ladder Network (IAA) ... DLN
Digital Land Mass Simulation (MCD) ... DLMS
Digital Land Mass System [*Directorate of Military Survey*] [*British*] ... DLMS
Digital LASER Printer (PDAA) ... DLP
Digital Library Project ... DLP
Digital Library Systems, Inc. [*Database producer*] (IID) ... DLS
Digital Light and Color [*Computer science*] (PCM) ... DLC
Digital Light Deflector (PDAA) ... DLD
Digital Light Processing ... DLP
Digital Light Processing [*Texas Instruments*] (PCM) ... DLP
Digital Light Processing [*A projection system*] (PCM) ... DLP
Digital Line Engineering Program [*Telecommunications*] (TEL) ... DILEP
Digital Line Graph ... DLG
Digital Line Interface [*Computer science*] (NITA) ... DLI
Digital Line Interface Controller [*Telecommunications*] (NITA) ... DLIC
Digital Line System [*Telecommunications*] (TEL) ... DLS
Digital Line Termination [*Telecommunications*] (TEL) ... DLT
Digital Line Unit [*Telecommunications*] ... DLU
Digital Linear (IAA) ... DIGILIN
Digital Linear Slide Switch (MCD) ... DLSS
Digital Linear Slide Switch Assembly ... DLSA
Digital Linear Slide Switch Assembly (MCD) ... DLSSA
Digital Linear Tape [*Computer science*] (PCM) ... DLT
Digital Link [*NASDAQ symbol*] (TTSB) ... DLNK
Digital Link Corp. [*Associated Press*] (SAG) ... DgtlLnk
Digital Link Corp. [*NASDAQ symbol*] (SAG) ... DLNK
Digital Linking Module (NITA) ... DLM
Digital Local Exchange (PDAA) ... DLE
Digital Logic Circuit ... DLC
Digital Logic Module ... DLM
Digital Logic System ... DLS
Digital Loop Carrier [*Telecommunications*] (OSI) ... DLC
Digital Magnetic Tape Controller (CAAL) ... DMTC
Digital Magnetic Tape Controller Unit ... DMTU
Digital Magnetic Tape Plotting System ... DMTPS
Digital Magnetic Tape System (CAAL) ... DMTS
Digital Magnetic Tape Unit (MCD) ... DMTU
Digital Main Network Switching Unit (NITA) ... DMSU
Digital Major Alarm (MCD) ... DMA
Digital Management Unit (MCD) ... DMU
Digital Map Analyzer ... DMA
Digital Map Display ... DMD
Digital Map Generator (MCD) ... DMG
Digital Map Processor ... DMP
Digital Master Imager (DGA) ... DMI
Digital Matched Filter ... DMF
Digital Matrix Switch (MCD) ... DMS
Digital Message Device (AABC) ... DMD
Digital Message Device Group [*Later, SOICS*] [*Army*] (INF) ... DMDG
Digital Message Device/Processing and Communication Terminal (MCD) ... DMD/PACT
Digital Message Entry Device [*Computer science*] ... DMED
Digital Message Entry System ... DMES
Digital Message Terminal (MCD) ... DMT
Digital Message Terminal Computer (IEEE) ... DMTC
Digital Message Unit (MCD) ... DMU
Digital Message Voice [*Device*] (MCD) ... DMV
Digital Meter Reader (IAA) ... DMR
Digital Microcircuit ... DMC
Digital Microfilm Unit (NITA) ... DMU
Digital Micromirror Device [*Silicon chip*] [*Telecommunications*] (PCM) ... DMD
Digital Micromirror Display [*Electronics*] (PS) ... DMD
Digital Microprocessor Plotter Language (CDE) ... DMPL
Digital Microsystems [*Digital Microsystems Ltd.*] [*Software package*] (NCC) ... DMS
Digital Microwave [*NASDAQ symbol*] (TTSB) ... DMIC
Digital Microwave Corp. [*Associated Press*] (SAG) ... DigMic
Digital Microwave Corp. [*NASDAQ symbol*] (NQ) ... DMIC
Digital Milliwatt [*Telecommunications*] (TEL) ... DMW
Digital Missile Autopilot (MCD) ... DMAP
Digital Missile Controller Set ... DMCS
Digital Missile Device (MCD) ... DMD
Digital Mobilized Radio (BARN) ... DMR
Digital MODEM Command Language [*Computer science*] (BYTE) ... DMCL
Digital/Modular Avionics Program [*Aerospace*] (MCD) ... DIMAP
Digital Modular Avionics System ... DMAS
Digital Module [*Telecommunications*] (TEL) ... DM
Digital Module Automatic Tester ... DMAT
Digital Module Test Set ... DMTS
Digital Monitor Computer ... DMC
Digital Monitor Unit ... DMU
Digital Monolithic [*Electronics*] (OA) ... DM
Digital Motion System ... DMS
Digital Motor Electronics ... DME
Digital Muirhead Display (NOAA) ... DMD
Digital Multibeam Steering ... DIMUS
Digital Multibeam Steering System ... DMSS
Digital Multimeter (IAA) ... DM
Digital Multimeter ... DMM
Digital Multimeter (IDOE) ... dmm
Digital Multimeter Control ... DMMC
Digital Multiplex (LAIN) ... DM
Digital Multiplex Control (IAA) ... DMC
Digital Multiplex Equipment [*Telecommunications*] ... DME
Digital Multiplex Switch [*Trademark of Northern Telecom Ltd.*] ... DMS
Digital Multiplexed Interface (HGAA) ... DMI
Digital Multiplexer Unit [*Electronics*] (ECII) ... DMU

Digital Multiplexing and Formatting [*Computer science*] (MCD) ... DMF
Digital Multiplexing Synchronizer [*Computer science*] ... DMS
Digital Multiservice Module [*Telecommunications*] ... DMM
Digital Multistandard Decoding [*Computer science*] ... DMSD
Digital Music Tuner [*Cable television*] ... DM
Digital Musical Express (ECON) ... DMX
Digital Net Radio Interface Unit (MCD) ... DNRIU
Digital Network Access Unit [*Bytex Corp.*] ... DNAU
Digital Network Analyzer ... DINA
Digital Network Architecture [*Digital Equipment Corp.*] [*Computer science*] ... DNA
Digital Network Interface Circuit [*Telecommunications*] ... DNIC
Digital Network Service Centre (NITA) ... DNSC
Digital Network Simulation System (MCD) ... DIGINESS
Digital Network Terminator ... DNT
Digital Network-Defense Special Security Communications System [*National Security Agency*] ... DIN/DCSS
Digital Networking Unit [*Telecommunications*] (ACRL) ... DNU
Digital Noise Reduction [*Television*] ... DNR
Digital Non-Interpolated (LAIN) ... DNI
Digital Nonsecure Voice Telephone (DWSG) ... DNVT
Digital Nonsecure Voice Terminal (MCD) ... DNVT
Digital Null Command Generator ... DNCG
Digital Object Identifier [*Computer science*] ... DOI
Digital Object Identifier [*Computer science*] ... DOI
Digital Oceanographic Data Acquisition System (MCD) ... DODAS
Digital Offline Automatic Recording System ... DOLARS
Digital Ohmmeter ... DOM
Digital On-Line Cryptographic Equipment (NATG) ... DOLCE
Digital Operation System (IEEE) ... DOS
Digital Optical Cassette [*Information retrieval*] ... DOC
Digital Optical Disc [*Storage medium*] (NITA) ... DOD
Digital Optical Projection System (IEEE) ... DOPS
Digital Optical Record (IAA) ... DOR
Digital Optical Technology System (NITA) ... DOT
Digital Optical Technology System [*3-D television system*] ... DOTS
Digital Optical Transceiver [*Citifax Corp.*] ... DOT
Digital Oscillator Chip [*Apple Computer, Inc.*] ... DOC
Digital Output [*Computer science*] ... DO
Digital Output Adapter ... DOA
Digital Output Channel (MCD) ... DOC
Digital Output Control ... DOC
Digital Output/Input Translator [*Computer science*] ... DO/IT
Digital Output Multiplexer (CAAL) ... DOM
Digital Output Relay ... DOR
Digital Output Timer [*Computer science*] ... DOT
Digital Oxygen Metering Device [*Aerospace*] ... DOMD
Digital Panel Meter [*Computer science*] ... DPM
Digital Panel Meter (IDOE) ... dpm
Digital Panel Meter [*Electronics*] (ECII) ... DPS
Digital Parallel Processing Array ... DIPPA
Digital Parallel Processor ... DPP
Digital Patch Unit ... DPU
Digital Pattern Generator ... DPG
Digital Phase Comparator ... DPC
Digital Phase Difference ... DPD
Digital Phase Lock Loop (NITA) ... DPLL
Digital Phase Shifter ... DPS
Digital Phase-Locked Loop [*Space communication*] ... DPLL
Digital Picture Terminal (NOAA) ... DPT
Digital Piezoelectric Translator [*Instrumentation*] ... DPT
Digital Planimetric Compiler [*Computer science*] (PDAA) ... DPC
Digital Plotter ... DP
Digital Plotter Map [*Military British*] ... DPM
Digital Plotter System ... DPS
Digital Power Meter (IAA) ... DPM
Digital Power Meter (IDOE) ... dpm
Digital Power Supply ... DPS
Digital Pressure Converter ... DPC
Digital Pressure Transducer ... DPT
Digital Principal Local Exchange ... DPLE
Digital Private Network Signalling System (NITA) ... DPNSS
Digital Process Controller ... DPC
Digital Process Instrument [*Computer science*] (IEEE) ... DPI
Digital Processing and Control Unit ... DPCU
Digital Processing Oscilloscope (MCD) ... DPO
Digital Processing Unit ... DPU
Digital Processor (MCD) ... DP
Digital Processor Assembly (MCD) ... DPA
Digital Program Selection (IAA) ... DIPS
Digital Programming Test Set (SAA) ... DPTS
Digital Projection Readout (CAAL) ... DPRO
Digital Propellant Level Control System (KSC) ... DPLCS
Digital Pseudorandom Inspection (IEEE) ... DPI
Digital Quadrature Detection [*Instrumentation*] ... DQD
Digital Quality Monitor ... DQM
Digital Quartz Servo [*Thomson video control system*] (NITA) ... DQS
Digital RADAR Altimeter (MUGU) ... DIGIRALT
Digital RADAR Landmass Simulator ... DRLMS
Digital RADAR Relay ... DRR
Digital RADAR Relay Link ... DRRL
Digital RADAR Signal Processor (MCD) ... DRSP
Digital RADAR Simulator ... DRS
Digital RADAR System ... DRS
Digital RADIAC ... DIGIRAD
Digital Radio and Multiplexer Acquisition (MCD) ... DRAMA
Digital, Radio Frequency (MCD) ... DRF
Digital Radiography ... DR
Digital Radiometer ... DRM
Digital Range Data Processor (MCD) ... DRDP
Digital Range Machine ... DIRAM
Digital Range Machine ... DRM
Digital Range Safety (NASA) ... DRS
Digital Range Safety Command Receiver [*NASA*] (KSC) ... DRSCR
Digital Range Safety Command System [*NASA*] (MCD) ... DRSCS
Digital Range Unit ... DRU
Digital Ranging Generator [*Apollo*] [*NASA*] ... DRG
Digital Rate-Integrating Gyro (MCD) ... DRIG
Digital Ray and Intensity Projector ... DRIP
Digital Read-In Assembly [*Computer science*] ... DRA
Digital Read-In Subsystem [*Computer science*] ... DRISS
Digital Read-In System [*Computer science*] (DNAB) ... DRIS
Digital Readout [*Computer science*] (AAG) ... DIGRO
Digital Readout [*Computer science*] ... DRO
Digital Readout Box [*Computer science*] ... DRB
Digital Readout Head [*Computer science*] ... DRH
Digital Readout Light [*Computer science*] ... DRL
Digital Readout Oscilloscope [*Computer science*] ... DRO
Digital Readout Oscilloscope [*Computer science*] ... DROO
Digital Readout System [*Computer science*] ... DRS
Digital Readout Timer [*Computer science*] ... DRT
Digital Readout Unit and Interactive Displays (MCD) ... DRUID
Digital Receiver Station [*Computer science*] ... DRS
Digital Recorder Analyzer [*Computer science*] ... DRA
Digital Recorder Signal Generator [*Computer science*] ... DRSG
Digital Recorders [*NASDAQ symbol*] (TTSB) ... TBUS
Digital Recorders, Inc. [*Associated Press*] (SAG) ... DigitR
Digital Recorders, Inc. [*Associated Press*] (SAG) ... DigitRec
Digital Recorders, Inc. [*NASDAQ symbol*] (SAG) ... TBUS
Digital Recorders Wrrt [*NASDAQ symbol*] (TTSB) ... TBUSW
Digital Recording and Measurement [*Computer science*] (MHDI) ... DREAM
Digital Recording and Measuring System ... DRAMS
Digital Recording and Playback Equipment (MCD) ... DRAPE
Digital Recording Process ... DRP
Digital Recording System ... DRS
Digital Rectal [*Proctoscopy*] ... DR
Digital Rectal Examination [*Medicine*] ... DRE
Digital Register Unit ... DRU
Digital Remote Antenna Driver [*Telecommunications*] (ACRL) ... DRAD
Digital Remote Unit [*Computer science*] (MCD) ... DRU
Digital Remote Unit Buffer [*Computer science*] (MCD) ... DRUB
Digital Research, Inc. ... DRI
Digital Resolver ... DR
Digital Road Map [*Digital Equipment Corp.*] (PCM) ... DRM
Digital Road Map ... DRM
Digital Rod Position Indication [*Nuclear energy*] (NRCH) ... DRPI
Digital Rotary Transducer ... DRT
Digital Satellite Image Processing System (MCD) ... DSIPS
Digital Satellite Radio (PS) ... DSR
Digital Satellite System [*TV signal transmission*] ... DSS
Digital Satellite System ... DSS
Digital Satellite System ... DSS
Digital Scan Converter (MCD) ... DSC
Digital Scanning Electron Microscope ... DSM
Digital Scene Matching Area Correlator [*Military*] (MCD) ... DIGISMAC
Digital Scene Matching Area Correlator [*Navy*] ... DSMAC
Digital Scene Simulation [*Computer graphics used in cinematography*] (WDMC) ... DSS
Digital Science [*Kodak*] [*Computer science*] ... ds
Digital Scrambler/Encoder (NITA) ... DS/E
Digital Secure Voice Telephone [*Telecommunications*] (TEL) ... DSVT
Digital Seismic Listing Device (DWSG) ... DSLD
Digital Select Emitter (IAA) ... DSE
Digital Select Matrix ... DSM
Digital Select Module (KSC) ... DSM
Digital Selective Calling ... DSC
Digital Selective Communications ... DISCOM
Digital Sense Multiple Access [*Telecommunications*] (ACRL) ... DSMA
Digital Service Planning Analysis [*Telecommunications*] (TEL) ... DISPLAY
Digital Service Unit [*Signal converting device*] [*Telecommunications*] (TSSD) ... DSU
Digital Serving Area [*Telecommunications*] (TEL) ... DSA
Digital Set Point Control (IAA) ... DSC
Digital Shaft Encoder ... DSE
Digital Shift Register ... DSR
Digital Signal ... DS
Digital Signal 1 [*Telecommunications*] ... DS1
Digital Signal Analyzer (IEEE) ... DSA
Digital Signal Conditioner (MCD) ... DSC
Digital Signal Cross-Connect [*Telecommunications*] ... DSX
Digital Signal Cross-Connect Level 1 (CDE) ... DSX-1
Digital Signal Generator ... DSG
Digital Signal Processing [*Telecommunications*] (ACRL) ... DSP
Digital Signal Processing Chip [*Computer science*] (MHDB) ... DSP
Digital Signal Processing System ... DSPS
Digital Signal Processor [*Computer science*] (IAA) ... DIGSIGPROC
Digital Signal Processor [*Computer science*] ... DSP
Digital Signal Processor Resource Manager [*Computer science*] ... DSPRM
Digital Signal Processors [*Computer science*] ... DSPS
Digital Signal Sinusoidal Modulation (PDAA) ... DSSM
Digital Signal Standard [*Telecommunications*] (ACRL) ... DSS

Digital Signal Synchronizer ..... DSS
Digital Signal Transfer Unit (DWSG) ..... DSTU
Digital Signature Algorithm [*Telecommunications*] ..... DSA
Digital Signature Initiative [*Computer science*] ..... DSig
Digital Signature Standard [*National Institute of Standards and Technology*] ..... DSS
Digital Simulated Analog Computer (MCD) ..... DYSAC
Digital Simulation Computer System (SAA) ..... DISC
Digital Simulation Language [*Computer science*] (CSR) ..... DSL
Digital Simulation Model (KSC) ..... DSM
Digital Simulation of Continuous Processes ..... DISCOP
Digital Simulator and Computer (IEEE) ..... DISAC
Digital Simulator Computer System ..... DSCS
Digital Simulator System ..... DSS
Digital Simultaneous Voice and Data (CDE) ..... DSVD
Digital Sine/Cosine Generator (IAA) ..... DSCG
Digital Solar Aspect Indicator (IIA) ..... DSAI
Digital Solutions [*NASDAQ symbol*] (TTSB) ..... DGSI
Digital Solutions, Inc. [*NASDAQ symbol*] (NQ) ..... DGSI
Digital Solutions, Inc. [*Associated Press*] (SAG) ..... DigtlSol
Digital Sound Corp. [*NASDAQ symbol*] (SAG) ..... DGSD
Digital Sound Corp. [*Associated Press*] (SAG) ..... DigtSd
Digital Sound Corp. [*Telecommunications service*] (TSSD) ..... DSC
Digital Space Trajectory Measurement System [*Raytheon Co.*] ..... DISTRAM
Digital Spectrum Analyzer (NVT) ..... DSA
Digital Spectrum Compatible (PS) ..... DSC
Digital Speech Interpolation [*Telephone channels*] ..... DSI
Digital Speech Interpretation ..... DSI
Digital Stabilization Console ..... DSC
Digital Stepping Recorder ..... DSR
Digital Stimulation [*Of rectal sphincter*] [*Gastroenterology*] (DAVI) ..... DL
Digital Storage and Retrieval of Engineering Data System [*Army*] (MCD) ..... DSREDS
Digital Storage Architecture ..... DSA
Digital Storage Buffer (IAA) ..... DSB
Digital Storage Media [*Computer science*] ..... DSM
Digital Storage Oscilloscope [*Gould, Inc.*] ..... DSO
Digital Storage Oscilloscope ..... DSO
Digital Storage System ..... DSS
Digital Storage Systems Interconnect ..... DSSI
Digital Storage Unit (DIT) ..... DSU
Digital Strain Indicator ..... DSI
Digital Strip Printer ..... DSP
Digital Subscriber Controller [*Telecommunications*] ..... DSC
Digital Subscriber Line [*Telecommunications*] (ACRL) ..... DSL
Digital Subscriber Line [*Telecommunications*] (PCM) ..... DSL
Digital Subscriber Modem [*Telecommunications*] (NITA) ..... DSM
Digital Subscriber Signaling One [*Telecommunications*] (OSI) DSS1
Digital Subscriber Signaling System [*Telecommunications*] (ACRL) ..... DSS
Digital Subscriber Terminal ..... DST
Digital Subscriber Terminal Equipment (AFM) ..... DSTE
Digital Subscriber Voice Terminal (MCD) ..... DSVT
Digital Subset [*or Subsystem*] ..... DSS
Digital Subtraction Angiography [*or Angiogram*] [*Medicine*] ..... DSA
Digital Subtraction Echocardiogram [*Cardiology*] (DAVI) ..... DSE
Digital Subtraction Imaging [*Cardiology*] (DAVI) ..... DSI
Digital Subtraction Phlebography [*Medicine*] (DMAA) ..... DSP
Digital Sum Variation [*Telecommunications*] ..... DSV
Digital Switched Services [*Telecommunications*] (ACRL) ..... DSS
Digital Switching [*Telecommunications*] (IAA) ..... DS
Digital Switching Network [*Telecommunications*] ..... DSN
Digital Switching System [*Telecommunications*] (TEL) ..... DSS
Digital Symbology Generator (MCD) ..... DSG
Digital Synchro Data Source ..... DSDS
Digital Synchronization Unit (HGAA) ..... DSU
Digital Synchronizing Load Sensing Control [*Electronic controls*] [*Diesel engines*] ..... DSLC
Digital System ..... DS
Digital System Cross-Connect [*Telecommunications*] (ACRL) ..... DSX
Digital System Design (IEEE) ..... DSD
Digital System Diagram ..... DSD
Digital Systems International, Inc. [*NASDAQ symbol*] (SAG) ..... DGTL
Digital Systems International, Inc. [*Associated Press*] (SAG) ..... DigtlSy
Digital Systems Intl. [*NASDAQ symbol*] (TTSB) ..... DGTL
Digital Systems Operations Panel (MCD) ..... DSOM
Digital Tactical Automatic Control (IEEE) ..... DIGITAC
Digital Tactical System (PDAA) ..... DITACS
Digital Talk-Out Module ..... DTM
Digital Tandem Switch ..... DTS
Digital Tape Conversion ..... DTC
Digital Tape Recorder ..... DTR
Digital Tape Unit (IEEE) ..... DTU
Digital Tape Unit Test Facility [*NASA*] ..... DTUTF
Digital Technique ..... DT
Digital Telemetering (IAA) ..... DT
Digital Telemetering Register ..... DTR
Digital Telemetry Analog Recording ..... DITAR
Digital Telemetry System ..... DTS
Digital Telemetry Unit ..... DTU
Digital Telephone System ..... DTS
Digital Television (NITA) ..... DIGIVISION
Digital Television (MSA) ..... DTV
Digital Television Camera (MCD) ..... DITEC
Digital Television Camera ..... DTC
Digital Television Display System ..... DTDS
Digital Television Encoder ..... DTE
Digital Television Encoding ..... DITEC
Digital Television Equipment (KSC) ..... DTE
Digital Television Equipment Cluster Control Unit (MCD) ..... DCCU
Digital Television Equipment Cluster Control Unit [*Military*] ..... DTVECCU
Digital Television Monitor ..... DTM
Digital Television Network ..... DTN
Digital Television Spectrometer (NG) ..... DITS
Digital Television System (MCD) ..... DTS
Digital Terminal Line Unit [*Telecommunications*] (ACRL) ..... DTLU
Digital Termination Service [*Data transmission*] ..... DTS
Digital Termination System [*Telecommunications*] ..... DTS
Digital Terrain Data [*Army*] ..... DTD
Digital Terrain Elevation Data [*Military*] ..... DTED
Digital Terrain Model (MCD) ..... DTM
Digital Test Command System ..... DTCS
Digital Test Indicator (IAA) ..... DTI
Digital Test Measurement System (NASA) ..... DT
Digital Test Measurement [*or Monitor*] **System** ..... DTMS
Digital Test Program Generation System (MCD) ..... DTPGS
Digital Test System (MCD) ..... DTS
Digital Testing Oscilloscope (IEEE) ..... DTO
Digital Test-Oriented Language [*Computer science*] (PDAA) ..... DTOL
Digital Theater Systems [*Surround-sound technology*] (PS) ..... DTS
Digital Time Assignment Speech Interpolation (PDAA) ..... DTASI
Digital Time Base Corrector (PDAA) ..... DTBC
Digital Tire Uniformity Optimizer Computer (PDAA) ..... DTUOC
Digital Titration System ..... DTS
Digital to Analog (MCD) ..... DGANL
Digital to Television (NITA) ..... DTV
Digital to Tone Converter ..... DTC
Digital Topographic Data (MCD) ..... DTD
Digital Topographic Support System [*Army*] (RDA) ..... DTSS
Digital Tracker ..... DT
Digital Tracking System [*or Subsystem*] ..... DTS
Digital Transfer Function Analyzer (IAA) ..... DTFA
Digital Transmission and Verification Converter (KSC) ..... DTVC
Digital Transmission Equipment (IAA) ..... DTE
Digital Transmission Sys Unit [*NASDAQ symbol*] (TTSB) ..... DTSXU
Digital Transmission System ..... DTSY
Digital Transmission Systems [*Telecommunications*] (ACRL) ..... DTS
Digital Transmission Systems, Inc. [*Associated Press*] (SAG) ..... DgTrns
Digital Transmission Systems, Inc. [*NASDAQ symbol*] (SAG) ..... DTSX
Digital Transmission Unit (IEEE) ..... DTU
Digital Transmitting and Routing System (IEEE) ..... DTARS
Digital Troposcatter MODEM (MCD) ..... DTM
Digital Trunk Module [*Telecommunications*] ..... DTM
Digital Tune Enable (IAA) ..... DTE
Digital Tune in Progress (IAA) ..... DTIP
Digital Tuning Unit (IAA) ..... DTU
Digital UHF [*Ultra-High Frequency*] **ECCM Radio** [*Electronic Counter-Countermeasures*] [*Army*] ..... DUER
Digital Unit ..... DU
Digital Universal Test Equipment (MCD) ..... DUTE
Digital Uplink Assembly ..... DUA
Digital Uplink Command (MCD) ..... DUC
Digital Vacuum-Tube Voltmeter (IAA) ..... DVTVM
Digital Valve Controller (ACII) ..... DVC
Digital Variable Increment Computer ..... DIVIC
Digital Variable-Frequency Oscillator (IEEE) ..... DVFO
Digital Vascular Imaging [*Roentgenology*] ..... DVI
Digital Vascular Imaging System [*Roentgenology*] (MCD) ..... DVIS
Digital Velocity Meter ..... DVM
Digital Versatile Disc ..... DVD
Digital Versatile Disc [*Computer science*] ..... DVD
Digital Versatile Disk ..... DVD
Digital Versatile Disk (PCM) ..... DVD
Digital Versatile Disk (PCM) ..... DVD
Digital Vibration Survey Instrument ..... DVSI
Digital Video ..... DV
Digital Video Bandwidth ..... DVB
Digital Video Cassette (DOM) ..... DVC
Digital Video Communication [*Military*] (CAAL) ..... DVC
Digital Video Compression ..... DVC
Digital Video Disk ..... DVD
Digital Video Display System ..... DVDS
Digital Video Effect [*Video technology*] (PCM) ..... DVE
Digital Video Express [*Computer science*] ..... Divx
Digital Video Generator [*Computer science*] ..... DVG
Digital Video Imagery Transmission System (DOMA) ..... DVITS
Digital Video Imaging (CPH) ..... DVI
Digital Video Integrator and Processor (MCD) ..... DVIP
Digital Video Interactive [*CD-ROM technology*] [*General Electric Co.*] ..... DVI
Digital Video Interactive (CDE) ..... DVI
Digital Video Optic MODEM [*Modulate/Demodulate*] (DWSG) ..... DVOM
Digital Video Producer [*Asymetrix Co.*] (PCM) ..... DVP
Digital Video Recording (NTCM) ..... DVR
Digital Video Sys Unit [*NASDAQ symbol*] (TTSB) ..... DVIDU
Digital Video Sys Wrrt'A' [*NASDAQ symbol*] (TTSB) ..... DVIDW
Digital Video Sys Wrrt'B' [*NASDAQ symbol*] (TTSB) ..... DVIDZ
Digital Video Systems [*NASDAQ symbol*] (TTSB) ..... DVID
Digital Video Systems, Inc. [*Associated Press*] (SAG) ..... DigVd
Digital Video Systems, Inc. [*Associated Press*] (SAG) ..... DigVid
Digital Video Systems, Inc. [*Associated Press*] (SAG) ..... DigVideo
Digital Video Systems, Inc. [*NASDAQ symbol*] (SAG) ..... DVID

Digital Video Tape Recorder (NITA) ... DVTR
Digital Video Terminal [Telecommunications] (ACRL) ... DVT
Digital Videocassette Recorder (CDE) ... DVCR
Digital Videodisc (CDE) ... DVD
Digital Videodisk ... DVD
Digital Voice (MCD) ... DV
Digital Voice Communications ... DVC
Digital Voice Communications System (MCD) ... DVCS
Digital Voice Controller (MCD) ... DVC
Digital Voice Exchange [Telecommunications] (TEL) ... DVX
Digital Voice Privacy [Telecommunications] ... DVP
Digital Voice System (MCD) ... DVS
Digital Volt Ohm Milliammeter (IDOE) ... DVOM
Digital Volt Ohm Milliammeter (IDOE) ... dvom
Digital Voltage Source ... DVS
Digital Voltmeter ... DVM
Digital Voltmeter (IDOE) ... dvm
Digital Volt-Ohmmeter ... DVOM
Digital Volt-Ohmmeter Display (IAA) ... DVMD
Digital Watch Association (EA) ... DWA
Digital Waveform Generator (MCD) ... DWG
Digital Wideband Transmission System (MCD) ... DWTS
Digital Wired Recorder ... DWR
Digital World-Wide Standardised Seismograph Network [Australia] ... DWWSSN
Digital-Analog Servo System [Computer science] (SAA) ... DASS
Digitale Telekabel AG [Associated Press] (SAG) ... DigitTel
Digitale Telekabel AG [NASDAQ symbol] (SAG) ... DTAG
Digital-Image-Generated [Computer science] (IEEE) ... DIG
Digitalis [Foxglove] [Pharmacy] ... DIG
Digitalis [Foxglove] [Pharmacy] (ROG) ... DIGIT
Digitalis [Foxglove] [Pharmacy] (ROG) ... DIGITAL
Digitalis Toxicity [Medicine] (DAVI) ... Dig Tox
Digitalis-Like Factor [Biochemistry] ... DLF
Digitalized Electronics MARC [Machine-Readable Cataloging] and Non-MARC Display [Machine-Readable Cataloging] [Library of Congress] ... DEMAND
Digitally Archived Library Images ... DALI
Digitally Controlled Delta Modulator (MCD) ... DCDM
Digitally Controlled Power Source (IEEE) ... DCPS
Digitally Directed Analog (MSA) ... DDA
Digitally Directed Control (MSA) ... DDC
Digitally Fuel-Injected [Automotive engineering] ... DFI
Digitally Implemented Communications Experiment (MCD) ... DICE
Digitally Integrated Fleet Air Defense ... DIFAD
Digitally Programmed (IAA) ... DP
Digitally Scanned Image Display (MCD) ... DIGISPLAY
Digitally Sensed Image (DGA) ... DSI
Digitally-Controlled Oscillator [Electronics] ... DCO
Digitally-Implemented Analogue Processing (IAA) ... DIAP
Digitally-Programmed Voltage Source (IAA) ... DPVS
Digital-to-Analog (IDOE) ... d/a
Digital-to-Analog (IDOE) ... D/A
Digital-to-Analog (ACRL) ... D/A
Digital-to-Analog (IDOE) ... DA
Digital-to-Analog [Converter] [Computer science] ... D-A
Digital-to-Analog [Converter] [Computer science] ... D-to-A
Digital-to-Analog Circuit [Computer science] (IAA) ... DAC
Digital-to-Analog Control [Computer science] (IAA) ... DAC
Digital-to-Analog Control Apparatus [Computer science] (IAA) ... DACA
Digital-to-Analog Converter [Computer science] ... DAC
Digital-to-Analog Converter [Computer science] ... DACON
Digital-to-Analog Converter [Electronics] (ECII) ... DACS
Digital-to-Analog Converter, Alternating Current [Computer science] (IAA) ... DACAC
Digital-to-Analog Converter, Direct Current [Computer science] (IAA) ... DACDIC
Digital-to-Analog Converter Unit [Computer science] ... DACU
Digital-to-Analog Deck Angle Converter [Computer science Navy] ... DADAC
Digital-to-Analog Function Table [Packard Bell Computer Corp.] ... DAFT
Digital-to-Analog Interface Unit [Computer science] ... DAIU
Digital-to-Analog Multiplier (IEEE) ... DAM
Digital-to-Analog Synchro Converter (DNAB) ... DASCO
Digital-to-Binary (NTCM) ... D/B
Digital-to-Binary Converter [Computer science] ... DBC
Digital-to-Digital ... D-to-D
Digital-to-Digital Converter [Electronics] (IAA) ... DDC
Digital-to-Teletype ... DTTY
Digital-to-Voice Translator ... DIVOT
Digitaria Striate Virus [Plant pathology] ... DSV
Digitech Ltd. [Toronto Stock Exchange symbol] ... DGT
Digitized Information Transfer [Air/ground] (GAVI) ... DATALINK
Digitized Message Link ... DML
Digitized Moving Target Indicator (CET) ... DMTI
Digitized RADAR Experiment ... D/RADEX
Digitizer (MSA) ... DGTZR
Digitizer Logic Unit ... DLU
Digitizing and Control Unit ... DACU
Digitoxin ... DIG
Digitronics Equipment Users Association ... DEUA
Digitronics Users Association [Later, IUA] (EA) ... DUA
Digit-Symbol Substitution Test [Psychiatry] ... DST
Diglyceride [Clinical chemistry] ... DG
Diglycidyl Ether of Bisphenol A [Monomer] [Organic chemistry] ... DGEBA
Diglycidyl Ether of Methyloiresorcinol [Organic chemistry] (MCD) ... DGEMER
Diglycolamine [Organic chemistry] ... DGA
Dignitary Protective Division [US Secret Service] ... DPD

Dignitatis Humanae [Declaration on Religious Freedom] [Vatican II document] ... DH
Dignity after Death (EA) ... DAD
Dignity Battalion [Paramilitary group formed to bolster the regime of Panamanian strongman, Manuel Noriega] ... DB
Dignity in Death Alliance [British] ... DIDA
Dignity Partners [NASDAQ symbol] (TTSB) ... DPNR
Dignity Partners, Inc. [Associated Press] (SAG) ... Dignity
Dignity Partners, Inc. [NASDAQ symbol] (SAG) ... DPNR
Dignum Deo Donum Dedit [Latin] (DLA) ... DDDD
Digoxigenin [Biochemistry] ... DG
Digoxigenin Bisdigitoxoside [Biochemistry] ... DBD
Digoxigenin Monodigitoxoside [Biochemistry] ... DMD
Digoxin ... DIG
Digoxin [Pharmacology] (DAVI) ... DIGOXN
Digoxin Reduction Products [Clinical chemistry] ... DRP
Digoxin-Like Factor [Biochemistry] ... DLF
Digoxin-Like Immunoreactive Factor [Laboratory analysis] ... DLIF
Digoxin-Like Immunoreactive Substance [Biochemistry] ... DLIS
Digroup Data Reduction [Telecommunications] (MCD) ... DDR
Digroup Terminal [Telecommunications] (TEL) ... DT
DiGuglielmo's Disease [Medicine] (AAMN) ... DD
Dihaloacetonitrile [Organic chemistry] ... DHAN
Dihematoporphyrin Ether [Pharmacology] ... DHE
Diheptyl Phthalate [Organic chemistry] ... DHP
Dihexadecyl Phosphate [Organic chemistry] ... DHP
Dihexadecyldimethylammonium Acetate [Organic chemistry] ... DHDAA
Dihomo-Gammalinoleic Acid [Biochemistry] (DAVI) ... DLL
Dihydralazine [Antihypertensive agent] ... DHZ
Dihydrate ... DIHY
Dihydro [As substituent on nucleoside] [Biochemistry] ... h
Dihydroactinidiolide [Organic chemistry] ... DHA
Dihydroalprenolol [Pharmacochemistry] ... DHA
Dihydroanthracene [Organic chemistry] ... DHA
Dihydrocapaicin [Biochemistry] ... DCAP
Dihydrochalcone [Sweetening agent] ... DHC
Dihydrocodeine [An analgesic] ... DC
Dihydrocodeine [An analgesic] [Pharmacology] ... DHC
Dihydrocollidine [Organic chemistry] (DAVI) ... DDC
Dihydrodeoxycorticosterone [Endocrinology] ... DH-DOC
Dihydrodigoxin [Biochemistry] ... DHD
Dihydro-Dimethyl-Benzopyranbutyric Acid ... DBA
Dihydroepiandrosterone Loading Test [Endocrinology] ... DLT
Dihydroergocornine [Endocrinology] ... DHE
Dihydroergocryptine [Organic chemistry] ... DHEC
Dihydroergosine [Biochemistry] ... DHESN
Dihydroergotamine [Pharmacology] ... DHE
Dihydroergotoxine [Organic chemistry] ... DHET
Dihydroflavonol Reductase [An enzyme] ... DFR
Dihydrofolate [Biochemistry] ... DHF
Dihydrofolate Reductase [An enzyme] ... DHFR
Dihydrogenated Tallow Dimethylammonium Chloride [Fabric softener] [Organic chemistry] ... DHTDMAC
Dihydroheptaprenol [Biochemistry] ... DHP
Dihydroisocodeine [Pharmacology] ... DHIC
Dihydrokaempferol [Botany] ... DHK
Dihydrolevobunolol [Biochemistry] ... DHLB
Dihydro(methyl)benzodiazepinone [Biochemistry] ... DMB
Dihydromorphine [Analgesic compound] [Organic chemistry] ... DHM
Dihydromuscimol [Biochemistry] ... DHM
Dihydromycoplanecin A [Biochemistry] ... DHMPA
Dihydronaphthacene [Organic chemistry] ... DHN
Dihydronicotinamide Adenine Dinucleotide (AD) ... NADH
Dihydronicotinamide Adenine Dinucleotide Phosphate (AD) ... nadph
Dihydronicotinamide Adenine Dinucleotide Phosphate (AD) ... NADPH
Dihydroouabain [Biochemistry] ... DHO
Dihydropteridine Reductase [An enzyme] ... DHPR
Dihydropyrane [Organic chemistry] ... DHP
Dihydropyridine [Organic chemistry] ... DHP
Dihydropyridine [Organic chemistry] ... DPR
Dihydropyridine Receptor [Biochemistry] ... DHPR
Dihydroqinghaosu [Organic chemistry] ... DHQHS
Dihydroquercetin [Botany] ... DHQ
Dihydroquercetin Reductase [An enzyme] ... DQR
Dihydroquinidine [Organic chemistry] ... DHQ
Dihydrostreptomycin [Also, DHSM, DST] [Antimicrobial agent] ... DHS
Dihydrostreptomycin [Also, DHS, DST] [Antimicrobial agent] ... DHSM
Dihydrostreptomycin [Also, DHS, DHSM] [Antimicrobial agent] ... DST
Dihydrostreptomycin Sulfate [Antimicrobial agent] ... DHSS
Dihydrotachysterol [Same as ATL-IO] [Biochemistry] ... DHT
Dihydroteleocidin B [Biochemistry] ... DHTB
Dihydrotestosterone [Also, DHT] [Endocrinology] ... D
Dihydrotestosterone [Also, D] [Endocrinology] ... DHT
Dihydrotestosterone, Corticosterone, and Thyroxine [Endocrinology] ... DCT
Dihydrotestosterone, Corticosterone, Thyroxine, and Growth Hormone [Endocrinology] ... DCTG
Dihydrotestosterone Propionate [Endocrinology] ... DHTP
Dihydrotestosterone Receptor [Endocrinology] ... DR
Dihydrothymine (MAE) ... DHT
Dihydrouridine [One-letter symbol; see H_2Urd] ... D
Dihydrouridine [Also, D, hU] [A nucleoside] ... H_2Urd
Dihydrouridine [Two-letter symbol; see H_2Urd] ... hU
Dihydroxy Benoxazin One [Organic chemistry] ... DIBOA
Dihydroxyacetone [Organic chemistry] ... DHA
Dihydroxyacetone Phosphate [Also, DHAP] [Organic chemistry] ... DAP

Dihydroxyacetone Phosphate [*Also, DAP*] [*Organic chemistry*] ...... DHAP
Dihydroxyanthracenedione [*Quinazarin*] [*Organic chemistry*] ...... DHAD
Dihydroxybenzoic Acid [*Organic chemistry*] ...... DHB
Dihydroxybenzophenone [*Organic chemistry*] ...... DHBP
Dihydroxybenzoylserine [*Organic chemistry*] ...... DHBS
Dihydroxybenzylamine [*Organic chemistry*] ...... DHBA
Dihydroxybiphenyl Dioxygenase [*An enzyme*] ...... DHBD
Dihydroxyborylaminoethyl [*Organic chemistry*] ...... DBAE
(Dihydroxybutyl)guanine [*Biochemistry*] ...... DHBG
Dihydroxycholecalciferol [*Vitamin D_3*] ...... DHCC
Dihydroxycholestanoic Acid [*Biochemistry*] ...... DHCA
Dihydroxydichlorodiphenylmethane [*Fungicide*] ...... DDDM
Dihydroxy(dimethyl)imidazolidinone [*Organic chemistry*] ...... DHDMI
Dihydroxydinaphthyl Disulfide [*Analytical chemistry*] ...... DDD
Dihydroxydiphenyl [*Antioxidant*] [*Organic chemistry*] ...... DOD
(Dihydroxyethylene)bisacrylamide [*Organic chemistry*] ...... DHEBA
Di(hydroxyethyl)glycinate [*Organic chemistry*] ...... DHG
Di(hydroxyethyl)glycine [*Organic chemistry*] ...... DHEG
Dihydroxyflavone [*Organic chemistry*] ...... DHF
Dihydroxy(hydroxydisulfonaphthylazo)naphthalenedisulfonic Acid [*An indicator*] [*Chemistry*] ...... DSNADNS
Dihydroxyindol ...... DHI
Dihydroxylysinonorleucine [*Biochemistry*] ...... DHLNL
Dihydroxymandelic Acid [*Also, DMA, DOMA*] [*Organic chemistry*] ...... DHMA
Dihydroxymandelic Acid [*Also, DHMA, DOMA*] [*Organic chemistry*] ...... DMA
Dihydroxymandelic Acid [*Also, DHMA, DMA*] [*Organic chemistry*] ...... DOMA
Dihydroxymethoxybenzoxazinone [*Organic chemistry*] ...... DIMBOA
Dihydroxymethoxyphenylalanine [*Biochemistry*] ...... DHMPA
Dihydroxyphenethyleneglycol [*Organic chemistry*] ...... DHPG
Dihydroxyphenol [*Organic chemistry*] ...... DHP
Dihydroxyphenylacetic Acid [*Biochemistry*] ...... DOPAC
Dihydroxyphenylalanine [*Biochemistry*] ...... DOPA
Dihydroxyphenylalanine Oxidase [*Organic chemistry*] (DMAA) ...... DOPASE
Dihydroxyphenylethanol [*Organic chemistry*] ...... DHPE
Dihydroxyphenylethanol [*Organic chemistry*] ...... DOPET
Dihydroxyphenylglycol [*Also, DHPG*] [*Organic chemistry*] ...... DOPEG
(Dihydroxyphenylimino)imidazolidine [*Biochemistry*] ...... DPI
Dihydroxyphenylserine [*Biochemistry*] ...... DOPS
(Dihydroxypropoxymethyl)guanine [*Biochemistry*] ...... DHPG
(Dihydroxypropoxymethyl)guanine Triphosphate [*Antiviral compound*] .... DHPGTP
Dihydroxypropyl Methacrylate [*Organic chemistry*] ...... DHPMA
Dihydroxypropyladenine [*Biochemistry*] ...... DHPA
Dihydroxytryptamine [*Biochemistry*] ...... DHT
DII Group [*NASDAQ symbol*] (TTSB) ...... DIIG
Diimidazolinophenylindole [*Biochemistry*] ...... DIPI
Diiminosuccinonitrile [*Organic chemistry*] ...... DISN
Diiodofluorescein [*Organic chemistry*] ...... DIF
Diiodo(Hydroxyphenyl)pyruvic Acid [*Organic chemistry*] ...... DIHPPA
Diiodonitrophenol [*Pharmacology*] ...... DNP
Diiodothyroacetic Acid [*Biochemistry*] ...... DIAC
Diiodothyronine [*Endocrinology*] ...... T_2
Diiodotyrosine [*Biochemistry*] ...... DIT
Diis Manibus [*To the Manes, i.e., Departed Souls*] [*Latin*] ...... DM
Diis Manibus Sacrum [*Sacred to the Manes, i.e., Departed Souls*] [*Latin*] ...... DMS
Di(isoamyloxy)thiocarbanilide [*Pharmacology*] ...... DAT
Diisobutyl Adipate [*Organic chemistry*] ...... DIBA
Diisobutyl Ketone [*Organic chemistry*] ...... DIBK
Diisobutyl Phthalate ...... DIBP
Diisobutylaluminum Chloride [*Organic chemistry*] ...... DIBAC
Diisobutylaluminum Hydride [*Also, DIBAH*] [*Organic chemistry*] ...... DBAH
Diisobutylaluminum Hydride [*Also, DBAH*] [*Organic chemistry*] ...... DIBAH
Diisobutylamine [*Organic chemistry*] ...... DIBA
Diisodecyl Adipate [*Organic chemistry*] ...... DIDA
Diisodecyl Glutarate [*Organic chemistry*] ...... DIDG
Diisodecyl Phthalate [*Organic chemistry*] ...... DIDP
Diisoheptyl Phthalate ...... DIHP
Diisononyl Adipate ...... DINA
Diisononyl Phthalate [*Organic chemistry*] ...... DINP
Diisooctyl Adipate [*Organic chemistry*] ...... DIOA
Diisooctyl Phthalate [*Organic chemistry*] ...... DIOP
Diisooctyl Sebacate [*Organic chemistry*] ...... DIOS
Diisopropanolamine [*Organic chemistry*] ...... DIPA
Diisopropyl Carbodiimide [*Organic chemistry*] ...... DIPC
Diisopropyl Ether [*Organic chemistry*] ...... DIPE
Diisopropyl Ether [*Gasoline*] [*Organic chemistry*] ...... DIPE
Diisopropyl Fluorophosphate [*or Diisopropyl Fluorophosphonate*] [*Also, DIFP Ophthalmic drug*] ...... DFP
Diisopropyl Fluorophosphonate [*Also, DFP*] [*Toxic compound*] ...... DIFP
Diisopropyl Methylphosphonate [*Organic chemistry*] ...... DIMP
Diisopropyl Percarbonate [*Organic chemistry*] ...... DIPP
Di-Isopropyl Phosphate [*Organic chemistry*] (DAVI) ...... DIP
Di-isopropyl Phosphorofluoridase [*An enzyme*] ...... DFPase
Di-Isopropyl Phosphorofluoridate [*Organic chemistry*] (DAVI) ...... DFD
Diisopropyl Tartrate [*Organic chemistry*] ...... DIPT
Diisopropylamine [*Also, DIPAM*] [*Organic chemistry*] ...... DIPA
Diisopropylamine [*Also, DIPA*] [*Organic chemistry*] ...... DIPAM
Diisopropylamine [*or Diisopropylammonium*] **Dichloroacetate** [*Pharmacology*] ...... DADA
Diisopropylaminoethyl Chloride [*Organic chemistry*] ...... DIC
Diisopropylbenzene [*Organic chemistry*] ...... DIPB
Diisopropylbenzene Hydroperoxide [*Organic chemistry*] ...... DIBHP
Diisopropylethanediol [*Organic chemistry*] ...... DIPED
(Diisopropyl)ethylamine [*Organic chemistry*] ...... DIEA
Diisopropylnaphthalene [*Organic chemistry*] ...... DIPN
Diisopropylphenol [*Anesthetic*] ...... DIP
Diisothiocyano (Disulfonic Acid) Stilbene [*Organic chemistry*] ...... DIDS
Diisotridecyl Phthalate ...... DTDP
Diisoundecyl Phthalate ...... DIUP
Dijon [*France*] [*Airport symbol*] (AD) ...... DIJ
Dijon/Longvic [*France ICAO location identifier*] (ICLI) ...... LFSD
Dijon/Val Suzon [*France ICAO location identifier*] (ICLI) ...... LFGI
Dikalium Phosphate [*Pharmacology*] ...... DKP
Diketogluconic Acid [*Organic chemistry*] ...... DKG
Diketogulonic Acid [*Organic chemistry*] ...... DKA
Diketopiperazine [*Organic chemistry*] ...... DKP
Diketopyrrolopyrrole [*Organic chemistry*] ...... DPP
Dikungu [*Zaire*] [*ICAO location identifier*] (ICLI) ...... FZVP
Dilantin [*Diphenylhydantoin*] [*Anticonvulsant*] ...... Dil
Dilantin [*Parke, Davis & Co.*] [*Pharmacology*] (DAVI) ...... DILAN
Dilapidated (ROG) ...... DILAPD
Dilapidation (ROG) ...... DILAPIDN
Dilaram [*Afghanistan*] [*ICAO location identifier*] (ICLI) ...... OARM
Dilatation and Evacuation [*Medicine*] ...... D & E
Dilated Cardiomyopathy [*Cardiology*] ...... DC
Dilated Cardiomyopathy [*Cardiology*] ...... DCM
Dilation [*Medicine*] ...... DILAT
Dilation [*or Dilatation*] **and Curettage** [*of the uterus*] [*Obstetrics*] ...... D & C
Dilation, Curettage, and Biopsy [*Gynecology*] (DAVI) ...... DC & B
Dilatus [*Dissolve*] [*Pharmacy*] (DHSM) ...... DIL
Dilaudid [*or Hydromorphone*] [*Knoll Pharmaceutical Co. Chemical dependency Slang*] (DAVI) ...... dL'S
Dilauroylphosphatidylcholine [*Biochemistry*] ...... DLPC
Dilauryl Thiodipropionate [*Also, DLTDP, DLTP*] [*Food preservative*] ...... DLT
Dilauryl Thiodipropionate [*Also, DLT, DLTP*] [*Food preservative*] ...... DLTDP
Dilauryl Thiodipropionate [*Also, DLT, DLTDP*] [*Food preservative*] ...... DLTP
Dilaurylphosphatidylethanolamine [*Biochemistry*] ...... DLPE
Dilettante (ROG) ...... DILET
Dili [*Zaire*] [*Airport symbol*] (AD) ...... DIC
Dili [*Indonesia*] [*Airport symbol*] (OAG) ...... DIL
Dili [*East Timor*] [*ICAO location identifier*] (ICLI) ...... WPDL
Diligence ...... DLGNC
Dillard Department Stores [*Associated Press*] (SAG) ...... Dillard
Dillard Department Stores, Inc. Class A [*NYSE symbol*] (SPSG) ...... DDS
Dillard Dept Str'A' [*NYSE symbol*] (TTSB) ...... DDS
Dillard University, New Orleans, LA [*OCLC symbol*] (OCLC) ...... DIL
Dillard University, New Orleans, LA [*Library symbol Library of Congress*] (LCLS) ...... LND
Dilling [*Sudan*] [*ICAO location identifier*] (ICLI) ...... HSDL
Dillingham [*Alaska*] [*Airport symbol*] (OAG) ...... DLG
Dillingham [*Alaska*] [*ICAO location identifier*] (ICLI) ...... PADL
Dillingham Air Force Base, Oahu Island [*Hawaii*] [*ICAO location identifier*] (ICLI) ...... PHDH
Dillingham, AK [*AM radio station call letters*] ...... KDLG
Dillingham, AK [*FM radio station call letters*] (RBYB) ...... KRUP
Dillingham Public Library, Dillingham, AK [*Library symbol Library of Congress*] (LCLS) ...... AkDil
Dillon (ROG) ...... DIL
Dillon Bay [*Vanuatu*] [*Airport symbol*] (OAG) ...... DLY
Dillon City Library, Dillon, MT [*Library symbol*] [*Library of Congress*] (LCLS) ...... MtDi
Dillon, CO [*AM radio station call letters*] ...... KHTH
Dillon County Library, Latta, SC [*Library symbol*] [*Library of Congress*] (LCLS) ...... ScLat
Dillon, MT [*Location identifier FAA*] (FAAL) ...... DLN
Dillon, MT [*AM radio station call letters*] ...... KDBM
Dillon, MT [*FM radio station call letters*] ...... KDBM-FM
Dillon on Municipal Bonds [*A publication*] (DLA) ...... Dill Mun Bonds
Dillon on Municipal Corporations [*A publication*] (DLA) ...... Dill Mun Cor
Dillon on Municipal Corporations [*A publication*] (DLA) ...... Dill Mun Corp
Dillon on Municipal Corporations [*A publication*] (DLA) ...... Dillon Mun Corp
Dillon on the Irish Judicature Act [*A publication*] (DLA) ...... Dill Ir Jud A
Dillon on the Removal of Causes [*A publication*] (DLA) ...... Dill Rem Caus
Dillon Ranch [*California*] [*Seismograph station code, US Geological Survey*] (SEIS) ...... DIL
Dillon, SC [*Location identifier FAA*] (FAAL) ...... DLC
Dillon, SC [*AM radio station call letters*] ...... WDSC
Dillong, SC [*FM radio station call letters*] ...... WEGX
Dillon's Bay [*Vanuatu*] [*ICAO location identifier*] (ICLI) ...... NVVD
Dillon's Laws and Jurisprudence of England and America [*A publication*] (DLA) ...... Dill Laws Eng & Am
Dillon's United States Circuit Court Reports [*A publication*] (DLA) ...... Dil
Dillon's United States Circuit Court Reports [*A publication*] (DLA) ...... Dil Cir Court Rep
Dillon's United States Circuit Court Reports [*A publication*] (DLA) ...... Dill
Dillon's United States Circuit Court Reports [*A publication*] (DLA) ...... Dill Rep
Dillon's United States Circuit Court Reports [*A publication*] (DLA) ...... Dillon
Dillon's United States Circuit Court Reports [*A publication*] (DLA) ...... Dillon CC
Dillon's United States Circuit Court Reports [*A publication*] (DLA) ...... Dillon Cir Court Rep
Dilloway (ROG) ...... DIL
Dilly [*Portuguese Timor*] [*Airport symbol*] (AD) ...... DIL
Dilolo [*Zaire*] [*ICAO location identifier*] (ICLI) ...... FZSI
Diltiazem [*Pharmacology*] ...... DIL
DiLucia Chinese Alphabet [*57-character Chinese type font created for typewriter keyboards*] ...... DCA
Diluculo [*At Daybreak*] [*Pharmacy*] ...... DILUC
Dilute ...... DIL
Dilute Blood Clot Lysis Method [*Hematology*] (MAE) ...... DBCL
Dilute Homogeneous Charge ...... DHC
Dilute Strength [*Chemistry*] ...... DS

Dilute Volume [*Chemistry*] .... DV
Diluted .... DILD
Dilutin Attenuation Factor [*Metallurgy*] .... DAF
Dilution .... DILN
Dilution Factor [*Also, Fd*] [*Nuclear energy*] (NRCH) ... DF
Dilution Factor [*Also, DF*] [*Nuclear energy*] (NRCH) ... Fd
Dilution of Precision .... DOP
Dilutional Cardiopulmonary Bypass [*Cardiology*] (AAMN) ... DCB
Dilutions to Threshold [*Olfactory*] .... D/T
Dilutus [*Dilute*] [*Pharmacy*] .... DILUT
DIMAC Corp. [*Associated Press*] (SAG) .... DIMAC
DIMAC Corp. [*AMEX symbol*] (SAG) .... DMC
Dimapur [*India*] [*Airport symbol*] (OAG) .... DMU
DiMark, Inc. [*Associated Press*] (SAG) .... Dimark
Dimark, Inc. [*Formerly, Mars Graphic Services, Inc.*] [*AMEX symbol*]
   (SPSG) .... DMK
Dimbokro [*Ivory Coast*] [*ICAO location identifier*] (ICLI) ... DIDK
DIMDI [*Deutsches Institut fuer Medizinische Dokumentation und Information*]
   Database Generator [*Index to Scientific Reviews*] (NITA) ... DDBG
DIMDI Information Retrieval System (NITA) .... DIRS
DIMDI [*Deutsches Institut fuer Medizinische Dokumentation und Information*]
   List Program Generator (NITA) .... DLPG
DIMDI's [*Deutsches Institut fuer Medizinische Dokumentation und Information*]
   Administration System (NITA) .... DIAS
DIMDI's [*Deutsches Institut fuer Medizinische Dokumentation und Information*]
   Input and Updata System (NITA) .... DINUPS
Dime [*Monetry unit*] .... D
Dime Bancorp [*NYSE symbol*] (TTSB) .... DME
Dime Bancorp, Inc. [*Formerly, Dime Savings Bank NY*] [*Associated Press*]
   (SAG) .... DimeBcp
Dime Community Bancorp, Inc. [*NASDAQ symbol*] (SAG) ... DIME
Dime Community Bancorp, Inc. [*Associated Press*] (SAG) ... DimeCo
Dime Financial Corp. [*NASDAQ symbol*] (NQ) .... DIBK
Dime Financial Corp. [*Associated Press*] (SAG) .... DimeFn
Dime Finl (CT) [*NASDAQ symbol*] (TTSB) .... DIBK
Dime Savings Bank of New York [*NYSE symbol*] (SPSG) ... DME
Dimension (KSC) .... DIM
Dimension (VRA) .... dim
Dimension (WDMC) .... dim
Dimension .... DIM
Dimension .... DIMEN
Dimension (ROG) .... DIMON
Dimension (AABC) .... DMN
Dimension Control Memory .... DCM
Dimension House [*Vancouver Stock Exchange symbol*] ... DMH
Dimensional .... D
Dimensional .... DIML
Dimensional Control Drawing .... DCD
Dimensional Control Standard (MCD) .... DCS
Dimensional Flowcharting [*Computer science*] .... DF
Dimensional Fund Advisors [*Fund-management firm*] (ECON) ... DFA
Dimensional Motion Time .... DMT
Dimensional Special Tooling (NASA) .... DST
Dimensionality of Nations Project [*Hawaii*] .... DON
Dimensionally Stabilized Anode .... DSA
Dimensionally Stabilized Electrode [*Electrochemistry*] ... DSE
Dimensionally-Stable Polyester [*Tire manufacturing*] ... DSP
Dimensioning Unit [*Telecommunications*] (TEL) .... DU
Dimensionless Power Spectral Density .... DPSD
Dimensions Description Questionnaire .... DDQ
Dimensions of Self-Concept [*Personality test*] .... DOSC
Dimer-Adatom-Stacking [*Fault model*] .... DAS
Dimercaptopropanesulfonate [*Salt*] [*Organic chemistry*] ... DMPS
Dimercaptopropanol [*Also, BAL: British Anti-Lewisite*] [*Detoxicant*] [*Organic
   chemistry*] .... DMP
Dimercaptosuccinic Acid [*Organic chemistry*] .... DMS
Dimercaptosuccinic Acid [*Organic chemistry*] .... DMSA
Dimercaptothiadiazole [*Organic chemistry*] .... DMTD
Dimethadione [*Biochemistry*] .... DMD
Dimethadone [*Pharmacology*] (DAVI) .... DMO
Dimethl(ethyl)chlorosilane [*Organic chemistry*] .... DMECS
Dimethoxy(amino)stilbene [*Organic chemistry*] .... DMBAS
Dimethoxyanthracene Sulfonate [*Organic chemistry*] ... DAS
Dimethoxybenzene [*Organic chemistry*] .... DMB
Dimethoxychalcone [*Organic chemistry*] .... DMC
Dimethoxydiphenyl Trichloroethane [*Organic chemistry*] (DMAA) ... DMDT
Dimethoxyethane [*Also known as GLYME*] [*Organic chemistry*] ... DME
Dimethoxyethyl Amphetamine [*A hallucinogenic drug, more commonly known
   as STP*] (MAH) .... DOET
Dimethoxyethylcarboline Carboxylate [*Organic chemistry*] (DAVI) ... DMCM
Dimethoxymethane [*Organic chemistry*] .... DMM
Dimethoxymethylamphetamine [*A hallucinogenic drug, more commonly known
   as STP*] .... DOM
Dimethoxyphenyl Penicillin [*Medicine*] (MAE) .... DPP
Dimethoxyphenylacetophenone [*Organic chemistry*] ... DMPA
(Dimethoxyphenyl)ethylamine [*Also, DMPE, DMPEA*] [*Psychomimetic
   compound*] .... DIMPEA
(Dimethoxyphenyl)ethylamine [*Also, DIMPEA, DMPEA*] [*Psychomimetic
   compound*] .... DMPE
(Dimethoxyphenyl)ethylamine [*Also, DIMPEA, DMPE*] [*Psychomimetic
   compound*] .... DMPEA
Dimethoxyphenylisopropylamine [*Organic chemistry*] ... DMPIA
Dimethoxypropane [*Organic chemistry*] .... DMP
Dimethoxytrityl [*As substituent on nucleoside*] [*Biochemistry*] ... dmt
Dimethoxytryptamine [*Possible central nervous system neuroregulator*] ... DMT

Dimethyl Adipimidate [*Biochemistry*] .... DMA
Dimethyl Aminoethyl Acetate [*Organic chemistry*] ...... DAEA
Dimethyl Aminoethyl Methacrylate [*Organic chemistry*] ... DMAM
Dimethyl Arsonic Acid [*Organic chemistry*] .... DMA
Dimethyl Carbinol [*Organic chemistry*] .... DMC
Dimethyl Carbonate [*Organic chemistry*] .... DMC
Dimethyl Dicarbonate [*Fungistatic agent*] .... DMDC
Dimethyl Dichlorovinyl Phosphate [*An insecticide*] ... DDVP
Dimethyl Disulfide [*Organic chemistry*] .... DMDS
Dimethyl Ether [*Organic chemistry*] .... DME
Dimethyl Ether .... DME
Dimethyl ether [*Gasoline*] [*Organic chemistry*] .... DME
Dimethyl Ether of Tetraethylene Glycol [*Organic chemistry*] ... DMETEG
Dimethyl Isophthalate [*Organic chemistry*] .... DMIP
Dimethyl Isosorbide [*Organic chemistry*] .... DMI
Dimethyl Methylphosphonate [*Organic chemistry*] ...... DMMP
Dimethyl Phthalate [*Organic chemistry*] .... DMP
Dimethyl Pyrocarbonate [*Organic chemistry*] .... DMP
Dimethyl Silicone [*Organic chemistry*] .... DMS
Dimethyl Sulfate-Hydrazine [*Organic chemistry*] .... DMS-HZ
Dimethyl Sulfide [*Organic chemistry*] .... DMS
Dimethyl Sulfoniopropionate [*Organic chemistry*] ...... DMSP
Dimethyl Sulfoxide [*Also, DMSO*] [*Organic chemistry*] ... DMS
Dimethyl Sulfoxide [*Also, DMS*] [*Organic chemistry*] ... DMSO
Dimethyl Sulfoxide [*Topical anti-inflammatory*] [*Medicine*] (DAVI) ... DSMO
Dimethyl Terephthalate [*Organic chemistry*] .... DMT
Dimethyl Terephthalate [*Organic chemistry*] (NUCP) ... DMTIK
Dimethyl Tetrachloroterephthalate [*Herbicide*] .... DCPA
Dimethyl Trisulfide [*Organic chemistry*] .... DMTS
Dimethylacetamide [*Also, DMAC*] [*Organic chemistry*] ... DMA
Dimethylacetamide [*Also, DMA*] [*Organic chemistry*] ... DMAC
Dimethylacetoacetamide [*Organic chemistry*] .... DMAA
Dimethylacetylenedicarboxylate [*Organic chemistry*] ... DMAD
Dimethyladenosine [*Organic chemistry*] (MAE) .... DMA
Dimethylallyl Pyrophosphate [*Organic chemistry*] ...... DMAPP
Dimethylamine [*Organic chemistry*] .... DMA
Dimethylamino Azobenzene Sulfonyl Chloride [*Organic chemistry*] ... DABSCI
Dimethylamino Isopropyl Chloride [*Organic chemistry*] ... DIC
Dimethylamino Pyridiniumtoluenesulfonic Acid [*Organic chemistry*] ... DPTS
Dimethylaminoazobenzene [*Organic chemistry*] .... DAB
(Dimethylaminoazobenzene)iodoacetamide [*Organic chemistry*] ... DABIA
(Dimethylaminoazobenzene)isothiocyanate [*Organic chemistry*] ... DABITC
Dimethylaminobenzaldehyde [*Ehrlich's reagent*] [*Analytical chemistry*] ... DMAB
Dimethylaminobenzaldehyde [*Analytical chemistry*] (AAMN) ... DMABA
Dimethylaminobenzenethiohydantoin [*Organic chemistry*] ... DABTH
Dimethylaminoborane [*Organic chemistry*] .... DMAB
Dimethylaminoethanol [*Antidepressant*] .... DMAE
Dimethylaminoethyl Chloride [*Organic chemistry*] ...... DMC
Dimethylaminoethyl Methacrylate [*Organic chemistry*] ... DMAEMA
(Dimethylamino)isoborneol [*Organic chemistry*] .... DAIB
Dimethylaminomethylcoumarin [*Organic chemistry*] ... DAMC
(Dimethylamino(methyl)coumarinyl)maleimide [*Organic chemistry*] ... DACM
(Dimethylaminomethyl)phenol [*Organic chemistry*] ...... DMAMP
Dimethylamino(methyl)propanol [*Organic chemistry*] ... DMAMP
Dimethylaminonaphthalenesulfonamide [*Organic chemistry*] ... DNSA
Dimethylaminonaphthalenesulfonyl [*Also, Dns, DNS*] [*Biochemical
   analysis*] .... Dansyl
Dimethylaminonaphthalenesulfonyl [*Also, Dansyl, dns*] [*Biochemical
   analysis*] .... DNS
Dimethylaminonaphthalenesulfonyl Chloride [*Also, DNSC*] [*Fluorescent
   reagent*] .... DANS
Dimethylaminonaphthalenesulfonyl Chloride [*Also, DANS*] [*Fluorescent
   reagent*] .... DNSC
Dimethylaminonaphthalenesulfonyl Phosphatidylserine [*Biochemistry*] ... DNS-PS
Dimethylamino(naphthoyl)cyclohexanoic Acid [*Organic chemistry*] ... DANCA
Dimethylamino(nitro)stilbene [*Organic chemistry*] ...... DMANS
(Dimethylaminophenyl)phenylnitrone [*Organic chemistry*] ... DMAPN
Dimethylaminopropionitrile [*Organic chemistry*] .... DMAPN
Dimethylaminopropyl Chloride [*Organic chemistry*] ... DMPC
Dimethylaminopropyl Methacrylamide [*Organic chemistry*] ... DMAPMA
Dimethylaminopropylamine [*Also, DMAPA*] [*Organic chemistry*] ... DIMAPA
Dimethylaminopropylamine [*Also, DIMAPA*] [*Organic chemistry*] ... DMAPA
Dimethylaminopurine [*Organic chemistry*] .... DMAP
Dimethylaminopyridine [*Organic chemistry*] .... DMAP
Di(methylamyl) Maleate [*Organic chemistry*] .... DMAM
Dimethylaniline [*Organic chemistry*] .... DEA
Dimethylaniline [*Organic chemistry*] .... DMA
Dimethylanisole [*Organic chemistry*] .... DMA
Dimethylarginine [*Biochemistry*] .... DMA
Dimethylarsenonic Acid [*Organic chemistry*] .... DMAA
Dimethylbarbituric Acid [*Organic chemistry*] .... DMBA
Dimethylbenzamil [*Organic chemistry*] .... DMB
Dimethylbenzanthracene [*Carcinogen*] .... DMBA
Dimethylbenzanthraceneoxide [*Organic chemistry*] ... DMBAO
Dimethylbenzimidazole [*Organic chemistry*] .... DMBZ
Dimethylbenzimidazolylcobamide [*Biochemistry*] ...... DBC
Dimethylbenzylcarbinol [*Organic chemistry*] .... DMBC
Dimethylbenzylcarbinol Acetate [*Organic chemistry*] ... DMBCA
Dimethylbusulfan [*Organic chemistry*] .... DMB
Dimethyl(butyl)amine [*Organic chemistry*] .... DMBA
Dimethylcadmium .... DMCd
Dimethylcarbamoyl Chloride [*Organic chemistry*] ...... DMCC
Dimethylcarboxypsoralen [*Metabolite of TMeP*] .... DMeCP
Dimethylcetylbenzylammonium Chloride [*Antiseptic*] [*Organic
   chemistry*] .... DMCBAC

Dimethylchlortetracycline [*Antimicrobial compound*] (DAVI) ...... DMCTC
Dimethylcyclohexamine [*Organic chemistry*] ...... DMCHA
Dimethylcyclohexanedione [*Analytical chemistry*] ...... DIMEDONE
Dimethylcyclooctadiene [*Organic chemistry*] ...... DMCOD
Dimethylcysteine (Penicillamine) [*Pharmacology*] ...... DMC
Dimethyldiallylammonium Chloride [*Organic chemistry*] ...... DMDAAC
Dimethyldichlorosilane [*Organic chemistry*] ...... DMCS
Dimethyldiethyllead [*Organic chemistry*] ...... DMDEL
Dimethyldithiocarbamate [*Organic chemistry*] ...... DMDC
Dimethylethanolamine [*Organic chemistry*] ...... DME
Dimethylformal [*Organic chemistry*] ...... DMFL
Dimethylformamide [*Also, DMFA*] [*Organic chemistry*] ...... DMF
Dimethylformamide [*Also, DMF*] [*Organic chemistry*] ...... DMFA
Dimethyl-gamma-butyrolactone [*Biochemistry*] ...... DMGBL
Dimethylglycine [*Biochemistry*] ...... DMG
Dimethylglyoxime [*Organic chemistry*] ...... DMG
Dimethylhexane [*Organic chemistry*] ...... DMH
Dimethylhydantoin Formaldehyde [*Organic chemistry*] ...... DMHF
Dimethylhydrazine [*Rocket fuel base, convulsant poison*] ...... DMH
Dimethylimidazolidinone [*Organic chemistry*] ...... DMI
Dimethylindoaniline [*Organic chemistry*] ...... DIA
Dimethylmercury [*Toxicology*] ...... DMM
Dimethylmethylene Blue [*Organic chemistry*] ...... DMB
Dimethyl(methylthio)sulfonium Fluoroborate [*Organic chemistry*] ...... DMTSF
Dimethylmonochlorosilane [*Organic chemistry*] ...... DMMCS
Dimethylmuconic Acid [*Organic chemistry*] ...... DMMA
Dimethylmyleran [*Organic chemistry*] (DAVI) ...... DMM
Dimethylnaphthalene [*Organic chemistry*] ...... DMN
Dimethyl(nitrophenylazo)anisole [*Organic chemistry*] ...... DMNPAA
Dimethylnitrosamine [*Also, DMNA, NDMA*] [*Organic chemistry*] ...... DMN
Dimethylnitrosamine [*Also, DMN, NDMA*] [*Organic chemistry*] ...... DMN
Dimethyloctadecanamine N-Oxide [*Organic chemistry*] ...... DONO
Dimethyloctadiene [*Organic chemistry*] ...... DMOD
Dimethyloctatriene [*Organic chemistry*] ...... DMOT
Dimethylol Dihydroxyethyleneurea [*Used to provide durable press finish in fabrics*] ...... DMDHEU
Dimethylol dimethylhydantoin [*Organic chemistry*] ...... DMDMH
Dimethylolethyleneurea [*Organic chemistry*] ...... DMEU
Dimethylolpropionic Acid [*Organic chemistry*] ...... DMPA
Dimethylolpropyleneurea [*Organic chemistry*] ...... DMPU
Dimethylolurea [*Organic chemistry*] ...... DMU
Dimethyloxacarbocyanine [*Organic chemistry*] ...... DIOC
Dimethyloxazolidinedione [*Pharmacology*] ...... DMO
Dimethyl-para-phenylenediamine [*Organic chemistry*] ...... DMPPD
Dimethylphenol [*Organic chemistry*] ...... DMP
Dimethylphenylenediamine [*Organic chemistry*] ...... DMPD
Dimethyl(phenyl)piperazinium [*Organic chemistry*] ...... DMPP
Dimethylphosphorodithioate [*Organic chemistry*] ...... DMPDT
Dimethylphthalate Indalone Dimethylcarbonate [*Insect repellant*] (IIA) ...... DID
Dimethylpiperazine [*Also, DMPP*] [*Organic chemistry*] ...... DMP
Dimethylpiperazine [*Also, DMP*] [*Organic chemistry*] ...... DMPP
Dimethylpolysiloxane [*Organic chemistry*] ...... DMPS
Dimethylpolysiloxane [*Organic chemistry*] (MAE) ...... DPS
Dimethylpropanediol [*Organic chemistry*] ...... DMP
Dimethylpyrrole [*Organic chemistry*] ...... DMP
Dimethylpyrrolineoxide [*Organic chemistry*] ...... DMPO
Dimethylquinoline [*Organic chemistry*] ...... DMQ
Dimethylsilapentane Sulfonate [*Organic chemistry*] ...... DSS
Dimethylstilbestrol [*Biochemistry*] ...... DMS
Dimethylsuberimidate [*Organic chemistry*] ...... DMS
Dimethylsulfoniopropionate [*Organic chemistry*] ...... DMSP
Dimethyl(Tetracyano)Quinodimethane ...... DMTCNQ
Dimethyltetrahydrothiadiazinethione [*Pesticide*] [*Organic chemistry*] ...... DMTT
Dimethylthiourea [*Organic chemistry*] ...... DMTU
Dimethyl-Triazeno-Acetanilide (DICI) ...... DTA
(Dimethyltriazenol)benzoic Acid [*Antineoplastic drug*] ...... DTBA
(Dimethyltriazenyl)imidazolecarboxamide [*Dacarbazine*] [*Also, DTIC Antineoplastic drug*] ...... DIC
(Dimethyltriazenyl)imidazolecarboxamide [*Dacarbazine*] [*Also, DIC Antineoplastic drug*] ...... DTIC
Dimethyltryptamine [*A hallucinogenic drug*] ...... DET
Dimethyltryptamine [*Hallucinogenic agent*] ...... DMT
Dimethyltryptamine [*Hallucinogenic agent*] (DAVI) ...... DPT
Dimethyluracil [*Biochemistry*] ...... DMU
Dimethylzinc ...... DMZn
Dimethynaphthidine [*An indicator*] [*Chemistry*] ...... DMN
Dimidius [*One-Half*] [*Pharmacy*] ...... DIM
Dimidius [*One-Half*] [*Pharmacy*] ...... DIMID
Diminish (FAAC) ...... DMSH
Diminish ...... DIM
Diminished (WDMC) ...... dim
Diminished Radix Complementation (DICI) ...... DRC
Diminished Visual Acuity ...... DVA
Diminishing Error Method of Optimization for Networks [*Computer science*] (RDA) ...... DEMON
Diminishing Manufacturing Service (MCD) ...... DMS
Diminishing Manufacturing Sources ...... DMS
Diminishing Manufacturing Sources and Material Shortages (MCD) ...... DMSM
Diminishing Manufacturing Sources/Material Shortages (MCD) ...... DMS/MS
Diminshed Breath Sound [*Medicine*] (DAVI) ...... DBS
Diminuendo [*Getting Softer*] [*Music*] ...... DIM
Diminuendo [*Getting Softer*] [*Music*] (WGA) ...... DIMIN
Diminutive ...... DIM
Diminutive (WDAA) ...... DIMIN
Dimissory [*Ecclesiastical*] (ROG) ...... DIM

Dimitrovgrad [*Bulgaria*] [*Seismograph station code, US Geological Survey*] (SEIS) ...... DIM
Dimmer ...... DIM
Dimmer (MSA) ...... DMR
Dimmer Switch [*Automotive engineering*] ...... D/SW
Dimmitt, TX [*AM radio station call letters*] ...... KDHN
Dimmitt, TX [*FM radio station call letters*] ...... KDIU
Dimmitt, TX [*FM radio station call letters*] (RBYB) ...... KLVK
Dimmitt, TX [*FM radio station call letters*] (RBYB) ...... KNNK-FM
Dimokratiki Ananeossi [*Greece*] [*Political party*] (ECED) ...... DIANA
Dimokratikos Synagermos [*Democratic Rally*] [*Political party*] (EAIO) ...... DISY
Dimon, Inc. [*Associated Press*] (SAG) ...... Dimon
Dimon, Inc. [*NYSE symbol*] (SAG) ...... DMN
Dimondale, MI [*AM radio station call letters*] ...... WXLA
Dimple Die ...... DPDI
DIMUS [*Digital Multibeam Steering*] Narrow-Band Accelerated (NVT) ...... DNA
Dimyristoyl Phosphatidic Acid [*Biochemistry*] ...... DMPA
Dimyristoyl Phosphatidylcholine [*Biochemistry*] ...... DMPC
Dimyristoyl Phosphatidylethanolamine ...... DMPE
Dimyristoyl Phosphatidylinositol ...... DMPI
Dimyristoyl-Lecithin [*Biochemistry*] ...... DML
Dimyristoylphosphatidylglycerol [*Biochemistry*] ...... DMPG
Dinah Shore Fan Club (EA) ...... DSFC
Dinan/Trelivan [*France ICAO location identifier*] (ICLI) ...... LFEB
Di(naphthyl)phenylenediamine [*Organic chemistry*] ...... DNPD
Dinar [*Monetary unit*] [*Tunisia*] ...... D
Dinar [*Monetary unit*] [*Algeria*] ...... DA
Dinar [*Monetary unit*] [*Former Yugoslavia*] ...... DIN
Dinar SA [*Argentina ICAO designator*] (FAAC) ...... RDN
Dinard [*France*] [*Airport symbol*] (OAG) ...... DNR
Dinard/Pleurtuit-Saint-Malo [*France ICAO location identifier*] (ICLI) ...... LFRD
Di(N-carbazoly)hexadiyne [*Organic chemistry*] ...... DCHD
Dinder/Galegu [*Sudan*] [*ICAO location identifier*] (ICLI) ...... HSGG
Diner ...... DNR
Dinero Contante [*Cash*] [*Spanish Business term*] ...... DC
Diners Club, Inc. (ADA) ...... DC
Dinette [*Classified advertising*] (ADA) ...... D'ETTE
Dingele [*Zaire*] [*ICAO location identifier*] (ICLI) ...... FZVD
Dinghy [*Coast Guard*] (DNAB) ...... DIN
Dinheiro [*Monetary unit*] [*Portugal*] ...... dro
Dining ...... DNG
Dining Facilities Administration Center (MCD) ...... DFAC
Dining Permit [*Slang*] ...... DP
Dining Room ...... DR
Dining Room Orderly [*Military*] (VNW) ...... DRO
Dinitroanilino Amino-Methylpropylamine ...... DAMP
Dinitrobenzene [*Organic chemistry*] ...... DNB
Dinitrobenzenesulfenyl Chloride [*Organic chemistry*] ...... DNBSC
Dinitrobenzenesulfonic [*Organic chemistry*] ...... DNBS
Dinitrobenzidine [*Organic chemistry*] ...... DNB
Dinitrobenzoic Acid [*Organic chemistry*] ...... DNBA
Dinitrobenzoyl Chloride [*Organic chemistry*] ...... DNBC
Dinitrobenzoylphenylglycine [*Biochemistry*] ...... DNBPG
Dinitrobutyphenol [*Biochemistry*] (DAVI) ...... DNBP
Dinitrocarbanilide [*Organic chemistry*] ...... DNC
Dinitrocellulose [*Organic chemistry*] ...... DNC
Dinitrochlorobenzene [*Organic chemistry*] (DAVI) ...... DNB
Dinitrochlorobenzene [*Organic chemistry*] ...... DNCB
Dinitrocyclohexylphenol [*Insecticide*] ...... DNOCHP
Dinitrodiphenyl Disulfide [*Organic chemistry*] ...... DNDS
Dinitrofluoroaniline [*Organic chemistry*] ...... DNFA
Dinitrofluorobenzene [*Also, DNFB, FDNB*] [*Organic chemistry*] ...... DFB
Dinitrofluorobenzene [*Also, DFB, FDNB*] [*Organic chemistry*] ...... DNFB
Dinitronapholsulfonic Acid [*Organic chemistry*] ...... DNNS
Dinitro-ortho-Cresol [*Also, DNOC*] [*Herbicide*] ...... DN
Dinitro-ortho-Cresol [*Also, DN*] [*Herbicide*] ...... DNOC
Dinitro-ortho-secondary-butylphenol [*Also, DNOSBP, DNSBP*] [*Herbicide*] ...... DNBP
Dinitro-ortho-secondary-butylphenol [*Also, DNBP, DNSBP*] [*Herbicide*] ...... DNOSBP
Dinitro-ortho-secondary-butylphenol [*Also, DNBP, DNOSBP*] [*Herbicide*] ...... DNSBP
Dinitro-p-cresol [*Organic chemistry*] ...... DNPC
Dinitroperoxybenzoic Acid [*Organic chemistry*] ...... DNPBA
Dinitrophenol [*Organic chemistry*] ...... DNP
Dinitrophenyl [*Biochemistry*] ...... Dnp
Dinitrophenyl Phosphate [*Organic chemistry*] ...... DNPP
Dinitrophenylated Keyhole Limpet Hemocyanin [*Immunology*] ...... DNP-KLK
(Dinitrophenylazo)phenol [*Organic chemistry*] ...... DNAP
Dinitrophenylhydrazine [*Also, DNPH*] [*Organic chemistry*] ...... DNP
Dinitrophenylhydrazine [*Also, DNP*] [*Organic chemistry*] ...... DNPH
Dinitrophenylmorphine [*Biochemistry*] (AAMN) ...... DNPM
Dinitropropyl Acrylate [*An explosive*] ...... DNPA
Dinitroquinoxalinedione [*Organic chemistry*] ...... DNQX
Dinitrosalicylate [*Organic chemistry*] ...... DNSA
Dinitrosalicylic [*Organic chemistry*] ...... DNS
Dinitrosopentamethylenetetramine [*Organic chemistry*] ...... DNPT
Dinitrosopiperazine [*Animal carcinogen*] ...... DNPZ
Dinitrosoterephthalamide [*Organic chemistry*] ...... DNTA
Dinitrostilbenedisulfonic Acid [*Antimalarial*] ...... DNDS
Dinitrotoluene [*Organic chemistry*] ...... DNT
Dinitrotrifluoromethyl [*Organic chemistry*] ...... DNT
Dinka [*MARC language code Library of Congress*] (LCCP) ...... din
Dinkelmeyer Elementary School, North Bellmore, NY [*Library symbol Library of Congress*] (LCLS) ...... NNbeDE

Dinking Die [*Tool*] (AAG) ... DKDI
Dinner (ADA) ... DIN
Dinner Ale [*British*] (ADA) ... DA
Dinner, Bed, and Breakfast ... DBB
Dinner Jacket (ADA) ... DJ
Dinner Theater ... D-T
Dinonyl Phthalate [*Organic chemistry*] ... DNP
Dinonyl Sebacate [*Organic chemistry*] ... DNS
Di-normal-butylamine [*Organic chemistry*] ... DNBA
Di-normal-Butylmagnesium [*Organic chemistry*] ... DNBM
Di-Normal-Hexyl Sulfide [*Organic chemistry*] ... DNHS
Di-normal-Hexylmagnesium [*Organic chemistry*] ... DNHM
Di-normal-propylamine [*Organic chemistry*] ... DNPA
Dinosaur National Monument ... DINO
Dinosaur Society (EA) ... DS
Dinshah Health Society (EA) ... DHS
Dinslaken/Schwarze Heide [*Germany ICAO location identifier*] (ICLI) ... EDLD
Dinuba, CA [*FM radio station call letters*] ... KJOI
Dinuba, CA [*AM radio station call letters*] ... KRDU
Dinuclear (IAA) ... DIN
Dinus de Mugello [*Flourished, 1278-98*] [*Authority cited in pre-1607 legal work*] (DSA) ... Di
Dio Cassius [*Third century AD*] [*Classical studies*] (OCD) ... Dio Cass
Dio Chrysostomus [*First century AD*] [*Classical studies*] (OCD) ... Dio Chrys
Diocesan (ROG) ... DIOCN
Diocesan Advisory Committee [*Church of England*] ... DAC
Diocesan Carmelites of Maine (TOCD) ... DCM
Diocesan Consistory Court [*Legal term*] (DLA) ... DCC
Diocesan Director of Ordinands [*Church of England*] ... DDO
Diocesan Home Missionary ... DHM
Diocesan Labor Priests (TOCD) ... DLP
Diocesan Labor Priests (TOCD) ... dlp
Diocesan Lay Ministry Adviser [*Church of England*] ... DLMA
Diocesan Library, Boston, MA [*Library symbol Library of Congress*] (LCLS) ... MBDio
Diocesan Library, Milwaukee, WI [*Library symbol Library of Congress Obsolete*] (LCLS) ... WMDio
Diocesan Library, Philadelphia, PA [*Library symbol Library of Congress Obsolete*] (LCLS) ... PPDio
Diocesan Sisters of Mercy (TOCD) ... RSM
Diocesan Travelling Mission [*Roman Catholic*] ... DTM
Diocesan Youth Officer [*Church of England*] ... DYO
Diocese ... DIO
Diocese ... DIO
Diocese [*or Diocesean*] ... DIOC
Diocese of Boise, Resource Center, Boise, ID [*Library symbol*] [*Library of Congress*] (LCLS) ... IdBDB
Diocese of Central New York, Syracuse, NY [*Library symbol Library of Congress*] (LCLS) ... NSYDCN
Diocese of Kootenay Archives, Kelowna, BC, Canada [*Library symbol*] [*Library of Congress*] (LCLS) ... CaBKKA
Diocese of Kootenay Archives, Kelowna, British Columbia [*Library symbol National Library of Canada*] (NLC) ... BKKA
Diocese of St. Cloud, St. Cloud, MN [*Library symbol*] [*Library of Congress*] (LCLS) ... MnStclD
Dioctadecyldimethylammonium Chloride [*Organic chemistry*] ... DODAC
Dioctanoylglycerol [*Organic chemistry*] ... DOG
Dioctyl Adipate [*Also, DEHA*] [*Organic chemistry*] ... DOA
Dioctyl Azelate [*Organic chemistry*] ... DOZ
Dioctyl Fumarate [*Organic chemistry*] ... DOF
Dioctyl Isophthalate [*Organic chemistry*] ... DOIP
Dioctyl Phosphate [*Organic chemistry*] ... DOP
Dioctyl Phthalate [*Also, DEHP*] [*Organic chemistry*] ... DOP
Dioctyl Sebacate [*Organic chemistry*] ... DOS
Dioctyl Sodium Sulfosuccinate [*Organic chemistry*] ... DOSS
Dioctyl Sodium Sulfosuccinate [*Organic chemistry*] ... DSS
Dioctyl Terephthalate [*Organic chemistry*] ... DOTP
Dioctylphenyl Phosphonate [*Organic chemistry*] ... DOPP
Dioctyltin [*Organic chemistry*] ... DOT
Diode (MDG) ... D
Diode (IAA) ... DI
Diode (KSC) ... DIO
Diode ... DIOD
Diode, Alternating Current (IAA) ... DIAC
Diode Array Multichannel Analyzer [*Instrumentation*] ... DAMA
Diode Array Rapid Scan Spectrometer ... DARSS
Diode Automatic Reliability Tester (IAA) ... DART
Diode Cathode (IAA) ... DC
Diode Curve Tracer ... DCT
Diode Emitter Follower Logic ... DEFL
Diode Flat Pack ... DFP
Diode Function Generator ... DFG
Diode Gate ... DG
Diode Interrogation, Navigation, and Detection (IAA) ... DINADE
Diode Ion Injector ... DII
Diode Ion Source Injector ... DISI
Diode Logic ... DL
Diode Microwave Oscillator ... DMO
Diode Outline (IAA) ... DO
Diode Phase Shifter ... DPS
Diode Phase Shifter Module ... DPSM
Diode Plate (IAA) ... DP
Diode Qualification Program ... DQP
Diode Qualification Test ... DQT
Diode Qualification Test Program ... DQTP
Diode Recovery Tester ... DRT
Diode Resistor Logic (IAA) ... DRL
Diode Resistor Transistor Logic (MSA) ... DRTL
Diode Semiconductor Device ... DSD
Diode Switch ... DS
Diode Test Program ... DTP
Diode Transistor (IAA) ... DT
Diode Transistor Compound Pair [*Electronics*] (OA) ... DTCP
Diode Under Test (IAA) ... DUT
Diode Zener Diode Transistor Logic [*Electronics*] (IAA) ... DZTL
Diode-Assisted Commutation (PDAA) ... DAC
Diode-Capacitor Gate ... DCG
Diode-Capacitor-Diode ... DCD
Diode-Capacitor-Diode Gate ... DCDG
Diode-Capacitor-Transistor Logic [*Electronics*] (ECII) ... DCTL
Diode-Coupled Gate Flip-Flop ... DCGFF
Diode-Diode Logic [*Physics*] ... DDL
Diode-Diode Transistor Logic [*Electronics*] (IAA) ... DDTL
Diode-Emitter-Coupled Logic ... DECL
Diodes, Inc. [*AMEX symbol*] (SPSG) ... DIO
Diodes, Inc. [*Associated Press*] (SAG) ... Diodes
Diode-Transistor Logic ... DTL
Diode-Transistor Logic with Zener Diode [*Electronics*] (IAA) ... DTLZ
Diode-Transistor Micrologic (IAA) ... DTML
Diodorus Siculus [*First century BC*] [*Classical studies*] (OCD) ... Diod
Diodorus Siculus [*First century BC*] [*Classical studies*] (OCD) ... Diod Sic
Diogenes Laertius [*Third century AD*] [*Classical studies*] (OCD) ... Diog Laert
Diogenes Laertius [*Third century AD*] [*Classical studies*] (OCD) ... DL
Dioila [*Mali*] [*ICAO location identifier*] (ICLI) ... GADA
Dioleoyl Trimethylammonium Propane [*Organic chemistry*] ... DOTAP
Dioleoylphosphatidylcholine [*Organic chemistry*] ... DOPC
Dioleoylphosphatidylserine [*Biochemistry*] ... DOPS
Dioleylphosphatidylethanolamine [*Organic chemistry*] ... DOPE
Diomedes Mariconda [*Deceased, 1511*] [*Authority cited in pre-1607 legal work*] (DSA) ... Diomed Mari
Dionex Corp. [*Associated Press*] (SAG) ... Dionex
Dionex Corp. [*NASDAQ symbol*] (NQ) ... DNEX
Dionysius [*Authority cited in pre-1607 legal work*] (DSA) ... Dio
Dionysius [*Authority cited in pre-1607 legal work*] (DSA) ... Dios
Dionysius Halicarnassensis [*First century BC*] [*Classical studies*] (OCD) ... Dion Hal
Diopside [*CIPW classification*] [*Geology*] ... di
Diopter [*Also, DIOPT*] [*Optics*] ... D
Diopter [*Also, D*] [*Optics*] ... DIOPT
Diopter Spherical ... DSPH
Dioptric Strength ... DS
Di-ortho-toylguanidine [*Organic chemistry*] ... DOTG
Diospyrin Dimethyl Ether [*Biochemistry*] ... DDE
Di-o-tolylthiourea [*Organic chemistry*] ... DOTT
Diourbel [*Senegal*] [*ICAO location identifier*] (ICLI) ... GOOD
Dioxane-Methanol [*Scintillation solvent*] [*Bray solution*] ... DM
Dioxide [*Freight*] ... DIOX
Dip ... D
Dip Brazing ... DB
Dip Coating ... DC
Dip Soldering ... DS
Dip Tube ... DT
Dipalmitoyl Lecithin [*Biochemistry*] ... DPL
Dipalmitoyl Phosphatidylcholine [*Biochemistry*] ... DPPC
Dipalmitoyl Phosphatidylethanolamine [*Biochemistry*] ... DPPE
Di(p-chlorophenyl)trichloromethylcarbinol [*Miticide*] ... DTMC
Dipentamethylenethiuram Hexasulfide [*Organic chemistry*] ... DPTH
Dipeptidyl Aminopeptidase [*An enzyme*] ... DAP
Dipeptidyl Aminopeptidase [*An enzyme*] ... DPAP
Dipeptidyl Carboxypeptidase [*An enzyme*] ... DCP
Dipeptidyl Peptidase [*An enzyme*] ... DPP
Diphenamid [*or Diphenyl-dimethylacetamide*] [*Organic chemistry*] (DAVI) ... DPD
Diphenhydramine [*Organic chemistry*] (DAVI) ... DPH
Diphenolic Acid [*Organic chemistry*] ... DPA
Diphenyl [*Organic chemistry*] ... DP
Diphenyl Carbonate [*Organic chemistry*] ... DPC
Diphenyl Diazomalonate [*Organic chemistry*] ... DPDM
Diphenyl Oxide [*Organic chemistry*] ... DPO
Diphenyl Phosphorochloridate [*or Diphenylphosphoric Acid Monochloride*] [*Organic chemistry*] ... DPPC
Diphenyl Phthalate [*Organic chemistry*] ... DPP
Diphenyl Sulfone [*Organic chemistry*] ... DPS
Diphenylamine [*Organic chemistry*] ... DPA
Diphenylaminecarboxylate [*Organic chemistry*] ... DPC
Diphenylaminechloroarsine [*Tear gas*] [*Military*] ... DM
Diphenylanthracene [*Organic chemistry*] ... DPA
Diphenylanthracene Endoperoxide [*Organic chemistry*] ... DAE
Diphenylarsine Cyanide ... DC
Diphenylbutadiene [*Organic chemistry*] ... DPB
Diphenylcarbazide [*Organic chemistry*] ... DPC
Diphenylcarbene [*Organic chemistry*] ... DPC
Diphenylchlorarsine [*Toxic smoke used in warfare, also called Clark I*] (DAVI) ... AD
Diphenylchloroarsine [*Tear gas*] [*Army symbol*] ... DA
Diphenylcyanoarsine [*A war gas*] ... DC
Diphenylcyclopentylamine [*Organic chemistry*] ... DPCA
Diphenyldiazomethane [*Organic chemistry*] ... DDM
Diphenyldiazomethane [*Organic chemistry*] ... DPDM
Diphenylethylene [*Organic chemistry*] ... DPE
Diphenylguanidine [*Organic chemistry*] ... DPG

Diphenylhexatriene [*A fluorophore*] [*Organic chemistry*] ... DPH
Diphenylhydantoin [*Anticonvulsant*] ... DPH
Diphenylhydantoin [*Also, DPH*] [*Anticonvulsant*] (DAVI) ... DPU
Diphenyliodonium Hexafluorophosphate [*Biochemistry*] ... DIFP
Diphenylisobenzofuran [*Organic chemistry*] ... DIB
Diphenylisobenzofuran [*Organic chemistry*] ... DPIBF
Diphenylmethane [*Organic chemistry*] ... DPM
Diphenyloxazole [*Organic chemistry*] ... DPO
Diphenyloxazole [*Chemistry*] (DAVI) ... PPO
Diphenylphenylenediamine [*Organic chemistry*] ... DPPD
Diphenylphosphoryl Azide [*Organic chemistry*] ... DPPA
Diphenylpicrylhydrazyl [*Analytical chemistry*] ... DPPH
Diphenylstilbene [*Organic chemistry*] ... DPS
Diphenylthiohydantoin [*Organic chemistry*] ... DPTH
Diphenyltrichloroethane [*Also, DPT*] [*Organic chemistry*] ... DPE
Diphenyltrichloroethane [*Also, DPE*] [*Organic chemistry*] ... DPT
Diphloretin Phosphate [*Biochemistry*] ... DPP
Diphosgene [*Poison gas*] [*Army symbol*] ... DP
Diphosphate [*Biochemistry*] ... DP
Diphosphoglycerate [*Also, DPGA*] [*Biochemistry*] ... DPG
Diphosphoglycerate [*Also, DPG*] [*Biochemistry*] ... DPGA
Diphosphoglycerate Phosphatase [*An enzyme*] (DAVI) ... DPGP
Diphosphoglyceromutase [*An enzyme*] ... DPGM
Diphosphoinositide [*Biochemistry*] ... DPI
Diphosphopyridine Nucleotide [*Also, ARPPRN, NAD*] [*Biochemistry*] ... DPN
Diphosphopyridine Nucleotide Glycohydrolase [*Also, NaDase*] [*An enzyme*] ... DPNase
Diphosphopyridine Nucleotide, Reduced Form [*Biochemistry*] ... DPNH
Diphosphothiamine [*Also, TDP, TPP*] [*Biochemistry*] ... DPT
Diphtheria [*Medicine*] ... DIP
Diphtheria [*Medicine*] ... DIPH
Diphtheria and Tetanus Toxoid [*or Toxin*] [*Immunology*] (DAVI) ... dt
Diphtheria Antitoxin [*Immunology*] ... DAT
Diphtheria, Pertussis, and Tetanus [*Also, DTP*] [*Immunology*] ... DPT
Diphtheria Pertussis Prophylactic [*Medicine*] ... DPP
Diphtheria/Tetanus [*Immunology*] ... DIPH/TET
Diphtheria, Tetanus [*Medicine*] ... DT
Diphtheria, Tetanus, Pertussis [*Also, DPT*] [*Immunology*] ... DTP
Diphtheria, Tetanus, Poliovirus [*Vaccine*] [*Medicine*] ... DTP
Diphtheria Toxin [*Biochemistry*] ... DT
Diphtheria Toxin, A Strain [*Immunology*] ... DTA
Diphtheria Toxin Normal [*Medicine*] ... DTN
Diphtheria Toxoid [*Immunology*] ... DIPH TOX
Diphtheria Toxoid, Alum Precipitated [*Immunology*] ... DIPH TOX AP
Diphtheria-Tetanus Toxoid [*Medicine*] ... DTT
Diphtheria-Tetanus Vaccine [*Medicine*] ... DT/VAC
Diphthong [*Linguistics*] ... DIPH
Diphthong (WDAA) ... DIPHTH
Dipicolinic Acid [*Organic chemistry*] ... DPA
Dipivaloylmethanate [*Organic chemistry*] ... DPM
Dipix Systems Ltd., Nepean, Ontario [*Library symbol National Library of Canada*] (NLC) ... ONDS
Diplex [*Electronics*] (MSA) ... DIPX
Diplexer [*Electronics*] ... DIPLXR
Diploid Number [*Genetics*] ... 2N
Diploma ... DIP
Diploma (DD) ... Dip
Diploma (EY) ... DIPL
Diploma (PGP) ... Dipl
Diploma (ROG) ... DIPLOM
Diploma (ROG) ... DPL
Diploma, Australian Risk Management ... Dip ARM
Diploma de Droit Notarial [*Canada*] (DD) ... DDN
Diploma in Accounting ... DipAcc
Diploma in Accounting and Finance ... DipAcctgFin
Diploma in Administration (Nursing) ... DipAdmin(Nursing)
Diploma in Administrative Science (ADA) ... DipAdminSc
Diploma in Adult Education [*British*] (DI) ... DipAE
Diploma in Advanced Accounting (ADA) ... DipAdvAcc
Diploma in Advanced Education (ADA) ... DAE
Diploma in Advanced Educational Studies, University of Newcastle [*British*] (DBQ) ... DAES
Diploma in Advanced Engineering [*British*] ... DAE
Diploma in Advanced Studies in Education [*British*] (DI) ... DASE
Diploma in Advanced Studies in Education ... DipAdStudEd
Diploma in Agricultural Chemistry (ADA) ... DipAgrChem
Diploma in Agricultural Economics ... DipAgE
Diploma in Agricultural Economics (ADA) ... DipAgEc
Diploma in Agricultural Economics (ADA) ... DipAgrEc
Diploma in Agricultural Entomology (ADA) ... DipAgrEnt
Diploma in Agricultural Extension ... DipAgExt
Diploma in Agricultural Extension (ADA) ... DipAgrExt
Diploma in Agricultural Extension (ADA) ... DipAgrExtn
Diploma in Agricultural Genetics (ADA) ... DipAgrGen
Diploma in Agricultural Microbiology (ADA) ... DipAgrMicro
Diploma in Agricultural Science (ADA) ... DipAgrSc
Diploma in Agriculture (ADA) ... DipAg
Diploma in Agriculture ... DipAgr
Diploma in Anaesthetics [*British*] ... DA
Diploma in Analytical Chemistry ... DipA
Diploma in Anatomy ... DipAnat
Diploma in Animal Husbandry (ADA) ... DipAnHus
Diploma in Anthropology (ADA) ... DipAnth
Diploma in Anthropology ... DipAnthr
Diploma in Anthropology (ADA) ... DipAnthrop
Diploma in Applicable Mathematics ... DipAppMath
Diploma in Applied Chemistry ... DipAppChem
Diploma in Applied Child Psychology ... DipAppChildPsych
Diploma in Applied Farm Management ... DipAppFarmMgmt
Diploma in Applied Kinesiology ... DipAK
Diploma in Applied Linguistics (ADA) ... DipALing
Diploma in Applied Linguistics ... DipAppLing
Diploma in Applied Mechanics [*British*] ... Dip AM
Diploma in Applied Parasitology and Entomology [*British*] ... DAP & E
Diploma in Applied Psychology (ADA) ... DipAppPsych
Diploma in Applied Science (NADA) ... DipAppSci
Diploma in Applied Science (Nursing) ... DipAppSc(Nursing)
Diploma in Applied Statistics ... DipAppSt
Diploma in Architectural Administration ... DipArchAdm
Diploma in Architectural Computing ... DipArchComp
Diploma in Architectural Design (ADA) ... DipArchDes
Diploma in Architecture [*British*] ... D Arch
Diploma in Architecture [*British*] ... Dip Arch
Diploma in Archives Administration (ADA) ... DipArchivAdmin
Diploma in Art ... DA
Diploma in Art ... DipArt
Diploma in Art and Design ... Dip AD
Diploma in Art Education ... DipArtEd
Diploma in Art Film and Television ... DipArtFilmTV
Diploma in Arts (NADA) ... DipArs
Diploma in Arts (ADA) ... DipArts
Diploma in Astrology ... DipAst
Diploma in Audiology ... DipAud
Diploma in Automobile Engineering [*British*] ... D Au E
Diploma in Avian Medicine ... DipAvMed
Diploma in Aviation Medicine [*British*] ... D Av Med
Diploma in Aviation Medicine (ADA) ... DipAvMed
Diploma in Bacteriology [*British*] ... Dip Bact
Diploma in Bacteriology (NADA) ... DipBac
Diploma in Bacteriology [*British*] (DBQ) ... DpBact
Diploma in Basic Medical Sciences (ADA) ... DipBMS
Diploma in Biometry (ADA) ... DipBiom
Diploma in Buddhist Studies ... DBS
Diploma in Building Science ... DipBdgSc
Diploma in Building Science (Energy-Conservative Design) (ADA) ... DipBdgSc(ECD)
Diploma in Business (ADA) ... DipBus
Diploma in Business Administration ... DipBusAdmin
Diploma in Business Administration [*British*] ... Dp BA
Diploma in Business Management (NADA) ... DBM
Diploma in Business Management (ADA) ... DipBM
Diploma in Business Management (ADA) ... DipBusMangt
Diploma in Business Studies (ADA) ... DipBusStud
Diploma in Business Studies (ADA) ... DipBusStudies
Diploma in Cardiology (ADA) ... DipCard
Diploma in Cardiovascular Disease ... DipCVD
Diploma in Careers ... DipCareers
Diploma in Careers Guidance [*British*] (DI) ... DCG
Diploma in Chemistry [*Medicine*] (DMAA) ... Dip Chem
Diploma in Chemistry [*British*] ... Dipl Chem
Diploma in Chest Diseases [*British*] ... DCD
Diploma in Chest Diseases ... DipChD
Diploma in Child Dental Health [*British*] (DBQ) ... DCDH
Diploma in Child Health [*British*] ... DCH
Diploma in Child Psychiatry ... DipCPsy
Diploma in Children's Literature ... DipChiLit
Diploma in Christian Studies (PGP) ... Dip CS
Diploma in Civic Design [*British*] ... DipCD
Diploma in Clinical Epidemiology ... DipCEpi
Diploma in Clinical Hypnosis ... DipClinHyp
Diploma in Clinical Hypnotherapy (ADA) ... DipCH
Diploma in Clinical Hypnotherapy ... DipClinHypno
Diploma in Clinical Medicine of the Tropics [*British*] ... DCMT
Diploma in Clinical Nutrition ... DipClinNut
Diploma in Clinical Pathology [*British*] ... DCP
Diploma in Clinical Pathology [*British*] ... Dip Clin Path
Diploma in Clinical Pharmacology ... DipClinPharm
Diploma in Clinical Psychology [*British*] ... DCP
Diploma in Clinical Psychology ... DipClinPsych
Diploma in Clinical Science (ADA) ... DipClinSc
Diploma in Coal Geology ... DipCoalGeol
Diploma in Commerce (ADA) ... DipComm
Diploma in Commerce [*German*] ... Dipl Kaufm
Diploma in Commerce [*German*] ... Dipl Kfm
Diploma in Commerce [*German*] ... Dkfm
Diploma in Commerce (Accounting) ... DipComm(Acc)
Diploma in Commercial Art ... DipCommArt
Diploma in Commercial Data Processing ... DipComDP
Diploma in Communications ... DipCommun
Diploma in Community Child Health ... DipCommChildHealth
Diploma in Community Health in Tropical Countries [*British*] (DBQ) ... DCHT
Diploma in Community Medicine ... DipCM
Diploma in Community Science ... DipCommSc
Diploma in Computer Education ... DipCompEd
Diploma in Computer Science (ADA) ... DipCompSc
Diploma in Computer Studies ... DipComp
Diploma in Computer Studies ... DipCompSt
Diploma in Computers and Control ... DipCom & Con
Diploma in Conservation Studies ... DipConsStud
Diploma in Contact Lens Fitting [*British*] (DBQ) ... DCLF

Diploma in Contact Lens Fitting of the Association of Dispensing Opticians [*British*] (DBQ) ... CL(ADO)
Diploma in Contact Lens Practice [*British*] (DBQ) ... DCLP
Diploma in Continuing Education (ADA) ... DipContEd
Diploma in Counselling ... DipCoun
Diploma in Criminology (ADA) ... DipCrim
Diploma in Cultural Studies ... DipCultSt
Diploma in Dairy Husbandry (ADA) ... DipDHus
Diploma in Dental Health [*British*] ... DDH
Diploma in Dental Health, University of Birmingham [*British*] (DI) ... DDHBirm
Diploma in Dental Orthopaedics [*British*] ... DDO
Diploma in Dental Orthopaedics of the Royal College of Physicians and Surgeons (Glasgow) (DI) ... DDOrthRCPS(Glas)
Diploma in Dental Public Health [*British*] ... DDPH
Diploma in Dental Public Health, Royal College of Surgeons of England ... DDPHRCS Eng
Diploma in Dental Public Health, Royal College of Surgeons of England [*British*] (DBQ) ... DPHRCSEng
Diploma in Dental Surgery (NADA) ... DipDS
Diploma in Dental Therapy ... DipDentTherapy
Diploma in Dermatological Medicine [*British*] ... DDM
Diploma in Dermatological Medicine (DAVI) ... DM
Diploma in Dermatology [*British*] (DI) ... DD
Diploma in Dermatology ... DipDermat
Diploma in Design ... DipDes
Diploma in Design and Crafts ... DipDesCra
Diploma in Developmental Disabilities ... DipDevDis
Diploma in Diagnostic Radiography ... DipRadDiagnostic
Diploma in Diagnostic Radiology [*British*] ... DDR
Diploma in Diagnostic Ultrasound ... DDU
Diploma in Dietetics (ADA) ... DipDiet
Diploma in Distance Education ... DipDistEd
Diploma in Divinity ... DipDiv
Diploma in Domestic Arts ... DipDomArts
Diploma in Domestic Science ... DipDomSc
Diploma in Drama Education ... DipDramEd
Diploma in Dramatic Art ... DipDramArt
Diploma in Drawing and Painting (NADA) ... DipDP
Diploma in Drug Development and Clinical Pharmacology ... DipDDCP
Diploma in Economic Statistics (ADA) ... DipEconStats
Diploma in Economic Studies ... DipEcStud
Diploma in Economics (ADA) ... DipEc
Diploma in Economics (NADA) ... DipEco
Diploma in Education Administration ... DipEdAdm
Diploma in Education Administration and Supervision ... D Ed AS
Diploma in Education Research ... DipEdRes
Diploma in Education Studies ... DipEdSt
Diploma in Education Studies ... DipEdStud
Diploma in Education Technology ... DipEdTech
Diploma in Educational Administration (ADA) ... DipEdAdmin
Diploma in Educational Management ... DipEdMan
Diploma in Educational Psychology (ADA) ... DipEdPsych
Diploma in Electrical Engineering (ADA) ... DEE
Diploma in Elementary Education ... D El Ed
Diploma in Engineering [*British*] ... Dip Eng
Diploma in Engineering [*British*] ... Dipl Eng
Diploma in Engineering Geology ... DipEngGeol
Diploma in Engineering Management (ADA) ... DipEngMgt
Diploma in Environmental Engineering ... DipEnvironEng
Diploma in Environmental Health [*British*] (DBQ) ... DipEH
Diploma in Environmental Health ... DipEnvHlth
Diploma in Environmental Impact Assessment ... DipEnvIA
Diploma in Environmental Science ... DipEnvSc
Diploma in Environmental Studies (ADA) ... DipEnvironStud
Diploma in Environmental Studies ... DipEnvSt
Diploma in Environmental Studies ... DipEnvStud
Diploma in Epidemiology ... DipEpid
Diploma in Executive Finance [*British*] (DBQ) ... DipEF
Diploma in Executive Finance for Non-Accountants [*British*] (DBQ) ... DipEMA
Diploma in Family Medicine ... DipFamMed
Diploma in Family Planning ... DipFP
Diploma in Family Therapy ... DipFamT
Diploma in Fashion Art ... DipFashArt
Diploma in Film and Television ... DipFTV
Diploma in Film Studies ... DipFSt
Diploma in Financial Management ... DipFinMan
Diploma in Financial Management (ADA) ... DipFinMangt
Diploma in Financial Management ... DipFM
Diploma in Financial Planning ... DipFP
Diploma in Fine Arts (ADA) ... DipFA
Diploma in Food and Drug Analysis (ADA) ... DipFDA
Diploma in Foreign Affairs (ADA) ... DFA
Diploma in Forensic Medicine (ADA) ... DFM
Diploma in French Studies ... DipFrenchStud
Diploma in Funeral Directing, National Association of Funeral Directors [*British*] (DBQ) ... DipFD
Diploma in Furniture and Interior Architecture ... DipFIA
Diploma in Gemmology ... DipGem
Diploma in General Linguistics ... DipGenLing
Diploma in Genito-Urinary Medicine ... DipGUM
Diploma in Geography ... DipGeog
Diploma in Geotechnical Engineering ... DipGeotEng
Diploma in German ... DipGerm
Diploma in Glass Technology (ADA) ... DipGT
Diploma in Government Administration [*British*] ... DGA
Diploma in Graduate and Professional Studies (PGP) ... DGP
Diploma in Graduate Studies [*British*] ... DGS
Diploma in Graphic Arts ... DipGA
Diploma in Graphic Design ... DipGD
Diploma in Guidance and Counselling (ADA) ... DGC
Diploma in Gynaecology and Obstetrics (NADA) ... DipG&O
Diploma in Gynecology and Obstetrics [*British*] ... DGO
Diploma in Health Administration (ADA) ... DipHA
Diploma in Health and Human Relations Education ... DipHHRE
Diploma in Health Education ... DipHlthE
Diploma in Health Science ... DHlthSc
Diploma in Health Science ... DipHealthSc
Diploma in Health Science ... DipHlthSc
Diploma in Health Sciences ... DipHS
Diploma in Higher Chiropodial Theory of the Institute of Chiropodists [*British*] (DBQ) ... HChD
Diploma in Higher Education ... DipHEd
Diploma in Higher Education (ADA) ... DipHigherEd
Diploma in Highway Engineering (ADA) ... DipHE
Diploma in History Studies ... DipHistStud
Diploma in Home Economics ... DipHomEc
Diploma in Home Science (ADA) ... DipHSc
Diploma in Homeopathy ... DipHom
Diploma in Horticultural Science (ADA) ... DHS
Diploma in Horticultural Science (ADA) ... DipHortSc
Diploma in Horticulture, Royal Botanic Garden, Edinburgh [*British*] (DBQ) ... DHE
Diploma in Hospital Administration ... DipHospAdm
Diploma in Hospital Administration (ADA) ... DipHospAdmin
Diploma in Hospital Pharmacy (ADA) ... DipHPharm
Diploma in Hotel and Catering Management ... DipHCM
Diploma in Human Biology ... DipHumBiol
Diploma in Human Movement Studies ... DipHMS
Diploma in Human Nutrition ... DipHumNut
Diploma in Human Relations Education ... DipHumRelEd
Diploma in Humanities ... DipHum
Diploma in Husbandry (NADA) ... DipHus
Diploma in Hydraulic Engineering ... DipHE
Diploma in Hypnosis ... DipHyp
Diploma in Hypnosis and Psychotherapy [*British*] (DBQ) ... DHP
Diploma in Illumination Design ... DipIllumDes
Diploma in Illustration ... DipIllus
Diploma in Immunology ... DipImm
Diploma in Industrial Chemistry ... DIC
Diploma in Industrial Chemistry [*British*] ... Dip Ind Chem
Diploma in Industrial Engineering (ADA) ... DIE
Diploma in Industrial Health [*British*] ... DIH
Diploma in Industrial Management (ADA) ... DIM
Diploma in Industrial Pharmacy (ADA) ... DipIPharm
Diploma in Industrial Studies, Loughborough University of Technology [*British*] (DBQ) ... DIS
Diploma in Information Management ... DipInfMan
Diploma in Information Management - Archives Administration (ADA) ... DipIM-ArchivAd
Diploma in Information Management - Librarianship (ADA) ... DipIM-Lib
Diploma in Information Processing (ADA) ... DipInfmProcessing
Diploma in Internal Medicine ... DipIntMed
Diploma in International Affairs (ADA) ... DIA
Diploma in International Affairs ... DipIntAffs
Diploma in Journalism (ADA) ... DipJour
Diploma in Journalism (ADA) ... DipJourn
Diploma in Journalism (ADA) ... DJ
Diploma in Journalism (ADA) ... JD
Diploma in Jurisprudence ... DipJur
Diploma in Kindergarten Teaching ... DipKindT
Diploma in Labor Law and Industrial Relations ... DipLLIRel
Diploma in Laboratory Animal Science ... DipLabAnimSc
Diploma in Labour Relations ... DipLabRel
Diploma in Labour Relations and the Law ... DipLabRelations and the Law
Diploma in Land Economy ... DipLE
Diploma in Landscape Architecture ... DipLA
Diploma in Landscape Design ... DipLDes
Diploma in Language (NADA) ... DipL
Diploma in Laryngology and Otolaryngology [*British*] ... DLO
Diploma in Law ... DipLaw
Diploma in Legal Studies ... DipLegStud
Diploma in Librarianship (ADA) ... DipLib
Diploma in Library and Information Studies ... DipLIS
Diploma in Library Information Services ... DLIS
Diploma in Library Science ... DipLibSc
Diploma in Library Science (NADA) ... DipLibSci
Diploma in Library Science (ADA) ... DipLSc
Diploma in Library Studies (ADA) ... DipLibStud
Diploma in Linguistics ... DipLing
Diploma in Literacy and Language Education ... DipLitLangEd
Diploma in Local Government ... DipLocGovt
Diploma in Local Government Administration ... DipLocGovtAdmin
Diploma in Management ... DipMan
Diploma in Management (NADA) ... DipMgmt
Diploma in Management Studies [*British*] ... DMS
Diploma in Manufacturing Management [*British*] ... DMM
Diploma in Manufacturing Technology ... DipManTech
Diploma in Marketing ... DipMark
Diploma in Marketing, Institute of Marketing [*British*] (DBQ) ... DipM
Diploma in Materials Engineering ... DipMatEng

Diploma in Maternity and Child Welfare	DM & CW
Diploma in Mathematical Studies	DipMathStud
Diploma in Mathematics [*British*]	Dipl Math
Diploma in Mathematics Education	DipMathsEd
Diploma in Maxial, Facial, and Oral Surgery (ADA)	DipMFOS
Diploma in Mechanical and Electrical Engineering	DipMEE
Diploma in Mechanical Engineering (NADA)	DipME
Diploma in Mechanical Engineering (ADA)	DME
Diploma in Media	DipMedia
Diploma in Medical Acupuncture	DipMedAc
Diploma in Medical Hypnosis	DipMedHyp
Diploma in Medical Jurisprudence [*British*]	DMJ
Diploma in Medical Jurisprudence (Clinical)	DipMJ (Clin)
Diploma in Medical Jurisprudence (Clinical) [*British*]	DMJ (Clin)
Diploma in Medical Jurisprudence (Pathological) [*British*]	DMJ (Path)
Diploma in Medical Laboratory Technology	DipMLT
Diploma in Medical Laboratory Technology (ADA)	DMLT
Diploma in Medical Practice Management	DipPM
Diploma in Medical Psychology (ADA)	DMP
Diploma in Medical Radiation Therapy	DipMRT
Diploma in Medical Radio-Diagnosis [*British*]	DMRD
Diploma in Medical Radiography	DipMedRad
Diploma in Medical Radiology [*British*]	DMR
Diploma in Medical Radiology and Electrology [*British*]	DMRE
Diploma in Medical Radio-Therapy [*British*]	DMRT
Diploma in Medical Rehabilitation [*British*] (DBQ)	DMedRehab
Diploma in Medical Rehabilitation	DMR
Diploma in Medical Services Administration [*British*]	DMSA
Diploma in Medical Surgery (ADA)	DipMedSurg
Diploma in Medical Ultrasound	DMU
Diploma in Medicine	DipMed
Diploma in Medicine, Surgery, Obstetrics and Gynecology	DMSOG
Diploma in Mental Health	DipMH
Diploma in Metallurgy	DipMet
Diploma in Microbiology [*British*]	Dip Microbiol
Diploma in Microbiology	DipMic
Diploma in Microbiology	DipMicro
Diploma in Midwifery	DipMid
Diploma in Migrant Studies	DipMigStud
Diploma in Migrant Teaching	DipMigTeach
Diploma in Military Studies	DipMilStudies
Diploma in Mineral Science	DipMinSc
Diploma in Municipal Accounting (ADA)	DMA
Diploma in Municipal Administration [*British*]	DMA
Diploma in Museum Studies	DipMS
Diploma in Museum Studies	DipMuseumStud
Diploma in Music (ADA)	DipMus
Diploma in Musical Composition	DipMusComp
Diploma in Musical Education (NADA)	DipMusEdu
Diploma in Musical Education, Royal Scottish Academy of Music and Drama	Dip (Mus Ed) RSAM
Diploma in Natural Resources (ADA)	DipNatRes
Diploma in Natural Therapeutics [*British*]	DNTh
Diploma in Natural Therapies	DipNatTh
Diploma in Naturopathy [*British*]	ND
Diploma in Nuclear Engineering (ADA)	DipNucEng
Diploma in Nuclear Science (ADA)	DipNucSc
Diploma in Numerical Analysis and Automatic Computing (ADA)	DipNA & AC
Diploma in Nursery School Education (ADA)	DipNEd
Diploma in Nursery School Education (NADA)	DipNSEdu
Diploma in Nursing	DipNurs
Diploma in Nursing	DN
Diploma in Nursing Administration	DipNA
Diploma in Nursing Administration (ADA)	DNSA
Diploma in Nursing Education	DipNE
Diploma in Nursing Education	DipNEd
Diploma in Nursing Education (ADA)	DNE
Diploma in Nutrition [*British*]	DN
Diploma in Nutrition and Dietetics (ADA)	DipND
Diploma in Nutrition and Dietetics	DipNut & Diet
Diploma in Nutrition and Dietetics	DipNutrDiet
Diploma in Obstetrics	DObst
Diploma in Obstetrics and Gynaecology (ADA)	Dip O & G
Diploma in Obstetrics, Royal College of Obstetricians and Gynaecologists [*British*]	D Obst RCOG
Diploma in Occupational Hazard Management	DipOccHazMan
Diploma in Occupational Health	DipOccHlth
Diploma in Occupational Health	DOH
Diploma in Occupational Health and Safety	DipOHS
Diploma in Occupational Hygiene [*British*]	DO Hyg
Diploma in Occupational Medicine	DipOccMed
Diploma in Occupational Therapy (ADA)	DipOccThy
Diploma in Occupational Therapy	DipOT
Diploma in Operatic Art	DipOpArt
Diploma in Operational Salesmanship [*British*] (DI)	DipOS
Diploma in Operations Research	DipOpsRes
Diploma in Ophthalmic Medicine	DOM
Diploma in Ophthalmic Medicine and Surgery [*British*]	DOMS
Diploma in Ophthalmics	DOpt
Diploma in Ophthalmology	DO
Diploma in Opthalmic Surgery [*British*]	D Ch O
Diploma in Oral Surgery	DipOS
Diploma in Oriental Learning (ADA)	DipOL
Diploma in Orthodontics (ADA)	DipOrth
Diploma in Orthodontics [*British*]	DOrth

Diploma in Orthopaedic Surgery (ADA)	DOS
Diploma in Orthopedics	DOrth
Diploma in Orthoptics [*British*]	D Orth
Diploma in Osteopathy	DipOsteo
Diploma in Osteopathy [*British*]	DO
Diploma in Osteopathy [*Australia*]	DOst
Diploma in Otorhinolaryngology	DORL
Diploma in Outdoor Education	DipOutEd
Diploma in Paediatrics	DipPaed
Diploma in Palliative Care	DipPall
Diploma in Parent Education and Counselling	DPEC
Diploma in Pathology [*British*]	D Path
Diploma in Pediatrics	DP
Diploma in Performing Arts	DipPerfArt
Diploma in Personnel Management	DipPersMan
Diploma in Petroleum and Reservoir Engineering	DipPetResEng
Diploma in Pharmaceutical Medicine [*British*] (DBQ)	DipPharmMed
Diploma in Pharmacology (NADA)	DipPhar
Diploma in Pharmacy (ADA)	DipPharm
Diploma in Philosophy of Medicine	DipPhilMed
Diploma in Photogrammetry (ADA)	DipPhot
Diploma in Physical and Occupational Therapy (NADA)	DipP&OT
Diploma in Physical Anthropology	DipPhysAnth
Diploma in Physical Education [*British*]	Dip PE
Diploma in Physical Education (ADA)	DipPhysEd
Diploma in Physical Education (NADA)	DipPhysEdu
Diploma in Physical Education [*British*]	DPE
Diploma in Physical Medicine [*British*]	D Phys Med
Diploma in Physics [*British*]	Dipl Phys
Diploma in Physiology	DPhysiol
Diploma in Physiotherapy (ADA)	DipPhty
Diploma in Plant Pathology (ADA)	DipPlPath
Diploma in Plant Pathology (ADA)	DPP
Diploma in Poultry Husbandry (ADA)	DipPHus
Diploma in Power Engineering	DipPowEng
Diploma in Practical Dermatology	DipPrDerm
Diploma in Primary Education	DipPrimEd
Diploma in Primary Teaching	DipPrimT
Diploma in Process Systems Engineering	DipProcessSystemsEng
Diploma in Production	DipProd
Diploma in Professional Art Studies	DipProArtS
Diploma in Professional Management	DipPM
Diploma in Psychiatric Medicine and Neurology	DPsyMedNeuro
Diploma in Psychiatry [*British*]	D Psych
Diploma in Psychiatry	DipPsy
Diploma in Psychiatry	DipPsy
Diploma in Psychological Medicine (ADA)	DipPsyMed
Diploma in Psychological Medicine [*British*]	DPM
Diploma in Psychology [*British*]	Dip Psych
Diploma in Psychology	DipPsychol
Diploma in Psychotherapy	DipPsy
Diploma in Psychotherapy	DipPT
Diploma in Public Administration [*British*]	Dipl PA
Diploma in Public Administration (ADA)	DipPubAd
Diploma in Public Administration (NADA)	DipPubAdm
Diploma in Public Administration (ADA)	DipPubAdmin
Diploma in Public Administration [*British*]	DPA
Diploma in Public and Social Administration	DipPSA
Diploma in Public and Social Administration (ADA)	DPSA
Diploma in Public Dentistry [*British*]	DPD
Diploma in Public Dentistry, University of Dundee [*British*]	DPDU Dund
Diploma in Public Health	DipPH
Diploma in Public Health [*British*]	DPH
Diploma in Public Health Dentistry (ADA)	DPHDent
Diploma in Public Health Nursing (ADA)	DPHN
Diploma in Public Policy	DipPubPol
Diploma in Public Policy Studies	DipPPS
Diploma in Quantity Surveying (ADA)	DipQS
Diploma in Radio and Television Production	DipRadTVProd
Diploma in Radio Engineering	DipRadEng
Diploma in Radiology [*British*]	DR
Diploma in Recreation Management	DipRectMan
Diploma in Regional and Town Planning (ADA)	DipRTP
Diploma in Rehabilitation Studies	DipRehabStud
Diploma in Religious Education	DipRE
Diploma in Religious Studies	DipRelStud
Diploma in Remedial Electrolysis, Institute of Electrolysis [*British*] (DBQ)	DRE
Diploma in Resource Geology	DipResGeol
Diploma in Resource Management (ADA)	DRM
Diploma in Restorative Dentistry, Royal College of Surgeons of Edinburgh [*British*] (DBQ)	DRDRCSEd
Diploma in Rural Accounting (ADA)	DipRurAcc
Diploma in Sanitary Science (ROG)	DSS
Diploma in Sanitary Science [*British*]	DSSc
Diploma in School Administration	DipSchoolAdmin
Diploma in Science in Agriculture (ADA)	DipScAg
Diploma in Secondary Education (ADA)	DipSecEd
Diploma in Secretarial Studies	DipSecStud
Diploma in Shared Obstetric Care	DipSObC
Diploma in Social Administration [*British*]	Dip Soc Ad
Diploma in Social Administration	DSA
Diploma in Social and Public Administration (ADA)	DipS & PA
Diploma in Social Communication	DipSocCommun
Diploma in Social Medicine [*British*]	Dip Soc Med
Diploma in Social Medicine [*British*]	DSM

Diploma in Social Science ... DipSocSc
Diploma in Social Studies [*British*] ... Dip Soc Studies
Diploma in Social Studies (ADA) ... DipSocStud
Diploma in Social Studies (ADA) ... DipSS
Diploma in Social Work (ADA) ... DipSW
Diploma in Sociology (ADA) ... DipSoc
Diploma in Sociology ... DipSociol
Diploma in Soil Science ... DipSoilSc
Diploma in Sound Preservation ... DipSP
Diploma in Special Education ... DipSpecEd
Diploma in Speech Therapy (ADA) ... DipSpThy
Diploma in Sport Science ... DipSpSc
Diploma in Sports Medicine ... DipSM
Diploma in Sports Science ... DipSpSci
Diploma in State Medicine (ROG) ... DSM
Diploma in Statistics ... DipStats
Diploma in Statistics (WDAA) ... SD
Diploma in Structural and Foundation Engineering ... DipStructFoundEng
Diploma in Structural Engineering ... DipStructEng
Diploma in Surgery Medicine ... DpSM
Diploma in Surveying Science (ADA) ... DipSurvSc
Diploma in Tax Law ... DipTaxLaw
Diploma in Teacher Librarianship (ADA) ... DipTchrLib
Diploma in Teacher Librarianship ... DipTeachLib
Diploma in Teachers Librarianship (ADA) ... DipTLiB
Diploma in Teaching (ADA) ... DipT
Diploma in Teaching ... DipTeach
Diploma in Teaching ... DTeaching
Diploma in Teaching (Early Childhood Education) ... DipTeach(ECE)
Diploma in Teaching English to the Migrant (ADA) ... DipTEM
Diploma in Teaching (Nursing) ... DipTeach(Nursing)
Diploma in Teaching of English as a Foreign Language (ADA) ... DipTEFL
Diploma in Teaching (Primary) ... DipTeach(Primary)
Diploma in Technical Business Administration ... DipTechBusAdmin
Diploma in Technical Teaching ... DipTechT
Diploma in Technology [*British*] ... Dip Tech
Diploma in Technology (NADA) ... DipTec
Diploma in Technology (Architecture) (ADA) ... DipTech(Arch)
Diploma in Technology (Building) (ADA) ... DipTech(Buil)
Diploma in Technology (Commerce) (ADA) ... DipTech(Comm)
Diploma in Technology (Information Processing) (ADA) ... DipTech(InfProc)
Diploma in Technology (Management) (ADA) ... DipTech(Mgt)
Diploma in Technology (Public Administration) (ADA) ... DipTech(PubAdm)
Diploma in Technology (Public Relations) (ADA) ... DipTech(PubRel)
Diploma in Technology (Science) (ADA) ... DipTech(Sci)
Diploma in Telecommunications ... DipTelecomm
Diploma in Tertiary Education ... DipTertEd
Diploma in Tertiary Education (ADA) ... DipTertiary Ed
Diploma in Tertiary Studies ... DipTertStud
Diploma in Textile Chemistry (ADA) ... DTC
Diploma in the History of Medicine, Society of Apothecaries of London [*British*] (DBQ) ... DHMSA
Diploma in Theological Studies ... DTS
Diploma in Theology [*British*] ... D Theol
Diploma in Theology (ADA) ... DipTh
Diploma in Theology (NADA) ... DipThe
Diploma in Theology (ADA) ... ThDip
Diploma in Theory and Practice of Teaching [*British*] ... DipTPT
Diploma in Theory and Practice of Teaching (Durham University) [*British*] ... DThPT
Diploma in Therapeutic Radiology [*British*] ... DTR
Diploma in Therapeutic Radiology and Electrology ... DTRE
Diploma in Town and Country Planning (ADA) ... DipTCP
Diploma in Town and Regional Planning (ADA) ... DipTRP
Diploma in Town and Regional Planning (ADA) ... DTRP
Diploma in Town Planning [*British*] ... DipTP
Diploma in Traditional Chinese Medicine ... DipTChM
Diploma in Training Management, the Institute of Training and Development [*British*] (DBQ) ... DipTM
Diploma in Transportation Engineering [*British*] (DBQ) ... DipTE
Diploma in Tropical Agriculture (ADA) ... DTA
Diploma in Tropical Agronomy (ADA) ... DipTropAgron
Diploma in Tropical Child Health [*British*] ... DTCH
Diploma in Tropical Health ... DTH
Diploma in Tropical Hygiene [*British*] ... DTH
Diploma in Tropical Medicine [*British*] ... DTM
Diploma in Tropical Medicine and Hygiene [*British*] ... DTM & H
Diploma in Tropical Medicine and Hygiene ... DTMH
Diploma in Tropical Medicine and Public Health ... DTMPH
Diploma in Tropical Public Health [*British*] ... DTPH
Diploma in Tropical Veterinary Health ... DTV
Diploma in Tropical Veterinary Medicine [*British*] ... DTVM
Diploma in Tuberculosis and Chest Diseases ... DipTCD
Diploma in Tuberculosis and Chest Diseases [*British*] ... DTCD
Diploma in Tuberculous Diseases [*British*] ... DTD
Diploma in Urban and Regional Studies ... DipUrbRegSt
Diploma in Urban and Social Planning ... DipUSP
Diploma in Urban Design ... DipUrbDes(Arch)
Diploma in Urban Estate Management ... DipUEMan
Diploma in Urban Sociology ... DipUrbSoc
Diploma in Urban Studies ... DipUrbStud
Diploma in Urology (DD) ... DU
Diploma in Valuation and Farm Management (ADA) ... DipVFM
Diploma in Venereology [*British*] ... Dip Ven
Diploma in Venereology (ADA) ... DV
Diploma in Venereology and Dermatology (ADA) ... DV & D
Diploma in Venereology and Dermatology ... DVD
Diploma in Veterinary Anaesthesia ... DipVetAn
Diploma in Veterinary Anaesthesia [*British*] ... DVA
Diploma in Veterinary Clinical Studies ... DipVetClinStud
Diploma in Veterinary Hygiene [*British*] ... DVH
Diploma in Veterinary Pathology (ADA) ... DipVetPath
Diploma in Veterinary Public Health (ADA) ... DVPH
Diploma in Veterinary Radiology ... DipVetRad
Diploma in Veterinary State Medicine ... DVSM
Diploma in Visual Arts ... DipVisArt
Diploma in Wildlife Medicine and Husbandry ... DipWildlifeMed & Hus
Diploma in Women's Health ... DWH
Diploma in Women's Studies ... DipWomSt
Diploma Member of the Institute of Baths and Recreation Management [*British*] (DBQ) ... MInstBRMDip
Diploma of Advanced Education (ADA) ... DipAdvEd
Diploma of Advanced Studies in Teaching (PGP) ... DAST
Diploma of Applied Physics ... DipAppPhys
Diploma of Applied Science (ADA) ... DipAppSc
Diploma of British Orthoptics ... DBO
Diploma of Building Science ... DipBuildSc
Diploma of Chelsea College [*British*] (DI) ... DCC
Diploma of Chemical Engineering ... DipChemE
Diploma of Chemistry in Industry ... DipChemInd
Diploma of Child and Educational Psychology (ADA) ... DCEP
Diploma of Choir Master of the Royal College of Organists [*British*] ... CHM
Diploma of Civil Engineering (ADA) ... DipCE
Diploma of College of Obstetricians and Gynecologists ... DCOG
Diploma of Commerce (ADA) ... DipCom
Diploma of Community Management ... DipCommunityMgmt
Diploma of Curative Education [*British*] ... DCE
Diploma of Designer, Royal College of Art [*British*] ... Des RCA
Diploma of Economic Geography (ADA) ... DipEconGeog
Diploma of Economics (ADA) ... Dip Econ
Diploma of Education [*British*] (EY) ... DipEd
Diploma of Electrical Engineering (ADA) ... DipEEng
Diploma of Electrical Engineering (ADA) ... DipElecEng
Diploma of Financial Planning ... DFP
Diploma of Fine Art [*British*] ... DFA
Diploma of Forestry (ADA) ... DipFor
Diploma of Graphic Design ... DipGraphicDes
Diploma of Heriot-Watt University [*British*] (DI) ... DipH-WU
Diploma of Higher Education ... DipHE
Diploma of Industrial Chemistry (ADA) ... DIChem
Diploma of Interior Design (ADA) ... DipIntDes
Diploma of Jewellery Design ... DipJewDes
Diploma of Journalism (ADA) ... DipJ
Diploma of Jurisprudence ... DipJ
Diploma of Jurisprudence (ADA) ... DipJuris
Diploma of Landscape Design (ADA) ... DipLD
Diploma of Landscape Design (ADA) ... DLD
Diploma of Law ... DipL
Diploma of Law (Barristers' Admission Board) ... DipL(BAB)
Diploma of Law (Solicitors' Admission Board) ... DipL(SAB)
Diploma of Legal Studies ... DipLS
Diploma of Loughborough College [*British*] ... DLC
Diploma of Mechanical Engineering (ADA) ... DipMechE
Diploma of Medical Technology (ADA) ... DipMT
Diploma of Membership of Imperial College of Science and Technology, University of London [*British*] ... DIC
Diploma of Nursing (ADA) ... Dip of N
Diploma of Nursing Administration (ADA) ... DipNAdmin
Diploma of Occupational Health and Safety ... DOHS
Diploma of Occupational Therapy ... DOT
Diploma of Physical and Rehabilitation Medicine (ADA) ... DPRM
Diploma of Physiotherapy (ADA) ... DipPhysio
Diploma of Physiotherapy [*British*] ... DPhys
Diploma of Physio-Therapy [*British*] ... DPT
Diploma of Practitioners in Advertising [*British*] ... DipPA
Diploma of Prehistoric Archaeology (ADA) ... DipPrehistArch
Diploma of Professional Competence in Comprehensive Ocupational Hygiene [*British*] (DBQ) ... DipOccHyg
Diploma of Psychology (PGP) ... D Ps
Diploma of Religious Education ... DipREd
Diploma of Remedial Education ... DipRemEd
Diploma of Royal Academy of Dramatic Art [*British*] (EY) ... DipRADA
Diploma of Royal Australasian [*Medicine*] (DMAA) ... DRACR
Diploma of Royal Australian College of Obstetricians and Gynaecologists (BABM) ... DRACOG
Diploma of Social Administration (ADA) ... DipSocAdmin
Diploma of Social Science (ADA) ... DipSocSci
Diploma of Social Work ... DipSocWk
Diploma of Special Education ... DipSpEd
Diploma of Special Subject Teaching ... DipSpecSubjTeach
Diploma of Teacher of Physiotherapy ... DipTP
Diploma of Teaching ... DipTchg
Diploma of Teaching English as a Second Language (ADA) ... DipTESL
Diploma of Teaching (Nursing) ... DTN
Diploma of Teaching (Tertiary) ... DipTeach(Tert)
Diploma of Technology (Engineering) [*British*] ... Dip Tech (Eng)
Diploma of Tertiary Studies ... DOTS
Diploma of Textile Industry ... DipTexInd
Diploma of the Advertising Association (DGA) ... DAA

Diploma of the Architectural Association School of Architecture [British] .... AA Dip
Diploma of the Chamber of Shipping [Australia] .... DipCS
Diploma of the College of Aeronautics [British] .... DCAe
Diploma of the College of Occupational Therapists [British] (DBQ) .... DipCOT
Diploma of the College of Optics [British] (EY) .... DCO
Diploma of the College of Pathologists [British] .... DC Path
Diploma of the College of Radiographers in Medical Ultra Sound [British] (DBQ) .... DCR MU
Diploma of the College of Radiographers in Nuclear Medicine [British] (DI) .... DCRNM
Diploma of the College of Radiographers in Radionuclide Imaging [British] (DBQ) .... DCR RNI
Diploma of the Communication Advertising and Marketing Education Foundation [British] (DBQ) .... DipCAM
Diploma of the Faculty of Homoeopathy [British] .... DF Hom
Diploma of the Imperial College of Science, Technology, and Medicine [Canada] (DD) .... DIC
Diploma of the Institute of Engineering [British] .... DIE
Diploma of the Institute of Private Secretaries [Australia] .... DipPrivSec
Diploma of the Nursery School Teachers' College [Australia] .... DipNSTC
Diploma of the Orthoptic Board of Australia .... DOBA
Diploma of the Plastics Institute [British] (DI) .... DPI
Diploma of the Royal Academy of Music [British] (DBQ) .... DipRAM
Diploma of the Royal College of Music [British] (DBQ) .... DipRCM
Diploma of the Royal College of Obstetricians and Gynaecologists [Australia] .... DRCOG
Diploma of the Royal College of Obstetrics and Gynaecology [British] .... DRCOG
Diploma of the Royal College of Pathologists [British] .... DRC Path
Diploma of the Royal College of Science and Technology, Glasgow [British] .... DRC
Diploma of the Royal Microscopical Society [British] (DBQ) .... DipRMS
Diploma of the Royal Scottish Academy of Music and Dance (BARN) .... DRSAMD
Diploma of the Royal Scottish Academy of Music and Drama .... DRSAM
Diploma of the Royal Technical College [British] .... DRTC
Diploma of the Sydney Conservatorium of Music [Australia] .... DSC
Diploma of the Sydney Kindergarten Teachers' College [Australia] .... DipSKTC
Diploma of the Teachers Guild (ADA) .... DipTG
Diploma of the University of Paris .... DUP
Diploma of the University of Southampton [British] .... DUS
Diploma of the Worshipful Company of Farriers [British] (DI) .... DipWCF
Diploma of Theology (ADA) .... Dip Theol
Diploma of Town and Country Planning (ADA) .... DipT & CP
Diploma of Visual Arts .... DipVA
Diploma Scam [FBI investigation of mail-order colleges] .... DIPSCAM
Diplomacy Test of Empathy [Psychology] .... DTE
Diplomat [License plate code assigned to foreign diplomats in the US] .... D
Diplomat (WDAA) .... DIP
Diplomat [or Diplomacy] .... dipl
Diplomat (WGA) .... DPL
Diplomat Corp. [NASDAQ symbol] (SAG) .... DIPL
Diplomat Corp. [Associated Press] (SAG) .... Diplm
Diplomat Corp. [Associated Press] (SAG) .... Diplomat
Diplomat Corp. Wrrt [NASDAQ symbol] (TTSB) .... DIPLW
Diplomat Resources [Vancouver Stock Exchange symbol] .... DIP
Diplomate (MAE) .... D
Diplomate .... DIPT
Diplomate, American Board of Allergy and Immunology (DHSM) .... D-AI
Diplomate, American Board of Anesthesiology (DHSM) .... D-AN
Diplomate, American Board of Colon and Rectal Surgery (DHSM) .... D-CRS
Diplomate, American Board of Dermatology (DHSM) .... D-D
Diplomate, American Board of Family Practice (DHSM) .... D-FP
Diplomate, American Board of Internal Medicine (DHSM) .... D-M
Diplomate, American Board of Neurological Surgery (DHSM) .... D-NS
Diplomate, American Board of Nuclear Medicine (DHSM) .... D-NuM
Diplomate, American Board of Obstetrics and Gynecology (DHSM) .... D-OG
Diplomate, American Board of Ophthalmology (DHSM) .... D-OP
Diplomate, American Board of Orthopaedic Surgery (DHSM) .... D-OS
Diplomate, American Board of Otolaryngology (DHSM) .... D-OT
Diplomate, American Board of Pathology (DHSM) .... D-P
Diplomate, American Board of Pediatrics (DHSM) .... D-Pd
Diplomate, American Board of Physical Medicine and Rehabilitation (DHSM) .... D-PMR
Diplomate, American Board of Plastic Surgery (DHSM) .... D-PlS
Diplomate, American Board of Preventive Medicine (DHSM) .... D-PrM
Diplomate, American Board of Psychiatry and Neurology (DAVI) .... DipAmerBdP & N
Diplomate, American Board of Psychiatry and Neurology (DHSM) .... D-PN
Diplomate, American Board of Radiology (DHSM) .... D-R
Diplomate, American Board of Surgery (DHSM) .... D-S
Diplomate, American Board of Thoracic Surgery (DHSM) .... D-TS
Diplomate, American Board of Urology (DHSM) .... D-U
Diplomate in Dental Orthoptics of the Royal College of Physicians and Surgeons of Glasgow [British] .... DDORCPS Glas
Diplomate in Orthodontics, Royal College of Surgeons of England .... D Orth RCS Eng
Diplomate of Acupuncture [Medicine] .... DipAc
Diplomate of Homeopathic Academy of Naturopathic Physicians [Medicine] .... DHANP
Diplomate of the Institute of Bankers in Scotland [British] (DBQ) .... DipIB(Scot)
Diplomate of the National Board of Medical Examiners (AAMN) .... DNB
Diplomatic (ADA) .... DIPL
Diplomatic and Consular Officers, Retired (EA) .... DACOR
Diplomatic Conference of International Maritime Law .... DCML

Diplomatic Corps .... DC
Diplomatic Correspondence of the United States [A publication] (DLA) .... Dip Cor
Diplomatic Immunity (ADA) .... DI
Diplomatic Security [U.S. Department of State] (BARN) .... DS
Diplomatic Service [or Servant] [British] .... DS
Diplomatic Service Administration Office [British] .... DSAO
Diplomatic Services Bureau .... DSB
Diplomatic Telecommunications Service (FAAC) .... DTS
Diplomatist (WDAA) .... DIPL
Diplome d'Etudes Collegiales [Canada] .... DEC
Diplome d'Etudes Superieures [Canada] (DD) .... DES
Diplome en Droit Civil (DD) .... DipDN
Diplome en Sciences Administratives (DD) .... DSA
Dipole (DEN) .... DP
Dipole (KSC) .... DPL
Dipole Antenna System .... DAS
Dipole Antenna with Feed-Points Displaced Transverse to Its Axis (PDAA) .... DAFDTA
Dipole Flat Plate .... DFP
Dipole Xerography .... DIXY
Dipolog [Philippines] [Airport symbol] (OAG) .... DPL
Dipolog, Zamboanga Del Norte [Philippines] [ICAO location identifier] (ICLI) .... RPWG
Dipping-Reflector Sequence [Geology] .... DRS
Dipropionate [Pharmacology] (MAE) .... DP
Dipropylacetate (MAE) .... DPA
Dipropylacetic Acid [Also, VPA] [Valproic acid Anticonvulsant compound] .... DPA
Dipropylamine [Organic chemistry] .... DPA
(Dipropylaminoethyl)indole [Organic chemistry] .... DPAI
Dipropylene Glycol Dibenzoate [Organic chemistry] .... DGDB
Dipropylnitrosamine [Also, DPNA, NDPA] [Organic chemistry] .... DPN
Dipropylnitrosamine [Also, DPN, NDPA] [Organic chemistry] .... DPNA
Dipropyl(sulfophenyl)xanthine [Organic chemistry] .... DPSX
Dipropyltryptamine [Hallucinogenic agent] .... DPT
Diprose and Gammon's Reports of Law Affecting Friendly Societies [1801-97] [England] [A publication] (DLA) .... D & G
Dipstick .... DPSTK
Diptera [Entomology] .... Dip
Diptheria, Pertussis [Whooping Cough], and Tetanus Vaccine [Also, called DTP vaccine] (PAZ) .... DPT vaccine
Diptheria, Tetanus, and Pertussis [Whooping Cough] Vaccine [Also, called the DPT vaccine] (PAZ) .... DTP vaccine
Diptych (VRA) .... dpty
Dipyridyl [Also, DIPY] [Organic chemistry] .... DIP
Dipyridyl [Also, DIP] [Organic chemistry] .... DIPY
Dirac Aviation [France ICAO designator] (FAAC) .... DAV
Dirac-Fock Theory [Electrodynamics] .... DF
Dire Dawa [Ethiopia] [Airport symbol] (OAG) .... DIR
Dire Dawa/Aba Tenna Dejazmatch Yilma [Ethiopia] [ICAO location identifier] (ICLI) .... HADR
Direccion General de la Inteligencia [Intelligence agency] [Cuba] .... DGI
Direccion General de Normas [National Standards Organization] [Mexico] .... DGN
Direccion Nacional de Turismo [National Direction of Tourism] [Bolivia] (EAIO) .... DINATUR
Direct [In relation to flight plan clearances and type of approach] [Aviation] .... DCT
Direct .... DIR
Direct (AFM) .... DRCT
Direct Access (BUR) .... DA
Direct Access [Computer science] (MHDB) .... DIRAC
Direct Access Arrangement [Telecommunications] .... DAA
Direct Access Beacon System (MCD) .... DABS
Direct Access Capability (MCD) .... DAC
Direct Access Communications (MCD) .... DAC
Direct Access Communications Channels .... DACC
Direct Access Computing (MCD) .... DAC
Direct Access Control (MCD) .... DAC
Direct Access Data Channel (IAA) .... DADC
Direct Access Desktop [Fifth Generation Systems] (PCM) .... DAD
Direct Access Device Space Management (MCD) .... DADSM
Direct Access Education System (AEBS) .... DAES
Direct Access File Manager .... DAFM
Direct Access Information .... DAI
Direct Access Intelligence System (PDAA) .... DAIS
Direct Access Management System .... DAMS
Direct Access Memory [Computer science] (BUR) .... DAM
Direct Access Method [Sperry UNIVAC] [Computer science] .... DAM
Direct Access, Multi-User, Synchrocyclotron Computer (PDAA) .... DAMUSC
Direct Access Performance Software (IAA) .... DAPS
Direct Access Programming System [Computer science] .... DAPS
Direct Access Signalling System .... DASS
Direct Access Storage Device [Pronounced "daz-dee"] [Computer science] .... DASD
Direct Access Storage Device Initialization Program [Computer science] (IAA) .... DASDI
Direct Access Storage Drive [Computer science] (NITA) .... DASD
Direct Access Storage Dump Restore .... DASDR
Direct Access Storage Facility [Computer science] .... DASF
Direct Access Storage Handler [Telecommunications] (TEL) .... DASH
Direct Access Storage Media [Computer science] .... DASM
Direct Access Store [Computer science] (IAA) .... DAS
Direct Access Terminal Application [Computer science] (BUR) .... DATA
Direct Access to Members [Trade union membership database] [British] .... DATOM
Direct Access to Reference Information [Xerox Corp.] .... DATRIX
Direct Access to Remote Data Bases Overseas [Italy Telecommunications] .... DARDO

Direct Acting .... DACT
Direct Acting Steam (MSA) .... DAS
Direct Action [*Bomb or shell fuze*] .... DA
Direct Action Team (MCD) .... DAT
Direct Address [*Telecommunications*] (NITA) .... DA
Direct Address Line [*Telecommunications*] (NITA) .... DAL
Direct Adjacent Channel Interference .... DACI
Direct Admission [*Medicine*] (DAVI) .... DA
Direct Advisory of Recorded Transactions (AABC) .... DART
Direct Aerial Fire Support [*Military*] (AABC) .... DAFS
Direct Agglutination [*Clinical chemistry*] .... DA
Direct Agglutination Pregnancy Test [*Clinical chemistry*] .... DAPT
Direct Agglutination Test [*Clinical chemistry*] (MAE) .... DAT
Direct Aid for Full Yaw .... DAFFY
Direct Aid Program .... DAP
Direct Air [*British ICAO designator*] (FAAC) .... DAJ
Direct Air [*ICAO designator*] (AD) .... UO
Direct Air Cycle .... DAC
Direct Air, Inc. [*Germany ICAO designator*] (FAAC) .... DIA
Direct Air Inc. [*ICAO designator*] (FAAC) .... XAP
Direct Air Support [*Military*] (AFM) .... DAS
Direct Air Support Center [*Later, ASOC*] .... DASC
Direct Air Support Center Squadron [*Air Force*] .... DASCS
Direct Air Support Center-Airborne (DOMA) .... DASC-A
Direct Air Support Flight [*Military*] (AFM) .... DASF
Direct Air Support Squadron [*Military*] (AFM) .... DASq
Direct Air Support Squadron [*Air Force*] .... DASS
Direct Air Support Squadron [*Air Force*] .... DASSq
Direct Air Support Team [*Military*] (CINC) .... DAST
Direct Airfield Attack Combined Munition [*Air Force*] (DOMA) .... DAACM
Direct Airline Reservations Ticketing .... DART
Direct Altitude and Identification Readout [*Aviation*] (MCD) .... DAIR
Direct Altitude and Identification Readout Equipment [*Aviation*] (FAAC) .... DAIRE
Direct Amylase Test [*Clinical chemistry*] .... DAT
Direct Analog-to-Digital Input-Output System [*Computer science*] (MHDB) .... DADIOS
Direct and Consensual [*Neurology and ophthalmology*] (DAVI) .... DC
Direct and Distribution [*Postal Service*] .... D & D
Direct Answer (HGAA) .... DA
Direct Antiglobulin Coombs' Test [*Medicine*] .... DCT
Direct Antiglobulin Test [*Clinical chemistry*] (MAE) .... DAGT
Direct Antiglobulin Test [*Clinical chemistry*] .... DAT
Direct Ascent (AAG) .... DA
Direct Assistance and Training Command [*Navy*] (NVT) .... DATC
Direct Automotive Support .... DAS
Direct Bilirubin [*Medicine*] (DMAA) .... DB
Direct Bilirubin [*Also, DBili*] [*Clinical chemistry*] .... DBIL
Direct Bilirubin [*Also, DBIL*] [*Clinical chemistry*] .... DBili
Direct Bilirubin [*Also, DBIL, DBili*] [*Clinical chemistry*] (DAVI) .... DBR
Direct Billing .... DB
Direct Branch Mode .... DBM
Direct Broadcast Access (MCD) .... DIBRAC
Direct Broadcast Satellite [*Television transmission system in which signals are transmitted by satellite directly to individual locations*] (MCD) .... DBS
Direct Broadcast Satellite Association [*Later, SBCA*] (EA) .... DBSA
Direct Broadcast Satellite Corp. [*Bethesda, MD*] [*Telecommunications*] (TSSD) .... DBSC
Direct Broadcast System .... DBS
Direct Broadcasting Ltd. [*British*] .... DBL
Direct Business Lines [*Telecom Canada*] [*Telecommunications service*] (TSSD) .... DBL
Direct Cable Connection [*Computer science*] .... DCC
Direct Calorimetric Analysis (OA) .... DCA
Direct Carbon Transfer .... DCT
Direct Carrier Injection .... DCI
Direct Centrifugal Flotation [*Parasitology*] .... DCF
Direct Channel Interface .... DCI
Direct Channel Interface Option .... DCIO
Direct Clinical Observation [*Psychology*] .... DCO
Direct Coal Liquefaction [*Fuel science*] .... DCL
Direct Command .... DC
Direct Commercial Contracts (AAGC) .... DCC
Direct Commissary Support System [*DoD*] .... DICOMSS
Direct Communications Link [*US/USSR*] .... DCL
Direct Computer Control .... DCC
Direct Computer Input (MCD) .... DCI
Direct Computer Input Load Module (MCD) .... DCILM
Direct Conductor-to-Circuit [*Advanced Circuit Technology, Inc.*] [*Electronics*] .... DCC
Direct Connect Intl Wrrt [*NASDAQ symbol*] (TTSB) .... KIDWE
Direct Connection [*Telecommunications*] (OA) .... DC
Direct Connection Module [*Computer science*] .... DCM
Direct Contact Desulfation .... DCD
Direct Contact Evaporator [*Chemical engineering*] .... DCE
Direct Control (IAA) .... DC
Direct Control Channel .... DCC
Direct Control Feature (CMD) .... DCF
Direct Control Oriented Language [*Computer science*] .... DCOL
Direct Conversion Reactor .... DCR
Direct Cortical Response .... DCR
Direct Cosine Transform (SSD) .... DCT
Direct Couple Operating System .... DCOS
Direct Couple System .... DCS
Direct Coupled .... DC
Direct Coupled Loop Network [*Computer science*] .... DCLN
Direct Critical Response (MEDA) .... DCR
Direct Current .... DC
Direct Current (IDOE) .... dc
Direct Current Clamp (IAA) .... DCC
Direct Current Motor and Generator Facility [*General Electric Co.*] .... DCM & G
Direct Current Network [*Solutions for resistive components and voltage sources*] .... DCNET
Direct Current Panel .... DCP
Direct Current to Direct Current [*Telecommunications*] .... DC/DC
Direct Current-Current Transformer (IAA) .... DCCT
Direct Cycle .... DC
Direct Cycle Diphenyl Reactor .... DCDR
Direct Cylinder Injection [*Engine design*] .... DCI
Direct Data Attachment .... DDA
Direct Data Channel .... DDC
Direct Data Entry [*Computer science*] (BUR) .... DDE
Direct Data Entry Replacement System .... DDERS
Direct Data Entry Station (NITA) .... DDES
Direct Data Entry System .... DDES
Direct Data Link (CDE) .... DDL
Direct Debit [*Banking*] .... DD
Direct Debit [*Banking*] (DCTA) .... DDR
Direct Deposit / Electronic Fund Transfer .... DD/EFT
Direct Deposit of Dividends .... DDD
Direct Deposit of Payroll .... DDP
Direct Development [*Phylogeny*] .... DD
Direct Device Attachment (NITA) .... DDA
Direct Dial In (BUR) .... DDI
Direct Dial Response Marketing, Inc. [*Information service or system*] (IID) .... DDRM
Direct Dial Service [*Telecommunications*] (HGAA) .... DDS
Direct Dial Telephone System .... DDTS
Direct Dialing [*or Dialed*] [*Telecommunications*] (TEL) .... DD
Direct Digital Analysis (IAA) .... DDA
Direct Digital Color Proofing [*Graphic arts*] (DGA) .... DDCP
Direct Digital Computer (IAA) .... DDC
Direct Digital Control .... DDC
Direct Digital Control System .... DDCS
Direct Digital Encoder .... DDE
Direct Digital Interface .... DDI
Direct Digital Interface Equipment [*Telecommunications*] (TEL) .... DDIE
Direct Digital Numerical Controller .... DDNC
Direct Digital Synthesizer (MCD) .... DDS
Direct Digital Writer .... DDW
Direct Disk Attachment .... DDA
Direct Display Console (MAE) .... DDC
Direct Distance Dialing [*of telephone numbers for toll calls*] .... DDD
Direct Distance Service .... DDS
Direct Drawing Change (AAG) .... DDC
Direct Drive .... DD
Direct Drive .... DDR
Direct Effective Fire Line [*Military*] (INF) .... DEFL
Direct Electrical Heating (PDAA) .... DEH
Direct Electrical Linkage .... DEL
Direct Electrical Linkage System (MCD) .... DELS
Direct Electronic Fourier Transform [*Camera*] .... DEFT
Direct Electronic Mail Marketing Association .... DEMMA
Direct Encounter (KSC) .... DE
Direct Energy Conversion .... DEC
Direct Energy Conversion Laboratory [*Johnson Space Center*] [*NASA*] (NASA) .... DECL
Direct Energy Conversion Operation .... DECO
Direct Energy Transfer .... DET
Direct Engineering Estimate (MCD) .... DEE
Direct Engineering Hours (MCD) .... DEH
Direct English Access and Control [*Computer science*] .... DEACON
Direct English Statement Information Retrieval [*Military*] .... DESIR
Direct Environmental Warming Impact .... DEWI
Direct Epifluorescence Filter Technique [*Microbiology*] .... DEFT
Direct Evaluation of Indexed Language (IAA) .... DEVIL
Direct Exchange [*Army*] (AABC) .... DX
Direct Exchange Activity (AABC) .... DXA
Direct Exchange Item [*Army*] (AABC) .... DXI
Direct Exchange Line [*Telecommunications*] .... DEL
Direct Exchange - Wholesale (MCD) .... DX-W
Direct Expansion .... DX
Direct Fire Antitank Weapon .... DFAW
Direct Fire Antitank Weapon System (SAA) .... DFAWS
Direct Fire Plan [*Army*] (INF) .... DFP
Direct Fire Simulator .... DFS
Direct Fire System .... DFS
Direct Fire Weapons Effect Simulator [*Military*] (PDAA) .... DFWES
Direct Flight (MCD) .... DF
Direct Flight Ltd. [*British ICAO designator*] (FAAC) .... DCT
Direct Flight Mode .... DFM
Direct Flight Test (KSC) .... DFT
Direct Flow .... DF
Direct Flow Sampler [*Meteorology*] .... DFS
Direct Fluorescence .... DF
Direct Fluorescent Antibody (Stain) [*Clinical medicine*] .... DFA
Direct Fluorescent Antibody Technique [*Clinical chemistry*] .... DFAT
Direct Forces Support [*Military*] .... DFS
Direct Foreign Investment .... DFI
Direct Formed Supergroup [*Telecommunications*] (TEL) .... DFSG
Direct Fourier Inversion [*Mathematics*] .... DFI

Direct Fuel Injection [*Automotive engineering*] ... DFI
Direct Function Search (PDAA) ... DFS
Direct Grant ... DG
Direct Graphics Interface Specification ... DGIS
Direct Graphics Interface Standard (CDE) ... DGIS
Direct Heat Removal Service [*or System*] [*Nuclear energy*] (IEEE) ... DHRS
Direct High-Level Language Processor ... DHLLP
Direct Hit ... D/H
Direct Ignition System [*Automotive engineering*] ... DIS
Direct Imaging Mass Analyzer ... DIMA
Direct Immunofluorescence [*Analytical biochemistry*] (CPH) ... DIF
Direct Immunofluorescent Assay [*Analytical biochemistry*] ... DFA
Direct Immunoperoxidase [*Clinical medicine*] ... DIP
Direct Impulse (DNAB) ... DI
Direct Information Access Link [*Computer science*] ... DIAL
Direct Information Access Network for Europe [*Commission of the European Communities*] [*Information service or system Defunct*] (IID) ... DIANE
Direct Injection [*Automotive engineering*] ... DI
Direct Injection Diesel [*Automotive engineering*] ... DID
Direct Injection Enthalpimetry ... DIE
Direct Injection Nebulization [*For spectrometry*] ... DIN
Direct Input/Output [*Telecommunications*] (TEL) ... DIO
Direct Insertion Probe ... DIP
Direct Instant Response Electronic Composition ... DIREC
Direct Instructional System for Teaching Arithmetic and Reading ... DISTAR
Direct Instructional Systems to Arithmetic and Reading (AIE) ... DISTAR
Direct Interaction with Product Repulsion [*Chemical kinetics*] ... DIPR
Direct Intercept (GAVI) ... DIR/INTC
Direct Interface Adapter ... DIA
Direct Internal Noise Amplification (NG) ... DINA
Direct Intraperitoneal Insemination [*Alternative to traditional in-vitro fertilization (IVF)*] (PAZ) ... DIP
Direct Investigation Group on Aerial Phenomena [*British*] (DBA) ... DIGAP
Direct Investor ... DI
Direct Inward Dialing [*Telecommunications*] ... DID
Direct Inward Dialling ... DID
Direct Inward System Access (HGAA) ... DISA
Direct Keying System ... DKS
Direct Labor ... DL
Direct Labor Charges by Organization (MCD) ... DLCO
Direct Labor Hours (DNAB) ... DLH
Direct Labor Man-Hours (RDA) ... DLMH
Direct Labor Organization ... DLO
Direct Labor Rate ... DLR
Direct Labor Time ... DLT
Direct Laboratories Estimate (MCD) ... DLE
Direct Laryngoscopy [*Otorhinolaryngology*] (DAVI) ... DL
Direct Laryngoscopy and Bronchoscopy [*Medicine*] (DAVI) ... DL & B
Direct LASER Vaporization ... DLV
Direct Latex Agglutination Pregnancy [*Test*] [*Medicine*] ... DAP
Direct Least Squares [*Econometrics*] ... DLS
Direct Letter Perfect [*Actors' slang*] ... DLP
Direct Liaison Authorized [*Military*] (NVT) ... DIRLAUTH
Direct Lift Control ... DLC
Direct Line [*Followed by telephone number*] ... DL
Direct Linear Loop Detector [*Computer science*] (IAA) ... DLLD
Direct Linear Transformation (PDAA) ... DLT
Direct Liquid Inlet [*Interface*] [*Analytical instrumentation*] ... DLI
Direct Listening (CAAL) ... DL
Direct Load ... DL
Direct Loan Revolving Fund [*Department of Veterans Affairs*] ... DLRF
Direct Logistic Support System (MCD) ... DLSS
Direct Logistical Support (RDA) ... DLS
Direct Lunar Transport (IIA) ... DLT
Direct Lytic Factor [*Polypeptide from cobra venom*] ... DLF
Direct Machine Environment ... DME
Direct Magnification Radiography ... DMR
Direct Mail ... DM
Direct Mail Advertising Association [*Later, DMMA*] ... DMAA
Direct Mail Fundraisers Association (EA) ... DMFA
Direct Mail Manager [*Software package*] ... DMM
Direct Mail/Marketing Association (EA) ... DMMA
Direct Mail/Marketing Educational Foundation (EA) ... DMMEF
Direct Mail Producers Association [*British*] (DBA) ... DMPA
Direct Mail Services Standards Board [*British*] ... DMSSB
Direct Mail Shelter Development System [*Civil Defense*] ... DMSDS
Direct Maintenance Cost (NASA) ... DMC
Direct Maintenance Man-Hours per Flight Hour [*Navy*] (NG) ... DMMH/FH
Direct Maintenance Man-Hours per Maintenance Action ... DMMH/MA
Direct Maintenance Man-Hours per Maintenance Event ... DMMH/ME
Direct Maintenance Man-Minutes (MCD) ... DMMM
Direct Man-Hours ... DMH
Direct Manufacturing Cost [*Marketing*] ... DMC
Direct Marketing ... DM
Direct Marketing Association [*New York, NY*] (EA) ... DMA
Direct Marketing Association Catalog Council [*New York, NY*] (EA) ... DMACC
Direct Marketing Computer Association [*Defunct*] (EA) ... DMCA
Direct Marketing Creative Guild [*New York, NY*] (EA) ... DMCG
Direct Marketing Credit Association [*Defunct*] (EA) ... DMCA
Direct Marketing Educational Foundation [*New York, NY*] (EA) ... DMEF
Direct Marketing Insurance Council [*New York, NY*] (EA) ... DMIC
Direct Marketing Market Place [*A publication*] ... DMMP
Direct Marketing Minorities Opportunities [*Defunct*] (EA) ... DMMO
Direct Marketing Writers Guild [*Later, DMCG*] (EA) ... DMWG
Direct Match Screening ... DMS
Direct Material Balance Control ... DMBC
Direct Material Inventory (DNAB) ... DMI
Direct Matrix Abstraction Process ... DMAP
Direct Maximum Principle (IAA) ... DMP
Direct Measurements Explorer [*Satellite*] ... DME
Direct Measurements Explorer A [*Satellite*] ... DME-A
Direct Memory Access [*Computing method*] ... DMA
Direct Memory Access Channel [*Pronounced "DEEmack"*] [*Computer science*] ... DMAC
Direct Memory Access Communications Processor ... DMACP
Direct Memory Access Control [*Computer science*] ... DMAC
Direct Memory Access Input/Output Subsystem (MCD) ... DIOS
Direct Memory Access Input/Output System [*Computer science*] (NITA) ... DIOS
Direct Memory Access Interface ... DMAI
Direct Memory Address [*Computer science*] ... DMA
Direct Memory Channel ... DMC
Direct Memory Exchange ... DMX
Direct Memory Interface ... DMI
Direct Memory Interface [*Computer science*] (NITA) ... DMI
Direct Memory Line (IAA) ... DML
Direct Memory Management [*Computer science*] (NITA) ... DMM
Direct Memory Processor ... DMP
Direct Memory Queue [*Computer science*] ... DMQ
Direct Memory Transfer [*Computer science*] ... DMT
Direct Metal Mastering [*System for manufacturing phonograph records*] ... DMM
Direct Metal Reaction [*Soap making*] ... DMR
Direct Methanol Fuel Cell ... DMFC
Direct Microscopic Clump Count ... DMCC
Direct Microscopic Count [*Biochemistry*] (DAVI) ... DMC
Direct Microscopic Somatic Cell Count (OA) ... DMSCC
Direct Mineral Water Supply (ROG) ... DMWS
Direct Mission Support Equipment (MCD) ... DMSE
Direct Modulation Technique ... DMT
Direct Molded Sole [*Boot*] [*Military*] ... DMS
Direct Multiplexed Control ... DMC
Direct Multiplexor Channel ... DMC
Direct Normalized [*Steel*] ... DN
Direct Notice of Cancellation [*Insurance*] ... DNC
Direct Numerical Control [*Automation method*] [*Computer science*] ... DNC
Direct Obligation ... DO
Direct Observation Evaluation [*Medicine*] (DMAA) ... DOE
Direct Operating Cost (DA) ... DC
Direct Operating Cost [*Accounting*] ... DOC
Direct Operating System [*Computer technology*] ... DOS
Direct Optical Position Sensor [*Instrumentation*] ... DOPS
Direct Order ... DO
Direct Order Entry System [*Computer science*] (MHDB) ... DOES
Direct Order Recording and Invoicing System [*A computer-based system of British petroleum companies*] ... DORIS
Direct Outward Dialing [*Telecommunications*] ... DOD
Direct Overwrite [*Computer science*] ... DOW
Direct Participation (ADA) ... DP
Direct Particle Rolling (PDAA) ... DPR
Direct Path (NVT) ... DP
Direct Patient Care [*Medicine*] ... DPC
Direct Payroll Deposit ... DPD
Direct Plaque-Forming Cell [*Immunology*] ... dPFC
Direct Plate Exposer [*Printing*] (NITA) ... DPE
Direct Plate Exposure (DGA) ... DPE
Direct Port [*Transportation*] ... DP
Direct Positive [*Photography*] (WDMC) ... DP
Direct Power Conversion [*Nuclear energy*] (AAG) ... DPC
Direct Price ... DP
Direct Procurement Method [*Personal property*] ... DPM
Direct Procurement Petty Officer ... DPPO
Direct Product Actual Hours (MCD) ... DPAH
Direct Product Profitability [*Analysis*] ... DPP
Direct Product Standard Hours (AFIT) ... DPSH
Direct Productive Annual Maintenance Manhours (MCD) ... DPAMMH
Direct Productive Man-Hours (AFIT) ... DPMH
Direct Program Control (BUR) ... DPC
Direct Program Search System (IAA) ... DPSS
Direct Provider Agreement ... DPA
Direct Purchasing Organisation [*Commercial firm British*] ... DPO
Direct Question [*Legal testimony*] ... DQ
Direct RADAR Scope Camera ... DRSC
Direct RADAR Scope Recorder (MCD) ... DRSR
Direct Radiative Forcing [*Atmospheric science*] ... DRF
Direct Read after Write [*Computer science*] ... DRAW
Direct Reading [*Spectroscopy*] ... DR
Direct Reading Azimuth Protractor [*Bureau of Mines*] ... DRAP
Direct Reading Emission Spectrograph (NRCH) ... DRES
Direct Reading Encoder ... DRE
Direct Reading Pocket Chamber ... DRPC
Direct Reading Range Assessor (DNAB) ... DRRA
Direct Reading Receiver ... DRR
Direct Reading Scope Camera ... DRSC
Direct Reading Telemeter (IAA) ... DRT
Direct Reading Thinking Activity [*Education*] (AEE) ... DRTA
Direct Reading Totalizer ... DRT
Direct Readout [*Computer science*] ... DRO
Direct Readout Equatorial Weather Satellite ... DREWS
Direct Readout Ground Station ... DRGS
Direct Readout Image Dissector [*Camera system*] ... DRID
Direct Read-Out Infrared (PDAA) ... DRI

Direct Readout Infrared Radiometer	DRIR
Direct Readout Miss Distance Indicator	DROMDI
Direct Readout Satellite	DROS
Direct Readout Weather Satellite	DROWS
Direct Reckoning Analyzer (MUGU)	DRA
Direct Recording (IAA)	DR
Direct Recording Oscillograph	DRO
Direct Reduction [Ironmaking process]	DR
Direct Reduction Iron [Ironmaking process]	DRI
Direct Reduction Mortgage [Banking]	DRM
Direct Reentry Telemetry [Air Force] (MCD)	DRET
Direct Reentry Telemetry System [Air Force]	DRETS
Direct Relief Foundation [Later, DRI]	DRF
Direct Relief International (EA)	DRI
Direct Repair Program [Automotive collision repairs]	DRP
Direct Repeat [Genetics]	DR
Direct Reporting Program Manager [Navy] (DOMA)	DRPM
Direct Reporting Unit	DRU
Direct Requisitioning Procedure (DNAB)	DRP
Direct Retrieval Language (NITA)	DRL
Direct/Reverse	D/R
Direct Rooming In [Medicine] (DAVI)	DRI
Direct Route	DR
Direct Satellite Communications	DSC
Direct Satellite System	DSS
Direct Scan Operating with Integrated Delay (MCD)	DISCOID
Direct Scope Recording System (MCD)	DSRS
Direct Screw Transfer	DST
Direct Selling Association (EA)	DSA
Direct Selling Association of Australia	DSAA
Direct Selling Education Foundation (EA)	DSEF
Direct Sequence [Telecommunications] (TEL)	DS
Direct Sequence Encoding [Telecommunications]	DSE
Direct Sequence Spread Spectrum [Telecommunications] (IAA)	DSSS
Direct Service Activities (MCD)	DSA
Direct Services Dialing Capability [Telecommunications] (OSI)	DSDC
Direct Ship (MCD)	D/S
Direct Ship Release (MCD)	DSR
Direct Ship Requirements (MCD)	DSR
Direct Shipment Order (AAG)	DSO
Direct Side Force Control [Aviation]	DSFC
Direct Signal Monitoring [Telecommunications] (TEL)	DSM
Direct Simulation Monte Carlo Technique [Statistics]	DMSC
Direct Sinoatrial Conduction Time [Medicine] (DMAA)	DSACT
Direct Sound Broadcast	DSB
Direct Sounding Transmission [Meteorology]	DST
Direct Space Refinement	DSR
Direct Stage Recorder (MCD)	DSR
Direct Static Logic (SAA)	DSL
Direct Station Selection [Telecommunications]	DSS
Direct Steamer	DS
Direct Storage Access	DSA
Direct Storage Recorder	DSR
Direct Subsystem (MCD)	DSS
Direct Suggestion under Hypnosis	DSUH
Direct Supply Support [Military]	DSS
Direct Supply Support Activity [Army] (AABC)	DSSA
Direct Supply Support Depot [Military] (AFM)	DSSD
Direct Supply Support Point [Military]	DSSP
Direct Supply Unit [Army] (VNW)	DSU
Direct Support [Army]	DS
Direct Support Aviation Section [Army]	DSAS
Direct Support Battery [Army] (ADDR)	DSB
Direct Support Element [Military] (NVT)	DSE
Direct Support/General Support (MCD)	DS/GS
Direct Support Group [Army] (AABC)	DSG
Direct Support Imagery Interpretation Report (MCD)	DSIIR
Direct Support Item [Army]	DSI
Direct Support Maintenance [Army]	DSM
Direct Support Maintenance Activity [Army] (MCD)	DSMA
Direct Support Operations (NVT)	DSOPS
Direct Support Plan (MCD)	DSP
Direct Support Platoon	DSP
Direct Support Real Property Installed Equipment (AFIT)	DS/RPIE
Direct Support System [Army]	DSS
Direct Support Unit [Army]	DSU
Direct Support Unit/General Support Unit [Computer system]	DSU/GSU
Direct Support Unit Standard Supply System [Army] (AABC)	DS4
Direct Support Weapon System (MCD)	DSWS
Direct Switching Equipment (NITA)	DSE
Direct Switching Exchange [Telecommunications] (NITA)	DSE
Direct System Output [Computer science] (MCD)	DSO
Direct System Platemaker	DSP
Direct Tape Access [Computer science]	DTA
Direct Tape Processor [Computer science] (ECII)	DTP
Direct Termination Overflow [MCI Communications Corp.] [Telecommunications]	DTO
Direct to Film [Printing technology]	DTF
Direct to Home [Satellite broadcast mode] [Canada]	DTH
Direct to Licensee	DTL
Direct Trader Input [Customs term] (DCTA)	DTI
Direct Transverse Traction [Orthopedics] (DAVI)	DTT
Direct Turn-Over (NG)	DTO
Direct Ultrasonic Visualization of Defects (PDAA)	DUVD
Direct User Access Terminal (DA)	DUAT

Direct User Access Terminal System [Aviation] (FAAC)	DUATS
Direct Variable Cost	DVC
Direct Vendor Delivery [DoD]	DVD
Direct View Console (MCD)	DVC
Direct View Filament Display (MCD)	DVFD
Direct View Optics	DVO
Direct View RADAR Indicator [Military] (CAAL)	DVRI
Direct Virtual Memory Access [Computer science]	DVMA
Direct Vision [Aviation]	DV
Direct Vision Internal Urethrotomy [Medicine] (MAE)	DVIU
Direct Vision Times One [Medicine] (DAVI)	DVXI
Direct Voice (NTCM)	DV
Direct Voice Input (DA)	DVI
Direct Voice Line (CET)	DVL
Direct Voltage (IAA)	DV
Direct Wire Burglar Alarm	DWBA
Direct Writing (MUGU)	D/W
Direct Writing Oscillograph	DWO
Direct-Access RADAR Channel [System] [Aviation]	DARC
Direct-Access Test Unit [Computer science]	DATU
Direct-Ascent Powered-Flight Simulation [NASA]	DAPFS
Direct-Connected [Mechanical engineering] (IAA)	DIRCONN
Direct-Contact Aftercooler [Engineering]	DCA
Direct-Contact Heat Transfer [Chemical engineering]	DCHT
Direct-Coupled FET [Field Effect Transistor] Logic [Integrated circuitry]	DCFL
Direct-Coupled Inverter (IAA)	DCI
Direct-Coupled Logic	DCL
Direct-Coupled System (IAA)	DCS
Direct-Coupled Transistor (IAA)	DCT
Direct-Coupled Transistor Logic	DCTL
Direct-Coupled Unipolar Transistor Logic	DCUTL
Direct-Coupling Transistor Logic Circuit	DCTLC
Direct-Current / Alternating-Current (IAA)	DCAC
Direct-Current Amplifier	DCA
Direct-Current Analog Input (MCD)	DCAI
Direct-Current Arc	DCA
Direct-Current Circuit Analysis Program [Computer science]	DICAP
Direct-Current Dialing (IAA)	DCD
Direct-Current Differential Transformer	DCDT
Direct-Current Displacement Transducer (IAA)	DCDT
Direct-Current Dump	DCD
Direct-Current Electroluminescence	DCEL
Direct-Current Experiments [Nuclear energy] (NRCH)	DCX
Direct-Current Flip-Flop [Electronics] (IAA)	DCFF
Direct-Current Free Gyro	DCFG
Direct-Current Generator	DCG
Direct-Current Key Pulsing (IEEE)	DCKP
Direct-Current, Main (IAA)	DCM
Direct-Current Milliamp (IAA)	DCMA
Direct-Current Operational Amplifier [Electronics]	DCOA
Direct-Current Peak Voltage (IAA)	DCPV
Direct-Current Plasma [Spectrometry]	DCP
Direct-Current Plasma Torch	DCPT
Direct-Current Plasma-LASER Ablation	DCP-LA
Direct-Current Potential Drop (MCD)	DCPD
Direct-Current Power Supply Panel (AAG)	DCPSP
Direct-Current Restorer	DCR
Direct-Current Reverse Polarity [Electronics]	DCRP
Direct-Current Sensor	DCS
Direct-Current Servo Amplifier	DCSA
Direct-Current Straight Polarity (MCD)	DCSP
Direct-Current Test Volts	VDCT
Direct-Current Torque Motor	DCTM
Direct-Current Voltage Reference	DCVR
Direct-Current Voltage Regulator	DCVR
Direct-Current Volts	DCV
Direct-Current Working Volts	DCWV
Direct-Current Working Volts	VDCW
Directed Acyclic Graph (MCD)	DAG
Directed Audit Program (AFM)	DAP
Directed Change (MCD)	DC
Directed Chopped Fiber [Plastics technology]	DCF
Directed Deployable Maintenance Concept (MCD)	DDMC
Directed Drawing Instrument	DDI
Directed Duty Assignment [Military] (AFM)	DDA
Directed Energy [Weaponry] (INF)	DE
Directed Energy Warfare [Army] (INF)	DEW
Directed Energy Weapon	DEW
Directed Energy Weapons - Vehicle [Army]	DEW-V
Directed Fan Engine	DFE
Directed Format Option [Rapid access management information system]	DFO
Directed Listening-Language Experience Approach (EDAC)	DL-LEA
Directed Metalation Group [Organic chemistry]	DMG
Directed Military Overstrength (GFGA)	DMO
Directed Proliferation	DP
Directed Reading Activity [Education]	DRA
Directed Reading-Thinking Activity (EDAC)	DR-TA
Directed Rocket Engine Demonstrator	DRED
Directed Stationing System [DoD]	DSS
Directed Studies Group [Air Force] (AFM)	DSG
Directed Studies Group [Air Force] (AFM)	DSGp
Directed to Request Termination of Inactive Duty Training Orders [Navy]	TERMINACTRAORD
Directed Verdict [Legal term]	DV
Directie Overheids-Personeelsbeleid [Netherlands]	DIR OP

Direct-Indirect .... DI
Direct-Induced High-Explosive Simulation Technique (MCD) .... DIHEST
Directing Ordnance Officer [*Military British*] .... DOO
Directing Point .... DP
Directing Staff (NATG) .... DISTAFF
Directing Staff .... DS
Directing Station (IAA) .... DS
Direct-Injected Stratified Charge [*Engine*] (RDA) .... DISC
Direction [*Computer science*] .... D
Direction .... DIRCTN
Direction .... DIRON
Direction (FAAC) .... DRCTN
Direction Action [*Bomb fuze*] .... DA
Direction and Range Acquisition System (MCD) .... DARAS
Direction Center [*SAGE*] [*RADAR*] .... DC
Direction Center Active [*SAGE*] [*RADAR*] .... DCA
Direction Center - Ground Controlled Intercept [*SAGE*] [*RADAR*] (CINC) .... DC/GCI
Direction Center Initial Appearance (SAA) .... DCIA
Direction Center Processor for Remote Combat Center (SAA) .... DCPR
Direction Center Programming Group [*Semiautomatic Ground Environment*] (IAA) .... DCPG
Direction Center Standby [*SAGE*] [*RADAR*] .... DCS
Direction Cosine (KSC) .... DC
Direction Cosine Linkage .... DIRCOL
Direction Cosine Matrix (MCD) .... DCM
Direction Cycle (MDG) .... DC
Direction de la Classification et de l'Evaluation des Emplois, Ministere de la Fonction Publique, Quebec, Quebec [*Library symbol National Library of Canada*] (NLC) .... QQFPCE
Direction de la Documentation, Office des Promotions du Quebec, Quebec, Quebec [*Library symbol National Library of Canada*] (NLC) .... QQOPD
Direction de la Surveillance du Territoire [*Directorate of Territorial Surveillance*] [*France*] .... DST
Direction de l'Analyse Economique et Regionale [*Economic and Regional Analysis Branch*] [*Transport Canada*] .... DERA
Direction de l'Environnement, Hydro-Quebec, Montreal, PQ, Canada [*Library symbol Library of Congress*] (LCLS) .... CaQMHDE
Direction de l'Information de la Valorisation [*Information and Valorization Directorate*] [*National Institute of Agronomic Research*] [*Information service or system*] (IID) .... DIV
Direction des Applications Militaries [*France*] .... DAM
Direction des Communications, Tourisme Quebec, Montreal, Quebec [*Library symbol National Library of Canada*] (BIB) .... QMTQ
Direction des Journaux Officiels Service de Microfiches, Paris, France [*Library symbol*] [*Library of Congress*] (LCLS) .... FrPJO
Direction Finder [*or Finding*] [*Radio aid to navigation*] .... DF
Direction Finder [*or Finding*] [*Radio aid to navigation*] .... DIF
Direction Finder Operator (IAA) .... DFOP
Direction Finder Team (IAA) .... DFTM
Direction Finding [*JETDS nomenclature*] .... DA
Direction Finding (IDOE) .... df
Direction Finding [*Radio*] [*Military*] .... DFING
Direction Finding and Tracking of Frequency Agile Communications Emitter (MCD) .... DFTFACE
Direction Finding Antenna .... DFA
Direction Finding Control Station (MCD) .... DF/CS
Direction Finding Equipment .... DFE
Direction Finding Frequency Measuring Equipment (IAA) .... DFFME
Direction Finding, Phase I [*Course*] [*Military*] (DNAB) .... DF I
Direction Finding, Phase II [*Course*] [*Military*] (DNAB) .... DF II
Direction Finding Receiver .... DFR
Direction Finding Set [*or System*] .... DFS
Direction Finding Station [*Aviation*] (FAAC) .... DFSTN
Direction for Army Logistic (MCD) .... DIALOG
Direction Generale de la Securite Exterieure [*Formerly, SDECE*] [*French intelligence agency*] .... DGSE
Direction Generale des Telecommunications [*Telecommunications administration*] [*France*] .... DGT
Direction Generale des Telecommunications [*Government of Quebec*] [*Canada*] (TSSD) .... DGT
Direction Generale du Cinema et de l'Audio-Visuel, Ministere des Communications du Quebec, Montreal, Quebec [*Library symbol National Library of Canada*] (NLC) .... QMCAV
Direction Indicator .... DI
Direction Level Detector (IAA) .... DLD
Direction Light [*Navigation*] .... DirLt
Direction of Arrival .... DOA
Direction of Arrival/Time of Arrival (MCD) .... DOA/TOA
Direction of Fire [*Weaponry*] (INF) .... DOF
Direction of Flight (KSC) .... DOF
Direction of President .... DP
Direction of Relative Movement [*Navigation*] .... DRM
Direction of Systems Management .... DSM
Direction of Trade (NITA) .... DOT
Direction of Trade Statistics [*International Monetary Fund*] [*Information service or system*] (CRD) .... DOTS
Direction Sports (EA) .... DS
Direction Technique des Constructions Navales [*French naval design bureau*] (DOMA) .... DTCN
Directional .... DIRCTNL
Directional Aerial Disposal [*Insecticide spray*] .... DAD
Directional Antenna .... DA
Directional Antenna (WDMC) .... da
Directional Antenna Day and Night [*Broadcasting term*] DA-1
Directional Antenna Daytime Only [*Broadcasting term*] .... DA-D
Directional Antenna Nighttime Only [*Broadcasting term*] .... DA-N
Directional Antenna Phasing Network .... DAPN
Directional Antenna with Changing Patterns, Day and Night [*Broadcasting term*] DA-2
Directional Antenna with Changing Patterns, Day and Night with Additional Pattern Change [*Broadcasting term*] DA-3
Directional Arm Lock .... DAL
Directional Automatic Realignment of Trajectory (NG) .... DART
Directional Command Activated Sonobuoy [*System*] [*Navy*] (NVT) .... DICAS
Directional Command Activated Sonobuoy System [*Navy*] .... DICASS
Directional Control [*Rocket*] (RDA) .... DC
Directional Control and Warning Communications System (MCD) .... DCWCS
Directional Control Antitank [*Missile*] .... DCAT
Directional Control Valve .... DCV
Directional Controlled Rocket-Assisted Projectile (MCD) .... DICORAP
Directional Controlled-Automatic Meteorological Compensation (DNAB) .... DC-AUTOMET
Directional Coupler .... DC
Directional Coupler (IAA) .... DIRCOUP
Directional Coupler Oscillator (IAA) .... DCO
Directional Coupler Synthesis (MCD) .... DICOSY
Directional Discontinuity Ring Radiator .... DDRR
Directional Doppler (MCD) .... DIDO
Directional Doppler Sonography [*Medicine*] (DMAA) .... DDS
Directional Emittance Measurement .... DEM
Directional Explosive Echo Ranging .... DEER
Directional Frequency Analysis and Recording System (MCD) .... DIFAR
Directional Grid (IAA) .... DG
Directional Gyro .... DG
Directional Gyro Mode .... DGM
Directional Gyro Operation .... DGO
Directional Gyro Unit .... DGU
Directional Horizon Indicator .... DHI
Directional Infrared Intrusion Detector (MCD) .... DIRID
Directional Multibeam Steering .... DIMUS
Directional Policty Matrix .... DPM
Directional Preponderance (MAE) .... DP
Directional Radiated Power [*Telecommunications*] (TEL) .... DRP
Directional Radio .... D/R
Directional Radio Beacon [*ITU designation*] (CET) .... RD
Directional Reference Locator .... DRL
Directional Reservation Equipment [*Telecommunications*] (TEL) .... DRE
Directional Solidification Crystal (SSD) .... DSC
Directional Solidification Crystal Growth (SSD) .... DSCG
Directional Solidification Furnace .... DSF
Directional Variable Microphone .... DVM
Directional Warhead Fuze .... DWF
Directional Wireless Installation [*British military*] (DMA) .... DWI
Directionally Solidified [*Metallurgy*] .... DS
Directionally-Controlled Rocket-Assisted Projectile .... DISCORAP
Directionally-Controlled-Medium Anti-Tank Assault Weapon (SAA) .... DC-MAW
Directione [*Directions*] [*Latin*] (DAVI) .... dir
Directione Propria [*With Proper Direction*] [*Pharmacy*] .... DIR PROP
Directione Propria [*With Proper Direction*] [*Pharmacy*] .... DP
Direction-Finding and Ranging .... DIFAR
Directions and Program Review [*American Library Association*] .... DPR
Directions for Education in Nursing via Technology .... DENT
Directions For Use [*Packaging*] .... DFU
Directive .... DIR
Directive Antenna with Reflector .... DR
Directive Coordinated and Approved by Budget Director [*Air Force*] .... DICAB
Directive Parental Counseling .... DPC
Directive-Organic [*Designation for biologically oriented, authoritarian psychiatrists*] .... D-O
Directives Control [*Employment and Training Administration*] [*Department of Labor*] .... DC
Directives Documentation [*NASA*] (NASA) .... DD
Directivity Index .... DI
Directly (MSA) .... DRCTY
Directly Authorised Body [*Securities and Investments Board*] [*British*] .... DAB
Directly Employed Labour [*British*] .... DEL
Directly Executable Language (MCD) .... DEL
Directly Executable Representation .... DER
Directly Executable Test-Oriented Language [*1968*] [*Computer science*] (CSR) .... DETOL
Directly Heated (DEN) .... DH
Directly Managed Unit [*Hospital administration*] .... DMU
Directly Observed Treatment Short-Course [*Therapy regime*] .... DOTS
Directly Operable Input/Output .... DOIO
Directly-Observed Therapy .... DOT
Director [*Films, television, etc.*] .... D
Director [*or Directorate*] (AFM) .... DIR
Director (DD) .... dir
Director (WDMC) .... dir
Director .... DIR
Director (ROG) .... DIREC
Director (ROG) .... DIROR
Director (ADA) .... DR
Director [*MARC relator code*] [*Library of Congress*] (LCCP) .... drt
Director Action for Rehabilitation and Employment [*Ex-offenders*] (OICC) .... DARE
Director, Admiralty Surface Weapons Establishment [*Navy British*] .... DASWE
Director, Admiralty Underwater Weapons Establishment [*Navy British*] .... DAUWE
Director, Advanced Base Logistics Control [*Navy*] .... DABLC

Director, Advanced Base Office, Atlantic [*Navy*] .... DABOA

Director, Advanced Base Office, Pacific [*Navy*] .... DABOP

Director aircraft capable of controlling drones or missiles [*Designation for all US military aircraft*] .... D

Director and Response Tester (KSC) .... DART

Director, Anti-Submarine Division [*British military*] (DMA) .... DASD

Director, Armament Engineering [*Canada*] [*Military*] .... DARME

Director, Armed Forces Courier Service (DNAB) .... DIRARFCOS

Director, Armed Forces Information and Education Division (DNAB) .... DIRAFIED

Director Assign Panel (MCD) .... DAP

Director Assignment Console (NVT) .... DAC

Director, Atlantic Division, Bureau of Yards and Docks [*Obsolete*] .... DIRLANTDOCKS

Director Attack Mine [*Air Force*] (MCD) .... DAM

Director, Auxiliary Territorial Service [*British military*] (DMA) .... DATS

Director Bomber [*Air Force*] .... DB

Director Communications Material Security (MCD) .... DCMS

Director Comptroller Systems (AABC) .... DCS

Director, Control Tower [*British military*] (DMA) .... DCT

Director, Defense Communications Agency (CINC) .... DDCA

Director (Defense Intelligence Agency) [*DoD*] .... D(DIA)

Director (Defense Nuclear Agency) [*DoD*] .... D(DNA)

Director, Defense Test and Evaluation (DOMA) .... DDT & E

Director, Defense Test and Evaluation [*Army*] (RDA) .... DDTE

Director Deputy of Communications-Electronics (AFIT) .... DC

Director Design Engineering (KSC) .... DDE

Director, Development and Operations (MUGU) .... DDO

Director, Division of Health [*New Zealand*] .... DDH

Director, Division of Traffic .... DD of T

Director Error [*Military*] (AFM) .... DE

Director Evaluation Feasibility [*or Flight*] **Test** (MCD) .... DEFT

Director Field Maintenance [*Army*] (AABC) .... DIRFM

Director, Field Support Activity .... DIRFLDSUPPACT

Director Fire Control System [*Air Force*] (MCD) .... DFCS

Director, Fleet Training .... DFT

Director, Flight Operations [*NASA*] (KSC) .... DFO

Director, Food Management [*Army*] (AABC) .... DFM

Director for Civil Disturbance Planning and Operations .... CDPO

Director for Individual Training (MCD) .... DIT

Director for Military Assistance (NATG) .... DFMA

Director for Mutual Security .... DMS

Director General for Vocational Training (AIE) .... DGVT

Director General of Water Engineering (DCTA) .... DGWE

Director, Gunnery Division [*British military*] (DMA) .... DGD

Director Historical Section [*World War I*] [*Canada*] .... DHS

Director/Illuminator (CAAL) .... D/I

Director, Industry and University Programs [*Military Canada*] .... DIUP

Director, International Military Staff Memorandum [*NATO*] (NATG) .... DIMS

Director, International Research and Development [*Military Canada*] .... DIRD

Director, Joint Oil Analysis Program [*Military*] (DNAB) .... DIRJOAP

Director, Joint Oil Analysis Program Technical Support Center [*Military*] (DNAB) .... DIRJOAPTSC

Director, Joint Staff [*Military*] (AABC) .... DJS

Director, Joint Staff Memorandum [*Military*] .... DJM

Director, Joint Staff Memorandum [*Military*] (AABC) .... DJSM

Director, Launch Operations [*NASA*] (KSC) .... DLO

Director Layer [*British military*] (DMA) .... DL

Director Major Staff Office (MCD) .... DMSO

Director, Management Information Systems [*Later, ADD*] [*Army*] (AABC) .... DMIS

Director, Marine Corps Reserve .... DMCR

Director Meteorological Officer, Ministry of Defence, London [*British*] (NATG) .... DMO

Director, National Security Agency [*Pronounced "dern-za"*] .... DIRNSA

Director National Security Agency / Chief Central Security Service .... DIRNSA/CHCSS

Director, Naval Audit Service .... NAVAUDSVC

Director, Naval Communications Instruction .... DNCINST

Director, Naval Communications Notice .... DNCNOTE

Director, Naval Council of Personnel Boards (DNAB) .... DIRNCPB

Director, Naval Council of Personnel Boards Detachment (DNAB) .... DIRNCPBDET

Director, Naval Courier Service (DNAB) .... DIRNAVCURSERV

Director, Naval Dental Services [*British*] .... DNDS

Director, Naval Future Policy Staff [*British*] .... DNFPS

Director, Naval Investigative Service (DNAB) .... DIRNAVINSERV

Director, Naval Research Laboratory (SAA) .... DIRNRL

Director, Naval Reserve Intelligence Program (DNAB) .... DIRNAVRESINTPRO

Director, Naval Security Group, Atlantic (DNAB) .... DIRNAVSECGRULANT

Director, Naval Security Group, Europe (DNAB) .... DIRNAVSECGRUEUR

Director, Naval Security Group, Pacific (DNAB) .... DIRNAVSECGRUPAC

Director, Naval Transportation Service [*Later, CNTS*] .... DNTS

Director, Navy Configuration Survival and Safety .... DNCSS

Director, Navy Petroleum Reserves .... DNPR

Director, Navy Program Planning .... DNPP

Director, Navy Publication and Printing Service .... DIRNAVPUBPRINTSERV

Director, Navy Secretariat Civilian Personnel Office (DNAB) .... DIRNSCPO

Director, Navy-Marine Corps Military Affiliate Radio Service (DNAB) .... DIRNAVMARCORMARS

Director of Acquisition Career Mangement [*DoD*] .... DACM

Director of Administration and Management [*DoD*] (DOMA) .... DA & M

Director of Administrative Services [*US Military Government, Germany*] .... DAS

Director of Advanced Systems Management .... DASM

Director of Advanced Systems Planning .... DASP

Director [*or Directorate*] **of Advanced Technology** [*Air Force*] .... DAT

Director of Aeronautical Inspection [*British*] .... DAI

Director of Aeroplane Production [*Air Ministry*] [*British World War II*] .... DAP

Director of Air Material [*Navy British*] .... DAM

Director of Air Ministry Factories [*British World War II*] .... DAMF

Director of Air Organisation and Training [*British military*] (DMA) .... DAOT

Director of Air Personnel [*Air Force British*] .... DAP

Director of Air Training Corps [*British*] .... DATC

Director of Aircraft (MUGU) .... DA

Director of Aircraft Equipment [*Ministry of Aircraft Production*] [*British*] .... DAE

Director of Aircraft Maintenance and Repair [*Navy British*] .... DAMR

Director of Aircraft Maintenance and Repair (Naval) [*British*] .... DAMR(N)

Director of Aircraft Maintenance and Repair (Washington) [*Navy*] .... DAMR(W)

Director of Airfield and Carrier Requirements [*British*] .... DACR

Director of Allied Air Cooperation [*World War II*] .... DAAC

Director of Ammunition Production [*Ministry of Supply*] [*British World War II*] .... DAP

Director of Antisubmarine Material [*British*] .... DA/SM

Director of Antisubmarine Warfare [*British*] .... DA/SW

Director of Anti-U-Boat Division [*British World War II*] .... DAUD

Director of Armament Supplies [*British World War II*] .... DAS

Director of Army Automation .... DAA

Director of Army Dental Services [*British*] .... DADS

Director of Army Education [*British*] .... DAE

Director of Army Fire Services [*British*] .... DAFS

Director of Army Instruction .... DAI

Director [*or Directorate*] **of Army Legal Services** [*British*] .... DALS

Director of Army Nursing Services [*British military*] (DMA) .... DANS

Director of Army Postal Services [*British*] .... DAPS

Director of Army Programs (AABC) .... DAP

Director of Army Psychiatry [*British*] .... DAP

Director of Army Requirements [*British*] .... DAR

Director of Army Research and Technology [*Washington, DC*] (GRD) .... DART

Director of Army Staff Duties [*British*] (RDA) .... DASD

Director of Army Technical Information (AABC) .... DATI

Director of Army Training [*British*] .... DAT

Director of Army Transportation .... DAT

Director of Army Veterinary and Remount Services [*British*] .... DAVRS

Director of Army Welfare Services [*British*] .... DAWS

Director of Artillery [*British*] .... D of A

Director [*or Directorate*] **of Audiovisual Activities** [*Army*] .... DAVA

Director of Barrack Construction [*British military*] (DMA) .... DBC

Director of Base Medical Services .... DBMS

Director of Biological Research [*Military British*] .... DBR

Director of Bombing Operations [*Air Ministry*] [*British World War II*] .... DBOps

Director of Camouflage [*British*] .... DOC

Director of [*Air*] **Campaign Plans** [*Central Command*] [*Military*] (DOMA) .... DCP

Director of Central Intelligence .... DCI

Director of Central Intelligence Directive .... DCID

Director of Central Intelligence Document .... DCID

Director of Ceremonies [*Freemasonry*] (ROG) .... DC

Director of Civil Affairs [*Military British*] .... DCA

Director [*or Directorate*] **of Civil Engineering** [*Air Force*] .... DCE

Director of Civilian Marksmanship [*Army*] .... DCM

Director of Civilian Personnel [*Navy*] .... DCP

Director of Clothing and Stores [*Military British*] .... DCS

Director of Coastal Forces Material Department [*British*] .... DCFMD

Director of Combat Development [*British*] (RDA) .... DCD

Director of Combat Intelligence (MCD) .... DCI

Director of Combat Operations .... DCO

Director of Combined Operations [*British Army*] [*World War II*] .... DCO

Director of Combined Operations (India) .... DCO(I)

Director of Combined Operations (Middle East) .... DCO(ME)

Director of Communications Development [*Ministry of Aircraft Production*] [*British*] .... DCD

Director [*or Directorate*] **of Communications - Electronics** [*ADC*] .... DCE

Director of Compass Department [*British military*] (DMA) .... DCD

Director of Contract Labour [*Admiralty*] [*British*] .... DCL

Director of Contracts [*Military British*] .... DOC

Director of Corporate Information .... DCI

Director of Craft and Amphibious Material [*British military*] (DMA) .... DCAM

Director of Defense Information (DNAB) .... DDI

Director of Defense Information (DOMA) .... DDI

Director [*or Directorate*] **of Defense Research and Engineering** [*DoD*] .... DDR & E

Director [*or Directorate*] **of Defense Research and Engineering** [*DoD*] .... DDRE

Director of Dental Services [*British*] .... DDS

Director [*or Directorate*] **of Development Planning** [*Air Force*] .... DDP

Director of Dockyard Manpower and Productivity [*Navy British*] .... DMPD

Director of Dockyards [*Admiralty*] [*British*] .... D of D

Director of Dockyards [*Admiralty*] [*British*] .... DOD

Director of Drafting and Records [*British military*] (DMA) .... DODAR

Director of Economics, Civil Affairs [*War Office*] [*British World War II*] .... DE(CA)

Director of Educational Services [*Air Force British*] .... DES

Director of Electrical and Mechanical Engineering [*Military British*] .... DEME

Director of Engine Development [*Ministry of Aircraft Production*] [*British*] .... DED

Director of Engineer Stores Service [*British*] .... DES

Director of Engineering [*Navy British*] .... DE

Director of Engineering and Industrial Services [*Edgewood Arsenal, MD*] .... DEIS

Director of Engineering (Naval) [*British military*] (DMA) .... DE(N)

Director of Equal Employment Opportunity [*Department of Labor*] .... DEEO

Director of Equipment and Ordnance Stores [*British military*] (DMA) .... DEOS

Director [*or Directorate*] **of Evaluation** [*Army*] .... DEV

Director of Facilities and Engineering [*Military*] (AABC) .... DFAE

Director of Fleet Maintenance [*Navy British*] .... DFM

Director of Fleet Management Services [*Navy British*] .... DFManS

Director of Flight Safety [*Air Force*] .... DFS

Director [*or Directorate*] **of Flight Safety Research** [*Air Force*] .... DFSR

Director of Fortifications and Works [*British*] .... DFW
Director of Graves Registration [*British*] .... DGR
Director of Ground Defence [*Military British*] .... DGD
Director of Ground Safety [*Air Force*] .... DGS
Director of Guided Weapons Trials [*British military*] (DMA) .... DTGW
Director of Health and Safety (PGP) .... HS Dir
Director of Health Services [*Army*] (AABC) .... DHS
Director of Home Operations [*Air Ministry*] [*British World War II*] .... DHO
Director of Hygiene [*British military*] (DMA) .... DH
Director of Industrial Operations [*Military*] (AABC) .... DIO
Director of Industrial Planning [*War Office*] [*British World War II*] .... DIP
Director of Infantry [*Military British*] .... DI
Director of Infantry [*Military British*] .... D-INF
Director [*or Directorate*] **of Information Management** [*DoD*] .... DOIM
Director of Information Systems for Command, Control, Communications, and Computers [*DoD*] DISC4
Director of Inland Water Transport Service [*British*] .... DIWT
Director [*or Directorate*] **of Installations** [*Abolished 1953, functions transferred to Department of Defense*] [*Air Force*] .... DI
Director of Intelligence [*RAF*] [*British*] .... D of I
Director of Intelligence, Division of the Admiralty [*British*] .... DIDA
Director of International Logistics [*Military*] .... DIL
Director of Laboratories [*AFSC*] .... DL
Director of Laboratories (MCD) .... DOL
Director of Laboratory Programs [*Navy*] .... DLP
Director of Labour [*Military British*] .... DL
Director of Legal Services [*British military*] (DMA) .... DLS
Director of Liaison and Munitions [*Military British*] .... DLM
Director [*or Directorate*] **of Logistics** [*DoD*] .... DOL
Director of Machine Tools [*Ministry of Aircraft Production and Ministry of Supply*] [*British*] .... DMT
Director of Management [*Military*] .... DM
Director of Manning [*British military*] (DMA) .... D of M
Director of Manpower and Organization [*Air Force*] .... DMO
Director of Manpower Planning [*British*] .... DMP
Director of Marine Services (Naval) [*British*] .... DMS(N)
Director of Maritime Operations [*RAF*] [*British*] .... DMO
Director of Materials Research (Naval) [*British*] .... DMR(N)
Director of Materiel Readiness [*Army*] .... DMR
Director of Mechanical Engineering [*War Office*] [*British World War II*] .... DME
Director of Mechanical Maintenance [*British military*] (DMA) .... DMM
Director of Medical Activities (AABC) .... DMEDA
Director of Medical Affairs (HCT) .... DMA
Director of Medical and Health Services [*British*] .... DMHS
Director of Medical and Sanitary Services [*British*] .... DMSS
Director of Medical Education .... DME
Director of Medical Services [*British*] .... DMS
Director of Meteorological and Oceanographical Services (Naval) [*British*] .... DMOS(N)
Director of Military Assistance .... DMA
Director of Military Intelligence [*US, British*] .... DMI
Director [*or Directorate*] **of Military Operations** .... DMO
Director of Military Operations and Intelligence .... DMOI
Director of Military Personnel [*Air Force*] .... DMP
Director of Military Training .... DMT
Director of Missile Safety Research [*Air Force*] .... DMSR
Director of Mission Safety Research [*Air Force*] .... DMSR
Director of Mobilization [*British military*] (DMA) .... DM
Director of Movements and Quartering [*British*] .... DMQ
Director of Music [*British military*] (DMA) .... DM
Director of Naval Accounts [*Obsolete British*] .... DNA
Director of Naval Air Division .... DNAD
Director of Naval Air Organization [*British*] .... DNAO
Director of Naval Air Warfare [*British military*] (DMA) .... DAW
Director of Naval Air Warfare and Flying Training [*British*] .... DAWT
Director of Naval Construction [*British*] .... DNC
Director of Naval Education and Training Support .... DENTS
Director of Naval Education Service [*British*] .... DNEDS
Director of Naval Education Service [*British*] (DMA) .... DNES
Director of Naval Engineering Training [*British military*] (DMA) .... DNET
Director of Naval Equipment .... DNE
Director of Naval Foreign and Commonwealth Training [*British*] .... DNFCT
Director of Naval Guided Weapons [*British*] .... DNGW
Director of Naval History (DNAB) .... DIRNAVHIS
Director of Naval History .... DIRNAVHIST
Director of Naval Intelligence [*US, British*] .... DNI
Director of Naval Laboratories .... DNL
Director of Naval Management and Organization [*British military*] (DMA) .... DNMO
Director of Naval Manning [*British military*] (DMA) .... DNM
Director of Naval Manning and Training [*British*] .... DNMT
Director of Naval Manpower Planning [*British*] .... DNMP
Director of Naval Manpower Requirements [*or Resources*] [*British*] .... DNMR
Director of Naval Manpower Structure Planning [*British military*] (DMA) .... DNMSP
Director of Naval Oceanography and Meteorology [*British*] .... DNOM
Director of Naval Officer Appointments [*British*] .... DNOA
Director of Naval Officer Procurement .... DNOP
Director of Naval Operational Studies [*British*] .... DNOS
Director of Naval Operations .... DNO
Director of Naval Ordnance [*Admiralty*] [*Obsolete British*] .... DNO
Director of Naval Physical Training and Sport [*British*] .... DNPTS
Director of Naval Records and History .... DNRH
Director of Naval Recruiting [*British*] .... D of NR
Director of Naval Recruiting [*British*] .... DNR
Director of Naval Service Conditions [*British*] .... DNSC
Director of Naval Signals [*British military*] (DMA) .... DNS
Director of Naval Telecommunications .... DNT
Director of Naval Training [*British military*] (DMA) .... DNT
Director of Naval Weapons Contracts [*British*] .... DNWC
Director of Naval Weather Service, Ministry of Defence [*British*] (NATG) .... DNWS
Director of Navigation and Direction [*British military*] (DMA) .... DND
Director of Navy Communications .... DNC
Director of Nuclear Safety [*Air Force*] .... DNS
Director of Nuclear Safety Research [*Air Force*] .... DNSR
Director of Nursing .... DON
Director of Nursing Education .... DNE
Director of Office of Programming [*Military*] .... DOP
Director of Officer Appointments [*British military*] (DMA) .... DOA
Director of Operational Requirements [*Air Ministry*] [*British*] .... DOR
Director of Operational Training [*RAF*] [*British*] .... DOT
Director of Operations .... DO
Director of Operations Division [*Navy British*] .... DOD
Director of Operations Division (Foreign) [*Navy British*] .... DOD(F)
Director of Operations Division (Home) [*Navy British*] .... DOD(H)
Director of Operations Narcotics Control Reports [*CIA*] .... DONCS
Director of Operations, Operational Plans Officer (MUGU) .... DOOPO
Director of Operations, Training and Intelligence [*Army*] (AABC) .... DOTI
Director of Ordnance Factories [*Ministry of Supply*] [*British World War II*] .... DOF
Director of Ordnance Factories, Engineering Factories [*Ministry of Supply*] [*British World War II*] .... DOF(E)
Director of Ordnance Factories, Explosives Factories [*Ministry of Supply*] [*British World War II*] .... DOF(X)
Director of Ordnance Services [*Military British*] .... DOS
Director of Overseas Civil Aviation [*British*] .... DOCA
Director of Pathology .... DP
Director of Personal Services [*Navy British*] .... DPS
Director of Personnel (MCD) .... DP
Director of Personnel and Administration [*Army*] (AABC) .... DIRPA
Director of Personnel and Community Activities [*Army*] (AABC) .... DPCA
Director of Personnel and Training [*Army*] .... D/P & T
Director of Personnel, Marine Corps .... DPMC
Director of Personnel Planning [*Air Force*] .... DPP
Director of Personnel Procurement and Training [*Air Force*] .... DPPT
Director of Photography [*Cinematography*] (WDMC) .... DP
Director of Physical Education (PGP) .... PE Dir
Director of Physical Training and Sports [*Navy British*] .... DPTS
Director of Planes [*Admiralty*] [*British*] .... D of P
Director of Planning of War Production [*Air Ministry*] [*British World War II*] .... DPWP
Director of Plans and Programs [*Army*] (RDA) .... DP & P
Director of Plans and Training [*Military*] (AABC) .... DPT
Director of Plans Division [*Navy British*] .... DPD
Director of Plans Division (Quartering) [*Navy British*] .... D of PD(Q)
Director of Plans, Training, and Mobilization [*DoD*] .... DPTM
Director of Postal and Courier Communications [*British military*] (DMA) .... DPCC
Director of Postal Services [*British*] .... DPS
Director of Postings [*RAF*] [*British*] .... DP
Director of Printing and Stationery Services [*Military British*] .... DPSS
Director of Prisoners of War [*British World War II*] .... DPW
Director of Procurement and Production [*Army*] .... DPP
Director of Program Analysis and Evaluation (RDA) .... DPAE
Director of Programs [*Air Force, Army*] .... DP
Director of Public Instruction .... DPI
Director of Public Prosecutions [*British*] .... DPP
Director of Public Prosecutions for Western Australia .... DPPWA
Director of Public Relations .... DPR
Director of Public Service .... D of PS
Director of Quartering [*British military*] (DMA) .... D of Q
Director of Radio Equipment [*Navy British*] .... DRE
Director of Radio Production [*Air Ministry*] [*British World War II*] .... DRP
Director of Railway Transport [*British military*] (DMA) .... DRT
Director of Recreation (PGP) .... Re Dir
Director of Recruiting and Organization [*Military British*] .... DRO
Director of Religious Education .... DRE
Director of Remounts [*Military British*] .... D of R
Director of Repair and Service [*British military*] (DMA) .... DRS
Director [*or Directorate*] **of Research and Development** [*Air Force*] .... DRD
Director [*or Directorate*] **of Research and Engineering** [*Military*] .... DRE
Director of Royal Artillery [*British*] .... DRA
Director of Sales .... DOS
Director of Salvage Department [*Navy British*] .... DS/VD
Director [*or Directorate*] **of Scientific Information Service** [*Canada*] .... DSIS
Director of Scientific Research [*British*] .... DSR
Director of Sea Transport [*British military*] (DMA) .... DST
Director of Security (AABC) .... DSEC
Director of Selection and Personnel [*British*] .... DSP
Director of Services [*Air Force*] .... DS
Director of Signal Department [*Obsolete Navy British*] .... DSD
Director of Signals [*British military*] (DMA) .... DS
Director of Site Operations [*Nuclear energy*] (NRCH) .... DSO
Director of Small Vessels Pool [*Admiralty*] [*British*] .... DSVP
Director of Special Weapons [*Army*] .... DSW
Director of Special Weapons and Vehicles [*Military British*] .... DSWV
Director of Staff Duties [*Military British*] .... DSD
Director [*or Directorate*] **of Statistical Services** [*Air Force*] .... DSS
Director of Stores [*Navy British*] .... DOS
Director of Stores (Washington) [*Navy*] .... D of S (W)
Director of Stores (Washington) [*Navy*] (DNAB) .... DOFS(W)
Director of Strategic Target Planning [*Military*] .... DSTP
Director of Strategic Target Planning Staff [*Offutt AFB*] [*Military*] (CINC) .... DSTPS

Director of Supplies and Quartering [*British military*] (DMA) .... DSQ
Director of Supplies and Transport [*British*] .... DST
Director of Supply and Maintenance [*Army*] .... DSM
Director of Supply and Secretariat Training [*British military*] (DMA) .... DSST
Director [*or Directorate*] **of Support** [*Army*] .... DOS
Director of Surface Weapons Projects [*Navy British*] .... DSWP
Director of Surveillance and Reconnaissance [*Army*] .... DSR
Director of Survey [*British military*] (DMA) .... DSVY
Director of Tactical and Staff Duties Division [*British military*] (DMA) .... DTSD
Director of Tactical Division [*Navy British*] .... D of TD
Director of Tactical Investigation [*Military British*] .... DTI
Director of Technical Training [*British military*] (DMA) .... DTT
Director of Telecommunications Management [*Abolished, 1970*] [*Air Force*] .... DTM
Director of the Army Budget .... DAB
Director of the Army National Guard .... DANG
Director of the Army National Guard .... DARNG
Director of the Army Staff .... DAS
Director of the Education Department [*Navy British*] .... DED
Director of the Intelligence Division [*British military*] (DMA) .... DID
Director of the Naval Reserve (DOMA) .... DNR
Director of the Naval Service [*Canada, 1910-1926*] .... DNS
Director of the Royal Armoured Corps [*British*] .... DRAC
Director of the Women's Royal Air Force [*British military*] (DMA) .... DWRAF
Director of Traffic .... D of T
Director [*or Directorate*] **of Training** [*Army*] .... DOT
Director of Training and Staff Duties Division [*Navy British*] .... DTSD
Director of Transport [*British military*] (DMA) .... DT
Director of Transport and Movements [*British military*] (DMA) .... DTM
Director of Undersea Warfare, Ministry of Defence, London (NATG) .... DUSW
Director of Underwater Weapons [*British*] .... DUW
Director of Underwater Weapons Projects [*Navy British*] .... DUWP
Director of Unexploded Bomb Disposal Department [*Navy British*] .... DUBDD
Director of Veterinary Services [*Military British*] .... DVS
Director of Victualling [*British military*] (DMA) .... D of V
Director of War Archives [*British*] .... DWA
Director of Weapon Systems Analysis [*Army*] (AABC) .... DWSA
Director of Weapons Coordination (Naval) [*British*] .... DWCOORD(N)
Director of Weapons Equipment, Surface [*British military*] (DMA) .... DWES
Director of Weapons Equipment, Underwater [*British military*] (DMA) .... DWEU
Director of Weapons Navigation (Naval) [*British*] .... DWNAV(N)
Director of Weapons Production [*British military*] (DMA) .... DWP
Director of Weapons Production (Naval) [*British*] .... DWP(N)
Director of Weapons Production (Naval) [*British*] .... DWPROD(N)
Director of Weapons Resources and Programmes [*British military*] (DMA) .... DWRP
Director of Weapons Surface Projects (Naval) [*British*] .... DWSP(N)
Director of Welfare and Service Conditions [*British military*] (DMA) .... DWSC
Director of Women Marines .... DIRW
Director of Women's Auxiliary Air Force [*British*] .... DWAAF
Director of Works [*Air Ministry*] [*British*] .... DW
Director of Works and Buildings [*British*] .... DOWB
Director of Wreck Disposal .... DWD
Director, Office of Civil Defense (AABC) .... DIROCD
Director, Office of Oceanography [*UNESCO*] .... DOO
Director, Office of Transport and Communications [*Department of State*] (AAG) .... DOTC
Director on Target [*Military*] (CAAL) .... DOT
Director, Operation and Maintenance, Army .... DOMA
Director, Operational Test and Evaluation [*OSD*] (AAGC) .... DOT&E
Director, Pacific and Alaskan Divisions, Bureau of Yards and Docks [*Obsolete*] .... DIRPACALDOCKS
Director, Pacific Division, Bureau of Yards and Docks [*Obsolete*] .... DIRPACDOCKS
Director, Personnel Department [*Marine Corps*] .... DPD
Director, Planning and Operations (MCD) .... DPO
Director, Polaris Technical [*Missiles*] .... DPT
Director Program Evaluation [*Navy*] (CAAL) .... DPE
Director, Research and Development, Air [*Military Canada*] .... DRDA
Director, Research and Development, Communications and Space [*Military Canada*] .... DRDCS
Director, Research and Development, Human Performance [*Military Canada*] .... DRDHP
Director, Research and Development, Land [*Military Canada*] .... DRDL
Director, Research and Development, Maritime [*Military Canada*] .... DRDM
Director, Research and Development, Program Control [*Military Canada*] .... DRDP
Director, Research and Development, Resource Management [*Military Canada*] .... DRDRM
Director, Research, Development, Test, and Evaluation [*Military*] (DNAB) .... DRDT & E
Director, San Diego [*California*] **Intermediate Maintenance Activity** [*Military*] (DNAB) .... DIRSDIMA
Director Selector Panel .... DSP
Director, Special Projects/Project Manager, Fleet Ballistic Missile (MCD) .... DIRSP/PROJMGRFBM
Director Standing Group Memorandum [*NATO*] (NATG) .... DSGM
Director, Strategic Defense Initiative Organization [*Military*] (SDI) .... DSDIO
Director, Strategic Systems Project Office [*Navy*] .... DIRSSP
Director, Submarine Policy and Warfare [*Military*] .... DSMPW
Director/Telecommunications and Command and Control System (MCD) .... DTACCS
Director to Commissary Operations [*Military*] (AABC) .... DOCO
Director, Torpedo, Anti-Submarine, and Mine Warfare [*British military*] (DMA) .... DTASW
Director Train Indicator .... DTI
Director, United States Naval Weather Service .... DUSNWS
Director, Vehicle and Field Engineering [*Canada*] [*Military*] .... DVFE
Director, Weapons Research and Development, Surface [*British military*] (DMA) .... DWRDS
Director, Weapons Research and Development, Underwater [*British military*] (DMA) .... DWRDU
Director, Weapons Systems Evaluation Group (CINC) .... DIRWSEG
Director, Women's Army Corps (AABC) .... DWAC
Directorate .... DIRCTRT
Directorate, Army MAP [*Military Assistance Program*] **Logistics** .... DAML
Directorate for Advanced Systems [*Army*] (RDA) .... DAS
Directorate for Armed Forces Information and Education [*Military*] .... DAFIE
Directorate for Civil Disturbance Planning and Operations [*Army*] (AABC) .... DCDPO
Directorate for Classification Management [*DoD*] .... DCM
Directorate for Industrial Security Clearance (AAGC) .... DISCR Review
Directorate for Information, Operation, and Patents (AAGC) .... DIOP
Directorate for Information Operations and Reports [*Washington, DC*] [*DoD*] .... DIOR
Directorate for Inspection Services [*Assistant Secretary of Defense for Administration*] (CINC) .... DINS
Directorate for Resource Management [*CIA*] .... DRM
Directorate for the Freedom of Information [*Formerly, Directorate for Security Review*] [*DoD*] .... DFI
Directorate General of Highways [*Vietnam*] .... DGOH
Directorate General of Telecommunications [*Taipei, Taiwan*] .... DGT
Directorate Notice (AAG) .... DN
Directorate of Accident Prevention [*RAF*] [*British*] .... DAP
Directorate of Advanced Systems Technology .... DAST
Directorate of Aeronautical Inspection Services [*British*] .... DAIS
Directorate of Aerospace Studies [*Kirtland Air Force Base, NM*] .... DAS
Directorate of Air Force Welfare [*British*] .... DAFW
Directorate of Aircraft Engineering and Maintenance (MCD) .... DAEM
Directorate of Aircraft Production Development [*British*] (DEN) .... DAPD
Directorate of Airlift [*Air Force*] (MCD) .... DOAL
Directorate of Ammunition [*Canada*] [*Military*] .... DAMMO
Directorate of Ancient Monuments and Historic Buildings [*Department of the Environment*] [*British*] (DI) .... DAMHB
Directorate of Armament Development [*British*] (MCD) .... DAD
Directorate of Armament Development [*Ministry of Aircraft Production*] [*British World War II*] .... DArmD
Directorate of Armament Requirements [*RAF*] [*British*] .... DAR
Directorate of Army Research (GRD) .... DAR
Directorate of Atomic Research [*Canada*] (BARN) .... DAR
Directorate of Atomic Warfare .... DAW
Directorate of Aviation Safety Regulation [*Australia*] .... DASR
Directorate of Ballistic Missiles .... D/BM
Directorate of Biological Operations [*Pine Bluff Arsenal, AR*] .... DBO
Directorate of Civil Aviation .... DCA
Directorate of Combat Developments [*Army*] .... DCD
Directorate of Contracting [*Military*] (RDA) .... DOC
Directorate of Covert Collection [*South African secret military-intelligence unit*] (ECON) .... DCC
Directorate of Design Engineering [*NASA*] (KSC) .... DE
Directorate of Documentation and Drawing Services (MCD) .... DDDS
Directorate of Engineering, Aeronautical Systems (SAA) .... DEAS
Directorate of Engineering and Housing [*Army*] (RDA) .... DEH
Directorate of Engineering, Ballistic Missiles (SAA) .... DEBM
Directorate of Evaluation, Standardization, Concepts, Studies and Doctrine [*Army*] .... DESCSD
Directorate of Facilities Engineering [*Military*] .... DFE
Directorate of Fleet Supply Duties [*Navy British*] .... DFSD
Directorate of Flight and Missile Safety Research [*Air Force*] .... DFMSR
Directorate of Flight Standards and Qualification Research [*St. Louis, MO*] [*Army*] .... FS/Q
Directorate of Geophysics Research [*Air Research and Development Command*] (AAG) .... DGR
Directorate of History, Department of National Defence [*Bureau du Service Historique, Ministere de la Defense Nationale*] **Ottawa, Ontario** [*Library symbol National Library of Canada*] (NLC) .... OONDH
Directorate of Industrial Security Clearance Review [*DoD*] .... DISCR
Directorate of Information Services, Department of National Defence [*Servicesd'Information, Ministere de la Defense Nationale*] **Ottawa, Ontario** [*Library symbol National Library of Canada*] (NLC) .... OONDIS
Directorate of Installation Services (MCD) .... DIS
Directorate of Intelligence (Operations) [*RAF*] [*British*] .... DI(O)
Directorate of Intelligence (Research) [*RAF*] [*British*] .... DI(R)
Directorate of Intelligence (Security) [*RAF*] [*British*] .... DI(S)
Directorate of Internal Affairs and Communications [*Allied German Occupation Forces*] .... DIAC
Directorate of Licensing [*AEC*] (NUCP) .... DOL
Directorate of Logistic Support Management [*or Manager*] (AAG) .... D/LSM
Directorate of Maintenance (AFIT) .... DM
Directorate of Materials and Structures Research and Development [*British*] .... D-MAT/S
Directorate of Materials and Structures Research and Development [*British*] .... DMSRD
Directorate of Materials Research and Development [*Aviation British*] .... D-MAT
Directorate of Materiel Management (MCD) .... DMM
Directorate of Medical Research [*Army*] .... DMR
Directorate of Microgram Services [*RAF*] [*British*] .... DMS
Directorate of Military Aid Overseas [*British*] .... DMAO
Directorate of Military Satellite Systems (AAG) .... DMSS
Directorate of Military Support (AABC) .... DOMS

Directorate of Missile Captive Test (AAG) .... DMCT
Directorate of National Coordination (CINC) .... DNC
Directorate of Naval Administration Planning [British] .... DNAP
Directorate of Naval Air Warfare [British] .... DNAW
Directorate of Naval Command, Control and Communications ... DNCCC
Directorate of Naval Communications Engineering .... DNCE
Directorate of Naval Operational Requirements [British] .. DNOR
Directorate of Naval Operations and Trade [British] ...... DNOT
Directorate of Naval Plans [British] .... DNPlans
Directorate of Naval Security [British] .... DNSy
Directorate of Naval Signals [British] .... DNS
Directorate of Naval Survival and Safety .... DONSS
Directorate of Naval Warfare [British] .... DNW
Directorate of Operational Support Services - Air Force ... DOSS-AF
Directorate of Overseas Surveys [Overseas Development Administration] [British] (DS) .... DOS
Directorate of Policy [Air Ministry] [British] .... DPA
Directorate of Post War Building [British] (DAS) .... PWB
Directorate of Project Management B - Air Force .... DPMB-AF
Directorate of Public Relations (Naval) [British] .... DPR(N)
Directorate of Quartering (Navy) [British] .... D of Q(N)
Directorate of Ranges and Targets [Army] .... DART
Directorate of Reserve Component Support [DoD] .... DRCS
Directorate of Science and Technology [CIA] (LAIN) .... DDS&T
Directorate of Scientific and Technical Intelligence [British] .... DSTI
Directorate of Scientific Information Service, Defence Research Board, Ottawa, ON, Canada [Library symbol Library of Congress] (LCLS) ..... CaOONDR
Directorate of Scientific Information Services, Department of National Defence [Services d'Information Scientifique, Ministere de la Defense Nationale] Ottawa, Ontario [Library symbol National Library of Canada] (NLC) .... OODSIS
Directorate of Scientific Intelligence (SAA) .... DSI
Directorate of Security and Law Enforcement [Military] (DNAB) .... DSLE
Directorate of Stores and Clothing Development [British] .... DSCD
Directorate of Supply Operations (AFIT) .... DSO
Directorate of Systems Engineering (AAG) .... DSE
Directorate of Technical Development (MCD) .... DTD
Directorate of Technical Research [Navy Canada] .... DTR
Directorate of Training and Development [Army] .... DOTD
Directorate of Training Developments [Army] .... DTD
Directorate of War Organization [RAF] [British] .... DWO
Directorate of Weapons and Engineering Research [Canada] ... DWER
Directorate of Weapons and Vehicle Procurement - Army ... DWVP-A
Directorate of Weapons and Vehicle Procurement - Army - Vehicles .... DWVP-A-VEH
Directorate of Weapons Effect Tests (MCD) .... DWET
Directorate Office Instruction .... DOI
Directorate-General (Section XIII) [Council of European Communities] (NITA) .... DG XIII
Director-General .... DG
Director-General (WDAA) .... DIR-GEN
Director-General Engineering, Land [Canada] .... DGEL
Director-General, Home Guard [British military] (DMA) ... DGHG
Director-General of Aerospace and Engineering Maintenance (MCD) ...... DGAEM
Director-General of Aircraft Equipment [Ministry of Aircraft Production] [British] .... DGAE
Director-General of Aircraft (Naval) [British military] (DMA) .... DGA(N)
Director-General of Armoured Vehicles [British] .... DGAV
Director-General of Army Education [British] .... DGAE
Director-General of Army Medical Services [British] ... DGAMS
Director-General of Army Requirements [British] .... DGAR
Director-General of [Quality] Assurance .... DGOA
Director-General of Civil Aviation [British] .... DGCA
Director-General of Civilian Clothing [British] .... DGCC
Director-General of Engine Production [British] .... DGEP
Director-General of Equipment [Air Force British] ..... DGE
Director-General of Explosives Production [Ministry of Supply] [British World War II] .... DGX
Director-General of Fighting Vehicles [British military] (DMA) .... DGFV
Director-General of Fighting Vehicles and Engineer Equipment [British] (RDA) .... DGFVE
Director-General of Filling Factories [Formerly, DGOF(F)] [Ministry of Supply] [British] [World War II] .... DGFF
Director-General of Ground Defence [Military British] ... DGGD
Director-General of Guided Weapons and Electronics [British] (RDA) ...... DGGWL
Director-General of Intelligence and Security (MCD) ... DGIS
Director-General of Internal Audit [British] (RDA) .... DGIA
Director-General of Manpower [Ministry of Labour] [British] ... DGM
Director-General of Mechanical Engineering, Supply [Ministry of Supply] [British] .... DGMechE(S)
Director-General of Medical Services [British] .... DGMS
Director-General of Military Railways [British military] (DMA) ... DGMR
Director-General of Military Training [British] .... DGMT
Director-General of Military Works [British military] (DMA) ...... DGMW
Director-General of Munitions Production [Ministry of Supply] [British World War II] .... DGMP
Director-General of Naval Manpower and Training [British] ...... DGNMT
Director-General of Naval Personnel Services [British] .... DGNPS
Director-General of Ordnance Factories [Ministry of Supply] [British World War II] .... DGOF
Director-General of Ordnance Factories (Filling) [Later, DGFF] [Ministry of Supply] [British] [World War II] .... DGOF(F)
Director-General of Organization [RAF] [British] ...... DGO
Director-General of Personnel [British] .... DGP
Director-General of Production [British Air Ministry] ... DGP

Director-General of Quality Assurance [British] .... DGQA
Director-General of Raw Materials [Ministry of Supply] [British] ... DGRM
Director-General of Royal Air Force Medical Services [British] ..... DGRAFMS
Director-General of Scientific Research and Development [Ministry of Supply] [British] .... DGSRD
Director-General of Servicing and Maintenance [RAF] [British] ... DGSM
Director-General of Small Arms Ammunition Production [Ministry of Supply] [British World War II] .... DGSAA
Director-General of Statistics and Planning [Ministry of Supply] [British] ... DGSP
Director-General of Supplies and Transport (Naval) [British] .... DGST(N)
Director-General of the Army Veterinary Service [British military] (DMA) .... DGAVS
Director-General of the Territorial Army [British] ..... DGTA
Director-General of the Territorial Force [British military] (DMA) ...... DGTF
Director-General of Training [British military] (DMA) ... DGT
Director-General of Transportation [British military] (DMA) .... DGT
Director-General of Transportation Services [British] .... DG Tn
Director-General of Weapons [British military] (DMA) ... DGW
Director-General of Weapons and Instruments Production [Military British] .... DGWIP
Director-General of Weapons (Army) [British military] (RDA) .... DGW(A)
Director-General of Weapons Department (Naval) [British] .... DGW(N)
Director-General of Works [RAF] [British] .... DGW
Director-General, Ordnance Systems [Canada] .... DGOS
Director-General, Personal Services (Naval) [British military] (DMA) ... DGPS(N)
Director-General, Quality Assurance Library, Department of National Defence [Bibliotheque du Directeur General-Assurance de la Qualite, Ministere de la Defense Nationale], Ottawa, Ontario [Library symbol National Library of Canada] (NLC) .... OOQA
Director-General, Research and Development Policy [Military Canada] ...... DGRD
Director-General, Research and Development Services [Military Canada] .... DGRDS
Director-General, Ship Refitting [Ministry of Defence] [British] .... DGSR
Director-General, Ships [Navy British] .... DGShips
Director-General, Supply and Transport [British military] (DMA) .... DGST
Directories in Print [Formerly, DOD] [A publication] ... DIP
Directorio Nacional Unido [Guerrilla forces] [Honduras] (EY) ...... DNU
Directorio Revolucionario Iberico de Liberta [Revolutionary Directorate for Iberian Liberation] .... DRIL
Directors Advisory Committee [National Institutes of Health] ...... DAC
Directors' and Officers' [Liability insurance] .... D & O
Director's Assistant (WDMC) .... da
Director's Discretionary Fund .... DDF
Directors Guild of America (EA) .... DGA
Directors Guild of Canada .... DGC
Directors Guild of Great Britain .... DGGB
Director's Instant Reversible Talkback [Device enabling contact between director in control room and crew in studio] .... DIRT
Director's Office .... DO
Directors-in-Exile [British] .... DIE
Directory .... DIR
Directory .... DIRCTRY
Directory (AFM) .... DRCTY
Directory Access Protocol [Telecommunications] (OSI) ... DAP
Directory Access Service Element [Telecommunications] (OSI) ... DASE
Directory and Equipment Number Status System (MCD) ... DENS
Directory Assistance [Telecommunications] (TEL) ...... DA
Directory Assistance System [Telecommunications] (TEL) ... DAS
Directory Assistance System/Microfilm [Bell System] ... DAS/M
Directory Assistance Systems / Computer and Microfilm [Bell System] .... DAS/CM
Directory Clearinghouse [Defunct] (EA) .... DC
Directory Control Module [Computer science] (HGAA) ... DCM
Directory Development Study .... DDS
Directory Enquiry Computerized Information Retrieval System [BT] (NITA) .... DQCIR
Directory Enquiry Service [Telecommunications] (TEL) ... DQ
Directory Information [Newsletter] .... DI
Directory Information Base [Computer science] (TNIG) ... DIB
Directory Information Base (CDE) .... DIB
Directory Information Service [A publication] .... DIS
Directory Information Tree (TNIG) .... DIT
Directory Number [Computer science] .... DN
Directory of American Book Workers [A publication] .... DABW
Directory of American Research and Technology [R. R. Bowker Co.] [Information service or system A publication] ...... DART
Directory of Associations in Canada [Micromedia, Ltd.] [Information service or system A publication] (IID) .... DAC
Directory of Australian Academic and Research Libraries [Australia A publication] .... DAARL
Directory of Australian Directories [A publication] .... DAD
Directory of Australian Public Libraries [Australia A publication] ... DAPL
Directory of Automated Information Systems (MCD) .... DAIS
Directory of Bankruptcy Attorneys [Information service or system] (IID) .... Bkr-Dir
Directory of Biotechnology Information/Resources [American Type Culture Collection] [Information service or system] (CRD) ...... DBIR
Directory of British Associations [A publication] ...... DBA
Directory of Computerized Information in Science and Technology [Leonard Cohen, ed., New York: Science Associates International, 1968] [A publication] .... DCIST
Directory of Directories [Later, DIP] [A publication] ... DOD
Directory of Education Research and Researchers in Australia (NITA) ...... DERA
Directory of Educational Software [British] (NITA) ... DOES
Directory of Engineering Document Services [A publication] ...... DEDS
Directory of Environmental Research Projects in the European Communities [EURONET] [Information service or system] .... ENREP

Directory of European Associations [*A publication*] ... DEA
Directory of Executive Recruitment Consultants [*A publication*] ... DERC
Directory of Foreign Investors in the US [*A publication*] ... DFI
Directory of Independent Training and Tutorial Organisations (AIE) ... DITTO
Directory of Information Sources Online [*National Library of Medicine*] [*Database*] ... DIRLINE
Directory of International and Corporate Giving in America and Abroad [*A publication*] ... ICGA
Directory of International Mail [*A publication*] ... DIM
Directory of International Mail [*A publication*] ... DOIM
Directory of Item Names for the Gas Industry [*A publication*] ... DING
Directory of Library and Information Professionals [*Gale Research, Inc.*] [*Information service or system*] (CRD) ... DLIP
Directory of Mortuary Operations [*Army*] (AABC) ... DMO
Directory of National Women's Organizations [*A publication*] ... NWO
Directory of Numerical Databases [*Database*] [*NASA Information service or system*] (CRD) ... DND
Directory of Occupational Titles (DNAB) ... DOT
Directory of Online Databases [*A publication*] ... DOD
Directory of Online Databases Produced in Sweden [*Database*] [*Royal Institute of Technology Library*] [*Information service or system*] (CRD) ... DOLDIS
Directory of Opportunities for Graduates [*A publication*] ... DOG
Directory of Outpatient Ostomy Resources and Services [*International Association for Enterostomal Therapy*] ... DOORS
Directory of Paper Makers [*A publication*] (DGA) ... DPM
Directory of Portable Databases [*A publication*] ... DPD
Directory of Post Office (AFM) ... DPO
Directory of Rare Analyses [*A publication*] ... DORA
Directory of Religious Organizations [*A publication*] ... DRO
Directory of Special Libraries and Information Centers [*A publication*] ... DSL
Directory of Special Libraries in Australia [*A publication*] ... DASL
Directory of Special Libraries in Australia [*A publication*] ... DSLA
Directory of Texas Manufacturers [*University of Texas at Austin*] [*Information service or system*] (CRD) ... DTM
Directory of Title Pages Indexes and Contents Pages [*UK Serials Group*] (NITA) ... DOTIC
Directory of United Nations Information Systems [*Database*] [*Inter-Organisation Board of the United Nations*] [*Information service or system*] (CRD) ... DUNIS
Directory of Visual Arts Organizations [*Arts Midwest*] [*Information service or system*] (CRD) ... DVA
Directory of Women's Media [*A publication*] ... DWM
Directory on Disk [*Information service or system*] (IID) ... DOD
Directory Project [*Bell Laboratories*] ... DIR/ECT
Directory Publishers Alliance (EA) ... DPA
Directory Publishers Association [*British England*] (EAIO) ... DPA
Directory Scope Analysis Program [*Bell System*] ... DSAP
Directory Service Agent (OSI) ... DSA
Directory Service Protocol [*Telecommunications*] (OSI) ... DSP
Directory Synchronization (ACRL) ... DS
Directory System Agent (ACRL) ... DSA
Directory System Service Element [*Telecommunications*] (OSI) ... DSSE
Directory Tape Processor ... DTP
Directory User Agent [*Computer science*] (TNIG) ... DUA
Directory Verification Processor [*Computer science*] ... DIRVIR
Directory Yellow Pages [*Telecommunications*] (TEL) ... DYP
Direct-Reaction Calculation ... DRC
Direct-Recording Electronic [*Technology*] ... DRE
Direct-Search Discretized [*Computer science*] ... DSD
Direct-Step-on-the-Wafer [*Microelectronics*] ... DSW
Direct-to-Consumer [*Sales*] ... DTC
Direct-to-Disc [*Recording system*] (WDAA) ... DTD
Direct-View Device [*Night vision*] ... DVD
Direct-View Diagnostic Region ... DVDR
Direct-View Navigation Aid ... DVNA
Direct-View Storage Tube [*Princeton Electronic Products*] ... DVST
Direct-Viewing Storage Tube ... DST
DirectVision [*Home-information service of KPIX-TV*] ... DV
Dirgantara Air Service PT [*Indonesia*] [*ICAO designator*] (FAAC) ... DIR
Dirham [*Monetary unit*] [*Morocco*] ... DH
Dirham [*Monetary unit*] [*Iraq*] ... DIRH
Dirigo [*I Guide*] [*Latin*] (ROG) ... DIR
Dirkou [*Niger*] [*ICAO location identifier*] (ICLI) ... DRZD
Dirksen Senate Office Building [*Washington, DC*] (DLA) ... DSOB
Dirleton's Decisions, Court of Sessions [*Scotland*] [*A publication*] (DLA) ... Dirl
Dirleton's Decisions, Court of Sessions [*Scotland*] [*A publication*] (DLA) ... Dirl Dec
Dirleton's Doubts and Questions in the Law [*A publication*] (DLA) ... Dirl D
Dirranbandi [*Australia Airport symbol Obsolete*] (OAG) ... DRN
Dirt [*Gossip*] [*Slang*] ... D
Dirt [*or Dust*] **Collector** (AAG) ... DC
Dirty Book ... DB
Dirty Liquid Radioactive Waste System [*Nuclear energy*] (NRCH) ... DLRWS
Dirty Lubricating Oil (AAG) ... DLO
Dirty Old Man [*Slang*] ... DOM
Dirty RADWASTE [*Nuclear energy*] (NRCH) ... DRW
Dirty Rotten Form [*Slang*] (ADA) ... DRF
Dirty Word Remover [*Graffiti-removing chemical*] ... DWR
Dirty Writers of America [*Satirical*] ... DWA
Disabilities Aids Collective [*Australia*] ... DAC
Disabilities and Gifted Education [*Educational Resources Information Center (ERIC) Clearinghouse*] [*Council for Exceptional Children*] (PAZ) ... EC
Disabilities, Opportunities, Internetworking, and Technology ... DO-IT
Disabilities Task Force [*Australia*] ... DTF
Disability (MAE) ... DB
Disability ... DIS
Disability (ADA) ... DISAB
Disability ... DSBLTY
Disability ... DSBLTY
Disability Adviser's Officer (South Australia) [*Medicine*] ... DAO
Disability Alliance Educational and Research Association [*British*] ... DAERA
Disability Assistance ... DA
Disability Benefit Law [*Insurance*] ... DBL
Disability Case Management [*Insurance*] (WYGK) ... DCM
Disability Council of New South Wales [*Australia*] ... DCNSW
Disability Determination [*Social Security Administration*] (OICC) ... DD
Disability Determination Service [*Social Security Administration*] (GFGA) ... DDS
Disability Hearings Unit [*Social Security Administration*] (OICC) ... DHU
Disability Income [*Insurance*] ... DI
Disability Information Network of South Australia ... DINSA
Disability Insurance (AAG) ... DI
Disability Insurance Benefits [*Social Security Administration*] (OICC) ... DIB
Disability Insurance Letter [*Social Security Administration*] (OICC) ... DIL
Disability Insurance Sales Course [*LUTC*] ... DISC
Disability Insurance Training Council [*Washington, DC*] (EA) ... DITC
Disability Officer ... DO
Disability Pension (MAE) ... DP
Disability Policy Board [*Veterans Administration*] ... DPB
Disability Retirement [*Military*] (DNAB) ... DIS RET
Disability Retirement Branch [*BUPERS*] ... DRB
Disability Review Council [*Military*] (AABC) ... DRC
Disability Rights Center (EA) ... DRC
Disability Rights Education and Defense Fund (EA) ... DREDF
Disability Severance Pay ... DSABLSEVP
Disability Veiling Brightness [*Optics*] (IAA) ... DVB
Disability-Adjusted Life Year [*Public health*] (ECON) ... DALY
Disable (AABC) ... DSABL
Disable (MSA) ... DSBL
Disable Transmit (NITA) ... DIS TX
Disabled (ECII) ... DIS
Disabled (FAAC) ... DISABLD
Disabled Adult Child [*Social Security Administration*] (OICC) ... DAC
Disabled Adults Residential Establishments [*Australian Capital Territory*] ... DARE
Disabled American Veterans (EA) ... DAV
Disabled American Veterans Auxiliary (EA) ... DAVA
Disabled Businesspersons Association (EA) ... DBA
Disabled Child [*Title XVI*] [*Social Security Administration*] (OICC) ... DC
Disabled Drivers' Action Group [*British*] (DI) ... DDAG
Disabled Drivers' Association [*British*] ... DDA
Disabled Drivers' Motor Club [*British*] ... DDMC
Disabled in Action National [*Defunct*] (EA) ... DIA
Disabled Individual [*Title XVI*] [*Social Security Administration*] (OICC) ... DI
Disabled Interest Group Electronic Exchange (HGAA) ... DIGEX
Disabled Journalists of America (EA) ... DJA
Disabled List [*Athletics*] ... DL
Disabled [*or Disability*] **Living Foundation** [*British*] (DI) ... DLF
Disabled Motorists Federation [*British*] (DBA) ... DMF
Disabled Officers Association (EA) ... DOA
Disabled Peoples' Association [*Singapore*] (EAIO) ... DPA
Disabled Peoples' International (EAIO) ... DPI
Disabled Peoples' International [*Australia*] ... DPIA
Disabled Peoples' International USA (EA) ... DPIUSA
Disabled Person (ADA) ... DP
Disabled Persons Bureau [*Northern Territory*] [*Australia*] ... DPB
Disabled Persons Organization [*Bahamas*] (EAIO) ... DPO
Disabled Persons Railcard [*British*] ... DPR
Disabled Persons Unit [*United Nations*] (DUND) ... DPU
Disabled Spouse [*Title XVI*] [*Social Security Administration*] (OICC) ... DS
Disabled Student Services ... DSS
Disabled Students' Programs and Services ... DSPS
Disabled Veterans Outreach Program [*Department of Labor*] ... DVOP
Disabled Veterans Outreach Program Specialist [*Veterans Administration*] ... DVOPS
Disabled Widow [*or Widower*] [*Social Security Administration*] (OICC) ... DW
Disabled Widow [*or Widower*] **Benefits** [*Social Security Administration*] (OICC) ... DWB
Disabled Workers' Union of Western Australia ... DWUWA
Disabled Young People's Services Program [*Australia*] ... DYPSP
Disablement Advisory Committee [*Department of Employment*] [*British*] ... DAC
Disablement Income Group [*British*] ... DIG
Disablement Information Advice Lines [*British*] ... DIAL
Disablement Resettlement Office [*or Officer*] [*British*] ... DRO
Disaccharide Repeating Unit [*Biochemistry*] ... DRU
Disaccommodation Factor ... DF
Disadvantaged Business Enterprise [*Business term*] ... DBE
Disadvantaged Business Utilization (MCD) ... DBU
Disadvantaged Children Series [*A publication*] ... DCS
Disadvantaged Person ... DP
Disaggregated (MAE) ... DA
Disagree (NASA) ... DIS
Disalicylidenepropanediamine [*Organic chemistry*] ... DSPD
Disallowance [*Legal*] [*British*] (ROG) ... DISALLCE
Disallowed [*Legal*] [*British*] (ROG) ... DISALLD
Disappearance of Single Cell [*Assay*] [*Cytology*] ... DSC
Disappearing ... DISAPG
Disappearing Automatic Retaliatory Target [*Military*] (RDA) ... DART
Disappearing RADAR Contact (MCD) ... DRC
Disapprove (AABC) ... DISAP
Disapproved In [*or Disapproving*] [*Legal term*] (DLA) ... Disappr
Disarm Education Fund (EA) ... DEF

Disarmament	DSARMNT
Disarmament Commission [*Also, DC (UN), UNDC*]	DC
Disarmament Commission of the United Nations [*Also, DC, UNDC*]	DC (UN)
Disarmament Resource Center [*Defunct*] (EA)	DRC
Disarmed Military Personnel	DMP
Disassemble	DA
Disassemble	DISASSM
Disassemble (IAA)	DSASBL
Disassemble Sequence Parameter (IAA)	DSP
Disassembly (KSC)	DISASSY
Disassembly and Inspection (DNAB)	D & I
Disassembly Facility [*NASA*] (NASA)	DF
Disassembly Inspection Report	DIR
Disassembly Manual (MCD)	DM
Disassembly Manual [*NASA*]	DM
Disassembly/Reassembly Equipment [*Nuclear energy*] (NRCH)	D/RE
Disassembly/Reassembly Station [*Nuclear energy*] (NRCH)	D/RS
Disaster Action Team [*Red Cross*]	DAT
Disaster Aid Association of the International Union of Gospel Missions (EA)	DAAIUGM
Disaster Assistance Center [*Federal Emergency Management Agency*]	DAC
Disaster Assistance Recovery Teams [*Military*]	DART
Disaster Control (AAG)	DC
Disaster Control Center (AAG)	DCC
Disaster Control Force	DCF
Disaster Control Group	DCG
Disaster Control Officer (AAG)	DCO
Disaster Control Plan (AFM)	DCP
Disaster Control Recovery Plan	DCRP
Disaster Control Team (AFM)	DCT
Disaster Field Office [*Federal Emergency Management Agency*] (GFGA)	DFO
Disaster Loan Corp. [*Dissolved 1945, functions transferred to Reconstructi on Finance Corp.*]	DLC
Disaster Nursing Chairman [*Red Cross*]	DNC
Disaster Operations Center (GNE)	DOC
Disaster Operations Plan [*Nuclear energy*] (NRCH)	DOP
Disaster Operations Room [*Public safety*]	DOR
Disaster Plan [*Australia*]	DISPLAN
Disaster Preparedness (NVT)	DP
Disaster Preparedness Bill (DNAB)	DPB
Disaster Preparedness Plan (DNAB)	DPP
Disaster Preparedness Planning Board (AFM)	DPPB
Disaster Prevention and Preparedness [*Marine science*] (OSRA)	DPP
Disaster Recovery (DA)	DR
Disaster Recovery Plan [*Computer systems*]	DRP
Disaster Recovery Training (DNAB)	DRT
Disaster Representative [*Red Cross*]	DR
Disaster Research Center [*Ohio*] (AEBS)	DRC
Disaster Research Group [*National Academy of Sciences*]	DRG
Disaster Research Institute (EAIO)	DRI
Disaster Response Force [*Military*]	DRF
Disaster Services [*Red Cross*]	DS
Disaster Services Liaison Officer	DSLO
Disaster Support Area (GNE)	DSA
Disaster Unemployment Assistance [*Disaster Relief Act*]	DUA
Disaster Warning Satellite [*NASA*] (NASA)	DWS
Disaster Warning System [*National Weather Service*]	DWS
Disaster Welfare Inquiry Center [*Federal disaster planning*]	DWIC
Disaturated Phosphatidylcholine [*Biochemistry*]	DSPC
Disbandment Control Unit [*Allied Military Government of Occupied Territory*] [*Post-World War II*]	DCU
Disburse (AABC)	DISB
Disbursement (AFM)	DISBMT
Disbursement	DISBMT
Disbursement	DSB
Disbursement Voucher (AFM)	DV
Disbursements [*Business term*]	DISBS
Disbursing (AFM)	DSBG
Disbursing and Transportation Office	DATO
Disbursing Clerk [*Navy rating*]	DK
Disbursing Clerk, Chief [*Navy rating*]	DKC
Disbursing Clerk, First Class [*Navy rating*]	DK1
Disbursing Clerk, Master Chief [*Navy rating*]	DKCM
Disbursing Clerk, Second Class [*Navy rating*]	DK2
Disbursing Clerk, Senior Chief [*Navy rating*]	DKCS
Disbursing Clerk, Third Class [*Navy rating*]	DK3
Disbursing Office Serial Number	DOSN
Disbursing Officer [*Military*] (DNAB)	DISBO
Disbursing Officer	DISBOFF
Disbursing Officer	DO
Disbursing Officer Making Payment on These Orders Forward Copy [*Military*] (DNAB)	DISBOFFCOP
Disbursing Officer Making Payment Submit Monthly Letter Reports [*Military*] (DNAB)	DISBSUBREPT
Disbursing Officers Liaison Office	DOLO
Disbursing Officers' Relief Act [*1982*]	DORA
Disbursing Officer's Voucher	DOV
Disbursing Order	DO
Disbursing Station Symbol Number [*Military*] (AFM)	DSSN
Disc and Drum Input/Output Routines [*Honeywell, Inc.*]	DIPDOP
Disc Brake Wear Indicator [*Automotive engineering*]	DBWI
Disc Brakes [*Automotive engineering*]	DB
Disc Controller [*Computer science*] (HGAA)	DC
Disc Diameter (BABM)	DD
Disc File Controller [*Computer science*] (NITA)	DFC

Disc Graphics [*NASDAQ symbol*] (TTSB)	DSGR
Disc Graphics, Inc. [*AMEX symbol*] (SAG)	DGI
Disc Graphics, Inc. [*Associated Press*] (SAG)	DiscGph
Disc Graphics, Inc. [*Associated Press*] (SAG)	DscGph
Disc Graphics, Inc. [*NASDAQ symbol*] (SAG)	DSGR
Disc Graphics Wrrt [*NASDAQ symbol*] (TTSB)	DSGRW
Disc Grind [*Technical drawings*]	DG
Disc Harrowing [*Agriculture*]	DH
Disc Harrowing and Ridging [*Agriculture*]	DHR
DISC Inc. [*NASDAQ symbol*] (TTSB)	DCSR
DISC Inc. Wrrt [*NASDAQ symbol*] (TTSB)	DCSRW
Disc Issuer and Assistant [*Sports*]	D
Disc Jockey	DJ
Disc Jockey (WDMC)	dj
Disc Jockey Association (NTCM)	DJA
Disc Jockeys (Mobile) [*Public-performance tariff class*] [*British*]	DJ
Disc Plowing [*Agriculture*]	DP
Disc Ridge Splitting [*Agriculture*]	DR
Disc Storage Facility (NITA)	DSF
Disc Storage Terminal (NITA)	DST
Disc Support System (NITA)	DSS
Disc Turntable [*A record player*] (WDMC)	DT
Disc User Multi-Access Unit (NITA)	DUM
Disc Width [*Pisciculture*]	DW
Discalced Carmelite Fathers (TOCD)	OCD
Discalced Carmelite Friars (TOCD)	ocd
Discalced Carmelite Nuns [*Italy*] (EAIO)	DCN
Discalced Carmelite Nuns (TOCD)	OCD
Discard at Failure (MCD)	DAF
Discard Message (CET)	DM
Discard-at-Failure Maintenance (IEEE)	DAFM
Discard-Eligibility [*Computer science*]	DE
Discarding Rotating Band [*Military*] (CAAL)	DRB
Discarding Sabot [*Navy*]	DS
Discarding Sabot/Training [*British military*] (DMA)	DS/T
Discharge [*or Discharged*]	DC
Discharge	DIS
Discharge (AFM)	DISCH
Discharge (ROG)	DISCHE
Discharge Afloat	DA
Discharge and Advise [*Medicine*]	D/A
Discharge by Operator (DNAB)	DISOP
Discharge Certificate Mailed Subsequent to Separation [*Navy*] (DNAB)	DCMAILSUB
Discharge Certificate/Naval Reserve Appointment Mailed Subsequent to Separation [*Navy*] (DNAB)	DCRESMAILSUB
Discharge Certificate/Notification Mailed Subsequent to Separation [*Navy*] (DNAB)	DCNOTEMAILSUB
Discharge Flow [*Chemical kinetics*]	DF
Discharge Gratuity [*Military*]	DISGRAT
Discharge Ionization Detector	DID
Discharge Monitoring Report [*Environmental Protection Agency*] (EG)	DMR
Discharge Multimedia Environmental Goals [*Environmental Protection Agency*]	DMEG
Discharge Plan (MEDA)	DCP
Discharge Planning Coordinator [*Medicine*] (DMAA)	DPC
Discharge Readiness Inventory (MAE)	DRI
Discharge Ringing Frequency	DRF
Discharge Summary Dictated [*Medicine*] (DMAA)	DSD
Discharge Tomorrow [*Medicine*] (DMAA)	DT
Discharge Tube (IAA)	DT
Discharge [*from Military Service*] under Honorable Conditions, Convenience of Government	HCCG
Discharge [*from Military Service*] under Honorable Conditions, Convenience of Man	HCCM
Discharge [*from Military Service*] under Honorable Conditions, Dependency Existing Prior to Enlistment	HCDP
Discharge [*from Military Service*] under Honorable Conditions, Expiration of Enlistment	HCEE
Discharge [*from Military Service*] under Honorable Conditions, Medical Survey	HCMS
Discharge [*from Military Service*] under Honorable Conditions, Minor Enlisted Without Consent, under Eighteen at Time of Discharge	HCMW
Discharge [*from Military Service*] under Honorable Conditions, under Age ofAuthorized Enlistment	HCMU
Discharge [*from Military Service*] under Honorable Conditions, Unsuitable	HCUS
Discharged	D
Discharged [*Military*]	DISC
Discharged Dead [*On a serviceman's papers*]	DD
Discharged During Referral [*Medicine*] (MEDA)	DDR
Discharged on Own Recognizance (IIA)	DOR
Discharged on Visit [*Psychiatry*]	DOV
Discharged Patient [*British*]	DP
Discharged Prisoners' Aid [*British*]	DPA
Discharged Prisoners' Aid Society [*British*]	DPAS
Discharged Servicemen's Employment Board [*Victoria*] [*Australia*]	DSEB
Discharged to Sick Quarters	DSQ
Discharge-Line Air Temperature [*Nuclear energy*] (NRCH)	DLAT
Discharge-Line Length [*Nuclear energy*] (NRCH)	DLL
Discharge-Line Volume [*Nuclear energy*] (NRCH)	DLV
Discharge-Line Water-Leg Length [*Nuclear energy*] (NRCH)	DLWL
Discharging Resistor	DR
Disc-Indexed Sequential File Package [*Computer science*] (PDAA)	DISFP
Disciple	DIS

Disciple (ADA) ... DISC
Disciple ... DP
Disciples Ecumenical Consultative Council (EA) ... DECC
Disciples of Christ ... DC
Disciples of Christ Historical Society (EA) ... DCHS
Disciples of Christ Historical Society, Nashville, TN [*Library symbol Library of Congress*] (LCLS) ... TNDC
Disciples of the Divine Master [*Roman Catholic women's religious order*] ... PDDM
Disciples of the Lord Jesus Christ (TOCD) ... DLJC
Disciples Peace Fellowship (EA) ... DPF
Disciplinary (DSUE) ... DISCIP
Disciplinary ... DSPL
Disciplinary Action Notice (DNAB) ... DAN
Disciplinary Barracks ... DB
Disciplinary Control Board [*Air Force*] ... DCB
Disciplinary Training Center ... DTC
Discipline ... DIS
Discipline (WDAA) ... DISC
Discipline (AFM) ... DSPLN
Discipline Oriented Information Retrieval (NITA) ... DIR
Disclosure of Classified Military Information [*to foreign governments*] (AFM) ... DCMI
Disclosure Statement (AAGC) ... DS
Disclosure-Online [*Information service or system*] ... DSCLO
Disco S.A. ADS [*NYSE symbol*] (TTSB) ... DXO
Disco Vision Associates [*Videodisc manufacturer*] (NITA) ... DVA
Discoid Lupus Erythematosus [*Medicine*] ... DLE
Discolored ... Discol
Discolored Wood Columns [*Plant pathology*] ... DWC
Discomfiture Index [*Weather*] ... DI
Discomfort Relief Quotient [*Medicine*] (AAMN) ... DRQ
Discommensurate Model [*Physics*] ... DC
Discone (NASA) ... DISC
Discone Antenna ... DSC
Disconnect (NTCM) ... DC
Disconnect ... DCN
Disconnect (DEN) ... DIS
Disconnect (KSC) ... DISC
Disconnect (KSC) ... DISCON
Disconnect [*Disorderly Conduct*] (BARN) ... discort
Disconnect Actuating Tools [*Nuclear energy*] (NRCH) ... DAT
Disconnect and Make Busy [*Telecommunications*] (TEL) ... DMB
Disconnect at Lift-Off [*NASA*] (KSC) ... DALO
Disconnect, End of Transmission ... DEOT
Disconnect Switch (MSA) ... DS
Disconnected Mode [*Telecommunications*] ... DM
Disconnecting Device (MSA) ... DD
Disconnecting Manhole ... DM
Disconnection Pending [*Telecommunications*] (TEL) ... DP
Disconnector Trap ... DT
Discontinue ... DC
Discontinue (AFM) ... DISC
Discontinue ... DISCON
Discontinue (BUR) ... DS
Discontinue (MSA) ... DSCONT
Discontinue Previous Medication [*Pharmacology*] ... DPM
Discontinued ... DIS
Discontinued ... discontd
Discontinued [*Medicine*] (DAVI) ... Dxd
Discontinued Depreciation Function ... DDF
Discontinued Post Office [*Deltiology*] ... DPO
Discontinuity [*Geology*] (BARN) ... dis
Discontinuous Variational Method ... DVM
Discontinuously Reinforced Plastic ... DRP
Discophiles Francais [*Record label*] [*France*] ... DFr
Discotheque (DSUE) ... DISCO
Discount ... D
Discount ... DIS
Discount ... DISC
Discount (WDMC) ... disc
Discount ... DISC
Discount ... DISCT
Discount ... DIST
Discount [*Stock exchange*] [*British*] (ROG) ... DIX
Discount Auto Parts [*NYSE symbol*] (SPSG) ... DAP
Discount Auto Parts Co. [*Associated Press*] (SAG) ... DiscAut
Discount Communications Services [*Telecommunications service*] (TSSD) ... DCS
Discount Long Distance [*Larose, LA*] [*Telecommunications*] (TSSD) ... DLD
Discount Rate [*Banking*] ... DR
Discount Schedule and Marketing Data ... DSMD
Discounted Cash Equivalent (ADA) ... DCE
Discounted Cash Equivalent Flow (ADA) ... DCEF
Discounted Cash Flow ... DCF
Discounted Cash Flow Method ... DCFM
Discounted Cash Flow Rate of Return [*Business term*] ... DCFRR
Discounted Rate of Return [*Marketing*] (PDAA) ... DRR
Discounting Analysis Model for Investment Decisions (PDAA) ... DAMID
Discourse (ROG) ... DISC
Discourse Analysis Research Group [*University of Calgary*] [*Research center*] (RCD) ... DARG
Discourse Comprehension Abilities Test (EDAC) ... DCAT
Discover [*or Discoverer*] ... DISC
Discover America Travel Organizations, Inc. [*Later, TIA*] ... DATO
Discovered (ROG) ... DISCOVD
Discoverer Recovery Capsule [*NASA*] ... DRC
Discoverer Research Program [*NASA*] (IAA) ... DRP
DISCovering Careers and Jobs [*Database*] ... DCJ
Discovery (ROG) ... DISCOVY
Discovery (ROG) ... DISCOY
Discovery Activities Related to Science ... DART
Discovery Airlines [*ICAO designator*] (AD) ... DH
Discovery Airways [*ICAO designator*] (FAAC) ... DVA
Discovery Channel [*Cable television channel*] ... DISC
[*The*] **Discovery Channel** [*Television*] ... TDC
Discovery Channel Online [*Computer science*] ... DCOL
Discovery Gold Explorations Ltd. [*Vancouver Stock Exchange symbol*] ... DYG
Discovery Mines Ltd. [*Toronto Stock Exchange symbol*] ... DSM
Discovery [*or Dissemination*] **of Information through Cooperative Organization** ... DICO
Discovery Value Accounting (ADA) ... DVA
Discovery West Corp. [*Toronto Stock Exchange symbol*] ... DSW
Discovery Zone, Inc. [*Associated Press*] (SAG) ... DiscZone
Discovery Zone, Inc. [*NASDAQ symbol*] (SAG) ... ZONE
Discreet Logic [*NASDAQ symbol*] (TTSB) ... DSLGF
Discreet Logic, Inc. [*Associated Press*] (SAG) ... Discreet
Discreet Logic, Inc. [*NASDAQ symbol*] (SAG) ... DSLG
Discreet Operations Vehicle [*Military*] (LAIN) ... DOV
Discrepancy (GAVI) ... DISCR
Discrepancy (AABC) ... DISCRP
Discrepancy and Corrective Action Report ... DCAR
Discrepancy Check (KSC) ... DC
Discrepancy Check Request Memorandum (SAA) ... DCRM
Discrepancy Control Area (SAA) ... DCA
Discrepancy Identification and System Checkout (DNAB) ... DISC
Discrepancy in Shipment Cargo Outturn Reporting System [*DoD*] (DNAB) ... DISCORS
Discrepancy in Shipment Confirmation [*DoD*] ... DISCON
Discrepancy in Shipment Report [*DoD*] (AABC) ... DISREP
Discrepancy Notice [*NASA*] (NASA) ... DN
Discrepancy Record [*or Report*] (KSC) ... DR
Discrepancy Report ... DISCREP
Discrepancy Report Squawk [*NASA*] (SAA) ... DRS
Discrepancy Report Squawk Sheet [*NASA*] (NASA) ... DRSS
Discrepancy Reporting System [*NASA*] ... DRS
Discrepancy Tag ... DT
Discrepant Item - Ships Record ... DISR
Discrete (IAA) ... DC
Discrete (AAG) ... DIS
Discrete (KSC) ... DISC
Discrete Activity Indicator [*NASA*] (KSC) ... DAI
Discrete Address ... DA
Discrete Address Beacon System ... DABS
Discrete Address Beacon System with Intermittent Positive Control (PDAA) ... DABS-IPC
Discrete Address Communications System ... DACS
Discrete Analog Signal Processing ... DASP
Discrete Automatic Address System ... DAAS
Discrete Autoregressive-Moving Average Model [*Statistics*] ... DARMA
Discrete Command ... DC
Discrete Component Part ... DCP
Discrete Control Unit [*American Solenoid Co.*] [*Somerset, NJ*] ... DCU
Discrete Correlation Function [*Mathematics*] ... DCF
Discrete Cosine Transform [*Telecommunications*] ... DCT
Discrete Data Input (MCD) ... DDI
Discrete Data Management (MCD) ... DDM
Discrete Data Output (MCD) ... DDO
Discrete Depth Plankton Sampler ... DDPS
Discrete Depth Sampler ... DDS
Discrete Differential Dynamic Programming [*Computer science*] ... DDDP
Discrete Digital Input (NASA) ... DDI
Discrete Digital Output (MCD) ... DDO
Discrete Dipole Approximation [*Physics*] ... DDA
Discrete Elastic System ... DES
Discrete Event Evaluator (KSC) ... DEE
Discrete Fourier Transform ... DFT
Discrete Frequency Generator ... DFG
Discrete Hartley Transform (BYTE) ... DHT
Discrete Hilbert Transform (IEEE) ... DHT
Discrete Horizon Sensor (MCD) ... DHS
Discrete Increment Filter (NASA) ... DIF
Discrete Input [*Computer science*] (KSC) ... DI
Discrete Input High (MCD) ... DIH
Discrete Input Low (MCD) ... DIL
Discrete Integrated Circuit (IAA) ... DIC
Discrete Integrator (IAA) ... DISINT
Discrete Main Memory Unit [*Computer bus*] ... DMMU
Discrete Memoryless Channel [*Computer science*] ... DMC
Discrete Memoryless Source [*Computer science*] (HGAA) ... DMS
Discrete Metal-Oxide Semiconductor (HGAA) ... DMOS
Discrete Monitoring (MCD) ... DMON
Discrete Network Simulation ... DNS
Discrete Network Simulation ... DNWS
Discrete Ordinate Transport ... DOT
Discrete Orthonormal Sequence ... DOS
Discrete Out Blockhouse [*NASA*] (KSC) ... DOB
Discrete Out Vehicle [*NASA*] (KSC) ... DOV
Discrete Output [*Computer science*] (KSC) ... DO
Discrete Output High (MCD) ... DOH
Discrete Output Low (MCD) ... DOL
Discrete Phase Loop (IAA) ... DPL

Discrete Process Variable Measurement [*Process control*] ... DPVM
Discrete Rate Command (MCD) ... DRC
Discrete Recovery Area (KSC) ... DRA
Discrete Register (MCD) ... DR
Discrete Sample Analyzer ... DSA
Discrete Signal Interface Unit (DWSG) ... DSIU
Discrete Signal Moving Target Indicator ... DSMTI
Discrete Sine Transform (PDAA) ... DST
Discrete Sliding Fourier Transform (PDAA) ... DSFT
Discrete Sonic Jet ... DSJ
Discrete Source with Memory [*Computer science*] (HGAA) ... DSM
Discrete Space and Discrete Time ... DSDT
Discrete Subaortic Stenosis [*Medicine*] ... DSAS
Discrete System Concept ... DSC
Discrete Time Pulse Frequency Modulation (IAA) ... DPFM
Discrete Time Sample [*Medicine*] (MEDA) ... DTS
Discrete Timesystems, Inc. [*Toronto Stock Exchange symbol*] ... DSC
Discrete Variation Method ... DVM
Discrete Wavelet Transformation (DOM) ... DWT
Discretion ... DISCRON
Discretionary Access Control (CDE) ... DAC
Discretionary Account [*Investment term*] ... DA
Discretionary Capital Expenditure System [*Bell System*] ... DCES
Discretionary Credit Limit [*Business term*] (MHDB) ... DCL
Discretionary Population Effects for Riot and Stability Employment [*Crowd control*] ... DISPERSE
Discretionary Program (OICC) ... DP
Discriminant Analysis with Shrunken Coveriances [*Mathematics*] ... DASCO
Discriminant Function [*Physiology*] ... DF
Discriminate (AABC) ... DISCR
Discriminate (MUGU) ... DISCRM
Discriminate Function [*Physiology*] ... DIF
Discriminate Function Analysis ... DFAn
Discriminating Digit [*Telecommunications*] (TEL) ... DD
Discriminating Selector Repeater (DEN) ... DSR
Discriminating Stimulus [*Psychology*] (AEE) ... DS
Discrimination Acuity ... DA
Discrimination Analysis [*Agronomy*] ... DA
Discrimination Analysis Technique Adapted and Refined at Kwajalein [*Army*] (AABC) ... DARK
Discrimination and Control Computer (MUGU) ... DCC
Discrimination by Identification of Pictures [*Psychiatry*] (DAVI) ... DBIP
Discrimination Data Processing System (AABC) ... DDPS
Discrimination Difficulty [*Psychometrics*] ... DD
Discrimination Filter (AAG) ... DF
Discrimination RADAR ... DR
Discrimination RADAR Control Group (AAG) ... DRCG
Discrimination RADAR Transmitter (IAA) ... DRT
Discrimination Reversal [*Neurophysiology*] ... DR
Discriminative Avoidance Conditioning [*Biochemistry*] ... DAC
Discriminator (IAA) ... DISC
Discriminator (MSA) ... DSCRM
Discuriosities [*Record label*] ... Discur
Discussion Group on Information Technology in Library and Information Studies Schools (AIE) ... DIGITALIS
Discussion in Groups ... DIG
Discussion Paper ... DP
Discutient [*Dissolving*] [*Pharmacy*] (ROG) ... DIS
Disease ... D
Disease ... DIS
Disease (DAVI) ... DZ
Disease Activity Index [*Medicine*] ... DAI
Disease and Environmental Alert Report [*Army*] [*A publication*] (INF) ... DEAR
Disease and Nonbattle Injury [*Military*] (NVT) ... DNBI
Disease Detection Information Bureau [*Medicine*] (DMAA) ... DDIB
Disease Index [*Botany*] ... DI
Disease Intervention Specialist [*Medicine*] ... DIS
Disease Management ... DM
Disease Variable [*Medicine*] ... DV
Disease Vector Ecology and Control Center [*Military*] (NVT) ... DVECC
Disease-Controlling Antirheumatic Therapy [*Medicine*] ... DCART
Diseased Kidney [*Medicine*] (MAE) ... DK
Diseased Mucosa [*Oncology*] ... DM
Disease-Free Intervals ... DFI
Disease-Free Survival (MEDA) ... DFS
Disease-Modifying Antirheumatic Drug [*Medicine*] ... DMARD
Di-Secondary Octyl Phthalate (GFGA) ... DOP
Di-secondary-butyl Ether [*Organic chemistry*] ... DSBE
Disembark (AABC) ... DISEMB
Disengage ... DISENG
Disengaging ... DSENGA
Disequilibrium Syndrome [*Medicine*] ... DES
Disestablish ... DISESTAB
Disestablish (NVT) ... DISTAB
Disgruntled Old Graduate [*West Point*] ... DOG
Dishman, WA [*AM radio station call letters*] ... KEYF
Dishman, WA [*FM radio station call letters*] ... KWQL
Dishonest John [*In TV series "Time for Beany"*] ... DJ
Dishonorable (ADA) ... DISHON
Dishonorable Discharge ... DD
Dishonorable Discharge, General Court-Martial, after Confinement in Prison [*Navy*] ... DDGC
Dishonorable Discharge, General Court-Martial, after Violation of Probation [*Navy*] ... DDGP
Dishonorable Discharge, General Court-Martial, Immediate [*Navy*] ... DDGI
Dishonored (ROG) ... DISHOND
Dishonored Check [*IRS*] ... DC
Dishonored Check File [*IRS*] ... DCF
Dishonored Check Name File [*IRS*] ... DCNF
Dish-Rinsing ... DSHR
Dishwasher [*Classified advertising*] ... DW
Disillusioned, Overcharged, Outraged Buyers Explode [*Computer hacker's terminology*] (PCM) ... DOOBE
Disinfectants & Disinfection By-Products Rule (ACII) ... D/DBP
Disinfected Mail Study Circle (EA) ... DMSC
Disinfection By-Product [*Enviromental chemistry*] ... DBP
Disintegration ... DIS
Disintegrations per Hour ... DPH
Disintegrations per Minute ... D/M
Disintegrations per Minute ... D/MIN
Disintegrations per Minute ... DIS/MIN
Disintegrations per Minute ... DPM
Disintegrations per Minute (IDOE) ... dpm
Disintegrations per Minute/Second (DEN) ... DPM/S
Disintegrations per Second ... D/S
Disintegrations per Second ... DIS/S
Disintegrations per Second ... DIS/SEC
Disintegrations per Second ... DPS
Disjunctive (ROG) ... DISJ
Disjunctive [*Linguistics*] ... DISJUNCT
Disjunctive Normal Formula ... DNF
Disjunctive Syllogism [*Rule of inference*] [*Logic*] ... DS
Disjunctively Linear ... DL
Disk [*Computer science*] (IAA) ... DK
Disk [*Computer science*] ... DSK
Disk Allocation Table [*Computer science*] (IBMDP) ... DAT
Disk Automation Storage Control Hardware [*Macintosh computer*] ... DASCH
Disk Auxiliary Storage [*Computer science*] (ECII) ... DAS
Disk, Balls, and Roller ... DBR
Disk Buffer Area Access Method ... DBAAM
Disk Cartridge Initialization Program (CMD) ... DCIP
Disk Cartridge Unit [*Computer science*] (ECII) ... DCU
Disk Communications Area (CMD) ... DCOM
Disk Compare [*Computer science*] ... DISKCOMP
Disk Control Unit [*Computer science*] (IAA) ... DCU
Disk Controller [*Computer science*] (IEEE) ... DC
Disk Controller/Formatter [*Computer science*] ... DCF
Disk Copy Restore and Backup System ... DCRABS
Disk Core Image (CMD) ... DCI
Disk Data File Conversion Program [*IBM Corp.*] ... DFCNV
Disk Data Unit ... DDU
Disk Diameter [*Ophthalmology*] ... dd
Disk Direct Memory Access ... DDMA
Disk Drive Dry Cleaner (NITA) ... DDDC
Disk Electrophoresis ... DE
Disk File [*Computer science*] (BUR) ... DF
Disk File Check [*Computer science*] ... DFC
Disk File Control [*Computer science*] ... DFC
Disk File Control Unit [*Computer science*] ... DFCU
Disk File Descriptor Control [*Computer science*] ... DFDC
Disk File Electronics Unit [*Computer science*] ... DFEU
Disk File Interrogate [*Computer science*] ... DFI
Disk File Optimizer [*Computer science*] (BUR) ... DFO
Disk File Protection Table [*Computer science*] (IAA) ... DFPT
Disk File Read [*Computer science*] (OA) ... DFR
Disk File Storage Unit [*Computer science*] ... DFSU
Disk File Write [*Computer science*] (OA) ... DFW
Disk Gap Band [*Parachute*] ... DGB
Disk Interrogation Alternation and Loading (IAA) ... DIAL
Disk Island [*Alaska*] [*Seismograph station code, US Geological Survey*] (SEIS) ... DSK
Disk Management Facility [*Computer science*] ... DMF
Disk Memory Controller [*Computer science*] ... DMC
Disk Monitor [*Computer science*] (IAA) ... DM
Disk Monitor System [*Computer science*] ... DMS
Disk On-Line Accounts Receivable System [*Computer science*] (MHDB) ... DOLARS
Disk Operating Monitor [*Computer science*] ... DOM
Disk Operating System [*Computer science*] (IID) ... DOS
Disk Operating System - Enhanced [*Computer science*] (MCD) ... DOSE
Disk Operating System - Large Volumes [*Computer science*] ... DOS-LV
Disk Operating System - Module Tester [*Computer science*] (IAA) ... DMT
Disk Operating System - Small Volumes [*Computer science*] ... DOS-SV
Disk Operating System/Virtual Storage [*IBM Corp.*] [*Computer science*] (MCD) ... DOS/VS
Disk Pack [*Computer science*] (IEEE) ... DP
Disk Pack Controller [*Computer science*] (IAA) ... DPC
Disk Pack Handler [*Computer science*] (IAA) ... DPH
Disk Pack Unit [*Computer science*] ... DPU
Disk Preparation Processor [*Computer science*] ... DPREP
Disk Processing System (IAA) ... DPS
Disk Programming System [*IBM Corp.*] (IEEE) ... DPS
Disk Real-Time and Programming System [*Computer science*] ... DRPS
Disk Real-Time Monitor [*Computer science*] ... DRTM
Disk Recorder (DEN) ... DR
Disk Resident Operating System [*Computer science*] (IEEE) ... DROS
Disk Resident System [*Computer science*] (IAA) ... DRS
Disk Space Management [*Computer science*] ... DSM
Disk Storage [*Computer science*] (NASA) ... DS
Disk Storage Allocation Table (MCD) ... DSAT

Disk Storage Controller [*Computer science*] (CMD) .... DSC
Disk Storage Device [*Computer science*] .... DSD
Disk Storage Facility [*Computer science*] .... DSF
Disk Storage System [*or Subsystem*] [*Computer science*] (IAA) .... DSS
Disk Storage Unit [*Computer science*] (MSA) .... DSU
Disk System .... DS
Disk Tape [*Computer science*] (IEEE) .... D/T
Disk Technician [*Computer science*] .... DT
Disk to Card [*Computer science*] (IAA) .... DC
Disk to Printer (IAA) .... DP
Disk Transfer Area [*Computer science*] (BYTE) .... DTA
Disk Turbine Assembly .... DTA
Disk Unit (IAA) .... DU
Disk Utility Program [*IBM Corp.*] [*Computer science*] .... DUP
Disk-Based Operating System [*Computer science*] (IEEE) .... DBOS
Disk-Insulated Quad [*Telecommunications*] (TEL) .... DIQD
Disk-Oriented Computer System (IEEE) .... DOCS
Disk-Oriented Engineering System [*Computer science*] .... DOES
Disk-Oriented Supply System [*Computer science*] (DNAB) .... DOSS
Disk-to-Disk (IAA) .... DD
Dislocated Farmer [*Job Training and Partnership Act*] (OICC) .... DF
Dislocated Homemaker [*Job Training and Partnership Act*] (OICC) .... DH
Dislocated Worker [*Job Training and Partnership Act*] (OICC) .... DW
Dislocated Worker Center [*Job Training and Partnership Act*] (OICC) .... DWC
Dislocation (DAVI) .... dis
Dislocation (DAVI) .... Disl
Dislocation [*Medicine*] .... DISLOC
Dislocation Allowance [*Military*] (AFM) .... DA
Dislocation Allowance [*Military*] .... DLA
Dismantle (MSA) .... DISM
Dismiss (AABC) .... DISM
Dismissed [*Legal term*] (DLA) .... D
Dismissed [*Legal shorthand*] (LWAP) .... DISMD
Dismissed (MHDB) .... dsmd
Dismissed for Want of Bond [*Legal term*] (DLA) .... DWB
Dismissed for Want of Prosecution [*Legal term*] (DLA) .... DWP
Dismissed with Prejudice [*Legal shorthand*] (LWAP) .... DWP
Dismissed without Prejudice [*Legal shorthand*] (LWAP) .... DWOP
Dismounted .... DSMTD
Dismounted Battlespace Battle Lab [*Army*] (INF) .... DBBL
Dismounted Infantry Battle Space Battle Lab [*Army*] (RDA) .... DIBBL
Dismounted Marksmanship Test [*Military*] (INF) .... DMT
Dismounted Reconnaissance Team [*Army*] (INF) .... DRT
Dismounted Training Day [*Military*] (INF) .... DTD
Dismounted Warfighting Battle Laboratory (INF) .... DWBL
[*The*] **Disney** [*Walt*] **Co.** [*Wall Street slang name: "Mickey Mouse"*] [*NYSE symbol*] (SPSG) .... DIS
[*The*] **Disney** [*Walt*] **Co.** [*Wall Street slang name: "Mickey Mouse"*] [*Associated Press*] (SAG) .... Disney
Disney. Gaming [*1806*] [*A publication*] (DLA) .... Disn Gam
Disney Television [*Animated music video program*] [*Cable-television*] .... DTV
Disney's Ohio Superior Court Reports [*A publication*] (DLA) .... D
Disney's Ohio Superior Court Reports [*A publication*] (DLA) .... Dis
Disney's Ohio Superior Court Reports [*A publication*] (DLA) .... Disn (Ohio)
Disney's Superior Court of Cincinnati Reports [*Ohio*] [*A publication*] (DLA) .... Dis R
Disney's Superior Court of Cincinnati Reports [*Ohio*] [*A publication*] (DLA) .... Disn
Disodium .... DISOD
Disodium Cromoglycate [*Pharmacology*] (MAE) .... DCG
Disodium Cromoglycate [*Pharmacology*] .... DSC
Disodium Cromoglycate [*Pharmacology*] .... DSCG
Disodium Hydrophosphate [*Inorganic chemistry*] [*Also, DSP*] .... DSHP
Disodium Iminodiacetate [*Organic chemistry*] .... DID
Disodium Iminodiacetate [*Organic chemistry*] .... DSIDA
Disodium Methyl Arsonate [*Herbicide*] .... DSMA
Disodium Phosphate [*or Dibasic Sodium Phosphate*] [*Also, DSHP Inorganic chemistry*] .... DSP
Disodium Phosphoglycerate [*Organic chemistry*] .... DPG
Disopyramide Phosphate [*Cardiac depressant*] (AAMN) .... DP
Disorder (DAVI) .... D/O
Disorder of Initiating and Maintaining Sleep [*Medicine*] .... DIMS
Disordered Action of the Heart [*Medicine*] .... DAH
Disorderly [*FBI standardized term*] .... DIS
Disorderly Conduct .... DC
Disorderly House .... DH
Disorderly House [*Legal term*] (DLA) .... DISORD H
Disorderly Person .... DP
Disorders .... DSORDRS
Disorders of Excessive Somnolence [*Medicine*] (MEDA) .... DOES
Disparity Reduction Rate [*Measures progress a country has made toward reconciling its current Physical Quality of Life Index with its optimum projected PQLI for the year 2000*] [*Overseas Development Council*] .... DRR
Dispatch .... DISP
Dispatch (AABC) .... DSPCH
Dispatch Critical System (MCD) .... DCS
Dispatch Discharging Only [*Shipping*] (DS) .... DDO
Dispatch Inoperative List (MCD) .... DIL
Dispatch Loading Only .... DLO
Dispatch, New Providence, NJ [*Library symbol Library of Congress*] (LCLS) .... NjNpD
Dispatch News Service (IIA) .... DNS
Dispatch Note [*Shipping*] .... D/N
Dispatch Payable Both Ends [*Shipping*] (DS) .... DBE
Dispatch Payable Both Ends All Time Saved [*Shipping*] (DS) .... DBEATS
Dispatch Payable Both Ends on Laytime Saved [*Shipping*] (DS) .... DBELTS
Dispatch Point .... DP
Dispatch Reliability (NASA) .... DR
Dispatch Rider [*Marine Corps*] .... D/R
Dispatch Services, Inc. [*ICAO designator*] (FAAC) .... XDS
Dispatch, Union City, NJ [*Library symbol Library of Congress*] (LCLS) .... NjUcD
Dispatcher (MSA) .... DISP
Dispatcher .... DISPR
Dispensary (AFM) .... DISP
Dispensary (ADA) .... DISPENS
Dispensary (DNAB) .... DSP
Dispensary .... DSPN
Dispensation .... DISP
Dispensatory (DAVI) .... disp
Dispense as Directed [*Medicine*] (MEDA) .... DA
Dispense as Directed [*Pharmacy*] .... DAD
Dispense as Written [*Prescription cannot be filled using a generic equivalent*] [*Pharmacy*] .... DAW
Dispensed (ADA) .... DIS
Dispenser (MCD) .... D
Dispenser [*Unit of issue*] [*Military*] (DNAB) .... DI
Dispenser .... DISP
Dispenser [*Technical drawings*] .... DPR
Dispenser Control Unit (RDA) .... DCU
Dispensetur [*Dispense*] [*Pharmacy*] .... DISP
Dispensing .... DISPNSG
Dispensing .... DSPNSG
Dispensing Allowance [*British military*] (DMA) .... DA
Dispensing Opticians Manufacturing Organisation [*British*] (BI) .... DOMO
Dispensing Precaution .... DP
Dispensing Tablet [*Medicine*] (DMAA) .... DT
Dispersal (FAAC) .... DSPRL
Dispersal Anchorage [*Navy*] (NVT) .... DSA
Dispersal Base [*Military*] (AFM) .... DB
Dispersal Point .... DP
Disperse .... DISP
Dispersed Electro-Magnetic Pulse (PDAA) .... DEMP
Dispersed Emergency Station (NATG) .... DES
Dispersed Emission [*Spectroscopy*] .... DE
Dispersed Human Parathyroid Cell [*Clinical chemistry*] .... dPTC
Dispersed Operating Base [*Air Force*] (AFM) .... DOB
Dispersed Organic Matter [*Chemistry*] .... DOM
Dispersed Phase (OA) .... DP
Dispersed Phase Hold Up [*Chemical engineering*] .... DPHU
Dispersion (WDAA) .... DISP
Dispersion (VRA) .... disp
Dispersion Against Concealed Targets [*Experiment*] [*Army*] (RDA) .... DACTS
Dispersion Coated Fabric [*Plastics technology*] .... DCF
Dispersion Coefficient .... DC
Dispersion Flattened Single Mode (IAA) .... DFSM
Dispersion Measure [*Astronomy*] .... DM
Dispersion Staining [*Analytical chemistry*] .... DS
Dispersion Strengthened [*Metallurgy*] .... DS
Dispersion Time (NATG) .... DT
Dispersive Delay Line .... DDL
Dispersive Fourier Spectroscopy (PDAA) .... DFS
Dispersive Fourier Transform Spectroscopy (MCD) .... DFTS
Dispersive Infrared [*Automotive engineering*] .... DIR
Dispersive Mechanism Test (NRCH) .... DMT
Dispersive Surface Acoustic Wave (MCD) .... DSAW
Dispersive Ultraviolet [*Automotive engineering*] .... DUV
Displace (FAAC) .... DSPLC
Displaced .... DSPLCD
Displaced Business Loan [*Small Business Administration*] .... DBL
Displaced Civilian [*Military*] (INF) .... DC
Displaced Cosine Pulse Function (IAA) .... DCPF
Displaced Employee Program [*Department of Labor*] .... DEP
Displaced Equipment Training [*DoD*] .... DET
Displaced Equipment Training Plan [*DoD*] .... DETP
Displaced Homemakers Network (EA) .... DHN
Displaced Person [*Post-World War II*] .... DP
Displaced Personnel [*Military*] .... DP
Displaced Persons Assembly Center Camp Staffs [*Allied Military Government of Occupied Territory*] [*Post-World War II*] .... DPACCS
Displaced Persons' Camps .... DPC
Displaced Persons Commission [*Terminated, 1952*] .... DPC
Displaced Persons Executive [*Allied Military Government detachments, Red Cross teams, and UN Relief and Rehabilitation Administration Corps*] [*Post-World War II*] .... DPX
Displaced Phase Center Antenna .... DPCA
Displaced System Support Item Identification .... DSSII
Displaced Virtual Machine .... DVM
Displaced Worker Program (OICC) .... DWP
Displacement .... D
Displacement .... DISP
Displacement (AAG) .... DISPL
Displacement .... DP
Displacement [*Physics*] (BARN) .... S
Displacement Cardiograph [*Medicine*] .... DCG
Displacement Contour Analyzer (MCD) .... DCA
Displacement Ducted Vessel [*Marine architecture*] .... DDV
Displacement Gyro [*Aerospace*] .... DG
Displacement Loop [*Genetics*] (DOG) .... D loop
Displacement Method Matrix Generator .... DMMG
Displacement Placentogram [*Medicine*] (MAE) .... DPG

Displacement to Length [*Ratio*] .... D/L
Displacement ton (BARN) .... DT
Displacement Transducer (KSC) .... DT
Displacement Water Line .... DWL
Displacement-Oriented Transducer .... DOT
Displacements per Atom (MCD) .... DPA
Display (MDG) .... D
Display (KSC) .... DIS
Display (KSC) .... DISP
Display .... DSPL
Display (IAA) .... DSPLY
Display .... DSPLY
Display (GAVI) .... DSPY
Display Adapter .... DA
Display Adjust Panel (MCD) .... DAP
Display/AGAP [*Attitude Gyro Accelerometer Package*] **Electronic Control Assembly** (KSC) .... DECA
Display Aided Maintenance [*Army*] .... DAM
Display Aided Maintenance Control System [*Army*] .... DAMCS
Display Analysis Console .... DAC
Display and Command Unit [*Military*] .... DCU
Display and Control (KSC) .... D & C
Display and Control Module (MCD) .... DCM
Display and Control Station .... DCS
Display and Control/Storage and Retrieval .... DC/SR
Display and Control Subsystem (NASA) .... D & CS
Display and Control Unit (CET) .... DCU
Display and Controls Input Processor .... DCIP
Display and Debriefing Subsystem (MCD) .... DDS
Display and Debug Unit [*Computer science*] (MDG) .... DDU
Display and Decision Area .... DDA
Display and Information Distribution System [*or Subsystem*] (MCD) .... DISIDS
Display and Keyboard [*Computer science*] .... DSKY
Display and Multi-Purpose Processor [*Computer science*] .... DMPP
Display and Sight Helmet System (MCD) .... DASH
Display and Storage (MSA) .... D & S
Display and Weapon Control (DNAB) .... DWC
Display Arrangement Bits (NITA) .... DAB
Display Assembly Unit (MCD) .... DAU
Display Assignment BITS [*Binary Digits*] .... DAB
Display Attention BITS [*Binary Digits*] [*Computer science*] .... DAB
Display Automated Telemetry Analyzer (MCD) .... DATA
Display Blocks Configuration [*Computer science*] (ECII) .... DBC
Display Buffer [*Computer science*] .... DB
Display Channel Complex [*FAA*] (TAG) .... DCC
Display Code .... DC
Display Compartments [*Freight*] .... DC
Display Computer .... DC
Display Computer Control Unit (MCD) .... DCCU
Display Console (KSC) .... DC
Display Control Console (KSC) .... DCC
Display Control Interface [*Computer science*] (PCM) .... DCI
Display Control Panel .... DCP
Display Control Program (NTCM) .... DCP
Display Coupler (MCD) .... DC
Display Crosstell Zone (SAA) .... DXTZ
Display Data Channel [*Computer science*] (PCM) .... DDC
Display Data Channel (PCM) DDC1
Display Data Controller (IAA) .... DDC
Display Decoder Drive (MCD) .... DDD
Display Driver .... DD
Display Driver Unit (NASA) .... DDU
Display Electronics (KSC) .... DE
Display Electronics Assemblies (KSC) .... DEA
Display Electronics Unit (NASA) .... DEU
Display Element .... DE
Display Equipment .... DE
Display Evaluation Flight Testing (MCD) .... DEFT
Display Evaluation Index .... DEI
Display Exercise for Battle Staff (SAA) .... DEBS
Display Format Facility .... DFF
Display Format Generator (MCD) .... DFG
Display Formatting Language .... DFL
Display Formatting System .... DFS
Display Generation System .... DGS
Display Generator (NASA) .... DG
Display Generator Unit (DNAB) .... DGU
Display Hold .... DH
Display Image Manipulation (IAA) .... DIM
Display Information Facility (CDE) .... DIF
Display Information Processor [*Air Force*] .... DIP
Display Initial Program Load (MCD) .... DIPL
Display Input Processor (NASA) .... DIP
Display Integrated Software System and Plotting Language [*Computer science*] .... DISSPLA
Display Interaction Enhancing Computer-Aided Shape Technique (PDAA) .... DIECAST
Display Interactive Assembly Language [*Computer science*] (IEEE) .... DIAL
Display Interface (NASA) .... DI
Display Interface Computer System (MCD) .... DICS
Display Interface Device [*Telecommunications*] (TEL) .... DID
Display Interface Processing (MCD) .... DIP
Display/Keyboard [*Computer science*] (MCD) .... DK
Display Language [*Computer science*] (MHDB) .... DISLAN
Display List Driver [*Computer science*] (PCM) .... DLD
Display Logic Unit .... DLU
Display Maintenance Program .... DMP
Display Makeup (IAA) .... DMP
Display Management System [*IBM Corp.*] .... DMS
Display Monitor and Control Unit .... DMCU
Display Octal Debugging Technique .... DODT
Display of Chromosome Statistics System .... DOCSYS
Display of Extracted RADAR Data (DA) .... DERD
Display of Synoptic Data .... DISYNDA
Display, Oral, Printed, and Electronic [*Media*] .... DOPE
Display Oriented Macro Expander [*Computer science*] (PDAA) .... DOMEX
Display Package .... DP
Display Panel .... DP
Display Power Control .... DPC
Display Power Management Signaling [*Computer science*] (PCM) .... DPMS
Display Power Management Support [*Computer science*] (PCM) .... DPMS
Display Power Supply .... DPS
Display Presentation Subsystem (IAA) .... DPSS
Display Processor .... DP
Display Processor Code .... DPC
Display Processor Program (MCD) .... DPP
Display Processor Unit (IAA) .... DPU
Display Producers' and Screen Printers' Association (DGA) .... DP & SPA
Display Racks [*Freight*] .... DR
Display Random Access Memory [*Computer science*] (IAA) .... DRAM
Display Request Keyboard (KSC) .... DRK
Display Result .... DR
Display Retrieval and Formatting Technique (MCD) .... DRAFT
Display Screen .... DS
Display Section .... DS
Display Select Computer Input Multiplexer (MCD) .... DSCIM
Display Simulation Program .... DSP
Display Started (IAA) .... DS
Display Station (IAA) .... DS
Display Storage Tube (CET) .... DST
Display Subsystem (MCD) .... DS
Display Support Unit (MCD) .... DSU
Display Switching Oscilloscope .... DSO
Display System Computer Input Multiplexer (MCD) .... DCIM
Display System Computer Input Multiplexer [*NASA*] (NASA) .... DSCIM
Display System Protocol [*Telecommunications*] (ACRL) .... DSP
Display System Replacement [*FAA*] (TAG) .... DSR
Display Technologies, Inc. (PCM) .... DTI
Display Terminal (IAA) .... DT
Display Terminal Interchange .... DTI
Display Terminal Unit (CMD) .... DTU
Display Test Chamber .... DTC
Display Timing Control .... DTC
Display Translator (MCD) .... DT
Display Translator Program (MCD) .... DTP
Display Transmission Generator .... DTG
Display Unit (NASA) .... DU
Display Unit Control System (IAA) .... DUCS
Display Unit Test Assembly (MCD) .... DUTA
Display, Upper .... DU
Display Write [*Software*] .... DW
Displayed Composition [*Graphic arts*] (DGA) .... DISP
Displayed Data Video Recorder .... DDTA
Displayed Impact Line (MCD) .... DIL
Displayed Impact Point (MCD) .... DIP
Displayed under Program Control .... DUPC
Display-List Processor [*Computer science*] .... DLP
Display-Oriented Computer Usage System .... DOCUS
Display-Oriented Language [*Computer science*] (IEEE) .... DOL
Displays, Controls, and Operation Procedures (NASA) .... DCOP
Disposable Absorption Collection Trunk (MCD) .... DACT
Disposable Baby Napkin Manufacturers Association [*British*] (DBA) .... DBNMA
Disposable Barrel Cartridge Area Target Ammunition [*Weapon launcher*] .... DBCATA
Disposable Extraction Column .... DEC
Disposable Hypodermic and Allied Equipment Manufacturers Association of Europe (EAIO) .... DHAEMAE
Disposable Personal Income .... DPI
Disposable Plotter Pen [*Koh-I-Noor Rapidograph, Inc.*] .... DPP
Disposable Seismic Intrusion Detector (MCD) .... DSID
Disposable Tape Reel [*Computer science*] .... DTR
[*The*] **Disposables Association** .... TDA
Disposal .... DISP
Disposal .... DSPL
Disposal .... DSPSL
Disposal Accounting Management System [*DoD*] .... DAMS
Disposal Analysis Network for New York [*U.S. Army Corps of Engineers*] .... DAN-NY
Disposal and Collection User Simulation (PDAA) .... DISCUS
Disposal Area Monitoring System .... DAMOS
Disposal from an Instantaneous Dump [*US Army Corps of Engineers*] .... DIFID
Disposal List Ship Unit Portsmouth [*Navy British*] .... DILSUP
Disposal Notification Area [*Community Land Act*] [*British*] (DI) .... DNA
Disposal Rate [*Of hormone metabolism*] .... DR
Disposal Regional Inventory File [*Military*] (AFIT) .... DRIF
Disposal Release Order [*DoD*] .... DRO
Disposal Turn-In Document [*Military*] .... DTID
Disposal Unit (DAC) .... DU
Dispose [*or Destroy*] [*Routing slip*] .... D
Dispose (AABC) .... DSPO

Disposite d'Aide a la Designation d'Objectif [*Target Designation Aid System*] [*French*] ... DALDO
Disposition (MSA) ... DISPN
Disposition (DAVI) ... dispo
Disposition (ROG) ... DISPOSN
Disposition (AFM) ... DSPN
Disposition and Findings (AAG) ... D & F
Disposition Form [*Army*] ... DF
Disposition Instructions ... DI
Disposition of Contract Request (SAA) ... DCR
Disposition of Inactive Parts List ... DIP
Disposition of Surplus Highly Enriched Uranium Environmental Impact Statement ... HEU EIS
Disposition of Vessel by Department of the Interior (DNAB) ... DI/INT
Disposition of Vessel by Scrapping (DNAB) ... DI/SCP
Disposition One Only (MCD) ... DOO
Disposition Pennant [*Navy British*] ... DN
Disposition Record (NASA) ... DR
Disposition Record Unsatisfactory Condition (MCD) ... DRUC
Disproportionation ... DISP
Disputation between Bird and Fish (BJA) ... BF
Disqualification Not Discardable [*Yacht racing*] (IYR) ... DND
Disqualified [*Horse racing*] ... D
Disqualified ... DQ
Disqualified [*Racing*] (IYR) ... DSQ
Disqualify (AABC) ... DISQUAL
Disque pour l'Analyse Economique (IID) ... DIANE
Disquisition (ROG) ... DISQ
Disregard (AABC) ... DISRE
Disregard (FAAC) ... DSRGD
Disregard Previous Assignment Instructions and Assign as Indicated [*Army*] (AABC) ... DPAIAI
Disrotatory [*Chemistry*] ... DIS
Disruption Zone [*Military*] (INF) ... DZ
Disruptive Pattern Material [*British military*] (DMA) ... DPM
Dissatisfied Parents Together (EA) ... DPT
Dissatisfied Peugeot Owners of America (EA) ... DPOA
Dissaying [*Slang*] (WDMC) ... dis
Dissector Camera Tube ... DCT
Dissemin/Action [*Defunct*] (EA) ... D/A
Disseminate (AABC) ... DISEM
Disseminated ... DISSEM
Disseminated Cryptococcus Neoformans Infection [*Medicine*] ... DCI
Disseminated Foci [*Medicine*] ... DF
Disseminated Gonococcal Infection [*Clinical chemistry*] ... DGI
Disseminated Histoplasmosis [*Medicine*] ... DH
Disseminated Idiopathic Skeletal Hyperostosis [*Medicine*] (DAVI) ... DISH
Disseminated Intravascular Blood Coagulation [*Medicine*] (DMAA) ... DIVBC
Disseminated Intravascular Coagulation [*Hematology*] (DAVI) ... D/C
Disseminated Intravascular Coagulation [*Hematology*] ... DIC
Disseminated Intravascular Coagulation [*Medicine*] (BARN) ... DIS
Disseminated Lupus Erythematosus [*Hematology*] ... DLE
Disseminated Mycobacterium Avium Complex [*Medicine*] ... DMAC
Disseminated Nontuberculous Mycobacterial Infection ... DNTM
Disseminated Sclerosis [*Medicine*] ... DS
Disseminated Superficial Actinic Porokeratosis [*Medicine*] (MAE) ... DSAP
Dissemination Capacity Building Project (EDAC) ... DCBP
Dissemination Network for Adult Educators (EDAC) ... DNAE
Dissent [*A publication*] (BRI) ... Dis
Dissenter ... DISS
Dissenting Opinion [*Legal term*] (DLA) ... Dis Op
Dissenting Opinion Citation in Dissenting Opinion [*Used in Shepard's Citations*] [*Legal term*] (DLA) ... j
Dissertation (BJA) ... D
Dissertation ... DISS
Dissertation ... DISSERT
Dissertation Inquiry Service [*Xerox Corp.*] ... DIS
Dissertationes ad Historiam Religionum Pertinentes [*A publication*] (BJA) ... DissadHRP
Dissertations on Chemical Oceanography ... DISCO
Dissimilar Air Combat Maneuvers ... DACM
Dissimilar Air Combat Tactics [*Navy*] (MCD) ... DACT
Dissimilar Air Combat Training (MCD) ... DACT
Dissimilarity Coefficient [*Numerical taxonomy*] ... DC
Dissimilar-Metal Weld ... DMW
Dissimulation [*Psychology*] ... Ds
Dissipate [*NWS*] (FAAC) ... DSIPT
Dissipation (IAA) ... D
Dissipation (IDOE) ... d
Dissipation ... DISSIP
Dissipation Factor ... DF
Dissociate ... DISSOC
Dissociated Double Hypertropia [*Ophthalmology*] ... DDH
Dissociated Vertical Deviation [*Ophthalmology*] ... DVD
Dissociated Vertical Divergence [*Ophthalmology*] (DAVI) ... DVD
Dissociated Zircon (PDAA) ... DZ
Dissociation Constant [*Physics*] (DAVI) ... K_d
Dissociation Constant [*Chemistry*] (DAVI) ... pK
Dissociation Constant of Water [*Physics*] (DAVI) ... K_w
Dissociation Enhanced Lanthanide Fluoroimmunoassay [*Clinical chemistry*] ... DELFIA
Dissociative Recombination [*Chemistry*] ... DR
Dissociative Return Electron Transfer ... DRET
Dissociative Surface Ionization [*Organic chemistry*] ... DSI
Dissociator [*Genetics*] ... DS
Dissolution Inhibitor Solubilizable by Chemical Amplification [*Chemistry*] ... DISCA
Dissolution of Acetaminophen [*Clinical chemistry*] ... DISACET
Dissolution Patterns [*Physics*] ... DP
Dissolve (NTCM) ... D
Dissolve [*Optical technique*] [*Filmmaking*] (WDMC) ... DIS
Dissolve ... DISS
Dissolve (NTCM) ... DIZ
Dissolved ... Dis
Dissolved ... DISLVD
Dissolved ... dissd
Dissolved (NVT) ... DSLV
Dissolved Acetylene ... DA
Dissolved Adenosine Triphosphate [*Oceanography*] ... DATP
Dissolved Air Flotation ... DAF
Dissolved Combined Amino Acid [*Marine biology*] ... DCAA
Dissolved Free Amino Acids ... DFAA
Dissolved Gaseous Mercury [*Environmental chemistry*] ... DGM
Dissolved Inorganic Carbon [*Also, DIOC*] ... DIC
Dissolved Inorganic Carbon [*Also, DIC*] ... DIOC
Dissolved Inorganic Nitrogen [*Chemistry*] ... DIN
Dissolved Inorganic Phosphorus [*Chemistry*] ... DIP
Dissolved Manganese [*Chemistry*] ... DMn
Dissolved Organic Carbon ... DOC
Dissolved Organic Matter ... DOM
Dissolved Organic Nitrogen [*Analytical chemistry*] ... DON
Dissolved Organic Phosphorus ... DOP
Dissolved Oxygen ... DO
Dissolved Oxygen Analyzer (DNAB) ... DOA
Dissolved Oxygen Deficit [*Water pollution*] ... DOD
Dissolved Oxygen Electrode ... DOE
Dissolved Oxygen Tension [*Chemistry*] ... DOT
Dissolved Reactive Phosphorus [*Environmental science*] ... DRP
Dissolved Reactive Silica [*Environmental science*] ... DRS
Dissolved Solids ... DS
Dissolved Transport Index [*Geochemistry*] ... DTI
Dissolved Water Color [*Environmental chemistry*] ... DWC
Dissolver Off-Gas [*Nuclear energy*] (NRCH) ... DOG
DISSOS [*Distributed Office Support System*] **Document Exchange Facility** [*IBM Corp.*] (NITA) ... DDXF
Distal [*Medicine*] ... D
Distal [*Medicine*] ... Di
Distal [*Medicine*] ... DIST
Distal Accessory Flexor Muscle [*of a lobster*] ... DAFM
Distal Articular Set Angle [*Orthopedics*] (DAVI) ... DASA
Distal Convoluted Tubule [*Nephrology*] ... DCT
Distal Effective Potassium Secretion [*Medicine*] (DMAA) ... DEPS
Distal Femoral Epiphysis [*Orthopedics*] (DAVI) ... DFE
Distal Interphalangeal [*Joints*] [*Anatomy*] (DAVI) ... D/P
Distal Interphalangeal [*Joint*] [*Anatomy*] ... DIP
Distal Interphalangeal Joint [*Anatomy*] ... DIPJ
Distal Main Pulmonary Artery [*Anatomy*] ... DMPA
Distal Muscular Dystrophy [*Medicine*] ... DisMD
Distal Over-Shoulder Strap ... DOSS
Distal Palmar Crease [*Anatomy*] ... DPC
Distal Pancreatectomy [*Medicine*] (AAMN) ... DP
Distal Radioulnar Joint [*Anatomy*] ... DRUJ
Distal Sequence Element [*Genetics*] ... DSE
Distal Splenorenal Shunt [*Medicine*] ... DSRS
Distal Subungual Onychomyosis ... DSO
Distal Tingling on Percussion [*Medicine*] ... DTP
Distance ... D
Distance (IDOE) ... d
Distance (IAA) ... DC
Distance (MUGU) ... DIS
Distance [*or Distant*] (AFM) ... DIST
Distance (WDMC) ... dist
Distance (FAAC) ... DSTC
Distance [*Radio term*] (EA) ... DX
Distance (DAVI) ... s
Distance Aids School (SAA) ... DAS
Distance Amplitude Correction (OA) ... DAC
Distance and Angularity Measurement Equipment [*Navy*] (MCD) ... DAME
Distance at Which a Watch Is Heard with Left Ear [*Medicine*] ... HDLW
Distance at Which a Watch Is Heard with Right Ear [*Medicine*] ... HDRW
Distance Azimuth Measuring Equipment [*Navy*] (MCD) ... DAME
Distance between Iliac Spines [*Anatomy*] (DAVI) ... ISP
Distance between Shaft Ends [*Mechanical engineering*] ... DBSE
Distance Education and Training Counsel [*Formerly National Home Study Council (NHSC)*] (PAZ) ... DETC
Distance Education Research Centre Library, Alberta Correspondence School, Barrhead, Alberta [*Library symbol National Library of Canada*] (BIB) ... ABACS
Distance Finding Station ... DFS
Distance - Force - Resistance [*Instrumentation*] ... DFR
Distance from Threshold Indicator (PDAA) ... DFTI
Distance from Touchdown Indicator [*Aviation*] (DA) ... DFTI
Distance in Error ... DIE
Distance Indicating Automatic Navigation Equipment ... DIANE
Distance Instruction for Adult Learning [*New School for Social Research, New York*] ... DIAL
Distance Learning Project [*Joint program of the Center for Talented Youth (Johns Hopkins University) and the Education Program for Gifted Youth (Stanford University)*] (PAZ) ... DLP
Distance Least-Squares [*Mathematics*] ... DLS

Distance Measuring Equipment [*Navigation*] .... DME
Distance Measuring Equipment [*Ground navigational aid that can provide display of distance to selected ground navigational radio transmitter*] (GAVI) .... DME
Distance Measuring Equipment Collocated With Glide Slope [*Aviation*] (FAAC) .... DMEG
Distance Measuring Equipment Collocated With Localizer [*Aviation*] (FAAC) .... DMEL
Distance Measuring Equipment Command and Navigation .... DECAN
Distance Measuring Equipment/Correlation Tracking and Ranging .... DME/COTAR
Distance Measuring Equipment TACAN [*Tactical Air Navigation*] (NG) .... DMET
Distance Measuring Equipment Tactical Air Navigation With DME Only Commissioned [*Aviation*] (FAAC) .... DMER
Distance Measuring Equipment Terminal (CET) .... DMET
Distance Measuring Instrument .... DMI
Distance Measuring System .... DMS
Distance Monitoring Equipment [*Military*] .... DME
Distance Root Mean Square (FAAC) .... DRMS
Distance Runners Club of South Australia .... DRCSA
Distance Test .... DT
Distance to Empty [*Automotive driver information display*] .... DTE
Distance to Nearest Male Plant [*Botany*] .... DNM
Distance University Education via Television [*Mount Saint Vincent University*] [*Halifax, NS*] [*Telecommunications service*] (TSSD) .... DUET
Distance Velocity Laboratory .... DVL
Distance Visual Acuity [*Ophthalmology*] .... DVA
Distance Winner [*Horse racing*] .... D
Distanced [*Horse racing*] .... DIS
Distanced [*Horse racing*] .... DIST
Distance-Measuring Unit (IAA) .... DMU
Distance-to-Go (GAVI) .... DTG
Distant .... DIS
Distant (VRA) .... dist
Distant (WDMC) .... dist
Distant (IAA) .... DS
Distant Aiming Point .... DAP
Distant Area Reduced Toll [*Telecommunications*] (TSSD) .... DART
Distant Central Office Transceivers .... DCOT
Distant Deployment (DNAB) .... DISDEP
Distant Early Warning [*North American RADAR system*] [*Obsolete*] .... DEW
Distant Early Warning Identification Zone [*North American RADAR system*] [*Obsolete*] .... DEWIZ
Distant Early Warning Line [*North American RADAR system*] [*Obsolete*] .... DEW LINE
Distant Early Warning Project Office [*North American RADAR System*] [*Obsolete*] (IAA) .... DEWPO
Distant Early Warning Summary (MCD) .... DEWSUM
Distant Electric Control (IAA) .... DEC
Distant Element (MDG) .... DE
Distant End Cross-Talk [*Telecommunications*] (NITA) .... DEXT
Distant End Disconnect [*Telecommunications*] (TEL) .... DED
Distant Object Attitude Measuring System (MCD) .... DOAMS
Distant Range .... DR
Distant Reading (IAA) .... DR
Distant Reading Compass .... DRC
Distant Reception (IAA) .... DR
Distant Remote Transceiver (IAA) .... DRT
Distant Space Radio Center (IAA) .... DSRC
Distant Station Connected [*Computer science*] (BUR) .... DSC
Distant Surveillance .... DS
Distant Transmission (IAA) .... DT
Distant-Control Boat .... DCB
Distearoyl Phosphatidylcholine [*Biochemistry*] .... DSPC
Distearyl Thiodipropionate [*Organic chemistry*] .... DSTDP
Distemper (VRA) .... temp
Distemper Virus .... DV
Distending Pressure .... DP
Distill .... DSTL
Distilla [*Distill*] [*Pharmacy*] (ROG) .... DIST
Distillate .... Dist
Distillate .... DSTLT
Distillate Assistance/Advisory Team [*Military*] (DNAB) .... DAT
Distillate Burner Manufacturers Association (EA) .... DBMA
Distillate plus Loss .... D & L
Distillation [*Calorimetry*] .... DI
Distillation .... DISTN
Distillation Desalination System .... DDS
Distilled [*or Distillery*] .... DIST
Distilled .... DISTD
Distilled .... DSTLD
Distilled Deionized [*Chemistry*] .... DDI
Distilled Fuel Oil .... DFO
Distilled Oil of Vitriol .... DOV
Distilled Spirits Council of the United States (EA) .... DISCUS
Distilled Spirits Industry Council of Australia .... DSICA
Distilled Spirits Institute [*Later, DISCUS*] (EA) .... DSI
Distilled Spirits Plant .... DSP
Distilled Water [*Pharmacology*] (DAVI) .... Aq Dist
Distilled Water .... DW
Distiller .... DISTLR
Distiller and Rectifier .... D & R
Distillers Dried Grain .... DDG
Distillers' Dried Grain with Solubles [*Feedstuff*] .... DDGS
Distillers Dried Solubles (OA) .... DDS
Distillers Feed Research Council (EA) .... DFRC
Distillery .... DISTLLRY
Distillery, Rectifying, Wine, and Allied Workers International Union of America [*Later, DWAW*] (EA) .... DRWAW
Distillery, Wine, and Allied Workers International Union (EA) .... DWAW
Distillery, Wine, and Allied Workers International Union .... DWW
Distillery, Wine, and Allied Workers Union (BARN) .... DWU
Distilling Ship [*Navy symbol*] .... AW
Distinctio [*Decretum Gratiani*] [*A publication*] (DSA) .... D
Distinctio [*Decretum Gratiani*] [*A publication*] (DSA) .... Di
Distinctio [*Decretum Gratiani*] [*A publication*] (DSA) .... Dis
Distinctio [*Decretum Gratiani*] [*A publication*] (DSA) .... Dist
Distinction .... D
Distinction (ROG) .... DIST
Distinctive .... DISTNCTV
Distinctive Insignia [*Military*] .... DI
Distinctive Ovarian Tumor with Sexual Precocity .... DOTSP
Distinctive Unit Insignia [*Military*] (INF) .... DUI
[*A*] **Distinctly Empirical Prover of Theorems** .... ADEPT
Distinctness of Image [*Mobay Corp.*] .... DOI
Distinguish .... DIST
Distinguish .... DISTING
Distinguished (ADA) .... D
Distinguished [*Case at bar different either in law or fact from case cited for reasons given*] [*Used in Shepard's Citations*] [*Legal term*] (DLA) .... d
Distinguished (ROG) .... DISTING
Distinguished Conduct Medal [*British*] .... DCM
Distinguished Federal Civilian Service [*Award*] (RDA) .... DFCS
Distinguished Flying Cross [*US and British*] [*Military decoration*] .... DFC
Distinguished Flying Medal [*British*] .... DFM
Distinguished From [*Medicine*] (DAVI) .... Dist F
Distinguished Graduate [*Military*] .... DG
Distinguished Guest [*Hotel term*] .... DG
Distinguished Guest Lecturer (DOMA) .... DGL
Distinguished Marksmanship Badge .... DMB
Distinguished Member of the Regiment .... DMOR
Distinguished Members of the Corps [*Army*] .... DMOC
Distinguished Military Graduate .... DMG
Distinguished Military Students .... DMS
Distinguished Naval Graduate .... DNG
Distinguished Pistol Badge .... DPB
Distinguished Pistol Shot Badge [*Military decoration*] (GFGA) .... DDB-P
Distinguished Pistol Shot Badge [*Military decoration*] (AABC) .... DPSBad
Distinguished Public Service Award (MUGU) .... DPSA
Distinguished Rifleman Badge [*Military decoration*] (GFGA) .... DDB-R
Distinguished Rifleman Badge [*Military decoration*] (AABC) .... DRflmnBad
Distinguished Service Cross [*US and British*] [*Military decoration*] .... DSC
Distinguished Service Medal [*US and British*] [*Military decoration*] .... DSM
Distinguished Service Order [*British*] .... DSO
Distinguished Unit Citation [*Military decoration*] .... DUC
Distinguished Unit Citation Emblem [*Military decoration*] .... DUCE
Distinguished Unit Emblem [*Military decoration*] .... DUE
Distinguished University Professor .... DUP
Distinguished Visitor .... DV
Distinguished Visitor Program [*Army*] .... DVP
Distinguished Visitor Quarters [*Military*] (DOMA) .... DVQ
Distobuccal [*Dentistry*] .... DB
Distobuccal Developmental Groove [*Medicine*] (DMAA) .... DBDG
Distobucco-Occlusal [*Dentistry*] .... DBO
Distobuccopulpal [*Dentistry*] .... DBP
Distocervical [*Dentistry*] .... DC
Distogingival [*Dentistry*] .... DG
Distoincisal [*Dentistry*] .... DI
Distolabial [*Dentistry*] .... DLA
Distolabioincisal [*Dentistry*] .... DLAI
Distolabiopulpal [*Dentistry*] .... DLaP
Distolingual [*Dentistry*] .... DL
Distolingual Groove [*Medicine*] (DMAA) .... DLG
Distolinguoincisal [*Dentistry*] .... DLI
Distolinguo-Occlusal [*Dentistry*] .... DLO
Distolinguopulpal [*Dentistry*] .... DLP
Disto-Occlusal [*Dentistry*] .... DO
Distopulpal [*Dentistry*] .... DP
Distopulpolabial [*Dentistry*] .... DPLa
Distopulpolingual [*Dentistry*] .... DPL
Distort (IAA) .... DIST
Distort (FAAC) .... DST
Distorted Communication (IAA) .... DC
Distorted Wave Impulse Approximation .... DWIA
Distorted Wave-Borne Approximation .... DWBA
Distortion (IAA) .... D
Distortion (MSA) .... DISTN
Distortion Factor [*Telecommunications*] (IAA) .... DF
Distortion Factor Meter [*Telecommunications*] (IAA) .... DFM
Distortion Transmission Impairment [*Telecommunications*] (TEL) .... DTI
Distortion-Eliminating Voltage Regulator .... DEVR
Distortionless Enhancement by Polarization Transfer [*Spectroscopy*] .... DEPT
Distracted .... DISTR
Distress (MSA) .... DTRS
Distress Alarm for Severely Handicapped [*British*] .... DASH
Distress Alerting and Locating System .... DALS
Distress Phase [*Aviation*] .... DETRESFA
Distress Radio Call System [*Telecommunications*] (TEL) .... DRCS
Distress Signal (IAA) .... DISSIG
Distressed Airman Recovery Beacon (IAA) .... DARB

Distressed British Seaman [*Granted a free passage home*] .... DBS
Distressed Gentlefolks' Aid Association [*British*] (DI) .... DGAA
Distressed Vehicle (KSC) .... DV
Distribuidora de Impresos, Sociedad Anonima [*Mexico*] .... DIMSA
Distributable Net Income .... DNI
Distributable Union Catalog [*Harvard University*] [*Microfiche*] (NITA) .... DUC
Distribute (ROG) .... DIS
Distribute .... DIST
Distribute (VRA) .... distrb
Distributed Access Unit [*Computer science*] .... DAU
Distributed Acquisition Facility (NITA) .... DAF
Distributed Active Archive Center [*NASA*] .... DAAC
Distributed Ada Interface Set (SSD) .... DAIS
Distributed Analysis Program (MCD) .... DAP
Distributed Application [*Automotive engineering*] .... DA
Distributed Application Processing System .... DAPS
Distributed Applications Architecture [*Computer science*] (BTTJ) .... DAA
Distributed Area Jamming System [*Air Force*] .... DAJS
Distributed Array Processor [*Sperry UNIVAC*] [*Telecommunications*] .... DAP
Distributed Array RADAR (MCD) .... DAR
Distributed Artificial Intelligence [*Computer science*] .... DAI
Distributed Audio Network [*Sound Apprentice*] .... DAN
Distributed Automation Edition [*Computer science*] (BTTJ) .... DAE
Distributed Bragg Reflector [*LASER*] .... DBR
Distributed Budget at Completion .... DBAC
Distributed Budget Variance (MCD) .... DBV
Distributed Call Center [*Telecommunications*] .... DCC
Distributed Capacity Computing System (NITA) .... DCCS
Distributed Command and Control System .... DCCS
Distributed Command, Control, and Communications [*Army*] .... DC^3
Distributed Command, Control, Communications, and Intelligence [*Army*] (RDA) .... DC^3I
Distributed Commercial System (IAA) .... DCS
Distributed Communications Architecture (BUR) .... DCA
Distributed Communications Processor [*Sperry UNIVAC*] .... DCP
Distributed Communications System [*Telecommunications*] (CDE) .... DCS
Distributed Component Object Model [*Computer science*] .... DCOM
Distributed Computer Design System (SDI) .... DCDS
Distributed Computer Network .... DCN
Distributed Computer Systems (MDG) .... DCS
Distributed Computer Telephony .... DCT
Distributed Computing Environment .... DCE
Distributed Computing Services .... DCS
Distributed Control Programming Language [*Computer science*] (CSR) .... DCPL
Distributed Control System [*Engineering*] .... DCS
Distributed Data Entry .... DDE
Distributed Data Manager .... DDM
Distributed Data Processing [*Computer science Telecommunications*] .... DDP
Distributed Data Processing Model (MCD) .... DDPM
Distributed Database .... DDB
Distributed Database Connection Service [*IBM Corp.*] (PCM) .... DDCS
Distributed Database Management System [*Computer science*] .... DDBMS
Distributed Database Testbed System (MCD) .... DDTS
Distributed Defense Study [*DoD*] .... DDS
Distributed Digital Control [*Computer science*] .... DDC
Distributed Double Loop Computer Network (MCD) .... DDLCN
Distributed Electronic Telephone Exchange [*Telecommunications*] (PDAA) .... DETE
Distributed Electronic Test and Analysis .... DELTA
Distributed Emission Crossed Field Amplifier (IAA) .... DECFA
Distributed Emission Magnetron Amplifier (MSA) .... DEMA
Distributed Emission Magnetron Amplifier .... DEMATRON
Distributed Energy Release [*Computer program*] .... DER
Distributed Executive (SSD) .... DE
Distributed Explosive Mine Neutralization System (DOMA) .... DEMNS
Distributed Explosive Technologies [*Military*] (DOMA) .... DET
Distributed Feedback .... DFB
Distributed Feedback LASER Diode .... DFB-LD
Distributed File System .... DFS
Distributed Floating Gate Amplifier (MCD) .... DFGA
Distributed Foundation Wireless Media Access Control [*Computer science*] .... DFWMAC
Distributed Function Architecture .... DFA
Distributed Function Terminal (ACRL) .... DFT
Distributed Graphics Support Subroutines [*Tektronix, Inc.*] (NITA) .... DGSS
Distributed Graphics System (MCD) .... DGS
Distributed Host Command Facility (NITA) .... DHCF
Distributed Illuminated Electronic System (DWSG) .... DIES
Distributed Impressed Current Cathodic Protection [*Anticorrosion system*] .... DICCAP
Distributed Information Processing .... DIP
Distributed Information Processing Network Architecture .... DINA
Distributed Information Processing Service System (NITA) .... DISS
Distributed Information System [*Computer science*] .... DIS
Distributed Input/Output System .... DIOS
Distributed Instructional System [*Military*] .... DIS
Distributed Intelligence Acquisition and Control (PDAA) .... DIAC
Distributed Intelligence Microcomputer System .... DIMS
Distributed Intelligent Actuators and Sensors (ACII) .... DIAS
Distributed Interactive Operating System (IAA) .... DINOS
Distributed Interactive Secure Telecommunications Area Network (MCD) .... DISTAN
Distributed Interactive Simulation [*Army*] (RDA) .... DIS
Distributed Interactive Simulation General Officer Steering Committee [*Army*] (RDA) .... DIS GOSC
Distributed Jamming (MCD) .... DJ
Distributed Knowledge Base [*Computer science*] (ODBW) .... DKB
Distributed Lab (MDG) .... DL
Distributed Language Translation [*Project being developed by BSO, a Dutch computer company*] .... DLT
Distributed Lock Manager (ACRL) .... DLM
Distributed Loop Computer Network (PDAA) .... DLCN
Distributed Loop Message Communication Protocol .... DLMCP
Distributed Loop Operating System .... DLOS
Distributed Lumped Active [*Electronics*] (OA) .... DLA
Distributed Maintenance Services (NITA) .... DMS
Distributed Management Environment .... DME
Distributed Message Router (NITA) .... DMR
Distributed Microcomputer Network for Avionics (MCD) .... DMNA
Distributed Microprocessor Unit .... DMU
Distributed Minicomputer Systems (AAGC) .... DMINS
Distributed Models and Simulation [*Army*] .... DMS
Distributed Monitoring System (ACII) .... DMS
Distributed Nesting System (MCD) .... DNS
Distributed Network Architecture (IAA) .... DNA
Distributed Network Control System .... DNCS
Distributed Network Server - Media Interface Module [*Cabletron Systems, Inc.*] .... DNS-MIM
Distributed Network System .... DNS
Distributed Numerical Control [*Computer science*] (ODBW) .... DNC
Distributed Object Management [*Computer science*] .... DOM
Distributed Object Management Environment [*Computer science*] (BTTJ) .... DOME
Distributed Object-Management Facility .... DOMF
Distributed Objects Everywhere [*Computer science*] .... DOE
Distributed Office Application Model [*Telecommunications*] (OSI) .... DOAM
Distributed Office Support Executive [*IBM Corp.*] (IAA) .... DOSE
Distributed Office Support System [*IBM Corp.*] .... DISOSS
Distributed Operating Multi-Access Interactive Network [*Apollo Computer, Inc.*] [*Chelmsford, MA*] [*Telecommunications*] (TSSD) .... DOMAIN
Distributed Operating System Kernel [*Computer science*] .... DOSK
Distributed Operation System [*Computer science*] (IAA) .... DOS
Distributed Operator Console [*Environmental science*] .... DOC
Distributed Parallel Processing [*Computer science*] .... DPP
Distributed Phase Plate [*LASER technology*] .... DPP
Distributed Present Services [*IBM*] (NITA) .... DPS
Distributed Presentation Services [*IBM Corp.*] .... DPS
Distributed Processing Communications Module .... DPCM
Distributed Processing Contractual Input [*Computer science*] .... DPCI
Distributed Processing Control Executive [*IBM Corp.*] .... DPCX
Distributed Processing Environment .... DPE
Distributed Processing Executive Program .... DPEX
Distributed Processing Programming Executive [*IBM*] (NITA) .... DPPX
Distributed Processing Programming Executive Base [*IBM Corp.*] .... DPPX
Distributed Processing System [*Honeywell, Inc.*] .... DPS
Distributed Processing Technology [*Computer science*] .... DPT
Distributed Processing Terminal Exchange [*Prime Computers*] (NITA) .... DPTX
Distributed Program Design Language .... DPDL
Distributed Programming System (IAA) .... DPS
Distributed Query and Retrieval System [*Telecommunications*] (PS) .... DQRS
Distributed Queue Dual Bus [*Telecommunications*] (PCM) .... DQDB
Distributed Read Address Counter .... DRAC
Distributed Real-Time Ever Available Microcomputing Laboratory [*University of California, Irvine*] [*Research center*] (RCD) .... DREAM
Distributed Real-Time Groove Network [*Computer science*] .... DRGN
Distributed Relational Database Access [*Computer science*] (TNIG) .... DRDA
Distributed Relational Database Architecture [*IBM Corp.*] [*Computer protocol*] [*Computer science*] (PCM) .... DRDA
Distributed Relational DBMS [*Database Management System*] (CDE) .... DRDBMS
Distributed Resource System (IAA) .... DRS
Distributed Scheduling Mulitiple Access [*Telecommunications*] (OSI) .... DSMA
Distributed Sensor Network (MCD) .... DSN
Distributed Shared Memory [*Computer science*] .... DSM
Distributed/Stand-Alone [*Pricing*] .... D/S
Distributed State Response .... DSR
Distributed Support Information Standard (PCM) .... DSIS
Distributed System .... DS
Distributed System Object Model [*Computer science*] (PCM) .... DSOM
Distributed System Program [*Computer science*] .... DSP
Distributed System Satellite (IAA) .... DSS
Distributed System Simulator .... DSS
Distributed Systems Architecture [*Computer science*] (HGAA) .... DSA
Distributed Systems Environment [*Honeywell, Inc.*] (BUR) .... DSE
Distributed Systems Executive [*IBM Corp.*] .... DSX
Distributed Systems Licensing Option [*IBM Corp.*] .... DSLO
Distributed Systems Management [*Computer science*] .... DSM
Distributed Systems Network [*Hewlett-Packard Co.*] .... DSN
Distributed Time (KSC) .... DIST
Distributed Time Division Multiple Access [*System*] [*DoD*] .... DTDMA
Distributed Transaction Processing (HGAA) .... DTP
Distributed Update Algorithm (ACRL) .... DUAL
Distributed Virtual Memory [*Computer science*] .... DVM
Distributed Write Address Counter .... DWAC
Distributed-Loop Database System (PDAA) .... DLDBS
Distributes .... DISTRB
Distributing .... DISTRG
Distributing Post Office .... DPO
Distributing Terminal Assembly [*Electronics*] .... DTA
Distribution (DCTA) .... DISBN
Distribution (IEEE) .... dist

Distribution (AAG) .... DISTN
Distribution [or Distributor] (AFM) .... DISTR
Distribution .... DISTRB
Distribution .... DISTRIB
Distribution (MCD) .... DSTR
Distribution Amplifier .... DA
Distribution Amplifier (MSA) .... DAMP
Distribution Analysis for Power Planning, Evaluation, and Reporting
 [Computer science] .... DAPPER
Distribution and Illumination System, Electrical [Army] (INF) .... DISE
Distribution and Switching System (MCD) .... DSS
Distribution Assembly [Ground Communications Facility, NASA] .... DA
Distribution Assembly [Ground Communications Facility, NASA] .... DSTA
Distribution Authority [Army] (AABC) .... DISTRA
Distribution Authority List (MCD) .... DAL
Distribution Automation (ACII) .... DA
Distribution Automation and Control (MCD) .... DAC
Distribution Box [Technical drawings] .... DB
Distribution Centers .... DC
Distribution Chart File .... DCF
Distribution Code .... DC
Distribution Codes Institute [Defunct] (EA) .... DCI
Distribution Coefficient .... DC
Distribution Coefficient [Partition coefficient] [Physics] (DAVI) .... K$_d$
Distribution Common Point [Telecommunications] (TEL) .... DCP
Distribution Construction Information System [IBM Corp.] .... DCIS
Distribution Contractors Association [Tulsa, OK] (EA) .... DCA
Distribution Control Analysis File [NASA] (MCD) .... DECAF
Distribution Control Assembly (MCD) .... DCA
Distribution Control Center (AAG) .... DCC
Distribution Control Unit .... DCU
Distribution Cost Analysis System (MCD) .... DCAS
Distribution Disk Builder [Computer science] .... DDB
Distribution Drop Point (AABC) .... DDP
Distribution, Excretion, and Metabolism [Environmental chemistry] .... DEM
Distribution Factor .... DF
Distribution Feeder [Telecommunications] (OA) .... DF
Distribution Frame (KSC) .... DF
Distribution Function [Statistics] .... DF
Distribution Function Terminal [Computer science] .... DFT
Distribution Fuse Board (IEEE) .... DFB
Distribution Fuse Panel .... DFP
Distribution Industry Training Board [Terminated British] .... DITB
Distribution, Information, and Optimizing System (OA) .... DIOS
Distribution Information System .... DIS
Distribution Intsruction .... DI
Distribution List .... DL
Distribution Management Accounting System (IEEE) .... DMAS
Distribution Media Format (CDE) .... DMF
Distribution Module [Telecommunications] .... DM
Distribution Navy Enlisted Classification (DNAB) .... DNEC
Distribution Networks, Edmonton, AB, Canada [Library symbol Library of
 Congress] (LCLS) .... CaAEDN
Distribution Networks, Edmonton, Alberta [Library symbol National Library of
 Canada] (NLC) .... AEDN
Distribution Number Bank .... DNB
Distribution Octane Number [Engineering] (IAA) .... DON
Distribution of Exact Classical Energy Transfer [Physics] .... DECENT
Distribution of Industry [British] .... DI
Distribution of Oceanographic Data at Isentropic Levels System .... DODIS
Distribution of Stockage Code (AABC) .... DSC
Distribution Office (DCTA) .... DO
Distribution Order Entry System (IAA) .... DOES
Distribution Panel .... DPNL
Distribution Plan (AFIT) .... DP
Distribution Plan Authorization [Military] (AFIT) .... DPA
Distribution Plot List .... DPL
Distribution Point .... DP
Distribution Point .... DSP
Distribution Processing Center (MCD) .... DPC
Distribution Programmer (IAA) .... DP
Distribution Register of Organic Pollutants [In Water] [Environmental
 Protection Agency] .... DROP
Distribution Regulation [Office of Price Stabilization] (DLA) .... DR
Distribution Reinvestment Program [Stock exchange term] .... DRP
Distribution Request .... DR
Distribution Requirement Table (MCD) .... DRT
Distribution Research and Education Foundation (EA) .... DREF
Distribution Resource Planning .... DRP
Distribution Sciences, Inc. [Information service or system] (IID) .... DSI
Distribution Space .... DS
Distribution Stock Control System (MHDB) .... DISC
Distribution Switchboard .... DSB
Distribution System (IAA) .... DISSYS
Distribution Tape Reel [Computer science] .... DTR
Distribution/Transportation Management Information System [Computer
 science] (PDAA) .... DMIS
Distribution Unit (KSC) .... DU
Distribution-Abundance [Ecology] .... DA
Distribution-Free Doppler Processor (PDAA) .... DFDP
Distribution-Free Logic Design .... DFLD
Distribution-Free Statistics .... DISFREE
Distribution-Oriented Management Information Analyzer [Computer
 science] (MHDI) .... DOMINA
Distributive Education .... DE

Distributive Education Clubs of America (EA) .... DECA
Distributive Principle of Multiplication over Addition [Mathematics] .... DPMA
Distributive, Processing, and Office Workers Union of America .... DPOWA
Distributive Trades [Department of Employment] [British] .... DT
Distributive Trades' Alliance [British] (BI) .... DTA
Distributive Trades Technology Advisory Centre [University of Stirling]
 [British] (CB) .... DTTAC
Distributor (KSC) .... DIST
Distributor .... DISTR
Distributor .... DR
Distributor [MARC relator code] [Library of Congress] (LCCP) .... dst
Distributor Electronic Control .... DEC
Distributor Gasket [Automotive engineering] .... DIS
Distributor Modulator System [Automotive engineering] .... DMS
Distributor Nesting System [Military] .... DNS
Distributor Quality rating Index [Chemical engineering] .... DQI
Distributor Retard Control Valve [Automotive engineering] .... DRCV
Distributor Thermo-Vacuum Switch [Automotive engineering] .... DTVS
Distributor Vacuum Advance Control [Automotive engineering] .... DVAC
Distributor Vacuum Vent Valve [Automotive engineering] .... DVVV
Distributorless Ignition [Automotive engineering] .... DLI
Distributorless Ignition System [Automotive engineering] .... DIS
Distributor-Manufacturer-Representative .... DMR
Distributor-to-Group Display Generator .... DGDG
Distributor-to-Group Display Generator Electronics (IAA) .... DGDGE
Distributor-to-Printer Electronics .... DPE
District .... D
District .... DIS
District .... DISC
District .... DISCT
District (AFM) .... DIST
District .... DIST
District (WDMC) .... dist
District (ROG) .... DISTR
District (VRA) .... distr
District .... DST
District Accounting Office [or Officer] [Navy] .... DAO
District Administrator .... DA
District Administrator (CINC) .... DISTAD
District Advisory Team [Military] (VNW) .... DAT
District Agent [Insurance] .... DA
District Air Support Center (MCD) .... DASC
District Airport Engineer .... DAE
District and County Reports [Pennsylvania] [A publication] (DLA) .... D & C
District and County, Second Series [A publication] (DLA) .... D & C2d
District Armament Supply Officer [British] .... DASO
District Assembly [British] .... DA
District Attorney .... DA
District Attorney (WGA) .... Dist Atty
District Authorities [British] .... DA
District Aviation Gas Office [Navy] .... DAGO
District Aviation Office [or Officer] [Navy] .... DAO
District Barrack Officer [British military] (DMA) .... DBO
District Base Service Office .... DBSO
District Building Officer [National Health Service] [British] (DI) .... DBO
District Business Conduct Committee [of the National Association of
 Securities Dealers] .... DBCC
District Camouflage Office [or Officer] .... DCO
District Chaplain [Navy] .... DCH
District Chief Ranger [Ancient Order of Foresters] .... DCR
District Civil Readjustment Office [or Officer] .... DCRO
District Civilian Personnel Office [or Officer] .... DCPO
District Clothing Office [or Officer] .... DCO
District Coast Guard Officer .... DCGO
District Commissioner [British government] .... DC
District Communication Officer .... DCO
District Communications Center [Navy] .... DCC
District Community Physician .... DCP
District Contracts Board [Australia] .... DCB
District Council [British] .... DC
District Council Office [British] (ROG) .... DCO
District Court [Federal] (DLA) .... D
District Court [Usually federal] (DLA) .... D Ct
District Court .... DC
District Court (DLA) .... Dist C
District Court [State] (DLA) .... Dist Ct
District Court, District of Columbia (DLA) .... DDC
District Court Judge .... DCJ
District Court Law Library, Second Judicial District, Denver, CO [Library
 symbol Library of Congress] (LCLS) .... CoDDC
District Court Law Reports [Hong Kong] [A publication] (ILCA) .... DCLR
District Court Law Reports [Hong Kong] [A publication] (DLA) .... District Court LR
District Court of Appeal (DLA) .... Dist Ct App
District Court of New South Wales [Australia] .... DCNSW
District Court-Martial [Facetious translation: "Don't Come Monday," in
 reference to a one-day suspension] [British] .... DCM
District Cub Master [Scouting] .... DCM
District Degaussing Vessel [Navy symbol] .... YDG
District Dental Office [or Officer] [Navy] .... DDO
District Deputy Grand Master [Freemasonry] (ROG) .... DDGM
District Deputy Grand Master [Freemasonry] .... DisDGM
District Director .... DD
District Directors of Internal Revenue [IRS] .... DDIR
District Domestic Transportation Office [or Officer] .... DDTO
District Educational Services Officer [Navy] .... DESO

District Emergency Operations Controller [*Australia*] .... DEOC
District Engineer [*Army*] .... DE
District Engineer [*Army*] (AABC) .... DISTENGR
District Engineer Officer [*Army*] .... DEO
District Enrolled Nurse [*British*] .... DEN
District Finance Officer .... DFO
District General Hospital .... DGH
District Guard [*British military*] (DMA) .... DG
District Headquarters .... DHQ
District Headquarters Induction and Recruiting Station [*Marine Corps*] .... DHIRS
District Health Authority [*British*] .... DHA
District Health Authority (Teaching) [*National Health Service*] [*British*] (DI) .... DHA(T)
District Health Council [*Australia*] .... DHC
District Heating Association [*British*] .... DHA
District Historical Office [*or Officer*] [*Navy*] .... DHO
District Industrial Incentive Office [*or Officer*] [*Navy*] .... DIIO
District Industrial Manager [*Navy*] .... DIM
District Industrial Relations Officer [*Navy*] .... DIRO
District Inspector [*Navy*] .... DI
District Inspector of Musketry [*Military British*] (ROG) .... DIM
District Instructional Media Center, Brentwood, NY [*Library symbol Library of Congress*] (LCLS) .... NBrenIMC
District Intelligence and Operations Coordination Center [*Vietnam*] (VNW) .... DIOCC
District Intelligence Officer .... DIO
District Intelligence Operations Centers [*Vietnam*] .... DIOC
District Judge .... DJ
District Labor Relations Office [*or Officer*] [*Navy*] .... DLRO
District Legal Office [*or Officer*] [*Navy*] .... DLO
District Management Office .... DMO
District Manager .... DM
District Manager's Assistant [*British*] (DCTA) .... DMA
District Marine Officer [*Navy*] .... DMO
District Material Officer [*Navy*] .... DMO
District Medical Officer [*Military*] (DNAB) .... DISTMEDO
District Medical Officer [*Navy*] .... DMO
District Members [*Also, EN for secrecy*] [*Fenian Brotherhood*] (ROG) .... DM
District Naval Material Office .... DNMO
District Naval Officer [*British*] (ADA) .... DNO
District Nurse [*British*] .... DN
District Nursing Association [*British*] (DBA) .... DNA
District Nursing Officer .... DNO
District of Colu8mbia Rules and Regulations [*A publication*] (AAGC) .... DCRR
District of Columbia [*Postal code*] .... DC
District of Columbia [*MARC country of publication code Library of Congress*] (LCCP) .... dcu
District of Columbia [*MARC geographic area code Library of Congress*] (LCCP) .... n-us-dc
District of Columbia Appeals Cases Reports [*1-5 United States*] [*A publication*] (DLA) .... Cranch CC
District of Columbia Appeals Reports [*A publication*] (DLA) .... DC App
District of Columbia Archives, Washington, DC [*Library symbol*] [*Library of Congress*] (LCLS) .... DAr
District of Columbia Bar Association. Journal [*A publication*] (DLA) .... Distr Col BAJ
[*Court of Appeals for the*] **District of Columbia Circuit** (AAGC) .... DC Cir
District of Columbia Circuit Court Rules [*A publication*] (DLA) .... DC Cir R
District of Columbia Code [*A publication*] (DLA) .... DC Code
District of Columbia Code, Annotated [*A publication*] (DLA) .... DC Code Ann
District of Columbia Code Encyclopedia [*A publication*] (DLA) .... DC Code Encycl
District of Columbia Code Encyclopedia [*A publication*] (DLA) .... DCCE
District of Columbia Code Legislative and Administrative Service (West) [*A publication*] (DLA) .... DC Code Legis & Admin Serv
District of Columbia Compensation Act (DLA) .... DCCA
District of Columbia Contract Appeals Board (AAGC) .... DCCAB
District of Columbia Council of Engineering and Architecture (SRA) .... DCCEAS
District of Columbia Court of Appeals (DLA) .... CADC
District of Columbia Court of Appeals (DLA) .... Dist Col App
District of Columbia Court of Appeals Cases [*A publication*] (DLA) .... DC Cir
District of Columbia Health Sciences Information Network [*Library network*] .... DOCHSIN
District of Columbia Manpower Administration .... DCMA
District of Columbia Military District (AABC) .... DCMD
District Of Columbia Municipal Regulations [*A publication*] .... DCMR
District of Columbia National Guard (AABC) .... DCNG
District of Columbia Public Library .... DCPL
District of Columbia Public Library, Washington, DC [*OCLC symbol*] (OCLC) .... DWP
District of Columbia Reports [*A publication*] (DLA) .... DC
District of Columbia Rules and Regulations [*A publication*] (DLA) .... DCR & Regs
District of Columbia Society of Internal Medicine (SRA) .... DCSIM
District of Columbia Supreme Court Reports [*1-5 District of Columbia*] [*1801-40*] [*A publication*] (DLA) .... Cranch CC
District of Columbia Teachers College [*Later, University of the District of Columbia*] .... DCTC
District of Columbia Teachers College [*Later, University of the District of Columbia*], Washington, DC [*Library symbol Library of Congress Obsolete*] (LCLS) .... DJOWT
District of Europe [*Proposed location of an EEC federal capital*] .... DE
District of North Vancouver Library, British Columbia [*Library symbol National Library of Canada*] (NLC) .... BNVD
District of North Vancouver Library, North Vancouver, BC, Canada [*Library symbol Library of Congress*] (LCLS) .... CaBNvD
District Office [*or Officer*] .... DO
District Office/Area Office [*IRS*] .... DO/AO
District Office Direct Input [*Social Security computerized system*] .... DODI
District Office of Jurisdiction [*IRS*] .... DJ
District Office of Location [*IRS*] .... DL
District Officer Commanding .... DOC
District Officer for Reserve Communication Supplementary Activities .... DORCSA
District One Technical Institute, Eau Claire, Eau Claire, WI [*OCLC symbol*] (OCLC) .... WEC
District Operations Office [*or Officer*] [*Navy*] .... DOO
District Ordnance Office [*or Officer*] [*Navy*] .... DOO
District Personnel Office [*or Officer*] [*Navy*] .... DPO
District Planning Officers Society [*British*] .... DPOS
District Port Director [*Navy*] .... DPD
District Postal Liaison Officer [*Navy*] .... DPLO
District Postal Office [*or Officer*] [*Navy*] .... DPO
District Postmaster [*British*] (DCTA) .... DPMR
District Power Equalizer [*Formula for school grants*] .... DPE
District Probate Registry .... DPR
District Property Transportation Office [*or Officer*] [*Navy*] .... DPTO
District Public Affairs Officer [*Military*] .... DPAO
District Public Information Office [*or Officer*] [*Navy*] .... DPIO
District Public Relations Office [*or Officer*] [*Navy*] .... DPRO
District Public Works Office .... DPWO
District Publications and Printing Office .... DPPO
District Railway [*London*] .... DR
District Records Management Office [*or Officer*] .... DRMO
District Recruiting Command [*Army*] (AABC) .... DRC
District Registry .... DR
District Relief Exercise [*Military*] (DNAB) .... DISTEX
District Reports [*A publication*] (DLA) .... Dist Rep
District Reserve Electronics Program Officer .... DREPO
District Reserve Equipment [*Army*] (AABC) .... DRE
District Reserve Supply Corps Program Officer (DNAB) .... DRSCPO
District Sales Manager .... DSM
District Sales Office .... DSO
District Scout Master [*Scouting*] .... DSM
District Secretary [*British*] .... DS
District Security Office [*or Officer*] [*Navy*] .... DSO
District Senior Advisory (MCD) .... DSA
District Service Office [*or Officer*] [*Navy*] .... DSO
District Ships Service Office [*or Officer*] [*Navy*] .... DSSO
District Signal Officer [*Navy*] (IAA) .... DSO
District Sorting Office [*British*] (ROG) .... DSO
District Staff Officer [*British*] (ROG) .... DSO
District Sub-Chief Ranger [*Ancient Order of Foresters*] .... DSCR
District Supply and Transport Officer [*British military*] (DMA) .... DSTO
District Supply Office [*or Officer*] [*Navy*] .... DSO
District Switching Center [*Telecommunications*] .... DSC
District Switching Centre [*Telecommunications network*] (NITA) .... DSC
District Traffic Agent .... DTA
District Traffic Superintendent [*British railroad term*] .... DTS
District Training Office [*or Officer*] [*Navy*] .... DTO
District Transportation Officer .... DTO
District Trust Co. [*Toronto Stock Exchange symbol*] .... DT
District War Bond Office [*or Officer*] [*Navy*] .... DWBO
District War Plans Officer .... DWPO
Disturbance [*FBI standardized term*] .... DIST
Disturbance Accommodation Standard-Deviation Optimal Controller [*Space telescope*] [*NASA*] .... DASOC
Disturbance Analysis and Surveillance System [*NRC*] .... DASS
Disturbance Analysis System [*Nuclear energy*] (NRCH) .... DAS
Disturbance Compensation System [*Navy satellite navigation*] .... DISCOS
Disturbance Lines [*Marine science*] (OSRA) .... DL
Disturbance Lines (USDC) .... DL
Disturbed Bowel Function [*Medicine*] (MEDA) .... DBF
Disturbed Gum [*Philately*] .... DG
Disturbed-Rock Zone [*Geology*] .... DRZ
Disturbing Behavior Checklist [*Psychology*] (EDAC) .... DBC
Disuccinimidyl Glutarate [*Organic chemistry*] .... DSG
Disuccinimidyl Tartrate [*Organic chemistry*] .... DST
Disuccinimydyl Suberate [*Organic chemistry*] .... DSS
Disulfiram [*Organic chemistry*] .... DSF
Disulfiram-Ethanol Reaction [*Medicine*] (DMAA) .... DER
Disused (ROG) .... DISUS
Disyllable .... DISY
Disyllable (ROG) .... DISYLL
Ditaurobilirubin [*Biochemistry*] .... DTB
Di-T-butyl Nitroxide [*Organic chemistry*] .... DTBN
Ditch Mile [*Newmarket Racecourse*] [*Horseracing*] [*British*] .... DM
Ditchley Foundation (EA) .... DF
Di-tert-amylhydroquinone [*Organic chemistry*] .... DAHQ
Di-tert-butyl Peroxide [*Organic chemistry*] .... DTBP
Di-tert-butylcatechol [*Organic chemistry*] .... DTBC
Di-tert-butylcresol [*Organic chemistry*] .... DTBC
Di-tert-butylhydroquinone [*Organic chemistry*] .... DTBHQ
Di-tert-butyl-m-cresol [*Organic chemistry*] .... DBMC
Di-tert-butylnaphthalene [*Organic chemistry*] .... DTBN
Di-tert-butyl-p-cresol [*Also, BHT*] [*Antioxidant*] .... DBPC
Di-Tert-Butylphenol [*Biochemistry*] .... DTBP
Di-Tertiary-Butylbiphenyl [*Organic chemistry*] .... DTBB
Dither .... DTER
Dithered Infrared Configuration .... DIRC
Dithiobis(nitrobenzoic acid) [*Analytical biochemistry*] .... DTNB
Dithiobis(nitrohydroxyethylbenzamide) [*Biochemistry*] .... DTNHEB

Dithiobis(succinimidylpropionate) [*Organic chemistry*] ... DSP
Dithiobiuret [*Organic chemistry*] ... DTB
Dithiocarbamate [*Organic chemistry*] ... DTC
Dithioerythritol [*Organic chemistry*] ... DTE
Dithionite-Citrate-Bicarbonate [*Extractive chemistry*] ... DCB
Dithionitrobenzoic Acid [*Organic chemistry*] ... DTNB
Dithiothreitol [*Organic chemistry*] ... DIT
Dithiothreitol [*Organic chemistry*] ... DTT
Ditley-Simonsen, Halfdan & Co. [*Steamship*] (MHDB) ... D-S
DiTomasso Methodology Inventory (EDAC) ... DMI
Ditridecyl Phthalate [*Organic chemistry*] ... DTDP
Di-Tryptophan Aminal Acetaldehyde [*Biochemistry*] ... DTAA
Ditta Transavio di I. Ballerio [*Italy ICAO designator*] (FAAC) ... TVO
Dittberner Associates, Inc. [*Bethesda, MD*] [*Information service or system Telecommunications*] (TSSD) ... DAI
Dittingen [*Switzerland ICAO location identifier*] (ICLI) ... LSPD
Dittler Airline Data Systems [*Information service or system*] (IID) ... DADS
Dittler Brothers, Inc [*Printer of U.S. postage stamps*] (BARN) ... DBI
Ditto (AFM) ... DO
Ditto (WDMC) ... do
Diundecyl Phthalate [*Organic chemistry*] ... DUP
Diuretic [*Increasing Discharge of Urine*] [*Pharmacy*] (ROG) ... DIU
Diuretic Hormone [*Endocrinology*] ... DH
Diurnal (MAE) ... d
Diurnal Rhythm [*Medicine*] (MEDA) ... DR
Diurnal Temperature Range [*Climatology*] ... DTR
Diva Foundation (EA) ... DF
DIVAD Systems Controller (MCD) ... DSC
Divalent Ion Metabolism (MAE) ... DIM
Divanillylidenecyclohexanone [*or Divanillalcyclohexanone*] [*Pharmacology*] ... DVC
Dive and Release Trajectory (MCD) ... DART
Dive Auditory Location System (MCD) ... DALS
Dive Bank ... DB
Dive Bomb ... DB
Dive Bomber Aircraft ... DB
Dive Bomber Squadron [*Navy symbol*] ... VB
Diver [*British military*] (DMA) ... D
Diver (MSA) ... DVR
Diver Alternative Work System ... DAWS
Diver Biographical Inventory [*Navy*] ... DBI
Diver Communication Research System (PDAA) ... DICORS
Diver Equipment Information Center [*Battelle Memorial Institute*] [*Information service or system*] (IID) ... DEIC
Diver Equivalent Manipulator System [*General Electric*] ... DEMS
Diver Escape Capsule (MCD) ... DEC
Diver Operated Plug (MCD) ... DOP
Diver Propulsion Vehicle (DNAB) ... DPV
Diver, Salvage [*Navy rating*] ... DS
Diver, Second Class [*Navy rating*] ... DT
Diver Transport Vehicle (PDAA) ... DTV
Diverge (FAAC) ... DVRG
Divergence ... DIV
Divergence Source-Image Distortion [*Crystal*] ... DSID
Divergent Exhaust Nozzle Control (MCD) ... DENC
Divergent Lobed Suppressor [*NASA*] ... DLS
Divers Alert Network [*Marine science*] (OSRA) ... DAN
Diver's Alert Network ... DAN
Divers Alert Network (USDC) ... DAN
Diverse (ROG) ... DIV
Diverse Use of Communication Technology ... DUCT
Diverse Vector Area [*FAA*] (TAG) ... DVA
Diversey Wyandotte, Inc., Mississauga, Ontario, [*Library symbol National Library of Canada*] (NLC) ... OMDW
Diversifax, Inc. [*NASDAQ symbol*] (SAG) ... DFAX
Diversifax, Inc. [*Associated Press*] (SAG) ... Divrs
Diversifax, Inc. [*Associated Press*] (SAG) ... Divrsfax
Diversified ... DVSFD
Diversified Composite Material (PDAA) ... DCM
Diversified Computer Technology, Inc. (MCD) ... DCT
Diversified Data Resources, Inc. [*Information service or system*] (IID) ... DDRI
Diversified Economic and Planning Associates ... DEPA
Diversified Entertainment [*Vancouver Stock Exchange symbol*] ... DDE
Diversified Foods, Inc. (MHDW) ... DIFSD
Diversified Pharmaceutical Services (ECON) ... DPS
Diversified Processed Foods [*Vancouver Stock Exchange symbol*] ... DPF
Diversified Techs Inc. [*Vancouver Stock Exchange symbol*] ... DIT
Diversion (DD) ... divers
Diversion (FAAC) ... DVRSN
Diversion Investigative Unit [*Drug Enforcement Administration*] ... DIU
Diversion Order [*Military*] (NVT) ... DIVERTORD
Diversion Path Analysis (PDAA) ... DPA
Diversional Therapy [*Psychiatry*] (DAVI) ... DT
Diversional Therapy Association of Australia ... DTAA
Diversity [*Genetics*] ... D
Diversity Combiner System ... DCS
Diversity Factor ... DF
Diversity Interfacility Link (LAIN) ... DIL
Diversity Receiving Instrumentation for Telemetry ... DRIFT
Diversity Reception Equipment ... DRE
Diversity Reception Receiver ... DRR
Diversity University [*On-line education*] [*Information retrieval*] ... DU
Diversity-Joining [*Genetics*] ... DJ
Diverted Force (CINC) ... DF
Diverted into Low-Velocity Layer (OA) ... DLVL
Diverter (KSC) ... DIV
Diverter Injection Tokamak [*Toroidal Kamera Magnetic*] **Experiment** (MCD) ... DITE
Diverter Valve (KSC) ... DV
Diverticular Disease of the Colon [*Medicine*] (DMAA) ... DDC
Diverticulum [*Anatomy*] (AAMN) ... D
Diverticulum [*Medicine*] (DAVI) ... divertic
Diverticulum [*Gastroenterology*] (DAVI) ... tic
Diverting Ileostomy [*Medicine*] ... DI
Divested Operating Company ... DOC
Divestiture Implementation Committee [*Ghana*] ... DIC
Dividatur [*Let It Be Divided*] [*Latin*] [*Pharmacy*] (BARN) ... divid
Dividatur in Partes Aequales [*Divide into Equal Parts*] [*Pharmacy*] ... D in P AEQ
Dividatur in Partes Aequales [*Divide into Equal Parts*] [*Pharmacy*] ... DIV in PAR AEQ
Dividatur in Partes Aequales [*Divide into Equal Parts*] [*Pharmacy*] ... DIV in PT AEQ
Divide (MSA) ... DIV
Divide [*Commonly used*] (OPSA) ... DIVIDE
Divide ... DV
Divide ... DV
Divide [*Commonly used*] (OPSA) ... DVD
Divide Check Test [*Computer science*] (IAA) ... DCT
Divide County Library, Crosby, ND [*Library symbol Library of Congress*] (LCLS) ... NdCr
Divide or Halt (IAA) ... DVH
Divide or Proceed (IAA) ... DVP
Divide Time Pulse (IAA) ... DVTP
Divided Access Line Circuit ... DALC
Divided Ringing (IAA) ... DR
Divided Spouses Coalition [*Defunct*] (EA) ... DSC
Divided Winding-Rotor ... DWR
Dividend [*Investment term*] ... D
Dividend [*Investment term*] (IAA) ... DD
Dividend [*Investment term*] ... DIV
Dividend (ODBW) ... div
Dividend [*Investment term*] ... DIVD
Dividend Disbursing Agent (DLA) ... DDA
Dividend Franking Account ... DFA
Dividend Investment Plan [*Stock purchase*] [*Investment term*] ... DIP
Dividend Payout Ratio [*Stock exchange term*] ... dpo
Dividend per Share [*Investment term*] (ADA) ... DPS
Dividend Received Deduction [*Finance*] ... DRD
Dividend Reinvestment Plan [*Also, DRP*] ... DRIP
Dividend Reinvestment Plan [*Also, DRIP*] ... DRP
Dividend Warrant (ROG) ... DW
Dividende [*Dividend*] [*French Business term*] (ILCA) ... Divde
Dividends and Earnings in Canadian Dollars [*Investment term*] (DFIT) ... G
Dividends from Space [*Defunct*] (EA) ... DFS
Divider Time Pulse Distributor Board (MCD) ... DTPB
Divinatio in Caecilium [*of Cicero*] [*Classical studies*] (OCD) ... Div Caec
Divinatory Arts World Association [*See also AMAD*] [*Rillieux-La-Pape, France*] (EAIO) ... DAWA
Divine [*or Divinity*] ... DIV
Divine Light Mission [*A cult*] ... DLM
Divine Name (BJA) ... DN
Divine Saviour Seminary, Lanham, MD [*Library symbol Library of Congress*] (LCLS) ... MdLaD
Divine Science Bachelor ... DSB
Divine Science Doctor ... DSD
Divine Science Federation International (EA) ... DSFI
Divine Science Ministers Organization (EA) ... DSMA
Divine Word College, Epworth, IA [*Library symbol Library of Congress*] (LCLS) ... IaEpD
Divine Word Missionaries [*See also SVD*] [*Italy*] (EAIO) ... DWM
Divine Word Seminary, Bay St. Louis, MS [*Library symbol Library of Congress*] (LCLS) ... MsBsS
Diving [*British military*] (DMA) ... Dg
Diving ... DIV
Diving ... DVNG
Diving Air Embolism [*Medicine*] (DAVI) ... DAE
Diving Dentists Society (EA) ... DDS
Diving Duty [*Military*] ... DVDY
Diving Duty [*Military*] (DNAB) ... DVNG DY
Diving Equipment Manufacturers Association (EA) ... DEMA
Diving Information Center [*Navy*] ... DIC
Diving Instrumentation Vehicle for Environmental and Acoustic Research (MCD) ... DIVAR
Diving Officer ... DO
Diving Officer-of-the-Watch [*Navy*] (DNAB) ... DOOW
Diving Pay [*Navy*] ... DIVPAY
Diving Saucer ... DS
Diving Support Vessel (DS) ... DSV
Diving Tender [*Non-self-propelled*] [*Navy symbol*] ... YDT
Diving Yeoman [*British military*] (DMA) ... DIVYEO
Divinitas (BJA) ... DV
Divinitatis Doctor [*Doctor of Divinity*] [*Latin*] ... DD
Divinity (BARN) ... Div
Divinity Calf [*Bookbinding*] (DGA) ... DIV CF
Divinity Circuit Edges [*Bookbinding*] (DGA) ... DIV CIRC
Divinity Edges [*Bookbinding*] (DGA) ... DIV E
Divinyl Ether-Maleic Anhydride [*Organic chemistry*] ... DIVEMA
Divinylacetylene [*Organic chemistry*] ... DVA
Divinylbenzene [*Organic chemistry*] ... DVB
Divinyloxydimethylsilane [*Organic chemistry*] ... DVOSI
(Divinyl)tetramethyldisilazane [*Organic chemistry*] ... DVTMDS
Divisao de Exploracao dos Transportes Aereos [*Angolan airline*] ... DETA

Divisao de Exploracao dos Transportes Aereos [*Angolan airline*] ... DTA
Divisi [*Divide*] [*Music*] ... DIV
Division ... D
Division (EY) ... DIV
Division (DD) ... div
Division ... DIV
Division ... DIVN
Division [*Mathematics*] (ROG) ... DV
Division Accounting and Finance Office [*Air Force*] (AFIT) ... DAFO
Division Adaptation Personnel (SAA) ... DIAPER
Division Administrative Assistant ... DAA
Division Advisory Group (MCD) ... DAG
Division Air Defense ... DIVAD
Division Air Defense Artillery (MCD) ... DIVADA
Division Air Defense Command and Control (MCD) ... DAD-C2
Division Air Defense Command, Control, and Communications [*Study*] (MCD) ... DAD-C3
Division Air Defense Study (MCD) ... DIVADS
Division Air Defense System [*Military*] ... DADS
Division Air Officer ... DAO
Division Airspace Management Element [*Military*] (INF) ... DAME
Division Ammunition Office [*or Officer*] [*Army*] ... DAO
Division Artillery [*Army*] ... DA
Division Artillery [*Army*] ... DIVART
Division Artillery [*Army*] (INF) ... DIVARTY
Division Artillery Group [*Military*] (AABC) ... DAG
Division Artillery Tactical Operations Center (MCD) ... DATOC
Division Avenue High School, Levittown, NY [*Library symbol*] [*Library of Congress*] (LCLS) ... NLevDH
Division Aviation Officer ... DAVNO
Division Base [*Army*] ... DB
Division Base [*Army*] ... DIVBASE
Division Battle Model (MCD) ... DBM
Division Battle Simulation ... DBS
Division Beachhead [*Army*] ... DBH
Division Classification Officer ... DCO
Division Clearing Station [*Medicine Army*] ... DCS
Division Commander [*Navy*] ... DIVCOM
Division Communications-Electronics Officer [*Military*] (AABC) ... DCEO
Division Contract Termination Team (AAG) ... DCTT
Division Court [*Canada*] (DLA) ... Div C
Division Crime Buffer ... DCB
Division Damage Control Petty Officer [*Navy*] (DNAB) ... DDCPO
Division Data Center [*Army*] (RDA) ... DDC
Division de Chimie Physique [*Division of Physical Chemistry - DPC*] (EAIO) ... DCP
Division Early Warning [*Army*] (INF) ... DEW
Division Engineer (MCD) ... DIVE
Division Engineer [*Army*] (AABC) ... DIVENGR
Division Engineering Planning Document ... DEPD
Division Entry (BUR) ... DE
Division Equivalent (MCD) ... DE
Division Final Appearance (SAA) ... DFA
Division Final Fade ... DFF
Division Flag [*Navy British*] ... DV
Division Follow-On ... DFO
Division for Advanced Systems Technology (SAA) ... DAST
Division for Children with Behavioral Disorders [*of Council for Exceptional Children*] (EA) ... DCBD
Division for Children with Communication Disorders [*Council for Exceptional Children*] ... DCCD
Division for Early Childhood (EA) ... DEC
Division for Girls' and Women's Sports [*of American Association for Health, Physical Education, and Recreation; also used in a book title*] [*Later, NAGUS*] ... DGWS
Division for Ocean Affairs and the Law of the Sea [*United Nations*] (OSRA) ... DOALOS
Division for Physically Handicapped (EA) ... DPH
Division for the Blind and Physically Handicapped [*Later, NLS*] [*Library of Congress*] ... DBPH
Division for the Visually Handicapped (EA) ... DVH
Division for Women in Medicine [*Defunct*] (EA) ... DWIM
Division Force Equivalents [*Army*] (AABC) ... DFE
Division Forms Control (AAG) ... DFC
Division Freight Agent ... DFA
Division Funding Control Point ... DFCP
Division Headquarters [*Military*] ... DHQ
Division Headquarters [*Army*] ... DIVHED
Division Increment [*DoD*] ... DI
Division Integrated Record System (SAA) ... DIRS
Division Level [*Combat model*] (MCD) ... DIVLEV
Division Level Data Entry Device (MCD) ... DLDED
Division Level Financial Management [*System*] (MCD) ... DLFM
Division Liaison Officer ... DLO
Division Logistical Operation Center ... DLOC
Division Logistics Control Center ... DLCC
Division Logistics Model (MCD) ... DIVLOGMOD
Division Logistics Organization Structure (MCD) ... DLOS
Division Logistics System (MCD) ... DLOGS
Division Logistics System Test [*Army*] (AABC) ... DLST
Division Logistics System Test/Seventh Army Card Processor System ... DLST/SEACAPS
Division Maintenance Battalion (MCD) ... DMB
Division Materiel Management Center [*Military*] (AABC) ... DMMC
Division Notice (AAG) ... DN
Division of Adult and Management Review [*United Nations*] (ECON) ... DAMR
Division of Adult and Vocational Research [*Office of Education*] ... DAVR
Division of Adult Corrections (OICC) ... DAC
Division of Adult Education [*Office of Education*] ... DAE
Division of Adult Education Service [*of NEA*] ... DAES
Division of Advanced Automotive Power Systems [*Energy Research and Development Administration*] ... DAAPS
Division of Air Pollution [*Public Health Service*] [*Obsolete*] ... DAP
Division of Allied Health Manpower [*Bureau of Health Professions Education and Manpower Training, HEW*] ... DAHM
Division of Ambulatory Care [*Later, DACHP*] (EA) ... DAC
Division of Ambulatory Care and Health Promotion [*of the American Hospital Association*] (EA) ... DACHP
Division of Applied Experimental and Engineering Psychologists (EA) ... DAEEP
Division of Applied Sciences [*Harvard University*] [*Research center*] (RCD) ... DAS
Division of Applied Technology [*Coast Guard*] ... DAT
Division of Assistance to States [*Department of Education*] ... DAS
Division of Associated Health Professions [*DHHS*] ... DAHP
Division of Atmospheric Surveillance [*Environmental Protection Agency*] ... DAS
Division of Basic Grants [*Office of Education*] ... DBG
Division of Biological Effects [*Bureau of Radiological Effects*] ... DBE
Division of Biologics Standards [*FDA*] ... DBS
Division of Biomedical and Environmental Research [*Later, Office of Health and Environmental Research*] [*Department of Energy*] ... DBER
Division of Biomedical Engineering [*University of Virginia*] [*Research center*] (RCD) ... BME
Division of Biometry and Applied Sciences [*Department of Health and Human Services*] (GFGA) ... DBAS
Division of Biometry and Epidemiology [*Department of Health and Human Services*] (GFGA) ... DBE
Division of Cancer Biology and Diagnosis [*National Cancer Institute*] ... DCBD
Division of Cancer Prevention and Control [*National Cancer Institute*] ... DCPC
Division of Cancer Treatment [*Department of Health and Human Services*] (GFGA) ... DCT
Division of Career Education [*Office of Education*] ... DCE
Division of Cataloging and Classification [*Later, CCS, RTSD*] [*American Library Association*] ... DCC
Division of Chemical Information [*American Chemical Society*] [*Information service or system*] (IID) ... CINF
Division of Chemical Information [*American Chemical Society*] [*Information service or system*] (IID) ... DCI
Division of Chemical Literature [*ACS*] ... DCL
Division of Church World Service [*Later, CWSW*] (EA) ... DCWS
Division of Civilian Marksmanship [*Army*] ... DCM
Division of Classification [*Energy Research and Development Administration*] ... DC
Division of College and University Assistance [*HEW*] ... DCUA
Division of Computer Research [*Formerly, OCA*] [*National Science Foundation*] ... DCR
Division of Computer Research and Technology [*Bethesda, MD*] [*National Institutes of Health*] ... DCRT
Division of Consumer Credit [*Federal Trade Commission*] ... DCC
Division of Contracts ... DC
Division of Controlled Thermonuclear Research [*Energy Research and Development Administration*] ... DCTR
Division of Defense Aid Reports [*Abolished, 1941*] [*Military*] ... DDAR
Division of Dental Health [*Bureau of Health Professions Education and Manpower Training, HEW*] ... DDH
Division of Drug Advertising [*FDA*] ... DDA
Division of Drug Biology [*Department of Health and Human Services*] (GRD) ... DDB
Division of Drug Chemistry [*Department of Health and Human Services*] (GRD) ... DDC
Division of Drug Information Resources [*Public Health Service*] [*Information service or system*] (IID) ... DDIR
Division of Drug Marketing, Advertising, and Communications [*Food and Drug Administration*] ... DDMAC
Division of Earth Sciences [*Marine science*] (OSRA) ... DES
Division of Earth Sciences [*National Research Council*] (USDC) ... DES
Division of Economic and Business Research [*University of Arizona*] [*Tucson*] [*Information service or system*] (IID) ... DEBR
Division of Economic Research [*Social Security Administration*] [*Washington, DC*] (GRD) ... DER
Division of Ecumenical Affairs [*Church of England*] ... DEA
Division of Educational and Research Facilities [*Bureau of Health Professions Education and Manpower Training, HEW*] ... DERF
Division of Educational Research Services [*University of Alberta*] [*Research center*] (RCD) ... DERS
Division of Educational Services [*Department of Education*] ... DES
Division of Electric Power Transmission and Distribution [*Energy Research and Development Administration*] ... DEPTD
Division of Eligibility and Agency Evaluation [*OE*] ... DEAE
Division of End Use Conservation [*Energy Research and Development Administration*] ... DEUC
Division of Energy Storage [*Energy Research and Development Administration*] ... DES
Division of Engineering and Applied Physics [*Harvard University*] (MCD) ... DEAP
Division of Engineering Research [*Michigan State University*] [*Research center*] (RCD) ... DER
Division of Environmental Biology [*National Science Foundation*] ... DEB
Division of Environmental Science [*Marine science*] (OSRA) ... DES
Division of Environmental Sciences [*National Science Foundation*] (USDC) ... DES
Division of Epidemiology and Statistical Analysis [*Department of Health and Human Services*] (GFGA) ... DESA

Division of Evaluation and Research [*Department of Labor*] (GRD) ... DER
Division of Foreign Labor Conditions [*Department of Labor*] ... DFLC
Division of General Medical Sciences [*National Institutes of Health*] ... DGMS
Division of Geothermal Research [*Energy Research and Development Administration*] ... DGR
Division of Government Research [*University of New Mexico*] [*Research center*] (RCD) ... DGR
Division of Graduate Education in Science [*National Science Foundation*] ... DGES
Division of Handicapped Children and Youth [*HEW*] ... DHCY
Division of Health Examination Statistics [*HEW*] ... DHES
Division of Health Interview Statistics [*Department of Health and Human Services*] (GFGA) ... DHIS
Division of Improved Conversion Efficiency [*Energy Research and Development Administration*] ... DICE
Division of Industrial Cooperation [*MIT*] (MCD) ... DIC
Division of Industrial Participation [*AEC*] ... DIP
Division of Information [*Marine Corps*] ... DIVINFO
Division of Information Management and Compliance [*Department of Education*] (GFGA) ... DIMC
Division of Information Science and Technology [*National Science Foundation*] ... DIST
Division of Information Services [*Council for Scientific and Industrial Research*] [*South Africa*] (IID) ... DIS
Division of Information Services [*Council of State Governments*] [*Information service or system*] (IID) ... DIS
Division of Innovation and Development [*Department of Education*] ... DID
Division of Institutional Development [*Office of Education*] ... DID
Division of Insured Loans [*Office of Education*] ... DIL
Division of Integration and Environmental Testing [*Social Security Administration*] ... DIET
Division of International Affairs [*An association*] (EA) ... DIA
Division of International Education [*Office of Education*] ... DIE
Division of International Education (of the American Council on Education) (EA) ... DIE (ACE)
Division of International Finance [*of FRS*] ... DIF
Division of International Medical Education [*Association of American Medical Colleges*] ... DIME
Division of International Security Affairs [*Energy Research and Development Administration*] ... DISA
Division of Isotopes Development [*AEC*] ... DID
Division of Juvenile Delinquency Service [*of SSA*] ... DJDS
Division of Labor Relations [*Energy Research and Development Administration*] ... DLR
Division of Labor Studies [*Indiana University*] [*Research center*] (RCD) ... DLS
Division of Law Enforcement Sciences [*Bureau of Indian Affairs*] (BARN) ... DLES
Division of Learning Disabilities [*Council for Exceptional Children*] ... DLD
Division of Library Automation [*University of California, Berkeley*] [*Information service or system*] (IID) ... DLA
Division of Library Services and Educational Facilities [*Office of Education*] ... DLSEF
Division of Logic, Methodology, and Philosophy of Science [*International Council of Scientific Unions*] ... DLMPS
Division of Materials Research [*National Science Foundation*] ... DMR
Division of Mechanical Engineering [*National Research Council of Canada*] ... DME
Division of Medicaid Cost Estimates [*Department of Health and Human Services*] (GFGA) ... DMCE
Division of Medical Radiation Exposure [*Bureau of Radiological Health*] ... DMRE
Division of Military Application [*Energy Research and Development Administration*] ... DMA
Division of Motor Vehicles (MCD) ... DMV
Division of Narcotic Addiction and Drug Abuse [*National Institute of Mental Health*] ... DNADA
Division of Naval Intelligence ... DNI
Division of Naval Reactors [*Energy Research and Development Administration*] ... DNR
Division of Nuclear Education and Training [*AEC*] ... DNET
Division of Nuclear Materials Management [*AEC*] ... DNMM
Division of Nuclear Materials Safeguards [*AEC*] ... DNMS
Division of Operational Safety [*Energy Research and Development Administration*] (MCD) ... DOS
Division of Organ Transplantation [*Department of Health and Human Services*] (PAZ) ... DOT
Division of Overseas Ministries [*National Council of Churches*] ... DOM
Division of Peaceful Nuclear Explosives [*AEC*] ... DPNE
Division of Personnel Preparation [*Department of Education*] ... DPP
Division of Physical Chemistry (EA) ... DPC
Division of Physical Research [*Energy Research and Development Administration*] ... DPR
Division of Physics, Canada Institute for Scientific and Technical Information [*Division de Physique, Institute Canadien de l'Information Scientifique et Technique*] **Ottawa, Ontario** [*Library symbol National Library of Canada*] (NLC) ... OONP
Division of Polar Programs [*National Science Foundation Information service or system*] (IID) ... DPP
Division of Policy Research and Analysis [*National Science Foundation*] ... PRA
Division of Production and Materials Management [*Energy Research and Development Administration*] ... DPMM
Division of Quality Assurance [*Department of Education*] (GFGA) ... DQA
Division of Quality Enhancement (AIE) ... DQF
Division of Reactor Development [*AEC*] ... DRD
Division of Reactor Development and Technology [*AEC*] ... DRDT
Division of Reactor Licensing [*AEC*] ... DRL
Division of Reactor Research and Development [*Energy Research and Development Administration*] ... DRRD
Division of Records and Archives, City of Toronto (NLC) ... OTCTAR
Division of Regional Operations (AAGC) ... DRO
Division of Rehabilitation Counseling [*of the APGA*] ... DRC
Division of Research [*Indiana University*] [*Research center*] (RCD) ... DOR
Division of Research [*Navy*] ... DR
Division of Research and Demonstrations Systems Support [*Department of Health and Human Services*] (GFGA) ... DRDSS
Division of Research and Evaluation in Medical Education [*Ohio State University*] [*Research center*] (RCD) ... DREME
Division of Research and Improvement, Vocational Education, and Rehabilitation [*Department of Education*] ... DRIVER
Division of Research Development and Administration [*University of Michigan*] [*Information service or system*] (IID) ... DRDA
Division of Research Facilities and Resources [*National Institutes of Health*] ... DRFR
Division of Research Grants [*National Institutes of Health*] ... DRG
Division of Research Information System (SAA) ... DORIS
Division of Research Resources [*Bethesda, MD*] [*National Institutes of Health*] ... DRR
Division of Research Services [*Bethesda, MD*] [*National Institutes of Health*] ... DRS
Division of Resources, Centers, and Community Activities [*National Cancer Institute*] ... DRCCA
Division of Retail Food Protection [*Food and Drug Administration*] ... DRFP
Division of Retirement and Survivors Studies [*Social Security Administration*] (GRD) ... DRSS
Division of Safeguards and Security [*Energy Research and Development Administration*] ... DSS
Division of Science Information [*National Science Foundation*] (IID) ... DSI
Division of Scientific and Technical Information [*International Atomic Energy Agency*] (DIT) ... DSTI
Division of Scientific Personnel and Education [*National Science Foundation*] ... DSPE
Division of Security Affairs [*ERDA*] (AAGC) ... DISA
Division of Ship Operations and Marine Technical Support [*Research center*] (RCD) ... SOMTS
Division of Small Manufacturers Assistance [*FDA*] ... DSMA
Division of Solar Research [*Energy Research and Development Administration*] ... DSR
Division of Space Nuclear Systems [*Energy Research and Development Administration*] ... DSNS
Division of Special Schools and Services (OICC) ... DSSS
Division of Sponsored Research [*Massachusetts Institute of Technology*] (MCD) ... DSR
Division of Sponsored Research [*University of South Florida*] [*Research center*] (RCD) ... DSR
Division of State Systems Management [*Social and Rehabilitation Service, HEW*] ... DSSM
Division of Student Support and Special Programs [*Office of Education*] ... DSSSP
Division of Supplemental Security Studies [*Department of Health and Human Services*] (GRD) ... DSSS
Division of Tax Research ... DTR
Division of Technical Information [*AEC*] ... DTI
Division of Technical Information Extension [*Later, Technical Information Center*] [*AEC*] ... DTIE
Division of Technology and Environmental Education [*Office of Education*] ... DTEE
Division of the AIDS [*Acquired Immune Deficiency Syndrome*] [*National Institutes of Health*] (EGAO) ... DAIDS
Division of Training and Facilities [*Office of Education*] ... DTF
Division of Unemployment Compensation [*A publication*] (DLA) ... DUC
Division of Validation [*Social Security Administration*] ... DV
Division of Veterinary Medical Research [*Department of Health and Human Services*] (GRD) ... DVMR
Division of Vital Statistics [*Department of Health and Human Services*] (DAVI) ... DVS
Division of Vocational and Technical Education [*Formerly, DVR*] [*Office of Education*] ... DVTE
Division of Vocational Education [*Department of Education*] (GFGA) ... DVE
Division of Waste Management and Transportation [*Energy Research and Development Administration*] ... DWMT
Division Officer's Guide [*A publication*] (DNAB) ... DOG
Division on Career Development and Transition [*Council for Exceptional Children*] (PAZ) ... DCDT
Division on Career Development of the Council for Exceptional Children (EA) ... DCDCEC
Division on Mental Retardation of the Council for Exceptional Children (EA) ... CEC-MR
Division on Physically Handicapped, Homebound, and Hospitalized [*Later, DPH*] (EA) ... DOPHHH
Division On-Line Tool System [*Allan Collautt Associates, Inc.*] [*Automotive engineering*] ... DOTS
Division Operating Instruction [*Air Force*] ... DOI
Division Ordnance Officer ... DIVOO
Division Ordnance Officer ... DOO
Division Piece [*Rotary piston meter*] ... DV
Division Police Petty Officer [*Navy*] (DNAB) ... DPPO
Division Primary Standards (AAG) ... DPS
Division Property Book Officer [*Military*] (AABC) ... DPBO
Division Quality Team (DOMA) ... DQT
Division Quartermaster ... DQM
Division Rapid Reaction Force [*Army*] (AABC) ... DRRF

Division Ready Force [*Army*] (MCD) ... DRF
Division Reconnaissance Team [*Warsaw Pact forces*] ... DRT
Division Reference Standards (AAG) ... DRS
Division Register (IAA) ... DR
Division Reliability Policy Committee (AAG) ... DRPC
Division Restructuring Study [*TRADOC*] [*Army*] (INF) ... DRS
Division Restructuring Study Group [*TRADOC*] [*Army*] (RDA) ... DRSG
Division Senior Advisor [*US advisor to the Army of the Republic of Vietnam*] (VNW) ... DSA
Division Service Area [*Army*] ... DSA
Division Signal Officer [*Army*] ... DSO
Division Standard Practice (AAG) ... DSP
Division/Station Code [*Searchable field*] [*Dialog*] (NITA) ... DS
Division Supply Control Point ... DSCP
Division Supply Officer [*Army*] ... DSO
Division Supply Point ... DIVSP
Division Support Area (AABC) ... DSA
Division Support Command [*Army*] (AABC) ... DISCOM
Division Support Control Center [*Army*] ... DSCC
Division Support Operations Center (MCD) ... DSOC
Division Support Slice Program (MCD) ... DSSP
Division Support Weapon System (MCD) ... DSWS
Division System Training Leader (SAA) ... DSTL
Division Tactical Area [*Army*] ... DTA
Division Tactical Operations Center ... DTOC
Division Tactical Operations System (MCD) ... DIVTOS
Division Tactical Zone [*Army*] (AABC) ... DTZ
Division through Army Group ... DIVTAG
Division Transportation Office [*or Officer*] ... DTO
Division War Game (MCD) ... DIVWAG
Divisional (ADA) ... DIVNL
Divisional ... DIVSNL
Divisional Administrative Area [*Military British*] ... DAA
Divisional Administrative Contracting Officer [*Military*] ... DACO
Divisional Agricultural Officer [*Ministry of Agriculture, Fisheries, and Food*] [*British*] ... DAO
Divisional Air Defense System (AAGC) ... DIVADS
Divisional Ammunition Column (ADA) ... DAC
Divisional and Full Court Judgments [*1911-1916*] [*A publication*] (DLA) ... D & F 11-16
Divisional Artillery Intelligence Officer [*British*] ... DAIO
Divisional Chief Superintendent [*British police*] ... DCS
Divisional Controls Group [*British*] (NITA) ... DCG
Divisional Court [*Legal term*] (DLA) ... DC
Divisional Court of Appeal [*Legal term*] (ILCA) ... DCA
Divisional Court Selected Judgments, Divisional Courts of the Gold Coast Colony [*A publication*] (DLA) ... Div Ct
Divisional Detective Inspector [*British police*] ... DDI
Divisional Education Officer [*British*] ... DEO
Divisional Electronic Warfare Combat (MCD) ... DEWCOM
Divisional Electronic Warfare Combat Model Test and Evaluation ... DEWCOM T & E
Divisional Electronic Warfare Intelligence Functional Analysis (MCD) ... DEWIFAS
Divisional Entertainments Officer [*British*] ... DEO
Divisional Executive Officer [*British*] ... DEO
Divisional Inspector [*Education*] (AIE) ... DI
Divisional Interests Special Committee [*American Library Association*] ... DISC
Divisional Land Agent [*Ministry of Agriculture, Fisheries, and Food*] [*British*] ... DLA
Divisional Machine Gun Officer [*British military*] (DMA) ... DMGO
Divisional Maintenance Area [*Military British*] ... DMA
Divisional Medical Officer [*British*] ... DMO
Divisional Naval Transport Officer [*British military*] (DMA) ... DNTO
Divisional Officer [*Agricultural Development and Advisory Service*] [*British*] ... DO
Divisional Orders ... DO
Divisional Pests Officer [*Ministry of Agriculture, Fisheries, and Food*] [*British*] ... DPO
Divisional Records Office [*British military*] (DMA) ... DRO
Divisional Routine Order ... DRO
Divisional Safety Inspector [*Ministry of Agriculture, Fisheries, and Food*] [*British*] ... DSI
Divisional Sergeant-Major [*British military*] (DMA) ... DSM
Divisional Superintendent [*British police*] ... DS
Divisional Vendor Data Coordinator (MCD) ... DVDC
Divisional Veterinary Officer [*Ministry of Agriculture, Fisheries, and Food*] [*British*] ... DVO
Divisional Work Request (AAG) ... DWR
Divisional-General [*British*] ... D-G
Divisionalized Analytical Ground Rule Exception Report ... DANGER
Divisions of Naval Staff Plans Division [*British*] ... DNSPD
Divisionsverfuegung [*or Divisionsverordnung*] [*Divisional Order*] [*German military - World War II*] ... DV
Divisor [*Mathematics*] (ROG) ... DIV
Divisor [*Mathematics*] ... DR
Divisor [*Mathematics*] (IAA) ... DV
Divisor Latch Access BIT [*Computer science*] ... DLAB
Divo [*Ivory Coast*] [*ICAO location identifier*] (ICLI) ... DIDV
Divorce [*Facetious translation of DV, Deo Volente (God Willing)*] (DSUE) ... DV
Divorce and Matrimonial Causes Court (DLA) ... Div & Mat Ct
Divorce and Separation (DLA) ... DIV & S
Divorce Anonymous [*Defunct*] (EA) ... DA
Divorce Help Sourcebook [*A publication*] ... DHS
Divorce Judge (DAS) ... DJ
Divorce Law Reform Association [*British*] (DBA) ... DLRA
Divorce Proceedings [*Legal term*] (DLA) ... Div
Divorce Registration Area [*Department of Health and Human Services*] (GFGA) ... DRA
Divorce Support [*An association*] (EA) ... DS
Divorced ... D
Divorced ... DIV
Divorced ... DV
Divorced Black Female [*Classified advertising*] (CDAI) ... DBF
Divorced Black Male [*Classified advertising*] (CDAI) ... DBM
Divorced Jewish Female [*Classified advertising*] ... DJF
Divorced Jewish Male [*Classified advertising*] ... DJM
Divorced White Female [*Classified advertising*] ... DWF
Divorced White Male [*Classified advertising*] ... DWM
Divrei Berakhot [*or Blessings*] **from Qumran. Cave One** (BJA) ... 1QS
Divrei Berakhot [*or Blessings*] **from Qumran. Cave One** (BJA) ... 1QSb
Divus [*The Late*] [*Latin*] ... D
Divus Augustus [*of Suetonius*] [*Classical studies*] (OCD) ... Aug
Divus Claudius [*of Suetonius*] [*Classical studies*] (OCD) ... Claud
Divus Iulius [*of Suetonius*] [*Classical studies*] (OCD) ... Iul
Divus Thomas [*Piacenza*] (BJA) ... DThom
Divus Thomas [*Piacenza*] (BJA) ... DThomP
Divus Titus [*of Suetonius*] [*Classical studies*] (OCD) ... Tit
Diwag [*Germany*] [*Research code symbol*] ... WV
Diwan [*France*] [*FAA designator*] (FAAC) ... DWA
Dixie [*Australia Airport symbol Obsolete*] (OAG) ... DXD
Dixie College, St. George, UT [*Library symbol Library of Congress*] (LCLS) ... UStgD
Dixie Council of Authors and Journalists (EA) ... DCAJ
Dixie National Corp. [*Associated Press*] (SAG) ... DixieN
Dixie National Corp. [*NASDAQ symbol*] (NQ) ... DNLC
Dixie Natl [*NASDAQ symbol*] (TTSB) ... DNLC
Dixie Regional Library, Pontotoc, MS [*Library symbol Library of Congress*] (LCLS) ... MsPon
Dixie Yarns [*NASDAQ symbol*] (TTSB) ... DXYN
Dixie Yarns, Inc. [*Associated Press*] (SAG) ... DixieYr
Dixie Yarns, Inc. [*NASDAQ symbol*] (NQ) ... DXYN
Dixieline Products, Inc. (MHDW) ... DIX
Dixmont State Hospital, Sewickley, PA [*OCLC symbol*] (OCLC) ... PHD
Dixmont State Hospital, Sewickley, PA [*Library symbol Library of Congress*] (LCLS) ... PSewD
Dixon [*Former USSR Geomagnetic observatory code*] ... DIK
Dixon, CA [*Location identifier FAA*] (FAAL) ... DIX
Dixon Correctional Institute, Jackson, LA [*Library symbol Library of Congress*] (LCLS) ... LJaD
Dixon, IL [*AM radio station call letters*] ... WIXN
Dixon, IL [*FM radio station call letters*] ... WIXN-FM
Dixon on General Average [*A publication*] (DLA) ... Dix Av
Dixon on Partnership [*1866*] [*A publication*] (DLA) ... Dix Part
Dixon on Title Deeds [*A publication*] (DLA) ... Dix Tit D
Dixon Springs Agricultural Center [*University of Illinois*] [*Research center*] (RCD) ... DSAC
Dixon Ticonderoga [*AMEX symbol*] (TTSB) ... DXT
Dixon Ticonderoga Co. [*Associated Press*] (SAG) ... DixnTic
Dixon Ticonderoga Co. [*AMEX symbol*] (SPSG) ... DXT
Dixon Unified School District Library, Dixon, CA [*Library symbol Library of Congress*] (LCLS) ... CDi
Dixon's Abridgment of the Maritime Law [*A publication*] (DLA) ... Dix Mar Law
Dixon's Law of Shipping [*A publication*] (DLA) ... Dix Ship
Dixon's Law of Subrogation [*A publication*] (DLA) ... Dix Subr
Dixon's Law of the Farm [*6th ed.*] [*1904*] [*A publication*] (DLA) ... Dix Farm
Dixon's Marine Insurance and Average [*A publication*] (DLA) ... Dix Mar Ins
Dixon's Mills, AL [*FM radio station call letters*] ... WMBV
Dixon's Probate and Administration Law and Practice [*3rd ed.*] [*1912*] [*A publication*] (DLA) ... Dix Pr
Dixonville School, Alberta [*Library symbol National Library of Canada*] (BIB) ... ADVS
Dix's School Law Decisions [*New York*] [*A publication*] (DLA) ... D Dec
Dix's School Law Decisions [*New York*] [*A publication*] (DLA) ... Dix Dec
Dix's School Law Decisions [*New York*] [*A publication*] (DLA) ... Dix Dec (NY)
Dixylylethane [*Organic chemistry*] ... DXE
DIY Home Warehouse [*NASDAQ symbol*] (SAG) ... DIYH
D.I.Y. Home Warehouse [*NASDAQ symbol*] (TTSB) ... DIYH
DIY Home Warehouse Co [*Associated Press*] (SAG) ... DIY Hme
Diyarbakir [*Turkey*] [*Airport symbol*] (OAG) ... DIY
Diyarbakir [*Turkey ICAO location identifier*] (ICLI) ... LTCC
Dizionario Epigrafico di Antichita Romana [*A publication*] (OCD) ... Diz Epigr
Dizygotic [*Genetics*] ... DZ
Dizygotic Twins Reared Apart [*Genetics*] ... DZA
Dizziness (KSC) ... DZ
Djajapura [*West Irian, Indonesia*] [*Airport symbol*] (AD) ... DJJ
Djakarta [*Batavia*] [*Java*] [*Seismograph station code, US Geological Survey*] (SEIS) ... DJA
Djakarta [*Java, Indonesia*] [*Airport symbol*] (AD) ... JKT
Djambala [*Congo*] [*Airport symbol*] (AD) ... DJM
Djambala [*Congo*] [*ICAO location identifier*] (ICLI) ... FCBD
Djambi [*Indonesia*] [*Airport symbol*] (AD) ... DJB
Djanet [*Algeria*] [*ICAO location identifier*] (ICLI) ... DAAJ
Djanet [*Algeria*] [*Airport symbol*] (OAG) ... DJG
Django Reinhardt Appreciation Society [*Inactive*] (EA) ... DRAS
Django Reinhardt Society (EA) ... DRS
Djelfa/Tletsi [*Algeria*] [*ICAO location identifier*] (ICLI) ... DAFI
Djerba [*Tunisia*] [*Airport symbol*] (OAG) ... DJE
Djibo [*Burkina Faso*] [*ICAO location identifier*] (ICLI) ... DHCJ
Djibouti [*IYRU nationality code*] [*ANSI two-letter standard code*] (CNC) ... DJ
Djibouti [*Aircraft nationality and registration mark*] (FAAC) ... J2
Djibouti [*Airport symbol*] (OAG) ... JIB

Djibouti/Ambouli [*Djibouti*] [*ICAO location identifier*] (ICLI) .... HFFF
Djoemoe [*Surinam*] [*Airport symbol*] (OAG) .... DOE
Djoemoe [*Surinam*] [*ICAO location identifier*] (ICLI) .... SMDJ
Djokele [*Zaire*] [*ICAO location identifier*] (ICLI) .... FZBL
Djougou [*Benin*] [*ICAO location identifier*] (ICLI) .... DBBD
Djupivogur [*Iceland*] [*ICAO location identifier*] (ICLI) .... BIDV
DK Platinum Corp. [*Vancouver Stock Exchange symbol*] .... DKP
DLB Oil & Gas [*NASDAQ symbol*] (TTSB) .... DLBI
DLB Oil & Gas, Inc. [*NYSE symbol*] (SAG) .... DLB
DLB Oil & Gas, Inc. [*Associated Press*] (SAG) .... DLB OG
DLB Oil & Gas, Inc. [*NASDAQ symbol*] (SAG) .... DLBI
DLJ Capital Trust I [*NYSE symbol*] (SAG) .... DLJ
DLJ Capital Trust I [*Associated Press*] (SAG) .... DLJ Ca
dl-Phenylalanine [*Biochemistry*] .... DLPA
DLSC [*Defense Logistics Services Center*] **Integrated Data System** [*Military*] .... DIDS
DLT Deutsche Regional [*ICAO designator*] (AD) .... DW
DLT Luftverkehrsgesellschaft mbH [*Germany ICAO designator*] (ICDA) .... DW
DM Management [*NASDAQ symbol*] (TTSB) .... DMMC
DM Management Co. [*Associated Press*] (SAG) .... DM Mgt
DM Management Co. [*NASDAQ symbol*] (SAG) .... DMMC
DMI Furniture [*NASDAQ symbol*] (TTSB) .... DMIF
DMI Furniture, Inc. [*Associated Press*] (SAG) .... DMI Frn
DMI Furniture, Inc. [*NASDAQ symbol*] (NQ) .... DMIF
DMI International Airlines [*Ukraine*] [*FAA designator*] (FAAC) .... DMI
DMR Group, Inc. [*Toronto Stock Exchange symbol*] .... DR
DMR Group, Inc. Class A SV [*Toronto Stock Exchange symbol*] .... DRA
DMR Group, Inc., Ottawa, Ontario [*Library symbol National Library of Canada*] (BIB) .... OODMR
DMX, Inc. [*Associated Press*] (SAG) .... DMX Inc
DMX, Inc. [*NASDAQ symbol*] (SAG) .... TUNE
DNA [*Deoxyribonucleic Acid*] **Adenine Methylation** [*Biochemistry*] .... DAM
DNA [*Deoxyribonucleic Acid*] **Affinity Precipitation** [*Analytical biochemistry*] .... DNAP
DNA Amplification Assay .... DAA
DNA [*Deoxyribonucleic Acid*] **Binding Domain** [*Genetics*] .... DBD
DNA [*Deoxyribonucleic Acid*]-Binding Protein [*Genetics*] .... DBP
DNA [*Deoxyribonucleic Acid*] **Data Bank of Japan** .... DDBJ
DNA Plant Tech $2.25 Cv Ex Pfd [*NASDAQ symbol*] (TTSB) .... DNAPP
DNA Plant Technology [*NASDAQ symbol*] (TTSB) .... DNAP
DNA Plant Technology Corp. [*Associated Press*] (SAG) .... DNA
DNA Plant Technology Corp. [*Associated Press*] (SAG) .... DNA Pl
DNA Plant Technology Corp. [*NASDAQ symbol*] (NQ) .... DNAP
DNA [*Deoxyribonucleic Acid*] **Unwinding Element** [*Genetics*] .... DUE
DNA[*Deoxyribonucleic Acid*]-like RNA[*Ribonucleic Acid*] [*Genetics*] (DOG) .... dRNA
Dnepa-Air [*Ukraine*] [*FAA designator*] (FAAC) .... DNE
Dnepropetrovsk Commodity Exchange [*Ukraine*] (EY) .... DCE
DNI Holdings, Inc. [*Vancouver Stock Exchange symbol*] .... DNI
Dnieproavia [*Ukraine*] [*FAA designator*] (FAAC) .... UDN
DNX Corp. [*Associated Press*] (SAG) .... DNX
DNX Corp. [*NASDAQ symbol*] (SPSG) .... DNXX
Do All Possible .... DAP
Do Anything Very Easily [*Computer science*] (PCM) .... DAVE
Do It Now [*Category of service call for maintenance or repair work*] [*Air Force*] .... DIN
Do It Now Foundation [*An association*] .... DIN
Do It Now Foundation (EA) .... DINF
Do Not Answer .... DA
Do Not Attempt Resuscitation [*Medicine*] (HCT) .... DNAR
Do Not Duplicate .... DND
Do Not Intubate [*Medicine*] (DAVI) .... DNI
Do Not Invite .... DNI
Do Not Like .... DNL
Do Not List .... DNL
Do Not Load [*Instruction re a freight car*] .... DNL
Do Not Pass to Air Defense RADAR [*Air Traffic Control*] (FAAC) .... NOPAR
Do Not Publish .... DNP
Do Not Reduce .... DNR
Do Not Renew [*A policy*] [*Insurance*] .... DNR
Do Not Report [*Medicine*] (DAVI) .... DNR
Do Not Resuscitate [*Medicine*] .... DNR
Do Not Set [*Printing*] (DICI) .... DNS
Do Not Transmit by Radio (NATG) .... NOTWT
Do Not Use .... DNU
Do the Right Thing [*Also, DWIM*] [*In data processing context, translates as "Guess at the meaning of poorly worded instructions"*] .... DTRT
Do What I Mean [*Also, DTRT*] [*In data processing context, translates as "Guess at the meaning of poorly worded instructions"*] .... DWIM
Do What I Mean, Correctly [*Computer hacker terminology*] (NHD) .... DWIMC
Do What I Need Done [*Also, DWIM*] [*In data processing context, translates as "Guess at the meaning of poorly worded instructions"*] (PCM) .... DWIND
Do What I Say [*Computer science*] .... DWIS
Do What You Say You Will Do .... DWYSYWD
Doane College, Crete, NE [*Library symbol Library of Congress*] (LCLS) .... NbCrD
Doane College, Crete, NE [*OCLC symbol*] (OCLC) .... NBD
Doany [*Madagascar*] [*Airport symbol*] (OAG) .... DOA
Dobbiaco [*Italy ICAO location identifier*] (ICLI) .... LIVD
Dobbs Ferry Public Library, Dobbs Ferry, NY [*Library symbol Library of Congress*] (LCLS) .... NDf
Dobbs Ferry Public Library, Dobbs Ferry, NY [*Library symbol*] [*Library of Congress*] (LCLS) .... NDfL
Doberman Pinscher Club of America (EA) .... DPCA
Dobie High School, Houston, TX [*Library symbol*] [*Library of Congress*] (LCLS) .... TxHDH
Dobie Public Library, Dobie, ON, Canada [*Library symbol*] [*Library of Congress*] (LCLS) .... CaODob
Dobie Public Library, Ontario [*Library symbol National Library of Canada*] (BIB) .... ODOB
DOBIS (Dortmunder Bibliothekssystem), Ottawa, Ontario [*Library symbol National Library of Canada*] (NLC) .... OODBS
Dobo [*Indonesia*] [*ICAO location identifier*] (ICLI) .... WAPD
Dobra [*Monetary unit*] (ODBW) .... Db
Dobrolet Airlines [*Russian Federation*] [*ICAO designator*] (FAAC) .... DOB
Dobrovol'noe Obshchestvo Sodeistvila Armii, Aviatsii, i Flotu [*Voluntary Society for Cooperation with the Army, Aviation, and the Fleet*] [*Former USSR*] .... DOSAAF
Dobson, NC [*AM radio station call letters*] .... WYZD
Dobson Unit (USDC) .... DU
Dobson Unit [*Measure of ozone*] .... DU
Dobutamine [*Pharmacology*] (DAVI) .... DOB
DOC (Doctors Ought to Care) (EA) .... DOC
DOC [*Department of Commerce*]/NASA Satellite Program Review Board (NOAA) .... DNSPRB
DOCARE International (EA) .... DI
Docent .... Doc
Dock .... DK
Dock and Harbour Authorities' Association [*British*] (ODBW) .... D & HAA
Dock Brief [*British*] (ADA) .... DB
Dock Dues and Shipping (DLA) .... DD & Shpg
Dock Junction, GA [*FM radio station call letters*] .... WXMK
Dock Mounted Loader (RDA) .... DML
Dock Office (ROG) .... DO
Dock Operations (DS) .... DO
Dock Receipt .... DR
Dock Service .... DS
Dock Warehouse [*Shipping*] (ROG) .... DW
Dock Warrant .... DW
Dock, Wharf, Riverside, and General Labourers' Union [*British*] .... DWRGLU
Docked Configuration Transfer (MCD) .... DCT
Dockers' Union [*British*] .... DU
Docket [*Law, Packaging*] .... DKT
Docket .... DOC
Docket (DLA) .... DOCK
Docket and the Barrister [*1889-98*] [*Canada*] [*A publication*] (DLA) .... Docket
[*The*] **DocketSearch Network, Inc.** [*Information service or system*] (IID) .... DSNI
Docking (MSA) .... DCKG
Docking [*Aerospace*] (NASA) .... DCKNG
Docking .... DK
Docking [*Aerospace*] (KSC) .... DKG
Docking Adapter [*Aerospace*] (MCD) .... DA
Docking Alignment Target [*NASA*] (MCD) .... DAT
Docking and Berthing (SSD) .... D & B
Docking and Crew Transfer [*Aerospace*] .... D & CT
Docking Initiate .... DKI
Docking Lock Handle .... DLH
Docking Mechanism (MCD) .... DM
Docking Mechanism System [*or Subsystem*] [*NASA*] (NASA) .... DMS
Docking Module [*NASA*] .... DM
Docking Module Subsystem (MCD) .... DMS
Docking Protein [*Biochemistry*] .... DP
Docking Survey .... DS
Docking System .... DS
Docklands Enterprise Zone [*British*] .... DEZ
Docklands Light Railway [*British*] (ECON) .... DLR
Docklands Taskforce [*Victoria*] [*Australia*] .... DT
Dockside Proofing Vehicle .... DPV
Dockside Training Simulator .... DSTS
Dockside Underway Replenishment Simulator [*Navy*] (DNAB) .... DURS
Dockside Underway Replenishment Simulator [*Navy*] (NVT) .... DUS
Dockyard .... DY
Dockyard .... DYD
Dockyard Department [*Navy British*] .... DD
Dockyard Ship Riggers' Association [*A union*] [*British*] .... DSRA
Docosahexaenoic Acid [*Organic chemistry*] .... DHA
Docteur de l'Universite de Paris [*Doctor of the University of Paris*] [*French*] (BARN) .... DUP
Docteur d'Universite [*Doctor of the University*] [*Canada*] (DD) .... DU
Docteur en Droit [*Doctor of Law*] [*French*] .... D en D
Docteur en Droit Canonique [*Doctor of Canon Law*] [*French*] (ILCA) .... DDC
Docteur es Sciences Agricole [*Doctor of Agricultural Sciences*] (DD) .... DSA
Docteur es Sciences Economiques (DD) .... DesScEco
Doctor .... D
Doctor (EY) .... DOC
Doctor .... Doct
Doctor (EY) .... DR
Doctor (DD) .... Dr
Doctor .... DR
Doctor and Martyr (ROG) .... D & M
Dr. & Mrs. (VRA) .... D/M
Doctor and Student [*A publication*] (DLA) .... D & S
Doctor and Student [*A publication*] (DSA) .... Dr & S
Doctor Blade [*Photogravure*] (DGA) .... DOC
Dr. Brown Elementary School, Pipestone, MN [*Library symbol*] [*Library of Congress*] (LCLS) .... MnPpBES
Dr. Charles A. Janeway Child Health Centre, St. John's, Newfoundland [*Library symbol National Library of Canada*] (NLC) .... NFSCJ
Doctor Chirurgiae Dentalis [*Doctor of Dental Surgery*] [*British*] .... DChD
Doctor Divinitatis [*Doctor of Divinity*] [*Latin*] .... DD

Dr. Dobb's Journal [*M & T Publishing, Inc.*] [*Information service or system*] (CRD) ... DDJ
Dr. Dvorkovitz & Associates [*Information service or system*] (IID) ... DDA
Dr. Edward Bach Healing Society [*Defunct*] (EA) ... DEBHS
Doctor Edward Bach Society of Australia ... DEBSA
Dr. Everett Chalmers Hospital, Fredericton, New Brunswick [*Library symbol National Library of Canada*] (NLC) ... NBFDEC
Dr. Harry Paikin Library, Hamilton Board of Education, Ontario [*Library symbol National Library of Canada*] (NLC) ... OHEC
Doctor Honoris Causa [*Honorary Doctor*] [*Latin*] (BARN) ... Drhc
Doctor in Administrative Sciences ... DScAdm
Doctor in Agricultural Sciences ... DASc
Doctor in Clinical Pathology ... DCP
Doctor in Missionology ... DMs
Doctor in Veterinary Radiology ... DVR
Doctor Ingeniariae [*Doctor of Engineering*] ... D Ing
Doctor Ingeniariae [*Doctor of Engineering*] ... Dr Ing
Dr. John W. Tintera Memorial Hypoglycemia Lay Group (EA) ... HLG
Doctor Juris [*Doctor of Law*] ... DJ
Doctor Juris [*Doctor of Law*] (EY) ... Dr Jur
Doctor Juris [*Doctor of Law*] ... DrJ
Doctor Juris Canonici [*Doctor of Canon Law*] [*Latin*] ... Dr Jur Can
Doctor Juris et Rerum Politicarum [*Doctor of Law and Politics*] [*Latin*] ... D Jur et Rer Pol
Doctor Juris Utriusque [*Doctor of Both Laws*] ... DrJU
Dr. Karl Thomae GmbH [*Germany*] [*Research code symbol*] ... N
Dr. Karl Thomae GmbH [*Germany*] [*Research code symbol*] ... PB
Dr. Madaus & Co. [*Germany*] [*Research code symbol*] ... AS
Doctor Martens [*Footwear*] ... DM
Doctor Martin Luther College, New Ulm, MN [*OCLC symbol*] (OCLC) ... DML
Doctor Martin Luther College, New Ulm, MN [*Library symbol Library of Congress*] (LCLS) ... MnNeuL
Doctor Medicinae Universae [*Latin*] ... DrMedUniv
Doctor Medicinae Veterinariae [*Doctor of Veterinary Medicine*] [*Latin*] ... DMedVer
Doctor Medicinae Veterinariae [*Doctor of Veterinary Medicine*] [*Latin*] ... Dr Med Vet
Doctor Oeconomiae [*Doctor of Economics*] ... D Oec
Doctor of Accountancy [*or Accounting*] ... D Acc
Doctor of Accounting (PGP) ... DA
Doctor of Accounts ... D Ac
Doctor of Acupuncture [*British*] (DBQ) ... DrAc
Doctor of Administration ... D Adm
Doctor of Administrative Engineering ... D Adm Eng
Doctor of Aeronautical Engineering ... D Ae E
Doctor of Aeronautical Engineering ... D Ae Eng
Doctor of Aeronautical Engineering ... D Aero E
Doctor of Aeronautical Science ... D Ae S
Doctor of Aeronautical Science ... D Ae Sc
Doctor of Aeronautical Science ... Dr Ae S
Doctor of Aeronautical Science ... Dr Ae Sc
Doctor of Aeronautics ... D Ae
Doctor of Agricultural Engineering ... D Agr E
Doctor of Agricultural Engineering ... D Agr Eng
Doctor of Agricultural Science ... D Agr S
Doctor of Agricultural Science ... D Agr Sc
Doctor of Agricultural Science (ADA) ... DAgSc
Doctor of Agricultural Sciences (DD) ... DSA
Doctor of Agriculture ... D Ag
Doctor of Agriculture ... D Agr
Doctor of Agriculture ... D Agric
Doctor of Agriculture ... Dr Agr
Doctor of Air Conditioning Engineering ... DAC Eng
Doctor of Air Conditioning Engineering ... DACE
Doctor of Applied Arts ... DAA
Doctor of Applied Chemistry ... DA Chem
Doctor of Applied Science ... DA Sc
Doctor of Applied Science (ADA) ... DAppSc
Doctor of Applied Science ... DAS
Doctor of Archaeology ... D Ark
Doctor of Archaeology ... DA
Doctor of Architectural Design ... D Arch Des
Doctor of Architectural Engineering ... D Arch E
Doctor of Architectural Engineering ... D Arch Eng
Doctor of Architecture ... D Arch
Doctor of Art Education ... DAE
Doctor of Art of Oratory ... DAO
Doctor of Arts ... AD
Doctor of Arts ... Art D
Doctor of Arts ... Arts D
Doctor of Arts ... DA
Doctor of Arts and Sciences ... D Ar Sc
Doctor of Arts in Education (PGP) ... DA Ed
Doctor of Arts in Information Science (GAGS) ... DAIS
Doctor of Arts in Training and Learning (GAGS) ... DATL
Doctor of Association Science ... D As S
Doctor of Association Science ... D As Sc
Doctor of Astronomy ... D As
Doctor of Automobile Engineering ... D Au E
Doctor of Automobile Engineering ... D Au Eng
Doctor of Aviation ... Dr Ae
Doctor of Ayurvedic Medicine ... DAyM
Doctor of Beauty Culture ... DBC
Doctor of Bible Philosophy ... Ph BD
Doctor of Biochemistry ... D Bi Ch
Doctor of Biochemistry ... D Bi Chem
Doctor of Biological Chemistry (NADA) ... DBiChem
Doctor of Biological Chemistry ... Dr Bi Ch
Doctor of Biological Chemistry (NADA) ... DrBiChem
Doctor of Biological Engineering ... D Bi E
Doctor of Biological Engineering ... D Bi Eng
Doctor of Biological Physics ... D Bi Phy
Doctor of Biological Sciences ... D Bi S
Doctor of Biological Sciences ... D Bi Sc
Doctor of Biophysics ... Dr Bi Phy
Doctor of Bio-Psychology ... BPD
Doctor of Business (ADA) ... DBus
Doctor of Business Administration ... DB Ad
Doctor of Business Administration ... DB Adm
Doctor of Business Administration ... DBA
Doctor of Business Administration (NADA) ... DrBusAdm
Doctor of Business Administration ... DrBusAdmin
Doctor of Business Education ... DB Ed
Doctor of Business Management ... DBM
Doctor of Business Science ... DB Sc
Doctor of Business Science ... DBS
Doctor of Canon Law ... D Can L
Doctor of Canon Law ... D Cn L
Doctor of Canon Law ... DCL
Doctor of Canon Law ... Dr Can L
Doctor of Celtic Literature ... DLC
Doctor of Cement Engineering ... D Ce Eng
Doctor of Ceramic Engineering ... D Cer E
Doctor of Ceramic Engineering ... D Cer Eng
Doctor of Chemical Engineering ... D Ch E
Doctor of Chemical Engineering ... D Ch Eng
Doctor of Chemical Engineering ... D Che E
Doctor of Chemical Engineering ... D Chem E
Doctor of Chemistry ... Ch D
Doctor of Chemistry (PGP) ... D Chem
Doctor of Chemistry (GAGS) ... DChem
Doctor of Chemistry (WDAA) ... DR CHEM
Doctor of Chiropody ... Cp D
Doctor of Chiropractic ... DC
Doctor of Chiropractic and Physiological Therapeutics ... DCPT
Doctor of Chiropraxis ... DC
Doctor of Christian Archeology ... DoctArch
Doctor of Christian Education ... D Chr Ed
Doctor of Christian Science [*Used by teachers who received instruction directly from Mary Baker Eddy*] ... CSD
Doctor of Christian Science ... DCS
Doctor of Christian Science ... DSC
Doctor of Christian Service ... DCS
Doctor of Christian Theology ... DCT
Doctor of Christian Training ... DCT
Doctor of Church History ... DHE
Doctor of Church Music (PGP) ... DCM
Doctor of City Forestry ... DCF
Doctor of City Planning ... DCP
Doctor of Civil Engineering ... DCE
Doctor of Civil Law ... CLD
Doctor of Civil Law (NADA) ... DCivL
Doctor of Civil Law ... DCL
Doctor of Classical Literature ... DCL
Doctor of Clinical Medicine of the Tropics [*British*] (DAVI) ... DCMT
Doctor of Clinical Science (ADA) ... DClSc
Doctor of Clinical Science (NADA) ... DClSci
Doctor of Commerce ... D Com
Doctor of Commerce ... DComm
Doctor of Commerce ... Dr Com
Doctor of Commercial Administration ... D Com Adm
Doctor of Commercial Arts ... DCA
Doctor of Commercial Education ... DC Ed
Doctor of Commercial Law ... DCL
Doctor of Commercial Law (ADA) ... DComL
Doctor of Commercial Science ... D Com Sc
Doctor of Commercial Science ... DC Sc
Doctor of Commercial Science ... DCS
Doctor of Commercial Science ... Dr CS
Doctor of Commercial Science ... DrComSc
Doctor of Commercial Science ... DSC
Doctor of Commercial Science ... SCD
Doctor of Commercial Service ... DC Se
Doctor of Comparative Law ... D Comp L
Doctor of Comparative Law (DLA) ... DCL
Doctor of Comparative Medicine ... DCM
Doctor of Comparative Medicine ... MCD
Doctor of Comparative Religion ... DCR
Doctor of Computer Science (PGP) ... DCS
Doctor of Cosmology ... D Co
Doctor of Creative Arts ... DCA
Doctor of Criminal Jurisprudence ... CJD
Doctor of Criminal Jurisprudence ... DCJ
Doctor of Criminal Jurisprudence ... Dr Cr Jus
Doctor of Criminology ... D Cr
Doctor of Criminology (GAGS) ... DCrim
Doctor of Cultural Science ... Dr Cul S
Doctor of Cultural Science ... Dr Cul Sc
Doctor of Dental Medicine ... DDM
Doctor of Dental Medicine (DAVI) ... DM
Doctor of Dental Medicine ... DMD

Doctor of Dental Medicine	MDD
Doctor of Dental Science	DD Sc
Doctor of Dental Science	DDS
Doctor of Dental Surgery	DD Sur
Doctor of Dental Surgery	DDS
Doctor of Design	D Des
Doctor of Design	D Dn
Doctor of Design (PGP)	Dr DES
Doctor of Didactics	D Did
Doctor of Diesel Engineering	D Di E
Doctor of Diesel Engineering	D Di Eng
Doctor of Diplomacy	D Dipl
Doctor of Divine Literature	DDL
Doctor of Divinity (DD)	DD
Doctor of Divinity	DDiv
Doctor of Divinity (EY)	DDr
Doctor of Divinity	Dr D
Doctor of Divinity in Metaphysics	DD
Doctor of Dramatic Art	DDA
Doctor of Drugless Therapy	DDT
Doctor of Economic Science	D Econ Sc
Doctor of Economic Science (DD)	DESc
Doctor of Economics	D Ec
Doctor of Economics (EY)	D Econ
Doctor of Economics (NADA)	DE
Doctor of Economics	Dr Ec
Doctor of Education	D Ed
Doctor of Education (AIE)	DEd
Doctor of Education (ADA)	DEduc
Doctor of Education	Ed D
Doctor of Educational Studies	DEdStudies
Doctor of Electrical Engineering	DE Eng
Doctor of Electrical Engineering	DEE
Doctor of Electro-Chemical Engineering	DE Ch E
Doctor of Electro-Chemical Engineering	DE Ch Eng
Doctor of Elements	D El
Doctor of Elocution	D Elo
Doctor of Engineering	D Eng
Doctor of Engineering	DE
Doctor of Engineering	DEngg
Doctor of Engineering	Doc Eng
Doctor of Engineering	Dr Eng
Doctor of Engineering	Dr of Eng
Doctor of Engineering	ED
Doctor of Engineering	Eng D
Doctor of Engineering	Engr D
Doctor of Engineering Physics	D Eng P
Doctor of Engineering Physics	DE Phy
Doctor of Engineering Science	D Eng Sc
Doctor of Engineering Science	DE Sc
Doctor of Engineering Science	DES
Doctor of Engineering Science	Eng Sc D
Doctor of English	D En
Doctor of English	Dr En
Doctor of English Divinity	DED
Doctor of English Literature	DEL
Doctor of Entomology	D Ent
Doctor of Entomology	DE
Doctor of Entomology	Dr Ent
Doctor of Environment (PGP)	D Env
Doctor of Environmental Design (GAGS)	DED
Doctor of Environmental Design (GAGS)	DEnvDes
Doctor of Environmental Studies (DD)	DES
Doctor of European Law (DD)	DEurL
Doctor of Expression	D Ex
Doctor of Family Life	DFL
Doctor of Finance	Dr Fi
Doctor of Financial Science	DFSc
Doctor of Financial Science	DScFin
Doctor of Fine Arts	AFD
Doctor of Fine Arts	DFA
Doctor of Foreign Science	DFS
Doctor of Foreign Service	DFS
Doctor of Forest Engineering	DF Eng
Doctor of Forest Engineering	DFE
Doctor of Forest Science (ADA)	DForSc
Doctor of Forest Science	DFS
Doctor of Forestry	DF
Doctor of Forestry	Dr F
Doctor of Forestry and Environmental Studies (PGP)	DFES
Doctor of Forestry and Environmental Systems (GAGS)	DFES
Doctor of Geography	Dr Geo
Doctor of Geological Engineering	D Ge E
Doctor of Geological Engineering	D Ge Eng
Doctor of Geology	Dr Ge
Doctor of Geopolitics	Dr GP
Doctor of Health and Safety (PGP)	HSD
Doctor of Health Science	DHS
Doctor of Hebrew Letters [or Literature]	DH Litt
Doctor of Hebrew Letters	DHL
Doctor of Hebrew Letters (BJA)	LittHD
Doctor of Hebrew Literature	DH Lit
Doctor of Hebrew Literature	DHL
Doctor of Hebrew Studies (BJA)	DHS
Doctor of Home Economics	DH Ec

Doctor of Honorary Humanities	DHH
Doctor of Honorary Humanities	HHD
Doctor of Horticulture	D Hor
Doctor of Horticulture	Dr Hor
Doctor of Hospital Administration	DH Adm
Doctor of Hospital Administration	DHA
Doctor of Household Economy	DH Ec
Doctor of Household Science	D Ho Sc
Doctor of Human Services (GAGS)	DHS
Doctor of Humane Letters	D Hu L
Doctor of Humane Letters	DHL
Doctor of Humane Letters (NADA)	DHumL
Doctor of Humane Letters	DHumLitt
Doctor of Humane Letters	HLD
Doctor of Humane Letters (DD)	LHD
Doctor of Humanics	DH
Doctor of Humanitarian Service	DHS
Doctor of Humanitarian Service	Dr HS
Doctor of Humanities	D Hu
Doctor of Humanities	D Hum
Doctor of Humanities	DH
Doctor of Humanities	HHD
Doctor of Humanities of Learning	Dr HL
Doctor of Hygiene	D Hy
Doctor of Hygiene	D Hyg
Doctor of Hygiene	DHg
Doctor of Hygiene	Dr Hy
Doctor of Hygiene (DAVI)	DrHyg
Doctor of Industrial Arts	DIA
Doctor of Industrial Engineering	DI Eng
Doctor of Industrial Engineering	DIE
Doctor of Industrial Engineering	DInd
Doctor of Industrial Science	SID
Doctor of Industrial Technology (GAGS)	DIT
Doctor of Industry	D Ind
Doctor of Industry	Dr Ind
Doctor of Interior Architectural Engineering	DI Arch E
Doctor of Interior Architectural Engineering	DI Arch Eng
Doctor of Interior Architecture	DI Arch
Doctor of International Business Administration (GAGS)	DIBA
Doctor of International Law	DIL
Doctor of Irrigation Engineering	D Ir E
Doctor of Irrigation Engineering	D Ir Eng
Doctor of Jewish Education (PGP)	DJ Ed
Doctor of Jewish Literature (BJA)	DJL
Doctor of Jewish Pedagogy	DJP
Doctor of Jewish Studies (PGP)	DJS
Doctor of Jewish Theology	DJ Th
Doctor of Jewish Theology	DJT
Doctor of Judicial Science	DJ Sc
Doctor of Judicial Science	DJS
Doctor of Judicial Science	Dr J Sc
Doctor of Judicial Science	Dr JS
Doctor of Judicial [or Juridical] Science [or Doctor of the Science of Law]	JSD
Doctor of Judicial Science (GAGS)	JSD
Doctor of Judicial Science [or Doctor of the Science of Jurisprudence]	Jur Sc D
Doctor of Judicial Science (GAGS)	SJD
Doctor of Juridical Science	D Jur Sc
Doctor of Juridical Science	DJS
Doctor of Juridical Science	J Sc D
Doctor of Juridical Science	JDS
Doctor of Juridical Science [or Doctor of the Science of Jurisprudence or Doctor of the Science of Law]	SJD
Doctor of Jurisprudence	D Jur
Doctor of Jurisprudence	DJuris
Doctor of Jurisprudence (DD)	JD
Doctor of Jurisprudence (GAGS)	JD
Doctor of Landscape Architecture	DL Arch
Doctor of Landscape Design	DL Des
Doctor of Landscape Engineering	DL Eng
Doctor of Landscape Management	DLM
Doctor of Languages	D Lang
Doctor of Late Laws	DLL
Doctor of Latin Letters	D La L
Doctor of Law (PGP)	D Law
Doctor of Laws	DL
Doctor of Laws	Dr Iur
Doctor of Laws	Dr LL
Doctor of Laws (PGP)	LL D
Doctor of Laws (DD)	LLD
Doctor of Laws (GAGS)	LLD
Doctor of Laws and Political Science	Dr Jur et Rer Pol
Doctor of Letters	D Let
Doctor of Letters	D Lit
Doctor of Letters	DL
Doctor of Letters	DLitt
Doctor of Letters	Dr Litt
Doctor of Letters	LD
Doctor of Letters	Let D
Doctor of Letters in Economic Studies	DLES
Doctor of Letters in Economic Studies (ADA)	LittD(Econ)
Doctor of Letters of Journalism	LJD
Doctor of Liberal Arts	DLA
Doctor of Library and Information Sciences (GAGS)	DLIS
Doctor of Library Economics	DL Ec

Doctor of Library Science	DL Sc
Doctor of Library Science	DLS
Doctor of Library Science (GAGS)	DLS
Doctor of Library Science	Dr LS
Doctor of Library Science	LSD
Doctor of Life Science	LSD
Doctor of Literary Interpretation	DLI
Doctor of Literature	D Lit
Doctor of Literature	DL
Doctor of Literature	DLitt
Doctor of Literature	Dr Lit
Doctor of Literature (DD)	LHD
Doctor of Lithuanian Philology	Phil LD
Doctor of Management (PGP)	DM
Doctor of Management Sciences	DManSc
Doctor of Marine Engineering	D Ma E
Doctor of Marine Engineering	D Ma Eng
Doctor of Marriage and Family Therapy (PGP)	DMFT
Doctor of Mathematics	DM
Doctor of Mathematics (NADA)	DMath
Doctor of Mathematics	Math D
Doctor of Mathematics and Didactics	DMD
Doctor of Mechanical Engineering	DM Eng
Doctor of Mechanical Engineering	DME
Doctor of Mechanical Engineering (NADA)	DMecE
Doctor of Mechanical Science	DMS
Doctor of Mechanics	D Mech
Doctor of Mechanotherapy	Dr MT
Doctor of Medical Dentistry	DMD
Doctor of Medical Jurisprudence	MJD
Doctor of Medical Science (PGP)	D Med Sc
Doctor of Medical Science	DM Sc
Doctor of Medical Science [or Sciences]	DMS
Doctor of Medical Science	M Sc D
Doctor of Medical Science [or the Science of Medicine]	Med Sc D
Doctor of Medical Science (DAVI)	MScD
Doctor of Medical Science	MSD
Doctor of Medical Science	Sc D (Med)
Doctor of Medical Technology	DMT
Doctor of Medicine	D Med
Doctor of Medicine	DM
Doctor of Medicine	Dr Med
Doctor of Medicine (PGP)	MD
Doctor of Medicine (WDMC)	MD
Doctor of Medicine and Master of Surgery (DD)	MDCM
Doctor of Metallurgical Engineering	D Met E
Doctor of Metallurgical Engineering	D Met Eng
Doctor of Metallurgy	D Met
Doctor of Metaphysics	D Me
Doctor of Metaphysics	Ms D
Doctor of Meteorology (ADA)	DMet
Doctor of Meterology (NADA)	DMeteor
Doctor of Microbiology	D Mic
Doctor of Microbiology	Mic D
Doctor of Military Science	D Mil S
Doctor of Military Science	DMS
Doctor of Military Science (ADA)	DScMil
Doctor of Mining Engineering	D Mi E
Doctor of Mining Engineering	D Mi Eng
Doctor of Ministry	DMin
Doctor of Missiology (PGP)	D Miss
Doctor of Missionary Science	DMSc
Doctor of Modern Languages	DML
Doctor of Municipal Administration	DM Adm
Doctor of Municipal Administration	DMA
Doctor of Music	D Mus
Doctor of Music	DM
Doctor of Music	Dr Mus
Doctor of Music Education (PGP)	DME
Doctor of Music Education (GAGS)	DMusEd
Doctor of Music Education	Mus Ed D
Doctor of Music Ministry (PGP)	DMM
Doctor of Musical Arts (GAGS)	AMusD
Doctor of Musical Arts	D Mus A
Doctor of Musical Arts	DMA
Doctor of Musical Arts (GAGS)	DMA
Doctor of Musical Arts	Mus AD
Doctor of Musical Education	D Mus Ed
Doctor of Musical Education	DM Ed
Doctor of Musicology (NADA)	DM
Doctor of Natural History (WDAA)	NHD
Doctor of Natural Philosophy	Dr N Ph
Doctor of Natural Philosophy	Dr Phil Nat
Doctor of Natural Philosophy	NPhD
Doctor of Natural Science	DrNatSc
Doctor of Natural Science (NADA)	DrNatSci
Doctor of Natural Science (WDAA)	NAT SC D
Doctor of Natural Science (AD)	Nat ScD
Doctor of Natural Sciences	D N Sc
Doctor of Natural Sciences	Dr Sci Nat
Doctor of Natural Sciences	RNDr
Doctor of Naturopathic Medicine (PGP)	ND
Doctor of Naturopathy	D Nat
Doctor of Naturopathy	ND
Doctor of Naval Architecture	DN Arch

Doctor of Naval Engineering	DN Eng
Doctor of Naval Engineering	DNE
Doctor of Naval Science	D Na S
Doctor of Naval Science	D Na Sc
Doctor of Navigation	D Na
Doctor of Nursing	DN
Doctor of Nursing (PGP)	ND
Doctor of Nursing Education	DN Ed
Doctor of Nursing Education (DAVI)	DNE
Doctor of Nursing Science	DN Sc
Doctor of Nursing Science	DNS
Doctor of Nursing Science (GAGS)	DNSc
Doctor of Occupational Therapy (PGP)	Dr OT
Doctor of Occupational Therapy (PGP)	OTD
Doctor of Ocular Science	D Oc S
Doctor of Ocular Science	D Oc Sc
Doctor of Ocular Science	DOS
Doctor of Ophthalmology (WDAA)	D OPH
Doctor of Ophthalmology	D Opth
Doctor of Ophthalmology	DO
Doctor of Ophthalmology (NADA)	DOphth
Doctor of Ophthalmology (WDAA)	OD
Doctor of Ophthalmology	Oph D
Doctor of Optical Science	DOS
Doctor of Optometric Science	DO Sc
Doctor of Optometric Science	DOS
Doctor of Optometry (WDAA)	D OPT
Doctor of Optometry	DO
Doctor of Optometry	OD
Doctor of Optometry	Opt D
Doctor of Oral English	DOE
Doctor of Oratory	D Or
Doctor of Oratory	DO
Doctor of Oriental Languages	DOL
Doctor of Oriental Learning	DOL
Doctor of Oriental Medicine	OMD
Doctor of Orthopaedic Medicine and Surgery	DOMS
Doctor of Osteopathy	DO
Doctor of Osteopathy (WDAA)	OD
Doctor of Paediatrics [Medicine]	DPaed
Doctor of Painting	D Pa
Doctor of Painting	Dr Pa
Doctor of Pastoral Counseling (PGP)	DPC
Doctor of Patent Law	DPL
Doctor of Pedagogy	D Pd
Doctor of Pedagogy	D Ped
Doctor of Pedagogy	DPaed
Doctor of Pedagogy	PD
Doctor of Pedagogy	Pd D
Doctor of Pedagogy	Ped D
Doctor of Pediatric Medicine (NADA)	DPM
Doctor of Petroleum Engineering	D Pe E
Doctor of Petroleum Engineering	D Pe Eng
Doctor of Pharmaceutical Chemistry	D Ph C
Doctor of Pharmaceutical Chemistry	D Phar C
Doctor of Pharmacology	D Phc
Doctor of Pharmacy	D Phar
Doctor of Pharmacy	DP
Doctor of Pharmacy (ADA)	DPharm
Doctor of Pharmacy	PD
Doctor of Pharmacy	Ph D
Doctor of Pharmacy	Pharm D
Doctor of Philanthropy	D Phil
Doctor of Philanthropy	Dr Phi
Doctor of Philanthropy	Phi D
Doctor of Philology	Fil Dr
Doctor of Philosophy	D Ph
Doctor of Philosophy	D Phil
Doctor of Philosophy	DP
Doctor of Philosophy	DPhy
Doctor of Philosophy	Dr Philos
Doctor of Philosophy (WDAA)	PD
Doctor of Philosophy	PH D
Doctor of Philosophy (GAGS)	PhD
Doctor of Philosophy	PHDr
Doctor of Philosophy in Education [British] (ADA)	PhDEd
Doctor of Philosophy in Mechanics and Hydraulics	PhDMH
Doctor of Philosophy in Metaphysics	D Ph M
Doctor of Philosophy in Otolaryngology (PGP)	PhD Otol
Doctor of Philosophy in Surgery (PGP)	PhD Surg
Doctor of Philosophy (Medicine) (ADA)	PhD(Med)
Doctor of Philosophy (Royal College of Art) [British] (DBQ)	PhD(RCA)
Doctor of Photography	D Pho
Doctor of Photography	Dr Pho
Doctor of Physical Biology	DPB
Doctor of Physical Education	DPE
Doctor of Physical Education (GAGS)	DPE
Doctor of Physical Education	Dr of PE
Doctor of Physical Education (PGP)	PED
Doctor of Physical Medicine	DPM
Doctor of Physical Medicine and Rehabilitation (PGP)	PhDPM Rehab
Doctor of Physical Science	D Ph S
Doctor of Physical Science	D Ph Sc
Doctor of Physical Science	Dr P Sc
Doctor of Physical Therapy (PGP)	DPT

Doctor of Physics	D Phy
Doctor of Physics	Dr Phy
Doctor of Podiatric Medicine	DPM
Doctor of Podiatry (WGA)	DP
Doctor of Podiatry	Pod D
Doctor of Political Economy	DPEc
Doctor of Political Economy (NADA)	DPolEco
Doctor of Political Science	D Pol Sc
Doctor of Political Science	DP Sc
Doctor of Political Science (NADA)	DPolSci
Doctor of Political Science	DPS
Doctor of Political Science	Dr Pol Sci
Doctor of Political Science (NADA)	DrPolSc
Doctor of Political Science	DScP
Doctor of Political Science (NADA)	DScPol
Doctor of Political Science	PSD
Doctor of Political Science	SPD
Doctor of Political Sciences (EY)	Dr Sc Pol
Doctor of Preventative Medicine	DPM
Doctor of Preventative Medicine	Dr Pr M
Doctor of Professional Studies (PGP)	DPS
Doctor of Psychiatric Medicine	DPM
Doctor of Psychological Science (ADA)	DPsSc
Doctor of Psychological Science (NADA)	DPsySci
Doctor of Psychology	D Ps
Doctor of Psychology (WDAA)	D PSYCH
Doctor of Psychology	DPsychol
Doctor of Psychology	Ps D
Doctor of Psychology	PsyD
Doctor of Psychology in Metaphysics	Ps D
Doctor of Psycho-Therapy	D Ps Th
Doctor of Public Administration	D Pub Adm
Doctor of Public Administration	DP Adm
Doctor of Public Administration	DPA
Doctor of Public Administration	Dr PA
Doctor of Public Health	DPH
Doctor of Public Health	Dr PH
Doctor of Public Health (GAGS)	DrPH
Doctor of Public Health [British] (DAS)	PHD
Doctor of Public Health and Hygiene	Dr PH Hy
Doctor of Public Health Education	DPH Ed
Doctor of Public Health Engineering	DPH Eng
Doctor of Public Health Engineering	DPHE
Doctor of Public Health Nursing	DPHN
Doctor of Public Hygiene	DPH
Doctor of Public Hygiene	DPHy
Doctor of Public Hygiene	Dr PH
Doctor of Public School Art	DPSA
Doctor of Public School Music	DPSM
Doctor of Public Service	DPS
Doctor of Public Service	PSD
Doctor of Radio and Television Engineering	DRT Eng
Doctor of Radio and Television Engineering	DRTE
Doctor of Radio Engineering	D Ra E
Doctor of Radio Engineering	D Ra Eng
Doctor of Radio Engineering (NADA)	DrRaEng
Doctor of Recreation	Dr of Rec
Doctor of Recreation (NADA)	DrRec
Doctor of Recreation (PGP)	Re D
Doctor of Recreation (GAGS)	ReD
Doctor of Recreation Education (GAGS)	DRE
Doctor of Refrigeration Engineering	D Re E
Doctor of Refrigeration Engineering	D Re Eng
Doctor of Refrigeration Engineering (NADA)	DrReEng
Doctor of Regional Planning	DRP
Doctor of Rehabilitation (PGP)	Rh D
Doctor of Rehabilitation (GAGS)	RhD
Doctor of Religion	D Re
Doctor of Religion	DR
Doctor of Religious Education	DR Ed
Doctor of Religious Education	DRE
Doctor of Religious Education	DRelEd
Doctor of Religious Education	Ed RD
Doctor of Rural Engineering	D Ru E
Doctor of Rural Engineering	D Ru Eng
Doctor of Rural Science (ADA)	DRurSc
Doctor of Rural Science (NADA)	DRurSci
Doctor of Sacred Letters	DLittS
Doctor of Sacred Literature	DSL
Doctor of Sacred Literature	Sac Lit D
Doctor of Sacred Music	DSM
Doctor of Sacred Music	S Mus D
Doctor of Sacred Music	SMD
Doctor of Sacred Sciences	D Sa Sc
Doctor of Sacred Scripture	SSD
Doctor of Sacred Theology	DST
Doctor of Sacred Theology (NADA)	STD
Doctor of Sanitary Engineering	DS Eng
Doctor of Sanitary Engineering	DSE
Doctor of Sanitary Science	DSS
Doctor of Sanitation	San D
Doctor of School Music	D Sch Mus
Doctor of Science	D Sc
Doctor of Science	D Sci
Doctor of Science	Dr Sc
Doctor of Science	Dr Sci
Doctor of Science	DS
Doctor of Science (GAGS)	DSc
Doctor of Science	Sc D
Doctor of Science (GAGS)	ScD
Doctor of Science	Sci D
Doctor of Science (PGP)	SD
Doctor of Science and Didactics (ADA)	DScD
Doctor of Science and English Literature	DSEL
Doctor of Science and Hygiene	D Sci H
Doctor of Science (Engineering) (EY)	D Sc (Eng)
Doctor of Science in Agriculture	D Sc Agr
Doctor of Science in Agriculture	DScA
Doctor of Science in Agriculture (ADA)	DScAg
Doctor of Science in Agriculture (ADA)	DSc(Agric)
Doctor of Science in Business Administration	DS in BA
Doctor of Science in Commerce	D Sc Com
Doctor of Science in Commerce (NADA)	SciDCom
Doctor of Science in Commerce	SD Comm
Doctor of Science in Dentistry (GAGS)	DScD
Doctor of Science in Dentistry (WGA)	DScD
Doctor of Science in Economics	D Sc Econ
Doctor of Science in Economics (NADA)	DScEco
Doctor of Science in Economics	DSE
Doctor of Science in Education	Sc D in Ed
Doctor of Science in Education	Sc Ed D
Doctor of Science in Engineering	DScE
Doctor of Science in Forestry (ADA)	DScFor
Doctor of Science in Geological Engineering	DS in Ge Engr
Doctor of Science in Geophysical Engineering	DS in Gp Engr
Doctor of Science in Government	Sc D Govt
Doctor of Science in Hygiene	D Sc Hyg
Doctor of Science in Hygiene	Sc D in Hyg
Doctor of Science in Hygiene (GAGS)	SDHyg
Doctor of Science in Industrial Medicine	DSIM
Doctor of Science in Industry (NADA)	DScI
Doctor of Science in Medicine (DAVI)	MScD
Doctor of Science in Metallurgical Engineering	DS in Met Engr
Doctor of Science in Metallurgical Engineering (NADA)	DSMetEng
Doctor of Science in Metallurgy (NADA)	SciDMet
Doctor of Science in Metallurgy	SD (Met)
Doctor of Science in Nursing (PGP)	DSN
Doctor of Science in Petroleum Engineering	DS in PE
Doctor of Science in Petroleum Refining Engineering	DS in PRE
Doctor of Science in Surgery	DSS
Doctor of Science in the Social Sciences, University of Southampton [British] (DBQ)	DSc(Social Sciences)
Doctor of Science in Veterinary Medicine	D Sc in VM
Doctor of Science in Veterinary Medicine (GAGS)	DScVM
Doctor of Science of Jurisprudence (NADA)	DScJur
Doctor of Scientific Didactics	DS Di
Doctor of Scientology	D Scn
Doctor of Secretarial Arts	D Se A
Doctor of Secretarial Science	D Se Sc
Doctor of Secretarial Science	DSS
Doctor of Secretarial Studies	D Se St
Doctor of Social Science	D So Sc
Doctor of Social Science	D Soc Sc
Doctor of Social Science	Dr So Sc
Doctor of Social Science	DS Sc
Doctor of Social Science	DScS
Doctor of Social Science	DScSoc
Doctor of Social Science	DSocS
Doctor of Social Science	DSocSci
Doctor of Social Science (GAGS)	DSSc
Doctor of Social Science (WDAA)	S SC D
Doctor of Social Science	ScSocD
Doctor of Social Sciences (NADA)	DSS
Doctor of Social Sciences	Sc SD
Doctor of Social Service	D So Se
Doctor of Social Service	DSS
Doctor of Social Welfare	DSW
Doctor of Social Work	DSW
Doctor of Sociology	D So
Doctor of Sociology	Dr So
Doctor of Speech	D Sp
Doctor of Statistics	D St
Doctor of Structural Engineering	D St E
Doctor of Structural Engineering	D St Eng
Doctor of Surgery	D Sur
Doctor of Surgery	DS
Doctor of Surgical Chiropody	DSC
Doctor of Surgical Podiatry (WGA)	DSP
Doctor of Systematic Theology	D Sy Th
Doctor of Technical Chemistry (EY)	D Tech Chem
Doctor of Technical Chemistry (NADA)	DTChem
Doctor of Technical Science	D Sc Tech
Doctor of Technical Science	Dr Rer Tech
Doctor of Technical Science	Dr Sc Techn
Doctor of Technology	D Tech
Doctor of Technology	Dr Tech
Doctor of Technology	Dr Techn
Doctor of Technology	DT
Doctor of Technology	DTechnol
Doctor of Textile Chemistry	DT Ch

Doctor of Textile Chemistry ... DTC
Doctor of Textile Design ... DT Des
Doctor of Textile Dyeing ... DTD
Doctor of Textile Engineering ... DT Eng
Doctor of Textile Engineering ... DTE
Doctor of Textile Science ... DTS
Doctor of Textile Technology ... DTT
Doctor of the Humanities (DD) ... LHD
Doctor of the Royal College of Art ... Dr RCA
Doctor of the Science of Forestry ... DSF
Doctor of the Science of Jurisprudence ... Dr Sc Jur
Doctor of the Science of Jurisprudence ... DSJ
Doctor of the Science of Law ... D Sc L
Doctor of the Science of Law ... L Sc D
Doctor of the Science of Medicine ... M Sc D
Doctor of the Science of Oratory ... D Or Sc
Doctor of the Science of Oratory ... D Sc O
Doctor of the Science of Oratory ... Dr O Sc
Doctor of the Science of Oratory ... DSO
Doctor of the Science of Osteopathy ... D Sc Os
Doctor of the Science of Theology ... STD
Doctor of the University ... DU
Doctor of the University ... DUniv
Doctor of the University ... Univ D
Doctor of the University of Calgary ... DUC
Doctor of the University of Essex [*British*] (DI) ... DU
Doctor of the University of Paris (ROG) ... DR UNIV PAR
Doctor of Theology ... D Th
Doctor of Theology ... D Theol
Doctor of Theology ... Dr Theol
Doctor of Theology ... DT
Doctor of Theology ... THDr
Doctor of Thinkology [*Honorary degree awarded the scarecrow by the wizard in 1939 film "The Wizard of Oz"*] ... ThD
Doctor of Tropical Medicine ... Dr T Med
Doctor of Tropical Medicine ... DTM
Doctor of Veterinary Medicine ... D Vet Med
Doctor of Veterinary Medicine (NADA) ... DMV
Doctor of Veterinary Medicine ... DVM
Doctor of Veterinary Medicine ... MDV
Doctor of Veterinary Medicine ... MVD
Doctor of Veterinary Medicine ... VMD
Doctor of Veterinary Medicine and Science (NADA) ... DVMS
Doctor of Veterinary Medicine and Surgery ... DVMS
Doctor of Veterinary Science ... DV Sc
Doctor of Veterinary Science ... DV Sci
Doctor of Veterinary Science (ADA) ... DVetSc
Doctor of Veterinary Science ... DVS
Doctor of Veterinary Surgery ... DVS
Doctor of Veterinary Surgery ... DVSC
Doctor of Visual Aids (NADA) ... DVA
Doctor of Vocational Education ... DV Ed
Doctor of Zoology ... DZ
Doctor of Zoology (ADA) ... DZool
Dr. Otto Schaefer Health Resource Centre, Yellowknife, Northwest Territories [*Library symbol National Library of Canada*] (NLC) ... NWYOS
Doctor Otto Schaefer Health Resource Centre, Yellowknife, NT, Canada [*Library symbol*] [*Library of Congress*] (LCLS) ... CaNWYOS
Dr. Pepper Bottlers Association (EA) ... DPBA
Dr. Pepper Co. (IIA) ... DOC
Doctor Pharmaciae [*Latin*] ... Dr Pharm
Doctor Philosophiae [*Doctor of Philosophy*] ... Dr Phil
Doctor Philosophiae Facultatis Theologicae [*Latin*] ... Dr Phil Fac Theol
Doctor Rerum Commercialium [*Latin*] ... Dr Rer Comm
Doctor Rerum Montanarum [*Latin*] ... Dr Mont
Doctor Rerum Naturalium [*Doctor of Natural Science*] [*Latin*] ... Dr Rer Nat
Doctor Rerum Naturalium Technicarum [*Latin*] ... DrNatTechn
Doctor Rerum Politicarum [*Doctor of Political Science*] [*Latin*] ... DocRerPol
Doctor Rerum Politicarum [*Doctor of Political Science*] [*Latin*] ... Dr Rer Pol
Doctor Rerum Socialium [*Doctor of Social Sciences*] [*Latin*] ... RSDr
Doctor Rerum Socialium Oeconomicarumque [*Latin*] ... Dr Rer Soc Oec
Doctor Sacrae Scripturae [*Doctor of Holy Scripture*] ... DSS
Dr. Schwarz Arzneimittelfabrik GmbH [*Germany*] [*Research code symbol*] ... SM
Doctor Scientiae [*Doctor of Science*] [*Latin*] ... D Sc
Doctor Who Information Network [*Canada*] (EAIO) ... DWIN
Dr. William M. Scholl College of Podiatric Medicine, Chicago, IL [*Library symbol*] [*Library of Congress*] (LCLS) ... ICSPM
Dr. William M. Scholl College of Podiatric Medicine, Chicago, IL [*OCLC symbol*] (OCLC) ... JAV
Doctoral Dissertations Accepted by American Universities [*A bibliographic publication*] ... DDAU
Doctorat en Medecin Veterinaire (DD) ... DMV
Doctorat Honoris Causa [*Canada*] (DD) ... DHC
Doctorate in audiology ... AuD
Doctorate of Military Science (DD) ... DMil Sc
Doctorate Records File [*National Research Council*] [*Information service or system*] (CRD) ... DRF
Doctores Bononienses [*Latin*] (DSA) ... Doc
Doctores Bononienses [*Latin*] (DSA) ... Doc Bon
Doctores Bononienses [*Latin*] (DSA) ... Docs
Doctores Bononienses [*Latin*] (DSA) ... Doct
Doctores Tholosani [*Latin*] (DSA) ... Doc To
Doctores Veteres [*Latin*] (DSA) ... Doc Ve
Doctors' and Dentists' Review Body [*British*] (DI) ... DDRB
Doctors Emergency Service [*New York City*] ... DES
Doctors for Artists (EA) ... DFA
Doctors for Disaster Preparedness (EA) ... DDP
Doctors Health Advisory Service [*Australia*] ... DHAS
Doctors Hospital, Alexander Raxlen Memorial Library, Toronto, ON, Canada [*Library symbol Library of Congress*] (LCLS) ... CaOTDAR
Doctors Hospital, Freeport, NY [*Library symbol Library of Congress*] (LCLS) ... NFreeDH
Doctors Hospital, Medical Library, Coral Gables, FL [*Library symbol Library of Congress*] (LCLS) ... FCgDH
Doctors Hospital, Milwaukee, WI [*Library symbol Library of Congress*] (LCLS) ... WMD
Doctor's Hospital, Modesto, CA [*Library symbol*] [*Library of Congress*] (LCLS) ... CMDH
Doctors Hospital, Tacoma, WA [*Library symbol Library of Congress*] (LCLS) ... WaTD
Doctor's Order Book ... DOB
Doctor's Orders ... DO
Doctors' Reform Society of New South Wales [*Australia*] ... DRSNSW
Doctors to the World [*An association*] (EA) ... DTTW
Doctrina Placitandi [*A publication*] (DLA) ... Doct Pl
Doctrinal and Organization Test Support Package [*Army*] ... DOTSP
Doctrinal and Organizational Training Team [*Army*] ... DOTT
Doctrinal and Tactical Training [*Army*] (INF) ... DTT
Doctrinal Audio-Visual Program [*Military*] ... DAVP
Doctrinal Literature Program [*Military*] ... DLP
Doctrine (ROG) ... DOCT
Doctrine ... DOCTRN
Doctrine and Command Systems [*Army*] (RDA) ... DCS
Doctrine and Command Systems Directorate [*Army*] (RDA) ... DCSD
Doctrine and Systems Directorate [*Army*] (RDA) ... DSD
Doctrine Improvement Program ... DIP
Doctrine of Demurrers [*A publication*] (DLA) ... Doct Dem
Doctrine of Incremental Reduction ... DIR
Doctrine, Organizations, Training, Leaders, Material, and Soldiers [*Military*] (RDA) ... DOTLMS
Doctrine, Training, Leader Development, Organization, and Materiel [*Army*] (INF) ... DTLOM
Doctrine, Training, Leader Development, Organization, Materiel, and the Soldier [*Army education program*] (INF) ... DTLOMS
Doctrine, Training, Leader [*Development*] **Organizations Materiel Soldi ers** [*Army*] ... DTLOMS
DocuCon, Inc. [*NASDAQ symbol*] (NQ) ... DOCU
DocuCon, Inc. [*Associated Press*] (SAG) ... DocuCn
Document ... D
Document (ADA) ... DCT
Document [*or Documentation*] (AFM) ... DOC
Document [*Computer science*] ... doc
Document (WDMC) ... doc
Document ... DOCT
Document (AABC) ... DOCU
Document Abstract Retrieval Equipment (IEEE) ... DARE
Document Accession Number (IAA) ... DAN
Document Acquisition File (DNAB) ... DAF
Document Analysis Sheet (MCD) ... DAS
Document and Information Center of the Chinese Academy of Social Sciences ... DICCASS
Document Availability Code (MCD) ... DAC
Document Center of the Patent Office of China [*Library*] ... DCPOC
Document Change Analysis (SAA) ... DCA
Document Change Authorization (SAA) ... DCA
Document Change List (MCD) ... DCL
Document Change Notice ... DCN
Document Change Notice Proposal (MCD) ... DCNP
Document Change Record (NASA) ... DCR
Document Change Release ... DCR
Document Code [*Computer science*] ... DC
Document Composition Facility [*IBM Corp.*] ... DCF
Document Content Architecture [*IBM Corp.*] ... DCA
Document Control ... DC
Document Control Assistant [*Environmental Protection Agency*] (EPA) ... DCA
Document Control Book (MCD) ... DCB
Document Control Center ... DCC
Document Control Chief [*NASA*] ... DCC
Document Control File ... DCF
Document Control Number (AFM) ... DCN
Document Control Officer [*Environmental Protection Agency*] (EPA) ... DCO
Document Control Remote Station ... DCRS
Document Control Services ... DCS
Document Control Software (CDE) ... DCS
Document Control System [*Computer science*] ... DCS
Document Data Indexing Set ... DDIS
Document de Transport Combine [*Combined Transport Document*] [*French Business term*] ... DTC
Document Delivery [*Computer science*] (NITA) ... DD
Document Delivery [*Information service or system*] ... DOCDEL
Document Depository Index System (MCD) ... DDIS
Document Description Language [*Computer science*] ... DDL
Document Disposal Indicator ... DDI
Document Distribution (SAA) ... DD
Document Distribution and Reproduction Branch [*NTIS*] ... DD & RB
Document Effected Code (IAA) ... DEC
Document Enabled Networking [*Computer science*] ... DEN
Document Engineering Co., Inc. [*Information service or system*] (IID) ... DECO
Document Error/Clarification Request (SAA) ... DECR
Document Error Report ... DER

Document Evaluation Center (IAA) DEC
Document Exchange Architecture [*Data General*] (NITA) DXA
Document Exchange Format File (CDE) DXF file
Document Exploitation DOCEX
Document Facsimile Transmission (NITA) DOCFAX
Document File Transfer [*Computer science*] DFT
Document Filing and Retrieval [*Telecommunications*] (OSI) DIA
Document Flow Component [*Computer science*] (IAA) DFC
Document Generator DOCGEN
Document Handler Processor DHP
Document Handler Unit DHU
Document Handling (IAA) DH
Document Handling and Information Services Facility [*General Accounting Office*] (IID) DHISF
Document History File (MCD) DHF
Document Identification and Description Macros [*IBM Corp.*] DIDM
Document Identification Number (NG) DIN
Document Identifier [*Military*] (AFM) DI
Document Identifier [*Military*] (MCD) DOCID
Document Identifier Code [*Military*] (AFM) DIC
Document Image Processing [*Computer science*] DIP
Document Imaging Systems Corp. [*NASDAQ symbol*] (SAG) DCSR
Document Imaging Systems Corp. [*Associated Press*] (SAG) DocIm
Document Imaging Systems Corp. [*Associated Press*] (SAG) DocImg
Document Indexing and Listing of Graphic Information Codes System [*Jet Propulsion Laboratory, NASA*] DIA-LOGICS
Document Information Directory System [*NIOSH*] [*Database*] DIDS
Document Information Record (KSC) DIR
Document Information Retrieval (NITA) DIR
Document Interchange Architecture [*Telecommunications*] (OSI) DIA
Document Interchange Facility (IAA) DIF
Document Interchange Format DIF
Document Library Facility [*Computer science*] DLF
Document Locator Number [*Computer science*] DLN
Document Locator Number Counter File [*IRS*] DLNC
Document Log (AABC) DL
Document Management Software [*Computer science*] DMS
Document Management System DMS
Document Number (NITA) DN
Document Object Model [*Computer science*] DOM
Document of Industrial Engineering (KSC) DIE
Document Ordering Online [*Document delivery system, MEDLARS*] (NITA) DOCLINE
Document Ordres et Reglements Statutaires [*Statutory Orders and Regulations - SOR*] [*Database Federal Department of Justice*] [*Canada*] [*Information service or system*] (CRD) DOR
Document Organization and Control System [*Telecommunications*] (TEL) DOCS
Document Printing Network Signaling System [*Telecommunications*] (OSI) DPA
Document Processing Branch [*NTIS*] DPB
Document Processing Language (IAA) DPL
Document Processing System [*IBM Corp.*] [*Computer science*] DPS
Document Processing Unit [*Computer science*] (IAA) DPU
Document Publishing (IAA) DP
Document Read and Format Translator DRAFT
Document Read, Information Verify, and Edit DRIVE
Document Record Card DRC
Document Register (MCD) DR
Document Release Authorization (KSC) DRA
Document Release Notice [*Jet Propulsion Laboratory, NASA*] DRN
Document Release Order (NASA) DRO
Document Release Record (NRCH) DRR
Document Report DR
Document Reproduction Unit DRU
Document Requirement Description (KSC) DRD
Document Requirement List (KSC) DRL
Document Research Center, Bedford, MA [*Library symbol Library of Congress*] (LCLS) MBdD
Document Retention Unit [*IRS*] DRU
Document Retrieval Index DRI
Document Retrieval Services [*Information service or system*] (IID) DRS
Document Retrieval System DRS
Document Revision Notice (MCD) DRN
Document Sciences Corp. [*Associated Press*] (SAG) DocuSci
Document Sciences Corp. [*NASDAQ symbol*] (SAG) DOCX
Document Search and Research [*Xerox Corp.*] DSR
Document Service Center DSC
Document Service Management System (NITA) DSMS
Document Services for Printing [*Xerox Co.*] (PCM) DSP
Document Signed DS
Document Status Bulletin (MCD) DSB
Document Status Report [*Military*] DSR
Document Storage Search and Retrieval [*Air Force*] DSS & R
Document Storage System (NITA) DSS
Document Style Semantics and Specification Language [*ISO/IEC*] [*Computer science*] DSSSL
Document Summary List DSL
Document Survey Data Sheet (KSC) DSDS
Document Title [*European Space Agency-Information Retrieval System*] [*Searchable fields*] (NITA) DT
Document Transformation Component (IAA) DTC
Document Transmittal Record (NRCH) DTR
Document Type [*Online database field identifier*] DT
Document Type Definition [*Computer science*] (PCM) DTD
Document Validation Audit [*NASA*] (MCD) DVA
Document Validation Report DVR
Documenta et Monumenta [*A publication*] (BJA) DM
Documentacion Iglesial America Latina [*France*] DIAL
Documentacion Internacional de Carreteras [*International Road Research Documentation*] [*Database Ministerio de Obras Publicas y Urbanismo*] [*Spanish*] [*Information service or system*] (CRD) DIC
Documentacion y Comunicacion Publicitaria Espanola [*Database*] [*Universidad Complutense de Madrid*] [*Spanish*] [*Information service or system*] (CRD) DCPE
Document-and-Image Management System [*Computer science*] (PCM) DIMS
Documentary (WDMC) doc
Documentary (BARN) docum
Documentary Bill (ADA) D/B
Documentary Bill for Acceptance DA
Documentary Draft (ADA) D/D
Documentary Management System [*for citations*] DMS
Documentary Relations of the South West [*Arizona State Museum*] [*Tucson*] [*Information service or system*] (IID) DRSW
Documentary Research Division [*Air Force*] DRD
Documentation DCMNTN
Documentation DM
Documentation Accountability Sheet (MCD) DAS
Documentation Aid System (IAA) DAS
Documentation and Automatization of Researches for Correlations [*For molecular structure*] [*Chemical physics*] DARC
Documentation and Configuration Management Office (SSD) DCMO
Documentation and Integration of Software into the Classroom Project (EDAC) DISC
Documentation and Status (AAG) D & S
Documentation Associates Information Services, Inc. (IID) DA
Documentation Associates, Los Angeles, CA [*Library symbol Library of Congress*] (LCLS) CLDo
Documentation Automated Retrieval Equipment [*System*] [*Army*] DARE
Documentation Centre, Canadian Advisory Council on the Status of Women [*Centre de Documentation, Conseil Consultatif Canadien de la Situation de la Femme*]Ottawa, Ontario [*Library symbol National Library of Canada*] (NLC) OOCACSW
Documentation Centre, Canadian Intergovernmental Conference Secretariat [*Centre de Documentation, Secretariat des Conferences Intergouvernementales Canadiennes*], Ottawa, Ontario [*Library symbol National Library of Canada*] (NLC) OOCIC
Documentation Centre, Communications and Informatics, Transport Canada [*Centre de Documentation, Communications et Informatique, Transports Canada*], Ottawa, Ontario [*Library symbol National Library of Canada*] (BIB) OOTCI
Documentation Centre, Family Action [*Centre de Documentation, Action Famille*], Ottawa, Ontario [*Library symbol National Library of Canada*] (NLC) OOFA
Documentation Centre, George Etienne Cartier House, Parks Canada [*Centre de Documentation, Maison George-Etienne Cartier, Parcs Canada*], Montreal, Quebec [*Library symbol National Library of Canada*] (NLC) QMPCG
Documentation Centre, Goss, Gilroy & Associates, Ottawa, Ontario [*Library symbol National Library of Canada*] (BIB) OOGG
Documentation Change Control Report DCCR
Documentation Change Instruction (KSC) DCI
Documentation Change Notice DCN
Documentation Development Notification (KSC) DDN
Documentation Distribution List (KSC) DDL
Documentation Distribution System (NASA) DDS
Documentation et Information Africaines [*African Documentation and Information*] [*Catholic News Agency*] DIA
Documentation Group [*Range Commanders Council*] [*NASA*] DG
Documentation Implementation Team [*Deep Space Network, NASA*] DIT
Documentation Index System (MCD) DIS
Documentation Information and Control System [*Military*] DIACS
Documentation Information Transmittal (NVT) DIT
Documentation Informatisee pour les Comptables [*CEDIC*] [*Database*] DICOMTA
Documentation Management Officer [*Air Force*] (AFM) DMO
Documentation Manager [*Air Force*] (AFM) DM
Documentation Modernization [*Program*] [*Army*] (INF) DOCMOD
Documentation of Molecular Spectroscopy DMS
Documentation of Programs in Core [*Computer science*] (IEEE) DOPIC
Documentation on Social Security [*ILO*] [*Information service or system United Nations*] (DUND) DOSS
Documentation Processing Center [*British*] DPC
Documentation Request Form (MCD) DRF
Documentation Research and Training Centre DRTC
Documentation Research Project [*American Institute of Physics*] DRP
Documentation Service [*Swiss Academy of Medical Sciences*] [*Information service or system*] (IID) DOKDI
Documentation Staging Area [*Military*] DSA
Documentation Standards Committee (ECII) DSB
Documentation Standards Committee [*British*] (DIT) DSC
Documentation Support Services (NASA) DSS
Documentation Unit DU
Document-Based Indexing System (ADA) DBIS
Documented Discount Notes [*Banking*] DDN
Documented Material Processed DMP
Documented Sample (KSC) DS
Documenter's Workbench [*AT & T*] [*Computer science*] DWB
Documenti Contro Accettazione [*Documents Against Acceptance*] [*Italian Business term*] D/A

Documenti Contro Pagamento [*Documents Against Payment*] [*Italian Business term*] ..... D/P
Document-Management Systems ..... DMSes
Documento de Transporte Combinado [*Combined Transport Document*] [*Spanish Business term*] ..... DTC
Documento di Trasporto Combinato [*Combined Transport Document*] [*Italian Business term*] ..... DTC
Document-Oriented Interface [*Computer science*] ..... DOI
Documentos Contra Aceptacion [*Documents Against Acceptance*] [*Spanish Business term*] ..... D/A
Documentos Contra Pago [*Documents Against Payment*] [*Spanish Business term*] ..... D/P
Documents ..... DOCS
Documents Against Acceptance [*Banking*] ..... D/A
Documents against Acceptance [*Investment term*] (DFIT) ..... DA
Documents Against Acceptance [*Banking*] ..... DAA
Documents Against Discretion [*Banking*] ..... DAD
Documents Against Payment [*Banking*] ..... D/P
Documents Against Payment [*Banking*] (ADA) ..... DAP
Documents against Payment (DFIT) ..... DP
Documents Attached ..... DA
Documents Contre Acceptation [*Documents Against Acceptance*] [*French Banking*] ..... D/A
Documents Contre Paiement [*Documents Against Payment*] [*French Banking*] ..... D/P
Documents for Acceptance [*Banking*] (ROG) ..... D/A
Documents from Old Testament Times [*A publication*] (BJA) ..... DOTT
Documents Information Accessing (BUR) ..... DIA
Documents of Essex England Data Set [*System for the analysis of medieval charters*] [*Canada*] (NITA) ..... DEEDS
Documents of Limited Significance (MCD) ..... DLS
Documents of Limited Significance - Limited Distribution (MCD) ..... DLSLD
Documents on Acceptance [*Banking*] ..... DOA
Documents on Payment [*Banking*] ..... DOP
Documents On-Line [*Medicine*] (DMAA) ..... DOCLINE
Documents Parlementaires [*A publication*] (DLA) ..... Doc Parl
Documents per Minute [*Computer science*] (BUR) ..... DPM
Documents Presargoniques [*A publication*] (BJA) ..... DP
Documents Review Committee [*American Occupational Therapy Association*] ..... DRC
Documents Signed ..... DSS
Documents to the People [*Government Documents Round Table*] [*American Library Association*] ..... DTTP
Documentum, Inc. [*NASDAQ symbol*] (SAG) ..... DCTM
Documentum Inc. [*NASDAQ symbol*] (TTSB) ..... DCTM
Documentum, Inc. [*Associated Press*] (SAG) ..... Documnt
Docusate Sodium [*Medicine*] (DMAA) ..... DOSS
DoD [*Department of Defense*]/Army Information Architecture (RDA) ..... D/AIA
DoD [*Department of Defense*] **ATE Language Standardization Committee** ..... DALSCOM
DoD [*Department of Defense*] **Audiovisual Activities** ..... DAVA
DoD [*Department of Defense*] **Automatic Addressing System** (NG) ..... DAAS
DOD [*Department of Defense*] **Document** (DOMA) ..... DODD
DOD [*Department of Defense*] [*Intelligence Information System*] **Extension** (DOMA) ..... DODEX
DoD [*Department of Defense*] **Gateway Information System** [*Defense Technical Information Center*] (TSSD) ..... DGIS
DoD [*Department of Defense*] **Industrial Security Program** (AABC) ..... DISP
DoD [*Department of Defense*] **Information Security Advisory Board** ..... DISAB
DOD [*Department of Defense*] **Joint Intelligence Center** (DOMA) ..... DOD-JIC
DoD [*Department of Defense*] **Logistics Data Element Standardization and Management Office** ..... DESMO
DoD [*Department of Defense*] **Manager for Space Shuttle Support** (MCD) ..... DDMS
DoD [*Department of Defense*] **Nuclear Information and Analysis Center** [*Defense Atomic Support Agency Information and Analysis Center*] [*Kaman Tempo*] [*Acronym is based on former name,*] [*Information service or system*] (IID) ..... DASIAC
DoD [*Department of Defense*] **Officer Record Examination** ..... DORE
DoD [*Department of Defense*] **Standard Data Repository System** ..... DSDRS
DoD [*Department of Defense*] **Value Engineering Services Office** (IEEE) ..... DVESO
DoD [*Department of Defense*] **Worldwide Energy Information System** (MCD) ..... DEIS
DODAAC [*Department of Defense Activity Address Code*] **Edit/Validation System** [*Military*] ..... DEVS
Dodaira [*Japan*] [*Seismograph station code, US Geological Survey*] (SEIS) ..... DDR
Dodd and Brook. Probate Practice [*A publication*] (ILCA) ..... D & B Pr Pr
Dodd and Brooks' Probate Court Practice [*A publication*] (DLA) ..... Dodd & Br Pr Pr
Dodd Junior High School, Freeport, NY [*Library symbol Library of Congress*] (LCLS) ..... NFreeDJ
Dodd on Burial and Other Church Fees [*A publication*] (DLA) ..... Dodd Bur Fees
Dodds Publishing Co., Hawthorne, NJ [*Library symbol Library of Congress*] (LCLS) ..... NjHawD
Dodecadienyl Acetate [*Pheromone*] [*Organic chemistry*] ..... DDDA
Dodecahedron [*Golf ball design*] ..... DDH
Dodecandienol [*Pheromone*] [*Organic chemistry*] ..... DDDOL
Dodecanedioic Acid [*Organic chemistry*] ..... DDDA
Dodecanethiolate [*Organic chemistry*] ..... DDT
Dodecanoylsarcosyltaurine [*Crustacean detergent*] ..... DST
Dodecenyl Acetate [*Pheromone*] [*Organic chemistry*] ..... DDA
Dodecenylsuccinic Anhydride [*Organic chemistry*] ..... DDSA
Dodecyl Benzenesulfonate [*Organic chemistry*] ..... DBS
Dodecyl Benzenesulfonate [*Organic chemistry*] ..... DDBS
Dodecyl Sulfate [*Medicine*] (DMAA) ..... DDS
Dodecyl Sulfate [*Organic chemistry*] ..... $DodSO_4$
Dodecylamine [*Organic chemistry*] ..... DDA
Dodecylammonium Propionate [*Organic chemistry*] ..... DAP
Dodecylbenzene [*Organic chemistry*] ..... DDB
Dodecylbenzenesulfonic Acid [*Organic chemistry*] ..... DDBSA
(Dodecylbenzyl)trimethylammonium Chloride [*Organic chemistry*] ..... DBT
Dodecyldimethylamine [*or Dimethyldodecylamine*] [*Organic chemistry*] ..... DDA
Dodecyldimethylamine [*or Dimethyldodecylamine*] **N-Oxide** [*Organic chemistry*] ..... DDNO
Dodecylimidazole [*Antifungal*] ..... DDI
DodecylMaltoside [*Organic chemistry*] ..... DM
Dodecylmorpholine [*Antifungal*] ..... DDM
Dodecyloxyhydroxybenzophenone [*Organic chemistry*] ..... DOBP
Dodecylpyrene [*Organic chemistry*] ..... DDP
Dodecylpyridinium Bromide [*Organic chemistry*] ..... DPB
Dodecylpyridinium Chloride [*Also, LPC*] [*Organic chemistry*] ..... DPC
Dodecylsuccinic Anhydride [*Organic chemistry*] ..... DSA
Dodecyltrimethylammonium Bromide [*Organic chemistry*] ..... DTAB
Dodecyltrimethylammonium Chloride [*Organic chemistry*] ..... DTAC
Doderidge on the Antiquity and Power of Parliaments [*A publication*] (DLA) ..... Dod Ant Parl
Doderidge's English Lawyer [*A publication*] (DLA) ..... Dod Eng Law
Doderidge's Nobility [*A publication*] (DLA) ..... Dod Nobility
Doderidge's The Lawyer's Light [*A publication*] (DLA) ..... Dod Law L
Dodge ..... DDG
Dodge Brothers Club (EA) ..... DBC
Dodge City [*Kansas*] [*Airport symbol*] (OAG) ..... DDC
Dodge City [*Diocesan*] [*Kansas*] (TOCD) ..... DOD
Dodge City College [*Kansas*] ..... DCC
Dodge City, KS [*AM radio station call letters*] ..... KDCC
Dodge City, KS [*FM radio station call letters*] ..... KDGB
Dodge City, KS [*AM radio station call letters*] ..... KGNO
Dodge City, KS [*FM radio station call letters*] ..... KOLS
Dodge City, KS [*FM radio station call letters*] ..... KONQ
Dodge City Public Library, Dodge City, KS [*Library symbol Library of Congress*] (LCLS) ..... KDc
Dodge County Mental Health Center, Juneau, WI [*Library symbol Library of Congress*] (LCLS) ..... WJuMe
Dodge Revolutionary Union Movement ..... DRUM
Dodge Wayfarer Sportabout Registry [*Defunct*] (EA) ..... DWSR
Dodgeville, WI [*AM radio station call letters*] ..... WDMP
Dodgeville, WI [*FM radio station call letters*] ..... WDMP-FM
Dodola [*Ethiopia*] [*ICAO location identifier*] (ICLI) ..... HADO
Dodollo [*Ethiopia*] [*Airport symbol*] (AD) ..... DDL
Dodoma [*Tanzania*] [*Airport symbol*] (OAG) ..... DOD
Dodoma [*Tanzania*] [*Seismograph station code, US Geological Survey Closed*] (SEIS) ..... DOD
Dodoma [*Tanzania*] [*ICAO location identifier*] (ICLI) ..... HTDO
Dodrill, Charles T., Hurricane WV [*STAC*] ..... DCT
Dod's Parliamentary Companion. Annual [*A publication*] (DLA) ..... Dod
Dodson's English Admiralty Reports [*A publication*] (DLA) ..... Dod
Dodson's English Admiralty Reports [*A publication*] (DLA) ..... Dod Adm
Dodson's English Admiralty Reports [*A publication*] (DLA) ..... Dods
Dodson's English Admiralty Reports [*A publication*] (DLA) ..... Dodson Adm (Eng)
Dodumentation Medizinische Technik [*Medical Technology Documentation*] [*TechnicalInformation Center*] [*Germany*] [*Information service or system*] (IID) ..... MEDITEC
DOE [*Department of Engery*] **Albuquerque Operations Office, Albuquerque, NM** (GAAI) ..... DOE/AL
DOE [*Department of Energy*] **Carlsbad Area Office, Carlsbad, NM** (GAAI) ..... DOE/CAO
DOE [*Department of Energy*] **Chicago Operations Office** [*Illinois*] (GAAI) ..... DOE/CH
DOE [*Department of Energy*] **Energy Information Administration** (GAAI) ..... DOE/EIA
DOE [*Department of Energy*] **Fernald Area Office** [*Ohio*] (GAAI) ..... DOE/FN
DOE [*Department of Energy*] **Headquarters** (GAAI) ..... DOE/HQ
DOE [*Department of Energy*] **Idaho Operations Office** (GAAI) ..... DOE/ID
DOE [*Department of Energy*] **Nevada Operations Office** (USDC) ..... DOE/NV
DOE [*Department of Energy*] **Oak Ridge Operations Office** [*Oak Park Ridge, TN*] (GAAI) ..... DOE/OR
DOE [*Department of Energy*] **Oakland Operations Office** [*Oakland, CA*] (GAAI) ..... DOE/OAK
DOE [*Department of Energy*] **Office of Defense Programs** (GAAI) ..... DOE/DP
DOE [*Department of Energy*] **Office of Environmental Management** (GAAI) ..... DOE/EM
DOE [*Department of Energy*] **Office of Scientific and Technical Information** [*Tennessee*] (GAAI) ..... DOE/OSTI
DOE [*Department of Energy*] **Ohio Field Office** (GAAI) ..... DOE/OH
DOE [*Department of Energy*] **Richland Operations Office** [*Richland, WA*] (GAAI) ..... DOE/RI
DOE [*Department of Energy*] **Rocky Flats Office** [*Colorado*] (GAAI) ..... DOE/RF
DOE [*Department of Energy*] **Savannah River Operations Office** [*Aiken, South Carolina*] (GAAI) ..... DOE/SR
DOE [*Department of Energy*] **West Valley Area Office** [*West Valley, NY*] (GAAI) ..... DOE/WVAO
DOE [*Department of Energy*] **WIPP** [*Waste Isolation Pilot Plant*] **Project Office** [*Carlsbad, NM*] (GAAI) ..... DOE/WIPP
Doerfler-Stewart [*Test*] [*Medicine*] (MEDA) ..... D-S
Does Everything but Eat [*Superseded by DITTO*] [*Computer science*] ..... DEBE
Does Not Answer [*Telephone operator's designation*] ..... DNA
Does Not Apply (MSA) ..... DNA
Does Not Run ..... DNR
Doesn't Answer (ADA) ..... DA
Doesn't Answer [*Telephone marketing*] (WDMC) ..... da

Dofasco, Inc. [*Toronto Stock Exchange symbol*] ... DFS
Dofasco, Inc., Hamilton, Ontario [*Library symbol National Library of Canada*] (NLC) ... OHDF
DOFASCO, Inc., Research Information Center, Hamilton, ON, Canada [*Library symbol*] [*Library of Congress*] (LCLS) ... CaOHDFR
Dofor Inc. [*Toronto Stock Exchange symbol*] ... DFR
Dog [*Veterinary science*] (DAVI) ... D
Dog [*Phonetic alphabet*] [*World War II*] (DSUE) ... D
Dog and Pony Show ... D & PS
Dog at Large [*Humorous notation put on letters that cannot be delivered*] [*British postmen's slang*] ... DAL
Dog Bite-Related Fatality ... DBRF
Dog Fancy [*A publication*] (BRI) ... Dog Fan
Dog Judges Association of America [*Defunct*] (EA) ... DJAA
Dog Kidney (MAE) ... DK
Dog Kidney Tissue Culture ... DKTC
Dog Lymphocytotoxicity ... DLA
Dog Owners' Guild ... DOG
Dog Owners League of America [*Defunct*] (EA) ... DOLA
Dog Pound [*Multistory parking lot*] [*Slang British*] ... D-P
Dog Unit [*Veterinary medicine*] ... DU
Dog Unit Negative (DAVI) ... DUNG
Dog Unit Positive [*Biochemistry*] (DAVI) ... DU+
Dog Vomit on Toast [*Creamed beef or tuna on toast*] [*Military slang*] ... DVOT
Dog Wags Tail [*Airspace effects*] ... DWT
Dog Writers' Association of America (EA) ... DWAA
Dogged ... DG
Dogger [*Ship's rigging*] (ROG) ... DR
Dog-Leg Severity Factor [*Well drilling technology*] ... DLSF
Dog-Leg-to-Orbit (SAA) ... DLTO
Dogman and the Shepherds Fan Club (EA) ... DSFC
Dogmatic ... DOGM
Dogondoutchi [*Niger*] [*ICAO location identifier*] (ICLI) ... DRRC
Dogri [*MARC language code Library of Congress*] (LCCP) ... doi
Dogru Yol Partisi [*Correct Way Party*] [*Turkey Political party*] (EY) ... DYP
Dogs for Defense [*Organization which trained dogs for armed services*] [*World War II*] ... DFD
Dogs for the Deaf (EA) ... DD
Dogs on Stamps Study Unit (EA) ... DOSSU
Dogwood [*Missouri*] [*Seismograph station code, US Geological Survey*] (SEIS) ... DWM
Dogwood Lakes Estate, FL [*FM radio station call letters*] ... WJED
Dogwood Library System [*Library network*] ... DLS
Dogwood, MO [*Location identifier FAA*] (FAAL) ... DGD
Doha [*Qatar*] [*Airport symbol*] (OAG) ... DOH
Doha/International [*Qatar*] [*ICAO location identifier*] (ICLI) ... OTBD
Dohle Bodies [*Biochemistry*] (DAVI) ... DOHL
Dohle Body Panmyelopathy [*Medicine*] (DMAA) ... DBP
Doing Business As [*Followed by company name*] ... DBA
Doing Business As (AAGC) ... dba
Doit [*Debit*] [*French*] ... DT
Do-It-Yourself (MCD) ... DITY
Do-It-Yourself ... DIY
Do-It-Yourself Economics ... DIYE
Do-It-Yourself Research Institute [*Later, HIRI*] (EA) ... DIYRI
Doklady Chemical Technology ... DCT
Doklady Physical Chemistry ... DPC
Doko [*Zaire*] [*ICAO location identifier*] (ICLI) ... FZJB
Dokumentation Kraftfahrwesen [*Motor Vehicle Documentation*] [*Germany Information service or system*] (IID) ... DKF
Dokumentation Maschinenbau [*Mechanical Engineering Documentation*] [*Technical Information Center*] [*Information service or system*] ... DOMA
Dokumentation Schweisstechnik [*Welding Documentation*] [*Federal Institute for Materials Testing*] [*Information service or system*] (IID) ... DS
Dokumentation Zerstorungsfreie Pruefung [*Nondestructive Testing Documentation*] [*Federal Institute for Materials Testing*] [*Information service or system*] (IID) ... ZfP
Dokumentations- und Ausbildungszentrum fuer Theorie und Methode der Regionalforschung [*Documentation and Training Center for Theory and Methods of Regional Research*] [*Germany*] ... DATUM
Dokumentations - und Informationsgesellschaft fuer Wirtschaft und Touristik mbH [*Database producer*] ... DIWT
Dokumentations- und Informationssystem fuer Parlamentsmaterial [*Documentation and Information System for Parliamentary Materials*] [*German Federal Diet Division of Scientific Documentation*] [*Information service or system*] (IID) ... DIP
Dokumentationsring Elektrotechnik [*Database*] ... DRE
Dokumentationszentrale Feinwerktechnik [*Precision Technology Documentation Center*] [*Originator, operator, and database*] [*Germany*] [*Information service or system*] (IID) ... DZF
Dokumentationszentrum des Bundes Judischer Verfolgter des Naziregimes [*Jewish Documentation Centre - JDC*] (EAIO) ... BJVN
Dokumente Gegen Akzept [*Documents Against Acceptance*] [*German Banking*] ... D/A
Dolar [*Dollar*] [*Monetary unit*] [*Portugal*] ... dol
Dolar [*Dollar*] [*Monetary unit*] [*Poland*] ... dol
Dolares [*Dollars*] [*Monetary unit*] [*Spanish*] ... dls
Dolbeau, PQ [*AM radio station call letters*] ... CHVD
Dolbeau, PQ [*FM radio station call letters*] ... CHVD-FM
Dolce [*Sweet*] [*Music*] ... DOL
Dolcemente [*Sweetly, Softly*] [*Music*] (ROG) ... DOLCEM
Dolcissimo [*Very Sweetly*] [*Music*] ... DOLCIS
Dolcissimo [*Very Sweetly*] [*Music*] (ROG) ... DOLCISS
Dolco Packaging Corp. [*Associated Press*] (SAG) ... Dolco
Dolco Packaging Corp. [*NASDAQ symbol*] (SAG) ... DPKG
Dole [*France*] [*Airport symbol Obsolete*] (OAG) ... DLE
Dole Food Co. [*AMEX symbol*] (SAG) ... DLA
Dole Food Co. [*NYSE symbol*] (SAG) ... DOL
Dole Food Co. [*Associated Press*] (SAG) ... DolAutEx
Dole Food Co. [*Associated Press*] (SAG) ... Dole
Dole/Tavaux [*France ICAO location identifier*] (ICLI) ... LFGJ
Dolenti Parti [*To the Afflicted Part*] [*Pharmacy*] ... DOLENT PART
Dolichol [*Biochemistry*] ... DOL
Dolichos [*Plant commonly known as Cowitch*] [*Pharmacology*] (ROG) ... DOLICH
Dolichos biflorus Agglutinin [*Immunology*] ... DBA
Do-List Item [*Military*] ... DLI
Doll Artisan Guild (EA) ... DAG
Doll Collectors of America (EA) ... DCA
Doll Supply Manufacturers Association (EA) ... DSMA
Dollar [*Monetary unit*] ... D
Dollar ... DLLR
Dollar [*Monetary unit*] ... DLR
Dollar [*Monetary unit*] ... DO
Dollar [*Monetary unit*] [*French*] ... dol
Dollar [*Monetary unit*] (ROG) ... DOLL
Dollar [*Monetary unit*] (ROG) ... DR
Dollar Air Services Ltd. [*British ICAO designator*] (FAAC) ... DAS
Dollar Averaging Cost [*Investment term*] ... DA
Dollar Error Limit (DICI) ... DEL
Dollar General [*NYSE symbol*] (TTSB) ... DG
Dollar General Corp. [*NYSE symbol*] (SAG) ... DG
Dollar General Corp. [*Associated Press*] (SAG) ... DollrGn
Dollar Penny Coalition (EA) ... DPC
Dollar Time Group(New) [*NASDAQ symbol*] (TTSB) ... DLRTD
Dollar Tradeoff ... DTO
Dollar Tree Stores [*NASDAQ symbol*] (TTSB) ... dltr
Dollar Tree Stores, Inc. [*Associated Press*] (SAG) ... DllrTree
Dollar Tree Stores, Inc. [*NASDAQ symbol*] (SAG) ... DLTR
Dollar Tree Stores, Inc. [*Associated Press*] (SAG) ... DolrTr
Dollar Unit Sampling (ADA) ... DUS
Dollar Value of Annual Demands (AFIT) ... DVAD
Dollars [*Monetary unit*] (ROG) ... DLLRS
Dollars [*Monetary unit*] ... DLS
Dollars & Sense [*Economic Affairs Bureau*] [*A publication*] ... D & S
Dollars per Flight Hour (MCD) ... DFH
Dollars per Share [*Investment term*] (MHDW) ... DLS/SHR
Dollman Electronics Canada Ltd., Brampton, Ontario [*Library symbol National Library of Canada*] (NLC) ... OBDE
Dollman Electronics Ltd., Brampton, ON, Canada [*Library symbol Library of Congress*] (LCLS) ... CaBraDE
Dollman Electronics Ltd., Brampton, ON, Canada [*Library symbol*] [*Library of Congress*] (LCLS) ... CaOBraDE
Dolly (MSA) ... DLY
Dolly Back [*Films, television, etc.*] ... DB
Dolly In [*Films, television, etc.*] ... DI
Dolly Out [*Cinematography*] (NTCM) ... DO
Dolly Parton Fan Club (EA) ... DPFC
Dolly Shot [*Cinematography*] (NTCM) ... DS
Dolly Varden Minerals [*Vancouver Stock Exchange symbol*] ... DYV
Dolomite [*Lithology*] ... DOL
Dolor [*Unit of Pain*] [*Medicine*] (BARN) ... dol
Dolore Urgente [*When the Pain Is Severe*] [*Pharmacy*] ... DOL URG
Dolores [*Argentina ICAO location identifier*] (ICLI) ... SAZD
Dolores County Public Library, Dove Creek, CO [*Library symbol Library of Congress*] (LCLS) ... CoDc
Dolores County Public Library, Dove Creek, CO [*Library symbol*] [*Library of Congress*] (LCLS) ... CoDcL
Dolores County School District, Rico, CO [*Library symbol Library of Congress*] (LCLS) ... CoRicD
Dolores Public Library, Dolores, CO [*Library symbol Library of Congress*] (LCLS) ... CoDol
Doloroso [*Mournfully*] [*Music*] (ROG) ... DOLO
Dolpa [*Nepal*] [*Airport symbol*] (OAG) ... DOP
Dolpa [*Nepal*] [*ICAO location identifier*] (ICLI) ... VNDP
Dolphin [*Mooring post*] [*British*] ... Dn
Dolphin ... Dol
Dolphin Explorations Ltd. [*Vancouver Stock Exchange symbol Toronto Stock Exchange symbol*] ... DOX
Dolphin Express Airlines, Inc. [*FAA designator*] (FAAC) ... IXX
Dolphin Morbillivirus ... DMV
Dolphin Research Center (EA) ... DRC
Dolphin Society (EA) ... DS
Dolph-Tchebyscheff Pattern ... DTP
Dolton Public Library District, Dolton, IL [*Library symbol Library of Congress*] (LCLS) ... IDol
Dom [*Port*] [*Latin*] (ROG) ... D
Dom Perignon [*Champagne*] ... DP
Domain [*Telecommunications*] ... D
Domain Directory (ACRL) ... DD
Domain Name Service ... DNS
Domain Name System [*or Service*] [*Computer science*] ... DNS
Domain Naming System ... DNS
Domain Software Engineering Environment ... DSEE
Domain Specific Part [*Telecommunications*] (OSI) ... DSP
Domain Specific Part Format Identifier [*Telecommunications*] (ACRL) ... DFI
Domain Tip (PDAA) ... DOT
Domain Tip Propagation Logic (MCD) ... DTPL
Domain Tip Random Access Memory [*Computer science*] ... DOTRAM
Domain Tip Technology (IAA) ... DTT
Domaine de la Romanee-Conti [*French vintner*] ... DRC

Domain-Originated Functional Integrated Circuit (IEEE) ... DOFIC
Domain-Referenced Test [*Education*] (AEE) ... DRT
Doman Industries Ltd. [*Toronto Stock Exchange symbol Vancouver Stock Exchange symbol*] ... DOM
Domat-Ems [*Switzerland ICAO location identifier*] (ICLI) ... LSXD
Domat's Civil Law [*A publication*] (DLA) ... Dom Civ Law
Domat's Civil Law [*A publication*] (DLA) ... Domat Civ Law
Dombas [*Norway*] [*Geomagnetic observatory code*] ... DOB
Dome ... D
Dome Lamp [*Automotive engineering*] ... D/LP
Dome Petroleum Ltd. [*Canada ICAO designator*] (FAAC) ... DPL
Dome Petroleum Ltd., Calgary, AB, Canada [*Library symbol Library of Congress*] (LCLS) ... CaACDP
Dome Petroleum Ltd., Calgary, Alberta [*Library symbol National Library of Canada*] (NLC) ... ACDP
Dome Removal Tool ... DRT
Domego Resources Ltd. [*Toronto Stock Exchange symbol*] ... DGO
Domesday [*British*] (ROG) ... DOM
Domesday Book [*Census-like record of the lands of England, 1085-86*] ... DB
Domesday Book [*Census-like record of the lands of England, 1085-86*] [*A publication*] (DLA) ... Dom Book
Domesday Book [*Census-like record of the lands of England, 1085-86*] [*A publication*] (DLA) ... Domes
Domesday Book [*Census-like record of the lands of England, 1085-86*] (ROG) ... DOMESD
Domesday Book [*Census-like record of the lands of England, 1085-86*] [*A publication*] (DLA) ... Domesday
Domesday Survey [*Census-like record of the lands of England, 1085-86*] ... DS
Domestic ... D
Domestic (AFM) ... DOM
Domestic ... DOM
Domestic Action Program [*Army*] (INF) ... DAP
Domestic Affairs Council [*Replaced Urban Affairs Council, Rural Affairs Council, and Cabinet Committee on Environment*] [*White House*] ... DAC
Domestic Afflictions [*Menstruation*] [*Slang*] (DSUE) ... DA's
Domestic and Foreign Missionary Society [*British*] ... DFMS
Domestic and International Business (MCD) ... DIB
Domestic and International Business Administration [*Terminated 1977, functions assumed by Industry and Trade Administration*] [*Department of Commerce*] ... DIBA
Domestic and International Scientific Planning and Cooperation ... DISPAC
Domestic Android [*Quasar Industries*] ... DA
Domestic Annual Fishing Capacity [*Fishery management*] (MSC) ... DAC
Domestic Annual Harvest ... DAH
Domestic Annual Processing ... DAP
Domestic Appliance (IAA) ... DOMAPP
Domestic Appliance Service Association [*British*] (DBA) ... DASA
Domestic Base Factor Report [*Army*] ... DBFR
Domestic Coal Consumers' Council [*British*] (DI) ... DCCC
Domestic Communications Satellite (DOAD) ... DOMSAT
Domestic Council [*Executive Office of the President*] [*Abolished 1978, functions transferred to the President*] ... DC
Domestic Council Committee on Veterans Services [*Veterans Administration*] ... DCCVS
Domestic Credit Expansion ... DCE
Domestic Door-to-Door [*Personal property*] ... DDD
Domestic Duties (ADA) ... DD
Domestic Emergency Plan (AAG) ... DEP
Domestic Escorted Tour [*Travel*] ... DET
Domestic European Ferret Breeders Association (EA) ... DEFBA
Domestic Exchange (MHDW) ... Dom Ex
Domestic Heating Society [*British*] (DBA) ... DHS
Domestic Hot Water ... DHW
Domestic Icebreaking [*USCG*] (TAG) ... DOM ICE
Domestic Independent Tour [*or Travel*] ... DIT
Domestic Information Display System [*Computer graphics*] ... DIDS
Domestic International Sales Corp. [*See also Foreign Sales Corp. - FSC*] ... DISC
Domestic Library Automation Functions [*Computer science*] ... DOMLIB
Domestic Mail Manual [*US Postal Service*] [*A publication*] ... DMM
Domestic Oil Burning Equipment Testing Association [*British*] (DI) ... DOBETA
Domestic Policy Association [*Later, NIF*] (EA) ... DPA
Domestic Policy Council [*Executive Office of the President*] (GFGA) ... DPC
Domestic Policy Review ... DPR
Domestic Prelate ... DP
Domestic Presidential Directive [*Jimmy Carter Administration*] ... DPD
DOMESTIC [*Development of Microcomputers in an Environment of Scientific and Technological Information Centers*] **Print Generator** [*Computer science*] ... DOMPRINT
Domestic Product of Industry (MHDB) ... DPI
Domestic Public Land Mobile [*Telecommunications*] (TEL) ... DPLM
Domestic Refrigeration Development Committee [*British*] (BI) ... DORDEC
Domestic Revenue Cost Coefficient [*Economics*] ... DRC
Domestic Route Order ... DRO
Domestic Satellite [*Australia*] (NITA) ... DOMSAT
Domestic Satellite Carrier [*Computer science*] (TNIG) ... DSC
Domestic Science [*Freight*] ... DOM SC
Domestic Service [*Equipment specification*] ... DS
Domestic Sewage Exclusion ... DSE
Domestic Solid Fuel Appliances Approval Scheme (PDAA) ... DSFAAS
Domestic Substances List [*Canada*] ... DSL
Domestic Technology Institute (EA) ... DTI
Domestic Textiles Federation [*British*] (BI) ... DTF
Domestic Transmission System [*ITT*] [*Telecommunications*] (TEL) ... DTS
Domestic Violence Crisis Service [*Australian Capital Territory*] [*Australia*] ... DVCS
Domestic Violence Project (EA) ... DVP
Domestic Water (AAG) ... DW
Domestic Water Tank Manufacturers Council [*Defunct*] ... DWTMC
Domglas, Inc., Corporate Library, Mississauga, ON, Canada [*Library symbol Library of Congress*] (LCLS) ... CaOMDO
Domicile ... DOM
Domiciliary Care for Homeless Veterans [*Department of Veterans Affairs*] ... DCHV
Domiciliary Visit [*Medicine*] ... DV
Dominance [*Psychology*] ... Do
Dominance [*Psychology*] ... DOM
Dominance and Submission ... D & S
Dominance Index [*Neurology*] ... DI
Dominant [*Applied to a species*] ... D
Dominant (FAAC) ... DMNT
Dominant ... DOM
Dominant Bubble Frequency [*Nuclear energy*] (NRCH) ... DBF
Dominant Control Region [*Genetics*] ... DCR
Dominant Exudative Vitreoretinopathy [*Ophthalmology*] (DAVI) ... DEVR
Dominant Feature Analysis ... DFA
Dominant Hand [*Psychometrics*] ... DH
Dominant Obstacle Allowance (MCD) ... DOA
Dominant Wavelength ... DWL
Dominantly Inherited Juvenile Optic Atrophy [*Ophthalmology*] (DAVI) ... DIJOA
Dominant-Subordinate Conflict [*Biology*] ... DSC
Dominco Industry Corp. [*Vancouver Stock Exchange symbol*] ... DMQ
Domingo [*Sunday*] [*Spanish*] ... Dom
Domingo [*Sunday*] [*Spanish*] ... domo
Dominguez Services Corp. [*Associated Press*] (SAG) ... Domng
Dominguez Services Corp. [*NASDAQ symbol*] (NQ) ... DOMZ
Domini de Rota [*Authority cited in pre-1607 legal work*] (DSA) ... Do de Ro
Domini Social Index [*Stock exchange term*] ... DSI
Domini Sportswear [*Vancouver Stock Exchange symbol*] ... DMS
Dominica [*ANSI two-letter standard code*] (CNC) ... DM
Dominica [*ANSI three-letter standard code*] (CNC) ... DMA
Dominica [*West Indies*] [*Airport symbol*] (OAG) ... DOM
Dominica [*West Indies*] [*Seismograph station code, US Geological Survey*] (SEIS) ... DOM
Dominica [*Leeward Islands*] [*Airport symbol*] (AD) ... DOM
Dominica [*MARC country of publication code Library of Congress*] (LCCP) ... dq
Dominica [*Aircraft nationality and registration mark*] (FAAC) ... J7
Dominica [*MARC geographic area code Library of Congress*] (LCCP) ... nwdq--
Dominica Democratic Alliance [*Political party*] (PPW) ... DDA
Dominica Freedom Party [*Political party*] (PPW) ... DFP
Dominica Labor Party [*Political party*] (PPW) ... DLP
Dominica Liberation Movement [*Political party*] (EY) ... DLM
Dominica/Melville Hall [*Dominica*] [*ICAO location identifier*] (ICLI) ... TDPD
Dominica Tourist Board (EAIO) ... DTB
Dominica United Workers' Party [*Political party*] (EY) ... UWP
Dominica-Cane [*West Indies*] [*Airport symbol*] (OAG) ... DCF
Dominical Letter ... DL
Dominican Campaign Medal ... DCM
Dominican College, Blauvelt, NY [*Library symbol Library of Congress*] (LCLS) ... NBlaD
Dominican College, Houston, TX [*Library symbol Library of Congress*] (LCLS) ... TxHDom
Dominican College of San Rafael [*California*] ... DCSR
[*The*] **Dominican College of San Rafael** (GAGS) ... Dominican C San Rafael
Dominican College of San Rafael, San Rafael, CA [*Library symbol Library of Congress*] (LCLS) ... CSrD
Dominican Contemplative Nuns (Cloistered) (TOCD) ... OP
Dominican Contemplative Sisters (TOCD) ... OP
Dominican Contemplative Sisters (Cloistered) (TOCD) ... OP
Dominican Educational Association [*Defunct*] (EA) ... DEA
Dominican House of Studies, Immaculate Conception Convent Library, Washington, DC [*Library symbol Library of Congress OCLC symbol*] (LCLS) ... DDC
Dominican Junior College of Blauvelt [*Later, Dominican College*] [*New York*] ... DJCB
Dominican Mission Foundation (EA) ... DMF
Dominican Oblates of Jesus [*Roman Catholic women's religious order*] ... DOJ
Dominican Oblates of Jesus (Spain) (TOCD) ... JSOP
Dominican Republic [*ANSI two-letter standard code*] (CNC) ... DO
Dominican Republic [*ANSI three-letter standard code*] (CNC) ... DOM
Dominican Republic (VRA) ... Dom Rep
Dominican Republic (AFM) ... DOMREP
Dominican Republic [*IYRU nationality code*] [*MARC country of publication code Library of Congress*] (LCCP) ... dr
Dominican Republic [*MARC geographic area code Library of Congress*] (LCCP) ... nwdr--
Dominican Republic Study Group [*Defunct*] (EA) ... DRSG
Dominican Rural Missionaries (TOCD) ... OP
Dominican Sisters (Adrian, MI) (TOCD) ... OP
Dominican Sisters (Akron, OH) (TOCD) ... OP
Dominican Sisters (Amityville, NY) (TOCD) ... OP
Dominican Sisters (Blauvelt, NY) (TOCD) ... OP
Dominican Sisters (Caldwell, PA) (TOCD) ... OP
Dominican Sisters (Colombia) (TOCD) ... OP
Dominican Sisters (Columbus, OH) (TOCD) ... OP
Dominican Sisters (Ecuador) (TOCD) ... OP
Dominican Sisters (Edmonds, WA) (TOCD) ... OP
Dominican Sisters (Fall River, MA) (TOCD) ... OP
Dominican Sisters (Grand Rapid, MI) (TOCD) ... OP
Dominican Sisters (Great Bend, KS) (TOCD) ... OP
Dominican Sisters (Hawthorne, NY) (TOCD) ... OP
Dominican Sisters (Houston, TX) (TOCD) ... OP

Dominican Sisters (Justice, IL) (TOCD) .... OP
Dominican Sisters (Kenosha, WI) (TOCD) .... OP
Dominican Sisters (Media, PA) (TOCD) .... OP
Dominican Sisters (Nashville, TN) (TOCD) .... OP
Dominican Sisters (New Orleans, LA) (TOCD) .... OP
Dominican Sisters (Newburgh, NY) (TOCD) .... OP
Dominican Sisters of Carondelet (TOCD) .... OP
Dominican Sisters of Charity of the Presentation of the Blessed Virgin (TOCD) .... OP
Dominican Sisters of Mt. Thabor (TOCD) .... OP
Dominican Sisters of Our Lady of the Most Holy Rosary (TOCD) .... OP
Dominican Sisters of Our Lady of the Rosary and of Saint Catherine of Siena, Cabra (TOCD) .... OP
Dominican Sisters of the Roman Congregation (TOCD) .... OP
Dominican Sisters (Ossining, NY) (TOCD) .... OP
Dominican Sisters (Oxford, MI) (TOCD) .... OP
Dominican Sisters (Oxford, South Africa) (TOCD) .... OP
Dominican Sisters (Racine, WI) (TOCD) .... OP
Dominican Sisters (St. Catherine, KY) (TOCD) .... OP
Dominican Sisters (San Jose, CA) (TOCD) .... OP
Dominican Sisters (San Rafael, CA) (TOCD) .... OP
Dominican Sisters (Sinsinawa, WI) (TOCD) .... OP
Dominican Sisters (Sparkill, NY) (TOCD) .... OP
Dominican Sisters (Spokane, WA) (TOCD) .... OP
Dominican Sisters (Springfield, IL) (TOCD) .... OP
Dominican Sisters (Tacoma, WA) (TOCD) .... OP
Dominican Sisters (Vietnam) (TOCD) .... OP
Dominicana de Aviacion [*ICAO designator*] (AD) .... DO
Dominicus de Sancto Geminiano [*Flourished, 1407-09*] [*Authority cited in pre-1607 legal work*] (DSA) .... Do
Dominicus de Sancto Geminiano [*Flourished, 1407-09*] [*Authority cited in pre-1607 legal work*] (DSA) .... Do de San Gemi
Dominicus de Sancto Geminiano [*Flourished, 1407-09*] [*Authority cited in pre-1607 legal work*] (DSA) .... Domi
Dominicus de Sancto Geminiano [*Flourished, 1407-09*] [*Authority cited in pre-1607 legal work*] (DSA) .... Domi de San Gemi
Dominion .... DOM
Dominion .... DOMNN
Dominion Arsenal [*World War I*] [*Canada*] .... DA
Dominion Astrophysical Observatory, Victoria, BC, Canada [*Library symbol Library of Congress*] (LCLS) .... CaBViO
Dominion Atlantic Railway Co. [*Absorbed into CP Rail*] [*AAR code*] .... DA
Dominion Board of Insurance Underwriters [*Canada*] (ODBW) .... DBIU
Dominion Bridge Co. Ltd., Montreal, PQ, Canada [*Library symbol Library of Congress*] (LCLS) .... CaQMDom
Dominion Bridge Co. Ltd., Montreal, Quebec [*Library symbol National Library of Canada*] (NLC) .... QMDOM
Dominion Bridge Co. Ltd., Ottawa, Ontario [*Library symbol National Library of Canada*] (NLC) .... OODB
Dominion Bureau of Statistics [*Canada*] .... DBS
Dominion Colour Ltd., Toronto, Ontario [*Library symbol National Library of Canada*] (NLC) .... OTDC
Dominion Companies Law Reports [*Canada*] [*A publication*] (DLA) .... DCLR(Can)
Dominion Drama Festival [*Canada*] .... DDF
Dominion Engineering Works Ltd., Montreal, PQ, Canada [*Library symbol Library of Congress*] (LCLS) .... CaQMDE
Dominion Engineering Works Ltd., Montreal, Quebec [*Library symbol National Library of Canada*] (NLC) .... QMDE
Dominion Explorers, Inc. [*Toronto Stock Exchange symbol*] .... DMN
Dominion Explorers, Inc. [*Vancouver Stock Exchange symbol*] .... DMN
Dominion Foundries & Steel Ltd., Hamilton, ON, Canada [*Library symbol Library of Congress*] (LCLS) .... CaOHDF
Dominion Glass Co. Ltd., Mississauga, ON, Canada [*Library symbol Library of Congress*] (LCLS) .... CaOMDG
Dominion Glass Co. Ltd., Mississauga, Ontario [*Library symbol National Library of Canada*] (NLC) .... OMDG
Dominion Government Survey [*Canada*] .... DGS
Dominion Land Surveyor [*Canada*] .... DLS
Dominion Law Reporter [*India*] [*Usually with a province abbreviation, as DLR (AM), Ajmer-Merwara*] [*A publication*] (DLA) .... DLR
Dominion Naval Forces .... DNF
Dominion of Canada Labour Service [*Commerce Clearing House*] [*A publication*] (DLA) .... DC Lab S
Dominion of Canada Rifle Association .... DCRA
Dominion of Canada Statutes in the Reign of Victoria [*A publication*] (DLA) .... C Vict
Dominion Radio Astrophysical Observatory [*Herzberg Institute of Astrophysics, National Research Council of Canada*] [*Research center*] (RCD) .... DRAO
Dominion Radio Astrophysical Observatory, Penticton, BC, Canada [*Library symbol Library of Congress*] (LCLS) .... CaBPO
Dominion Res Black Warrior Tr [*NYSE symbol*] (TTSB) .... DOM
Dominion Resources [*NYSE symbol*] (TTSB) .... D
Dominion Resources Black Warrior Trust [*Associated Press*] (SAG) .... DmRsBW
Dominion Resources Black Warrior Trust [*Associated Press*] (SAG) .... DmRsEW
Dominion Resources Black Warrior Trust [*NYSE symbol*] (SAG) .... DOM
Dominion Resources, Inc. [*NYSE symbol*] (SPSG) .... D
Dominion Resources, Inc. [*Associated Press*] (SAG) .... DomRes
Dominion Rubber Co. [*Canada*] [*Research code symbol*] .... D
Dominion Rubber Co. [*Research code symbol*] [*Canada*] .... F
Dominion Securities Ltd. [*Toronto Stock Exchange symbol Vancouver Stock Exchange symbol*] .... DS
Dominion Tax Cases [*CCH Canadian Ltd.*] [*Information service or system A publication*] (DLA) .... D Tax
Dominion Tax Cases [*CCH Canadian Ltd.*] [*Information service or system A publication*] (DLA) .... DTC
Dominion Textile [*NASDAQ symbol*] (TTSB) .... DTX
Dominion Textile, Inc. [*Toronto Stock Exchange symbol*] .... DTX
Dominion Textile, Montreal, PQ, Canada [*Library symbol Library of Congress*] (LCLS) .... CaQMDT
Dominion Textile, Montreal, Quebec [*Library symbol National Library of Canada*] (NLC) .... QMDT
Dominion Traffic Association [*Canada*] .... DTA
Dominion Yarn Co., St. Laurent, Quebec [*Library symbol National Library of Canada*] (BIB) .... QSTLD
Dominions, Colonies, and Overseas [*British*] (DI) .... DCO
Dominions Office [*British*] .... DO
Dominion-Scottish Investments Ltd. [*Toronto Stock Exchange symbol*] .... DSI
Dominis Nostris [*To Our Lords*] [*Latin*] .... DDNN
Domino Nostro [*Our Lord*] [*Latin*] .... DN
Dominquez Seminary, Compton, CA [*Library symbol Library of Congress*] (LCLS) .... CComD
Dominquez Services [*NASDAQ symbol*] (TTSB) .... DOMZ
Dominus [*The Lord*] [*Latin*] (GPO) .... D
Dominus [*The Lord*] [*Latin*] .... DN
Dominus [*The Lord*] [*Latin*] .... DOM
Dominus [*The Lord*] [*Latin*] .... DS
Dominus Noster [*Our Lord*] [*Latin*] .... DN
Dominus Noster Jesus Christus [*Our Lord Jesus Christ*] [*Latin*] .... DNJC
Dominus Noster Papa Pontifex [*Our Lord the Pope*] [*Latin*] .... DNPP
Dominus Omnium Magister [*God the Master, or Lord, of All*] [*Motto of the Benedictine Order*] [*Latin*] .... DOM
Domitianus [*of Suetonius*] [*Classical studies*] (OCD) .... Dom
Domodedovo Civil Air Production Association [*Former USSR*] [*FAA designator*] (FAAC) .... DMO
Domodossola [*Italy*] [*Seismograph station code, US Geological Survey Closed*] (SEIS) .... DMD
DOMSAT [*Domestic Satellite*] **Interface Facility** (MCD) .... DIF
Domtar, Inc. [*NYSE symbol Toronto Stock Exchange symbol Vancouver Stock Exchange symbol*] (SPSG) .... DTC
Domtar Ltd. [*Associated Press*] (SAG) .... Domtar
Domtar Ltd., Montreal, PQ, Canada [*Library symbol Library of Congress*] (LCLS) .... CaQMDL
Domtar Ltd., Montreal, Quebec [*Library symbol National Library of Canada*] (NLC) .... QMDL
Domtar Ltd., Research Centre, Senneville, PQ, Canada [*Library symbol Library of Congress*] (LCLS) .... CaQSeD
Domus Procerum [*The House of Lords*] [*Latin*] (ROG) .... DOM PROC
Domus Procerum [*The House of Lords*] [*Latin*] .... DP
Don [*Phonetic alphabet*] [*Pre-World War II*] (DSUE) .... D
Don [*Sir*] [*Spanish*] .... D
Don Airlines [*Former USSR*] [*FAA designator*] (FAAC) .... DNV
Don Bosco College [*Newton, NJ*] .... DBC
Don Bosco College, Newton, NJ [*Library symbol Library of Congress*] (LCLS) .... NjNetDB
Don Diego [*Costa Rica*] [*ICAO location identifier*] (ICLI) .... MRDD
Don King Sports and Entertainment Network [*Cable-television system*] .... DKSEN
Don Winters and the Winters Brothers Fan Club [*Defunct*] (EA) .... DWWBFC
Don Youngblood and the Hoosier Bears International Fan Club [*Defunct*] (EA) .... DYHBIFC
Dona [*Mrs.*] [*Spanish*] (BARN) .... Dna
Donahue Elementary School, Lawrence, NY [*Library symbol Library of Congress*] (LCLS) .... NLawDE
Donahue Library [*Catholic Library of San Francisco*], San Francisco, CA [*Library symbol Library of Congress*] (LCLS) .... CSfD
Donair Flying Club Ltd. [*British ICAO designator*] (FAAC) .... DON
Donaker's Reports [*165 Indiana*] [*A publication*] (DLA) .... Donaker
Donakonda [*India*] [*ICAO location identifier*] (ICLI) .... VODK
Donald C. Cook Nuclear Power Plant (NRCH) .... DCNP
Donald C. Cook Plant [*Nuclear energy*] (NRCH) .... DCP
Donald Mitchell Healey [*Designer of Healey sports cars*] [*British*] .... DMH
Donald W. Douglas Laboratory [*McDonnell Douglas Corp.*] .... DWDL
Donalda and District Museum, Donalda, Alberta [*Library symbol National Library of Canada*] (BIB) .... ADOD
Donalda Public Library, Alberta [*Library symbol National Library of Canada*] (BIB) .... ADO
Donaldon Co., Inc. [*Associated Press*] (SAG) .... Donaldsn
Donaldson Co. [*NYSE symbol*] (TTSB) .... DCI
Donaldson Co., Inc. [*NYSE symbol*] (SPSG) .... DCI
Donaldson Lufkin & Jenrette [*NYSE symbol*] (SAG) .... DLJ
Donaldson Lufkin & Jenrette [*Associated Press*] (SAG) .... DonLJ
Donaldsonville, LA [*FM radio station call letters*] .... KKAY
Donalsonville, GA [*Location identifier FAA*] (FAAL) .... ONG
Donalsonville, GA [*FM radio station call letters*] .... WGMK
Donalsonville, GA [*AM radio station call letters*] .... WSEM
Donath-Landsteiner [*Hemolysin*] [*Hematology*] .... D-L
Donath-Landsteiner Antibody [*Immunology*] (MAE) .... D-L Ab
Donation Land Claim [*Legal term*] (DLA) .... DLC
Donation on Discharge .... D/D
Donative (ROG) .... D
Donative .... DON
Donaueschingen/Villingen [*Germany ICAO location identifier*] (ICLI) .... EDTD
Donauflug Bedarfsfluggesellschaft GmbH [*Austria ICAO designator*] (FAAC) .... DFL
Donauworth/Genderkingen [*Germany ICAO location identifier*] (ICLI) .... EDMQ
Doncaster [*British ICAO location identifier*] (ICLI) .... EGCI
Doncaster Public Library, Doncaster, United Kingdom [*Library symbol Library of Congress*] (LCLS) .... UkDo
Doncourt-Les-Conflans [*France ICAO location identifier*] (ICLI) .... LFGR

Donderskamp [*Surinam*] [*ICAO location identifier*] (ICLI) ... SMDK
Dondino Fan Club (EA) ... DFC
Donec [*Until*] [*Pharmacy*] (ROG) ... DON
Donec Alvus Bis Dejiciatur [*Until the Bowels Have Been Twice Evacuated*] [*Pharmacy*] (ROG) ... DONEC ALV BIS DEJ
Donec Alvus Soluta Fuerit [*Until the Bowels Are Opened*] [*Latin Medicine*] (DAVI) ... don alv sol fuerit
Donec Alvus Soluta Fuerit [*Until the Bowels Are Opened*] [*Pharmacy*] (ROG) ... DONEC ALV SOL FUER
Donec Alvus Soluta Fuerit [*Until the Bowels Are Opened*] [*Pharmacy*] ... DONEC ALV SOL FUERIT
Donec Dolor Nephriticus Exulaverit [*Until the Nephritic Pain Is Removed*] [*Pharmacy*] (ROG) ... DONEC DOL NEPH EXULAV
Donegal [*County in Ireland*] ... DON
Donegal [*County in Ireland*] (ROG) ... DONEG
Donegal Group [*NASDAQ symbol*] (TTSB) ... DGIC
Donegal Group, Inc. [*NASDAQ symbol*] (NQ) ... DGIC
Donegal Group, Inc. [*Associated Press*] (SAG) ... Donegal
Donelson, TN [*AM radio station call letters*] ... WAMB
Donelson, TN [*FM radio station call letters*] ... WAMB-FM
Donetsk [*Former USSR Airport symbol Obsolete*] (OAG) ... DOK
Dong [*Monetary unit*] [*Vietnam*] (BARN) ... D
Dong Feng [*East Wind*] [*Chinese missile*] ... DF
Dongara [*Australia Airport symbol*] (OAG) ... DOX
Donggang [*China*] [*ICAO location identifier*] (ICLI) ... RCMJ
Dongola [*Sudan*] [*Airport symbol*] (OAG) ... DOG
Dongola [*Missouri*] [*Seismograph station code, US Geological Survey*] (SEIS) ... DON
Dongola [*Sudan*] [*ICAO location identifier*] (ICLI) ... HSDN
Dongshi [*China*] [*ICAO location identifier*] (ICLI) ... RCNO
Doniphan, Kensett & Searcy Railway [*AAR code*] ... DKS
Doniphan, MO [*AM radio station call letters*] ... KDFN
Doniphan, MO [*FM radio station call letters*] ... KOEA
Donizetti Society (EA) ... DonSoc
Donkey Boiler [*of a ship*] (DS) ... DKY
Donkey Breed Society [*British*] (DBA) ... DBS
Donkey Red Cell [*s*] ... DRC
Donkey Society of Australia ... DSA
Donna Fargo Fan Club [*Later, DFIFC*] (EA) ... DFFC
Donna Fargo International Fan Club (EA) ... DFIFC
Donna Karan New York [*Sportswear*] ... DKNY
Donnelley [*R. R.*] **& Sons Co.** [*NYSE symbol*] (SPSG) ... DNY
Donnelley [*R.R.*] **& Sons Co.** [*Associated Press*] (SAG) ... Donlley
Donnelley Corp. [*Associated Press*] (SAG) ... Donelly
Donnelley Marketing Information Services [*Database producer*] (IID) ... DMIS
Donnelley(RR)& Sons [*NYSE symbol*] (TTSB) ... DNY
Donnell's Irish Land Cases [*1871-76*] [*A publication*] (DLA) ... Donn
Donnell's Irish Land Cases [*1871-76*] [*A publication*] (DLA) ... Donn Ir Land Cas
Donnellson Public Library, Donnellson, IA [*Library symbol Library of Congress*] (LCLS) ... IaDon
Donnellson Star, Donnellson, IA [*Library symbol Library of Congress*] (LCLS) ... IaDonS
Donnelly College, Kansas City, KS [*Library symbol*] [*Library of Congress*] (LCLS) ... KKcD
Donnelly Corp. [*AMEX symbol*] (SPSG) ... DON
Donnelly Corp. Cl'A' [*AMEX symbol*] (TTSB) ... DON
Donnelly Municipal Library, Alberta [*Library symbol National Library of Canada*] (NLC) ... ADOM
Donnelly Municipal Library, Donnelly, AB, Canada [*Library symbol*] [*Library of Congress*] (LCLS) ... CaADoM
Donnelly Official Airline Reservation Service (SAA) ... DOARS
Donnelly's English Chancery Reports [*A publication*] (DLA) ... Donn
Donnelly's English Chancery Reports [*A publication*] (DLA) ... Donn Eq
Donnelly's English Chancery Reports [*A publication*] (DLA) ... Donnelly
Donnelly's English Chancery Reports [*A publication*] (DLA) ... Donnelly (Eng)
Donnely Dome [*Alaska*] [*Seismograph station code, US Geological Survey*] (SEIS) ... DDM
Donnkenny, Inc. [*NASDAQ symbol*] (SAG) ... DNKY
Donnkenny, Inc. [*Associated Press*] (SAG) ... Donkeny
Donny Osmond Fan Club (EA) ... DOFC
Dono Dedit Dedicavit [*He Gave and Dedicated as a Gift*] [*Latin*] ... DDD
Donohue, Inc. [*Toronto Stock Exchange symbol*] ... DHC
Donor ... D
Donor [*MARC relator code*] [*Library of Congress*] (LCCP) ... dnr
Donor [*Searchable field, Dialog*] [*Information service or system*] (NITA) ... DO
Donor Energy Level ... DEL
Donor Horse Serum [*Pharmaceutical manufacture*] ... DHS
Donor Insemination [*Medicine*] ... DI
Donor Procurement Efficiency Rating [*Medicine*] ... DPER
Donor Specific Transfusion ... DST
Donor Specific Transfusion [*Hematology*] (DAVI) ... DTS
Donora Southern R. R. [*AAR code*] ... DSO
Donor-Acceptor ... DA
Donor-Acceptor-Donor [*Physiology*] ... DAD
Donor-Insulator-Acceptor Device [*Electronics*] ... DIAD
Donor's Cells [*Medicine*] ... DC
Donors' Offspring [*An association*] (EA) ... DO
Donor's Plasma [*Medicine*] ... DP
Donor's Serum [*Medicine*] ... DS
Donovan Data Systems [*A company*] [*New York, NY*] (WDMC) ... DDS
Donovan, Gerard J., Co., Inc., North Attleboro MA [*STAC*] ... DGJ
Donovan's Modern Jury Trials [*A publication*] (DLA) ... Don Tr
Donrey Media Group, Fort Smith, AR [*Library symbol Library of Congress*] (LCLS) ... ArFsD
Don't Ditch a Buddy [*Promise made by members of the Junior Woodchucks, organization to which comic strip character Donald Duck's nephews belonged*] ... DDB
Don't Fragment [*Telecommunications jargon*] (ACRL) ... DF
Don't Get Sucked In ... DGSI
Don't Give a Spit [*Slang*] [*Bowdlerized version*] ... DGS
Don't Knock It [*Slang*] ... DKI
Don't Know ... DK
Don't Overlook Mature Expertise, South Australia ... DOMESA
Don't Overlook Mature Expertise, Victoria [*Australia*] ... DOMEV
Don't Want [*Telecommunications*] (TEL) ... DW
Don't-Care-a-Damn [*British naval slang term for torpedo-boat destroyer*] [*World War I*] ... DCD
Donum Dedit [*Gave, Dedicated*] [*Latin*] ... DD
Donwood Institute, Toronto, Ontario [*Library symbol National Library of Canada*] (BIB) ... OTDO
Do-Object-Oriented-Development-Yourself [*Computer science*] ... DOODY
Doolan Road [*California*] [*Seismograph station code, US Geological Survey*] (SEIS) ... DOO
Doom and Gloom ... D & G
Doomadgee Mission [*Australia Airport symbol*] (OAG) ... DMD
Doon Pioneer Village, Kitchener, Ontario [*Library symbol National Library of Canada*] (BIB) ... OKITD
Door ... DR
Door (VRA) ... dr
Door and Hardware Institute (EA) ... DHI
Door and Operator Dealers Association (EA) ... DODA
Door and Shutter Manufacturers' Association [*British*] ... DSMA
Door Closer (AAG) ... DC
Door Closer ... DCL
Door County Library, Sturgeon Bay, WI [*Library symbol Library of Congress*] (LCLS) ... WSbD
Door Gunner [*Military*] ... DGR
Door in Flat [*Theater*] ... DF
Door Insulating Systems Index ... DISI
Door Lock Rotary Actuator ... DLRA
Door Mounted Junction Panel ... DMJP
Door Operator and Remote Controls Manufacturers Association (EA) ... DORCMA
Door or Window [*Freight*] ... DR WIND
Door Stop (AAG) ... DST
Door Switch ... DSW
Doors of Hope [*An association*] (EA) ... DH
Dopa Decarboxylase [*An enzyme*] ... DDC
Dopachrome Conversion Factor [*Medicine*] (DMAA) ... DCF
Dopamine [*Pharmacology*] (DAVI) ... D
Dopamine [*Biochemistry*] ... DA
Dopamine [*Biochemistry*] (AAMN) ... DM
Dopamine [*Pharmacology*] (DAVI) ... DOP
Dopamine [*Pharmacology*] (DAVI) ... DOPA
Dopamine- and Cyclic AMP-Regulated Phosphoprotein [*Biochemistry*] ... DARPP
Dopamine Beta-Hydroxylase [*An enzyme*] ... DBH
Dopamine Transporter [*Biochemistry*] ... DAT
Dope and Wimp [*Term used by Ross Thomas in his book, "Briarpatch"*] ... DOMP
Doped Deposited Silical [*Corning process*] ... DDS
Doped Erbium Oxide ... DEO
Doped Glass LASER ... DGL
Doped Polysilicon Diffusion Source [*Electronics*] (IAA) ... DOPOS
Doped Polysilicon Diffusion Technology [*Electronics*] (IAA) ... DOPODT
Dopo Cristo [*After Christ*] [*Italian*] ... DC
Doppellafette [*Two-barreled mount*] [*German military - World War II*] ... DL
Doppelposten [*Double Sentry*] [*German military - World War II*] ... DP
Doppio Pedale [*Double Pedal*] [*Music*] ... DOPP PED
Doppler (IAA) ... DO
Doppler (KSC) ... DOP
Doppler (MUGU) ... DOPP
Doppler (MCD) ... DPLR
Doppler Acoustic Vortex Sensing System [*FAA*] (MCD) ... DAVSS
Doppler Acoustic Vortex Sensing Equipment [*Meteorology*] (DA) ... DAVSS
Doppler and Range Evaluation ... DARE
Doppler Arrival Angle Spectral Measurement System [*Geophysics*] ... DAASM
Doppler Attitude Heading Reference System (MCD) ... DAHRS
Doppler Automatic Reduction Equipment (MCD) ... DARE
Doppler Azimuth Discrimination (MCD) ... DAD
Doppler Beam Rider (MCD) ... DBR
Doppler Beam Sampling [*Air navigation*] ... DBS
Doppler Beam Shaping ... DBS
Doppler Beam Sharpener ... DBS
Doppler Bearing Tracker [*Military*] (CAAL) ... DBT
Doppler Broadening Spectroscopy ... DBS
Doppler Broadening Velocity [*Spectroscopy*] (OA) ... DBV
Doppler Color Flow Mapping [*Cardiology*] (DAVI) ... DCFM
Doppler Control Gain (IAA) ... DCG
Doppler Count Accumulator (IAA) ... DCA
Doppler Data Translator ... DDT
Doppler Detection Station [*Detection station on the Mid-Canada Line*] ... DDS
Doppler Detection System ... DDS
Doppler Ekelund Ranging [*Navy*] (CAAL) ... DEKE
Doppler Electrophoretic Light Scanning Analyzer ... DELSA
Doppler Evaluated Attack Depth [*Navy*] (CAAL) ... DEAD
Doppler Extractor (MCD) ... DE
Doppler Filter Mixer-Oscillator [*Electronics*] (AABC) ... DFMO
Doppler Frequency Converter (MCD) ... DFC
Doppler Frequency Rate (MCD) ... DFR
Doppler Hover System (MCD) ... DHS

Doppler Imaging System [*Physics*] ... DIS
Doppler Inertial ... DI
Doppler Inertial LORAN ... DIL
Doppler Inertial LORAN System ... DILS
Doppler Inertial Omega (IAA) ... DIO
Doppler Inertial System (AAG) ... DIS
Doppler Landing Guidance System ... DLGS
Doppler LASER RADAR ... DLR
Doppler Location (IAA) ... DOPLOC
Doppler Location and Ranging System ... DOLARS
Doppler Martin RADAR [*Air Force*] ... DOMAR
Doppler Measurement System ... DMS
Doppler Microwave Landing System ... DMLS
Doppler Missile (MUGU) ... DM
Doppler Moving Target Indicator (IAA) ... DMTI
Doppler Navigation Satellite System (PDAA) ... DNSS
Doppler Navigation Sensor ... DNS
Doppler Navigation System ... DNS
Doppler on Wheels [*Instrumentation*] ... DOW
Doppler Ophthalmic Test (CPH) ... DOT
Doppler Optical Navigation ... DON
Doppler Optical Surveillance System ... DOSS
Doppler Orbitography and Radiopositioning Integrated by Satellite [*Marine science*] (OSRA) ... DORIS
Doppler Orbitography Integrated by Satellite ... DORIS
Doppler Phase Lock ... DOPLOC
Doppler Predict Voltage ... DPV
Doppler RADAR ... DRA
Doppler RADAR and Storm Electricity Research Group [*Norman, OK*] [*Department of Commerce*] (GRD) ... DRASER
Doppler RADAR Equipment ... DRE
Doppler RADAR Set (DNAB) ... DRS
Doppler RADAR Velocity Sensor ... DRVS
Doppler Range and Navigation [*Electronics*] ... DORAN
Doppler Ranging and Information System [*Navy*] (MCD) ... DORIS
Doppler Shift [*Physics*] ... DS
Doppler Shift Compensation [*Physics*] ... DSC
Doppler Shift Frequency Spectrum ... DSFS
Doppler Software Package (ADA) ... DOPACK
Doppler SONAR (IAA) ... DS
Doppler SONAR Velocity Log (MCD) ... DSVL
Doppler Spectrum Analyzer ... DSA
Doppler Spectrum Processor ... DSP
Doppler Techniques Proposal ... DTP
Doppler Tracking and Ranging [*Military*] (CAAL) ... DOPTAR
Doppler Tracking Station ... DTS
Doppler Translation Channel ... DTC
Doppler Ultrasound Stethoscope (MEDA) ... DUS
Doppler Unbeamed Search RADAR ... DOUSER
Doppler Velocity Altimeter RADAR Set [*Military*] (CAAL) ... DVARS
Doppler, Velocity and Position [*NASA*] ... DOVAP
Doppler Velocity Sensor ... DVS
Doppler Very High Frequency Omnidirectional Range [*FAA*] (TAG) ... DVOR
Doppler VHF [*Very High Frequency*] **Omnirange** ... DVOR
Doppler Zeeman Analyser [*British*] ... DZA
Doppler-Balloon [*Marine science*] (OSRA) ... DOPLIGHT
Doppler-Balloon (USDC) ... DOPLOON
Doppler-Enhanced RADAR Intensity Profiling System (MCD) ... DERIPS
Doppler-Inertial Gyrocompass (PDAA) ... DIG
Doppler-Lighting (USDC) ... DOPLIGHT
Doppler-Shifted Constant Frequency [*Biosonar research*] ... DSCF
Doppler-Shifted Ultrasonic Cyclotron Resonance (PDAA) ... DSUCR
Dopyera Brothers [*Guitar*] (IIA) ... DOBRO
D'Or Val Mines Ltd. [*Toronto Stock Exchange symbol Vancouver Stock Exchange symbol*] ... DQA
Dora, AL [*AM radio station call letters*] ... WPYK
Dora Explorations Ltd. [*Vancouver Stock Exchange symbol*] ... DO
Dorado [*Puerto Rico*] [*Airport symbol*] (OAG) ... DDP
Dorado [*Constellation*] ... Dor
Dorado [*Constellation*] ... Dora
Dorado Air [*Dominican Republic*] [*ICAO designator*] (FAAC) ... DAD
Dorado Resources Ltd. [*Vancouver Stock Exchange symbol*] ... DRR
Dorado Wings [*Airline code*] ... KW
Dorcas Welfare Society [*Later, Community Services*] (EA) ... DWS
Dorchester [*City in England*] (ROG) ... DORCH
Dorchester County Library, St. George, SC [*Library symbol*] [*Library of Congress*] (LCLS) ... ScStg
Dorchester County Public Library, Cambridge, MD [*Library symbol Library of Congress*] (LCLS) ... MdCam
Dorchester Hotels, Inc. [*Vancouver Stock Exchange symbol*] ... DOH
Dorchester Hugoton [*NASDAQ symbol*] (TTSB) ... DHULZ
Dorchester Hugoton Ltd. [*NASDAQ symbol*] (NQ) ... DHUL
Dorchester Hugoton Ltd. [*Associated Press*] (SAG) ... DrchHu
Dorchester Terrace-Brentwood, SC [*AM radio station call letters*] ... WTMZ
Dordabis [*Namibia*] [*ICAO location identifier*] (ICLI) ... FADS
Dordt College, Sioux Center, IA [*Library symbol Library of Congress*] (LCLS) ... IaSceD
Dordt College, Sioux Center, IA [*OCLC symbol*] (OCLC) ... IOT
Dore-Norbaska Resources, Inc. [*Toronto Stock Exchange symbol*] ... DN
Dori [*Burkina Faso*] [*ICAO location identifier*] (ICLI) ... DHEE
Dori [*Burkina Faso*] [*Airport symbol*] (OAG) ... DOR
Dori [*Upper Volta*] [*Airport symbol*] (AD) ... DOR
Doria's Law and Practice in Bankruptcy [*2nd ed.*] [*1873*] [*A publication*] (DLA) ... Dor Bank
Doric ... DOR
Doriden [*Glutethimide*] [*Sedative*] ... D
Doriden [*Rhone-Poulenc Rorer Consumer Pharmaceuticals*] [*Pharmacology*] (DAVI) ... DORIDN
Dorion Public Library, Ontario [*Library symbol National Library of Canada*] (NLC) ... ODOR
Dorion's Quebec Queen's Bench Reports [*A publication*] (DLA) ... Dor QB
Dorion's Quebec Queen's Bench Reports [*A publication*] (DLA) ... Dorion
Dorion's Quebec Queen's Bench Reports [*A publication*] (DLA) ... Dorion QB
Dorion's Quebec Queen's Bench Reports (Canada) [*A publication*] (DLA) ... Dorion (Can)
Dorion's Quebec Reports [*A publication*] (DLA) ... Dor
Dorion's Queen's Bench Reports [*Canada*] [*A publication*] (DLA) ... DCA
Doris Day Animal League (EA) ... DDAL
Doris Day Collectors (EA) ... DDC
Dorling Kindersley, Ltd. [*British*] ... DK
Dormant Account [*Banking*] ... DA
Dormant Equipping of Merchant Ships [*Organization*] (MCD) ... DEMS
Dormant Inertial Navigation System (MCD) ... DINS
Dormit in Pace [*Sleeps in Peace*] [*Latin*] ... DIP
Dormitory ... DOR
Dormitory ... DORM
Dormitory (VRA) ... dorm
Dornier [*German airplane type*] ... DO
Dornier 228 [*Airplane code*] ... Do8
Dornier Recoverable Instrument Sonde (MCD) ... DORIS
Dornier Reparaturwerft GmbH [*Germany ICAO designator*] (FAAC) ... DOR
Dornier-Werke GmbH [*Germany ICAO aircraft manufacturer identifier*] (ICAO) ... DO
Dorobisoro [*Papua New Guinea*] [*Airport symbol*] (OAG) ... DOO
Doron Exploration, Inc. [*Vancouver Stock Exchange symbol*] ... DNE
Dorothy L. Sayers Historical and Literary Society [*British*] ... DLSHLS
Dorothy L. Sayers Society (EAIO) ... DLS Soc
Dorozhno-Transportnyy Upravleniye [*Road and Transportation Directorate*] [*Former USSR*] (LAIN) ... DTU
Dorr Township Library, Dorr, MI [*Library symbol Library of Congress*] (LCLS) ... MiDo
Dorsal ... D
Dorsal Accessory Olive [*Neuroanatomy*] ... DAO
Dorsal Aorta [*Anatomy*] ... DA
Dorsal Area [*Anatomy*] ... DA
Dorsal Cardiac Nerve [*Anatomy*] ... DCN
Dorsal Column Stimulator [*Pain killer*] ... DCS
Dorsal Cortex [*Neuroanatomy*] ... DC
Dorsal Cutaneous Nerve ... DCN
Dorsal Fin, Depressed Length [*Pisciculture*] ... DFDL
Dorsal Fold ... DF
Dorsal Fold (Oesophagus) ... DFO
Dorsal Hippocampus [*Neuroanatomy*] ... DHPC
Dorsal Intercalary Segment Instability [*Medicine*] ... DISI
Dorsal Intermediate Tract [*Anatomy*] ... DIT
Dorsal Intersegmental Muscles [*Anatomy*] ... DIM
Dorsal Kidney ... DK
Dorsal Lateral Geniculate Nucleus [*Also, LGd*] [*Anatomy*] ... dLGN
Dorsal Lateral Geniculate Nucleus [*Also, dLGN*] [*Anatomy*] ... LGd
Dorsal Lip ... DL
Dorsal Longitudinal ... DL
Dorsal Longitudinal Muscle [*Anatomy*] ... DLM
Dorsal Median Pallium [*Neuroanatomy*] ... DMP
Dorsal Median Tract [*Anatomy*] ... DMT
Dorsal Midline Precursor [*Neuroanatomy*] ... dMP
Dorsal Motor Nucleus [*of the vagus*] ... DMN
Dorsal (Nephridial Gland) ... DNG
Dorsal Nerve [*Anatomy*] ... DN
Dorsal Pallium [*Neuroanatomy*] ... DP
Dorsal Peristomial Collar Fold ... DPCF
Dorsal Pioneer Cell [*Cytology*] ... DP
Dorsal Pitt ... DP
Dorsal Pressure Neuron [*of a leech*] ... Pd
Dorsal Raphe [*Brain anatomy*] ... DR
Dorsal Raphe Nucleus [*Brain anatomy*] ... DRN
Dorsal Respiratory Group [*Medicine*] ... DRG
Dorsal Root [*of spinal nerve*] [*Anatomy*] ... DR
Dorsal Root Entry Zone [*Medicine*] ... DREZ
Dorsal Root Ganglion [*Neuroanatomy*] ... DRG
Dorsal Root Neurons [*Neuroanatomy*] ... DRN
Dorsal Root Potential [*Anatomy*] ... DRP
Dorsal Spine [*Anatomy*] (DAVI) ... D
Dorsal Striatum [*Neuroanatomy*] ... DSTR
Dorsal Touch Neurons [*of a leech*] ... Td
Dorsal Unpaired Median (PDAA) ... DUM
Dorsal Unpaired Median Extensor-Tibiae (PDAA) ... DUMETI
Dorsal Velar Lobe ... DVL
Dorsal Vertebra [*Anatomy*] (DAVI) ... D
Dorsal-Axial [*Embryology*] ... DMZ
Dorsalis Pedis [*Pulse*] [*Medicine*] ... DP
Dorsay's Law of Insolvency [*A publication*] (DLA) ... Dor Ins
Dorsch Memorial Public Library, Monroe, MI [*Library symbol Library of Congress*] (LCLS) ... MiMD
Dorset [*County in England*] (ODBW) ... Dors
Dorset Exploration Ltd. [*Toronto Stock Exchange symbol*] ... DXL
Dorset Resources Ltd. [*Toronto Stock Exchange symbol*] ... DOT
Dorsetshire [*County in England*] (ROG) ... DORS
Dorsetshire [*County in England*] ... DORSET
Dorsey Laboratories [*Research code symbol*] ... HF
Dorsey Trailers [*NASDAQ symbol*] (TTSB) ... DSYT

Dorsey Trailers, Inc. [*Associated Press*] (SAG) ... DorseyTr
Dorsey Trailers, Inc. [*NASDAQ symbol*] (SAG) ... DSYT
Dorsey's Maryland Laws [*A publication*] (DLA) ... Dor MD Laws
Dorsiflexion [*Medicine*] ... DF
Dorsolateral Fascicle [*Muscular anatomy, neuroanatomy*] ... DLF
Dorsolateral Funiculus [*Neuroanatomy*] ... DLF
Dorsolateral Nucleus [*Neuroanatomy*] ... DLN
Dorsolateral Prefrontal Cortex [*Brain anatomy*] ... dlPFC
Dorsolateral Prefrontal Cortex [*Brain anatomy*] ... DLPFC
Dorsolateral Septal Nucleus [*Neuroanatomy*] ... DLSN
Dorsomedial Nucleus [*Brain anatomy*] ... DMN
Dorsoventral [*Anatomy*] ... DV
Dorsoventral Abdominal Vibration [*Entomology*] ... DVAV
Dortmund [*Germany Airport symbol*] (OAG) ... DTM
Dortmund Data Bank [*University of Dortmund*] [*Germany Information service or system*] (IID) ... DDB
Dortmund/Wickede [*Germany ICAO location identifier*] (ICLI) ... EDLW
Dortmunder Bibliothekssystem [*Dortmund Bibliographic Information System*] [*Cataloguing system developed in Germany*] ... DOBIS
Dorunda Station [*Australia Airport symbol Obsolete*] (OAG) ... DRD
Dos Bocas Dam [*Puerto Rico*] [*Seismograph station code, US Geological Survey*] (SEIS) ... DOS
Dos De Mayo [*Peru*] [*ICAO location identifier*] (ICLI) ... SPMY
Dos Equis [*Beer*] [*Standard Brands, Inc.*] ... XX
DOS LAN Requester [*Computer science*] ... DLR
Dos Mundos [*Dominican Republic*] [*ICAO designator*] (FAAC) ... DOM
Dos Passos on Stock-Brokers and Stock Exchanges [*A publication*] (DLA) ... Dos Passos Stock-Brok
DOS [*Disk Operating System*] **Protected Mode Interface** [*Computer science*] (PCM) ... DPMI
DOS [*Disk Operating System*] **Protected Mode Service** (PCM) ... DPMS
DOS [*Disk Operating System*] **under OS** [*Operating System*] ... DUO
Dosage [*Medicine*] ... DOS
Dosage-Sensitive Sex [*Reversal*] [*Genetics*] [*Medicine*] ... DSS
Dose Assessment [*Nuclear energy*] (NRCH) ... DA
Dose Assessment Advisory Group [*Department of Energy*] [*Las Vegas, NV*] (EGAO) ... DAAG
Dose Commitment Factor [*Radioactivity calculations*] ... DCF
Dose Conversion Factor [*Radioactivity calculations*] (NRCH) ... DCF
Dose Detector System ... DDS
Dose Equivalent [*Radioactivity calculations*] ... DE
Dose Equivalent [*Radioactivity calculations*] (IEEE) ... DEQ
Dose Equivalent Iodine [*Nuclear energy*] (NRCH) ... DEI
Dose Factor [*Radioactivity calculations*] ... DF
Dose Modifying Factor [*Medicine*] ... DMF
Dose Rate Effectiveness Factor [*Toxicology of radiation*] ... DREF
Dose Rate Instrumentation ... DRI
Dose Ratio [*Medicine*] ... DR
Dose Reduction Factor (DEN) ... DRF
Dose Response Curve [*Medicine*] ... DRC
Dosemeter Issue and Record Keeping ... DIRK
Doshisha Law Journal. International Edition [*A publication*] (DLA) ... Doshisha LJ
Doshisha Law Review [*A publication*] (DLA) ... Doshisha L Rev
Dosimeter (NASA) ... DOSIM
Dosimeter Corp. of America [*Nuclear energy*] (NRCH) ... DCA
Dosimetry Acquisition and Display System ... DADS
Dosimetry Applications Research Facility [*AEC*] ... DOSAR
Dosis [*Dose*] [*Pharmacy*] ... D
Dosis [*Dose*] [*Pharmacy*] (ROG) ... DOS
Dosis Letalis [*Lethal Dose*] [*Latin*] ... Dos Let
Dosso [*Niger*] [*ICAO location identifier*] (ICLI) ... DRRD
Dot and Dash (IAA) ... DD
Dot Cycle [*Telecommunications*] (IAA) ... DC
Dot Immunobinding Assay [*Immunology*] ... DIB
Dot Matrix ... DM
Dot Pitch (CDE) ... DP
Dot Sequential Transmission (IAA) ... DST
Dot System [*Mitre Corp.*] [*Braille translation system*] (NITA) ... DOTSYS
Dothan [*Alabama*] [*Airport symbol*] (OAG) ... DHN
Dothan [*Alabama*] [*ICAO location identifier*] (ICLI) ... KDHN
Dothan, AL [*Location identifier FAA*] (FAAL) ... RRS
Dothan, AL [*AM radio station call letters*] ... WAGF
Dothan, AL [*FM radio station call letters*] (RBYB) ... WAGF-FM
Dothan, AL [*Television station call letters*] ... WDHN
Dothan, AL [*FM radio station call letters*] ... WESP
Dothan, AL [*FM radio station call letters*] ... WGTF
Dothan, AL [*AM radio station call letters*] ... WGZS
Dothan, AL [*FM radio station call letters*] ... WJJN
Dothan, AL [*AM radio station call letters*] ... WOOF
Dothan, AL [*FM radio station call letters*] ... WOOF-FM
Dothan, AL [*FM radio station call letters*] ... WRWA
Dothan, AL [*FM radio station call letters*] ... WTVY
Dothan, AL [*Television station call letters*] ... WTVY-TV
Dothan, AL [*FM radio station call letters*] ... WVOB
Dothan, AL [*AM radio station call letters*] ... WWNT
Doti [*Nepal*] [*ICAO location identifier*] (ICLI) ... VNDT
Dotronics, Inc. [*Associated Press*] (SAG) ... Dotrnix
Dotronics, Inc. [*NASDAQ symbol*] (SAG) ... DOTX
Dotronix, Inc. [*NASDAQ symbol*] (NQ) ... DOTX
Dots Per Inch (WDMC) ... DPI
Dots-per-Inch [*Printing technology*] ... dpi
Dottore Ingenieur [*Doctor of Engineering*] [*Italian*] ... Dott Ing
Dottoressa [*Female Doctor*] [*Italian*] ... Dssa
Dottrina Giuridica [*Consiglio Nazionale delle Ricerche*] [*Italy Information service or system*] (CRD) ... DOGI
Douala [*Cameroon*] [*Airport symbol*] (OAG) ... DLA
Douala [*Cameroon*] [*ICAO location identifier*] (ICLI) ... FKKD
Douala [*Cameroon*] [*ICAO location identifier*] (ICLI) ... FKKK
Douane [*Customs*] [*French*] ... D
Douay Bible ... D Bib
Douay Version [*Bible*] ... DV
Double ... D
Double (AAG) ... DBL
Double (VRA) ... dbl
Double (WDMC) ... dbl
Double ... DBL
Double (ROG) ... DBLE
Double ... DUBL
Double Absorption Photofragment Spectroscopy ... DAPS
Double Aged [*Metals*] ... DA
Double Aluminized Mylar (NASA) ... DAM
Double Amplitude (KSC) ... DA
Double Anode Zener Diode ... DAZD
Double Antibody Solid-Phase [*Clinical chemistry*] (AAMN) ... DASP
Double Antibody Solid-Phase Radioimmunoassay [*Clinical chemistry*] ... DASP
Double Antiparallel [*Molecular biology*] ... DAP
Double Arm Magnetic Spectrometer ... DASP
Double Armor [*Telecommunications*] (TEL) ... DA
Double Balanced Mixer ... DBM
Double Bass [*Music*] ... DB
Double Bass [*Music*] ... DBS
Double Bassoon [*Music*] ... DBN
Double Bayonet Base [*Electronics*] (IAA) ... DB
Double Beam Spectrophotometer ... DBS
Double Bed ... db
Double Beta Decay ... DBD
Double Biased (CET) ... DB
Double Bituminous Surface Treatment ... DBST
Double Black [*Pencil*] ... BB
Double Blind Study [*Medicine*] (DMAA) ... DB
Double Blind Study ... DBS
Double Bond Equivalent [*Analytical chemistry*] ... DBE
Double Book Form [*Photography*] (ROG) ... DBF
Double Bottom (MSA) ... DB
Double Bottom Center [*of a ship*] (DS) ... DBC
Double Bounce [*Electronics*] (IAA) ... DB
Double Bounce, Circularly Polarized ... DBCP
Double Bowl Stainless Steel Sink [*Classified advertising*] (ADA) ... DBSSS
Double Braid (AAG) ... DB
Double Braid Weatherproof [*Wire insulation*] (IAA) ... DBWP
Double Break ... DB
Double Breasted [*Clothing industry*] ... DB
Double British Standard Time (IAA) ... DBST
Double British Summer Time ... DBST
Double Byte Interleaved ... DBI
Double Cantilever Beam [*Stress condition of aluminum alloy*] ... DCB
Double Cap [*or Crown*] [*Paper size*] ... DC
Double Cash Ruled [*Stationery*] ... DX
Double Chain Branch-Oblong Master Link-Grab Hook ... DOG
Double Channel Duplex ... DCD
Double Channel Simplex ... DCS
Double Column [*Advertising*] (ODBW) ... d col
Double Column [*Publishing*] (NTCM) ... DC
Double Column (ADA) ... D-COL
Double Column Inch [*Typography*] (DGA) ... DCI
Double Column Ion Chromotography ... DCIC
Double Common Meter [*Music*] ... DCM
Double Common Multiple [*Mathematics*] (ROG) ... DCM
Double Compton Scattering ... DCS
Double Concave [*Medicine*] ... DCc
Double Conductor ... DC
Double Conductor, Shipboard General Use, Armor [*Cable*] (IAA) ... DSGA
Double Contact [*Switch*] ... DC
Double Contact [*Lamp base type*] (NTCM) ... DC
Double Contact Switch (IAA) ... DBLCN
Double Contrast Barium Enema [*X-ray procedure*] (CPH) ... DCBE
Double Contrast Shoulder Arthrography [*Radiology*] (DAVI) ... DCSA
Double Conversion Adapter ... DCA
Double Convex ... DCx
Double Coronary Artery Bypass Graft [*Medicine*] ... DCABG
Double Cotton [*Wire insulation*] (AAG) ... DC
Double Cotton Covered [*Wire insulation*] ... DCC
Double Cotton Double Silk [*Wire insulation*] ... DCDS
Double Cotton Single Silk [*Wire insulation*] (AAG) ... DCS
Double Cotton Varnish [*Wire insulation*] (AAG) ... DCV
Double Crochet ... DC
Double Cropped [*Agriculture*] ... DC
Double Cross-Polarization, Magic Angle Spinning [*Spectroscopy*] ... DCPMAS
Double Crown [*Paper*] (DGA) ... DC
Double Crown [*Monetary unit*] [*British*] ... DC
Double Crown [*Monetary unit*] [*British*] (ADA) ... DCN
Double Crystal Monochromator ... DCM
Double Current (IAA) ... DC
Double Current Cable Code [*Telecommunications*] ... DCCC
Double Current Generator ... DCG
Double Cylinder Deadlock ... DCDL
Double Dacron Braid Lacquered (MDG) ... DD
Double Dark [*Photography*] (ROG) ... DD
Double Decidual Sac [*Medicine*] (DMAA) ... DDS
Double Deck ... DD

Double Declining Balance [Depreciation method] [Accounting]	DDB
Double Deflection Tube (BUR)	DDT
Double Demy [Paper] (DGA)	DD
Double Density	DD
Double Density Modular Core Memory (MCD)	DMCM
Double Derivatized Guar [Chemical technology]	DDG
Double Diamond (MSA)	DD
Double Differential Cross Section	DDCS
Double Diffused Mesa	DDM
Double Diffused Transistor Logic [Electronics] (IAA)	DDTL
Double Diffusion [Test]	DD
Double Diffusion Epitaxial Plane	DDEP
Double Diffusion Epitaxial Process (IAA)	DDE
Double Diode	DD
Double Diode-Pentode	DDP
Double Diode-Triode	DDT
Double Dominance [Ethology]	DD
Double Draft [Banking] (ROG)	DD
Double Draw-Off [Crystallizer] [Chemical engineering]	DDO
Double Drift [As used in a navigator's log]	DD
Double Drift Region (IEEE)	DDR
Double Dual Tandem [Aviation] (DA)	DDT
Double Eagle Energy [Vancouver Stock Exchange symbol]	DET
Double Eagle Pete & Mng [NASDAQ symbol] (TTSB)	DBLE
Double Eagle Petroleum & Mining Co. [NASDAQ symbol] (NQ)	DBLE
Double Eagle Petroleum & Mining Co. [Associated Press] (SAG)	DblEgl
Double Edge Receiver (MCD)	DER
Double Electron Muon Resonance (MCD)	DEMUR
Double Electron Transfer (MCD)	DET
Double Elephant [Paper] (ADA)	DE
Double Enamel [Insulation] (MSA)	DE
Double End [Technical drawings]	DE
Double End Trimmed (DAC)	DET
Double Entry [Bookkeeping]	DE
Double Entry [Bookkeeping] (ODBW)	de
Double Error Detection	DED
Double Escape Peak Efficiency [Nuclear science] (OA)	DEPE
Double Excellent	XX
Double Exposure	DEX
Double Exposure Endpoint Detection Technique (IAA)	DEEPDET
Double Extension [Camera stand] (ROG)	DE
Double Extra Hard Black [Pencil leads] (ROG)	DEHB
Double Extra Heavy (DAC)	XXH
Double Extra Strong	XXSTR
Double Face	DBLF
Double Failure Matrix [Hazard quantification method]	DFM
Double Feeder [Line] [Technical drawings]	DF
Double First Class	D1
Double Foolscap [Paper] (ADA)	DCAP
Double Foolscap [Paper] (ADA)	DF
Double Four Valve [Cosworth racing engines]	DFV
Double Four-Valve Long Distance [Cosworth racing engines]	DFL
Double Frequency	DF
Double Frequency Change (IAA)	DFC
Double Frequency Recording (HGAA)	DFR
Double Frequency Shift Keying [Radio]	DFSK
Double Front Contact [Photovoltaic energy systems]	DFC
Double Gear [Engineering] (ROG)	DG
Double Glass (AAG)	DG
Double Glass Door [Classified advertising] (ADA)	DGD
Double Glass Sliding Doors [Classified advertising] (ADA)	DGSD
Double Green Silk Covered [Wire insulation]	DGS
Double Groove [Insulators]	DG
Double Groove, Double Petticoat [Insulators]	DGDP
Double Gypsy Winch	DGW
Double Hard [Pencil leads]	HH
Double Heat-Sink Diode (CET)	DHD
Double Heave Amplitude	DHA
Double Helix [Cytology, genetics]	DH
Double Heterostructure [Physics]	DH
Double Hexagonal Close-Packed [Metallography]	DHCP
Double High-Resolution File [Computer science]	DHR
Double Hollow Fork [Bicycle part or a fool] [Slang British] (DSUE)	DHF
Double Homology [Biochemistry]	DH
Double Hydrant [On fire insurance maps]	DH
Double Imperial [Paper] (ADA)	DI
Double Incidence Technique	DIT
Double [or Dual] Income, Children, and Everything [Term coined by William F. Doescher, publisher of "D & B Reports"] [Lifestyle classification]	Dice
Double [or Dual] Income, Kids [Lifestyle classification]	Dik
Double [or Dual] Income, Lots of Kids [Lifestyle classification]	DILK
Double [or Dual] Income, No Children [Lifestyle classification]	Dinc
Double [or Dual] Income, No Kids [Lifestyle classification]	Dink
Double [or Dual] Income, No Kids Yet [Lifestyle classification]	Dinky
Double [or Dual] Income, Separate Homes [Lifestyle classification]	Dish
Double Income Tax [Insurance] (ODBW)	DIT
Double Indemnity [Insurance]	DI
Double Injection	DI
Double Injection Effect	DIE
Double Injection Field Effect Transistor [Electronics]	DIFET
Double Injection Luminescence	DIL
Double In-Line Package [Computer science]	DIP
Double Inverse Pinch Device [Physics] (OA)	DIPD
Double Isobaric Analogue State [Physics]	DIAS
Double Isomorphous Replacement [Medicine] (DMAA)	DIR
Double Isotope Derivative	DID
Double Jeopardy	DJ
Double Knockout [Genetics]	DKO
Double Known Addition Method [Analytical electrochemistry]	DKAM
Double Label Index [Medicine] (DMAA)	DLI
Double Large Post (ADA)	DLP
Double Layer Polysilicon (IAA)	DLP
Double Ledger [Accounting]	DL
Double Left Shift	DLS
Double Leg Elbow Amplifier	DLEA
Double Length Line	DLL
Double Length Number	DLN
Double Local Oscillator	DLO
Double Lock Up Garage	DLUG
Double Long Meter [Music]	DLM
Double Make (IAA)	DM
Double Mannitol Isolation Method [Microscopy]	DMIM
Double Many-Body Expansion [Kinetics]	DMBE
Double Mark Blank Column (BUR)	DMBC
Double Mars Loiter	DML
Double Master [LORAN stations]	DM
Double Medium (ADA)	DM
Double Meridian Distance (PDAA)	DMD
Double Minute [Cytology]	DM
Double Motor Alternator	DMA
Double Mouldboard [Ploughing]	DMB
Double Negation [Rule of replacement] [Logic]	DN
Double Odd Pass Even [System in game of bridge]	DOPE
Double Offset [Engineering]	DO
Double Offset Tactic (SAA)	DOT
Double Oil of Vitriol	DOV
Double Outlet Left Ventricle [Cardiology] (DAVI)	DOLV
Double Outlet Right Ventricle [Cardiology]	DORV
Double Overhead Camshaft [Automotive term]	DOHC
Double Paper [Wire insulation] (AAG)	DP
Double Paper, Double Cotton [Wire insulation]	DPDC
Double Paper, Single Cotton [Wire insulation] (AAG)	DPSC
Double Paper-Covered [Wire insulation] (DEN)	DPC
Double Parallel [Molecular biology]	DP
Double Petticoat [Insulators]	DP
Double Plasma	DP
Double Play [Baseball]	DP
Double Plug Diode (IAA)	DPD
Double Pole [Switch]	DP
Double Pole, Double Throw [Switch]	DPDT
Double Pole, Front Connected [Switch]	DPFC
Double Pole, Single Throw [Switch]	DPST
Double Pole, Triple Throw [Switch]	DPTT
Double Precision (NASA)	DP
Double [or Dual] Propellant Loading (AFM)	DPL
Double Pulse Duration Modulation (KSC)	DPDM
Double Pulse Operation	DPO
Double Pulse Ranging (NG)	DPR
Double Pumped Parametric Amplifier	DPPA
Double Pure Rubber (IAA)	DPR
Double Radial Immunodiffusion [Medicine] (DMAA)	DRID
Double Reduced [Tinplate]	DR
Double Reduction Gearing (DS)	Dr
Double Reduction-Locked Train	DLT
Double Right Shift	DRS
Double Roll Out Arrays (MCD)	DORA
Double Rotation [Spectroscopy]	DOR
Double Royal [Paper] (ADA)	DR
Double Sandwich	DS
Double Sandwich Indirect	DSI
Double Secondary Current Transformer (MSA)	DSCT
Double Sheath Bronchial Brushing [Medicine] (DAVI)	DSBB
Double Short Meter [Music]	DSM
Double Sideband	DSB
Double Sideband Reduced Carrier [Telecommunications] (IAA)	DSRC
Double Sideband with Carrier [Modulation] (IAA)	DSBWC
Double Sided Double Density [Magnetic disc format] (NITA)	DSDD
Double Sided High-Density Disk [Computer software] (PCM)	DS/HD
Double Silk [Wire insulation] (AAG)	DS
Double Silk, Cotton Covered [Wire insulation] (IAA)	DSCC
Double Silk Covered [Wire insulation]	DSC
Double Silk Covered (IDOE)	dsc
Double Silk, Single Cotton [Wire insulation] (IAA)	DSSC
Double Silk Varnish [Wire insulation] (AAG)	DSV
Double Silver Plate	DSP
Double Single-Sideband (MSA)	DSSB
Double Slave [LORAN stations]	DS
Double Spot System	DSS
Double Spot Tuning	DST
Double Stitch [Bookbinding]	DS
Double Stout [Brewing] (ROG)	DS
Double Strand Break [Genetics]	DSB
Double Stranded (OA)	DS
Double Strength [Medicine]	DS
Double Strokes per Minute (MSA)	DSPM
Double Subdominance [Ethology]	DS
Double Summer Time [Daylight Saving Time two hours ahead of Standard Time] [British]	DST
Double Supertwisted Nematic [Video technology] (PCM)	DSTN
Double Tachycardia [Cardiology]	DT

Double Tape Armored [*Heavy-duty telephone buried cable*] .... DTA
Double Test Position .... DTP
Double Thermostat and Safety [*Nuclear energy*] (OA) .... DTS
Double Throw [*Switch*] .... DT
Double Throw Switch .... DTS
Double Time .... DT
Double Tinned (IDOE) .... DTn
Double Tongue and Groove (DAC) .... DT & G
Double Track [*Engineering acoustics*] (IAA) .... DT
Double Tube .... DT
Double Twin Tube [*Fluorescent lighting*] .... DTT
Double Uptake [*Boilers*] .... DU
Double Vacuum Melting (PDAA) .... DVM
Double Valve [*Stutz car model designation*] .... DV
Double Valve Replacement [*Medicine*] .... DVR
Double Velocity Transit Time [*Physics*] .... DOVETT
Double Vessel Disease with an Abnormal Left Ventricle [*Cardiology*] .... DVDALV
Double Vibrations [*Cycles*] .... DV
Double Vibrations [*Cycles*] .... VD
Double Vision .... DV
Double Wall .... DBLW
Double Wall .... DW
Double Weight .... DW
Double White Silk Covered [*Wire insulation*] .... DWS
Double Whole-Cell Recording [*Neurophysiology*] .... DWCR
Double Wipe Slide Switch .... DWSS
Double with Bath [*Hotel room*] .... DWB
Double Word [*Computer science*] .... DW
Double Zigzag Rectifier .... DZR
Double-Acting .... DA
Double-Acting (IAA) .... DBLACT
Double-Acting Door [*Technical drawings*] .... DAD
Double-Acting Limit Switch .... DALS
Double-Acting Steam .... DASTM
Double-Action Cylinder .... DAC
Double-Air Movement Valve .... DAMV
Double-Amplitude Displacement (MCD) .... DAD
Double-Amplitude Peak (DEN) .... DAP
Double-Aperture Speckle Camera .... DASC
Double-Aperture Speckle Shearing Camera (PDAA) .... DASSC
Double-Barreled (ADA) .... DB
Double-Barrier Resonant Tunneling Structure [*Physics*] .... DBRTS
Double-Base Diode .... DBD
Double-Base Propellant (AAG) .... DBP
Double-Base Solid Propellant (MSA) .... DBSP
Double-Base Transistor .... DBT
Double-Byte Character Set [*Computer science*] (PCM) .... DBCS
Double-Channel Planar Buried Heterostructure .... DC-PBH
Double-Charge Exchange .... DCX
Double-Charge-Transfer Spectroscopy (MCD) .... DCTS
Double-Check Valve .... DCV
Double-Coated Foam Tape .... DCFT
Double-Concentric .... DC
Double-Conductor, Heat and Flame-Resistant, Armored [*Cable*] .... DHFA
Double-Conductor, Radio, High-Tension, Lead-Armored [*Cable*] (IAA) .... DRHLA
Doublecross [*i.e., to betray*] [*Criminal slang*] .... Y
Doublecross Committee [*British military*] (DMA) XX
Double-Crucible [*Optics*] (EECA) .... DC
Double-Cylinder Tank [*Liquid gas carriers*] .... dc
Doubled .... DD
Double-Declining-Balance Depreciation Method [*Finance*] (DFIT) .... DDB
Double-Density Disk Drive Input/Output Processor [*Computer science*] (NITA) .... DIOP
Double-Diffused Medal Oxide Semiconductor Technology [*Microelectronics*] (PDAA) .... DMOST
Double-Diffused Metal-Oxide Semiconductor [*Microelectronics*] (MCD) .... DMOS
Double-Dipper [*Retired military-government employee*] .... DD
Double-Doped Crystal .... DDC
Double-Dose Gallbladder [*Medicine*] (MEDA) .... DDGB
Double-Ended Boiler [*Shipping*] (DS) .... DB
Double-Ended Cold Leg Guillotine [*Nuclear energy*] (NRCH) .... DECLG
Double-Ended Guillotine [*Nuclear energy*] (NRCH) .... DEG
Double-Ended Guillotine Break [*Nuclear energy*] (NRCH) .... DEGB
Double-Ended Pivot .... DEP
Double-Ended Pump Suction [*Nuclear energy*] (NRCH) .... DEPS
Double-Ended Rupture [*Nuclear energy*] (NRCH) .... DER
Double-Ended Suction Leg Slot [*Nuclear energy*] (NRCH) .... DESL
Double-Exposure Prevention [*Advanced photo system*] .... DEP
Double-Fronted .... D-F
Double-Gimbaled Momentum Wheel .... DGMW
Double-Gummed [*Envelopes*] .... DG
Double-Headed Ceiling (DAC) .... DB Clg
Double-Hung [*Construction*] .... DH
Double-Hung Windows [*Technical drawings*] .... DHW
Double-Inlet Ventricle [*Cardiology*] (DAVI) .... DIV
Double-Loop Magnetic Mine Sweep [*Navy British*] LL
Double-Modified Lysine Iron Agar [*Microorganism medium*] .... DMLIA
Double-Phase Hologram .... DPH
Double-Pole, Back Connected [*Switch*] (MCD) .... DPBC
Double-Pole, Both Connected [*Switch*] .... DPBC
Double-Pole, Double-Throw (IDOE) .... dpdt
Double-Pole, Double-Throw Switch .... DPDTSW
Double-Pole, Single-Throw (IDOE) .... dpst
Double-Pole, Single-Throw, Normally Closed Switch (IAA) .... DPSTNC
Double-Pole, Single-Throw, Normally Open Switch (IAA) .... DPSTNO
Double-Pole, Single-Throw Switch .... DPSTSW
Double-Pole, Snap Switch (IAA) .... DPS
Double-Pole, Snap Switch (IAA) .... DPSS
Double-Pole Switch .... DPSW
Double-Precision Arithmetic (AAG) .... DPA
Double-Precision Automatic Interpretive System .... DAISY
Double-Precision Floating Point [*Computer science*] .... DPFP
Double-Precision Orbit Determination Program [*NASA*] .... DPODP
Double-Precision Quantity .... DPQ
Double-Precision Trajectory Program [*NASA*] .... DPTRAJ
Double-Purpose Gun .... DP
Doubler (KSC) .... DBLR
Double-Ring Storage [*Particle accelerator*] .... DORIS
Double-Round Nose .... DRN
Double-Screened [*Coal*] .... D/S
Double-Sealed Ball Valve .... DSBV
Double-Sideband Amplitude Modulation [*Telecommunications*] (TEL) .... DSBAM
Double-Sideband Amplitude Modulation Reduced Carrier [*Telecommunications*] (IEEE) .... DSBAMRC
Double-Sideband Doppler Very-High-Frequency Omnidirectional Range [*FAA*] .... DSDVOR
Double-Sideband Emitted Carrier [*Telecommunications*] (TEL) .... DSBEC
Double-Sideband Reduced Carrier [*Telecommunications*] (TEL) .... DSBRC
Double-Sideband Suppressed Carrier [*Modulation*] .... DSBSC
Double-Sideband Suppressed Carrier [*Modulation*] (IEEE) .... DSSC
Double-Sideband Transmitted Carrier [*Telecommunications*] .... DSBTC
Double-Sideband Transmitted Carrier [*Telecommunications*] (IAA) .... DSTC
Double-Sided [*Disks*] [*Computer science*] .... DS
Double-Sided, Double-Density Disk [*Computer science*] .... DSDD
Double-Sided Inter-Symbol Interference (PDAA) .... DSISI
Double-Sided Linear Induction Motor (PDAA) .... DSLIM
Double-Sided Pulse-Width Modulation [*Telecommunications*] .... DPWM
Double-Sided Quad-Density [*Disk drive*] [*Scottsdale Systems*] [*Computer science*] .... DSQD
Double-Sided Single-Density Disk [*Computer science*] .... DSSD
Double-Sided, Triple-Deposit .... DSTD
Double-Single-Dummy [*in game of bridge*] .... DSD
Double-Strand Break Repair [*Genetics*] .... DSBR
Double-Stranded Ribonuclease .... dsRNase
Double-Stranded Ribonucleic Acid [*Biochemistry, genetics*] .... dsRNA
Double-Submerged Arc (PDAA) .... DSA
Doublet .... D
Double-Taxation Relief (ODBW) .... DTR
Doubletree Corp. [*Associated Press*] (SAG) .... Dbletree
Doubletree Corp. [*NASDAQ symbol*] (SAG) .... TREE
Double-Wall Fiberboard .... DWLFBD
Double-Weight [*Paper*] .... DWT
Double-Wire Armor .... DWA
Doubly Asymptotic Approximation (MCD) .... DAA
Doubly Auto-Ionizing (PDAA) .... DAI
Doubly Buffered Ringer [*Physiology*] .... DBR
Doubly Refractile Fat Bodies [*Biochemistry*] (DAVI) .... DRFB
Doubly Resonant Oscillator (IEEE) .... DRO
Doubly-Labelled Water [*Analytical chemistry*] .... DLW
Doubtful .... D
Doubtful (FAAC) .... DBTF
Doubtful-Very [*Theatrical term*] [*Facetious translation of DV, Deo Volente (God Willing)*] (DSUE) .... DV
Douentza [*Mali*] [*ICAO location identifier*] (ICLI) .... GADZ
Dough Rate of Reaction [*Food science*] .... DRR
Dougherty County Court House, Albany, GA [*Library symbol Library of Congress*] (LCLS) .... GAID
Dough-Molding Compound [*Plastics technology*] .... DMC
Doughnut .... DONUT
Doughtie's Foods [*NASDAQ symbol*] (TTSB) .... DOBG
Doughtie's Foods, Inc. [*Associated Press*] (SAG) .... Dghtie
Doughtie's Foods, Inc. [*NASDAQ symbol*] (NQ) .... DOBQ
Douglas [*Arizona*] [*Airport symbol*] (OAG) .... DUG
Douglas Advanced Research Laboratories [*Obsolete*] (KSC) .... DARL
Douglas Aircraft Co. [*of McDonnell Douglas Corp.*] .... DAC
Douglas Aircraft Co. of Canada [*of McDonnell Douglas Corp.*] (MCD) .... DACAN
Douglas Aircraft Co. Overseas [*Obsolete*] .... DACO
Douglas Aircraft Co., Santa Monica Division, Santa Monica, CA [*Library symbol Library of Congress*] (LCLS) .... CStmoD
Douglas Aircraft Co., Technical Library, Long Beach, CA [*Library symbol Library of Congress*] (LCLS) .... CLobD
Douglas Aircraft Corporation (AAGC) .... DAC
Douglas Airways [*ICAO designator*] (AD) .... DZ
Douglas & Lomason [*NASDAQ symbol*] (TTSB) .... DOUG
Douglas & Lomason Co. [*Associated Press*] (SAG) .... DglsLom
Douglas & Lomason Co. [*NASDAQ symbol*] (NQ) .... DOUG
Douglas, AZ [*Location identifier FAA*] (FAAL) .... DGL
Douglas, AZ [*AM radio station call letters*] .... KAPR
Douglas, AZ [*AM radio station call letters*] .... KDAP
Douglas, AZ [*FM radio station call letters*] .... KDAP-FM
Douglas, AZ [*FM radio station call letters*] (RBYB) .... KEAL-FM
Douglas, AZ [*FM radio station call letters*] .... KKRK
Douglas, AZ [*FM radio station call letters*] (RBYB) .... KRMC
Douglas/Bisbee International [*Arizona*] [*ICAO location identifier*] (ICLI) .... KDUG
Douglas College Learning Resources Centre [*UTLAS symbol*] .... DOC
Douglas College, New Westminster, BC, Canada [*Library symbol Library of Congress*] (LCLS) .... CaBNWD
Douglas College, New Westminster, British Columbia [*Library symbol National Library of Canada*] (NLC) .... BNWD
Douglas Colliery [*South Africa*] [*ICAO location identifier*] (ICLI) .... FADC

Douglas Commercial [*Airplane*] (IIA) .... DC
Douglas County Hospital, Health Science Library, Alexandria, MN [*Library symbol*] [*Library of Congress*] (LCLS) .... MnAleDH
Douglas County Jarman Memorial Hospital, Tuscola, IL [*Library symbol Library of Congress*] (LCLS) .... ITuCoH
Douglas County Library, Minden, NV [*Library symbol Library of Congress*] (LCLS) .... NvMiD
Douglas County Library, Roseburg, OR [*Library symbol Library of Congress*] (LCLS) .... OrRoD
Douglas County Museum, Roseburg, OR [*Library symbol Library of Congress*] (LCLS) .... OrRoM
Douglas County Public Library, Castle Rock, CO [*Library symbol Library of Congress*] (LCLS) .... CoCr
Douglas County Public Library, Castle Rock, CO [*OCLC symbol*] (OCLC) .... DAD
Douglas County Public Library, Parker Branch, Parker, CO [*Library symbol Library of Congress*] (LCLS) .... CoParD
Douglas Development Co. - Irvine [*California*] .... DDCI
Douglas Elementary School, Princeton, IL [*Library symbol Library of Congress*] (LCLS) .... IPriDS
Douglas' English Election Cases [*A publication*] (DLA) .... Doug
Douglas' English Election Cases [*A publication*] (DLA) .... Doug El Ca
Douglas' English Election Cases [*A publication*] (DLA) .... Doug El Cas
Douglas' English Election Cases [*A publication*] (DLA) .... Dougl El Cas
Douglas' English King's Bench Reports [*A publication*] (DLA) .... Doug
Douglas' English King's Bench Reports [*A publication*] (DLA) .... Doug KB
Douglas' English King's Bench Reports [*A publication*] (DLA) .... Dougl KB
Douglas' English King's Bench Reports [*A publication*] (DLA) .... Dougl KB (Eng)
Douglas Equipment Specification .... DES
Douglas Fir (MSA) .... DF
Douglas Fir Export Co. [*Defunct*] (EA) .... DFEC
Douglas Fir Larch [*Lumber*] .... DOUG FIR-L
Douglas Fir Plywood Association [*Later, APA*] (EA) .... DFPA
Douglas Furnished Material [*DAC*] .... DFM
Douglas, GA [*Location identifier FAA*] (FAAL) .... DQH
Douglas, GA [*AM radio station call letters*] .... WDMG
Douglas, GA [*FM radio station call letters*] .... WDMG-FM
Douglas, GA [*FM radio station call letters*] .... WKZZ
Douglas, GA [*AM radio station call letters*] .... WOKA
Douglas, GA [*FM radio station call letters*] .... WOKA-FM
Douglas Hospital Centre [*Centre Hospitalier Douglas*] **Montreal, Quebec** [*Library symbol National Library of Canada*] (NLC) .... QMDH
Douglas Hospital, Montreal, PQ, Canada [*Library symbol Library of Congress*] (LCLS) .... CaQMDH
Douglas Hospital Research Centre [*McGill University, Douglas Hospital*] [*Canada Research center*] (RCD) .... DHRC
Douglas Inspection Standard (SAA) .... DIS
Douglas Material Qualification Report [*DAC*] .... DMQR
Douglas' Michigan Supreme Court Reports [*A publication*] (DLA) .... Doug
Douglas' Michigan Supreme Court Reports [*A publication*] (DLA) .... Doug (Mich)
Douglas' Michigan Supreme Court Reports [*A publication*] (DLA) .... Dougl (Mich)
Douglas Missile - Model XX (MCD) .... DM-XX
Douglas Model (SAA) .... DM
Douglas [*Arizona*] **Municipal** [*Airport symbol*] (OAG) .... DGL
Douglas Point Nuclear Station (GFGA) .... DPNS
Douglas Point Project Nuclear Generating Station (NRCH) .... DPPNGS
Douglas Process Standard Development Record [*DAC*] .... DPSDR
Douglas Public Library, Douglas, AZ [*Library symbol*] [*Library of Congress*] (LCLS) .... AzD
Douglas' Reports [*A publication*] (DLA) .... Doug
Douglas Sleeper Transport [*Aviation*] .... DST
Douglas Space Physics Laboratory (MUGU) .... DSPL
Douglas Space Vehicle .... DSV
Douglas Township Library, Gilman, IL [*Library symbol Library of Congress*] (LCLS) .... IGil
Douglas United Nuclear, Inc. (KSC) .... DUN
Douglas, WY [*Location identifier FAA*] (FAAL) .... DGW
Douglas, WY [*AM radio station call letters*] .... KKTY
Douglas, WY [*FM radio station call letters*] .... KKTY-FM
Douglas-Fir Tussock Moth .... DFTM
Douglasville, GA [*AM radio station call letters*] .... WDCY
Doukhobor Village Museum, Castelgar, British Columbia [*Library symbol National Library of Canada*] (NLC) .... BCDVM
Doukhobor Village Museum, Castlegar, BC, Canada [*Library symbol*] [*Library of Congress*] (LCLS) .... CaBCDVM
Doulas of North America [*An association*] (PAZ) .... DONA
Doullens/Lucheux [*France ICAO location identifier*] (ICLI) .... LFXD
Doulton Ware [*Ceramics*] (ROG) .... DOULT
Dounreay Experimental Reactor Establishment [*British*] .... DERE
Dounreay Fast Reactor [*British*] .... DFR
Dounreay Materials Testing Reactor [*British*] .... DMTR
Dounreay/Thurso [*British ICAO location identifier*] (ICLI) .... EGPY
Dourados [*Brazil*] [*Airport symbol*] (OAG) .... DOU
Dourbes [*Belgium*] [*Seismograph station code, US Geological Survey*] (SEIS) .... DOU
Douro Public Library, Ontario [*Library symbol National Library of Canada*] (BIB) .... ODOU
Doutre. Procedure Civile de Bas Canada [*A publication*] (DLA) .... Dout Pr
Douzaine [*Dozen*] [*French*] .... DZNE
DOVAP [*Doppler Velocity and Position*] **Automatic Reduction Equipment** (AAG) .... DARE
Dovas Nordiske Rad [*Nordic Council for the Deaf - NCD*] (EAIO) .... DNR
DOVatron International [*Associated Press*] (SAG) .... Dovatrn
Dovatron International [*NASDAQ symbol*] (SAG) .... DOVT
Dove and Hawk [*One who took a moderate position on the Vietnam War*] .... DAWK
Dove Audio [*NASDAQ symbol*] (TTSB) .... DOVE
Dove Audio, Inc. [*NASDAQ symbol*] (SAG) .... DOVE
Dove Audio, Inc. [*Associated Press*] (SAG) .... DoveAud
Dove Creek, CO [*Location identifier FAA*] (FAAL) .... DVC
Dover [*Delaware*] [*Airport symbol*] (AD) .... DOV
Dover Air Force Base [*Delaware*] [*ICAO location identifier*] (ICLI) .... KDOV
Dover Corp. [*NYSE symbol*] (SPSG) .... DOV
Dover Corp. [*Associated Press*] (SAG) .... Dover
Dover, DE [*Location identifier FAA*] (FAAL) .... DOV
Dover, DE [*Location identifier FAA*] (FAAL) .... LIR
Dover, DE [*AM radio station call letters*] .... WDOV
Dover, DE [*FM radio station call letters*] .... WDSD
Dover, DE [*AM radio station call letters*] .... WKEN
Dover, DE [*FM radio station call letters*] .... WRTX
Dover Downs Entertainment, Inc. [*Associated Press*] (SAG) .... DoverD
Dover Downs Entertainment, Inc. [*NYSE symbol*] (SAG) .... DVD
Dover Downs International Speedway [*Auto racing facility*] .... DDIS
Dover Industries Ltd. [*Toronto Stock Exchange symbol*] .... DVI
Dover, NH [*FM radio station call letters*] .... WOKQ
Dover, NH [*AM radio station call letters*] .... WTSN
Dover, NJ [*FM radio station call letters*] .... WDHA
Dover, OH [*FM radio station call letters*] .... WJER
Dover Public Library, Dover, DE [*OCLC symbol*] (OCLC) .... DOV
Dover Public Library, Dover, NH [*Library symbol Library of Congress*] (LCLS) .... NhDo
Dover Public Library, Dover, NJ [*Library symbol Library of Congress*] (LCLS) .... NjD
Dover Public Library, Newfoundland [*Library symbol National Library of Canada*] (BIB) .... NFD
Dover Publications, New York, NY [*Library symbol Library of Congress*] (LCLS) .... NND
Dover Township, NJ [*FM radio station call letters*] .... WWNJ
Dover-Foxcroft, ME [*FM radio station call letters*] .... WDME-FM
Doveri Pulvis [*Dover's Powder*] [*Pharmacy*] (ROG) .... DOV PULV
Dover-New Philadelphia, OH [*AM radio station call letters*] .... WJER
Doverton Oils Ltd. [*Vancouver Stock Exchange symbol*] .... DOV
Dovetail (MSA) .... DVTL
Dovetail Anchor [*Technical drawings*] .... DTA
Dovetail Anchor Slot [*Technical drawings*] .... DTS
Dow and Clark's English House of Lords Cases [*A publication*] (DLA) .... D & C
Dow and Clark's English House of Lords Cases [*A publication*] (DLA) .... Dow & C
Dow and Clark's English House of Lords Cases [*A publication*] (DLA) .... Dow & C (Eng)
Dow and Clark's English House of Lords Cases [*A publication*] (DLA) .... Dow & Cl
Dow and Clark's English House of Lords Cases [*A publication*] (DLA) .... Dow NS
Dow and Clark's Reports [*A publication*] (DLA) .... D & Cl
Dow Chemical [*NYSE symbol*] (TTSB) .... DOW
Dow Chemical Co. [*Research code symbol*] .... A-E
Dow Chemical Co. .... DCC
Dow Chemical Co. [*Research code symbol*] .... DH
Dow Chemical Co. [*NYSE symbol Toronto Stock Exchange symbol*] .... DOW
Dow Chemical Co. [*Associated Press*] (SAG) .... DowCh
Dow Chemical Co., E and CS Information Center, Houston, TX [*Library symbol Library of Congress*] (LCLS) .... TxHDC
Dow Chemical Co., Granville Research Center, Granville, OH [*OCLC symbol*] (OCLC) .... DOW
Dow Chemical Co., Library, Midland, MI [*OCLC symbol*] (OCLC) .... MDC
Dow Chemical Co., Midland, MI [*Library symbol Library of Congress*] (LCLS) .... MiMidD
Dow Chemical Co., Rocky Flats Division, Golden, CO [*Library symbol Library of Congress*] (LCLS) .... CoGD
Dow Chemical Co., Sarnia, ON, Canada [*Library symbol Library of Congress*] (LCLS) .... CaOSD
Dow Chemical Co., Sarnia, Ontario [*Library symbol National Library of Canada*] (NLC) .... OSD
Dow Chemical Co., Texas Division, Freeport, TX [*OCLC symbol*] (OCLC) .... DTF
Dow Chemical Co., Texas Division, Freeport, TX [*Library symbol Library of Congress*] (LCLS) .... TxFrD
Dow Chemical USA, Western Division Library, Walnut Creek, CA [*Library symbol Library of Congress*] (LCLS) .... CWcD
Dow Corning Corp., Midland, MI [*Library symbol Library of Congress*] (LCLS) .... MiMidDC
Dow Corning Corp., TIS Library, Carrollton, KY [*Library symbol Library of Congress*] (LCLS) .... KyCarD
Dow Dividend Strategy .... DDS
Dow Education Systems [*Dow Chemical Corp.*] .... DES
Dow Epoxy Novolac .... DEN
Dow Gardens, Midland, MI [*Library symbol*] [*Library of Congress*] (LCLS) .... MiMidDG
Dow Jones & Co. [*NYSE symbol*] (TTSB) .... DJ
Dow Jones & Co., Inc. [*Also, the stock market averages compiled by this co mpany*] [*NYSE symbol*] (SPSG) .... DJ
Dow Jones & Co., Inc. [*Associated Press*] (SAG) .... DowJns
Dow Jones & Co., Inc., Chicopee, MA [*Library symbol Library of Congress*] (LCLS) .... MChiD
Dow Jones Averages [*Information retrieval*] .... DJA
Dow Jones Books, Princeton, NJ [*Library symbol Library of Congress*] (LCLS) .... DjB
Dow Jones Cable News [*Cable-television system*] .... DJCN
Dow Jones Index [*Stock market*] [*Investment term*] .... DJI
Dow Jones Index - Commodity [*Stock market*] .... CDJI
Dow Jones Index - Composite [*Stock market*] [*Investment term*] .... DJIC
Dow Jones Index - Industrials [*Stock market*] [*Investment term*] .... DJII
Dow Jones Index - Transport [*Stock market*] [*Investment term*] .... DJIT
Dow Jones Index - Utilities [*Stock market*] [*Investment term*] .... DJIU

Dow Jones Industrial Average [*Stock market*] [*Investment term*] ... DJIA
Dow Jones Information Retrieval System (HGAA) ... DJIRS
Dow Jones Investor Network ... DJIN
Dow Jones News [*Dow Jones & Co., Inc.*] [*Information service or system*] (CRD) ... DJN
Dow Jones News/Retrieval [*Princeton, NJ*] [*Bibliographic database*] [*Information service or system*] ... DJNR
Dow Jones Newspaper Fund (EA) ... DJNF
Dow Jones Transportation Average [*Information retrieval*] ... DJTA
Dow Jones Utility Average [*Information retrieval*] ... DJUA
Dow. New Series [*Dow and Clark, English House of Lords Cases*] [*A publication*] (DLA) ... DNS
Dow Theory [*Stock market analysis*] ... DT
Dowager ... D
Dowagiac, MI [*AM radio station call letters*] ... WDOW
Dowagiac, MI [*FM radio station call letters*] ... WVHQ
Dowagiac Public Library, Dowagiac, MI [*Library symbol Library of Congress*] (LCLS) ... MiDow
Dowdeswell on Life and Fire Insurance [*A publication*] (DLA) ... Dowd Ins
Dowel ... DWL
DOWELANCO, Indianapolis, IN [*Library symbol*] [*Library of Congress*] (LCLS) ... InIDow
Dowell's Income Tax Acts [*9th ed.*] [*1934*] [*A publication*] (DLA) ... Dow Inc
Dowell's Stamp Duties [*1873*] [*A publication*] (DLA) ... Dow St
Dower [*or Dowager*] ... DOW
Dowlais Central [*Cardiff*] [*Welsh depot code*] ... DLIS
Dow-Lepetit [*Research code symbol*] ... DL
Dowling and Lowndes' English Bail Court Reports [*A publication*] (DLA) ... D & L
Dowling and Lowndes' English Bail Court Reports [*A publication*] (DLA) ... Dow & L
Dowling and Lowndes' English Bail Court Reports [*A publication*] (DLA) ... Dowl & L
Dowling and Lowndes' English Bail Court Reports [*A publication*] (DLA) ... Dowl & Lownd
Dowling and Lowndes' English Practice Cases [*A publication*] (DLA) ... Dow & Lownd
Dowling and Ryland's English King's Bench Reports [*A publication*] (DLA) ... D & R
Dowling and Ryland's English King's Bench Reports [*A publication*] (DLA) ... Dow & Ry
Dowling and Ryland's English King's Bench Reports [*A publication*] (DLA) ... Dow & Ry KB
Dowling and Ryland's English King's Bench Reports [*A publication*] (DLA) ... Dowl & R
Dowling and Ryland's English King's Bench Reports [*A publication*] (DLA) ... Dowl & R (Eng)
Dowling and Ryland's English King's Bench Reports [*A publication*] (DLA) ... Dowl & Ryl
Dowling and Ryland's English King's Bench Reports [*A publication*] (DLA) ... New Term Rep
Dowling and Ryland's English Magistrates' Cases [*A publication*] (DLA) ... D & R Mag Cas
Dowling and Ryland's English Magistrates' Cases [*A publication*] (DLA) ... D & RMC
Dowling and Ryland's English Magistrates' Cases [*A publication*] (DLA) ... Dow & Ry MC
Dowling and Ryland's English Magistrates' Cases [*A publication*] (DLA) ... Dowl & R Mag Cas (Eng)
Dowling and Ryland's English Magistrates' Cases [*A publication*] (DLA) ... Dowl & Ryl MC
Dowling and Ryland's English Nisi Prius Cases [*A publication*] (DLA) ... D & RNP
Dowling and Ryland's English Nisi Prius Cases [*A publication*] (DLA) ... D & RNPC
Dowling and Ryland's English Nisi Prius Cases [*A publication*] (DLA) ... Dow & Ry
Dowling and Ryland's English Nisi Prius Cases [*A publication*] (DLA) ... Dow & Ry KB
Dowling and Ryland's English Nisi Prius Cases [*A publication*] (DLA) ... Dow & Ry NP
Dowling and Ryland's English Nisi Prius Cases [*A publication*] (DLA) ... Dowl & R NP
Dowling and Ryland's English Nisi Prius Cases [*A publication*] (DLA) ... Dowl & R NP (Eng)
Dowling and Ryland's English Nisi Prius Cases [*A publication*] (DLA) ... Dowl & Ryl NP
Dowling Branch, Onaping Falls Public Library, Ontario [*Library symbol National Library of Canada*] (NLC) ... ODOF
Dowling College, Des Moines, IA [*Library symbol Library of Congress*] (LCLS) ... IaDmDC
Dowling College, Oakdale, NY [*Library symbol Library of Congress*] (LCLS) ... NOaD
Dowling College, Oakdale, NY [*OCLC symbol*] (OCLC) ... VXZ
Dowling's Common Law Practice [*A publication*] (DLA) ... Dowl Pr
Dowling's English Bail Court (Practice) Cases [*A publication*] (DLA) ... Dowl
Dowling's English Bail Court (Practice) Cases [*A publication*] (DLA) ... Dowl (Eng)
Dowling's English Bail Court (Practice) Cases [*A publication*] (DLA) ... Dowl PC
Dowling's English Bail Court (Practice) Cases [*A publication*] (DLA) ... Dowl PC (Eng)
Dowling's English Bail Court Reports, New Series [*1841-43*] [*A publication*] (DLA) ... DNS
Dowling's English Bail Court Reports, New Series [*1841-43*] [*A publication*] (DLA) ... Dow NS
Dowling's English Bail Court Reports, New Series [*1841-43*] [*A publication*] (DLA) ... Dowl NS
Dowling's English Bail Court Reports, New Series [*1841-43*] [*A publication*] (DLA) ... Dowl NS (Eng)
Dowling's English Practice Cases [*A publication*] (DLA) ... Dow
Dowling's English Practice Cases [*A publication*] (DLA) ... Dow PC
Dowling's English Practice Cases [*A publication*] (DLA) ... Dow PC (Eng)
Dowling's English Practice Cases [*A publication*] (DLA) ... Dow Pr
Dowling's English Practice Cases [*A publication*] (DLA) ... Dowl Pr Cas
Dowling's English Practice Cases [*A publication*] (DLA) ... DPC
Dowling's English Practice Cases, New Series [*A publication*] (DLA) ... Dowl PC NS
Dowling's English Practice Cases, New Series [*A publication*] (DLA) ... Dowl Pr C NS
Dowling's Practice Reports [*A publication*] (DLA) ... Dowl PR
Down ... DN
Down (WDMC) ... dn
Down (KSC) ... DWN
Down Center [*Theater*] (WDMC) ... DC
Down Control (IAA) ... DNCTL
Down Drain [*Medicine*] (DAVI) ... DD
Down Feeding Spindle ... DFS
Down Hours to Operating Hours Ratio [*Quality control*] ... DH/OH
Down Left [*The front left portion of a stage*] [*A stage direction*] ... DL
Down Left Center (IAA) ... DLC
Down Link [*Computer science*] ... DL
Down (Quark) [*Atomic physics*] ... d
Down Right [*The front right portion of a stage*] [*A stage direction*] ... DR
Down Sensor Assembly (PDAA) ... DSA
Down Syndrome Association of Metropolitan Toronto ... DSAMT
Down Syndrome Association of New South Wales [*Australia*] ... DSANSW
[*The*] **Down Syndrome Association of Queensland** ... DSAQ
Down Through [*Clairvoyance experiment*] ... DT
Down through Sealed Packs [*Clairvoyance experiment*] ... DTSP
Downbeat [*A publication*] (BRI) ... Dbt
Downcomer Flow Resistance Plate [*Nuclear energy*] (NRCH) ... DFRP
Downconverter [*Satellite communications*] ... DC
Downdraft (DA) ... DFT
Downdraft ... DNDFT
Downdraft (DA) ... DWN
Downdrafts [*NWS*] (FAAC) ... DWNDFTS
Downeast Airlines [*ICAO designator*] (AD) ... DE
Downeast Association of Physician Assistants (SRA) ... DEAPA
Downeast Flying Service, Inc. [*FAA designator*] (FAAC) ... DOW
Downed Aircraft (NVT) ... DAC
Downed Aircraft Locator [*Military*] (PDAA) ... DAL
Downed Aircraft Recovery Team [*Army*] (DOMA) ... DART
Downed Airman Power Source [*Navy*] ... DAPS
Downers Grove, IL [*FM radio station call letters*] ... WDGC
Downers Grove Public Library [*Illinois*] ... DGPL
Downers Grove Public Library, Downers Grove, IL [*Library symbol Library of Congress*] (LCLS) ... IDow
Downey, CA [*Location identifier FAA*] (FAAL) ... JDY
Downey City Library, Downey, CA [*Library symbol Library of Congress*] (LCLS) ... CDo
Downey Financial [*NYSE symbol*] (TTSB) ... DSI
Downey Financial Corp. [*Formerly, Downey S & L Association*] [*Associated Press*] (SAG) ... DowneyF
Downey Financial Corp. [*NYSE symbol*] (SAG) ... DSL
Downey Hand Center Hand Sensitivity Test ... DHCHST
Downflow Stationary Fixed-Film [*Chemical engineering*] ... DSFF
Downgrade (NVT) ... DG
Downgrade in Lieu of Layoff ... DGILLO
Downgrade to Unclassified [*Military*] (MCD) ... DGU
Downhill [*Bicycle handlebars*] ... DH
Down-Hole Safety Valve ... DHSV
Downing College [*Cambridge University*] (ROG) ... DOWN
Down-Island Communication System [*Taiwan*] (CINC) ... DICS
Downline Loading ... DLL
Downlink ... D/K
Downlink (MCD) ... DNLK
Downlink Channel Assignment (CAAL) ... DCA
Down-Link Communications [*Antisubmarine warfare*] (MCD) ... DOLCO
Downlink Frequency ... DLF
Down-Link Multipath (MCD) ... DLMP
Down-Link Television Terminal ... DLTT
Downlist (NASA) ... D/L
Downlist (NASA) ... DNLT
Download [*Computer science*] [*Telecommunications*] ... D
Downloadable Sample [*Computer science*] ... DLS
Downrange ... D/R
Downrange [*NASA*] (KSC) ... DNR
Downrange Antimissile Measurement Program [*RADAR*] ... DAMP
Downrange Antimissile Program [*Army*] ... DAM
Downrange Computer Input System (MUGU) ... DCIS
Downrange Computer Output System (MUGU) ... DCOS
Downrange Data Report ... DDR
Downrange Distance during Launch [*NASA*] ... D
Downrange Error [*NASA*] ... DRE
Downrange Ship (SAA) ... DRS
Downrange Support Ship ... DRSS
Downrange Up Link [*Apollo*] [*NASA*] ... DRUL
Downs [*Maps and charts*] (ROG) ... DNS
Downs, KS [*FM radio station call letters*] ... KDNS
Down's Syndrome [*Medicine*] ... DS
Down's Syndrome Association [*British*] ... DSA
Down's Syndrome Congress [*Later, NDSC*] (EA) ... DSC

Down's Syndrome International (EA) .... DSI
Downslope (FAAC) .... DNSLP
Downspout (AAG) .... DS
Downspout Rechargement Infusion Program [Energy development program] .... DRIP
Downstage [Toward audience] [A stage direction] .... DS
Downstage Center [Toward audience] [A stage direction] .... DSC
Downstage Left [Toward audience] [A stage direction] .... DSL
Downstage Right [Toward audience] [A stage direction] .... DSR
Downstate Medical Center, SUNY [State University of New York], Brooklyn, NY [OCLC symbol] (OCLC) .... VVD
Downstream (FAAC) .... DNSTRM
Downstream (AAG) .... DS
Downstream Control Region [Biochemistry] .... DCR
Downstream Heat Exchanger (AAG) .... DSHE
Downstream Physical Unit [Computer science] .... DSPU
Downstream Venous Pressure [Physiology] (MAH) .... DSVP
Downtime [Computer science Telecommunications] .... DNT
Downtime [Computer science Telecommunications] (AAG) .... DT
Downtime between Sorties [Military] (AFIT) .... DS
Downtime Code [Military] (AFIT) .... DTC
Downtime Costs [Quality control] .... DC
Downtime Ratio [Computer science Telecommunications] (TEL) .... DTR
Downton and Luder's English Election Cases [A publication] (DLA) .... Down & Lud
Downton Castle Sandstone Formation [England] [Geology] .... DCSF
Downtown .... DWNTN
Downtown Area Short Hops [Battery-powered bus service in Long Beach, California] .... DASH
Downtown Copy Center [Washington, DC] [Telecommunications] (TSSD) .... DCC
Downtown Development Foundation [Washington, DC Defunct] (EA) .... DDF
Downtown General Hospital, Chattanooga, TN [Library symbol Library of Congress] (LCLS) .... TCGH
Downtown People Mover .... DPM
DownTrack Fix (GAVI) .... DNTKFX
Downward Ejection Bomblet (MCD) .... DEB
Downward Light Output Ratio (PDAA) .... DLOR
Downward Vertical Velocity [NWS] (FAAC) .... DVV
Downward-Looking Infrared [Air Force] .... DLIR
Downward-Looking Infrared System [Air Force] (MCD) .... DLIS
Downwardly Mobile [Lifestyle classification] .... DOMO
Downwind [Aviation] (FAAC) .... DNWND
Downwind Safety Limit .... DSL
Downy Mildew Resistant (GNE) .... DMR
Downy Woodpecker [Ornithology] .... DW
Dows Community Library, Dows, IA [Library symbol Library of Congress] (LCLS) .... IaDo
Dow's House of Lords (Parliamentary) Cases [Same as Dow's Reports] [3 English Reprint] [A publication] (DLA) .... Dow
Dow's House of Lords (Parliamentary) Cases [Same as Dow's Reports] [3 English Reprint] [A publication] (DLA) .... Dow PC
Dow's House of Lords (Parliamentary) Cases [Same as Dow's Reports] [3 English Reprint] [A publication] (DLA) .... Dow PC (Eng)
Doxographi Graeci [A publication] (OCD) .... Dox Graec
Doxology (ROG) .... DOX
Doxorubicin [Also, DOX, DXR] [Formerly, ADR, Adriamycin] [Antineoplastic drug] .... D
Doxorubicin [Also, D, DXR] [Formerly, ADR, Adriamycin] [Antineoplastic drug] .... DOX
Doxorubicin [Also, D, DOX] [Formerly, ADR, Adriamycin] [Antineoplastic drug] .... DXR
Doxorubicin [Adriamycin], Vincristine, Cyclophosphamide, Methotrexate, Fluorouracil [Antineoplastic drug regimen] .... DVCMF
Doxorubicinol [Antineoplastic drug] .... DOXOL
Doxurubicin [Adriamycin], Vincristine, Methotrexate [Antineoplastic drug regimen] .... DVM
Doyle Dane Bernbach, Inc. [Advertising agency] .... DDB
Doyle Holly International Fan Club [Defunct] (EA) .... DHIFC
Doylestown, PA [Location identifier FAA] (FAAL) .... DYL
Doylestown, PA [AM radio station call letters] .... WBUX
Doyon, AK [Location identifier FAA] (FAAL) .... ADI
Dozen (ROG) .... DN
Dozen (AFM) .... DOZ
Dozen .... DZ
Dozenal Society of America (EA) .... DSA
Dozen-Year White House Foul-Up Cycle [Reference to the 1949 "mess in Washington," 1961 Bay of Pigs disaster, 1973 Watergate scandal, and 1985 Iran-CONTRA affair] [Term coined by William Safire] .... D-YWHF
Dozier, AL [Television station call letters] .... WDIQ
D-Pantothenyl Alcohol [Biochemistry] .... DPA
D-Penicillamine [Pharmacology] .... DPCN
DPL, Inc. [Formerly, Dayton Power & Light Co.] [NYSE symbol] (SPSG) .... DPL
DQE [NYSE symbol] (TTSB) .... DQE
DQE Co. [Associated Press] (SAG) .... DQE
DQE, Inc. [NYSE symbol] (SPSG) .... DQE
DR Horton, Inc. [NYSE symbol] (SAG) .... DHI
DR Horton, Inc. [Associated Press] (SAG) .... DR Hort
DR Horton, Inc. [Associated Press] (SAG) .... DR Horton
Dr Solomon's Anti-Virus [Software] .... DSAV
Drab [Philately] .... db
Drachenbronn [France ICAO location identifier] (ICLI) .... LFYA
Drachm [Unit of weight] [German] .... dr
Drachm Apothecaries' Weight [Pharmacology] (DAVI) .... dr ap
Drachma [Monetary unit in Greece] .... D
Drachma [Monetary unit] [Greece] (EY) .... DR

Drachma [Monetary unit in Greece] (EY) .... DRE
Drachma [Monetary unit] [Greece] .... DRX
Drachten [Netherlands ICAO location identifier] (ICLI) .... EHDR
Drackett Co., Research and Development Library, Cincinnati, OH [Library symbol Library of Congress] (LCLS) .... OCDr
Draco [Constellation] .... Dra
Draco [Constellation] .... Drac
Draco [Sweden] [Research code symbol] .... KWD
Draco Gold Mines [Vancouver Stock Exchange symbol] .... DGM
Dracula and Co. [An association] (EA) .... DC
Dracula Society (EA) .... DS
Draepelin-Morel [Disease] [Psychiatry] (DAVI) .... KM
Draft [or Drafting] (ROG) .... D
Draft (ADA) .... DF
Draft .... DFT
Draft (WDMC) .... dft
Draft .... DR
Draft Action [Defunct] (EA) .... DA
Draft Addendum (OSI) .... DAD
Draft Amendment (OSI) .... DAM
Draft Attached [Business term] .... DFT/A
Draft Change Notice (MCD) .... DCN
Draft Collection Only [Business term] .... DCO
Draft Concept Paper .... DCP
Draft Development Concept Paper (RDA) .... DDCP
Draft Environmental Impact Statement [NRC] (MSC) .... DEIS
Draft Environmental Statement [Bureau of Outdoor Recreation] .... DES
Draft Equipment Publication Technical Manual (MCD) .... DEPTM
Draft Experiment Publication (MCD) .... DEP
Draft for Development (OSI) .... DD
Draft Horse and Mule Association of America (EA) .... DHMAA
Draft International Standard [International Standards Organization] .... DIS
Draft International Standardized Profile [OSI] (OSI) .... DISP
Draft Legislation .... DL
Draft Letter of Agreement (MCD) .... DLOA
Draft Letter Requirement (MCD) .... DLR
Draft Living Table of Organization and Equipment [Military] (INF) .... DLTOE
Draft Materiel Fielding Plan [Army] .... DMFP
Draft on Demand [Banking] (ROG) .... DOD
Draft Plan Table of Organization and Equipment (MCD) .... DPTOE
Draft Presidential Memorandum [DoD] .... DPM
Draft Proposal .... DP
Draft Proposal Qualitative Materiel Requirement .... DPQMR
Draft Proposed Letter of Agreement .... DPLOA
Draft Proposed Required Operational Capability (MCD) .... DPROC
Draft Proposed Training Device Requirement (MCD) .... DPTDR
Draft Recommendation [International Standards Organization] .... DR
Draft Release (MCD) .... DR
Draft Request for Proposal (MCD) .... DRFP
Draft Requirements Package (MCD) .... DRP
Draft Safety Evaluation (NRCH) .... DSE
Draft Ships Manpower Document [Navy] (CAAL) .... DSMD
Draft Site Treatment Plan [Department of Energy] .... DSTP
Draft Site Treatment Plan .... DSTP
Draft Stop [Technical drawings] .... DS
Draft Table of Organization and Equipment [Military] (INF) .... DTOE
Draft Technical Corrigendum [Correction] [Telecommunications] (OSI) .... DTC
Draft Technical Manual .... DTM
Draft Technical Report [Telecommunications] (OSI) .... DTR
Draft Training Device Requirement (MCD) .... DTDR
Drafting (KSC) .... DFTG
Drafting .... DRFTNG
Drafting and Records Office, Royal Marines [British military] (DMA) .... DRORM
Drafting Machine .... DFMACH
Drafting Manual (AABC) .... DM
Drafting, Pay and Records Office, Royal Marines [British] .... DPRORM
Drafting Practice Manual .... DPM
Drafting Program [Association of Independent Colleges and Schools specialization code] .... D
Drafting Request (MSA) .... DR
Drafting [or Drawing] Room Manual .... DRM
Drafting Site [NFPA pre-fire planning symbol] (NFPA) .... DS
Draftsman (AFM) .... DFTMN
Draftsman (KSC) .... DFTSMN
Draftsman .... DFTSMN
Draftsman, Electrical (IAA) .... DME
Draftsman, First Class, Illustrator [Navy] (DNAB) DM1
Draftsman, Second Class, Illustrator [Navy] (DNAB) DM2
Draftsman, Third Class, Illustrator [Navy] (DNAB) DM3
Drag (MCD) .... D
Drag .... DRG
Drag Coefficient [Automotive engineering] .... Cd
Drag Coefficient .... DC
Drag Disk-Turbine Transducer [Nuclear energy] (NRCH) .... DTT
Drag Friction .... DF
Drag Racing Association of Women .... DRAW
Drag Reducing Agent [Petroleum pipeline transport] .... DRA
Drag Your Feet (DAVI) .... DYF
Dragon .... DRGN
Dragon Airways Ltd. .... DA
Dragon Flight Simulator [Military] (MCD) .... DFS
Dragon Jump [Pack] [Military] (MCD) .... DJ
Dragon Jump Pack [Military] (MCD) .... DJP
Dragon [Missile] Maintenance Set [Military] .... DMS
Dragon Missile Jump Pack [Military] (MCD) .... DMJP

Dragon Missile Special Jump Pack [*Military*] (MCD) ... DMSP
Dragon Night Tracker [*Military*] (MCD) ... DNT
Dragon Remote Launch System [*Military*] (MCD) ... DRLS
Dragon Terminal Night Sight [*Military*] (MCD) ... DTNS
Dragon under Cover (MCD) ... DUC
Dragonfly Distillers [*Vancouver Stock Exchange symbol*] ... DGF
Dragonfly Society of America (EA) ... DSA
Dragoon [*British military*] (DMA) ... Dn
Dragoon (ROG) ... DR
Dragoon Guards [*Military unit*] [*British*] ... DG
Dragoon Resources Ltd. [*Vancouver Stock Exchange symbol*] ... DGN
Dragoons [*Military unit*] [*British*] ... D
Dragoons [*Military unit*] [*British*] (DMA) ... Dragns
Drain [*Electron device*] (MSA) ... D
Drain (IDOE) ... d
Drain (MSA) ... DR
Drain (NASA) ... DRN
Drain ... DRN
Drain and Purge (NASA) ... D & P
Drain Channel (NRCH) ... DC
Drain Collection Header [*Nuclear energy*] (NRCH) ... DCH
Drain Cutoff Current ... DCOC
Drain on Day One [*Classification for new newspaper*] ... DODO
Drain Panel (AAG) ... DP
Drain Resistance (IDOE) ... R_D
Drain Saturation Current ... DSC
Drain Source Protected (IAA) ... DSP
Drain Tile [*Technical drawings*] ... DT
Drain Voltage (IDOE) ... V_D
Drain, Waste, and Vent [*System*] ... DWV
Drainage [*Medicine*] (DAVI) ... drng
Drainage ... DRNG
Drainage and Water Supply Officer [*Ministry of Agriculture, Fisheries, and Food*] [*British*] ... DWSO
Drainage Fixture Unit (DNAB) ... DFU
Drainage Fluid [*Medicine*] (DAVI) ... DRFL
Drainage Unions and Trusts [*Australia*] ... DUT
Drainboard [*Technical drawings*] ... DRB
Drain-Induced Barrier Lowering (IAA) ... DIBL
Drake Beam Morin, Inc. ... DBM
Drake on Attachment [*A publication*] (DLA) ... Dr Att
Drake on Attachment [*A publication*] (DLA) ... Drake Att
Drake on Attachment [*A publication*] (DLA) ... Drake Attachm
Drake Public Library, Centerville, IA [*Library symbol Library of Congress*] (LCLS) ... IaCenv
Drake University (GAGS) ... Drake U
Drake University, Des Moines, IA [*Library symbol Library of Congress*] (LCLS) ... IaDmD
Drake University, Des Moines, IA [*OCLC symbol*] (OCLC) ... IOD
Drake University, Law Library, Des Moines, IA [*OCLC symbol*] (OCLC) ... IWD
Drake University, Law School, Des Moines, IA [*Library symbol Library of Congress*] (LCLS) ... IaDmD-L
Dram (MCD) ... DM
Dram ... DR
Dram (IDOE) ... dr
Dram, Apothecary ... DRAP
Dram, Avoirdupois ... DRAV
Drama ... D
Drama (ADA) ... DR
Drama (ADA) ... DRAM
Drama [*Greece*] [*Airport symbol*] (AD) ... DRM
Drama ... DRMA
Drama and Comedy [*Slice-of-life television show*] ... DRAMEDY
Drama Book Specialists ... DBS
Drama Criticism [*A publication*] ... DC
Drama Desk (EA) ... DD
Drama Tree (EA) ... DT
Dramatic ... DRAM
Dramatic and Lyric Theatres Association [*British*] (BI) ... DALTA
Dramatic, Artistic, and Literary Rights Organization (DGA) ... DALRO
Dramatic Authors' Society [*British*] ... DAS
Dramatic Criticism Index [*A publication*] ... DCI
Dramatic Interpretation of the Ghetto through Improvisational Theater [*Washington, DC*] ... DIG-IT
Dramatic Order Knights of Khorassan (EA) ... DOKK
Dramatis Personae [*Characters of the Play*] [*Latin*] ... DRAM PERS
Dramatist (WDAA) ... DRAM
Dramatists Guild (EA) ... DG
Dramatists of the Restoration [*British*] (ROG) ... DotR
Draped [*Numismatics*] ... DR
Draper Aden Environmental Modeling ... DAEM
Draper Industrial Assembly Language [*Computer science*] ... DIAL
Draper on Dower [*A publication*] (DLA) ... Dra Dow
Draper Public Library, Draper, SD [*Library symbol Library of Congress*] (LCLS) ... SdDr
Draperies [*Astronomy*] (BARN) ... D
Draper's Upper Canada King's Bench Reports [*A publication*] (DLA) ... Dra
Draper's Upper Canada King's Bench Reports [*A publication*] (DLA) ... Draper
Draper's Upper Canada King's Bench Reports [*A publication*] (DLA) ... Draper (Can)
Draper's Upper Canada King's Bench Reports [*A publication*] (DLA) ... Draper (Ont)
Drapery ... DRAP
Drapery Hardware Manufacturers Association [*Defunct*] (EA) ... DHMA
Draught ... DT
Draught Moulded [*British*] (IAA) ... DTMLD
Draught Proofing Advisory Association [*British*] (DBA) ... DPAA
Draughting Software System [*Gould Electronics Ltd. Computer Systems*] [*Software package*] (NCC) ... DSS
Draughtsmen's and Allied Technicians' Association [*British*] (DI) ... DATA
Dravida Munnetra Kazhagam [*India*] [*Political party*] (PPW) ... DMK
Dravidian [*MARC language code Library of Congress*] (LCCP) ... dra
Dravidian [*Family of languages from southern India and Sri Lanka*] (BARN) ... Drav
Dravidian Air Services Ltd. [*British ICAO designator*] (FAAC) ... DRA
Dravo Corp. [*Associated Press*] (SAG) ... Dravo
Dravo Corp. [*NYSE symbol*] (SPSG) ... DRV
Draw ... D
Draw (WDAA) ... DR
Draw and Re-Draw [*Tin can manufacturing*] ... DRD
Draw Bar (ADA) ... DB
Draw Die [*Tool*] (MCD) ... DRD
Draw Die [*Tool*] (AAG) ... DWDI
Draw Form [*Tool*] (AAG) ... DWFM
Draw International Resources Corp. [*Formerly, Draw Resources Corp.*] [*Vancouver Stock Exchange symbol*] ... DRA
Draw Out (KSC) ... DO
Draw Ratio [*Plastics technology*] ... DR
Draw-a-Family [*Test*] [*Psychology*] (DAVI) ... DAF
Draw-A-Family Test (MEDA) ... DAFT
Draw-a-Person [*Psychology*] ... D-A-P
Draw-a-Person Quality Scale [*Psychology*] ... DPQS
Draw-A-Person Test (MEDA) ... DAPT
Drawback [*Business term*] ... DBK
Drawback Accounting and Computing System [*Australia*] ... DBACS
Drawbar Horsepower ... DBHP
Drawbar Horsepower ... DHP
Drawbar Pull ... DBP
Drawer ... DR
Drawer (MSA) ... DWR
Drawing ... DRG
Drawing (NATG) ... DRWG
Drawing (AFM) ... DWG
Drawing (VRA) ... dwg
Drawing (WDMC) ... dwg
Drawing Analysis Record (MCD) ... DAR
Drawing and Assembly Release Record (AAG) ... DARR
Drawing and Specification Listing (NRCH) ... DSL
Drawing Assembly List (MCD) ... DAL
Drawing Breakdown List ... DBL
Drawing Center (EA) ... DC
Drawing Change (AAG) ... DC
Drawing Change List ... DCL
Drawing Change Notice ... DCN
Drawing Change Order (MUGU) ... DCO
Drawing Change Request ... DCR
Drawing Change Summary ... DCS
Drawing Control Manual (MCD) ... DCM
Drawing Copy Request (MCD) ... DCR
Drawing Data Required for Change (KSC) ... DDRC
Drawing Data Requirement (IAA) ... DDR
Drawing Departure Authorization (KSC) ... DDA
Drawing Deviation (MCD) ... DD
Drawing Error Report (NASA) ... DER
Drawing Exchange File [*Computer science*] (PCM) ... DXF
Drawing File Processor (MCD) ... DFP
Drawing for Army Training Aids ... DATA
Drawing List [*Engineering*] ... DL
Drawing Office Graphics System [*Deltacam Systems Ltd.*] [*Software package*] (NCC) ... DOGS
Drawing Office Material Manufacturers' and Dealers' Association [*British*] (BI) ... DOMMDA
Drawing Paper Having a Medium Rough Surface (BARN) ... BB
Drawing Parts Release Ticket (MCD) ... DPRT
Drawing Practice (NG) ... DRPR
Drawing Quality (DNAB) ... DQ
Drawing Quality Audit (MCD) ... DQA
Drawing Quality, Special-Killed [*Metallurgy*] ... DQSK
Drawing Quality Steel ... DQS
Drawing Record Card (MCD) ... DRC
Drawing Release Authorization ... DRA
Drawing Release Ticket (MCD) ... DRT
Drawing Requirement Outline ... DRO
Drawing Requirements Manual [*NASA*] (NASA) ... DRM
Drawing Sign Out (MCD) ... DSO
Drawing Society (EA) ... DS
Drawing Stimulus Strategy Measure ... DSSM
Drawing Submittal Monitoring System [*MAC*] ... DSMS
Drawing Summary (AAG) ... DS
Drawing Web Format [*Computer science*] (PCM) ... DWF
Drawn (AABC) ... DR
Drawn [*Cricket*] (ROG) ... DRN
Drawn (MSA) ... DWN
Drawn and Ironed ... D & I
Drawn and Wall Ironed [*Metal printing*] (DGA) ... DWI
Drawn Cup Roller Bearing ... DCRB
Drawn over Mandrel [*Tubes*] ... DOM
Drawn-on-Cover [*Graphic arts*] (DGA) ... DOC
Drawout Circuit Breaker [*Electronics*] (OA) ... DCB
Draxis Health [*NASDAQ symbol*] (TTSB) ... DRAXF
Draxis Health, Inc. [*NASDAQ symbol*] (SAG) ... DRAX

Draxis Health, Inc. [*Associated Press*] (SAG) ... Draxis
Drayage Carriers Inc., Fort Wayne IN [*STAC*] ... DCR
Drayton Valley, AB [*FM radio station call letters*] (RBYB) ... CIBW-FM
Drayton Valley Public Library, Alberta [*Library symbol National Library of Canada*] (NLC) ... ADV
DRC Resources Corp. [*Vancouver Stock Exchange symbol*] ... DRC
DRCA Medical Corp. [*AMEX symbol*] (SPSG) ... DRC
DRCA Medical Corp. [*Associated Press*] (SAG) ... DRCA
Dread Zeppelin Fan Club (EA) ... DZFC
Dreaded Lake Effect [*Weather condition, resulting in increased precipitation, produced by Utah's Great Salt Lake*] ... DLE
Dream ... DRM
Dream Element [*Psychology*] (MAE) ... DE
Dream Factory (EA) ... DF
Dream Time [*Neurology and psychiatry*] (DAVI) ... D
Dreco Energy Services Ltd. [*NASDAQ symbol*] (SAG) ... DREA
Dreco Energy Services Ltd. [*Associated Press*] (SAG) ... DrecoE
Dreco Energy Svcs 'A' [*NASDAQ symbol*] (TTSB) ... DREAF
Dredge [*Self-propelled*] [*Navy symbol*] ... YM
Dredged Material Research Program [*Waterways Experiment Station*] [*Army*] (RDA) ... DMRP
Dredged Material Spatial Management Analysis Resolution Tool [*U.S. Army Corps of Engineers*] ... DMSMART
Dredger (MSA) ... DRGR
Dredging Industry Size Standard Committee (EA) ... DISSC
Dredging Operations and Environmental Research [*U.S. Army Corps of Engineers*] ... DOER
Dredging Operations and Environmental Research [*US Army Corps of Engineers*] ... DOER
Dredging Operations Technical Support (RDA) ... DOTS
Dredging Range [*Nautical charts*] ... DRDG RGE
Dredging Research Program [*U.S. Army Corps of Engineers*] ... DRP
D-Related [*Antigen*] [*Immunology*] ... DR
Drenair [*Spain ICAO designator*] (FAAC) ... DRS
Dresden [*City in East Germany*] (ROG) ... DRES
Dresden [*Germany Airport symbol*] (OAG) ... DRS
Dresden [*Germany ICAO location identifier*] (ICLI) ... ETDN
Dresden Nuclear Power Station (NRCH) ... DNPS
Dresden, TN [*FM radio station call letters*] ... WCDZ
Dresdner International Financial Markets (Australia) Ltd. ... DIFMA
Dress ... DRS
Dress Barn [*NASDAQ symbol*] (SAG) ... DBRN
Dress Barn, Inc. [*Associated Press*] (SAG) ... DresB
Dress Rehearsal (MUGU) ... DR
Dresse on Internal Revenue Laws [*A publication*] (DLA) ... Dres Int Rev
Dressed [*Fish processing*] ... DR
Dressed [*Lumber*] ... DRS
Dressed and Center Matched [*Lumber*] (DAC) ... D & CM
Dressed and Headed [*Lumber*] ... D & H
Dressed and Matched [*Technical drawings*] ... D & M
Dressed and Matched Beaded [*Lumber*] (DAC) ... C & MB
Dressed and Standard Matched [*Lumber*] (DAC) ... D & SM
Dressed Four Sides [*Lumber*] (DAC) ... D4S
Dressed One Side [*Lumber*] (DAC) ... D1S
Dressed or Tanned [*Freight*] ... DT
Dressed Sides [*of lumber*] (BARN) ... DS
Dressed Two Sides [*Lumber*] (DAC) ... D2S
Dressed Two Sides and Center Matched [*Lumber*] (DAC) ... D2S & CM
Dressed Two Sides and Matched [*Lumber*] (DAC) ... D2S & M
Dressed Two Sides and Standard Matched [*Lumber*] (DAC) ... D2S & SM
Dresser ... DR
Dresser (MSA) ... DRSR
Dresser Industries [*NYSE symbol*] (TTSB) ... DI
Dresser Industries, Inc. [*NYSE symbol*] (SPSG) ... DI
Dresser Industries, Inc. [*Associated Press*] (SAG) ... Dressr
Dresser Industries, Inc., Dresser Clark Division, Olean, NY [*Library symbol Library of Congress*] (LCLS) ... NOID
Dresser Industries, Inc., Garland, TX [*Library symbol Library of Congress*] (LCLS) ... TxGarD
Dresser Industries, Inc., Harbison-Walker Refractories Co., West Mifflin, PA [*Library symbol Library of Congress*] (LCLS) ... PWesD
Dresser Industries, Inc., Lane-Wells Co., Houston, TX [*Library symbol Library of Congress*] (LCLS) ... TxHDE
Dressing [*Medicine*] ... D
Dressing [*Medicine*] ... DR
Dressing (MSA) ... DREG
Dressing [*Medicine*] ... DRSG
Dressing [*Medicine*] ... dsg
Dressing after Finish [*Manufacturing term*] ... DAF
Dressing before Finish [*Manufacturing term*] ... DBF
Dressing Dry and Intact [*Medicine*] (DAVI) ... DDI
Dressing Room (DAC) ... DR
Dressing Table [*Classified advertising*] (ADA) ... DT
Dreux/Vernouillet [*France ICAO location identifier*] (ICLI) ... LFON
Drew Industries [*AMEX symbol*] (TTSB) ... DW
Drew Industries, Inc. [*Associated Press*] (SAG) ... DrewInd
Drew Industries, Inc. (MHDW) ... DRWI
Drew Industries, Inc. [*AMEX symbol*] (SAG) ... DW
Drew Institute for Archaeological Research [*Drew University*] [*Research center*] (RCD) ... DIAR
Drew, MS [*FM radio station call letters*] (RBYB) ... WOHT
Drew University (GAGS) ... Drew U
Drew University, Madison, NJ [*OCLC symbol*] (OCLC) ... DRU
Drew University, Madison, NJ [*Library symbol Library of Congress*] (LCLS) ... NjMD
Drew University, Theological School, Madison, NJ [*Library symbol Library of Congress*] (LCLS) ... NjMD-T
Drewry and Smale's English Chancery Reports [*A publication*] (DLA) ... D & S
Drewry and Smale's English Chancery Reports [*A publication*] (DLA) ... D & Sm
Drewry and Smale's English Chancery Reports [*A publication*] (DLA) ... Drew & S
Drewry and Smale's English Chancery Reports [*A publication*] (DLA) ... Drew & S (Eng)
Drewry and Smale's English Chancery Reports [*A publication*] (DLA) ... Drew & Sm
Drewry and Smale's English Vice Chancellors' Reports [*1860-65*] [*A publication*] (DLA) ... Dr & Sm
Drewry on Injunctions [*1841*] [*A publication*] (DLA) ... Drew Inj
Drewry's Chancery Forms [*1876*] [*A publication*] (DLA) ... Drew Ch F
Drewry's English Chancery Reports [*A publication*] (DLA) ... Drew (Eng)
Drewry's English Vice Chancellors' Reports [*A publication*] (DLA) ... Dr
Drewry's English Vice Chancellors' Reports [*A publication*] (DLA) ... Drew
Drewry's Equity Pleading [*A publication*] (DLA) ... Drew Eq Pl
Drewry's Patent Law Amendment Act [*1838*] [*A publication*] (DLA) ... Drew Pat
Drewry's Trade Marks [*1878*] [*A publication*] (DLA) ... Drew Tr M
Drew's Reports [*13 Florida*] [*A publication*] (DLA) ... Drew
Drexel Elementary School, Westbury, NY [*Library symbol*] [*Library of Congress*] (LCLS) ... NWeDE
Drexel Institute of Technology [*Pennsylvania*] (MCD) ... DIT
Drexel University (GAGS) ... Drexel U
Drexel University, Philadelphia, PA [*OCLC symbol*] (OCLC) ... DXU
Drexel University, Philadelphia, PA [*Library symbol Library of Congress*] (LCLS) ... PPD
Drexel University, School of Library and Information Science, Philadelphia, PA [*OCLC symbol*] (OCLC) ... DRX
Drexler Technology [*NASDAQ symbol*] (TTSB) ... DRXR
Drexler Technology Corp. [*Associated Press*] (SAG) ... Drexlr
Drexler Technology Corp. [*NASDAQ symbol*] (NQ) ... DRXR
Drexore Developments, Inc. [*Vancouver Stock Exchange symbol*] ... DXD
Dreyer's Gr Ice Cr [*NASDAQ symbol*] (TTSB) ... DRYR
Dreyer's Grand Ice Cream, Inc. [*Associated Press*] (SAG) ... DreyerG
Dreyer's Grand Ice Cream, Inc. [*NASDAQ symbol*] (NQ) ... DRYR
Dreyfus Cal Muni Income [*AMEX symbol*] (TTSB) ... DCM
Dreyfus California Municipal Income Fund [*Associated Press*] (SAG) ... DryCal
Dreyfus California Municipal Income, Inc. [*AMEX symbol*] (CTT) ... DCM
Dreyfus Muni Income [*AMEX symbol*] (TTSB) ... DMF
Dreyfus Municipal Income Fund [*AMEX symbol*] (CTT) ... DMF
Dreyfus Municipal Income Fund [*Associated Press*] (SAG) ... DryfMu
Dreyfus New York Municipal Income Fund [*AMEX symbol*] (CTT) ... DNM
Dreyfus New York Municipal Income Fund [*Associated Press*] (SAG) ... DryfNY
Dreyfus N.Y. Muni Income [*AMEX symbol*] (TTSB) ... DNM
Dreyfus Strategic Government [*NYSE symbol*] (SPSG) ... DSI
Dreyfus Strategic Government Income Fund [*Associated Press*] (SAG) ... DryStG
Dreyfus Strategic Gvts [*NYSE symbol*] (TTSB) ... DSI
Dreyfus Strategic Municipal Bond Fund, Inc. [*Associated Press*] (SAG) ... DrySM
Dreyfus Strategic Municipals [*Associated Press*] (SAG) ... DryStrt
Dreyfus Strategic Municipals [*NYSE symbol*] (SPSG) ... LEO
Dreyfus Strategic Municipals, Inc. [*NYSE symbol*] (SPSG) ... DSM
Dreyfus Strategic.Muni Bd Fd [*NYSE symbol*] (TTSB) ... DSM
DRG, Inc. [*Toronto Stock Exchange symbol*] ... DRG
D.R.Horton [*NYSE symbol*] (TTSB) ... DHI
DRI [*Data Resources, Inc.*] **Bank Analysis Service** [*Information service or system*] (CRD) ... DRI-BAS
DRI [*Data Resources, Inc.*] **Commodities** [*Information service or system*] (CRD) ... DRICOM
DRI [*Data Resources, Inc.*] **Current Economic Indicators Data Bank** [*Information service or system*] (CRD) ... DRI-CEI
DRI [*Data Resources, Inc.*] **Financial and Credit Statistics** [*Information service or system*] (CRD) ... DRI-FACS
DRI [*Data Resources, Inc.*] **US Equity and Debt Securities** [*Information service or system*] (CRD) ... DRI-SEC
Dried Bakery Products [*An animal feed*] ... DBP
Dried Coffee Residue ... DCR
Dried Fruit Association of California [*Later, DFA of California*] (EA) ... DFA
Dried Fruit Association of California [*Later, DFA of California*] ... DFAC
Dried Fruits Board [*New South Wales, South Australia, Western Australia*] ... DFB
Dried Fruits Research and Development Council [*Australia*] ... DFRDC
Dried Poultry Manure ... DPM
Dried Skim Milk ... DSM
Dried Tree Fruit ... DTF
Dried Vine Fruit ... DVF
Dried Weight of Cell Mass (OA) ... DWCM
Driefontein Consolidated [*NASDAQ symbol*] (NQ) ... DRFN
Driefontein Consolidated Ltd. [*Associated Press*] (SAG) ... DriefC
Dries [*Maps and charts*] [*British*] ... Dr
Dries Below a Century [*Ink*] (DGA) ... DBC
Drietabbetje [*Surinam*] [*ICAO location identifier*] (ICLI) ... SMDA
Drift (MSA) ... DFT
Drift [*NWS*] (FAAC) ... DRFT
Drift and Ground-Speed Measuring Airborne RADAR ... DAGMAR
Drift Angle [*Navigation*] ... DA
Drift Angle Indicator [*Navigation*] ... DAI
Drift Chamber (MCD) ... DC
Drift Correction ... D/C
Drift Correction Angle ... DCA
Drift Cyclotron Loss Cone [*Plasma physics*] ... DCLC
Drift Down (GAVI) ... D/D
Drift Field-Effect Transistor [*Electronics*] ... DFET
Drift Rate ... DR
Drift Voltage ... DV
Drifters, Inc. (EA) ... DI

Drifting Automatic Radiometeorological Station .... DARMS
Drifting Electron Hole .... DEH
Drifting Low-Capability Buoys [*National Oceanic and Atmospheric Administration*] (MCD) .... DLCB
Drifting Snow [*Meteorology*] .... DRSN
Driftwood Bay Air Force Station [*Alaska*] [*ICAO location identifier*] (ICLI) .... PADF
Drill (MSA) .... DR
Drill .... DRLL
Drill Adapter .... DRAD
Drill and Ceremony [*Military*] (ADDR) .... D & C
Drill and Transfer System .... DATS
Drill Attendance Monitoring Procedure and Report [*National Guard*] .... DAMPRE
Drill Attendance Reporting Test [*National Guard*] .... DART
Drill Bushing .... DRBG
Drill Cluster Plate (MCD) .... DCP
Drill, Command, and Ceremony [*Military*] (DNAB) .... DCC
Drill Fixture .... DRFX
Drill Guidance System .... DGS
Drill Head .... DRHD
Drill Instructor [*Marine Corps*] .... DI
Drill Jig (MSA) .... DJ
Drill Jig .... DRJG
Drill Jig (AAG) .... DRJI
Drill Jig Bushing .... DJB
Drill Leader [*British military*] (DMA) .... DL
Drill Minelaying and Recovery Vessel [*Navy symbol*] (DNAB) .... ACM
Drill Nonpay Status [*Naval Reserve*] .... DNP
Drill Pay .... DP
Drill Plate [*Tool*] (MSA) .... DP
Drill Plate [*Tool*] (MCD) .... DRP
Drill Plate [*Tool*] (AAG) .... DRPE
Drill Plate [*Tool*] .... DRPL
Drill Press Feed .... DPF
Drill Purposes [*British military*] (DMA) .... DP
Drill Regulations .... DR
Drill Rod .... DR
Drill Sergeant [*British military*] (DMA) .... D/Sgt
Drill Sergeant [*Army*] .... DS
Drill Sergeant [*Army skill qualification identifier*] (INF) X
Drill Sergeant Identification Badge [*Military decoration*] (GFGA) .... DSIDBAD
Drill Sergeant Identification Badge [*Military decoration*] (AABC) .... DSIdentBad
Drill Sergeant School [*Army*] (AABC) .... DSS
Drill Service in Paygrade [*Military*] (DNAB) .... DSPG
Drill Shell .... DRSH
Drill Spacer Block (MCD) .... DSB
Drill Stem Test (ADA) .... DST
Drill Template (MCD) .... DRT
Drill Template .... DRTP
Drill Time in Service [*Military*] (DNAB) .... DTIS
Drill Vise .... DRVS
Drilled (WDAA) .... DD
Drilling .... DRILL
Drilling Activity Analysis System [*Petroleum Information Corp.*] [*Information service or system*] (NITA) .... DAAS
Drilling and Sawing Association [*British*] (DBA) .... DSA
Drilling Cost Estimates Model [*Department of Energy*] (GFGA) .... DCEM
Drilling Individual Mobilization Augmentation [*Army*] (DOMA) .... DIMA
Drilling Information Service Co. [*Houston, TX*] [*Telecommunications*] (TSSD) .... DISC
Drilling Information Services [*Adams Engineering, Inc.*] [*Information service or system*] (IID) .... DIS
Drilling Mud Emulsifier (BARN) .... DME
Drilling Mud Surfactant (BARN) .... DMS
Drillsite Supervisors Association (EA) .... DSA
Drink Skim Milk [*Dietetics*] (DAVI) .... DSM
Drinker Library of Choral Music (EA) .... DLCM
Drinkers Against Mad Mothers (EA) .... DAMM
Drinking Behavior Scale [*Test*] .... DBS
Drinking Fountain (AAG) .... DF
Drinking Straw Institute [*Defunct*] (EA) .... DSI
Drinking Water (AAG) .... DW
Drinking Water Equivalent Level [*Environmental Protection Agency*] .... DWEL
Drinking Water Quality Guideline Value [*World Health Organization*] .... DWQGV
Drinking Water Quality Research Center [*Florida International University*] .... DWQRC
Drinking Water Standard .... DWS
Drinkwater's English Common Pleas Reports [*1840-41*] [*A publication*] (DLA) .... Drink
Drinkwater's English Common Pleas Reports [*1840-41*] [*A publication*] (DLA) .... Drinkw
Drinkwater's English Common Pleas Reports [*1840-41*] [*A publication*] (DLA) .... Drinkw (Eng)
Drinkwater's English Common Pleas Reports [*1840-41*] [*A publication*] (DLA) .... Drinkwater
Drip Infusion Pyelography [*Radiography*] .... DIP
Drip Pan Pot [*of closed-loop ex-vessel machine*] [*Nuclear energy*] (NRCH) .... DPP
Dripolene Pyrolysis Gasoline [*Lummus Crest, Inc. process*] .... DPG
Drip-Proof (AAG) .... DP
Dripproof and Ratproof .... DPRP
Dripproof Open .... DPO
Dripproof Protected .... DPP
Dripproof Semienclosed .... DPS
Dripproof Totally Enclosed .... DPT
Driptank .... DRTA
Driscoll Play Kit [*Psychological testing*] .... DPK
Drishat Shalom [*Best Regards*] [*Hebrew*] .... DASH
Dritte Welt Frauensinformationszentrum [*Information Center for Third World Women*] [*Zurich, Switzerland*] (EAIO) .... FIZ
Drive [*State*] [*Psychology*] .... D
Drive (IDOE) .... d
Drive .... DR
Drive [*or Driver*] (AFM) .... DR
Drive (DD) .... Dr
Drive .... DRI
Drive [*Automotive engineering*] .... DRIV
Drive [*Commonly used*] (OPSA) .... DRIVE
Drive [*Commonly used*] (OPSA) .... DRV
Drive .... Dve
Drive by Wire [*Electronics Automotive engineering*] .... DBW
Drive Control Equipment .... DCE
Drive End (MSA) .... DE
Drive Fit [*Technical drawings*] .... DF
Drive Front Axle .... DFA
Drive Magnet .... DM
Drive Motor Assembly (MCD) .... DMA
Drive Other Cars [*Insurance*] .... DOC
Drive Parameter Block [*Computer science*] (PCM) .... DPB
Drive Parameter Tracking [*Computer science*] (PCM) .... DPT
Drive System .... DS
Drive Tube .... DT
Drive Unit .... DRU
Drive Voltage (IDOE) .... V_{drive}
Driveability Test Chamber [*Automotive engineering*] .... DTC
Drive-Gearhead Package .... DGHP
Drive-Gearhead Package .... DGP
Driven [*Automotive engineering*] .... DRVN
Driven Equilibrium Fourier Transform [*Mathematics*] .... DEFT
Driver [*Navy rating*] (MUGU) .... CD
Driver [*British military*] (DMA) .... D
Driver (MSA) .... DRVR
Driver (AABC) .... DVR
Driver Aid, Information, and Routing [*Computer science*] .... DAIR
Driver Amplifier Module (NASA) .... DAM
Driver and Mechanic Badge, Amphibious Vehicles [*Military decoration*] (AABC) .... DvrMechBadA
Driver and Mechanic Badge, Mechanic [*Military decoration*] (AABC) .... DvrMechBadMech
Driver and Mechanic Badge, Motorcycles [*Military decoration*] (AABC) .... DvrMechBadM
Driver and Mechanic Badge, Operator [*Military decoration*] (AABC) .... DvrMechBadOp
Driver and Mechanic Badge, Tracked Vehicles [*Military decoration*] (AABC) .... DvrMechBadT
Driver and Mechanic Badge, Wheeled Vehicles [*Military decoration*] (AABC) .... DvrMechBadW
Driver and Vehicle Licensing Agency [*Formerly, Driver and Vehicle Licensing Centre*] [*British*] (ECON) .... DVLA
Driver and Vehicle Licensing Centre [*British*] (DCTA) .... DVLC
Driver Augmented Readout [*Computer science*] .... DAR
Driver Badge, Amphibious Vehicles [*Military decoration*] .... DVRABAD
Driver Badge, Motorcycles [*Military decoration*] .... DVRMBAD
Driver Badge, Tracked Vehicles [*Military decoration*] .... DVRTBAD
Driver Badge, Wheeled Vehicles [*Military decoration*] .... DVRWBAD
Driver Cell (IAA) .... DC
Driver Control Area [*Computer science*] (BUR) .... DCA
Driver Control Area Region Extension [*Computer science*] (BUR) .... DCARE
Driver Development Centre [*South Australia*] .... DDC
Driver Energy Conservation Awareness Training [*US government program*] .... DECAT
Driver Evaluation Assembly [*Nuclear energy*] (NRCH) .... DEA
Driver Fuel Assembly [*Nuclear energy*] (NRCH) .... DFA
Driver Improvement Program [*American Automobile Association*] .... DIP
Driver Information Center [*Automotive engineering*] .... DIC
Driver Information Experimenting with Communication Technology [*FHWA*] (TAG) .... DIRECT
Driver Leasing Council of America (EA) .... DLCA
Driver, Master .... DM
Driver Mechanic [*British military*] (DMA) .... DM
Driver of Automobile (MAE) .... DOA
Driver Oriented New Ultimate Tire Science .... DONUTS
Driver Performance Measurement and Analysis System (MCD) .... DPMAS
Driver Propulsion Unit .... DPU
Driver Reaction Time .... DRT
Driver Screening Evaluator .... DSE
Driver Stage Silicon Transistor .... DSST
Driver Training Platoon [*British military*] (DMA) .... DTP
Driver Units Speaker .... DUS
Driver Vehicle Inspection Report [*FHWA*] (TAG) .... DVIR
DriverHarris [*AMEX symbol*] (TTSB) .... DRH
Driver-Harris Co. [*AMEX symbol*] (SPSG) .... DRH
Driver-Harris Co. [*Associated Press*] (SAG) .... DrivHar
Driver-Only Operation [*Railroad*] [*British*] .... DOO
Driver-Only Operation, Freight [*Railroad*] [*British*] .... DOOF
Driver-Only Operation, Passenger [*Railroad*] [*British*] .... DOOP
Drivers' Independent Race Tracks [*An association*] .... DIRT
Drivers Integrated Display [*Military*] (RDA) .... DID
Driver's Thermal Viewer [*Tank technology*] [*Army*] .... DTV
Driver's Vision Enhancer [*Military*] .... DVE
Driver's Vision Enhancer .... DVE
Drives [*Commonly used*] (OPSA) .... DRIVES

Drives [*Postal Service standard*] (OPSA) .... DRS
Drives .... DRS
Drives, Motors, Controls, and Programmable Controllers Exhibition [*British*] (ITD) .... DMC/PC
Drives You Nuts [*Coined by Erma Bombeck*] .... DYN
Driving .... D
Driving .... DRIVE
Driving after License Revoked .... DLR
Driving after License Suspended .... DLS
Driving and Maintenance (IAA) .... DM
Driving Away Auto without Owner's Permission [*FBI standardized term*] .... DAA w/o OP
Driving Car Intoxicated .... DCI
Driving Control Indicator .... DCI
Driving Instructors Association [*British*] (DBA) .... DIA
Driving Licence [*British*] (ADA) .... DL
Driving Licences Regulations [*British*] (ILCA) .... DLR
Driving Point Admittance .... DPA
Driving Point Function [*Control system*] (IAA) .... DPF
Driving Power .... DP
Driving School Association of America (EA) .... DSAA
Driving under the Influence (DHSM) .... DUI
Driving under the Influence of Liquor .... DUIL
Driving While Drugged .... DWD
Driving While Drunk [*Police term*] .... DWD
Driving While Intoxicated [*Legal term*] .... DWI
Driving While under the Influence (OICC) .... DWUI
Drizzle [*Meteorology*] .... DZ
Drizzle [*Meteorology*] L
Drizzle [*Meteorology*] .... zl
Drizzling [*Meteorology*] .... D
Drocourt-Queant Line [*World War I*] [*Canada*] .... D-Q
Drogue (KSC) .... DRG
Drogue .... DROG
Drogue Parachute Deployment .... DPR
Drogue Parachute System (SAA) .... DPS
Droit [*Right*] [*French*] .... D
Droit Civil Canadien [*A publication*] (DLA) .... Droit CC
Droit Civil Ecclesiastique [*A publication*] (DLA) .... Dr C Ec
Droit Commercial [*Commercial Law*] [*French*] (DLA) .... Dr Com
Droit du Travail: Revue Mensuelle [*French A publication*] (DLA) .... Dr Trav
Droit International Prive [*Private International Law*] [*French*] (DLA) .... DIP
Dromoland Development [*Vancouver Stock Exchange symbol*] .... DLD
Dromore [*District in Northern Ireland*] (ROG) .... DROM
Drone [*Designation for all US military aircraft*] .... Q
Drone Aircraft Catapult Control Craft [*Navy symbol Obsolete*] .... YV
Drone Anti-RADAR [*German military - World War II*] .... DAR
Drone Antisubmarine Helicopter [*Air Force, Navy*] .... DASH
Drone Assisted Torpedo .... DAT
Drone Control and Data Retrieval System [*Later, CDRS*] [*Air Force*] (MCD) .... DCDRS
Drone Control Center [*Military*] (MCD) .... DCC
Drone Control System [*Military*] .... DCS
Drone Deceptive Self-Screening Jammer [*Military*] (MCD) .... DDSSJ
Drone Employment Value Analysis (MCD) .... DEVA
Drone Formation Control System [*Military*] .... DFCS
Drone Generation Squadron .... DGS
Drone Launch Platform [*Navy*] (CAAL) .... DLP
Drone Maintenance Squadron .... DMS
Drone Noise Jammers [*Military*] .... DNJ
Drone on Copyrights [*A publication*] (DLA) .... Drone Cop
Drone Plane [*Navy symbol*] .... D
Drone Recovery Platform (NVT) .... DRP
Drone Squadron .... DS
Drone Target [*Navy symbol British*] .... AQM
Drone Target Control System [*Military*] (MCD) .... DTCS
Drone Target Facility [*Military*] .... DTF
Drone Test Facility [*Military*] .... DTF
Drone Tracking and Control System [*Military*] (MCD) .... DTCS
Drones for Aerodynamic and Structural Testing (MCD) .... DAST
Drooped Leading Edge .... DLE
Drop .... D
Drop Altitude .... DALT
Drop and Block Wire [*Telecommunications*] (TEL) .... DW
Drop Box (LAIN) .... DB
Drop Build-Out Capacitor [*Telecommunications*] (TEL) .... DBO
Drop Dead .... DD
Drop Dynamics Module (MCD) .... DDM
Drop Everything and Read .... DEAR
Drop Forge (KSC) .... DF
Drop Forged Clamp .... DFC
Drop Forging Association [*Later, FIA*] (EA) .... DFA
Drop Forging Research Association [*British*] .... DFRA
Drop Head Coupe [*Convertible automobile*] [*British*] .... DHC
Drop Landing Zone [*Air Force*] (AFM) .... DLZ
Drop Manhole [*Technical drawings*] .... DMH
Drop Off .... D/O
Drop on Demand Jet Printing [*Carpet manufacturing*] (ECON) .... DODJET
Drop Out (KSC) .... DPO
Drop Out Generator (NG) .... DOG
Drop Point [*Air Force*] (AFM) .... DP
Drop Siding .... DS
Drop Survival Time .... DST
Drop Tank (KSC) .... DT
Drop Test Report .... DT
Drop Test Vehicle (IAA) .... DTV
Drop Top (OA) .... DT
Drop Tube/Drop Tower [*Facility*] .... DT/DT
Drop Wire .... DW
Drop Wood Siding [*Technical drawings*] .... DWS
Drop Zone [*For parachute troops and gliders*] [*Military*] .... DZ
Drop Zone Area [*Military*] .... DZA
Drop Zone Assembly Aid System [*Military*] (INF) .... DZAAS
Drop Zone Control Officer [*Military*] (AFM) .... DZCO
Drop Zone Safety Officer [*Military*] (AABC) .... DZSO
Drop Zone Study [*Military*] (MCD) .... DZS
Drop Zone Support Team [*Army*] (INF) .... DZST
Drop-By [*Brief social appearance*] .... DB
Drop-Hammer Die (MSA) .... DHD
Drop-Hammer Die .... DHDI
Drop-In Care Partners (EA) .... DICP
Drop-In Skills Centre [*British*] (AIE) .... DISC
Drop-In-Maintenance (MCD) .... DIM
Droplet Combustion Facility .... DCF
Droplet Countercurrent Chromatography .... DCCC
Drop-on-Demand [*Computer printer*] .... DOD
Dropout (AAG) .... DO
Dropout Compensator (NTCM) .... DOC
Dropout Connector .... DOC
Dropout Rate (DNAB) .... DOR
Droppable Fuel Tank [*Suffix to plane designation*] .... D
Dropped [*Army*] .... Drpd
Dropped from Rolls .... DFR
Dropped Own Request [*Navy*] .... DOR
Dropped Rod Control [*Nuclear energy*] (NRCH) .... DRC
Dropped Shipped (DNAB) .... D/S
Dropping Mercury Electrode [*Electrochemistry*] .... DME
Dropsie University, Philadelphia, PA [*Library symbol Library of Congress*] (LCLS) .... PPDrop
Drop-Weight .... DW
Drop-Weight Tear Test .... DWTT
Drop-Weight Test [*Nuclear energy*] (NRCH) .... DWT
Dror Young Zionist Organization [*Later, YKM*] (EA) .... DYZO
Drosophila Information Service [*Genetics*] .... DIS
Drought Policy Review Task Force [*Australia*] .... DPRTF
Drought Preparedness [*US Army Corps of Engineers*] .... DPS
Droughtmaster Stud Breeders' Society [*Australia*] .... DSBS
Drowning Prevention and Beach Safety Program (EA) .... DPBSP
Drowsiness (KSC) .... DRS
Druckzuender [*Pressure Igniter*] [*German military - World War II*] .... DZ
Drucox Petroleum [*Vancouver Stock Exchange symbol*] .... DRX
Drug .... D
Drug Abuse Control Amendment (DAVI) .... DACA
Drug Abuse Council [*Defunct*] .... DAC
Drug Abuse Education Act (OICC) .... DAEA
Drug Abuse Education Specialist (DNAB) .... DAES
Drug Abuse Epidemiology Data Center [*Ceased operation*] [*Texas Christian University*] (IID) .... DAEDAC
Drug Abuse Law Enforcement [*Department of Justice*] .... DALE
Drug Abuse Law Review [*A publication*] (DLA) .... Drug Abuse L Rev
Drug Abuse Law Review [*A publication*] (DLA) .... Drug Abuse LR
Drug Abuse Prevention Resource Unit [*National Institute on Drug Abuse*] [*Databank*] .... DAPRU
Drug Abuse Prevention, Treatment, and Rehabilitation Act [*1972*] .... DAPTRA
Drug Abuse Reporting Program (EDAC) .... DARP
Drug Abuse Resistance Education .... DARE
Drug Abuse Team [*Military*] (DNAB) .... DAT
Drug Abuse Treatment Outcome Study [*National Institute on Drug Abuse*] .... DATOS
Drug Abuse Warning Network [*Public Health Service*] [*Rockville, MD*] .... DAWN
Drug Addict .... DA
Drug Addiction and Alcoholism [*Title XVI*] [*Social Security Administration*] (OICC) .... DA & A
Drug Addiction Rehabilitation Enterprise (EA) .... DARE
Drug Addicts Yield to Persuasion [*of Daytop Village, Inc., a narcotics-addiction rehabilitation facility*] .... DAYTOP
Drug Administration Device [*Pharmacology*] (DAVI) .... DAD
Drug Amendments Act (BARN) .... DAA
Drug Analysis Laboratory (DAVI) .... DAL
Drug and Alcohol Abuse (OICC) .... DAA
Drug and Alcohol Abuse Program Advisor [*Navy*] (NVT) .... DAPA
Drug and Alcohol Dependent Offenders' Treatment Act of 1986 .... DADOTA
Drug and Alcohol Directorate [*New South Wales*] [*Australia*] .... DAD
Drug and Alcohol Multicultural Education Centre [*Medicine Australia*] .... DAMEC
Drug and Alcohol Nursing Association (EA) .... DANA
Drug and Alcohol Rehabilitation Testing System [*Navy*] (NVT) .... DARTS
Drug and Allied Products Guild [*Later, NAPM*] .... DAPG
Drug and Cosmetic Colors .... D & C
Drug and Poison Information Centre [*University of British Columbia*] [*Information service or system*] (IID) .... DPIC
Drug and Therapeutic Information [*Later, Medical Letter*] (EA) .... DTI
Drug, Chemical, and Allied Trades Association (EA) .... DCAT
Drug Coefficient [*Pharmacology*] (DAVI) .... Cd
Drug Delivery System [*Pharmacy*] .... DDS
Drug Detection Dog (DNAB) .... DDD
Drug Detector Dog Unit .... DDDU
Drug Development (Scotland) Ltd. [*British*] (IRUK) .... DDS
Drug Discrimination [*Psychopharmacology*] .... DD
Drug Dynamics Institute [*University of Texas at Austin*] [*Research center*] (RCD) .... DDI

Drug Education Specialist [*Military*] (AABC) ... DES
Drug Effects on Laboratory Tests: Attention [*Worldwide Medical Information Ltd.*] [*Database*] ... DELTABANK
Drug Efficacy Study Implementation Notice [*Food and Drug Administration*] ... DESI
Drug Emporium [*NASDAQ symbol*] (TTSB) ... DEMP
Drug Emporium, Inc. [*NASDAQ symbol*] (NQ) ... DEMP
Drug Emporium, Inc. [*Associated Press*] (SAG) ... DrugE
Drug Enforcement Administration [*Formerly, Bureau of Narcotics and Dangerous Drugs*] ... DEA
Drug Enforcement Administration - Special Operations Group ... DEA-SOG
Drug Evaluation ... DE
Drug Evaluation and Classification [*NHTSA*] (TAG) ... DEC
Drug Evaluation Branch [*Therapeutic Goods Administration*] [*Australia*] ... DEB
Drug Evaluation Center ... DEC
Drug Hypersensitivity [*Medicine*] (DAVI) ... DH
Drug Identification Kit ... DIK
Drug Induced Agranulocytosis [*Medicine*] ... DIA
Drug Information ... DI
Drug Information Association (EA) ... DIA
Drug Information Fulltext [*American Society of Hospital Pharmacists*] [*Bethesda, MD Database*] ... DIF
Drug Information Service [*Memorial Medical Center of Long Beach*] [*Information service or system*] (IID) ... DIS
Drug Information Services [*University of Minnesota, Minneapolis*] (IID) ... DIS
Drug Information Systems Network ... DISNET
Drug Interactions ... DI
Drug Interdiction Assistance Program [*FHWA*] (TAG) ... DIAP
Drug Literature Microfilm File (NITA) ... DLMF
Drug Marketing, Advertising, and Communications [*FDA*] ... DOMAC
Drug Master File ... DMF
Drug Mending Zone [*Drug abuse center*] ... DMZ
Drug Overdose [*Emergency Medicine*] (DAVI) ... OD
Drug Policy Foundation (EA) ... DPF
Drug Price Review ... DPR
Drug Product Information File [*American Society of Hospital Pharmacists*] [*Information service or system*] (IID) ... DPIF
Drug Product Reference File [*US Public Health Service*] [*Information service or system*] (IID) ... DPRF
Drug Rehabilitation ... DR
Drug Specific Oral Delivery System [*Pharmacy*] ... DSODS
Drug Supervisory Body ... DSB
Drug Supervisory Body of the United Nations ... DSB (UN)
Drug Trade News [*A publication*] ... DTN
Drug Usage Review (MEDA) ... DUR
Drug Use Evaluation ... DUE
Drug Use Index [*Psychology*] ... DUI
Drug Utilisation Sub-Committee [*Australia*] ... DUSC
Drug Utilization Review [*Medicine*] ... DUR
Drug Wholesalers Association [*Later, NWDA*] (EA) ... DWA
Drug-Appropriate Responding [*Biochemistry*] ... DAR
Drug-Free Workplace Act of 1988 (WYGK) ... DFWA
Druggist's Guild of St. James [*Defunct*] (EA) ... DGSJ
Drug-Induced Antinuclear Antibodies [*Immunology*] (DAVI) ... DANA
Drug-Induced Lupus Erythematosus [*Rheumatology*] (DAVI) ... DILE
Drug-Induced Pneumonitis [*Medicine*] ... DIP
Drug-Quaternary Carrier [*Biochemistry*] ... D-QC
Drugs Advisory Committee [*Australian Capital Territory, South Australia*] ... DAC
Drugs and Cosmetics [*Pharmacology*] (DAVI) ... D & C
Drugs Anonymous (EA) ... DA
Drugs Available Abroad [*A publication*] ... DAA
Drugs, Debt, Deforestation, and Democracy [*US foreign policy concerns in Latin America*] ... 4D's
Drugs of Abuse in Urine [*Toxicology*] ... DAU
Drug-Seeking Index (MEDA) ... DSI
Drugstore [*US maps*] ... DS
Druids [*Freemasonry*] ... D
Druk Air [*Bhutan*] [*ICAO designator*] (FAAC) ... DRK
Drum (MDG) ... D
Drum ... DM
Drum (MUGU) ... DR
Drum [*Shipping*] ... DRM
Drum and Display [*Computer science*] (ADA) ... DAD
Drum Control Unit (AABC) ... DCU
Drum Corps International (EA) ... DCI
Drum Demand ... DD
Drum Experimental Automatic Computer (IAA) ... DREAC
Drum Information Assembler and Dispatcher ... DIAD
Drum Information Display ... DID
Drum Input to Digital Automatic Computer ... DRIDAC
Drum Interrogation, Alteration, and Loading System [*Honeywell, Inc.*] (IEEE) ... DIAL
Drum Major [*Marine Corps*] ... DRMAJ
Drum Memory Assembly [*Computer science*] ... DMA
Drum Memory System [*Computer science*] ... DMS
Drum Module [*Computer science*] (IAA) ... DM
Drum Out of Service (CET) ... DOS
Drum Processor [*Computer science*] (IEEE) ... DP
Drum Safety Valve (DS) ... DSV
Drum Seiners Association [*Defunct*] (EA) ... DSA
Drum Storage [*Computer science*] (IEEE) ... DS
Drum Storage System ... DSS
Drum Storage Unit ... DSU
Drum Switch ... DS
Drum Switch ... DSW
Drum Timing Pulse ... DTP
Drum Transfer (CET) ... DT
Drum Trap (DAC) ... DT
Drum Write [*Computer science*] ... DW
Drum Write Driver [*Computer science*] ... DWD
Drumheller, AB [*Television station call letters*] ... CFCN-TV-1
Drumheller, AB [*AM radio station call letters*] ... CKDQ
Drumheller, AB [*FM radio station call letters*] ... CKUA-13
Drumheller Municipal Library, Alberta [*Library symbol National Library of Canada*] (NLC) ... ADRM
Drumheller Municipal Library, Drumheller, AB, Canada [*Library symbol Library of Congress*] (LCLS) ... CaADrM
Drum-Major [*British military*] (DMA) ... D/Maj
Drummer [*Military British*] ... DMR
Drummer (WDAA) ... DR
Drummond Island, MI [*Location identifier FAA*] (FAAL) ... DRM
Drummond Lighterage [*AAR code*] ... DLC
Drummond, MT [*Location identifier FAA*] (FAAL) ... DRU
Drummond Petroleum Ltd. [*Toronto Stock Exchange symbol*] ... DRU
Drummondville, PQ [*AM radio station call letters*] ... CHRD
Drummondville, PQ [*FM radio station call letters*] ... CJDM
Drum-Programmed Automatic Tester ... D-PAT
Drum-Read Amplifier [*Computer science*] (CET) ... DRA
Drum-Read Driver [*Computer science*] ... DRD
Drunk [*FBI standardized term*] ... DRK
Drunk and Dirty [*Military*] ... D & D
Drunk and Disorderly ... D & D
Drunk and Disorderly Conduct ... D & DC
Drunk and Proud ... D & P
Drunk Driving Defense (LAIN) ... DDR
Drunk in Charge ... DIC
Drury and Walsh's Irish Chancery Reports [*1837-40*] [*A publication*] (DLA) ... D & W
Drury and Walsh's Irish Chancery Reports [*1837-40*] [*A publication*] (DLA) ... D & Wal
Drury and Walsh's Irish Chancery Reports [*1837-40*] [*A publication*] (DLA) ... Dr & Wal
Drury and Walsh's Irish Chancery Reports [*1837-40*] [*A publication*] (DLA) ... Dru & Wal
Drury and Walsh's Irish Chancery Reports [*1837-40*] [*A publication*] (DLA) ... Drury & Wal
Drury and Walsh's Irish Chancery Reports [*1837-40*] [*A publication*] (DLA) ... Drury & Wal (Ir)
Drury and Warren's Irish Chancery Reports [*1841-43*] [*A publication*] (DLA) ... D & W
Drury and Warren's Irish Chancery Reports [*1841-43*] [*A publication*] (DLA) ... D & War
Drury and Warren's Irish Chancery Reports [*1841-43*] [*A publication*] (DLA) ... Dr & War
Drury and Warren's Irish Chancery Reports [*1841-43*] [*A publication*] (DLA) ... Dru & War
Drury and Warren's Irish Chancery Reports [*1841-43*] [*A publication*] (DLA) ... Drury & War
Drury and Warren's Irish Chancery Reports [*1841-43*] [*A publication*] (DLA) ... Drury & War (Ir)
Drury College (GAGS) ... Drury C
Drury College, Springfield, MO [*OCLC symbol*] (OCLC) ... MOD
Drury College, Springfield, MO [*Library symbol Library of Congress*] (LCLS) ... MoSpD
Drury College, Springfield, MO [*Library symbol*] [*Library of Congress*] (LCLS) ... MoSpDC
Drury Military Extension, Springfield, MO [*OCLC symbol*] (OCLC) ... MFT
Drury's Irish Chancery Reports [*A publication*] (DLA) ... Drury
Drury's Irish Chancery Reports [*A publication*] (DLA) ... Drury (Ir)
Drury's Irish Chancery Reports Tempore Napier [*1858-59*] [*A publication*] (DLA) ... Ca T Nap
Drury's Irish Chancery Reports Tempore Napier [*1858-59*] [*A publication*] (DLA) ... Cas T Nap
Drury's Irish Chancery Reports Tempore Napier [*1858-59*] [*A publication*] (DLA) ... Dr
Drury's Irish Chancery Reports Tempore Napier [*1858-59*] [*A publication*] (DLA) ... Dr & Nap
Drury's Irish Chancery Reports Tempore Napier [*1858-59*] [*A publication*] (DLA) ... Dr R T Nap
Drury's Irish Chancery Reports Tempore Napier [*1858-59*] [*A publication*] (DLA) ... Dr T Nap
Drury's Irish Chancery Reports Tempore Napier [*1858-59*] [*A publication*] (DLA) ... Dru & Nap
Drury's Irish Chancery Reports Tempore Napier [*1858-59*] [*A publication*] (DLA) ... Dru T Nap
Drury's Irish Chancery Reports Tempore Napier [*1858-59*] [*A publication*] (DLA) ... Drury T Nap
Drury's Irish Chancery Reports Tempore Sugden [*A publication*] (DLA) ... Ca T Sugd
Drury's Irish Chancery Reports Tempore Sugden [*A publication*] (DLA) ... Dr
Drury's Irish Chancery Reports Tempore Sugden [*A publication*] (DLA) ... Dr & Sug
Drury's Irish Chancery Reports Tempore Sugden [*A publication*] (DLA) ... Dr R T Sug
Drury's Irish Chancery Reports Tempore Sugden [*A publication*] (DLA) ... Dr T Sug
Drury's Irish Chancery Reports Tempore Sugden [*A publication*] (DLA) ... Dru
Drury's Irish Chancery Reports Tempore Sugden [*A publication*] (DLA) ... Dru & Sug

Drury's Irish Chancery Reports Tempore Sugden [*A publication*] (DLA) ... Dru T Sug
Drury's Irish Chancery Reports Tempore Sugden [*A publication*] (DLA) ... Dru T Sugden
Drury's Irish Chancery Reports Tempore Sugden [*A publication*] (DLA) ... Drury T Sug
Dry (NFPA) ... D
Dry Active Waste [*Nuclear energy*] (NUCP) ... DAW
Dry Adiabatic Lapse Rate [*Heat transfer*] ... DALR
Dry Air [*Meterology*] (BARN) ... Y
Dry Air Equivalent [*Engineering*] ... DAE
Dry and Ash-Free [*Coal*] ... DAF
Dry and Mineral Matter Free [*Coal*] ... DMMF
Dry Basis ... DB
Dry Bath [*Instrumentation*] ... DB
Dry Bed Training [*Medicine*] ... DBT
Dry Blood Temperature (MAE) ... DBT
Dry Bulb [*Thermometer, of a psychrometer*] [*Meteorology*] ... DB
Dry Bulb Temperature ... DBT
Dry Bulk Material ... DBM
Dry Carbon Dioxide ... DCO2
Dry Carbon Monoxide ... DCO
Dry Cargo Loading Technical Committee [*NATO*] (NATG) ... DCLTC
Dry Cell Mass ... DCM
Dry Chemical ... DCHEM
Dry Chemical Powder (PDAA) ... DCP
Dry Chemical System [*NFPA pre-fire planning symbol*] (NFPA) ... DC
Dry Cleaning Information Bureau [*British*] (CB) ... DIB
Dry Color Manufacturers Association (EA) ... DCMA
Dry Contact Acoustic Transmission [*Automotive engineering*] ... DCAT
Dry Crease Recovery Angle [*Textile technology*] ... DCRA
Dry Creek [*Idaho*] [*Seismograph station code, US Geological Survey*] (SEIS) ... DCI
Dry Cubic Feet (ERG) ... DCF
Dry Cubic Meter (EG) ... DCM
Dry Days [*Ecology*] ... DD
Dry Deck Shelter [*Navy*] (DOMA) ... DDS
Dry Deposition Inferential Method (USDC) ... DDIM
Dry Deposition Inferential Method [*Marine science*] (OSRA) ... DDIM
Dry Discharge Pump ... DDP
Dry Diver Transport Vehicle [*Navy*] ... DDTV
Dry Dock Companion Craft [*Non-self-propelled*] [*Navy symbol*] ... YFND
Dry Dressing [*Medicine*] ... DD
Dry Electrolytic Capacitor ... DEC
Dry Etching Station Computerized [*Graphic arts*] (DGA) ... DESC
Dry Film Binder ... DFB
Dry Film Lubricant ... DFL
Dry Film Processor ... DFP
Dry Filter Processing ... DFP
Dry Gas Pump ... DGP
Dry Heat Sterilization ... DHS
Dry Honing Machine ... DHM
Dry Hydrocarbon ... DHC
Dry Lining and Partition Association [*British*] (DBA) ... DLPA
Dry Mass ... DM
Dry Matter ... DM
Dry Matter Accumulation (OA) ... DMA
Dry Matter Disappearance (OA) ... DMD
Dry Matter Loss ... DML
Dry Non-Polish ... DNP
Dry Oxides of Nitrogen ... DNOX
Dry Peridotite Solidus [*Geochemistry*] ... DPS
Dry Photo Process ... DPP
Dry Pipe Valve ... DPV
Dry Point ... DP
Dry Powder Inhaler [*Pharmacy*] ... DPI
Dry Process Ceramic and Steatite Manufacturers Association [*Later, TECMA*] (EA) ... DPCSMA
Dry Prong, LA [*FM radio station call letters*] ... KVDP
Dry Rectifier ... DRF
Dry Reed Pushbutton Switch ... DRPS
Dry Reed Switch ... DRS
Dry Rod Consolidation Technology (GAAI) ... DRCT
Dry Rotor Inertial Reference Unit [*NASA*] (NASA) ... DRIRU
Dry Rubber Content ... DRC
Dry Standard Cubic Feet (GFGA) ... DSCF
Dry Standard Cubic Meter (EG) ... DSCM
Dry Sterile Dressing [*Medicine*] ... DSD
Dry Stone Walling Association [*British*] (DBA) ... DSWA
Dry Sunk (ROG) ... DS
Dry Swallow [*Medicine*] ... DS
Dry Tank Weight ... DTW
Dry Toned [*Copier*] [*Reprography*] ... DT
Dry Tortugas Island, FL [*Location identifier FAA*] (FAAL) ... DTF
Dry Vacuum Pump Discharge Filter ... DVPDF
Dry Vacuum Pump Filter ... DVPF
Dry Valley Drilling Project [*National Science Foundation*] ... DVDP
Dry Wall (DAC) ... Drwl
Dry Weather Flow (IAA) ... DWF
Dry Weight ... DW
Dry Workshop [*NASA*] (KSC) ... DWS
Dry Wrinkle Recovery Angle [*Textile technology*] ... DWRA
Dry-Bulk Container [*Packaging*] (DCTA) ... D
Dry-Column Chromatography ... DCC
Dryden [*Canada*] [*Airport symbol*] (OAG) ... YHD
Dryden Flight Research Center [*NASA*] ... DFRC
Dryden, ON [*Television station call letters*] ... CBWDT
Dryden, ON [*AM radio station call letters*] ... CKDR
Dryden, ON [*ICAO location identifier*] (ICLI) ... CYHD
Dryden Public Library, Dryden, ON, Canada [*Library symbol Library of Congress*] (LCLS) ... CaODr
Dryden Public Library, Ontario [*Library symbol National Library of Canada*] (NLC) ... ODR
Dryden Resources Corp. [*Vancouver Stock Exchange symbol*] ... DRY
Dryden Township Library, Dryden, MI [*Library symbol Library of Congress*] (LCLS) ... MiDry
Drydock ... DD
Drydock Launch Facility ... DLF
Dry-Filled Capsules [*Pharmacy*] ... DFC
Drying ... DYG
Drying Control Chemical Additive [*Ceramic technology*] ... DCCA
Dryland Research Unit [*Washington State University*] [*Research center*] (RCD) ... DLRU
Drypers Corp. [*Associated Press*] (SAG) ... Drypers
Drypers Corp. [*NASDAQ symbol*] (SAG) ... DYPR
Drypoint (VRA) ... dryp
Dry-Type Self-Cooled [*Transformer*] (IEEE) ... AA
Drywall ... DRYWL
Drywell (NRCH) ... DW
Drywell (NRCH) ... DWL
Drywell Equipment Drain (IEEE) ... DWED
Drywell Equipment Drain Sump (NRCH) ... DWEDS
Drywell Floor Drain (IEEE) ... DWFD
Drywell Floor Drain Sump (NRCH) ... DWFDS
DS Bancor [*NASDAQ symbol*] (TTSB) ... DSBC
DS Bancor, Inc. [*Associated Press*] (SAG) ... DS Bnc
DS Bancor, Inc. [*NASDAQ symbol*] (NQ) ... DSBC
DSA [*Defense Supply Agency*] **Augmentation Element** ... DAE
DSA [*Defense Supply Agency*] **Central Regional Audit Office** ... DMRA
DSA [*Defense Supply Agency*] **Central Regional Telecommunications Office** ... DCRTO
DSA [*Defense Supply Agency*] **Civil Preparedness Office** ... DCPO
DSA [*Defense Supply Agency*] **Command Security Support Office** ... DCSO
DSA [*Defense Supply Agency*] **Disposal Operating Procedures** ... DDOP
DSA [*Defense Supply Agency*] **Eastern Regional Telecommunications Office** ... DERTO
DSA [*Defense Supply Agency*] **Objective Document** ... DPOD
DSA [*Defense Supply Agency*] **Performance Standards Support Office** ... DPSSO
DSA [*Defense Supply Agency*] **Planning Objective** ... DPO
DSC Communications [*NASDAQ symbol*] (TTSB) ... DIGI
DSC Communications Corp. [*NASDAQ symbol*] (NQ) ... DIGI
DSC Communications Corp. [*Associated Press*] (SAG) ... DSC
Dschang [*Cameroon*] [*ICAO location identifier*] (ICLI) ... FKKS
DSCS [*Defense Satellite Communication System*] **Operational Support System** [*DoD*] ... DOSS
DSCS [*Defense Satellite Communication System*] **Operations Control System** [*DoD*] ... DOCS
DSG International Ltd. [*Associated Press*] (SAG) ... DSG Int
DSG International Ltd. [*NASDAQ symbol*] (SAG) ... DSGI
DSG International Ltd [*NASDAQ symbol*] (TTSB) ... DSGIF
DSI Industries [*Associated Press*] (SAG) ... DSI Ind
DSI Industries [*NASDAQ symbol*] (SAG) ... DSIC
DSIF [*Deep Space Instrumentation Facility*] **Maintenance Facility** [*NASA*] ... DMF
DSIF [*Deep Space Instrumentation Facility*] **Monitor and Control Subsystem** [*NASA*] ... DMC
DSIF [*Deep Space Instrumentation Facility*] **Supply Depot** [*NASA*] ... DSD
DSIF [*Deep Space Instrumentation Facility*] **Telemetry and Command Subsystem** [*NASA*] ... DTC
DSIF [*Deep Space Instrumentation Facility*] **Tracking and Monitor-Control Subsystem** [*NASA*] ... DTS
DSMA Acton Ltd., Toronto, Ontario [*Library symbol National Library of Canada*] (NLC) ... OTDA
DSP Communications [*NASDAQ symbol*] (SAG) ... DSPC
DSP Communications [*Associated Press*] (SAG) ... DSPCm
DSP Group [*NASDAQ symbol*] (TTSB) ... DSPG
DSP Group, Inc. [*Associated Press*] (SAG) ... DSP Gp
DSP Group, Inc. [*NASDAQ symbol*] (SAG) ... DSPG
DSP Technology [*NASDAQ symbol*] (TTSB) ... DSPT
DSP Technology, Inc. [*Associated Press*] (SAG) ... DSP
DSP Technology, Inc. [*NASDAQ symbol*] (NQ) ... DSPT
DSS [*Deep Space Station*] **Communications Equipment Subsystem** ... DCES
DSS [*Deep Space Station*] **Communications Terminal Subsystem** ... DCT
DST Systems [*NYSE symbol*] (TTSB) ... DST
DST Systems, Inc. [*NYSE symbol*] (SAG) ... DST
DST Systems, Inc. [*Associated Press*] (SAG) ... DST Sys
DT Industries, Inc. [*Associated Press*] (SAG) ... DT Inds
DT Industries, Inc. [*NASDAQ symbol*] (SAG) ... DTII
DTE Energy [*NYSE symbol*] (TTSB) ... DTE
DTIC [*Dacarbazine*], Actinomycin D [*Dactinomycin*] [*Antineoplastic drug regimen*] ... DTIC-ACT-D
DTIC [*Dacarbazine*], BCNU , and Hydroxyurea [*Carmustine*] [*Antineoplastic drug regimen*] (DAVI) ... DBH
DTIC [*Dacarbazine*], BCNU , and Vincristine [*Carmustine*] [*Antineoplastic drug regimen*] (DAVI) ... DBV
DTIC [*Dacarbazine*], CCNU , Vincristine [*Lomustine*] [*Antineoplastic drug regimen*] (DAVI) ... DCV
DTIC Retrieval and Indexing Terminology [*DoD*] ... DRIT
DTIC [*Defense Technical Information Center*] **Technical Awareness Circular** [*Information service or system*] (CRD) ... TRAC
D-Tubocurarine [*Pharmacology*] (DAVI) ... DTBC
d-Tubocurarine [*Muscle relaxant*] ... dTC

Du Bois [Pennsylvania] [Airport symbol] (OAG) ...... DUJ
Du Bois, PA [AM radio station call letters] .... WCED
Du Bois, PA [FM radio station call letters] .... WDBA
Du Cange's Glossarium [A publication] (DLA) ...... Du Cange
Du Pont Canada, Inc. [Toronto Stock Exchange symbol] ...... DUP
Du Pont Canada, Inc., Kingston, Ontario [Library symbol National Library of Canada] (NLC) ...... OKDC
Du Pont Canada, Inc., Maitland, Ontario [Library symbol National Library of Canada] (NLC) ...... OMD
Du Pont Canada, Inc., Mississauga, Ontario [Library symbol National Library of Canada] (NLC) ...... OMDC
Du Pont Canada, Inc., Patent and Legal Library, Mississauga, ON, Canada [Library symbol] [Library of Congress] (LCLS) ...... CaOMDCPL
Du Pont [E. I.] De Nemours & Co., Inc. [NYSE symbol] (SPSG) ...... DD
Du Pont [E. I.] De Nemours & Co., Inc. [Research code symbol] ...... EXP
Du Pont [E. I.] De Nemours & Co., Inc. [Research code symbol] ...... GP
Du Pont of Canada Ltd., Economist's Office Library, Montreal, PQ, Canada [Library symbol Library of Congress] (LCLS) ...... CaQMDP
Du Pont of Canada Ltd., Legal Library, Montreal, PQ, Canada [Library symbol Library of Congress] (LCLS) ...... CaQMDPL
Du Pont of Canada Ltd., Maitland, ON, Canada [Library symbol Library of Congress] (LCLS) ...... CaOMD
Du Pont of Canada Ltd., Research Centre Library, Kingston, ON, Canada [Library symbol Library of Congress] (LCLS) ...... CaOKD
du Pont(E.I.),$3.50 Pfd [NYSE symbol] (TTSB) ...... DDPrA
du Pont(E.I.),$4.50 Pfd [NYSE symbol] (TTSB) ...... DDPrB
Du Quoin, IL [AM radio station call letters] ...... WDQN
Du Quoin, IL [FM radio station call letters] ...... WDQN-FM
Du Variant [Laboratory science] (DAVI) ...... RHOV
Dual (BJA) ...... Du
Dual Absorption Model [Nuclear physics] (OA) ...... DAM
Dual Access Array (MCD) ...... DAA
Dual Access Feature (IAA) ...... DAF
Dual Access Storage Handling ...... DASH
Dual Action ...... DA
Dual Aerospace Servo Amplifier (NASA) ...... DASA
Dual Air Density [Explorer satellite] [NASA] ...... DAD
Dual Air Density Explorer [Satellite] [NASA] ...... DADE
Dual Air Density Satellite [NASA] (NASA) ...... DADS
Dual Approach Temperatures Method [Heat exchange design] ...... DATM
Dual Area Nozzle (KSC) ...... DAN
Dual Attached Station [Computer science] (TNIG) ...... DAS
Dual Attachment Concentrator [Telecommunications] (ACRL) ...... DAC
Dual Audio Cassette Interface ...... DACI
Dual Axis Rate Transducer [A gyroscope] ...... DART
Dual Beam Oscilloscope ...... DBO
Dual Binary Non-Uniform Simple Surface Evaporation Model [US Army Chemical Research, Development, and Engineering Center] (RDA) ...... DBNUSSE
Dual Bowl Feeder ...... DBF
Dual Bowl Vibratory Feeder ...... DBVF
Dual Cam Clutch ...... DCC
Dual Camshaft Four-Valve [Engine] [Automotive engineering] ...... DFV
Dual Camshafts and Electronic Management [Automotive engineering] ...... DE
Dual Capable (NATG) ...... DC
Dual Capacity [London Stock Exchange] ...... D
Dual Catalyst System [Automotive engineering] ...... DCS
Dual Chamber Preliminary Design Code (MCD) ...... DCPDC
Dual Chamber Shock Absorbers (MCD) ...... DCSA
Dual Channel ...... DC
Dual Channel Dual Speed ...... DCDS
Dual Channel Port Controller (MHDI) ...... DCPC
Dual Channel Port Controller [Computer science] (NITA) ...... DCPC
Dual Channel Radiometer ...... DCR
Dual Channel Receiver (MCD) ...... DCR
Dual Checkout Station (MCD) ...... DCS
Dual Combined Brake System [Motorcycle engineering] ...... DCBS
Dual Combustor Ramjet (MCD) ...... DCR
Dual Current Layer (OA) ...... DCL
Dual Cycle Rifle ...... DCR
Dual Deflection Tube (IAA) ...... DDT
Dual Diaphragm [Automotive engineering] ...... DD
Dual Diaphragm Distributor [Automotive engineering] ...... DDD
Dual Discrimination Ratio (IAA) ...... DDR
Dual Displacement Engine ...... DDE
Dual Diversity Comparator ...... DDC
Dual Diversity Unit ...... DDU
Dual Doctor Families (EA) ...... DDF
Dual Drilling [NASDAQ symbol] (TTSB) ...... DUAL
Dual Drilling Co. [NASDAQ symbol] (SAG) ...... DUAL
Dual Drilling Co. [Associated Press] (SAG) ...... DualDrl
Dual Driver Protective Service [MTMC] (TAG) ...... DDPS
Dual Electron Injector Structure (MCD) ...... DEIS
Dual Element Pump ...... DEP
Dual Emitter Transistor [Electronics] ...... DUET
Dual Employed Coping Scale [Psychology] (EDAC) ...... DECS
Dual Employed, No Kids [Lifestyle classification] ...... DENK
Dual Employed, with Kids [Lifestyle classification] ...... DEWK
Dual Employed With Kids (DFIT) ...... DEWKS
Dual Energy Gamma Group [Nuclear energy] (NRCH) ...... DUEGG
Dual Energy Use System ...... DEUS
Dual Energy X-Ray Absorptiometry [Analytical chemistry] ...... DEXA
Dual Energy X-Ray Absorptiometry [Painless bone mass test] [Medicine] ...... DXA
Dual Exchangeable Disc Storage (NITA) ...... DEDS
Dual Exciter System ...... DES
Dual Exhaust [Automotive engineering] ...... D/EXH

Dual Facility ...... DF
Dual Fault Correction Actuator ...... DFCA
Dual Field-of-View ...... DFOV
Dual Filament Ion Source ...... DFIS
Dual Filter Hybrid ...... DFH
Dual Frequency GPS Receiver ...... DFGR
Dual Frequency Signaling Units (MCD) ...... DFSU
Dual Fuel Quantity Indicating System (MCD) ...... DFQIS
Dual Function Jammer ...... DFJ
Dual Gauge Expander ...... DGE
Dual Image System ...... DIS
Dual Impact Prediction System [Aerospace] (IAA) ...... DIPS
Dual Income, Money Problems [Lifestyle Classification] ...... Dimps
Dual Income, No Kids (TAG) ...... DINK
Dual Independent Map Encoding [Transportation] ...... DIME
Dual Independent Map Encoding File of Countries [Harvard University] [A databank] (NITA) ...... DIMECO
Dual In-Line [Electronic components] ...... DIL
Dual In-Line Case [Computer science] (IAA) ...... DIC
Dual In-Line Flatpack (CDE) ...... DIF
Dual In-Line Integrated Circuit [Electronics] (IAA) ...... DILIC
Dual In-Line Memory Module [Computer science] ...... DIMM
Dual In-Line Memory Module [Computer science] (DOM) ...... DIMM
Dual In-Line Package [Computer science] ...... DILP
Dual In-Line Package [Computer science] ...... DIP
Dual In-Line Package Switch [Electronics] (DOM) ...... DIP switch
Dual In-Line Package Switch (CDE) ...... DIP switch
Dual In-Line Pin ...... DIP
Dual Input Describing Function [Computer science] ...... DIDF
Dual Input Discrete Describing Function [Computer science] (IAA) ...... DIDDF
Dual Input Null Network ...... DINN
Dual Input Transponder ...... DIT
Dual Interface Adapter ...... DIA
Dual Language ...... DL
Dual Language Translation [Chinese University of Hong Kong] (NITA) ...... DLT
Dual Launching Adaptor (DNAB) ...... DLA
Dual Loop Oscillator ...... DLO
Dual Maneuvering Simulator (MCD) ...... DMS
Dual Maneuvering Unit [A spacecraft] ...... DMU
Dual Mechanical Seal [Engineering] ...... DMS
Dual Miniature Inertial Navigation Systems (MCD) ...... DMINS
Dual Mode Display ...... DMD
Dual Mode Hydrazine ...... DMH
Dual Mode Imbedded Munitions (MCD) ...... DMIM
Dual Mode LASER ...... DML
Dual Mode Lunar Roving Vehicle [NASA] ...... DLRV
Dual Mode Recognizer (MCD) ...... DMR
Dual Mode Tracker (MCD) ...... DMT
Dual Modular Magnetic Tape Unit (CAAL) ...... DMTU
Dual Multiplexer Interface Adapter (NASA) ...... DMIA
Dual Output Linear Power Supply (DWSG) ...... DOLPS
Dual Path Protection Arrangement [AT & T] ...... DUPPA
Dual Pen Recorder ...... DPR
Dual Phase (MCD) ...... DP
Dual Photon Absorptiometry [Analytical chemistry] ...... DPA
Dual Pilot (MUGU) ...... DP
Dual Point Memorandum ...... DPM
Dual Porosity Sinter ...... DPS
Dual Processing Unit [Computer science] (WGA) ...... DPU
Dual Program Feature ...... DPF
Dual Progress Plan [Education] (AEE) ...... DPP
Dual Propellant Loading ...... DPL
Dual Pulse LASER Microwelder ...... DPLM
Dual Pulse Ranging Fuse ...... DPRF
Dual Purpose (NG) ...... DP
Dual Purpose (DOMA) ...... DP
Dual Purpose Missile (KSC) ...... DP
Dual Purpose Weapon System ...... DPWS
Dual Radio Magnetic Indicator (MCD) ...... DRMI
Dual Readout Devices (MCD) ...... DRD
Dual Resources Ltd. [Vancouver Stock Exchange symbol] ...... DUA
Dual Role Fighter (MCD) ...... DRF
Dual Roll Idler ...... DRI
Dual Roll Trough Idler ...... DRTI
Dual Salvo Attack Tactic [Navy] (NVT) ...... DUALEXTAC
Dual Shift Left (SAA) ...... DSL
Dual Shift Right (IAA) ...... DSR
Dual Speed ...... DSP
Dual System Estimator [Demography] ...... DSE
Dual Tandem [Aviation] (DA) ...... DT
Dual Tandem Wheels [Aviation] ...... DTW
Dual Thrust Rocket Motor ...... DTRM
Dual Tires ...... DT
Dual Tone Modulated Frequency [Telecommunications] ...... DTMF
Dual Tone Multifrequency [Telecommunications] ...... DTMF
Dual Tone Multifrequency Signalling (NITA) ...... DTMF
Dual Trace Amplifier ...... DTA
Dual Trace Display ...... DTD
Dual Track Etcher ...... DTE
Dual Track Geneva ...... DTG
Dual Transport Module (NOAA) ...... DTM
Dual Universal Asynchronous Receiver/Transmitter [Motorola, Inc.] ...... DUART
Dual Universal Serial Communicator Controller [Signetics Corp.] (NITA) ...... DUCC
Dual Valve ...... DV
Dual Walking Beam ...... DWB

Dual Wheels [*Aviation*] .... DW
Dual Wide Avionics Van (DWSG) .... DWAV
Duala [*MARC language code Library of Congress*] (LCCP) .... dua
Dual-Axis Radiographic Hydrotest [*For evaluating nuclear weapons*] .... DAHRT
Dual-Axis Radiographic Hydrotest Facility [*For simulation of nuclear weapons*] .... DAHRT
Dual-Beam-Sputtering [*Coating technology*] .... DBS
Dual-Bed Monolith [*Automotive engineering*] .... DBM
Dualbowl Vibratory Feeder .... DVF
Dual-Call Auto Answer (HGAA) .... DCAA
Dual-Capable Aircraft (MCD) .... DCA
Dual-Energy X-Ray Absorptiometry [*Physiology*] .... DXA
Duales System Deutschland [*German recycling organization*] .... DSD
Dual-Expanded Plastic-Insulated Conductor [*Telecommunications*] (TEL) .... DEPIC
Dual-Feed Carriage (IAA) .... DFC
Dual-Feed Channel (IAA) .... DFC
Dual-Feed Coupler .... DFC
Dual-Frequency Method .... DFM
Dual-Frequency Receiver .... DFR
Dual-Hardness Steel .... DHS
Dual-Income, No Kids (DFIT) .... DINKS
Dual-Injection Floating-Gate Metal Oxide Semiconductor (PDAA) .... DIFMOS
Dual-Mode Vehicle (PDAA) .... DMV
Dual-Object Electronic Tracking System .... DOETS
Dual-Port Memory [*Computer science*] (MCD) .... DPM
Dual-Port Memory Control [*Computer science*] .... DPMC
Dual-Port Network Adapter [*Telecommunications*] (PCM) .... DPNA
Dual-Ported Dynamic Random Access Memory [*Computer science*] .... DPDRAM
Dual-Purpose Improved Conventional Munition (AABC) .... DPICM
Dual-Purpose Submunitions [*Military*] (INF) .... DPSM
Dual-Source Dynamic Synchronous (DNAB) .... DSDS
Dual-Speed Drive .... DSD
Dual-Speed Magnetic Transducer .... DSMT
DualStar Technologies Corp. [*NASDAQ symbol*] (SAG) .... DSTR
DualStar Technologies Corp. [*Associated Press*] (SAG) .... DualStar
DualStar Technologies Corp. [*Associated Press*] (SAG) .... DualStr
DualStar Technologies Unit [*NASDAQ symbol*] (TTSB) .... DSTRU
DualStar Technologies Wrrt'A' [*NASDAQ symbol*] (TTSB) .... DSTRW
Dual-Surface Attenuation Module (MCD) .... DSAM
Dual-Tone Multifrequency [*Telephone*] (WDMC) .... DTMT
Duane Arnold Energy Center (NRCH) .... DAEC
Duane Eddy Circle, United Kingdom (EAIO) .... DECUK
Duane Eddy Circle, USA (EA) .... DECUS
Duane Information Center Indexing Service [*Database compilers*] (NITA) .... DICIS
Duane on the Law of Nations [*A publication*] (DLA) .... Duane Nat
Duane's Road Laws of Pennsylvania [*A publication*] (DLA) .... Duane Road L
Duarte [*California*] [*Seismograph station code, US Geological Survey*] (SEIS) .... DUC
Duarte Variant Allele [*Genetics*] (DAVI) .... Gt^D
Dubach, LA [*FM radio station call letters*] .... KPCH
Dubai [*IYRU nationality code*] (IYR) .... AE
Dubai [*United Arab Emirates*] [*Airport symbol*] (OAG) .... DXB
Dubai [*Trucial Oman*] [*Airport symbol*] (AD) .... DXB
Dubai [*United Arab Emirates*] [*ICAO location identifier*] (ICLI) .... OMDB
Dubai Airwing [*United Arab Emirates*] [*ICAO designator*] (FAAC) .... DUB
Dubai International Airport .... DIA
Dubai Marine Areas (BJA) .... DUMA
Dubai Riyal [*Monetary unit*] .... QDR
Dubbo [*Australia ICAO location identifier*] (ICLI) .... ASDU
Dubbo [*Australia Airport symbol*] (OAG) .... DBO
Dubbo [*New South Wales*] [*Airport symbol*] (AD) .... DBO
Dubendorf [*Switzerland ICAO location identifier*] (ICLI) .... LSMD
Dubin-Johnson Syndrome [*Medicine*] (CPH) .... DJS
Dubious (ADA) .... DUB
Dubitans [*or Dubius*] [*Doubting or Dubious*] [*Latin*] .... DUB
Dubitatur [*It Is Doubted*] [*Legal term*] (DLA) .... DUB
Dublin [*City and county in Ireland*] (ROG) .... DN
Dublin [*City and county in Ireland*] .... DUB
Dublin [*Ireland*] [*Airport symbol*] (OAG) .... DUB
Dublin [*City and county in Ireland*] .... DUBL
Dublin [*Ireland*] [*ICAO location identifier*] (ICLI) .... EIDB
Dublin [*Ireland*] [*ICAO location identifier*] (ICLI) .... EIDW
Dublin Area Rapid Transit [*Ireland*] .... DART
Dublin Castle .... DC
Dublin City University (ACII) .... DCU
Dublin, GA [*Location identifier FAA*] (FAAL) .... DBN
Dublin, GA [*FM radio station call letters*] .... WKKZ
Dublin, GA [*AM radio station call letters*] .... WMLT
Dublin, GA [*FM radio station call letters*] .... WQZY
Dublin, GA [*AM radio station call letters*] .... WXLI
Dublin Institute for Advanced Studies .... DIAS
Dublin Institute of Technology (ACII) .... DIT
Dublin Pharmacopoeia .... PD
Dublin Rathfarnham Castle [*Ireland*] [*Seismograph station code, US Geological Survey Closed*] (SEIS) .... DUB
Dublin University Mission .... DUM
Dublin, VA [*Location identifier FAA*] (FAAL) .... PSK
Dublin, VA [*AM radio station call letters*] .... WKNV
Dublin, VA [*FM radio station call letters*] .... WPIN
Dubois County Historical Society, Jasper, IN [*Library symbol Library of Congress*] (LCLS) .... InJDHi
Dubois, ID [*Location identifier FAA*] (FAAL) .... DBS
Dubois Oleic Albumin Complex [*Microbiology*] .... DOAC
Dubois Oleic Serum Complex [*Bacteriology*] .... DOSC
DuBois, PA [*FM radio station call letters*] .... WOWQ
Dubowitz [*Score*] [*Obstetrics*] (DAVI) .... DUB
Dubrovnik [*Yugoslavia*] [*Seismograph station code, US Geological Survey Closed*] (SEIS) .... DBR
Dubrovnik [*Former Yugoslavia*] [*Airport symbol*] (OAG) .... DBV
Dubrovnik [*Former Yugoslavia*] [*ICAO location identifier*] (ICLI) .... LYDU
Dubuque [*Iowa*] [*Airport symbol*] (OAG) .... DBQ
Dubuque [*Iowa*] [*Seismograph station code, US Geological Survey*] (SEIS) .... DBQ
Dubuque [*Diocesan abbreviation*] [*Iowa*] (TOCD) .... DUB
Dubuque Area Library Consortium [*Library network*] .... DALC
Dubuque, IA [*FM radio station call letters*] .... KATF
Dubuque, IA [*AM radio station call letters*] .... KDTH
Dubuque, IA [*Television station call letters*] (RBYB) .... KFXB
Dubuque, IA [*FM radio station call letters*] .... KGGY
Dubuque, IA [*FM radio station call letters*] .... KLYV
Dubuque, IA [*AM radio station call letters*] .... WDBQ
Dubuque Leader, Dubuque, IA [*Library symbol Library of Congress*] (LCLS) .... IaDuLe
Dubuque Witness, Dubuque, IA [*Library symbol Library of Congress*] (LCLS) .... IaDuWi
Ducange's Glossarium [*A publication*] (DLA) .... Duc Gl
Ducati International Owners Club (EA) .... DIOC
Ducati Owners' Club of Canada (EA) .... DOCC
Duchenne Muscular Dystrophy .... DMD
Duchesne College, Omaha, NE [*Library symbol Library of Congress*] (LCLS) .... NbOD
Duchess .... D
Duchess .... DCHSS
Duchess (ROG) .... DSS
Duchess .... DUC
Duchess (ROG) .... DUCH
Duchess of Brittany (Jersey) Ltd. [*British ICAO designator*] (FAAC) .... DBJ
Duchess Public Library, Alberta [*Library symbol National Library of Canada*] (NLC) .... ADU
Duchy .... D
Duchy .... DU
Duchy of Cornwall [*British*] (ROG) .... DC
Duchy of Lancaster [*British*] (ILCA) .... D of L
Duck (VRA) .... dc
Duck .... DK
Duck Book Communications Ltd. [*Vancouver Stock Exchange symbol*] .... DBC
Duck Egg Lysozyme [*Biochemistry*] .... DEL
Duck Egg Virus [*or Duck Embryo Vaccine*] [*Immunology*] .... DEV
Duck Embryo Fibroblasts (PDAA) .... DEF
Duck Experiment on Low-Frequency and Incident-Band Longshore and Across-Shore Hydrodynamics [*Coastal Engineering Research Center*] .... DELILAH
Duck Hepatic B Virus .... DHBV
Duck Hepatitis Virus .... DHV
Duck Producers Association [*British*] (DBA) .... DPA
Duck Virus Enteritis .... DVE
Ducks Unlimited (EA) .... DU
Ducks Unlimited, Winnipeg, Manitoba [*Library symbol National Library of Canada*] (NLC) .... MWDU
Ducks Unlimited, Winnipeg, MB, Canada [*Library symbol Library of Congress*] (LCLS) .... CaMWDU
Ducktail [*Hair style*] [*Bowdlerized version*] .... DA
Duckwall-Alco Stores [*NASDAQ symbol*] (TTSB) .... DUCK
Duckwall-Alco Stores, Inc. [*NASDAQ symbol*] (SAG) .... DUCK
Duckwall-Alco Stores, Inc. [*Associated Press*] (SAG) .... Duckwall
Ducommun, Inc. [*AMEX symbol*] (SPSG) .... DCO
Ducommun, Inc. [*Associated Press*] (SAG) .... Ducom
Ducosyn Excitation Switch .... DES
Ducretet-Thomson [*Formerly, Ducretet Selmer*] [*Record label*] [*France*] .... Sel
Duct (NFPA) .... D
Duct Burner Augmentation .... DBA
Duct Carcinoma [*Oncology*] .... DC
Duct Carcinoma In Situ [*Oncology*] .... DCIS
Duct Detector [*NFPA pre-fire planning symbol*] (NFPA) .... DD
Duct Integrity and Nozzle Efficiency (MCD) .... DIANE
Duct Keel [*of a ship*] (DS) .... DK
Duct Transmission Loss [*Facility*] (MCD) .... DTL
Duct Type .... DCTP
Ductal Glandular Mastectomy [*Medicine*] (DAVI) .... DGM
Ductal Hyperplasia [*Medicine*] (DMAA) .... DH
Ducted Propellers [*Aviation*] (AAG) .... DP
Ducted Rocket (MCD) .... DR
Ducted Rocket Engine Development (MCD) .... DRED
Ducted Rocket Motor .... DRM
Ducted Rocket Propulsion Test Vehicle (MCD) .... DRPTV
Ducted-Air Medium Underground Transmission (PDAA) .... DAMUT
Ductile Cast Iron .... DCI
Ductile Fracture Propagation [*Engineering*] .... DFP
Ductile Iron Pipe (PDAA) .... DIP
Ductile Iron Pipe Research Association (EA) .... DIPRA
Ductile Iron Society (EA) .... DIS
Ductile to Brittle Transition Temperature .... DBTT
Ductus Arteriosus [*Anatomy*] .... DA
Ductus Deferens Tumor [*Type of cell line*] .... DDT
Ductwork Services [*Focus Software Consultants*] [*Software package*] (NCC) .... DUCTS
Dude Ranchers' Association (EA) .... DRA
Dudley Herbarium of Stanford University [*San Francisco, CA*] .... DS
Dudley, Kenneth F., Ottumwa IA [*STAC*] .... DKF
Dudley, MA [*FM radio station call letters*] .... WNRC

Dudley Observatory, Albany, NY [*Library symbol Library of Congress*] (LCLS) ... NAID
Dudley's Georgia Reports [*A publication*] (DLA) ... Dud
Dudley's Georgia Reports [*A publication*] (DLA) ... Dud (GA)
Dudley's Georgia Reports [*A publication*] (DLA) ... Dud (Geo)
Dudley's Georgia Reports [*A publication*] (DLA) ... Dud R
Dudley's Georgia Reports [*A publication*] (DLA) ... Dudl
Dudley's Georgia Reports [*A publication*] (DLA) ... Dudley (GA)
Dudley's Georgia Reports [*A publication*] (DLA) ... GA Dec (Dudley)
Dudley's Georgia Reports [*A publication*] (DLA) ... GM Dud
Dudley's Georgia Reports [*A publication*] (DLA) ... GM Dudl
Dudstone and King's Barton [*England*] ... DUDST & K'S BART
Due ... Du
Due and Ancient Form [*Freemasonry*] ... DAF
Due Date ... DD
Due Date ... DUDAT
Due In ... DI
Due in Assets ... DIA
Due in from Overhaul (AFIT) ... DIOH
Due Out [*Army*] ... DO
Due Process ... DP
Due Process of Law [*Legal shorthand*] (LWAP) ... DPL
Due to Arrive ... DTA
Due to Void (MAE) ... DTV
Due West Motor Line [*AAR code*] ... DWML
Dueim [*Sudan*] [*ICAO location identifier*] (ICLI) ... HSDM
Due-In - Due-Out File (AFIT) ... DDF
Due-In from Maintenance [*Military*] (AFM) ... DIFM
Due-In from Overhaul [*Military*] (MCD) ... DIFO
Due-In Quantity ... DIQ
Due-Out Cancellation [*Military*] (AFM) ... DOC
Due-Out of Group [*Military*] (MCD) ... DOG
Due-Out to Maintenance [*Military*] (MCD) ... DOTM
Duer on Insurance [*A publication*] (DLA) ... Duer Ins
Duer on Marine Insurance [*A publication*] (DLA) ... Duer Mar Ins
Duer on Representation [*A publication*] (DLA) ... Duer Rep
Duer's Constitutional Jurisprudence [*A publication*] (DLA) ... Duer Const Jur
Duer's New York Superior Court Reports [*A publication*] (DLA) ... Duer
Duer's New York Superior Court Reports [*A publication*] (DLA) ... Duer (NY)
Dues ... D
Duesseldorf [*Germany ICAO location identifier*] (ICLI) ... EDDL
Duesseldorf [*Germany ICAO location identifier*] (ICLI) ... EDLL
Duetto [*Duet*] [*Music*] (ROG) ... DUO
Duff [*Phonetic alphabet*] [*Royal Navy World War I*] (DSUE) ... D
Duff & Phelps Corp. [*NYSE symbol*] (SPSG) ... DUF
Duff and Phelps Credit Rating [*NYSE symbol*] (TTSB) ... DCR
Duff & Phelps Credit Rating Co. [*NYSE symbol*] (SAG) ... DCR
Duff & Phelps Credit Rating Co. [*Associated Press*] (SAG) ... DufPCr
Duff & Phelps Credit Rating Co. [*Associated Press*] (SAG) ... DufPhCr
Duff & Phelps Utilities & Corporate Bond Trust [*NYSE symbol*] (SPSG) ... DUC
Duff & Phelps Utilities & Income, Inc. [*Associated Press*] (SAG) ... DufPUtil
Duff & Phelps Utilities Tax Free Income [*Associated Press*] (SAG) ... DufPTF
Duff & Phelps Utility & Corporate Bond Trust [*Associated Press*] (SAG) ... DufPUC
Duff/Phelps Util & Cp Bd Tr [*NYSE symbol*] (TTSB) ... DUC
Duff/Phelps Util Income [*NYSE symbol*] (TTSB) ... DNP
Duff/Phelps Util Tax-Free Inc. [*NYSE symbol*] (TTSB) ... DTF
Duff/Phelps Utilities Income [*NYSE symbol*] (SPSG) ... DNP
Duff/Phelps Utilities Tax-Free Income [*NYSE symbol*] (SPSG) ... DTF
Duffel Bag Delivery System [*Military*] (INF) ... DBDS
Duffield Public Library, Alberta [*Library symbol National Library of Canada*] (NLC) ... ADUF
Duffield, VA [*AM radio station call letters*] ... WDUF
Duffryn Yard [*Welsh depot code*] ... PT
Duff's Feudal Conveyancing [*Scotland*] [*A publication*] (DLA) ... Duff
Duff's Feudal Conveyancing [*Scotland*] [*A publication*] (DLA) ... Duff Conv
Duffy [*Blood group*] ... Fy
Duffy A Negative [*Blood type*] [*Hematology*] (DAVI) ... FYAN
Duffy A Positive [*Blood type*] [*Hematology*] (DAVI) ... FYA
Duffy B Negative [*Blood type*] [*Hematology*] (DAVI) ... FYBN
Duffy B Positive [*Blood type*] [*Hematology*] (DAVI) ... FYB
Dufresne's Glossary [*A publication*] (DLA) ... Dufresne
Dugdale on Summons [*A publication*] (DLA) ... Dug Sum
Dugdale's Monasticon [*A publication*] (DLA) ... Dug Mon
Dugway [*Utah*] [*Seismograph station code, US Geological Survey*] (SEIS) ... DUG
Dugway Proving Ground [*Dugway, UT*] [*Army*] (AABC) ... DPG
Dugway Proving Ground [*Utah*] [*Army*] ... DPGR
Dugway Proving Ground Studies Branch [*Utah*] [*Army*] ... DPG-S
Dugway Proving Ground Technical Analysis and Information Office [*Utah*] [*Army*] ... DPG/TA
Dugway/Tooele, UT [*Location identifier FAA*] (FAAL) ... DPG
Dugway/Tooele, UT [*Location identifier FAA*] (FAAL) ... MIJ
Duisburg [*Germany*] [*Airport symbol*] (AD) ... DUI
Duke ... D
Duke (ROG) ... DK
Duke ... DU
Duke Bar Association. Journal [*A publication*] (DLA) ... Duke B Ass'n J
Duke Bar Association. Journal [*A publication*] (DLA) ... Duke BAJ
[*The*] Duke Ellington Society (EA) ... TDES
Duke Minerals Ltd. [*Vancouver Stock Exchange symbol*] ... DKM
Duke, Nat, New York NY [*STAC*] ... DUK
Duke of Buccleuch [*British*] (ROG) ... DB
Duke of Cambridge's Own [*Military unit*] [*British*] ... DCO
Duke of Connaught's Own [*Military unit*] [*British*] ... DCO
Duke of Connaught's Royal Canadian Hussars [*British military*] (DMA) ... DCRCH
Duke of Cornwall's Light Infantry [*Military unit*] [*British*] (ROG) ... D of CORN LI
Duke of Cornwall's Light Infantry [*Military unit*] [*British*] ... DCLI
Duke of Edinburgh Award Scheme [*Australia*] ... DEAS
Duke of Edinburgh's Own [*Military unit*] [*British*] ... DEO
Duke of Edinburgh's Own Volunteer Rifles [*Military unit*] [*British*] ... DEOVR
Duke of Edinburgh's Royal Regiment [*Military unit*] [*British*] ... DERR
Duke of Edinburgh's Wiltshire Regiment [*Military unit*] [*British*] (ROG) ... DE
Duke of Lancaster's Own [*British military*] (DMA) ... DLO
Duke of Lancaster's Own Yeomanry [*Military unit*] [*British*] ... DLOY
Duke of Northumberland [*British*] (ROG) ... DN
Duke of Wellington's Regiment [*Military unit*] [*British*] ... DWR
Duke of Wellington's West Riding Regiment [*Military unit*] [*British*] ... DW
Duke of York's Own [*British military*] (DMA) ... DYO
Duke of York's Royal Military School [*British military*] (DMA) ... DYS
Duke on Charitable Uses [*1676*] [*A publication*] (DLA) ... Duke Ch Us
Duke Power [*NYSE symbol*] (TTSB) ... DUK
Duke Power Co. [*NYSE symbol*] (SPSG) ... DUK
Duke Power Co. [*Associated Press*] (SAG) ... Duke
Duke Power Co. [*Associated Press*] (SAG) ... DukeP
Duke Power Co., David Nabow Library, Charlotte, NC [*Library symbol*] [*Library of Congress*] (LCLS) ... NcCDD
Duke Power Co., Information Resource Center, Cornelius, NC [*Library symbol Library of Congress*] (LCLS) ... NcCorD
Duke Power Co., Information Systems Library, Charlotte, NC [*Library symbol*] [*Library of Congress*] (LCLS) ... NcCD
Duke Primate Center [*North Carolina*] ... DPC
Duke Pwr 7.72%'A'Pfd [*NYSE symbol*] (TTSB) ... DUKPrS
Duke Pwr 6.375%'A'Pfd [*NYSE symbol*] (TTSB) ... DUKPrA
Duke Realty Inv [*NYSE symbol*] (TTSB) ... DRF
Duke Realty Investments Capital Shares [*Associated Press*] (SAG) ... DukeR
Duke Realty Investments Capital Shares [*Associated Press*] (SAG) ... DukeRlty
Duke Realty Investments, Inc. [*NYSE symbol*] (SPSG) ... DRE
Duke Severity of Illness [*Checklist*] ... DUSOI
Duke University (GAGS) ... Duke U
Duke University Bar Association. Journal [*A publication*] (DLA) ... Duke BA Jo
Duke University Clinical Cardiology Study [*Cardiology study*] ... DUCCS
Duke University, Divinity School, Durham, NC [*Library symbol Library of Congress*] (LCLS) ... NcD-D
Duke University, Durham, NC [*Library symbol Library of Congress*] (LCLS) ... NcD
Duke University, Fuqua School of Business, Durham, NC [*Library symbol Library of Congress*] (LCLS) ... NcD-B
Duke University, Law Library, Durham, NC [*OCLC symbol*] (OCLC) ... NDL
Duke University Library, Durham, NC [*OCLC symbol*] (OCLC) ... NDD
Duke University, Medical Center, Durham, NC [*Library symbol Library of Congress*] (LCLS) ... NcD-MC
Duke University Preventive Approach to Cardiovascular Disease ... DUPAC
Duke University, School of Law, Durham, NC [*Library symbol Library of Congress*] (LCLS) ... NcD-L
Duke University, Woman's College, Durham, NC [*Library symbol Library of Congress*] (LCLS) ... NcD-W
Dukes County Historical Society, Edgartown, MA [*Library symbol Library of Congress*] (LCLS) ... MEdDHi
Duke's Law of Charitable Uses [*A publication*] (DLA) ... Duke
Dulbecco's Minimum Essential Medium ... DMEM
Dulbecco's Modified Eagle's Medium [*Also, DMEM, DMM*] [*Medium for cell growth*] ... DME
Dulbecco's Modified Eagle's Medium [*Also, DME, DMM*] [*Medium for cell growth*] ... DMEM
Dulbecco's Modified Eagle's Medium [*Also, DME, DMEM*] [*Medium for cell growth*] ... DMM
Dulbecco-Vogt Modified Eagle's [*Medium for cell growth*] ... DVME
Dulcamara Mottle Virus [*Plant pathology*] ... DUMV
Dulce [*New Mexico*] [*Seismograph station code, US Geological Survey Closed*] (SEIS) ... DNM
Dulce, NM [*FM radio station call letters*] ... KCIE
Dulcis [*Dear One*] [*Latin*] ... D
Dulcis [*Sweet*] [*Pharmacy*] ... DULC
Dulcitol Lysine Lactose Iron [*Agar*] [*Microbiology*] ... DLLI
Dulcken's Eastern District Reports [*Cape Colony, South Africa*] [*A publication*] (DLA) ... Dulck
Dull ... D
Dull [*Philately*] ... dl
Dull Black Finish Slate (KSC) ... DBFS
Dull but Important [*Wall Street Journal slang*] (WDMC) ... DBI
Dull Knife Memorial College Library, Lame Deer, MT [*Library symbol*] [*Library of Congress*] (LCLS) ... MtLdD
Dull Men's Club (EA) ... DMC
Dulles International Airport [*FAA*] ... DIA
Duluth [*Minnesota*] [*Airport symbol*] (OAG) ... DLH
Duluth [*Minnesota-Superior, Wisconsin*] [*Airport symbol*] (AD) ... DLH
Duluth [*Minnesota*] [*Seismograph station code, US Geological Survey Closed*] (SEIS) ... DUL
Duluth & Iron Range Railway Co. ... D & IR
Duluth & Northeastern Railroad Co. [*AAR code*] ... DNE
Duluth Environmental Research Laboratory [*Minnesota*] [*Environmental Protection Agency*] (GRD) ... ERL/DUL
Duluth/International [*Minnesota*] [*ICAO location identifier*] (ICLI) ... KDLH
Duluth, Missabe & Iron Range Railroad (MHDB) ... DM & IRR
Duluth, Missabe & Iron Range Railway Co. ... DM & IR
Duluth, Missabe & Iron Range Railway Co. [*AAR code*] ... DMIR
Duluth, Missabe & Northern Railway ... DM & N
Duluth, MN [*Location identifier FAA*] (FAAL) ... JUD
Duluth, MN [*AM radio station call letters*] ... KDAL
Duluth, MN [*FM radio station call letters*] ... KDAL-FM
Duluth, MN [*Television station call letters*] ... KDLH

Duluth, MN [*FM radio station call letters*] ... KDNI
Duluth, MN [*FM radio station call letters*] ... KDNW
Duluth, MN [*FM radio station call letters*] (RBYB) ... KKCB-FM
Duluth, MN [*FM radio station call letters*] (RBYB) ... KLDJ-FM
Duluth, MN [*FM radio station call letters*] ... KLXK
Duluth, MN [*Television station call letters*] ... KNLD
Duluth, MN [*AM radio station call letters*] ... KQDS
Duluth, MN [*FM radio station call letters*] ... KQDS-FM
Duluth, MN [*FM radio station call letters*] ... KTCO
Duluth, MN [*FM radio station call letters*] ... KUMD
Duluth, MN [*Location identifier FAA*] (FAAL) ... LKI
Duluth, MN [*FM radio station call letters*] ... WAVC
Duluth, MN [*Television station call letters*] ... WDIO
Duluth, MN [*Television station call letters*] ... WDSE
Duluth, MN [*AM radio station call letters*] ... WEBC
Duluth, MN [*FM radio station call letters*] ... WNCB
Duluth, MN [*FM radio station call letters*] ... WSCD
Duluth, MN [*AM radio station call letters*] ... WWJC
Duluth Prison Camp, Duluth, MN [*Library symbol*] [*Library of Congress*] (LCLS) ... MnDuPC
Duluth Public Library, Duluth, MN [*Library symbol Library of Congress*] (LCLS) ... MnDu
Duluth, South Shore & Atlantic Railroad [*AAR code Obsolete*] ... DSA
Duluth, South Shore & Atlantic Railroad [*Nickname: Damned Slow Service and Abuse*] [*Obsolete*] ... DSS & A
Duluth Technical Institute, Duluth, MN [*Library symbol*] [*Library of Congress*] (LCLS) ... MnDuTI
Duluth Weapons Calibration System ... DUWCAL
Duluth, Winnipeg & Pacific Railway ... DW & P
Duluth, Winnipeg & Pacific Railway [*AAR code*] ... DWP
Duly Authorized Officer ... DAO
Dumagami Mines Ltd. [*Toronto Stock Exchange symbol*] ... DMI
Dumaguete [*Philippines*] [*Airport symbol*] (OAG) ... DGT
Dumaguete/Sibulan Negros Oriental [*Philippines*] [*ICAO location identifier*] (ICLI) ... RPVD
Dumai/Pinangkampai [*Indonesia*] [*ICAO location identifier*] (ICLI) ... WIBD
Dumas, AR [*AM radio station call letters*] ... KDDA
Dumas, AR [*FM radio station call letters*] ... KXFE
Dumas, TX [*Location identifier FAA*] (FAAL) ... DUX
Dumas, TX [*AM radio station call letters*] ... KDDD
Dumas, TX [*FM radio station call letters*] ... KMRE
Dumb [*Auxiliary craft suffix*] [*British Navy*] ... N
Dumb Driver [*Auto-racing*] ... DD
Dumbarton Oaks Research Library of Harvard University, Washington, DC [*Library symbol Library of Congress OCLC symbol*] (LCLS) ... DDO
Dumbwaiter (MSA) ... DW
Dumbwaiter Door ... DWD
Dumfries and Galloway [*Region of Southern Scotland, established in 1975*] (WGA) ... Dumf Gal
Dumfriesshire [*County in Scotland*] ... DUMF
Dumfries-Triangle, VA [*AM radio station call letters*] ... WPWC
Dummy [*in game of bridge*] ... D
Dummy (KSC) ... DMY
Dummy (MSA) ... DUM
Dummy Antenna ... DA
Dummy Control Section [*Computer science*] ... DSECT
Dummy Delivery Order (DNAB) ... DDO
Dummy Director Set ... DDS
Dummy Firing Unit ... DFU
Dummy Fuel Assembly [*Nuclear energy*] (NRCH) ... DFA
Dummy Guide Assembly [*Nuclear energy*] (NRCH) ... DGA
Dummy Guided Missile ... DGM
Dummy Load [*JETDS nomenclature*] [*Military*] (CET) ... DA
Dummy Load [*Military*] (MCD) ... DL
Dummy Missile Firing ... DMF
Dummy Nose Plug ... DNP
Dummy Part (MCD) ... DP
Dummy Part (MCD) ... DPT
Dummy Part Master (MCD) ... DPMA
Dummy Rip Cord Pulls (DICI) ... DRCP
Dummy Round (MCD) ... DM
Dummy Stowage Receptacle ... DSR
Dummy Surface-to-Air Missile ... DUSAM
Dummy Target (OA) ... DT
Dumont D'Urville [*Pointe Geologie, Adelie*] [*Antarctica*] [*Seismograph station code, US Geological Survey*] (SEIS) ... DRV
Dumont D'Urville [*France*] [*Geomagnetic observatory code*] ... DUM
Dumont Journal, Hampton, IA [*Library symbol Library of Congress*] (LCLS) ... IaHampJ
DuMont Television Network [*1946-55*] ... DTN
Dump ... D
Dump [*Computer science*] ... DMP
Dump Data Line Switch (MCD) ... DDLS
Dump Heat Exchanger [*Nuclear energy*] (OA) ... DHE
Dump Heat Exchanger [*Nuclear energy*] (NRCH) ... DHX
Dump Heat Exchanger Control System [*Nuclear energy*] (NRCH) ... DHXCS
Dump Revenues [*Solid waste management*] ... DR
Dump Telemetry ... DT
Dump Valve (IEEE) ... DV
Dumping (MSA) ... DMPG
Dumping ... DPG
Dumping at Sea Act [*1974*] ... DASA
Dumptruck (AABC) ... DPTRK
Dumpu [*New Guinea*] [*Airport symbol*] (AD) ... DPU
Dun [*Thoroughbred racing*] ... D
Dun (WGA) ... DN
Dun & Bradstreet (AAGC) ... D&B
Dun & Bradstreet [*NYSE symbol*] (TTSB) ... DNB
Dun & Bradstreet [*Associated Press*] (SAG) ... DunBrd
Dun & Bradstreet (AAGC) ... DUNS
Dun & Bradstreet France Marketing [*Dun & Bradstreet France*] [*Database*] ... DBFM
Dun & Bradstreet Guide to Canadian Manufacturers [*Information service or system*] (IID) ... DBGCM
Dun & Bradstreet, Inc. ... D & B
Dun & Bradstreet, Inc. [*NYSE symbol*] (SPSG) ... DNB
Dun & Bradstreet United States [*STM Systems Corp.*] [*Canada Information service or system*] (CRD) ... DBUS
Dunbar [*Australia Airport symbol Obsolete*] (OAG) ... DNB
Dunbar, WV [*FM radio station call letters*] ... WBES
Dunbarton College of Holy Cross [*Closed, 1973*] [*Washington, DC*] ... DCHC
Dunbartonshire [*County in Scotland*] ... DUNB
Dunblane (ROG) ... DUNBL
Duncan [*Oklahoma*] [*Airport symbol Obsolete*] (OAG) ... DUC
Duncan & Associates Library Management Consultants and Looseleaf Filing Service, Los Gatos, CA [*Library symbol*] [*Library of Congress*] (LCLS) ... CLgD
Duncan Aviation, Inc. [*ICAO designator*] (FAAC) ... PHD
Duncan, BC [*AM radio station call letters*] ... CKAY
Duncan Gold Resources [*Vancouver Stock Exchange symbol*] ... DGI
Duncan Memorial Library, Casey, IA [*Library symbol Library of Congress*] (LCLS) ... IaCa
Duncan, OK [*AM radio station call letters*] ... KRHD
Duncan, OK [*FM radio station call letters*] ... KRHD-FM
Duncan/Quamichan Lake [*Canada*] [*Airport symbol Obsolete*] (OAG) ... DUQ
Duncan Town, Exuma Island [*Bahamas*] [*ICAO location identifier*] (ICLI) ... MYRD
Duncan's Manual of Summary Procedure [*A publication*] (DLA) ... Dunc Man
Duncan's Mercantile Cases [*1885-86*] [*Scotland*] [*A publication*] (DLA) ... Dunc Mer Cas
Duncan's Mercantile Cases [*1885-86*] [*Scotland*] [*A publication*] (DLA) ... Dunc Merc Cas
Duncan's New Multiple Range Test (OA) ... DNMRT
Duncan's Scotch Entail Cases [*A publication*] (DLA) ... Dunc Ent Cas
Duncan's Scotch Parochial Ecclesiastical Law [*A publication*] (DLA) ... Dunc Eccl L
Duncanville Public Library, Duncanville, TX [*Library symbol Library of Congress*] (LCLS) ... TxDunv
Duncombe on the Law of Evidence [*A publication*] (DLA) ... Dunc Ev
Duncombe's Nisi Prius [*A publication*] (DLA) ... Dunc NP
Dundalk Public Library, Dundalk, ON, Canada [*Library symbol*] [*Library of Congress*] (LCLS) ... CaODUN
Dundalk Public Library, Ontario [*Library symbol National Library of Canada*] (NLC) ... ODUN
Dundarave Resources [*Vancouver Stock Exchange symbol*] ... DOR
Dundas [*Greenland*] [*ICAO location identifier*] (ICLI) ... BGDU
Dundas Historical Society Museum, Ontario [*Library symbol National Library of Canada*] (BIB) ... ODHS
Dundas Public Library, Dundas, ON, Canada [*Library symbol Library of Congress*] (LCLS) ... CaOD
Dundas Public Library, Ontario [*Library symbol National Library of Canada*] (NLC) ... OD
Dundee [*Scotland*] [*Airport symbol*] (OAG) ... DND
Dundee [*Scotland*] [*Seismograph station code, US Geological Survey*] (SEIS) ... EDU
Dundee [*South Africa*] [*ICAO location identifier*] (ICLI) ... FADD
Dundee, IL [*FM radio station call letters*] ... WABT
Dundee, IL [*FM radio station call letters*] (RBYB) ... WZCH-FM
Dundee Law Chronicle [*1853-58*] [*A publication*] (DLA) ... Dund LC
Dundee Library, Dundee, NY [*Library symbol Library of Congress*] (LCLS) ... NDd
Dundee, NY [*AM radio station call letters*] ... WFLR
Dundee, NY [*FM radio station call letters*] ... WFLR-FM
Dundee Resources [*Vancouver Stock Exchange symbol*] ... DNU
Dundee (Riverside Park) [*British ICAO location identifier*] (ICLI) ... EGPN
Dundee University Numerical Method Information Retrieval Experiment [*British*] (NITA) ... DUNMIRE
Dundee-Palliser Resources, Inc. [*Toronto Stock Exchange symbol*] ... DPR
Dundigul [*India*] [*ICAO location identifier*] (ICLI) ... VODG
Dundo [*Angola*] [*Airport symbol*] (OAG) ... DUE
Dundo [*Angola*] [*Seismograph station code, US Geological Survey*] (SEIS) ... DUN
Dune Resources Ltd. [*Toronto Stock Exchange symbol*] ... DNL
Dunedin [*New Zealand*] [*Airport symbol*] (OAG) ... DUD
Dunedin [*New Zealand*] (ROG) ... DUN
Dunedin [*New Zealand*] [*ICAO location identifier*] (ICLI) ... NZDN
Dunedin, FL [*AM radio station call letters*] ... WGUL
Dunedin, FL [*AM radio station call letters*] ... WLVU
Dunedin Public Library, Dunedin, FL [*Library symbol Library of Congress*] (LCLS) ... FDu
Duneland Post Card Club [*Defunct*] (EA) ... DPCC
Duneland School Corp., Chesterton, IN [*OCLC symbol*] (OCLC) ... ISC
Dunellon, FL [*FM radio station call letters*] ... WTRS
Dunelmensis [*Of Durham*] [*Signature of Bishops of Durham*] [*Latin*] (ROG) ... DUNELM
Dunford BAE [*British ICAO designator*] (FAAC) ... DUN
Dungannon Explorations Ltd. [*Vancouver Stock Exchange symbol*] ... DGX
Dungeon Master [*In game Dungeons and Dragons*] ... DM
Dungeons and Dragons [*Game*] ... D & D
Dunglison. Dictionary of Medical Science and Literature [*A publication*] (DLA) ... Dungl Med Dict
Dungpit (ROG) ... DP
Dungun [*Malaysia*] [*ICAO location identifier*] (ICLI) ... WMAG

Dunhuang [*China*] [*Airport symbol*] (OAG) .... DNH
Dunk Island [*Australia Airport symbol*] (OAG) .... DKI
Dunkeld (ROG) .... DUNK
Dunkerque-Ghyvelde [*France ICAO location identifier*] (ICLI) .... LFAK
Dunkeswell [*England*] .... DUNK
Dunkirk, NY [*Location identifier FAA*] (FAAL) .... DKK
Dunkirk, NY [*AM radio station call letters*] .... WDOE
Dunkirk Veterans Association [*Leeds, England*] (EAIO) .... DVA
Dunlap & Associates, Inc. (MCD) .... DA
Dunlap Public Library District, Dunlap, IL [*Library symbol Library of Congress*] (LCLS) .... IDun
Dunlap Public Library District, Dunlap, IL [*OCLC symbol*] (OCLC) .... IDV
Dunlap Reporter, Dunlap, IA [*Library symbol Library of Congress*] (LCLS) .... IaDunR
Dunlap Society, Essex, NY [*Library symbol Library of Congress*] (LCLS) .... NEssDS
Dunlap, TN [*AM radio station call letters*] .... WSDQ
Dunlap's Abridgment of Coke's Reports [*A publication*] (DLA) .... Dunl Abr
Dunlap's Forms [*A publication*] (DLA) .... Dunl F
Dunlap's Paley on Agency [*A publication*] (DLA) .... Dunl Paley Ag
Dunlop Art Gallery, Regina, Saskatchewan [*Library symbol National Library of Canada*] (NLC) .... SRDA
Dunlop Art Gallery, Regina, SK, Canada [*Library symbol Library of Congress*] (LCLS) .... CaSRDA
Dunlop, Bell, and Murray's Scotch Court of Session Cases, Second Series [*1838-62*] [*A publication*] (DLA) .... D
Dunlop, Bell, and Murray's Scotch Court of Session Cases, Second Series [*1838-62*] [*A publication*] (DLA) .... DB & M
Dunlop, Bell, and Murray's Scotch Court of Session Cases, Second Series [*1838-62*] [*A publication*] (DLA) .... Dunl
Dunlop, Bell, and Murray's Scotch Court of Session Cases, Second Series [*1838-62*] [*A publication*] (DLA) .... Dunl B & M
Dunlop, Bell, and Murray's Scotch Court of Session Cases, Second Series [*1838-62*] [*A publication*] (ILCA) .... Dunl (Ct of Sess)
Dunlop, Bell, and Murray's Scotch Court of Session Cases, Second Series [*1838-62*] [*A publication*] (DLA) .... Dunlop
Dunlop on Parochial Law [*Scotland*] [*A publication*] (DLA) .... Dunl Par
Dunlop Research Centre, Sheridan Park, Mississauga, ON, Canada [*Library symbol Library of Congress*] (LCLS) .... CaOMDR
Dunlop Research Centre, Sheridan Park, Mississauga, Ontario [*Library symbol National Library of Canada*] (NLC) .... OMDR
Dunlop's Admiralty Practice [*A publication*] (DLA) .... Dunl Adm Pr
Dunlop's Admiralty Practice [*A publication*] (DLA) .... Dunl Pr
Dunlop's Laws of Pennsylvania [*A publication*] (DLA) .... Dunl L PA
Dunlop's Laws of the United States [*A publication*] (DLA) .... Dunl L US
Dunlop's Parochial Law [*A publication*] (DLA) .... DPL
Dunn, NC [*AM radio station call letters*] .... WCKB
Dunn, NC [*FM radio station call letters*] .... WRCQ
Dunn Public Library, Dunn, NC [*Library symbol Library of Congress*] (LCLS) .... NcDu
Dunnage .... DUN
Dunnage Board .... DB
Dunnigan, CA [*FM radio station call letters*] (RBYB) .... KLNA-FM
Dunning's English King's Bench Reports [*1753-54*] [*A publication*] (DLA) .... Dunn
Dunning's English King's Bench Reports [*1753-54*] [*A publication*] (DLA) .... Dunning
Dunnottar [*South Africa*] [*ICAO location identifier*] (ICLI) .... FADR
Dunnville Public Library, Dunnville, ON, Canada [*Library symbol Library of Congress*] (LCLS) .... CaODu
Dunnville Public Library, Ontario [*Library symbol National Library of Canada*] (NLC) .... ODU
Dunoir, WY [*Location identifier FAA*] (FAAL) .... DNW
Dunphy and Cummins' Remarkable Trials [*A publication*] (DLA) .... Dun & Cum
Dunquesne Lt cm$2.10 Pfd [*NYSE symbol*] (TTSB) .... DQUPrA
Dunraine Mines Ltd. [*Toronto Stock Exchange symbol*] .... DRM
Dun's Financial Profiles Report [*Dun & Bradstreet Credit Services*] [*Information service or system*] (CRD) .... DFP
Dun's Financial Records [*Dun's Marketing Services*] [*Parsippany, NJ*] [*Information service or system*] (IID) .... DFR
Dun's Financial Records Plus [*Dun's Marketing Services*] [*Information service or system*] (IID) .... DFR+
DUNS [*Data Universal Numbering System*] **Industrial Affiliations Service** (IID) .... DIAS
Dun's Landlord and Tenant in Ireland [*A publication*] (DLA) .... Dun L & T
Dun's Market Identifiers [*Dun's Marketing Services*] [*Information service or system*] (CRD) .... DMI
Dun's Marketing Services [*Dun & Bradstreet, Inc.*] [*Parsippany, NJ*] [*Information service or system*] (IID) .... DMS
Duns Scotus College [*Detroit, MI*] .... DSC
Duns Scotus College, Detroit, MI [*Library symbol Library of Congress*] (LCLS) .... MiDDS
Dunserve II [*Canada Systems Group*] [*Information service or system*] (IID) ...... DBII
Dunsfold [*British ICAO location identifier*] (ICLI) .... EGTD
Dunsink Observatory [*Ireland*] [*Seismograph station code, US Geological Survey*] (SEIS) .... DDK
Dunsmuir, CA [*FM radio station call letters*] .... KZRO
Dunstable [*Municipal borough in England*] .... DUNST
Duodecimal Society of America (AEBS) .... DSA
Duodecimo [*Book up to 20 centimeters in height*] .... D
Duodecimo [*Book up to 20 centimeters in height*] .... DUO
Duodenal Ulcer [*Medicine*] .... DU
Duodenum [*Anatomy*] .... D
Duodenum [*Anatomy*] .... DUOD
Duolateral .... DL
Duolateral Coil [*Electromagnetism*] (IAA) .... DLC
Duo-Mode Electric Transport System, Inc. .... DUETS

Duoplasmation Ion .... DPI
Duoplasmation Ion Source .... DPIS
Duotone (VRA) .... DUTN
DuPage Library System [*Library network*] .... DLS
DuPage Library System, Geneva, IL [*Library symbol Library of Congress*] (LCLS) .... IGenD
Duplex .... D
Duplex (IAA) .... DPL
Duplex (BARN) .... dplx
Duplex (ADA) .... DPX
Duplex [*Radio*] (NATG) .... DU
Duplex [*Watchmaking*] (ROG) .... DUP
Duplex [*Signaling*] (NASA) .... DUPLX
Duplex [*Signaling*] [*Telecommunications*] (MSA) .... DX
Duplex Bearing [*Military*] .... DB
Duplex Controller (IAA) .... DUCO
Duplex Line Control (BUR) .... DLC
Duplex One-Tape System .... DOT
Duplex Products, Inc. [*AMEX symbol*] (SPSG) .... DPX
Duplex Products, Inc. [*Associated Press*] (SAG) .... Duplex
Duplex-Drive [*Amphibious tank*] .... DD
Duplex-Drive Tank .... DDT
Duplexed Display Distributor .... DDD
Duplexer (MSA) .... DPLXR
Duplexer (NASA) .... DUPLXR
Duplicate (AFM) .... DUP
Duplicate (VRA) .... dup
Duplicate (WDMC) .... dup
Duplicate (AABC) .... DUPE
Duplicate (BJA) .... dupl
Duplicate Aperture Card .... DAC
Duplicate Copy .... DC
Duplicate Filing [*IRS*] .... DUP-FIL
Duplicate Negative (MCD) .... DN
Duplicate Positive (MCD) .... DP
Duplicate Title Transferred [*Library science*] .... DTT
Duplicates Exchange Union (EA) .... DEU
Duplicating .... DUPNG
Duplicating Pattern Production (MCD) .... DPP
Duplicating Pattern Tooling (MCD) .... DPT
Duplicating Requisition (MCD) .... DR
Duplication .... DUP
Duplication Technician, Photolithography [*Navy rating*] .... DUT
Duplin County, Dorothy Wightman Library, Kenansville, NC [*Library symbol Library of Congress*] (LCLS) .... NcKeD
Dupo Junior-Senior High School, Dupo, IL [*Library symbol Library of Congress*] (LCLS) .... IDupHS
Duponceau on Jurisdiction of United States Courts [*A publication*] (DLA) .... Dup Jur
Duponceau on Jurisdiction of United States Courts [*A publication*] (DLA) .... Duponceau US Cts
Duponceau on the Constitution [*A publication*] (DLA) .... Dup Const
Dupont Canada, Inc. [*Toronto Stock Exchange symbol*] .... DUP
DuPont [*E. I.*] de Nemours [*Associated Press*] (SAG) .... DuPnt
DuPont [*E. I.*] de Nemours [*Associated Press*] (SAG) .... DuPont
DuPont Photomasks, Inc. [*NASDAQ symbol*] (SAG) .... DPMI
DuPont Photomasks, Inc. [*Associated Press*] (SAG) .... DuPontP
duPont(EI)deNemours [*NYSE symbol*] (TTSB) .... DD
Dupree, SD [*Location identifier FAA*] (FAAL) .... DPR
Duqesne Cap L.P.8.375%'MIPS' [*NYSE symbol*] (TTSB) .... DQPrA
Duquesne Capital [*NYSE symbol*] (SAG) .... DQ
Duquesne Capital [*Associated Press*] (SAG) .... DuqCap
Duquesne Light Co. [*Later, DQE*] [*NYSE symbol*] (SPSG) .... DQU
Duquesne Light Co. [*Associated Press*] (SAG) .... Duq
Duquesne Lt 4% Pfd [*NYSE symbol*] (TTSB) .... DQUPrC
Duquesne Lt 3.75% Pfd [*NYSE symbol*] (TTSB) .... DQUPrB
Duquesne Lt 4.15% Pfd [*NYSE symbol*] (TTSB) .... DQUPrE
Duquesne Lt 4.20% Pfd [*NYSE symbol*] (TTSB) .... DQUPrG
Duquesne Lt4.10% Pfd [*NYSE symbol*] (TTSB) .... DQUPrD
Duquesne University (GAGS) .... Duquesne U
Duquesne University Library, Pittsburgh, PA [*OCLC symbol*] (OCLC) .... DUQ
Duquesne University, Pittsburgh, PA [*Library symbol Library of Congress*] (LCLS) .... PPiD
Duquesne University, School of Law, Pittsburgh, PA [*Library symbol Library of Congress*] (LCLS) .... PPiD-L
Dura Pharmaceuticals [*NASDAQ symbol*] (TTSB) .... DURA
Dura Pharmaceuticals, Inc. [*NASDAQ symbol*] (SAG) .... DURA
Dura Pharmaceuticals, Inc. [*Associated Press*] (SAG) .... DuraPh
Durability (MCD) .... DURA
Durability and Damage Tolerance Analysis [*Air Force*] .... DADTA
Durability/Damage Tolerance Analysis [*Air Force*] .... D/DTA
Durable Goods Industries Advisory Board [*New Deal*] .... DGIAB
Durable Goods Manufacturer [*DoD*] .... DGM
Durable Medical Equipment .... DME
Durable Power of Attorney for Health Care .... DPAHC
Durable Press [*Textile technology*] .... DP
Durable Sprayed Cladding (PDAA) .... DSCl
Durable Woods Institute (EA) .... DWI
Duracell International [*NYSE symbol*] (SPSG) .... DUR
Duracell International [*Associated Press*] (SAG) .... Duracel
Duracell Intl. [*NYSE symbol*] (TTSB) .... DUR
Duracraft Co. [*Associated Press*] (SAG) .... Duracrft
Duracraft Corp. [*NASDAQ symbol*] (SAG) .... DUCR
Durakon Industries [*NASDAQ symbol*] (TTSB) .... DRKN
Durakon Industries, Inc. [*NASDAQ symbol*] (NQ) .... DRKN

Durakon Industries, Inc. [*Associated Press*] (SAG) .... Durkn
Duramed Phamaceutical [*NASDAQ symbol*] (TTSB) .... DRMD
Duramed Pharmaceuticals, Inc. [*NASDAQ symbol*] (SAG) .... DRMD
Duramed Pharmaceuticals, Inc. [*Associated Press*] (SAG) .... Duramed
Durand Free Library, Durand, WI [*Library symbol Library of Congress*] (LCLS) .... WDu
Durand, WI [*AM radio station call letters*] .... WRDN
Durand, WI [*FM radio station call letters*] .... WRDN-FM
Durandi. Speculum Judiciale [*A publication*] (DSA) .... Spe
Durango [*Colorado*] [*Seismograph station code, US Geological Survey Closed*] (SEIS) .... DGC
Durango [*Mexico*] [*Airport symbol*] (OAG) .... DGO
Durango [*Colorado*] [*Airport symbol*] (OAG) .... DRO
Durango [*Mexico ICAO location identifier*] (ICLI) .... MMDO
Durango, CO [*AM radio station call letters*] .... KDGO
Durango, CO [*FM radio station call letters*] .... KDUR
Durango, CO [*FM radio station call letters*] .... KIQX
Durango, CO [*AM radio station call letters*] .... KIUP
Durango, CO [*Television station call letters*] .... KREZ
Durango, CO [*FM radio station call letters*] .... KRSJ
Durango, CO [*FM radio station call letters*] .... KWXA
Durango Public Library, Durango, CO [*Library symbol Library of Congress*] (LCLS) .... CoDu
Durango Public Library, Durango, CO [*Library symbol*] [*Library of Congress*] (LCLS) .... CoDuL
Durant Family Registry (EA) .... DFR
Durant, OK [*Location identifier FAA*] (FAAL) .... DUA
Durant, OK [*FM radio station call letters*] .... KHIB
Durant, OK [*FM radio station call letters*] .... KLAK
Durant, OK [*FM radio station call letters*] .... KLBC
Durant, OK [*AM radio station call letters*] .... KSEO
Durant, OK [*FM radio station call letters*] (RBYB) .... KSSU-FM
Durante Dolore [*While Pain Lasts*] [*Pharmacy*] .... DUR DOL
Durante Dolore [*While Pain Lasts*] [*Pharmacy*] .... DUR DOLOR
Duranton's Droit Francais [*A publication*] (DLA) .... Dur Dr Fr
Duration .... D
Duration .... DUR
Duration (FAAC) .... DURN
Duration Adjusting Type .... DAT
Duration Mines Ltd. [*Toronto Stock Exchange symbol Vancouver Stock Exchange symbol*] .... DAN
Duration of Disease Control .... DDC
Duration of Ejection (MAE) .... DE
Duration of Hospital Stay .... DHS
Duration of Systole (MAE) .... DS
Duration of Tetany [*Medicine*] .... DT
Duration of the Present Emergency [*British World War II*] .... DPE
Duration of Voluntary Apnea [*Physiology*] .... DVA
Duration of War .... DOW
Duration Time Modulation (IAA) .... DTM
Durazno/Santa Bernardina Internacional de Alternativa [*Uruguay*] [*ICAO location identifier*] (ICLI) .... SUDU
Durban [*South Africa*] (ILCA) .... Dbn
Durban [*South Africa*] [*Airport symbol*] (OAG) .... DUR
Durban City Council, Durban, South Africa [*Library symbol Library of Congress*] (LCLS) .... SaDDC
Durban/Louis Botha [*South Africa*] [*ICAO location identifier*] (ICLI) .... FADN
Durban Roodepoort Deep Ltd. [*NASDAQ symbol*] (SAG) .... DROO
Durban Roodepoort Deep Ltd. [*Associated Press*] (SAG) .... Durb ADR
Durban/Virginia [*South Africa*] [*ICAO location identifier*] (ICLI) .... FAVG
Durbin-Watson [*Procedure*] [*Statistics*] .... DW
Durchfuehrungsverordnung [*Executive Decree*] [*German*] (ILCA) .... DVO
Durchgangsvermittlung [*Long-distance telephone exchange*] [*German military - World War II*] .... DV
Durene Association of America (EA) .... DAA
Durex Abrasives Corp. [*Defunct*] (EA) .... DAC
Durfee's Reports [*2 Rhode Island*] [*A publication*] (DLA) .... Durf
Durfee's Reports [*2 Rhode Island*] [*A publication*] (DLA) .... Durfee
Durham [*City and county in England*] .... DRHM
Durham [*England*] [*Seismograph station code, US Geological Survey*] (SEIS) .... DUR
Durham [*City and county in England*] .... DUR
Durham [*City and county in England*] .... DURH
Durham Air Monitoring Demonstration Facility [*Environmental Protection Agency*] (GFGA) .... DAMDF
Durham & Southern Railway Co. [*AAR code*] .... DS
Durham City-County Public Library, Durham, NC [*Library symbol Library of Congress*] (LCLS) .... NcDur
Durham College of Applied Arts and Technology, Oshawa, ON, Canada [*Library symbol Library of Congress*] (LCLS) .... CaOOshD
Durham College of Applied Arts and Technology, Oshawa, Ontario [*Library symbol National Library of Canada*] (NLC) .... OOSHD
Durham County General Hospital, Medical Library, Durham, NC [*Library symbol Library of Congress*] (LCLS) .... NcDurGH
Durham Downs [*Australia Airport symbol*] (OAG) .... DHD
Durham Light Infantry [*Military unit*] [*British*] .... DLI
Durham Light Infantry [*Military unit*] [*British*] (ROG) .... DURH LI
Durham, NC [*FM radio station call letters*] .... WDCG
Durham, NC [*AM radio station call letters*] .... WDNC
Durham, NC [*AM radio station call letters*] .... WDUR
Durham, NC [*FM radio station call letters*] .... WFXC
Durham, NC [*FM radio station call letters*] .... WNCU
Durham, NC [*Television station call letters*] .... WRDC
Durham, NC [*AM radio station call letters*] .... WSRC
Durham, NC [*AM radio station call letters*] .... WTIK
Durham, NC [*Television station call letters*] .... WTVD
Durham, NC [*FM radio station call letters*] .... WXDU
Durham, NH [*Television station call letters*] .... WENH
Durham, NH [*FM radio station call letters*] .... WUNH
Durham Public Library, Durham, ON, Canada [*Library symbol Library of Congress*] (LCLS) .... CaODur
Durham Public Library, Ontario [*Library symbol National Library of Canada*] (NLC) .... ODUR
Durham Resources, Inc. [*Toronto Stock Exchange symbol*] .... DUR
Durham Technical Institute [*Durham, NC*] .... DTI
Durham Technical Institute, Durham, NC [*Library symbol Library of Congress*] (LCLS) .... NcDurT
Durham University Business School .... DUBS
Durie's Scotch Court of Session Decisions [*1621-42*] [*A publication*] (DLA) .... Durie
During .... DRG
During .... DUR
During (FAAC) .... DURG
During Climb [*Aviation*] (FAAC) .... DURC
During Descent [*Aviation*] (FAAC) .... DURD
During Reporting Period .... DRP
During the Temporary Absence Of [*Military*] .... DTAO
Duriron Co. [*NASDAQ symbol*] (SAG) .... DURI
Duriron Co. [*Associated Press*] (SAG) .... Duriron
Durium [*Record label*] [*Italy*] .... Dur
Durnacol [*South Africa*] [*ICAO location identifier*] (ICLI) .... FADH
Durnford and East's (Term) Reports [*1785-1800*] [*England*] [*A publication*] (DLA) .... Durn & E
Durnford and East's (Term) Reports, English King's Bench [*1785-1800*] [*A publication*] (DLA) .... D & E
Duroxide Uptake [*Radiology*] (DAVI) .... DU
Durrie [*Australia Airport symbol Obsolete*] (OAG) .... DRR
Dursley [*England*] .... DURS
Dursunbey [*Turkey*] [*Seismograph station code, US Geological Survey Closed*] (SEIS) .... DRB
Dursunbey [*Turkey*] [*Seismograph station code, US Geological Survey*] (SEIS) .... DST
Durum Growers Association of the United States (EA) .... DGA
Durum Wheat Institute [*Later, MNF*] (EA) .... DWI
Durus [*Hard*] [*Pharmacy*] .... DUR
DUSA Pharmaceuticals [*NASDAQ symbol*] (TTSB) .... DUSA
DUSA Pharmaceuticals, Inc. [*Associated Press*] (SAG) .... DUSA
DUSA Pharmaceuticals, Inc. [*NASDAQ symbol*] (SAG) .... DUSA
Dushanbe [*Stalinabad*] [*Former USSR Seismograph station code, US Geological Survey*] (SEIS) .... DSH
Dushanbe [*Former USSR Airport symbol*] (OAG) .... DYU
Dushanbe [*Former USSR ICAO location identifier*] (ICLI) .... UTDD
Dusheti [*Former USSR Seismograph station code, US Geological Survey*] (SEIS) .... DUS
Dusing [*New York*] [*Seismograph station code, US Geological Survey Closed*] (SEIS) .... DSN
Dusio [*In Cisitalia car model "D46"*] .... D
Dusseldorf [*Germany Airport symbol*] (OAG) .... DUS
Dusseldorf-Main RR [*Germany Airport symbol*] (OAG) .... QDU
Dusseldorf's Institution Art Network Application (IID) .... DIANA
Dust [*Meteorology*] .... D
Dust [*Tea trade*] (ROG) .... DST
Dust [*ICAO*] (FAAC) .... DU
Dust and Moisture .... DUMR
Dust Cover [*Automotive engineering*] .... D/CVR
Dust Erosion Tunnel (MCD) .... DET
Dust Haze [*Aviation*] .... HZ
Dust Haze [*Meteorology*] (WDAA) .... Z
Dust Impact Detection System [*Astrophysics*] .... DID
Dust Impact Detection System [*Astrophysics*] .... DIDSY
Dust Infall Predominant (AAG) .... DIP
Dust Infrared Test (MCD) .... DIRT
Dust Jacket [*Paper cover for a hardbound book*] .... DJ
Dust Jacket (WDMC) .... dj
Dust/Sand Storm [*Meteorology*] (WDAA) .... KZ
Dust Shield [*Automotive engineering*] .... D/SHLD
Dust Storm [*Astronomy*] .... DS
Dust, Thermal, and Radiation Engineering Measurements Package [*NASA*] .... DTREM
Dust Turn (OA) .... DT
Dust Veil Index [*of atmosphere*] .... DVI
Dust Wrapper [*Paper cover for a hardbound book*] .... DW
Dust Wrapper [*Also, Dust Jacket*] (WDMC) .... dw
Duster Class Yacht Racing Association (EA) .... DCYRA
Dust-Free Chamber .... DFC
Dust-Free Room .... DFR
Dust-Induced Electromagnetic Noise .... DIEMN
DUSTOFF [*Dedicated Unhesitating Service to Our Fighting Forces*] **Association** (EA) .... DA
Dust-Tight (MSA) .... DT
Dusty Gas Enveloped [*Astronomy*] .... DGE
Dusty Mac Mines Ltd. [*Vancouver Stock Exchange symbol*] .... DUS
Dusty Mac Oil & Gas Ltd. [*NASDAQ symbol*] (SAG) .... DMAC
Dusty Mac Oil & Gas Ltd. [*Associated Press*] (SAG) .... DustyM
Dutch .... D
Dutch .... DTCH
Dutch .... DU
Dutch .... DUT
Dutch [*MARC language code Library of Congress*] (LCCP) .... dut
Dutch Actiongroup for Indians of North America .... NANAI

Dutch Australian Society .... DAS
Dutch Belted [*Rabbits*] .... DB
Dutch Belted Cattle Association of America (EA) .... DBCAA
Dutch Broadway Elementary School, Elmont, NY [*Library symbol*] [*Library of Congress*] (LCLS) .... NElmoDE
Dutch Dairy Bureau (EA) .... DDB
Dutch Door [*Technical drawings*] .... DD
Dutch East Indies .... DEI
Dutch Elm Disease .... DED
Dutch Family Heritage Society (EA) .... DFHS
Dutch Florin [*Monetary unit*] (IMH) .... Dfl
Dutch Guilder [*Monetary unit*] (NATG) .... DG
Dutch Harbor [*Alaska*] [*Seismograph station code, US Geological Survey Closed*] (SEIS) .... DHA
Dutch Harbor [*Alaska*] [*Airport symbol*] (OAG) .... DUT
Dutch Harbour [*Alaska*] [*ICAO location identifier*] (ICLI) .... PADU
Dutch Interchurch Aid and Service to Refugees [*Netherlands*] .... DIA
Dutch Lane Elementary School, Hicksville, NY [*Library symbol Library of Congress*] (LCLS) .... NHickDLE
Dutch, Middle [*MARC language code Library of Congress*] (LCCP) .... dum
Dutch New Guinea [*Later, Irian Barat*] .... DNG
Dutch RCA [*Victor*] [*Record label*] .... DV
Dutch Reformed Church (IIA) .... DR
Dutch Reformed Church .... DRC
Dutch State Mines .... DSM
Dutch Warmblood Association (EA) .... DWA
Dutch West Indies .... DWI
Dutch-American Historical Commission (EA) .... DAHC
Dutch-Auction-Rate Transferable Securities [*Investment term*] .... DARTS
Dutch-Australian Community Assistance Bureau .... DACAB
Dutcher's Law Reports [*25-29 New Jersey*] [*A publication*] (DLA) .... Dutch
Dutchess Community College, Poughkeepsie, NY [*Library symbol Library of Congress*] (LCLS) .... NPDC
Dutchess County Mental Health Center, Poughkeepsie, NY [*Library symbol Library of Congress*] (LCLS) .... NPDCM
Dutchess County Mental Health Center, Poughkeepsie, NY [*Inactive*] [*OCLC symbol*] (OCLC) .... RVD
Duties Other than Teaching (ADA) .... DOTT
Duties Require Parachuting [*Army*] (AABC) .... DYRQRPRCHT
Dutton and Cowdrey's Revision of Swift's Digest of Connecticut Laws [*A publication*] (DLA) .... Dut & Cowd Rev
Duty [*Navy*] .... D
Duty (AFM) .... DY
Duty Air Force Specialty .... DAFS
Duty Air Force Specialty Code .... DAFSC
Duty Air Traffic Control Officer (DA) .... DATCO
Duty as an Operator or Crewmember of an Operational Self-Propelled Submersible Including Underseas Exploration and Research Vehicles [*Military*] (DNAB) .... DSVOPS
Duty as His Relief [*Military*] (DNAB) .... DURELAS
Duty as Technical Observer in a Flying Status Involving Operational or Training Flights [*Military*] (DNAB) .... DIFTECH
Duty Connection .... DUCON
Duty Controller [*Tactical Air Command*] .... DC
Duty Controller [*Air Force*] .... DYCONTR
Duty Cycle [*Engineering*] .... DC
Duty Cycle [*Military*] .... DU
Duty Cycle (IAA) .... DUCY
Duty Cycle Modulation Alternator .... DCMA
Duty Cypher Officer [*Military British*] .... DCO
Duty Deferment Account [*Customs*] (DS) .... DDA
Duty Deposit Account [*Customs*] (DS) .... DDA
Duty Directed in Order Is Being Performed For .... DOPF
Duty Directed Is Being Performed for Unit Issuing Order .... DPUO
Duty Driver [*Military*] .... DD
Duty Factor [*Military*] (CAAL) .... DF
Duty Flying Control Officer [*Navy*] .... DFCO
Duty Free [*Customs*] .... DF
Duty Free International, Inc. [*NYSE symbol*] (SPSG) .... DFI
Duty Free International, Inc. [*Associated Press*] (SAG) .... DutyF
Duty Free Intl. [*NYSE symbol*] (TTSB) .... DFI
Duty in a Flying Status Involving Operational or Training Flights [*Air Force*] (NVT) .... DIFOPS
Duty in a Flying Status Involving Operational or Training Flights as a TechnicalObserver [*Air Force*] .... DIFOTECH
Duty in a Flying Status Involving Operational or Training Flights as His Relief [*Air Force*] .... DIFOTRELAS
Duty in a Flying Status Involving Operational or Training Flights Effective Such Date as Endorsed [*Military*] (DNAB) .... DIFOTDORSE
Duty in a Flying Status Involving Operational or Training Flights Effective SuchDate as Endorsed [*Military*] (DNAB) .... DIFOPSDORSE
Duty in a Flying Status Involving Operational or Training Flights Revoked [*Air Force*] .... DIFOTRVK
Duty in a Flying Status Involving Operational or Training Flights under Instruction [*Air Force*] .... DIFOTINS
Duty in a Flying Status Involving Proficiency Flying [*Air Force*] (NVT) .... DIFPRO
Duty in a Flying Status Not Involving Flying [*Air Force*] (NVT) .... DIFDEN
Duty in a Flying Status Not Involving Flying as His Relief [*Military*] (DNAB) .... DIFDENRELAS
Duty Intelligence Officer [*Air Force*] .... DIO
Duty Involving Flying [*Military*] .... DIF
Duty Involving Flying [*Military*] .... DUFLY
Duty Involving Flying as a Technical Observer [*Military*] .... DUFLYTECH
Duty Involving Flying Crewman [*Military*] (NVT) .... DIFCREW
Duty Involving Operational or Training Flights [*Air Force*] .... DIFOT
Duty Involving Underway Operations in Submarines .... DISUB
Duty Military Occupational Specialty .... DMOS
Duty Military Occupational Specialty Qualified [*Army*] (DOMA) .... DMSQ
Duty Not Involving Flying .... DNIF
Duty Officer [*Military*] .... DO
Duty Officer [*Military*] .... DTYO
Duty on Board that Vessel when Placed in Commission [*Navy*] .... ONBOWCOM
Duty on Board that Vessel when Placed in Service [*Navy*] .... ONBOWSERV
Duty Operational Test Director .... DOTP
Duty Orbital Analyst (IAA) .... DOA
Duty Paid [*International trade*] .... DP
Duty Paid Value [*Business term*] .... DPV
Duty Pay .... DP
Duty Petty Officer [*Navy*] (DNAB) .... DPO
Duty Preference Card (DNAB) .... DPC
Duty Salvage Ship [*Navy*] (NVT) .... SALV
Duty Section [*Air Force*] (AFM) .... DS
Duty Security Petty Officer [*Navy*] (DNAB) .... DSPO
Duty Space Surveillance Officer [*Air Force*] (AFM) .... DSSO
Duty Station [*Navy*] .... DUSTA
Duty Status [*Air Force*] (AFM) .... DS
Duty Steam Boat [*British military*] (DMA) .... DSB
Duty under Instruction .... DUINS
Duty under Instruction in a Flying Status Involving Operational or Training Flights [*Military*] (DNAB) .... DIFINSOPS
Duty under Instruction in a Flying Status Involving Proficiency Flying [*Military*] (DNAB) .... DIFINSPRO
Duty under Instruction in a Flying Status Not Involving Flying [*Military*] (DNAB) .... DIFDENIS
Duty under Instruction or Temporary Duty under Instruction as a Student [*Military*] (DNAB) .... DUINS/TEMDUINS STU
Duty Weather Forecaster (SAA) .... DWF
Duty-Free Into-Store Cost .... DFIST
Duvall's Canada Supreme Court Reports [*A publication*] (DLA) .... Duv
Duvall's Canada Supreme Court Reports [*A publication*] (DLA) .... Duv (Can)
Duvall's Canada Supreme Court Reports [*A publication*] (DLA) .... Duval
Duvall's Canada Supreme Court Reports [*A publication*] (DLA) .... Duvall
Duvall's Reports [*62, 63 Kentucky*] [*A publication*] (DLA) .... Duv
Du-Well Resources Ltd. [*Vancouver Stock Exchange symbol*] .... DWR
Duxbury Rural and Historical Society, Duxbury, MA [*Library symbol Library of Congress*] (LCLS) .... MDuHi
Duxbury's High Court Reports [*South African Republic*] [*A publication*] (DLA) .... D
Duxbury's High Court Reports [*South African Republic*] [*1895*] [*A publication*] (DLA) .... Dux
DVI Corp. [*NYSE symbol*] (SPSG) .... DVI
DVI, Inc. [*Associated Press*] (SAG) .... DVI
DVI, Inc. [*Associated Press*] (SAG) .... DVI Inc
DVI, Inc. [*NASDAQ symbol*] (SAG) .... DVIC
Dviefontein Consol ADR [*NASDAQ symbol*] (TTSB) .... DRFNY
Dvoracek Memorial Library, Wilber, NE [*Library symbol Library of Congress*] (LCLS) .... NbWi
Dvorak International (EAIO) .... DI
Dvorak International Federation (EA) .... DIF
Dvorak Simplified Keyboard [*Typewriter keyboard developed by August Dvorak in the 1920's*] .... DSK
Dwanga [*Malawi*] [*ICAO location identifier*] (ICLI) .... FWDW
Dwarf .... D
Dwarf [*Horticulture*] .... Dwf
Dwarf Aster Yellows [*Plant pathology*] .... DAY
Dwarf Fruit Trees Association [*Later, International Dwarf Fruit Trees Association*] (EA) .... DFTA
Dwarf Iris Society of America (EA) .... DISA
Dwarf Mouse [*Medicine*] (DMAA) .... dw
Dwarf Shoot [*Botany*] .... DS
Dwarris on Statutes [*A publication*] (DLA) .... Dw Stat
Dwarris on Statutes [*A publication*] (DLA) .... Dwar
Dwarris on Statutes [*A publication*] (DLA) .... Dwar St
Dwell Time (AAG) .... DT
Dwelling (MSA) .... DWEL
Dwelling (ADA) .... DWG
Dwelling (VRA) .... dwl
Dwelling (AABC) .... DWLG
Dwelling .... DWLLNG
Dwelling Sculpture Institute [*Defunct*] (EA) .... DSI
Dwelling Unit [*Household census*] .... DU
Dwight Branch, Lake Of Bays Township Public Library, Ontario [*Library symbol National Library of Canada*] (BIB) .... ODLB
Dwight D. Eisenhower Army Medical Center [*Fort Gordon, GA*] .... DDEAMC
Dwight D. Eisenhower Library .... DDEL
Dwight D. Eisenhower Library, Abilene, KS [*Library symbol Library of Congress*] (LCLS) .... KAbE
Dwight D. Eisenhower Philatelic and Historical Society (EA) .... DDEPHS
Dwight David Eisenhower [*US general and president, 1890-1969*] .... DDE
Dwight, IL [*Location identifier FAA*] (FAAL) .... DTG
Dwight, IL [*FM radio station call letters*] .... WDWT
Dwight T. Parker Public Library, Fennimore, WI [*Library symbol Library of Congress*] (LCLS) .... WFe
Dwight's Charity Cases [*England*] [*A publication*] (DLA) .... Dwight
Dwingeloo Obscured Galaxy Survey .... DOGS
Dworkin/Culatta Oral Mechanism Examination [*Speech and language therapy*] (DAVI) .... DCOME
Dwyer Aircraft Sales, Inc. [*ICAO designator*] (FAAC) .... DFS
Dwyer Community Hospital, Medical Library, Milwaukie, OR [*Library symbol Library of Congress*] (LCLS) .... OrMiD
Dwyer Group [*NASDAQ symbol*] (TTSB) .... DWYR

Dwyer Group, Inc. [*Associated Press*] (SAG) ... DwyerGp
Dwyer Group, Inc. [*NASDAQ symbol*] (SAG) ... DWYR
Dwyer on the Militia Laws [*A publication*] (DLA) ... Dw Mil
Dwyer-Mercer County District Library, Celina, OH [*Library symbol Library of Congress*] (LCLS) ... OCel
D-Xylose [*In urine*] [*Gastroenterology*] (DAVI) ... D-XYL
Dyad Services Ltd. [*British ICAO designator*] (FAAC) ... SKT
Dyad Symmetry Element [*Genetics*] ... DSE
Dyadic Adjustment Scale [*Psychology*] (EDAC) ... DAS
Dyadic Interaction Analysis ... DIA
Dyadic Parent-Child Interaction Coding System [*Psychology*] ... DPICS
Dycam, Inc. [*AMEX symbol*] (SAG) ... DYC
Dycam, Inc. [*Associated Press*] (SAG) ... Dycam
Dyche and Pardon's Dictionary [*A publication*] (DLA) ... Dyche & P Dict
Dycom Industries [*NYSE symbol*] (TTSB) ... DY
Dycom Industries, Inc. [*NYSE symbol*] (SPSG) ... DY
Dycom Industries, Inc. [*Associated Press*] (SAG) ... Dycom
Dye [*Classification key in textile printing*] ... D
Dye Diffusion Thermal Transfer [*Printer technology*] (PCM) ... D2T2
Dye Testing ... DT
Dye Transfer Print (VRA) ... DYTRPT
Dye-Binding Capacity ... DBC
Dye-Free [*Pharmacy*] ... DF
Dyeing ... DYNG
Dyer Hill [*Washington*] [*Seismograph station code, US Geological Survey*] (SEIS) ... DHW
Dyer Library, Saco, ME [*Library symbol Library of Congress*] (LCLS) ... MeSaco
Dyer, TN [*FM radio station call letters*] ... WLSQ
Dyers' and Cleaners' Research Association (BI) ... DCRA
Dyer's Edition of Valiant's English King's Bench Reports [*1513-82*] [*A publication*] (DLA) ... D
Dyer's English King's Bench Reports [*73 English Reprint*] [*A publication*] (DLA) ... Dy
Dyer's English King's Bench Reports [*73 English Reprint*] [*A publication*] (DLA) ... Dyer
Dyer's English King's Bench Reports [*73 English Reprint*] [*A publication*] (DLA) ... Dyer (Eng)
Dyers of Man-Made Fibre Fabrics Federation [*British*] (BI) ... DMF
Dyersburg [*Tennessee*] [*Seismograph station code, US Geological Survey Closed*] (SEIS) ... DY1
Dyersburg Corp. [*NYSE symbol*] (SPSG) ... DBG
Dyersburg Corp. [*Associated Press*] (SAG) ... Dyersbg
Dyersburg, TN [*Location identifier FAA*] (FAAL) ... DYR
Dyersburg, TN [*FM radio station call letters*] ... WASL
Dyersburg, TN [*FM radio station call letters*] ... WKNQ
Dyersburg, TN [*AM radio station call letters*] ... WTRO
Dyersville Commercial, Dyersville, IA [*Library symbol Library of Congress*] (LCLS) ... IaDyC
Dyersville, IA [*FM radio station call letters*] ... KDST
Dyess Air Force Base [*Texas*] (AAG) ... DAFB
Dyestuffs ... DS
Dyestuffs Environmental and Toxicology Organization ... DETO
Dyett's Summary Proceedings [*A publication*] (DLA) ... Dy Sum Proc
Dying ... DYG
Dyke College, Cleveland, OH [*Library symbol Library of Congress*] (LCLS) ... OCID
Dylan Flight Service SA [*Switzerland ICAO designator*] (FAAC) ... DFX
Dylex Ltd. [*Toronto Stock Exchange symbol*] ... DLX
Dymo LASER Composer (DGA) ... DLC
Dymond's Death Duties [*15th ed.*] [*1973*] [*A publication*] (DLA) ... Dym Death Dut
Dyna Group International, Inc. [*NASDAQ symbol*] (NQ) ... DGIX
Dyna Group International, Inc. [*Associated Press*] (SAG) ... DynaGp
Dyna Group Intl. [*NASDAQ symbol*] (TTSB) ... DGIX
Dynacq International, Inc. [*NASDAQ symbol*] (SAG) ... DYII
Dynacq International, Inc. [*Associated Press*] (SAG) ... Dynacq
Dynacq Intl. [*NASDAQ symbol*] (TTSB) ... DYIL
Dynaflow [*Automotive engineering*] ... DYNA
Dynagen, Inc. [*NASDAQ symbol*] (SAG) ... DYGN
Dynagen, Inc. [*Associated Press*] (SAG) ... Dynag
Dynagen, Inc. [*Associated Press*] (SAG) ... Dynagn
Dynagen, Inc. [*Associated Press*] (SAG) ... Dyng
DynaGen Inc. Wrrt [*NASDAQ symbol*] (TTSB) ... DYGNW
DynAir Services, Inc. [*ICAO designator*] (FAAC) ... XDY
Dynamair Aviation, Inc. [*Canada ICAO designator*] (FAAC) ... DNR
Dynamar Energy Ltd. [*Toronto Stock Exchange symbol*] ... DNA
Dynamex, Inc. [*NASDAQ symbol*] (SAG) ... DYMX
Dynamex, Inc. [*Associated Press*] (SAG) ... Dynamx
Dynamic ... DYN
Dynamic (WGA) ... DYNAM
Dynamic ... DYNMC
Dynamic Accelerated Cooling [*Sumitomo Metals*] ... DAC
Dynamic Accuracy Test Set [*or System*] ... DATS
Dynamic Accuracy Tester [*General Electric Co.*] ... DYNAT
Dynamic Acoustic Response Trigger (IEEE) ... DART
Dynamic, Acoustic, Thermal Environment (MCD) ... DATE
Dynamic Action Management Operations [*BSD*] ... DYNAMO
Dynamic Active Index Matrix (BUR) ... DAIM
Dynamic Address Table [*Computer science*] (IAA) ... DAT
Dynamic Address Translation [*Computer science*] ... DAT
Dynamic Air [*Netherlands ICAO designator*] (FAAC) ... DYE
Dynamic Air Blast Simulator (MCD) ... DABS
Dynamic Air War Game [*Military*] ... DAWG
Dynamic ALGOL [*Algorithmic Language*] **String Handling** [*Computer science*] (IAA) ... DASH
Dynamic Allocation Interface Routine [*Computer science*] (BUR) ... DAIR
Dynamic Allocation of Manufacturing Inventory and Time (MHDB) ... DYNAMIT
Dynamic Allocation Translator [*Computer science*] (IAA) ... DAT
Dynamic Analog Differential Equation Equalizer ... DADEE
Dynamic Analog of Vocal Tract ... DAVO
Dynamic Analysis (NRCH) ... DYNAL
Dynamic Analysis and Control Laboratory [*MIT*] (MCD) ... DACL
Dynamic Analysis and Design of Systems (RDA) ... DADS
Dynamic Analysis and Design Software ... DADS
Dynamic Analysis and Replanning Tool ... DART
Dynamic Analysis Branch [*Redstone Arsenal*] ... DA
Dynamic Analysis of Mechanical Networks (PDAA) ... DAMN
Dynamic Analytic Replanning Tools [*DoD*] ... DARTS
Dynamic Analyzer ... DYANA
Dynamic Analyzer (MCD) ... DYNA
Dynamic Analyzer (HGAA) ... DYNANA
Dynamic Angle Spinning [*Spectroscopy*] ... DAS
Dynamic Antiresonant Vibration Isolator ... DAVI
Dynamic Application Integration [*Computer science*] (PCM) ... DAI
Dynamic Arm Programmer [*Computer science*] ... DYNARM
Dynamic Assertion Processor [*Computer science*] ... DAP
Dynamic Assignation Interface Routine [*Electronics*] (ECII) ... DAIR
Dynamic Asynchronous Logic Circuit ... DALC
Dynamic Audio Video Interactive Device [*Hearing aid*] ... DAVID
Dynamic Automatic Monitoring (CET) ... DYNAMO
Dynamic Automatic RADAR Tester (SAA) ... DART
Dynamic Axial Fatigue (PDAA) ... DAF
Dynamic Balancing and Tracking System (MCD) ... DBATS
Dynamic Balancing Equipment ... DBE
Dynamic Bandwidth Allocation [*Computer science*] ... DBA
Dynamic Braking ... DB
Dynamic Braking ... DYB
Dynamic Capital Corp. [*Toronto Stock Exchange symbol*] ... D
Dynamic Cardiogram ... DCG
Dynamic Channel Allocation (PDAA) ... DCA
Dynamic Channel Exchange (NITA) ... DCW
Dynamic Characteristic Load ... DCL
Dynamic Checkout [*Aerospace*] (IAA) ... DCO
Dynamic Checkout Unit [*Aerospace*] (AAG) ... DCU
Dynamic Cloud Free Line of Sight (MCD) ... DCFLOS
Dynamic Coercive Force ... DCF
Dynamic Color Rendition [*Computer science*] ... DCR
Dynamic Combat System Test [*Military*] (CAAL) ... DCST
Dynamic Complementary Metal Oxide Semiconductor (IAA) ... DYCMOS
Dynamic Compliance [*Of lung on pulmonary function tests*] [*Medicine*] (DAVI) ... CDYN
Dynamic Component Change (MCD) ... DCC
Dynamic Compression-Plate ... DCP
Dynamic Computer Display (IEEE) ... DCD
Dynamic Console for Operations Planners ... DYCOP
Dynamic Control ... DYCON
Dynamic Crew Procedures Simulator ... DCPS
Dynamic Crossed-Field Electron Multiplication ... DCFEM
Dynamic Crossed-Field Photomultiplier ... DCFP
Dynamic Data Allocator (DNAB) ... DYDAT
Dynamic Data Exchange [*Message protocol*] [*Computer science*] (BYTE) ... DDE
Dynamic Data Exchange Management Library [*Microsoft, Inc.*] (PCM) ... DDEML
Dynamic Debugger ... DYDE
Dynamic Debugging Tape (IAA) ... DDT
Dynamic Debugging Technique (DEN) ... DDT
Dynamic Demand Assignment [*Army*] (MCD) ... DDA
Dynamic Depletion Mode (IAA) ... DDM
Dynamic Design Analysis Method [*Navy*] ... DDAM
Dynamic Design Analysis Method System [*Navy*] ... DDAMS
Dynamic Device Reconfiguration [*IBM Corp.*] [*Computer science*] (MDG) ... DDR
Dynamic Diagnostic System (MCD) ... DDS
Dynamic Display Tester ... DDT
Dynamic Docking Test Facility [*NASA*] (NASA) ... DDTF
Dynamic Docking Test System [*NASA*] (NASA) ... DDTS
Dynamic Dummy Director ... DDD
Dynamic Econometric Retention Model (MCD) ... DERM
Dynamic Effect Induction [*Automotive engineering*] ... DEI
Dynamic Electromagnetic Environment Simulator ... DEES
Dynamic Electrospeaker ... DES
Dynamic Energy [*Foglight*] [*Hella, Inc.*] [*Automotive engineering*] ... DE
Dynamic Energy Conversion ... DEC
Dynamic Engineer ... DE
Dynamic Environment Simulator [*Air Force*] ... DES
Dynamic Environmental Conditioning [*Cycling*] [*Medicine*] (DAVI) ... DEC
Dynamic Environmental Laboratory Test ... DELT
Dynamic Ephemeral Bodies [*Planetary science*] ... DEB
Dynamic Equilibrium Cycling (IAA) ... DEC
Dynamic Error-Free Transmission ... DEFT
Dynamic Fault Diagnosis Technique (MCD) ... DFDT
Dynamic Fermenter [*Microbiology*] ... DF
Dynamic File Allocation System ... DFAST
Dynamic Flight Simulator ... DFS
Dynamic Flow Control Unit [*Chromatography*] ... DFCU
Dynamic Flow Parameter ... DFP
Dynamic Force Analysis ... DFA
Dynamic Forcing Function [*Information*] **Report** [*Nuclear energy*] (NRCH) ... DFFR
Dynamic Functional Interaction (EDAC) ... DFI
Dynamic Fuze Simulator [*RADAR*] ... DYFUS
Dynamic Gas Disengagement [*Chemical engineering*] ... DGD
Dynamic Gravity Detector ... DGD
Dynamic Gravity Generator ... DGG
Dynamic Hardness Number ... DHN

Dynamic Healthcare Tech [*NASDAQ symbol*] (TTSB) .... DHTI
Dynamic Healthcare Technologies, Inc. [*NASDAQ symbol*] (SAG) ..... DHTI
Dynamic Healthcare Technologies, Inc. [*Associated Press*] (SAG) .... DynHlth
Dynamic High-Speed Functional Tester (MCD) .... DHSFT
Dynamic Hip Screw [*System*] [*Orthopedics*] (DAVI) .... DHS
Dynamic Homes [*NASDAQ symbol*] (TTSB) .... DYHM
Dynamic Homes, Inc. [*NASDAQ symbol*] (SAG) .... DYHM
Dynamic Homes, Inc. [*Associated Press*] (SAG) .... DynHm
Dynamic Homes, Inc. [*Associated Press*] (SAG) .... DynHom
Dynamic Host Configuration Program [*Computer science*] .... DHCP
Dynamic Host Configuration Protocol [*Computer science*] .... DHCP
Dynamic Host Control Protocol [*Computer science*] .... DHCP
Dynamic HTML [*Hyper Text Markup Language*] [*Computer science*] .... DHTML
Dynamic HTML [*HyperText Markup Language*] [*Computer science*] .... dHTML
Dynamic Imagery Viewer .... DIV
Dynamic Impedance Measurement .... DIM
Dynamic Inclined Plane (PDAA) .... DIP
Dynamic Inducer Rotor (MCD) .... DIR
Dynamic Input to Control Center Equipment (IAA) .... DICE
Dynamic Input-Output Analysis [*Economics*] .... DIOA
Dynamic Instrumentation Data Automobile System [*Telemetering system for auto test tracks*] .... DIDAS
Dynamic Instrumentation Digital Analyzer .... DIDA
Dynamic Integrated Data Display .... DIDD
Dynamic Integrated Data Display System .... DIDDS
Dynamic Integrated Test (MCD) .... DIT
Dynamic Intelligent Scheduling [*Computer science*] .... DISC
Dynamic International Access to Databases and Economic Models [*Economic Models Ltd.*] [*British*] (NITA) .... DIADEM
Dynamic Inventory Analysis System [*Computer science*] .... DIAS
Dynamic Isotope Power System .... DIPS
Dynamic Job Description Entity [*For Xerox printer*] (NITA) .... DJDE
Dynamic Lead Guidance (PDAA) .... DLG
Dynamic Light Scattering .... DLS
Dynamic Light Scattering [*Physics*] .... DLS
Dynamic Limit Programming (MHDB) .... DLP
Dynamic Line Regulation .... DLR
Dynamic Link Library [*Software*] [*Computer science*] (BYTE) .... DLL
Dynamic Load Characteristic (MDG) .... DL
Dynamic Load Characteristic .... DLC
Dynamic Load Regulation .... DLR
Dynamic Load Simulator (NASA) .... DLS
Dynamic Load Thermo-Mechanical Analysis [*Thermal analysis*] .... DLTMA
Dynamic Logic Chassis Analyzer .... DLCA
Dynamic Lung Compliance [*Medicine*] (BABM) .... Cdyn
Dynamic Magnetic Resonant Imaging [*Medicine*] .... DMRI
Dynamic Magneto-Optical Correlator [*Instrumentation*] .... DYNAMO
Dynamic Manned Orbital Weapon System (IAA) .... DYNAMOWS
Dynamic Map Display .... DMD
Dynamic Mapping System [*Hewlett-Packard Co.*] .... DMS
Dynamic Materials [*NASDAQ symbol*] (TTSB) .... BOOM
Dynamic Materials Corp. [*NASDAQ symbol*] (SAG) .... BOOM
Dynamic Materials Corp. [*Associated Press*] (SAG) .... DynMatl
Dynamic Matrix Control [*Chemical engineering*] [*Computer science*] .... DMC
Dynamic Mechanical Analysis .... DMA
Dynamic Mechanical Testing .... DMT
Dynamic Mechanical Thermal Analysis .... DMTA
Dynamic Melting [*Chemistry*] .... DM
Dynamic Memory [*Computer science*] .... DRAM
Dynamic Memory Control [*Computer science*] .... DMC
Dynamic Memory Interface [*Computer science*] (NITA) .... DMI
Dynamic Memory Relocation and Protection System (NITA) .... DRPS
Dynamic Microprocessor Associates (PCM) .... DMA
Dynamic Mid-Ride Controls [*Truck seating*] .... DMRC
Dynamic Missile Simulator .... DMS
Dynamic Mission Equivalent (IAA) .... DME
Dynamic Mixing Model [*Marine science*] (OSRA) .... DYNMX
Dynamic Mixing Model (USDC) .... DYNMX
Dynamic Mockup .... DMU
Dynamic Model Continuous Time Simulation (BUR) .... DYNAMO
Dynamic Model Operations Section .... DMOS
Dynamic Modelling System (AIE) .... DMS
Dynamic Module Replacement .... DMR
Dynamic Motion Simulator (MCD) .... DMS
Dynamic Multipoint Bridging [*Computer science*] (ACRL) .... DMB
Dynamic Multi-Tasking System (DNAB) .... DMTS
Dynamic Noise Limiter [*Electronics*] (IAA) .... DNL
Dynamic Noise Reduction [*Video technology*] .... DNR
Dynamic Noise Suppression [*Electronics*] .... DNS
Dynamic Nuclear Magnetic Resonance .... DNMR
Dynamic Nuclear Polarization .... DNP
Dynamic Ocean Track System (DA) .... DOTS
Dynamic Octal Load .... DOL
Dynamic Oil Ltd. [*Vancouver Stock Exchange symbol*] .... DOL
Dynamic Oil Ltd. [*Associated Press*] (SAG) .... DynOil
Dynamic Oil Ltd. [*NASDAQ symbol*] (NQ) .... DYOL
Dynamic Oil Ltd. [*NASDAQ symbol*] (TTSB) .... DYOLF
Dynamic Operation Test .... DOT
Dynamic Operational Requirements and Cost Analysis [*Computer program*] [*NASA*] .... DORCA
Dynamic Operator Response Apparatus .... DORA
Dynamic Operator Response System .... DORS
Dynamic Order Quantity .... DOQ
Dynamic Output Printer Analyzer (IAA) .... DOPA
Dynamic Overload Controls [*Telecommunications*] .... DOC

Dynamic Personality Inventory [*Psychology*] .... DPI
Dynamic Phase Error .... DPE
Dynamic Philatelic Society .... DPS
Dynamic Plume Test .... DPT
Dynamic Preferential Runway System [*Aviation*] .... DPRS
Dynamic Pressure [*NASA*] .... Q
Dynamic Pressure Feedback .... DPF
Dynamic Pressure Measurements .... DPM
Dynamic Processing System [*Mitsubishi*] (NITA) .... DPS
Dynamic Processor Overload Control [*Telephone technology*] .... DPOC
Dynamic Programming [*Computer science*] .... DP
Dynamic Programming System [*Computer science*] (IAA) .... DYPS
Dynamic Pulse Position Modulation [*LASER technology*] .... DPPM
Dynamic Quality Control .... DQC
Dynamic Radius [*Tires*] .... DR
Dynamic RAM [*Random Access Memory*] (NITA) .... DRAM
Dynamic Random Access Mechanization .... DRAM
Dynamic Random Access Memory [*Computer science*] .... d-RAM
Dynamic Random Access Memory [*Computer science*] (ACRL) .... DRAM
Dynamic Range .... DR
Dynamic Real-Time Information Processing System (MCD) .... DRIPS
Dynamic Recipe Control Table .... DRCT
Dynamic Reflectance Spectroscopy .... DRS
Dynamic Reliability, Availability, and Maintainability .... DRAM
Dynamic Reliability Instantaneous Forecasting Technique .... DRIFT
Dynamic Reprocessing (NITA) .... DR
Dynamic Research Console .... DRC
Dynamic Resolver Angle Digitizer .... DYRAD
Dynamic Response Index .... DRI
Dynamic Response of Articulate Machinery [*MDI*] (NITA) .... DRAM
Dynamic Runout [*Automotive engineering*] .... DRO
Dynamic Safety Suspension [*Automotive engineering*] .... DSA
Dynamic Scattering Mode (IEEE) .... DSM
Dynamic Self-Verification (IAA) .... DSV
Dynamic Sequence Parameters (SAA) .... DSP
Dynamic Sequencing and Segregation Model [*Computer science*] (OA) ..... DSSM
Dynamic Sequential Control (AAG) .... DSC
Dynamic Shear Adhesion (PDAA) .... DSA
Dynamic Shift Register .... DSR
Dynamic Sideband Regulator .... DSR
Dynamic Signal Analyzer .... DSA
Dynamic Simulated Optimized Contact .... DSOC
Dynamic Simulation Language [*Computer science*] .... DSL
Dynamic Simulation of Auto and Passenger Rail Transports .... DART
Dynamic Simulation System (MCD) .... DSS
Dynamic Slide Compensator .... DSC
Dynamic Soaring [*Space flight*] .... DYNA-SOAR
Dynamic Spatial Reconstructor [*X-ray scanning machine*] .... DSR
Dynamic Speaker .... DSP
Dynamic Special-Use Airspace [*FAA*] (TAG) .... DSUA
Dynamic Spring Analysis .... DSA
Dynamic Stability Control [*Automotive*] .... DSC
Dynamic Stability Test (NASA) .... DST
Dynamic Standby Computer (KSC) .... DSC
Dynamic Steady State .... DSS
Dynamic Stiffness Modulus (PDAA) .... DSM
Dynamic Storage Allocation Language [*in FORTRAN*] [*Computer science*] .... DYSTAL
Dynamic Storage Analog Computer (IEEE) .... DYSAC
Dynamic Storage Analog Computer .... DYSTAC
Dynamic Storage Area (CMD) .... DSA
Dynamic Subscription Promotion .... DSP
Dynamic Support Program [*Computer science*] .... DSP
Dynamic Support System (MCD) .... DSS
Dynamic Synchro Data Service [*or Source*] (MCD) .... DSDS
Dynamic System Electronics .... DSE
Dynamic System Synthesizer .... DSS
Dynamic Systems Analyzer [*General Electric Co.*] (IEEE) .... DYNASAR
Dynamic Systems Test Rig [*Helicopters*] [*Army*] (RDA) .... DSTR
Dynamic Tactical Area File [*Military*] (CAAL) .... DTAF
Dynamic Tactical Simulator - Enhanced .... DYNTACS-X
Dynamic Tear (OA) .... DT
Dynamic Tear Energy (PDAA) .... DTE
Dynamic Tensile Modulus [*Materials testing*] .... DTM
Dynamic Test Fixture [*Military*] (MCD) .... DTF
Dynamic Test Model [*Spacecraft*] .... DTM
Dynamic Test Panel .... DTP
Dynamic Test System .... DTS
Dynamic Test Target [*Military*] (CAAL) .... DTT
Dynamic Test Vehicle .... DTV
Dynamic Tester .... DT
Dynamic Testing Program (AAG) .... DTP
Dynamic Time Warping .... DTW
Dynamic to Static .... D/S
Dynamic Tongue and Palatometric Shapes [*System to help the deaf speak*] .... DYTAPS
Dynamic Track Following [*Electronics*] .... DTF
Dynamic Tracking Suspension System [*Automotive engineering*] .... DTSS
Dynamic Track-Tensioning System [*Army*] (RDA) .... DTTS
Dynamic Translation Buffer .... DTB
Dynamic Universal Assembly Language [*Computer science*] .... DUAL
Dynamic Vacuum Seal .... DVS
Dynamic Velocity Taper (PDAA) .... DVT
Dynamic Ventures, Inc. [*ICAO designator*] (FAAC) .... DYN
Dynamic Vertical Sensor (IAA) .... DVS

Dynamic Visual Acuity (IEEE) .... DVA
Dynamic Visual Camouflage [*Army*] (INF) .... DVC
Dynamic Weather Display .... DWD
Dynamic X-Ray Diffraction [*Physics*] .... DXRD
Dynamical Extended Range Forecasting [*Meteorology*] .... DERF
Dynamical Tactical Simulator .... DYNTACS
Dynamically Adaptive Multicarrier Quadrative Amplitude Modulation [*Computer science*] .... DAMQAM
Dynamically Adaptive Receiver Transmitter (CAAL) .... DART
Dynamically Decoupled Steering [*Automotive engineering*] .... DDS
Dynamically Equivalent Equal-Volume Ellipsoid .... DEEVE
Dynamically Positioned .... DP
Dynamically Redefinable Character Set [*Computer science*] .... DRCS
Dynamically Tuned Gyro [*Inertial sensor*] (IEEE) .... DTG
Dynamically-Correlated Domain [*Physics*] .... DCD
Dynamically-Loaded Engineering Bearing Analysis (PDAA) .... DEBA
Dynamiclly Alterable System (PDAA) .... DAS
Dynamics, Acoustics, and Thermal Environment (NASA) .... DATE
Dynamics Analyzer Programmer [*Computer program*] (NITA) .... DYANA
Dynamics Augmentation Experiment (MCD) .... DAE
Dynamics Corp. Amer [*NYSE symbol*] (TTSB) .... DYA
Dynamics Corp. of America [*NYSE symbol*] (SPSG) .... DYA
Dynamics Corp. of America [*Associated Press*] (SAG) .... DynAm
Dynamics Differential Analyzer (IEEE) .... DDA
Dynamics Explorer [*NASA*] .... DE
Dynamics International Gardening Association (EA) .... DIGA
Dynamics Research [*NASDAQ symbol*] (TTSB) .... DRCO
Dynamics Research Corp. .... DRC
Dynamics Research Corp. [*NASDAQ symbol*] (NQ) .... DRCO
Dynamics Research Corp. [*Associated Press*] (SAG) .... DynRsh
Dynamite (MSA) .... DYNMT
Dynamiting [*FBI standardized term*] .... DYN
Dynamo (IAA) .... DM
Dynamo (MSA) .... DYN
Dynamo Alert System (AAG) .... DAS
Dynamo Electric Amplifier .... DEA
Dynamo Management System (AAG) .... DMS
Dynamo Resources [*Vancouver Stock Exchange symbol*] .... DYR
Dynamogram .... DG
Dynamometer [*Engineering*] (DEN) .... DYN
Dynamometer [*Engineering*] .... DYNMT
Dynamometer [*Engineering*] (KSC) .... DYNO
Dynamotion/ATI [*NASDAQ symbol*] (TTSB) .... DYMO
Dynamotion ATI Corp. [*NASDAQ symbol*] (SAG) .... DYMO
Dynamotion ATI Corp. [*NASDAQ symbol*] (SAG) .... DYMP
Dynamotion ATI Corp. [*NASDAQ symbol*] (SAG) .... DYMZ
Dynamotion ATI Corp. [*Associated Press*] (SAG) .... Dyna
Dynamotion ATI Corp. [*Associated Press*] (SAG) .... Dynam
Dynamotion ATI Corp. [*Associated Press*] (SAG) .... Dynamo
Dynamotion/ATI Wrrt'A' [*NASDAQ symbol*] (TTSB) .... DYMOZ
DynaMotive Technologies [*NASDAQ symbol*] (TTSB) .... DYMTF
Dynamotor (IAA) .... D
Dynamotor (IAA) .... DM
Dynamotor (IAA) .... DYN
Dynamotor .... DYNM
Dynamotors [*JETDS nomenclature*] [*Military*] (CET) .... DY
Dynasty (BJA) .... Dyn
Dynasty Fan Club (EA) .... DFC
Dynasty Resources, Inc. [*Vancouver Stock Exchange symbol*] .... DYN
Dynatec International, Inc. [*Associated Press*] (SAG) .... Dyntcl
Dynatec International, Inc. [*NASDAQ symbol*] (NQ) .... DYNX
Dynatec Intl. [*NASDAQ symbol*] (TTSB) .... DYNX
Dynatech Corp. [*NASDAQ symbol*] (NQ) .... DYTC

Dynatech Corp. [*Associated Press*] (SAG) .... DytchC
Dynatech Research/Development Co., Cambridge, MA [*Library symbol Library of Congress*] (LCLS) .... MCD
Dynatronics Corp. [*NASDAQ symbol*] (TTSB) .... DYNT
Dynatronics Corp. [*Associated Press*] (SAG) .... DyntrCp
Dynatronics Laser Corp. [*NASDAQ symbol*] (NQ) .... DYNT
Dynatronics Laser Corp. [*Vancouver Stock Exchange symbol*] .... DYT
Dynayoke Deflection Yoke .... DDY
Dyne [*Unit of force*] [*Also, Dy, dyn Preferred unit is N, Newton*] .... D
Dyne [*Unit of force*] [*Also, D, dyn Preferred unit is N, Newton*] .... Dy
Dyne [*Unit of force*] [*Also, D Preferred unit is N, Newton*] (DEN) .... dyn
Dynein Defective Cilia [*Medicine*] .... DDC
Dynes per Centimeter .... DYN/CM
Dynes per Square Centimeter .... DYN/CM^2
Dynex Petroleum Ltd. [*Toronto Stock Exchange symbol*] .... DPL
Dynode (IAA) .... DY
Dynorphin [*Biochemistry*] .... DP
Dyonix Greentree Technologies, Inc. [*Vancouver Stock Exchange symbol*] .... DXG
D'Youville College, Buffalo, NY [*Library symbol Library of Congress*] (LCLS) .... NBuD
Dysart [*Australia Airport symbol*] (OAG) .... DYA
Dysart Branch, Haliburton County Public Library, Ontario [*Library symbol National Library of Canada*] (BIB) .... OHAD
Dysart Reporter, Dysart, IA [*Library symbol Library of Congress*] (LCLS) .... IaDysR
Dysautonomia Foundation (EA) .... DF
Dysbaric Osteonecrosis [*Scuba diving disorder*] .... DON
Dysfunctional Uterine Bleeding [*Gynecology*] (DAVI) .... DFB
Dysfunctional Uterine Bleeding [*Medicine*] .... DUB
Dysgerminoma [*Oncology*] .... DYS
Dyskaryosis, Index of [*Cytopathology*] .... DI
Dyskeratosis Congenita [*Medicine*] (DMAA) .... DC
Dyslexia Determination Test [*Educational test*] .... DDT
Dyslexia Screening Survey [*Psychology*] .... DSS
Dysmenorrhea [*Medicine*] .... DYSM
Dysplasia Epiphysealis Hemimelica [*Medicine*] (DMAA) .... DEH
Dysplasia-Associated Lesion or Mass [*Medicine*] .... DALM
Dysplastic Nevus Syndrome [*Medicine*] .... DNS
Dyspnea Index [*Medicine*] (DAVI) .... DI
Dyspnea on Exercise [*or Exertion*] [*Medicine*] .... DOE
Dyspnea on Exertion [*Medicine*] (DMAA) .... DOE
Dysprosium [*Chemical element*] .... Dy
Dysrhythmic Aggressive Behavior .... DAB
Dyssynergia Cerebellaris Myoclonica [*Medicine*] (DMAA) .... DCM
Dystonia Medical Research Foundation (EA) .... DMRF
Dystonia Musculorum Deformans [*Medicine*] .... DMD
Dystrophia Myotonica Protein Kinase [*An enzyme*] .... DMPK
Dystrophia Myotonica-Associated Homeodomain Protein [*Biochemistry*] .... DMAHP
Dystrophic Epidermolysis Bullosa [*Medicine*] .... DEB
Dystrophic Epidermolysis Bullosa Research Association of America (EA) .... DEBRA
Dystrophin Protein Complex [*Biochemistry*] .... DPC
Dystrophin-Associated Glycoprotein [*Biochemistry*] .... DAG
Dystrophin-Associated Protein [*Biochemistry*] .... DAP
Dystrophin-Glycoprotein Complex [*Biochemistry*] .... DGC
Dystrophin-Related Protein [*Biochemistry*] .... DRP
Dystrophy-Dystocia Syndrome [*Medicine*] (MAE) .... DDS
Dzaoudzi [*Comoro Islands*] [*Airport symbol*] (OAG) .... DZA
Dzaoudzi/Pamanzi [*Mayotte*] [*ICAO location identifier*] (ICLI) .... FMCZ
Dzhafr [*Former USSR Seismograph station code, US Geological Survey Closed*] (SEIS) .... DZH
Dzhergetal [*Former USSR Seismograph station code, US Geological Survey Closed*] (SEIS) .... DZT
Dzhizak [*Former USSR ICAO location identifier*] (ICLI) .... UTED

E

By Meaning

E & B Marine, Inc. [*NASDAQ symbol*] (SAG) ... EBMA
E. & J. Gallo Winery, Modesto, CA [*Library symbol Library of Congress*] (LCLS) ... CMGW
E. B. Eddy Co., Hull, Quebec [*Library symbol National Library of Canada*] (NLC) ... QHE
E. B. Eddy Co., Research and Technical Library, Hull, PQ, Canada [*Library symbol Library of Congress*] (LCLS) ... CaQHE
E. C. Brown Foundation (EA) ... ECBF
E. D. Jones Branch, Gloucester Public Library, Ontario [*Library symbol National Library of Canada*] (NLC) ... OGEDJ
E. D'Appolonia Consulting Engineers, Pittsburgh, PA [*Library symbol Library of Congress*] (LCLS) ... PPiE
E. E. Oliver School, Fairview, Alberta [*Library symbol National Library of Canada*] (BIB) ... AFVES
E. F. Benson Society (EAIO) ... EFBS
E. F. Hutton & Co., Philadelphia, PA [*Library symbol Library of Congress Obsolete*] (LCLS) ... PPEFH
E. F. Schumacher Society (EA) ... EFSS
E for M Corp. [*NASDAQ symbol*] (SAG) ... EFMC
E. I. Du Pont de Nemours & Co., Aiken, SC [*Library symbol Library of Congress*] (LCLS) ... ScAiD
E. I. Du Pont de Nemours & Co., Benger Laboratory, Waynesboro, VA [*Library symbol Library of Congress*] (LCLS) ... ViWbD
E. I. Du Pont de Nemours & Co., Carney's Point Development Laboratory, Carney's Point, NJ [*Library symbol Library of Congress*] (LCLS) ... NjCarpD
E. I. Du Pont de Nemours & Co., Eastern Laboratory Library, Gibbstown, NJ [*Library symbol Library of Congress*] (LCLS) ... NjGiD
E. I. Du Pont de Nemours & Co., Electrochemical Department, Niagara Falls, NY [*Library symbol Library of Congress*] (LCLS) ... NNiaD
E. I. Du Pont de Nemours & Co., Haskell Laboratory, Newark, DE [*OCLC symbol*] (OCLC) ... DLI
E. I. Du Pont de Nemours & Co., Jackson Laboratory, Wilmington, DE [*Library symbol Library of Congress*] (LCLS) ... DeWDJ
E. I. Du Pont de Nemours & Co., Jackson Laboratory, Wilmington, DE [*OCLC symbol*] (OCLC) ... DUJ
E. I. Du Pont de Nemours & Co., Lavoisier Library, Wilmington, DE [*Library symbol Library of Congress*] (LCLS) ... DeWDL
E. I. Du Pont de Nemours & Co., Marshall Laboratory, Philadelphia, PA [*Library symbol Library of Congress*] (LCLS) ... PPDM
E. I. Du Pont de Nemours & Co., Martinsville, VA [*Library symbol Library of Congress*] (LCLS) ... ViMvD
E. I. Du Pont de Nemours & Co., Sabine River Works, Orange, TX [*Library symbol Library of Congress*] (LCLS) ... TXOrD
E. I. Du Pont de Nemours & Co., Stine Laboratory, Newark, DE [*Library symbol Library of Congress*] (LCLS) ... DeND
E. I. Du Pont de Nemours & Co., Technical Library, Wilmington, DE [*Library symbol Library of Congress*] (LCLS) ... DeWDT
E. I. Du Pont de Nemours & Co., Yerkes Research Laboratory, Buffalo, NY [*Library symbol Library of Congress*] (LCLS) ... NBuDY
E. I. DuPont de Nemours & Co., Lavoisier Library, Wilmington, DE [*OCLC symbol*] (OCLC) ... DUP
E. J. Noble Hospital, Medical Library, Alexandria Bay, NY [*Library symbol Library of Congress*] (LCLS) ... NAleNH
E. J. Wilson High School Library, Spencerport, NY [*OCLC symbol*] (OCLC) ... RWA
E. Jack Sharpe Public Library, White Cloud, MI [*Library symbol Library of Congress*] (LCLS) ... MiWhc
E Lacte [*With Milk*] [*Pharmacy*] ... E LACT
E Magazine [*A publication*] (BRI) ... E Mag
E. Merck [*Laboratories*] ... EM
E. Merck AG [*Germany*] [*Research code symbol*] ... AK
E. Merck AG [*Germany*] [*Research code symbol*] ... St
E. Merck AG, Darmstadt, Germany [*Library symbol Library of Congress*] (LCLS) ... GyDaM
E. O. Hulburt Center for Space Research (MCD) ... HCSR
E Quolibet Vehiculo [*In Any Vehicle*] [*Pharmacy*] ... E QUOL VEH
E Quovis Liquido [*In Any Liquid*] [*Pharmacy*] ... E QUOV LIQ
E. R. Squibb & Sons [*Research code symbol*] ... C
E. R. Squibb & Sons [*Research code symbol*] ... SF
E. R. Squibb & Sons [*Research code symbol*] ... SQ
E. R. Squibb & Sons Ltd., Montreal, Quebec [*Library symbol National Library of Canada*] (NLC) ... QMERS
E. R. Squibb & Sons, Princeton, NJ [*Library symbol Library of Congress*] (LCLS) ... NjPERS
E. R. Squibb & Sons, Princeton, NJ [*OCLC symbol*] (OCLC) ... SQU
E Vino [*In Wine*] [*Pharmacy*] ... E VIN
E Vivis Discessit [*Departed from Life*] [*Latin*] (BARN) ... E VIV DISC
EA Engineering Systems [*Associated Press*] (SAG) ... EA Eng
EA Engineering Systems [*NASDAQ symbol*] (NQ) ... EACO
EA Engr Science/Tech [*NASDAQ symbol*] (TTSB) ... EACO
EA Industries [*NYSE symbol*] (TTSB) ... EA
EAA [*Experimental Aircraft Association*] **Antique/Classic Division** (EA) ... EAAACD
EAA [*Experimental Aircraft Association*] **Aviation Foundation** (EA) ... EAAAF
EAA [*Experimental Aircraft Association*] **Ultralight Association** [*Defunct*] (EA) ... EAAUA
Each ... EA
Each Accident [*Insurance*] ... EA ACC
Each and Every Accident [*Insurance*] (AIA) ... E & EA
Each and Every Loss [*Insurance*] (AIA) ... E & EL
Each and Every Occurrence [*Insurance*] (AIA) ... E & EO
Each Community Helps Others [*Environmental Protection Agency*] ... ECHO
Each Face [*Technical drawings*] ... EF
Each Layer [*Technical drawings*] ... EL
Each Less Than ... ELT
Each Military Department (LAIN) ... EMD
Each More Than ... EMT
Each Pays Own Postage ... EPOP
Each Person [*Insurance*] ... EA PER
Each Thousand Foot Level (FAAC) ... ETFL
Each Vehicle [*Insurance*] ... EA VEH
Each Way (MSA) ... EW
EADAS [*Engineering and Administrative Data Acquisition System*] **Traffic Data Center** [*Bell System*] ... ETDC
Eadem [*The Same*] [*Pharmacy*] ... EAD
Eagar, AZ [*FM radio station call letters*] (RBYB) ... KTHQ-FM
Eager to Grab Your Pretty Top [*Correspondence*] [*Bowdlerized version*] (DSUE) ... EGYPT
Eagle [*Alaska*] [*Airport symbol*] (OAG) ... EAA
Eagle [*Colorado*] [*Seismograph station code, US Geological Survey Closed*] (SEIS) ... EGC
Eagle ... EGL
Eagle Aero, Inc. [*ICAO designator*] (FAAC) ... ICR
Eagle Air [*ICAO designator*] (AD) ... IS
Eagle Air Ltd. [*Switzerland ICAO designator*] (FAAC) ... EAB
Eagle Air Ltd. [*Iceland*] [*ICAO designator*] (FAAC) ... ISL
Eagle Airways Ltd. [*British ICAO designator*] (FAAC) ... EGT
Eagle and Younge's English Tithe Cases [*A publication*] (DLA) ... E & Y
Eagle and Younge's English Tithe Cases [*A publication*] (DLA) ... Eag & Y
Eagle and Younge's English Tithe Cases [*A publication*] (DLA) ... Eag & Yo
Eagle Aviation [*ICAO designator*] (AD) ... EX
Eagle Aviation [*British*] [*FAA designator*] (FAAC) ... GYP
Eagle Aviation Luftfahrt Ges.MbH [*Austria*] [*FAA designator*] (FAAC) ... EAV
Eagle BancGroup, Inc. [*NASDAQ symbol*] (SAG) ... EGLB
Eagle BancGroup, Inc. [*Associated Press*] (SAG) ... EglBGp
Eagle Bancorp, Inc. [*Associated Press*] (SAG) ... EagleBcp
Eagle Bancorp, Inc. [*NASDAQ symbol*] (NQ) ... EBCI
Eagle Bancshares [*NASDAQ symbol*] (TTSB) ... EBSI
Eagle Bancshares [*Associated Press*] (SAG) ... EglBsh
Eagle Bancshares, Inc. [*NASDAQ symbol*] (NQ) ... EBSI
Eagle Bend Public Library, Eagle Bend, MN [*Library symbol*] [*Library of Congress*] (LCLS) ... MnEb
Eagle Bend School, Eagle Bend, MN [*Library symbol*] [*Library of Congress*] (LCLS) ... MnEbS
Eagle Butte [*South Dakota*] [*Seismograph station code, US Geological Survey*] (SEIS) ... EBS
Eagle Butte, SD [*Television station call letters*] ... KPSD-TV
Eagle, CO [*Location identifier FAA*] (FAAL) ... EGE
Eagle, CO [*FM radio station call letters*] (RBYB) ... KTUN-FM
Eagle, CO [*Location identifier FAA*] (FAAL) ... OWE
Eagle Commuter Airlines [*ICAO designator*] (AD) ... EE
Eagle, Eagle Grove, IA [*Library symbol Library of Congress*] (LCLS) ... IaEE
Eagle Elementary Consolidated School District 43, Streator, IL [*Library symbol Library of Congress*] (LCLS) ... IStrESD
Eagle European Airways [*British*] [*FAA designator*] (FAAC) ... EAU
Eagle Finance [*NASDAQ symbol*] (TTSB) ... EFCW
Eagle Finance Corp. [*Associated Press*] (SAG) ... EaglFnce
Eagle Finance Corp. [*NASDAQ symbol*] (SAG) ... EFCW
Eagle Financial [*Associated Press*] (SAG) ... EaglFncl
Eagle Financial [*NASDAQ symbol*] (SAG) ... EGFC
Eagle Financial Corp. (MHDW) ... EAGL
Eagle Flying Services Ltd. [*British ICAO designator*] (FAAC) ... EAG
Eagle Food Centers [*NASDAQ symbol*] (SAG) ... EGLE

Eagle Food Centers, Inc. [*Associated Press*] (SAG) EglFd
Eagle Forum (EA) EF
[*The*] **Eagle Foundation** [*Defunct*] (EA) TEF
Eagle Grove, IA [*FM radio station call letters*] KJYL
Eagle Grove Junior College [*Iowa*] EGJC
Eagle Grove Public Library, Eagle Grove, IA [*Library symbol Library of Congress*] (LCLS) IaE
Eagle Hardware & Garden [*NASDAQ symbol*] (TTSB) EAGL
Eagle Hardware & Garden, Inc. [*NASDAQ symbol*] (SAG) EAGL
Eagle Hardware & Garden, Inc. [*Associated Press*] (SAG) EglHrd
Eagle, ID [*AM radio station call letters*] KIDH
Eagle, ID [*FM radio station call letters*] KXLT
Eagle Industry [*Vancouver Stock Exchange symbol*] EAL
Eagle Jet Charter, Inc. [*FAA designator*] (FAAC) EGJ
Eagle Lake, TX [*Location identifier FAA*] (FAAL) ELA
Eagle Pacific Indus [*NASDAQ symbol*] (TTSB) EPII
Eagle Pacific Industries, Inc. [*Associated Press*] (SAG) EaglPac
Eagle Pacific Industries, Inc. [*NASDAQ symbol*] (SAG) EPII
Eagle Pass [*Texas*] [*Airport symbol Obsolete*] (OAG) EGP
Eagle Pass/Municipal [*Texas*] [*ICAO location identifier*] (ICLI) KEGP
Eagle Pass Resources [*Vancouver Stock Exchange symbol*] EGP
Eagle Pass, TX [*FM radio station call letters*] (RBYB) KEPI
Eagle Pass, TX [*AM radio station call letters*] KEPS
Eagle Pass, TX [*FM radio station call letters*] KEPX
Eagle Pass, TX [*FM radio station call letters*] KINL
Eagle Pass, TX [*Television station call letters*] KVAW
Eagle Point, OR [*FM radio station call letters*] (RBYB) KZZE
Eagle Point Software [*NASDAQ symbol*] (TTSB) EGPT
Eagle Point Software Corp. [*Associated Press*] (SAG) EagPnt
Eagle Point Software Corp. [*NASDAQ symbol*] (SAG) EGPT
Eagle Precision Technologies, Inc. [*Toronto Stock Exchange symbol*] EGL
Eagle Public Library, Eagle, CO [*Library symbol Library of Congress*] (LCLS) CoEag
Eagle Public Library, Eagle, ID [*Library symbol*] [*Library of Congress*] (LCLS) IdEa
Eagle Ridge Resources Ltd. [*Vancouver Stock Exchange symbol*] ERR
Eagle River, AK [*AM radio station call letters*] KFFR
Eagle River Interactive [*NASDAQ symbol*] (TTSB) ERIV
Eagle River Interactive, Inc. [*Associated Press*] (SAG) EgleRiv
Eagle River Interactive, Inc. [*NASDAQ symbol*] (SAG) ERIV
Eagle River Mines [*Vancouver Stock Exchange symbol*] EGR
Eagle River, WI [*Location identifier FAA*] (FAAL) EGV
Eagle River, WI [*AM radio station call letters*] WERL
Eagle River, WI [*FM radio station call letters*] WRJO
Eagle River, WI [*TV station call letters*] (RBYB) WYOW-TV
Eagle Rock Public Library, Eagle Rock, CA [*Library symbol Library of Congress*] (LCLS) CEr
Eagle Squadron [*British military*] (DMA) ES
Eagle USA Airfreight [*NASDAQ symbol*] (TTSB) EUSA
Eagle USA Airfreight, Inc. [*Associated Press*] (SAG) EgleUSA
Eagle USA Airfreight, Inc. [*NASDAQ symbol*] (SAG) EUSA
Eagle Valley Environmentalists (EA) EVE
Eagle's Basal Medium with Earle's Salts [*Culture medium*] EBME
Eagle's Law of Tithes [*2nd ed.*] [*1836*] [*A publication*] (DLA) Eag T
Eagle's Law of Tithes [*2nd ed.*] [*1836*] [*A publication*] (ILCA) ELT
Eagle's Magistrate's Pocket Companion [*A publication*] (DLA) Eag Mag Com
Eagle's Minimum Essential Medium [*Culture medium*] EMEM
Eagle's Nest [*New York*] [*Seismograph station code, US Geological Survey*] (SEIS) EGN
Eaglesham Municipal Library, Alberta [*Library symbol National Library of Canada*] (NLC) AEAM
Eaglesham Municipal Library, Eaglesham, AB, Canada [*Library symbol*] [*Library of Congress*] (LCLS) CaAEaM
Eaglesham School, Alberta [*Library symbol National Library of Canada*] (BIB) AEAGLS
Eaglet Mines Ltd. [*Toronto Stock Exchange symbol Vancouver Stock Exchange symbol*] EAG
Ealing College of Higher Education [*England*] ECHE
Ealing Electro-Optics [*British*] EEO
E&B Marine [*NASDAQ symbol*] (TTSB) EBMA
Ear and Mouth E&M
Ear and Mouth Lead [*A headpiece unit used by telephone operators and broadcasters*] (WDMC) E&M leads
Ear Clamp [*Medicine*] EC
Ear Falls Public Library, Ear Falls, ON, Canada [*Library symbol Library of Congress*] (LCLS) CaOEf
Ear Falls Public Library, Ontario [*Library symbol National Library of Canada*] (NLC) OEF
Ear Foundation (EA) EF
Ear, Nose, and Throat [*Medical Officer designation*] [*British*] E
Ear Research Institute [*Later, HEI*] (EA) ERI
Earl E
Earl K. Long Hospital, Medical Library, Baton Rouge, LA [*Library symbol Library of Congress*] (LCLS) LBrLH
Earl L. Vandermeulen High School, Port Jefferson, NY [*Library symbol Library of Congress*] (LCLS) NPjVH
Earl Marshal [*British*] EM
Earl Marshal's Secretary [*Pseudonym used by James Dalloway*] EMS
Earl of Chester's Imperial Yeomanry [*British military*] (DMA) ECIY
Earl of Chester's Yeomanry Cavalry [*British military*] (DMA) ECYC
Earl of March Secondary School, Kanata, Ontario [*Library symbol National Library of Canada*] (NLC) OKEMS
Earl Park, IN [*FM radio station call letters*] WIBN
Earl Park Public Library, Earl Park, IN [*Library symbol Library of Congress*] (LCLS) InEaP
Earl Thomas Conley Fan Club (EA) ETCFC
Earl Township Public Library, Earlville, IL [*Library symbol Library of Congress*] (LCLS) IEar
Earl Warren Legal Training Program (EA) EWLTP
Earl Weaver Baseball [*Computer game*] EWB
Earles Balanced Salt Solution [*Media for cell culture*] EBSS
Earle's Salt Solution (OA) ESS
Earlham College, Richmond, IN [*OCLC symbol*] (OCLC) IEC
Earlham College, Richmond, IN [*Library symbol Library of Congress*] (LCLS) InRE
Earlham Echo, Earlham, IA [*Library symbol Library of Congress*] (LCLS) IaEarE
[*The*] **Earlham Review** [*A publication*] ER
Earliest Arrival Date (AABC) EAD
Earliest Arrival Time EAT
Earliest Delivery Date [*Navy*] (DOMA) EDD
Earliest Due Date EDD
Earliest Finish Date EFD
Earliest Possible Arrival Time (MCD) EPAT
Earliest Possible Date EPD
Earliest Practicable Date EARLPRADATE
Earliest Practicable Date (AFIT) EPD
Earliest Scram Set Point [*Nuclear energy*] (NRCH) ESSP
Earliest Start Date ESD
Earliest Time [*Business term*] ET
Earliest Time to Launch [*Navy*] (CAAL) ETL
Earliest Work Listed EWL
Earlimart, CA [*FM radio station call letters*] (RBYB) KNAC
Earls Colne [*British ICAO location identifier*] (ICLI) EGSR
Earlton [*Canada*] [*Airport symbol*] (OAG) YXR
Earlton, ON [*ICAO location identifier*] (ICLI) CYXR
Earlville Community Unit, School District 9, Earlville, IL [*Library symbol Library of Congress*] (LCLS) IEarSD
Early [*Genetics*] E
Early (ROG) EA
Early (VRA) ea
Early ERLY
Early (FAAC) ERY
Early Acquisition System [*Army*] (AABC) EASY
Early American EA
Early American Coppers (EA) EAC
Early American Industries Association (EA) EAIA
Early American Life Insurance Association (EA) EAL
Early American Society (EA) EAS
Early and Periodic Screening, Diagnosis, and Treatment EPSDT
Early Antigen [*Immunochemistry*] EA
Early Apollo Scientific Experiments Package [*or Payload*] [*NASA*] EASEP
Early Assistance Unit EAU
Early Babylonian Personal Names [*A publication*] (BJA) EBPN
Early Bargain [*Stock exchange term British*] (DCTA) EB
Early B-cell Factor [*Biochemistry*] EBF
Early Bedtime (DAVI) EBT
Early Birds of Aviation [*Defunct*] (EA) EBA
Early Bronze [*Age*] EB
Early Burst [*Premature explosion of a warhead*] EB
Early Capability Orbital Manned Station ECOMS
Early Childhood (ADA) EC
Early Childhood Center, Freeport, NY [*Library symbol*] [*Library of Congress*] (LCLS) NFreeEC
Early Childhood Day Care Center [*University of Alabama*] [*Research center*] (RCD) ECDCC
Early Childhood Education ECE
Early Childhood Education Journal [*A publication*] (BRI) ECEJ
Early Childhood Embedded Figures Test (EDAC) ECEFT
Early Childhood Health ECH
Early Childhood/Primary EC/P
Early Childhood Resource Center ECRC
Early Childhood Services (ADA) ECS
Early Childhood Teachers' Association [*Australia*] ECTA
Early Churches in Palestine [*A publication*] (BJA) ECP
Early Closing Association [*British*] ECA
Early College Mathematics Placement Testing Program EMPT
Early Comparability Analysis (RDA) ECA
Early Comparability Analysis Time Requirement [*Army*] ECATR
Early Day Motion [*British*] (BARN) edm
Early Decision Plan [*Medical school entrance program*] EDP
Early Departure Authorized EDA
Early Departure Release At (SAA) EDR
Early Deploying Armored Bridge (MCD) EDAB
Early Deploying Unit (MCD) EDU
Early Development Planning EDP
Early Diastolic Murmur [*Medicine*] EDM
Early Docking Demonstration System (IAA) EDDS
Early Docking Demonstration System (SAA) EES
Early Dry Breakfast [*Medicine*] EDB
Early Education for Children with Disabilities Program Project [*Established under the Individuals with Disabilities Education Act (IDEA)*] (PAZ) EEPCD
Early Emissions Reduction [*Environmental science*] EER
Early English [*Language, etc.*] EE
Early English [*Language*] (DGA) EENG
Early English Text Society [*Oxford, England*] EETS
Early Entry Lethality and Survivability [*Military*] (INF) EELS
Early Evening Nautical Twilight [*Navigation*] (MCD) EENT
Early Failure Detection EFD
Early Finish EF
Early Finish Time EFT

Early Four Cylinder Chevrolet Club, International [*Defunct*] (EA) .... EFCCCI
Early Fuel Evaporation [*Automotive technology*] .... EFE
Early Grand Knight Templar [*Freemasonry*] (ROG) .... EGKT
Early Greek Philosophy [*1930*] [*A publication*] (OCD) .... EGP
Early Growth Response [*Biochemistry*] .... EGR
Early Heart Attack Care .... EHAC
Early Hebrew (BJA) .... EH
Early Hebrew Orthography [*A publication*] (BJA) .... EHO
Early Hemi Association (EA) .... EHA
Early History of Assyria [*A publication*] (BJA) .... EHA
Early Initial Operational Capability (MCD) .... EIOC
Early Initial Operational-Information Management System (MCD) .... EIO-IMS
Early Intervention .... EI
Early Intervention Developmental Profile [*Speech and language therapy*] (DAVI) .... EIDP
Early Intervention Program .... EIP
Early Intervention Research Institute [*Utah State University*] [*Research center*] (RCD) .... EIRI
Early Iron Age [*Archeology*] (BJA) .... EI
Early Iron Age [*Archeology*] .... EIA
Early Labeled-Fragment Hybridization [*Analytical biochemistry*] .... ELFH
Early Landed Cognac [*British*] .... ELC
Early Language Milestone Scale (MEDA) .... ELM
Early Latent [*Medicine*] .... EL
Early Latent Infection [*Medicine*] .... ELI
Early Launch Air Defense System (MCD) .... ELADS
Early Life History [*Marine science*] (OSRA) .... ELH
Early Life History (USDC) .... ELH
Early Light Breakfast [*Medicine*] .... ELB
Early Lunar Flare .... ELF
Early Lunar Shelter [*NASA*] (KSC) .... ELS
Early Manned Planetary-Interplanetary Round Trip Experiment .... EMPIRE
Early Medical School Acceptance Program (GAGS) .... EMSAP
Early Minoan [*Archeology*] (BJA) .... EM
Early Missile Test .... EMT
Early Modern English (BARN) .... E Mod E
Early Modern English [*Language, etc.*] .... EMNE
Early Money Is Like Yeast [*Political fund raising campaign for female Democrats running for the US Senate*] .... EMILY
Early Morning Specimen [*Medicine*] .... EMS
Early Negative .... EN
Early Neonatal Neurobehavior Scale (MEDA) .... ENNS
Early News, Early, IA [*Library symbol Library of Congress*] (LCLS) .... IaEaryN
Early Onset Cerebellar Ataxia [*Medicine*] .... EOCA
Early Operational Assessment [*Military*] .... EOA
Early Philosophies [*A publication*] .... EP
Early Positive .... EP
Early Postsurgical Fitting [*Medicine*] .... EPSF
Early Pregnancy Factor [*Medicine*] (DMAA) .... EPF
Early Pregnancy Test .... EPT
Early Prenatal Karyotype [*Medicine*] (DAVI) .... EPK
Early Programming Language [*Computer science*] .... EPL
Early Prolific Straightneck Summer Squash .... EPS
Early Psychosis Prevention and Intervention Centre [*Australia*] .... EPPIC
Early Receptor Potential [*of the eye*] .... ERP
Early Release (MCD) .... ER
Early Renal Failure [*Medicine*] .... ERF
Early Retirement Adjustment (EERA) .... ERA
Early Retirement Incentive Program [*Generic term*] .... ERIP
Early Retirement Opportunity [*Business term*] .... ERO
Early School Personality Questionnaire [*Psychology*] .... ESPQ
Early Screening Inventory [*Child development test*] .... ESI
Early Settlers Association of the Western Reserve (EA) .... ESAWR
Early Shock [*Medicine*] .... ES
Early Site Review [*Nuclear energy*] (NRCH) .... ESR
Early Site Review Report [*Nuclear energy*] (NRCH) .... ESRR
Early Site Safety Analysis Report [*Nuclear energy*] (NRCH) .... ESSAR
Early Sites Research Society (EA) .... ESRS
Early Start Time .... EST
Early Storage Reserve .... ESR
Early Successional [*Botany*] .... ES
Early Supplier Involvement (AAGC) .... ESI
Early Support Program (HGAA) .... ESP
Early Suppression Fast Response [*Sprinkler program for fire protection*] .... ESFR
Early Systolic Paradox [*Cardiology*] (DAVI) .... ESP
Early Thrust Termination .... ETT
Early to Mid-Holocene Transition .... EMHT
Early Token Release [*Computer science*] .... ETR
Early Treatment Diabetic Retinopathy Study .... ETDRS
Early Typewriter Collectors Association (EA) .... ETC
Early User Test and Evaluation [*Army*] .... EUTE
Early User Test and Experimentation [*DoD*] .... EUTE
Early Valve Actuation [*or Actuator*] [*Nuclear energy*] (NRCH) .... EVA
Early Vendor Involvement Program [*Automotive engineering*] .... EVI
Early Warning [*Air Force*] .... EW
Early Warning Adjunct .... EWA
Early Warning Air Defense (NATG) .... EWAD
Early Warning Aircraft (MCD) .... EWAC
Early Warning and Control Aircraft System (IEEE) .... EWCAS
Early Warning and Control Squadron [*Air Force*] .... EW & CSq
Early Warning and Monitoring System (MCD) .... EWAMS
Early Warning/Attack Assessment .... EWA
Early Warning Broadcast Net [*DoD*] .... EWBN
Early Warning Change Proposal (MCD) .... EWCP
Early Warning/Control and Reporting Post .... EW/CRP
Early Warning Data Transmission (NATG) .... EWDT
Early Warning Fighter .... EWF
Early Warning/Ground Control Intercept [*RADAR*] .... EW/GCI
Early Warning Notification .... EWN
Early Warning Observation Teams (CINC) .... EWOTS
Early Warning RADAR [*Air Force*] .... EWR
Early Warning Receiver (DWSG) .... EWR
Early Warning Squadron [*Symbol*] (MCD) .... VW
Early Warning System .... EWS
Early Warning Threat Analysis Display .... EWTAD
Early Warning/Threat Assessment .... EW/TA
Early-Break-Make [*Computer science*] .... EBM
Early-Closing Day [*British*] .... EC
Early-Closing Day [*British*] .... ECD
Early-Make-Break [*Computer science*] .... EMB
Early-Morning Fuzzy Thinking .... EMFT
Earlysville, VA [*AM radio station call letters*] .... WKTR
Earned Average [*Baseball*] .... Er Av
Earned Growth Rate [*Finance*] (ODBW) .... EGR
Earned Hour Ratio (NASA) .... EHR
Earned Income .... EI
Earned Income Credit .... EIC
Earned Income Tax Credit .... EITC
Earned Loss Ratio [*Insurance*] .... ELR
Earned Premium [*Insurance*] .... EP
Earned Premium to Incurred Loss Ratio [*Insurance*] .... E/I
Earned Run [*Baseball*] .... ER
Earned Run Average [*Baseball*] .... ERA
Earned Self-Image [*Psychology*] .... ESI
Earned Surplus .... ES
Earned Value .... EV
Earned Value Analysis (NASA) .... EVA
Earning Power [*Business term*] .... EP
Earnings [*Finance*] .... E
Earnings and Profit (ADA) .... E & P
Earnings and Profits Calculation System .... EPCS
Earnings Before Interest .... EBI
Earnings Before Interest and After Taxes [*Accounting*] (PDAA) .... EBIAT
Earnings before Interest and Taxes [*Accounting*] .... EBIT
Earnings before Interest Taxes and Depreciation .... EBITD
Earnings before Interest, Taxes, Depreciation, and Amortization [*Investment term*] (DFIT) .... EBITA
Earnings before Interest, Taxes, Depreciation, and Amortization [*Business term*] .... EBITDA
Earnings per Share [*Finance*] .... EPS
Earnings per Share Issued [*Finance*] .... EPSI
Earnings Price [*Investment term*] .... EP
Earnings Price Ratio .... EPR
Earnings Record (Wage Record) [*Social Security Administration*] (OICC) .... ER(WR)
Earnings Report [*Business term*] .... ER
Earnings-at-Risk [*Incentive pay plan*] .... EAR
Earnings-Before Interest, Taxes, Depreciation, and Amortization [*Finance*] .... EBITDA
Earnings-Related National Insurance Contribution [*British*] (DCTA) .... ERNIC
Earnings-Related Supplement [*British*] .... ERS
Earnshaw's Gold Coast Judgments [*1909-10*] [*Ghana*] [*A publication*] (DLA) .... Earn
Earp, Joseph O., Seattle WA [*STAC*] .... EJO
Earphone Amplifier .... EA
Ears, Nose, and Throat .... EN & T
Ears, Nose, and Throat .... ENT
Earth [*Wind triangle problems and relative movement problems*] .... E
Earth (IAA) .... EA
Earth [*Freight*] .... ERTH
Earth .... ERTH
Earth and Ocean Dynamic Applications Program [*NASA*] (PDAA) .... EODAP
Earth and Ocean Physics [*NASA*] (NASA) .... EOP
Earth and Ocean Physics Applications Program [*NASA*] .... EOPAP
Earth Aspect Sensor .... EAS
Earth Awareness Foundation (EA) .... EAF
Earth Central Angle .... ECA
Earth Closet [*British*] (ROG) .... EC
Earth Communications Office (EERA) .... ECO
Earth Conservation Corps .... ECC
Earth Continuity Conductor [*Electronics*] (BARN) .... ECC
Earth Council [*Costa Rica*] (EERA) .... EC
Earth Coverage Horizon Measurement (PDAA) .... ECHM
Earth Coverage Horn [*Satellite communications*] .... ECH
Earth Crust Formation .... ECF
Earth Departure Window [*Aerospace*] .... EDW
Earth Dynamics Program [*Smithsonian Astrophysical Observatory*] .... EDP
Earth Ecology Foundation (EA) .... EEF
Earth Entry Module [*NASA*] (KSC) .... EEM
Earth Environment University Roundtable [*of America*] .... EEUR
Earth Equatorial Plane .... EEP
Earth Exchange Museum [*Sydney, New South Wales, Australia*] .... EEM
Earth Far Horizon [*NASA*] (KSC) .... EFH
Earth First (EA) .... EF
Earth Garden [*A publication*] .... Earth G
Earth Geodetic Satellite [*Air Force*] .... ERGS
Earth Horizon Scanner .... EHS
Earth Inductor Compass .... EIC
Earth Information System [*Commercial firm*] .... EISYS
Earth Island Institute (EA) .... EII

Earth Laboratory Applications Software ..... ELAS
Earth Landing Control Assembly [*NASA*] (KSC) ..... ELCA
Earth Landing Sequence Controller [*NASA*] (NASA) ..... ELSC
Earth Landing System [*or Subsystem*] [*NASA*] ..... ELS
Earth Landmark [*NASA*] ..... ELDMK
Earth Launch Date [*Aerospace*] ..... ELD
Earth Launch Vehicle [*NASA*] ..... ELV
Earth Launch Window [*Aerospace*] (AAG) ..... ELW
Earth Leakage Circuit Breaker ..... ELCB
Earth Limb Measurement Satellite [*NASA/Air Force*] ..... ELMS
Earth Limb Measurement System [*NASA*] (SSD) ..... ELMS
Earth Mass ..... EM
Earth Mean Orbital Speed ..... EMOS
Earth, Moon, and Mars [*Astronomy*] ..... EMM
Earth Near Horizon [*NASA*] (KSC) ..... ENH
Earth Net Dial ..... END
Earth Observation ..... EO
Earth Observation Data Centre (EERA) ..... EODC
Earth Observation Mission [*NASA*] ..... EOM
Earth Observation Research Center [*Japan*] ..... EORC
Earth Observation Satellite [*NASA*] (OSRA) ..... EOS
Earth Observation Satellite [*France*] [*Marine science*] (OSRA) ..... SPOT
Earth Observation Satellite Co. [*Joint venture of RCA Corp. and Hughes Aircraft Co.*] ..... EOSAT
Earth Observations Aircraft Program [*NASA*] ..... EOAP
Earth Observations Division [*Johnson Space Center*] [*NASA*] ..... EOD
Earth Observations Programs [*NASA*] ..... EOP
Earth Observatory Satellite [*NASA*] ..... EOS
Earth Observing System [*NASA*] ..... EOS
Earth Observing System Data and Information System ..... EOSDIS
Earth or Geocentric Radius (AAG) ..... Re
Earth Orbit [*NASA*] (KSC) ..... EO
Earth Orbit Ejection [*Aerospace*] (MCD) ..... EOE
Earth Orbit Equipment [*Aerospace*] ..... EOE
Earth Orbit Escape Device [*Aerospace*] ..... EOED
Earth Orbit Insertion [*NASA*] (KSC) ..... EOI
Earth Orbit Launch [*NASA*] (KSC) ..... EOL
Earth Orbit Plane [*Aerospace*] (AAG) ..... EOP
Earth Orbit Rendezvous [*NASA*] ..... EOR
Earth Orbit Station ..... EOS
Earth Orbital Flight [*Aerospace*] (AAG) ..... EOF
Earth Orbital Launch Configuration [*NASA*] (KSC) ..... EOLC
Earth Orbital Military Satellite [*NASA*] (IAA) ..... EOMS
Earth Orbital Military Space Force (MCD) ..... EOMSF
Earth Orbital Mission [*NASA*] ..... EOM
Earth Orbital Shuttle [*NASA*] (KSC) ..... EOS
Earth Orbital Space Station [*NASA*] (MCD) ..... EOSS
Earth Orbiting Recoverable Biological Satellite ..... EORBS
Earth Orbiting Teleoperator System [*Spacecraft*] [*NASA*] ..... EOTS
Earth Parking Orbit [*Apollo*] [*NASA*] ..... EPO
Earth Path Indicator ..... EPI
Earth Penetrating Maneuverable Reentry Vehicle [*Military*] ..... EPMaRV
Earth Penetrator [*Weapon*] ..... EP
Earth Penetrator Weapon (MCD) ..... EPW
Earth Physics and Physical Oceanography Program [*NASA*] ..... EPPO
Earth Physics Branch, Energy, Mines and Resources Canada [*Direction de la Physique du Globe, Energie, Mines et Resources Canada*] **Ottawa, Ontario** [*Library symbol National Library of Canada*] (NLC) ..... OOO
Earth Physics Library [*Canada Energy Mines and Resources*] [*UTLAS symbol*] ..... EMO
Earth Physics Program ..... EPP
Earth Potential Compensation [*Telecommunications*] (TEL) ..... EPC
Earth Potential Difference (IAA) ..... EPD
Earth Prelaunch Calibration [*NASA*] (KSC) ..... EPC
Earth Preservation Fund (GNE) ..... EPF
Earth Pressure Balance [*Civil engineering*] ..... EPB
Earth Pressure Balance Machine [*Excavation*] ..... EPBM
Earth Probe near Limb of Venus [*Angle*] ..... EPV
Earth Protectors (GNE) ..... EP
Earth Radiation Budget Experiment [*NASA*] ..... ERBE
Earth Radiation Budget Instrument ..... ERBI
Earth Radiation Budget Observation Satellite (PDAA) ..... ERBOS
Earth Radiation Budget Satellite [*NASA*] (MCD) ..... ERBS
Earth Radiation Budget Satellite System [*NASA*] (MCD) ..... ERBSS
Earth Radii ..... ER
Earth Rate ..... ER
Earth Rate Compensation ..... ERC
Earth Rate Directional Reference ..... ERDR
Earth Rate Unit [*NASA*] (KSC) ..... ERU
Earth Received Time [*Astronomy*] ..... ERT
Earth Recovery Subsystem [*NASA*] (KSC) ..... ERS
Earth Re-Entry Module (MCD) ..... ERM
Earth Reference Pulse (IAA) ..... ERP
Earth Regeneration Society (EA) ..... ERS
Earth Remote Sensing Satellite (EERA) ..... ERS
Earth Remote Sensing Satellite-1 (MCD) ERS-1
Earth Resistivity Meter ..... ERM
Earth Resource Survey Operational System (TEL) ..... ERSOS
Earth Resource Survey Satellite (PDAA) ..... ERSATS
Earth Resources (MCD) ..... ER
Earth Resources Aircraft Facility [*NASA*] ..... ERAF
Earth Resources Aircraft Program [*NASA*] ..... ERAP
Earth Resources Applications Mission [*NASA*] (KSC) ..... ERAM
Earth Resources Budget Satellite ..... ERBS
Earth Resources Data Center [*NASA*] ..... ERDC
Earth Resources Digital Analysis System Software [*Computer science*] (EERA) ..... ERDAS
Earth Resources Experiment Package [*Skylab*] [*NASA*] ..... EREP
Earth Resources Experiment Package Program [*Skylab*] [*NASA*] ..... EREPP
Earth Resources Flight Data Processor [*NASA*] ..... ERFDP
Earth Resources Image [*or Interactive*] **Processing System** ..... ERIPS
Earth Resources Information Storage, Transformation, Analysis, and Retrieval ..... ERISTAR
Earth Resources Laboratory [*Later, NSTL*] [*NASA*] (KSC) ..... ERL
Earth Resources Laboratory Application Software ..... ELAS
Earth Resources Observation System [*United States of America*] [*Military*] (EERA) ..... EROS
Earth Resources Observation Systems [*US Geological Survey*] ..... EROS
Earth Resources Observing Satellite [*Marine science*] (OSRA) ..... EROS
Earth Resources Observing Satellite (USDC) ..... EROS
Earth Resources Package [*NASA*] (NASA) ..... EREP
Earth Resources Project Office (MCD) ..... ERPO
Earth Resources Research Data Facility ..... ERRDF
Earth Resources Satellite [*NASA*] ..... ERS
Earth Resources Satellite Data Analysis Center [*Japan*] (EERA) ..... ERSDAC
Earth Resources Satellite System (IEEE) ..... ERSS
Earth Resources Shuttle Imaging RADAR ..... ERSIR
Earth Resources Survey [*NASA*] ..... ERS
Earth Resources Survey Flights Program [*NASA*] ..... ERSFP
Earth Resources Survey Program [*NASA*] ..... ERSP
Earth Resources Survey Program Review Committee [*NASA*] (NOAA) ..... ERSPRC
Earth Resources Survey Satellite [*NASA*] (IAA) ..... ERSS
Earth Resources Technology Satellite [*Later, LANDSAT*] [*NASA*] ..... ERTS
Earth Resources-2 [*Aircraft*] [*NASA*] (OSRA) ER-2
Earth Resources-2 [*Satellite*] [*NASA*] (USDC) ER2
Earth Return Module [*NASA*] (KSC) ..... ERM
Earth Satellite Vehicle [*Air Force*] ..... ESV
Earth Satellite Weapon Systems ..... ESWS
Earth Save [*An association*] (EA) ..... ES
Earth Science and Applications Data System [*National Oceanic and Atmospheric Administration*] ..... ESADS
Earth Science Curriculum Project [*Education*] ..... ESCP
Earth Science Data Directory (EERA) ..... ESDD
Earth Science Research (SSD) ..... ESR
Earth Science Teachers Association [*British*] (DBA) ..... ESTA
Earth Sciences [*NASDAQ symbol*] (TTSB) ..... ESCI
Earth Sciences and Resources Institute [*University of South Carolina at Columbia*] [*Research center*] (RCD) ..... ESRI
Earth Sciences Assistance Office [*Department of the Interior*] (GRD) ..... ESAO
Earth Sciences Division [*Army Natick Laboratories*] ..... ES
Earth Sciences Division [*Army Natick Laboratories*] (NOAA) ..... ESD
Earth Sciences, Inc. [*Associated Press*] (SAG) ..... EarthSc
Earth Sciences, Inc. [*NASDAQ symbol*] (NQ) ..... ESCI
Earth Sciences Laboratory [*Boulder, CO*] [*National Oceanic and Atmospheric Administration*] ..... ESL
Earth Society Foundation (EA) ..... ESF
Earth Spring (OA) ..... ES
Earth Station ..... ES
Earth Station - Arabia ..... ESA
Earth Station - Brazil ..... ESB
Earth Station - Chile ..... ESCH
Earth Station - Colombia ..... ESCO
Earth Station - Congo ..... ESC
Earth Station - Ecuador ..... ESEC
Earth Station - Egypt ..... ESEG
Earth Station - Greece ..... ESG
Earth Station - Hong Kong ..... ESHK
Earth Station - Iran ..... ESI
Earth Station - Israel ..... ESIS
Earth Station - Ivory Coast ..... ESIC
Earth Station - Jordan ..... ESJ
Earth Station - Kenya ..... ESK
Earth Station - Libya ..... ESL
Earth Station - Mexico ..... ESM
Earth Station - Morocco ..... ESMO
Earth Station - Scandinavia ..... ESSC
Earth Station - Senegal ..... ESSE
Earth Station - South Africa ..... ESSA
Earth Station - Sudan ..... ESS
Earth Station - Syria ..... ESSY
Earth Station - Turkey ..... EST
Earth Station - Venezuela ..... ESV
Earth Station - Yugoslavia ..... ESY
Earth Surveillance and Rendezvous Simulator ..... ESARS
Earth Switch (IAA) ..... ES
Earth System Data and Information Management [*Marine science*] (OSRA) ..... ESDIM
Earth System Data and Information Management [*National Oceanic and Atmospheric Administration*] (USDC) ..... ESDIM
Earth System Science Committee [*US governmental interagency group*] ..... ESSC
Earth Systems Model [*Climatology*] ..... ESM
Earth Systems Science Committee (EERA) ..... ESSC
Earth Technology Corp. [*Associated Press*] (SAG) ..... EarthT
[*The*] **Earth Technology Corp. (USA)** [*NASDAQ symbol*] (NQ) ..... ETCO
Earth Terminal (HGAA) ..... ET
Earth Terminal Complex ..... ETC
Earth Terrain Camera [*NASA*] (MCD) ..... ETC
Earth to Space (IAA) ..... ES
Earth Venus Transit [*Aerospace*] ..... EVT
Earth Viewing Applications Laboratory (MCD) ..... EVAL

Earth Viewing Module ... EVM
Earth Vote Network (EA) ... EN
Earth, Wind, and Fire [*Rock music group*] ... EWF
Earth Works Group Inc. (EERA) ... EWG
EarthBank Association of North America (EA) ... EB
Earth-Based Radio Guidance ... EBRG
Earth-Based Tug [*NASA*] ... EBT
Earthcare Network (EA) ... EN
Earth-Centered, Earth-Fixed ... ECEF
Earth-Centered Inertial [*System*] ... ECI
Earth-Centered Inertial System (SAA) ... ECIS
Earth-Centered True ... ECT
Earth-Crossing Asteroid [*Astronomy*] ... ECA
Earth-Crossing Asteroid ... ECAS
Earthenware (VRA) ... erthwr
Earthenware [*Freight*] ... ERWRE
Earthenware ... EW
Earth-Fixed Coordinate (MCD) ... EFC
Earth-Fixed Coordinate System (MCD) ... EFCS
Earth-Fixed System ... EFS
Earthgrains Co. [*Associated Press*] (SAG) ... Earthgr
Earthgrains Co. [*NYSE symbol*] (SAG) ... EGR
Earthgrains Co. [*NYSE symbol*] (TTSB) ... EGR
Earth-Ionosphere Cavity ... EIC
Earth-Jupiter Orbiter Transfer Flight (PDAA) ... EJOTF
Earthlink Network, Inc. [*NASDAQ symbol*] (SAG) ... ELNK
Earthlink Network, Inc. [*Associated Press*] (SAG) ... Erthlink
Earth-Lunar Horizon Sensor ... EHS
Earth-Mars-Earth ... EME
Earth-Moon Space Exploration Study ... ESES
Earth-Moon-Earth [*Extraterrestrial communications*] ... EME
Earth-Observed Time [*NASA*] ... EOT
Earth-orbit-Crossing Asteroid ... ECA
Earth-Orientated Applications Experiment (MCD) ... EOAE
Earth-Penetrating Warhead (RDA) ... EPW
Earth-Physics Satellite Observation [*or Observing*] **Campaign** [*Smithsonian Astrophysical Observatory*] ... EPSOC
Earth-Pointing Error (MCD) ... EPE
Earth-Pointing Instrument Carrier [*A satellite*] ... EPIC
Earth-Probe-Mars [*Angle*] ... EPM
Earth-Probe-Sun [*Angle*] ... EPS
Earthquake Data File [*Marine science*] (MSC) ... EDF
Earthquake Early Reporting System [*Marine science*] (MSC) ... EERS
Earthquake Engineering Research Center [*University of California, Berkeley*] (IID) ... EERC
Earthquake Engineering Research Institute (EA) ... EERI
Earthquake Light ... EQL
Earthquake Monitoring System (NRCH) ... EMS
Earthquake Phenomena Observation System [*Japan*] [*Marine science*] (OSRA) ... EPOS
Earthquake Phenomena Observation System [*Japan*] (USDC) ... EPOS
Earthquake Reporting and Prediction (NOAA) ... ERP
Earthquake Risk Analysis (PDAA) ... ERA
Earth-Reflecting Ionospheric Sounder [*Air Force*] (MCD) ... ERIS
Earth's Armed Forces (SAA) ... EAF
Earth's Physical Features Study Unit (EA) ... EPFSU
Earth's Polar Axis (KSC) ... EPA
Earth's Radiation Budget [*Meteorology*] ... ERB
Earth-Sighting Simulator [*NASA*] ... ESS
Earthspirit Community (EA) ... ESC
Earth-Sun Coordinate System ... ESN
Earth-Surface Potential ... ESP
Earth-to-Space Railgun Launcher (MCD) ... ESRL
Earthwatch [*United Nations Environment Program*] ... EW
Earthwork (VRA) ... erthwk
Earthwork/Center for Rural Studies (EA) ... ECRS
Earwalker's Manchester Court-Leet Records [*England*] [*A publication*] (DLA) ... Earw
Easco, Inc. [*Associated Press*] (SAG) ... Easco
Easco, Inc. [*NASDAQ symbol*] (SAG) ... ESCO
Eased Edge (DAC) ... EE
Eased Up [*Horse racing*] ... U
Easel Corp. [*NASDAQ symbol*] (SAG) ... EASL
Easement [*Legal term*] (DLA) ... EASE
Easement [*British Legal term*] (ROG) ... EASEMT
Easement [*British Legal term*] (ROG) ... EASMT
Easily ... E
Easily Used Computer Language for Illustration and Drawing [*European Community*] (MHDB) ... EUCLID
Easley, SC [*AM radio station call letters*] ... WLWZ
Easley, SC [*FM radio station call letters*] (RBYB) ... WOLI-FM
Easley, SC [*AM radio station call letters*] (RBYB) ... WRAH-AM
Easley, SC [*FM radio station call letters*] ... WXWX
East (WDMC) ... e
East [*or Eastern*] ... E
East Africa ... E Afr
East Africa ... EA
East Africa Association (EA) ... EAA
East Africa Court of Appeals Reports [*A publication*] (DLA) ... East Af
East Africa Law Reports [*A publication*] (DLA) ... E Afr LR
East Africa Law Reports [*A publication*] (DLA) ... EALR
East Africa Law Reports [*A publication*] (DLA) ... East Afr L Rep
East Africa Protectorate [*Later, Kenya*] ... EAP
East Africa Protectorate Law Reports [*A publication*] (DLA) ... EA Prot LR
East Africa Protectorate Law Reports [*A publication*] (DLA) ... EAPLR
East Africa Wins Again [*Used by US Diplomatic Corps in Nairobi, Kenya, to express dispair at bureaucratic obstacles*] ... EAWA
East African Agricultural and Forestry Journal [*A publication*] ... EAAJ
East African Agriculture and Forestry Research Organization ... EAAFRO
East African Airways Corp. [*African airline*] ... EAA
East African Airways Corp. [*African airline*] ... EAAC
East African Armoured Corps [*British military*] (DMA) ... EAAC
East African Army Educational Corps [*British military*] (DMA) ... EAAEC
East African Army Medical Corps [*British military*] (DMA) ... EAAMC
East African Army Ordnance Corps [*British military*] (DMA) ... EAAOC
East African Artillery [*British military*] (DMA) ... EAA
East African Cargo Handling Services (PDAA) ... EACHS
East African Common Services Organization [*Later, EAC*] ... EACSO
East African Community [*Formed in 1967*] [*Formerly, EACSO*] (AF) ... EAC
East African Development Bank [*Uganda*] (AF) ... EADB
East African Economic Community ... EAEC
East African Electrical and Mechanical Engineers [*British military*] (DMA) ... EAEME
East African External Telecommunications Co. (PDAA) ... EAET
East African Freshwater Fisheries Research Organization ... EAFFRO
East African Geographical Review [*A publication*] ... EAGR
East African Horn [*MARC geographic area code Library of Congress*] (LCCP) ... fh----
East African Institute of Malaria and Vector-Borne Disease [*Tanzania*] (PDAA) ... EAMVBD
East African Journal of Criminology [*A publication*] (DLA) ... EAJ Criminol
East African Journal of Criminology [*A publication*] (DLA) ... East Afr J Criminol
East African Law Journal [*A publication*] (DLA) ... E African LJ
East African Law Journal [*A publication*] (DLA) ... EALJ
East African Law Journal [*A publication*] (DLA) ... East Afr LJ
East African Literature Bureau ... EALB
East African Management Journal [*A publication*] ... EAMJ
East African Marine Fisheries Research Organization [*Marine science*] (OSRA) ... EAMFRO
East African Marine Fisheries Research Organization (USDC) ... EAMFRO
East African Military Labour Service [*British military*] (DMA) ... EAMLS
East African Natural History Society (EAIO) ... EANHS
East African Natural Resources Research Council [*Kenya*] (PDAA) ... EANRRC
East African Pesticides Control Organization (PDAA) ... EAPCO
East African Pioneer Corps [*British military*] (DMA) ... EAPC
East African Publishing House [*Kenya*] ... EAPH
East African Reconnaissance Corps [*British military*] (DMA) ... EARC
East African Reconnaissance Squadron [*British military*] (DMA) ... EARS
East African Regional Committee for Conservation and Utilisation of Soil ... EARCCUS
East African School of Aviation [*Kenya*] (PDAA) ... EASA
East African School of Aviation [*Kenya*] [*ICAO location identifier*] (ICLI) ... HKSA
East African Service Corps [*British military*] (DMA) ... EASC
East African Shilling [*Monetary unit*] ... EAs
East African Society of African Culture ... EASTASAC
East African Tea Trade Association (EA) ... EATTA
East African Time ... EAT
East African Tuberculosis Investigation Centre [*Kenya*] (PDAA) ... EATIC
East African Wild Life Society (GNE) ... EAWLS
East Albemarle Regional Library, Elizabeth City, NC [*Library symbol Library of Congress*] (LCLS) ... NcElc
East Alton Elementary 13, Alton, IL [*Library symbol Library of Congress*] (LCLS) ... IAIE
East Alton Public Library, East Alton, IL [*Library symbol Library of Congress*] (LCLS) ... IEa
East Alton-Wood River Community High School 14, Wood River, IL [*Library symbol Library of Congress*] (LCLS) ... IWorHS
East and West India Dock Co. [*Shipping*] (ROG) ... E & WIDC
East and West London Railway [*British*] (ROG) ... E & WLR
East Anglia [*England*] (ROG) ... EA
East Anglia Tourist Board [*British*] (DCTA) ... EATB
East Anglian Examinations Board (AIE) ... EAEB
East Anglian Regional Advisory Council for Further Education (AIE) ... EARAC
East Asia Blocking Ridge [*Meteorology*] ... EABR
East Asia Christian Conference [*Later, Christian Conference of Asia - CCA*] ... EACC
East Asia Hydrographic Commission [*Marine science*] (OSRA) ... EAHC
East Asia Journalism Program (EA) ... EAJP
East Asia Regional Council of Overseas Schools (EA) ... EARCOS
East Asia Regional Organization for Planning and Housing ... EAROPH
East Asia Strategy Initiative [*Military*] ... EASI
East Asia Travel Association (EAIO) ... EATA
East Asian and Pacific [*Series*] [*A publication*] ... EA & P
East Asian Art Society ... EAAS
East Asian Art Society Chinese School ... EAASCS
East Asian Economic Caucus ... EAEC
East Asian Economic Group [*Australia*] ... EAEG
East Asian Growth Area [*International Trade*] ... EAGA
East Asian Library Resources Group of Australia ... EALRGA
East Asian Studies Center [*Indiana University*] [*Research center*] (RCD) ... EASC
East Asian-North Pacific Regional Experiment (USDC) ... APARE
East Atlantic [*Satellite*] (DOMA) ... ELANT
East Australian Current [*Oceanography*] ... EAC
East Australian Pipeline Ltd. [*Commercial firm*] ... EAPL
East Australian Standard Time ... EAST
East Auxiliary Airborne Command Post (MCD) ... EAUXCP
East Baton Rouge Parish Public Library, Baton Rouge, LA [*Library symbol Library of Congress*] (LCLS) ... LBr
East Baton Rouge Parish Public Library, Baton Rouge, LA [*OCLC symbol*] (OCLC) ... LEB

East Bay Fan Guild (EA) .... EBFG
East Bay Information Service [*Library network*] .... EBIS
East Bend Public Library, East Bend, NC [*Library symbol*] [*Library of Congress*] (LCLS) .... NcEb
East Bengal State Railway Volunteer Rifles [*British military*] (DMA) .... EBSRVR
East Bonner County District Library, Clark Fork Branch, Clark Fork, ID [*Library symbol*] [*Library of Congress*] (LCLS) .... IdSan-C
East Bonner County Free Public Library District, Sandpoint, ID [*Library symbol*] [*Library of Congress*] (LCLS) .... IdSan
East Brewton, AL [*FM radio station call letters*] .... WZEW
East Brunswick Public Library, East Brunswick, NJ [*Library symbol Library of Congress*] (LCLS) .... NjEb
East by North .... EbN
East by South .... EbS
East Camden & Highland Railroad Co. [*AAR code*] .... EACH
East Cape [*New Zealand*] [*Seismograph station code, US Geological Survey*] (SEIS) .... ECZ
East Caribbean .... EC
East Caribbean Common Market (DS) .... ECCM
East Caribbean Natural Area Management Program (EAIO) .... ECNAMP
East Carolina College [*Later, ECU*] [*North Carolina*] .... ECC
East Carolina Railway [*AAR code*] .... EC
East Carolina University (GAGS) .... East Car U
East Carolina University [*Formerly, ECC*] [*Greenville, NC*] .... ECU
East Carolina University, Department of Library Science, Greenville, NC [*OCLC symbol*] (OCLC) .... NEL
East Carolina University, Greenville, NC [*OCLC symbol*] (OCLC) .... ERE
East Carolina University, Greenville, NC [*Library symbol Library of Congress*] (LCLS) .... NcGrE
East Carolina University, Health Sciences Library, Greenville, NC [*Library symbol Library of Congress*] (LCLS) .... NcGrE-H
East Carolina University, Health Sciences Library, Greenville, NC [*OCLC symbol*] (OCLC) .... NEH
East Carroll Parish Library, Lake Providence, LA [*Library symbol Library of Congress*] (LCLS) .... LLpEC
East Central [*Refers especially to London postal district*] .... EC
East Central Area Reliability Coordination Agreement [*Regional power council*] .... ECAR
East Central Europe (ECON) .... ECE
East Central Junior College [*Decatur, MS*] .... ECJC
East Central Nuclear Group .... ECNG
East Central Oklahoma State University (GAGS) .... East Cent Okla St U
East Central Oklahoma State University, Ada, OK [*OCLC symbol*] (OCLC) .... ECO
East Central Regional Library, Cambridge, MN [*Library symbol Library of Congress*] (LCLS) .... MnCaE
East Central Regional Library System [*Library network*] .... ECRL
East Central Reservoir Investigation [*Department of the Interior*] (GRD) .... ECRI
East Central State College [*Later, East Central Oklahoma State University*] .... ECSC
East Central State College [*Later, East Central Oklahoma State University*], Ada, OK [*Library symbol Library of Congress*] (LCLS) .... OkAdE
East Chicago Public Library, East Chicago, IN [*OCLC symbol*] (OCLC) .... INE
East Chicago Public Library, East Chicago, IN [*Library symbol Library of Congress*] (LCLS) .... InEc
East China Sea and Area [*MARC geographic area code Library of Congress*] (LCCP) .... an----
East Cleveland Public Library, East Cleveland, OH [*OCLC symbol*] (OCLC) .... ECP
East Cleveland Public Library, East Cleveland, OH [*Library symbol Library of Congress*] (LCLS) .... OEac
East Coast .... EASTCO
East Coast .... EC
East Coast Airlines [*Australia ICAO designator*] (FAAC) .... ECO
East Coast Airlines [*ICAO designator*] (AD) .... UN
East Coast Airlines Ltd. [*Kenya*] [*ICAO designator*] (FAAC) .... ECK
East Coast Base .... EASTCOBASE
East Coast Carriers Conference, New York NY [*STAC*] .... ECC
East Coast Coal Port [*Shipping*] [*British*] .... ECCP
East Coast Conference on Aerospace and Navigational Electronics (MCD) .... ECCANE
East Coast Documents Distribution Center .... EDDC
East Coast Fever [*Veterinary medicine*] .... ECF
East Coast Flying Service (SAA) .... ECFS
East Coast Hang Out [*Computer network*] .... ECHO
East Coast Hazards Observation [*Sampling program*] .... ECHO
East Coast Joint Service, Stock [*Railroad*] [*British*] (ROG) .... ECJS
East Coast Laboratory [*Environmental Science Services Administration*] .... ECL
East Coast Magnetic Anomaly [*Geophysics*] .... ECMA
East Coast Migrant Health Project (EA) .... ECMHP
East Coast of Great Britain [*Shipping*] .... ECGB
East Coast of Ireland [*Shipping*] .... ECI
East Coast of the United Kingdom [*Shipping*] .... ECUK
East Coast Telecommunications Center [*Defense Communications System*] (RDA) .... ECTC
East Coast Trawl Management Advisory Committee (EERA) .... ECTMAC
East Coast Tuna Management Advisory Committee (EERA) .... ECTUNAMAC
East Connecticut State University (GAGS) .... East Conn St U
East Coulee Community Library, Alberta [*Library symbol National Library of Canada*] (NLC) .... AEACC
East Coulee Community Library, East Coulee, AB, Canada [*Library symbol*] [*Library of Congress*] (LCLS) .... CaAEacC
East Coulee Community Library, East Coulee, AB, Canada [*Library symbol Library of Congress*] (LCLS) .... CaAEacC
East Daggafontein [*Vancouver Stock Exchange symbol*] .... EDF
East Detroit Memorial Library, East Detroit, MI [*Library symbol Library of Congress*] (LCLS) .... MiEad
East Eifel Volcanic Field [*Geology*] [*Germany*] .... EEVF
East Eight [*Zambia*] [*ICAO location identifier*] (ICLI) .... FLEH
East Elementary School, Hicksville, NY [*Library symbol Library of Congress*] (LCLS) .... NHickEE
East Erie Commercial Railroad [*AAR code*] .... EEC
East European Chemical Monitor [*Business International*] [*Vienna, Austria*] [*Information service or system*] (IID) .... EECM
East European Development Bank [*Acronym is based on foreign phrase*] .... BERD
East European Family History Association (EA) .... EEFHA
East European Program (EERA) .... EEP
East European Solidarity Committee [*Defunct*] (EAIO) .... EESC
East Five [*Zambia*] [*ICAO location identifier*] (ICLI) .... FLEE
East Florida [*Obsolete*] (ROG) .... EF
East Fork, AK [*Location identifier FAA*] (FAAL) .... EFO
East Four [*Zambia*] [*ICAO location identifier*] (ICLI) .... FLED
East German Army (CINC) .... EGA
East Germany .... E GER
East Germany [*License plate code assigned to foreign diplomats in the US*] .... TJ
East Gippsland Coalition (EERA) .... EGC
East Grand Forks High School, East Grand Forks, MN [*Library symbol*] [*Library of Congress*] (LCLS) .... MnEgfH
East Grand Forks, MN [*AM radio station call letters*] .... KCNN
East Grand Forks, MN [*FM radio station call letters*] .... KZLT
East Grand Forks Technical Institute, East Grand Forks, MN [*Library symbol*] [*Library of Congress*] (LCLS) .... MnEgfTI
East Greenland Polar Front [*Oceanography*] .... EGPF
East Griqualand Mounted Rifles [*British military*] (DMA) .... EGMR
East Gwillimbury Public Libraries, Holland Landing, ON, Canada [*Library symbol Library of Congress*] (LCLS) .... CaOHIEG
East Gwillimbury Public Libraries, Holland Landing, Ontario [*Library symbol National Library of Canada*] (NLC) .... OHLEG
East Hampton [*New York*] [*Airport symbol*] (OAG) .... HTO
East Hampton Air [*ICAO designator*] (AD) .... IN
East Hampton Aire [*ICAO designator*] (FAAC) .... EHA
East Hampton Free Library, East Hampton, NY [*Library symbol Library of Congress*] (LCLS) .... NEh
East Hampton, NY [*FM radio station call letters*] .... WEHM
East Hampton Public Library, East Hampton, CT [*Library symbol*] [*Library of Congress*] (LCLS) .... CtEham
East Hanover Public Library, East Hanover, NJ [*Library symbol Library of Congress*] (LCLS) .... NjEh
East Hartford, CT [*Location identifier FAA*] (FAAL) .... EHT
East Hartford, CT [*Location identifier FAA*] (FAAL) .... RFX
East Hartford, CT [*Location identifier FAA*] (FAAL) .... UAZ
East Hartford Public Library, East Hartford, CT [*Library symbol Library of Congress*] (LCLS) .... CtEh
East Helena, MT [*AM radio station call letters*] .... KHKR
East Helena, MT [*FM radio station call letters*] .... KHKR-FM
East Hertshire Archaeological Society [*British*] .... EHAS
East High School, Duluth, MN [*Library symbol*] [*Library of Congress*] (LCLS) .... MnDuEH
East High School, Rockford, IL [*Library symbol*] [*Library of Congress*] (LCLS) .... IRoEH
East Hills Intermediate School, Roslyn Heights, NY [*Library symbol*] [*Library of Congress*] (LCLS) .... NRoslhEI
East India (ROG) .... EI
East India Civil Service [*British*] (ROG) .... EICS
East India Co. [*1600-1858*] [*British*] (ROG) .... EI CO
East India Co. [*1600-1858*] [*British*] .... EIC
East India Company's Service [*British*] .... EICS
East India Dock .... EID
East India House (ROG) .... EIH
East Indian Defence Committee .... EIDC
East Indian Railway .... EIR
East Indies .... E Ind
East Indies .... EI
East Integrated Test Stand (KSC) .... EITS
East Islip Public Library, East Islip, NY [*Library symbol Library of Congress*] (LCLS) .... NEi
East Jersey Railroad & Terminal Co. [*AAR code*] .... EJR
East Jordan & Southern R. R. [*AAR code*] .... EJS
East Jordan, MI [*FM radio station call letters*] .... WIZY
East Junior High School, Brentwood, NY [*Library symbol*] [*Library of Congress*] (LCLS) .... NBrenEJ
East Junior High School, Grand Junction, CO [*Library symbol Library of Congress*] (LCLS) .... CoGjEJ
East Junior/Senior High School Library, Rochester, NY [*OCLC symbol*] (OCLC) .... RWC
East Kansas City Aviation, Inc. [*ICAO designator*] (FAAC) .... EKC
East Kent Regiment [*Military unit*] [*British*] (ROG) .... E KENT R
East Kent Regiment [*Military unit*] [*British*] .... EKR
East Kent Volunteer Fencibles [*British military*] (DMA) .... EKVF
East Kimberley Impact Assessment Program (EERA) .... EKIAP
East Kootenay Community College, Cranbrook, BC, Canada [*Library symbol Library of Congress*] (LCLS) .... CaBCrEK
East Kootenay Community College, Cranbrook, British Columbia [*Library symbol National Library of Canada*] (NLC) .... BCREK
East Kootenay Community College Library [*UTLAS symbol*] .... EAK
East Kurupa, AK [*Location identifier FAA*] (FAAL) .... ACU
East Lake Ainslie Historical Society, Nova Scotia [*Library symbol National Library of Canada*] (BIB) .... NSELH
East Lake Elementary School, Massapequa, NY [*Library symbol Library of Congress*] (LCLS) .... NMassELE

East Lancashire Regiment [*Military unit*] [*British*] (DAS) .... E Lan R
East Lancashire Regiment [*Military unit*] [*British*] (ROG) .... E LANC R
East Lansing, MI [*FM radio station call letters*] .... WDBM
East Lansing, MI [*FM radio station call letters*] .... WFMK
East Lansing, MI [*AM radio station call letters*] .... WKAR
East Lansing, MI [*FM radio station call letters*] .... WKAR-FM
East Lansing, MI [*Television station call letters*] .... WKAR-TV
East Lansing, MI [*AM radio station call letters*] .... WVFN
East Lansing, MI [*FM radio station call letters*] .... WVIC
East Lansing Public Library, East Lansing, MI [*Library symbol Library of Congress*] (LCLS) .... MiE
East Las Vegas, NV [*Radio expansion station*] (RBYB) .... KLSQ EXP STN
East Liverpool Carnegie Public Library, East Liverpool, OH [*Library symbol Library of Congress*] (LCLS) .... OEal
East Liverpool, OH [*Location identifier FAA*] (FAAL) .... EVO
East Liverpool, OH [*FM radio station call letters*] .... WELA
East Liverpool, OH [*AM radio station call letters*] .... WOHI
East London [*South Africa*] [*Airport symbol*] (OAG) .... ELS
East London/Ben Schoeman [*South Africa*] [*ICAO location identifier*] (ICLI).... FAEL
East London Railway (ROG) .... ELR
East London Telecommunications [*Commercial firm British*] .... ELT
East Longitude .... E Lon
East Longitude (HGAA) .... E Long
East Longitude (ROG) .... EL
East Longitude Date .... ELD
East Longmeadow, MA [*AM radio station call letters*] .... WAQY
East Los Angeles College, Los Angeles, CA [*Library symbol Library of Congress*] (LCLS) .... CLELJ
East Lothian Yeomanry Cavalry [*British military*] (DMA) .... ELYC
East Lyme, CT [*FM radio station call letters*] .... WXZR
East Machias [*Maine*] [*Seismograph station code, US Geological Survey*] (SEIS) .... EMM
East Main [*Canada*] [*Airport symbol*] (OAG) .... ZEM
East Malling Research Station [*British*] (ARC) .... EMRS
East Mark [*Monetary unit*] [*Germany*] .... EM
East Meadow High School, East Meadow, NY [*Library symbol*] [*Library of Congress*] (LCLS) .... NEmMH
East Meadow Public Library, East Meadow, NY [*Library symbol Library of Congress*] (LCLS) .... NEm
East Meadow Public Library, East Meadow, NY [*Library symbol*] [*Library of Congress*] (LCLS) .... NEmL
East Memorial Elementary School, Farmingdale, NY [*Library symbol Library of Congress*] (LCLS) .... NFarEE
East Midland Regional Advisory Committee on Special Education [*British*] (AIE) .... EMRACSE
East Midlands [*British ICAO location identifier*] (ICLI) .... EGNX
East Midlands [*England*] .... EM
East Midlands [*England*] [*Airport symbol*] (OAG) .... EMA
East Midlands [*England*] .... EMDL
East Midlands Airport [*England*] .... EMA
East Midlands Allied Press [*British*] (DI) .... EMAP
East Midlands Education Union [*British*] (AIE) .... EMEU
East Midlands Helicopters [*British*] [*FAA designator*] (FAAC) .... CTK
East Mississippi Junior College [*Scooba, MS*] .... EMJC
East Missoula, MT [*AM radio station call letters*] .... KLCY
East Moline, IL [*AM radio station call letters*] .... WDLM
East Moline, IL [*FM radio station call letters*] .... WDLM-FM
East Moline, IL [*FM radio station call letters*] .... WLLR
East Of [*In outdoor advertising*] (WDMC) .... E/O
East of Scotland Brass Founders' Society [*A union*] .... ESBFS
East One [*Zambia*] [*ICAO location identifier*] (ICLI) .... FLEA
East Orange Free Public Library, East Orange, NJ [*Library symbol Library of Congress*] (LCLS) .... NjEo
East Orange, NJ [*FM radio station call letters*] .... WFMU
East Pacific Barrier [*Oceanography*] .... EPB
East Pacific Rise [*Geology*] .... EPR
East Pennsylvania Psychiatric Institute, Philadelphia, PA [*OCLC symbol*] (OCLC) .... PIU
East Peoria Elementary School District, East Peoria, IL [*Library symbol Library of Congress*] (LCLS) .... IEpE
East Peoria Elementary Schools, East Peoria, IL [*OCLC symbol*] (OCLC) .... ILN
East Point, GA [*AM radio station call letters*] (RBYB) .... WERD
East Point, GA [*AM radio station call letters*] .... WTJH
East Porterville, CA [*FM radio station call letters*] .... KOJJ
East Prairie, MO [*AM radio station call letters*] .... KYMO
East Prairie, MO [*FM radio station call letters*] .... KYMO-FM
East Promontory [*Utah*] [*Seismograph station code, US Geological Survey*] (SEIS) .... EPU
East Region Development Corp. .... ERDC
East Ridge, TN [*FM radio station call letters*] .... WOGT
East Riding of Yorkshire [*Administrative county in England*] .... ER
East Riding of Yorkshire [*Administrative county in England*] (ROG) .... ERY
East Riding of Yorkshire Imperial Yeomanry [*British military*] (DMA) .... ERYIY
East Riding Yeomanry [*Military unit*] [*British*] .... ERY
East River [*New York*] .... ER
East Rockaway High School, East Rockaway, NY [*Library symbol*] [*Library of Congress*] (LCLS) .... NErHS
East Rockaway Public Library, East Rockaway, NY [*Library symbol Library of Congress*] (LCLS) .... NEr
East St. Louis, IL [*Location identifier FAA*] (FAAL) .... CPS
East St. Louis, IL [*AM radio station call letters*] .... WESL
East St. Louis, IL [*Television station call letters*] .... WHSL
East St. Louis, IL [*FM radio station call letters*] .... WVRV
[*The*] **East St. Louis Junction R. R.** [*AAR code*] .... ESLJ
East St. Louis Public Library, East St. Louis, IL [*Library symbol Library of Congress*] (LCLS) .... IEs
East Saint Louis Public School District 189, East St. Louis, IL [*Library symbol Library of Congress*] (LCLS) .... IEsSD
East Sale [*Australia ICAO location identifier*] (ICLI) .... AMES
East Saxon [*Dialect of Old English*] [*Language, etc.*] .... ESAX
East School, Long Beach, NY [*Library symbol Library of Congress*] (LCLS) .... NLobES
East Seven [*Zambia*] [*ICAO location identifier*] (ICLI) .... FLEG
East Siberian Region, RSFSR [*MARC geographic area code Library of Congress*] (LCCP) .... e-ure-
East Side [*In outdoor advertising*] (WDMC) .... E/S
East Six [*Zambia*] [*ICAO location identifier*] (ICLI) .... FLEF
East Stroudsburg, PA [*Location identifier FAA*] (FAAL) .... ESP
East Stroudsburg, PA [*FM radio station call letters*] .... WESS
East Stroudsburg State College, East Stroudsburg, PA [*OCLC symbol*] (OCLC) .... ETS
East Stroudsburg State College, East Stroudsburg, PA [*Library symbol Library of Congress*] (LCLS) .... PEsS
East Stroudsburg University .... ESU
East Stroudsburg University of Pennsylvania (GAGS) .... East Stroudsburg U
East Surrey Militia [*British military*] (DMA) .... ESM
East Surrey Regiment [*Military unit*] [*British*] (ROG) .... E SURR R
East Surrey Regiment [*Military unit*] [*British*] .... ESR
East Syracuse, NY [*AM radio station call letters*] .... WSIV
East Tennessee & Western North Carolina Railroad Co. (IIA) .... ET & WNC
East Tennessee & Western North Carolina Railroad Co. [*AAR code*] .... ETWN
East Tennessee Baptist Hospital, Knoxville, TN [*Library symbol Library of Congress*] (LCLS) .... TKEBH
East Tennessee Children's Hospital, Pediatric Library, Knoxville, TN [*Library symbol*] [*Library of Congress*] (LCLS) .... TKECH
East Tennessee Historical Society, Knoxville, TN [*Library symbol Library of Congress*] (LCLS) .... TKETHi
East Tennessee State College [*Later, East Tennessee State University*] .... ETSC
East Tennessee State University (GAGS) .... East Tenn St U
East Tennessee State University [*Formerly, East Tennessee State College*] .... ETSU
East Tennessee State University, Johnson City, TN [*OCLC symbol*] (OCLC) .... TET
East Tennessee State University, Johnson City, TN [*Library symbol Library of Congress*] (LCLS) .... TJoS
East Tennessee State University, Medical Library, Johnson City, TN [*OCLC symbol*] (OCLC) .... MET
East Tennessee State University, Medical Library, Johnson City, TN [*Library symbol Library of Congress*] (LCLS) .... TJoS-M
East Texas Baptist College .... ETBC
East Texas Baptist University, Marshall, TX [*Library symbol*] [*Library of Congress*] (LCLS) .... TxMaEB
East Texas Financial Services, Inc. [*Associated Press*] (SAG) .... EstTX FS
East Texas Financial Services, Inc. [*NASDAQ symbol*] (SAG) .... ETFS
East Texas Financial Svcs [*NASDAQ symbol*] (TTSB) .... ETFS
East Texas, PA [*Location identifier FAA*] (FAAL) .... ETX
East Texas State College [*Later, East Texas State University*] .... ETSC
East Texas State University (GAGS) .... East Tex St U
East Texas State University [*Formerly, East Texas State College*] .... ETSU
East Texas State University at Texarkana, Texarkana, TX [*Library symbol Library of Congress*] (LCLS) .... TxTeS
East Texas State University, Commerce, TX [*OCLC symbol*] (OCLC) .... IEA
East Texas State University, Commerce, TX [*Library symbol Library of Congress*] (LCLS) .... TxComS
East Texas State University, Metroplex Center, Commerce, TX [*OCLC symbol*] (OCLC) .... IEM
East Texas State University, Metroplex Center, Dallas, TX [*Library symbol Library of Congress*] (LCLS) .... TxDaET
East Texas State University, Museum, Commerce, TX [*Library symbol Library of Congress*] (LCLS) .... TxComS-M
East Texas State University, Texarkana, Texarkana, TX [*OCLC symbol*] (OCLC) .... IET
East Texas State University, Texarkana, TX [*Library symbol Library of Congress*] (LCLS) .... TxTeET
East Three [*Zambia*] [*ICAO location identifier*] (ICLI) .... FLEC
East Timor [*ISO three-letter standard code*] (CNC) .... TMP
East Timor [*ISO two-letter standard code*] (CNC) .... TP
East Timor Human Rights Committee (EA) .... ETHRC
East Timor News Agency .... ETNA
East Timor Project [*Defunct*] (EA) .... ETP
East Traverse Mountains [*Utah*] [*Seismograph station code, US Geological Survey*] (SEIS) .... ETU
East Troy Public Library, East Troy, WI [*Library symbol Library of Congress*] (LCLS) .... WEa
East Two [*Zambia*] [*ICAO location identifier*] (ICLI) .... FLEB
East Washington Railway Co. [*AAR code*] .... EW
East Wenatchee, WA [*FM radio station call letters*] .... KYSN
East West Academy of Healing Arts (EA) .... EWAHA
East West Center, Honolulu, HI [*OCLC symbol*] (OCLC) .... HWE
East West European [*Bulgaria*] [*ICAO designator*] (FAAC) .... EWE
East West Resources [*Vancouver Stock Exchange symbol*] .... EWR
East Wind Trade Associates [*Defunct*] (EA) .... EWTA
East York Public Library [*UTLAS symbol*] .... EYP
East York Public Library, Toronto, ON, Canada [*Library symbol Library of Congress*] (LCLS) .... CaOTEY
East York Public Library, Toronto, Ontario [*Library symbol National Library of Canada*] (NLC) .... OTEY
East Yorkshire Militia [*British military*] (DMA) .... EY
East Yorkshire Regiment [*Military unit*] [*British*] (ROG) .... E YORK R

East Yorkshire Regiment [*Military unit*] [*British*] .... EYR
Eastbay, Inc. [*Associated Press*] (SAG) .... Eastbay
Eastbay, Inc. [*NASDAQ symbol*] (SAG) .... EBAY
Eastbound .... EB
Eastbound (FAAC) .... EBND
Eastbound Basing and Billing Book .... EB & BB
Eastchester Public Library, Eastchester, NY [*Library symbol Library of
Congress*] (LCLS) .... NEa
Eastco Indl Safety Wrrt [*NASDAQ symbol*] (TTSB) .... ESTOW
Eastco Industrial Safety [*Associated Press*] (SAG) .... Estco
Eastco Industrial Safety [*NASDAQ symbol*] (TTSB) .... ESTO
Eastco Industrial Safety Corp. [*Associated Press*] (SAG) .... Eastco
Eastco Industrial Safety Corp. [*NASDAQ symbol*] (NQ) .... ESTO
Eastcoast Petroleum Operators' Association [*Canada*] .... EPOA
Easter .... E
Easter Island [*Seismograph station code, US Geological Survey*] (SEIS) .... EIC
Easter Island [*Chile*] [*Airport symbol*] (OAG) .... IPC
Easter Island [*MARC geographic area code Library of Congress*] (LCCP) ..... poea--
Easter Island Committee (EA) .... EIC
Easter Offerings [*to a church*] .... EO
Easter Seal Research Foundation of the National Easter Seal Society
(EA) .... ESRF
Easter Term .... ET
Easterline Angus (SAA) .... EA
Easterling Family Genealogical Society (EA) .... EFGS
Easterly (WDAA) .... E
Easterly .... ELY
Eastern (WDAA) .... EAST
Eastern .... EASTN
Eastern .... ERN
Eastern .... ESTN
Eastern .... ESTRN
Eastern Academy of Sexual Therapy [*Later, SSTAR*] (EA) .... EAST
Eastern Administrative Support Center [*Marine science*] (OSRA) .... EASC
Eastern Administrative Support Center (USDC) .... EASC
Eastern Aerospace Rescue and Recovery Center [*Air Force*] ...... EARC
Eastern Africa Law Reports [*A publication*] (DLA) .... EA
Eastern Africa Law Reports [*Durban*] [*A publication*] (DLA) .... East Afr L Rep
Eastern Africa Law Review [*A publication*] (DLA) .... E Afr L Rev
Eastern Air Command [*CBI Theater*] [*World War II*] .... EAC
Eastern Air Defense Command (SAA) .... EADC
Eastern Air Defense Control Center (SAA) .... EADCC
Eastern Air Defense Force .... EADF
Eastern Air Executive Ltd. [*British ICAO designator*] (FAAC) ...... EAX
Eastern Air Lines, Inc. [*ICAO designator*] .... EA
Eastern Air Procurement District .... EAPD
Eastern Air Transport .... EAT
Eastern Air Transport, Inc. [*FAA designator*] (FAAC) .... EAH
Eastern Airlines [*ICAO designator*] (AD) .... RI
Eastern Airways [*British ICAO designator*] (ICDA) .... EN
Eastern American Natural Gas Trust [*Associated Press*] (SAG) ... EstANG
Eastern American Natural Gas Trust [*NYSE symbol*] (SAG) .... NGT
Eastern AmerNatlGasTr'SPERs' [*NYSE symbol*] (TTSB) .... NGT
Eastern Analytical Symposium .... EAS
Eastern & Midlands Railway [*British*] (ROG) .... EMR
Eastern and Southern African Initiative in Debt and Reserves
Management (ECON) .... ESAIDARM
Eastern and Southern African Mineral Resources Development
Center .... ESAMRDC
Eastern and Southern African Regional Branch of the International Council
on Archives [*Nairobi, Kenya*] (EAIO) .... ESARBICA
Eastern Apicultural Society of North America (EA) .... EAS
Eastern Arctic Research Laboratory, Indian and Northern Affairs Canada
[*Laboratoire de Recherches Arctique de l'Est, Affaires Indiennes et du Nord
Canada*], Igloolik, Northwest Territories [*Library symbol National Library of
Canada*] (BIB) .... NWIIE
Eastern Area .... EA
Eastern Area Frequency Coordinator .... EAFC
Eastern Area Library Cooperative, Cedar Falls, IA [*Library symbol Library of
Congress*] (LCLS) .... IaCfE
Eastern Area, Military Traffic Management and Terminal Service
(AABC) .... EAMTMTS
Eastern Area Military Traffic Management Command (AFIT) .... EAMTMC
Eastern Arizona College [*Formerly, EAJC*] [*Thatcher*] .... EAC
Eastern Arizona College, Thatcher, AZ [*Library symbol Library of Congress*]
(LCLS) .... AzThE
Eastern Arizona Junior College [*Later, EAC*] .... EAJC
Eastern Arts Association (AEBS) .... EAA
Eastern Association of College Deans and Advisers of Students
(AEBS) .... EADAS
Eastern Association of Rowing Colleges (EA) .... EARC
Eastern Atlantic and Mediterranean [*Military*] .... ELM
Eastern Atlantic and Mediterranean Command [*Military*] .... EAMC
Eastern Atlantic and Mediterranean Command [*Military*] .... EASTLANTMEDCOM
Eastern Atlantic Area [*NATO*] .... EASTLANT
Eastern Atlantic, Channel and North Sea Orders for Ships [*NATO*]
(NATG) .... ECNOS
Eastern Atlantic Planning Guidance [*NATO*] (NATG) .... EAPG
Eastern Atlantic War Plan [*NATO*] (NATG) .... EAWP
Eastern Authorities Orchestral Association [*British*] .... EAOA
Eastern Bakeries Ltd. [*Toronto Stock Exchange symbol*] .... EBK
Eastern Bancorp [*NASDAQ symbol*] (TTSB) .... EBCP
Eastern Bancorp, Inc. [*NASDAQ symbol*] (SAG) .... EBCP
Eastern Bancorp, Inc. [*Associated Press*] (SAG) .... EstnBc

Eastern Baptist Theological Seminary, Philadelphia, PA [*OCLC symbol*]
(OCLC) .... EBS
Eastern Baptist Theological Seminary, Philadelphia, PA [*Library symbol
Library of Congress*] (LCLS) .... PPEB
Eastern Base Section [*Mediterranean and England*] [*Army World War II*] .... EBS
Eastern Basketball League .... EBL
Eastern Bering Sea .... EBS
Eastern Bird Banding Association (EA) .... EBBA
Eastern Building Material Dealers Association (SRA) .... EBMDA
Eastern California Shear Zone [*Geology*] .... ECSZ
Eastern Caribbean Central Bank [*Formerly, East Caribbean Currency
Authority*] [*Basseterre, St. Christopher*] (GEA) .... ECCB
Eastern Caribbean Natural Area Management Program (EERA) ..... ECNAP
Eastern Caribbean States Export Development Agency [*Dominica*]
(EY) .... ECSEDA
Eastern Carolina Aviation, Inc. [*ICAO designator*] (FAAC) .... ECI
Eastern Catholic Life, Passaic, NJ [*Library symbol Library of Congress*]
(LCLS) .... NjPasE
Eastern Cedar [*Utility pole*] [*Telecommunications*] (TEL) .... EC
Eastern Central .... EC
Eastern Central Motor Carriers Association .... ECMCA
Eastern Central Motor Carriers Association, Agent, Akron OH [*STAC*] .. ECA
Eastern Claims Conference (EA) .... ECC
Eastern Coach Works [*British*] (DCTA) .... ECW
Eastern Coal Transportation Conference (EA) .... ECTC
Eastern Coast Breweriana Association (EA) .... ECBA
Eastern College Athletic Conference (EA) .... ECAC
Eastern College Basketball Association (EA) .... ECBA
Eastern College Hockey Association (EA) .... ECHA
Eastern College Personnel Officers .... ECPO
Eastern College, St. Davids, PA [*OCLC symbol*] (OCLC) .... EAS
Eastern College, St. Davids, PA [*Library symbol Library of Congress*]
(LCLS) .... PstdE
Eastern College Soccer Association (EA) .... ECSA
Eastern College Soccer Officials Bureau [*Later, ECSA*] .... ECSOB
Eastern Command [*World War II*] .... EASCOM
Eastern Command [*British*] .... EC
Eastern Communications Region [*Military*] (AFM) .... EASTCOMMRGN
Eastern Communications Region [*Air Force*] .... ECOMMRGN
Eastern Co. [*AMEX symbol*] (SPSG) .... EML
Eastern Co. [*Associated Press*] (SAG) .... EstnCo
Eastern Connecticut Clam Diggers Association [*Defunct*] (EA) ... ECCDA
Eastern Connecticut State College, J. Eugene Smith Library, Willimantic,
CT [*OCLC symbol*] (OCLC) .... CTW
Eastern Connecticut State College, Willimantic, CT [*Library symbol Library of
Congress*] (LCLS) .... CtWillN
Eastern Construction Co. in Laos (CINC) .... ECCOIL
Eastern Continental Air Defense Region (DNAB) .... EASTCONRADREG
Eastern Contract Management Region [*Air Force*] .... ECMR
Eastern Cooperative Oncology Group [*Research center*] (RCD) ... ECOG
Eastern Cosmetic Manufacturers Association .... ECMA
Eastern Counties Newspapers Ltd., Norwich, United Kingdom [*Library
symbol Library of Congress*] (LCLS) .... UkNrE
Eastern Counties Omnibus Co. Ltd. [*British*] .... ECO
Eastern Counties Omnibus Co. Ltd. [*British*] (DCTA) .... ECOC
Eastern Counties Operational Research Society (PDAA) .... ECORS
Eastern Counties Railway [*British*] (ROG) .... ECR
Eastern Counties Regional Library, Mulgrave, Nova Scotia [*Library symbol
National Library of Canada*] (NLC) .... NSME
Eastern Counties Regional Library, Mulgrave, NS, Canada [*Library symbol
Library of Congress*] (LCLS) .... CaNSME
Eastern Dark-Fired Tobacco Growers Association (EA) .... ED-FTGA
Eastern Daylight Saving Time .... EDST
Eastern Daylight Time .... EDT
Eastern Deciduous Forest Biome [*Ecological biogeographic study*] .... EDFB
Eastern Defense Command [*Army*] .... EDC
Eastern Development Division [*Air Force*] .... EDD
Eastern District [*ATSC*] .... ED
Eastern District Court Reports [*South Africa*] [*A publication*] (DLA) .... East DC
Eastern District Court Reports [*South Africa*] [*A publication*] (DLA) .... ED
Eastern District Court Reports [*South Africa*] [*A publication*] (DLA) .... EDC
Eastern District Court Reports [*South Africa*] [*A publication*] (DLA) .... Gane
Eastern Districts, Local Division, South African Law Reports
[*A publication*] (DLA) .... East DL
Eastern Diverging Volcanism [*Geology*] .... EDV
Eastern Dry Cleaning and Laundry Machinery Distributors Association
[*Defunct*] (EA) .... EDCLMDA
Eastern Economic Association .... EEA
Eastern Educational Television Network [*Boston, MA*] [*Telecommunications
service*] (TSSD) .... EEN
Eastern Electricity Board [*British*] .... EEB
Eastern Energy and Land Use Team [*Kearneysville, WV*] [*Department of the
Interior*] (GRD) .... EELUT
Eastern Enterprises [*Associated Press*] (SAG) .... EastEn
Eastern Enterprises [*NYSE symbol*] (SPSG) .... EFU
Eastern Environmental Radiation Facility [*Environmental Protection
Agency*] (IID) .... EERF
Eastern Environmental Radiation Laboratory [*Environmental Protection
Agency*] .... EERL
Eastern Environmental Services [*Associated Press*] (SAG) .... EstnEn
Eastern Environmental Services, Inc. [*NASDAQ symbol*] (NQ) ... EESI
Eastern Environmental Svc [*NASDAQ symbol*] (TTSB) .... EESI
Eastern Equatorial Pacific .... EEP
Eastern Equatorial Pacific Sea Surface Temperature [*Oceanography*] .... ESST
Eastern Equine Encephalitis [*Virus*] (DAVI) .... EEE

Eastern Equine Encephalomyelitis [*Virus*] ... EEE
Eastern Equine Encephalomyelitis Virus [*Medicine*] (DMAA) ... EEEV
Eastern Establishment [*Politics*] ... EE
Eastern Europe Bible Mission (EA) ... EEBM
Eastern Europe Business Information Center [*Department of Commerce*] ... EEBIC
Eastern Europe Solidarity Campaign (EAIO) ... EESC
Eastern European Mission [*Later, SGA*] ... EEM
Eastern European Time (DCTA) ... EET
Eastern Executive Air Charter Ltd. [*British*] [*FAA designator*] (FAAC) ... GNS
Eastern Federation of Building Trades' Employers [*British*] (BI) ... EFBTE
Eastern Federation of Feed Merchants (SRA) ... EFFM
Eastern Finance Association (EA) ... EFA
Eastern Fishermen's Federation [*See also FPE*] [*Canada*] ... EFF
Eastern Flying Service Ltd. [*Canada ICAO designator*] (FAAC) ... SPR
Eastern Football Conference ... EFC
Eastern Freight Inspection Bureau ... EFIB
Eastern Group of Painters, Montreal [*1938*] [*Canada*] (NGC) ... EGP
Eastern Gulf of Mexico ... EGMEX
Eastern Historical Commission, Prospect Park, NJ [*Library symbol Library of Congress*] (LCLS) ... NjPpE
Eastern Hockey League ... EHL
Eastern Hockey League (BARN) ... EHL
Eastern Idaho Regional Medical Center, Medical Library, Idaho Falls, ID [*Library symbol*] [*Library of Congress*] (LCLS) ... IdIfH
Eastern Illinois State College [*Later, EIU*] ... EISC
Eastern Illinois University (GAGS) ... East Ill U
Eastern Illinois University [*Formerly, EISC*] [*Charleston*] ... EIU
Eastern Illinois University, Charleston, IL [*OCLC symbol*] (OCLC) ... IAD
Eastern Illinois University, Charleston, IL [*Library symbol Library of Congress*] (LCLS) ... ICharE
Eastern Independent Collegiate Basketball League ... EICBL
Eastern Intercollegiate Gymnastic League (EA) ... EIGL
Eastern Joint Computer Conference ... EJCC
Eastern Journal of International Law [*A publication*] (DLA) ... East J Int L
Eastern Journal of International Law [*A publication*] (ILCA) ... Eastern J Int L
Eastern Journal of International Law [*A publication*] (DLA) ... Eastern J In'tl L
Eastern Journal of International Law [*A publication*] (DLA) ... Eastern J of Internat L
Eastern Kentucky State College [*Later, EKU*] ... EKSC
Eastern Kentucky University (GAGS) ... East Ky U
Eastern Kentucky University [*Formerly, EKSC*] [*Richmond*] ... EKU
Eastern Kentucky University, Richmond, KY [*OCLC symbol*] (OCLC) ... KEU
Eastern Kentucky University, Richmond, KY [*Library symbol Library of Congress*] (LCLS) ... KyRE
Eastern King's Memorial Hospital, Wolfville, Nova Scotia [*Library symbol National Library of Canada*] (NLC) ... NSWEK
Eastern Knight [*Freemasonry*] (ROG) ... EK
Eastern Lamp and Lighting Association (EA) ... ELLA
Eastern Launch Site (MCD) ... ELS
Eastern Law Reporter [*Canada*] [*A publication*] (DLA) ... East LR
Eastern Law Reporter [*Canada*] [*A publication*] (DLA) ... East LR (Can)
Eastern Law Reporter [*Canada*] [*A publication*] (DLA) ... ELR
Eastern League [*Baseball*] ... EL
Eastern Lights Resources Ltd. [*Vancouver Stock Exchange symbol*] ... ETL
Eastern Line of Communication [*World War II*] ... ELOC
Eastern Lines ... EL
Eastern Long Island Hospital, Greenport, NY [*Library symbol Library of Congress*] (LCLS) ... NGrpEH
Eastern Management Group (HGAA) ... EMG
Eastern Marathon Swimming Association (EA) ... EMSA
Eastern Massachusetts Regional Library System [*Information service or system*] (IID) ... EMRLS
Eastern Mediterranean Area [*NATO*] (NATG) ... MEDEAST
Eastern Mediterranean Regional Office [*World Health Organization*] [*Information service or system*] (IID) ... EMRO
Eastern Mediterranean Special Service Intelligence Bureau [*World War I*] [*British*] ... EMSIB
Eastern Megalopolis [*Proposed name for possible "super-city" formed by growth and mergers of other cities*] ... EM
Eastern Mennonite College [*Virginia*] ... EMC
Eastern Mennonite College, Harrisonburg, VA [*OCLC symbol*] (OCLC) ... VEM
Eastern Mennonite College, Harrisonburg, VA [*Library symbol Library of Congress*] (LCLS) ... ViHarEM
Eastern Metropolitan Fruit Growers' Association [*Australia*] ... EMFGA
Eastern Michigan University (GAGS) ... East Mich U
Eastern Michigan University [*Ypsilanti*] ... EMU
Eastern Michigan University, Ypsilanti, MI [*OCLC symbol*] (OCLC) ... EYE
Eastern Michigan University, Ypsilanti, MI [*Library symbol Library of Congress*] (LCLS) ... MiYEM
Eastern Microwave, Inc. [*Telecommunications service*] (TSSD) ... EMI
Eastern Mineral Law Foundation (EA) ... EMLF
Eastern Mines Ltd. [*Vancouver Stock Exchange symbol*] ... EAN
Eastern Montana College (GAGS) ... East Mont C
Eastern Montana College, Billings, MT [*Library symbol Library of Congress*] (LCLS) ... MtBilE
Eastern Museum of Motor Racing (EA) ... EMMR
Eastern Nazarene College, Wollaston, MA [*OCLC symbol*] (OCLC) ... ENC
Eastern Nazarene College, Wollaston, MA [*Library symbol Library of Congress*] (LCLS) ... MWollE
Eastern New Mexico University (GAGS) ... East N Mex U
Eastern New Mexico University ... ENMU
Eastern New Mexico University, Portales, NM [*OCLC symbol*] (OCLC) ... IPU
Eastern New Mexico University, Portales, NM [*Library symbol Library of Congress*] (LCLS) ... NmPE
Eastern New Mexico University, Roswell Campus, Roswell, NM [*Library symbol Library of Congress*] (LCLS) ... NmRE
Eastern News Agency [*Bangladesh*] (FEA) ... ENA
Eastern Nigeria Law Reports [*1956-60*] [*A publication*] (DLA) ... ENLR
Eastern Nigeria Legal Notice [*A publication*] (DLA) ... ENLN
Eastern Oklahoma District Library, Muskogee, OK [*OCLC symbol*] (OCLC) ... OEA
Eastern Oklahoma District Library, Muskogee, OK [*Library symbol Library of Congress*] (LCLS) ... OkMuE
Eastern Ontario Regional Library, Ottawa, ON, Canada [*Library symbol Library of Congress*] (LCLS) ... CaOOEO
Eastern Ontario Regional Library, Ottawa, Ontario [*Library symbol National Library of Canada*] (NLC) ... OOEO
Eastern Orchestral Board [*British*] [*An association*] (DBA) ... EOB
Eastern Oregon College (GAGS) ... East Ore C
Eastern Oregon College ... EOC
Eastern Oregon College, La Grande, OR [*Library symbol Library of Congress*] (LCLS) ... OrLgE
Eastern Oregon State College ... EOSC
Eastern Orthodox ... E Orth
Eastern Orthodox ... EO
Eastern Owyhee County District Library, Grand View, ID [*Library symbol*] [*Library of Congress*] (LCLS) ... IdGv
Eastern Pacific Area (MUGU) ... EASTPAC
Eastern Pacific Aviation Ltd. [*Canada ICAO designator*] (FAAC) ... EPB
Eastern Pacific Command [*Navy*] ... EASTPAC
Eastern Pacific Hurricane Center [*San Francisco*] [*National Weather Service*] (NOAA) ... EPHC
Eastern Pacific Oceanic Conference ... EPOC
Eastern Pacific Tuna Fishing Organization [*Marine science*] (OSRA) ... OAPO
Eastern Pakistan Rifles [*British military*] (DMA) ... EPR
Eastern Peninsula Library System [*Library network*] ... EPLS
Eastern Pennsylvania Psychiatric Institute ... EPPI
Eastern Pennsylvania Psychiatric Institute, Philadelphia, PA [*Library symbol Library of Congress*] (LCLS) ... PPEP
Eastern Pentecostal Bible College, Peterborough, ON, Canada [*Library symbol Library of Congress*] (LCLS) ... CaOPeEPB
Eastern Pentecostal Bible College, Peterborough, Ontario [*Library symbol National Library of Canada*] (NLC) ... OPEPB
Eastern Pilgrim College [*Later, United Weslayan College*] [*Pennsylvania*] ... EPC
Eastern Plains Regional Library, Tucumcari, NM [*Library symbol Library of Congress*] (LCLS) ... NmTuE
Eastern Primary Standards Laboratory ... EPSL
Eastern Procurement Division [*Navy*] ... EPD
Eastern Production District [*Navy*] ... EPD
Eastern Professional Hockey League ... EPHL
Eastern Professional River Outfitters Association (EA) ... EPRO
Eastern Professional Ski Instructors Association [*Formerly, EPSTI*] (EA) ... EPSIA
Eastern Professional Ski Touring Instructors [*Later, EPSIA*] (EA) ... EPSTI
Eastern Provincial Airways [*Labrador*] ... EPA
Eastern Provincial Airways [*Labrador*] [*ICAO designator*] (OAG) ... PV
Eastern Psychiatric Research Association (EA) ... EPRA
Eastern Psychological Association ... EPA
Eastern Public Radio Network (NTCM) ... EPRN
Eastern Railroad Association [*Defunct*] (EA) ... ERA
Eastern Railroad Presidents Conference [*Later, ERA*] (EA) ... ERPC
Eastern Range Ships ... ERS
Eastern Recruiting Division ... ERD
Eastern Region of Nigeria Law Reports [*A publication*] (DLA) ... ERLR
Eastern Region of Nigeria Law Reports [*A publication*] (DLA) ... ERNLR
Eastern Region Public Notice [*Nigeria*] [*A publication*] (DLA) ... ERPN
Eastern Region SEATO [*Southeast Asia Treaty Organization*] **Field Forces** (CINC) ... ERSFF
Eastern Region Teacher Education Consortium (AIE) ... ERTEC
Eastern Regional Institute for Education ... ERIE
Eastern Regional Office Machine Dealers Association Convention (TSPED) ... EROMDA
Eastern Regional Organization for Public Administration GG2 [*Manila, Philippines*] [*See also OROAP*] ... EROPA
Eastern Regional Research Center [*Department of Agriculture*] [*Philadelphia, PA*] (GRD) ... ERRC
Eastern Reporter [*A publication*] (ILCA) ... East
Eastern Reporter [*A publication*] (DLA) ... East Rep
Eastern Rift Zone [*Geology*] ... ERZ
Eastern Rite News Service ... ER
Eastern Rugby Union of America (EA) ... ERU
Eastern School Law Review [*A publication*] (DLA) ... E School L Rev
Eastern Sea Frontier ... EASTSEAFRON
Eastern Sea Frontier ... ESF
Eastern Sea Frontier Control Local of Shipping in Gulf of Maine ... EASTCON
Eastern Secondary Standards Laboratory ... ESSL
Eastern Shore Community College, Learning Resources Center, Melfa, VA [*Library symbol Library of Congress*] (LCLS) ... ViMelE
Eastern Shore Public Library, Accomac, VA [*Library symbol Library of Congress*] (LCLS) ... ViAc
Eastern Shore Regional Library Resource Center [*Library network*] ... ESRL
Eastern Signal Corps Replacement Training Center ... ESCRTC
Eastern Simulation Council ... ESC
Eastern Ski Area Operators Association (EA) ... ESAOA
Eastern Ski Association [*Later, USSA*] (EA) ... ESA
Eastern Ski Representatives Association (EA) ... ESRA
Eastern Soccer Officials Bureau [*Later, ECSA*] (EA) ... ESOB
Eastern Sociological Society (AEBS) ... ESS
Eastern Sovereign Base Area [*British military*] (DMA) ... ESBA

Eastern Space and Missile Center [*Patrick Air Force Base, FL*] [*Also, ETR*] [*Air Force*] ... ESMC
Eastern Special Passenger [*Eastern Airlines*] ... ESP
Eastern Standard Summer Time [*Australia*] ... ESST
Eastern Standard Time ... E
Eastern Standard Time ... EST
Eastern State Hospital, Medical Lake, WA [*Library symbol Library of Congress*] (LCLS) ... WaMeH
Eastern State School and Hospital, Trevose, PA [*OCLC symbol*] (OCLC) ... PHE
Eastern States (ADA) ... ES
Eastern States Blast Furnace and Coke Oven Association (EA) ... ESBFCOA
Eastern States International Construction Expo and Conference [*Associated General Contractors of America - Carolinas Branch*] (TSPED) ... EASTCON
Eastern Summer Time (IAA) ... EST
Eastern Surfing Association (EA) ... ESA
Eastern Tank Carrier Conference ... ETCC
Eastern Task Force ... ETF
Eastern Technical Net [*Air Force*] ... ETN
Eastern Telecommunications Philippines, Inc. [*Manila*] ... ETPI
Eastern Telegraph (IAA) ... ET
Eastern Tennessee Seismic Zone [*Geology*] ... ETSV
Eastern Tennis Patrons (EA) ... ETP
Eastern Test Range [*See also ESMC*] [*Air Force*] ... ETR
Eastern Test Range [*Formerly, Atlantic Missile Range*] [*Air Force*] ... ETRA
Eastern Test Range Instrumentation Ship (DNAB) ... ETRIS
Eastern Test Range Operations Directive [*Air Force*] (NASA) ... ETROD
Eastern Time (GPO) ... ET
Eastern Transport Air Force ... EASTAF
Eastern Tropical North Pacific Sea ... ETNP
Eastern Tropical Pacific [*Oceanographic expedition*] ... EASTROPAC
Eastern Tropical Pacific [*Marine science*] (OSRA) ... ETP
Eastern Tropical Pacific (USDC) ... ETP
Eastern Tropical Pacific Ocean ... ETP
Eastern Trunk Line (IAA) ... ETL
Eastern Underwriters Association [*Later, ISO*] ... EUA
Eastern United States ... EUS
Eastern United States Business Law Review [*A publication*] (DLA) ... East US Bus L Rev
Eastern Upper Peninsula [*Michigan*] ... EUP
Eastern Util Assoc [*NYSE symbol*] (TTSB) ... EUA
Eastern Utilities Associates [*NYSE symbol*] (SPSG) ... EUA
Eastern Utilities Association [*Associated Press*] (SAG) ... EastUtl
Eastern Verbal Investigators League ... EVIL
Eastern Virginia Medical Authority, Norfolk, VA [*OCLC symbol*] (OCLC) ... VNN
Eastern Virginia Medical School, Norfolk, VA [*Library symbol Library of Congress*] (LCLS) ... ViNE
Eastern Virginia Medical School, Norfolk, VA [*Library symbol*] [*Library of Congress*] (LCLS) ... ViNEVM
Eastern Virginia Medicine School (GAGS) ... East Va Med Sch
Eastern War Time [*World War II*] ... EWT
Eastern Washington State College, Cheney, WA [*Library symbol Library of Congress*] (LCLS) ... WaChenE
Eastern Washington State College, Cheney, WA [*OCLC symbol*] (OCLC) ... WEA
Eastern Washington State Historical Society, Museum Library, Spokane, WA [*Library symbol Library of Congress*] (LCLS) ... WaSpHiE
Eastern Washington University (GAGS) ... East Wash U
Eastern Washington University (PDAA) ... EWU
Eastern Women's Amateur Basketball League of the AAU [*Amateur Athletic Union of the United States*] (EA) ... EWABL/AAU
Eastern Women's Center (EA) ... EWC
Eastern Women's Headwear Association [*Later, AMMA*] (EA) ... EWHA
Eastern Wyoming College, Torrington, WY [*Library symbol Library of Congress*] (LCLS) ... WyToE
Eastern Yiddish (BJA) ... EY
Eastern Zone ... EZ
Eastfield College, Mesquite, TX [*Library symbol Library of Congress*] (LCLS) ... TxMeE
Eastfield Resources [*Vancouver Stock Exchange symbol*] ... ETF
Eastgroup Properties [*Associated Press*] (SAG) ... Estgp
Eastgroup Properties, Inc. [*NYSE symbol*] (SAG) ... EGP
EastGroup Properties SBI [*NYSE symbol*] (TTSB) ... EGP
Eastham Public Library, Eastham, MA [*Library symbol*] [*Library of Congress*] (LCLS) ... MEa
Easthamstead [*England*] ... EASTH
Eastind Airlines, Inc. [*FAA designator*] (FAAC) ... BBE
Eastland Air [*Australia ICAO designator*] (FAAC) ... ELA
Eastland, TX [*Location identifier FAA*] (FAAL) ... ETN
Eastland, TX [*AM radio station call letters*] ... KEAS
Eastland, TX [*FM radio station call letters*] ... KEAS-FM
Eastland, TX [*FM radio station call letters*] ... KVMX
Eastland, TX [*Location identifier FAA*] (FAAL) ... OIP
Eastmain Resources, Inc. [*Toronto Stock Exchange symbol*] ... EMN
Eastman Chemical [*NYSE symbol*] (TTSB) ... EMN
Eastman Chemical Co. [*Associated Press*] (SAG) ... EastChm
Eastman Chemical Co., Inc. [*NYSE symbol*] (SPSG) ... EMN
Eastman Dental Center [*University of Rochester*] [*Research center*] (RCD) ... EDC
Eastman Dental Center, Basil G. Bibby Library, Rochester, NY [*Library symbol Library of Congress*] (LCLS) ... NREd
Eastman Dental Center, Basil G. Bibby Library, Rochester, NY [*OCLC symbol*] (OCLC) ... VQG
Eastman, GA [*AM radio station call letters*] ... WUFF
Eastman, GA [*FM radio station call letters*] ... WUFF-FM
Eastman Kodak [*NYSE symbol*] (TTSB) ... EK
Eastman Kodak Co. [*NYSE symbol*] (SPSG) ... EK
Eastman Kodak Co. ... EKC
Eastman Kodak Co. [*Associated Press*] (SAG) ... EKodak
Eastman Kodak Co., Apparatus Division, Rochester, NY [*Library symbol Library of Congress*] (LCLS) ... NRE-A
Eastman Kodak Co., Business Library, Rochester, NY [*OCLC symbol*] (OCLC) ... VQI
Eastman Kodak Co., Engineering Division, Library, Rochester, NY [*OCLC symbol*] (OCLC) ... VQJ
Eastman Kodak Co., Engineering Division, Rochester, NY [*Library symbol Library of Congress*] (LCLS) ... NRE-E
Eastman Kodak Co., Health and Safety Laboratory, Library, Rochester, NY [*OCLC symbol*] (OCLC) ... VQK
Eastman Kodak Co., Health and Safety Laboratory, Rochester, NY [*Library symbol Library of Congress*] (LCLS) ... NRE-M
Eastman Kodak Co., KAD Library, Rochester, NY [*OCLC symbol*] (OCLC) ... VQH
Eastman Kodak Co., Photographic Technology Library, Rochester, NY [*Library symbol Library of Congress*] (LCLS) ... NRE-P
Eastman Kodak Co., Photographic Technology Library, Rochester, NY [*OCLC symbol*] (OCLC) ... VQL
Eastman Kodak Co., Research Laboratories, Library, Rochester, NY [*OCLC symbol*] (OCLC) ... VQM
Eastman Kodak Co., Research Laboratories, Rochester, NY [*Library symbol Library of Congress*] (LCLS) ... NRE-R
Eastman Kodak Co., Rochester, NY [*Library symbol Library of Congress*] (LCLS) ... NRE
Eastman Kodak Inst. Print Film (VRA) ... EKIP
Eastman Kodak/Navy Ordnance District (AAG) ... EK/NOD
Eastman School of Music, Rochester, NY [*OCLC symbol*] (OCLC) ... RES
Eastmaque Gold Mines Ltd. [*Toronto Stock Exchange symbol Vancouver Stock Exchange symbol*] ... EMG
Eastmont High School, East Wenatchee, WA [*Library symbol*] [*Library of Congress*] (LCLS) ... WaEawE
East-Northeast ... ENE
East-Northeastern (FAAC) ... ENERN
East-Ocean Meeting Point ... EASTOMP
Easton [*Maryland*] [*Airport symbol*] (AD) ... ESN
Easton Area Public Library, Easton, PA [*OCLC symbol*] (OCLC) ... EAP
Easton Area Public Library, Easton, PA [*Library symbol Library of Congress*] (LCLS) ... PE
Easton, MA [*FM radio station call letters*] ... WSHL
Easton, MD [*Location identifier FAA*] (FAAL) ... ESN
Easton, MD [*AM radio station call letters*] ... WCEI
Easton, MD [*FM radio station call letters*] ... WCEI-FM
Easton Minerals [*Vancouver Stock Exchange symbol*] ... EM
Easton, PA [*AM radio station call letters*] (RBYB) ... WEEX-AM
Easton, PA [*AM radio station call letters*] ... WEST
Easton, PA [*AM radio station call letters*] ... WIPI
Easton, PA [*FM radio station call letters*] ... WJRH
Easton, PA [*FM radio station call letters*] ... WLEV
Easton, PA [*FM radio station call letters*] ... WODE
Eastover Corp. [*NASDAQ symbol*] (NQ) ... EAST
Eastplain Elementary School, North Massapequa, NY [*Library symbol*] [*Library of Congress*] (LCLS) ... NNomEE
Eastport High School, Eastport, NY [*Library symbol Library of Congress*] (LCLS) ... NEaspHS
Eastport, ME [*FM radio station call letters*] ... WSHD
Eastridge High School Library, Rochester, NY [*OCLC symbol*] (OCLC) ... RWD
East's English King's Bench Term Reports [*A publication*] (DLA) ... E
East's English King's Bench Term Reports [*A publication*] (DLA) ... Ea
East's English King's Bench Term Reports [*A publication*] (DLA) ... East
East's English King's Bench Term Reports [*A publication*] (DLA) ... East (Eng)
East's English King's Bench Term Reports [*A publication*] (DLA) ... ER
East's Notes of Cases [*1785-1821*] [*Bengal, India*] [*A publication*] (DLA) ... Ea
East's Notes of Cases in Morley's East Indian Digest [*A publication*] (DLA) ... East
East's Notes of Cases in Morley's East Indian Digest [*A publication*] (DLA) ... East N of C
East's Pleas of the Crown [*A publication*] (DLA) ... East PC
East's Pleas of the Crown [*A publication*] (DLA) ... East Pl Cr
East's Pleas of the Crown [*A publication*] (DLA) ... EPC
East's Pleas of the Crown (England) [*A publication*] (DLA) ... East PC (Eng)
Eastside ... ESTSD
Eastside Medical Laboratory, Redmond, WA [*Library symbol*] [*Library of Congress*] (LCLS) ... WaRedEM
Eastsound [*Washington*] [*Airport symbol*] (OAG) ... ESD
East-Southeast ... ESE
East-Southeastern (FAAC) ... ESERN
East-Southeastward (FAAC) ... ESEWD
Eastward Position ... EP
East-West ... EW
East-West Acceleration ... EWA
East-West Airlines [*ICAO designator*] (AD) ... EW
Eastwest Airlines, Erfurt [*Germany*] [*FAA designator*] (FAAC) ... EWT
East-West Airlines Ltd. [*Australia ICAO designator*] (FAAC) ... EWA
East-West Center (EA) ... EWC
East-West Center, Population Institute, Honolulu, HI [*Library symbol Library of Congress*] (LCLS) ... HHE-P
East-West Communication Institute [*Later, East-West Institute of Culture and Communication*] [*Research center*] (RCD) ... EWCI
East-West Cultural Center (EA) ... EWCC
East-West Environment and Policy Institute [*East-West Center*] [*Research center*] (RCD) ... EAPI
East-West Fine, Hundreds ... EWFH
East-West Fine, Tens ... EWFT
East-West Fine, Units ... EWFU

East-West Institute of Culture and Communication [*Research center*] (RCD) .... EW-CLI
East-West Population Institute .... EWPI
East-West Resource Systems Institute [*Research center*] (RCD) .... RSI
East-West Sign Language Association [*Japan*] (SLS) .... EWSLA
East-West Speed .... EWS
East-West Trade Council [*Defunct*] (EA) .... EWTC
East-West Trade Policy Committee .... EWTPC
Eastwind Group [*NASDAQ symbol*] (TTSB) .... EWND
Eastwind Group, Inc. (The) [*Associated Press*] (SAG) .... Estwind
Eastwind Group, Inc. (The) [*NASDAQ symbol*] (SAG) .... EWND
Eastwood Hospital, Memphis, TN [*Library symbol Library of Congress*] (LCLS) .... TME
Easy [*Phonetic alphabet*] [*World War II*] (DSUE) .... E
Easy [*Slang*] .... EZ
Easy Access .... EZACC
Easy Access Data Interchange [*Unisys Corp.*] (IT) .... EaDI
Easy Access Ordering System [*Automated book ordering system, Blackwells North America*] (NITA) .... EAOS
Easy Access Report Language [*Computer science*] (MHDB) .... EARL
Easy Application Language [*Computer science*] (MHDB) .... EASAL
Easy Bleaching Kraft [*Pulp and paper technology*] .... EBK
Easy Instruction Automatic Computer (IAA) .... EASIAC
Easy Listening [*Radio*] (NTCM) .... EZ
Easy Magic Cookery Council [*Defunct*] (EA) .... EMCC
Easy Processing Channel .... EPC
Easy Projection (PDAA) .... EP
Easy to Move [*Horticulture*] .... E
Easy to Reach [*Telecommunications*] (TEL) .... ER
Easy to Test [*Audiology*] .... ETT
Easy Washer [*Laboratory science*] .... EAW
Eat Right and Slim Easily [*Weight Watchers, Inc., competition*] .... ERASE
Eateries, Inc. [*Associated Press*] (SAG) .... Eaterie
Eateries, Inc. [*NASDAQ symbol*] (NQ) .... EATS
Eatery .... ETRY
Eat-In [*Kitchen*] [*Classified advertising*] .... EI
Eat-In Kitchen [*Classified advertising*] .... EIK
Eating Attitude Test (EDAC) .... EAT
Eating Disorder Inventory [*Psychology*] .... EDI
Eating Disorder Unit [*Medicine*] (DAVI) .... EDU
Eating Disorders Association (EAIO) .... EDA
Eaton Corp. [*Associated Press*] (SAG) .... Eaton
Eaton Corp. [*NYSE symbol*] (SPSG) .... ETN
Eaton Corp. Engineering Research Center, Southfield, MI [*Library symbol*] [*Library of Congress*] (LCLS) .... MiSfE
Eaton Corp., Milwaukee, WI [*Library symbol Library of Congress*] (LCLS) .... WME
Eaton Corp., Milwaukee, WI [*Library symbol*] [*Library of Congress*] (LCLS) .... WMEC
Eaton Laboratories, Inc. [*Research code symbol*] .... F
Eaton Laboratories, Inc. [*Research code symbol*] .... NF
Eaton Laboratories, Inc. [*Research code symbol*] .... U
Eaton, OH [*AM radio station call letters*] .... WCTM
Eaton, OH [*FM radio station call letters*] .... WGTZ
Eaton Public Library, Eaton, CO [*Library symbol Library of Congress*] (LCLS) .... CoEa
Eaton Rapids Public Library, Eaton Rapids, MI [*Library symbol Library of Congress*] (LCLS) .... MiEat
Eaton Trust Co. [*Toronto Stock Exchange symbol*] .... ET
Eaton Vance [*NASDAQ symbol*] (TTSB) .... EAVN
Eaton Vance Corp. [*Associated Press*] (SAG) .... EatnVan
Eaton Vance Corp. [*NASDAQ symbol*] (NQ) .... EAVN
Eaton-Lambert Syndrome [*Medicine*] (MEDA) .... E-L
Eaton-Lambert Syndrome [*Medicine*] (DMAA) .... ELS
Eaton's Motor Machine Gun Battery [*British military*] (DMA) .... EMMGB
Eaton's Supplement to Chipman on Contracts [*A publication*] (DLA) .... Eat Cont
Eatonton [*Georgia*] [*Seismograph station code, US Geological Survey*] (SEIS) .... ETG
Eatonton, GA [*AM radio station call letters*] .... WKVQ
Eatontown, NJ [*AM radio station call letters*] .... WHTG
Eatontown, NJ [*FM radio station call letters*] .... WHTG-FM
Eatontown Public Library, Eatontown, NJ [*Library symbol Library of Congress*] (LCLS) .... NjEa
Eatonville, FL [*AM radio station call letters*] .... WHBS
Eatonville, FL [*AM radio station call letters*] (RBYB) .... WRLZ-AM
Eatonville, WA [*FM radio station call letters*] .... KJUN
Eatonville, WA [*FM radio station call letters*] (RBYB) .... KKBY-FM
Eau Claire [*Wisconsin*] [*Airport symbol*] (OAG) .... EAU
Eau Claire County Hospital, Eau Claire, WI [*Library symbol Library of Congress*] (LCLS) .... WEC
Eau Claire District Library, Eau Claire, MI [*Library symbol Library of Congress*] (LCLS) .... MiEc
Eau Claire Public Library, Eau Claire, WI [*OCLC symbol*] (OCLC) .... GZF
Eau Claire Public Library, Eau Claire, WI [*Library symbol Library of Congress*] (LCLS) .... WE
Eau Claire, WI [*FM radio station call letters*] .... WAXX
Eau Claire, WI [*AM radio station call letters*] .... WBIZ
Eau Claire, WI [*FM radio station call letters*] .... WBIZ-FM
Eau Claire, WI [*AM radio station call letters*] .... WEAQ
Eau Claire, WI [*Television station call letters*] .... WEAU
Eau Claire, WI [*AM radio station call letters*] .... WEIO
Eau Claire, WI [*FM radio station call letters*] .... WHEM
Eau Claire, WI [*FM radio station call letters*] .... WIAL
Eau Claire, WI [*Television station call letters*] .... WQOW
Eau Claire, WI [*FM radio station call letters*] .... WUEC
Eau Claire, WI [*FM radio station call letters*] (RBYB) .... WVCF-FM
Eau Gallie Public Library, Melbourne, FL [*Library symbol Library of Congress*] (LCLS) .... FMeE
Eau-de-Vie [*Taken from the French pronunciation and used to refer to brandy*] .... ODV
Eavesdropping (DLA) .... EAVES
Eave-to-Eave Width [*of boxcar*] .... EW
EB, Inc. [*NASDAQ symbol*] (SAG) .... EBEB
EBASCO Services, Inc. Site Support Engineering [*Nuclear energy*] (NRCH) .... ESSE
EBASCO Standard Safety Analysis Report [*Nuclear energy*] (NRCH) .... ESSAR
Ebbinghaus Test [*Psychology*] (DAVI) .... ET
Ebenda (BJA) .... ebd
Ebenezer Society (EA) .... ES
Ebensburg, PA [*FM radio station call letters*] .... WQKK
Ebensburg, PA [*AM radio station call letters*] .... WRDD
Ebers-MOLL [*Metallo-Organic Liquid LASER*] **Model** [*Electronics*] (OA) .... EMM
Ebersole's Reports [*59-80 Iowa*] [*A publication*] (DLA) .... Ebersole
Ebersole's Reports [*59-80 Iowa*] [*A publication*] (DLA) .... Ebersole (IA)
Ebini [*Guyana*] [*ICAO location identifier*] (ICLI) .... SYEB
Eblanencis [*Signature of the Bishops of Dublin*] (ROG) .... EBLAN
Ebolowa [*Cameroon*] [*Airport symbol*] (AD) .... EBW
Ebolowa [*Cameroon*] [*ICAO location identifier*] (ICLI) .... FKKW
Ebonized (VRA) .... ebn
Ebony (VRA) .... ebn
Ebony Gold Corp. [*Vancouver Stock Exchange symbol*] .... EGC
Ebony Man [*Johnson Publishing Co., Inc.*] [*A publication*] .... EM
Eboracensis [*Signature of the Bishop of York*] (ROG) .... EBOR
Eboracum [*York*] [*County in England*] [*Latin*] (ROG) .... EBOR
Ebrei nell'Europa Orientale (BJA) .... ENEO
EBRI [*Employee Benefit Research Institute*] **Quarterly Pension Investment Report** [*A publication*] .... QPIR
Ebro Roquetas [*Spain*] [*Seismograph station code, US Geological Survey*] (SEIS) .... EBR
EBSCO Electronic Information [*EBSCO Industries, Inc.*] [*Information service or system*] (IID) .... EEI
Ebsco, Inc. [*ICAO designator*] (FAAC) .... DOL
EBSCO Publishing & EBSCO Subscription Service Service, Birmingham, AL [*Library symbol*] [*Library of Congress*] (LCLS) .... EbpS
Ebstein's Anomaly [*Cardiology*] .... EA
Ebsworth on the Law of Infants [*A publication*] (DLA) .... Ebs Inf
Eburnetoxin [*Biochemistry*] .... ETX
Eburneus [*Made of Ivory*] [*Pharmacy*] (ROG) .... EBURN
Ebury Press [*Publisher*] [*British*] .... EP
EBV [*Epstein-Barr Virus*] **Nuclear Antigen** [*Immunochemistry*] .... EBNA
Eby Elementary Identification Instrument [*Educational test*] .... EEII
EC Digital Evaluation System (MCD) .... ECDES
EC02, Inc. [*NASDAQ symbol*] (SAG) .... TIRE
ECC [*Emergency Control Center*] **Bypass Test Facility** [*Nuclear energy*] (NRCH) .... EBTF
ECC Group ADR [*Formerly, English China Clays ADR*] [*NYSE symbol*] (SPSG) .... ENC
ECC International [*NYSE symbol*] (TTSB) .... ECC
ECC International Ltd. [*Formerly, Educational Computer Corp.*] [*NYSE symbol*] (SPSG) .... ECC
ECC International Ltd. [*Formerly, Educational Computer Corp.*] [*Associated Press*] (SAG) .... ECC Int
Ecce Homo [*Behold the Man*] [*Latin*] (ROG) .... ECC HOM
Eccentric (AAG) .... ECC
Eccentric (IAA) .... ECCEN
Eccentric Geophysical Observatory [*Also, EOGO*] [*NASA*] .... EGO
Eccentric Mailbox User [*Electronic mail systems*] (NITA) .... EMU
Eccentric Orbital Geophysical Observatory [*Also, EGO*] [*NASA*] (MUGU) .... EOGO
Eccentric Variable-Angle Thermionic Rheostat .... EVATRON
Eccentrically Stiffened Cylindrical Shell .... ESCS
Eccentricity [*of application of load*] [*Aerospace*] (AAG) .... e
Eccentricity (ABBR) .... ECTCT
Eccentricity, Tilt, Precession [*Oceanography*] .... ETP
Eccles Public Library, Central Library, Eccles, United Kingdom [*Library symbol Library of Congress*] (LCLS) .... UkEc
Ecclesiastes [*Old Testament book*] (BJA) .... Ec
Ecclesiastes [*Old Testament book*] (BJA) .... Ecc
Ecclesiastes [*Old Testament book*] .... Eccl
Ecclesiastes [*Old Testament book*] .... Eccles
Ecclesiastes Rabbah (BJA) .... EcclesR
Ecclesiastical (DLA) .... E
Ecclesiastical .... ECCL
Ecclesiastical .... ECCLES
Ecclesiastical (VRA) .... eccles
Ecclesiastical (ABBR) .... ECLSTCL
Ecclesiastical and Admiralty [*Legal term*] (DLA) .... Eccl & Ad
Ecclesiastical and Admiralty Reports [*1853-55*] [*A publication*] (DLA) .... E & A
Ecclesiastical Archivists Association [*Italy*] (EAIO) .... EAA
Ecclesiastical Commissioner [*British*] (DAS) .... EC
Ecclesiastical District [*Maps*] (ROG) .... E
Ecclesiastical History Society (EAIO) .... EHS
Ecclesiastical Parish .... EP
Ecclesiastical Relations Branch [*BUPERS*] .... ERB
Ecclesiastical Reports [*England*] [*A publication*] (DLA) .... Eccl Rep
Ecclesiastical Statutes [*A publication*] (DLA) .... Eccl Stat
Ecclesiasticus [*Old Testament book*] [*Apocrypha*] .... Ecclus
Ecclesiazusae [*of Aristophanes*] [*Classical studies*] (OCD) .... Eccl
Eccles-Jordan Circuit [*Electronics*] .... EJC
Eccles-Jordan Trigger [*Electronics*] .... EJT
ECCS, Inc. [*NASDAQ symbol*] (SAG) .... ECCS
Ecdysteroid Glucosyl Transferase [*An enzyme*] .... EGT

Ecgonine Methyl Ester [*Organic chemistry*] ... EME
Ech-Cheliff [*Algeria*] [*ICAO location identifier*] (ICLI) ... DAOI
Echelon ... ECH
Echelon Above Corps [*Military*] (RDA) ... EAC
Echelon Above Corps Communications [*Army*] (DOMA) ... EAC COMM
Echelon Above Division [*Military*] (MCD) ... EAD
Echelon International Corp. [*Associated Press*] (SAG) ... Echelon
Echelon International Corp. [*NYSE symbol*] (SAG) ... EIN
Echeloned Series Processor (PDAA) ... ESP
Echelons Above Division - Expanded [*Military*] (MCD) ... EADX
Echelons Above Division Study [*Military*] (AABC) ... EADS
Echelons Below Corps [*Army*] (DOMA) ... EBC
Echelons Below Theater [*Military*] (MCD) ... EBT
Echelons Corps Level and Below [*Military*] ... ECB
Echery [*France*] [*Seismograph station code, US Geological Survey*] (SEIS) ... ECH
Echinococcus [*Microorganism*] (DAVI) ... ECHIN
Echlin, Inc. [*NYSE symbol*] (SPSG) ... ECH
Echlin, Inc. [*Associated Press*] (SAG) ... Echlin
Echo [*Phonetic alphabet*] [*International*] (DSUE) ... E
Echo Bay Finance Corp. [*AMEX symbol*] (SPSG) ... EBI
Echo Bay Finance Corp. [*Associated Press*] (SAG) ... EchBF
Echo Bay Mines [*AMEX symbol*] (TTSB) ... ECO
Echo Bay Mines Ltd. [*Associated Press*] (SAG) ... EchoBay
Echo Bay Mines Ltd. [*AMEX symbol*] (SPSG) ... ECO
Echo Cancellation Hybrid [*Telecommunications*] (NITA) ... ECH
Echo Control Equipment [*Telecommunications*] (TEL) ... ECE
Echo Control Factor [*Telecommunications*] (TEL) ... ECF
Echo Control Subsystem [*Telecommunications*] (TEL) ... ECS
Echo Controller [*Telecommunications*] (TEL) ... EC
Echo Depth Sounder ... EDS
Echo Doppler Indicator [*Telecommunications*] (IAA) ... EDI
Echo Equalizer (IAA) ... EE
Echo Free Room ... EFR
Echo Glen Children's Center, Resident Library, Snoqualmie, WA [*Library symbol Library of Congress*] (LCLS) ... WaSnqE-R
Echo Glen Children's Center, Staff Library, Snoqualmie, WA [*Library symbol Library of Congress*] (LCLS) ... WaSnqE
Echo Integration-Mid Water Trawl [*Marine science*] (OSRA) ... EIMWT
Echo Integration-MidWater Trawl (USDC) ... EIMWT
Echo Intensity [*Marine science*] (OSRA) ... EI
Echo Mountain Resources Ltd. [*Vancouver Stock Exchange symbol*] ... EMR
Echo Public Library, Echo, OR [*Library symbol*] [*Library of Congress*] (LCLS) ... OrEc
Echo Range Equipment ... ERE
Echo Ranging ... ER
Echo Ranging Operated Acoustic Torpedo [*Military*] (IAA) ... EROAT
Echo Return Loss [*Telecommunications*] ... ERL
Echo Return Loss Enhancement ... ERLE
Echo Sounding ... ES
Echo Sounding Device [*Navigation*] ... ESD
Echo Suppression Subsystem [*Telecommunications*] (TEL) ... ESS
Echo Suppressor [*Telecommunications*] (TEL) ... ES
Echo Suppressor Control [*Telecommunications*] (TEL) ... ESC
Echo Suppressor, Originating End [*Telecommunications*] (TEL) ... ESO
Echo Suppressor, Terminating End [*Telecommunications*] (TEL) ... EST
Echo Suppressor Testing System [*Telecommunications*] (TEL) ... ESTS
Echo-Cancellation [*Data transmission*] (BYTE) ... EC
Echocardiogram [*Cardiology*] (DAVI) ... ECG
Echocardiogram [*Cardiology*] ... ECHO
EchoCath, Inc. [*Associated Press*] (SAG) ... EchoC
EchoCath, Inc. [*Associated Press*] (SAG) ... EchoCth
EchoCath, Inc. [*NASDAQ symbol*] (SAG) ... ECHT
EchoCath Inc.'A' [*NASDAQ symbol*] (TTSB) ... ECHTA
EchoCath Inc. Unit [*NASDAQ symbol*] (TTSB) ... ECHTU
EchoCath Inc. Wrrt [*NASDAQ symbol*] (TTSB) ... ECHTW
EchoCath Inc. Wrrt'B' [*NASDAQ symbol*] (TTSB) ... ECHTZ
Echoencephalogram [*Neurology*] ... ECHO
Echo-Free Hole [*Meterology*] ... EFH
Echogram [*Radiology*] (DAVI) ... echo
Echo-Planar Imaging [*Physics*] ... EPI
Echoplex [*Telecommunications protocol*] (CDE) ... echo
Echo-Ranging Masked Acoustic Communications ... ERMAC
Echo-Rhino-Coryza [*Virus*] [*Usage obsolete*] ... ERC
EchoStar Communications Corp. [*NASDAQ symbol*] (SAG) ... DISH
EchoStar Communications Corp. [*Associated Press*] (SAG) ... EchoStar
EchoStar Communications Corp. [*Associated Press*] (SAG) ... EchoStr
EchoStar Communications'A' [*NASDAQ symbol*] (TTSB) ... DISH
Echovirus 28 [*Virology*] (DAVI) ... JH
Echo-Wood Lake Elementary School, Echo, MN [*Library symbol*] [*Library of Congress*] (LCLS) ... MnEcES
Echo-Wood Lake High School, Wood Lake, MN [*Library symbol*] [*Library of Congress*] (LCLS) ... MnWIHS
Echterdingen [*Germany ICAO location identifier*] (ICLI) ... EDOC
ECI Environmental, Inc. [*Associated Press*] ... ECI Env
ECI Telecom Ltd. [*Associated Press*] (SAG) ... ECI Tel
ECI Telecom Ltd. [*NASDAQ symbol*] (NQ) ... ECIL
ECI Telecom Ltd. (MHDW) ... ECILF
Eckels Memorial Library, Oakland, IA [*Library symbol Library of Congress*] (LCLS) ... IaOak
Eckerd College, St. Petersburg, FL [*OCLC symbol*] (OCLC) ... FEC
Eckerd College, St. Petersburg, FL [*Library symbol Library of Congress*] (LCLS) ... FSpE
Eckerd Corp. [*NYSE symbol*] (SPSG) ... ECK
Eckerd Corp. [*Associated Press*] (SAG) ... Eckerd
Eckhart Public Library, Auburn, IN [*Library symbol Library of Congress*] (LCLS) ... InAub
Eckler Industries [*NASDAQ symbol*] (TTSB) ... ECKL
Eckler Industries, Inc. [*NASDAQ symbol*] (SAG) ... ECKL
Eckler Industries, Inc. [*Associated Press*] (SAG) ... Eckler
Eckler Industries Unit [*NASDAQ symbol*] (TTSB) ... ECKLU
Eckler Industries Wrrt [*NASDAQ symbol*] (TTSB) ... ECKLW
Eckley Public Library, Eckley, CO [*Library symbol Library of Congress*] (LCLS) ... CoEck
Eckville Public Library, Alberta [*Library symbol National Library of Canada*] (NLC) ... AECK
Eclairage [*Illumination*] [*French*] ... E
Eclectic (WGA) ... ECL
Eclectic (ROG) ... ECLEC
Eclectic Grand Lodge [*Freemasonry*] (ROG) ... EGL
Eclecticism (ABBR) ... ECLTM
Eclipse ... EC
Eclipse (WDAA) ... ECL
Eclipse (BARN) ... ecli
Eclipse (ABBR) ... ECLPS
Eclipse Airlines, Inc. [*ICAO designator*] (FAAC) ... BRN
Eclipse Capital Corp. [*Toronto Stock Exchange symbol*] ... ECP
Eclipse Mining [*Vancouver Stock Exchange symbol*] ... ECL
Eclipse Surgical Tech [*NASDAQ symbol*] (TTSB) ... ESTI
Eclipse Surgical Technologies, Inc. [*Associated Press*] (SAG) ... EclpSurg
Eclipse Surgical Technologies, Inc. [*NASDAQ symbol*] (SAG) ... ESTI
Eclipsed (ABBR) ... ECLPSD
Eclipse-News-Review, Parkersburg, IA [*Library symbol Library of Congress*] (LCLS) ... IaParE
Eclipsing (ABBR) ... ECLPSG
Eclogues [*of Vergil*] [*Classical studies*] (OCD) ... Ecl
Eclosion Hormone [*Entomology*] ... EH
ECM Paytel [*Vancouver Stock Exchange symbol*] ... ECM
ECM [*Electronic Countermeasures*] **- Resistant Voice** ... ERV
Eco 2 Inc. [*NASDAQ symbol*] (TTSB) ... TIRE
Eco 2 Inc. Wrrt'A' [*NASDAQ symbol*] (TTSB) ... TIREW
Eco Corp. [*Toronto Stock Exchange symbol*] ... EC
Eco Soil Systems, Inc. [*Associated Press*] (SAG) ... EcoSoil
Eco Soil Systems, Inc. [*NASDAQ symbol*] (SAG) ... ESSI
ECO2, Inc. [*Associated Press*] (SAG) ... ECO2
Ecobank Ghana (EY) ... EBG
Eco-Energy System ... EES
Ecoforestry Institute - United States (EA) ... EI
Ecogen, Inc. [*Associated Press*] (SAG) ... Ecogen
Ecogen, Inc. [*Associated Press*] (SAG) ... Ecogn
Ecogen, Inc. [*NASDAQ symbol*] (SPSG) ... EECN
Ecogen Inc. Wrrt [*NASDAQ symbol*] (TTSB) ... EECNW
Ecogeographer (ABBR) ... ECOGEO
Ecogeographer (ABBR) ... ECOGEOR
Ecogeographic (ABBR) ... ECOGEOC
Eco-Justice Working Group [*Joint Strategy and Action Committee and National Council of the Churches of Christ in the USA*] (EA) ... EJWG
Ecolab, Inc. [*NYSE symbol*] (SPSG) ... ECL
Ecolab, Inc. [*Associated Press*] (SAG) ... Ecolab
Ecole Africaine de la Meterologie et de d'Aviation Civile [*East African School of Meteorology and Civil Aviation*] [*Republic of Niger*] (PDAA) ... EMAC
Ecole d'Aviation Civile [*Belgium ICAO designator*] (FAAC) ... BSA
Ecole de Bibliotheconomie, Universite de Montreal, Quebec [*Library symbol National Library of Canada*] (NLC) ... QMUEB
Ecole de Chimie, Geneva, Switzerland [*Library symbol Library of Congress*] (LCLS) ... SzGE
Ecole de Technologie Superieure, Universite de Quebec, Montreal, Quebec [*Library symbol National Library of Canada*] (NLC) ... QMUQET
Ecole des Arts Visuels, Universite Laval, Quebec, Quebec [*Library symbol National Library of Canada*] (NLC) ... QQLAAV
Ecole des Beaux Arts [*Paris, France*] ... EBA
Ecole des Beaux-Arts, Montreal, PQ, Canada [*Library symbol Library of Congress*] (LCLS) ... CaQMBA
Ecole des Beaux-Arts, Montreal, Quebec [*Library symbol National Library of Canada*] (NLC) ... QMBA
Ecole des Hautes Etudes Commerciales, Bibliotheque [*UTLAS symbol*] ... HEC
Ecole des Hautes Etudes Commerciales, Montreal, PQ, Canada [*Library symbol Library of Congress*] (LCLS) ... CaQMHE
Ecole des Hautes Etudes Commerciales, Montreal, Quebec [*Library symbol National Library of Canada*] (NLC) ... QMHE
Ecole Francaise d'Extreme Orient [*French School of the Far East*] ... EFEO
Ecole Nationale d'Administration [*France*] (ECON) ... ENA
Ecole Nationale d'Administration Publique, Universite du Quebec, Montreal, Quebec [*Library symbol National Library of Canada*] (NLC) ... QMUQEN
Ecole Nationale d'Administration Publique, Universite du Quebec, Quebec, Quebec [*Library symbol National Library of Canada*] (NLC) ... QQUQEN
Ecole Nationale de Theatre, Montreal, PQ, Canada [*Library symbol Library of Congress*] (LCLS) ... CaQMENT
Ecole Nationale des Ponts et Chaussees [*Graduate School of International Business*] [*France*] ... ENPC
Ecole Normale M. L. Duplessis, Trois-Rivieres, PQ, Canada [*Library symbol Library of Congress*] (LCLS) ... CaQTE
Ecole Normale M. L. Duplessis, Trois-Rivieres, Quebec [*Library symbol National Library of Canada*] (NLC) ... QTE
Ecole Normale Superieure, Laboratoire de Chimie, Paris, France [*Library symbol Library of Congress*] (LCLS) ... FrPE-C
Ecole Polytechnique, Bibliotheque [*Montreal*] [*UTLAS symbol*] ... EPM
Ecole Polytechnique Federale de Lausanne [*Swiss Federal Institute of Technology, Lausanne*] (ECON) ... EPFL

Ecole Polytechnique, Montreal, PQ, Canada [*Library symbol Library of Congress*] (LCLS) .... CaQMEP
Ecole Polytechnique, Montreal, Quebec [*Library symbol National Library of Canada*] (NLC) .... QMEP
Ecole Polytechnique, Publications Officielles [*UTLAS symbol*] ..... EPG
Ecole Quebecoise du Meuble et du Bois Ouvre, College de Victoriaville, Quebec [*Library symbol National Library of Canada*] (NLC) .... QVCEMBO
Ecole Secondaire Champlain, Ottawa, Ontario [*Library symbol National Library of Canada*] .... OOESC
Ecole Secondaire le Caron, Penetanguishene, ON, Canada [*Library symbol*] [*Library of Congress*] (LCLS) .... CaOPenE
Ecole Secondaire le Caron, Penetanguishene, Ontario [*Library symbol National Library of Canada*] (BIB) .... OPENE
Ecole Secondaire Louis-Riel, Gloucester, Ontario [*Library symbol National Library of Canada*] (BIB) .... OGELR
Ecole Secondaire Nicolas-Gatineau, Gatineau, Quebec [*Library symbol National Library of Canada*] (BIB) .... QGNG
Ecole Secondaire St.-Francois, Sherbrooke, Quebec [*Library symbol National Library of Canada*] (NLC) .... QSHERSF
Ecole Secondaire St. Joseph, Hull, PQ, Canada [*Library symbol*] [*Library of Congress*] (LCLS) .... CaQHESJ
Ecole Secondaire St.-Joseph, Hull, Quebec [*Library symbol National Library of Canada*] (BIB) .... QHESJ
Ecole Secondaire Saint-Francois, Sherbrooke, PQ, Canada [*Library symbol Library of Congress*] (LCLS) .... CaQSherSF
Ecole Secondaire Saint-Stanislas, Montreal, PQ, Canada [*Library symbol Library of Congress*] (LCLS) .... CaQMES
Ecole Secondaire Saint-Stanislas, Montreal, Quebec [*Library symbol National Library of Canada*] (NLC) .... QMES
Ecole Superieure des Affaires [*High Business School*] [*Information service or system*] (IID) .... ESA
Ecoles Sans Frontieres [*Education Without Frontiers*] [*An association*] (EAIO) .... ESF
Ecologic (ABBR) .... ECOLC
Ecological (ABBR) .... ECOLCL
Ecological Agriculture Projects [*See also PAE*] [*Sainte Anne De Bellevue, PQ*] (EAIO) .... EAP
Ecological and Toxicological Association of the Dyestuffs Manufacturing Industry [*Basel, Switzerland*] (EAIO) .... ETAD
Ecological Consortium (EERA) .... ECOCO
Ecological Information and Analysis Center .... EIAC
Ecological Life Systems Institute [*San Diego, CA*] (CROSS) .... ELSI
Ecological Management of Arid and Semi Arid Rangelands (EERA) ...... EMASAR
Ecological Mediterranean [*An association Turkey*] (EAIO) .... ECOMED
Ecological Sabotage [*Tactic used by radical environmentalists*] .... ECOTAGE
Ecological Sciences Division [*Oak Ridge National Laboratory*] .... ESD
Ecological Sciences Information Center [*Oak Ridge National Laboratory*] ..... ESIC
Ecological Society of America (BARN) .... Ecol Soc Am
Ecological Society of America (EA) .... ESA
Ecological Study Center [*Oak Ridge National Laboratory*] .... ESC
Ecological Vegetation Class (EERA) .... EVC
Ecologically (ABBR) .... ECOLCLY
Ecologically Responsive Tractor Transmission Oil [*Lubricants*] .... ERTTO
Ecologically Sustainable Development Intersectoral Issues Report (EERA) .... ESDIIR
Ecologically Sustainable Development Steering Committee [*Commonwealth*] (EERA) .... ESDSC
Ecologically Sustainable Society (EERA) .... ESS
Ecologically-Sustainable Development .... ESD
Ecologist (ABBR) .... ECOLST
Ecology (WDAA) .... ECO
Ecology .... ECO
Ecology .... ECOL
Ecology Action/Common Ground [*An association*] .... EA/CG
Ecology Action East [*An association*] (EA) .... EAE
Ecology Action Educational Institute (EA) .... EAEI
Ecology and Analysis of Trace Contaminants [*Program*] [*Oak Ridge National Laboratory*] (IID) .... EATC
Ecology & Environment [*Associated Press*] (SAG) .... EcolEn
Ecology & Environment [*AMEX symbol*] (SPSG) .... EEI
Ecology and Environment, Inc., Buffalo, NY [*Library symbol Library of Congress*] (LCLS) .... NBuEE
Ecology and Evolutionary Biology [*A discipline division*] .... EEB
Ecology Center (EA) .... EC
Ecology Center Communications Council [*Defunct*] (EA) .... ECCC
Ecology/Environment 'A' [*AMEX symbol*] (TTSB) .... EEI
Ecology of Knowledge Network (EA) .... EKN
Eco-Management Audit Scheme (ACII) .... EMAS
Ecomat, Inc. [*NASDAQ symbol*] (SAG) .... ECMT
Ecomat, Inc. [*Associated Press*] (SAG) .... Ecomat
Econolite Automatic Sensing Equipment .... EASE
Econometric (ABBR) .... ECONOMET
Econometric Research Program [*Princeton University*] [*Research center*] (RCD) .... ERP
Econometric Society (EA) .... ES
Econometric Time-Series [*Computer program*] (PCM) .... ETS
Economic .... ECNMC
Economic (ABBR) .... ECO
Economic (ABBR) .... ECONC
Economic Abstracts International [*Database*] (NITA) .... EAI
Economic Activity [*A publication*] .... Econ Act
Economic Activity [*A publication*] .... Econ Activ
Economic Activity Analysis .... EAA
Economic Adjustment Committee (MCD) .... EAC
Economic Adviser .... EA

Economic Advisers .... ECONADS
Economic Advisory Board [*Department of Commerce Washington, DC*] (EGAO) .... EAB
Economic Affairs Bureau (EA) .... EAB
Economic Analysis .... EA
Economic Analysis [*Program*] [*Department of State*] .... EC
Economic Analysis Division [*Federal Emergency Management Agency*] [*Information service or system*] (IID) .... EAD
Economic Analysis Group [*General Accounting Office*] [*Washington, DC*] (GRD) .... EAG
Economic Analysis Staff [*Department of Agriculture*] (GFGA) .... EAS
Economic and Budget Review Committee [*Victoria, Australia*] .... EBRC
Economic and Business Foundation .... EBF
Economic and Contingency Reserve Stock [*Military*] .... ECRS
Economic and Employment Development Officer .... EEDO
Economic and Financial [*Plans*] [*British*] .... E & F
Economic and Financial Council of Ministers [*EC*] (ECED) .... ECOFIN
Economic and Monetary Union .... EMU
Economic and Regulatory Analysis Division [*Environmental Protection Agency*] (GFGA) .... ERAD
Economic and Sector Work .... ESW
Economic and Social Commission for Asia and the Pacific [*UN division*] (NITA) .... ESCAP
Economic and Social Commission for Western Asia [*Iraq*] [*United Nations Research center*] (IRC) .... ESCWA
Economic and Social Committee [*EC*] (ECED) .... ECOSOC
Economic and Social Committee [*EC*] (ECED) .... ESC
Economic and Social Council [*ICSU*] [*United Nations*] .... ECOSOC
Economic and Social Council [*United Nations*] .... ESC
Economic and Social Data System [*Agency for International Development*] [*Database*] .... ESDS
Economic and Social Research Council [*British*] .... ESRC
Economic and Social Research Council [*British*] .... ESRC
Economic and Social Research Institute (ACII) .... ESRI
Economic and Social Science Research Association [*British*] .... ESSRA
Economic and Youth Opportunity Agency (IIA) .... EYOA
Economic Awareness Teacher Training (AIE) .... EcATT
Economic Batch Determination .... EBD
Economic Bulletin Board [*Information service or system*] (IID) .... EBB
Economic Bulletin of Ghana [*A publication*] .... EBG
Economic Cabinet [*British*] .... ECOCAB
Economic Census Advertising and Response Behavior Study [*Bureau of the Census*] (GFGA) .... ECARBS
Economic Census Staff [*Census*] (OICC) .... ECS
Economic Classification Policy Committee [*BTS*] (TAG) .... ECPC
Economic Commission for Africa [*Addis Ababa, Ethiopia*] [*See also CEA*] [*United Nations*] (EAIO) .... ECA
Economic Commission for Asia and the Far East [*Later, ESCAP*] [*United Nations*] .... ECAFE
Economic Commission for Europe [*United Nations*] (IRC) .... ECE
Economic Commission for Europe [*United Nations*] (DS) .... ECOCOM
Economic Commission for Latin America [*Database originator*] [*Later, ECLAC*] [*United Nations*] .... ECLA
Economic Commission for Latin America and the Caribbean [*See also CEPAL*] [*Santiago, Chile*] [*United Nations*] (EAIO) .... ECLAC
Economic Commission for the Middle East [*United Nations*] (DS) .... ECME
Economic Commission for Western Asia [*Later, ESCWA*] [*United Nations*] .... ECWA
Economic Commission of West African States (EERA) .... ECOWAS
Economic Community for Livestock and Meat [*See also CEBV*] (EAIO) ...... ECLM
Economic Community Monitoring Group [*West Africa*] .... ECOMOG
Economic Community of Central African States [*See also CEEAC*] [*Bangui, Central African Republic*] (EAIO) .... ECCAS
Economic Community of the Great Lakes Countries [*See also CEPGL*] [*Gisenye, Rwanda*] (EAIO) .... ECGLC
Economic Community of West African States [*Treaty signed May 28, 1975*] .... ECOWAS
Economic Community of West African States [*Treaty signed May 28, 1975*] .... ECWAS
Economic Control Agency [*Allied German Occupation Forces*] .... ECA
Economic Cooperation Act [*of 1948*] .... ECA
Economic Cooperation Administration [*Administered aid under Marshall Plan; abolished, 1951*] .... ECA
Economic Cooperation Agreement (EERA) .... ECA
Economic Cooperation among Developing Countries [*United Nations*] .... ECDC
Economic Cooperation Organization .... ECO
Economic Council of Canada .... ECC
Economic Council of Canada, Ottawa, ON, Canada [*Library symbol Library of Congress*] (LCLS) .... CaOOEC
Economic Council of Canada [*Conseil Economique du Canada*] Ottawa, Ontario [*Library symbol National Library of Canada*] (NLC) .... OOEC
Economic Coverage Endorsement .... ECE
Economic Data Retrieval and Application System (BUR) .... EDRAS
Economic Defense Board [*Later, Board of Economic Warfare*] [*World War II*] .... EDB
Economic Development [*A publication*] .... ED
Economic Development Administration [*Formerly, Office of Appalachian Assistance*] [*Terminated Department of Commerce*] .... EDA
Economic Development Board [*Singapore*] .... EDB
Economic Development Committee [*Nickname: "Little Neddie"*] [*British*] .... EDC
Economic Development District [*EDA*] .... EDD
Economic Development Division, Metro Toronto Chairman's Office, Toronto, Ontario [*Library symbol National Library of Canada*] (BIB) .... OTMTC
Economic Development Financing Organization [*Greece*] .... EDFO

Economic Development Information Network [*Indiana University*] [*Information service or system*] (IID) .... EDIN
Economic Development Institute [*of the International Bank for Reconstruction and Development*] .... EDI
Economic Development of Equatorial and Southern Africa .... EDESA
Economic Development Operations .... EDO
Economic Development Opportunity Committee [*Department of Labor*] .... EDOC
Economic Development Program .... EDP
Economic Dislocation and Worker Adjustment Assistance [*Department of Labor*] .... EDWAA
Economic Dislocation and Worker Adjustment Assistance Act of 1988 (WYGK) .... EDWAAA
Economic Dislocation Loans [*Small Business Administration*] .... EDL
Economic Distribution Quantity (AFIT) .... EDQ
Economic Documentation and Information Centre Ltd. [*British Database producer*] (IID) .... EDIC
Economic Education for Clergy (EA) .... EEC
Economic Education Foundation for Clergy [*Later, EEC*] (EA) .... EEFC
Economic Education Project [*Public Media Center*] (EA) .... EEP
Economic Engineering Branch [*Army Tank Automotive Command*] [*Warren, MI*] .... EEB
Economic Evaluation of Natural Resources (EERA) .... EENR
Economic Feasibility of Projects and Investments .... EFOP
Economic Feeder Administration and Relief (TEL) .... EFAR
Economic Forestry Group [*British*] .... EFG
Economic General Staff [*British*] .... EGS
Economic Geography [*A publication*] (BRI) .... EG
Economic Growth Center [*Yale University*] (PDAA) .... EGC
Economic History Association (EA) .... EHA
Economic Hundred Call Seconds [*Telecommunications*] (TEL) .... ECCS
Economic Impact Assessment .... EIA
Economic Impact Budget .... EIB
Economic Impact Forecast System [*Army*] (RDA) .... EIFS
Economic Indicator's Handbook [*A publication*] .... EIH
Economic Information System [*International Monetary Fund*] [*Information service or system*] (IID) .... EIS
Economic Information Systems-Plants [*Information service or system*] (NITA) .... EIS Plants
Economic Injury Disaster Loan [*Small Business Administration*] .... EIDL
Economic Intelligence Committee [*Military*] .... EIC
Economic Inventory Policy .... EIP
Economic Inventory Procedures [*Army*] (AABC) .... EIP
Economic Investment Trust Ltd. [*Toronto Stock Exchange symbol*] .... EVT
Economic Journal [*A publication*] (BRI) .... Econ J
Economic League [*British*] .... EL
Economic Literature Index [*American Economic Association*] [*Information service or system*] (IID) .... ELI
Economic Load Dispatching (BUR) .... ELD
Economic Lot Scheduling Problem .... ELSP
Economic Lot Size (MHDW) .... ELS
Economic Manufacturing Quality .... EMQ
Economic Models Ltd. [*British*] (NITA) .... EML
Economic Monographs [*A publication*] .... Econ Monog
Economic News [*A publication*] .... Econ N
Economic Objectives Department [*Ministry of Economic Warfare*] [*British World War II*] .... EOD
Economic Opportunity Act [*1964*] [*Repealed, 1974*] .... EOA
Economic Opportunity Act Loan .... EOL
Economic Order and Stockage Policy (AFIT) .... EO & SP
Economic Order and Stockage Procedure .... EOSP
Economic Order Quality Techniques [*Course*] [*Military*] (DNAB) .... EOQT
Economic Order Quantity .... EOQ
Economic Order Van (AABC) .... EOV
Economic Papers [*A publication*] .... Econ Paps
Economic Performance Indicator [*New York Stock Exchange*] .... EPI
Economic Performance Monitoring (OA) .... EPM
Economic Planning (MCD) .... EP
Economic Planning Advisory Council (EERA) .... EPAC
Economic Planning. Journal for Agriculture and Related Industries [*A publication*] .... EP
Economic Planning Machine [*British*] .... EPM
Economic Planning Unit [*Generic term*] (DS) .... EPU
Economic Policy [*British*] .... EP
Economic Policy Board [*Department of the Treasury*] .... EPB
Economic Policy Committee [*OECD*] .... EPC
Economic Policy Council [*UNA-USA*] .... EPC
Economic Policy Group .... EPG
Economic Policy Institute (EA) .... EPI
Economic Policy towards Eire [*British*] .... EPE
Economic Power Dispatch Computer .... EPDC
Economic Power Transmission .... EPT
Economic Pressure on Germany Committee [*War Cabinet*] [*British World War II*] .... EPG
Economic Price Adjustment .... EPA
Economic Procurement Item (NATG) .... EPI
Economic Production Quantity (AAGC) .... EPQ
Economic Production Rate (MCD) .... EPR
Economic Quotient .... EQ
Economic [*or Economical*] **Radioisotope Thermoelectric Generator** .... ERTG
Economic Rate of Return .... ERR
Economic Record [*A publication*] .... Ec Rec
Economic Recovery Tax Act [*1981*] .... ERTA
Economic Regulations [*Civil Aeronautics Board*] .... ER
Economic Regulatory Administration (MCD) .... ERA
Economic Release Lot-Size .... ERLS

Economic Reorder Quantity (ADA) .... ERQ
Economic Repair Quantity .... ERQ
Economic Requirement Batching .... ERB
Economic Research Action Project [*Students for a Democratic Society*] [*Defunct*] .... ERAP
Economic Research Council [*Research center British*] (IRC) .... ERC
Economic Research Institute [*Utah State University*] [*Research center*] (RCD) .... ERI
Economic Research Round Table (EA) .... ERRT
Economic Research Service [*Department of Agriculture*] [*Washington, DC*] .... ERS
Economic Resource Impact Statement .... ERIS
Economic Resources Corp. [*OEO-Department of Labor project*] (EA) .... ERC
Economic Retention Level (AFIT) .... ERL
Economic Retention Requirement (AFIT) .... ERR
Economic Retention Stock .... ERS
Economic Review Period .... ERP
Economic Rights Program [*Later, WERP*] (EA) .... ERP
Economic Sciences Corp. [*Information service or system*] (IID) .... ESC
Economic Security Employees' National Association [*Canada*] .... ESNA
Economic Society of Australia .... ESA
Economic Society of Australia and New Zealand. Economic Monograph [*A publication*] .... Econ Monogr Econ Soc Aust NZ
Economic Society of Australia and New Zealand, Melbourne University, Parkville, V, Australia [*Library symbol Library of Congress*] (LCLS) .... AuPaE
Economic Stabilization Act [*Wage-price controls*] [*Expired April 30, 1974*] .... ESA
Economic Stabilization Administration .... ESA
Economic Stabilization Agency [*Terminated, 1953*] .... ESA
Economic Stabilization Board [*World War II*] .... ESB
Economic Stabilization Office (OICC) .... ESO
Economic Stabilization Program [*Internal Revenue Service*] .... ESP
Economic Standards (Commerce Clearing House) [*A publication*] (DLA) .... Econ Stand (CCH)
Economic Stimulus Appropriations Act (OICC) .... ESAA
Economic Strategy Institute (RDA) .... ESI
Economic Studies [*Bureau of the Census*] .... ES
Economic Subregion [*Bureau of the Census*] .... ESR
Economic Sufficiency Plan (OICC) .... ESP
Economic Support Fund [*Agency for International Development*] .... ESF
Economic Support Funds (GNE) .... ESP
Economic Survey of Ancient Rome [*A publication*] (OCD) .... Econ Survey
Economic Surveys Division [*Census*] (OICC) .... ESD
Economic Transactions Framework .... ETF
Economic Value [*Accounting*] .... EV
Economic Value Added .... EVA
Economic Verification Experiments [*Marine science*] (MSC) .... EVE
Economic Warfare [*British*] .... EW
Economical (ABBR) .... ECONCL
Economical (ABBR) .... ECONL
Economical Methods [*A line of Varian spectrometers*] .... EM
Economical Storage and Access System [*Computer science*] .... ECSTASY
Economically (ABBR) .... ECONCLY
Economically Disadvantaged (OICC) .... ED
Economically Disadvantaged Income (ADA) .... EDI
Economically-Targeted Investment .... ETI
Economic-Damage Index [*Environmental technology*] .... EDI
Economics (ADA) .... E
Economics .... EC
Economics (EY) .... ECON
Economics (DD) .... Econ
Economics (ABBR) .... ECS
Economics and Government [*Office of Management and Budget*] .... EG
Economics and Statistics Administration [*Marine science*] (OSRA) .... ESA
Economics and Statistics Administration (USDC) .... ESA
Economics and Technology Division [*Environmental Protection Agency*] (GFGA) .... ETD
Economics & Technology, Inc. [*Telecommunications service*] (TSSD) .... ETI
Economische Division [*US Military Government, Germany*] .... ED
Economics Information Centre, Bell Canada, Hull, Quebec [*Library symbol National Library of Canada*] (NLC) .... QHB
Economics Information Resources Directory [*A publication*] .... EIRD
Economics Laboratory, Inc. .... EL
Economics Management Staff [*Department of Agriculture*] (GFGA) .... EMS
Economics Minerals (NITA) .... ECOMINE
Economics News Broadcasters Association (EA) .... ENBA
[*The*] **Economics of Ancient Greece** [*A publication*] (OCD) .... Econom Anc Gr
Economics of Distribution Foundation (EA) .... EDF
Economics, Statistics, and Cooperatives Service [*Later, ERS, SRS*] [*Department of Agriculture*] .... ESCS
Economie et Humanism [*Economy and Humanism*] [*An association*] (EAIO) .... EH
Economies in Transition (ACII) .... EIT
Economische Commissie voor Africa [*Economic Commission for Africa*] [*United Nations*] .... ECA
Economische Voorlichtingsdienst [*Economic Information Service*] [*Information service or system*] (IID) .... EVD
Economist [*A publication*] (BRI) .... Econ
Economist .... ECONMST
Economist (ABBR) .... ECONST
Economist Intelligence Unit [*British*] .... EIU
Economist Newspapers, Chicago, IL [*Library symbol Library of Congress*] (LCLS) .... ICE
Economists Allied for Arms Reduction [*An association*] (EA) .... ECAAR
Economists' National Committee on Monetary Policy (EA) .... ENCMP
Economists', Sociologists', and Statisticians' Association .... ESSA
Economize (ABBR) .... ECONZ
Economized (ABBR) .... ECONZD

Economizer (ABBR) ... ECONZR
Economizing (ABBR) ... ECONZG
Economy (AFM) ... ECON
Economy ... ECON
Economy (ABBR) ... ECONY
Economy Act Order ... EAO
Economy Cylinder Rating [*Engine technology*] ... ECR
Economy Inns, Inc. [*Vancouver Stock Exchange symbol*] ... ECY
Economy Systems Plate ... ESP
Economy-Class Syndrome [*Medicine*] ... ECS
Ecophysiologic (ABBR) ... ECOPHYS
Ecoropa UK [*An association*] (EAIO) ... EUK
Ecos Resources [*Vancouver Stock Exchange symbol*] ... ECS
EcoScience Corp. [*Associated Press*] (SAG) ... EcoSci
EcoScience Corp. [*NASDAQ symbol*] (SAG) ... ECSC
Ecossais [*Scottish*] [*Freemasonry*] [*French*] ... Ec
Ecosystem (ABBR) ... ECOSYS
Ecosystem (ABBR) ... ECSYT
Ecosystem Conservation Group [*Marine science*] (MSC) ... ECG
Ecosystem Evaluation (GNE) ... EE
Ecosystem of Machines Information System ... EMIS
Ecosystem Processes and Effects Branch [*Army*] ... EPEB
Ecosystems Conservation Group (EERA) ... ECG
Ecosystems Research Center [*Cornell University, EPA*] [*Research center*] (RCD) ... ERC
ECO-TEC Ltd., Pickering, ON, Canada [*Library symbol*] [*Library of Congress*] (LCLS) ... CaOPicET
Eco-Tec Ltd., Pickering, Ontario [*Library symbol National Library of Canada*] (NLC) ... OPIET
EcoTyre Technologies [*NASDAQ symbol*] (TTSB) ... ETTI
EcoTyre Technologies, Inc. [*Associated Press*] (SAG) ... EcoTyre
EcoTyre Technologies, Inc. [*NASDAQ symbol*] (SAG) ... ETTI
EcoTyre Technologies, Inc. [*Associated Press*] (SAG) ... ETyre
EcoTyre Technologies Wrrt [*NASDAQ symbol*] (TTSB) ... ETTIW
ECRM, Inc. [*NASDAQ symbol*] (SAG) ... ECRM
ECS [*Energy Conversion Systems*] **Power Systems, Inc., Ottawa, Ontario** [*Library symbol National Library of Canada*] (NLC) ... OOECS
Ecsoft Group [*NASDAQ symbol*] (SAG) ... ECSGY
Ecsoft Group [*Associated Press*] (SAG) ... Ecsoft
Ecstacy [*Synthetic stimulant*] ... E
Ecstasy (ABBR) ... ECST
Ecstasy [*Synthetic stimulant*] ... X
Ecstatic (ABBR) ... ECSTC
Ecstatically (ABBR) ... ECSTCY
Ectodermal Dysplasia [*Medicine*] ... ED
Ectodermal Dysplasia, Ectrodactyly, Macular Dystrophy Syndrome [*Medicine*] (DMAA) ... EEM
Ectohormone (ABBR) ... ECTOHORM
Ectoparasitic [*Biology*] ... Ec
Ectoparasitic [*Biology*] ... Ecto
Ectopic Atrial Tachycardia [*Cardiology*] (DAVI) ... EAT
Ectopic Depolarization [*Medicine*] (DMAA) ... ED
Ectopic Focus [*Cardiology*] ... EF
Ectopic Junctional Beat [*Cardiology*] ... EJB
Ectopic Pregnancy [*Obstetrics*] ... EP
Ectoplacental Cone [*Embryology*] ... EPC
Ector County Public Library, Odessa, TX [*Library symbol Library of Congress*] (LCLS) ... TxOE
Ectrodactylia, Ectodermal Dysplasia, Cleft Lip and Palate ... EEC
Ectrodactyly, Ectodermal Dysplasia Elefting [*Syndrome*] [*Medicine*] (DAVI) ... EEC
Ecuador [*ANSI two-letter standard code*] (CNC) ... EC
Ecuador [*IYRU nationality code*] [*MARC country of publication code Library of Congress*] (LCCP) ... ec
Ecuador [*ANSI three-letter standard code*] (CNC) ... ECU
Ecuador (VRA) ... Ecu
Ecuador ... ECUA
Ecuador [*International civil aircraft marking*] (ODBW) ... HC
Ecuador [*MARC geographic area code Library of Congress*] (LCCP) ... s-ec--
Ecuadorean American Association (EA) ... EAA
Ecuato Guineana de Aviacion [*Equatorial Guinea*] [*ICAO designator*] (FAAC) ... EGA
Ecumania (ABBR) ... ECU
Ecumenic (ABBR) ... ECUM
Ecumenic (ABBR) ... ECUMN
Ecumenical (ABBR) ... ECUMEN
Ecumenical (ABBR) ... ECUML
Ecumenical (ABBR) ... ECUMNL
Ecumenical Association of Laity Centres and Academies in Europe [*See also OVATE*] [*Germany*] (EAIO) ... EALCAE
Ecumenical Association of Third World Theologies [*India*] ... EATWOT
Ecumenical Celebrations (EA) ... EC
Ecumenical Church Loan Fund ... ECLOF
Ecumenical Clergy Association [*Later, AGEI*] (EA) ... ECA
Ecumenical Coalition on Third World Tourism (EA) ... ECTWT
Ecumenical Committee on the Andes [*Defunct*] (EA) ... ECO
Ecumenical Development Cooperative Society (EAIO) ... EDCS
Ecumenical Institute [*World Council of Churches*] (EA) ... EI
Ecumenical Program for Inter American Communication and Action [*Later, EPCAC*] (EA) ... EPICA
Ecumenical Program on Central America and the Caribbean (EA) ... EPCAC
Ecumenical Review [*A publication*] (BRI) ... ER
Ecumenical Satellite Commission ... ECUSAT
Ecumenical Society of the Blessed Virgin Mary (EA) ... ESBVM
Ecumenical Study and Action Centre on Investment [*Netherlands*] ... OSACI
Ecumenical Voluntary Service [*Defunct*] ... EVS
Ecumenical Youth Council in Europe (EAIO) ... EYCE
Ecumenicalism (ABBR) ... ECUMLSM
Ecumenically (ABBR) ... ECUMLY
Ecumenically (ABBR) ... ECUMNLY
Ecumenism (WDAA) ... ECU
Ecumenism (ABBR) ... ECUMNM
Ecurie Ecosse Association Ltd. [*British*] (BI) ... EEA
Ecuvillens [*Switzerland ICAO location identifier*] (ICLI) ... LSGE
Eczema (ABBR) ... ECZM
Eczema [*Medicine*] ... EZ
Eczema, Asthma, Hay Fever [*Medicine*] ... EAHF
Eczematous Allergic Contact Dermatitis [*Dermatology*] ... EACD
Ed Bruce Fan Club [*Defunct*] (EA) ... EBFC
Edac Technologies [*NASDAQ symbol*] (TTSB) ... EDAC
Edac Technologies Corp. [*NASDAQ symbol*] (NQ) ... EDAC
Edac Technologies Corp. [*Associated Press*] (SAG) ... Edac
Edathamil (MAE) ... EDTA
Edatrexate [*Antineoplastic drug*] (CDI) ... EDAM
Edatrexate, Vinblastine, Mutamycin [*Antineoplastic drug*] (CDI) ... EVM
Eday [*Orkney Islands*] [*Airport symbol*] (OAG) ... EOI
Edberg Municipal Library, Alberta [*Library symbol National Library of Canada*] (NLC) ... AEDM
EDCO, Springfield, MO [*Library symbol Library of Congress*] (LCLS) ... EdC
Eddie Rabbitt Fan Club (EA) ... ERFC
Eddied (ABBR) ... EDD
Eddie-Dampened Quasi-Normal Markovian [*Equation*] [*Marine science*] (OSRA) ... EDQNM
Eddie-Dampened Quasi-Normal Markovian [*Equation*] (USDC) ... EDQNM
Eddis. Administration of Assets [*1880*] [*A publication*] (DLA) ... Ed Ass
Eddis on Bills of Exchange [*A publication*] (DLA) ... Ed Bills
Eddy Current [*Electromagnetism*] (NRCH) ... EC
Eddy Current Brake [*Mechanical engineering*] ... ECB
Eddy Current Clutch [*Mechanical engineering*] ... ECC
Eddy Current Energy ... ECE
Eddy Current Flow Meter [*Nuclear energy*] (NRCH) ... ECFM
Eddy Current Loss [*Electromagnetism*] ... ECL
Eddy Current Test [*Nuclear energy*] (NRCH) ... ECT
Eddy Current Testing Instrument ... ECTI
Eddy Family Association (EA) ... EFA
Eddy Hot Plate Test [*Clinical chemistry*] (AAMN) ... EHPT
Eddy-Current Heating (EECA) ... ECH
Eddy-Current Killed Oscillator [*Engineering instrumentation*] ... ECKO
Eddy-Current Testing [*Electromagnetism*] ... ET
Eddying (ABBR) ... EDYG
Eddyville, IA [*FM radio station call letters*] ... KKSI
Eddyville, KY [*AM radio station call letters*] ... WWLK
Eddyville Public Library, Eddyville, IA [*Library symbol Library of Congress*] (LCLS) ... IaEdd
Eddyville Tribune, Eddyville, IA [*Library symbol Library of Congress*] (LCLS) ... IaEddT
Edelbrock Corp. [*NASDAQ symbol*] (SAG) ... EDEL
Edelbrock Corp. [*Associated Press*] (SAG) ... Edelbrck
Edema [*Medicine*] ... E
Edema, Clubbing, and Cyanosis [*Medicine*] (DAVI) ... ECC
Edema Disease of Swine [*Medicine*] (DMAA) ... EDS
Edema Factor [*Medicine*] ... EF
Eden, NC [*AM radio station call letters*] ... WCLW
Eden, NC [*AM radio station call letters*] (RBYB) ... WETR-AM
Eden, NC [*AM radio station call letters*] ... WLOE
Eden, NC [*AM radio station call letters*] ... WWMO
Eden, NC [*FM radio station call letters*] ... WXRA
Eden on Injunctions [*1821*] [*A publication*] (DLA) ... Ed Inj
Eden Prairie, MN [*FM radio station call letters*] ... KCFE
Eden Public Library, Eden, NC [*Library symbol*] [*Library of Congress*] (LCLS) ... NcEd
Eden Public Library, Eden, NC [*Library symbol Library of Congress*] (LCLS) ... NcRf
Eden Resources Ltd. [*Vancouver Stock Exchange symbol*] ... EEN
Eden Theological Seminary, Webster Groves, MO [*Library symbol Library of Congress*] (LCLS) ... MoWgT
Eden Valley-Watkins High School, Eden Valley, MN [*Library symbol*] [*Library of Congress*] (LCLS) ... MnEvH
Eden's Bankrupt Law [*A publication*] (DLA) ... Ed BL
Eden's Bankrupt Law [*A publication*] (DLA) ... Eden Bankr
Eden's Edition of Brown's English Chancery Reports [*1757-66*] [*A publication*] (DLA) ... Ed Bro
Eden's English Chancery Reports [*28 English Reprint*] [*A publication*] (DLA) ... Eden
Eden's English Chancery Reports [*28 English Reprint*] [*A publication*] (DLA) ... Eden (Eng)
Eden's English Chancery Reports Tempore Northington [*28 English Reprint*] [*1757-66*] [*A publication*] (DLA) ... Ca T N
Eden's English Chancery Reports Tempore Northington [*28 English Reprint*] [*1757-66*] [*A publication*] (DLA) ... Ca T North
Eden's English Chancery Reports Tempore Northington [*28 English Reprint*] [*1757-66*] [*A publication*] (DLA) ... Cas T North
Eden's English Chancery Reports Tempore Northington [*28 English Reprint*] [*1757-66*] [*A publication*] (DLA) ... Ed
Eden's Principles of Penal Law [*A publication*] (DLA) ... Ed PL
Eden's Principles of Penal Law [*A publication*] (DLA) ... Eden Pen Law
Eden's Principles of Penal Law [*A publication*] (DLA) ... Eden's Prin PL
Eden's Principles of Penal Law [*A publication*] (DLA) ... Prin PL
Edentate (ABBR) ... EDENT
Edenton, NC [*Location identifier FAA*] (FAAL) ... EDE

Edenton, NC [*FM radio station call letters*] ... WBXB
Edenton, NC [*FM radio station call letters*] ... WERX
Edenton, NC [*AM radio station call letters*] ... WZBO
Edentulous [*Toothless*] [*Dentistry*] (DAVI) ... edent
Edetic Acid [*Organic chemistry*] (AAMN) ... EDTA
Edgar Allan Poe [*Initials used as pseudonym*] ... EAP
Edgar Allan Poe Society of Baltimore (EA) ... EAPSB
Edgar County Film Library, Paris, IL [*Library symbol*] [*Library of Congress*] (LCLS) ... IparF
Edgar Dale Media Center, Columbus, OH [*OCLC symbol*] (OCLC) ... EDM
Edgar L. M. Roberts Memorial Library, Woodypoint, Newfoundland [*Library symbol National Library of Canada*] (NLC) ... NFWE
Edgar L. M. Roberts Memorial Library, Woodypoint, NF, Canada [*Library symbol Library of Congress*] (LCLS) ... CaNfWE
Edgar Lee Masters Memorial Museum, Petersburg, IL [*Library symbol Library of Congress*] (LCLS) ... IPetM
Edgar Rice Burroughs [*1875-1950*] [*Author of Tarzan books*] ... ERB
Edgar Rice Burroughs Domain [*as in organization, Friends of ERB-Dom*] ... ERB-Dom
Edgar Rice Burroughs, Inc., Tarzana, CA [*Library symbol Library of Congress*] (LCLS) ... CTarB
Edgar Wallace Society (EAIO) ... EWS
Edgar Z. Steever IV [*Designer's mark when appearing on US coins*] ... EZS
Edgar's Decisions, Scotch Court of Session [*1724-25*] [*A publication*] (DLA) ... Ed
Edgar's Reports, Scotch Court of Session [*1724-25*] [*A publication*] (DLA) ... Edg
Edgar's Reports, Scotch Court of Session [*1724-25*] [*A publication*] (DLA) ... Edgar
Edgartown Air, Inc. [*ICAO designator*] (FAAC) ... SLO
Edge [*Lumber*] ... E
Edge Act [*Banking*] ... EA
Edge and Center Bead on One Side [*Technical drawings*] ... E & CB1S
Edge and Center Bead on Two Sides [*Technical drawings*] ... E & CB2S
Edge and Center V on One Side [*Technical drawings*] ... E & CV1S
Edge and Center V on Two Sides [*Technical drawings*] ... E & CV2S
Edge Bead One Side [*Lumber*] (DAC) ... EB1S
Edge Connector ... EC
Edge Connector Programmable Cartridge ... ECPC
Edge Crush Test [*Packaging*] ... ECT
Edge Distance ... ED
Edge Enhancement Technology [*Tandy*] ... EET
Edge Finishing (DNAB) ... EF
Edge Gradient Analysis ... EGA
Edge Grain ... EG
Edge Guide System ... EGS
Edge Light Emitting Diode (IAA) ... ELED
Edge Number [*Film stock identification number*] (NTCM) ... EN
Edge of Cutter (MSA) ... EOC
Edge of Earth (IAA) ... EOE
Edge Oya [*Norway*] [*Seismograph station code, US Geological Survey*] (SEIS) ... EO1
Edge Path Adapter (CDE) ... EPA
Edge Punched Card (IAA) ... EPC
Edge Reading Controller ... ERC
Edge Reading Meter ... ERM
Edge Salicornia Zone [*Ecology*] ... ES
Edge Thickness [*Technical drawings*] ... ET
Edge Tool Cutters' Association [*A union*] [*British*] ... ETCA
Edge Tool Grinders' Society [*A union*] [*British*] ... ETGS
Edge Tool Trade Society [*A union*] [*British*] ... ETTS
Edge Vee One Side [*Lumber*] (DAC) ... EV1S
Edge Wear [*Deltiology*] ... ED/WR
Edgecliff College, Cincinnati, OH [*Library symbol Library of Congress*] (LCLS) ... OCE
Edgecomb General Hospital Library, Tarboro, NC [*Library symbol*] [*Library of Congress*] (LCLS) ... NcTaH
Edgecombe County Memorial Library, Pinetops Branch, Pinetops, NC [*Library symbol Library of Congress*] (LCLS) ... NcTa-P
Edgecombe County Memorial Library, Tarboro, NC [*Library symbol Library of Congress*] (LCLS) ... NcTA
Edgecombe County Technical Institute, Tarboro, NC [*Library symbol Library of Congress*] (LCLS) ... NcTaE
Edgecombe Technical College, Learning Resources Center, Rocky Mount, NC [*Library symbol Library of Congress*] (LCLS) ... NcRmE
Edged (ABBR) ... EDGD
Edge-Defined Film-Fed Growth [*Photovoltaics*] ... EFG
Edgefield County Genealogical and Historical Society, Edgefield, SC [*Library symbol*] [*Library of Congress*] (LCLS) ... ScEHi
Edgefield County Library, Edgefield, SC [*Library symbol Library of Congress*] (LCLS) ... ScE
Edge-Lighted Display ... ELD
Edge-Lighted Status Board [*Navy*] ... ELSB
Edge-Lit Panel (DNAB) ... ELP
Edgell Communications, Inc. [*Database producer*] (IID) ... ECI
Edgemont High School, Edgemont, SD [*Library symbol Library of Congress*] (LCLS) ... SdEdH
Edgemont Public Library, Edgemont, SD [*Library symbol Library of Congress*] (LCLS) ... SdEd
Edgemont Resources [*Vancouver Stock Exchange symbol*] ... EDR
Edge-Mounted Threaded Inserts ... EMTI
Edgerton Public Library, Alberta [*Library symbol National Library of Canada*] (NLC) ... AEDG
Edgerton Public Library, Edgerton, AB, Canada [*Library symbol*] [*Library of Congress*] (LCLS) ... CaAEdg
Edges Bevelled [*Printing*] (DGA) ... E/B
Edges Cut [*Printing*] (DGA) ... E/C
Edges' Forms of Leases [*A publication*] (DLA) ... Edg Leas
Edges Gilt [*Bookbinding*] (BARN) ... eg
Edges Opened [*Publishing*] (DGA) ... E/O
Edges Red [*Publishing*] (DGA) ... E/R
Edges Rolled [*Publishing*] (DGA) ... E/RLD
Edges Rounded [*Publishing*] (DGA) ... E/RD
Edges Trimmed [*Publishing*] (DGA) ... E/T
Edges Untouched [*Publishing*] (DGA) ... E/U
Edge-Stabilized Ribbon [*Photovoltaic energy systems*] ... ESR
Edge-Supported Pulling [*Photovoltaic energy systems*] ... ESP
Edge-Triggered (IEEE) ... ET
Edgewater, FL [*FM radio station call letters*] (RBYB) ... WKRO-FM
Edgewater Public Library, Edgewater, CO [*Library symbol Library of Congress*] (LCLS) ... CoEdg
Edgewater Resources Ltd. [*Vancouver Stock Exchange symbol*] ... EGW
Edgewise (MSA) ... EDGW
Edgewise (ABBR) ... EDGWS
Edgewise Meter ... EWM
Edgewood Arsenal [*Aberdeen Proving Ground, MD*] [*Army*] ... EA
Edgewood Arsenal [*Maryland*] [*Army*] (AABC) ... EWA
Edgewood Arsenal, MD [*Location identifier FAA*] (FAAL) ... EDG
Edgewood Arsenal Nuclear Defense Center [*Maryland*] [*Army*] ... EANDC
Edgewood Arsenal Special Publication [*Army*] ... EASP
Edgewood Arsenal Technical Memorandum [*Army*] ... EATM
Edgewood Arsenal Technical Report [*Army*] ... EATR
Edgewood College of the Sacred Heart [*Wisconsin*] ... ECSH
Edgewood, NM [*Location identifier FAA*] (FAAL) ... EDO
Edgewood, OH [*FM radio station call letters*] ... WZOO
Edgewood Reminder, Edgewood, IA [*Library symbol Library of Congress*] (LCLS) ... IaEdgR
Edgewood Research, Development and Engineering Center [*Army*] (RDA) ... ERDEC
Edgeworth Kuiper Belt Object [*Planetary science*] ... EKO
Edgeworth-Kuiper Belt [*Panetary science*] ... EKB
Edgier (ABBR) ... EDGR
Edgier (ABBR) ... EDGYR
Edgiest (ABBR) ... EDGST
Edgiest (ABBR) ... EDGYST
Edginess (ABBR) ... EDGNS
Edging (ABBR) ... EDGG
Edgmoor & Manetta Railway [*AAR code*] ... EM
Edible (ABBR) ... EDB
Edible ... EDBL
Edible Portion [*of a food*] ... EP
Edible Structure Material ... ESM
Edible Whip Technology [*Aerosol technology*] ... EWT
Edict (ABBR) ... EDT
Edicts of Justinian [*A publication*] (DLA) ... Edict
Edification (ABBR) ... EDFCN
Edifice (ABBR) ... EDFC
Edifice ... EDFC
Edificio ... EDIF
Edified (ABBR) ... EDFD
Edified (ABBR) ... EDFYD
Edify Corp. [*NASDAQ symbol*] (TTSB) ... EDFY
Edifying (ABBR) ... EDFG
Edifying (ABBR) ... EDFYG
Edimbourg [*Edinburgh*] (ROG) ... EDIMB
Edinaia Tovarnaia Nomenklatura Vneshney Torgovli [*Commodity nomenclature system used in international trade*] ... ETNVT
Edinaya Systema [*Unified System*] [*Russian Computer science*] ... ES
Edinboro, PA [*FM radio station call letters*] ... WFSE
Edinboro, PA [*FM radio station call letters*] ... WXTA
Edinboro State College, Edinboro, PA [*OCLC symbol*] (OCLC) ... EIB
Edinboro State College, Edinboro, PA [*Library symbol Library of Congress*] (LCLS) ... PEdiS
Edinboro University of Pennsylvania (GAGS) ... Edinboro U
Edinburg Public Library, Edinburg, IN [*Library symbol*] [*Library of Congress*] (LCLS) ... InEd
Edinburg, TX [*FM radio station call letters*] ... KBFM
Edinburg, TX [*FM radio station call letters*] ... KOIR
Edinburg, TX [*AM radio station call letters*] ... KURV
Edinburg, TX [*FM radio station call letters*] ... KVLY
Edinburg, VA [*FM radio station call letters*] ... WOTC
Edinburgensis [*Signature of Bishops of Edinburgh*] (ROG) ... EDINBURG
Edinburgh [*Australia ICAO location identifier*] (ICLI) ... AAED
Edinburgh [*Australia ICAO location identifier*] (ICLI) ... APED
Edinburgh [*City in Scotland*] (ROG) ... E
Edinburgh [*City in Scotland*] ... ED
Edinburgh [*Scotland*] [*Airport symbol*] (OAG) ... EDI
Edinburgh [*Scotland*] [*Seismograph station code, US Geological Survey*] (SEIS) ... EDI
Edinburgh [*City in Scotland*] ... EDIN
Edinburgh [*British ICAO location identifier*] (ICLI) ... EGPH
Edinburgh [*British ICAO location identifier*] (ICLI) ... EGPQ
Edinburgh [*British ICAO location identifier*] (ICLI) ... EGQP
Edinburgh [*British ICAO location identifier*] (ICLI) ... EGQT
Edinburgh Artillery Volunteer Corps [*British military*] (DMA) ... EAVC
Edinburgh Centre of Rural Economy [*British*] (CB) ... ECRE
Edinburgh County Police [*British*] (ROG) ... ECP
Edinburgh Home Guard [*British military*] (DMA) ... EHG
Edinburgh Law Journal [*A publication*] (DLA) ... Ed LJ
Edinburgh Law Journal [*A publication*] (DLA) ... Edinb LJ
Edinburgh Multiaccess System (HGAA) ... EMAS

Edinburgh Network [*Edinburgh Regional Computer Centre*] [*British*] (NITA) ... EDNET
Edinburgh Paperback [*A publication*] ... EUP
Edinburgh Pharmacopoeia [*British*] (DAVI) ... PE
Edinburgh Public Library, Edinburgh, United Kingdom [*Library symbol Library of Congress*] (LCLS) ... UkE
Edinburgh Regional Computing Center [*British*] ... ERCC
Edinburgh University Library Online for General Information Access (NITA) ... EULOGIA
Edinburgh University Press [*Publisher*] [*Scotland*] ... EUP
Edincik [*Turkey*] [*Seismograph station code, US Geological Survey*] (SEIS) ... EDC
Edinger-Westphal Nucleus [*Neuroanatomy*] ... EW
Edingtonite [*A zeolite*] ... EDI
Edison Animal Biotechnology Center [*Ohio University*] [*Research center*] (RCD) ... EABC
Edison Birthplace Association (EA) ... EBA
Edison Bros Stores [*NYSE symbol*] (TTSB) ... EBS
Edison Brothers Stores [*Associated Press*] (SAG) ... EdisBr
Edison Brothers Stores, Inc. [*NYSE symbol*] (SPSG) ... EBS
Edison Community College, ECC/USF Learning Resources, Fort Meyers, FL [*Library symbol Library of Congress*] (LCLS) ... FFmE
Edison Control [*NASDAQ symbol*] (TTSB) ... EDCO
Edison Control Corp. [*NASDAQ symbol*] (NQ) ... EDCO
Edison Control Corp. [*Associated Press*] (SAG) ... EdisCtr
Edison Electric Institute (EA) ... EEI
Edison Elementary School, Moorhead, MN [*Library symbol*] [*Library of Congress*] (LCLS) ... MnMohEE
Edison Institute [*Henry Ford Museum and Greenfield Village*] **Library, Dearborn, MI** [*Library symbol Library of Congress*] (LCLS) ... MiDbEI
Edison Intl. [*NYSE symbol*] (TTSB) ... EIX
Edison Materials Technology Center [*Military*] ... EMTEC
Edison National Historic Site ... EDIS
Edison National Historic Site, West Orange, NJ [*Library symbol Library of Congress*] (LCLS) ... NjWoE
Edison Responsive Environment [*Automated learning system*] ... ERE
Edison Sault Electric Co. (MHDW) ... EDSE
Edison Screw ... ES
Edison Screw Cap [*Electronics*] (EECA) ... ESC
Edison State Community College, Piqua, OH [*Library symbol Library of Congress*] (LCLS) ... OPiE
Edison Technical and Occupational Educational Center Library, Rochester, NY [*OCLC symbol*] (OCLC) ... RWE
Edison Welding Institute (EA) ... EWI
Edisto Resources [*AMEX symbol*] (TTSB) ... EDT
Edisto Resources Corp. [*Associated Press*] (SAG) ... Edisto
Edisto Resources Corp. [*AMEX symbol*] (SPSG) ... EDS
Edisto Resources Corp. [*AMEX symbol*] (SAG) ... EDT
Edisto Resources Wrrt [*AMEX symbol*] (TTSB) ... EDSWS
Edit [*or Edited*] ... ED
Edit (ABBR) ... EDT
Edit, Count, Recode (IAA) ... ECR
Edit Decision List ... EDL
Edit Error [*Military*] (AFIT) ... EE
Edit Master and Activity Review List (MCD) ... EMARL
Edit Program Generator ... EPG
Edit Sync Guide (NTCM) ... ESG
EDITEC, Chicago, IL [*Library symbol Library of Congress*] (LCLS) ... ICEdit
Edited (ROG) ... EDIT
Edited (ABBR) ... EDTD
Edited By (WDMC) ... ed
Edited Collections Report File [*IRS*] ... ECRF
Editek, Inc. [*AMEX symbol*] (SPSG) ... EDI
Editek, Inc. [*Associated Press*] (SAG) ... Editek
Edith and Dana Bennett Agricultural Roundtable (EA) ... EDBAR
Edith Stein Guild (EA) ... ESG
Editing (ABBR) ... EDTG
Editing, Arranging, and Sequencing Environment [*Computer science*] (BYTE) ... EASE
Editing Macros [*Computer science*] (NHD) ... EMACS
Editing Specifications (MCD) ... EDITSPEC
Editio Citata [*Edition Cited*] [*Latin*] ... ed cit
Edition ... E
Edition (AFM) ... ED
Edition (VRA) ... ed
Edition ... ED
Edition ... EDIT
Edition ... EDN
Edition (ABBR) ... EDTN
Edition Bookbinders of New York (EA) ... EBNY
Edition Deluxe ... EDL
Editions (ROG) ... EDD
Editions [*A publication*] ... Edns
Editions (WDMC) ... Eds
Editions du Boreal Express, Montreal, PQ, Canada [*Library symbol Library of Congress*] (LCLS) ... CaQTB
Editions Nouveaux Horizons [*US government imprint*] ... NH
Editions Phonographiques Parisiennes - Allegro Label [*Record label*] [*France*] ... EPP
Edit-Level Video (NTCM) ... ELV
Edito Princeps [*First edition*] [*Latin*] (WDAA) ... EP
Editor (EY) ... ED
Editor [*Computer science*] ... EDI
Editor (ROG) ... EDIT
Editor ... EDIT
Editor ... EDT
Editor (ABBR) ... EDTR
Editor, 6, 9, and 10, Heiskell's Tennessee Reports [*A publication*] (DLA) ... Malone
Editor and Compiler ... EDCOM
Editor & Publisher (WDMC) ... E&P
Editor "Hebrew Christians' Magazine" [*Pseudonym used by Nathan Davis*] ... EHCM
Editora y Distribuidora Hispano-Americana Sociedad Anonima [*Publisher's imprint*] [*Spain*] ... EDHASA
Editorial (WDAA) ... EDIT
Editorial (ABBR) ... EDTL
Editorial Alteration [*Publishing*] (WDMC) ... EA
Editorial Assistant [*Publishing*] ... EA
Editorial Code and Data, Inc. (IID) ... ECDI
Editorial Comment (DLA) ... Ed Comment
Editorial Data Systems ... EDS
Editorial Freelancers Association (EA) ... EFA
Editorial Layout Display System ... ELDS
Editorial Management System (DGA) ... EMS
Editorial Processing Center ... EPC
Editorial Production Branch [*BUPERS*] ... EPB
Editorial Projects in Education (EA) ... EPE
Editorial Staff (DGA) ... ED STAFF
Editorial Status Report ... ESR
Editorial Support Group ... ESG
Editorial Word Processing International Network (DGA) ... EDWIN
Editorialize (ABBR) ... EDTLZ
Editorialized (ABBR) ... EDTLZD
Editorializing (ABBR) ... EDTLZG
Editor-in-Chief (WDAA) ... ED IN CH
Editors (ROG) ... EDD
Editors (WDMC) ... Eds
Editors Organizing Committee and Writers' and Publishers' Alliance for Disarmament (EA) ... EOC and WPA
Editor's Presentation Copy ... EPC
Editorship (ABBR) ... EDTRSP
Editorship (ABBR) ... EDTSP
Edits et Ordonnances [*Lower Canada*] [*A publication*] (DLA) ... Ed et Ord
Edmark Corp. [*Associated Press*] (SAG) ... Edmark
Edmark Corp. [*NASDAQ symbol*] (SAG) ... EDMK
Edmond James Rothschild Memorial Group [*Foundation*] ... EJRMG
Edmond, OK [*FM radio station call letters*] ... KCSC
Edmond, OK [*FM radio station call letters*] ... KOKF
Edmonds Community College, Edmonds, WA [*Library symbol Library of Congress*] (LCLS) ... WaEdE
Edmond's Learning Style Identification Exercise (EDAC) ... ELSIE
Edmonds' New York Select Cases [*A publication*] (DLA) ... Edm Sel Ca
Edmonds' New York Select Cases [*A publication*] (DLA) ... Edm Sel Cas
Edmonds' New York Statutes at Large [*A publication*] (DLA) ... Edm Stat
Edmonds' New York Statutes at Large [*A publication*] (DLA) ... Edmonds' St at Large
Edmonds, WA [*AM radio station call letters*] ... KCIS
Edmonds, WA [*FM radio station call letters*] ... KCMS
Edmonton [*Alberta*] [*Seismograph station code, US Geological Survey*] (SEIS) ... EDM
Edmonton [*Canada*] (ABBR) ... EDMN
Edmonton [*Canada*] [*Airport symbol*] (OAG) ... YEG
Edmonton, AB [*AM radio station call letters*] ... CBX
Edmonton, AB [*FM radio station call letters*] ... CBX-FM
Edmonton, AB [*Television station call letters*] ... CBXFT
Edmonton, AB [*Television station call letters*] ... CBXT
Edmonton, AB [*FM radio station call letters*] ... CFBR
Edmonton, AB [*AM radio station call letters*] ... CFRN
Edmonton, AB [*Television station call letters*] ... CFRN-TV
Edmonton, AB [*AM radio station call letters*] ... CHED
Edmonton, AB [*AM radio station call letters*] ... CHFA
Edmonton, AB [*AM radio station call letters*] ... CHQT
Edmonton, AB [*FM radio station call letters*] ... CIRK
Edmonton, AB [*FM radio station call letters*] ... CISN
Edmonton, AB [*Television station call letters*] ... CITV
Edmonton, AB [*Television station call letters*] ... CJAL
Edmonton, AB [*AM radio station call letters*] ... CJCA
Edmonton, AB [*FM radio station call letters*] ... CJSR
Edmonton, AB [*AM radio station call letters*] ... CKER
Edmonton, AB [*FM radio station call letters*] ... CKNG
Edmonton, AB [*FM radio station call letters*] ... CKRA
Edmonton, AB [*AM radio station call letters*] ... CKUA
Edmonton, AB [*FM radio station call letters*] ... CKUA-FM
Edmonton, AB [*ICAO location identifier*] (ICLI) ... CWEG
Edmonton, AB [*ICAO location identifier*] (ICLI) ... CZEG
Edmonton Catholic School District, Edmonton, AB, Canada [*Library symbol Library of Congress*] (LCLS) ... CaAECSD
Edmonton Catholic School District, Professional Library, Edmonton, AB, Canada [*Library symbol Library of Congress*] (LCLS) ... CaAEPL
Edmonton General Hospital, Alberta [*Library symbol National Library of Canada*] (NLC) ... AEGH
Edmonton General Hospital, Edmonton, AB, Canada [*Library symbol Library of Congress*] (LCLS) ... CaAEGH
Edmonton International, AB [*ICAO location identifier*] (ICLI) ... CYEG
Edmonton, KY [*FM radio station call letters*] (RBYB) ... WKNK
Edmonton/Municipal, AB [*ICAO location identifier*] (ICLI) ... CYXD
Edmonton [*Canada*] **Municipal Airport** [*Airport symbol*] (OAG) ... YXD
Edmonton/Namao Canadian Forces Base, AB [*ICAO location identifier*] (ICLI) ... CYED
Edmonton Oilers Booster Club [*Defunct*] (EA) ... EOBC

Edmonton Power Co., Alberta [*Library symbol National Library of Canada*] (NLC) ... AEEP

Edmonton Power Co., Edmonton, AB, Canada [*Library symbol Library of Congress*] (LCLS) ... CaAEEP

Edmonton Public Library [*UTLAS symbol*] ... EPL

Edmonton Public Library, Alberta [*Library symbol National Library of Canada*] (NLC) ... AE

Edmonton Public Library, Edmonton, AB, Canada [*Library symbol Library of Congress*] (LCLS) ... CaAE

Edmund, OK [*FM radio station call letters*] ... KTNT

Edmund Scientific Consumer Science Division ... es

Edmund Sixtus Muskie [*American politician*] ... ESM

Edmund Walker [*Car parts distribution company*] [*British*] ... EW

Edmund's Exchequer Practice [*A publication*] (DLA) ... Edm Exch Pr

Edmundston, NB [*FM radio station call letters*] ... CFAI

Edmundston, NB [*AM radio station call letters*] ... CJEM

Edna I. Murphy School, Grand Rapids, MN [*Library symbol*] [*Library of Congress*] (LCLS) ... MnGrEMS

Edna, TX [*Location identifier FAA*] (FAAL) ... EDX

Edna, TX [*AM radio station call letters*] ... KTMR

Edna Zybell Memorial Library, Clarence, IA [*Library symbol Library of Congress*] (LCLS) ... IaClar

EDO Corp. [*NYSE symbol*] (SPSG) ... EDO

EDP [*Electronic Data Processing*] **Auditors' Association** ... EAA

EDP [*Electronic Data Processing*] **Auditors Association** (EA) ... EDPAA

EDP [*Electronic Data Processing*]-Microfilm-Integrated-Retrieval [*German Patent Office*] ... EMIR

Edrophonium [*A cholinergic*] [*Anesthesiology*] ... E

Edsbyn [*Sweden ICAO location identifier*] (ICLI) ... ESUY

Edsel Owner's Club (EA) ... EOC

Edson, AB [*AM radio station call letters*] ... CJYR

Edson, AB [*ICAO location identifier*] (ICLI) ... CYET

Edson Public Library, Alberta [*Library symbol National Library of Canada*] (NLC) ... AED

Educable (ABBR) ... EDCAB

Educable (ABBR) ... EDCBL

Educable (ABBR) ... EDUCB

Educable Mentally Handicapped ... EMH

Educable Mentally Retardate [*or Retarded*] ... EMR

Educable Neurologically Handicapped ... ENH

Educate (ABBR) ... EDCA

Educate People - Protect Innocent Children [*Defunct*] (EA) ... EPPIC

Educated ... E

Educated (ABBR) ... EDCAD

Educated [*or Education*] (AFM) ... EDUC

Educated (ABBR) ... EDUCD

Educating (ABBR) ... EDCAG

Educating (ABBR) ... EDCG

Educating (ABBR) ... EDUCG

Education ... ED

Education (DD) ... Ed

Education (ABBR) ... EDCAN

Education (ADA) ... EDCN

Education ... EDN

Education (ADA) ... EDU

Education (VRA) ... educ

Education ... EDUC

Education ... EDUCN

Education Administration Specialist (PGP) ... EAS

Education Alternative, Inc. [*NASDAQ symbol*] (SAG) ... EAIN

Education Alternative, Inc. [*Associated Press*] (SAG) ... EdcAlt

Education Alternatives ... EA

Education Alternatives [*NASDAQ symbol*] (TTSB) ... EAIN

Education and Behavioral Sciences Section [*Association of College and Research Libraries*] ... EBSS

Education and Development ... E & D

Education and Enrichment Section of the National Council on Family Relations (EA) ... EES/NCFR

Education and Experience in Engineering [*Illinois Institute of Technology program*] ... E^3

Education and Information Dissemination ... E & ID

Education and Information Technology [*Educational viewdata service*] (NITA) ... ED.IT

Education and Neighborhood Action for Better Living Environment ... ENABLE

Education and Religious Affairs [*US Military Government, Germany*] ... ERA

Education and Research Institute [*Washington, DC*] (EA) ... ERI

Education and Research Network [*India*] [*Computer science*] (TNIG) ... ERNET

Education and Resource Centre [*South Australia*] ... ERC

Education and Training [*Navy*] ... E & T

Education and Training Advisory Team (CINC) ... ETAT

Education and Training in Quality Assurance Practices [*American Society for Quality Control*] (NRCH) ... ETQAP

Education and Training Support Detachment [*Military*] (DNAB) ... EDTRASUPPDET

Education and Training Support Detachment [*Military*] (DNAB) ... ETSD

Education and Training Support Training Device Field Engineering Office [*Military*] (DNAB) ... EDTRASUPPTRADEV FEO

Education and Vocational Training [*British military*] (DMA) ... EVT

Education and World Affairs [*Later, ICED*] ... EWA

Education Appeal Board [*Department of Education*] (GFGA) ... EAB

Education Association (AIE) ... EA

Education Audit Institute [*Washington, DC*] ... EAI

Education Cataloguing Support System [*UTLAS symbol*] ... EDUCATSS

Education Center [*Army*] (AABC) ... EDCEN

Education Center Publications (MCD) ... ECP

Education Centre, Toronto Board of Education, Ontario [*Library symbol National Library of Canada*] (NLC) ... OTEC

Education Code (OICC) ... EC

Education Commission of the States (EA) ... ECS

Education Commission of the States, Denver, CO [*Library symbol Library of Congress*] (LCLS) ... CoDE

Education Consolidation and Improvement Act [*1981*] ... ECIA

Education Council of the Graphic Arts Industry [*Later, GATF*] (EA) ... ECGAI

Education Credit Union Council (EA) ... ECUC

Education Department [*British military*] (DMA) ... ED

Education Department Acquisition Regulation (AAGC) ... EDAR

Education Department General Administrative Regulations [*Department of Education*] (GFGA) ... EDGAR

Education Development Associates [*Information service or system*] ... EDA

Education Development Center [*Defunct*] (EA) ... EDC

Education Document Reproduction Service ... EDRS

Education Equivalency Test ... EET

Education Evaluation and Remedial Assistance Program [*Connecticut*] (EDAC) ... EERA

Education Excellence Partnership ... EEP

Education Exploration Center ... EEC

Education for All Handicapped Children Act (AIE) ... EHA

Education for all Handicapped Children act [*1975 federal law*] (PAZ) ... EHC

Education for All Handicapped Children Act ... EHCA

Education for Economic Security Act [*1988*] ... EESA

Education for Enterprise Network (AIE) ... EEN

Education for Librarianship - Australia [*A publication*] ... EFLA

Education for Public Management [*Program*] [*Civil Service Commission*] (RDA) ... EPM

Education Funding Research Council (EA) ... EFRC

Education Improvement Act of 1984 ... EIA

Education in Asia and Oceania [*A publication*] ... Ed Asia Oceania

Education in Asia and the Pacific [*A publication*] ... Ed Asia Pacif

Education in Personal Relationships (AIE) ... EPR

Education in Science (AIE) ... EIS

Education Industries Association [*Later, NSSEA*] (EA) ... EIA

Education Information Center [*Georgia State Department of Education*] [*Information service or system*] (IID) ... EIC

Education Information Network in the European Community [*Commission of the European Communities*] [*Belgium Information service or system*] (IID) ... EURYDICE

Education Instruction Network (WDAA) ... EDINET

Education Law Advisers Service (AIE) ... ELAS

Education Learning Services (AIE) ... ELS

Education Level ... EL

Education Liberation Front ... ELF

Education Libraries Sharing of Resources [*Network*] ... ELSOR

Education Library [*A publication*] ... EL

Education Library, Memorial University, St. John's, Newfoundland [*Library symbol National Library of Canada*] (NLC) ... NFSMED

Education Library, University of Regina, Saskatchewan [*Library symbol National Library of Canada*] (BIB) ... SRUE

Education Library, Wellington County Board of Education, Guelph, Ontario [*Library symbol National Library of Canada*] (NLC) ... OGWE

Education Management Corp. [*Associated Press*] (SAG) ... EdcMge

Education Management Corp. [*NASDAQ symbol*] (SAG) ... EDMC

Education Management System [*Military*] ... EMS

Education Manual [*Military*] ... EM

Education Network [*EDUCOM*] ... EDUNET

Education Network for Environment and Development (AIE) ... ENED

Education of Girls in Mathematics and Science ... EGMS

Education of the Handicapped Act [*1968*] ... EHA

Education Officer [*Military*] ... EO

Education Opportunity Center of the State University of New York, Syracuse, NY [*OCLC symbol*] (OCLC) ... ZUH

Education Otherwise [*British*] [*An association*] (DBA) ... EO

Education Outcomes Division [*Washington, DC Department of Education*] (GRD) ... EOD

Education Professions Development Act [*1965*] ... EPDA

Education Projects Fund [*British Council/Overseas Development Administration*] (DS) ... EPF

Education Reform Act [*1988*] (AIE) ... ERA

Education Research and Perspectives [*A publication*] ... Ed Res Perspectives

Education Research Assistant (ADA) ... ERA

Education Research Branch (AIE) ... ERB

Education Research Unit News [*Australian Union of Students*] [*A publication*] (ADA) ... ERUN

Education Resource Allocation in Schools Project [*Australia*] ... ERASP

Education Resource Centre, Oshawa General Hospital, Ontario [*Library symbol National Library of Canada*] (BIB) ... OOSHH

Education Review Association [*Australia*] ... ERA

Education Review Unit [*South Australia*] ... ERU

Education Service Advisory Committee (AIE) ... ESAC

Education Service Group [*Bibliographic Retrieval Services*] [*Information service or system*] (IID) ... ESG

Education Service of the Plastics Industry (AIE) ... ESPI

Education Services Officer (AAGC) ... ESO

Education Society [*Later, Psychology Society - PS*] (EA) ... EMSO

Education Specialist ... Ed Sp

Education Specialist ... Ed Spec

Education Student Assistance System ... ESAS

Education Support Centre [*Australia*] ... ESB

Education Support Staff (AIE) ... ESS

Education Task Force [*Government Documents Round Table*] [*American Library Association*] ... ETF

Education Technology and Equipment Manufacturing Association (AIE) ... ETEMA
Education through Aviation ... ETA
Education, Training, and Military Operations [*Army*] (RDA) ... ET & MO
Education, Training and Qualifications Committee (ACII) ... ETQ
Education, Training and Research Associates (EA) ... ETR
Education, Volunteerism, Employment Opportunities ... EVE
Education Voucher Institute [*Defunct*] (EA) ... EVI
Education Welfare Officers' National Association [*British*] (DI) ... EWONA
Education with Industry ... EWI
Education Without Frontiers [*An association*] (EAIO) ... EWF
Education Writers Association (EA) ... EWA
Educational [*FCC*] (NTCM) ... ED
Educational (ABBR) ... EDCANL
Educational (WGA) ... EDNL
Educational ... EDUCL
Educational ... EDUCL
Educational ... Educnl
Educational Accountability Function (OICC) ... EAF
Educational Activities (ACII) ... EAP
Educational Administration Resource Centre [*Information service or system*] (IID) ... EARC
Educational Advice Service Project (AIE) ... EASP
Educational Advisor ... EA
Educational Advisory Board [*British*] ... EAB
Educational Advisory Committee [*AIAA*] ... EAC
Educational Age ... EA
Educational Alliance (EA) ... EA
Educational Analog Simulator ... EAS
Educational and Cultural Development Program ... ECD
Educational and Health Career Services (EA) ... EHCS
Educational and Industrial Testing Service ... EDITS
Educational and Industrial Testing Service ... EITS
Educational and Scientific Establishment (IIA) ... EASE
Educational and Training Establishment [*Military British*] ... ETE
Educational Art ... EA
Educational Assessment Center [*University of Washington*] [*Research center*] (RCD) ... EAC
Educational Assessment Guidelines Leading [*Toward*] **Excellence** ... EAGLE
Educational Assistance Ltd. (PCM) ... EAL
Educational Awareness Project (EA) ... EAP
Educational Broadcast Satellite (MCD) ... EBS
Educational Broadcasting Corp. (EA) ... EBC
[*The*] **Educational Broadcasting Institute** [*National Association of Educational Broadcasters*] (NTCM) ... EBI
Educational Broadcasting Services Trust (AIE) ... EBST
Educational Cable Television (NTCM) ... ECATV
Educational Career Service [*Later, EHCS*] [*An association*] (EA) ... ECS
Educational Career Service/Health Career Service [*Later, EHCS*] [*An association*] (EA) ... ECS/HCS
Educational Center for Applied Ekistics (EA) ... ECAE
Educational Centres Association [*British*] ... ECA
Educational Commission for Foreign Medical Graduates (EA) ... ECFMG
Educational Communication Association (EA) ... ECA
Educational Communications [*An association*] (EA) ... EC
Educational Communications on Exhibit [*Commercial firm*] ... ECOX
Educational Computer Consortium of Ohio (SRA) ... ECCO
Educational Computing Organization of Ontario (EDAC) ... ECOO
Educational Concern for Hunger Organization (EA) ... ECHO
[*The*] **Educational Corp. of America** (ECON) ... ECA
Educational Council for Foreign Medical Students (DAVI) ... ECFMS
Educational Counselling and Credit Transfer Information Service [*Information service or system*] (IID) ... ECCTIS
Educational Counselling Service [*British Council*] (AIE) ... ECS
Educational Data Bank (IEEE) ... EDB
Educational Data Base Management System [*Computer science*] (MHDB) ... EDBS
Educational Data Information Ltd. [*Information service or system*] (IID) ... EDI
Educational Data Processing (NITA) ... EDP
Educational Data System (IAA) ... EDS
Educational Database System [*Computer System Research Group*] [*University of Toronto*] (NITA) ... EDBS
Educational Dealers and Suppliers Association International (EA) ... EDSAI
Educational Delivery System (OICC) ... EDS
Educational Development [*NASDAQ symbol*] (TTSB) ... EDUC
Educational Development Corp. [*Defunct*] (EA) ... EDCo
Educational Development Corp. [*NASDAQ symbol*] (NQ) ... EDUC
Educational Development Corp. [*Associated Press*] (SAG) ... EduDv
Educational Development of Military Personnel ... EDOMP
Educational Developmental Laboratories [*of McGraw Hill, Inc.*] ... EDL
Educational Document Management and Retrieval System [*Database*] [*Japan*] ... EDMARS
Educational Drama ... ED
Educational Drama Association [*Defunct*] (EAIO) ... EDA
Educational Employment Service ... EES
Educational Equity Concepts [*An association*] (EA) ... EEC
Educational Events [*Timeplace, Inc.*] [*Waltham, MA*] [*Information service or system*] (IID) ... EdVENT
Educational Exhibitors' Association [*British*] (BI) ... EEA
Educational Expeditions International [*Later, Earthwatch*] ... EEI
Educational Facilities Laboratories [*Defunct*] (EA) ... EFL
Educational Film Library Association (EA) ... EFLA
Educational Film Library Association, New York, NY [*Library symbol Library of Congress*] (LCLS) ... NNEF
Educational FM Station (NTCM) ... EDFM
Educational Forum [*A publication*] (BRI) ... Ed F
Educational Foundation for Foreign Study (EA) ... EF Foundation
Educational Foundation for Jewish Girls [*Later, Jewish Foundation for Educationof Women*] (EA) ... EFJG
Educational Foundation for Nuclear Science (EA) ... EFNS
Educational Foundation for the Apparel Industry [*Later, EFFI*] (EA) ... EFAI
Educational Foundation for the Fashion Industries (EA) ... EFFI
Educational Foundation for Visual Arts [*British*] ... EFVA
Educational Foundation of the National Restaurant Association (EA) ... EFNRA
Educational Freedom Foundation (EA) ... EFF
Educational Fund for Individual Rights [*Defunct*] (EA) ... EFIR
Educational Fund to End Handgun Violence (EA) ... EFEHV
Educational Futures, Inc. (EA) ... EFI
Educational Grants Advisory Service (AIE) ... EGAS
Educational Group of the Music Industries Association [*British*] (BI) ... EGMIA
Educational Growth Group (DICI) ... EGG
Educational Guidance Associates School and College Advisory Center [*Formerly, SCAC*] (EA) ... EGASCAC
Educational Guidance Center for the Mentally Retarded [*Defunct*] (EA) ... EGC
Educational Improvement Center - Northeast [*Information service or system*] ... EIC-NE
Educational Improvement Process [*Indiana*] (EDAC) ... EIP
Educational Incentive Plan [*Red Cross*] ... EIP
Educational Information Center [*Office of Education*] ... EIC
Educational Information Network [*Princeton, NJ*] ... EIN
Educational Insights [*NASDAQ symbol*] (TTSB) ... EDIN
Educational Insights ... EI
Educational Insights, Inc. [*NASDAQ symbol*] (SAG) ... EDIN
Educational Insights, Inc. [*Associated Press*] (SAG) ... EducIns
Educational Institute of Design, Craft, and Technology [*British*] ... EIDCT
Educational Institute of Scotland ... EIS
Educational Institution Program (NTCM) ... ED
Educational Jewelry Manufacturers Association [*Defunct*] (EA) ... EJMA
Educational Leadership [*A publication*] (BRI) ... EL
Educational Leadership Institute (EA) ... ELI
Educational Management [*Educational Resources Information Center (ERIC) Clearinghouse*] [*University of Oregon*] (PAZ) ... EA
Educational Management Information System ... EMIS
Educational Marketer [*A publication*] ... EM
Educational Materials Laboratory ... EML
Educational Media and Technology Center ... EMC
Educational Media Association of Canada ... EMAC
Educational Media Centre, Sudbury Board of Education, Ontario [*Library symbol National Library of Canada*] (NLC) ... OSUBE
Educational Media Council [*Defunct*] (EA) ... EMC
Educational Media Institutes Evaluation [*Project*] ... EMIE
Educational Media Producers and Distributors Association of Canada ... EMPDAC
Educational Media Producers Council [*of the National Audio-Visual Association*] [*Later, NAVA Materials Council*] ... EMPC
Educational Media Research Information Center ... EMRIC
Educational Media Selection Center [*National Book Committee*] ... EMSC
Educational Modulation Center ... EMC
Educational Opportunity Bank ... EOB
Educational Opportunity Center [*Higher Education Act*] ... EOC
Educational Opportunity Center, Syracuse, NY [*Library symbol Library of Congress*] (LCLS) ... NSyEd
Educational Opportunity Grant ... EOG
Educational Organization [*Internet address domain name*] (CDE) ... edu
Educational Organizations and Agencies Directory [*A publication*] ... EOAD
Educational Orientation Questionnaire (EDAC) ... EOQ
Educational Paperback Association (EA) ... EPA
Educational Planning Institute (EA) ... EPI
Educational Policies Commission [*Defunct*] (EA) ... EPC
Educational Premises [*Public-performance tariff class*] [*British*] ... N
Educational Press Association of America (EA) ... EDPRESS
Educational Press Association of America [*Later, EDPRESS*] (EA) ... EPAA
Educational Priority Indices (AIE) ... EPI
Educational Products Information Exchange (HGAA) ... EPIC
Educational Products Information Exchange ... EPIE
Educational Products Information Exchange Institute [*Later, EPIE Institute*] (EA) ... EPIEI
Educational Professional Development Assistance [*Office of Education*] ... EPDA
Educational Program in Systems Analysis (RDA) ... EPSA
Educational Programming of Cultural Heritage (AEBS) ... EPOCH
Educational Programs that Work [*Department of Education*] [*Information service or system*] (IID) ... EPTW
Educational Publication [*NASA*] ... EP
Educational Publishers Association ... EPA
Educational Publishers Council [*British*] ... EPC
Educational Puppetry Association [*British*] (BI) ... EPA
Educational Quality Assessment Program [*Pennsylvania*] (EDAC) ... EQA
Educational Quotient [*Psychology*] ... EQ
Educational Radio Network ... ERN
Educational Rankings Annual [*A publication*] ... ERA
Educational Ratio ... ER
Educational Records Bureau (EA) ... ERB
Educational Reference Center [*National Institute of Education*] ... ERC
Educational Reimbursement Program (SAA) ... ERP
Educational Reptiles in Captivity Zoological Compound (EA) ... ERICZC
Educational Requirements Test ... ERT
Educational Research Analysts (EA) ... EdReAn
Educational Research Center [*New Mexico State University*] [*Research center*] (RCD) ... ERC
Educational Research Centre [*Australia*] ... ERC
Educational Research Council of America (AEBS) ... ERC

Educational Research Council of America [*Defunct*] (EA) .... ERCA
Educational Research Information .... ERI
Educational Research Service (EA) .... ERS
Educational Resources [*Auckland, NZ*] .... ER
Educational Resources Allocation Systems .... ERAS
Educational Resources Center (AEBS) .... ERC
Educational Resources [*formerly, Research*] Information Center [*Department of Education*] [*Bibliographic database Washington, DC*] .... ERIC
Educational Resources Information Center/Adult Education [*Department of Education*] (AEBS) .... ERIC/AE
Educational Resources Information Center/Clearinghouse for Information Resources [*Department of Education*] [*Syracuse University*] [*Research center*] (IID) .... ERIC/IR
Educational Resources Information Center/Clearinghouse for Library Information Sciences .... ERIC/CLIS
Educational Resources Information Center/Clearinghouse for Science, Mathematics,and Environmental Education [*Department of Education*] [*Information service or system*] (IID) .... ERIC/SMEAC
Educational Resources Information Center/Clearinghouse for Social Studies/SocialScience Education [*Department of Education*] [*Information service or system*] (IID) .... ERIC/CHESS
Educational Resources Information Center/Clearinghouse in Career Education [*Ohio State University*] (IID) .... ERIC/CE
Educational Resources Information Center/Clearinghouse on Adult, Career, and Vocational Education [*Department of Education*] (IID) .... ERIC/ACVE
Educational Resources Information Center/Clearinghouse on Counseling and Personnel Services [*Department of Education*] [*University of Michigan*] [*Research center*] (IID) .... ERIC/CAPS
Educational Resources Information Center/Clearinghouse on Educational Administration [*University of Oregon*] [*Department of Education*] (AEBS) .... ERIC/CEA
Educational Resources Information Center/Clearinghouse on Educational Management [*Department of Education*] [*University of Oregon Eugene*] [*Research center*] .... ERIC/CEM
Educational Resources Information Center/Clearinghouse on Elementary and Early Childhood Education [*Department of Education*] [*University of Illinois*] (IID) .... ERIC/EECE
Educational Resources Information Center/Clearinghouse on Handicapped and GiftedChildren [*Department of Education*] [*Information service or system*] (IID) .... ERIC/EC
Educational Resources Information Center/Clearinghouse on Higher Education (IID) .... ERIC/CHE
Educational Resources Information Center/Clearinghouse on Higher Education [*George Washington University*] [*Research center*] (EA) .... ERIC/HE
Educational Resources Information Center/Clearinghouse on Languages and Linguistics [*Department of Education*] [*Center for Applied Liguistics*] (IID) .... ERIC/CLL
Educational Resources Information Center/Clearinghouse on Reading and Communication Skills [*Department of Education*] [*Urbana, IL*] .... ERIC/RCS
Educational Resources Information Center/Clearinghouse on Retrieval of Information and Evaluation on Reading [*Indiana University*] [*Department of Education*] (AEBS) .... ERIC/CRIER
Educational Resources Information Center/Clearinghouse on Rural Education and Small Schools [*Department of Education*] [*New Mexico State University*] [*Research center*] (IID) .... ERIC/CRESS
Educational Resources Information Center/Clearinghouse on Teacher Education .... ERIC/TE
Educational Resources Information Center/Clearinghouse on Tests, Measurement, and Evaluation [*Department of Education*] [*Educational Testing Service*] (IID) .... ERIC/TM
Educational Resources Information Center/Clearinghouse on Urban Education [*Department of Education*] [*Columbia University*] (IID) .... ERIC/CUE
Educational Resources Information Center, Elementary and Early Childhood Education (ERIC/ECE), Urbana, IL [*Library symbol Library of Congress*] (LCLS) .... IUrE-E
Educational Resources Information Center/Information Retrieval Center on the Disadvantaged [*Horace Mann-Lincoln Institute Teachers College*] [*Columbia University*] [*Department of Education*] (AEBS) .... ERIC/IRCD
Educational Resources Information Center, National Council of Teachers of English, Urbana, IL [*Library symbol Library of Congress*] (LCLS) .... IUrE-NC
Educational Resources Information Center/School Personnel [*Department of Education*] [*Washington, DC*] .... ERIC/SP
Educational Rewards Bureau .... ERB
Educational Satellite (KSC) .... EDUSAT
Educational, Scientific, and Cultural Organization (BARN) .... ESCO
Educational Service and Demonstration Centers [*Washington*] (EDAC) .... ESD
Educational Service Branch [*BUPERS*] .... ESB
Educational Services [*Publisher*] .... ES
Educational Services, Inc. [*Later, EDC*] .... ESI
Educational Services, International (EA) .... ESI
Educational Services Office [*or Officer*] [*Navy*] .... ESO
Educational Services Section [*Navy*] .... ESS
Educational Services, Seven Oaks General Hospital, Winnipeg, Manitoba [*Library symbol National Library of Canada*] (NLC) .... MWSOGH
Educational Software Products [*Commercial firm*] (PCM) .... ESP
[*The*] Educational Software Selector [*Database*] (AEE) .... TESS
Educational Specialist .... Ed S
Educational Specialist .... ES
Educational Sport Institute (EA) .... ESI
Educational Statistics [*Search system*] .... EDSTAT
Educational Statistics Information Access Service [*Databank*] (NITA) .... EDSTAT
Educational Statistics, National Center (OICC) .... ESNC
Educational Studies [*A publication*] (BRI) .... ES
Educational Subscription Service, Inc. .... ESS

Educational Support Personnel .... ESP
Educational Systems Corp. [*Defunct*] (EA) .... ESC
Educational Talent Search (EA) .... ETS
Educational Technology and Language Learning (AIE) .... ETLL
Educational Technology Center [*Harvard University*] [*Department of Education Research center*] (RCD) .... ETC
Educational Technology Language [*University of Western Ontario*] [*Canada*] (NITA) .... ETL
Educational Telecommunications Network .... ETN
Educational Teleconference System [*University of Missouri - Columbia*] [*Telecommunications*] (TSSD) .... ETS
Educational Telephone Network [*University of North Dakota*] [*Grand Forks*] (TSSD) .... ETN
Educational Television [*FCC*] (NTCM) .... ET
Educational Television .... ETV
Educational Television and Radio Center [*Later, EBC*] .... ETRC
Educational Television Association (EAIO) .... ETA
Educational Television by Satellite (NTCM) .... ETVS
Educational Television for the Metropolitan Area .... ETMA
Educational Television Stations [*National Association of Educational Broadcasters*] (AEBS) .... ETS
Educational Test [*British military*] (DMA) .... ET
Educational Testing Service (EA) .... ETS
Educational Testing Service, Princeton, NJ [*Library symbol Library of Congress*] (LCLS) .... NjPE
Educational Testing Service Test Collection (IID) .... ETSTC
Educational Testing Service Test Collection File (EDAC) .... ETSF
Educational Theater Association (EA) .... ETA
Educational Theory [*A publication*] (BRI) .... Ed Theory
Educational Therapy .... ET
Educational Training .... ET
Educational Training Material (MCD) .... ETM
Educational Travel Connection [*Oracle Corp.*] [*Information service or system*] (IID) .... ETC
Educational Travel, Inc. .... ETI
Educational TV Services [*Oklahoma State University*] [*Stillwater*] (TSSD) .... ETS
Educational Use of Computers .... EDUCOM
Educational Video Corp. .... EVC
Educational Welfare Officer [*British*] (DI) .... EWO
Educational Workers' International (AIE) .... EWI
Educationalist (ABBR) .... EDUCNLST
Educationally Disadvantaged Youth (EDAC) .... EDY
Educationally Handicapped .... EH
Educationally Impaired .... EI
Educationally Mentally Impaired .... EMI
Educationally Subnormal .... ESN
Educationally Subnormal-Moderate [*Medicine*] (DMAA) .... ESN(M)
Educative (ABBR) .... EDCAV
Educative (ABBR) .... EDUCV
Educator (ABBR) .... EDCATR
Educator (ABBR) .... EDUCR
Educators' Ad Hoc Committee on Copyright Law (EA) .... EAHCCL
Educator's Desk Reference [*A publication*] .... EDR
Educators for Social Responsibility (EA) .... ESR
Educators Forum [*Columbus, OH*] [*Information service or system*] (IID) .... EDFORUM
Educators Fund Management Corp. [*of NEA*] .... EFMC
Educators of Library Media Specialists Section [*American Association of School Librarians*] .... ELMS
Educators of Library Media Specialists Section [*American Association of School Librarians*] [*American Library Association*] .... ELMSS
Educators of Professional Personnel for the Hearing Impaired .... EPPHI
Educator's Purchasing Master [*A publication*] .... EPM
Educators to Africa [*Later, ETAA*] (EA) .... EA
Educators to Africa (EA) .... ETAA
Educators'-Employers' Tests and Services Associate (AEBS) .... ETSA
Educo [*Record label*] .... Edu
Educreative Systems, Inc. .... ESI
Educt Vent .... EV
Eductor (MSA) .... EDUC
Edulcorata [*Sweetened*] [*Pharmacy*] (ROG) .... ED
Edunetics Ltd. [*NASDAQ symbol*] (SAG) .... EDNT
Edunetics Ltd. [*Associated Press*] (SAG) .... Edunetic
Edusoft Ltd. [*NASDAQ symbol*] (SAG) .... EDUS
Edusoft Ltd. [*Associated Press*] (SAG) .... Edusoft
Edusoft Ltd [*NASDAQ symbol*] (TTSB) .... EDUSE
Eduworld Society [*Later, CFB*] (EA) .... EWS
'Eduyyoth (BJA) .... 'Ed
'Eduyyoth (BJA) .... 'Eduy
Edvard Grieg Memorial Foundation (EA) .... EGMF
Edwald-Kornfeld Method .... EKM
Edward [*Phonetic alphabet*] [*Royal Navy World War I*] (DSUE) .... E
Edward Elgar [*Publisher*] [*British*] .... EE
Edward Grey Institute of Field Ornithology (BARN) .... EGIFO
Edward Hamilton Aitken [*Author*] [*Initials used as pseudonym*] .... EHA
Edward J. Meyer Memorial Hospital Medical Library, Buffalo, NY [*Library symbol Library of Congress*] (LCLS) .... NBuEMH
Edward Medal [*British*] .... EM
Edward Moore Kennedy [*American politician*] .... EMK
Edward Mulhare's Foundation of Friends (EA) .... EMFF
Edward River [*Australia Airport symbol*] (OAG) .... EDR
Edward the Confessor (King of England) (DLA) .... Edw Conf
Edward Waters College [*Jacksonville, FL*] .... EWC
Edwardian Drama and Literature Circle (EA) .... EDLC
Edwards [*California*] [*Airport symbol Obsolete*] (OAG) .... EDW

Edwards' Abridgment of Prerogative Court Cases [*A publication*] (DLA) Edw Abr
Edwards' Abridgment of Prerogative Court Cases [*A publication*] (DLA) Edw Pr Ct Cas
Edwards' Abridgment, Privy Council [*A publication*] (DLA) Edw Abr
Edwards' Admiralty Jurisdiction [*1847*] [*A publication*] (DLA) Edw Adm Jur
Edwards Air Force Base [*California*] EAFB
Edwards Air Force Base [*California*] [*TACAN station*] (NASA) EDW
Edwards Air Force Base [*California*] [*ICAO location identifier*] (ICLI) KEDW
Edwards Air Force Base Library, Edwards AFB, CA [*OCLC symbol*] (OCLC) CEB
Edwards [*A. G.*] **& Sons, Inc.** [*NYSE symbol*] (SPSG) AGE
Edwards [*A. G.*] **& Sons, Inc.** [*Associated Press*] (SAG) Edwards
Edwards' Chester Palatine Courts [*England*] [*A publication*] (DLA) Edw
Edwards' English Admiralty Reports [*A publication*] (DLA) Edw
Edwards' English Admiralty Reports [*A publication*] (DLA) Edw Adm
Edwards' English Admiralty Reports [*A publication*] (DLA) Edw Adm (Eng)
Edwards' English Admiralty Reports [*A publication*] (DLA) Edw (Tho)
Edwards' English Prize Cases [*A publication*] (DLA) Edw PC
Edwards' English Prize Cases [*A publication*] (DLA) Edw Pr Cas
Edwards Flight Research Center [*NASA*] EFRC
Edwards Flight Test Center [*NASA*] EFTC
Edwards' Juryman's Guide [*A publication*] (DLA) Edw Jur
Edwards' Law of Gaming [*A publication*] (DLA) Edw Gam
Edwards' Leading Decisions in Admiralty [*Edwards' Admiralty Reports*] [*A publication*] (DLA) Edw Lead Dec
Edwards' New York Chancery Reports [*A publication*] (DLA) Ed Ch
Edwards' New York Chancery Reports [*A publication*] (DLA) Ed Ch R
Edwards' New York Chancery Reports [*A publication*] (DLA) Ed CR
Edwards' New York Chancery Reports [*A publication*] (DLA) Edw
Edwards' New York Chancery Reports [*A publication*] (DLA) Edw Ch
Edwards' New York Chancery Reports [*A publication*] (DLA) Edw Ch (NY)
Edwards' New York Chancery Reports [*A publication*] (DLA) Edw Chan
Edwards' New York Chancery Reports [*A publication*] (DLA) Edw (NY)
Edwards' New York Chancery Reports [*A publication*] (DLA) Edw Rep
Edwards' New York Chancery Reports [*A publication*] (DLA) Edwards' Chr R
Edwards' New York Chancery Reports [*A publication*] (DLA) Edwards' Rep
Edwards on Bills and Notes [*A publication*] (DLA) Edw Bills
Edwards on Bills and Notes [*A publication*] (DLA) Edw Bills & N
Edwards on Ecclesiastical Jurisdiction [*A publication*] (DLA) Edw Eccl Jur
Edwards on Factors and Brokers [*A publication*] (DLA) Edw Brok & F
Edwards on Factors and Brokers [*A publication*] (DLA) Edw Fac
Edwards on Parties in Chancery [*A publication*] (DLA) Edw Part
Edwards on Receivers in Equity [*A publication*] (DLA) Edw Rec
Edwards on the Law of Bailments [*A publication*] (DLA) Edw Bail
Edwards on the Law of Bailments [*A publication*] (DLA) Edw Bailm
Edwards on the Law of Referees [*A publication*] (DLA) Edw Ref
Edwards on the Stamp Act [*A publication*] (DLA) Edw St Act
Edwards Personal Preference Scale [*or Schedule*] [*Psychology*] EPPS
Edwards Personality Inventory [*Psychology*] EPI
Edwards' Pleasantries of the Courts of New York [*A publication*] (DLA) Edw Pleas
Edwards Public Library, Henrietta, TX [*Library symbol Library of Congress*] (LCLS) TxHe
Edwards Public Library, Henrietta, TX [*Library symbol*] [*Library of Congress*] (LCLS) TxHeE
Edwards' Reports [*2, 3 Missouri*] [*A publication*] (DLA) Edw
Edwards' Reports [*2, 3 Missouri*] [*A publication*] (DLA) Edw MO
Edwards Rocket Base (MUGU) ERB
Edwards Rocket Engine Test Station [*NASA*] (IAA) ERETS
Edwards Rocket Test Site (KSC) ERTS
Edwards Test Station [*NASA*] ETS
Edwardsburg Township Public Library, Spencerville, ON, Canada [*Library symbol*] [*Library of Congress*] (LCLS) CaOSE
Edwardsburg Township Public Library, Spencerville, Ontario [*Library symbol National Library of Canada*] (BIB) OSE
Edwardsville Community Unit, School District 7, Edwardsville, IL [*Library symbol Library of Congress*] (LCLS) IEdSD
Edwardsville Free Public Library, Edwardsville, IL [*Library symbol Library of Congress*] (LCLS) IEd
Edwardsville, IL [*AM radio station call letters*] WRYT
Edwardsville, IL [*FM radio station call letters*] WSIE
Edwardus Rex [*King Edward*] [*Latin*] ER
Edwardus Rex et Imperator [*Edward King and Emperor*] [*Latin*] ER et I
Edwin A. Bemis Public Library, Littleton, CO [*Library symbol Library of Congress*] (LCLS) CoLi
Edwin I. Hatch Nuclear Plant (NRCH) EHNP
EEC Advisory Council of the Asbestos International Association (EAIO) EAC-AIA
EEC [*European Economic Community*] **Ship Owners Association** [*Belgium*] (EAIO) ECSA
EEC Wheat Starch Manufacturers Association [*Defunct*] (EAIO) EWSA
EEG Aperiodic-Interval Spectrum Analysis [*Neurology*] EISA
Eek [*Alaska*] [*Airport symbol*] (OAG) EEK
Eelam National Democratic Liberation Front [*Sri Lanka*] [*Political party*] (EY) ENDLF
Eelam National Liberation Front [*Sri Lanka*] ENLF
Eelam People's Democratic Party [*Sri Lanka*] [*Political party*] (EY) EPDP
Eelam People's Revolutionary Liberation Front [*Sri Lanka*] [*Political party*] EPRLF
Eelam Revolutionary Organization [*Sri Lanka*] [*Political party*] EROS
Eelam Tamils Association of America (EA) ETAA
Eerie (ABBR) EER
Eerier (ABBR) EERR
Eeriest (ABBR) EERST
Eerily (ABBR) EERY
Eeriness (ABBR) EERNS
Eesti Lennukompani [*Estonia*] [*ICAO designator*] (FAAC) ELK
Eesti Rahvusliku Soltumatuse Partei [*Estonian National Independence Party*] [*Political party*] (EAIO) ERSP
Eestimaa Kommunistlik Partei EKP
Efamol Research Institute, Kentville, Nova Scotia [*Library symbol National Library of Canada*] (NLC) NSKER
Efamol Research Institute, Kentville, NS, Canada [*Library symbol*] [*Library of Congress*] (LCLS) CaNSKER
Efface (ABBR) EFC
Effaceable (ABBR) EFACB
Effaced (ABBR) EFACD
Effaced (ABBR) EFCD
Effacement (ABBR) EFACT
Effacement (ABBR) EFCNT
Effacement [*Obstetrics*] (DAVI) Eff
Effacer (ABBR) EFACR
Effacer (ABBR) EFCR
Effacing (ABBR) EFACG
Effacing (ABBR) EFCG
Effect (WDMC) E
Effect (ABBR) EFCT
Effect (AFM) EFF
Effect (MSA) EFT
Effect Corona (IAA) EFCOR
Effect of Gravity on Methane-Air Combustion EGOMAC
Effect on Guarantees EOG
Effect on System EOS
Effected (ABBR) EFCTD
Effected Radioactive Power ERP
Effectible (ABBR) EFCTB
Effecting (ABBR) EFCTG
Effecting (ABBR) EFTAG
Effecting Promotion, Procedure Outlined [*Military*] (DNAB) EFPROUT
Effective (ABBR) EF
Effective (ABBR) EFCTV
Effective [*Legal term*] (DLA) Eff
Effective (ABBR) EFFECT
Effective Acoustic Center EAC
Effective Address [*Computer science*] (MDG) EA
Effective Address Register [*Computer science*] (IAA) EAR
Effective Air Distance EAD
Effective Air Path EAP
Effective Alveolar Ventilation [*Medicine*] (DAVI) $V_{A}eff$
Effective Angular Velocity EAV
Effective Area EA
Effective Arterial Blood Volume EABV
Effective Atomic Charge EAC
Effective Atomic Number EAN
Effective Attenuation Coefficient (PDAA) EAC
Effective Bandwidth EBW
Effective Billing Date (TEL) EBD
Effective Buying Income [*Portion of gross income after subtracting taxes, food, clothing, and housing expenditures*] EBI
Effective Calls Meter [*Telecommunications*] (NITA) ECM
Effective Candlepower Second [*Photography*] (WDMC) ECPS
Effective Capillary Flow [*Medicine*] (MAE) ECF
Effective Carbon Number [*Chemistry*] ECN
Effective Cation and Exchange Capacity [*Soil science*] ECEC
Effective Cell Pair Area [*Electrochemistry*] ECPA
Effective Circulating Blood Volume [*Physiology*] ECBV
Effective Citizens Organization [*Later, PAC*] (EA) ECO
Effective Common Mode Rejection [*Electronics*] (IAA) ECMR
Effective Complex Modulus ECM
Effective Concentration [*Instrumentation*] EC
Effective Concentration at which Light Emission Is Reduced by 50% [*Instrumentation*] EC_{50}
Effective Concentration, Median Value $EC_{5}0$
Effective Concentration of Substance for 50% Survival of Organism ECSO
Effective Conductivity EC
Effective Control of Manpower (AFM) ECONOMAN
Effective Conversion Efficiency ECE
Effective Creep Compliance ECC
Effective Cutoff Diameter [*Particulate measurement*] ECD
Effective Cutoff Frequency ECF
Effective Damage Risk Level EDRL
Effective Date [*Military*] (AFIT) EDTE
Effective Date of Change (MCD) EDC
Effective Date of Change (AFM) EDOC
Effective Date of Change in Station Assignment [*Military*] EDSA
Effective Date of Change of Morning Report [*Military*] EDCMR
Effective Date of Change of Strength Accountability [*Military*] EDCSA
Effective Date of Federal Recognition [*Military*] EDFR
Effective Date of Release from Training EDRT
Effective Date of Supply EDOS
Effective Date of Training EDT
Effective Diagenetic Temperature [*Geology*] EDT
Effective Diameter [*TII*] (TAG) ED
Effective Diameter of Objective [*Optics*] EDO
Effective Direct Radiation EDR
Effective Directives and Plans (MUGU) EDP
Effective Dose ED
Effective Dose, Median ED_{50}
Effective Doubleword Address [*Computer science*] (IAA) EDA

Effective Drug Duration [*Medicine*] (MAE) .... EDD
Effective Dynamic Compliance (MEDA) .... EDC
Effective Elastic Modulus .... EEM
Effective Engineering Management .... EEM
Effective Equal Opportunity .... EEO
Effective Equivalent Chlorine [*Analytical chemistry*] .... EECL
Effective Exposure Method (KSC) .... EEM
Effective External Boundary [*Forestry*] .... EEB
Effective Filtration Area .... EFA
Effective Filtration Pressure [*Physiology*] .... EFP
Effective Filtration Rate [*Physiology*] .... EFR
Effective Focal Length [*Optics*] .... EFL
Effective Full Power Day (KSC) .... EFPD
Effective Full Power Month (NRCH) .... EFPM
Effective Full-Charge [*Weaponry*] (RDA) .... EFC
Effective Full-Power Years (NRCH) .... EFPY
Effective Government Committee (EA) .... EGC
Effective Halflife [*Nuclear science*] .... EHL
Effective Horsepower .... EHP
Effective Hydration Temperature [*Archeology, geology*] .... EHT
Effective Index Method (PDAA) .... EIM
Effective Initial Value .... EIV
Effective Inlet Valve Closing [*Automotive engineering*] .... EIC
Effective Instantaneous Field of View .... EIFOV
Effective Instantaneous [*or Isotropic*] Radiated Power
  [*Telecommunications*] .... EIRP
Effective Isotropic Radiated Power [*Telecommunications*] (WDMC) .... EIRP
Effective Kilogram (NRCH) .... EKG
Effective Management Responsibility .... EMR
Effective Management Systems [*Associated Press*] (SAG) .... EffMgt
Effective Management Systems [*NASDAQ symbol*] (SAG) .... EMSI
Effective Marginal Tax Rate .... EMTR
Effective Mass Approximation .... EMA
Effective Mechanical Advantage [*Bone-muscle physiology*] .... EMA
Effective Mgmt Sys Wrrt [*NASDAQ symbol*] (TTSB) .... EMSIW
Effective Mgmt Systems [*NASDAQ symbol*] (TTSB) .... EMSI
Effective Monopole-Radiated Power (TEL) .... EMRP
Effective National Action to Control Tobacco .... ENACT
Effective Networks, Inc. [*Telecommunications service*] (TSSD) .... ENI
Effective On or About [*Business term*] .... EOA
Effective Oxygen Transport (MAE) .... EOT
Effective Par [*Investment term*] .... EP
Effective Perceived Noise [*Aviation*] .... EPN
Effective Perceived Noise-Level Decibel [*Aviation*] (IIA) .... EPNLDB
Effective Privilege Level [*Computer science*] .... EPL
Effective Production .... EP
Effective Production Coefficient .... EPC
Effective Program Projections .... EPP
Effective Radiated Power [*Radio transmitting*] .... ERP
Effective Rate of Assistance [*International trade*] .... ERA
Effective Rate of Interest and Charges .... ERIC
Effective Rating Point (WDMC) .... ERP
Effective Reading in Content Areas (EDAC) .... ERICA
Effective Reference Time .... ERT
Effective Refractory Length [*Ophthalmology*] (DAVI) .... ERL
Effective Refractory Period .... ERP
Effective Relaxation Modulus .... ERM
Effective Renal Blood Flow [*Medicine*] .... ERBF
Effective Renal Plasma Flow [*Medicine*] .... ERPF
Effective Resistance (IDOE) .... R_{eff}
Effective Sample Base [*Advertising*] (DOAD) .... ESB
Effective School Battery [*Educational test*] .... ESB
Effective Search Radius (MCD) .... ESR
Effective Segment Number (IAA) .... ESN
Effective Sensory Projection [*Neurology*] (DAVI) .... ESP
Effective Series Resistance [*Electronics*] (IAA) .... ESR
Effective Shunt Resistance [*Electronics*] (IAA) .... ESR
Effective Signal Radiated .... ESR
Effective SONAR Range [*Navy*] (NVT) .... ESR
Effective Standard Deviation [*of chemical standardized solutions*] .... ESD
Effective Study Test [*Study skills test*] .... EST
Effective Sunrise .... ESR
Effective Sunset .... ESS
Effective Systolic Pressure [*Cardiology*] (DAVI) .... ESP
Effective T$_4$ Ratio [*Endocrinology*] .... ET$_4$R
Effective Tax Rate .... ETR
Effective Technical and Human Implementation of Computer Systems
  [*Implementation methodology*] (NITA) .... ETHICS
Effective Temperature .... ET
Effective Testing Loss [*Telecommunications*] (TEL) .... ETL
Effective Thermal Expansion Coefficient .... ETEC
Effective Thyroxine Ratio [*Medicine*] .... ETR
Effective Transfer Date [*Military*] (AFM) .... ETD
Effective True Airspeed (AFM) .... ETAS
Effective United States Control Fleet .... EUSC
Effective Visual Transmission (NATG) .... EVT
Effective Warmth (IAA) .... EW
Effective Wavelength .... EWL
Effective Word Address (IAA) .... EWA
Effectively (ABBR) .... EFCTVY
Effectively (ABBR) .... EFTVY
Effectiveness (CAAL) .... E
Effectiveness (ABBR) .... EFCTVNS
Effectiveness (ABBR) .... EFTVNS
Effectiveness and Maintainability (MCD) .... E & M

Effectiveness Evaluation System .... EES
Effectiveness Index (MCD) .... EI
Effectiveness of Navy Electronic Warfare Systems .... ENEWS
Effectiveness Ratio (MCD) .... ER
Effectiveness Report [*Military*] .... ER
Effectiveness Report - Performance Report [*Air Force*] (AFM) .... ER-PR
Effectiveness Simulation Model .... ESM
Effectiveness Training Associates .... ETA
Effectiveness Training for Women [*A course of study*] .... ETW
Effective-Perceived-Noise Decibel Level [*Aviation*] .... EPNdB
Effective-Perceived-Noise Level [*Aviation*] .... EPNL
Effectivity (ABBR) .... EFFECT
Effectivity (ABBR) .... EFTV
Effector [*Biology*] .... E
Effector (ABBR) .... EFCTR
Effector Cell Precursor [*Medicine*] (DMAA) .... ECP
Effector-Cell Protease Receptor [*Biochemistry*] .... EPR
Effects (WDMC) .... E
Effects [*Automotive advertising*] .... EFFCTS
Effects [*Filmmaking and television*] [*Also title of a movie about special
  effects*] .... F/X
Effects of Initial Entry Conditions (SAA) .... EOIEC
Effects of Nuclear Weapons [*AEC-DoD book*] .... ENW
Effects of Subsurface Explosions [*Project*] [*Army and DNA*] (RDA) .... ESSEX
Effects Test Area [*Army*] .... ETA
Effectual (ABBR) .... EFCTL
Effectual (ABBR) .... EFTL
Effectuality (ABBR) .... EFCTLT
Effectually (ABBR) .... EFCTLY
Effectualness (ABBR) .... EFCTLNS
Effectuate (ABBR) .... EFCTA
Effectuate (ABBR) .... EFTA
Effectuated (ABBR) .... EFCTAD
Effectuated (ABBR) .... EFTAD
Effectuating (ABBR) .... EFCTAG
Effectuating (ROG) .... EFFG
Effeminacy (ABBR) .... EFEMC
Effeminate (ABBR) .... EFEM
Effeminately (ABBR) .... EFEMAY
Effeminately (ABBR) .... EFEMY
Effeminateness (ABBR) .... EFEMNS
Efferent [*Anatomy*] .... EFF
Efferent (ABBR) .... EFFER
Efferent Branchial Vein [*Anatomy*] .... EBV
Efferent Cochlear Bundle (PDAA) .... ECB
Efferent Renal Sympathetic Nerve Activity [*Physiology*] .... ERSNA
Efferent Renal Vein [*Anatomy*] .... ERV
Efferent Vein from Nephridial Gland [*Anatomy*] .... ENVG
Efferent Vessel [*Anatomy*] .... EV
Effervesce (ABBR) .... EFERVS
Effervesce (ABBR) .... EFRVS
Effervesced (ABBR) .... EFERVSD
Effervesced (ABBR) .... EFRVSD
Effervescence (ABBR) .... EFERVSNC
Effervescence (ABBR) .... EFRVSNC
Effervescent (ABBR) .... EFERVST
Effervescent [*Pharmacy*] (ROG) .... EFF
Effervescent (ABBR) .... EFRVST
Effervescent Magnetic Peroxoborate .... EMPB
Effervescing (ABBR) .... EFERVSG
Effervescing (ABBR) .... EFRVSG
Effete (ABBR) .... EFFT
Efficacious (ABBR) .... EFICU
Efficacy (ABBR) .... EFIC
Efficiency [*or Efficient*] .... E
Efficiency .... EFF
Efficiency (AABC) .... EFFCY
Efficiency (ROG) .... EFFIC
Efficiency (ABBR) .... EFICNC
Efficiency (ABBR) .... EFICNY
Efficiency [*Physics*] (BARN) .... N
Efficiency Decoration [*Military British*] .... ED
Efficiency Full Load (IAA) .... EFFFL
Efficiency Medal .... EM
Efficiency Modulation .... EM
Efficiency of Conversion of Digested Material [*Physiology*] .... ECD
Efficiency of Conversion of Ingested Material [*Physiology*] .... ECI
Efficiency of Plating [*Microbiology*] .... EOP
Efficiency of Survival [*Genetics*] .... EOS
Efficiency Review [*DoD*] .... ER
Efficient (ABBR) .... EFICNT
Efficient Assembly System [*Honeywell, Inc.*] [*Assembler language*] .... EASY
Efficient Component Pricing [*Business term*] (ECON) .... ECP
Efficient Consumer Response [*Marketing incentive*] (ECON) .... ECR
Efficient Deck Hand (NATG) .... EDH
Efficient Growth [*Computer program*] (NASA) .... EFFGRO
Efficient Logic Reduction Analysis of Fault Trees (PDAA) .... ELRAFT
Efficient Market Hypothesis (ADA) .... EMH
Efficient Personal-Experimental [*Concept vehicle*] .... EP-X
Efficient Reliable High-Power Amplifier (MCD) .... ERHPA
Efficient Vulcanizing [*Rubber processing*] .... EV
Efficiently (ABBR) .... EFICNTY
Efficiently (ABBR) .... EFICY
Effie School, Effie, MN [*Library symbol*] [*Library of Congress*] (LCLS) .... MnEfS
Effigies (ROG) .... EFFIG

Effigy (ROG) ... EFF
Effigy (VRA) ... efg
Effigy (ABBR) ... EFGY
Effigy Mounds National Monument ... EFMO
Effingham, IL [*AM radio station call letters*] ... WCRA
Effingham, IL [*FM radio station call letters*] ... WCRC
Effingham, IL [*FM radio station call letters*] ... WXEF
Effloresce (ABBR) ... EFLOR
Effloresced (ABBR) ... EFLORD
Efflorescence (ABBR) ... EFLORNC
Efflorescent (ABBR) ... EFFL
Efflorescent (ABBR) ... EFLORT
Efflorescing (ABBR) ... EFLORG
Effluence (ABBR) ... EFLUNC
Effluent ... EFF
Effluent (MSA) ... EFL
Effluent (ABBR) ... EFLU
Effluent [*or Evolved*] **Gas Analysis** ... EGA
Effluent Gas Detection (BARN) ... EGD
Effluent Guidelines Division [*Environmental Protection Agency*] ... EGD
Effluent Inventory System [*Nuclear energy*] (NRCH) ... EIS
Effluent Management Information System [*Computer science*] (PDAA) ... EMIS
Effluent Standards and Water Quality Information Advisory Committee (DICI) ... ES & WQIAC
Effluent Thermal Effect (IAA) ... ETE
Effluent Treatment Cell (PDAA) ... ETC
Effluent Treatment Facility ... ETF
Effluent Treatment Plant (PDAA) ... ETP
Effluvia (ABBR) ... EFLUVA
Effluvial (ABBR) ... EFLUVL
Effluvium (ABBR) ... EFLUVM
Effort (CDAI) ... E
Effort (ABBR) ... EFRT
Effort Adjustment Factor ... EAF
Effort Adjustment Factor, Development [*Military*] ... EAFDEV
Effort Adjustment Factor, Maintenance [*Military*] ... EAFMAIN
Effort Net Return [*Motivation model*] [*Business term*] ... ENR
Effortless (ABBR) ... EFRTLS
Effortlessly (ABBR) ... EFRTLSY
Effortlessness (ABBR) ... EFRTLSNS
Effrontery (ABBR) ... EFRNT
Effulgence (ABBR) ... EFULGNC
Effulgent (ABBR) ... EFULG
Effundatur [*Let It Be Poured Out*] [*Pharmacy*] (ROG) ... EFFUNDAT
Effuse (ABBR) ... EFUS
Effused (ABBR) ... EFUSD
Effusing (ABBR) ... EFUSG
Effusion (ABBR) ... EFUSN
Effusive (ABBR) ... EFUSV
Effusively (ABBR) ... EFUSVY
Effusiveness (ABBR) ... EFUSVNS
EFI Electronics [*NASDAQ symbol*] (TTSB) ... EFIC
EFI Electronics Corp. [*NASDAQ symbol*] (SAG) ... EFIC
EFI Electronics Corp. [*Associated Press*] (SAG) ... EFIEI
Efik [*MARC language code Library of Congress*] (LCCP) ... efi
Efird's Reports [*45-56 South Carolina*] [*A publication*] (DLA) ... Efird
Efogi [*Papua New Guinea*] [*Airport symbol*] (OAG) ... EFG
Efs-Flugservice GmbH [*Germany ICAO designator*] (FAAC) ... FSD
EFTA [*European Free Trade Association*] **Brewing Industry Council** (EAIO) ... EBIC
EG & G Idaho, Inc., INEL Technical Library, Idaho Falls, ID [*Library symbol*] [*Library of Congress*] (LCLS) ... IdIfEG
EG & G, Inc. [*NYSE symbol*] (SPSG) ... EGG
Egalitarian ... EGAL
Egalitarian (ABBR) ... EGALTR
Egalitarianism (ABBR) ... EGALSM
Egalitarianism (ABBR) ... EGALTRM
Egan. Bills of Sale [*4th ed.*] [*1882*] [*A publication*] (DLA) ... Egan Bills
Egan on Extradition [*1846*] [*A publication*] (DLA) ... Eg Ext
EG&G Idaho, Inc. (GAAI) ... EG&G/ID
Eganville Public Library, Ontario [*Library symbol National Library of Canada*] (NLC) ... OEG
Egedesminde [*Greenland*] [*ICAO location identifier*] (ICLI) ... BGEM
Egegik [*Alaska*] [*Airport symbol*] (OAG) ... EGX
Egelsbach [*Germany ICAO location identifier*] (ICLI) ... EDFE
Eger's Yellow ... EY
EGF [*Epidermal Growth Factor*] **Receptor-Related Protein** [*Biochemistry*] ... ERRP
EGFR [*Epidermal Growth Factor Receptor*] **Related Inhibitor** [*Biochemistry*] ... ERI
Egg Albumin ... EA
Egg Diameter [*Pisciculture*] ... ED
Egg Drop Syndrome [*Medicine*] (DMAA) ... EDS
Egg Harbor City, NJ [*FM radio station call letters*] ... WRDR
Egg Harbor News, Egg Harbor City, NJ [*Library symbol Library of Congress*] (LCLS) ... NjEgN
Egg Harbor Township, NJ [*FM radio station call letters*] (RBYB) ... WXGN-FM
Egg Industry Licensing Committee [*Victoria, Australia*] ... EILC
Egg Length ... EL
Egg Lethal Dose ... ELD
Egg Marketing Board of Western Australia ... EMBWA
Egg Phosphatidylcholine [*Biochemistry*] ... EPC
Egg Research and Consumer Information Act [*1974*] ... ERCIA
Egg Stalk Length ... ESL
Egg White Lysozyme (OA) ... EWL
Egg White Serum [*Immunology*] ... EWS
Egg Width ... EW
Egg Yok-Pyruvate-Tellurite-Glycine Agar [*Microbiology*] (DAVI) ... EYA
Egg Yolk ... EY
Egg Yolk-Pyruvate-Tellurite-Glycine Agar [*Medicine*] (BABM) ... EYA
Eggebek [*Germany ICAO location identifier*] (ICLI) ... EDCG
Eggenfelden, Nieder Bayern [*Germany ICAO location identifier*] (ICLI) ... EDME
Eggerton [*England*] ... EGG
Egghead, Inc. [*Associated Press*] (SAG) ... Egghead
Egghead, Inc. [*NASDAQ symbol*] (NQ) ... EGGS
Egg-Infective Dose [*Clinical chemistry*] ... EID
Egg-Laying Hormone [*Endocrinology*] ... ELH
Egg-Laying Release Hormone [*Endocrinology*] ... ERH
Eggleston on Damages [*A publication*] (DLA) ... Egg Dam
Eggplant Mosaic Virus [*Plant pathology*] ... EMV
Eggplant Mottled Crinkle Virus [*Plant pathology*] ... EMCV
Eggplant Mottled Dwarf Virus [*Plant pathology*] ... EMDV
Egg-Release Pheromone [*Biology*] ... ERF
Eggs in Hatching [*Parcel Post*] ... EH
Eggs per Gram [*Parasitology*] ... EPG
Egidius Bellamera [*Deceased, 1407*] [*Authority cited in pre-1607 legal work*] (DSA) ... Egid Bellam
Egidius de Fuscarariis [*Deceased, 1289*] [*Authority cited in pre-1607 legal work*] (DSA) ... Eg
Egidius de Fuscarariis [*Deceased, 1289*] [*Authority cited in pre-1607 legal work*] (DSA) ... Egid
Egidius de Losano [*Authority cited in pre-1607 legal work*] (DSA) ... Egi
Egilsstadir [*Iceland*] [*ICAO location identifier*] (ICLI) ... BIEG
Egilsstadir [*Iceland*] [*Seismograph station code, US Geological Survey*] (SEIS) ... EGI
Egilsstadir [*Iceland*] [*Airport symbol*] (OAG) ... EGS
Egletons [*France ICAO location identifier*] (ICLI) ... LFDE
Eglin Air Force Base [*Florida*] ... EAFB
Eglin Air Force Base [*Florida*] (SAA) ... EGL
Eglin Air Force Base [*Florida*] [*Airport symbol*] (AD) ... VPS
Eglin Air Force Base, Eglin, FL [*OCLC symbol*] (OCLC) ... FEA
Eglin Field [*Florida*] [*Air Force*] (MCD) ... EF
Eglin Gulf Missile Test Range [*Florida*] [*Air Force*] ... EGMTR
Eglin Gulf Test Range [*Florida*] [*Air Force*] ... EGTR
Eglin RADAR Control Facility [*Florida*] [*Air Force*] (MCD) ... ERCF
Eglin Refugee Processing Center [*Florida*] [*Air Force*] (MCD) ... ERPC
Eglin Regional Hospital Library, Eglin AFB, FL [*OCLC symbol*] (OCLC) ... SCV
Eglin Test Facility [*Florida*] [*NASA*] (KSC) ... ETF
Egmont, BC [*FM radio station call letters*] ... CIEG
Ego Boost ... EGOBOO
Ego Control [*Psychology*] ... EC
Ego Overcontrol [*Psychology*] ... EO
Ego Resiliency [*Psychology*] ... ER
Ego Resources Ltd. [*Toronto Stock Exchange symbol*] ... EGO
Ego Strength [*Psychology*] ... Es
Ego Strength Q-Sort Test [*Psychology*] ... ESQST
Ego Stress [*Test*] [*Psychology*] (DAVI) ... ES
Ego Support Value [*Psychology*] ... ESV
Ego-Ideal and Conscience Development Test [*Personality development test*] [*Psychology*] ... EICDT
, Egon [*Keil*] [*Haydee Madsen In ballet title, "Initials RBME." Refers to the four starring dancers.*] ... RBME
Egremont on the Law of Highways [*A publication*] (DLA) ... Egr High
Egress (KSC) ... EGRS
Egress Maintenance Vehicle ... EMV
Egress Node (ACRL) ... EN
Egress Router (ACRL) ... ER
Eguinarius Baro [*Deceased, 1550*] [*Authority cited in pre-1607 legal work*] (DSA) ... Eguin Baro
Egypt [*IYRU nationality code*] (IYR) ... AR
Egypt [*ANSI two-letter standard code*] (CNC) ... EG
Egypt (ROG) ... EGP
Egypt ... EGT
Egypt [*ANSI three-letter standard code*] (CNC) ... EGY
Egypt (VRA) ... Egy
Egypt ... ET
Egypt [*International civil aircraft marking*] (ODBW) ... SU
Egypt Air [*ICAO designator*] (FAAC) ... MSR
Egypt Exploration Society (EA) ... EES
Egyptair [*ICAO designator*] (AD) ... MS
Egyptian ... E
Egyptian (ROG) ... EG
Egyptian [*MARC language code Library of Congress*] (LCCP) ... egy
Egyptian (ROG) ... EGY
Egyptian (ROG) ... EGYP
Egyptian (ROG) ... EGYPT
Egyptian Air Force ... EAF
Egyptian Air Force [*FAA designator*] (FAAC) ... EGY
Egyptian American Chamber of Commerce [*Defunct*] (EA) ... EACC
Egyptian Antiquities Organization (EA) ... EAO
Egyptian Army ... EA
Egyptian Aviation Co. [*ICAO designator*] (FAAC) ... EMA
[*The*] **Egyptian Book of the Dead** (BJA) ... BD
[*The*] **Egyptian Coffin Texts** [*A publication*] (BJA) ... ECT
Egyptian Communist Party [*Political party*] (PD) ... ECP
Egyptian Communist Workers' Party [*Political party*] (PD) ... ECWP
Egyptian Confederation of Labor ... ECL
[*The*] **Egyptian Era** [*Beginning 747BC*] (ROG) ... AEG
[*The*] **Egyptian Expedition. Metropolitan Museum of Art** [*New York*] [*A publication*] (BJA) ... EEMM
Egyptian Expeditionary Force [*Military British*] ... EEF
Egyptian Exploration Fund. Memoirs [*A publication*] (ROG) ... EEFM

Egyptian Federation of Labor - United Arab Republic [*Obsolete*] ... EFL-UAR
Egyptian General Petroleum Corp. ... EGPC
Egyptian Government Organization for Tourism and Hotels ... EGOTH
Egyptian International Bank (IMH) ... EIB
Egyptian International Line (DS) ... EIL
Egyptian Moslem Association [*Australia*] ... EMA
Egyptian Mysteries [*Freemasonry*] (ROG) ... EM
Egyptian National Scientific and Technical Information Network ... ENSTINET
Egyptian Order of Merit ... EOM
Egyptian Pattern [*British military*] (DMA) ... EP
Egyptian Railways (DCTA) ... ER
Egyptian Religious Texts and Representations [*New York*] [*A publication*] (BJA) ... ERT
Egyptian Research Account [*London*] [*A publication*] (BJA) ... ERA
Egyptian Society for Information Technology (NITA) ... ESIT
Egyptian State Railway (ROG) ... ESR
Egyptology ... EGY
Egyptology (ROG) ... EGYPTOL
Egyseg Partja [*Party of Unity*] [*Hungary*] (PPE) ... EP
E.H. Darby Aviation [*FAA designator*] (FAAC) ... EHD
Eha-Kibbuts ha-Artsi (BJA) ... KA
Ehegesetz [*Marriage Law*] [*German*] (ILCA) ... EheG
Ehlers-Danlos National Foundation (EA) ... EDNF
Ehlers-Danlos Syndrome [*Medicine*] (MAE) ... ED
Ehlers-Danlos Syndrome [*Medicine*] ... EDS
Ehrenfest Adiabatic Law [*Physics*] ... EAL
Ehrenreich Photo-Optical Industries, Inc. ... EPI
Ehrenreich Photo-Optical Industries, Inc. ... EPOI
Ehrlich Ascites Carcinoma [*Cells*] [*Oncology*] ... EAC
Ehrlich Ascites Tumor [*Oncology*] ... EAT
Ehrlich Ascites Tumor Cell [*Oncology*] ... EATC
Ehrlich Unit [*Laboratory*] (DAVI) ... EU
Ehrlich Units [*Clinical chemistry*] ... EU
Ehrlich-Lettre Hyperdiploid [*Mouse ascites tumor*] ... ELD
El Air Exports Ltd. [*Ireland*] [*ICAO designator*] (FAAC) ... EIX
El Paso Electric [*AMEX symbol*] (TTSB) ... EE
Eicosanoyl(trifluoroacetyl)kanamycin [*Antiviral*] ... ETK
Eicosapentaenoic Acid [*Biochemistry*] ... EPA
Eicosatetraynoic Acid [*Organic chemistry*] ... ETYA
Eider Resources Minieres, Inc. [*Toronto Stock Exchange symbol*] ... EID
Eidgenoessische Technische Hochschule, Zurich, Switzerland [*Library symbol Library of Congress*] (LCLS) ... SzZE
Eiffe on the Irish Judicature Act [*A publication*] (DLA) ... Eif Jud Act
Eigenmode Expansion Method (PDAA) ... EEM
Eigenvalue [*Mathematics*] ... EV
Eigenvalue Change Analysis ... ECA
Eight Card Redrawing Test [*Psychology*] ... 8CRT
Eight Fathom Bight [*Alaska*] [*Airport symbol*] (OAG) ... EFB
Eight Sheet Outdoor Advertising Association [*Independence, MO*] (EA) ... ESOAA
Eight to Fourteen Modulation (IAA) ... EFM
Eighteen "Great" Choral Preludes [*Bach*] ... E
Eighteen Thirty Eight Bond Fund [*Associated Press*] (SAG) ... 1838BdF
Eighteen Thirty Eight Bond Fund [*NYSE symbol*] (SAG) ... BDF
Eighteen-Nation Disarmament Committee [*or Conference*] [*Later, CCD Convened March 14, 1962; actually attended by 17 nations, with France absent*] ... ENDC
Eighteenth Century Scottish Studies Society (EA) ... ECSSS
Eighteenth Century Short Title Catalogue [*British Library*] [*Bibliographic database London, England*] ... ESTC
Eighteenth-Century Studies [*A publication*] (BRI) ... Eight-C St
Eightfold (ABBR) ... EGHTFD
Eighth Air Force Historical Society (EA) ... EAFHS
Eighth Armored Division Association (EA) ... EADA
Eighth Army (MCD) ... EA
Eighth Coast Guard District [*New Orleans, LA*] [*USCG*] (TAG) ... D8
Eighth Lively Art [*Advertising award*] ... ELA
Eighth United States Army ... EUSA
Eighth United States Army (CINC) ... USAEIGHT
Eighth United States Army in Korea ... EUSAK
Eighth United States Army Rear ... EUSAR
Eightieth (ABBR) ... EGHTH
Eight-Parallel-Form Anxiety Battery [*Psychology*] ... 8PFAB
EightXEight, Inc. [*Associated Press*] (SAG) ... 8X8
EightXEight, Inc. [*NASDAQ symbol*] (SAG) ... EGHT
Eil [*Somalia*] [*ICAO location identifier*] (ICLI) ... HCME
Eilat [*Israel*] [*Seismograph station code, US Geological Survey*] (SEIS) ... EIL
Eilat [*Israel*] [*Airport symbol*] (AD) ... EIT
Eiloart's Laws Relating to Women [*1878*] [*A publication*] (DLA) ... Eil Wom
Eimac, Division of Varian Associates, Technical Library, San Carlos, CA [*Library symbol*] [*Library of Congress*] (LCLS) ... CScE
Eimac [*Division of Varian Associates*] **Technical Library, San Carlos, CA** [*Library symbol Library of Congress*] (LCLS) ... JScE
Ein Grosser Komponist [*A Great Composer*] **or Ein Genialer Komponist** [*A Great Genius of a Composer*] [*Suggested interpretations for the adopted surname of German composer Werner Egk. Egk maintained that he chose the name in honor of his wife*] ... EGK
EIN [*Employer Identification Number*] **Research and Assignment System** [*IRS*] ... ERAS
Ein Yahav [*Israel*] [*Airport symbol Obsolete*] (OAG) ... EIY
Eindhoven [*Netherlands ICAO location identifier*] (ICLI) ... EHEH
Eindhoven [*Netherlands*] [*Airport symbol*] (OAG) ... EIN
Eineiige Zwillinge [*Monozygotic Twins*] [*Psychology*] ... EZ
Einfache Lafette [*Single-barreled mount*] [*German military - World War II*] ... EL
Eingang Vorbehalten [*Rights reserved, i.e., copyrighted*] [*German*] ... EV
Eingetragene Gesellschaft mit Beschraenkter Haftung [*Registered Company with Limited Liability*] [*German*] (ILCA) ... eGmbH
Eingetragenes Warenzeichen [*Registered Trademark*] [*German*] ... EW
Einheitliche Systematik [*Library science*] ... ES
Einkommensteuergesetz [*Income Tax Law*] [*German*] (DLA) ... EStG
Einleitung in die Assyrischen Koenigsinschriften [*A publication*] (BJA) ... EAK
Einschluss-Korper [*Inclusion body*] [*Medicine*] ... EK
Einsehower Middle School, Rockford, IL [*Library symbol*] [*Library of Congress*] (LCLS) ... IRoEM
Einspritz [*Fuel-injection*] [*As in 280 E, the model number of a Mercedes-Benz automobile*] ... E
Einspruch [*Objection, Opposition, Caveat*] [*German*] (ILCA) ... Einspr
Einstein Equivalence Principle [*Gravity*] ... EEP
Einstein Extended Medium Sensitive Survey [*Cosmology*] ... EMSS
Einstein Noah Bagel Corp. [*Associated Press*] (SAG) ... EinstnN
Einstein Noah Bagel Corp. [*NASDAQ symbol*] (SAG) ... ENBX
Einstein Stoke Radius [*Medicine*] (DMAA) ... ESR
Einstein Viscosity Equation ... EVE
Einsteinium [*Also see Es*] [*Chemical element*] ... E
Einsteinium [*Preferred form, but also see E*] [*Chemical element*] ... Es
Einsteinium (IDOE) ... E_s
Einstein-Podolsky-Rosen [*Quantum mechanics*] ... EPR
Einzelkommentar [*A publication*] (BJA) ... EK
Einzelsphaltrohrversuchsanlage [*Hydrogen generating reactor*] ... EVA
EIP Microwave [*NASDAQ symbol*] (TTSB) ... EIPM
EIP Microwave, Inc. [*Associated Press*] (SAG) ... EIP
EIP Microwave, Inc. [*NASDAQ symbol*] (NQ) ... EIPM
Eire Army Corps ... EAC
Eire Philatelic Association (EA) ... EPA
Eirunepe [*Brazil ICAO location identifier*] (ICLI) ... SBER
EIS International [*Associated Press*] (SAG) ... EIS Intl
EIS International [*NASDAQ symbol*] (TTSB) ... EISI
Eisai Co. Ltd. [*Japan*] [*Research code symbol*] ... PP
EISCAT [*European Incoherent Scatter Scientific Association*] **Svalbard Radar** ... ESR
Eisenbahnkesselwagen [*Railway tank car*] [*German military - World War II*] ... EKW
Eisenbahn-Verkehrsordnung [*Germany*] ... EVO
Eisenhower Exchange Fellowships (EA) ... EEF
Eisenhower Foundation for the Prevention of Violence [*Later, Milton S. Eisenhower Federation*] (EA) ... EFPV
Eisenhower Institute (EA) ... EI
Eisenhower Institute for Historical Research [*Smithsonian Institution*] ... EIHR
Eisenhower Public Library District, Harwood Heights, IL [*Library symbol Library of Congress*] (LCLS) ... IHh
Eisenhower World Affairs Institute [*Later, EI*] (EA) ... EWAI
Either (ROG) ... EIR
EJA/Newport [*ICAO designator*] (AD) ... NF
Eject (KSC) ... EJ
Eject ... EJCT
Eject Rocket Container ... ERC
Ejection ... EJN
Ejection Click [*Cardiology*] ... EC
Ejection Escape Suit (NASA) ... EES
Ejection Factor [*Cardiology*] (DAVI) ... EF
Ejection Fraction [*Cardiology*] ... EF
Ejection Launch Test Vehicle (NG) ... ELTV
Ejection Murmur [*Cardiology*] ... EM
Ejection Rate [*Medicine*] ... ER
Ejection Seat (MSA) ... EJN ST
Ejection Sound [*Cardiology*] ... ES
Ejection Systolic Murmur [*Cardiology*] ... ESM
Ejection Test Vehicle (NG) ... ETV
Ejection Time ... ET
Ejector ... EJCTR
Ejector Release Unit (MCD) ... ERU
Ejector Thrust Augmentation [*Air Force*] ... ETA
Ejector Unit (MCD) ... EU
Ejector-Launcher, Guided Missile, Transporter ... EGLMT
Ejercito de Liberacion Nacional [*National Liberation Army*] [*Colorado*] (PD) ... ELN
Ejercito de Liberacion Nacional [*National Liberation Army*] [*Bolivia*] (PD) ... ELN
Ejercito de Liberacion Nacional [*National Liberation Army*] [*Peru*] (PD) ... ELN
Ejercito del Pueblo Costarricense [*Costa Rica*] [*Political party*] (EY) ... EPC
Ejercito Guerrillero de los Pobres [*Guerrilla Army of the Poor*] [*Guatemala*] ... EGP
Ejercito Nacional de Liberacion [*National Liberation Army*] [*Nicaragua*] (PD) ... ENL
Ejercito Popular Boricua [*Puerto Rican Popular Army*] (PD) ... EPB
Ejercito Popular Catalan [*Catalan Popular Army*] [*Spain*] (PD) ... EPC
Ejercito Popular de Liberacion [*Popular Liberation Army*] [*El Salvador*] (PD) ... EPL
Ejercito Revolucionario del Pueblo [*People's Revolutionary Army*] [*Argentina*] (PD) ... ERP
Ejercito Revolucionario del Pueblo [*People's Revolutionary Army*] [*El Salvador*] (PD) ... ERP
Ejercito Rojo Catalan de Liberacion [*Spain Political party*] (EY) ... ERCA
Ejercito Salvadoreno Anticomunista [*Salvadoran Anti-Communist Army*] (PD) ... ESA
Ejercito Segredo Anti-Comunista [*Secret Anti-Communist Army*] [*Guatemala*] (PD) ... ESA
EJS/ECP Automated Status Information and Exception System (MCD) ... EASIE
Ejus [*Of Him, or Of Her*] [*Latin*] ... EJ
Ejusdem [*Of the Same*] [*Latin*] ... EJUSD
Ejusdem Generis [*Of the Same Kind*] [*Latin*] ... EG
Ek Chor China Motorcycle [*Associated Press*] (SAG) ... EK Chor

Ek Chor Ching Motorcycle [*NYSE symbol*] (SPSG) .... EKC
Ekah Rabbah (BJA) .... EkahR
Ekalaka Public Library, Ekalaka, MT [*Library symbol*] [*Library of Congress*] (LCLS) .... MtE
Ekaton Industries, Inc. [*Toronto Stock Exchange symbol*] .... EKI
Ekco Group [*Associated Press*] (SAG) .... EKCO
Ekco Group [*NYSE symbol*] (SPSG) .... EKO
Ekereku [*Guyana*] [*Airport symbol*] (OAG) .... EKE
Ekimcham [*Former USSR ICAO location identifier*] (ICLI) .... UHBP
Eko [*Record label*] [*France*] .... Eko
Ekofisk [*Norway ICAO location identifier*] (ICLI) .... ENEK
Ekranolytny Spassatyelny Kater Amphibiya [*Screen-Effect Amphibious Lifeboat*] [*Former USSR*] .... ESKA
Eksharad [*Sweden ICAO location identifier*] (ICLI) .... ESKH
Eksportfinans Capital Securities [*NYSE symbol*] (SAG) .... EKP
Eksportfinans Capital Securities [*Associated Press*] (SAG) .... Eksprt
Ektachrome (VRA) .... EKT
Ekuk [*Alaska*] [*Airport symbol*] (OAG) .... KKU
Ekwal Reading Inventory (EDAC) .... ERI
Ekwok [*Alaska*] [*Airport symbol*] (OAG) .... KEK
El Aaiun [*Morocco*] [*Airport symbol*] (AD) .... EUN
El Aaiun [*Western Sahara*] [*ICAO location identifier*] (ICLI) .... GSAI
El Adem [*Libya*] [*Airport symbol*] (AD) .... ELE
El Al Israel Airlines [*ICAO designator*] (AD) .... LY
El Al-Israel Airlines Ltd. [*ICAO designator*] (FAAC) .... ELY
El Arish [*Egypt*] [*Airport symbol*] (AD) .... EAH
El Arish/El Arish [*Egypt*] [*ICAO location identifier*] (ICLI) .... HEAR
El Bagre [*Colombia*] [*Airport symbol*] (OAG) .... EBG
El Banco [*Colombia*] [*Airport symbol*] (OAG) .... ELB
El Banco/Los Flores [*Colorado ICAO location identifier*] (ICLI) .... SKBC
El Batan [*Ecuador*] [*ICAO location identifier*] (ICLI) .... SEBT
El Bato [*Bolivia*] [*ICAO location identifier*] (ICLI) .... SLYB
El Beida/Labraq [*Libya*] [*ICAO location identifier*] (ICLI) .... HLLQ
El Bireh Palestine Society of the USA (EA) .... EBPSUSA
El Bolson [*Argentina*] [*Airport symbol*] (OAG) .... EHL
El Bolson [*Argentina ICAO location identifier*] (ICLI) .... SAVB
El Borma [*Tunisia*] [*ICAO location identifier*] (ICLI) .... DTTR
El Bur [*Somalia*] [*ICAO location identifier*] (ICLI) .... HCML
El Cairo [*Bolivia*] [*ICAO location identifier*] (ICLI) .... SLEC
El Cajon [*California*] [*Airport symbol Obsolete*] (OAG) .... CJN
El Cajon [*California*] [*Seismograph station code, US Geological Survey Closed*] (SEIS) .... ECA
El Cajon, CA [*AM radio station call letters*] .... KECR
El Cajon, CA [*FM radio station call letters*] (RBYB) .... KHTS
El Camino College [*Torrance, CA*] .... ECC
El Camino College, Torrance, CA [*Library symbol Library of Congress*] (LCLS) .... CEcaE
El Camino Resources, Inc. [*Vancouver Stock Exchange symbol*] .... ECA
El Campo, TX [*Location identifier FAA*] (FAAL) .... ECE
El Campo, TX [*FM radio station call letters*] .... KIOX
El Campo, TX [*AM radio station call letters*] .... KULP
El Cap Gold Mines [*Vancouver Stock Exchange symbol*] .... ELG
El Caribe [*Cuba ICAO location identifier*] (ICLI) .... MUBE
El Carmen [*Costa Rica*] [*ICAO location identifier*] (ICLI) .... MREC
El Centro [*California*] [*Seismograph station code, US Geological Survey Closed*] (SEIS) .... ECC
El Centro [*Colombia*] [*Seismograph station code, US Geological Survey*] (SEIS) .... ETC
El Centro, CA [*AM radio station call letters*] .... KAMP
El Centro, CA [*Television station call letters*] (RBYB) .... KECY
El Centro, CA [*Television station call letters*] .... KLXO
El Centro, CA [*TV station call letters*] (RBYB) .... KVYE-TV
El Centro, CA [*AM radio station call letters*] .... KXO
El Centro, CA [*FM radio station call letters*] .... KXO-FM
El Centro, CA [*Location identifier FAA*] (FAAL) .... NJK
El Centro College, Dallas, TX [*Library symbol Library of Congress*] (LCLS) .... TxDaE
El Centro Free Public Library, El Centro, CA [*Library symbol Library of Congress*] (LCLS) .... CEc
El Centro/Imperial [*California*] [*Airport symbol*] (OAG) .... IPL
El Centro Naval Air Station [*California*] [*ICAO location identifier*] (ICLI) .... KNJK
El Cerrito, CA [*FM radio station call letters*] .... KECG
El Chico Restaurants [*NASDAQ symbol*] (TTSB) .... ELCH
El Chico Restaurants, Inc. [*NASDAQ symbol*] (SPSG) .... ELCH
El Chico Restaurants, Inc. [*Associated Press*] (SAG) .... ElChico
El Coco Explorations Ltd. [*Vancouver Stock Exchange symbol*] .... ELC
El Condor Resources [*Vancouver Stock Exchange symbol*] .... ECN
El Condor Resources Ltd. [*NASDAQ symbol*] (SAG) .... ECNC
El Condor Resources Ltd. [*Associated Press*] (SAG) .... ElCondor
El Debba [*Sudan*] [*Airport symbol Obsolete*] (OAG) .... EDB
El Desengano [*Bolivia*] [*ICAO location identifier*] (ICLI) .... SLDN
El Dorado [*Arkansas*] [*Airport symbol*] (OAG) .... ELD
El Dorado [*Venezuela*] [*Airport symbol*] (AD) .... EOR
El Dorado [*Argentina ICAO location identifier*] (ICLI) .... SATD
El Dorado [*Bolivia*] [*ICAO location identifier*] (ICLI) .... SLED
El Dorado & Wesson Railway Co. [*AAR code*] .... EDW
El Dorado, AR [*FM radio station call letters*] (RBYB) .... KAGL
El Dorado, AR [*FM radio station call letters*] .... KBSA
El Dorado, AR [*FM radio station call letters*] .... KBYB
El Dorado, AR [*AM radio station call letters*] .... KDMS
El Dorado, AR [*AM radio station call letters*] .... KELD
El Dorado, AR [*FM radio station call letters*] .... KIXB
El Dorado, AR [*FM radio station call letters*] .... KLBQ
El Dorado, AR [*Television station call letters*] .... KTVE
El Dorado, Bolivar [*Venezuela ICAO location identifier*] (ICLI) .... SVED
El Dorado County Free Library, Placerville, CA [*Library symbol Library of Congress*] (LCLS) .... CPla
El Dorado County Historical Museum, Placerville, CA [*Library symbol*] [*Library of Congress*] (LCLS) .... CPlaHi
El Dorado/Goodwin Field [*Arkansas*] [*ICAO location identifier*] (ICLI) .... KELD
El Dorado, KS [*Location identifier FAA*] (FAAL) .... EQA
El Dorado, KS [*AM radio station call letters*] .... KSRX
El Dorado, KS [*FM radio station call letters*] .... KTLI
El Dorado Springs, MO [*AM radio station call letters*] .... KESM
El Dorado Springs, MO [*FM radio station call letters*] .... KESM-FM
El Dorado Systems Canada [*Vancouver Stock Exchange symbol*] .... EDS
El Fasher [*Sudan*] [*Airport symbol*] (OAG) .... ELF
El Fasher [*Sudan*] [*ICAO location identifier*] (ICLI) .... HSFS
E-L Financial Corp. Ltd. [*Toronto Stock Exchange symbol*] .... ELF
El Geneina [*Sudan*] [*Airport symbol*] (OAG) .... EGN
El Golea [*Algeria*] [*ICAO location identifier*] (ICLI) .... DAUE
El Golea [*Algeria*] [*Airport symbol*] (AD) .... ELG
El Golfo De Santa Clara [*Mexico*] [*Seismograph station code, US Geological Survey*] (SEIS) .... EGM
El Hato [*Venezuela*] [*Seismograph station code, US Geological Survey*] (SEIS) .... EHV
El Indio, TX [*Location identifier FAA*] (FAAL) .... TOV
El Jadida [*Morocco*] [*ICAO location identifier*] (ICLI) .... GMMJ
El Jordan [*Bolivia*] [*ICAO location identifier*] (ICLI) .... SLJD
El Jovi [*Bolivia*] [*ICAO location identifier*] (ICLI) .... SLEJ
El Maiten [*Argentina*] [*Airport symbol*] (OAG) .... EMX
El Maiten [*Argentina ICAO location identifier*] (ICLI) .... SAVD
El Monte, CA [*Location identifier FAA*] (FAAL) .... EMT
El Morro National Monument .... ELMO
El Mundo Publishing Co., San Juan, PR [*Library symbol Library of Congress*] (LCLS) .... PrSE
El Nakab/El Nakab [*Egypt*] [*ICAO location identifier*] (ICLI) .... HEKB
El Nino and Southern Oscillation [*Coupled oceanic-atmospheric change*] .... ENSO
EL Nino-Southern Moniotoring Center [*Marine science*] (OSRA) .... ENMOC
El Nino-Southern Oscillation [*Experiment*] .... ELSO
El Obeid [*Sudan*] [*Airport symbol*] (OAG) .... EBD
El Obeid [*Sudan*] [*ICAO location identifier*] (ICLI) .... HSOB
El Oued [*Algeria*] [*Airport symbol*] (OAG) .... ELU
El Oued/Guemar [*Algeria*] [*ICAO location identifier*] (ICLI) .... DAUO
El Palomar [*Argentina ICAO location identifier*] (ICLI) .... SADP
El Pangue [*Chile*] [*Seismograph station code, US Geological Survey*] (SEIS) .... ELP
El Paraiso [*Bolivia*] [*ICAO location identifier*] (ICLI) .... SLEO
El Paraiso Resources Ltd. [*Vancouver Stock Exchange symbol*] .... EPR
El Paso [*Texas*] [*Airport symbol*] (OAG) .... ELP
El Paso [*Texas*] [*Seismograph station code, US Geological Survey*] (SEIS) .... EPT
El Paso/Biggs Air Force Base [*Texas*] [*ICAO location identifier*] (ICLI) .... KBIF
El Paso Community College, Colorado Springs, CO [*Library symbol Library of Congress*] (LCLS) .... CoCE
El Paso Community College, El Paso, TX [*OCLC symbol*] (OCLC) .... TXE
El Paso Community College, El Paso, TX [*Library symbol Library of Congress*] (LCLS) .... TxEC
El Paso Electric Co. [*AMEX symbol*] (SAG) .... EE
El Paso Electric Co. [*NASDAQ symbol*] (NQ) .... ELPA
El Paso Electric Co. [*Associated Press*] (SAG) .... ElPasoE
El Paso Energy Corp. [*Vancouver Stock Exchange symbol*] .... ELE
El Paso [*Texas*] **Intelligence Center** [*Drug Enforcement Administration; Border Patrol; US Customs Service; Bureau of Alcohol, Tobacco, and Firearms; FAA; US Coast Guard*] .... EPIC
El Paso/International [*Texas*] [*ICAO location identifier*] (ICLI) .... KELP
El Paso Natural Gas [*NYSE symbol*] (TTSB) .... EPG
El Paso Natural Gas Co. [*Associated Press*] (SAG) .... ElPasNG
El Paso Natural Gas Co. [*NYSE symbol*] (SPSG) .... EPG
El Paso Natural Gas Co., Technical Information Center, El Paso, TX [*Library symbol Library of Congress*] (LCLS) .... TxENG
El Paso Products Co., Odessa, TX [*Library symbol Library of Congress*] (LCLS) .... TxOEP
El Paso Public Library, El Paso, TX [*Library symbol Library of Congress*] (LCLS) .... TxE
El Paso Public Library, El Paso, TX [*OCLC symbol*] (OCLC) .... TXP
El Paso Southern Railway Co. [*AAR code*] .... EPS
El Paso Tennessee Pipeline [*Associated Press*] (SAG) .... ElPasT
El Paso Tennessee Pipeline [*NYSE symbol*] (SAG) .... EPG
El Paso Trial Lawyers Review [*A publication*] (DLA) .... El Paso Trial Law Rev
El Paso, TX [*Location identifier FAA*] (FAAL) .... BIF
El Paso, TX [*Location identifier FAA*] (FAAL) .... ELP
El Paso, TX [*AM radio station call letters*] .... KAMA
El Paso, TX [*AM radio station call letters*] .... KBNA
El Paso, TX [*FM radio station call letters*] .... KBNA-FM
El Paso, TX [*Television station call letters*] .... KCOS
El Paso, TX [*Television station call letters*] .... KDBC
El Paso, TX [*AM radio station call letters*] .... KELP
El Paso, TX [*AM radio station call letters*] .... KFNA
El Paso, TX [*Television station call letters*] .... KFOX-TV
El Paso, TX [*AM radio station call letters*] .... KHEY
El Paso, TX [*FM radio station call letters*] .... KHEY-FM
El Paso, TX [*Television station call letters*] .... KINT
El Paso, TX [*FM radio station call letters*] .... KINT-FM
El Paso, TX [*Television station call letters*] .... KJLF
El Paso, TX [*FM radio station call letters*] .... KLAQ
El Paso, TX [*FM radio station call letters*] .... KOFX
El Paso, TX [*FM radio station call letters*] .... KPRR
El Paso, TX [*AM radio station call letters*] .... KROD
El Paso, TX [*Television station call letters*] .... KSCE
El Paso, TX [*FM radio station call letters*] .... KSET
El Paso, TX [*FM radio station call letters*] (RBYB) .... KSII

El Paso, TX [*AM radio station call letters*] ... KSVE
El Paso, TX [*FM radio station call letters*] ... KTEP
El Paso, TX [*AM radio station call letters*] ... KTSM
El Paso, TX [*FM radio station call letters*] ... KTSM-FM
El Paso, TX [*Television station call letters*] ... KTSM-TV
El Paso, TX [*FM radio station call letters*] ... KVER
El Paso, TX [*Television station call letters*] ... KVIA
El Paso, TX [*AM radio station call letters*] ... KVIV
El Paso, TX [*FM radio station call letters*] ... KXCR
El Peru [*Bolivia*] [*ICAO location identifier*] (ICLI) ... SLEP
El Pinto [*Mexico*] [*Seismograph station code, US Geological Survey*] (SEIS) ... IIP
El Porvenir [*Panama*] [*ICAO location identifier*] (ICLI) ... MPVR
El Qahira [*Cairo*] [*Egyptian Arabic*] (AD) ... Qahira
El Quisco [*Chile*] [*Seismograph station code, US Geological Survey Closed*] (SEIS) ... ELQ
El Real [*Panama*] [*Airport symbol*] (OAG) ... ELE
El Recreo [*Colombia*] [*Airport symbol*] (OAG) ... ELJ
El Remate [*Bolivia*] [*ICAO location identifier*] (ICLI) ... SLRE
El Reno College [*Oklahoma*] ... ERC
El Reno Junior College Learning Resource Center, El Reno, OK [*Library symbol*] [*Library of Congress*] (LCLS) ... OkErC
El Reno, OK [*AM radio station call letters*] ... KZUE
El Rio, CA [*FM radio station call letters*] (RBYB) ... KMLA-FM
El Ron Ron [*Costa Rica*] [*ICAO location identifier*] (ICLI) ... MRER
El Roseda [*Bolivia*] [*ICAO location identifier*] (ICLI) ... SLEL
El Sal Air [*El Salvador*] [*ICAO designator*] (FAAC) ... ELS
El Salvador (VRA) ... E Sal
El Salvador ... El Salv
El Salvador [*MARC country of publication code Library of Congress*] (LCCP) ... es
El Salvador [*Chile*] [*Seismograph station code, US Geological Survey Closed*] (SEIS) ... ESC
El Salvador [*Chile*] [*Airport symbol*] (OAG) ... ESR
El Salvador [*MARC geographic area code Library of Congress*] (LCCP) ... nces--
El Salvador [*Bolivia*] [*ICAO location identifier*] (ICLI) ... SLEV
El Salvador [*ANSI three-letter standard code*] (CNC) ... SLV
El Salvador [*ANSI two-letter standard code*] (CNC) ... SV
El Salvador and Guatemala Committees for Human Rights [*British*] (EAIO) ... CACHR
El Salvador Committee for Human Rights (EAIO) ... ESCHR
El Salvador Film and Video Projects [*Later, El Salvadore Media Projects*] (EA) ... EFVP
El Salvador Media Projects (EA) ... ESMP
EL Salvador Solidarity Campaign [*British*] ... ELSSOC
El Segundo Public Library, El Segundo, CA [*Library symbol Library of Congress*] (LCLS) ... CEs
El Senoussi Multiphasic Marital Inventory [*Psychology*] ... SMMI
El Tocuyo [*Venezuela*] [*Seismograph station code, US Geological Survey*] (SEIS) ... TOV
El Toro Marine Corps Air Station [*California*] [*ICAO location identifier*] (ICLI) ... KNZJ
El Triunfo [*Bolivia*] [*ICAO location identifier*] (ICLI) ... SLEF
El Yopal [*Colombia*] [*Airport symbol*] (OAG) ... EYP
El Yunque [*Puerto Rico*] [*Seismograph station code, US Geological Survey Closed*] (SEIS) ... EYP
Ela Area Public Library District, Lake Zurich, IL [*OCLC symbol*] (OCLC) ... IHY
Ela Area Public Library, Lake Zurich, IL [*Library symbol Library of Congress*] (LCLS) ... ILz
Elaborate [*Used in correcting manuscripts, etc.*] ... E
Elaborately-Transformed Manufacture ... ETM
Elaine Music Shop [*Record label*] ... EMS
El-Amarna (BJA) ... EA
Elamex SA de CV [*Associated Press*] (SAG) ... Elamex
Elamex SA de CV [*NASDAQ symbol*] (SAG) ... ELAMP
Elamex S.A.de C.V. Cl I [*NASDAQ symbol*] (TTSB) ... ELAMF
Elamite (BJA) ... El
Elamite [*MARC language code Library of Congress*] (LCCP) ... elx
Elan Corp. [*Associated Press*] (SAG) ... Elan
Elan Corp. [*NYSE symbol*] (SAG) ... ELN
Elan Corp. ADS [*NYSE symbol*] (TTSB) ... ELN
Elan Corp. ADS Wrrt'98 [*NYSE symbol*] (TTSB) ... ELN.WS A
Elan Corp. PLC (MHDW) ... ELANY
Elan Industries, Inc. [*Vancouver Stock Exchange symbol*] ... ENI
Elan Populaire pour l'Unite Nationale [*Popular Impulse for National Unity*] [*Malagascar*] [*Political party*] (PPW) ... VONJY
Elantec Semiconductor [*NASDAQ symbol*] (TTSB) ... ELNT
Elantec Semiconductor, Inc. [*Associated Press*] (SAG) ... Elantec
Elantec Semiconductor, Inc. [*NASDAQ symbol*] (SAG) ... ELNT
Elapsed Greenwich Mean Time (KSC) ... EGMT
Elapsed Ground Time (MCD) ... EGT
Elapsed Maintenance Time ... EMT
Elapsed Method of Training (MCD) ... EMT
Elapsed Spacecraft Time ... ESCT
Elapsed Time ... ET
Elapsed Time [*Aviation*] (FAAC) ... ETIM
Elapsed Time Code ... ETC
Elapsed Time Distribution System (MCD) ... ETDS
Elapsed Time/Maintenance Action (MCD) ... ETMA
Elapsed Time Multiprogramming Factor ... ETMF
Elapsed Time Multiprogramming Factor (NITA) ... ETMF
Elapsed-Time Code Generator ... ETCG
Elapsed-Time Indicator (MCD) ... ELTI
Elapsed-Time Indicator ... ETI
Elapsed-Time Meter ... ETM
Elastance (MAE) ... E
Elastance [*Electricity*] (BARN) ... S
Elastase Inhibitory Capacity [*Physiology*] ... EIC
Elastase-Neomycin Gene [*Genetics*] ... ELNEO
Elastic (MSA) ... ELAS
Elastic Active Aerodynamics [*Mitsubishi*] [*Automotive engineering*] ... EAA
Elastic Analysis for Structural Engineering (NRCH) ... EASE
Elastic Braid Manufacturers Association [*Later, EFMC or EFMCNTA*] (EA) ... EBMA
Elastic Diaphragm Switch Technology [*IBM Corp.*] (MCD) ... EDST
Elastic Energy Density (WDAA) ... EED
Elastic Fabric Manufacturers Council of the Northern Textile Association ... EFMC
Elastic Fabric Manufacturers Council of the Northern Textile Association (EA) ... EFMCNTA
Elastic Fabric Manufacturers Institute [*Later, EFMC or EFMCNTA*] (EA) ... EFMI
Elastic Fibril [*Medicine*] (DMAA) ... EF
Elastic Frame Analysis Program [*Structures & Computers Ltd.*] [*Software package*] (NCC) ... EFAP
Elastic Hysteresis Constant ... EHC
Elastic Incoherent Structure Factor [*of spectra*] ... EISF
Elastic Limit ... EL
Elastic Loop Mobility System [*NASA*] ... ELMS
Elastic Low-Energy Electron Diffraction (PDAA) ... ELEED
Elastic Performance Coefficient [*Textile testing*] ... EPC
Elastic Plastic Membrane ... EPM
Elastic Recoil Detection ... ERD
Elastic Recoil Detection Analysis [*Physics*] ... ERDA
Elastic Reservoir Molding (DICI) ... ERM
Elastic Resist Weld (DNAB) ... ERW
Elastic Space Vehicle ... ESV
Elastic Stop Nut [*Hardware*] ... ESN
Elastic Stop Nut Corp. of America ... ESNA
Elastic Structural Analysis System - Two Dimensional [*Structures & Computers Ltd.*] [*Software package*] (NCC) ... ESAS-2
Elastic Surface Transformation (IAA) ... EST
Elastic Suspensor ... ES
Elastic Top and Bottom [*Military-issue clothing*] [*British*] (DSUE) ... ETB
Elasticities of Substitution [*Statistics*] ... ES
Elasticity of Demand [*Economics*] (DCTA) ... ED
Elasticity of Supply [*Economics*] (DCTA) ... ES
Elasticity, Viscosity, and Thixotropy ... EVT
Elastohydrodynamic ... EHD
Elastohydrodynamic Lubrication ... EHL
Elastomeric Insulation Material ... EIM
Elastomeric Molding Tooling Compound (MCD) ... EMC
Elastomeric Reusable Surface Insulation (NASA) ... ERSI
Elastomeric Rotary-Wing Head [*Military*] (CAAL) ... ERH
Elastomeric Shield Material [*Plastic technology*] ... ESM
Elastomeric Solid Material ... ESM
Elastomeric Thermoplastic [*Organic chemistry*] ... ETP
Elastomeric-Oriented Copolyester (PDAA) ... ELOC
Elastomer-Modified Cast Double-Base (MCD) ... EMCDB
Elastometric Thermoplastic ... ETP
Elastosis Perforans Serpiginosa [*Medicine*] ... EPS
Elat [*Israel*] [*Airport symbol*] (OAG) ... ETH
Elat/J. Hozman [*Israel*] [*ICAO location identifier*] (ICLI) ... LLET
Elaterium [*To Stimulate or Incite*] [*Pharmacy*] (ROG) ... ELAT
Elazig [*Turkey*] [*Seismograph station code, US Geological Survey Closed*] (SEIS) ... ELA
Elazig [*Turkey*] [*Seismograph station code, US Geological Survey*] (SEIS) ... ELZ
Elazig [*Turkey*] [*Airport symbol*] (OAG) ... EZS
Elazig [*Turkey ICAO location identifier*] (ICLI) ... LTCA
Elba, AL [*AM radio station call letters*] ... WELB
Elba, AL [*FM radio station call letters*] ... WZTZ
Elba Island [*Italy*] [*Airport symbol Obsolete*] (OAG) ... EBA
El-Baha [*Saudi Arabia*] [*ICAO location identifier*] (ICLI) ... OEBA
Elberfelder Bibel [*1905*] (BJA) ... El
Elbert County Public Library, Kiowa, CO [*Library symbol Library of Congress*] (LCLS) ... CoK
Elbert Hubbard Library Museum, East Aurora, NY [*Library symbol Library of Congress*] (LCLS) ... NEAuH
Elbert Ivey Memorial Library, Hickory, NC [*Library symbol Library of Congress*] (LCLS) ... NcHy
Elberta Public Library, Elberta, MI [*Library symbol Library of Congress*] (LCLS) ... MiElb
Elberton, GA [*AM radio station call letters*] ... WWRK
Elberton, GA [*FM radio station call letters*] ... WWRK-FM
Elbit Ltd. [*Associated Press*] (SAG) ... Elbit
Elbit Ltd. [*Associated Press*] (SAG) ... ElbitLtd
Elbit Ltd. [*NASDAQ symbol*] (NQ) ... ELBT
Elbit Ltd. [*NASDAQ symbol*] (TTSB) ... ELBTF
Elbit Medical Imaging Ltd. [*Associated Press*] (SAG) ... ElbitMd
Elbit Medical Imaging Ltd. [*NASDAQ symbol*] (SAG) ... EMIT
Elbit Systems Ltd. [*Associated Press*] (SAG) ... ElbitSys
Elbit Systems Ltd. [*NASDAQ symbol*] (SAG) ... ESLT
Elbit Vision Systems Ltd. [*Associated Press*] (SAG) ... ElbitVis
Elbit Vision Systems Ltd. [*NASDAQ symbol*] (SAG) ... EVSN
Elbow (DAC) ... E
Elbow (MSA) ... ELB
Elbow Disarticulation [*Orthopedics*] ... E/D
Elbow Extension [*Sports medicine*] ... ELXT
Elbow Jerk [*Medicine*] ... EJ
Elbow Orthosis [*Medicine*] ... EO
Elbow Pitch (MCD) ... EP
Elbow-Wrist-Hand-Orthosis [*Medicine*] ... EWHO
Elchies. Court of Session Cases [*Scotland*] [*A publication*] (DLA) ... Elch

Elchies. Court of Session Cases [*Scotland*] [*A publication*] (DLA) .... Elchies
Elchies' Dictionary of Decisions, Scotch Court of Session [*A publication*] (DLA) .... El
Elchies' Dictionary of Decisions, Scotch Court of Session [*A publication*] (DLA) .... El Dict
Elchies' Dictionary of Decisions, Scotch Court of Session [*A publication*] (DLA) .... Elchies' Dict
Elcho Island [*Australia Airport symbol*] (OAG) .... ELC
Elco [*Illinois*] [*Seismograph station code, US Geological Survey*] (SEIS) .... ELC
Elco Industries, Inc. [*NASDAQ symbol*] (NQ) .... ELCN
Elcom International [*NASDAQ symbol*] (SAG) .... ELCO
Elcom International [*Associated Press*] (SAG) .... Elcom
Elcom Intl. [*NASDAQ symbol*] (TTSB) .... ELCO
Elcor Corp. [*Associated Press*] (SAG) .... Elcor
Elcor Corp. [*NYSE symbol*] (SPSG) .... ELK
Elcotel, Inc. [*NASDAQ symbol*] (NQ) .... ECTL
Elcotel, Inc. [*Associated Press*] (SAG) .... Elcotel
Elder (VRA) .... eld
Elder .... ELDR
Elder .... ER
Elder and Fyfes Ltd. [*Shipping*] (ROG) .... E & F
Elder Cottage Housing Opportunity .... ECHO
Elder Craftsmen (EA) .... EC
Elder Flowers, Peppermint, and Composition Essense [*Patent medicine ingredients*] [*British*] .... EPC
Elder Statesman .... ES
Elder Tech Ltd. [*Vancouver Stock Exchange symbol*] .... ELD
Elderberry Carlavirus [*Plant pathology*] .... ECV
Elderberry Latent Virus [*Plant pathology*] .... EBLV
Elderhostel, Inc. (EA) .... EI
Elderly .... ELDRLY
Elderly and Handicapped [*TRB*] (TAG) .... E&H
Elderly Care Research Center [*Case Western Reserve University*] [*Research center*] (RCD) .... ECRC
Elderly Citizens Homes of South Australia .... ECHSA
Elderly Onset Rheumatoid Arthritis [*Medicine*] (DAVI) .... EORA
Elders IXL Canada, Inc. [*Toronto Stock Exchange symbol*] .... EIX
Eldest .... E
Eldest (ROG) .... EL
Eldest .... ELD
Eldest Son .... ES
Eldinder Aviation [*Sudan*] [*ICAO designator*] (FAAC) .... DND
Eldisine [*Also, VDS*] [*Antineoplastic drug*] .... E
Eldisine [*Vindesine*], BCNU , Adriamycin, Prednisone [*Carmustine*] [*Antineoplastic drug regimen*] .... EBAP
Eldon Avenue Revolutionary Union Movement .... ELRUM
Eldon Carnegie Library, Eldon, IA [*Library symbol Library of Congress*] (LCLS) .... IaEld
Eldon Forum, Eldon, IA [*Library symbol Library of Congress*] (LCLS) .... IaEldF
Eldon, IA (RBYB) .... KRKN
Eldon, MO [*FM radio station call letters*] .... KBMX
Eldon, MO [*FM radio station call letters*] .... KLOZ
Eldon Resources Ltd. [*Vancouver Stock Exchange symbol*] .... ELR
Eldora, IA [*FM radio station call letters*] .... KDAO-FM
Eldorado [*Cadillac automobile*] .... ELDO
Eldorado Bancorp [*AMEX symbol*] (SPSG) .... ELB
Eldorado Bancorp [*Associated Press*] (SAG) .... Eldorad
Eldorado, IL [*FM radio station call letters*] .... WEBQ
Eldorado Minerals & Petroleum [*Vancouver Stock Exchange symbol*] .... ELO
Eldorado Mining & Refining Co., Port Hope, ON, Canada [*Library symbol Library of Congress*] (LCLS) .... CaOPhE
Eldorado Nuclear Ltd., Ottawa, ON, Canada [*Library symbol Library of Congress*] (LCLS) .... CaOOEN
Eldorado Nuclear Ltd., Port Hope, Ontario [*Library symbol National Library of Canada*] (NLC) .... OPE
Eldorado Resources Ltd., Blind River Refinery, Blind River, ON, Canada [*Library symbol Library of Congress*] (LCLS) .... CaOBrER
Eldoret [*Kenya*] [*Airport symbol Obsolete*] (OAG) .... EDL
Eldoret [*Kenya*] [*ICAO location identifier*] (ICLI) .... HKEL
Eldred Rock, AK [*Location identifier FAA*] (FAAL) .... ERO
Eldredge Public Library, Chatham, MA [*Library symbol*] [*Library of Congress*] (LCLS) .... MCha
ELE Energy, Inc. [*Vancouver Stock Exchange symbol*] .... ELI
Eleanor Association (EA) .... EA
Eleanor Roosevelt [*1884-1962*] .... ER
Eleanor Roosevelt Institute (EA) .... ERI
Eleanor Roosevelt Institute for Cancer Research .... ERICR
Eleanor Roosevelt's Centennial Observance Committee of Friends and Admirers (EA) .... ERCOCFA
Eleanor Steber Music Foundation [*Defunct*] (EA) .... ESMF
Elecrical Council of Florida (SRA) .... ECF
Elect [*or Election*] .... EL
Elect .... ELEC
Elect of Fifteen [*Freemasonry*] (ROG) .... EF
Elected .... ELCTD
Elected Members Board of General Purposes [*Freemasonry*] (ROG) .... EMB of GP
Elected Public Official .... EPO
Elected Spanish Speaking Officials (EA) .... ESSO
Election (ROG) .... ELEC
Election (AABC) .... ELECT
Election Cases [*A publication*] (DLA) .... EC
Election Cases [*A publication*] (DLA) .... El Cas
Election Cases [*A publication*] (DLA) .... Elect Cas
Election District .... ED
Election Knight of Nine [*Freemasonry*] (ROG) .... EK of N
Election Law Reports [*India*] [*A publication*] (DLA) .... Elec LR
Election Law Reports [*India*] [*A publication*] (DLA) .... ELR
Election Laws .... EL
Election Reports [*Ontario*] [*A publication*] (DLA) .... Elect Rep
Election Reports [*Ontario*] [*A publication*] (DLA) .... ER
Elections Canada, Ottawa, Ontario [*Library symbol National Library of Canada*] (BIB) .... OOELC
Elections Code [*A publication*] (DLA) .... Elec C
Elections Research Center (EA) .... ERC
Elective Abortion [*Obstetrics*] (DAVI) .... EAB
Elective Cosmetic Surgery .... ECS
Elective Low Forceps [*Delivery*] [*Obstetrics*] (DAVI) .... ELF
Elective Masonry [*Freemasonry*] (ROG) .... EM
Elective Node Dissection [*Medicine*] .... ELND
Elective Repeat Cesarean Section [*Obstetrics*] .... ERCS
Electocon International, Inc. [*Associated Press*] (SAG) .... ElcIntl
Electocon International, Inc. [*NASDAQ symbol*] (SAG) .... EPLT
[*The*] **Electonic Clearing House, Inc.** [*NASDAQ symbol*] (NQ) .... ECHO
Electonic Remote Control [*Automotive electronic systems*] .... ERC
Elector [*or Electoral*] (WDAA) .... ELEC
Electoral Boundaries Commission [*Victoria, Australia*] .... EBC
Electoral Education Centre [*Australia*] .... EEC
Electoral Funding Authority of New South Wales [*Australia*] .... EFANSW
Electoral Office [*Australia*] .... EO
Electoral Reform Society [*British*] .... ERS
Electorate (ROG) .... ELEC
Electra [*of Euripides*] [*Classical studies*] (OCD) .... El
Electra Data Management System .... EDMS
Electra North West [*Vancouver Stock Exchange symbol*] .... ETA
Electra Title Corp. [*Vancouver Stock Exchange symbol*] .... ETC
Electret-Passive Environmental Radon Monitor [*Rad-Elec, Inc.*] .... E-PERM
Electric (ADA) .... E
Electric .... EL
Electric (AFM) .... ELEC
Electric (AAGC) .... Elec
Electric .... ELECTR
Electric (IAA) .... ELTRC
Electric Accounting Machine and Electronic Data Processing Machine .... EAMEDPM
Electric Accounting Machine Unit .... EAMU
Electric Affinity [*Physics*] (DAVI) .... EA
Electric Affinity [*Symbol*] [*Physics*] (DAVI) .... E_0
Electric & Gas Technology [*NASDAQ symbol*] (TTSB) .... ELGT
Electric & Gas Technology, Inc. [*Associated Press*] (SAG) .... ElcGas
Electric & Gas Technology, Inc. [*NASDAQ symbol*] (NQ) .... ELGT
Electric and Hybrid Vehicles .... EHV
Electric and Magnetic Field .... EMF
Electric & Musical Industries [*later, EMI Ltd.*] **Analogue Computer** (DEN) .... EMIAC
Electric Antenna [*Automobile accessory*] .... EA
Electric Arc Furnace [*Steelmaking*] .... EAF
Electric Arc Metallizing Gun .... EAMG
Electric Arc Shock Tunnel [*NASA*] .... EAST
Electric Arc Weld .... EAW
Electric Auto Association (EA) .... EAA
Electric Battery (IAA) .... ELB
Electric Beam Exposure System [*Integrated circuit*] [*Bell Laboratories*] .... EBES
Electric Bilge Pump .... EBP
Electric Boat (MCD) .... EB
Electric Boat Association [*British*] (DBA) .... EBA
Electric Bomb Fuze (NG) .... EBF
Electric Bond and Share (IAA) .... EBS
Electric Brain Stimulator .... EBS
Electric Cable (IAA) .... ELC
Electric Cable Makers' Confederation [*British*] (BI) .... ECMC
Electric Car Racing Association .... ECRA
Electric Charge [*Electricity*] (DAVI) .... e
Electric Charge to Mass (IEEE) .... e/m
Electric [*or Electronic*] **Cipher Machine** [*or Coding*] .... ECM
Electric Cipher [*or Coding*] **Machine Repairman** [*Navy rating*] .... EC
Electric Circuit Analysis Program (NITA) .... ECAP
Electric Circuit Test Set .... ECTS
Electric Clock Valve .... ECV
Electric Companies' Advertising Program .... ECAP
Electric Companies' Public Information Program .... ECPIP
Electric Consumer Protection Act of 1986 .... ECPA
Electric Consumers Information Committee (EA) .... ECIC
Electric Contact .... ELCTC
Electric Contact Brush .... ELCTCBR
Electric Contact Ring .... ELCTRG
Electric Control and Manufacturing (IAA) .... ECAM
Electric Control Drive .... ECD
Electric Controller and Manufacturing (IAA) .... ECM
Electric Cooperative of Oklahoma .... ECO
Electric Current .... EC
Electric Current [*Symbol*] [*IUPAC*] I
Electric Current Density [*Symbol*] [*IUPAC*] (DEN) .... J
Electric Current Perturbation [*Method*] [*Southwest Research Institute*] .... ECP
Electric Current Relay .... RT
Electric Delay Line .... EDL
Electric Depth Finder .... EDF
Electric Dipole Moment [*Physics*] .... EDM
Electric Dipole Moment (BARN) .... P
Electric Discharge Mixing LASER (PDAA) .... EDML
Electric Displacement [*Symbol*] .... D

Electric Displacement Density .... EDD
Electric Double Layer .... EDL
Electric Drive Mechanism (KSC) .... EDM
Electric Dynamic [*Motors*] .... ED
Electric Dynamometer [*Engineering*] .... EDYNMT
Electric Energy Association [*Later, EEI*] (EA) .... EEA
Electric Feedback .... EFB
Electric Field and Waves .... EFW
Electric Field Gradient [*of crystals*] .... EFG
Electric Field Integral Equation (PDAA) .... EFIE
Electric Field Meter .... EFM
Electric Field Strength [*Symbol*] .... E
Electric Field Strength .... EFS
Electric Field Vector .... E
Electric Field Vector .... EFV
Electric Field-Induced Second Harmonic Generation [*Physics*] .... EFISH
Electric Field-Induced Spectra .... EFS
Electric Fire Pump [*Nuclear energy*] (NRCH) .... EFP
Electric Flow Field .... EFF
Electric Flux Density .... EFD
Electric Fuel [*NASDAQ symbol*] (TTSB) .... EFCX
Electric Fuel Control [*Automotive engineering*] .... EFC
Electric Fuel Corp. [*Associated Press*] (SAG) .... ElcFuel
Electric Fuse Manufacturers Guild [*Defunct*] (EA) .... EFMG
Electric Glue Gun .... EGG
Electric Ground Power System [*Aerospace*] (AAG) .... EGPS
Electric Heart Vector [*Cardiology*] .... EHV
Electric Heat Tracing (ACII) .... EHT
Electric Heat Vector [*Physics*] (DAVI) .... EHV
Electric Heated Back Light [*Automotive engineering*] .... EBL
Electric Heater (AAG) .... EH
Electric Heating Association (EA) .... EHA
Electric Heating Unit .... EHU
Electric Hoist (IAA) .... EH
Electric Home and Farm Authority [*Terminated, 1947*] .... EHFA
Electric Horsepower .... EHP
Electric Horsepower Hour (IAA) .... EHPH
Electric Hot Water Service [*Classified advertising*] (ADA) .... EHWS
Electric Hot Water Service [*Classified advertising*] (ADA) .... ELHWS
Electric Induction Oven .... EIO
Electric Induction Steel (IAA) .... EIS
Electric Junction Equation .... EJE
Electric Lamp Industry Council [*British*] (BI) .... ELIC
Electric Lamp Manufacturers' Association of Great Britain Ltd. (BI) .... ELMA
Electric LASER (MCD) .... EL
Electric League of Arizona (SRA) .... ELA
Electric League of Indiana (SRA) .... ELI
Electric League of the Pacific Northwest (SRA) .... ELPN
Electric Light .... EL
Electric Light (IAA) .... ELLT
Electric Light and Power Group .... ELPG
Electric Light Fittings Association [*British*] (BI) .... ELFA
Electric Light Orchestra [*Rock music group*] .... ELO
Electric Light Pole .... ELP
Electric Limit Switch .... ELS
Electric Motor Driven .... EMD
Electric Motor-Operated (NRCH) .... EMO
Electric Motors (MCD) .... EM
Electric Multiple Unit [*Passenger trains*] (DCTA) .... EMU
Electric Music Instrument (SAA) .... EMI
Electric Organ Discharge [*Electrophysiology*] .... EOD
Electric Overhead Crane Institute [*Later, Crane Manufacturers Association of America*] (EA) .... EOCI
Electric Overhead Travelling .... EOT
Electric Plant Control Panel .... EPCP
Electric Polarization Vector .... EPV
Electric Potential [*Symbol*] [*IUPAC*] V
Electric Potential Difference .... EPD
Electric Power (NRCH) .... EP
Electric Power Database [*Electric Power Research Institute*] [*Information service or system*] (IID) .... EPD
Electric Power Database/Research and Development Information System [*Electric Power Research Institute*] [*Information service or system*] (IID) .... EPD/RDIS
Electric Power Distribution .... EPD
Electric Power Generation and Distribution (MCD) .... EGAD
Electric Power Generation System .... EPGS
Electric Power Industry Abstracts [*Utility Data Institute*] [*Information service or system*] .... EPIA
Electric Power Monthly [*A publication*] (GFGA) .... EPM
Electric Power Plant (MCD) .... EPP
Electric Power Plant Engineer (IAA) .... ELECPWRPLNTENGR
Electric Power Research Institute [*Palo Alto, CA*] (ECON) .... EPRI
Electric Power Research Institute (USDC) .... EPRI
Electric Power Research Institute, High Voltage Transmission Research Center [*Research center*] (RCD) .... EPRI-HVTRC
Electric Power Research Institute, Palo Alto, CA [*Library symbol Library of Congress*] (LCLS) .... CPaE
Electric Power Research Laboratory [*Arizona State University*] [*Research center*] (RCD) .... EPRL
Electric Power Source (MCD) .... EPS
Electric Power Steering System [*Automotive engineering*] .... EPS
Electric Power System [*or Subsystem*] (NRCH) .... EPS
Electric Power Transmission (ADA) .... EPT
Electric Powered Vehicle .... EPV

Electric Pressure Wave .... EPW
Electric Primer .... EP
Electric Process Heating (MCD) .... EPH
Electric Programmer, Evaluator, Controller (SAA) .... EPEC
Electric Propulsion System .... EPS
Electric Propulsion Trajectory Analysis .... EPTA
Electric Quadrupole-Quadrupole .... EQQ
Electric Railroaders Association (EA) .... ERA
Electric Railway Society (EAIO) .... ERS
Electric Regulation Co. .... ERC
Electric Reliability Council of Texas [*Regional power council*] .... ERCOT
Electric Remote Speed Indicator (IAA) .... ERSI
Electric Resonance Optothermal Spectroscopy .... EROS
Electric Response Audiometry (AAMN) .... ERA
Electric Seats [*Automotive accessory*] .... ES
Electric Service Dealers Association of Illinois (SRA) .... EDSA-IL
Electric Shutoff [*NFPA pre-fire planning symbol*] (NFPA) .... E
Electric Skin Resistance [*Neurology*] (DAVI) .... ESR
Electric Sliding Roof [*Automotive accessory*] .... ESR
Electric Space Heating and Air Conditioning (MCD) .... ESHAC
Electric Starting (ADA) .... ES
Electric Storage Battery .... ESB
Electric Storage Battery Co., Yardley, PA [*Library symbol Library of Congress*] (LCLS) .... PYarE
Electric Strip Heater (OA) .... ESH
Electric Surface Current .... ESC
Electric Target Intermediate Marksmanship Range .... ETIMR
Electric Telegraph .... ET
Electric Tension [*Symbol*] [*IUPAC*] .... U
Electric Test Installation .... ETI
Electric Test Vehicle [*Department of Energy*] .... ETV
Electric Tool Institute [*Later, Power Tool Institute*] (EA) .... ETI
Electric Trace Heating Industry Council [*British*] (DBA) .... ETHIC
Electric Utilities Fleet Managers Conference .... EUFMC
Electric Utility Industrial Power Association (EA) .... EUIPA
Electric Utility Pump .... EUP
Electric Vacuum Gyro .... EVG
Electric Vehicle .... EV
Electric Vehicle Association of Canada .... EVAC
Electric Vehicle Association of Great Britain Ltd. (BI) .... EVA
Electric Vehicle Association of the Americas (EA) .... EVAA
Electric Vehicle Capsulated Contact [*Automotive electrical systems*] .... EVCC
Electric Vehicle Council [*Defunct*] (EA) .... EVC
Electric Vehicle Development Group Ltd. [*British*] .... EVDG
Electric Vehicle Exposition (ADA) .... EVE
Electric Vehicle Total Energy Cycle Analysis .... EVTECA
Electric Vehicles (EERA) .... EVs
Electric Wall Oven and Hot Plates [*Classified advertising*] (ADA) .... EWO & HP
Electric Water Cooler .... EWC
Electric Water Systems Council .... EWSC
Electric Wave Section Filter .... EWSF
Electric Weld (IAA) .... ELW
Electric Winch Drive (DWSG) .... EWD
Electric Windows [*Automotive accessory*] .... EW
Electrical (IAA) .... ECL
Electrical .... ELECT
Electrical .... ELECTL
Electrical .... ELECTRCL
Electrical .... ELECTRL
Electrical [*in British naval officers' ranks*] L
Electrical Accounting for the Security Industry [*IBM Corp.*] (IEEE) .... EASI
Electrical Accounting Machine (NITA) .... EAM
Electrical Aerosol Analyzer [*Instrumentation*] .... EAA
Electrical Aerospace Ground Equipment (TEL) .... EAGE
Electrical and Electromagnetic Interference (KSC) .... EEI
Electrical and Electronic Insulation Association [*British*] (DBA) .... EEIA
Electrical and Electronic Manufacturers Association of Canada (EAIO) .... EEMAC
Electrical and Electronic Manufacturers Joint Education Board .... EEMJEB
Electrical and Electronic Measurement and Test Instrumentation Conference (MCD) .... EEMTIC
Electrical and Electronic Properties of Materials .... EEPM
Electrical and Electronics Commission .... EEC
Electrical and Electronics Standards Board [*American National Standards Institute*] [*Telecommunications*] .... EESB
Electrical and Electronics Standards Management Board .... EESMB
Electrical and Engineering Staff Association [*British*] .... EESA
Electrical and Instrument Shop (NRCH) .... EIS
Electrical and Instrumentation Verification Tests [*NASA*] (NASA) .... EIVT
Electrical and Mechanical (KSC) .... E & M
Electrical and Mechanical Assistant Engineer [*British military*] (DMA) .... EMAE
Electrical and Mechanical Capability Committee .... E & MCC
Electrical and Mechanical Capability Working Group .... E & MCWG
Electrical and Mechanical Compatibility [*Military*] .... E & MC
Electrical and Mechanical Engineering [*or Engineers*] .... EME
Electrical and Mechanical Engineering [*British*] .... EMEC
Electrical and Mechanical Instrument Makers' Association [*A union*] [*British*] .... EMIMA
Electrical and Mechanical Interface Working Group [*Strategic Defense Initiative*] .... E & MIWG
Electrical and Mechanical Maintenance (IAA) .... EMM
Electrical & Musical Industries Ltd. [*British*] .... EMI
Electrical and Wireless Operators [*Air Force British*] .... EWO
Electrical Apparatus Service Association (EA) .... EASA
Electrical Approvals Board (Victoria) .... EAB
Electrical Armaments Program Office [*Army*] .... EAPO

Electrical Artificer [*Navy British*] ... EA
Electrical Artificer, Air [*British military*] (DMA) ... EA(A)
Electrical Artificer (Air), Apprentice [*British military*] (DMA) ... EA(A)APP
Electrical Assembly Order (MCD) ... EAO
Electrical Association for Women [*British*] ... EAW
Electrical Automatic Support Equipment ... EASE
Electrical Auxiliary Power Unit (DNAB) ... EAPU
Electrical Cable Test Set ... ECTS
Electrical Cell-Substrate Impedance Sensing [*for cell-culture study*] ... ECIS
Electrical Charge (WDAA) ... Q
Electrical Checkout Equipment (KSC) ... ECE
Electrical Check-Out System ... ECOS
Electrical [*or Electronic*] **Circuit Analysis Program** ... ECAP
Electrical Circuit Interrupter (KSC) ... ECI
Electrical Coding (WDAA) ... EC
Electrical Command and Stability System (PDAA) ... ECSS
Electrical Commuter Car ... ECC
Electrical Conductivity ... EC
Electrical Conductivity Measurement ... ECM
Electrical Connector Subassembly ... ECS
Electrical Contact Analyzer (IAA) ... ECA
Electrical Contact Plate ... ECP
Electrical Contact Resistance (PDAA) ... ECR
Electrical Continuous Cloth (IAA) ... ECC
Electrical Contractors' Association [*British*] (BI) ... ECA
Electrical Contractors' Association of New South Wales [*Australia*] ... ECANSW
Electrical Contractors' Association of Scotland (EAIO) ... ECAS
Electrical Control Activity (MCD) ... ECA
Electrical Control Package ... ECP
Electrical Control Unit (PDAA) ... ELCU
Electrical Conversion Unit ... ECU
Electrical Coupling Display Unit (KSC) ... ECDU
Electrical, Defective, Government [*Government-furnished equipment*] (DNAB) ... ELDG
Electrical Deflection Indicator ... EDI
Electrical Department [*Navy British*] ... ED
Electrical Description of Operation Chart (IAA) ... EDOC
Electrical Design Engineering ... EDE
Electrical Development Association ... EDA
Electrical Development Association of New South Wales [*Australia*] ... EDANSW
Electrical Development Association of Queensland [*Australia*] ... EDAQ
Electrical Development Association of Victoria [*Australia*] ... EDAV
Electrical Development Association of Western Australia [*Australia*] ... EDAWA
Electrical Differential ... ED
Electrical Discharge Forming [*Manufacturing term*] (IAA) ... EDF
Electrical Discharge Grinding [*Manufacturing term*] ... EDG
Electrical Discharge LASER (MCD) ... EDL
Electrical Discharge [*or Electrodischarge*] **Machine** [*or Machining*] ... EDM
Electrical Discharge Tube (MSA) ... EDT
Electrical Discharge Wire Cutting [*Manufacturing term*] ... EDWC
Electrical Disconnect (MCD) ... ELDISC
Electrical Disintegration Machining [*Nuclear energy*] (NRCH) ... EDM
Electrical Distance Recorder [*British military*] (DMA) ... EDR
Electrical Distribution Center [*Army*] ... EDC
Electrical Distribution System (MCD) ... EDS
Electrical Distribution Unit ... EDU
Electrical Distributor [*A publication*] (EAAP) ... TED
Electrical Drawing (IAA) ... ED
Electrical/Electronic ... E/E
Electrical, Electronic, and Electromechanical ... EEE
Electrical, Electronic, Telecommunication, and Plumbing Union [*British*] (DCTA) ... EETPU
Electrical/Electronics Insulation Conference (EA) ... EEIC
Electrical Energy [*Symbol*] (DEN) ... W
Electrical Engineer [*or Engineering*] ... EE
Electrical Engineer (FAAC) ... EENGR
Electrical Engineering (DD) ... EEng
Electrical Engineering Division, Canada Institute for Scientific and Technical Information [*Division de Genie Electrique, Institut Canadien de l'Information Scientifique et Technique*] **Ottawa, Ontario** [*Library symbol National Library of Canada*] (NLC) ... OONRE
Electrical Engineering Exposition ... EEE
Electrical Engineering Research Laboratory (KSC) ... EERL
Electrical Enhancement Factor ... EEF
Electrical, Environmental, and Communications ... EECOM
Electrical, Environmental, Consumables, and Mechanical Systems (MCD) ... EECOM
Electrical, Environmental Control, and Instrumentation Systems Specialist [*NASA*] ... EECIS
Electrical Equipment [*Fire classification*] ... C
Electrical Equipment Bay Cooling System ... EEBCS
Electrical Equipment List (MCD) ... EEL
Electrical Equipment Protection Room Ventilation System [*Nuclear energy*] (NRCH) ... EEPVS
Electrical Equipment Representatives Association (EA) ... EERA
Electrical Equipment Shelter ... EES
Electrical Equipment Trailer ... EET
Electrical Equipment Users Association (OSI) ... EEUA
Electrical Export Corp. [*Defunct*] ... EEC
Electrical Field Current ... EFC
Electrical Field-Flow Fractionation [*Electrochemical separation method*] ... EFFF
Electrical Fitting Inventory Control Branch ... EFICO
Electrical Floor Warming Association [*British*] (BI) ... EFA
Electrical Frequency Control (MCD) ... EFC
Electrical Fuel Corp. [*NASDAQ symbol*] (SAG) ... EFCX
Electrical Galvanic Stimulation [*Physiology*] ... EGS
Electrical, General Instrumentation, and Lighting Engineer (MCD) ... EGIL
Electrical Generating Systems Association (EA) ... EGSA
Electrical Generating Systems Marketing Association [*Later, EGSA*] (EA) ... EGSMA
Electrical Grapple Fixture (MCD) ... EGF
Electrical [*or Electronic*] **Ground-Support Equipment** ... EGSE
Electrical Harness Assembly (KSC) ... EHA
Electrical Heating Control (MCD) ... EHC
Electrical Height Calculator (IAA) ... EHC
Electrical Historical Foundation [*Defunct*] (EA) ... EHF
Electrical Horology Society (EA) ... EHS
Electrical Housewares Distributors Association [*Defunct*] (EA) ... EHDA
Electrical Hull Penetration ... EHP
Electrical Impedance Tomography [*Medicine*] (BARN) ... EIT
Electrical Industries Association ... EIA
Electrical Industries Benevolent Association [*British*] (BI) ... EIBA
Electrical Industries Federation of Ireland (BI) ... EIFI
Electrical Industry Study Board (EA) ... EISB
Electrical Information Test ... EIT
Electrical Inspection Directorate (IAA) ... EID
Electrical Installation Equipment Manufacturers Association [*British*] (DBA) ... EIEMA
Electrical Installation Test [*or Technician*] ... EIT
Electrical Insulating Liquid (PDAA) ... EIL
Electrical Insulation (MCD) ... EI
Electrical Insulation Committee [*Military*] ... EIC
Electrical Insulation Conference [*Later, EEIC*] (MCD) ... EIC
Electrical Insulation Tape ... EIT
Electrical Integration System (NASA) ... EIS
Electrical Interface Building [*NASA*] (KSC) ... EIB
Electrical Interface Control Document (MCD) ... EICD
Electrical Interface Verification Test [*NASA*] (NASA) ... EIVT
Electrical Intersystems Test ... EIT
Electrical Joint Compound (IAA) ... EJC
Electrical Kilowatts ... EKW
Electrical Latching (IAA) ... EL
Electrical Launch Support Equipment [*NASA*] (KSC) ... ELSE
Electrical Length Measurement (IAA) ... ELM
Electrical Maintenance Test Equipment ... MTEE
Electrical Manufacturers' Association of South Australia ... EMASA
Electrical Manufacturers Standards Council (BARN) ... EMSC
Electrical Mate Test (KSC) ... EMT
Electrical Measurements and Standards Division [*National Institute of Standards and Technology*] (GRD) ... EMSD
Electrical Measuring Instrument (IAA) ... EMI
Electrical Mechanic (Air) [*British military*] (DMA) ... EM(A)
Electrical Mechanic (Air Weapon) [*British military*] (DMA) ... EM(AW)
Electrical Mechanical (IAA) ... ELECMECH
Electrical, Mechanical, and Environmental Systems (MCD) ... EMES
Electrical/Mechanical Power Generation Subsystem ... EMPG
Electrical/Mechanical Power Generation Subsystem (MCD) ... EMPGS
Electrical Mechanical Tubing ... EMT
Electrical Mechanician (Air) [*Navy rating British*] ... ELMN(A)
Electrical Mechanician (Air Weapon) [*British military*] (DMA) ... ELMN(AW)
Electrical Megawatt ... EMW
Electrical Metallic Conduit (DAC) ... EMC
Electrical Metallic Tubing ... EMT
Electrical Meter Kit ... EMK
Electrical Metrology Laboratory (MCD) ... EML
Electrical Multiplex ... EMUX
Electrical Muscle Stimulation [*Physiology*] ... EMS
Electrical Nonmetallic Tubing ... ENT
Electrical Objective Loudness Rating (IEEE) ... EOLR
Electrical Overstress/Electrostatic Discharge Association (EA) ... EOS/ESD
Electrical Panel (NG) ... EP
Electrical Potential Gradient Radiosonde [*Meteorology*] ... EPGR
Electrical Power and Distribution (CET) ... EP & D
Electrical Power Conditioning, Distribution, and Control (MCD) ... EPCDC
Electrical Power Control Unit (MCD) ... EPCU
Electrical Power Distribution and Control (NASA) ... EPDC
Electrical Power Distribution and Control System (KSC) ... EPDCS
Electrical Power Distribution Box (MCD) ... EPDB
Electrical Power Distribution System [*or Subsystem*] (KSC) ... EPDS
Electrical Power Engineers' Association [*A union*] [*British*] ... EPEA
Electrical Power Generator (NASA) ... EPG
Electrical Power Level (MCD) ... EPL
Electrical Power Panel (MCD) ... EPP
Electrical Power Production Technician (IAA) ... EPPT
Electrical Power Production Technician/Specialist (AAG) ... EPPT/S
Electrical Power/Pyro Sequential System (MCD) ... EPPS
Electrical Power Requirements Data ... EPRD
Electrical Power Storage (ROG) ... EPS
Electrical Power Supply ... EPS
Electrical Power System [*or Subsystem*] ... EPS
Electrical Power System Test Facility [*NASA*] (KSC) ... EPSTF
Electrical Power Unit ... EPU
Electrical Pressure Regulator (IEEE) ... EPR
Electrical Programmed Stimulation [*Medicine*] (CPH) ... EPS
Electrical Propulsion (AAG) ... EP
Electrical Prototype ... EP
Electrical Quality Assurance Directorate [*British Ministry of Defense*] [*Research center*] ... EQD
Electrical Quantity (IDOE) ... q
Electrical Ram Air Turbine (PDAA) ... ELRAT

Electrical [or Electronic] Replaceable Assembly	ERA
Electrical Representatives Association	ERA
Electrical Research Association [British]	ERA
Electrical Research Memorandum	ERM
Electrical Resistance (MSA)	ER
Electrical Resistance Strain (OA)	ERS
Electrical Resistance Temperature	ERT
Electrical Resistance Temperature (MCD)	TEMP
Electrical Resistance Weld	ERW
Electrical Response Activity	ERA
Electrical Rule Checker [For integrated circuitry]	ERC
Electrical Section (IAA)	ES
Electrical Sign Manufacturers Association	ESMA
Electrical Sounding (PDAA)	ES
Electrical Spark Erosion	ELOX
Electrical Specification	ESPEC
Electrical Spinal Orthosis	ESO
Electrical Standards Set	ESS
Electrical Stimulating and Recording Unit	ESRU
Electrical Stimulation - Hot Boning [Meat processing]	ESHB
Electrical Stimulation of the Brain	ESB
Electrical Stimulation of the Lateral Hypothalamus [Medicine]	ESLH
Electrical Stimulation of the Midbrain	ESM
Electrical Stimulus	ES
Electrical Stress Analysis	ESA
Electrical Supervisory Subassembly (IAA)	ESS
Electrical Supply Industry Training Committee (AIE)	ESITC
Electrical Support Equipment	ESE
Electrical Survey-Net Adjuster	ESNA
Electrical System	ELS
Electrical System Design Report	ESDR
Electrical System Integration (MCD)	ESI
Electrical System-Integrated Test (SSD)	ESIT
Electrical Systems and Controls (ACII)	ESAC
Electrical Systems Branch [NASA] (KSC)	ESB
Electrical Systems Panel [Apollo Spacecraft Program Office] [NASA]	ESP
Electrical Systems Repair Facilities (MCD)	ESRF
Electrical Tactical Map	ETM
Electrical Technician (IAA)	ET
Electrical Technician/Electrician (AAG)	ET/E
Electrical Techniques in Medicine and Biology (MCD)	ETMB
Electrical Terminal Distributor (KSC)	ETD
Electrical Terminal Nut	ETN
Electrical Test Group (NRCH)	ETG
Electrical Test Setup [NASA] (KSC)	ETS
Electrical Testing Laboratory [Portsmouth Naval Shipyard, NH]	ETL
Electrical Thermal Analysis	ETA
Electrical Thermal Generators (KSC)	ETG
Electrical Time	ET
Electrical Time Base	ETB
Electrical Time Measurement	ETM
Electrical Time, Superquick	ETSQ
Electrical Tough Pitch [Copper]	ETP
Electrical Trade Council (EA)	ETC
Electrical Trades' Commercial Travellers' Association [British] (BI)	ETCTA
Electrical Trades Union [British]	ETU
Electrical Transcription	ET
Electrical/Transformer Room [NFPA pre-fire planning symbol] (NFPA)	ET
Electrical Typewriter (CMD)	ET
Electrical Utility Application (IAA)	EUA
Electrical Weekly [A publication]	Electl Wkly
Electrical Welding (IAA)	EW
Electrical Welding Machine	EWM
Electrical Wholesalers' Association, Victoria [Australia]	EWAV
Electrical Wholesalers Federation [British] (BI)	EWF
Electrical Wiring Component Application Partnership	EWCAP
Electrical Women's Round Table (EA)	EWRT
Electrical Workers and Contractors' Board [Queensland, Australia]	EWCB
Electrical Zero	EZ
Electrical-Electronics Materials Distributors Association [Later, LEMDA] (EA)	EEMDA
Electrically	ELECTLY
Electrically Activated Bank Release Device (IEEE)	EABRD
Electrically Alterable Device (NASA)	EAD
Electrically Alterable Memory [Computer science]	EAM
Electrically Alterable Programmable Read-Only Memory [Computer science]	EAPROM
Electrically Alterable Read-Only Memory [Computer science]	EAROM
Electrically Alterable Read-Only Store [Computer science]	EAROS
Electrically Augmented Gravity Filter [Chemical engineering]	EAGF
Electrically Augmented Pressure Filter [Chemical engineering]	EAPF
Electrically Augmented Vacuum Filter [Chemical engineering]	EAVF
Electrically Calibrated Pyroelectric Radiometer	ECPR
Electrically Compensated Pyrometer	ECP
Electrically Conductive Film (MCD)	ECF
Electrically Controlled Birefringence [Telecommunications] (TEL)	ECB
Electrically Erasable, Programmable, Read-Only Memory [Computer science]	EEPROM
Electrically Erasable Read-Only Memory [Computer science] (MDG)	EEROM
Electrically Heated Catalyst	EHC
Electrically Initiated Explosive Device	EIED
Electrically Insulated Coating	EIC
Electrically Modulated Control Clutch	ELPHEV
Electrically Operated Depressurization Valve (MCD)	ELDV
Electrically Operated Valve	ELV

Electrically Operated Valve	EOV
Electrically Polarized [Relay]	EP
Electrically Programmable Logic Device [Computer science]	EPLD
Electrically Programmable Read-Only Memory [Computer science] (MCD)	EPROM
Electrically Reconfigurable Array (CDE)	ERA
Electrically Scanned Microwave Radiometer [NASA]	ESMR
Electrically Steerable Antenna Feed Techniques (NG)	ESAFT
Electrically Supported [or Suspended] Accelerometer	ESA
Electrically Supported [or Suspended] Gyro Accelerometer	ESGA
Electrically [or Electrostatically] Suspended Gyro (MSA)	ESG
Electrically Suspended Gyro Navigation	ESGN
Electrically Trainable Analog Neural Network [Intel Corp.] [Computer science] (PCM)	ETANN
Electrically Transmitted Message	ETM
Electrically Transmitted Unsatisfactory Report	EUR
Electrically Tuned Antenna Coupler	ETAC
Electrically-Alterable Non-Destructive Read Out [Computer science] (IAA)	EANDRO
Electrically-Commutated Motor [General Electric Co.] (PS)	ECM
Electrically-Conducting Polymer	ECP
Electrically-Erasable Floating Gate Avalanche-Injection Metal-Oxide Semiconductor [Computer science] (IAA)	EEFAMOS
Electrically-Erasable Programmable Logic Device [Computer science] (IAA)	EEPOL
Electrically-Erasable Programmable Read-Only Memory [Computer science] (EECA)	E$_2$PROM
Electrically-Excited Thermally-Stimulated Current	ETSC
Electrically-Pulsed Chamber (PDAA)	EPC
Electrical-to-Optical (ACRL)	E/O
Electrical-to-Pneumatic [Converter] (NRCH)	E/P
Electric-Discharge Convection LASER [Navy]	EDCL
Electric-Drive Fan [Automotive engineering]	EDF
Electric-Field-Induced Infrared Absorption (PDAA)	EFIRA
Electric-Field-Induced Second-Harmonic Generation	EFISHG
Electrician [British military] (DMA)	EL
Electrician (AFM)	ELECN
Electrician	ELECTRCN
Electrician (IAA)	ELECTRN
Electrician's Mate [Navy rating]	EM
Electrician's Mate, Chief [Navy rating]	EMC
Electrician's Mate, Construction Battalion [Navy rating Obsolete]	EMCB
Electrician's Mate, Construction Battalion, Communications [Navy rating Obsolete]	EMCBC
Electrician's Mate, Construction Battalion, Draftsman [Navy rating Obsolete]	EMCBD
Electrician's Mate, Construction Battalion, General [Navy rating Obsolete]	EMCBG
Electrician's Mate, Construction Battalion, Line and Station [Navy rating Obsolete]	EMCBL
Electrician's Mate, Fireman [Navy rating]	EMFN
Electrician's Mate, Fireman Apprentice [Navy rating]	EMFA
Electrician's Mate, First Class [Navy rating]	EM1
Electrician's Mate, Master Chief [Navy rating]	EMCM
Electrician's Mate, Seaman [Navy rating]	EMSN
Electrician's Mate, Seaman Apprentice [Navy rating]	EMSA
Electrician's Mate, Second Class [Navy rating]	EM2
Electrician's Mate, Senior Chief [Navy rating]	EMCS
Electrician's Mate, Ship Repair [Navy rating Obsolete]	EMSR
Electrician's Mate, Ship Repair, General Electrician [Navy rating Obsolete]	EMSRG
Electrician's Mate, Ship Repair, I.C. Repairman [Navy rating Obsolete]	EMSRT
Electrician's Mate, Ship Repair, Shop Electrician [Navy rating Obsolete]	EMSRS
Electrician's Mate, Telephone [Coast Guard rating] [Obsolete]	EMT
Electrician's Mate, Third Class [Navy rating]	EM3
Electricite de France (ECON)	EDF
Electricite de France [Database originator] (NITA)	EDF
Electricite de France [Bibliographic database] [French]	EDF-DOC
Electricity (NTCM)	E
Electricity (WDAA)	ELEC
Electricity	ELECTRCTY
Electricity	ELECTY
Electricity Board [British]	EB
Electricity Board for Northern Ireland (BI)	EBNI
Electricity Commission [British] (DAS)	EC
Electricity Consumers' Council [British]	ECC
Electricity Consumers Resource Council (EA)	ELCON
Electricity Council [British]	EC
Electricity Council Research Center [British] (MCD)	ECRC
Electricity Development Fund [Australia]	EDF
Electricity, Electronics, and Hydraulics School (DNAB)	EE & H
Electricity Market Model [Department of Energy] (GFGA)	EMM
Electricity Supply Association of Australia (EERA)	ESAA
Electricity Supply Board (ACII)	ESB
Electricity Supply Board [Republic of Ireland] (BI)	ESB
Electricity Supply Industry Building Energy Estimating Program [Electricity Council] [British]	ESIBEEP
Electricity Supply Item Name Directory [A publication]	ESIND
Electricity Supply Union [British]	ESU
Electricity Trust of South Australia [State] (EERA)	ETSA
[The] Electrification Council	EC
[The] Electrification Council (EA)	TEC
Electrinium Foundation of America (EA)	EFA
Electro [Record label] [Finland]	Elec

Electro Catheter Corp. [*NASDAQ symbol*] (SAG) .... ECTH
Electro Catheter Corp. [*Associated Press*] (SAG) .... ElCath
Electro Chemical Inds. (Frutarom) Ltd. [*AMEX symbol*] (SAG) .... EIL
Electro Chemical Industries (Frutarom) Ltd. [*Associated Press*] (SAG) ..... ElcChm
Electro Mechanical .... EIMECH
Electro Optical .... EO
Electro Optical / Electronic Warfare [*DoD*] .... EO/EW
Electro Optics Division (ACII) .... ELEOP
Electro Rent [*NASDAQ symbol*] (TTSB) .... ELRC
Electro Rent Corp. [*Associated Press*] (SAG) .... ElcRnt
Electro Rent Corp. [*NASDAQ symbol*] (NQ) .... ELRC
Electro Science Laboratory [*Ohio State University*] .... ESL
Electro Scientific Ind [*NASDAQ symbol*] (TTSB) .... ESIO
Electro Scientific Industries, Inc. [*Associated Press*] (SAG) .... ElcSci
Electro Scientific Industries, Inc. [*NASDAQ symbol*] (NQ) .... ESIO
Electro Sensor Panel [*Toyota*] .... ESP
Electro Sensors [*Associated Press*] (SAG) .... ElcSen
Electro Sensors [*NASDAQ symbol*] (SAG) .... ELSE
Electro-Absorption Avalanche Photodiode [*Instrumentation*] .... EAP
Electroabsorption Photodiode [*Electronics*] (EECA) .... EAPD
Electroacoustic (IAA) .... ELAC
Electro-Acoustic Music Association of Great Britain (EAIO) .... EMAS
Electro-Acoustic Rating System (PDAA) .... EARS
Electroacoustic Systems Laboratory .... EASL
Electroacoustic Torpedo Countermeasure (MCD) .... ETC
Electroacoustic Transmission Measuring System [*Telecommunications*]
(TEL) .... EATMS
Electroacupuncture .... EAP
Electroaerosol Therapy [*Medicine*] .... EAT
Electroanesthesia [*Medicine*] (AAMN) .... EA
Electroantennogram [*Entomology*] .... EAG
Electrocapiogram [*Medicine*] .... ECG
Electrocardioanalyzer [*Medicine*] (AAMN) .... ECA
Electrocardiocorder [*Medicine*] .... ECC
Electrocardiogram [*Also, EK, EKG*] [*Medicine*] .... ECG
Electrocardiogram [*Also, ECG, EKG*] [*Medicine*] .... EK
Electrocardiogram [*Also, ECG, EK*] [*Medicine*] .... EKG
Electrocardiogram Simulator .... EKS
Electrocardiograph [*Also, EKG*] (MSA) .... ECG
Electrocardiograph [*Also, ECG*] (NASA) .... EKG
Electrocardiographic Amplifier .... EA
Electrocardiography and Basal Metabolism Technician [*Navy*] .... ELT
Electrocardioscanner .... ECS
Electro-Catalytic Hyper-Heaters (GNE) .... ECHH
Electro-Catheter [*NASDAQ symbol*] (TTSB) .... ECTH
Electro-Catheter Corp. [*NASDAQ symbol*] (NQ) .... ECTH
Electrocerebral Inactivity (MAE) .... ECI
Electrocerebral Silence [*Medicine*] (CPH) .... ECS
Electrochemical [*or Electrochemistry*] .... EC
Electrochemical and Electrical Discharge Machining (PDAA) .... ECDM
Electrochemical Cathodes (MCD) .... ECC
Electrochemical Cell (MCD) .... ECELL
Electrochemical, Chemical, Electrochemical [*Chemical mechanism*] .... ECE
Electrochemical Concentration Cell (MCD) .... ECC
Electrochemical Deburring .... ECD
Electrochemical Deburring (IAA) .... ECDB
Electro-Chemical Degradation .... ECD
Electrochemical Depolarization CO_2 [*Carbon Dioxide*] (**Module**) .... EDC (M)
Electrochemical Depolarized Carbon Dioxide (Module) [*NASA*] (NASA).... EDC(M)
Electrochemical Deposition [*Metallurgy*] .... ECD
Electrochemical Detector [*Instrumentation*] .... ED
Electrochemical Diffused (IAA) .... ED
Electrochemical Diffused-Collector Transistor .... ECDC
Electrochemical Diffused-Transistor (IAA) .... ECDT
Electrochemical Discharge Grinding [*Manufacturing term*] .... ECDG
Electrochemical Discharge Machining [*Manufacturing term*] (IAA) .... ECDM
Electro-Chemical Engine .... ECE
Electrochemical Equipment Committee [*Military*] .... EEC
Electrochemical Equivalent (IAA) .... ECE
Electrochemical Equivalent (IDOE) .... z
Electrochemical Fluorination [*Chemical synthesis*] .... ECF
Electrochemical Forming [*Manufacturing term*] (IAA) .... ECF
Electrochemical Fuel Cell .... EFC
Electrochemical Grinding (IEEE) .... ECG
Electrochemical Honing [*Manufacturing term*] .... ECH
Electrochemical Ind(Frutarom) [*AMEX symbol*] (TTSB) .... EIF
Electrochemical Industries (Frutarom) Ltd. [*AMEX symbol*] (SPSG) .... EIF
Electrochemical Machining .... ECM
Electrochemical Photocapacitance Spectroscopy .... EPS
Electrochemical Plating and Honing [*Manufacturing term*] (IAA) .... EPH
Electrochemical Potential Gradient .... ECPOG
Electrochemical Potentiokinetic Reactivation [*Metallurgical test*] .... EPR
Electrochemical Quartz-Crystal Microbalance [*Biochemistry*] .... EQCM
Electrochemical Reaction .... ECR
Electrochemical Relaxation Methods .... ERM
Electrochemical Society (EA) .... ECS
Electrochemical Society .... ES
Electrochemical Time Indicator [*Army*] (MCD) .... ETI
Electrochemical Turning [*Manufacturing term*] .... ECT
Electrochemical Unit .... ECU
Electrochemically Modulated Infrared Reflectance Spectroscopy .... EMIRS
Electrochemically Regenerable Carbon Dioxide Absorber (NASA) .... ERCA
Electrochemichromic [*Optoelectronics*] .... ECC
Electrochemiluminescence .... ECL
Electrochemistry .... ELECTROCHEM

Electrochromic [*Optics*] .... EC
Electrochromic Display [*Instrumentation*] .... ECD
Electrocoating .... EC
Electrocon International, Inc. [*NASDAQ symbol*] (NQ) .... EPLT
Electrocon Intl. [*NASDAQ symbol*] (TTSB) .... EPLTF
Electroconductivity .... EC
Electro-Continuously Variable Transmission [*Subaru*] [*Automotive
engineering*] .... ECVT
Electroconvulsive Shock .... ECS
Electroconvulsive Therapy [*or Treatment*] [*Medicine*] .... ECT
Electrocorticogram [*Neurology*] (DAVI) .... ECC
Electrocorticogram [*or Electrocorticographic*] .... ECOG
Electrode (MSA) .... ELCTD
Electrode Dark Current .... EDC
Electrode Electrostatic Precipitator .... EEP
Electrode Film Barrier .... EFB
Electrode Heater Kit .... EHK
Electrode per Bit (EECA) .... E/B
Electrode Plasma [*Energy source*] .... EP
Electrode Potential .... E
Electrode Signalling [*British military*] (DMA) .... E/S
Electrode Track .... ET
Electrodeless Discharge Lamp .... EDL
Electrodeless Discharge Tube .... EDT
Electrodeposition (EG) .... EDP
Electrodeposition Memo .... EM
Electrodermal Audiometry [*Otolaryngology*] .... EDA
Electrodermal Diagnosis [*Controversial medical technique*] .... EDD
Electrodermal Response .... EDR
Electrodesiccation [*Medicine*] .... EDN
Electrodesiccation and Curettage [*Medicine*] (AAMN) .... ED & C
Electrodiagnosis [*Medicine*] .... EDX
Electrodialysis [*Medicine*] .... ED
Electrodialysis Reversing .... EDR
Electrodynamic (DEN) .... ED
Electrodynamic Balance [*Physical chemistry*] .... EDB
Electrodynamic Explorer [*NASA*] .... EE
Electrodynamic Gradient Freeze [*Crystal growing technique*] .... EDG
Electrodynamic Levitation (PDAA) .... EDL
Electrodynamic Suspension [*Railway technology*] (PS) .... EDS
Electro-Dynamic Venturi (PDAA) .... EDV
Electrodynogram [*For evaluation of walking gait*] .... EDG
Electroencephalic Audiometry [*Medicine*] (MAE) .... EEA
Electroencephalic Response [*Medicine*] (MAE) .... EER
Electroencephalogram [*or Electroencephalography*] [*Medicine*] .... EEG
Electroencephalographic Technologist [*Neurology*] (DAVI) .... EEG T
Electroencephalography Technician [*Navy*] .... ENC
Electroencephalophony [*Medical electronics*] (IEEE) .... EEP
Electroendosmosis [*Analytical biochemistry*] .... EEO
Electro-Epitaxial Crystal Growth [*Materials processing*] .... ECG
Electroexplosive Device .... EED
Electroflotation (PDAA) .... EF
Electrofluid Converter .... EFC
Electrofluid Dynamic [*Process*] (MCD) .... EFD
Electrofluidized Bed [*Chemical engineering*] .... EFB
Electro-Flux Remelting [*Metal industry*] .... EFR
Electrogalvanized Steel .... EGS
Electrogalvanizing [*Automotive engineering*] .... EG
Electrogas Welding .... EGW
Electrogasdynamic [*Generator*] .... EGD
Electrogastrogram [*Medicine*] .... EGG
Electro-Generated Chemiluminescene (PDAA) .... EGCL
Electroglas, Inc. [*NASDAQ symbol*] (SAG) .... EGLS
Electroglas Inc. [*Associated Press*] (SAG) .... Elctrgls
Electrogram (MAE) .... EGM
Electrograph (KSC) .... EOG
Electrographic Recorder (CAAL) .... EGR
Electrographic Seizure [*Neurophysiology*] .... EGS
Electrohemodynamics .... EHD
Electrohome Ltd. [*Toronto Stock Exchange symbol*] .... EL
Electrohydraulic [*Nuclear energy*] (NRCH) .... EH
Electrohydraulic (KSC) .... ELECTHYDR
Electrohydraulic .... ELHYD
Electrohydraulic Actuator .... EHA
Electrohydraulic Control (NRCH) .... EHC
Electrohydraulic Forming .... EHF
electrohydraulic Fragmentation [*Medicine*] (DAVI) .... EHF
Electrohydraulic Lithotripsy [*Medicine*] (HCT) .... EHL
Electrohydraulic Lithotriptor [*Nephrology and urology*] (DAVI) .... EHL
Electrohydraulic Motor .... EHM
Electro-Hydraulic Proportional Control [*Automotive engineering*] .... EHPC
Electrohydraulic Pulse Motor .... EHPM
Electrohydraulic Servo Valve (MCD) .... EHSV
Electrohydraulic Valve (MCD) .... EHV
Electrohydraulic Valve Actuator (IAA) .... EHVA
Electrohydrodimerization [*Organic chemistry*] .... EHD
Electrohydrodynamic Convection [*Physics*] .... EHC
Electrohydrodynamic Heat Pipe [*NASA*] .... EHDHP
Electrohydrodynamic Ionization .... EH
Electrohydrodynamic Ionization Mass Spectrometry .... EHMS
Electroimmunoassay [*Clinical medicine*] .... EIA
Electroimmunodiffusion [*Clinical medicine*] (MAE) .... EID
Electrojet (IAA) .... EJ
Electrokinetic Chromatography .... EKC
Electrokinetic Sonic Amplitude [*Determination of electrokinetic potential*] ...... ESA

Electrokymogram	EKY
Electroless Nickel	EN
Electroless Nickel Plating	ENP
Electrologic Language (IAA)	ELAN
Electrologist	ELCTRLGST
Electroluminescence	EL
Electroluminescent (IDOE)	EL
Electroluminescent Diode	ELD
Electroluminescent Display [Computer science]	ELD
Electroluminescent Ferroelectric	ELF
Electroluminescent Ferroelectric Cell	ELFC
Electroluminescent Quantum Counter	ELQC
Electroluminescent Runway Marking System [Aviation]	ERMS
Electroluminescent Vertical Indication System	ELVIS
Electroluminescent-Photoconductive (MCD)	EL-PC
Electroluminescent-Photoelectric	ELPE
Electroluminescent-Photoresponsive (IAA)	ELPR
Electrolux AB [NASDAQ symbol] (NQ)	ELUX
Electrolux AB [Associated Press] (SAG)	EluxAB
Electrolux AB CI'B'ADR [NASDAQ symbol] (TTSB)	ELUXY
Electrolysis	ELCTRYLS
Electrolysis (IAA)	ELECTROL
Electrolysis Cell (SSD)	EC
Electrolysis Society of America [Later, SCME] (EA)	ESA
Electrolyte	ELCTLT
Electrolyte (KSC)	ELECT
Electrolyte (IAA)	ELECTRL
Electrolyte and Steroid-Produced Cardiopathy Characterized by Necrosis [Medicine]	ESCN
Electrolyte Imbalance [Physiology]	EI
Electrolyte Insulator Semiconductor (IAA)	EIS
Electrolyte Replacement with Glucose [Medicine] (MEDA)	ERG
Electrolytes [Medicine] (BABM)	Lytes
Electrolytes on Urine Spot [Test] [Biochemistry] (DAVI)	EL-SPT
Electrolytic	ELECTL
Electrolytic Biological Oxygen Demand	E/BOD
Electrolytic Capacitor (DEN)	ELCO
Electrolytic Chloride Generator (DWSG)	ECG
Electrolytic Conductivity Detector	ELCD
Electrolytic Display (PDAA)	ELD
Electrolytic Fused-Salt Process	EFSP
Electrolytic Grinding (IEEE)	ELG
Electrolytic Manganese Dioxide [For use in batteries]	EMD
Electrolytic Oxidation	EO
Electrolytic Oxygen Generator (DNAB)	EOG
Electrolytic Plunge Grinder	EPG
Electrolytic Polishing (MCD)	ELP
Electrolytic Reactants Production System (IAA)	ERPS
Electrolytic Refining and Smelting Company [Australia Commercial firm]	ERS
Electrolytic Sewage Treatment (IAA)	EST
Electrolytic Tinning Line (PDAA)	ETL
Electrolytic Tough-Pitch [Copper grade]	ETP
Electrolytic-in-Process-Dressing [Optics manufacturing] (RDA)	ELID
Electro-Machine Fixture (MCD)	EMF
Electromagnet Radiance [Astronomy] (BARN)	L
Electromagnetic	ELECTMG
Electromagnetic	EM
Electromagnetic Accelerometer [Navigation]	EMA
Electromagnetic Acoustic Transducer [Engineering]	EMAT
Electromagnetic Acoustic Transducer Testing (PDAA)	EMAT
Electromagnetic Activity Receiver (DNAB)	EAR
Electromagnetic Air Launch System	EMALS
Electromagnetic Amplifying Lens	EAL
Electromagnetic Analysis (NASA)	EMA
Electromagnetic Bone Stimulator [Orthopedics] (DAVI)	EBI
Electromagnetic Capability	EMC
Electromagnetic Centimeter Gram Second (IAA)	EMCGS
Electromagnetic Compatibility	EMC
Electromagnetic Compatibility Advisory Board (MCD)	EMCAB
Electromagnetic Compatibility Analysis Center [Illinois Institute of Technology] [Annapolis, MD]	ECAC
Electro-Magnetic Compatibility Data Acquisition System [Telecommunications] (PDAA)	EMCDAS
Electromagnetic Compatibility Figure of Merit [Telecommunications] (TEL)	EMCFOM
Electromagnetic Compatibility Frequency Analysis (SSD)	EMCFA
Electromagnetic Compatibility Operational System (PDAA)	EMCOPS
Electromagnetic Compatibility Program [Air Force]	ECP
Electromagnetic Compatibility Program [Air Force] (AFM)	EMCP
Electromagnetic Compatibility Standardization [Program] [Telecommunications] (IEEE)	EMCS
Electromagnetic Compatibility Test Plan (IEEE)	EMCTP
Electromagnetic Containerless Processing [Materials processing]	ECP
Electromagnetic Contamination (MCD)	EMCON
Electromagnetic Control	EMC
Electromagnetic Control Compatibility	EMCC
Electromagnetic Cover and Deception (MCD)	EC & D
Electromagnetic Cyclotron	EMC
Electromagnetic Defense (CAAL)	EMD
Electromagnetic Dent Removal [Aviation]	EDR
Electro-Magnetic Design System [Computer simulation]	EMDS
Electromagnetic Distance Measurement [Geology]	EDM
Electromagnetic Effect	EME
Electromagnetic Effects Capability (NASA)	EMEC
Electromagnetic Effects Compatibility [NASA] (NASA)	EMEC

Electromagnetic Effects Laboratory [Army] (RDA)	EEL
Electromagnetic Emission Control (IEEE)	ECON
Electromagnetic Energy (IEEE)	EME
Electromagnetic Energy Environment Criteria [Army] (AABC)	EEEC
Electromagnetic Energy Policy Alliance (EA)	EEPA
Electromagnetic Environment (MCD)	EME
Electromagnetic Environment Analysis	EEA
Electromagnetic Environment Effects	E³
Electromagnetic Environment Experiment [NASA] (MCD)	EEE
Electromagnetic Environment Generator	EMEG
Electromagnetic Environment Recorder (MCD)	EMER
Electromagnetic Environment Simulator	EES
Electromagnetic Environment Synthesizer (NVT)	ENSYN
Electromagnetic Environment Synthesizer (DNAB)	ENSYS
Electromagnetic Environmental Effect (CAAL)	E³
Electromagnetic Environmental Effects	E3
Electromagnetic Environmental Test Facility [Fort Huachuca, AZ] [Army] (AABC)	EMETF
Electromagnetic Field	ELF
Electromagnetic Field	EMF
Electromagnetic Flow [or Florometer] [Cardiology]	EMF
Electromagnetic Flow Probe [Analytical biochemistry]	EMFP
Electromagnetic Flowmeter (MAE)	EMF
Electromagnetic Flowmeter	EMFM
Electromagnetic Force [Physics] (DAVI)	E
Electromagnetic Force (NASA)	EMF
Electromagnetic Form Factor	EMFF
Electromagnetic Frequency	EMF
Electromagnetic Gun Weapon System	EMGWS
Electromagnetic Gyro	EMG
Electromagnetic Impulse (IAA)	EMI
Electromagnetic Impulse Capability	EMIC
Electromagnetic Impulse Deicing [System under development by NASA]	EID
Electromagnetic Induction Tweeter	EMIT
Electromagnetic Instrument Test System (MCD)	EMITS
Electromagnetic Intelligence	ELINT
Electromagnetic Intelligence	ELMINT
Electromagnetic Intelligence (MSA)	EMINT
Electromagnetic Intelligence Collection System	EICS
Electromagnetic Intelligence System	EIS
Electromagnetic Intelligence System	EMIS
Electromagnetic Interface	EMI
Electromagnetic Interference	EI
Electromagnetic Interference	EMI
Electromagnetic Interference (SAA)	EMIT
Electromagnetic Interference and Compatibility	EMIC
Electromagnetic Interference Control (IAA)	EIC
Electromagnetic Interference Control Engineer (IEEE)	EMICE
Electromagnetic Interference Control Group (AAG)	EICG
Electromagnetic Interference Test System [Navy] (MCD)	EMITS
Electromagnetic Interference Testing	EIT
Electromagnetic Interference Testing	EMIT
Electromagnetic Intrusion Detector (NVT)	EMID
Electromagnetic Isotope Separation [Uranium enrichment]	EMIS
Electromagnetic Laboratory [NASA] (GFGA)	EML
Electromagnetic Launcher [Military] (SDI)	EML
Electromagnetic Levitator	EML
Electromagnetic Measurement (IEEE)	EMM
Electromagnetic Molecular Electronic Resonance (PDAA)	EMER
Electromagnetic Motion Detector (PDAA)	EMD
Electromagnetic Moving Coil and Neutralized Winding (IAA)	EMN
Electromagnetic Performance Information Research (PDAA)	EMPIRE
Electromagnetic Performance of Air and Ship Systems	EMPASS
Electromagnetic Phenomena Interference Repository (PDAA)	EMPIRE
Electromagnetic Position Sensor	EPS
Electromagnetic Power [or Pulse]	EMP
Electromagnetic Principle Investigators Council [An association]	EPIC
Electromagnetic Propagation	EMP
Electromagnetic Propagation Working Group [Army]	EPWG
Electro-Magnetic Pulse	EMP
Electromagnetic Pulse Radiation Environment Simulator for Ships [Navy] (MCD)	EMPRESS
Electromagnetic Pulse Simulator (MCD)	EMPS
Electromagnetic Quiet	EMQ
Electromagnetic Radiation (AFM)	EMR
Electromagnetic Radiation Advisory Council	ERAC
Electromagnetic Radiation Effect [Military]	EMRE
Electromagnetic Radiation Generator	EMRG
Electromagnetic Radiation Generator	ERG
Electromagnetic Radiation Hazard (MCD)	EMRH
Electromagnetic Radiation Management Advisory Council [US Government]	ERMAC
Electromagnetic Radiation Operational	EMRO
Electromagnetic Radiation Project Office [Naval Medical Research and Development Command] [Bethesda, MD]	EMRPO
Electromagnetic Radiation Source Elimination (NVT)	ERASE
Electromagnetic Radiation System (MCD)	EMRS
Electro-Magnetic Release Unit (PDAA)	EMRU
Electromagnetic Relief Valve [Engineering instrumentation] (IAA)	EMAV
Electromagnetic Relief Valve [Engineering instrumentation]	ERV
Electromagnetic Resonance (WDAA)	EMR
Electromagnetic Riveting (PDAA)	EMR
Electromagnetic Sci [NASDAQ symbol] (TTSB)	ELMG
Electromagnetic Sciences, Inc. [Associated Press] (SAG)	Elctmg
Electromagnetic Sciences, Inc. [NASDAQ symbol] (NQ)	ELMG

Electromagnetic Servoactuator System (NASA)	EMSS
Electromagnetic Simulation Unit (MCD)	EMSU
Electromagnetic Spectrum (NITA)	EMS
Electromagnetic Spectrum Allocation Request [Army] (RDA)	ESAR
Electromagnetic Storage	ES
Electromagnetic Submarine [Navy]	EMS
Electromagnetic Surveillance [Air Force]	EMS
Electromagnetic Susceptibility (IEEE)	EMS
Electromagnetic Suspension [Railway technology] (PS)	EMS
Electromagnetic Switching (IEEE)	ES
Electromagnetic Systems Laboratories, Inc.	ESL
Electromagnetic Technology	EMTECH
Electromagnetic Test and Evaluation Data (IAA)	EMTED
Electromagnetic Test Environment	EMTE
Electromagnetic Test Environment (MCD)	ETE
Electromagnetic Test Environment Data System (MCD)	EMTEDS
Electromagnetic Test Environment Data System	ETEDS
Electromagnetic Thickness Tool [Gas well]	ETT
Electromagnetic Thrust [Propulsion for ship or submarine]	EMT
Electromagnetic Unit	EMU
Electromagnetic Vector Potential [Physics] (BARN)	EVP
Electromagnetic Velocity (KSC)	EMV
Electro-Magnetic Velocity Profiler [Oceanography] (MSC)	EMVP
Electromagnetic Vibrating Feeder	EVF
Electromagnetic Voltage (CAAL)	EMV
Electromagnetic Volume (IAA)	EMV
Electromagnetic Vulnerability	EMV
Electromagnetic Warfare (MCD)	EMW
Electromagnetic Warfare and Communications Laboratory	EWCL
Electromagnetic Wave	EMW
Electromagnetic Wave Amplification by Stimulated Emission of Radiation	EWASER
Electromagnetic Wave Energy Converter [Solar energy conversion]	EWEC
Electromagnetic Wave Filter	EWF
Electromagnetic Wave Form	EMWF
Electromagnetic Window	EMW
Electro-Magnetically Controlled Differential [Powertrain] [Automotive engineering]	EMCD
Electromagnetically Induced Transparency [Optics]	EIT
Electromagnetically Operated Valve (NRCH)	EMOV
Electromantle	EMA
Electromantle Extraction	EME
Electromatic Speed Meter (IAA)	ESM
Electromechanical	ELCTRMCHNCL
Electromechanical (KSC)	ELECTMECH
Electromechanical	ELMCH
Electromechanical (NASA)	ELMECH
Electromechanical	EM
Electromechanical [JETDS nomenclature]	J
Electromechanical Averaging Circuit	EMAC
Electromechanical Control Diagram (MCD)	EMCD
Electromechanical Dissociation	EMD
Electromechanical Laboratories (MUGU)	EML
Electromechanical Linear Actuator	EMLA
Electromechanical Machining [Manufacturing term]	EMM
Electromechanical Mockup (KSC)	EMM
Electromechanical Optical (AAG)	EMO
Electromechanical Potentiokinetic Reactivation Test [Nuclear energy] (NRCH)	EPR
Electromechanical Power [or Pulse]	EMP
Electromechanical Relay [Power switchgear] (IEEE)	EMR
Electromechanical Research (IEEE)	EMR
Electromechanical Slope Computer (MAE)	ESC
Electromechanical Stop Clock	EMSC
Electromechanical Stop Clock	ESC
Electromechanical Team	EMT
Electromechanical Technology	EMT
Electromechanical Test (NASA)	EMT
Electromechanochemical	EMC
Electromedical	ELCMED
Electro-Medical Trade Association [British] (BI)	EMTA
Electrometallurgical	ELCMTLG
Electrometer (DEN)	ELT
Electromicroscopic [or Electromicroscopy]	EM
Electromolecular Instrument Space Simulator	EMISS
Electromolecular Propulsion [Electrochemistry]	EMP
Electromotive Difference of Potential	EMDP
Electro-Motive Division [General Motors Corp.]	EMD
Electromotive Force [Symbol] [See also EMF, V Electrochemistry]	E
Electromotive Force [Electrochemistry] (IAA)	ELF
Electromotive Force [See also E, V] [Electrochemistry]	EMF
Electromotive Force (IDOE)	emf
Electromotive Force [Symbol] [See also E, EMF Electrochemistry] (DEN)	V
Electromotive Surface [Electrochemistry]	EMS
Electro-Motorische Kraft [Electromotive Force] [German]	EMK
Electromyelography [or Electromyelogram] [Neurology] (DAVI)	EMG
Electromyogram [or Electromyographic, Electromyography]	EMG
Electromyogram Sensors [For control of artificial limbs]	EMGORS
Electromyosignal [Computer science]	EMS
Electromyostimulation [Medicine] (DAVI)	EMS
Electron [A nuclear particle]	e
Electron [A nuclear particle]	ELCTRN
Electron	ELCTRN
Electron (WDAA)	ELEC
Electron [A nuclear particle]	ELTRN

Electron Accelerator System (IAA)	EAS
Electron Affinity [Chemistry]	EA
Electron Arc Furnace (IAA)	EAF
Electron Backscattering Pattern (MCD)	EBSP
Electron Beam	EB
Electron Beam Accelerator	EBA
Electron Beam Access Method (PDAA)	EBAM
Electron Beam Activated Switch (PDAA)	EBAS
Electron Beam Coating	EBC
Electron Beam Control	EBC
Electron Beam Control Electronics	EBCE
Electron Beam Curing [Chemical technology]	EBC
Electron Beam Cutting [Engraving] [Welding]	EBC
Electron Beam Engraving System (NITA)	EBES
Electron Beam Evaporation Equipment	EBEE
Electron Beam Evaporation Module	EBEM
Electron Beam Evaporator	EBE
Electron Beam Fusion Accelerator	EBFA
Electron Beam Generator	EBG
Electron Beam Gun	EBG
Electron Beam Inert Gas (PDAA)	EBIG
Electron Beam Ion Source (IEEE)	EBIS
Electron Beam Ion Trap [Developed at Lawrence Livermore and Lawrence Berkeley National Laboratories] [Atomic physics]	EBIT
Electron Beam Ionization of Semiconductor Devices (PDAA)	EBIRD
Electron Beam Lithography (IAA)	EBL
Electron Beam Lithography Facility [British]	EBLF
Electron Beam Machining [Manufacturing term]	EBM
Electron Beam Melting (IAA)	EBM
Electron Beam Membrane Light Modulator [Army] (MCD)	EBMLM
Electron Beam Method	EBM
Electron Beam Microanalysis	EBM
Electron Beam Microanalysis	EMB
Electron Beam Microfabricator (IAA)	EBMF
Electron Beam Mode Discharge	EBMD
Electron Beam Multiplier (IAA)	EBM
Electron Beam Parametric Amplifier	EBPA
Electron Beam Pattern Generator	EBPG
Electron Beam Readout	EBR
Electron Beam Recorder [or Recording]	EBR
Electron Beam Regulator	EBR
Electron Beam Remelting (IAA)	EBR
Electron Beam Semiconductor	EBS
Electron Beam System	EBS
Electron Beam [Fluorescence] Technique	EBT
Electron Beam Tomography [Imaging science]	EBT
Electron Beam Transmission	EBT
Electron Beam Welding (MUGU)	EBW
Electron Beam Welding - High Vacuum	EBW-HV
Electron Beam Welding - Medium Vacuum	EBW-MV
Electron Beam Welding - Nonvacuum	EBW-NV
Electron Beam-Induced Oxide Charging	EBIOC
Electron Binding Energy	EBE
Electron Capture [Radioactivity]	EC
Electron Capture Gas-Liquid Chromatography	ECGLC
Electron Channeling Pattern (MCD)	ECP
Electron Charge (IDOE)	e
Electron Coupled (DEN)	EC
Electron Cyclotron Harmonic [Planetary Physics]	ECH
Electron Cyclotron Heating [Nuclear energy]	ECH
Electron Cyclotron Resonance (IEEE)	ECR
Electron Cyclotron Resonance Heating (MCD)	ECRH
Electron Decay Profile	EDP
Electron Decay Rate	EDR
Electron Dense Particles [Chemistry] (DAVI)	EDP
Electron Density Map [Crystallography]	EDM
Electron Device (MCD)	ED
Electron Devices Data Service [National Institute of Standards and Technology]	EDDS
Electron Devices Laboratory	EDL
Electron Devices Society (EA)	EDS
Electron Diffraction	ED
Electron Diffraction Instrument	EDI
Electron Diffraction Pattern	EDP
Electron Dipole-Dipole Polarization	EDDP
Electron Dipole-Dipole Reservoir (NASA)	EDDR
Electron Donor Acceptor Complex	EDAC
Electron Donor-Acceptor	EDA
Electron Drift Instrument	EDI
Electron Electron Double Resonance [Physics]	ELDOR
Electron Energy Loss Fine Structure	EELFS
Electron Energy Loss Spectroscopy [Also, ELS]	EELS
Electron Energy Loss Spectroscopy [Also, EELS]	ELS
Electron Engineering Co. of California, Santa Ana, CA [Library symbol Library of Congress] (LCLS)	CStaE
Electron Gun (OA)	EG
Electron Image Animation System [Computer science]	EIAS
Electron Impact [Mass spectrometry]	EI
Electron Impact [or Induced] Desorption	EID
Electron Impact Emission Spectroscopy [Photovoltaic energy systems]	EIES
Electron Impact Mass Spectrometry	EIMS
Electron Impact Selected Ion Monitoring [Instrumentation]	EISIM
Electron Injection LASER	EIL
Electron Ionization [Spectrometry]	EI
Electron Ionization Cross Section	EIC

Electron Ionization Mass Spectrometry	EIMS
Electron Irradiation and Neutron Irradiation (IAA)	EINI
Electron Kilovolt (EY)	eKv
Electron LASER Facility [Physics]	ELF
Electron Linear Accelerator	ELA
Electron Loss Near Edge Structure [Electron microscopy]	ELNES
Electron Manual Metal Arc (OA)	EMMA
Electron Megavolt (EY)	eMv
Electron Microprobe	EM
Electron Microprobe	EMP
Electron Microprobe Analysis [Also, EMA]	EMPA
Electron Microprobe Analyzer [Also, EMPA]	EMA
Electron Microprobe X-Ray Analyzer	EMX
Electron Microprobe X-Ray Analyzer	EMXA
Electron Microprobe X-Ray Fluorescence	EMXRF
Electron Microscope	EM
Electron Microscope Surface Area (PDAA)	EMSA
Electron Microscope Technique Meeting (PDAA)	EMTM
Electron Microscope Tomography	EMT
Electron Microscopy (MAE)	EMC
Electron Microscopy [Organic chemistry] (DAVI)	E-MICR
Electron Microscopy and Microanalysis (IEEE)	EMMA
Electron Microscopy Center for Materials Research [Argonne, IL] [Argonne National Laboratory] [Department of Energy] (GRD)	EMC
Electron Microscopy Congress	EMCON
Electron Microscopy Society of America (EA)	EMSA
Electron Mirror Microscope (IAA)	EMM
Electron Multiplex Switch	EMS
Electron News Service [Evans Economics, Inc.] [Information service or system] (CRD)	ENS
Electron N-Type Semiconductor Material	N
Electron Optic Tracking System (MUGU)	EOTS
Electron Optical Recording Facility	EORF
Electron Paramagnetic	EP
Electron Paramagnetic Resonance [Also, ESR] [Physics]	EPR
Electron Paramagnetic Resonance Spectroscopy	EPRS
Electron Photon	EP
Electron Photon Cascade	EPC
Electron Photon Interaction	EPI
Electron Plasma Oscillation [Astrophysics]	EPO
Electron Plasma Wave [Physics]	EPW
Electron Polar Zone	EPZ
Electron Probe Analysis Society of America [Later, MAS] (EA)	EPASA
Electron Probe Analyzer	EPA
Electron Probe Microanalysis [Also, EPMA]	EPM
Electron Probe Microanalysis [Also, EPM]	EPMA
Electron Probe X-Ray Microanalyzer	EPXMA
Electron/Proton (MCD)	E/P
Electron Radiography (IAA)	ERG
Electron Readout Measurement (MCD)	EROM
Electron Reflection Coefficient	ERC
Electron Ring Accelerator	ERA
Electron Scan Antenna [FAA]	ESA
Electron Speckle Pattern Interferometry	ESPI
Electron Spectrographic Diffraction	ESD
Electron Spectroscopic Imaging	ESI
Electron Spectroscopy for Chemical Analysis	ESCA
Electron Spin Echo [Physics]	ESE
Electron Spin Echo Envelope Modulation [Physics]	ESEEM
Electron Spin Echo Modulation [Physics]	ESEM
Electron Spin Polarization	ESP
Electron Spin Resonance [Also, EPR] [Physics]	ESR
Electron Spin Spectra [Physics] (IAA)	ESS
Electron Steady-State Fermi Level	ESSFL
Electron Stream Potential (MSA)	ESP
Electron Synchrotron [Nuclear energy]	ES
Electron Temperature [Plasma physics] (OA)	TE
Electron Temperature Probe	ETP
Electron Transfer	ET
Electron Transfer Ionization Mass Spectroscopy (MCD)	ETIMS
Electron Transfer [or Transporting] Particle	ETP
Electron Transmission Spectroscopy	ETS
Electron Transparent Zone [Biochemistry]	ETZ
Electron Transport Rate [Physical chemistry]	ETR
Electron Transport System	ETS
Electron Trapping Optical Memory [Computer science]	ETOM
Electron [or Electronic] Tube (MCD)	ET
Electron Tube Klystron	ETK
Electron Tube Management Group (SAA)	ETMG
Electron Tube Panel	ETP
Electron Tube Rectifier	ETR
Electron Tube, Triode	ETT
Electron Unit	EU
Electron Volt	eV
Electron Yield	EY
Electron Yield Measurement	EYM
Electron Yield Measurement System	EYMS
Electron-Assisted Chemical Vapor Deposition [Coating technology]	EACVD
Electron-Beam Addressed Light Modulator (PDAA)	EALM
Electron-Beam-Addressed Memory [Air Force]	EBAM
Electron-Beam-Induced Current [Photovoltaic energy systems]	EBIC
Electron-Beam-Induced Voltage [Photovoltaic energy systems]	EBIV
Electron-Bombarded Semiconductor	EBS
Electron-Bombardment (SAA)	E-B
Electron-Bombardment Furnace	EBF

Electron-Bombardment Ion Thrustor	EIT
Electron-Bombardment Silicon (KSC)	EBS
Electron-Bombardment Vehicle	EBV
Electron-Bombardment-Induced Conductivity	EBIC
Electron-Bombardment-Induced Conductivity	EBICON
Electron-Bombardment-Induced Response	EBIR
Electron-Capture Detection [Instrumentation]	ECD
Electron-Capture Gas Chromatography	ECGC
Electron-Capture Negative Chemical Ionization [Spectrometry]	EC-NCI
Electron-Coupled Control (IAA)	ECC
Electron-Coupled Oscillator	ECO
Electron-Coupled Oscillator (IDOE)	eco
Electron-Dense Amorphous Material [Medicine] (DMAA)	EDAM
Electron-Dense Mitochondrial Inclusions [Oncology]	EDMI
Electron-Dense Region [in Microorganisms]	EDR
Electronegative Gas Detector	EGAD
Electronet Information Systems, Inc. [Information service or system] (IID)	EIS
Electroneurodiagnostic Technologist (HCT)	ENDT
Electroneuromyographic (PDAA)	ENMG
Electron-Hole Drop [Semiconductor physics]	EHD
Electron-Hole Liquid Model [Physics]	EHL
Electron-Hole Pairs (ACRL)	EHP
Electron-Hole Potential Method [Physics]	EHP
Electronic [Automotive engineering]	E
Electronic (AABC)	ELCT
Electronic (VRA)	elctr
Electronic (NASA)	ELEC
Electronic (MCD)	ELECT
Electronic	ELECT
Electronic (MSA)	ELEK
Electronic	ELTRNC
Electronic Access Project	EAP
Electronic Access to Medieval Manuscripts	EAMM
Electronic Accounting Machine [Computer science]	EAM
Electronic Acquisition Systems Instrumentation [Vehicle testing] [Automotive engineering]	EASI
Electronic Actuation System	EAS
Electronic Address Light Modulator	EALM
Electronic Aerospace Systems Convention	EASTCON
Electronic Air Cleaner	EAC
Electronic Air Control [Automotive engineering]	EAC
Electronic Air Control Valve [Automotive emissions]	EACV
Electronic Air Inlet Controller (MCD)	EAIC
Electronic Air Particle Separator	EAPS
Electronic Air Suspension [Automotive engineering]	EAS
Electronic Air Switching [Automotive engineering]	EAS
Electronic Altitude Sensor (DNAB)	EAS
Electronic Analog Resolver (WDAA)	EAR
Electronic Analog Simulating Equipment [Computer science]	EASE
Electronic and Aerospace Report (IAA)	EAR
Electronic and Chaff Jamming (IEEE)	JAFF
Electronic and Control Technology (NITA)	ECT
Electronic and Desktop Publishing	EP
Electronic and Editing Layout System [Telecommunications] (DGA)	EELS
Electronic and Geodetic Ranging Satellite (IAA)	EGRS
Electronic Angle Tracking (PDAA)	EAT
Electronic Anti-Intrusion Device (DNAB)	EAID
Electronic Area Support Base [Air Force]	EASB
Electronic Array (IAA)	EA
Electronic Article Surveillance	EAS
Electronic Arts	EA
Electronic Arts [Commercial firm] (NQ)	ERTS
Electronic Arts [NASDAQ symbol] (TTSB)	ERTS
Electronic Arts, Inc. [Associated Press] (SAG)	ElcArt
Electronic Arts, Inc. [NASDAQ symbol] (SAG)	ERTS
Electronic Assembly	EA
Electronic Asset Control Center (AFM)	EACC
Electronic Assisted Solicitation Exchange (AAGC)	EASE
Electronic Associates, Inc. [NYSE symbol] (SPSG)	EA
Electronic Associates, Inc.	EAI
Electronic Associates, Inc. [Associated Press] (SAG)	ElecAs
Electronic Associates Limited (NITA)	EAL
Electronic Attitude and Direction Indicator	EADI
Electronic Attitude Director Indicator	EADI
Electronic Audio Recognition	EAR
Electronic Audit Gauger	EAGER
Electronic Aural Responder (IAA)	EAR
Electronic Autocollimator [Optics] (IAA)	EAC
Electronic Automatic Chart System (OA)	EACS
Electronic Automatic Exchange [See also ESS] [General Telephone & Electronics] [Telecommunications]	EAX
Electronic Automatic Machinery	EAM
Electronic Automatic Switch (IAA)	EAS
Electronic Automatic Switch (ECII)	EAX
Electronic Automatic Temperature Control [Automotive engineering]	EATC
Electronic Automatic Transaxle [Automotive engineering]	EATX
Electronic Band Spectra	EBS
[The] Electronic Banking Economics Society [New York, NY] (EA)	THEBES
Electronic Batch Control	EBC
Electronic Batch Record	EBR
Electronic Beam [Electronics]	EB
Electronic Beam Activated Switch (IAA)	EBAS
Electronic Bearing Line [RADAR technology]	EBL
Electronic Bearing Marker [Navigation] (OA)	EBM
Electronic Bearing-Time Recorder	EBTR

Electronic Benefits Transfer [Department of Agriculture] (GFGA) ...... EBT
Electronic Bombarded Silicon ...... EBS
Electronic Book Technologies, Inc. (PCM) ...... EBT
Electronic Bourse (ECON) ...... EB
Electronic Brake Control Module [Automotive engineering] ...... EBCM
Electronic Brake-Force Distribution [Anti-lock brake systems] [Automotive
   engineering] ...... EBD
Electronic Braking Control - Four Wheel Hybrid [Automotive
   engineering] ...... EBC-IVH
Electronic Braking System ...... EBS
Electronic Bulletin Board [Department of Commerce Washington, DC
   Information service or system] (IID) ...... EBB
Electronic Business Communications System ...... EBCS
Electronic Business Document Interchange ...... EBDI
Electronic Business Solutions [Computer science] ...... EBS
Electronic Cabling Unit ...... ECU
Electronic Calculating Punch ...... ECP
Electronic Calculator [or Computer] (BUR) ...... EC
Electronic Calibration ...... EC
Electronic Calibration and Normalization (KSC) ...... ECAN
Electronic Calibration Center [National Institute of Standards and
   Technology] ...... ECC
Electronic Capability [Designation for all US military aircraft] ...... E
Electronic Carburetor Control [Automotive engineering] ...... ECC
Electronic Cascade Impactor [For aerosol analysis] ...... ECI
Electronic Cash and Credit Register (HGAA) ...... ECCR
Electronic Cash Register ...... ECR
Electronic Central Office [Within network] [Telecommunications] (TEL) ...... ECO
Electronic Centralized Aircraft Monitoring System ...... ECAM
Electronic Change Notice (HGAA) ...... ECN
Electronic Character Generation [Electronography] (DGA) ...... ECG
Electronic Character Generator [Television] (WDMC) ...... ECG
Electronic Character Recognition Machine (DGA) ...... ECRM
Electronic Chart Display and Information System [Computer science] ...... ECDIS
Electronic Chart System ...... ECS
Electronic Check Presentment [Finance] ...... ECP
Electronic Checkout ...... ECO
Electronic Checkout Maintenance Equipment (IAA) ...... ECME
Electronic Cinematography (WDMC) ...... EC
Electronic Circuit Analysis Program (ECII) ...... ECAP
Electronic Circuit Designer (IAA) ...... ELECTCIRDESGNR
Electronic Circuit Plug-In Unit ...... ECPIU
Electronic Circuit Protector ...... ECP
Electronic Circuit-Making Equipment [Computer science] ...... ECME
Electronic Claims Billing (HGAA) ...... ECB
Electronic Claims Submission (MEDA) ...... ECS
Electronic Clearing House [NASDAQ symbol] (TTSB) ...... ECHO
Electronic Clearing House, Inc. [Associated Press] (SAG) ...... ElClear
Electronic Climate Control [Automotive engineering] ...... ECC
Electronic Clipping Service (HGAA) ...... ECLIPSE
Electronic Coding ...... EC
Electronic Color Prepress (DGA) ...... ECP
Electronic Combat ...... EC
Electronic Combat Measures [Military] (LAIN) ...... ECM
Electronic Combat Squadron ...... ECS
Electronic Combat Wing [Military] ...... ECW
Electronic Command Signal Programmer (MCD) ...... ECSP
Electronic Commerce [Computer science] (RDA) ...... EC
Electronic Commerce Acquisition (AAGC) ...... ECA
[Federal] Electronic Commerce Acquisition Team (AAGC) ...... ECAT
Electronic Commerce Acquisition-Program Management Office
   (AAGC) ...... ECA-PMO
Electronic Commerce / Electronic Data Interchange [DoD] ...... EC/EDI
Electronic Common Control [Telecommunications] (TEL) ...... ECC
Electronic Communications Division [Air Force] (AFM) ...... ECD
Electronic Communications for the Home and Office [Marina Del Ray, CA]
   [Telecommunications service] (TSSD) ...... ECHO
Electronic Communications, Inc. ...... ECI
Electronic Communications Index ...... ECI
Electronic Communications Piracy Act of 1986 ...... ECPA
[The] Electronic Communications Privacy Act ...... ECPH
Electronic Community Deal Office [Telecommunications] (TEL) ...... ECDO
Electronic Company Filing Index [Disclosure Information Group] [Information
   service or system] (IID) ...... ECFI
Electronic Comparator ...... EC
Electronic Compass Logic Module [Automotive navigation systems] ...... ECLM
Electronic Component Checkout Area (AAG) ...... ECCA
Electronic Component Group ...... ECG
Electronic Component Industries Association ...... ELCINA
Electronic Component Reliability Center [Battelle Memorial Institute]
   (MCD) ...... ECRC
Electronic Component Research and Development Grant [Canada] ...... ECRDG
Electronic Components (NITA) ...... ELECOMPS
Electronic Components Certification Board (EA) ...... ECCB
Electronic Components Code (NATG) ...... ECC
Electronic Components Conference ...... ECC
Electronic Components Industry Federation [British] ...... ECIF
Electronic Components Information Center [Battelle Memorial Institute] ...... ECIC
Electronic Components Laboratory ...... ECL
Electronic Components Quality Assurance Committee (BARN) ...... ECQAC
Electronic Components Research Center ...... ECRC
Electronic Composing System ...... ECS
Electronic Computer (MCD) ...... EC
Electronic Computer Concepts (HGAA) ...... ECC
Electronic Computer Ignition [Automotive engineering] ...... ECI

Electronic Computer Manufacturers Association ...... ECMA
Electronic Computer Programming Institute [Ceased operation, 1976] ...... ECPI
Electronic Computer-Aided Design [Computer science] (BYTE) ...... ECAD
Electronic Computer-Originated Mail [Postal Service] ...... E-COM
Electronic Computer-Originated Mail Services [Postal Service] [United
   States] [Defunct] (WDMC) ...... E-Com
Electronic Computing ...... ELECOM
Electronic Computing, Hospital-Oriented (IEEE) ...... ECHO
Electronic Computing Unit (IAA) ...... ECU
Electronic Concentrated Control System [Computerized car fuel system] ...... ECCS
Electronic Concentrated Control System ...... ECCS
Electronic Conductivity ...... EC
Electronic Conference on Trends in Organic Chemistry ...... ECTOC
Electronic Confusion Area ...... ECA
Electronic Connector Study Group (EA) ...... ECSG
Electronic Consumer Advertising Network [Data Corp. of America] ...... ECAN
Electronic Contact Operate ...... ECO
Electronic Control ...... ELECTC
Electronic Control Amplifier (MCD) ...... ECA
Electronic Control Analyzer and Programmer [Automotive engineering] ...... ECAP
Electronic Control Assembly [Ford Motor Co.] ...... ECA
Electronic Control Assembly - Engine Thrust (KSC) ...... ECET
Electronic Control Assembly - Pitch (IAA) ...... ECAP
Electronic Control Assembly - Pitch and Yaw (KSC) ...... ECPY
Electronic Control Assembly - Roll (KSC) ...... ECAR
Electronic Control Assembly - Thrust Vector, Pitch and Yaw (IAA) ...... ETPY
Electronic Control Assembly - Yaw (IAA) ...... ECAY
Electronic Control for Switching and Telemetering Automobile Systems
   [Automotive engineering] ...... ECSTASY
Electronic Control Instrumentation ...... ECI
Electronic Control Module [Instrumentation] ...... ECM
Electronic Control of Spark Timing (PDAA) ...... ECST
Electronic Control of the Mixture Ratio ...... ECMR
Electronic Control Products (MUGU) ...... ECP
Electronic Control Relay (IEEE) ...... ECR
Electronic Control Sensor (MCD) ...... ECS
Electronic Control Switch (IEEE) ...... ECS
Electronic Control Unit ...... ECU
Electronic Controlled Injection [Automotive engineering] ...... ECI
Electronic Conversion Unit (IEEE) ...... ECU
Electronic Converter Electric Power Supply (PDAA) ...... ECEPS
Electronic Cooling Distilled Water (DNAB) ...... ECDW
Electronic Cooling Water (DNAB) ...... ECW
Electronic Coordinatograph and Readout System ...... ECARS
Electronic Counter ...... EC
Electronic Counter Control Measure ...... ECC
Electronic Counter Services ...... ECS
Electronic Counter-Countermeasures [Military] ...... ECCM
Electronic Counter-Countermeasures Operator [Military] (CET) ...... ECCMO
Electronic Countermeasure [Military] ...... ECM
Electronic Countermeasure Transmitter Frequency Set Up [Military]
   (IAA) ...... ETFS
Electronic Countermeasures [Military] ...... E
Electronic Countermeasures [Military] (IAA) ...... ECCCM
Electronic Countermeasures and Reconnaissance ...... ECR
Electronic Countermeasures Ballistic Reentry Vehicle [Military] ...... ECM/BRV
Electronic Countermeasures Electronic Intelligence [Military] (IAA) ...... ECMELINT
Electronic Countermeasures Environment [Military] ...... ECME
Electronic Countermeasures Exercise [Military] (NVT) ...... ECMEX
Electronic Countermeasures Malfunction [Military] (IAA) ...... EM
Electronic Countermeasures Mission [Military] ...... ECMSN
Electronic Countermeasures Observer [Military] ...... ECMob
Electronic Countermeasures Officer [Navy] (NVT) ...... ECMO
Electronic Countermeasures Program [Military] ...... ECMP
Electronic Countermeasures Squadron [Military] (IAA) ...... ECMRON
Electronic Countermeasures System [Military] ...... ECS
Electronic Countermeasures Training [Military] (NVT) ...... ECMTNG
Electronic Coupling Unit (MCD) ...... ECU
Electronic Courier Systems [Eatontown, NJ] (TSSD) ...... ECS
Electronic Cover and Deception (PDAA) ...... EC & D
Electronic Current Analysis Program (IAA) ...... ECAP
Electronic Custom Telephone Set [or System] (NRCH) ...... ECTS
Electronic Cycling Clutch Switch [Automotive engineering] ...... ECCS
Electronic Damping Control [Automotive engineering] ...... EDC
Electronic Data Communications ...... EDC
Electronic Data Display ...... EDD
Electronic Data Exchange [DoD] ...... EDE
Electronic Data Gathering, Analysis, and Retrieval [Securities and Exchange
   Commission pilot project] (IID) ...... EDGAR
Electronic Data Gathering Equipment ...... EDGE
Electronic Data Gathering System [Computer science] (ECII) ...... EDGS
Electronic Data Information Technical Service (DIT) ...... EDITS
Electronic [Warfare] Data Integration Test System (MCD) ...... EDITS
Electronic Data Intelligence (DOMA) ...... EDI
Electronic Data Interchange [Computer science Telecommunications] ...... EDI
Electronic Data Interchange ...... EDI
Electronic Data Interchange Association (EA) ...... EDIA
Electronic Data Interchange/Electronic Commerce [Computer science
   Army] (RDA) ...... EDI/EC
Electronic Data Interchange for Administration, Commerce, and Transport
   [Economic Commission for Europe] ...... EDIFACT
Electronic Data Interchange Network (TSSD) ...... EDI-NET
Electronic Data Interchanges Council of Canada (EAIO) ...... EDICC
Electronic Data Local Communications Central [or Complex] ...... EDLCC
Electronic Data Processing ...... EDP

Electronic Data Processing Center .... EDPC
Electronic Data Processing Device (IAA) .... EDPD
Electronic Data Processing Education Program (MHDI) .... EDPEP
Electronic Data Processing Equipment .... EDPE
Electronic Data Processing Equipment Office (IAA) .... EDPEO
Electronic Data Processing/Industry Report .... EDP/IR
Electronic Data Processing - Information Retrieval .... EDP-IR
Electronic Data Processing Institute (HGAA) .... EDPI
Electronic Data Processing Machine [Also translated by some users of such equipment as "Every Damn Problem Multiplied"] .... EDPM
Electronic Data Processing Magnetic [Tape] .... EDPM
Electronic Data Processing Operations Research (IAA) .... EDPOR
Electronic Data Processing System .... EDAPS
Electronic Data Processing System .... EDPS
Electronic Data Processing Test (AFM) .... EDPT
Electronic Data Remote Communications Complex .... EDRCC
Electronic Data Storage (IAA) .... EDS
Electronic Data Storage Automatic Computer (IAA) .... EDSAC
Electronic Data Switching System [Computer science] (TEL) .... EDS
Electronic Data System (IEEE) .... EDS
Electronic Data Systems Federal Corp. .... EDS
Electronic Data Systems Federal Corp. .... EDSFC
Electronic Data Systems Ltd. [Information service or system] (IID) .... EDS
Electronic Data Traffic Control Center [or Complex] .... EDTCC
Electronic Data Transmission (AAG) .... EDT
Electronic Data Transmission Communications Central .... EDTCC
Electronic Data Transmission Working Party [Army] (AABC) .... ELDATRAWP
Electronic Decoy Rocket .... EDR
Electronic Defense Evaluator .... EDE
Electronic Defense Laboratory .... EDL
Electronic Dehydration Dryer .... EDD
Electronic Delay Storage Automatic Calculator [or Computer] [1949] .... EDSAC
Electronic Dental Anesthesia .... EDA
Electronic Depressurizing Valve (MCD) .... EDV
Electronic Design and Manufacture (IAA) .... EDAM
Electronic Design and Manufacture (IAA) .... EDM
Electronic Design Automation [Computer science] .... EDA
Electronic Design Automation Research Center [University of California] .... EDARC
Electronic Design for Manufacture .... EDFM
Electronic Design Interchange Format [Computer science] .... EDIF
Electronic Design Section (SAA) .... EDS
Electronic Designs [NASDAQ symbol] (TTSB) .... EDIX
Electronic Designs, Inc. [NASDAQ symbol] (SAG) .... EDIX
Electronic Designs, Inc. [Associated Press] (SAG) .... ElDes
Electronic Designs, Inc. [Associated Press] (SAG) .... ElecDes
Electronic Designs Wrrt [NASDAQ symbol] (TTSB) .... EDIXW
Electronic Desk Calculator (IEEE) .... EDC
Electronic Detection (LAIN) .... ED
Electronic Detection Machine (PDAA) .... ELDEMA
Electronic Development (MCD) .... ED
Electronic Development and Compatibility Test Unit .... EDCTU
Electronic Development Group [Military] (AFIT) .... EDG
Electronic Devices Quality Assurance .... EDQA
Electronic Dew Point Sensor .... EDPS
Electronic Diagnostic and Technical Information Tools [Army] .... EDIT
Electronic Dial Tone Speed Register [Bell System] .... EDTSR
Electronic Diesel Control [Automotive engineering] .... EDC
Electronic Differential [Analyzer] .... ED
Electronic Differential Analyzer .... EDA
Electronic Differential Analyzer (MSA) .... EDFA
Electronic Differential Lock System [Automotive engineering] .... EDS
Electronic Digital [Analyzer] .... ED
Electronic Digital Analyzer (MCD) .... EDA
Electronic Digital Computer .... EDC
Electronic Digital Pipette [Instrumentation] .... EDP
Electronic Digital Slide Rule (IAA) .... EDSR
Electronic Digital System Cross-Connect (ACRL) .... EDSX
Electronic Digital Tracking and Ranging .... EDITAR
Electronic Digital-Vernier Analog Computer (SAA) .... EDVAC
Electronic Digital-Vernier Analog Plotter (MUGU) .... EDVAP
Electronic Directory of German Databases [Information service or system] (IID) .... EDDA
Electronic Discharge LASER (MCD) .... EDC
Electronic Discrete Sequential Automatic Computer [University of Manchester, 1949] [British] (IEEE) .... EDSAC
Electronic Discrete Variable Automatic Calculator [or Computer] (MCD) .... EDVAC
Electronic Display .... ED
Electronic Display Assembly (NASA) .... EDA
Electronic Display of Indexing Association and Content (PDAA) .... EDIAC
Electronic Display Panel .... EDP
Electronic Display Unit .... EDU
Electronic Dissemination of Information (GFGA) .... EDI
Electronic Distance Measurement (NITA) .... EDM
Electronic Distance Measuring .... EDM
Electronic Distance Measuring Equipment (MCD) .... EDME
Electronic Distance-Measuring Instrument .... EDMI
Electronic Distribution Measurement .... EDM
Electronic Distribution of Software [Consumer market] (NITA) .... EDOS
Electronic Distribution Show (ITD) .... EDS
Electronic Distribution System (MCD) .... EDS
Electronic Distributor Modulator [Automotive engineering] .... EDM
Electronic Distributor Unit [Automotive engineering] .... EDU
Electronic Distributorless Ignition System [Automotive engineering] .... EDIS

Electronic Distributors' Research Institute .... EDRI
Electronic Dive Angle Control .... EDAC
Electronic Document .... ED
Electronic Document Authorization (CDE) .... EDA
Electronic Document Collection .... EDC
Electronic Document Delivery [Software] .... EDD
Electronic Document Delivery: Integrated Solutions [Project] (AIE) .... EDDIS
Electronic Document Gathering Environment [A.B. Dick] [Updatable fiche system] (NITA) .... EDGE
Electronic Document Interchange .... EDI
Electronic Document Management System .... EDMS
Electronic Document Management System .... EDMS
Electronic Document Service .... EDS
Electronic Document Storage Systems (NITA) .... EDS
Electronic Dot Generation (DGA) .... EDG
Electronic Drafting Machine .... EDM
Electronic Dummy [Engineering acoustics] (IAA) .... ED
Electronic Editing [Telecommunications] .... EE
Electronic Editions [Cowles Publishing Co.] [Information service or system] (IID) .... EE
Electronic Egg Exchange [Computer program] .... EEX
Electronic EGR [Exhaust Gas Recirculation] Transducer [Automotive engineering] .... EET
Electronic, Electrical, and Electromechanical Parts List (NASA) .... EPL
Electronic Electrical Termination Building [NASA] (NASA) .... EETB
Electronic Emission Intelligence [Military] .... EEI
Electronic Emission Security (NATG) .... EES
Electronic Emitter Location System (MCD) .... EELS
Electronic Engine Control .... EEC
Electronic Engine Control - 5th Generation [Automotive engineering] .... EEC-V
Electronic Engine Control Module .... EECM
Electronic Engine Control System [OC Johnson & Associates, Inc.] [Automotive engineering] .... EECS
Electronic Engine Management System .... EEMS
Electronic Engineer (IAA) .... ELECTENGR
Electronic Engineering .... EE
Electronic Engineering (DD) .... ElEng
Electronic Engineering Association [British] .... EEA
Electronic Engineering Division [Coast Guard] .... EED
Electronic Engineers Master (MUGU) .... EEM
Electronic Environment Simulator .... EES
Electronic Environmental Test Facility (MUGU) .... EETF
Electronic Equipment Committee [NASA] (KSC) .... EEC
Electronic Equipment Engineering [A publication] .... EEE
Electronic Equipment Environment Survey (AFM) .... EEES
Electronic Equipment Maintainability Datebook (MCD) .... EEMD
Electronic Equipment Maintenance Kit .... EEMK
Electronic Equipment Maintenance Trainer (MCD) .... EEMT
Electronic Equipment Modification .... EEM
Electronic Equipment Monitoring (IEEE) .... EEM
Electronic Equipment Reliability Databook (MCD) .... EERD
Electronic Equipment Representative (MCD) .... EER
Electronic Equipment Technical Committee [NASA] (KSC) .... EETC
Electronic Evaluation and Procurement (MHDB) .... EEP
Electronic Event Programmer (MHDB) .... EEP
Electronic Evidence Discovery [Company] .... EED
Electronic Explosive Device (NVT) .... EED
Electronic Export Documentation [Australia] .... EXDOC
Electronic Exposure Timer (KSC) .... EET
Electronic Fab Technology [NASDAQ symbol] (SAG) .... EFTC
Electronic Fab Technology [Associated Press] (SAG) .... ElecFab
Electronic Facial Identification Technique .... EFIT
Electronic Facility Instruction (SAA) .... EFI
Electronic Facsimile (AAGC) .... Fax
Electronic Failure Report .... EFR
Electronic Failure Report Only .... EFRO
Electronic Family Security Program [of Sun Life Assurance Co. of Canada] .... EFSP
Electronic Fetal Monitoring [Medicine] .... EFM
Electronic Fiber Fineness Indicator .... EFFI
Electronic Field Production (IEEE) .... EFP
Electronic Field Seaman Recruit [Military] (IAA) .... EFSR
Electronic Fighting Vehicle System [Army] .... EFVS
Electronic Filing (NITA) .... EF
Electronic Final Zero .... EFZ
Electronic Financial Control .... EFICON
Electronic Firing Switches [Military] (NG) .... EFS
Electronic Flash Approach Light (IAA) .... EFAL
Electronic Flash Approach System .... EFAS
Electronic Flash Illuminator .... EFI
Electronic Flight Control System .... EFCS
Electronic Flight Data Accumulation Service .... EFDAS
Electronic Flight Data and Recording System (MCD) .... EFDARS
Electronic Flight Information Systems [FAA] (TAG) .... EFIS
Electronic Flight Instrument Control Panel (MCD) .... EFICP
Electronic Flight Instrument System .... EFIS
Electronic Flight Instruments (WDAA) .... EFI
Electronic Flow Control .... EFC
Electronic Forms Designer [Microsoft Corp.] (PCM) .... EFD
Electronic Forum for Industry [British] .... EFFI
Electronic Freedom Foundation [Telecommunications] .... EFF
Electronic Frequency Control .... EFC
Electronic Frequency Selection (IEEE) .... EFS
Electronic Frontier Foundation (EA) .... EFF
Electronic Fuel Control System .... EFCS

Electronic Fuel Injection	EFI
Electronic Fuel Injection (Metering) [*Automotive engineering*]	EFI (M)
Electronic Fuel Metering [*Automotive engineering*]	EFM
Electronic Fund Tape [*Banking*]	EFT
Electronic Fund Transfer Act [*1978*]	EFTA
Electronic Funds Transfer [*Banking*]	EFT
Electronic Funds Transfer Association [*Washington, DC*] (EA)	EFTA
Electronic Funds Transfer at Point of Banking	EFTPOB
Electronic Funds Transfer at Point of Sale	EFTPOS
Electronic Funds Transfer at Point of Sales (EERA)	EFTPoS
Electronic Funds Transfer System [*or Service*] [*Banking National Science Foundation*]	EFTS
Electronic Gear Selection [*Heavy-duty vehicles*]	EGS
Electronic Geographic Coordinate Navigation (MCD)	EGECON
Electronic Glossary and Symbol Panel (IAA)	EGSP
Electronic Gourmet Guide [*America Online Greenhouse program*]	eGG
Electronic Governor Control [*Automotive engineering*]	EGC
Electronic Governor Module (IEEE)	EGM
Electronic Governor Regulator (IEEE)	EGR
Electronic Governor System [*Heavy-duty automotive engines*]	EGS
Electronic Governor System	EGS
Electronic Grading Operator	EGO
Electronic Ground Automatic Destruct [*Air Force*]	EGAD
Electronic Ground Automatic Destruct Sequencer [*Air Force*]	EGADS
Electronic Guidance (AAG)	EG
Electronic Guides for Standardizing Items of Procurement and Supply (MCD)	EGSIPS
Electronic Gyro Compass	EGC
Electronic Hair Styling [*NASDAQ symbol*] (TTSB)	EHST
Electronic Hair Styling, Inc. [*NASDAQ symbol*] (SAG)	EHST
Electronic Hair Styling, Inc. [*Associated Press*] (SAG)	ElecHair
Electronic Height Indicator (MCD)	EHI
Electronic Horizontal Director Indicator [*Aviation*] (PDAA)	EHDI
Electronic Horizontal Situation Display [*Aviation*] (PDAA)	EHSD
Electronic Horizontal Situation Indicator	EHSI
Electronic Ignition [*Automotive engineering*]	EI
Electronic Ignition System [*Automotive engineering*]	EIS
Electronic Image Generator	EIG
Electronic Image Stabilizer [*Photography*]	EIS
Electronic Imaging Conference and Exposition (ITD)	EI
Electronic Imaging in Medicine [*Computer graphics*]	EIM
Electronic Imaging System [*Computer graphics*]	EIS
Electronic Industries Association [*Formerly, RETMA*] (EA)	EIA
Electronic Industries Association - Japan	EIA-J
Electronic Industries Association of Canada	EIAC
Electronic Industries Foundation (EA)	EIF
Electronic Industry Production and Test Equipment (IMH)	EIPT
Electronic Industry Show Corp. [*Defunct*] (EA)	EISC
Electronic Information Bulletin [*Navy*]	EIB
Electronic Information Delivery Online System [*Information retrieval*]	EIDOS
Electronic Information Delivery System [*Individual learning center equipped with head sets and video monitors*]	EIDS
Electronic Information Delivery System - Authoring Software System for Instructive Simulation and Training	EIDS-ASSIST
Electronic Information Display System	EIDS
Electronic Information Exchange [*National Message Center, Inc.*] [*Overland Park, KS*] [*Telecommunications service*] (TSSD)	EIE
Electronic Information Exchange System [*Pronounced "eyes"*] [*New Jersey Institute of Technology Computer network*] [*Telecommunications*]	EIES
Electronic Information Series [*Information service or system*] (IID)	EIS
Electronic Information Services [*Industry*] (IT)	EIS
Electronic Information Systems, Inc. [*NASDAQ symbol*] (SAG)	EISI
Electronic Information Technology [*Hardware manufacturer*]	EIT
Electronic Infusion Device [*Pharmacology*] (DAVI)	EID
Electronic Ink and Moisture System [*Printing*] (DGA)	EIMS
Electronic Inquiry System (PDAA)	EIS
Electronic Installation	EI
Electronic Installation Change and Maintenance (DNAB)	EICAM
Electronic Installation Design [*Navy*]	EID
Electronic Installation Plan (NG)	EIP
Electronic Installation Technician	EIT
Electronic Installation Verification Test [*NASA*] (NASA)	EIVT
Electronic Institute of Canada (HGAA)	EIC
Electronic Institutional [*or Integrated*] Media System	EIMS
Electronic Instruction (MCD)	EI
Electronic Instrument Manufacturers Exhibit (MUGU)	EIME
Electronic Instruments Limited [*as in EIL electrode, used in biochemistry*] [*British*]	EIL
Electronic Intelligence [*or Intercept*] [*Meaning of ELINT determined by reference to before (Intercept) and after (Intelligence) analysis of reconnaissance mission results*]	ELINT
Electronic Intelligence Analysis Processing Subsystem (MCD)	EAPSS
Electronic Intelligence Parameter Limits	EPL
Electronic Intelligence Satellite (NITA)	ELINT
Electronic Intelligence Support System (MCD)	ESS
Electronic Intelligence Technical Guidance Unit (MCD)	ELINT TGU
Electronic Interface (MCD)	EI
Electronic Interface Unit	EIU
Electronic Interference	EI
Electronic Intrusion Detection	EID
Electronic Jamming	EJ
Electronic Journal (TNIG)	E-Journal
Electronic Journalism	EJ
Electronic Journalism (WDMC)	EJ
Electronic Key System [*Telecommunications*] (NITA)	EKS
Electronic Key Telephone System	EKTS
Electronic Keyboard	EKB
Electronic Keyboard System	EKBS
Electronic Keyboard System	EKS
Electronic Keyboarding, Inc. [*Information service or system*] (IID)	EKI
Electronic Knowledge Bank	EKB
Electronic Label Printing [*Diagraph Corp.*]	ELP
Electronic Laboratories and Services	EL & S
Electronic Laboratory Animal Monitoring System	ELAMS
Electronic Laboratory Notebook	ELN
Electronic Launching Equipment	ELE
Electronic Lean Burn (ADA)	ELB
Electronic Legislative Search System [*Commerce Clearing House, Inc.*] [*Information service or system*]	ELSS
Electronic Letter Sorting and Indicator Equipment	ELSIE
Electronic Level Control [*General Motors Corp.*] [*Automotive engineering*]	ELC
Electronic Library Association [*Defunct*] (EA)	ELA
Electronic Library Computer	ELC
Electronic Library Inc. (IID)	EL
Electronic Library Information Service at the Australian National University	ELISA
Electronic Library Information System [*Library network*] (IT)	ELIS
Electronic Library Membership Initiative Group [*ALA*] (NITA)	ELMIG
Electronic Library System [*Aviation*]	ELS
Electronic Library System Cabinet	ELSC
Electronic Lie Detector	ELD
Electronic Line Indicator [*Tennis*]	ELI
Electronic Line Printer	ELP
Electronic Line Replacement [*Cinematography*] (WDMC)	ELR
Electronic Linear Circuit Analysis (PDAA)	ELCA
Electronic Line-of-Sight [*Military*]	ELOS
Electronic Load Controller	ELC
Electronic Lobe Switching Antenna (PDAA)	ELSA
Electronic Location and Status Indicating Equipment (IAA)	ELSIE
Electronic Location Finder	ELF
Electronic Magnetic Slip Couplings (DS)	EM
Electronic Mail [*Telecommunications*]	EM
Electronic Mail [*Internet language*] [*Computer science*]	email
Electronic Mail [*Computer science*]	e-mail
Electronic Mail (WDMC)	E-mail
Electronic mail [*Computer science*] (EERA)	E-mail
Electronic Mail (TNIG)	EMAIL
Electronic Mail and Message Systems	EMMS
Electronic Mail Association (EA)	EMA
Electronic Mail Broadcast to a Roaming Computer [*Telecommunications*] (PCM)	EMBARC
Electronic Mail Communication Center [*Naples, FL*] [*Telecommunications service*] (TSSD)	Emc²
Electronic Mail Courier	EMC
Electronic Mail Facility [*Postal Service*]	EMF
Electronic Mail Handling	EMH
Electronic Mail Service [*Telecommunications*]	EMS
Electronic Mail System [*Postal Service*]	EMS
Electronic Maintenance Assembly	EMA
Electronic Maintenance Book (IAA)	EMB
Electronic Maintenance Co. [*Military*] (DNAB)	ELECTMAINTCO
Electronic Maintenance Engineering Association	EMEA
Electronic Maintenance Engineering Center [*Military*] (IEEE)	EMEC
Electronic Maintenance Ground Equipment (KSC)	EMGE
Electronic Maintenance Inspector	EMI
Electronic Maintenance Proficiency Test	EMPT
Electronic Maintenance Publication System (MCD)	EMPS
Electronic Maintenance Technician [*FAA*]	EMT
Electronic Management System	EMS
Electronic Manifold Card [*Clippard Instrument Laboratory, Inc.*] [*Cincinnati, OH*]	EMC
Electronic Manufacturing Facility (IAA)	EMF
Electronic Manufacturing Manual (IAA)	EMM
Electronic Manuscript Project [*Association of American Publishers*] [*Information service or system*] (IID)	EMP
Electronic Map Display	EMD
Electronic Marcel Dassault [*France*]	EMD
Electronic Market-Research Terminal	EMRT
Electronic Markets and Information Systems, Inc. [*Information service or system*]	EMIS
Electronic Mask-Making Apparatus (IAA)	EMMA
Electronic Material Bulletin [*Army*] (MCD)	EMB
Electronic Material Change	EMC
Electronic Material Data Service (MUGU)	EMDS
Electronic Material Sciences Laboratory	EMSL
Electronic Material Shipment Request [*Navy*]	EMSR
Electronic Materials Information Service [*Institution of Electrical Engineers*] [*Database*] (IID)	EMIS
Electronic Mathematic Automation (IAA)	EMA
Electronic Mathematic Model-Analog (PDAA)	EMMA
Electronic Measurement (IAA)	EM
Electronic Measuring Apparatus (IAA)	EMA
Electronic Mechanic Technician	ELMT
Electronic Media Claims [*Department of Health and Human Services*] (GFGA)	EMC
Electronic Media Rating Council (EA)	EMRC
Electronic Medical System [*or Service*]	EMS
Electronic Meeting Services [*Clinton, MD*] [*Telecommunications*] (TSSD)	EMS
Electronic Memory and Magnetics (IAA)	EMM
Electronic Memory Systems Organization [*Burroughs Corp.*]	EMSO

Electronic Message Service Center (IAA) ...... EMSC
Electronic Message Service System [Telecommunications] (TEL) ...... EMSS
Electronic Message System ...... EMS
Electronic Microsystem (IAA) ...... EMS
Electronic Mind Tester ...... EMT
Electronic Missile Acquisition ...... EMA
Electronic Mock-Up [Computer-aided design] ...... EMU
Electronic Mode Control (IAA) ...... EMC
Electronic Modular Control Panel [Motor-generator set design] ...... EMCP
Electronic Module Retard [Automotive engineering] ...... EMR
Electronic Moisture Recorder ...... EMR
Electronic Money Transfer System ...... EMTS
Electronic Motion Control Association [Defunct] (EA) ...... EMCA
Electronic MRO [Maintenance Repair Operation] Distributors Association (EA) ...... EMRODA
Electronic Multiplying Punches (DEN) ...... EMP
Electronic Multipurpose Intelligence Retaliatory Equipment (IAA) ...... EMPIRE
Electronic Muscle Stimulator [Medicine] (CPH) ...... EMS
Electronic Music Consortium (EA) ...... EMC
Electronic Networking Association [Defunct] (IID) ...... ENA
Electronic News Gathering [Television news coverage] ...... ENG
Electronic Nuclear Instrumentation Group (MCD) ...... ENIG
Electronic Null Detector ...... END
Electronic Numerical Integrator and Calculator [Early computer, 1946] (DCTA) ...... ENAC
Electronic Numerical Integrator and Calculator [Early computer, 1946] ...... ENIAC
Electronic Numerical Integrator and Computer (IDOE) ...... ENIAC
Electronic Office Centers of America, Inc. [Schaumburg, IL] [Telecommunications] (TSSD) ...... EOCA
Electronic Oil Pressure Sensor [Automotive engineering] ...... EOPS
Electronic Operating Instructions (DNAB) ...... EOI
Electronic Operations Center [Military] ...... EOC
Electronic Order of Battle (MSA) ...... EOB
Electronic Order of Battle Control Center ...... EOBCC
Electronic Original Equipment Market ...... EOEM
Electronic Overload Protection ...... EOP
Electronic Pacemaker [Cardiology] (DAVI) ...... EPM
Electronic Package ...... EP
Electronic Package Housing ...... EPH
Electronic Packaging Engineer (IAA) ...... ELECTPKGENGR
Electronic Page Composition (DGA) ...... EPC
Electronic Page Image Composer (DGA) ...... EPIC
Electronic Pain Control [Apparatus] [Neurology] (DAVI) ...... EPC
Electronic Parties List [On-line version of List of Parties Excluded from Federal Procurement and Non-Procurement Programs] (AAGC) ...... EPL
Electronic Parts and Equipment (NATG) ...... EPE
Electronic Parts Distributors' Show ...... EPDS
Electronic Parts Manual ...... EPM
Electronic Parts Reliability ...... EPR
Electronic Patrol, Experimental (MCD) ...... EPX
Electronic Payments System ...... EPS
Electronic Performance Support System (CDE) ...... EPSS
Electronic Personnel Information Network [Data Corp. of America] ...... EPIN
Electronic Pest Control Association (EA) ...... EPCA
Electronic Photochromic Integrating Cathode-Ray [Tube] ...... EPIC
Electronic Photocomposing Machine (DGA) ...... EPM
Electronic Plan Position Indicator (IAA) ...... EPPI
Electronic Plate Scanner (DGA) ...... EPS
Electronic Point-of-Sale [Computer science] ...... EPOS
Electronic Portable Information Center [Computer science] ...... EPIC
Electronic Position Indicator ...... EPI
Electronic Post [British Post Office] [Defunct] (TSSD) ...... EP
Electronic Postproduction (NTCM) ...... EPP
Electronic Power Conditioner ...... EPC
Electronic Power Control [Off-highway equipment] [Hydraulics] ...... EPC
Electronic Power Feed (NITA) ...... EPF
Electronic Power Steering [Mitsubishi] [Automotive engineering] ...... EPS
Electronic Power Unit (IDOE) ...... EPU
Electronic Preferred Parts List [Jet Propulsion Laboratory, NASA] ...... EPPL
Electronic Prepress System (DGA) ...... EPS
Electronic Press Kit ...... EPK
Electronic Price Information Computer ...... EPIC
Electronic Printer (MCD) ...... ELP
Electronic Printer ...... EP
Electronic Printer Image Construction (DGA) ...... EPIC
Electronic Privacy Information Center ...... EPIC
Electronic Private Automatic Branch Exchange [Telecommunications] (MCD) ...... EPABX
Electronic Private Branch Exchange [Telecommunications] ...... EPBX
Electronic Processing (IAA) ...... EP
Electronic Processing and Dissemination System [Computer science] (DOMA) ...... EPDS
Electronic Processors Inc. (NITA) ...... EPI
Electronic Procurement Regulation [Defense Supply Agency] ...... EPR
Electronic Product Information Center [Buick's computerized information network and database] ...... EPIC
Electronic Production and Inventory Control (IAA) ...... EPIC
Electronic Production Resources Agency [Military] ...... EPRA
Electronic Products Laboratory (IAA) ...... EPL
Electronic Program Control ...... EPC
Electronic Program Guide [Cable-television system] ...... EPG
Electronic Programmable Transmission Control [Off-highway vehicles] ...... EPTC
Electronic Programmed Procurement Information (NG) ...... EPPI
Electronic Properties Information Center [DoD] ...... EPIC
Electronic Protection System (IIA) ...... EPS

Electronic Proving Ground [Army] (MCD) ...... EPG
Electronic Proximity Detector (MCD) ...... EPD
Electronic Publication Technology Group [Defunct] (EA) ...... EPTG
Electronic Publishing Abstracts [Information service or system] (NITA) ...... EPA
Electronic Publishing Abstracts [The Research Association for the Paper and Board, Printing and Packaging Industries] [Database] ...... EPUBS
Electronic Publishing and Prepress Systems (DGA) ...... EPPS
Electronic Publishing Business [Electronic Publishing Ventures, Inc.] [Information service or system] (IID) ...... EPB
Electronic Publishing Committee [Association of American Publishers] [Information service or system] (IID) ...... EPC
Electronic Publishing Special Interest Group [Association of American Publishers] ...... EPSIG
Electronic Publishing Specialist Group (NITA) ...... EPSG
Electronic Publishing System (BYTE) ...... EPS
Electronic Publishing System [ITT Dialcom] [Database] ...... EPUB
Electronic Purchasing Agent Network [Service of Data Corp. of America] ..... EPAN
Electronic Quality Assurance Test Equipment [System] [Army] (RDA) .... EQUATE
Electronic RADAR ...... ELRA
Electronic RADAR Navigation (DNAB) ...... ERN
Electronic Radiated Power (PDAA) ...... ERP
Electronic Random Action Control ...... ERAC
Electronic Random Number and Indicating Equipment [Used for selecting winning premium bond numbers] [British] ...... ERNIE
Electronic Range Scoring Device (MCD) ...... ERSD
Electronic Reading Automation [Information retrieval] ...... ERA
Electronic Rear Steering [Automotive engineering] ...... ERS
Electronic Reconnaissance ...... ER
Electronic Reconnaissance (MCD) ...... EREC
Electronic Reconnaissance Access Set ...... ERAS
Electronic Reconnaissance Accessory ...... ELRAC
Electronic Reconnaissance Procurement Division ...... ERPD
Electronic Reconnaissance Set ...... ERS
Electronic Reconnaissance System ...... ERS
Electronic Reconnaissance Unit (MCD) ...... ERU
Electronic Recording Beam (MDG) ...... ERB
Electronic Recording Machine Accounting ...... ERMA
Electronic Reference Document ...... ERD
Electronic Reflected Energy System [Acoustics] ...... ERES
Electronic Register-Sender [Telecommunications] (TEL) ...... ERS
Electronic Remittance Advice ...... ERA
Electronic Remote and Independent Control ...... ERIC
Electronic Remote Switching (MCD) ...... ERS
Electronic Remote Switching (IAA) ...... ERX
Electronic Rentals Association [British] (BI) ...... ERA
Electronic Rentals Group [Commercial firm] [British] ...... ERG
Electronic Repair Facility [Military] ...... ERF
Electronic Repair Order [Automobile service] ...... ERO
Electronic Repair Parts Allowance List [Navy] ...... ERPAL
Electronic Repair Station ...... ERS
Electronic Repair Vehicle (PDAA) ...... ERV
Electronic Representatives Association (EA) ...... ERA
Electronic Requirement Plan [Navy] ...... ERP
Electronic Requirements Report (DNAB) ...... ERR
Electronic Research and Development Command [Army] ...... ERDC
Electronic Research and Development Laboratory [Army] (MCD) ...... ERDL
Electronic Research and Development Technician (IAA) ...... ERDT
Electronic Research and Support Organization [Taiwan] (NITA) ...... ERSO
Electronic Research Association [British] ...... ERA
Electronic Research Directorate [Air Force] ...... ERD
Electronic Research Supply Agency ...... ERSA
Electronic Resources Development Agency ...... ERDA
Electronic Retailing Investment Corp. [Acronym is also the name of an electronic vending kiosk] ...... ERIC
Electronic Retailing Sys [NASDAQ symbol] (TTSB) ...... ERSI
Electronic Retailing Systems International [Associated Press] (SAG) .... ElcRetl
Electronic Retailing Systems International [NASDAQ symbol] (SAG) .... ERSI
Electronic Retina Computing Reader ...... ERCR
Electronic Revision and Approval [Computer science] ...... ERA
Electronic Ride Control [Automotive engineering] ...... ERC
Electronic Rig Stats [Pennwell Publishing Co.] [Information service or system] (IID) ...... ERS
Electronic Road Pricing (PDAA) ...... ERP
Electronic Room (IAA) ...... ELCTRM
Electronic Route Guidance System (OA) ...... ERGS
Electronic Safe Arming and Firing Device (DWSG) ...... ESAF
Electronic Sales-Marketing Association [Defunct] (EA) ...... ESMA
Electronic Satellite Image Analysis Console [NASA] ...... ESIAC
Electronic Scan Converter ...... ESC
Electronic Scanning and Stabilizing Antenna ...... ESSA
Electronic Scanning Microwave Radiometer [Marine science] (OSRA) .... ESMR
Electronic Scanning RADAR ...... ESR
Electronic Scanning RADAR System (MCD) ...... ESRS
Electronic Scanning Spectrometer ...... ESS
Electronic Science Section (IAA) ...... ESS
Electronic Section [National Weather Service] ...... ES
Electronic Security [Air Force] ...... ELSEC
Electronic Security Alarm [Automobile theft preventive] ...... ESA
Electronic Security Alaska [Air Force] ...... ESA
Electronic Security Combat Operations Staff [Military] ...... ESCOS
Electronic Security Command (MCD) ...... ESC
Electronic Security Group [Military] ...... ESG
Electronic Security Number [Cellular telephones] (WDMC) ...... ESN
Electronic Security Profile [of Equitable Life Assurance Society] ...... ESP
Electronic Security Squadron [Military] ...... ESS

Electronic Security Strategic [*Military*] .... ESS
Electronic Security Surveillance .... ESS
Electronic Security System .... ESS
Electronic Security Tactical [*Military*] .... EST
Electronic Seismic Photography .... ESP
Electronic Selection and Bar Operating (IAA) .... ESBO
Electronic Selective Archives [*Swiss News Agency*] [*Information service or system*] (IID) .... ELSA
Electronic Selective Switching Unit .... ESSU
Electronic Send/Receive .... ESR
Electronic Sequence Switching .... ESS
Electronic Sequencer Timer .... EST
Electronic Sequencing Module .... ESM
Electronic Sequencing Unit [*for helicopters*] [*Army*] (RDA) .... ESU
Electronic Serial Number .... ESN
Electronic Server Pad [*Restaurant computer device manufactured by Remanco Systems, Inc.*] .... ESP
Electronic Services Unlimited [*New York, NY*] [*Telecommunications*] (TSSD) .... ESU
Electronic Setup (WDMC) .... ESU
Electronic Shift Automatic Transmission [*Automotive engineering*] .... ESAT
Electronic Shock Absorber Control .... ESAC
Electronic Shop Computer .... ESC
Electronic Shop Major [*Coast Guard*] .... ES
Electronic Shop Major Telephone and Teletype [*Coast Guard*] .... EST
Electronic Shop Minor [*Coast Guard*] .... ESM
Electronic Shop Minor Telephone and Teletype [*Coast Guard*] .... ESMT
Electronic Shop, Shelter-Mounted [*Army*] .... ESSM
Electronic Signal Monitoring (PDAA) .... ESM
Electronic Signaling and Indicating Equipment (IEEE) .... ELSIE
Electronic Simulated Image Generation .... ESIG
Electronic Sky Screen Equipment [*Air Force*] .... ELSSE
Electronic Slide Rule (WDAA) .... ESR
Electronic Smart Power [*Automotive engineering*] .... ESP
Electronic Social Transformation .... EST
Electronic Software Distribution .... ESD
Electronic Software Distribution and Licensing (CDE) .... ESDL
Electronic Software Licensing [*Software*] (CDE) .... ESL
Electronic Solid-State Wide-Angle Camera System (MCD) .... ESSWACS
Electronic Spacecraft Simulator (IAA) .... ESCS
Electronic Spark Control [*Automotive*] .... ESC
Electronic Spark Timing [*Automotive engineering*] .... EST
Electronic Specialist .... ECSP
Electronic Speciality (IAA) .... ELS
Electronic Specialty (IAA) .... ES
Electronic Specification Package (BTTJ) .... ESP
Electronic Specifications [*Databank of specifications issued by national agencies*] (NITA) .... ELSPECS
Electronic Speckle-Pattern Interferometer (OA) .... ESPI
Electronic Speech Information Equipment [*System developed by Britain's Department of Transport to facilitate bus transit*] .... ELSIE
Electronic Speech Synthesis (IAA) .... ESS
Electronic Speed Switch .... ESS
Electronic Sports Gathering [*Television*] (WDMC) .... ESG
Electronic Spreadsheet (CDE) .... ESS
Electronic Stability Program [*Automotive*] .... ESP
Electronic Stability Program [*Automotive*] .... ESP
Electronic Standard .... ES
Electronic Standard (MSA) .... ESTD
Electronic Standard Procedure (MCD) .... ESP
Electronic Standards Office [*Navy*] .... ESO
Electronic Still Camera .... ESC
Electronic Still Photography (CDE) .... ESP
Electronic Still Photography at Rochester Institute of Technology [*A publication*] .... ESPRIT
Electronic Still Store [*Television*] (WDMC) .... ESS
Electronic Stock Evaluator Corp. .... ESE
Electronic Store Information System (IAA) .... ESIS
Electronic Structure of Materials Centre [*Flinders University, Australia*] .... ESMC
Electronic Subsystems Analysis (MCD) .... ESA
Electronic Summation Device (MAE) .... ESD
Electronic Supervisory Control (MCD) .... ESC
Electronic Supervisory Panel (MCD) .... ESP
Electronic Supply Segment of the Navy Supply System .... ESSNSS
Electronic Supply Support Base [*Air Force*] .... ESSB
Electronic Support Equipment (MCD) .... ESE
Electronic Support Laboratory .... ESL
Electronic Support Measure / Non-Cooperative Target Recognition .... ESM/NCTR
Electronic Support Measures [*Instrumentation*] (IEEE) .... ESM
Electronic Supporting Systems Project Office [*Air Force*] .... ESSPO
Electronic Surface Recorder (PDAA) .... ESR
Electronic Surge Arrester .... ESA
Electronic Surveillance Index [*FBI file of persons overheard on wiretaps*] .... ELSUR
Electronic Surveillance Measures .... ESM
Electronic Surveillance System .... ESS
Electronic Sweep Generator .... ESG
Electronic Switch Module .... ESM
Electronic Switching [*Telecommunications*] .... ES
Electronic Switching Center (CET) .... ESC
Electronic Switching Programming Language .... ESPL
Electronic Switching System [*See also EAX*] [*Telecommunications*] .... ESS
Electronic Switching System Arranged with Data Features .... ESS ADF
Electronic Switching System Control [*Telecommunications*] (TEL) .... EL-SSC
Electronic Switching System Flow Chart .... ESSFLO
Electronic Switching Systems Programming Language [*Computer science*] (MHDB) .... EPL
Electronic Switching Unit [*Telecommunications*] (MCD) .... ESU
Electronic Synchro-Shift .... ESS
Electronic System Evaluator .... ESE
Electronic System for Control of Receipt Transactions (MCD) .... ESCORT
Electronic System Integration (KSC) .... ESI
Electronic System Precision Orbit Determination [*Air Force*] (MCD) .... ESPOD
Electronic System Test Facility (IAA) .... ESTF
Electronic System Test Unit .... ESTU
Electronic Systems .... ES
Electronic Systems Assistance Center [*Telecommunications*] (TEL) .... ESAC
Electronic Systems Center [*Air Force*] .... ESC
Electronic Systems Command [*Also, NESC*] [*Navy*] .... ELECSYSCOM
Electronic Systems Command [*Also, NESC*] [*Navy*] .... ESC
Electronic Systems Compatibility Facility [*NASA*] .... ESCF
Electronic Systems Compatibility Laboratory [*NASA*] .... ESCL
Electronic Systems Division [*Hanscom Air Force Base, MA*] .... ESD
Electronic Systems Division Eastwing [*Hanscom Air Force Base, MA*] .... ESD/EW
Electronic Systems Division, Technical Documentary Reports [*AFSC*] .... ESD TDR
Electronic Systems Engineering Department [*Naval Weapons Support Center*] [*Crane, IN*] .... ESED
Electronic Systems Engineering Group (SAA) .... ESEG
Electronic Systems Laboratory (MCD) .... ESL
Electronic Systems Library, Westinghouse Canada Ltd., Burlington, Ontario [*Library symbol National Library of Canada*] (NLC) .... OHW
Electronic Systems Mockup (KSC) .... ESMU
Electronic Systems Planning (RDA) .... ESP
Electronic Systems Reliability (MCD) .... ESR
Electronic Systems Sector (AAGC) .... ESS
Electronic Systems Test Laboratory [*NASA*] .... ESTL
Electronic Systems Test Program [*NASA*] .... ESTP
Electronic Systems Test Set (MCD) .... ESTS
Electronic Tactical Action Report (AFM) .... ECTAR
Electronic Tactical Display [*Military*] .... ETD
Electronic Tandem Network (ACRL) .... ETN
Electronic Tandem Switching [*Telecommunications*] (TEL) .... ETS
Electronic Tape Printer (IAA) .... ETP
Electronic Target Generator [*Military*] (DA) .... ETG
Electronic Technical Institute (EA) .... ETI
Electronic Technical Publishing (IAA) .... ETP
Electronic Technical Suitability Test .... ETST
Electronic Technical Support Center [*DiagSoft*] .... ETSC
Electronic Technician .... ELT
Electronic Technician .... ET
Electronic Technology [*Automotive engineering*] .... Eltec
Electronic Technology & Devices Laboratory [*Army*] (RDA) .... EDTL
Electronic Technology Laboratory [*Air Force*] (MCD) .... ETL
Electronic Telcommunications, Inc. [*Associated Press*] (SAG) .... ElecTel
Electronic Tele Comm'A' [*NASDAQ symbol*] (TTSB) .... ETCIA
Electronic Telecommunication Switching System (MCD) .... ETSS
Electronic Tele-Communications, Inc. [*NASDAQ symbol*] (NQ) .... ETCI
Electronic Telegraph System .... ETS
Electronic Teleprinter Cryptographic Regenerative Repeater Mixer (NATG) .... ETCRRM
Electronic Temperature Control .... ETC
Electronic Temperature Offset .... ETO
Electronic Tensile Tester .... ETT
Electronic Terms for Space Age Language .... ETSAL
Electronic Test .... ET
Electronic Test and Maintenance (IAA) .... ETM
Electronic Test and Measurement (MCD) .... ETM
Electronic Test Block .... ETB
Electronic Test Equipment .... ETE
Electronic Test Set .... ETS
Electronic Test Stand .... ETS
Electronic Test Station .... ETS
Electronic Text .... E-Text
Electronic Text and Graphics Transfer System .... ETGTS
Electronic Text Corp. [*Information service or system*] (IID) .... ETC
Electronic Thickness Gauge .... ETG
Electronic Three-Vortex Control System .... ETVCS
Electronic Throttle Control [*Automotive engineering*] .... ETC
Electronic Throttle Control System [*Automotive engineering*] .... ETCS
Electronic Time [*Fuze*] (MCD) .... ET
Electronic Time and Alarm Control System [*Mitsubishi*] [*Automotive engineering*] .... ETACS
Electronic Time Delay .... ETD
Electronic Timing Set .... ETS
Electronic Toll and Traffic Management [*Highway engineering*] .... ETTM
Electronic Toll Center [*AT & T*] .... ETC
Electronic Toll Collection [*FHWA*] (TAG) .... ETC
Electronic Tolls and Traffic Management (PS) .... ETTM
Electronic Tool and Traffic Management .... ETTM
Electronic Tool Company (NITA) .... ETC
Electronic Torque Split [*Automotive engineering*] .... ETS
Electronic Tough Pitch [*Copper*] (NITA) .... ETP
Electronic Traction Control [*Automotive engineering*] .... ETC
Electronic Train Number System (PDAA) .... ETNS
Electronic Trajectory Measurements Working Group [*IRIG*] [*Range Commanders Council White Sands Missile Range, NM*] .... ETMWG
Electronic Transaction Cycle (HGAA) .... ETC
Electronic Transcription [*Radio*] (WDMC) .... ET
Electronic Transfer Vehicle [*MTMC*] (TAG) .... ETV

Electronic Transformers (MCD) ..... ET
Electronic Translator System [Bell System] ..... ETS
Electronic Translator Unit [Telecommunications] ..... ETU
Electronic Trouble Report ..... ETR
Electronic Truck Engine Control System [Automotive engineering] ..... ETEC
Electronic Truck Governor [Cummins Engine] [Automotive engineering] ..... ETG
Electronic Tuning Control (IAA) ..... ETC
Electronic Tuning Fork ..... ETF
Electronic Turbine Governor ..... ETG
Electronic Typewriter ..... ET
Electronic Typing Calculator (IAA) ..... ETC
Electronic Unit ..... ETU
Electronic Unit ..... EU
Electronic Unit Design Section ..... EUDS
Electronic Unit Injector [or Injection] [Automotive Engineering] ..... EUI
Electronic University Network [TeleLearning Systems] [San Francisco, CA] [Computer science] ..... EUN
Electronic Vacuum Regulator Valve [Automotive engineering] ..... EVRV
Electronic Valve and Semiconductor Manufacturers' Association (IAA) ..... VASCA
Electronic Valve Specification (MCD) ..... EVS
Electronic Valve Timing [Automobile engine design] ..... EVT
Electronic Variable Delay Line [Automotive engineering] (IAA) ..... EVDL
Electronic Variable Orifice [Automotive engineering] ..... EVO
Electronic Variable Power-Assist Steering System Controller [Automotive engineering] ..... EVPASSC
Electronic Variable Shock Absorber [Automotive engineering] ..... EVSA
Electronic Variable-Orifice Steering ..... EVOS
Electronic Vehicle Information Center [Automotive engineering] ..... EVIC
Electronic Velocity Analyzer ..... EVA
Electronic Verification of Account Number [Social Security] ..... EVAN
Electronic Vibration Cutoff [Aerospace] (AAG) ..... EVC-O
Electronic Video Recording [or Recorder] (NTCM) ..... EVR
Electronic Video Reproduction (IAA) ..... EVR
Electronic Viewfinder [Photography] ..... EV
Electronic Viewfinder [Photography] (WDMC) ..... EVF
Electronic Vision System [Saab] (NITA) ..... EVS
Electronic Vision Systems Development ..... EVSD
Electronic Visual Communications (DNAB) ..... EVC
Electronic Visual Display Subsystem ..... EVDS
Electronic Voice Alert [Automotive engineering] ..... EVA
Electronic Voice Exchange [Commterm, Inc.] [Billerica, MA] [Telecommunications] (TSSD) ..... EVX
Electronic Voice Phenomena [Parapsychology] ..... EVP
Electronic Voice Switching (AFM) ..... EVS
Electronic Voltmeter (IEEE) ..... EVM
Electronic Voltohmmeter (IEEE) ..... EVOM
Electronic Vote Analysis [Election poll] ..... EVA
Electronic Warfare (CAAL) ..... ELW
Electronic Warfare ..... ELWAR
Electronic Warfare ..... EW
Electronic Warfare ..... EWF
Electronic Warfare and Intelligence [Military] ..... EW & I
Electronic Warfare and Intelligence Operations Center [Military] (MCD) ..... EWIOC
Electronic Warfare Anechoic Chamber ..... EWAC
Electronic Warfare Center (MCD) ..... EWC
Electronic Warfare/Close-Air Support (MCD) ..... EW/CAS
Electronic Warfare, Close-Air Support, Joint Task Force (MCD) ..... EW-CAS-JTF
Electronic Warfare Control Ship [Navy] (NVT) ..... EWCS
Electronic Warfare Coordinating Staff ..... EWCS
Electronic Warfare Coordination Center ..... EWCC
Electronic Warfare Coordination Module (DOMA) ..... EWCM
Electronic Warfare Coordinator (NVT) ..... EWC
Electronic Warfare Counter Response (MCD) ..... EWCR
Electronic Warfare Cover and Deception (MCD) ..... EWCD
Electronic Warfare Cover and Deception Management Subsystem (MCD) ..... EWCDMS
Electronic Warfare Element (AABC) ..... EWE
Electronic Warfare Evaluation Simulator ..... EWES
Electronic Warfare Exercise (NVT) ..... EWEX
Electronic Warfare Exercise in Port (NVT) ..... EWEXIPT
Electronic Warfare Ground Environment Threat Simulator ..... EWGETS
Electronic Warfare Information System (MCD) ..... EWIS
Electronic Warfare Integrated Reprogramming Concept (MCD) ..... EWIRC
Electronic Warfare Intelligence Facility [Fort Huachuca, AZ] [United States Army Electronic Proving Ground] (GRD) ..... EWIF
Electronic Warfare/Intercept (MCD) ..... EW/I
Electronic Warfare Interface Connection Box ..... EWICB
Electronic Warfare Laboratory [Army] ..... EWL
Electronic Warfare Management Information System [Air Force] (MCD) ..... EWMIS
Electronic Warfare Office [or Officer] ..... EWO
Electronic Warfare Officer Training (AFM) ..... EWOT
Electronic Warfare Operational Support Establishment [Royal Air Force] [British] (PDAA) ..... EWOSE
Electronic Warfare Operational System [Air Force] ..... EWOS
Electronic Warfare Operations (NVT) ..... EWOPS
Electronic Warfare Plans [NATO] (NATG) ..... EWP
Electronic Warfare Quick Reaction Capability (MCD) ..... EWQRC
Electronic Warfare/Radioelectronic Parity Study ..... E-PAR
Electronic Warfare Response Monitor (MCD) ..... EWRM
Electronic Warfare Scenario Generator ..... EWSG
Electronic Warfare/Signal Intelligence (MCD) ..... EW/SIGINT
Electronic Warfare Signal Intelligence Material Management Realignment Implementation Task Group ..... EMMRIT
Electronic Warfare Supervisor [Navy] (DOMA) ..... EWS

Electronic Warfare Support Element [Army] (DOMA) ..... EWSE
Electronic Warfare Support Measures [Formerly, EWSM] (AABC) ..... ESM
Electronic Warfare Support Measures [Later, ESM] (AABC) ..... EWSM
Electronic Warfare Support Measures / Electronic Warfare Warning System [Army] ..... ESSM/EWWS
Electronic Warfare System (MCD) ..... EWS
Electronic Warfare Tactical [or Threat] Environment Simulation (NG) ..... EWTES
Electronic Warfare Tactics Analysis Program [Military] (CAAL) ..... EWTAP
Electronic Warfare Tactics Trainer ..... EWTT
Electronic Warfare Technician, First Class (DNAB) EW1
Electronic Warfare Technician, Seaman (DNAB) ..... EWSN
Electronic Warfare Technician, Seaman Apprentice (DNAB) ..... EWSA
Electronic Warfare Technician, Second Class (DNAB) EW2
Electronic Warfare Technician, Third Class (DNAB) EW3
Electronic Warfare Technology (MCD) ..... EWT
Electronic Warfare Test Range [Military] ..... EWTR
Electronic Warfare Trainer ..... EWT
Electronic Warfare Training Squadron [Air Force] ..... EWTNGSq
Electronic Warfare Training Squadron [Air Force] ..... EWTS
Electronic Warfare Vulnerability Assessment [DoD] (RDA) ..... EWVA
Electronic Warfare Warning System ..... EWWS
Electronic White Pages [Information service or system] (IID) ..... EWP
Electronic Wholesaler ..... EW
Electronic Wide-Angle Camera System ..... EWACS
Electronic Wind Direction Indicator ..... EWDI
Electronic Wind Speed Indicator ..... EWSI
Electronic Wiring Intercommunication ..... EWI
Electronic Yellow Pages [Dun's Marketing Services] [Information service or system] (IID) ..... EYP
Electronic-Aided Instruction (IAA) ..... EAI
Electronically Accessible Russian Lexicon ..... EARL
Electronically Adjustable Proportionally Pressure Compensated Flow Control ..... EAPPCFC
Electronically Agile RADAR ..... EAR
Electronically Commutated [Motor] [Electrical engineering] ..... EC
Electronically Controlled Automatic Transmission [Mazda] [Automotive engineering] ..... EC-AT
Electronically Controlled Automatic-Switching System (DEN) ..... ECASS
Electronically Controlled Continuously Variable Transmission ..... ECVT
Electronically Controlled Gasoline Injection [Automotive fuel systems] ..... ECGI
Electronically Controlled Suspension [Mitsubishi] [Automotive engineering] ..... ECS
Electronically Controlled Telephone Exchange (DEN) ..... ECX
Electronically Controlled Transmission [Automotive engineering] ..... ECT
Electronically Heated Catalysts [Automotive engineering] ..... EHC
Electronically Invisible Interconnect [Computer science] ..... EII
Electronically Limited Braking ..... ELB
Electronically Programmed Injection Control [Automotive engineering] ..... EPIC
Electronically Proportioned Braking ..... EPB
Electronically Scanned Array RADAR (IEEE) ..... ESAR
Electronically Scanned Stacked Beam RADAR [Program] ..... ESSBR
Electronically Scanned Thinned Array Radiometer (MCD) ..... ESTAR
Electronically Scanning Airborne Intercept RADAR Antenna ..... ESAIRA
Electronically Steerable Antenna System [Navy] (CAAL) ..... ESAS
Electronically Steerable Array (MCD) ..... ESA
Electronically Steerable Array RADAR ..... ESAR
Electronically Steerable Phased Array [SPADATS] (MCD) ..... ESPA
Electronically Steerable Phased Array RADAR [SPADATS] ..... ESPAR
Electronically Stimulated Incarnation Recall ..... ESIR
Electronically Tunable Filter ..... ETF
Electronically Tunable Parametric Amplifier ..... ETPA
Electronically Tuned Receiver ..... ETR
Electronically Tuned Receiver Tuner ..... ETRT
Electronically Tuned Tuner ..... ETT
Electronically Variable Attenuator (NITA) ..... EVA
Electronically-Agile Solid-State Universal Surveillance (PDAA) ..... ESUS
Electronically-Controlled Throttle Valve [Automotive engineering] ..... ECTV
Electronically-Processed Inter-Unit Cabling (PDAA) ..... EPIC
Electronically-Scanned Optical Receiver (PDAA) ..... ESOR
Electronically-Scanned Thin Array RADAR (SSD) ..... ESTAR
Electronically-Synchronised Transmission Assembly (PDAA) ..... ESTA
Electronic-Courier Circuit (DNAB) ..... ECC
Electronic-Forms (CDE) ..... e-forms
Electronic-Glide Slope (NG) ..... EGS
Electronic-Making Apparatus (IAA) ..... EMA
Electronic-Media Literacy [or Literate] ..... E-ML
Electronic-Optic-Electronic (IAA) ..... EOE
Electronics ..... ELEC
Electronics (NASA) ..... ELECTR
Electronics (KSC) ..... ELECTRO
Electronics (MSA) ..... ELEX
Electronics and Aerospace Systems Convention (MCD) ..... EASCON
Electronics and Avionics Requirements Board (ACII) ..... EARB
Electronics and Computers [Cambridge Scientific Abstracts] [Bethesda, MD Bibliographic database] ..... ELCOM
Electronics and Control ..... EC
Electronics and Power Sources Directorate [Army] (RDA) ..... EPSD
Electronics and Telecommunications Literature Analysis Retrieval System [Computer science] (IID) ..... ETLARS
Electronics Assembly Plant [College Station, TX] [Westinghouse Electric Corp.] ..... EAP
Electronics Association of South Australia ..... EASA
Electronics Buyers' Guide [A publication] (NITA) ..... EBG
Electronics Chassis ..... EC
Electronics Combat Reconnaissance ..... ECR

Electronics Command [*Fort Monmouth, NJ*] [*Army*] ... ECOM
Electronics Command [*Army*] (MCD) ... EL
Electronics Command Meteorological Support Agency [*Army*] (MCD) ... ECMSA
Electronics Command R & D [*Research and Development*] **Laboratories** [*Army*] (MCD) ... ECOM LABS
Electronics Communications [*NASDAQ symbol*] (TTSB) ... ELCC
Electronics Communications Corp. [*NASDAQ symbol*] (SAG) ... ELCC
Electronics Communications Corp. [*Associated Press*] (SAG) ... ElcCm
Electronics Communications Corp. [*Associated Press*] (SAG) ... ElecCm
Electronics Communications Wrrt'A' [*NASDAQ symbol*] (TTSB) ... ELCCW
Electronics Component Test Area (AAG) ... ECTA
Electronics Control Signal Processor [*HELLFIRE*] ... ECSP
Electronics Control System ... ECS
Electronics Coordinating Group [*Army*] (RDA) ... ECOG
Electronics Data Interchange For Administration, Commerce, and Trade [*Telecommunications*] (ACRL) ... EDIFACT
Electronics Design Center [*Case Western Reserve University*] [*Research center*] (RCD) ... EDC
Electronics Engineer ... ELECTRONENGR
Electronics Engineering Division [*Coast Guard*] ... EE
Electronics Engineering Group [*Military*] ... EEG
Electronics Engineering Squadron [*Military*] ... EES
Electronics Exercise [*Military*] (NVT) ... ELEX
Electronics Field Activity ... EFA
Electronics For Imaging (PCM) ... EFI
Electronics For Imaging [*NASDAQ symbol*] (TTSB) ... EFII
Electronics for Imaging [*NASDAQ symbol*] (SAG) ... EFII
Electronics for Imaging, Inc. [*Associated Press*] (SAG) ... EFII
Electronics for Medicine ... EFM
Electronics for Peace (PDAA) ... EIP
Electronics Hardover Monitor (SAA) ... EHOM
Electronics Industry Association and the Telecommunications Industry Association (PCM) ... EIA/TIA
Electronics Information Branch [*Navy*] (MCD) ... EIB
Electronics Information Test ... ELIT
Electronics Installation and Maintenance Bulletin ... EIMB
Electronics Installation Bulletin ... EIB
Electronics Installations Group [*Military*] ... EIG
Electronics Installations Squadron [*Military*] ... EIS
Electronics Interface Integrated Validation (KSC) ... EIIV
Electronics Laboratory ... EL
Electronics Logistics Research Office ... ELRO
Electronics Manufacturers Association [*Defunct*] (EA) ... EMA
Electronics Manufacturing Productivity Facility (MCD) ... EMPF
Electronics Material Officer ... EMO
Electronics Materials Engineering ... EME
Electronics Materiel Agency [*Army*] ... EMA
Electronics Materiel Readiness Activity [*Army*] ... EMRA
Electronics Materiel Support Agency [*Army*] ... EMSA
Electronics Panel ... EP
Electronics Performance and Operational Report (DNAB) ... EPOR
Electronics Precedence List Agency ... EPLA
Electronics Program [*Association of Independent Colleges and Schools specialization code*] ... E
Electronics Research and Development Activity [*Army*] ... ERDA
Electronics Research and Development Activity Analysis [*Army*] (MCD) ... ERDAA
Electronics Research and Development Command [*Later, LABCOM*] [*Adelphi, MD*] [*Army*] ... ERADCOM
Electronics Research and Development Command Atmospheric Sciences Laboratory [*Army*] ... ERADCOM/ASL
Electronics Research Center [*NASA*] ... ERC
Electronics Research Laboratory [*Montana State University*] [*Research center*] (RCD) ... ERI
Electronics Research Laboratory [*Massachusetts Institute of Technology*] [*Research center*] (MCD) ... ERL
Electronics Research Laboratory [*University of California, Berkeley*] [*Research center*] (RCD) ... ERL
Electronics Sea Trials (MCD) ... EST
Electronics Small Business Council ... ESBC
Electronics Supply Office [*or Officer*] ... ESO
Electronics System Measures Operator (MCD) ... ESMO
Electronics Systems Division [*Air Force*] (DOMA) ... ESD
Electronics Systems Source (MCD) ... ESS
Electronics Technical Applications Center [*Air Force*] ... ETAC
Electronics Technical Field Office [*FAA*] ... ETFO
Electronics Technician (DNAB) ... ELECTECH
Electronics Technician (NOAA) ... ELTEC
Electronics Technician [*Navy rating*] ... ET
Electronics Technician, Communications [*Navy rating*] ... ETN
Electronics Technician, Communications, First Class [*Navy rating*] (DNAB) ... ETN1
Electronics Technician, Communications Seaman [*Navy rating*] ... ETNSN
Electronics Technician, Communications Seaman Apprentice [*Navy rating*] ... ETNSA
Electronics Technician, Communications, Second Class [*Navy rating*] (DNAB) ... ETN2
Electronics Technician, Communications, Third Class [*Navy rating*] (DNAB) ... ETN3
Electronics Technician, First Class [*Navy rating*] ... ET1
Electronics Technician, Master Chief [*Navy rating*] ... ETCM
Electronics Technician, (RADAR) [*Navy rating*] ... ETR
Electronics Technician, (RADAR), First Class [*Navy rating*] (DNAB) ... ETR1
Electronics Technician, (RADAR) Seaman [*Navy rating*] ... ETRSN
Electronics Technician, (RADAR) Seaman Apprentice [*Navy rating*] ... ETRSA
Electronics Technician, (RADAR), Second Class [*Navy rating*] (DNAB) ... ETR2
Electronics Technician, (RADAR), Third Class [*Navy rating*] (DNAB) ... ETR3
Electronics Technician, Second Class [*Navy rating*] ... ET2
Electronics Technician, Senior Chief [*Navy rating*] ... ETCS
Electronics Technician, Third Class [*Navy rating*] ... ET3
Electronics Technicians Association, International (EA) ... ETA-I
Electronics Technician's Mate [*Navy rating*] ... ETM
Electronics Technician's Mate, Ship Repair [*Navy rating*] ... ETMSR
Electronics Technology and Devices Laboratory [*Fort Monmouth, NJ*] [*Army*] (RDA) ... ETDL
Electronics Test Equipment Coordination Group [*Military*] ... ETECG
Electronics to Electronics ... EE
Electronics-To-Electronics (WDMC) ... E-to-E
Electronic-Theodolite Naval Alignment ... ETNA
Electronic-Visual-Auditory Training Aid ... EVATA
Electron-Induced Conduction (IAA) ... EIC
Electron-Ion Recombination ... EIR
Electronique Aerospatiale [*France*] ... EAS
Electronique Serge Dassault [*French manufacturer*] (NITA) ... ESD
Electron-Momentum Spectrometer ... EMS
Electron-Nuclear Coupling (IAA) ... ENC
Electron-Nuclear Double Resonance ... ENDOR
Electron-Positron Intersecting Complex (PDAA) ... EPIC
Electron-Proton Spectrometer ... EPS
Electron-Ray Tuning Indicator (DEN) ... ERTI
Electrons per Atom ... E/AT
Electrons per Cubic Centimeter ... E/CM3
Electron-Stimulated Desorption [*Spectroscopy*] ... ESD
Electron-Stimulated Desorption Ion Angular Distribution [*For study of surfaces*] ... ESDIAD
Electron-Transferring Flavoprotein [*Biochemistry*] ... ETF
Electronystagmogram [*or Electrostagmography*] [*Neurology*] (DAVI) ... ENG
Electronystagmography [*Medicine*] ... ENG
Electroocular Symbol Display ... ESD
Electrooculogram [*or Electrooculography*] [*Medicine*] ... EOG
Electroolfactogram [*Medicine*] ... EOG
Electro-Optic Digital Deflector (IEEE) ... EODD
Electro-Optic Direction Sensor ... EODS
Electro-Optic Display ... EOD
Electro-Optic Display Test Chamber ... EODTC
Electro-Optic Force ... EOF
Electro-Optic/Infrared (RDA) ... EO/IR
Electro-Optic Light Valve ... EOLV
Electro-Optic Phase Change (IEEE) ... EOPC
Electro-Optic Projector ... EOP
Electro-Optic Test Chamber ... EOTC
Electro-Optical ... EO
Electro-Optical Alignment Unit (AAG) ... EOAU
Electro-Optical Area Correlator [*Missile guidance system*] ... EAC
Electro-Optical Assembly (MCD) ... EOA
Electro-Optical Bench [*Army*] ... EOB
Electro-Optical Collection and Analysis Reporting System (MCD) ... ELOCARS
Electro-Optical Collection and Analysis Targeting System ... ELO-CATS
Electro-Optical Counter-Countermeasures (MCD) ... EOCCM
Electro-Optical Countermeasures (MCD) ... EOCM
Electro-Optical Direction and Ranging System (IAA) ... EODARS
Electro-Optical Fire Control [*Military*] (PDAA) ... EOFC
Electro-Optical Fire Control System [*Military*] (CAAL) ... EOFCS
Electro-Optical Glide Bomb (MCD) ... EOGB
Electro-Optical Guided Bomb (VNW) ... EOGB
Electro-Optical Guided Weapons ... EO/GW
Electro-Optical Identification and Tracking System (MCD) ... EOITS
Electro-Optical Imaging (PDAA) ... EOI
Electro-Optical Imaging System (IEEE) ... EOIS
Electro-Optical Infrared ... EOIR
Electrooptical Intelligence [*DoD*] ... ELECTRO-OPTINT
Electro-Optical Ion Detection [*Spectroscopy*] ... EOID
Electro-Optical Light Modulator ... EOLM
Electro-Optical Long-Range Protection System [*Military*] (DWSG) ... EOLORPS
Electro-Optical Modulator ... EOM
Electro-Optical Rectifier (MCD) ... EOR
Electro-Optical Research ... EOR
Electro-Optical Sensor System [*Navy*] (MCD) ... EOSS
Electro-Optical Sensors Atmospheric Effects Library (RDA) ... E-O SAEL
Electro-Optical Signal Processing Computer ... EOSPC
Electro-Optical Simulation [*or Sighting*] **System** [*for missiles*] [*Army*] (MCD) ... EOSS
Electro-Optical System [*Electronics*] (ECII) ... EOS
Electro-Optical Systems, Inc. [*Subsidiary of Xerox Corp.*] ... EOS
Electro-Optical Systems, Inc., Pasadena, CA [*Library symbol Library of Congress*] (LCLS) ... CPEI
Electro-Optical Target Acquisition and Designation System [*Military*] ... EOTADS
Electro-Optical Target Locating System (MCD) ... ELOTARLOCS
Electro-Optical Technology Program Office [*Navy*] (GRD) ... EOPTO
Electro-Optical Tracking Device ... EOTD
Electro-Optical Tracking System (IDOE) ... EOTS
Electro-Optical Unit ... EOU
Electro-Optical Viewing System (MCD) ... EOVS
Electro-Optical Viewing System ... EVS
Electro-Optical Visual Sensors [*Hughes Aircraft Co.*] ... EVS
Electro-Optical Weapons System ... EOWS
Electro-Optics and Laser International Exhibition and Conference [*British*] (ITD) ... EOL
Electro-Optics Augmentation ... EOA
Electro-Optics Industries Ltd. ... EL-OP

Electro-Optics Laboratory [*University of Michigan*] [*Research center*]
(RCD) .... EOLAB
Electro-Optics Test Facility .... EOTF
Electroosmotic Flow [*Physical chemistry*] .... EOF
Electropharmacology, Inc. [*Associated Press*] (SAG) .... Elctph
Electropharmacology, Inc. [*Associated Press*] (SAG) .... Elctphr
Electropharmacology, Inc. [*NASDAQ symbol*] (SAG) .... EPHI
Electropharmacology Inc. Wrrt [*NASDAQ symbol*] (TTSB) .... EPHIW
Electrophenesis Operations in Space .... EOS
Electrophoresis [*Laboratory*] (DAVI) .... ELP
Electrophoresis .... EP
Electrophoresis Duplicating Film [*For analytical chemistry*] ...... EDF
Electrophoresis Duplicating Paper [*For analytical chemistry*] .... EDP
Electrophoresis Equipment Test Verification [*Military*] .... EETV
Electrophoresis Equipment Verification Test .... EEVT
Electrophoresis Experiment [*NASA*] (MCD) .... EPE
Electrophoretic Analysis [*Botany*] .... E
Electrophoretic Image Display [*Analytical chemistry*] (IAA) .... EPID
Electrophoretic Light Scattering [*Analytical chemistry*] .... ELS
Electrophoretic Mobility [*Analytical biochemistry*] .... EM
Electrophoretic Mobility Shift Assay [*Analytical biochemistry*] .. EMSA
Electrophoretic Operations in Space [*Without gravity*] .... EOS
Electro-Phosphate Coating [*Metallurgical engineering*] .... ELPO
Electrophotographic Display (DGA) .... EPD
Electrophrenic Respiration [*Medicine*] .... EPR
Electrophysics (IAA) .... ELECTROPHYS
Electrophysiologic Study .... EPS
Electrophysiological Study Versus Electrocardiographic Monitoring
[*Medical study*] .... ESVEM
Electrophysiological Technologists' Association (EAIO) .... EPTA
Electrophysiology .... EP
Electroplate (VRA) .... elctrpl
Electroplate .... EP
Electroplate (MSA) .... EPL
Electroplate White Metal (IAA) .... EPWM
Electroplated Britannia Metal (IIA) .... EPBM
Electroplated Nickel Silver .... EPNS
Electroplating .... ELCPLTG
Electropneumatic .... ELPNEU
Electropneumatic .... EP
Electropneumatic Gear Shift [*System*] .... EPS
Electropneumatic Service System [*Truck engineering*] .... ESS
Electropneumatic Valve .... EPV
Electropneumogram [*Medicine*] .... EPG
Electropsychometer [*Device for measuring emotional response through
electrical conductivity of subject's skin*] .... E (Meter)
Electroradioimmunoassay [*Clinical chemistry*] .... ERIA
Electroretinogram [*Medicine*] .... ERG
Electro-Rheological .... ER
Electro-Rheological Fluids [*American Cyanamid Co.*] .... ERF
Electrorheology [*Physics*] .... ER
Electroscience Laboratory [*Ohio State University*] [*Research center*]
(RCD) .... ESL
Electroselective Pattern Metering [*Olympus cameras*] .... ESP
Electrosensitive Paper (MHDB) .... ESP
Electrosensitive Programming .... ESP
Electro-Sensors [*NASDAQ symbol*] (TTSB) .... ELSE
Electro-Sensors, Inc. [*NASDAQ symbol*] (NQ) .... ELSE
Electrosensory Lateral Line [*Invertebrate zoology*] .... ELLL
Electrosensory Lateral Line-Lobe [*Biology*] .... ELL
Electroshock [*Psychology*] .... ES
Electroshock Protection (MCD) .... ESP
Electroshock Research Association [*Later, International Psychiatric Library
Service*] .... ERA
Electroshock Therapy [*Psychology*] .... EST
Electroshock Therapy Apparatus [*Psychology*] .... ESTA
Electroslag Refining Technology [*Chemical engineering*] (IAA) .. ESRT
Electroslag Remelting [*Steel alloy*] .... ESR
Electro-Slag Remelting .... ESR
Electroslag Remelting (PDAA) .... ESRM
Electroslag Welding .... ESW
Electroslag Welding .... EW
Electrosonic Profiler .... ESP
Electrosource, Inc. [*Associated Press*] (SAG) .... Elctsrc
Electrosource, Inc. [*NASDAQ symbol*] (NQ) .... ELSI
Electrospinogram [*Medicine*] (MEDA) .... ESG
Electrospray [*Ionization*] [*Physics*] .... ES
Electrospray Ionization [*Physics*] .... ESI
Electrospray Ionization Mass Spectrometry .... ESI-MS
Electrospray Ionization Mass Spectrometry .... ES-MS
ElectroStar Inc. [*NASDAQ symbol*] (TTSB) .... ESTR
Electrostatic .... ES
Electrostatic (IDOE) .... stat-
Electrostatic Air Filter (PDAA) .... ESF
Electrostatic Analyzer (IAA) .... EA
Electrostatic Analyzer .... ESA
Electrostatic Capacity [*Symbol*] (AAMN) .... K
Electrostatic Centimeter Gram Second (IAA) .... ESCGS
Electrostatic Collector .... ESC
Electrostatic Compatibility (IEEE) .... ESC
Electrostatic Deflecting Lens (PDAA) .... EDL
Electrostatic Discharge (IAA) .... ED
Electrostatic Discharge (MCD) .... ESD
Electrostatic Discharge Effects (MCD) .... ESDE
Electrostatic Discharge Sensitive (MCD) .... ESDS

Electrostatic Electron Microscope .... EEM
Electrostatic Energy Analyzer [*Instrumentation*] .... EEA
Electrostatic Focusing [*Electronics*] .... ESF
Electrostatic Gyroscope (IEEE) .... ESG
Electrostatic Ion Cyclotron [*Seismology*] .... EIC
Electrostatic Ion Cyclotron Waves [*Seismology*] .... EICW
Electrostatic Klystron .... ESK
Electrostatic Latent Image Development (IAA) .... ELID
Electrostatic Latent Image Photography (IEEE) .... ELIP
Electrostatic Levitator Facility (SSD) .... ELF
Electrostatic Loudspeaker (DEN) .... ELS
Electrostatic Particle Guide (OA) .... EPG
Electrostatic Particle Size Analyzer .... EPSA
Electrostatic Plasma Oscillator .... EPO
Electrostatic Powder .... EP
Electrostatic Power Generator .... EPG
Electrostatic Precipitator [*Also, ESP*] .... EP
Electrostatic Precipitator [*Also, EP*] .... ESP
Electrostatic Primer [*Automotive manufacturing*] .... ELPO
Electrostatic Print (VRA) .... ELSTPT
Electrostatic Printing Tube .... EPT
Electrostatic Probe (IAA) .... ESP
Electrostatic Probe Experiment .... EPE
Electrostatic Process (IAA) .... ELECPROC
Electrostatic Reversal Printing .... ERP
Electrostatic Sensitive Device (PDAA) .... ESD
Electrostatic Spray .... ES
Electrostatic Spraying .... ES
Electrostatic Storage .... ES
Electrostatic Storage Deflection (IAA) .... ED
Electrostatic Storage Deflection .... ESD
Electrostatic Storage Display Tube (IAA) .... ESDT
Electrostatic Storage Tube .... EST
Electrostatic Transistorized Voltmeter .... ETVM
Electrostatic Unit .... ESU
Electrostatic Unit (IDOE) .... esu
Electrostatic Units (IDOE) .... esu
Electrostatic Vector Grid .... EVG
Electrostatic Voltmeter (DEN) .... ESV
Electrostatic Water Treaters (DICI) .... EWT
Electrostatically Enhanced Fabric Filtration .... EEFF
Electrostatically Focused Tube .... EFT
Electrostatically Supported Gyro Monitor [*Navy*] .... ESGM
Electrostatically Supported Gyro Monitor/Ships Inertial Naviation System
[*Navy*] .... ESGM/SINS
Electrostatically-Focused Kylstron (IAA) .... ESFK
Electrostatische Einheit [*Electrostatic unit*] [*Physics*] (DAVI) ... ESE
Electrosurgical Unit [*Medicine*] .... ESU
[*The*] Electro-Technical Council of Ireland (ACII) .... ETCI
Electrotechnical Laboratory (MCD) .... ETL
Electrothermal [*Gun classification*] .... ET
Electrothermal Atomic Absorption [*Physics*] (DAVI) .... EAA
Electrothermal Atomic Absorption [*Analytical technique*] ...... ETAA
Electrothermal Atomic Absorption Spectrometry .... ETAAS
Electrothermal Atomization [*For spectrometry*] .... ETA
Electrothermal Engine .... ETE
Electrothermal Filter .... ETF
Electrothermal Gun .... ETG
Electrothermal Hydrazine Thruster .... EHT
Electrothermal Vaporization .... ETV
Electrothermal-Chemical (RDA) .... ETC
Electrotype (ROG) .... ELECTRO
Electrotypers' and Stereotypers' Managers and Overseers Association
[*British*] (BI) .... ESMOA
Electroultrafiltration .... EUF
Electrovacuum Drive .... EVD
Electro-Viscous Fluid [*Electrical engineering*] .... EVF
Electrovisual Sensors .... EVS
Electrovisual System (MUGU) .... ELVIS
Electrum [*Numismatics*] .... EL
Electuarium [*Electuary*] [*Pharmacy*] (ROG) .... ELEC
Electuarium [*Electuary*] [*Pharmacy*] .... ELECT
Eledoisin [*Biochemistry*] .... Ele
Eleele, HI [*AM radio station call letters*] .... KUAI
Elefsis [*Greece*] [*ICAO location identifier*] (ICLI) .... LGEL
Eleftherofronon [*Free Opinion Party*] [*Greek*] (PPE) .... EF
Elegance .... ELGNC
Elegant .... ELGNT
Elegant Illusions, Inc. [*NASDAQ symbol*] (SAG) .... EILL
Elegant Illusions, Inc. [*Associated Press*] (SAG) .... ElegIll
Elek Tek, Inc. [*NASDAQ symbol*] (SAG) .... ELEK
Elek Tek, Inc. [*Associated Press*] (SAG) .... ElekTek
Elektra [*Record label*] .... Elek
Elektra Power, Inc. [*Vancouver Stock Exchange symbol*] .... EPW
Elektromotroischer Systembaukasten .... ESB
Elektronische Datenverarbeitung [*Electronic Data Processing - EDP*]
[*German*] .... EDV
Elektronisches Dokumentations und Informations System [*Information
retrieval system*] [*France*] (NITA) .... EDIS
Elektronisches Worterbuch der Fachsprachen [*Technische Universitat
Dresden*] [*Multilingual terminology bank*] (NITA) .... EWF
Elektronno-Vychislitel'naya Mashina [*Electronic Calculating Machine*]
[*Russian*] .... EVM
Element (IAA) .... E
Element .... EL

Element (MSA) ... ELEM
Element (VRA) ... elem
Element (AABC) ... ELM
Element ... ELMNT
Element ... ELT
Element ... L
Element Change Factor (MCD) ... ECF
Element Characteristics Equation ... ECE
Element Code (MCD) ... ELECD
Element Contractor (NASA) ... EC
Element Count [*Searchable field*] [*Dialog*] [*Information service or system*] (NITA) ... EC
Element Interface Functional Analysis (NASA) ... EIFA
Element Load Model ... ELM
Element Management System [*Computer science*] (TNIG) ... EMS
Element Number [*Computer science*] ... EN
Element Numbers [*On urinalysis*] [*Biochemistry*] (DAVI) ... ELMTNO
Element of Expense ... EOE
Element of Expense/Investment Code (AFM) ... EEIC
Element Processor (NITA) ... ELP
Element Project Office [*NASA*] (NASA) ... EPO
Element Signal [*Dialog*] [*Searchable field*] [*Information service or system*] (NITA) ... ES
Elemental Analysis Research Center [*Department of Health and Human Services*] (GRD) ... EARC
Elemental Chlorine-Free [*Pulp and paper processing*] ... ECF
Elemental Method of Training ... EMT
Elemental Standard Data System (NG) ... ESDS
Elemental Time Monitor (PDAA) ... ETM
Elemental X-Ray Analysis of Materials ... EXAM
Elementary ... EL
Elementary (MSA) ... ELEM
Elementary ... ELEM
Elementary Access Method (IAA) ... EAM
Elementary Adult Sex Education (EDAC) ... EASE
Elementary and Early Childhood Education [*Educational Resources Information Center (ERIC) Clearinghouse*] [*University of Illinois*] (PAZ) ... PS
Elementary and High School [*Acronym refers to books published for this market*] ... ELHI
Elementary and High School Levels [*Textbook publishing*] (WDMC) ... el-hi
Elementary and Reserve Flying Training School [*British military*] (DMA) ... E & RFTS
Elementary and Secondary Education Act [*1965*] ... ESEA
Elementary and Secondary Education General Information Survey [*Department of Education*] (GFGA) ... ELSEGIS
Elementary and Secondary Education Longitudinal Studies [*Department of Education*] (GFGA) ... ESLS
Elementary and Secondary Education Statistics Division [*Department of Education*] (GFGA) ... ESESD
Elementary and Secondary School Index [*Research test*] [*Psychology*] ... ESI
Elementary Assignment (IAA) ... EA
Elementary Body [*Hematology*] ... EB
Elementary Charge [*of a proton*] [*Symbol IUPAC*] ... e
Elementary Charge [*of a Proton*] (IAA) ... ELEMCH
Elementary Circulation Mechanism ... ECM
Elementary Electrical and Radio Material [*Training School*] [*Navy*] ... EE & RM
Elementary Flying Training College [*British*] ... EFTC
Elementary Flying Training School [*British*] ... EFTS
Elementary Flying Training School [*British*] (MCD) ... ELE
Elementary Gliding School [*British military*] (DMA) ... EGS
Elementary Imprint Assistance [*Writing system for the blind*] ... ELIA
Elementary Language [*Programming language*] (NITA) ... ELAN
Elementary Math Library [*IBM Corp.*] ... EML
Elementary Operated Control (PDAA) ... EOC
Elementary Operation (IAA) ... EO
Elementary Perceiver and Memorizer [*University of California*] [*Learning theory Computer device*] ... EPAM
Elementary Potential Digital Computing Component ... EPDCC
Elementary Potential Digital Computing Element (IAA) ... EPDCE
Elementary Processing Centers ... EPC
Elementary Relaxation Oscillator [*Instrumentation*] ... ERO
Elementary Reliability Unit Parameter Technique (PDAA) ... ERUPT
Elementary Renewal Theorem ... ERT
Elementary School Administrative Supervisory Certificate ... ESASC
Elementary School Behavior Rating Scale [*Devereaux*] [*Psychology*] ... ESBRS
Elementary School Center [*An association*] (EA) ... ESC
Elementary School No. 2, Inwood, NY [*Library symbol*] [*Library of Congress*] (LCLS) ... NInDE
Elementary School No. 4, Inwood, NY [*Library symbol*] [*Library of Congress*] (LCLS) ... NInWE
Elementary School Science Project ... ESSP
Elementary Science Study [*National Science Foundation*] ... ESS
Elementary Symmetric Function (MCD) ... ESF
Elementary Wiring Diagram ... EWD
Elements ... ELMS
Elements [*on Urinalysis*] [*Biochemistry*] (DAVI) ... ELMT
Elements of Data (MSA) ... EOD
Elements of Expense [*Army*] (AABC) ... EE
Elenchus Suppletorius ad Elenchum Bibliographicum Biblicum [*A publication*] (BJA) ... ES
Elephant & Castle Group [*NASDAQ symbol*] (TTSB) ... PUBSF
Elephant & Castle Group, Inc. [*Associated Press*] (SAG) ... ElepCstl
Elephant & Castle Group, Inc. [*NASDAQ symbol*] (SAG) ... PUBS
Elephant Folio (WGA) ... El Fo
Elephant Interest Group (EA) ... EIG
Elephant Memory System [*Computer science*] ... EMS
Elephant Species Survival Plan ... ESSP
Elephantine Papyri (BJA) ... EP
Elephantine Papyri [*A publication*] (OCD) ... PEleph
Eleutherian Mills Historical Library, Greenville, DE [*Library symbol Library of Congress*] (LCLS) ... DeGE
Elevate (DAVI) ... elev
Elevate Head of Bed [*Medicine*] (DAVI) ... EHB
Elevated [*Railway*] [*Also, L*] ... EL
Elevated [*Railway*] [*Also, EL*] ... L
Elevated Acquisition RADAR (PDAA) ... ELEVAR
Elevated Causeway System (CAAL) ... ELCAS
Elevated Electric Railway [*South London Railway*] (ROG) ... EER
Elevated Electrode Integrated Circuit (MHDI) ... EEIC
Elevated Glandular Epidermis ... EGE
Elevated Kinetic Energy Weapon ... ELKE
Elevated Radiation Seeking Rocket ... ERASER
Elevated Radio System ... ERS
Elevated Release Point [*Nuclear energy*] (NRCH) ... ERP
Elevated Stabilized Platform [*Aircraft*] ... ESP
Elevated Target Acquisition System ... ETAS
Elevated Temperature (MCD) ... ET
Elevated Temperature Polyethylene ... ETPE
Elevated Temperature Strain Gauge ... ETSG
Elevated Training Platform ... ETP
Elevated Water Storage Tank [*Nuclear energy*] (NRCH) ... EWST
Elevated Work Cage Improvement Program (DWSG) ... EWCIP
Elevating Transfer Vehicle (PDAA) ... ETV
Elevation [*Angle*] ... E
Elevation (AAG) ... EL
Elevation (AFM) ... ELEV
Elevation (VRA) ... elv
Elevation Angle (NASA) ... E
Elevation Angle Guidance Landing Equipment ... EAGLE
Elevation Console ... EC
Elevation Data Edit Terminals (RDA) ... EDET
Elevation Drive Assembly (MCD) ... EDA
Elevation Finder [*Military*] ... EF
Elevation Guidance for Approach and Landing [*Aviation*] ... EGAL
Elevation Model (NRCH) ... EM
Elevation Position Indicator [*Aviation*] ... EPI
Elevation Versus Amplitude (SAA) ... EVA
Elevation Versus Integrated Log ... EVIL
Elevator [*Technical drawings*] (NFPA) ... E
Elevator ... ELEV
Elevator ... ELEV
Elevator Code (NFPA) ... EIC
Elevator Code ... EIC
Elevator Equipment Room [*NFPA pre-fire planning symbol*] (NFPA) ... EE
Elevator Industries Association (EA) ... EIA
Elevator Load Feel (MCD) ... ELF
Eleven (NASA) ... ELVN
Eleven Years of Bible Bibliography [*A publication*] (BJA) ... ElevenYBB
Eleventh Coast Guard District [*Los Angeles, CA*] [*USCG*] (TAG) ... D11
Eleventh Commandment Fellowship (EA) ... ECF
Elevon [*Aviation*] (NASA) ... ELEV
Elevon Load System [*Aviation*] (MCD) ... ELS
Elexsys International, Inc. [*NASDAQ symbol*] (SAG) ... ELEX
Elexsys International, Inc. [*Associated Press*] (SAG) ... Elexsys
ELEXSYS Intl. [*NASDAQ symbol*] (TTSB) ... ELEX
Eley-Rideal Mechanism [*Chemistry*] ... ER
Elf Air Ltd. [*Russian Federation*] [*ICAO designator*] (FAAC) ... EFR
Elf Aquitaine [*NYSE symbol*] (SAG) ... ELF
Elf Aquitaine [*Associated Press*] (SAG) ... ElfAquit
Elf Aquitaine ADS [*NYSE symbol*] (TTSB) ... ELF
Elf Overseas Ltd. [*Associated Press*] (SAG) ... ElfOv
Elf Overseas Ltd. [*NYSE symbol*] (SPSG) ... EOL
Elf Overseas Ltd 8.50% Pfd'A' [*NYSE symbol*] (TTSB) ... EOLPrA
Elf Overseas Ltd 7.625% Pfd'B' [*NYSE symbol*] (TTSB) ... EOLPrB
Elfin Cove [*Alaska*] [*Airport symbol*] (OAG) ... ELV
Elfin Cove, AK [*Location identifier FAA*] (FAAL) ... ELV
Elfquest Fan Club (EA) ... EFC
Elgaz [*Poland ICAO designator*] (FAAC) ... LGA
Elgin Branch, Rideau Lakes Union Library, Ontario [*Library symbol National Library of Canada*] (NLC) ... OERL
Elgin Community College [*Illinois*] ... ECC
Elgin Community College, Elgin, IL [*Library symbol Library of Congress*] (LCLS) ... IElgC
Elgin County Public Library, St. Thomas, ON, Canada [*Library symbol Library of Congress*] (LCLS) ... CaOStTE
Elgin County Public Library, St. Thomas, Ontario [*Library symbol National Library of Canada*] (NLC) ... OSTTE
Elgin Echo, Elgin, IA [*Library symbol Library of Congress*] (LCLS) ... IaElgE
Elgin, IL [*FM radio station call letters*] ... WEPS
Elgin, IL [*FM radio station call letters*] ... WJKL
Elgin, IL [*AM radio station call letters*] ... WRMN
Elgin, Joliet & Eastern Railway Co. [*AAR code*] ... EJE
Elgin, TX [*AM radio station call letters*] ... KELG
Elgin, TX [*FM radio station call letters*] ... KKLB
Elginfield [*Ontario*] [*Seismograph station code, US Geological Survey*] (SEIS) ... ELF
El-Gora [*Egypt*] [*ICAO location identifier*] (ICLI) ... HEGR
Eli Lilly & Co. [*Research code symbol*] ... A
Eli Lilly & Co. [*Research code symbol*] ... EL
Eli Lilly & Co. [*Research code symbol*] [*Canada*] ... VC-K

Eli Lilly & Co., Agricultural Library, Greenfield, IN [*OCLC symbol*] (OCLC) .... ILD
Eli Lilly & Co., Business Library, Indianapolis, IN [*OCLC symbol*] (OCLC) .... ILB
Eli Lilly & Co., Business Library, Indianapolis, IN [*Library symbol Library of Congress*] (LCLS) .... InILB
Eli Lilly & Co., Indianapolis, IN [*OCLC symbol*] (OCLC) .... IES
Eli Lilly & Co., Law Library, Indianapolis, IN [*Library symbol*] [*Library of Congress*] (LCLS) .... InILL
Eli Lilly & Co., Library Agricultural Services, Greenfield, IN [*Library symbol Library of Congress*] (LCLS) .... InGrefL
Eli Lilly & Co., Scientific Library, Indianapolis, IN [*Library symbol Library of Congress*] (LCLS) .... InIL
Eli Whitney Metrology Center .... EWMC
Eliadamello SPA [*Italy ICAO designator*] (FAAC) .... LLO
Eliciantur [*Let Be Drawn*] [*Pharmacy*] (ROG) .... ELICIANT
Eli-Fly SpA [*Italy ICAO designator*] (FAAC) .... EBS
Eligibility On-Site (MEDA) .... EOS
Eligibility Review and Reemployment Assistance Program [*Employment Service*] [*Department of Labor*] .... ERP
Eligibility Review Committee [*Social security*] [*Australia*] .... ERC
Eligible (AFM) .... ELIG
Eligible for Overseas Service .... EOS
Eligible for Retirement (DNAB) .... ELIG RET
Eligible for Separation .... ES
Eligible Individual [*Social Security Administration*] .... EI
Eligible Layout .... EL
Eligible Legalized Alien (GFGA) .... ELA
Eligible Liability [*British*] .... EL
Eligible Participant (OICC) .... EP
Eligible Rollover Distribution [*Business term*] .... ERD
Eligible Spouse [*Social Security Administration*] .... ES
Eligible Termination Payment (ADA) .... ETP
Elim [*Alaska*] [*Airport symbol*] (OAG) .... ELI
Eliminate (AFM) .... ELIM
Eliminate and Count [*Coding*] [*Computer science*] .... ELCO
Eliminate Legal-Size Files [*An association*] .... ELF
Eliminate the National Debt (EA) .... END
Elimination of Discharge of Pollutants (DICI) .... EDOP
Elimination of Purchase Requirement [*Department of Agriculture*] .... EPR
Elimination of Range Zero System [*Aviation*] .... EROS
Elimination of Solvation Procedure [*Chemistry*] .... ESP
Eliminator [*Automotive engineering*] .... ELIM
Eline .... EI
ELINT [*Electronic Intelligence*] Advisory Group (AABC) .... EAG
ELINT [*Electronic Intercept*] Collection/Analysis Guide [*Air Force*] .... ELCAG
ELINT [*Electronic Intelligence*] - Ocean Reconnaissance Satellite (MCD) .... EORSAT
ELINT [*Extended-Range Interceptor Technology*] Ocean Reconnaissance Satellite (DOMA) .... EROSAT
ELINT [*Electronic Intelligence*] Receiver Test System (MCD) .... ERTS
ELINT [*Electronic Intelligence*] Requirements and Capabilities Management System (MCD) .... ERCMS
ELINT [*Electronic Intelligence*] Support System (DWSG) .... ESS
ELINT [*Electronic Intelligence*], Technical (MCD) .... ELTEC
Elipse of Skin [*Medicine*] (DAVI) .... EOS
Elisabeth Bruyere Health Center [*Centre de Sante Elisabeth Bruyere*] Ottawa, Ontario [*Library symbol National Library of Canada*] (NLC) .... OOEB
Elisabeth Kubler-Ross Center (EA) .... EKRC
Elisabeth Sladen Information Network [*Actress featured in TV series "Dr. Who"*] [*British*] (EA) .... ESIN
Elisha D. Smith Public Library, Menasha, WI [*Library symbol Library of Congress*] (LCLS) .... WMe
Elison Air Force Base [*Alaska*] (KSC) .... EAFB
Elite [*Record label*] [*Europe*] .... Eli
Elite Insurance Management Ltd. [*Toronto Stock Exchange symbol Vancouver Stock Exchange symbol*] .... EIM
Elite Resources Corp. [*Vancouver Stock Exchange symbol*] .... ERE
Elitos SpA [*Italy ICAO designator*] (FAAC) .... EHS
Elixir [*Pharmacology*] (MAE) .... el
Elixir [*Pharmacology*] .... ELIX
Elixir Terpin Hydrate [*Pharmacy*] .... ETH
Elixir Terpin Hydrate with Codeine [*Pharmacy*] .... ETH/C
Eliye Springs [*Kenya*] [*ICAO location identifier*] (ICLI) .... HKES
[*An*] Elizabeth Barrett Browning Concordance [*A publication*] .... BRCN
Elizabeth City [*North Carolina*] [*Airport symbol*] (AD) .... ECG
Elizabeth City Coast Guard Air Base/Municipal [*North Carolina*] [*ICAO location identifier*] (ICLI) .... KECG
Elizabeth City, NC [*Location identifier FAA*] (FAAL) .... ECG
Elizabeth City, NC [*Location identifier FAA*] (FAAL) .... IZE
Elizabeth City, NC [*Location identifier FAA*] (FAAL) .... NOZ
Elizabeth City, NC [*AM radio station call letters*] .... WCNC
Elizabeth City, NC [*AM radio station call letters*] .... WGAI
Elizabeth City, NC [*FM radio station call letters*] .... WKJX
Elizabeth City, NC [*FM radio station call letters*] .... WRVS
Elizabeth City State University, Elizabeth City, NC [*Library symbol Library of Congress*] (LCLS) .... NcElcE
Elizabeth City State University, Elizabeth City, NC [*OCLC symbol*] (OCLC) .... NPE
Elizabeth Free Public Library, Elizabeth, NJ [*Library symbol Library of Congress*] (LCLS) .... NjEli
Elizabeth Garrett Anderson Hospital [*British*] (DI) .... EGA
Elizabeth Jones [*Designer's mark, when appearing on US coins*] .... EJ
Elizabeth Linington Society (EA) .... ELS
Elizabeth Macarthur Agricultural Institute [*Australia*] .... EMAI
Elizabeth McRae Associates, Toronto, ON, Canada [*Library symbol*] [*Library of Congress*] (LCLS) .... CaOTEMC

Elizabeth McRae Associates, Toronto, Ontario [*Library symbol Obsolete National Library of Canada*] (NLC) .... OTEMC
Elizabeth, NJ [*AM radio station call letters*] .... WJDM
Elizabeth Public Library, Elizabeth, CO [*Library symbol Library of Congress*] (LCLS) .... CoEli
Elizabeth Regina [*Queen Elizabeth*] (DLA) .... ER
Elizabeth S. Priori-1 [*Virus named after one of the scientists who isolated it*] ESP-1
Elizabeth Seton College, Yonkers, NY [*Library symbol Library of Congress*] (LCLS) .... NYES
Elizabeth Watson Library, Teck Mining Group Ltd., Vancouver, British Columbia [*Library symbol National Library of Canada*] (NLC) .... BVATE
Elizabetha Regina [*Queen Elizabeth*] [*Latin*] .... ER
Elizabethan (ROG) .... ELIZ
Elizabethan Club of Yale University (EA) .... ECYU
Elizabethan Railway Society [*British*] (BI) .... ERS
Elizabethton, TN [*Location identifier FAA*] (FAAL) .... EZT
Elizabethton, TN [*FM radio station call letters*] (RBYB) .... WAEZ
Elizabethton, TN [*AM radio station call letters*] .... WBEJ
Elizabethton, TN [*AM radio station call letters*] (RBYB) .... WKPP
Elizabethtown College, Elizabethtown, PA [*OCLC symbol*] (OCLC) .... ELZ
Elizabethtown College, Elizabethtown, PA [*Library symbol*] [*Library of Congress*] (LCLS) .... PEIC
Elizabethtown College, Elizabethtown, PA [*Library symbol Library of Congress*] (LCLS) .... PEIC
Elizabethtown, KY [*AM radio station call letters*] .... WIEL
Elizabethtown, KY [*FM radio station call letters*] .... WKUE
Elizabethtown, KY [*Television station call letters*] .... WKZT
Elizabethtown, KY [*FM radio station call letters*] .... WQXE
Elizabethtown, NC [*AM radio station call letters*] .... WBLA
Elizabethtown, NC [*FM radio station call letters*] .... WGQR
Elizabethtown, PA [*AM radio station call letters*] .... WPDC
Elizabethtown, PA [*FM radio station call letters*] .... WWEC
Elizabethville [*Zaire*] [*Later, KVA*] [*Geomagnetic observatory code*] .... ELI
Elizabethville, PA [*FM radio station call letters*] .... WYGL
Elizabth Taber Library, Marion, MA [*Library symbol*] [*Library of Congress*] (LCLS) .... MMn
Eljer Industries [*NASDAQ symbol*] (TTSB) .... ELJ
Eljer Industries, Inc. [*NYSE symbol*] (SPSG) .... ELJ
Eljer Industries, Inc. [*Associated Press*] (SAG) .... Eljer
Elk Chute Ditch [*Missouri*] [*Seismograph station code, US Geological Survey*] (SEIS) .... ECD
Elk City, OK [*Location identifier FAA*] (FAAL) .... ELK
Elk City, OK [*Location identifier FAA*] (FAAL) .... EZY
Elk City, OK [*AM radio station call letters*] .... KADS
Elk City, OK [*FM radio station call letters*] .... KECO
Elk City, OK [*FM radio station call letters*] .... KTIJ
Elk City, OK [*FM radio station call letters*] (RBYB) .... KXOO
Elk City School/Community Library, Elk City, ID [*Library symbol*] [*Library of Congress*] (LCLS) .... IdEcL
Elk Horn-Kimballton Review, Elk Horn, IA [*Library symbol Library of Congress*] (LCLS) .... IaElkhR
Elk Lake Public Library, Elk Lake, ON, Canada [*Library symbol*] [*Library of Congress*] (LCLS) .... CaOElk
Elk Lake Public Library, Ontario [*Library symbol National Library of Canada*] (BIB) .... OELk
Elk Mound, WI [*FM radio station call letters*] .... WECL
Elk Point Public Library, Alberta [*Library symbol National Library of Canada*] (NLC) .... AELK
Elk Point Public Library, Elk Point, AB, Canada [*Library symbol*] [*Library of Congress*] (LCLS) .... CaAElk
Elk Rapids District Library, Elk Rapids, MI [*Library symbol Library of Congress*] (LCLS) .... MiElk
Elk River Public Library, Elk River, MN [*Library symbol*] [*Library of Congress*] (LCLS) .... MnEr
Elk River Reactor .... ERR
Elk River School/Community Library, Elk River, ID [*Library symbol*] [*Library of Congress*] (LCLS) .... IdEr
Elk River Senior High School, Elk River, MN [*Library symbol*] [*Library of Congress*] (LCLS) .... MnErS
Elk Township Library, Peck, MI [*Library symbol Library of Congress*] .... MiPec
Elkader Historical Society, Elkader, IA [*Library symbol Library of Congress*] (LCLS) .... IaElkHi
Elkader, IA [*AM radio station call letters*] .... KADR
Elkader Public Library, Elkader, IA [*Library symbol Library of Congress*] (LCLS) .... IaElk
Elkan N. Adler Collection [*Jewish Theological Seminary of America, New York*] (BJA) .... ENA
Elkem Metals Co., Niagara Falls, NY [*Library symbol Library of Congress*] (LCLS) .... NNiaEM
Elkford Public Library, British Columbia [*Library symbol National Library of Canada*] (NLC) .... BELK
Elkhart [*Indiana*] [*Airport symbol*] (OAG) .... EKI
[*The*] Elkhart Carriage & Motor Car Co. [*Automobile manufacturer (1909-1915), later, Elcar Motor Co. (1916-1931)*] [*Acronym also used as car name*] .... ELCAR
Elkhart County Historical Society, Bristol, IN [*Library symbol Library of Congress*] (LCLS) .... InBriEHi
Elkhart, IN [*Location identifier FAA*] (FAAL) .... EKM
Elkhart, IN [*FM radio station call letters*] .... WBYT
Elkhart, IN [*AM radio station call letters*] .... WFRN
Elkhart, IN [*FM radio station call letters*] .... WFRN-FM
Elkhart, IN [*Television station call letters*] .... WSJV
Elkhart, IN [*AM radio station call letters*] .... WTRC

Elkhart, IN [*FM radio station call letters*] ... WVPE
Elkhart, KS [*Location identifier FAA*] (FAAL) ... EHA
Elkhart Public Library, Elkhart, IN [*OCLC symbol*] (OCLC) ... IEB
Elkhart Public Library, Elkhart, IN [*Library symbol Library of Congress*] (LCLS) ... InElk
Elkhart Truth, Elkhart, IN [*Library symbol Library of Congress*] (LCLS) ... InElkT
Elkhorn City, KY [*AM radio station call letters*] ... WBPA
Elkhorn City, KY [*FM radio station call letters*] ... WPKE
Elkhorn Ranch [*California*] [*Seismograph station code, US Geological Survey*] (SEIS) ... EKH
Elkin, NC [*AM radio station call letters*] (RBYB) ... WIFM
Elkin, NC [*FM radio station call letters*] ... WIFM-FM
Elkin, NC [*Location identifier FAA*] (FAAL) ... ZEF
Elkin Public Library, Elkin, NC [*Library symbol Library of Congress*] (LCLS) ... NcElk
Elkins [*West Virginia*] [*Airport symbol*] (OAG) ... EKN
Elkins, WV [*Location identifier FAA*] (FAAL) ... OUW
Elkins, WV [*Location identifier FAA*] (FAAL) ... RQY
Elkins, WV [*FM radio station call letters*] ... WCDE
Elkins, WV [*AM radio station call letters*] ... WDNE
Elkins, WV [*FM radio station call letters*] ... WDNE-FM
Elkins, WV [*FM radio station call letters*] ... WELK
Elko [*Nevada*] [*Airport symbol*] (OAG) ... EKO
Elko [*Nevada*] [*Seismograph station code, US Geological Survey Closed*] (SEIS) ... EKO
Elko [*Nevada*] [*Seismograph station code, US Geological Survey*] (SEIS) ... ELK
Elko County Library, Elko, NV [*Library symbol Library of Congress*] (LCLS) ... NvE
Elko, NV [*Television station call letters*] (RBYB) ... KANL
Elko, NV [*AM radio station call letters*] ... KELK
Elko, NV [*TV station call letters*] (RBYB) ... KENV-TV
Elko, NV [*FM radio station call letters*] ... KLKO
Elko, NV [*FM radio station call letters*] ... KNCC
Elko, NV [*FM radio station call letters*] ... KRJC
Elko, NV [*AM radio station call letters*] (RBYB) ... KTSN-AM
Elks, Inc. [*Toronto Stock Exchange symbol*] ... EKS
Elkton, KY [*AM radio station call letters*] ... WEKT
Elkton, MD [*FM radio station call letters*] ... WOEL
Elkton, MD [*AM radio station call letters*] ... WSER
Elkton Public Library, Elkton, SD [*Library symbol Library of Congress*] (LCLS) ... SdEl
Elkton, VA [*FM radio station call letters*] ... WPKZ
Ell ... E
Ell, Flemish [*Unit of measure*] (ROG) ... E FL
Ell, French [*Unit of measure*] (ROG) ... E FR
Ellagic Acid ... EA
Elle Va [*She Goes*] [*Racing car*] [*French*] ... ELVA
Ellef Ringnes Island [*Canada*] ... ERI
Ellendale, ND [*Television station call letters*] ... KJRE
Ellenikos Laikos Apeleutherotikos Stratos [*Hellenic People's Army of Liberation*] [*Military arm of EAM*] [*Greek*] ... ELAS
Ellensburg Public Library, Ellensburg, WA [*Library symbol Library of Congress*] (LCLS) ... WaEl
Ellensburg, WA [*Location identifier FAA*] (FAAL) ... ELN
Ellensburg, WA [*FM radio station call letters*] (RBYB) ... KNWR
Ellensburg, WA [*FM radio station call letters*] ... KQBE
Ellensburg, WA [*AM radio station call letters*] ... KXLE
Ellensburg, WA [*FM radio station call letters*] ... KXLE-FM
Ellenville, NY [*AM radio station call letters*] ... WELV
Ellenville, NY [*FM radio station call letters*] (RBYB) ... WTHN-FM
Ellenville, NY [*FM radio station call letters*] ... WWWK
Ellenville Public Library, Ellenville, NY [*Library symbol Library of Congress*] (LCLS) ... NElle
Ellerman & Bucknall Steamship Co. (MHDW) ... E & B
Eller's Minnesota Digest [*A publication*] (DLA) ... El Dig
Eller's Minnesota Digest [*A publication*] (ILCA) ... Ell Dig
Ellesmere & Glyn Valley Railway [*Later, GVR*] [*Wales*] ... E & GVR
Ellesmere's Post Nati [*A publication*] (DLA) ... Ellesm Post N
Ellet on the Laws of Trade [*A publication*] (DLA) ... Ell Trade
Ellett Brothers [*NASDAQ symbol*] (TTSB) ... ELET
Ellett Brothers, Inc. [*NASDAQ symbol*] (SAG) ... ELET
Ellett Brothers, Inc. [*Associated Press*] (SAG) ... EllettBr
Ellettsville, IN [*FM radio station call letters*] ... WGCT
Ellettsville Journal, Ellettsville, IN [*Library symbol Library of Congress*] (LCLS) ... InEllJ
Ellijay, GA [*AM radio station call letters*] ... WLJA
Ellijay, GA [*FM radio station call letters*] ... WLJA-FM
Ellinghausen, McCullough, Johnson, Harris [*Medium*] [*Microbiology*] ... EMJH
Ellington Air Force Base [*Texas*] (KSC) ... EAFB
Ellington Air Force Base, TX [*Location identifier FAA*] (FAAL) ... HKX
Ellington Navigators/Observers Association (EA) ... ENOA
Elliniki Aristera [*Greek Left Party*] [*Political party*] (EY) ... EAR
Elliniki Radiophonia [*Greek radio*] (EY) ... ERA
Elliot [*South Africa*] [*ICAO location identifier*] (ICLI) ... FAET
Elliot Automation RADAR System (IAA) ... EARS
Elliot Lake [*Canada*] [*Airport symbol*] (OAG) ... YEL
Elliot Lake, ON [*Television station call letters*] ... CBLFT-6
Elliot Lake, ON [*Television station call letters*] ... CICI-1
Elliot Lake, ON [*Television station call letters*] ... CKNC-1
Elliot Lake Public Library, Elliot Lake, ON, Canada [*Library symbol Library of Congress*] (LCLS) ... CaOEL
Elliot Lake Public Library, Ontario [*Library symbol National Library of Canada*] (NLC) ... OEL
Elliot Lake Secondary School, Elliot Lake, ON, Canada [*Library symbol Library of Congress*] (LCLS) ... CaOELS
Elliot Lake Secondary School, Ontario [*Library symbol National Library of Canada*] (NLC) ... OELS
Elliotdale Sheepbreeders' Society of Australia ... ESSA
Elliot's American Diplomatic Code [*A publication*] (DLA) ... Ell Dip Code
Elliot's Debates on the Federal Constitution [*A publication*] (DLA) ... Ell Deb
Elliot's Debates on the Federal Constitution [*A publication*] (DLA) ... Elliot Deb Fed Const
Elliott Automation Space and Advanced Military Systems (MCD) ... EASAMS
Elliott Automation Space and Advanced Military Systems ... ESAMS
Elliott Beechcraft of Omaha, Inc. [*ICAO designator*] (FAAC) ... ELT
Elliott District Community Government Council [*Australia*] ... EDCGC
Elliott Forbes-Robinson [*Race car driver*] ... EFR
Elliott Lake, ON [*AM radio station call letters*] ... CKNR
Elliott on Roads and Streets [*A publication*] (DLA) ... Elliott Roads & S
Elliott Public Library, Elliott, IA [*Library symbol Library of Congress*] (LCLS) ... IaEll
Elliott's Appellate Procedure [*A publication*] (DLA) ... Elliott App Proc
Elliott's Supplement to the Indiana Revised Statutes [*A publication*] (DLA) ... Elliott Supp
Ellipsoid Collector Mirror ... ECM
Ellipsoidal Reflector Floodlight (WDMC) ... ERF
Ellipsometry [*Surface analysis*] ... ELL
Ellipsometry, Low Field [*Microscopy*] ... ELF
Ellipsomicroscopy for Surface Imaging ... EMSI
Elliptic [*or Exact*] **Differential Equation** ... EDE
Elliptic Function First-Order Ripple Phase Approximation ... EFFORPA
Elliptic Function Second-Order Ripple Phase Approximation ... EFSORPA
Elliptical (FAAC) ... ELIP
Elliptical ... ELLIPT
Elliptical (MSA) ... ELP
Elliptical Cavity Pump ... ECP
Elliptical Earth Orbit ... EEO
Elliptical Error Probability (CAAL) ... EEP
Elliptical Gear Planetary ... EGP
Elliptical Head (IEEE) ... ELPH
Elliptical Orbit [*Aerospace*] (AAG) ... EO
Elliptical Zone Plate (PDAA) ... EZP
Elliptically Polarized Light ... EPL
Elliptically Polarized Wave ... EPW
Elliptocytes [*Biochemistry*] (DAVI) ... ELLP
Ellis Air Lines ... ES
Ellis and Blackburn's English Queen's Bench Reports [*118-120 English Reprint*] [*A publication*] (DLA) ... E & B
Ellis and Blackburn's English Queen's Bench Reports [*118-120 English Reprint*] [*A publication*] (DLA) ... El & B
Ellis and Blackburn's English Queen's Bench Reports [*118-120 English Reprint*] [*A publication*] (DLA) ... El & Bl
Ellis and Blackburn's English Queen's Bench Reports [*118-120 English Reprint*] [*A publication*] (DLA) ... El & Bl (Eng)
Ellis and Blackburn's English Queen's Bench Reports [*118-120 English Reprint*] [*A publication*] (DLA) ... Ell & Bl
Ellis and Blackburn's English Queen's Bench Reports [*118-120 English Reprint*] [*A publication*] (DLA) ... Ellis & Bl
Ellis and Ellis' English Queen's Bench Reports [*A publication*] (DLA) ... E & E
Ellis and Ellis' English Queen's Bench Reports [*A publication*] (DLA) ... El & El
Ellis and Ellis' English Queen's Bench Reports [*A publication*] (DLA) ... El & El (Eng)
Ellis and Ellis' English Queen's Bench Reports [*A publication*] (DLA) ... Ell & Ell
Ellis, Best, and Smith's English Queen's Bench Reports [*A publication*] (DLA) ... EB & S
Ellis, Best, and Smith's English Queen's Bench Reports [*A publication*] (DLA) ... El B & S
Ellis, Best, and Smith's English Queen's Bench Reports [*A publication*] (DLA) ... El B & S (Eng)
Ellis, Best, and Smith's English Queen's Bench Reports [*A publication*] (DLA) ... Ell B & S
Ellis, Blackburn, and Ellis' English Queen's Bench Reports [*1858*] [*A publication*] (DLA) ... EB & E
Ellis, Blackburn, and Ellis' English Queen's Bench Reports [*A publication*] (DLA) ... El B & E
Ellis, Blackburn, and Ellis' English Queen's Bench Reports [*A publication*] (DLA) ... El B & El
Ellis, Blackburn, and Ellis' English Queen's Bench Reports [*A publication*] (DLA) ... El Bl & El
Ellis, Blackburn, and Ellis' English Queen's Bench Reports [*A publication*] (DLA) ... El Bl & El (Eng)
Ellis, Blackburn, and Ellis' English Queen's Bench Reports [*A publication*] (ILCA) ... Ell B & Ell
Ellis, Blackburn, and Ellis' English Queen's Bench Reports [*A publication*] (DLA) ... Ell Bl & Ell
Ellis College, Newtown, PA [*Library symbol Library of Congress Obsolete*] (LCLS) ... PNtE
Ellis. Debtor and Creditor [*1822*] [*A publication*] (DLA) ... Ell D & Cr
Ellis. Debtor and Creditor [*1822*] [*A publication*] (DLA) ... Ellis Dr & Cr
Ellis Elementary School, Rockford, IL [*Library symbol*] [*Library of Congress*] (LCLS) ... IRoEE
Ellis Enterprises, Inc. (IID) ... EEI
Ellis Hospital, Schenectady, NY [*Library symbol Library of Congress*] (LCLS) ... NSchE
Ellis on Fire and Life Insurance and Annuities [*A publication*] (DLA) ... Ell Ins
Ellis on Insurance [*A publication*] (DLA) ... Ellis
Ellison. Law of Annuities [*A publication*] (DLA) ... Ell Ann
Ellison, R. A., Cincinnati OH [*STAC*] ... ERA
Ellisras [*South Africa*] [*ICAO location identifier*] (ICLI) ... FAER

Ellisras Control Reporting Point [*South Africa*] [*ICAO location identifier*] (ICLI) ... FAEA
Ellisville, MS [*FM radio station call letters*] ... WJKX
Elloree, SC [*FM radio station call letters*] ... WORG
Elloree-Santee, SC [*AM radio station call letters*] ... WMNY
Ells Scotch (ROG) ... ES
Ellsworth [*Connecticut*] [*Seismograph station code, US Geological Survey*] (SEIS) ... ECT
Ellsworth Air Force Base [*South Dakota*] (SAA) ... EAFB
Ellsworth Air Force Base [*South Dakota*] (KSC) ... ELAFB
Ellsworth Commumity College, Iowa Falls, IA [*Library symbol Library of Congress*] (LCLS) ... IaIfE
Ellsworth Community College [*Iowa*] [*Formerly, EJC*] ... ECC
Ellsworth Convertible Growth & Income Fund, Inc. [*AMEX symbol*] (SPSG) ... ECF
Ellsworth Cv Growth/Income [*AMEX symbol*] (TTSB) ... ECF
Ellsworth Junior College [*Iowa*] [*Later, ECC*] ... EJC
Ellsworth, ME [*AM radio station call letters*] ... WDEA
Ellsworth, ME [*FM radio station call letters*] ... WKSQ
Ellsworth, ME [*FM radio station call letters*] ... WWMJ
Ellsworth Public Library, Ellsworth, IA [*Library symbol Library of Congress*] (LCLS) ... IaEls
Ellsworth's Copyright Manual [*A publication*] (DLA) ... Ells Cop Man
Ellwood, CA [*FM radio station call letters*] (RBYB) ... KSPE-FM
Ellwood City Area Public Library, Ellwood City, PA [*Library symbol Library of Congress*] (LCLS) ... PEc
Ellwood City, PA [*Location identifier FAA*] (FAAL) ... EWC
Ellwood City, PA [*FM radio station call letters*] ... WKST
Elm [*Alabama*] [*Seismograph station code, US Geological Survey*] (SEIS) ... EMA
Elm Leaf Scorch [*Plant pathology*] ... ELS
Elm Mottle Virus [*Plant pathology*] ... EMOV
Elm Research Institute (EA) ... ERI
Elma [*New York*] [*Seismograph station code, US Geological Survey Closed*] (SEIS) ... ELM
Elma Reminder, Elma, IA [*Library symbol Library of Congress*] (LCLS) ... IaElmR
Elma Township Public Library, Atwood, Ontario [*Library symbol National Library of Canada*] (NLC) ... OAET
Elma, WA [*FM radio station call letters*] (RBYB) ... KAPV-FM
Elmali [*Turkey*] [*Seismograph station code, US Geological Survey*] (SEIS) ... ELL
Elmbrook Memorial Hospital, Brookfield, WI [*Library symbol Library of Congress*] (LCLS) ... WBrE
Elmer Bird International Fan Club (EA) ... EBIFC
Elmer Times, Elmer, NJ [*Library symbol Library of Congress*] (LCLS) ... NjElT
Elmer's New Jersey Digest of Laws [*A publication*] (DLA) ... Elm Dig
Elmer's New Jersey Digest of Laws [*A publication*] (DLA) ... Elm NJ Laws
Elmer's Practice in Lunacy [*A publication*] (DLA) ... Elm Lun
Elmer's Practice in Lunacy [*A publication*] (DLA) ... Elmer Lun
Elmers Restaurants [*NASDAQ symbol*] (TTSB) ... ELMS
Elmers Restaurants, Inc. [*Associated Press*] (SAG) ... Elmers
Elmer's Restaurants, Inc. [*NASDAQ symbol*] (NQ) ... ELMS
Elmes' Executive Departments of the United States [*A publication*] (DLA) ... Elm Exec Dep
Elmes on Architectural Jurisprudence [*A publication*] (DLA) ... Elm Arch Jur
Elmes on Ecclesiastical Civil Dilapidation [*A publication*] (DLA) ... Elm Dilap
Elmhurst College, Elmhurst, IL [*OCLC symbol*] (OCLC) ... ICV
Elmhurst College, Elmhurst, IL [*Library symbol Library of Congress*] (LCLS) ... IElmC
Elmhurst, IL [*AM radio station call letters*] ... WJJG
Elmhurst, IL [*FM radio station call letters*] ... WRSE
Elmhurst Public Library, Elmhurst, IL [*Library symbol Library of Congress*] (LCLS) ... IElm
Elmira [*New York*] [*Airport symbol*] (OAG) ... ELM
Elmira and Williamsport Railway [*British*] (ROG) ... E & WR
Elmira College (GAGS) ... Elmira C
Elmira College, Elmira, NY [*Library symbol Library of Congress*] (LCLS) ... NElmC
Elmira College, Elmira, NY [*OCLC symbol*] (OCLC) ... VXE
Elmira Heights-Horseheads, NY [*AM radio station call letters*] ... WEHH
Elmira, NY [*Location identifier FAA*] (FAAL) ... ALP
Elmira, NY [*Location identifier FAA*] (FAAL) ... UEK
Elmira, NY [*FM radio station call letters*] ... WCIH
Elmira, NY [*FM radio station call letters*] ... WECW
Elmira, NY [*AM radio station call letters*] ... WELM
Elmira, NY [*AM radio station call letters*] ... WENY
Elmira, NY [*FM radio station call letters*] ... WENY-FM
Elmira, NY [*Television station call letters*] ... WENY-TV
Elmira, NY [*Television station call letters*] ... WETM
Elmira, NY [*FM radio station call letters*] ... WLVY
Elmira Psychiatric Center, Elmira, NY [*Library symbol Library of Congress*] (LCLS) ... NElmP
[*The*] **Elmira Savings Bank** [*NASDAQ symbol*] (NQ) ... ESBK
Elmira Savings Bank FSB [*Associated Press*] (SAG) ... ElmrSv
Elmira Svgs Bk FSB NY [*NASDAQ symbol*] (TTSB) ... ESBK
Elmo Bumpy Torus [*Nuclear energy*] ... EBT
Elmo Bumpy Torus Reactor [*Conceptual design study*] [*Nuclear energy*] ... EBT-R
Elmo Bumpy Torus Reactor [*Nuclear energy*] (MCD) ... EBTR
Elmo Bumpy Torus-One (MCD) ... EBT-1
Elmo Bumpy Torus-Proof of Principle (MCD) ... EBT-P
Elmo Bumpy Torus-Scale (MCD) ... EBT-S
Elmo Snakey Torus (MCD) ... EST
Elmont Memeorial High School, Elmont, NY [*Library symbol*] [*Library of Congress*] (LCLS) ... NElmoMH
Elmont Memorial High School, Sewanhaka, NY [*Library symbol Library of Congress*] (LCLS) ... NSewEH
Elmont Public Library, Elmont, NY [*Library symbol Library of Congress*] (LCLS) ... NElmo
Elmore Memorial Hospital, Medical Library, Mountain Home, ID [*Library symbol*] [*Library of Congress*] (LCLS) ... IdMhH
Elms Unlimited [*Superseded by ERI*] ... EU
Elmsett [*British ICAO location identifier*] (ICLI) ... EGST
Elmwood (VRA) ... elmwd
Elmwood Branch, Bruce County Public Library, Ontario [*Library symbol National Library of Canada*] (NLC) ... OELM
Elmwood, IL [*FM radio station call letters*] ... WFYR
Elmwood Institute (EA) ... EI
Elmwood Park, IL [*FM radio station call letters*] ... WCKG
Elmwood Park Public Library, Elmwood Park, IL [*Library symbol Library of Congress*] (LCLS) ... IElwp
Elmwood Public Library, Providence, RI [*Library symbol Library of Congress*] (LCLS) ... RPE
Elmwood Township, MI [*AM radio station call letters*] ... WLJN
Elmworth School, Alberta [*Library symbol National Library of Canada*] (BIB) ... AELMS
Elnora Public Library, Alberta [*Library symbol National Library of Canada*] (NLC) ... AELNO
Elocution ... E
Elocution ... Eloc
Elodoisin-Related Peptide [*Medicine*] (DMAA) ... ERP
Elohist Source [*Biblical scholarship*] ... E
Elon College, Elon College, NC [*Library symbol Library of Congress*] (LCLS) ... NcElon
Elon College, NC [*FM radio station call letters*] ... WSOE
Elongatable Dow Fiber [*Dow Chemical Co.*] ... EDF
Elongate (MSA) ... ELNG
Elongate (FAAC) ... ELNGT
[*The*] **Elongated Collectors** [*An association*] (EA) ... TEC
Elongated Die Bushing ... EDB
Elongated Punch ... EP
Elongated Single Domain ... ESD
Elongating Hypocotyl Section [*Botany*] ... EHS
Elongation (WDAA) ... EL
Elongation (MSA) ... ELONG
Elongation, Derotation, and Lateral Flexion [*Medicine*] ... EDF
Elongation Factor [*Biochemistry, genetics*] ... EF
Elongation in Two Inches ... EL2
Elongation-at-Break [*Textile technology*] ... EAB
Elongation-Sensitive Cell (PDAA) ... ESC
Eloquence [*or Eloquent*] (ROG) ... ELOQ
Elorza [*Venezuela*] [*Airport symbol*] (OAG) ... EOZ
Elorza, Apure [*Venezuela ICAO location identifier*] (ICLI) ... SVEZ
Elphinstone, Norton, and Clark. Interpretation of Deeds [*1885*] [*A publication*] (DLA) ... Elph
Elphinstone's Introduction to Conveyancing [*A publication*] (DLA) ... Elph Conv
Elphinstone's Rules for Interpretation of Deeds [*A publication*] (DLA) ... Elph Interp Deeds
Elrick & Lavidge, Inc. (WDMC) ... E & L
Elrom Aviation & Investments [*Israel*] [*ICAO designator*] (FAAC) ... ELR
Elron Electric Ind Wrrt [*NASDAQ symbol*] (TTSB) ... ELRWF
Elron Electrn Ind Ord [*NASDAQ symbol*] (TTSB) ... ELRNF
Elron Electronic Industries [*Associated Press*] (SAG) ... Elron
Elron Electronic Industries Ltd. [*NASDAQ symbol*] (NQ) ... ELRN
Elron Electronic Industries Ltd. (MHDW) ... ELRNF
Elron Electronic Industries, Ltd. [*Associated Press*] (SAG) ... ElronEl
Elron Elektronic Industries [*NASDAQ symbol*] (SAG) ... ELRW
Elsa Clubs of America [*Defunct*] (EA) ... ECA
Elsa Wild Animal Appeal - USA (EA) ... EWAA-USA
Elsaess-Lothringen Partei [*Alsace-Lorraine Party*] [*German*] (PPE) ... ELSASSER
Elsag Bailey Process Auto NV [*NYSE symbol*] (SPSG) ... EBY
Elsag Bailey Process Automation [*Associated Press*] (SAG) ... ElsagB
Elsah, IL [*FM radio station call letters*] ... WTPC
Elscint Ltd. [*Associated Press*] (SAG) ... Elscint
Elscint Ltd. [*NYSE symbol*] (SPSG) ... ELT
Else Good [*In good condition except for defects mentioned*] [*Antiquarian book trade*] ... EG
Elsenborn [*Belgium ICAO location identifier*] (ICLI) ... EBLB
Elsevier [*Published by the Elsevier family*] (ROG) ... ELS
Elsevier NV [*Associated Press*] (SAG) ... Elsevier
Elsevier NV [*NYSE symbol*] (SAG) ... ENL
Elsevier NV ADS [*NYSE symbol*] (TTSB) ... ENL
Elsevier Science Publishers ... ESP
Elsewhere [*Manuscripts*] (ROG) ... ELSEWH
Elsewhere (FAAC) ... ELSW
Elsewhere (MAE) ... ew
Elsinore Corp. [*AMEX symbol*] (SPSG) ... ELS
Elsinore Corp. [*Associated Press*] (SAG) ... Elsinor
Elsinore Free Public Library, Elsinore, CA [*Library symbol Library of Congress*] (LCLS) ... CEl
Elsley's Edition of William Blackstone's English King's Bench Reports [*A publication*] (DLA) ... Els W Bl
Elstree [*British ICAO location identifier*] (ICLI) ... EGTR
Elswick Quick-Firing Gun ... EQF
Elsworth Convertible Growth & Income Fund, Inc. [*Associated Press*] (SAG) ... Elswth
Elsynge on Parliaments [*A publication*] (DLA) ... Elsyn Parl
Elting Memorial Library, New Paltz, NY [*Library symbol Library of Congress*] (LCLS) ... NNepa
Elton on Commons and Waste Lands [*A publication*] (DLA) ... Elt Com
Elton on Commons and Waste Lands [*A publication*] (DLA) ... Elton Com
Elton on Copyholds [*A publication*] (DLA) ... Elt Copyh
Elton on Copyholds [*A publication*] (DLA) ... Elton Copyh
Elton's Tenures of Kent [*A publication*] (DLA) ... Elt Ten of Kent

Eltopia [*Washington*] [*Seismograph station code, US Geological Survey*] (SEIS) ... ETP
El-Tor [*Egypt*] [*ICAO location identifier*] (ICLI) ... HETR
Eltrax Sys [*NASDAQ symbol*] (TTSB) ... ELTX
Eltrax System, Inc. [*Associated Press*] (SAG) ... Eltrax
Eltrax Systems, Inc. [*NASDAQ symbol*] (SAG) ... ELTX
Eltron International, Inc. [*NASDAQ symbol*] (SAG) ... ELTN
Eltron International, Inc. [*Associated Press*] (SAG) ... Eltron
Eltron Intl. [*NASDAQ symbol*] (TTSB) ... ELTN
Eltsovka [*Former USSR Seismograph station code, US Geological Survey*] (SEIS) ... ELT
Elucidatio Terrae Sanctae (BJA) ... ETS
Elva Owners Club [*Worthing, West Sussex, England*] (EAIO) ... EOC
Elves', Gnomes', and Little Men's Science Fiction, Chowder, and Marching Society (EA) ... EGLMSFCMS
Elvington [*British ICAO location identifier*] (ICLI) ... EGYK
Elvira Fan Club (EA) ... EFC
Elvis Brothers Fan Club (EA) ... EBFC
Elvis Forever TCB [*Taking Care of Business*] **Fan Club** (EA) ... EFTCBFC
Elvis in Canada [*An association*] (EAIO) ... EC
Elvis Is King Fan Club (EAIO) ... EKFC
Elvis Lives On Fan Club (EA) ... ELFC
Elvis Now Fan Club (EA) ... ENFC
Elvis Presley Burning Love Fan Club (EA) ... EPBLFC
Elvis Presley Circle City Fan Club (EA) ... EPCCFC
Elvis Presley Enterprises ... EPE
Elvis Presley Fan Club of Luxembourg (EAIO) ... EPFCL
Elvis Presley Memorial Society of Syracuse, New York (EA) ... EMS
Elvis Presley Performing Arts Scholarship Foundation (EA) ... EPPASF
Elvis Presley Performing Arts Scholarship Foundation of Virginia [*Later, EPPASF*] (EA) ... EPPASFV
Elvis Presley Tribute Fan Club [*Defunct*] (EA) ... EPTFC
Elvis Special Photo Association (EA) ... ESPA
Elvis Teddy Bears (EA) ... ETB
Elvis, This One's for You Fan Club (EA) ... ETOFY
Elvis We Care Campaign [*Later, EPIAI*] (EA) ... EWCC
Elvis Worldwide Memorial Fan Club (EA) ... EWMFC
Elvish Linguistic Fellowship (EA) ... ELF
Elvisly Yours [*Fan club*] (EAIO) ... EY
Elwell on Malpractice and Medical Jurisprudence [*A publication*] (DLA) ... Elw Mal
Elwell on Malpractice and Medical Jurisprudence [*A publication*] (DLA) ... Elw Med Jur
Elwood Call-Leader, Elwood, IN [*Library symbol Library of Congress*] (LCLS) ... InElwCL
Elwood, IN [*FM radio station call letters*] ... WLHN
Elwood Junior High School, Huntington, NY [*Library symbol Library of Congress*] (LCLS) ... NHuEJ
Elwood Public Library, Elwood, IN [*Library symbol Library of Congress*] (LCLS) ... InElw
Elwood Township Carnegie Library, Ridge Farm, IL [*Library symbol Library of Congress*] (LCLS) ... IRid
Elwyn Institute, Elwyn, PA [*OCLC symbol*] (OCLC) ... PIE
ELXSI Corp. [*NASDAQ symbol*] (NQ) ... ELXS
ELXSI Corp. [*Associated Press*] (SAG) ... ELXSI
Ely [*Nevada*] [*Airport symbol*] (OAG) ... ELY
Ely [*Nevada*] [*Seismograph station code, US Geological Survey Closed*] (SEIS) ... ELY
Ely Junior College [*Minnesota*] [*Later, Vermilion Community College*] ... EJC
Ely, MN [*Location identifier FAA*] (FAAL) ... ELO
Ely, MN [*AM radio station call letters*] ... WELY
Ely, MN [*FM radio station call letters*] ... WELY-FM
Ely, NV [*Location identifier FAA*] (FAAL) ... ELY
Ely, NV [*FM radio station call letters*] ... KDSS
Ely, NV [*AM radio station call letters*] ... KELY
Ely, NV [*FM radio station call letters*] ... KELY-FM
Ely Public Library, Ely, MN [*Library symbol*] [*Library of Congress*] (LCLS)... MnEly
Elyria Library, Elyria, OH [*Library symbol Library of Congress*] (LCLS) ... OEly
Elyria, OH [*AM radio station call letters*] ... WEOL
Elyria, OH [*FM radio station call letters*] ... WNWV
Elyria Project for Innovative Curriculum (EDAC) ... EPIC
Elysium Mons [*A filamentary mark on Mars*] ... E
Elzevir [*Elsevier*] [*Published by the Elsevier family*] (ROG) ... ELZ
Em [*Printing*] (WDMC) ... m
Em [*Printing*] (WDMC) ... M
Emae [*Vanuatu*] [*Airport symbol*] (OAG) ... EAE
Emae [*Vanuatu*] [*ICAO location identifier*] (ICLI) ... NVSE
Emalangeni [*Monetary unit*] [*Swaziland*] (BARN) ... E
Emam Shahr [*Iran*] [*ICAO location identifier*] (ICLI) ... OIMJ
Emanation (ADA) ... EM
Emanation Thermal Analysis ... ETA
Emanations Security (AABC) ... EMSEC
[*The*] **Emanu El Single Person** (BJA) ... ESP
Emanuel County Junior College, Swainsboro, GA [*Library symbol Library of Congress*] (LCLS) ... GSwE
Emanuel Einstein Free Public Library, Pompton Lakes, NJ [*Library symbol Library of Congress*] (LCLS) ... NjPl
Emanuel Foundation for Hungarian Culture (EA) ... EFHC
Emanuel Hospital, Portland, OR [*Library symbol Library of Congress*] (LCLS) ... OrPEH
Emaus Internacional [*Emmaus International*] (EA) ... EI
Emba Mink Breeders Association (EA) ... EMBA
Embaba [*Egypt*] [*ICAO location identifier*] (ICLI) ... HEEM
Embalmer [*Navy rating*] ... EMT
Embalming Chemical Manufacturers Association [*Westport, CT*] (EA) ... ECMA
Embalse Rio Tercero [*Argentina ICAO location identifier*] (ICLI) ... SAOE
Embankment ... EMB
Embankment ... EMBKMT
Embar Information Consultants [*Information service or system*] (IID) ... EIC
Embarc [*Electronic Mail Broadcast to a Roaming Computer*] **Communications Service** [*Boyton Beach, FL*] (CDE) ... EMBARC
Embargo (ADA) ... EM
Embargo (ADA) ... EMB
Embark (AABC) ... EMB
Embarkation (DSUE) ... EMBARK
Embarkation Commandant [*Military British*] ... EC
Embarkation/Disembarkation ... E/D
Embarkation Medical Official [*Military British*] ... EMO
Embarkation Officer [*Marine Corps*] ... EMBO
Embarkation Order [*Marine Corps*] ... EMBO
Embarkation Staff Officer [*Military British*] ... ESO
Embarkation Supply and Stores Officer [*Military British*] ... ESSO
Embarked Mine Countermeasures Force ... EMCMF
Embarked Personnel Material Report [*Navy*] (ANA) ... EPMR
Embarrassing Personal Question [*National Security Agency screening procedure*] ... EPQ
Embassador Extraordinary [*Diplomacy*] [*British*] (ROG) ... EE
Embassy ... E
Embassy (AFM) ... EMB
Embassy ... EMBSSY
Embassy Home Entertainment [*Video distributor*] ... EHE
Embassy of Argentina, Ottawa, Ontario [*Library symbol National Library of Canada*] (BIB) ... OOEA
Embassy of Brazil, Ottawa, Ontario [*Library symbol National Library of Canada*] (BIB) ... OOEMB
Embassy of Ghana, Washington, DC [*Library symbol Library of Congress*] (LCLS) ... DGhE
Embassy of Korea, Ottawa, Ontario [*Library symbol National Library of Canada*] (BIB) ... OOEK
Embassy of Zaire, Washington, DC [*Library symbol Library of Congress*] (LCLS) ... DZaE
Embassy Officer ... EMBOFF
Embassy Social Secretaries Association (EA) ... ESSA
Embassy Telegram (NATG) ... EMBTEL
Embden-Meyerhof [*Glycolytic pathway*] [*Biochemistry*] ... E-M
Embden-Meyerhof-Parnas [*Hexose metabolic pathway*] [*Biochemistry*] ... EMP
Embedded Advance Sampling Environment [*Hewlett-Packard Co.*] ... EASE
Embedded Computer Resources (MCD) ... ECR
Embedded Computer Systems ... ECS
Embedded Data Processor (SSD) ... EDP
Embedded Design Language [*Computer science*] (PDAA) ... EDL
Embedded Document Architecture [*PenPoint*] [*Computer science*] ... EDA
Embedded Figures [*Psychometrics*] ... EF
Embedded Figures Test [*Psychology*] ... EFT
Embedded Micro-Interface Technoloy [*Telecommunications*] ... EMIT
Embedded Operations Channel [*Telecommunications*] (ACRL) ... EOC
Embedded Post-Beamformer Interference Canceler (CAAL) ... EPIC
Embedded Print Command [*Computer science*] (HGAA) ... EPC
Embedded Sensor Technique ... EST
Embedded Structured Query Language and Tools for C Language [*Computer science*] (HGAA) ... ESQL/C
Embedded Temperature Detector (IAA) ... ETD
Embedded Training [*Army*] (RDA) ... ET
Embedded Training Material [*Military*] ... ETM
Embedded Training Requirement [*Military*] ... ETR
Embedded Wiring Board (MSA) ... EWB
Embedded-Alumina-Particle Aluminide [*Chemical coating*] ... EAPA
Embedded-Atom Method [*Model of interatomic interaction*] ... EAM
Embessa [*Papua New Guinea*] [*Airport symbol*] (OAG) ... EMS
Embezzlement (DLA) ... EMBEZ
Embezzlement of Government Property ... EGP
Emboss (MSA) ... EMB
Embossed [*Deltiology*] ... EMBS
Embossed (VRA) ... embs
Embossed Character Reader [*Banking*] ... ECR
Embossed Groove Recording ... EGR
Embossing Press Station ... EPS
Embotelladora Andina ADS [*NYSE symbol*] (TTSB) ... AKO
Embotelladora Andina SA [*NYSE symbol*] (SAG) ... AKO
Embotelladora Andina SA [*Associated Press*] (SAG) ... EAandina
Embotelladora Andina SA [*Associated Press*] (SAG) ... EAndina
Embracery [*Legal term*] (DLA) ... EMBRAC
EMBRAER [*Empresa Brasileira Aeronautica SA*] [*Brazil ICAO aircraft manufacturer identifier*] (ICAO) ... E
Embrasure (VRA) ... embrs
Embrex, Inc. [*Associated Press*] (SAG) ... Embrex
Embrex, Inc. [*Associated Press*] (SAG) ... Embrx
Embrex, Inc. [*NASDAQ symbol*] (SPSG) ... EMBX
Embrex Inc. Wrrt [*NASDAQ symbol*] (TTSB) ... EMBXW
Embrittlement Index (PDAA) ... EI
Embroidered ... EMB
Embroiderers' Guild of America (EA) ... EGA
Embroiderers' Guild of New South Wales [*Australia*] ... EGNSW
Embroiderers' Guild of Queensland [*Australia*] ... EGQ
Embroiderers' Guild of South Australia ... EGSA
Embroiderers' Guild of Tasmania [*Australia*] ... EGT
Embroiderers' Guild of the Australian Capital Territory ... EGACT
Embroiderers' Guild of Victoria [*Australia*] ... EGV
Embroiderers' Guild of Western Australia ... EGWA
Embroidery [*Quilting*] ... E

Embroidery ... EMB
Embroidery ... EMBR
Embroidery (VRA) ... embr
Embroidery Council of America (EA) ... ECA
Embroidery Manufacturers Promotion Board [*Later, SEMPB*] (EA) ... EMPB
Embroidery Trade Association (EA) ... ETA
Embryo [*Botany*] ... E
Embryo ... EMBR
Embryo Development [*NASDAQ symbol*] (TTSB) ... EMBR
Embryo Development Corp. [*NASDAQ symbol*] (SAG) ... EMBR
Embryo Development Corp. [*Associated Press*] (SAG) ... Embryo
Embryo Extract ... EE
Embryo Fibroblast [*Medicine*] (DMAA) ... EF
Embryo Infective Dose ... EID
Embryo Lethal Dose (OA) ... ELD
Embryo Replacement [*Gynecology*] ... ER
Embryo Sac [*Botany*] ... ES
Embryo Stem Cell ... ES
Embryo Transfer ... ET
Embryo-Fetal [*Neonatology and obstetrics*] (DAVI) ... EF
Embryology (ROG) ... EMB
Embryology ... EMBRY
Embryology ... EMBRYOL
Embryonal Carcinoma [*Medicine*] ... EC
Embryonal Carcinoma Derived Growth Factor [*Biochemistry*] ... ECDGF
Embryonal Cell Carcinoma [*Medicine Medicine*] (DMAA) ... ECC
Embryonal Stem [*Cell line*] ... ES
Embryonic ... E
Embryonic Bovine Kidney ... EBK
Embryonic Chicken Kidney ... ECK
Embryonic Chicken Muscle ... ECM
Embryonic Day ... ED
Embryonic Growth and Development Factor [*Biochemistry*] ... EGDF
Embryonic Shield ... ES
Embryonic Stem Cell [*Cytology*] ... ESC
Embryonic Turkey Kidney ... ETK
Embry-Riddle Aeronautical University [*Formerly, ERSA*] [*Daytona Beach, FL*] ... E-RAU
Embry-Riddle Aeronautical University, Prescott Campus, Prescott, AZ [*Library symbol*] [*Library of Congress*] (LCLS) ... AzPrER
Embry-Riddle School of Aviation [*Later, E-RAU*] [*Florida*] ... ERSA
Embu [*Kenya*] [*ICAO location identifier*] (ICLI) ... HKEM
EMC Corp. [*NYSE symbol*] (SPSG) ... EMC
EMC Insurance Group [*NASDAQ symbol*] (TTSB) ... EMCI
EMC Insurance Group, Inc. [*Associated Press*] (SAG) ... EMC In
EMC Insurance Group, Inc. [*NASDAQ symbol*] (NQ) ... EMCI
EmCare Holdings [*NASDAQ symbol*] (TTSB) ... EMCR
EmCare Holdings, Inc. [*Associated Press*] (SAG) ... EmCare
EmCare Holdings, Inc. [*NASDAQ symbol*] (SAG) ... EMCR
EMCEE Broadcast Products [*NASDAQ symbol*] (TTSB) ... ECIN
EMCEE Broadcast Products, Inc. [*NASDAQ symbol*] (SAG) ... ECIN
EMCEE Broadcast Products, Inc. [*Associated Press*] (SAG) ... EMCEE
EMCLASS Terms [*Online database field identifier*] ... ET
EMCO Ltd. [*Associated Press*] (SAG) ... EMCO
Emco Ltd. [*Toronto Stock Exchange symbol*] ... EML
EMCO Ltd. [*NASDAQ symbol*] (SAG) ... EMLTF
EMCON [*NASDAQ symbol*] (TTSB) ... MCON
EMCON Associates [*NASDAQ symbol*] (NQ) ... MCON
EMCON, Corp. [*Associated Press*] (SAG) ... EMCON
EMCORE Group [*NASDAQ symbol*] (TTSB) ... EMCG
Emden [*Germany ICAO location identifier*] (ICLI) ... EDWE
Emden [*Germany Airport symbol*] (OAG) ... EME
Emendatio [*Emendation*] [*Latin*] ... EMEND
Emerald [*Australia Airport symbol*] (OAG) ... EMD
Emerald [*Philately*] ... emer
Emerald (ROG) ... EMLD
Emerald (VRA) ... emrl
Emerald Agricultural College ... EAC
Emerald Air [*British*] [*FAA designator*] (FAAC) ... EYE
Emerald Airlines [*ICAO designator*] (AD) ... OD
Emerald Airways Ltd. [*British*] [*FAA designator*] (FAAC) ... JAN
Emerald Capital Holdings, Inc. [*NASDAQ symbol*] (SAG) ... EMRL
Emerald Capital Holdings, Inc. [*Associated Press*] (SAG) ... EmrldCH
Emerald Isle Bancorp, Inc. [*NASDAQ symbol*] (SAG) ... EIRE
Emerald Isle Bancorp, Inc. [*Associated Press*] (SAG) ... EmrldIsle
Emerald Isle Resources, Inc. [*Vancouver Stock Exchange symbol*] ... EIR
Emerald Lake Resources, Inc. [*Toronto Stock Exchange symbol*] ... ELK
Emerald Star Mining [*Vancouver Stock Exchange symbol*] ... ESM
Emergence [*Biology*] ... Em
Emergence and Establishment [*Agriculture*] ... EM/ES
Emergency [*Symbol placed in neighborhood windows to indicate that resident will aid passing schoolchildren in the event of an emergency*] ... E
Emergency (NASA) ... EM
Emergency (KSC) ... EMER
Emergency ... EMER
Emergency (AABC) ... EMERG
Emergency (DS) ... Emy
Emergency Accommodation Unit (ADA) ... EAU
Emergency Action (MCD) ... EA
Emergency Action Communications (MCD) ... EAC
Emergency Action Console [*Navy*] (CINC) ... EAC
Emergency Action Coordination Team [*Department of Energy*] ... EACT
Emergency Action File [*Air Force*] (AFM) ... EAF
Emergency Action Level [*Nuclear energy*] (NRCH) ... EAL
Emergency Action Message [*Navy*] (NVT) ... EAM
Emergency Action Message Authentication System [*Military*] ... EAMAS
Emergency Action Message/Selected Release (MCD) ... EAM/SELREL
Emergency Action Notification [*Civil Defense*] ... EAN
Emergency Action Notification System [*White House Teletype network*] [*Civil Defense*] ... EANS
Emergency Action Procedure [*Military*] (NVT) ... EAP
Emergency Action Report [*Military*] ... EAR
Emergency Action Reporting for Logistics Action Programming [*Military*] (AFM) ... EARFLAP
Emergency Actions Book ... EAB
Emergency Actions Noncommissioned Officer [*Army*] (AABC) ... EANCO
Emergency Actions Officer [*Army*] (AABC) ... EAO
Emergency Addressee [*Aeromedical evacuation*] ... EA
Emergency Advisory Committee for Natural Gas [*Terminated, 1977*] [*Department of the Interior*] (EGAO) ... EACNG
Emergency Advisory Committee for Political Defense ... EACPD
Emergency Air Breathing System (DNAB) ... EAB
Emergency Air Staff Actions (AFM) ... EASA
Emergency Airborne Reaction System (MCD) ... EARS
Emergency Alternate Command Center (CINC) ... EACC
Emergency and Humanitarian Assistance ... EHA
Emergency and Remedial Response Division [*Environmental Protection Agency*] (GFGA) ... ERRD
Emergency and Trauma Unit ... ETU
Emergency Area (AFM) ... EA
Emergency Assembly Point ... EAP
Emergency Assistance [*Medicine*] (DAVI) ... EMA
Emergency Assistance Dispatch System ... EADS
Emergency Assistant [*Medicine*] (DAVI) ... EMA
Emergency Automated Response Subsystem [*National Oceanic and Atmospheric Administration*] ... EARS
Emergency Ballast Tank (DNAB) ... EMBT
Emergency Banking Relief Act ... EBRA
Emergency Bed Request System [*Computer science*] ... EMBERS
Emergency Bed Service [*Medicine*] ... EBS
Emergency Bomb Release (CINC) ... EBR
Emergency Borating System (IEEE) ... EBS
Emergency Box (MCD) ... EB
Emergency Brake (WDAA) ... EB
Emergency Breathing Apparatus ... EBA
Emergency Breathing Subsystem (MCD) ... EBS
Emergency Breathing System ... EBS
Emergency Broadcast System [*Formerly, CONELRAD*] ... EBS
Emergency Call (IAA) ... EC
Emergency Call Announcer [*Hearing technology*] ... ECA
Emergency Call System [*AT & T*] ... ECS
Emergency Capability ... EC
Emergency Capability System (SAA) ... ECAPS
Emergency Carbon Dioxide Limit (SAA) ... ECDL
Emergency Cardiac Care ... ECC
Emergency Care Research Institute (EA) ... ECRI
Emergency Cargo [*Vessel*] (IIA) ... EC
Emergency Category Designation ... ECD
Emergency Centre for Locust Operations (EERA) ... ECLO
Emergency Chaplain [*Army British*] ... EC
Emergency Charges ... E/C
Emergency Chemical Restraint (DAVI) ... ECR
Emergency Civil Liberties Committee [*Later, NECLC*] (EA) ... ECLC
Emergency Coalition for Haitian Refugees (EA) ... ECHR
Emergency Combat Capability ... ECC
Emergency Combat Readiness (AAG) ... ECR
Emergency Command Control Communications System ... ECCCS
Emergency Command Precedence (DNAB) ... ECP
Emergency Commission [*British*] ... EC
Emergency Commissioned Officer [*British military*] (DMA) ... ECO
Emergency Committee for American Trade (EA) ... ECAT
Emergency Committee to Boycott Mother's Day ... ECBMD
Emergency Committee to Save America's Marine Resources (EA) ... ECSAMR
Emergency Committee to Suspend Immigration (EA) ... ECSI
Emergency Communication Network [*Highway*] [*Telecommunications*] (TEL) ... ECN
Emergency Communications Control [*Fictitious military unit in film "Seven Days in May"*] ... ECOMCON
Emergency Communications Key ... ECK
Emergency Communications Plan (NUCP) ... ECP
Emergency Communications Research Unit [*Carleton University*] [*Canada Research center*] (RCD) ... ECRU
Emergency Communications Working Group [*DoD*] ... ECWG
Emergency Community Facilities Act of 1970 ... ECFA
Emergency Condensate Storage Tank [*Nuclear energy*] (NRCH) ... ECST
Emergency Condition [*Navy*] (ANA) ... EMERGCON
Emergency Conservation Committee [*Defunct*] ... ECC
Emergency Conservation Measures ... ECM
Emergency Conservation Program [*Department of Agriculture*] (EGAO) ... ECP
Emergency Conservation Work [*Succeeded by CCC, 1937, now obsolete*] ... ECW
Emergency Control Center (CINC) ... ECC
Emergency Control Officer (IAA) ... ECO
Emergency Control Station [*Nuclear energy*] (NRCH) ... ECS
Emergency Controlling Authority (DA) ... ECA
Emergency Coolant Injection [*Nuclear energy*] (NRCH) ... ECI
Emergency Coolant Recirculation [*Nuclear energy*] (NRCH) ... ECR
Emergency Coolant System (MSA) ... ECS
Emergency Cooling Function [*Nuclear energy*] (NRCH) ... ECF
Emergency Cooling Tower [*Nuclear energy*] (NRCH) ... ECT
Emergency Cooling Water [*Nuclear energy*] (NRCH) ... ECW

Emergency Cooling Water Pond [*Nuclear energy*] (NRCH) .... ECWP
Emergency Cooling Water Pumphouse [*Nuclear energy*] (NRCH) .... ECWPH
Emergency Coordination Group [*Military*] .... ECG
Emergency Coordinator (CET) .... EC
Emergency Core Cooling [*or Coolant*] [*Nuclear energy*] .... ECC
Emergency Core-Cooling System [*Nuclear energy*] .... ECCS
Emergency Council of Jewish Families (EA) .... ECJF
Emergency Court of Appeals [*United States*] (DLA) .... Em App
Emergency Court of Appeals [*United States*] (DLA) .... Em Ct App
Emergency Court of Appeals [*United States*] (DLA) .... Emer Ct App
Emergency Crop and Feed Loans [*New Deal*] .... ECFL
Emergency Decelerating [*Relay*] (IEEE) .... EDE
Emergency Declaration Area [*Environmental Protection Agency*] .... EDA
Emergency Decontamination Center [*Nuclear energy*] (NRCH) .... EDC
Emergency Decontamination Facility [*Energy Research and Development
  Administration*] .... EDF
Emergency Defense Plan [*Later, GDP*] (NATG) .... EDP
Emergency Deorbit System [*NASA*] (KSC) .... EDS
Emergency Department [*of a hospital*] .... ED
Emergency Department Nurses Association [*Later, ENA*] (EA) .... EDNA
Emergency Deployment Readiness Exercise [*Army*] (INF) .... EDRE
Emergency Destruction (MCD) .... ED
Emergency Detection and Decision System .... EDDS
Emergency Detection System .... EDS
Emergency Diesel Engine Cooling Water System [*Nuclear energy*]
  (NRCH) .... EDECWS
Emergency Diesel Engine Lubrication System [*Nuclear energy*] (NRCH) .... EDELS
Emergency Diesel Engine Starting System [*Nuclear energy*] (NRCH) ...... EDESS
Emergency Diesel Generator (NRCH) .... EDG
Emergency Diesel Generator Combustion Air Intake and Exhaust System
  [*Nuclear energy*] (NRCH) .... EDGCAIES
Emergency Digital Computer .... EDC
Emergency Digital Information Service (INF) .... EDIS
Emergency Disablement System .... EDS
Emergency Dispersal Bases (NATG) .... EDB
Emergency Distance [*Aviation*] (DA) .... ED
Emergency Distance Available [*Aviation*] (AIA) .... EDA
Emergency Distance Available [*Aviation*] .... EMDA
Emergency Distance Required [*Aviation*] (AIA) .... EDR
Emergency Distribution Plan [*DoD*] (AFIT) .... EDP
Emergency Distribution System (MCD) .... EDS
Emergency Drill in the Home [*Fire Department drill exercise*] .... EDITH
Emergency Earth Orbital Escape Device (KSC) .... EEOED
Emergency Economic Committee for Europe [*A "Western Nation"
  organization*] [*Post-World War II*] .... EECE
Emergency Education Network [*Federal Emergency Management Agency*]
  (GFGA) .... EENET
Emergency Egress Air Pack [*NASA*] (KSC) .... EEAP
Emergency Ejection Suits (MCD) .... EES
Emergency Electrical Power System (MCD) .... EEPS
Emergency Employment Act [*1971*] .... EEA
Emergency Energy Conservation Act [*1979*] .... EECA
Emergency Energy Conservation Program (OICC) .... EECP
Emergency Engineering Notice (MCD) .... EEN
Emergency English for Refugees [*Pennsylvania*] (EDAC) .... EER
Emergency Equipment Service Water System [*Nuclear energy*] (NRCH) .... EESWS
Emergency Escape Breathing Device [*Navy*] (CAAL) .... EEBD
Emergency Escape Device .... EED
Emergency Escape Ramp for Runaway Heavy Vehicle (PDAA) .... EERRHV
Emergency Essential Personnel (AFM) .... EEP
Emergency Establishment [*Military*] (NATG) .... EE
Emergency Establishment Supplement Table of Personnel Distribution
  [*NATO*] (NATG) .... EEST/PD
Emergency Establishment Supplements (NATG) .... EES
Emergency Evacuation Study [*Military*] (MCD) .... EES
Emergency Evaluation Study [*Military*] .... EES
Emergency Evaporative Coolant Garment System (PDAA) .... EECGS
Emergency Exchanger Cooling Water (IEEE) .... EECW
Emergency Expected Approach Time (DNAB) .... EEAT
Emergency Exposure Limits (AFM) .... EEL
Emergency Facilities (AAG) .... EF
Emergency Farm Mortgage Act of 1933 .... EFMA
Emergency Feed Baron Detector (IEEE) .... EFBD
Emergency Feeding Service [*Civil Defense*] .... EFS
Emergency Feedwater [*System*] [*Nuclear energy*] (NRCH) .... EFW
Emergency Feedwater Actuation Signal [*Nuclear energy*] (NRCH) .... EFAS
Emergency Feedwater Storage Tank [*Nuclear energy*] (NRCH) .... EFWST
Emergency Feedwater System [*Nuclear energy*] (NRCH) .... EFS
Emergency Feedwater System [*Nuclear energy*] (NRCH) .... EFWS
Emergency Field Arresting Gear (MCD) .... EFAG
Emergency Financial Control Board [*Later, FCB*] .... EFCB
Emergency Firing Panel .... EFP
Emergency Fix .... EF
Emergency Fleet Corp. [*Defunct, 1936*] .... EFC
Emergency Flight Termination (AFM) .... EFT
Emergency Food and Medical Program .... EFMP
Emergency Food and Shelter Program [*FEMA*] .... EFSP
Emergency Food Supply Scheme [*World Food Program*] .... EFSS
Emergency Foster Care (ADA) .... EFC
Emergency Fund Request .... EFR
Emergency Gas Treatment System [*Nuclear energy*] (NRCH) .... EGTS
Emergency General Account of Advances .... EGAA
Emergency Generator (NRCH) .... EG
Emergency Generator Room [*NFPA pre-fire planning symbol*] (NFPA) .... EG
Emergency Global Rescue, Escape, and Survival System [*NASA*] .... EGRESS

Emergency Grade [*Automotive engineering*] [*Polymer Steel Corp.*] .... EG
Emergency Ground Egress (MCD) .... EGE
Emergency Health Preparedness Advisory Committee [*Terminated, 1973*]
  (EA) .... EHPAC
Emergency Health Service [*HEW*] .... EHS
Emergency Heat Removal [*Nuclear energy*] (NRCH) .... EHR
Emergency Highway Energy Conservation Act [*1974*] .... EHECA
Emergency Highway Traffic Regulation [*Federal disaster planning*] .... EHTR
Emergency Highway Traffic Regulation Center [*Federal disaster planning*]
  (AABC) .... EHTRC
Emergency Homes, Inc. .... EHI
Emergency Hospital Scheme .... EHS
Emergency Housing Corp. .... EHC
Emergency Hurricane Information Center [*Marine science*] (MSC) .... EHIC
Emergency Identification Light [*Aerospace*] (AAG) .... EIDLT
Emergency Immigrant Education Act [*1984*] (GFGA) .... EIEA
Emergency Implementation Procedure (NRCH) .... EIP
Emergency Incident of Environmental Contamination [*Environmental
  Protection Agency*] .... EIEC
Emergency Information and Coordination Center [*Federal Emergency
  Management Agency*] .... EICC
Emergency Information Officer [*Civil Defense*] .... EIO
Emergency Information Readiness [*Civil Defense*] .... EIR
Emergency Information System [*Software package*] [*Research Alternatives,
  Inc.*] .... EIS
Emergency Infusion Device [*Medicine*] .... EID
Emergency Injection [*Nuclear energy*] (NRCH) .... EI
Emergency Injection System [*Nuclear energy*] (NRCH) .... EIS
Emergency International (EA) .... EI
Emergency Jobs and Unemployment Assistance Act .... EJUAA
Emergency Jobs Programs Extension Act of 1976 .... EJPEA
Emergency Land Fund [*Later, FSC/LAF*] (EA) .... ELF
Emergency Landing Ground .... ELG
Emergency Landing Site (SSD) .... ELS
Emergency Lead-Zinc Committee [*Later, Lead-Zinc Producers Committee*]
  (EA) .... ELZC
Emergency Legal Assistance Project .... ELAP
Emergency Legislation .... EL
Emergency Letter of Instructions .... ELOI
Emergency Librarian [*A publication*] (BRI) .... Emerg Lib
Emergency Life Support Apparatus (PDAA) .... ELSA
Emergency Life Support System .... ELSS
Emergency Life-Saving Instant Exit [*Aircraft*] [*Air Force*] .... ELSIE
Emergency Lighting Equipment .... ELE
Emergency Lighting Manufacturers Association [*Defunct*] (EA) .... ELMA
Emergency Lighting Supply (DNAB) .... ELS
Emergency Lighting System (DNAB) .... ELS
Emergency List [*Navy British*] .... EMY
Emergency Loading Procedure .... ELP
Emergency Loan Guarantee Board .... ELGB
Emergency Location Beacon - Aircraft (PDAA) .... ELB-A
Emergency Locator Beacon .... ELB
Emergency Locator Transmitter .... ELT
Emergency Locator Transmitter Automatic Deployable [*Navigation*]
  (OA) .... ELTAD
Emergency Locator Transmitter Automatic Portable [*Navigation*] (OA) ..... ELTAP
Emergency Locator Transmitter Receiver .... ELTR
Emergency Machine Tool Armament Corps [*British World War II*] .... EMTAC
Emergency Maintenance (BUR) .... EM
Emergency Management .... EM
Emergency Management Agency .... EMA
Emergency Management Assistance [*Federal Emergency Management
  Agency*] (GFGA) .... EMA
Emergency Management Coordinator [*Nuclear energy*] (NRCH) .... EMC
Emergency Management Institute .... EMI
Emergency Management System [*Computer science*] (EERA) .... EMS
Emergency Management Team [*Nuclear energy*] (GFGA) .... EMT
Emergency Manning Level (CET) .... EML
Emergency Manual Release Handle (MCD) .... EMRH
Emergency Manual Switching System [*Telecommunications*] (NITA) ..... EMSS
Emergency Maternity and Infant Care .... EMIC
Emergency Measures Organization [*Canada*] .... EMO
Emergency Mechanical Restraint [*Medicine*] (DAVI) .... EMR
Emergency Medical Care (DAVI) .... EMC
Emergency Medical Care and Rescue .... EMC & R
Emergency Medical Center .... EMC
Emergency Medical Command and Communications System .... EMCCS
Emergency Medical Information .... EMI
Emergency Medical Information Devices .... EMID
Emergency Medical Kit (MCD) .... EMK
Emergency Medical Personnel (MCD) .... EMP
Emergency Medical Responders .... EMR
Emergency Medical Service .... EMS
Emergency Medical Service System .... EMSS
Emergency Medical Tag .... EMT
Emergency Medical Technician .... EMT
Emergency Medical Technician, Ambulance (DHSM) .... EMT-A
Emergency Medical Technician, Intermediate [*Also, IEMT*] (DHSM) ...... EMT-I
Emergency Medical Technician, Paramedic (DHSM) .... EMT-P
Emergency Medical Treatment [*Military*] (AABC) .... EMT
Emergency Medical Treatment and Active Labor Act (AAGC) .... EMTALA
Emergency Medical Treatment and Active Labor Act .... EMTALA
Emergency Medicine [*Medical specialty*] (DHSM) .... EM
Emergency Medicine and Crisis Care [*Database*] .... EMCC
Emergency Medicine Foundation (EA) .... EMF

Emergency Medicine Management Association [*Defunct*] (EA) .... EMMA
Emergency Medicine Research Society [*Manchester, England*] (EAIO) .... EMRS
Emergency Medicine Residents' Association (EA) .... EMRA
Emergency Message (CINC) .... EM
Emergency Message - Alert Message (CINC) .... EM/AM
Emergency Message Authentication System [*USEUCOM*] (AABC) .... EMAS
Emergency Message Automatic Transmission System [*Military*] .... EMATS
Emergency Message Automatic Transmission System - Air Force ...... EMATS-AF
Emergency Message Automatic Transmission System - Joint Chiefs of
  Staff .... EMATS-JCS
Emergency Message Changes (MCD) .... EMC
Emergency Message Initiation Terminal (MCD) .... EMIT
Emergency Military Construction Program .... EMCP
Emergency Military Manpower Procurement System (MCD) .... EMMPS
Emergency Minerals Administration [*Department of the Interior*] .... EMA
Emergency Mission Control Center [*NASA*] .... EMCC
Emergency Mission Support [*Air Force*] .... EMS
Emergency Mission Support System [*Air Force*] .... EMSS
Emergency Mobilization Preparedness Board [*DoD*] .... EMPB
Emergency Movements Atomic [*Military*] (AABC) .... EMA
Emergency Mulitple Person Rescue Apparatus (PDAA) .... EMPRA
Emergency National Council Against US Intervention in Central America/
  The Caribbean (EA) .... ENC
Emergency Natural Gas Act of 1977 .... ENGA
Emergency Negative Thrust .... ENT
Emergency Network Control Center (MCD) .... ENCC
Emergency Network Operations Control Center (MCD) .... ENOCC
Emergency Notification System [*Nuclear energy*] (NRCH) .... ENS
Emergency Notification System .... ENS
Emergency Nurses Association (EA) .... ENA
Emergency Observation Bed [*Medicine*] .... EOB
Emergency Off (SAA) .... EMO
Emergency Officer [*Nuclear energy*] (NRCH) .... EO
Emergency Officers' Retired List [*Army*] .... EORL
Emergency Operating Center [*Civil Defense*] .... EOC
Emergency Operating Facility [*Civil Defense*] .... EOF
Emergency Operating Procedure [*Nuclear energy*] (NRCH) .... EOP
Emergency Operating Program (OICC) .... EOP
Emergency Operation Headquarters [*Army*] (AABC) .... EOH
Emergency Operational Capability (AAG) .... EOC
Emergency Operational Sequencing System (MCD) .... EOSS
Emergency Operations Center [*Military*] .... EOC
Emergency Operations Control Center [*Environmental Protection
  Agency*] .... EOCC
Emergency Operations Facility [*Nuclear energy*] (NRCH) .... EOF
Emergency Operations Plan [*Civil Defense*] .... EOP
Emergency Operations Research Center .... EORC
Emergency Operations Simulation [*Civil Defense*] .... EOS
Emergency Operations Simulation Techniques [*Civil Defense*] .... EOST
Emergency Operations Staff (MCD) .... EOS
Emergency Operations System .... EOS
Emergency Operations Systems Development [*Civil Defense*] .... EOSD
Emergency Operations Team [*Environmental Protection Agency*] (GFGA) ... EOT
Emergency Ordnance Disposal .... EOD
Emergency Out of Commission for Parts .... EOCP
Emergency Outpatient [*Medicine*] (HGAA) .... EOP
Emergency Oxygen Mask Assembly (KSC) .... EOMA
Emergency Oxygen Pack [*NASA*] (KSC) .... EOP
Emergency Oxygen Supply [*or System*] .... EOS
Emergency Parts Requisition (KSC) .... EPR
Emergency Passenger Exit .... EPE
Emergency Petroleum Allocation Act .... EPAA
Emergency Petroleum and Gas Administration [*Department of the
  Interior*] .... EPGA
Emergency Petroleum Supply Committee [*Terminated, 1976*] (EA) .... EPSC
Emergency Physical Restraint [*Medicine*] (DAVI) .... EPR
Emergency Plan Implementing Procedure [*Nuclear energy*] (NRCH) .... EPIP
Emergency Planning (NATG) .... EP
Emergency Planning and Community Right to Know Act, 1986 (EERA) .... EPCR
Emergency Planning and Community Right-to-Know Act [*1986*] .... EPCRA
Emergency Planning and Community Right-to-Know Act [*1986*] .... EPCRTK
Emergency Planning Canada .... EPC
Emergency Planning Canada, Ottawa, ON, Canada [*Library symbol Library of
  Congress*] (LCLS) .... CaOOEPC
Emergency Planning Canada [*Planification d'Urgence Canada*] Ottawa,
  Ontario [*Library symbol National Library of Canada*] (NLC) .... OOEPC
Emergency Planning Committee for Civil Transportation [*US and
  Canada*] .... EPCCT
Emergency Planning Officer [*Army*] .... EPO
Emergency Planning Review Guideline [*Nuclear energy*] (NRCH) .... EPRG
Emergency Planning Zone [*Nuclear emergency planning*] .... EPZ
Emergency Plans and Readiness Division [*of OEP*] [*Terminated*] .... EPRD
Emergency Plant Facilities .... EPF
Emergency Position Indicating Radio Beacons (AAGC) .... EPIRBs
Emergency Position-Indicating Radio Beacon (MCD) .... EPIRB
Emergency Positive Control Communications System .... EPCCS
Emergency Power .... EPWR
Emergency Power Cutoff [*NASA*] (KSC) .... EPCO
Emergency Power Engineering (HGAA) .... EME
Emergency Power Generator .... EPG
Emergency Power Level (KSC) .... EPL
Emergency Power Off .... EPO
Emergency Power Package (NG) .... EPP
Emergency Power Ride through Capability System [*Nuclear energy*]
  (NUCP) .... EPRICS

Emergency Power Ride-Through Capability System [*Nuclear energy*]
  (NRCH) .... EPRTCS
Emergency Power Supply (MSA) .... EMPS
Emergency Power Supply .... EPS
Emergency Power Switching Logic (NRCH) .... EPSL
Emergency Power System .... EPS
Emergency Power Unit .... EPU
Emergency Power Unit (IDOE) .... EPU
Emergency Power Unit Test Set .... EPUTS
Emergency Powers Act [*British World War II*] .... EPA
Emergency Powers Defence Act [*British World War II*] .... EPDA
Emergency Preparedness [*Nuclear energy*] (NRCH) .... EP
Emergency Preparedness at Local Level (EERA) .... EPALL
Emergency Preparedness Evaluation [*Nuclear energy*] (NRCH) .... EPE
Emergency Pressurization System .... EPS
Emergency Pressurization Valve (MCD) .... EPV
Emergency Price Control Act of 1942 .... EPCA
Emergency Priorities and Allocations Manual [*DoD*] .... EPAM
Emergency Procedure Guidelines (IAA) .... EPG
Emergency Procedure Trainer [*NASA*] (NASA) .... EPT
Emergency Procedures (MCD) .... EP
Emergency Procedures Document (MCD) .... EPD
Emergency Procurement Service [*Later, Defense Materials Service*] .... EPS
Emergency Production Planning List [*Army*] .... EPPL
Emergency Production Planning Program [*Navy*] (NG) .... EPPP
Emergency Production Weapons Schedule [*Navy*] (NG) .... EPWS
Emergency Program Release Notice [*NASA*] (NASA) .... EPRN
Emergency Programs Information Center [*Database*] .... EPIC
Emergency Project for Equal Rights (EA) .... EPER
Emergency Propaganda Committee [*London*] [*World War II*] .... EPC
Emergency Propellant Venting System .... EPVS
Emergency Proposal (NATG) .... EMPRO
Emergency Propulsive Propellant Venting System .... EPPVS
Emergency Public Information [*Civil Defense*] .... EPI
Emergency Radiation Monitor .... ERM
Emergency Radiation Monitoring System (GNE) .... ERMS
Emergency Radio Beacon .... ERB
Emergency Railroad Transportation Act, 1933 .... ERTA
Emergency [*or Essential*] Raw Cooling Water [*Nuclear energy*] (NRCH) .... ERCW
Emergency Recorder Plot (IAA) .... ERP
Emergency Recovery Display [*Bell System*] .... ERD
Emergency Recovery Force .... ERF
Emergency Recovery Group .... ERG
Emergency Recovery Section .... ERS
Emergency Recovery Unit .... ERU
Emergency Reference Level [*Nuclear energy*] (NRCH) .... ERL
Emergency Refugee and Migration Assistance [*Department of State*] .... ERMA
Emergency Relief .... ER
Emergency Relief Administration .... ERA
Emergency Relief and Construction Act .... ERCA
Emergency Relocation Center (NRCH) .... ERC
Emergency Relocation Point (DOMA) .... ERP
Emergency Relocation Site [*Military*] .... ERS
Emergency Relocation Site Afloat (MCD) .... ERSA
Emergency Remote Tracking Station [*Navy*] (ANA) .... ERTS
Emergency Repair Overseer [*Navy*] .... ERO
Emergency Repair Team [*Nuclear energy*] (GFGA) .... ERT
Emergency Reporting System [*Telecommunications*] (TEL) .... ERS
Emergency Request .... ER
Emergency Rescue .... ER
Emergency Rescue Equipment .... ERE
Emergency Rescue Team Chief [*Air Force*] .... ERTC
Emergency Reserve .... ER
Emergency Reserve Decoration [*British*] .... ERD
Emergency Resources Identification Equipment (IAA) .... ERIS
Emergency Response [*Nuclear energy*] (NRCH) .... ER
Emergency Response Cleanup Services (GNE) .... ERCS
Emergency Response Commission (GNE) .... ERC
Emergency Response Data System (ODBW) .... ERDS
Emergency Response Division [*Environmental Protection Agency*] (GFGA) ... ERD
Emergency Response Facility (MCD) .... ERF
Emergency Response Facility Information System [*Nuclear energy*]
  (NRCH) .... ERFIS
Emergency Response Guide [*RSPA*] (TAG) .... ERG
Emergency Response Guidelines [*Nuclear energy*] (NRCH) .... ERG
Emergency Response Indictor .... ERI
Emergency Response Information System [*Nuclear Regulatory
  Commission*] (GFGA) .... ERIS
Emergency Response Notification System [*Environmental Protection
  Agency*] (EPA) .... ERNS
Emergency Response Planning Guideline [*Environmental science*] .... ERPG
Emergency Response Team (NRCH) .... ERT
Emergency Response Training .... ERT
Emergency Return Device [*Aerospace*] .... ERD
Emergency Road Service [*American Automobile Association*] .... ERS
Emergency Rocket Communications System .... ERCS
Emergency Room [*Medicine*] .... ER
Emergency Rubber Project [*National Research Council*] .... ERP
Emergency Safe Altitude (MCD) .... ESA
Emergency Safeguards System Activation (IEEE) .... ESSA
Emergency Satellite Communications System .... ESCS
Emergency School Aid Act [*1972*] .... ESAA
Emergency School Assistance Program .... ESAP
Emergency Security Control of Air Traffic (AFM) .... ESCAT
Emergency Security Operations (AFM) .... ESO

Emergency Service	ES
Emergency Service Water [*Nuclear energy*] (NRCH)	ESW
Emergency Service Water Discharge [*Nuclear energy*] (NRCH)	ESWD
Emergency Service Water Intake [*Nuclear energy*] (NRCH)	ESWI
Emergency Service Water Screening [*Nuclear energy*] (NRCH)	ESWS
Emergency Service Water Supply System [*Nuclear energy*] (NRCH)	ESWSS
Emergency Service Water System [*Nuclear energy*] (IEEE)	ESWS
Emergency Services Bureau [*Queensland, Australia*]	ESB
Emergency Services Unit (LAIN)	ESU
Emergency Shelter Grant Program [*HUD*]	ESGP
Emergency Shelter Grants Program [*Department of Housing and Urban Development*] (GFGA)	ESG
Emergency Ship Handling Unit [*Navy*]	ESHU
Emergency Ship Repair Act of 1954	ESRA
Emergency Ship Salvage Material [*Navy*] (NG)	ESSM
Emergency Ship Service [*Navy*] (MSA)	ESS
Emergency Shipment Memorandum	ESM
Emergency Shipping Information System [*MARAD*] (TAG)	EMSIS
Emergency Short Stay [*in hospital*] [*British*]	ESS
Emergency Shutdown (MCD)	ESD
Emergency Shutoff Valve (KSC)	ESV
Emergency Signal (BUR)	EMS
Emergency Situations That Occur Outside of a Health Care Facility	ESTOOOAHCF
Emergency Social Services [*Civil Defense*]	ESS
Emergency Solid Fuels Administration	ESFA
Emergency Standby Order - Federal Highway Administration [*Federal disaster planning*]	ESO-FHWA
Emergency Standoff Range (NVT)	ESOR
Emergency Status Precedence Code [*DoD*]	ESPC
Emergency Stop Indicator [*Aerospace*] (AAG)	ESI
Emergency Strike Effort [*Military*]	ESE
Emergency Substitute in a Regular Position [*Education*]	ESRP
Emergency Supply Operations Center [*Defense Supply Agency*] (MCD)	ESOC
Emergency Support Organization (NRCH)	ESO
Emergency Survival System	ESS
Emergency System of Control Allowing Pilot Escape and Recovery (MCD)	ESCAPER
Emergency Takeover	ET
Emergency Tank [*Nuclear energy*] (NRCH)	ET
Emergency Target Relay Unit (MCD)	ETRU
Emergency Task Force for Indochinese Refugees [*Defunct*] (EA)	ETFIR
Emergency Technical Operations Center [*DoD*]	ETOC
Emergency Technical Provisions Act of 1976	ETPA
Emergency Technology Program [*Oak Ridge National Laboratory*]	ETP
Emergency Telephone Service	ETS
Emergency Temporary Standard [*OSHA*]	ETS
Emergency Tension Retractor [*Mercedes Benz*] [*Automotive engineering*]	ETR
Emergency Terrain Clearance Altitude	ETCA
Emergency Test Operation	ETO
Emergency Time Limit	ETL
Emergency Traffic Coordinating Officer [*Army*] (AABC)	ETCO
Emergency Traffic Disposition Plan [*Military*]	ETDP
Emergency Training Centre [*British*]	ETC
Emergency Transceiver Equipment	ETE
Emergency Treatment [*Dentistry*]	ET
Emergency Treatment Unit	ETU
Emergency Unemployment Compensation [*Account*]	EUC
Emergency Unit (CPH)	EU
Emergency Unitized Cargo Unloading System [*Navy*] (CAAL)	EUCUS
Emergency Unsatisfactory Material Report (MCD)	EUMR
Emergency Unsatisfactory Report [*Military*] (AFM)	EUR
Emergency Urgent Change Package [*Army*] (AABC)	EUCP
Emergency Utility Building (NRCH)	EUB
Emergency Vehicle [*Medicine*] (DAVI)	EV
Emergency Venting System	EVS
Emergency Veterinary Tag	EVT
Emergency Virus Isolation Facility [*National Cancer Institute*]	EVIF
Emergency War Operations	EWO
Emergency War Order [*Air Force*]	EWO
Emergency War Plan	EWP
Emergency War Surgery Training Program [*Army*]	EWSTP
Emergency Ward	EW
Emergency Warnings Branch [*National Weather Service*]	EWB
Emergency Water Supply	EWS
Emergency Welfare Registration and Inquiry [*Civil Defense*]	EWR & I
Emergency Welfare Service [*Civil Defense*]	EWS
Emergency Window Escape [*NASA*] (NASA)	EWE
Emergency-Room Physician (MEDA)	ERP
Emergent Group, Inc. [*NASDAQ symbol*] (SAG)	EMER
Emergent Group, Inc. [*Associated Press*] (SAG)	Emergnt
Emergent Hydrophyte Treatment System	EHTS
Emergent Reading Ability Judgements for Favorite Storybooks Scale (EDAC)	ERAJFS
Emergent S Wave [*Earthquakes*]	e(S)
Emerging and Reemerging Infectious Diseases [*Medicine*]	ERID
Emerging Company Marketplace (DFIT)	ECM
Emerging Ethnic Engineers [*An association*]	E³
Emerging Flux Region (OA)	EFR
Emerging Germany Fund [*Associated Press*] (SAG)	EmgGer
Emerging Germany Fund [*NYSE symbol*] (SPSG)	FRG
Emerging Issues Task Force (TDOB)	EITF
Emerging Market Economy (ECON)	EME
Emerging Markets Floating Rate Fund [*NYSE symbol*] (SAG)	EFL
Emerging Markets Floating Rate Fund [*Associated Press*] (SAG)	EmMkFlt

Emerging Markets Income Fund [*NYSE symbol*] (SPSG)	EDF
Emerging Markets Income Fund [*NYSE symbol*] (SPSG)	EMD
[*The*] Emerging Markets Income Fund [*Associated Press*] (SAG)	EMInco
Emerging Markets Income Fund II, Inc. [*Associated Press*] (SAG)	EMInco2
[*The*] Emerging Markets Infrastructure Fund [*NYSE symbol*] (SPSG)	EMG
[*The*] Emerging Markets Infrastructure Fund [*Associated Press*] (SAG)	EmgMkt
Emerging Markets Telecommunications Fund [*Associated Press*] (SAG)	EMTel
Emerging Markets Telecommunications Fund [*NYSE symbol*] (SAG)	ETF
Emerging Markets Traders Association (EA)	EMTA
Emerging Mexico Fund [*Associated Press*] (SAG)	EmMex
Emerging Mexico Fund [*NYSE symbol*] (SPSG)	MEF
Emerging Mkts Fltg Rt Fd [*NYSE symbol*] (TTSB)	EFL
Emerging Mkts Income Fund II [*NYSE symbol*] (TTSB)	EDE
Emerging Mkts Infrastructure [*NYSE symbol*] (TTSB)	EMG
Emerging Mkts Telcommun Fd [*NYSE symbol*] (TTSB)	ETF
Emerging Small Business (AAGC)	ESB
Emerging Small Business Reserve Amount (AAGC)	ESBRA
Emerging Technologies Advisory Board	ETAB
Emerging Technology	ET
Emerging Tigers Fund [*Associated Press*] (SAG)	EmgTgr
Emerging Tigers Fund [*NYSE symbol*] (SAG)	TGF
Emerigon on Insurance [*A publication*] (DLA)	Emer Ins
Emerigon on Insurance [*A publication*] (DLA)	Emerig Ins
Emerigon on Maritime Loans [*A publication*] (DLA)	Emer Mar Lo
Emerigon on Maritime Loans [*A publication*] (DLA)	Emerig Mar Loans
Emeritus [*Obtain by Service*] [*Latin*]	em
Emeritus	EMER
Emeritus Corp. [*Associated Press*] (SAG)	Emerit
Emeritus Corp. [*Associated Press*] (SAG)	Emeritus
Emeritus Corp. [*AMEX symbol*] (SAG)	ESC
Emerson and Haber's Political and Civil Rights in the United States [*A publication*] (DLA)	Emerson & Haber Pol & Civ Rits
Emerson Books, Inc. (DGA)	EBI
Emerson College (GAGS)	Emerson C
Emerson College, Boston, MA [*OCLC symbol*] (OCLC)	ECL
Emerson College, Boston, MA [*Library symbol Library of Congress*] (LCLS)	MBE
Emerson Electric [*NYSE symbol*] (TTSB)	EMR
Emerson Electric Co. (MCD)	EE
Emerson Electric Co.	EEC
Emerson Electric Co. [*NYSE symbol*] (SPSG)	EMR
Emerson Electric Co. [*Associated Press*] (SAG)	EmrsEl
Emerson, Lake & Palmer [*Rock music group*]	ELP
Emerson Programmer-Evaluator-Controller [*Computer science*]	EPEC
Emerson Radio [*AMEX symbol*] (TTSB)	MSN
Emerson Radio & Phonograph Corp. [*Later, Emerson Radio Corp.*]	ERPC
Emerson Radio Corp. [*Associated Press*] (SAG)	EmerR
Emerson Radio Corp. [*AMEX symbol*] (SAG)	MSN
Emery [*Germany ICAO location identifier*] (ICLI)	EDOH
Emery Control (IAA)	EMCON
Emery County High School, Castle Dale, UT [*Library symbol Library of Congress*] (LCLS)	UCdH
Emery County Library, Castle Dale, UT [*Library symbol Library of Congress*] (LCLS)	UCdE
Emery Industries, Inc. [*Research code symbol*]	Emfac
Emery Industries, Inc., Research Library, Cincinnati, OH [*Library symbol Library of Congress*] (LCLS)	OCEmI
Emery Testing Machine [*Nineteenth-century hydraulic testing machine*] (RDA)	ETM
Emery Worldwide Airlines, Inc. [*ICAO designator*] (FAAC)	EWW
Emeryville Public Library, Emeryville, CA [*Library symbol Library of Congress*] (LCLS)	CEv
Emetic [*Pharmacy*] (ROG)	EME
Emetine [*Antiamebic compound*]	EME
Emetine Bismuth Iodide [*Pharmacology*]	EBI
Emhart Manufacturing Co. [*Later, Emhart Corp.*], Bloomfield, CT [*Library symbol Library of Congress*] (LCLS)	CtBIE
EMI [*formerly, Electric & Musical Industries Ltd.*] Data Electronic Computer [*British*]	EMIDEC
EMI [*formerly, Electric & Musical Industries Ltd.*] Special Issues [*Record label*] [*Great Britain*]	EMI
Emigrant Gap, CA [*Location identifier FAA*] (FAAL)	BLU
Emigrant Institute [*Sweden*]	EI
Emigrant's Assured Savings Estate [*Banking program*]	EASE
Emigration Portfolio Manager [*Investment term*]	EPM
Emil Gilels Society (EA)	EGS
Emil Verban Memorial Society (EA)	EVMS
[*The*] Emily Carr College of Art, Vancouver, British Columbia [*Library symbol National Library of Canada*] (NLC)	BVAVSA
EMILY's List (EA)	EL
Eminence (DLA)	E
Eminence	EM
Eminence, KY [*AM radio station call letters*]	WKXF
Eminence, KY [*FM radio station call letters*] (RBYB)	WXLM-FM
Eminence, KY [*FM radio station call letters*]	WXLN
Eminent [*Freemasonry*]	E
Eminent (ROG)	EM
Eminent (ROG)	EMIN
Eminent Chaplain [*Freemasonry*] (ROG)	EC
Eminent Commander [*Freemasonry*] (ROG)	EC
Eminent Conductor [*Freemasonry*] (ROG)	EC
Eminent Domain [*Legal term*]	EM DOM
Eminent Domain Procedure Law [*New York, NY A publication*]	EDPL
Eminent Grand Almoner [*Freemasonry*] (ROG)	EGA
Eminent Grand Commander [*Freemasonry*] (ROG)	EGC

Eminent Grand Treasurer [Freemasonry] (ROG)	EGT
Eminent Herald [Freemasonry] (ROG)	EH
Eminent Junior Grand Steward [Freemasonry] (ROG)	EJGS
Eminent Persons Group [Group of elder statesmen from Commonwealth countries]	EPG
Eminent Women [A publication]	EW
Eminentra Granularis Posterior [Anatomy]	EGP
Emir Oils Ltd. [Vancouver Stock Exchange symbol]	EOL
Emirates Airlines [United Arab Emirates] (MENA)	EA
Emirates Airlines [ICAO designator] (AD)	EX
Emirates Flight Information Region [United Arab Emirates] [ICAO location identifier] (ICLI)	OMAE
Emirates News Agency [United Arab Emirates] (MENA)	WAM
Emirates Telecommunications Corp. Ltd. (TEL)	EMIRTEL
Emirates Telecommunications Corp. Ltd. [Telecommunications service] (TSSD)	ETISALAT
Emirau [Papua New Guinea] [Airport symbol] (OAG)	EMI
Emisphere Technologies [NASDAQ symbol] (TTSB)	EMIS
Emisphere Technologies, Inc. [NASDAQ symbol] (SAG)	EMIS
Emisphere Technologies, Inc. [Associated Press] (SAG)	EmisTch
Emissary Foundation International (EA)	EFI
Emission	EM
Emission (KSC)	EMIS
Emission (MSA)	EMSN
Emission/Absorption Inversion Codes (MCD)	EMABIC
Emission Characteristics Monitor	ECM
Emission Circular Intensity Differential [Spectroscopy]	ECID
Emission Computed Tomography	ECT
Emission Computerized Axial Tomography	ECAT
Emission Contribution Fraction (OA)	ECF
Emission Control (CAAL)	EMCON
Emission Control 1 Gasoline [ARCO]	EC-1
Emission Control Device [Automotive engineering]	ECD
Emission Control Experimental	EC-X
Emission Control Information Label [Automotive engineering]	ECIL
Emission Control System (MCD)	ECS
Emission Control Technology Division [Environmental Protection Agency] (GFGA)	ECTD
Emission Data Vehicle [Exhaust emissions testing] [Automotive engineering]	EDV
Emission Density Zoning [Environmental Protection Agency] (GFGA)	EDZ
Emission Electron Microscope (IAA)	EEM
Emission Electron Miscroscope (PDAA)	EEM
Emission Factor [Environmental Protection Agency] (GFGA)	EF
Emission History Information System [Environmental Information Agency]	EHIS
Emission Index	EI
Emission Inventory Questionnaire [Environmental science] (FFDE)	EIQ
Emission Maintenance Reminder [Automotive engineering]	EMR
Emission Monochromator [Spectroscopy]	EM
Emission Policy (NATG)	EP
Emission Reduction Credit [Environmental Protection Agency] (GFGA)	ERC
Emission Release (NVT)	EMREL
Emission Security (AFM)	EMISEC
Emission Security	EMSEC
Emission Spectrograph	EMS
Emission Spectrum [Spectroscopy]	ES
Emission Standards and Engineering Division [Environmental Protection Agency] (GFGA)	ESED
Emissions Balancing [Environmental Protection Agency] (GFGA)	EB
Emissions Impact Statement [Environmental Protection Agency] (GFGA)	EIS
Emissions Inventory [Environmental Protection Agency] (GFGA)	EI
Emissions Inventory System [Environmental Protection Agency] (GFGA)	EIS
Emissions Inventory System/Area Source [Environmental Protection Agency] (GFGA)	EIS/AS
Emissions Inventory System/Point Source [Environmental Protection Agency] (GFGA)	EIS/PS
Emissions of Light and Very Low Frequency Perturbations Due to Electromagnetic Pulse Sources	ELVES
Emissions Opportunity Cost	EOC
Emissions Trading [Environmental Protection Agency]	ET
Emissions Trading Policy [Environmental Protection Agency] (GFGA)	ETP
Emissora Nacional de Radiodifusao [Radio network] [Portugal]	ENR
Emittatur [Let It Be Discharged] [Pharmacy] (ROG)	EMITT
Emitted Coherent Radiation	ECR
Emitted Radiation from Special Engines (MCD)	ERASE
Emitted Radio Power (IAA)	ERP
Emitter (MSA)	E
Emitter (IDOE)	e
Emitter (MSA)	EM
Emitter (MSA)	EMTR
Emitter Base (IAA)	EB
Emitter Capacitance (IDOE)	C_E
Emitter Dip Effect (IEEE)	EDE
Emitter Follower [Electronics] (MCD)	EF
Emitter Follower Current Switch [Electronics] (IAA)	EFCS
Emitter Follower Logic [Electronics]	EFL
Emitter Follower Transistor Logic [Electronics] (IAA)	ETL
Emitter Identification (MCD)	EID
Emitter Identification Guide (NG)	EIG
Emitter Identification Program [RADAR] (MCD)	EIP
Emitter Isolated Difference Amplifier Paralleling [Bell System]	EIDAP
Emitter Location and Analysis System (MCD)	ELAS
Emitter Location and Identification	ELI
Emitter Location Method	ELM
Emitter Location Method	ELME

Emitter Location System [Air Force]	ELS
Emitter Position Location	EPL
Emitter Program Library (CAAL)	EPL
Emitter Resistance (IDOE)	R_E
Emitter Voltage (IDOE)	V_E
Emitter-Controlled Negative Resistance Triode	ECNRT
Emitter-Coupled Circuit [Electronics] (HGAA)	ECC
Emitter-Coupled Current-Steered Logic [Electronics] (MSA)	ECCSL
Emitter-Coupled Logic [Electronics]	ECL
Emitter-Coupled Logic Operator [Electronics]	ECLO
Emitter-Coupled Pair [Electronics] (IAA)	ECP
Emitter-Coupled Transistor Logic [Electronics]	ECTL
Emitter-Emitter Coupled Logic [Electronics] (IEEE)	EECL
Emitter-Emitter Coupled Logic [Electronics] (IAA)	EEL
Emitter-Region Width (IDOE)	W_E
Emitter-Voltage Supply (IDOE)	V_{EE}
Emma [Novel by Jane Austen]	E
Emma [Phonetic alphabet] [In use in 1904 and 1914] (DSUE)	M
Emma Dorothy Nevitte Southworth [American novelist, 1818-99] [Acronym used as pseudonym]	EDEN
Emmaboda [Sweden ICAO location identifier] (ICLI)	ESMA
Emmanuel College [Boston, MA] (ROG)	EMM
Emmanuel College, Boston, MA [OCLC symbol] (OCLC)	EMC
Emmanuel College, Boston, MA [Library symbol Library of Congress] (LCLS)	MBEmm
Emmanuel College, Victoria University, Toronto, ON, Canada [Library symbol Library of Congress] (LCLS)	CaOTE
Emmanuel College, Victoria University, Toronto, Ontario [Library symbol National Library of Canada] (NLC)	OTE
Emmanuel Radnitsky [American artist, 1890-1976]	Man Ray
Emmanuel School of Religion, Johnson City, TN [OCLC symbol] (OCLC)	TEJ
Emmanuel School of Religion, Johnson City, TN [Library symbol Library of Congress] (LCLS)	TJoE
Emmeloord/Noord-Oostpolder [Netherlands ICAO location identifier] (ICLI)	EHNP
Emmen [Switzerland ICAO location identifier] (ICLI)	LSME
Emmenagogue [Promoting Menstruation] [Pharmacy] (ROG)	EMM
Emmet [California] [Seismograph station code, US Geological Survey] (SEIS)	EMT
Emmetropia [Also, EM] [Ophthalmology]	E
Emmetropia [Also, E] [Ophthalmology]	EM
Emmetsburg Democrat, Emmetsburg, IA [Library symbol] [Library of Congress] (LCLS)	IaEmD
Emmetsburg, IA [Location identifier FAA] (FAAL)	EGQ
Emmetsburg, IA [FM radio station call letters]	KEMB
Emmetsburg Public Library, Emmetsburg, IA [Library symbol Library of Congress] (LCLS)	IaEm
Emmetsburg Reporter, Emmetsburg, IA [Library symbol] [Library of Congress] (LCLS)	IaEmR
Emmett, ID [FM radio station call letters]	KJHY
Emmett Public Library, Emmett, ID [Library symbol] [Library of Congress] (LCLS)	IdEm
Emmis Broadcasting Corp. [Associated Press] (SAG)	EmmisBd
Emmis Broadcasting Corp. [NASDAQ symbol] (SAG)	EMMS
Emmis Broadcasting 'A' [NASDAQ symbol] (TTSB)	EMMS
Emmitsburg, MD [FM radio station call letters]	WMTB
Emmonak [Alaska] [Airport symbol] (OAG)	EMK
Emmonak, AK [Location identifier FAA] (FAAL)	ENM
Emmylou Harris Fan Club (EA)	EHFC
Emo [Papua New Guinea] [Airport symbol] (OAG)	EMO
Emo Public Library, Ontario [Library symbol National Library of Canada] (NLC)	OEM
Emo Questionnaire [Psychology]	EQ
Emolliens [Mollifying, Healing] [Pharmacy] (ROG)	EMOLL
Emollient (ROG)	EMO
Emons Holding, Inc. [Associated Press] (SAG)	Emons
Emons Transportation Group [NASDAQ symbol] (TTSB)	EMON
Emory and Henry College [Virginia]	EHC
Emory and Henry College, Emory, VA [OCLC symbol] (OCLC)	VEH
Emory and Henry College, Emory, VA [Library symbol Library of Congress] (LCLS)	ViEmoE
Emory Center for International Studies [Emory University] [Research center] (RCD)	ECIS
Emory University (GAGS)	Emory U
Emory University, A. W. Calhoun Medical Library, Atlanta, GA [OCLC symbol] (OCLC)	EMM
Emory University, A. W. Calhoun Medical Library, Atlanta, GA [Library symbol Library of Congress] (LCLS)	GEU-M
Emory University, Atlanta, GA [OCLC symbol] (OCLC)	EMU
Emory University, Atlanta, GA [Library symbol Library of Congress] (LCLS)	GEU
Emory University, Candler School of Theology, Atlanta, GA [Library symbol Library of Congress] (LCLS)	GEU-T
Emory University Division of Librarianship, Atlanta, GA [OCLC symbol] (OCLC)	EML
Emory University, Division of Librarianship, Atlanta, GA [Library symbol Library of Congress] (LCLS)	GEU-LS
Emory University, Division of Librarianship, Atlanta, GA [OCLC symbol] (OCLC)	LEU
Emory University, Lamar School of Law, Atlanta, GA [Library symbol Library of Congress] (LCLS)	GEU-L
Emory University, Pitts Theological Library, Atlanta, GA [OCLC symbol] (OCLC)	EMT
Emory University, School of Business Administration, Atlanta, GA [Library symbol Library of Congress] (LCLS)	GEU-B

Emory University School of Dentistry, Atlanta, GA [*OCLC symbol*] (OCLC) .... EMD

Emory University, School of Dentistry, Atlanta, GA [*Library symbol Library of Congress*] (LCLS) .... GEU-D

Emory University, Special Collections Department, Atlanta, GA [*Library symbol*] [*Library of Congress*] (LCLS) .... GEU-S

Emory University, Yerkes Primate Research Center, Atlanta, GA [*Library symbol Library of Congress*] (LCLS) .... GEU-Y

Emory, VA [*FM radio station call letters*] .... WEHC

Emosson [*Switzerland*] [*Seismograph station code, US Geological Survey*] (SEIS) .... EMO

Emotional .... EMOT

Emotional and Behavioural Difficulties (AIE) .... EBD

Emotional Disturbance .... ED

Emotional Factor [*Psychology*] (DAVI) .... EF

Emotional Health Anonymous (EA) .... EHA

Emotional Icon [*Expression of emotion typed into a message using standard keyboard characters*] (CDE) .... emoticon

Emotional Violence .... EV

Emotional-Ethical Attitudes Test [*Psychometrics*] .... EEAT

Emotionally Deprived .... ED

Emotionally Disabled (OICC) .... ED

Emotionally Disturbed .... EM

Emotionally Disturbed/Learning Disabled .... ED/LD

Emotionally Disturbed Person (LAIN) .... EDP

Emotionally Handicapped [*Psychology*] .... EH

Emotionally Impaired .... EI

Emotionally Mentally Retarded [*Psychology*] .... EMR

Emotionally Unstable Character Disorder (MEDA) .... EUCD

Emotions Anonymous (EA) .... EA

Empada [*Guinea-Bissau*] [*ICAO location identifier*] (ICLI) .... GGEP

Empathy Inventory [*Teacher evaluation test*] .... EI

Empathy Test [*Psychology*] .... ET

Empennage [*Aerospace engineering*] .... EMP

Empennage Support Beam [*Aerospace engineering*] (MCD) .... ESB

Emperor (ROG) .... E

Emperor [*or Empress*] .... EMP

Emperor (VRA) .... emp

Emperor Gold [*VS Symbol*] (TTSB) .... EMR

Emperor of the East and West [*Freemasonry*] (ROG) .... EE & W

Emperor's Clothes Syndrome .... ECS

Empfindichkeit [*Susceptibility to Stimulation*] [*Psychology*] .... E

Empfindlicher Aufschlagzuender [*Superquick impact fuze*] [*German military - World War II*] .... EAZ

Emphatic [*Linguistics*] .... e

[*The*] Emphatic Diaglott [*1942*] [*A publication*] (BJA) .... ED

Emphysema [*Medicine*] .... EMPH

Emphysema Anonymous, Inc. (EA) .... EAI

Emphysema plus Asthma [*Medicine*] .... EMPHAS

Emphysematous Bullae [*Pulmonary medicine*] .... EB

EMPI, Inc. [*NASDAQ symbol*] (NQ) .... EMPI

Empire .... EMP

Empire .... EMP

Empire Air Service, Inc. [*ICAO designator*] (FAAC) .... EMP

Empire Air Training Scheme [*British military*] (DMA) .... EATS

Empire Airlines [*ICAO designator*] (AD) .... EM

Empire Airlines [*ICAO designator*] (AD) .... UR

Empire Airlines, Inc. [*ICAO designator*] (FAAC) .... CFS

Empire Co. Ltd. [*Toronto Stock Exchange symbol*] .... EMP

Empire Cotton Growing Corp. [*British*] (BI) .... ECGC

Empire Dist El,4 3/4% Pfd [*NYSE symbol*] (TTSB) .... EDEPrA

Empire Dist El,5% Pfd [*NYSE symbol*] (TTSB) .... EDEPrB

Empire Dist Elec [*NYSE symbol*] (TTSB) .... EDE

Empire District Electric Co. [*NYSE symbol*] (SPSG) .... EDE

Empire District Electric Co. [*Associated Press*] (SAG) .... Emp

Empire District Electric Co. [*Associated Press*] (SAG) .... EmpDist

Empire Gallantry Medal [*British*] .... EGM

Empire Gold Resources Ltd. [*Vancouver Stock Exchange symbol*] .... EPG

Empire Grade Road [*California*] [*Seismograph station code, US Geological Survey*] (SEIS) .... EGR

Empire Journal of Experimental Agriculture [*A publication*] .... EJEA

Empire Lines, Inc. .... EML

Empire Marketing Board [*For motion pictures in England*] .... EMB

Empire of Carolina [*AMEX symbol*] (TTSB) .... EMP

Empire of Carolina, Inc. [*AMEX symbol*] (SPSG) .... EMP

Empire of Carolina, Inc. [*Associated Press*] (SAG) .... EmpCar

Empire Parliamentary Association [*Later, CPA*] [*Australia*] .... EPA

Empire Press Agency (DGA) .... EPA

Empire Press Union (DGA) .... EPU

Empire Resources [*Vancouver Stock Exchange symbol*] .... EMT

Empire Social Telegram (IAA) .... EST

Empire State Atomic Development Associates, Inc. .... ESADA

Empire State College, Saratoga Springs, NY [*Library symbol Library of Congress*] (LCLS) .... NSsE

Empire State College, Saratoga Springs, NY [*Inactive*] [*OCLC symbol*] (OCLC) .... YEM

Empire State Forest Products Association (SRA) .... ESFPA

Empire State Historical Publications [*Series*] .... ESHP

Empire State Paper Research Associates .... ESPRA

Empire State Paper Research Institute .... ESPRI

Empire State Paper Research Institute [*College of Environmental Science and Forestry at Syracuse*] [*Research center*] (RCD) .... ESPRI

Empire State Tattoo Club of America (EA) .... ESTCA

Empire Telecommunications [*British World War II*] .... ETS

Empire Test Pilots School [*British ICAO designator*] (FAAC) .... ETP

Empire Test Pilots' School [*British*] .... ETPS

Empiric Studies Group (SAA) .... ESG

Empiric Studies Group Simulated SAC [*Strategic Air Command*] Force Data Base (SAA) .... ESGSSFDB

Empirical Distribution Function [*Statistics*] .... EDF

Empirical Force Field [*Physical chemistry*] .... EFF

Empirical Kinetic Modeling Approach [*Air pollution research*] .... EKMA

Empirical Mathematics (ECON) .... EM

Empirical Orthogonal Function [*Statistics*] .... EOF

Empirical Pseudopotential Method [*Physics*] .... EPM

Empirical Research Group (HGAA) .... ERG

Empirically Supported Algorithm Driven [*Computer science*] .... ESAD

Emplaced Instrument Complex [*Aerospace*] .... EIC

Emplaced Lunar Scientific Station [*Aerospace*] .... ELSS

Emplaced Scientific Station [*Aerospace*] .... ESS

Emplacement (AABC) .... EMPL

Emplacement, Installation, and Test (CET) .... EI & T

Emplane [*British*] .... EMPL

Emplastrum [*Plaster*] [*Pharmacy*] .... EMP

Emplastrum [*Plaster*] [*Pharmacy*] (ROG) .... EMP

Emplastrum [*Plaster*] [*Pharmacy*] (ROG) .... EMPLAST

Emplastrum Vesicatorum [*A Blister*] [*Medicine*] .... Emp Vesic

Employ [*or Employee*] (AABC) .... EMPL

Employ the Physically Handicapped .... EPH

Employability Development (OICC) .... ED

Employability Development Model (OICC) .... EDM

Employability Development Services [*US Employment Service*] [*Department of Labor*] .... EDS

Employability Development Team (OICC) .... EDT

Employables (OICC) .... EMP

Employed .... EMPL

Employed Full Time [*Chiropody*] [*British*] .... EF

Employee [*Legal shorthand*] (LWAP) .... E

Employee (OICC) .... EE

Employee [*or Employer*] (DCTA) .... EMP

Employee .... EMPLEE

Employee .... EMPLYE

Employee Appraisal Record .... EAR

Employee Aptitude Survey [*Psychology*] (AEBS) .... EAS

Employee Assistance Personnel [*Psychology*] (DAVI) .... EAP

Employee Assistance Program [*Health care*] (HCT) .... EAP

Employee Assistance Society of North America (EA) .... EASNA

Employee Attitude Research (IEEE) .... EAR

Employee Auxiliary Service Personnel (MCD) .... EASP

Employee Auxiliary Services (MCD) .... EAS

Employee Benefit Research Institute (EA) .... EBRI

Employee Benefits Cases (DLA) .... EBC

Employee Benefits Infosource [*International Foundation of Employee Benefit Plans*] [*Information service or system*] (CRD) .... EBIS

Employee Charity and Community Services .... ECCS

Employee Cost Index .... ECI

Employee Counseling and Assistance Program [*Environmental Protection Agency*] (EPA) .... ECAP

Employee Daily Labor Distribution (AAG) .... EDLD

Employee Data Record .... EDR

Employee Development and Assistance Programme (AIE) .... EDAP

Employee Development Officer .... EDO

Employee Educational Assistance Act of 1978 (WYGK) .... EEAA

Employee Exposure Guidelines [*General Motors Corp.*] .... EEG

Employee Health Assurance Group [*Medicine*] .... EHAG

Employee Health Insurance .... EHI

Employee Health Insurance Plan (DHSM) .... EHIP

Employee Health Maintenance Examination .... EHME

Employee Home Ownership Plan [*Human resources*] (WYGK) .... EHOP

Employee Incident Report (MCD) .... EIR

Employee Information System (MCD) .... EIS

Employee Involvement [*Human resources*] (WYGK) .... EI

Employee Involvement Association .... EIA

Employee Not on Duty [*FRA*] (TAG) .... ENOD

Employee Number (MCD) .... EMPNO

Employee on Duty [*FRA*] (TAG) .... EOD

Employee Ownership Plan (WGA) .... EOP

Employee Participation (ADA) .... EP

Employee Participation Group .... EPG

Employee Plan [*IRS*] .... EP

Employee Plan Administrators .... EPA

Employee Plans/Exempt Organization [*IRS*] .... EP/EO

Employee Polygraph Protection Act of 1988 .... EPPA

Employee Profile Security File [*IRS*] .... EPSF

Employee Record Change Notice .... ERCN

Employee Relations Index .... ERI

Employee Relations Law Review [*A publication*] (AAGC) .... Employee Rel L Rev

Employee Relocation Council (EA) .... E-R-C

Employee Relocation Real Estate Advisory Council [*Later, E-R-C*] (EA) .... ERREAC

Employee Retirement Income Security Act [*of 1994*] (AAGC) .... ERISA

Employee Retirement Income Security Act of 1974 [*Also facetiously translated as Every Ridiculous Idea Since Adam*] .... ERISA

Employee Satisfaction .... ESAT

Employee Savings Program .... ESP

Employee Skills Upgrade .... ESU

Employee Solutions [*NASDAQ symbol*] (TTSB) .... ESOL

Employee Solutions, Inc. [*Associated Press*] (SAG) .... EmplySI

Employee Solutions, Inc. [*NASDAQ symbol*] (SAG) .... ESOL

Employee Standards Administration .... ESA

Employee Stock Option [*or Ownership*] **Plan** [*Tax plan*] ... ESOP
Employee Stock Ownership Plan (AAGC) ... ESOP
Employee Stock Ownership Trust ... ESOT
Employee Stock Purchase [*Software*] ... ESP
Employee Stock Purchase Plan (AAGC) ... ESPP
Employee Suggestion (AAG) ... ES
Employee Support Services Company [*Military*] ... ESSCO
Employee Transportation Coordinator [*MOCD*] (TAG) ... ETC
Employee-Management Cooperation ... EMC
Employees' Compensation Appeals Board [*Department of Labor*] ... ECAB
Employees' Compensation Commission ... ECC
Employees' Compensation Fund (NG) ... ECF
Employees of Diplomatic Missions [*A publication*] ... EDMI
Employees' Plan Master File [*IRS*] ... EPMF
Employee's Withholding Allowance Certificate [*IRS*] ... W-4
Employer (ROG) ... EMPL
Employer ... EMPLR
Employer (OICC) ... ER
Employer Dentists Federation of Australia ... EDFA
Employer Group Health Plan [*Department of Health and Human Services*] (GFGA) ... EGHP
Employer Health Insurance Cost Survey [*Department of Health and Human Services*] (GFGA) ... EHICS
Employer Identification Code (AABC) ... EIC
Employer Identification Number [*IRS*] ... EIN
Employer Identification Number Assignment Control Card File [*IRS*] ... EACF
Employer Identification Number Key Index File [*IRS*] ... EKIF
Employer Identification Number Name and Address File [*IRS*] ... ENAF
Employer Identification Number Taxpayer Information File [*IRS*] ... ETIF
Employer Master Control File [*State Employee Security Agency*] (OICC) ... EMCF
Employer Relations Officer ... ERO
Employer Relations Representative ... ERR
Employer School Program (OICC) ... ESP
Employer Services [*State Employee Security Agency*] (OICC) ... ES
Employer Support of the Guard and Reserve ... ESGR
Employer Trip Reduction [*Environmental Protection Agency*] ... ETR
Employer-Paid Advertising ... EPA
Employers' Association [*British*] (DCTA) ... EA
Employers Association of South Carolina (SRA) ... EASC
Employers Council on Flexible Compensation (EA) ... ECFC
Employers' Federation of Paper Makers (DGA) ... EFPM
Employer's Inventory of Critical Manpower ... EICM
Employers Labor Relations Information Committee (EA) ... ELRIC
Employers' Liability (DLA) ... Empl'rs Liab
Employers' Mutual Indemnity Association Ltd. [*Australia Commercial firm*] ... EMIA
Employers Mutual Indemnity Ltd. ... EMI
Employers Organization (DCTA) ... EO
Employers' Perceptions of Colleges (AIE) ... EPOC
Employer's Return File [*IRS*] ... ERF
Employers' Review [*A publication*] ... Empl R
Employers' Review [*A publication*] ... Employers' Rev
Employers' Unemployment Compensation Council (EA) ... EUCC
Employing Photo-Engravers Association of America [*Defunct*] (EA) ... EPEAA
Employing Printers Association of America [*Defunct*] (EA) ... EPAA
Employment ... EMPLMNT
Employment ... EMPLMNT
Employment [*Economics*] ... N
Employment Act (OICC) ... EA
Employment Agencies Protective Association of the United States [*Later, National Employment Association*] ... EAPAUS
Employment Agency (WDAA) ... EMP AGCY
Employment Agents' Federation of Great Britain (BI) ... EAF
Employment and Enterprise Group (AIE) ... EEG
Employment and Immigration Canada, Edmonton, AB, Canada [*Library symbol*] [*Library of Congress*] (LCLS) ... CaAEEI
Employment and Immigration Canada [*Emploi et Immigration Canada*] **Edmonton,Alberta** [*Library symbol National Library of Canada*] (NLC) ... AEEI
Employment and Immigration Canada Library [*UTLAS symbol*] ... EIC
Employment and Immigration Canada [*Emploi et Immigration Canada*] **Ottawa, Ontario** [*Library symbol National Library of Canada*] (NLC) ... OOMI
Employment and Immigration Canada [*Emploi et Immigration Canada*] **Toronto, Ontario** [*Library symbol National Library of Canada*] (NLC) ... OTMIO
Employment and Immigration Canada [*Emploi et Immigration Canada*] **Vancouver, British Columbia** [*Library symbol National Library of Canada*] (NLC) ... BVAMI
Employment and Suitability Test [*Aerospace*] (AAG) ... E & ST
Employment and Training ... E & T
Employment and Training Administration [*Formerly, Manpower Administration*] [*Department of Labor*] ... ETA
Employment and Training Administration Management System [*Department of Labor*] ... ETAMS
Employment and Training Administration Regional Office [*Department of Labor*] ... ETARO
Employment and Training Automated Information and Retrieval System [*Department of Labor*] [*Database*] ... ETAIRS
Employment and Training Institute [*University of Wisconsin-Milwaukee*] ... ETI
Employment and Training Service Center (EA) ... ETSC
Employment and Training Unit [*Work Incentive Program*] ... ETU
Employment Appeal Tribunal [*British*] ... EAT
Employment at Will ... EAW
Employment at Will Reporter [*A publication*] (DLA) ... EAWR
Employment Barrier Identification Scale [*Employment test*] ... EBIS
Employment Code [*IRS*] ... EC
Employment Conditions Abroad [*British*] [*An association*] (DBA) ... ECA
Employment Cost Index (OICC) ... ECI
Employment Counseling (OICC) ... EC
Employment Department Clerks' Association [*A union*] [*British*] ... EDCA
Employment Development Plan [*Job Training and Partnership Act*] (OICC) ... EDP
Employment Guide (CAAL) ... EG
Employment Incentive Scheme ... EIS
Employment Management Association (EA) ... EMA
Employment Market Research Unit (AIE) ... EMRU
Employment Medical Advisory Service [*Department of Employment*] [*British*] ... EMAS
Employment of Naval Forces [*Course*] (DNAB) ... ENF
Employment of Personnel in Computing (PDAA) ... EPIC
Employment of Very Low Yield Nuclear Weapons ... EVELYN
Employment Office Manager (ADA) ... EOM
Employment Officer ... EO
Employment Opportunities Pilot Program [*Department of Labor*] ... EOPP
Employment Policy and Organization Committee [*British*] (DCTA) ... EPOC
Employment Policy Grievance Review Staff [*OSA*] ... EPGRS
Employment Practices Decisions [*Commerce Clearing House*] [*A publication*] (DLA) ... Empl Prac Dec
Employment Practices Guide [*Commerce Clearing House*] [*A publication*] (DLA) ... Empl Prac Guide
Employment Prospects by Industry and Occupation [*A publication*] (ADA) ... EPIO
Employment Protection [*Act*] [*British*] ... EP
Employment Protection Act [*1975*] [*British*] (DCTA) ... EPA
Employment Protection Consolidation Act [*1978*] [*British*] (DLA) ... EPCA
Employment Rehabilitation Divisional Manager (AIE) ... ERDM
Employment Relations Board [*Usually preceded by abbreviation of state name*] ... ERB
Employment Relations Resource Centre [*British*] (AIE) ... ERRC
Employment Resources Group [*British*] ... ERG
Employment Safety and Health Guide [*A publication*] (DLA) ... Empl Saf'y & Health Guide
Employment Schedule [*Navy*] (ANA) ... EMPSKD
Employment Schedule (NVT) ... EMPSKED
Employment Schedule ... EMSKED
Employment Security Administration Account ... ESAA
Employment Security Administrative Financing Act of 1954 ... ESAFA
Employment Security Automation Project [*Department of Labor*] ... ESAP
Employment Security Manual (OICC) ... ESM
Employment Security System [*Department of Labor*] ... ESS
Employment Security Systems Institute ... ESSI
Employment Service [*US*] (KSC) ... ES
Employment Service Agency [*Department of Employment*] [*British*] ... ESA
Employment Service Automated [*or Automatic*] **Reporting System** [*Department of Labor*] ... ESARS
Employment Service Improvement Program [*Department of Labor*] ... ESIP
Employment Service Online Placement System [*Computer science*] ... ESOPS
Employment Service Potential [*Department of Labor*] ... ESP
Employment Service Representative ... ESR
Employment Service Review [*A publication*] ... EMSR
Employment Services Regulatory Authority [*Australia*] ... ESRA
Employment Standards Administration [*Department of Labor*] ... ESA
Employment Status Recode [*Bureau of the Census*] (GFGA) ... ESR
Employment Studies Centre [*University of Newcastle, Australia*] ... ESC
Employment Support Center (EA) ... ESC
Employment Taxes, Social Security Act Rulings [*Internal Revenue Service*] [*A publication*] (DLA) ... Em T
Employment Training [*British*] ... ET
Employment Transfer Scheme [*British*] ... ETS
Employment-Corrected Double Factorial Terms of Trade [*Economics*] ... ECDFTT
Emporia, KS [*Location identifier FAA*] (FAAL) ... EMP
Emporia, KS [*FM radio station call letters*] ... KFFX
Emporia, KS [*FM radio station call letters*] ... KGZF
Emporia, KS [*FM radio station call letters*] ... KNGM
Emporia, KS [*AM radio station call letters*] ... KVOE
Emporia, KS [*FM radio station call letters*] ... KVOE-FM
Emporia Public Library, Emporia, KS [*Library symbol Library of Congress*] (LCLS) ... KEm
Emporia State University (GAGS) ... Emporia St U
Emporia State University, Emporia, KS [*Library symbol Library of Congress*] (LCLS) ... KEmU
Emporia State University, Emporia, KS [*OCLC symbol*] (OCLC) ... KKR
Emporia State University, School of Library Science, Emporia, KS [*OCLC symbol*] (OCLC) ... KEE
Emporia, VA [*Location identifier FAA*] (FAAL) ... EMV
Emporia, VA [*AM radio station call letters*] ... WEVA
Emporia, VA [*FM radio station call letters*] ... WEVA-FM
Emporium ... EMPOR
Emporium, PA [*AM radio station call letters*] ... WLEM
Emporium, PA [*FM radio station call letters*] ... WQKY
Empower Self through Education and Eating Management ... ESTEEM
Empowering Individuals with Disabilities Through Education, Information, and Opportunity [*Farmer outreach program*] [*Montana State University*] ... EIEIO
Empowerment Project (EA) ... EP
Empowerment Zones/Enterprise Communities [*Medicine*] ... EZ/EC
Empresa Aero Uruguay SA [*ICAO designator*] (FAAC) ... AUO
Empresa Aerocaribbean SA [*Cuba*] [*ICAO designator*] (FAAC) ... CRN
Empresa Aeromar [*Dominican Republic*] [*ICAO designator*] (FAAC) ... ROM
Empresa Aero-Servicios Parrague Ltd. [*Chile*] [*ICAO designator*] (FAAC) ... PRG
Empresa Aerotuy [*Venezuela*] [*ICAO designator*] (FAAC) ... TUY
Empresa AVIAIMPORT [*Cuba ICAO designator*] (ICDA) ... IP
Empresa Brasileira de Aeronautica SA [*Brazil*] [*ICAO designator*] (FAAC) ... EMB

Empresa Brasileira de Correios e Telegrafos [*State enterprise*] [*Brazil*] (EY) ... EBCT
Empresa Brasileira de Telecomunicacoes [*Brazilian Telecommunications Enterprises*] ... EMBRATEL
Empresa Commercial Latinoamericana de Telecommunicaciones [*Latin America Commercial Telecommunications Enterprise*] (PDAA) ... ECLATEL
Empresa Cubana de Aviacion [*Cuba*] [*ICAO designator*] (FAAC) ... CUB
Empresa de Aviacion Aerogaviota, SA [*Cuba*] [*FAA designator*] (FAAC) ... GTV
Empresa de Servicios Aeronauticos [*Cuba ICAO designator*] (ICDA) ... XR
Empresa de Servicios Maritima y Aerea SA [*Peru*] [*FAA designator*] (FAAC) ... ASP
Empresa de Suministros Industriales [*Import-export board*] [*Cuba*] (EY) ... Esi
Empresa de Transporte Aereo del Peru [*ICAO designator*] (FAAC) ... PLI
Empresa Ecuatoriana de Aviacion [*Ecuador*] [*ICAO designator*] (FAAC) ... EEA
Empresa Ecuatoriana de Aviacion [*Ecuador*] [*ICAO designator*] (ICDA) ... EU
Empresa Guatemalteca de Aviacion [*Airline*] [*Guatemala*] ... AVIATECA
Empresa Guatemalteca de Aviacion [*Guatemala*] [*ICAO designator*] (FAAC) ... GUG
Empresa Importadora y Exportadora de Suministros Tecnicos [*Import-export board*] [*Cuba*] (EY) ... Emiat
Empresa Nacional de Autocamiones SA [*National Truck Manufacturing Company*] [*Spain*] ... ENASA
Empresa Nacional de Electricidad SA ADS [*NYSE symbol*] (SPSG) ... ELE
Empresa Nacional de Electridad de Chile [*Associated Press*] (SAG) ... EEIChil
Empresa Nacional de Electridad de Chile [*NYSE symbol*] (SAG) ... EOC
Empresa Nacional de Servicios Aereos [*Cuba*] [*FAA designator*] (FAAC) ... CNI
Empresa Nacionale de Espana SA [*NYSE symbol*] (SAG) ... ELE
Empresa Nacionale de Espana SA [*Associated Press*] (SAG) ... Endesa
Empresa Nac'l De Electric ADS [*NYSE symbol*] (TTSB) ... EOC
Empresa Nac'l Elec ADS [*NYSE symbol*] (TTSB) ... ELE
Empresa Naviera Boliviana [*Shipping company*] [*Bolivia*] (EY) ... ENABOL
Empresa Servicicious Avensa SA [*Venezuela*] [*ICAO designator*] (FAAC) ... SERVIVENSA
Empresa Servicicious Avensa SA [*Venezuela*] [*ICAO designator*] (FAAC) ... SVV
Empresario de Transporte Combinado [*Combined Transport Operator*] [*Business term Spanish*] ... ETC
Empresas Ica Sociedad Controladora [*Associated Press*] (SAG) ... Emplca
Empresas ICA Socledad ADS [*NYSE symbol*] (SPSG) ... ICA
Empresas La Moderna SA [*Associated Press*] (SAG) ... ELaMod
Empresas La Moderna SA [*NYSE symbol*] (SAG) ... ELM
Empresas La Moderna SAADS [*NYSE symbol*] (TTSB) ... ELM
Empresas Telex-Chile ADS [*NYSE symbol*] (TTSB) ... TL
Empress Chinchilla Breeders Cooperative (EA) ... ECBC
Empress Municipal Library, Alberta [*Library symbol National Library of Canada*] (NLC) ... AEM
Empress Municipal Library, Empress, AB, Canada [*Library symbol Library of Congress*] (LCLS) ... CaAEM
Empty ... E
Empty ... EMT
Empty [*Slang*] ... MT
Empty ... MTY
Empty Bed Contact Time [*Environmental Protection Agency*] ... EBCT
Empty Body Weight (OA) ... EBW
Empty Coaching Stock [*Railway term*] (DCTA) ... ECS
Empty, Measure, and Record [*Nursing*] (DAVI) ... EMR
Empty Net Goals [*Hockey*] ... ENG
Empty Sella Syndrome [*Medicine*] ... ESS
Empty Signal Unit [*Telecommunications*] (TEL) ... ESU
Empty Weight ... EW
EMS Systems Ltd. [*Vancouver Stock Exchange symbol*] ... EMS
EMU [*Extra-Vehicular Mobility Unit*] **Electrical Harness** ... EEH
Emulated Buffer Computer (MCD) ... EBC
Emulated-Disk (CDE) ... e-disk
Emulation Design Language [*Computer science*] (MHDB) ... EDL
Emulation Program [*IBM Corp.*] (BUR) ... EP
Emulation Sensing Processor [*Quality Micro Systems*] ... ESP
Emulator (IAA) ... EML
Emulator (MSA) ... EMU
Emulator Application Program (MHDB) ... EAP
Emulator Control (IAA) ... EC
Emulator Control Program (IAA) ... ECP
Emulator High-Level Language Application Programming Interface [*Computer science*] (PCM) ... EHLLAPI
Emulator Interface Program (IAA) ... EIP
Emulator Machine Language [*Computer science*] (MHDB) ... EML
Emulator Monitor System (IAA) ... EMS
Emulator Program (IAA) ... EU
Emulator/Simulator (MCD) ... EM/SIM
Emulator Trap (MHDB) ... EMT
Emulex Corp. [*NASDAQ symbol*] (NQ) ... EMLX
Emulex Corp. [*Associated Press*] (SAG) ... Emulex
Emulex SCSI [*Small Computer System Interface*] **Processor** (CDE) ... ESP
Emulsible Concentrate ... EC
Emulsified Liquid Propellant ... ELP
Emulsifying Activity Index [*Food analysis*] ... EAI
Emulsifying Capacity [*Food technology*] ... EC
Emulsifying Salts [*Food technology*] ... ES
Emulsion (VRA) ... eml
Emulsion (MSA) ... EMUL
Emulsion Butadiene Rubber ... EBR
Emulsion In [*Photography*] (WDMC) ... EI
Emulsion Liquid Membrane [*Chemical separation technology*] ... ELM
Emulsion Out [*Photography*] (WDMC) ... EO
Emulsion Polymers Institute (EA) ... EPI
Emulsion Stability Index [*Food analysis*] ... ESI
Emulsum [*Emulsion*] [*Medicine*] (ROG) ... EMULS
Emunah Women of America (EA) ... EWA
En [*Typography*] (WDAA) ... N
En [*Printing measurement*] (WDMC) ... n
En Cuenta [*On Account*] [*Spanish Business term*] ... EC
En Foco [*An association*] (EA) ... EF
En Nahud [*Sudan*] [*Airport symbol*] (AD) ... NUD
En Passant [*In Passing*] [*Chess*] ... EP
En Pointe Tech [*NASDAQ symbol*] (TTSB) ... ENPT
En Route ... E/R
En Route (NVT) ... ENR
En Route ... ENRT
En Route Advisory Service [*Aeromedical evacuation*] ... ERAS
En Route Air Traffic Control [*A publication*] ... ENAT
En Route Analysis and Reporting System [*FAA*] (TAG) ... EARS
En Route and Provide Service to Units Indicated [*Military*] (NVT) ... ENRSVC
En Route, Arrival at ____ [*Military*] (NVT) ... ENRAT
En Route Automated Radar Tracking System [*FAA*] (TAG) ... EARTS
En Route Automated RADAR Tracking System [*Aviation*] (FAAC) ... EARTS
En Route Chart [*Aviation*] ... ERC
En Route Computer Identification (KSC) ... ECID
En Route Flight Advisory Services [*FAA*] ... EFAS
En Route Guidance System (IEEE) ... ERGS
En Route High Altitude ... EHA
En Route Low Altitude ... ELA
En Route Metering [*FAA*] (TAG) ... ERM
En Route Minimum Safe Altitude Warning [*FAA*] (TAG) ... EMSAW
En Route Penetration [*Aviation*] (FAAC) ... EP
En Route Spacing Program [*FAA*] (TAG) ... ESP
En Route Stand-Alone Radar Training System [*FAA*] (TAG) ... ESARTS
En Route Supplement ... E-S
En Route Support Team [*Military*] (AFIT) ... EST
En Route Surveillance RADAR ... RSR
En Route This Station from Oversea Command ... ENRFOSCOMD
En Route to/from Public Affairs Event [*Military*] (NVT) ... ENRPAE
En Route Weather Forecast [*Navy*] (NVT) ... WEAX
En Suite (ADA) ... E/S
Enable (NASA) ... ENA
Enable (MSA) ... ENBL
Enable Application Developer [*Computer science*] (PCM) ... EAD
Enable Control System ... ECS
Enable Interrupt (MHDB) ... EI
Enable Level Group (MHDB) ... ENLG
Enable Output [*Davey Air Services*] [*Computer science*] (MHDB) ... EO
Enable This Level Group [*Computer science*] (MHDI) ... ETLG
Enable Transmit [*Status activation code*] (NITA) ... EN TX
Enabled Artists United [*An association*] (EA) ... EAU
Enabling Objective [*Military training*] ... EA
Enacie Demokratiki Aristera [*United Democratic Left Party*] [*Greek*] (BARN) ... EDA
Enamel (AAG) ... E
Enamel (KSC) ... ENAM
Enamel (ROG) ... ENL
Enamel (VRA) ... enl
Enamel ... ENL
Enamel Bonded Double Cotton [*Wire insulation*] ... EBDC
Enamel Bonded Double Paper [*Wire insulation*] ... EBDP
Enamel Bonded Double Silk [*Wire insulation*] ... EBDS
Enamel Bonded Single Cotton [*Wire insulation*] (AAG) ... EBC
Enamel Bonded Single Silk [*Wire insulation*] (AAG) ... EBS
Enamel Covered ... EC
Enamel Double Cotton [*Wire insulation*] (AAG) ... EDC
Enamel Double Cotton Varnish [*Wire insulation*] ... EDCV
Enamel Double Silk [*Wire insulation*] (AAG) ... EDS
Enamel Double Silk Varnish [*Wire insulation*] ... EDSV
Enamel Guild: West (EA) ... EGW
Enamel Insulated Wire ... EIW
Enamel Insulating Compound ... EIC
Enamel Single Cotton [*Wire insulation*] (AAG) ... EC
Enamel Single, Cotton Covered [*Wire insulation*] (IAA) ... ESCC
Enamel Single Cotton Varnish [*Wire insulation*] (AAG) ... ECV
Enamel Single Glass [*Wire insulation*] (IAA) ... EG
Enamel Single Silk [*Wire insulation*] (AAG) ... ES
Enamel Single Silk Varnish [*Wire insulation*] (AAG) ... ESV
Enamel Single-Covered [*Wire insulation*] (DEN) ... ESC
Enamel-Bonded Single Paper [*Wire insulation*] (IAA) ... EBP
Enamel-Covered (IDOE) ... ec
Enameled (ROG) ... ENAMD
Enameled ... ENMLD
Enameled Copper [*Wire insulation*] (IAA) ... EC
Enameling ... ENMLNG
Enamelist Society (EA) ... ES
Enamelled Blotter (DGA) ... ENAM BLR
Enamelled Board (DGA) ... ENAM BD
Enantiomeric Excess [*Organic chemistry*] ... EE
Enarotali [*Indonesia*] [*Airport symbol*] (OAG) ... EWI
Enarotali [*Indonesia*] [*ICAO location identifier*] (ICLI) ... WABT
Encad, Inc. [*Associated Press*] (SAG) ... Encad
Encad, Inc. [*NASDAQ symbol*] (SAG) ... ENCD
Encampment for Citizenship [*An association*] (EA) ... EFC
Encapsulated Harpoon Command and Launch System (MCD) ... EHCLS
Encapsulated Light Diffusion (IAA) ... ELD
Encapsulated Post-Script [*Computer science*] ... EPS
Encapsulated Post-Script Draw Format [*Computer science*] ... EPSF
Encapsulated PostScript File [*Computer science*] (EERA) ... EPS

Encapsulated Toroidal Inductor ... ETI
Encapsulated Torpedo [*Antisubmarine*] [*Navy*] ... CAPTOR
Encapsulated Variable Inductor ... EVI
Encapsulating Security Payload [*Computer science*] ... ESP
Encapsulation (MSA) ... ENCAP
Encarnacion [*Paraguay*] [*ICAO location identifier*] (ICLI) ... SGEN
Encased (MSA) ... ENCSD
Encased Elastic Cylinder ... EEC
Encaustic (VRA) ... enc
Encephalitogenic Factor (MAE) ... EF
Encephalization Quotient ... EQ
Encephalomyocarditis [*Virus*] ... EMC
Encephalomyocarditis Virus ... EMCV
Encercorp Inc. [*NASDAQ symbol*] (TTSB) ... ENCP
Enchant Public Library, Alberta [*Library symbol National Library of Canada*] (NLC) ... AEN
Enchiridion Locorum Sanctorum [*A publication*] (BJA) ... ELS
Enciclopedia Cattolica [*Vatican City*] [*A publication*] (BJA) ... EC
Enciclopedia Judaica Castellana [*A publication*] (BJA) ... EJC
Enciclopedia Universal Illustrada, Espasa [*A publication*] ... EUI
Enciphered Facsimile Communications ... CIFAX
Enciphered Television (MCD) ... CIVISION
Encircled Energy Function (PDAA) ... EEF
Encircling Endocardial Ventriculotomy [*Cardiology*] ... EEV
Enclose [*Technical drawings*] ... ENC
Enclose (KSC) ... ENCL
Enclosed (WDMC) ... enc
Enclosed (WDMC) ... encl
Enclosed (ROG) ... ENCLD
Enclosed (ROG) ... ENCLOD
Enclosed and Ventilated (IAA) ... EV
Enclosed Cryocondenser for Air Recovery ... ENCAR
Enclosed Operating Station [*Military*] (CAAL) ... EOS
Enclosed Track Conveyor ... ETC
Enclosed-Frame Low Voltage (IEEE) ... ELV
Enclosing (ROG) ... ENCLOSG
Enclosure ... ENC
Enclosure (WDMC) ... enc
Enclosure (WDMC) ... encl
Enclosure (ROG) ... ENCL
Enclosure ... ENCLO
Enclosure Building Filtration System (IEEE) ... EBFS
Encode (NASA) ... ENC
Encode (MSA) ... ENCD
Encode ... ENCD
Encoded Item Identifier (CAAL) ... EII
Encoder (MSA) ... ENCDR
Encoder Address Translator ... EAT
Encoder Buffer (IAA) ... EB
Encoder Coupler (NASA) ... E/C
Encoder/Decoder Assembly (MCD) ... EDA
Encoder Power Supply ... EPS
Encoder Programming Language [*Computer science*] ... EPL
Encoder-Receiver-Transmitter [*Telecommunications*] ... ERT
Encon Systems [*Commercial firm Associated Press*] (SAG) ... Encon
Encon Systems [*NASDAQ symbol*] (SAG) ... NCON
Encor Energy Corp. Inc. [*Toronto Stock Exchange symbol Vancouver Stock Exchange symbol*] ... ECI
Encore Australia [*A publication*] ... Encore Aust
Encore Computer [*NASDAQ symbol*] (TTSB) ... ENCC
Encore Computer Corp. [*NASDAQ symbol*] (SAG) ... ENCC
Encore Computer Corp. [*Associated Press*] (SAG) ... Encore
Encore Marketing International [*AMEX symbol*] (SAG) ... EMI
Encore Marketing International [*Associated Press*] (SAG) ... Encore
Encore Marketing International [*Associated Press*] (SAG) ... Encr
Encore Marketing Intl. [*ECM Symbol*] (TTSB) ... EMLEC
Encore Mkt Intl Cv Partic Pfd [*ECM Symbol*] (TTSB) ... EMIPr
Encore Wire Corp. [*Associated Press*] (SAG) ... EncoreW
Encore Wire Corp. [*NASDAQ symbol*] (SAG) ... WIRE
Encounter [*Time*] ... E
Encounter (FAAC) ... ENCTR
Encounter Energy Resources Ltd. [*Toronto Stock Exchange symbol*] ... EER
Encounter in Health Education ... ENHE
Encourage (DAVI) ... enc
Encourage Coughing and Deep Breathing [*Medicine*] ... EC & DB
Encrypt for Transmission Only [*Military*] ... EFTO
Encrypted (MCD) ... ENCR
Encrypted for Transmission Overseas (MCD) ... EFTO
Encrypted Traffic Report (CET) ... ETR
Encryptic Secure Tracking RADAR Identification Friend or Foe (NATG) ... ESTRIFF
Encyclopaedia Biblica [*A publication*] ... EB
Encyclopaedia Biblica [*A publication*] (BJA) ... EBI
Encyclopaedia Biblica [*A publication*] (ROG) ... EBL
Encyclopaedia Biblica [*Jerusalem*] [*A publication*] (BJA) ... EncBibl
Encyclopaedia Britannica [*A publication*] (ROG) ... E BR
Encyclopaedia Britannica Educational Corp. ... EBEC
Encyclopaedia Britannica Film (IIA) ... EBF
Encyclopaedia Britannica, Inc. ... EB
Encyclopaedia Britannica, Inc., Chicago, IL [*Library symbol*] [*Library of Congress*] (LCLS) ... ICEnB
Encyclopaedia Hebraica [*Jerusalem*] [*A publication*] (BJA) ... EH
Encyclopaedia Judaica [*A publication*] ... EJ
Encyclopaedia Judaica [*Jerusalem*] [*A publication*] (BJA) ... EncJud
Encyclopaedia Judaica [*Jerusalem*] [*A publication*] (BJA) ... EnJu
Encyclopaedia Judaica: Das Judentum in Geschichte und Gegenwart [*Berlin*] [*A publication*] (BJA) ... EJud
Encyclopaedia Sefardica Neerlandica [*A publication*] (BJA) ... ESN
Encyclopedia ... ENC
Encyclopedia ... ENCY
Encyclopedia ... ENCY
Encyclopedia ... ENCYC
Encyclopedia ... encycl
Encyclopedia Britannica [*A publication*] ... Encyc Brit
Encyclopedia Canadiana [*A publication*] ... EC
Encyclopedia Dictionary, Edited by Robert Hunter [*1879-88*] [*A publication*] (DLA) ... Enc Dict
Encyclopedia of Afterlife Beliefs and Phenomena [*A publication*] ... EABP
Encyclopedia of American Associations [*Later, EA*] [*A publication*] ... EAA
Encyclopedia of American Industries [*A publication*] ... EAI
Encyclopedia of American Religions [*A publication*] ... EAR
Encyclopedia of Associations [*Information service or system A publication*] ... EA
Encyclopedia of Associations: Association Periodicals [*A publication*] ... EA-AP
Encyclopedia of Associations: International Organizations [*A publication*] ... EA-IO
Encyclopedia of Associations: Regional, State, and Local Organizations [*A publication*] ... EA-RSL
Encyclopedia of Associations: Updating Service [*A publication*] ... EA-UPDS
Encyclopedia of Business [*A publication*] ... EOB
Encyclopedia of Business Information Sources [*A publication*] ... EBIS
Encyclopedia of Chemical Technology [*A publication*] ... ECT
Encyclopedia of College Basketball [*A publication*] ... ECB
Encyclopedia of Consumer Brands [*A publication*] ... ECB
Encyclopedia of Endangered Species [*A publication*] ... EES
Encyclopedia of Environmental Information Sources [*A publication*] ... EEIS
Encyclopedia of European Community Law [*A publication*] (DLA) ... EECL
Encyclopedia of Evidence [*A publication*] (DLA) ... Ency of Ev
Encyclopedia of Forms [*A publication*] (DLA) ... Enc Forms
Encyclopedia of Forms and Precedents [*A publication*] (DLA) ... Ency of Forms
Encyclopedia of Geographic Information Sources [*A publication*] ... EGIS
Encyclopedia of Georgia Law [*A publication*] (DLA) ... EGL
Encyclopedia of Governmental Advisory Organizations [*A publication*] ... EGAO
Encyclopedia of Health Information Sources [*A publication*] ... EHIS
Encyclopedia of Hoaxes [*A publication*] ... EOH
Encyclopedia of Holistic Medicine [*A publication*] ... EHM
Encyclopedia of Information Systems and Services [*Later, IID*] [*A publication*] ... EISS
Encyclopedia of Law and Practice [*A publication*] (DLA) ... Ency of L & Pr
Encyclopedia of Legal Information Sources [*A publication*] ... ELIS
Encyclopedia of Medical Organizations and Agencies [*A publication*] ... EMOA
Encyclopedia of Occultism and Parapsychology [*A publication*] ... EOP
Encyclopedia of Pennsylvania Law [*A publication*] (DLA) ... PLE
Encyclopedia of Physical Sciences and Engineering Information Sources [*A publication*] ... EPSEIS
Encyclopedia of Pleading and Practice [*A publication*] (DLA) ... Enc Pl & Pr
Encyclopedia of Pleading and Practice [*A publication*] (DLA) ... Ency of Pl & Pr
Encyclopedia of Pleading and Practice [*A publication*] (DLA) ... Ency P & P
Encyclopedia of Pleading and Practice. Supplement [*A publication*] (DLA) ... Ency US Sup Ct Rep
Encyclopedia of Polymer Science and Technology [*A publication*] ... EPST
Encyclopedia of Protest Movements [*A publication*] ... EPM
Encyclopedia of Public Affairs Information Sources [*A publication*] ... EPAIS
Encyclopedia of Senior Citizens Information Sources [*A publication*] ... ESCIS
Encyclopedia of the Laws of England [*2 eds.*] [*1897-1919*] [*A publication*] (DLA) ... Encyc
Encyclopedia of the Social Sciences [*A publication*] ... ESS
Encyclopedia of United States Reports [*A publication*] (DLA) ... USE
Encyclopedia of United States Supreme Court Reports [*A publication*] (DLA) ... Enc US Sup Ct Rep
Encyclopedia of United States Supreme Court Reports [*A publication*] (DLA) ... Ency US Sup Ct
Encyclopedia of US Foreign Relations [*A publication*] ... EUSFR
Encyclopedia of Women's Associations Worldwide [*A publication*] ... EWAW
Encyclopedia of World Biography [*A publication*] ... EWB
Encyclopedic Dictionary of Mathematics [*A publication*] ... EDM
Encyclopedic Dictionary of Religion ... EDR
Encyclopedie des Citations [*A publication*] ... EDC
End [*Football*] ... E
End Address [*of Main Memorix Section*] [*Computer science*] (IAA) ... ENDADR
End Article (DNAB) ... EA
End Article Identity Record ... EAIR
End Article Item Manager (AFIT) ... EAIM
End Breguet Cruise [*SST*] ... EBC
End Cell Switch (IAA) ... ECS
End Center Matched [*of lumber*] (BARN) ... EMC
End Child Prostitution in Asian Tourism [*An association*] ... ECPAT
End Date of an Exercise (MCD) ... ENDEX
End Delimiter (TNIG) ... ED
End Delivery Date (AAG) ... EDD
End Door ... ED
End Effector (MCD) ... EE
End Effector ... END EFF
End Effector Electronics Unit (MCD) ... EEEU
End, Evening Astronomical Twilight (MCD) ... EEAT
End, Evening Civil Twilight [*Navigation*] ... EECT
End, Evening Nautical Twilight [*Navigation*] ... EENT
End Exercise Point (FAAC) ... EEP
End Expiratory Pressure (AAMN) ... EEP
End Forming Press ... EFP
End Game Analysis ... EGA

End Game Analysis Program (MCD)	EGAP
End Half	EHF
End Hunger Network (EA)	EHN
End Injection (IEEE)	EI
End Interruption Sequence [Computer science]	EIS
End Item	EI
End Item Allocation Document (AAG)	EIAD
End Item Application (MCD)	EIA
End Item Assembly Sequence Number (NASA)	EIASN
End Item Code	EIC
End Item Contract	EIC
End Item Data Package (NASA)	EIDP
End Item Delivery (AAG)	EID
End Item Description (AAG)	EID
End Item Designators	EID
End Item Documentation (MCD)	EID
End Item Equipment	EIE
End Item Failure	EIF
End Item Maintenance Form	EIMF
End Item Maintenance Sheets (MCD)	EIMS
End Item Maintenance Transmittal Sheet	EIMTS
End Item Manager (AFIT)	EIM
End Item Parameter	EIP
End Item Requirement (AAG)	EIR
End Item Specification (AAG)	EIS
End Item Subdivision (MCD)	EIS
End Item Test Plan (MCD)	EITP
End Item/Weapon System [Army]	EI/WS
End Loans to Southern Africa [An association] (EAIO)	ELTSA
End Matched	EM
End Mill	ENML
End Node (ACRL)	EN
End Notch Discrimination (EA)	END
End of Address [Computer science]	EOA
End of Arm Tooling [Robotics]	EAOT
End of Battle [Time] (MCD)	EOB
End of Battle Control Center (MCD)	EOBCC
End of Block [Computer science]	EOB
End of Bombardment	EOB
End of Buffer (MCD)	EOB
End of Burn (MCD)	EOB
End of Bus (ACRL)	EOB
End of Calendar Year	EOCY
End of Card [Computer science] (CMD)	EOC
End of Construction (NG)	EOC
End of Contract (AAG)	EOC
End of Conversation (ECII)	EOC
End of Conversion	EOC
End of Course (AFM)	EOC
End of Cycle (NRCH)	EOC
End of Data [Computer science] (IAA)	ED
End of Data [Computer science] (SAA)	END
End of Data [Computer science]	EOD
End of Data Address [Computer science] (HGAA)	EODAD
End of Data Block [Computer science] (CET)	EDB
End of Data Block [Computer science] (MCD)	EODB
End of Day (AFM)	EOD
End of Dialing [Telecommunications] (TEL)	EOD
End of Equilibrium Cycle [Nuclear energy] (NRCH)	EEC
End of Equilibrium Cycle [Nuclear energy] (NRCH)	EOEC
End of Equilibrium Life [Nuclear energy] (NUCP)	EOEL
End of Extent [Computer science] (IBMDP)	EOE
End of File [Computer science]	EOF
End of Fiscal Year (AFM)	EFY
End of Fiscal Year	EOFY
End of Form [Computer science] (IAA)	EOF
End of Frame Sequence [Telecommunications] (ACRL)	EFS
End of Identity [Computer science] (IAA)	EOI
End of Information (NITA)	EOI
End of Information Marker [Computer science] (IAA)	EIM
End of Input [Computer science]	EOI
End of Inquiry [Computer science]	EOI
End of Job [Computer science]	EOJ
End of Life	EOL
End of Line (CDE)	EOL
End of Line [Computer science]	EOLN
End of Line Block [Computer science] (CET)	EOLB
End of Line Marker [Computer science]	EOLM
End of List [Computer science] (IAA)	EOL
End of Logical Tape [Computer science]	EOLT
End of Magnetic Tape [Computer science] (MDG)	EMT
End of Major Cycle [Military]	EMC
End of Medium [Computer science]	EM
End of Medium [Computer science] (BUR)	EOM
End of Message [Computer science] (IAA)	EM
End of Message [Computer science]	EOM
End of Message Incomplete [Computer science] (IAA)	EOMI
End of Message Sequence [Computer science] (CET)	EOMS
End of Minor Frame (MCD)	EOMF
End of Mission	EOM
End of Month [Business term]	EOM
End Of Month [Billing] (WDMC)	eom
End of Month Payment [Business term]	EMP
End of Number [Computer science] (IAA)	EON
End of Operation [Computer science] (IAA)	EO

End of Overhaul	EOH
End of Paragraph	EOP
End of Part (MCD)	EOP
End of Period	EOP
End of Powered Flight	EOPF
End of Procedure [Computer science]	EOP
End of Program [Computer science]	EOP
End of Program [Computer science]	EP
End of Programmed Flight (MCD)	EPF
End of Push [Spectroscopy]	EOP
End of Quarter (AFM)	EOQ
End of Record [Computer science]	EOR
End of Recorded Information [Computer science]	ERI
End of Reel	EOR
End of Run [Telecommunications] (TEL)	EOR
End of Run (IAA)	ER
End of Screening Date [DoD]	ESD
End of Season [Business term]	EOS
End of Segment [Computer science] (IAA)	EOS
End of Segment Pulse [Military]	ESP
End of Service (MCD)	EOS
End of String [Computer science] (IAA)	EOS
End of Study	ES
End of Tape [Computer science]	EOT
End of Tape [Computer science] (CET)	ET
End of Tape Marker [Computer science] (IAA)	ETM
End of Tape Test [Computer science]	ETT
End of Tape Warning [Computer science] (CET)	ETW
End of Task [Computer science]	EOT
End of Test [Computer science]	EOT
End of Text [Computer science]	EOT
End of Text [Computer science]	ET
End of Text [Computer science]	ETX
End of Text Block [Computer science] (ACRL)	ETB
End of the Initial Operating Period [Department of Housing and Urban Development] (GFGA)	EIOP
End of Tour [Air Force] (AFM)	EOT
End of Track	EOT
End of Track [Electronics] (ECII)	ETR
End of Transmission [Computer science]	EOT
End of Transmission (GAVI)	ETX
End of Transmission Block [Computer science]	ETB
End of User [Computer hacker terminology] (NHD)	EOU
End of Valid Message [Computer science] (IAA)	EOVM
End of Volume [Computer science]	EOV
End of Word [Computer science]	EOW
End of Year	EOY
End of Year Financial Statement	EOYFS
End Office [Telecommunications] (TEL)	EO
End Output [Computer science] (IEEE)	EOP
End Paragraph [Typesetting command] (WDMC)	ep
End Piece of Equipment	EPOE
End Plate Current	EPC
End Plate Potential	EPP
End Point [Distilling]	EP
End Point Prediction	EPP
End Poverty in America Society (EA)	EPIA
End Poverty in California [Slogan used by Upton Sinclair during campaign as Democratic candidate for governor of California, 1934]	EPIC
End Products Committee [of WPB] [World War II]	EPC
End Refueling and Start Climb Point (SAA)	ERSCP
End Reporting Period	ERP
End Request (IAA)	ERQ
End Response (IAA)	ERP
End Results Evaluation Program [Later, SEER] [National Cancer Institute]	EREP
End Routing Domain [Computer science] (TNIG)	ERD
End Sheet [Publishing]	ES
End Stage Heart Disease [Medicine] (CPH)	ESHD
End Stage Renal Disease [Medicine]	ESRD
End Stage Renal Failure [Medicine]	ESRF
End Strength	ES
End Sweep Support Carrier [Navy] (DNAB)	ESSC
End System [Computer science] (TNIG)	ES
End System Hello [Computer science] (TNIG)	ESH
End System Identifier [Telecommunications] (ACRL)	ESI
End System-Intermediate System [Computer science] (TNIG)	ES-IS
End Systolic Pressure [Cardiology]	ESP
End to End [Telecommunications]	E to E
End to End [Technical drawings] (NASA)	E-E
End to End (NASA)	ETE
End to End Protocol (IAA)	EEP
End to Side [Portacaval shunt] [Medicine] (AAMN)	ES
End Translation Time Indicator (IAA)	ETTI
End Use Check	EUC
End User Computing [AT & T]	EUC
End User Facility	EUF
End Viewing Tube	EVT
End Violence Against the Next Generation (EA)	EVAN-G
End Wall [Of a cell] [Botany]	EW
End Warning Area [Computer science] (BUR)	EWA
ENDA [Envoroment and Development] Caribe [An association] (EAIO)	ENDA
Endangered and Vulnerable (EERA)	E&V
Endangered Animal [Medicine] (DMAA)	E
Endangered Species Act [1973]	ESA

Endangered Species Act Reauthorization Coordinating Committee (EA) ... ESARCC
Endangered Species Advisory Committee [*Commonwealth*] (EERA) ... ESAC
Endangered Species Committee [*Environmental Protection Agency*] (EPA) ... ESC
Endangered Species Conservation Act of 1969 ... ESCA
Endangered Species Program [*Australia*] ... ESP
Endangered Species Protection Act 1992 [*Commonwealth*] (EERA) ... ESP Act
Endangered Species Scientific Authority [*US Fish and Wildlife Service*] [*Terminated 1979, functions transferred to Department of the Interior*] ... ESSA
Endangered Species Scientific Subcommittee [*Commonwealth*] (EERA) ... ESSS
Endangered Species Unit [*Commonwealth*] (EERA) ... ESU
Endangerment Assessment (GNE) ... EA
Endangerment Information Report [*Environmental Protection Agency*] (ERG) ... EIR
End-Around Carry ... EAC
End-Around Shift ... EAS
End-Around Test ... EAT
End-Article Application Code [*Military*] ... EAA
Endatcom Ventures [*Vancouver Stock Exchange symbol*] ... EVC
End-Detonating Cartridge [*Explosive*] ... EDC
End-Diastole [*Cardiology*] ... ED
End-Diastolic Area [*Cardiology*] ... EDA
End-Diastolic Chamber Stiffness [*Medicine*] (DMAA) ... EDCS
End-Diastolic Circumferential Stress [*Medicine*] (DMAA) ... EDCS
End-Diastolic Count [*Cardiology*] ... EDC
End-Diastolic Diameter [*Cardiology*] ... EDD
End-Diastolic Dimension [*Cardiology*] ... EdD
End-Diastolic Length [*Cardiology*] ... EDL
End-Diastolic Pressure [*Cardiology*] ... EDP
End-Diastolic Segment Length [*Cardiology*] ... EDSL
End-Diastolic Volume [*Cardiology*] ... EDV
End-Diastolic Volume Index [*Cardiology*] (DAVI) ... EDVI
End-Diastolic Wall Thickness [*Cardiology*] ... EDWTH
Ende [*Indonesia*] [*Airport symbol*] (OAG) ... ENE
Ende/Ipi [*Indonesia*] [*ICAO location identifier*] (ICLI) ... WRKE
Endeavor ... ENDVR
Endeavour Forum [*Australia*] ... EF
Endeavour Foundation [*Australia*] ... EF
Endemic Bird Area ... EBA
Endemic Burkitt's Lymphoma [*Medicine*] ... EBL
Endemic Nephropathy (PDAA) ... EN
Enderby and District Museum, Enderby, BC, Canada [*Library symbol*] [*Library of Congress*] (LCLS) ... CaBEM
Enderby and District Museum, Enderby, British Columbia [*Library symbol National Library of Canada*] (NLC) ... BEM
Enderby, BC [*ICAO location identifier*] (ICLI) ... CYNY
End-Expiratory Esophageal Pressure [*Medicine*] (MAE) ... EEEP
Endicott Junior College [*Beverly, MA*] ... EJC
Endicott, NY [*AM radio station call letters*] ... WENE
Endicott, NY [*FM radio station call letters*] ... WMRV
Ending (FAAC) ... ENDG
Ending Delimiter [*Telecommunications*] (ACRL) ... ED
Ending Event - Beginning Event (SAA) ... EE-BE
Ending Flag Value for Data Input [*Computer science*] ... EF
Ending Period (AABC) ... EP
Ending Sequence Done ... ESD
Ending Tape Label [*Computer science*] (BUR) ... ETL
Endings [*of nerves*] **to Lip Muscle** ... ELM
End-Inspiratory Pause [*Respiration*] ... EIP
Endless Tangent Screw ... ETS
Endless Vacation [*A publication*] ... Endl Vac
Endlich on Building Associations [*A publication*] (DLA) ... End Bdg Ass
Endlich on Building Associations [*A publication*] (DLA) ... Endl Bldg Ass'ns
Endlich's Commentaries on the Interpretation of Statutes [*A publication*] (DLA) ... End Interp St
Endlich's Commentaries on the Interpretation of Statutes [*A publication*] (ILCA) ... End Interp Stat
Endo Laboratories, Inc. [*Research code symbol*] ... EN
Endo Laboratories, Inc., Garden City, NY [*Library symbol Library of Congress*] (LCLS) ... NGcE
Endo-Atmospheric Decoy ... EAD
Endoatmospheric/Exoatmospheric Interceptor [*Army*] (DOMA) ... E^2I
Endoatmospheric Non-Nuclear Defense Application Review ... ENDAR
Endoatmospheric Non-Nuclear Definition and Requirements Study [*Military*] ... ENDER
Endo-Atmospheric Non-Nuclear Kill (MCD) ... ENNK
Endoatmospheric Non-Nuclear Kill Applications Study [*DoD*] ... ENNKAS
Endoatmospheric Non-Nuclear Kill Controls Implementation Study [*DoD*] ... ENNKCIS
Endo-Atmospheric Penetration Aids Concept ... ENDO-PAC
Endoatmospheric Summer Study ... ESS
Endocardial Cushion Defect ... ECD
Endocardial Fibroelastosis [*Medicine*] ... EFE
Endocardial Resection Procedure [*Cardiology*] ... ERP
Endocervical Cone [*or Conization*] [*Gynecology*] (DAVI) ... ECC
Endocervical Curettage [*or Curretings*] [*Gynecology*] (DAVI) ... ECC
Endocervical Ecchymosis [*Gynecology*] (DAVI) ... ECE
Endocrine [*or Endocrinology*] (WDAA) ... ENDO
Endocrine and Infertility [*Endocrinology and obstetrics*] (DAVI) ... E & I
Endocrine and Metabolism [*Medicine*] (DAVI) ... E & M
Endocrine Research Group [*University of Calgary*] [*Research center*] (RCD) ... ERG
Endocrine Society (EA) ... ES
Endocrinologist ... ENDCRNLGST
Endocrinology ... E
Endocrinology [*Medical specialty*] (DHSM) ... END
Endocrinology ... Endoc
Endocrinology ... ENDOCRIN
Endocrinology ... ENDOCRINOL
Endodermal Sinus Tumor [*Oncology*] ... EST
Endodontic ... EDDNTC
Endodontics [*Dentistry*] (DAVI) ... Endo
End-of-Course Comprehensive Testing ... EOCCT
End-of-Cycle Test [*Army training*] (INF) ... EOCT
End-of-Descent (GAVI) ... E/D
End-of-File Mark [*Computer science*] ... EOF mark
End-of-Mix Viscosity (MCD) ... EOMV
End-of-Screen [*Computer science*] (MHDB) ... EOS
End-of-Sequence [*Computer science*] (MHDB) ... EOS
End-of-Step [*Computer science*] (MHDB) ... EOS
End-of-Text/Acknowledge [*Computer science*] (MHDB) ... ETX/ACK
End-of-Treatment Response [*Medicine*] ... ETR
Endogen, Inc. [*NASDAQ symbol*] (SAG) ... ENDG
Endogen, Inc. [*Associated Press*] (SAG) ... Endogen
Endogenous Circadian Phase [*Physiology*] ... ECP
Endogenous Circadian Rhythm (PDAA) ... ECR
Endogenous Digitalis-Like Factor [*Biochemistry*] ... EDLF
Endogenous Fecal Calcium [*Medicine*] (MAE) ... EFC
Endogenous Hyperlipidemia [*Medicine*] (MAE) ... EHL
Endogenous Inhibitor of Prostaglandin Synthase [*Biochemistry*] ... EIPS
Endogenous Limbic Potentials [*Neurophysiology*] ... ELP
Endogenous Morphine [*or Endomorphin*] [*Also, ENM Brain peptide*] ... ENDORPHIN
Endogenous Morphine [*or Endomorphin*] [*Also, ENDORPHIN Brain peptide*] ... ENM
Endogenous Opioid Peptides [*Medicine*] (MEDA) ... EOP
Endogenous Pyrogen [*Immunology*] ... EP
Endogenous Retrovirus ... ERV
Endogenous Substance [*Biology*] ... ES
Endogenous Transcript [*Genetics*] ... ET
Endoglucanases [*An enzyme*] ... EG
Endoglucosaminidase-H [*An enzyme*] ... endo-H
Endolymphatic Hydrops [*Medicine*] (DAVI) ... ELH
Endolymphatic Sac Tumors [*Oncology*] ... ELST
Endomethylenetetrahydrophthalic Acid [*Organic chemistry*] ... EMTA
Endometrial Biopsy [*Gynecology*] (DAVI) ... EMB
Endometrial Carcinoma [*Oncology*] ... EnCa
Endometrial LASER Ablation [*Medicine*] ... ELA
Endometriosis Association (EA) ... EA
Endometritis-Salpingitis [*Medicine*] (DMAA) ... ES
Endometrium [*Anatomy*] ... ENDOMET
Endomorphin-Like Immunoreactivity ... ELI
Endomyocardial Biopsy [*Medicine*] ... EMB
Endomyocardial Fibrosis [*Cardiology*] ... EMF
Endoneurial Fluid Pressure (PDAA) ... EFP
Endoplasmic [*Freeze etching in microscopy*] ... E
Endoplasmic Fracture [*Freeze etching in microscopy*] ... EF
Endoplasmic Reticulum [*Cytology*] ... ER
Endoplasmic Reticulum (DOG) ... er
Endoplasmic Reticulum of Golgi [*Cytology*] ... ERG
Endoplasmic Surface [*Freeze etching in microscopy*] ... ES
Endoreduplication (MAE) ... end
Endorphin [*Biochemistry*] ... EP
Endorsed [*or Endorsement*] [*Business term*] ... END
Endorsee [*Legal shorthand*] (LWAP) ... ENDEE
Endorsement [*Legal shorthand*] (LWAP) ... ENDMT
Endorsement (ROG) ... ENDORST
Endorsement ... ENDT
Endorsement Guaranteed (MHDW) ... End Guar
Endorsement Irregular [*Banking*] ... E/I
Endorser [*Legal shorthand*] (LWAP) ... ENDER
Endorser Potential [*Advertising term*] ... EP
Endorsers Conference for Veterans Affairs Chaplaincy (EA) ... ECVAC
Endoscopic Esophageal Sclerotherapy [*Medicine*] ... EES
Endoscopic LASER Therapy [*Medicine*] ... ELT
Endoscopic Pancreatocholangiography [*Medicine*] (AAMN) ... EPCG
Endoscopic Papillotomy [*Medicine*] ... EPT
Endoscopic Paravariceal Sclerotherapy [*Medicine*] ... EPS
Endoscopic Retrograde Cannulation of Pancreatic Duct [*Medicine*] (DAVI) ... ERCP
Endoscopic Retrograde Cholangiography [*Medicine*] ... ERC
Endoscopic Retrograde Cholangiopancreatographic [*Exam*] [*Medicine*] ... ERCP
Endoscopic Retrograde Pancreatography [*Medicine*] ... ERP
Endoscopic Retrograde Sphincterotomy [*Medicine*] ... ERS
Endoscopic Sclerosis [*Medicine*] (DAVI) ... ES
Endoscopic Sclerotherapy [*Medicine*] ... ES
Endoscopic Sphincterotomy [*Medicine*] ... ES
Endoscopic Sphincterotomy [*Medicine*] ... EST
Endoscopic Ultrasonography [*Medicine*] ... EUS
Endoscopic Variceal Sclerosis [*Medicine*] ... EVS
Endoscopy [*or Endoscope*] [*Medicine*] (DAVI) ... ENDO
Endoscopy/Cystoscopy [*Medicine*] (MAE) ... E/C
Endosonics Corp. [*Associated Press*] (SAG) ... Endsonc
Endosonics Corp. [*NASDAQ symbol*] (SAG) ... ESON
Endosperm [*Botany*] ... En
Endosperm Balance Number [*Genetics*] ... EBN
Endosteal Marrow [*Hematology*] ... EM
Endothelial Cell [*Medicine*] ... EC
Endothelial Cell Density [*Anatomy*] ... ECD
Endothelial Cell Growth Factor [*Cytochemistry*] ... ECGF
Endothelial Cell Growth Supplement [*Cytochemistry*] ... ECGS

Endothelial Cell-Derived Growth Factor [*Biochemistry*] ... ECDGF
Endothelial Leukocyte Adhesion Molecule [*Cytology*] ... ELAM
Endothelial Proliferating Factor [*Biochemistry*] ... EPF
Endothelial-Derived Growth Factor [*Biochemistry*] ... EDGF
Endothelial-Derived Relaxing Factor [*Biochemistry*] ... EDRF
Endothelial-Epithelial Corneal Dystrophy [*Medicine*] (DMAA) ... EECD
Endothelin [*Biochemistry*] ... ET
Endothelin-Converting Enzyme [*Biochemistry*] ... ECE
Endothelium-Derived Vascular Relaxant Factor [*Biochemistry*] ... EDRF
Endothia parasitica [*Plant pathology*] ... EP
Endotoxin [*Microbiology*] ... E
Endotoxin [*Microbiology*] ... ET
Endotoxin Inactivating Agent (OA) ... EIA
Endotoxin Neutralizing Protein [*Biochemistry*] ... ENP
Endotoxin Unit [*Clinical chemistry*] ... EU
Endotracheal [*Medicine*] (DAVI) ... ENDO
Endotracheal [*Medicine*] (AAMN) ... ET
Endotracheal Aspirates [*Medicine*] (MEDA) ... ETA
Endotracheal Tube [*Medicine*] ... ET
Endotracheal Tube [*Medicine*] ... ETT
EndoVascular Technologies [*NASDAQ symbol*] (TTSB) ... EVTI
Endovascular Technologies, Inc. [*Associated Press*] (SAG) ... Endovas
Endovascular Technologies, Inc. [*NASDAQ symbol*] (SAG) ... EVTI
Endowed (ROG) ... END
Endowment (ABBR) ... EDWNT
Endowment (ROG) ... ENDOW
End-Paper [*Bibliography*] ... E/P
Endpaper (ADA) ... ENDP
Endpaper Map [*Publishing*] ... ENDPRM
End-Paper Rubbed, Else Good [*Condition*] [*Antiquarian book trade*] ... EPR/G
End-Point Temperature [*Food science*] ... EPT
Ends and Rings [*Architecture*] (ROG) ... E & R
End-Stage Liver Disease [*Medicine*] ... ESLD
Endstone [*Horology*] ... ESTN
End-Systole [*Cardiology*] ... ES
End-Systolic Areas [*Cardiology*] ... ESA
End-Systolic Count [*Cardiology*] ... ESC
End-Systolic Diameter [*or Dimension*] [*Cardiology*] ... ESD
End-Systolic Length [*Cardiology*] ... ESL
End-Systolic Volume [*Cardiology*] ... ESV
End-Systolic Volume Index [*Cardiology*] (DMAA) ... ESVI
End-Tidal [*Physiology*] ... ET
End-to-End [*Anastomosis*] [*Medicine*] (DAVI) ... EE
End-to-End Anastomosis [*Medicine*] ... EEA
End-to-End Information System (NASA) ... EEIS
Endue (ABBR) ... EDU
Endurance (IAA) ... END
Endurance (FAAC) ... ENDCE
Endurance Factor [*Cardiology*] (DAVI) ... EF
Endurance Horse Registry of America (EA) ... EHRA
Endurance Limit [*Mechanical engineering*] ... EL
Endurance Minerals [*Vancouver Stock Exchange symbol*] ... END
End-Use Product [*Environmental Protection Agency*] ... EP
End-User [*Computer science*] ... EU
End-User Certificate ... EUC
End-Users of Derivatives Association, Inc. (ECON) ... EUDA
Endwell, NY [*FM radio station call letters*] ... WRGG
Eneabba [*Australia Airport symbol*] (OAG) ... ENB
Enema [*Medicine*] ... E
Enema [*Medicine*] ... EN
Enema [*Medicine*] (ROG) ... ENEM
Enema Saponis [*Medicine*] ... ES
Enemy (ADA) ... E
Enemy (AABC) ... EN
Enemy Activities Branch [*British military*] (DMA) ... EAB
Enemy Aircraft ... EA
Enemy Ammunition Disposal and Collection Unit [*Military British*] ... EADCU
Enemy and Occupied Territories Department [*Ministry of Economic Warfare*] [*British World War II*] ... E & OT
Enemy Area (IAA) ... EA
Enemy Capabilities (MCD) ... EC
Enemy Civilian Internee Information Bureau [*Military*] (AABC) ... ECIIB
Enemy Civilian Internee Information Bureau (Branch) [*Military*] (AABC) ... ECIIB(Br)
Enemy Contact Report [*NATO*] (NATG) ... ECR
Enemy Countries Intelligence [*Ministry of Economic Warfare*] [*British World War II*] ... ECI
Enemy Dead ... ED
Enemy Equipment Identification Service [*World War II*] ... EEIS
Enemy Equipment Intelligence Branch [*World War II*] ... EEIB
Enemy Equipment Intelligence Service Team [*World War II*] ... EEIST
Enemy Exports Committee [*British World War II*] ... EEC
Enemy Forward Disposition [*Military*] ... EFD
Enemy/Friendly (MCD) ... E/F
Enemy Fuels and Lubricants Technical Committee ... EF & LTC
Enemy Identification Friend or Foe ... EIFF
Enemy Initiated Incident [*Vietnam*] ... ENI
Enemy Initiated Incident Responded to by Friendly Forces [*Vietnam*] ... ENIRF
Enemy Intelligence ... EI
Enemy Objective Unit [*of US*] [*in London*] ... EOU
Enemy Occupied Europe [*World War II*] ... EOE
Enemy Oil Committee [*US*] ... EOC
Enemy Oil Intelligence Group [*Ministry of Economic Warfare*] [*British World War II*] ... EOIG
Enemy Order of Battle (AFM) ... EOB
Enemy Position ... EP
Enemy Prisoner of War [*Army*] (AABC) ... EPW
Enemy Prisoner of War Information Bureau [*Army*] (AABC) ... EPWIB
Enemy Prisoner of War Information Bureau (Branch) [*Army*] (AABC) ... EPWIB(Br)
Enemy Situation (MCD) ... ENSIT
Enemy Situation Correlation Element [*DoD*] ... ENSCE
Enemy Situation Correlation Element [*Air Force*] ... ESCE
Enemy Status (MCD) ... ES
Enemy Unit Identification [*Military*] ... EUI
Enemy War Materials Branch [*Supreme Headquarters, Allied Expeditionary Force*] [*World War II*] ... EWMB
Enemy Wireless Monitoring Unit (IAA) ... EWMU
Enemy-Occupied Territory ... EOT
Enentarzid (BJA) ... EE
Energas Co. (MHDW) ... EGAS
Energen Corp. [*NYSE symbol*] (SPSG) ... EGN
Energen Corp. [*Associated Press*] (SAG) ... Engn
Energetic Dynamic Cardiac Insufficiency [*Cardiology*] (DMAA) ... EDCI
Energetic Gamma Ray Experiment Telescope [*NASA*] ... EGRET
Energetic Heavy Ion Composition Experiment [*NASA*] ... EHIC
Energetic Ion Analysis [*Surface analysis*] ... EIA
Energetic Komprimierendes System [*Nuclear science*] (OA) ... EKS
Energetic Neutral Atom [*Imaging*] ... ENA
Energetic Particle Anisotropy Spectrometer ... EPAS
Energetic Particle Composition Instrument [*Astrophysics*] ... EPAC
Energetic Particles Analyzer [*Astrophysics*] ... EPA
Energetic Particles Detector [*Geophysics*] ... EPD
Energetic Particles Explorer [*Satellite*] [*NASA*] ... EPE
Energetic Particles Satellite [*NASA*] (MUGU) ... EPS
Energetic Pion Channel and Spectrometer (PDAA) ... EPICS
Energetic Storm Particle ... ESP
Energetic Ultra-Violet ... EUV
Energetic X-Ray Imaging Telescope Experiment (MCD) ... EXITE
Energex Minerals Ltd. [*Toronto Stock Exchange symbol Vancouver Stock Exchange symbol*] ... EGX
Energia e Industrias Aragonesas Sociedad Anonima [*Spain*] ... EIASA
Energicamente [*With Energy*] [*Music*] ... ENERG
Energicamente [*With Energy*] [*Music*] (ROG) ... ENERGE
Energie Atomique du Canada, Limitee [*Atomic Energy of Canada Ltd.*] ... EACL
Energize (IAA) ... ENE
Energize (AAG) ... ENER
Energize (MSA) ... ENRGZ
Energize Output M [*Symbol language*] ... EOM
Energy [*Symbol*] [*IUPAC*] ... E
Energy ... ENGRY
Energy (MSA) ... ENGY
Energy (ABBR) ... NRG
Energy (IDOE) ... W
Energy Absorbing ... EA
Energy Absorbing Capacity (NASA) ... EAC
Energy Absorbing Gas Lithium Ejector (MCD) ... EAGLE
Energy Absorbing Steering ... EAS
Energy Absorbing Unit [*Automotive engineering*] ... EAU
Energy Absorption (AAG) ... EA
Energy Absorption ... EAB
Energy Absorption Characteristics (AAG) ... EAC
Energy Abstracts for Policy Analysis [*National Science Foundation A publication*] (MCD) ... EAPA
Energy Action Educational Foundation [*Later, EAEP*] (EA) ... EAEF
Energy Action Educational Project of C/LEC [*Defunct*] (EA) ... EAEP
Energy Analysis and Diagnostic Center [*Department of Energy*] ... EADC
Energy and Air Division [*Office of Research and Development*] [*Environmental Protection Agency*] (EPA) ... EAD
Energy and Chemical Workers Union [*See also STEC*] ... ECWU
Energy and Economics Data Bank [*IAEA*] [*United Nations*] (DUND) ... EEDB
Energy and Economics Data Bank [*IAEA*] [*Information service or system*] ... ENEC
Energy and Environment Data Base [*Oak Ridge National Laboratory*] [*Database*] ... EEDB
Energy and Environmental Analysis [*Environmental Protection Agency*] (GFGA) ... EEA
Energy and Environmental Policy Center [*Harvard University*] [*Research center*] (RCD) ... EEPC
Energy and Environmental Research Center [*University of North Dakota*] ... EERC
Energy & Fuels [*A publication*] ... ENFUEM
Energy and Industry Subgroup (EERA) ... EIS
Energy and Man's Environment [*Utility-funded curriculum program*] ... EME
Energy & Mineral Resources [*Business Publishers, Inc.*] [*No longer available online*] [*Information service or system*] (CRD) ... E & MR
Energy and Mineral Resources Research Institute [*Iowa State University*] [*Research center*] (RCD) ... EMRRI
Energy and Minerals Division [*GAO*] (AAGC) ... EMD
Energy and Natural Resources (DLA) ... ENR
Energy and Power Evaluation Program [*Computer science*] ... ENPEP
Energy and Resource Development Institute [*Clemson University*] [*Research center*] (RCD) ... ERDI
Energy and the Environment [*A publication*] ... EAE
Energy Association of New York State (SRA) ... EANYS
Energy Audit Report [*Navy*] ... EAR
Energy Balance Model [*Climatology*] ... EBM
Energy Balance Models (EERA) ... EBMS
Energy Band Structure (IAA) ... EBS
Energy Bibliography and Index [*Center for Energy and Mineral Resources - Texas A & M University*] [*College Station, TX Bibliographic database*] ... EBIB
Energy BioSystems [*NASDAQ symbol*] (TTSB) ... ENBC

Energy Biosystems Corp. [*NASDAQ symbol*] (SAG) .... ENBC
Energy Biosystems Corp. [*Associated Press*] (SAG) .... EngBiosy
Energy Budget Level .... EBL
Energy Charge .... EC
Energy Charge Potential .... ECP
Energy Company [*Slogan and brand name used by Humble Oil & Refining Co.*] [*Later, Exxon*] .... ENCO
Energy Conservation and Management (MCD) .... ECAM
Energy Conservation and Production Act [*1976*] (MCD) .... ECPA
Energy Conservation and Solar Centre [*British*] (CB) .... ECSC
Energy Conservation Assessment of Systems, Technologies, and Requirements .... ECASTAR
Energy Conservation Caucus [*Defunct*] (EA) .... ECC
Energy Conservation Coalition (EA) .... ECC
Energy Conservation Council .... ECC
Energy Conservation in Existing Buildings Act of 1976 .... ECEBA
Energy Conservation Investment Program [*DoD*] (MCD) .... ECIP
Energy Conservation Measure (AAGC) .... ECM
Energy Conservation Opportunities [*Federal Energy Administration*] ... ECO
Energy Conservation Program Guide for Industry and Commerce [*Department of Commerce*] .... EPIC
Energy Conservation Update [*A publication*] .... ECU
Energy Conservation Using Better Engineering (PDAA) .... ECUBE
Energy Conservation Vehicle [*British Leyland*] .... ECV
Energy Conserving - Second Generation [*Automotive engineering*] ... ECII
Energy Consumers and Producers Association (EA) .... ECPA
Energy Consumption Rate .... ECR
Energy Content Curve (NOAA) .... ECC
Energy Control Report [*Navy*] .... ECR
Energy Controls (Prentice-Hall, Inc.) [*A publication*] (DLA) .... Energy Cont (P-H)
Energy Conv Devices [*NASDAQ symbol*] (TTSB) .... ENER
Energy Conversion Alternatives Study [*NASA*] .... ECAS
Energy Conversion and Utilization Technologies Program [*Department of Energy*] .... ECUT
Energy Conversion Devices, Inc. .... ECD
Energy Conversion Devices, Inc. [*Associated Press*] (SAG) ... EgyCny
Energy Conversion Devices, Inc. [*NASDAQ symbol*] (SAG) ... ENER
Energy Conversion Laboratory [*MIT*] (MCD) .... ECL
Energy Conversion Subsystem (SSD) .... ECS
Energy Conversion System (PDAA) .... ECS
Energy Conversion Systems, Ottawa, ON, Canada [*Library symbol*] [*Library of Congress*] (LCLS) .... CaOOECS
Energy Coordinating Group [*Twelve-nation coalition*] .... ECG
Energy Crisis Assistance Program [*Federal government*] .... ECAP
Energy Data and Modeling Center [*Institute of Energy Economics*] [*Japan Database producer*] (IID) .... EDMC
Energy Data System [*Databank*] [*Environmental Protection Agency*] (IID) ... EDS
Energy Database [*Department of Energy*] [*Information service or system*] ... EDB
Energy Depot Systems .... EDS
Energy Detente International Price/Tax Series [*Lundberg Survey, Inc.*] [*No longer available online*] [*Information service or system*] (CRD) ... EDPRICE
Energy Disaggregated Input-Output Model [*Department of Energy*] (GFGA) ... EDIO
Energy Discharge Capacitor (IAA) .... EDC
Energy Dispersive Analysis by X-Ray [*Photovoltaic energy systems*] ... EDAX
Energy Dispersive Spectroscopy .... EDS
Energy Dispersive System [*Microscopy*] .... EDS
Energy Dispersive X-Ray .... EDX
Energy Dispersive X-Ray Analysis [*or Analyzer*] [*Also, EDXRA*] ... EDXA
Energy Dispersive X-Ray Analysis [*or Analyzer*] [*Also, EDXA*] ... EDXRA
Energy Dispersive X-Ray Analysis Computation Technique [*X-Ray fluorescence software*] [*Kevex Corp.*] .... EXACT
Energy Dispersive X-Ray Diffraction [*Atomic structure determination*] ... EDXD
Energy Dispersive X-Ray Fluorescence [*Spectrometry*] .... EDXF
Energy Dispersive X-Ray Fluorescence [*Spectrometry*] .... EDXRF
Energy Dispersive X-Ray Spectrometry .... EDXRS
Energy Dispersive X-Ray Spectrum .... EDXS
Energy Dissipation Tests (NRCH) .... EDT
Energy Distribution Curve [*Electron*] .... EDC
Energy, Economics and Environment Institute [*Defunct*] (EA) ... EEEI
Energy Efficiency [*Electrochemistry*] .... EE
Energy Efficiency Ratio [*Home appliance electric output*] .... EER
Energy Efficient Building Association (EA) .... EEBA
Energy Efficient Design .... EED
Energy Efficient Engine .... EEE
Energy Efficient Services and Equipment .... EESE
Energy Efficient Transport (MCD) .... EET
Energy Emergency Management Information System (PDAA) ... EEMIS
Energy Engineering Program [*Navy*] .... EEP
Energy Enterprises [*Information service or system*] (IID) .... EE
Energy Expenditure .... EE
Energy Extension Service [*Department of Energy*] .... EES
Energy Facilities Contractors Group (AAGC) .... EFCOG
Energy Filtering Electron Microscope .... EFEM
Energy Flux Density .... EFD
Energy from the Forest Program [*Canada*] .... ENFOR
Energy/Gross National Product [*Fuel use ratio*] .... E/GNP
Energy Guideline Factors .... EGF
Energy Incorp., Idaho Falls, ID [*Library symbol*] [*Library of Congress*] (LCLS) ... IdIfE
Energy Independence Authority .... EIA
Energy Industries Council [*British*] (DS) .... EIC
Energy Industry Information System (IEEE) .... EIIS
Energy Information Administration [*Department of Energy*] (IID) ... EIA
Energy Information Administration Clearinghouse .... EIAC

Energy Information Administration Electronic Publication System [*Database*] [*Department of Energy Information service or system*] (CRD) ... EIA/EPUB
Energy Information Center [*Battelle Memorial Institute*] (IID) ... EIC
Energy Information Centre [*Australia*] .... EIC
Energy Information Guide [*A publication*] .... EIG
Energy Information Resource (MCD) .... EIR
Energy Information Resources Inventory [*Database*] [*Department of Energy Information service or system*] (CRD) ... EIRI
Energy Information Systems [*UNIDO*] [*United Nations*] (DUND) ... EIS
Energy Information Systems Group [*Department of Energy Also, an information service or system*] (IID) ... EISG
Energy Journal [*A publication*] (BRI) .... En Jnl
Energy Law Institute (EA) .... ELI
Energy Law Service [*A publication*] (DLA) .... Energy L Serv
Energy Level Diagram .... ELD
Energy Loss (IAA) .... EL
Energy Loss Peak [*Physics*] .... ELP
Energy Management .... EM
Energy Management and Control System .... EMCS
Energy Management and Controls Society (EA) .... EMCS
Energy Management Bumper System [*Automobile safety*] ...... EMBS
Energy Management Center .... EMC
Energy Management (Commerce Clearing House) [*A publication*] (DLA) ... Energy Mgmt (CCH)
Energy Management Display Indicator .... EMDI
Energy Management in Lighting Award Scheme [*British*] .... EMILAS
Energy Management Plan (MCD) .... EMP
Energy Management System .... EMS
Energy Management Unit (PCM) .... EMU
Energy Managers' Association [*Australia*] .... EMA
Energy Managers' Group [*Australia*] .... EMG
Energy Maneuverability (MCD) .... EM
Energy, Mines, and Resources [*Canadian government department*] ... EMR
Energy, Mines, and Resources Canada, CANMET, BCC Library, Nepean, ON, Canada [*Library symbol*] [*Library of Congress*] (LCLS) ... CaONpEMRCM
Energy, Mines, and Resources Canada, CNP Resource Centre, Ottawa, ON, Canada [*Library symbol Library of Congress*] (LCLS) ... CaOOCNP
Energy, Mines and Resources Canada, Conservation and Renewable Energy Office, Toronto, ON, Canada [*Library symbol*] [*Library of Congress*] (LCLS) ... CaOTEMR
Energy, Mines and Resources Canada, National Air Photo Library, Ottawa, ON, Canada [*Library symbol*] [*Library of Congress*] (LCLS) ... CaOOMNA
Energy, Mines, and Resources Canada, Western Research Laboratory, CANMET Library, Sherwood Park, AB, Canada [*Library symbol Library of Congress*] (LCLS) ... CaASpEMRCM
Energy Mobilization Board .... EMB
Energy North, Inc. [*NYSE symbol*] (SAG) .... EI
Energy North, Inc. [*Associated Press*] (SAG) .... Engynth
Energy Nova Scotia [*Database*] [*Nova Scotia Research Foundation Corp.*] [*Information service or system*] (CRD) ... ENS
Energy of Activation [*Medicine*] (DAVI) .... AE
Energy of Crush Factor [*Automotive safety*] .... ECF
Energy of State .... EOS
Energy Office [*Department of Agriculture*] (OICC) .... EOA
Energy Optimized Technology [*German-manufactured car tire*] [*Continental Gummi-Werke AG*] ... EOT
Energy over Weight .... E/W
Energy over Weight (MCD) .... EOW
Energy Policy Act of 1992 [*BTS*] (TAG) .... EPACT
Energy Policy and Conservation Act [*1975*] .... EPCA
Energy Policy Information Center [*Defunct*] (EA) .... EPIC
Energy Policy Office [*Formerly, National Energy Office*] [*Executive Office of the President Abolished, 1974*] ... EPO
Energy Probe Research Foundation [*Canada*] (IRC) .... EPRF
Energy Production and Delivery (IAA) .... EEPD
Energy Production Working Group [*Australia*] .... EPWG
Energy Programs [*Database*] [*Energy, Mines, and Resources, Canada*] [*Information service or system*] (CRD) ... ENP
Energy Pulse Bonding [*Electronics*] .... EPB
Energy Quotient .... EQ
Energy Rate Input Controller (IEEE) .... ERIC
Energy Recovery Ventilators .... ERV
Energy Reorganization Act [*1974*] .... ERA
Energy Research [*NASDAQ symbol*] (TTSB) .... ERCC
Energy Research Advisory Board [*Department of Energy*] ..... ERAB
Energy Research and Development .... ER & D
Energy Research and Development (DNAB) .... ERAD
Energy Research and Development Administration [*Superseded by Department of Energy, 1977*] ... ERDA
Energy Research and Development Administration Board of Contract Appeals (AAGC) ... ERDABCA
Energy Research and Development Administration, Division of Reactor Development and Demonstration (PDAA) ... ERDA-RDD
Energy Research and Development Administration Manual [*A publication*] (IEEE) ... ERDAM
Energy Research and Development Advisory Council .... ERDAC
Energy Research and Development Agency [*Information service or system*] (NITA) ... ERDA
Energy Research and Development Inventory [*Information service or system*] (NITA) ... ERD
Energy Research and Development Inventory [*Marine science*] (MSC) ... ERDI
Energy Research and Education Foundation .... EREF
Energy Research Centre (EERA) .... ERC
Energy Research Corp. [*Associated Press*] (SAG) .... EngyRsh

Energy Research Corp. [*NASDAQ symbol*] (SAG) .... ERCC
Energy Research for the Governors .... ERG
Energy Research Institute (EA) .... ERI
Energy Research Laboratories (EERA) .... ERL
Energy Research Management (MCD) .... ERM
Energy Research Management Project [*Federal interagency group*] .... ERMP
Energy Research Office [*Department of Energy*] (OICC) .... ERO
Energy Research Video Network [*Video conferencing*] .... ERVIN
Energy Resources Center [*University of Illinois at Chicago*] [*Research center*] (RCD) .... ERC
Energy Resources Council [*Terminated, 1977*] .... ERC
Energy Resources Institute [*University of Oklahoma*] [*Research center*] (RCD) .... ERI
Energy Resources of Australia (EERA) .... ERA
Energy Resources Research, Calgary, AB, Canada [*Library symbol Library of Congress*] (LCLS) .... CaACERR
Energy Resources Research, Calgary, Alberta [*Library symbol National Library of Canada*] (NLC) .... ACERR
Energy Return on Investment .... EROI
Energy Return System [*In ERS 2000, brand name of Reebok International Ltd.*] .... ERS
Energy Rich Glucose Optimized Drink [*Military*] (INF) .... ERGO
Energy Saving Trust (AIE) .... EST
Energy Sciences Network [*Department of Energy*] .... ESnet
Energy Sciences Network [*DOE-funded network*] (AAGC) .... ESNET
Energy Security Act [*1980*] .... ESA
Energy Service Co. [*Associated Press*] (SAG) .... ENSCO
Energy Service Co. .... ESCO
Energy Service Co. [*AMEX symbol*] (SPSG) .... ESV
Energy Services Planning .... ESP
Energy Soft Computer-Aided Design [*Energy Soft Computer Systems Ltd.*] [*Software package*] (NCC) .... ESCAD
Energy Sources Technology Conference and Exhibition (ITD) .... ETCE
Energy Specific Carbon Dioxide [*Automotive emissions*] ESCO2
Energy Storage Device (IAA) .... ESD
Energy Storage Modulator .... ESM
Energy Storage System .... ESS
Energy Studies Unit [*University of Strathclyde*] [*Scotland*] (IRC) ... ESU
Energy Supplies Allocation Board .... ESAB
Energy Supply and Environmental Coordination Act of 1974 .... ESECA
Energy Supply Planning Model [*National Science Foundation*] .... ESPM
Energy Systems and Policy Research Program [*University of Wisconsin - Madison*] [*Research center*] (RCD) .... ESPRP
Energy Systems Center [*University of Nevada*] [*Research center*] (RCD) .... ESC
Energy Systems Trade Association [*British*] (DBA) .... ESTA
Energy Tax Act [*1978*] .... ETA
Energy Technology Center .... ETC
Energy Technology Data Exchange [*Department of Energy*] (GFGA) .... ETDE
Energy Technology Engineering Center [*Canoga Park, CA*] [*Department of Energy*] (GRD) .... ETEC
Energy Technology Office [*Department of Energy*] (OICC) .... ETO
Energy Technology Support Unit at Harwell [*British*] .... ETSU
Energy Telecommunications and Electrical Association (EA) .... ENTELEC
Energy Test Reactor .... ETR
Energy Transfer (IAA) .... ET
Energy Transfer Control [*Aviation*] .... ETC
Energy Transfer Module [*Aviation*] (MCD) .... ETM
Energy Transfer System (MCD) .... ETS
Energy Transmission System [*Automotive engineering*] .... ETS
Energy Transportation Systems, Inc. .... ETSI
Energy Unit (IAA) .... EU
Energy Use Working Group [*Australia*] .... EUWG
Energy Users Report [*Commerce Clearing House*] [*A publication*] (DLA) .... En Users Rep
Energy Users Reports (Bureau of National Affairs) [*A publication*] (DLA) .... Energy Users Rep (BNA)
Energy Utilization and Conversation Exhibition and Conference (PDAA) .... EUCON
Energy Ventures [*Associated Press*] (SAG) .... EngyVen
Energy Ventures [*NYSE symbol*] (SAG) .... EVI
Energy Victoria [*Australia*] .... EV
Energy West [*NASDAQ symbol*] (TTSB) .... EWST
Energy West, Inc. [*Associated Press*] (SAG) .... EngWst
Energy West, Inc. [*NASDAQ symbol*] (SAG) .... EWST
Energy-Absorbing Resin (PDAA) .... EAR
Energy-Dependent Photoelectron Diffraction (PDAA) .... EDPD
Energy-Information Database [*International Research and Evaluation*] [*Information service or system*] (CRD) .... E-ID
Energy-Loss Electron Spectroscopy .... ELES
Energy-Loss Spectroscopy .... ELS
EnergyNorth, Inc. [*NASDAQ symbol*] (NQ) .... ENNI
Energy-Protein Malnutrition .... EPM
Energy-Related General [*National Science Foundation research office*] .... ERG
Energy-Related Graduate [*National Science Foundation trainee program*] .... ERG
Energy-Related Inventions Program [*Department of Energy and National Bureau of Standards*] .... ERIP
Energy-Related Laboratory Equipment [*Defunct*] .... ERLE
Energy-Related Minority-Owned Business Enterprise .... ERMBE
Energy-Separating Agent [*Chemical engineering*] .... ESA
Energy-to-Weight Ratio (MCD) .... EW
Energy-Variant Sequential Detection (CET) .... EVSD
Enerplus Resources Corp. [*Toronto Stock Exchange symbol*] .... ENP
Enerplus Resources Fund Series 'B' Trust Units [*Toronto Stock Exchange symbol*] .... ERF
Enershare Technology Corp. [*Vancouver Stock Exchange symbol*] .... ERT

Enersis Co. [*Associated Press*] (SAG) .... Enersis
Enersis SA [*NYSE symbol*] (SPSG) .... ENI
Enersis S.A. ADS [*NYSE symbol*] (TTSB) .... ENI
Enertec Corp. [*Toronto Stock Exchange symbol*] .... ENR
Enerteck Energy Technologies Corp. [*Vancouver Stock Exchange symbol*] .... ENK
Enesco Precious Moments Collectors' Club (EA) .... EPMCC
Eneteractive, Inc. [*NASDAQ symbol*] (SAG) .... ENTR
Eneteractive, Inc. [*Associated Press*] (SAG) .... Entract
Eneteractive, Inc. [*Associated Press*] (SAG) .... Entractv
ENEX Resources [*NASDAQ symbol*] (TTSB) .... ENEX
Enex Resources Corp. [*NASDAQ symbol*] (NQ) .... ENEX
Enex Resources Corp. [*Associated Press*] (SAG) .... EnexRs
Enexco International Ltd. [*Vancouver Stock Exchange symbol*] .... ENX
Enfield [*Borough of London*] .... ENFD
Enfield Corp. Ltd. [*Toronto Stock Exchange symbol*] .... ENF
Enfield, CT [*FM radio station call letters*] .... WPKX
Enfield Resources [*Vancouver Stock Exchange symbol*] .... EFD
Enflurane [*Also, ENF*] [*An anesthetic*] .... E
Enflurane [*Also, E*] [*An anesthetic*] .... ENF
Enforced [*Legal term*] (DLA) .... Enf'd
Enforced Dipole Moment .... EDM
Enforcement (DCTA) .... ENF
Enforcement .... ENFCMNT
Enforcement Action [*Nuclear energy*] (NRCH) .... EA
Enforcement Agreement [*Environmental Protection Agency*] (GFGA) ..... EA
Enforcement Compliance Schedule Letter [*Environmental Protection Agency*] (EG) .... ECSL
Enforcement Decision Document [*Environmental Protection Agency*] (ERG) .... EDD
Enforcement Division [*Environmental Protection Agency*] (GFGA) ...... ED
Enforcement Document Retrieval System [*Environmental Protection Agency*] (EPA) .... EDRS
Enforcement Management and Accountability System [*Environmental Protection Agency*] (GFGA) .... EMAS
Enforcement Management Subsystem [*Environmental Protection Agency*] .... EMS
Enforcement Management System (GNE) .... EMS
Enforcement Notification (NRCH) .... EN
Enforcement of Laws and Treaties [*Program*] [*Coast Guard*] .... ELT
Enforcement Response Policy [*Environmental Protection Agency*] (GFGA) ..... ERP
Enforcement Response Policy (GNE) .... ERP
Enforcement Stategy [*Environmental Protection Agency*] (GFGA) .... ES
Engage (MSA) .... ENGA
Engage Enemy Target .... EET
Engage High Yield .... EHY
Engage Intercept (CAAL) .... ENG INT
Engage Missile Orders [*Military*] (CAAL) .... EMO
Engage Test [*Manual exchanges*] [*Telecommunications*] (NITA) .... ET
Engaged Tone [*Telecommunications*] (TEL) .... ET
Engagement (ADA) .... ENG
Engagement (ROG) .... ENGAGMT
Engagement Area [*Military*] (INF) .... EA
Engagement Control Center [*Army*] .... ECC
Engagement Control Panel (MCD) .... ECP
Engagement Control System [*Navy*] (MCD) .... ECS
Engagement Controller [*Navy*] (NVT) .... EC
Engagement Controller Set .... ECS
Engagement Controller Software .... ECSW
Engagement Data Display (MCD) .... EDD
Engagement Decision Analysis Process [*DoD*] .... EDAP
Engagement Direction Center (SAA) .... EDC
Engagement Direction Station (SAA) .... EDs
Engagement Effectiveness [*Army*] (AABC) .... EE
Engagement Sensor Set .... ESS
Engagement Simulation [*Military*] (INF) .... ES
Engagement Tracking Station (SAA) .... ETS
Engagement Zone [*Army*] (ADDR) .... EZ
Engelbert's Aquarians (EA) .... EA
Engelbert's "Goils" [*An association*] (EA) .... EG
Engelbert's Golden Eagles (EA) .... EGE
[*The*] Engelettes [*An association Defunct*] (EA) .... TE
Engelhard Corp. [*Formerly, ENG*] [*NYSE symbol*] (SPSG) .... EC
Engelhard Corp. [*Associated Press*] (SAG) .... EnglhCp
Engelhard Minerals & Chemicals Corp. [*Later, Engelhard Corp.*] ...... EM & C
Engelhard Minerals & Chemicals Corp. [*Later, Engelhard Corp.*], Research Library, Edison, NJ [*Library symbol Library of Congress*] (LCLS) ... NjEdE
Engellireth-Holm Swarm Tumor [*Medicine*] .... EHST
Engel's Angels in Humperdinck Heaven Fan Club (EA) .... EAHHFC
Enge's Entourage (EA) .... EE
Enge's Flaming Hearts (EA) .... EFH
Engex, Inc. [*AMEX symbol*] (SPSG) .... EGX
Engex, Inc. [*Associated Press*] (SAG) .... Engex
Enghien-Moisselles [*France ICAO location identifier*] (ICLI) .... LFFE
Engin Teleguide Anti-Char [*Antitank Missile*] [*French*] .... ENTAC
Engine .... E
Engine (AFM) .... ENG
Engine .... ENG
Engine Acceleration Temperature Schedule .... EATS
Engine Air Intake Duct [*Hovercraft*] .... EAID
Engine Air Particle Separator .... EAPS
Engine Analytical Maintenance Program [*Navy*] (NVT) .... EAMP
Engine Analyzer Systems [*Air Force*] (MCD) .... EASY
Engine Analyzer Unit (DWSG) .... EAU
Engine and Electrical Engineering [*Automotive engineering*] .... EEE
Engine and Propeller Factor [*IOR*] [*Yacht racing*] .... EPF
Engine Angular Speed Variation [*Automotive engineering*] .... EASV

Engine Assembly ... EA
Engine Assembly Vehicle ... EAV
Engine Automatic Stop and Start System (PDAA) ... EASS
Engine Bleed Air Precooler System ... EBAPS
Engine Block Heater [*Automotive engineering*] ... EBH
Engine, Booster Maintenance Area ... EBMA
Engine Breather Separator ... EBS
Engine Bulletin (MCD) ... EB
Engine Burn [*NASA*] ... EB
Engine Calibration Unit [*Automotive engineering*] ... ECU
Engine Change (MCD) ... EC
Engine Change Kit ... ECK
Engine Change Unit (MCD) ... ECU
Engine Checkout System [*Aerospace*] (AAG) ... ECO
Engine Combustion (NASA) ... ECO
Engine Compartment Heater (AAG) ... ECH
Engine Computer Assembly [*Automotive engineering*] ... ECA
Engine Condition Monitoring ... ECM
Engine Configuration Management System ... ECMS
Engine Control (MCD) ... EC
Engine Control Development Area (KSC) ... ECDA
Engine Control Module [*General Motors' computer system*] ... ECM
Engine Control System [*Facetious translation: Expect Catastrophe Soon*] ... ECS
Engine Control Unit ... ECU
Engine Coolant Temperature [*Automotive engineering*] ... ECT
Engine Coolant Temperature Sensor [*Automotive engineering*] ... ECTS
Engine Cutoff [*Aerospace*] (MCD) ... EC
Engine Cutoff [*Aerospace*] (MCD) ... ECO
Engine Cutoff Timer [*Aerospace*] (KSC) ... ECT
Engine Deflector Nozzle ... EDN
Engine Designer (DS) ... ED
Engine Detector (MCD) ... EDET
Engine Diagnostic System ... EDS
Engine Drive (MSA) ... ED
Engine Driven Fire Pump (IEEE) ... EDFP
Engine Driven Hydraulic Pump (MCD) ... EDHP
Engine Drivers' Board of South Australia ... EDBSA
Engine Dynamometer Schedule [*Automotive emissions testing*] ... EDS
Engine Electronic Control (MCD) ... EEC
Engine Failure Sensing and Shutdown System [*NASA*] (KSC) ... EFSSS
Engine Firing Rate (NVT) ... EFR
Engine Flat Rate ... EFR
Engine Flight Hours ... EFH
Engine Fuel Economy Control System [*Automotive engineering*] ... EFECS
Engine Health Monitoring (MCD) ... EHM
Engine Health Monitoring System ... EHMS
Engine Heater [*Automotive accessory*] ... EH
Engine Hoods ... EH
Engine Identification Number [*Automotive engineering*] ... EIN
Engine Identification Report [*Air Force*] ... ENGID
Engine Indication and Crew Advisory System ... EICAS
Engine Indication and Crew Alerting System (MCD) ... EICAS
Engine In-Flight Condition Monitoring System (MCD) ... EICMS
Engine Installation Vehicle ... EIV
Engine Interface Unit (NASA) ... EIU
Engine Inventory Manager [*Air Force*] (AFIT) ... EIM
Engine Life Expectancy (NG) ... ELE
Engine Life Management Group [*Navy*] ... ELMG
Engine Life Management Simulation Model (PDAA) ... ELMSIM
Engine Logistics Planning Board [*Air Force*] (AFIT) ... ELPB
Engine Lube and Purge [*System*] ... ELP
Engine Lube Filter ... ELF
Engine Maintenance ... EM
Engine Maintenance Area (AAG) ... EMA
Engine Maintenance Assembly and Disassembly (GAAI) ... EMAD
Engine Maintenance Center (AAG) ... EMC
Engine Maintenance Reminder [*Automotive engineering*] ... EMR
Engine Management Display (MCD) ... EMD
Engine Management System [*Army*] ... EMS
Engine Manufacturers Association (EA) ... EMA
Engine Manufacturers' Committee (EAIO) ... EMC
Engine Mixture Ratio ... EMR
Engine Model Derivative Program [*Air Force*] (DOMA) ... EMDP
Engine Modification [*Automotive engineering*] ... EM
Engine Monitor Computer ... EMC
Engine Monitor Display (MCD) ... EMD
Engine Monitoring and Control System ... EMACS
Engine Monitoring System ... EMS
Engine Monitoring Unit [*Automotive electronics*] ... EMU
Engine Multiplexing Unit (MCD) ... EMU
Engine Negative Torque Control (MSA) ... ENTC
Engine Not Mission Capable - Supply (AFIT) ... ENG-NMCS
Engine Not Operationally Ready - Supply [*Air Force*] ... ENORS
Engine Oil ... EO
Engine Oil Filterability Test ... EOFT
Engine Oil Licensing and Certification System [*American Petroleum Institute*] ... EOLCS
Engine Oil Temperature [*Automotive engineering*] ... EOT
Engine Order ... EOR
Engine Order Capability (NASA) ... EOC
Engine Order Telegraph (DNAB) ... EOT
Engine Out (NASA) ... EO
Engine Out Capability (MCD) ... EOC
Engine Out of Commission for Parts ... EOCP
Engine Out Warning ... EOW
Engine over the Wing ... EOW
Engine Parts Coordinating Office [*Navy*] ... EPCO
Engine Performance Computer (PDAA) ... EPC
Engine Performance Indicator (NG) ... EPI
Engine Performance Monitoring System (MCD) ... EPMS
Engine Power [*or Pressure*] **Ratio** ... EPR
Engine Power Trim System ... EPTS
Engine Powertrain Management [*Automotive engineering*] ... EPM
Engine Pressure Ratio (GAVI) ... EPR
Engine Pressure Ratio Indicator ... EPRI
Engine Production and Information Control System (PDAA) ... EPICS
Engine Project Office [*NASA*] (KSC) ... EPO
Engine Propeller Order (MSA) ... EPO
Engine Relay Box (MCD) ... ERB
Engine Removal Report ... ERR
Engine Repair and Overhaul Squadron [*British Royal Air Force*] ... EROS
Engine Requisition and Build-Up Time (MCD) ... ERBUT
Engine Room (WDAA) ... ENG RM
Engine Room [*Force*] ... ER
Engine Room ... ERM
Engine Room Supervisor (DNAB) ... ERS
Engine Rotor Tester ... ERT
Engine Sequence Panel (AAG) ... ESP
Engine Service Association (EA) ... ESA
Engine Service Platform (KSC) ... ESP
Engine Service Unit (AAG) ... ESU
Engine Speed Synchronizer ... ESS
Engine Start after Launch [*Navy*] (CAAL) ... ESAL
Engine Start before Launch [*Navy*] (CAAL) ... ESBL
Engine Start Command (KSC) ... ESC
Engine Start Panel ... ESP
Engine Start Signal ... ESS
Engine Start System Maintenance Trainer (DWSG) ... ESSMT
Engine Status Report [*Air Force*] ... ENGSTAT
Engine Status Word (MCD) ... ESW
Engine Technical and Administrative Data System (PDAA) ... ETAADS
Engine Technical Commission ... ETC
Engine Test Chamber (MCD) ... ETC
Engine Test Facility [*Arnold Air Force Base, TN*] [*Air Force*] (MCD) ... ETF
Engine Test Information ... ETI
Engine Test Panel [*Aerospace*] (AAG) ... ETP
Engine Test Panel [*Aerospace*] (AAG) ... ET-PNL
Engine Test Stand [*Nevada*] [*Seismograph station code, US Geological Survey Closed*] (SEIS) ... ETS
Engine Test Stands [*NERVA program*] ... ETS
Engine Test Technology Centre [*Worcester, England*] ... ETTC
Engine Transaction Report (NVT) ... ETR
Engine Turned [*Watchmaking*] (ROG) ... ET
Engine V-Belt ... ENGV
Engine/Vehicle Test Stand ... E/VTS
Engine Vertical Scale ... EVS
Engine Vibration Monitor (MCD) ... EVM
Engine-Drive Compressor (DNAB) ... EDC
Engineer [*or Engineering*] ... E
Engineer [*or Engineering*] (EY) ... ENG
Engineer (GAGS) ... Eng
Engineer ... ENGNR
Engineer ... ENGR
Engineer (PGP) ... Engr
Engineer Acquisition Letter (AAGC) ... EAL
Engineer Agency for Resources Inventories [*Army Corps of Engineers*] ... EARI
Engineer Amphibian Command [*World War II*] ... EAC
Engineer and Railway Volunteer Staff Corps [*Army British*] ... ERVSC
Engineer/Architect (DAC) ... E/A
Engineer Automation Support Activity [*Army Corps of Engineers*] ... EASA
Engineer Aviation Battalion [*Military*] ... EABN
Engineer Aviation Unit Training Center [*Military*] ... EAUTC
Engineer Battalion [*Military*] ... EB
Engineer Battalion [*Military*] ... ENGBAT
Engineer Battalion [*Military*] ... ENGRBN
Engineer Battlefield Assessment [*Military*] (INF) ... EBA
Engineer Boat and Shore Regiment [*Army*] ... EB & SR
Engineer Boat and Shore Regiment [*Army*] ... EBSR
Engineer Buyers' and Representatives' Association [*British*] ... EBRA
Engineer Captain [*Navy British*] ... EC
Engineer Change Order Request (AAG) ... ECOR
Engineer Circular [*Army Corps of Engineers*] ... EC
Engineer Cognizant Authority ... ECA
Engineer Combat Battalions (CINC) ... ECBS
Engineer Command [*Army*] (DOMA) ... ENCOM
Engineer Command and Control Automation System [*Army*] (RDA) ... ECCAS
Engineer Command and Control System [*Software*] ... ECCS
Engineer Commander [*Navy British*] (ROG) ... E CR
Engineer Commissioner, District of Columbia [*Military*] (AABC) ... ENGCOMDC
Engineer Construction Battalion (CINC) ... ECB
Engineer Construction Command [*Army*] ... ENCOM
Engineer Control and Advisory Detachment [*Air Force*] ... ECAD
Engineer District, Far East (CINC) ... EDFE
Engineer Element ... ENGRE
Engineer Equipment Maintenance Repair Platoon (DNAB) ... ENGREQUIPMAINTRPRPLT
Engineer Family of Systems Study (MCD) ... EFOSS
Engineer Federal Acquisition Regulation Supplement [*A publication*] (AAGC) ... EFARS
Engineer Functional Components System (AABC) ... EFCS

Engineer, Furnish, and Install ... EF & I
Engineer Group, Construction [*Military*] ... EGC
Engineer Hill [*Alaska*] [*Seismograph station code, US Geological Survey*] (SEIS) ... ENG
Engineer Historical Division [*Army*] ... EHD
Engineer in Aeronautics and Astronautics ... EAA
Engineer in Electrical Engineering ... E in EE
Engineer in Mechanical Engineering ... E in ME
Engineer Information and Data Systems Office [*Army*] (AABC) ... EIDSO
Engineer Inspector [*Navy British*] (ROG) ... E INS
Engineer Intelligence Note ... EIN
Engineer Lieutenant [*Navy British*] ... EL
Engineer Lieutenant [*Navy British*] (DMA) ... En L
Engineer Lieutenant [*Navy British*] (ROG) ... ENG-LT
Engineer Lieutenant-Commander [*Navy British*] ... ELCR
Engineer Lieutenant-Commander [*Navy British*] (DMA) ... En L Cr
Engineer Maintenance Center ... EMC
Engineer Maintenance Co. [*Military*] (DNAB) ... ENGRMAINTCO
Engineer Maintenance Control [*Army*] ... EMC
Engineer Manager ... EM
Engineer Manual [*Army Corps of Engineers*] ... EM
Engineer of Metallurgy ... E Met
Engineer of Mines [*or Mining*] ... EM
Engineer Officer [*Navy British*] ... ENG
Engineer Officer [*Navy British*] ... EO
Engineer Officers Reserve Corps ... ENGORC
Engineer Packaging Technical Office [*Merged with General Equipment Command*] ... EPTO
Engineer Pamphlet [*Army Corps of Engineers*] ... EP
Engineer Performance Description Form [*Test*] ... EPDF
Engineer Personnel [*Marine Corps*] ... EP
Engineer Photographic and Reproduction [*Marine Corps*] ... EPR
Engineer Platoon (DNAB) ... ENGRPLT
Engineer Procurement Office [*Army*] ... EPCO
Engineer Reactors Group [*Army*] ... ERG
Engineer Rear-Admiral [*Navy British*] ... EA
Engineer Rear-Admiral [*Navy British*] ... ERA
Engineer Rear-Admiral [*Navy British*] (DMA) ... RA(E)
Engineer Relations [*ACE*] (AAGC) ... ER
Engineer Repair Parts Packaging Office [*Merged with General Equipment Command*] ... ERPPO
Engineer Replacement Training Center ... ERTC
Engineer Restructuring Initiative [*Army*] ... ERI
Engineer, Royal Naval Artillery [*Navy British*] (ROG) ... ERNA
Engineer/Service [*Aerospace*] (AAG) ... E/S
Engineer/Service Test [*Aerospace*] (MCD) ... EST
Engineer/Service Test Office [*Aerospace*] ... ESTO
Engineer Special Brigade [*Military*] ... ESB
Engineer Specialized Services ... ESS
Engineer Stores Assignment [*British*] ... ESA
Engineer Strategic Studies Group [*Army*] (AABC) ... ESSG
Engineer Studies Center (MCD) ... ESC
Engineer Studies Group [*Office of the Chief of Engineers*] ... ESG
Engineer Sub-Lieutenant [*Navy British*] (DMA) ... En SL
Engineer Sub-Lieutenant [*Navy British*] (ROG) ... ESL
Engineer Support Battalion (DNAB) ... ENGRSPTBN
Engineer Surveyors' Association [*A union*] [*British*] ... ESA
Engineer Technical Letter [*Army Corps of Engineers*] ... ETL
Engineer Technical Letter [*ACE*] (AAGC) ... ETR
Engineer Test/Service Test [*Aerospace*] ... ET/ST
Engineer Topographic Laboratories [*Fort Belvoir, VA*] [*Army*] (MCD) ... ETL
Engineer Training ... ET
Engineer/User [*Aerospace*] (AAG) ... E/U
Engineer Vice-Admiral [*British*] ... EVA
Engineer Volunteer Corps [*British*] ... EVC
Engineer Volunteers [*British military*] (DMA) ... EV
Engineered ... ENGRD
Engineered Australia Plan Party [*Political party*] ... EAPP
Engineered Average Monthly Demand [*Military*] ... EAMD
Engineered Barrier System [*Waste disposal*] ... EBS
Engineered Fasteners Division [*Townsend Co.*] ... EFD
Engineered Materials Abstracts [*Materials Information*] [*Information service or system A publication*] ... EMA
Engineered Military Circuit [*Leased long lines established in continental US*] [*Military*] ... EMC
Engineered Operating Cycle ... EOC
Engineered Polypropylene [*Plastics*] [*Automotive engineering*] ... EPP
Engineered Restoration Procedure ... ERP
Engineered Safeguards [*Nuclear energy*] (NRCH) ... ES
Engineered Safeguards Actuation System [*Nuclear energy*] (NRCH) ... ESAS
Engineered Safety Feature [*Nuclear energy*] (NRCH) ... ESF
Engineered Safety Feature Actuation [*Nuclear energy*] (NRCH) ... ESFA
Engineered Safety Feature Ventilation System [*Nuclear energy*] (NRCH) ... ESFVS
Engineered Safety Features Actuation System [*Nuclear energy*] (NRCH) ... ESFAS
Engineered Safety Features System [*Nuclear energy*] (NRCH) ... ESFS
Engineered Safety System (IEEE) ... ESS
Engineered Support Sys [*NASDAQ symbol*] (TTSB) ... EASI
Engineered Support Systems, Inc. [*NASDAQ symbol*] (NQ) ... EASI
Engineered Support Systems, Inc. [*Associated Press*] (SAG) ... EngnSu
Engineered Time Standards (NG) ... ETS
Engineer-in-Charge [*Army*] ... E in C
Engineer-in-Charge ... EIC
Engineer-In-Charge [*Television*] (WDMC) ... E-I-C
Engineer-in-Chief ... E in C
Engineer-in-Chief's Department [*British military*] (DMA) ... E-in-CD
Engineering (DD) ... eng
Engineering [*A publication*] (DLA) ... Eng'g
Engineering (WGA) ... ENGG
Engineering ... ENGIN
Engineering ... ENGING
Engineering ... ENGN
Engineering ... ENGNG
Engineering ... ENGRG
Engineering ... ENGRG
Engineering ... ENGRING
Engineering Abstract Report [*Defense Supply Agency*] ... EAR
Engineering Accreditation Commission of the Accreditation Board for Engineering Technology ... EAC/ABET
Engineering Administration and Operations Control [*Military*] ... EA & OC
Engineering Administrative Data Systems (MCD) ... EADS
Engineering Advance Material Release (KSC) ... EAMR
Engineering Aid [*Navy rating*] ... EA
Engineering Aid, Chief [*Navy rating*] ... EAC
Engineering Aid, Draftsman [*Navy rating Obsolete*] ... EAD
Engineering Aid, First Class [*Navy rating*] ... EA1
Engineering Aid, Master Chief [*Navy rating*] ... EACM
Engineering Aid, Second Class [*Navy rating*] ... EA2
Engineering Aid, Senior Chief [*Navy rating*] ... EACS
Engineering Aid, Surveyor [*Navy rating Obsolete*] ... EAS
Engineering Aid, Third Class [*Navy rating*] ... EA3
Engineering Alumni Recruiting Network ... EARN
Engineering Analysis and Simulation Language [*Computer science*] ... EASL
Engineering Analysis Data System ... EADS
Engineering Analysis Facility (SSD) ... EAF
Engineering Analysis Report (KSC) ... EAR
Engineering Analysis Services [*Auto industry supplier*] ... EAS
Engineering Analysis Team [*NASA*] ... EAT
Engineering and Acquisition ... E & A
Engineering and Administrative Data Acquisition System [*Bell System*] ... EADAS
Engineering and Architects Association ... EAA
Engineering and Architecture, Indian and Northern Affairs Canada [*Genie et Architecture, Affaires Indiennes et du Nord Canada*], Edmonton, Alberta [*Library symbol National Library of Canada*] (BIB) ... AEINE
Engineering & Business (DD) ... Eng&Bus
Engineering and Construction ... E & C
Engineering and Development Directorate [*Johnson Space Center*] [*NASA*] (NASA) ... E & D
Engineering and Development Directorate [*Johnson Space Center*] [*NASA*] ... EDD
Engineering and Development Services Department [*Naval Air Development Center*] ... EDSD
Engineering and Development Support Services (KSC) ... EDSS
Engineering and Economic Research Technologies, Inc., Ottawa, Ontario [*Library symbol National Library of Canada*] (BIB) ... OOEE
Engineering and Industrial Research Station [*Mississippi State University*] [*Research center*] (RCD) ... EIRS
Engineering and Industrial Software Directory [*Engineering Information, Inc.*] [*Information service or system*] (CRD) ... EISD
Engineering and Laboratory (KSC) ... E & L
Engineering and Logistics Management Office [*MERDC*] [*Army*] ... ELMO
Engineering and Manufacturing Development [*Military*] ... EMD
Engineering and Manufacturing Instructions (NRCH) ... EMI
Engineering and Mine Warfare [*Army*] ... EMW
Engineering and Operations Building [*NASA*] ... EOB
Engineering and Operations Training [*Navy*] ... EOT
Engineering and Physical Sciences Research Council [*British*] ... EPSRC
Engineering and Product Development Work Order ... EPDWO
Engineering and Public Policy [*Graduate program, Carnegie-Mellon University*] ... EPP
Engineering and Repair [*Department*] [*Navy*] ... E & R
Engineering and Research (IAA) ... EAR
Engineering and Science Network on Thinking (EA) ... ESNETT
Engineering and Scientific Career Continuation Pay [*Air Force*] ... ESCCP
Engineering and Scientific Interpreter (IEEE) ... ESI
Engineering and Scientific Support System [*IBM Corp.*] ... E/S^3
Engineering and Services Laboratory [*Tyndall Air Force Base, FL*] [*Air Force*] (GRD) ... ESL
Engineering and Society ... ES
Engineering and Statistical Research Centre, Agriculture Canada [*Centre de Recherche Technique et de Statistique, Agriculture Canada*] **Ottawa, Ontario** [*Library symbol National Library of Canada*] (NLC) ... OOAGER
Engineering and Statistical Research Institute [*Canada*] (ARC) ... ESRI
Engineering and Stores Association [*A union*] [*British*] ... F & SA
Engineering and Systems Analysis for the Control of Toxics Technology Center [*University of California at Los Angeles*] [*Research center*] (RCD) ... ESACT
Engineering and Technical Service (AFM) ... ETS
Engineering and Technical Services Specialist [*DoD*] ... ETSS
Engineering and Training Center [*NASA*] (KSC) ... ETC
Engineering and Water Supply Department [*South Australia*] ... EWSD
Engineering Animation [*NASDAQ symbol*] (TTSB) ... EAII
Engineering Application of Computer Technology ... ENACT
Engineering Applications Centre [*University of Strathclyde*] [*British*] (CB) ... EAC
Engineering Applications for Support Engineers [*British*] ... EASE
Engineering Approved Source List ... EASL
Engineering Aspects of Magnetohydrodynamics [*A publication*] (MCD) ... EAMHD
Engineering Assembly Parts List ... EAPL
Engineering Assignment ... EA
Engineering Assistant ... EGA

Engineering Associate of the Society of Engineers, Inc. [British] (DBQ) .... ESE
Engineering Automated Release and Record System (MCD) .... EARRS
Engineering Automated Systems (MCD) .... EAS
Engineering Automatic System for Solving Equations .... EASE
Engineering Automation and Control (PCM) .... EAC
Engineering Bulletin (MCD) .... EB
Engineering Bulletin Board System .... EBBS
Engineering Capacity Exchange (IEEE) .... ECE
Engineering Careers Information Service (AIE) .... ECIS
Engineering Careers Information System .... ECIS
Engineering Casualty Control [Military] (NVT) .... ECC
Engineering Casualty Control Evaluation Team [Navy] (ANA) .... ECCET
Engineering Casualty Control Training Team [Navy] .... ECCTT
Engineering CATT [Army] (RDA) .... ENCATT
Engineering Center .... ENGRCEN
Engineering Center for Automated Manufacturing Technology [Clemson University] [Research center] (RCD) .... CAM
Engineering Central Files .... ECF
Engineering Change (MCD) .... EC
Engineering Change Analysis .... ECA
Engineering Change Announcement .... ECA
Engineering Change Authorization .... ECA
Engineering Change Automation System .... ECAS
Engineering Change Control .... ECC
Engineering Change Control Board (NASA) .... ECCB
Engineering Change Coordination (MCD) .... ECC
Engineering Change Identity Parts List [McDonnell Douglas Aircraft Corp.] .... ECIPL
Engineering Change Incorporation (AAG) .... ECI
Engineering Change Information .... ECI
Engineering Change Instruction .... ECI
Engineering Change List (MCD) .... ECL
Engineering Change Management-Development .... ECM-D
Engineering Change Memo (KSC) .... ECM
Engineering Change Notice .... ECN
Engineering Change Order .... ECO
Engineering Change Order Factor (MCD) .... ECOF
Engineering Change Program .... ECP
Engineering Change Proposal .... ECP
Engineering Change Proposal Service Action Status (AAG) .... EXPSAS
Engineering Change Proposal System (DNAB) .... ECPS
Engineering Change Proposal Work Statement (AAG) .... ECPWS
Engineering Change Proposal-Software .... ECP-S
Engineering Change Report (KSC) .... ECR
Engineering Change [or Correction] Request [or Requirement] .... ECR
Engineering Change Request and Record (MCD) .... ECRR
Engineering Change Request/Authorization (AFM) .... ECR/A
Engineering Change Schedule (AAG) .... ECS
Engineering Change Sheet (NATG) .... ECS
Engineering Change Summary .... ECS
Engineering Cognizant Authority (MCD) .... EC
Engineering College Administrative Council .... ECAC
Engineering College Magazines Associated (EA) .... ECMA
Engineering College Research Council (EA) .... ECRC
Engineering Command (AAG) .... ENC
Engineering Command (MCD) .... ENGCOM
Engineering Committee for the American Bicentennial .... ECAB
Engineering Committee on Oceanic Research (USDC) .... ECOR
Engineering Committee on Oceanic Resources [Later, SUT] [United Nations] .... ECOR
Engineering Computer Laboratory [University of Southern California] [Research center] (RCD) .... ECL
Engineering Concept Review .... ECR
Engineering Concepts Curriculum Project .... ECCP
Engineering Concern Action Report [Industrial engineering] .... ECAR
Engineering Configuration Data Control (AAG) .... ECDC
Engineering Configuration List (MCD) .... ECL
Engineering Construction .... EC
Engineering Construction and Related Industries Manpower [British] .... ECRIM
Engineering Contractors Association (EA) .... ECA
Engineering Control Board (AAG) .... ECB
Engineering Control Distribution Report (MCD) .... ECDR
Engineering Control Drawing (MCD) .... ECD
Engineering Control Office [Telecommunications] (TEL) .... ECO
Engineering Control Proposal .... ECP
Engineering Control System .... ECS
Engineering Coordination Memorandum [Military] .... ECM
Engineering Corps .... EC
Engineering Council (ACII) .... EC
Engineering Council Regional Organisation Committee (ACII) .... ECROC
Engineering Craftsmen's Guild [A union] [British] .... ECG
Engineering Critical (MCD) .... EC
Engineering Critical Component (KSC) .... ECC
Engineering Data .... ED
Engineering Data Bank [GIDEP] .... EDB
Engineering Data Bank System (MCD) .... EDBS
Engineering Data Computer-Assisted Retrieval System [Air Force] (GFGA) .... EDCARS
Engineering Data Control .... EDC
Engineering Data Depository (MSA) .... EDD
Engineering Data File .... EDF
Engineering Data Information System (IEEE) .... EDIS
Engineering Data Management .... EDM
Engineering Data Management Information Control System [DoD] .... EDMICS

Engineering Data Management System [Jet Propulsion Laboratory, NASA] .... EDMS
Engineering Data Microreproduction System [DoD] .... EDMS
Engineering Data Package [Air Force] (AFIT) .... EDP
Engineering Data Plotting [Computer science] .... EDPLOT
Engineering Data Requirements (AAG) .... EDR
Engineering Data Retrieval System [Military] .... EDRS
Engineering Data Service Center [Air Force] .... EDSC
Engineering Data Sheet .... EDS
Engineering Data Software .... EDS
Engineering Data Storage and Retrieval [Military] .... EDS & R
Engineering Data Storage and Retrieval Project [Picatinny Arsenal] [Dover, NJ] [Military] .... EDS/R
Engineering Data Support Center [Air Force] (CET) .... EDSC
Engineering Data Systems [DoD] .... EDS
Engineering Decision Integrator and Communicator .... EDIAC
Engineering Demonstrated Inspection (AAG) .... EDI
Engineering Department [Navy British] .... ED
Engineering Department Interface Control Task [or Technique] .... EDICT
Engineering Department Notice (AAG) .... EDN
Engineering Department [or Division] Report .... EDR
Engineering Department Sketch (MSA) .... ED SK
Engineering Depot .... ED
Engineering Description Tape (IAA) .... EDT
Engineering Design .... ED
Engineering Design Advance Information (DNAB) .... EDAI
Engineering Design and Analysis Laboratory [University of New Hampshire] [Research center] (RCD) .... EDAL
Engineering Design and Analysis Laboratory Habitat .... EDALHAB
Engineering, Design, and Inspection .... ED & I
Engineering Design and Simulation System [Graphic Data Ltd.] [Software package] (NCC) .... EDAS
Engineering Design Change .... EDC
Engineering Design Change Proposal .... EDCP
Engineering Design Change Request (MCD) .... EDCR
Engineering Design Change Schedule .... EDCS
Engineering Design Data (AAG) .... EDD
Engineering Design Data Package (AAG) .... EDDP
Engineering Design Documentation Procedures (MCD) .... EDDP
Engineering Design Handbook (MCD) .... EDH
Engineering Design Handbook Series (MCD) .... EDHS
Engineering Design Integration System [NASA] (MCD) .... EDIN
Engineering Design Machine .... EDM
Engineering Design Memorandum .... EDM
Engineering Design Plan .... EDP
Engineering Design Proposal (AAG) .... EDP
Engineering Design Research Center [Pittsburgh, PA] [National Science Foundation] (GRD) .... EDRC
Engineering Design Review (NASA) .... EDR
Engineering Design Review Board (SAA) .... EDRB
Engineering Design Support to Production (MCD) .... EDSP
Engineering Design Test .... EDT
Engineering Design Test and Evaluation Program .... EDTEP
Engineering Design Test, Contractor (MCD) .... EDTC
Engineering Design Test, Government (MCD) .... EDTG
Engineering Development .... ED
Engineering Development and Test Center [Mack Trucks, Inc.] [Allentown, PA] .... EDTC
Engineering Development Division [Marine science] (OSRA) .... EDD
Engineering Development Division [Pacific Marine Environmental Laboratory] (USDC) .... EDD
Engineering Development Establishment [Australia] .... EDE
Engineering Development Integration Test .... EDIT
Engineering Development Integration Test Program (IAA) .... EDITP
Engineering Development Laboratory .... EDL
Engineering Development Laboratory Program (KSC) .... EDLP
Engineering Development Logic Network (NASA) .... EDLN
Engineering Development Model .... EDM
Engineering Development Part Release (KSC) .... EDPR
Engineering Development Phase (OAG) .... EDP
Engineering Development Systems Integration Laboratory .... EDSIL
Engineering Development Test .... EDT
Engineering Development Unit [NASA] (NASA) .... EDU
Engineering Directive (NASA) .... ED
Engineering Discrepancy Notice [Nuclear energy] (NRCH) .... EDN
Engineering Division .... ED
Engineering Document .... ED
Engineering Document Control System (HGAA) .... EDCS
Engineering Document [or Drawing] Information Collection Task [or Technique] .... EDICT
Engineering Document Management System [Computer science] .... EDMS
Engineering Documentation Center [NASA] (KSC) .... EDC
Engineering Drafting Machine .... EDM
Engineering Drafting Manual [Air Force] .... EDM
Engineering Drafting Software [Calcomp Ltd.] [Software package] (NCC) .... EDS
Engineering Draftsman .... ED
Engineering Drawing and Assembly Release Record (AAG) .... EDARR
Engineering Drawing Change Notice [Nuclear energy] (NRCH) .... EDCN
Engineering Drawing List .... EDL
Engineering Drawing Microfilm (MCD) .... EDM
Engineering Drawing Release .... EDR
Engineering Drawing Release Authorization .... EDRA
Engineering Drawing Status and Release (DNAB) .... EDSAR
Engineering Drawing Tree .... EDT
Engineering Drawing Usage Record [DAC] .... EDUR

Engineering Drawings to Automatic Control Tapes (PDAA) ...... EDACT
Engineering Duty [Navy] .... ED
Engineering Duty Officer [Military] .... EDO
Engineering Duty Officer School [Military] (DNAB) .... EDOSCOL
Engineering Duty Only [Aerospace] .... EDO
Engineering Economic Cost Analysis (MCD) .... EECA
Engineering Economics .... EE
Engineering Electronics Laboratory .... EEL
Engineering Employers' Association, South Australia .... EEASA
Engineering Employers' Federation [British] (DCTA) .... EEF
Engineering Equation Solver [Macintosh] [Computer science] ...... EES
Engineering Equipment and Materials User's Association [British] .... EEMUA
Engineering Equipment Users' Association [British] (BI) ...... EEUA
Engineering Error (WDAA) .... ENG ERR
Engineering Estimate .... EE
Engineering Evaluation Article (AAG) .... EEA
Engineering Evaluation/Cost Analysis (DOGT) .... EE/CA
Engineering Evaluation Model (KSC) .... EEM
Engineering Evaluation Test (NG) .... EET
Engineering Experiment Station [University of Missouri, Columbia] [Research center] (RCD) .... EES
Engineering Experimental Memo .... EEM
Engineering Experimental Phase [National Data Buoy Project] .... EEP
Engineering Facilities Depot .... EFD
Engineering Facility .... ENGRFAC
Engineering Factory Support Equipment (SAA) .... EFSE
Engineering Feasibility Model (MCD) .... EFM
Engineering Feasibility Test (CAAL) .... EFT
Engineering Field Activity (MCD) .... EFA
Engineering Field Bulletin (MCD) .... EFB
Engineering Field Change (MSA) .... EFC
Engineering Field Divisions [Military] .... EFD
Engineering Flight Test .... EFT
Engineering Flight Test Inspector .... EFTI
Engineering Flight Test Instrumentation (AAG) .... EFTI
Engineering Flight Test Report .... EFTR
Engineering Flow Diagram (NRCH) .... EFD
Engineering Foundation (EA) .... EF
Engineering Geologist .... EG
Engineering Headquarters, Canadian Broadcasting Corp. [Service de l'Ingenierie, Societe Radio-Canada] Montreal, Quebec [Library symbol National Library of Canada] (NLC) .... QMCBE
Engineering in Medicine and Biology (MCD) .... EMB
Engineering Index (ECII) .... EI
Engineering Index Thesaurus [A publication] .... EIT
Engineering Industries Association [British] (EAIO) .... EIA
Engineering Industries Export Intelligence Officer [British] (DI) ...... EIEIO
Engineering Industries Internalisation Program [Australia] ...... EIIP
Engineering Industry Training Board [British] .... EITB
Engineering Information [An association Also, an information service or system] (EA) .... Ei
Engineering Information Center .... EIC
Engineering Information Meetings (NITA) .... EIMET
Engineering Information Report [Telecommunications] (TEL) ...... EIR
Engineering Information Report Date [Telecommunications] (TEL) ...... EIRD
Engineering Information Request [Nuclear energy] (NRCH) ...... EIR
Engineering Information System (MCD) .... EIS
Engineering Inspectors' Association [A union] [British] ...... EIA
Engineering Installation Center [Military] .... EIC
Engineering Installation Division [Military] .... EID
Engineering Installation Group [Military] .... EIG
Engineering Installation Management System [Air Force] (CET) ...... EIMS
Engineering Installation Plan (CET) .... EIP
Engineering Installation Workload Schedule (CET) .... EIWS
Engineering Institute of Canada .... EIC
Engineering Institute of Canada, Montreal, PQ, Canada [Library symbol Library of Congress Obsolete] (LCLS) ...... CaQME
Engineering Instruction .... EI
Engineering Instruction Bulletin (KSC) .... EIB
Engineering Instrumentation Requirements Document ...... EIRD
Engineering Investigation (MCD) .... EI
Engineering Investigation Request .... EIR
Engineering Item (MCD) .... EI
Engineering Item Description (AAG) .... EID
Engineering Item Identification .... EII
Engineering Job Analysis (KSC) .... EJA
Engineering Job Order (MCD) .... EJO
Engineering Job Sheet (MCD) .... EJS
Engineering Job Ticket .... EJT
Engineering Joint Council Thesaurus (NITA) .... EJCT
Engineering Laboratories [Army] (MCD) .... EL
Engineering Laboratory Report .... ELR
Engineering Laboratory Technician .... ELT
Engineering Letter [Telecommunications] (TEL) .... EL
Engineering Liaison Request (KSC) .... ELR
Engineering Library, Bell Helicopter Textron, Ste. Therese, Quebec [Library symbol National Library of Canada] (NLC) ...... QSTTB
Engineering Library, Canadair Ltd., Montreal, Quebec [Library symbol National Library of Canada] (NLC) ...... QMCA
Engineering Library, City of Calgary, Alberta [Library symbol National Library of Canada] (BIB) ...... ACE
Engineering Library, Garrett Canada, Rexdale, Ontario [Library symbol National Library of Canada] (BIB) ...... OTGAR
Engineering Library, University of New Brunswick, Fredericton [Library symbol National Library of Canada] (BIB) ...... NBFUE

Engineering Library, University of Toronto, Ontario [Library symbol National Library of Canada] (NLC) ...... OTUE
Engineering Library, University of Western Ontario, London, Ontario [Library symbol National Library of Canada] (BIB) ...... OLUE
Engineering Logic Diagram .... ELD
Engineering Lunar Model Obstacle [NASA] (PDAA) .... ELMO
Engineering Lunar Model Surface .... ELMS
Engineering Maintenance Officer (DNAB) .... EMO
Engineering Malfunction Report (MCD) .... EMR
Engineering Management (MCD) .... EM
Engineering Management Information System [Defense Supply Agency] ..... EMIS
Engineering Management Information Technique .... EMIT
Engineering Management Manual .... EMM
Engineering Management Network (NASA) .... EMN
Engineering Management Requirements Special [McAir] ...... EMRS
Engineering Manpower Commission (EA) .... EMC
Engineering Manual (IEEE) .... EM
Engineering Manual Preparation Instruction [Army Materiel Command] ...... EMPI
Engineering Manufacturing Liaison Release (KSC) .... EMLR
Engineering Master Drawing (MCD) .... EMD
Engineering Master Parts List (KSC) .... EMPL
Engineering Master Schedule .... EMS
Engineering Material Specification .... ESM
Engineering Materials Characterization Research Facility [Louisiana State University] [Research center] (RCD) ...... EMCRF
Engineering Materials List [Nuclear energy] .... EML
Engineering Materials Research Laboratory [Brown University] (PDAA) ...... EMRL
Engineering, Mathematics, and Physical Sciences [Military] ...... EMP
Engineering Measurements Co. [NASDAQ symbol] (NQ) ...... EMCO
Engineering Measurements Co. [Associated Press] (SAG) ...... EngMea
Engineering Measure't [NASDAQ symbol] (TTSB) .... EMCO
Engineering Mechanician .... EM
Engineering Mechanics Division [American Society of Civil Engineers] (MCD) ...... EMD
Engineering Mechanics Laboratory [National Institute of Standards and Technology] (IEEE) ...... EML
Engineering Mechanics Research Laboratory [Texas University] (MCD) ...... EMRL
Engineering Memorandum .... EM
Engineering Methods Analysis (MCD) .... EMA
Engineering Mock-Up .... EMU
Engineering Mock-Up and Manufacturing Aid (MCD) ...... EMMA
Engineering Mock-Up Critical Experiment [Nuclear energy] (NRCH) ...... EMC
Engineering Mock-Up Work Order .... EMWO
Engineering Model .... EM
Engineering Model Configuration Inspection (MCD) .... EMCI
Engineering Model Transport .... EMT
Engineering Model Unit [NASA] (NASA) .... EMU
Engineering Modification Proposal (NG) .... EMP
Engineering Modification Requirements (MCD) .... EMR
Engineering Module (NASA) .... EM
Engineering Narrative Report [Defense Supply Agency] ...... ENR
Engineering Next Assembly (MCD) .... ENA
Engineering Note [or Notice] .... EN
Engineering of Complex Computer Systems .... ECCS
Engineering Officer of the Watch [Navy] .... EEOW
Engineering Officer of the Watch [Navy] (NVT) .... EOOW
Engineering Officers Reserve Corps .... EORC
Engineering Officers' (Telecommunications) Association [British] ...... EO(T)A
Engineering Operating Directives (MCD) .... EOD
Engineering Operating Procedure (MCD) .... EOP
Engineering Operating Station [Military] (CAAL) .... EOS
Engineering Operating System .... EOS
Engineering Operational Casualty Control (NVT) .... EOCC
Engineering Operational Sequence System (DNAB) .... EOSS
Engineering/Operations [NASA] (NASA) .... E/O
Engineering Operations Control (MCD) .... EOC
Engineering Operations Division [Environmental Protection Agency] (GFGA) ...... EOD
Engineering/Operations - Information Management System (NASA) ...... E/O-IMS
Engineering Operations Manual [NASA] (NASA) .... EOM
Engineering Order .... EO
Engineering Order .... EO
Engineering Order Delayed for Parts .... EODP
Engineering Order List of Material Revision (MCD) .... EOMR
Engineering Order Map Correction (MCD) .... EOMC
Engineering Order Material Revision Data Collection (MCD) ...... EOMC
Engineering Order Purchase Request (SAA) .... EOPR
Engineering Order Request for Quotation (SAA) .... EORQ
Engineering Order Worksheet .... EOW
Engineering Paper .... EP
Engineering Part Card .... EPC
Engineering Part Number [Automotive engineering] .... EPN
Engineering Parts List (KSC) .... EPL
Engineering Parts List/Drawing Release List (KSC) ...... EPL/DRL
Engineering Parts Release (KSC) .... EPR
Engineering Performance Management System (NASA) ...... EPMS
Engineering Performance Measurement System (MCD) ...... EPMS
Engineering Performance Standards .... EPS
Engineering Personnel [Coast Guard] .... EP
Engineering Phase (MCD) .... EP
Engineering, Planning, and Analysis Systems [Telecommunications] (TEL) ...... EPLANS
Engineering Planning Document .... EPD
Engineering Planning Report .... EPR
Engineering Planning Skeleton (MCD) .... EPS

Engineering Power Reactor ... EPR
Engineering Practice (NG) ... EP
Engineering Practice Amendment (AAG) ... EPA
Engineering Print (KSC) ... EP
Engineering Print System [*Xerox*] ... EPS
Engineering Procedure ... EP
Engineering Procedure Directive ... EPD
Engineering Procedure Memorandum [*Nuclear Regulatory Commission*] (GFGA) ... EPM
Engineering Procedures Manual ... EPM
Engineering Procedures Services (MCD) ... EPS
Engineering Process Bulletin ... EPB
Engineering, Procurement, and Construction ... EPC
Engineering Product Assumptions ... EPA
Engineering Program Definition Plan (MCD) ... EPDP
Engineering Program Notice (AFIT) ... EPN
Engineering Project ... EP
Engineering Project Management System (MCD) ... EPMS
Engineering Proposal ... EP
Engineering Purchase Specification ... EPS
Engineering Qualification Test ... EQT
Engineering Qualification Trials (DOMA) ... EPQ
Engineering Quality ... EQ
Engineering Quality Improvement ... EQUIP
Engineering Record ... ER
Engineering Records Organisation System [*Applied Research of Cambridge Ltd.*] [*Software package*] (NCC) ... EROS
Engineering Reference Branch [*Department of the Interior*] ... ERB
Engineering Reference Number ... ERN
Engineering Regional Organisation (ACII) ... ERO
Engineering Regulations [*A publication*] ... ER
Engineering Release (MCD) ... ER
Engineering Release ... ER
Engineering Release Authorization ... ERA
Engineering Release Change Record ... ERCR
Engineering Release for Vendor Article Data [*Later, PRVD*] (AAG) ... ERVAD
Engineering Release Group (AAG) ... ERG
Engineering Release Notice (MSA) ... ERN
Engineering Release Operations (NASA) ... ERO
Engineering Release Order [*Formerly, ROD*] ... ERO
Engineering Release Package ... ERP
Engineering Release Record (AAG) ... ERR
Engineering Release System ... ERS
Engineering Release Ticket ... ERT
Engineering Release Work Sheet (AAG) ... ERWS
Engineering Reliability and Quality Control (AAG) ... ERQC
Engineering Reliability Review (MCD) ... ERR
Engineering Rental Agreement ... ERA
Engineering Report ... ER
Engineering Reprographic Management Association [*Later, ERS*] ... ERMA
Engineering Reprographic Society (EA) ... ERS
Engineering Request Authorization (AAG) ... ERA
Engineering Requirements and Procedures Manual (MCD) ... ERPM
Engineering Requirements Plan [*for Military Assistance Programs*] ... ERP
Engineering Research and Development Center [*University of Nevada, Reno*] [*Research center*] (RCD) ... ERDC
Engineering, Research and Development Service [*FAA*] (TAG) ... ACD
Engineering Research Associates (MCD) ... ERA
Engineering Research Center [*New Mexico State University*] (RCD) ... ERC
Engineering Research Center for Composites Manufacturing Science and Engineering [*Newark, DE*] [*Army*] (GRD) ... CCM
Engineering Research Council (NRCH) ... ERC
Engineering Research Initiation Program [*National Science Foundation*] ... ERIP
Engineering Research Institute [*Iowa State University*] [*Research center*] (AAG) ... ERI
Engineering Research Report ... ERR
Engineering Research Services Division [*North Carolina State University*] [*Research center*] (RCD) ... ERSD
Engineering Research Station [*British*] ... ERS
Engineering Resins Information System [*General Electric Co.*] ... ERIS
Engineering Review Board [*NASA*] (NASA) ... ERB
Engineering Route [*Telecommunications*] (TEL) ... ER
Engineering Schedule Memorandum ... ESM
Engineering Schedule Plan ... ESP
Engineering Schoolship [*Navy*] (NVT) ... ENGSS
Engineering Science (DD) ... EngSc
Engineering, Science, and Management War Training ... ESMWT
Engineering, Science, and Management War Training Program (HGAA) ... ESMWTP
Engineering Sciences Data Unit ... ESDU
Engineering Sequential Camera (KSC) ... ESC
Engineering Sequential Camera Coverage (KSC) ... ESCC
Engineering Service Circuit ... ESC
Engineering Service [*or Support*] **Group** (AAG) ... ESG
Engineering Service Memorandum (MCD) ... ESM
Engineering Service Order (AAG) ... ESO
Engineering Service Project (MCD) ... ESP
Engineering Service Publications (AAG) ... ESP
Engineering Service Requests (MUGU) ... ESR
Engineering/Service Test and Independent Evaluation Program [*Army*] (AABC) ... E/S TIEP
Engineering Services ... ES
Engineering Services and Safety (NRCH) ... ES & S
Engineering Setup [*Television*] (WDMC) ... ESU
Engineering Shipping Notice (AAG) ... ESN
Engineering Shop Work Authorization (SAA) ... ESWA
Engineering Signal Processor ... ESP
Engineering Sign-Off ... ESO
Engineering Sketch ... ESK
Engineering Societies Commission on Energy [*Defunct*] (EA) ... ESCOE
Engineering Societies Library (MCD) ... ESL
Engineering Societies Library, New York, NY [*Library symbol Library of Congress*] (LCLS) ... NNE
Engineering Society of Baltimore, Baltimore, MD [*Library symbol Library of Congress*] (LCLS) ... MdBREC
Engineering Society of Detroit (EA) ... ESD
Engineering Software Package ... ESP
Engineering Source Selection ... ESS
Engineering Special Test Equipment (AAG) ... ESTE
Engineering Specification [*Air Force*] ... ENSP
Engineering Specification ... ES
Engineering Specification Control Document (AAG) ... ESCD
Engineering Specification Files ... ESF
Engineering Specification Worksheet ... ESW
Engineering Standard ... ES
Engineering Standard Practice Instruction (MCD) ... ESPI
Engineering Standard Specification (MCD) ... ESS
Engineering Standardization Directives ... ESD
Engineering Statement of Work (NASA) ... ESOW
Engineering Statement of Work (MCD) ... ESW
Engineering Stop and Release Order [*Aerospace*] ... ESRO
Engineering Stop Order (AAG) ... ESO
Engineering Structural Foam ... ESF
Engineering Student Officer Program [*Air Force*] ... ESOP
Engineering Study ... ES
Engineering Study Authorization Division [*NASA*] (KSC) ... ESA
Engineering Sub Task (MCD) ... EST
Engineering Summary Report ... ESR
Engineering Supply Area (NASA) ... ESA
Engineering Support Activity [*Military*] ... ESA
Engineering Support Assembly (NASA) ... ESA
Engineering Support Documentation ... ESD
Engineering Support Equipment (KSC) ... ESE
Engineering Support Field Office [*Federal disaster planning*] ... ESFO
Engineering Support Request (NASA) ... ESR
Engineering Support Team (KSC) ... EST
Engineering Support Test Equipment [*Deep Space Instrumentation Facility, NASA*] ... ETE
Engineering Surveillance Report (MCD) ... ENSURE
Engineering Systems and Procedures (MCD) ... ES & P
Engineering Systems Flight [*Military*] ... ESF
Engineering Tactical System ... ETS
Engineering Task Assignment ... ETA
Engineering Technical Change Package (MCD) ... ETCP
Engineering Technical Operating Procedure ... ETOP
Engineering Technician (ACII) ... EngTech
Engineering Technologist Certification Institute (EA) ... ETCI
Engineering Technology (DD) ... EngTech
Engineering Technology (MCD) ... ET
Engineering Television Mode ... ETV
Engineering Test ... ET
Engineering Test and Evaluation (MCD) ... ET & E
Engineering Test Area Working Group (SAA) ... ETAWG
Engineering Test Base Office (AAG) ... ETBO
Engineering Test Basis (KSC) ... ETB
Engineering Test Capsule ... ETC
Engineering Test Center (MCD) ... ETC
Engineering Test Directive ... ETD
Engineering Test Equipment (CAAL) ... ETE
Engineering Test Evaluation (AAG) ... ETE
Engineering Test / Expanded Service Test [*Military*] ... ET/EST
Engineering Test Laboratory (AAG) ... ETL
Engineering Test Model (KSC) ... ETM
Engineering Test Part Release (SAA) ... ETPR
Engineering Test Program [*NASA*] (KSC) ... ETP
Engineering Test Program Spares (SAA) ... ETPS
Engineering Test Reactor ... ETR
Engineering Test Reactor Critical Facility ... ETRC
Engineering Test Record (IAA) ... ETR
Engineering Test Request [*NASA*] (KSC) ... ETR
Engineering Test Satellite ... ETS
Engineering Test Support Equipment (SAA) ... ETSE
Engineering Test Unit ... ETU
Engineering Test Vehicle (KSC) ... ETV
Engineering Thermoplastic [*Plastics technology*] ... ETP
Engineering Time Estimate ... ETE
Engineering Time Standards [*Navy*] (NVT) ... ETS
Engineering Time Study (MCD) ... ETS
Engineering Tooling Coordination ... ETC
Engineering Trades' Joint Council [*British*] (DCTA) ... ETJC
Engineering Unit (MCD) ... EU
Engineering Unsatisfactory Report [*Military*] (AFIT) ... EUR
Engineering Use ... EU
Engineering Verification Order (MCD) ... EVO
Engineering Verification Test ... EVT
Engineering Watch Supervisor (DNAB) ... EWS
Engineering Waterways Experiment Station [*Army*] ... EWES
Engineering Weekly Labor Distribution (AAG) ... EWLD
Engineering Work Assignment ... EWA
Engineering Work Authorization [*Aerospace*] ... EWA

Engineering Work Order EWO
Engineering Work Order - Drawing Summary (AAG) EWODS
Engineering Work Report [*or Request*] EWR
Engineering Work Schedule (MCD) EWS
Engineering Work Statement (MCD) EWS
Engineering Work-Station [*Yokogawa Hewlett Packard Ltd.*] [*Japan*] EWS
Engineering Writer EGW
Engineering Writing and Speech (MCD) EWS
Engineering Youth Day EYD
Engineering-Installation (AFM) E-I
Engineer-in-Training EIT
Engineer-Maintenance Assembly-Disassembly [*NERVA program*] E-MAD
Engineers Adhesive Selector Program EASel
Engineers' and Allied Hand Tool Makers' Association [*British*] (BI) EAHTMA
Engineers and Architects Institute [*Defunct*] EAI
Engineers' and Managers' Association [*A union*] [*British*] (DCTA) EMA
Engineers and Scientists Non-Construction [*Army*] (RDA) E & S NC
Engineers and Scientists of America [*Defunct*] ESA
Engineers Australia [*A publication*] Engrs Aust
Engineers' Club of Dayton, Dayton, OH [*Library symbol Library of Congress*] (LCLS) ODaE
Engineers' Club, Philadelphia, PA [*Library symbol Library of Congress Obsolete*] (LCLS) PPEng
Engineers Council for Professional Development [*Later, ABET*] (EA) ECPD
Engineers Foreign Language Circle (PDAA) EFLC
Engineers Joint Contract Documents Committee (AAGC) EJCDC
Engineers Joint Council [*Superseded by AAES*] (EA) EJC
Engineers Joint Council Nuclear Congress (IEEE) EJCNC
Engineers' Language for Automatic Test Equipment ELATE
Engineers Manual for Emergency Construction [*Army Corps of Engineers*] EMEC
Engineers Manual for Military Construction [*Army Corps of Engineers*] [*A publication*] (AAGC) EMMC
Engineer's Order Wire EOW
Engineers Registration Board [*Council of Engineering Institutions*] [*British*] ERB
[*The*] **Engineers School** (MCD) TES
Engineers Society of Norway ESN
Engineers Supply Control Office [*Army*] ESCO
Engineer's Writer [*British military*] (DMA) EW
Engine-Generator E/G
Engineman [*Navy rating*] EN
Engineman, Chief [*Navy rating*] ENC
Engineman, First Class [*Navy rating*] EN1
Engineman, Master Chief [*Navy rating*] ENCM
Engineman, Second Class [*Navy rating*] EN2
Engineman, Senior Chief [*Navy rating*] ENCS
Engineman, Third Class [*Navy rating*] EN3
Enginemen and Firemen's Association [*A union*] [*British*] EFA
Engine-Mounted Gear Box (MCD) EMGB
Engine-Room Artificer [*Obsolete Navy British*] ERA
Engine-Sized [*Paper*] ES
Enginesmith [*British military*] (DMA) ES
England (ROG) E
England [*or English*] ENG
England (VRA) Eng
England ENGL
England ENGLD
England [*MARC country of publication code Library of Congress*] (LCCP) enk
England [*MARC geographic area code Library of Congress*] (LCCP) e-uk-en
England AFB (Alexandria), LA [*Location identifier FAA*] (FAAL) HTE
England and Wales E & W
England, AR [*AM radio station call letters*] KLRA
England, AR [*FM radio station call letters*] KLRA-FM
England Football Supporters Association (DBA) EFSA
England, France, Ireland, Scotland, Germany, and Aborigines [*See also TUPONA*] [*Suggested early name for Canada*] EFISGA
Engle Homes [*NASDAQ symbol*] (SPSG) ENGL
Engle Homes, Inc. [*Associated Press*] (SAG) EnglHm
Englefield Resources [*Vancouver Stock Exchange symbol*] EGF
Englehard, NC [*Location identifier FAA*] (FAAL) EQP
Englehart Public Library, Englehart, ON, Canada [*Library symbol*] [*Library of Congress*] (LCLS) CaOEng
Englehart Public Library, Ontario [*Library symbol National Library of Canada*] (BIB) OENG
Englewood, CO KCUV
Englewood, FL [*FM radio station call letters*] (RBYB) WEDD-FM
Englewood, FL [*AM radio station call letters*] WENG
Englewood, FL [*FM radio station call letters*] WSEB
Englewood Library, Englewood, NJ [*Library symbol Library of Congress*] (LCLS) NjEn
Englewood, OH [*FM radio station call letters*] (RBYB) WBTT-FM
Englewood, OH [*FM radio station call letters*] WDOL
Englewood Press, Englewood, NJ [*Library symbol Library of Congress*] (LCLS) NjEnP
Englewood Public Library, Englewood, CO [*Library symbol Library of Congress*] (LCLS) CoEn
Englewood, TN [*AM radio station call letters*] WENR
English [*Language*] (BARN) A
English E
English [*MARC language code Library of Congress*] (LCCP) eng
English (ROG) ENGL
English (DD) Engl
English ENGL
English Actors [*A publication*] EA
English Admiralty Reports [*A publication*] (DLA) Eng Adm
English Admiralty Reports [*A publication*] (DLA) Eng Adm R
English & American Literature Section [*Association of College and Research Libraries*] [*American Library Association*] EALS
English and Empire Digest [*A publication*] (DLA) E & E Dig
English and Empire Digest [*A publication*] (DLA) E & ED
English and Foreign Philosophical Library [*A publication*] EFPL
English and Germanic Studies [*A publication*] EAGS
English and Irish Appeals, House of Lords [*A publication*] (DLA) E & I
English and Scotch Ecclesiastical Reports [*A publication*] (DLA) Eng Sc Ecc
English as a Foreign Language EFL
English as a Second Language ESL
English as a Second Language (EDAC) ESLAT
English as a Second Language Allowance [*Australia*] ESLA
English as a Secondary Dialect ESD
English Association [*British*] (EAIO) EA
English Association of American Bond and Share Holders [*Commercial firm*] (EA) EAABSH
English Baron (ROG) EB
English Basket Ball Association EBBA
English Bay, AK [*Location identifier FAA*] (FAAL) EGY
English Bay, AK [*Location identifier FAA*] (FAAL) KEB
English Beet Molasses (PDAA) EMB
English Bible EB
English Bookplate Society (BARN) EBS
English Bowling Association EBA
English Bowling Federation (DBA) EBF
English Bridge Union (BI) EBU
English Centre of PEN (EAIO) ECP
English Ceramic Circle [*An Association*] [*British*] (EAIO) ECC
English Chamber Choir ECC
English Chamber Orchestra ECO
English Chancery (DLA) EC
English Chancery [*Legal term*] (DLA) Eng Ch
English Chancery Reports [*American Reprint*] [*A publication*] (DLA) EC
English Chancery Reports [*American Reprint*] [*A publication*] (DLA) Eng Ch
English Chancery Reports Tempore Finch [*A publication*] (DLA) Finch
English Chancery Reports Tempore Finch [*A publication*] (DLA) Finch (Eng)
English China Clays ADR [*NYSE symbol*] (TTSB) ENC
English China Clays International Ltd. [*British*] (IRUK) ECL
English China Clays Ltd. (ECON) ECC
English China Clays Ltd. [*Associated Press*] (SAG) EngChin
English Church Leaders [*A publication*] ECL
English Church Union ECU
English Citizen Series [*A publication*] ECS
English Civil War Society [*British*] (DBA) ECWS
English Cocker Spaniel Club of America (EA) ECSCA
English Collective of Prostitutes (DI) ECP
English Common Bench Reports [*1840-56*] [*A publication*] (DLA) CB
English Common Bench Reports (Manning, Granger, and Scott) [*135-139 English Reprint*] [*A publication*] (DLA) CB (Eng)
English Common Bench Reports, New Series [*A publication*] (DLA) Com BNS
English Common Bench Reports, New Series (Manning, Granger, and Scott) [*140-144 English Reprint*] [*A publication*] (DLA) CB (NS)
English Common Bench Reports, New Series (Manning, Granger, and Scott) [*140-144 English Reprint*] [*A publication*] (DLA) CB NS (Eng)
English Common Law Procedure Act (DLA) CLP Act
English Common Law Reports [*A publication*] (DLA) CL
English Common Law Reports [*A publication*] (DLA) Com Law R
English Common Law Reports [*A publication*] (DLA) Com Law Rep
English Common Law Reports [*A publication*] (DLA) Com LR
English Common Law Reports [*A publication*] (DLA) Eng CL
English Common Law Reports [*A publication*] (DLA) Eng Com LR
English Common Law Reports, Edited by Sergeant and Lowber [*A publication*] (DLA) Serg & Lowb
English Common Law Reports, Edited by Sergeant and Lowber [*A publication*] (DLA) Serg & Lowb Rep
English Composition Test [*Education*] (AEBS) ECT
English Comprehension Level [*Army*] (AABC) ECL
English Comprehensive Level Test [*DoD*] ECLT
English Conditions [*Insurance*] EC
English Connemara Pony Society (DBA) ECPS
English Consistorial Reports, by Haggard [*1788-1821*] [*A publication*] (DLA) Consist
English Consistorial Reports, by Haggard [*1788-1821*] [*A publication*] (DLA) Consist Rep
English Constitution (ADA) EC
English Council of California Two-Year Colleges (EDAC) ECCTYC
English Country Cheese Council (BI) ECCC
English Cross Country Union (BI) ECCU
English Crown Cases [*American Reprint*] [*A publication*] (DLA) Eng CC
English Crown Cases [*American Reprint*] [*A publication*] (DLA) Eng Cr Cas
English Curling Association ECA
English Dialect Dictionary [*A publication*] EDD
English Dialect Society EDS
English Draughts Association (DBA) EDA
English Duke (ROG) ED
English Earl (ROG) EE
English Ecclesiastical Reports [*A publication*] (DLA) Eccl R
English Ecclesiastical Reports [*A publication*] (DLA) EER
English Ecclesiastical Reports [*A publication*] (DLA) Eng Ecc R
English Ecclesiastical Reports [*A publication*] (DLA) Eng Eccl
English Electric [*Commercial firm British*] EE
English Electric Computers [*British*] (NITA) EEC
English Electric Valve [*Electronics company*] EEV
English Ell [*Unit of measure*] (ROG) EE

English Estates [British] (GEA) ... EE
English Exchequer Reports [A publication] (DLA) ... EE
English Exchequer Reports [A publication] (DLA) ... Eng Exch
English Exchequer Reports [A publication] (DLA) ... Ex
English Exchequer Reports [A publication] (DLA) ... Exch
English Exchequer Reports [A publication] (DLA) ... Exch Rep
English Finish [Paper] ... EF
English Folk Dance and Song Society [British] ... EFDSS
English for Foreigners ... EFF
English for Occupational Purposes (AIE) ... EOP
English for Scientific Purposes [Education] [British] ... ESP
English for Specific Purposes [Education] (PDAA) ... ESP
English Goethe Society [British] ... EGS
English Golf Union (BI) ... EGU
English Guernsey Cattle Society [British] ... EGCS
English Historical Review [A publication] (BRI) ... EHR
English Horn ... EH
English Horn (BARN) ... eng hn
English House of Lords Cases, by Clark [A publication] (DLA) ... Clark
English House of Lords Reports [A publication] (DLA) ... HL Rep
English Hymnal [Episcopalian] ... EH
English in Action (EA) ... EiA
English Indoor Bowling Association [British] (DBA) ... EIBA
English Industrial Estates Corp. ... EIEC
English Inshore Traffic Zone (DS) ... EITZ
English Institute (EA) ... EI
English Institute Materials Center ... EIMC
English Journal [A publication] (BRI) ... EJ
English King's Bench Modern Reports [86-88 English Reprint] [A publication] (DLA) ... Mod (Eng)
English King's Bench Reports [72 English Reprint] [A publication] (DLA) ... F Moore
English King's Bench Reports, by Sir Francis Moore [1512-1621] [A publication] (DLA) ... Moor
English Lacrosse Union (BI) ... ELU
English Language Amendment [Proposed] ... ELA
English Language Aptitude Test (DNAB) ... ELAT
English Language Book Society [British] ... ELBS
English Language Books Abroad [A publication] ... ELBA
English Language Books by Title [A publication] ... ELBT
English Language Institute [University of Michigan] [Research center] (RCD) ... ELI
English Language Institute of America (WDAA) ... ELIA
English Language Interpreter (NITA) ... ELI
English Language Laboratory ... ELL
English Language Learning and Improvement Service [State Library of South Australia] ... ELLIS
English Language Proficiency Survey [Department of Education] (GFGA) ... ELPS
English Language Program (MCD) ... ELP
English Language Skills Assessment in a Reading Context [Educational test] ... ELSA
English Language Teaching ... ELT
English Law and Equity Reports [American Reprint] [A publication] (DLA) ... EL & Eq
English Law and Equity Reports [American Reprint] [A publication] (DLA) ... Eng L & Eq
English Law and Equity Reports [American Reprint] [A publication] (DLA) ... Eng L & Eq R
English Law and Equity Reports [American Reprint] [A publication] (DLA) ... Eng Law & Eq
English Law and Equity Reports [American Reprint] [A publication] (DLA) ... L & E
English Law and Equity Reports [American Reprint] [A publication] (DLA) ... L & E Rep
English Law Journal. Exchequer in Equity [A publication] (DLA) ... LJ Exch in Eq (Eng)
English Law Reports, Admiralty and Ecclesiastical [A publication] (DLA) ... Adm & Ecc
English Law Reports, Admiralty and Ecclesiastical [A publication] (DLA) ... Adm & Eccl
English Law Reports, Admiralty and Ecclesiastical [A publication] (DLA) ... LRA & E
English Law Reports, Appeal Cases [A publication] (DLA) ... LRAC
English Law Reports, Appeal Cases, House of Lords [A publication] (DLA) ... LR App
English Law Reports, Appeal Cases, House of Lords [A publication] (DLA) ... LR App Cas
English Law Reports, Appeal Cases, House of Lords [A publication] (DLA) ... LR App Cas (Eng)
English Law Reports, Chancery Appeals [1891 onwards] [A publication] (DLA) ... Ch
English Law Reports, Chancery Division [A publication] (DLA) ... Ch
English Law Reports, Chancery Division [A publication] (DLA) ... Ch D
English Law Reports, Chancery Division [A publication] (DLA) ... Ch Div
English Law Reports, Chancery Division [A publication] (DLA) ... Ch Div (Eng)
English Law Reports, Chancery Division [A publication] (DLA) ... LR Ch D
English Law Reports, Chancery Division, Second Series [A publication] (DLA) ... Ch D 2d
English Law Reports, Common Pleas Division [A publication] (DLA) ... LRCP Div (Eng)
English Law Reports, Common Pleas Division [A publication] (DLA) ... LRCPD
English Law Reports, Crown Cases Reserved [2 vols.] [1865-75] [A publication] (DLA) ... LRCC
English Law Reports, Crown Cases Reserved [2 vols.] [1865-75] [A publication] (DLA) ... LRCC (Eng)
English Law Reports, Equity [1866-75] [A publication] (DLA) ... LR Eq
English Law Reports, Equity [1866-75] [A publication] (DLA) ... LR Eq (Eng)
English Law Reports, Exchequer [1866-75] [A publication] (DLA) ... Exch
English Law Reports, Exchequer [1866-75] [A publication] (DLA) ... LR Ex
English Law Reports, Exchequer [1866-75] [A publication] (DLA) ... LR Ex Cas
English Law Reports, Exchequer [1866-75] [A publication] (DLA) ... LR Exch
English Law Reports, Exchequer [1866-75] [A publication] (DLA) ... LR Exch (Eng)
English Law Reports, Exchequer Division [A publication] (DLA) ... LR Ex Div
English Law Reports, Exchequer Division [A publication] (DLA) ... LR Exch D
English Law Reports, Exchequer Division [A publication] (DLA) ... LR Exch Div (Eng)
English Law Reports, House of Lords, Scotch and Divorce Appeal Cases [1866-75] [A publication] (DLA) ... HL Sc App Cas
English Law Reports, House of Lords, Scotch and Divorce Appeal Cases [1866-75] [A publication] (DLA) ... LR Sc & D
English Law Reports, House of Lords, Scotch and Divorce Appeal Cases [1866-75] [A publication] (DLA) ... LRHL Sc
English Law Reports, House of Lords, Scotch and Divorce Appeal Cases [1866-75] [A publication] (DLA) ... LRHL Sc App Cas (Eng)
English Law Reports, Indian Appeals [A publication] (DLA) ... LR Ind App
English Law Reports, Indian Appeals [A publication] (DLA) ... LR Indian App
English Law Reports, Indian Appeals [A publication] (DLA) ... LR Indian App (Eng)
English Law Reports, Indian Appeals [A publication] (DLA) ... LRIA
English Law Reports, Indian Appeals, Supplement [A publication] (DLA) ... LR Ind App Supp
English Law Reports, Indian Appeals, Supplementary Volume [A publication] (DLA) ... IA Sup Vol
English Law Reports, King's Bench Division [1901-52] [A publication] (DLA) ... KB
English Law Reports, King's Bench Division [1901-52] [A publication] (DLA) ... KB (Eng)
English Law Reports, King's Bench Division [1901-52] [A publication] (DLA) ... LRKB
English Law Reports, Privy Council, Appeal Cases [1866-75] [A publication] (DLA) ... LRPC
English Law Reports, Privy Council, Appeal Cases [1866-75] [A publication] (DLA) ... LRPC (Eng)
English Law Reports, Probate Division [A publication] (DLA) ... LRP
English Law Reports, Probate, Divorce, and Admiralty Division [A publication] (DLA) ... LR Prob & M (Eng)
English Law Reports, Probate, Divorce, and Admiralty Division [A publication] (DLA) ... LR Prob Div
English Law Reports, Probate, Divorce, and Admiralty Division [A publication] (DLA) ... LR Prob Div (Eng)
English Law Reports, Probate, Divorce, and Admiralty Division [A publication] (DLA) ... LRP Div
English Law Reports, Queen's Bench Division [1865-75] [A publication] (DLA) ... LRQB
English Law Reports, Queen's Bench Division [1865-75] [A publication] (DLA) ... LRQB Div
English Law Reports, Queen's Bench Division [1865-75] [A publication] (DLA) ... LRQB Div (Eng)
English Law Reports, Queen's Bench Division [1865-75] [A publication] (DLA) ... LRQB (Eng)
English Law Reports, Queen's Bench Division [1865-75] [A publication] (DLA) ... LRQBD
English Law Reports, Queen's Bench Division [1865-75] [A publication] (DLA) ... QB Div
English Law Reports, Sessions Cases [A publication] (DLA) ... LR Sess Cas
English Law Reports, Statutes [A publication] (DLA) ... LR Stat
English Literature (WDAA) ... ENG LIT
English Literature in Transition 1880-1920 [A publication] (BRI) ... ELT
English Maritime Law Reports, Published by Crockford [1860-71] [A publication] (DLA) ... Crockford
English Market ... EM
English Market Selection [Cigars] ... EMS
English Marquess (ROG) ... EM
English Men of Action [A publication] ... EMA
English Men of Letters [A publication] ... EML
English Men of Science [A publication] ... EMS
English/Metric ... E/M
English, Middle [MARC language code Library of Congress] (LCCP) ... enm
English National Ballet School ... ENBS
English National Board Careers Advisory Centre [British] (CB) ... ENB
English National Opera ... ENO
English New Education Fellowship (BI) ... ENEF
English Newspaper Association ... ENA
English Nisi Prius Reports [171 English Reprint] [A publication] (DLA) ... Starkie's
English [Communion] Office [Episcopalian] ... EO
English Olympic Wrestling Association ... EOWA
English on Church Pews [A publication] (DLA) ... Eng Pews
English Orienteering Association (BI) ... EOA
English Patent (IAA) ... EP
English Philips [Record label] ... EPhi
English Picture Vocabulary Test [Educational test] (EDAC) ... EPVT
English Picture Vocabulary Tests [Educational test] ... EPVTS
English Placement Test [Education] ... EPT
English Place-Name Society ... EPNS
English Playing-Card Society (DBA) ... EPCS
English Pleader [A publication] (DLA) ... Eng Pl
English Pool Association [British] (DBA) ... EPA
English Prayer Book Version (BJA) ... PBV
English Privy Council Reports [A publication] (DLA) ... PC Rep
English Prize Cases [Legal] ... EPC
English Probate and Admiralty Reports for Year Cited [A publication] (DLA) ... Prob

English Racing Automobiles Ltd. [*British*] ..... ERA
English Railway and Canal Cases [*A publication*] (DLA) ..... Eng R & C Cas
English Railway and Canal Cases [*A publication*] (DLA) ..... Eng RR Ca
English Railway and Canal Cases [*A publication*] (DLA) ..... Eng Ry & C Cas
English Railway and Canal Cases [*A publication*] (DLA) ..... Ra Ca
English Railway and Canal Cases [*A publication*] (DLA) ..... Rail & Can Cas
English Railway and Canal Cases, by Beavan and Others [*A publication*]
(DLA) ..... Beav R & C Cas
English Railway and Canal Cases, by Carrow, Oliver, and Others [*1835-55*]
[*A publication*] (DLA) ..... Car & O
English Railway and Canal Cases, by Carrow, Oliver, and Others [*1835-55*]
[*A publication*] (DLA) ..... Car & Ol
English Railway and Canal Cases, by Carrow, Oliver, Beavan, and Others
[*1835-55*] [*A publication*] (DLA) ..... Car O & B
English Reports [*Legal*] ..... ER
English Reports, Annotated [*A publication*] (DLA) ..... Eng Rep Anno
English Reports, Annotated [*A publication*] (DLA) ..... ERA
English Reports, Full Reprint [*A publication*] (DLA) ..... Eng Re
English Reports, Full Reprint [*A publication*] (DLA) ..... Eng Rep
English Reports, Full Reprint [*A publication*] (DLA) ..... Eng Rep R
English Reports, Full Reprint [*A publication*] (DLA) ..... Eng Rep Re
English Reports, Full Reprint [*A publication*] (DLA) ..... ER
English Reports, Full Reprint [*A publication*] (DLA) ..... Reprint
English Reports (N. C. Moak) [*A publication*] (DLA) ..... Eng
English Reports (N. C. Moak) [*American Reprint*] [*A publication*] (DLA) ..... Eng Rep
English Revised Version [*of the Bible*] [*A publication*] (BJA) ..... ER
English Revised Version [*of the Bible*] [*A publication*] (BJA) ..... ERV
English Revised Version [*of the Bible*], Margin ..... ERVm
English Rugby Union ..... ERU
English Ruling Cases [*A publication*] (DLA) ..... Eng Ru Ca
English Ruling Cases [*A publication*] (DLA) ..... Eng Rul Cas
English Ruling Cases [*A publication*] (DLA) ..... ERC
English Schools' Athletic Association (BI) ..... ESAA
English Schools Cricket Association (BI) ..... ESCA
English Schools' Rugby Union (BI) ..... ESRU
English Schools' Swimming Association (BI) ..... ESSA
English, Scottish & Australian Bank Ltd. (ADA) ..... ESA
English Setter Association of America (EA) ..... ESAA
English Settlement and Removal Cases [*Burrow's Settlement Cases*]
[*A publication*] (DLA) ..... Set
English Shakespeare Co. (ECON) ..... ESC
English Shepherd Club (EA) ..... ESC
English Shilling (WDAA) ..... E
English Ski Council [*British*] (DBA) ..... ESC
English Socialism [*From George Orwell's novel, "1984"*] ..... INGSOC
English Speaking Union [*British*] (EAIO) ..... ESU
English Speaking Union International Council (EAIO) ..... ESUIC
English Speaking Union of the Commonwealth (EAIO) ..... ESUC
English Springer Spaniel Field Trial Association (EA) ..... ESSFTA
English Standard Gauge ..... ESG
English Table Soccer Association (DBA) ..... ETSA
English Table Tennis Association ..... ETTA
English Teachers' Association of Western Australia ..... ETAWA
English Teachers in University Departments of Education (AIE) ..... ETUDE
English Text ..... ET
English the New Way [*Education*] (AEBS) ..... ENW
English Tiddlywinks Association (DBA) ..... ETWA
English Timber Merchants' Association (BI) ..... ETMA
English Title [*Online database field identifier*] ..... ET
English to Speakers of Other Languages [*Program*] ..... ESOL
English Tourist Board ..... ETB
English Toy Spaniel Club of America (EA) ..... ETSCA
English Translation ..... ET
English Universities Press ..... EUP
English Version ..... EV
English Versions ..... EVV
English Villages Housing Association (ECON) ..... EVHA
English Vineyards Association (DBA) ..... EVA
English Viscount (ROG) ..... EV
English Volleyball Association ..... EVA
English Vox [*Record label*] ..... EVox
English Westerners Society [*British*] ..... EWS
English Winter Index ..... EWI
English Women's Bowling Association (DBA) ..... EWBA
English Women's Bowling Federation (DBA) ..... EWBF
English Women's Indoor Bowling Association (DBA) ..... EWIBA
English-Pressed Allegro [*Record label*] ..... EA
English's Digest of the Statutes [*Arkansas*] [*A publication*] (DLA) ..... Dig St
English's Reports [*6-13 Arkansas*] [*A publication*] (DLA) ..... Eng
English's Reports [*6-13 Arkansas*] [*A publication*] (DLA) ..... Eng Rep
English's Reports [*6-13 Arkansas*] [*A publication*] (DLA) ..... English
English-Speaking Background (ADA) ..... ESB
English-Speaking Board (International) [*British*] ..... ESB
English-Speaking Country ..... ESC
English-Speaking Nations [*of NATO*] ..... ESN
English-Speaking Tape Respondents Association [*British*] (BI) ..... ESTRA
English-Speaking Union of the United States (EA) ..... ESU
English-Teaching Information Center [*British Council*] (PDAA) ..... ETIC
Engpasskonzentrierte Strategie [*Bottleneck-focused strategy*] [*German*]
[*Business term*] ..... EKS
Engrave ..... ENG
Engrave ..... ENGRV
Engraved ..... ENGR
Engraved (WDMC) ..... engr
Engraved Stationery Manufacturers Association (EA) ..... ESMA

Engraved Stationery Manufacturers Research Institute (EA) ..... ESMRI
Engraver [*MARC relator code*] [*Library of Congress*] (LCCP) ..... egr
Engraver (ROG) ..... ENG
Engraver (ROG) ..... ENGR
Engraver (WDMC) ..... engr
Engraver ..... ENGRVR
Engraving (WDMC) ..... engr
Engraving (VRA) ..... engr
Engraving ..... ENGRV
Engraving Master (MCD) ..... EM
Engravings (ROG) ..... ENGR
Engross (ROG) ..... ENGS
Engrossed (ROG) ..... ENGD
Engrossment (ROG) ..... ENGT
Enhance Financial Services Group [*NYSE symbol*] (SAG) ..... EFS
Enhance Financial Services Group [*Associated Press*] (SAG) ..... Enhance
Enhance Financial Svcs Grp [*NYSE symbol*] (TTSB) ..... EFS
Enhanced [*ICAO designator*] (FAAC) ..... ENHNCD
Enhanced Airline Communications and Reporting System (DA) ..... E-CARS
Enhanced Apple Digital Sound Chip [*Computer science*] ..... EADSC
Enhanced AT Attachment [*Computer science*] ..... EATA
Enhanced Bottom Pressure Recorder [*Marine science*] (OSRA) ..... E-BPR
Enhanced Bottom Pressure Recorder (USDC) ..... E-BPR
Enhanced Capabilities Port [*Computer science*] ..... ECP
Enhanced Character Set/All Purpose Interface [*Xerox Corp.*] ..... ECS/API
Enhanced Chemiluminescence [*Analytical chemistry*] ..... ECL
Enhanced Cobra Armament Program [*Military*] ..... ECAP
Enhanced Cobra/TOW [*Tube-Launched, Optically-Tracked, Wire-Guided*]
Armament System [*Military*] (MCD) ..... ECAS
Enhanced Color Display [*Computer monitor*] ..... ECD
Enhanced Compact Disk (PCM) ..... ECD
Enhanced Comprehensive Asset Management System (MCD) ..... ECAMS
Enhanced Computer Tomography [*Radiology*] (DAVI) ..... ECT
Enhanced Connectivity Facilities (CDE) ..... ECF
Enhanced Console Driver [*Computer science*] ..... ECD
Enhanced Consumer Spending Patterns [*National Planning Data Corp.*]
[*Information service or system*] (CRD) ..... ECSP
Enhanced Control Cellular [*Telecommunications*] ..... ECC
Enhanced Cubic Grain [*Photography*] ..... ECB
Enhanced Cytotoxicity Factor [*Biochemistry*] ..... ECF
Enhanced Data Output Dynamic Access Random [*Computer
science*] ..... EDO DRAM
Enhanced Data-Acquisition System [*Computer science*] (ODBW) ..... EDAS
Enhanced Defense Logistics Agency Distribution System (AAGC) ..... EDDS
Enhanced [*or Extended*] Definition Television (PCM) ..... EDTV
Enhanced Distant Early Warning ..... EDEW
Enhanced Drive Parameter Table [*Computer science*] ..... EDPT
Enhanced Dynamic Random Access Memory [*Computer science*] ..... EDRAM
Enhanced Engine Starting Control and Monitor ..... EESCM
Enhanced Enlisted Master Tape Record (AABC) ..... EEMTR
Enhanced Expanded Memory Specifications [*AST, Quadram*] ..... EEMS
Enhanced Fiber-Optic-Guided Missiles [*DoD*] ..... EFOGM
Enhanced Fighter Maneuverability (MCD) ..... EFM
Enhanced Flight Screening (DOMA) ..... EFS
Enhanced Forecaster Tools [*Forecast Systems Laboratory*] [*Branch*]
(USDC) ..... EFT
Enhanced Forecaster Tools [*Branch*] [*Marine science*] (OSRA) ..... EFT
Enhanced Graphics Acquisition and Analysis [*Computer science*] ..... EGAA
Enhanced Graphics Adapter [*Computer technology*] ..... EGA
Enhanced Graphics Monitor [*Computer technology*] ..... EGM
Enhanced Greenhouse Effect (EERA) ..... EGE
Enhanced Guardrail (MCD) ..... EGR
Enhanced Heat Transfer Reformer [*Engineering*] ..... EHTR
Enhanced Industry Standard Architecture [*Computer hardware*] (PCM) ..... EISA
Enhanced Integral Drive Electronics (DOM) ..... EIDE
[*The*] Enhanced Integrated Soldier System [*Army*] ..... TEISS
Enhanced Interior Gateway Routing Protocol [*Telecommunications*]
(ACRL) ..... EIGRP
Enhanced JTIDS [*Joint Tactical Information Distribution System*] **System** [*Air
Force*] ..... EJS
Enhanced Land Warrior [*Military*] (RDA) ..... ELW
Enhanced Logistics Information Management System ..... ELIMS
Enhanced Logistics Intratheater Support Tool [*DoD*] ..... ELIST
Enhanced Luminescent Immunoassay [*Analytical biochemistry*] ..... ELIA
Enhanced Main Display Unit (DWSG) ..... EMDU
Enhanced Manpack UHF [*Ultra High Frequency*] **Terminal** ..... EMUT
Enhanced Manual SHORAD [*Short Range Air Defense*] **Control System**
[*Army*] ..... E/MSCS
Enhanced Master Terminal Unit ..... EMTU
Enhanced MEECN [*Minimum Essential Emergency Communications Network*]
Message Processing System ..... EMMPS
Enhanced Memory Specifications [*Computer science*] ..... EMS
Enhanced Metafile [*Computer science*] ..... EMF
Enhanced Metafile Format [*Microsoft Corp.*] (PCM) ..... EMF
Enhanced Microbial Degradation [*Biochemistry*] ..... EMD
Enhanced Mobility System [*LTV Aerospace and Defense Co.*] ..... EMS
Enhanced Modular Signal Processor (MCD) ..... EMSP
Enhanced Monitoring [*Environmental Protection Agency*] ..... EM
Enhanced Monitoring Rule [*For industrial plant emissions*] ..... EMR
Enhanced Mortar Fire Control System [*Military*] (INF) ..... EMFCS
Enhanced Moving Target Indicator [*Air Force*] (DOMA) ..... EMTI
Enhanced Naval Warfare Gaming System (GFGA) ..... ENWGS
Enhanced Network Administration System [*Telecommunications*] (TEL) ..... ENADS
Enhanced Non-Return to Zero (IAA) ..... ENRZ
Enhanced Oil Recovery [*Petroleum engineering*] ..... EOR

Enhanced Operating System [*Computer science*] (PDAA) .... EOS
Enhanced Parallel Port [*PCM*] .... EPP
Enhanced Parallel Ports [*Computer science*] .... EPPs
Enhanced Performance Architecture [*Computer science*] (TNIG) .... EPA
Enhanced Performance Engine (MCD) .... EPE
Enhanced Performance Implanted CMOS [*Texas Instruments, Inc.*] .... EPIC
Enhanced Perimeter Acquisition RADAR Characterization System
 (PDAA) .... EPARCS
Enhanced Peripheral Communication Interface [*Motorola, Inc.*] .... EPCI
Enhanced PLRS [*Position Location Reporting System*] **User Unit** [*Air Force*] .... EPUU
Enhanced Position Location Reporting System [*Army*] (INF) .... EPLRS
Enhanced Private Switched Communications Service [*Pronounced "ep-sis"*] [*AT & T*] .... EPSCS
Enhanced Radiation/Reduced Blast .... ER/RB
Enhanced Radiation Weapon .... ER
Enhanced Radiation Weapon .... ERW
Enhanced Reactivation [*Medicine*] (DMAA) .... ER
Enhanced Remote Target System [*Military*] (INF) .... E-RETS
Enhanced Run Length Limited [*Computer science*] (BYTE) .... ERLL
Enhanced Self-Propelled Artillery Weapon System (MCD) .... ESPAWS
Enhanced Self-Propelled Artillery Weapon System Study (MCD) .... ESPAWSS
Enhanced Serial Interface [*Communication protocol*] [*Computer science*]
 (PCM) .... ESI
Enhanced Serial Port (PCM) .... ESP
Enhanced Serial Processor [*Communication protocol*] [*Computer science*]
 (PCM) .... ESP
Enhanced Service Provider [*Online database service*] .... ESP
Enhanced Small Device [*or Disk*] **Interface** [*Computer science*] .... ESDI
Enhanced SMMC [*FAA*] (TAG) .... ESMMC
Enhanced Station-Keeping Equipment [*Air Force*] (DOMA) .... ESKE
Enhanced Structural Adjustment Facility [*IMF*] (ECON) .... ESAF
Enhanced Tactical Fighter (MCD) .... ETF
Enhanced Tactical Fighter Engineering (MCD) .... ETE
Enhanced Tactical User Terminal (DOMA) .... ETUT
Enhanced Telephone .... ET
Enhanced Telephone Unit .... ETU
Enhanced Terminal Voice Switching [*FAA*] (TAG) .... ETVS
Enhanced Thematic Mapper [*Geoscience*] .... ETM
Enhanced Thermionically Supported Discharge [*Materials technology*] .... ETSD
Enhanced Throughput Cellular [*AT & T*] [*Telecommunications*] (PCM) .... ETC
Enhanced Timing Module (IEEE) .... ETM
Enhanced Traffic Management System [*FAA*] (TAG) .... ETMS
Enhanced Transportation Automated Data System [*Air Force*] .... ETADS
Enhanced VERDIN [*Antijam Modem, Very-Low Frequency*] **Processor**
 [*Military*] (CAAL) .... EVP
Enhanced VERDIN [*Antijam Modem, Very-Low Frequency*] **System** [*Military*]
 (CAAL) .... EVS
Enhanced Videotex Service (LAIN) .... EVS
Enhanced Vortex Advisory System [*FAA*] (TAG) .... EVAS
Enhanced Winkler Processor .... EWP
Enhanced Winkler Processor Autopilot [*Military*] .... EWPA
Enhanced-Technology Fighter (MCD) .... ETF
Enhancement [*ICAO designator*] (FAAC) .... ENHNCMNT
Enhancement Depletion (IAA) .... ED
Enhancement Depletion Metal-Oxide Semiconductor Field-Effect
 Transistor (IAA) .... EDMOSFET
Enhancement Metal-Oxide Semiconductor (BUR) .... EMOS
Enhancement Mode Field Effect Transistor (IAA) .... EFET
Enhancement of Life Support, Europe (MCD) .... ELIFE
Enhancement Ratio .... ER
Enhancement-Depletion Logic (NITA) .... E-D
Enhancement-Metal Semiconductor Field Effect Transistor (HGAA) .... E-MESFET
Enhancement-Mode Junction Field-Effect Transistor [*Electronics*] .... E-JFET
ENI S.p.A.ADS [*NYSE symbol*] (TTSB) .... E
Enid [*Oklahoma*] [*Airport symbol*] (OAG) .... WDG
Enid Board of Trade (EA) .... EBT
Enid, OK [*Location identifier FAA*] (FAAL) .... EIU
Enid, OK [*Location identifier FAA*] (FAAL) .... END
Enid, OK [*Television station call letters*] .... KAFU
Enid, OK [*FM radio station call letters*] .... KBVV
Enid, OK [*AM radio station call letters*] .... KCRC
Enid, OK [*AM radio station call letters*] .... KGWA
Enid, OK [*FM radio station call letters*] .... KNID
Enid, OK [*FM radio station call letters*] .... KOFM
Enid, OK [*Location identifier FAA*] (FAAL) LVC
Enid, OK [*Location identifier FAA*] (FAAL) .... ODG
Enid, OK [*Location identifier FAA*] (FAAL) .... WDG
Enid/Vance Air Force Base [*Oklahoma*] [*ICAO location identifier*] (ICLI) .... KEND
Eniwetok [*Marshall Islands*] [*Airport symbol*] (OAG) .... ENT
Eniwetok [*Marshall Islands*] [*ICAO location identifier*] (ICLI) .... PKMA
Eniwetok Marine Biological Laboratory [*Marine science*] (MSC) .... EMBL
Eniwetok Proving Ground [*AEC*] .... EPG
Enjoin [*Legal shorthand*] (LWAP) .... ENJ
Enjoyment (ROG) .... ENJOYT
Enjoyment of Music Series, EMI [*Record label*] [*Great Britain*] .... EOM
Enkephalin [*Brain peptide, subclass of endorphin*] .... EK
Enkephalin [*Brain peptide, subclass of Endorphin*] .... ENK
Enkephalin-Containing Polypeptide [*Physiological chemistry*] .... ECP
Enkephalin-Hydrolyzing Activity .... EHA
Enki and Eridu (BJA) .... EE
Enki and Ninhursag (BJA) .... EN
Enki and the World Order [*A publication*] (BJA) .... EWO
Enlarge [*or Enlargement*] .... ENL
Enlarge (MSA) .... ENLG

Enlarge .... ENLRG
Enlarged (WDMC) .... enl
Enlarged .... ENLGD
Enlarged Committee for Program and Coordination [*United Nations
 Development Program*] .... ECPC
Enlarged Compact by Response (IAA) .... ENCORE
Enlarged Heart [*Medicine*] .... EH
Enlargement (VRA) .... enlgmnt
Enlighten Software Solutions [*Associated Press*] (SAG) .... ENlghtS
Enlighten Software Solutions [*NASDAQ symbol*] (SAG) .... SFTW
Enlil Hymn (BJA) .... EH
Enlisted [*Often in combination with numbers to denote serviceman's grade*] .... E
Enlisted Assignment Document [*Military*] (DNAB) .... EAD
Enlisted Assignment System .... EAS
Enlisted Association of the National Guard of the United States .... EANGUS
Enlisted Classification Code .... ECC
Enlisted Commissioning Program [*Military*] (DNAB) .... ECP
Enlisted Correspondence Course .... ECC
Enlisted Development and Distribution Support System [*Military*]
 (DNAB) .... ENLDEVDISTSYS
Enlisted Dining Facility [*Military*] .... EDF
Enlisted Distribution and Assignment System [*DoD*] .... EDAS
Enlisted Distribution and Verification Report .... EDAVR
Enlisted Distribution and Verification Report .... EDVR
Enlisted Education Advancement Program [*Military*] (DNAB) .... EEAP
Enlisted Efficiency Report Weighted Average [*Army*] .... EERWA
Enlisted Evaluation Center [*Army*] .... EEC
Enlisted Evaluation Report [*DoD*] (GFGA) .... EER
Enlisted Evaluation System [*Army*] .... EES
Enlisted Loss Inventory Model (MCD) .... ELIM
Enlisted Loss to Commissioned Status [*Military*] .... ELTC
Enlisted Loss to Warrant Status [*Military*] .... ELTW
Enlisted Man [*or Men*] .... EM
Enlisted Manning Report [*Air Force*] .... EMR
Enlisted Master File [*Army*] (INF) .... EMF
Enlisted Master Tape Record [*Army*] (AABC) .... EMTR
Enlisted Member (AABC) .... EM
Enlisted Men on Duty with the Counter Intelligence Corps [*Army*] .... DEML(CIC)
Enlisted Men on Duty with the National Guard [*Army*] .... DEML(NG)
Enlisted Men on Duty with the Organized Reserves [*Army*] .... DEML(OR)
Enlisted Men on Duty with the Reserve Officers' Training Corps
 [*Army*] .... DEML(ROTC)
Enlisted Navy Career Options for Reenlistment (DOMA) .... ENCORE
Enlisted/Officer Combined Correspondence Course [*Military*] (DNAB) ..... ECC-OCC
Enlisted Personnel (AABC) .... EP
Enlisted Personnel (DNAB) .... E-PERS
Enlisted Personnel Assignment Document [*Navy*] (NVT) .... EPAD
Enlisted Personnel Directorate [*Army*] .... EPD
Enlisted Personnel Distribution Office [*Navy*] .... EPDO
Enlisted Personnel Distribution Office, Atlantic Fleet [*Navy*] .... EPDOLANT
Enlisted Personnel Distribution Office, Continental United States
 [*Navy*] .... EPDOCONUS
Enlisted Personnel Distribution Office, Pacific Fleet [*Navy*] (MUGU) ..... EPDOPAC
Enlisted Personnel Division [*Navy*] .... EPD
Enlisted Personnel Enlistment Eligibility Activity [*Army*] .... EPEEA
Enlisted Personnel Individualized Career System [*Military*] (MCD) .... EPICS
Enlisted Personnel Management Center [*Navy*] (DNAB) .... ENLPERMGTCEN
Enlisted Personnel Management Center [*Navy*] (NVT) .... EPMAC
Enlisted Personnel Management Directorate .... EPMD
Enlisted Personnel Management System [*Army*] (AABC) .... EPMS
Enlisted Programs Branch [*BUPERS*] .... EPB
Enlisted Programs Officer (DNAB) .... EPO
Enlisted Record Brief [*Army*] (AABC) .... ERB
Enlisted Records and Evaluation Center [*Fort Benjamin Harrison, IN*]
 [*Army*] .... EREC
Enlisted Reserve Corps [*Later, Army Reserve*] .... ERC
Enlisted Separation Questionnaire [*Military*] (DNAB) .... ESQ
Enlisted Signal Corps School .... ESCS
Enlisted Surface Warfare Specialist (DNAB) .... ESWS
Enlisted Surface Warfare Specialist (DOMA) .... EWS
Enlisted Tactical Air Controller [*Army*] (INF) .... ETAC
Enlisted Tactical Application (DOMA) .... ETAC
Enlisted Training Branch [*BUPERS*] .... ETB
Enlisted Transfer Manual [*Military*] .... TRANSMAN
Enlisted Woman [*or Women*] .... EW
Enlisted Women's Quarters [*Military*] .... EWQ
Enlistment (AFM) .... ENL
Enlistment Allowance [*Military*] .... EA
Enlistment Bonus [*Military*] (AABC) .... EB
Enlistment Canceled [*Military*] .... ENC
Enlistment Screening Test [*Military*] .... EST
Enlow Public Library, West Branch, IA [*Library symbol Library of Congress*]
 (LCLS) .... IaWb
Enlya Ruzgariya Netwa Kurdistan [*National Front for the Liberation of
 Kurdistan*] [*Turkey Political party*] .... ERNK
Enmekar and the Lord of Aratta (BJA) .... ELA
Enna [*Italy ICAO location identifier*] (ICLI) .... LICE
Enneades [*of Plotinus*] [*Classical studies*] (OCD) .... Enn
Ennis Business Forms [*NYS*] (TTSB) .... EBF
Ennis Business Forms, Inc. [*NYSE symbol*] (SPSG) .... EBF
Ennis Business Forms, Inc. [*Associated Press*] (SAG) .... EnisBu
Enniskillen [*Northern Ireland*] [*Airport symbol*] .... ENK
Enniskillen/St. Angelo [*British ICAO location identifier*] (ICLI) .... EGAB
Ennismore Township Public Library, Ontario [*Library symbol National Library
 of Canada*] (BIB) .... OEN

Ennisteel Corp. [*Toronto Stock Exchange symbol*] ... ENN
Eno Foundation for Transportation (EA) ... EFT
Enoch (BJA) ... En
Enoch Pratt Free Library, Baltimore, MD [*OCLC symbol*] (OCLC) ... MDB
Enoch Pratt Free Library, Baltimore, MD [*Library symbol Library of Congress*] (LCLS) ... MdBE
Enoch Pratt Free Library, George Peabody Branch, Baltimore, MD [*Library symbol Library of Congress*] (LCLS) ... MdBP
Enolase [*An enzyme*] ... ENO
Enology ... ENOL
Enolpyruvate [*Biochemistry*] ... ePrv
Enolpyruvylshikimatephosphate Synthase [*An enzyme*] ... EPSPS
Enolpyruvylshikimic Acid Phosphate [*Organic chemistry*] ... EPSP
Enontekio [*Finland ICAO location identifier*] (ICLI) ... EFET
Enormous State University [*Fictitious school often featured in comic strip "Tank McNamara"*] ... ESU
Enormously Entertaining Prodigy ... EEP
Enose Demokratikou Hellinikou Kentrou [*Union of the Greek Democratic Center*] (PPE) ... EDHK
Enose Demokratikou Kentrou [*Union of the Democratic Center*] [*Greek*] (PPW) ... EDK
Enosis Laikou Kommatos [*Union of Populist Parties*] [*Greek*] (PPE) ... ELK
Enossi Dimokratikou Kentrou [*Union of Democratic Centre Party*] [*Greece*] [*Political party*] (EY) ... EDIK
Enough ... ENO
Enough Is Enough Club [*Defunct*] (EA) ... EEC
Enova Corp. [*NASDAQ symbol*] (TTSB) ... ENA
Enoyl Reductase [*An enzyme*] ... ENR
Enoyl Reductase [*An enzyme*] ... ER
Enquiries [*Telecommunications*] (TEL) ... EQ
Enquiry [*Transmission control character*] ... ENQ
Enquiry Agency [*British*] ... EA
Enquiry Terminal System [*International Computers Ltd.*] ... ETS
Enriched Brucella Blood Agar [*Culture media*] ... EBA
Enriched Mantle [*Geology*] ... EM
Enriched Pulverised Refuse (PDAA) ... EPR
Enriched Uranium Extraction (PDAA) ... EUREX
Enrichment of Nutrients on Coral Reefs Experiment [*Australia*] ... ENCORE
Enrichment Science and Technology for Exceptionally Able and Motivated Pupils (AIE) ... ESTEAM
Enrico Fermi Atomic Power Plant [*Decommissioned*] (NRCH) ... EFAPP
Enrico Fermi Fast Breeder Power Reactor ... EFFBR
Enrico Fermi Institute [*University of Chicago*] ... EFI
Enrico Fermi Institute for Nuclear Studies [*University of Chicago*] ... EFINS
Enriquillo [*Dominican Republic*] [*ICAO location identifier*] (ICLI) ... MDEN
Enroles de Force [*Forced Conscripts*] [*Luxembourg*] (PPE) ... EdF
Enrolled Agent [*IRS*] ... EA
Enrolled Federal Tax Accountant [*EFTA Institute*] [*Designation awarded by*] ... EFTA
Enrolled Nurse ... EN
Enrolled Nurse (General) [*British*] (DBQ) ... EN(G)
Enrolled Nurse, General (Mental Nursing) [*British*] (DI) ... ENG(M)
Enrolled Nurse, General (Mental Sub-Normal Nursing) [*British*] (DI) ... ENG(MS)
Enrolled Nurse Interest Group [*Australia*] ... ENIG
Enrolled Nurse (Mental) [*British*] (DBQ) ... EN(M)
Enrolled Nurse (Mental Handicap) [*British*] (DBQ) ... EN(MH)
Enrolled Nursing Aide (ADA) ... ENA
Enrollment (ROG) ... ENR
Enrollment (AABC) ... ENRL
ENRON $10.50 Cv 2nd Pfd [*NYSE symbol*] (TTSB) ... ENEPrJ
Enron Cap Res 9% 'A' Pfd [*NYSE symbol*] (TTSB) ... ENEPrA
Enron Capital Corp. LLC [*Associated Press*] (SAG) ... EnrLLC
Enron Capital LLC'MIPS' [*NYSE symbol*] (TTSB) ... ENEPrC
Enron Capital Resources Ltd. [*Associated Press*] (SAG) ... EnrCR
Enron Capital Trust I TOPRS [*NYSE symbol*] (SAG) ... ENE
Enron Capital Trust I TOPRS [*Associated Press*] (SAG) ... EnrnC
Enron Corp. [*NYSE symbol Toronto Stock Exchange symbol*] (SPSG) ... ENE
Enron Corp. [*Associated Press*] (SAG) ... Enrn
Enron Corp. [*Associated Press*] (SAG) ... Enron
Enron Corp. [*Associated Press*] (SAG) ... Enron98
Enron Corp. [*NYSE symbol*] (SAG) ... EXG
Enron Cp 6.25% Exch Nts'98 [*NYSE symbol*] (TTSB) ... EXG
Enron Global Power & Pipeline [*Associated Press*] (SAG) ... EnrGP
Enron Global Power & Pipeline Co. [*NYSE symbol*] (SAG) ... EPP
Enron Global Pwr/Pipeln LLC [*NYSE symbol*] (TTSB) ... EPP
Enron Liquids Pipeline [*Associated Press*] (SAG) ... EnronLq
Enron Liquids Pipeline L.P. [*NYSE symbol*] (TTSB) ... ENP
Enron Liquids Pipiline Ltd. [*NYSE symbol*] (SPSG) ... ENP
Enron Oil & Gas [*NYSE symbol*] (SPSG) ... EOG
Enroute Air Traffic Regulation (MCD) ... EATR
Enroute Communications [*Aviation*] (FAAC) ... RCOM
Enroute Control Center [*Aviation*] (DA) ... ERCC
Enroute Metering [*Aviation*] (FAAC) ... ERMG
Enroute RADAR [*Aviation*] (FAAC) ... ERAD
Enroute Reporting Point [*MTMC*] (TAG) ... ERP
Enroute Spacing Program [*Aviation*] (FAAC) ... ERSP
Enroute Support Team (SAA) ... EST
Enroute Tracking Automatic RADAR Service [*Aviation*] (FAAC) ... ETARS
Enschede [*Netherlands*] [*Airport symbol*] (OAG) ... ENS
Enschede/Twenthe [*Netherlands ICAO location identifier*] (ICLI) ... EHTW
ENSCO Intl. [*NYSE symbol*] (TTSB) ... ESV
Enscor, Inc. [*NASDAQ symbol*] (NQ) ... ENCR
Enscor Inc. [*NASDAQ symbol*] (TTSB) ... ENCRF
Enscor, Inc. [*Associated Press*] (SAG) ... Enscor
Enscor, Inc. [*Toronto Stock Exchange symbol*] ... ENZ
Ensemble [*Group*] [*French*] ... ens
Ensemble (VRA) ... ensb
Ensemble for Early Music ... EEM
Ensenada [*Mexico ICAO location identifier*] (ICLI) ... MMES
ENSERCH Corp. [*NYSE symbol*] (TTSB) ... ENS
Enserch Corp. [*Associated Press*] (SAG) ... Ensc
Enserch Corp. [*Associated Press*] (SAG) ... Ensrch
ENSERCH Dep Adj cm E Pfd [*NYSE symbol*] (TTSB) ... ENSPrE
ENSERCH Dep Adj cm F Pfd [*NYSE symbol*] (TTSB) ... ENSPrF
Enserch Exploration [*NYSE symbol*] (TTSB) ... EEX
Enserch Exploration [*NYSE symbol Toronto Stock Exchange symbol*] ... ENS
Enserch Exploration, Inc. [*NYSE symbol*] (SAG) ... EEX
Enserch Exploration, Inc. [*Associated Press*] (SAG) ... EnsExp
Enserv Corp. [*Toronto Stock Exchange symbol*] ... ESV
Enshi [*China*] [*Airport symbol*] (OAG) ... ENH
Ensign (AABC) ... ENS
Ensign ... ENS
Ensign [*Navy*] ... 01
Ensign, Canadian Forces Base, Cornwallis, Nova Scotia [*Library symbol National Library of Canada*] (NLC) ... NSCCFE
Ensign Class Association [*Defunct*] (EA) ... ECA
Ensign, KS [*Television station call letters*] ... KBSD
Ensor Air [*Czechoslovakia*] [*ICAO designator*] (FAAC) ... ENR
Enstatite [*CIPW classification*] [*Geology*] ... en
Enstatite, Magnesite, Olivine, Graphite [*Geology*] ... EMOG
Ensuing (ROG) ... ENSG
Ensured Data Integrity ... EDI
EnSys Environmental Products [*NASDAQ symbol*] (TTSB) ... ENSY
EnSys Environmental Products, Inc. [*NASDAQ symbol*] (SAG) ... ENSY
EnSys Environmental Products, Inc. [*Associated Press*] (SAG) ... EnSys
Entablature (VRA) ... entbl
Entamoeba [*Microbiology*] (MAE) ... E
Entamoeba Histolytica-Complement Fixation [*Immunochemistry*] (DAVI) ... EH-CF
Entanglement Network (EA) ... EN
Entartungs-Reaktion [*Reaction of Degeneration*] [*German*] ... EaR
Entayant Institute (EA) ... EI
Ente de Radiodiffusion y Television [*Radio and television network*] [*Argentina*] ... ERT
Ente Nazionale Italiano per il Turismo [*Italian National Tourist Board*] ... ENIT
Entebbe [*Uganda*] [*Seismograph station code, US Geological Survey Closed*] (SEIS) ... ENT
Entebbe Area Control Center [*Uganda*] [*ICAO location identifier*] (ICLI) ... HUEC
Entebbe/International [*Uganda*] [*ICAO location identifier*] (ICLI) ... HUEN
Entebbe/Kampala [*Uganda*] [*Airport symbol*] (OAG) ... EBB
Entek Oil & Gas [*Vancouver Stock Exchange symbol*] ... ETK
Entente Council [*See also CE*] (EAIO) ... EC
Entente Europeenne du Commerce en Gros des Deux-Roues (EA) ... EECGDR
Entente Medicale Mediterraneenne [*Mediterranean Medical Entente*] (EAIO) ... EMM
Entente Nationale Democratique [*National Democratic Entente*] [*Monaco*] [*Political party*] (PPE) ... END
Enter (MUGU) ... ENT
Enter Control Area [*Aviation*] ... ECA
Enter Controlled Airspace [*Air Traffic Control*] (FAAC) ... ECAS
Enter Exponent [*Computer science*] ... EE
Enter Key [*Computer science*] (IAA) ... ENK
Enter Trapping Mode (SAA) ... ETM
Enteractive Inc. Wrrt [*NASDAQ symbol*] (TTSB) ... ENTRW
Enteral Nutrition [*Medicine*] ... EN
Enteral Nutrition Council (EA) ... ENC
Entered ... ENTD
Entered Apprentice [*Freemasonry*] ... EA
Entered Apprentice [*Freemasonry*] (ROG) ... EAP
Entered Apprentice Mason [*Freemasonry*] (ROG) ... EAM
Entered at Stationers' Hall [*British*] (BARN) ... Ent Sta Hall
Entered Employment Rate [*Job Training and Partnership Act*] (OICC) ... EER
Entered From (SAA) ... EF
Entered in Service [*Military*] ... EIS
Entered on Duty (SAA) ... EOD
Entered without Inspection [*Usually applies to aliens who enter at other than a port of entry*] ... EWI
Entergy Arkansas $2.40cmPfd [*NYSE symbol*] (TTSB) ... AKPPr
Entergy Arkansas, Inc. Capital I [*NYSE symbol*] (SAG) ... EAI
Entergy Arkansas, Inc. Capital I [*Associated Press*] (SAG) ... EntArk
Entergy Corp. [*Associated Press*] (SAG) ... Entergy
Entergy Corp. [*NYSE symbol*] (SPSG) ... ETR
Entergy Corp. [*NYSE symbol*] (TTSB) ... ETR
Entergy Gulf States [*Associated Press*] (SAG) ... EntGlf
Entergy Gulf States [*NYSE symbol*] (SAG) ... GSU
Entergy Gulf States $1.75 Pref [*NYSE symbol*] (TTSB) ... GSUPr
Entergy Gulf States $4.40 Pfd [*NYSE symbol*] (TTSB) ... GSUPrB
Entergy Gulf States $4.52 Pfd [*NYSE symbol*] (TTSB) ... GSUPrG
Entergy Gulf States $5.08 Pfd [*NYSE symbol*] (TTSB) ... GSUPrE
Entergy Gulf States $8.80 Pfd [*NYSE symbol*] (TTSB) ... GSUPrK
Entergy Gulf States Dep Adj B Pfd [*NYSE symbol*] (TTSB) ... GSUPrD
Entergy Louisiana 9.68% cm Pfd [*NYSE symbol*] (TTSB) ... LPLPrA
Entergy Louisiana 12.64% cmPfd [*NYSE symbol*] (TTSB) ... LPLPr
Entergy Louisiana, Inc. [*Associated Press*] (SAG) ... EntLA
Entergy Louisiana, Inc. [*NYSE symbol*] (SAG) ... LPL
Entergy Louisiana, Inc. Capital I [*Associated Press*] (SAG) ... EntLA
Entergy Louisiana, Inc. Capital I [*NYSE symbol*] (SAG) ... LPL
Entergy Services, Inc. [*ICAO designator*] (FAAC) ... ENS
Enteric Coated [*Pharmacy*] ... EC
Enteric Coated Tablet [*Pharmacology*] ... ECT
Enteric Cytopathic Human Orphan-Rhino-Coryza Virus (DMAA) ... ERC

Enteric Cytopathogenic Porcine Orphan Virus	ECPO
Enteric Ganglion [Neurology]	EG
Enteric [or Epidemic] NANB Hepatitis [Non-A, Non-B] [Medicine]	ENANB
Enteric Nervous System [Neurobiology]	ENS
Enterically Transmitted [Medicine]	ET
Enterically Transmitted Non-A, Non-B Hepatitis [Medicine]	ET-NANBH
Enteric-Coated Microspheres of Pancrelipase	ECMP
Entering [FBI standardized term]	E
Entering [FBI standardized term]	ENT
Entering (ROG)	ENTG
Entering Air Defense Identification Zone [Aviation] (FAAC)	EADIZ
Entering Complaint [Medicine]	EC
Entering Office Date (DNAB)	EOD
Enterobacterial Common Antigen [Immunology]	ECA
Enterobacterial Repetitive Intergenic Consensus [Genetics]	ERIC
Enterochromaffin Cells [Medicine]	EC
Enterochromaffin-Like [Biochemistry]	ECL
Enterocytopathogenic Bovine Virus	ECBO
Enterocytopathogenic Dog Orphan Virus	ECDO
Enterocytopathogenic Human Orphan Virus	ECHO
Enterocytopathogenic Monkey Orphan Virus	ECMO
Enterocytopathogenic Swine Orphan Virus	ECSO
Enterohepatic Circulation [Medicine]	EHC
Enterohepatic Clearance [Biochemistry] (DAVI)	EHC
Enteropathogenic Escherichia Coli [Also, EPEC] [Medicine]	EEC
Enteropathogenic Escherichia coli [Also, EEC] [Medicine]	EPEC
Enterostomal Therapist [Gastroenterology]	ET
Enterotoxigenic Escherichia coli [Water pollution indicator]	ETEC
Enterprise	Ent
Enterprise (DLA)	ENTER
Enterprise	ENTRPRS
Enterprise Airlines [ICAO designator] (AD)	BE
Enterprise, AL [Location identifier FAA] (FAAL)	BVG
Enterprise, AL [Location identifier FAA] (FAAL)	EDN
Enterprise, AL [FM radio station call letters]	WDJR
Enterprise, AL [FM radio station call letters]	WKMX
Enterprise Allowance (ODBW)	EA
Enterprise Allowance Scheme [for the self-employed] [British]	EAS
Enterprise America (EA)	EA
Enterprise and Deregulation Unit (AIE)	EDU
Enterprise Association of the United States (EA)	EAUS
Enterprise Branch, Lennox and Addington County Library, Ontario [Library symbol National Library of Canada] (NLC)	OENLA
Enterprise Business Model [Australia]	EBM
Enterprise Data Access/SQL [Structured Query Language] (CDE)	EDA/SQL
Enterprise Development Programme [University of Glasgow] (AIE)	EDP
Enterprise, Family, and Freedom [Australia Political party]	EFF
Enterprise Federal Bancorp [NASDAQ symbol] (TTSB)	EFBI
Enterprise Federal Bancorp, Inc. [NASDAQ symbol] (SAG)	EFBI
Enterprise Federal Bancorp, Inc. [Associated Press] (SAG)	EntFedB
Enterprise Flexibility Agreement [Australia]	EFA
Enterprise for the Americas Initiative [Bush administration]	EAI
Enterprise Foundation (EA)	EF
Enterprise Information Systems	EIS
Enterprise Integration Network [Information service or system] (IID)	EINET
Enterprise Integration Technologies [Commercial firm]	EIT
Enterprise Investment Scheme [British] (ECON)	EIS
Enterprise Investments Trust [Australia]	EIT
Enterprise Learning through Information Technology [University of Durham] (AIE)	ELITE
Enterprise Mail Exchange [Soft-Switch, Inc.]	EMX
Enterprise Management Architecture [Computer science] (TNIG)	EMA
Enterprise Messaging Server (CDE)	EMS
Enterprise Modeling Server (PCM)	EMS
Enterprise Naming Service [Banyan Systems, Inc.] [Telecommunications] (PCM)	ENS
Enterprise Network Data Interconnectivity Family [Telecommunications]	ENDIF
Enterprise Network Services [Banyan] [Computer science]	ENS
Enterprise Networking Event [Telecommunications] (OSI)	ENE
Enterprise Oil [NYSE symbol] (SPSG)	ETP
Enterprise Oil ADS [NYSE symbol] (TTSB)	ETP
Enterprise Oil Co. [Associated Press] (SAG)	EntOil
Enterprise Oil Pref 'B' ADS [NYSE symbol] (TTSB)	ETPPrB
Enterprise Oil Pref'A'ADS [NYSE symbol] (TTSB)	ETPPr
Enterprise, OR [AM radio station call letters]	KWVR
Enterprise, OR [FM radio station call letters]	KWVR-FM
Enterprise Quality Improvement Program [Australia]	EQUIP
Enterprise Resource Planning (ACII)	ERP
Enterprise Resources [Vancouver Stock Exchange symbol]	ERI
Enterprise State Junior Colleg, Enterprise, AL [Library symbol] [Library of Congress] (LCLS)	AEnC
Enterprise Statistics [A publication]	ES
Enterprise Support Service	ESS
Enterprise Support Services for Africa [Funded by CIDA - Canadian International Development Agency]	ESSA
Enterprise Support Unit	ESU
Enterprise Systems [NASDAQ symbol] (TTSB)	ESIX
Enterprise Systems Connection [IBM Corp.]	ESCON
Enterprise Systems, Inc. [Associated Press] (SAG)	EntrSys
Enterprise Systems, Inc. [NASDAQ symbol] (SAG)	ESIX
Enterprise Thesaurus [Database]	LTH
Enterprise Value [Finance] (ECON)	EV
Enterprise Workshops Ltd.	EWL
Enterprise Zone [British]	EZ
Enterprise-Based Agreement	EBA
Enterprise-Based Committee [Australia]	EBC
Enterprises (AAGC)	Enters
Enterprises Systems, Inc. [NASDAQ symbol] (SAG)	ESIX
Enterprise-Specific Agreement	ESA
Enterprise-Wide Application Network	EWAN
Enterprise-Wide Web (ACII)	EWW
Entertaining Allowance [British military] (DMA)	EA
Entertainment [Wire service code] (NTCM)	E
Entertainment	ENT
Entertainment	ENTRTN
Entertainment Agents Association [British]	EAA
Entertainment and Sports Lawyer [A publication] (DLA)	Ent & Sports Law
Entertainment and Sports Programming Network [Television]	ESPN
[The] Entertainment Channel [Pay-television network] [Obsolete]	TEC
Entertainment Duty (DLA)	ED
Entertainment Industries Council (EA)	EIC
Entertainment Industry Employers' Association [Australia]	EIEA
Entertainment Industry Interim Council [Australia]	EIIC
Entertainment Industry Referral and Assistance Center (EA)	EIRAC
Entertainment Industry Support Committee [Defunct] (EA)	EISC
Entertainment Law Journal [A publication] (DLA)	Entertainment LJ
Entertainment Production Services [British]	EPS
Entertainment Satellite [Proposed] (MCD)	ENT/SAT
Entertainment Software Rating Board	ESRB
Entertainment Systems International [Database producer] (IID)	ESI
Entertainment Tax (DLA)	ET
Entertainment Television [Also, E! Entertainment] [A cable network] [Los Angeles, California] (WDMC)	E!
Entertainment Television [Also, E! Entertainment] [A cable network] [Los Angeles, California] (WDMC)	ET
Entertainment This Week [TV program]	ETW
Entertainment Tonight [Television program]	ET
Entertainment Trades Alliance [British]	ETA
Entertainment Weekly [A publication] (BRI)	Ent W
Entertainments National Service Association [Facetiously translated as "Every Night Something Awful"] [Military British]	ENSA
Entertainments Officer [Military British]	EO
Entgegen [Opposed] [Chemistry] [German]	(E)
Enthalpimetric Analysis [Analytical chemistry]	EA
Enthalpy [Symbol] [IUPAC] (DEN)	H
Enthronement of the Sacred Heart in the Home (EA)	ESHH
Entire [Philately]	Ent
Entire	ENTR
Entire Field Available (FAAC)	EFA
Entire Treatment Period [Medicine]	ETP
Entitle (AABC)	ENTL
Entitled to Severance Pay	ETSP
Entity	ENT
Entity Module [Computer science]	EM
Entity Relationship [Computer science] (PCM)	ER
Entity Relationship Diagram [Computer science] (EERA)	ERD
Entity Relationship for Windows (CDE)	Erwin
Entity-Relationships Diagram [Computer science]	ERD
Entity-Relationships Model (HGAA)	ERM
Entner-Doudoroff [Hexose metabolic pathway]	ED
Entomologic	ENTOMOL
Entomological Research Institute	ERI
Entomological Society of America (EA)	ESA
Entomological Society of Australia	ESA
Entomological Society of Canada (BARN)	ESC
Entomological Society of New South Wales (EERA)	ESNSW
Entomological Society of Ontario, Guelph, ON, Canada [Library symbol Library of Congress] (LCLS)	CaOGE
Entomological Society of Ontario, Guelph, Ontario [Library symbol National Library of Canada] (NLC)	OGE
Entomological Society of Queensland (EERA)	ESO
Entomological Society of Victoria [Australia]	ESV
Entomology	ENT
Entomology (AABC)	ENTO
Entomology	ENTOM
Entomology Research Library, Biosystematics Research Institute, Agriculture Canada [Bibliotheque de Recherches Entomologiques, Institut de Recherches Biosystematiques, Agriculture Canada] Ottawa, Ontario [Library symbol National Library of Canada] (NLC)	OOAGE
Entorhinal Cortex [Brain anatomy]	EC
Entrada	ENT
Entraide Universitaire Mondial du Canada [World University Service of Canada - WUSC]	EUMC
Entraide Universitaire Mondiale [World University Service - WUS] (EAIO)	EUM
Entrained Air Volume	EV
Entrained-Flow Gasification Test Facility	EFGTF
Entrained-Flow Reactor [Chemical engineering]	EFR
Entraineurs en Patinage Artistique du Canada [Figure Skating Coaches of Canada - FSCC]	EPAC
Entrainment Pressure	EP
Entrainment Release Factor [Nuclear energy] (NRCH)	ERF
Entrance	E
Entrance (ROG)	ENT
Entrance [A stage direction] (WDMC)	ent
Entrance (ROG)	ENTCE
Entrance [Maps and charts] (MSA)	ENTR
Entrance (VRA)	entr
Entrance (ROG)	ENTRACE
Entrance Complaint [Medicine] (MEDA)	EC
Entrance Left [A stage direction] [Theater] (WDMC)	EL

Entrance National Agency Check [*Military*] (AABC) .... ENTAC
Entrance National Agency Check [*Military*] (NVT) .... ENTNAC
Entrance Right [*A stage direction*] [*Theater*] (WDMC) .... ER
EntreMed, Inc. [*NASDAQ symbol*] (SAG) .... ENMD
EntreMed, Inc. [*Associated Press*] (SAG) .... EntreMd
Entrenching Tool [*Shovel/pick combination*] [*Military*] (VNW) .... ET
Entrepot .... ENTRPT
Entrepreneur .... ENTRPRNR
Entrepreneur de Transport Combine [*Combined Transport Operator*]
  [*Business term French*] .... ETC
[*The*] Entrepreneurial Economy [*Corporation for Enterprise Development*]
  [*A publication*] .... TEE
Entrepreneurial Institute [*Australia*] .... EI
Entrepreneurial Leadership Center (EA) .... ELC
[*The*] Entrepreneurship Institute (EA) .... TEI
Entreprise de Gestion Touristique [*Algeria*] (EY) .... EGT
Entries Closed (ROG) .... EC
Entropy [*Symbol*] [*IUPAC*] .... S
Entropy Unit .... EU
Entrucking Point [*Military*] .... EP
Entry [*Horse racing*] .... E
Entry (NASA) .... ENT
Entry .... ENT
Entry Acceptance Data (DS) .... EAD
Entry and Postlanding [*NASA*] (KSC) .... E & PL
Entry and Recovery Simulation (MCD) .... ERS
Entry Clearance Officer [*Immigration*] (DLA) .... ECO
Entry Closed Loop (NASA) .... ECL
Entry Code [*Computer science*] .... EC
Entry Computer .... ECU
Entry Control Point (MCD) .... ECP
Entry Control Roster (MCD) .... ECR
Entry Controller .... EC
Entry Corridor Display (KSC) .... ECD
Entry Data Subsystem .... EDS
Entry Date [*British Library Automated Information Service and National Library
  of Medicine*] [*Searchable field*] [*Information service or system*] (NITA) .... ED
Entry Elapsed Time (MCD) .... EET
Entry Guidance [*NASA*] (NASA) .... EG
Entry Interface (NASA) .... EI
Entry Interface Time (MCD) .... EIT
Entry/Landing (NASA) .... E/L
Entry Level Interactive Applications Systems [*Computer science*] .... ELIAS
Entry Level Item [*Bureau of Labor Statistics*] (GFGA) .... ELI
Entry Level System [*Computer science*] .... ELS
Entry Level Training .... ELT
Entry Lock [*Diving apparatus*] .... EL
Entry Military Occupational Specialty (AABC) .... EMOS
Entry Monitor Display (KSC) .... EMD
Entry Monitor System [*or Subsystem*] [*NASA*] .... EMS
Entry on Active Duty [*Army*] .... EAD
Entry on Duty (MUGU) .... EOD
Entry Point (BUR) .... EP
Entry Point Control Item (MHDB) .... EPCI
Entry Point Interface Control .... EPIC
Entry Processing Unit [*Computer science*] (DCTA) .... EPU
Entry Query Control Console [*Computer science*] .... EQCC
Entry Research Vehicle .... ERV
Entry Sequence Data Set (HGAA) .... ESDS
Entry Survival System .... ESS
Entry Systems Division [*IBM division*] (CDE) .... ESD
Entry Systems Technology [*IBM*] (PCM) .... EST
Entry Time-Sharing System [*IBM Corp.*] [*Computer science*] .... ETSS
Entry to Anesthesia Record by Speech .... EARS
Entry Year [*Information retrieval*] (NITA) .... EY
Entscheidung [*Decision, Judgment*] [*German*] (ILCA) .... E
Entscheidung [*Decision, Judgment*] [*German*] (ILCA) .... Entsch
Entsiklopedyah 'Ivrit [*or Enziklopedyah 'Ivrit*] (BJA) .... EI
Entsiklopedyah 'Ivrit [*or Enziklopedyah 'Ivrit*] (BJA) .... EIV
Entsiqlopedia Miqra'it-Encyclopaedia Biblica [*Jerusalem*] [*A publication*]
  (BJA) .... EM
Entsiqlopedia Miqra'it-Encyclopaedia Biblica [*Jerusalem*] [*A publication*]
  (BJA) .... EMiqr
Entsprechend [*Corresponding*] [*German*] .... ENTSPR
Entwicklungsalter [*Developmental Age*] [*Psychology*] .... EA
Entwicklungsring Nord Organisation [*Space Division of European
  Consortium*] .... ERNO
Entwistle Public Library, Alberta [*Library symbol National Library of
  Canada*] (NLC) .... AENT
Entwurf [*Draft*] [*German*] (ILCA) .... E
Entwurf [*Draft*] [*German*] (ILCA) .... Entw
Enugu [*Nigeria*] [*ICAO location identifier*] (ICLI) .... DNEN
Enugu [*Nigeria*] [*Airport symbol*] (OAG) .... ENU
Enuma Elis (BJA) .... EnEl
Enumclaw Public Library, Enumclaw, WA [*Library symbol*] [*Library of
  Congress*] (LCLS) .... WaEn
Enumclaw, WA [*AM radio station call letters*] .... KENU
Enumeration (MSA) .... ENUM
Enumeration Area [*Statistics*] .... EA
Enumeration District [*Census*] .... ED
Enunciation (ROG) .... ENUN
Envelope [*Unit of issue*] [*Military*] (DNAB) .... EN
Envelope [*Refers to the envelope that surrounds cells*] [*Biochemistry*] (DAVI) .... env
Envelope (KSC) .... ENV
Envelope .... ENV

Envelope (WDMC) .... ep
Envelope Delay Distortion .... EDD
Envelope Drawing (MSA) .... ED
Envelope Elimination and Restoration .... EER
Envelope Institute of America .... EIA
Envelope Makers' and Manufacturing Stationers' Association (DGA) .... EMMSA
Envelope Manufacturers Association [*Later, EMAA*] (EA) .... EMA
Envelope Manufacturers Association of America (EA) .... EMAA
Envipco Canada [*Vancouver Stock Exchange symbol*] .... ECW
Envirocare Facility [*Clive, UT*] (GAAI) .... ENVR
Enviroon Ltd., Vancouver, BC, Canada [*Library symbol Library of
  Congress*] (LCLS) .... CaBVaEN
Enviroon Ltd., Vancouver, British Columbia [*Library symbol National Library
  of Canada*] (NLC) .... BVAEN
Envirodyne Inds [*NASDAQ symbol*] (TTSB) .... EDYN
Envirodyne Industries, Inc. [*NASDAQ symbol*] (SAG) .... EDYN
Envirodyne Industries, Inc. [*Associated Press*] (SAG) .... EnvirIn
Envirogen, Inc. [*NASDAQ symbol*] (SAG) .... ENVG
Envirogen, Inc. [*Associated Press*] (SAG) .... Envrg
Envirogen, Inc. [*Associated Press*] (SAG) .... Envrgen
Envirogen Inc. Wrrt [*NASDAQ symbol*] (TTSB) .... ENVGW
Enviromental Index (USDC) .... ENDEX
Envirometrics Inc. [*Associated Press*] (SAG) .... Envmt
Envirometrics, Inc. [*Associated Press*] (SAG) .... Envmtrc
Envirometrics, Inc. [*NASDAQ symbol*] (SAG) .... EVRM
Envirometrics Inc. Wrrt [*NASDAQ symbol*] (TTSB) .... EVRMW
Environ [*About*] [*French*] .... ENV
Environic Foundation International (EA) .... EFI
Environment [*Psychology*] .... E
Environment [*A publication*] (BRI) .... Env
Environment (VRA) .... envir
Environment (MSA) .... ENVIR
Environment .... ENVIR
Environment .... ENVIRN
Environment (AFM) .... ENVMT
Environment Actions Plan [*Commonwealth*] (EERA) .... EAP
Environment and Consumer Protection Service [*EEC*] (DS) .... ECPS
Environment and Energy Study Institute (GNE) .... EESI
Environment and Heredity .... E & H
Environment and RADAR Operations Simulator .... EROS
Environment and Resource Management Division [*World Wildlife Fund-
  United States*] .... ERMD
Environment and School Initiatives Project (EERA) .... ENSI
Environment and Special Measurement System (MCD) .... ESMS
Environment Assistance Program (EERA) .... EAP
Environment Canada .... EC
Environment Canada, AES Regina Weather Office, Regina, SK, Canada
  [*Library symbol*] [*Library of Congress*] (LCLS) .... CaSREAE
Environment Canada, AES Regional Library, Bedford, NS, Canada [*Library
  symbol*] [*Library of Congress*] (LCLS) .... CaNSBeAE
Environment Canada, Air Pollution Technology Centre, Ottawa, ON,
  Canada [*Library symbol Library of Congress*] (LCLS) .... CaOOEAPT
Environment Canada, Archaeological Research, Ottawa, ON, Canada
  [*Library symbol Library of Congress*] (LCLS) .... CaOOEAR
Environment Canada, Atmospheric Environment Service, Central Region
  Headquarter, Winnipeg, MB,Canada [*Library symbol*] [*Library of
  Congress*] (LCLS) .... CaMWEAE
Environment Canada, Atmospheric Environment Service, Dorval, PQ,
  Canada [*Library symbol Library of Congress*] (LCLS) .... CaQMEA
Environment Canada, Atmospheric Environment Service, Edmonton, AB,
  Canada [*Library symbol Library of Congress*] (LCLS) .... CaAEEAE
Environment Canada, Atmospheric Environment Service, Vancouver, BC,
  Canada [*Library symbol*] [*Library of Congress*] (LCLS) .... CaBVaEAE
Environment Canada, Atmospheric Environment Service, Ville St. Laurent,
  PQ, Canada [*Library symbol*] [*Library of Congress*] (LCLS) .... CaQVsLEA
Environment Canada, Canadian Wildlife Service, National Wildlife
  Research Centre, Ottawa, ON, Canada [*Library symbol*] [*Library of
  Congress*] (LCLS) .... CaOOECWN
Environment Canada, Canadian Wildlife Service, Winnipeg, MB, Canada
  [*Library symbol Library of Congress*] (LCLS) .... CaMWECW
Environment Canada, Canadian Wildlife Service, Yellowknife, NT, Canada
  [*Library symbol Library of Congress*] (LCLS) .... CaNWYECW
Environment Canada, Conservation Division, Ottawa, ON, Canada [*Library
  symbol Library of Congress*] (LCLS) .... CaOOECD
Environment Canada [*Environnement Canada*] Dartmouth, Nova Scotia
  [*Library symbol National Library of Canada*] (NLC) .... NSDE
Environment Canada, Dartmouth, NS, Canada [*Library symbol Library of
  Congress*] (LCLS) .... CaNSDE
Environment Canada, Environmental Protection Service, Assessment and
  Coordination, Yellowknife, NT, Canada [*Library symbol*] [*Library of
  Congress*] (LCLS) .... CaNWYEEP
Environment Canada, Environmental Protection Service, Environmental
  Emergency Library, Toronto, ON, Canada [*Library symbol Library of
  Congress*] (LCLS) .... CaOTEPSE
Environment Canada, Environmental Protection Service, Northwest
  Region, Edmonton, AB, Canada [*Library symbol Library of Congress*]
  (LCLS) .... CaAEEPS
Environment Canada, Environmental Protection Service, Regina, SK,
  Canada [*Library symbol*] [*Library of Congress*] (LCLS) .... CaSREEP
Environment Canada, Environmental Protection Service, Toronto, ON,
  Canada [*Library symbol Library of Congress*] (LCLS) .... CaOTEPS
Environment Canada, Environmental Protection Service, Whitehorse, YT,
  Canada [*Library symbol*] [*Library of Congress*] (LCLS) .... CaYWEEP
Environment Canada, Environmental Protection Service, Winnipeg, MB,
  Canada [*Library symbol*] [*Library of Congress*] (LCLS) .... CaMWEEP

Environment Canada, Hull, PQ, Canada [*Library symbol Library of Congress*] (LCLS) .... CaQHEn
Environment Canada, Inland Waters Directorate, Regina, SK, Canada [*Library symbol Library of Congress*] (LCLS) .... CaSREIW
Environment Canada, Legal Services, Ottawa, ON, Canada [*Library symbol*] [*Library of Congress*] (LCLS) .... CaOOELS
Environment Canada, National Hydrology Research Centre, Saskatchewan, SK, Canada [*Library symbol*] [*Library of Congress*] (LCLS) .... CaSSEH
Environment Canada, Pacific and Yukon Region Canadian Wildlife Service, Delta, BC, Canada [*Library symbol*] [*Library of Congress*] (LCLS) .... CaBDeCW
Environment Canada, Parks Canada, Ottawa, ON, Canada [*Library symbol Library of Congress*] (LCLS) .... CaOOPAC
Environment Centre, New South Wales [*Australia*] .... ECNSW
Environment Centre, Northern Territory [*Australia*] .... ECNT
Environment Centre (Northern Territory) [*State*] (EERA) .... EC(NT)
Environment Centre of the Northern Territory [*State*] (EERA) .... ECNT
Environment Centre of Western Australia [*Australia*] .... ECWA
Environment Code of Ethics for Rangeland Managers (EERA) .... ECERM
Environment Concept Car [*Volvo Motor Co.*] .... ECC
Environment Condition (CAAL) .... EC
Environment Conditioning Unit (MCD) .... ECU
Environment, Conservation, and Hunting Outreach [*An association*] .... ECHO
Environment Coordination Board [*United Nations*] .... ECB
Environment Council of Alberta, Edmonton, AB, Canada [*Library symbol Library of Congress*] (LCLS) .... CaAECA
Environment Council of Alberta, Edmonton, Alberta [*Library symbol National Library of Canada*] (NLC) .... AEECA
Environment Decision-Making Support System [*Computer science*] (EERA) .... EDSS
Environment Determination Program (SAA) .... EDP
Environment Division, Newfoundland Department of Consumer Affairs and Environment, St. John's, Newfoundland [*Library symbol National Library of Canada*] (NLC) .... NFSCAEE
Environment Effects Statement (EERA) .... EES
Environment Encyclopedia [*A publication*] .... ENE
Environment Generator [*Computer software*] .... EG
Environment Generator [*Computer software*] .... ENVGEN
Environment in Latin-America Network (EERA) .... ELAN
Environment Information Center, Inc. [*Database producer*] .... EIC
Environment Information Centre (EERA) .... EIC
Environment Information On-Line [*Database*] [*Environment Information Center, Inc. New York, NY*] .... ENVIROLINE
Environment Institute of Australia (EERA) .... EIA
Environment Lapse Rate (DA) .... ELR
Environment Law and Machinery Unit (EERA) .... ELMU
Environment Liaison Board [*British*] (DI) .... ELB
Environment Liaison Centre [*Later, ELCI*] (EAIO) .... ELC
Environment Liaison Centre International (EAIO) .... ELCI
Environment Libraries Automated System [*Environment Canada*] [*Database*] [*Information service or system*] (IID) .... ELIAS
Environment Management and Review Program (EERA) .... ERMP
Environment Management Committee [*Australia*] .... EMC
Environment Management Industries (EERA) .... EMI
Environment Management Industry .... EMI
Environment Management Industry Association of Australia (EERA) .... EMIAA
Environment Management Program (EERA) .... EMP
Environment Matters [*A publication*] .... EM
Environment Model .... ENVM
Environment Modification Convention (EERA) .... ENMOD
Environment News [*A publication*] .... Envir News
Environment News Digest [*A publication*] (EAAP) .... END
Environment Noise Control Committee (EERA) .... ENCC
Environment One Corp. [*Associated Press*] (SAG) .... EnvrOne
Environment One Corp. [*NASDAQ symbol*] (SAG) .... EONE
Environment Planning Authority (EERA) .... EPA
Environment Policy Coordinating Committee [*Commonwealth*] (EERA) .... EPCC
Environment Pollutions Agency [*British*] .... EPA
Environment Programme Library [*Database*] [*UNEP*] [*United Nations*] (DUND) .... EPLIB
Environment Protection Agency [*USA*] (EERA) .... EPA
Environment Protection Agency [*Australia*] (EERA) .... EPA
Environment Protection Authority [*Western Australia*] [*State*] (EERA) .... EPA
Environment Protection (Impact of Proposals) [*Act 1974*] [*Commonwealth Act*] (EERA) .... EP (IP)
Environment Protection Policy (EERA) .... EPOC
Environment Protection Program (EERA) .... EPP
Environment Regulation Handbook [*A publication*] (DLA) .... Env't Reg Handbook
Environment Reporter [*Bureau of National Affairs*] [*A publication*] (DLA) .... Envir Rep
Environment Reporter (Bureau of National Affairs) [*A publication*] (DLA) .... Env't Rep (BNA)
Environment Round Table (EERA) .... ERT
Environment Strategies Division [*Commonwealth*] (EERA) .... ESD
Environment Supply Sensing Device (MCD) .... ESSD
Environment Table Simulation (SAA) .... ETS
Environment Teachers' Association (EERA) .... ETA
Environment Technical Advisory Committee (EERA) .... ETAC
Environment Variable [*Computer science*] (PCM) .... E-VAR
Environment Visualization System [*Computer science*] .... EVS
Environmental (DD) .... envirl
Environmental .... ENVIRON
Environmental .... ENVIRON
Environmental .... ENVMTL
Environmental (KSC) .... ENVR
Environmental .... ENVRNMTL
Environmental .... ENVT
Environmental Acceptance Test (NASA) .... EAT
Environmental Acoustics Laboratory [*Pennsylvania State University*] [*Research center*] (RCD) .... EAL
Environmental Action (EA) .... EA
Environmental Action Coalition (EA) .... EAC
Environmental Action for Survival [*Defunct*] (EA) .... ENACT
Environmental Action Foundation (EA) .... EAF
Environmental Action Plan [*Environmental Protection Agency*] (ERG) .... EAP
Environmental Activities Staff [*Automotive industry*] .... EAS
Environmental Affairs [*A publication*] (DLA) .... Envtl Affairs
Environmental Analog Recording System .... EARS
Environmental Analysis [*Program*] .... ENVANAL
Environmental Analysis and Planning (PDAA) .... EAP
Environmental Analysis Group [*Army*] .... EAG
Environmental and Conservation Bureau [*Australian Capital Territory*] .... ECB
Environmental and Energy Study Conference (EA) .... EESC
Environmental and Energy Systems .... E & ES
Environmental and Molecular Science Laboratory (DOMA) .... EMSL
Environmental and Morale Leave [*Military*] .... E & ML
Environmental and Planning Law Journal [*Australia A publication*] .... EPLJ
Environmental and Safety Business Opportunities [*Bureau of National Affairs*] .... ESBO
Environmental and Social Systems Analysts Ltd. .... ESSA
Environmental and Societal Impacts Group [*National Center for Atmospheric Research*] .... ESIG
Environmental and Water Quality Operational Studies [*Army Corps of Engineers*] .... EWQOS
Environmental Assessment (MCD) .... EA
Environmental Assessment Command Center [*Nuclear energy*] (NRCH) .... EACC
Environmental Assessment Data Systems [*Discontinued*] [*Environmental Protection Agency Information service or system*] (IID) .... EADS
Environmental Assessment/Environmental Impact Statement [*Army*] (RDA) .... EA/EIS
Environmental Assessment of Great Lakes Ecosystems [*United States Fish and Wildlife Service*] (ASF) .... EAGLE
Environmental Assessment Scale [*Occupational therapy*] .... EAS
Environmental Assistance Procedure .... EAP
Environmental Audit [*Environmental Protection Agency*] (GFGA) .... EA
Environmental Auditing Roundtable [*Environmental Protection Agency*] (EPA) .... EAR
Environmental Awareness Reading List [*Department of the Interior*] .... EARL
Environmental Bankers Association .... EBA
Environmental Buoy [*Marine science*] (MSC) .... EB
Environmental Business Council .... EBC
Environmental Business Publishing, Inc. (IID) .... EBPI
Environmental Capacity (EERA) .... EC
Environmental Carcinogen Information [*Department of Energy*] [*Information service or system*] (IID) .... ECI
Environmental Chamber (KSC) .... EC
Environmental Characterization Working Group .... ECWG
Environmental Chemicals Data and Information Network [*Commission of the European Communities*] [*Chemical databank*] (IID) .... ECDIN
Environmental Chemistry and Biology [*Marine science*] (OSRA) .... ECB
Environmental Chemistry and Biology (USDC) .... ECB
Environmental Chemistry Laboratory [*Environmental Protection Agency*] (GFGA) .... ECL
Environmental Choice Australia .... ECA
Environmental Cleanup and Responsibility Act [*1983*] (ERG) .... ECRA
Environmental Clearinghouse, Inc. [*An association*] (EA) .... ECI
Environmental Coalition on Nuclear Power (EA) .... ECNP
Environmental Communications Network [*Proposed environmental information exchange network*] .... ECN
Environmental Communicators Organisation [*British*] (DBA) .... ECO
Environmental Compatibility Assurance Program [*Navy*] .... ECAP
Environmental Complexity .... EC
Environmental Compliance Assessment and Management Program [*Air Force*] (DOMA) .... ECAMP
Environmental Conditions Determination (AAG) .... ECD
Environmental Consequences of Nuclear War [*International Council of Scientific Unions*] .... ENUWAR
Environmental Conservation Acreage Reserve Program [*Department of Agriculture*] .... ECARP
Environmental Conservation Law [*New York, NY A publication*] .... ECL
Environmental Conservation Organization .... ECO
Environmental Conservation Service [*Canada*] .... ECS
Environmental Contaminant Evaluation [*Fish and Wildlife Service program*] .... ECE
Environmental Contaminants Authority (EERA) .... ECA
Environmental Control (KSC) .... EC
Environmental Control Administration [*Later, EPA*] .... ECA
Environmental Control and Life Support [*NASA*] (NASA) .... ECLS
Environmental Control and Life Support Subsystem [*NASA*] (MCD) .... ECLSS
Environmental Control and Mechanism (SAA) .... EC & M
Environmental Control Canister .... ECC
Environmental Control Equipment .... ECE
Environmental Control Group (CAAL) .... ECG
Environmental Control Organization [*Proposed in 1970 by Walter J. Hickel, Secretary of the Interior*] .... ECO
Environmental Control Report [*A publication*] (EAAP) .... ECR
Environmental Control Shroud [*Nuclear energy*] (NRCH) .... ECS
Environmental Control System [*NASA*] .... ECS
Environmental Control Table .... ECT
Environmental Control Unit .... ECU
Environmental Control Unit (MCD) .... ENCU

Environmental Cooperation with Asia Program (EERA) ... ECAP
Environmental Council of Concrete Organizations ... ECCO
Environmental Crimes Unit [*Environmental Protection Agency*] (GFGA) ... ECU
Environmental Crisis Operation [*University of British Columbia*] ... ECO
Environmental Criteria and Assessment Office [*Environmental Protection Agency*] (GRD) ... ECAO
Environmental Criteria and Assessment Office, Cincinnati [*Ohio*] [*Environmental Protection Agency*] (GRD) ... ECAO/CIN
Environmental Criteria and Assessment Office, Research Triangle Park [*North Carolina*] [*Environmental Protection Agency*] (GRD) ... ECAO/RTP
Environmental Damage (EERA) ... ED
Environmental Data Access and Control System (HGAA) ... EDACS
Environmental Data and Ecological Parameters Data Base [*International Societyof Ecological Modelling*] [*Information service or system*] (IID) ... EDE
Environmental Data and Information Management Systems [*Marine science*] (OSRA) ... EDIMS
Environmental Data and Information Management Systems (USDC) ... EDIMS
Environmental Data and Information Service [*Later, NESDIS*] ... EDIS
Environmental Data Base Directory [*National Oceanographic Data Center*] [*Database*] (MSC) ... EDBD
Environmental Data Book (NASA) ... EDB
Environmental Data Collection and Processing Facility [*Tucson, AZ*] [*Army*] (AABC) ... EDCPF
Environmental Data Directory [*Database*] (EERA) ... EDD
Environmental Data Index [*National Oceanic and Atmospheric Administration*] (MCD) ... ENDEX
Environmental Data Records ... EDR
Environmental Data Resources, Inc. (IID) ... EDR
Environmental Data Service [*Later, NESDIS*] [*Washington, DC National Oceanic and Atmospheric Administration*] (EA) ... EDS
Environmental Data Service Technical Memoranda [*National Oceanic and Atmospheric Administration*] (NOAA) ... EDSTM
Environmental Data Services [*Publisher*] [*British*] ... ENDS
Environmental Data Support System (MCD) ... EDSS
Environmental Defender's Office, New South Wales [*Australia*] ... EDONSW
Environmental Defense Fund (EA) ... EDF
Environmental Design Alignment Process ... EDAP
Environmental Design of Waterways [*U.S. Army Corps of Engineers*] ... ENDOW
Environmental Design Research Association (EA) ... EDRA
Environmental Deterioration Rating (PDAA) ... EDR
Environmental Diagnostics, Inc. ... EDI
Environmental Disruption ... ED
Environmental Distribution of Dynamic Item Entries (SAA) ... EDDIE
Environmental Diving Unit [*Marine science*] (MSC) ... EDU
Environmental Easement Program [*Department of Agriculture*] ... EEP
Environmental Ecological and Support Laboratory [*Environmental Protection Agency*] (GFGA) ... EESL
Environmental Economics ... EE
Environmental Economics (EERA) ... ENVEC
Environmental Education Advisers Association [*British*] (DBA) ... EEAA
Environmental Education and Information Committee (EERA) ... EEIC
Environmental Education Group [*Defunct*] (EA) ... EEG
Environmental Effects for Distributed Interactive Simulation [*Army*] ... E^{2}DIS
Environmental Effects Group [*Army*] (RDA) ... EEG
Environmental Effects Laboratory [*Army*] ... EEL
Environmental Effects on Space Systems ... EESS
Environmental Effects Report [*Military*] ... EER
Environmental Effects Statement [*Australia*] ... EES
Environmental Elements [*NYSE symbol*] (TTSB) ... EEC
Environmental Elements Corp. [*NYSE symbol*] (SPSG) ... EEC
Environmental Elements Corp. [*Associated Press*] (SAG) ... EnvEle
Environmental Emergency Library, Environmental Protection Service, Environment Canada [*Bibliotheque des Incidences Environnementales, Service de la Protection de l'Environnement, Environnement Canada*] **Toronto, Ontario** [*Library symbol National Library of Canada*] (NLC) ... OTEPSE
Environmental Encyclopedia [*A publication*] ... EE
Environmental Engineering Intersociety Board ... EEIB
Environmental Engineering Management Team ... EEMT
Environmental Engineering Section ... EES
Environmental Enhancement Program ... EEP
Environmental Epidemiology and Cancer Centre [*British*] (IRUK) ... EECC
Environmental Equipment Institute [*Defunct*] (EA) ... EEI
Environmental Expenditure on Protection and Abatement (EERA) ... EEPA
Environmental Experiments Program [*National Science Foundation*] ... EEP
Environmental Exposure Level [*Toxicology*] ... EEL
Environmental Extremists ... ENVEX
Environmental Factor ... EF
Environmental Fate [*Environmental Protection Agency Information service or system*] (CRD) ... ENVIROFATE
Environmental Financial Advisory Board [*Environmental Protection Agency*] (EGAO) ... EFAB
Environmental Financing Authority [*Expired, 1975*] [*Environmental Protection Agency*] ... EFA
Environmental Flow Requirements of Australia's Waterways (EERA) ... EFR
Environmental Fluid Mechanics Foundation [*Monash University*] [*Australia*] ... EFMF
Environmental Forum [*A publication*] (DLA) ... Envtl F
[*The*] **Environmental Fund** [*Later, PEB*] (EA) ... TEF
Environmental, General Instrumentation, Life Support [*NASA*] (KSC) ... EGIL
Environmental Group, Pacific Command (CINC) ... EGPACOM
Environmental Hazard Communication ... EHC
Environmental Hazards Management Institute [*University of New Hampshire*] [*Research center*] (RCD) ... EHM
Environmental Hazards Management Institute (GNE) ... EHMI
Environmental, Health, and Safety ... EH & S
Environmental Health Association (WDAA) ... EHA
Environmental Health Committee [*Environmental Protection Agency*] (GFGA) ... EHC
Environmental Health Directorate, Health Protection Branch, Department of National Health and Welfare [*Direction de l'Hygiene du Milieu, Direction Generale de la Protection de la Sante, Ministere de la Sante Nationale et du Bien-Etre Social*] **Ottawa, Ontario** [*Library symbol National Library of Canada*] (NLC) ... OONHH
Environmental Health Engineering Services [*Army*] (AABC) ... EHES
Environmental Health Institute [*Pittsfield, MA*] ... EHI
Environmental Health Laboratory [*Air Force*] ... EHL
Environmental Health Laboratory, Kelly Air Force Base ... EHL(K)
Environmental Health Laboratory, McClellan Air Force Base ... EHL-M
Environmental Health Laboratory Sciences Division [*Atlanta, GA*] [*Department of Health and Human Services*] (GRD) ... EHLS
Environmental Health Network [*Defunct*] (EA) ... EHN
Environmental Health News [*Database*] [*Occupational Health Services, Inc.*] [*Information service or system*] (CRD) ... EHN
Environmental Health Officer [*British*] (DCTA) ... EHO
Environmental Health Service [*US Government*] ... EHS
Environmental Health Specialist ... EHS
Environmental Health Standards (EERA) ... EHS
Environmental Hygiene Agency [*Army*] (MCD) ... EHA
Environmental Impact (NASA) ... EI
Environmental Impact Analysis Program [*or Project*] [*Department of the Interior*] (GRD) ... EIAP
Environmental Impact Appraisal [*Nuclear Regulatory Commission*] (GFGA) ... EIA
Environmental Impact Assessment [*Environmental Protection Agency*] (MCD) ... EIA
Environmental Impact Assessment (EERA) ... EIA
Environmental Impact Assessment/Environmental Impact Statement ... EIA/EIS
Environmental Impact Assessment for Life Cycle [*Army*] ... EIALC
Environmental Impact Computer System [*Database*] [*Army Corps of Engineers*] ... EICS
Environmental Impact Report [*Environmental Protection Agency*] ... EIR
Environmental Impact Research Program [*Army*] (RDA) ... EIRP
Environmental Impact Review ... EIR
Environmental Impact Service (USDC) ... EIS
Environmental Impact Statement [*Environmental Protection Agency*] ... EIS
Environmental Impact Statement (EERA) ... EIS
Environmental Impact Statements [*Heiner and Co.*] (NITA) ... EIS
Environmental Impact Study ... EIS
Environmental Impairment Liability ... EIL
Environmental Index [*Marine science*] (OSRA) ... ENDEX
Environmental Industries Directory [*A publication*] ... ENID
Environmental Industries Marketplace [*A publication*] ... EIM
Environmental Industry Council (EA) ... EIC
Environmental Information Analysis Center [*Battelle Memorial Institute*] (IID) ... EIAC
Environmental Information and Documentation Centres Database [*Commission of the European Communities*] [*Information service or system*] (CRD) ... ENDOC
Environmental Information and Support Network (EERA) ... EISN
Environmental Information Directory [*Later, Gale Environmental Sourcebook*] [*A publication*] ... EID
Environmental Information Division [*Air Force Air Training Command*] (IID) ... EID
Environmental Information Management System ... EIMS
Environmental Information Management Unit (EERA) ... EIMU
Environmental Information Networks Inc. [*Database producer*] (IID) ... EIN
Environmental Information Retrieval On-Line [*Environmental Protection Agency*] ... ENVIRON
Environmental Information System [*National Science Foundation*] ... EIS
Environmental Information System Office [*National Science Foundation*] ... EISO
Environmental Instrumentation Measurement and Monitoring (IAA) ... EIMAM
Environmental Interaction Theory of Personality (PDAA) ... EIT
Environmental Interference Effects Model (MCD) ... EIEM
Environmental Inventory System (GNE) ... EIS
Environmental Investigation Agency (BARN) ... EIA
Environmental Issues Test (EDAC) ... EIT
Environmental Labelling Schemes (EERA) ... ELS
Environmental Laboratories Information Retrieval Technique (PDAA) ... ELIRT
Environmental Laboratory ... EL
Environmental Laboratory Advisory Board [*Environmental Protection Agency*] ... ELAB
Environmental Language Inventory [*Speech and language therapy*] (DAVI) ... ELI
Environmental Law Centre (EERA) ... ELC
Environmental Law Institute (EA) ... ELI
Environmental Law Reporter [*A publication*] (DLA) ... Envtl L Rptr
Environmental Law Review [*A publication*] (DLA) ... Envtl L Rev
Environmental Life-Support Assembly [*NASA*] (KSC) ... ELSA
Environmental Life-Support System (MCD) ... ELSS
Environmental Load Unit [*Recycling, emissions*] [*Automotive engineering*] ... ELU
Environmental Management (NRCH) ... EM
Environmental Management and Control System (AAGC) ... EMCS
Environmental Management Association (EA) ... EMA
Environmental Management Committee (EERA) ... EMC
Environmental Management of Enclosed Coastal Seas (EERA) ... EMECS
Environmental Management Office (DOMA) ... EMO
Environmental Management Plan ... EMP
Environmental Management Report [*Environmental Protection Agency*] (GFGA) ... EMR
Environmental Management Subsystem [*Environmental Protection Agency*] (GFGA) ... EMS
Environmental Measurement Unit (MCD) ... EMU
Environmental Measurements Experiment ... EME

Environmental Measurements Laboratory [*Department of Energy*] (GRD) ..... EML
Environmental Measurements Laboratory Impactor [*Sampling instrument*] ..... EMLI
Environmental Mediation International [*Defunct*] (EA) ..... EMI
Environmental Medical Centre [*Australia*] ..... EMC
Environmental Medicine Branch [*NASA*] (KSC) ..... EMB
Environmental Medicine Officer [*Military*] ..... EMO
Environmental Meteorological Support Unit [*National Weather Service*] ..... EMSU
Environmental Methods Testing Site [*Environmental Protection Agency*] (GFGA) ..... EMTS
Environmental Modeling Systems, Inc. [*Computer science*] ..... EMS-I
Environmental Modification ..... ENMOD
Environmental Monitoring ..... EM
Environmental Monitoring and Assessment Program [*Environmental Protection Agency*] ..... EMAP
Environmental Monitoring and Prediction [*Subcommittee*] [*Marine science*] (OSRA) ..... EMP
Environmental Monitoring and Prediction [*Subcommittee*] (USDC) ..... EMP
Environmental Monitoring and Support Laboratory, Cincinnati [*Ohio*] [*Environmental Protection Agency*] (GRD) ..... EMSL/CIN
Environmental Monitoring & Testing Corp. [*NASDAQ symbol*] (NQ) ..... EMON
Environmental Monitoring Program ..... EMP
Environmental Monitoring Systems Division [*Environmental Protection Agency*] (GFGA) ..... EMSD
Environmental Monitoring Systems Laboratory, Las Vegas [*Nevada*] [*Environmental Protection Agency*] (GRD) ..... EMSL/LV
Environmental Monitoring Systems Laboratory, Research Triangle Park [*North Carolina*] [*Environmental Protection Agency*] (GRD) ..... EMSL/RTP
Environmental Mutagen Information [*Department of Energy*] [*Information service or system*] (IID) ..... EMI
Environmental Mutagen Information Center [*Environmental Information System Office*] ..... EMIC
Environmental Mutagen Society (EA) ..... EMS
Environmental Mutagen Test Development Program [*National Institute of Environmental Health Sciences*] ..... EMTDP
Environmental Park [*Australia*] ..... EP
Environmental Periodicals Bibliography [*Environmental Studies Institute*] [*Information service or system*] ..... ENVIROBIB
Environmental Periodicals Bibliography [*Environmental Studies Institute*] [*Information service or system*] ..... EPB
Environmental Photographic Interpretation Center [*Environmental Protection Agency*] ..... EPIC
Environmental Physiology Unit [*Simon Fraser University*] [*Canada Research center*] (RCD) ..... EPU
Environmental Planning and Management (EERA) ..... EPM
Environmental Policy and Law [*A publication*] (DLA) ..... Envtl Pol'y & L
Environmental Policy Center (EA) ..... EPC
Environmental Policy Institute (EA) ..... EPI
Environmental Pollution [*A publication*] (NOAA) ..... EP
Environmental Pollution Control (PDAA) ..... ENPOCON
Environmental Pollution Control ..... EPC
Environmental, Population, and Organismic Biology ..... EPO
Environmental Power [*NASDAQ symbol*] (SAG) ..... POWR
Environmental Power Corp. [*Associated Press*] (SAG) ..... EnvPwr
Environmental Prediction Research Facility [*Monterey, CA*] [*Navy*] ..... ENVPREDRSCHF
Environmental Prediction Research Facility [*Monterey, CA*] [*Navy*] ..... EPRF
Environmental Pre-Language Battery [*Speech and language therapy*] (DAVI) ..... EPB
Environmental Pre-Language Battery [*Speech and language therapy*] (DAVI) ..... EPLB
Environmental Priorities Initiative ..... EPI
Environmental Priorities Strategies [*Volvo*] [*Automotive engineering*] ..... EPS
Environmental Processes and Effects Division [*Army*] ..... EPED
Environmental Profile [*Environmental Protection Agency*] (GFGA) ..... EP
Environmental Programs Assistance Act (GFGA) ..... EPAA
Environmental Project Manager (NRCH) ..... EPM
Environmental Project on Central America [*Defunct*] (EA) ..... EPOCA
Environmental Projects Working Group [*NASA*] (NASA) ..... EPWG
Environmental Proof Test (IAA) ..... EPT
Environmental Protection Agency [*Government agency formed in 1970*] ..... EPA
Environmental Protection Agency Acquisition Regulations (GFGA) ..... EPAAR
Environmental Protection Agency/Air Resources Board ..... EPA/ARB
Environmental Protection Agency Analytical Operations Branch ..... AOP
Environmental Protection Agency Chemical Activities Status Report [*Databa se*] [*Environmental Protection Agency*] ..... EPACASR
Environmental Protection Agency Composite Model for Landfills [*Formerly, EPASMOD*] ..... EPACML
Environmental Protection Agency, Environmental Monitoring and Support Laboratory, Las Vegas, NV [*OCLC symbol*] (OCLC) ..... ERB
Environmental Protection Agency, Environmental Research Laboratory, Athens, GA [*OCLC symbol*] (OCLC) ..... EKD
Environmental Protection Agency, Environmental Research Laboratory, Gulf Breeze,FL [*OCLC symbol*] (OCLC) ..... EKC
Environmental Protection Agency, Environmental Research Laboratory, Narragansett, RI [*OCLC symbol*] (OCLC) ..... EHB
Environmental Protection Agency, ERC [*Environmental Research Center*] Library, Corvallis, OR [*OCLC symbol*] (OCLC) ..... ESB
Environmental Protection Agency, ESRL [*Environmental Sciences Research Laboratory*], Meteorology Laboratory, Research Triangle Park, NC [*OCLC symbol*] (OCLC) ..... EKF
Environmental Protection Agency Grants Administration Manual ..... EPAGM
Environmental Protection Agency, Headquarters Library, Washington, DC [*OCLC symbol*] (OCLC) ..... EJB

Environmental Protection Agency, Law Library, Washington, DC [*OCLC symbol*] (OCLC) ..... EJC
Environmental Protection Agency, Library, Environmental Research Center, Cincin nati, OH [*OCLC symbol*] (OCLC) ..... ELB
Environmental Protection Agency, Library, Environmental Research Laboratory, Du luth, MN [*OCLC symbol*] (OCLC) ..... ELD
Environmental Protection Agency, Library, Research Triangle Park, NC [*OCLC symbol*] (OCLC) ..... EKE
Environmental Protection Agency, Library Services, Research Triangle Park, NC [*OCLC symbol*] (OCLC) ..... EKB
Environmental Protection Agency, Motor Vehicle Emission Laboratory, Ann Arbor, MI [*OCLC symbol*] (OCLC) ..... ELC
Environmental Protection Agency, NEIC Library, Denver, CO [*OCLC symbol*] (OCLC) ..... EOB
Environmental Protection Agency, OTS [*Office of Toxic Substances*] Technical Information Center, Washington, DC [*OCLC symbol*] (OCLC) ..... EJE
Environmental Protection Agency Payroll System (GFGA) ..... EPAYS
Environmental Protection Agency - Pesticide Regional Division ..... EPA-PRD
Environmental Protection Agency Procurement Regulations [*A publication*] (AAGC) ..... EPPR
Environmental Protection Agency, R. S. Kerr Environmental Research Laboratory, Ada, OK [*OCLC symbol*] (OCLC) ..... EMB
Environmental Protection Agency, Region I Library, Boston, MA [*OCLC symbol*] (OCLC) ..... EHA
Environmental Protection Agency, Region II Field Office, Edison, NJ [*OCLC symbol*] (OCLC) ..... EIC
Environmental Protection Agency, Region II Library, New York, NY [*OCLC symbol*] (OCLC) ..... EIA
Environmental Protection Agency, Region III Field Office, Annapolis, MD [*OCLC symbol*] (OCLC) ..... EJD
Environmental Protection Agency, Region III Library, Philadelphia, PA [*OCLC symbol*] (OCLC) ..... EJA
Environmental Protection Agency, Region IV Library, Atlanta, GA [*OCLC symbol*] (OCLC) ..... EKA
Environmental Protection Agency, Region IX Library, San Francisco, CA [*OCLC symbol*] (OCLC) ..... ERA
Environmental Protection Agency, Region V Library, Chicago, IL [*OCLC symbol*] (OCLC) ..... ELA
Environmental Protection Agency, Region VI Library, Dallas, TX [*OCLC symbol*] (OCLC) ..... EMA
Environmental Protection Agency, Region VII Library, Kansas City, MO [*OCLC symbol*] (OCLC) ..... ENA
Environmental Protection Agency, Region VIII Library, Denver, CO [*OCLC symbol*] (OCLC) ..... EOA
Environmental Protection Agency, Region X Library, Seattle, WA [*OCLC symbol*] (OCLC) ..... ESA
Environmental Protection Agency Subsurface Fate and Transport Model [*Later, EPACML*] ..... EPASMOD
Environmental Protection Board [*British*] (BARN) ..... EPB
Environmental Protection Council [*Tasmania, Australia*] ..... EPC
Environmental Protection Data Base [*Environmental Protection Agency*] ..... EPDB
Environmental Protection Devices (MCD) ..... EPD
Environmental Protection Division (EERA) ..... EDP
Environmental Protection Limit (NRCH) ..... EPL
Environmental Protection Oil Sands Systems (PDAA) ..... EPOSS
Environmental Protection Program (CAAL) ..... EPP
Environmental Protection Research Institute ..... EPRI
Environmental Protection Service, Environment Canada [*Service de la Protection de l'Environnement, Environment Canada*] **Montreal, Quebec** [*Library symbol National Library of Canada*] (NLC) ..... QMEE
Environmental Protection Service, Environment Canada/Pacific Region [*Service de la Protection de l'Environnement, Environnement Canada/Region du Pacifique*] **West Vancouver, British Columbia** [*Library symbol National Library of Canada*] (NLC) ..... BVAEP
Environmental Protection Service, Environment Canada [*Service de la Protection de l'Environnement, Environment Canada*] **Regina, Saskatchewan** [*Library symbol National Library of Canada*] (NLC) ..... SREEP
Environmental Protection Service, Environment Canada [*Service de la Protection de l'Environnement, Environment Canada*] **Toronto, Ontario** [*Library symbol National Library of Canada*] (NLC) ..... OTEPS
Environmental Protection Service, Environment Canada [*Service de la Protection de l'Environnement, Environment Canada*] **Whitehorse, Yukon** [*Library symbol National Library of Canada*] (NLC) ..... YWEEP
Environmental Protection Service, Environment Canada [*Service de la Protection de l'Environnement, Environment Canada*] **Winnipeg, Manitoba** [*Library symbol National Library of Canada*] (NLC) ..... MWEEP
Environmental Protection Service, West Vancouver [*Environment Canada*] [*Research center*] (RCD) ..... EPS
Environmental Protection Shelter (MCD) ..... EPS
Environmental Protection System (AAG) ..... EPS
Environmental Protective Plan (MCD) ..... EP
Environmental Psychology [*City University of New York*] [*Defunct Information service or system*] (CRD) ..... Envpsych
Environmental Purification Systems, Inc. ..... EPS
Environmental Qualification Test ..... EQT
Environmental Quality ..... EQ
Environmental Quality Control ..... EQC
Environmental Quality Control Committee ..... EQCC
Environmental Quality Council [*Terminated, 1970*] (MCD) ..... EQC
Environmental Quality Improvement Act of 1970 ..... EQIA
Environmental Quality Index (PDAA) ..... EQI
Environmental Quality Information Services Program [*Navy*] ..... EQIS
Environmental Quality Laboratory [*California Institute of Technology*] ..... EQL
Environmental Quality Objective [*British*] (DCTA) ..... EQO

Environmental Quality Office [*HUD*] (OICC) ... EQO
Environmental Quality Staff [*Tennessee Valley Authority*] [*Knoxville, TN*] (GRD) ... EQS
Environmental Quality Standard [*British*] (DCTA) ... EQS
Environmental Radiation Ambient Monitoring System [*Environmental Protection Agency*] ... ERAMS
Environmental Radiation Data System [*Environmental Protection Agency*] (GFGA) ... ERDS
Environmental Radiation Protection Standard (NUCP) ... ERPS
Environmental Radiological Technical Specifications [*Nuclear energy*] (NRCH) ... ERTS
Environmental Record Editing and Statistics [*Fujitsu*] [*Japan*] (NITA) ... ERES
Environmental Recording, Editing, and Printing Program (BUR) ... EREP
Environmental Remote Sensing Applications Laboratory [*Oregon State University*] [*Research center*] (RCD) ... ERSAL
Environmental Report (NRCH) ... ER
Environmental Reporter Cases [*Bureau of National Affairs*] [*A publication*] (DLA) ... ERC
Environmental Requirement ... ER
Environmental Requirements/Capabilities Management Information System (MCD) ... ERCMIS
Environmental Research Aircraft and Sensor Technology ... ERAST
Environmental Research and Information Centre [*Commercial*] (EERA) ... ERIC
Environmental Research and Technology, Inc. [*Concord, MA*] (MCD) ... ERT
Environmental Research and Technology, Information Center, Concord, MA [*OCLC symbol*] (OCLC) ... ERT
Environmental Research Assessment Committee [*National Research Council*] ... ERAC
Environmental Research Center [*Environmental Protection Agency*] ... ERC
Environmental Research Consortium ... ERC
Environmental Research Development and Demonstration Authorization Act (GFGA) ... ERDDAA
Environmental Research Group ... ERG
Environmental Research Institute (EA) ... ERI
Environmental Research Institute of Michigan [*Research center*] (RCD) ... ERIM
Environmental Research Institute of Michigan, Ann Arbor, MI [*Library symbol Library of Congress*] (LCLS) ... MiAaE
Environmental Research Laboratories [*Boulder, CO*] [*National Oceanic and Atmospheric Administration*] ... ERL
Environmental Research Laboratory, Narragansett [*Environmental Protection Agency*] ... ERL-N
Environmental Research Laboratory, University of Arizona ... ERLUA
Environmental Research Papers (MCD) ... ERP
Environmental Research Satellite [*NASA*] ... ERS
Environmental Research Ship [*Navy symbol*] ... AGER
Environmental Resistance ... ER
Environmental Resistance Inherent in Equipment ... ERIE
Environmental Resource Information Services [*Australia*] ... ERIS
Environmental Resources Center ... ERC
Environmental Resources Information Network [*Australia*] ... ERIN
Environmental Resources Information System [*Computer science*] (EERA) ... ERIS
Environmental Resources Ltd. [*British*] ... ERL
Environmental Resources Management ... ERM
Environmental Resources Management, Inc. [*Database producer*] (IID) ... ERM
Environmental Resources Mapping System [*Computer science*] (EERA) ... ERMS
Environmental Resources of Australia [*Commercial*] (EERA) ... ERA
Environmental Resources Research and Assistance Program [*US Army Corps of Eng ineers*] ... ERRAP
Environmental Resources Research Institute [*Pennsylvania State University*] [*Information service or system*] (IID) ... ERRI
Environmental Resources Technology [*Information service or system*] (IID) ... ERTH
Environmental Resources Technology Satellite (NRCH) ... ERTS
Environmental Response and Referral Service [*Oak Ridge National Laboratory*] (IID) ... ERRS
Environmental Response Center [*Department of Energy*] (IID) ... ERC
Environmental Response Inventory [*Research test*] [*Psychology*] ... ERI
Environmental Response Policy ... ERP
Environmental Response Team [*Environmental Protection Agency*] ... ERT
Environmental Response Team Air Quality Model [*Environmental Protection Agency*] (GFGA) ... ERTAQ
Environmental Responsibility Program [*An association*] (EA) ... ERP
Environmental Restoration [*Metallurgy*] ... ER
Environmental Restoration and Waste Management (EGAO) ... EM
Environmental Restoration and Waste Management Advisory Committee [*Department of Energy*] (EGAO) ... EMAC
Environmental Restoration Opportunities Conference ... EROC
Environmental Review Guide for Operations [*US Army Corps of Engineers*] ... ERGO
Environmental Safety (EA) ... ES
Environmental Safety and Health [*Environmental Protection Agency*] (EPA) ... ES & H
Environmental Safety Facility [*Stanford University*] ... ESF
Environmental Safety Systems, Inc. [*Toronto Stock Exchange symbol*] ... ENV
Environmental Sanitation Information Center [*Asian Institute of Technology*] [*Thailand*] [*Information service or system*] (IID) ... ENSIC
Environmental Satellite Data [*National Oceanic and Atmospheric Administration*] (GFGA) ... ESD
Environmental Scanning Electron Microscope ... ESEM
Environmental Science (AABC) ... EVS
Environmental Science Education (AIE) ... ESE
Environmental Science Index [*Environmental Information Center Inc.*] [*Database*] (NITA) ... ESI
Environmental Science Information Center [*National Oceanic and Atmospheric Administration*] ... ESIC
Environmental Science Research [*Concept car*] [*Automotive engineering*] ... ESR
Environmental Science Services Administration [*Later, National Oceanic and Atmospheric Administration*] ... ESSA
Environmental Sciences Division [*Oak Ridge National Laboratory*] ... ESD
Environmental Sciences Group [*Boulder, CO*] [*Department of Commerce*] (GRD) ... ESG
Environmental Sciences Research Laboratory [*Environmental Protection Agency*] (GRD) ... ESRL
Environmental Sciences Research Laboratory/Research Triangle Park [*Environmental Protection Agency*] ... ESRL/RTP
Environmental Sciences Research Unit [*Cranfield Institute of Technology*] ... ESRU
Environmental Security Technology Certification Program [*Army*] (RDA) ... ESTCP
Environmental Self-Assessment Program ... ESAP
Environmental Sensing Device (IAA) ... ESD
Environmental Sensor Kit (MCD) ... ESK
Environmental Services (EERA) ... ES
Environmental Services Division [*Environmental Protection Agency*] (GFGA) ... ESD
Environmental Services of America, Inc. [*NASDAQ symbol*] (SAG) ... ENSA
Environmental Services of America, Inc. [*Associated Press*] (SAG) ... EnvSvc
Environmental Severity Index ... ESI
Environmental Sex Determination [*Biology*] ... ESD
Environmental Simulation Unit (PDAA) ... ESU
Environmental Simulator (IAA) ... ENSIM
Environmental Sketches in Perspective [*Computer program*] ... ESP
Environmental Standard Review Plan (NRCH) ... ESRP
Environmental Stress Crack [*or Cracking*] [*Plastics*] ... ESC
Environmental Stress Screening (MCD) ... ESS
Environmental Stress Sensing [*Automotive engineering*] ... ESS
Environmental Stress-Crack Resistance [*Plastics*] ... ESCR
Environmental Studies Association of Canada (EERA) ... ESAC
Environmental Studies Board [*National Academy of Sciences*] ... ESB
Environmental Studies Center [*State University of New York at Buffalo*] [*Research center*] (RCD) ... ESC
Environmental Studies Library, University of Waterloo, Ontario [*Library symbol National Library of Canada*] (NLC) ... OWTUE
Environmental Study Area ... ESA
Environmental Study Conference [*House of Representatives*] ... ESC
Environmental Support System (MCD) ... ESS
Environmental Survey ... ES
Environmental Survey Satellite (TEL) ... ESSA
Environmental Sustainment Laboratory (RDA) ... ESL
Environmental Symptoms Questionnaire (PDAA) ... ESQ
Environmental Synthesizer [*Navy*] ... ENSYN
Environmental System (MCD) ... ENV-SYS
Environmental System and Effects Division [*NASA*] ... ESED
Environmental System Management Controller (MCD) ... ESMC
Environmental System Module (MCD) ... ESM
Environmental System Resources [*National Science Foundation*] (MCD) ... ESR
Environmental Systems Applications Center [*NASA*] ... ESAC
Environmental Systems Division [*Army*] ... ESD
Environmental Systems Laboratory [*Virginia Polytechnic Institute and State University*] [*Research center*] (RCD) ... ESL
Environmental Systems Monitor (IAA) ... ESM
Environmental Systems Research Institute ... ESRI
Environmental Systems Research Institute Pty Ltd [*Commercial*] (EERA) ... ESRI
Environmental Systems Test Facility (KSC) ... ESTF
Environmental Task Force (EA) ... ETF
Environmental Team Leader [*Nuclear energy*] (NRCH) ... ELT
Environmental Tech USA [*NASDAQ symbol*] (TTSB) ... ENVR
Environmental Tech USA, Inc. [*Associated Press*] (SAG) ... EnTUSA
Environmental Tech USA Inc. [*NASDAQ symbol*] (SAG) ... ENVR
Environmental Tech USA, Inc. [*Associated Press*] (SAG) ... EnvT
Environmental Tech USA Wrrt [*NASDAQ symbol*] (TTSB) ... ENVRW
Environmental Technical Applications Center [*Air Force*] ... ETAC
Environmental Technical Information System [*Army Information service or system*] (IID) ... ETIS
Environmental Technical Specifications (NRCH) ... ETS
Environmental Technician ... ET
Environmental Technologies [*NASDAQ symbol*] (TTSB) ... EVTC
Environmental Technologies Group ... ETG
Environmental Technology and Economics [*A publication*] ... ET & E
Environmental Technology Corp. [*Associated Press*] (SAG) ... EnvrTch
Environmental Technology Corp. [*Associated Press*] (SAG) ... EnvTcCp
Environmental Technology Corp. [*NASDAQ symbol*] (SAG) ... EVTC
Environmental Technology Initiative [*Environmental Protection Agency*] ... ETI
Environmental Technology Laboratory [*Environmental Research Laboratories*] (USDC) ... ETL
Environmental Technology Laboratory [*Marine science*] (OSRA) ... ETL
Environmental Technology Seminar (EA) ... ETS
Environmental Tectonics [*AMEX symbol*] (TTSB) ... ETC
Environmental Tectonics Corp. [*Associated Press*] (SAG) ... EnvrTc
Environmental Tectonics Corp. (MHDW) ... ENVT
Environmental Tectonics Corp. [*AMEX symbol*] (SPSG) ... ETC
Environmental Teratology Information [*Department of Energy*] [*Information service or system*] (IID) ... ETI
Environmental Teratology Information Center [*Department of Energy*] (IID) ... ETIC
Environmental Test (MCD) ... ENT
Environmental Test ... ET
Environmental Test Article (NASA) ... ETA

Environmental Test Chamber ... ETC
Environmental Test Control Center (AAG) ... ETCC
Environmental Test Facility [*Fort Huachuca, AZ*] [*United States Army Electronic Proving Ground*] (GRD) ... ETF
Environmental Test Laboratory [*Jet Propulsion Laboratory, NASA*] ... ETL
Environmental Test Program (AAG) ... ETP
Environmental Test Report ... ETR
Environmental Test Specification (IEEE) ... ETS
Environmental Test Vacuum Center (SAA) ... ETVC
Environmental Testing Advisory Board [*Dow Chemical Co.*] ... ETAB
Environmental Testing Section [*Social Security Administration*] ... ETS
Environmental Thermal Infrared ... ETIR
Environmental Threat and Opportunity Profile ... ETOP
Environmental Threshold of Measurement Accuracy ... ETOMA
Environmental Tobacco Smoke ... ETS
Environmental Toxicology Research Laboratory [*National Environmental Research Center*] ... ETRL
Environmental Training Project [*World Wildlife Fund-United States*] ... ETP
Environmental Treatment & Technologies Corp. (MHDW) ... ETT
Environmental Use Permit (HGAA) ... EUP
Environmental Variance (DAVI) ... V_E
Environmental Viewpoints [*A publication*] ... EV
Environmental Weapons Effects Prediction System (MCD) ... EWEPS
Environmental Workforce Coordinating Committee [*Environmental Protection Agency*] (GFGA) ... EWCC
Environmental Working Group [*An advocacy group*] ... EWG
Environmental-Ecological Education [*Office of Education program*] ... EEE
Environmentalists for Full Employment [*Defunct*] (EA) ... EFFE
Environmentally Assisted Crack [*Metallurgy*] ... EAC
Environmentally Conscious Oil [*A trademark*] [*Automotive lubricant*] ... ECO
Environmentally Correct (PS) ... EC
Environmentally Friendly Accreditation Program [*Australia*] ... EFAP
Environmentally Hazardous Chemical ... EHC
Environmentally Ill [*Medicine*] ... EI
Environmentally Safe Oil Change [*Automobile service*] ... ESOC
Environmentally Sensitive Area [*British*] ... ESA
Environmentally Sound and Appropriate Technology (PDAA) ... ESAT
Environmentally Sound and Sustainable Development (EERA) ... ESSD
Environmentally Sound Management of Inland Water [*United Nations*] ... EMINWA
Environmentally Sound Management of Inland Waters (EERA) ... EMINWAR
Environmentally Sound Technology Assessment (GNE) ... ESTA
Environmentally-Responsive Workstation ... ERW
Environmentaly Benign Processing [*Engineering*] ... EBP
Environment-One [*NASDAQ symbol*] (TTSB) ... EONE
Environments and Threats Directorate [*Army*] ... ETD
Environment-Sensitive Fracture Processes (PDAA) ... ESFP
Environnement et Developpement du Tiers Monde [*Environment and Development of the Third World*] (EAIO) ... ENDA-TM
Enviropur Waste Refining & Technology, Inc. [*Associated Press*] (SAG) ... EnvWste
Enviropur Waste Refining & Technology, Inc. [*NASDAQ symbol*] (SAG) ... EPUR
Enviropur Waste Refining/Tech [*NASDAQ symbol*] (TTSB) ... EPUR
Envirosource, Inc. [*NASDAQ symbol*] (SAG) ... ENSO
Envirosource, Inc. [*Associated Press*] (SAG) ... Envsrc
Envirotest Systems, Inc. [*NASDAQ symbol*] (SAG) ... ENVI
Envirotest Systems, Inc. [*Associated Press*] (SAG) ... Envirotst
Envirotest Systems'A' [*NASDAQ symbol*] (TTSB) ... ENVI
Envoy (ROG) ... ENV
Envoy Corp. [*Associated Press*] (SAG) ... Envoy
Envoy Corp. [*NASDAQ symbol*] (SPSG) ... ENVY
Envoy Extraordinary [*Department of State*] ... EE
Envoy Extraordinary (DLA) ... Env Extr
Envoy Extraordinary and Minister Plenipotentiary [*Department of State*] ... EE & MP
Enziklopedyah la-Hafirot ha-Arkheologiyot be-Erez Yisrael [*A publication*] (BJA) ... EHA
Enziklopedyah Shel Galuyot (BJA) ... EG
Enziklopedyah shel ha-Ziyonut ha-Datit [*A publication*] (BJA) ... EZD
Enziklopedyah [*or Entsiklopedyah*] **Talmudit** (BJA) ... ET
Enzo Biochem [*AMEX symbol*] (TTSB) ... ENZ
Enzo Biochem, Inc. [*AMEX symbol*] (SPSG) ... ENZ
Enzo Biochem, Inc. [*Associated Press*] (SAG) ... EnzoBi
Enzon, Inc. [*NASDAQ symbol*] (NQ) ... ENZN
ENZON Inc. [*NASDAQ symbol*] (TTSB) ... ENZN
Enzon, Inc. [*Associated Press*] (SAG) ... Enzon
Enzootic Bovine Leukemia ... EBL
Enzymatic [*or Enzyme*] (MAE) ... enz
Enzymatic Deficiencies ... ED
Enzymatics, Inc. [*NASDAQ symbol*] (SAG) ... ENZY
Enzymatics, Inc. [*Associated Press*] (SAG) ... Enzymat
Enzyme (AAMN) ... E
Enzyme and Microbore Immobilization [*Biochemistry*] ... EMI
Enzyme Commission [*of the International Union of Biochemistry*] ... EC
Enzyme Field Effect Transistor [*Electrochemistry*] ... ENFET
Enzyme, Free [*Enzyme kinetics*] ... E
Enzyme Immunoassay [*Analytical biochemistry*] ... EIA
Enzyme Immunochromatography ... EIC
Enzyme Inhibitor [*Biochemistry*] ... EI
Enzyme Membrane Immunoassay [*Biochemistry*] ... EMIA
Enzyme Multiplied Immunoassay Technique [*Clinical chemistry*] [*Syva Co. trade mark*] ... EMIT
Enzyme Multiplied Immunoassay Test [*Clinical chemistry*] [*Generic*] ... EMIT
Enzyme Presoak [*for laundry*] ... EP
Enzyme Rate Analyzer ... ERA
Enzyme Unit [*Analytical biochemistry*] ... EU
Enzyme-Digested Delta Endotoxin [*of Bacillus thuringiensis*] [*Biological control*] ... EDD
Enzyme-Linked Antiglobulin Test [*Immunology*] (DAVI) ... ELAT
Enzyme-Linked Coagulation Assay [*Clinical chemistry*] ... ELCA
Enzyme-Linked Fluorescence Assay ... ELFA
Enzyme-Linked [*or Labeled*] **Immunoadsorbent Assay** [*Immunochemistry*] ... ELISA
Enzyme-Linked Immunocytochemical Technique [*Clinical chemistry*] (DMAA) ... ELICT
Enzyme-Linked Immunoelectric Diffusion Assay [*Clinical chemistry*] ... ELIEDA
Enzyme-Linked Immunoelectrotransfer Blot (Technique) [*Clinical chemistry*] ... EITB
Enzyme-Linked Immunosorbent Assay [*Clinical chemistry*] ... EIA
Enzyme-Linked Ligand Sorbent Assay [*Analytical biochemistry*] ... ELLSA
Enzyme-Modified Cheese ... EMC
Enzyme-Product [*Biochemistry*] (DAVI) ... EP
Enzyme-Product Complex [*Enzyme kinetics*] ... EP
Enzyme-Substrate Complex [*Enzyme kinetics*] ... ES
Enzymic Radiochemical Assay [*Clinical chemistry*] ... ERA
Eocene [*Second epoch of the Cenozoic Era*] (BARN) ... Eoc
Eocene/Oligocene [*Geological boundary zone*] ... E/O
EOD Control Center ... EODCC
Eodem [*In the Same Place, Title Explained*] [*Latin*] (ILCA) ... e
EOLAS - the Irish Science and Technology Agency (EAIO) ... EOLAS - ISTA
Eosin-Methylene Blue [*Dye combination*] ... EMB
Eosinophil [*Hematology*] ... E
Eosinophil [*Hematology*] ... eo
Eosinophil [*Hematology*] (WGA) ... Eosin
Eosinophil Cationic Protein [*Immunology*] ... ECP
Eosinophil Chemotactic Factor [*Hematology*] ... ECF
Eosinophil Chemotactic Factor of Anaphylaxis [*Immunochemistry*] ... ECF-A
Eosinophil Count [*Hematology*] (DAVI) ... EO CT
Eosinophil Derived Neurotoxin [*Immunology*] ... EDN
Eosinophil Peroxidase [*An enzyme*] ... EPO
Eosinophil Stimulation Promoter [*Medicine*] (MAE) ... ESP
Eosinophil-Activating Factor [*Immunology*] ... EAF
Eosinophilia Myalgia Syndrome [*Medicine*] ... EMS
Eosinophilic Fasciitis [*Medicine*] ... EF
Eosinophilic Gastroenteropathy [*Medicine*] ... EGE
Eosinophilic Granuloma [*Medicine*] ... EG
Eosinophilic Granuloma of the Lung [*Medicine*] ... EGL
Eosinophilic Index [*Medicine*] (MAE) ... EI
Eosinophilic Lymphfolliculosis of the Skin [*Kimura disease*] [*Dermatology*] ... ELS
Eosinophilic Nonallergic Rhinitis [*Medicine*] ... ENR
Eosinophils [*Hematology*] ... EOS
Eott Energy Partners [*NYSE symbol*] (SAG) ... EOT
Eott Energy Partners [*Associated Press*] (SAG) ... EottEn
EOTT Energy Partners L.P. [*NYSE symbol*] (TTSB) ... EOT
Eotvos Number [*Fluid mechanics*] ... Eo
EP/EO [*Employee Plans/Exempt Organization*] **Application Control System** [*IRS*] ... EACS
EP Group of Companies, Microform Division, Wakefield, Yorkshire, United Kingdom [*Library symbol Library of Congress*] (LCLS) ... EpG
EP [*Elvis Presley*] **Impersonators Association International** (EA) ... EPIAI
EP Technologies, Inc. [*Associated Press*] (SAG) ... EP Tech
EP Technologies, Inc. [*NASDAQ symbol*] (SAG) ... EPTK
EPAG - Group Air France [*ICAO designator*] (FAAC) ... IAF
Epag-Group Air France [*FAA designator*] (FAAC) ... IAG
Epaminondas [*of Nepos*] [*Classical studies*] (OCD) ... Epam
Epanastatiko Kommunistiko Komma Ellados [*Revolutionary Communist Party of Greece*] (PPW) ... EKKE
Eparchy (ROG) ... EP
Eparchy of St. Maron of Brooklyn [*Diocesan abbreviation*] [*United States of America*] (TOCD) ... SAM
Eparchy of Saint Thomas the Apostle [*Diocesan abbreviation*] (TOCD) ... EST
Epatite Degenerative-Proliferativa [*A strain of mouse hepatitis virus*] ... EDP
EPCOT [*Experimental Prototype Community of Tomorrow*] **Center** [*Walt Disney World*] ... EC
Epec Consulting Western Ltd., Edmonton, Alberta [*Library symbol National Library of Canada*] (NLC) ... AEEPCW
Epena [*Congo*] [*Airport symbol*] (OAG) ... EPN
Epernay/Plivot [*France ICAO location identifier*] (ICLI) ... LFSW
Ephemera Society [*British*] ... EPHSOC
Ephemera Society of America (EA) ... EPSOC
Ephemerides Lovanienses (BJA) ... EL
Ephemerides Mariologicae (BJA) ... EM
Ephemerides of the Minor Planets (DICI) ... EMP
Ephemeris Epigraphica [*A publication*] (OCD) ... Eph Epigr
Ephemeris fuer Semitische Epigraphik [*A publication*] (BJA) ... ESE
Ephemeris - Orbit ... EPHO
Ephemeris - Reentry ... EPHR
Ephemeris Time [*Astronomy*] ... ET
Ephemeris-Tuned Oscillator ... ETO
Ephesians [*New Testament book*] (BJA) ... Ep
Ephesians [*New Testament book*] ... Eph
Ephesians [*New Testament book*] (ROG) ... Ephes
Ephinstone Pioneer Museum, Gibsons, BC, Canada [*Library symbol*] [*Library of Congress*] (LCLS) ... CaBGIPM
Ephinstone Pioneer Museum, Gibsons, British Columbia [*Library symbol National Library of Canada*] (NLC) ... BGIPM
Ephphatha Services (EA) ... ES
Ephphatha Services - Division for Service and Mission in America (EA) ... ES-DSMA

Ephraim ..... EPH
Ephraim (BJA) ..... Ephr
Ephraim, UT [*FM radio station call letters*] ..... KAGJ
Ephrata [*Washington*] [*Seismograph station code, US Geological Survey*] (SEIS) ..... EPW
Ephrata, PA [*FM radio station call letters*] ..... WIOV
Ephrata, PA [*FM radio station call letters*] ..... WRTL
Ephrata Public Library, Ephrata, WA [*Library symbol Library of Congress*] (LCLS) ..... WaEp
Ephrata, WA [*Location identifier FAA*] (FAAL) ..... EPH
Ephrata, WA [*FM radio station call letters*] (RBYB) ..... KTAC
Ephrata, WA [*AM radio station call letters*] ..... KTBI
Ephrata, WA [*AM radio station call letters*] ..... KULE
Ephrata, WA [*FM radio station call letters*] ..... KULE-FM
Epiallopregnanolone [*Endocrinology*] ..... EAP
Epibromohydrin [*Organic chemistry*] ..... EBH
Epibromohydrin (GNE) ..... EPH
Epic Angim Dimma (BJA) ..... Angim
EPIC Center for Adhesives, Sealants, and Coatings [*Research center*] (RCD) ..... ECASC
Epic Data, Inc. [*Toronto Stock Exchange symbol Vancouver Stock Exchange symbol*] ..... EKD
Epic Design Technology [*NASDAQ symbol*] (TTSB) ..... EPIC
Epic Design Technology, Inc. [*NASDAQ symbol*] (SAG) ..... EPIC
Epic Design Technology, Inc. [*Associated Press*] (SAG) ..... EpicDes
[*The*] **Epic of Gilgamesh** [*R. C. Thompson*] [*A publication*] (BJA) ..... GETh
Epic Record Co. [*Record label*] [*New York*] ..... ERC
Epic Resources (BC) Ltd. [*Vancouver Stock Exchange symbol*] ..... ERB
Epicardial Breakthrough [*Cardiology*] ..... EBT
Epicardial Electrogram [*Cardiology*] (DMAA) ..... EP
Epicathechin Gallate [*Biochemistry*] ..... ECG
Epichlorohydrin [*Organic chemistry*] ..... ECH
Epichlorohydrin Copolymer [*Organic chemistry*] ..... ECO
Epichlorohydrin Ethylene Oxide [*Organic chemistry*] (RDA) ..... ECO
Epichlorohydrin Ethylene Oxide [*Organic chemistry*] ..... EPO
Epichlorohydrin Triethanolamine [*Organic chemistry*] ..... ECTEOLA
Epicorum Graecorum Fragmenta [*A publication*] (OCD) ..... EGF
Epicteti Dissertationes [*of Arrian*] [*Classical studies*] (OCD) ..... Epict Diss
Epidemic ..... EPID
Epidemic Acute Nonbacterial Gastroenteritis [*Medicine*] (MEDA) ..... EANG
Epidemic [*or Epizootic*] **Diarrhea of Infant Mice** ..... EDIM
Epidemic Hemorrhagic Fever [*Disease encountered by American troops during the Korean War*] ..... EHF
Epidemic Hepatitis-Associated Antigen [*Immunochemistry*] ..... EHAA
Epidemic Intelligence Service [*of the Centers for Disease Control*] ..... EIS
Epidemic Keratoconjunctivitis [*Ophthalmology*] ..... EKC
Epidemic Keratoconjunctivitis [*Ophthalmology*] (DAVI) ..... EKG
Epidemic Observation Unit [*Medicine*] ..... EOU
Epidemiologic Catchment Area [*Department of Health and Human Services*] (GFGA) ..... ECA
Epidemiological (ADA) ..... EPIDEM
Epidemiological Flight [*Military*] ..... EPF
Epidemiological Laboratory [*Air Force*] ..... EL
Epidemiological Report ..... EPIREPT
Epidemiology [*or Epidemiological*] ..... EPDML
Epidemiology ..... EPDMLGY
Epidemiology and Oral Disease Prevention Program [*Bethesda, MD*] [*National Institute of Dental Research*] [*Department of Health and Human Services*] (GRD) ..... EODPP
Epidemiology and Sanitation Technician [*Navy*] ..... EST
Epidemiology, Demography, and Biometry Program [*National Institute on Aging*] [*Department of Health and Human Services*] ..... EDBP
Epidemiology Information System [*Database*] [*Oak Ridge National Laboratory*] [*Information service or system*] (CRD) ..... EIS
Epidemiology Program Office [*Department of Health and Human Services*] (GRD) ..... EPO
Epidermal Cell ..... EC
Epidermal Cell Derived Factor [*Biochemistry*] ..... EDF
Epidermal Cytokeratin [*Cytology*] ..... ECK
Epidermal Growth Factor [*Endocrinology*] ..... EGF
Epidermal Growth Factor Receptor [*Biochemistry*] ..... EGFR
Epidermal Growth Factor Receptor Kinase [*An enzyme*] ..... EGFRK
Epidermal Growth Factor - Urogastrone [*Endocrinology*] ..... EGF-URO
Epidermal Melanin Pigmentation [*Dermatology*] ..... EMP
Epidermal Proliferative Unit (PDAA) ..... EPU
Epidermal Soluble Protein [*Biochemistry*] (DAVI) ..... ESP
Epidermatophyton ..... TOE
Epidermic Hepatitis-Associated Antigen [*Immunology*] (DAVI) ..... EHAA
Epidermis ..... E
Epidermodysplasia Verruciformis [*Medicine*] ..... EDV
Epidermolysis Bullosa [*Dermatology*] ..... EB
Epidermolysis Bullosa Acquisita [*Dermatology*] ..... EPA
Epidermolysis Bullosa Dystrophia [*Dermatology*] ..... EBD
Epidermolysis Bullosa Dystrophic Dominant [*Dermatology*] ..... EBDD
Epidermolysis Bullosa Dystrophic Recessive [*Dermatology*] ..... EBDR
Epidermolysis Bullosa Simplex [*Dermatology*] ..... EBS
Epidermolysis Bullosa Simplex - Weber Cockayne [*Dermatology*] ..... EBSWC
Epidermolysis Bullosa Simplex-Koebner [*Dermatology*] ..... EBSK
Epidermolytic Hyperkeratosis [*Dermatology*] ..... EHK
Epidermolytic Palmoplantar Keratoderma [*Medicine*] ..... EPPK
Epidote [*Petrology*] ..... EPI
Epidoxorubicin, Bleomycin, Vinblastine, Prednisone [*Antineoplastic drug regimen*] ..... EBVP
Epidural [*Brain anatomy*] ..... ED
Epidural [*Medicine*] (DAVI) ..... epi
Epidural Anesthesia [*Medicine*] ..... EA
Epidural Blood Patch [*Medicine*] ..... EBP
Epifanio de los Santos [*Avenue where Philippine President Marcos' government tanks were stopped by unarmed citizens*] [*In the EDSA Revolution of February, 1986*] ..... EDSA
Epifluorescence Microscopy ..... EFM
Epigallocatechin Gallate [*Biochemistry*] ..... EGCG
Epigallocathechin [*Biochemistry*] ..... EGC
Epigastrium [*The part above the stomach*] [*Pharmacy*] (ROG) ..... EPIGAS
Epigram (WDAA) ..... EPIG
Epigrammata [*Classical studies*] (OCD) ..... Epigr
Epigrammata Graeca ex Lapidibus Conlecta [*A publication*] (OCD) ..... Epigr Gr
Epigrammata Super Exilio [*of Seneca the Younger*] [*Classical studies*] (OCD) ..... Epigr
Epigraphic Society (EA) ..... ES
Epigraphic South Arabian (BJA) ..... ESA
Epigraphical Museum [*Epigraphic notation*] ..... EM
Epikeraprosthesis [*Ophthalmology*] ..... EKP
Epilepsy ..... EPIL
Epilepsy Abstracts Retrieval Service (NITA) ..... EARS
Epilepsy Abstracts Retrieval System (PDAA) ..... EARS
Epilepsy Association of America [*Later, EFA*] ..... EAA
Epilepsy Concern Service Group (EA) ..... EC
Epilepsy Foundation of America (EA) ..... EFA
Epilepsy Foundation of Victoria [*Australia*] ..... EFV
Epilepsy International (EAIO) ..... EI
Epilepsy Partialis Continua [*Medicine*] ..... EPC
Epilepsy Research Center [*Baylor College of Medicine*] [*Research center*] (RCD) ..... ERC
Epileptic (AIE) ..... EP
Epileptic Attentional Deficit Disorder [*Medicine*] (DMAA) ..... E-ADD
Epileptic Syndrome [*Medicine*] (DMAA) ..... ES
Epilogue (ROG) ..... EPI
Epilogue ..... EPIL
Epilogue to (a Designated Part or Volume of) Coke's Institutes [*A publication*] (DLA) ..... Inst Epil
Epiluminescence Microscopy ..... ELM
Epinal/Dogneville [*France ICAO location identifier*] (ICLI) ..... LFSE
Epinal/Mirecourt [*France ICAO location identifier*] (ICLI) ..... LFSG
Epinephrine [*Endocrinology*] ..... E
Epinephrine [*Endocrinology*] ..... EPI
Epinephrine [*Endocrinology*] (DAVI) ..... epineph
Epinomis [*of Plato*] [*Classical studies*] (OCD) ..... Epin
Epiotic [*Ear anatomy*] ..... EP
Epiphany ..... EPIPH
Epiphany Apostolic College [*New York*] ..... EAC
Epiphany Apostolic College, Newburgh, NY [*Library symbol Library of Congress*] (LCLS) ..... NNebgE
Epiphyllum Society of America (EA) ..... ESA
Epiphyllum Society of America ..... ESOA
Epiphytic Plant Study Group [*British*] (DBA) ..... EPSG
Epiretinal Membrane [*Ophthalmology*] ..... ERM
Episcopal ..... EPIS
Episcopal [*or Episcopalian*] (WDAA) ..... EPISC
Episcopal ..... EPISCPL
Episcopal Actor's Guild of America (EA) ..... EAGA
Episcopal Center for Evangelism (EA) ..... ECE
Episcopal Church ..... EC
Episcopal Church Building Fund (EA) ..... ECBF
Episcopal Church Missionary Community (EA) ..... ECMC
Episcopal Church Women ..... ECW
Episcopal Churchmen for South Africa (EA) ..... ECSA
Episcopal Churchpeople for a Free Southern Africa (EA) ..... ECFSA
Episcopal Commission for Black Ministries (EA) ..... ECBM
Episcopal Communicators (EA) ..... EC
Episcopal Conference of the Deaf (EA) ..... ECD
Episcopal Council for Foreign Students and Other Visitors [*Defunct*] (EA) ..... ECFSOV
Episcopal Council for Global Mission (EA) ..... ECGM
Episcopal Diocese of Massachusetts, Boston, MA [*Library symbol Library of Congress*] (LCLS) ..... MBD
Episcopal Diocese of Massachusetts, Diocesan Library and Archives, Boston, MA [*Library symbol*] [*Library of Congress*] (LCLS) ..... MBED
Episcopal Diocese of Mississippi, Jackson, MS [*Library symbol Library of Congress*] (LCLS) ..... MsJPED
Episcopal Divinity School, Cambridge, MA [*OCLC symbol*] (OCLC) ..... BPS
Episcopal Divinity School, Cambridge, MA [*Library symbol Library of Congress*] (LCLS) ..... MCE
Episcopal Divinity School, Cambridge, MA [*Library symbol*] [*Library of Congress*] (LCLS) ..... MCED
Episcopal Guild for the Blind (EA) ..... EGB
Episcopal Peace Fellowship (EA) ..... EPF
Episcopal Service for Youth (EA) ..... ESY
Episcopal Society for Cultural and Racial Unity [*Defunct*] (EA) ..... ESCRU
Episcopal Society for Ministry on Aging (EA) ..... ESMA
Episcopal Synod of America (EA) ..... ESA
Episcopal Theological School ..... ETS
Episcopal Theological Seminary of the Southwest, Austin, TX [*Library symbol Library of Congress*] (LCLS) ..... TxAuE
Episcopal Women's Caucus (EA) ..... EWC
Episcopal World Mission (EA) ..... EWM
Episcopalian ..... EP
Episcopalians and Others for Responsible Social Action (EA) ..... EORSA
Episcopalians United (EA) ..... EU
Episcopus [*Bishop*] [*Latin*] ..... EP

Episcopus [*Bishop*] [*Latin*] ... Episc
Episcopus [*Bishop*] [*Latin*] ... EPUS
Episcopus et Martyr [*Bishop and Martyr*] [*Latin*] ... EM
Episiotomy [*Obstetrics*] ... EPIS
Episkopi [*Cyprus*] [*ICAO location identifier*] (ICLI) ... LCRO
Epistilbite [*A zeolite*] ... EPI
Epistle ... E
Epistle ... EP
Epistle ... EPIS
Epistle of Barnabas (BJA) ... EpBarn
Epistle of Jeremy [*Apocrypha*] (BJA) ... EpJer
Epistola [*Epistle, Letter*] [*Latin*] (ROG) ... EP
Epistolae [*Epistles, Letters*] [*Latin*] (ROG) ... EPP
Epistolographi Graeci [*A publication*] (OCD) ... Epistolog Graec
Epistomium [*A Stopper*] [*Pharmacy*] ... EPISTOM
Epistula ad Pompeium [*of Dionysius Halicarnassensis*] [*Classical studies*] (OCD) ... Pomp
Epistula ad Tryphonem [*of Quintilian*] [*Classical studies*] (OCD) ... Ep ad Tryph
Epistulae [*of Augustine*] [*Classical studies*] (OCD) ... Ep
Epistulae [*of Epicurus*] [*Classical studies*] (OCD) ... Ep
Epistulae [*of St. Jerome*] [*Classical studies*] (OCD) ... Ep
Epistulae [*Classical studies*] (OCD) ... Epist
Epistulae ad Atticum [*of Cicero*] [*Classical studies*] (OCD) ... Att
Epistulae ad Brutum [*of Cicero*] [*Classical studies*] (OCD) ... ad Brut
Epistulae ad Familiares [*of Cicero*] [*Classical studies*] (OCD) ... Fam
Epistulae ad Quintum Fratrem [*of Cicero*] [*Classical studies*] (OCD) ... QFr
Epistulae ad Traianum [*of Pliny the Younger*] [*Classical studies*] (OCD) ... Tra
Epistulae ex Ponto [*of Ovid*] [*Classical studies*] (OCD) ... Pont
Epitaph ... EPIT
Epitaxial (IAA) ... EPI
Epitaxial Mesa ... EM
Epitaxial Passivated Integrated Circuits (MCD) ... EPIC
Epitaxial Planar [*Electronics*] ... EP
Epitaxial Silicon Films on Insulators (MCD) ... ESFI
Epitaxial Tuning Varactor ... ETV
Epitek International, Inc. [*Toronto Stock Exchange symbol*] ... EPK
Epithelial [*or Epithelioid*] [*Histology*] (DAVI) ... EP
Epithelial [*or Epithelium*] [*History*] (DAVI) ... EPI
Epithelial Cell [*Cytology*] ... EpC
Epithelial Focus-Forming Unit [*Oncology*] ... EFFU
Epithelial Force (Assay) [*Oncology*] ... EF
Epithelial Membrane Antigen [*Immunology*] ... EMA
Epithelial Possibly Precancerous Lesion ... EPPL
Epithelial Proliferation [*Histology*] ... EP
Epithelial Stromal Junction [*Anatomy*] ... ESJ
Epithelioid A Globoid Cell [*Medicine*] (AAMN) ... EGC
Epithelioma [*Medicine*] ... EOA
Epithelium [*Anatomy*] ... E
Epithelium [*Medicine*] ... EPITH
Epithermal Critical Experiment Laboratory [*Nuclear energy*] ... ECEL
Epithermal Neutron Activation Analysis [*Analytical chemistry*] ... ENAA
Epithet (ROG) ... EPITH
Epitomae [*of Livy*] [*Classical studies*] (OCD) ... Epit
Epitome ... EPIT
Epitome [*Classical studies*] (OCD) ... Epit
Epitome Oxyrhynchica [*of Livy*] [*Classical studies*] (OCD) ... Epit Oxyrh
Epitope, Inc. [*Associated Press*] (SAG) ... Epitope
Epitope, Inc. [*AMEX symbol*] (SPSG) ... EPT
Epitympanic Recess [*Medicine*] (DAVI) ... ETR
Epizootic Bovine Abortion ... EBA
Epizootic Epitheliotropic Disease [*Ichthyology*] ... EED
Epizootic Hemorrhagic Disease [*Veterinary medicine*] ... EHD
Epizootic Hemorrhagic Disease Virus [*Veterinary medicine*] (DMAA) ... EHDV
Eplett Dairies Ltd. [*Toronto Stock Exchange symbol*] ... EPD
EPLRS [*Enhanced Position Location Reporting System*] **User Unit/Microwave Landing System** (MCD) ... EPUU/MLS
EPO [*Erythroprotein*] **Mimetic Peptide** [*Biochemistry*] ... EMP
Epoch Capital Corp. [*Vancouver Stock Exchange symbol*] ... EPH
Epochs of Ancient History [*A publication*] ... EAH
Epochs of Church History [*A publication*] ... ECH
Epochs of History [*A publication*] ... EH
Epochs of Modern History [*A publication*] ... EMH
Epodi [*of Horace*] [*Classical studies*] (OCD) ... Epod
Eponyms Dictionaries Index [*A publication*] ... EDI
Epoxide Hydrolase [*An enzyme*] ... EH
Epoxide Plastic ... EP
Epoxidized Linseed Oil [*Organic chemistry*] ... ELO
Epoxidized Natural Rubber ... ENR
Epoxidized Soybean Oil [*Organic chemistry*] ... ESO
Epoxy Bond Coating ... EBC
Epoxy Bridge Rectifier ... EBR
Epoxy Creosol Novolac [*Resin*] ... ECN
Epoxy Curing Agent ... ECA
Epoxy Experimental Kit ... EEK
Epoxy Field Effect Transistor ... EFET
Epoxy Spray Coater ... ESC
Epoxy Vinyl Ester [*Plastics technology*] ... EVE
Epoxy-Beta-Ionone [*Biochemistry*] ... EPBI
Epoxy-Encapsulated Transistor ... EET
Epoxyfarnesyl Diazoacetate [*Organic chemistry*] ... EFDA
Epoxy(nitrophenoxy)propane [*Organic chemistry*] ... EPNP
Epping [*Urban district in England*] ... EP
Epping Realty Corp. [*Vancouver Stock Exchange symbol*] ... ERC
Eppley Airfield [*FAA*] (TAG) ... OMA
Epps Air Service, Inc. [*ICAO designator*] (FAAC) ... EPS
EPRI [*Electric Power Research Institute*] **Database for Environmentally Assisted Cracking** [*Battelle Memorial Institute*] [*Information service or system*] (IID) ... EDEAC
EPRI Research and Development Information System (NITA) ... EPRI RDS
Eprova Ltd. [*Switzerland*] [*Research code symbol*] ... ES
Epsilon (NUCP) ... E
Epsilon ... EPSLN
Epsilon Eta Phi [*Later, Phi Chi Theta*] ... EEP
Epsilon Flight Data Acquisition System (IAA) ... EFDAS
Epsilon Pi Tau (EA) ... EPT
Epsilon-Aminocaproic Acid [*Pharmacology*] ... EACA
Epstein and Macintosh, Oxford [*Ether inhaler and Oxford bellows*] [*Anesthesiology*] (DAVI) ... EMO
Epstein-Barr [*Virus*] ... EB
Epstein-Barr Nuclear Antigen [*Virus*] [*Immunology*] ... EBNA
Epstein-Barr Virus ... EBV
Eptein-Barr Virus Capsid Antigen [*Medicine*] (PDAA) ... EBVCA
Epworth, IA [*FM radio station call letters*] ... KGRR
EQK Realty Inv I SBI [*NYSE symbol*] (TTSB) ... EKR
EQK Realty Investors [*Associated Press*] (SAG) ... EQK Rt
EQK Realty Investors I SBI [*NYSE symbol*] (SPSG) ... EKR
Equal ... EQ
Equal [*Copyediting*] (WDMC) ... eq
Equal ... EQL
Equal (MSA) ... EQL
Equal Access to Justice Act [*1980*] ... EAJA
Equal Access to Softward and Information ... EASI
Equal and reactive [*Ophthalmology*] (DAVI) ... E & R
Equal and Regular [*Ophthalmology*] (DAVI) ... E & R
Equal Area SSM/I [*Special Sensor Microwave/Imager*] **Earth** [*Grid*] (USDC) ... EASE
Equal Area SSMI [*Special Sensor Microwave Imager*] **Earth Grid** [*Marine science*] (OSRA) ... EASE
Equal Area SSMI [*Special Sensor Microwave Imager*] **Earth Grid** [*Marine science*] (OSRA) ... EASE Grid
Equal Brake (OA) ... EB
Equal Charge Displacement [*Fission*] ... ECD
Equal Credit Opportunity Act [*1974, 1976*] ... ECOA
Equal Educational Opportunities Program [*HEW*] ... EEOP
Equal, Effective, Elected [*Canada's Triple E Senate movement*] ... EEE
Equal Employment Act ... EEA
Equal Employment Advisory Council (EA) ... EEAC
Equal Employment Compliance Section [*Employment and Training Administration*] (OICC) ... EECS
Equal Employment Officer ... EEO
Equal Employment Opportunity ... EEO
Equal Employment Opportunity Act (TDOB) ... ECOA
Equal Employment Opportunity Act (OICC) ... EEOA
Equal Employment Opportunity Advisory Council (DNAB) ... EEOAC
Equal Employment Opportunity Agency ... EEOA
Equal Employment Opportunity Commission ... EEOC
Equal Employment Opportunity Commission Compliance Manual [*Commerce Clearing House*] (DLA) ... EEOC Compl Man
Equal Employment Opportunity Directives System (DNAB) ... EEODIRSYS
Equal Employment Opportunity Officer [*DoD*] ... EEOO
Equal Employment Opportunity Officer Activity ... EEOOA
Equal Employment Opportunity Program (MCD) ... EEOP
Equal Interval [*Isophase navigation light*] ... E Int
Equal Justice Foundation (EA) ... EJF
Equal Life Group [*Depreciation class*] ... ELG
Equal Listener Response [*Scale*] ... ELR
Equal Matrix Languages [*Computer science*] (PDAA) ... EML
Equal Mental Age [*Psychometrics*] ... EMA
Equal Ocular Movement [*Medicine*] (DMAA) ... EOM
Equal Opportunities Commission [*British*] ... EOC
Equal Opportunity ... EO
Equal Opportunity [*A publication*] ... Equal Opp
Equal Opportunity Advisor [*DoD*] ... EOA
Equal Opportunity and Full Employment Act (OICC) ... EOFEA
Equal Opportunity and Treatment [*Army program*] ... EOT
Equal Opportunity Board [*Victoria, Australia*] ... EOB
Equal Opportunity Cases [*Australia A publication*] ... EOC
Equal Opportunity Commission [*Western Australia*] ... EOC
Equal Opportunity Compliance (SSD) ... EOC
Equal Opportunity Employer ... EOE
Equal Opportunity Employer, Male/Female (OICC) ... EOE M/F
Equal Opportunity Employer, Male-Female-Handicapped ... EOE M-F-H
Equal Opportunity Information and Support System (DNAB) ... EOISS
Equal Opportunity Information and Support System (DNAB) ... EQOPPINFOSYS
Equal Opportunity Policy (OICC) ... EOP
Equal Opportunity Program Office [*Kennedy Space Center Directorate*] [*NASA*] (NASA) ... EO
Equal Opportunity Program Specialist [*Navy*] (NVT) ... EOPS
Equal Opportunity Programs (MCD) ... EOP
Equal Opportunity Quality Indicator [*Navy*] (NVT) ... EOQI
Equal Opportunity/Race Relations [*Navy*] (NVT) ... EO/RR
Equal Opportunity Specialist (AAGC) ... EOS
Equal Pay Act [*US*] (OICC) ... EPA
Equal Pay Act [*1970*] [*British*] (DCTA) ... Eq PA
Equal Payment Plan ... EPP
Equal Pressure Point (MAE) ... EPP
Equal Protection of the Law [*Legal shorthand*] (LWAP) ... EPL
Equal Rights Advocates (EA) ... ERA
Equal Rights Amendment [*Proposed constitutional amendment which supports equal rights regardless of sex*] ... ERA
Equal Rights Congress (EA) ... ERC

Equal Rights in Clubs Campaign for Action [British] (DI) ..... ERICCA
Equal Section [Technical drawings] ..... ES
Equal Taper (OA) ..... ET
Equal Time Point ..... ETP
Equal Time Spacing ..... ETS
Equal To or Greater Than ..... ETGT
Equal To or Less Than ..... ETLT
Equal Zero (MDG) ..... E/Z
Equal-Appearing Intervals (EDAC) ..... EAI
Equality (ROG) ..... EQ
Equality of Educational Opportunity Survey [1965] ..... EEOS
Equalization [Electronics] ..... EQ
Equalized Assessed Valuation ..... EAL
Equalized Maintenance, Maximum Availability (PDAA) ..... EMMA
Equalized Sidelobe Antenna ..... ESA
Equalizer ..... EQ
Equalizing Line Amplifier (IAA) ..... EA
Equally [Legal term] (ROG) ..... EQLY
EqualNet Holding [NASDAQ symbol] (TTSB) ..... ENET
EqualNet Holding Corp. [NASDAQ symbol] (SAG) ..... ENET
EqualNet Holding Corp. [Associated Press] (SAG) ..... EqualN
Equal-Time Commutation ..... ETC
Equate (MDG) ..... EQU
Equation (KSC) ..... EQ
Equation ..... EQN
Equation Cruncher [Computer science] ..... EC
Equation of Motion (NASA) ..... EOM
Equation of State ..... EOS
Equation of Time (ROG) ..... E
Equation of Time [Navigation] ..... EQT
Equation of Time [Navigation] ..... ET
Equational Prover ..... EOP
Equato-Guinean de Aviacion [Airline] [Equatorial Guinea] ..... EGA
Equator (WDAA) ..... E
Equator (WDAA) ..... EQ
Equator Airlines Ltd. [Kenya] [ICAO designator] (FAAC) ..... PKA
Equator Crossing ..... EQX
Equator Earth Terminal ..... EET
Equatorial [Air mass] ..... E
Equatorial ..... EQ
Equatorial (ROG) ..... EQUAT
Equatorial Airlines of Sao Tome and Principe [ICAO designator] (FAAC) ..... EQL
Equatorial Atlantic (MSC) ..... EQUALANT
Equatorial Atlantic Survey [Marine science] (OSRA) ..... EQUALANT
Equatorial Communications Co. [Mountain View, CA] [Telecommunications]
(TSSD) ..... ECC
Equatorial Countercurrent [Oceanography] ..... ECC
Equatorial Currents System [Oceanography] ..... ECS
Equatorial Dynamics Study [Marine science] (MSC) ..... EDS
Equatorial Electrojet ..... EEJ
Equatorial Guinea [Aircraft nationality and registration mark] (FAAC) 3C
Equatorial Guinea [MARC country of publication code Library of Congress]
(LCCP) ..... eg
Equatorial Guinea (WDAA) ..... EQUAT GUI
Equatorial Guinea [MARC geographic area code Library of Congress]
(LCCP) ..... f-eg--
Equatorial Guinea [ANSI three-letter standard code] (CNC) ..... GNQ
Equatorial Guinea [ANSI two-letter standard code] (CNC) ..... GQ
Equatorial Magnetosphere Laboratory (MCD) ..... EML
Equatorial Mesoscale Experiment [National Oceanic and Atmospheric
Administration] ..... EMEX
Equatorial Pacific [Project] [Marine science] (OSRA) ..... EqPac
Equatorial Pacific (USDC) ..... EQPAC
Equatorial Pacific ..... EQUAPAC
Equatorial Pacific Information Collection [Marine science] (OSRA) ..... EPIC
Equatorial Pacific Information Collection (USDC) ..... EPIC
Equatorial Pacific Ocean Climate Studies [National Oceanic and Atmospheric
Administration] ..... EPOCS
Equatorial Pitch Angle [Geophysics] ..... EPA
Equatorial Ring Current (IEEE) ..... ERC
Equatorial Scatter ..... EQS
Equatorial Undercurrent [Marine science] ..... EU
Equatorial Undercurrent [Marine science] (MSC) ..... EUC
Equerry ..... EQ
Eques [Knight] [Latin] (ROG) ..... EQ
Eques Auratus [Knight Bachelor] [Latin] (ROG) ..... EQ AUR
Equestrian (ROG) ..... EQ
Equestrian ..... EQSTTRN
Equestrian Federation of Ireland (EAIO) ..... EFI
Equestrian Federation of Victoria [Australia] (EFV) ..... EFV
Equi Ventures, Inc. [Vancouver Stock Exchange symbol] ..... EVS
Equidistant Letter Sequences [Computer analysis of texts] ..... ELS
Equifax, Inc. [Formerly, Retail Credit Co.] [NYSE symbol] (SPSG) ..... EFX
Equifax, Inc. [Formerly, Retail Credit Co.] [Associated Press] (SAG) ..... Equifx
Equifax, Inc., Atlanta, GA [Library symbol Library of Congress] (LCLS) ..... GAEI
Equilibrated Metal Surface [Catalyst science] ..... EMS
Equilibrium (MSA) ..... EQUIL
Equilibrium (AAMN) ..... equilib
Equilibrium Air Distillation (AAG) ..... EAD
Equilibrium Air Total Radiation ..... EATR
Equilibrium Constant [Symbol] [Chemistry] ..... K
Equilibrium Dialysis [Analytical chemistry] ..... ED
Equilibrium Equivalent Concentration [Nuclear energy] (NUCP) ..... EEC
Equilibrium Field (MCD) ..... EF
Equilibrium Flash Vaporization (PDAA) ..... EFV

Equilibrium Float Altitude [Balloon flight] ..... EFA
Equilibrium Mode Simulator (TEL) ..... EMS
Equilibrium Moisture Content ..... EMC
Equilibrium Peritoneal Dialysis [Medicine] (BARN) ..... EPD
Equilibrium Porous Flow [Chemistry] ..... EPF
Equilibrium Problem Solver (IEEE) ..... EPS
Equilibrium Problems of Linear Structures ..... ELAS
Equilibrium Radiation Spectra ..... ERS
Equilibrium Radionuclide Angiography [Cardiology] (CPH) ..... ERNA
Equilibrium Reflux Boiling Point [Brake fluid] ..... ERBP
Equilibrium Surface Thermochemistry ..... EST
Equilibrium Yield [Fishery management] (MSC) ..... EY
Equilibrium-Gated Radionuclide Angiography [Medicine] (DMAA) ..... EGRA
Equilibrium-Grated Blood Pool Study [Hematology] (DAVI) ..... EGBPS
Equilibrium-Line Altitude [Glaciation] ..... ELA
EquiMed [NASDAQ symbol] (SAG) ..... EQMD
EquiMed [Associated Press] (SAG) ..... EquiMed
EquiMed Inc. [NASDAQ symbol] (TTSB) ..... EQMD
Equine ..... EQN
Equine Abortion Virus [Medicine] (DMAA) ..... EAV
Equine Antihuman Lymphoblast Globulin [Immunochemistry] (MAE) ..... EAHLG
Equine Antihuman Lymphoblast Serum [Immunochemistry] (MAE) ..... EAHLS
Equine Chorionic Gonadotropin [Endocrinology] ..... ECG
Equine Encephalitis ..... EE
Equine Follicle Stimulating Hormone [Endocrinology] ..... EFSH
Equine Herpes Virus ..... EHV
Equine Infectious Anemia ..... EIA
Equine Infectious Anemia Virus ..... EIAV
Equine Luteinizing Hormone [Endocrinology] ..... ELH
Equine Lymphocyte Alloantigen [Genetics, immunochemistry] ..... ELA
Equine Morbillivirus [Veterinary medicine] ..... EM
Equine Morbillivirus ..... EMV
Equine Piroplasmosis (PDAA) ..... EP
Equine Research Laboratory [University of California, Davis] ..... ERL
Equine Resources Ltd. [Vancouver Stock Exchange symbol] ..... EQN
Equine Rhinopneumonia [Medicine] (DMAA) ..... ER
Equine Rhinopneumonitis [Medicine] (MAE) ..... ERP
Equinox Resources Ltd. [Associated Press] (SAG) ..... Equinox
Equinox Resources Ltd. [Toronto Stock Exchange symbol Vancouver Stock
Exchange symbol] ..... EQX
Equinox Systems [NASDAQ symbol] (TTSB) ..... EQNX
Equinox Systems, Inc. [NASDAQ symbol] (SAG) ..... EQNX
Equip and Install (MSA) ..... E & I
Equip and Install (IAA) ..... EAI
Equipage Category Number (MSA) ..... ECN
Equipage Repair Part Consumable (AFIT) ..... ERC
Equipe de Recherche Interdisciplinaire en Sante [Universite de Montreal,
Quebec] [Canada] ..... ERIS
Equipes Notre-Dame [Teams of Our Lady - TOOL] [Paris, France] (EAIO) ..... END
Equipment (NFPA) ..... E
Equipment (BUR) ..... EQ
Equipment (CINC) ..... EQP
Equipment (MDG) ..... EQPMT
Equipment ..... EQPT
Equipment ..... EQUIP
Equipment (DD) ..... equip
Equipment ..... EQUIP
Equipment (AAGC) ..... Equip
Equipment (WGA) ..... EQUIPT
Equipment Acceptance Requirements and Inspections (AAG) ..... EARI
Equipment Acceptance Test (MCD) ..... EAT
Equipment Accuracy Test Station ..... EATS
Equipment Acquisition Manual (DNAB) ..... EAM
Equipment Acquisition Strategy (ADA) ..... EAS
Equipment Advisory Group ..... EAG
Equipment Air Lock [Nuclear energy] (NRCH) ..... EAL
Equipment Alignment ..... EA
Equipment Alignment Procedure (MCD) ..... EAP
Equipment Allocation Document (MCD) ..... EAD
Equipment and Component Configuration Listing (DNAB) ..... ECCL
Equipment and Component Index (DNAB) ..... ECI
Equipment and Floor Drainage System [Nuclear energy] (NRCH) ..... EFDS
Equipment and Spare Parts ..... E & SP
Equipment and Tool Institute [Glenview, IL] ..... EATI
Equipment and Tool Institute (EA) ..... ETI
Equipment Antiriot Projector [British] (MCD) ..... EARP
Equipment Applications List (MCD) ..... EAL
Equipment Approval Authority (AFM) ..... EAA
Equipment Authorization Inventory Data [Air Force] (AFM) ..... EAID
Equipment Authorization Inventory Data Listing [Air Force] (AFM) ..... EAIDL
Equipment Authorization Inventory Data System [Air Force] (AFIT) ..... EAIDS
Equipment Authorization Review Activity (MCD) ..... EARA
Equipment Availability Constant (MCD) ..... EAC
Equipment Availability Date (MCD) ..... EAD
Equipment Bay (KSC) ..... EB
Equipment Blockages and Failures [Telecommunications] (TEL) ..... EB & F
Equipment Branch [Air Force British] ..... EB
Equipment Building (AAG) ..... EB
Equipment Calibration [Military] (NVT) ..... ECAL
Equipment Calibration Maintenance Record (MCD) ..... ECMR
Equipment Category ..... ECAT
Equipment Category Code [Military] (AABC) ..... ECC
Equipment Category Rollup Code [Army] ..... ECRC
Equipment Certified (FAAC) ..... EQCRT
Equipment Change Analysis Group (SAA) ..... ECAG

Equipment Change Information	ECI
Equipment Code Department Master (MCD)	EDM
Equipment Collecting Point [Military British]	ECP
Equipment Compiler System (IAA)	ECS
Equipment Component List [Army] (AABC)	ECL
Equipment Concentration Site System [Army]	ECSS
Equipment Concentration Sites [Military] (AABC)	ECS
Equipment Condition Analysis (MSA)	ECA
Equipment Condition Monitoring	ECM
Equipment Configuration Control (AAG)	ECC
Equipment Construction Site (MCD)	ECS
Equipment Control Board (KSC)	ECB
Equipment Control Officer [Air Force] (AFM)	ECO
Equipment Control Record (MCD)	ECR
Equipment Control Record System [Army]	ECRS
Equipment Control Unit (AFIT)	ECU
Equipment Controller (CET)	EC
Equipment Conversion Package [Telecommunications] (TEL)	ECP
Equipment Data Display	EDD
Equipment Data Package (MCD)	EDP
Equipment Deadlined for Maintenance [Army] (AABC)	EDM
Equipment Deadlined for Parts [Army]	EDP
Equipment Decontamination Room [Nuclear energy] (NUCP)	EDR
Equipment Decontamination Station [Military]	EDS
Equipment Delay (CAAL)	ED
Equipment Density Data	EDD
Equipment Density Data (AABC)	EQDD
Equipment Deployment and Storage System [MTMC] (TAG)	EDSS
Equipment Description	ED
Equipment Design Agent	EDA
Equipment Design Information Memo	EDIM
Equipment Development and Test Report [Forest Service]	ED & T
Equipment Development Division [Britain's national phone-tapping center]	EDD
Equipment Dictionary [Navy] (MCD)	EDIC
Equipment Disposition Authorization	EDA
Equipment Distribution and Condition [Statistical reporting system] [Military] (AFM)	EDAC
Equipment Distribution Plan (MCD)	EDP
Equipment Distribution Planning Studies [Army] (AABC)	EDPS
Equipment/Document Change Proposal (NATG)	E/DCP
Equipment Downtime	EDT
Equipment Drain Tank [Nuclear energy] (NRCH)	EDT
Equipment Drain Treatment System [Nuclear energy] (NRCH)	EDTS
Equipment Engaged Tone [Telecommunications] (IAA)	EE
Equipment Engaged Tone [Telecommunications] (TEL)	EET
Equipment, Environment, Velocity, Technique, Conditioning [Sports medicine]	EEVeTec
Equipment Evaluation Report (NG)	EER
Equipment Factor (CAAL)	EF
Equipment Failure Rate	EFR
Equipment for Charity Hospitals Overseas [British] (DI)	ECHO
Equipment Foreman	EQPFOR
Equipment Functional Check (KSC)	EFC
Equipment Ground Wire	EGW
Equipment Group Design Specifications (NATG)	EGDS
Equipment Group Interface	EGIF
Equipment Group Laboratories (MCD)	EGL
Equipment Growth Fund 1 (PLM) [Associated Press] (SAG)	EqGth1
Equipment Growth Fund 2 (PLM) [Associated Press] (SAG)	EqGth2
Equipment Growth Fund III (PLM) [Associated Press] (SAG)	EQGth3
Equipment Guide List (NVT)	EGL
Equipment Handover Agreement [Shipping] (DS)	EHA
Equipment Historical Availability Trend [Military]	EHAT
Equipment Identification Code	EIC
Equipment Identification Coded System (DNAB)	EICS
Equipment Identification List (DNAB)	EIL
Equipment Identification Register	EIR
Equipment Improvement Recommendations [Military]	EIR
Equipment Improvement Report [DoD]	EIR
Equipment in Place (MCD)	EIP
Equipment Inoperable Record [Nuclear energy] (NRCH)	EIR
Equipment Installation and Checkout (MUGU)	EIC
Equipment Installation Notice (AAG)	EIN
Equipment Installation Procedure [Telecommunications] (TEL)	EIP
Equipment Installation Record (MCD)	EIR
Equipment Integration Design Section	EIDS
Equipment Interchange Association [Defunct] (EA)	EIA
Equipment Interface Document (CAAL)	EID
Equipment Interstage Container	EIC
Equipment Inventory Update [Telecommunications] (TEL)	EIU
Equipment Item (MCD)	EI
Equipment Item Material Requirements	EIMR
Equipment Item Out of Balance (AFIT)	EIOBL
Equipment Leasing Association [British] (DBA)	ELA
Equipment Loss Consolidator	ELCON
Equipment Maintenance Agreement	EMA
Equipment Maintenance and Control [Online database]	EMAC
Equipment Maintenance and Support (MHDB)	EM & S
Equipment Maintenance Change Record (MCD)	EMCR
Equipment Maintenance Council [Defunct] (EA)	EMC
Equipment Maintenance Facility [Deep Space Instrumentation Facility, NASA]	EMF
Equipment Maintenance Log [Army] (AABC)	EML
Equipment Maintenance Management Program [Air Force]	EMMP
Equipment Maintenance Record [Army] (AABC)	EMR
Equipment Maintenance Requirements List (MCD)	EMRL
Equipment Maintenance Squadron [POMO] (MCD)	EMS
Equipment Maintenance Squadron [Air Force]	EMSq
Equipment Major Subdivision	EMSD
Equipment Management (MCD)	EM
Equipment Management Balance Register (AFIT)	EMBR
Equipment Management Code [Air Force] (AFIT)	EMC
Equipment Management Exception Indicator (AFIT)	EMEI
Equipment Management Group	EMG
Equipment Management Office [Air Force] (AFIT)	EMO
Equipment Management Subsystem (DNAB)	EMSUBS
Equipment Management System Training Requirements Program [Navy] (NG)	EMSTRP
Equipment Manufacturers Design	EMD
Equipment Manufacturers Workmanship	EMW
Equipment Market Abstracts [Predicast Inc.] [Database] (NITA)	EMA
Equipment Modification List (MCD)	EML
Equipment Modification Procurement Costs (MCD)	EMPC
Equipment Mounting Plate (NASA)	EMP
Equipment Move Order (AAG)	EMO
Equipment Not Operationally Ready to Fire [Military] (MCD)	ENF
Equipment Number (NITA)	EN
Equipment Oil Analysis Program [Air Force] (MCD)	EOAP
Equipment on Hand (AABC)	EOH
Equipment on Station Date [Army] (AABC)	EOSD
Equipment Operating Instructions	EOI
Equipment Operating [or Operational] Procedure (AAG)	EOP
Equipment Operational Control	EOC
Equipment Operational Readiness Trends [Report] (MCD)	EORT
Equipment Operationally Ready (AABC)	EOR
Equipment Operator [Navy rating]	EO
Equipment Operator, Construction Equipment [Navy rating]	EON
Equipment Operator, First Class [Navy rating]	EO1
Equipment Operator, Hauling [Navy rating]	EOH
Equipment Operator, Master Chief [Navy rating]	EOCM
Equipment Operator, Second Class [Navy rating]	EO2
Equipment Operator, Senior Chief [Navy rating]	EOCS
Equipment Operator, Third Class [Navy rating]	EO3
Equipment or Component	E/C
Equipment Parts Bin	EPB
Equipment Performance Log	EPL
Equipment Performance Report	EPR
Equipment Performance Report Management System (MCD)	EPRM
Equipment Piece (NRCH)	EP
Equipment Policy Statement [Army] (AABC)	EPS
Equipment Practice [Telecommunications] (TEL)	EP
Equipment Procurement and Installation Team (PDAA)	EPIT
Equipment Publication (AABC)	EP
Equipment Qualification (NRCH)	EQ
Equipment Qualification Data Bank [Information service or system] (IID)	EQDB
Equipment Quality Analysis	EQA
Equipment Readiness [DoD]	ER
Equipment Readiness Codes [or Criteria] (MCD)	ERC
Equipment Readiness Data	ERD
Equipment Readiness Date [Army] (AABC)	ERD
Equipment Readiness Drawing (MCD)	ERD
Equipment Recall Data System (MCD)	ERDS
Equipment Record	ER
Equipment Record Card (AAG)	ERC
Equipment Record System (KSC)	ERS
Equipment Related (DNAB)	ER
Equipment Release Priority System [DoD]	ERPS
Equipment Reliability Status Report	ERSR
Equipment Removal/Material Review Tag [Military] (MCD)	ER/MRT
Equipment Removal Tag (MCD)	ERT
Equipment Rental Agreement	ERA
Equipment Repair Order (DNAB)	ERO
Equipment Repair Parts	ERP
Equipment Repair Parts List	ERPL
Equipment Repair Time	ERT
Equipment Repairer [British military] (DMA)	ER
Equipment Replacement and Enhancement Program [Computer science]	EREP
Equipment Replacement Program [Computer science]	ERP
Equipment Report (MCD)	EQREP
Equipment Required on Site (MCD)	EROS
Equipment Requirement	ER
Equipment Requirement List (MCD)	ERL
Equipment Requirement Program (MCD)	ERP
Equipment Requirement Specification	ERS
Equipment Requirements Data [Army]	ERD
Equipment Requisitioning Priority System [Military]	ERPS
Equipment Review and Authorization Activity [Military] (AFM)	ERAA
Equipment Revision Level (IAA)	ERL
Equipment Section	ES
Equipment Section Container	ESC
Equipment Section Leakage Test	ESLT
Equipment Section/Loaded Equipment Section	ES/LES
Equipment Section Shell	ESS
Equipment Serial Number (ACRL)	ESN
Equipment Service Association (EA)	ESA
Equipment Serviceability (MCD)	ES
Equipment Serviceability Criteria [Military]	ESC
Equipment Shipment Ready Date [Army] (AABC)	ESRD
Equipment Sliding Drawer Cabinet	ESDC

Equipment Spare Package/Ground Communications and Electronic Equipment .... ESP/GC & EE
Equipment Specialist [Military] (AFIT) .... ES
Equipment Specification (AAGC) .... E SPEC
Equipment Specification .... ES
Equipment Specification [Nuclear energy] (NRCH) .... E-Spec
Equipment Statistical Data .... ESD
Equipment Statistical Data Card .... ESDC
Equipment Status (MCD) .... ES
Equipment Status Log (DNAB) .... ESL
Equipment Status Panel (AAG) .... ESP
Equipment Status Report [Air Force] .... ESR
Equipment Storage Container (KSC) .... ESC
Equipment Supervisory Rack [Telecommunications] (TEL) .... ESR
Equipment Supply Depot [British military] (DMA) .... ESD
Equipment Support Center, Mannheim [Germany] .... ESCM
Equipment Support Plan (MCD) .... ESP
Equipment Table Nomenclature (AFM) .... ETN
Equipment Task Time .... ETT
Equipment Technical Director (MCD) .... ETD
Equipment Temporarily Removed (MCD) .... ETR
Equipment Test .... ET
Equipment Test Plan (NASA) .... ETP
Equipment Time .... ET
Equipment to Computer Converter Buffer (DNAB) .... ECCB
Equipment Transfer Aisle (NRCH) .... ETA
Equipment Transfer Bag [NASA] .... ETB
Equipment Transfer or Change Order (NASA) .... ETCO
Equipment Transfer or Loan Order (NASA) .... ETLO
Equipment Trials Wing [Military British] .... ETW
Equipment Trust Certificate .... ETC
Equipment under Test .... EUT
Equipment Unsatisfactory Report .... EUR
Equipment Upgrade Program [Army] .... EUP
Equipment Visibility File (NASA) .... EVF
Equipment Visibility System (NASA) .... EVS
Equipment Working Group .... EWG
Equipmentman [Military] (DNAB) .... EQ
Equipo de Conferencias Sindicales de America Latina [Committee for Latin American Trade Union Conferences] .... ECOSAL
Equipotential Cathode .... EPC
Equipotential Kathode .... EPK
Equipotential Region .... EPR
Equipotential Surface .... EPS
Equippage Category Numbered Allowance Parts List (DNAB) .... ECN-APL
Equipped with Search Light [Suffix to plane designation] [Navy] L
EQuIS for Windows [Computer science] .... EQWin
Equisure, Inc. [Associated Press] (SAG) .... Equisure
Equitable [Legal term] (DLA) .... Eq
Equitable [Legal term] (ROG) .... EQBLE
Equitable .... EQTBL
Equitable Benefit-Based Financing .... EBBF
Equitable Companies, Inc. [Associated Press] (SAG) .... EqtCos
Equitable Co. [NYSE symbol] (SPSG) .... EQ
Equitable Conversion (DLA) .... EQ CONV
Equitable Cos. [NYSE symbol] (TTSB) .... EQ
Equitable Fed Svgs Bank [NASDAQ symbol] (TTSB) .... EQSB
Equitable Federal Savings Bank [NASDAQ symbol] (SAG) .... EQSB
Equitable Federal Savings Bank [Associated Press] (SAG) .... EqtFedl
Equitable Handicap [Sailing] .... EH
Equitable Handicap Associated-Measured Rating [Boating] .... EHA-MR
Equitable Life Assurance Society of the United States, General Library, New York, NY [OCLC symbol] (OCLC) .... YEL
Equitable Life Assurance Society of the United States, Medical Library, New Yor k, NY [OCLC symbol] (OCLC) .... ZEL
Equitable Life Assurance Society of the United States, Medical Library, New York, NY [Library symbol Library of Congress] (LCLS) .... NNEL
Equitable Life Assurance Society of the United States, Medical Library, New York, NY [Library symbol Library of Congress] (LCLS) .... NNEL-M
Equitable Life Interpreter [Computer] .... ELI
Equitable of Iowa [NYSE symbol] (TTSB) .... EIC
Equitable of Iowa Companies [Associated Press] (SAG) .... EqIowa
Equitable Real Estate Shopping [Later, Midwest Real Estate Shopping Center Ltd.] [NYSE symbol] (SPSG) .... EQM
Equitable Reserve Association [Neenah, WI] (EA) .... ERA
Equitable Resources [NYSE symbol] (TTSB) .... EQT
Equitable Resources, Inc. [Formerly, Equitable Gas Co.] [NYSE symbol] (SPSG) .... EQT
Equitable Resources, Inc. [Formerly, Equitable Gas Co.] [Associated Press] (SAG) .... EqtResc
Equites [Knights] [of Aristophanes] [Classical studies] (OCD) .... Eq
Equitex, Inc. [NASDAQ symbol] (NQ) .... EQTX
Equitex, Inc. [Associated Press] (SAG) .... Equitex
Equitrac Corp. [Associated Press] (SAG) .... Equitrc
Equitrac Corp. [NASDAQ symbol] (SAG) .... ETRC
Equitrac's Professional Internet Client [Computer science] .... EPIC
Equitum Magister [Master of the Horse] [British] .... EM
Equity (DLA) .... E
Equity .... EQ
Equity .... EQTY
Equity [Business term] .... Equ
Equity Access Account [Revolving mortgage-credit account] [Merrill Lynch & Co.] .... EAA
[The] Equity and Choice Act .... TEACH
Equity & Law [Brokerage group] [British] .... E & L

Equity Appreciation Certificate [Investment term] .... EAC
Equity Capital for Industry [British] .... ECI
Equity Cases [A publication] (DLA) .... Eq Cas
Equity Cases [A publication] (DLA) .... Eq Cas Mod
Equity Cases Abridged [2 vols.] [21, 22 English Reprint] [A publication] (DLA) .... Abr Cas Eq
Equity Cases Abridged [2 vols.] [21, 22 English Reprint] [A publication] (DLA) .... Abr Eq Cas
Equity Cases Abridged [A publication] (DLA) .... Eq Ca Ab
Equity Cases Abridged [2 vols.] [21, 22 English Reprint] [A publication] (DLA) .... Eq Cas Abr
Equity Cases Abridged [2 vols.] [21, 22 English Reprint] [A publication] (DLA) .... Eq Cas Abr (Eng)
Equity Corporation International [NASDAQ symbol] (SAG) .... ECII
Equity Corporation International [Associated Press] (SAG) .... EquityCp
Equity Corp. Intl. [NASDAQ symbol] (TTSB) .... ECII
Equity Court [or Division] [Legal term] .... Eq
Equity Draftsman (Van Heythuysen's, Edited by Hughes) [A publication] (DLA) .... Eq Draft
Equity Earnings [Accounting] .... EE
Equity Exchequer [Legal term] (DLA) .... EE
Equity Income [Finance] .... EqI
Equity Income Fund [AMEX symbol] (TTSB) .... ATF
Equity Inns [NASDAQ symbol] (SAG) .... ENNS
Equity Inns [Associated Press] (SAG) .... EqtyInn
Equity Joint Venture [Business term] .... EJV
Equity Judgments, by A'Beckett [New South Wales] [A publication] (DLA) .... Eq Judg
Equity Linked Life Insurance Policy with an Asset Value Guarantee (DICI) .... ELPAVG
Equity Market Analysis [MMS International] [Information service or system] (CRD) .... EMA
Equity Marketing [NASDAQ symbol] (TTSB) .... EMAK
Equity Marketing, Inc. [NASDAQ symbol] (SAG) .... EMAK
Equity Marketing, Inc. [Associated Press] (SAG) .... EqtyMkt
Equity Oil [NASDAQ symbol] (TTSB) .... EQTY
Equity Oil Co. [Associated Press] (SAG) .... EqtOil
Equity Oil Co. [NASDAQ symbol] (NQ) .... EQTY
Equity Policy Center (EA) .... EPOC
Equity Preservation Corp. [Toronto Stock Exchange symbol Vancouver Stock Exchange symbol] .... EQP
Equity Principle Auditions (BARN) .... EPA
Equity Reports [A publication] (DLA) .... Eq
Equity Reports [England] [A publication] (DLA) .... Eq R (Eng)
Equity Reports [A publication] (DLA) .... Eq Rep
Equity Reports (Gilbert) [England] [A publication] (DLA) .... Equity Rep
Equity Reports, Published by Spottiswoode [A publication] (DLA) .... Eq Rep
Equity Res Prop Tr 9.125%Pfd [NYSE symbol] (TTSB) .... EQRPrB
Equity Res Prop Tr 9.375% Pfd [NYSE symbol] (TTSB) .... EQRPrA
Equity Reserve Corp. [Toronto Stock Exchange symbol] .... EQR
Equity Residential Prop Tr [NYSE symbol] (TTSB) .... EQR
Equity Residential Property Trust [NYSE symbol] (SPSG) .... EQR
Equity Residential Property Trust [Associated Press] (SAG) .... EqtR
Equity Residential Property Trust [Associated Press] (SAG) .... EqtyRsd
Equity Silver Mines Ltd. [Toronto Stock Exchange symbol Vancouver Stock Exchange symbol] .... EST
Equivalence (IAA) .... EQV
Equivalence Class Mask .... ECM
Equivalence Principle [Physics] .... EP
Equivalency Capability File (MCD) .... ECF
Equivalency Class [Statistical algorithm] .... EC
Equivalent .... E
Equivalent .... EQ
Equivalent (AFM) .... EQUIV
Equivalent (IDOE) .... Equiv
Equivalent .... EQUIV
Equivalent Aerodynamic Median Diameter [of atmospheric particulates] .... EAMD
Equivalent Age Load (IAA) .... EAL
Equivalent Air Depth [Deep-sea diving] .... EAD
Equivalent Air Pressure .... EAP
Equivalent Air Speed .... EAS
Equivalent Alkane Carbon Number [of crude oil] .... EACN
Equivalent Annual Cost .... EAC
Equivalent Atomic Number .... EAN
Equivalent Availability Factor (IEEE) .... EAF
Equivalent Average Word [Mathematics] (IAA) .... EAW
Equivalent Background Input .... EBI
Equivalent Binary Digit .... EBD
Equivalent Carbon Dioxide [Climatology] .... ECD
Equivalent CEP .... ECEP
Equivalent Chain Length [of fatty acids] [Biochemistry] .... ECL
Equivalent Chlorine [Analytical Chemistry] .... ECL
Equivalent Circulating Density [Well drilling] .... ECD
Equivalent Continuous Perceived Noise Level (PDAA) .... ECPNL
Equivalent Current Dipole [Magnetism] .... ECD
Equivalent Daylight Visibility (PDAA) .... EDV
Equivalent Delivered Source Instructions .... EDSI
Equivalent Direct Radiation .... EDR
Equivalent Effective Temperature Corrected for Radiation (PDAA) .... ETCR
Equivalent Exposure Time (KSC) .... EET
Equivalent Fatality Unit [National Highway Traffic Safety Administration] .... EFU
Equivalent Focal Length [Optics] .... EF
Equivalent Focal Length [Optics] .... EFL
Equivalent Focus [Medicine] (DAVI) .... EF
Equivalent Forced Outage Rate (IEEE) .... EFOR

Equivalent Fuel Efficiency Improvement .... EFEI
Equivalent Full Charge .... EFC
Equivalent Full Power Hour [*FCC*] .... EFPH
Equivalent Full-Time Student Unit .... EFTSU
Equivalent Gear Train .... EGT
Equivalent Heat Transfer Dimensionality [*Process engineering*] .... EHTD
Equivalent Hertz (SSD) .... EH
Equivalent Horsepower (DOMA) .... ehp
Equivalent Industrial Standard Process (MCD) .... EISP
Equivalent Input Offset Current .... EIOC
Equivalent Input Offset Voltage .... EIOV
Equivalent Instruction or Duty .... EIOD
Equivalent Insulated Gate Field Effect Transistor (IAA) .... EIGFET
Equivalent Isotropic Radiated Power [*Telecommunications service*]
  (BARN) .... EIRT
Equivalent Isotropically Radiated Power [*Microwave transmission*] ..... EIRP
Equivalent Length [*Engineering*] .... EL
Equivalent Load Duration Curve .... ELDC
Equivalent Logic Element .... ELE
Equivalent Loudness Level .... ELL
Equivalent Martin Day (PDAA) .... EMD
Equivalent Mean Time to Failure .... EMTTF
Equivalent Means Investment Period .... EMIP
Equivalent Megatonnage [*Military weapon index*] (MCD) .... EMGTN
Equivalent Megatonnage [*Military weapon index*] .... EMT
Equivalent Mission Cycle .... EMC
Equivalent Monthly Payment .... EMP
Equivalent Mud Weight [*Well drilling technology*] .... EMW
Equivalent Neutral Density (DGA) .... END
Equivalent Noise Charge .... ENC
Equivalent Noise Input (DEN) .... ENI
Equivalent Noise Level .... ENL
Equivalent Noise Ratio [*or Resistance*] [*Electronics*] (IEEE) .... ENR
Equivalent Noise Sideband .... ENSB
Equivalent Noise Sideband Input (MCD) .... ENSI
Equivalent Noise Temperature [*Electronics*] .... ENT
Equivalent Noise Voltage .... ENV
Equivalent Orifice (IAA) .... EO
Equivalent Parallel Resistance (DEN) .... EPR
Equivalent Passband (MCD) .... EPB
Equivalent Pension Benefit [*British*] .... EPB
Equivalent per Million (IAA) .... EPM
Equivalent Prior Sample [*Information*] [*Statistics*] .... EPS
Equivalent Quantum Efficiency (MCD) .... EQE
Equivalent Radiated Power .... ERP
Equivalent Residual Dose .... ERD
Equivalent Roentgen .... ER
Equivalent Round (MCD) .... ER
Equivalent Series Resistance .... ESR
Equivalent Service Rounds [*A standard for indicating gun erosion*] ...... ESR
Equivalent Shaft Horsepower [*Air Force*] .... ESHP
Equivalent Single Axle Load .... ESAL
Equivalent Single Wheel Load (MCD) .... ESWL
Equivalent Snowline Altitude .... ESA
Equivalent Solar Hour [*NASA*] .... ESH
Equivalent Specific Fuel Consumption (NG) .... ESFC
Equivalent Spherical Diameter [*of a particle*] .... ESD
Equivalent Spherical Illumination (PDAA) .... ESI
Equivalent Square Miles of Mapping (NOAA) .... ESMM
Equivalent Standard Hours (MCD) .... ESH
Equivalent State Subset (IAA) .... ESS
Equivalent Station Location Error .... ESLE
Equivalent Stylized Day [*Of wartime combat*] .... ESD
Equivalent Target Area (MCD) .... ETA
Equivalent Target Size (SAA) .... ETS
Equivalent Threshold Sound Pressure Level .... ETSPL
Equivalent to Sheathed Explosive (IAA) .... EQS
Equivalent Top Product .... ETP
Equivalent Training (AFM) .... EQT
Equivalent Training (AABC) .... ET
Equivalent Transmission Density [*Photography*] (OA) .... ETD
Equivalent Ultraviolet Solar Hour [*NASA*] .... EUVSH
Equivalent Unavailability Factor (IEEE) .... EUF
Equivalent Uniform Annual Cost .... EUAC
Equivalent Uniform Cash Flow .... EUCF
Equivalent Uranium .... eU
Equivalent Weapons [*Military*] .... EW
Equivalent Weight [*Chemistry*] .... equiv wt
Equivalent Zero-Emission Vehicle .... EZEV
Equivalent-Continuous Noise Level (PDAA) .... ECNL
Equivalents per Million (DNAB) .... EPM
Equivalent-Weight Factor .... EWF
Equivest Finance, Inc. [*NASDAQ symbol*] (SAG) .... EQUI
Equivest Finance, Inc. [*Associated Press*] (SAG) .... Equivst
Equivest International Financial Corp. [*Vancouver Stock Exchange
  symbol*] .... EQV
Equiviscous Temperature [*Chemical engineering*] (IAA) .... EVT
Equivision, Inc. [*Associated Press*] (SAG) .... Equivsn
Equuleus [*Constellation*] .... Equ
Equus Gaming Co. Ltd. [*NASDAQ symbol*] (SAG) .... EQUUS
Equus Gaming Co., Ltd. [*Associated Press*] (SAG) .... EquusG
Equus Gaming LP [*NASDAQ symbol*] (TTSB) .... EQUUS
Equus II, Inc. [*AMEX symbol*] (SPSG) .... EQS
Equus II, Inc. [*Associated Press*] (SAG) .... EquusII
Equus Petroleum [*Vancouver Stock Exchange symbol*] .... EQU

ERA Helicopters, Inc. [*ICAO designator*] (FAAC) .... ERH
ERA [*Equal Rights Amendment*] Impact Project [*Defunct*] (EA) .... EIP
[*The*] Era of Persia [*Beginning 632AD*] (ROG) .... A PERS
ERADCOM [*Electronics Research and Development Command*] Flight Test
  Activity .... EFTA
ERADCOM [*Electronics Research and Development Command*] Tactical
  Software Support Center (MCD) .... ETSSC
Eramosa Community Library, Rockwood, ON, Canada [*Library symbol*]
  [*Library of Congress*] (LCLS) .... CaOREC
Eramosa Community Library, Rockwood, Ontario [*Library symbol National
  Library of Canada*] (NLC) .... OREC
Eras of Nonconformity [*A publication*] .... EN
Eras of the Christian Church [*A publication*] .... ECC
Erasable Direct Read After Write [*Computer science*] (IAA) .... EDRAW
Erasable LASER Optical Disk [*Computer science*] (IAA) .... ELOD
Erasable Magneto-Optical Disk [*Computer science*] (IAA) .... EMOD
Erasable Memory [*Computer science*] (KSC) .... EM
Erasable Memory Octal Dump [*Computer science*] .... EMOD
Erasable Memory Program [*Computer science*] .... EMP
Erasable Programmable Logic Device (NITA) .... EPLD
Erasable Programmable Read-Only Memory [*Computer science*]
  (MCD) .... EPROM
Erasable Read-Only Memory [*Computer science*] .... EROM
Erasable ROM [*Computer science*] (ECII) .... EROM
Erase [*British naval signaling*] .... EEEEE
Erase Digital [*Signal*] .... ED
Erase Gap [*Computer science*] .... ERG
Erase, Record, and Playback (NTCM) .... ERP
Erased (MSA) .... ERS
Erasmus Press, Lexington, KY [*Library symbol Library of Congress*] (LCLS) ..... EP
Erath, LA [*FM radio station call letters*] .... KPEL-FM
Erato [*Record label*] [*France*] .... Era
Erato (Discophiles de Paris Series) [*Record label*] [*France*] .... DDP
Eratosthenes [*275-194BC*] [*Classical studies*] (OCD) .... Eratosth
Erave [*Papua New Guinea*] [*Airport symbol*] (OAG) .... ERE
Erbil [*Iraq*] [*ICAO location identifier*] (ICLI) .... ORBA
Erbium [*Chemical element*] [*Symbol is ER*] (ROG) .... E
Erbium [*Symbol is Er*] [*Chemical element*] (ROG) .... EB
Erbium [*Chemical element*] .... Er
Erbium Oxide Crystal .... EOC
ERC Industries [*NASDAQ symbol*] (SAG) .... ERCI
ERC Industries, Inc. [*Associated Press*] (SAG) .... ERC Ind
Ercan [*Cyprus*] [*Airport symbol*] (OAG) .... ECN
Erck's Ecclesiastical Register [*1608-1825*] [*England*] [*A publication*] (DLA)..... Erck
ERCO Industries Ltd., Islington, ON, Canada [*Library symbol Library of
  Congress*] (LCLS) .... CaOIsE
Ercoupe Owners Club (EA) .... EOC
ERD Waste Corp. [*Associated Press*] (SAG) .... ERD
ERD Waste Corp. [*NASDAQ symbol*] (SAG) .... ERDI
ERDA [*Energy Research and Development Agency*] Energy Database
  [*Database*] (NITA) .... EEDB
Erdbeernekrosevirus .... ENV
Erdek [*Turkey*] [*Seismograph station code, US Geological Survey*] (SEIS) .... ERD
Erdelyi Vilagszovetseg [*Transylvanian World Federation - TWF*] (EAIO) .... EV
Erding [*Germany ICAO location identifier*] (ICLI) .... EDSE
Ere Vulgaire [*Common Era*] [*Freemasonry*] [*French*] (ROG) .... EV
Erect Posterior-Anterior [*Radiology*] .... EPA
Erecting .... ERCG
Erecting .... ERCT
Erection (ROG) .... EREC
Erection .... ERECT
Erection (ROG) .... ERECTN
Erection and Maintenance .... E & M
Erection Computer .... EC
Erection Counter Readout .... ECRO
Erection Digital Assembly .... EDA
Erection, Holddown, and Release [*Aerospace*] (AAG) .... EHDR
Erection Mechanism Motor Control Center .... EMMCC
Erection Subsystem .... ESS
Erection Timing Unit .... ETU
Erection Torquer (SAA) .... ET
Erection Unit .... EU
Erector .... ERCR
Erector .... ERCTR
Erector-Launcher Ground Interface Electronics Unit (MCD) .... EL-GIEU
Erector-Launcher, Guided Missile, Transportable .... ELGMT
Eremitarum Camaldulensium [*Monk Hermits of Camaldoli*] [*Roman Catholic
  religious order*] .... ER CAM
Erevan [*Former USSR Seismograph station code, US Geological Survey*]
  (SEIS) .... ERE
Erevan [*Former USSR Airport symbol*] (OAG) .... EVN
Erfurt [*Germany Airport symbol*] (OAG) .... ERF
Erfurt [*Germany ICAO location identifier*] (ICLI) .... ETEF
Erg [*Unit of work*] (GPO) .... E
Erg (IDOE) .... e
ERG Resources, Inc. [*Formerly, Energy & Resources (CAM) Ltd.*] [*Toronto
  Stock Exchange symbol*] .... ERG
Ergaenzung [*Amendment, Supplement*] [*German*] (DLA) .... Erg
Ergli [*Former USSR ICAO location identifier*] (ICLI) .... UMRG
Ergo Science [*NASDAQ symbol*] (TTSB) .... ERGO
Ergocryptine [*Organic chemistry*] .... EC
Ergometer (MCD) .... ERG
Ergonomic Accident Model [*Engineering*] .... EAM
Ergonomic Digitally Generated Environments [*Chrysler Corp.*] .... EDGE
Ergonomics (ADA) .... ERGON

Ergonomics Information Analysis Centre [University of Birmingham] [British] (CB) .... EIAC
Ergonomics Research Society [British] (BI) .... ERS
Ergonomics Society [British] .... ES
Ergonomics Society of Australia .... ESA
Ergonomy Data [Information service or system] [France] (NITA) .... ERGODATA
Ergosterol Biosynthesis Inhibitor [Biochemistry] .... EBI
Ergotamine Tartrate (DICI) .... ET
Ergs per Second [Unit of work] .... ERG/S
Ergs per Square Centimeter Second [Unit of work] .... ERG/(CM² S)
Erhard Seminars Training .... est
Erhardt Development Prehension Assessment .... EDPA
Eric and Parrish Making Dollars [Rap recording group] .... EPMD
Eric Braeden Fan Club (EA) .... EBFC
ERIC [Educational Resources Information Center] Data Access System [Search system] .... EDAS
ERIC [Educational Resources Information Center] Document .... ED
ERIC [Educational Resources Information Center] Document Reproduction Service [Stanford University] (NTCM) .... EDRS
ERIC [Educational Resources Information Center] Document Reproduction Service [Department of Education] [Alexandria, VA] ...... EDRS
Erickson Educational Foundation [Later, J2CP Information Services] .... EEF
Eric's Wasted Worldwide Repair Society (EA) .... EWWRS
Ericson Class Association (EA) .... ECA
Ericson Public Library, Boone, IA [Library symbol Library of Congress] (LCLS) .... IaBo
Ericsson L M Tel [NASDAQ symbol] (TTSB) .... ERICZ
Ericsson Manufacturing Systems [Commercial firm] [British] ...... EMS
Ericsson Telephone [Associated Press] (SAG) .... EricTel
Ericsson [L. M.] Telephone Co. [NASDAQ symbol] (NQ) ...... ERIC
Ericsson [L.M.] Telephone Co. [Associated Press] (SAG) ...... EricT
Ericsson(LM) Tel'B'ADR [NASDAQ symbol] (TTSB) .... ERICY
Eridamus [Constellation] .... Eri
Eridamus [Constellation] .... Erid
Eridania-Beghin Say [France] (ECON) .... EBS
Eridu Hymn (BJA) .... EH
Erie [Diocesan abbreviation] [Pennsylvania] (TOCD) .... E
Erie [Pennsylvania] [Airport symbol] (OAG) .... ERI
Erie Airways, Inc. [ICAO designator] (FAAC) .... ERE
Erie Area Health Information Library Cooperative [Library network] .... EAHILC
Erie Army Depot .... ERAD
Erie Community College-North, Buffalo, NY [Library symbol Library of Congress] (LCLS) ...... NBuEC
Erie Community College-North, Buffalo, NY [OCLC symbol] (OCLC) .... VVE
Erie Community College-North, City Campus, Buffalo, NY [Library symbol Library of Congress] (LCLS) .... NBuEC-C
Erie Community College-North, Urban Center, Buffalo, NY [Library symbol Library of Congress] (LCLS) ...... NBuEC-U
Erie Community College-South, Orchard Park, NY [Library symbol Library of Congress] (LCLS) ...... NOrcE
Erie County Historical Society, Erie, PA [Library symbol Library of Congress] (LCLS) ...... PerHi
Erie County Law Journal (Pennsylvania) [A publication] (DLA) ...... Erie Co L J (PA)
Erie County Legal Journal [Pennsylvania] [A publication] (DLA) .... Erie
Erie County Legal Journal [Pennsylvania] [A publication] (DLA) .... Erie Co Leg J
Erie County Legal Journal [Pennsylvania] [A publication] (DLA) .... Erie LJ
Erie County Library, Erie, PA [OCLC symbol] (OCLC) .... EPL
Erie County Technical Institute [New York] .... ECTI
Erie Indemnity 'A' [NASDAQ symbol] (TTSB) .... ERIE
Erie Indemnity Co. [NASDAQ symbol] (SAG) .... ERIE
Erie Indemnity Co. [Associated Press] (SAG) .... ErieInd
Erie No. 1 Board of Coopertive Educational Services, Lancaster, NY [Library symbol] [Library of Congress] (LCLS) .... NLanEB
Erie, PA [Location identifier FAA] (FAAL) .... AWY
Erie, PA [Location identifier FAA] (FAAL) .... CQD
Erie, PA [Location identifier FAA] (FAAL) .... ERI
Erie, PA [FM radio station call letters] .... WEFR
Erie, PA [FM radio station call letters] .... WERG
Erie, PA [FM radio station call letters] .... WFGO
Erie, PA [AM radio station call letters] .... WFLP
Erie, PA [Television station call letters] (RBYB) .... WFXP
Erie, PA [Television station call letters] .... WICU
Erie, PA [FM radio station call letters] .... WJET
Erie, PA [Television station call letters] .... WJET-TV
Erie, PA [AM radio station call letters] .... WLKK
Erie, PA [FM radio station call letters] .... WMCE
Erie, PA [AM radio station call letters] .... WPSE
Erie, PA [FM radio station call letters] .... WQLN
Erie, PA [Television station call letters] .... WQLN-TV
Erie, PA [AM radio station call letters] .... WRIE
Erie, PA [FM radio station call letters] .... WRTS
Erie, PA [Television station call letters] .... WSEE
Erie, PA [FM radio station call letters] .... WXKC
Erie Public Library, Erie, CO [Library symbol Library of Congress] (LCLS) ...... CoEr
Erie Public Library, Erie, PA [Library symbol Library of Congress] (LCLS) .... PEr
Erie Railroad .... ERR
Erie Western Railway Co. [AAR code] .... ERES
Erie-Cattaraugus Board of Cooperative Educational Services, Orchard Park, NY [Library symbol] [Library of Congress] (LCLS) ...... NorcEB
Erie-Lackawanna Railway Co. [Absorbed into Consolidated Rail Corp.] [AAR code] ...... EL
Erient Resources, Inc. [Vancouver Stock Exchange symbol] ...... ETR
Erigavo [Somalia] [Airport symbol] (AD) .... ERA
Erigavo [Somalia] [ICAO location identifier] (ICLI) .... HCMU
Erika Slezak Official Fan Club (EA) .... ESOFC

Erikson Psychosocial Stage Inventory [Psychology] .... EPSI
Erimo [Japan] [Seismograph station code, US Geological Survey] (SEIS) .... ERM
Erin District High School, Erin, ON, Canada [Library symbol] [Library of Congress] (LCLS) ...... CaOErD
Erin District High School, Erin, Ontario [Library symbol National Library of Canada] (NLC) ...... OERD
ERIN On-line Service [Commonwealth] (EERA) .... EOS
Erin Township Public Library, Hillsburgh, ON, Canada [Library symbol] [Library of Congress] (LCLS) ...... CaOHET
Erin Township Public Library, Hillsburgh, Ontario [Library symbol National Library of Canada] (NLC) ...... OHET
Erindale Campus Library, University of Toronto [UTLAS symbol] ...... ERI
Erindale College, University of Toronto, Mississauga, Ontario [Library symbol National Library of Canada] (NLC) ...... OME
Eriodictyol [Organic chemistry] .... E
Erionite [A zeolite] .... ERI
ERISA [Employee Retirement Income Security Act] Industry Committee (EA) ...... ERIC
Erith Herbarium [Borough Museum] [British] .... ERH
Eritrea .... Erit
Eritrean Liberation Front [Ethiopia] (PD) .... ELF
Eritrean Liberation Front - Popular Liberation Forces [Ethiopia] (PD) ..... ELF-PLF
Eritrean Liberation Front - Revolutionary Command [Ethiopia] (PD) .... ELF-RC
Eritrean People's Liberation Army [Ethiopia] [Political party] (EY) ...... EPLA
Eritrean People's Liberation Front [Ethiopia] (PD) .... EPLF
Eritrean Relief Committee (EA) .... ERC
Erkennungssignal [Recognition signal] [German military - World War II] .... ES
Erkowit/Carthago [Sudan] [ICAO location identifier] (ICLI) ...... HSCG
Erksine Public School, Erkskine, MN [Library symbol] [Library of Congress] (LCLS) ...... MnErsS
Erlang [Unit] [Statistics] [Telecommunications] .... E
Erlangen [Germany ICAO location identifier] (ICLI) .... EDET
Erlanger, KY [FM radio station call letters] .... WIZF
Erlanger Medical Center, I. C., Thompson's Children's Pediatric Library, Chattanooga, TN [Library symbol Library of Congress] (LCLS) ...... TCEC-P
Erlanger Medical Center, Medical Library, Chattanooga, TN [Library symbol Library of Congress] (LCLS) ...... TCEC
Erlanger Medical Center, Nursing School, Chattanooga, TN [Library symbol Library of Congress] (LCLS) ...... TCEC-N
Erlanger Rechner-Entwurfs-Sprache [Programming language] [1974] ...... ERES
Erlass [Decree, Edict, Order] [German] (ILCA) .... Erl
Erle on the Law of Trade-Unions [A publication] (DLA) .... Erle Tr Un
ERLY Indus [NASDAQ symbol] (TTSB) .... ERLY
ERLY Industries, Inc. [NASDAQ symbol] (SAG) .... ERLY
Ermelo [South Africa] [ICAO location identifier] (ICLI) ...... FAEO
Ermine [Heraldry] .... ERM
Ermington [England] .... ERMING
Ermolino Flying Test Research Enterprise [Former USSR] [FAA designator] (FAAC) ...... EFE
Ernaehrungs-, Land-, und Forstwissenschaftliches Informations-System [German Information System on Food, Agriculture, and Forestry] [Zentralstelle fuer Agrardokumentation und -Information] [Information service or system] ...... ELFIS
Ernaehrungswissenschaften Giessen [Nutrition Sciences - Giessen University] [Database] ...... EWG
Ernest Bloch Society (EA) .... EBS
Ernest Fan Club [Defunct] (EA) .... EFC
Ernest Hemingway Home, Key West, FL [Library symbol Library of Congress] (LCLS) ...... FKwH
Ernest K. Lehmann & Associates, Inc. [Also, an information service or system] (IID) ...... ELA
Ernest Orland Lawrence Livermore Laboratory [University of California] (KSC) ...... EOLLL
Ernest Read Music Association [British] (DBA) .... ERMA
Ernest Tubb Fan Club (EA) .... ETFC
Ernestine [Alaska] [Seismograph station code, US Geological Survey Closed] (SEIS) ...... ERN
Ernst & Whinney, Audit Management Services, New York, NY [Library symbol Library of Congress] (LCLS) ...... NNEW
Ernst & Whinney, Cleveland, OH [OCLC symbol] (OCLC) ...... OEE
Ernst Home Center [NASDAQ symbol] (TTSB) .... ERNS
Ernst Home Center, Inc. [NASDAQ symbol] (SAG) .... ERNS
Ernst Home Center, Inc. [Associated Press] (SAG) .... ErnstHm
Ernst Toller Memorial Society [Later, ISSE] (EA) .... ETMS
ERO, Inc. [Associated Press] (SAG) .... ERO
ERO, Inc. [NASDAQ symbol] (SAG) .... EROI
Erogenic .... E
Eromanga [New Hebrides] [Airport symbol] (AD) .... ERG
EROS [Earth Resources Observation Systems] Data Center [Marine science] (MSC) ...... EDC
Eros Resources [Vancouver Stock Exchange symbol] .... ERS
Erosion and Sediment .... E & S
Erosion Control [Type of water project] .... EC
Erosion Productivity Impact Calculator (GNE) .... EPIC
Erosive Osteoarthritis [Medicine] .... EOA
Erotic Art Book Society [Commercial firm] (EA) .... EABS
Erox Corp. [NASDAQ symbol] (SAG) .... EROX
Erox Corp. [Associated Press] (SAG) .... EroxCp
Er-Rachidia [Morocco] [ICAO location identifier] (ICLI) ...... GMFK
Errata .... ER
Errata [Error] [Latin] (NVT) .... ER
Errata and Addenda (NRCH) .... E & A
Errata Data [Dialog] [Searchable field] [Information service or system] (NITA) .... ED
Errata Sheet .... ES

Errata Volume [*Dialog*] [*Searchable field*] [*Information service or system*]
(NITA) .... EV
Errett Lobban Cord [*Auto industrialist*] .... ELC
Erreur ou Omission Exceptee [*Error or Omission Excepted*] [*French*] .... EOOE
Errol, NH [*Location identifier FAA*] (FAAL) .... ERR
Erroneous .... ER
Erroneous .... ERRON
Error [*Computer science*] (BUR) .... E
Error [*International telex abbreviation*] (WDMC) .... EEE
Error [*Baseball*] .... ER
Error (MCD) .... ERR
Error Adaptive Control Computer (IEEE) .... EACC
Error Adjusted (WDAA) .... EAD
Error Alert Control (OA) .... EAC
Error Analysis Study .... EAS
Error and Appeal [*Legal term*] (DLA) .... E & A
Error and Appeal Reports [*Canada A publication*] (DLA) .... E & AR
Error and Appeal Reports [*Canada A publication*] (DLA) .... Err & App
Error and Dispersion Analysis (MCD) .... EDA
Error Cause Identification [*Military*] (AFM) .... ECI
Error Cause Register [*Computer science*] (IAA) .... ERCR
Error Cause Removal [*Quality control*] .... ECR
Error Check Analysis Diagram (IAA) .... ECAD
Error Check Analysis Program (IAA) .... ECAP
Error Checking and Correction [*Computer science*] .... ECC
Error Checking and Correction (NITA) .... ECC
Error Checking and Correction [*Computer science*] .... ERCC
Error Checking and Correction Logic [*Computer science*] (IAA) .... ECCL
Error Checking Code (NITA) .... ECC
Error Classification, Omission, or Deficiency (MCD) .... ECOD
Error Code [*Computer science*] .... EC
Error Control Circuitry [*Algorithm to verify data*] [*Computer science*] (PCM) .... ECC
Error Control Device (TEL) .... ECD
Error Control Receiver (IEEE) .... ECR
Error Control Register [*Computer science*] (IAA) .... ECOR
Error Control Translator .... ECT
Error Control Transmitter .... ECT
Error Correcting [*or Correction*] [*Computer science*] .... E/C
Error Correction .... ERRC
Error Correction and Control .... ECC
Error Correction Capability [*Computer software quality*] .... ECC
Error Correction Code .... ECC
Error Correction Console Technician (IAA) .... ECCT
Error Correction Information System [*NASA*] .... ECIS
Error Correction Mode [*Computer science*] .... ECM
Error Correction Mode/Binary File Transfer [*Computer science*]
(PCM) .... ECM/BFT
Error Correction Servo [*or Signals*] (AAG) .... ECS
Error Counter (OA) .... EC
Error Counter .... ERR CNTR
Error Deletion by Iterative Transmission .... EDIT
Error Demodulator [*or Determination*] Output (MCD) .... EDO
Error Detecting [*or Detection*] [*Computer science*] .... ED
Error Detecting Code .... EDC
Error Detection (PDAA) .... ERDET
Error Detection and Correction .... EDAC
Error Detection and Correction (NATG) .... EDC
Error Detection and Decision Feedback .... EDDF
Error Detection Code Generator .... EDCG
Error Detection Encoder-Decoder [*Ground Communications Facility, NASA*] .... EDED
Error Detection Instrument (IAA) .... EDI
Error Detection System (KSC) .... EDS
Error Detection Unit Input/Output .... EDUI/O
Error Detector Assembly .... EDA
Error Expected (IAA) .... EE
Error Factor (IEEE) .... EF
Error Factor Analysis and Reduction (ADA) .... EFAR
Error File Teaching Package (NITA) .... EFTP
Error, Freak, Oddity .... EFO
Error Free Interval (NITA) .... EFI
Error Free Seconds (TEL) .... EFS
Error Frequency Limit [*Computer science*] (IAA) .... EFL
Error Function .... ERF
Error Function Complementary .... ERFC
Error Function, Inverse .... ERFI
Error Gap Probability Mass Function .... EGPMF
Error in Spelling [*Used in correcting manuscripts, etc.*] .... SP
Error in Use of Numbers [*Used in correcting manuscripts, etc.*] .... NUM
Error Indicator [*Computer science*] .... EI
Error Likely Situation (IEEE) .... ELS
Error Logging Device .... ELD
Error Logging Register (MHDB) .... ELR
Error Mean Square .... EMS
Error Model Best Estimate of Trajectory (PDAA) .... EMBET
Error Monitor Register (KSC) .... EMR
Error Multiplier .... EM
Error of Closure .... EOC
Error of Measurement (WDAA) .... E of M
Error, Omission, Clarification, or Deficiency (MCD) .... EOCD
Error Pattern Register .... EPR
Error Protecting Packet Assembler/Disassembler [*Telecommunications*]
(OSI) .... EPAD
Error Protection Code (NASA) .... EPC
Error Rate [*Statistics*] .... ER

Error Rate Test Set (TEL) .... ERTS
Error Recorder .... ER
Error Recording Device .... ERD
Error Recovery (BUR) .... ER
Error Relay .... ER
Error Retrieval [*Computer science*] (ECII) .... ER
Error Retry Count [*Computer science*] (IAA) .... ERC
Error Return Point (MCD) .... ERRET
Error Sequence Number [*Computer science*] .... ESN
Error Statistics by Tape Volume [*Computer science*] (IBMDP) .... ESTV
Error Statistics by Volume [*Computer science*] (BUR) .... ESV
Error Status Word [*Computer science*] (BUR) .... ESW
Error Terminate Interrupt Handler (MCD) .... ETIH
Error Time Word (KSC) .... ETW
Error Trap Handling [*Military*] .... ETH
Error Unavoidable .... EU
Error Variance Dependent on Level [*Statistical test*] .... ERRDEP
Error Vector Computer (NG) .... EVC
Error Voltage [*Electricity*] (IAA) .... EV
Error Volume Analysis [*Computer science*] (IBMDP) .... EVA
Error-Correcting Circuitry [*Computer science*] (IAA) .... ECC
Error-Correcting Tree Automation [*Computer science*] .... ECTA
Error-Free Communication Link (IAA) .... EFCL
Error-Free Performance .... EFP
Error-Prone Repair (GNE) .... EPR
Error-Recovery Package [*Computer science*] (MDG) .... ERP
Error-Recovery Procedure [*Computer science*] .... ERP
Errors [*Baseball*] .... E
Errors and Omissions (AAGC) .... E&O
Errors and Omissions [*Insurance*] .... EO
Errors and Omissions Excepted [*Insurance*] .... E and OE
Errors and Omissions Excepted [*Insurance*] .... EOE
Errors Excepted [*Business term*] .... EE
Errors, Freaks and Oddities Collector's Club (EA) .... EFOCC
Error-Sensitive Test Case Analysis (MCD) .... ESTCA
Errors-in-Variables Model [*Statistics*] .... EVM
Erros & Omissions (TDOB) .... E&O
Erskine College, Due West, SC [*Library symbol Library of Congress*]
(LCLS) .... ScDwE
Erskine College, Erskine Theological Seminary, Due West, SC [*Library symbol Library of Congress*] (LCLS) .... ScDwE-T
Erskine Register (EA) .... ER
Erskine's Institutes of the Law of Scotland [*A publication*] (DLA) .... Ersk
Erskine's Institutes of the Law of Scotland [*8 eds.*] [*1773-1871*]
[*A publication*] (DLA) .... Ersk Inst
Erskine's Institutes of the Law of Scotland [*8 eds.*] [*1773-1871*]
[*A publication*] (DLA) .... Erskine I
Erskine's Institutes of the Law of Scotland [*8 eds.*] [*1773-1871*]
[*A publication*] (DLA) .... Erskine Inst
Erskine's Principles of the Law of Scotland [*A publication*] (DLA) .... Ersk
Erskine's Principles of the Law of Scotland [*A publication*] (DLA) .... Ersk Prin
Erskine's Speeches [*A publication*] (DLA) .... Ersk Speech
Erskine's Speeches [*A publication*] (DLA) .... Ersk Speeches
Erskine's United States Circuit Court, Etc., Decisions [*35 Georgia*]
[*A publication*] (DLA) .... Ersk Dec
Erstfeld [*Switzerland ICAO location identifier*] (ICLI) .... LSXE
Erthrocyte Mass [*Hematology*] (CPH) .... EM
Ertl Collectors Club [*Commercial firm*] (EA) .... ECC
ERTS Command Auxiliary Memory (MCD) .... ECAM
'Erubin [*or 'Eruvin*] (BJA) .... 'Er
'Erubin (BJA) .... 'Erub
Erume [*Papua New Guinea*] [*Airport symbol*] (OAG) .... ERU
Erwin, NC [*FM radio station call letters*] .... WUAW
Erwin Public Library, Erwin, NC [*Library symbol Library of Congress*]
(LCLS) .... NcEr
Erwin, TN [*AM radio station call letters*] .... WEMB
Erwin, TN [*FM radio station call letters*] .... WXIS
Erwinville, LA [*FM radio station call letters*] .... KPAE
Erysimum Latent Virus [*Plant pathology*] .... ERLV
Erysipelas [*Medicine*] .... ERY
Erysipelothrix [*A bacteria*] (DAVI) .... Ery
Erythema Chronicum Migrans [*Dermatology*] .... ECM
Erythema Dose [*Medicine*] .... ED
Erythema Multiforme [*Hematology*] (CPH) .... EM
Erythema Nodosum [*Medicine*] .... EN
Erythema Nodosum Leproticum [*Medicine*] .... ENL
Erythema-Inducing Factor [*Hematology*] .... EIF
Erythematous-Edematous [*Reaction*] [*Medicine*] .... E-E
Erythroblastosis Fetalis [*Hematology*] .... EBF
Erythrocyte [*Hematology*] .... E
Erythrocyte [*Hematology*] .... ER
Erythrocyte [*Hematology*] (DAVI) .... erythro
Erythrocyte Acid Phosphatase [*Hematology*] .... EAP
Erythrocyte Amboceptor [*Immunology*] .... EA
Erythrocyte Amboceptor Complement [*Immunology*] .... EAC
Erythrocyte Binding Antigen [*Immunology*] .... EBA
Erythrocyte Coproporphyrin [*Hematology*] (MAE) .... ECP
Erythrocyte Creatine [*Clinical chemistry*] .... EC
Erythrocyte Glutamic Oxaloacetic Transaminase (AAMN) .... EGOT
Erythrocyte Glutatione Reductase [*An enzyme*] .... EGR
Erythrocyte Initiation Factor .... EIF
Erythrocyte Mass [*Hematology*] (MAE) .... EM
Erythrocyte Maturation Factor [*Hematology*] .... EMF
Erythrocyte Membrane Protein [*Biochemistry*] .... EMP

Erythrocyte Membrane Protein Electrophoretic Pattern [*Clinical chemistry*] (AAMN) ..... EMPEP
Erythrocyte Particle Counter [*Hematology*] ..... Epc
Erythrocyte Protoporphyrin [*Hematology*] ..... EP
Erythrocyte Rosette [*Hematology*] ..... ER
Erythrocyte Rosette-Forming Cells [*Hematology*] ..... ERFC
Erythrocyte Sedimentation Rate [*Hematology*] ..... ESR
Erythrocyte Superoxide Dismutase [*An enzyme*] ..... ESOD
Erythrocyte Tri-Iodothyronine [*Hematology*] (DAVI) ET-3
Erythrocyte Tri-Iodothyronine [*Endocrinology*] (DAVI) ..... T-e
Erythrocyte-Antibody [*Complex*] [*Immunochemistry*] ..... EA
Erythrocyte-Antibody Complement [*Immunochemistry*] ..... EAC
Erythrocyte-Sensitizing Substance [*Hematology*] ..... ESS
Erythrocytic Fragmentation (AAMN) ..... EF
(Erythrofuranosyl)imidazolinethione [*Antineoplastic drug*] ..... EIT
Erythro(hydroxynonyl)adenine [*Biochemistry*] ..... EHNA
Erythroid Colony Formation [*Hematology*] (DMAA) ..... ECF
Erythroid Differentiation Factor [*Endocrinology*] ..... EDF
Erythroid Iron Turnover [*Hematology*] ..... EIT
Erythroid Kruppel-Like Factor [*Medicine*] ..... EKLF
Erythroid Potentiating Activity [*Hematology*] ..... EPA
Erythroid Progenitor Cells [*Hematology*] ..... EPC
Erythrokinase [*Biochemistry*] (DAVI) ..... EK
Erythroleukemia [*Medicine*] (MAE) ..... EL
Erythromycin [*Also, ERY, ERYC, ETM*] [*Antibacterial compound*] ..... E
Erythromycin [*Also, E, ERYC, ETM*] [*Antibacterial compound*] ..... ERY
Erythromycin [*Also, E, ERY, ETM*] [*Antibacterial compound*] ..... ERYC
Erythromycin [*Also, E, ERY, ETM, ERYC*] [*An antibacterial compound*] (DAVI) ..... ERYTHR
Erythromycin [*Also, E, ERY, ERYC*] [*Antibacterial compound*] ..... ETM
Erythromycin Acistrate [*Antibacterial*] ..... EA
Erythromycin Ethylsuccinate [*Antimicrobial compound*] ..... EES
Erythromycylamine [*Antibacterial*] ..... EA
Erythrophagocytosis [*Hematology*] ..... EP
Erythropoietic Porphyria [*A genetic disorder*] ..... EP
Erythropoietic Protoporphyria [*A genetic disorder*] ..... EPP
Erythropoietic Stimulating [*or Erythropoietin Switching*] **Factor** [*Hematology*] ..... ESF
Erythropoietin [*Also, EPO*] [*Hematology*] ..... Ep
Erythropoietin [*Also, Ep*] [*Hematology*] ..... EPO
Erythropoietin Receptor [*Hematology*] ..... EPOR
Erythropoietin-Producing Enzyme [*Hematology*] (MAE) ..... EPE
Erythropoietin-Responsive Cell [*Hematology*] ..... ERC
Erythropoietin-Sensitive Stem Cell [*Hematology*] ..... ESC
Erythrose Phosphate [*Biochemistry*] (BARN) ..... EP
Erzincan [*Turkey*] [*Airport symbol*] (AD) ..... ERC
Erzincan [*Turkey ICAO location identifier*] (ICLI) ..... LTCD
Erzurum [*Turkey*] [*Airport symbol*] (OAG) ..... ERZ
Erzurum [*Turkey*] [*Seismograph station code, US Geological Survey*] (SEIS) ..... ERZ
Erzurum [*Turkey ICAO location identifier*] (ICLI) ..... LTCE
Esa Ala [*Papua New Guinea*] [*Airport symbol*] (OAG) ..... ESA
Esa Ala [*Papua New Guinea*] [*Seismograph station code, US Geological Survey*] (SEIS) ..... ESA
Esa Ala [*D'Entrecasteaux Islands*] [*Seismograph station code, US Geological Survey*] (SEIS) ..... ESB
ESA Furnished Property (MCD) ..... EFP
ESA [*European Space Agency*] **Furnished Property** ..... EFP
ESA [*European Space Agency*] **Network** [*Information service or system*] (NITA) ..... ESANET
ESA [*European Space Agency*] **Remote Sensing Satellite** ..... ERS
ESADA [*Empire State Atomic Development Associates, Inc.*] **Vallecitos Experimental Superheat Reactor** ..... EVESR
Esaki Diode [*Electronics*] ..... ED
Esalen Institute (EA) ..... EI
Esarhaddon (BJA) ..... Esarh
Esbjerg [*Denmark*] [*Airport symbol*] (OAG) ..... EBJ
Esbjerg [*Denmark ICAO location identifier*] (ICLI) ..... EKEB
ESC Medical Systems [*NASDAQ symbol*] (TTSB) ..... ESCMF
ESC Medical Systems Ltd. [*NASDAQ symbol*] (SAG) ..... ESCM
ESC Medical Systems Ltd. [*Associated Press*] (SAG) ..... ESCMed
Escadrille [*Military*] (BARN) ..... Esc
Escala Inteligencia Wechsler Para Adultes [*Weschler Adult Intelligence Scale*] [*Psychology*] (DAVI) ..... EIWA
Escalade, Inc. [*NASDAQ symbol*] (NQ) ..... ESCA
Escalade, Inc. [*Associated Press*] (SAG) ..... Escalde
Escalation during Construction (MCD) ..... EDC
Escalator [*Technical drawings*] ..... ESC
Escalator (MSA) ..... ESCL
Escalon Med Corp. Wrrt'A' [*NASDAQ symbol*] (TTSB) ..... ESMCW
Escalon Med Corp. Wrrt'B' [*NASDAQ symbol*] (TTSB) ..... ESMCL
Escalon Medical Corp. [*Associated Press*] (SAG) ..... Escalon
Escalon Medical Corp. [*Associated Press*] (SAG) ..... Escln
Escalon Medical Corp. [*NASDAQ symbol*] (SAG) ..... ESMC
Escalon Medical Corp. [*NASDAQ symbol*] (TTSB) ..... ESMC
Escanaba [*Michigan*] [*Airport symbol*] (OAG) ..... ESC
Escanaba & Lake Superior Railroad Co. [*AAR code*] ..... ELS
Escanaba, MI [*Location identifier FAA*] (FAAL) ..... ESC
Escanaba, MI [*AM radio station call letters*] ..... WCHT
Escanaba, MI [*AM radio station call letters*] ..... WDBC
Escanaba, MI [*FM radio station call letters*] ..... WGLQ
Escanaba, MI [*Television station call letters*] ..... WJMN
Escanaba, MI [*FM radio station call letters*] ..... WYKX
Escanaba Public Library, Escanaba, MI [*Library symbol Library of Congress*] (LCLS) ..... MiEsc
ESCAP [*Economic and Social Commission for Asia and the Pacific*] **Bibliographic Information System** [*Thailand*] [*United Nations Information service or system*] (IID) ..... EBIS
ESCAP [*Economic and Social Commssion for the Asia and Pacific*] **Division for Shipping, Ports, and Inland Waterways** (EAIO) ..... SPIW
ESCAP [*Economic and Social Commission for Asia and the Pacific*] **Maritime Transport Database** [*United Nations*] (DUND) ..... EMTDB
ESCAP [*Economic and Social Commission for Asia and the Pacific*] **Pacific Operations Center** [*Vanuatu*] ..... EPOC
Escape (ROG) ..... E
Escape (NASA) ..... ESC
Escape and Evasion ..... E & E
Escape and Rescue ..... EAR
Escape and Survival Equipment (PDAA) ..... EASE
Escape Aviation [*ICAO designator*] (FAAC) ..... TCL
Escape Character [*Keyboard*] (KSC) ..... ESC
Escape Motor ..... EM
Escape PAC (MCD) ..... ESCAPAC
Escape Road [*Hawaii*] [*Seismograph station code, US Geological Survey*] (SEIS) ..... ESR
Escape Suit Ventilation System (MCD) ..... ESVS
Escape System (MCD) ..... ES
Escape System Test Article (MCD) ..... ESTA
Escape System Ventilation System (NASA) ..... ESVS
Escape Tower [*NASA*] (KSC) ..... E/T
Escaped Federal Prisoner ..... EFP
Escapees, Inc. (EA) ..... S-K-P's
Eschatological (ADA) ..... ESCHAT
Escherichia [*Bacterial strain*] ..... E
Escherichia [*Bacterial strain*] ..... ESCH
Escherichia Coli (DOG) ..... E coli
Escherichia Coli [*Microorganism*] ..... EC
Escherichia Coli [*Microorganism*] ..... ECC
Escherichia Coli [*Microorganism*] ..... Eco
Escherichia Coli Database [*Genetics*] ..... ECD
Escherichia Coli Phosphoribosyl Anthranilate Isomerase ..... ePRAI
Escherichia Coli Polypeptides ..... ECP
Escherichia Coli Single-Stranded Protein ..... EcoSSP
ESCO Electronics [*Associated Press*] (SAG) ..... Esco
ESCO Electronics [*NYSE symbol*] (SPSG) ..... ESE
Escobilla [*Little Broom*] [*Flamenco dance term*] [*Spanish*] ..... ESC
Escompte [*Discount, Rebate*] [*French*] ..... ESC
Escondido, CA [*FM radio station call letters*] ..... KOWF
Escondido, CA [*AM radio station call letters*] ..... KSPA
Escondido Public Library, Escondido, CA [*Library symbol Library of Congress*] (LCLS) ..... CEsc
Escort [*Record label*] ..... Esc
Escort (AABC) ..... ESC
Escort Aircraft (CINC) ..... EA
Escort Aircraft Carrier [*Navy symbol*] ..... CVE
Escort Carrier Force ..... ESCARFOR
Escort Convoy (CINC) ..... EC
Escort Cost Model ..... ESCOMO
Escort Destroyer [*Navy symbol*] ..... DDE
Escort Division ..... CORTDIV
Escort Division ..... ESCORTDIV
Escort Fighter Squadron ..... ESCORTFIGHTRON
Escort Fighter Squadron [*Navy symbol*] ..... VGF
Escort Force Commander [*NATO*] (NATG) ..... EFC
Escort Group ..... EG
Escort Guard ..... ESCRG
Escort Helicopter (CINC) ..... EH
Escort Helicopter Aircraft Carrier [*Navy symbol*] ..... CVHE
Escort Mission ..... ESM
Escort Oilers Supervising Officer [*Navy*] ..... EOSO
Escort Research Ship [*Navy symbol*] ..... AGDE
Escort Screening Jammer [*Military*] ..... ESJ
Escort Ship [*Destroyer Escort*] [*Navy symbol*] ..... DE
Escort Ship (CINC) ..... ES
Escort Squadron ..... CORTRON
Escort Towed Array Sensor [*Later, TACTAS*] [*Navy*] (MCD) ..... ETAS
Escort Towed Array SONAR System [*Navy*] (PDAA) ..... ETASS
Escort Trains (CINC) ..... ET
Escort Vessel [*Enemy*] ..... EV
Escort Vessel Administration [*World War II*] ..... EVA
Escort-Scouting Squadron ..... ESCORON
Escort-Scouting Squadron [*Navy symbol*] ..... VGS
Escriche's Dictionary of Jurisprudence [*A publication*] (DLA) ..... Escriche Dict
Escrow [*Legal term*] (DLA) ..... Esc
Escrowed to Maturity [*Finance*] ..... ETM
Escuadron de la Muerte Nuevo [*New Death Squad*] [*El Salvador*] (PD) ..... EMN
Escudo [*Monetary unit*] [*Chile, Portugal*] ..... E
Escudo [*Monetary unit*] [*Chile, Portugal*] ..... ESC
Escuela Interamericana de Educacion Democratica ..... EIDED
Escuela Superior de Economia y Negocios [*El Salvador*] ..... ESEN
Escutcheon ..... ESC
Esdras [*Apocrypha*] (BJA) ..... Esd
E-Section Escape Suit [*Military*] ..... EES
Eseka [*Cameroon*] [*ICAO location identifier*] (ICLI) ..... FKKE
ESELCO, Inc. [*NASDAQ symbol*] (SPSG) ..... EDSE
ESELCO, Inc. [*Associated Press*] (SAG) ..... ESELCO
Esen Bulak [*Mongolia*] [*Seismograph station code, US Geological Survey Closed*] (SEIS) ..... EBM
Esfahan [*Iran*] [*ICAO location identifier*] (ICLI) ..... OIFH
Esfahan [*Iran*] [*ICAO location identifier*] (ICLI) ..... OIFM

Esfahan [*Iran*] [*ICAO location identifier*] (ICLI) ... OIFT
Esfarayen [*Iran*] [*ICAO location identifier*] (ICLI) ... OIME
Eshed Robotec 1982 Ltd. [*Associated Press*] (SAG) ... EshedR
Eshed Robotec 1982 Ltd [*NASDAQ symbol*] (TTSB) ... ROBOF
Eshed Robotec Ltd. [*NASDAQ symbol*] (SAG) ... ROBO
Eshkashem [*Afghanistan*] [*ICAO location identifier*] (ICLI) ... OAEM
Eshowe [*South Africa*] [*ICAO location identifier*] (ICLI) ... FAES
ESI International [*Washington, D.C.*] (AAGC) ... ESI
Eskdalemuir [*Scotland*] [*Seismograph station code, US Geological Survey*] (SEIS) ... ESK
Eskdalemuir Array [*Scotland*] [*Seismograph station code, US Geological Survey*] (SEIS) ... EKA
Eski Sark Eserleri Muezesi [*Istanbul*] (BJA) ... ESEM
Eskilstuna [*Sweden*] [*Airport symbol*] ... EKT
Eskilstuna [*Sweden ICAO location identifier*] (ICLI) ... ESSU
Eskilstuna/Ekeby [*Sweden ICAO location identifier*] (ICLI) ... ESSC
Eskimo [*Language, etc.*] ... ESK
Eskimo [*MARC language code Library of Congress*] (LCCP) ... esk
Eskimo Dog Society of the Northwest Territories [*Defunct*] (EA) ... EDS-NWT
Eskimo Museum, Churchill, Manitoba [*Library symbol National Library of Canada*] (NLC) ... MCHE
Eskimo Museum, Churchill, MB, Canada [*Library symbol Library of Congress*] (LCLS) ... CaMChE
Eskimo Pie [*NASDAQ symbol*] (TTSB) ... EPIE
Eskimo Pie Corp. [*NASDAQ symbol*] (SAG) ... EPIE
Eskimo Pie Corp. [*Associated Press*] (SAG) ... Eskimo
Eskimo Point [*Canada*] [*Airport symbol*] (OAG) ... YEK
Eskimo Point, NT [*ICAO location identifier*] (ICLI) ... CYEK
Eskisehir [*Turkey ICAO location identifier*] (ICLI) ... LTBI
Esko High School, Esko, MN [*Library symbol*] [*Library of Congress*] (LCLS) ... MnEskH
Eskridge Family Association (EA) ... EFA
ESL, Inc., Sunnyvale, CA [*Library symbol Library of Congress*] (LCLS) ... CSvE
Eslov [*Sweden ICAO location identifier*] (ICLI) ... ESME
Esmeraldas [*Ecuador*] [*Airport symbol*] (OAG) ... ESM
Esmeraldas/General Rivadeneira [*Ecuador*] [*ICAO location identifier*] (ICLI) ... SEES
Esmor Correctional Services [*Commercial firm Associated Press*] (SAG) ... Esmor
Esmor Correctional Services [*NASDAQ symbol*] (SAG) ... ESMR
Esmor Correctional Svcs [*NASDAQ symbol*] (TTSB) ... ESMR
Esmor Correct'l Svcs Wrrt [*NASDAQ symbol*] (TTSB) ... ESMRW
Esophageal Atrial Pacing [*Medicine*] ... EAP
Esophageal Gastric Tube Airway [*Medicine*] ... EGTA
Esophageal Hiatal Hernia [*Medicine*] (MEDA) ... EHH
Esophageal Motility Disorder [*Medicine*] ... EMD
Esophageal Obturator Airway [*Medicine*] (DMAA) ... EOA
Esophageal Pressure [*Used to estimate intrapleural pressure*] (DAVI) ... Pes
Esophageal Scintigraphy [*Medicine*] (DAVI) ... ES
Esophageal Valve [*Anatomy*] ... ESV
Esophageal Varices [*Medicine*] ... EV
Esophageal Varices Hemorrhage [*Medicine*] ... EVH
Esophagogastrectomy [*Medicine*] ... EG
Esophagogastric Junction [*Anatomy*] (DAVI) ... EGJ
Esophagogastroduodenoscopy [*Medicine*] ... EGD
Esophagoscopy [*Medicine*] (DAVI) ... eso
Esophagus [*Anatomy*] ... E
Esophagus [*Anatomy*] (DAVI) ... ES
Esophagus [*Anatomy*] (DAVI) ... ESO
Esophagus [*Anatomy*] ... ESOPH
Esophagus, Stomach, and Duodenum [*Gastroenterology*] (DAVI) ... ESD
Esophoria [*Ophthalmology*] (DAVI) ... ES
Esophoria [*Ophthalmology*] (DAVI) ... s
Esophoria for Distance [*Ophthalmology*] ... E
Esoteric [*Record label*] ... Eso
Esoteric [*or Esoterica*] (WDAA) ... ESOT
Esotropia [*Ophthalmology*] (DAVI) ... ET
Esotropia [*Ophthalmology*] (MAE) ... ST
Esotropia for Distance [*Ophthalmology*] ... ET
Esotropia, Left [*Ophthalmology*] (DAVI) ... STI
Esotropia, Right [*Ophthalmology*] (DAVI) ... STr
ESP [*Extrasensory Perception*] **Research Associates Foundation** [*Defunct*] (EA) ... ESPRAF
Espana [*Spain*] ... E
Espana, Direccion General de Aviacion Civil [*Spain ICAO designator*] (FAAC) ... ENA
Espanola, NM [*AM radio station call letters*] ... KDCE
Espanola, NM [*FM radio station call letters*] (RBYB) ... KPZA
Espanola, NM [*FM radio station call letters*] (RBYB) ... KYBR-FM
Espanola, ON [*AM radio station call letters*] ... CKNS
Espanola Public Library, Espanola, NM [*Library symbol Library of Congress*] (LCLS) ... NmE
Espanola Public Library, Ontario [*Library symbol National Library of Canada*] (NLC) ... OES
Esparros [*France*] [*Seismograph station code, US Geological Survey*] (SEIS) ... EPF
Esparto, CA [*FM radio station call letters*] (RBYB) ... KZAC
Espe [*Germany*] [*Research code symbol*] ... OMP
Espeair [*Chechoslovakia*] [*FAA designator*] (FAAC) ... ESP
Especial [*Designation on brandy labels*] ... E
Especialidades Consumidas por la Seguridad Social [*Ministerio de Sanidad y Consumo*] [*Spain Information service or system*] (CRD) ... ECOM
Especialidades Farmaceuticas en Tramite de Registro [*Ministerio de Sanidad y Consumo*] [*Spain Information service or system*] (CRD) ... TRAMIT
Especialidades Farmaceuticas Espanolas Data Bank [*Spanish Pharmaceutical Specialities Data Bank*] [*Spanish Drug Information Center*] [*Information service or system*] (IID) ... ESPES
Especially ... ESP
Especially (VRA) ... esp
Especially (WDMC) ... esp
Especially ... ESPEC
Especially (FAAC) ... SPCLY
Esperance [*Australia Airport symbol*] (OAG) ... EPR
Esperanta Jura Asocio [*Esperanto Law Association*] [*See also ELA*] [*British*] [*England*] (EAIO) ... EJA
Esperantic Studies Foundation (EA) ... ESF
Esperantist Club of Veterans [*See also VEK*] [*Wolfhagen, Federal Republic of Germany*] (EAIO) ... ECV
Esperantist Movement for World Peace [*See also MEM*] [*Tours, France*] (EAIO) ... EMWP
Esperantista Go-Ligo Internacia [*International Esperantist League for Go - IELG*] (EAIO) ... EGLI
Esperantista Sak-Ligo Internacia [*International Esperantist Chess League - IECL*] (EAIO) ... ESLI
Esperantlingva Verkista Asocio [*Esperanto Writers Association - EWA*] [*Netherlands*] (EA) ... EVA
Esperanto [*MARC language code Library of Congress*] (LCCP) ... esp
Esperanto Association of North America [*Defunct*] (EA) ... EANA
Esperanto en Komerco Kaj Industrio [*Institute for Esperanto in Commerce and Industry*] (EA) ... EKI
Esperanto Family History Association [*Later, EEFHA*] (EA) ... EFHA
Esperanto Federation of New South Wales [*Australia*] ... EFNSW
Esperanto Law Association [*British England*] (EAIO) ... ELA
Esperanto League for North America (EA) ... ELNA
Esperanto Teachers Association [*British*] ... ETA
Esperanto Writers Association (EA) ... EWA
Esperanto-Asocio de Britujo [*British*] ... EAB
Esperanto-Ligo Filatelista [*Philatelic Esperanto League - PEL*] (EAIO) ... ELF
Esperanza Explorations Ltd. [*Vancouver Stock Exchange symbol*] ... EEP
Espey Manufacturing & Electronics, Inc. [*AMEX symbol*] (SPSG) ... ESP
Espey Manufacturing & Electronics, Inc. [*Associated Press*] (SAG) ... Espey
Espey Mfg & Electr [*AMEX symbol*] (TTSB) ... ESP
Espinasse. Actions on Statutes [*A publication*] (ILCA) ... Esp Act
Espinasse on Penal Evidence [*A publication*] (DLA) ... Esp Ev
Espinasse on Penal Evidence [*A publication*] (DLA) ... Esp Pen Ev
Espinasse on Penal Statutes [*A publication*] (DLA) ... Esp P St
Espinasse's Digest of the Law of Actions at Nisi Prius [*1812*] [*A publication*] (ILCA) ... Esp Dig
Espinasse's English Nisi Prius Reports [*1793-1810*] [*A publication*] (DLA) ... Esp
Espinasse's English Nisi Prius Reports [*1793-1810*] [*A publication*] (DLA) ... Esp NP
Espinasse's Law of Bankrupts [*1825*] [*A publication*] (DLA) ... Esp Bank
Espinho [*Portugal ICAO location identifier*] (ICLI) ... LPIN
Espinosa [*Brazil*] [*Airport symbol*] (OAG) ... ESI
Espionage [*FBI standardized term*] ... ESP
Espionage (AABC) ... ESPG
Espirito Santo Financial [*NYSE symbol*] (SPSG) ... ESF
Espirito Santo Financial Holding [*Associated Press*] (SAG) ... EspirSan
Espirito Santo Financial Holding [*Associated Press*] (SAG) ... EsprSan
Espirito Santo Finl ADS [*NYSE symbol*] (TTSB) ... ESF
Espirito Santo Overseas [*NYSE symbol*] (SPSG) ... ESB
Espirito Santo Overseas Ltd. [*Associated Press*] (SAG) ... EspSan
Espirito Santo Oversecs 8.50% Pref [*NYSE symbol*] (TTSB) ... ESBPrA
Espiritu [*Bolivia*] [*ICAO location identifier*] (ICLI) ... SLES
Espiritu Santo [*Vanuatu*] [*Airport symbol*] (OAG) ... SON
Esplanade (DD) ... Espl
Esplanade Centre Holdings [*Vancouver Stock Exchange symbol*] ... ESC
Espoir de la Jeunesse Camerounaise [*Hope of the Cameroonese Youth*] ... EJC
Espressivo [*With Expression*] [*Music*] ... ESP
Espressivo [*With Expression*] [*Music*] ... Espr
Espressivo [*With Expression*] [*Music*] ... Espres
Espressivo [*With Expression*] [*Music*] ... ESPRESS
Esquel [*Argentina*] [*Airport symbol*] (OAG) ... EQS
Esquel [*Argentina ICAO location identifier*] (ICLI) ... SAVE
Esquerda Democratica Estudantil [*Democratic Student Left*] [*Portugal Political party*] (PPE) ... EDE
Esquerra Democratica [*Democratic Left*] [*Spain Political party*] (PPE) ... ED
Esquerra Gallega [*Galician Left*] [*Political party*] (PPW) ... EG
Esquerra Republicana de Catalunya [*Catalan Republican Left*] [*Spain Political party*] (PPE) ... ERC
Esquimalt & Nanaimo Railway Co. [*AAR code*] ... EN
Esquimalt, BC [*ICAO location identifier*] (ICLI) ... CYPF
Esquipulas [*Guatemala*] [*ICAO location identifier*] (ICLI) ... MGES
Esquire [*A publication*] [*New York, NY*] (WDMC) ... Esky
Esquire ... ESQ
Esquire [*Record label*] [*British*] ... Esq
Esquire ... ESQ
Esquire ... ESQR
Esquire [*Gentleman*] (ROG) ... ESQRE
Esquire Communications [*Commercial firm Associated Press*] (SAG) ... EsqCm
Esquire Communications [*Commercial firm Associated Press*] (SAG) ... EsqCom
Esquire Communications [*NASDAQ symbol*] (SAG) ... ESQS
Esquire Communications Wrrt [*NASDAQ symbol*] (TTSB) ... ESQSW
Esquirol on Insanity [*A publication*] (DLA) ... Esq Ins
Esquisure, Inc. [*AMEX symbol*] (SAG) ... EQE
ESRO [*European Space Research Organization*] **Advanced Imaging Detector** [*Satellite*] ... EAID
ESS Technology [*NASDAQ symbol*] (TTSB) ... ESST
ESS Technology, Inc. [*NASDAQ symbol*] (SAG) ... ESST
ESS Technology, Inc. [*Associated Press*] (SAG) ... ESSTech
Essa Centennial Library, Angus, Ontario [*Library symbol National Library of Canada*] (BIB) ... OAEC

ESSA [*Environmental Science Services Administration*] **Research Laboratories** .... ERL

ESSA [*Environmental Science Services Administration*] **Research Laboratories. Technical Memorandum** [*A publication*] .... ERLTM

ESSA [*Environmental Science Services Administration*] **Weather Wire Service** .... EWWS

ESSA [*Environmental Science Services Administration*] **World** [*A publication*] .... ESW

Essai Orgel [*Orgel test reactor*] [*Italy*] .... ESSOR

Essaouira [*Morocco*] [*ICAO location identifier*] (ICLI) .... GMMI

Essay-Proof Society (EA) .... EPS

Essays on Anglo-Saxon Law [*A publication*] (DLA) .... Ess Ang Sax Law

Essays on Canadian Writing [*A publication*] (BRI) .... Essays CW

Essays on International Law [*A publication*] (ILCA) .... EIL

ESSEF Corp. [*Associated Press*] (SAG) .... ESSEF

ESSEF Corp. [*NASDAQ symbol*] (NQ) .... ESSF

Essen [*Germany ICAO location identifier*] (ICLI) .... EDLQ

Essen/Muelheim [*Germany ICAO location identifier*] (ICLI) .... EDLE

Essence .... ESS

Essence Biotech [*Vancouver Stock Exchange symbol*] .... ESN

Essence Export Group [*British*] (BI) .... EEG

Essences et Lubrifiants de France - Entreprise de Recherches et d'Activites Petrolieres [*French oil company*] .... ELF-ERAP

Essential (AABC) .... ESN

Essential .... ESNTL

Essential .... ESS

Essential .... ESSEN

Essential .... ESSNTL

Essential Access Community Hospital .... EACH

Essential Air Servicer [*Department of Transportation*] .... EAS

Essential Amino Acid [*Nutrition*] .... EAA

Essential Amino Acids plus Histidine [*Nutrition*] .... EAAH

Essential Auxiliary Support [*Nuclear energy*] (NRCH) .... EAS

Essential Controls and Instrumentation [*Nuclear energy*] (NRCH) .... ECI

Essential Data Duplicator [*Utilico Microware*] .... EDD

Essential Elements of Analysis .... EEA

Essential Elements of Friendly Information [*Army*] (AABC) .... EEFI

Essential Elements of Information [*Military*] .... EEI

Essential Energy (MCD) .... ESSERGY

Essential Fatty Acid [*Biochemistry*] .... EFA

Essential Fatty Acid Deficiency [*Medicine*] .... EFAD

Essential High Blood Pressure [*Cardiology*] (DAVI) .... EHBF

Essential Hypercholesterolemia [*Medicine*] (MAE) .... EHC

Essential Hypertension [*Medicine*] .... EH

Essential Information [*An association*] (EA) .... EI

Essential Light Chain .... ELC

Essential Maintenance Action (MCD) .... EMA

Essential Manning .... ESMA

Essential Metabolism Ratio [*Medicine*] (DMAA) .... EMR

Essential Motor Control Center (AAG) .... EMCC

Essential/Nonessential/Update [*Telecommunications*] (TEL) .... ENU

Essential Oil Association of the United States (EA) .... EOA

Essential Oils Research and Development Committee [*Tasmania, Australia*] .... EORDC

Essential Performance Requirements (NATG) .... EPR

Essential Pharmacy Allowance .... EPA

Essential Program Information, Technologies or Systems [*DoD*] (RDA) .... EPITS

Essential Repair Part Stockage List [*Military*] (AABC) .... ERPSL

Essential Service Cooling Water System [*Nuclear energy*] (NRCH) .... ESCWS

Essential Service Line [*Telecommunications*] (TEL) .... ESL

Essential Service Value [*Telecommunications*] (IEEE) .... ESV

Essential Service Water [*Nuclear energy*] (NRCH) .... ESW

Essential Service Water System [*Nuclear energy*] (NRCH) .... ESWS

Essential Sight Words Program [*EDAC*] .... ESWP

Essential Subjects Test [*Marine Corps*] (DOMA) .... EST

Essential Support Items List .... ESIL

Essential Sustainment Items (DOMA) .... ESI

Essential Switching Box (MCD) .... ESB

Essential Technical Medical Data .... ETMD

Essential Thrombocythemia [*Hematology*] .... ET

Essential Tremor [*Neurophysiology*] .... ET

Essential Tremor and Parkinson's Disease [*Neurophysiology*] .... ETPD

Essential Work Order .... EWO

Essentiality Code (NASA) .... EC

Essentially Negative (MAE) .... ess neg

Essentials Review Committee [*American Occupational Therapy Association*] .... ERC

Esses [*Phonetic alphabet*] [*Pre-World War II*] (DSUE) .... S

Essex [*County in England*] .... ESS

Essex Bancorp [*AMEX symbol*] (TTSB) .... ESX

Essex Bancorp, Inc. [*Associated Press*] (SAG) .... EssxBc

Essex Bancorp, Inc. [*AMEX symbol*] (SPSG) .... ESX

Essex, CA [*FM radio station call letters*] .... KHWY

Essex Community College, Baltimore, MD [*Library symbol Library of Congress*] (LCLS) .... MdBEs

Essex Community College, James A. Newpher Library, Baltimore, MD [*OCLC symbol*] (OCLC) .... ECC

Essex Corp. [*NASDAQ symbol*] (NQ) .... ESEX

Essex Corp. [*Associated Press*] (SAG) .... Essex

Essex County College, Newark, NJ [*OCLC symbol*] (OCLC) .... ESX

Essex County College, Newark, NJ [*Library symbol Library of Congress*] (LCLS) .... NjNE

Essex County Cooperating Libraries [*Library network*] .... ECCL

Essex County Gas [*NASDAQ symbol*] (TTSB) .... ECGC

Essex County Gas Co. [*NASDAQ symbol*] (NQ) .... ECGC

Essex County Gas Co. [*Associated Press*] (SAG) .... EsxCty

Essex County Newspapers Ltd., Colchester, United Kingdom [*Library symbol Library of Congress*] (LCLS) .... UkCoE

Essex County Public Library, Essex, ON, Canada [*Library symbol Library of Congress*] (LCLS) .... CaOEsE

Essex County Public Library, Essex, Ontario [*Library symbol National Library of Canada*] (NLC) .... OEE

Essex Independent, Essex, IA [*Library symbol Library of Congress*] (LCLS) .... IaEsxI

Essex Institute, Salem, MA [*Library symbol Library of Congress*] (LCLS) .... MSaE

Essex International [*Microprocessor manufacturer*] (NITA) .... ESI

Essex, NY [*FM radio station call letters*] .... WCPV

Essex Petroleum [*Vancouver Stock Exchange symbol*] .... EEX

Essex Property Trust [*NYSE symbol*] (TTSB) .... ESS

Essex Property Trust, Inc. [*NYSE symbol*] (SAG) .... ESS

Essex Property Trust, Inc. [*Associated Press*] (SAG) .... EssxPT

Essex Scottish Regiment of Canada [*Military unit*] .... ESR

[*The*] **Essex Terminal Railway Co.** [*AAR code*] .... ETL

Essex Volunteer Artillery [*British military*] (DMA) .... EVA

Essex Yeomanry [*British military*] (DMA) .... EY

Essexville, MI [*FM radio station call letters*] .... WIXC

Essider [*Libya*] [*ICAO location identifier*] (ICLI) .... HLSD

Esso Australia Resources Ltd. [*Commercial firm*] .... EARL

ESSO Building Products of Canada Ltd., La Salle, Quebec [*Library symbol National Library of Canada*] (NLC) .... QLSE

ESSO [*Standard Oil*] **Minerals of Canada, Toronto, ON, Canada** [*Library symbol Library of Congress*] (LCLS) .... CaOTEM

ESSO [*Standard Oil*] **Minerals of Canada, Toronto, Ontario** [*Library symbol National Library of Canada*] (NLC) .... OTEM

ESSO [*Standard Oil*] **Resources Canada Ltd.** [*UTLAS symbol*] .... ERC

ESSO [*Standard Oil*] **Resources Canada Ltd., Calgary, AB, Canada** [*Library symbol Library of Congress*] (LCLS) .... CaACERC

ESSO [*Standard Oil*] **Resources Canada Ltd., Calgary, Alberta** [*Library symbol National Library of Canada*] (NLC) .... ACI

ESSO [*Standard Oil*] **Resources Canada Ltd., Library Information Center, Calgary, AB, Canada** [*Library symbol Library of Congress*] (LCLS) .... CaACERI

ESSO [*Standard Oil*] **Resources Canada Ltd., Production Research Division, Calgary, AB, Canada** [*Library symbol Library of Congress*] (LCLS) .... CaACIPRD

Esso Rosources Canada Ltd. [*ICAO designator*] (FAAC) .... ERC

ESSO [*Standard Oil*] **Turbo Oil** .... ETO

Esstra Industries Corp. [*Vancouver Stock Exchange symbol*] .... ESS

Establish [*or Establishment*] (KSC) .... ESTAB

Establish [*or Establishment*] (AFM) .... ESTB

Established (EY) .... EST

Established (VRA) .... est

Established (ROG) .... ESTABD

Established .... ESTBD

Established (ADA) .... ESTD

Established Church .... EC

Established Church of Scotland (ROG) .... ECS

Established Market Economy .... EME

Established Onset of Disability (OICC) .... EOD

Established Pattern of Psychodynamic Adaptation .... EPPA

Established Populations for Epidemiologic Studies of the Elderly [*Department of Health and Human Services*] (GFGA) .... EPESE

Established Program Financing .... EPF

Established Quarter of Disability [*Social Security Administration*] (OICC) .... EQD

Established Reliability (MCD) .... ER

Established Risk Factor (PDAA) .... ERF

Establishing Multimedia Authoring Skills in Higher Education (AIE) .... EMASHE

Establishment (WDAA) .... EST

Establishment .... ESTAB

Establishment (ROG) .... ESTABLT

Establishment [*British military*] (DMA) .... Estt

Establishment Date [*IRS*] .... ED

Establishment Inspection [*Federal government*] .... EI

Establishment Inspection Report [*Federal government*] .... EIR

Establishment License Application [*Food & Drug Administration*] .... ELA

Establishment Reporting Plan [*Social Security Administration*] (GFGA) .... ERP

Estacada High School, Estacada, OR [*Library symbol Library of Congress*] (LCLS) .... OrEsHS

Estacada Public Library, Estacada, OR [*Library symbol Library of Congress*] (LCLS) .... OrEs

Estados Unidos Americanos [*United States of America*] [*Spanish*] .... EUA

Estados Unidos do Brasil [*United States of Brazil*] [*Portuguese*] .... EUB

Estahbanat [*Iran*] [*ICAO location identifier*] (ICLI) .... OISE

Estancia [*New Mexico*] [*Seismograph station code, US Geological Survey*] (SEIS) .... EST

Estate .... EST

Estate .... EST

Estate .... ESTE

Estate Agency [*London Stock Exchange*] .... E

Estate Agents' Council [*British*] (BI) .... EAC

Estate and Gift Tax Ruling [*A publication*] (DLA) .... ET

Estate Duties Investment Taxes [*British*] .... EDITH

Estate Duties Investment Trust (DLA) .... EDIT

Estate Duty (DLA) .... ED

Estate Duty Office [*British*] .... EDO

Estate Gazette [*A publication*] (DLA) .... EG

Estate Planning for Persons with Disabilities [*An association*] (PAZ) .... EPPD

Estate Planning Review [*A publication*] (DLA) .... Est Plan Rev

Estate Tax .... ET

Estate-Bottling [*Wine*] .... E-B

Estates [*Commonly used*] (OPSA) .... ESTATES

Estates [*Postal Service standard*] (OPSA) ... ESTS
Estates ... ESTS
Estates and Trusts [*Legal term*] (DLA) ... Est & Trusts
Estates Gazette Digest of Cases [*A publication*] (DLA) ... EGD
Estates Gazette Digest of Cases [*A publication*] (DLA) ... EGDC
Estates, Gifts, and Trusts Journal [*A publication*] (DLA) ... Est Gifts & Tr J
Estates, Powers, and Trusts [*Legal term*] (DLA) ... Est Powers & Trusts
Estates, Powers, and Trusts Law [*A publication*] ... EPTL
Estates Property Investment Co. [*British*] ... EPIC
Estcourt [*South Africa*] [*ICAO location identifier*] (ICLI) ... FAEC
Estec Systems [*Vancouver Stock Exchange symbol*] ... ESE
Estee Lauder Companies, Inc. [*NYSE symbol*] (SAG) ... EL
Estee Lauder Companies, Inc. [*Associated Press*] (SAG) ... EsteeL
Esteemed (ADA) ... EST
Estee's Code Pleading, Practice, and Forms [*A publication*] (DLA) ... Est Prac
Estee's Code Pleading, Practice, and Forms [*A publication*] (DLA) ... Est Prac Pl
Estee's District Court of Hawaii [*A publication*] (DLA) ... Estee
Estee's District Court of Hawaii [*A publication*] (DLA) ... Estee (Hawaii)
Estelline Public Library, Estelline, SD [*Library symbol Library of Congress*] (LCLS) ... SdEs
Ester [*Organic chemistry*] (MAE) ... E
Esterase [*An enzyme*] ... EST
Esterase D [*An enzyme*] ... ESD
Esterified Cholesterol (OA) ... EC
Esterified Propoxylated Glycerol [*Organic chemistry*] ... EPG
Esterillos [*Costa Rica*] [*ICAO location identifier*] (ICLI) ... MRET
Esterline Corp. [*Associated Press*] (SAG) ... Estrlne
Esterline Technologies [*NYSE symbol*] (TTSB) ... ESL
Ester-Linked Phospholipid Membrane Analysis [*Analytical biochemistry*] ... ELPFA
Estern American Natural Gas Trust [*Associated Press*] (SAG) ... EstANG
Estero Azul [*Costa Rica*] [*ICAO location identifier*] (ICLI) ... MREA
Estes Park, CO [*AM radio station call letters*] ... KRKI
Estes Park Institute ... EPI
Estes Park Public Library, Estes Park, CO [*Library symbol Library of Congress*] (LCLS) ... CoEp
Estetrol [*Endocrinology*] (DAVI) ... E_4
Estevan Point, BC [*ICAO location identifier*] (ICLI) ... CYEP
Estevan, SK [*AM radio station call letters*] ... CJSL
Estevan, SK [*ICAO location identifier*] (ICLI) ... CYEN
Esther [*Old Testament book*] ... ES
Esther [*Old Testament book*] ... Est
Esther [*Old Testament book*] ... Esth
Esther Rabbah (BJA) ... EsthR
Esther Rabbah (BJA) ... EstR
Estherville Daily News, Estherville, IA [*Library symbol Library of Congress*] (LCLS) ... IaEsN
Estherville, IA [*Location identifier FAA*] (FAAL) ... EST
Estherville, IA [*AM radio station call letters*] ... KILR
Estherville, IA [*FM radio station call letters*] ... KILR-FM
Estherville Junior College [*Iowa*] ... EJC
Estherville Public Library, Estherville, IA [*Library symbol Library of Congress*] (LCLS) ... IaEs
Esthetic ... ESTH
Estima [*Mozambique*] [*ICAO location identifier*] (ICLI) ... FQES
Estimate ... E
Estimate (ROG) ... ES
Estimate [*or Estimation*] (EY) ... EST
Estimate (WDMC) ... est
Estimate at Completion (NASA) ... EAC
Estimate Change Request (NRCH) ... ECR
Estimate of Adversary Sequence Interruption [*Nuclear energy*] (NRCH) ... EASI
Estimate of Properties for Industrial Chemistry [*Universite de Liege*] [*Database*] ... EPIC
Estimate Range Zero System (SAA) ... EROS
Estimate to Complete [*Cost*] (AAGC) ... ETC
Estimated ... ESTD
Estimated (ROG) ... ESTIMD
Estimated (DLA) ... Estm
Estimated Acquisition Cost [*of drug products*] [*HEW*] ... EAC
Estimated Additional Resources ... EAR
Estimated Air Speed (MCD) ... EAS
Estimated Arrival Carrier (MCD) ... EAC
Estimated Arrival Date ... ESTAR
Estimated Arrival Time (WDAA) ... EAT
Estimated Assumed Resources [*Minerals*] ... EAR
Estimated Availability Date [*Military*] (AFM) ... EAD
Estimated [*or Expected*] **Average Life** ... EAL
Estimated Blood Loss [*Medicine*] ... EBL
Estimated Blood Volume [*Hematology*] ... EBV
Estimated Breeding Value [*Agricultural science*] ... EBV
Estimated Cloud Time [*Drinking slang*] ... ECT
Estimated Completion Date ... ECD
Estimated Completion Time [*Business term*] ... ECT
Estimated Consumption [*of gasoline*] [*Computer model*] ... ESCON
Estimated Correction Cost (MCD) ... ECC
Estimated Cost of Damage (MCD) ... ECOD
Estimated Critical Position [*Nuclear energy*] (NRCH) ... ECP
Estimated Daily Intake [*Toxicology*] ... EDI
Estimated Date (AAG) ... ED
Estimated Date of Arrival (NG) ... EDA
Estimated Date of Availability (AAG) ... EDA
Estimated Date of Completion ... EDC
Estimated Date of Conception [*Obstetrics*] (DAVI) ... EDC
Estimated [*or Expected*] **Date of Confinement** [*Obstetrics*] ... EDC
Estimated Date of Departure [*or Detachment*] [*Military*] (DNAB) ... EDD
Estimated Date of Departure Far East Command [*Military*] ... EDDFEC
Estimated Date of Labor [*Obstetrics*] (DMAA) ... EDL
Estimated Date of Publication (AAG) ... EDP
Estimated Date of Resumption (AAG) ... EDR
Estimated Date of Separation ... EDS
Estimated Daughter Superiority [*Genetics*] (OA) ... EDS
Estimated Delivery Date ... EDD
Estimated Delivery Dates of Supply [*Army*] (INF) ... EDOS
Estimated Delivery Times ... EDT
Estimated Departure Clearance Time [*FAA*] (TAG) ... EDCT
Estimated Departure Clearance Time [*Aviation*] (FAAC) ... EDCT
Estimated Departure from Pacific (CINC) ... EDPAC
Estimated Departure Time ... EDT
Estimated Discharge Time ... EDT
Estimated Dry Weight [*Nephrology*] (DAVI) ... EDW
Estimated Earnings before Interest and Taxes ... EBITS
Estimated Effective Perceived Noise Level ... EEPNL
Estimated Elapsed Time [*ICAO*] (FAAC) ... EET
Estimated Expenditure of Ammunition (AABC) ... EEA
Estimated Exposure Concentration [*Toxicology*] ... EEC
Estimated Exposure Dose [*Toxicology*] ... EED
Estimated Fetal Weight [*Obstetrics*] (DAVI) ... EFW
Estimated Final Cost ... EFC
Estimated Gestational Age ... EGA
Estimated Ground Time (MCD) ... EGT
Estimated Hepatic Blood Flow [*Medicine*] ... EHBF
Estimated Horsepower ... EHP
Estimated Information (FAAC) ... ETI
Estimated Junction Frequency [*Telecommunications*] (TEL) ... EJF
Estimated Latitude (FAAC) ... ELAT
Estimated Learning Potential ... ELP
Estimated Length of Program [*Medicine*] (DAVI) ... ELOP
Estimated Length of Stay [*Medicine*] (DAVI) ... ELOS
Estimated Life Expectancy (MCD) ... ELE
Estimated Man Hours (DNAB) ... EM
Estimated Man-Hours (AFIT) ... EMH
Estimated Maximum Daily Intake [*Toxicology*] ... EMDI
Estimated Maximum Heart Rate [*Aerobic dance*] ... EMHR
Estimated Mean Time to Failure ... EMTF
Estimated Minimum Operating Temperature [*Engineering*] ... EMOT
Estimated Month of Loss ... EML
Estimated Net Energy (OA) ... ENE
Estimated [*Time At or Over*] **Next Position** (BARN) ... ENP
Estimated Off-Block Time [*ICAO designator*] (FAAC) ... EOBT
Estimated on Berth ... EOB
Estimated on Dock (KSC) ... EOD
Estimated Operational Date (CINC) ... EOD
Estimated Position [*Navigation*] ... EP
Estimated Position Arc [*Navy*] (NVT) ... EPA
Estimated Price Request (MCD) ... EPR
Estimated Project Duration Time ... EPDT
Estimated Receival Date (KSC) ... ERD
Estimated Release Date (AAG) ... ERD
Estimated Release Schedule (AAG) ... ERS
Estimated Rental (ROG) ... ER
Estimated Repair Time [*Telecommunications*] (TEL) ... ERT
Estimated Reseller Price ... ERP
Estimated Resident Population [*Demographics*] [*Australia*] ... ERP
Estimated Shipping Date ... ESD
Estimated Standard [*Statistics*] (DAVI) ... ES
Estimated Standard Deviation [*Mathematics*] ... ESD
Estimated Standard Labor Hours (AAGC) ... ESLH
Estimated Surface Wheel Load (CINC) ... ESWL
Estimated Takeoff (KSC) ... ETO
Estimated Target Assurance ... ETA
Estimated Task Completion Date (AAG) ... ETCD
Estimated Tax [*IRS*] ... ES
Estimated Tax Penalty [*IRS*] ... ESPEN
Estimated Time ... ET
Estimated Time En Route ... ETE
Estimated Time in Commission [*Army*] (AABC) ... ETIC
Estimated Time of Acquisition (KSC) ... ETA
Estimated Time of Arrival (DAVI) ... ET
Estimated [*or Expected*] **Time of Arrival** ... ETA
Estimated Time of Berthing [*Navigation*] ... ETB
Estimated Time of Completion ... ETC
Estimated Time of Conception [*Obstetrics*] (DAVI) ... ETC
Estimated Time of Correction ... ETC
Estimated Time of Correction [*NASA*] (KSC) ... ETOC
Estimated Time of Crew's Return ... ETCR
Estimated [*or Expected*] **Time of Departure** ... ETD
Estimated Time of Flight ... ETF
Estimated Time of Interception ... ETI
Estimated Time of Operations [*NASA*] (KSC) ... ETO
Estimated Time of Ovulation [*Gynecology*] ... ETO
Estimated Time of Parachute Deployment (MUGU) ... ETPD
Estimated Time of Repair (NG) ... ETR
Estimated Time of Return ... ETR
Estimated Time of Return to Operation [*Military*] (AFM) ... ETRO
Estimated Time of Sailing [*Navigation*] ... ETS
Estimated Time of Separation [*Military Slang*] ... ETS
Estimated Time of Track ... ETT
Estimated Time Off ... ETO
Estimated Time Out of Commission ... ETOC
Estimated Time Over [*Aviation*] (FAAC) ... ETOV

Estimated Time Over Target ... ETOT
Estimated Time to Next Failure (MCD) ... ETNF
Estimated Time to Reach Altitude ... ETRA
Estimated Total Shelf Life (OA) ... ETSL
Estimated Total Target Cost ... ETTC
Estimated Travel Time [*Army*] (AABC) ... ETT
Estimated Turnaround Point ... ETP
Estimated Turnover Date (MCD) ... ETD
Estimated Unit Price (MCD) ... EUP
Estimated Warehouse Arrival (NASA) ... EWA
Estimated Weapon Release (MCD) ... EWRL
Estimated Weight [*Measurement*] (DAVI) ... Est Wt
Estimated Weight Report ... EWR
Estimated Will Ship ... EWS
Estimated Yearly Cost of Operation [*of electrical appliance*] ... EYCO
Estimated Yearly Operating Cost [*of electrical appliance*] ... EYOC
Estimates Safety Factors Against Embarkment Sliding [*Military*] ... ESFAES
Estimating (IAA) ... ESTG
Estimating Price Policy ... EPP
Estimating Relationship (AFIT) ... ER
Estimating System Survey (AAGC) ... ESS
Estimation ... ESTMTN
Estimation ... ESTN
Estimation-before-Modeling (MCD) ... EBM
Estimator ... ESTMTR
Estivoautumnal [*Malaria*] ... EA
Estonia ... EST
Estonia (VRA) ... Esto
Estonian [*MARC language code Library of Congress*] (LCCP) ... est
Estonian Aid (EA) ... EA
Estonian Air [*ICAO designator*] (FAAC) ... ELL
Estonian American National Council (EA) ... EANC
Estonian Association of Scientists ... EAS
Estonian Educational Society (EA) ... EHS
Estonian Learned Society of America (EA) ... ELSA
Estonian Music Center, USA (EA) ... EMC USA
Estonian National Independence Party [*Political party*] ... ENIP
Estonian Relief Committee (EA) ... ERC
Estonian School Center in the United States (EA) ... CESUS
Estonian Soviet Socialist Republic [*MARC country of publication code Library of Congress*] (LCCP) ... err
Estonian Soviet Socialist Republic ... EstSSR
Estonian Soviet Socialist Republic [*MARC geographic area code Library of Congress*] (LCCP) ... e-ur-er
Estonian Student Association in the United States of America [*Defunct*] (EA) ... ESAUSA
Estonian World Festival ... ESTO
Estoppel [*Legal shorthand*] (LWAP) ... ESTOP
Estoppel and Waiver [*Legal term*] (DLA) ... ESTOP & W
Estrada Nacional [*National Highway*] [*Spanish*] (BARN) ... EN
Estradiol [*Medicine*] (DAVI) ... E
Estradiol [*Also, E-diol, ES*] [*Endocrinology*] ... E2
Estradiol [*Also, E2, ES*] [*Endocrinology*] ... E-Diol
Estradiol [*Also, E_2, E-diol*] [*Endocrinology*] ... ES
Estradiol [*Biochemistry*] (DAVI) ... ESTRA
Estradiol Benzoate [*Endocrinology*] ... EB
Estradiol Binding Index [*Biochemistry*] (DMAA) ... EBI
Estradiol Cyclopentanepropionate [*Endocrinology*] ... ECP
Estradiol Production Rate [*Endocrinology*] (MAE) ... EPR
Estradiol Receptor [*Endocrinology*] ... ER
Estradiol-Binding Protein [*Biochemistry*] ... EBP
Estrellas del Aire SA de CV [*Mexico ICAO designator*] (FAAC) ... ETA
Estriol [*Endocrinology*] ... E_3
Estriol [*Endocrinology*] (AAMN) ... Es
Estriol [*or Estrogen*]/Creatinine [*Ratio*] [*Clinical chemistry*] (AAMN) ... E/C
Estriol-3-Glucosiduronate [*Pharmacology*] (DAVI) ... E_3-3Gl
Estrogen [*Endocrinology*] (AAMN) ... ESG
Estrogen [*Biochemistry*] (DAVI) ... Est
Estrogen Conjugate [*Endocrinology*] ... EC
Estrogen Receptor [*Endocrinology*] ... ER
Estrogen Receptor Assay [*Clinical chemistry*] ... ERA
Estrogen Receptor, Cytosolic [*Endocrinology*] ... ERC
Estrogen Receptor Knockout [*Mouse strain*] ... ERKO
Estrogen Receptor Protein [*Endocrinology*] ... ERP
Estrogen Receptor-Related ... ERR
Estrogen Replacement Therapy [*Medicine*] ... ERT
Estrogen Withdrawal Bleeding [*Medicine*] ... EWB
Estrogen-Responsive Element [*Endocrinology*] ... ERE
Estrogen-Stimulated Neurophysin [*Endocrinology*] ... ESN
Estrone [*Endocrinology*] ... E_1
Estrone Glucuronide [*Endocrinology*] ... EG
Estuarine and Brackish-Water Sciences Association (EAIO) ... EBSA
Estuarine and Coastal Sciences Association [*Scotland*] (EAIO) ... ECSA
Estuarine Living Marine Resources Program [*National Oceanic and Atmospheric Administration*] ... ELMR
Estuarine Programs Office [*National Oceanic and Atmospheric Administration*] ... EPO
Estuarine Research Federation (EA) ... ERF
Estuary [*Maps and charts*] ... EST
Estudios Conjuntos sobre Integracion Economica Latinoamericana [*Program*] ... ECIEL
Esutoru [*Uglegorsk*] [*Former USSR Seismograph station code, US Geological Survey Closed*] (SEIS) ... ESU
Et Alibi [*And Elsewhere*] [*Latin*] ... ET AL
Et Alii [*or Et Aliae or Et Alia*] [*And Others*] [*Latin*] (GPO) ... et al
Et Alii Frequentis [*And in Many Other (Passages)*] [*Latin*] (ROG) ... ET AL FREQ
Et Cetera [*And So Forth*] [*Latin*] ... ETC
Et Inter Alia [*And Among Others*] [*Latin*] (ROG) ... ET INT AL
Et Sequens [*or Et Sequentes, Et Sequentia*] [*And the Following*] [*Latin*] ... ET SEQ
Et Sequens [*or Et Sequentes, Et Sequentia*] [*And the Following*] [*Latin*] ... ET SQQ
Et Sequentes [*And the Following*] [*Latin*] (BARN) ... et seqq
Et Suivants [*And Following*] [*French*] (ILCA) ... et s
Et Uxor [*And Wife*] [*Latin*] ... ET UX
Et Viri [*And Husband*] [*Latin*] ... Et Vir
Eta (NUCP) ... E
Eta Kappa Nu [*Fraternity*] ... EKN
Etablissement Donnacona, Quebec [*Library symbol National Library of Canada*] (BIB) ... QDE
Etac Sales Ltd. [*Toronto Stock Exchange symbol*] ... ESL
Etain/Rouvres [*France ICAO location identifier*] (ICLI) ... LFQE
Etaiyapuram [*India*] [*Geomagnetic observatory code*] ... ETT
Etampes/Mondesir [*France ICAO location identifier*] (ICLI) ... LFOX
Etana Tech Corp. [*Vancouver Stock Exchange symbol*] ... ETT
Etasable Optical Storage [*Computer science*] (ODBW) ... EOS
Etat-Major [*Headquarters*] [*French military*] ... E-M
Etat-Major General [*General Headquarters*] [*French military*] ... E-MG
Etats Africains et Malgache Associes [*Associated African and Malagasy States*] ... EAMA
Etats-Unis [*United States*] [*French*] ... E-U
Etch Back Process (IAA) ... EBP
Etch Back Uniformity Calculation (IAA) ... EBUC
Etch Pitch Density (PDAA) ... EPD
Etch Template [*Tool*] (AAG) ... ETTP
Etch-Bleach [*Photography*] (DGA) ... E-B
Etched Card Assembly (IAA) ... ECA
Etched Circuit Board ... ECB
Etched Circuit Society [*Defunct*] (EA) ... ECS
Etched Flexible Circuitry ... EFC
Etched Lead (IAA) ... EL
Etched Metal Circuit ... EMC
Etched Multiple Vertical Junction [*Photovoltaic energy systems*] ... EMVJ
Etched Plate ... EP
Etched Sensitized Projected Image [*Circuit board manufacture*] ... ESPI
Etcher [*MARC relator code*] [*Library of Congress*] (LCCP) ... etr
Etching (MSA) ... ETCH
Etching (VRA) ... etch
Etching by Transmitted Light ... ETL
Etchingham Family Tree (EA) ... EFT
Etec Systems [*NASDAQ symbol*] (TTSB) ... ETEC
Etec Systems, Inc. [*NASDAQ symbol*] (SAG) ... ETEC
Etec Systems, Inc. [*Associated Press*] (SAG) ... EtecSys
E-Tech Speedy Protocol (CDE) ... ESP
Eterna [*Record label*] [*Germany*] ... Eta
Eterna [*Record label*] [*Germany*] ... Ete
Eterna International Foundation for Disabled Children (EA) ... EIFDC
Eternal Word Television Network [*Cable-television system*] ... EWTN
Eternally Elvis TCB [*Taking Care of Business*] (EA) ... EETCB
Ethacrynic Acid [*A diuretic*] [*Pharmacology*] (DAVI) ... EA
Ethacrynic Acid [*Biochemistry*] ... ECA
Ethambutol [*An antituberculosis drug*] ... EMB
Ethambutol Hydrochloride [*Pharmacology*] ... EMB
Ethamoxytriphetol [*An antiestrogen*] (DAVI) ... MER
Ethan Allen Interiors [*NYSE symbol*] (TTSB) ... ETH
Ethan Allen Interiors, Inc. [*NYSE symbol*] (SPSG) ... ETH
Ethan Allen Interiors, Inc. [*Associated Press*] (SAG) ... EthanAln
Ethanehydroxydiphosphonate [*or -diphosphonic Acid*] [*Also, HEDP*] [*Organic chemistry*] ... EHDP
Ethanol [*DOE*] (TAG) ... C2H5OH
Ethanol ... E
Ethanol [*or ethyl alcohol*] [*Organic chemistry*] (DAVI) ... ETH
Ethanolamine [*Also, Etn, OLAMINE*] [*Organic chemistry*] ... EA
Ethanolamine [*Also, EA, OLAMINE*] [*Organic chemistry*] ... Etn
Ethanolamine [*Also, EA, Etn*] [*USAN*] [*Organic chemistry*] ... OLAMINE
Ethanolamine Ammonia Lyase [*An enzyme*] ... EAL
Ethanolamineperchlorate (MCD) ... EAP
Ethanol-Disulfiram Reaction [*Pharmacology*] ... EDR
Ethel Delaney International Fan Club (EA) ... EDIFC
Ethelda Bay, BC [*ICAO location identifier*] (ICLI) ... CYTC
Ether (AAMN) ... eth
Ether Ester Block Copolymer ... EEBC
Ether-Chloroform [*Mixture*] ... E-C
Ether-Isopentane-Ethanol [*Solvent system*] ... EPA
Ethernet Alto Research Generator Scanning Laser Output Terminal [*Laser printer*] (NITA) ... EARS
Ethernet Management Module [*Telecommunications*] ... EMME
Ethernet Needing Zero Overhead ... ENZO
Ethernet Packet Processor (CDE) ... EPP
Ethernet Specification [*Computer science*] (BTTJ) ... ESPEC
EtherTalk Link Access Protocol [*Computer science*] (ACRL) ... ELAP
Ether-Water (PDAA) ... EW
Ethete, WY [*FM radio station call letters*] (RBYB) ... KWRR-FM
Ethica Eudemia [*of Aristotle*] [*Classical studies*] (OCD) ... Eth Eud
Ethica Nicomachea [*of Aristotle*] [*Classical studies*] (OCD) ... Eth Nic
Ethical Holdings Ltd. [*NASDAQ symbol*] (SAG) ... ETHC
Ethical Holdings Ltd. [*Associated Press*] (SAG) ... EthicHld
Ethical Holdings Ltd ADS [*NASDAQ symbol*] (TTSB) ... ETHCY
Ethical Investment Research Service [*British Information service or system*] ... EIRIS
Ethical Investment Research Service [*London, England*] [*Information service or system*] (IID) ... EIRS

Ethical Judgement Scale (EDAC) .... EJS
Ethical, Legal and Social Implications [*Genetic research*] .... ELSI
Ethical Library [*A publication*] .... ELA
Ethical Reasoning Inventory (EDAC) .... ERI
Ethical Society of Washington (EA) .... ESW
Ethicon, Inc., Somerville, NJ [*Library symbol Library of Congress*] (LCLS) .... NjSoE
Ethics .... ETH
Ethics Advisory Board [*HEW*] .... EAB
Ethics and Public Policy Center (EA) .... EPPC
Ethics and Values in Science and Technology [*National Science Foundation*] .... EVIST
Ethics in Government Act .... EIGA
Ethics Officer Association .... EOA
Ethics Resource Center (EA) .... ERC
Ethics Works Group (EERA) .... EWG
Ethidium Bromide [*Trypanocide*] [*Also, ETB, Etd Br Biochemical analysis*] .... EB
Ethidium Bromide [*Trypanocide*] [*Also, EB, Etd Br Biochemical analysis*] .... ETB
Ethidium Bromide [*Trypanocide*] [*Also, EB, ETB Biochemical analysis*] .... Etd Br
Ethinylestradiol Methyl Ether (MAE) .... EEME
Ethinyloestradiol-3-Methyl Ether [*or Mestranol*] [*Pharmacology*] (DAVI) EE3ME
Ethiodized Oil Emulsion [*Clinical chemistry*] .... EOE
Ethionamide [*An antibacterial compound*] (DAVI) .... ET
Ethionamide [*Antibacterial*] .... ETA
Ethiopia [*ANSI two-letter standard code*] (CNC) .... ET
Ethiopia [*MARC country of publication code Library of Congress*] (LCCP) .... et
Ethiopia [*ANSI three-letter standard code*] (CNC) .... ETH
Ethiopia (VRA) .... Eth
Ethiopia [*MARC geographic area code Library of Congress*] (LCCP) .... f-et--
Ethiopia Air Lines .... EAL
Ethiopian Airlines [*ICAO designator*] (AD) .... ET
Ethiopian Airlines Corp. [*ICAO designator*] (FAAC) .... ETH
Ethiopian Birr [*Monetary Unit*] (BARN) .... EB
Ethiopian Collectors Club (EA) .... ECC
Ethiopian Communist Party [*Political party*] (PD) .... ECP
Ethiopian Community Development Council (EA) .... ECDC
Ethiopian Community Mutual Assistance Association (EA) .... ECMAA
Ethiopian Democratic Union [*Political party*] (PD) .... EDU
Ethiopian Democratic Unity Party [*Political party*] (EY) .... EDUP
Ethiopian News Agency .... ENA
Ethiopian People's Democratic Movement [*Political party*] .... EPDM
Ethiopian People's Democratic Union (EA) .... EPDU
Ethiopian People's Revolutionary Democratic Front [*Political party*] (ECON) .... EPRDF
Ethiopian People's Revolutionary Party [*Political party*] (PD) .... EPRP
Ethiopian Philatelic Society (EA) .... EPS
Ethiopian Refugee Help-Line (EAIO) .... ERH
Ethiopian Standards Institution .... ESI
Ethiopian Students Union of North America .... ESUNA
Ethiopic [*MARC language code Library of Congress*] (LCCP) .... eth
Ethiopic [*Language, etc.*] (ROG) .... ETHIOP
Ethiopic Book of Enoch [*A publication*] (BJA) .... EthEnoch
Ethmoid Sinus [*Medicine*] (DAVI) .... E
Ethnic Affairs Commission of New South Wales .... EACNSW
Ethnic Aged Worker .... EAW
Ethnic Aged Working Party [*Australia Political party*] .... EAWP
Ethnic American Coalition (of Eastern Europeans) (EA) .... EAC
Ethnic and Genealogical Sourcebook Series [*A publication*] .... EGSS
Ethnic Anonymous (EA) .... EA
Ethnic Archives of Canada, Public Archives [*Archives Ethniques du Canada, Archives Publiques*] **Ottawa, Ontario** [*Library symbol National Library of Canada*] (NLC) .... OOAEA
Ethnic Children's Service [*Australia*] .... ECS
Ethnic Communities Council of New South Wales [*Australia*] .... ECCNSW
Ethnic Communities Council of South Australia .... ECCSA
Ethnic Cultural Preservation Council [*Also known as Association of North American Museums, Libraries, Archives, Cultural Centers, and Fraternal Organizations*] (EA) .... ECPC
Ethnic Employees of the Library of Congress (EA) .... EELC
Ethnic Health Worker [*Australia*] .... EHW
Ethnic Identification Index (BJA) .... EII
Ethnic Materials and Information Exchange Round Table [*American Library Association*] (EA) .... EMIERT
Ethnic Materials Information Exchange .... EMIE
Ethnic Materials Information Exchange Task Force [*Later, EMIERT*] (EA) .... EMIETF
Ethnic Millions Political Action Committee (EA) .... EMPAC
Ethnic Minorities Action Group [*Australia*] .... EMAG
Ethnic Minorities and Women in Science [*National Science Foundation*] .... EMWS
Ethnic Minority Business Development Unit [*British*] .... EMBDU
Ethnic, Nationalist, and Separatist [*Conflicts or wars*] .... ENS
Ethnic NewsWatch [*Softline Information Co.*] .... ENW
Ethnic Quotient .... EQ
Ethnic Schools Association of South Australia .... ESASA
Ethnic Schools Liaison Officer [*Australia*] .... ESLO
Ethnic Schools Program [*Australia*] .... ESP
Ethnike Organosis Kypriakou Agonos [*National Organization of Cypriot Fighters*] [*Greece*] .... EOKA
Ethniki Enosis [*National Unity Party*] [*Greek*] (PPE) .... EE
Ethniki Politiki Enosis [*National Political Union*] [*Greek*] (PPE) .... EPE
Ethniko Laiko Komma [*National Populist Party*] [*Greek*] (PPE) .... ELK
Ethniko Rizospastiko Komma [*National Radical Party*] [*Greek*] (PPE) .... ERK
Ethnikon Agrotikon Komma Xiton [*National Agrarian Party "X"*] [*Political party*] (PPE) X
Ethnikon Apelephtherotikon Metopon [*National Liberation Front*] [*Greek*] (PPE) .... EAM
Ethnikon Phileleftheron Komma [*National Liberal Party*] [*Greek*] (PPE) .... EPK
Ethnikos Demokratikos Ellinikos Stratos [*National Democratic Greek Army*] (PPE) .... EDES
Ethnobotany Specialist Group (EA) .... ESG
Ethnography (ADA) .... ETHNOG
Ethnology .... ETHNOL
Ethnology Division, British Columbia Provincial Museum, Victoria, British Columbia [*Library symbol National Library of Canada*] (NLC) .... BVIPME
Ethology .... ethol
Ethos Foundation (EA) .... EF
Ethosuximide [*Medicine*] (DMAA) .... ESM
(Ethoxybenylidene)butylaniline [*Organic chemistry*] .... EBBA
Ethoxybenzoic Acid [*Dental cement*] .... EBA
(Ethoxybenzylidene)cyanoaniline [*Also, PEBAB*] [*Organic chemistry*] .... EBCA
Ethoxycarbonylethoxydihydroquinone [*Pharmacology*] .... EEDQ
Ethoxycoumarin Deethylase [*An enzyme*] .... ECD
Ethoxycoumarin O-Deethylase [*An enzyme*] .... ECOD
Ethoxylated Bisphenol A Dimethacrylate [*Organic chemistry*] .... EBPAD
Ethoxylated Monoglyceride (OA) .... EM
Ethoxy-meta-phenylenediamine [*Organic chemistry*] .... EMPD
Ethoxymethyl [*Organic chemistry*] .... EOM
Ethoxymethylfluorouracil [*Antineoplastic drug*] .... EMFU
Ethoxyquin [*Antioxidant*] [*Organic chemistry*] .... EMQ
Ethoxyresorufin O-Deethylase [*An enzyme*] .... EROD
Ethoxy(trichloromethyl)thiadiazole [*Fungicide*] .... ETMT
Ethrane, Oxygen, and Gas [*Nitrous oxide*] [*Anesthesiology*] (DAVI) .... EOG
Ethycarbazole [*Organic chemistry*] .... ECZ
Ethyl [*As substituent on nucleoside*] [*Biochemistry*] .... e
Ethyl [*Organic chemistry*] .... Et
Ethyl 2-(Diisopropylamino)ethylmethylphosphonite [*See EDMP*] [*Army symbol*] .... QL
Ethyl Acetamidocinnamate [*Organic chemistry*] .... EAC
Ethyl Acetimidate [*Biochemistry*] .... EAI
Ethyl Acetoacetate [*Organic chemistry*] .... EAA
Ethyl Acrylate [*Organic chemistry*] .... EA
Ethyl Alcohol [*Organic chemistry*] (DAVI) .... Et Alc
Ethyl Alcohol [*or Ethanol*] .... ETOH
Ethyl Amyl Ketone [*Organic chemistry*] .... EAK
Ethyl Azodicarboxylate [*Organic chemistry*] .... EAD
Ethyl Biscoumacetate [*Organic chemistry*] (DAVI) .... BOEA
Ethyl Bromoacetate [*Organic chemistry*] .... EBA
Ethyl Cellulose .... EC
Ethyl Cellulose and Caster Oil (SAA) .... ECCO
Ethyl Cellulose Perfluorobutyrate .... ECFB
Ethyl Centralite (OA) .... EC
Ethyl Corp. (KSC) .... EC
Ethyl Corp. [*Associated Press*] (SAG) .... Ethyl
Ethyl Corp. [*NYSE symbol Toronto Stock Exchange symbol*] (SPSG) .... EY
Ethyl Corp., Chemical Development Library, Baton Rouge, LA [*Library symbol Library of Congress*] (LCLS) .... LBrE
Ethyl Corp., Pasadena, TX [*Library symbol Library of Congress*] (LCLS) .... TxPE
Ethyl Diazoacetate [*Organic chemistry*] .... EDA
Ethyl Dichlorophosphate [*Organic chemistry*] .... EDCP
Ethyl (Diisopropylamino)ethylmethyl-phosphonite [*Nerve gas intermediate*] [*Organic chemistry*] .... EDMP
Ethyl Dinitropentanoate [*An explosive*] .... EDNP
Ethyl Dipropylthiocarbamate [*Organic chemistry*] .... EPTC
Ethyl Enthanesulfate [*Organic chemistry*] (MAE) .... EES
Ethyl Ethoxypropionate [*Organic chemistry*] .... EEP
Ethyl Group [*Organic chemistry*] (DAVI) .... Et
Ethyl Mercury Phosphate (BARN) .... EMP
Ethyl Methacrylate [*Organic chemistry*] .... EMA
Ethyl Methanesulfonate [*or Ethyl Methanesulfonic Acid*] [*Experimental mutagen*] .... EMS
Ethyl Michler's Ketone Oxime (PDAA) .... EMKO
Ethyl N-Phenylcarbamoylazoformate [*Organic chemistry*] .... ENPCAF
Ethyl Phenylcarbamate [*Plant regulator*] [*Organic chemistry*] .... EPC
Ethyl Tertiary Amyl Ether [*Gasoline blending*] .... ETAE
Ethyl Tertiary-Butyl Ether [*Fuel additive*] .... ETBE
Ethyl Trimethylsilylacetate [*Organic chemistry*] .... ETSA
Ethyl Vinyl Alcohol (PDAA) .... EVAL
Ethyl Vinyl Ether [*Organic chemistry*] .... EVE
Ethyl Vinyl Ketone [*Organic chemistry*] .... EVK
Ethyl Violet-Azide [*Broth*] [*Microbiology*] .... EVA
Ethylaluminum Dichloride [*Organic chemistry*] .... EADC
Ethylaluminum Sesquichloride [*Organic chemistry*] .... EASC
Ethylaminoethanol [*Organic chemistry*] .... EAE
Ethylanthrahydroquinone [*Organic chemistry*] .... EAHQ
Ethylanthranilic Acid [*Organic chemistry*] .... EAA
Ethylanthraquinone [*Organic chemistry*] .... EAQ
Ethylbenzene [*Organic chemistry*] .... EB
Ethylbenzene Hydroperoxide [*Organic chemistry*] .... EBHP
Ethylbenzene Producers Association (EA) .... EBPA
Ethylbenzene Producers Association (EA) .... EPA
Ethylbenzenesulfonic Acid [*Organic chemistry*] .... EBSA
Ethyl(benzyl)aniline [*Organic chemistry*] .... EBA
Ethyl(benzyl)anilinesulfonic Acid [*Organic chemistry*] .... EBASA
Ethyl(butyl)amine [*Organic chemistry*] .... EBA
Ethylcamptothecin [*Antineoplastic drug*] .... ECPT
Ethylcarboxylate Adenosine [*Biochemistry*] .... ECA
Ethyl(chloroethyl)aniline [*Organic chemistry*] .... ECEA
Ethylcholine Mustard Aziridinium [*Picrate*] [*Biochemistry*] .... ECMA
Ethyldichloroarsine [*Organic chemistry*] (DAVI) .... dick
Ethyldichloroarsine [*Medicine*] (ADDR) .... ED

Ethyl(dimethylaminopropyl)carbodiimide [*Also, EDC, EDCI*] [*Organic chemistry*] ..... EDAC

Ethyl(dimethylaminopropyl)carbodiimide [*Also, EDAC, EDCI*] [*Organic chemistry*] ..... EDC

Ethyl(dimethylaminopropyl)carbodiimide [*Also, EDAC, EDC*] [*Organic chemistry*] ..... EDCI

Ethylene Acrylic Acid [*Organic chemistry*] ..... EAA

Ethylene Bistearamide [*Organic chemistry*] ..... EBS

Ethylene Bromide [*Same as DBE, EDB*] [*Organic chemistry*] ..... EB

Ethylene Butyl Acrylate [*Organic chemistry*] ..... EBA

Ethylene Diacrylate [*Organic chemistry*] ..... EDA

Ethylene Diamine Tartrate (IDOE) ..... EDT

Ethylene Diaminetetracetic Acid (DOG) ..... EDTA

Ethylene Dibromide [*Same as DBE, EB*] [*Organic chemistry*] ..... EDB

Ethylene Dichloride [*Organic chemistry*] ..... EDC

Ethylene Dimethacrylate [*Organic chemistry*] ..... EDMA

Ethylene Glycol [*Organic chemistry*] ..... EG

Ethylene Glycol Bis(aminoethyl ether)tetraacetic Acid [*Also, EBONTA*] [*Organic chemistry*] ..... EGTA

Ethylene Glycol Diacetate [*Organic chemistry*] ..... EGDA

Ethylene Glycol Dimethacrylate [*Organic chemistry*] ..... EDMA

Ethylene Glycol Dimethacrylate [*Organic chemistry*] ..... EGDMA

Ethylene Glycol Dimethyl Ether [*Also, DME, GLYME*] [*Organic chemistry*] .... EGDE

Ethylene Glycol Dimethyl Ether [*Also, DME,EGDE*] [*Organic chemistry*] .... GLYME

Ethylene Glycol Dinitrate [*Organic chemistry*] ..... EGDN

Ethylene Glycol Monomethyl Ether [*A poison*] [*Organic chemistry*] ..... EGME

Ethylene Glycol Succinate [*Organic chemistry*] ..... EGS

Ethylene Glycol Tetra-Acetic Acid [*Organic chemistry*] (DAVI) ..... EGTA

Ethylene Interpolymer Alloy ..... EIP

Ethylene Methacrylic Acid [*Organic chemistry*] ..... EMAA

Ethylene Methyl Acetate [*Plastic technology*] ..... EMA

Ethylene Methyl Acrylate [*Photovoltaic energy systems*] ..... EMA

Ethylene Methyl Methacrylate [*Organic chemistry*] ..... EMMA

Ethylene Oxide [*Organic chemistry*] ..... EO

Ethylene Oxide [*Organic chemistry*] (KSC) ..... ETHO

Ethylene Oxide [*Organic chemistry*] ..... ETO

Ethylene Oxide [*Organic chemistry*] (MAE) ..... ETOX

Ethylene Oxide Industry Council (EA) ..... EOIC

Ethylene Oxide Number [*Surfactant technology*] ..... EON

Ethylene Oxide Sterilizer (MCD) ..... EOS

Ethylene Propylene Rubber [*Organic chemistry*] ..... EPR

Ethylene Propylene Terpolymer [*Organic chemistry*] ..... EPT

Ethylene Response Sensor [*Botanical genetics*] ..... ERS

Ethylene Thiourea [*Organic chemistry*] ..... ETU

Ethylene Vinyl Alcohol [*Plastics*] ..... EVOH

Ethylenebis(dithiocarbamate) [*Organic chemistry*] ..... EBDC

Ethylenebis(hydroxyphenylglycine) [*Organic chemistry*] ..... EHPG

Ethylenebisisothiocyanate Sulfide [*Organic chemistry*] ..... EBIS

(Ethylenebis(oxyethylenenitrilo))tetraacetic Acid [*Also, EGTA*] [*Organic chemistry*] ..... EBONTA

Ethylene-Chlorotrifluoroethylene [*Organic chemistry*] ..... ECTFE

Ethylenediamenetetraacetic Acid ..... EDA

Ethylenediamine [*Organic chemistry*] ..... EDA

Ethylenediamine [*Organic chemistry*] ..... EN

Ethylenediamine Dihydriodide [*Organic chemistry*] ..... EDDI

Ethylene-Diamine Dinitrate/Ammonium Nitrate Explosive ..... EA

Ethylenediamine Tartrate [*Organic chemistry*] ..... EDT

Ethylenediaminebis(hydroxyphenylacetic acid) [*Also, EDDHA, EDHPA*] [*Organic chemistry*] ..... EDBHPA

Ethylenediaminediacetic Acid [*Organic chemistry*] ..... EDDA

Ethylenediaminedi-O-Hydroxyphenylacetate [*or -hydroxyphenylacetic Acid*] [*Also, EDBHPA, EDHPA*] [*Organic chemistry*] ..... EDDHA

Ethylenediaminedi-O-Hydroxyphenylacetic Acid [*Also, EDBHPA, EDDHA*] [*Organic chemistry*] ..... EDHPA

Ethylenediaminedisuccinic [*Organic chemistry*] ..... EDDS

Ethylenediamine-Pyrocatechol-Water [*Mixture for etching silicon sensors*] ..... EDPW

Ethylenediaminetetraacetate [*Also, EDTA, enta*] [*USAN*] [*Organic chemistry*] ..... EDETATE

Ethylenediaminetetraacetate [*Also, EDETATE, enta*] [*Organic chemistry*] ..... EDTA

Ethylenediaminetetraacetate [*Also, EDETATE, EDTA*] [*Organic chemistry*] ..... enta

Ethylenediaminetetra-Acetic Acid [*Also called edathamil and edetic acid*] [*Organic chemistry*] (DAVI) ..... EDTA

Ethylenediaminetetraacetonitrile [*Also, EDTN*] [*Organic chemistry*] ..... EDTAN

Ethylenediaminetetraacetonitrile [*Also, EDTAN*] [*Organic chemistry*] ..... EDTN

Ethylenediaminetetra(methylenephosphonic Acid) [*Organic chemistry*] ..... EDTPO

Ethylenedihydrazine (MCD) ..... EDH

Ethylenedinitrilo Tetraacetic Acid [*Organic chemistry*] (NRCH) ..... EDTA

(Ethylenedinitrilo)tetrakis(propanol) [*Organic chemistry*] ..... ENTPROL

Ethylene-Ethyl Acetate [*Organic chemistry*] ..... EEA

Ethylene-Ethyl Acrylate [*Copolymer*] [*Organic chemistry*] ..... EEA

Ethylenehydroxydiphosphonate [*Organic chemistry*] ..... EHDP

Ethyleneimine [*Organic chemistry*] ..... EI

Ethylene-(Isobutyl Acrylate) [*Organic chemistry*] ..... EIBA

Ethylene-Maleic Anhydride [*Copolymer*] [*Organic chemistry*] ..... EMA

Ethylene-Propylene-Diene Monomer [*Rubber, ASTM nomenclature*] ..... EPDM

Ethylene-Responsive Element [*Biochemistry*] ..... ERE

Ethylene-Tetrafluoroethylene [*Organic chemistry*] ..... ETFE

Ethylenetetrafluoroethylene [*Organic chemistry*] ..... ETFE

Ethyleneurea [*Organic chemistry*] ..... EU

Ethylene-Vinyl Acetate [*Copolymer*] [*Organic chemistry*] ..... EVA

Ethylene-Vinyl Acetate [*Copolymer*] [*Organic chemistry*] ..... EVAC

Ethylene-Vinyl Chloride [*Fire-retardant resin*] [*Organic chemistry*] ..... EVCI

Ethylhexadecyldimethylammonium Bromide [*Blood count diluent*] ..... EHDA

Ethylhexyl Acrylate [*Organic chemistry*] ..... EHA

Ethylhexyl Diphenyl Phosphate [*Organic chemistry*] ..... EHDPP

Ethyl(hydroxyethyl)cellulose [*Organic chemistry*] ..... EHEC

Ethylidenebis(tryptophan) [*Biochemistry*] ..... EBT

Ethylidenenorborene [*Organic chemistry*] ..... ENB

Ethyl(isopropyl)amiloride [*Organic chemistry*] ..... EIPA

Ethylisopropylaniline [*Organic chemistry*] ..... EIPA

Ethylketocyclazocine [*Biochemistry*] ..... EKC

Ethylmercurithiosalicylate [*Organic chemistry*] ..... EMTS

Ethylmercury-P-Toluenesulfonamide [*Organic chemistry*] ..... EMTS

Ethyl(methyl)-Gamma-Butyrolactone [*Biochemistry*] ..... EMGBL

Ethyl(methyl)(piperidyl)barbituric Acid [*Biochemistry*] ..... EMPB

EthylInitrolic Acid [*Organic chemistry*] ..... ENA

Ethyl-nitronitrosoguanidine [*Organic chemistry*] ..... ENNG

Ethylnitrosourea [*Organic chemistry*] ..... ENU

Ethylnorepinephrine [*Also, ENS*] [*Pharmacology*] ..... ENE

Ethylnorsuprarenin [*Also, ENE*] [*Pharmacology*] ..... ENS

Ethyloxaergoline [*Biochemistry*] ..... EOE

Ethyl-Para-Nitrophenyl Phenylphosphonothioate [*An insecticide*] ..... EPN

Ethyl(para-Nitrophenyl)methylphosphonate [*Biochemistry*] ..... EPMP

Ethylphosphonothioicdichloride [*Organic chemistry*] ..... EPTD

Ethyl-P-Nitrophenylthiobenzene Phosphate [*Organic chemistry*] (DAVI) ..... ENP

Ethylpyridinium Bromide [*Organic chemistry*] ..... EPB

Ethyl-sec-butylamiline [*Organic chemistry*] ..... ESBA

Ethyl-Terminated Polyarylene Ether [*Organic chemistry*] ..... ETPAE

Ethylthioribose [*Biochemistry*] ..... ETR

Ethyltoluene [*Organic chemistry*] ..... ET

Ethynodiol [*Pharmacology*] ..... ED

Ethynyl Estradiol [*Endocrinology*] ..... EE

Etidronate Sodium [*Pharmacology*] (DAVI) ..... EHDA

Etiocholanolone [*A pyrogen*] [*Medicine*] (MAE) ..... ETIO

Etiology [*Medicine*] (DAVI) ..... E

Etiology (AAMN) ..... et

Etiology ..... ETIOL

ETIS [*European Technical Information Service*] in Machine Readable For m (NITA) ..... ETIS-MARFO

Etling Clearinghouse (EA) ..... EC

Etna & Montrose R. R. [*AAR code*] ..... EM

Etna Free Library, Etna, CA [*Library symbol Library of Congress*] (LCLS) ..... CEt

Etobicoke Public Library [*UTLAS symbol*] ..... ETB

Etobicoke Public Library, Etobicoke, ON, Canada [*Library symbol Library of Congress*] (LCLS) ..... CaOTEtPL

Etobicoke Public Library, Ontario [*Library symbol National Library of Canada*] (NLC) ..... OTEPL

Eton College [*British*] (ROG) ..... EC

Eton College Chronicle [*A publication British*] ..... ECC

Eton College, Windsor, Berks, United Kingdom [*Library symbol Library of Congress*] (LCLS) ..... UkWE

Eton Volunteer Rifle Corps [*British military*] (DMA) ..... EVRC

Etoposide, Cyclophosphamide, Hydroxydaunomycin [*Adriamycin*], Oncovin [*Vincristine*] [*Antineoplastic drug regimen*] ..... ECHO

Etoposide (VP-16), Vincristine, Adriamycin, Cyclophosphamide [*Antineoplastic drug regimen*] ..... EVAC

Etopside, Cisplatin, Arabinosylcytosine, Methylprednisolone [*Antineoplastic drug*] (CDI) ..... E-SHAP

Etowah, TN [*AM radio station call letters*] ..... WCPH

Etowah, TN [*FM radio station call letters*] ..... WDRZ

E'Town Corp. [*Formerly, Elizabethtown Water*] [*Associated Press*] (SAG) ..... ETown

E'town Corp. [*Formerly, Elizabethtown Water*] [*NYSE symbol*] (SPSG) ..... ETW

Etrepagny [*France ICAO location identifier*] (ICLI) ..... LFFY

Etruria (VRA) ..... Etru

[The] Etruscan Cities and Rome [*A publication*] (OCD) ..... Etr Cities

Etruscan Enterprises Ltd. [*Vancouver Stock Exchange symbol*] ..... EET

Etruscan Foundation (EA) ..... EF

Ets Haim Seminary [*Amsterdam*] (BJA) ..... EH

ETS International, Inc. [*Vancouver Stock Exchange symbol*] ..... ETS

ETS International, Inc. [*AMEX symbol*] (SAG) ..... ETS

ETS International, Inc. [*Associated Press*] (SAG) ..... ETS Int

Etting's American Admiralty Jurisdiction [*A publication*] (DLA) ..... Ett Ad

Ettore Bugatti [*Auto engineer*] [*French*] ..... EB

Etude ..... ETD

Etude [*Record label*] ..... Etu

Etude de la Protection des Usagers de la Route et de l'Environement [*St udy of Road User Safety and Environmental Protection*] [*French Automotive engineering*] ..... EPURE

Etude en Commun de la Mediterranee [*Cooperative Investigations in the Mediterranean - CIM*] [*French*] (MSC) ..... ECM

Etudes d'Urbanisme de Developpement et d'Amenagement [*du Territoire*] ..... EURDA

Etudes et Expansion (EA) ..... Et Ex

Etudes Preliminaires aux Religions Orientales dans l'Empire Romain [*A publication*] (BJA) ..... EPRO

Etudes Publies par des Peres de la Compagnie de Jesus [*A publication*] (BJA) ..... ECJ

Etudes sur le Judaisme Medieval [*A publication*] (BJA) ..... EJM

Etudes Techniques et Constructions Aerospatiales [*Belgium*] ..... ETCA

Etymologicum Magnum [*Twelfth century AD*] [*Classical studies*] (OCD) ..... Etym Magn

Etymology [*or Etymologist*] (WGA) ..... ety

Etymology [*or Etymologist*] ..... ETYM

Etymology ..... Etymol

Etz Lavud Ltd. [*AMEX symbol*] (SPSG) ..... ETZ

Etz Lavud Ltd. [*Associated Press*] (SAG) ..... EtzLav

Etz Lavud Ltd. [*Associated Press*] (SAG) ..... EtzLv

Etz Lavud Ltd 'A' [*AMEX symbol*] (TTSB) ..... ETZA

Etz Lavud Ltd Ord [*AMEX symbol*] (TTSB) ..... ETZ

Eua [*Tonga*] [*ICAO location identifier*] (ICLI) .... NFTE
Eua Tonga Island [*South Pacific*] [*Airport symbol*] (OAG) .... EUA
Eucaliptos [*Bolivia*] [*ICAO location identifier*] (ICLI) .... SLEU
Eucaloric Balanced Diet .... EBD
Eucaloric Ketogenic Diet .... EKD
Eucalyptus Improvement Association (EA) .... EIA
Eucharist (ROG) .... EUCH
Eucharistic Franciscan Missionary Sisters (TOCD) .... EFMS
Eucharistic Guard for Nocturnal Adoration [*Defunct*] (EA) .... EGNA
Eucharistic Missionaries of St. Dominic (TOCD) .... OP
Eucharistic Missionaries of St. Theresa (Mexico) (TOCD) .... MEST
Eucharistic Missionaries of the Most Holy Trinity (TOCD) .... MESST
Eucharistic Missionary Society (TOCD) .... EMS
Euclid [*Second century BC*] [*Classical studies*] (OCD) .... Euc
Euclid Public Library, Euclid, OH [*OCLC symbol*] (OCLC) ...... ECU
Euclid Public Library, Euclid, OH [*Library symbol Library of Congress*]
   (LCLS) .... OEu
Euclid R. R. [*AAR code*] .... EUC
Euclidean [*Mathematics*] .... EUC
Euclidean Distance Matrix [*Statistics*] .... ED
Euer [*Your*] [*German*] .... EW
Euer. Doctrina Placitandi [*England*] [*A publication*] (DLA) ...... Euer
Euer Ehrwuerden [*Your Reverence*] [*German*] .... EE
Eufaula, AL [*Location identifier FAA*] (FAAL) .... EUF
Eufaula, AL [*FM radio station call letters*] .... WDMT
Eufaula, AL [*AM radio station call letters*] .... WULA
Eufaula, AL [*FM radio station call letters*] .... WULA-FM
Eufaula BancCorp [*NASDAQ symbol*] (TTSB) .... EUFA
Eufaula BancCorp, Inc. [*NASDAQ symbol*] (SAG) .... EUFA
Eufaula BancCorp, Inc. [*Associated Press*] (SAG) .... Eufaula
Eufaula, OK [*FM radio station call letters*] .... KCES
Eufaula, OK [*Television station call letters*] .... KOET
Eugene [*Oregon*] [*Airport symbol*] (OAG) .... EUG
Eugene Ballet Company [*Eugene, OR*] .... EBC
Eugene Field House, St. Louis, MO [*Library symbol Library of Congress*]
   (LCLS) .... MoSFi
Eugene Isle, LA [*Location identifier FAA*] (FAAL) .... VUW
Eugene O'Neill Memorial Theater Center (EA) .... EOMTC
Eugene O'Neill Society (EA) .... EOS
Eugene, OR [*Location identifier FAA*] (FAAL) .... EUG
Eugene, OR [*AM radio station call letters*] .... KDUK
Eugene, OR [*AM radio station call letters*] (RBYB) .... KEED
Eugene, OR [*Television station call letters*] .... KEPB
Eugene, OR [*Television station call letters*] .... KEVU
Eugene, OR [*Television station call letters*] .... KEZI
Eugene, OR [*AM radio station call letters*] (RBYB) .... KKNX-AM
Eugene, OR [*AM radio station call letters*] .... KKXO
Eugene, OR [*FM radio station call letters*] .... KLCC
Eugene, OR [*AM radio station call letters*] .... KMGE
Eugene, OR [*Television station call letters*] .... KMTR
Eugene, OR [*FM radio station call letters*] .... KODZ
Eugene, OR [*AM radio station call letters*] .... KPNW
Eugene, OR [*FM radio station call letters*] .... KRVM
Eugene, OR [*AM radio station call letters*] .... KUGN
Eugene, OR [*FM radio station call letters*] .... KUGN-FM
Eugene, OR [*Television station call letters*] .... KVAL
Eugene, OR [*AM radio station call letters*] .... KWAX
Eugene, OR [*FM radio station call letters*] .... KWVA
Eugene, OR [*FM radio station call letters*] .... KZEL
Eugene, OR [*AM radio station call letters*] (RBYB) .... KZTU
Eugene, OR [*AM radio station call letters*] (RBYB) .... KZTU-AM
Eugene Public Library, Eugene, OR [*OCLC symbol*] (OCLC) ...... OEL
Eugene Public Library, Eugene, OR [*Library symbol Library of Congress*]
   (LCLS) .... OrE
Eugene V. Debs Foundation (EA) .... EVDF
Eugene V. Debs Foundation, Terre Haute, IN [*Library symbol Library of
   Congress*] (LCLS) .... InTD
Eugenic Insemination by Donor .... EID
Eugenics (ADA) .... EUGEN
Eugenics Special Interest Group [*Defunct*] (EA) .... ESIG
Euglobulin Clot Lysis [*Hematology*] .... ECL
Euglobulin Clot Lysis Time [*Clinical chemistry*] .... ECLT
Euglobulin Clot Test [*Clinical chemistry*] (MAE) .... ECT
Euglobulin Lysis [*Also, fibrinolysin and plasmin*] [*Biochemistry*] (DAVI) ...... EUG LY
Euglobulin Lysis Time [*Clinical chemistry*] .... ELT
Eukaryotic Initiation Factors [*Biochemistry*] .... eIF
Euler Number [*Fluid mechanics*] .... E
Euler Number [*IUPAC*] [*Fluid mechanics*] .... Eu
Eulerian Iterative Nonsteady [*Method*] [*Mathematics*] .... EIN
Euler-Rodrigues Parameter [*Physics*] .... ERP
Eumenides [*of Aeschylus*] [*Classical studies*] (OCD) .... Eum
Eu-Mers/Le Treport [*France ICAO location identifier*] (ICLI) ...... LFAE
Eunice, LA [*AM radio station call letters*] .... KEUN
Eunice, LA [*FM radio station call letters*] .... KJJB
Eunice, NM [*FM radio station call letters*] (RBYB) .... KYRK-FM
Eunice Public Library, Eunice, LA [*Library symbol Library of Congress*]
   (LCLS) .... LE
Eunuchus [*of Terence*] [*Classical studies*] (OCD) .... Eun
Euphemism (ROG) .... EUPHEM
Euphonium [*Musical instrument*] .... EUPH
Euphonix, Inc. [*NASDAQ symbol*] (SAG) .... EUPH
Euphonix, Inc. [*Associated Press*] (SAG) .... Euphnx
Euphorbia Mosaic Virus [*Plant pathology*] .... EUMV
Euphrasia Township Public Library, Kimberley, Ontario [*Library symbol
   National Library of Canada*] (NLC) .... OKET

Eupolis [*Fifth century BC*] [*Classical studies*] (OCD) .... Eup
Eupora, MS [*AM radio station call letters*] .... WEPA
Eura [*Finland ICAO location identifier*] (ICLI) .... EFEU
EURAIL [*European Railway*] Community (EAIO) .... EC
Euralair [*France ICAO designator*] (FAAC) .... ERL
Euralair International [*France ICAO designator*] (FAAC) .... EUL
Eurasia [*MARC geographic area code Library of Congress*] (LCCP) ...... me----
Eurasian Communist Countries (MCD) .... ECC
Eurasian Ice Sheet [*Climatology*] .... EIS
Eurasian Target Data Inventory [*File*] (MCD) .... ETDI
EURATOM [*European Atomic Energy Community*] Classified Information .... ECI
Euravia [*Spain ICAO designator*] (FAAC) .... EUI
Eureka [*Nevada*] [*Seismograph station code, US Geological Survey*] (SEIS) .... EUR
Eureka [*Washington*] [*Seismograph station code, US Geological Survey*]
   (SEIS) .... EUW
Eureka Aero Industries [*ICAO designator*] (AD) .... IK
Eureka/Arcata [*California*] [*Airport symbol*] (OAG) .... ACV
Eureka/Arcata [*California*] Murray Field [*Airport symbol Obsolete*] (OAG) .... EKA
Eureka, CA [*FM radio station call letters*] (RBYB) .... KAKD
Eureka, CA [*Television station call letters*] .... KBVU
Eureka, CA [*Television station call letters*] .... KEET
Eureka, CA [*FM radio station call letters*] .... KEKA
Eureka, CA [*FM radio station call letters*] .... KFMI
Eureka, CA [*FM radio station call letters*] .... KGOE
Eureka, CA [*Television station call letters*] .... KIEM
Eureka, CA [*AM radio station call letters*] .... KINS
Eureka, CA [*FM radio station call letters*] (RBYB) .... KKHB-FM
Eureka, CA [*FM radio station call letters*] (RBYB) .... KMUE-FM
Eureka, CA [*FM radio station call letters*] (RBYB) .... KRED-FM
Eureka, CA [*Television station call letters*] .... KVIQ
Eureka, CA [*Television station call letters*] .... KWSW
Eureka Canyon [*California*] [*Seismograph station code, US Geological
   Survey*] (SEIS) .... EUC
Eureka City Library, Eureka, CA [*Library symbol Library of Congress*]
   (LCLS) .... CE
Eureka College, Eureka, IL [*OCLC symbol*] (OCLC) .... IBU
Eureka College, Eureka, IL [*Library symbol Library of Congress*] (LCLS) .... IEuC
Eureka, IL [*FM radio station call letters*] .... WIVR
Eureka, KS [*FM radio station call letters*] .... KOTE
Eureka Mesa [*New Mexico*] [*Seismograph station code, US Geological
   Survey*] (SEIS) .... EUM
Eureka, MT [*Location identifier FAA*] (FAAL) .... EUR
Eureka, NT [*ICAO location identifier*] (ICLI) .... CYEU
Eureka Public Library, Eureka, SD [*Library symbol Library of Congress*]
   (LCLS) .... SdEu
Eureka Resources, Inc. [*Vancouver Stock Exchange symbol*] .... EUK
Eureka Ridge [*Idaho*] [*Seismograph station code, US Geological Survey
   Closed*] (SEIS) .... ERI
Eureka Society (EA) .... ES
Eureka Springs, AR [*FM radio station call letters*] .... KTCN
Euripides [*Fifth century BC*] [*Classical studies*] (OCD) .... Eur
Euro Air Helicopter Service AB [*Sweden ICAO designator*] (FAAC) .... SCO
Euro American Cultural Exchange (EA) .... EACE
Euro Direct Airlines UK Ltd. [*British*] [*FAA designator*] (FAAC) ...... EUD
Euro Disneyland [*France*] .... EDL
Euro/NATO .... E/N
Euro Petroleum Corp. [*Toronto Stock Exchange symbol Vancouver Stock
   Exchange symbol*] .... EPT
Euro Travellers Cheque [*Thomas Cook International*] .... ETC
Euro-Abstracts [*Commission of the European Communities*] [*Information
   service or system*] .... EABS
Euroair Transport Ltd. [*British ICAO designator*] (FAAC) .... EUZ
Euro-American Alliance (EA) .... EAA
Euro-American Financial [*Vancouver Stock Exchange symbol*] .... EFN
Euro-Arab Management School [*Granada, Spain*] (ECON) .... EAMS
Euro-Asia Capital Ltd. [*Vancouver Stock Exchange symbol*] .... EAC
Euro-Asia Trade Organisation .... EATO
Euroberlin [*France ICAO designator*] (FAAC) .... EEB
Eurobike Limited (EA) .... ELTD
Eurocan Ventures Ltd. [*Vancouver Stock Exchange symbol*] .... EUR
Eurocard [*Credit card*] [*British*] .... £ E
Eurocard [*Credit card*] [*British*] (ADA) .... EC
Eurocheque [*Credit card*] [*British*] .... EC
Euro-Children (EAIO) .... EC
Eurochord [*Record label*] [*France*] .... Eur
EuroCity [*Railroad*] .... EC
Eurocity Express [*Airline*] [*British*] .... EE
Eurocommander SA [*Spain ICAO designator*] (FAAC) .... ERA
Euro-Commercial Paper [*Finance*] .... ECP
Euro-Commercial Paper and Certificates of Deposit Programme
   [*Finance*] .... ECPCDP
Eurocontrol [*Belgium ICAO designator*] (FAAC) .... EUC
Eurocopter [*France ICAO designator*] (FAAC) .... ECF
Eurocypria Airlines Ltd. [*Cyprus*] [*ICAO designator*] (FAAC) .... ECA
Eurodata Foundation (EAIO) .... EF
Eurodefence .... ED
Euroflight Sweden, AB [*ICAO designator*] (FAAC) .... EUW
Eurofly [*Italy ICAO designator*] (FAAC) .... EEU
Eurofly SPA [*Italy ICAO designator*] (FAAC) .... EEZ
Eurogroup Committee of National Armaments Directors .... EURONAD
Eurojet Aviation Ltd. [*British ICAO designator*] (FAAC) .... GOJ
Eurojet Compagnie [*British ICAO designator*] (FAAC) .... RIK
Eurojet Italia [*Italy ICAO designator*] (FAAC) .... ERJ
Eurojet SA [*Spain ICAO designator*] (FAAC) .... EUR
Euro-Latin America Bank Ltd. [*British*] (EY) .... EULABANK

Euro-Latin American Bank Ltd. .... EULA
Eurolaw Commercial Intelligence [*A publication*] (DLA) .... Eurolaw Com Intel
Euroline, Ottawa, Ontario [*Library symbol National Library of Canada*]
    (BIB) .... OOEU
Euromarket Federation of Animal Protein Importers and Traders
    (EAIO) .... EFAPIT
EuroMed Inc. [*NYSE symbol*] (TTSB) .... EMED
Euromin Canada Ltd. [*Vancouver Stock Exchange symbol*] .... ENC
Euromissile Dynamics Group (PDAA) .... EMDG
Euromissiles Working Group [*Defunct*] (EA) .... EWG
Euro-NATO Joint Jet Pilot Training .... ENJJPT
Euro-NATO Training Group [*An association*] (EAIO) .... ENTG
Euro-Nevada Mining Corp. Ltd. [*Toronto Stock Exchange symbol*] ...... EN
Euronorm Certified Reference Material .... ECRM
Europa Cruises [*NASDAQ symbol*] (TTSB) .... KRUZ
Europa Cruises Corp. [*Associated Press*] (SAG) .... EuroCr
Europa Cruises Corp. [*NASDAQ symbol*] (SAG) .... KRUZ
Europa Esperanto-Centro [*European Esperanto Centre - EEC*] (EAIO) ...... EEC
Europa, MS [*FM radio station call letters*] .... WLZA
Europa Nostra [*Historic preservation organization*] (EA) .... EN
Europa Petroleum [*Vancouver Stock Exchange symbol*] .... EUP
Europa Study Unit (EA) .... ESU
Europa Year Book [*A publication*] .... EURYB
Europa Year Book [*A publication*] (MHDB) .... EYB
Europaeiche Mittelstands-Union [*European Medium and Small Business
    Union*] [*EC*] (ECED) .... EMSU
Europaeische Arbeiterpartei [*European Workers' Party*] [*Germany Political
    party*] (PPE) .... EAP
Europaeische Baptistische Foderation [*European Baptist Federation - EBF*]
    (EAIO) .... EBF
Europaeische Baptistische Frauenunion [*European Baptist Women's Union -
    EBWU*] (EAIO) .... EBF
Europaeische Baptistische Mission [*European Baptist Mission*] [*Germany*]
    (EAIO) .... EBM
Europaeische Demokratische Union [*European Democratic Union*] [*Austria*]
    (EAIO) .... EDU
Europaeische Evangelische Allianz [*European Evangelical Alliance - EEA*]
    (EAIO) .... EEA
Europaeische Foderation Biotechnologie [*European Federation of
    Biotechnology*] (EAIO) .... EFB
Europaeische Foderation fuer Chemie-Ingenieur-Wesen [*European
    Federation of Chemical Engineering - EFCE*] (EAIO) .... EFCIW
Europaeische Foederalistische Partei [*European Federalist Party*] [*Austria*]
    (PPE) .... EFP
Europaeische Gemeinschaft fuer Kohle und Stahl [*European Coal and Steel
    Community*] [*German*] (DCTA) .... EGKS
Europaeische Gesellschaft fuer Schriftpsychologie und Schriftexpertise
    [*European Society of Handwriting Psychology - ESHP*] (EAIO) ...... EGS
Europaeische Go Foderation [*European Go Federation - EGF*] [*Austria*]
    (EAIO) .... EGF
Europaeische Kernenergie-Gesellschaft [*European Nuclear Society - ENS*]
    (EAIO) .... ENS
Europaeische Maerchengesellschaft [*European Fairytale Association - EFA*]
    [*Germany*] (EAIO) .... EMG
Europaeische Motel Foderation [*European Motel Federation*] (EA) ...... EMF
Europaeische Musikschul-Union [*European Music School Union*] [*Linz,
    Austria*] (SLS) .... EMU
Europaeische Organisation der Militarverbande [*European Organization of
    Military Associations*] (EAIO) .... EUROMIL
Europaeische Studentenvereinigung in Osterreich .... ESTO
Europaeische Union Gegen den Missbrauch der Tiere [*European Union for
    the Prevention of Cruelty to Animals*] [*Switzerland*] (EAIO) .... EUMT
Europaeische Vereinigung der Allgemeinarzte [*European Union of General
    Practitioners*] (EAIO) .... EVA
Europaeische Vereinigung der Briefumschlagfabrikanten [*European
    Association of Envelope Manufacturers*] (EAIO) .... FEPE
Europaeische Vereinigung der Veterinaranatomen [*European Association of
    Veterinary Anatomists - EAVA*] (EAIO) .... EVVA
Europaeische Wahrungsabkommen [*European Monetary Agreement*]
    [*German*] (DCTA) .... EWA
Europaeische Wandervereinigung [*European Ramblers' Association - ERA*]
    [*Germany*] (EAIO) .... EW
Europaeische Wirtschaftsgemeinschaft [*European Economic Community*] ...... EWG
Europaeischer Tabakwaren-Grosshandels-Verband [*European Tobacco
    Wholesalers' Union*] (EAIO) .... ETV
Europaeischer Verband fuer Zellstoff und Papiertechnik [*European Liaison
    Committee for Pulp and Paper*] (EAIO) .... EUCEPA
Europaeisches Netzwerk fuer den Ost-West-Dialog [*European Network for
    East-West Dialogue - ENEWD*] (EAIO) .... ENOWD
Europaeisches Patentamt [*European Patent Office - EPO*] (EAIO) ...... EPA
Europaische Foderation Junger Chore [*European Federation of Young
    Choirs*] (EAIO) .... EFJC
Europaische Frauen Union [*Austria*] (EAIO) .... EFU
Europaische Gesellschaft fuer Herbologie [*European Weed Research
    Society*] (EAIO) .... EGH
Europaische Gesellschaft fur Kartoffelforschung [*Netherlands*] (EAIO) ...... EAPR
Europaische Konferenz der Industrie Elektrischer Kondensatoren
    [*European Conference of the Industry of Electrical Capacitors*] [*EC*]
    (ECED) .... EUCONEC
Europaische Musikschul-Union [*European Union of Music Schools*]
    (EAIO) .... EMU
Europaische Vereinigung der Allgemeinartze [*European Union of General
    Practitioners*] [*Denmark*] (EAIO) .... UEMO
Europaische Vereinigung der Keramik-Industrie [*Europeean Federation of
    the Electro-Ceramic Industry*] (PDAA) .... EVKI

Europaische Verteidigungsgemeinschaft [*European Defense Community*]
    [*German*] (BARN) .... EVG
Europaischer Holzhandelsverband [*European Timber Association*] [*EC*]
    (ECED) .... EHV
Europaischer Holzhandelsverband [*European Timber Association*] [*EC*]
    (ECED) .... ETA
Europe [*MARC geographic area code Library of Congress*] (LCCP) ...... e-----
Europe .... EU
Europe [*or European*] (AFM) .... EUR
Europe (VRA) .... Eur
Europe (AAGC) .... Eur
Europe Aero Service .... EAS
Europe Aero Service [*ICAO designator*] (AD) .... EY
Europe Aero Service [*France ICAO designator*] (FAAC) .... EYT
Europe Air [*France ICAO designator*] (FAAC) .... EUA
Europe and Africa .... EURAFRICA
Europe, Asia, and Africa .... EURASAFRICA
Europe, Australia, and Far East .... EAFE
Europe, Central [*MARC geographic area code Library of Congress*]
    (LCCP) .... ec----
Europe China Association (EA) .... ECA
Europe Computer Systems [*Computer leasing company*] (NITA) ...... ECS
Europe, East Central [*MARC geographic area code Library of Congress*]
    (LCCP) .... et----
Europe, Eastern [*MARC geographic area code Library of Congress*]
    (LCCP) .... ee----
Europe Falcon Service [*France ICAO designator*] (FAAC) .... EFS
[*The*] Europe Fund [*NYSE symbol*] (SPSG) .... EF
Europe Fund [*NYSE symbol*] (TTSB) .... EF
[*The*] Europe Fund [*Associated Press*] (SAG) .... EuroFd
Europe Industry and Technology Division [*Department of Trade*] [*British*] ...... EIT
Europe, Northern [*MARC geographic area code Library of Congress*]
    (LCCP) .... en----
Europe, Southeastern [*MARC geographic area code Library of Congress*]
    (LCCP) .... ed----
Europe, Southern [*MARC geographic area code Library of Congress*]
    (LCCP) .... es----
Europe, Western [*MARC geographic area code Library of Congress*]
    (LCCP) .... ew----
Europeaero Service National [*France ICAO designator*] (FAAC) ...... EXN
Europeaero Service National [*France*] [*FAA designator*] (FAAC) ...... EYN
European [*British military*] (DMA) .... E
European .... ERPN
European (AAGC) .... Eur
European Academic Association for Financial Research (EAIO) ...... EAAFR
European Academic Research Network [*A computer network*] ...... EARN
European Academy of Allergology and Clinical Immunology (EAIO) ...... EAACI
European Academy of Anaesthesiology (EA) .... EAA
European Academy of Arts, Sciences, and Humanities (EAIO) ...... EAASH
European Academy of Facial Surgery (EAIO) .... EAFS
European Academy of History (EA) .... EAH
European Academy of Science and Technology .... EAST
European Access to Seafloor Survey Systems [*Southampton Oceanography
    Centre*] [*British*] .... EASSS
European Accident Statement .... EAS
European Accountancy Students Study Group (PDAA) .... EASSG
European Accounting Association [*Brussels, Belgium*] (EAIO) ...... EAA
European Advanced Technology Programme [*British*] .... EUREKA
European Advertising Tripartite [*Brussels, Belgium*] (EA) .... EAT
European Advisory Committee [*Allied German Occupation Forces*] ...... EAC
European Advisory Council (EAIO) .... EAC
European Advisory Council of the Asbestos International Association
    [*EC*] (ECED) .... AIA/EAC
European Agricultural Aviation Centre [*Later, International Agricultural
    Aviation Centre*] .... EAAC
European Agricultural Guidance and Guarantee Fund [*Also known as
    FEOGA*] .... EAGGF
European Air Chemistry Network .... EACN
European Air Combat Operations Staff [*Military*] .... EACOS
European Air Lines .... EURAL
European Air Navigation Plan [*ICAO*] (DA) .... EUR ANP
European Air Operations Staff [*Military*] .... EUROPS
European Air Taxi [*British*] [*FAA designator*] (FAAC) .... ETX
European Air Traffic Control Harmonization and Integration Program
    [*Eurocontrol*] .... EATCHIP
European Air Transport [*ICAO designator*] (FAAC) .... BCS
European Air Transport Service .... EATS
European Airlines [*France ICAO designator*] (FAAC) .... TAT
European Airlines Electronic Committee .... EAEC
European Airlines Electronics Meeting (PDAA) .... EAEM
European Airlines Research Bureau .... EARB
European Airways Ltd. [*British*] [*FAA designator*] (FAAC) .... EAW
European Alliance of News Agencies .... EANA
European Allied Contacts Section [*Supreme Headquarters, Allied
    Expeditionary Force*] [*World War II*] .... EACS
European Aluminium Association [*Germany*] (EA) .... EAA
European Amateur Baseball Confederation (EA) .... EABC
European American Bank (NITA) .... EAB
European and Mediterranean Association of Coloproctology (EAIO) ...... EMAC
European and Mediterranean Cereal Rusts Foundation (EAIO) ...... EMCRF
European and Mediterranean Plant Protection Organization [*See also
    OEPP*] (EAIO) .... EPPO
European and Near East Section [*Friends World Committee for Consultation*]
    [*Luxembourg*] .... ENES
European and Pacific Weather Graphics Switch [*Air Force*] (GFGA) ...... EWGS

European Application Satellite Systems .... EUROSAT
European Aquaculture Society (EA) .... EAS
European Arbitration [*A publication*] (DLA) .... Eur Arb
European Architectural Heritage Year [*1975*] .... EAHY
European Area Communications Plan [*Military*] (AABC) .... EACP
European Area Headquarters [*Red Cross*] .... EUA
European Article Number [*Equivalent of Universal Product Code*] ...... EAN
European Article Numbering System (PDAA) .... EANS
European/ASEAN [*Association of Southeast Asian Nations*] **Business Council** (DS) .... EABC
European Asphalt Pavement Association (EA) .... EAPA
European Association for American Studies [*Italy*] (EAIO) .... EAAS
European Association for Animal Production [*ICSU*] [*Italian*] (SLS) ...... EAAP
European Association for Aquatic Mammals (EA) .... EAAM
European Association for Behavior Therapy (EA) .... EABT
European Association for Business Research, Planning, and Development in the Chemical Industry [*Formerly, European Chemical Market Research Association*] [*British*] .... ECMRA
European Association for Cancer Research (EAIO) .... EACR
European Association for Chinese Law (EAIO) .... EACL
European Association for Co-Operation .... EAC
European Association for Cranio-Maxillo-Facial Surgery (EAIO) ... EACMFS
European Association for Earthquake Engineering (PDAA) .... EAEE
European Association for Grey Literature Exploitation [*Database producer*] (EAIO) .... EAGLE
European Association for Marine Sciences and Techniques [*Marine science*] (OSRA) .... EASTM
European Association for Maxillo-Facial Surgery (EA) .... EAMFS
European Association for Microprocessing and Microprogramming (PDAA) .... EUROMICRO
European Association for National Productivity Centers [*See also AECNP*] (EAIO) .... EANPC
European Association for Population Studies (EA) .... EAPS
European Association for Potato Research (EAIO) .... EAPR
European Association for Research on Plant Breeding (EAIO) ..... EUCARPIA
European Association for Signal Processing [*Lausanne, Switzerland*] (MCD) .... EASP
European Association for Signal Processing (EAIO) .... EURASIP
European Association for Software Access and Infomation Transfer (PDAA) .... EASIT
European Association for Special Education .... EASE
European Association for Textile Polyolefins (EAIO) .... EATP
European Association for the Exchange of Technical Literature in the Field of Ferrous Metallurgy [*Luxembourg*] (EA) .... EAETLFFM
European Association for the Promotion of Poetry (EA) .... EAPP
European Association for the Science of Air Pollution (EAIO) .... EURASAP
European Association for the Study of Diabetes [*See also AEED*] (EAIO) .... EASD
European Association for the Study of Economic, Commercial, and Industrial Motivation [*Belgium*] (PDAA) .... EUMOTIV
European Association for the Trade in Jute Products (EA) .... EATJP
European Association for the Transfer of Technologies, Innovation, and Industrial Information [*Information service or system*] (IID) ...... TII
European Association for Theoretical Computer Science (EAIO) ... EATCS
European Association of Advertising Agencies .... EAAA
European Association of Agricultural Economists (EA) .... EAAE
European Association of Audiophonological Centres (EA) .... EAAC
European Association of Automobile Manufacturers [*Belgium*] (EAIO) ...... EAAM
European Association of Cardiothoracic Anaesthesiologists [*Cambridge, England*] (EAIO) .... EACTA
European Association of Charter Airlines (EAIO) .... EACA
European Association of Chinese Studies (EA) .... EACS
European Association of Classification Societies (EAIO) .... EurACS
European Association of Cognitive Ergonomics (EAIO) .... EACE
European Association of Conservatories (EA) .... EAC
European Association of Consumer Electronic Manufacturers [*EEC*] (PDAA) .... EACEM
European Association of Country Planning Institutions (EAIO) .... EACPI
European Association of Decaffeinators [*France*] (EAIO) .... EAD
European Association of Development Research and Training Institutes (EAIO) .... EADI
European Association of Development Research and Training Institutes .... EADRI
European Association of Directory Publishers (EA) .... EADP
European Association of Editors of Biological Periodicals (DIT) ... EAEBP
European Association of Environmental and Resource Economists (EERA) .... EAERE
European Association of Experimental Social Psychology (EA) .... EAESP
European Association of Exploration Geophysicists (EAIO) ...... EAEG
European Association of Exploration Geophysics [*International Council of Scientific Unions*] .... EAGS
European Association of Health Information and Libraries [*Stockholm, Sweden*] (EAIO) .... EAHIL
European Association of Hospital Administrators (EA) .... EAHA
European Association of Hospital Managers [*France*] (EAIO) ... EAHM
European Association of Hospital Pharmacists (EAIO) .... EAHP
European Association of Information Services [*Formerly, European Association of Scientific Information Dissemination Centers*] [*Information service or system*] (IID) .... EUSIDIC
European Association of Jewish Community Centres (EAIO) ..... EAJCC
European Association of Livestock Markets [*See also AEMB*] [*Belgium*] (EAIO) .... EALM
European Association of Machine Tool Merchants [*British*] (EAIO) .... EAMTM
European Association of Makers of Corrugated Base Papers (EAIO) .... EAMCBP
European Association of Management Training Centres .... EAMTC

European Association of Manufacturers and Distributors of Education Materials (PDAA) .... EURODIDAC
European Association of Manufacturers of Business Machines and Data Processing Equipment [*Frankfurt, Federal Republic of Germany*] (EAIO) .... EUROBIT
European Association of Manufacturers of Radiators (EA) .... EURORAD
European Association of Museums of the History of Medical Sciences [*See also AEMHSM*] (EAIO) .... EAMHMS
European Association of Music Festivals (EA) .... EAMF
European Association of Netting Manufacturers (EA) .... EURONEM
European Association of Neurosurgical Societies (EAIO) .... EANS
European Association of Organic Geochemists (EAIO) .... EAOG
European Association of Perinatal Medicine (EAIO) .... EAPM
European Association of Personnel Management [*Paris, France*] (EA) .... EAPM
European Association of Poison Control Centers (EAIO) .... EAPCC
European Association of Poisons Control Centers and Clinical Toxicologists [*Sweden*] (EAIO) .... EAPCCCT
European Association of Professional Fire Brigade Officers (EA) ..... EAPFBO
European Association of Professional Secretaries [*Paris, France*] (EAIO) .... EAPS
European Association of Programmes in Health Services Studies (EAIO) .... EAPHSS
European Association of Radiology (EA) .... EAR
European Association of Remote Sensing Laboratories (EA) ..... EARSEL
European Association of Schools and Colleges of Optometry (EA) ..... EASCO
European Association of Science Editors [*European Association of Earth Science Editors and European Life Sciences Editors*] [*Formed by a merger of*] (EAIO) .... EASE
European Association of Science Information Referral Centres (NITA) .... EUSIREF
European Association of Securities Dealers Automated Quotation [*System*] .... EASDAQ
European Association of Senior Hospital Physicians (PDAA) ..... EASHP
European Association of Shipping Informatics [*Brussels, Belgium*] (EAIO) .... EASI
European Association of South Asian Archaeologists [*British*] (EAIO) ..... EASAA
European Association of Teachers [*See also AEDE*] (EAIO) .... EAT
European Association of Testing Institutions (PDAA) .... EUROSTEST
European Association of Testing Institutions [*Belgium*] (PDAA) ... EUROTEST
European Association of the Textile Wholesale Trade [*EC*] (ECED) ..... OECT
European Association of Urology .... EAU
European Association of Users of Satellites in Training and Education Programmes (AIE) .... EUROSTEP
European Association of Veterinary Anatomists (EA) .... EAVA
European Assurance Arbitration [*1872-75*] [*A publication*] (DLA) ..... Eur Ass Arb
European Astronomical Society .... EAS
European Atex Users Group [*Deventer, Netherlands*] (EAIO) .... EAUG
European Atherosclerosis Society (EA) .... EAS
European Athletic Association [*Paris, France*] .... EAA
European Athletics Coaches Association (EAIO) .... EACA
European Atlantic Group [*British*] (DBA) .... E-AG
European Atomic Commission (NATG) .... EAC
European Atomic Energy Community [*Also, EURATOM*] (DCTA) ... EAEC
European Atomic Energy Community [*Also, EAEC*] .... EURATOM
European Atomic Energy Society .... EAES
European Audiovisual Entrepeneurs [*EC*] (ECED) .... EAVE
European Automated Dictionary .... EURODICAUTOM
European Automated Manufacturing Exhibition and Conference [*British Robot Association*] .... AUTOMAN
European Automotive Engineers Cooperation .... EAEC
European Aviation Air Charter Ltd. [*British*] [*FAA designator*] (FAAC) ... EAF
European Aviation Services Ltd. [*British ICAO designator*] (FAAC) CCC
European Badminton Union (EA) .... EBU
European Bank for Reconstruction and Development [*Economic assistance for Eastern Europe*] [*Proposed*] .... EBRD
European Bank of Frozen Blood of Rare Groups [*Amsterdam, Netherlands*] (EAIO) .... EBFBRG
European Baptist Federation Youth Committee (EAIO) .... EBFYC
European Baptist Mission (EAIO) .... EBM
European Baptist Press Service [*of the European Baptist Federation*] (EAIO) .... EBPS
European Baptist Theological Teachers' Conference [*Germany*] (EAIO) .... EBTTC
European Baptist Women's Union (EAIO) .... EBWU
European Barge Carrier System (PDAA) .... EBCS
European Bibliographical Center .... EBC
European Billiards Confederation .... EBC
European Bioinformatics Institute .... EBI
European Biological Control Laboratory (ECON) .... EBCI
European Biotech Partnering Event .... EBPE
European Biotechnology Information Project [*British Library*] [*Information service or system*] (IID) .... EBIP
European Bird Strike Committee (PDAA) .... EBSC
European Bitumen Association (EA) .... EUROBITUME
European Blind Union (EA) .... EBU
European Blue Cross Youth Association (EAIO) .... EBY
European Bone Marrow Transplantation .... EBMT
European Boxing Union .... EBU
European Brain and Behaviour Society (PDAA) .... EBBS
European Brazilian Bank [*London, England*] .... EBB
European Brazilian Bank .... EUROBRAZ
European Brewery Convention .... EBC
European Bridge League (EAIO) .... EBL
European Broadcasting Union [*Switzerland*] .... EBU
European Bureau for Lesser Used Languages (EA) .... EBLUL

European Bureau for the Allocation of International Long Lines (NATG) .... EBAILL

European Bureau for Youth and Childhood .... EBYC

European Bureau of Adult Education (EAIO) .... EBAE

European Bureau of Library Information and Documentation Associations (AIE) .... EBLIDA

European Business Associates [Information systems marketing organization] (NITA) .... EBA

European Business Aviation Association (EAIO) .... EBAA

European Business Information .... CGE

European Business Journal [A publication] .... EBJ

European Business School Librarians Group [London Business School] [Information service or system] (IID) .... EBSLG

European Business Services Directory [A publication] .... EBSD

European Businessmen Readership Study [Database] [Research Services Ltd.] [Information service or system] (CRD) .... EBRS

European Button Industries Federation [British] (EAIO) .... EBIF

European CAD Integration Project (NITA) .... ECIP

European CAD [Computer-Aided Design] Standardization Initiative [Computer science] .... ECSI

European Calcified Tissue Society (EA) .... ECTS

European Calibration Line .... ECL

European Capsules Association [EC] (ECED) .... EUCAPA

European Car and Truck Rental Association (EA) .... ECATRA

European Caravan Federation (EA) .... ECF

European Carton Makers Association (PDAA) .... ECMA

European Catalysts Manufacturers Association [of the European Council of Chemical Manufacturers' Federation] (EAIO) .... ECMA

European Catering Association [Germany] (EAIO) .... ECA

European Cell Biology Organization (EAIO) .... ECBO

European Cell Death Organisation .... ECDO

European Cellars [Commercial firm British] .... EC

European Cement Association (EAIO) .... CEMBUREAU

European Center for Medium-Range Weather Forecasting .... ECMWF

European Center for Research and Information Exchange [Belgium] (EAIO) .... ECRIE

European Center for the Validation of Alternative Methods [To animals for biological testing, Italy] .... ECVAM

European Central Bank .... ECB

European Central Inland Movements of Transport .... ECIMOT

European Central Inland Transport Organization .... ECITO

European Central NOTAM [Notice to Airmen] Facility [Military] .... ECNF

European Centre for Automatic Translation [Luxembourg] (NITA) .... ECAT

European Centre for Leisure and Education (EA) .... ECLE

European Centre for Medical Application and Research (EAIO) .... CERAMBRUX

European Centre for Medium Range Weather Forecasts (EERA) .... ECMWF

European Centre for Medium-Range Weather Forecasts (PDAA) .... ECMRWF

European Centre for Nature Conservation (EERA) .... ECNC

European Centre for Parliamentary Research and Documentation [See also CERDP] [Luxembourg, Luxembourg] (EAIO) .... ECPRD

European Centre for Population Studies (EA) .... ECPS

European Centre for Social Welfare Training and Research [See also CEFRAS] [United Nations] (EAIO) .... ECSWTR

European Centre for Studies of Sulfuric Acid (EAIO) .... ECSSA

European Centre for Work and Society (EA) .... ECWS

European Centre of Public Enterprise (EAIO) .... ECPE

European Centre of Studies on Linear Alkylbenzene [Belgium] (EAIO) .... ECOSOL

European Centre of Studies on Linear Alkylbenzene (EAIO) .... ECSLA

European Chamber of Extra-Judicial Adjudicators and Expert Technical Advisers [See also CEASPECT] (EA) .... ECEJAETA

European Channel Tunnel Group [Planning a proposed tunnel between England and France under the English Channel] .... ECTG

European Chemical Coastal Tanker Owners .... ECCTO

European Chemical Data and Infomation Network [EURATOM] (PDAA) ..... ECDIN

European Chemical Industry Ecology and Toxicology Centre [Belgium] (PDAA) .... ECETOC

European Chemical News [Reed Business Publishing Ltd.] [Information service or system] (CRD) .... ECN

European Chemical Society .... ECS

European Chemoreception Research Organization [Research center Switzerland] (IRC) .... ECRO

European Chips and Snacks Association [British] (EAIO) .... ECSA

European Chiropractors' Union .... ECU

European Chlorinated Solvent Association (EAIO) .... ECSA

European Choral Association (EA) .... ECA

European Christian Democratic Union [Brussels, Belgium Political party] (EAIO) .... ECDU

European Christian Mission .... ECM

European Citric Acid Manufacturers Association [of the European Council of Chemical Manufacturers' Federations] (EAIO) .... ECAMA

European Civil Affairs .... ECA

European Civil Affairs Division [US Military Government, Germany] .... ECAD

European Civil Affairs Regiment .... ECAR

European Civil Aviation Conference [See also CEAC] (EAIO) .... ECAC

European Civil Service Federation (EAIO) .... ECSF

European Clamping Tools Association [EC] (ECED) .... EUROCLAMP

European Clothing Association [Belgium] (EAIO) .... ECLA

European Coal and Steel Community [France, West Germany, Italy, BENELUX] .... ECSC

European Coal Data Bank [DECHEMA] [Germany Information service or system] (IID) .... COALDATA

European Coal Organization .... ECO

European Coffee Federation (EAIO) .... ECF

European Coil Coating Association .... ECCA

European Collaborative Interspecies Backcross [Genetic mapping resource] .... EUCIB

European Collaborative Linkage of Agriculture and Industry through Research [EC] (ECED) .... ECLAIR

European Collection of Animal Cell Cultures [Cell bank] (ECON) .... ECACC

European Collectors and Modellers Association (EAIO) .... ECMA

European Colloid and Interface Society .... ECIS

European Colloquium on Heterocyclic Chemistry .... ECHC

European Combat Aircraft (PDAA) .... ECA

European Command [Military] .... EUCOM

European Command [Military] .... EURCOM

European Command and Control Console System [DoD] .... ECCCS

European Command Coordination Committee [Military] (AABC) .... ECCC

European Command Nuclear Interface Element Fastbreak (MCD) .... EUNICEF

European Commercial Register [EC] (ECED) .... ECR

European Commission .... EC

European Commission for the Control of Foot-and-Mouth Disease .... ECCFD

European Commission Host Organization [Commission of the European Communities] [Host system] [Luxembourg] [Information service or system] (IID) .... ECHO

European Commission Library Automated System [Database] [EC] (ECED) .... ECLAS

European Commission of Human Rights (EA) .... ECHR

European Commission on Agriculture [FAO] [United Nations] .... ECA

European Committee for Agricultural and Horticultural Tools and Implements (EA) .... ECAHTI

European Committee for Building Technical Equipment [See also CEETB] (EAIO) .... ECBTE

European Committee for Clinical Laboratory Standards [Kent, England] .... ECCLS

European Committee for Cocoa Trade Organisations (EERA) .... ECCTO

European Committee for Consultant Services (EA) .... ECCS

European Committee for Future Activities (PDAA) .... ECFA

European Committee for IT [Information Technology] Testing and Certification (OSI) .... ECITC

European Committee for Mini-Basketball [See also CEMB] [Germany] (EAIO) .... ECMB

European Committee for the Development of the Meuse and Meuse/Rhine Links (EAIO) .... ECDMMRL

European Committee for the Study of Salt (EA) .... ECSS

European Committee for the Valves and Fittings Industry [Germany] (EAIO) .... ECVFI

European Committee for Young Farmers and 4H Clubs (EA) .... ECYFC

European Committee for Young Farmers and 4H Clubs [Germany] (EAIO) ECYFC4HC

European Committee of Associations of Manufacturers of Gears and Transmission Parts [EC] (ECED) .... EUROTRANS

European Committee of Associations of Manufacturers of Internal Combustion Engines (EA) .... EUROMOT

European Committee of Associations of Manufacturers of Welding Products (EA) .... ECAMWP

European Committee of Associations of Printing and Paper Converting Machinery (EA) .... EUMAPRINT

European Committee of Chemical Plant Manufacturers [EC] (ECED) .... EUCHEMAP

European Committee of Crop Protection .... ECP

European Committee of Food, Catering, and Allied Workers' Unions within the IUF [International Union of Food and Allied Workers' Associations] (EAIO) .... ECF-IUF

European Committee of Forging and Stamping Industries (EAIO) .... EUROFORGE

European Committee of Industrial Furnace and Heating Equipment Associations [EC] [Germany] (EAIO) .... CECOF

European Committee of Machinery Manufacturers for Plastics and Rubber Industries [EC] (ECED) .... EUROMAP

European Committee of Machinery Manufacturers for the Plastics and Rubber Industries (PDAA) .... EUROMPAP

European Committee of Manufacturers of Compressors, Vacuum Pumps, and Pneumatic Tools (EA) .... PNEUROP

European Committee of Manufacturers of Electrical Machines and Power Electronics [France] (EAIO) .... CEMEP

European Committee of Private Hospitals [Belgium] (EAIO) .... ECPH

European Committee of Pump Manufacturers (EA) .... EUROPUMP

European Committee of the International Ozone Association [See also CEAIO] (EA) .... EC-IOA

European Committee of Ventilating Equipment Manufacturers (PDAA) .... EUROVENT

European Committee of Weighing Instrument Manufacturers (EAIO) .... ECWIM

European Committee on Crime Problems .... ECCP

European Committee on Future Accelerators [Nuclear energy] .... ECFA

European Committee on Milk-Butter-Fat Recording .... ECMBR

European Committee on Ocean and Polar Science .... ECOPS

European Commmunity of Cooperative Societies (PDAA) .... EUROCOOP

European Commodities Exchange [of the European Economic Community] (EA) .... ECE

European Commodities Exchange Statistical Database [United Nations] (DUND) .... ECESDB

European Common Market .... ECM

European Common Market .... EUROMART

European Communication Satellite .... ECS

European Communication Satellite System .... ECSS

European Communication Security Agency .... ECSA

European Communications .... EUROCOM

European Communications Area [Military] .... ECA

European Communications Division [Military] .... ECD

European Communications Security and Evaluation Agency of the Military Committee, London [*US Army*] (AABC) .... EUSEC
[*US*] **European** [*Command*] **Communications Zone** (DOMA) .... EUCOMM-Z
European Communist Countries (MCD) .... ECC
European Communist Party Conference .... ECPC
European Communities Biologists Association [*Belgium*] (EAIO) .... ECBA
European Communities Biologists Organization [*University of Bremen*] (EAIO) .... ECBA
European Communities Chemistry Committee (EA) .... ECCC
European Communities Court of Justice (DLA) .... ECCJ
European Community [*Collective name given to the consolidation of the European Coal and Steel Community, the Common Market, and the European Atomic Energy Community*] .... EC
European Community Banking Federation [*Belgium*] (EAIO) .... ECBF
European Community Bureau of Reference (ACII) .... BCR
European Community Cocoa Trade Organization (EAIO) .... ECCTO
European Community Commission (MCD) .... ECC
European Community Convention on the Jurisdiction of the Courts and Enforcement of Judgments in Civil and Commercial Matters [*27 Sept. 1968*] (DLA) .... Conv FJ
European Community Information Service (EA) .... ECIS
European Community Marketing Authorisation Number (ECON) .... ECMA
European Community Mortgage Federation [*Brussels, Belgium*] (EA) .... ECMF
European Community Research Council .... ECRC
European Community Shipowners' Associations [*Belgium*] (EAIO) .... ECSA
European Community Visitors Program .... ECVP
European Community Youth Exchange Bureau (AIE) .... ECYEB
European Community Youth Orchestra [*British*] (EAIO) .... ECYO
European Companions (EAIO) .... EC
European Company for the Chemical Processing of Irradiated Fuels (DS) .... EURO CHEMIC
European Competition Law Review [*A publication*] (DLA) .... ECLR
European Composite Unit [*European Economic Community*] .... EURCO
European Compression Technique [*Bone screw and internal fixation*] [*Orthopedics*] (DAVI) .... ECT
European Computer Industry Research Centre (PDAA) .... ECIRC
European Computer Industry Research Centre .... ECRC
European Computer Industry Research Centre [*Munich (FRG)*] (NITA) .... ECRC
European Computer Lessors and Trading Association (PDAA) .... ECLAT
European Computer Manufacturers Association [*Switzerland*] .... ECMA
European Computer Manufacturers Association Algorithmic Language .... ECMALGOL
European Computer Measurement Association .... ECOMA
European Computer Program Information Centre [*Databank*] (NITA) .... EUROCOPI
European Computing Congress .... EUROCOMP
European Computing Services Association .... ECSA
European Confederation for Physical Therapy (EAIO) .... ECPT
European Confederation for Trade in Paint, Wall- and Floorcoverings (EAIO) .... ECTPWF
European Confederation of Agriculture .... ECA
European Confederation of Free Trade Unions [*Later, ETUC*] .... ECFTU
European Confederation of Independents [*Germany*] (EAIO) .... ECI
European Confederation of Iron and Steel Industries [*EC*] (ECED) .... EUROFER
European Confederation of Medical Suppliers Associations (EA) .... EUCOMED
European Confederation of Plastics Convertors [*EC*] (ECED) .... EPC
European Confederation of Public Relations [*France*] (EAIO) .... ECPR
European Confederation of Retail Tobacconists [*Luxembourg*] (EA) .... ECRT
European Confederation of Scouts (EAIO) .... ECS
European Confederation of Youth Clubs (EA) .... ECYC
European Conference in Social Science Information and Documentation (NITA) .... ECSSID
European Conference of Associations of Telecommunications Cables Industries [*EC*] (ECED) .... EUROTELCAB
European Conference of Associations of Telecommunications Industries (OSI) .... EUCATEL
European Conference of Associations of Telecommunications Industries (NITA) .... EUCATEL
European Conference of Conscripts Organisations (EAIO) .... ECCO
European Conference of Meteorological Experts for Aeronautics .... ECMEA
European Conference of Ministers of Transport (EAIO) .... ECMT
European Conference of Postal and Telecommunications Administration (OSRA) .... CEPT
European Conference of Radiotelegraphy Experts for Aeronautics .... ECREA
European Conference on Flammability and Fire Retardants .... EUCOFF
European Conference on LASER Interaction with Matter and LASER Thermonuclear Fusion (PDAA) .... ECLIM
European Conference on Mixing and Centrifugal Separation .... ECMCS
European Conference on Molecular Biology .... ECMB
European Conference on Optical Systems and Applications (PDAA) .... ECOSA
European Conference on Research into Management of Information (NITA) .... EURIM
European Conference on Research into the Management of Information Systems and Libraries (PDAA) .... EURIM
European Conference on Satellite Communications (MCD) .... ECSC
European Conference on Surface Science .... ECOSS
European Conference on Telecommunications by Satellite .... ECTS
European Conflict Analysis Project [*NATO*] .... ECAP
European Congress of Biotechnology .... ECB
European Congress on Metallic Corrosion (PDAA) .... EUROCOR
European Consortium Communications Satellite (MCD) .... EUROCOMSAT
European Consortium for Political Research [*Colchester, Essex, England*] (EAIO) .... ECPR
European Consultants Directory [*A publication*] .... ECD
European Consultation on Refugees and Exiles .... ECRE
European Consumer Law Group (EA) .... ECLG
European Consumer Product Safety Association [*EC*] (ECED) .... ECPSA
European Consumers Organization [*Belgium*] (EAIO) .... ECO
European Contact Group on Urban Industrial Mission (EAIO) .... ECG
European Container Glass Federation (EA) .... ECGF
European Container Manufacturers Committee (EA) .... ECMC
European Control Data User's Organization (EA) .... ECODU
European Cooperation in Information Processing (PDAA) .... ECIP
European Cooperation in Social Science Information and Documentation .... ECSSID
European Cooperation on Science and Technology [*British*] .... ECOST
European Cooperation Research Group [*European parliamentarians*] .... EUCORG
European Cooperation Space Environment Committee .... ECOSEC
European Cooperative Longterm Initiative for Defense [*NATO*] .... EUCLID
European Coordinating Committee .... ECC
European Coordinating Committee for Artificial Intelligence (EAIO) .... ECCAI
European Coordination Bureau for International Youth Organizations G2 [*See also BEC*] (EAIO) .... ECB
European Copper Sulphate Manufacturers' Association (EAIO) .... ECSMA
European Core Inventory of Existing Substances [*Chemicals which are exempt from new product regulations*] .... ECOIN
European Corn Borer [*Agronomy*] .... ECB
European Council for Animal Welfare (EA) .... ECAW
European Council for Education by Correspondence .... CEC
European Council for Environmental Law (PDAA) .... ECEL
European Council for Nondestructive Testing (EA) .... ECNDT
European Council for Nuclear Research (DCTA) .... ECNR
European Council for Payments Systems .... ECPS
European Council of International Schools (EA) .... ECIS
European Council of Jewish Community Services (EA) .... ECJCS
European Council of National Associations of Independent Schools [*Denmark*] (EAIO) .... ECNAIS
European Council of Women [*Belgium*] (EAIO) .... ECW
European Council on Refugees and Exiles .... ECRE
European Court Reports [*European Communities*] [*A publication*] (DLA) .... ECR
European Crystallographic Committee [*International Council of Scientific Unions*] .... ECC
European Cultural Centre [*Geneva, Switzerland*] .... ECC
European Cultural Foundation (EAIO) .... ECF
European Culture Collections' Organization (EAIO) .... ECCO
European Currency Unit [*European monetary system*] (AF) .... ECU
European Cutting Tools Association (EA) .... ECTA
European Data Relay Satellite .... EDRS
European Database [*Databank on election results*] (NITA) .... EUROBASE
European Datamanager Users Group [*London, England*] (CSR) .... EDUG
European Deaf Swimming Championships [*British*] .... EDSC
European Defense Analysis Center (MCD) .... EUDAC
European Defense Community [*NATO*] .... EDC
European Defense Force (NATG) .... EDF
European Defense Improvement Program [*NATO*] (MCD) .... EDIP
European Democratic Alliance [*Political movement*] (ECON) .... EDA
European Democratic Group [*European Parliament*] (ECED) .... ED
European Democratic Group in the European Parliament [*Brussels, Belgium*] [*Political party*] (EAIO) .... EDGEP
European Demolition Association (EA) .... EDA
European Demonstrtion Reprocessing Plant [*Nuclear energy*] (NUCP) .... EDRP
European Depositary Receipt [*Investment term*] .... EDR
European Desalination Association [*Glasgow, Scotland*] (EAIO) .... EDA
European Dessert Mixes Manufacturers' Association [*EC*] (ECED) .... EDMMA
European Development Education Curriculum Network .... EDECN
European Development Fund (EY) .... EDF
European Diabetes Pregnancy Study Group [*of the European Association for the Study of Diabetes*] (EAIO) .... EDPSG
European Dialysis and Transplant Nurses Association/European Renal Care Association [*Formerly, European Dialysis and Transplant Nurses Associaton*] (EA) .... EDTNA/ERCA
European Digital Road-mapping Association .... EDRA
European Direct Marketing Association [*Jona/SG, Switzerland*] (EAIO) .... EDMA
European Direct Marketing Association List Council [*Jona/SG, Switzerland*] [*Inactive*] (EA) .... EDMALC
European Directory of Marine Environmental Data [*Marine science*] (OSRA) .... EDMED
European Disarmament Conference .... EDC
European Disposables and Nonwovens Association .... EDANA
European Disposables Association [*Belgium*] (PDAA) .... EDA
European Distribution and Accounting Agency of the Military Committee, London [*US Army*] (AABC) .... EUDAC
European Distribution System [*DoD*] .... EDS
European Distribution System Aircraft [*DoD*] .... EDSA
European Division Naval Facilities Engineering Command .... DIREURDOCKS
European Division Naval Facilities Engineering Command .... EURNAVFACENGCOM
European Documentation [*Research Service*] .... EURODOC
European Documentation and Information System for Education [*Council of Europe*] [*Database*] (IID) .... EUDISED
European Documentation Centre [*University of Dundee*] [*Dundee, Scotland*] (DLA) .... EDC
European Dun's Market Identifiers [*Information service or system*] (IID) .... EDMI
European DX Council [*Huntingdon, Cambridgeshire, England*] (EAIO) .... EDXC
European Economic Area (ECON) .... EEA
European Economic Community (TDOB) .... ECC
European Economic Community [*Common Market*] .... EEC
European Economic Community - Liaison Committee of Midwives (EAIO) .... EEC-LCM
European Economic Community - Shipbuilders' Linking Committee [*Brussels, Belgium*] (EAIO) .... EEC-SLC

European Economic Interest Grouping ... EEIG
European Economic Research and Advisory Consortium [*Belgium*] (EAIO) ... ERECO
European Economic Space ... EES
European Ecumenical Commission for Church and Society [*Formerly, Ecumenical Commission for Church and Society*] (EA) ... EECCS
European Ecumenical Organization for Development [*Brussels, Belgium*] (EAIO) ... EECOD
European Electronic Component Manufacturers Association (EAIO) ... EECA
European Electronic Intelligence Center (MCD) ... EEIC
European Electronic Security Division [*Military*] ... EESD
European Electro-Optics Conference and Exhibition ... EEO
European Electrostatic Discharge Association [*British*] (EAIO) ... EEDS
European Enterprises Development Co. [*Luxembourg*] ... EED
European Environment Agency ... EEA
European Environment Bureau (EERA) ... EEB
European Environmental Bureau [*Belgium*] ... EEB
European Environmental Mutagen Society [*Leiden, Netherlands*] (EAIO) ... EEMS
European Environmental Research Organization ... EERO
European Esperanto Union (EA) ... EEU
European Exchange System ... EES
European Expedition Guild (EA) ... EEG
European Expidite [*Belgium ICAO designator*] (FAAC) ... EUX
European Faculty Directory [*A publication*] ... EFD
European Fair Trade Association [*Netherlands*] (EAIO) ... EFTA
European Fairytale Association [*See also EMG*] [*Rheine, Federal Republic of Germany*] (EAIO) ... EFA
European Fast Reactor [*Physics*] ... EFR
European Federalist Movement ... EFM
European Federation for AIDS Research ... EFAR
European Federation for Company Sports (EAIO) ... EFCS
European Federation for Intercultural Learning (EAIO) ... EFIL
European Federation for Medical Informatics (EAIO) ... EFMI
European Federation for Medical Informatics [*Sweden*] (EAIO) ... MIE
European Federation for Retirement Provision (ECON) ... EFRP
European Federation for the Advancement of Anaesthesia in Dentistry [*Italy*] (EAIO) ... EFAAD
European Federation for the Protection of Waters ... EFPW
European Federation of Agricultural Workers' Unions [*EC*] (ECED) ... EFA
European Federation of Air Traffic Controllers Association ... EFATCA
European Federation of Associations of Coffee Roasters (EA) ... EUCA
European Federation of Associations of Health Product Manufacturers (EAIO) ... EHPM
European Federation of Building and Woodworkers (EA) ... EFBWW
European Federation of Building Societies (EAIO) ... EFBS
European Federation of Catalysis Societies ... EFCATS
European Federation of Catering Equipment Manufacturers (EA) ... EFCEM
European Federation of Ceramic Sanitaryware Manufacturers (EA) ... EFCSM
European Federation of Chemical and General Workers Unions (EAIO) ... EFCGU
European Federation of Chemical Engineering [*See also EFCIW*] (EAIO) ... EFCE
European Federation of Chemical Engineering ... EFChE
European Federation of Corrosion (EA) ... EFC
European Federation of Cytology Societies (EAIO) ... EFCS
European Federation of Earthenware, China and Tableware, and Ornamental Ware (EAIO) ... FEPF
European Federation of Employees in Public Services (EAIO) ... EUROFEDOP
European Federation of Fiber Cement Manufacturers [*EC*] (ECED) ... EFFM
European Federation of Finance Houses Association [*Belgium*] (PDAA) ... EUROFINAS
European Federation of Financial Analysts' Societies (EA) ... EFFAS
European Federation of Flight Engineers ... EFFE
European Federation of Food Science and Technology (EA) ... EFFoST
European Federation of Investment Funds and Companies (ECON) ... EFIFC
European Federation of Liberal, Democratic, and Reform Parties (EAIO) ... ELDR
European Federation of Manufacturers of Multi-wall Paper Sacks [*France*] (PDAA) ... EUROSAC
European Federation of Medicinal Chemistry (EAIO) ... EFMC
European Federation of National Maintenance Societies [*Sweden*] ... EFNMS
European Federation of Optical and Precision Instruments Industry [*EC*] (ECED) ... EUROM
European Federation of Organizations for Medical Physics [*EC*] (ECED) ... EFOMP
European Federation of Pallet and Wooden Crate Manufacturers (EA) ... EFPWCM
European Federation of Parasitologists (EAIO) ... EFP
European Federation of Pharmaceutical Industries' Associations (EA) ... EFPIA
European Federation of Productivity Services [*Stockholm, Sweden*] (EA) ... EFPS
European Federation of Professional Florists' Unions [*Italy*] (EAIO) ... FEUPF
European Federation of Professional Psychologists Associations (EA) ... EFPPA
European Federation of Purchasing (PDAA) ... EFP
European Federation of Quick Frozen Food Manufacturers [*Belgium*] (EAIO) ... EFQFFM
European Federation of Retail Traders [*Belgium*] (EAIO) ... EFRT
European Federation of Sea Anglers (EAIO) ... EFSA
European Federation of Societies of Ultrasound in Medicine and Biology (EAIO) ... EFSUMB
European Federation of the Associations of Dietitians (EAIO) ... EFAD
European Federation of the Brush and Paint Brush Industries (EA) ... EFBPBI
European Federation of the Plywood Industry (EA) ... EFPI
European Federation of Tobacco Retail Organizations (EAIO) ... EFTRO
European Federation of Trade Unions for Energy, Chemical, and Miscellaneous Industries (EA) ... ECI
European Federation of Trade Unions of Non-Manual Workers [*Belgium*] (EY) ... EFTUNMW
European Federation of Vending Associations (EA) ... EFVA
European Federation of Young Choirs [*See also EFJC*] (EA) ... EFYC
European Fertilizer Importers' Associations (EAIO) ... EFIA
European Fertilizer Manufacturers Association (EAIO) ... EFMA
European Fiber Optic Communications and Local Area Network Exposition [*Information Gatekeepers, Inc.*] ... EFOC/LAN
European Fighter Aircraft ... EFA
European Finance Association (EAIO) ... EFA
European Financial Management and Marketing Association (EAIO) ... EFMA
European Fishing Tackle Trade Association (EAIO) ... EFTTA
European Fittings Manufacturers Association (EAIO) ... EFMA
European Flavour and Fragrance Association [*Belgium*] (EAIO) ... EFFA
European Flexible Intermediate Bulk Container Association (PDAA) ... EFIBCA
European Flexographic Technical Association (PDAA) ... EFTA
European Fluorocarbon Technical Committee [*Belgium*] (EAIO) ... EFCTEC
European Fluorocarbon Technical Committee [*of the European Council of Chemical Manufacturers' Federations*] [*Belgium*] (EAIO) ... EFTC
European Fluorocarbon Technical Committee [*of the European Council of Chemical Manufacturers' Federations*] (EAIO) ... EFTEC
European Folk Art and Craft Federation [*Zurich, Switzerland*] (EAIO) ... EFACF
European Food Distributors Association (PDAA) ... EUFODA
European Food Phosphates Producers' Association (EAIO) ... EFPA
European Food Service and Packaging Association [*British*] (EAIO) ... EFPA
European Football Commentators Association Television (EA) ... EFCAT
European Foreign Trade Association ... EFTA
European Forest Institute ... EFI
European Forestry Commission ... EFC
European Formula Drivers Association (EAIO) ... EFDA
European Foundation (DS) ... EF
European Foundation for Landscape Architecture [*EC*] (ECED) ... EFLA
European Foundation for Management Development (EAIO) ... EFMD
European Franchise Federation [*France*] (EAIO) ... EFF
European Free Alliance [*See also ALE*] [*Brussels, Belgium Political party*] (EAIO) ... EFA
European Free Exchange Area (NATG) ... EFEA
European Free Trade Area (DS) ... EFTA
European Free Trade Association [*Known as the "Outer Seven" as opposed to the "Inner Six" Common Market nations*] [*Switzerland*] ... EFTA
European Free Trade Association (EERA) ... EFTA
European Freight Timetable Conference (EAIO) ... EFTC
European Frequency Coordinating Body [*ICAO*] (DA) ... EUR FCB
European Fuel Oxygenates Association (EAIO) ... EFOA
European Funeral Directors' Association (EAIO) ... EFDA
European Furniture Federation ... EFF
European Future Advanced Rotocraft (MCD) ... EUROFAR
European General Galvanizers Association (EA) ... EGGA
European Geographical Information Systems Symposia (EERA) ... EGIS
European Geophysical Society (EAIO) ... EGS
European Geophysical Society Working Group on Tsunami [*Marine science*] (OSRA) ... EGSWG
European Geostationary Navigation Overlay System ... EGNOS
European Geostationary Navigation Overlay System ... EGNOS
European Geotraverse [*A collaborative lithosphere study*] ... EGT
European Glass Container Manufacturers' Committee [*British*] (EAIO) ... EGCMC
European Glass Container Manufacturers' Committee [*British*] ... EGM
European Good Templar Youth Federation [*Norway*] (EAIO) ... EGTYF
European Grassland Federation (EA) ... EGF
European Greens [*Brussels, Belgium Political party*] (EAIO) ... EG
European Group for Atomic Spectroscopy (EAIO) ... EGAS
European Group for Cooperation in Management (PDAA) ... EGCM
European Group for Organizational Studies [*British*] (SLS) ... EGOS
European Group of Artists of the Ardennes and the Eifel (EAIO) ... EGAAE
European Group of Cellulose Manufacturers [*Defunct*] (EA) ... EGCM
European Group of Corrugated Paper Makers (EAIO) ... EGCPM
European Group of Journalists/International Federation of Journalists [*EC*] (ECED) ... EGJ/IFJ
European Group of Lymphology [*Belgium*] (EAIO) ... EGL
European Group of Public Administration [*See also GEAP*] [*Brussels, Belgium*] (EAIO) ... EGPA
European Group of Television Advertising (EA) ... EGTA
European Guide to Industrial Trading Regulations and Practice [*EC*] (ECED) ... GINTRAP
European Heads of Research Councils ... Eurohorc
European Health Policy Forum (EAIO) ... EHPF
European Health Policy Research Network [*British*] (ECON) ... EHPRN
European Healthcare Management Association (EAIO) ... EHMA
European Helicopter Association (PDAA) ... EHA
European Herbal Infusions Association (EA) ... EHIA
European High Pressure Research Group (EA) ... EHPRG
European High Temperature Nuclear Power Stations Society (EAIO) ... EURO-HKG
European Histamine Research Society (EAIO) ... EHRS
European Host Network [*Computer science*] ... EHN
European Host Operators Group [*EURONET*] [*Luxembourg*] ... EHOG
European Hotel Managers Association (EA) ... EHMA
European Human Rights (EAIO) ... EHR
European Humanities Research Centre [*University of Warwick*] [*British*] (CB) ... EHRC
European Incoherent Scattering Scientific Association ... EISCAT
[*Association of the*] **European Independent Information Industry** (NITA) ... EIII
European Independent Steelworks Association (EAIO) ... EISA
European Independents Confederation (EAIO) ... EIC
European Industrial Fasteners Institute [*EC*] (ECED) ... EIFI
European Industrial Planning Group [*NATO*] ... EIPG
European Industrial Research Management Association [*France*] ... EIRMA

European Industrial Space Study Group .... EUROSPACE
European Informatics Network (NITA) .... EIN
European Information Association [EC] (ECED) .... EIA
European Information Centre (AIE) .... EIC
European Information Industry Association [Database producer] (IID) .... EIIA
European Information Industry Association [Formerly, European Information
  Providers Association] [Information retrieval] (IID) .... EURIPA
European Information Network [Telecommunications] (TEL) .... EIN
European Information Providers Association (NITA) .... EURIPA
European Information Researchers Network (IID) .... EIRENE
European Information Service [Belgium] (NITA) .... EURIS
European Inland Fisheries Advisory Commission [Food and Agriculture
  Organization] [United Nations] (ASF) .... EIFAC
European Institute for Advanced Studies in Management [Information
  service or system] (IID) .... EIASM
European Institute for the Media (EA) .... EIM
European Institute for Trans-National Studies in Group and Organizational
  Development (EA) .... EIT
European Institute for Water (EAIO) .... EIW
European Institute of Ecology and Cancer [Formerly, European Institute of
  Cancerology] (EA) .... EIEC
European Institute of Education and Social Policy (AIE) .... EIESP
European Institute of Hunting and Sporting Weapons (EAIO) .... EIHSW
European Institute of Printed Circuits (EA) .... EIPC
European Institute of Public Administration (EA) .... EIPA
European Institute of Technology [International Consortium of Industrial
  Firms] .... EIT
European Insulation Manufacturers Association (PDAA) .... EURIMA
European Insurance Committee [Paris, France] (EA) .... EIC
European Integrated Network of Image and Services (EAIO) .... EINIS
European Integrated Services Digital Network [Telecommunications]
  (ECON) .... EuroISDN
European Intelligent Actuation and Measurement User Group (ACII) ..... EIAMUG
European Interactive Media [Joint venture of Philips International and
  PolyGram BV International] .... EIM
European International Business Association [Brussels, Belgium] (EA) ...... EIBA
European Interprofessional Market (ECON) .... EIM
[The] European Interuniversity Association on Society, Science, and
  Technology [Lausanne, Switzerland] (ECON) .... ESST
European Inventory of Existing Commercial Chemical Substances [Which
  will be exempt from new product regulations] .... EINECS
European Investment Bank (AF) .... EIB
European Investment Bank (GNE) .... EID
European Investment Casters Federation [Netherlands] (PDAA) ...... EICF
European Investment Research Bureau [Information service or system]
  (NITA) .... EIRB
European Jet Ltd. [British ICAO designator] (FAAC) .... JET
European Joint Committee of Scientific Cooperation [Council of Europe]
  (PDAA) .... EJCSC
European Joint Optical Bistability Programme [To develop an optical
  computer] .... EJOB
European Judo Union (EAIO) .... EJU
European Justice and Peace Commissions (EAIO) .... EJPC
European Kompass Online [Reed Information Services Ltd.] [Information
  service or system] .... EKOL
European Laboratory for Particle Physics .... CERN
European Landowning Organization Group (EAIO) .... ELOG
European Landscape Contractors Association (EAIO) .... ELCA
European Landworkers Federation .... ELF
European Large Orbiting Instrumentation for Solar Experiments .... ELOISE
European Laser Association (EA) .... ELA
European Late Effects Project Group (PDAA) .... EULEP
European Launcher Development Organization [Superseded by European
  Space Agency] .... ELDO
European Laundry and Dry Cleaning Machinery Manufacturers
  Organization (EA) .... ELMO
European Law Digest [A publication] (DLA) .... Eur L Dig
European Law Newsletter [A publication] (DLA) .... Eur L Newsl
European Law Review [A publication] (DLA) .... Eur L Rev
European Lead Development Committee [EC] (EA) .... ELDC
European Lead Development Committee [EC] (ECED) .... ELDEC
European League Against Rheumatism (EAIO) .... EULAR
European League for a New Society [See also LIENS] [Paris, France]
  (EAIO) .... ELNS
European League for Economic Cooperation .... ELEC
European League of Institutes of the Arts [British] .... ELIA
European Learning Technology Association (AIE) .... ELTA
European Legal Literature Information Service [London, England] ...... ELLIS
European Leisure and Recreation Association (EAIO) .... elra
European Letter Telegram .... ELT
European Liaison Committee for Osteopaths (EA) .... ELCO
European Liaison Committee for the Sewing Machine Industries [Defunct]
  (EA) .... ELCSMI
European Liaison Group [Army] (AABC) .... ELG
European Library Automation Group (PDAA) .... ELAG
European Light Infantry [British military] (DMA) .... ELI
European Liquefied Petroleum Gas Association (EA) .... ELPGA
European Logistics Task Group (MCD) .... ELTG
European Long Lines Agency [NATO] .... ELLA
European Lubricant Testing Committee .... ELTC
European Lubricating Grease Institute [An association] .... ELGI
European Lymphology Group [See also GEL] [Brussels, Belgium] (EAIO) ..... ELG
European Machine Tool Exhibition (PDAA) .... EMTE
European Mail Order Traders' Association [EC] (ECED) .... EMOTA

European MAP [Manufacturing Automation Protocol] Users Group [Automotive
  engineering] .... EMUG
European Mariculture Society (EAIO) .... EMS
European Market Development .... EMD
European Marketing Academy (EAIO) .... EMAC
European Marketing Association [Brixham, Devonshire, England] (EA) .... EMA
European Marketing Research Board [British] .... EMRB
European Master in Society, Science, and Technology [Swiss Federal
  Institute of Technology, Lausanne] (ECON) .... ESST
European Master's in International Business .... EMIB
European Mastic Asphalt Association (EA) .... EMAA
European Mathematical Council (EA) .... EMC
European Mechanics Colloquia (PDAA) .... EUROMECH
European Mechanics Committee (EAIO) .... EMC
European Mechanics Committee [ICSU] .... EUROMECH
European Medical Research Councils [ESF] (PDAA) .... EMRC
European Medicines Evaluation Agency [London] .... EMEA
European Mediterranean Aeronautical Fixed Telecommunications
  Network (PDAA) .... EUM-AFTN
European Mediterranean Commission on Water Planning (EA) ...... EMCWP
European Mediterranean Troposphere (IEEE) .... EMT
European Medium and Small Business Union (PDAA) .... EMSU
European Metalworkers' Federation in the Community [EC] (ECED) ...... EMF
European Meteorological Satellite (MCD) .... EUMETSAT
European Meteorological Telecommunications Network (PDAA) ...... EMTN
European Microwave Conference and Exhibition [British] (ITD) ..... EUMC
European Microwave Signature Laboratory [Italy] .... EMSL
European Military Communication (IEEE) .... EMC
European Military Communications Co-Ordinating Committee [NATO] ..... EMCCC
European Mills Association [EC] (ECED) .... AEM
European Mineworkers' Union [Zambia] .... EMU
European Missionary Fellowship .... EMF
European Mobility Service Office [Army] (AABC) .... EMSO
European Molecular Biology Conference .... EMB
European Molecular Biology Laboratory .... EMBI
European Molecular Biology Laboratory [Research center Germany]
  (IRC) .... EMBL
European Molecular Biology Laboratory Data Library (DOG) ..... EMBL Data Library
European Molecular Biology Organization [ICSU] [Germany] .... EMBO
European Monetary Agreement .... EMA
European Monetary Co-Operation Fund [Bank for International Settlements]
  (EY) .... EMCF
European Monetary Co-Operation Fund .... EMCOF
European Monetary Fund [Proposed] .... EMF
European Monetary Institute (ECON) .... EMI
European Monetary Reserve Fund [Common Market] .... EMRF
European Monetary System (AF) .... EMS
European Monetary Union .... EMU
European Monetary Unit [Proposed] .... EMU
European Monetary Unit of Account .... EMUA
European Monitoring and Evaluation Programme [Environmental
  research] .... EMEP
European Motor Products, Inc. [Auto industry supplier] .... EMPI
European Motorcycle Association [Defunct] (EA) .... EMA
European Movement .... EM
European Multifunction Phased-Array RADAR (MCD) .... EMPAR
European Municipal Credit Community .... EMCC
European Muon Collaboration [Nuclear research] .... EMC
European Muon Collaboration [Nuclear physics] .... EMC
European Natural Hygiene Society (EAIO) .... ENHS
European Natural Sausage Casings Association (EA) .... ENSCA
European Naval Communications Agency [NATO] .... ENCA
European Naval Communications Plan [NATO] (NATG) .... ENCP
European Navigation Satellite System .... ENSS
European Nervous System .... ENS
European Network - Direct Information Access Network for Europe
  [Computer science] (HGAA) .... EURONET-DIANE
European Network for East-West Dialogue (EA) .... ENEWD
European Network for Science [Marine science] (OSRA) .... ENS
European Network for the Exchange of Information on Local Employment
  Initiatives [EC] (ECED) .... ELISE
European Networking Center (HGAA) .... ENC
European Neurological Society [Switzerland] .... ENS
European Neuroscience Association (EAIO) .... ENA
European Neuroscience Programme [Defunct France] (EAIO) .... ENP
European Neurosciences Association [Bussum, Netherlands] (SLS) ...... ENA
European Nuclear Disarmament [British] .... END
European Nuclear Documentation System [Information service or
  system] .... ENDS
European Nuclear Energy Agency (DS) .... ENEA
European Nuclear Medical Society (EAIO) .... ENMS
European Nuclear Research Centre (NUCP) .... ENRC
European Nuclear Society (NUCP) .... ENS
European Nuclear Steelmaking Club [British] (NUCP) .... ENSEC
European Oceanic Association [Monaco, Monaco] (EAIO) .... EUROCEAN
European Office of Aerospace Research .... EOAR
European Office of Aerospace Research and Development .... EOARD
European Offshore Petroleum Conference and Exhibition (PDAA) ..... EUROPEC
European Oil Hydraulic and Pneumatic Committee [Italy] (EAIO) ...... EOHPC
European Olive Oil Federation [Italy] (EAIO) .... EOOF
European On-Line Information Network [Commission of the European
  Communities] [Information service or system] (IID) .... EURONET
European Options Exchange [Netherlands] .... EOE
European Options Market (DCTA) .... EOM

European Organisation for the Control of Circulatory Diseases (PDAA) .... EOCCD
European Organization for Cancer Prevention Studies .... ECP
European Organization for Civil Aviation Electronics [France] (PDAA) .... EUROCAE
European Organization for Nuclear Reserch (NUCP) .... EONR
European Organization for Quality [Switzerland] (EAIO) .... EOQ
European Organization for Research on the Treatment of Cancer [Research center Switzerland] (IRC) .... EORTC
European Organization for the Exploitation of Meteorological Satellites .... EUMETSAT
European Organization for the Promotion of New Techniques and Methods in Building (EA) .... EUROBUILD
European Organization for the Promotion of Prefabrication and other Industralized Building (PDAA) .... EUROPREFAB
European Organization for the Safety of Air Navigation .... EUROCONTROL
European Original New York Seltzer Ltd. [Vancouver Stock Exchange symbol] .... ENY
European Orthodontic Society (PDAA) .... EOS
European Packaging Federation [Denmark] (SLS) .... EPF
European Pallet Pool (PDAA) .... EPP
European Pan-Keltic League (EA) .... EPKL
European Paper Institute [Research center] .... EPI
European Parent Association (AIE) .... EPA
European Parliament .... EP
European Parliament Delegations for Latin America [Luxembourg] (EAIO) .... ELAIA
European Parliament Working Documents [A publication] (DLA) .... Eur Parl Doc
European Parliament Working Documents [A publication] (DLA) ...... Eur Parl Docs
European Parliamentary Assembly Debates [A publication] (DLA) ..... Eur Parl Deb
European Parliamentary Labor Party [European Community] [Political party] .... EPLP
European Participating Governments [In the F-16 fighter program] .... EPG
European Participating Industry .... EPI
European Partnership for Insurance Co-operation [Proposed] (ECON) .... EPIL
European Passenger Services [British] (ECON) .... EPS
European Passenger Train Timetable Conference (EA) .... EPTTC
European Patent Convention .... EPC
European Patent Office [Germany] (PDAA) .... EPO
European Patents Administration System [Information service or system] (NITA) .... EPASYS
European Payments Union .... EPU
European Pension Committee [France] (EAIO) .... EPC
European People's Party - Federation of Christian Democratic Parties of the European Community [Brussels, Belgium] .... EPP
European Petrochemical Association [Database producer] .... EPCA
European Petrochemical Industry Computerized System [Parpinelli Tecnon] [Italy Information service or system] (IID) .... EPICS
European Pharmaceutical Marketing Research Association (EAIO) .... EPhMRA
European Photochemistry Association (EAIO) .... EPA
European Physical Society (EAIO) .... EPS
European Piano Teachers Association (EAIO) .... EPTA
European Pineal Study Group (EAIO) .... EPSG
European Plan [Hotel room rate] .... EP
European Planning Federation [British] (EA) .... EPLAF
European Plantmakers Committee (EA) .... EUROPLANT
European Plasma Fractionation Association .... EPFA
European Plastics Converters [Belgium] (EAIO) .... EuPC
European Policies Research Centre [University of Strathclyde] [Glasgow, Scotland] [Database producer] (IID) .... EPRC
European Political Community (NATG) .... EPC
European Political Cooperation .... EPC
European Political Cooperation [EC] (ECED) .... POCO
European Popular Circle (EAIO) .... EPC
European Portable Battery Association .... EPBA
European Power Tool Association (EAIO) .... EPTA
European Press Group .... EPG
European Pressure Die Casting Committee (EA) .... EPDCC
European Primary Aluminum Association [Later, European Aluminium Association - EAA] (IID) .... EPAA
European Primate Resources Network .... EUPREN
European Printer Performance Test (ODBW) .... EPPT
European Producer Price .... EPP
European Productivity Agency .... EPA
European Professional Fair for Industry and Handicraft of Bakery, Confectionery,Pastry, Biscuits, Chocolate, and Ice Cream Making .... EUROBA
European Program for Ice Coring in Antarctica [Proposed start up date, 1997] .... EPICA
European Programme Group [NATO] .... EPG
European Programme of Advanced Continuing Education .... EuroPACE
European Progressive Democrats (PPE) .... EPD
European Proliferation Information Centre [British] (CB) .... EPIC
European Proprietary Medicines Manufacturers Association [Belgium] (EAIO) .... EPMMA
European Psycho-Analytical Federation (EA) .... EPF
European Public Relations Advisory Committee .... EUPRAC
European Publishers' Markup User Group .... EPMARKUP
European Pure Phosphoric Acid Producers' Association [Belgium] (EAIO) .... EPPAA
European Pure Phosphoric Acid Producers' Association [Belgium] (EAIO) .... EPPAPA
European Quality Alliance [Proposed merger between four European airlines] (ECON) .... EQA
European Radio Frequency Agency [Later, ARFA] [NATO] .... ERFA

European Radio Messaging System .... ERMES
European Railway Passenger [Ticket] .... EURAILPASS
European Railway Wagon Pool (EA) .... ERWP
European Ramblers' Association (EAIO) .... ERA
European Read Only Memory (NITA) .... EUROM
European Ready Mixed Concrete Organization (EAIO) .... ERMCO
European Recovery Program .... ERP
European Red Mite [Insect] .... ERM
European Redistribution Facility .... ERF
European Region [USTTA] (TAG) .... EUR
European Regional Airlines (PDAA) .... ERA
European Regional Airlines Association [British] (EAIO) .... ERA
European Regional Clearing House for Community Work (EAIO) .... ERCHCW
European Regional Development Fund [See also FEDER] [Brussels, Belgium] (EAIO) .... ERDF
European Regional Organization of the ICFTU .... ERO
European Regional Organization of the International Dental Federation (EAIO) .... ERO
European Regional Test Center (NATG) .... ERTC
European Registration Plate Association (EA) .... EUROPLATE
European Registry of Commerce (DS) .... ERC
European Registry of Congenital Abnormalities and Twins .... EUROCAT
European Reliability Data Association .... EuReDatA
European Remote Sensing Satellite-1 (EERA) ERS-1
European Remote Sensing Satellite-2 [Marine science] (OSRA) ERS-2
European Renderers Association (EAIO) .... EURA
European Requirements and Army Capabilities (AABC) .... EURAC
European Requirements List [Military] (AABC) .... ERL
European Research Associates .... ERA
European Research Cooperation Agency [Non-defense research study group including eighteen European countries] .... EUREKA
European Research Group for Alternatives in Toxicity Testing .... EGRATT
European Research Institute for Welding (PDAA) .... ERIW
European Research into Consumer Affairs [England] [Research center] (IRC) .... ERICA
European Research National Organization (MCD) .... ERNO
European Research Office [British] .... ERO
European Research on Advanced Materials .... EURAM
European Retrievable Carrier [Space shuttle experiment] .... EURECA
European Review of Native American Studies [A publication] .... ERNAS
European Rhinologic Society (EA) .... ERS
European Right [European Parliament] (ECED) .... DR
European Right [Political movement] (ECON) .... ER
European Road Transport Agreement (ILCA) .... ERTA
European Rotogravure Association [Germany] (PDAA) .... ERA
European Round Table (EAIO) .... ERT
European Rum Association (EAIO) .... ERA
European Satellite Agency [Marine science] (OSRA) .... ESA
European Satellite Agency/European Space Agency (USDC) .... ESA
European Satellite Consulting Organization [France Telecommunications] .... ESCO
European Satellite Launching Organization (MCD) .... ESLO
European Savings Bank Group [EC] (ECED) .... ESBG
European Schoolbooks Ltd. [British] .... ESB
European Schools Federation (EA) .... ESF
European Science and Environment Forum [An association] .... ESEF
European Science and Technology Assembly .... ESTA
European Science Foundation (EAIO) .... ESF
European Science Research Council (NUCP) .... ESRC
European Scientific Information Referral [EUSIDIC] [Information service or system] (IID) .... EUSIREF
European Scientific Information Retrieval Working Group (NITA) .... EUSIREF
European Scientific Notes [Office of Naval Research, London] (PDAA) .... ESN
European Security Conference [Soviet-sponsored] .... ESC
European Security Forum .... ESF
European Security Region [Military] .... ESR
European Security Transport Association (EA) .... ESTA
European Seismological Commission (EAIO) .... ESC
European Semiconductor Device Research Conference .... ESCERC
European Semiconductor Device Research Conference (PDAA) .... ESDERC
European Shielding Information Service [EURATOM] [Databank] (IID) .... ESIS
European Shippers' Councils [Netherlands] (DS) .... ESC
European Shock Absorber Manufacturers Association (PDAA) .... EUSAMA
European Showmen's Union [EC] (ECED) .... ESU
European Showmen's Union/Union Foraine Europeenne (EA) .... ESU/UFE
European Side Impact Dummy [Automotive engineering] .... EUROSID
European Silicon Structures (NITA) ES2
European Silicon Structures (NITA) .... ESS
European Simmental Federation (EAIO) .... ESF
European Single Service Association (EA) .... ESSA
European Social Fund .... ESF
European Society for Animal Cell Technology (EA) .... ESACT
European Society for Artificial Organs (EA) .... ESAO
European Society for Blue Cross Youth (EA) .... ESBCY
European Society for Cardiovascular Surgery (EAIO) .... ESCVS
European Society for Clinical Investigation (EAIO) .... ESCI
European Society for Engineering and Medicine .... ESEM
European Society for Engineering Education .... ESEE
European Society for Market and Opinion Research .... EOSMOR
European Society for Medical Oncology (EA) .... ESMO
European Society for Microcirculation (EA) .... ESM
European Society for Mycobacteriology (EA) .... ESM
European Society for Neurochemistry (EA) .... ESN
European Society for Noninvasive Cardiovascular Dynamics (EA) .... ESNCD
European Society for Noninvasive Cardiovascular Dynamics (EAIO) .... ESNICVD

European Society for Opinion and Market Research [*Netherlands*] .... ESOMAR
European Society for Paediatric Haematology and Immunology (EAIO)..... ESPHI
European Society for Pediatric Endocrinology (EAIO) .... ESPE
European Society for Pediatric Nephrology [*Switzerland*] (SLS) .... ESPN
European Society for Radiation Biology [*Formerly, Association of Radiobiologists from EURATOM Countries*] (EA) .... ESRB
European Society for Rural Sociology .... ESRS
European Society for the History of Photography (EA) .... ESHPH
European Society for Therapeutic Radiology and Oncology (EAIO) .... ESTRO
European Society of Air Safety Investigators (PDAA) .... ESASI
European Society of Association Executives (EA) .... ESAE
European Society of Biomechanics (EA) .... ESB
European Society of Cardiology (MCD) .... ESC
European Society of Child and Adolescent Psychiatry (EA) .... ESCAP
European Society of Climatotherapy [*See also FEC*] [*Briancon, France*] (EAIO) .... ESC
European Society of Comparative Physiology and Biochemistry (EAIO) .... ESCPB
European Society of Corporate and Strategic Planners [*Belgium*] (PDAA) .... ESCSP
European Society of Culture [*See also SEC*] (EAIO) .... ESC
European Society of Gastrointestinal Motility [*Louvain, Belgium*] (EAIO) .... ESGM
European Society of Handwriting Psychology (EAIO) .... ESHP
European Society of Membrane Science and Technology (EA) .... ESMST
European Society of Nematologists (EAIO) .... ESN
European Society of Neuroradiology (EA) .... ESN
European Society of Ophthalmic Plastic and Reconstructive Surgery (EAIO) .... ESOPRS
European Society of Osteoarthrology [*Former Czechoslovakia*] (SLS) .... ESOA
European Society of Paediatric Radiology (EA) .... ESPR
European Society of Pathology (EAIO) .... ESP
European Society of Regional Anaesthesia (EA) .... ESRA
European Society of Toxicology (EAIO) .... EST
European Society of Veterinary Pathology (EA) .... ESVP
European Solid State Device Research Conference (PDAA) .... ESSDERC
European Solid-State-Circuits Conference (PDAA) .... ESSCIRC
European Southern Observatory [*ICSU*] [*Research center Germany*] (IRC) .... ESO
European Space Agency [*See also ASE*] (EAIO) .... ESA
European Space Agency Information Network (PDAA) .... ESANET
European Space Agency Information Retrieval Service [*Italy*] .... ESA-IRS
European (Space Agency) Remote Sensing Satellite System (EERA) .... ERS
European Space Association .... ESA
European Space Conference .... ESC
European Space Data Center (MCD) .... ESDAC
European Space Information System .... ESIS
European Space Laboratory .... ESLAB
European Space Launcher Organization .... ESLO
European Space Operations Center .... ESOC
European Space Range [*Sweden*] (MCD) .... ESRANGE
European Space Research Institute .... ESRIN
European Space Research Organization [*Superseded by ESA*] .... ESRO
European Space Satellite Tracking and Telemetry Network (MCD) .... ESTRAC
European Space Satellite Tracking and Telemetry Network (BARN) ...... ESTRACK
European Space Science Committee .... ESSC
European Space Technology Center [*Netherlands*] (KSC) .... ESTC
European Space Technology Center [*Netherlands*] .... ESTEC
European Space Tribology Laboratory .... ESTL
European Space Vehicle Launcher Development Organization (MCD) .... EUR/SV/LDO
European Spallation Source [*High-energy physics*] (ECON) .... ESS
European Special Activities Area [*Military*] .... ESAA
European Special Situations Fund [*EEC*] .... ESS
European Specialist Publishers Dictionary [*A publication*] .... ESP
European Spice Association [*EC*] (ECED) .... ESA
European Sport Shooting Confederation (EAIO) .... ESC
European Sport Shooting Confederation (EAIO) .... ESSC
European Squash Rackets Federation (EA) .... ESRF
European Standard Inventory List (NATG) .... ESIL
European Standards on Nuclear Electronics Committee [*Switzerland*] ...... ESONE
[*The*] **European Static Protection and Shielding Exhibition** [*British*] (ITD) .... EUROSTAT
European Stock Exchange .... ESE
European Strabismological Association (EAIO) .... ESA
European Strategic Planning Federation [*British*] (EAIO) .... ESPLAF
European Strategic Program for Research and Development in Information Technology and Telecommunications [*Research center Belgium*] (IRC) .... ESPRIT
European Stroke Prevention Study .... ESPS
European Study Group on Lysosomal Diseases (EAIO) .... ESGLD
European Supply Agency (NATG) .... ESA
European Support Groups for Liberation and Nonviolence in Latin America (EAIO) .... ESGLNLA
European Surface-to-Air Missile [*NATO*] .... EUROSAM
European Surfing Federation (EAIO) .... ESF
European Suzuki Association [*British*] (EAIO) .... ESA
European Symposium of Independent Inspecting Organizations (EA) .... ESIIO
European Symposium on Computer Aided Process Engineering .... ESCAPE
European Synchroton Radiation Source (PDAA) .... ESRS
European Synchrotron Radiation Facility [*High-energy physics*] (ECON) ...... ESRF
European Synchrotron Radiation Facility .... ESRF
European Synchrotron Radiation Source [*High-energy physics*] .... ESRS
European System for the International Clearing of Vacancies and Applications forEmployment [*EC*] (ECED) .... SEDOC
European Systems Language (IAA) .... ESL
European Table Tennis Union (EA) .... ETTU
European Tape Industry Associaton (PDAA) .... ETIA
European Tax Confederation (EAIO) .... ETC
European Taxi Confederation [*Belgium*] (EAIO) .... ETC
European Taxpayers Association (EA) .... ETA
European Tea Committee (EA) .... ETC
European Teachers Association (BARN) .... ETA
European Teachers Trade Union Committee [*EC*] (ECED) .... ETTUC
European Technical Association for Furniture Finishes [*Defunct*] .... ETAFF
European Technical Association for Protective Coatings [*Belgium*] (SLS) .... ETAPC
European Technical Caramel Association [*EC*] (ECED) .... EUTECA
European Technical Committee for Fluorine [*of the European Council of Chemical Manufacturers' Federations*] [*Belgium*] (EAIO) .... ETCF
European Technical Information Service [*Information broker and database originator*] (NITA) .... ETIS
European Technical Network [*EC*] (ECED) .... EUROTECNET
European Technical Operations Area [*Military*] .... EURTOA
European Technical Operations Group .... ETOG
European Technical Rim and Tyre Organisation (PDAA) .... ETRTO
European Technological Forecasting Association (PDAA) .... ETFA
European Telecommunications and Professional Electronics Industry [*Europe an Conference of Associations of Telecommunications Industries and European Conference of Radio and Electronic Equipment Associations*] [*Formed by a merger of*] (EAIO) .... ECTEL
European Telecommunications Satellite [*Agency*] (BARN) .... EUTELSAT
European Telecommunications Satellite Organization [*France Telecommunications*] .... EUTELSAT
European Telecommunications Standard (OSI) .... ETS
European Telecommunications Standards Institute .... ETSI
European Telephone Marketing Council [*of the European Direct Marketing Organization*] [*Jona, Switzerland*] (EA) .... ETMC
European Telephone System [*DoD*] .... ETS
European Television .... EUROVISION
European Tennis Association (EAIO) .... ETA
European Teratology Society (EA) .... ETS
European Testing and Certification for Office and Manufacturing Protocol (OSI) .... ETCOM
European Theater .... ET
European Theater Air Command and Control Study [*DoD*] .... ETACCS
European Theater Bureau of Public Relations [*World War II*] .... ETBPR
European Theater Network Analysis Model (MCD) .... ETNAM
European Theater of Operations [*World War II*] .... ETO
European Theater of Operations, United States Army [*Pronounced "ee-too-sah"*] [*World War II*] .... ETOUSA
European Throwsters Association (EA) .... ETA
European Throwsters Association [*Italy*] (EAIO) .... FTA
European Thyroid Association (EAIO) .... ETA
European Tick-Borne Encephalitis [*Medicine*] (PDAA) .... ETASS
European Tissue Repair Society .... ETRS
European Tool Committee (EA) .... ETC
European Touring Car .... ETC
European Toy Confederation [*France*] (EAIO) .... ETC
European Toy Institute (EAIO) .... ETI
European Trade Committee [*British Overseas Trade Board*] (DS) .... ETC
European Trade Promotion Organization (DS) .... ETPO
European Trade Union Committee for Textiles, Clothing, and Leather [*Belgium Belgium*] (EAIO) .... ETUCTCL
European Trade Union Confederation [*Formerly, ECFTU*] .... ETUC
European Trade Union Institute [*Belgium*] .... ETUI
European Traffic Committee .... ETC
European Training and Development Centre for Farming and Rural Life (EA) .... ETDCFRL
European Training Foundation [*EC*] (ECED) .... ETF
European Training Programme in Brain and Behavior Research [*of the European Science Foundation*] [*France*] (EA) .... ETP
European Training Programme in Brain and Behavior Research [*of the European Science Foundation*] [*France*] (EAIO) .... ETPBBR
European Translations Centre [*Later, International Translations Centre*] .... ETC
European Transonic Wind-Tunnel .... ETW
European Transport Law [*Belgium*] [*A publication*] (DLA) .... Eur TL
European Transport Law [*Belgium A publication*] (DLA) .... Eur Trans L
European Transport Law [*Belgium A publication*] (DLA) .... Eur Transp L
European Transport Organization [*ECE*] .... ETO
European Transuranium Institute [*Germany*] .... ETI
European Trans-Uranium Institute [*Karlsruhe, Germany*] .... ETUI
European Travel Commission (EA) .... ETC
European Treaty Series [*Council of Europe*] [*A publication*] (DLA) .... ETS
European Treaty Series [*Council of Europe*] [*A publication*] (DLA) .... Europ TS
European Triathlon Union (EA) .... ETU
European Troop Strength (DOMA) .... ETS
European Tropical Forest Research Network (EERA) .... ETFRN
European Tropospheric-Scatter Army [*Communications system*] .... ETA
European Tube Association [*EC*] (ECED) .... ETA
European Tugowners Association (EAIO) .... ETA
European Tumour Virus Group (EAIO) .... ETVG
[*The*] **European Turf Management Exhibition** [*British*] (ITD) .... ETME
European Tyre and Rim Technical Organisation [*Belgium*] .... ETRTO
European Tyre Stud Manufacturers Association (PDAA) .... ETSMA
European Underseas Bio-Medical Society (EAIO) .... EUBS
European Unified Research on Educational Development (AIE) .... EURED
European Union [*Formerly, European Community*] .... EU
European Union Football Associations .... EUFA
European Union for Bird Ringing [*Europe*] (EERA) .... EURING
European Union for Packaging and the Environment [*EEC*] (PDAA) .... EUPE
European Union for the Prevention of Cruelty to Animals (EAIO) .... UEMTA

European Union for the Protection of Animals (PDAA) .... EUPA
European Union for the Scientific Study of Glass (EA) .... EUSSG
European Union of Arab and Islamic Studies [See also UEAI] (EAIO) .... EUAIS
European Union of Coachbuilders (EA) .... EUC
European Union of Dentists (PDAA) .... EUD
European Union of Developers and House Builders [Belgium] (EAIO) .... EUDH
European Union of Federalists .... EUF
European Union of Film and Television Technicians (BARN) .... EUFTT
European Union of Geosciences [Strasbourg, France] .... EUG
European Union of Jewish Students (EA) .... EUJS
European Union of Music Schools [See also EMU] (EA) .... EUMS
European Union of Paediatric Surgical Associations (PDAA) .... EUPSA
European Union of Public Relations - International Service Organization
   [See also UERP] (EAIO) .... EUPRISO
European Union of Public Relations - International Service Organization
   [Hungary] (EA) .... EURPISO
European Union of Science Journalists Associations (EAIO) .... EUSJA
European Union of Social Medicine (EA) .... EUSM
European Union of Societies for Experimental Biology .... EUSEB
European Union of Tourist Officers (EAIO) .... EUTO
European Union of Wholesale Eggs, Egg-Products, Poultry and Game
   [EC] (ECED) .... EUWEP
European Union of Women [Stockholm, Sweden] .... EUW
European Union of Young Christian Democrats [Belgium] (EY) .... EUYCD
European Units of Account [Economics] .... EUA
European University Institute [Florence, Italy] (AIE) .... EUI
European UNIX Network [Computer science] (ACRL) .... EUNET
European UNIX User Group [Computer science] .... EUUG
European Urban Driving Cycle [Automotive emissions] .... EUDC
European Vaccine Against AIDS [Acquired Immune Deficiency Syndrome]
   [Medicine] .... EVA
European Vegetable Protein Federation (EAIO) .... EUVEPRO
European Venture Capital Association .... EVCA
European Vinyl Asbestos Tile Manufacturers Institute (PDAA) .... EVATMI
European Volcanological Project .... EVOP
European Voluntary Worker .... EVW
European Warrant Fund [Associated Press] (SAG) .... EurWtFd
European Warrant Fund [NYSE symbol] (SPSG) .... EWF
European Water Pollution Control Association (EAIO) .... EWPCA
European Wax Association (EAIO) .... EWA
European Wax Federation [Belgium] (EAIO) .... EWF
European Weed Research Council [Later, EWRS] .... EWRC
European Weed Research Society [See also EGH] [Research center
   Germany] (IRC) .... EWRS
European Weightlifting Federation (EA) .... EWF
European Welding Association (EAIO) .... EWA
European Wholesalers and Distributors Directory [Pronounced "eewed"]
   [A publication] .... EWDD
European Wideband Communications System [Army] .... EWCS
European Wideband Transmission Media Improvement Program .... EWTMI
European Wind Energy Association (EAIO) .... EWEA
European Wings [Czechoslovakia] [ICAO designator] (FAAC) .... EWS
European Wire Rope Information Service [EC] (ECED) .... EWRIS
European Women's Judo Championships [British] .... EWJC
European Women's Lobby [Belgium] (EAIO) .... EWL
European Women's Management Development Network (EAIO) .... EWMD
European Working Party on Hypertension in the Elderly [An
   association] .... EWPHE
European Workshop for Open Systems [British] .... EWOS
European Workshop of Industrial Computer Systems (NITA) .... EWICS
European X-Ray Observatory .... EXO
European X-Ray Observatory Satellite (MCD) .... EXOSAT
European Year of Older People and Solidarity Between Generations .... EYOP
European Year of the Environment [Beginning March 23, 1987] .... EYE
European Yearbook [A publication] (DLA) .... Eur YB
European Young Christian Democrats [Formerly, European Union of Young
   Christian Democrats] (EA) .... EYCD
European Youth Campaign .... EYC
European Youth Centre [Council of Europe] (EY) .... EYC
European Youth Foundation (EA) .... EYF
European Zinc Institute (EA) .... EZI
European Zone Charge (DS) .... EZC
European-African-Middle Eastern [Communications area] [NASA]
   (KSC) .... E-A-ME
European-African-Middle Eastern Campaign Medal [Military
   decoration] .... EAMECM
European-American Bank [Databank on activities of non-US banks]
   (NITA) .... EURABANK
European-American Chamber of Commerce in the United States .... EACC-USA
European-American Committee on Reactor Physics .... EACRP
European-American Nuclear Data Committee [OECD] .... EANDC
[The] European-Atlantic Movement [British] .... TEAM
European-Materials Research Society (EAIO) .... E-MRS
European-Mediterranean [Military] .... EUM
European-Mediterranean Siesmology Center .... EMSC
Europeene Norme [European Standard] .... EN
Europeene Norme Vorausgabe [European Prestandard] (OSI) .... ENV
Europees Muziekfestival voor de Jeugd [European Music Festival for the
   Youth] (EAIO) .... EMFJ
Europees Studie en Informatie Centrum [Later, European Center for
   Research and Information] [Belgium] (EAIO) .... ESIC
Europe-Latin America Interparliamentary Assembly [See also DPERPLA]
   [Luxembourg, Luxembourg] (EAIO) .... ELAIA
Europe's Largest Companies [ELC International] [Information service or
   system] (CRD) .... ELC

Europese Economische Gemeenschap [European Economic Community] ..... EEG
Europese Investeringsbank [European Investment Bank] .... EIB
Europese Rum Vereniging [European Rum Association] [EC] (ECED) .... ERV
Europese Vereniging voor Haveninformatica [European Port Data Processing
   Association] [Belgium] (EA) .... EVHA
Europese Vereniging voor Pediatrische Hematologie en Immunologie
   [European Society for Paediatric Haematology and Immunology - ESPHI]
   (EAIO) .... EVPHI
Europium [Chemical element] .... Eu
Europium Iron Garnet (PDAA) .... EuIG
Europrime Capital [Vancouver Stock Exchange symbol] .... EP
Eurosky Airlines [Austria] [FAA designator] (FAAC) .... ESK
Eurotec Consultants Ltd. [Information service or system] (IID) .... ECL
Eurotransplant Foundation (EA) .... EF
EuroVision [Later, SGA] (EA) .... EV
Eurowings, AG, Nurnberg [Germany] [FAA designator] (FAAC) .... EWG
Eurowings (NFD & RFG Luftverhehrs AG) [Germany ICAO designator]
   (FAAC) .... NFD
Eurythmics Fan Club (EA) .... EFC
Eusebius [Ecclesiastical historian, c. 260-340AD] [Classical studies] (OCD) ..... Eus
Eusebius [Ecclesiastical historian, c. 260-340AD] [Classical studies]
   (ROG) .... EUSEB
Euskal Iraultzako Alderdia [Basque Revolutionary Party] (PPW) .... EIA
Eusko Alkartasuna [Basque Solidarity] [Spain Political party] .... EA
Eustachian Tube [Anatomy] .... ET
Eustachian Tube Function [Medicine] .... ETF
Eustachian Tube Obstruction [Medicine] .... ETO
Eustachian Tube Pressure [Medicine] (MAE) .... ETP
Eustis, FL [AM radio station call letters] .... WKIQ
Eustis Memorial Library, Eustis, FL [Library symbol Library of Congress]
   (LCLS) .... FE
Euston Railway Station [British] (ROG) .... E
Eutaw, AL [FM radio station call letters] .... WQLW
Eutectic Mixture of Local Anesthetics [A cream that reduces electrolysis
   pain] [Dermatology] .... EMLA
Eutectic Mixture of Local Anesthetics [Topical anesthetic cream] .... EMLA
Euterpe [Record label] .... Eut
Euthanasia Society of America [Later, SRD] (EA) .... ESA
Euthanize for Humane Reasons [ASPCE terminology] .... EHR
Euthroid [Endocrinology] (DAVI) .... EU
Euthyphro [of Plato] [Classical studies] (OCD) .... Euthphr
Euthyroid Sick Syndrome [Medicine] (DMAA) .... ESS
Euzkadi ta Azkatasuna [Basque Fatherland and Freedom] [Spain] (PD) .... ETA
Euzkadi ta Azkatasuna [Basque Fatherland and Freedom] Military Fr ont
   [Spain] .... ETA-M
Euzkadi ta Azkatasuna [Basque Fatherland and Freedom] Political-Military
   Front [Spain] .... ETA-PM
Euzkadiko Ezkerra [Basque Left] [Spain Political party] (PPE) .... EE
EV Environmental [NASDAQ symbol] (TTSB) .... EVEN
EV Environmental, Inc. [Associated Press] (SAG) .... EV En
EV Environmental, Inc. [Associated Press] (SAG) .... EV Env
EV Environmental, Inc. [NASDAQ symbol] (SAG) .... EVEN
EV Environmental Wrrt'A' [NASDAQ symbol] (TTSB) .... EVENW
Ev. [Evangelical] Lutheran Good Samaritan Society (EA) .... ELGSS
Eva Brook Donly Museum, Simcoe, ON, Canada [Library symbol Library of
   Congress] (LCLS) .... CaOSiDM
Eva Brook Donly Museum, Simcoe, Ontario [Library symbol National Library
   of Canada] (NLC) .... OSIDM
EVA [Extravehicular Activity] Life-Support System [NASA] .... ELSS
EVA [Extravehicular Activity] Support Equipment [NASA] (NASA) .... ESE
Evacuation (AFM) .... EVAC
Evacuation and Evasion .... E & E
Evacuation Coordination Center (DOMA) .... ECC
Evacuation Hospital Semimobile (VNW) .... EVACS
Evacuation Hospital Ship [Navy symbol Obsolete] .... AHP
Evacuation Mission [Air Force] .... EVM
Evacuation/Replacement [Jar technique] [Microbiology] .... E/R
Evacuation Ship [Navy] (NVT) .... EVACSHIP
Evacuation Unit [Army] .... EU
Evacuator (MSA) .... EVAC
Evadale, TX [Location identifier FAA] (FAAL) .... ETO
Evadale, TX [Location identifier FAA] (FAAL) .... EVA
Evaluate .... EV
Evaluate [or Evaluation or Evaluator] (AFM) .... EVAL
Evaluated Disposition toward the Environment [Student attitude test] .... EDEN
Evaluated Maintenance Programming .... EMP
Evaluated Nuclear Data File [National Nuclear Data Center] [Information
   service or system] .... ENDF
Evaluated Nuclear Structure Data File [National Nuclear Data Center]
   [Information service or system] .... ENSDF
Evaluated Testbed System (SSD) .... ETS
Evaluating Acquired Skills in Communication [Language ability test] .... EASIC
Evaluating Fallout Protection in Homes [Later, HFPS] [Civil Defense] .... EFPH
Evaluating New Technologies for Roads Program Initiatives in Safety and
   Efficiency [FHWA] (TAG) .... ENTERPRISE
Evaluation .... EVAL
Evaluation (MSA) .... EVLTN
Evaluation Agree [Canada] (DD) .... EA
Evaluation and Advisory Service [Educational testing service] (AEBS) .... EAS
Evaluation and Analysis Group [Bureau of Ordnance] [Washington, DC]
   [Navy] (MCD) .... EAG
Evaluation and Analysis Staff [Bureau of Ordnance] [Washington, DC Navy]
   (MCD) .... EAS
Evaluation and Development (IAA) .... EAD
Evaluation and Development (IAA) .... ED

Evaluation and Optimization .... EVOP
Evaluation and Planning Centre for Health Care [*London School of Hygiene and Tropical Medicine*] [*British*] (CB) .... EPC
Evaluation & Sale of Assets Agency .... VVA
Evaluation and Subsystem Training (SAA) .... EAST
Evaluation and Warning Team (CINC) .... EWT
Evaluation Branch [*BUPERS*] .... EB
Evaluation by Computer of the Learning Environment (PDAA) .... ECOLE
Evaluation Center (NATG) .... EC
Evaluation Contractors Estimating System .... ECES
Evaluation Coordination Working Group [*Navy*] .... ECWG
Evaluation, Decision and Weapon Assignment [*Army*] .... EDWA
Evaluation, Dissemination, and Assessment Center for Bilingual Education (EDAC) .... EDAC
Evaluation Documentation Center [*Department of Health and Human Services*] [*Information service or system*] (IID) .... EDC
Evaluation Elements of Analysis (MCD) .... EEA
Evaluation, Experimental and Development Projects (OICC) .... EEDP
Evaluation Instrumentation (AAG) .... EI
Evaluation Kit [*American Microsystems Inc.*] (NITA) .... EVK
Evaluation Management Using Past History Analysis for Scientific Inventory Simulation .... EMPHASIS
Evaluation Modality Test [*Psychology*] .... EMT
Evaluation Model (NRCH) .... EM
Evaluation Monitoring Team (MCD) .... EMT
Evaluation Network [*An association*] (EA) .... ENET
Evaluation of Air Defense Effectiveness .... EVADE
Evaluation of Foreign Weapons Systems (MCD) .... EFWS
Evaluation of Glide Reentry Structural Systems .... EGRESS
Evaluation of Oxygen Interaction with Materials (MCD) .... EOIM
Evaluation of Small Unit Training (MCD) .... ESUT
Evaluation of Testing in Schools Project (AIE) .... ETSP
Evaluation of the Army Study System (MCD) .... ETASS
Evaluation of Total System Survivability (MCD) .... ETSS
Evaluation of Unitary Programs for Effecting Plural Tasks in Index Construction (NITA) .... EUPEPTIC
Evaluation of Uranium Resources and Economic Analysis [*Department of Energy*] (GFGA) .... EUREKA
Evaluation of Women in the Army (MCD) .... EWITA
Evaluation Plan .... EP
Evaluation Project Report [*Air Force*] .... EPR
Evaluation Record [*LIMRA*] .... ER
Evaluation Record Sheet (MCD) .... ERS
Evaluation Report .... ER
Evaluation Research Center [*University of Virginia*] [*Research center*] (RCD) .... ERC
Evaluation Review Committee (EERA) .... ERC
Evaluation SAGE [*Semiautomatic Ground Environment*] **Sector** (IAA) .... ESS
Evaluation Staff, War College [*Air Force*] .... ESAWC
Evaluation Task Force [*Defunct*] (EA) .... ETF
Evaluation Test (IAA) .... ET
Evaluation Test Plan .... ETP
Evaluation Test Specification .... ETS
Evaluation Trainers .... ETS
Evaluation Vector Table .... EVT
Evaluator Programmer Integrated Circuit [*NASA*] .... EPIC
Evanescent Access Method [*Sperry UNIVAC*] .... EAM
Evanescent Space Charge (PDAA) .... ESC
Evanescent Wave Dynamic Light Scattering [*Physics*] .... EWDLS
Evangel College, Springfield, MO [*OCLC symbol*] (OCLC) .... MOE
Evangel College, Springfield, MO [*Library symbol Library of Congress*] (LCLS) .... MoSpE
Evangeli Christi Proedicatur [*Preacher of the Gospel of Christ*] [*Latin*] (ROG) .... ECP
Evangelical [*or Evangelist*] .... EVAN
Evangelical [*or Evangelist*] .... EVANG
Evangelical .... EVNGLCL
Evangelical Alliance [*British*] (BI) .... EA
[*The*] **Evangelical Alliance Mission** [*An association*] (NTCM) .... EAM
[*The*] **Evangelical Alliance Mission** (EA) .... TEAM
[*The*] **Evangelical Alliance Relief** [*of The TEAR Fund*] (EA) .... TEAR
Evangelical and Catholic Mission (EA) .... ECM
Evangelical and Reformed Historical Society .... ERHS
Evangelical and Reformed Historical Society and Archives, United Church of Christ (EA) .... ERHSA-UCC
Evangelical and Reformed Historical Society, United Church of Christ [*Later, ERHSA-UCC*] (EA) .... ERHS-UCC
Evangelical Association of the Caribbean (EAIO) .... EAC
Evangelical Christian Publishers Association (EA) .... ECPA
Evangelical Church Alliance (EA) .... ECA
Evangelical Church Library Association (EA) .... ECLA
Evangelical Congregational School of Theology, Myerstown, PA [*Library symbol Library of Congress*] (LCLS) .... PMyE
Evangelical Council for Financial Accountability (EA) .... ECFA
Evangelical Education Society of the Protestant Episcopal Church (EA) .... EES
Evangelical Foreign Missions Association (EA) .... EFMA
Evangelical Free Church of Australia .... EFCA
Evangelical Friends Alliance [*Later, EFI*] (EA) .... EFA
Evangelical Friends International (EA) .... EFI
Evangelical Literature Overseas (EA) .... ELO
Evangelical Lutheran (ROG) .... EL
Evangelical Lutheran Church [*Later, ELCA*] .... ELC
Evangelical Lutheran Church in America [*Formed by merger of ALC, ELC, and LCA*] .... ELCA
Evangelical Lutheran Church in America (BARN) .... ELCH
Evangelical Lutheran Education Association (EA) .... ELEA
Evangelical Lutheran Synod .... ELS
Evangelical Lutheran Theological Seminary, Columbus, OH [*Library symbol Library of Congress*] (LCLS) .... OCoE
Evangelical Lutherans in Mission [*Group opposing the Missouri Synod of the Lutheran Church*] .... ELIM
Evangelical Ministries, Inc. (EA) .... EMI
Evangelical Missionary Alliance [*British*] .... EMA
Evangelical Missions Information Service (EA) .... EMIS
Evangelical Movement of Wales .... EMW
Evangelical Press Association (EA) .... EPA
Evangelical Radio Alliance [*British*] (BI) .... ERA
Evangelical School of Nursing, Oak Lawn, IL [*Library symbol Library of Congress*] (LCLS) .... IOIE
Evangelical Seminary, Rio Piedras, PR [*Library symbol Library of Congress*] (LCLS) .... PrRe
Evangelical Social Action Commission (EA) .... ESAC
Evangelical Teacher Training Association [*Later, ETA*] (EA) .... ETTA
Evangelical Theological Society (EA) .... ETS
Evangelical Tract Society [*British*] (DBA) .... ETS
Evangelical Training Association (EA) .... ETA
Evangelical Union [*British*] .... EU
Evangelical United Brethren [*Church*] .... EUB
Evangelical Women's Caucus, International (EA) .... EWCI
Evangelicals Concerned (EA) .... EC
Evangelicals for Social Action (EA) .... ESA
Evangeline Parish Library, Ville Platte, LA [*Library symbol Library of Congress*] (LCLS) .... LVpE
Evangeline Railway Co. [*AAR code*] .... EVNG
Evangelische Arbeitsgemeinschaft fuer Erwachsenenbildung in Europa [*Protestant Association for Adult Education in Europe*] (EAIO) .... EAEE
Evangelische Freiheit [*A publication*] (BJA) .... EF
Evangelische Kirche Deutschlands .... EKD
Evangelische Progressieve Volkspartij [*Evangelical Progressive People's Party*] [*Netherlands*] (PPW) .... EPV
Evangelische Volkspartei der Schweiz [*Swiss Evangelical People's Party*] [*Political party*] (PPW) .... EVP
Evangelische Volkspartij [*Evangelical People's Party*] [*Netherlands Political party*] (EY) .... EVP
Evangelisches Kirchenlexikon. Kirchlich-Theologisches Handwoerterbuch [*A publication*] (BJA) .... EKL
Evangelisch-Katholischer Kommentar zum Neuen Testament [*A publication*] (BJA) .... EKK
Evangelism and Home Missions Association (EA) .... EHMA
Evangelism Center International (EA) .... ECI
Evangelist [*Church calendars*] .... E
Evangelist .... EV
Evangelist (VRA) .... evang
Evangelist .... EVNGLST
Evangelist and Martyr [*Church calendars*] .... EM
Evangelistic Faith Missions (EA) .... EFM
Evangelization Society (EA) .... ES
"Evangelize China" Fellowship (EA) .... ECF
Evangelstic .... EVNGLSTC
Evangile [*Paris*] [*A publication*] (BJA) .... Ev
Evangile [*Paris*] [*A publication*] (BJA) .... Evan
Evans & Sutherland Computer Corp. .... E & S
Evans & Sutherland Computer Corp. [*NASDAQ symbol*] (NQ) .... ESCC
Evans & Sutherland Computer Corp. [*Associated Press*] (SAG) .... EvnSut
Evan's Blue [*Fluorescent dye*] .... EB
Evans Blue Dye [*Radiology*] (DAVI) T-1824
Evans Clear Tunnel (OA) .... ECT
Evans' Collection of Statutes [*A publication*] (DLA) .... Ev Stat
Evans Economics, Inc. [*Database producer*] [*Information service or system*] (IID) .... EEI
Evans' Edition of Harris' Modern Entries [*A publication*] (DLA) .... Ev Harr
Evans Electroselenium Limited [*as in EEL analyzer, used in biochemical analysis*] [*British*] .... EEL
Evans Environmental [*NASDAQ symbol*] (TTSB) .... ECOS
Evans, GA [*FM radio station call letters*] .... WAEG
Evans, Inc. [*NASDAQ symbol*] (NQ) .... EVAN
Evans, Inc. [*Associated Press*] (SAG) .... Evans
Evans' King's Bench Reports [*1756-88*] [*A publication*] (DLA) .... Evans
Evans, Kitchel, Jenckes P.C. Library, Phoenix, AZ [*Library symbol*] [*Library of Congress*] (LCLS) .... AzPhE
Evans' Maryland Practice [*A publication*] (DLA) .... Ev Md Pr
Evans Medical Ltd. [*Great Britain*] [*Research code symbol*] .... EM
Evans Memorial Library, Aberdeen, MS [*Library symbol Library of Congress*] (LCLS) .... MsAb
Evans on Agency [*A publication*] (DLA) .... Ev Ag
Evans on Pleading [*A publication*] (DLA) .... Ev Pl
Evans on the Law of Principal and Agent [*A publication*] (DLA) .... Ev Pr & Ag
Evans' Practice of the Supreme Court of Judicature [*A publication*] (DLA) .... Ev Jud Pr
Evans Public Library, Vandalia, IL [*Library symbol Library of Congress*] (LCLS) IV
Evans' Road Laws of South Carolina [*A publication*] (DLA) .... Ev RL
Evans Signal Laboratory [*Army*] .... ESL
Evans Systems [*NASDAQ symbol*] (TTSB) .... EVSI
Evans Systems, Inc. [*Associated Press*] (SAG) .... EvansSys
Evans Systems, Inc. [*NASDAQ symbol*] (SAG) .... EVSI
Evans' Translation of Pothier on Obligations [*A publication*] (DLA) .... Ev Poth
Evans' Trial [*A publication*] (DLA) .... Ev Tr
Evans Withycombe Res [*NYSE symbol*] (TTSB) .... EWR
Evans Withycombe Residential, Inc. [*Associated Press*] (SAG) .... Evnwth

Evans Withycombe Residential, Inc. [*NYSE symbol*] (SAG) .... EWR
Evans&Sutherl'd Computer [*NASDAQ symbol*] (TTSB) .... ESCC
Evansburg Public Library, Alberta [*Library symbol National Library of Canada*] (NLC) .... AEV
Evanston Early Identification Scale [*Psychology*] .... EEIS
Evanston, IL [*AM radio station call letters*] .... WKTA
Evanston, IL [*FM radio station call letters*] .... WNUR
Evanston, IL [*FM radio station call letters*] .... WOJO
Evanston, IL [*FM radio station call letters*] .... WONX
Evanston Public Library, Evanston, IL [*Library symbol Library of Congress*] (LCLS) .... IE
Evanston Public Library, Evanston, IL [*OCLC symbol*] (OCLC) .... IHE
Evanston Public Library, Extension (Bookmobile), Evanston, IL [*Library symbol Library of Congress*] (LCLS) .... IE-Ex
Evanston Public Library, North Branch, Evanston, IL [*Library symbol Library of Congress*] (LCLS) .... IE-N
Evanston Public Library, South Branch, Evanston, IL [*Library symbol Library of Congress*] (LCLS) .... IE-S
Evanston Public Library, West Branch, Evanston, IL [*Library symbol Library of Congress*] (LCLS) .... IE-W
Evanston Township High School, Evanston, IL [*Library symbol*] [*Library of Congress*] (LCLS) .... IEHS
Evanston, WY [*Location identifier FAA*] (FAAL) .... EVW
Evanston, WY [*AM radio station call letters*] .... KEVA
Evanston, WY [*FM radio station call letters*] .... KOTB
Evansville [*Diocesan abbreviation*] [*Indiana*] (TOCD) .... EVN
Evansville [*Indiana*] [*Airport symbol*] (OAG) .... EVV
Evansville Elementary School, Evansville, MN [*Library symbol*] [*Library of Congress*] (LCLS) .... MnEvaE
Evansville High School, Evansville, MN [*Library symbol*] [*Library of Congress*] (LCLS) .... MnEvaH
Evansville, IN [*Location identifier FAA*] (FAAL) .... DSO
Evansville, IN [*Location identifier FAA*] (FAAL) .... PDW
Evansville, IN [*Location identifier FAA*] (FAAL) .... PXV
Evansville, IN [*Television station call letters*] .... WEHT
Evansville, IN [*Television station call letters*] .... WEVV
Evansville, IN [*Television station call letters*] .... WFIE
Evansville, IN [*AM radio station call letters*] (RBYB) .... WGBF
Evansville, IN [*FM radio station call letters*] .... WIKY
Evansville, IN [*AM radio station call letters*] .... WJPS
Evansville, IN [*FM radio station call letters*] .... WNIN
Evansville, IN [*Television station call letters*] .... WNIN-TV
Evansville, IN [*FM radio station call letters*] .... WPSR
Evansville, IN [*AM radio station call letters*] .... WSWI
Evansville, IN [*Television station call letters*] .... WTVW
Evansville, IN [*FM radio station call letters*] .... WUEV
Evansville, IN [*AM radio station call letters*] .... WVHI
Evansville, IN [*FM radio station call letters*] .... WYNG
Evansville Press and Courier, Evansville, IN [*Library symbol Library of Congress*] (LCLS) .... InEP
Evansville Public Library and Vanderburgh County Public Library, Evansville, IN [*OCLC symbol*] (OCLC) .... IEP
Evansville Public Library and Vanderburgh County Public Library, Evansville, IN [*Library symbol Library of Congress*] (LCLS) .... InE
Evansville, WI [*FM radio station call letters*] .... WMJB
Evansville, WY [*AM radio station call letters*] .... KUYO
Evansville-Vanderburgh School Corp., Evansville, IN [*OCLC symbol*] (OCLC) .... IVA
Evansville-Vanderburgh School Corp., Library Services Center, Evansville, IN [*Library symbol Library of Congress*] (LCLS) .... InESC
Evaporate (KSC) .... EVAP
Evaporate Rate Monitor (IAA) .... ERM
Evaporated (IAA) .... EVAPD
Evaporated .... EVPD
Evaporated Milk Association (EA) .... EMA
Evaporated Milk Formula [*Dietetics*] (DAVI) .... EMF
Evaporation .... E
Evaporation (IAA) .... EVAPN
Evaporation Control System [*Automobile antipollution device*] .... ECS
Evaporation [*or Evaporative*] Emission Control [*Automobile antipollution device*] .... EEC
Evaporation/Solidification System [*Nuclear energy*] (NRCH) .... ESS
Evaporative Air Cooler .... EAC
Evaporative Cooling Garment [*Spacesuit*] [*NASA*] .... ECG
Evaporative Cooling Garment System [*NASA*] .... ECGS
Evaporative Cooling Institute (EA) .... ECI
Evaporative Cooling Processor .... ECP
Evaporative Cooling Techniques .... ECT
Evaporative Emission Control System [*Automotive engineering*] .... EECS
Evaporative Emission SHED [*Sealed Housing for Evaporative Determinations*] System [*Automotive engineering*] .... EESS
Evaporative Emission System [*Automotive engineering*] .... EES
Evaporative Emissions Generator [*Gasoline testing*] [*Organic chemistry*] .... EEG
Evaporative Light Scattering Detector [*Chemistry*] .... ELSD
Evaporative Loss Control Device [*Automobile antipollution device*] .... ELCD
Evaporative Pattern Casting [*Automotive engineering*] .... EPC
Evaporative Rate Analysis [*Surface technology*] .... ERA
Evaporative Water Chiller [*Engineering*] .... EWC
Evaporative Water Loss .... EWL
Evaporator .... EVAP
Evaporator [*Freight*] .... EVAPTR
Evaporator Pressure Regulator (DNAB) .... EPR
Evaporator Vessel (NRCH) .... EV
Evapotranspiration [*Hydrology*] .... ET

Evart Public Library, Evart, MI [*Library symbol Library of Congress*] (LCLS) .... MiEv
Evasion and Escape [*Military*] .... E & E
Evasion and Escape Fingerprint Identification System .... EEFIS
Evasive Aircraft System (MCD) .... EASY
Evasive Combat Maneuver (MCD) .... ECM
Evasive Maneuvering .... EVM
Evasive Target Tank [*Army*] (RDA) .... ETT
Eveleth Junior College [*Later, Mesabi Community College*] [*Minnesota*] .... EJC
Eveleth, MN [*Location identifier FAA*] (FAAL) .... EVM
Eveleth, MN [*AM radio station call letters*] .... WEVE
Eveleth, MN [*FM radio station call letters*] .... WEVE-FM
Eveleth Public Library, Eveleth, MN [*Library symbol*] [*Library of Congress*] (LCLS) .... MnEvl
Eveleth-Gilbert Senior High School, Eveleth, MN [*Library symbol*] [*Library of Congress*] (LCLS) .... MnEvlSH
Evelyn Waugh Society (EA) .... EWS
Even ha-'Ezer, Shulhan 'Arukh (BJA) .... EH
Even Lot [*Investment term*] .... EL
Even Parity Select .... EPS
Even Positive Acknowledgment [*Computer science*] (IBMDP) .... ACKO
Even Resources [*Vancouver Stock Exchange symbol*] .... EVN
Even Side Flat .... ESF
Even Small Caps [*Publishing*] (WDMC) .... ESC
Even Transversal Magnetic (IAA) .... ETM
Evenes [*Norway ICAO location identifier*] (ICLI) .... ENEV
Evenes [*Norway*] [*Airport symbol*] (OAG) .... EVE
Even-Even Nucleus .... EEN
Evening .... E
Evening (ROG) .... E'EN
Evening .... EV
Evening .... EVE
Evening (ROG) .... EVEN
Evening .... EVG
Evening (WDMC) .... evg
Evening .... EVNG
Evening .... EVNNG
Evening College Characteristics Index (EDAC) .... ECCI
Evening News Association .... ENA
Evening News, New Glasgow, Nova Scotia [*Library symbol National Library of Canada*] (NLC) .... NSNGE
Evening Newspaper Advertising Bureau [*Business term*] .... ENAB
Evening Prayer .... EP
Evening Primrose Oil Capsules [*Trade name*] [*British*] .... EPOC
Evening Student Personnel Association [*Later, Evening Student Association*] (EA) .... ESPA
Even-Odd .... EO
Evensong .... E
Evensong (ROG) .... EVEN
Event .... EVNT
Event Block [*Computer science*] (IAA) .... EB
Event Capture Storage Mode .... ECSM
Event Code [*Searchable field*] [*Dialog*] [*Information service or system*] (NITA) .... EC
Event Control Block [*Computer science*] (BUR) .... ECB
Event Control Block [*Computer science*] (EECA) .... EVCB
Event Control Module [*Chromatography*] .... ECM
Event Count (NITA) .... EC
Event Counter (NITA) .... EC
Event Data Distributor (MCD) .... EDD
Event Database .... EDB
Event Driven Component .... EDC
Event Driven Executive [*IBM Corp.*] .... EDX
Event Elapsed Time (MCD) .... EET
Event Index Log [*NASA*] (KSC) .... EIL
Event Marketing Funds [*Business term*] .... EMF
Event Name [*Dialog*] [*Searchable field*] [*Information service or system*] (NITA) .... EN
Event Processing System .... EPS
Event Queue Element [*Computer science*] (MCD) .... EQE
Event Record Log .... ERL
Event Recorder [*NASA*] .... ERC
Event Scheduling System .... ESS
Event Sensing and Analysis System (DNAB) .... ESAS
Event Sequence Override .... ESO
Event Storage and Distribution Unit .... ESDU
Event Storage Record (SAA) .... ESR
Event Time Digitizer .... ETD
Event Timer (NASA) .... ET
Event Tree Analysis [*Engineering*] .... ETA
Event Verification System [*Technology that encripts time and location on video recordings*] .... EVS
Event-Based Discrete Simulation (PDAA) .... EDSIM
Event-Based Language [*1979*] [*Computer science*] (CSR) .... EBL
Event-by-Event Recording and Sorting [*Electronics*] .... EBERAS
Event-Related Optical Signal [*Imaging science*] .... EROS
Event-Related Potential [*Neurophysiology*] .... ERP
Event-Related Slow-Brain Potential [*Neurophysiology*] .... ERSP
Events Control [*Subsystem*] [*NASA*] (NASA) .... EVCON
Events Control Buffer [*NASA*] (NASA) .... ECB
Events Controller (MCD) .... EC
Events Coupler (MCD) .... EC
Events History Recorder (MCD) .... EHR
Events per Time Unit [*NASA*] .... EPTU
Events per Unit Time (NASA) .... EPUT
Events Recorder Console (MCD) .... ERC

Events Select Logic and Rates (MCD) .... ESLR
Ever (ROG) .... E'ER
Ever Heard of Him [*Facetious criterion for determining insignificance of Supreme Court Justices*] [*Proposed by University of Chicago professor David P. Currie*] .... EHH
Everen Cap 13.50%'A'Ex Pfd [*NYSE symbol*] (TTSB) ..... EVRPrA
Everen Capital Corp. [*Associated Press*] (SAG) .... Everen
Everen Capital Corp. [*Associated Press*] (SAG) .... EverenC
Everen Capital Corp. [*NYSE symbol*] (SAG) .... EVR
Everest & Jennings International [*AMEX symbol*] (SPSG) .... EJ
Everest & Jennings International [*Associated Press*] (SAG) ... EverJen
Everest/Jennings Intl. [*AMEX symbol*] (TTSB) .... EJ
Everest Med [*NASDAQ symbol*] (TTSB) .... EVMD
Everest Medical Corp. [*Associated Press*] (SAG) ...... EverMd
Everest Medical Corp. [*NASDAQ symbol*] (SAG) .... EVMD
Everest Reinsurance Hldgs [*NYSE symbol*] (TTSB) .... RE
Everest Reinsurance Holdings, Inc. [*Associated Press*] (SAG) ... EverestRe
Everest Reinsurance Holdings, Inc. [*NYSE symbol*] (SAG) .... RE
Everest Resources Ltd. [*Vancouver Stock Exchange symbol*] ... EVR
Everett Community College [*Formerly, EJC*] [*Washington*] ... ECC
Everett Community College, Everett, WA [*Library symbol Library of Congress*] (LCLS) .... WaEE
Everett General Hospital, Medical Library, Everett, WA [*Library symbol Library of Congress*] (LCLS) .... WaEG
Everett I. Brown Co., Indianapolis, IN [*Library symbol*] [*Library of Congress*] (LCLS) .... InlBr
Everett Junior College [*Later, ECC*] [*Washington*] .... EJC
Everett, PA [*AM radio station call letters*] .... WSKE
Everett, PA [*FM radio station call letters*] .... WSKE-FM
Everett Public Library, Everett, WA [*Library symbol Library of Congress*] (LCLS) .... WaE
[*The*] Everett Railroad Co. [*AAR code*] .... EV
Everett/Snohomish County-Paine Field [*Washington*] [*ICAO location identifier*] (ICLI) .... KPAE
Everett, WA [*Television station call letters*] .... KONG
Everett, WA [*AM radio station call letters*] .... KRKO
Everett, WA [*FM radio station call letters*] .... KSER
Everett, WA [*AM radio station call letters*] .... KWYZ
Everett, WA [*Location identifier FAA*] (FAAL) .... PAE
Everett, WA [*Location identifier FAA*] (FAAL) .... SNJ
Everglades National Park .... EVER
Evergold Resources [*Vancouver Stock Exchange symbol*] ... EVG
Evergreen .... EVRGRN
Evergreen, AL [*AM radio station call letters*] .... WIJK
Evergreen, AL [*FM radio station call letters*] .... WPGG
Evergreen Bancorp [*NASDAQ symbol*] (TTSB) .... EVGN
Evergreen Bancorp, Inc. [*NASDAQ symbol*] (NQ) .... EVGN
Evergreen Bancorp, Inc. [*Associated Press*] (SAG) .... EvrgrnB
Evergreen, CO [*FM radio station call letters*] .... KXPK
Evergreen Foundation (EA) .... EF
Evergreen General Hospital Library, Kirkland, WA [*Library symbol*] [*Library of Congress*] (LCLS) .... WaKiE
Evergreen Helicopters of Alaska [*ICAO designator*] (AD) .... OT
Evergreen International Airlines [*ICAO designator*] (FAAC) ... EIA
Evergreen International Corp. [*Toronto Stock Exchange symbol*] ... EVI
Evergreen Marine Corp. [*Taiwan*] .... EM
Evergreen Media $3.00 Cv Pfd [*NASDAQ symbol*] (TTSB) ... EVGMP
Evergreen Media Corp'A' [*NASDAQ symbol*] (TTSB) ...... EVGM
Evergreen Media Corp. [*NASDAQ symbol*] (SAG) .... EVGM
Evergreen Media Corp. [*Associated Press*] (SAG) .... EvgrM
Evergreen Media Corp. [*Associated Press*] (SAG) ..... EvgrMda
Evergreen Media Corp. [*Associated Press*] (SAG) ..... EvgrMed
Evergreen Park Public Library, Evergreen Park, IL [*Library symbol Library of Congress*] (LCLS) .... IEvp
Evergreen Regional Library, Gimli, Manitoba [*Library symbol National Library of Canada*] (NLC) .... MGE
Evergreen Regional Library, Gimli, MB, Canada [*Library symbol Library of Congress*] (LCLS) .... CaMGE
Evergreen Resources [*NASDAQ symbol*] (TTSB) .... EVER
Evergreen Resources, Inc. [*NASDAQ symbol*] (NQ) ..... EVER
Evergreen Resources, Inc. [*Associated Press*] (SAG) ... EvgrnRs
[*The*] Evergreen State College [*Olympia, WA*] .... TESC
Evergreen State College, Olympia, WA [*Library symbol Library of Congress*] (LCLS) .... WaOE
Evergreen Valley College, San Jose, CA [*OCLC symbol*] (OCLC) ... CEV
Evergreen Valley College, San Jose, CA [*Library symbol Library of Congress*] (LCLS) .... CSjE
Everitt-Metzger-Flanders [*Early automobile*] [*Facetious translation: Every Mechanical Failure*] .... EMF
Everlasting Heritage [*A variety of sweet corn*] .... EH
Ever-Lock .... EVRLK
Everly Brothers International [*Defunct*] (EA) .... EBI
Everly News, Everly, IA [*Library symbol Library of Congress*] (LCLS) ... IaEveN
Eversion [*Medicine*] (DAVI) .... ev
Eversion [*Medicine*] (DAVI) .... ever
Eversley Series [*A publication*] .... ES
Everted [*or Eversion*] [*Medicine*] .... EV
Everton's Genealogical Helper [*A publication*] .... EGH
Every .... EV
Every .... EVY
Every Block is a Village [*Chicago community development program*] ... EBV
Every Day .... ED
Every Day Low Pricing [*Business term*] .... EDLP
Every Good Boy Deserves Favour [*Title of play by Tom Stoppard*] ... EGBDF

Every Good Boy Does Fine [*or Deserves Favor*] [*Mnemonic guide to notes on the treble clef*] .... EGBDF
Every Hand an Adventure [*Bridge bidding method*] .... EHAA
Every Hour around the Clock [*Q2⁰ is evey 2 hours, etc.*] [*Pharmacy*] (DAVI) .... $Q1^0$
Every Landing, Always Late [*Humorous interpretation of El Al Airlines*] ... EL AL
Every Member Canvas [*Fundraising*] .... EMC
Every Member Canvas [*Fundraising term*] (NFD) .... EMC
Every Member Visit [*Fundraising term*] (NFD) .... EMV
Every Member Visit [*Fundraising*] .... EMV
Every Minute Fix-It (IIA) .... EMF
Every Morning Fixum [*An old car*] [*Slang*] .... EMF
Every Other Day .... EOD
Every Other Month (ADA) .... EOM
Every Other Week .... EOW
Every Other Week Til Forbid [*Advertising*] (DOAD) ..... EOWTF
Every Other Week Till Forbid (NTCM) .... EOWTF
Every Pupil Achievement Test (EDAC) .... EPAT
Every Shift [*Nursing*] (DAVI) .... QS
Every Test Known to Man [*or Mankind*] [*Medicine*] (CPH) ... ETKM
Everybody Loves Fudge [*in Keebler Co. brand of cookies "E. L. Fudge"*] ... ELF
Everybody's Law Magazine [*A publication*] (DLA) .... Everybody's LM
Everybody's Magazine [*A publication*] (ROG) .... EVERY M
Every-Day Life [*Psychological testing*] .... EDL
Everyman's Contingency Table Analyzer (PDAA) .... ECTA
Everyman's Fiction [*Series published by J. M. Dent & Sons*] [*British*] ... EF
Everyman's Library [*A publication*] .... EVL
Everything But the Girl [*British band*] .... EBTG
Everything's Going to Be All Right .... EGBAR
Evets Communications Ltd. [*Telecommunications service*] (TSSD) ... ECL
Evidence [*Law*] .... E
Evidence [*Legal term*] (DLA) .... Ev
Evidence .... EVCE
Evidence .... EVID
Evidence of Disease (DAVI) .... ED
Evidence of Insurability .... EOI
Evidence Photographers International Council (EA) ..... EPIC
Evidences [*Paris*] [*A publication*] (BJA) .... Evid
Evington, VA [*Location identifier FAA*] (FAAL) .... EVI
Evisceration [*Medicine*] (MAE) .... evisc
Evoked Action Potential [*Neurophysiology*] .... EAP
Evoked Compound Electromyography [*Neurology*] (DAVI) ... ECEMG
Evoked Electrospinogram [*Medicine*] (AAMN) .... EESG
Evoked Muscle Action Potential [*Neurophysiology*] ..... EMAP
Evoked Potential [*Neurophysiology*] .... EP
Evoked Potential Index [*Neurophysiology*] .... EPI
Evoked Potential Technique [*Neurophysiology*] .... EPT
Evoked Response [*Neurophysiology*] .... ER
Evoked Response [*Neurophysiology*] (MAE) .... EV
Evoked Response [*Neurology*] (DAVI) .... EVR
Evoked Response Audiometry [*Neurophysiology*] .... ERA
Evoked Response Detector [*Neurophysiology*] (MCD) ... ERD
Evoked Sensory Action Potential [*Neurophysiology*] ... ESAP
Evoked Synaptic Currents [*Neurophysiology*] .... ESC
Evoked Synaptic Potential [*Neurophysiology*] .... ESP
Evoked Vascular Response [*Physiology*] .... EVR
Evoked Visual Potential [*Neurophysiology*] .... EVP
Evolution .... EV
Evolution [*or Evolutionist*] (WDAA) .... EVOL
Evolution of Competing Hierarchical Organizations ..... ECHO
Evolutionarily Stable Strategy .... ESS
Evolutionary Acquisition (AAGC) .... EA
Evolutionary Acquisition Strategy [*Army*] .... EA
Evolutionary Data Management System (IAA) .... EDMS
Evolutionary Defense Acquisition (AAGC) .... EDA
Evolutionary Distance .... ED
Evolutionary Factor Analysis [*Statistics*] .... EFA
Evolutionary Operation [*Statistical technique*] .... EVOP
Evolutionary Stable Strategy .... ESS
Evolutionary Surface-to-Air Missile [*Military*] .... ESAM
Evolutionary System for Data Processing (IAA) .... ESDP
[*An*] Evolutionary System for On-Line Processing [*Computer science*] ... AESOP
Evolved .... EVOL
Evolved Expendable Launch Vehicle [*NASA*] (ECON) ... EELV
Evolved Gas Analysis [*Chemistry*] .... EGA
Evolved Gas Analysis Mass Spectrometry (MCD) ...... EGAMS
Evolved Gas Detection [*Chemistry*] .... EGD
Evolved Gas Profile [*Chemistry*] .... EGP
Evolved Sea Sparrow Missile (DOMA) .... ESSM
Evolving Magnetic Feature (OA) .... EMF
Evolving Natural Language Information Model [*Computer science*] (MHDI) .... ENALIM
Evora [*Portugal ICAO location identifier*] (ICLI) .... LPEV
Evreiskaia Entsiklopediia [*A publication*] (BJA) .... EE
Evreiskaia Kommunisticheskaia Partiia [*Political party*] (BJA) ... EKP
Evreiskaia Sektsiia (BJA) .... EvSektsiia
Evreiskaia Sotsialdemokraticheskaia Rabochaia Partiia (BJA) ... ESDRP
Evreiskaia Sotsialisticheskaia Rabochaia Partiia (BJA) ... ESRP
Evreiskii Komitet Pomoshchi [*Shanghai*] (BJA) .... EKOPO
Evreiskii Kommunisticheskii Soiuz Molodezhi (BJA) ... EKSM
Evreiskii Kommunisticheskii Soiuz Molodezhi (BJA) ... EvKoMoe
Evreiskii Obshchestvennyi Komitet Pomoshchi Pogromlennym (BJA) ... EvObshchestKom
Evreiskii Soiuz Kommunisticheskoi Rabochei Molodezhi (BJA) ... ESKRM
Evreux/Fauville [*France ICAO location identifier*] (ICLI) ... LFOE

EVRO Corp. [*NASDAQ symbol*] (TTSB) ... EVRO
EVRO Financial Corp. [*Formerly, Envirosearch Corp.*] [*NASDAQ symbol*] (NQ) ... EVRO
Evrytanian Association of America (EA) ... EAA
E.W. Blanch Holdings [*NYSE symbol*] (TTSB) ... EWB
Ewa, HI [*Location identifier FAA*] (FAAL) ... NAX
Ewald Ernst Air-Service [*Germany*] [*FAA designator*] (FAAC) ... EAM
Ewe [*MARC language code Library of Congress*] (LCCP) ... ewe
Ewell on the Law of Fixtures [*A publication*] (DLA) ... Ewell Fix
Ewell's Edition of Blackstone [*A publication*] (DLA) ... Ewell Bl
Ewell's Edition of Evans on Agency [*A publication*] (DLA) ... Ewell Evans Ag
Ewell's Essentials of the Law [*A publication*] (DLA) ... Ewell Ess
Ewell's Leading Cases on Infancy, Etc. [*A publication*] (DLA) ... Ewell Cas Inf
Ewell's Leading Cases on Infancy, Etc. [*A publication*] (DLA) ... Ewell LC
Ewell's Leading Cases on Infancy, Etc. [*A publication*] (DLA) ... LC
Ewing, NJ [*AM radio station call letters*] ... WIMG
Ewing's Justice [*A publication*] (DLA) ... Ewing Just
Ewing's Sarcoma [*Oncology*] ... EWS
Ewo [*Congo*] [*Airport symbol*] (OAG) ... EWO
Ewo [*Congo*] [*ICAO location identifier*] (ICLI) ... FCOE
Ex [*From*] [*Latin*] (MAE) ... e
Ex Affinis [*Of Affinity*] [*Latin*] ... EX AFF
Ex Air Ministry [*British*] (DEN) ... ExAM
Ex Aqua [*Out of Water*] [*Pharmacy*] ... EX AQ
Ex Authenticis Pandectis [*Digest of Justinian*] [*A publication*] (DSA) ... Ex Aut
Ex Caelis Oblatus ... ECO
Ex Capitalisation [*Finance*] ... xc
Ex Commissione [*Upon Order*] ... EC
Ex Dividendum [*Without the right to dividend*] [*Finance*] (ROG) ... EX D
Ex Dividendum [*Without (or Exclusive) of Dividend*] [*Finance*] (ROG) ... X/D
Ex Grege [*Among the Rest*] [*Latin*] ... EG
Ex Grege [*Among the Rest*] [*Latin*] (ROG) ... EX G
Ex Grupa [*Of The Group Of*] [*Latin*] (DAVI) ... ex gr
Ex Idoneo Crasso Liquido [*In a Suitable Thick Liquid*] [*Pharmacy*] ... EX IDON CRASS LIQ
Ex Idoneo Liquido [*In a Suitable Liquid*] [*Pharmacy*] ... EX IDON LIQ
Ex Libris [*From the Library Of*] [*Book plate*] [*Latin*] (ROG) ... EX LIB
Ex Modo Praescripto [*In the Manner Prescribed*] [*Pharmacy*] ... EMP
Ex New Issue [*Without the right to new stocks or shares*] [*Stock exchange term*] ... XNEW
Ex Officina [*From the Workshop Of*] [*Latin*] (ROG) ... EX OFFICIN
Ex Officio [*By Virtue of Office*] [*Latin*] ... EO
Ex Officio [*By Virtue of Office*] [*Latin*] (ROG) ... EX OFF
Ex Oriente Lux [*A publication*] (BJA) ... EOL
Ex Parte [*One-Sided Statement*] [*Latin Legal term*] (ROG) ... EX P
Ex Parte [*One-Sided Statement*] [*Latin Legal term*] (ROG) ... EXPTE
Ex Patriates Association [*British*] (DBA) ... EPA
Ex Quay [*Seller's responsibility is to make goods available on the wharf at destination named*] [*"INCOTERM," International Chamber of Commerce official code*] ... EXQ
Ex Relatione [*On the Report Of*] [*Latin*] (ADA) ... EX REL
Ex Senatus Consulto [*By Decree of the Senate*] [*Latin*] ... ESC
Ex Senatus Consulto [*By Decree of the Senate*] [*Latin*] (ROG) ... EX SC
Ex Senatus Decreto [*By Decree of the Senate*] [*Latin*] (ROG) ... EX SD
Ex Ship [*Seller's responsibility is to make goods available on board ship at destination named*] [*"INCOTERM," International Chamber of Commerce official code*] ... EXS
Ex Testamento [*In Accordance with the Testament Of*] [*Latin*] ... EXTM
Ex Voto [*In Fulfillment of a Vow*] [*Latin*] ... EV
Ex Works [*Seller's only responsibility is to make goods available at his premises*] [*"INCOTERM," International Chamber of Commerce official code*] ... EXW
Exa [*A prefix meaning multiplied by 10^{18}*] [*SI symbol*] ... E
Exabyte Corp. [*Associated Press*] (SAG) ... Exabyte
Exabyte Corp. [*NASDAQ symbol*] (NQ) ... EXBT
Exact ... EXCT
Exact Cubic Search [*Mathematics*] ... ECS
Exact Finite Range ... EFR
Exact Interest [*Banking*] ... EI
Exact Manning Table (SAA) ... EMT
Exact Match (IAA) ... EM
Exact Quadratic Search [*Mathematics*] ... EQS
Exact Repeat Mission [*of GEOSAT*] [*Navy*] (GFGA) ... ERM
Exactech Inc. [*NASDAQ symbol*] (TTSB) ... EXAC
Exador Resources, Inc. [*Toronto Stock Exchange symbol*] ... EXX
Exaggerated (DAVI) ... ex
Exaggeration ... EXAG
Exall Resources Ltd. [*Toronto Stock Exchange symbol*] ... EXL
Exaltation Newcastle Disease ... END
Exaltation of Inanna [*A publication*] (BJA) ... EI
EXAMETNET [*Experimental Inter-American Meteorological Rocket Network*] **Executive Committee** [*NASA*] ... EEC
Examination (AFM) ... EXAM
Examination (DSUE) ... EXAMINA
Examination ... EXAMN
Examination ... EXMNTN
Examination [*Slang*] ... X
Examination and Diagnosis (DAVI) ... X & D
Examination and Inventory (AFIT) ... E & I
Examination Before Trial (DHSM) ... EBT
Examination Division Planning Tape [*IRS*] ... EPT
Examination, Opinion, and Advice [*Medicine*] ... EOA
Examination Procedure Outline [*Weighing equipment*] ... EPO
Examination Status Verification Report (NVT) ... ESVR
Examination under Anesthesia [*Medicine*] ... EUA
Examine ... EXAM
Examine and Repair as Necessary ... ERAN
Examine Your Birthday Suit on Your Birthday [*To detect potentially malignant moles*] [*Skin Cancer Foundation*] ... EYBSOYB
Examine Your Zipper ... XYZ
Examined ... EX
Examined ... EXAMD
Examined ... EXD
Examined (ROG) ... XD
Examined and Found Correct (ADA) ... E & FC
Examiner [*Legal term*] (DLA) ... Exam
Examiner ... EXAMR
Examiner ... EXMNR
Examiner ... EXMR
Examiner (ROG) ... XR
Examiner, Middleton, Nova Scotia [*Library symbol National Library of Canada*] (NLC) ... NSMEX
Examiner, Middleton, NS, Canada [*Library symbol*] [*Library of Congress*] (LCLS) ... CaNSMiEX
Examiner's Decision [*Legal term*] (DLA) ... Ex
Examining (BARN) ... Examg
Examining and Entrance Station [*Air Force*] ... EES
Examining and Validating Body (AIE) ... EVB
Examining Circulars ... EC
Examining, Diagnosis, Identification, and Training (PDAA) ... EDIT
Examining for Aphasia [*Psychology*] ... EA
Examining Officer (ROG) ... EO
Example ... EX
Example (VRA) ... ex
Examples ... EXX
Exar Corp. [*NASDAQ symbol*] (NQ) ... EXAR
Excalibur Aviation [*British ICAO designator*] (FAAC) ... EXC
Excalibur Technologies [*NASDAQ symbol*] (TTSB) ... EXCA
Excalibur Technologies Corp. [*Associated Press*] (SAG) ... Excalb
Excalibur Technology Corp. [*NASDAQ symbol*] (NQ) ... EXCA
Excavate (MSA) ... EXC
Excavate [*Technical drawings*] ... EXCA
Excavate ... EXCVT
Excavating ... EXCAVTG
Excavation ... EXCVTN
Excavation Engineering and Earth Mechanics Institute [*Colorado School of Mines*] [*Research center*] (RCD) ... EMI
Excavator ... EXCVTR
Exceeding ... EX
Exceeding [*Weight*] [*Postage*] [*British*] (ROG) ... EXC
Exceeding Speed Limit ... ESL
Exceedingly Rare [*Numismatics*] ... RRR
Exceeds Limits of Procedure (DAVI) ... XS-LIM
Excel ... EXCL
EXCEL Communications [*NYSE symbol*] (TTSB) ... ECI
Excel Communications, Inc. [*NYSE symbol*] (SAG) ... ECI
Excel Communications, Inc. [*Associated Press*] (SAG) ... ExcelCm
Excel Energy, Inc. [*Toronto Stock Exchange symbol*] ... EEI
Excel Industries [*NYSE symbol*] (TTSB) ... EXC
Excel Industries, Inc. [*AMEX symbol*] (SPSG) ... EXC
Excel Industries, Inc. [*Associated Press*] (SAG) ... Excel
Excel Realty Trust [*Associated Press*] (SAG) ... ExcelRl
Excel Realty Trust [*NYSE symbol*] (TTSB) ... XEL
Excel Realty Trust, Inc. [*NYSE symbol*] (SPSG) ... XEL
Excel Tech $0.40 Cv Pfd [*NASDAQ symbol*] (TTSB) ... XLTCP
Excel Technology [*Associated Press*] (SAG) ... ExclTch
Excel Technology [*NASDAQ symbol*] (TTSB) ... XLTC
Excel Technology, Inc. [*Associated Press*] (SAG) ... ExclT
Excel Technology, Inc. [*Associated Press*] (SAG) ... ExclTc
Excel Technology, Inc. [*NASDAQ symbol*] (SAG) ... XLTC
Excel Technology Wrrt'B' [*NASDAQ symbol*] (TTSB) ... XLTCW
Excellence in Education Act (GFGA) ... EEA
"Excellence in Production" [*Army-Navy "E" awarded manufacturers*] [*World War II*] ... E
Excellence-in-Competition Badge (Pistol) [*Military decoration*] ... ECB-P
Excellence-in-Competition Badge (Rifle) [*Military decoration*] ... ECB-R
Excellency ... E
Excellency ... EXC
Excellent ... E
Excellent [*Condition*] [*Deltiology*] ... EX
Excellent (AABC) ... EXC
Excellent (ADA) ... EXCELL
Excellent (WGA) ... XLNT
Excellent Companion [*Freemasonry*] ... E COMP
Excellent Companion [*Freemasonry*] (ROG) ... EC
Excellent Condition [*Doll collecting*] ... EC
Excellent Grand Master [*Freemasonry*] (ROG) ... EGM
Excellent Grand Master of Ceremonies [*Freemasonry*] (ROG) ... EGM of C
Excellent Grand Orator [*Freemasonry*] (ROG) ... EGO
Excellent Grand Recorder [*Freemasonry*] (ROG) ... EGR
Excellent Grand Secretary [*Freemasonry*] (ROG) ... EGS
Excellent Grand Tabernacle [*Freemasonry*] (ROG) ... EGT
[*The*] **Excellent Lodge Leader** [*Freemasonry*] ... TELL
Excellent Masons [*Freemasonry*] (ROG) ... EM
Excellent Skiing Conditions ... E
Excellentissime Vestre Reverendissime Dominationis [*Of Your Most Excellent and Reverend Lordship*] [*Latin*] (ECON) ... EVRD
Excelsior ... EXCLSR
Excelsior Airlines Ltd. [*Ghana*] [*ICAO designator*] (FAAC) ... ESR
Excelsior Income Shares, Inc. [*NYSE symbol*] (SAG) ... EIS

Excelsior Income Shares, Inc. [*Associated Press*] (SAG) .... Excelsr
Excelsior Inc. Shares [*NYSE symbol*] (TTSB) .... EIS
Excelsior Life Insurance Co. [*Toronto Stock Exchange symbol*] .... XEL
Excelsior Springs Genealogical Society, Excelsior Springs, MO [*Library symbol Library of Congress*] (LCLS) .... MoExGS
Excelsior Springs, MO [*AM radio station call letters*] .... KEXS
Except .... EX
Except .... EXC
Except (ROG) .... EXT
Except (DAVI) X
Except (KSC) .... XCPT
Except Approach Clearance [*Aviation*] (OA) .... EAC
Except as Otherwise Herein Provided .... EOHP
Except as Otherwise Noted .... EAON
Except Change Departure to Read [*Aviation*] (FAAC) .... ECD
Except Change Route to Read [*Aviation*] (FAAC) .... ECR
Except Sixth Form [*For the wearing of schoolgirls' uniforms*] [*British*] .... Y
Except What Turns Up (DI) .... EWTU
Excepted (WDMC) .... ex
Excepted (WDMC) .... Ex
Excepted Net Income .... ENI
Exception .... EXCPT
Exception Analysis System (IAA) .... EASY
Exception Management System .... EMS
Exception Monitor (NASA) .... EM
Exception Monitoring (MCD) .... EMON
Exception Noted .... EN
Exception Reporting (MCD) .... ER
Exception Time Accounting .... ETA
Exception to National Disclosure Policy .... ENDP
Exceptional Cancer Patients [*Therapy program*] .... ECaP
Exceptional Child Center [*Utah State University*] [*Research center*] (RCD) .... ECC
Exceptional Child Education Resources [*Formerly, ECEA*] [*Council for Exceptional Children Bibliographic database*] [*A publication*] .... ECER
Exceptional Children [*A publication*] .... Ex Child
Exceptional Children [*A publication*] (BRI) .... Ex Child
Exceptional Children Abstracts [*A publication*] (IID) .... EC
Exceptional Circumstances Allowance [*Legal term*] (DLA) .... ECA
Exceptional Civilian Service Award (RDA) .... ECSA
Exceptional Family Member Program [*Army*] (INF) .... EFMP
Exceptional Merit Media Awards [*National Women's Political Caucus*] .... EMMA
Exceptional Needs Payment [*Legal term*] (DLA) .... ENP
Exceptionally Well Qualified (AFM) .... EWQ
Excerpta Criminologica [*A publication*] (DLA) .... Excerpta Crim
Excerpta e Rotulis Finium [*Extracts of Boundary Records*] [*A publication*] (ROG) .... EXCERP e ROT FIN
Excerpta Medica Database [*Trademark*] [*Elsevier Bibliographic database*] .... EMBASE
Excerpta Medica/EMBASE Publishing Group (IID) .... EMPG
Excerpta Medica Foundation [*Database producer*] .... EM
Excerpta Medica Foundation [*Database producer*] (EA) .... EMF
Excerpta Medica Online [*Information service or system*] (NITA) .... EMOL
Excerpta Medica Physicians Information Retrieval and Education Service [*Elsevier Science Publishers*] [*Information service or system*] .... EMPIRES
Excerpta Medica Vocabulary [*Elsevier Science Publishers BV*] [*Netherlands Information service or system*] (CRD) .... EVOC
Excess (AABC) .... EX
Excess .... EXCSS
Excess .... XS
Excess and Casualty Reinsurance Association (EA) .... ECRA
Excess and Surplus Business [*Insurance*] .... E & S
Excess Carrier Ratio (IAA) .... ECR
Excess Charge Adjudication [*Health insurance*] (GHCT) .... ECA
Excess Chiasma Frequency [*Genetics*] .... ECF
Excess Cost Adjudication Function [*Army*] .... ECAF
Excess Current Liabilities [*Insurance*] XCL
Excess Defense Article (AFIT) .... EDA
Excess Disposition System (MCD) .... EDS
Excess Distribution (ADA) .... ED
Excess Ejection Fraction [*Cardiology*] (DAVI) .... XEF
Excess Eleven [*1967 group of scientist-astronauts selected by NASA*] XS-11
Excess Emission Report (GNE) .... EER
Excess Emission Report [*Environmental Protection Agency*] (ERG) .... EER
Excess Exception Code [*Air Force*] (AFIT) .... EEX
Excess Exchange Material (AFIT) .... EEM
Excess Fare Allowance .... EFA
Excess Flow Check Valve [*Nuclear energy*] (NRCH) .... EFCV
Excess Flow Valve .... EFV
Excess Information Rate [*Telecommunications*] (ACRL) .... EIR
Excess Lactate XL
Excess Leave [*Military*] .... EXLV
Excess Limit .... EL
Excess Minority Carrier [*Electronics*] (OA) .... EMC
Excess Noise Ratio .... ENR
Excess Personal Property .... EPP
Excess Personal Property List .... EPPL
Excess Profits .... EP
Excess Profits Duty .... EPD
Excess Profits Levy [*British*] .... EPL
Excess Profits Tax .... EPT
Excess Profits Tax Council Ruling or Memorandum [*Internal Revenue Bureau*] [*A publication*] (DLA) .... EPC
Excess Rent Allowance [*British*] .... ERA
Excess Reserves (MHDB) .... ER
Excess Reserves .... RX
Excess Speed of Advance Authorized [*Navy*] (NVT) .... XSOA
Excess Three [*Code*] XS3
Excess Three Code (IAA) .... XTC
Excess Transit Time .... XSTT
Excess Travelling Time .... ETT
Excess Weight Loss [*Morbid obesity surgical treatment*] .... EWL
Excessive (MSA) .... EXCSV
Excessive Daytime Sleepiness .... EDS
Excessive Duty Cycle [*Military*] .... EDC
Excessive Heat Production (MAE) .... EHP
Excessive Key Strokes [*Computer science*] (PCM) .... EKS
Excessive Requirements Cost (EERA) .... ERC
Excessive Soil Moisture (PDAA) .... EXSM
Excessively Included [*Colored gemstone grade*] .... EI
Exchange .... EX
Exchange .... EXC
Exchange .... Excg
Exchange [*Telecommunications*] (AFM) .... EXCH
Exchange .... EXCH
Exchange X
Exchange (AAG) .... XCH
Exchange [*Business term*] .... Xge
Exchange Access (ACRL) .... XA
Exchange Bill of Lading (MHDW) .... Ex B/L
Exchange Carrier Association (EA) .... ECA
Exchange Carriers Standards Association (EA) .... ECSA
Exchange Certificate [*Rate*] [*Value of the English pound*] .... EX/C
Exchange Chromatography .... EC
Exchange Clearing House Organization [*European bank coalition*] (ECON) .... ECHO
Exchange Control Copy [*Business term*] (DS) .... ECC
Exchange Control Logic (KSC) .... ECL
Exchange Data Format [*Computer science*] (EERA) .... XDF
Exchange Feeder Route Analysis Program [*Bell System*] .... EFRAP
Exchange for Physicals [*Commodities exchange*] .... EFP
Exchange Identification .... XID
Exchange Information Group (NATG) .... EIG
Exchange Jump .... EJP
Exchange Key [*Word processing*] .... EXC
Exchange Line [*Telecommunications*] (TEL) .... EL
Exchange Line Multiplexing Analysis Program (TEL) .... ELMAP
Exchange Line Relay [*Telecommunications*] (IAA) .... ELR
Exchange Line Selector [*Telecommunications*] (IAA) .... ELS
Exchange Network Facilities for Interstate Access [*Computer science*] (TNIG) .... ENFIA
Exchange Network Facilities Interconnecting Arrangement [*Tariffs*] [*Telecommunications*] .... ENFIA
Exchange of Authenticated Electronic Component Performance Test Data [*European counterpart of GIDEP*] .... EXACT
Exchange of Information, Visits, and Reports .... EIVR
Exchange of Medical Information [*Program*] [*Veterans Administration*] .... EMI
Exchange of Property (DLA) .... EXCH P
Exchange of Ready for Issue in Lieu of Concurrent Overhaul .... ERILCO
Exchange of Technical Apollo Simulation Information [*NASA*] (IEEE) .... XTASI
Exchange Officer [*Air Force*] .... EXCHO
Exchange Option Rental .... EOR
Exchange Parameter Definitions [*Telecommunications*] (TEL) .... EPD
Exchange Price Indicators [*Database*] [*British*] .... EPIC
Exchange Price Information Computer (MHDB) .... EPIC
Exchange Price Information Service [*Finance British*] .... EPIS
Exchange Rate [*Economics*] .... XR
Exchange Rate Agreement [*Banking*] [*British*] .... ERA
Exchange Ratio (MCD) .... ER
Exchange Reference File (ADA) .... ERF
Exchange Rolls .... ER
Exchange Sale Property .... ESP
Exchange Servicing Center [*Telecommunications*] (TEL) .... ESC
Exchange Software Generator (TEL) .... ESG
Exchange Stabilization Fund (ECON) .... ESF
Exchange Stock Portfolio [*Investment term*] (MHDW) .... ESP
Exchange Telegraph [*Press agency*] [*British*] (DCTA) .... EXTEL
Exchange Terminal Circuit (ACRL) .... ETC
Exchange Termination [*Telecommunications*] .... ET
Exchange Transfusion [*Medicine*] (DMAA) .... ET
Exchange Two Registers [*Computer science*] .... EXG
Exchange, Unlimited (DNAB) .... EU
Exchange Users Association (EA) .... EUA
Exchange Voltage Regulator [*Telecommunications*] (TEL) .... XVR
Exchange Work List [*Telecommunications*] (TEL) .... EWL
Exchangeable Body Potassium [*Biochemistry*] (DAVI) .... K_e
Exchangeable Body Sodium (AD) .... Na
Exchangeable Body Sodium (MAE) .... Nae
Exchangeable Disc Stores (NITA) .... EDS
Exchangeable Disk Storage [*Computer science*] .... EDS
Exchangeable General Linear Model [*Statistics*] .... EGLM
Exchangeable Potassium per Kilogram of Body Weight [*Biochemistry*] (DAVI) .... Ke/Kg
Exchangeable Sodium (OA) .... ES
Exchangeable-Potassium-Percentage .... EPP
Exchangeable-Sodium-Percentage .... ESP
Exchange-Oriented Operator Control (IAA) .... EOOC
Exchanger (AAG) .... XCNGR
Exchange-Rate Mechanism [*European Economic Union*] (ECON) .... ERM
Exchange-Traded Option .... ETO
Exchequer [*British*] (DLA) .... E

Exchequer [British]	EX
Exchequer [British]	EXCH
Exchequer and Audit Department [British government]	E and A
Exchequer and Audit Department [British government] (RDA)	E & AD
Exchequer Cases [Legacy duties, etc.] [Scotland] [A publication] (DLA)	Exch Cas
Exchequer Chamber [Legal term] (DLA)	EXCH CHAM
Exchequer Court Reports [Canada Department of Justice] [Information service or system] (CRD)	ECR
Exchequer Division, English Law Reports [A publication] (DLA)	ED
Exchequer Division, English Law Reports [A publication] (DLA)	Exch Div
Exchequer Division, English Law Reports [A publication] (DLA)	Exch Div (Eng)
Exchequer Division, High Court [1875-80] [A publication] (DLA)	Exch
Exchequer Master's Associate [British] (ROG)	EMA
Exchequer Reports [A publication]	EX
Exchequer Reports (Welsby, Hurlstone, and Gordon) [A publication] (DLA)	Exch
Exchequer Reports (Welsby, Hurlstone, and Gordon) [A publication] (DLA)	Exch Rep
Exchequer Reports (Welsby, Hurlstone, and Gordon) [A publication] (DLA)	Exch Rep WH & G
Excimer LASER Lithography	ELL
Excimer, Mid-Range [or Moderate-Power], Raman-Shifted LASER Device	EMRLD
Excise (DSUE)	EX
Excise Act [Canada]	EA
Excise Duty Bulletins [Revenue Canada - Customs and Excise] [Information service or system] (CRD)	EDB
Excise Officer (ROG)	EO
Excise Tax [Canada]	ET
Excise Tax Act [Canada]	ETA
Excise Tax Memoranda [Revenue Canada - Customs and Excise] [Information service or system] (CRD)	ETM
Excise Tax Reduction Act	ETRA
Excision [Medicine] (MAE)	ex
Excision [Medicine]	EXC
Excitability-Inducing Material [Biochemistry]	EIM
Excitation (MSA)	EXC
Excitation (IDOE)	exc
Excitation (AAG)	XCIT
Excitation Dispersive X-Ray Fluorescence [Chemical analysis]	EDXRF
Excitation Energy (IDOE)	Ex
Excitation Energy Transfer	EET
Excitation Monochromator	XM
Excitation Power Supply (MCD)	EPS
Excitation-Contraction [Physiology]	E-C
Excitation-Emission Matrix [Fluorometry]	EEM
Excitatory Amino Acid [Neurophysiology]	EAA
Excitatory Amino-Acid Transporter [Neurochemistry]	EAAT
Excitatory Center [Neurology] (DAVI)	EC
Excitatory Interneuron [Neurophysiology]	EIN
Excitatory Junctional Potential [Neurophysiology]	EJP
Excitatory Postsynaptic Current [Neurophysiology]	EPSC
Excitatory Postsynaptic Potential [Neurophysiology]	EPSP
Excitatory Premotor Neuron [Neurology]	EPN
Excitatory Receptive Field [Physiology]	ERF
Excitatory Tendency [Psychology]	E
Excite Inc. [NASDAQ symbol] (TTSB)	XCIT
Excited Dimmer (IAA)	EXCIMER
Excited Skin Syndrome [Dermatology]	ESS
Excited State Complex [LASER] (IEEE)	EXCIPLEX
Excited State Mass Energy	ESME
Excited-State Absorption	ESA
Excitement, Choreiform Movements, and Circling [Characterizations of a medical syndrome]	ECC
Exciter (IDOE)	exc
Exciter [Electricity]	EXCTR
Exciter Power Amplifier Assembly [Electricity] (DWSG)	EPAA
[The] Exciting Game Without Any Rules [Card game]	TEGWAR
Excitor Substance (DAVI)	E-Sub
Exclamation	EXCL
Exclamation (WDMC)	excl
Exclamatory (ROG)	EXCLAM
Exclude	EXC
Exclude (MSA)	EXCL
Exclude	EXCLD
Excluded from General Declassification Schedule (MCD)	XCL
Excluded Goods Schedule	EGS
Excluding	EX
Excluding (EY)	EXCL
Excluding (ROG)	EXCLG
Excluding Interest [Finance] (WDAA)	EX INT
Exclusion	E
Exclusion Area Boundary [Nuclear energy] (NRCH)	EAB
Exclusive (ADA)	EX
Exclusive (AFM)	EXCL
Exclusive [News media] (WDMC)	excl
Exclusive (MDG)	EXCLU
Exclusive (FAAC)	EXCLV
Exclusive [Concession in a circus or carnival]	X
Exclusive Air P Ltd. [South Africa] [FAA designator] (FAAC)	EXL
Exclusive Distribution [Military security classification] (AFM)	EXDIS
Exclusive Economic Zone [Offshore sovereignty] [ICSU]	EEZ
Exclusive Exchange Line [Telecommunications]	EEL
Exclusive Fishing Zone	EFZ
Exclusive of Covering and Uncovering	XC & UC

Exclusive of Loading and Unloading	XL & UL
Exclusive of Sheeting	ES
Exclusive Operating Room [Medicine] (DAVI)	EOR
Exclusive Operating Room [Medicine] (MAE)	XOR
Exclusive Operation [Computer single-key cryptosystem] (PCM)	XOR
Exclusive Or [Gates] [Computer science]	EO
Exclusive Or [Gates] [Computer science]	EOR
Exclusive Or [Gates] [Computer science]	EXOR
Exclusive Or [Gates] [Computer science]	XOR
Exclusive Provider Organization [Medicine]	EPO
Exclusive Read, Exclusive Write [Computer science]	EREW
Exclusive-Nor Gate (HGAA)	EXNOR
Exco Capital Markets [Money brokers] [British]	ECM
Exco Technologies Ltd. [Toronto Stock Exchange symbol]	XTC
Ex-Communist Country	ECC
Ex-Coupon [Investment term]	EC
Ex-Coupon [Without the right to coupons, as of a bond] [Finance]	X-C
Ex-Coupon [Without the right to coupons, as of a bond] [Finance]	XCP
Excreted Fraction of Filtered Sodium [Test] (DAVI)	FE$_{Na}$
Excretory Amino Acid	EAA
Excretory Cell	EC
Excretory Cystogram [Medicine] (MAE)	XC
Excretory Urogram [Radiology] (DAVI)	EU
Excretory Urogram [Medicine] (DMAA)	EXU
Excretory Urogram [Medicine]	XU
Excretory-Secretory	ES
Excudit [Made] [Latin] (ROG)	EX
Excudit [Made] [Latin]	EXC
Excudit [Made] [Latin] (ROG)	EXUD
Excursion [Also, BE] [Airline fare code]	B
Excursion [Also, B] [Airline fare code]	BE
Excursion	EX
Excursion (ROG)	EXC
Excursion (KSC)	EXCUR
Excursion Inlet [Alaska] [Airport symbol] (OAG)	EXI
Excursion Inlet, AK [Location identifier FAA] (FAAL)	EXI
Excursus (ROG)	EX
Excuse (WGA)	EXC
Excused from Duty	ED
Excused from Duty	EFD
Excutive Aerospace (Pty) Ltd. [South Africa ICAO designator] (FAAC)	EAS
Ex-Directory [Telecommunications] (TEL)	XD
Ex-Directory/Calls Offered [Telephone service] (DI)	XD/CO
Ex-Directory/No Connections [Telephone service] (DI)	XD/NC
Ex-Distribution	X-Dis
Ex-Dividend [Without the right to dividend] [Finance]	ED
Ex-Dividend [Without the right to dividend] [Finance]	EX DIV
Ex-Dividend [Without the right to dividend] [Finance] (SPSG)	X-D
Ex-Dividend [Without the right to dividend] [Finance]	X-Div
Ex-Dividend and Sales in Full [Investment term] (DFIT)	Y
Exec Express [ICAO designator] (AD)	AD
Exec Express II, Inc. [ICAO designator] (FAAC)	LSS
Execaire Aviation Ltd. [Canada ICAO designator] (FAAC)	EXA
ExecuFirst Bancorp [NASDAQ symbol] (SAG)	FXBC
Execujet [British ICAO designator] (FAAC)	EXQ
Executable File (CDE)	EXE file
Executable Program File [Computer science]	EXE
Executair Ltd. [Nigeria] [ICAO designator] (ICDA)	EE
Execute	EX
Execute (FAAC)	EXCT
Execute (ROG)	EXE
Execute (MSA)	EXEC
Execute (IAA)	XCT
Execute	XEC
Execute	XEQ
Execute and Repeat	EXR
Execute Channel Program [Computer science]	EXCP
Execute Command Request (KSC)	ECR
Execute Control Cycle (IAA)	ECC
Execute Input/Output (DEN)	XI/O
Execute Input-Output (IAA)	EIO
Execute Reference Time (MCD)	ERT
Execute Stack [Computer science] (IAA)	EXST
Executed (ROG)	EXED
Executed (ROG)	XD
Executed Out Of [Business term]	EX
Execute-in-Place [Computer science]	XIP
Executing Agency Identifier (CINC)	EXA
Execution (MHDB)	E
Execution (ROG)	EX
Execution (WDAA)	EXEC
Execution (ROG)	EXON
Execution Cycle [Computer science] (IAA)	EC
Execution Cycle [Computer science] (NITA)	E-cycle
Execution Damage Assessment (SAA)	EDA
Execution Diagnostic Facility (HGAA)	EDF
Execution Language [Computer science]	XL
Execution List (MCD)	XLIST
Execution Time (CDE)	E-time
Execution Unit [Computer science]	EU
Execution Year	EY
Executive	EX
Executive (EY)	EXEC
Executive (DD)	exec
Executive	EXEC

Executive ... EXTVE
Executive Advisory Board [*Army*] (RDA) ... EAB
Executive Agent ... EXAGT
Executive Agreement Series [*A publication*] (DLA) ... EAS
Executive Air [*Zimbabwe*] [*ICAO designator*] (FAAC) ... AXE
Executive Air Charter [*ICAO designator*] (FAAC) ... EAC
Executive Air Fleet [*ICAO designator*] (FAAC) ... XAF
Executive Air Services Proprietary Ltd. [*Australia*] (ADA) ... EAS
Executive Air Transport Ltd. [*Switzerland ICAO designator*] (FAAC) ... EXV
Executive Airlines Services Ltd. [*Nigeria*] [*FAA designator*] (FAAC) ... EXW
Executive and Management Development Program [*Defense Mapping Agency*] (DNAB) ... EMDP
Executive and Scientific Appointments, Ltd. [*Commercial firm*] [*British*] ... EScA
Executive Assignment Service [*Civil Service Commission*] ... EAS
Executive Assistant ... EA
Executive Assistant (DNAB) ... EXECASST
Executive Audial Rehabilitation Society ... EARS
Executive Aviation Services Ltd. [*Nigeria*] [*ICAO designator*] (FAAC) ... ESY
Executive Board ... EB
Executive Bulletin ... EB
Executive Business Transport [*Aircraft*] ... EBT
Executive Career Trac [*A publication*] ... ECT
Executive Chef Association [*Defunct*] (EA) ... ECA
Executive Chefs de Cuisine Association of America [*Later, Chefs de Cuisine Association of America*] (EA) ... ECCAA
Executive Committee (NATG) ... EC
Executive Committee (IEEE) ... EXCO
Executive Committee [*National Security Council*] ... EXCOM
Executive Committee of the Army Board [*British*] ... ECAB
Executive Committee on Commercial Policy [*Abolished, 1944*] ... ECCP
Executive Committee on Economic Foreign Policy [*Terminated*] (EGAO) ... ECEFP
Executive Committee - Western Traffic Association (SAA) ... EC-WTA
Executive Committee's Panel on Meteorological Aspects of Ocean Affairs [*WMO*] (MSC) ... ECPMAOA
Executive Communications and Control (DOMA) ... ECC
Executive Communications Exchange (MHDI) ... ECE
Executive Compensation Service ... ECS
Executive Control (SSD) ... EXCON
Executive Control Language [*Computer science*] ... ECL
Executive Control Program [*Computer science*] ... ECP
Executive Control Program [*Computer science*] (MCD) ... XCP
Executive Control Routines ... ECR
Executive Control System [*Computer science*] ... ECS
Executive Council (ADA) ... EC
Executive Council (ADA) ... EXCO
Executive Council for National Recovery [*New Deal*] ... ECNR
Executive Council on Foreign Diplomats (EA) ... ECFD
Executive Council on Integrity and Efficiency (AAGC) ... ECIE
Executive Council, Regina, Saskatchewan [*Library symbol National Library of Canada*] (NLC) ... SREC
Executive Council, Regina, SK, Canada [*Library symbol Library of Congress*] (LCLS) ... CaSREC
Executive Counselling Service [*Australia*] ... ECS
Executive Data Display System (HGAA) ... EDDS
Executive Data Link [*IBM Corp.*] ... EDL
Executive Data System (DNAB) ... EDATS
[*The*] **Executive Desk Register** [*Information service or system*] (IID) ... EDR
Executive Development [*Civil Service Commission*] ... XD
Executive Director ... ED
Executive Director for Conventional Ammunition ... EDCA
Executive Director of Operations (IAA) ... EDO
Executive Directorate Industrial Security (MCD) ... EDIS
Executive Doctorate in Management [*Weatherhead School of Management, Case Western Reserve University*] (ECON) ... EDM
Executive Doctorate in Management ... EDM
Executive Document (BARN) ... Ex Doc
Executive Document [*Legal term*] (DLA) ... Exec Doc
Executive Engineer [*British*] (DCTA) ... EE
Executive Financial Woman [*National Association of Bank Women*] [*A publication*] ... EFW
Executive Flight Detachment (AAG) ... EFD
Executive Flight, Inc. [*ICAO designator*] (FAAC) ... EXE
Executive for National Military Representatives [*Supreme Headquarters Allied Powers Europe*] (NATG) ... ENMR
Executive for Small Business ... ESB
Executive Forum (EA) ... EF
Executive Generator ... EG
Executive Group of Companies [*Engineering Council*] (ACII) ... EGC
Executive Guide to Information Sources [*Later, EBIS*] [*A publication*] ... EGIS
Executive Independent Review Team (MCD) ... EIRT
Executive Information Service [*or Software or System*] ... EIS
Executive Input/Output (NITA) ... XIO
Executive Instruments [*Ghana*] [*A publication*] (DLA) ... EI
Executive Interface Program [*Computer science*] (HGAA) ... EIP
Executive Inventory File [*Civil Service Commission*] ... EIF
Executive Jet Aviation, Inc. [*ICAO designator*] (FAAC) ... EJA
Executive Jet Aviation SA [*Switzerland*] [*FAA designator*] (FAAC) ... EJE
Executive Jet Italiana SRL [*Italy ICAO designator*] (FAAC) ... EXJ
Executive Level Interactive Terminal Environment (RDA) ... ELITE
Executive Management Course (DOMA) ... EMC
Executive Management Office [*Kennedy Space Center Directorate*] [*NASA*] (NASA) ... EX
Executive Management Program (DD) ... EMP
Executive Management Responsibility (MCD) ... EMR
Executive Management Review (NG) ... EMR
Executive Management Team (NRCH) ... EMT
Executive Manpower Management Technical Assistance Center [*Civil Service Commission*] ... EMMTAC
Executive Manpower Management Technical Assistance Plan [*Civil Service Commission*] ... EMMTAP
Executive Mansion and Grounds [*i.e., the White House and its grounds*] [*Executive Office of the President*] ... EMG
Executive Master of Business Administration (GAGS) ... EMBA
Executive Master of Business Administration (PGP) ... Exec MBA
Executive Master of Business Administration (GAGS) ... XMBA
Executive Master of General Administration (PGP) ... Exec MGA
Executive Master of International Business Studies (PGP) ... EMIBS
Executive Master of International Management (PGP) ... Exec MIM
Executive Master of Public Administration (PGP) ... Exec MPA
Executive Master of Public Affairs (PGP) ... EMPA
Executive Master of Public Health (PGP) ... Exec MPH
Executive Master of Rehabilitation Administration (PGP) ... EMRA
Executive Master of Science (PGP) ... Exec MS
Executive Master of Science in Engineering (PGP) ... Ex MSE
Executive Master of Science in Industrial and Labor Relations (PGP) ... EMSILR
Executive Master of Science in Taxation (PGP) ... EMST
Executive Master's of Business Administration (RDA) ... ExMBA
Executive Master's of Science in Science and Technology Commercialization (RDA) ... ExMSE
Executive Memorandum ... EM
Executive Office [*or Officer*] ... EO
Executive Office Building [*Washington, DC*] ... EOB
Executive Office for Immigration Review [*Department of Justice*] (GFGA) ... EOIR
Executive Office for United States Attorneys [*Department of Justice*] ... EOUSA
Executive Office for United States Trustees [*Department of Justice*] (BARN) ... EOUST
Executive Office of the President ... EOP
Executive Office of the President ... EXOP
Executive Office of the President, Washington, DC [*OCLC symbol*] (OCLC) ... EOP
Executive Office of the Secretary [*Navy*] ... EXOS
Executive Office of the Secretary [*Navy*] ... NAVEXOS
Executive Officer ... EXECO
Executive Officer ... EXO
Executive Officer [*Military*] ... XO
Executive Officers Council of the National Association of Real Estate Boards (EA) ... EOC
Executive Operating System [*Military*] (CAAL) ... EXOS
Executive Order [*Rule or regulation having the force of law, issued by the President with congressional authorization*] ... EO
Executive Order (DNAB) ... EXECORD
Executive Order of the President (AAGC) ... Exec Order
Executive Pension [*British*] ... EP
Executive Pension Plan (ODBW) ... EPP
Executive Planning Section [*British military*] (DMA) ... EPS
Executive Policy Committee [*Western Australia*] [*State*] (EERA) ... EPC
[*The*] **Executive President's Council** [*New Deal*] ... TEC
Executive Privatization Commission ... CEP
Executive Processing Unit ... EPU
Executive Professional Leadership (AEBS) ... EPL
Executive Profile Survey [*Management and supervision test*] ... EPS
Executive Program (MCD) ... EP
Executive Program Initialize ... EPINT
Executive Program Task Assignment Queue Manager (MCD) ... EPTAQ
Executive Protective Service [*Formerly, White House Police; later, USSS/UD*] ... EPS
Executive Reference Time ... ERT
Executive Request [*Computer science*] ... ER
Executive Reserve ... ER
Executive Resource Associates (AAGC) ... ERA
Executive Resources Board [*NASA*] (RDA) ... ERB
Executive Resources International [*British*] ... ERI
Executive Review Group ... ERG
Executive Review of Overseas Programs [*Army*] (AABC) ... EROP
Executive Right of Way [*Telecommunications*] (TEL) ... EROW
Executive Risk [*NYSE symbol*] (TTSB) ... ER
Executive Risk, Inc. [*NYSE symbol*] (SAG) ... ER
Executive Risk, Inc. [*Associated Press*] (SAG) ... ExcRisk
Executive Risk, Inc. [*Associated Press*] (SAG) ... ExcRsk
Executive Schedule [*U.S. Civil Service*] (BARN) ... ES
Executive Schedule [*Job classification for certain Presidentially appointed executives*] ... EX
Executive Search Council [*Defunct*] (EA) ... ESC
Executive Secretariat (USDC) ... ES
Executive Secretary ... ES
Executive Security International [*Institute for training bodyguards*] [*Aspen, CO*] ... ESI
Executive Selection Inventory System ... ESIS
Executive Seminar Center [*Civil Service Commission*] ... ESC
Executive Sequence Parameter Table (SAA) ... ESPT
Executive Service Requests (MCD) ... ESR
[*The*] **Executive Speaker** (IID) ... TES
Executive Steering Committee (DOMA) ... ESC
Executive Stewards' and Caterers' Association [*Later, IFSEA*] ... ESCA
Executive Storage Area (IAA) ... ESA
Executive Strike Leader Attack Training School (DOMA) ... E-SLATS
Executive Subroutine [*NASA*] (IAA) ... EXSR
Executive Subroutines for Afterheat Temperature Analysis [*Computer program*] [*NASA*] ... ESATA

Executive Suite Network [*An association*] (EA)	ESN
Executive Suites and Services [*Business term*]	ESS
Executive Summary (MCD)	EXSUM
Executive Summary Requirements (MCD)	ESR
Executive Support Board [*Army*] (RDA)	ESB
Executive Support System	ESS
Executive System (NITA)	EXEC
Executive System Problem-Oriented Language [*Burroughs Corp.*] [*Computer science*] (BUR)	ESPOL
Executive Systems Corp. [*An association Defunct*] (EA)	ESC
Executive Team (NRCH)	ET
Executive Telecard Ltd. [*Associated Press*] (SAG)	ExecTl
Executive Telecard Ltd. [*NASDAQ symbol*] (SAG)	EXTL
Executive Telecard Ltd [*NASDAQ symbol*] (TTSB)	EXTL
Executive Telecom System, Inc. [*Database producer*] (IID)	ETSI
Executive Television Workshop [*New York, NY*]	ETW
Executive Tours International	ETI
Executive Transportation [*ICAO designator*] (AD)	XT
Executive Transports [*France ICAO designator*] (FAAC)	EXU
Executive Vice President	EVP
Executive Vice President	XVP
Executive Volunteer Corps	EVC
Executive Women International [*Salt Lake City, UT*] (EA)	EWI
Executive Working Group [*NATO*]	EWG
Executive-Legislative-Judicial	ELJ
Executives Association of Great Britain [*England*] (EAIO)	EAGB
Executives Consultants, Inc. [*An association*] (EA)	ECI
Executives on the Move [*A publication*]	EOM
Executives' Secretaries, Inc. [*Later, EWI*] (EA)	ESI
Executive's Shopping Service	ESS
Executive-Secure Voice Network	ESVN
Executone Info Sys [*NASDAQ symbol*] (TTSB)	XTON
Executone Information Systems, Inc. [*Associated Press*] (SAG)	EXTON
EXECUTONE Information Systems, Inc. [*NASDAQ symbol*] (SPSG)	XTON
Executor (ROG)	EX
Executor	Exctr
Executor	EXEC
Executor (ROG)	EXOR
Executor	EXR
Executor [*Business term*]	EXTR
Executor	EXTR
Executor and Administrator (DLA)	EX & AD
Executor and Trustee Institute [*Australia*]	ETI
Executrix	EXECX
Executrix (ROG)	EXIX
Executrix	EXOX
Executrix	EXRX
Executrix	EXTRIX
Executrix [*Business term*]	EXTRX
Executrix	EXX
Exegetisches Handbuch zum Alten Testament [*Muenster*] [*A publication*] (BJA)	EH
Exegetisches Handbuch zum Alten Testament [*Muenster*] [*A publication*] (BJA)	EHAT
EXEL Ltd. [*Associated Press*] (SAG)	Exel
EXEL Limited [*NYSE symbol*] (TTSB)	XL
EXEL Ltd. [*NYSE symbol*] (SPSG)	XL
EXEM, Inc. [*Associated Press*] (SAG)	EZEM
Exemplary Center for Reading Instruction [*Maine*] (EDAC)	ECRI
Exemplary Rehabilitation Certificate [*Department of Labor*]	ERC
Exemplary Service in Government	ESIG
Exempli Causa [*For the Sake of Example*] [*Latin*]	EC
Exempli Gratia [*For Example*] [*Latin*]	EG
Exempli Gratia [*For Example*] [*Latin*] (ROG)	EX G
Exempli Gratia [*For Example*] [*Latin*]	EX GR
Exempt [*from traceability*] [*NASA*] (NASA)	E
Exempt	EX
Exempt	EXM
Exempt	EXMPT
Exempt (NVT)	XMT
Exempt from General Declassification Schedule (MCD)	XGDS
Exempt Organization [*IRS*]	EO
Exempt Organization Master File [*IRS*]	EOMF
Exempt Security	ES
Exempted	EXMPTD
Exempted by Commanding Officer	ECO
Exemption (DLA)	EXEMP
Exercise (NVT)	EX
Exercise (AABC)	EXER
Exercise [*British military*] (DMA)	X
Exercise and Plans (CINC)	E & P
Exercise Angioscintigraphy [*Medicine*]	EAS
Exercise Benefit Zone [*Aerobic dance*]	EBZ
Exercise Code Word [*NATO*] (NATG)	CODEX
Exercise Commander [*NATO*] (NATG)	EC
Exercise Control Center [*Military*] (AABC)	EXCC
Exercise Control Centre [*Australia*]	ECC
Exercise Control Group [*Army*]	ECG
Exercise Control Group [*Military*] (AABC)	EXCG
Exercise Director (CINC)	EXDIR
Exercise Head	EH
Exercise Hyperemia Blood Flow [*Medicine*] (MAE)	EHBF
Exercise Hyperemia Blood Flow (MAE)	EXBF
Exercise Intelligence Center [*Military*] (CINC)	EIC
Exercise Limit [*Medicine*]	EL

Exercise Monitoring and Control (MCD)	EMC
Exercise Operating Area (NVT)	EOA
Exercise Order [*Military*] (AFM)	EXORD
Exercise Plan [*Military*] (AFM)	EXPLAN
Exercise Plan of Analysis (MCD)	EPOA
Exercise Planning Staff [*NATO*] (NATG)	EPS
Exercise Plans and Analysis Division (MCD)	EP & A
Exercise Readiness Condition [*Military*] (AABC)	EXREDCON
Exercise Simulation System for Flexible Nuclear Response (MCD)	ESSFNR
Exercise Specification [*NATO*] (NATG)	EXSPEC
Exercise Testing [*Medicine*]	ET
Exercise Tolerance Test [*Medicine*]	ETT
Exercise Torpedo (NVT)	EXTORP
Exercise Treadmill (AAMN)	ET
Exercise Treadmill Test [*Cardiology*] (DAVI)	ETT
Exercise Weapon (NVT)	EXWEP
Exercised/Not Repositioned [*Sports medicine*]	E/NR
Exercised/Repositioned [*Sports medicine*]	E/R
Exercise-Induced Anaphylaxis [*Medicine*]	EIA
Exercise-Induced Asthma [*Medicine*]	EIA
Exercise-Induced Bronchiospasm [*Medicine*]	EIB
Exercise-Induced Pulmonary Hemorrhage [*Veterinary medicine*]	EIPH
Exerque [*Numismatics*]	EX
Exer-Safety Association (EA)	ESA
Exertional Dyspnea [*Medicine*] (DAVI)	ED
Exeter [*British ICAO location identifier*] (ICLI)	EGTE
Exeter [*Post code*] (ODBW)	EX
Exeter [*British depot code*]	EXE
Exeter [*England*] [*Airport symbol*] (OAG)	EXT
[*The*] Exeter Abstract Reference System [*Exeter University*] [*Information service or system*] (IID)	TEARS
Exeter College [*Oxford University*] (ROG)	EXET
Exeter Domesday Book [*A publication*] (ROG)	EXON D
Exeter Industrial Archaeology Group [*British*] (DBA)	EIAG
Exeter, NH [*FM radio station call letters*]	WERZ
Exeter, NH [*AM radio station call letters*]	WMYF
Exeter, NH [*FM radio station call letters*]	WPEA
Exeter Public Library, Exeter, NE [*Library symbol Library of Congress*] (LCLS)	NbE
Exeter Public Library, Exeter, ON, Canada [*Library symbol Library of Congress*] (LCLS)	CaOE
Exeter Public Library, Ontario [*Library symbol National Library of Canada*] (NLC)	OE
Exeunt [*They Go Out*] [*Latin*] (ROG)	EX
Exhaust [*Automotive engineering*]	EX
Exhaust (KSC)	EXH
Exhaust	EXHST
Exhaust (AAG)	XHST
Exhaust Air (OA)	EA
Exhaust Air Control [*Automotive engineering*]	EAC
Exhaust Air Filter	EAF
Exhaust Back Pressure	EBP
Exhaust Closes [*Valve position*]	EC
Exhaust Control System	ECS
Exhaust Dampers [*Nuclear energy*] (NRCH)	ED
Exhaust Deflection Angle	EDA
Exhaust Emmission Control [*Automotive engineering*]	EEC
Exhaust Fan (AAG)	EF
Exhaust Gas Analyzer (MCD)	EGA
Exhaust Gas Check Valve [*Automotive engineering*]	EGCV
Exhaust Gas Ionization Sensor [*Automotive engineering*]	EGIS
Exhaust Gas Oxygen [*Automotive engineering*]	EGO
Exhaust Gas Oxygen Sensor [*Automotive engineering*]	EGOS
Exhaust Gas Oxygen Sensor Return [*Automotive engineering*]	EGOR
Exhaust Gas Pressure	EGP
Exhaust Gas Recirculation [*Engines*]	EGR
Exhaust Gas Recirculation Control [*Valve*] [*Automotive engineering*]	EGRC
Exhaust Gas Recirculation Control Valve [*Automotive engineering*]	EGRCV
Exhaust Gas Recirculation Sensor [*Automotive engineering*]	EGRS
Exhaust Gas Recirculation Vacuum Port [*Automotive engineering*]	EGRVP
Exhaust Gas Recirculation Valve [*Automotive engineering*]	EGRV
Exhaust Gas Recirculation Valve Actuator [*Automotive engineering*]	EGRVA
Exhaust Gas Recirculation Vent [*Automotive engineering*]	EGRV
Exhaust Gas System	EGS
Exhaust Gas Temperature	EGT
Exhaust Gas Temperature Indicator	EGTI
Exhaust Muffler	EXM
Exhaust Nozzle Control	ENC
Exhaust Nozzle Temperature (KSC)	ENT
Exhaust Opens [*Valve position*]	EO
Exhaust Outlet Temperature [*Automotive engineering*]	EOT
Exhaust Oxygen Sensor [*Automotive engineering*]	EOS
Exhaust Plume Interference Characterization [*NASA*] (KSC)	EPIC
Exhaust Port Combustion	EPC
Exhaust Pressure Governor [*Diesel engines*]	EPG
Exhaust Pressure Ratio	EPR
Exhaust Pressure Regulator [*Automotive engineering*]	EPR
Exhaust [*Oxygen Sensor*] Return [*Automotive engineering*]	ERTN
Exhaust System Terminal (KSC)	EST
Exhaust Systems Professional Association [*Defunct*] (EA)	ESPA
Exhaust Trail Indicator [*Military*] (NVT)	ETI
Exhaust Ultimate Power Valve [*Yamaha Motor Co.*]	EXUP
Exhaust Valve [*Nuclear energy*] (NRCH)	EV
Exhaust Valve Position [*Automotive engineering*]	EVP
Exhaust Valve Seat Recession [*Automotive engineering*]	EVSR

Exhaust Vent ... EXHV
Exhausted Publications Reference File (MCD) ... EPRF
Exhibeatur [*Let It Be Given*] [*Pharmacy*] ... EXHIB
Exhibit ... EX
Exhibit ... EXH
Exhibit (VRA) ... exh
Exhibit ... EXHBT
Exhibit ... xbt
Exhibit and Display Association of Canada ... EDAC
Exhibit Designers and Producers Association (EA) ... EDPA
Exhibit Line Item Number (MCD) ... ELIN
Exhibited [*or Exhibition*] ... EXHIB
Exhibition (DSUE) ... EX
Exhibition ... EXHBN
Exhibition ... EXHN
Exhibition Industry Federation [*British*] (DBA) ... EIF
Exhibition of Industrial Electronics, Electrical Engineering, and Technical Installation (TSPED) ... INELTEC
Exhibition of Sports and Leisure [*British*] (ITD) ... EXSL
Exhibitioner (ROG) ... EXHBNR
Exhibitioner (ROG) ... EXHIB
Exhibitions [*Trade fairs, etc.*] [*Public-performance tariff class*] [*British*] ... X
Exhibitor ... EXHBTR
Exhibitor (NTCM) ... EXHIB
Exhibitors Advisory Council ... EAC
Exhibitors in Cable [*An association*] (EA) ... EIC
Exhibits Round Table [*American Library Association*] ... ERT
Ex-Husband [*or Ex-Wife*] [*Slang*] ... X
Exide Corp. [*NYSE symbol*] (SAG) ... EX
Exide Corp. [*Associated Press*] (SAG) ... ExideCp
Exide Electronics Group [*NASDAQ symbol*] (TTSB) ... XUPS
Exide Electronics Group, Inc. [*Associated Press*] (SAG) ... ExideEl
Exide Electronics Group, Inc. [*NASDAQ symbol*] (SAG) ... XUPS
Exigencies of the Service Having Been Such as to Preclude the Issuance of Competent Written Orders in Advance ... ESPWO
Exile Fan Club (EA) ... EFC
Exin [*Poland ICAO designator*] (FAAC) ... EXN
Ex-Interest [*Without the right to interest*] [*Finance*] ... EI
Ex-Interest [*Without the right to interest*] [*Finance*] ... X
Ex-Interest [*Without the right to interest*] [*Finance*] ... X-I
Ex-Interest [*Without the right to interest*] [*Finance*] ... XIN
Ex-Interest [*Without the right to interest*] [*Finance*] ... XINT
Existed Prior to Enlistment [*Especially, dependency or physical defect*] [*Military*] ... EPTE
Existed Prior to Entry [*Military*] ... EPTE
Existed Prior to Entry Service [*Military*] ... EPTS
Existed Prior to Induction [*Especially, dependency or physical defect*] [*Military*] ... EPTI
Existence Doubtful [*Navigation charts*] ... ED
Existence, Relatedness, and Growth [*Basic human needs suggested by Clayton P. Alderfer*] ... ERG
Existential Generalization [*Rule of quantification*] [*Logic*] ... EG
Existential Instantiation [*Rule of quantification*] [*Logic*] ... EI
Existential Study [*Psychology*] ... ES
Existing [*Technical drawings*] ... EXG
Existing ... EXIST
Existing (MSA) ... EXST
Existing Chemical Assessment Division [*Environmental Protection Agency*] ... ECAD
Existing Documents Improvement and Updating (MCD) ... EDIUP
[*An*] **Existing Generalized Information System** [*Computer science*] ... AEGIS
Existing Lapse Rate (DA) ... ELR
Existing Light [*Photography*] (NTCM) ... XL
Existing Stationary Emission Source [*Environmental Protection Agency*] ... ESES
Exit [*He, or She, Goes Out*] [*Latin*] (ROG) ... EX
Exit [*Computer science*] [*Telecommunications*] ... X
Exit Guide Vane ... EGV
Exit List [*Computer science*] ... EXLST
Exmar Resources Ltd. [*Vancouver Stock Exchange symbol*] ... EXA
Ex-Meridian [*Navigation*] ... EX-MER
Exmore, VA [*FM radio station call letters*] ... WKRE
Ex-New [*Without the right to new stocks or shares*] [*Stock exchange term*] (SPSG) ... XN
Exoatmospheric Defense System [*DoD*] ... XDS
Exoatmospheric Interceptor Propulsion (MCD) ... EIP
Exoatmospheric Kill Vehicle [*Military*] ... EKV
Exoatmospheric Penetration Aid ... EPA
Exoatmospheric Penetration Aids Concept (MCD) ... EXO-PAC
Exoatmospheric Plume RADAR Cross Section (MCD) ... EXORCS
Exoatmospheric Reentry Vehicle Interceptor Subsystem [*Army*] (RDA) ... ERIS
Exobiology and Radiation Assembly (SSD) ... ERA
Exocellular Polysaccharide [*Biochemistry*] ... EPS
Exodus [*Old Testament book*] ... Ex
Exodus [*Old Testament book*] (DSA) ... Exo
Exodus [*Old Testament book*] ... Exod
Exodus International - North America (EA) ... EINA
Exodus Online Services [*Computer science*] ... EOS
Exodus Rabbah (BJA) ... ER
Exodus Rabbah (BJA) ... ExR
Exodus Trust (EA) ... ET
Exoelectron (PDAA) ... EE
Exoelectron Emission (PDAA) ... EE
Exoelectron Emission (PDAA) ... EEE
Exoerythrocytic [*Medicine*] ... EE
Exoerythrocytic Form [*Phase of malaria parasite*] ... EEF
Exogen, Inc. [*NASDAQ symbol*] (SAG) ... EXGN
Exogen, Inc. [*Associated Press*] (SAG) ... Exogen
Exogenous Substance [*Biology*] ... ExS
Exogenous Triglyceride Clearance Rate [*Medicine*] ... ETGCR
Exol Industries Ltd. [*Vancouver Stock Exchange symbol*] ... ELX
Exolon-Esk Co. [*BO Symbol*] (TTSB) ... EXL
Exomphalos, Macroglossia, and Giantism [*Syndrome*] [*Medicine*] ... EMG
Exonia [*Exeter*] [*British*] ... EXON
Exoniensis [*Of Exeter*] [*Latin*] (ILCA) ... Exon
Exonuclease [*An enzyme*] ... EXO
Exonuclease III [*An enzyme*] ... EXOIII
Exophoria [*Medicine*] (MEDA) ... XP
Exophoria Distance [*Ophthalmology*] ... X
Exophthalmos [*Ophthalmology*] (MAE) ... ex
Exophthalmos-Hyperthyroid Factor [*Endocrinology*] (AAMN) ... EHF
Exophthalmos-Producing Factor [*Endocrinology*] ... EPF
Exophthalmos-Producing Substance [*Endocrinology*] ... EPS
Exoplasmic [*Freeze etching in microscopy*] ... E
Exoplasmic Fracture [*Freeze etching in microscopy*] ... EF
Exoplasmic Surface [*Freeze etching in microscopy*] ... ES
Exospheric Composition Studies (MUGU) ... ECS
Exospheric Satellite [*Japan*] ... EXOS
Exothermic Bimetallic Ignition System (MCD) ... EBIS
Exotic Animal Disease Preparedness Consultative Committee [*Australia*] ... EXANDIS
Exotic Animal Disease Preparedness Trust Account ... EADPTA
Exotic Dancers League of America (EA) ... EDLA
Exotic Pathology Society [*Paris, France*] (EAIO) ... EPS
Exotic Vertebrate Animals Control Working Party [*Australia*] ... EVACWP
Exotropia Near [*Ophthalmology*] ... XT
Expand (NASA) ... EXP
Expand Nonstop Network (MHDB) ... ENN
Expandable Case ... XC
Expandable Computerized Automatic Test System (MCD) ... ECATS
Expandable File Family [*Computer science*] (MHDB) ... EFF
Expandable Level Interactive Application System (HGAA) ... ELIAS
Expandable Machine Accounting System (IAA) ... XMAS
Expandable Personnel Shelter (MCD) ... EXP
Expandable [*or Expanded*] **Polystyrene** [*Plastics Technology*] ... EPS
Expandable Precision Emitter Location System (MCD) ... EXPELS
Expandable Processor [*IBM Corp.*] [*Computer science*] ... XP
Expandable Shelter Containers (MCD) ... ESC
Expandable Stored Program ... ESP
Expandable Wing Tank ... EWT
Expandable Wing Tank Structure ... EWTS
Expanded Additional Skill Identifier [*Military*] (AABC) ... EASI
Expanded Advanced Terminal Defense Study ... EATD
Expanded Advanced Terminal Defense Study (MCD) ... EATDS
Expanded Alternative Minimum Tax ... EAMT
Expanded Background Investigation (AFM) ... EBI
Expanded Bed Capacity ... EXBEDCAP
Expanded Calculator Link Processing System [*Computer science*] ... ECLIPS
Expanded Capability (CAAL) ... EXCAP
Expanded Characteristics Option [*Metallurgy*] ... ECHO
Expanded Charted Visual Flight Procedures [*FAA*] (TAG) ... ECVFP
Expanded Clay and Shale Association [*Later, LAPA*] (EA) ... ECSA
Expanded Communications - Electronics System [*DoD*] ... EXCELS
Expanded Community Calling [*Telecommunications*] (TEL) ... ECC
Expanded Data Processing Unit (DNAB) ... XDPU
Expanded Data Reporting System (PDAA) ... EDRS
Expanded Direct Distance Dialing [*Telecommunications*] ... EDDD
Expanded Disability Status Scale [*Clinical medicine*] ... EDSS
Expanded Display ... ED
Expanded ESS (MCD) ... EXESS
Expanded Field [*Prism*] **Telescopes** [*Instrumentation*] ... EFT's
Expanded Flight Line Tester ... XFLT
Expanded Food and Nutrition Education Program [*Department of Agriculture*] ... EFNEP
Expanded Function Dental Auxiliary [*HEW program*] ... EFDA
Expanded Function Operator Panel (MHDB) ... EFOP
Expanded Helicopter Industries [*Military*] ... EHI
Expanded Inband Signaling [*Telecommunications*] (TEL) ... EIS
Expanded Infrared (DNAB) ... EIR
Expanded In-Home Services for the Elderly Program (BARN) ... EISEP
Expanded Kurtzke Disability Status Scale [*Medicine*] ... EDSS
Expanded Liquid Engine Simulation (MCD) ... ELES
Expanded Litton Automatic Test Station (MCD) ... ELATS
Expanded Memory ... XM
Expanded Memory Manager (BYTE) ... EM
Expanded Memory Manager ... EMM
[*The*] **Expanded Memory Print Program** (SAA) ... TEMP
Expanded Memory Specification [*Computer science*] ... EMS
Expanded Metal ... EM
Expanded Metal [*Heavy gauge*] ... XPM
Expanded Metal Lath ... EML
Expanded Metal Manufacturers Association [*Defunct*] (EA) ... EMMA
Expanded Metal Plate [*Technical drawings*] ... EXMP
Expanded Mobility Tactical Truck (MCD) ... EMTT
Expanded Mobility Truck (MCD) ... EMT
Expanded National Agency Check [*DoD*] ... ENAC
Expanded National Military Command Center (MCD) ... ENMCC
Expanded Near-Term Prepositioning Ships ... ENTPS
Expanded Partial Plan Position Indicator (IAA) ... EPPPI
Expanded Plan Indicator ... EPI
Expanded Polystyrene (ADA) ... EP

Expanded Polystyrene Cavity Insulation Association [British] (DBA) .... EPCIA
Expanded Polystyrene Product Manufacturers' Association [British]
  (BI) .... EPPMA
Expanded Polytetrafluoroethylene [Organic chemistry] .... EPTFE
Expanded Position Indicator .... EPI
Expanded Program Evaluation and Review Technique .... EXPERT
Expanded Program of Technical Assistance [United Nations] .... EPTA
Expanded Programme on Immunization [World Health Organization] .... EPI
Expanded Quota Flow [Aviation] (FAAC) .... EXOF
Expanded Quota Flow (FAAC) .... EXQF
Expanded RADAR Service (AFM) .... ERS
Expanded Range Bench Stock .... ERBS
Expanded Reactance Series Resonator .... ERSER
Expanded Relations Program [Army] (DOMA) .... ERP
Expanded Sample Frame (NTCM) .... ESF
Expanded Service Testing .... EST
Expanded Shale, Clay, and Slate Institute (EA) .... ESCSI
Expanded Spread Profile [Seismology] .... ESP
Expanded Sweep Generator (CET) .... ESG
Expanded Technical Assistance Board [United Nations] .... ETAB
Expanded Technical Assistance Program [United Nations] .... ETAP
Expanded Virtual Machine Assist [Computer science] (MHDI) .... EVMA
Expanded Water Column Characterization [Oceanography] (MSC) .... XWCC
Expanded with Computers and Information Technology .... EXCITE
Expander Cell (IAA) .... EC
Expander Input/Output [Microprocessing] (NITA) .... EXPIO
Expander Tube .... ET
Expanding and Specialty Paper Products Institute [Defunct] (EA) .... ESPPI
Expanding Shielded Mild Detonating Cord (MCD) .... XSMDC
Expansion (KSC) .... EXP
Expansion [Automotive engineering] .... EXPN
Expansion .... EXPSN
Expansion (AAG) .... XPN
Expansion Anchor Manufacturers Institute (EA) .... EAMI
Expansion Bolt [Technical drawings] .... EB
Expansion Bolt [Technical drawings] (DAC) .... EXP BT
Expansion Deflection (AAG) .... E-D
Expansion Interface [Electronics] (ACRL) .... EI
Expansion Joint .... EJ
Expansion Joint Institute .... EJI
Expansion Joint Manufacturers Association (EA) .... EJMA
Expansion Rate Measuring Apparatus .... ERMA
Expansion Symbolic Compiling Assembly Program for Engineers .... ESCAPE
Expansionist Party of the United States [Political party] (EA) .... XP
Expansive Classification .... EC
Exparc [Russian Federation] [ICAO designator] (FAAC) .... EPA
Ex-Partners of Servicemen (Women) for Equality (EA) .... EXPOSE
Expatriate (DSUE) .... EXPAT
Expatriate Resources Co. [British] .... ERC
Expect (DA) .... EX
Expect .... EXP
Expect (FAAC) .... EXPC
Expect (AABC) .... EXPT
Expect Approach Clearance [Aviation] (FAAC) .... EACLN
Expect Approach Clearance Not Later Than [Aviation] (FAAC) .... EACNL
Expect Delivery (FAAC) .... EXDLVY
Expect Departure Clearance At [Aviation] (FAAC) .... EDC
Expect Departure Release At [Aviation] (FAAC) .... EDR
Expect Further Clearance [FAA] (TAG) .... EFC
Expect Further Clearance At [Aviation] (FAAC) .... EFC
Expect Further Routing [Aviation] (FAAC) .... EFR
Expect Higher Altitude (FAAC) .... EHA
Expect to Arrive .... ETA
Expect Vector To [Aviation] (FAAC) .... EVT
Expectancy Age [Education] .... EA
Expectancy Phenomenon .... EP
Expectation .... E
Expectation Maximization [Statistics] .... EM
Expectation Score (MAE) .... ES
Expectations about Counseling Questionnaire (EDAC) .... EAC
Expected Amount of Sample Information [Statistics] .... EASI
Expected Approach Clearance [Aviation] (AFM) .... EAC
Expected Availability Date (MCD) .... EAD
Expected Average Life [Physics] (IAA) .... EAL
Expected Confidence Interval Length [Statistics] .... ECIL
Expected Date of Confinement [Medicine] (DHSM) .... EDC
Expected Date of Confinement .... EDOC
Expected Date of Delivery [Obstetrics] .... EDD
Expected Demand not Supplied (ODBW) .... EDNS
Expected/Dual-Command Travel Time .... E/DC
Expected Environmental Concentration [Environmental science] .... EEC
Expected Exceedance (GNE) .... ExEx
Expected Family Contribution [Department of Education] (GFGA) .... EFC
Expected Fraction of Casualties (MCD) .... EFC
Expected Further Clearance (GAVI) .... EFC
Expected Gentlemanly Behavior (DSUE) .... EGB
Expected Grade Level [Education] .... EGL
Expected Loss .... EL
Expected Loss Ratio [Insurance] .... ELR
Expected Measured Loss [Telecommunications] (TEL) .... EML
Expected Monetary Value .... EMV
Expected Number of Kills [Military] (MCD) .... ENK
Expected Occupancy Date .... EOD
Expected Operations Forecast [NWS] (FAAC) .... EOF
Expected [Patient] Outcome [Medicine] (DAVI) .... EO

Expected Output .... EO
Expected Pay-Off .... EP
Expected Period of Hospitalisation .... EPH
Expected Present Multiattribute Utility (IEEE) .... EPMAU
Expected Progeny Difference [Agricultural science] .... EPD
Expected Project Return on Investment [Finance] (PDAA) .... EPROI
Expected Provident Fund .... EPF
Expected Quality Level .... EQL
Expected Response File .... ERF
Expected Result (IAA) .... ER
Expected Run-Time .... ERT
Expected Sample Size Ratio [Statistics] .... ESSR
Expected Significance Level .... ESL
Expected/Single-Command Travel Time .... E/SC
Expected Test Time .... ETT
Expected Time of Arrival .... ETA
Expected Time of Response .... ETR
Expected Total Cost .... ETC
Expected Total Operating Cost (PDAA) .... ETOC
Expected Total Remnant Costs .... ETRC
Expected Total Utility .... ETU
Expected Turnaround [Computer science] .... ETA
Expected Upper Limit [Clinical psychology] .... EUL
Expected Utility .... EU
Expected Utility Hypothesis .... EUH
Expected Utility Value .... EUV
Expected Value [Statistics] .... EV
Expected Value Business Model (IAA) .... EVBM
Expected Value of Clinical Information [Medicine] (DMAA) .... EVCI
Expected Value of Perfect Information [Statistics] .... EVPI
Expected Value of Sample Information [Statistics] .... EVSI
Expected Value Saved .... EVS
Expected Value-Variance-Skewness [Statistics] .... E-V-S
Expected Working Hours (IAA) .... EWH
Expectorant [Pharmacy] (ROG) .... EXP
Expectorant [Pharmacology] (DAVI) .... expect
Expectorant [Pharmacy] .... EXPT
Expectorated [Medicine] .... EXP
Expects to Enter on Duty (NOAA) .... EXEOD
Expedient Demise [Used as title of novel by Len Deighton] .... XPD
Expedite (MUGU) .... XPD
Expedite Delivery by Telephone (FAAC) .... EXPHO
Expedite Departure Path [FAA] (TAG) .... EDP
Expedite Engineering Order (MCD) .... EEO
Expedite Mail Reply (FAAC) .... EXREP
Expedite Release Request Notice (MCD) .... ERRN
Expedite Requirement (KSC) .... ER
Expedite Shipment (NOAA) .... EXSHI
Expedite Shipping Request (MCD) .... ESR
Expedite Travel Order (NOAA) .... EXPTO
Expedited Air Munitions .... EX-AM
Expedited Engineering Change Proposal .... E ECP
Expedited Essential Required Operational Capability .... EEROC
Expedited Flow Indicator [Telecommunications] (ACRL) .... EFI
Expedited Movement Report [Army] (AABC) .... EXMOVREP
Expedited Non-Standard Urgent Requirements for Equipment [Army]
  (AABC) .... ENSURE
Expedited Qualitative and Quantitative Personnel Requirements
  Information [Army] .... EXQQPRI
Expedited Removal Action [Environmental science] (FFDE) .... ERA
Expedited Site Characterization [Argonne National Laboratory] [Environmental
  science] .... ESC
Expediting .... EXPED
Expediting Management Association (EA) .... EMA
Expedition (ADA) .... EXP
Expedition .... EXPDN
Expedition .... EXPDTN
Expedition Advisory Centre [Royal Geographical Society] [British] (CB) .... EAC
Expedition Internationale de l'Ocean Indien [International Indian Ocean
  Expedition - IIOE] [French] (MSC) .... EIOI
Expeditionary .... EXPED
Expeditionary Airfield (MCD) .... EAF
Expeditionary Equipment Report System .... EERS
Expeditionary Force .... EF
Expeditionary Force Canteens [Official supply organization] [World War I]
  [British] .... EFC
Expeditionary Force Institutions [Military British] .... EFI
Expeditionary Force Message [Low-rate cable or radio message selected from
  a list of standard wordings] .... EFM
Expeditionary Force Message [Usually, EFM] [Low-rate cable or radio
  message selected from a list of standard wordings] .... XFM
Expeditionary Logistics Facility (MCD) .... ELF
Expeditionary Shelters [Marine Corps] (MCD) .... EXSH
Expeditionary Test Set (MCD) .... ETS
Expeditious Discharge Program [Army] .... EDP
Expeditious Discharge Program for the Reserve Components [Army]
  (MCD) .... EDP-RC
Expeditious Monitor and Maintenance Analyst [Computer] [NASA] .... EMMA
Expeditious Sales, Catalog, and Property Evaluation [Defense Logistics
  Services Center project] [DoD] .... ESCAPE
Expeditor .... EXPD
Expeditor .... EXPDTR
Expeditor Resource Group Ltd. [Vancouver Stock Exchange symbol] .... EXD
Expeditors International of Washington [Associated Press] (SAG) .... ExpdInt
Expeditors International of Washington, Inc. [NASDAQ symbol] (NQ) ...... EXPD

Expeditors Intl,Wash [*NASDAQ symbol*] (TTSB) .... EXPD
Expend .... EXP
Expendability, Recoverability Cost Code (AAG) .... ERCC
Expendability/Recoverability/Repair Capability (NASA) .... ERRC
Expendability, Recoverability, Repairability Cost (NASA) .... ERRC
Expendability, Recoverability, Repairability Cost Category .... ERRCC
Expendability Repair Classification (AAG) .... ERC
Expendable (MSA) .... EXPEN
Expendable .... EXPEND
Expendable Acoustic Device [*Military*] (CAAL) .... EAD
Expendable Bathythermograph (EERA) .... XBT
Expendable Bathythermograph [*Oceanography*] .... XBT
Expendable Case (MCD) XC
Expendable Cluster Aircraft Rocket Launcher .... ECARL
Expendable Communications Jammer [*Army*] (INF) .... EXJAM
Expendable Conductivity-Temperature-Depth [*Probe*] [*Marine science*] (OSRA) .... XCTD
Expendable Conductivity-Temperature-Depth Probe (USDC) .... XCTD
Expendable Current Profiler [*Instrumentation, oceanography*] .... XCP
Expendable Current Temperature Density Profiler (EERA) .... XCTD
Expendable Dissipation Profiler [*Oceanography*] .... XDP
Expendable Electronic Markers (NVT) .... EEM
Expendable Instrument System .... EIS
Expendable Jammer (LAIN) .... EJ
Expendable LASER Jammer (MCD) .... ELJ
Expendable Launch Vehicle [*NASA*] (KSC) .... ELV
Expendable Light Markers (NVT) .... ELM
Expendable Mobile Acoustic Target (MCD) .... EMAT
Expendable Mobile ASW [*Antisubmarine Warfare*] **Tracking Target** [*Navy*] (CAAL) .... EMATT
Expendable Mobile ASW [*Air-to-Surface Weapon*] **Training Target** [*Navy*] (DWSG) .... EMATT
Expendable Ordnance Management [*Navy*] (DOMA) .... EOM
Expendable Parts Record and Structures System (IAA) .... EXPRESS
Expendable Radio Sonobuoy (IAA) .... ERSB
Expendable Recoverable Sound Projector [*Navy*] (CAAL) .... ERSP
Expendable Reliable Acoustic Path Sensor [*or Sonar or Sonobuoy*] (MCD) .... ERAPS
Expendable Remote Array (PDAA) .... EXRAY
Expendable Remote Operating Weather Station [*Air Force*] .... EROWS
Expendable Salinity/Temperature/Depth Probe [*Oceanography*] (MSC) .... XSTD
Expendable Second Stage [*Space shuttle*] [*NASA*] .... ESS
Expendable Sound Source .... ESS
Expendable Sound Velocimeter [*Oceanography*] (MSC) .... XSV
Expendable Stored Project Contract (DNAB) .... ESPC
Expendable Supplies and Materials List (MCD) .... ESML
Expendable Surface Current Probe [*Coast Guard*] .... ESCP
Expendable Threat Emitter (DWSG) .... ETE
Expendable Turbine Engine .... ETE
Expendable Vehicle (MCD) .... EV
Expendable-Expendable-Reusable .... EER
Expended Core Facility [*Nuclear energy*] .... ECF
Expenditious Discharge Program for the Reserve Components [*Military*] .... EDR-RC
Expenditure [*Economics*] .... E
Expenditure [*Dialog*] [*Searchable field*] [*Information service or system*] (NITA) .... EX
Expenditure .... EXPEND
Expenditure (AFM) .... EXPND
Expenditure Account .... EXACCT
Expenditure Account Number .... EAN
Expenditure Analysis Plan (TEL) .... EAP
Expenditure and Employment (OICC) .... EE
Expenditure Greater Than [*Dialog*] [*Searchable field*] [*Information service or system*] (NITA) .... EG
Expenditure Less Than [*Dialog*] [*Searchable field*] [*Information service or system*] (NITA) .... EL
Expenditure Order [*Military*] (AABC) .... XO
Expenditure Saved [*Economics*] .... S
Expenditure Targets [*Medical care proposal*] .... ET
Expense (AABC) .... EXP
Expense .... EXP
Expense Appropriation Management/Army Industrial Fund .... EAM/AIF
Expense for Return of Absentee [*Military*] .... ERA
Expense for Return of Deserter [*Military*] .... ERD
Expense Management and Control, Inc. [*Vancouver Stock Exchange symbol*] .... EXM
Expense Operating Budget (AFM) .... EOB
Expense Report (AAG) .... ER
Expenses .... E
Expenses (ROG) .... EXES
Expenses (ROG) .... EXPS
Expenses .... EXS
Expenses .... XS
Experessed Attitude Toward Confrontation Questionnaire (EDAC) .... EATCQ
Experience .... E
Experience (AABC) .... EXPC
Experience .... EXPRNC
Experience Analysis Mechanism [*Health insurance*] (GHCT) .... EXAM
Experience and Background Inventory [*Management and supervision test*] .... EBI
Experience and Background Questionnaire [*Test*] .... EBQ
Experience Critique Orgel [*Nuclear reactor*] [*Italy*] .... ECO
Experience Data Report (AAGC) .... EDR
Experience de Recherche d'Objects Sombres [*Astronomy*] .... EROS
Experience de Recherches d'Objets Sombres [*Experiment on Investigations int o Dark Objects*] .... EROS

Experience Demand Replacement Factor [*Navy*] .... EDRF
Experience Rating System [*Health insurance*] (GHCT) .... ERS
Experience Retention Action Request (SAA) .... ERAR
Experience Unit .... EU
Experience Usage Replacement Factor [*Navy*] .... EURF
Experience-Based Career Education .... EBCE
Experience-Based Career Education for Mentally Disabled Students (OICC) .... EBCE-MD
Experienced .... EXP
Experienced .... EXPER
Experienced Control Scales (EDAC) .... ECS
Experienced Export Manager [*American Society of International Executives*] [*Designation awarded by*] .... EEM
Experienced International Executive - Air Forwarding [*American Society of International Executives, Inc.*] [*Designation awarded by*] .... EIE-AF
Experienced International Executive - Banking [*American Society of Intern ational Executives, Inc.*] [*Designation awarded by*] .... EIEB
Experienced International Executive - Credit [*American Society of Interna tional Executives, Inc.*] [*Designation awarded by*] .... EIE-C
Experienced International Executive - Export Management [*American Society of International Executives, Inc.*] [*Designation awarded by*] .... EIE-EM
Experienced International Executive - Forwarding [*American Society of Int ernational Executives, Inc.*] [*Designation awarded by*] .... EIE-F
Experienced International Executive - Marketing [*American Society of Inte rnational Executives, Inc.*] [*Designation awarded by*] .... EIE-M
Experienced International Executive - Traffic Management [*American Societ y of International Executives, Inc.*] [*Designation awarded by*] .... EIE-TM
Experienced Librarians and Information Personnel in the Developing Countries of Asia and Oceania [*Korea Advanced Institute of Science and Technology*] [*Seoul*] [*Information service or system*] (IID) .... ELIPA
Experienced Playgoer [*Theatrical*] .... EP
Experienced Teacher Fellowship Program .... EXTFP
Experienced Worker Standard .... EWS
Experiences in Marketing Management (MCD) .... EMM
Experiences in Mathematical Ideas (EDAC) .... EMI
Experiential World Inventory [*Psychodiagnostic questionnaire*] .... EWI
Experimenal Forecast Facility [*Marine science*] (OSRA) .... EFF
Experiment [*or Experimental*] .... EX
Experiment (KSC) .... EXP
Experiment [*or Experimental*] (AFM) .... EXPER
Experiment (IAA) .... EXPR
Experiment .... EXPRMNT
Experiment .... EXPT
Experiment Analysis Form (KSC) .... EAF
Experiment and Development [*Flotilla*] [*Landing Craft*] .... X & D
Experiment and Guidance Loop Evaluator .... EAGLE
Experiment and Operations (KSC) .... EXOP
Experiment Apparatus Container .... EAC
Experiment Assembly (KSC) .... EA
Experiment Assurance System [*Nuclear energy*] (NRCH) .... EAS
Experiment Beryllium Oxide Reactor - Critical Assembly (SAA) .... EBOR-CX
Experiment Canister (MCD) .... EC
Experiment Checkout Equipment (MCD) .... ECE
Experiment Checkout Equipment Processor (NASA) .... ECEP
Experiment Compartment .... E
Experiment Computer (MCD) .... EC
Experiment Computer (MCD) .... EXC
Experiment Computer Application Software (MCD) .... ECAS
Experiment Computer Input/Output (NASA) .... ECIO
Experiment Computer Operating System (MCD) .... ECOS
Experiment Data Facility [*NASA*] (KSC) .... EDF
Experiment Data Record .... EDR
Experiment Data System .... EDS
Experiment Dedicated Heat Exchanger (MCD) .... EHX
Experiment Development Center [*NASA*] (KSC) .... EDC
Experiment Flight Applications (NASA) .... EFA
Experiment Implementation Plan [*NASA*] .... EIP
Experiment in Free-Form Education (AEBS) .... EFFE
Experiment in International Living/School for International Training (EA) .... EIL
Experiment, Inc., Richmond, VA [*Library symbol Library of Congress*] (LCLS) .... ViREx
Experiment Information System .... EIS
Experiment Integration Center (MCD) .... EIC
Experiment Integration Requirements Document [*NASA*] .... EIRD
Experiment Interface Definition Document (MCD) .... EIDD
Experiment Mock-Up Converters (KSC) .... EMC
Experiment on Rapidly Intensifying Cyclones over the Atlantic [*National Oceanic and Atmospheric Administration*] .... ERICA
Experiment Operations Handbook (KSC) .... EOH
Experiment Operations Panel .... EOP
Experiment Operator (MCD) .... EXO
Experiment Performance Option .... EPO
Experiment Point Control [*NASA*] .... EPC
Experiment Point Control System [*or Subsystem*] [*NASA*] (KSC) .... EPCS
Experiment Pointing Electronic Assembly [*NASA*] .... EPEA
Experiment Pointing System [*NASA*] .... EPS
Experiment Power Distribution Box (NASA) .... EPDB
Experiment Power Switching Panel (MCD) .... EPSP
Experiment Procedures (KSC) .... EXPRO
Experiment Requirements Document (KSC) .... ERD
Experiment Review Board [*Nuclear Regulatory Commission*] (NRCH) .... ERB
Experiment Segment (MCD) .... ES
Experiment Segment and Pallet Simulator [*NASA*] (NASA) .... ESPS
Experiment Sensing Platform (NASA) .... ESP
Experiment Subsystem Simulator [*NASA*] (NASA) .... ESS

Experiment Support Equipment ... ESE
Experiment Support System (MCD) ... ESS
Experiment Systems Division (MCD) ... ESD
Experiment Terminal (MCD) ... EXT
Experimental ... E
Experimental [*When preceding vessel classification*] [*Navy symbol*] ... E
Experimental (IDOE) ... exp
Experimental ... EXPTL
Experimental [*Military*] (AABC) ... X
Experimental (DOMA) ... Xmtl
Experimental Activity Proposal [*Nuclear energy*] (NRCH) ... EAP
Experimental Aerospace Multiprocessor ... EXAM
Experimental (Air Force) ... XA
Experimental Air Specification Weapons [*Navy*] (NG) ... XAS
Experimental Aircraft Association (EA) ... EAA
Experimental Aircraft Programme [*British*] ... EAP
Experimental Air-to-Air Missile [*Air Force, NASA*] ... XAAM
Experimental Air-to-Surface Missile [*Air Force, NASA*] ... XASM
Experimental Alcoholic Rhabdomyolysis [*Medicine*] ... EAR
Experimental Allergic Encephalomyelitis [*Medicine*] (AAMN) ... EAE
Experimental Allergic Neuritis [*Medicine*] ... EAN
Experimental Allergic Uveitis [*Ophthalmology*] ... EAU
Experimental and Demonstration Projects ... E & D
Experimental and Development ... XAD
Experimental and Development Flotilla [*Navy*] (DNAB) ... X & DFLOT
Experimental and Development Operations (MCD) ... E & DO
Experimental and Proving Establishment [*Canada*] (MCD) ... EPE
Experimental Arctic Data Buoy (MSC) ... EADB
Experimental Army Satellite Tactical ... EAST
Experimental Army Satellite Tactical Terminals ... EASTT
Experimental Array RADAR [*Army*] ... EAR
Experimental Assembly and Sterilization Laboratory [*NASA*] ... EASL
Experimental Assembly of Structures in Extravehicular Activity [*Space technology*] ... EASE
Experimental Assistant, Gunnery [*British military*] (DMA) ... EG
Experimental Autoimmune Encephalomyelitis [*Medicine*] ... EAE
Experimental Autoimmune Myasthenia Gravis [*Medicine*] ... EAMG
Experimental Autoimmune Neuritis [*Medicine*] ... EAN
Experimental Autoimmune Thymitis [*Medicine*] ... EAT
Experimental Autoimmune Uveoretinitis [*Immunology*] ... EAU
Experimental Autonomous Vehicle [*Underwater robot*] ... EAVE
Experimental Avionics Simulation and Integration Laboratory ... EASILY
Experimental Ballistics Associates [*Defunct*] (EA) ... EBA
Experimental Behavioral Analyzer ... EBA
Experimental Beryllium Oxide Reactor [*Later, BORE*] ... EBOR
Experimental Boiling Water Reactor ... EBWR
Experimental Bomber (MCD) ... XB
Experimental Breeder Reactor ... EBR
Experimental Breeder Reactor ... XBR
Experimental Bridging Establishment [*British*] ... EBE
Experimental Building Station ... EBS
Experimental Buoy [*Marine science*] (MSC) ... EB
Experimental Buried Collector Gauge ... EBCG
Experimental Cardiology [*Russian*] ... IEC
Experimental Cargo Aircraft ... XC
Experimental Cargo Glider ... XCG
Experimental Cartographic Facility [*Air Force*] ... ECF
Experimental Changes of Practice Committees [*British Post Office*] (PDAA) ... ECOPC
Experimental Cities, Inc. (EA) ... ECI
Experimental Cloud Lidar Polot Study (EERA) ... ECLIPS
Experimental Coherent RADAR (MCD) ... ECR
Experimental Communications Satellite [*NASA*] ... ECS
Experimental Computer Complex ... ECC
Experimental Computer-Aided Shop Scheduling (IAA) ... ECASS
Experimental Concentration-Percent (FFDE) ... ECx
Experimental Consultative Conference of Industrialists (NATG) ... ECCI
Experimental Contract Highlight Operation [*NASA*] ... ECHO
Experimental Control (MAE) ... EC
Experimental Cross Section Information Library [*University of California, Livermore*] ... ECSIL
Experimental Data Communications Network (MCD) ... EDCN
Experimental Data Gathering and Reduction (MCD) ... EDGAR
Experimental Data Handling Equipment ... EDHE
Experimental Data Management System [*Computer science*] (MHDI) ... XDMS
Experimental Demolition Establishment [*British*] ... EDE
Experimental Design ... ED
Experimental Development ... EDP
Experimental Development, Demonstration, and Integration Center [*Army*] ... EDDIC
Experimental Development Requirements (CINC) ... EDR
Experimental Development Specification [*Military*] (CAAL) ... XMS
Experimental, Developmental, Test, and Research ... EDTR
Experimental Digital Television System ... EDITS
Experimental Display Concept [*Space shuttle*] [*NASA*] ... EDC
Experimental Display Generator ... EDGE
Experimental Diving Unit [*Research center British*] ... EDU
Experimental Diving Unit ... EXPDIVUNIT
Experimental Division ... EXDIV
Experimental Dynamic Processor (MUGU) ... EDP
Experimental Ecological Reserves [*Project*] [*National Science Foundation*] ... EER
Experimental Education Program ... EEP
Experimental Engine [*NASA*] ... XE
Experimental Engine - Cold Flow Configuration [*NERVA*] ... XECF
Experimental Engineering Orders (DNAB) ... XEO
Experimental Environmental Research Buoy [*Marine science*] (MSC) ... XERB
Experimental Establishment [*RAF*] [*British*] ... EE
Experimental Farm, Agriculture Canada [*Ferme Experimentale, Agriculture Canada*], Indian Head, Saskatchewan [*Library symbol National Library of Canada*] (BIB) ... SIHAG
Experimental Farm, Agriculture Canada [*Ferme Experimentale, Agriculture Canada*] **La Pocatiere, Quebec** [*Library symbol National Library of Canada*] (NLC) ... QPAG
Experimental Farm, Agriculture Canada [*Ferme Experimentale, Agriculture Canada*] **L'Assomption, Quebec** [*Library symbol National Library of Canada*] (NLC) ... QASAG
Experimental Farm, Agriculture Canada [*Ferme Experimentale, Agriculture Canada*] **Normandin, Quebec** [*Library symbol National Library of Canada*] (NLC) ... QNOAG
Experimental Farm, Agriculture Canada [*Ferme Experimentale, Agriculture Canada*], Prince George, British Columbia [*Library symbol National Library of Canada*] (BIB) ... BPGAG
Experimental Fast Ceramic Reactor ... EFCR
Experimental Fighter ... XF
Experimental Fighting Biplane [*British military*] (DMA) ... EFB
Experimental Firing Ship ... EFS
Experimental Flight ... EF
Experimental Flight Management System [*Aviation*] (DA) ... EFMS
Experimental Flight Systems Section [*Langley*] ... EFSS
Experimental Flight Test ... EFT
Experimental Force [*Army*] (INF) ... EXFOR
Experimental Forecast Facility [*National Weather Service*] (USDC) ... EFF
Experimental Gas-Cooled Reactor ... EGCR
Experimental Geodetic Payload [*Japan*] ... EGP
Experimental Geophysical Orbiting [*Vehicle*] ... EGO
Experimental Geosynchronous Platform (SSD) ... XGP
Experimental Glider ... EG
Experimental Glomerulonephritis [*Medicine*] ... EGN
Experimental GOES [*Goestationary Operational Environmental Satellite*] **Platform** [*Marine science*] (MSC) ... EGP
Experimental Group ... EG
Experimental Guided Air Missiles ... XGAM
Experimental Health Services Delivery Systems [*HEW*] ... EHSDS
Experimental Helicopter ... XH
Experimental Horticulture Station [*British*] ... EHS
Experimental Housing Allowance Program [*Department of Housing and Urban Development*] (GFGA) ... EHAP
Experimental Husbandry Farm [*British*] ... EHF
Experimental Hybrid Computer Network (MHDB) ... EHCN
Experimental Information Service in Two Social Welfare Agencies (PDAA) ... EISSWA
Experimental Institute for Models and Structures [*Italy*] ... ISMES
Experimental Integrated Conformed Array ... EICA
Experimental Integrated Network ... EIN
Experimental Integrated Switched Network ... EISN
Experimental Inter-American Meteorological Rocket Network [*NASA*] ... EXAMETNET
Experimental Intercom (NASA) ... EIC
Experimental International Data Centre [*Australia*] ... EIDC
Experimental Jaguar [*Jaguar PLC*] ... XJ
Experimental Jaguar Racing ... XJR
Experimental Labor Control System (IAA) ... ELCS
Experimental Lakes Area [*A collection of 48 small lakes near the Ontario-Manitoba border*] [*Canada*] ... ELA
Experimental LASER Device (MCD) ... XLD
Experimental Launching Round (SAA) ... ELR
Experimental Library Management System ... ELMS
Experimental Light [*Navigation signal*] ... Exper
Experimental Liquid Rocket [*Air Force, NASA*] ... XLR
Experimental Logistics Module (SSD) ... ELM
Experimental Low-Temperature Process Heat Reactor ... ELPHR
Experimental Manned Interceptor Program (IAA) ... EMIP
Experimental Manned Space Station [*Air Force*] ... EMSS
Experimental Manpower Laboratory for Corrections (OICC) ... EMLC
Experimental Mathematical Programming System [*Computer science*] (MHDI) ... XMP
Experimental Medical Care Review Organization [*Program of the National Center for Health Services Research and Development*] ... EMCRO
Experimental Medical Research Support Center (SAA) ... EMRSC
Experimental Memo ... EM
Experimental Memory - Address Register ... EMAR
Experimental Meteorological Sounding Rocket Research Network (IEEE) ... EXMETNET
Experimental Meteorology Laboratory ... EML
Experimental Military Command Information System (MCD) ... EMCIS
Experimental Miscellaneous Auxiliary [*Navy symbol*] ... EAG
Experimental Missile [*Air Force, NASA*] ... XM
Experimental Missile Specifications ... XMS
Experimental Mobile Satellite System (DA) ... EMSS
Experimental Model ... XM
Experimental Model Basin [*Navy*] ... EMB
Experimental Monitoring Satellite (MCD) ... EMS
Experimental Navigation Ship ... ENS
Experimental (Navy) ... XN
Experimental Negotiating Agreement [*Steelworkers contract*] ... ENA
Experimental Network Operating System ... XNOS
Experimental Officer [*Also, ExO, XO*] [*Ministry of Agriculture, Fisheries, and Food*] [*British*] ... EO
Experimental Officer [*Also, EO, XO*] [*Ministry of Agriculture, Fisheries, and Food*] [*British*] ... ExO

Experimental Officer [*Also, EO, ExO*] [*Ministry of Agriculture, Fisheries, and Food*] [*British*] ... XO
Experimental On-Line Capabilities [*Computer science*] ... XOC
Experimental Operating Procedure (SAA) ... EOP
Experimental Operations Center ... EOC
Experimental Order (MSA) ... EXPO
Experimental Organic Cooled Reactor ... EOCR
Experimental Packet Switching System [*Telecommunications*] ... EPSS
Experimental Patrol Craft, Escort and Rescue ... EPCER
Experimental Power Reactor (MCD) ... EPR
Experimental Power Supply (NASA) ... EPS
Experimental Process System Development Unit [*Photovoltaic energy systems*] ... EPSDU
Experimental Procurement Service ... EPS
Experimental Program to Stimulate Competitive Research [*National Science Foundation*] ... EPSCoR
Experimental Project Apollo-Soyuz [*Acronym used as name of a cologne created to commemorate the first joint US/Russian manned space flight*] ... EPAS
Experimental Prototype Automatic Meteorological System (MCD) ... EPAMS
Experimental Prototype Community of Tomorrow [*Disney World*] [*Facetious translation: "Every Person Comes Out Tired"*] ... EPCOT
Experimental Prototype Gas-Cooled Reactor ... EPGCR
Experimental Prototype Silo (SAA) ... EPS
Experimental Prototype Test (MCD) ... EPT
Experimental Psychology Society [*British*] ... EPS
Experimental Publications System [*Defunct*] ... EPS
Experimental RADAR Prediction Device (MCD) ... ERPD
Experimental RADAR System ... ERS
Experimental Reflector Orbital Shot [*NASA project*] ... EROS
Experimental Remote Maneuvering Unit ... ERMU
Experimental Reproduction File [*Computer science*] (ECII) ... XRF
Experimental Reproduction Film (DIT) ... XRF
Experimental Research and Development Incentives Program [*National Science Foundation*] ... ERDIP
Experimental Research in Electronic Submission of Scientific Documents Program [*Washington, DC National Science Foundation*] ... EXPRES
Experimental Research Kit ... ERK
Experimental Research Society [*Defunct*] (EA) ... ERS
Experimental Rocket Engine Test Station (SAA) ... ERETS
Experimental Route Guidance System (IAA) ... ERGS
Experimental Safety Vehicle [*Later, Research Safety Vehicle*] [*Department of Transportation*] ... ESV
Experimental SAGE [*Semi-Automatic Ground Environment*] **Sector** ... ESS
Experimental Sheet Growth Unit [*Photovoltaic energy systems*] ... ESGU
Experimental Solid Propellant Vehicle ... XSPV
Experimental Solid-State Exchange [*Communication system*] (MCD) ... ESSEX
Experimental Sonic Azimuth Detector (MCD) ... X-SONAD
Experimental Space Communication Earth Station [*Telecommunications*] (TEL) ... ESCES
Experimental Space Laboratory ... XSL
Experimental Space Station [*NASA*] ... XSS
Experimental Squadron [*Symbol*] (MCD) ... VX
Experimental Station ... ES
Experimental Station [*ITU designation*] (CET) ... EX
Experimental Station ... EXSTA
Experimental Stations Committee on Organization and Policy [*National Association of State Universities and Land-Grant Colleges*] ... ESCOP
Experimental Stealth Tactical Demonstrator [*Air Force*] ... XST
Experimental STOL Transport Research ... ESTRA
Experimental Strategic Missile ... XSM
Experimental Study [*Research*] (DAVI) ... ES
Experimental Superconducting Accelerating Ring [*Atomic physics*] ... ESCAR
Experimental Superheat Reactor ... ESR
Experimental Surface Missile ... XSM
Experimental Surface-to-Air Missile [*Military*] (IAA) ... XSAM
Experimental Surface-to-Surface Missile [*Military*] (IAA) ... XSSM
Experimental Tactic (NVT) ... EXTAC
Experimental Target Designation Equipment ... ETDE
Experimental Target Drone [*Air Force, NASA*] ... XQ
Experimental Techniques Centre [*Brunel University*] [*British*] (CB) ... ETC
Experimental Technology Incentives Program [*National Institute of Standards and Technology*] ... ETIP
Experimental Test Accelerator [*Nuclear physics*] ... ETA
Experimental Test Bed (MCD) ... ETB
Experimental Test Bed [*Army*] (DOMA) ... XTB
Experimental Test Model (IAA) ... ETM
Experimental Test Model ... XTM
Experimental Test Procedure (MCD) ... ETP
Experimental Test Reactor [*Nuclear energy*] (OA) ... ETR
Experimental Translation Language (IAA) ... XTRAN
Experimental Transmitting Antenna Modular Model (MCD) ... ETAM
Experimental Tunneling Establishment [*British*] ... ETE
Experimental Underwater Pump Jet ... EUPJ
Experimental Unit (NASA) ... EU
Experimental Use Computer, London Integrated Display ... EUCLID
Experimental Use Permit [*Environmental Protection Agency*] ... EUP
Experimental Vehicle for Avionics Research (MCD) ... EVARS
Experimental Version (SDI) ... EV
Experimental Volunteer Army Training Program (RDA) ... EVATP
Experimental Warhead ... XW
Experimental Weapon Specification ... XWS
Experimental Weapon System ... XWS
Experimental Yacht Society [*Defunct*] (EA) ... EYS
Experimental-Eleventh Generation [*Jaguar*] [*Automotive engineering*] ... XK
Experimentation Command [*Army*] (MCD) ... EC
Experimenter [*Psychology*] ... E
Experimenter-Administered Stimulation [*Psychology*] ... EAS
Experimento Meteologico del Verano [*Marine science*] (OSRA) ... EMVER
Experimento Meteorologico del Verano (USDC) ... EMVER
Experiments, Drill, and Maintenance ... EDAM
Experiments Ground Computer [*NASA*] (NASA) ... EGC
Experiments in Art and Technology (EA) ... EAT
Experiments of Opportunity (NASA) ... EOP
Experiments Systems Branch [*NASA*] (KSC) ... ESB
Experiments Systems Monitor [*NASA*] (KSC) ... ESM
Expert ... EX
Expert ... EXP
Expert ... EXPR
Expert (WGA) ... EXPT
Expert Adaptive Controller Tuning (NITA) ... EXACT
Expert Bradley Infantry Squad Training Test [*Army*] (INF) ... EBIST
Expert Center for Taxonomic Identification [*The Netherlands*] (EERA) ... ETI
Expert Committee on Plant Gene Resources [*Canadian Agricultural Services Coordinating Committee*] ... ECPGR
Expert Committee on Post Adjustments [*United Nations*] ... ECPA
Expert Database Designer [*Computer science*] ... EDD
Expert Database System [*Computer science*] (ODBW) ... EDBS
Expert Decision-Support System [*Computer science*] (ODBW) ... EDSS
Expert Disclosure Analysis and Avoidance System [*Environmental protection agency*] (NITA) ... EDAAS
Expert Field Medical Badge [*Military decoration*] (AABC) ... EFMB
Expert Field Medical Badge [*Military decoration*] (GFGA) ... EXPFLDMB
Expert Gunner [*Army*] ... EG
Expert Infantryman Badge [*Military decoration*] ... EIB
Expert Infantryman Badge [*Military decoration*] ... EIBAD
Expert Information Systems Ltd. [*Information service or system*] (IID) ... EXIS
Expert Panel on the Facilitation of Tuna Research [*Marine science*] (MSC) ... EPFTR
Expert Qualification Badge [*Military decoration*] (AABC) ... ExpQualBad
Expert Requirements Expression and Systems Synthesis (SSD) ... EXPRESS
Expert Rifleman ... ER
Expert Slope [*Skiing*] ... E
Expert Software [*NASDAQ symbol*] (TTSB) ... XPRT
Expert Software, Inc. [*Associated Press*] (SAG) ... ExpSoft
Expert Software, Inc. [*NASDAQ symbol*] (SAG) ... XPRT
Expert Statistical System ... ESS
Expert System [*Computer science*] ... ES
Expert System [*Computer science*] (IAA) ... XPS
Expert System Building Tool [*Computer science*] ... ESBT
Expert System Environment/Virtual Machine [*Computer science*] ... ESE/VM
Expert Tsunami Database for the Pacific [*Marine science*] (OSRA) ... ETDP
Expert Vax Ethernet Interface [*Work station computer-network interface*] (NITA) ... EVE
Experts-Conseils Shawinigan, Montreal, PQ, Canada [*Library symbol*] [*Library of Congress*] (LCLS) ... CaQMECS
Experts-Conseils Shawinigan, Montreal, Quebec [*Library symbol National Library of Canada*] (NLC) ... QMECS
Expiration [*or Expiratory*] [*Medicine*] ... EXPIR
Expiration (ROG) ... EXPN
Expiration of Active Obligated Service [*Military*] ... EAOS
Expiration of Active Service [*Marine Corps*] ... EAS
Expiration of Enlistment ... E of E
Expiration of Enlistment ... EE
Expiration of Obligated Service [*Military*] ... EOS
Expiration of Service ... E of S
Expiration of Service Agreement [*Military*] (AABC) ... ESA
Expiration of Term of Obligation [*Military*] ... ETO
Expiration of Term of Service [*Military*] ... ETS
Expiration-Inspiration [*Ratio*] [*Physiology*] ... E/I
Expiratory [*Respiration*] (DAVI) ... exp
Expiratory Center [*Physiology*] ... EC
Expiratory Flow-Volume Curve [*Medicine*] ... EFVC
Expiratory Reserve Volume [*Physiology*] ... ERV
Expire [*Medicine*] (DAVI) ... E
Expire [*Medicine*] (DAVI) ... expir
Expire (AABC) ... EXPR
Expired [*Gas*] [*Medicine*] ... E
Expired (ROG) ... EXP
Expired (ROG) ... EXPD
Expired Air [*Medicine*] (DMAA) ... E
Expired Air Resuscitation (ADA) ... EAR
Expiring Law Continuance Acts (DLA) ... ELC Acts
Explain [*or Explanation*] (IAA) ... XPL
Explained [*Statement of import of decision in cited case, not merely a restatement of the facts*] [*Legal term*] (DLA) ... E
Explained [*Legal term*] (DLA) ... Exp
Explained (ROG) ... EXPLD
Explained Sum of Squares [*Data Analysis*] ... ESS
Explanation ... EX
Explanation ... EXPL
Explanation of Benefit Payment [*Insurance*] ... EBP
Explanation of Benefit Payment [*Insurance*] ... EOBP
Explanation of Benefits ... EOB
Explanation of Medicare [*or Medical*] **Benefits** ... EOMB
Explanation of Votes (EERA) ... EOVs
Explanation Report [*NASA*] (NASA) ... ER
Explanatory (ADA) ... EXPLAN
Explanatory Memorandum ... EM
Expletive (ROG) ... EXPLET
Explicit ... E

Explicit 2-D Patterns Local Operations and Randomness [*Programming language*] [*1975*] (CSR) .... EXPLOR
Explicit Call Transfer [*Telecommunications*] (DOM) .... ECT
Explicit Congestion Notification [*Telecommunications*] (ACRL) .... ECN
Explicit Forward Congestion Indicator [*Telecommunications*] (ACRL) .... EFCI
Explicitly Coded Program (MCD) .... ECP
Explode (MSA) .... EXPLD
Exploder .... EXPLR
Exploder Control Sensor (MCD) .... ECS
Exploding Bridge-Wire .... EBW
Exploding Bridge-Wire .... XB
Exploding Bridge-Wire System (KSC) .... EBWS
Exploding Wire Aerosol Generator [*Liquid suspension*] .... EWAG
Exploding Wire Phenomena .... EWP
Exploit (MUGU) .... XPLT
Exploitable Subcommittee [*Military*] .... EXSUBCOM
Exploitation de Renseignements Contenus dans les Brevets [*Patent Information Exploitation - PIE*] [*Canadian Patent Office*] .... ERCB
Exploitation Products File (MCD) .... EPF
Exploration (MAE) .... exp
Exploration (DD) .... explor
Exploration .... EXPLRN
Exploration and Production [*In organization name Oil Industry International Exploration & Production Forum*] .... E & P
Exploration Co. [*Associated Press*] (SAG) .... Explor
[*The*] Exploration Co. [*NASDAQ symbol*] (NQ) .... TXCO
Exploration Company of Louisiana, Inc. [*Later, XCL Ltd.*] [*AMEX symbol*] (SPSG) XCL
Exploration Lease (ADA) .... EL
Exploration Licence Application [*Australia*] : .... ELA
Exploration Map Data (RDA) .... EMD
Exploration of Alternative Concepts (MCD) .... EASC
Exploration of Common Bile Duct [*Medicine*] (DMAA) .... ECBD
Exploration Permit [*Australia*] .... EP
Exploration Science Working Group [*NASA*] (EGAO) .... EXSWG
Explorations in Eastern Palestine [*A publication*] (BJA) .... EEP
Exploratory [*Surgery*] (DAVI) .... expl
Exploratory Career Development (DNAB) .... ECD
Exploratory Committee on Assessing the Progress of Education [*Later, NAEP*] .... ECAPE
Exploratory Data Analysis [*Statistics*] .... EDA
Exploratory Development [*Military*] .... ED
Exploratory Development [*Military*] (MCD) .... XD
Exploratory Development Goal [*Military*] .... EDG
Exploratory Development Model [*Military*] .... EDM
Exploratory Development Objective [*Military*] .... EDO
Exploratory Development Program Summary [*Military*] .... EDPS
Exploratory Development Request [*Military*] .... EDR
Exploratory Development Requirement [*Military*] .... EDR
Exploratory Development Summary Report [*Military*] .... EDSR
Exploratory Group (NATG) .... EG
Exploratory Laparatomy [*Medicine*] .... Exp Lap
Exploratory Laparatomy [*Surgical procedure*] (DAVI) .... Expl Lap
Exploratory Project for Economic Alternatives (EA) .... EPEA
Exploratory Project on the Conditions of Peace [*Defunct*] (EA) .... ExPro
Exploratory Research for Advanced Technology [*Japan*] .... ERATO
Explore the World of Work [*Vocational guidance test*] .... E-WOW
Explorer .... EXPL
Explorer Plus Guidance Application Network [*Electronic college application*] .... ExPAN
Explorers Club (EA) .... EC
Explorers Club, New York, NY [*Library symbol Library of Congress*] (LCLS) .... NNEC
Exploring Human Nature [*National Science Foundation project*] .... EHN
Explosion (ECII) .... EXPL
Explosion (MSA) .... EXPLN
Explosion [*Military*] (CAAL) X
Explosion and Flame Laboratory [*British*] (IRUK) .... EFL
Explosion Collapse, Underground Operations .... XCU
Explosion of the Total Contents [*Insurance*] (DS) .... ETC
Explosion Release Factor [*Nuclear energy*] (NRCH) .... ERF
Explosion Release Factor [*Nuclear energy*] (NUCP) .... XPF
Explosion Release Factor [*Nuclear energy*] (NRCH) .... XRF
Explosion Tear Test [*Military*] .... ETT
Explosion Welding .... EXW
Explosion-Proof .... EP
Explosion-Proof Enclosure .... EPE
Explosion-Proof Housing .... EPH
Explosion-Proof Relay .... EPR
Explosion-Resistant Multi-Influence Sweep System (NATG) .... ERMISS
Explosive .... EXP
Explosive (KSC) .... EXPL
Explosive (AABC) .... EXPLO
Explosive .... explos
Explosive .... EXPLSV
Explosive (AAG) .... XPL
Explosive (FAAC) .... XPLOS
Explosive Anchorage [*Buoy*] .... Explos Anch
Explosive Detection Systems [*FAA*] (TAG) .... EDS
Explosive Device .... ED
Explosive Device System (KSC) .... EDS
Explosive Disposal Control .... EDC
Explosive Distributors Association [*Defunct*] (EA) .... EDA
Explosive Echo Ranging .... EER
Explosive Echo Ranging Charge (NG) .... EERC

Explosive Embedment Anchor (PDAA) .... EEA
Explosive Excavation Research Agency [*Formerly, NCG*] [*Army*] (RDA) .... EERA
Explosive Excavation Research Laboratory [*Army Engineer Waterways Experiment Station*] [*Livermore, CA*] .... EERL
Explosive Excavation Research Office [*Livermore, CA*] [*Army*] .... EERO
Explosive Foxhole Digger [*Army*] (INF) .... EXFOD
Explosive Gas Indicator .... EGI
Explosive Inventory Manager [*Military*] .... EIM
Explosive Investigation Manager .... EIM
Explosive Investigative Laboratory [*Navy*] .... EIL
Explosive Lens Flashbinder .... ELF
Explosive Mental Behavior (BABM) .... EMB
Explosive Metal Forming .... EMF
Explosive Motor Behavior [*Neurochemistry*] .... EMB
Explosive Ordinance Disposal [*Military*] (VNW) .... EOD
Explosive Ordnance [*Military*] (AFM) .... EO
Explosive Ordnance Components [*Military*] (MCD) .... EOC
Explosive Ordnance Detachment [*Army*] (RDA) .... EOD
Explosive Ordnance Device [*Military*] (MCD) .... EOD
Explosive Ordnance Disposal [*Military*] .... EOD
Explosive Ordnance Disposal Badge [*Military decoration*] (GFGA) .... EODBAD
Explosive Ordnance Disposal Bulletin [*Military*] .... EODB
Explosive Ordnance Disposal Center [*DoD*] .... EODC
Explosive Ordnance Disposal Control [*Military*] (AABC) .... EODC
Explosive Ordnance Disposal Evaluator .... EODE
Explosive Ordnance Disposal Flight [*Military*] .... EODF
Explosive Ordnance Disposal Group [*Military*] (NVT) .... EODG
Explosive Ordnance Disposal Group [*Military*] .... EODGRU
Explosive Ordnance Disposal Group, Atlantic [*Military*] .... EODGRULANT
Explosive Ordnance Disposal Group Detachment [*Military*] (DNAB) .... EODGRUDET
Explosive Ordnance Disposal Group, Pacific [*Military*] .... EODGRUPAC
Explosive Ordnance Disposal Mobile Unit [*Military*] (DNAB) .... EODMU
Explosive Ordnance Disposal, Nuclear [*Military*] (NVT) .... EODN
Explosive Ordnance Disposal School [*Indian Head, MD*] [*Military*] .... EODS
Explosive Ordnance Disposal Specialist Badge [*Military decoration*] (AABC) .... EODSBad
Explosive Ordnance Disposal Squadron [*Military*] .... EODS
Explosive Ordnance Disposal Supervisor Badge [*Military decoration*] (AABC) .... EODSupvBad
Explosive Ordnance Disposal Technical Center [*Military*] (DNAB) .... EODTECHCEN
Explosive Ordnance Disposal Technical Information Center [*Military*] (DNAB) .... EODTIC
Explosive Ordnance Disposal Technology and Training Center [*Military*] .... EODT & T
Explosive Ordnance Disposal Training and Evaluation Unit [*Military*] (DNAB) .... EODTEU
Explosive Ordnance Disposal Unit [*Military*] (NVT) .... EODU
Explosive Ordnance Reconnaissance [*Military*] .... EOR
Explosive Ordnance Reconnaissance Agent [*Military*] (AABC) .... EORA
Explosive Ordnance Safety Approval [*Military*] (MUGU) .... EOSA
Explosive Reactive Armor [*Tank design*] .... ERA
Explosive Research and Development Establishment [*British*] .... ERDE
Explosive Safe Area [*NASA*] .... ESA
Explosive Safety Approval (MUGU) .... ESA
Explosive Safety Board [*Military*] .... ESB
Explosive Safety Knowledge Improvement Operation (MCD) .... ESKIMO
Explosive Safety Survey (NVT) .... ESS
Explosive Set Circuit Test System (DWSG) .... ESCTS
Explosive Technology .... ET
Explosive Test Operator (RDA) .... ETO
Explosive Testing Kit (MCD) .... ETK
Explosive Transfer Assembly (MCD) .... ETA
Explosive Transfer Lines [*Military*] .... ETL
Explosive Transient Camera [*Astronomy*] .... ETC
Explosive Valve (KSC) .... EV
Explosive Vapor Detector (DA) .... EVD
Explosive Vapor Detector Systems (MCD) .... EVDS
Explosive-Actuated Light Filter (NG) .... ELF
Explosive-Actuated Valve .... EAV
Explosively-Formed Penetrator [*Army*] (RDA) .... EFP
Explosives Corp. of America (MCD) .... ECA
Explosives Corp. of America .... EXCOA
Explosives Detection Devices [*FAA*] (TAG) .... EDD
Explosives Information and Analysis Center [*Army*] (PDAA) .... EXIAC
Explosives Ingredients Sources Database [*Chemical Propulsion Information Agency*] .... EISD
Explosives Investigation Memorandum [*Navy*] (MCD) .... EIM
Explosives Report .... ER
Explosives Research Center [*Bruceton, PA*] [*Bureau of Mines*] .... ERC
Explosives Research Memorandum .... ERM
Explosives Research Note .... ERN
Explosives Safety Quality Distance (DNAB) .... ESQD
Explosives Storage Area .... ESA
Explosives Testing Facility (SAA) .... ETF
Explosive-Safe Facility .... ESF
Explosive-to-Electric Transducer .... EET
Expo Collectors - Historians Organization (EA) .... ECHO
Expo Line [*Expository line*] [*Photograph caption*] (WDMC) .... e-line
Expo Oil [*Vancouver Stock Exchange symbol*] .... EPO
Expo West Trade Association (EA) .... EWTA
Exponent .... E
Exponent [*Mathematics*] (IAA) .... EX
Exponent (MSA) .... EXPNT
Exponential .... EXP

Exponential (IDOE) ... exp
Exponential (MSA) ... EXPNT
Exponential Decay Unit [*Physics*] (IAA) ... EDU
Exponential Ensemble Mutagenesis [*Technique for studying genetic sequences*] ... EEM
Exponential Equation ... EE
Exponential Function [*Mathematics*] (DAVI) ... exp
Exponential Hazard Function ... EHF
Exponential Integral ... EI
Exponential Power Distribution [*Statistics*] ... EPD
Exponential Reliability Function ... ERF
Exponentially Modified Gaussian [*Mathematical function*] ... EMG
Exponentially Restored, Poisson-Released ... ERPR
Exponentially Retrograded Diode ... ERD
Exponentially Weighted Moving Average [*Statistics*] ... EWMA
Exponentially-Tapered Reactive Antenna (IAA) ... EXTRA
Exponential-Slope Difference [*Statistics*] ... ESD
Export ... E
Export ... EX
Export ... EXP
Export ... EXPRT
Export (WGA) ... EXPT
Export [*Economics*] ... X
Export ... XPT
Export Administration Act [*1979*] ... EAA
Export Administration Regulation [*Department of Commerce*] ... EAR
Export Administration Review Board ... EARB
Export Advertising Association (DGA) ... EAA
Export Air del Peru SA Cargo Air Lines [*ICAO designator*] (FAAC) ... EXD
Export Annual Data [*Department of Commerce*] (GFGA) ... EA
Export Business Relations Division [*Department of Commerce*] ... EBRD
Export Buying Offices Association [*British*] (DBA) ... EXBO
Export Cargo Form [*Shipping*] ... ECF
Export Cargo Packing Declaration (DS) ... ECPD
Export Cargo Shipping Instruction (DS) ... ECSI
Export Clearance Number ... ECN
Export Consignment Identifying Number (DS) ... ECI
Export Control Act (MCD) ... ECA
Export Control Automated Support System [*Department of Commerce*] ... ECASS
Export Control Bulletin [*Department of Commerce*] ... ECB
Export Control Commodity Number (AAGC) ... ECCN
Export Control Regulations [*Department of Commerce*] ... ECR
Export Control Review Board ... ECRB
Export Council for Europe (ILCA) ... ECE
Export Credit Enhanced Leverage ... EXCEL
Export Credit Facilitation Scheme [*Australia*] ... ECFS
Export Credit Guarantee (DLA) ... ECG
Export Credits Guarantee Department [*British*] ... ECGD
Export Credits Insurance Corp. [*Canada*] ... ECIC
Export Development Corp. [*Canada*] ... EDC
Export Development Corp., Ottawa, ON, Canada [*Library symbol Library of Congress*] (LCLS) ... CaOOEDC
Export Development Corp. [*Societe pour l'Expansion des Exportations*] **Ottawa, Ontario** [*Library symbol National Library of Canada*] (NLC) ... OOEDC
Export Development Group of New South Wales [*Australia*] ... EDGNSW
Export Development Office [*Department of Commerce*] (IMH) ... EDO
Export Enhancement Program [*Department of Agriculture*] ... EEP
Export Expansion Facility [*Export-Import Bank of the US*] ... EEF
Export Facilitation Scheme [*Motor vehicles*] [*Australia*] ... EFS
Export Finance and Insurance Fund ... EFIF
Export Finance Co. [*British*] ... EXFINCO
Export Free Processing Zone ... EFPZ
Export Grape and Plum Act [*1960*] ... EGPA
Export Group for the Construction Industries [*British*] ... EGCI
Export Guarantees Act ... EGA
Export Insurance Division [*of the Ministry of International Trade and Industry*] [*Japan*] ... EID
Export Integrated System ... EXIT
Export Intelligence Service (DS) ... EIS
Export Licensing Branch [*British Overseas Trade Board*] (DS) ... ELB
Export Licensing Regulations (ODBW) ... ELR
Export Management Company ... EMC
Export Market Development [*Grants*] ... EMD
Export Market Development Grants Act [*Australia*] ... EMDGA
Export Marketing Assistance Program [*Australia*] ... EMAP
Export Marketing Service [*Department of Agriculture*] ... EMS
Export Meat Order ... EMO
Export Monthly Data [*Department of Commerce*] (GFGA) ... EM
Export Network [*British Information service or system*] (CRD) ... EN
Export Office (ROG) ... EO
Export Packers Association of New York [*Defunct*] (EA) ... EPANY
Export Pound Account [*Special type of currency*] [*United Arab Republic*] ... EPA
Export Processing Industry Coalition ... EPIC
Export Processing Zone (ECON) ... EPZ
Export Processing Zone Authority ... EPZA
Export Promotion Bureau [*Pakistan*] ... EPB
Export Promotion Programme Budget [*British*] ... EPPB
Export Propensity ... EP
Export Reactor [*Nuclear energy*] (NRCH) ... XR
Export Return Scheme [*Australia*] ... ERS
Export Service [*Queen's award*] [*British*] ... E
Export Services and Promotions Division [*British Overseas Trade Board*] (DS) ... ESPD
Export Surpluses [*British*] ... ES
Export Task Force (EA) ... ETF
Export Tender Risk Advance [*British*] ... EXTRA
Export Trading Company [*Department of Commerce*] ... ETC
Export Trading Company Act of 1982 ... ETCA
Export Traffic Release ... ETR
Export Traffic Release Request [*MTMC*] (TAG) ... ETRR
Export Transport Release ... ETR
Exportable Training Package [*Army*] ... ETP
Exportation ... EXPN
Exporter ... EXPRTR
Exporter (ADA) ... EXPTR
Export-Import (WDAA) ... EXP-IMP
Export-Import Bank ... E-IB
Export-Import Bank ... EXIM
Export-Import Bank ... EXIMBANK
Export-Import Bank ... EXIMBK
Export-Import Bank of the United States [*Formerly, EIB(W)*] ... EIBUS
Export-Import Bank of the United States (TDOB) ... EXIMBANK
Export-Import Bank of the United States (USGC) ... Eximbank
Export-Import Bank of the United States, Washington, DC [*Library symbol Library of Congress*] (LCLS) ... DEI
Export-Import Bank (of Washington) [*Later, EIBUS*] ... EIB(W)
Exports Directorate [*British*] ... ED
Exports to Europe Branch [*British Overseas Trade Board*] (DS) ... EEB
Exports to Japan Unit [*British Overseas Trade Board*] (DS) ... EJU
Exports to North America Branch [*British Overseas Trade Board*] (DS) ... ENAB
Expose (KSC) ... EXP
Expose ... EXPS
Exposed ... EXPD
Exposed Facility (SSD) ... EF
Exposed Location Single-Buoy Mooring (DNAB) ... ELSBM
Exposed Uninfected [*Medicine*] ... EU
Expositer's Greek New Testament [*A publication*] ... EGNT
Expositio of Epistulae ad Romanos [*of Augustine*] [*Classical studies*] (OCD) ... Ad Rom
Exposition ... EXPN
Exposition ... EXPO
Exposition (VRA) ... expo
Exposition ... EXPO
Exposition (ODBW) ... Expo
Exposition and Conference Council (EA) ... ECC
Exposition Management Association (EA) ... EMA
Exposition of the Blessed Sacrament [*Roman Catholic*] ... EXP
Exposition Service Contractors Association (EA) ... ESCA
[*The*] **Expositor's Bible** [*A publication*] ... EB
[*The*] **Expositor's Bible** [*A publication*] (BJA) ... ExpB
Expositor's Bible Commentary [*A publication*] ... EBC
[*The*] **Expositor's Greek Testament** [*A publication*] (BJA) ... EGT
[*The*] **Expositor's Greek Testament** [*A publication*] (BJA) ... ExpGT
Exposure ... E
Exposure ... EX
Exposure (WGA) ... EXP
Exposure (VRA) ... exp
Exposure (WDMC) ... exp
Exposure (MSA) ... EXPSR
Exposure [*Symbol*] [*IUPAC*] ... H
Exposure Analysis Modeling System [*Environmental chemistry*] ... EXAMS
Exposure Assessment Group [*Environmental Protection Agency*] (GFGA) ... EAG
Exposure Control Limit [*Environmental science*] ... ECL
Exposure Control Technique ... ECT
Exposure Draft [*Business term*] ... ED
Exposure Evaluation Division [*Environmental Protection Agency*] (GFGA) ... EED
Exposure Growth Curve ... EGC
Exposure Index [*Photography*] ... EI
Exposure Intensity Distribution (IAA) ... EID
Exposure Level (GNE) ... EL
Exposure Meter (IAA) ... EM
Exposure Monitoring Test Site [*Environmental Protection Agency*] (ERG) ... EMTS
Exposure Value [*System*] [*Photography*] ... EV
Expreso Aereo [*Peru*] [*ICAO designator*] (FAAC) ... EPR
Express ... EX
Express (AABC) ... EXP
Express ... EXPRSS
Express (FAAC) ... EXPS
Express Air [*ICAO designator*] (AD) ... FX
Express Air, Inc. [*ICAO designator*] (FAAC) ... FXA
Express Airlines I, Inc. [*ICAO designator*] (FAAC) ... FLG
Express Airlines II, Inc. [*ICAO designator*] (FAAC) ... TWC
Express Airways [*ICAO designator*] (AD) ... CH
Express Airways Nigeria Ltd. [*ICAO designator*] (FAAC) ... EAN
Express America Hldgs [*NASDAQ symbol*] (TTSB) ... EXAM
Express America Holdings [*NASDAQ symbol*] (SAG) ... EXAM
Express America Holdings [*Commercial firm Associated Press*] (SAG) ... ExprAm
Express & Star Ltd., Wolverhampton, United Kingdom [*Library symbol Library of Congress*] (LCLS) ... UkWoE
Express Delivery Service ... EDS
Express/Direct Pack (DNAB) ... EX/DP
Express Group Newspapers [*British*] ... EGN
Express International Telex Service (MHDB) ... EITS
Express Mail Service [*Generic term*] ... EMS
Express One International, Inc. [*ICAO designator*] (FAAC) ... LHN
Express Order Wire [*Telecommunications*] (TEL) ... XOW
Express Paid ... XP
Express Paid Letter (ROG) ... XPP
Express Paid Telegraph ... XPT
Express Parcel Systems [*Europe*] ... XP

Express Passenger Coach ... XPC
Express Resources Ltd. [*Vancouver Stock Exchange symbol*] ... EXR
Express Scripts 'A' [*NASDAQ symbol*] (TTSB) ... ESRX
Express Scripts, Inc. [*NASDAQ symbol*] (SAG) ... ESRX
Express Scripts, Inc. [*Associated Press*] (SAG) ... ExpScpt
Express Transfer Protocol (ACRL) ... XTP
Express Transportation Order [*Army*] (AABC) ... ETO
Expressed Breast Milk [*Medicine*] ... EBM
Expressed Prostatic Secretion [*Physiology*] ... EPS
Expressed Reading Difficulty (EDAC) ... ERD
Expressed Sequence Tag [*Genetics*] ... EST
Expressible Moisture Index ... EMI
Expression (MHDI) ... E
Expression ... EXPR
Expression ... EXPRSSN
Expression Cassette Polymerase Chain Reaction [*Genetics*] ... ECPCR
Expression Library Immunisation [*Immunology*] ... ELI
Expression of Anger [*Psychology*] ... AnE
Expression of Interest ... EOI
Expression Site-Associated Genes ... ESAG
Expression Translator [*Computer science*] (MHDI) ... EXTRAN
Expressional Fluency [*Research test*] [*Psychology*] ... EF
Expression-Library Immunization [*To develop a vaccine*] ... ELI
Expression-Linked Extra Copy [*Genetics*] ... ELC
Expression-Oriented Language [*Computer science*] ... EOL
Expressive Language Age [*of the hearing-impaired*] ... ELA
Expressive One-Word Picture Vocabulary Test [*Intelligence test*] ... EOWPVT
Expressive One-Word Picture Vocabulary Test: Upper Extension [*Intelligence test*] ... EOWPVT:UE
Expressive-Regressive Index ... ERI
Expressivo [*With Expression*] [*Music*] (ROG) ... EXPO
Expressway [*Commonly used*] (OPSA) ... EXP
Expressway [*Commonly used*] (OPSA) ... EXPR
Expressway [*Commonly used*] (OPSA) ... EXPRESS
Expressway [*Commonly used*] (OPSA) ... EXPRESSWAY
Expressway [*Commonly used*] (OPSA) ... EXPW
Expressway (WDAA) ... EXPWY
Expressway (MCD) ... EXPY
Expressway (DD) ... Expy
Expressway [*Postal Service standard*] (OPSA) ... EXPY
Expressway ... EXPY
Expressway ... X-WAY
Exprisoner ... EP
Ex-Prisoners of War Association of Australia ... Ex-POWAA
Ex-Privileges [*Without the right to privileges*] [*Finance*] (DS) ... x pri
Ex-Privileges [*Without the right to privileges*] [*Finance*] ... XPR
Expropriation [*Legal term*] (DLA) ... Exp
Expulsion (KSC) ... EXP
Expurgated ... EXP
Expurgated (ADA) ... EXPURG
Ex-Rights [*Without Rights*] [*Investment term*] ... ER
Ex-Rights [*Without Rights*] [*Investment term*] ... Ex R
Ex-Rights [*Without Rights*] [*Investment term*] ... XR
Ex-Rights [*Without Rights*] [*Investment term*] (SPSG) ... XRT
Ex-Rights [*Without Rights*] [*Investment term*] ... X-RTS
Exsecant [*Mathematics*] (BARN) ... exsec
Exshaw Community Library, Alberta [*Library symbol National Library of Canada*] (NLC) ... AEXC
Exshaw Community Library, Exshaw, AB, Canada [*Library symbol Library of Congress*] (LCLS) ... CaAExC
Exsmoker (DAVI) ... ES
Exsorbet Industries [*NASDAQ symbol*] (TTSB) ... EXSO
Exsorbet Industries, Inc. [*NASDAQ symbol*] (SAG) ... EXSO
Exsorbet Industries, Inc. [*Associated Press*] (SAG) ... Exsorbet
Exstar Financial [*NASDAQ symbol*] (TTSB) ... EXTRE
Exstar Financial Corp. [*Associated Press*] (SAG) ... Exstar
Exstar Financial Corp. [*NASDAQ symbol*] (SAG) ... EXTR
Ex-Stock Dividend [*Investment term*] ... ESD
Extant ... EXT
Ex-Tapol [*Political Prisoner*] [*Indonesia*] ... ET
Extecapital Ltd. [*NYSE symbol*] (SPSG) ... BEX
Extecapital Ltd. [*Associated Press*] (SAG) ... Extecp
Extecapital Ltd'A'Pref [*NYSE symbol*] (TTSB) ... BEXPr
Extemporaneous (WDAA) ... EXTEMP
Extend [*or Extension*] (AFM) ... EXT
Extend [*or Extended*] (KSC) ... EXTD
Extend [*or Extended*] ... XTND
Extend of Cerebral Lesion [*Neurology*] (DAVI) ... ECL
Extendable Computer System Simulator [*Programming language*] [*1973*] ... ECSS
Extendable Debugging and Monitoring System [*Computer science*] ... EXDAMS
Extendable Exit Cone (MCD) ... EEC
Extendable Integration Support Environment [*Air Force*] ... EISE
Extendable Nozzle Cone ... ENCE
Extendable Nozzle Exit Cone (MCD) ... ENEC
Extendable Stiff Arm Manipulator [*NASA*] ... ESAM
Extendable Tubular Member Device [*Aerospace*] ... ETMD
Extende [*Spread*] [*Pharmacy*] ... EXT
Extende super Alutum Mollem [*Spread upon Soft Leather*] [*Pharmacy*] (ROG) ... EXT sup ALUT MOLL
Extended [*Automotive advertising*] ... EXTEN
Extended ... EXTND
Extended ... XT
Extended Accumulator (IAA) ... EA
Extended Active Duty ... EAD
Extended Aeration Process [*Sludge treatment*] ... EA
Extended Air Defense [*NATO*] ... EAD
Extended Air Defense Command and Control [*Army*] (RDA) ... EAD C2
Extended Air Defense Simulation [*Army*] (RDA) ... EADSIM
Extended Air Defense Test Bed [*Army*] (RDA) ... EADTB
Extended Air Surveillance Communications Intercept [*Air Force*] ... EASCOMINT
Extended Algorithmic "R" Language ... EARL
Extended Appearance Potential Fine Structure (PDAA) ... EAPFS
Extended Application of Ground LASER Equipment (MCD) ... EAGLE
Extended Architecture [*Computer science*] ... XA
Extended Area Instrumentation RADAR (MCD) ... EAIR
Extended Area Instrumentation System (MCD) ... EAIS
Extended Area Service [*Telecommunications*] ... EAS
Extended Area Test System [*Navy*] ... EATS
Extended Arithmetic Chip ... EAC
Extended Arithmetic Element ... EAE
Extended Arithmetic Processor (MHDB) ... EAP
Extended Arithmetic Unit (IAA) ... EAU
Extended Assembler Language Coding [*Computer science*] (MHDI) ... XALC
Extended Attribute [*Computer science*] ... EA
Extended Attribute Record [*Computer science*] (DOM) ... XAR
Extended Backus-Naur Form ... EBNF
Extended Basal Period ... EBP
Extended BASIC Mode [*International Computers Ltd.*] ... XBM
Extended Batch Language (CDE) ... EBL
Extended Battlefield Contact Team (MCD) ... EBCT
Extended Benefits [*Unemployment insurance*] ... EB
Extended Binary-Coded Decimal [*Computer science*] ... EBCD
Extended Binary-Coded Decimal Interchange [*Computer science*] (IAA) ... EBCDI
Extended Binary-Coded Decimal Interchange Code [*Computer science*] ... EBCDIC
Extended BIOS [*Basic Input/Output System*] [*Operating system*] ... XBIOS
Extended BIT [*Binary Digit*] **Read Only Memory** [*Computer science*] (IAA) ... EBROM
Extended Boundary Condition Method ... EBCM
Extended Branch Mode ... EBM
Extended Campus Library Services Section [*Association of College and Research Libraries*] ... ECLSS
Extended Capabilities Ports [*Computer science*] ... ECPs
Extended Capability Port [*Telecommunications*] (PCM) ... ECP
Extended Capacity Memory [*Computer science*] (IAA) ... ECM
Extended Care Facility [*Medicine Obsolete*] ... ECF
Extended Care Facility (WYGK) ... ECF
Extended Care Hospital (DAVI) ... ECH
Extended Care Nursery [*Neonatology*] (DAVI) ... ECN
Extended Care Unit [*Medicine*] (DHSM) ... ECU
Extended Center Line (WDAA) ... ECL
Extended Central Area (DOAD) ... ECA
Extended Channel Status Word [*Computer science*] (MHDB) ... ECSW
Extended Character Set [*Computer science*] (PCM) ... ECS
Extended Cold Weather Clothing System [*Army*] (INF) ... ECWCS
Extended Cold/Wet Clothing Systems [*Military*] (INF) ... ECWC
Extended Communications Access Method (WDAA) ... ECAM
Extended Communications Operating System (HGAA) ... ECOS
Extended Communications Search [*DoD*] ... EXCOM
Extended Communications Search [*Navy*] (NVT) ... EXCOMMS
Extended Connection Table Representation (NITA) ... ECTR
Extended Console System (MHDB) ... ECON
Extended Content-Addressable Memory [*Computer science*] (MHDB) ... ECAM
Extended Control [*Mode*] [*Computer science*] ... EC
Extended Control and Simulation Language [*Computer science*] (PDAA) ... ECSL
Extended Control Program Support [*IBM Corp.*] ... ECPS
Extended Conventional Memory [*Computer science*] ... ECM
Extended Core Barrel [*Drilling technology*] ... XCB
Extended Core Memory [*Computer science*] (MCD) ... ECM
Extended Core Memory Unit [*Computer science*] (NVT) ... ECMU
Extended Core Module [*Computer science*] (IAA) ... ECM
Extended Core Storage [*Computer science*] ... ECS
Extended Corresponding States Principle [*Physical chemistry*] ... ECSP
Extended Coverage [*Insurance*] ... EC
Extended Coverage Altitude (SAA) ... ECA
Extended Coverage Endorsement [*Insurance*] ... ECE
Extended Coverage Range [*Insurance*] (IAA) ... ECR
Extended Data Flow Graph ... EDFG
Extended Data Management Facility ... EDMF
Extended Data Management System [*Xerox Corp.*] ... EDMS
Extended Data Out [*Computer science*] ... EDO
Extended Data Out RAM [*Radom Access Memory*] (CDE) ... EDO RAM
Extended Data Stream [*Medicine*] (MEDA) ... EDS
Extended Defense Communication System (CINC) ... EDCS
Extended Definition Television [*in ED Beta*] [*Sony Corp.*] ... ED
Extended Device Control (MHDB) ... EDC
Extended Direct Memory Access [*Computer science*] ... EDMA
Extended Disability Status Scale [*Medicine*] ... EDSS
Extended Disc Operating System with Remote Job Entry (PDAA) ... EDOS/RJE
Extended Disc Operating System-Multistage Operations [*Fujitsu*] [*Japan*] (NITA) ... EDOS-MSO
Extended Disk Operating System [*Computer science*] (BUR) ... EDOS
Extended Disk Utilities Program [*Computer science*] ... XDUP
Extended Distance Feature (ACRL) ... XDF
Extended Duration (OICC) ... ED
Extended Duration Orbiter [*NASA*] ... EDO
Extended Edition [*IBM Corp.*] (BYTE) ... EE
Extended Education in Therapeutic Recreation Administration (EDAC) ... EXTRA
Extended Electron Loss Fine Structure [*Spectrometry*] ... EXELFS
Extended Eligibility Temporary Entry Permit ... EETEP

Extended Emission Line Region [*Spectrometry*] .... EELR
Extended Endocardial Resection [*Medicine*] .... EER
Extended Exercise [*Navy*] (ANA) .... EXTENDEX
Extended Facility [*IBM Corp.*] .... EF
Extended Family [*Unitarian Universalist program*] .... XF
Extended Field [*Radiation therapy*] (DAVI) .... EF
Extended File Attribute [*Software feature*] [*Computer science*] (PCM) .... EFA
Extended Fine Auger Structure [*Physics*] .... EXFAS
Extended Forecasts [*Symbol*] [*National Weather Service*] .... FE
Extended Function Code .... XFC
Extended Fund Facility [*International Monetary Fund*] .... EFF
Extended General Purpose Simulator [*National Electronics Conference*] (IEEE) .... EGPS
Extended Glaciological Timescale [*Climatology*] .... EGT
Extended Graphics Adapter [*Computer science*] (DOM) .... XGA
Extended Graphics Array [*Computer science*] (EERA) .... EGA
Extended Graphics Array [*IBM Corp.*] .... XGA
Extended Group Coded Recording [*Computer science*] (IBMDP) .... E/GCR
Extended Guide Projectile [*Navy*] (MCD) .... EGP
Extended Health Care [*Insurance*] .... EHC
Extended High-Level Language Application Program Interface [*Computer science*] .... EHLLAPI
Extended Hospital Care [*Veterans Administration*] (GFGA) .... EHC
Extended Huckel Theory [*Atomic physics*] .... EHT
Extended Hueckel [*Molecular orbit*] [*Atomic physics*] .... EH
Extended Hueckel Molecular Orbit [*Atomic physics*] .... EHMO
Extended Hueckel Molecular Orbit [*Atomic physics*] (IEEE) .... XHMO
Extended Hueckel Tight-Binding [*Quantum mechanics*] .... EHTB
Extended Industry Standard Architecture [*Computer science*] .... EISA
Extended Input-Output System (IAA) .... EIOS
Extended Instruction Set [*Honeywell, Inc.*] .... EIS
Extended Interaction Amplifier .... EIA
Extended Interaction Klystron [*Electronics*] (IAA) .... EIK
Extended Interactive Oscillator (PDAA) .... EIO
Extended Interprocess Communications Facilities .... XIPC
Extended Iterative Weighted Least Squares [*Statistics*] (PDAA) .... EIWLS
Extended Joint Test (MCD) .... EJT
Extended Lapped Transform [*Telecommunications*] .... ELT
Extended Length Message (DA) .... ELM
Extended Length Methods (MCD) .... ELM
Extended Length Super HIPPO [*High Internal Pressure Producing Orifice*] (MCD) .... ELSH
Extended Life Attitude Control System [*NASA*] .... ELACS
Extended Line Adapter (MHDB) .... ELA
Extended Linear Expenditure System .... ELES
Extended Line-of-Sight (CAAL) .... ELOS
Extended Local Area Network [*Defunct*] (TSSD) .... ELAN
Extended Long Tank (MCD) .... ELT
Extended Long-Range Integrated Technology Evaluation .... ELITE
Extended Lubrication Interval [*Automotive engineering*] .... ELI
Extended Lunar Mission [*NASA*] (KSC) .... ELM
Extended Lunar Orbital Rendezvous [*NASA*] (KSC) .... ELOR
Extended Lunar Orbital Rendezvous Mission [*NASA*] (KSC) .... ELORM
Extended Lymphadenopathy Syndrome [*Medicine*] .... ELAS
Extended Maintenance Service (IAA) .... EMS
Extended Management Improvement Program [*Military*] .... EMIP
Extended Math Coprocessor [*Computer science*] .... EMC
Extended Media List [*British*] .... EML
Extended Memory Block [*Computer science*] (PCM) .... EMB
Extended Memory Manager [*Computer science*] (PCM) .... XMM
Extended Memory Specification [*Computer science*] (PCM) .... XMS
Extended Memory Store [*Computer science*] (ECII) .... EMS
Extended Memory Unit (NASA) .... EMU
Extended Mercury Autocoder (IEEE) .... EMA
Extended Messaging Services [*Computer science*] (PCM) .... EMS
Extended Midcourse Mode [*Navy*] (CAAL) .... EMM
Extended Mission Apollo [*NASA*] .... EMA
Extended Mission Apollo Simulation [*NASA*] (IEEE) .... XMAS
Extended Mobility Tire [*Automotive technology*] (PS) .... EMT
Extended Model Checker [*Computer science*] .... EMC
Extended Multiplexer Channel (NITA) .... EMC
Extended Network Services (MHDB) .... ENS
Extended Non-Owned Automobile Coverage [*Insurance*] .... ENOA
Extended Nylon Shaft .... ENS
Extended Observation of Solar and Cosmic Radiation [*National Center for Atmospheric Research*] .... EOSCOR
Extended Operating System [*DoD*] .... EOS
Extended Operating System Card [*Computer science*] (IAA) .... EOSC
Extended Operating System for Magnetic Tapes (DNAB) .... EOS/MT
Extended Operating System Magnetic Drum [*Computer science*] (IAA) .... EOSMD
Extended Operation .... XOP
Extended Operations .... EO
Extended Overhaul Cycle (NVT) .... EOC
Extended Parliamentary Network .... EPN
Extended Performance and Increased Capability .... EPIC
Extended Period of Eligibility [*Social Security Administration*] (GFGA) .... EPE
Extended Personality Attributes Questionnaire (EDAC) .... EPAQ
Extended Planning Annex .... EPA
Extended Planning Guidance (MCD) .... EPG
Extended Play .... EP
Extended Play (IDOE) .... ep
Extended Power in Composition Systems (DGA) .... EPICS
Extended Processor (NITA) .... XT
Extended Quality Television (ACRL) .... EQTV
Extended Quasi-Static Approximation [*Materials research*] .... EQSA

Extended Range .... ER
Extended Range [*Film*] [*Briteline Corp.*] .... XR
Extended Range Ammunition (MCD) .... ERA
Extended Range Antiarmor Munition .... ERAM
Extended Range Antitank Mine (MCD) .... ERAM
Extended Range Cap [*Navy*] (ANA) .... ERC
Extended Range Data Link [*Bomb*] (MCD) .... ERDL
Extended Range Guided Projectiles (MCD) .... ERGP
Extended Range Guided Projectiles (MCD) .... XRGP
Extended Range Interceptor [*Air Force*] .... ERINT
Extended Range, Multiple Launch Rocket System [*Army*] .... ER-MLRS
Extended Range Rocket [*Aerospace*] .... ERR
Extended Range Twinjet Operation [*Aviation*] (DA) .... ETOPS
Extended Reconnaissance Zone [*Army*] (AABC) .... ERZ
Extended Recovery Facility (NITA) .... XRF
Extended Red Emission [*Spectroscopy*] .... ERE
Extended Red Multialkali [*Cathode*] .... ERMA
Extended Release [*Pharmacy*] .... ER
Extended Reliability Feature (HGAA) .... XRF
Extended Remote Job Entry .... ERJE
Extended Research Telescope .... ERT
Extended Response (WGA) .... XR
Extended Salvage Depth Capability (MCD) .... ESDC
Extended School Year .... ESY
Extended School Year Aid .... ESYA
Extended Self-Contained PROLOG [*Programming language*] .... ESP
Extended Service [*Automotive engineering*] .... ES
Extended Service Agreement .... ESA
Extended Service and Cooling Umbilical (NASA) .... ESCU
Extended Service Coverage [*Automotive engineering*] .... ESC
Extended Service Life [*Military*] (CAAL) .... ESL
Extended Service Plan [*Ford Motor Co.*] .... ESP
Extended Set Processor [*Computer science*] (MHDI) .... XSP
Extended Sleeper [*In truck name Aero ES*] [*Volvo White Truck Corp.*] [*Automotive engineering*] .... ES
Extended Software Defined Network [*Computer science*] (HGAA) .... ESDN
Extended Source Calibration Area [*Nuclear energy*] (NRCH) .... ESCA
Extended Specific Fuel Consumption (WDAA) .... ESFC
Extended Spooling Facility (IAA) .... ESF
Extended Standard Theory [*Linguistics*] .... EST
Extended State Machine .... ESM
Extended Stay Amer [*NASDAQ symbol*] (TTSB) .... STAY
Extended Stay America [*Associated Press*] (SAG) .... ExtStA
Extended Stay America [*NASDAQ symbol*] (SAG) .... STAY
Extended Sterilization Qualification Test .... ESQT
Extended Storage Platelet Pack [*Hematology*] .... ESP
Extended Streamflow Prediction (NOAA) .... ESP
Extended Subsequent Application Review (AAGC) .... ESAR
Extended Subset of Automatically Programmed Tools [*Manufacturing term*] .... EXAPT
Extended Super Frame [*Telecommunications*] .... ESF
Extended Superframe Format [*Telecommunications*] (ACRL) .... ESF
Extended Take [*Recording term*] .... ET
Extended Tape Operating System (BUR) .... ETOS
Extended Tape Processing (IAA) .... ETP
Extended Task Analysis Procedure [*Education*] (AIE) .... ETAP
Extended Telecommunications Modules .... EXTM
Extended Telephone Systems Programming Language [*Computer science*] (MHDB) .... ETSPL
Extended Temperature Range (IAA) .... ETR
Extended Term Plan (BUR) .... ETP
Extended Text Compositor [*Applied Data Research, Inc.*] .... ETC
Extended Three Letter Acronym .... ETLA
Extended Three-Letter Acronym [*Internet language*] [*Computer science*] .... ETLA
Extended Time Division Multiple Access [*Telecommunications*] (ACRL) .... E-TDMA
Extended Time Tests .... ETT
Extended Twin-Engine Over Water Operations [*OST*] (TAG) .... ETOPS
Extended Ultraviolet Transmission .... EUVT
Extended Unemployment Compensation Account .... EUCA
Extended Upper Deck .... EUD
Extended User Area [*Computer science*] .... EUA
Extended User Authentication [*Computer science*] .... EUA
Extended User Employment [*Military training*] .... EUE
Extended Video Graphics Array (PCM) .... EVGA
Extended Virtual Machine .... EVM
Extended Voluntary Departure [*Temporary status sometimes granted by the State Department as protection against deportation*] .... EVD
Extended Work Week .... EWW
Extended X-Ray Absorption Fine Structure [*Spectrometry*] .... EXAFS
Extended-Address [*Computer science*] .... EA
Extended-Definition Television [*in ED Beta*] [*Sony Corp.*] (PS) .... EDTV
Extended-Field Radiotherapy [*Radiology*] .... EFR
Extended-Height-to-Diameter [*Aviation*] .... EHD
Extended-Life Protection [*Automotive engineering*] .... XLP
Extended-Range Air-to-Air Missile (MCD) .... ERAAM
Extended-Range and Space Communication (MCD) .... ERSC
Extended-Range Antisubmarine Rocket [*Navy*] (SAA) .... ER ASROC
Extended-Range ASROC [*Antisubmarine Rocket*] [*Navy*] (NVT) .... ERA
Extended-Range Ballistic Missile .... ERBM
Extended-Range Doppler .... EXTRADOP
Extended-Range Doppler Velocity and Position (CET) .... EXTRADOVAP
Extended-Range Floating Point Interpretive System .... ERFPI
Extended-Range Floating Point Interpretive System (IAA) .... ERFPIS
Extended-Range Fuel System (DOMA) .... ERFS
Extended-Range Full Bore (PDAA) .... ERFB

Extended-Range Instrumentation RADAR (PDAA) ... ERIR
Extended-Range Intercept Technology Missile [*Army*] ... ERINT
Extended-Range Juno [*Survey meter for radiation*] ... ERJ
Extended-Range Lance [*Missile*] (MCD) ... ERL
Extended-Range Lance [*Missile*] ... XRL
Extended-Range Phase-Locked Demodulator (IEEE) ... ERPLD
Extended-Range Poseidon [*Missile*] [*Navy*] ... EXPO
Extended-Range Projectile ... ERP
Extended-Range Strike Aircraft [*for low-level missions*] [*Air Force*] ... ERSA
Extended-Range TOW [*Tube-Launched, Optically Tracked Wire-Guided (Weapon)*] (MCD) ... ERT
Extended-Range TOW ... XRT
Extended-Range TOW [*Tube-Launched, Optically Tracked, Wire-Guided*] [*Weapon*] (MCD) ... XRTOW
Extended-Range Twin-Engine Operation [*Aviation*] ... ETOP
Extended-Wear Lenses [*Optometry*] ... EW
Extended-Wear Soft Contact Lens [*Optometry*] ... EWSCL
Extender (MSA) ... EXTND
Extender ... EXTNR
Extendicare, Inc. [*NYSE symbol*] (SAG) ... EXE
Extendicare, Inc. [*Associated Press*] (SAG) ... Extend
Extending Concepts through Language Activities [*Education*] (AEE) ... ECOLA
Extensible Authentication Protocol [*Computer science*] ... EAP
Extensible Compound Document [*Programming language*] [*Computer science*] (PCM) ... Ecd
Extensible Language Facility [*Computer science*] (IEEE) ... ELF
Extensible Language I [*Computer science*] ... ELI
Extensible Machine (PDAA) ... EM
Extensible Markup Language [*Computer science*] ... XML
Extensible Microprogramming Language [*Computer science*] (MHDB) ... EMPL
Extensible Object Orientation ... EOO
Extensible Programming System [*Computer science*] (CSR) ... EPS
Extensible Structure Processing Language [*1969-71*] [*Computer science*] (CSR) ... ESPL
Extensible Video Interactive Language [*Computer science*] ... EVIL
Extensible Virtual Toolkit [*Computer science*] ... XVT
Extension (ADA) ... EX
Extension ... EXT
Extension ... EXT
Extension (WDMC) ... ext
Extension [*Commonly used*] (OPSA) ... EXTENSION
Extension (WDMC) ... extn
Extension ... EXTN
Extension ... EXTNS
Extension (VRA) ... extns
Extension [*Commonly used*] (OPSA) ... EXTNSN
Extension (MDG) ... EXTSN
Extension (AAG) ... X
Extension and Change of Immigration Status (ADA) ... ECIS
Extension and Conversion [*Public buildings*] ... EC
Extension Battery (IAA) ... EXTBAT
Extension Bell [*Telecommunications*] (TEL) ... XBL
Extension Committee on Organization and Policy [*Department of Agriculture*] (EA) ... ECOP
Extension Cord (IAA) ... EXTCD
Extension Course ... EC
Extension Course Institute [*Air Force*] ... ECI
Extension Course Institute [*Air Force*] (DOMA) ... ECI
Extension/Flexion [*Medicine*] ... E/F
Extension Frequency (IAA) ... EXTFREQ
Extension Hose/Mouthpiece (MCD) ... EH/M
Extension Lay Volunteers (EA) ... ELV
Extension Management Information System [*Department of Agriculture*] ... EMIS
Extension Module Group (ACRL) ... EMG
Extension of BASIC [*Computer science*] ... XBASIC
Extension of Enlistment [*Military*] ... EXTENL
Extension of Leave [*Military*] (AABC) ... EXTLV
Extension of LISP [*List Processor*] **1.5** [*Programming language*] (CSR) ... XLISP
Extension of the Gastric Shield ... EGS
Extension Pay [*British military*] (DMA) ... EP
Extension Producing Interneuron [*Neurology*] ... EPI
Extension Register ... XR
Extension Service [*Department of Agriculture*] ... ES
Extension Shaft [*Nuclear energy*] (NUCP) ... ES
Extension Shaft Disconnect [*Nuclear energy*] (IAA) ... ED
Extension Shaft Disconnect [*Nuclear energy*] (NRCH) ... ESD
Extension Society Volunteers [*Defunct*] ... ESV
Extension Station (IAA) ... ES
Extension Teleconferencing Network [*Texas A & M University*] [*College Station, TX*] [*Telecommunications service*] (TSSD) ... ETN
Extension Toxicology Network (GNE) ... EXTOXNET
Extension Training Management [*Military*] (INF) ... ETM
Extension Training Materials [*Army*] ... ETM
Extension Training Memorandum [*Civil Defense*] ... ETM
Extension Trunk Dialing [*Telecommunications*] (PDAA) ... ETEC
Extension Wire (IAA) ... EXTW
Extensions [*Commonly used*] (OPSA) ... EXTENSIONS
Extensions [*Postal Service standard*] (OPSA) ... EXTS
Extensions ... EXTS
Extensions and Restrictions of Operators (IEEE) ... EROP
Extensions for Independence [*An association*] (EA) ... EI
Extensive (FAAC) ... EXTSV
Extensive ... EXTV
Extensive Air Shower [*Cosmic ray physics*] ... EAS
Extensive Disease [*Medicine*] ... ED
Extensive Field Maintenance [*Military*] (NG) ... EFM
Extensive Landuse Zone [*Australia*] (EERA) ... ELZ
Extensive User Library ... EUL
Extensive Wound ... EW
Extensive-Dilatancy Anisotropy [*Geology*] ... EDA
Extensor [*Anatomy*] ... EXT
Extensor Carpi Radialis Brevis [*Anatomy*] ... ECRB
Extensor Carpi Radialis Longus [*Muscle or tendon*] [*Anatomy*] (DAVI) ... ECRL
Extensor Carpi Ulnaris [*Muscle or tendon*] [*Anatomy*] (DAVI) ... ECU
Extensor Digiti Quinti [*Muscle*] [*Anatomy*] (DAVI) ... EDQ
Extensor Digitorum [*Muscle or tendon*] [*Orthopedics*] (DAVI) ... ED
Extensor Digitorum Brevis [*Anatomy*] ... EDB
Extensor Digitorum Communis [*Muscle or tendon*] [*Anatomy*] (DAVI) ... EDC
Extensor Digitorum Longus [*Anatomy*] ... EDL
Extensor Hallucis Longus [*Anatomy*] ... EHL
Extensor Indicis Proprius [*Anatomy*] ... EIP
Extensor Pollicis Brevis [*Anatomy*] ... EPB
Extensor Pollicis Longus [*Anatomy*] ... EPL
Exterior (AABC) ... EXT
Exterior (VRA) ... ext
Exterior (WDMC) ... ext
Exterior (BARN) ... exte
Exterior Ballistic Verification Projectile (MCD) ... EBVT
Exterior Closet (ADA) ... EC
Exterior Communications [*Military*] (CAAL) ... EXCOMM
Exterior Communications [*Military*] (CAAL) ... XCOM
Exterior Communications System [*Military*] (CAAL) ... ECS
Exterior Gateway Protocol [*Computer science*] ... EGP
Exterior Insulation and Finish System [*Sto Industries*] ... EIFS
Exterior Insulation Manufacturers Association (EA) ... EIMA
Exterior Nodal Switching Subsystem [*Computer science*] (ACRL) ... ENSS
Exterior Surface ... ES
Exterior Vacuum Metallized (DICI) ... EVM
Exterminating ... EXTERM
External (WDMC) ... ext
External (AABC) ... EXT
External (KSC) ... EXTER
External (DLA) ... EXTL
External ... EXTNL
External (ROG) ... EXTR
External Address Modifier [*Computer science*] (MHDI) ... XAM
External Aerodynamic Diffusion ... EAD
External Affairs and International Trade Canada [*Government agency*] ... EAITC
External Affairs Canada, Trade Negotiations Office, Ottawa, ON, Canada [*Library symbol*] [*Library of Congress*] (LCLS) ... CaOOTN
External Affairs Department [*Canada*] ... EA
External Agency Simulator (MCD) ... EAS
External Air Transportability (MCD) ... EAT
External Architectural Students Association [*British*] (BI) ... EASA
External Archival Storage [*Computer science*] (BARN) ... EAS
External Armament Stores Management/Remote Set Fuze (MCD) ... EASM/RSF
External Auditory Canal [*Anatomy*] ... EAC
External Auditory Meatus [*Anatomy*] ... EAM
External Auxiliary Power Unit ... EAPU
External Baggage Container (DNAB) ... EBC
External Block Controller ... XBC
External Branch Condition Address [*Telecommunications*] (TEL) ... EBCA
External Branch Condition Input [*Telecommunications*] (TEL) ... EBCI
External Breathing Direct Injection [*Chrysler Corp.*] [*Automotive engineering*] ... EBDI
External Burning (RDA) ... EB
External Burning-Assisted Projectile [*Military*] (DNAB) ... EBAP
External Call Barring Circuit (IAA) ... ECBC
External Calling Sequence [*Computer science*] ... ECS
External Cardiac Compression ... ECC
External Cardiac Massage [*Medicine*] (ADA) ... ECM
External Cardiac Pressure [*Medicine*] (DMAA) ... ECP
External Carotid - Middle Cerebral Artery [*Anatomy*] ... EC-MCA
External Cephalic Version [*Gynecology*] ... ECV
External Channels Ratio ... ECR
External Chest Compression [*Medicine*] ... ECC
External Combustion ... EC
External Combustion Engine [*Steam bus*] ... ECE
External Combustion Piston Engine (PDAA) ... ECPE
External Command [*Computer science*] ... XCMD
External Command [*Computer science*] (CDE) ... XCMD
External Compliance Programs [*Environmental Protection Agency*] (GFGA) ... ECP
External Control [*Military*] (INF) ... EXCON
External Control Panel ... ECP
External Control Register (OA) ... ECR
External Countdown Clock ... ECDC
External Counterpulsation [*Medicine*] ... ECP
External Crystalline Massif [*Geology*] ... ECM
External Data Aiding [*Computer science*] (PDAA) ... EDA
External Data Channel Processor (NOAA) ... EDCP
External Data Controller (NITA) ... EXDC
External Data Representation [*Computer science*] ... XDR
External Delay [*Computer science*] (IAA) ... ED
External Delay Factor [*Computer science*] ... EDF
External Device [*Computer science*] ... ED
External Device [*Computer science*] ... EXD
External Diameter [*Measurement*] (DAVI) ... ED
External Disk/Drum Channel ... EDC
External Document Exchange (HGAA) ... EDE
External Drug and Cosmetic [*Color*] ... EXT D & C

External Ear Effect [*Audiology*] ... EEE
External Economic Policy [*British*] ... EEP
External Entity ... EE
External Environment ... EE
External Environment Interface [*Computer science*] ... EEI
External Evaluation [*Military*] (INF) ... EXEVAL
External Event Detection Module [*Computer science*] (MDG) ... EEDM
External Expansion Ramjet (PDAA) ... EERJ
External Fetal Heart Rate (MEDA) ... EXT FHR
External Fetal Monitoring [*Obstetrics*] (DAVI) ... EFM
External Field Emission ... EFE
External File System (BYTE) ... EFS
External Finance Limit ... EFL
External Finished Reports Information Subsystem [*Computer science*] ... EFRIS
External Flaps (AAG) ... EF
External Floating Roof Tank [*Engineering*] ... EFRT
External Function ... EXF
External Function [*Computer science*] (CDE) ... XFCN
External Function Translator ... EFT
External Gauge ... EXGA
External Genitalia [*Medicine*] (DAVI) ... EG
External Genitalia and Bartholin's, Urethral, and Skene's Glands [*Gynecology*] (DAVI) ... EXGBUS
External Genitalia, Bartholin, Urethral, Skene's Glands [*Medicine*] (DMAA) ... EGBUS
External Germinal Layer [*Cytology*] ... EGL
External Granular Layer (PDAA) ... EGL
External Guide Sequence [*Genetics*] ... EGS
External Hydrogen/Oxygen Tank (NASA) ... EHOT
External Input-Output Processor (IAA) ... EIOP
External Intelligence Bureau (MCD) ... EIB
External Interlace ... EIN
External Isovolumic Contraction Time [*Laboratory*] (DAVI) ... EICT
External Jugular Vein [*Anatomy*] ... EJV
External Lamina (OA) ... EL
External Lamina Substance (OA) ... ELS
External Lid [*Ophthalmology*] (DAVI) ... E-L
External Limiting Membrane ... ELM
External Link (MHDB) ... EL
External Locus of Control [*Psychology*] ... ELC
External Loop Air Lift Reactor [*Chemical engineering*] ... ELALR
External Loop Airlift Bioreactor [*Chemical engineering*] ... ELAB
External Memorandum ... EM
External Mixer Interface Module (NITA) ... EMIM
External Mold Release [*Plastic fabrications*] ... EMR
External Monitor [*Obstetrics*] (DAVI) ... EM
External Multiplexer Channel (MHDB) ... EMC
External Muon Identifier [*Atomic physics*] ... EMI
External Negative Differential (PDAA) ... END
External Ocular Movement [*Medicine*] ... EOM
External Oxygen and Hydrogen Tanks (NASA) ... EOHT
External Page Storage [*Computer science*] (BUR) ... EPS
External Page Table [*Computer science*] (BUR) ... XPT
External Payload Operations Center ... EPOC
External Phloem [*Botany*] ... EP
External Pipe Thread [*Technical drawings*] ... EPT
External Plant Operators' Association of South Australia ... EPOA
External Pneumatic Compression [*Medicine*] ... EPC
External Pneumatic Intermittent Compression ... EPIC
External Polarization Modulation (IEEE) ... EPM
External Power Contractor (NASA) ... EPC
External Power Monitor ... EMP
External Power Relay (MCD) ... EPR
External Pressure ... EP
External Pressure Circulatory Assist [*Cardiac treatment*] ... EPCA
External Pressure Vessel ... EPV
External Priority Number [*Computer science*] (OA) ... EPN
External Priority Number (ECII) ... XPN
External Processor Status Word ... XPSW
External Protection Material (MCD) ... EPM
External Proton Beam ... EPB
External Publication ... EP
External Radiation Therapy [*Medicine*] ... ERT
External Ramjet ... ERJ
External Reference (BUR) ... EXTRN
External Reflection Spectroscopy ... ERS
External Regulation System (IEEE) ... ERS
External Relational Memory ... XRM
External Release Agent ... ERA
External REM [*Roentgen-Equivalent-Man*] [*Radiology*] ... EXREM
External Report ... ER
External Representation of the Ukrainian Helsinki Group (EA) ... ERUHG
External Research Publication and Retrieval System [*Department of State*] ... XPARS
External Reset ... XR
External Resistance [*Physics*] ... ER
External Roentgem-Equivalent-Man Dose [*Radiation therapy*] (DAVI) ... EXTREM
External ROM [*Read Only Memory*] **Mode** [*Computer science*] (IAA) ... XRM
External Rotation [*Myology*] ... ER
External Rotation [*Myology*] (MAE) ... ext rot
External Rotation, Abduction Stress Test [*Medicine*] ... EAST
External Rotation in Extension [*Orthopedics*] (DAVI) ... ERE
External Rotation in Flexion [*Orthopedics*] (DAVI) ... ERF
External Run Unit (MHDB) ... ERU
External Segment Name (MHDB) ... ESN
External Services [*British Broadcasting Corp.*] ... ES
External Set Loop [*Electronics*] (ECII) ... ESL
External Shield (IAA) ... ES
External Source Format (CDE) ... ESF
External Standard Pulse [*Instrumentation*] ... ESP
External Standard Ratio ... ESR
External Store ... ES
External Stores Support System [*or Subsystem*] (MCD) ... ESSS
External Symbol Dictionary [*A publication*] ... ESD
External Tank [*NASA*] ... ET
External Tank Attachment (MCD) ... ETA
External Tank Door (MCD) ... ETD
External Tank Lift-Off Weight [*NASA*] (NASA) ... ETLOW
External Tank Rocket Motor ... ETRM
External Tank Separation [*NASA*] (NASA) ... ETSEP
External Tank Separation Subsystem [*NASA*] (NASA) ... ETSS
External Tank System (MCD) ... ETS
External Tank Vent Arm (MCD) ... ETVA
External Technical Memorandum ... ETM
External Technical Report ... ETR
External Telecommunications Executive (IAA) ... ETE
External Test Equipment (IAA) ... ETE
External Thermal Garment ... ETG
External Time-Sharing (IAA) ... ETS
External Timing Register ... ETR
External Torpedo [*Formerly, DEXTOR*] (MCD) ... EXTOR
External Transcribed Spacer [*Genetics*] ... ETS
External Transmit Clock ... XTC
External Tympaniform Membrane [*Zoology*] ... ETM
External Urethral Sphincter [*Anatomy*] ... EUS
External Visual Display (MCD) ... EVD
External Visual Display Equipment [*Used in Apollo mission*] [*NASA*] ... EVDE
External Visual Reference [*Motion sickness*] ... EVR
External Wall Insulation Association [*British*] (DBA) ... EWIA
External Work ... EW
External-Device Code [*Computer science*] (MDG) ... EDC
External-Device Control Word [*Computer science*] ... EDCW
Externally [*Medicine*] (BARN) ... extern
Externally Blown Flap [*Aviation*] ... EBF
Externally Caused Failure ... ECF
Externally Coupled Resonator Filter (MCD) ... ECRF
Externally Mounted Assembly ... EMA
Externally Mounted Electrical Device ... EED
Externally Powered [*Gun*] (MCD) ... EP
Externally Quenched Counter ... EQC
Externally Received Component ... ERC
Externally Specified Address (CAAL) ... ESA
Externally Specified Index ... ESI
Externally Supported Processor [*Mainframe computer*] (NITA) ... ESP
Externally-Specified Index Address (IAA) ... ESIA
External-Mix Spray Nut ... EMSN
External-to-Internal Interface (MCD) ... ETII
Externus [*External*] [*Latin*] ... ext
Extinct ... EXT
Extinct (WDMC) ... ext
Extinction [*Neurophysiology*] ... E
Extinguish (KSC) ... EXT
Extinguish (AAG) ... EXTG
Extinguish ... EXTGH
Extinguish (ROG) ... EXTIN
Extinguish (KSC) ... EXTING
Extinguished Light [*Navigation signal*] ... Exting
Extinguisher (AAG) ... EXTGR
Exton's Maritime Dicaeologie [*A publication*] (DLA) ... Exton Mar Dic
Extortion [*FBI standardized term*] ... EXT
Extortionate Credit Transactions [*FBI standardized term*] ... ECT
Extotal Resources, Inc. [*Vancouver Stock Exchange symbol*] ... EXO
Extra ... EX
Extra ... EXT
Extra (WDMC) ... ext
Extra (ROG) ... EXTR
Extra ... X
Extra (ROG) ... XTRA
Extra Best Best [*Steel wire*] ... EBB
Extra Control [*Wire*] [*Telecommunications*] (TEL) ... EC
Extra Control Wire (MSA) ... EC WIRE
Extra Coordination ... EC
Extra Dark Color (ADA) ... EDC
Extra Deep Drawing [*Metal industry*] ... EDD
Extra Deep Drawing Quality ... EDDQ
Extra Dense ... XD
Extra Dividend [*Banking*] (ADA) ... ED
Extra Duty [*Marine Corps*] ... ED
Extra Executive Transport [*Germany ICAO designator*] (FAAC) ... EXT
Extra Fine [*Threads*] ... EF
Extra Fine ... XF
Extra Gentleman Usher to His Majesty [*British*] ... EGUHM
Extra Gilt [*Bookbinding*] (ROG) ... EX
Extra Hard [*Pencil leads*] ... HH
Extra Hard Black [*Pencil leads*] (ROG) ... EHB
Extra Hazardous (AAG) ... EH
Extra Heavy ... XHVY
Extra [*or Extremely*] **High** ... EH
Extra Incidence Rate in Non-Vaccinated Groups [*Medicine*] (BABM) ... EIRNV
Extra Incidence Rate in Vaccinated Groups [*Biochemistry*] (DAVI) ... EIRv

Extra Incidence Rate of Vaccinated Groups [*Medicine*] (DMAA) .... EIRv
Extra Input Terminal .... XIT
Extra Large [*or Long*] [*Size*] XL
Extra Large Apertures [*Optics*] (ROG) .... ELA
Extra Large Capacity XLC
Extra Large Hinge [*Philately*] .... xlh
Extra Large-Scale Packaging (MHDI) .... XLP
Extra Licentiate of the Royal College of Physicians [*British*] (ROG) .... EXT LRCP
Extra Light Fast [*Ink*] (DGA) .... ELF
Extra Lightly Loaded (IAA) XLL
Extra Load [*Automotive engineering*] XL
Extra Long (WDMC) XL
Extra Long Range [*ICAO designator*] (FAAC) .... ELR
Extra Luxurious Chaparral XLC
Extra MARC [*Machine-Readable Catalog*] **Material** (NITA) .... EMMA
Extra Miler Club (EA) .... EMC
Extra Milers [*Later, EMC*] (EA) .... EM
Extra Military Instruction .... EMI
Extra Old [*Designation on brandy labels*] .... XO
Extra Output Terminal [*Computer science*] (MHDI) .... XOT
Extra Outsize [*Clothing*] .... XOS
Extra Parochial [*Geographical division*] [*British*] .... EXT P
Extra Person (WGA) .... XP
Extra Point [*Football*] .... EP
Extra Point (WGA) .... X PT
Extra Police Duty [*Extra cleaning chores*] [*Military*] .... EPD
Extra Prime Skills Program (DICI) .... EPSP
Extra Range Multigrade [*Automotive engineering*] .... XRM
Extra Restricted (ADA) .... ER
Extra Section (FAAC) .... EXSEC
Extra Segment [*Computer science*] .... ES
Extra Segment:Destination Index [*Computer science*] .... ES:DI
Extra Series .... ES
Extra Slow [*Photography*] (DGA) .... ES
Extra Small .... XS
Extra Soil Defense [*Fabric treatment*] .... ESD
Extra Strong .... XS
Extra Strong (MSA) .... XSTR
Extra Strong Bitter [*Beer*] [*British*] .... ESB
Extra Telecoms Service [*British*] .... ETS
Extra Time Allowance .... EXTAL
Extra Value Package [*Automotive marketing*] .... EVP
Extra Wide [*Women's shoe width*] [*More than one "E" indicates increasing wideness, up to EEE*] .... E
Extra Wide [*Size*] .... XW
Extra Years of Zest [*Gerontology*] .... XYZ
Extra-Anatomic Bypass [*Medicine*] (MEDA) .... EAB
Extrabold [*Type*] (WDMC) .... xbld
Extrabold [*Typography*] .... XBLD
Extracapillary Lesion [*Cardiology*] (DAVI) .... ECL
Extracapillary Proliferative Glomerulonephritis [*Nephrology*] .... ExPGN
Extracapillary Space .... ECS
Extracapsular (CPH) .... EC
Extracapsular Cataract Extraction [*Ophthalmology*] (DAVI) .... XCCE
Extracapular Cataract Extraction [*Ophthalmology*] .... ECCE
Extracellular [*Hematology*] .... EC
Extracellular Enveloped Virus .... EEV
Extracellular Fluid [*Physiology*] .... ECF
Extracellular Fluid Volume [*Physiology*] .... ECFV
Extracellular Fluid Volume [*Physiology*] .... EFV
Extracellular Material [*Physiology*] .... ECM
Extracellular Matrix [*Cytology*] .... ECM
Extracellular Products .... ECP
Extracellular Signaling Protein [*Biochemistry*] .... ESP
Extracellular Virus .... EV
Extracellular Volume [*Hematology*] .... ECV
Extracellular Volume Expansion [*Hematology*] (CPH) .... ECVE
Extracellular Volume Fraction [*Hematology*] .... EVF
Extracellular Water [*Physiology*] .... ECW
Extracellular-Like, Calcium-Free Solution [*Medicine*] .... ECS
Extrachromosomal Element [*Genetics*] .... ECE
Extracorporeal Circulation [*Medicine*] .... ECC
Extracorporeal Irradiation [*Medicine*] .... ECI
Extracorporeal Irradiation of Blood [*Medicine*] .... ECIB
Extracorporeal Irradiation of Lymph (MAE) .... ECIL
Extracorporeal Liver-Assist Device [*Medicine*] (ECON) .... ELAD
Extracorporeal Membrane Oxygenator [*Respirator*] .... ECMO
Extracorporeal Shockwave Lithotripsy [*Medicine*] .... ESWL
Extracorporeal Volume [*Medicine*] (MAE) .... ECV
Extracranial [*Medicine*] .... EC
Extracranial-Intracranial [*Medicine*] .... ECIC
Extract [*or Extracted*] .... EXT
Extract (WDMC) .... ext
Extract .... EXTR
Extract .... EXTRCT
Extract Bit String [*Computer science*] (PCM) .... XBTS
Extract of Requisition .... EXREQ
Extract Release Volume [*Food technology*] .... ERV
Extractable Fluorescence .... EF
Extractable Nuclear Antibody [*Immunology*] (DAVI) .... ENA
Extractable Nuclear Antigen [*Immunology*] .... ENA
Extractable Nucleoprotein [*Biochemistry*] .... ENP
Extractable Organic Halogen [*Environmental chemistry*] (FFDE) .... EOX
Extractable Organic Matter [*Environmental chemistry*] .... EOM
Extracted .... EXTD
Extracting (MSA) .... EXTG
Extraction [*Dentistry*] (DAVI) .... Ext
Extraction .... EXTN
Extraction Dialysis [*For separation of mixtures*] .... ED
Extraction Fraction (MAE) .... E
Extraction Procedure [*Chemical engineering*] .... EP
Extraction Procedure Toxicity .... EPT
Extraction Procedure Toxicity Characteristic [*Environmental Protection Agency*] .... EPTC
Extraction Steam [*System*] [*Nuclear energy*] (NRCH) .... ES
Extraction Tool Insert .... ETI
Extraction Zone [*Military*] (AFM) .... EZ
Extraction Zone Control Officer [*Military*] (AFM) .... EZCO
Extractive Distillation Column [*Chemical engineering*] .... EDC
Extractive Industries Association of South Australia .... EIASA
Extractive Industries Board [*Victoria, Australia*] .... EIB
Extractive Membrane Bioreactor [*Chemical engineering*] .... EMB
Extractive Metallurgy Institute (EA) .... EMI
Extractor .... EXTRCTR
Extractor Parachute Emergency Release Assembly (PDAA) .... EPERA
Extractor Tool .... ETTO
Extractum [*Extract*] [*Latin*] .... EX
Extractum [*Extract*] [*Latin*] .... EXT
Extractum Liquidum [*Liquid extract*] [*Latin Pharmacy*] (WDAA) .... EXT LIQ
Extra-Deep Armed Team Sweep [*Military*] .... EDATS
Extra-Deep-Drawing-Quality [*Steel*] .... EDDQ
Extradimensional Being .... EDB
Extradimensional Shift [*Psychometrics*] .... EDS
Extradition (ADA) .... EXTRAD
Extraepithelial Enterochromaffin Cells [*Cytology*] .... EEEC
Extra-Extra Large [*Size*] XXL
Extra-Extra Strong .... XXS
Extrafamily Adoptee (MAE) .... EFA
Extrafield Sensitivity [*Photonics*] .... EFS
Extrafloral Nectary [*Botany*] .... EFN
Extragalactic Cosmic Ray .... EGCR
Extragalactic Light .... EGL
Extragalactic Radio Source .... EGRS
Extra-Great Value [*In automobile name Yugo GVX*] .... GVX
Extrahatur [*Draw Out*] [*Pharmacy*] (ROG) .... EXTRAH
Extra-Heavy Crude [*Petroleum technology*] .... EHC
Extrahepatic Biliary Atresia [*Medicine*] .... EHBA
Extrahepatic Biliary Obstruction [*Medicine*] .... EBO
Extrahepatic Blood Flow [*Medicine*] .... EHBF
Extrahepatic Cholestasis [*Medicine*] .... EHC
Extrahepatic Distribution [*Gastroenterology*] (DAVI) .... V_{EH}
Extrahepatic Obstruction [*Medicine*] .... EHO
Extrahepatic Portal Hypertension [*Medicine*] (MAE) .... EHPH
Extrahepatic Shunt Ratio [*Medicine*] .... ESR
Extra-High Frequency (NVT) .... XHF
Extra-High Potency .... EHP
Extra-High Pressure (ROG) .... EHP
Extra-High Reliability .... EHR
Extra-High Reliability .... XHR
Extra-High Strength [*Steel*] [*Telecommunications*] (TEL) .... EHS
Extra-High Tension .... EHT
Extra-High Voltage [*FPC*] .... EHV
Extra-High-Density [*Floppy disk technology*] (PCM) .... ED
Extra-High-Frequency Satellite Communication .... EHF SATCOM
Extra-High-Tension Power Supply (EECA) .... EHTPS
Extra-Illustrated .... EI
Extra-Intracranial Arterial Bypass [*Cardiology*] (DMAA) .... EIAB
Extra-Intracranial Bypass [*Medicine*] (PDAA) .... EICB
Extra-Large-Scale Integration [*Computer science*] (TEL) .... ELSI
Extra-Long Distance .... ELD
Extra-Long Shot (WDMC) .... XLS
Extra-Long Staple [*Cotton*] .... ELS
Extra-Long Wheelbase .... XLWB
Extra-Long Working Distance [*Microscopy*] .... ELWD
Extra-Low Carbon .... ELC
Extra-Low Dispersion [*Instrumentation*] .... ED
Extra-Low Impurity [*Metals*] .... ELI
Extra-Low Interstitial [*Alloy*] .... ELI
Extra-Low Interstitial [*Alloy*] XLI
Extra-Low Voltage .... ELV
Extralymphatic [*Medicine*] .... E
Extralymphatic Organ Site [*Oncology*] (DAVI) .... ELOS
Extramedullary Hematopoiesis [*Hematology*] (DAVI) .... EH
Extramembranous Glomerulonephritis [*Medicine*] (AAMN) .... EMGN
Extra-Mural (AIE) .... EM
Extramural Absorption [*Fiber optics*] .... EMA
Extraneous Residue Limit [*Toxicology*] .... ERL
Extraocular Motion [*or Movement*] **Intact** [*Ophthalmology*] (DAVI) .... EOMI
Extraocular Movement [*or Motion*] [*Ophthalmology*] .... EOM
Extraocular Muscles [*Ophthalmology*] .... EOM
Extraocular Muscles Intact [*Ophthalmology*] .... EOMI
Extraoptic Photoreceptors .... EOP
Extraordinary .... EXT
Extraordinary (ROG) .... EXTR
Extraordinary (ROG) .... EXTRAOR
Extraordinary .... EXTRRDNRY
Extraordinary (ROG) .... XTRY
Extraordinary Administrative Radio Conference [*ITU*] .... EARC
Extraordinary and Plenipotentiary .... E & P
Extraordinary Contractual Relief (AAGC) .... ECR

Extraordinary Contractual Relief Reporter [*A publication*] (AAGC) ...... ECR
Extraordinary Contractual Relief Reporter [*A publication*] (AAGC) ...... ER
Extraordinary Electromagnetic Wave ...... EEW
Extraordinary General Meeting [*British*] (ADA) ...... EGM
Extraordinary Mode (MCD) ...... X (Mode)
Extraordinary Nuclear Occurrence (NRCH) ...... ENO
Extraordinary Occasion Service [*Associated Press*] (IIA) ...... EOS
Extraordinary Ray [*Direction of*] ...... E
Extraordinary Session [*A publication*] (DLA) ...... Extra Sess
Extraordinary Wave (IEEE) ...... XWAVE
Extra-Pair Copulation [*Biology*] ...... EPC
Extra-Pair Fertilization [*Biology*] ...... EPF
Extra-Pair Paternity [*Biology*] ...... EPP
Extra-Pair Young [*Biology*] ...... EPY
Extrapolated Alternating Direction Implicit (PDAA) ...... EACRP
Extrapolated End-Point Method [*Nuclear energy*] (NRCH) ...... EEM
Extrapolated Water Elevation (PDAA) ...... EWE
Extrapolation [*A publication*] (BRI) ...... Ext
Extrapyramidal Symptoms [*Medicine*] ...... EPS
Extrapyramidal Syndrome [*Neurology and psychiatry*] (DAVI) ...... EPS
Extra-Regimental Assignment [*Army*] (INF) ...... ERA
Extra-Regimentally Employed [*List*] [*Military British*] ...... ERE
Extraretinal Eye Position Information [*Ophthalmology*] ...... EEPI
Extrasensory Perception ...... ESP
Extra-Solar Giant Planet ...... EGP
Extra-Special Flexible Steel Wire Rope [*British*] ...... ESFSWR
Extra-Special Quality [*Steel cable*] [*Ship's equipment*] (DS) ...... ESQ
Extrastriate [*Neurology*] ...... ES
Extrastrong [*Technical drawings*] ...... EXS
Extrasystole [*Cardiology*] (DAVI) ...... ES
Extraterrestrial [*Also used in film title "ET - The Extra-Terrestrial"*] ...... ET
Extraterrestrial Activity ...... ETA
Extraterrestrial Actuality ...... ETA
Extraterrestrial Biological Entity ...... EBE
Extraterrestrial Civilization ...... ETC
Extraterrestrial Hypothesis ...... ETH
Extraterrestrial Intelligence ...... ETI
Extraterrestrial Material ...... ETM
Extraterrestrial Photographic Information Center [*NASA*] ...... EPIC
Extraterrestrial Research Agency [*Army*] (IEEE) ...... EXTERRA
Extra-Theoretical [*Telecommunications*] (TEL) ...... EXTHEO
Extrathoracic Assisted Breathing [*Medicine*] (DNAB) ...... ETAB
Extrathoracic Assisted Breathing and Circulation [*Medicine*] (DNAB) ...... ETABC
Extrathyroidal Neck Radioactivity [*Radiology*] ...... ENR
Extrathyroidal Thyroxine [*Endocrinology*] (MAE) ...... ETT
Extravagant (ROG) ...... EXTR
Extravagantes Communes [*A publication*] (DLA) ...... EX COM
Extravagantes Communes [*A publication*] (DSA) ...... Extr Comm
Extravagantes Communes [*A publication*] (DSA) ...... Extrav Com
Extravagantes Johannes XXII [*A publication*] (DSA) ...... Extr Joann XXII
Extravagantes Johannes XXII [*A publication*] (DSA) ...... Extrav Joann XXII
Extravagantes Johannes XXII [*A publication*] (DSA) ...... J XXII
Extravaganza (ROG) ...... EX
Extravaganza (ROG) ...... EXTRAV
Extravascular [*Anatomy*] ...... EV
Extravascular Extracellular Water [*Medicine*] ...... EVECW
Extravascular Lung Water [*Medicine*] ...... EVLW
Extravascular Thermal Volume [*Medicine*] ...... EVTV
Extravehicular (MCD) ...... EV
Extravehicular Activity [*Aerospace*] ...... EVA
Extravehicular Activity System (SSD) ...... EVAS
Extravehicular Activity Translational Aid (NASA) ...... EVATA
Extravehicular Aerospace Routing ...... EAR
Extravehicular Astronaut (SAA) ...... EVA
Extravehicular Communications [*Aerospace*] (NASA) ...... EVC
Extravehicular Communications System [*NASA*] ...... EVCS
Extravehicular Communications Umbilical [*Aerospace*] (MCD) ...... EVCU
Extravehicular Communicator [*NASA*] (KSC) ...... EVC
Extravehicular Crew Transfer [*NASA*] (MCD) ...... EVCT
Extravehicular Crew Transfer Device [*NASA*] (KSC) ...... EVCTD
Extravehicular Engineering Activity [*Aerospace*] ...... EVEA
Extravehicular Excursion Unit (SSD) ...... EEU
Extravehicular Glove [*NASA*] (KSC) ...... EVG
Extravehicular Life Support System [*NASA*] ...... EVLSS
Extravehicular Maneuvering Unit Decontamination System (SSD) ...... EMUDS
Extravehicular Mobility Unit [*NASA*] (KSC) ...... EMU
Extravehicular Mobility Unit [*NASA*] (NASA) ...... EVMU
Extravehicular Mobility Unit-Television ...... EMU-TV
Extravehicular Operation [*Aerospace*] ...... EVO
Extravehicular Reference Information [*NASA space program*] ...... ERI
Extravehicular Space Suit [*Aerospace*] (MCD) ...... EVSS
Extravehicular Space Unit [*Aerospace*] (MCD) ...... EVSU
Extravehicular Suit [*Aerospace*] (MCD) ...... EVS
Extravehicular Suit Communications [*Aerospace*] ...... EVSC
Extravehicular Suit Telemetry Communications [*Aerospace*] ...... EVSTC
Extravehicular Support Equipment (SSD) ...... ESE
Extravehicular Support Pack [*or Package*] [*NASA*] ...... ESP
Extravehicular System [*Aerospace*] ...... EVS
Extravehicular Transfer (KSC) ...... EVT
Extravehicular Visor Assembly [*NASA*] ...... EVVA
Extraversion [*Psychology*] ...... Ex
Extraversion-Introversion [*Psychology*] ...... E-I
Extremadura Unida [*Spain Political party*] (EY) ...... EU
Extremal Regulation System (PDAA) ...... ERS
Extreme ...... EXT

Extreme (MSA) ...... EXTM
Extreme ...... extr
Extreme ...... EXTRM
Extreme (FAAC) ...... EXTRM
Extreme ...... XTRM
Extreme Close-Up [*Television*] ...... ECU
Extreme Close-Up [*Also, VCU*] [*Cinematography*] (NTCM) ...... XCU
Extreme Close-Up Indeed [*Photography*] [*British*] (NTCM) ...... ECUI
Extreme Cold Weather Sleep System [*Army*] ...... ECWSS
Extreme Disablement Adjustment ...... EDA
Extreme Fuel - Critical, Unspecified Area [*NASA*] ...... EFCUA
Extreme High Shot [*Photography*] ...... EHS
Extreme High Vacuum ...... XHV
Extreme High Water ...... EHW
Extreme Limb Photometer [*Instrumentation*] ...... ELP
Extreme Long Shot [*Photography*] (WDMC) ...... ELS
Extreme Low Water ...... ELW
Extreme Low Water of Spring Tide ...... ELWS
Extreme Pressure (MSA) ...... EP
Extreme Pressure Ratio [*Military*] ...... EPR
Extreme Terrain Bike [*Military*] (INF) ...... ETB
Extreme Ultraviolet ...... EUV
Extreme Ultraviolet ...... XUV
Extreme Ultraviolet and X-Ray Survey Satellite (PDAA) ...... EXUV
Extreme Ultraviolet Explorer ...... EUVE
Extreme Ultraviolet Explorer (MCD) ...... EUVEX
Extreme Ultraviolet LASER [*Medicine*] (DAVI) ...... EUV
Extreme Ultraviolet Photometer (MCD) ...... EUVP
Extreme Ultraviolet Telescope ...... EUVT
Extreme Value Statistics ...... EVS
Extreme Width [*of flight deck*] ...... EW
Extreme Width ...... EXW
Extremely Elliptical Orbit [*Telecommunications*] (ACRL) ...... EEO
Extremely Fine [*Condition*] [*Antiquarian book trade and numismatics*] ...... EF
Extremely Fine [*Philately*] ...... xf
Extremely Hazardous Air Pollutant [*Environmental science*] ...... EHAP
Extremely Hazardous Substances ...... EHS
Extremely High Frequency [*Electronics, radio wave*] ...... EHF
Extremely Low Birth Weight [*Obstetrics*] (ADA) ...... ELBW
Extremely Low Frequency [*Electronics, radio wave*] ...... ELF
Extremely Low Frequency Radiation ...... ELFR
Extremely Low-Emitting Vehicle [*Automotive engineering*] ...... ELEV
Extremely Sensitive Information [*Army*] (AABC) ...... ESI
Extremely Severe [*Rock climbing*] ...... XS
Extremely Small (IDOE) ...... micro
Extreme-Ultraviolet Imaging Telescope [*Instrumentation*] ...... EIT
Extremity [*Medicine*] ...... EXT
Extremity (MAH) ...... extr
Extremity [*Medicine*] (WDAA) ...... EXTREM
Extrinsic Allergic Alveolitis [*Medicine*] ...... EAA
Extrinsic Alveolitis (PDAA) ...... EA
Extrinsic Factor [*Vitamin B$_{12}$*] [*Also, APA, APAF, LLD*] ...... EF
Extrinsic Hyperpolarizing Potential ...... EHP
Extrinsic Irradiated Silicon Vidicon ...... EISV
Extrinsic Plasminogen Activator [*Hematology*] ...... EPA
Extropy Institute (EA) ...... ExI
Extrovert, Intuitive, a Thinker, and Judger [*Keirsey Temperament Test Result*] [*Psychology*] ...... ENTJ
Extrovert, Intuitive, Feeling, Perceptive [*Meyers-Briggs Type Indicator*] ...... ENFP
Extrudate ...... Ext
Extrude (MSA) ...... EXTD
Extrude (MSA) ...... EXTR
Extruded Bar Solder ...... EBS
Extruded Vinyl Bumper ...... EVB
Extruded Vinyl Chamfer Strip ...... EVCS
Extrusion (MSA) ...... EXTRN
Extrusion Die (MCD) ...... ED
Extrusion Trim and Drill Template ...... ETDT
Extrusion Trim Template ...... ETT
Exudative Vitreoretinopathy [*Ophthalmology*] ...... EV
Ex-Vessel Core Catcher [*Nuclear energy*] (NRCH) ...... EVCC
Ex-Vessel Flux Monitor [*Nuclear energy*] (NRCH) ...... EVFM
Ex-Vessel Handling Machine [*Later, CLEM*] [*Nuclear energy*] (NRCH) ...... EVHM
Ex-Vessel Storage Tank [*Nuclear energy*] (NRCH) ...... EVST
Ex-Vessel Transfer Machine [*Nuclear energy*] (NRCH) ...... EVTM
Ex-Warrants [*Without Warrants*] [*Finance*] ...... EW
Ex-Warrants [*Without Warrants*] [*Finance*] ...... Ex W
Ex-Warrants [*Without Warrants*] [*Finance*] (SPSG) ...... XW
Ex-Warrants [*Without Warrants*] [*Finance*] ...... X-WARR
EXX, Inc. [*Formerly, SFM Corp.*] [*AMEX symbol*] (SAG) ...... EXX
Exxon Corp. [*Associated Press*] (SAG) ...... Exxon
Exxon Corp. [*NYSE symbol*] (SPSG) ...... XON
Exxon Corp., Exploration Library, Denver, CO [*Library symbol Library of Congress*] (LCLS) ...... CoDEx
Exxon Corp., Information Center, Technical Service Coordinator, New York, NY [*OCLC symbol*] (OCLC) ...... ZXX
Exxon Donor Solvent Process [*Coal liquefaction*] ...... EDS
Exxon Education Foundation ...... EEF
Exxon Research and Development Laboratories [*Formerly, Esso Research Laboratory*] ...... ERDL
Exxon Research and Engineering Co. [*Information service or system*] (IID) ...... EREC
Exxon Research & Engineering Co., Company and Literature Information Center Library, Linden, NJ [*Library symbol Library of Congress*] (LCLS) ...... NjLinEx

Exxon Research & Engineering Co., Engineering Information Center, Florham Park, NJ [*Library symbol Library of Congress*] (LCLS) .... NjFpEx
Exxon Research & Engineering Co., Medical Research Library, Linden, NJ [*Library symbol Library of Congress*] (LCLS) .... NjLinEx-M
Ex-Young-Lady [*Wife*] [*Amateur radio slang*] .... XYL
Exzellenz [*Excellency*] [*German*] .... EXZ
Eyberg Child Behavior Inventory (EDAC) .... ECBI
Eye .... E
Eye and Ear .... EE
Eye Artifact Potential .... EAP
Eye Ball Down (MCD) .... EBD
Eye Ball In .... EBI
Eye Ball Left (MCD) .... EBL
Eye Ball Out .... EBO
Eye Ball Right (MCD) .... EBR
Eye Ball Up (MCD) .... EBU
Eye Balls In (SAA) .... EI
Eye Balls In - Eye Balls Out (SAA) .... EI-EO
Eye Balls Out (SAA) .... EO
Eye Bank Association of America (EA) .... EBAA
Eye Care (EA) .... EC
Eye Contolled Focus [*Camera technology*] .... ECF
Eye Focus .... EF
Eye Guard .... EGRD
Eye Infection [*Classification system used by doctors on Ellis Island to detain, re-examine, and possibly deny entry to certain immigrants*] .... E
Eye Lens (MSA) .... EL
Eye Lens Obsolescence [*Ophthalmology*] .... ELO
Eye Notochord Length [*Fish anatomy*] .... ENL
Eye Point of Regard [*NASA*] .... EPR
Eye Protection Factor .... EPF
Eye Protection Shutter .... EPS
Eye Reference Point [*NASA*] (KSC) .... ERP
Eye Research [*Defunct*] (EA) .... ER
Eye Research Foundation (DAVI) .... ERF
Eye Research Laboratories [*University of Chicago*] [*Research center*] (RCD) .... ERL
Eye Stalk .... ES
Eye Standard Length [*Fish anatomy*] .... ESL
Eye Travel .... ET
Eye-Bank for Sight Restoration (EA) .... EBSR
Eye-Derived Growth Factor [*Biochemistry*] .... EDGF
Eye-Gaze Response Interface Computer Aid [*Computer designed for the physically handicapped that responds to user's eye movements*] [*Designed by Thomas Hutchinson*] .... ERICA
Eye-Hand-Muscle (SAA) .... EHM
Eyelet (MSA) .... EYLT
Eyelet-Installing Machine .... EIM
Eye-Motion Camera .... EMC
Eye-Movement Desensitization and Reprocessing [*Psychotherapy*] .... EMDR
Eye-Movement Device .... EMD
Eye-Movement Gauge .... EMG
Eye-Movement Measuring Apparatus [*Ophthalmology*] (DAVI) .... EMMA
Eyepiece (MSA) .... EYPC
Eyepiece Box .... EB
Eyepiece Focusing Adjustment [*Optics*] (ROG) .... EFA

Eyes Closed [*Ataxia*] .... EC
Eyes, Ears, Nose, and Throat [*Medicine*] .... EENT
Eyes in the Sky .... EIS
Eyes, Motor, Voice [*Glasgow Coma Scale*] [*Medicine*] .... EMV
[*The*] Eyes of the Army (AAG) .... TEOTA
Eyes Open [*Ataxia*] .... EO
Eyes Right (EA) .... ERI
Eye-Safe LASER Range Finder Training Device (MCD) .... ELRFTD
Eyesafe LASER Rangefinder (RDA) .... ELRF
Eye-Safe Simulated LASER Range Finder (MCD) .... ESSLR
Eye-Slaved Display Integration and Test .... EDIT
Eye-Slaved Projected Rafter Inset [*Simulator*] .... ESPRIT
Eye-Voice Span .... EVS
Eymard League (EA) .... EL
Eyn-Shemer [*Israel*] [*ICAO location identifier*] (ICLI) .... LLES
Eyre's English King's Bench Reports Tempore William III [*A publication*] (DLA) .... Eyre
Eyre's Manuscript Notes of Cases, King's Bench [*New York Law Institute Library*] [*A publication*] (DLA) .... Eyre MS
Eyretechnics Ltd., Ottawa, ON, Canada [*Library symbol Library of Congress*] (LCLS) .... CaOOEy
Eyretechnics Ltd., Ottawa, Ontario [*Library symbol National Library of Canada*] (NLC) .... OOEY
Eyrewell [*New Zealand*] [*Geomagnetic observatory code*] .... EYR
Eysenck Personality Inventory [*Psychology*] .... EPI
Eysenck Personality Profiler [*Psychology*] .... EPP
Eysenck Personality Questionnaire [*Personality development test*] [*Psychology*] .... EPQ
Eysenck-Withers Personality Inventory [*Psychology*] .... EWPI
EZ Communications, Inc. [*Associated Press*] (SAG) .... EZ Com
EZ Communications, Inc. [*NASDAQ symbol*] (SAG) .... EZCI
E-Z Communications'A' [*NASDAQ symbol*] (TTSB) .... EZCIA
EZ Serve [*Associated Press*] (SAG) .... EZ Serv
E-Z Serve Corp. [*AMEX symbol*] (SPSG) .... EZS
EZ Ventures Ltd. [*Vancouver Stock Exchange symbol*] .... EZV
Ezcony Interamerica [*NASDAQ symbol*] (TTSB) .... EZCOF
Ezcony Interamerica, Inc. [*NASDAQ symbol*] (SAG) .... EZCO
Ezcony Interamerica, Inc. [*Associated Press*] (SAG) .... Ezcony
Ezcorp, Inc. [*Associated Press*] (SAG) .... Ezcorp
EZCORP, Inc. [*NASDAQ symbol*] (SPSG) .... EZPW
EZCORP Inc.'A' [*NASDAQ symbol*] (TTSB) .... EZPW
Ezechiel [*Old Testament book*] [*Douay version*] .... EZECH
Ezegodnik Muzeja Istorii i Ateizma [*Moscow*] (BJA) .... EMIRA
Ezeiza [*Argentina ICAO location identifier*] (ICLI) .... SAEF
Ezeiza [*Argentina ICAO location identifier*] (ICLI) .... SAEV
Ezekiel [*Old Testament book*] .... Ez
Ezekiel [*Old Testament book*] .... Ezek
Ezekiel [*Old Testament book*] .... EZK
E-Z-EM, Inc. [*NASDAQ symbol*] (NQ) .... EZEM
EZEM, Inc. [*AMEX symbol*] (SAG) .... EZM
Ezine [*Turkey*] [*Seismograph station code, US Geological Survey*] (SEIS) .... EZN
Ezra [*Old Testament book*] .... Ez
Ezra [*Old Testament book*] .... Ezr
Ezra Pound Society (EA) .... EPS
Ezrat Nashim [*Defunct*] (EA) .... EN
Ezrin-Radixin-Moesin [*Cytology*] .... ERM

F
By Meaning

F & E Resource Systems Technology, Inc. [*Associated Press*] (SAG) .... F & E Res
F & E Resource Systems Technology, Inc. [*NASDAQ symbol*] (SAG) .... FERS
F & M Bancorp, Inc. [*Associated Press*] (SAG) .... F & M Bc
F & M Bancorp, Inc. [*Associated Press*] (SAG) .... F & M Bn
F & M Bancorp, Inc. [*NASDAQ symbol*] (SAG) .... FMBK
F & M Bancorp, Inc. [*NASDAQ symbol*] (SAG) .... FMBN
F & M National Corp. [*Associated Press*] (SAG) .... F & M Nat
F & M National Corp. [*NYSE symbol*] (SAG) .... FMN
F Antigen [*Immunochemistry*] .... F-Ag
F. E. Madill Secondary School, Wingham, Ontario [*Library symbol National Library of Canada*] (NLC) .... OWINF
F. F. Slaney & Co. Ltd., Vancouver, BC, Canada [*Library symbol Library of Congress*] (LCLS) .... CaBVaSLA
F. F. Slaney & Co. Ltd., Vancouver, British Columbia [*Library symbol National Library of Canada*] (NLC) .... BVASLA
F. Marion Crawford Memorial Society (EA) .... FMCMS
F. P. Ristine & Co., Philadelphia, PA [*Library symbol Library of Congress Obsolete*] (LCLS) .... PPFPR
F. S. Royster Guano Co., Norfolk, VA [*Library symbol Library of Congress*] (LCLS) .... ViNR
F. W. Faxon Co. [*ACCORD*] [*UTLAS symbol*] .... FXU
F. W. Minkler Library, North York Board of Education, Willowdale, Ontario [*Library symbol National Library of Canada*] (NLC) .... OTNYE
F_1 Adenosine Triphosphatase [*A protein*] [*Biochemistry*] (DAVI) .... F_1ATPase
F-15 Adapted Place Atlas Program (MCD) .... FAPA
FA Naval del Peru [*ICAO designator*] (FAAC) .... INP
Fa, Sol, and La [*Musical notation system*] .... FASOLA
FAA Air Traffic Activity Data Base [*BTS*] (TAG) .... ATADS
FAA Airline Data Exchange [*FAA*] (TAG) .... FADE
FAA Technical Center [*FAA*] (TAG) .... FAATC
FAAD [*Forward Area Air Defense*] **Data Link** [*Army*] .... FDL
Fab Eating at School Today [*Nutritional improvement group*] [*British*] .... FEAST
Fab Indus [*AMEX symbol*] (TTSB) .... FIT
Fab Industries, Inc. [*Associated Press*] (SAG) .... FabInd
Fab Industries, Inc. [*AMEX symbol*] (SPSG) .... FIT
Fabbrica Italiana Automobile, Torino [*Italian automobile manufacturer*] [*Facetious translations: "Fix It Again, Tony"; "Futile Italian Attempt at Transportation"*] .... FIAT
Fabens, TX [*FM radio station call letters*] .... KPAS
Fabian Society (BARN) .... Fab Soc
Fabian Society [*British*] (ILCA) .... FS
Fabien Exploration, Inc. [*Toronto Stock Exchange symbol*] .... FEX
Fabius Accorambonus [*Deceased, 1559*] [*Authority cited in pre-1607 legal work*] (DSA) .... Fab
Fable (ROG) .... FAB
Fabra [*Barcelona*] [*Spain*] [*Seismograph station code, US Geological Survey*] (SEIS) .... FBR
Fabray-Perot Infrared Grating Spectrometer [*Chemistry*] .... FIGS
Fabri Centers of America [*Associated Press*] (SAG) .... FabC
Fabri Centers of America [*NYSE symbol*] (SAG) .... FCA
Fabric .... FAB
Fabric (VRA) .... fab
Fabric .... FBRC
Fabric Care Research Association [*British*] (IRUK) .... FCRA
Fabric Insulation Material .... FIM
Fabric Laminators Association [*Defunct*] .... FLA
Fabric Retailers, Etc., Etc. [*Trade group*] .... FREE
Fabric Salesmen's Association (EA) .... FSA
Fabrica Uruguaya de Neumaticos, Sociedad Anonima [*A tire manufacturer*] .... FUNSA
Fabricants Canadiens de Produits Alimentaires [*Grocery Products Manufacturers of Canada - GPMC*] .... FCPA
Fabricate .... FAB
Fabricated .... FABD
Fabricated .... FABR
Fabricated Metal Goods .... FMG
Fabricated Steel Construction [*Bethlehem Steel Corp.*] .... FSC
Fabricating .... FABG
Fabrication .... FBRCN
Fabrication and Acceptance Checkout (MCD) .... FACO
Fabrication and Architecture of Single-Electron Memories [*Computer Science*] .... FASEM
Fabrication Assembly (MCD) .... FA
Fabrication, Assembly, and Inspection Record [*NASA*] (NASA) .... FAIR
Fabrication Assembly Order (MCD) .... FAO
Fabrication Equivalent Unit Reporting System (MCD) .... FEURS
Fabrication in Transit (ADA) .... FIT
Fabrication Instruction (NG) .... FI
Fabrication, Integration, and Test .... FIT
Fabrication Isometric (IAA) .... FABISO
Fabrication of Inflatable Reentry Structures for Test [*Air Force*] .... FIRST
Fabrication Operations Requirements System (MCD) .... FORS
Fabrication Order (MCD) .... FO
Fabrication Order Special Number .... FOSN
Fabrication Outline (MCD) .... FO
Fabrication Outline Special Purpose .... FOSP
Fabrication Performance Utilization System (MCD) .... FAPUS
Fabrication Quality Record .... FQR
Fabrication Reporting System (MCD) .... FABRS
Fabrication Statusing System (MCD) .... FSS
Fabrication Technology (MCD) .... FABTECH
Fabrication Tracking and Management System (MCD) .... FTMS
Fabricationless (CDE) .... fabless
Fabricator .... FAB
Fabricators and Manufacturers Association .... FMA
Fabricators and Manufacturers Association, International (EA) .... FMA
Fabricators and Manufacturers Association, International (EA) .... FMAI
Fabri-Centers of America, Inc. [*Associated Press*] (SAG) .... FabriC
Fabri-Centers of America, Inc. [*NYSE symbol*] (SPSG) .... FCA
Fabrichnaya [*Former USSR Seismograph station code, US Geological Survey Closed*] (SEIS) .... FAB
Fabryka Samochodow Malolotia [*Polish affiliate of Fiat Motors*] .... FSM
Fabryka Samochodow Osobowych [*Polish automobile manufacturer*] .... FSO
Fabry-Perot [*Etalon on interferometer*] [*Optics*] .... FP
Fabry-Perot Interferometer .... FPI
Fabry-Perot Recycling Spectrometer (PDAA) .... FPRS
FABS Electronic Bible [*FABS International, Inc.*] [*Information service or system*] (CRD) .... FEB
FABS Reference Bible [*FABS International, Inc.*] [*Information service or system*] (CRD) .... FRB
Fabulous (ROG) .... FAB
Fabulous Fifties Ford Club of America (EA) .... FFFCA
Fabulous Thunderbirds Fan Club (EA) .... FTFC
Fac [*Let There Be Made*] [*Pharmacy*] .... F
Facade (VRA) .... fac
Face .... F
Face Amount [*Business term*] .... FA
Face Brick [*Technical drawings*] .... FB
Face Immersion (DNAB) .... FI
Face Information Digested Online (NITA) .... FIDO
Face Lying [*Medicine*] (DMAA) .... fcly
Face Mask [*Medicine*] (DAVI) .... FM
Face Measurement .... FM
Face of Concrete [*Technical drawings*] .... FOC
Face of Drawing (AAG) .... FD
Face of Finish [*Technical drawings*] .... FOF
Face of Masonry [*Technical drawings*] .... FOM
Face of Studs [*Technical drawings*] .... FOS
Face of Template (MCD) .... FOT
Face to Face [*Technical drawings*] .... F to F
Face to Face .... F-F
Face to Face .... FTF
Face Value (ADA) .... FV
Face Width (MSA) .... FW
Face-Amount Certificate [*Banking*] (MHDB) .... FAC
Face-Bow [*Dentistry*] (DAVI) .... f-b
Face-Centered [*Crystallography*] .... FC
Face-Centered Cubic [*Crystallography*] .... FCC
Face-Centered Tetragonal [*Crystallography*] .... FCT
Facel Vega Owners Club [*Defunct*] (EA) .... FVOC
Facelifters Home Systems, Inc. [*NASDAQ symbol*] (NQ) .... FACE
Facelifters Home Systems, Inc. [*Associated Press*] (SAG) .... Fcelftr
Faceplate (IEEE) .... FP
Faceplate [*Electronics*] (IAA) .... FPL
Faceted Fixed Mirror Concentrator (PDAA) .... FFMC
Faceted Information Retrieval for Linguistics (PDAA) .... FIRL
Faceted Region Editor [*Software package*] [*Military*] (RDA) .... FRED
Facetious .... FACET
Face-to-Face [*Fundraising*] F2F
Facez, Rockford, IL [*Library symbol*] [*Library of Congress*] (LCLS) .... FcZ
Fachhochschule Esslingen - Hochschule fuer Technik [*Business Management Program*] [*Germany*] .... FHTE

Fachinformationssystem [*Information service or system*] [*Germany*] (NITA) ..... FIS
Fachinformationszentrum [*Information centre*] [*Germany*] (NITA) ..... FIZ
Fachinformationszentrum Technik [*Germany*] (NITA) ..... FIZ-technik
Fachinformationszentrum Werkstoffe [*Information Center for Materials*] [*Information service or system*] (IID) ..... FIZ-W
Fachverband Klebstoffindustrie [*Association of European Adhesives Manufacturers*] (EAIO) ..... FKI
Facial [*Chemistry*] ..... FAC
Facial Nerve Involvement [*Medicine*] ..... FNI
Facial Rash [*Classification system used by doctors on Ellis Island to detain, re-examine, and possibly deny entry to certain immigrants*] ..... F
Facial Surface [*Dentistry*] ..... F
Facies [*Medicine*] ..... F
Facilitated Transport Membrane [*Separation of chemicals*] ..... FTM
Facilitating Agency [*Business term*] ..... FA
Facilitation Awards for Handicapped Scientists and Engineers Program [*Washington, DC National Science Foundation*] (GRD) ..... FAH
Facilitation of International Air Transport [*Aviation*] ..... FAL
Facilitative Communication [*Autism*] ..... FC
Facilities (ADA) ..... FACS
Facilities Action Control Target System [*US Postal Service*] ..... FACTS
Facilities Administration Consolidated Tape System (MCD) ..... FACTS
Facilities Administration Control and Time Schedule ..... FACTS
Facilities Advisory Board (AAG) ..... FAB
Facilities Analysis Model [*Computer science*] ..... FAM
Facilities and Communication Evaluation [*Army*] (AABC) ..... FACE
Facilities and Design (KSC) ..... F & D
Facilities and Design (MCD) ..... FD
Facilities and Environmental Measurement Components Parts List [*NASA*] (NASA) ..... FEMCPL
Facilities and Environmental Measuring System [*NASA*] (KSC) ..... FEMS
Facilities and Equipment ..... F & E
Facilities and Equipment Department's Control Division [*Navy*] (DNAB) ..... F & EDCD
Facilities and Support Service Division [*Environmental Protection Agency*] (GFGA) ..... FSSD
Facilities Assets Catalog and Tracking System [*Army*] ..... FACTS
Facilities Assistance Program ..... FAP
Facilities Associate Contractor ..... FAC
Facilities Automation System ..... FAS
Facilities Capital Cost of Money (AAGC) ..... FCCM
Facilities Capital Cost of Money (AAGC) ..... FCCOM
Facilities Capital Cost of Money Factors Computation [*DoD*] ..... CMF
Facilities Capital Employed [*DoD*] ..... FCE
Facilities Computer Monitoring System [*Johnson Controls, Inc.*] ..... FCMS
Facilities Construction (AAG) ..... FC
Facilities Contract ..... FC
Facilities Control [*Military*] ..... F/C
Facilities Control [*Radio Central*] [*Navy*] (CAAL) ..... FACCON
Facilities Control Center [*Army*] (AABC) ..... FACCONCEN
Facilities Control Console (AAG) ..... FCC
Facilities Control Relay Unit [*Army*] (AABC) ..... FCRU
Facilities Control System ..... FACS
Facilities Engineer (MCD) ..... FE
Facilities Engineer Apprentice Program [*Army*] (MCD) ..... FEAP
Facilities Engineer Equipment Maintenance System [*Army*] ..... FEEMS
Facilities Engineer Supply System [*Army*] ..... FESS
Facilities Engineering and Construction Agency [*HEW*] ..... FECA
Facilities Engineering Command [*Also, NFEC*] [*Formerly, Bureau of Yards and Docks*] [*Navy*] ..... FEC
Facilities Engineering Items [*Military*] (AABC) ..... FEI
Facilities Engineering Management System (MCD) ..... FEMS
Facilities Engineering Support Agency [*Army*] (MCD) ..... FESA
Facilities Engineering Support Agency Technology Support Division [*Fort Belvoir, VA*] [*Army*] ..... FESA-TS
Facilities Forecast Obligations Summary ..... FFOS
Facilities Installation Monitoring Group (MUGU) ..... FIMG
Facilities Installation Study Program [*Navy*] (NVT) ..... FACSTEAM
Facilities Interface Data Requirements Sheets (MCD) ..... FIDRS
Facilities Inventory Study ..... FIS
Facilities Item ..... FI
Facilities Laboratory [*National Center for Atmospheric Research*] ..... FAL
Facilities Maintenance ..... FM
Facilities Maintenance Operations and Computerized Systems Show (TSPED) ..... FMO
Facilities Maintenance Team [*Military*] ..... FMT
Facilities Management ..... FM
Facilities Management Analysis ..... FMA
Facilities Management and Services Division [*Environmental Protection Agency*] (GFGA) ..... FMSD
Facilities Management Contract ..... FMC
Facilities Management System ..... FMS
Facilities Matrix (MCD) ..... FAC MAT
Facilities Planning and Development Branch [*BUPERS*] ..... FP & DB
Facilities Procurement Application (AAG) ..... FPA
Facilities Procuring Contracting Officer [*Military*] (AFIT) ..... FPCO
Facilities Report [*or Request*] ..... FR
Facilities Requirements Documents (MCD) ..... FRD
Facilities Requirements Study ..... FRS
Facilities Rule-Based Model Management Environment ..... FRAMME
Facilities Supply Office ..... FACSO
Facilities System Engineer ..... FSE
Facilities Technology Application Test [*Army*] (RDA) ..... FTAT
Facility (AAG) ..... FAC
Facility ..... FACIL
Facility ..... FACLTY
Facility (AFM) ..... FCLTY
Facility Activation [*or Activity*] **Schedule** ..... FAS
Facility Air Supply ..... FAS
Facility Analysis Plan [*Telecommunications*] (TEL) ..... FAP
Facility and Design (IAA) ..... FAD
Facility and Environment (NASA) ..... F & E
Facility and Equipment Design Plan (MCD) ..... FEDP
Facility and Equipment Requirements Document (NASA) ..... FERD
Facility Block Table (IAA) ..... FBT
Facility Board [*Air Force*] (CET) ..... FB
Facility Capability Report [*Military*] ..... FCR
Facility Capability Review ..... FCR
Facility Capital Funds (AAG) ..... FCF
Facility Chance Initiation Request (AAGC) ..... FCIR
Facility Change Authorization (AAG) ..... FCA
Facility Change Group (KSC) ..... FCG
Facility Change Initiation Request ..... FCIR
Facility Change Order (AAG) ..... FCO
Facility Change Request ..... FCR
Facility Checking Flight - Service Evaluation [*Air Force*] (MCD) ..... FCF SE
Facility Checking Squadron [*Air Force*] ..... FCLTYCHECKINGSq
Facility Checking Squadron [*Air Force*] ..... FCS
Facility Checkout ..... FAC/CO
Facility Checkout Vehicle [*NASA*] (KSC) ..... FCOV
Facility Checkout Vehicle [*NASA*] (KSC) ..... FCV
Facility Chief (FAAC) ..... FACF
Facility [*Security*] **Clearance** ..... FCL
Facility Clearance Board [*WPB*] ..... FCB
Facility Communication System (IAA) ..... FCS
Facility Communications Criteria (IAA) ..... FCC
Facility Contract (AAGC) ..... FAC
Facility Contract End Item ..... FCEI
Facility Control / Power Management (MHDB) ..... FC/PM
Facility Coordination Officer (FAAC) ..... FCO
Facility Data Report [*Nuclear energy*] ..... FDR
Facility Density Mapper ..... FDM
Facility Design Criteria (AAG) ..... FDC
Facility Design Criteria Document (AAG) ..... FDCD
Facility Development Design and Review System [*Veterans Administration*] (GFGA) ..... FDDRS
Facility Division [*Marine science*] (OSRA) ..... FD
Facility Division [*Forecast Systems Laboratory*] (USDC) ..... FD
Facility Drawing ..... FD
Facility Emergency Organization [*Nuclear energy*] (NRCH) ..... FEO
Facility Engineering and Systems Development Library, Transport Canada [*Bibliotheque de l'Ingenierie des Installations et de la Mise au Point des Systemes, Transports Canada*], Edmonton, Alberta [*Library symbol National Library of Canada*] (NLC) ..... AETATE
Facility Engineering and Systems Development Sub-Library, Edmonton InternationalAirport, Transport Canada [*Succursale de la Bibliotheque de l'Ingenierie des Installations et de la Mise au Point des Systemes, Aeroport International d'Edm onton, Transports Canada*], Alberta [*Library symbol National Library of Canada*] (NLC) ..... AETATES
Facility Engineering Change Proposal ..... FECP
Facility Engineering Command ..... FACENGCOM
Facility Engineering Job Estimating [*Military*] (GFGA) ..... FEJE
Facility for Accelerated Service Testing ..... FAST
Facility for Analyzing Surface Texture [*National Bureau of Standards*] (MCD) ..... FAST
Facility for Automatic Software Production [*Computer science*] (CAAL) ..... FASP
Facility for Automatic Sorting and Testing ..... FAST
Facility for Automation, Control and Test (PDAA) ..... FACT
Facility for Integrated Data Organization ..... FIDO
Facility for Interrogating the National Directory of Australian Resources (EERA) ..... FINDAR
Facility for the Analysis of Chemical Thermodynamics [*McGill University*] [*Information service or system*] (IID) ..... FACT
Facility Forecast (MCD) ..... FF
Facility Gauge (AAG) ..... FCGA
Facility Ground ..... FG
Facility Group Control [*Military*] (AFM) ..... FGC
Facility Index System [*Environmental Protection Agency*] (EPA) ..... FINDS
Facility Indexing System ..... FINDS
Facility Information Management System (MCD) ..... FIMS
Facility Installation Review ..... FIR
Facility Interface Sheet ..... FIS
Facility Interface Unit [*Telecommunications*] ..... FIU
Facility Interference Review ..... FIR
Facility Intrusion Detection System (RDA) ..... FIDS
Facility Laboratory for Ablative Materials Evaluation (SAA) ..... FLAME
Facility Manager ..... FM
Facility Need Date (NASA) ..... FND
Facility Operating License [*Nuclear energy*] (NRCH) ..... FOL
Facility Planning and Design (KSC) ..... FP & D
Facility Portable Test Equipment (AAG) ..... FPTE
Facility Power Control (AAG) ..... FPC
Facility Power Monitor (AAG) ..... FPM
Facility Power Out Test (KSC) ..... FPOT
Facility Power Panel (AAG) ..... FPP
Facility Remote Control Panel (AAG) ..... FRCP
Facility Requirements Division [*Environmental Protection Agency*] (EPA) ..... FRD
Facility Review Committee ..... FRC
Facility Security Officer ..... FSO
Facility Security Profile [*Military*] (GFGA) ..... FSP

Facility Security Program [*World War II*] .... FSP
Facility Security Supervision (MCD) .... FSS
Facility Support Equipment .... FSE
Facility Support Plan [*Military*] .... FSP
Facility Tape Loading (SAA) .... FTL
Facility Terminal Cabinet (AAG) .... FTC
Facility Training Equipment .... FTE
Facility Utilization Board (AFM) .... FUB
Facility Utilization Plan (AFM) .... FUP
Facility Verification Vehicle .... FVV
Facility Working Group .... FWG
Facing (WDAA) .... F
Facing .... FCG
Facing East [*In outdoor advertising*] (WDMC) .... F/E
Facing History and Ourselves National Foundation (EA) .... FHONF
Facing Identification Mark [*Postal Service*] .... FIM
Facing North [*In outdoor advertising*] (WDMC) .... F/N
Facing South [*In outdoor advertising*] (WDMC) .... F/S
Facing Tile Institute (EA) .... FTI
Facing West [*In outdoor advertising*] (WDMC) .... F/W
Facioscapulohumeral Muscular Dystrophy [*Neurology*] (DAVI) .... FSHMD
Faciundum Curavit [*He Caused To Be Made*] [*Latin*] .... FC
Facsimile .... FAC
Facsimile (KSC) .... FACS
Facsimile .... FACSIM
Facsimile (AFM) .... FAX
Facsimile (IDOE) .... fax
Facsimile (ADA) .... FS
Facsimile (KSC) .... FX
Facsimile Broadcast Service .... FBS
Facsimile Communications System [*Telecommunications*] .... FCS
Facsimile Data Converter [*Facilitates communication between facsimile terminal and computer*] (NITA) .... FDC
Facsimile Information Network Development .... FIND
Facsimile Infromation Field [*Telecommunications*] (OSI) .... FIF
Facsimile Packet [*ITT*] [*Telecommunications*] (TEL) .... FAXPAK
Facsimile Switching Unit .... FSU
Facsimile System [*Western Union trade name*] .... INTRAFAX
Facsimile Test Society .... FTS
Facsimile Transmission [*Telecommunications*] (MCD) .... FAX
Facsimile Transmission (WDMC) .... fax
Facsimile Transmission [*Telecommunications*] (NOAA) .... FAXTM
Facsimile Transmission [*Telecommunications*] .... TRANSFAX
Facsimile Transmission over AUTODIN [*Telecommunications*] .... FAXDIN
Facsimile Transmission System [*Telecommunications*] .... FACTS
Fact, Discussion, Recommendations .... FDR
Fact Issue Paper .... FIP
Facteur Respiratoire Equilibre [*Ingredient in a cosmetic by Chanel*] .... FRE
Facteur Thymique Serique [*Synthetic Serum Thymic Factor*] [*Immunochemistry*] [*French*] .... FTS
Fact-Finding Bodies .... FFB
Factitious Fever [*Medicine*] (CPH) .... FF
Factor (DAVI) .... F
Factor (MSA) .... FAC
Factor .... FCTR
Factor (KSC) .... FTR
Factor Analysis [*Mathematics*] .... FA
Factor Analysis Chart Technique [*Business term*] .... FACT
Factor Information Retrieval Data System [*Information service or system*] (IID) .... FIRE
Factor IX [*Hematology*] .... FIX
Factor of Merit [*Telecommunications*] (TEL) .... FOM
Factor of Production [*Economics*] .... F/Pn
Factor of Safety (IAA) .... FOS
Factor of Safety .... FS
Factor Storage (IAA) .... FS
Factor/Test Procedure (MCD) .... FTP
Factorial Correspondence Analysis [*Mathematics*] .... FCA
Factorial Moment Generating Function [*Statistics*] .... FMGF
Factories and Workshops Acts [*Law*] [*British*] (ROG) .... FWA
Factories Inspectorate [*British*] (NUCP) .... FI
Factories Journal Reports [*India*] [*A publication*] (DLA) .... FJR
Factoring Services Group [*British*] (DBA) .... FSG
Factory .... FAC
Factory [*Automotive engineering*] .... FACT
Factory (VRA) .... fact
Factory .... Facty
Factory (KSC) .... FCT
Factory .... FCTRY
Factory (MUGU) .... FCTY
Factory Acceptance Checkout (MCD) .... FACO
Factory Acceptance Test .... FAT
Factory Acceptance Test Procedure .... FATP
Factory Acceptance Test Specification .... FATS
Factory Act [*British*] (ILCA) .... FA
Factory Aerospace Ground Equipment (MCD) .... FAGE
Factory Assembly and Checkout .... FACO
Factory Automatic Checkout Equipment .... FACE
Factory Automation .... FA
Factory Automation, Control, and Test Facility .... FACT
Factory Automation Systems Technology [*British*] .... FAST
Factory Card Outlet Corp. [*Associated Press*] (SAG) .... FactCrd
Factory Card Outlet Corp. [*NASDAQ symbol*] (SAG) .... FCPY
Factory Checkout Equipment (MCD) .... FCE
Factory Damaged [*Slang*] .... FD'd
Factory Data Processing (IAA) .... FDP
Factory Equipment Transfer Order .... FETO
Factory Experimental [*Class of drag racing cars*] .... FX
Factory Finish [*Technical drawings*] .... FF
Factory Ground Equipment (KSC) .... FGE
Factory Information Control System (MHDB) .... FICS
Factory Insurance Association [*Later, Industrial Risk Insurers*] (EA) .... FIA
Factory Layout Analysis [*PERA*] [*Software package*] (NCC) .... FLAN
Factory Management and Control [*Computer Automation Ltd.*] [*Software package*] (NCC) .... FM & C
Factory Management Information System [*British*] (NITA) .... FAMIS
Factory Management System [*General Electric Co.*] .... FMS
Factory Manual .... FM
Factory Marriage Test .... FMT
Factory Materials Association .... FMA
Factory Mechatronics (TSPED) .... FACTRO
Factory Monitoring and Control System [*Computer science*] .... FMCS
Factory Mutual Engineering and Research .... FMER
Factory Mutual Engineering and Research Organization (EA) .... FMERO
Factory Mutual System [*Formerly, AFMFIC*] [*Group of four insurance companies and an engineering organization*] .... FM
Factory Mutual System [*Formerly, AFMFIC*] [*Group of four insurance companies and an engineering organization*] .... FMS
Factory Mutuals' Combined Fire-Boiler Policy [*Insurance*] .... FMB
Factory on Dock (SAA) .... FOD
Factory Order .... FO
Factory Pass (AAG) .... FP
Factory Programmable Read Only Memory [*Computer science*] (IAA) .... FROM
Factory Serial Number (MCD) .... FSN
Factory Space Allocation Plan (MCD) .... FSAP
Factory Special Test Equipment (NASA) .... FSTE
Factory Stores of America [*NYSE symbol*] (TTSB) .... FAC
Factory Stores of America, Inc. [*Associated Press*] (SAG) .... FacStr
Factory Support Equipment (KSC) .... FSE
Factory Test .... FT
Factory Test Equipment (MCD) .... FTE
Factory Test Equipment Manufacturing .... FTEM
Factory Test Set .... FTS
Factory Training School .... FTS
Factory Training Unit (KSC) .... FTU
Factory Work Group .... FWG
Factory-Installed Maintenance Automatic Test Equipment .... FIMATE
Factory-of-the-Future .... FOF
Factotum Initial [*Typography*] (DGA) .... FACT INIT
Facts and Logic about the Middle East [*An association*] .... FLAME
Facts Bulletin Board System [*Database*] [*Fast Agricultural Communications Terminal System*] [*Information service or system*] (CRD) .... FBBS
Facts Location and Summarized History [*General Motors Corp.*] [*Computer science*] .... FLASH
Facts of Bayonne Publishing Co., Bayonne, NJ [*Library symbol Library of Congress*] (LCLS) .... NjBaF
[*The*] **Facts of Life** [*NBC television program*] .... FOL
Facts on Aging Quiz (EDAC) .... FAO
Facts on File, Inc. .... FOF
Factset Research Systems, Inc. [*Associated Press*] (SAG) .... FactsetR
Factset Research Systems, Inc. [*NYSE symbol*] (SAG) .... FDS
Factual Compiler .... FACT
Factual Lines about Submarine Hazards (DNAB) .... FLASH
Factum Similis [*Facsimile*] [*Latin*] .... FAC
Facture [*Invoice*] [*Business term French*] .... FRE
Facultad Latinoamericana de Ciencias Sociales [*Latin American Faculty of Social Sciences*] [*San Jose, Costa Rica*] .... FLACSO
Facultative Wetland Plant (ERG) .... FACW
Faculte de Droit, Universite Laval, Quebec, Quebec [*Library symbol National Library of Canada*] (NLC) .... QQLAD
Faculte de Medecine Veterinaire de l'Universite de Montreal, St.-Hyacinthe, PQ, Canada [*Library symbol Library of Congress*] (LCLS) .... CaQStHV
Faculte Saint-Jean Library, University of Alberta [*UTLAS symbol*] .... FSJ
Faculte Saint-Jean, University of Alberta, Edmonton, Alberta [*Library symbol National Library of Canada*] (NLC) .... AEUSJ
Faculty (AABC) .... FAC
Faculty .... FCLTY
Faculty Author Development [*Software development program*] .... FAD
Faculty Christian Fellowship [*National Council of Churches*] (AEBS) .... FCF
Faculty Directory of Higher Education [*A publication*] .... FDHE
Faculty Exchange Center (EA) .... FEC
Faculty for Human Rights in El Salvador and Central America (EA) .... FACHRES-CA
Faculty of Actuaries [*British*] (BI) .... FA
Faculty of Advocates [*British*] (ILCA) .... FA
Faculty of Advocates [*British*] (DAS) .... FOA
Faculty of Advocates Collection of Decisions, Scotch Court of Sessions [*A publication*] (DLA) .... F
Faculty of Advocates Collection of Decisions, Scotch Court of Sessions [*A publication*] (DLA) .... Fac
Faculty of Advocates Collection of Decisions, Scotch Court of Sessions [*A publication*] (DLA) .... Fac Coll NS
Faculty of Advocates Collection of Decisions, Scotch Court of Sessions [*A publication*] (DLA) .... FC
Faculty of Advocates Collection of Decisions, Scotch Court of Sessions [*A publication*] (DLA) .... FC (Scott)
Faculty of Advocates Collection of Decisions, Scotch Court of Sessions, First and Second Series [*38 vols.*] [*A publication*] (DLA) .... Fac Coll
Faculty of Advocates Collection of Decisions, Scotch Court of Sessions, First and Second Series [*38 vols.*] [*A publication*] (DLA) .... Fac Dec

Faculty of Architects and Surveyors [*British*] (DAS) .... FAS
Faculty of Building [*British*] .... FB
Faculty of Building (PDAA) .... FOB
Faculty of Civil Law, University of Ottawa [*Faculte de Droit Civil, Universite d'Ottawa*] **Ontario** [*Library symbol National Library of Canada*] (NLC) .... OOUD
Faculty of Community Medicine [*British*] .... FCM
Faculty of Dentistry, University of Toronto, Ontario [*Library symbol National Library of Canada*] (NLC) .... OTUFD
Faculty of Dispensing Opticians [*British*] .... FDO
Faculty of Education, Lakehead University, Thunder Bay, Ontario [*Library symbol National Library of Canada*] (NLC) .... OPALE
Faculty of Education, University of Calgary, Alberta [*Library symbol National Library of Canada*] (NLC) .... ACUFE
Faculty of Education, University of Toronto, Ontario [*Library symbol National Library of Canada*] (NLC) .... OTC
Faculty of Fine Arts, University of Regina, Saskatchewan [*Library symbol National Library of Canada*] (NLC) .... SRUFA
Faculty of Law Library, University of Toronto [*UTLAS symbol*] .... KLW
Faculty of Law, University of Manitoba, Winnipeg, Manitoba [*Library symbol National Library of Canada*] (NLC) .... MWLS
Faculty of Law, University of Toronto, Ontario [*Library symbol National Library of Canada*] (NLC) .... OTUL
Faculty of Library and Information Science (Teaching), University of Toronto [*UTLAS symbol*] .... FLT
Faculty of Library and Information Science, University of Toronto [*EDUCATSS*] [*UTLAS symbol*] .... EUT
Faculty of Library and Information Science, University of Toronto [*UTLAS symbol*] .... FLS
Faculty of Library and Information Science, University of Toronto [*UTLAS symbol*] .... KLS
Faculty of Library Science, University of Alberta [*EDUCATSS*] [*UTLAS symbol*] .... EUA
Faculty of Library Science, University of Alberta, Edmonton, Alberta [*Library symbol National Library of Canada*] (NLC) .... AEULS
Faculty of Library Science, University of British Columbia [*EDUCATSS*] [*UTLAS symbol*] .... EUU
Faculty of Library Science, University of Toronto, Ontario [*Library symbol National Library of Canada*] (NLC) .... OTULS
Faculty of Management Studies, University of Toronto, Ontario [*Library symbol National Library of Canada*] (NLC) .... OTUMS
Faculty of Music, University of Toronto, Ontario [*Library symbol National Library of Canada*] (NLC) .... OTUFM
Faculty of Nursing, University of Toronto, Ontario [*Library symbol National Library of Canada*] (NLC) .... OTUN
Faculty of Ophthalmologists [*British*] .... FO
Faculty of Pharmacy, University of Toronto, Ontario [*Library symbol National Library of Canada*] (NLC) .... OTUFP
Faculty of Physicians and Surgeons [*British*] (ROG) .... FPS
Faculty of Radiologists .... FR
Faculty of Surgeons of England .... FSE
Faculty Rating .... FR
Faculty Research Participation [*National Science Foundation program*] .... FRP
Faculty Review Group [*Education*] (AIE) .... FRG
Faculty White Pages [*A publication*] .... FWP
Fada [*Chad*] [*ICAO location identifier*] (ICLI) .... FTTF
Fada N'Gourma [*Burkina Faso*] [*ICAO location identifier*] (ICLI) .... DHEF
Fada N'Gourma [*Burkina Faso*] [*Airport symbol*] (OAG) .... FNG
FADAC [*Field Artillery Digital Automatic Computer*] **Automatic Logic Tester** .... FALT
FADAC [*Field Artillery Digital Automatic Computer*] **Automatic Test AnalysisLanguage** (IEEE) .... FATAL
Fade In [*Films, television, etc.*] .... FI
Fade In, Fade Out [*Films, television, etc.*] .... FIFO
Fade Out [*Films, television, etc.*] .... FO
Fade Sound and Picture Out [*Cinematography*] (NTCM) .... FSAPO
Faded [*Bookselling*] (DGA) .... FAD
Faded Prior to Interception [*RADAR*] .... FPI
Fading Safety Factor [*Telecommunications*] (TEL) .... FSF
Faenza [*Italy*] [*Seismograph station code, US Geological Survey Closed*] (SEIS) .... FAE
Faeroese Krone [*Monetary unit*] (ODBW) .... Fkr
Fagaitua, AS [*FM radio station call letters*] (RBYB) .... KPRI
Fagali'I [*Western Samoa*] [*ICAO location identifier*] (ICLI) .... NSFI
Fagerhult [*Sweden ICAO location identifier*] (ICLI) .... ESMF
Fagernes/Leirin [*Norway ICAO location identifier*] (ICLI) .... ENFG
Faggan Studio Industries [*Database producer*] (IID) .... FSI
Faggot [*Derogatory term for male homosexual*] [*Slang*] (DSUE) .... FAG
Fagotto [*Bassoon*] [*Music*] .... FAG
Fagurholsmyri [*Iceland*] [*ICAO location identifier*] (ICLI) .... BIFM
Fagurholsmyri [*Iceland*] [*Airport symbol*] (AD) .... FAG
Fahnestock Viner Hldgs'A' [*NASDAQ symbol*] (TTSB) .... FAHNF
Fahnestock Viner Holdings, Inc. [*NASDAQ symbol*] (NQ) .... FAHN
Fahnestock Viner Holdings, Inc. [*Associated Press*] (SAG) .... FahnVin
Fahnestock Viner Holdings, Inc. [*Toronto Stock Exchange symbol Vancouver Stock Exchange symbol*] .... FHV
Fahrdienstregelement [*Traffic Service Regulations*] [*German*] .... FDR
Fahrenheit [*German*] (EG) .... F
Fahrenheit [*Temperature scale*] (DAVI) .... Fa
Fahrenheit (KSC) .... FAH
Fahrenheit .... FAHR
Fahrenheit Dry Bulb (KSC) .... FDB
Fahrenheit Wet Bulb (KSC) .... FWB
Fahrzeugtestdatenbank [*Dokumentation Kraftfahwesen eV*] [*Germany Information service or system*] (CRD) .... TDKF
Fahud [*Oman*] [*ICAO location identifier*] (ICLI) .... OOFD
FAI Airservice, Nurnberg [*Germany*] [*FAA designator*] (FAAC) .... IFA
FAI Insurances Ltd. [*NYSE symbol Toronto Stock Exchange symbol*] (CTT) .... FAI
FAI Insurances Ltd. [*Associated Press*] (SAG) .... FAI In
FAI Insurances Ltd ADS [*NYSE symbol*] (TTSB) .... FAI
Faience (VRA) .... fai
Faience Mosaics (DICI) .... FM
Faience Tile (DICI) .... FT
Fail (NASA) .... FL
Fail As-Is [*Nuclear energy*] (NRCH) .... FAI
Fail Closed [*Nuclear energy*] (NRCH) .... FC
Fail in Place [*Nuclear energy*] (NRCH) .... FI
Fail Open [*Nuclear energy*] (NRCH) .... FO
Fail Operation [*NASA*] (KSC) .... FO
Fail Sheer Ultimate (MCD) .... FSU
Fail Tension Ultimate (MCD) .... FTU
Fail to Synchronize (MCD) .... FS
Fail Type [*Military*] (AFIT) .... FT
Failed Element Detection and Location [*In nuclear power reactors*] .... FEDAL
Failed Fuel Location Subsystem [*Nuclear energy*] (NRCH) .... FFLS
Failed Handover [*NASA*] (NASA) .... FHO
Failed Item (AAG) .... F/I
Failed Item Analysis Report (MCD) .... FIAR
Failed Item Report .... FIR
Failed to Attend (ADA) .... FTA
Failed to Make (IAA) .... FTM
Failed to Open (IEEE) .... FTO
Failed to Return [*British military*] (DMA) .... FTR
Failed UNI BUS Address Register [*Computer science*] (NHD) .... FUBAR
Failed Vector Number (OA) .... FVN
Fail-Operational, Fail-Operational, Fail-Safe .... FO/FO/FS
Fail-Operational, Fail-Safe (NASA) .... FO/FS
Fail-Passive Autoland System [*Aviation*] .... FPAS
Fails to Break .... FTB
Fails to Drain .... FTD
Fails to Drive (DNAB) .... FTD
Fails to Reproduce .... FTR
Fails to Respond (DNAB) .... FTR
Fail-Safe (NASA) .... FS
Failure .... F
Failure .... FAIL
Failure (MSA) .... FLR
Failure Analysis (AAG) .... FA
Failure Analysis and Associates (RDA) .... FaAA
Failure Analysis Board .... FAB
Failure Analysis by Statistical Techniques [*Data processing code*] .... FAST
Failure Analysis Coordinator .... FAC
Failure Analysis Information Retrieval (IAA) .... FAIR
Failure Analysis Laboratory (MCD) .... FAL
Failure Analysis of Material Systems (MCD) .... FAMS
Failure Analysis Program .... FAP
Failure Analysis Report .... FAR
Failure Analysis Report Summary [*Bell System*] .... FARS
Failure Analysis Section .... FAS
Failure and Accident Technical Information System .... FACTS
Failure and Consumption Data (AAG) .... F & CD
Failure and Consumption Data Form (AAG) .... FCDF
Failure and Consumption Data Inspection Report (AAG) .... F & CD/IR
Failure and Consumption Data Report (IAA) .... FCDR
Failure and Consumption Inspector's Report (AAG) .... F-CIR
Failure and Consumption Sheets (AAG) .... FCS
Failure and Discrepancy Reporting (KSC) .... F & DR
Failure and Malfunction Report [*NASA*] (KSC) .... FMR
Failure and Rejection Report (MCD) .... FARR
Failure and Rejection Report .... FRR
Failure and Usage Data Report (IEEE) .... FUDR
Failure Cause Data Report .... FCDR
Failure Correction Decoding (IAA) .... FCD
Failure Correction Panel (NASA) .... FCP
Failure Count .... FC
Failure Definition (MCD) .... FD
Failure Definitions/Scoring Criteria (AABC) .... FD/SC
Failure Density Function .... FDF
Failure Detection and Isolation .... FD & I
Failure Detection and Isolation (MCD) .... FDI
Failure Detection and Location Analysis (MCD) .... FADALA
Failure Detection Identification and Control System Reconfiguration (MCD) .... FDI & R
Failure Detector Indicator (NASA) .... FDI
Failure Diagnostic Code [*Military*] (AFIT) .... FDC
Failure Diagnostic Team [*Aerospace*] (AAG) .... FDT
Failure Effect Analysis .... FEA
Failure Effects Evaluation (IAA) .... FEE
Failure Effects Summary List (NASA) .... FESL
Failure Equation .... FE
Failure Equation .... FEQ
Failure Experience Data Bank [*GIDEP*] .... FEDB
Failure Factor (NG) .... FF
Failure Factor Update Request .... FFUR
Failure Free Warranty [*Military*] (AFIT) .... FFW
Failure Frequency Report [*Military*] (AFIT) .... FFR
Failure Group [*NASDAQ symbol*] (TTSB) .... FAIL
Failure Group, Inc. [*NASDAQ symbol*] (SAG) .... FAIL
Failure Group, Inc. [*Associated Press*] (SAG) .... FailGrp
Failure Identification (MCD) .... FID
Failure in Time [*Telecommunications*] (TEL) .... FIT

Failure Indicating Fuse ... FIF
Failure Indication Modules ... FIM
Failure Investigation Action Report [*NASA*] (NASA) ... FIAR
Failure Mode (MCD) ... FM
Failure Mode Analysis ... FMA
Failure Mode and Effects ... FME
Failure Mode and Effects Analysis ... FMEA
Failure Mode and Effects Management [*Engineering*] ... FMEM
Failure Mode Effects and Criticality Analysis ... FMECA
Failure Mode Indicator (MUGU) ... FMI
Failure Notification Sheet (KSC) ... FNS
Failure Notification Telex (MCD) ... FNT
Failure of All Vital Forces (MAE) ... FOAVF
Failure or Unsatisfactory Report ... FUR
Failure or Unsatisfactory Report System ... FURS
Failure Outage Rate [*Electronics*] (IAA) ... FOR
Failure Probability Analysis (MCD) ... FPA
Failure/Problem Report ... FPR
Failure Rate ... FR
Failure Rate Assessment Machine (PDAA) ... FRAM
Failure Rate Data (KSC) ... FRD
Failure Rate Data Bank [*GIDEP*] ... FRDB
Failure Rate Data Program [*Navy*] (NG) ... FARADA
Failure Recurrence Control (SAA) ... FRC
Failure Report ... FR
Failure Reporting, Analyses, and Corrective Action (MCD) ... FRACA
Failure Reporting and Corrective Action System (MCD) ... FRACAS
Failure Reporting Review (KSC) ... FRR
Failure Reporting System (MCD) ... FRS
Failure Review Board [*NASA*] (NASA) ... FRB
Failure to Appear [*Court case*] ... FTA
Failure to Descend [*Obstetrics and urology*] (DAVI) ... FTD
Failure to Eject (MCD) ... FE
Failure to Feed (MCD) ... FF
Failure to Obtain Action (AAG) ... FOA
Failure to Pay [*IRS*] ... FTP
Failure to Pay Child Support ... FTPCS
Failure to Progress [*In labor*] [*Obstetrics*] (DAVI) ... FTP
Failure to Return to Battery [*Study*] (MCD) ... FRB
Failure to Thrive [*Syndrome*] [*Medicine*] ... FTT
Failure Warning and Analysis System ... FWAS
Failures per Hour [*Military*] ... FPH
Failures per Million Hours [*Telecommunications*] (TEL) ... FPMH
Failures per Year [*Telecommunications*] (TEL) ... FPY
Faint ... FT
Faint Blue Galaxy [*Astronomy*] ... FBG
Faint Object Red Spectrograph [*Astronomy*] ... FORS
Faint Object Spectrograph [*Astronomy*] ... FOS
Faint Object Telescope (PDAA) ... FOT
Faint-Object Camera [*Astronomy*] ... FOC
Faint-Object Classification and Analysis System [*Astronomy*] ... FOCAS
Faint-Object Grism Spectrograph [*Astronomy*] ... FOGS
Fair ... F
Fair (ROG) ... FR
Fair Access to Insurance Requirements [*Government insurance program*] ... FAIR
Fair [*Isaac*] **& Co.** [*Associated Press*] (SAG) ... FairIsc
Fair [*Isaac*] **& Co., Inc.** [*NASDAQ symbol*] (NQ) ... FICI
Fair and Impartial Random Selection [*System*] [*Military draft*] ... FAIR
Fair and Simple Tax [*Type of flat tax proposed by Rep. Jack Kemp and Sen. Bob Kasten*] ... FAST
F-Air AS [*Denmark ICAO designator*] (FAAC) ... FRP
Fair Average Quality ... FAQ
Fair Average Quality of Season [*Business term*] ... FAQS
Fair Bluff, NC [*AM radio station call letters*] ... WJHB
Fair Bluff, NC [*AM radio station call letters*] (RBYB) ... WNCR-AM
Fair Budget Action Campaign (EA) ... FBAC
Fair Campaign Practices Committee (EA) ... FCPC
Fair Condition [*Doll collecting*] ... fc
Fair Copy ... FCO
Fair Credit Billing Act ... FCBA
Fair Credit Reporting Act [*1971*] ... FCRA
Fair Cutting [*Brick*] (DICI) ... FC
Fair Debt Collection Practices Act ... FDCPA
Fair Educational Practice Act [*New York, New Jersey, Massachusetts*] ... FEPA
Fair Employment Board [*of Civil Service Commission*] [*Abolished, 1955*] ... FEB
Fair Employment Practice ... FEP
Fair Employment Practices Act [*1964*] ... FEPA
Fair Employment Practices Cases (DLA) ... Fair Empl Prac Cas
Fair Employment Practices Code ... FEPC
Fair Employment Practices Committee [*or Commission*] ... FEPC
Fair, Fat, Fertile, and Forty [*Medical slang describing women most susceptible to gallbladder attacks*] ... 4F
Fair Housing and Equal Opportunity [*HUD*] (OICC) ... FHEO
Fair Housing Assistance Program [*HUD*] ... FHAP
Fair Housing Initiatives Program [*Department of Housing and Urban Development*] (GFGA) ... FHIP
Fair International Trade Employment Committee ... FITE
Fair Isaac & Co. [*NYSE symbol*] (TTSB) ... FIC
Fair Isle [*Scotland*] [*Airport symbol*] (OAG) ... FIE
Fair Labor Standards Act [*1938*] ... FLSA
Fair Lawn Free Public Library, Fair Lawn, NJ [*Library symbol Library of Congress*] (LCLS) ... NjF
Fair Market Price (AAGC) ... FMP
Fair Market Rent (GFGA) ... FMR
Fair Market Value [*Bargaining term*] ... FMV
Fair Organ Preservation Society [*British*] ... FOPS
Fair Packaging and Labeling Act [*1966*] ... FPLA
Fair Play [*Signature used on warning letters sent by George Metesky, the "Mad Bomber" of New York City in 1940's and 1950's*] ... FP
Fair Play for Cuba Committee [*Defunct*] ... FPCC
Fair Political Practices Commission (OICC) ... FPPC
Fair Public Key Cryptosystem [*Telecommunications*] ... FPKC
Fair Rents Board [*New South Wales, Australia*] ... FRB
Fair Skiing Conditions ... F
Fair Tax Education Fund (EA) ... FTEF
Fair Tax Foundation [*Defunct*] (EA) ... FTF
Fair Trade Commission [*Japan*] (ECON) ... FTC
Fair Trade Laws [*A publication*] (DLA) ... Fair Tr
Fair Wear and Tear ... FWT
Fair Wear and Tear (ODBW) ... fwt
Fair Weather Current ... FWC
Fairbairn-Sykes [*British military*] (DMA) ... FS
Fairbanks [*Alaska*] [*Airport symbol*] (OAG) ... FAI
Fairbanks [*Alaska*] [*Seismograph station code, US Geological Survey Closed*] (SEIS) ... FBK
Fairbanks [*Alaska*] [*ICAO location identifier*] (ICLI) ... PAZF
Fairbanks Air Service [*Alaska*] [*Air carrier designation symbol*] ... FASX
Fairbanks, AK [*Location identifier FAA*] (FAAL) ... CNA
Fairbanks, AK [*Location identifier FAA*] (FAAL) ... CUN
Fairbanks, AK [*Location identifier FAA*] (FAAL) ... EAF
Fairbanks, AK [*Location identifier FAA*] (FAAL) ... EIL
Fairbanks, AK [*Location identifier FAA*] (FAAL) ... FAI
Fairbanks, AK [*FM radio station call letters*] ... KAKQ
Fairbanks, AK [*FM radio station call letters*] ... KAKQ-FM
Fairbanks, AK [*Television station call letters*] ... KATN
Fairbanks, AK [*AM radio station call letters*] ... KCBF
Fairbanks, AK [*AM radio station call letters*] ... KFAR
Fairbanks, AK [*Television station call letters*] (RBYB) ... KFXF
Fairbanks, AK [*AM radio station call letters*] ... KIAK
Fairbanks, AK [*FM radio station call letters*] ... KIAK-FM
Fairbanks, AK [*Television station call letters*] ... KTVF
Fairbanks, AK [*FM radio station call letters*] ... KUAC
Fairbanks, AK [*Television station call letters*] ... KUAC-TV
Fairbanks, AK [*FM radio station call letters*] ... KUWL
Fairbanks, AK [*FM radio station call letters*] ... KWLF
Fairbanks, AK [*FM radio station call letters*] ... KXLR
Fairbanks, AK [*Location identifier FAA*] (FAAL) ... MTF
Fairbanks, AK [*Location identifier FAA*] (FAAL) ... PII
Fairbanks/Eielson Air Force Base [*Alaska*] [*ICAO location identifier*] (ICLI) ... PAEI
Fairbanks/International [*Alaska*] [*ICAO location identifier*] (ICLI) ... PAFA
Fairbanks Law Library, Fairbanks, AK [*Library symbol Library of Congress*] (LCLS) ... AkFL
Fairbanks' Marriage and Divorce Laws of Massachusetts [*A publication*] (DLA) ... Fair M & D
Fairbanks Memorial Hospital, Fairbanks, AK [*Library symbol Library of Congress*] (LCLS) ... AkFM
Fairbanks [*Alaska*] **Metro Field** [*Airport symbol Obsolete*] (OAG) ... MTX
Fairbanks Museum of Natural Science, St. Johnsbury, VT [*Library symbol Library of Congress*] (LCLS) ... VtStjF
Fairbanks North Star Borough Library, Fairbanks, AK [*Library symbol Library of Congress*] (LCLS) ... AkF
Fairbanks North Star Borough School District, Fairbanks, AK [*Library symbol*] [*Library of Congress*] (LCLS) ... AkFSD
Fairbanks Rhyme Test [*Hearing*] ... FRT
Fairbanks/Wainwright, AK [*Location identifier FAA*] (FAAL) ... FBK
Fairbanks/Wainwright Army Air Field [*Alaska*] [*ICAO location identifier*] (ICLI) ... PAFB
Fairborn, OH [*AM radio station call letters*] ... WGNZ
Fairbourne Miniature Railway [*Wales*] ... FMR
Fairbury Junior College [*Nebraska*] ... FJC
Fairbury, NE [*Location identifier FAA*] (FAAL) ... FBY
Fairbury, NE [*AM radio station call letters*] ... KGMT
Fairbury, NE [*FM radio station call letters*] ... KUTT
Fairbury Public Library, Fairbury, NE [*Library symbol Library of Congress*] (LCLS) ... NbFb
Fairchild Advanced CMOS Technology [*Fairchild Semiconductor Corp.*] ... FACT
Fairchild Advanced Schottky T2L [*Transistor-Transistor Logic*] ... FAST
Fairchild Air Force Base [*Washington*] (AAG) ... FAFB
Fairchild Aircraft ... FA
Fairchild Aircraft Ltd. [*Canada*], Fairchild/Republic [*ICAO aircraft manufacturer identifier*] (ICAO) ... FA
Fairchild & Northeastern Railway ... F & NE
Fairchild Automatic Intercept and Response System (MCD) ... FAIRS
Fairchild Camera & Instrument Corp. (MCD) ... FCIC
Fairchild Club (EA) ... FC
Fairchild Communications Networks & Services Co. [*Chantilly, VA*] [*Later, FCS*] [*Telecommunications service*] (TSSD) ... FCNS
Fairchild Communications Services Co. [*Washington, DC*] (TSSD) ... FCS
Fairchild Corp. [*Associated Press*] (SAG) ... FairCp
Fairchild Corp.'A' [*NYSE symbol*] (TTSB) ... FA
Fairchild Engine & Airplane Corp. ... FEAC
Fairchild Gold [*Vancouver Stock Exchange symbol*] ... FLD
Fairchild Guided Missile Division (SAA) ... FGMD
Fairchild Industries, Inc. [*Associated Press*] (SAG) ... Fairc
Fairchild Industries, Inc. [*NYSE symbol*] (SPSG) ... FEN
Fairchild/Republic [*ICAO aircraft manufacturer identifier*] (ICAO) ... HH
Fairchild Satellite Operations Complex (MCD) ... FSOC
Fairchild Semiconductor ... FCS
Fairchild Space and Defense System, Syosset, NY [*Library symbol Library of Congress*] (LCLS) ... NSyoF

Fairchild Tropical Garden ... FTG
Fairchild-Hiller Corp. [*Later, Fairchild Industries, Inc.*] (KSC) ... FHC
Fairchild-Hiller Corp. [*Later, Fairchild Industries, Inc.*], Republic Aviati on Division, Farmingdale, NY [*Library symbol Library of Congress*] (LCLS) ... NFarF
Faircross [*England*] ... FAIRC
Faire Reporter [*Carry Over*] [*Stock exchange term French*] ... fr
Faire Suivre [*Please Forward*] [*French*] ... FS
Fairest One [*Genotype of Phlox paniculata*] ... FO
Fairfax Bank & Trust Co. [*NASDAQ symbol*] (SAG) ... FBTC
Fairfax Bank & Trust Financial Corp. [*Associated Press*] (SAG) ... FB&T Fn
Fairfax County Public Library, Fairfax, VA [*Library symbol Library of Congress*] (LCLS) ... ViF
Fairfax County Public Library, Services for the Blind and Physically Handicapped, Alexandria, VA [*Library symbol Library of Congress*] (LCLS) ... ViF-BPH
Fairfax Financial Holdings Ltd. [*Toronto Stock Exchange symbol*] ... FFH
Fairfax Hall Junior College, Waynesboro, VA [*Library symbol Library of Congress*] (LCLS) ... ViWbF
Fairfax, VA [*AM radio station call letters*] ... WDCT
Fairfax, VA [*Television station call letters*] ... WNVC
Fairfield, AL [*AM radio station call letters*] ... WJLD
Fairfield Bay, AR [*FM radio station call letters*] ... KFFB
Fairfield, CA [*Location identifier FAA*] (FAAL) ... SUU
Fairfield, CA [*Location identifier FAA*] (FAAL) ... TXV
Fairfield Communities [*NYSE symbol*] (TTSB) ... FFD
Fairfield Communities, Inc. [*Associated Press*] (SAG) ... FairCm
Fairfield Communities, Inc. [*NASDAQ symbol*] (SAG) ... FFCI
Fairfield County District Library, Lancaster, OH [*OCLC symbol*] (OCLC) ... OFA
Fairfield County District Library, Lancaster, OH [*Library symbol Library of Congress*] (LCLS) ... OLanF
Fairfield County Library, Winnsboro, SC [*Library symbol*] [*Library of Congress*] (LCLS) ... ScWn
Fairfield, CT [*FM radio station call letters*] ... WSHU
Fairfield, CT [*FM radio station call letters*] ... WVOF
Fairfield Daily Ledger, Fairfield, IA [*Library symbol Library of Congress*] (LCLS) ... IaFairL
Fairfield Elementary School, Massapequa, NY [*Library symbol Library of Congress*] (LCLS) ... NMassFE
Fairfield Free Public Library, Fairfield, NJ [*Library symbol Library of Congress*] (LCLS) ... NjFf
Fairfield, IA [*Location identifier FAA*] (FAAL) ... FFL
Fairfield, IA [*FM radio station call letters*] ... KHOE
Fairfield, IA [*FM radio station call letters*] ... KIIK
Fairfield, IA [*AM radio station call letters*] ... KMCD
Fairfield, IL [*Location identifier FAA*] (FAAL) ... FWC
Fairfield, IL [*AM radio station call letters*] ... WFIW
Fairfield, IL [*FM radio station call letters*] ... WFIW-FM
Fairfield, IL [*FM radio station call letters*] (RBYB) ... WOKZ-FM
Fairfield, ME [*FM radio station call letters*] ... WCTB
Fairfield Minerals Ltd. [*Vancouver Stock Exchange symbol*] ... FFD
Fairfield, OH [*AM radio station call letters*] ... WCNW
Fairfield, OH [*FM radio station call letters*] ... WOFX
Fairfield, OH [*FM radio station call letters*] (RBYB) ... WVAE
Fairfield Public Library, Fairfield, CT [*Library symbol Library of Congress*] (LCLS) ... CtFa
Fairfield Public Library, Fairfield, IA [*Library symbol Library of Congress*] (LCLS) ... IaFair
Fairfield Public Library, Fairfield, IL [*Library symbol Library of Congress*] (LCLS) ... IFaf
Fairfield Public Library, Supervisor of Technical Services, Fairfield, CT [*OCLC symbol*] (OCLC) ... FRP
Fairfield/Travis Air Force Base [*California*] [*ICAO location identifier*] (ICLI) ... KSUU
Fairfield, TX [*FM radio station call letters*] ... KNES
Fairfield University (GAGS) ... Fairfield U
Fairfield University, Fairfield, CT [*Library symbol Library of Congress*] (LCLS) ... CtFaU
Fairfield University, Fairfield, CT [*OCLC symbol*] (OCLC) ... FAU
Fairfield's Reports [*10-12 Maine*] [*A publication*] (DLA) ... Fairf
Fairfield's Reports [*10-12 Maine*] [*A publication*] (DLA) ... Fairf (ME)
Fairfield's Reports [*10-12 Maine*] [*A publication*] (DLA) ... Fairfield
Fairflight Ltd. [*British ICAO designator*] (FAAC) ... FGT
Fairford [*British ICAO location identifier*] (ICLI) ... EGVA
Fairgrove Township Library, Fairgrove, MI [*Library symbol Library of Congress*] (LCLS) ... MiFg
Fairhaven, MA [*FM radio station call letters*] ... WFHN
Fairhaven, MA [*AM radio station call letters*] ... WLAW
Fairhope, AL [*AM radio station call letters*] ... WABF
Fairhope, AL [*AM radio station call letters*] ... WBLX
Fairhope, AL [*FM radio station call letters*] ... WGCX
Fairhope, AL [*AM radio station call letters*] (RBYB) ... WHOZ-AM
Fairing ... FAIR
Fairlady Energy [*Vancouver Stock Exchange symbol*] ... FRY
Fairlane Club of America (EA) ... FCA
Fairlawn, VA [*AM radio station call letters*] ... WCQR
Fairlead (MSA) ... FLD
Fairleigh Dickinson University (GAGS) ... Fairleigh Dickinson U
Fairleigh Dickinson University [*New Jersey*] ... FDU
Fairleigh Dickinson University, Madison, NJ [*Library symbol Library of Congress*] (LCLS) ... NjMF
Fairleigh Dickinson University, Rutherford, NJ [*OCLC symbol*] (OCLC) ... FDR
Fairleigh Dickinson University, Rutherford, NJ [*Library symbol Library of Congress*] (LCLS) ... NjRuF
Fairleigh Dickinson University, Teaneck, NJ [*OCLC symbol*] (OCLC) ... FDU
Fairleigh Dickinson University, Teaneck, NJ [*Library symbol Library of Congress*] (LCLS) ... NjTeaF
Fairleigh Dickinson University, Wayne, NJ [*Library symbol Library of Congress*] (LCLS) ... NjWF
Fairlines, BV [*Netherlands*] [*FAA designator*] (FAAC) ... FLS
Fairly Fearless Flier ... FFF
Fairly Important Person ... FIP
Fairly Reliable Source of Intelligence Information ... C
Fairmont [*Minnesota*] [*Airport symbol*] (OAG) ... FRM
Fairmont [*Washington*] [*Seismograph station code, US Geological Survey*] (SEIS) ... FTW
Fairmont, MN [*Location identifier FAA*] (FAAL) ... FRM
Fairmont, MN [*FM radio station call letters*] ... KFMC
Fairmont, MN [*AM radio station call letters*] ... KSUM
Fairmont, NC [*AM radio station call letters*] ... WFMO
Fairmont, NC [*FM radio station call letters*] ... WSTS
Fairmont State College [*West Virginia*] ... FSC
Fairmont State College, Fairmont, WV [*OCLC symbol*] (OCLC) ... WVF
Fairmont State College, Fairmont, WV [*Library symbol Library of Congress*] (LCLS) ... WvFS
Fairmont, WV [*FM radio station call letters*] ... WFGM
Fairmont, WV [*AM radio station call letters*] ... WMMN
Fairmont, WV [*FM radio station call letters*] ... WRLF
Fairmont, WV [*AM radio station call letters*] ... WTCS
Fairmount News, Fairmount, IN [*Library symbol Library of Congress*] (LCLS) ... InFaiN
Fairmount Public Library, Fairmount, IN [*Library symbol Library of Congress*] (LCLS) ... InFai
Fairness and Accuracy in Reporting (EA) ... FAIR
Fairness Fund (EA) ... FF
Fairness in Media (EA) ... FIM
Fairness of Opportunity [*Competitive bidding*] ... FOO
Fairoaks [*British ICAO location identifier*] (ICLI) ... EGTF
Fairplay Information [*Fairplay Publications Ltd.*] [*Information service or system*] (IID) ... FI
Fairplay Information Systems Ltd. (IID) ... FISYS
Fairport High School Library, Fairport, NY [*OCLC symbol*] (OCLC) ... RWF
Fairport, Painesville & Eastern Railway Co. [*AAR code*] ... FPE
Fairview College, Fairview, AB, Canada [*Library symbol Library of Congress*] (LCLS) ... CaAFAC
Fairview Elementary Library, Mora, MN [*Library symbol*] [*Library of Congress*] (LCLS) ... MnMrFE
Fairview High School, Alberta [*Library symbol National Library of Canada*] (BIB) ... AFVS
Fairview Hospital, Minneapolis, MN [*Library symbol Library of Congress*] (LCLS) ... MnMF
Fairview, NC [*AM radio station call letters*] (RBYB) ... WLVM-AM
Fairview, NC [*AM radio station call letters*] ... WMIY
Fairview, OK [*Location identifier FAA*] (FAAL) ... FAU
Fairview, OR [*AM radio station call letters*] (RBYB) ... KZTW
Fairview Park [*Nevada*] [*Seismograph station code, US Geological Survey Closed*] (SEIS) ... FPN
Fairview Park Regional Library, Fairview Park, OH [*Library symbol Library of Congress*] (LCLS) ... OFavp
Fairview Preschool, Rockford, IL [*Library symbol*] [*Library of Congress*] (LCLS) ... IRoFP
Fairview Public Library, Alberta [*Library symbol National Library of Canada*] (NLC) ... AFV
Fairview Public Library, Fairview, AB, Canada [*Library symbol*] [*Library of Congress*] (LCLS) ... CaAFV
Fairview State Hospital, Waymart, PA [*OCLC symbol*] (OCLC) ... PHF
Fairview, TN [*AM radio station call letters*] ... WPFD
Fairwater Planes ... FWPLN
Fairway, KS [*AM radio station call letters*] ... KCNW
Fairways Corp. [*Air carrier designation symbol*] ... FAIX
Fairways Corp. [*ICAO designator*] (FAAC) ... FWY
Fair-Witness Project (EA) ... FWP
Fairy Investigation Society [*Inactive*] (EA) ... FIS
Fairy Tale-Folklore Study Unit [*American Topical Association*] (EA) ... FTFLSU
Fairy Tale-Folklore Study Unit [*American Topical Association*] (EA) ... FTFSU
Faisalabad [*Pakistan*] [*Airport symbol*] (OAG) ... LYP
Faisalabad [*Pakistan*] [*ICAO location identifier*] (ICLI) ... OPFA
Faisceaux Nationalistes Europeens [*European Nationalist Alliances*] [*France*] (PD) ... FNE
Faith ... FTH
Faith Alive (EA) ... FA
Faith at Work (EA) ... FAW
Faith Baptist Bible College, Ankeny, IA [*Library symbol Library of Congress*] (LCLS) ... IaAnkFB
Faith, Hope, and Charity [*Freemasonry*] (ROG) ... FH & C
Faith, Hope, and Charity [*Freemasonry*] ... FHC
Faith Mines Ltd. [*Vancouver Stock Exchange symbol*] ... FHM
Faith, SD [*FM radio station call letters*] ... KPSD
Faith Theological Seminary ... FTS
Faithful Performance ... FP
Faithfully ... FFLY
Faithfully ... FFY
Faith-Man-Nature [*from F/M/N Papers, National Council of Churches*] ... F/M/N
Faizabad [*Afghanistan*] [*ICAO location identifier*] (ICLI) ... OAFZ
Fajardo [*Puerto Rico*] [*Airport symbol*] (OAG) ... FAJ
Fajardo [*Puerto Rico*] [*ICAO location identifier*] (ICLI) ... TJFA
Fajardo, PR [*Location identifier FAA*] (FAAL) ... FAJ
Fajardo, PR [*FM radio station call letters*] ... WDOY
Fajardo, PR [*AM radio station call letters*] ... WMDD
Fajardo, PR [*Television station call letters*] ... WMTJ
Fajardo, PR [*Television station call letters*] ... WPRV
Fajardo, PR [*Television station call letters*] ... WRUA

Fak Fak/Torea [*Indonesia*] [*ICAO location identifier*] (ICLI) ... WASF
Fakahina [*French Polynesia*] [*ICAO location identifier*] (ICLI) ... NTGL
Fakarava [*French Polynesia*] [*Airport symbol*] (OAG) ... FAV
Fakarava [*French Polynesia*] [*ICAO location identifier*] (ICLI) ... NTGF
Faker Track (MUGU) ... FK
Fak-Fak [*Indonesia*] [*Airport symbol*] (OAG) ... FKQ
Fako Transport Shipping Lines [*Joint venture between Cameroon and the US*] [*Shipping line*] (EY) ... FTSC
Faladie [*Mali*] [*ICAO location identifier*] (ICLI) ... GAFD
Falaise-Monts-D'Eraines [*France ICAO location identifier*] (ICLI) ... LFAS
Falange Espanola de las Juntas de Ofensiva Nacional Sindicalista [*Spanish Phalange of the Syndicalist Juntas of the National Offensive*] [*Political party*] (PPE) ... FE de las JONS
Falange Espanola Tradicionalista y de las Juntas de Ofensiva Nacional Sindicalista [*Traditionalist Spanish Phalange of the Syndicalist Juntas of the NationalOffensive*] [*Political party*] (PPE) ... FET de las JONS
Falange Patria Nova [*New Fatherland Phalange*] [*Brazil*] (PD) ... FPN
Falange Socialista Boliviana [*Bolivian Socialist Phalange*] [*Political party*] (PPW) ... FSB
Falange Socialista Boliviana de Izquierda [*Bolivian Socialist Phalange of the Left*] [*Political party*] (PPW) ... FSBI
Falciparum Interspersed Repeat Antigen [*Genetics*] ... FIRA
Falciparum Sporozoite Vaccine [*Antimalarial*] ... FSV
Falciparum Uganda - Palo Alto [*Plasmodium strain causing malaria*] ... FUP
Falck [*When used in identifying W. F. Bach's compositions, refers to cataloging of his works by musicologist Falck*] ... F
Falcks Redningskorps Beldringe AS [*Denmark ICAO designator*] (FAAC) ... FLK
Falcon Air, Inc. [*ICAO designator*] (FAAC) ... FAI
Falcon Airlines [*ICAO designator*] (AD) ... AB
Falcon Airlines [*Yugoslavia*] [*ICAO designator*] (FAAC) ... FLO
Falcon Aviation AB [*Sweden ICAO designator*] (FAAC) ... FCN
Falcon Building Products, Inc. [*Associated Press*] (SAG) ... FalconBP
Falcon Building Products, Inc. [*NYSE symbol*] (SAG) ... FB
Falcon Building Products'A' [*NYSE symbol*] (TTSB) ... FB
Falcon Cable Sys L.P. [*AMEX symbol*] (TTSB) ... FAL
Falcon Cable Systems Ltd. [*AMEX symbol*] (SPSG) ... FAL
Falcon Cable Systems Ltd. [*Associated Press*] (SAG) ... FalcCbl
Falcon Club of America (EA) ... FCA
Falcon Drilling [*NASDAQ symbol*] (TTSB) ... FLCN
Falcon Drilling Co. [*Associated Press*] (SAG) ... FalcDr
Falcon Drilling Co. [*Associated Press*] (SAG) ... FalconDr
Falcon Drilling Co. [*NYSE symbol*] (SAG) ... FLC
Falcon Drilling Co. [*NASDAQ symbol*] (SAG) ... FLCN
Falcon Jet Centre [*British ICAO designator*] (FAAC) ... FJC
Falcon Launching Saber System ... FLSS
Falcon Products [*NYSE symbol*] (TTSB) ... FCP
Falcon Products, Inc. [*Associated Press*] (SAG) ... FalcnPr
Falcon Products, Inc. [*Associated Press*] (SAG) ... FalconPd
Falcon Products, Inc. [*NYSE symbol*] (SAG) ... FCP
Falcon Products, Inc. [*NASDAQ symbol*] (NQ) ... FLCP
Falcon Research & Development, Inc., Buffalo, NY [*Library symbol Library of Congress*] (LCLS) ... NBuF
Falconbridge Branch, Nickel Centre Public Library, Ontario [*Library symbol National Library of Canada*] (NLC) ... OFANC
Falconbridge Gold Corp. [*Toronto Stock Exchange symbol*] ... FCG
Falconbridge Ltd. [*Toronto Stock Exchange symbol Vancouver Stock Exchange symbol*] ... FL
Falconbridge Ltd., Mining Library, Onaping, ON, Canada [*Library symbol*] [*Library of Congress*] (LCLS) ... CaOOFM
Falconbridge Nickel Mines Ltd., Information Centre, Toronto, ON, Canada [*Library symbol Library of Congress*] (LCLS) ... CaOTFN
Falconbridge Nickel Mines Ltd., Metallurgical Laboratory, Thornhill, ON, Canada [*Library symbol Library of Congress*] (LCLS) ... CaOThorF
Falconbridge Nickel Mines Ltd., Metallurgical Research Library, Falconbridge, ON, Canada [*Library symbol Library of Congress*] (LCLS) ... CaOFaF
Falconer and Fitzherbert's English Election Cases [*1835-39*] [*A publication*] (DLA) ... F & Fitz
Falconer and Fitzherbert's English Election Cases [*1835-39*] [*A publication*] (DLA) ... Falc & F
Falconer and Fitzherbert's English Election Cases [*1835-39*] [*A publication*] (DLA) ... Falc & Fitz
Falconer's Decisions, Scotch Court of Session [*1744-51*] [*A publication*] (DLA) ... Pres Fal
Falconer's English County Court Cases [*A publication*] (DLA) ... Falc Co Cts
Falconer's Marine Dictionary [*A publication*] (DLA) ... Falc Marine Dict
Falconer's Scotch Court of Session Cases [*1744-51*] [*A publication*] (DLA) ... Falc
Faleolo/International [*Western Samoa*] [*ICAO location identifier*] (ICLI) ... NSFA
Falfurrias, TX [*Location identifier FAA*] (FAAL) ... BKS
Falfurrias, TX [*Location identifier FAA*] (FAAL) ... FFR
Falfurrias, TX [*AM radio station call letters*] ... KPSO
Falfurrias, TX [*FM radio station call letters*] ... KPSO-FM
Falher, AB [*FM radio station call letters*] (RBYB) ... CKRP-FM
Falkirk [*Postcode*] (ODBW) ... FK
Falkland Islands (ROG) ... FALK I
Falkland Islands (WDAA) ... FALK IS
Falkland Islands (ROG) ... FALKLD I
Falkland Islands ... FI
Falkland Islands [*ANSI two-letter standard code*] (CNC) ... FK
Falkland Islands [*MARC country of publication code Library of Congress*] (LCCP) ... fk
Falkland Islands [*ANSI three-letter standard code*] (CNC) ... FLK
Falkland Islands [*MARC geographic area code Library of Congress*] (LCCP) ... lsfk--
Falkland Islands [*International civil aircraft marking*] (ODBW) ... VP-F
Falkland Islands and Dependencies Aerial Survey Expedition [*1955-57*] ... FIDASE
Falkland Islands Dependencies Survey [*1943-62*] ... FIDS
Falkland Islands Government Air Service (EY) ... FIGAS
Falkland Islands Philatelic Study Group [*of the American Philatelic Society*] [*Fordingbridge, Hampshire, England*] (EAIO) ... FIPSG
Falkoping [*Sweden ICAO location identifier*] (ICLI) ... ESGK
Fall [*Postal Service standard*] (OPSA) ... FALL
Fall ... FL
Fall Back Network Control Center (MCD) ... FBNCC
Fall [*Autumn*] **Exercise** [*Military NATO*] (NATG) ... FALLEX
Fall Joint Computer Conference [*Replaced by National Computer Conference - NCC*] ... FJCC
Fall of Shot (NVT) ... FOS
Fall Planting Council (EA) ... FPC
Fall Reaction Spheres (AAG) ... FRS
Fall River [*Massachusetts*] [*Seismograph station code, US Geological Survey*] (SEIS) ... FLR
Fall River [*Diocesan abbreviation*] [*Massachusetts*] (TOCD) ... FR
Fall River, MA [*Location identifier FAA*] (FAAL) ... FLR
Fall River, MA [*AM radio station call letters*] ... WHTB
Fall River, MA [*AM radio station call letters*] ... WSAR
Fall River Public Library, Fall River, MA [*Library symbol Library of Congress*] (LCLS) ... MF
Fall River-New Bedford [*Massachusetts*] [*Airport symbol*] (AD) ... EWB
Fall Yearling [*Pisciculture*] ... FY
Fallbrook, CA [*FM radio station call letters*] ... KBAX
Fallbrook, CA [*FM radio station call letters*] (RBYB) ... KSYY-FM
Fallen (ABBR) ... FLN
Fallen Angels International (EA) ... FA
Fallen Building Clause ... FBC
Fallen Building Clause Waiver [*Legal term*] (DLA) ... FBCW
Fallfors [*Sweden ICAO location identifier*] (ICLI) ... ESUF
Falling [*NWS*] (FAAC) ... FLG
Falling Dilute-Phase (PDAA) ... FDP
Falling Film Evaporation ... FFE
Falling Mass Hazard ... FMH
Falling Object Protective Structure [*For mining machines*] ... FOPS
Falling Sphere Trajectory Measurement (MUGU) ... FASTRAM
Falling to Pieces [*Slang*] ... FTP
Falling Weight Deflectometer [*FHWA*] (TAG) ... FWD
Fallon County Library, Baker MT [*Library symbol*] [*Library of Congress*] (LCLS) ... MtBaF
Fallon, NV [*Location identifier FAA*] (FAAL) ... FLX
Fallon, NV [*FM radio station call letters*] (RBYB) ... KRNG
Fallon, NV [*FM radio station call letters*] ... KVCE
Fallon, NV [*AM radio station call letters*] ... KVLV
Fallon, NV [*FM radio station call letters*] ... KVLV-FM
Fallon, NV [*Location identifier FAA*] (FAAL) ... NFL
Fallopian [*Gynecology*] (DAVI) ... FALL
Fallout (IIA) ... FO
Fallout Assessment System ... FAS
Fallout Decay Simulation (OA) ... FDS
Fallout Forecast Data [*Civil Defense*] ... DF
Fallout Intensity Detector Oscillator ... FIDO
Fallout Monitoring Station [*Civil Defense*] ... FMS
Fallout Protection in Houses ... FPHS
Fallout Shelter Analysis [*or Analyst*] [*Civil Defense*] ... FSA
Fallout Studies Branch [*AEC*] ... FSB
Falls (ROG) ... F
Falls [*Commonly used*] (OPSA) ... FALLS
Falls ... FLS
Falls (MCD) ... FLS
Falls Church, VA [*AM radio station call letters*] ... WFAX
Falls City, NE [*Location identifier FAA*] (FAAL) ... FNB
Falls City, NE [*AM radio station call letters*] ... KTNC
Falls City Press, Louisville, KY [*Library symbol Library of Congress*] (LCLS) ... FCP
Falls City Public Library, Falls City, OR [*Library symbol Library of Congress*] (LCLS) ... OrFc
Fallschirm [*Parachute*] [*German military*] ... FS
Fallschirmjaeger-Gewehr [*Parachutist's rifle*] [*German military - World War II*] ... FG
Fallschirmtruppen [*Parachute Troops*] [*German military*] ... FSTR
Falmouth [*Municipal borough in England*] ... FALM
Falmouth Co-Operative Bank [*Associated Press*] (SAG) ... FalmBk
Falmouth Co-Operative Bank [*AMEX symbol*] (SAG) ... FCB
Falmouth Co-operative Bank [*AMEX symbol*] (TTSB) ... FCB
Falmouth Historical Society, Falmouth, MA [*Library symbol Library of Congress*] (LCLS) ... MFalHi
Falmouth, KY [*Location identifier FAA*] (FAAL) ... FLM
Falmouth, KY [*FM radio station call letters*] ... WIOK
Falmouth, MA [*Location identifier FAA*] (FAAL) ... BNX
Falmouth, MA [*Location identifier FAA*] (FAAL) ... CPD
Falmouth, MA [*Location identifier FAA*] (FAAL) ... FMH
Falmouth, MA [*FM radio station call letters*] ... WCIB
Falmouth, MA [*FM radio station call letters*] (RBYB) ... WFPB-FM
Falmouth, MA [*FM radio station call letters*] (RBYB) ... WUNZ
Falmouth/Otis Air Force Base [*Massachusetts*] [*ICAO location identifier*] (ICLI) ... KFMH
Falmouth Petroleum [*Vancouver Stock Exchange symbol*] ... FAU
Falmouth Public Library, Falmouth, MA [*Library symbol Library of Congress*] (LCLS) ... MFal
Falsa Lectio [*False Reading, in a text*] [*Latin*] ... FL
False ... F

False [*FBI standardized term*] ..... FLS
False Alarm Avoidance ..... FAA
False Alarm Rate ..... FAR
False Aneurysm [*Cardiology*] (DAVI) ..... FA
False Calves [*Padding worn under tights by actors, to improve shape of their legs*] ..... FC's
False Cape [*NASA*] (KSC) ..... FC
False Claims Act (AAGC) ..... FCA
False Contact Rate (CAAL) ..... FCR
False Deck [*Stowage*] (DNAB) ..... FD
False Entries in Records of Interstate Carriers [*FBI standardized term*] ..... FERIC
False Identification Crime Control Act of 1982 ..... FICCA
False Negative [*Medicine*] ..... FN
False Negative [*Medicine*] ..... FNEG
False Negative Rate [*Medicine*] (DAVI) ..... FNB
False Neurochemical Transmitter [*Medicine*] (DMAA) ..... FNT
False Pass [*Alaska*] [*Airport symbol*] (OAG) ..... KFP
False Positive [*Medicine*] ..... FP
False Pretenses ..... FP
False Removal Rate (CAAL) ..... FRR
False Signal Recognition [*RADAR technology*] ..... FSR
False Target Can [*Navy*] (NVT) ..... FTC
False Target Rate [*Military*] (CAAL) ..... FTR
False Transmitter [*Neurology*] (DAVI) ..... FT
False-Flag Recruitment [*CIA*] (LAIN) ..... FFR
Falsely (ABBR) ..... FLSLY
Falsely (ABBR) ..... FLSY
Falsely Claiming [*US*] **Citizenship** ..... FCC
Falseness (ABBR) ..... FLSNS
Falser (ABBR) ..... FLSR
Falsest (ABBR) ..... FLSST
Falsest (ABBR) ..... FLST
Falsetto [*Music*] ..... FALSET
Falsification (ABBR) ..... FLSFCAN
Falsification (ABBR) ..... FLSFN
Falsification, Fabrication, and Plagiarism [*Scientific misconduct*] ..... FF & P
Falsified (ABBR) ..... FLSFD
Falsifier (ABBR) ..... FLSFR
Falsify (ABBR) ..... FLSFY
Falsifying (ABBR) ..... FLSFG
Falsity (ABBR) ..... FLST
Falsity (ABBR) ..... FLSTY
Falwell Aviation, Inc. [*ICAO designator*] (FAAC) ..... FAW
FAMECE [*Family of Military Engineer Construction Equipment*] **Computer Simulator for Independent and Logical Evaluation** [*or Simulation*] (MCD) ..... FACSIMILE
Familia Nova [*New Family*] [*Biology*] ..... fam nov
Familial Adenamatosis Coli [*Medicine*] ..... FAC
Familial Adenomatous Polyposis [*Formerly, FPC*] [*Medicine*] ..... FAP
Familial Adenomatous Polyposis Coli [*Medicine*] ..... FAPC
Familial Alzheimer's Disease [*Medicine*] ..... FAD
Familial Amyloid Polyneuropathy [*Medicine*] ..... FAP
Familial Amyotrophic Lateral Sclerosis [*Medicine*] ..... FALS
Familial Atypical Multiple Mole Melanoma [*Oncology*] ..... FAMMM
Familial Autonomic Dysfunction [*Medicine*] (DMAA) ..... FAD
Familial Benign Hypocalciuric Hypercalcaemia [*Medicine*] (BABM) ..... FBH
Familial Benign Hypocalciuric Hypercalcemia [*Nephrology*] (DAVI) ..... FBH
Familial Colonic Cancer [*Gastroenterology and oncology*] (DAVI) ..... FCC
Familial Combined Hyperlipidaemia [*Medicine*] ..... FCHL
Familial Combined Hyperlipidemia [*Cardiology*] (DAVI) ..... FCH
Familial Dysalbuminemic Hyperthyroxinemia [*Medicine*] ..... FDH
Familial Dysautonomia [*Medicine*] ..... FD
Familial Erythrophagocytic Lymphohistocytosis [*Medicine*] ..... FEL
Familial Exudative Vitreoretinopathy [*Ophthalmology*] ..... FEV
Familial Hemiplegic Migraine [*Medicine*] ..... FHM
Familial Hemiplegic Migraine ..... FHM
Familial Hypercholesteremia [*or Hypercholesterolemia*] [*Medicine*] ..... FH
Familial Hypertriglyceridemia [*Medicine*] (DMAA) ..... FHTG
Familial Hypertrophic Cardiomyopathy [*Medicine*] ..... FHC
Familial Hypocalciuric Hypercalcemia [*Medicine*] ..... FHH
Familial Hypophosphatemic Rickets ..... FHR
Familial Idiopathic Gonadotropin Deficiency [*Medicine*] (DMAA) ..... FIGD
Familial Juvenile Nephrophthisis [*Medicine*] ..... FJN
Familial Male Precocious Puberty [*Medicine*] ..... FMPP
Familial Mediterranean Fever ..... FMF
Familial Medullary Thyroid Carcinoma [*Oncology*] ..... FMTC
Familial Periodic Paralysis [*Medicine*] (BABM) ..... FAM PER PAR
Familial Periodic Paralysis [*Neurology*] (DAVI) ..... Fam per par
Familial Polyposis Coli [*Later, FAP*] [*Medicine*] ..... FPC
Familial Pulmonary Fibrosis ..... FPF
Familial Pure Depressive Disease ..... FPDD
Familial Spastic Paraplegia [*Medicine*] (DMAA) ..... FSP
Familial Uveal Melanoma [*Oncology*] ..... FUM
Familiar (AABC) ..... FAM
Familiarization Exercise [*Military*] (NVT) ..... FAMEX
Familiarization Firing (DNAB) ..... FAMFIRE
Familiarization Flight (FAAC) ..... FFLT
Familiarization Job Training (AFIT) ..... FJT
Familiarization Training Data (MCD) ..... FTD
Families Adopting Children Everywhere (EA) ..... FACE
Families Against Intimidation and Terror [*An association*] ..... FAIT
Families Against Mandatory Minimums Foundation (EA) ..... FAMM
Families Against Meat in New England [*Worcester, Massachusetts, group protesting high cost of food, 1973*] ..... FAMINE
Families Against the Bomb [*British*] (DI) ..... FAB
Families and Work Institute (EA) ..... FWI
Families Anonymous (EA) ..... FA
Families for Private Adoption (EA) ..... FPA
Families for the Homeless (EA) ..... FFH
Families in Action [*Later, NFA*] (EA) ..... FIA
Families in Action National Drug Information Center [*Later, NFA*] (EA) ..... FIANDIC
Families in Society [*A publication*] (BRI) ..... Fam in Soc
Families Including Kids [*Lifestyle classification*] ..... Fik
Families Leaving Quebec [*Humorous interpretation for Front de Liberation du Quebec*] ..... FLQ
Families Need Fathers [*British*] [*An association*] (DBA) ..... FNF
Families of Australia Foundation ..... FAF
Families of Resisters for Amnesty (EA) ..... FORA
Families of SMA [*Spinal Muscular Atrophy*] [*An association*] (EA) ..... FSMA
Families of Structurally Similar Proteins [*A database*] ..... FSSP
Families of Vietnamese Political Prisoners Association (EA) ..... FVPPA
Families within Orders (DICI) ..... F/O
Family ..... F
Family (AFM) ..... FAM
Family (ROG) ..... FAMY
Family ..... FMLY
Family ..... FMLY
Family Action Information and Rescue [*British*] (DI) ..... FAIR
Family Action Section (EA) ..... FAS
Family Adaptability and Cohesion Evaluation Scale [*Psychology*] ..... FACES
Family Adjustment Test [*Psychology*] ..... FAT
Family Advancement Resources Cooperative [*Australia*] ..... FARC
Family Agency ..... FA
Family Allowance [*Navy*] ..... FA
Family Allowance, Class A [*Navy*] ..... FAA
Family Allowance, Class A and B [*Navy*] ..... FAAB
Family Allowance, Class B [*Navy*] ..... FAB
Family America [*An association*] (EA) ..... FA
Family and Children's Services Agency [*New South Wales, Australia*] ..... FCSA
Family and Commercial [*Hotels*] [*British*] (ROG) ..... F & C
Family and Community Services (WDAA) ..... FACS
Family and Community Treatment Services ..... FACTS
Family and Demographic Research Institute [*Brigham Young University*] [*Research center*] (RCD) ..... FDRI
Family and Health Section (EA) ..... FHS
Family and Intimate Assault [*Criminology*] ..... FIA
Family and Medical Leave Act of 1993 (WYGK) ..... FMLA
Family and Neighborhood Services ..... FNS
Family Assessment Adjustment Pass [*Psychology*] (DAVI) ..... FAAP
Family Assessment Device ..... FAD
Family Assessment Tool [*Kit*] [*Medicine*] ..... FAT
Family Assistance Management Information System [*Department of Health and Human Services*] (GFGA) ..... FAMIS
Family Assistance Plan [*or Program*] [*Proposed during Nixon administration*] ..... FAP
Family Auto Policy [*Insurance*] ..... FAP
Family Bancorp [*Associated Press*] (SAG) ..... FamBc
Family Bancorp [*NASDAQ symbol*] (NQ) ..... FMLY
Family Bargain [*NASDAQ symbol*] (TTSB) ..... FBAR
Family Bargain 9.5% Cv'A'Pfd [*NASDAQ symbol*] (TTSB) ..... FBARP
Family Bargain Corp. [*Associated Press*] (SAG) ..... FamB
Family Bargain Corp. [*Associated Press*] (SAG) ..... FamBarg
Family Bargain Corp. [*NASDAQ symbol*] (SAG) ..... FBAR
Family Bible [*Genealogy*] ..... FB
Family Business Network [*Switzerland*] ..... FBN
Family Camping Federation [*Later, FCFA*] (EA) ..... FCF
Family Camping Federation of America [*Formerly, FCF*] [*Defunct*] (EA) ..... FCFA
Family Care Home (HCT) ..... FCH
Family Care Program [*Insurance*] (WYGK) ..... FCP
Family Centered Learning Alternatives (EA) ..... FCLA
Family Communications, Inc. [*Public television*] (NTCM) ..... FCI
Family Communion Crusade [*Defunct*] (EA) ..... FCC
Family Continuation of Coverage [*Health insurance*] (GHCT) ..... FC
Family Contribution [*Department of Education*] (GFGA) ..... FC
Family Court of Australia ..... FCA
Family Court, Western Australia ..... FCWA
Family Crisis Intervention Unit [*New York Police Department*] ..... FCIU
Family Day Care Centre [*Australia*] ..... FDCC
Family Day Care Development Service [*Australia*] ..... FDCDS
Family Day Care Program [*Australia*] ..... FDCP
Family Discussion Bureau [*Later, Institute of Marital Studies*] [*British*] (DI) ..... FDB
Family Division, High Court, England and Wales (DLA) ..... Fam
Family Doctor (AAMN) ..... fam doc
Family Doctor (MEDA) ..... FD
Family Dollar Stores [*Associated Press*] (SAG) ..... FamDlr
Family Dollar Stores [*NYSE symbol*] (TTSB) ..... FDO
Family Dollar Stores, Inc. [*NYSE symbol*] (SPSG) ..... FDO
Family Economics Research Group [*Department of Agriculture*] (GRD) ..... FERG
Family Education and Information Council of the United States (EA) ..... FEICUS
Family Education Network [*Computer science*] ..... FEN
Family Education Unit [*Australia*] ..... FEU
Family Educational Rights and Privacy Act [*1974*] ..... FERPA
Family Emission Level [*Automotive engineering*] ..... FEL
Family Empowerment Network [*Support for Families Affected by FAS/FAE*] [*Organization concerned with families affected by fetal alcohol syndrome or fetal alcohol effects*] (PAZ) ..... FEN
Family Environment Scale ..... FES
Family Expenditure Survey [*Department of Employment*] [*British*] ..... FES
Family Farm Movement (EA) ..... FFM

Family Financial Statement ... FFS
Family Fitness Council ... FFC
Family Functioning Index ... FFI
Family Golf Centers [*NASDAQ symbol*] (TTSB) ... FGCI
Family Golf Centers, Inc. [*Associated Press*] (SAG) ... FamGolf
Family Golf Centers, Inc. [*NASDAQ symbol*] (SAG) ... FGCI
Family Grocer Alliance Ltd. [*British*] (BI) ... FGA
Family Group Number ... FGN
Family Groups [*Aid to Families with Dependent Children*] (OICC) ... FG
Family Hands Off [*Indicates that a certain dish is not to be eaten by members of the family at a meal where guests are present*] ... FHO
Family Health Insurance Plan ... FHIP
Family Health International [*Family Health International/International Fe rtility Research Program*] [*Acronym is based on former name,*] (EA) ... FHI/IFRP
Family Health - Service Authority [*British*] (ECON) ... FHSA
Family Heart Association [*British*] (DBA) ... FHA
Family History [*Medicine*] ... FH
Family History (DAVI) ... FHx
Family History Library, Church of Jesus Christ of Latter-Day Saints, Cranbrook, British Columbia [*Library symbol National Library of Canada*] (BIB) ... BCC
Family History-Research Diagnostic Criteria [*Medicine, Psychiatry*] ... FH-RDC
Family Hold Back [*Indicates family should take small portions at a meal where guests are present*] ... FHB
Family Hold Off [*Indicates that a certain dish is not to be eaten by members of the family at a meal where guests are present*] ... FHO
Family Home Entertainment [*Division of International Video Entertainment*] ... FHE
Family Housing [*Army*] (AABC) ... FHSG
Family Housing Assignment Application System [*Military*] (DNAB) ... FAMHSGASSIGNSY
Family Housing Division [*Army*] (AABC) ... FHD
Family Housing Management Account [*Army*] (AABC) ... FHMA
Family Housing Management Appropriation ... FHMA
Family Housing Officer ... FHO
Family Housing Requirements Survey Record System (DNAB) ... FAMHSGRQMTSURVSYS
Family Income Security Plan ... FISP
Family Income Supplement (ODBW) ... FIS
Family Information Facility (MHDB) ... FIF
Family Interaction Summary Format ... FISF
Family Interest Group - Head Trauma (EA) ... FIGHT
Family Inventory of Life Events and Changes ... FILE
Family Involvement Process [*Used to encourage parental support in the education of handicapped children*] ... FIP
Family Keep Off [*Food, in presence of company*] [*British*] (DI) ... FKO
Family Law Bar Association [*British*] (DBA) ... FLBA
Family Law Council (EA) ... FLC
Family Law Division (New South Wales Supreme Court) [*Australia*] ... FLD
Family Law Practitioners' Association of Queensland [*Australia*] ... FLPAQ
Family Law Reform Association [*Australia*] ... FLRA
Family Law Reform Association of New South Wales [*Australia*] ... FLRANSW
Family Law Reform Party [*Political party Australia*] ... FLR
Family Law Review [*A publication*] ... Family Law Rev
Family Liaison Action Group [*Inactive*] (EA) ... FLAG
Family Liaison Office ... FLO
Family Life and Population Program/Church World Service [*Defunct*] (EA) ... FLPP/CWS
Family Life Bureau (EA) ... FLB
Family Life Communications Line ... FLCL
Family Life Income Patterns [*Economics simulation game*] ... FLIP
Family Life Mission [*An association*] (EAIO) ... FLM
Family Life Movement of Australia ... FLMA
Family Limited Partnership ... FLP
Family Location and Legal Service [*Formerly, FLS*] (EA) ... FLLS
Family Location Service [*Later, FLLS*] (EA) ... FLS
Family Manned Planetary Mission ... FMPM
Family Mediation Association (EA) ... FMA
Family Mediation Centre [*Australia*] ... FMC
Family Medical Doctor (DAVI) ... FMD
Family Medical History [*Medicine*] (HGAA) ... FMH
Family Medicine Program Certificate ... FMPCert
Family Member Prefix (DNAB) ... FMP
Family Motor Coach Association (EA) ... FMCA
Family Nurse Practitioner ... FNP
Family Nursing Unit ... FNU
Family of Antiair Missile Systems (MCD) ... FAAMS
Family of Army Aircraft System ... FAAS
Family of Army Vehicles Study ... FAVS
Family of Battle Simulators [*Army*] ... FAMSIM
Family of Faith Foundation [*Later, FFM*] (EA) ... FFF
Family of Frequencies [*Aviation*] (DA) ... FAM
Family of Heavy Tactical Vehicles [*MTMC*] (TAG) ... FHTV
Family of Humanists [*An association*] (EA) ... FH
Family of Light-Armed Vehicle [*Saudi Arabian National Guard*] (DWSG) ... FOLAV
Family of Medium Tactical Vehicles [*Military*] (RDA) ... FMTV
Family of Military Engineer Construction Equipment ... FAMECE
Family of Military Engineer Construction Equipment/Universal Engineer Tractor (RDA) ... FAMECE/UET
Family of Operational Rations [*Army*] ... FOR
Family of Scatterable Mines [*Army*] (RDA) ... FASCAM
Family of Simulations [*Computer science Army*] (RDA) ... FAMSIM
Family of Small Arms [*Military*] (MCD) ... FOS
Family of Small Arms [*Military*] ... FOSA
Family of Special Weapons Atomic Contractors ... FOSWAC
Family of Systems Studies [*Military*] (RDA) ... FOSS
Family of the Americas Foundation (EA) ... FAF
Family of Vehicles ... FOV
Family of Weapons (MCD) ... FOW
Family Personal Computer (PCM) ... FPC
Family Physician (CPH) ... fam phys
Family Pitch In [*Indicates family may eat freely of a certain dish at a meal where guests are present*] ... FPI
Family Planning ... FP
Family Planning and Information Service ... FPIS
Family Planning Association ... FPA
Family Planning Association of Kenya (EERA) ... FPAK
Family Planning Association of New South Wales [*Australia*] ... FPANSW
Family Planning Center (WDAA) ... FPC
Family Planning Clinic [*British*] ... FPC
Family Planning Evaluation Branch [*Public Health Service*] (IID) ... FPEB
Family Planning Evaluation Division [*HEW*] (IID) ... FPED
Family Planning Federation of Australia Inc. (EERA) ... FPFA
Family Planning International Assistance (EA) ... FPIA
Family Planning Program (WDAA) ... FPP
Family Planning Training Institute, Baltimore, MD [*Library symbol Library of Congress*] (LCLS) ... MdBFamP
Family Policy Studies Centre [*British*] (CB) ... FPSC
Family Practice [*or Practioner*] ... FP
Family Practice Center (MEDA) ... FPC
Family Practitioner Committee [*British*] ... FPC
Family Protection League of USA [*Defunct*] (EA) ... FPL
Family Quarters, Navy (DNAB) ... FQN
Family Radio Service ... FRS
Family Radio Service ... FRS
Family Relations [*A publication*] (BRI) ... Fam Relat
Family Relations Indicator [*Psychology*] ... FRI
Family Relations Test [*Psychology*] ... FRT
Family Relationship Inventory [*Psychology*] ... FRI
Family Relationships Institute [*Australia*] ... FRI
Family Research Council (EA) ... FRC
Family Research Council of America [*Later, FRC*] (EA) ... FRCA
Family Research Institute (EA) ... FRI
Family Resource and Network Support [*Australia*] ... FRANS
Family Resource and Referral Center [*National Council on Family Relations*] [*Information service or system*] (IID) ... FR & RC
Family Resource Coalition (EA) ... FRC
Family Respite and Network Support [*Australia*] ... FRNS
Family Rights and Privacy Act [*1974*] (OICC) ... FRPA
Family Rights Group [*British*] (DBA) ... FRG
Family Room [*Real estate*] ... FR
Family Rosary (EA) ... FR
Family Rosary Crusade [*Later, FR*] (EA) ... FRC
Family Security Friendly Society [*Australia*] ... FSFS
Family Security Service ... FSS
Family Separation Allowance [*Military*] (AABC) ... FSA
Family Separation Allowance (Restricted Station) [*Military*] (DNAB) ... FSA-R
Family Separation Allowance (Shipboard Operations) [*Military*] (DNAB) ... FSA-S
Family Separation Allowance (Temporary Duty) [*Military*] (DNAB) ... FSA-T
Family Service America (EA) ... FSA
Family Service Association of America [*Later, FSA*] (EA) ... FSAA
Family Service Unit [*Medicine British*] ... FSU
Family Services and Assistance Officer (AABC) ... FSAO
Family Services Branch [*Australian Capital Territory*] ... FSB
Family Services Center [*Military*] ... FSC
Family Services Program [*Military*] ... FSP
Family Status (OICC) ... FS
Family Steak Houses Fla [*NASDAQ symbol*] (TTSB) ... RYFL
Family Steak Houses of Florida, Inc. [*Associated Press*] (SAG) ... FamStk
Family Steak Houses of Florida, Inc. [*Neptune Beach, FL*] [*NASDAQ symbol*] (NQ) ... RYFL
Family Stop Eating [*A table signal at a meal where guests are present*] ... FSE
Family Strike Light [*Indicates family should take small portions at a meal where guests are present*] ... FSL
Family Suffering Index [*Economic measurement based on unemployment rate, plus costs of food, fuel, and housing*] ... FSI
Family Support Act of 1988 (WYGK) ... FSA
Family Support Administration [*Department of Health and Human Services*] ... FSA
Family Support Association of New South Wales [*Australia*] ... FSANSW
Family Support Group [*Military*] (INF) ... FSG
Family Support Service [*Australia*] ... FSS
Family Support Services Association of New South Wales [*Australia*] ... FSSANSW
Family Therapy ... FT
Family Therapy Institute of Australia ... FTIA
Family Therapy Network (EA) ... FTN
Family Viewing Time [*FCC rule*] (NTCM) ... FV
Family Viewing Time [*Television*] ... FVT
Family Violence Prevention Fund ... FUND
Family Welfare Association [*British*] (ILCA) ... FWA
Family Worker Development Program [*Australia*] ... FWDP
Family-Centered Maternity Care [*Obstetrics*] (DAVI) ... FCMC
Family-Centered Maternity Nursing [*Obstetrics*] (DAVI) ... FCMN
Family-Related Emotional Trauma - Anonymous ... FRET-ANON
Famine Early Warning System [*US Agency for International Development*] ... FEWS
Famous (WGA) ... FAM
Famous ... FMS
Famous Artists Schools [*Later, FAS International, Inc.*] ... FAS

Famous Cases of Circumstantial Evidence, by Phillips [*A publication*] (DLA) ... Fam Cas Cir Ev
Famous Daves of America, Inc. [*NASDAQ symbol*] (SAG) ... DAVE
Famous Daves of America, Inc. [*Associated Press*] (SAG) ... FamDv
Famous Daves of America, Inc. [*Associated Press*] (SAG) ... FmDaves
Famous Fone Friends (EA) ... FFF
Famous Personalities' Business Card Collectors of America [*Defunct*] (EA) ... FPBCCA
Famous Records of the Past [*Record label*] ... FRP
Famous Sayings [*Psychological testing*] ... FS
Famous Scots [*A publication*] ... FS
Famous Spock Neck Pinch [*From television show "Star Trek"*] ... FSNP
Fan Air Valve (MCD) ... FAV
Fan Association of North America (EA) ... FANA
Fan Beam Scatterometer ... FBS
Fan Circle International (EA) ... FCI
Fan Club Associates [*Later, IFCA*] (EA) ... FCA
Fan Coil Unit (NRCH) ... FCU
Fan Control Module [*Automotive engineering*] ... FCM
Fan Control Relay [*Automotive engineering*] ... FCR
Fan Douche [*Medicine*] ... FD
Fan In [*Electronics*] (IAA) ... FI
Fan In ... FNI
Fan Inlet Variable Guide Vanes (MCD) ... FIVGV
Fan Lift ... FL
Fan Magazine [*Generic term for a publication of interest to science fiction fans*] ... FANZINE
Fan Manufacturers Association [*British*] (DBA) ... FMA
Fan Marker [*Aviation*] ... FM
Fan Marker [*Aviation*] (IAA) ... FMKR
Fan Marker Approach [*Aviation*] ... FMAP
Fan Marker Located with Radio Beacon [*Aviation*] (FAAC) ... FMH
Fan Out ... FNO
Fan Out ... FO
Fan Pressure Ratio [*Aviation*] ... FPR
Fan Tek (EA) ... FT
Fan Thrust Reverser ... FTR
Fan Turbine Inlet Temperature (MCD) ... FTIT
Fanaroff-Riley [*Radio galaxy*] ... FR
Fan-Assisted Drug Detector ... FADD
Fanatic (WDMC) ... fan
Fancamp Resources Ltd. [*Vancouver Stock Exchange symbol*] ... FNM
Fanconi Syndrome [*Medicine*] (DMAA) ... FS
Fanconi's Anemia [*Medicine*] ... FA
Fanconi's Anemia Support Group (EA) ... FASG
Fancy (ROG) ... FCY
Fancy ... FNCY
Fancy Cane, Wicker, and Bamboo Workers' Union [*British*] ... FCWBWU
Fancy Goods Store [*British military*] (DMA) ... FGS
F&E Resource Systems Tech [*NASDAQ symbol*] (TTSB) ... FERS
F&M Bancorp [*NASDAQ symbol*] (TTSB) ... FMBN
F&M Bancorporation, Inc. [*NASDAQ symbol*] (TTSB) ... FMBK
Fandom Is a Way of Life [*Science-fiction-fan slogan*] ... FIAWOL
Fane [*Papua New Guinea*] [*Airport symbol*] (OAG) ... FNE
Fane's Horse [*British military*] (DMA) ... FH
Fanfare [*A publication*] (BRI) ... FF
Fang [*MARC language code Library of Congress*] (LCCP) ... fan
Fangatau [*French Polynesia*] [*Airport symbol*] (OAG) ... FGU
Fangatau [*French Polynesia*] [*ICAO location identifier*] (ICLI) ... NTGB
Fangmeyer's Utility, a Basic Algorithm for Revision (PDAA) ... FUBAR
Fanned Beam Antenna ... FBA
Fannie Major Pool [*FNMA*] [*Business term*] (EMRF) ... FMP
Fannie Smith School, Bridgeport, CT [*Library symbol Library of Congress*] (LCLS) ... CtBFAST
Fanning Island [*Line Islands*] [*Seismograph station code, US Geological Survey Closed*] (SEIS) ... FAN
Fanny Adams [*Canned mutton stew*] [*Slang*] (DSUE) ... FA
Fanny Fern [*Pseudonym used by Sara Payson Parton*] ... FF
Fanout-Observed Output Function (MHDB) ... FOOF
Fan-Powered Terminal (DAC) ... FPT
Fans Against Indian Racism (EA) ... FAIR
Fans Against the Strike (EA) ... FAST
Fans of Bentsen [*Treasury Secretary, Lloyd Bentsen*] (ECON) ... FOB
Fans of General Hospital (EA) ... FGH
Fanshawe College of Applied Arts and Technology, London, ON, Canada [*Library symbol Library of Congress*] (LCLS) ... CaOLFC
Fanshawe College of Applied Arts and Technology, London, Ontario [*Library symbol National Library of Canada*] (NLC) ... OLFC
Fansteel, Inc. [*Associated Press*] (SAG) ... Fanstel
Fansteel, Inc. [*NYSE symbol*] (SPSG) ... FNL
Fantail Darter [*Ichthyology*] ... Fd
Fantastic ... FNTSTIC
Fantasy ... FNTSY
Fantasy Amateur Press Association ... FAPA
Fantasy and Science Fiction [*A publication*] ... F & SF
Fantasy Association (EA) ... FA
Fantasy Bowling League ... FBL
Fantasy Unrestricted Network [*Cable-television system*] ... FUN
Fantasy Wrestling Leagues ... FWL
Fanton's Tables of Roman Law [*A publication*] (DLA) ... Fan Rom Law
Fan-Type Marker ... FTM
FAO [*Food and Agriculture Organization of the United Nations*] **Association of Professional Staff** [*Rome, Italy*] (EAIO) ... FAO/APS
Far Advanced [*Medicine*] (MAE) ... FA
Far Airlines [*Italy*] [*FAA designator*] (FAAC) ... FAR
Far and Wide Tape Club (EA) ... FWTC
Far East ... FE
Far East Air Force ... FEAF
Far East Air Logistical Force ... FEALOGFOR
Far East Air Materiel Command ... FEAMCOM
Far East Air Transport Association ... FEATA
Far East and Australasia [*A publication*] ... FEA
Far East and South Pacific ... FESPIC
Far East Area (CINC) ... FEAREA
Far East Army and Air Force Exchange Service ... FEAAES
Far East Auto Owners Association (EA) ... FEAOA
Far East Broadcasting Association ... FEBA
Far East Broadcasting Co. ... FEBC
Far East Combined Bureau [*Singapore, 1940*] [*Military*] ... FECB
Far East Command [*Military*] ... FEC
Far East Command [*Military*] ... FECOM
Far East Communications Region [*Air Force*] (MCD) ... FECR
Far East Conference [*Defunct*] (EA) ... FEC
Far East Job International [*Former USSR*] (ECON) ... FEJI
Far East Land Forces (CINC) ... FARELF
Far East Land Forces [*British military*] (DMA) ... FELF
Far East Liaison Group (CINC) ... FELG
Far East Merchants Association [*Defunct*] (EA) ... FEMAS
Far East National Bank [*Associated Press*] (SAG) ... FarEst
Far East National Bank [*AMEX symbol*] (SAG) ... FEB
Far East National Bank [*AMEX symbol*] (TTSB) ... FEB
Far East National Bank [*NASDAQ symbol*] (SAG) ... FENB
Far East Network [*US Armed Forces radio station*] [*Japan*] ... FEN
Far East/Pacific ... FEAP
Far East Prisoner of War ... FEPOW
Far East Research Office ... FERO
Far East Science Center ... FESC
Far East Time (IAA) ... FET
Far Eastern Advisory Council ... FEAC
Far Eastern Air Transport [*ICAO designator*] (AD) ... EF
Far Eastern Air Transport Corp. [*Taiwan*] [*ICAO designator*] (FAAC) ... FEA
Far Eastern Cargo Airlines [*Former USSR*] [*FAA designator*] (FAAC) ... FEW
Far Eastern Commission ... FEC
Far Eastern Department, Royal Ontario Museum, Toronto, Ontario [*Library symbol National Library of Canada*] (NLC) ... OTRMF
Far Eastern Economic Review [*A publication*] (BRI) ... FEER
Far Eastern Freight Conference ... FEFC
Far Eastern Law Review [*A publication*] (DLA) ... Far East L Rev
Far Eastern Region, RSFSR [*MARC geographic area code Library of Congress*] (LCCP) ... e-urf-
Far Eastern Resources Corp. [*Vancouver Stock Exchange symbol*] ... FST
Far Eastern Shipping Co. [*Former USSR*] ... FESCO
Far Eastern Technical Unit [*World War II*] ... FETU
Far Eastern Textile Ltd. [*Associated Press*] (SAG) ... FarETxt
Far Eastern Textile Ltd. [*NYSE symbol*] (SAG) ... FET
Far Eastern Tick-Borne Encephalitis [*Medicine*] (DMAA) ... FETE
Far End Block Error [*Telecommunications*] (ACRL) ... FEBE
Far End Receive Failure [*Telecommunications*] (ACRL) ... FERF
Far Field (MCD) ... FF
Far Horizons Newsletter [*A publication*] ... FHNL
Far Infrared ... FIR
Far Infrared and Submillimeter Space Telescope [*Proposed European*] ... FIRST
Far Infrared Space Telescope ... FIRST
Far Infrared Target Indicator [*Military*] ... FIRTI
Far North Queensland Regiment [*Australia*] ... FNQR
Far Point of Accommodation [*Ophthalmology*] ... FPA
Far Side ... FS
Far Ultraviolet Detector ... FUVD
Far Ultraviolet Satellite Experiment (MCD) ... FUSE
Far Ultraviolet Space Telescope ... FAUST
Far Ultraviolet Spectrometer [*NASA*] ... FUS
Far Ultraviolet Spectroscopy Explorer [*NASA*] (SSD) ... FUSE
Far West Airlines, Inc. [*ICAO designator*] (FAAC) ... FWA
Far West Industries, Inc. [*Toronto Stock Exchange symbol Vancouver Stock Exchange symbol*] ... FWT
Far West Laboratory for Educational Research and Development [*San Francisco, CA*] [*Department of Education*] (GRD) ... FWL
Far West Laboratory for Educational Research and Development [*Department of Education*] ... FWLERD
Far West Regional Educational Laboratory [*San Francisco, CA*] [*Department of Education*] (AEBS) ... FWREL
Farabundo Marti National Liberation Front [*Brazil Political party*] (ECON) ... FMLN
Farad [*Symbol*] [*Unit of electric capacitance*] (GPO) ... F
Farad [*Unit of electric capacitance*] (ROG) ... FAR
Faraday (WDAA) ... FAR
Faraday Constant [*Electrochemistry*] ... F
Faraday Cup Array [*Electronics*] (OA) ... FCA
Faraday Dark Space ... FDS
Faraday Disc Machine ... FDM
Faraday Resources, Inc. [*Toronto Stock Exchange symbol*] ... CFY
Faradje [*Zaire*] [*ICAO location identifier*] (ICLI) ... FZJK
Farads per Meter ... F/M
Farafangana [*Madagascar*] [*ICAO location identifier*] (ICLI) ... FMSG
Farafangana [*Madagascar*] [*Airport symbol*] (OAG) ... RVA
Farah [*Afghanistan*] [*ICAO location identifier*] (ICLI) ... OAFR
Farah, Inc. [*Associated Press*] (SAG) ... Farah
Farah, Inc. [*NYSE symbol*] (SPSG) ... FRA
Farallon Islands (GAAI) ... FIS
Faranah/Badala [*Guinea*] [*ICAO location identifier*] (ICLI) ... GUFH
Farashband [*Iran*] [*ICAO location identifier*] (ICLI) ... OISH

Faratahi [*Tuamotu Archipelago*] [*Seismograph station code, US Geological Survey*] (SEIS) .... FRT
Faraway Gold Mines Ltd. [*Vancouver Stock Exchange symbol*] .... FRW
Faraz Qeshm Airlines [*Iran*] [*FAA designator*] (FAAC) .... IRQ
Farband Labor Zionist Order [*Later, Labor Zionist Alliance*] (EA) .... FLZO
Farbenfabriken Bayer [*Germany*] [*Research code symbol*] .... B
Farbenfabriken Bayer [*Germany*] [*Research code symbol*] .... BAY
Farbenfabriken Bayer [*Germany*] [*Research code symbol*] .... E
Farbenfabriken Bayer [*Germany*] [*Research code symbol*] .... FB
Farbenfabriken Bayer [*Germany*] [*Research code symbol*] .... FBA
Farbenfabriken Bayer [*Germany*] [*Research code symbol*] .... GEA
Farbenfabriken Bayer [*Germany*] [*Research code symbol*] .... P
Farbwerke Hoechst AG [*Germany*] [*Research code symbol*] .... HB
Farbwerke Hoechst AG [*Germany*] [*Research code symbol*] .... LB
Farce (ROG) .... F
Fare Automated Search Technique [*Airline travel service information system*] .... FAST
Fare Construction Unit [*Airlines*] .... FCU
Fare Quotation [*Airline*] .... FQ
Fare Reduction Enhancement Device [*Travel industry software*] [*CompuCheck Corp.*] .... FRED
Far-East-America Council of Commerce and Industry [*Defunct*] (EA) .... FEACCI
Far-Eastern Prehistory Association [*Later, IPPA*] (EA) .... FEPA
Far-Encounter Planet Sensor .... FEPS
Far-End Crosstalk [*Telecommunications*] .... FEXT
Far-End Suppressor (IAA) .... FES
Fares Calculating Unit (OA) .... FCU
Farewell [*Alaska*] [*Airport symbol*] (OAG) .... FWL
Farewell [*Alaska*] [*ICAO location identifier*] (ICLI) .... PAFW
Farewell, AK [*Location identifier FAA*] (FAAL) .... FWL
Farfield Acoustic Measuring System (KSC) .... FAMS
Far-Field Pressure .... FFP
Far-Field Visibility [*Aviation*] .... FFV
Fargo [*North Dakota*] [*Airport symbol*] (OAG) .... FAR
Fargo House Movement [*Trinidad and Tobago*] [*Political party*] (PPW) .... FHM
Fargo, ND [*Location identifier FAA*] (FAAL) .... AAM
Fargo, ND [*Location identifier FAA*] (FAAL) .... FAR
Fargo, ND [*Location identifier FAA*] (FAAL) .... HAW
Fargo, ND [*FM radio station call letters*] .... KDSU
Fargo, ND [*AM radio station call letters*] .... KFGO
Fargo, ND [*FM radio station call letters*] .... KFGO-FM
Fargo, ND [*Television station call letters*] .... KFME
Fargo, ND [*FM radio station call letters*] .... KFNW-FM
Fargo, ND [*FM radio station call letters*] .... KPFX
Fargo, ND [*AM radio station call letters*] (RBYB) .... KQFN
Fargo, ND [*Television station call letters*] (RBYB) .... KVLY-TV
Fargo, ND [*Television station call letters*] .... KVRR
Fargo, ND [*AM radio station call letters*] .... WDAY
Fargo, ND [*FM radio station call letters*] .... WDAY-FM
Fargo, ND [*Television station call letters*] .... WDAY-TV
Fargo Public Library, Fargo, ND [*Library symbol Library of Congress*] (LCLS) .... NdF
Fargo Resources Ltd. [*Vancouver Stock Exchange symbol*] .... FR
Faribault, MN [*Location identifier FAA*] (FAAL) .... FBL
Faribault, MN [*AM radio station call letters*] .... KDHL
Faribault, MN [*FM radio station call letters*] .... KQCL
Faridkot [*India*] [*ICAO location identifier*] (ICLI) .... VIFD
Faridpur [*Bangladesh*] [*Airport symbol*] (AD) .... FDP
Farila [*Sweden ICAO location identifier*] (ICLI) .... ESNF
Farim [*Guinea-Bissau*] [*ICAO location identifier*] (ICLI) .... GGFR
Fariman [*Iran*] [*ICAO location identifier*] (ICLI) .... OIMR
Farina [*Flour*] [*Pharmacy*] (ROG) .... FAR
Farina-LaGrove Community Unit, School District 206, Farina, IL [*Library symbol Library of Congress*] (LCLS) .... IFaSD
Far-Infrared Absolute Spectrophotometer .... FIRAS
Far-Infrared Detector .... FID
Far-Infrared Detector .... FIRD
Far-Infrared MASER [*Microwave Amplification by Stimulated Emission of Radiation*] .... FIM
Far-Infrared Observation .... FIO
Far-Infrared Observation .... FIRO
Far-Infrared Pointer .... FIP
Far-Infrared Pointer .... FIRP
Far-Infrared Pointer Package .... FIPP
Far-Infrared Pointer Package .... FIRPP
Far-Infrared Radiometer .... FIR
Far-Infrared Search .... FIS
Far-Infrared Search and Track .... FIRST
Far-Infrared Spectrometer .... FIRS
Far-Infrared Spectrometer .... FIS
Far-Infrared Target Detector .... FITD
Far-Infrared Target Indicator .... FITI
Far-Infrared Technical Area [*Night Vision Laboratories*] [*Army*] (RDA) .... FIRTA
Far-Infrared Track .... FIT
Farinon Canada, Dorval, Quebec [*Library symbol National Library of Canada*] (NLC) .... QMFAC
Farm .... FM
Farm (ADA) .... FRM
Farm .... FRM
Farm Acreage Base .... FAB
Farm Advisory Committee [*MAFF*] [*British*] .... FAC
Farm Aid (EA) .... FA
Farm and Food Society [*British*] .... FAFS
Farm and Industrial Equipment Institute (EA) .... FIEI
Farm and Land Institute [*Later, RLI*] (EA) .... FLI

Farm Animal Practice Teaching Unit [*Royal Veterinary College*] [*British*] (IRUK) .... FAPTU
Farm Animal Reform Movement (EA) .... FARM
Farm Animal Welfare Coordinating Executive [*British*] (DI) .... FAWCE
Farm Audience Readership Measurement Service [*Starch INRA Hooper, Inc.*] [*Information service or system*] (IID) .... FARMS
Farm Bankruptcy Act [*1933*] .... FBA
Farm Buildings Advisory Officer [*Ministry of Agriculture, Fisheries, and Food*] [*British*] .... FBAO
Farm Buildings Association [*British*] .... FBA
Farm Buildings Information Centre Ltd. [*British*] (CB) .... FBIC
Farm Bureau Services .... FBS
Farm Business Management Branch, Alberta Agriculture, Olds, Alberta [*Library symbol National Library of Canada*] (NLC) .... AOAF
Farm Cash Operating Surplus .... FCOS
Farm, Construction, and Industrial Machinery (PDAA) .... FCIM
Farm Costs and Returns [*A publication*] .... FCR
Farm Costs and Returns Survey [*Department of Agriculture*] (GFGA) .... FCRS
Farm Credit Administration [*Independent government agency*] .... FCA
Farm Credit Corp. [*Canada*] .... FCC
Farm Credit Corp. Canada [*Ottawa, ON*] .... FCCC
Farm Credit Corp., Ottawa, Ontario [*Library symbol Obsolete National Library of Canada*] (NLC) .... OOFCC
Farm Credit Council (EA) .... FCC
Farm Credit System [*of FCA*] .... FCS
Farm Crisis Committee [*Defunct*] (EA) .... FCC
Farm Economics Research Division [*of ARS, Department of Agriculture*] .... FE
Farm Equipment Institute [*Later, FIEI*] (EA) .... FEI
Farm Equipment Manufacturers Association (EA) .... FEMA
Farm Equipment Wholesalers Association (EA) .... FEWA
Farm Family Holdings, Inc. [*Associated Press*] (SAG) .... FarmFH
Farm Family Holdings, Inc. [*NYSE symbol*] (SAG) .... FFH
Farm Film Foundation [*Later, Grange-Farm Film Foundation*] (EA) .... FFF
Farm Financial Counselling Program [*of Queensland*] (EERA) .... FFCP
Farm Financial Management Skills Program Advisory Committee [*Australia*] .... FFMSPAC
Farm Forestry Program (EERA) .... FFP
Farm Foundation (EA) .... FF
Farm Household Support Scheme [*Australia*] .... FHS
Farm Improvement Loans Act [*Canada*] .... FILA
Farm Income Situation .... FIS
Farm Labor Coalition (EA) .... FLC
Farm Labor Contractor Registration Act [*1963*] [*US Employment Service Department of Labor*] .... FLCRA
Farm Labor Information [*US Employment Service*] [*Department of Labor*] .... FLI
Farm Labor Interstate Clearance System [*US Employment Service*] [*Department of Labor*] .... FLICS
Farm Labor Organizing Committee (EA) .... FLOC
Farm Labor Research Committee [*Defunct*] (EA) .... FLRC
Farm Labor Research Project (EA) .... FLRP
Farm Labor Service [*of USES*] .... FLS
Farm Machinery Dealers' Association of Australia .... FMDAA
Farm Management and Finance [*British*] .... FMF
Farm Management Association [*British*] .... FMA
Farm Management Extension Initiative (EERA) .... FMEI
Farm Market Infodata Service [*Department of Agriculture*] [*Database*] .... FMIS
Farm Mortgage Corp. [*New Deal*] .... FMC
Farm Publications Reports (EA) .... FPR
Farm Sanctuary (EA) .... FS
Farm Scow [*Navy symbol*] (DNAB) .... YWN
Farm Security Administration [*Succeeded by Farmers Home Administration, 1946*] .... FSA
Farm Shop and Pick Your Own Association [*British*] (DBA) .... FSPA
Farm Storage Facility Loan Program .... FSFLP
Farm Store Merchandising Association [*Defunct*] (EA) .... FSMA
Farm Structure Survey Retrieval System [*Information service or system*] (IID) .... FSSRS
Farm to Market .... FM
Farm Underwriters Association [*Defunct*] .... FUA
Farm Verified Organic .... FVO
Farm Workers Family Health Center .... FWFHC
Farm Writers and Broadcasters' Society [*Australia*] .... FWBS
Farman Experimental [*British military*] (DMA) .... FE
Farmer (ROG) .... FAR
Farmer .... FRMR
Farmer Bros. [*NASDAQ symbol*] (TTSB) .... FARM
Farmer Brothers Co. [*NASDAQ symbol*] (NQ) .... FARM
Farmer Brothers Co. [*Associated Press*] (SAG) .... FarmBr
Farmer City, IL [*FM radio station call letters*] (RBYB) .... WEZO
Farmer City, IL [*FM radio station call letters*] (RBYB) .... WWHP-FM
Farmer Cooperative Service [*Later, ESCS*] [*Department of Agriculture*] .... FCS
Farmer-Owned Reserve [*Business term*] .... FOR
Farmers' Allied Meat Enterprises Cooperative .... FAME
Farmers and Manufacturers Beet Sugar Association .... FAMBSA
Farmers and Manufacturers Beet Sugar Association (EA) .... FMBSA
Farmers & Mechanics Bank [*Associated Press*] (SAG) .... FarmMch
Farmers & Mechanics Bank [*NASDAQ symbol*] (SAG) .... FMCT
Farmers & Merchants Bank .... F & M
Farmers and World Affairs [*An association Defunct*] (EA) .... FWA
Farmers Assistance Relief Mission (EA) .... FARM
Farmers' Bulletin [*A publication*] .... FB
Farmers Capital Bank [*NASDAQ symbol*] (TTSB) .... FFKT
Farmers Capital Bank Corp. [*Associated Press*] (SAG) .... FarmCB
Farmers Capital Bank Corp. [*NASDAQ symbol*] (NQ) .... FFKT
Farmers Chinchilla Cooperative of America [*Later, ECBC*] (EA) .... FCCA

Farmers' Educational and Cooperative Union of America (EA) .... FECUA
Farmers Federation Cooperative .... FFC
Farmers Group Capital [*Associated Press*] (SAG) .... FrmG
Farmers Group Capital II [*NYSE symbol*] (SAG) .... FIG
Farmers Group Capital II [*Associated Press*] (SAG) .... FrmG
Farmers Group Captial [*NYSE symbol*] (SAG) .... FIG
Farmers Grp Cap 8.45% 'QUIPS' [*NYSE symbol*] (TTSB) .... FIGPrA
Farmers Grp Cap II 8.25% 'QUIPS' [*NYSE symbol*] (TTSB) .... FIGPrB
Farmers Home Administration [*Later, FmHA*] [*Department of Agriculture*] .... FHA
Farmers Home Administration [*Formerly, FHA*] [*Department of Agriculture*] .... FmHA
Farmers Home Administration (USGC) .... FMHA
Farmer's Insurance Group, Los Angeles, CA [*Library symbol Library of Congress*] (LCLS) .... CLF
Farmers' Union of Wales (BI) .... FUW
Farmerville, LA [*Location identifier FAA*] (FAAL) .... FWV
Farmerville, LA [*FM radio station call letters*] .... KWJM
Farming .... FRMNG
Farming and Wildlife Advisory Group [*British*] (DI) .... FWAG
Farming and Wildlife Advisory Groups (EERA) .... FWAG
Farming and Wildlife Trust [*British*] (DBA) .... FWT
Farming Elementary School, Albany, MN [*Library symbol*] [*Library of Congress*] (LCLS) .... MnAlFE
Farming for Agriculturally Sustainable Systems in Tasmania (EERA) .... FASST
Farming Systems Research .... FSR
Farming Systems Trial (GNE) .... FST
Farmingdale, NY [*Location identifier FAA*] (FAAL) .... FRG
Farmingdale Public Library, Farmingdale, NY [*Library symbol Library of Congress*] (LCLS) .... NFar
Farmingdale Senior High School, Farmingdale, NY [*Library symbol*] [*Library of Congress*] (LCLS) .... NFarSH
Farmington [*New Mexico*] [*Seismograph station code, US Geological Survey*] (SEIS) .... FARG
Farmington [*New Mexico*] [*Airport symbol*] (OAG) .... FMN
Farmington [*New Mexico*] [*ICAO location identifier*] (ICLI) .... KFMN
Farmington, AR [*AM radio station call letters*] .... KFAY
Farmington East High School, Farmington, IL [*OCLC symbol*] (OCLC) .... IQZ
Farmington East Unit District No. 324, Farmington, IL [*Library symbol Library of Congress*] (LCLS) .... IFarE
Farmington Hills, MI [*FM radio station call letters*] .... WORB
Farmington, ME [*FM radio station call letters*] .... WKTJ
Farmington, ME [*FM radio station call letters*] .... WUMF
Farmington, MN [*Location identifier FAA*] (FAAL) .... FGT
Farmington, MO [*Location identifier FAA*] (FAAL) .... FAM
Farmington, MO [*AM radio station call letters*] .... KREI
Farmington, MO [*FM radio station call letters*] .... KTJJ
Farmington, MO [*Location identifier FAA*] (FAAL) .... PRI
Farmington, NM [*Location identifier FAA*] (FAAL) .... FMN
Farmington, NM [*FM radio station call letters*] .... KDAG
Farmington, NM [*AM radio station call letters*] .... KENN
Farmington, NM [*AM radio station call letters*] .... KNDN
Farmington, NM [*FM radio station call letters*] .... KNMI
Farmington, NM [*Television station call letters*] .... KOBF
Farmington, NM [*FM radio station call letters*] .... KPCL
Farmington, NM [*FM radio station call letters*] .... KRWN
Farmington, NM [*AM radio station call letters*] .... KRZE
Farmington, NM [*FM radio station call letters*] .... KSJE
Farmington, NM [*FM radio station call letters*] .... KTRA
Farmington Public Library, Farmington, NM [*OCLC symbol*] (OCLC) .... FAR
Farmington Public Library, Farmington, NM [*Library symbol Library of Congress*] (LCLS) .... NmF
Farmington State Teachers College [*Merged with University of Maine*] .... FSTC
Farmington Village Library, Farmington, CT [*Library symbol Library of Congress*] (LCLS) .... CtF
Farmitalia [*Italy*] [*Research code symbol*] .... FI
Farmitalia [*Italy*] [*Research code symbol*] .... P
Farmland Industries (EA) .... FI
Farmland Industries Inc., Communications Services, Kansas City, MO [*Library symbol Library of Congress*] (LCLS) .... MoKF
Farmland Protection Policy Act (GNE) .... FPPA
Farmland Public Library, Farmland, IN [*Library symbol Library of Congress*] (LCLS) .... InFarl
Farm-Related Service Industries [*FHWA*] (TAG) .... FRSI
FARMS International, Inc. (EA) .... FII
Farmstead Equipment Association (EA) .... FEA
Farmstead Tel Group [*NASDAQ symbol*] (TTSB) .... FONE
Farmstead Tel Group Wrrt [*NASDAQ symbol*] (TTSB) .... FONEW
Farmstead Telephone Group [*AMEX symbol*] (SAG) .... FTG
Farmstead Telephone Group, Inc. [*Associated Press*] (SAG) .... FarmT
Farmstead Telephone Group, Inc. [*Associated Press*] (SAG) .... FarmTel
Farmstead Telephone Group, Inc. [*NASDAQ symbol*] (NQ) .... FONE
Farm-to-Market [*Texas highway*] .... FM
Farmville, NC [*AM radio station call letters*] .... WGHB
Farmville, NC [*FM radio station call letters*] (RBYB) .... WGPM-FM
Farmville, NC [*FM radio station call letters*] .... WRQR
Farmville Public Library, Farmville, NC [*Library symbol Library of Congress*] (LCLS) .... NcFv
Farmville, VA [*Location identifier FAA*] (FAAL) .... FVX
Farmville, VA [*AM radio station call letters*] .... WFLO
Farmville, VA [*FM radio station call letters*] .... WFLO-FM
Farmville, VA [*FM radio station call letters*] .... WLCX
Farmville, VA [*AM radio station call letters*] .... WPAK
Farmworker Justice Fund (EA) .... FJF
Farnas Aviation Services [*Sudan*] [*FAA designator*] (FAAC) .... RAF
Farnborough [*British ICAO location identifier*] (ICLI) .... EGUF
Farnborough Rae [*British*] [*FAA designator*] (FAAC) .... RAE
Farner Air Transport AG [*Switzerland ICAO designator*] (FAAC) .... FAT
Farner Air Transport Hungary [*FAA designator*] (FAAC) .... FAH
Farnesyl Methyl Ether [*Juvenile hormone analog*] .... FME
Farnesyl Pyrophosphate [*Biochemistry*] .... FPP
Farnesyltransferase [*An enzyme*] .... FNTA
Farnesyltransferase [*An enzyme*] .... FTase
Farnesynic Acid [*Juvenile hormone analog*] .... FA
Farnsworth-Munsell [*One hundred hue test*] [*Ophthalmology*] (DAVI) .... FM
Faro [*Portugal*] [*Airport symbol*] (OAG) .... FAO
Faro [*Portugal*] [*Seismograph station code, US Geological Survey*] (SEIS) .... FAR
Faro [*Portugal ICAO location identifier*] (ICLI) .... LPFR
FARO [*Federation of AIDS Related Organizations*] **AIDS Action Council** [*Acquired Immune Deficiency Syndrome*] (EA) .... FAAC
Faro, YT [*ICAO location identifier*] (ICLI) .... CZFA
Faroe Islands [*MARC country of publication code Library of Congress*] (LCCP) .... fa
Faroe Islands [*Denmark*] [*Airport symbol*] (OAG) .... FAE
Faroe Islands .... FI
Faroe Islands [*ANSI two-letter standard code*] (CNC) .... FO
Faroe Islands [*ANSI three-letter standard code*] (CNC) .... FRO
Faroe Islands [*MARC geographic area code Library of Congress*] (LCCP) .... infa--
Faroese [*MARC language code Library of Congress*] (LCCP) .... far
Faron Young Fan Club (EA) .... FYFC
Farquharson's Court of Chancery [*A publication*] (DLA) .... Farq Chy
Farr Co. [*NASDAQ symbol*] (NQ) .... FARC
Farr Co. [*Associated Press*] (SAG) .... Farr
Farragut, TN [*AM radio station call letters*] .... WTNN
Farrah Resources [*Vancouver Stock Exchange symbol*] .... FAH
Farrand Optical Co., Inc. .... FOCI
Farrar, Straus & Giroux [*Publisher*] .... FS & G
Farrar's Manual of the United States Constitution [*A publication*] (DLA) .... Farr Const
Farrel Corp. [*NASDAQ symbol*] (SAG) .... FARL
Farrel Corp. [*Associated Press*] (SAG) .... Farrel
Farrell, PA [*AM radio station call letters*] .... WRQQ
Farren on Life Assurance [*A publication*] (DLA) .... Farr Life Ass
Farren's Bill in Chancery [*A publication*] (DLA) .... Farr Bill
Farren's Masters in Chancery [*A publication*] (DLA) .... Farr Mas
Farrer Memorial Trust [*Australia*] .... FMT
Farresley's Cases in Holt's King's Bench Reports [*A publication*] (DLA) .... Far
Farresley's Reports [*7 Modern Reports*] [*87 English Reprint 1733-45*] [*A publication*] (DLA) .... Far
Farresley's Reports [*7 Modern Reports*] [*87 English Reprint 1733-45*] [*A publication*] (DLA) .... Farr
Farresley's Reports [*7 Modern Reports*] [*87 English Reprint 1733-45*] [*A publication*] (DLA) .... Farresley
Farrier (ROG) .... FAR
Farrier Corporal-Major [*British military*] (DMA) .... FCM
Farrier Quartermaster-Sergeant [*British military*] (DMA) .... FQMS
Farriers Co. of London [*British*] (DI) .... FCL
Farris, Vaughan, Wills & Murphy Law Firm, Vancouver, BC, Canada [*Library symbol Library of Congress*] (LCLS) .... CaBVaFV
Farris, Vaughan, Wills & Murphy Law Firm, Vancouver, British Columbia [*Library symbol National Library of Canada*] (NLC) .... BVAFV
Farr's Medical Jurisprudence [*A publication*] (DLA) .... Farr Med Jur
Farrukhabad [*India*] [*ICAO location identifier*] (ICLI) .... VIFB
Farsund [*Norway*] [*Airport symbol*] (OAG) .... FAN
Farthest on Point .... FOP
Farthest-On Circle (NVT) .... FOC
Farthing [*Monetary unit*] [*British*] .... F
Farthing [*Monetary unit*] [*British*] .... FAR
Far-Ultraviolet [*Spectra*] .... FUV
Farwell on Powers [*3 eds.*] [*1874-1916*] [*A publication*] (DLA) .... Farw Pow
Farwell on Powers [*3 eds.*] [*1874-1916*] [*A publication*] (DLA) .... Farwell
Farwell Public Library, Farwell, MI [*Library symbol Library of Congress*] (LCLS) .... MiFaw
Farwell, TX [*FM radio station call letters*] .... KICA
Farwell, TX [*AM radio station call letters*] .... KIJN
Farwell, TX [*FM radio station call letters*] .... KIJN-FM
Farwell, TX [*Television station call letters*] .... KMZN
FAS [*Fixed Airlock Shroud*] **Work Station** .... FWS
Fasa [*Iran*] [*ICAO location identifier*] (ICLI) .... OISF
Fascia Dentata [*Brain anatomy*] .... FD
Fascicle .... FASC
Fascicular Area [*Neurology*] .... FA
Fascicule [*Installment*] [*A publication*] (DLA) .... Fasc
Fasciculus [*Little Bundle*] [*Latin*] (ROG) .... FASC
Fasciculus Longitudinalis Medialis [*Medicine*] (DMAA) .... FLM
Fascimile (VRA) .... fasc
Fascimile Communications (EECA) .... FAXCOM
Fascinating Womanhood [*Title of book by Helen Andelin and of antifeminist seminars*] .... FW
Fascioscapulohumeral [*Medicine*] .... FSH
Fashion .... FASHN
Fashion Aid (EA) .... FA
Fashion Coordination Institute [*Defunct*] (EA) .... FCI
Fashion, Features, and Fluff [*Subject assignments to which female journalists were once limited*] .... 3F's
Fashion Foot Wear Association .... FFANY
Fashion Glamour Set .... FGS
Fashion Group [*Later, TFG*] (EA) .... FG
[*The*] **Fashion Group** (EA) .... TFG
Fashion Group International (EAIO) .... FGI
Fashion Institute of Technology .... FIT

Fashion Institute of Technology, New York, NY [*Library symbol Library of Congress*] (LCLS) ... NNFIT
Fashion Integrated Merchandising Planning and Control System (BUR) ... FIMPACS
Fashion Jewelry Association of America (EA) ... FJAA
Fashion Merchandising, Fashion Design, and/or Interior Design Programs [*Association of Independent Colleges and Schools specialization code*] ... FM
Fashion Originators Guild of America [*Defunct*] (EA) ... FOGA
Fashion Reporters Award - New York ... FRANY
Fashion Sales and Marketing Association [*Australia*] ... FSMA
Fashion Sales and Marketing Association of Western Australia ... FSMAWA
Fashion Teacher's Certificate ... FashTeachCert
Fashion Television [*TV program*] ... FT
Fashion Television [*Video sales technique in the apparel industry*] ... FTV
Fashion Victim [*Women's Wear Daily*] ... FV
Fassberg [*Germany ICAO location identifier*] (ICLI) ... EDNF
Fassey Aviation Ltd. [*Nigeria*] [*FAA designator*] (FAAC) ... FSY
Fast ... F
Fast [*Horse racing*] ... FST
Fast [*Track condition*] [*Thoroughbred racing*] ... FT
Fast Access Current Text ... FACT
Fast Access Current Text Bank [*University of Missouri*] [*Electronic library*] (NITA) ... FACT
Fast Access Information Retrieval ... FAIR
Fast Access Memory [*Computer science*] (HGAA) ... FAM
Fast Access Scan Talker [*Occupational therapy*] ... FAST
Fast Access Storage Technology [*Computer science*] (MHDB) ... FAST
Fast Access to Computerized Technical Sources [*Information service or system*] (IID) ... FACTS
Fast Access to Insurance Requirement (PDAA) ... FAIR
Fast Access to Systems Technical Information ... FASTI
Fast Accurate Refraction Correction [*NASA*] (KSC) ... FARC
Fast Acess Coded Small Image [*Computer science*] (PDAA) ... FACSI
Fast Acquisition Search and Track (MCD) ... FAST
Fast Action on Comments of Technical Significance ... FACTS
Fast Action Procedures (NVT) ... FAP
Fast Aerial Mine [*British military*] (DMA) ... FAM
Fast Affinity Chromatography ... FAC
Fast Agricultural Communication Terminal System [*Purdue University*] [*Information service or system*] ... FACTS
Fast Air Ltda. [*Chile*] [*ICAO designator*] (FAAC) ... FST
Fast Airways BV [*Netherlands ICAO designator*] (ICDA) ... OF
Fast Analog Scanner for Data Acquisition [*Computer science*] (PDAA) ... FASDA
Fast Analysis of Tape and Recovery ... FATAR
Fast and Systematic [*Predicasts Inc.*] [*Set of databases*] (NITA) ... F and S
Fast Anion Exchange [*Chromatography*] ... FAX
Fast Announcement Service [*NTIS publication*] ... FAS
Fast as Can [*Business term*] ... FAC
Fast Asymptotic Coherent Transmission (NVT) ... FACT
Fast Asymptotic Coherent Transmission Extended (MCD) ... FACTEX
Fast at Sea Transfer [*Equipment*] ... FAST
Fast Atmospheric Pulsation ... FAP
Fast Atom Bombardment [*Mass spectrometry*] ... FAB
Fast Atom Bombardment Mass Spectroscopy ... FABMS
Fast Atom Capillaritron Source [*Instrumentation*] ... FACS
Fast Attack Ammunition Support Vehicle [*Army*] (RDA) ... FAASV
Fast Attack Class Submarine [*Navy*] ... FACS
Fast Attack Craft ... FAC
Fast Attack Submarine (MCD) ... FASSN
Fast Attack Vehicle [*Army*] (INF) ... FAV
Fast Automatic Gain Control ... FAGC
Fast Automatic Shuttle Transfer [*System*] [*Navy*] ... FAST
Fast Automatic Transfer ... FAT
Fast Auxiliary Memory (IEEE) ... FAM
Fast Axonal Transport [*Neurobiology*] ... FAT
Fast Blue [*Biological stain*] ... FB
Fast Breeder Reactor [*Nuclear energy*] ... FBR
Fast Breeder Test Reactor [*Nuclear energy*] ... FBTR
Fast Burn Rate ... FBR
Fast Burst Reactor [*Nuclear energy*] ... FBR
Fast Burst Reactor Facility [*Nuclear energy*] ... FBRF
Fast Capacitor Bank ... FCB
Fast Carry Iterative Network (IAA) ... FCIN
Fast Carry-Propagation Iterative Network (PDAA) ... FCIN
Fast Ceramic Reactor [*Program*] ... FCR
Fast Coastal Interceptor [*US Coast Guard vessel*] ... FCI
Fast Combat Support Ship [*Navy symbol*] ... AOE
Fast Component ... FC
Fast Conversion Ratio (NRCH) ... FCR
Fast Cosine Transform [*Mathematics*] ... FCT
Fast Critical Assembly [*Nuclear reactor*] [*Japan*] ... FCA
Fast Cycle Time [*Business term*] ... FCT
Fast Cyclotron Wave [*Electromagnetism*] (IAA) ... FCW
Fast Death Factor [*Medicine*] ... FDF
Fast Delivery Processor [*Computer science*] (EERA) ... FDP
Fast Deployment Logistics Ship [*Navy symbol*] ... FDL
Fast Deployment Logistics Ship [*Navy*] ... FDLS
Fast Digital Processor [*Computer science*] ... FDP
Fast Diode Switch ... FDS
Fast Discrete Cosine Transform (MCD) ... FDCT
Fast Dump Restore (IAA) ... FDR
Fast Economic Language [*Computer science*] (BUR) ... FASTEL
Fast Eigensolution Extraction Routine [*Computer program*] ... FEER
Fast Erect System ... FES
Fast Escape Recallable Missile ... FERM
Fast Evening Persons Report [*Nielsen Television Index*] (NTCM) ... FEP
Fast Extrusion Furnace ... FEF
Fast Fatigue [*Type of muscle contraction*] ... FF
Fast Field Program (KSC) ... FFP
Fast File Manager (NITA) ... FFM
Fast Fission Factor ... FFF
Fast Fleet Replenishment Ship ... FFRS
Fast Floating Point [*Computer science*] ... FFP
Fast Flow ... FF
Fast Flux Test Facility [*Nuclear energy*] ... FFTF
Fast Flux Test Facility Project Office [*Nuclear energy*] (GFGA) ... FFTFPO
Fast Flux Test Reactor [*Nuclear energy*] (OA) ... FFTR
Fast Flying Vestibule [*Old railroad term for a deluxe coach*] ... FFV
Fast Forward [*Audio-visual technology*] ... FF
Fast Forward [*Audio-visual technology*] ... FFWD
Fast Forward-Air-Control [*Marine Corps*] (DOMA) ... FASFAC
Fast Fourier Analyzer (MCD) ... FFA
Fast Fourier Transform [*Mathematics*] ... FFT
Fast Fourier Transform Processor [*Mathematics*] (IAA) ... FFTP
Fast Fourier Transformation [*Noise reduction technique*] (NITA) ... FFT
Fast Fourier-Hadamard Transform (PDAA) ... FFHT
Fast Fractional Gaussian Noise [*Mathematics*] ... ffGn
Fast Free-Form Fabrication [*Engineering design and modeling*] ... FFFF
Fast Freight Line [*Shipping*] ... FFL
Fast Freight Train ... FFT
Fast Frequency on Target ... FFOT
Fast Frequency Shift Keying (MCD) ... FFSK
Fast Gas-Cooled Reactor [*Nuclear energy*] (NUCP) ... FGCR
Fast Glycolytic [*Muscle*] ... FG
Fast Gunboat [*Navy British*] ... FGB
Fast Hartley Transform (BYTE) ... FHT
Fast Heavy Ion Induced Desorption [*Analytical chemistry*] ... FHIID
Fast Hydrofoil Escort ... FHE
Fast Implementation of Real Time Signal Transforms [*University of Edinburgh*] [*Silicone compiler*] [*British*] (NITA) ... FIRST
Fast Index Location Educators ... FILE
Fast Information Retrieval for Surface Transportation [*IBM Corp.*] ... FIRST
Fast Interactive Retrieval System Technology ... FIRST
Fast Interbroker Delivery Service [*Australian Stock Exchange*] ... FIDS
Fast Inter-Library Loans and Statistics [*MacNeal Hospital*] [*Information service or system*] (IID) ... FILLS
Fast Interline Nonactivate Automatic Control [*AT & T*] ... FINAC
Fast Interrupt Request (IAA) ... FIRQ
Fast Ion Bombardment ... FIB
Fast Ion Conduction (PDAA) ... FIC
Fast Library Maintenance ... FLIM
Fast Library Maintenance (NITA) ... FLIM
Fast Linear Displacement Transducer [*Electronics*] ... FLDT
Fast Liner Reactor (MCD) ... FLR
Fast Linkage Editor [*Computer science*] (MHDI) ... FLEE
Fast, Low-Ionization Emission-Line Region [*Planetary science*] ... FLIER
Fast Luciferase Automated Assay of Specimens for Hospitals [*Bacteria analysis*] [*NASA*] ... FLASH
Fast Magnetosonic Wave (PDAA) ... FMW
Fast Memory (IAA) ... FM
Fast Memory Parity Error (IAA) ... FMPE
Fast Missile Boat [*Navy*] ... FMB
Fast Motor Launches (NATG) ... MLF
Fast Moving Object ... FMO
Fast Multiply ... FM
Fast Multiply/Divide Unit (NITA) ... FMDU
Fast Multipole Method [*Physics*] ... FMM
Fast Multitasking Operating System [*MVT Microcomputer Systems, Inc.*] ... FAMOS
Fast Neutron Activation Analysis [*Analytical chemistry*] ... FNAA
Fast Neutron Breeder Reactor [*Nuclear energy*] (DEN) ... FNBR
Fast Neutron Cavity ... FNC
Fast Neutron Dose ... FND
Fast Night Striking Force [*British military*] (DMA) ... FNSF
Fast Operating [*Relay*] ... FO
Fast Orbital Recording of Transient Events Satellite [*Department of Energy*] ... FORTE
Fast Order Radiation Effects Sampling Technique ... FOREST
Fast Oxidative Glycolytic [*Fibers*] [*Neuroanatomy*] ... FOG
Fast Packet Switching [*Telecommunications*] ... FPS
Fast Patrol Boat [*Navy*] (NVT) ... FPB
Fast Patrol Boat [*Ship symbol*] [*NATO*] (NATG) ... PBF
Fast Performance Liquid Chromatography [*Analytical chemistry*] ... FPLC
Fast Prepotential [*Neurophysiology*] ... FPP
Fast Processor [*Instrumentation*] ... FP
Fast Processor Interface [*Computer chip*] ... FPI
Fast Protein, Peptide, and Polynucleotide Liquid Chromatography ... FPLC
Fast Pulse Electron Gun [*NASA*] (NASA) ... EGUN
Fast Pulse Electron Gun (MCD) ... FPEG
Fast Queuing System [*Computer science*] ... FAQS
Fast Reaction Automatic Lightweight Inertial North-Seeking Equipment (PDAA) ... FRALINE
Fast Reaction Fighting System (NATG) ... FRFS
Fast Reaction Integrated Submarine Control [*Navy*] ... FRISCO
Fast Reactivity Exclusion Device [*Nuclear energy*] ... FRED
Fast Reactor Core Test Facility [*Nuclear energy*] ... FRCTF
Fast Reactor Experiment Test [*Proposed but never built*] [*Nuclear energy*] ... FARET
Fast Reactor Safety [*Nuclear energy*] (NRCH) ... FRS
Fast Reactor Thermal Engineering Facility [*Nuclear energy*] (NRCH) ... FRTEF

Fast Reactor Training Center [*Nuclear energy*] (NUCP) .... FRTC
Fast Reading and Understanding Memory Program [*Computer science*] .... FRUMP
Fast Realistic Editor [*Word processing program*] (ADA) .... FRED
Fast Recovery .... FR
Fast Recovery Epitaxial Diode FET [*Field Effect Transistor*] (NITA) .... FRED FET
Fast Recovery Rectifier (IAA) .... FRR
Fast Reference for Engineering Drawings (IAA) .... FRED
Fast Release [*Relay*] .... FR
Fast Relocatable Editing Dump (SAA) .... FRED
Fast Response Action Potential [*Psychology*] .... FRAP
Fast Response Flame Ionization Detector [*Automotive emissions testing*] .... FRFID
Fast Response Survey System [*Washington, DC Department of Education*] (GRD) .... FRSS
Fast Retrieval and Data Manipulator (MCD) .... FRDM
Fast Retrieval Storage [*Computer science*] .... FRS
Fast Rise Balloon .... FRB
Fast Rise Pulse .... FRP
Fast Rise RADAR Reflective Balloon .... FRRRB
Fast Rise Reflective Balloon .... FRRB
Fast Rope Insertion/Extraction System [*for rappeling*] [*Military*] (RDA) .... FRIES
Fast Scan Cutoff (CAAL) .... FASCO
Fast Scan Television [*Computer science*] (IAA) .... FSTV
Fast Screening .... FS
Fast Sealift Ship [*Navy*] (DOMA) .... FSS
Fast Sealift Ship .... TAKRX
Fast Settle Mode .... FSM
Fast Settle Operation .... FSO
Fast Slew .... FS
Fast Slew Rate .... FSR
Fast Space Charge Wave (IAA) .... FSCW
Fast Steering Mirror [*Optical instrumentation*] .... FSM
Fast Store [*Computer science*] (TEL) .... FS
Fast Supercritical Pressure Power Reactor .... FSPPR
Fast Supply [*Ships*] .... FS
Fast Test Reactor .... FTR
Fast Time Analysis .... FTA
Fast Time Analyzer System .... FTAS
Fast Time Constant [*RADAR*] .... FTC
Fast Time Control (IAA) .... FTC
Fast Torpedo Boat [*NATO*] .... FTB
Fast Track [*Insurance*] .... FT
Fast Transient Loader .... FTL
Fast Transit Link [*Rapid-transit term*] .... FTL
Fast Walsh Transform [*Spectrometry*] .... FWT
Fast Wave Simple Harmonic Motion [*A microwave tube device*] ..... FAWSHMOTRON
Fast Weekly Household Audience Report [*Nielsen Television Index*] (NTCM) .... FWH
Fast-Acess Charge-Coupled Memory [*Computer science*] (WDAA) .... FACCM
Fast-Acting Fuse .... FAF
Fast-Binding Target-Attaching Globulin [*Medicine*] (MEDA) .... F-TAG
Fast-Burn Booster [*Rocketry*] .... FBB
FastComm Communications [*NASDAQ symbol*] (TTSB) .... FSCX
FastComm Communications Corp. [*Associated Press*] (SAG) .... FastCm
FastComm Communications Corp. [*NASDAQ symbol*] (NQ) .... FSCX
Fasten [*Technical drawings*] .... FAS
Fastenal Co. [*NASDAQ symbol*] (NQ) .... FAST
Fastenal Co. [*Associated Press*] (SAG) .... Fastenal
Fastener .... FAS
Fastener .... FSTNR
Fastener Installation Procedure [*Manual*] (MCD) .... FIP
Fastener Testing Development (MCD) .... FTD
Fasteners and Hardware (SAA) .... FH
Fasteners Institute of Australia .... FIA
Fasteners Research Council [*Defunct*] (EA) .... FRC
Fastening [*or Fastener*] [*Automotive engineering*] .... FAST
Faster Adoption of Superior Technologies .... FAST
Faster and Safer Travel/Traffic Routing and Advanced Control [*FHWA*] (TAG) .... FAST-TRAC
FASTER [*Filing and Source Data Entry Techniques for Easier Retrieval*] Language Translation System (MHDI) .... FLTS
Faster Than Light [*Science fiction*] (AAG) .... FTL
Faster-Than-Light Drive (AAG) .... FTLD
Fastest Lap [*Auto racing*] .... FL
Fastest Time of the Day [*Auto racing*] .... FTD
Fast-Fourier Transforms (DAVI) .... FFT
Fast-Frequency Hopping (MCD) .... FFH
Fasti [*of Ovid*] [*Classical studies*] (OCD) .... Fast
Fasting [*Test*] [*Medicine*] .... F
Fasting Blood Glucose [*Physiology*] (AAMN) .... FBG
Fasting Blood Sugar [*Physiology*] (DAVI) .... FB
Fasting Blood Sugar [*Physiology*] .... FBS
Fasting Blood Work [*Biochemistry*] (DAVI) .... FBW
Fasting Chemistry Profile (DAVI) .... FCP
Fasting Glucose [*Endocrinology*] (DAVI) .... FGLU
Fasting Glycocholic Acid [*Clinical chemistry*] .... FGA
Fasting Hyperbilirubinemia [*Medicine*] (DMAA) .... FH
Fasting Intestinal Contents [*Gastroenterology*] (DAVI) .... FIC
Fatima Intestinal Flow Rate (MAE) .... FIFR
Fasting Metabolic Panel [*Biochemistry*] (DAVI) .... FMP
Fasting Metabolic Rate (PDAA) .... FMR
Fasting Plasma Glucose [*Medicine*] .... FPG
Fasting Serum Glucose [*Clinical chemistry*] .... FSG
Fasting-Total Bile Acids [*Physiology*] .... F-TBA
Fast-Moving Consumer Goods (DS) .... FMCG

Fast-Moving Industrializing Country .... FIC
Fast-Page-Mode [*Computer science*] (PCM) .... FPM
Fast-Payback Capital Investment Program [*Air Force*] .... FASCAP
Fast-Payback System (MCD) .... FPS
Fast-Rate Electro-Deposition Plating [*Automotive engineering*] .... FRED
Fast-Response Relief Valve (MCD) .... FRRV
Fast-Response Solar Array Simulator .... FRSAS
Fat .... F
Fat Binding Capacity [*Food technology*] .... FBC
Fat Embolism Syndrome [*Medicine*] (CPH) .... FES
Fat Free [*Biochemistry*] .... FF
Fat Globules [*Biochemistry*] (DAVI) .... FATG
Fat Head Minnow .... FHM
Fat Lip Readers Theater (EA) .... FLRT
Fatah Revolutionary Council [*Libyan-based terrorist organization*] .... FRC
Fatal Accident Circumstances and Epidemiology [*National Institute for Occupational Safety and Health*] .... FACE
Fatal Accident Frequency Rate .... FAFR
Fatal Accident Reduction Effort [*or Enforcement*] [*Department of Transportation*] .... FARE
Fatal Accident Reporting System [*National Highway Traffic Safety Administration*] [*Washington, DC*] (GRD) .... FARS
Fatal Casualties Vulnerability Number (SAA) .... FCVN
Fatal Dose .... FD
Fatal Familial Insomnia [*Medicine*] .... FFI
Fatal Granulomatous Disease (MAE) .... FGD
Fatal Heart Sound [*Medicine*] (DHSM) .... FHS
Fatalities [*Military*] (DOMA) .... FAT
Fat-Corrected Milk .... FCM
Fate of Atmospheric Pollutants Study [*National Science Foundation*] .... FAPS
Fat-Free Body .... FFB
Fat-Free Body Mass .... FFBM
Fat-Free Dry Weight .... FFDW
Fat-Free Mass (MAE) .... FFM
Fat-Free Solids .... FFS
Fat-Free Supper [*Medicine*] .... FFS
Fat-Free Wet Weight .... FFWW
Father .... F
Father (DSUE) .... FA
Father .... FR
Father .... FR
Father Factor [*Medicine*] (MAE) .... FF
Father Moriarty Asylum Project [*Defunct*] (EA) .... FMAP
Father Moriarty Central American Refugee Program [*Later, FMAP*] (EA) .... FMCARP
Father of Baby (DAVI) .... FOB
Father of Chapel [*Shop steward*] [*British*] .... FOC
Father of Chapel [*Shop steward*] [*British*] (ODBW) .... FoC
Father of Child (DAVI) .... FOC
Father of Sion [*Roman Catholic*] .... FS
Father R. Perin School, Chard, Alberta [*Library symbol National Library of Canada*] (BIB) .... ACHFS
Fatherhood Project (EA) .... FP
Fatherland Party of Labor [*Bulgaria*] [*Political party*] .... FPL
Fathers Are Forever [*Defunct*] (EA) .... FAF
Fathers Day Council (EA) .... FDC
Fathers for Equal Rights (EA) .... FER
Father's Grandfather (MAE) .... FGF
Father's Grandmother (MAE) .... FGM
Fathers of Sion [*An association British*] (BI) .... FS
Fathers Rights and Equality Exchange (EA) .... FREE
Father's Rights of America (EA) .... FRA
Fathom .... F
Fathom (NATG) .... FAT
Fathom .... FATH
Fathom .... FM
Fathom .... FTH
Fathom (ROG) .... FTHM
Fathom Oceanology Ltd. [*Toronto Stock Exchange symbol*] .... FAM
Fathometer Depth Sounder .... FDS
Fatigue [*Slang*] (DSUE) .... FAG
Fatigue (WDAA) .... FAT
Fatigue Crack Growth [*Metals*] (PDAA) .... FCG
Fatigue Crack Growth Rate [*Metals*] .... FCGR
Fatigue Crack Propagation (OA) .... FCP
Fatigue Cracking Test .... FCT
Fatigue Index [*Aircraft strain/fatigue scale*] [*British*] .... FI
Fatigue Indicating Meter Attachment .... FATIMA
Fatigue Life Assessment Expert [*Automotive engineering*] .... FLAE
Fatigue Life Expectancy [*or Expended*] (MCD) .... FLE
Fatigue Life Modification Expert [*Automotive engineering*] .... FLME
Fatigue Limit .... FL
Fatigue Monitoring System (MCD) .... FMS
Fatigue Resistant .... FR
Fatigue Scales Kit [*Psychology*] .... FSK
Fatigue Test Article (NASA) .... FTA
Fatigue Time [*Sports medicine*] .... FT
Fatigue-Decreased Proficiency Boundary .... FDPB
Fatima [*Bolivia*] [*ICAO location identifier*] (ICLI) .... SLFA
Fat-Induced Hyperglycemia [*Medicine*] .... FIH
Fat-Mobilizing Hormone [*Medicine*] .... FMH
Fat-Mobilizing Substance [*Medicine*] .... FMS
Fatphobia Awareness Training .... FAT
Fats and Oils Situation .... FOS
Fats and Proteins Research Foundation (EA) .... FPRF

Fats, Oils, and Grease [Food plant effluent] .... FOG
Fat-Specific Element [Genetics] .... FSE
Fatstock Marketing Corp. [British] .... FMC
Fat-Storing Cell [Liver anatomy] .... FSC
Fatty Acid [Biochemistry] (HGAA) .... F
Fatty Acid [Biochemistry] .... FA
Fatty Acid Alkanolamide [Organic chemistry] .... FAA
Fatty Acid Amide Hydrolase [An enzyme] .... FAAH
Fatty Acid Binding Protein [Biochemistry] .... FABP
Fatty Acid Ethyl Ester .... FAEE
Fatty Acid Methyl Ester [Biochemistry] .... FAME
Fatty Acid Producers' Council (EA) .... FAPC
Fatty Acid Synthase [An enzyme] .... FAS
Fatty Acid-Free [Biochemistry] .... FAF
Fatty Amine Oxide [Organic chemistry] .... FAO
Fatty Oil .... FO
Fatty-Acid Cellulos Esters [Organic chemistry] .... FACE
Fatundu [Zaire] [ICAO location identifier] (ICLI) .... FZCT
Faucet .... FCT
Faucett [ICAO designator] (AD) .... CF
Faucett Peruvian Airlines [Airline flight code] (ODBW) .... CF
Faucher Aviation [France ICAO designator] (FAAC) .... FAU
Faujasite [A zeolite] .... FAU
Faulding, Inc. [NASDAQ symbol] (SAG) .... FAUL
Faulding Inc. [NASDAQ symbol] (TTSB) .... FAUL
Faulding, Inc. [Associated Press] (SAG) .... Faulding
Faulkner University, Jones School of Law, Montgomery, AL [Library
symbol] [Library of Congress] (LCLS) .... AMF-L
Fault .... FLT
Fault Analysis Process (TEL) .... FAP
Fault and Facility Control (IAA) .... FFC
Fault Control Management [Automotive diagnostics] .... FCM
Fault Control Module (TEL) .... FCM
Fault Detect Verification .... FDV
Fault Detection (MCD) .... FD
Fault Detection and Annunciation (NASA) .... FDA
Fault Detection and Diagnosis System [Automotive service electronics] .... FDDS
Fault Detection and Identification (MCD) .... FDI
Fault Detection and Isolation (NASA) .... FDI
Fault Detection and Isolation Subsystem (RDA) .... FDIS
Fault Detection/Fault Location [Military] (CAAL) .... FD/FL
Fault Detection Identification/Isolation and Recovery/Recognition
(NASA) .... FDIR
Fault Detection, Isolation, Identification, and Recompensation (NASA) ...... FDIIR
Fault Detection/Location Subsystem .... FD/LS
Fault Detection Tester .... FDT
Fault Directory .... FD
Fault Hazard Analysis [Hazard quantification method] .... FHA
Fault Identification (MCD) .... FI
Fault Inferring Nonlinear Detection System [NASA] .... FINDS
Fault Isolater and Exerciser [Honeywell] (NITA) .... FIX
Fault Isolation .... FI
Fault Isolation Analysis (MCD) .... FIA
Fault Isolation and Monitoring System [NGT] (MCD) .... FIMS
Fault Isolation by Nodal Dependency (MCD) .... FIND
Fault Isolation by Semiautomatic Techniques [National Institute of Standards
and Technology] .... FIST
Fault Isolation Checkout System .... FICS
Fault Isolation Code .... FIC
Fault Isolation Detection (MCD) .... FID
Fault Isolation Diagnostics (MCD) .... FID
Fault Isolation Equipment (MCD) .... FIE
Fault Isolation Maintainability Analysis (MCD) .... FIMA
Fault Isolation Meter (MCD) .... FIM
Fault Isolation Module (CAAL) .... FIM
Fault Isolation Procedure .... FIP
Fault Isolation Requirement Document (MCD) .... FIRD
Fault Isolation Routine .... FIR
Fault Isolation Software (CAAL) .... FIS
Fault Isolation Test .... FIT
Fault Isolation Test Adapter (MCD) .... FITA
Fault Isolation Time (MCD) .... FIT
Fault Localization (CAAL) .... FL
Fault Localization .... FLOC
Fault Location and Monitoring (AABC) .... FLAM
Fault Location and Repair (AABC) .... FLAR
Fault Location Facility [Aircraft] .... FLF
Fault Location Indicating Console (AABC) .... FLIC
Fault Location Indicator .... FLI
Fault Location Panel [Aerospace] (AAG) .... FLP
Fault Location Technology [or Test] (IEEE) .... FLT
Fault Location Test (IAA) .... FLT
Fault Location through Interpretive Testing [Computer science] .... FLIT
Fault Location Unit [Aerospace] (AAG) .... FLU
Fault Location Word (MCD) .... FLW
Fault Locator Cable .... FLC
Fault Locator System (AABC) .... FLS
Fault Logic Diagram .... FLD
Fault Message Line (MCD) .... FML
Fault Monitor (TEL) .... FM
Fault of Management .... FOM
Fault Repair Service [Telecommunications British] .... FRS
Fault Report Point (TEL) .... FRP
Fault Reporting Module (TEL) .... FRM
Fault Servicing Process (TEL) .... FSP

Fault Simulation Comparator .... FSC
Fault Summary (MCD) .... FS
Fault Summary Page (MCD) .... FSP
Fault Tolerance System .... FTS
Fault Tolerant (HGAA) .... FT
Fault Tolerant Compiler (NITA) .... FTC
Fault Tolerant Multiprocessor System [Computer science] (HGAA) .... FTM
Fault Tolerant Multiprocessor System [Computer science] .... FTMP
Fault Tolerant/Online Transaction Processing (NITA) .... FT/OLTP
Fault Tolerant Spaceborne Computer .... FTSC
Fault Tolerant System Architecture [Computer science] .... FTSA
Fault Tolerant UNIX (CDE) .... FTX
Fault Transfer Facility (NITA) .... FTR
Fault Tree (MCD) .... FT
Fault Tree Analysis (NASA) .... FTA
Fault Warning Computer [Aviation] (DA) .... FWC
Faulte de Medecine Veterinaire de l'Universite de Montreal, Saint-
Hyacinthe, Quebec [Library symbol National Library of Canada]
(NLC) .... QSTHV
Faulted Circuit (IAA) .... FC
Fault-Location Oscillator [Bell System] .... FLO
Faultsman's Ring Back [Telecommunications] (NITA) .... FRB
Fault-Tolerant Computing .... FTC
Faulty Abbreviation [Used in correcting manuscripts, etc.] .... AB
Faulty Agreement [Used in correcting manuscripts, etc.] .... AGR
Faulty Capitalization [Used in correcting manuscripts, etc.] .... CAP
Faulty Diction [Used in correcting manuscripts, etc.] .... D
Faulty Magazine [Military] (MCD) .... FM
Faulty Punctuation [Used in correcting manuscripts, etc.] .... P
Faulty Sentence Structure [Used in correcting manuscripts, etc.] .... SS
Fauna and Flora Preservation Society (EA) .... FFPS
Fauna and Flora Reserve [State] (EERA) .... FFR
Fauna Impact Statement .... FIS
Fauna Preservation Society [Later, FFPS] (EA) .... FPS
Fauquier-Strickland Public Library, Fauquier, ON, Canada [Library symbol]
[Library of Congress] (LCLS) .... CaOFauS
Fauquier-Strickland Public Library, Fauquier, Ontario [Library symbol
National Library of Canada] (BIB) .... OFS
Faust Community Library, Alberta [Library symbol National Library of
Canada] (NLC) .... AFC
Faust's Compiled Laws [Scotland] [A publication] (DLA) .... Faust
Favor (WDAA) .... FAV
Favorable (AFM) .... FAV
Favorite (ADA) .... FAV
Favorite Picture Selection [Photo CD feature] (PCM) .... FPS
Favrile Glass (VRA) .... fvrl gls
Fawcett Association [A union] [British] .... FA
Fawcett. Court of Referees [1866] [A publication] (DLA) .... Fawc Ref
Fawcett on Landlord and Tenant [3 eds.] [1870-1905] [A publication]
(DLA) .... Fawc
Fawcett on Landlord and Tenant [3 eds.] [1870-1905] [A publication]
(DLA) .... Fawc L & T
Fawcett on Landlord and Tenant [3rd ed.] [1905] [A publication] (ILCA) .... Fawcett
Fawcett Public Library, Alberta [Library symbol National Library of Canada]
(NLC) .... AFAW
Fawn (WGA) .... F
Fax Like You Print [3X USA] (PCM) .... FLYP
FaxSav Inc. [Associated Press] (SAG) .... FaxSav
FaxSav Inc. [NASDAQ symbol] (SAG) .... FAXX
Faya Largeau [Chad] [Airport symbol] (AD) .... FYA
Faya-Largeau [Chad] [ICAO location identifier] (ICLI) .... FTTY
Fayalite [CIPW classification] [Geology] .... fa
Fayalite Magnetite Quartz (Buffer) [Geophysics] .... FMQ
Fayban Air Services [Nigeria] [FAA designator] (FAAC) .... FAY
Fayence [France ICAO location identifier] (ICLI) .... LFMF
Fayette, AL [AM radio station call letters] .... WLDX
Fayette, AL [FM radio station call letters] .... WTXT
Fayette Community Library, Fayette, IA [Library symbol Library of
Congress] (LCLS) .... IaFay
Fayette County Bancshares, Inc. [Associated Press] (SAG) .... Fayette
Fayette County Bancshares, Inc. [NASDAQ symbol] (SAG) .... FCBS
Fayette County Bancshrs [NASDAQ symbol] (TTSB) .... FCBS
Fayette County Court House, Fayette, AL [Library symbol Library of
Congress] (LCLS) .... AFC
Fayette County Courthouse, West Union, IA [Library symbol Library of
Congress] (LCLS) .... IaWuCoC
Fayette County Free Library, Somerville, TN [Library symbol Library of
Congress] (LCLS) .... TSo
Fayette County Helpers Club and Historical Society, Fayette, IA [Library
symbol Library of Congress] (LCLS) .... IaFayHHi
Fayette County Public Library, Fayetteville, WV [Library symbol Library of
Congress] (LCLS) .... WvFa
Fayette County Union, West Union, IA [Library symbol Library of Congress]
(LCLS) .... IaWuU
Fayette Leader, Fayette, IA [Library symbol Library of Congress] (LCLS) ...... IaFayL
Fayette Legal Journal [Pennsylvania] [A publication] (ILCA) .... Fay LJ
Fayette Legal Journal [Pennsylvania] [A publication] (DLA) .... Fayette Leg J (PA)
Fayette, MO [FM radio station call letters] (RBYB) .... KLSC-FM
Fayette, MS [FM radio station call letters] .... WTYJ
Fayetteville [Arkansas] [Seismograph station code, US Geological Survey]
(SEIS) .... FAV
Fayetteville [Arkansas] [Seismograph station code, US Geological Survey
Closed] (SEIS) .... FAY
Fayetteville [North Carolina] [Airport symbol] (OAG) .... FAY
Fayetteville [Arkansas] [Airport symbol] (OAG) .... FYV

Fayetteville, AR [*Location identifier FAA*] (FAAL) ... DAK
Fayetteville, AR [*Location identifier FAA*] (FAAL) ... FYV
Fayetteville, AR [*Television station call letters*] ... KAFT
Fayetteville, AR [*FM radio station call letters*] ... KEZA
Fayetteville, AR [*Television station call letters*] ... KHOG
Fayetteville, AR [*FM radio station call letters*] ... KKEG
Fayetteville, AR [*FM radio station call letters*] ... KKIX
Fayetteville, AR [*AM radio station call letters*] ... KOFC
Fayetteville, AR [*FM radio station call letters*] ... KUAF
Fayetteville, AR [*Location identifier FAA*] (FAAL) ... RZC
Fayetteville Area Health Education Foundation, Inc., Fayetteville, NC [*Library symbol Library of Congress*] (LCLS) ... NcFayH
Fayetteville/Drake Field [*Arkansas*] [*ICAO location identifier*] (ICLI) ... KFYV
Fayetteville Flying Service & Scheduled Skyways System [*ICAO designator*] (FAAC) ... SKM
Fayetteville/Fort Bragg, NC [*Location identifier FAA*] (FAAL) ... FBG
Fayetteville/Fort Bragg, NC [*Location identifier FAA*] (FAAL) ... UPI
Fayetteville/Fort Bragg, NC [*Location identifier FAA*] (FAAL) ... VRY
Fayetteville Free Library, Fayetteville, NY [*Library symbol Library of Congress*] (LCLS) ... NFay
Fayetteville, GA [*FM radio station call letters*] (RBYB) ... WHTA
Fayetteville, NC [*Location identifier FAA*] (FAAL) ... FAY
Fayetteville, NC [*Location identifier FAA*] (FAAL) ... GRA
Fayetteville, NC [*Location identifier FAA*] (FAAL) ... POB
Fayetteville, NC [*AM radio station call letters*] ... WFAI
Fayetteville, NC [*AM radio station call letters*] ... WFLB
Fayetteville, NC [*AM radio station call letters*] ... WFNC
Fayetteville, NC [*FM radio station call letters*] ... WFSS
Fayetteville, NC [*AM radio station call letters*] ... WIDU
Fayetteville, NC [*Television station call letters*] ... WKFT
Fayetteville, NC [*FM radio station call letters*] ... WQSM
Fayetteville/Pope Air Force Base [*North Carolina*] [*ICAO location identifier*] (ICLI) ... KPOB
Fayetteville State Teachers College [*Later, Fayetteville State University*] [*North Carolina*] ... FSTC
Fayetteville State University, Fayetteville, NC [*Library symbol Library of Congress*] (LCLS) ... NcFayS
Fayetteville State University, Fayetteville, NC [*OCLC symbol*] (OCLC) ... NFS
Fayetteville Technical Institute, Fayetteville, NC [*Library symbol Library of Congress*] (LCLS) ... NcFayT
Fayetteville, TN [*Location identifier FAA*] (FAAL) ... FYM
Fayetteville, TN [*AM radio station call letters*] ... WEKR
Fayetteville, TN [*FM radio station call letters*] ... WYTM
Fayetville, NC [*Television station call letters*] ... WFAY
Fay's, Inc. [*NYSE symbol*] (SPSG) ... FAY
Fays, Inc. [*Associated Press*] (SAG) ... FaysInc
FBA Pharmaceuticals Ltd. [*Great Britain*] [*Research code symbol*] ... FBA
FBL Financial Group [*Associated Press*] (SAG) ... FBL Fn
FBL Financial Group [*NYSE symbol*] (SAG) ... FFG
FBM [*Fleet Ballistic Missile*] **Support Ship** ... TAGS
FC Financial Corp. [*Vancouver Stock Exchange symbol*] ... FCN
FCA International Ltd. [*Toronto Stock Exchange symbol*] ... FC
FCB Financial [*NASDAQ symbol*] (TTSB) ... FCBF
FCB Financial Corp. [*Associated Press*] (SAG) ... FCB Fn
FCB Financial Corp. [*NASDAQ symbol*] (SAG) ... FCBF
FCES Automated Software Test (MCD) ... FAST
FCMI Financial Corp. [*Toronto Stock Exchange symbol*] ... FCM
FCNB Corp. [*NASDAQ symbol*] (SAG) ... FCNB
FDA [*Food and Drug Administration*] **Consumer** [*A publication*] (DLA) ... FDA Cons
F'Derick [*Mauritania*] [*ICAO location identifier*] (ICLI) ... GQPF
FDP Corp. [*Associated Press*] (SAG) ... FDP
FDP Corp. [*NASDAQ symbol*] (SAG) ... FDPC
FDresenius Medical Care AG [*Associated Press*] (SAG) ... FresM
FDTE Master (MCD) ... FM
Feachtas Dt-Armail Eithneach nah Eireann [*Irish Campaign for Nuclear Disarmament*] (EAIO) ... FDE
Fear, Love, Anger, and Pain [*Cognitive system*] ... FLAP
Fear of Death ... FOD
Fear of Negative Evaluation Scale (EDAC) ... FNE
Fear of Obesity ... FOO
Fear Survey Schedule [*Psychology*] ... FSS
Fear, Tension, Pain [*Syndrome*] [*Psychology*] (BARN) ... FTP
Fear, Uncertainty, and Doubt [*Factors hindering sales of lesser-known products*] ... FUD
Fearful, Irritable, Tense, and Tremulous [*Combat behavior disorder*] [*Military*] (INF) ... F-I-T-T
Fearne on Contingent Remainders [*1722-1844*] [*A publication*] (DLA) ... FCR
Fearne on Contingent Remainders [*1722-1844*] [*A publication*] (DLA) ... Fear Rem
Fearne's Posthumous Works [*A publication*] (DLA) ... Fea Posth
Feasibility Ascension Cape Town [*Project*] [*Marine science*] (OSRA) ... FACT
Feasibility Ascension Cape Town [*Project*] (USDC) ... FACT
Feasibility Demonstration Model ... FDM
Feasibility Guidance Document ... FSGD
Feasibility of Rocket Energy Employment (MCD) ... FREE
Feasibility Study ... FS
Feasibility Study Change Proposal (MCD) ... FSCP
Feasibility Validation Program ... FVP
Feasible (MSA) ... FSBL
Feasible Ideal System (MHDI) ... FIS
Feasible Ideal System Target (MHDI) ... FIST
Feast ... F
Feather ... FE
Feather [*Aircraft engine*] (DNAB) ... FEA
Feather (MSA) ... FTR
Feather and Down Association (EA) ... FDA
Feather Falls [*California*] [*Seismograph station code, US Geological Survey Closed*] (SEIS) ... FEA
Feather River [*AAR code*] ... FR
Feather River Project ... FRP
Feather River Project Association (BARN) ... FRPA
Feather Weight Automotive [*Auto racing engine model designation*] [*British*] ... FWA
Feather Weight Marine [*Auto racing engine model designation*] [*British*] ... FWM
Feather Weight Marine Automotive [*Auto racing engine model designation*] [*British*] ... FWMA
Feather Weight Marine Twin Cam [*Auto racing engine model designation*] [*British*] ... FWMC
Feather Weight Pump [*Auto racing engine model designation*] [*British*] ... FWP
Feathered [*Aviation*] (FAAC) ... FTHRD
Feathered Pipe Foundation (EA) ... FPF
Featherlite Manufacturing, Inc. [*Associated Press*] (SAG) ... Feathrlte
Featherlite Manufacturing, Inc. [*NASDAQ symbol*] (SAG) ... FTHR
Featherlite Mfg [*NASDAQ symbol*] (TTSB) ... FTHR
Featherly Pass [*Alaska*] [*Seismograph station code, US Geological Survey*] (SEIS) ... FLP
Feathers (VRA) ... fthrs
Featherston Camp Trumpet Band [*British military*] (DMA) ... FCTB
Feature Analysis Comparison and Evaluation Library (PDAA) ... FACEL
Feature Analysis System [*Image analysis*] ... FAS
Feature Correlation ... FC
Feature Count [*Computer science*] ... FC
Feature Film Only (ADA) ... F/O
Feature Group ... FG
Feature Identification and Landmark Experiment [*NASA*] ... FILE
Feature Protection Area [*Conservation*] [*Australia*] ... FPA
Feature Recognition Processor ... FRP
Features, Advantages, Benefits [*of clothing*] [*Retailing*] ... FAB
Febre Durante [*During the Fever*] [*Pharmacy*] (ROG) ... FEB DUR
Febrifuge [*Allaying Fever Heat*] [*Pharmacy*] (ROG) ... FEB
Febrile [*Medicine*] (DAVI) ... feb
Febrile Agglutinin [*Serology*] (CPH) ... feb agglut
Febrile Agglutinins [*Immunochemistry*] (DAVI) ... FEBRIL
Febrile Antigen [*Immunology*] (MAE) ... FA
Febrile Battery-Acute [*Medicine*] (DAVI) ... FEBROA
Febrile Convulsion [*Medicine*] (DMAA) ... FC
Febris [*Fever*] [*Pharmacy*] ... FEB
February ... F
February (CDAI) ... Fb
February (ADA) ... FE
February (EY) ... FEB
February (ODBW) ... Feb
February and August [*Denotes semiannual payments of interest or dividends in these months*] [*Business term*] ... F & A
February Group [*An association*] (EA) ... FG
February, May, August, November [*Denotes quarterly payments of interest or dividends in these months*] [*Business term*] ... FMAN
Fecal [*Medicine*] (DAVI) ... FEC
Fecal Alpha 1 - Antitrypsin [*Clinical chemistry*] ... FA1AT
Fecal Blood Loss [*Medicine*] ... FBL
Fecal Coli [*Microbiology*] ... FC
Fecal Collection Device [*NASA*] ... FCD
Fecal Collection Receptacle Assembly [*NASA*] (KSC) ... FCRA
Fecal Containment System [*NASA*] ... FCS
Fecal Emesis ... FE
Fecal Energy [*Nutrition*] ... FE
Fecal Frequency (MAE) ... FF
Fecal Management System [*NASA*] (KSC) ... FMS
Fecal Occult Blood [*Medicine*] (MAE) ... FOB
Fecal Occult Blood Test [*Medicine*] ... FOBT
Fecal Pellet ... FP
Fecal Urobilinogen [*Clinical chemistry*] ... FU
Fecerunt [*They Did It*] [*Latin*] (ADA) ... FEC
Fecerunt [*They Did It*] [*Latin*] ... FF
Feces ... F
Fecit [*He, or She, Did It*] [*Latin*] ... F
Fecit [*He, or She, Did It*] [*Latin*] ... FEC
Fed One Bancorp [*Associated Press*] (SAG) ... FedOne
Fed One Bancorp [*NASDAQ symbol*] (SAG) ... FOBC
Fed One Bancorp [*NASDAQ symbol*] (TTSB) ... FOBC
Fed One Savings Bank [*Associated Press*] (SAG) ... FedOne
Fed One Savings Bank [*NASDAQ symbol*] (SAG) ... FOBC
Fedders Corp'A' [*NYSE symbol*] (TTSB) ... FJA
Fedders Corp. [*Associated Press*] (SAG) ... FederA
Fedders Corp. [*Associated Press*] (SAG) ... Feders
Fedders Corp. [*NYSE symbol*] (SAG) ... FJ
Fedders Corp. [*NYSE symbol*] (SAG) ... FJA
Fedders Corp. [*NYSE symbol*] (SAG) ... FJC
Federacion Cafetalera de America [*Central American Coffee Growers' Federation*] ... FEDECAME
Federacion de Comunidades Judias de Centroamerica y Panama [*Federation of Jewish Communities of Central America and Panama*] (EAIO) ... FEDECO
Federacion de Estudiantes Revolucionarios [*Federation of Revolutionary Students*] [*Uruguay*] (PD) ... FER
Federacion de Partidos Democraticas y Liberales [*Federation of Democratic and Liberal Parties*] [*Spain Political party*] (PPE) ... FPDL
Federacion de Sociedades Hispanas [*Defunct*] (EA) ... FSH
Federacion de Trabajadores Nicaraguenses [*Political party*] (EY) ... FTN
Federacion de Trabajadores Revolucionarios [*Revolutionary Workers' Federation*] [*El Salvador*] (PD) ... FTR

Federacion de Universidades Privadas de America Central .... FUPAC
Federacion de Universitarios de Uruguay [Federation of University Students of Uruguay] (PD) .... FUU
Federacion del Trabajo de Puerto Rico [Puerto Rican Federation of Labor] .... FTPR
Federacion Democrata Cristiana [Christian Democratic Federation] [Spain Political party] (PPE) .... FDC
Federacion Democratica Internacional de Mujeres [Women's International Democratic Federation] .... FDIM
Federacion Espeleologica de America Latina y el Caribe [Speleological Federation of Latin America and the Caribbean] (EAIO) .... FEALC
Federacion Interamericana de Abogados [Washington, DC] .... FIA
Federacion Interamericana de Asociaciones de Secretarias [Inter-American Federation of Secretaries] [San Salvador, El Salvador] (EAIO) .... FIAS
Federacion Interamericana de la Industria de la Construccion [Inter-American Federation of the Construction Industry - IAFCI] (EAIO) .... FIIC
Federacion Interamericana de Periodistas y Escritores de Turismo [Interamerican Federation of Journalists and Writers in the Tourist Trade] .... FIPET
Federacion Interamericana de Touring y Automovil Clubes [Inter-American Federation of Touring and Automobile Clubs - IFTAC] (EAIO) .... FITAC
Federacion Interamericana de Trabajadores de la Industria Textil, Vestuario, Cuero, y Calzado [Interamerican Textile, Leather, Garment, and Shoe Workers Federation - ITLGSWF] (EA) .... FITITVCC
Federacion Interamericana de Trabajadores de la Industria Textil, Vestuario , y Cuero [Interamerican Textile, Garment, and Leather Workers Federation] .... FITITV
Federacion Interamericana de Trabajadores del Espectaculo [Interamerican Federation of Entertainment Workers] .... FITE
Federacion Internacional de Asociaciones de Ferreteros y Almacenistas de Hierros [International Federation of Ironmongers and Iron Merchants Associations] .... FIDAF
Federacion Internacional de Documentacion [International Federation for Documentation - IFD] [Spanish Information service or system] (ASF) .... FID
Federacion Internacional de Medecina Fisica [International Federation of Physical Medicine] .... FIMF
Federacion Internacional de Oleicultura [International Olive Oil Federation] [Rome, Italy] [Defunct] (EA) .... FIO
Federacion Internacional de Pelota Vasca [International Federation of Pelota Vasca - IFPV] (EA) .... FIPV
Federacion Internacional de Periodistas [International Federation of Journalists] .... FIP
Federacion Internacional de Trabajadores de las Industrias Metalurgicas [International Metalworkers' Federation] .... FITIM
Federacion Internacional de Trabajadores Petroleros y Quimicos [International Federation of Petroleum and Chemical Workers] .... FITPQ
Federacion Internacional de Vivienda y Urbanismo [International Federation for Housing and Planning] .... FIVU
Federacion Latinoamericana de Asociaciones de Familiares de Detenidos-Desaparecidos [Federation of Associations of Families of Disappeared-Detainees] (EAIO) .... FEDEFAM
Federacion Latinoamericana de Bancos [Latin American Banking Federation - LABF] [Bogota, Colombia] (EAIO) .... FELABAN
Federacion Latinoamericana de Hospitales [Latin American Hospital Federation] (EAIO) .... FLH
Federacion Latinoamericana de Parasitologos .... FLAP
Federacion Latinoamericana de Termalismo [Latin American Federation of Thermalism and Climatism - LAFTC] [Buenos Aires, Argentina] (EAIO) .... FLT
Federacion Latinoamericana de Trajabadores de la Prensa [Latin American Federation of Press Workers] (EAIO) .... FELATRAP
Federacion Latinoamericana de Usuarios del Transporte [Latin American Federation of Shippers' Councils] (EAIO) .... FELACUTI
Federacion Mundial Cristiana de Estudiantes [World Student Christian Federation] .... FMCE
Federacion Mundial de Instituciones Financieras de Desarrollo [World Federation of Development Financing Institutions - WFDFI] [Madrid, Spain] (EAIO) .... FEMIDE
Federacion Mundial de Sindicatos de Industrias [World Federation of Industrial Workers' Unions] .... FEMUSI
Federacion Obrera Revolucionaria [Mexican political party] .... FOR
Federacion Odontologica Centro America y Panama [Odontological Federation of Central America and Panama] .... FOCAP
Federacion Panamericana de Asociaciones de Arquitectos [Panamerican Federation of Architects' Associations] (EA) .... FPAA
Federacion Panamericana de Asociacions de Facultades de Medicina [Pan American Federation of Associations of Medical Schools - PAFAMS] [Caracas, Venezuela] (EAIO) .... FEPAFEM
Federacion Popular Democratica [Popular Democratic Federation] [Spain Political party] (PPE) .... FPD
Federacion Progresista [Spain Political party] (EY) .... FP
Federacion Socialista Madrilena [Spain Political party] (EY) .... FSM
Federacion Unica de Trabajadores Campesinos [Single Federation of Peasant Workers] [Bolivia] (PD) .... FUTC
Federal (AAGC) .... F
Federal .... FED
Federal (AFM) .... FED
Federal .... FEDL
Federal Accounting Standards Advisory Board (AAGC) .... FASAB
Federal Acquisition Circular [DoD] .... FAC
Federal Acquisition Reform Act of 1996 (AAGC) .... FARA
Federal Acquisition Reform Act of 1996 (AAGC) .... FASA II
Federal Acquisition Reform Act-Information Technology Management Reform Act [Currently known as Clinger-Cohen Act] .... FARA-ITMRA
Federal Acquisition Regional Work Group [Army] .... FARWG
Federal Acquisition Regulation .... FAR

Federal Acquisition Regulation Project Office (MCD) .... FARPO
Federal Acquisition Regulatory Council (AAGC) .... FAR Council
Federal Acquisition Services for Technology [GSA] (AAGC) .... FAST
Federal Acquisition Streamlining Act of 1994 (AAGC) .... FASA
Federal Acquisitions Computer Network .... FACNET
Federal Acquisitions Institute [Formerly, FPI] (MCD) .... FAI
Federal Administrative Law Judges Conference (EA) .... FALJC
Federal ADP [Automatic Data Processing] Users Group .... FADPUG
Federal Advanced Superconducting Transportation Act .... FAST
Federal Advertising Committee on Ethics (MCD) .... FACE
Federal Advertising Services .... FAS
Federal Advisory Commision on Consolidation and Conversion [DoD] (RDA) .... FACCC
Federal Advisory Committee Act .... FACA
Federal Advisory Committee on False Identification [Department of Justice] [Terminated, 1976] .... FACFI
Federal Advisory Committee on Occupational Safety and Health [Department of Labor] [Washington, DC] .... FACOSH
Federal Advisory Council [Department of Labor] .... FAC
Federal Advisory Council on Employment Security .... FACES
Federal Advisory Council on Medical Training Aids .... FACMTA
Federal Advisory Council on Regional Economic Development .... FACRED
Federal Advisory Council on Scientific Information .... FACSI
Federal Advisory Council on Unemployment Insurance .... FACUI
Federal Agent [Slang] .... fed
Federal Agents Registration Act (OICC) .... FARA
Federal Agricultural Marketing Authority .... FAMA
Federal Agricultural Mortgage [Associated Press] (SAG) .... FdAgricA
Federal Agricultural Mortgage [Associated Press] (SAG) .... FdAgricC
Federal Agricultural Mortgage Corporation (USGC) .... Farmer Mac
Federal Agricultural Mortgage Corp. [Associated Press] (SAG) .... FdAgric
Federal Agricultural Mtge'A' [NASDAQ symbol] (TTSB) .... FAMICA
Federal Agricultural Mtge'C' [NASDAQ symbol] (TTSB) .... FAMCK
Federal Aid Primary System (GNE) .... FAPS
Federal Aid to Airports Program [FAA] .... FAAP
Federal Aid Urban System [Road improvement program] [Federal Highway Administration] .... FAUS
Federal Air P Ltd. [South Africa] [FAA designator] (FAAC) .... FDR
Federal Air Regulations [FAA] .... FAR
Federal Airlines [Sudan] [FAA designator] (FAAC) .... FLL
Federal Airmail (IAA) .... FAM
Federal Airport Service .... FAS
Federal Airworthiness Regulation .... FAR
Federal Alcohol Control Administration [Established, 1933; abolished, 1935] .... FACA
Federal Ambient Air Quality Studies .... FAAQS
Federal and Judicial Appointments Project [Defunct] (EA) .... FJAP
Federal and State Business Assistance Database [National Technical Information Service] [Information service or system] (CRD) .... FSBA
Federal and State Governments Assistance Programs [Database] [Australia] .... GAIN
Federal Anti-Trust Cases, Decrees, and Judgments [1890-1918] [A publication] (DLA) .... Fed Anti-Tr Cas
Federal Anti-Trust Decisions [A publication] (DLA) .... FAD
Federal Anti-Trust Decisions [A publication] (DLA) .... Fed Anti-Tr Dec
Federal Applied Technology Database [National Technical Information Service] [Information service or system] (CRD) .... FATD
Federal Archives and Records Center [Regional depository of the National Archives and Records Service] .... FARC
Federal Archives and Records Center, General Services Administration, Atlanta Region, East Point, GA [Library symbol Library of Congress] (LCLS) .... GEpFAR
Federal Archives and Records Center, General Services Administration, Bayonne, NJ [Library symbol Library of Congress] (LCLS) .... NjBaFAR
Federal Archives and Records Center, General Services Administration, Chicago, IL [Library symbol Library of Congress] (LCLS) .... ICFAR
Federal Archives and Records Center, General Services Administration, Philadelphia, PA [Library symbol Library of Congress] (LCLS) .... PPFAR
Federal Archives and Records Center, General Services Administration, Waltham, MA [Library symbol Library of Congress] (LCLS) .... MWalFAR
Federal Area Port Controller .... FAPC
Federal Armed Forces of Germany [ICAO designator] (FAAC) .... DCN
Federal Armored Service, Inc. [ICAO designator] (FAAC) .... FRM
Federal Art Project .... FAP
Federal Assets Disposition Association [Functions transferred to FDIC and RTC, 1989] .... FADA
Federal Assistance Award Data System [Bureau of the Census] [Washington, DC Information service or system] .... FAADS
Federal Assistance for Staff Training [Education] .... FAST
Federal Assistance Information Reporting .... FAIR
Federal Assistance Programs Retrieval System [General Services Administration] [Information service or system] (MCD) .... FAPRS
Federal Assistance Review [Program] .... FAR
Federal Assistance Review Board [Marine science] (OSRA) .... FARB
Federal Assistance Review Board (USDC) .... FARB
Federal Assistance Streamlining Taskforce [HEW] .... FAST
Federal Association of Management Analysts [Defunct] .... FAMA
Federal Association of Teachers of Dancing (Australia) .... FATD(A)
Federal Assumed Enforcement [State implementation plan by EPA] .... FAE
Federal Automated Career System .... FACS
Federal Automatic Data Processing (MHDI) .... FADP
Federal Aviation Act [1958] .... FAA
Federal Aviation Administration [ICAO designator] (FAAC) .... AYA
Federal Aviation Administration [Formerly, Federal Aviation Agency] [Department of Transportation] .... FAA

Federal Aviation Administration Aeronautical Center ... FAA-AC
Federal Aviation Administration Aeronautical Fixed Telecommunications Network (NOAA) ... FAA-AFTN
Federal Aviation Administration Air Traffic Service ... FAA-AT
Federal Aviation Administration Air Traffic Service (NOAA) ... FAA-ATS
Federal Aviation Administration Aircraft Development Service ... FAA-ADS
Federal Aviation Administration Airports Service ... FAA-AS
Federal Aviation Administration Airway Facilities Service ... FAA-AAF
Federal Aviation Administration Airway Facilities Service ... FAA-AF
Federal Aviation Administration and Air Force RADAR Replacement ... FARR
Federal Aviation Administration Area Regional Traffic Control Center (DNAB) ... FAAARTCC
Federal Aviation Administration Associate Administrator for Airports ... FAA-ARP
Federal Aviation Administration Canadian Air Services Committee ... FAA/CAS
Federal Aviation Administration Development Services ... FAA-DS
Federal Aviation Administration, Eastern Region Library, Jamaica, NY [*Library symbol Library of Congress*] (LCLS) ... NJFAA
Federal Aviation Administration Flight Standards National Field Office ... FAA-AFO
Federal Aviation Administration Flight Standards Service ... FAA-AFS
Federal Aviation Administration Flight Standards Service ... FAA-FS
Federal Aviation Administration Flight Standards Service National Flight Inspection Division ... FAA-FS-NFID
Federal Aviation Administration National Airspace System Program Office ... FAA-NS
Federal Aviation Administration National Aviation Facilities Experimental Center ... FAA-NA
Federal Aviation Administration Office of Airport Standards ... FAA-AAS
Federal Aviation Administration Office of Airports Programs ... FAA-AAP
Federal Aviation Administration Office of Airports Programs ... FAA-AP
Federal Aviation Administration Office of Aviation Medicine ... FAA-AM
Federal Aviation Administration Office of Aviation Policy ... FAA-AV
Federal Aviation Administration Office of Aviation Policy and Plans ... FAA-APO
Federal Aviation Administration Office of Aviation Policy and Plans ... FAA-AVP
Federal Aviation Administration Office of Aviation Safety ... FAA-ASF
Federal Aviation Administration Office of Aviation Systems Plans ... FAA-ASP
Federal Aviation Administration Office of Environment and Energy ... FAA-AEE
Federal Aviation Administration Office of Environment and Energy ... FAA-EE
Federal Aviation Administration Office of Environmental Quality ... FAA-AEQ
Federal Aviation Administration Office of Environmental Quality ... FAA-EQ
Federal Aviation Administration Office of Management Systems ... FAA-MS
Federal Aviation Administration Office of Noise Abatement ... FAA-NO
Federal Aviation Administration Office of Supersonic Transport Development ... FAA-SS
Federal Aviation Administration Office of Supersonic Transport Development ... FAA-SST
Federal Aviation Administration Office of Systems Engineering Management ... FAA-AEM
Federal Aviation Administration Office of Systems Engineering Management ... FAA-EM
Federal Aviation Administration Orders [*A publication*] (DLA) ... FAA Order
Federal Aviation Administration Quiet Short-Haul Air Transportation Systems Office ... FAA-QS
Federal Aviation Administration RADAR Air Traffic Control Facility (DNAB) ... FAARATCF
Federal Aviation Administration Regional Office (NOAA) ... FAARO
Federal Aviation Administration, Southern Region, East Point, GA [*OCLC symbol*] (OCLC) ... GFA
Federal Aviation Administration Systems Research and Development Service ... FAA-ARD
Federal Aviation Administration Systems Research and Development Service ... FAA-RD
Federal Aviation Administration Technical Development Center ... FAATDC
Federal Aviation Agency (AEBS) ... FAA
Federal Aviation Agency Contract Appeals Panel (AAGC) ... FAA CAP
Federal Aviation Commission [*Terminated, 1935*] ... FAC
Federal Aviation Information Retrieval System ... FAIRS
Federal Aviation Procurement Regulations ... FAPR
Federal Aviation Regulation ... FAR
Federal Aviation Science and Technological Association [*Defunct*] (EA) ... FASTA
Federal Aviation Service ... FAS
Federal Banking Law Reports [*Commerce Clearing House*] [*A publication*] (DLA) ... Fed Banking L Rep
Federal Banking Law Reports (Commerce Clearing House) [*A publication*] (DLA) ... CCH Fed Banking L Rep
Federal Bar Association (EA) ... FBA
Federal Bar News & Journal [*A publication*] (AAGC) ... Fed B News & J
Federal Barge Lines, Inc. [*AAR code*] ... FBL
Federal Barge Lines, Inc., St. Louis MO [*STAC*] ... FBG
Federal Board of Hospitalization [*Coordinated hospitalization activities of Army, Navy, and various agencies; terminated, 1948*] ... FBH
Federal Boating Safety Act of 1971 [*USCG*] (TAG) ... FBSA
Federal Bonding Program ... FBP
Federal Buildings Fund [*General Services Administration*] ... FBF
Federal Bureau of Advanced Paranoia [*Agency in film "Last Embrace"*] ... FBAP
Federal Bureau of Investigation ... FBI
Federal Bureau of Narcotics ... FBN
Federal Bureau of Prisons (WDAA) ... FBP
Federal Business Development Bank [*See also BFD*] [*Canada Database producer*] ... FBDB
Federal Business Development Bank, Montreal, PQ, Canada [*Library symbol Library of Congress*] (LCLS) ... CaQMFBD
Federal Business Development Bank [*Banque Federale de Developpement*] **Montreal, Quebec** [*Library symbol National Library of Canada*] (NLC) ... QMFBD
Federal Business Development Bank, St. John's, NF, Canada [*Library symbol Library of Congress*] (LCLS) ... CaNfSFBD
Federal Capital Press of Australia, Canberra, ACT, Australia [*Library symbol Library of Congress*] (LCLS) ... AuCF
Federal Carriers Cases [*Commerce Clearing House*] [*A publication*] (DLA) ... CC
Federal Carriers Cases [*Commerce Clearing House*] [*A publication*] (DLA) ... F Carr Cas
Federal Carriers Cases [*Commerce Clearing House*] [*A publication*] (DLA) ... F Carrier Cas
Federal Carriers Cases [*Commerce Clearing House*] [*A publication*] (DLA) ... Fed Carr Cas
Federal Carriers Reporter [*Commerce Clearing House*] [*A publication*] (DLA) ... Fed Carr Rep
Federal Carriers Reporter (Commerce Clearing House) [*A publication*] (DLA) ... CC
Federal Case Number [*Legal term*] (DLA) ... F Cas No
Federal Case Number [*Legal term*] (DLA) ... Fed Cas No
Federal Cases [*A publication*] (DLA) ... F Cas
Federal Cases [*A publication*] (DLA) ... FC
Federal Cases [*A publication*] (DLA) ... Fed Cas
Federal Catalog Number ... FCN
Federal Catalog System [*of GSA*] ... FCS
Federal Cataloging Handbook ... FCH
Federal Cataloging Program ... FCP
Federal Centre for AIDS [*Acquired Immune Deficiency Syndrome*], Health Protection Branch, Health and Welfare Canada , Ottawa, Ontario [*Centre Federal du SIDA, Direction Generale de la Protection de la Sante, Sante et Bien-Etre Social Canada*] [*Library symbol National Library of Canada*] (BIB) ... OONHAC
Federal Chamber of Automotive Industries (EERA) ... FCAI
Federal Circuit Bar Association (AAGC) ... FCBA
Federal City College [*Later, UDC*] [*Washington, DC*] ... FCC
Federal City College [*Later, UDC*], Washington, DC [*Library symbol Library of Congress Obsolete*] (LCLS) ... DFC
Federal Civil Defense Administration [*Transferred to Office of Defense and Civilian Mobilization, 1958; to Department of Defense and Office of Emergency Preparedness, 1961*] ... FCDA
Federal Civil Defense Guide ... FCDG
Federal Civil Service System ... FCSS
Federal Claims Settlement Commission of the United States ... FCSCUS
Federal Class Manager (AFIT) ... FCM
Federal Clean Air Act (WDAA) ... FCAA
Federal Clean Car Incentive Program [*Environmental Protection Agency*] (MCD) ... FCCI
Federal Clean Car Incentive Program [*Environmental Protection Agency*] ... FCCIP
Federal Coal Leasing Amendments Act [*1976*] ... FCLAA
Federal Coal Mine Safety Board of Review [*Independent government agency*] [*Inactive, 1970*] ... FCMSBR
Federal COBOL [*Common Business-Oriented Language*] **Compiler Testing Service** [*National Institute of Standards and Technology*] ... FCCTS
Federal Code, Annotated [*A publication*] (DLA) ... FCA
Federal Columbia River Power System ... FCRPS
Federal Committee for Meteorological Services and Supporting Research ... FCMS & SR
Federal Committee on Apprenticeship [*Department of Labor*] ... FCA
Federal Committee on Pest Control ... FCPC
Federal Communications Act ... FCA
Federal Communications Bar Association (EA) ... FCBA
Federal Communications Commission [*Independent government agency*] ... FCC
Federal Communications Commission Network ... FCCN
Federal Communications Commission, Washington, DC [*OCLC symbol*] (OCLC) ... FCC
Federal Communications Law Journal [*A publication*] (DLA) ... Fed Comm LJ
Federal Communications Systems (MCD) ... FCS
Federal Compiler Testing Center ... FCTC
Federal Complaint Coordinating Center [*US Office of Consumer Affairs*] ... FCCC
Federal Computer Performance Evaluation and Simulation Center [*General Services Administration*] ... FEDSIM
Federal Consistency Determination [*Environmental application*] ... FCD
Federal Constitutional Law ... FECL
Federal Construction Council (EA) ... FCC
Federal Consultative Council of South African Railways and Harbors Staff Association ... FCC
Federal Contract Compliance Program Office [*Department of Labor*] (IEEE) ... FCCPO
Federal Contract Research Center ... FCRC
Federal Contracts Report (Bureau of National Affairs) [*A publication*] (DLA) ... Fed Cont Rep (BNA)
Federal Contracts Reports (AAGC) ... FCR
Federal Conversion Support Center (MCD) ... FCSC
Federal Coordinating Council for Science and Technology ... FCCST
Federal Coordinating Council for Science, Engineering, and Technology [*Pronounced "fix it"*] [*Office of Science and Technology Policy*] ... FCCSET
Federal Coordinating Officer [*Federal disaster planning*] ... FCO
Federal Coordination Committee on Instrumentation and Measurement ... FCCIM
Federal Coordinator for Geology [*Marine science*] (OSRA) ... FCG
Federal Coordinator for Geology (USDC) ... FCG
Federal Coordinator for Marine Environmental Prediction (USDC) ... FCMAREP
Federal Coordinator for Marine Environmental Prediction [*Marine science*] (OSRA) ... FCMAREP
Federal Coordinator for Meteorological Services and Supporting Research [*Marine science*] (OSRA) ... FCMSSR

Federal Coordinator for Meteorological Services and Supporting Research (USDC) .... FCMSSR
Federal Coordinator for Ocean Mapping and Prediction [*Marine science*] (OSRA) .... ECOMP
Federal Coordinator for Ocean Mapping and Prediction (USDC) .... FCOMP
Federal Coordinator of Transportation [*New Deal*] .... FCT
Federal Correctional Institute Library, Sandstone, MN [*Library symbol*] [*Library of Congress*] (LCLS) .... MnSaF
Federal Correctional Institution (WDAA) .... FCI
Federal Council for Science and Technology [*Later, FSPC, FCCSET*] [*Executive Office of President*] .... FCST
Federal Council for Science and Technology - Committee on Water Resources Research (NOAA) .... FCST-CORR
Federal Council of Churches .... FCC
Federal Council of University Staff Associations. Bulletin [*A publication*] .... Fed Council Bull
Federal Council on Computer Storage Standards and Technology [*General Services Administration*] .... FCCSSAT
Federal Council on the Aging [*Succeeded by President's Council on Aging, 1962*] .... FCA
Federal Court Clerks Association (EA) .... FCCA
Federal Court Industrial Division [*Australia*] .... FCID
Federal Court Judgements [*Canada Department of Justice*] [*Information service or system*] (CRD) .... FCJ
Federal Court of Canada [*A publication*] (DLA) .... Can FC
Federal Court of Canada .... FCT
Federal Court of Canada, Ottawa, ON, Canada [*Library symbol Library of Congress*] (LCLS) .... CaOOFC
Federal Court of Canada [*Cour Federale du Canada*] Ottawa, Ontario [*Library symbol National Library of Canada*] (NLC) .... OOFC
Federal Court Procurement Decisions [*A publication*] (AAGC) .... FPD
Federal Court Reports [*Canada Department of Justice*] [*Information service or system*] (CRD) .... FCR
Federal Court Rules [*A publication*] .... FCR
Federal Courts Administration Act of 1992 (AAGC) .... FCAA
Federal Courts Improvement Act (AAGC) .... FCIA
Federal Credit Union Administration .... FCUA
Federal Credit Union System [*New Deal*] .... FCUS
Federal Credit Unions Bureau .... FCU
Federal Crime Insurance .... FCI
Federal Crime Insurance Program (WDAA) .... FCIP
Federal Criminal Investigators Association (EA) .... FCIA
Federal Crop Insurance .... FCI
Federal Crop Insurance Corp. [*Department of Agriculture*] .... FCIC
Federal Crop Insurance Program (GNE) .... FCIP
Federal Cultural Policy Review Committee [*Canada*] .... FCPRC
Federal Data Processing Centers .... FDPC
Federal Defense Laboratory (AAGC) .... FDI
Federal Defense Laboratory Diversification (AAGC) .... FDLD
Federal Defense Laboratory Diversification Program (RDA) .... FDLDP
Federal Democratic Movement [*Uganda*] [*Political party*] .... FEDEMO
Federal Deposit Insurance Corp. [*Independent government agency*] [*Database*] .... FDIC
Federal Deposit Insurance Corporation Improvement Act (ECON) .... FDICIA
Federal Deposit Insurance Corp., Washington, DC [*OCLC symbol*] (OCLC) .... FDI
Federal Depository Library Program .... FDLP
Federal Design Approval [*Nuclear energy*] (NUCP) .... FDA
Federal Design Council [*Defunct*] (EA) .... FDC
Federal Detention Center (BARN) .... FDC
Federal Directive .... FD
Federal Disaster Assistance Administration [*FEMA*] .... FDAA
Federal Document (AFM) .... FD
Federal Document Clearing House .... FDCH
Federal Document Retrieval [*Information service or system*] (IID) .... FDR
Federal Documents Task Force [*Government Documents Round Table*] [*American Library Association*] .... FDTF
Federal Domestic Assistance [*Catalog*] (OICC) .... FDA
Federal Drug Administration .... FDA
Federal Drug Enforcement Administration (WDAA) .... FDEA
Federal Economic Development Co-Ordinator [*Canada*] .... FEDC
Federal Editors Association [*Later, NAGC*] (EA) .... FEA
Federal Education Data Acquisition Council (OICC) .... FEDAC
Federal Education Project [*Defunct*] (EA) .... FEP
Federal Election Campaign Act of 1971 .... FECA
Federal Election Campaign Financing Guide (Commerce Clearing House) [*A publication*] (DLA) .... Fed Election Camp Fin Guide (CCH)
Federal Elections Commission [*Formerly, OFE*] .... FEC
Federal Electric Co. (KSC) .... FEC
Federal Emergency Administration of Public Works [*Consolidated into Federal Works Agency and administered as PWA, 1939*] .... FEAPW
Federal Emergency Housing Corp. [*New Deal*] .... FEHC
Federal Emergency Management Agency (ECON) .... FEMA
Federal Emergency Management Agency Acquisition Regulation (AAGC) .... FEMAAR
Federal Emergency Management Agency Office of Mitigation and Research [*Washington, DC*] .... FEMA-M/R
Federal Emergency Management Agency Procurement Regulations (AAGC) .... FEMAPR
Federal Emergency Relief Act of 1933 .... FERA
Federal Emergency Relief Administration [*Liquidated, 1937*] .... FERA
Federal Emission Test Sequence and Selective Enforcement Audit [*General Motors Corp.*] .... FETS/SEA
Federal Employee Direct Corporate Stock Ownership Plan (GFGA) .... FED Co-OP
Federal Employee Education and Assistance Fund .... FEEA
Federal Employee Program .... FEP

Federal Employees' Appeal Authority [*Civil Service Commission*] .... FEAA
Federal Employees Association (Independent) .... FEA(I)
Federal Employees Benefits Improvement Act of 1986 .... FEBIA
Federal Employees Compensation Act [*1908*] (AFM) .... FECA
Federal Employees' Compensation System (GFGA) .... FECS
Federal Employees Coordinating Committee (EA) .... FECC
Federal Employees for a Democratic Society [*Defunct*] .... FEDS
Federal Employees' Group Life Insurance .... FEGLI
Federal Employees Health Benefits .... FEHB
Federal Employees Health Benefits Act .... FEHBA
Federal Employees Health Benefits Program (AFM) .... FEHBP
Federal Employees Pay Act .... FEPA
Federal Employees Pay Comparability Act [*1990*] .... FEPCA
Federal Employees' Retirement System .... FERS
Federal Employees' Retirement System Act of 1986 .... FERSA
Federal Employees Salary Act of 1970 .... FESA
Federal Employees Salary Increase Act .... FESIA
Federal Employees Veterans Association [*Later, NAGE*] (EA) .... FEVA
Federal Employer Identification Number .... FEIN
Federal Employers' Liability Act (Railroads) [*1906*] .... FELA
Federal Employment Activity Report .... FEAR
Federal Employment Decision Search [*Database*] [*Labor Relations Press*] [*Information service or system*] (CRD) .... FEDS
Federal Employment [*or Employees*] Retirement System .... FERS
Federal Employment Service Act [*1933*] .... FESA
Federal Employment Stabilization Office [*Functions transferred to National Resources Planning Board, 1939*] .... FESO
Federal Energy Administration [*Formerly, FEO*] [*Superseded by Department of Energy, 1977*] .... FEA
Federal Energy Bar Association (EA) .... FEBA
[*The*] Federal Energy Data Index [*Department of Energy Information service or system Defunct*] (CRD) .... FEDEX
Federal Energy Data System [*Department of Energy*] (GFGA) .... FEDS
Federal Energy Data System (GNE) .... FEDS
Federal Energy Emergency Administration (MCD) .... FEEA
Federal Energy Information Locator Systems .... FEILS
Federal Energy Management Program [*Department of Energy*] .... FEMP
Federal Energy Office [*Later, FEA*] .... FEO
Federal Energy Policy and Conservation Act (GNE) .... FEPCA
Federal Energy Regulatory Commission [*Department of Energy*] .... FERC
Federal Environmental Assessment Review Office [*Canada*] .... FEARO
Federal Environmental Assessment Review Office [*Bureau Federal d'Examen des Evaluations Environnementales*], Ottawa, Ontario [*Library symbol National Library of Canada*] (BIB) .... OOFE
Federal Environmental Pesticide Control Act [*1972*] .... FEPCA
Federal Equal Employment Opportunity Recruitment Program (GFGA) .... FEEOR
Federal Equal Opportunity Recruitment Program .... FEORP
Federal Estate Tax (DLA) .... FET
Federal Excise Tax .... FET
Federal Excise Tax Council [*Defunct*] (EA) .... FETC
Federal Excise Tax Reporter [*Commerce Clearing House*] [*A publication*] (DLA) .... Fed Ex Tax Rep
Federal Executive and Professional Association [*Defunct*] (EA) .... FEPA
Federal Executive Association .... FEA
Federal Executive Board .... FEB
Federal Executive Board (USGC) .... FEB
Federal Executive Committee (OICC) .... FEC
Federal Executive Development Program [*Civil Service Commission*] .... FEDP
Federal Executive Drug Abuse Council .... FEDAC
Federal Executive Institute .... FEI
Federal Executive Pay Act, 1956 .... FEPA
Federal Executive Salary Act of 1964 .... FESA
Federal Executive Service .... FES
Federal Expenditures by State .... FES
Federal Express [*NYSE symbol*] (TTSB) .... FDX
Federal Express [*Parcel Service*] (AAGC) .... FedEx
Federal Express Corp. [*NYSE symbol Toronto Stock Exchange symbol*] (SPSG) .... FDX
Federal Express Corp. [*ICAO designator*] (FAAC) .... FDX
Federal Express Corp. [*Service mark and trade name*] .... FEDEX
Federal Express Corp. [*Associated Press*] (SAG) .... FedExp
Federal Extension Service [*Department of Agriculture*] .... FES
Federal Facilities Compliance Agreement .... FFCA
Federal Facilities Corp. [*Dissolved, 1961*] .... FFC
Federal Facilities Information System (EPA) .... FFIS
Federal Facility (GFGA) .... FF
Federal Facility Compliance Act .... FFCA
Federal Facility Compliance Act (DOGT) .... FFCAct
Federal Facility Compliance Act .... FFCAct
Federal Facility Compliance Act of 1992 (GAAI) .... FFCA
Federal Facility Compliance Agreement .... FFCA
Federal Facility Compliance Agreement (DOGT) .... FFCA
Federal Facility Environmental Restoration (AAGC) .... FFER
Federal Family Education Loan [*Program*] .... FFEL
Federal Farm Board [*Name changed to Farm Credit Administration, 1933*] .... FFB
Federal Farm Credit Board [*of FCA*] .... FFCB
Federal Farm Credit System .... FFCS
Federal Farm Loan Act [*1916*] .... FFLA
Federal Farm Mortgage Corp. [*Established, 1934; assets transferred to Secretary of the Treasury, 1961*] .... FFMC
Federal Financial Institutions Examination Council (OICC) .... FFIEC
Federal Financial Participation .... FFP
Federal Financing Bank .... FFB
Federal Fire Council [*Defunct*] (EA) .... FFC
Federal Fire Fighters' Union [*Australia*] .... FFFU

Federal Firearms Act ... FFA
Federal Firearms License ... FFL
Federal Fiscal Liability ... FFL
Federal Fiscal Year Quarters (OICC) ... FFYQ
Federal Food Advisory Committee [*Cost of Living Council*] ... FFAC
Federal Food, Drug, and Cosmetic Act ... FFDCA
Federal Geodetic Control Committee [*Department of Commerce*] ... FGCC
Federal Geographic Data Committee [*of the USA*] (EERA) ... FGDC
Federal Geographic Data Committee ... FGDC
Federal German Navy ... FGN
Federal Gift Tax (DLA) ... FGT
Federal Government (WDAA) ... FG
Federal Government Accountants Association [*Later, AGA*] (EA) ... FGAA
Federal Grain Inspection Service [*Department of Agriculture*] ... FGIS
Federal Grant and Cooperative Agreement Act (AAGC) ... FGCAA
Federal Grants & Contracts Weekly [*Capital Publications*] (AAGC) ... FG&CW
Federal Group Code (MCD) ... FGC
Federal Hall National Memorial ... FEHA
Federal Hazardous Materials Regulations (TAG) ... FMHR
Federal Hazardous Substances Act ... FHSA
Federal Health Insurance Plan [*Proposed*] (DHSM) ... FHIP
Federal Health Programs Service [*Health Services and Mental Health Administration, HEW*] ... FHPS
Federal Highway Administration [*Department of Transportation*] ... FHA
Federal Highway Administration [*Department of Transportation*] ... FHWA
Federal Highway Cost Allocation Study [*Also, HCAS*] ... FHCAS
Federal Highway Projects [*Department of Transportation*] ... FHP
Federal Home Bank ... FHB
Federal Home Loan [*NYSE symbol*] (TTSB) ... FRE
Federal Home Loan Bank ... FHLB
Federal Home Loan Bank Administration (IIA) ... FHLBA
Federal Home Loan Bank Board [*Functions transferred to Office of Thrift Supervision, 1989*] ... FHLBB
Federal Home Loan Bank Board, Accounts Payable, Washington, DC [*OCLC symbol*] (OCLC) ... HLB
Federal Home Loan Bank System ... FHLBS
Federal Home Loan Mortgage [*NYSE symbol*] (SPSG) ... FRE
Federal Home Loan Mortgage Corp. [*Associated Press*] (SAG) ... FdHL
Federal Home Loan Mortgage Corp. [*Associated Press*] (SAG) ... FdHLn
Federal Home Loan Mortgage Corp. [*Associated Press*] (SAG) ... FdHmLn
Federal Home Loan Mortgage Corp. [*Federal Home Loan Bank Board*] [*Nickname: "Freddie Mac"*] ... FHLMC
Federal Home Loan Mortgage Corp. (ECON) ... FREDDIE MAC
Federal Housing Administration [*HUD*] ... FHA
Federal Housing Administration Matters [*FBI standardized term*] ... FHAM
Federal Housing Authority (TDOB) ... FHA
Federal Housing Authority Insurance (AABC) ... FHAI
Federal Housing Commission [*HUD*] (OICC) ... FHC
Federal Housing Corp. ... FHC
Federal Housing Finance Board [*Pronounced "foof-ba"*] ... FHFB
Federal Identification Number ... FIN
Federal Identity Program [*Canada*] ... FIP
Federal Implementation Plan [*Environmental Protection Agency*] (ERG) ... FIP
Federal Income Tax ... FIT
Federal Income Tax Withholding ... FITW
Federal Independent Democratic Alliance [*South Africa Political party*] (EY) ... FIDA
Federal Index [*Capitol Services International*] (NITA) ... FEDEX
Federal Industries Ltd. [*Toronto Stock Exchange symbol*] ... FIL
Federal Information Center Program (EA) ... FIC
Federal Information Centers (USGC) ... FIC
Federal Information Exchange System (DNAB) ... FIES
Federal Information Locator System ... FILS
Federal Information Network ... FEDNET
Federal Information Procedures System [*Environmental Protection Agency*] (ERG) ... FIPS
Federal Information Processing [*ANSI*] (EECA) ... FIP
Federal Information Processing Standard (EERA) ... FIPS
Federal Information Processing Standards [*Gaithersburg, MD*] [*National Institute of Standards and Technology*] ... FIPS
Federal Information Processing Standards (DOMA) ... FIST
Federal Information Processing Standards Coordinating and Advisory Committee [*National Institute of Standards and Technology*] ... FIPSCAC
Federal Information Processing Standards Publication [*National Institute of Standards and Technology*] ... FIPS-PUB
Federal Information Processing Standards Register [*National Institute of Standards and Technology*] ... FIPSR
Federal Information Relay Service (USGC) ... FIRS
Federal Information Requirements Management Council ... FIRMCO
Federal Information Research Science and Technology (DICI) ... FIRST
Federal Information Research Science and Technology Network (NITA) ... FIRST
Federal Information Resource Management Regulations Interagency Advisory Council [*Information Resources Management Service*] [*General Services Administration*] ... FIMR
Federal Information Resources Management Regulation [*A publication*] (AAGC) ... FIRMR
Federal Information Resources Management Regulation Interagency Advisory Council [*Information Resources Management Service*] [*General Services Administration*] (EGAO) ... FIRMR
Federal Information Systems Corp. (IID) ... FISC
Federal Insecticide, Fungicide, and Rodenticide Act [*1947*] [*Department of Agriculture*] ... FIFRA
Federal Insecticide, Fungicide, and Rodenticide Act ... FIFRA
Federal Institute for Snow and Avalanche Research ... FISAR
Federal Insurance Administration [*HUD*] ... FIA
Federal Insurance Contribution (MHDW) ... FIC
Federal Insurance Contributions Act [*1954*] [*Under which collections are made from employers and employees for OASDI benefits*] ... FICA
Federal Insurance Counsel Quarterly [*A publication*] (DLA) ... Fed Ins Counsel Q
Federal Insurance Tax (DLA) ... FIT
Federal Insured Student Loan Program ... FISLP
Federal Interagency Broadcast Committee ... FIBC
Federal Interagency Committee on Education ... FICE
Federal Interagency Coordinating Council ... FICC
Federal Interagency Day Care Requirements ... FIDCR
Federal Interagency Media Committee (EGAO) ... FIMC
Federal Inter-Agency Sedimentation Conference [*Department of Agriculture*] ... FIASC
Federal Interagency Task Force on Inadvertent Modification of the Stratosphere ... FITFIMS
Federal Intermediate Credit Bank ... FICB
Federal Internal Security Board [*Formerly, Subversive Activities Control Board*] ... FISB
Federal Internet Exchange (TNIG) ... FIX
Federal Internetworking Requirements Panel [*Telecommunications*] (ACRL) ... FIRP
Federal Inventory Accounting ... FIA
Federal Investigative Strike Team ... FIST
Federal Item Identification ... FII
Federal Item Identification Guide System ... FIIGS
Federal Item Identification Guides ... FIIG
Federal Item Identification Guides for Supply Cataloging (AABC) ... FIIGSC
Federal Item Identification Number ... FIIN
Federal Item Inventory Group ... FIIG
Federal Item Logistics Data ... FILD
Federal Item Logistics Data Record ... FILDR
Federal Item Name ... FIN
Federal Item Name Directory ... FIND
Federal Judicial Center ... FJC
Federal Junior Fellowship [*Army*] (RDA) ... FJF
Federal Labor Laws ... FELL
Federal Labor Relations Authority [*Independent government agency*] ... FLRA
Federal Labor Relations Council [*Later, FLRA*] ... FLRC
Federal Labor Standard Act [*Marine science*] (OSRA) ... FLSA
Federal Labor Standards Act (AAGC) ... FLSA
Federal Labor Standards Act (USDC) ... FLSA
Federal Laboratory Consortium for Technology Transfer ... FLC
Federal Lake Survey Center ... FLSC
Federal Land Bank ... FLB
Federal Land Bank Association ... FLBA
Federal Land Development Authority [*Malaysia*] ... FLDA
Federal Land Manager (GNE) ... FILM
Federal Land Manager [*Department of the Interior*] (GFGA) ... FLM
Federal Land Policy and Management Act [*1976*] ... FLPMA
Federal Law Enforcement Officers Association (EA) ... FLEOA
Federal Law Enforcement Training Center [*Department of the Treasury*] ... FLETC
Federal Law Enforcement Training Center, Glynco, GA [*Library symbol Library of Congress*] (LCLS) ... GGIF
Federal Law Journal [*1939*] [*A publication*] (DLA) ... FLJ
Federal Law Journal of India [*A publication*] (DLA) ... Fed LJ
Federal Law Journal of India [*A publication*] (DLA) ... Fed LJ Ind
Federal Law Journal of India [*A publication*] (DLA) ... FLJ
Federal Law Journal of India [*A publication*] (ILCA) ... FLJ Ind
Federal Law Quarterly [*A publication*] (DLA) ... Fed LQ
Federal Law Review [*A publication*] ... Fed Law Rev
Federal Law Review [*A publication*] ... FLRev
Federal League [*Major league in baseball, 1914-15*] ... F
Federal League [*Major league in baseball, 1914-15*] ... FL
Federal Legal Information through Electronics [*Air Force*] (IID) ... FLITE
Federal Lesbians and Gays (EA) ... FLAG
Federal Liberal Agency of Canada Library [*UTLAS symbol*] ... LIB
Federal Liberal Agency of Canada, Ottawa, ON, Canada [*Library symbol*] [*Library of Congress*] (LCLS) ... CaOOFL
Federal Liberal Agency of Canada, Ottawa, Ontario [*Library symbol National Library of Canada*] (NLC) ... OOFL
Federal Librarians Association [*Defunct*] ... FLA
Federal Librarians Round Table [*American Library Association*] ... FLIRT
Federal Librarians Round Table [*American Library Association*] (EA) ... FLRT
Federal Libraries' Experiment in Cooperative Cataloging [*Later, FEDLINK*] ... FLECC
Federal Libraries Information Network - New South Wales [*Australia*] ... FLIN-NSW
Federal Libraries Information Network - Northern Territory [*Australia*] ... FLIN-NT
Federal Libraries Information Network - Queensland [*Australia*] ... FLIN-QLD
Federal Libraries Information Network - Victoria [*Australia*] ... FLIN-VIC
Federal Libraries Information Network - Western Australia ... FLIN-WA
Federal Library and Information Center Committee [*Library of Congress Also, an information service or system*] (IID) ... FLICC
Federal Library and Information Network [*Formerly, FLECC*] [*Library of Congress Washington, DC Library network*] ... FEDLINK
Federal Library Committee [*Later, FLICC*] [*Library of Congress Washington, DC*] ... FLC
Federal Library Network Prototype Project (NITA) ... FLNPP
Federal Licensed Officers Association (EA) ... FLOA
Federal Licensing Examination [*for physicians*] ... FLEX
Federal Loan Administration ... FLA
Federal Loan Agency [*Abolished 1947, records transferred to Reconstruction Finance Corp.*] ... FLA
Federal Loan Bank ... FLB
Federal Local Port Controller ... FLPC

Federal Low-Emission Vehicle [*Automotive engineering*] .... FEDLEV
Federal Management Circular .... FMC
Federal Management Officer (GFGA) .... FMO
Federal Management System (GFGA) .... FMS
Federal Managers Association (EA) .... FMA
Federal Managers Financial Integrity Act [*1982*] .... FMFIA
Federal Manual for Supply Cataloging (AABC) .... FMSC
Federal Manufacturers Code (MCD) .... FMC
Federal Maritime Adminstration (WDAA) .... FMA
Federal Maritime Board [*1950-1961; functions transferred to FMC*] .... FMB
Federal Maritime Board (AAGC) .... FMB
Federal Maritime Board Reports [*United States Maritime Administration, Department of Commerce*] [*A publication*] (DLA) .... FMB
Federal Maritime Commission [*Independent government agency*] .... FMC
Federal Meat Inspection Act .... FMIA
Federal Mediation and Conciliation Service [*Independent government agency*] .... FMCS
Federal Mediation and Reconciliation Service (MHDB) .... FMRS
Federal Medical Assistance Percentage [*Department of Health and Human Services*] (GFGA) .... FMAP
Federal Merit Promotion Program .... FMPP
Federal Meteorological Handbook .... FMH
Federal Mine Safety and Health Review Commission (EG) .... FMSHRC
Federal Mine Safety and Health Review Decisions [*A publication*] (DLA) .... FMSHRD
Federal Mortgage Bank [*Nigeria*] .... FMB
Federal Motor Carrier Safety Regulation .... FMCSR
Federal Motor Vehicle Control Program (GNE) .... FMVCP
Federal Motor Vehicle Safety Standard .... FMVSS
Federal Motor Vehicle Theft Prevention Standard [*Automotive engineering*] .... FMVTPS
Federal Music Society (EA) .... FMS
Federal National Democratic Front [*Myanmar*] [*Political party*] (PD) .... FNDF
Federal National Mortgage Association [*Wall Street slang name: "Fannie Mae"*] [*Associated Press*] (SAG) .... FedNM
Federal National Mortgage Association [*Wall Street slang name: "Fannie Mae"*] [*NYSE symbol*] (SPSG) .... FNM
Federal National Mortgage Association .... FNMA
Federal National Railroad Association [*Proposed railroad corporation*] [*Nickname: Fannie Rae*] .... FNRA
Federal Natl Mtge [*NYSE symbol*] (TTSB) .... FNM
Federal Natl Mtge 6.41% Pfd [*NYSE symbol*] (TTSB) .... FNMPrA
Federal Natl Mtge 6.50% Pfd [*NYSE symbol*] (TTSB) .... FNMPrB
Federal Network [*Computer network*] (NITA) .... FEDNET
Federal Networking Council [*Computer science*] (TNIG) .... FNC
Federal News Service [*Database*] (IID) .... FNS
Federal Noxious Weed Act .... FNWA
Federal Oceanographic Fleet Coordination Council .... FOFCC
Federal Office Automation Conference (HGAA) .... FOAC
Federal Office Building .... FOB
Federal Office Systems Expo [*National Trade Productions*] (TSPED) .... FOSE
Federal Official .... FO
Federal Oil & Gas Corp. .... FOGCO
Federal Oil and Gas Royalty Management Act .... FOGRMA
Federal On-Scene Commander (DNAB) .... FOSC
Federal Open Market Committee [*Also, OMC*] [*Federal Reserve System*] .... FOMC
Federal Pacific Electric Co. (KSC) .... FPEC
Federal Pacific Lakes Lines [*Steamship*] (MHDW) .... FEDPAC
Federal Paper Board Co., Inc. [*NYSE symbol*] (SPSG) .... FBO
Federal Paper Board Co., Inc. [*Associated Press*] (SAG) .... FedPB
Federal Paper Board Co., Inc. [*Associated Press*] (SAG) .... FPap
Federal Parent Locator Service [*HEW*] .... FPLS
Federal Parliament (DLA) .... FP
Federal Party [*Namibia*] (PPW) .... FP
Federal Party of Australia [*Political party*] .... FPA
Federal Pattern Description (AAG) .... FPD
Federal Pecan Growers .... FPG
Federal Penal and Correctional Institution (WDAA) .... FPCI
Federal Personnel and Compensation Division (AAGC) .... FPCD
Federal Personnel Council [*Abolished, 1954*] [*Civil Service Commission*] .... FPC
Federal Personnel Intern [*Program*] [*Civil Service Commission*] .... FPI
Federal Personnel Management Information System [*Civil Service Commission*] .... FPMIS
Federal Personnel Management Letters [*Office of Personnel Management*] (GFGA) .... FPML
Federal Personnel Manual .... FPM
Federal Personnel Manual Systems (OICC) .... FPMS
Federal Pesticide Act (GNE) .... FPA
Federal Petroleum Board [*Department of the Interior*] .... FPB
Federal Photovoltaics Utilization Program [*Department of Energy*] .... FPUP
Federal Physicians Association (EA) .... FPA
Federal Pioneer Ltd. [*Toronto Stock Exchange symbol*] .... FPE
Federal Plant Quarantine Inspectors National Association [*Later, NAAE*] .... FPQI
Federal Plant Quarantine Inspectors National Association [*Later, NAAE*] (EA) .... FPQINA
Federal Police Disciplinary Tribunal [*Australia*] .... FPDT
Federal Post Card Application [*For an absentee ballot*] (AABC) .... FPCA
Federal Potato Co-ordinating Committee [*Australia*] .... FPCC
Federal Power Commission (IAA) .... FEDPOWCOMM
Federal Power Commission [*Superseded by Department of Energy, 1977*] .... FPC
Federal Power Commission Reports [*A publication*] (DLA) .... FPC
Federal Power Commission Reports .... FPCR
Federal Powers Act (GNE) .... FPA
Federal Practice and Procedure [*A publication*] (DLA) .... Fed Prac
Federal Preparedness Agency [*FEMA*] .... FPA
Federal Preparedness Agency/General Services Administration .... FPA/GSA
Federal Prevailing Rate Advisory Committee [*Washington, DC*] (EGAO) .... FPRAC
Federal Prison Industries (AAGC) .... UNICOR
Federal Prison Industries Acquisition Regulation (AAGC) .... FPIAR
Federal Prison Industries, Inc. [*Department of Justice*] .... FPI
Federal Prison System (MCD) .... FPS
Federal Probation [*A publication*] (BRI) .... Fed Prob
Federal Probation Newsletter [*A publication*] (DLA) .... Fed Prob NL
Federal Probation Officers Association (EA) .... FPOA
Federal Procurement Data Center [*Database*] .... FPDC
Federal Procurement Data System [*Database*] (IID) .... FPDS
Federal Procurement Disc [*Alde Publishing*] [*Information service or system*] (IID) FPS1117
Federal Procurement Eligibility .... FPE
Federal Procurement Institute [*Later, FAI*] (MCD) .... FPI
Federal Procurement Regulations .... FPR
Federal Productivity Measurement System [*Bureau of Labor Statistics*] (GFGA) .... FPMS
Federal Professional Association [*Later, FEPA*] .... FPA
Federal Property and Administrative Services Act [*1949*] .... FPASA
Federal Property Assistance [*Department of Health and Human Services*] .... FPA
Federal Property Council [*Terminated, 1977*] .... FPC
Federal Property Management Regulations .... FPMR
Federal Property Resources Service [*General Services Administration*] .... FPRS
Federal Protective Officer [*General Services Administration*] .... FPO
Federal Protective Service [*General Services Administration*] .... FPS
Federal/Provincial Committee on Atlantic Region Transportation [*Canada*] .... FP-CART
Federal Public Housing Authority [*Functions transferred to Public Housing Administration, 1947*] .... FPHA
Federal Publications, Inc. (AAGC) .... Fed Pubs
Federal Publications, Inc. (AAGC) .... FPI
Federal Publisher's Committee (EA) .... FPC
Federal Quality Institute [*Office of Management and Budget*] (GFGA) .... FQI
Federal Quarantine Service (BARN) .... FQS
Federal Radiation Council [*Defunct*] (EA) .... FRC
Federal Radio Act (NITA) .... FRA
Federal Radio Commission [*Functions transferred to FCC, 1934*] .... FRC
Federal Radio Education Committee .... FREC
Federal Radiological Management Assessment Center (USDC) .... FRMAC
Federal Radiological Monitoring and Assessment Center [*Department of Energy*] .... FRMAC
Federal Radionavigation Plan .... FRP
Federal Railroad Administration .... FRA
Federal Railway Administration [*DOT*] (AAGC) .... FRA
Federal Ranch [*British Columbia*] [*Seismograph station code, US Geological Survey Closed*] (SEIS) .... FRC
Federal Real Estate Board [*Abolished, 1951*] .... FREB
Federal Realty Investment Trust [*Associated Press*] (SAG) .... FedRlty
Federal Realty Investment Trust SBI [*NYSE symbol*] (SPSG) .... FRT
Federal Records Center [*General Services Administration*] (AABC) .... FRC
Federal Records Center, San Francisco, CA [*Library symbol Library of Congress*] (LCLS) .... CSfFRC
Federal Records Center, Seattle, WA [*Library symbol Library of Congress*] (LCLS) .... WaSFRC
Federal Records Council .... FRC
Federal Reference Method .... FRM
Federal Region [*Dialog*] [*Searchable field*] [*Information service or system*] (NITA) .... FR
Federal Regional Center [*Office of Civil Defense*] .... FRC
Federal Regional Council [*for federal-state-local interchange*] [*Abolished, 1983*] .... FRC
Federal Regional Reconstitutional Area .... FRRA
Federal Register [*A publication*] (AAGC) .... Fed Reg
Federal Register [*Capitol Services International*] (NITA) .... FEDREG
Federal Register [*A publication*] .... FR
Federal Register Abstracts [*Capitol Services, Inc.*] [*Washington, DC Database*] .... FEDREG
Federal Register Act (GFGA) .... FRA
Federal Register Electronic News Delivery .... FREND
Federal Register Notice (NRCH) .... FRN
Federal Register Office [*National Archives and Records Administration*] (GFGA) .... FRO
Federal Register Reprint .... FRR
Federal Register Search System [*Chemical Information Systems, Inc.*] [*Information service or system*] (CRD) .... FRSS
Federal Regular Army [*Federation of South Arabia*] .... FRA
Federal Regulation of Employment Service [*A publication*] (DLA) .... FRES
Federal Regulation of Lobbying Act .... FRLA
Federal Regulatory Flexibility Act (IEEE) .... FRFA
Federal Regulatory Plan [*Database*] (IID) .... FRP
Federal Reporter [*A publication*] (DLA) .... F
Federal Reporter [*A publication*] (DLA) .... Fed
Federal Reporter [*A publication*] (DLA) .... Fed R
Federal Reporter [*A publication*] (DLA) .... Fed Rep
Federal Reporter [*A publication*] (DLA) .... FR
Federal Reporter, Second Series [*A publication*] (DLA) .... F 2d
Federal Reporter, Second Series [*A publication*] (DLA) .... Fed 2d
Federal Reporter, Third Series [*A publication*] .... F 3d
Federal Reporting Data System (EPA) .... FRDS
Federal Reporting Data System (GNE) .... FRDS
Federal Reports Act (DLA) .... FRA
Federal Representative [*Job Training and Partnership Act*] (OICC) .... FR
Federal Republic (EY) .... FR
Federal Republic of Germany [*ANSI two-letter standard code*] (CNC) .... DE

Federal Republic of Germany [*ANSI three-letter standard code*] (CNC) .... DEU
Federal Republic of Germany (AABC) .... FRG
Federal Republic of Germany [*IYRU nationality code*] (IYR) .... G
Federal Republic of Germany [*NATO*] .... GE
Federal Research Contract Center .... FRCC
Federal Research Division [*Library of Congress*] (GFGA) .... FRD
Federal Research in Progress [*NTIS*] [*Department of Commerce Information service or system*] (IID) .... FEDRIP
Federal Research in Progress Database (USGC) .... FEDRIP
Federal Research Internet Coordinating Committee [*National Science Foundation*] .... FRICC
Federal Research on Biological and Health Effects of Ionizing Radiations .... FREIR
Federal Research Report [*Business Publishers, Inc.*] [*Information service or system*] (CRD) .... FRR
Federal Reserve .... FR
Federal Reserve Act [*1913*] .... FRA
Federal Reserve Bank of Atlanta, Atlanta, GA [*OCLC symbol*] (OCLC) .... GFR
Federal Reserve Bank of Atlanta, Research Library, Atlanta, GA [*Library symbol Library of Congress*] (LCLS) .... GAFR
Federal Reserve Bank of Boston, Boston, MA [*Library symbol Library of Congress*] (LCLS) .... MBFR
Federal Reserve Bank of Boston, Boston, MA [*OCLC symbol*] (OCLC) RF1
Federal Reserve Bank of Chicago, Chicago, IL [*Library symbol Library of Congress*] (LCLS) .... ICFRB
Federal Reserve Bank of Chicago Library, Chicago, IL [*OCLC symbol*] (OCLC) .... ITT
Federal Reserve Bank of Cleveland, Cleveland, OH [*Library symbol Library of Congress*] (LCLS) .... OClFRB
Federal Reserve Bank of Dallas, Dallas, TX [*OCLC symbol*] (OCLC) .... FRD
Federal Reserve Bank of Dallas, Dallas, TX [*Library symbol Library of Congress*] (LCLS) .... TxDaFR
Federal Reserve Bank of Kansas City, Kansas City, MO [*OCLC symbol*] (OCLC) .... FRK
Federal Reserve Bank of Kansas City, Kansas City, MO [*Library symbol Library of Congress*] (LCLS) .... MoKFR
Federal Reserve Bank of Philadelphia, Philadelphia, PA [*OCLC symbol*] (OCLC) .... FRC
Federal Reserve Bank of Philadelphia, Philadelphia, PA [*Library symbol Library of Congress*] (LCLS) .... PPFRB
Federal Reserve Bank of Richmond, Richmond, VA [*OCLC symbol*] (OCLC) .... FRR
Federal Reserve Bank of Richmond, Richmond, VA [*Library symbol Library of Congress*] (LCLS) .... ViRFR
Federal Reserve Bank of St. Louis, St. Louis, MO [*OCLC symbol*] (OCLC)..... FRS
Federal Reserve Bank of San Francisco, San Francisco, CA [*Library symbol Library of Congress*] (LCLS) .... CSfFB
Federal Reserve Banks [*of FRS*] .... FRB
Federal Reserve Board [*Later, BGFRS*] .... FRB
Federal Reserve Board Weekly [*Database*] [*I. P. Sharp Associates*] [*Information service or system*] (CRD) .... FRBW
Federal Reserve Communications System .... FRCS
Federal Reserve District (MHDB) .... FR DIST
Federal Reserve District .... FRD
Federal Reserve Note .... FRN
Federal Reserve System [*Banking*] .... FED
Federal Reserve System [*Independent government agency*] .... FRS
Federal Reserve System Bank .... FRSB
Federal Reserve System, Board of Governors, Washington, DC [*OCLC symbol*] (OCLC) .... FRG
Federal Retirement Thrift Investment Board (GFGA) .... FRTIB
Federal Revenue Forms (Prentice-Hall, Inc.) [*A publication*] (DLA) .... Fed Revenue Forms (P-H)
Federal Rlty Inv Tr SBI [*NYSE symbol*] (TTSB) .... FRT
Federal Rules of Appellate Procedure [*A publication*] (DLA) .... Fed R App P
Federal Rules of Appellate Procedure [*A publication*] .... FRAP
Federal Rules of Civil Procedure [*A publication*] (DLA) .... Fed R Civ P
Federal Rules of Civil Procedure [*A publication*] (HGAA) .... Fed R Civ Proc
Federal Rules of Civil Procedure [*A publication*] (DLA) .... Fed R Civil P
Federal Rules of Civil Procedure [*A publication*] (DLA) .... Fed Rules Civ Proc
Federal Rules of Civil Procedure [*A publication*] (DLA) .... FRCP
Federal Rules of Civil Procedure [*A publication*] (AAGC) .... FRCP
Federal Rules of Criminal Procedure [*A publication*] (DLA) .... Fed R Crim P
Federal Rules of Criminal Procedure [*A publication*] (HGAA) .... Fed R Crim Proc
Federal Rules of Criminal Procedure [*A publication*] (DLA) .... Fed Rules Cr Proc
Federal Rules of Evidence [*A publication*] (DLA) .... Fed Evid R
Federal Rules of Evidence [*A publication*] (DLA) .... Fed R Evid
Federal Rules of Evidence .... FRE
Federal Rules of Evidence Service [*A publication*] (DLA) .... Fed R Evid Serv
Federal Rules Service [*A publication*] (DLA) .... Fed Rules Serv
Federal Rules Service, Second Series [*A publication*] (DLA) .... Fed R Serv 2d (Callaghan)
Federal Rules Service, Second Series [*A publication*] (DLA) .... Fed Rules Serv 2d
Federal Safety Advisory Council [*Later, FACOSH*] .... FSAC
Federal Safety Council .... FSC
Federal Sales Tax [*Canada*] .... FST
Federal Savings and Loan Association [*New Deal*] .... FSLA
Federal Savings & Loan Insurance Corp. [*of FHLBB*] [*Pronounced "FIZ-lick" Functions transferred to SAIF, 1989*] .... FSLIC
Federal Savings Bank .... FSB
Federal Science Policy Council [*Later, FCCSET*] .... FSPC
Federal Screw Works [*Associated Press*] (SAG) .... FdScrw
Federal Screw Works [*NASDAQ symbol*] (NQ) .... FSCR
Federal Secure Telephone Service [*or System*] [*DoD*] .... FSTS
Federal Securities and Exchange Commission [*New Deal*] .... FSEC
Federal Securities Law Reporter [*Commerce Clearing House*] [*A publication*] (DLA) .... Fed Sec L Rep
Federal Securities Law Reporter (Commerce Clearing House) [*A publication*] (DLA) .... CCH Fed Sec L Rep
Federal Security Agency [*Functions and units transferred to HEW, 1953*] .... FSA
Federal Security Agency, Health, Education, and Welfare .... FSHEW
Federal Security Forces .... FSF
Federal Service Campaign for National Health Agencies [*Later, National Health Agencies for the Combined Federal Campaign*] (EA) .... FSCNHA
Federal Service Entrance Examination [*Later, PACE*] [*Civil Service*] .... FSEE
Federal Service Impasses Panel .... FSIP
Federal Services Podiatric Medical Association (EA) .... FSPMA
Federal Sewage Research Association [*Later, Federal Water Quality Association*] .... FSRA
Federal Shelter Incentive Program .... FSIP
Federal Signal [*NYSE symbol*] (TTSB) .... FSS
Federal Signal Corp. [*Associated Press*] (SAG) .... FedSignl
Federal Signal Corp. [*Formerly, Federal Sign & Signal Corp.*] [*NYSE symbol*] (SPSG) .... FSS
Federal Simulation Center .... FSC
Federal Software Exchange Center .... FSEC
Federal Software Exchange Center .... FSWEC
Federal Software Exchange Program (AAGC) .... FSEP
Federal Solar Energy Research Institute [*Energy Research and Development Administration*] .... FSERI
Federal South East Asia Line [*Steamship*] (MHDW) .... FEDSEA
Federal Specification .... FED
Federal Specification .... FEDSPEC
Federal Specification .... FS
Federal Specification Board .... FSB
Federal Specifications Executive Committee .... FSEC
Federal Sports Club [*Australia*] .... FSC
Federal Standard .... FEDSTD
Federal Standard .... FS
Federal Standard Requisitioning and Issue Procedure .... FEDSTRIP
Federal Standard Stock Catalog .... FSSC
Federal/State Cooperative Program for Population Estimates and Projections (OICC) .... FSCP
Federal/State Initiative Coordinating Committee [*Department of Commerce*] (GFGA) .... F/SICC
Federal/State Programs [*Social Security Administration*] (OICC) .... FSP
Federal Statistical Data Center (IEEE) .... FSDC
Federal Statistical Policy and Standards Office (OICC) .... FSPSO
Federal Statistics Users' Conference [*Defunct*] (EA) .... FSUC
Federal Statutes, Annotated [*A publication*] (DLA) .... Fed Stat Ann
Federal Statutes, Annotated [*A publication*] (DLA) .... FSA
Federal Stock [*or Supply*] **Catalog** (NG) .... FSC
Federal Stock [*or Supply*] **Classification** [*Army*] .... FSC
Federal Stock Control .... FSC
Federal Stock Group .... FSG
Federal Stock Item .... FSI
Federal Stock Listings .... FSL
Federal Stock Number [*Later, NSN*] .... FSN
Federal Stock Number [*later, NSN*] **Master Data Record** .... FSNMDR
Federal Student Aid Program [*Department of Education*] (GFGA) .... FSAP
Federal Student Financial Aid [*Department of Education*] (GFGA) .... FSFA
Federal Subsistence Homesteads Corp. [*New Deal*] .... FSHC
Federal Supplement [*A publication*] (DLA) .... Fed Sup
Federal Supplement [*A publication*] (DLA) .... Fed Supp
Federal Supplement [*A publication*] (DLA) .... FS
Federal Supplement Reporter [*West*] [*A publication*] (AAGC) .... F Supp
Federal Supplemental Benefits .... FSB
Federal Supplemental Compensation [*Unemployment insurance*] (OICC) .... FSC
Federal Supply Catalog (MCD) .... FSC
Federal Supply Catalog Identification List (MSA) .... FSCIL
Federal Supply Classification [*DoD*] (MCD) .... FSC
Federal Supply Classification Code .... FSCC
Federal Supply Classification Group (AFM) .... FSCG
Federal Supply Classification Listing .... FSCL
Federal Supply Classification/Material Management Aggregation (MCD) .... FSC/MMAC
Federal Supply Classification System .... FSCS
Federal Supply Code (MCD) .... FSC
Federal Supply Code for Manufacturers .... FSCM
Federal Supply Code for Non-Manufacturers .... FSCNM
Federal Supply Group [*Air Force*] .... FSG
Federal Supply Group [*Air Force*] (AFM) .... FSGp
Federal Supply Manufacturers' Code [*DoD*] .... FSMC
Federal Supply Schedule .... FSS
Federal Supply Service (USGC) .... FSS
Federal Supply Storage Depot .... FSSD
Federal Surplus Commodities Corp. .... FSCC
Federal Systems Division (SAA) .... FSD
Federal Tax Coordinator Second (Tax Research Institute of America) [*A publication*] (DLA) .... Fed Tax Coordinator 2d (RIA)
Federal Tax Deposit [*IRS*] .... FTD
Federal Tax Enforcement [*A publication*] (DLA) .... Fed Tax Enf
Federal Tax Included .... FTI
Federal Taxes [*Prentice-Hall, Inc.*] [*A publication*] (DLA) .... Fed Taxes
Federal Taxes: Estate and Gift Taxes [*Prentice-Hall, Inc.*] [*A publication*] (DLA) .... Fed Taxes Est & Gift
Federal Taxes (Prentice-Hall, Inc.) [*A publication*] (DLA) .... Fed Taxes (P-H)
Federal Taxes (Prentice-Hall, Inc.) [*A publication*] (DLA) .... P-H Fed Taxes
Federal Taxes (Prentice-Hall, Inc.) [*A publication*] (DLA) .... P-H Tax
Federal Telecommunications Center (NUCP) .... FTC

Federal Telecommunications Laboratory [*Air Force*] ..... FTL
Federal Telecommunications Records Center (NRCH) ..... FTRC
Federal Telecommunications Standards (AAGC) ..... FED-STDS
Federal Telecommunications Standards Committee ..... FTSC
Federal Telecommunications System [*of GSA*] (NOAA) ..... FTC
Federal Telecommunications System [*of GSA*] ..... FTS
Federal Telephone and Radio ..... FTR
Federal Telephone System (KSC) ..... FTS
Federal Teleprocessing Service [*GSA*] ..... FTS
Federal Test Method Standards (MCD) ..... FTMS
Federal Test Procedure ..... FTP
Federal Test Procedure Revision Project ..... FTPRP
Federal Theater Project ..... FTP
Federal Timber Purchasers Association (EA) ..... FTPA
Federal Tobacco Inspectors Mutual Association ..... FTIMA
Federal Tort Claims Act ..... FTCA
Federal Trade Commission [*Independent government agency*] [*OCLC symbol*] ..... FTC
Federal Trade Commission Decisions [*A publication*] (DLA) ..... FTC
Federal Trade Reporter [*A publication*] (DLA) ..... Fed Tr Rep
Federal Trade Union Congress [*European*] ..... FTUC
Federal Trade Zone ..... FTZ
Federal Train Wreck Statute ..... FTWS
Federal Training Centre, Penitentiary, Ministry of the Solicitor General [*Centre Federal de Formation, Penitencier, Ministere du Solliciteur General*] **Laval, Quebec** [*Library symbol National Library of Canada*] (NLC) ..... QLASGPT
Federal Transit Administration [*Formerly, UMTA*] [*Department of Transportation*] ..... FTA
Federal Travel Regulations (NRCH) ..... FTR
Federal Trial Examiners Conference [*Later, FALJC*] (EA) ..... FTEC
Federal Trial Reports [*Maritime Law Book Co. Ltd.*] [*Canada Information service or system*] (CRD) ..... FTR
Federal Triangle [*Washington, DC*] ..... FT
Federal Underground Injection Control Reporting System [*Environmental Protection Agency*] (ERG) ..... FURS
Federal Unemployment Account [*Unemployment insurance*] ..... FUA
Federal Unemployment Benefit and Allowance Account [*Unemployment insurance*] ..... FUBA
Federal Unemployment Tax (MCD) ..... FUT
Federal Unemployment Tax Act [*1954*] ..... FUTA
Federal Union (DAS) ..... FU
Federal Union of European Nationalities [*Political party*] (PPW) ..... FUEN
Federal Union of Wire Weavers of the United Kingdom ..... FUWW
Federal Urban Driving Schedule ..... FUDS
Federal Utility Regulation, Annotated [*A publication*] (DLA) ..... FURA
Federal Visibility Monitoring Program (GNE) ..... FVMP
Federal Voting Assistance Program ..... FVAP
Federal Wage Systems [*DoD*] ..... FWS
Federal Warning Center (NATG) ..... FWC
Federal Waste Repository (NUCP) ..... FWR
Federal Water Pollution Control Act [*1965*] (NRCH) ..... FWPCA
Federal Water Pollution Control Administration [*Later, OWP*] [*Department of the Interior*] ..... FWPCA
Federal Water Quality Administration [*Later, OWP*] [*Environmental Protection Agency*] ..... FWQA
Federal Water Quality Association (EA) ..... FWQA
Federal Water Resources Assistance Program (EERA) ..... FWRAP
Federal Water Resources Council ..... FWRC
Federal Way School District Central Library, Federal Way, WA [*Library symbol Library of Congress*] (LCLS) ..... WaFwS
Federal Wholesale Druggists Association [*Later, DWA*] (EA) ..... FWDA
Federal Wildlife Permit Office [*Department of the Interior*] ..... FWPO
Federal Women's Interagency Board (EA) ..... FWIB
Federal Women's Program ..... FWP
Federal Women's Program Advisory Committee (GFGA) ..... FWPAC
Federal Women's Program Committee/Coordinator (AABC) ..... FWOP
Federal Women's Program Committee/Coordinator ..... FWPC
Federal Works Agency [*Abolished, 1949*] ..... FWA
Federal Writers' Project [*Obsolete*] ..... FWP
Federalist ..... FED
[*The*] **Federalist, by Hamilton** [*A publication*] (DLA) ..... Fed
Federalist Caucus (EA) ..... FC
Federalist Society for Law and Public Policy Studies (EA) ..... FSLPPS
Federally Assisted Code Enforcement [*Proposed HUD program*] ..... FACE
Federally Chartered Research Centers (AAGC) ..... FCRC
Federally Employed Women (EA) ..... FEW
Federally Funded Research and Development Center [*National Science Foundation*] ..... FFRDC
Federally Insured Student Loan ..... FISL
Federal-Mogul ..... F-M
Federal-Mogul [*NYSE symbol*] (TTSB) ..... FMO
Federal-Mogul Corp. [*Associated Press*] (SAG) ..... FedMog
Federal-Mogul Corp. [*NYSE symbol*] (SPSG) ..... FMO
Federal-Provincial Relations Office [*Canada*] ..... FPRO
Federal-Provincial Taxation and Fiscal Relations Library, Nova Scotia Departmentof Finance, Halifax, Nova Scotia [*Library symbol National Library of Canada*] (NLC) ..... NSHFIF
Federalsburg, MD [*FM radio station call letters*] (RBYB) ..... WTDK
Federal-State Cooperative for Public Library Data ..... FSCS
Federal-State Emergency Unemployment Compensation Act [*1970*] ..... FSEUCA
Federated ..... FDRTD
Federated (WDAA) ..... FED
Federated Antisubmarine Combat System [*Navy*] (CAAL) ..... FASCS
Federated Association of Australian Housewives, Tasmania ..... FAAHT
Federated Brick, Tile, and Pottery Industrial Union of Australia ..... FBTPIU
Federated Cold Storage and Meat Preserving Employees' Union of Australia ..... FCSMPEUA
Federated Computing Research Conference ..... FCRC
Federated Council of Beth Jacob Schools (EA) ..... FCBJS
Federated Council of Israel Institutions (EA) ..... FCII
Federated Department Stores, Inc. [*NYSE symbol*] (SAG) ..... FD
Federated Department Stores, Inc. [*Associated Press*] (SAG) ..... FdDS
Federated Department Stores, Inc. [*Associated Press*] (SAG) ..... FedrDS
Federated Dept Stores [*NYSE symbol*] (TTSB) ..... FD
Federated Engineering Union ..... FEU
Federated Funeral Directors of America [*Commercial firm*] ..... FFD of A
Federated Funeral Directors of America [*Commercial firm*] (EA) ..... FFDA
Federated Furnishing Trades Society [*Australia*] ..... FFSTA
Federated Gas Employees' Industrial Union [*Australia*] ..... FGEIU
Federated Liquor and Allied Industries Employees Union of Australia ..... FLAIEUA
Federated Malay States ..... FMS
Federated Malay States Reports [*A publication*] (DLA) ..... FMSR
Federated Malay Straits Volunteer Reserve [*British military*] (DMA) ..... FMSVR
Federated Millers and Manufacturing Grocers' Employees' Union of Australia ..... FMMGEUA
Federated Mining Mechanics Association of Australia ..... FMMAA
Federated Miscellaneous and Hospital Service Union [*Australia*] ..... FMHSU
Federated Miscellaneous Workers' Union of Australia ..... FMWU
Federated Municipal and Shire Council Employees' Union of Australia ..... FMSCEUA
Federated Music Clubs of Australia ..... FMCA
Federated Pecan Growers' Associations of the United States (EA) ..... FPGAUS
Federated Russian Orthodox Clubs (EA) ..... FROC
Federated Ship Painters and Dockers' Union of Australia ..... FSPDUA
Federated States of Micronesia [*ANSI two-letter standard code*] (CNC) ..... FM
Federated States of Micronesia [*ANSI three-letter standard code*] (CNC) ..... FSM
Federated Superannuation Scheme for Universities [*British*] ..... FSSU
Federated Tanners' Association of Australia ..... FTA
Federated Tanners' Association of Australia ..... FTAA
Federated Teachers' Union of Victoria [*Australia*] ..... FTUV
Federated Tobacco and Cigarette Workers' Union [*Australia*] ..... FTCWU
Federated Tobacco Workers' Union of Australia ..... FTWUA
Federated Union of Employers [*Ireland*] (IMH) ..... FUE
Federated Wire Drawers' Association [*A union*] [*British*] ..... FWDA
Federated Women in Timber (EA) ..... FWIT
Federated Women's Institutes of Canada ..... FWIC
Federation (EY) ..... FED
Federation ..... FEDN
Federation ..... FEDRN
Federation Abolitionniste Internationale [*International Abolitionist Federation*] [*India*] ..... FAI
Federation Aeronautique Internationale [*International Aeronautical Federation*] [*France*] ..... FAI
Federation Africaine des Chambres de Commerce [*Federation of African Chambersof Commerce*] [*Ethiopia*] (EAIO) ..... FACC
Federation Africaine des Syndicats du Petrole et Assimiles [*African Federation of Trade Unions of Oil and Petrochemicals*] [*Tripoli, Libya*] (EAIO) ..... FASPA
Federation Against Copyright Theft [*British*] ..... FACT
Federation Against Software Theft ..... FAST
Federation Americaine du Travail et Congres des Organisations Industrielles [*American Federation of Labor and Congress of Industrial Organizations - AFL-CIO*] [*Canada*] ..... FAT-COI
Federation Baden-Powell [*Canada*] (EAIO) ..... FBP
Federation Bancaire de la Communaute Europeenne [*Banking Federation of the European Community*] (EAIO) ..... FBCE
Federation Canadien des Societes de Biologie (AC) ..... FCSB
Federation Canadienne de Gymnastique Rythmique Sportive [*Canadian Modern Rhythmic Gymnastics Federation - CMRGF*] ..... FCGRS
Federation Canadienne de Handball Olympique [*Canadian Team Handball Federation - CTHF*] ..... FCHO
Federation Canadienne de l'Agriculture [*Canadian Federation of Agriculture - CFA*] ..... FCA
Federation Canadienne de Sport Scolaire [*Canadian Federation of Provincial School Athletic Associations*] ..... FCSS
Federation Canadienne de Yachting [*Canadian Yachting Association*] ..... FCY
Federation Canadienne des Amis de Musees (AC) ..... FCAM
Federation Canadienne des Archers [*Federation of Canadian Archers*] ..... FCA
Federation Canadienne des Cine-Clubs [*Canada*] ..... FCCC
Federation Canadienne des Communications [*Canadian Federation of Communications Workers - CFCW*] ..... FCC
Federation Canadienne des Echecs [*Chess Federation of Canada*] ..... FCE
Federation Canadienne des Enseignants [*Canadian Teachers' Federation - CTF*] ..... FCE
Federation Canadienne des Etudes Humaines [*Canadian Federation for the Humanities - CFH*] ..... FCEH
Federation Canadienne des Etudiantes et Etudiants (AC) ..... FCEE
Federation Canadienne des Etudiants [*Canadian Federation of Students*] ..... FCE
Federation Canadienne des Femmes Diplomees des Universites [*Canadian Federation of University Women*] ..... FCFDU
Federation Canadienne des Maires et des Municipalites [*Canadian Federation of Mayors and Municipalities*] ..... FCMM
Federation Canadienne des Municipalites [*Federation of Canadian Municipalities*] ..... FCM
Federation Canadienne des Sciences Sociales [*Social Science Federation of Canada - SSFC*] ..... FCSS
Federation Canadienne des Services de Garde a l'Enfance [*Formerly, Canadian Child Day Care Federation*] (AC) ..... FCSGE

Federation Canadienne du Sport Automobile [*Canadian Automobile Sport Clubs*] ..... FCSA
Federation Canadienne du Sport Boules [*An association*] (EAIO) ..... FCSB
Federation Canadienne du Travail [*Canadian Federation of Labour - CFL*] ..... FCT
Federation Canadienne du Travail (AC) ..... FCT
Federation Canadienne Nationale des Syndicats Independants [*Canadian National Federation of Independent Unions - CNFIU*] ..... FCNSI
Federation Colombophile Internationale [*International Pigeon Federation - IPF*] (EAIO) ..... FCI
Federation Costing System (DGA) ..... FCS
Federation Council (EA) ..... FC
Federation Cynologique Internationale [*International Federation of Kennel Clubs*] [*Thuin, Belgium*] (EA) ..... FCI
Federation d'Action Nationale et Europeene [*Federation of National and European Action*] [*France Political party*] (PPE) ..... FANE
Federation d'Associations de Techniciens des Industries de Peintures, Vernis, Emaux, et Encres d'Imprimerie de l'Europe [*Federation of the Associations of Technicians of the Paint, Varnish, and Ink Industries of Continental Europe*] (EAIO) ..... FATIPEC
Federation d'Associations d'Ingenieurs et de Scientifiques [*Federation of Engineering and Scientific Associations*] [*Canada*] (EAIO) ..... FAIS
Federation de Bourses de la Communaute Europeenne [*Federation of Stock Exchanges in the European Community*] (EAIO) ..... FBCE
Federation de la Fonction Publique Europeenne [*European Civil Service Federation*] (EAIO) ..... FFPE
Federation de l'Industrie de l'Huile d'Olive de la CEE [*Federation of the European Economic Community Olive Oil Industry*] ..... FEDOLIVE
Federation de l'Industrie de l'Huilerie de la CEE [*EEC Seed Crushers and Oil Processors' Federation*] [*Belgium*] (EAIO) ..... FEDIOL
Federation de l'Industrie Dentaire en Europe [*Federation of the European Dental Industry*] ..... FIDE
Federation de l'Industrie Europeenne de la Construction [*European Construction Industry Federation*] (EAIO) ..... FIEC
Federation de l'Industrie Granitiere Europeenne [*Federation of the European Granite Industry*] (EAIO) ..... FIGE
Federation de l'Industrie Marbriere de la Communaute Economique Europeenne [*Federation of the Marble Industry of the European Economic Community*] (EAIO) ..... FIMCEE
Federation Democratique Internationale des Femmes [*Women's International Democratic Federation - WIDF*] [*Germany*] (EAIO) ..... FDIF
Federation Dentaire Internationale [*International Dental Federation*] [*British*] (EA) ..... FDI
Federation des Affaires Sociales, Inc. [*Federation of Social Affairs*] [*Canada*] ..... FAS
Federation des Alliances Francaises en Australie [*Federation of Alliances Francaises (Institutes for the study of French language and culture) in Australia*] ..... FAFA
Federation des Associations Canadiennes sur l'Environnement [*Federation of Associations on the Canadian Environment*] ..... FACE
Federation des Associations d'Antiquaires du Marche Commun (EA) ..... FAAMC
Federation des Associations de Chasseurs de la CEE [*Federation of Hunters' Associations of the European Economic Community*] [*Brussels, Belgium*] ..... FACE
Federation des Associations de Fabricants de Produits Alimentaires Surgeles d e la CE [*European Federation of Quick Frozen Food Manufacturers*] [*Belgium*] (EAIO) ..... FAFPAS
Federation des Associations d'Editeurs de Periodiques de la CE [*Brussels, Belgium*] (EAIO) ..... FAEPC
Federation des Associations Europeennes des Constructeurs de Fenetres [*Federation of European Window Manufacturers Associations - FEWMA*] (EA) ..... FAECF
Federation des Associations Internationales Etablies en Belgique [*Federation of International Associations Established in Belgium*] ..... FAIB
Federation des Associations Roumaines du Canada [*Federation of Romanian Associations of Canada*] ..... FAR
Federation des Caisses Populaires Desjardins, Levis, Quebec [*Library symbol National Library of Canada*] (NLC) ..... QLFCP
Federation des Clubs Cooperatifs de Consommation [*Federation of Consumer Cooperative Associations*] [*Canada*] ..... FCCC
Federation des Concours Internationaux de Musique [*Federation of International Music Competitions - FIMC*] (EAIO) ..... FCIM
Federation des Employes Congolais des Banques [*Federation of Congolese Bank Clerks*] ..... FECB
Federation des Enseignants d'Afrique Noire [*Federation of Teachers of Black Africa*] ..... FEAN
Federation des Etudiants Revolutionnaires [*Federation of Revolutionary Students*] [*France*] ..... FER
Federation des Femmes Canadiennes-Francaises [*Federation of French-Canadian Women*] ..... FFCF
Federation des Foires et Salons du Benelux [*Federation of Fairs and Trade Shows of BENELUX - FFTSB*] (EA) ..... FFSB
Federation des Fondations pour la Sante Mondiale [*Federation of World Health Foundations - FWHF*] [*Geneva, Switzerland*] (EA) ..... FFSM
Federation des Gynecologues et Obstetriciens de Langue Francaise [*Federation of French-Language Gynaecologists and Obstetricians*] [*Paris, France*] (EAIO) ..... FGOLF
Federation des Importateurs et Producteurs d'Adjuvants et Additifs pour Coulis Mortier et Beton de Ciment [*Association of Importers and Producers of Admixtures*] (EAIO) ..... FIPAH
Federation des Industries de Ficellerie et Corderie de l'Europe Occidentale [*Federation of Western European Rope and Twine Industries*] (EA) ..... EUROCORD
Federation des Industries de Matieres Premieres et des Ameliorants pour la Boulangerie et la Patisserie dans la CEE [*European Federation of Manufacturers of Bakers' and Confectioners' Ingredients and Additives*] [*Common Market*] ..... FEDIMA
Federation des Ingenieurs des Telecommunications de la Communaute Europeenne [*Federation of Telecommunications Engineers in the European Community*] ..... FITCE
Federation des Institutions Internationales Semi-Officielles et Privees Etabliesa Geneve [*Federation of Semi-Official and Private International Institutions Established in Geneva*] [*Switzerland*] (EA) ..... FIIG
Federation des Jeunes Canadiens-Francais [*Federation of French-Canadian Youth*] ..... FJCF
Federation des Jeunes Chefs d'Entreprises d'Europe [*European Federation of Young Managers*] ..... FJCEE
Federation des Jeunes Progressistes-Conservateurs du Canada [*Progressive Conservative Youth Federation of Canada*] ..... FJPC
Federation des Medecins Omnipracticiens du Quebec, Montreal, PQ, Canada [*Library symbol Library of Congress*] (LCLS) ..... CaQMFMO
Federation des Medecins Omnipraticiens du Quebec, Montreal, Quebec [*Library symbol National Library of Canada*] (NLC) ..... QMFMO
Federation des Medecins Specialistes du Quebec, Montreal, PQ, Canada [*Library symbol Library of Congress*] (LCLS) ..... CaQMFMS
Federation des Medecins Specialistes du Quebec, Montreal, Quebec [*Library symbol National Library of Canada*] (NLC) ..... QMFMS
Federation des Mouvements Socialistes Regionalistes de la Reunion [*Federation of Socialist Regionalist Movements of Reunion*] [*Political party*] (PPW) ..... FMSR
Federation des Pecheurs de l'Est [*Eastern Fishermen's Federation - EFF*] [*Canada*] ..... FPE
Federation des Personnels Africains de Police [*Federation of African Police*] ..... FAPAP
Federation des Republicains de Progres [*Federation of Progressive Republicans*] [*France Political party*] (PPW) ..... FRP
Federation des Scouts du Congo ..... FEBOSCO
Federation des Socialistes Democrates [*Federation of Democratic Socialists*] [*France Political party*] (PPE) ..... FSD
Federation des Societes d'Assurances de Droit National Africains [*Federation of African National Insurance Companies*] [*Dakar, Senegal*] (EAIO) ..... FANAF
Federation des Societes Suisses d'Employes [*Federation of Swiss Employees' Societies*] ..... FSSE
Federation des Syndicats du Secteur de l'Aluminium, Inc. [*Federation of Aluminum Sector Unions, Inc.*] [*Canada*] ..... FSSA
Federation des Syndicats Libres des Travailleurs Luxembourgeois [*Free Luxembourg Workers' Federation*] ..... FSL
Federation des Travailleurs du Papier et de la Foret [*Federation of Paper and Forest Workers*] [*Canada*] ..... FTPF
Federation des Travailleurs et Travailleuses du Quebec [*Canada*] (CROSS) ..... FTQ
Federation des Unions de Familles [*Federation of Family Unions*] [*Canada*] ..... FUF
Federation des Unions Royalistes de France [*Federation of Royalist Unions of France*] (PPW) ..... FURF
Federation Employment and Guidance Service (EA) ..... FEGS
Federation Equestre Internationale [*International Equestrian Federation*] [*Berne, Switzerland*] (EAIO) ..... FEI
Federation Europeene des Fabricants de Caisses et Emballages en Bois [*European Federation of Manufacturers of Timber Crates and Packing Cases*] (PDAA) ..... FEFCEB
Federation Europeenne d'Associations Nationales d'Ingenieurs [*European Federation of National Engineering Associations*] (EAIO) ..... FEANI
Federation Europeenne de Climatotherapie [*European Society of Climatotherapy - ESC*] [*French*] (EAIO) ..... FEC
Federation Europeenne de la Ganterie de Peau [*European Federation of Leather Glove-Making*] [*EC*] (ECED) ..... FEGAP
Federation Europeenne de la Manutention [*European Federation of Handling Industries*] (EAIO) ..... FEM
Federation Europeenne de la Publicite Exterieure [*European Federation of Outdoor Advertising*] [*France*] ..... FEPE
Federation Europeenne de la Salmoniculture [*Federation of the European Trout and Salmon Industry*] [*Formerly, European Salmon Breeding Federation*] (EA) ..... FES
Federation Europeenne de la Sante Animale [*European Federation of Animal Health*] [*Belgium*] (ECED) ..... FEDESA
Federation Europeenne de l'Emballage Souple (EAIO) ..... FEDES
Federation Europeenne de l'Industrie de la Brosserie et de la Pinceuterie [*European Federation of the Brush and Paint Brush Industries - EFBPBI*] (EAIO) ..... FEIBP
Federation Europeenne de l'Industrie des Aliments pour Animaux Familiers [*European Petfood Industry Federation*] (EAIO) ..... FEDIAF
Federation Europeenne de l'Industrie du Contreplaque [*European Federation of the Plywood Industry - EFPI*] (EA) ..... FEIC
Federation Europeenne de Psychanalyse [*European Psycho-Analytical Federation - EPF*] (EAIO) ..... FEP
Federation Europeenne de Zootechnie [*European Association for Animal Production - EAAP*] [*France*] (ASF) ..... FEZ
Federation Europeenne des Associations Aerosols [*Federation of European Aerosol Associations*] (EA) ..... FEA
Federation Europeenne des Associations d'Analystes Financiers [*European Federation of Financial Analysts' Societies - EFFAS*] (EAIO) ..... FEAAF
Federation Europeenne des Associations de Conseils en Organisation [*European Federation of Management Consultants Associations*] [*France*] ..... FEACO
Federation Europeenne des Associations de Dieteticiens [*European Federation of the Associations of Dietitians - EFAD*] (EAIO) ..... FEAD

Federation Europeenne des Associations des Psychologues [*European Federation of Professional Psychologists Associations - EFPPA*] (EA) .... FEAP
Federation Europeenne des Associations d'Ingenieurs de Securite et de Chefs de Service de Securite [*European Federation of Associations of Engineers and Heads of Industrial Safety Services*] .... FEAICS
Federation Europeenne des Associations d'Instruments a Ecrire [*Federation of European Writing Instruments Associations*] (EAIO) .... FEAIE
Federation Europeenne des Associations Nationales des Negociants en Materiaux deConstruction [*European Association of National Builders Merchants Associations*] (EAIO) .... UFEMAT
Federation Europeenne des Constructeurs d'Equipement de Grandes Cuisines [*European Federation of Catering Equipment Manufacturers - EFCEM*] (EA) .... FECEGC
Federation Europeenne des Constructeurs d'Equipement Petrolier [*European Federation of Petroleum Equipment Manufacturers*] .... FECEP
Federation Europeenne des Ecoles [*Later, European Schools Federation*] (EAIO) .... FEDE
Federation Europeenne des Emballeurs et Distributeurs de Miel [*European Federation of Honey Packers and Distributors*] [*British*] (EAIO) .... FEEDM
Federation Europeenne des Fabricants d'Adjuvants pour la Nutrition Animale [*European Federation of Manufacturers of Feed Additives*] (EAIO) .... FEFANA
Federation Europeenne des Fabricants d'Aliments Composes [*European Federation of Compound Animal Feedingstuff Manufacturers*] (EAIO) .... FEFAC
Federation Europeenne des Fabricants de Carton Ondule [*European Federation of Manufacturers of Corrugated Board*] [*France*] .... FEFCO
Federation Europeenne des Fabricants de Ceramiques Sanitaires [*European Federation of Ceramic Sanitaryware Manufacturers - EFCSM*] (EAIO) .... FECS
Federation Europeenne des Fabricants de Palettes et Emballages en Bois [*European Federation of Pallet and Wooden Crate Manufacturers - EFPWCM*] (EAIO) .... FEFPEB
Federation Europeenne des Fabricants de Panneaux de Fibres [*European Federation of Fireboard Manufacturers*] [*EC*] (ECED) .... FEROPA
Federation Europeenne des Fabricants de Produits Abrasifs [*European Federation of the Manufacturers of Abrasive Products*] [*France*] .... FEPA
Federation Europeenne des Fabricants de Produits Refractaires [*Zurich, Switzerland*] (EAIO) .... PRE
Federation Europeenne des Fabricants de Sacs en Papier a Grande Contenance [*European Federation of Multiwall Paper Sacks Manufacturers*] (EAIO) .... EUROSAC
Federation Europeenne des Fabricants de Tuiles et de Briques [*European Association of Brick and Tile Manufacturers*] (EAIO) .... TBE
Federation Europeenne des Fabricants de Tuyaux en Gre [*European Federation of Manufacturers of Salt Glazed Pipes*] (PDAA) .... FEUGRES
Federation Europeenne des Importateurs de Fruits Secs, Conserves, Epices et Miels [*European Federation of Importers of Dried Fruits, Preserves, Spices, and Honey*] .... FRUCOM
Federation Europeenne des Importateurs de Machines et d'Equipements de Bureau [*European Federation of Importers of Business Equipment*] (EAIO) .... FEIM
Federation Europeenne des Industries de Colles et Adhesifs [*Association of European Adhesives Manufacturers*] (EA) .... FEICA
Federation Europeenne des Industries Techniques du Cinema .... FEITC
Federation Europeenne des Jeunesse Bons Templiers [*European Good Templar Youth Federation*] [*Norway*] (EAIO) .... FEJBT
Federation Europeenne des Mandataires de l'Industrie en Propriete Industrielle [*European Federation of Agents of Industry in Industrial Property*] (EAIO) .... FEMIPI
Federation Europeenne des Masseurskinesitherapeutes Praticiens en Physiotherapie .... FEMK
Federation Europeenne des Metallurgistes dans la Communaute [*European Metalworkers' Federation in the Community*] [*EC*] (ECED) .... FEM
Federation Europeenne des Motels [*European Motel Federation*] .... FEM
Federation Europeenne des Organisations des Detaillants en Tabacs [*European Federation of Tobacco Retail Organizations*] (EAIO) .... FEODT
Federation Europeenne des Parfumeurs Detaillants [*European Federation of Perfumery Retailers*] (EAIO) .... FEPD
Federation Europeenne des Personnes Agees [*European Federation for the Welfare of the Elderly*] (EAIO) .... EURAG
Federation Europeenne des Producteurs Autonomes et des Consommateurs Industrielsd'Energie [*European Federation of Autoproducers and Industrial Consumers of Energy*] (EAIO) .... FEPACE
Federation Europeenne des Societes d'Acoustique [*Federation of Acoustical Societies of Europe*] (EAIO) .... FASE
Federation Europeenne des Sports Corporatifs [*European Federation for Company Sports - EFCS*] (EAIO) .... FESC
Federation Europeenne des Syndicats de Fabricants de Menuiseries Industrielles de Batiment [*European Federation of Building Joinery Manufacturers*] (EAIO) .... FEMIB
Federation Europeenne des Syndicats de Fabricants de Panneaux de Particules [*European Federation of Associations of Particleboard Manufacturers*] (EAIO) .... FESYP
Federation Europeenne des Syndicats de Fabricants de Parquets [*European Federation of Parquet Manufacturers Unions*] .... FESFP
Federation Europeenne des Syndicats de la Chimie et des Industries Diverses [*European Federation of Chemical and General Workers Unions*] (EAIO) .... FESCID
Federation Europeenne des Syndicats d'Entreprises d'Isolation [*European Federation of Associations of Insulation Contractors*] (EA) .... FESI
Federation Europeenne des Synicats de Panneaux de Fibres [*European Federation of Manufacturers Associations of Fiber Panels*] (PDAA) .... FEROPA
Federation Europeenne des Transports Aeriens Prives [*European Federation of Independent Air Transport*] .... FETAP
Federation Europeenne des Travailleurs du Batiment et du Bois [*European Federation of Building and Woodworkers - EFBWW*] (EAIO) .... FETBB
Federation Europeenne des Unions Professionelles de Fleuristes [*European Federation of Professional Florists' Unions*] (EAIO) .... FEUPF
Federation Europeenne du Commerce Chimique [*Federation of European Chemical Merchants - FECM*] (EAIO) .... FECC
Federation Europeenne du Mobilier de Bureau [*European Federation of Office Furniture*] [*EC*] (ECED) .... FEMB
Federation Europeenne du Verre d'Emballage [*European Container Glass Federation - ECGF*] (EA) .... FEVE
Federation Europeenne Halterophile [*European Weightlifting Federation - EWF*] (EA) .... FEH
Federation Europeenne pour la Vente et le Service a Domicile [*European Direct Selling Federation*] [*Brussels, Belgium*] (EA) .... FEVSD
Federation Europeenne pour l'Education Catholique des Adultes [*European Associaton for Catholic Adult Education*] (EAIO) .... FEECA
Federation Feminine Franco-Americaine [*Federation of French American Women*] (EA) .... FFFA
Federation for a Democratic China [*Australia*] .... FDC
Federation for a Democratic China, Sydney Branch [*Australia*] .... FDCSB
Federation for Accessible Nursing Education and Licensure (EA) .... FANEL
Federation for American Afghan Action (EA) .... FAAA
Federation for American Immigration Reform (EA) .... FAIR
Federation for Children with Special Needs (EA) .... FCSN
Federation for Constitutional Government [*Defunct*] (EA) .... FCG
Federation for Industrial Retention and Renewal (CROSS) .... FIRR
Federation for Progress [*Defunct*] (EA) .... FFP
Federation for Unified Science Education (EA) .... FUSE
Federation for Universal French (EAIO) .... FUF
Federation Francaise des Cooperatives Agricoles d'Approvisionnement .... FFCAA
Federation Francaise des Cooperatives Agricoles de Cereales .... FFCAC
Federation Francaise du Sport Automobile [*French Federation of Motorsport*] .... FFSA
Federation Generale du Congo [*Congolese General Federation*] .... FGC
Federation Graphique Internationale [*International Graphical Federation - IGF*] [*Berne, Switzerland*] (EAIO) .... FGI
Federation Guadeloupeenne de l'Union pour la Democratie Francaise [*Guadeloupe Federation of the Union for French Democracy*] [*Political party*] (PPW) .... UDF
Federation Guadeloupeenne du Rassemblement pour la Republique [*Guadeloupe Federation of the Rally for the Republic*] [*Political party*] (PPW) .... RPR
Federation Halterophile Internationale [*International Weightlifting Federation - IWF*] (EAIO) .... FHI
Federation Interalliee des Anciens Combattants [*World War I*] [*French*] ..... FIDAC
Federation Interalliee des Evades de Guerre et des Passeurs .... FIDEGEP
Federation International des Societes d'Ingenieurs des Techniques de l'Automobile .... FISITA
Federation International Triathlon (EA) .... FIT
Federation Internationale Amateur de Cyclisme [*International Amateur Cycling Federation*] [*Rome, Italy*] (EA) .... FIAC
Federation Internationale Amateur de Sambo [*Anglet, France*] (EAIO) .... FIAS
Federation Internationale Catholique d'Education Physique et Sportive [*Catholic International Federation for Physical and Sports Education - CIFPSE*] [*Paris, France*] (EAIO) .... FICEP
Federation Internationale Culturelle Feminine [*Women's International Cultural Federation - WICF*] (EAIO) .... FICF
Federation Internationale d'Athletisme Amateur [*International Amateur Athletic Federation - IAAF*] [*British*] (EAIO) .... FIAA
Federation Internationale de Badminton [*International Badminton Federation - IBF*] (EA) .... FIB
Federation Internationale de Baseball [*International Baseball Federation*] .... FIB
Federation Internationale de Basketball Amateur [*International Amateur Basketball Federation*] [*Germany*] (EA) .... FIBA
Federation Internationale de Bobsleigh et de Tobogganing [*International Bobsledding and Tobogganing Federation*] [*Milan, Italy*] (EAIO) .... FIBT
Federation Internationale de Boules [*International Bocce Federation*] [*Turin, Italy*] (EAIO) .... FIB
Federation Internationale de Camping et de Caravanning [*International Federation of Camping and Caravanning*] [*Brussels, Belgium*] (EA) .... FICC
Federation Internationale de Canoe [*International Canoe Federation - ICF*] [*Florence, Italy*] (EAIO) .... FIC
Federation Internationale de Centres Touristiques [*International Federation of Tourist Centres*] (EAIO) .... FICT
Federation Internationale de Chimie Clinique [*International Federation of Clinical Chemistry*] .... FICC
Federation Internationale de Communautes de Jeunesse Catholique Paroissiales [*International Federation of Catholic Parochial Youth Communities*] [*Antwerp, Belgium*] (EAIO) .... FIMCAP
Federation Internationale de Cremation [*International Cremation Federation*] (EAIO) .... FIC
Federation Internationale de Documentation (NITA) .... FID
Federation Internationale de Football Association [*International Federation of Association Football*] [*Zurich, Switzerland*] (EA) .... FIFA
Federation Internationale de Football-Rugby Amateur [*International Amateur Rugby Foundation*] (EA) .... FIRA
Federation Internationale de Genetique [*International Genetics Federation*] (EAIO) .... FIG
Federation Internationale de Gymnastique [*International Gymnastic Federation - IGF*] [*Lyss, Switzerland*] (EAIO) .... FIG
Federation Internationale de Gynecologie et d'Obstetrique [*International Federation of Gynecology and Obstetrics*] [*British*] (EAIO) .... FIGO

Federation Internationale de Gynecologie Infantile et Juvenile [*International Federation of Infantile and Juvenile Gynecology - IFIJG*] [*Sierre, Switzerland*] (EAIO) ... FIGIJ
Federation Internationale de Handball [*International Handball Federation*] ... FIH
Federation Internationale de Hockey [*International Hockey Federation*] [*Brussels, Belgium*] (EA) ... FIH
Federation Internationale de Judo [*International Judo Federation*] ... FIJ
Federation Internationale de la Croix-Bleue [*International Federation of the Blue Cross*] [*Switzerland*] (EAIO) ... FICB
Federation Internationale de la Filterie [*International Thread Federation*] [*EC*] (ECED) ... FIF
Federation Internationale de la Jeunesse Catholique ... FIJC
Federation Internationale de la Philatelie Maritime [*International Federation of Maritime Philately - IFMP*] (EA) ... FIPM
Federation Internationale de la Precontrainte [*International Federation of Prestressed Concrete*] (EAIO) ... FIP
Federation Internationale de la Presse Agricole ... FIPRA
Federation Internationale de la Presse Cinematographique [*International Federation of the Cinematographic Press - IFCP*] (EAIO) ... FIPRESCI
Federation Internationale de la Presse de Langue Francaise (EA) ... FIPLF
Federation Internationale de la Presse Gastronomique et Vinicole [*International Federation of Gastronomical and Vinicultural Press*] ... FIPREGA
Federation Internationale de la Presse Periodique [*International Federation of the Periodical Press*] (EAIO) ... FIPP
Federation Internationale de la Presse Technique et Periodique [*International Federation of the Technical and Periodical Press*] ... FIPTP
Federation Internationale de la Vieillesse [*International Federation on Ageing - IFA*] (EAIO) ... FIV
Federation Internationale de l'Action des Chretiens pour l'Abolition de la Torture [*International Federation of Action of Christians for the Abolition of Torture*] (EAIO) ... FIACAT
Federation Internationale de Laiterie [*International Dairy Federation - IDF*] (EAIO) ... FIL
Federation Internationale de l'Art Photographique [*International Federation of Photographic Art*] (EAIO) ... FIAP
Federation Internationale de l'Artisanat [*International Federation of Master-Craftsmen*] ... FIA
Federation Internationale de l'Automobile [*International Automobile Federation*] (EAIO) ... FIA
Federation Internationale de Lawn Tennis [*International Lawn Tennis Federation*] ... FILT
Federation Internationale de l'Enseignement Menager ... FIEM
Federation Internationale de l'Habitation et de l'Urbanisme ... FIHU
Federation Internationale de l'Industrie du Medicament [*International Federation of Pharmaceutical Manufacturers Associations - IFPMA*] (EAIO) ... FIIM
Federation Internationale de l'Industrie Phonographique ... FIIP
Federation Internationale de Luge de Course [*International Luge Federation - ILF*] [*Rottenmann, Austria*] (EA) ... FIL
Federation Internationale de Lutte Amateur [*International Amateur Wrestling Federation*] [*Lausanne, Switzerland*] (EAIO) ... FILA
Federation Internationale de Medecine Physique [*International Federation of Physical Medicine*] ... FIMP
Federation Internationale de Medecine Preventive et Sociale [*International Federation for Preventive and Social Medicine*] (EAIO) ... FIMPS
Federation Internationale de Medicine Manuelle [*International Federation of Manual Medicine*] [*Zurich, Switzerland*] (EAIO) ... FIMM
Federation Internationale de Natation Amateur [*International Amateur Swimming Federation*] [*Vancouver, BC*] ... FINA
Federation Internationale de Petanque et Jeu Provencal [*Marseille, France*] (EAIO) ... FIPJP
Federation Internationale de Philatelie [*International Federation of Philately*] (EAIO) ... FIP
Federation Internationale de Podologie [*International Federation of Podology*] ... FIP
Federation Internationale de Psychotherapie Medicale [*International Federation for Medical Psychotherapy*] ... FIPM
Federation Internationale de Roller-Skating [*International Roller Skating Federation*] (EAIO) ... FIRS
Federation Internationale de Sauvetage Aquatique [*Germany*] ... FIS
Federation Internationale de Ski [*International Ski Federation*] [*Gumlingen, Switzerland*] (EA) ... FIS
Federation Internationale de Skibob [*Germany*] (EAIO) ... FISB
Federation Internationale de Stenographie et de Dactylographie [*International Federation of Shorthand and Typewriting*] ... FISD
Federation Internationale de Stenographie et de Dactylographie [*International Federation of Shorthand and Typewriting*] [*Bonn, Federal Republic of Germany*] (EAIO) ... INTERSTENO
Federation Internationale de Tennis de Table [*International Table Tennis Federation*] ... FITT
Federation Internationale de Tir a l'Arc [*International Archery Federation*] [*Milan, Italy*] (EA) ... FITA
Federation Internationale de Tir aux Arms Sportives de Chasse [*International Federation for Sport Shooting*] [*Paris, France*] (EAIO) ... FITASC
Federation Internationale de Trampoline [*International Trampoline Federation*] (EA) ... FIT
Federation Internationale de Vo Viet Nam [*An association*] (EAIO) ... FIVV
Federation Internationale de Volleyball [*International Volleyball Federation*] [*Switzerland*] ... FIVB
Federation Internationale d'Education Physique [*International Federation for Physical Education*] (EAIO) ... FIEP
Federation Internationale des Acteurs [*International Federation of Actors*] (EAIO) ... FIA
Federation Internationale des Agences de Voyages [*International Federation of Travel Agencies*] ... FIAV
Federation Internationale des Amies de la Jeune Fille ... FIAJF
Federation Internationale des Archives de Television [*International Federation of Television Archives - IFTA*] (EAIO) ... FIAT
Federation Internationale des Archives du Film [*International Federation of Film Archives*] (EAIO) ... FIAF
Federation Internationale des Assistantes Sociales [*International Federation of Social Workers*] [*Switzerland*] (EAIO) ... FIAS
Federation Internationale des Associations Contre la Lepre [*International Federation of Anti-Leprosy Associations - ILEP*] (EAIO) ... ILEP
Federation Internationale des Associations de Bibliothecaires [*International Federation of Library Associations*] ... FIAB
Federation Internationale des Associations de Chefs de Publicite d'Annonceurs [*International Federation of Advertising Managers Associations*] ... FIAPA
Federation Internationale des Associations de Controleurs du Trafic Aerien [*International Federation of Air Traffic Controllers' Associations*] (EAIO) ... FIACTA
Federation Internationale des Associations de Distributeurs de Films [*International Federation of Associations of Film Distributors*] (EAIO) ... FIAD
Federation Internationale des Associations de Fabricants de Produits d'Entretien [*International Federation of Associations of Manufacturers of Household Products*] (EAIO) ... FIFE
Federation Internationale des Associations de l'Electronique de Securite du Trafic Aerien [*International Federation of Air Traffic Safety Electronic Associations*] (EAIO) ... FIAESTA
Federation Internationale des Associations de Patrons de Navires [*International Federation of Shipmasters Associations*] (EAIO) ... FIAPN
Federation Internationale des Associations de Pilotes de Ligne ... FIAPL
Federation Internationale des Associations de Producteurs de Films [*International Federation of Film Producers' Associations*] ... FIAPF
Federation Internationale des Associations de Professeurs de Sciences [*International Council of Associations for Science Education - ICASE*] (EAIO) ... FIAPS
Federation Internationale des Associations de Quincailliers et Marchands de Fer [*International Federation of Ironmongers and Iron Merchants Associations - IFIA*] (EAIO) ... FIDAQ
Federation Internationale des Associations de Thanatopraxie [*International Federation of Thanatopractic Associations*] ... FIAT
Federation Internationale des Associations de Transitaires et Assimilies [*International Federation of Freight Forwarders Associations*] [*Zurich, Switzerland*] (EAIO) ... FIATA
Federation Internationale des Associations de Travailleurs Evangeliques ... FIATE
Federation Internationale des Associations de Vexillologie [*International Federation of Vexillological Associations*] (EA) ... FIAV
Federation Internationale des Associations d'Entrepots Publics [*International Federation of Public Warehousing Associations - IFPWA*] (EAIO) ... FIAEP
Federation Internationale des Associations des Chimistes du Textile et da la Couleur ... FIACTC
Federation Internationale des Associations d'Etudes Classiques [*International Federation of the Societies of Classical Studies*] (EAIO) ... FIEC
Federation Internationale des Associations d'Etudiants en Medecine [*International Federation of Medical Students Associations - IFMSA*] [*Vienna, Austria*] (EAIO) ... FIAEM
Federation Internationale des Associations d'Instituteurs [*International Federation of Teachers' Associations - IFTA*] (EAIO) ... FIAI
Federation Internationale des Associations Medicales Catholiques [*International Federation of Catholic Medical Associations*] (EA) ... FIAMC
Federation Internationale des Associations Nationales de Negociants en Aciers, Tubes, et Metaux [*International Federation of Associations of Steel, Tube, and Metal Merchants*] (EAIO) ... FIANATM
Federation Internationale des Associations Nationales d'Eleves Ingenieurs [*International Federation of National Associations of Engineering Students*] ... FIANEI
Federation Internationale des Associations Touristiques de Cheminots [*International Federation of Railwaymen's Travel Associations - IFRTA*] [*France*] ... FIATC
Federation Internationale des Auberges de la Jeunesse [*International Youth Hostel Federation - IYHF*] [*Welwyn Garden City, Hertfordshire, England*] (EAIO) ... FIAJ
Federation Internationale des Aveugles [*International Federation of the Blind*] ... FIA
Federation Internationale des Bourses de Valeurs [*International Federation of Stock Exchanges*] (EAIO) ... FIBV
Federation Internationale des Bureaux d'Extraits de Presse [*International Federation of Press Cutting Agencies - IFPCA*] (EAIO) ... FIBEP
Federation Internationale des Cadres de la Chimie et des Industries Annexes ... FICCIA
Federation Internationale des Cadres des Mines ... FICM
Federation Internationale des Centres d'Entrainement aux Methodes d'Education Active [*International Federation of Training Centres in Methods of Active Education*] (EAIO) ... FICEMEA
Federation Internationale des Centres Sociaux et Communautaires [*International Federation of Settlements and Neighborhood Centers*] ... FIS
Federation Internationale des Chasseurs de Son [*International Federation of Sound Hunters - IFSH*] (EAIO) ... FICS
Federation Internationale des Cheminots Antialcooliques [*International Railway Temperance Union*] ... FICA
Federation Internationale des Choeurs de Garcons (EAIO) ... FICG
Federation Internationale des Choeurs d'Enfants [*International Federation of Children's Choirs*] (EA) ... FICE
Federation Internationale des Chronometreurs [*Rome, Italy*] (EAIO) ... FIC
Federation Internationale des Cine-Clubs [*International Federation of Film Societies*] ... FICC

Federation Internationale des Clubs de Camping-Cars [*Montreuil, France*] (EAIO) .... FICCC

Federation Internationale des Clubs de Publicite [*International Federation of Advertising Clubs*] [*Lille, France*] (EAIO) .... FICP

Federation Internationale des Communautes d'Enfants [*International Federation of Children's Communities*] .... FICE

Federation Internationale des Communautes Educatives [*International Federation of Educative Communities*] [*Zurich, Switzerland*] (EAIO) .... FICE

Federation Internationale des Conseils en Propriete Industrielle [*International Federation of Industrial Property Attorneys*] (EAIO) .... FICPI

Federation Internationale des Conseils Juridiques et Fiscaux [*International Federation of Legal Fiscal Consultants*] .... FICJF

Federation Internationale des Corps et Associations Consulaires [*Federation of International Consular Corps and Associations*] (EAIO) .... FICAC

Federation Internationale des Demenageurs Internationaux [*International Federation of International Furniture Removers - IFIFR*] (EAIO) .... FIDI

Federation Internationale des Diffuseurs d'Oeuvres d'Art Originales [*International Federation of Original Art Diffusors*] [*France*] (EAIO) .... FIDOAO

Federation Internationale des Directeurs de Journaux Catholiques .... FIDJC

Federation Internationale des Distributeurs de Presse [*International Federation of Wholesale Newspaper, Periodical, and Book Distributors*] .... DISTRIPRESS

Federation Internationale des Droits de l'Homme [*International Federation for Human Rights*] [*Paris, France*] (EA) .... FIDH

Federation Internationale des Echecs [*International Chess Federation*] [*Switzerland*] .... FIDE

Federation Internationale des Echecs [*International Chess Federation*] .... FIE

Federation Internationale des Editeurs de Journaux [*International Federation of Newspaper Publishers*] [*Paris, France*] (EAIO) .... FIEJ

Federation Internationale des Editeurs de Medailles [*International Federation of Medal Producers*] .... FIDEM

Federation Internationale des Employes, Techniciens, et Cadres [*International Federation of Commercial, Clerical, Professional, and Technical Employees*] [*Geneva, Switzerland*] (EAIO) .... FIET

Federation Internationale des Enseignants de Rythmique [*International Federation of Teachers of Rhythmics - IFTR*] (EA) .... FIER

Federation Internationale des Etudiants en Pharmacie .... FIEP

Federation Internationale des Etudiants en Sciences Politiques .... FIESP

Federation Internationale des Experts en Automobiles [*International Federation of Automobile Experts*] [*Rhode St. Genese, Belgium*] (EAIO) ..... FIEA

Federation Internationale des Fabricants de Papiers Gommes [*International Federation of Manufacturers of Gummed Paper*] (EAIO) .... FIPAGO

Federation Internationale des Fabricants et Transformateurs d'Adhesifs et Thermocollants sur Papiers et Autres Supports [*International Federation of Manufacturers and Converters of Pressure-Sensitive and Heatseals on Paper and Other Base Materials*] (EAIO) .... FINAT

Federation Internationale des Femmes de Carrieres Liberales et Commerciales [*International Federation of Business and Professional Women*] .... FIFCLC

Federation Internationale des Femmes des Carrieres Juridiques [*France*] .... FIFCJ

Federation Internationale des Femmes Diplomees des Universites [*International Federation of University Women - IFUW*] (EAIO) .... FIFDU

Federation Internationale des Fonctionnaires Superieurs de Police [*International Federation of Senior Police Officers*] [*France*] .... FIFSP

Federation Internationale des Geometres [*International Federation of Surveyors - IFS*] [*Edmonton, AB*] (EAIO) .... FIG

Federation Internationale des Grandes et Moyennes Entreprises de Distribution [*International Federation of Retail Distributors*] [*Belgium*] (EAIO) .... FEMGED

Federation Internationale des Grandes et Moyennes Entreprises de Distribution [*International Federation of Retail Distributors*] (EAIO) .... FIGED

Federation Internationale des Grossistes, Importateurs, et Exportateurs Fournitures Automobiles [*International Federation of Wholesalers, Importers, and Exporters in Automobile Fittings*] (EAIO) .... FIGIEFA

Federation Internationale des Hommes Catholiques [*International Council of Catholic Men - ICCM*] [*Vatican City, Vatican City State*] (EAIO) .... FIHC

Federation Internationale des Hopitaux [*International Hospital Federation*] .... FIH

Federation Internationale des Horlogers, Bijoutiers, Joailliers, Orfevres Detaillants de la CE [*International Federation of Retailers in Horology, Jewellery, Gold and Silverware of the EC*] (ECED) .... FIHBJO

Federation Internationale des Ingenieurs Conseils [*International Federation of Consulting Engineers*] (EAIO) .... FIDIC

Federation Internationale des Ingenieurs Municipaux [*International Federation of Municipal Engineers - IFME*] (EAIO) .... FIIM

Federation Internationale des Ingenieurs-Conseils en Propriete Industrielle .... FIICPI

Federation Internationale des Instituts de Hautes Etudes [*International Federation of Institutes for Advanced Study*] (EAIO) .... FIIHE

Federation Internationale des Instituts de Recherches Socio-Religieuses [*International Federation of Institutes for Socio-Religious Research*] .... FERES

Federation Internationale des Intellectuels Aveugles .... FIDIA

Federation Internationale des Jeunesse Bons Templiers [*International Good Templar Youth Federation*] (EAIO) .... FIJBT

Federation Internationale des Jeunesses Musicales [*International Federation of Jeunesses Musicales*] (EAIO) .... FIJM

Federation Internationale des Journalistes [*International Federation of Journalists - IFJ*] [*Brussels, Belgium*] (EAIO) .... FIJ

Federation Internationale des Journalistes et Ecrivains du Tourisme [*World Federation of Travel Journalists and Writers*] [*Paris, France*] (EA) .... FIJET

Federation Internationale des Journalistes Libres [*International Federation of Free Journalists*] .... FIJL

Federation Internationale des Journalistes Professionnels de l'Aeronautique .... FIJPA

Federation Internationale des Langues et Litteratures Modernes [*International Federation for Modern Languages and Literatures*] (EAIO) .... FILLM

Federation Internationale des Maisons de l'Europe [*International Federation of Europe Houses - IFEH*] (EAIO) .... FIME

Federation Internationale des Mineurs [*Miners' International Federation - MIF*] [*Brussels, Belgium*] (EAIO) .... FIM

Federation Internationale des Mouvements d'Adultes Ruraux Catholiques [*International Federation of Adult Rural Catholic Movements*] .... FIMARC

Federation Internationale des Mouvements d'Ecole Moderne (EAIO) .... FIMEM

Federation Internationale des Mouvements Ouvriers Chretiens [*International Federation of Christian Workers Movements*] .... FIMOC

Federation Internationale des Musiciens [*International Federation of Musicians*] [*Zurich, Switzerland*] (EAIO) .... FIM

Federation Internationale des Mutiles, des Invalides du Travail, et des Inval ides Civils [*International Federation of Disabled Workmen and Civilian Handicapped*] (EAIO) .... FIMITIC

Federation Internationale des Organisateurs de Festivals [*International Federation of Festival Organizations*] (EAIO) .... FIDOF

Federation Internationale des Organisations de Correspondances et d'Echanges Scolaires [*International Federation of Organizations for School Correspondence and Exchange*] [*Paris, France*] (EA) .... FIOCES

Federation Internationale des Organisations de Donneurs de Sang Benevoles [*International Federation of Blood Donor Organizations - IFBDO*] [*Dole, France*] (EAIO) .... FIODS

Federation Internationale des Organisations de Sciences Sociales [*International Federation of Social Science Organizations - IFSSO*] (EAIO) .... FIOSS

Federation Internationale des Organisations de Travailleurs de la Metallurgie [*International Metalworkers Federation - IMF*] [*Geneva, Switzerland*] (EAIO) .... FIOM

Federation Internationale des Organisations d'Hoteliers, Restaurateurs, et Cafetiers [*International Organization of Hotel and Restaurant Associations*] (EAIO) .... HO-RE-CA

Federation Internationale des Organisations Syndicales du Personnel des Transporte [*International Federation of Trade Unions of Transport Workers - IFTUTW*] (EAIO) .... FIOST

Federation Internationale des Organismes de Psychologie Medicale [*International Federation of the Psychological-Medical Organizations - IFPMO*] (EAIO) .... FIOPM

Federation Internationale des Ouvriers de la Chaussure et du Cuir [*International Shoe and Leather Worker's Federation*] .... FIOCC

Federation Internationale des Ouvriers sur Metaux [*International Metalworkers' Federation*] .... FIOM

Federation Internationale des Petites et Moyennes Entreprises Commerciales [*International Federation of Small and Medium-Sized Commercial Enterprises*] .... FIPMEC

Federation Internationale des Petits Freres des Pauvres [*International Federation of the Little Brothers of the Poor - IFLBP*] (EAIO) .... FIPFP

Federation Internationale des Pharmaciens Catholiques [*International Federation of Catholic Pharmacists*] [*Eupen, Belgium*] (EAIO) .... FIPC

Federation Internationale des Phonotheques [*International Federation of Record Libraries*] .... FIP

Federation Internationale des Pietons [*International Federation of Pedestrians*] [*Netherlands*] .... FIP

Federation Internationale des Producteurs Agricoles [*International Federation of Agricultural Producers*] .... FIPA

Federation Internationale des Producteurs Auto-Consommateurs Industriels d'Electricite [*International Federation of Industrial Producers of Electricity for Own Consumption*] .... FIPACE

Federation Internationale des Producteurs de Jus de Fruits [*International Federation of Fruit Juice Producers - IFFJP*] (EAIO) .... FIJU

Federation Internationale des Producteurs de Jus de Fruits [*International Federation of Fruit Juice Producers - IFFJP*] .... FIPJF

Federation Internationale des Professeurs de Francais [*International Federation of Teachers of French - IFTF*] (EAIO) .... FIPF

Federation Internationale des Professeurs de Langues Vivantes [*International Federation of Modern Language Teachers*] [*Switzerland*] ..... FIPLV

Federation Internationale des Professeurs de l'Enseignement Secondaire Officiel [*International Federation of Secondary Teachers*] (EAIO) .... FIPESO

Federation Internationale des Professions Immobilieres [*International Real Estate Federation*] (EAIO) .... FIABCI

Federation Internationale des Quillieurs [*International Federation of Bowlers*] [*Espoo, Finland*] (EA) .... FIQ

Federation Internationale des Reconstructeurs de Moteurs [*International Federation of Engine Reconditioners - IFER*] (EAIO) .... FIRM

Federation Internationale des Redacteurs en Chef .... FIREC

Federation Internationale des Resistants [*International Federation of Resistance Movements*] .... FIR

Federation Internationale des Semaines d'Art .... FISA

Federation Internationale des Societes Aerophilateliques [*International Federation of Aero-Philatelic Societies*] [*Zurich Airport, Switzerland*] (EAIO) .... FISA

Federation Internationale des Societes Artistiques et Intellectuelles de Cheminots [*International Federation of Railwaymen's Art and Intellectual Societies*] .... FISAIC

Federation Internationale des Societes d'Amateurs d'Exlibris [*British*] (EAIO) .... FISAE

Federation Internationale des Societes d'Aviron [*International Rowing Federation*] [*Neuchatel, Switzerland*] (EAIO) .... FISA

Federation Internationale des Societes de Philosophie [*International Federation of Philosophical Societies - IFPS*] (EAIO) .... FISP

Federation Internationale des Societes de Recherche Operationelle [*International Federation of Operational Research Societies*] [*Denmark*] (EAIO) .... FISRO

Federation Internationale des Societes d'Ecrivains-Medecins .... FISEM
Federation Internationale des Societes d'Histochimie et de Cytochimie [*International Federation of Societies for Histochemistry and Cytochemistry*] (EAIO) .... FISHC
Federation Internationale des Societes d'Ingenieurs des Techniques de l'Automobile [*International Federation of Automobile Engineers' and Technicians' Associations*] .... FISITA
Federation Internationale des Societes et Instituts pour l'Etude de la Renaissance [*International Federation of Societies and Institutes for the Study of the Renaissance*] (EA) .... FISIER
Federation Internationale des Societes Magiques [*International Federation of Magical Societies - IFSM*] [*Paris, France*] (EAIO) .... FISM
Federation Internationale des Societes Scientifiques (EERA) .... FISS
Federation Internationale des Syndicats Chretiens de la Metalurgie [*International Federation of Christian Metalworkers Unions*] .... FISCM
Federation Internationale des Syndicats Chretiens d'Employes, Techniciens, Cadres, et Voyageurs de Commerce [*International Federation of Christian Trade Unions of Salaried Employees, Technicians, Managers, and Commercial Travellers*] .... FISCETCV
Federation Internationale des Syndicats Chretiens des Travailleurs du Textile etde l'Habillement [*International Federation of Christian Trade Unions of Textile and Clothing Workers*] .... FISCTTH
Federation Internationale des Syndicats Chretiens d'Ouvriers Agricoles [*International Federation of Christian Agricultural Workers Unions*] .... FISCOA
Federation Internationale des Syndicats Chretiens d'Ouvriers du Batiment et du Bois [*International Federation of Christian Trade Unions of Building and Wood Workers*] .... FISCOBB
Federation Internationale des Syndicats des Travailleurs Audiovisuel [*International Federation of Audio-Visual Workers Unions - IFAVWU*] (EAIO) .... FISTA
Federation Internationale des Techniciens de la Bonneterie [*International Federation of Knitting Technologists - IFKT*] (EAIO) .... FITB
Federation Internationale des Traducteurs [*International Federation of Translators - IFT*] (EAIO) .... FIT
Federation Internationale des Transports Aeriens Prives [*International Federation of Private Air Transport*] .... FITAP
Federation Internationale des Travailleurs de la Terre .... FITT
Federation Internationale des Travailleurs de l'Habillement .... FITH
Federation Internationale des Travailleurs des Industries du Textile, de l'Habillement, et du Cuir [*International Textile, Garment, and Leather Workers' Federation*] [*Brussels, Belgium*] .... FITITHC
Federation Internationale des Travailleurs des Industries du Textile, de l'Habillement, et du Cuir [*International Textile, Garment, and Leather Workers' Federation - ITGLWF*] (EAIO) .... FITTHC
Federation Internationale des Travailleurs des Plantations .... FITP
Federation Internationale des Travailleurs des Plantations, de l'Agriculture, etdes Secteurs Connexes [*International Federation of Plantation, Agricultural, and Allied Workers*] .... FITPASC
Federation Internationale des Travailleurs du Batiment et du Bois [*International Federation of Building and Woodworkers*] .... FITBB
Federation Internationale des Travailleurs du Petrole .... FITP
Federation Internationale des Travailleurs du Petrole et de la Chimie [*International Federation of Petroleum and Chemical Workers*] .... FITPC
Federation Internationale des Universites Catholiques [*International Federation of Catholic Universities - IFCU*] (EAIO) .... FIUC
Federation Internationale des Vehicules Anciens (EA) .... FIVA
Federation Internationale des Vins et Spiritueux [*International Federation of Wines and Spirits - IFWS*] (EAIO) .... FIVS
Federation Internationale d'Escrime [*International Fencing Federation*] .... FIE
Federation Internationale d'Etudes Medievales (EAIO) .... FIDEM
Federation Internationale d'Eutonie Gerda Alexander [*International Federation for Gerda Alexander Eutony*] [*Belgium*] (EAIO) .... FIEGA
Federation Internationale d'Information et de Documentation [*International Federation for Information and Documentation*] [*Netherlands Information service or system*] (IID) .... FID
Federation Internationale d'Information et de Documentation [*International Federation for Information and Documentation - IFID*] (EAIO) .... FIID
Federation Internationale d'Oleiculture [*International Olive Growers Federation*] .... FIO
Federation Internationale du Batiment et des Travaux Publics .... FIBTP
Federation Internationale du Commerce des Semences [*International Federation of the Seed Trade*] .... FIS
Federation Internationale du Commerce et des Industries du Camping ..... FICIC
Federation Internationale du Cyclisme Professionel [*International Federation of Professional Cycling*] .... FICP
Federation Internationale du Diabete [*International Diabetes Federation - IDF*] [*Brussels, Belgium*] (EAIO) .... FID
Federation Internationale du Film sur d'Art [*International Federation of Films on Art*] .... FIFA
Federation Internationale du Personnel d'Encadrement des Industries et CommercesAgricoles et Alimentaires [*International Federation of Managerial Staff of Agricultural and Alimentary Industry and Commerce*] (EAIO) .... FICICA
Federation Internationale du Sport Automobile [*Paris, France*] (EAIO) .... FISA
Federation Internationale du Sport Medical pour l'Aide a la Recherche Cancerologique [*International Medical Sports Federation for Aid to Cancer Research*] [*Beziers, France*] (EAIO) .... FISMARC
Federation Internationale du Sport Universitaire [*International University Sports Federation*] [*Brussels, Belgium*] (EAIO) .... FISU
Federation Internationale du Thermalisme et du Climatisme [*International Federation of Thermalism and Climatism*] .... FITEC
Federation Internationale du Tourisme Social [*International Social Travel Federation - ISTF*] (EAIO) .... FITS
Federation Internationale et Syndicale des Employes de Madagascar [*International Federation and Union of Malagasy Employees*] [*WFTU affiliate*] .... FISEMA
Federation Internationale Halterophile et Culturiste .... FIHC
Federation Internationale Libre des Deportes et Internes de la Resistance [*International Free Federation of Deportees and Resistance Internees*] .... FILDIR
Federation Internationale Medecine Sportive [*International Federation of Sportive Medicine*] .... FIMS
Federation Internationale Motocycliste [*International Motorcycle Federation*] [*Geneva, Switzerland*] (EAIO) .... FIM
Federation Internationale Pharmaceutique [*International Pharmaceutical Federation*] [*The Hague, Netherlands*] (EAIO) .... FIP
Federation Internationale pour la Protection des Populations .... FIPP
Federation Internationale pour la Recherche Theatrale [*International Federation for Theatre Research - IFTR*] (EAIO) .... FIRT
Federation Internationale pour la Sante [*International Federation for Health*] [*France*] (EAIO) .... FIS
Federation Internationale pour le Droit Europeen [*International Federation for European Law*] [*Benelux*] (EAIO) .... FIDE
Federation Internationale pour l'Economie Familiale [*International Federation for Home Economics - IFHE*] (EAIO) .... FIEF
Federation Internationale pour l'Education Artistique .... FEA
Federation Internationale pour l'Education des Parents [*International Federation for Parent Education - IFPE*] [*Sevres, France*] (EAIO) .... FIEP
Federation Internationale pour l'Habitation, l'Urbanisme et l'Amenagement des Territoires [*International Federation for Housing and Planning - IFHP*] [*The Hague, Netherlands*] (EA) .... FIHUAT
Federation Internationale pour l'Organisation de Rencontres de Handicapes [*International Federation for the Organization of Meetings for the Handicapped*] .... FIORH
Federation Internationale Sportive de l'Enseignement Catholique .... FISEC
Federation Internationale Syndicale de l'Enseignement [*World Federation of Teachers' Unions*] [*Berlin, Federal Republic of Germany*] (EAIO) .... FISE
Federation Internationale Una Voce (EA) .... FIUV
Federation Internationale Veterinaire de Zootechnie .... FIVZ
Federation Lainiere Internationale [*International Wool Textile Organization - IWTO*] (EAIO) .... FLI
Federation Life Insurance of America [*Milwaukee, WI*] (EA) .... FLIA
Federation Lutherienne Mondiale [*Lutheran World Foundation - LWF*] [*Geneva, Switzerland*] (EAIO) .... FLM
Federation Mondiale de Jeunesse Catholique [*World Federation of Catholic Youth*] .... FMJC
Federation Mondiale de la Jeunesse Democratique [*World Federation of Democratic Youth - WFDY*] [*Budapest, Hungary*] (EAIO) .... FMJD
Federation Mondiale de l'Hemophilie [*World Federation of Hemophilia*] (EAIO) .... FMH
Federation Mondiale de Neurologie [*World Federation of Neurology*] .... FMN
Federation Mondiale de Travailleurs Agricoles [*World Federation of Agricultural Workers - WFAW*] (EAIO) .... FMTA
Federation Mondiale de Travailleurs des Industries Alimentaires, du Tabac, et del'Hotellerie [*World Federation of Workers in Food, Tobacco, and Hotel Industries - WFFTH*] (EAIO) .... FMATH
Federation Mondiale des Amis de Musees [*World Federation of Friends of Museums - WFFM*] (EAIO) .... FMAM
Federation Mondiale des Anciens Combattants [*World Veterans Federation - WVF*] [*Paris, France*] (EAIO) .... FMAC
Federation Mondiale des Annonceurs [*World Federation of Advertisers - WFA*] [*Brussels, Belgium*] (EAIO) .... FMA
Federation Mondiale des Associations, Centres, et Clubs UNESCO [*World Federation of UNESCO Clubs and Associations*] [*France*] (EAIO) .... FMACCU
Federation Mondiale des Associations pour les Nations Unies [*World Federation of United Nations Associations - WFUNA*] [*Geneva, Switzerland*] (EA) .... FMANU
Federation Mondiale des Communautes de Vie Chretienne [*World Federation of Christian Life Communities - WFCLC*] [*Rome, Italy*] (EAIO) .... FMCVC
Federation Mondiale des Concours Internationaux de Musique [*World Federation of International Music Competitions - WFIMC*] (EAIO) .... FMCIM
Federation Mondiale des Jeunesses Feminines Catholiques .... FMJFC
Federation Mondiale des Jeunesses Liberales et Radicales [*World Federation of Liberal and Radical Youth*] .... FMJLR
Federation Mondiale des Organisations d'Ingenieurs [*World Federation of Engineering Organizations*] .... FMOI
Federation Mondiale des Societes de Cuisiniėrs [*World Association of Cooks Societies - WACS*] (EA) .... FMSC
Federation Mondiale des Sourds [*World Federation of the Deaf - WFD*] [*Rome, Italy*] (EA) .... FMS
Federation Mondiale des Syndicats d'Industries [*World Federation of Industrial Workers' Unions*] .... FEMOSI
Federation Mondiale des Travailleurs Non-Manuels [*World Federation of Trade Unions of Non-Manual Workers - WFNMW*] [*Antwerp, Belgium*] (EAIO) .... FMTNM
Federation Mondiale des Travailleurs Scientifiques [*World Federation of Scientific Workers - WFSW*] (EAIO) .... FMTS
Federation Mondiale des Villes Jumelees-Cites Unies [*United Towns Organisation - UTO*] (EA) .... FMVJ
Federation Mondiale du Jeu de Dames [*World Draughts (Checkers) Federation - WDF*] [*Dordrecht, Netherlands*] (EAIO) .... FMJD
Federation Mondiale pour la Protection des Animaux [*World Federation for the Protection of Animals*] [*Also known as WFPA and WTB*] .... FMPA
Federation Mondiale pour la Sante Mentale [*World Federation for Mental Health*] .... FMSM
Federation Mondiale pour l'Enseignement Medical [*World Federation for Medical Education - WFME*] (EA) .... FMEM

Federation Nationale d'Achats des Cadres [*Initials alone now used as name of discount-store chain in France*] [*Pronounced "f-nak"*] ..... FNAC
Federation Nationale des Centres d'Etudes Techniques Agricoles ..... FNCETA
Federation Nationale des Communications [*National Federation of Communication*] [*Canada*] (EAIO) ..... FNC
Federation Nationale des Cooperatives de Cereales ..... FNCC
Federation Nationale des Cooperatives d'Utilisation de Materiel Agricole ..... FNCUMA
Federation Nationale des Etudiants des Universites Canadiennes [*National Federation of Canadian University Students*] ..... FNEUC
Federation Nationale des Gaullistes de Progres [*National Federation of Progressive Gaullists*] [*France Political party*] (PPW) ..... FNGP
Federation Nationale des Groupements Agricoles d'Approvisionnement ..... FNGAA
Federation Nationale des Republicains Independants [*National Federation of Independent Republicans*] [*France Political party*] (PPW) ..... FNRI
Federation Nationale des Syndicats d'Infirmieres et d'Infirmiers [*National Federation of Nurses' Unions - NFNU*] ..... FNSII
Federation Nationale des Syndicats du Batiment et du Bois, Inc. [*National Federation of Shipyard and Woodworkers Unions*] ..... FNSBB
Federation Nationale des Syndicats du Commerce Ouest Africain [*National Federation of Commerce Unions - West Africa*] ..... FENASYCOA
Federation Nationale du Batiment [*France*] (NITA) ..... FNB
Federation Naturiste Internationale [*International Naturist Federation*] ..... FNI
Federation Nordique des Travailleurs du Batiment et du Bois [*Nordic Federation of Building and Wood Workers - NFBWW*] (EAIO) ..... FNTBB
Federation of Acoustical Societies of Europe (EAIO) ..... FASE
Federation of African Organisations of Engineers (PDAA) ..... FAOE
Federation of Agricultural Cooperatives [*British*] (DBA) ..... FAC
Federation of Air Transport User Representatives in the European Community (DA) ..... FATUREC
Federation of Alcoholic Residential Establishments [*British*] (DI) ..... FARE
Federation of All Okinawan Labor Unions ..... FAOLU
Federation of All Okinawan Military Employees' Labor Unions ..... FAOMELU
Federation of Alpine and Schuhplattler Clubs in North America (EA) ..... FASCNA
Federation of American Arab Organizations (EA) ..... FAAO
Federation of American Citizens of German Descent [*Later, DANK*] (EA) ..... FACGD
Federation of American Consumers and Travelers (EA) ..... FACT
Federation of American Controlled Shipping [*New York, NY*] (EA) ..... FACS
Federation of American Cultural and Language Communities (EA) ..... FACLC
Federation of American Health Systems (EA) ..... FAHS
Federation of American Hospitals [*Later, FAHS*] ..... FAH
Federation of American Research Networks [*Computer science*] (TNIG) ..... FARNET
Federation of American Scientists (EA) ..... FAS
Federation of American Societies for Experimental Biology (EA) ..... FASEB
Federation of American Women's Clubs Overseas (EA) ..... FAWCO
Federation of Americans Supporting Science and Technology ..... FASST
Federation of Analytical Chemistry and Spectroscopy Societies (EA) ..... FACSS
Federation of Apparel Manufacturers (EA) ..... FAM
Federation of Armenian Students Clubs of America (EA) ..... FASCA
Federation of Army Wives Clubs [*British*] ..... FAWC
Federation of ASEAN [*Association of South East Asian Nations*] **Shipowners' Associations** [*Kuala Lumpur, Malaysia*] (EAIO) ..... FASA
Federation of Asian Pharmaceutical Associations ..... FAPA
Federation of Asian Photographic Art ..... FAPA
Federation of Asian Scientific Academies and Societies [*India*] (EY) ..... FASAS
Federation of Asian Women's Associations [*San Marcelino, Philippines*] ..... FAWA
Federation of Associations of Health Regulatory Boards [*Later, FARB*] (EA) ..... FAHRB
Federation of Associations of Materials Handling Equipment Manufacturers (MHDI) ..... FAMHEM
Federation of Associations of Medical Technology [*British*] (DBA) ..... FAMT
Federation of Associations of Mental Health Workers [*British*] (BI) ..... FAMHW
Federation of Associations of Mining Equipment Manufacturers (MHDB) ..... FAMEM
Federation of Associations of Periodical Publishers (DGA) ..... FAPP
Federation of Associations of Periodical Publishers in the EC (EAIO) ..... FAPPEC
Federation of Associations of Regulatory Boards (EA) ..... FARB
Federation of Associations of Specialists and Subcontractors [*British*] (BI) ..... FASS
Federation of Associations on the Canadian Environment ..... FACE
Federation of Astronomical and Geophysical Services [*Research center France*] (IRC) ..... FAGS
Federation of Astronomical Societies [*British*] (EAIO) ..... FAS
Federation of Australian historical Societies ..... FAHS
Federation of Australian Kung Fu and Wun Shu Organisations ..... FAKFWSO
Federation of Australian Muslim Students and Youth ..... FAMSY
Federation of Australian Scientific and Technical Societies (EERA) ..... FASTS
Federation of Automated Coding Technologies (EA) ..... FACT
Federation of Automatic Transmission Engineers [*British*] (DBA) ..... FATE
Federation of Bank Employers [*British*] (DCTA) ..... FBE
Federation of Behavioral, Psychological, and Cognitive Sciences (EA) ..... FBPCS
Federation of Bloodstock Agents [*British*] (DBA) ..... FBA
Federation of Bloodstock Agents Australia ..... FBAA
Federation of Brickwork Contractors [*British*] (DBA) ..... FBC
Federation of British Aquatic Societies (DBA) ..... FBAS
Federation of British Artists (EAIO) ..... FBA
Federation of British Astrologers Ltd. (BI) ..... FBA
Federation of British Audio (DBA) ..... FBA
Federation of British Bonsai Societies (DBA) ..... FOBBS
Federation of British Columbia Writers [*Canada*] (WWLA) ..... FBCW
Federation of British Cremation Authorities (BI) ..... FBCA
Federation of British Engineers Tool Manufacturers [*British*] (DBA) ..... FBETM
Federation of British Fire Organisations ..... FBFO
Federation of British Fire Organisations (BI) ..... FOBFO
Federation of British Hand Tool Manufacturers (EAIO) ..... FBHTM
Federation of British Industries [*Later, CBI*] ..... FBI
Federation of British Tape Recording Clubs (BI) ..... FBTRC
Federation of Broadcasting Unions [*British*] ..... FBU
Federation of Builders Contractors and Allied Employers of Ireland (BI) ..... FBCAEI
Federation of Building Block Manufacturers [*British*] (BI) ..... FBBM
Federation of Building Societies of Western Australia ..... FBSWA
Federation of Building Specialist Contractors [*British*] (DBA) ..... FBSC
Federation of Calico Printers (DGA) ..... FCP
Federation of Cambodian Associations in North America (EA) ..... FCANA
Federation of Canadian Archers ..... FCA
Federation of Canadian Artists ..... FCA
Federation of Canadian Municipalities ..... FCM
Federation of Cash Grain Commission Merchants Associations [*Defunct*] (EA) ..... FCGCMA
Federation of Catholic Physicians Guilds ..... FCPG
Federation of Children's Book Groups [*British*] ..... FCBG
Federation of Chinese Organizations in America (EA) ..... FCOA
Federation of Civil Engineering Contractors [*British*] (BI) ..... FCEC
Federation of Civil Service and Primary Aided School Teachers' Unions [*Mauritius*] ..... FCSPASTU
Federation of Civil Service Unions of Mauritius ..... FCSUM
Federation of Clinker Block Manufacturers [*British*] (BI) ..... FCBM
Federation of Clothing Designers and Executives [*British*] (DBA) ..... FCDE
Federation of Coated Macadam Industries [*British*] (BI) ..... FCMI
Federation of Commodity Associations (EAIO) ..... FCA
Federation of Commonwealth Chambers of Commerce (BI) ..... FCCC
Federation of Communication Services [*British*] (TSSD) ..... FCS
Federation of Community Sporting and Workers' Clubs [*Australia*] ..... FCSWC
Federation of Computer Users in the Medical Sciences (EA) ..... FCUMS
Federation of Crafts and Commerce [*British*] (DBA) ..... FCC
Federation of Danish Trade Unions ..... FDTU
Federation of Deer Management Societies [*British*] (DBA) ..... FDMS
Federation of Democratic Turkish Associations of Australia ..... FDTAA
Federation of Dental Diagnostic Sciences [*Defunct*] (EA) ..... FDDS
Federation of Digestive Disease Societies [*Defunct*] (EA) ..... FDDS
Federation of Documentary Film Units [*British*] (BI) ..... FDFU
Federation of Dredging Contractors [*British*] (BI) ..... FDC
Federation of Drum Reconditioners [*British*] (DBA) ..... FDR
Federation of Eastern Stars (EA) ..... FES
Federation of Eastern Stars of the World (EA) ..... FESW
Federation of Egalitarian Communities (EA) ..... FEC
Federation of Engine Re-Manufacturers [*Chigwell, Essex, England*] (EAIO) ..... FER
Federation of Engineering and Scientific Associations ..... FESA
Federation of Engineering and Shipbuilding Trades of the United Kingdom [*A union*] ..... FESTUK
Federation of Engineering Design Companies [*British*] (DBA) ..... FEDC
Federation of Engineering Design Consultants (BARN) ..... FEDC
Federation of English Language Course Organisation [*British*] ..... FELCO
Federation of English-Writers in Quebec [*Canada*] (WWLA) ..... FEWQ
Federation of Environmental Technologists (EA) ..... FET
Federation of Environmental Trade Associations [*British*] (DBA) ..... FETA
Federation of Ethical Stage Hypnotists [*British*] (DBA) ..... FESH
Federation of European American Organizations (EA) ..... FEAO
Federation of European Bearing Manufacturers Associations (EAIO) ..... FEBMA
Federation of European Biochemical Societies [*France*] ..... FEBS
Federation of European Chemical Merchants (EA) ..... FECM
Federation of European Chemical Societies (EAIO) ..... FECS
Federation of European Chemical Trade (EAIO) ..... FECT
Federation of European Coin Machine Associations [*EC*] (ECED) ..... EUROMAT
Federation of European Coin-Machine Associations (EAIO) ..... FECMA
Federation of European Delegation Associations of Scientific Equipment Manufacturers, Importers, and Dealers in the Laboratory, Industrial and Medical Fields (PDAA) ..... FEDAS
Federation of European Direct Selling Associations [*Belgium*] (EAIO) ..... FEDSA
Federation of European Heating and Ventilating Associations (EA) ..... FEHVA
Federation of European Helicopter Operators (PDAA) ..... FEHO
Federation of European Industrial Co-Operative Research Organizations (EA) ..... FEICRO
Federation of European Industrial Editors' Associations ..... FEIEA
Federation of European Manufacturers of Friction Materials (EA) ..... FEMFM
Federation of European Pencil Manufacturers Associations [*See also FEFM*] (EA) ..... FEPMA
Federation of European Petroleum Equipment Manufacturers [*Netherlands*] ..... FEPEM
Federation of European Producers of Abrasives (PDAA) ..... FEPAP
Federation of European Publishers [*Belgium*] (EAIO) ..... FEP
Federation of European Rigid Polyurethane Foam Associations (EAIO) ..... BING
Federation of European Screen Printers Associations (PDAA) ..... FESPA
Federation of European Veterinarians in Industry and Research (EA) ..... FEVIR
Federation of European Wholesale and International Trade Associations [*Common Market*] [*Belgium*] ..... FEWITA
Federation of European Window Manufacturers Associations (EA) ..... FEWMA
Federation of European Writing Instruments Associations [*See also FEAIE*] (EA) ..... FEWIA
Federation of Fairs and Trade Shows of BENELUX [*Formerly, Federation of Fairs and Exhibitions in BENELUX - FFSB*] (EA) ..... FFTSB
Federation of Family History Societies (EA) ..... FFHS
Federation of Feminist Women's Health Centers (EA) ..... FFWHC
Federation of Film Unions [*British*] ..... FFU
Federation of Flatmen, Watermen, and Canal Boatmen [*A union*] [*British*] ..... FFWCB

Federation of Fly Fishers (EA) ... FFF
Federation of Fly Fishers ... FFF
Federation of Former Jewish Fighters (EA) ... FFJF
Federation of Franco-American Genealogical and Historical Societies [*Defunct*] (EA) ... FFAGHS
Federation of Free African Trade Unions of South Africa ... FOFATUSA
Federation of Free Byelorussian Journalists (EA) ... FFBJ
Federation of Free Farmers [*Philippines*] ... FFF
Federation of Free Labor [*Philippines*] ... FFL
Federation of Free Workers [*Philippines*] ... FFW
Federation of French Alliances in the United States [*Later, FIAF*] (EA) ... FFAUS
Federation of French American Women (EA) ... FFFA
Federation of French War Veterans (EA) ... FFWV
Federation of Gelatine and Glue Manufacturers [*British*] (BI) ... FGGM
Federation of Genealogical Societies (EA) ... FGS
Federation of German Industries (EA) ... FGI
Federation of Government Information Processing Councils, Inc. (EA) ... FGIPCI
Federation of Health Funds - International [*British*] (EAIO) ... FHF
Federation of Health Funds - International [*International Federation of Voluntary Health Service Funds*] [*Later, FHF*] [*Acronym is based on former name,*] (EAIO) ... IFVHSF
Federation of Heathrow Anti-Noise Groups [*British*] (DI) ... FHANG
Federation of Hellenic American Societies of Greater New York (EA) ... FHAS
Federation of High Frequency Welders [*British*] (DBA) ... FHFW
Federation of Historical Bottle Clubs (EA) ... FOHBC
Federation of Holistic Therapists [*British*] ... FHT
Federation of Homemakers (EA) ... FH
Federation of Housing Societies of Victoria [*Australia*] ... FHSV
Federation of Independent Advice Centres [*British*] (DBA) ... FIAC
Federation of Independent British Optometrists (DBA) ... FIBO
Federation of Independent Nursing Organization (DICI) ... FINO
Federation of Independent Trade Unions [*Lebanon*] ... FITU
Federation of Independent Trade Unions of Russia (ECON) ... FNPR
Federation of Indian Export Organisations [*Canada*] ... FIEO
Federation of Information Users [*Defunct*] (EA) ... FIU
Federation of Insurance and Corporate Counsel [*Marblehead, MA*] (EA) ... FICC
Federation of Insurance Counsel (EA) ... FIC
Federation of International American Clubs [*Oslo, Norway*] (EAIO) ... FIAC
Federation of International Civil Servants' Associations [*Geneva, Switzerland*] (EA) ... FICSA
Federation of International Country Air Personalities [*Defunct*] (EA) ... FICAP
Federation of International Music Competitions (EA) ... FICM
Federation of International Poetry Associations (EA) ... FIPA
Federation of International Trade Associations (EA) ... FITA
Federation of International Trampoline Technical Committee (EA) ... FITTC
Federation of International Youth Travel Organizations [*Copenhagen, Denmark*] (EAIO) ... FIYTO
Federation of Interstate Truckers [*Acronym is title of film*] ... FIST
Federation of Irish Cyclists (EAIO) ... FIC
Federation of Irish Industries Ltd. (BI) ... FII
Federation of Islamic Associations in the US and Canada (EA) ... FIA
Federation of Jewish Charities, Philadelphia, PA [*Library symbol Library of Congress Obsolete*] (LCLS) ... PPFJC
Federation of Jewish Men's Clubs (EA) ... FJMC
Federation of Jewish Philanthropies of New York (EA) ... FJP
Federation of Jewish Philanthropies Task Force on Compulsive Gambling (EA) ... FJPTFCG
Federation of Jewish Student Organizations [*Defunct*] (EA) ... FJSTO
Federation of Jewish Women's Organizations (EA) ... FJWO
Federation of Korean Trade Unions [*South Korea*] ... FKTU
Federation of Labor Unions [*Lebanon*] ... FLU
Federation of Labor Unions in Lebanon ... FLUL
Federation of Latvian Organisations of Victoria [*Australia*] ... FLOV
Federation of Leisure Activity Groups [*Australia*] ... FLAG
Federation of Liberal and Democratic Parties (PPE) ... FLDP
Federation of Liberal and Democratic Parties of the European Community [*Brussels, Belgium Political party*] (EAIO) ... ELD
Federation of Libyan Labor Unions ... FLLU
Federation of Lutheran Clubs (EA) ... FLC
Federation of Malaya Volunteer Electrical and Mechanical Engineers [*British military*] (DMA) ... FMVEME
Federation of Malaya Volunteer Reconnaissance Corps [*British military*] (DMA) ... FMVRC
Federation of Manufacturers of Construction Equipment and Cranes [*British*] (EAIO) ... FMCEC
Federation of Manufacturing Opticians [*British*] (BI) ... FMO
Federation of Masons of the World (EA) ... FMW
Federation of Master Builders [*British*] (DAS) ... FMB
Federation of Master Organ Builders [*British*] (BI) ... FMOB
Federation of Master Painters and Signwriters of Australia ... FMPSA
Federation of Master Process Engravers [*British*] (BI) ... FMPE
Federation of Materials Societies (EA) ... FMS
Federation of Mental Health Centers [*Defunct*] (EA) ... FMHC
Federation of Mental Health Workers [*British*] ... FMHW
Federation of Merchant Tailors of Great Britain, Inc. (BI) ... FMT
Federation of Military and United Services Institutes of Canada ... FMUSIC
Federation of Mobile Home Owners (EA) ... FMO
Federation of Modern Painters and Sculptors (EA) ... FMPS
Federation of Motion Picture Councils (EA) ... FMPC
Federation of Moulders and Collateral Trades [*A union*] [*British*] ... FMCT
Federation of Municipal Passenger Transport Employers [*British*] (BI) ... FMPTE
Federation of Music Industries [*British*] (DBA) ... FMI
Federation of Mutual Fire Insurance Companies (EA) ... FMFIC
Federation of National AFS Organizations in Europe [*Brussels, Belgium*] (EAIO) ... FNAOE
Federation of National Associations (EA) ... FNA
Federation of National Associations of Shipbrokers and Agents [*British*] (EAIO) ... FONASBA
Federation of National Electrolysis Associations [*Defunct*] (EA) ... FNEA
Federation of National Professional Organizations for Recreation (EA) ... FNPOR
Federation of Nature and National Parks of Europe (EERA) ... FNNPE
Federation of NCR [*NCR Corp.*] **User Groups** (EA) ... FNUG
Federation of NCR [*NCR Corp.*] **User Groups** (EA) ... NUG
Federation of Needle Fish Hook and Fishing Tackle Makers [*British*] (BI) ... FNFHFTM
Federation of Netherlands Societies [*Australia*] ... FNS
Federation of Nordic Commercial Agents [*Stockholm, Sweden*] (EA) ... FNCA
Federation of Nuclear Shelter Consultants and Contractors [*British*] (DBA) ... FNSCC
Federation of Nurses and Health Professionals (EA) ... FNHP
Federation of Oils, Seeds, and Fats Associations [*British*] ... FOSFA
Federation of Old Cornwall Societies [*British*] (DBA) ... FOCS
Federation of Ontario Naturalists [*Canada*] ... FON
Federation of Ophthalmic and Dispensing Opticians [*British*] (DBA) ... FODO
Federation of Organizations for Professional Women (EA) ... FOPW
Federation of Orthodontic Associations (EA) ... FOA
Federation of Outdoor Recreationists [*Defunct*] (EA) ... FOR
Federation of Overseas Property Devlopers, Agents, and Consultants [*British*] (DBA) ... FOPDAC
Federation of Paint and Varnish Production Clubs [*Later, FSCT*] ... FPVPC
Federation of Pakistan Chambers of Commerce and Industry (ECON) ... FPCCI
Federation of Pan-African Cinema [*of the Organization of African Unity*] ... FEPACI
Federation of Parents and Citizens' Associations of New South Wales [*Australia*] ... FPCANSW
Federation of Parents and Friends of Lesbians and Gays (EA) ... P-FLAG
Federation of Performance Sheep Breeders [*Australia*] ... FPSB
Federation of Piling Specialists [*British*] (DBA) ... FPS
Federation of Playgoers Societies [*British*] (BI) ... FOPS
Federation of Podiatric Medical Boards (EA) ... FPMB
Federation of Podiatry Boards [*Later, FPMB*] (EA) ... FPB
Federation of Postal Police Officers [*Defunct*] (EA) ... FPPO
Federation of Postal Security Police [*Later, FPPO*] (EA) ... FPSP
Federation of Private Hospitals and Nursing Homes [*Australia*] ... FPHNH
Federation of Private Residents' Associations [*British*] (DBA) ... FPRA
Federation of Professional Athletes [*Later, NFLPA*] (EA) ... FPA
Federation of Professional Officers Association (AIE) ... FPOA
Federation of Professional Organisations [*British*] (DBA) ... FPO
Federation of Professional Railway Staff [*A union*] [*British*] ... FPRS
Federation of Professional Writers of America (EA) ... FPWA
Federation of Progressive Trade Unions [*Zanzibar*] ... FPTU
Federation of Prosthodontic Organizations (EA) ... FPO
Federation of Protestant Welfare Agencies (EA) ... FPWA
Federation of Public Passenger Transport Employees [*British*] (DCTA) ... FPPTE
Federation of Radical Booksellers [*British*] ... FRB
Federation of Radio and Television Retailers Association (MHDB) ... FORTRA
Federation of Reconstructionist Congregations and Fellowships [*Later, FRCH*] (EA) ... FRCF
Federation of Reconstructionist Congregations and Havurot (EA) ... FRCH
Federation of Recorded Music Societies [*British*] (EAIO) ... FRMS
Federation of Recruitment and Employment Services [*British*] (EAIO) ... FRES
Federation of Regional Accrediting Commissions of Higher Education [*Later, COPA*] (EA) ... FRACHE
Federation of Registered House-Builders [*British*] (BI) ... FRHB
Federation of Retail Merchants [*Defunct*] (EA) ... FRM
Federation of Right to Life Associations [*Australia*] ... FRLA
Federation of Rocky Mountain States ... FRMS
Federation of Russian Charitable Organizations of the United States of America [*Defunct*] (EA) ... FRCOUSA
Federation of Sailmakers of Great Britain and Ireland [*A union*] ... FSGBI
Federation of Serbian Sisters Circle [*Australia*] ... FSSC
Federation of Sewage and Industrial Wastes Associations [*Later, Water PollutionControl Federation*] ... FSIWA
Federation of Sidecar Clubs [*British*] (DBA) ... FOSC
Federation of Small Mines [*British*] (DBA) ... FSMGB
Federation of Societies for Coatings Technology (EA) ... FSCT
Federation of Societies for Paint Technology [*Later, FSCT*] (EA) ... FSPT
Federation of Soroptimist Clubs of Great Britain and Ireland (BI) ... FGBI
Federation of Southern Cooperatives [*Later, FSC/LAF*] (EA) ... FSC
Federation of Southern Cooperatives and Land Assistance Fund (EA) ... FSC/LAF
Federation of Specialised Film Associations [*British*] (BI) ... FSFA
Federation of Sports Goods Distributors [*British*] (DCTA) ... FSGD
Federation of State Associations of Independent Colleges and Universities [*Later, NAICU*] (EA) ... FSAICU
Federation of State Medical Boards of the United States (EA) ... FSMB
Federation of State Medical Boards of the United States (EA) ... FSMBUS
Federation of Sterea Hellas (EA) ... FSH
Federation of Stock Exchanges (WDAA) ... FSE
Federation of Stock Exchanges in the European Community [*Belgium*] (EAIO) ... FSEEEC
Federation of Straight Chiropractic Organizations (EA) ... FSCO
Federation of Sunday Newspaper Owners (DGA) ... FSNO
Federation of Swiss Employees' Societies ... FSES
Federation of Tax Administrators (EA) ... FTA
Federation of Telephone Workers ... FTW
Federation of the Association of College Lecturers in Scotland (AIE) ... FACLS
Federation of the European Cutlery and Flatware Industries (EA) ... FEC

Federation of the European Microbiological Societies (EAIO) ..... FEMS
Federation of the Marble Industry of the European Economic Community (EAIO) ..... FIMIG-CEE
Federation of the Scientific and Technical Organizations of the Socialist Countries [*Formerly, Permanent Council of Scientific and Technical Organizations of Socialist Countries*] (EA) ..... FeNTO
Federation of Theatre Unions [*British*] (DCTA) ..... FTU
Federation of Trade Associations [*Republic of Ireland*] (BI) ..... FTA
Federation of Trade Unions [*British*] (DAS) ..... FTU
Federation of Trainers and Training Programs in PsychoDrama (EA) ..... FTTPP
Federation of Turkish Revolutionary Youth ..... DEV GENC
Federation of Turkish-American Societies (EA) ..... FTAS
Federation of Ukrainians in Great Britain (DBA) ..... FUGB
Federation of Union Representatives (BARN) ..... FOUR
Federation of Unions of Workers and Employees of North Lebanon ..... FUNL
Federation of United Kingdom and Eire Malaysian and Singaporean Students [*British*] ..... FUEMSSO
Federation of University Women ..... FUW
Federation of Veterinarians of the EEC (EAIO) ..... FVE
Federation of Victorian School Administrators [*Australia*] ..... FVSA
Federation of Victorian Walking Clubs [*Australia*] ..... FVWC
Federation of Wall and Ceiling Contractors of Australia and New Zealand ..... FWCCANZ
Federation of West Indies ..... FWI
Federation of Western Outdoor Clubs (EA) ..... FWOC
Federation of Westinghouse Independent Salaried Unions (EA) ..... FWISU
Federation of Westinghouse Independent Salaried Unions ..... WISU
Federation of Wholefood Wholesalers [*British*] ..... FWW
Federation of Wholesale and Multiple Bakers [*British*] (BI) ..... FWMB
Federation of Wholesalers and Distributors [*British*] (DBA) ..... FWD
Federation of Wire Rope Manufacturers of Great Britain (BI) ..... FWRMGB
Federation of Woman's Exchanges (EA) ..... FWE
Federation of Women Clerks [*A union*] [*British*] ..... FWA
Federation of Women Lawyers', Judicial Screening Panel [*Defunct*] (EA) .... FWL
Federation of Women Shareholders in American Business [*New York, NY*] (EA) ..... FOWSAB
Federation of Women Shareholders in American Business (EA) ..... FWSAB
Federation of Women's Institutes [*British*] (DI) ..... FWI
Federation of Workers' Singing Societies of the USA (EA) ..... FWSSUSA
Federation of World Health Foundations (EA) ..... FWHF
Federation of Young Democrats [*Hungary*] [*Political party Acronym is based on foreign phrase*] (ECON) ..... FIDESZ
Federation of Young Democrats [*Hungary Political party*] (EY) ..... FYD
Federation on Computing in the US (CDE) ..... FOCUS
Federation Ouest Africaine des Associations pour la Promotion des Personnes Handicapees [*West African Federation of Associations for the Advancement of Handicapped Persons - WAFAH*] [*Bamako, Mali*] (EAIO) ..... FOAPH
Federation pour une Nouvelle Societe Caledonienne [*Federation for a New Caledonian Society*] [*Political party*] (PPW) ..... FNSC
Federation Prohibitionniste Internationale [*International Prohibition Federation*] ..... FPI
Federation Reserve Bank of Minneapolis, Minneapolis, MN [*Library symbol*] [*Library of Congress*] (LCLS) ..... MnMFR
Federation Sephardite Mondiale [*World Sephardi Federation - WSF*] [*Geneva, Switzerland*] (EAIO) ..... FSM
Federation Socialiste Caledonienne [*Caledonian Socialist Federation*] [*Political party*] (PPW) ..... FSC
Federation Socialiste de la Martinique [*Socialist Federation of Martinique*] [*Political party*] (PPW) ..... FSM
Federation Spirite Internationale [*International Spiritualist Federation*] ..... FSI
Federation Sportive et Gymnique du Travail ..... FSGT
Federation Syndicale Mondiale [*World Federation of Trade Unions - WFTU*] [*French*] (EAIO) ..... FSM
Federation Universelle des Associations Chretiennes d'Etudiants [*Universal Federation of Christian Students Associations*] ..... FUACE
Federation Universelle des Associations d'Agences de Voyages [*Universal Federation of Travel Agents' Associations - UFTAA*] (EAIO) ..... FUAAV
Federazione Autonoma Italiana Lavoratori Cemento Legno, Edilizia, ed Affini [*Workers in Cement, Wood, Construction, and Related Industries Federation*] [*Italy*] (EY) ..... FAILCLEA
Federazione Autonoma Italiana Lavoratori Elettrici [*Electrical Workers Federation*] [*Italy*] (EY) ..... FAILE
Federazione Autonoma Lavoratori Casse di Risparmio Italiane [*Savings Banks Workers Federation*] [*Italy*] (EY) ..... FALCRI
Federazione delle Associazioni Italiane Alberghi e Turismo [*Hotels and Tourism Federation*] [*Italy*] (EY) ..... FAIAT
Federazione Europea Fabbricanti Matite [*Federation of Eraser Pencil Manufacturers Associations*] (EAIO) ..... FEFM
Federazione Internazionale della Stampa Gastronomica e Vinicola [*International Federation of Gastronomical and Vinicultural Press*] ..... FISGV
Federazione Italiana Bancari e Assicuratori [*Italy*] (EY) ..... FIBA
Federazione Italiana Editori Giornali [*Italian Federation of Newspaper Publishing*] (EY) ..... FIEG
Federcion Interamericana del Cemento [*Inter American Cement Federation*] [*Colombia*] (EAIO) ..... FICEM
Federicus Petrucius de Senis [*Flourished, 1321-43*] [*Authority cited in pre-1607 legal work*] (DSA) ..... Fede de Sen
Fedgwick, Dettret, Moran & Arnold, San Francisco, CA [*Library symbol*] [*Library of Congress*] (LCLS) ..... CSfFDM
Fed'l Home Ln Mtg 6.72% Pfd [*NYSE symbol*] (TTSB) ..... FREPrA
Fed'l Home Ln Mtg 7.90% Pfd [*NYSE symbol*] (TTSB) ..... FREPr
Fed'l Home Ln Mtg Var Rt Pfd [*NYSE symbol*] (TTSB) ..... FREPrB
FEDLINK [*Federal Library and Information Network*], Washington, DC [*OCLC symbol*] (OCLC) ..... FLC
FEDLINK [*Federal Library and Information Network*], Washington, DC [*OCLC symbol*] (OCLC) ..... TPY
FEDLINK [*Federal Library and Information Network*], Washington, DC [*OCLC symbol*] (OCLC) ..... TPZ
Fedreal Atlantic-Lakes Line [*Steamship*] (MHDW) ..... FALLINE
Fee Determination Official (NASA) ..... FDO
Fee Factor (MCD) ..... FF
Fee for Service ..... FFS
Fee for Service [*Equivalency*] ..... FFS
Fee Paid [*Classified advertising*] ..... FP
Feed (MSA) ..... FD
Feed And Speed Technology (PDAA) ..... FAST
Feed Assembly Modification ..... FAM
Feed Control Panel (IAA) ..... FCP
Feed Drive Analysis [*Machine Tool Industry Research Association*] [*Software package*] (NCC) ..... FEDRAN
Feed Efficiency Ratio ..... FER
Feed Forward (IAA) ..... FF
Feed Forward (ECII) ..... FFW
Feed Forward Control (IAA) ..... FFC
Feed Forward Filter (IAA) ..... FFF
Feed Lines (NASA) ..... FL
Feed Materials Production Center [*AEC*] ..... FMPC
Feed Rate Number (MCD) ..... FRN
Feed Rate Override [*Mechanical engineering*] (IAA) ..... FRO
Feed System Maintenance Transfer (MCD) ..... FSMT
Feed the Children (EA) ..... FC
Feed Water (AAG) ..... FDW
Feed Water (KSC) ..... FW
Feed Water Heater Management ..... FHM
Feed Water Heater Manufacturers Association (EA) ..... FWHMA
Feed Water Pump (MSA) ..... FWP
Feed Water Regulation Valve (IEEE) ..... FPV
Feedback ..... F
Feedback (AAG) ..... FB
Feedback (MSA) ..... FDBK
Feedback Analysis for GCM Intercomparison and Observation (EERA) ..... FANGIO
Feedback and Analysis of Control Statistics (PDAA) ..... FACS
Feedback Carburetor [*Automotive engineering*] ..... FBC
Feedback Carburetor Actuator [*Automotive engineering*] ..... FBCA
Feedback Control [*Computer science*] (IAA) ..... FBC
Feedback Control Loop [*Computer science*] (BUR) ..... FCL
Feedback Control System ..... FCS
Feedback Controlled Heat Pipes (MCD) ..... FCHP
Feedback Filter (IAA) ..... FBF
Feedback Frequency Modulation ..... FBFM
Feedback Information Request Evidence (DNAB) ..... FIRE
Feedback Inhibition Factor [*Immunochemistry*] ..... FIF
Feedback Mechanism ..... FM
Feedback, Multiple Loop ..... FML
Feedback Network ..... FBN
Feedback Node Set ..... FNS
Feedback of Repair, Workshop, and Reliability Data (PDAA) ..... FORWARD
Feedback Positive [*Computer science*] ..... FP
Feedback Potentiometer ..... FP
Feedback Potentiometer (MSA) ..... FPOT
Feedback Report (NVT) ..... FBR
Feedback Resistance (IEEE) ..... FBR
Feedback Shift Register ..... FSR
Feedback Signal ..... FBS
Feedback, Stabilized ..... FS
Feedback Summing Junction [*Computer science*] ..... FSJ
Feedback System ..... FBS
Feedback Technology (SSD) ..... FBT
Feedback to Oral Reading Miscues Analysis System (EDAC) ..... FORMAS
Feedback Voltage (IDOE) ..... V_{FB}
Feed-Effluent Heat Exchanger [*Chemical engineering*] ..... FEHE
Feeder ..... FDR
Feeder Branch Edit (PDAA) ..... FBE
Feeder Control Logic [*Computer science*] (IAA) ..... FCL
Feeder Distribution Interface [*Bell System*] ..... FDI
Feeder Equipment Capacity (PDAA) ..... FECAP
Feeder Fault Analysis (PDAA) ..... FEFA
Feeder Fault Sensing (MCD) ..... FFS
Feeder Length in Feet (PDAA) ..... FELIF
Feeder Lighter Aboard Ship ..... FLASH
Feeder Load Search (PDAA) ..... FELOS
Feeder Meter Flow (PDAA) ..... FEMEF
Feed-Forward Signal Regeneration (PDAA) ..... FFSR
Feeding ..... FDG
Feeding ..... FDNG
Feeding and Watering [*Charge*] [*Business term*] ..... F & W
Feeding Interaction Report, Scale, and Treatment [*Occupational therapy*] ..... FIRST
Feedline (NASA) ..... FDLN
Feedlot Waste ..... FLW
Feedlot Waste Filtrate ..... FLWF
Feed-Only-Good Generator [*Nuclear energy*] (NRCH) ..... FOGG
Feedwater Control [*Nuclear energy*] (NRCH) ..... FWC
Feedwater Control System [*Nuclear energy*] (NRCH) ..... FWCS
Feedwater Coolant Injection [*Nuclear energy*] (NRCH) ..... FWCI
Feedwater Pipe Break [*Nuclear energy*] (NRCH) ..... FWPB
Feedwater Pump Turbine [*Nuclear energy*] (NRCH) ..... FPT
Feel Augmentation System [*Helicopters*] ..... FAS

Feel, Inspect, Tighten, Clean, Adjust, Lubricate [*A keyword representing operations in preventive maintenance of communications equipment*] [*Military*] .... FITCAL
Feeler .... FELR
Feeley-Gorman [*Agar*] [*Microbiology*] .... F-G
Feeling Rough Inside [*Slang*] .... FRI
Feeling-Oriented Discussion .... F-O Dis
Feels Like [*A term used by weather forecasters*] (WDMC) .... flslk
Feet [*or Foot*] .... F
Feet [*or Foot*] (AAG) .... FT
Feet .... ft
Feet (IDOE) .... ft
Feet Apart [*Dance terminology*] .... FA
Feet Board Measure .... FBM
Feet of Fresh Water .... FFW
Feet of Seawater [*Deep-sea diving*] .... FSW
Feet Out of Bed .... FOB
Feet per Day .... FT/D
Feet per Hour (WDAA) .... FPH
Feet per Hour .... FT/H
Feet per Minute (ADA) .... F/M
Feet per Minute .... FPM
Feet Per Minute (WDMC) .... fpm
Feet per Minute .... FT/MIN
Feet per Revolution .... FPR
Feet per Second .... FPS
Feet per Second (IDOE) .... fps
Feet per Second .... FS
Feet per Second .... FT/S
Feet per Second (MCD) .... FT/SEC
Feet per Second per Second .... FPS/S
Feet per Second per Second .... FPSPS
Feet per Year .... FT/A
Feet Together [*Dance terminology*] .... FT
Feffer & Simons [*Publisher*] .... F & S
FEI Co. [*Associated Press*] (SAG) .... FEI Co
FEI Co. [*NASDAQ symbol*] (SAG) .... FEIC
Feingold Association of the United States (EA) .... FAUS
Fein-Marquart Associates [*Chemical Information Systems, Inc.*] [*Information service or system*] (IID) .... FMA
Feint [*of account book rulings*] .... FT
Feint and Cash [*of account book rulings*] .... FC
Feint and Cash [*of account book rulings*] .... FT & C
Felavarjan [*Iran*] [*ICAO location identifier*] (ICLI) .... OIFL
Felbamate [*Organic chemistry*] .... FBM
FelCor Suite Hotels [*NYSE symbol*] (TTSB) .... FCH
FelCor Suite Hotels $1.95 Pfd [*NYSE symbol*] (TTSB) .... FCHPrA
FelCor Suite Hotels, Inc. [*NYSE symbol*] (SAG) .... FCH
FelCor Suite Hotels, Inc. [*Associated Press*] (SAG) .... FelCor
Feldberg In Schwarzwald [*Federal Republic of Germany*] [*Seismograph station code, US Geological Survey*] (SEIS) .... FEL
Feldenkrais Guild [*An association*] (EA) .... FG
Feldspar [*A mineral*] .... FI
Feldspar Subgroup [*Orthoclase, albite, anorthite*] [*CIPW classification Geology*] .... F
[*The*] **Felician College** [*Chicago, IL*] .... TFC
Felician College, Chicago, IL [*OCLC symbol*] (OCLC) .... IAE
Felician College, Chicago, IL [*Library symbol Library of Congress*] (LCLS) .... ICFC
Felician College, Lodi, NJ [*Library symbol Library of Congress*] (LCLS) .... NjLF
Felician Sisters (TOCD) .... CSSF
Feliciana Eastern Railroad Co. [*Later, FERR*] [*AAR code*] .... FE
Feliciana Eastern Railroad Co. [*Formerly, FE*] [*AAR code*] .... FERR
Felicidades Wildlife Foundation (EA) .... FWF
Felicis Memoriae [*Of Happy Memory*] [*Latin*] .... FEL MEM
Felicissimi Fratres [*Most Fortunate Brothers*] [*Latin*] .... FF
Felicissimus [*Most Happy*] [*Latin*] (ROG) .... FF
Feliciter [*Happily*] .... F
Feline (ABBR) .... FLN
Feline Acquired Immune Deficiency Syndrome [*Pathology*] .... FAIDS
Feline Advisory Bureau [*British*] (CB) .... FAB
Feline Advisory Bureau and Central Fund for Feline Studies (EAIO) .... FABCFFS
Feline and Canine Friends (EA) .... FCF
Feline Ataxia Virus (MAE) .... FAV
Feline Calicivirus .... FCV
Feline Central Retinal Degeneration [*Animal pathology*] .... FCRD
Feline Control Council of Victoria [*Australia*] .... FCCV
Feline Embryonic Fibroblast .... FEF
Feline Fibrosarcoma Virus .... FSV
Feline Gardner-Rasheed Virus .... FGR
Feline Immunodeficiency Virus .... FIV
Feline Infectious Peritonitis .... FIP
Feline Infectious Peritonitis Virus .... FIPV
Feline Leukemia Virus [*Also, FLV*] .... FELV
Feline Leukemia Virus [*Veterinary medicine*] .... FeV
Feline Leukemia Virus [*Also, FELV*] .... FLV
Feline Lung (Cell) [*Cytology*] .... FL
Feline McDonough Sarcoma [*Virus*] .... FMS
Feline Orcornavirus-Associated Cell Membrane Antigen [*Immunology*] .... FOCMA
Feline Panleukopenia .... FPL
Feline Panleukopenia Virus .... FPV
Feline Sarcoma Virus [*Also, FeSV*] .... FESV
Feline Syncytium-Forming Virus .... FeSFV
Feline T-Lymphotropic Lentivirus [*Later, FIV*] .... FTLV
Feline Urologic Syndrome .... FUS
Feline Viral Rhinotracheitis [*Vaccine*] .... FVR

Felinely (ABBR) .... FLNY
Felinity (ABBR) .... FLNT
Felinus Sandeus [*Deceased, 1503*] [*Authority cited in pre-1607 legal work*] (DSA) .... Fel
Felinus Sandeus [*Deceased, 1503*] [*Authority cited in pre-1607 legal work*] (DSA) .... Feli
Felinus Sandeus [*Deceased, 1503*] [*Authority cited in pre-1607 legal work*] (DSA) .... Felin
Felis Domesticus 1 [*Protein found in the saliva of cats*] .... Fel D1
Felix Schlag [*Designer's mark, when appearing on US coins*] .... FS
Felix-Weil [*Reaction*] [*Clinical chemistry*] .... FW
Felix-Weil Reaction [*Clinical chemistry*] (AAMN) .... FWR
Fell [*Horse racing*] .... F
Fell on Guaranty and Suretyship [*A publication*] (DLA) .... Fell Guar
Fell Out of Bed [*Medicine*] (DMAA) .... FOOB
Fell Pony Society [*British*] (BI) .... FPS
Fellatio (ABBR) .... FLTIO
Fellesradet for det Sorlige Afrika [*Norway*] .... FSA
Fellis [*Gall*] [*Pharmacy*] (ROG) .... FEL
Fellow .... F
Fellow .... FEL
Fellow .... FELL
Fellow, American Society of Appraisers [*American Society of Appraisers*] [*Designation awarded by*] .... FASA
Fellow Associate of the Institute of Chemistry .... FAIC
Fellow Association for Healthcare Philanthropy .... FAHP
Fellow, Association for Healthcare Philanthropy (NFD) .... FAHP
Fellow Chartered Accountant of New Zealand .... FCA(NZ)
Fellow Craft [*Freemasonry*] (ROG) .... FC
Fellow, Fundraising Institute-Australia, Inc. (NFD) .... FFIA
Fellow in Dental Surgery of the Royal College of Physicians and Surgeons of Glasgow .... FDSRCPS Glasg
Fellow in Dental Surgery of the Royal College of Physicians and Surgeons of Glasgow .... FDSRCPSGlas
Fellow in Dental Surgery of the Royal College of Surgeons of Edinburgh .... FDSRCS Edin
Fellow in Dental Surgery of the Royal College of Surgeons of Edinburgh .... FDSRCSE
Fellow in Dental Surgery of the Royal College of Surgeons of Edinburgh .... FDSRCSEd
Fellow in Dental Surgery of the Royal College of Surgeons of England .... FDSRCS
Fellow in Dental Surgery of the Royal College of Surgeons of England .... FDSRCS Eng
Fellow in the Faculty of Dentistry [*British*] .... FFD
Fellow in the Technology of Surface Coatings [*British*] (DBQ) .... FTSC
Fellow Lady Astronaut Trainee .... FLAT
Fellow, Life Management Institute [*Life Office Management Association*] [*Designation awarded by*] .... FLMI
Fellow, London Association of Accountants .... FLAA
Fellow, National College of Music [*London, England*] (ADA) .... FNCM
Fellow of Advertising [*British*] .... FOA
Fellow of Agricultural Institute of Canada .... FAIC
Fellow of American College of Emergency Physicians (DHSM) .... FACEP
Fellow of American College of Health Care Administrators (DHSM) .... FACHCA
Fellow of American College of Healthcare Executives (DHSM) .... FACHE
Fellow of American College of Organists .... FACO
Fellow of Business Administration (DD) .... FBA
Fellow of Catherine Hall, Cambridge [*British*] (ROG) .... FCHC
Fellow of College of Violinists [*British*] (ROG) .... FCV
Fellow of Commercial Actuaries (DD) .... FCommA
Fellow of Dental Surgery [*British*] .... FDS
Fellow [*or Fellowship*] **of Engineering** .... FEng
Fellow of Guildhall School of Music [*British*] (EY) .... FGSM
Fellow of Heriot-Watt College, Edinburgh .... FH-WC
Fellow of King's College [*London*] .... FKC
Fellow of King's College, London .... FKCL
Fellow of Operational Research [*British*] (DBQ) .... FOR
Fellow of Pembroke College [*British*] (ROG) .... FPC
Fellow of Sheffield Polytechnic [*British*] .... FSP
Fellow of Technological Sciences .... FTS
Fellow of the Academy of Arts and Sciences .... FAAS
Fellow of the Accountants' and Executives' Corp. of Canada .... FAE
Fellow of the Actuarial Society .... FAS
Fellow of the Acupuncture Association [*British*] (DBQ) .... FAcA
Fellow of the Administration Association (DD) .... FAdmA
Fellow of the Ambulance Service Institute [*British*] (DBQ) .... FASI
Fellow of the American Academy of Allergy .... FAAA
Fellow of the American Academy of Arts and Sciences .... FAAAS
Fellow of the American Academy of Nursing .... FAAN
Fellow of the American Academy of Orthopedic Surgeons .... FAAOS
Fellow of the American Academy of Pediatrics (WGA) .... FAAP
Fellow of the American Association for the Advancement of Science .... FAA
Fellow of the American Association for the Advancement of Science .... FAAAS
Fellow of the American Association of Criminology .... FAAC
Fellow of the American College of Abdominal Surgeons (DAVI) .... FACAS
Fellow of the American College of Allergists .... FACAl
Fellow of the American College of Anesthesiologists (WGA) .... FACAn
Fellow of the American College of Anesthesiologists .... FACAn
Fellow of the American College of Angiology .... FACA
Fellow of the American College of Apothecaries .... FACA
Fellow of the American College of Cardiology .... FACC
Fellow of the American College of Chest Physicians .... FACCP
Fellow of the American College of Chest Physicians .... FCCP

Fellow of the American College of Clinical Pharmacology and Chemotherapy (DAVI) .... FACCPC
Fellow of the American College of Dentists .... FACD
Fellow of the American College of Family Physicians .... FACFP
Fellow of the American College of Foot Surgeons .... FACFS
Fellow of the American College of Gastroenterology .... FACG
Fellow of the American College of Gastroenterology (DAVI) .... FACGE
Fellow of the American College of Health Administrators .... FACHA
Fellow of the American College of Legal Medicine (DAVI) .... FACLM
Fellow of the American College of Neuropsychopharmacology (DAVI) ..... FACNP
Fellow of the American College of Nutrition (DAVI) .... FACN
Fellow of the American College of Obstetricians and Gynecologists .... FACOG
Fellow of the American College of Orthopedic Surgeons (DAVI) .... FACOS
Fellow of the American College of Otolaryngology .... FACO
Fellow of the American College of Physician Executives (HCT) .... FACPE
Fellow of the American College of Physicians .... FACP
Fellow of the American College of Preventive Medicine .... FACPM
Fellow of the American College of Preventive Medicine (DAVI) .... FACPRM
Fellow of the American College of Radiology .... FACR
Fellow of the American College of Sports Medicine .... FACSM
Fellow of the American College of Surgeons .... FACS
Fellow of the American College of Trial Lawyers (DD) .... FACTL
Fellow of the American Geographical Society .... FAGS
Fellow of the American Guild of Organists .... FAGO
Fellow of the American Institute of Actuaries .... FAIA
Fellow of the American Institute of Aeronautics and Astronautics [Formerly, FIAes,FIAS] .... FAIAA
Fellow of the American Institute of Architects .... FAIA
Fellow of the American Institute of Criminology .... FAIC
Fellow of the American Institute of Electrical Engineers .... F Am IEE
Fellow of the American Institute of Electrical Engineers .... FAIEE
Fellow of the American Medical Association .... FAMA
Fellow of the American Neurological Association .... FANA
Fellow of the American Neurological Society .... FANS
Fellow of the American Occupational Therapy Association .... FAOTA
Fellow of the American Ornithologists Union .... FAOU
Fellow of the American Physical Society .... FAPS
Fellow of the American Psychiatric Association .... FAPA
Fellow of the American Psychoanalytic Association .... FAPA
Fellow of the American Psychological Association .... FAPA
Fellow of the American Public Health Association .... FAPHA
Fellow of the American Society of Civil Engineers .... FAmSCE
Fellow of the American Society of Civil Engineers .... FASCE
Fellow of the American Sociological Association .... FASA
Fellow of the Ancient Monuments Society [British] .... FAMS
Fellow of the Anthropological Society [British] (DAS) .... FAS
Fellow of the Anthropological Society, London (ROG) .... FASL
Fellow of the Antiquarian Society [British] .... FAS
Fellow of the Antiquarian Society, London (ROG) .... FASL
Fellow of the Antiquarian Society of Edinburgh (ROG) .... FASE
Fellow of the Art Galleries Association of Australia .... FAGAA
Fellow of the Asia-Oceania Federation of Obstetricians and Gynaecologists .... FAOFOG
Fellow of the Association of Business and Administrative Computing [British] (DBQ) .... FABAC
Fellow of the Association of Business Executives [British] (DCTA) .... FABE
Fellow of the Association of Certified Accountants (DD) .... FCCA
Fellow of the Association of Certified and Corporate Accountants [British] (EY) .... FACCA
Fellow of the Association of Computer Professionals [British] (DBQ) .... FACP
Fellow of the Association of Corporate Treasurers [British] (ODBW) .... FCT
Fellow of the Association of Cost and Executive Accountants [British] (DBQ) .... FCEA
Fellow of the Association of Dispensing Opticians [British] (DBQ) .... FADO
Fellow of the Association of Dispensing Opticians with Honours Diploma [British] (DBQ) .... FADO(Hons)
Fellow of the Association of Dispensing Opticians with Honours Diploma and Diploma in Contact Lens Fitting [British] (DBQ) .... FADO(Hons)CL
Fellow of the Association of Health Care Information and Medical Records Officers [British] (DBQ) .... FMR
Fellow of the Association of Home Economists [British] (DI) .... FAHE
Fellow of the Association of International Accountants [British] .... FAIA
Fellow of the Association of Medical Secretaries, Practice Administrators, and Receptionists [British] (DBQ) .... FAMS
Fellow of the Australian Academy of Optometry .... FAAO
Fellow of the Australian Academy of Paediatrics .... FAAP
Fellow of the Australian Academy of the Humanities .... FAAH
Fellow of the Australian Council of Educational Administration .... FACEA
Fellow of the Australian Grain Institute .... FAGI
Fellow of the Australian Institute of Export (ODBW) .... FAI Ex
Fellow of the Australian Institute of Management (ODBW) .... FAIM
Fellow of the Australian Institute of Parks and Recreation .... FAIPR
Fellow of the Australian Institute of Sales and Marketing Executives ..... FAISME
Fellow of the Australian Insurance Institute (ODBW) .... FAII
Fellow of the Australian Marketing Institute (ODBW) .... FAMI
Fellow of the Australian Psychology and Hypnotherapy Association .... FAPHA
Fellow of the Australian Society of Accountants (ODBW) .... FASA
Fellow of the Australian Society of Sports Administrators .... FASSA
Fellow of the Benesh Institute of Choreology [British] (DBQ) .... FIChor
Fellow of the Birmingham School of Music [British] .... FBSM
Fellow of the Boot and Shoe Institution [British] .... FBSI
Fellow of the Botanical Society [British] (ROG) .... FBS
Fellow of the Botanical Society, Edinburgh (ROG) .... FBSE
Fellow of the British Academy (ROG) .... FBA
Fellow of the British Arts Association (DBQ) .... FBA

Fellow of the British Association of Accountants and Auditors (EY) .... FBAA
Fellow of the British Association of Industrial Editors (DBQ) .... FAIE
Fellow of the British Association of Secretaries [British] (DAS) .... FBAS
Fellow of the British Ballet Organisation .... FBBO
Fellow of the British College of Obstetricians and Gynaecologists (DAS) .... FCOG
Fellow of the British College of Ophthalmic Opticians (DBQ) .... FBCO
Fellow of the British Computer Society .... FBCS
Fellow of the British Esperanto Association (DAS) .... FBEA
Fellow of the British Horological Institute .... FBHI
Fellow of the British Horse Society (DBQ) .... FBHS
Fellow of the British Hypnotherapy Association (DBQ) .... FBHA
Fellow of the British Institute of Embalmers (DBQ) .... FBIE
Fellow of the British Institute of Interior Design (DBQ) .... FBID
Fellow of the British Institute of Management [Formerly, FIIA] .... FBIM
Fellow of the British Institute of Non-Destructive Testing (DBQ) .... FInstNDT
Fellow of the British Institute of Professional Photography (DBQ) .... FBIPP
Fellow of the British Institute of Surgical Technologists (DBQ) .... FBIST
Fellow of the British Institution of Radio Engineers .... FBritIRE
Fellow of the British Insurance Brokers' Association (ODBW) .... FBIBA
Fellow of the British Interplanetary Society .... FBIS
Fellow of the British Optical Association .... FBOA
Fellow of the British Ornithologists' Union (ROG) .... FBOU
Fellow of the British Psychological Society .... FBPsS
Fellow of the British Society of Commerce .... FBSC
Fellow of the British Society of Commerce .... FBSComm
Fellow of the Building Societies Institute [British] .... FBS
Fellow of the Business Education Council (Scotland) (ODBW) .... FBEC(S)
Fellow of the Cambridge Philological Society [British] .... FCPS
Fellow of the Cambridge Philosophical Society [British] (ROG) .... FCPS
Fellow of the Canadian Academy of Engineering (DD) .... FCAE
Fellow of the Canadian Aeronautics and Space Institute .... FCASI
Fellow of the Canadian Bankers' Association .... FCBA
Fellow of the Canadian Certified General Accountants Association (DD) .... FCGA
Fellow of the Canadian College of Organists .... FCCO
Fellow of the Canadian College of Physicians (DD) .... FCCP
Fellow of the Canadian College of Teachers .... FCCT
Fellow of the Canadian Credit Institute .... FCI
Fellow of the Canadian Credit Union Institute (DD) .... FCCUI
Fellow of the Canadian Institute of Actuaries .... FCIA
Fellow of the Canadian Institute of Chemistry (DD) .... FCIC
Fellow of the Canadian Institute of Realtors .... FRI
Fellow of the Canadian Psychological Association .... FCPA
Fellow of the Canadian Securities Institute (DD) .... FCSI
Fellow of the Canadian Society of Civil Engineers (DD) .... FCSCE
Fellow of the Canadian Society of Radiological Technicians .... FCSRT
Fellow of the Casualty Actuarial Science (DD) .... FCAS
Fellow of the Casualty Actuarial Society [Casualty Actuarial Society] [Designation awarded by] .... FCAS
Fellow of the Chartered Auctioneers' and Estate Agents' Institute [British].... FAI
Fellow of the Chartered Building Societies Institute [British] (DBQ) .... FCBSI
Fellow of the Chartered Institute of Arbitrators [British] (DBQ) .... FCIArb
Fellow of the Chartered Institute of Bankers (DD) .... FCIB
Fellow of the Chartered Institute of Building [British] (DBQ) .... FCIOB
Fellow of the Chartered Institute of Cost and Work Accountants [British] (EY) .... FCWA
Fellow of the Chartered Institute of Loss Adjusters [British] (DBQ) .... FCILA
Fellow of the Chartered Institute of Marketing (DD) .... FCIM
Fellow of the Chartered Institute of Marketing [British] (ODBW) .... FCIM
Fellow of the Chartered Institute of Patent Agents [British] .... FCIPA
Fellow of the Chartered Institute of Secretaries [British] (ROG) .... FCIS
Fellow of the Chartered Institute of Secretaries and Administrators [Australia] (ODBW) .... FCOSA
Fellow of the Chartered Institute of Transport [British] .... FCIT
Fellow of the Chartered Institution of Building Services [British] (DBQ) ..... FCIBS
Fellow of the Chartered Insurance Institute [British] (EY) .... FCII
Fellow of the Chartered Land Agents' Society [British] .... FLAS
Fellow of the Chartered Society of Physiotherapy [British] .... FCSP
Fellow of the Chemical Institute of Canada .... FCIC
Fellow of the Chemical Society [British] .... FChemSoc
Fellow of the Chemical Society [British] (ROG) .... FCS
Fellow of the City and Guilds of London Institute [British] (ROG) .... FCGI
Fellow of the Clothing and Footwear Institute [British] (DI) .... FCFI
Fellow of the College of American Pathologists .... FCAP
Fellow of the College of Craft Education [British] (DI) .... FCCEd
Fellow of the College of Family Physicians (DD) .... FCFP
Fellow of the College of General Practitioners .... FCGP
Fellow of the College of Medicine and Surgery [British] .... FCMS
Fellow of the College of Obstetricians and Gynecologists .... FCOG
Fellow of the College of Organists [British] (ROG) .... FCO
Fellow of the College of Osteopathy [British] .... FCO
Fellow of the College of Pathologists [Later, Royal College of Pathologists] [British] .... FC Path
Fellow of the College of Physicians (DD) .... FCP
Fellow of the College of Physicians and Surgeons [British] .... FCPS
Fellow of the College of Physicians and Surgeons and Obstetricians of South Africa .... FCPSO (SoAf)
Fellow of the College of Physicians of South Africa .... FCP(SA)
Fellow of the College of Physicians of South Africa .... FCP(SoAf)
Fellow of the College of Preceptors [British] (ROG) .... FCP
Fellow of the College of Speech Therapists [British] .... FCST
Fellow of the College of Surgeons of South Africa .... FCS(SA)
Fellow of the College of Surgeons of South Africa .... FCS(SoAf)
Fellow of the College of Teachers of the Blind .... FCTB

Fellow of the Commonwealth Institute of Accountancy ... FICA
Fellow of the Communication Advertising and Marketing Education Foundation [*British*] (DBQ) ... FCAM
Fellow of the Confederation of Insurance Brokers of Australia ... FCIB
Fellow of the Confederation of Professional Management [*British*] (DBQ) ... FCPM
Fellow of the Construction Surveyors' Institute [*British*] (DBQ) ... FCSI
Fellow of the Coopers Hill College [*British*] ... FCH
Fellow of the Corporation of Certified Secretaries [*British*] (EY) ... FCCS
Fellow of the Corporation of Executives and Administrators [*British*] (DBQ) ... FFBA
Fellow of the Corporation of Insurance Agents [*British*] ... FCIA
Fellow of the Corporation of Insurance Brokers [*British*] ... FCIB
Fellow of the Corporation of Registered Accountants [*British*] (DAS) ... FCRA
Fellow of the Educational Institute of Scotland ... FEIS
Fellow of the Engineering Institute of Canada ... FEIC
Fellow of the Engineering Institution of Zambia ... FEIZ
Fellow of the English Association of Accountants and Auditors (DD) ... FEAA
Fellow of the English Association of Corporate Secretaries (DD) ... FEAS
Fellow of the Entomological Society [*British*] ... FES
Fellow of the Ethnological Society [*British*] ... FES
Fellow of the Faculty of Actuaries [*British*] ... FFA
Fellow of the Faculty of Anaesthetists of the Royal College of Surgeons in Ire land [*British*] (DBQ) ... FFARCSIrel
Fellow of the Faculty of Anaesthetists of the Royal College of Surgeons in Ireland ... FFARCSI
Fellow of the Faculty of Anaesthetists of the Royal College of Surgeons of England ... FFARCS
Fellow of the Faculty of Anaesthetists of the Royal College of Surgeons of England ... FFARCS Eng
Fellow of the Faculty of Anesthetists [*British*] ... FFA
Fellow of the Faculty of Architects and Surveyors [*British*] (DBQ) ... FFS
Fellow of the Faculty of Architects and Surveyors, London [*British*] ... FFAS
Fellow of the Faculty of Child and Adolescent Psychiatry ... FFCPsy
Fellow of the Faculty of Commerce and Industry [*British*] (DBQ) ... FFCI
Fellow of the Faculty of Community Medicine [*British*] ... FFCM
Fellow of the Faculty of Dental Surgery, Royal College of Surgeons [*British*] (DAVI) ... FFDSRCS
Fellow of the Faculty of Dentistry of the Royal College of Surgeons in Ireland ... FFDRCS Irel
Fellow of the Faculty of Dentistry of the Royal College of Surgeons in Ireland ... FFDRCSI
Fellow of the Faculty of Dispensing Opticians [*British*] (DBQ) ... FFDO
Fellow of the Faculty of Fire Loss Adjusters [*British*] (DAS) ... FFLA
Fellow of the Faculty of Homoeopathy [*British*] ... FF Hom
Fellow of the Faculty of Insurance [*French Forces of the Interior*] (DAS) ... FFI
Fellow of the Faculty of Occupational Medicine (DAVI) ... FFOM
Fellow of the Faculty of Physicians and Surgeons [*British*] ... FFPS
Fellow of the Faculty of Physiotherapists ... FFPh
Fellow of the Faculty of Radiologists [*British*] ... FFR
Fellow of the Faculty of Radiologists, Royal College of Surgeons of Ireland [*British*] (DBQ) ... FFRRCSIrel
Fellow of the Faculty of Secretaries [*British*] (DBQ) ... FFCS
Fellow of the Faculty of Teachers in Commerce [*British*] (DBQ) ... FFTCom
Fellow of the Franklin Society [*British*] ... FFS
Fellow of the Gemmological Association [*British*] ... FGA
Fellow of the Geographical Society ... FGS
Fellow of the Geographical Society of America ... FGSA
Fellow of the Geological Society [*British*] ... FGS
Fellow of the Geological Society of America ... FGSA
Fellow of the Greek Institute [*British*] (DI) ... FGI
Fellow of the Guild of Agricultural Journalists [*British*] (DGA) ... FGAJ
Fellow of the Guild of Cleaners and Launderers [*British*] (DBQ) ... FGCL
Fellow of the Guild of Industrial, Commercial, & Institutional Accounts (DD) ... FICIA
Fellow of the Guild of Organists [*British*] ... FGO
Fellow of the Guild of Professional Toastmasters [*British*] (DI) ... FGPT
Fellow of the Heraldry Society of Canada ... FHSC
Fellow of the Highland and Agricultural Society of Scotland ... FHAS
Fellow of the Highway and Traffic Technicians Association [*British*] (DBQ) ... FHTTA
Fellow of the Horological Guild of Australia ... FHGA
Fellow of the Horticultural Society [*British*] ... FHS
Fellow of the Hotel and Catering International Management Association (DD) ... FHIMA
Fellow of the Hotel, Catering, and Institutional Management Association [*British*] (DBQ) ... FHCIMA
Fellow of the Illuminating Engineering Society [*Later, FIllumES*] [*British*] ... FIES
Fellow of the Illuminating Engineering Society [*Formerly, FIES*] [*British*] ... FIllumES
Fellow of the Imperial Institute [*British*] (DAS) ... FII
Fellow of the Imperial Institute [*British*] ... FIInst
Fellow of the Imperial Society of Teachers of Dancing [*British*] (DBQ) ... FISTD
Fellow of the Incorporated Advertising Managers Association [*British*] (DAS) ... FIAMA
Fellow of the Incorporated Association of Architects and Surveyors [*British*] (DBQ) ... FIAA
Fellow of the Incorporated Association of Architects and Surveyors [*British*] ... FIAA & S
Fellow of the Incorporated Association of Architects and Surveyors [*British*] (DBQ) ... FIAS
Fellow of the Incorporated Guild of Church Musicians [*British*] ... FIGCM
Fellow of the Incorporated Phonographic Society [*British*] (ROG) ... FIPS
Fellow of the Incorporated Sales Managers' Association [*Later, F Inst MSM*] [*British*] ... FSMA
Fellow of the Incorporated Secretaries' Association [*British*] ... FISA
Fellow of the Incorporated Shorthand Teachers [*British*] (ROG) ... F INC ST
Fellow of the Incorporated Society of Accountants and Auditors [*British*] (DAS) ... FISAA
Fellow of the Incorporated Society of Advertisement Consultants [*British*] (DAS) ... FISAC
Fellow of the Incorporated Society of Auctioneers and Landed Property Agents [*British*] ... FALPA
Fellow of the Incorporated Society of Organ Builders [*British*] (DI) ... FISOB
Fellow of the Incorporated Society of Valuers and Auctioneers [*British*] (DBQ) ... FSVA
Fellow of the Indian Academy of Medical Sciences ... FIAMS
Fellow of the Indian College of Dentists ... FICD
Fellow of the Indian National Science Academy [*Formerly, FNI*] ... FNA
Fellow of the Institute of Actuaries [*British*] ... FIA
Fellow of the Institute of Actuaries of Australia (ODBW) ... FIAA
Fellow of the Institute of Actuaries of New Zealand ... FIANZ
Fellow of the Institute of Administrative Accounting and Data Processing [*British*] (DCTA) ... FAAI
Fellow of the Institute of Administrative Management [*British*] (ODBW) ... F Inst AM
Fellow of the Institute of Administrative Management [*British*] (ODBW) ... FIAM
Fellow of the Institute of Administrative Management [*British*] (DBQ) ... FInstAM
Fellow of the Institute of Aeronautical Sciences [*Later, FAIAA*] [*British*] (EY) ... FIAeS
Fellow of the Institute of Aeronautical Sciences [*Later, FAIAA*] [*British*] ... FIAS
Fellow of the Institute of Animal Technicians [*British*] (DBQ) ... FIAT
Fellow of the Institute of Arbitrators ... FIArb
Fellow of the Institute of Asphalt Technology [*British*] (DBQ) ... FIAT
Fellow of the Institute of Auctioneers [*British*] ... FIA
Fellow of the Institute of Automotive Engineer Assessors [*British*] (DBQ) ... FIAEA
Fellow of the Institute of Automotive Engineer Assessors [*British*] (DBQ) ... FInstAEA
Fellow of the Institute of Bankers [*British*] (EY) ... FIB
Fellow of the Institute of Bankers in Scotland [*British*] (DBQ) ... FIB(Scot)
Fellow of the Institute of Banking Associations ... FIBA
Fellow of the Institute of Baths and Recreation Management [*British*] (DBQ) ... FInstBRM
Fellow of the Institute of Biology [*Formerly, FInstBiol*] [*British*] ... FI Biol
Fellow of the Institute of Biology (DAVI) ... FIB
Fellow of the Institute of Biology [*Later, FI Biol*] [*British*] ... FInstBiol
Fellow of the Institute of British Bakers (DBQ) ... FInstBB
Fellow of the Institute of British Decorators ... FIBD
Fellow of the Institute of British Foundrymen (DBQ) ... FIBF
Fellow of the Institute of British Photographers ... FIBP
Fellow of the Institute of Builders [*British*] ... FIB
Fellow of the Institute of Builders [*British*] ... FIOB
Fellow of the Institute of Burial and Cremation Administration [*British*] (DBQ) ... FInstBCA
Fellow of the Institute of Business Administration [*British*] ... FIBA
Fellow of the Institute of Business and Technical Management [*British*] (DBQ) ... FInstBTM
Fellow of the Institute of Canadian Bankers (DD) ... FICB
Fellow of the Institute of Canadian Dentists ... FICD
Fellow of the Institute of Careers Officers [*British*] (DBQ) ... FICO
Fellow of the Institute of Carpenters [*British*] (DBQ) ... FIOC
Fellow of the Institute of Ceramics [*British*] ... FICeram
Fellow of the Institute of Certificated Grocers [*British*] ... FGI
Fellow of the Institute of Certified Administrative Managers (DD) ... FCAM
Fellow of the Institute of Certified Management Consultants (DD) ... FCMC
Fellow of the Institute of Certified Public Accountants [*British*] (DAS) ... FCPA
Fellow of the Institute of Chartered Accountants [*British*] (ROG) ... FCA
Fellow of the Institute of Chartered Accountants in Canada ... FCA(Can)
Fellow of the Institute of Chartered Accountants in Ireland (ODBW) ... FICAI
Fellow of the Institute of Chartered Architects [*British*] ... FCA
Fellow of the Institute of Chartered Secretaries and Administrators (DD) ... FCIS
Fellow of the Institute of Chartered Shipbrokers [*British*] ... FICS
Fellow of the Institute of Chemistry [*Later, FRIC*] [*British*] ... FIC
Fellow of the Institute of Chemistry of Ireland ... FICI
Fellow of the Institute of Chiropodists [*British*] ... FInstCh
Fellow of the Institute of Civil Defence [*British*] ... FICD
Fellow of the Institute of Clerks of Works of Great Britain, Inc. (DBQ) ... FICW
Fellow of the Institute of Commerce [*British*] ... FCI
Fellow of the Institute of Commerce ... FIC
Fellow of the Institute of Commerce [*British*] ... FInstC
Fellow of the Institute of Commercial Management [*British*] (DCTA) ... F Inst CM
Fellow of the Institute of Company Accountants [*British*] (DAS) ... FIAC
Fellow of the Institute of Cost and Management Accountants [*British*] ... FCMA
Fellow of the Institute of Cost and Management Accountants [*British*] (ODBW) ... FICMA
Fellow of the Institute of Credit Management [*British*] (DCTA) ... FICM
Fellow of the Institute of Data Processing (WDAA) ... FIDP
Fellow of the Institute of Directors [*British*] (ODBW) ... F Inst D
Fellow of the Institute of Directors [*British*] ... F Inst Dir
Fellow of the Institute of Directors [*British*] ... FID
Fellow of the Institute of Directors [*British*] ... FInstD
Fellow of the Institute of Directors, Australia (ODBW) ... FIDA
Fellow of the Institute of Electrical and Electronic Engineers ... FIEEE
Fellow of the Institute of Electrical Engineers [*British*] ... FIEE
Fellow of the Institute of Employment Consultants [*British*] (DBQ) ... FECI
Fellow of the Institute of Energy [*British*] (DBQ) ... FInstE
Fellow of the Institute of Engineers [*British*] ... FIE

Fellow of the Institute of Executive Engineers and Officers [*British*] (DBQ) ... FIExE
Fellow of the Institute of Executives and Managers [*British*] (DBQ) ... FIEM
Fellow of the Institute of Explosives Engineers [*British*] (DBQ) ... FIXExpE
Fellow of the Institute of Export [*British*] (DCTA) ... FIEx
Fellow of the Institute of Financial Accountants [*British*] (ODBW) ... FFA
Fellow of the Institute of Food Science and Technology [*British*] ... FIFST
Fellow of the Institute of Freight Forwarders [*British*] (ODBW) ... F Inst FF
Fellow of the Institute of Freight Forwarders [*British*] (ODBW) ... FIFF
Fellow of the Institute of Freight Forwarders [*British*] (DBQ) ... FInstFF
Fellow of the Institute of Fuel [*British*] ... F Inst F
Fellow of the Institute of Grocery Distribution [*British*] (DBQ) ... FIGD
Fellow of the Institute of Health Education [*British*] ... FIHE
Fellow of the Institute of Health Service [*formerly, Hospital*] **Administrators** [*British*] ... FHA
Fellow of the Institute of Heraldic and Genealogical Studies [*British*] (DBQ) ... FHG
Fellow of the Institute of Hospital Engineering [*British*] (DI) ... FIHospE
Fellow of the Institute of Hospital Secretaries [*British*] ... FIHS
Fellow of the Institute of Housing [*British*] (DBQ) ... FIH
Fellow of the Institute of Housing [*Later, FIHM*] [*British*] ... FIHsg
Fellow of the Institute of Housing Managers [*Formerly, FIHsg*] [*British*] ... FIHM
Fellow of the Institute of Hygiene [*British*] ... FIH
Fellow of the Institute of Industrial Administration [*Later, FBIM*] [*British*] ... FIIA
Fellow of the Institute of Industrial and Commercial Accountants [*British*] ... FIAI
Fellow of the Institute of Industrial Security [*British*] (DBQ) ... FIISec
Fellow of the Institute of Information Scientists [*British*] ... FIInfSc
Fellow of the Institute of Journalists [*British*] ... FIJ
Fellow of the Institute of Landscape Architects [*British*] ... FILA
Fellow of the Institute of Legal Executives [*British*] (DCTA) ... F Inst L Ex
Fellow of the Institute of Legal Executives [*British*] (DLA) ... FILE
Fellow of the Institute of Leisure and Amenity Management [*British*] (DBQ) ... FILAM
Fellow of the Institute of Linguists [*British*] (EY) ... FIL
Fellow of the Institute of Management (DD) ... FIMgt
Fellow of the Institute of Management Consultants [*British*] ... FIMC
Fellow of the Institute of Management Consultants (DD) ... FMC
Fellow of the Institute of Management Services [*British*] (DBQ) ... FMS
Fellow of the Institute of Management Specialists [*British*] (DBQ) ... FIMS
Fellow of the Institute of Manufacturing [*British*] (DBQ) ... FIManf
Fellow of the Institute of Marine Engineers [*British*] ... FIMarE
Fellow of the Institute of Marine Engineers [*British*] (DCTA) ... FIME
Fellow of the Institute of Marketing [*British*] ... FInstM
Fellow of the Institute of Marketing and Sales Management [*Formerly, FSMA*] [*British*] ... F Inst MSM
Fellow of the Institute of Materials (DD) ... FIM
Fellow of the Institute of Materials Handling [*British*] (DBQ) ... FIMH
Fellow of the Institute of Mathematics and its Application [*British*] ... FIMA
Fellow of the Institute of Measurement and Control [*British*] (DBQ) ... FInstMC
Fellow of the Institute of Meat [*British*] ... FInstM
Fellow of the Institute of Medical and Biological Illustration [*British*] (DBQ) ... FIMBI
Fellow of the Institute of Medical Laboratory Sciences [*British*] (DBQ) ... FIMLS
Fellow of the Institute of Medical Laboratory Technology [*British*] (DI) ... FIMLT
Fellow of the Institute of Metal Finishing [*British*] (DBQ) ... FIMF
Fellow of the Institute of Metallurgists [*British*] (EY) ... FIM
Fellow of the Institute of Metals [*British*] ... FIM
Fellow of the Institute of Metals [*British*] ... FInstMet
Fellow of the Institute of Motor Trade [*Later, FIMI*] [*British*] ... FIMT
Fellow of the Institute of Municipal Building Management [*British*] (DBQ) ... FIMBM
Fellow of the Institute of Municipal Treasurers and Accountants [*British*] ... FIMA
Fellow of the Institute of Municipal Treasurers and Accountants [*British*] ... FIMTA
Fellow of the Institute of Music Instrument Technology [*British*] ... FIMIT
Fellow of the Institute of Navigation [*British*] ... FIN
Fellow of the Institute of Operating Theatre Technicians [*British*] ... FIOT
Fellow of the Institute of Ophthalmic Opticians [*British*] ... FIO
Fellow of the Institute of Packaging [*British*] (DI) ... FInstPkg
Fellow of the Institute of Park and Recreation Administration [*British*] (DI) ... FInstPRA
Fellow of the Institute of Patentees and Inventors [*British*] (EY) ... F Inst PI
Fellow of the Institute of Personnel Management [*Later, CIPM*] [*British*] ... FIPM
Fellow of the Institute of Petroleum [*British*] ... F Inst Pet
Fellow of the Institute of Physics (DD) ... FInstP
Fellow of the Institute of Physics [*British*] ... FIP
Fellow of the Institute of Physics and the Physical Society [*British*] (EY) ... F Inst P
Fellow of the Institute of Plumbing [*British*] (DBQ) ... FIOP
Fellow of the Institute of Population Registration [*British*] (DBQ) ... FIR
Fellow of the Institute of Practitioners in Advertising [*British*] ... FIPA
Fellow of the Institute of Printing [*British*] (DBQ) ... FIOP
Fellow of the Institute of Printing Management [*British*] (DGA) ... FI PTG M
Fellow of the Institute of Production Control [*British*] (DBQ) ... FIPC
Fellow of the Institute of Professional Designers ... FIPD
Fellow of the Institute of Professional Investigators [*British*] (DBQ) ... FIPI
Fellow of the Institute of Public Administration [*British*] ... FIPA
Fellow of the Institute of Public Relations [*British*] ... FIPR
Fellow of the Institute of Purchasing and Supply [*British*] (ODBW) ... F Inst PS
Fellow of the Institute of Purchasing and Supply [*British*] ... FInstPS
Fellow of the Institute of Qualified Private Secretaries [*British*] (DI) ... FIQPS
Fellow of the Institute of Quality Assurance [*British*] (DBQ) ... FIQA
Fellow of the Institute of Quantity Surveyors [*British*] (DI) ... FIQS
Fellow of the Institute of Quarrying [*British*] (DBQ) ... FIQ
Fellow of the Institute of Railway Auditors and Accountants (India) ... FIRA(Ind)
Fellow of the Institute of Railway Signal Engineers [*British*] (DBQ) ... FIRSE
Fellow of the Institute of Recreation Management [*British*] (DI) ... FInstRM
Fellow of the Institute of Refrigeration [*British*] (DBQ) ... FInstR
Fellow of the Institute of Road Transport Engineers [*British*] ... FIRTE
Fellow of the Institute of Sales and Marketing Management [*British*] (ODBW) ... F Inst SMM
Fellow of the Institute of Sales Management [*British*] (DI) ... FInstSM
Fellow of the Institute of Sales Management [*British*] (DBQ) ... FInstSMM
Fellow of the Institute of Sales Technology and Management [*British*] (DBQ) ... FISTM
Fellow of the Institute of Science Technology [*British*] ... FIST
Fellow of the Institute of Scientific and Technical Communicators [*British*] (DBQ) ... FISTC
Fellow of the Institute of Sewage Purification (DAVI) ... FInstSP
Fellow of the Institute of Shipping and Forwarding Agents [*British*] (ODBW) ... FSF
Fellow of the Institute of Shorthand Teachers [*British*] (ROG) ... F INST ST
Fellow of the Institute of Social Welfare [*British*] (DBQ) ... FISW
Fellow of the Institute of Statisticians [*British*] ... FIS
Fellow of the Institute of Supervisory Management [*British*] (DBQ) ... FISM
Fellow of the Institute of Taxation [*British*] (DCTA) ... FTIT
Fellow of the Institute of Technical Journalists [*British*] (DGA) ... FITJ
Fellow of the Institute of the Motor Industry [*Formerly, FIMT*] [*British*] ... FIMI
Fellow of the Institute of Trading Standards Administration [*British*] (DBQ) ... FITSA
Fellow of the Institute of Training and Development [*British*] (DBQ) ... FITD
Fellow of the Institute of Transport Administration [*British*] (DCTA) ... F Inst TA
Fellow of the Institute of Valuers [*British*] ... FIV
Fellow of the Institute of Wastes Management [*British*] (DBQ) ... FInstWM
Fellow of the Institute of Water Engineers [*British*] ... FIWE
Fellow of the Institute of Welding [*British*] ... FInstW
Fellow of the Institute of Welfare Officers [*British*] ... FWI
Fellow of the Institute of Wireless Technology [*British*] (DAS) ... FIWT
Fellow of the Institute of Wood Science [*British*] ... FIWSc
Fellow of the Institution of Agricultural Engineers [*British*] ... FIAgrE
Fellow of the Institution of Analysts and Programmers [*British*] (DBQ) ... FIAP
Fellow of the Institution of Body Engineers [*British*] (DBQ) ... FBEI
Fellow of the Institution of Building Control Officers (DBQ) ... FIBCO
Fellow of the Institution of Chemical Engineers [*British*] ... FIChemE
Fellow of the Institution of Civil Engineers [*British*] ... FICE
Fellow of the Institution of Corrosion Science and Technology [*British*] (DBQ) ... FICorrST
Fellow of the Institution of Electrical and Electronics Incorporated Engineers [*British*] (DBQ) ... FIELecIE
Fellow of the Institution of Electrical Engineers (DD) ... FIEE
Fellow of the Institution of Electronic and Radio Engineers [*British*] ... FIERE
Fellow of the Institution of Engineering Designers [*British*] (DBQ) ... FIED
Fellow of the Institution of Engineering Inspection [*British*] ... FIEI
Fellow of the Institution of Engineers, India ... FIE(India)
Fellow of the Institution of Fire Engineers [*British*] (DCTA) ... FIFirE
Fellow of the Institution of Gas Engineers [*British*] ... FIGasE
Fellow of the Institution of Geologists [*British*] (DBQ) ... FIGeol
Fellow of the Institution of Heating and Ventilating Engineers [*British*] ... FIHVE
Fellow of the Institution of Highway Engineers [*British*] (DBQ) ... FIHT
Fellow of the Institution of Industrial Managers [*British*] (DCTA) ... FIIM
Fellow of the Institution of Mechanical and General Technician Engineers [*British*] (DBQ) ... FIMGTechE
Fellow of the Institution of Mechanical Engineers [*British*] ... FI Mech E
Fellow of the Institution of Mining and Metallurgy [*British*] (DBQ) ... FIMM
Fellow of the Institution of Mining Engineers [*British*] ... FIMinE
Fellow of the Institution of Municipal Engineers [*British*] ... FIMunE
Fellow of the Institution of Nuclear Engineers [*British*] ... FI Nucl E
Fellow of the Institution of Occupational Safety and Health [*British*] (DCTA) ... FIOSH
Fellow of the Institution of Plant Engineers [*British*] (DBQ) ... FIPlantE
Fellow of the Institution of Production Engineers [*British*] ... FIProdE
Fellow of the Institution of Public Health Engineers [*British*] ... FIPHE
Fellow of the Institution of Radio Engineers [*British*] ... FIRE
Fellow of the Institution of Sanitary Engineers [*British*] ... FISE
Fellow of the Institution of Structural Engineers [*British*] ... FIStructE
Fellow of the Institution of Surveyors [*British*] ... FIS
Fellow of the Institution of the Rubber Industry [*British*] ... FIRI
Fellow of the Institution of Water Engineers and Scientists [*British*] (DI) ... FIWES
Fellow of the Institution of Works and Highways Technician Engineers [*British*] (DBQ) ... FIWHTE
Fellow of the Institution of Works Managers [*British*] ... FIWM
Fellow of the Insurance Institute of Canada ... FIIC
Fellow of the International Academy of Management ... FIAM
Fellow of the International Academy of Wood Sciences ... FIAWS
Fellow of the International Association of Bookkeepers [*British*] (DCTA) ... FIAB
Fellow of the International College of Dentists ... FICD
Fellow of the International College of Surgeons ... FICS
Fellow of the International Colonial Institute [*British*] ... FICI
Fellow of the International Criminal Justice Association ... FICJA
Fellow of the International Dance Teachers' Association [*British*] (DBQ) ... FIDTA
Fellow of the International Institute of Arts and Letters ... FIAL
Fellow of the International Institute of Arts and Letters, Zurich [*1931*] (NGC) ... FIAL
Fellow of the International Institute of Social Economics [*British*] (DBQ) ... FIISE
Fellow of the International Institute of Sports Therapy [*British*] (DBQ) ... FISTC
Fellow of the Journalists' Institute [*British*] (ROG) ... FJI
Fellow of the King's and Queen's College of Physicians, Ireland ... FKQCP

Fellow of the King's and Queen's College of Physicians, Ireland [*Later,* FRCPI] (ROG) .... FKQCPI
Fellow of the Landscape Institute [*British*] (DBQ) .... FLI
Fellow of the Library Association [*British*] .... FLA
Fellow of the Life Insurance Association [*British*] (ODBW) .... FLIA
Fellow of the Life Management Institute (DD) .... FLMI
Fellow of the Linnaean Society [*British*] .... FLS
Fellow of the Local Government Association [*British*] .... FLGA
Fellow of the London and Counties Society of Physiologists [*British*] ...... FLCSP
Fellow of the London Associaton of Certified and Corporate Accountants (DAS) .... FLAA
Fellow of the London College of Music [*British*] .... FLCM
Fellow of the London Historical Society [*British*] .... FLHS
Fellow of the Master Photographers Association [*British*] (DBQ) ...... FMPA
Fellow of the Medical Council [*British*] .... FMC
Fellow of the Medical Society [*British*] .... FMS
Fellow of the Meteorological Society [*British*] .... FMS
Fellow of the Mineralogical Society of America .... FMSA
Fellow of the Museums Association [*British*] (EY) .... FMA
Fellow of the National Association of Estate Agents [*British*] (DBQ) ...... FNAEA
Fellow of the National Association of Opticians [*British*] (DAS) ...... FNAO
Fellow of the National College of Rubber Technology [*British*] ...... FNCRT
Fellow of the National Federation of Accountants [*British*] (DAS) ...... FNFA
Fellow of the National Institute of Arts and Letters [*British*] ...... FNIAL
Fellow of the National Institute of Hardware [*British*] (DBQ) ...... FNIH
Fellow of the National Institute of Medical Herbalists [*British*] ...... FNIMH
Fellow of the National Institute of Sciences in India [*Later, FNA*] ...... FNI
Fellow of the National Society of Art Education [*British*] ...... FSAE
Fellow of the National Society of Interior Designers .... FNSID
Fellow of the National University of Ireland (DI) .... FNUI
Fellow of the Nautical Institute [*British*] .... FNI
Fellow of the New Zealand Institute of Agricultural Science ...... FNZIAS
Fellow of the New Zealand Institute of Architects .... FNZIA
Fellow of the New Zealand Institute of Chemistry .... FNZIC
Fellow of the New Zealand Institution of Engineers .... FNZIE
Fellow of the New Zealand Library Association .... FNZLA
Fellow of the Non-Destructive Testing Society of Great Britain ...... FNDTS
Fellow of the North British Academy (DAS) .... FNBA
Fellow of the North East Coast Institution of Engineers and Shipbuilders [*British*] .... FNECInst
Fellow of the Ontario Hostelry Institute [*Canada*] (DD) ...... FHI
Fellow of the Ontario Teachers' Federation [*Canada*] (DD) ...... FOTF
Fellow of the Pakistan Academy of Sciences .... FPAS
Fellow of the Pathological Society of Great Britain .... FPS
Fellow of the Pensions Management Institute [*British*] (DBQ) ...... FPMI
Fellow of the Pharmaceutical Society [*British*] .... FPharmS
Fellow of the Pharmaceutical Society [*British*] .... FPS
Fellow of the Philological Society [*British*] .... FPS
Fellow of the Philosophical Society [*British*] .... F Ph S
Fellow of the Philosophical Society [*British*] .... FPS
Fellow of the Physical Society [*British*] .... F Phys S
Fellow of the Physical Society [*British*] .... FPS
Fellow of the Plastics and Rubber Institute [*British*] (DBQ) ...... FPRI
Fellow of the Plastics Institute [*British*] .... FPI
Fellow of the Rating and Valuation Association [*British*] (DBQ) ...... FRVA
Fellow of the Real Estate Institute (DD) .... FRI
Fellow of the Royal Academy of Dancing [*British*] .... FRAD
Fellow of the Royal Academy of Music [*British*] .... FRAM
Fellow of the Royal Academy of Physicians [*British*] .... FRAP
Fellow of the Royal Aeronautical Society [*British*] (EY) ...... FRAeS
Fellow of the Royal Agricultural Societies [*British*] .... FRAgSs
Fellow of the Royal Agricultural Society of England .... FRASE
Fellow of the Royal and Antiquarian Societies [*British*] ...... FR and ASS
Fellow of the Royal Anthropological Institute [*British*] ...... FRAI
Fellow of the Royal Architectural Institute of Canada .... FRAIC
Fellow of the Royal Asiatic Society [*British*] .... FRAS
Fellow of the Royal Asiatic Society of Bengal .... FRASB
Fellow of the Royal Astronomical Society [*British*] .... FRAS
Fellow of the Royal Australasian College of General Practitioners [*Medicine*] (DMAA) .... FRACGP
Fellow of the Royal Australasian College of Ophthalmologists [*Medicine*] (DMAA) .... FRACO
Fellow of the Royal Australasian College of Physicians ...... FRACP
Fellow of the Royal Australasian College of Radiologists .... FRACR
Fellow of the Royal Australasian College of Surgeons .... FRACS
Fellow of the Royal Australian and New Zealand College of Psychiatrists [*Medicine*] (DMAA) .... FRANZCP
Fellow of the Royal Botanic Society [*British*] .... FRBS
Fellow of the Royal Canadian Geographical Society (DD) ...... FRCGS
Fellow of the Royal College of Advanced Technology, Salford [*British*] .... FRCATS
Fellow of the Royal College of Art [*British*] .... FRCA
Fellow of the Royal College of Dentists [*British*] .... FRCD
Fellow of the Royal College of Dentists (Canada) .... FRCD(C)
Fellow of the Royal College of General Practitioners [*British*] ...... FRCGP
Fellow of the Royal College of Medicine [*Canada*] (DD) ...... FRCM
Fellow of the Royal College of Music [*British*] .... FRCM
Fellow of the Royal College of Obstetricians and Gynaecologists [*British*] .... FRCOG
Fellow of the Royal College of Organists [*British*] .... FRCO
Fellow of the Royal College of Organists (Choir-Training Diploma) [*British*] .... FRCO(CHM)
Fellow of the Royal College of Pathologists [*British*] ...... FRC Path
Fellow of the Royal College of Physicians [*British*] .... FRCP

Fellow of the Royal College of Physicians and Surgeons of Glasgow .... FRCPGlas
Fellow of the Royal College of Physicians and Surgeons of Glasgow [*British*] (BABM) .... FRCS(Glasg)
Fellow of the Royal College of Physicians and Surgeons of Glasgow qua Surgeon (DAVI) .... FRCS(Glasg)
Fellow of the Royal College of Physicians (Canada) .... FRCP(C)
Fellow of the Royal College of Physicians, Ireland (ROG) ...... FRCPI
Fellow of the Royal College of Physicians of Canada (DD) ...... FRCPC
Fellow of the Royal College of Physicians of Canada .... FRCPCan
Fellow of the Royal College of Physicians of Edinburgh ...... FRCP Edin
Fellow of the Royal College of Physicians of Edinburgh ...... FRCPE
Fellow of the Royal College of Physicians of Edinburgh ...... FRCPEd
Fellow of the Royal College of Physicians of Ireland .... FRCP Irel
Fellow of the Royal College of Physicians of London [*British*] ...... FRCP Lond
Fellow of the Royal College of Preceptors [*British*] .... FRCP
Fellow of the Royal College of Psychiatrists [*British*] ...... FRC Psych
Fellow of the Royal College of Radiologists [*British*] ...... FRCR
Fellow of the Royal College of Surgeons [*British*] .... FRCS
Fellow of the Royal College of Surgeons (Canada) .... FRCS(C)
Fellow of the Royal College of Surgeons in Ireland .... FRCS Irel
Fellow of the Royal College of Surgeons in Ireland .... FRCSI
Fellow of the Royal College of Surgeons of Canada (DD) ...... FRCSC
Fellow of the Royal College of Surgeons of Canada .... FRCSCan
Fellow of the Royal College of Surgeons of Edinburgh .... FRCS Ed
Fellow of the Royal College of Surgeons of Edinburgh .... FRCS Edin
Fellow of the Royal College of Surgeons of Edinburgh .... FRCSE
Fellow of the Royal College of Surgeons of Edinburgh, Specialising in Cardiothoracic Surgery [*British*] (DBQ) ...... FRCSEd(C/Th)
Fellow of the Royal College of Surgeons of Edinburgh, Specialising in Orthopaedic Surgery [*British*] (DBQ) ...... FRCSEd(Orth)
Fellow of the Royal College of Surgeons of Edinburgh, Specialising in Surgical Neurology [*British*] (DBQ) ...... FRCSEd(SN)
Fellow of the Royal College of Surgeons of England .... FRCS Eng
Fellow of the Royal College of Surgeons of Glasgow .... FRCSGlas
Fellow of the Royal College of Surgeons of London .... FRCSL
Fellow of the Royal College of University Surgeons [*Denmark*] ...... FRCUS
Fellow of the Royal College of Veterinary Surgeons [*British*] ...... FRCVS
Fellow of the Royal Colonial Institute [*British*] .... FRCI
Fellow of the Royal Commonwealth Society [*British*] .... FRCSoc
Fellow of the Royal Economic Society [*British*] .... FR Ec S
Fellow of the Royal Economic Society [*British*] .... FR Econ S
Fellow of the Royal Economic Society [*British*] (ROG) ...... FR Econ Soc
Fellow of the Royal Economic Society [*British*] .... FRES
Fellow of the Royal Empire Society [*British*] (EY) .... FRES
Fellow of the Royal Entomological Society [*British*] .... FR Ent S
Fellow of the Royal Entomological Society [*British*] (ROG) ...... FRES
Fellow of the Royal Faculty of Physicians and Surgeons [*British*] ...... FRFPS
Fellow of the Royal Faculty of Physicians and Surgeons of Glasgow .... FRFPS(G)
Fellow of the Royal Faculty of Physicians and Surgeons of Glasgow .... FRFPSGlas
Fellow of the Royal Geographical Society [*British*] (ROG) ...... FRGS
Fellow of the Royal Geographical Society (Canada) .... FRGS(C)
Fellow of the Royal Geographical Society, Scotland (ROG) ...... FRGSS
Fellow of the Royal Historical Society [*British*] (ROG) ...... FRHistS
Fellow of the Royal Historical Society [*British*] .... FRHistSoc
Fellow of the Royal Historical Society [*British*] (ROG) ...... FRHS
Fellow of the Royal Horticultural Society [*British*] .... FRHortS
Fellow of the Royal Horticultural Society [*British*] (ROG) ...... FRHS
Fellow of the Royal Incorporation of Architects of Scotland (DI) ...... FRIAS
Fellow of the Royal Institute of Architects of Ireland ...... FRIAI
Fellow of the Royal Institute of Architects of Scotland ..... FRIAS
Fellow of the Royal Institute of British Architects (ROG) ...... FRIBA
Fellow of the Royal Institute of Chartered Surveyors [*Canada*] (DD) ...... FRICS
Fellow of the Royal Institute of Chemistry [*Formerly, FIC*] [*British*] ...... FRIC
Fellow of the Royal Institute of Horticulture [*New Zealand*] ...... FRIH
Fellow of the Royal Institute of International Affairs [*British*] (DI) ...... FRIIA
Fellow of the Royal Institute of Naval Architects [*British*] ...... FRINA
Fellow of the Royal Institute of Public Administration [*British*] (ADA) ...... FRIPA
Fellow of the Royal Institute of Public Health [*British*] (ADA) ...... FRIPH
Fellow of the Royal Institute of Public Health and Hygiene [*British*] ...... FRIPHH
Fellow of the Royal Institution [*British*] .... FRI
Fellow of the Royal Institution of Chartered Surveyors [*Formerly, FSI*] [*British*] .... FRICS
Fellow of the Royal Institution of Navigation [*British*] (DBQ) ...... FRIN
Fellow of the Royal Manchester College of Music [*British*] ...... FRMCM
Fellow of the Royal Medical and Chirurgical Society, London (ROG) ...... FRMCSL
Fellow of the Royal Medical Society [*British*] .... FRMedSoc
Fellow of the Royal Meteorological Society [*British*] .... FR Met S
Fellow of the Royal Meteorological Society [*British*] (ROG) ...... FR Met Soc
Fellow of the Royal Meteorological Society [*British*] .... FRMS
Fellow of the Royal Microscopical Society [*British*] (ROG) ...... FRMS
Fellow of the Royal Northern College of Music [*British*] (DBQ) ...... FRNCM
Fellow of the Royal Numismatic Society [*British*] (EY) ...... FRNS
Fellow of the Royal Philatelic Society, London .... FRPSL
Fellow of the Royal Photographic Society [*British*] (ROG) ...... FRPS
Fellow of the Royal Sanitary Institute [*Later, FRSH*] [*British*] ...... FRSanI
Fellow of the Royal Sanitary Institute [*British*] (ROG) ...... FRSI
Fellow of the Royal School of Church Music [*British*] .... FRSCM
Fellow of the Royal School of Naval Architects [*British*] (ROG) ...... FRSNA
Fellow of the Royal Scottish Academy of Music and Drama [*British*] (DI) ...... FRSAMD
Fellow of the Royal Scottish Geographical Society (ROG) ...... FRSGS
Fellow of the Royal Scottish Society of Arts (ROG) .... FRSSA

Fellow of the Royal Society [British] (ROG) ... FRS
Fellow of the Royal Society, Canada (ROG) ... FRSC
Fellow of the Royal Society, Edinburgh (ROG) ... FRSE
Fellow of the Royal Society, London [British] ... FRSL
Fellow of the Royal Society of Antiquaries, Ireland (ROG) ... FRSAIrel
Fellow of the Royal Society of Antiquaries of Ireland ... FRSAI
Fellow of the Royal Society of Arts [British] (EY) ... FRSA
Fellow of the Royal Society of Arts, London [1909, founded 1754 as Society of Arts] (NGC) ... FRSA
Fellow of the Royal Society of British Sculptors ... FRBS
Fellow of the Royal Society of Canada ... FRSCan
Fellow of the Royal Society of Chemistry [British] (DBQ) ... FRSC
Fellow of the Royal Society of Edinburgh ... FRS Edin
Fellow of the Royal Society of Health [Formerly, FRSanI] [British] ... FRSH
Fellow of the Royal Society of Literature [British] (ROG) ... FRSL
Fellow of the Royal Society of London [1660] (NGC) ... FRS
Fellow of the Royal Society of Medicine [British] ... FRSM
Fellow of the Royal Society of Medicine [British] ... FRSocMed
Fellow of the Royal Society of New Zealand ... FRSNZ
Fellow of the Royal Society of Painter-Etchers and Engravers [British] (ROG) ... FRPE
Fellow of the Royal Society of Painter-Etchers and Engravers [British] ... RE
Fellow of the Royal Society of Radiographers ... FSR
Fellow of the Royal Society of South Africa ... FRSSAf
Fellow of the Royal Society of Teachers [British] ... FRST
Fellow of the Royal Society of Tropical Medicine and Hygiene [British] ... FRSTM & H
Fellow of the Royal Statistical Society [British] (ROG) ... FRSS
Fellow of the Royal Statistical Society [British] ... FSS
Fellow of the Royal Statistical Society [British] ... FSSR
Fellow of the Royal Statistical Society of Scotland (ROG) ... FRSSS
Fellow of the Royal Town Planning Institute [British] ... FRTPI
Fellow of the Royal University of Ireland (ROG) ... FRUI
Fellow of the Royal Veterinary College [British] (DI) ... FRVC
Fellow of the Royal Victorian Institute of Architects [British] (ROG) ... FRVIA
Fellow of the Royal Zoological Society [British] (DI) ... FRZS
Fellow of the Royal Zoological Society of Scotland ... FRZSScot
Fellow of the Sanitary Institute [British] (ROG) ... FSI
Fellow of the Savings Bank Institute [British] (ODBW) ... FSBI
Fellow of the Scottish Association of Opticians (DAS) ... FSAO
Fellow of the Society of Accountants and Auditors (DD) ... FSAA
Fellow of the Society of Actuaries [Society of Actuaries] [Designation awarded by] ... FSA
Fellow of the Society of Antiquaries [British] ... FSA
Fellow of the Society of Antiquaries, Edinburgh ... FSAE
Fellow of the Society of Antiquaries, Ireland (ROG) ... FSAI
Fellow of the Society of Antiquaries, London (ROG) ... FSAL
Fellow of the Society of Antiquaries of Scotland ... FSA Scot
Fellow of the Society of Antiquaries of Scotland ... FSAS
Fellow of the Society of Architects [British] ... FSArc
Fellow of the Society of Architects [British] ... FSArch
Fellow of the Society of Art Masters [British] ... FSAM
Fellow of the Society of Arts [British] (DAS) ... FAS
Fellow of the Society of Arts [British] ... FSA
Fellow of the Society of Cardiological Technicians [British] (DBQ) ... FSCT
Fellow of the Society of Certified Professionals [British] (DBQ) ... FSCP
Fellow of the Society of Chiropodists [British] ... FChS
Fellow of the Society of Commercial Teachers [British] (DBQ) ... FSCT
Fellow of the Society of Company and Commercial Accountants [British] (DCTA) ... FSCA
Fellow of the Society of Dyers and Colourists [British] ... FSDC
Fellow of the Society of Electronic and Radio Technicians [British] (DBQ) ... FSERT
Fellow of the Society of Engineers [British] ... FSE
Fellow of the Society of Genealogists [British] ... FSG
Fellow of the Society of Glass Technology [British] ... FSGT
Fellow of the Society of Health and Beauty Therapists [British] (DBQ) ... FSBTh
Fellow of the Society of Hearing Aid Audiologists [British] (DBQ) ... FSHAA
Fellow of the Society of Incorporated Accountants and Auditors [British] (EY) ... FSAA
Fellow of the Society of Industrial Artists [British] (EY) ... FSIA
Fellow of the Society of Industrial Artists and Designers [British] ... FSIAD
Fellow of the Society of Interior Designers ... FASID
Fellow of the Society of Investment Analysts [British] (DBQ) ... FSIA
Fellow of the Society of Licensed Aircraft Engineers and Technologists [British] ... FSLAET
Fellow of the Society of Management Accountants of Canada (DD) ... FCMA
Fellow of the Society of Management Accountants of Canada (DD) ... FSMAC
Fellow of the Society of Metaphysicians [British] ... FSM
Fellow of the Society of Remedial Gymnasts [British] ... FSRG
Fellow of the Society of Science and Art [British] ... FSSA
Fellow of the Society of Science and Arts, London [British] (ROG) ... FSSCA
Fellow of the Society of Typographic Designers [British] (DI) ... FSTD
Fellow of the Society of Typographic Designers of Canada (DGA) ... FTDC
Fellow of the South African Institute of Electrical Engineers ... F(SA)IEE
Fellow of the South African Institution of Civil Engineers ... F(SA)ICE
Fellow of the South African Institution of Mechanical Engineers ... F(SA)IME
Fellow of the South African Library Association ... FSALA
Fellow of the Spectacle Makers Co. ... FSMC
Fellow of the Statistical Society of Ireland (ROG) ... FSSI
Fellow of the Surveyors' Institute [Later, FRICS] [British] ... FSI
Fellow of the Surveyors' Institution (DD) ... FSI
Fellow of the Swimming Teachers' Association [British] (DBQ) ... FSTA
Fellow of the Taxation Institute, Inc. [British] (DBQ) ... FTII
Fellow of the Technical Publishing Society ... FTPS
Fellow of the Textile Institute [British] ... FTI
Fellow of the Theatrical Designers and Craftsmen's Association [British] ... FTDA
Fellow of the Toastmasters for Royal Occasions [British] (DI) ... FTRO
Fellow of the Town Planning Association [British] ... FTPA
Fellow of the University of Dublin (ROG) ... FUD
Fellow of the University of Manchester Institute of Science and Technology [British] ... FUMIST
Fellow of the Valuers' Association [British] (DAS) ... FVA
Fellow of the Victoria College of Music [London] [British] (ROG) ... FVCM
Fellow of the Welding Institute [British] ... FIW
Fellow of the Welding Institute [British] (DBQ) ... FWeldI
Fellow of the World Academy of Arts and Sciences ... FWA
Fellow of the Worshipful Company of Farriers [British] (DI) ... FWCF
Fellow of the Zoological Academy ... FZA
Fellow of the Zoological Society [British] ... FZS
Fellow of the Zoological Society, London [British] (ROG) ... FZSL
Fellow of Trinity College, Cambridge [British] (ROG) ... FTCC
Fellow of Trinity College, Dublin ... FTCD
Fellow of Trinity College of Music, London (EY) ... FTCL
Fellow of Trust Institute (DD) ... FTI
Fellow of University College, London [British] (ROG) ... FUCL
Fellow of University College, Oxford [British] (ROG) ... FUCO
Fellow, Physical Society [British] (ROG) ... F PHYS SOC
Fellow, Public Accountant, New Zealand ... FPANZ
Fellow, Registered Accountant, New Zealand ... FRANZ
Fellow, Royal College of Pathologists, Australasia ... FRCPA
Fellow, Society of Pension Actuaries [American Society of Pension Actuaries] [Designation awarded by] ... FSPA
Fellowes Athenaeum, Boston, MA [Library symbol Library of Congress] (LCLS) ... MBFA
Fellows, CA [Location identifier FAA] (FAAL) ... FLW
Fellows, CA [TACAN station] (NASA) ... FLW
Fellows in American Studies ... FAS
Fellows of the American Bar Foundation (EA) ... FABF
Fellowship ... FLLWSHP
Fellowship ... FSHIP
Fellowship Depressives Anonymous [British] (DBA) ... FDA
Fellowship Diploma of Architecture ... FDA
[The] Fellowship for Freedom in Medicine [British] ... FFM
Fellowship for Intentional Community (EA) ... FIC
Fellowship for Racial and Economic Equality [Later, Southeast Institute] (EA) ... FREE
Fellowship for Spiritual Understanding (EA) ... FSU
Fellowship in Israel for Arab-Jewish Youth (EA) ... FIAJY
Fellowship in Prayer (EA) ... FIP
Fellowship in Prayer [An association] (EA) ... FP
Fellowship of American Baptist Musicians (EA) ... FABM
Fellowship of Artists for Cultural Evangelism (EA) ... FACE
Fellowship of Associates of Medical Evangelism (EA) ... FAME
Fellowship of British Christian Esperantists ... FBCE
Fellowship of Catholic Scholars (EA) ... FCS
Fellowship of Christian Airline Personnel (EA) ... FCAP
Fellowship of Christian Athletes (EA) ... FCA
Fellowship of Christian Firefighters, International (EA) ... FCF
Fellowship of Christian Magicians (EA) ... FCM
Fellowship of Christian Motorcyclists [Welwyn Garden City, England] (EAIO) ... FCM
Fellowship of Christian Musicians (EA) ... FCM
Fellowship of Christian Peace Officers (EA) ... FCPO
Fellowship of Christian Racers [Defunct] (EA) ... FCR
Fellowship of Christians in the Arts, Media, and Entertainment (EA) ... FCAME
Fellowship of Companies for Christ [Later, FCCI] (EA) ... FCC
Fellowship of Companies for Christ International (EA) ... FCCI
Fellowship of Concerned Churchmen (EA) ... FCC
Fellowship of Conservative Southern Baptists (EA) ... FCSB
Fellowship of Engineering [British] (DBA) ... FoEng
Fellowship of Fire Chaplains (EA) ... FFC
Fellowship of First Fleeters ... FFF
Fellowship of Independent Evangelical Churches ... FIEC
Fellowship of Independent Missions (EA) ... FIM
Fellowship of Independent Schools [British] ... FIS
Fellowship of Interdenominational Missionary Societies ... FIMS
Fellowship of Makers and Researchers of Historical Instruments [Formerly, Fellowship of Makers and Restorers of Historical Instruments] (EA) ... FoMRHI
Fellowship of Missions (EA) ... FOM
Fellowship of Reconciliation (EA) ... FOR
Fellowship of Reconciliation Task Force on Latin America and Caribbean (EA) ... FORTFLAC
Fellowship of Reconciliation Task Force on Latin America and Caribbean (EA) ... TFLAC
Fellowship of Religious Humanists (EA) ... FRH
Fellowship of Religious Journalists (EA) ... FORJ
Fellowship of Riders (Motorcyclists) [British] (BI) ... FOR
Fellowship of St. James (EA) ... FSJ
Fellowship of St. Paul (EA) ... FSP
Fellowship of St. Paul (EA) ... FSSP
Fellowship of Southern Churchmen [Later, Committee of Southern Churchmen] (EA) ... FSC
Fellowship of the American Academy of Neurological and Orthopaedic Surgeons (EA) ... FAANaOS
Fellowship of the Golden Rule (EA) ... FGR
Fellowship of the London School of Polymer Technology [British] (DBQ) ... FLSPT
Fellowship of the Motor Industry [British] (BI) ... FMI

[*The*] **Fellowship of United Methodist Musicians** (EA) ... FUMM
Fellowship of Youth [*British*] (BI) ... FOY
Fellowship of Youth Development [*British*] (DBQ) ... FYD
Fellowship Party [*British*] ... FP
Fellowship Recorded Libraries of Sacred Music [*Record label*] [*Atlanta, GA*] ... FSM
Felmersham [*England*] ... FELM
Felon ... F
Felon (ABBR) ... FLN
Felonious (ABBR) ... FLNUS
Felonious Assault ... FA
Feloniously (ABBR) ... FLNUSY
Feloniousness (ABBR) ... FLNUSNS
Felony [*FBI standardized term*] ... FEL
Felony (ABBR) ... FLNY
Fels Institute of Local and State Governments [*University of Pennsylvania*] ... FILSG
Fels Parent Behavior Rating Scales [*Psychology*] ... FPBRS
Fels Research Institute, Yellow Springs, OH [*Library symbol Library of Congress*] (LCLS) ... OYesF
Felsic Granulite [*Geology*] ... fg
Felsted [*Record label*] [*Great Britain, etc.*] ... Fel
Felt (VRA) ... flt
Felt Manufacturers Council (EA) ... FMC
Felt Reusable Surface Insulation (MCD) ... FRSI
Felt Roofing Contractors' Advisory Board [*British*] (BI) ... FRCAB
Feltman Research and Engineering Laboratory [*Picatinny Arsenal*] [*Army*] ... FREL
Feltman Research Laboratory [*Picatinny Arsenal*] [*Army*] (RDA) ... FRL
Felton, CA [*FM radio station call letters*] ... KHIP
Felucca [*Ship's rigging*] (ROG) ... FEL
FEMA [*Federal Emergency Management Agency*] **National Radio System** (GFGA) ... FNARS
FEMA [*Federal Emergency Management Agency*] **Switched Network** (GFGA) ... FSN
Female ... F
Female (DD) ... f
Female ... FE
Female [*or Feminine*] (KSC) ... FEM
Female Bowhunter Fingers [*International Bowhunting Organization*] [*Class equipment*] ... FBF
Female Business Enterprise (AAGC) ... FBE
Female Chromosome ... X
Female Cigar Makers' Protective Union [*British*] ... FCMPU
Female Domination ... FD
Female Family Household [*Bureau of the Census*] (GFGA) ... FFH
Female Flared ... FFL
Female Genital Mutilation ... FGM
Female Groove ... FG
Female Headed Household ... FHH
Female Health [*AMEX symbol*] (TTSB) ... FHC
Female Health Co. [*Associated Press*] (SAG) ... FemHlth
Female Health Co. [*AMEX symbol*] (SAG) ... FHC
Female Liberal Arts Graduate ... FLAG
Female Penitentiary [*British*] (ROG) ... FP
Female Pipe Thread (MSA) ... FPT
Female Protein [*Biochemistry*] ... FP
Female Seniors [*International Bowhunting Organization*] [*Class Equipment*] ... FSR
Female Servant ... FS
Female Sex Chromosome [*Genetics*] (DAVI) ... X-chrom
Female Sexual Biomass [*Botany*] ... FSB
Female Soldered (MSA) ... FS
Female, Spayed ... FS
Female Treated with DOC [*Deoxycorticosterone*] ... FD
Female Urban Professional [*Lifestyle classification*] ... Fuppy
Female Voice Warning System (MCD) ... FVWS
Female with Eggs [*Pisciculture*] ... FE
Female-Day-Equivalent [*Entomology*] ... FDE
Female-Female Adaptor (MEDA) ... FFA
Females, Density Of [*Ecology*] ... FDEN
Females Opposed to Equality ... FOE
Femarfarmamide [*Biochemistry*] ... FMRF
Feminine ... F
Feminine Chromosome Pair ... XX
Feminine Congregation of the Passion (TOCD) ... CFP
Feminine Deodorant Spray [*Initialism used as brand name*] ... FDS
Feminine Hygiene Spray ... FHS
Femininity Study [*Psychology*] ... FS
Feminist Alliance Against Rape [*Defunct*] (EA) ... FAAR
Feminist Anti-Censorship Task Force ... FACT
Feminist Bureaucrat ... Femocrat
Feminist Business and Professional Network (EA) ... FBPN
Feminist Center for Human Growth and Development (EA) ... FCHGD
Feminist Karate Union (EA) ... FKU
Feminist Library and Resource Centre [*British*] (EAIO) ... FLRC
Feminist News Service ... FNS
Feminist Party of Canada ... FPC
Feminist Press [*An association*] (EA) ... FP
[*The*] **Feminist Press** (EA) ... TFP
Feminist Radio Network [*Defunct*] (EA) ... FRN
Feminist Resources on Energy and Ecology [*Defunct*] (EA) ... FREE
Feminist Teacher Editorial Collective (EA) ... FTEC
Feminist Uniting Women [*Australia*] ... FUN
Feminist Women's Health Center [*Later, FWHC/WCC*] (EA) ... FWHC
Feminist Women's Health Center/Women's Choice Clinic [*Defunct*] (EA) ... FWHC/WCC
Feminist Writers' Guild [*Defunct*] (EA) ... FWG
Feministas en Marcha [*Feminists on the March*] [*Puerto Rico*] (EAIO) ... FEM
Feministas Unidas [*An association*] (EA) ... FU
Feminists Against Benyon [*Pro-abortion group*] [*British*] (DI) ... FAB
Feminists Concerned for Better Feminist Leadership (EA) ... FCBFL
Feminists Fighting Pornography (EA) ... FFP
Feminists for Animal Rights (EA) ... FAR
Feminists for Life of America (EA) ... FFL
Feminists for Life of America [*Later, FFL*] (EA) ... FLA
Feminists on Children's Media [*Defunct*] (EA) ... FOCM
Feminizing Testis Syndrome [*Medicine*] (DMAA) ... FTS
Femmes [*or Feminin*] [*Initial used as title of a publication*] ... F
Femmes Chefs d'Entreprises Mondiales [*World Association of Women Entrepreneurs*] (EAIO) ... FCEM
Femoral [*Anatomy*] ... FEM
Femoral Artery [*Anatomy*] ... FA
Femoral Ash per Centimeter ... FAC
Femoral Blood Flow [*Physiology*] ... FBF
Femoral Blood Pressure [*Medicine*] ... FBP
Femoral Cortical Density ... FCD
Femoral Hypoplasia-Unusual Facies Syndrome [*Medicine*] (DMAA) ... FH-UFS
Femoral Popliteal Bypass [*Medicine*] ... FPB
Femoral Popliteal Vein Bypass [*Medicine*] ... FPVB
Femoral Total Density ... FTD
Femoral Vein [*Anatomy*] ... Fv
Femoral Vein Ligation [*Medicine*] ... FVL
Femoral-Popliteal [*Bypass*] [*Cardiology*] (DAVI) ... fem-pop
Femoral-Popliteal [*Medicine*] (MAE) ... F-P
Femoribus Internis [*To the Inner Part of the Thigh*] [*Pharmacy*] (ROG) ... FEM INTERN
FemRx, Inc. [*Associated Press*] (SAG) ... FemRx
FemRx, Inc. [*NASDAQ symbol*] (SAG) ... FMRX
FemRx Inc. [*NASDAQ symbol*] (TTSB) ... FMRX
Femto [*A prefix meaning divided by 10 to the 15th power*] [*SI symbol*] ... f
Femtoampere (IEEE) ... fA
Femtofarad [*One quadrillionth of a farad*] ... fF
Femtoliter [*One quadrillionth of a liter*] ... fl
Femtometer [*Formerly, Fermi*] (MCD) ... FM
Femtomole (MAE) ... fmol
Femtosecond [*One quadrillionth of a second*] ... FS
Femtosecond [*One quadrillionth of a second*] ... fsec
Femtosecond Field Emission Camera [*Physics*] ... FFEC
Femtosecond Photoelectron Spectroscopy ... FPES
Femtosecond Transition-State Spectroscope ... FTS
Femtosecond Transition-State Spectroscopy ... FTS
Femtovolt (MDG) ... FV
Fen [*Monetary unit*] [*China*] ... F
Fence [*Technical drawings*] ... FN
Fence ... FNC
Fence Against Satellite Threats ... FAST
Fence Disturbance System [*Military*] ... FDS
Fencing (ROG) ... FENC
Fencing Contractors Association [*British*] (DBA) ... FCA
Fenco Consultants Ltd., Toronto, Ontario [*Library symbol National Library of Canada*] (NLC) ... OTFEC
Fender [*s*] [*Freight*] ... FND
Fender [*Automotive engineering*] ... FNDR
Fendi [*Italian couturier*] ... F
Fenelon Falls Public Library, Ontario [*Library symbol National Library of Canada*] (BIB) ... OFFP
Fenestra Vestibuli [*Anatomy*] ... FV
Fenestration (VRA) ... fnstr
Fenestration Oval Window [*Otology*] ... FOW
Feng Yang-Pyongyang [*North Korea*] [*Airport symbol*] (AD) ... FNJ
Feng Yun - 2 [*Chinese geostationary satellite*] (EERA) ... FY-2
Fengshan [*China*] [*ICAO location identifier*] (ICLI) ... RCFZ
Fengtien [*Hoten, Shenyang*] [*Republic of China*] [*Seismograph station code, US Geological Survey*] (SEIS) ... FEN
Fenian Brotherhood [*Irish political movement, c. 1858-1914*] (ROG) ... FB
Fenix Airways [*Latvia*] [*FAA designator*] (FAAC) ... FNX
Fenland [*British ICAO location identifier*] (ICLI) ... EGCL
Fennimore, Craig, von Ammom, Udall & Powers, Phoneix, AZ [*Library symbol*] [*Library of Congress*] (LCLS) ... AzPhFC
Fenoterol [*Pharmacology*] ... F
Fentanyl Isothiocyanate [*Biochemistry*] ... FIT
Fentanyl/Pancuronium/Oxygen Anesthesia ... FPOA
Fenton Art Glass Collectors of America (EA) ... FAGCA
Fenton, MI [*AM radio station call letters*] ... WWON
Fenton's Important Judgments [*New Zealand*] [*A publication*] (DLA) ... Fent
Fenton's Important Judgments [*New Zealand*] [*A publication*] (DLA) ... Fent Imp Judg
Fenton's Important Judgments [*New Zealand*] [*A publication*] (DLA) ... Fenton
Fenton's New Zealand Reports [*A publication*] (DLA) ... Fent
Fenton's New Zealand Reports [*A publication*] (DLA) ... Fent (New Zealand)
Fenton's New Zealand Reports [*A publication*] (DLA) ... Fent NZ
Fentress, VA [*Location identifier FAA*] (FAAL) ... NFE
Fenway Library Consortium/Abbot Memorial Library [*Library network*] ... FLC
Fenway Resources Ltd. [*Vancouver Stock Exchange symbol*] ... FWY
Fenwick Island, DE [*FM radio station call letters*] ... WLBW
Feodosiya [*Former USSR Seismograph station code, US Geological Survey Closed*] (SEIS) ... FEO
Fera Island [*Solomon Islands*] [*Airport symbol*] (OAG) ... FRE
Feral Animals Committee [*Northern Territory, Australia*] ... FAC

Feral Pests Program (EERA) ... FPP
Ferard on Fixtures [*A publication*] (DLA) ... Fer Fixt
Ferber Mining Corp. [*Vancouver Stock Exchange symbol*] ... FBM
Ferdinand Marcos [*Former Philippine president*] ... FM
Ferdinand News, Ferdinand, IN [*Library symbol Library of Congress*] (LCLS) ... InFerN
Ferdinand Railroad Co. [*AAR code*] ... FRDN
Ferdous [*Iran*] [*ICAO location identifier*] (ICLI) ... OIMF
Fereidan [*Iran*] [*ICAO location identifier*] (ICLI) ... OIFU
Fergana [*Former USSR Seismograph station code, US Geological Survey*] (SEIS) ... FRG
Fergus Falls Community College, Fergus Falls, MN [*Library symbol Library of Congress*] (LCLS) ... MnFfC
Fergus Falls Middle School, Fergus Falls, MN [*Library symbol*] [*Library of Congress*] (LCLS) ... MnFfM
Fergus Falls, MN [*Location identifier FAA*] (FAAL) ... FFM
Fergus Falls, MN [*AM radio station call letters*] ... KBRF
Fergus Falls, MN [*AM radio station call letters*] ... KJJK
Fergus Falls, MN [*FM radio station call letters*] ... KJJK-FM
Fergus Falls, MN [*FM radio station call letters*] ... KZCR
Fergus Falls Public Library, Fergus Falls, MN [*Library symbol Library of Congress*] (LCLS) ... MnFf
Fergus Falls Regional Treatment Center, Fergus Falls, MN [*Library symbol*] [*Library of Congress*] (LCLS) ... MnFfRT
Fergus Falls Senior High School, Fergus Falls, MN [*Library symbol*] [*Library of Congress*] (LCLS) ... MnFfSH
Fergus Public Library, Fergus, ON, Canada [*Library symbol*] [*Library of Congress*] (LCLS) ... CaOFER
Fergus Public Library, Ontario [*Library symbol National Library of Canada*] (NLC) ... OFER
Ferguson Formula [*Four-wheel drive system*] [*Automotive engineering British*] ... FF
Ferguson Library for Print Handicapped Students, Patrick Power Library, St. Mary's University, Halifax, Nova Scotia [*Library symbol National Library of Canada*] (NLC) ... NSHSPT
Ferguson Library, Stamford, CT [*OCLC symbol*] (OCLC) ... FEM
Ferguson Memorial Library [*Presbyterian Church, Sydney, New South Wales, Australia*] ... FML
Ferguson, MO [*FM radio station call letters*] ... KCFV
Ferguson's Common Law Procedure Act [*Ireland*] [*A publication*] (DLA) ... Ferg Proc
Fergusson's Consistorial Decisions [*Scotland*] [*A publication*] (DLA) ... Ferg
Fergusson's Consistorial Decisions [*Scotland*] [*A publication*] (DLA) ... Fergusson
Fergusson's Consistorial Reports [*Scotland*] [*A publication*] (DLA) ... Ferg Cons
Fergusson's Divorce Decisions by Consistorial Courts [*Scotland*] [*A publication*] (DLA) ... Ferg M & D
Fergusson's Five Years' Railway Cases [*A publication*] (DLA) ... Ferg Ry Cas
Fergusson's Scotch Session Cases [*1738-52*] [*A publication*] (DLA) ... Fergusson
Feria Aviacion [*Spain ICAO designator*] (FAAC) ... FER
Feria Internacional de Artesania ... FINART
Ferkessedougou [*Ivory Coast*] [*ICAO location identifier*] (ICLI) ... DIFK
Fermanagh [*County in Northern Ireland*] (ROG) ... FERM
Fermanagh [*County in Northern Ireland*] ... FERMANH
Fermanagh, Armagh, Tyrone, Derry, Antrim, Down [*The six counties of Northern Ireland*] ... FATDAD
Fermanagh, Armagh, Tyrone, Londonderry, Antrim, Down [*Unionist mnemonic for the six counties of Northern Ireland*] ... FATLAD
Fermanagh County [*Ireland*] (BARN) ... Fer
Fermat's Last Theorem [*Mathematics*] ... FLT
Fermentation [*Biology*] ... F
Fermentation ... FRMNTN
Fermentation Biomass ... FB
Fermentation/Cell Culture [*Biology*] ... F/CC
Fermented Egg Product [*Animal repellent*] ... FEP
Fermet's Last Theorem [*Mathematics*] ... FLT
Fermi [*Later, Femtometer*] [*Unit of length Nuclear physics*] ... F
Fermi Contact [*Physics*] ... FC
Fermi Liquid Theory [*Physics*] ... FLT
Fermi National Accelerator Laboratory [*Also, FNAL*] [*Batavia, IL*] [*Department of Energy*] ... FERMILAB
Fermi National Accelerator Laboratory [*Also, FERMILAB*] [*Batavia, IL*] [*Department of Energy*] ... FNAL
Fermi Selection Rules ... FSR
Fermi-Dirac Gas ... FDG
Fermi-Dirac Statistics ... FDS
FERMILAB, Batavia, IL [*Library symbol Library of Congress*] (LCLS) ... IBatF
Fermi-Level Referenced Electron Spectroscopy for Chemical Analysis ... FRESCA
Fermium [*Chemical element*] ... Fm
Fermont, PQ [*FM radio station call letters*] ... CBMR
Fermont, PQ [*FM radio station call letters*] ... CFMF
Fern Ridge Community Library, Veneta, OR [*Library symbol Library of Congress*] (LCLS) ... OrV
Fernadina Beach, FL [*FM radio station call letters*] ... WNLE
Fernald Environmental Management Project [*Department of Energy*] ... FEMP
Fernald's English Synonyms [*A publication*] (DLA) ... Fernald Eng Synonyms
Fernandina Beach, FL [*AM radio station call letters*] ... WQAI
Fernando De Noronha [*Brazil ICAO location identifier*] (ICLI) ... SBFN
Fernbank Science Center, Atlanta, GA [*Library symbol Library of Congress*] (LCLS) ... GAFSC
Fernbank Science Center, Atlanta, GA [*OCLC symbol*] (OCLC) ... GFS
Ferndale [*Cardiff*] [*Welsh depot code*] ... FDL
Ferndale [*California*] [*Seismograph station code, US Geological Survey*] (SEIS) ... FER
Ferndale, CA [*FM radio station call letters*] ... KAJK-FM
Ferndale Internet Experiment [*Computer science*] ... FIX
Ferndale Public Library, Ferndale, CA [*Library symbol Library of Congress*] (LCLS) ... CFe
Ferndale, WA [*AM radio station call letters*] ... KNTR
Fernie [*British Columbia*] [*Seismograph station code, US Geological Survey Closed*] (SEIS) ... FRN
Fernie, BC [*AM radio station call letters*] ... CFEK
Fernie Museum, British Columbia [*Library symbol National Library of Canada*] (NLC) ... BFM
Fernie Museum, Fernie, BC, Canada [*Library symbol*] [*Library of Congress*] (LCLS) ... CaBFM
Fernie Public Library, British Columbia [*Library symbol National Library of Canada*] (NLC) ... BF
Fernschreiben [*or Fernschreiber*] [*Teletype Message or Teletype*] [*German military - World War II*] ... FS
Ferntree Computer Corp. ... FCC
Fernwood, Columbia & Gulf R. R. [*AAR code*] ... FCG
Ferojpur [*India*] [*ICAO location identifier*] (ICLI) ... VIFZ
Ferranti PLC [*British ICAO designator*] (FAAC) ... FFU
Ferranti Sonobuoy Processing System (MCD) ... FSPS
Ferrara [*Italy ICAO location identifier*] (ICLI) ... LIPF
Ferrari Club of America (EA) ... FCA
Ferrari Data Bank (EA) ... FDB
Ferrari Owners Club (EA) ... FOC
Ferredoxin [*Biochemistry*] ... Fd
Ferredoxin-Reducing Substance [*Biochemistry*] (MAE) ... FRS
Ferrellgas Partners Ltd. [*Associated Press*] (SAG) ... Ferllgs
Ferrellgas Partners Ltd. [*NYSE symbol*] (SAG) ... FGP
Ferrellgas Partners L.P. [*NYSE symbol*] (TTSB) ... FGP
Ferret Fanciers Club (EA) ... FFC
Ferret LASER Detector ... FLD
Ferric Ammonium Citrate [*Inorganic chemistry*] ... FAC
Ferric Dimethyldithiocarbamate [*A fungicide*] ... FDDC
Ferric Ion Free ... FIF
Ferric Oxide (CDE) ... Fe^2O^3
Ferrichrome Recording Tape (NTCM) ... FeCr
Ferric-Leach Bacterial Regeneration [*Uranium extraction process*] ... FBR
Ferriday, LA [*AM radio station call letters*] ... KFNV
Ferriday, LA [*FM radio station call letters*] ... KFNV-FM
Ferriere's Dictionary of Jurisprudence [*A publication*] (DLA) ... Ferriere Dict de Jr
Ferrierite [*A zeolite*] ... FER
Ferri-Gas Duplexer ... FGD
Ferriprotoporphyrin [*Biochemistry*] ... FP
Ferriprotoporphyrin IX [*Biochemistry*] ... FPIX
Ferris State College, Big Rapids, MI [*OCLC symbol*] (OCLC) ... EZF
Ferris State College, Big Rapids, MI [*Library symbol Library of Congress*] (LCLS) ... MiBrF
Ferris, TX [*AM radio station call letters*] ... KDFT
Ferrite Array Demonstration [*RADAR*] ... FAD
Ferrite Control Amplifier ... FCA
Ferrite Core ... FC
Ferrite Diode Limiter (IAA) ... FDL
Ferrite Driver Amplifier ... FDA
Ferrite Manufacturers Association ... FMA
Ferrite Memory Core ... FMC
Ferrite Metal ... FM
Ferrite Phase Driver ... FPD
Ferrite Phase Shifter ... FPS
Ferrite Pot Core ... FPC
Ferrite Resonance Switch ... FRS
Ferrite-Rod Antenna (IEEE) ... FERROD
Ferritin [*Hematology*] (DAVI) ... FERRIT
Ferritin [*Biochemistry*] (AAMN) ... Ft
Ferritin Repressor Protein [*Biochemistry*] ... FRP
Ferritin-Conjugated Antibody [*Biochemistry*] (MAE) ... FCA
Ferro Alloys and Metals Producers Association [*British*] (DBA) ... FAMPA
Ferro Corp. [*Associated Press*] (SAG) ... Ferro
Ferro Corp. [*NYSE symbol*] (SPSG) ... FOE
Ferro Corp., Chemical Library, Bedford, OH [*Library symbol Library of Congress*] (LCLS) ... OBedF
Ferro Corp., Independence, OH [*Library symbol Library of Congress*] (LCLS) ... OInF
Ferroacoustic Memory [*Electronics*] (IAA) ... FAME
[*The*] **Ferroalloys Association** (EA) ... FA
[*The*] **Ferroalloys Association** (EA) ... TFA
Ferroan Anorthosite [*Lunar geology*] ... FeAn
Ferrocarril de Chihuahua al Pacifico, SA de CV [*AAR code*] ... CHP
Ferrocarril de Minatitlan al Carmen [*AAR code*] ... FDMA
Ferrocarril de Nacozari [*AAR code*] ... FCDN
Ferrocarril del Pacifico, SA de CV [*AAR code*] ... FCP
Ferrocarril del Sureste [*AAR code*] ... SCOP
Ferrocarril Mexicano [*AAR code*] ... FCM
Ferrocarril Mexicano del Pacifico [*Mexican Pacific Railroad Co., Inc.*] [*AAR code*] ... MDP
Ferrocarril Nacional de Tehuantepec [*AAR code*] ... NDT
Ferrocarril Nor-Oeste de Mexico [*Mexico North Western Railroad*] [*AAR code*] ... NODM
Ferrocarril Sonora Baja California SA de CV [*AAR code*] ... SBC
Ferrocarriles Argentinos [*Railway*] [*Argentina*] (EY) ... FA
Ferrocarriles Nacionales de Colombia [*National Railways of Colombia*] (EY) ... FNC
Ferrocarriles Nacionales de Mexico [*National Railways of Mexico*] ... FNM
Ferrocarriles Nacionales de Mexico [*AAR code*] ... MGRS
Ferrocarriles Nacionales de Mexico [*AAR code*] ... NDM
Ferrocarriles Unidos del Sureste, SA de CV [*AAR code*] ... SE
Ferrocement ... FC

Ferrocene Polymer Cure Process	FPCP
Ferrocenedicarboxylic Acid [*Organic chemistry*]	FDA
Ferrochelatase [*An enzyme*]	FC
Ferroelectric	FE
Ferroelectric Ceramic	FEC
Ferroelectric Ceramic Picture Device (IEEE)	FERPIC
Ferroelectric Liquid Crystal [*Physical chemistry*]	FLC
Ferroelectric/Photoconductive (PDAA)	FE/PC
Ferroelectric Random Access Memory [*Computer science*]	FRAM
Ferroelectric Variable Capacitor	FEVAC
Ferroelectric-Dielectric Field Effect Transistor (IAA)	FEFET
Ferroelectric-Electroluminescent	FE-EL
Ferroelectronic RAM [*Random-Access Memory*] [*Ramtron*]	FRAM
Ferrofluidics Corp. [*NASDAQ symbol*] (NQ)	FERO
Ferrofluidics Corp. [*Associated Press*] (SAG)	Ferofl
Ferrohydrodynamic (IAA)	FHD
Ferromagnet [*Physics*]	FM
Ferromagnetic Contamination [*Medicine*]	FC
Ferromagnetic Fluid Levitation Accelerometer	FFLA
Ferromagnetic Material	FMM
Ferromagnetic Object Recognition Matrix	FORM
Ferromagnetic Resonance	FMR
Ferroresonance Servo Motor (PDAA)	FRSM
Ferrosan [*Sweden*] [*Research code symbol*]	F
Ferrosan [*Sweden*] [*Research code symbol*]	FG
Ferrosan [*Denmark*] [*Research code symbol*]	NSD
Ferrosilite [*CIPW classification*] [*Geology*]	fs
Ferrous	FER
Ferrous Metal Detector	FMD
Ferrous Metal Powder	FMP
Ferrous Scrap Consumers Coalition (EA)	FSCC
Ferrous Sulfate [*Organic chemistry*] (DAVI)	$FeSO_4$
Ferrovie dello Stato [*Italian State Railways*]	FS
Ferrox Cube [*Telecommunications*] (TEL)	FXC
Ferroxcube Corp., Suagerties, NY [*Library symbol Library of Congress*] (LCLS)	NSauF
Ferrule Contact [*Lamp base type*] (NTCM)	F
Ferrule Contact [*Design engineering*] (IAA)	FERCON
Ferrum [*Iron*] [*Chemical element*]	Fe
Ferrum [*Iron*] [*Pharmacy*]	FER
Ferrum [*Iron*] [*Pharmacy*] (ROG)	FERR
Ferrum College, Ferrum, VA [*OCLC symbol*] (OCLC)	VFC
Ferrum College, Ferrum, VA [*Library symbol Library of Congress*] (LCLS)	ViFerF
Ferrum, VA [*FM radio station call letters*]	WFFC
Ferruzzi Finanziaria	FERFIN
Ferry	FER
Ferry [*Commonly used*] (OPSA)	FERRY
Ferry [*Commonly used*] (OPSA)	FRRY
Ferry	FRY
Ferry	FRY
Ferry [*Nautical charts*]	Fy
Ferry Command [*RAF*] [*British*]	FC
Ferry Command Police [*British military*] (DMA)	FCP
Ferry Mission Equipment Store (MCD)	FMES
Ferry Movement Directive [*Navy*] (NVT)	FMD
Ferry Range (MCD)	FR
Ferry Service Unit	FSU
Ferry Squadron [*Navy*] (DNAB)	FERRON
Ferry Squadron [*Navy symbol*] (NVT)	VRF
Ferry Supply Vehicle	FSV
Ferry Training Unit [*British*]	FTU
Ferryboat or Launch [*Self-propelled*] [*Navy symbol*]	YFB
Ferry-Porter Law [*Physics*]	FPL
Fertile [*Medicine*]	F
Fertile Public Library, Fertile, MN [*Library symbol*] [*Library of Congress*] (LCLS)	MnFer
Fertile-Betrami School, Fertile, MN [*Library symbol*] [*Library of Congress*] (LCLS)	MnFerS
Fertiliser Board [*Tasmania, Australia*]	FB
Fertiliser Manufacturers Association [*British*]	FMA
Fertilisers from Organic Wastes Program (EERA)	FOWP
Fertility (WDAA)	FERT
Fertility Factor [*Genetics*]	F
Fertility Research Foundation (EA)	FRF
Fertilization Antigen [*Immunology*]	FA
Fertilized	F
Fertilized [*Medicine*] (DAVI)	fertd
Fertilized	FERTD
Fertilizer	FERT
Fertilizer	FERT
Fertilizer	FERTZ
Fertilizer Advisory Development Information Network for Asia and the Pacific	FADINAP
Fertilizer Dealers Association [*Defunct*] (EA)	FDA
Fertilizer Grade Ammonium Nitrate	FGAN
Fertilizer Industry Round Table (EA)	FIRT
[*The*] Fertilizer Institute	FI
[*The*] Fertilizer Institute (EA)	TFI
Fertility Factor [*Medicine*]	FF
Ferulic Acid [*Biochemistry*]	FA
Fervens [*Hot*] [*Pharmacy*]	FERV
Fes/Saiss [*Morocco*] [*ICAO location identifier*] (ICLI)	GMFF
Fes/Sefrou [*Morocco*] [*ICAO location identifier*] (ICLI)	GMFU
Fessenden on Patents [*A publication*] (DLA)	Fess Pat
Fessenden on Patents [*A publication*] (DLA)	Fessen Pat

Fest Resources [*Vancouver Stock Exchange symbol*]	FSC
Festival [*Record label*]	Fest
Festival	FEST
Festival [*Slang*] (WDMC)	fest
Festival (France) [*Record label*]	FestF
Festival International de Nouvelle Danse	FIND
Festival International de Programmes Audiovisuels	FIPA
Festival International du Film de la Critique Quebecoise [*International Festival of Quebec Film Critics*] [*Canada*]	FIFCQ
Festival International du Video-Clip [*The first festival entirely devoted to pop-music video, at San Tropez, October, 1984*]	FIVC
Festival of American Community Theatre [*American Community Theatre Association*]	FACT
Festival of European Anglophone Theatrical Societies	FEATS
Festival of Lights [*Hanukkah*] [*Commemoration of the rededication of the Temple by Judas Maccabeus in 165BC*] (ADA)	FOL
Festival of Sydney [*Australia*]	FOS
Festlegepunkt [*Reference point, a gunnery term*] [*German military - World War II*]	FLP
Festpunkt [*Reference point, a surveying term*] [*German military - World War II*]	FP
Festschrift [*A publication*] (BJA)	Fs
Festschrift fuer Otto Procksch (1934) [*A publication*] (BJA)	FOP
Festuca Cryptic Virus [*Plant pathology*]	FCV
Festuca Necrosis Virus [*Plant pathology*]	FNV
Festus, MO [*Location identifier FAA*] (FAAL)	FES
Festus, MO [*AM radio station call letters*]	KJCF
Festus, MO [*AM radio station call letters*] (RBYB)	KJFF-AM
Festus, MO [*FM radio station call letters*] (RBYB)	KTBJ-FM
Festus-St. Louis, MO [*AM radio station call letters*]	KXEN
Fetal [*Medicine*]	F
Fetal Activity Determination	FAD
Fetal Age [*Obstetrics*] (DAVI)	FA
Fetal Alcohol Effect [*Medicine*]	FAE
Fetal Alcohol Effects [*Medicine*]	FAE
Fetal Alcohol Syndrome [*Medicine*]	FAS
Fetal Blood Sample [*Hematology*]	FBS
Fetal Bovine Serum [*Medicine*]	FBS
Fetal Breathing Movements [*Gynecology*]	FBM
Fetal Calf [*or Cow*] Serum [*Medicine*]	FCS
Fetal Cord Serum [*Gynecology*]	FCoS
Fetal Cord Serum [*Embryology*]	FCS
Fetal Death in Utero [*Medicine*]	FDIU
Fetal Death Zone [*Medicine*]	FDZ
Fetal Electrocardiogram [*Medicine*]	FEKG
Fetal Electrocardiography [*or Electrocardiogram*] [*Medicine*]	FECG
Fetal Electroencephalogram [*Medicine*] (AAMN)	FEEG
Fetal Erythroblastosis [*Medicine*]	FE
Fetal Head [*Medicine*]	FH
Fetal Heart [*Medicine*]	FH
Fetal Heart [*Medicine*] (MAE)	FHT
Fetal Heart Heard [*Medicine*]	FHH
Fetal Heart Not Heard [*Medicine*]	FHNH
Fetal Heart Rate [*Medicine*]	FHR
Fetal Heart Sounds [*Medicine*]	FHS
Fetal Heart Tone [*Obstetrics*]	FHT
Fetal Hydantoin Syndrome [*Medicine*]	FHS
Fetal Intensive Care Unit [*Neonatology*] (DAVI)	FICU
Fetal Lamb Kidney [*A cell line*]	FLK
Fetal Lung Maturity [*Physiology*]	FLM
Fetal Maternal Hemorrhage [*Medicine*]	FMH
Fetal Mouse Liver Cell [*Bioassay*]	FMLC
Fetal Movement [*Gynecology*]	FM
Fetal Movement Count [*Obstetrics*] (DAVI)	FMC
Fetal Movement Felt [*Medicine*]	FMF
Fetal Movements [*Obstetrics*] (DAVI)	FM
Fetal Occult Blood [*Medicine*]	FOB
Fetal Protection Policy [*Insurance*] (WYGK)	FPP
Fetal Rhesus Monkey Kidney Cell [*Medicine*] (DMAA)	FRh
Fetal Scalp Blood [*Fetal monitoring*] (CPH)	FSB
Fetal Scalp Electrode [*Obstetrics*] (DAVI)	FSE
Fetal Sulfoglycoprotein Antigen [*Oncology*]	FSA
Fetal Thymic Organ Cultures [*Biochemistry*]	FTOC
Fetal Valproate Syndrome [*Medicine*] (DMAA)	FVS
Fetal Zone [*Medicine*]	FZ
Fetch [*Computer science*]	F
Fetch and Send [*Telecommunications*] (TEL)	F/S
Fetch and Set BIT [*Binary Digit*] [*Computer science*] (IAA)	FASB
Fetch, Generate [*or Generalize*], and Project [*Computer Program*]	FGP
Fetch/Load [*Computer science*] (MDG)	F/L
Fetlar [*Shetland Islands*] [*Airport symbol*] (OAG)	FEA
Fetoneonatal Estrogen-Binding Protein	FEBP
Feto-Pelvic Disproportion [*Medicine*] (DMAA)	FPD
Fetter's Treatise on Carriers of Passengers [*A publication*] (DLA)	Fett Carr
Fetus Active [*Obstetrics*] (DAVI)	F/A
Feucht [*Germany ICAO location identifier*] (ICLI)	EDIG
Feudal	FEUD
Feudalism (WDAA)	FEUD
Feudorum Liber [*Book of Feuds*] [*Latin A publication*] (DLA)	Feud Lib
Feuerstein's Instrumental Enrichment [*Education*] (AEE)	FIE
Feurs/Chambeon [*France ICAO location identifier*] (ICLI)	LFLZ
Fever (WDAA)	FEV
Fever and Chills [*Medicine*] (DAVI)	FC
Fever Caused by Infection (MAE)	FI

Fever, Chills, Sweating, Nausea, Vomiting, and Diarrhea [*Gastroenterology*] (DAVI) ... FCSNVD
Fever of Undetermined Etiology [*Medicine*] (DAVI) ... FUE
Fever of Undetermined [*or Unknown*] **Origin** [*Medicine*] ... FUO
Fever Therapy Technician [*Navy*] ... FTT
Few Civilian Casualties [*Persian Gulf War*] ... FCA
Few Large Platelets [*Hematology*] (DAVI) ... FLP
Few-Tube Test Model [*Nuclear energy*] (NRCH) ... FTTM
Feynman-Gellman Theory [*Nuclear physics*] ... F-G
Feynman-Kak Formula [*Particle physics*] ... F-K
Fez [*Morocco*] [*Airport symbol*] (OAG) ... FEZ
Fez [*Morocco*] [*Airport symbol*] (AD) ... FEZ
FFBS Bancorp [*NASDAQ symbol*] (TTSB) ... FFBS
FFBS Bancorp, Inc. [*NASDAQ symbol*] (SAG) ... FFBS
FFD Financial [*NASDAQ symbol*] (TTSB) ... FFDF
FFD Financial Corp. [*NASDAQ symbol*] (SAG) ... FFDFinl
FFD Financial Corp. [*Associated Press*] (SAG) ... FFDFinl
FFE Financial Corp. [*Associated Press*] (SAG) ... FFE Fn
FFE Financial Corp. [*NASDAQ symbol*] (SAG) ... FFEF
FFLC Bancorp [*NASDAQ symbol*] (SAG) ... FFLC
FFLC Bancorp [*Associated Press*] (SAG) ... FFLC Bc
F.F.O. Financial Group [*NASDAQ symbol*] (TTSB) ... FFFG
FFO Financial Group, Inc. [*NASDAQ symbol*] (CTT) ... FFFG
FFO Financial Group, Inc. [*Associated Press*] (SAG) ... FFO Fn
FFP Partners Ltd. [*AMEX symbol*] (SPSG) ... FFP
FFP Partners L.P. [*AMEX symbol*] (TTSB) ... FFP
FFS [*Flight Service Station*] **Guarding Service B** [*Aviation*] (FAAC) ... FGSB
FFTF [*Fast Flux Test Facility*] **Test Engineering** [*Nuclear energy*] (NRCH) ... FTE
FFTF [*Fast Flux Test Facility*] **Test Procedure** [*Nuclear energy*] (NRCH) ... FTP
FFVA Financial [*NASDAQ symbol*] (TTSB) ... FFFC
FFVA Financial Corp. [*NASDAQ symbol*] (SAG) ... FFFC
FFVA Financial Corp. [*Associated Press*] (SAG) ... FFVA Fn
FFW Corp. [*Associated Press*] (SAG) ... FFW Cp
FFW Corp. [*NASDAQ symbol*] (SAG) ... FFWC
FFY Financial [*NASDAQ symbol*] (TTSB) ... FFYF
FFY Financial Corp. [*Associated Press*] (SAG) ... FFY Fn
FFY Financial Corp. [*NASDAQ symbol*] (SAG) ... FFYF
FGGE [*First Global Atmospheric Research Program Global Experiment*] **Operational Year** [*Marine science*] (MSC) ... FOY
FHP International Corp. [*Associated Press*] (SAG) ... FHP
FHP International Corp. [*NASDAQ symbol*] (NQ) ... FHPC
FHP Intl $1.25 Cv Pfd'A' [*NASDAQ symbol*] (TTSB) ... FHPCA
FHP Int'l Corp. [*NASDAQ symbol*] (TTSB) ... FHPC
Fialcytosine [*Medicine*] ... FIAC
Fialuridine [*!Medicine*] ... FIAU
Fianarantsoa [*Madagascar*] [*ICAO location identifier*] (ICLI) ... FMSF
Fianarantsoa [*Madagascar*] [*Airport symbol*] (OAG) ... WFI
Fianna Fail [*Warriors of Destiny*] [*Political party Ireland*] ... FF
Fiant [*Let Them be Made*] [*Pharmacology*] (DAVI) ... f
Fiant [*Let Them Be Made*] [*Pharmacy*] (ROG) ... FT
Fiat [*Let It Be Made*] [*Pharmacy*] ... F
Fiat [*Make*] [*Pharmacy*] ... FT
Fiat Auto Recycling ... FARE
Fiat Cataplasma [*Let a Poultice Be Made*] [*Pharmacy*] ... FT CAT
Fiat Cataplasma [*Let a Poultice Be Made*] [*Pharmacy*] (DAVI) ... ft cataplasm
Fiat Ceratum [*Let a Cerate Be Made*] [*Pharmacy*] ... FT CERAT
Fiat Chartula [*Let a Powder Be Made*] [*Pharmacy*] ... FT CHART
Fiat Club of America (EA) ... FCA
Fiat Collyrium [*Let an Eyewash Be Made*] [*Pharmacy*] ... FT COLLYR
Fiat Emulsio [*Let an Emulsion Be Made*] [*Pharmacy*] ... FT EMULS
Fiat Enema [*Let an Injection (per Rectum) be Made*] [*Pharmacy*] (DAVI) ... ft enem
Fiat Gargarisma [*Let a Gargle Be Made*] [*Pharmacy*] ... FT GARG
Fiat Haustus [*Let a Drink Be Made*] [*Pharmacy*] ... FH
Fiat Haustus [*Let a Drink Be Made*] [*Pharmacy*] ... Ft Haust
Fiat Infusum [*Let an Infusion Be Made*] [*Pharmacy*] ... FT INFUS
Fiat Lege Artis [*Let It Be Done According to the Rules of the Art*] [*Pharmacy*] ... FLA
Fiat Linimentum [*Let a Linament Be Made*] [*Pharmacy*] ... FT LINIM
Fiat Massa [*Let a Mass Be Made*] [*Pharmacy*] ... FT MAS
Fiat Massa et Divide in Pilulae [*Let a Mass Be Made and Divided into Pills*] [*Pharmacy*] ... FT MAS DIV in PIL
Fiat Mistura [*Let a Mixture Be Made*] [*Pharmacy*] (ROG) ... F MIST
Fiat Mistura [*Let a Mixture Be Made*] [*Pharmacy*] ... FM
Fiat Mistura [*Let a Mixture Be Made*] [*Pharmacy*] ... FT MIST
Fiat Pilula [*Let a Pill Be Made*] [*Pharmacy*] ... F PIL
Fiat Pilula [*Let a Pill Be Made*] [*Pharmacy*] ... FP
Fiat Pilulae [*Let Pills Be Made*] [*Pharmacy*] (ROG) ... FT PIL
Fiat Potio [*Let a Potion Be Made*] [*Pharmacy*] ... FP
Fiat Pulvis [*Let a Powder Be Made*] [*Pharmacy*] ... FT PULV
Fiat Pulvis Subtilis [*Let a Fine Powder Be Made*] [*Pharmacy*] ... FT PULV SUBTIL
Fiat Secundum Artem [*Let It Be Done According to Art*] [*Pharmacy*] ... FSA
Fiat Secundum Artem Reglas [*Let It Be Done According to the Rules of the Art*] [*Pharmacy*] ... FSAR
Fiat Solutio [*Let a Solution Be Made*] [*Pharmacy Latin*] (MAE) ... ft solut
Fiat SpA [*NYSE symbol*] (CTT) ... FIA
Fiat SpA [*Associated Press*] (SAG) ... Fiat
Fiat SpA [*Italy ICAO aircraft manufacturer identifier*] (ICAO) ... FT
Fiat SpA ADR [*NYSE symbol*] (TTSB) ... FIA
Fiat SpA Preference ADR [*NYSE symbol*] (TTSB) ... FIAPr
Fiat SpA Savings ADR [*NYSE symbol*] (TTSB) ... FIAPrA
Fiat Suppositorium [*Let a Suppository Be Made*] [*Pharmacy*] (DAVI) ... ft suppos
Fiat Trochisci [*Make Lozenges*] [*Pharmacy*] ... FT TROCH
Fiat Unguentum [*Make an Ointment*] [*Pharmacy*] ... FT UNG
Fiat Venaesectio [*Let the Patient Be Bled*] [*Pharmacy*] (ROG) ... F VENOES
Fiat Venaesectio [*Let the Patient Be Bled*] [*Pharmacy*] ... F VS
Fibber McGee and Molly [*Radio program*] ... FM & M
Fiber (KSC) ... FBR
Fiber (VRA) ... fbr
Fiber ... FBR
Fiber ... FIB
Fiber ... FIBR
Fiber Almost to the Home [*Telecommunications*] ... FATTH
Fiber Bonded Carpet Manufacturers Association [*British*] (DBA) ... FBCMA
Fiber Composite Material ... FCM
Fiber Distributed Data Interface [*Telecommunications*] ... FDDI
Fiber Duct [*Telecommunications*] (TEL) ... FD
Fiber, Fabric, and Apparel Coalition for Trade (EA) ... FFACT
Fiber Fineness Distribution Analyzer (ADA) ... FFDA
Fiber Hub ... FH
Fiber in The Loop (ACRL) ... FITL
Fiber Interferometer Gyroscope (MCD) ... FIG
Fiber Node ... FN
Fiber Optic [*Data transmission*] (TEL) ... FO
Fiber Optic Cable System (DWSG) ... FOCS
Fiber Optic Communication and Information Society (MHDI) ... FOCIS
Fiber Optic Communications for Aerospace Systems (MCD) ... FOCAS
Fiber Optic Coordinating Committee [*American National Standards Institute*] [*Telecommunications*] ... FOCC
Fiber Optic Data Bus (SSD) ... FODB
Fiber Optic Guided Missile [*Army*] (RDA) ... FOG-M
Fiber Optic Helmet Mounted Display [*Computer generated imagery*] ... FOHMD
Fiber Optic Inter Repeater Link Standard [*Institute of Electrical and Electronics Engineers*] ... FOIRL
Fiber Optic Material Research Program [*Rutgers University*] ... FOMRP
Fiber Optic MODEM [*Modulator-Demodulator*] ... FOM
Fiber Optic Mortar Projectile [*Boeing Co.*] [*Military*] ... FOMP
Fiber Optic Rate Sensors [*Instrumentation*] ... FORS
Fiber Optic Sensor (IAA) ... FOS
Fiber Optic Sensor System (MCD) ... FOSS
Fiber Optic Terminal [*Electric*] (ACRL) ... FOT
Fiber Optic Test Procedure ... FOTP
Fiber Optic Transmission System [*Consists of modulated light signals sent through glass fibers and demodulated by photo-diodes*] [*Data transmission*] ... FOTS
Fiber Optics Board (MCD) ... FOB
Fiber Optics Borehole Earth Strainmeter [*Geology*] ... FOBES
Fiber Optics Borescope ... FOBS
Fiber Optics Communications [*Data transmission*] (TEL) ... FOC
Fiber Optics Data Link (MCD) ... FODL
Fiber Optics Guidance (MCD) ... FOG
Fiber Optics Guidance Demonstration (RDA) ... FOGD
Fiber Optics LASER ... FOL
Fiber Optics LASER Gyro (MCD) ... FOLG
Fiber Optics Light ... FOL
Fiber Optics Photo Pickup ... FOPP
Fiber Optics Photo Transfer ... FOPT
Fiber Optics Probe ... FOP
Fiber Optics SONAR System (MCD) ... FOSS
Fiber Plan [*Used in title of book advocating a high-fiber diet*] ... F (Plan)
Fiber Producers Credit Association (EA) ... FPCA
Fiber Reinforced (MCD) ... FR
Fiber Saturation Point [*Of drying lumber*] (BARN) ... FSP
Fiber Society (EA) ... FS
Fiber to the Curb [*Telecommunications*] ... FTTC
Fiber to the Home [*Telecommunications*] ... FTTH
Fiber to the Pedestal [*Telecommunications*] ... FTTP
Fiber Volume Ratio ... FVR
Fiberboard [*Technical drawings*] ... FB
Fiberboard ... FBRBD
Fiberboard (VRA) ... fibd
Fiberboard, Corrugated ... FBDC
Fiberboard, Double Wall ... FDWL
Fiberboard, Solid ... FBDS
Fiberchem, Inc. [*Associated Press*] (SAG) ... Fibchm
Fiberchem, Inc. [*NASDAQ symbol*] (NQ) ... FOCS
Fibercorp Intl. [*NASDAQ symbol*] (TTSB) ... FCII
Fiber-Embedding Approximation ... FEA
Fiberglas Canada, Inc., Sarnia, Ontario [*Library symbol National Library of Canada*] (NLC) ... OSFC
Fiberglass ... FBRGLS
Fiberglass (ADA) ... FG
Fiberglass [*Technical drawings*] ... FGL
Fiberglass (VRA) ... fibgl
Fiberglass Aerial Target (DNAB) ... FIGAT
Fiberglass Backed Vacuum Forming [*Fiberglass production*] ... FBVF
Fiberglass Brush ... FGB
Fiberglass Cone Brush ... FGCB
Fiberglass Covers (DCTA) ... FC
Fiberglass Curtain ... FGC
Fiberglass Fabrication Association (EA) ... FFA
Fiberglass Hull ... FGH
Fiberglass Ltd., Sarnia, ON, Canada [*Library symbol Library of Congress*] (LCLS) ... CaOSFC
Fiberglass Petroleum Tank and Pipe Institute (EA) ... FPTPI
Fiberglass Reinforced Panel Association [*Defunct*] (EA) ... FRPA
Fiberglass Rotor Blade (MCD) ... FRB
Fiberglass Stain Remover [*Cleaning product*] [*Jamie Industries*] ... FSR
Fiberglass-Insulated Wire ... FIW
Fiberglass-Reinforced Plastic ... FRP
Fiberglass-Reinforced Plywood ... FRP

Fiberglass-Reinforced Polyester [*Organic chemistry*] .... FRP
Fiberglass-Reinforced Thermoplastic .... FRTP
Fiber-in-Bending [*Lumber*] .... FB
Fiberoptic Bronchoscopy [*Also, FOB*] [*Medicine*] .... FB
Fiberoptic Bronchoscopy [*Also, FB*] [*Medicine*] .... FOB
Fiber-Optic Cable (SSD) .... FOC
Fiber-Optic Chemical Sensor [*Analytical chemistry*] .... FOCS
Fiber-Optic Digital Device Interface [*Computer science*] ...... FDDI
Fiber-Optic Gyroscope [*Automotive navigation systems*] .... FOG
Fiberoptic Link Around the Globe [*Undersea communications cable*] ...... FLAG
Fiber-Optic Scintillating [*Plate*] .... FOS
Fiber-Optics Tactical Local Area Network [*Army*] .... FOTLAN
Fiber-Reinforced Advanced Titanium (MCD) .... FRAT
Fiber-Reinforced Ceramic Matrix Composite [*Organic chemistry*] ...... FRCMC
Fiber-Reinforced Composite .... FRC
Fiber-Reinforced Composite Junction .... FRCJ
Fiber-Reinforced Material .... FRM
Fiber-Reinforced Metal [*Materials science*] .... FRM
Fiber-Reinforced Polyethylene Terephthalate [*Glass*] .... FR-PET
Fiber-Reinforced Polymer Honeycomb .... FRPH
Fibers per Cubic Centimeter .... F/cc
Fiberstars, Inc. [*NASDAQ symbol*] (SAG) .... FBST
Fiberstars, Inc. [*Associated Press*] (SAG) .... Fibrstrs
Fiberstock [*Firearms*] .... FS
Fibertech Industries Corp. [*Formerly, Essex Petroleum Corp.*] [*Vancouver
   Stock Exchange symbol*] .... FBT
Fiber-to-the Feeder [*Telecommunications*] .... FTTF
Fibonacci Association (EA) .... FA
Fibonacci Benchmark Program [*Computer science*] (BYTE) .... FBP
Fibre [*Classification key in textile printing*] .... F
Fibre Box Association (EA) .... FBA
Fibre Building Board Development Organisation Ltd. [*British*] (BI) ...... FIDOR
Fibre Cement Manufacturers Association [*British*] (DBA) ...... FCMA
Fibre Distribution Frame [*Optics*] (EECA) .... FDF
Fibre Drum Manufacturers Association [*Defunct*] .... FDMA
Fibre Drum Technical Council (EA) .... FDTC
Fibre Optic Cable Assembly (NITA) .... FOCA
Fibre Optic Line Dividers (NITA) .... FOLD
Fibre Optic Local Area Network [*Telecommunications*] (PDAA) ...... FOLAN
Fibre Trade Federation [*British*] (BI) .... FTF
Fibreboard [*Freight*] .... FIBRD
Fibreboard and Wood [*Freight*] .... FB WD
Fibreboard Corp. [*AMEX symbol*] (CTT) .... FBD
Fibreboard Corp. [*AMEX symbol*] (TTSB) .... FBD
Fibreboard Corp. [*Associated Press*] (SAG) .... Fibrbd
Fibreboard Packing Case Employers' Association [*British*] (BI) ...... FPCEA
Fibreboard Packing Case Manufacturers' Association [*British*] (BI) ...... FPCMA
Fibre-Optics-Coupled Image Amplifier (PDAA) .... FOCIA
Fibrequest International Ltd. [*Formerly, Trawler Petroleum Explorations Ltd.*]
   [*Vancouver Stock Exchange symbol*] .... FBQ
Fibrillating Action Potential [*Neurophysiology*] .... FAP
Fibrillation [*Medicine*] .... fib
Fibrillation [*Medicine*] (DAVI) .... fibrill
Fibrin [*Hematology*] (DAVI) .... FIB
Fibrin Breakdown Products [*Hematology*] .... FBP
Fibrin [*or Fibrinogen*] Degradation Products [*Hematology*] ...... FDP
Fibrin Monomer [*Hematology*] (DAVI) .... FM
Fibrin [*or Fibrinolytic*] Split Products (DAVI) .... FSP
Fibrinogen [*Factor 1*] [*Hematology*] .... FBG
Fibrinogen [*Factor 1*] [*Hematology*] .... Fg
Fibrinogen [*Factor 1*] [*Hematology*] .... FIB
Fibrinogen [*Hematology*] (DAVI) .... FIBRGN
Fibrinogen [*Factor 1*] [*Hematology*] .... fibrin
Fibrinogen Breakdown Products [*Hematology*] (DAVI) .... FBP
Fibrinogen Derivative [*Hematology*] (AAMN) .... FD
Fibrinogen Equivalent [*Hematology*] .... FE
Fibrinogen Factor 1 [*Hematology*] (MAE) .... FI
Fibrinogen Qualitative Test [*Hematology*] (DAVI) .... F-Y
Fibrinogen-Related [*Hematology*] (DAVI) .... FR
Fibrinogen-Related Antigen [*Immunology*] .... FRA
Fibrinogen-Split Products [*Hematology*] .... FSP
Fibrinolytic Activity [*Hematology*] .... FA
Fibrinopeptide .... FP
Fibrinopeptide A [*Biochemistry*] .... FPA
Fibrinopeptide B [*Biochemistry*] .... FBP
Fibrino-Peptide B [*Biochemistry*] (DMAA) .... FPB
Fibrin-Stabilizing Factor [*Factor XIII*] [*Also, LLF Hematology*] ...... FSF
Fibrin-Stabilizing Factor [*Hematology*] (DAVI) .... LLF
Fibro Cement (ADA) .... FC
Fibroadenoma [*Oncology*] .... FA
Fibroblast [*Medicine*] .... FB
Fibroblast Activating Factor [*Biochemistry*] .... FAF
Fibroblast Growth Factor [*Cytochemistry*] .... FGF
Fibroblast Growth Factor Receptor [*Biochemistry*] .... FGFA
Fibroblast Growth-Factor Receptor [*Biochemistry*] .... FGFR
Fibroblast Interferon [*Genetics*] .... FIF
Fibroblast Pneumonocyte Factor [*Biochemistry*] .... FPF
Fibroblast Populated Collagen Matrix [*Biology*] .... FPCM
Fibroblast-Derived Growth Factor [*Medicine*] (DMAA) .... FDGE
Fibroblast-Like Cell [*Cytology*] .... FBLC
Fibroblast-Migration Inhibitory Factor [*Immunochemistry*] ...... FIF
Fibrocystic Breast Disease [*Medicine*] .... FBD
Fibrocystic Disease [*Medicine*] (DMAA) .... FCD
Fibrocystic Disease of the Breast [*Gynecology*] (DAVI) ...... FCDB
Fibrodysplasia Ossificans Progressiva [*Medicine*] .... FOP

Fibroelastic Connective Tissue [*Medicine*] .... FECT
Fibrolamellar Carcinoma [*Oncology*] .... FLC
Fibromuscular Dysplasia [*Medicine*] .... FMD
Fibromuscular Hyperplasia [*Medicine*] (DMAA) .... FH
Fibromuscular Hyperplasia [*Neurology*] (DAVI) .... FMH
Fibronectin [*Biochemistry*] .... FBN
Fibronectin [*Biochemistry*] .... FN
Fibron-Related [*Hematology*] (DAVI) .... FR
Fibrosarcoma [*Oncology*] .... FSa
Fibrosing Alveolitis [*Medicine*] (DMAA) .... FA
Fibrosing Interstitial Pneumonitis [*Medicine*] (CPH) .... FIB
Fibrositis [*Medicine*] .... FIB
Fibrous .... F
Fibrous .... FBRS
Fibrous Body-Membrane Organelle [*Biochemistry*] .... FBMO
Fibrous Long-Spacing Collagen .... FLS
Fibrous Material .... FM
Fibrous Plaster (ADA) .... FP
Fibrous Plasterboard .... FPBD
Fibrous Refractory Composite Insulation .... FRCI
Fibrous Sausage Casing .... FSC
Fibrous Tissue [*Medicine*] .... FT
Fibula [*Medicine*] .... FIB
Fiche Information Selectively Held and Retrieved on Demand [*Computer
   science*] (PDAA) .... FISHROD
Fichier de Recherches Automatisees sur les Nouvautes, la Communication
   et l'Information en Sciences Sociales et Humaines [*French Retrieval
   Automated Network for Current Information in Social and Human Sciences*]
   [*Database*] .... FRANCIS
Fichier MARC [*Machine-Readable Cataloging*] Quebecois [*Source file*]
   [*UTLAS symbol*] .... FMQ
Fichier National des Etablissements Sanitaires et Sociaux .... FINESS
Fichtel & Sachs [*Auto industry supplier*] [*German*] .... FS
Fick Diffusion Law .... FDL
Fickle Hill [*California*] [*Seismograph station code, US Geological Survey*]
   (SEIS) .... FHC
Ficksburg [*South Africa*] [*ICAO location identifier*] (ICLI) ...... FAFB
Ficoll-Hypaque [*Clinical hematology*] .... FH
Ficoll-Hypaque Centrifugation [*Medicine*] (DMAA) .... FHC
Fictilis [*Made of Pottery*] [*Latin*] .... FICT
Fiction .... F
Fiction .... FICT
Fiction International [*A publication*] (BRI) .... Fic Int
Fiction Magazine [*Generic term for a publication covering science
   fiction*] .... FICTIONZINE
Fictional (WDAA) .... FICT
Fictitious (WDAA) .... FICT
FIDAC [*Film Input to Digital Automatic Computer*] System (NITA) ...... FIDACSYS
Fide Bona [*In Good Faith*] [*Latin*] (ROG) .... FI B
Fidei Commissum [*Bequeathed in Trust*] [*Latin*] .... FC
Fidei Defensor [*Defender of the Faith*] [*Latin*] .... FD
Fidei Defensor [*Defender of the Faith*] [*Latin*] (ROG) .... FID DEF
Fidelco [*Fidelity Cooperative*] Guide Dog Foundation (EA) ...... FGDF
Fidelity (WGA) .... FID
Fidelity .... FIDLTY
Fidelity Advisor Emer'g Asia [*NYSE symbol*] (TTSB) .... FAE
Fidelity Advisor Emerging Asia Fund [*NYSE symbol*] (SAG) ...... FAE
Fidelity Advisor Emerging Asia Fund [*Associated Press*] (SAG) ...... FAEmA
Fidelity Advisor Emerging Asia Fund [*Associated Press*] (SAG) ...... FAEmAs
Fidelity Advisor Korea Fund [*Associated Press*] (SAG) ...... FA Korea
Fidelity Advisor Korea Fund [*NYSE symbol*] (SAG) .... FAK
Fidelity Bancorp [*NASDAQ symbol*] (SAG) .... FBCI
Fidelity Bancorp [*Associated Press*] (SAG) .... FidBcp
Fidelity Bancorp [*Associated Press*] (SAG) .... FidBnCh
Fidelity Bancorp [*NASDAQ symbol*] (SAG) .... FSBI
Fidelity Bond [*Business term*] .... FB
Fidelity Fed Bancorp [*NASDAQ symbol*] (TTSB) .... FFED
Fidelity Federal Bancorp [*NASDAQ symbol*] (NQ) .... FFED
Fidelity Federal Bancorp [*Associated Press*] (SAG) .... FidFdB
Fidelity Federal Savings Bank [*NASDAQ symbol*] (SAG) ...... FFFL
Fidelity Federal Savings Bank (MHDW) .... FFMA
Fidelity Federal Savings Bank [*NASDAQ symbol*] (NQ) .... FFRV
Fidelity Federal Savings Bank [*Associated Press*] (SAG) ...... FidFdlSv
Fidelity Fedl Svgs Bk Fla [*NASDAQ symbol*] (TTSB) .... FFFL
Fidelity Financial Bankshares Corp. [*NASDAQ symbol*] (SAG) ...... FFRV
Fidelity Financial Bankshares Corp. [*Associated Press*] (SAG) ...... FidFnVA
Fidelity Financial Corp. [*Associated Press*] (SAG) .... FidelFin
Fidelity Financial Corp. [*NYSE symbol*] (SAG) .... FNF
Fidelity Financial of Ohio, Inc. [*Associated Press*] (SAG) ...... FedFOH
Fidelity Financial of Ohio, Inc. [*NASDAQ symbol*] (SAG) ...... FFOH
Fidelity Finl Bancshares [*NASDAQ symbol*] (TTSB) .... FFRV
Fidelity Finl Ohio [*NASDAQ symbol*] (TTSB) .... FFOH
Fidelity FSB [*Associated Press*] (SAG) .... FidFdVA
Fidelity [*to Living Condition*] Index [*Botany*] .... FI
Fidelity Mutual Life Insurance Co., Philadelphia, PA [*Library symbol Library
   of Congress*] (LCLS) .... PPFML
Fidelity National [*NASDAQ symbol*] (TTSB) .... LION
Fidelity National Corp. [*Associated Press*] (SAG) .... FidelNtl
Fidelity National Corp. [*NASDAQ symbol*] (SAG) .... LION
Fidelity Natl Finl [*NYSE symbol*] (TTSB) .... FNF
Fidelity Online Express [*Trading and investment tracking program*] (PCM) ...... FOX
Fidelity Trust Co. [*Toronto Stock Exchange symbol*] .... FDT
Fidelity Union Life Insurance Co. .... FULICO
Fidelity Union Trust Co. (MHDB) .... FUTC
Fidell's Precedents [*A publication*] (DLA) .... FI

Fides [*Faith*] [*Latin*] (ROG) .... FID
Fiducial Automated Measuring Machine [*Defunct*] .... FAMM
Fiduciary (ADA) .... FID
Fiduciary Activity Simulation Training [*Investment banking simulation game*] .... FAST
Fiduciary Identification Number [*IRS*] .... FIN
Fiduciary Law Chronicle [*A publication*] (DLA) .... Fid L Chron
Fiduciary Reporter [*Pennsylvania*] [*A publication*] (DLA) .... Fiduc Rep
Fiduciary Reporter [*Pennsylvania*] [*A publication*] (DLA) .... Fiduciary
Fiduciary Reporter [*Pennsylvania*] [*A publication*] (DLA) .... Fiduciary R (PA)
Fiduciary Reporter [*Pennsylvania*] [*A publication*] (DLA) .... Fiduciary Rptr
Field .... F
Field .... FD
Field [*Commonly used*] (OPSA) .... FIELD
Field .... FLD
Field [*Computer science*] (AFM) .... FLD
Field Accelerating Contactor or Relay [*Industrial control*] (IEEE) .... FA
Field Accelerator .... FAC
Field Action Unit (AEBS) .... FAU
Field Activities .... F/A
Field Activity Missile (MCD) .... FAM
Field Activity Missile Engineering (MCD) .... FAME
Field Activity Report .... FAR
Field Activity Squadron [*Air Force*] .... FLDACTYSq
Field Activity War and Emergency Support Plan [*DoD*] (MCD) .... FAWESP
Field Activity War Emergency Program [*DoD*] .... FAWEP
Field Address .... FA
Field Advisory Element (CINC) .... FAE
Field Aircraft Services Ltd. [*British ICAO designator*] (FAAC) .... FAS
Field Alert Status [*Army*] (AABC) .... FAS
Field Alert Status Verification [*Army*] (MCD) .... FASV
Field Allowance [*British military*] (DMA) .... FA
Field Alterable Control Element (MDG) .... FACE
Field Ambulance [*British military*] (DMA) .... F Amb
Field Ambulance [*Military*] .... FA
Field Ambulance [*British military*] (DMA) .... Fld Amb
Field Analysis Report .... FAR
Field and Dunn's Chancery Practice [*A publication*] (DLA) .... Field & D Ch Pr
Field and Game Federation of Australia .... FGFA
Field and Reservoir Reserve Estimate [*US Geological Survey*] .... FRRE
Field Application Engineer (IEEE) .... FAE
Field Application Panel (IEEE) .... FAP
Field Army .... FA
Field Army Air Defense System (MCD) .... FAADS
Field Army Ballistic Missile Defense System [*Later, AADS*] [*Antimissile missile*] .... FABMDS
Field Army Ballistic Missile Defense System [*Later, AADS*] [*Antimissile missile*] .... FABMIDS
Field Army Calibration Team Support .... FACTS
Field Army Communication System (AABC) .... FACS
Field Army Guided Missile (IAA) .... FAGM
Field Army Guided Missile System - Sergeant (SAA) .... FAGMS-S
Field Army Issuing Office .... FAIO
Field Army Messenger Service (AABC) .... FAMS
Field Army Petroleum Office (AABC) .... FAPO
Field Army Replacement System (AABC) .... FARS
Field Army Service Area (AABC) .... FASA
Field Army Support Command .... FASCOM
Field Army Tactical Operation Center .... FATOC
Field Army Tactical Random Access Communications System .... FATRACS
Field Artillery .... FA
Field Artillery Acoustic Locating System (MCD) .... FAALS
Field Artillery Aerial Observer .... FAAO
Field Artillery Airborne .... FAA
Field Artillery Ammunition Support Vehicle .... FAASV
Field Artillery Brigade (AABC) .... FAB
Field Artillery Cannon Basic Officer's Course [*Army*] .... FACBOC
Field Artillery CATT [*Army*] (RDA) .... FACATT
Field Artillery Computer Equipment .... FACE
Field Artillery Digital Automatic Computer (IEEE) .... FADAC
Field Artillery Fire Support Team [*Army*] (RDA) .... FIST
Field Artillery Group .... FLDARTYGRU
Field Artillery Guided Missile [*Air Force*] .... FAGMS
Field Artillery Intelligence Officer [*Military*] (AABC) .... FAIO
Field Artillery Logic Tester [*Army*] (AABC) .... FALT
Field Artillery Meteorological Acquisition System (MCD) .... FAMAS
Field Artillery Missile .... FAM
Field Artillery Missile System (RDA) .... FAMS
Field Artillery Missile Systems Evaluation Group (RDA) .... FAMSEG
Field Artillery Officer Advanced Course [*Military*] (INF) .... FAOAC
Field Artillery RADAR Crewman (IAA) .... FARDRCRM
Field Artillery Replacement Center .... FARC
Field Artillery Rocket (MCD) .... FAR
Field Artillery School (MCD) .... FAS
Field Artillery Survey Knowledge Acquisition Program [*Army*] .... FASKAP
Field Artillery Survey Team .... FAST
Field Artillery Survey Test (MCD) .... FAST
Field Artillery System [*Army*] (RDA) .... FAS
Field Artillery System Training Fire Direction Centers (MCD) .... FASTFIRE
Field Artillery System Training for the Common Battalion Command and Control System (MCD) .... FASTBACCS
Field Artillery System Training for the Fire Support Officer (MCD) .... FASTSUPPORT
Field Artillery Tactical Data Systems [*Army*] (RDA) .... FATDS
Field Artillery Target Acquisition Battalion [*Army*] (AABC) .... FATAB
Field Artillery Target Acquisition Group [*Army*] (AABC) .... FATAG
Field Artillery Tractor [*British*] .... FAT
Field Artillery Training Centre [*British military*] (DMA) .... FATC
Field Artillery Turret Maintenance Simulator (MCD) .... FATMS
Field Artillery Turret Maintenance Trainer (MCD) .... FATMAT
Field Assembly Test Point (IAA) .... FATP
Field Assessment Officer [*Military*] (AEBS) .... FAO
Field Assessment Review [*Military*] .... FAR
Field Assistance in Science and Technology Program [*US Army Materiel Command*] .... FAST
Field Assistance Support Team (MCD) .... FAST
Field Assistance Support Team for Calibration (DOMA) .... FASTCAL
Field Asymmetry Sensing Technique .... FAST
Field Audit [*IRS*] .... FA
Field Audit and Completion Test [*Market research*] .... FACT
Field Audit Office .... FAO
Field Automated Intelligence File (AFM) .... FAIF
Field Aviation GmbH & Co. [*Germany ICAO designator*] (FAAC) .... FIE
Field Aviation Supply Office .... FASO
Field Bake Oven [*Military*] .... FBO
Field Base Visit (NASA) .... FBV
Field Branch .... FLDBR
Field Branch, Bureau of Medicine and Surgery [*Navy*] (DNAB) .... FLDBRBUMED
Field Broadcasting Unit (IAA) .... FBU
Field by Information Blending and Smoothing [*Marine science*] (OSRA) .... FIBS
Field by Information Blending and Smoothing (USDC) .... FIBS
Field Cable Installation Platoon [*Army*] (AABC) .... FCIP
Field Camera .... FC
Field Camera Control .... FCC
Field Carrier Landing Passes [*or Practice*] .... FCLP
Field Cashier Military Accounts [*British military*] (DMA) .... FCMA
Field Challenge Test Plan .... FCTP
Field Champion [*Dog show term*] .... FCh
Field Champion [*Dog show term*] .... FldCH
Field Change .... FC
Field Change Analysis .... FCA
Field Change Authorization [*Nuclear energy*] (NRCH) .... FCA
Field Change Control Board .... FCCB
Field Change Identification Guide (IAA) .... FCIG
Field Change Kit .... FCK
Field Change Notification (KSC) .... FCN
Field Change Order .... FCO
Field Change Package [*Nuclear energy*] (NRCH) .... FCP
Field Change Proposal .... FCP
Field Change Request [*Nuclear energy*] (NRCH) .... FCR
Field Checkout Equipment .... FCE
Field Circular [*Military*] (INF) .... FC
Field Command [*Military*] .... FC
Field Command, Defense Atomic Support Agency .... FC/DASA
Field Command, Defense Atomic Support Agency (AABC) .... FLDCOMDASA
Field Command, Defense Nuclear Agency [*DoD*] .... FCDNA
Field Command, Defense Nuclear Agency [*DoD*] (AABC) .... FLDCOMDNA
Field Command Post .... FCP
Field Communication Unit [*Military*] .... FCU
Field Company [*British military*] (DMA) .... F Co
Field Computer Test Set .... FTS
Field Concept Evolution and Trials [*Army*] .... FCE & T
Field Condition Report [*Aviation*] (FAAC) .... FCRP
Field Configuration Control Board [*Army*] (AABC) .... FCCB
Field Contactor (IAA) .... FC
Field Contract Administration Division [*of ONM*] .... FCAD
Field Contracting Office (MCD) .... FCO
Field Control Center .... FCC
Field Control Division [*Military*] (LAIN) .... FCD
Field Controlled Thyristor [*Electronics*] .... FCST
Field Controller Component (MCD) .... FCC
Field Conversion [*Computer science*] (ECII) .... FC
Field Cook [*Marine Corps*] .... FLDCK
Field Cook (Baker) [*Marine Corps*] .... FLDCK(B)
Field Cook (Commissary) [*Marine Corps*] .... FLDCK(C)
Field Cooled .... FC
Field Coordination Group .... FCG
Field Crop Advisory Committee [*Western Australia*] .... FCAC
Field Crops Branch, Alberta Agriculture, Lacombe, Alberta [*Library symbol National Library of Canada*] (NLC) .... ALAAF
Field Data Acquisition System (DWSG) .... FDAS
Field Data Applications, Systems, and Techniques [*Computer science*] .... FAST
Field Data Computer .... FDC
Field Data Description Language (NITA) .... FDDL
Field Data Processing .... FDP
Field Decelerating Contactor or Relay [*Industrial control*] (IEEE) .... FD
Field Decelerator .... FDE
Field Definition (IAA) .... FD
Field Definition Record (IAA) .... FDR
Field Definition Table (IAA) .... FDT
Field Dependence/Independence (EDAC) .... FD/I
Field Depot Aviation Squadron [*Air Force*] .... FDAS
Field Depot Veterinary Stores [*British military*] (DMA) .... FDVS
Field Descriptor Block .... FDB
Field Designator Number [*Air Force*] (AFM) .... FDN
Field Desorption .... FD
Field Desorption - Mass Spectrometry .... FD-MS
Field Developed Programs [*Computer science*] .... FDPS
Field Development Program [*LIMRA*] .... FDP
Field Development Test and Evaluation (MCD) .... FDT & E

Field Deviation Disposition Request [*Nuclear energy*] (NRCH) ...... FDDR
Field Director .... FD
Field Director Indicator (OA) .... FDI
Field Director Overseas [*Red Cross*] .... FDO
Field Discharge .... FDI
Field Discharge Chip .... FDC
Field Displacement Isolator .... FDI
Field Disposition Instruction [*Nuclear energy*] (NRCH) ...... FDI
Field Division [*Census*] (OICC) .... FLD
Field Drainage Experimental Unit (PDAA) ...... FDEU
Field Dressing Station [*Military*] (NATG) ... FDS
Field Dynamic Braking .... FDB
Field Effect Amplifier .... FEA
Field Effect Device .... FED
Field Effect Diode (IAA) .... FED
Field Effect Thyristor (IAA) .... FETH
Field Effect Transistor .... FET
Field Electron Emission Microscope [*or Microscopy*] ...... FEEM
Field Electron Microscope [*or Microscopy*] .. FEM
Field Electronic Maintenance Section [*National Weather Service*] ...... FEMS
Field Emission [*Physics*] .... FE
Field Emission Deposition [*Coating technique*] ...... FED
Field Emission Display .... FED
Field Emission Microscope [*or Microscopy*] .. FEM
Field Emission Scanning Electron Microscopy .. FESEM
Field Emission Spectroscopy .... FES
Field Emitting Surface .... FES
Field Engineer [*or Engineering*] .... FE
Field Engineer Control System (PDAA) .... FECONS
Field Engineering and Equipment [*Military*] . FEE
Field Engineering Assistance Request (MCD) ... FEAR
Field Engineering Bulletin .... FEB
Field Engineering Bureau [*FCC*] (NTCM) ...... FEB
Field Engineering Change (KSC) .... FEC
Field Engineering Change Proposal .... FECP
Field Engineering Instruction [*British*] (DA) ...... FEI
Field Engineering Maintenance .... FEM
Field Engineering Order (KSC) .... FEO
Field Engineering Representative .... FER
Field Engineering Service .... FES
Field Engineering Theory of Operations .... FETO
Field Enterprises Educational Corp. [*Later, World Book-Childcraft International, Inc.*] ...... FEEC
Field Entry Standard [*Military*] (ADDR) ..... FES
Field Epidemiological Survey Team [*Army*] (LAIN) ...... FEST
Field Error Correction (MCD) .... FEC
Field Evaluation Agency [*Army*] .... FEA
Field Evaluation Model .... FEM
Field Exchange [*Computer science*] (PCM) .... FX
Field Excitatory Postsynaptic Potential [*Neurophysiology*] ...... FEPSP
Field Exercise [*Military*] (NVT) .... FEX
Field Exercise [*Military*] (MCD) .... FX
Field Exercise Data Collection [*Army*] (RDA) . FEDC
Field Exercise under Snow Conditions [*Military*] (NVT) ...... SNOWFLEX
Field Expedient (AABC) .... FE
Field Experimenter Detection [*or Detector*] Survivability (MCD) ...... FEDS
Field Exploitation of Elevation Data (RDA) ... FEED
Field Exploration Library, Inco Ltd., Copper Cliff, Ontario [*Library symbol National Library of Canada*] (NLC) ...... OOCIFE
Field Extension Office [*DoD*] .... FEO
Field Failure (AAG) .... FFL
Field Failure Voltage (IEEE) .... FFV
Field File (LAIN) .... FF
Field Firing Exercise [*Military*] (NVT) ..... FFEX
Field Flight Plan .... FPL
Field Focusing Nuclear Magnetic Resonance .... FONAR
Field Force, Vietnam (CINC) .... FFORCEV
Field Force, Vietnam .... FFV
Field Forces [*Military*] .... FF
Field Forcing (Decreasing) .... FFD
Field Forcing (Increasing) .... FFI
Field Forcing, Protective (IAA) .... FFP
Field Forcing, Reversing (IAA) .... FFR
Field Format .... FF
Field Format Index Reference Number .... FFIRN
Field Format Name .... FFN
Field Fresnel Lens Optical Platform .... FFLOP
Field Function [*Telecommunications*] (TEL) .. FF
Field Functional System Assembly and Checkout ...... FFSA
Field Functional System Assembly and Checkout (KSC) ...... FFSA & C
Field Functional Systems Assembly and Checkout (IAA) ...... FFSAC
Field Gain (IAA) .... FG
Field General Court-Martial .... FGCM
Field Goal [*Football, basketball*] .... FG
Field Goals Attempted [*Football, basketball*] ...... FA
Field Goals Attempted [*Football, basketball*] ...... FGA
Field Goals Made [*Football, basketball*] .... FGM
Field Goals Missed [*Football, basketball*] .. M
Field Grade .... FG
Field Gun .... FG
Field Handler (MHDB) .... FH
Field Handling Design Objective .... FHDO
Field Handling Trainer [*Army*] (INF) .... FHT
Field Hockey Association of America (EA) ...... FHAA
Field Hospital [*British military*] (DMA) .... FH

Field Howitzer [*British military*] (DMA) .... FH
Field Identifier [*Computer science*] .... FID
Field Image Feature Interface [*Photovoltaic energy systems*] ...... FIFI
Field Impact Insulation Class (DAC) .... FIIC
Field Imprisonment [*British military*] (DMA) ...... F Imp
Field Incident Radio System [*Nuclear energy*] (NRCH) ...... FIRS
Field Independent (EDAC) .... FI
Field Information Agency, Technical [*Under G-2, SHAEF*] ...... FIAT
Field Information Release (MCD) .... FIR
Field Information Report [*CIA*] .... FIR
Field Information System [*Computer science*] ...... FIS
Field Infrared Spectrometer .... FIS
Field Input/Output [*Computer science*] (ECII) ...... FIO
Field Insertion Unit [*Rational, California*] (NITA) ...... FIU
Field Inspection Manual (NRCH) .... FIM
Field Inspection Procedure (NRCH) .... FIP
Field Installation and Test .... FIT
Field Installation Branch Adaption Section (SAA) ...... FIBAS
Field Installation Branch Control Section (SAA) ...... FIBCS
Field Installation Change Order (MCD) .... FICO
Field Installation Simulator .... FIS
Field Installation Time (IAA) .... FIT
Field Installed Connector .... FIC
Field Instruction Memorandum .... FIM
Field Instruction System .... FIS
Field Instrumentation Division (SAA) .... FID
Field Integration Engineering Test (MCD) ..... FIET
Field Intelligence Department .... FID
Field Intelligence Non-Commissioned Officer [*British military*] (DMA) ...... FINCO
Field Intelligence Officer [*British military*] (DMA) ...... FIO
Field Intelligence Simulation Test (NATG) .... FIST
Field Intelligence Unit (MUGU) .... FIU
Field Intensity .... FI
Field Intensity Measuring System .... FIMS
Field Intensity Meter .... FIM
Field Intensity Receiver .... FIR
Field Interview .... FI
Field Inversion Gel Electrophoresis [*Analytical biochemistry*] ...... FIGE
Field Investigation Team [*Environmental Protection Agency*] (ERG) ...... FIT
Field Ion Microscope [*or Microscopy*] .... FIM
Field Ionization .... FI
Field Ionization Kinetics .... FIK
Field Ionization Mass Spectrometry [*Air-pollutant detector*] ...... FIMS
Field Ion-Scanning Tunneling Microscopy ...... FI-STM
Field Item (DNAB) .... FI
Field Judge [*Football*] .... FJ
Field Kitchen Trailer (MCD) .... FKT
Field Landing Practice .... FLP
Field Length .... FL
Field Length (IAA) .... FLDL
Field Length Condition Register (MHDB) .... FLCN
Field Length for Small Core Memory (IAA) ..... FLS
Field Level Repair (NVT) .... FLR
Field Level Training .... FLT
Field Liaison Division [*Military*] .... FLD
Field Library, Inc., Peekskill, NY [*Library symbol Library of Congress*] (LCLS) ...... NPee
Field Logistics Center, Navy Joint United States Military Assistance Group (DNAB) ...... FLCNAVJUSMAG
Field Loss Contactor or Relay [*Industrial control*] (IEEE) ...... FL
Field Loss Relay .... FLR
Field Magnet (ROG) .... FM
Field Main (AAG) .... FM
Field Maintenance (MCD) .... FM
Field Maintenance Activity (MCD) .... FMA
Field Maintenance Bulletin [*Army*] .... FMB
Field Maintenance Equipment [*Military*] ..... FME
Field Maintenance Party [*Aviation*] .... FMP
Field Maintenance Request .... FMR
Field Maintenance Shop [*Army*] (AABC) .... FLDMS
Field Maintenance Shop [*Army*] (NATG) .... FMS
Field Maintenance Squadron [*Air Force*] ..... FLDMAINTSq
Field Maintenance Squadron [*Air Force*] (MCD) ...... FMS
Field Maintenance Squadron [*Air Force*] (AFM) ...... FMSq
Field Maintenance System .... FMS
Field Maintenance Technician .... FMT
Field Maintenance Test Equipment .... FMTE
Field Maintenance Test Set .... FMTS
Field Maintenance Test Station [*Military*] (AFIT) ...... FMTS
Field Management Information System (AAGC) .... FMIS
Field Manual [*Military*] .... FM
Field Manufacture (AFIT) .... FM
Field Marching Pack .... FMP
Field Marshal .... FM
Field Marshal Commanding-in-Chief [*British military*] (DMA) ...... FMC-in-C
Field Materiel-Handling Robot Technology [*US Army Human Engineering Laboratory*] (RDA) ...... FMR-T
Field Medical Card [*Army*] (AABC) .... FMC
Field Medical Oxygen Generation/Distribution System (DOMA) ...... FMOGDS
Field Medical Service School (DNAB) .... FLDMEDSERVSCOL
Field Memorandum .... FM
Field Mirror Landing Practice .... FMLP
Field Missile Maintenance Squadron [*Air Force*] ...... FLDMSLMAINTSq
Field Missile Maintenance Squadron [*Air Force*] ...... FMMS
Field Missile Specification Test .... FMST

Field Missile System Test	FMST
Field Modification (AAG)	FM
Field Modification Report	FMR
Field Modification Request [Military]	FMR
Field Modification Task (MCD)	FMT
Field Moist Soil [Agronomy]	FM
Field Museum of Natural History [Chicago, IL]	FMNH
Field Museum of Natural History, Chicago, IL [OCLC symbol] (OCLC)	IBT
Field Museum of Natural History, Chicago, IL [Library symbol Library of Congress] (LCLS)	ICF
Field Museum of Natural History, Edward E. Ayer Ornithological Library, Chicago,IL [Library symbol Library of Congress] (LCLS)	ICF-A
Field Music [Marine Corps]	FM
Field Music Corporal [Marine Corps]	FMCORP
Field Music Corporal [Marine Corps]	FMCPL
Field Music School [Marine Corps]	FMS
Field Music Sergeant [Marine Corps]	FMSGT
Field Network Evaluation Study [Survey]	FNES
Field Observing Facility [National Center for Atmospheric Research]	FOF
Field Observing Support Facility [National Center for Atmospheric Research]	FOSF
Field of Drawing (AAG)	FD
Field of Fire [Military] (AABC)	F of F
Field of Fire [Military] (MCD)	FOF
Field of Regard	FOR
Field of Science (EERA)	FOS
Field of Science [Dialog] [Searchable field] [Information service or system] (NITA)	FS
Field of View [or Vision]	FOV
Field of Vision [Medicine]	F
Field of Vision Intact [Ophthalmology] (DAVI)	FOVI
Field Office [or Officer]	FO
Field Office Assistant [Red Cross]	FOA
Field Office Reporting-Management System [HUD]	FORMS
Field Office Sales and Service Costs Study [LIMRA]	FOSSCS
Field Officer	FLDO
Field Officer of the Day [Army] (AABC)	FOD
Field Officers School [Formerly, AOS] [LIMRA]	FOS
Field Oil Identification Laboratory [Marine science] (MSC)	FOIL
Field on Corporations [A publication] (DLA)	Field Corp
Field on Private Corporations [A publication] (DLA)	Field Pr Cor
Field on Protestant Curates and Incumbents [A publication] (DLA)	Field Cur
Field on the Common Law of England [A publication] (DLA)	Field Com Law
Field on the Hindu and Mohammedan Laws of Inheritance [A publication] (DLA)	Field on Inh
Field on the Law of Damages [A publication] (DLA)	Field Dam
Field Online Data Acquisition and Analysis System	FODAAS
Field Operating Activity (AAGC)	FOA
Field Operating Agencies [Air Force] (DOMA)	FOAS
Field Operating Agency (MCD)	FOA
Field Operating Cost Agency [Army]	FOCA
Field Operational [Test] (NATG)	FO
Field Operational Evaluation	FOE
Field Operations and Support Division [Environmental Protection Agency]	FOSD
Field Operations Bureau [FCC] (NTCM)	FOB
Field Operations Department	FOD
Field Operations Division (AAGC)	FOD
Field Operations Division (EERA)	FOD
Field Operations Group	FOG
Field Operations Intelligence	FOI
Field Operations Manual	FOM
Field Operations Memorandum	FOM
Field Order	FO
Field Ordering Officer [Army] (RDA)	FOO
Field Pack, Large, with Internal Frame [Army] (INF)	FPLIF
Field Personnel Record	FPERR
Field Personnel Record	FPR
Field Petroleum Corp. [Vancouver Stock Exchange symbol]	FPC
Field Placement Officer	FPO
Field Plated Diode (PDAA)	FPD
Field Post Office [Military British]	FDPO
Field Post Office [Military British]	FPO
Field Potential [Neuroelectricity]	FP
Field Power Supply	FPS
Field Presence Indicator	FPI
Field Press Censorship	FPC
Field Printing Squadron	FPS
Field Processing Language (IAA)	FPL
Field Profit Analysis	FPA
Field Programmable Gate Array [Computer science]	FPGA
Field Programmable Logic Array [Computer science]	FPLA
Field Programmable Logic Family (TEL)	FPLF
Field Programmable Logic Sequencer [Computer science] (HGAA)	FPLS
Field Programmable Read-Only Memory [Computer science] (EECA)	FROM
Field Project Officer	FPO
Field Protective (AAG)	FP
Field Punishment [Military]	FP
Field Quality Audit (IAA)	FQA
Field Rations (DNAB)	FLD RATS
Field Record Group [Air Force] (AFM)	FRGp
Field Records Administration Microform Mode	FRAM2
Field Reference Scene Equipment (MCD)	FIRSE
Field Relay (IAA)	FR
Field Remount Depot [British military] (DMA)	FRD
Field Repairable - Expendable Rotor Blade (RDA)	FREB
Field Replaceable Unit [IBM Corp.]	FRU
Field Report	FR
Field Representative Europe	FRE
Field Representative Far East	FRFE
Field Requirements List	FRL
Field Research Division [Marine science] (OSRA)	FRD
Field Research Facility [Army]	FRF
Field Reset Device [Army]	FRD
Field Reset Device [Army]	FRED
Field Resistance (DEN)	FR
Field Retrofit (MCD)	FR
Field Reversed Configuration	FRC
Field Reversed Mirror (MCD)	FRM
Field Reversing (AAG)	FR
Field Review Group [Army] (RDA)	FRG
Field Safety Activity (MCD)	FSA
Field Safety Agency (MCD)	FSA
Field Security [British Army detective police - a branch of Intelligence]	FS
Field Security Officer [Military]	FSO
Field Security Personnel	FSP
Field Security Police	FSP
Field Select Command Register	FSCR
Field Select Unit	FSU
Field Selection Board [Military]	FSB
Field Separator	FS
Field Sequential (IAA)	FS
Field Sequential System [Military] (IAA)	FSS
Field Service	FS
Field Service Addition (MCD)	FSA
Field Service Bulletin (AAG)	FSB
Field Service Engineer [Military]	FSE
Field Service Engineering (AAG)	FSER
Field Service Manual [British military] (DMA)	FSM
Field Service Marching Order [British military] (DMA)	FSMO
Field Service Modification Work Order	FSMWO
Field Service Operations (NATG)	FSO
Field Service Pocket Book [British military] (DMA)	FSPB
Field Service Regulations [Army]	FSR
Field Service Report	FSR
Field Service Representative (AFM)	FSR
Field Service Section [Military]	FSS
Field Service Support Group [USMC] (MCD)	FSSG
Field Service Technical Report (AAG)	FSTR
Field Service Technician (MCD)	FST
Field Service Trouble Report	FSTRE
Field Service Worker [Social Services] (DAVI)	FSW
Field Signal Battalion (IAA)	FSIGBN
Field Site Facility	FSF
Field Sound Transmission Class (DAC)	FSTC
Field Sparrow [Ornithology]	FS
Field Spectrometer System (MCD)	FSS
Field Standard Weight and Force System (AAG)	FSWFS
Field Station	FS
Field Station Materiel Requirements	FSMR
Field Storage List (MCD)	FSL
Field Storage Unit [Military]	FSU
Field Strength Meter	FSM
Field Strength Radio	FSR
Field Studies Council [British] (ARC)	FSC
Field Study Coordinator [Military] (MCD)	FSC
Field Suitability Test	FST
Field Supply and Maintenance Analysis Office (DNAB)	FSMAO
Field Supply Group	FSG
Field Supply Technician (MCD)	FST
Field Support Activity [Military] (DNAB)	FLDSUPPACT
Field Support Activity [Military] (NVT)	FSA
Field Support Center [Military] (IAA)	FSC
Field Support Diagram (IAA)	FSD
Field Support Engineering	FSE
Field Support Equipment [Military]	FSE
Field Support System	FSS
Field Support Test Equipment	FSTE
Field Surgical Team [Military British]	FST
Field Survey Association (BARN)	FSA
Field Survey Company [British military] (DMA)	FSC
Field Survey Team	FST
Field Switch (IAA)	FS
Field Switch	FSW
Field Tactical Trainer [Army] (INF)	FTT
Field Target Screen	FTS
Field Team Bulletin [Military] (CINC)	FTB
Field Technical Authority (NVT)	FTA
Field Technical Training Unit (MCD)	FTTU
Field Terminated Diode [Electronics]	FTD
Field Test (AAG)	FT
Field Test Administration (AAG)	FTA
Field Test Exercise [Military]	FTX
Field Test Kit	FTK
Field Test Office (MCD)	FTO
Field Test Operational Procedures [Aerospace] (AAG)	FTP
Field Test Operations [Aerospace] (KSC)	FTO
Field Test Operations Support [Aerospace] (AAG)	FTOS
Field Test Program [Aerospace] (IAA)	FTP
Field Test Support [Aerospace] (AAG)	FTS

Field Testing and Development Center .... FTDC
Field to Advise [Telecommunications] (TEL) .... FTA
Field Torpedo Unit .... FTU
Field Township Public Library, Ontario [Library symbol National Library of
  Canada] (NLC) .... OFT
Field Training [AFROTC] (AFM) .... FT
Field Training Command [Military] .... FTC
Field Training Detachment [Program] [Air Force] .... FTD
Field Training Equipment Concentration Site [Army] (AABC) .... FTECS
Field Training Exercise [Army] (INF) .... FTX
Field Training Feedback Components (MCD) .... FTFC
Field Training Flight (MCD) .... FTF
Field Training Group [Military] .... FLDTG
Field Training Services [Army] (AABC) .... FTS
Field Training Squadron .... FLDTS
Field Training Team [Military] (CINC) .... FTT
Field Trains .... FLDTNS
Field Trains Command Post [Army] (INF) .... FTCP
Field Transfer Charge-Coupled Device [Instrumentation] .... FTCCD
Field Transfusion Unit [Military British] .... FTU
Field Transport Pack (DNAB) .... FTP
Field Trial Champion [Sporting dogs] (IIA) .... FTC
Field Trip .... FT
Field Turn-Around Time (MCD) .... FTAT
Field Validation Test .... FVT
Field Verification Test Set (MCD) .... FVTS
Field Weakening .... FW
Field Weakening .... FWK
Field Weld (NRCH) .... FW
Field Winding [Electromagnetism] (IAA) .... FW
Field Wire Command Link [Army] (AABC) .... FWCL
Field Work Performance Report .... FWPR
Field Worship [Army British] .... FW
Field-Activated Promotion [Marketing] (DOAD) .... FAP
Fieldair Freight Ltd. [New Zealand] [ICAO designator] (FAAC) .... FLD
Fieldale, VA [AM radio station call letters] .... WODY
Field-Aligned Irregularity (MCD) .... FAI
Field-Collected Aster Yellows [Plant pathology] .... FAY
Field-Controlled Thyristor [Electronics] (IAA) .... FCT
Fieldcrest Cannon [NYSE symbol] (TTSB) .... FLD
Fieldcrest Cannon [NASDAQ symbol] (SAG) .... FLDC
Fieldcrest Cannon [Associated Press] (SAG) .... Fldcrst
Fieldcrest Cannon $3 Cv [NASDAQ symbol] (TTSB) .... FLDCP
Fieldcrest Cannon, Inc. [NYSE symbol] (SPSG) .... FLD
Fieldcrest Cannon, Inc. [Associated Press] (SAG) .... Fldcrst
Fielded Aircraft System .... FAS
Fielded Software Control Board [Army] .... FSCB
Fielded Software Support Center .... FSSC
Fielded System Review .... FSR
Field-Effect Modified (IEEE) .... FEM
Field-Effect Tetrode Transistor [Electronics] (OA) .... FETT
Field-Effect Transistor Volt Meter [Electronics] (DICI) .... FETVM
Field-Effect Transistor Volt-Ohm-Milliammeter (IDOE) .... FET VOM
Field-Effect-Transistor-Capacitor [Electronics] (PDAA) .... FETC
Field-Emission Display (ECON) .... FED
Field-Emitter Referenced Electron Spectroscopy for Chemical
  Analysis .... FRESCA
Field-Enhanced Secondary Emission .... FESE
Fielder's Choice [Baseball] .... FC
Field-Flow Fractionation [Chemical separation method] .... FFF
Field-Free Emission Current .... FFEC
Field-Gradient Voltage (PDAA) .... FGV
Field-Induced Delay [Astrophysics] .... FID
Field-Induced Negative Ion Formation .... FINIF
Field-Induced Spin Density Wave [Physics] .... FISDW
Fielding Average [Baseball] .... FA
Fielding Institute, Santa Barbara, CA [Library symbol Library of Congress]
  (LCLS) .... CStbF
Field-Koros-Noves [Physical chemistry] .... FKN
Field-of-Interest Register [DoD] .... FOIR
Field-Programmable Interconnect Component [Computer science] .... FPIC
Field-Programmable Logic Element [Military] .... FPLE
Field-Programmable Read-Only Memory [Computer science] (MCD) .... F-PROM
Fields [Commonly used] (OPSA) .... FIELDS
Fields [Postal Service standard] (OPSA) .... FLDS
Fields .... FLDS
Field's Analysis of Blackstone's Commentaries [A publication] (DLA) .... Field Anal
Field's International Code [A publication] (DLA) .... Field Int Code
Field's Law of Evidence in British India [A publication] (DLA) .... Field Ev
Field's Penal Law [A publication] (DLA) .... Field Pen L
Fields Point [Washington] [Seismograph station code, US Geological Survey]
  (SEIS) .... FPW
Field-Site Production and Reduction System (SAA) .... FSPRS
Field-Site Production Capability (SAA) .... FSPC
Field-Site Production Study Committee (SAA) .... FSPSC
Field-Site Production System (SAA) .... FSPS
Field-Stimulated Exoelectron Emission [Physics] .... FSEE
Fiendishly Rapid Electronic Device .... FRED
Fieramente [Boldly] [Music] (ROG) .... FIER
Fieri Curavit [Caused to Be Made] [Latin] .... FC
Fieri Facias [Cause to Be Made] [A writ commanding the sheriff to execute
  judgment] [Legal term] [Latin] .... FI FA
Fieri Fecit [Caused to Be Made] [Latin] .... FF
Fiero Owners Club of America (EA) .... FOCA
Fiero Owners Club of America (EA) .... FOCOA

Fieseler [Germany ICAO aircraft manufacturer identifier] (ICAO) .... FI
Fiesta-Air [Air carrier designation symbol] .... FIAX
Fife and Forfar Imperial Yeomanry [British military] (DMA) .... F & FIY
Fife and Forfar Yeomanry [British military] (DMA) .... F & FY
Fife and Forfar Yeomanry/Scottish Horse [British military] (DMA) .... FFY/SH
Fife and Kincardine Royal Garrison Artillery [British military] (DMA) .... F & K RGA
Fife/Glenrothes [British ICAO location identifier] (ICLI) .... EGPJ
Fife Lake Public Library, Fife Lake, MI [Library symbol Library of Congress]
  (LCLS) .... MiFil
Fife Light Horse [British military] (DMA) .... FLH
Fife Light Horse Volunteers [British military] (DMA) .... FLHV
Fife Mounted Rifles [British military] (DMA) .... FMR
Fifeshire [County in Scotland] .... FIFES
FIFRA [Federal Insecticide, Fungicide, and Rodenticide Act] and TSCA [Toxic
  Substances Control Act] Enforcement System (GNE) .... FATES
Fifteen [Lawn tennis] (DSUE) .... FIF
Fifteenth Field Artillery Regiment, Royal Canadian Artillery Museum and
  ArchivesSociety, Vancouver, British Columbia [Library symbol National
  Library of Canada] (NLC) .... BVAAM
Fifth Allied Tactical Air Force, Southern Europe (NATG) .... FIVEATAF
Fifth Amphibious Corps .... VAC
Fifth Avenue Ventures [Vancouver Stock Exchange symbol] .... FA
Fifth Coast Guard District [Portsmouth, VA] [USCG] (TAG) D5
Fifth Cranial Nerve, Mandibular Division (DAVI) .... V_3
Fifth Cranial Nerve, Maxillary Division (DAVI) .... V_2
Fifth Cranial Nerve, Opththalmic Division (DAVI) .... V_1
Fifth Dimension [NASDAQ symbol] (TTSB) .... FIVD
Fifth Dimension, Inc. [Associated Press] (SAG) .... FifthDim
Fifth Dimension, Inc. [NASDAQ symbol] (NQ) .... FIVD
Fifth Flux Experiment (USDC) .... PENTAFLUX
Fifth Generation Computer (NITA) .... FGC
Fifth Third Bancorp [Associated Press] (SAG) .... FifthT
Fifth Third Bancorp [NASDAQ symbol] (NQ) .... FITB
Fifth-Generation Computer Systems .... FGCS
Fifth-Order Theory .... FOT
Fifty [Roman numeral] L
Fifty Off Stores [Associated Press] (SAG) 50-Off
Fifty Off Stores [NASDAQ symbol] (SAG) .... FOFF
Fifty-Plus Runners Association (EA) .... FPRA
Figari [Corsica] [Airport symbol] (OAG) .... FSC
Figari, Sud-Corse [France ICAO location identifier] (ICLI) .... LFKF
Figeac/Livernon [France ICAO location identifier] (ICLI) .... LFCF
Figgie International [Associated Press] (SAG) .... FiggieA
Figgie International [Associated Press] (SAG) .... FiggieB
Figgie International, Inc. [Associated Press] (SAG) .... Figgie
Figgie International, Inc. [NASDAQ symbol] (NQ) .... FIGI
Figgie Intl Cl'A' [NASDAQ symbol] (TTSB) .... FIGIA
Figgie Intl Cl'B' [NASDAQ symbol] (TTSB) .... FIGI
Fight .... FGHT
Fight Against Dictating Designers [Group opposing below-the-knee fashions
  introduced in 1970] .... FADD
Fight for Sight [Also known as NCCB] (EA) .... FS
Fight Inflation Together [Group opposing high food prices in 1973] .... FIT
Fight Level (PDAA) .... FL
Fight to Advance the Nation's Sports [Defunct] (EA) .... FANS
Fight to Advertise the Truth about Saturates [Student legal action
  organization] .... FATS
Fighter [Russian aircraft symbol] .... DI
Fighter [Designation for all US military aircraft] .... F
Fighter .... FGHTR
Fighter (NATG) .... FH
Fighter (NATG) .... FIT
Fighter (AABC) .... FTR
Fighter [Russian aircraft symbol] I
Fighter [Russian aircraft symbol] .... JP
Fighter [Russian aircraft symbol] .... LA
Fighter [Russian aircraft symbol] .... LAGG
Fighter Air Direction Center .... FADC
Fighter Air Director [Military] (NVT) .... FAD
Fighter Aircraft Code Type (SAA) .... FACT
Fighter Aircraft Structural Loads [Program] [Air Force] .... FASTLODS
Fighter Alert (NATG) .... FA
Fighter, All Weather [British military] (DMA) .... FAW
Fighter Allocator (NATG) .... FA
Fighter Analysis Tactical Air Combat .... FANTAC
Fighter/Attack Simulator Visual System [Military] .... F/ASVS
Fighter Attack Squadron (DNAB) .... FITAKTRON
Fighter, Attacker, Reconnaissance [Requirements] [Air Force] .... FAR
Fighter Automatic Navigator .... FAN
Fighter Bomber .... FB
Fighter Bomber [Advanced] .... FBX
Fighter Bomber [Obsolete] .... FTB
Fighter Bomber Aircraft (NATG) .... FBA
Fighter Bomber Attack (NATG) .... FB/A
Fighter Bomber Program .... FBP
Fighter Bomber Strike (NATG) .... FB/S
Fighter Bombing Plane [Navy symbol] .... VFB
Fighter Catapult [Ship] .... FC
Fighter Catapult Ship [British military] (DMA) .... FCS
Fighter Command [Air Force] .... FC
Fighter Command School [Air Force] .... FCS
Fighter Control Area [Military] .... FCA
Fighter Control Center (MUGU) .... FCC
Fighter Control Unit [Military British] .... FCU
Fighter Conveyor .... FICON

Fighter Data Storage (IAA) .... FDS
Fighter Direction .... FD
Fighter Direction Net [Navy] .... FDNET
Fighter Director Control Schools [Navy] .... FDCS
Fighter Director Officer [Navy] .... FDO
Fighter Director Post .... FDP
Fighter Director Ship [Navy] .... FDS
Fighter Director Tender [Navy] .... FDT
Fighter Dive-Bomber .... FDB
Fighter Duty Officer .... FDO
Fighter Engagement Zone [Military] (NVT) .... FEZ
Fighter Escort .... FE
Fighter Experimental (MCD) .... FX
Fighter Export [Military] .... FX
Fighter Ground Attack (NATG) .... FGA
Fighter Identification System .... FIS
Fighter Inertial Navigation System .... FINE
Fighter Intercepter Group (MCD) .... FIG
Fighter Interception Unit [RAF] [British] .... FIU
Fighter Interceptor .... FI
Fighter Interceptor Training Squadron [Air Force] .... FITNGSq
Fighter Interceptor Training Squadron [Air Force] .... FITS
Fighter Jet .... FJ
Fighter Leader School [British military] (DMA) .... FLS
Fighter Missile System .... FMS
Fighter Multifunctional Inertial Reference Assembly (MCD) .... FMIRA
Fighter Officer for Interceptors [Member of the SAGE Command Post staff] .... FOI
Fighter Officer for Missiles [Member of the SAGE Command Post staff] .... FOM
Fighter Operations .... FTRO
Fighter Plane [Navy symbol] .... VF
Fighter Plane (Two-Engine) [Navy symbol] .... VF(M)
Fighter Plans .... FTRP
Fighter Prop .... FP
Fighter Reconnaissance [Air Force] .... FR
Fighter Squadron [Navy] (MUGU) .... FITRON
Fighter Squadron [Navy symbol] .... VF
Fighter Squadron - All Weather [Navy symbol] (MCD) .... VF AW
Fighter Squadron Detachment (DNAB) .... FITRONDET
Fighter Squadron, Photo [Navy symbol] (MCD) .... VFP
Fighter Support Experimental [Military] .... FSX
Fighter Tactical Wing (MCD) .... FTW
Fighter Weapons (MCD) .... FW
Fighter Weapons Instructor Course [Military] .... FWIC
Fighter Weapons School [Topgun] [Navy] (DOMA) .... FITWEPSCOL
Fighter Weapons School [Military] .... FWS
Fighter Weapons School [Military] .... FWSCH
Fighter Weapons Squadron [Air Force] .... FTRWPNSSq
Fighter Weapons Squadron [Air Force] .... FWS
Fighter Weapons Training Command (MCD) .... FWTC
Fighter Weapons Wing .... FWW
Fighter Wing [Navy] (NVT) .... FITWING
Fighter-Aircraft-Delivered Seismic Intrusion Detector (NVT) .... FADSID
Fighter-Interceptor Squadron [Air Force] .... FIS
Fighter-Interceptor Squadron [Air Force] (AFM) .... FISq
Fighter-Interceptor Wing (MCD) .... FIW
Fighting French .... FF
Fighting in Built-Up Areas [Military] (INF) .... FIBUA
Fighting Landplane .... FLP
Fighting Squadron .... FIGHTRON
Fighting Vehicle [Bradley] [Army] .... FV
Fighting Vehicle Armament (RDA) .... FVA
Fighting Vehicle Systems (RDA) .... FVS
Fighting Vehicles Design Establishment [British military] (DMA) .... FVDE
Fighting Vehicles Research and Development Establishment [British] (DMA) .... FVRDE
Figlie de San Paolo [Pious Society of the Daughters of Saint Paul - PSDSP] [Rome, Italy] (EAIO) .... FSP
Figura Etymologica [A publication] (BJA) .... FigEtym
Figural After-Effect .... FAE
Figural Bottle Association [Defunct] .... FBA
Figural Bottle Openers Collectors Club (EA) .... FBOC
Figurative .... FIG
Figurative (WDMC) .... fig
Figure (WDMC) .... fig
Figure (AFM) .... FIG
Figure (VRA) .... fig
Figure Drawing Test [Psychology] .... FDT
Figure Location Test (EDAC) .... FLT
Figure of Merit .... FM
Figure of Merit .... FOM
Figure of Merit [Symbol] (DEN) .... Z
Figure Reading Electronic Device [Information retrieval] .... FRED
Figure Skating Coaches of Canada [See also EPAC] .... FSCC
Figures or Images [Freight] .... FGIM
Figures Shift [Teleprinters] .... FIGS
Figwort Mosaic Virus [Plant pathology] .... FIMV
Fiji [Aircraft nationality and registration mark] (FAAC) .... DQ
Fiji (BARN) .... F
Fiji [MARC country of publication code Library of Congress] (LCCP) .... fj
Fiji [ANSI two-letter standard code] (CNC) .... FJ
Fiji [ANSI three-letter standard code] (CNC) .... FJI
Fiji [IYRU nationality code] (IYR) .... KF
Fiji [Fiji] [ICAO location identifier] (ICLI) .... NFOF
Fiji [MARC geographic area code Library of Congress] (LCCP) .... pofj--
Fiji Air [ICAO designator] (AD) .... PC
Fiji Air Services Ltd. [ICAO designator] (FAAC) .... FAJ

Fiji Disease Virus [Plant pathology] .... FDV
Fiji Federation of Labor .... FFL
Fiji Fracture Zone [Geology] .... FFZ
Fiji Hotel Association (EY) .... FHA
Fiji Industrial Workers' Congress .... FIWC
Fiji Labour Party [Political party] (FEA) .... FLP
Fiji Law Reports [A publication] (DLA) .... Fiji LR
Fiji Law Reports [A publication] (DLA) .... FLR
Fijian Nationalist Party [Political party] (PPW) .... FNP
Fijian-Australian Resource Centre .... FARC
Fiji-West Australian Association .... FWAA
Fike High School Library, Wilson, NC [Library symbol] [Library of Congress] (LCLS) .... NcWilF
Fila Holdings [NYSE symbol] (SPSG) .... FLH
Fila Holdings ADS [NYSE symbol] (TTSB) .... FLH
Fila Holdings SA [Associated Press] (SAG) .... FilaHold
Filadelfia [Paraguay] [ICAO location identifier] (ICLI) .... SGFI
Filament (AAG) .... F
Filament (KSC) .... FIL
Filament (IDOE) .... fil
Filament Atom Reservoir (PDAA) .... FAR
Filament Center Tap .... FCT
Filament Composite Material .... FCM
Filament Ground (MSA) .... FG
Filament Midtop .... FM
Filament Supply (IAA) .... FILSUP
Filament Wound .... FW
Filamentous Hemagglutinin [Medicine] .... FHA
Filament-Reinforced Plastic .... FRP
Filament-Wound Case (MCD) .... FWC
Filament-Wound Glass Fiber .... FGF
Filament-Wound Plastic (PDAA) .... FWP
Filament-Wound Structure .... FWS
Filaria [Microbiology] (MAE) .... F
Filarial Excretory Antigen [Immunology] .... FEA
Filariasis [Infectious disease] (DAVI) .... FILAR
File [Computer science] .... F
File [Document Locator Number] [IRS] .... TCDF
File Access Channel .... FAC
File Access Data Unit [Telecommunications] (OSI) .... FADU
File Access Keys (NITA) .... FAKS
File Access Listener .... FAL
File Access Manager .... FAM
File Access Protocol [Telecommunications] (OSI) .... FAP
File Access Subsystem [Computer science] (TEL) .... FAS
File Address Register .... FAR
File Allocation Table [Computer science] .... FAT
File Allocation Table 32-Bit [Computer science] FAT32
File Analysis and Selection Technique [Computer science] .... FAST
File Analysis for Random Access Storage [Computer science] (IAA) .... FARS
File Analyzer and Report Generator (DNAB) .... FIANA
File and Print Service for NetWare [Computer science] .... FPSNW
File and Report Information Processing Generator [Computer science] .... FRINGE
File Attribution Table [Computer science] (PCM) .... FAT
File Block .... FB
File Cabinet (AAG) .... FC
File Code [Computer science] (IEEE) .... FC
File Compare (PCM) .... FC
File Control (AFIT) .... FC
File Control [Microfilm] (MCD) .... FICO
File Control Block [Computer science] (BUR) .... FCB
File Control Package (NITA) .... FCP
File Control Processor [Computer science] (BUR) .... FCP
File Control Program [Computer science] .... FCP
File Control Services [Digital Equipment Corp.] .... FCS
File Control System (NITA) .... FCS
File Control Unit .... FCU
File Conversion [Computer science] (BUR) .... FC
File Conversion [Computer science] .... FICON
File Copy .... FC
File Create and Maintenance [Computer science] (MHDI) .... FCRAM
File Data Block [Computer science] .... FDB
File Data Description Language (MHDI) .... FDDL
File Data Register [Computer science] .... FDR
File Definition [Computer science] .... FD
File Description .... FD
File Description System [Computer science] (PDAA) .... FDS
File Directory .... FD
File Exchange .... FILEX
File Expansion Transport Magazine (SAA) .... FETM
File Extended Control Block [Computer science] (BUR) .... FECB
File Finish (MSA) .... FF
File Gap [Computer science] (BUR) .... FG
File Identification Control Block [Computer science] (IAA) .... FICB
File Indirect Register .... FIR
File Information Block .... FIB
File Information Language Executive Routine [Computer science] .... FILER
File Information Table [Computer science] .... FIT
File Interrogation Technique .... FIT
File Interrogation and Reporting System [Computer science] .... FIRS
File Interrogation of Nineteen-Hundred Data [Computer science] (DIT) .... FIND
File List Processor [Computer science] .... FLIST
File Location Code [Computer science] .... FLC
File Maintenance [Computer science] (BUR) .... FM
File Maintenance [Computer science] (IAA) .... FMAIN

File Maintenance System (MCD)	FMS
File Management	FM
File Management Loading Facility	FMLF
File Management Supervisor [Honeywell, Inc.]	FMS
File Management System (AFIT)	FMS
File Management Transaction Processor	FMTP
File Manipulation Language	FML
File Manufacturers Association [Defunct] (EA)	FMA
File Name Block [Computer science] (MHDB)	FNB
File Name Table [Computer science] (MHDB)	FNT
File Next Register	FNR
File of Enemies [British] [An association] (DBA)	FOE
File of Evaluated and Event Data [Nuclear energy] (NUCP)	FEED
File of Industrial Data [Computer science]	FIND
File Organization Evaluation Model	FOREM
File Organization Generator	FORGE
File Organization System (DIT)	FOS
File Organization Technique (BUR)	FORTE
File Parameter List [Computer science] (IAA)	FPL
File Parameter Table (IAA)	FPT
File Processor [Computer science] (BUR)	FP
File Protect	FP
File Protect Memory [Computer science] (BUR)	FPM
File Recovery Area [Computer science] (ECII)	FRA
File Register	FR
File Save [Computer science]	FS
File Segment [Searchable field] (NITA)	FS
File Separator [Computer science]	FS
File Sequence Number [Computer science] (IAA)	FSN
File Server Control [Computer science] (DOMA)	FSC
File Source [Computer science]	FS
File Status Table [Computer science] (IBMDP)	FST
File Storage Region [Digital Equipment Corp.]	FSR
File Structure Volume Descriptor Record (NTCM)	FSVDR
File System Agent [Telecommunications] (PCM)	FSA
File System Control [Computer science]	FSC
File System Control Block [Computer science] (IBMDP)	FSCB
File System Driver (PCM)	FSD
File System Helpers (PCM)	FSHLPS
File Systems Tree [Computer science]	FST
File Trade Association [British] (BI)	FTA
File Transfer, Access, and Management [Telecommunications] (TSSD)	FTAM
File Transfer Access Management [Computer science] (EERA)	FTAM
File Transfer Access Method [Computer science]	FTAM
File Transfer and Manipulation (NITA)	FTAM
File Transfer Facility [Telecommunications] (OSI)	FTF
File Transfer Facility (NITA)	FTR
File Transfer Packet [Computer science] (IAA)	FTP
File Transfer Program [or Protocol] [Computer science]	FTP
File Transfer Protocol	ftp
File Transfer Protocol (NITA)	FTP
File Transfer Service (DOMA)	FTS
File Utility Routines [Computer science]	FUR
File Utility Routines, Program Utility Routines [Computer science]	FURPUR
File Verification Utility [Computer science]	FVU
Filed a Petition [FDA]	FAP
Filed but Impracticable to Transmit [NWS] (FAAC)	FIBI
Filed Flight Plan (DA)	FPL
Filed Flight Plan Message [Aviation code]	FPL
Filene's [Boston] Automatic Bargain Basement	FABB
Filene's Basement [NASDAQ symbol] (TTSB)	BSMT
Filene's Basement Corp. [NASDAQ symbol] (SPSG)	BSMT
Filenes Basement Corp. [Associated Press] (SAG)	FilBsmt
File-Nesting Store [Computer science] (OA)	FNS
FileNet Corp. [NASDAQ symbol] (NQ)	FILE
FileNet Corp. [Associated Press] (SAG)	FileNet
File-Oriented Interpretive Language [1969] [Computer science]	FOIL
File-Oriented Programming System [Computer science] (PDAA)	FOPS
Filer, ID [Television station call letters]	KBGH
Filer Public Library, Filer, ID [Library symbol] [Library of Congress] (LCLS)	IdFi
Files Control Office	FCO
Files for Agricultural Science and Technology Literature [Database] [Agricultural Science Information Center] [Information service or system] (CRD)	FASTEL
Files for Agricultural Science and Technology Personnel [Database] [Agricultural Science Information Center] [Information service or system] (CRD)	FASTEP
Files Management Unit [Computer science]	FMU
File-Set Description [Computer science]	FSD
Filesmiths' Benefit Club [A union] [British]	FBC
Filestore Transfer Routine [Computer science] (PDAA)	FTR
Filiae a Caritate Sacri Corde Jesus [Daughters of Charity of the Sacred Heart of Jesus] [Roman Catholic religious order]	FCSCJ
Filiae Divinae Caritatis [Daughters of Divine Charity] [Roman Catholic religious order]	FDC
Filial Generation [Biology]	F
Filial Generation, First [Biology]	F_1
Filial Generation, Second [Biology]	F_2
Filiform and Follower [Instruments] [Urology] (DAVI)	F & F
Filigree [Jewelry] (ROG)	FIL
Filii Divinae Providentiae [Sons or Daughters of Divine Providence] [Roman Catholic religious order]	FDP
Filii Mariae Salutis Infirmorum [Sons of Mary, Health of the Sick] [Roman Catholic religious order]	FMSI
Filing (ROG)	FILG

Filing and Source Data Entry Techniques for Easier Retrieval [Computer science] (MHDI)	FASTER
Filing Requirement [IRS]	FR
Filing Status [IRS]	FS
Filing Status Code [IRS]	FSC
Filing Time [Time a message is presented for transmission]	FLT
Filing Time [Time a message is presented for transmission]	FT
Filipinas Americas Science and Art Foundation (EA)	FASAF
Filipinas Orient Airways, Inc. [Philippines] [ICAO designator] (FAAC)	FOA
Filipino American Political Association	FAPA
Filipino Association of South Australia	FASA
Filipino Community Cooperative [Australia]	FCC
Filipino Cultural Association [Australia]	FCA
Filipino Employment Policy Instruction (CINC)	FEPI
Filipino Forum in New South Wales [Australia]	FFNSW
Filipino Rehabilitation Commission [Post-World War II]	FRC
Filipino Women's Council [Australia]	FWC
Filipino-Australian Association of North Queensland [Australia]	FAANQ
Filius [Son] [Latin]	F
Filius [or Filia] et Hoeres [Latin] (ROG)	FIL et HOER
Fill and Bleed (SAA)	F & B
Fill and Drain (AAG)	F & D
Fill/Drain (MCD)	FD
Fill Exit Entry [Computer science]	FEE
Fill Factor [Photovoltaic energy systems]	FF
Fill/Full [or Full/Fill] (MCD)	F/F
Fill or Kill [Stock options] [Investment term]	FOK
Fill Producers' Association	FPA
Fill Start Entry [Computer science]	FSE
Filled Quartz Helix	FQH
Filled Thermal System [Temperature sensor]	FTS
Filler (AABC)	FLR
Filler for Smoke Shells [Weaponry] (NATG)	FS
Filler Sensor Nozzle	FSN
Filler Wire Addition	FWA
Filles de Jesus [Sons of Jesus] [Religious order]	FDJ
Filles de Jesus de Kermaria [Daughters of Jesus of Kermaria - DJK] [Paris, France] (EAIO)	FJ
Filles du Saint Esprit [Institute of the Franciscan Sisters of the Eucharist] [Roman Catholic religious order]	FSE
Fillet (MSA)	FIL
Filling	FILL
Filling, Storage, and Remelt System [Nuclear energy] (NRCH)	FS & R
Filling, Storage, and Remelt System [Nuclear energy] (IAA)	FSAR
Fillip (ABBR)	FLP
Fillister	FIL
Fillister Head [Screws]	FILH
Fillister Head Brass [Screw] (IAA)	FILHB
Fillister Head Steel [Screw] (IAA)	FILHS
Fillmore, CA [Location identifier FAA] (FAAL)	FIM
Fillmore City Library, Fillmore, UT [Library symbol Library of Congress] (LCLS)	UFi
Filly [Thoroughbred racing]	F
Film	FLM
Film Advisory Board (EA)	FAB
Film, Air, and Package Carriers Conference (EA)	FAPCC
Film and Equipment Exchange [Army] (AABC)	F & EE
Film and Literature Board of Review [Australia]	FLBR
Film and Sheet [Plastics technology]	F/S
Film and Television Correlation Assessment Technique (MCD)	FATCAT
Film and Television Documentation Center [State University of New York at Albany] [Information service or system] (IID)	FATDOC
Film and Television Group [Western Australia]	FTI
Film and Television Institute (Western Australia)	FTIWA
Film Artistes' Association [A union] [British] (DCTA)	FAA
Film Arts Foundation (EA)	FAF
Film Availability Services [British Film Institute]	FAS
Film Badge (IEEE)	FB
Film: British Documentary	FBD
Film: British Feature	FBF
Film: British Series	FBS
Film Bulletin	FB
Film Capability Laboratories [Bell System]	FCL
Film Carrousel Handle	FCH
Film Censorship Board [Australia]	FCB
Film Coalition [Defunct] (EA)	FILCO
Film Comment [A publication] (BRI)	FC
Film Compensated STN [Super Twisted Nematic] (CDE)	FSTN
Film Council Film Circuit [Library network]	FCFC
Film Criticism [A publication] (BRI)	Film Cr
Film Culture Non-Profit Corp. (EA)	FCNPC
Film Entertainments National Service Association (BARN)	FENSA
Film: Foreign Documentary	FFD
Film: Foreign Feature	FFF
Film: Foreign Series	FFS
Film Four International [Commercial firm British]	FFI
Film Industry Defence Organisation [British] (DI)	FIDO
Film Input/Output Unit	FIOU
Film Input to Digital Automatic Computer	FIDAC
Film Input to Digital Automatic Computer System	FIDACSYS
Film Inspection Apply Template (MCD)	FIAT
Film Integrated Circuit	FIC
Film Laboratory Association Ltd. [British] (BI)	FLA
Film Liaison Officer [Army]	FLO

Film Library, CBHT-TV, Halifax, Nova Scotia [Library symbol National Library of Canada] (NLC) .... NSHCBF
Film Library Information Council [EFLA] [Absorbed by] (EA) .... FLIC
Film Library Instantaneous Presentation [Computer science] .... FLIP
Film Library Inter-College Cooperative of Pennsylvania [Library network] .... FLIC
Film Library of Mesa County, School District 51, Grand Junction, CO [Library symbol] [Library of Congress] (LCLS) .... CoCjFL
Film Library of Mesa County, School, District 51, Grand Junction, CO [Library symbol] [Library of Congress] (LCLS) .... CoGjFL
Film Linearized Muffin-Tin Orbital [Physics] .... FLMTO
Film Load (KSC) .... F/L
Film Magazine Stowage Container (MCD) .... FMSC
Film Magnetic Counter .... FMC
Film Optical Scanning Device for Input to Computer (NITA) .... FOSDIC
Film Optical Sensing Device for Input to Computers [National Institute of Standards and Technology] .... FOSDIC
Film Pack [Photography] .... FP
Film Processing .... FLMPRS
Film Producers Association of New York [Defunct] (EA) .... FPANY
Film Production Association of Great Britain (BI) .... FPA
Film Production Unit [British military] (DMA) .... FPU
Film Quarterly [A publication] (BRI) .... FQ
Film Reading Machine .... FRM
Film Recording .... FR
Film Report (AFM) .... FR
Film Roman, Inc. [Associated Press] (SAG) .... FilmRm
Film Roman, Inc. [NASDAQ symbol] (SAG) .... ROMN
Film Society Review [A publication] .... FSR
Film Sound .... FLMSD
Film Stowage Container .... FSC
Film Strip Sound Projector .... FSSP
Film Studies Association of Canada .... FSAC
Film Supertwist .... FST
Film Thickness Indicator .... FTI
Film Thickness Monitor .... FTM
Film Tracing Reproduction .... FTR
Film Training Aid .... FTA
Film Transfer Boom [NASA] .... FTB
Film Unit Secretary .... FUS
Film Users Network [Cine Information] [Information service or system] (IID) .... Filmnet
Film/Video Arts (EA) .... FVA
Film/Video Producers and Distributors [National Film Board of Canada] [Information service or system] (CRD) .... FVPD
Film Weekly Award [British] .... FWA
Film-Coated [Pharmacy] .... FC
Film-Forming Fluoroprotein Formulation [Organic chemistry] .... FFFP
Filmier (ABBR) .... FLMR
Filmiest (ABBR) .... FLMST
Filminess (ABBR) .... FLMNS
Filmless Automatic Bond Inspection System .... FABIS
Filmless Dental Imager (RDA) .... FDI
Filmless Radiography (MCD) .... FR
Film-Makers' Cooperative (EA) .... FMC
Filmmakers United Against Apartheid (EA) .... FUAA
Films for Christ Association (EA) .... FCA
Films for Christ Association .... FFC
Films in Review [A publication] (BRI) .... FIR
Films, Inc. .... FI
Filmstrip .... FS
Filmstrip (VRA) .... fs
Filmstrip and Slide Laboratory .... FASLA
Filmy (ABBR) .... FLMY
Filoil Free Workers [Philippines] .... FFW
Fils de Marie Immaculee [Sons of Mary Immaculate] [Saint Fulgent, France] (EAIO) .... FMI
Filson Club (EA) .... FC
Filson Club, Louisville, KY [Library symbol Library of Congress] (LCLS) .... KyLoF
Filter .... F
Filter (AABC) .... FIL
Filter (CET) .... FL
Filter .... FLT
Filter (MSA) .... FLTR
Filter Address Correction .... FAC
Filter and Detect Chip (NITA) .... FAD
Filter Assembly Machine (MCD) .... FAM
Filter Center .... FC
Filter Center .... FILCEN
Filter Change Kit .... FCK
Filter/Demineralizer (NRCH) .... F/D
Filter Drain [Computer science] .... FD
Filter Factor (NRCH) .... FF
Filter Gate .... FG
Filter Manufacturers Council (EA) .... FMC
Filter Output (AAG) .... FO
Filter Paper .... FP
Filter Paper Activity .... FPA
Filter Paper Microscopic [Test] [Medicine] .... FPM
Filter Paper Units [Pulp and paper technology] .... FPU
Filter Replacement Fluid .... FRF
Filter Response Analysis for Continuously Accelerating Spacecraft [NASA] .... FRACAS
Filter Wedge Spectrometer .... FWS
Filter Wheels .... FW
Filterable Agent [Virology] .... FA

Filter-Band Eliminator (MUGU) .... FL-BE
Filter-Band High .... FLBH
Filter-Band Suppressor Assembly .... FBSA
Filter-Bandpass (MUGU) .... FL-BP
filtered Air (MEDA) .... FA
Filtered Air Supply (IAA) .... FAS
Filtered Back-Projection [Computer science] .... FBP
Filtered Detection Only Processor (CAAL) .... FDOP
Filtered Load (MAE) .... FL
Filtered Phosphate (MAE) .... Fp
Filtered Sodium (MAE) .... FNa
Filter-High Pass (MUGU) .... FL-HP
Filter-Low Pass (MUGU) .... FL-LP
Filthier (ABBR) .... FLTHR
Filthiest (ABBR) .... FLTHST
Filthiness (ABBR) .... FLTHNS
Filthy (ABBR) .... FLTHY
Filtra [Filter] [Pharmacy] .... FILT
Filtration Factor [Physiology] (DAVI) .... FF
Filtration Fraction [Physiology] .... FF
Filtration Society (EA) .... FS
Fimbria-Fornix [Neuroanatomy] .... FF
Fin Creek, AK [Location identifier FAA] (FAAL) .... FNK
Fin Prochain [At the End of Next Month] [Business term French] .... fp
Fin Stabilized [Rocketry] .... FS
Fin Stabilized Discarding Sabot (MCD) .... FSDS
Fin Stabilized Rockets .... FSR
Fina, Inc. [AMEX symbol] (SPSG) .... FI
Fina, Inc. [Associated Press] (SAG) .... Fina
Finagle-Factor .... FF
FINA,Inc. CI'A' [AMEX symbol] (TTSB) .... FI
Final [Telecommunications] (TEL) .... F
Final (WDAA) .... FIN
Final (NASA) .... FNL
Final Acceptance, Assembly Tests .... FAT
Final Acceptance Criteria (NRCH) .... FAC
Final Acceptance Inspection Test Equipment (MCD) .... FAITE
Final Acceptance Review [NASA] (NASA) .... FAR
Final Acquisition Action Approval (AAGC) .... FAAA
Final Address [Computer science] (ECII) .... FA
Final Address Message [Telecommunications] (TEL) .... FAM
Final Address Register [Computer science] (MDG) .... FA
Final Aerospace Trial .... FAT
Final Anthropic Principle [Term coined by authors John Barrow and Frank Tipler in their book, "The Anthropic Cosmological Principle"] .... FAP
Final Approach (GAVI) .... FA
Final Approach [Aviation] .... FNA
Final Approach and Takeoff Area [OST] (TAG) .... FATO
Final Approach Course [Aviation] (DA) .... FAC
Final Approach Display (MCD) .... FAD
Final Approach Equipment [Aviation] .... FAE
Final Approach Fix [Aviation] (DA) .... FAF
Final Approach Fix [Aviation] (FAAC) .... FAF
Final Approach Monitoring Equipment [Aviation] .... FAME
Final Approach Path [or Plane] [Aviation] .... FAP
Final Approach Spacing Assignment [Aviation] (IAA) .... FASA
Final Approach Spacing Tool [FAA] (TAG) .... FAST
Final Approach Spacing Tool (GAVI) .... FAST
Final Approach Track [Aviation] (DA) .... FAT
Final Approval [Automotive project management] .... FA
Final Assembly (MSA) .... FA
Final Assembly and Closeout System Installation (MCD) .... FA/COSI
Final Assembly Checkout [NASA] (NASA) .... FACO
Final Assembly Test .... FAT
Final Asset Screen [DoD] .... FAS
Final Average Earnings .... FAE
Final Average Salary .... FAS
Final Basis of Issue Plan [Army] .... FBOIP
Final Boiling Point .... FBP
Final Bomb Release Line .... FBRL
Final Braking (MCD) .... FB
Final CAPE [Capability and Proficiency Evaluation] Review Period .... FCRP
Final Checkout (MCD) .... FCO
Final Command and Sequencing [Viking lander mission] [NASA] .... FC & S
Final Common Pathway [Neurology] .... FCP
Final Configuration Review (KSC) .... FCR
Final Contract Trials [Navy] .... FCT
Final Contractor's Trial (NVT) .... FCTRL
Final Coordination Line [Military] .... FCL
Final Coordination Line [Military] .... FINALCL
Final Data Report .... FDR
Final Defense Guidance Memorandum [Navy] .... FDGM
Final Delivered Article .... FDA
Final Delivery Date (AAGC) .... FDD
Final Design Acceptance [or Approval or Authorization] .... FDA
Final Design Criteria .... FDC
Final Design Presentation (NOAA) .... FDP
Final Design Report [Nuclear Regulatory Commission] (GFGA) .... FDR
Final Design Review (MCD) .... FDR
Final Determination Letter (GNE) .... FDL
Final Development Test and Evaluation (MCD) .... FDTE
Final Draft Equipment Publication (MCD) .... FDEP
Final Draft Manuscript .... FDM
Final Draft, Presidential Memorandum [DoD] .... FDPM
Final Drug Evaluation [Pharmacology] (DAVI) .... FDE

Final Engineering Acceptance Test [*Apollo*] [*NASA*] ... FEAT
Final Engineering Report ... FER
Final Environmental Impact Statement ... FEIS
Final Environmental Statement [*Bureau of Outdoor Recreation*] ... FES
Final Estimation of Data [*Computer science*] ... FED
Final Feedwater Temperature [*Nuclear energy*] (NRCH) ... FFWT
Final Flight Certification [*Aerospace*] ... FFC
Final Grid (IAA) ... FG
Final Hazards Summary Report [*Nuclear energy*] (NRCH) ... FHSR
Final Implementation Plan (EPA) ... FIP
Final Initial Operational Capability [*Aerospace*] (AAG) ... FIOC
Final Inspection Record [*Army*] ... FIR
Final Inspection Report (MCD) ... FIR
Final Issue ... FI
Final Limit, Down ... FLDO
Final Limit, Forward ... FLF
Final Limit, Hoist ... FLH
Final Limit, Lower ... FLL
Final Limit, Reverse ... FLR
Final Limit, Up ... FLU
Final Marker Aid [*FAA*] (TAG) ... FMA
Final Materials List [*NASA*] (NASA) ... FML
Final Meteorological Radiation ... FMR
Final Meteorological Radiation Tape ... FMRT
Final Missile Deviation Report [*Aerospace*] (AAG) ... FMDR
Final Moisture Content (IAA) ... FMC
Final Multiple Score (NVT) ... FMS
Final Operating System (MCD) ... FOS
Final Operational Capability [*Military*] (AFM) ... FOC
Final Operational Capacity ... FOC
Final Opinion Inventory [*Psychometrics*] ... FOI
Final Parts List (MCD) ... FPL
Final Plan (DNAB) ... FP
Final Power Amplifier ... FPA
Final Prediction Error [*Statistics*] ... FPE
Final Processing Center ... FPC
Final Procurement Action Approval (MCD) ... FPAA
Final Program and Budget Guidance ... FPBG
Final Progress Report ... FPR
Final Project Design Description (NRCH) ... FPDD
Final Protective Fire [*Artillery term*] ... FPF
Final Protective Line [*Military*] ... FPL
Final Qualitative and Quantitative Personnel Requirements Information ... FQQPRI
Final Queue (IAA) ... FINQ
Final Release (AAG) ... FR
Final Report ... FINREP
Final Report ... FR
Final Routing Center [*Telecommunications*] (TEL) ... FRC
Final Rule [*RSPA*] (TAG) ... FR
Final Rulemaking [*Federal government*] (GFGA) ... FRM
Final Rulemaking Notice [*Federal government*] (GFGA) ... FRN
Final Safety Analysis Report [*NASA*] (KSC) ... FSAR
Final Selector [*Telecommunications*] ... FS
Final Semester Temporary Duty [*Air Force*] (AFM) ... FSTDY
Final Settlement ... FS
Final Signal Unit [*Telecommunications*] (TEL) ... FSU
Final Site Acceptance (NATG) ... FSA
Final Software Design Review ... FSDR
Final Stage Marker (IAA) ... FSM
Final Stage Vehicle ... FSV
Final Staging Base (AFM) ... FSB
Final Statement [*Army*] ... F/S
Final Station [*Computer science*] ... FINST
Final Status Word [*Computer science*] (IAA) ... FSW
Final Subcircuit [*An enzyme*] (IAA) ... FSC
Final System Release (MCD) ... FSR
Final System Run (KSC) ... FSR
Final Systems Check [*NASA*] (KSC) ... FSC
Final Systems Installation [*NASA*] (NASA) ... FSI
Final Target ... F
Final Technical Proposal (NATG) ... FTP
Final Technical Report ... FTR
Final Test Rack (KSC) ... FTR
Final Thermomechanical Treatment (MCD) ... FTMT
Final Turn Lead Pursuit (SAA) ... FTLP
Final Value ... FV
Final Voluntary Indefinite [*Status*] [*Army*] (INF) ... FVI
Final Work Statement (MCD) ... FWS
Final Working System Design Review [*Nuclear energy*] (NRCH) ... FWSDR
Final Year Temporary Duty [*Military*] (AFM) ... FYTDY
Finale [*Italy ICAO location identifier*] (ICLI) ... LICI
Finance [*or Financial*] ... F
Finance [*or Financial*] (AFM) ... FIN
Finance (DD) ... fin
Finance ... FIN
Finance (AAGC) ... Fin
Finance Act [*British*] (DCTA) ... FA
Finance and Accounting ... F & A
Finance and Accounting (MCD) ... FA
Finance and Accounting Group [*Air Force*] (AFM) ... FAG
Finance and Accounting Group [*Air Force*] (AFM) ... FAGp
Finance and Accounting Policy [*Army*] (AABC) ... FAP
Finance and Accounts Office [*Army*] ... FAAO
Finance and Accounts Office [*or Officer*] [*Army*] ... FAO
Finance and Accounts Office [*or Officer*], United States Army ... FAOUSA
Finance and Audit Committee [*American Library Association*] ... F & A
Finance and Comptroller Information Systems Command [*Army*] ... FINCISCOM
Finance and Comptroller Information Systems Command, United States Army ... FACISCOM USA
Finance and Control System (NASA) ... FACS
Finance and General Purposes Committee [*British*] (DCTA) ... F & GP
Finance and Leasing Association [*British*] (EAIO) ... FLA
Finance and Supply School [*Coast Guard*] ... FINSUPSCOL
Finance Brokers Supervisory Board [*Western Australia*] ... FBSB
Finance Center, United States Army ... FCUSA
Finance Charge ... FC
Finance Committee [*UN Food and Agriculture Organization*] ... FC
Finance Committee [*Institute of Electrical and Electronics Engineers*] (IEEE) ... FINCOM
Finance Corp. for Industry Ltd. [*British*] ... FCIL
Finance Corps ... FC
Finance Corps Board, United States Army ... FCBUSA
Finance Department ... FD
Finance Direction ... FD
Finance Disbursing Section [*Army*] ... FDS
Finance Docket ... FD
Finance for Industry [*Later, Investors in Industry International - 3I*] [*British*] ... FFI
Finance Group Office ... FGO
Finance Houses Association [*British*] ... FHA
Finance Image Processor [*Computer science*] (IBMDP) ... FIP
Finance, Insurance, and Real Estate [*Insurance*] ... FIRE
Finance, Insurance, and Real Estate USA [*A publication*] ... FIRE USA
Finance Ledger System [*Economics*] ... FLS
Finance Officer [*Army*] ... FINO
Finance Officer [*Army*] ... FO
Finance Officer, United States Army ... FOUSA
Finance Regulation [*Economics*] ... FR
Finance Replacement Training Center [*World War II*] ... FRTC
Finance School, United States Army ... FSUSA
Finance Sector Union of Australia ... FSUA
Finance Service, Army ... FSA
Finance Taxation and Co. Law [*Pakistan*] [*A publication*] (DLA) ... Fin Tax & Comp L
Finances of Selected Public Employee Retirement System [*Bureau of the Census*] (GFGA) ... FSPER
Financial (AAGC) ... Fin
Financial (WDMC) ... fin
Financial ... FINAN
Financial (BARN) ... Finci
Financial ... FINL
Financial (DD) ... finl
Financial [*Rate*] [*Value of the English pound*] ... FN
Financial ... NCL
Financial Accounting and Control System ... FACS
Financial Accounting and Control Techniques for Supply [*Army*] ... FACTS
Financial Accounting and Reporting System [*Federal Emergency Management Agency*] (GFGA) ... FARS
Financial Accounting Data ... FAD
Financial Accounting Foundation [*Stamford, CT*] (EA) ... FAF
Financial Accounting Institute [*Tenafly, NJ*] [*Telecommunications service*] (TSSD) ... FAI
Financial, Accounting Marketing Exercise (PDAA) ... FAME
Financial Accounting Office (AAGC) ... FAO
Financial Accounting Resource Management System ... FARMS
Financial Accounting Standard ... FAS
Financial Accounting Standards Advisory Council [*Financial Accounting Foundation*] (EDAC) ... FASAC
Financial Accounting Standards Board [*Formerly, Accounting Principles Board*] [*American Institute of Certified Public Accountants*] ... FASB
Financial Accounting Standards Board ... FASB
Financial Accounting System ... FAS
Financial Accounts Package New Data [*Torch Computers Ltd.*] [*Financial accounting software*] (NITA) ... FAPNEWDT
Financial Accounts Receivable ... FAR
Financial Administrative Control (AFM) ... FAC
Financial Advertising Committee on Ethics ... FACE
Financial Adviser ... FA
Financial Aid Administrator [*Department of Education*] (GFGA) ... FAA
Financial Aid Form [*Of College Board*] ... FAF
Financial Aid Planning Service [*College Scholarship Service*] ... FAPS
Financial AirExpress [*ICAO designator*] (FAAC) ... FAK
Financial Analysis and Planning System (IAA) ... FAPS
Financial Analysis and Reporting (MHDB) ... FINAR
Financial Analysis and Security Trading ... FAST
Financial Analysis Capability through Scanning ... FACTS
Financial Analysis Language [*Computer science*] (MCD) ... FAL
Financial Analysis Language [*Computer science*] ... FINAL
Financial Analysis of Management Effectiveness [*Department of Agriculture*] ... FAME
Financial Analysis Program [*IBM Corp.*] ... FAP
Financial Analysis System (MHDW) ... FAS
Financial Analysts Federation [*Later, AIMR*] (EA) ... FAF
Financial and Accounting Services Branch (AIE) ... FASB
Financial and Administrative Integrated Management System [*Department of Health and Human Services*] (GFGA) ... FAIMS
Financial and Administrative Support System [*Office of Personnel Management*] (GFGA) ... FASS
Financial and Business Administration Department [*American Occupational Therapy Association*] ... FBA

Financial and Business Management Division [*American Occupational Therapy Association*] .... FBM
Financial and Economic Analysis .... FAEA
Financial and Economic Board (NATG) .... FEB
Financial and Management Information System [*Naval Oceanographic Office*] .... FAMIS
Financial and Material Management System (SAA) .... FAMMS
Financial and Operating Data for Investor-Owned Water Companies [*A publication*] (EAAP) .... F & O
Financial and Operations Combined Uniform Single Report .... FOCUS
Financial Application Preprocessor System (MHDW) ... FAPS
Financial Assistance Grant .... FAG
Financial Assistance Program (AFM) .... FAP
Financial Automation Systems Team for Writing Programs for Standardized Army-Wide Applications .... FAST RIPSAW
Financial Bancorp [*NASDAQ symbol*] (TTSB) .... FIBC
Financial Bancorp, Inc. [*NASDAQ symbol*] (SAG) ...... FIBC
Financial Bancorp, Inc. [*Associated Press*] (SAG) ...... FinclBcp
Financial Benefit Group, Inc. [*NASDAQ symbol*] (NQ) .. FBGI
Financial Benefit Group, Inc. [*Associated Press*] (SAG) .. FnBen
Financial Business Package [*Computer science*] .... FBP
Financial Clearing and Services Ltd. [*Information service or system*] (IID) ..... FiCS
Financial Code (DLA) .... Fin C
Financial Compliance and Quality Assurance Staff [*Environmental Protection Agency*] (GFGA) .... FCQAS
Financial Control Research Institute [*British*] (DBA) ... FCRI
Financial Control System .... FCS
Financial Controller .... FC
Financial Corp. of America (ECON) .... FCA
Financial Corporations Act [*Australia*] .... FCA
Financial Correlation Table .... FCT
Financial/Cost Management System (MCD) .... F/CMS
Financial Crimes Enforcement Network [*Federal task force*] ...... FINCEN
Financial Data Planning .... FDA
Financial Data Records Folder (MUGU) .... FDRF
Financial Director .... FD
Financial Evaluation Program [*IBM Corp.*] .... FEP
Financial Executives Institute (EA) .... FEI
Financial Executives Institute of Australia .... FEIA
Financial Executives Institute of Canada (DD) .... FEI
Financial Executives Research Foundation (EA) .... FERF
Financial Federal [*AMEX symbol*] (TTSB) .... FIF
Financial Federal Corp. [*AMEX symbol*] (SPSG) .... FIF
Financial Federal Corp. [*Associated Press*] (SAG) ...... FinFdl
Financial Funds Control .... FFC
Financial General Ledger .... FGL
Financial Guaranty Insurance Corp. .... FGIC
Financial Inds [*NASDAQ symbol*] (TTSB) .... FNIN
Financial Industries Corp. [*Associated Press*] (SAG) ... FinIInd
Financial Industries Corp. [*NASDAQ symbol*] (NQ) .... FNIN
Financial Industry Information Service [*Database*] [*Bank Marketing Association*] [*Information service or system*] ...... FINI
Financial Industry Information Service [*Database*] [*Bank Marketing Association*] [*Information service or system*] (CRD) ..... FINIS
Financial Information and Accounting System .... FIAS
Financial Information Control System .... FICS
Financial Information for Resources Management (AFM) ... FIRM
Financial Information Management System [*Computer science*] (EERA) ...... FIMS
Financial Information Reporting System [*Computer science*] ...... FIRST
Financial Information Services Agency .... FISA
Financial Information System .... FIS
Financial Institution Data Base [*Cates Consulting Analysts, Inc.*] [*Information service or system*] (CRD) ...... FINDB
Financial Institutions Data File [*Rand McNally & Co.*] [*Information service or system*] (CRD) ...... FIDF
Financial Institutions in the Nation's Economy [*Study initiated by House of Representatives*] ...... FINE
Financial Institutions Insurance Group Ltd. [*NASDAQ symbol*] (SAG) .... FIRE
Financial Institutions Marketing Association [*Chicago, IL*] (EA) ...... FIMA
Financial Institutions Reform, Recovery, and Enforcement Act [*1989*] [*Also, FIRREA Pronounced "Fire"*] ...... FIRRE
Financial Institutions Reform, Recovery, and Enforcement Act [*1989*] [*Pronounced "fi-ree-a"*] ...... FIRREA
Financial Institutions Regulatory and Interest Rate Control Act of 1978 ...... FIRIRCA
Financial Institutions Resource Management [*Online database*] ...... FIRM
Financial Institutions Supervisory Act of 1966 .... FISA
Financial Interest and Syndication Rules [*FCC*] .... FIN-SYN
Financial Interest and Syndication Rules [*FCC*] .... FISR
Financial Intermediaries, Managers, and Brokers Association [*British*] (ECON) ...... FIMBRA
Financial Inter-Relations Ratio .... FIR
Financial Inventory Accounting .... FIA
Financial Inventory Control .... FIC
Financial Inventory Control Ledger (DNAB) .... FICL
Financial Inventory Control Report .... FICR
Financial Inventory Report .... FIR
Financial Inventory Subsidiary .... FIS
Financial Listing Service [*Prime Rating, Inc.*] [*Defunct Information service or system*] (CRD) ...... FLS
Financial Mail (Johannesburg) [*A publication*] .... FMJ
Financial Management (DD) .... FinlMgmt
Financial Management (MHDB) .... FINMAN
Financial Management .... FM
Financial Management Advisory Committee .... FMAC

Financial Management and Information System .... FINMIS
Financial Management Association [*Tampa, FL*] (EA) ... FMA
Financial Management Board [*Air Force*] (AFIT) .... FMB
Financial Management Center [*Marine science*] (OSRA) ... FMC
Financial Management Center (USDC) .... FMC
Financial Management Division [*Environmental Protection Agency*] (EPA) ..... FMD
Financial Management Executive Workshop .... FMEW
Financial Management for Data Processing [*An association*] (EA) ...... FMDP
Financial Management Improvement Program .... FMIP
Financial Management Information and Control System [*Navy*] ...... FMICS
Financial Management Information System [*Army*] ..... FIMIS
Financial Management Information System .... FMIS
Financial Management Initiative [*British*] .... FMI
Financial Management Manual [*NASA*] .... FMM
Financial Management Office (KSC) .... FMO
Financial Management Plan .... FMP
Financial Management Plan for Emergency Conditions [*Army*] ...... FMPEC
Financial Management Report (AABC) .... FMR
Financial Management Service (USGC) .... FMS
Financial Management System (USDC) .... FIMA
Financial Management System [*Marine science*] (OSRA) ... FIMA
Financial Management System .... FMS
Financial Management Systems [*A publication*] .... FMSS
Financial Management Systems Software (AAGC) .... FMSS
Financial Management Unit [*LIMRA*] .... FMU
Financial Managers Society (EA) .... FMS
Financial Managers' Statement [*Financial Managers' Society*] [*A publication*] ...... FMS
Financial Marketing Association (EA) .... FMA
Financial Markets Foundation .... FMF
Financial Network Manager (BUR) .... FNM
Financial News Composite Index [*Pronounced "fancy"*] [*Financial News Network*] ...... FNCI
Financial News Network [*Cable-television system*] ..... FNN
Financial On-Line Central Information System [*Computer science*] (MHDB) ...... FOCIS
Financial Operating Plan .... FOP
Financial Operations Association (EA) .... FOA
Financial Plan .... FP
Financial Planners and Planning Organizations Directory [*A publication*] ...... FPPOD
Financial Planning System [*IBM Corp.*] .... FPS
Financial Planning Volume .... FPV
Financial Post Canadian Corporate Database [*Financial Post Corporation Service Group*] [*Information service or system*] (CRD) ...... FPCORP
Financial Post Information Centre [*MacLean-Hunter Ltd.*] [*Information service or system*] (IID) ...... FPIC
Financial Post, Toronto, Ontario [*Library symbol National Library of Canada*] (NLC) ...... OTMH
Financial Print & Communications Ltd. [*British*] ...... FPC
Financial Printers Association (EA) .... FPA
Financial Products Standards Board (EA) .... FPSB
Financial Public Relations Association [*Later, BMA*] (EA) ...... FPRA
Financial Public Relations Consultants Retained .... FPR
Financial Real Estate Insurance .... FRI
Financial Relations Society [*Defunct*] (EA) .... FRS
Financial Reporting Council (ODBW) .... FRC
Financial Reporting Extender [*Computer science*] ..... FRX
Financial Reporting Releases [*SEC*] (TDOB) .... FRR
Financial Reporting Review Panel .... FRRP
Financial Reporting System .... FIRE
Financial Reporting System (MHDW) .... FRS
Financial Research Associates .... FRA
Financial Responsibility .... F/R
Financial Results Simulator (MHDB) .... FRS
Financial Results Simulator System (MHDB) .... FRSS
Financial Satellite Corp. [*Washington, DC Telecommunications service*] (TSSD) ...... FINANSAT
Financial Satellite Network .... FSN
Financial Scribe [*Freemasonry*] (ROG) .... FS
Financial Sec Assurance Hldg [*NYSE symbol*] (TTSB) .. FSA
Financial Secretary (WGA) .... Fin Sec
Financial Secretary .... FS
Financial Secretary to the War Office [*British*] .... FSWO
Financial Sector Adjustment Program [*West Africa*] ... FINSAP
Financial Security Assurance .... FSA
Financial Security Assurance Holdings [*Associated Press*] (SAG) ...... FnclSec
Financial Security Assurance Holdings [*NYSE symbol*] (SAG) ...... FSA
Financial Security Corp. [*Associated Press*] (SAG) ...... FinclSec
Financial Security Corp. [*NASDAQ symbol*] (SAG) ...... FNSC
Financial Services Acquisition Corp. [*Associated Press*] (SAG) ...... FnclSvcs
Financial Services Act [*British*] .... FSA
Financial Services Holding Co. .... FSHC
Financial Services Industry (TDOB) .... FSF
Financial Services Recorder [*Telecommunications*] [*British*] ...... FSR
Financial Services Society [*New York, NY*] (WDMC) ... FCS
Financial Services Technical Consortium .... FSTC
Financial Services Terminals Support [*IBM Corp.*] ..... FSTS
Financial Services Volunteer Corps [*An association*] (EA) ...... FSVC
Financial Statement .... F/S
Financial Statement and Budget Report [*British*] ...... FSBR
Financial Stationers Association (EA) .... FSA
Financial Status Report (OICC) .... FSR
Financial Status Summary (OICC) .... FSS
Financial Suppliers Association [*Later, FSF*] (EA) ...... FSA

Financial Suppliers Forum (EA) ..... FSF
Financial Support, Advocacy, Medical Management, Love, Information, Education, Structural Support (MEDA) ..... FAMLIES
Financial Suspense File [*Army*] ..... FSF
Financial Svcs. Acquisition Corp. [*Associated Press*] (SAG) ..... FncSv
Financial Svcs. Acquisition Corp. [*NASDAQ symbol*] (SAG) ..... FSAT
Financial Technology [*Publisher*] [*British*] ..... FinTech
Financial Terminal Application Language (IAA) ..... FITAL
Financial Times [*A publication*] (ODBW) ..... FT
Financial Times Actuaries (ODBW) ..... FTA
Financial Times Actuaries All-Share Index (ODBW) ..... FTASI
Financial Times Actuaries Share Indices [*Database*] [*Financial Times Business Enterprises Ltd.*] [*Information service or system*] (CRD) ..... FTACT
Financial Times Business Information [*British*] ..... FTBI
Financial Times Commercial Law Reports [*A publication British*] ..... FTCLR
Financial Times Company Information Database [*Financial Times Business Information Ltd. and Predicasts*] [*Bibliographic database*] [*British*] ..... FINTEL
Financial Times Database of Key Statistical Information (MHDB) ..... Finstat
Financial Times, Don Mills, Ontario [*Library symbol National Library of Canada*] (NLC) ..... OTFT
Financial Times, Don Mills, Toronto, ON, Canada [*Library symbol Library of Congress*] (LCLS) ..... CaOTFT
Financial Times Electronic Publishing [*Financial Times*] [*British*] (NITA) ..... FINTEL
Financial Times Index [*A publication*] (CDAI) ..... FTI
Financial Times Institute of Actuaries [*A publication*] (BARN) ..... FTIA
Financial Times Law Report [*A publication*] (DLA) ..... FTLR
Financial Times Ordinary Share Index (ODBW) FT-30
Financial Times - Stock Exchange [*Stock index*] [*Pronounced "footsie"*] [*British*] ..... FT-SE
Financial Times-Actuaries World Indices [*British*] ..... FT-AWI
Financial Times-Stock Exchange 100 (ODBW) ..... FT-SE 100
Financial Transaction Terminal [*Banking*] (MHDW) ..... FTT
Financial Trust Corp. [*Associated Press*] (SAG) ..... FinlTrust
Financial Trust Corp. [*NASDAQ symbol*] (NQ) ..... FITC
Financial Trustco Capital Ltd. [*Toronto Stock Exchange symbol*] ..... FTC
Financial Weekly [*A publication*] ..... FW
Financial Wire [*Wire service term*] (WDMC) ..... F wire
Financial Women's Association of New York [*New York, NY*] (EA) ..... FWA
Financial Working Arrangement ..... FWA
Financial Working Group [*Military*] (AFIT) ..... FWG
Financial Year (EERA) ..... FY
Financially Disadvantaged Person ..... FDP
Financially Limited Plan (NATG) ..... FLIP
Financially-Oriented Computer Updating Service (IAA) ..... FOCUS
Financial-Services Industry (TDOB) ..... FSI
Financier (WDAA) ..... FIN
Financier ..... FINR
Financiera Nacional Azucarera, SNC [*Mexico*] (EY) ..... FINASA
Financiers' Association of New South Wales [*Australia*] ..... FANSW
Financing ..... FING
Financing Adjustment Factor ..... FAF
Financing Analysis Cost and Testing Service [*LIMRA*] ..... FACTS
Financing Corp. [*Created by the Reagan administration in 1987 for the Fede ral Savings and Loan Insurance Corp.*] ..... FICO
Financing for Science International, Inc. [*NASDAQ symbol*] (SAG) ..... FFSI
Financing for Science International, Inc. [*Associated Press*] (SAG) ..... FinancSci
Financing for Science International, Inc. [*Associated Press*] (SAG) ..... FinSci
Financing for Science Intl [*NASDAQ symbol*] (TTSB) ..... FFSI
Financing for Science Intl Wrrt [*NASDAQ symbol*] (TTSB) ..... FFSIW
Finanzgericht [*Tax Court*] [*German*] (ILCA) ..... FG
Finca 10 (Nuevo Palmar Sur) [*Costa Rica*] [*ICAO location identifier*] (ICLI) ..... MRFI
Finca 63 [*Costa Rica*] [*ICAO location identifier*] (ICLI) ..... MRFS
Finca Delicias [*Costa Rica*] [*ICAO location identifier*] (ICLI) ..... MRFD
Finca La Promesa [*Costa Rica*] [*ICAO location identifier*] (ICLI) ..... MRFP
Finch Branch, Stormont, Dundas, and Glengarry County Public Library, Ontario [*Library symbol National Library of Canada*] (BIB) ..... OFSDG
Finch College, New York, NY [*Library symbol Library of Congress*] (LCLS) ..... NNFC
Fincha [*Ethiopia*] [*ICAO location identifier*] (ICLI) ..... HAFN
Finch's Cases on Contract [*1886*] [*A publication*] (DLA) ..... Finch Cas Cont
Finch's Cases on Contract [*1886*] [*A publication*] (DLA) ..... Finch Cas Contr
Finch's English Chancery Reports [*1673-81*] [*A publication*] (DLA) ..... Ca T F
Finch's English Chancery Reports [*1673-81*] [*A publication*] (DLA) ..... Fin
Finch's English Chancery Reports, by Nelson [*1673-81*] [*A publication*] (DLA) ..... Nels F
Finch's English Chancery Reports, by Nelson [*1673-81*] [*A publication*] (DLA) ..... Nels Fol
Finch's Insurance Digest [*A publication*] (DLA) ..... Finch Ins Dig
Finch's Land Cases [*A publication*] (DLA) ..... Finch LC
Finch's Nomotechnia [*A publication*] (DLA) ..... Finch Nomot
Finch's Precedents in Chancery [*England*] [*A publication*] (DLA) ..... Fin Pr
Finch's Precedents in Chancery [*England*] [*A publication*] (DLA) ..... Fin Prec
Finch's Precedents in Chancery [*England*] [*A publication*] (DLA) ..... Finch
Finch's Precedents in Chancery [*England*] [*A publication*] (DLA) ..... Finch (Eng)
Finch's Summary of the Common Law [*A publication*] (DLA) ..... Finch Sum CL
Find Called [*or Calling*] **Party** [*Telecommunications*] (TEL) ..... FC
Find Dead Dynamic Link Library [*Computer software*] (PCM) ..... FDDLL
Find, Fix and Finish [*Military slang*] (VNW) ..... FFF
Find Number (MSA) ..... FN
Find or List the Identifications (SAA) ..... FLID
Find SVP [*NASDAQ symbol*] (TTSB) ..... FSVP
Find SVP, Inc. [*Associated Press*] (SAG) ..... Fd SVP
FIND/SVP, Inc. [*New York, NY NASDAQ symbol*] (NQ) ..... FSVP
Finder (MSA) ..... FDR
Finder Matrix (IAA) ..... FM
Finding ..... FNDG
Finding in Transit ..... FIT
Finding of No Significant Impact ..... FNSI
Finding of No Significant Impact [*Office of Surface Mining*] ..... FONSI
Finding Our Own Ways [*An association*] (EA) ..... FOOW
Findings and Determination (AFM) ..... F & D
Findings and Determination (IAA) ..... FAD
Findlay College, Findlay, OH [*OCLC symbol*] (OCLC) ..... FIN
Findlay College, Findlay, OH [*Library symbol Library of Congress*] (LCLS) ..... OFiC
Findlay, OH [*Location identifier FAA*] (FAAL) ..... BNR
Findlay, OH [*Location identifier FAA*] (FAAL) ..... FDY
Findlay, OH [*Location identifier FAA*] (FAAL) ..... MAH
Findlay, OH [*AM radio station call letters*] ..... WFIN
Findlay, OH [*FM radio station call letters*] ..... WKXA
Findlay, OH [*FM radio station call letters*] ..... WLFC
Findlay-Hancock County District Public Library, Findlay, OH [*OCLC symbol*] (OCLC) ..... FPL
Findlay-Hancock County District Public Library, Findlay, OH [*Library symbol Library of Congress*] (LCLS) ..... OFi
Fine [*Designation on brandy labels*] ..... F
Fine [*Condition*] [*Antiquarian book trade, numismatics, etc.*] ..... F
Fine [*End*] [*Music*] ..... F
Fine [*Quality of the bottom*] [*Nautical charts*] ..... fne
Fine Aim Positioning ..... FAP
Fine Airlines, Inc. [*ICAO designator*] (FAAC) ..... FBF
Fine Alignment ..... FA
Fine Alignment Complete ..... FAC
Fine Alignment Equipment ..... FAE
Fine Alignment Subsystem ..... FASS
Fine Alignment Unit ..... FAU
Fine and Specialty Wire Manufacturers Association [*Later, Specialty Wire Association*] (EA) ..... FSWMA
Fine Art, Antique, and Philatelic Squad [*Scotland Yard*] [*British*] ..... FAAPS
Fine Art Development [*British*] ..... FAD
Fine Art Trade Guide [*British*] (DBA) ..... FATG
Fine Arts ..... FA
Fine Arts Foundation (EA) ..... FAF
Fine Arts Gallery of San Diego, San Diego, CA [*Library symbol Library of Congress*] (LCLS) ..... CSdA
Fine Arts Library, Northern District, Toronto Public Libraries, Ontario [*Library symbol National Library of Canada*] (NLC) ..... OTPFA
Fine Arts, Music, and Films Division, Vancouver Public Library, British Columbia [*Library symbol National Library of Canada*] (NLC) ..... BVAFA
Fine Arts Philatelists (EA) ..... FAP
Fine Attitude Control System [*Aerospace*] ..... FACS
Fine Bearing Servo ..... FBS
Fine Business [*i.e., excellent*] [*Amateur radio*] ..... FB
Fine Champagne ..... FC
Fine Chemicals Directory (NITA) ..... FCD
Fine Chemicals Directory Data Base [*Molecular Design Ltd.*] [*Information service or system*] ..... FCD
Fine Cognac ..... FC
Fine Control (DEN) ..... FC
Fine Control Damper [*Nuclear energy*] (NRCH) ..... FCD
Fine Crushed Rock (ADA) ..... FCR
Fine Erection ..... FE
Fine Erection Complete ..... FEC
Fine Error Sensor (KSC) ..... FES
Fine French Furniture ..... FFF
Fine Gardening [*A publication*] ..... Fine Gard
Fine Gardening [*A publication*] (BRI) ..... Fine Gard
Fine Grain ..... FG
Fine Grain Data [*Equipment*] [*RADAR*] ..... FGD
Fine Guidance Sensor (PDAA) ..... FGS
Fine Hardwoods American Walnut Association (EA) ..... FHAWA
Fine Hardwoods Association [*Later, FHAWA*] (EA) ..... FHA
Fine Homebuilding [*A publication*] (BRI) ..... FHB
Fine Hose Corp. [*NASDAQ symbol*] (SAG) ..... FINE
Fine Host Corp. [*Associated Press*] (SAG) ..... FineHost
Fine [*Condition*] **in Dust Wrapper** [*Antiquarian book trade*] ..... FDW
Fine Intestinal Needle [*Medicine*] (DMAA) ..... FIN
Fine Measurement ..... FM
Fine Mesh Cover Protected (IAA) ..... FMPROT
Fine Mesh Gauze [*Surgery*] (DAVI) ..... FMG
Fine Motor ..... FM
Fine Needle Aspiration Cytology (DAVI) ..... FNAC
Fine Needle Catheter Jejunostomy [*Medicine*] (DMAA) ..... FNCJ
Fine Old ..... FO
Fine Old Blend [*Wines and spirits*] ..... FOB
Fine Old Extra Special ..... FOES
Fine Old Very Extra Special [*Designation on brandy labels*] ..... FOVES
Fine Paper ..... FP
Fine Particle Society (EA) ..... FPS
Fine Particulate (GFGA) ..... FP
Fine Particulate Emissions Information System [*Environmental Protection Agency*] (GFGA) ..... FPEIS
Fine Particulate Emissions Information System (GNE) ..... FPEIS
Fine Particulate Matter [*Pisciculture*] ..... FPM
Fine Particulate Organic Matter ..... FPOM
Fine Pitch Technology [*Engineering*] ..... FPT
Fine Pointing (MCD) ..... FP
Fine Pointing Facility [*NASA*] (KSC) ..... FPF
Fine Range Tuning [*Military*] (CAAL) ..... FRT
Fine Resolution Antarctic Model [*Oceanography*] ..... FRAM
Fine Scale Modeler [*A publication*] ..... FSM
Fine Structure Analysis (IAA) ..... FSA

Fine Sun Sensor [*NASA*] .... FSS
Fine Sun Sensor/Signal Conditioner [*NASA*] (MCD) ..... FSS/S
Fine Test Dust [*Automotive engineering*] .... FTD
Fine Thermal [*Furnace*] .... FT
Fine to Very Fine [*Philately*] .... F-VF
Fine Track Sensor .... FTS
Finely Granular [*Laboratory*] (DAVI) .... FGRN
Fine-Needle Aspiration [*Medicine*] .... FNA
Fine-Needle Aspiration Biopsy [*Medicine*] .... FNAB
Fine-Needle Cholangiography [*Gastroenterology*] .... FNC
Fineness Modulus (DICI) .... FM
Fineness of Grind [*Materials science*] .... FOG
Fineness Ratio .... FR
Finest .... FNST
Finest Foods of Virginia [*Brand name*] .... FFV
Finfish Excluding Device [*Fishing technology*] .... FED
Finger .... F
Finger (MSA) .... FGR
Finger .... Fin
Finger Breadth [*Medicine*] .... FB
Finger Clubbing [*Medicine*] (MAE) .... FC
Finger Counting [*See also CF*] .... FC
Finger Lakes Library System [*Library network*] .... FLLS
Finger Lakes Library System, Ithaca, NY [*Library symbol Library of Congress*] (LCLS) .... NIFL
Finger Lakes Library System, Ithaca, NY [*OCLC symbol*] (OCLC) .... VYG
Finger Lakes Wine Growers Association (EA) .... FLWGA
Finger Millet Mosaic Virus [*Plant pathology*] .... FMMV
Finger of Death [*Fantasy gaming*] (NHD) .... FOD
Finger Sweat Print [*Psychometrics*] .... FSP
Finger to Finger [*Medicine*] .... FF
Finger to Nose [*Medicine*] (DMAA) .... FTN
Finger to Nose Test [*Neurology*] .... F to N
Finger to Nose Test [*Neurology*] .... F-N
Fingerbreadth Below Right Costal Margin [*Measurement*] [*Anatomy*] (DAVI) .... FBRCM
Fingerhut Companies [*NYSE symbol*] (TTSB) .... FHT
Fingerhut Companies, Inc. [*NYSE symbol*] (SPSG) .... FHT
Fingerhut Companies, Inc. [*Associated Press*] (SAG) .... Fingerht
Finger-Nose-Finger [*Test*] [*Neurology*] (DAVI) .... FNF
Fingerprint Access and Searching Technique [*Computer science*] (IAA) ...... FAST
Fingerprint Automatic Classification Technique [*Computer science*] .... FACT
Fingerprint Identification Unit [*Sony Corp.*] .... FIU
Fingerprint Reader .... FINDER
Fingerprint Reader .... FIRE
Fingers Below Umbilicus [*Measurement*] [*Anatomy*] (DAVI) .... FBU
Finger-Stick Blood Gas (MEDA) .... FSBG
Fingertip Blood [*Medicine*] .... FTB
Finger-to-Finger [*Neurology*] (DAVI) .... FTF
Finis [*The End*] [*Latin*] .... FIN
Finish .... F
Finish (KSC) .... FIN
Finish (VRA) .... fin
Finish (WDMC) .... fin
Finish .... FNSH
Finish (MSA) .... FNSH
Finish All Over [*Technical drawings*] .... FAO
Finish Exercise [*Military*] (NVT) .... FINEX
Finish Line 'A' [*NASDAQ symbol*] (TTSB) .... FINL
Finish Line, Inc. [*NASDAQ symbol*] (SAG) .... FINL
Finish Line, Inc. [*Associated Press*] (SAG) .... FinLine
Finish Moulding [*Automotive engineering*] .... F/MLDG
Finish One Side [*Technical drawings*] F1S
Finish One Side [*Technical drawings*] (IAA) .... FOS
Finish Specification .... FS
Finish Two Sides [*Technical drawings*] F2S
Finish Two Sides [*Technical drawings*] (IAA) .... FTS
Finished (VRA) .... fin
Finished Dialing [*Telecommunications*] (TEL) .... FD
Finished Floor Elevation [*Technical drawings*] .... FFE
Finished Floor Line [*Technical drawings*] .... FFL
Finished Goods Control .... FGC
Finished Goods Store .... FGS
Finished Intelligence (MCD) .... FI
Finished Lens Molding .... FLM
Finished with Engines .... FWE
Finished with Main Engines [*Navy*] .... FME
Finisher/Preserver/Cleaner (DGA) .... FPC
Finishers' Society [*A union*] [*British*] .... FS
Finishing .... FINISH
Finishmaster, Inc. [*Associated Press*] (SAG) .... FinsMst
Finishmaster, Inc. [*NASDAQ symbol*] (SAG) .... FMST
Finist' Air [*France ICAO designator*] (FAAC) .... FTR
Finite Area Solids Technology (MCD) .... FAST
Finite Automation .... FA
Finite Automation Language [*Computer science*] .... FAL
Finite Difference [*Metallurgy*] .... FD
Finite Difference [*Mathematics*] .... FD
Finite Difference Method [*Mathematics*] .... FDM
Finite Difference - Time Domain [*Computer simulation*] .... FD-TD
Finite Differential Equation (PDAA) .... FDE
Finite Elastic Body .... FEB
Finite Element Analysis [*Engineering*] .... FEA
Finite Element Analysis Basic Library [*MIT*] .... FEABL
Finite Element Analysis Program [*Nuclear energy*] (NRCH) .... FELAP

Finite Element Analysis Sensibly Implemented by Least Effort .... FEASIBLE
Finite Element Analysis System [*IBM UK Ltd.*] [*Software package*] (NCC) .... FEAS
Finite Element Data Generation [*Computer science*] .... FEDGE
Finite Element Mesh and Result Viewing [*Fegs Ltd.*] [*Software package*] (NCC) .... FEMVIEW
Finite Element Mesh Generation Program [*Fegs Ltd.*] [*Software package*] (NCC) .... FEMGEN
Finite Element Method .... FEM
Finite Element Modeling Optimization .... FEMO
Finite Element Mold-Filling Analysis Program [*General Electric Co.*] .... FEMAP
Finite Element Solution System (PDAA) .... FESS
Finite Element Solver (NITA) .... FES
Finite Element Structures Analysis Program [*Computer science*] .... FESAP
Finite Energy Sum Rules [*Physics*] .... FESR
Finite Flat Plate .... FFP
Finite Fourier Transform .... FFT
Finite Hilbert Transform (PDAA) .... FHT
Finite Impulse Response [*Filter*] (MCD) .... FIR
Finite Intermediate Storage [*Industrial engineering*] .... FIS
Finite Logical View (MHDB) .... FLV
Finite Mass Sum Rule [*Nuclear science*] (OA) .... FMSR
Finite Message Machine [*Telecommunications*] .... FMM
Finite Perturbation Theory [*Physics*] .... FPT
Finite Sampling Time .... FST
Finite Solution Set [*Mathematics*] (WDAA) .... FSS
Finite State Automation (HGAA) .... FSA
Finite State Channel (IAA) .... FSC
Finite State Grammar .... FSG
Finite State Language .... FSL
Finite State Machine .... FSM
Finite State Specification Language [*Computer science*] (MHDI) .... FISSL
Finite Volume [*Metallurgy*] .... FV
Finite-Element Meshing [*or Modeling*] [*Computer science*] (PCM) .... FEM
Finite-Life Real Estate Investment Trust .... FREIT
Finitely Repeated Prisoner's Dilemma [*Psychology*] .... FRPD
Finkel, et Alia. Lawyers' Medical Cyclopedia [*A publication*] (DLA) .... Finkel Medical Cyc
Finkelstein Memorial Library, Spring Valley, NY [*Library symbol Library of Congress*] (LCLS) .... NSv
Fink's Indian Evidence Act [*A publication*] (DLA) .... Fink Ev
Finl Institutions Insur Grp [*NASDAQ symbol*] (TTSB) .... FIRE
Finland [*MARC geographic area code Library of Congress*] (LCCP) .... e-fi---
Finland [*MARC country of publication code Library of Congress*] (LCCP) .... fi
Finland [*ANSI two-letter standard code*] (CNC) .... FI
Finland [*ANSI three-letter standard code*] (CNC) .... FIN
Finland (VRA) .... Finl
Finland [*IYRU nationality code*] (IYR) L
Finland [*International civil aircraft marking*] (ODBW) .... OH
Finland-European Free Trade Association Treaty .... FINEFTA
Finlandia Foundation (EA) .... FF
Finlands Folks Enhetsparti [*Finnish People's Unity Party*] (PPE) .... FFEP
Finlands Kommunistiska Parti [*Finnish Communist Party*] (PPE) .... FKP
Finlands Kristliga Foerbund [*Finnish Christian League*] (PPE) .... FKF
Finlands Landsbygdsparti [*Finnish Rural Party*] [*Political party*] (PPE) .... FLP
Finlason on Charitable Trusts [*A publication*] (DLA) .... Finl Ch Tr
Finlason on Commons [*A publication*] (DLA) .... Finl Com
Finlason's Commentaries on Martial Law [*A publication*] (DLA) .... Finl Mar L
Finlason's History of Law of Tenures of Land [*1870*] [*A publication*] (DLA) .... Finl Ld Ten
Finlason's History of Law of Tenures of Land [*1870*] [*A publication*] (DLA) .... Finl Ten
Finlason's Judicial System [*A publication*] (DLA) .... Finl Jud Sys
Finlason's Leading Cases on Pleading [*A publication*] (DLA) .... Finl LC
Finlason's Report of the Gurney Case [*A publication*] (DLA) .... Finl Rep
Finlay Enterprises [*NASDAQ symbol*] (TTSB) .... FNLY
Finlay Enterprises, Inc. [*Associated Press*] (SAG) .... Finlay
Finlay Enterprises, Inc. [*NASDAQ symbol*] (SAG) .... FNLY
Finlay Fork [*British Columbia*] [*Seismograph station code, US Geological Survey Closed*] (SEIS) .... FNC
Finlay on Renewals [*A publication*] (DLA) .... Fin Ren
Finlay on Repression of Riot or Rebellion [*A publication*] (DLA) ... Finl Riot
Finlay's Irish Digest [*A publication*] (DLA) .... Fin
Finlay's Irish Digest [*A publication*] (DLA) .... Fin Dig
Finlay's Irish Digest [*A publication*] (DLA) .... Finl Dig
Finlayson Elementary School, Finlayson, MN [*Library symbol*] [*Library of Congress*] (LCLS) .... MnFiE
Finlayson High School, Finlayson, MN [*Library symbol*] [*Library of Congress*] (LCLS) .... MnFiH
Finley Junior High School, Huntington, NY [*Library symbol Library of Congress*] (LCLS) .... NHuFJ
Finnair [*ICAO designator*] (AD) .... AY
Finnair [*Airline flight code*] (ODBW) .... AY
Finnair OY [*Finland ICAO designator*] (FAAC) .... FIN
Finnaviation OY [*Finland ICAO designator*] (FAAC) .... FAV
Finned Air Rocket (SAA) .... FAR
Finnemore and Dulcken's Natal Law Reports [*A publication*] (DLA) .... Fin & Dul
Finnemore's Notes and Digest of Natal Cases [*A publication*] (DLA) .... FND
Finning Ltd. [*Toronto Stock Exchange symbol Vancouver Stock Exchange symbol*] .... FTT
Finningley [*British ICAO location identifier*] (ICLI) .... EGXI
Finningley FTU [*British ICAO designator*] (FAAC) .... FYY
Finnish [*MARC language code Library of Congress*] (LCCP) .... fin
Finnish .... FINN
Finnish Air Force .... FinAF
Finnish Air Force Headquarters [*ICAO designator*] (FAAC) .... FNF

Finnish American Historical Society of Michigan (EA) .... FAHSM
Finnish American League for Democracy (EA) .... FALD
Finnish Association for Data Processing .... FADP
Finnish Center for Radiation and Nuclear Safety [Sateilyturvakeskus], Helsinki, Finland [Library symbol] [Library of Congress] (LCLS) .... FiHCRN
Finnish International Development Agency (International) (EERA) .... FINNIDA
Finnish Meteorological Institute [Helinski, Finland] .... FMI
Finnish Periodicals Index in Economics and Business [Helsinki School of Economics Library] [Information service or system] .... FINP
Finnish Plywood Development Association .... FPDA
Finnish Radio Industries Association .... FRIA
Finnish Reactor .... FIR
Finnish Sauna Society [British] (DBA) .... FSS
Finnish Society of Adelaide [South Australia] .... FSA
Finnish Society of Sydney [New South Wales, Australia] .... FSS
[The] Finnish University Network [Finland] [Computer science] (TNIG) .... FUNET
Finnish War Veterans in America (EA) .... FWVA
Finnish Workers' Educational Association [Defunct] (EA) .... FWEA
Finnish-American Historical Archives (EA) .... FAHA
Finnish-American Historical Society of the West (EA) .... FAHSW
Finnish-American Society [Later, LFAS] (EA) .... FAS
Finnmark [Finnish Mark] [Monetary unit] .... FIM
Finno-Ugrian [MARC language code Library of Congress] (LCCP) .... fiu
Finno-Ugrian Studies Association of Canada [See also ACEFO] .... FUSAC
Finnsheep Breeders Association (EA) .... FSBA
Finnsnes [Norway] [Airport symbol] (AD) .... FNE
FINOVA Group [NYSE symbol] (TTSB) .... FNV
Finova Group, Inc. [Associated Press] (SAG) .... FinovaGp
Finova Group, Inc. [NYSE symbol] (SAG) .... FNV
Finova Group, Inc. Finance Trust [Associated Press] (SAG) .... Finova
Fins per Inch [Heat exchangers] .... FPI
FINSAP Implementation Secretariat [West Africa] .... FIS
Finsbury Data Services Ltd. [Database] [London, England] .... FDS
Finsbury Group Ltd. [Vancouver Stock Exchange symbol] .... FBG
Finschhafen [Papua New Guinea] [Airport symbol] (OAG) .... FIN
Finsen Unit [for ultraviolet light] .... Fu
Finthen [Germany ICAO location identifier] (ICLI) .... EDOT
FIPS [Federal Information Processing Standard] Coordinating and Advisory Committee (NITA) .... FIPSCAC
Fir and Hemlock Door Association [Defunct] (EA) .... FHDA
Firan Corp. [Toronto Stock Exchange symbol] .... FNG
Firariana [Madagascar] [Seismograph station code, US Geological Survey] (SEIS) .... FRR
Fircrest Resources [Vancouver Stock Exchange symbol] .... FCH
Fircrest School, Resident Library, Seattle, WA [Library symbol Library of Congress] (LCLS) .... WaSF-R
Fircrest School, Staff Library, Seattle, WA [Library symbol Library of Congress] (LCLS) .... WaSF
Fire .... F
Fire Alarm (ROG) .... FA
Fire Alarm Bell .... FABL
Fire Alarm Box .... FABX
Fire Alarm Monitoring Panel (IEEE) .... FAMP
Fire and Allied Lines [Insurance] .... F & A
Fire and Bilge .... F & B
Fire and Casualty (WDAA) .... F & C
Fire and Casualty Cases [Commerce Clearing House] [A publication] (DLA) .... F & CC
Fire and Casualty Cases [A publication] (DLA) .... Fire & Cas Cas
Fire and Casualty Insurance Library Edition .... FACILE
Fire and Explosion Index [Hazard analysis] .... F & EI
Fire and Flushing (KSC) .... F & F
Fire and Forget Antitank System Technology (MCD) .... FFAST
Fire and Maneuver [Infantry strategy] (VNW) .... F and M
Fire and Safety [Technician] [Coast Guard] (DOMA) .... FS
Fire and Safety Test Detachment [Mobile, AL] [Coast Guard] (GRD) .... F & STD
Fire and Safety Unit [Coast Guard] (DOMA) .... FSU
Fire and Theft .... F & T
Fire Ant Venom [Immunology] .... FAV
Fire Ant Whole Body Extract [Immunology] .... FAWBE
Fire Apparatus Manufacturers Association [Defunct] (EA) .... FAMA
Fire Brick [Technical drawings] .... FBRK
Fire Brick Workers' Union [British] .... FBWU
Fire Brigade .... FB
Fire Brigade Hydrant .... FBH
Fire Brigade Society [British] (DBA) .... FBS
Fire Brigade Union .... FBU
Fire Brigades Board [Queensland, Australia] .... FBB
Fire Cause [Criminology] (LAIN) .... FC
Fire Clay .... FC
Fire Cock [British] (ROG) .... FC
Fire Collectors Club (EA) .... FCC
Fire Command (KSC) .... FCMD
Fire Command Vehicle .... FCV
Fire Commander [British military] (DMA) .... FC
Fire Control [of guns] .... FC
Fire Control [JETDS nomenclature] .... G
Fire Control and Small Caliber Weapon Systems Laboratory [Picatinny Arsenal, Dover, NJ] [Army] (RDA) .... FC & SCWSL
Fire Control and Small Caliber Weapon Systems Laboratory [Picatinny Arsenal, Dover, NJ] [Army] (INF) .... FSL
Fire Control Area [Army] .... FCA
Fire Control Armourer [British military] (DMA) .... FALD
Fire Control Check [Military] (NVT) .... FCCK
Fire Control Code .... FCC

Fire Control Computer .... FCC
Fire Control Computer Operational Program (MCD) .... FCCOP
Fire Control Console (NATG) .... FCC
Fire Control Control Console .... FCCC
Fire Control Control Subsystem .... FCCSS
Fire Control Data Converter (MCD) .... FCDC
Fire Control Electronics (MCD) .... FCE
Fire Control Electronics Unit [Military] (RDA) .... FCEU
Fire Control Element (MCD) .... FCE
Fire Control Engagement Controller [Military] (CAAL) .... FCEC
Fire Control Equipment .... FCE
Fire Control Group .... FCG
Fire Control Instruments (MCD) .... FCI
Fire Control, Line-of-Sight .... FC/LOS
Fire Control Navigation Panel (IEEE) .... FCNP
Fire Control Notes [A publication] .... FCN
Fire Control Operator [Army] .... FCO
Fire Control Optical Instrument .... FCOI
Fire Control Panel (MCD) .... FCP
Fire Control Personnel [Marine Corps] .... FCP
Fire Control Platoon [Army] .... FCP
Fire Control RADAR .... FCR
Fire Control Reference Frame (MCD) .... FCRF
Fire Control Sensor Group .... FCSG
Fire Control Sight System [Military] .... FCSS
Fire Control Simulation (MCD) .... FICS
Fire Control Simulator .... FCS
Fire Control Simulator Unit .... FCSU
Fire Control Switchboard .... FCSB
Fire Control Switchboard .... FCSWB
Fire Control Switchboard .... FCSWBD
Fire Control Switching Unit .... FCSU
Fire Control System .... FCS
Fire Control System Console [Military] (CAAL) .... FCSC
Fire Control System Coordinator .... FCSC
Fire Control System Laboratory .... FCSL
Fire Control System Module .... FCSM
Fire Control Technician [Navy rating Obsolete] .... FCT
Fire Control Technician [Navy rating] .... FT
Fire Control Technician, Ballistic Missile [Navy rating] .... FTB
Fire Control Technician, Ballistic Missile Fire Control, Chief [Navy rating] (DNAB) .... FTBC
Fire Control Technician, Ballistic Missile Fire Control, First Class [Navy rating] (DNAB) FTB1
Fire Control Technician, Ballistic Missile Fire Control, Seaman [Navy rating] .... FTBSN
Fire Control Technician, Ballistic Missile Fire Control, Seaman Apprentice [Navy rating] .... FTBSA
Fire Control Technician, Ballistic Missile Fire Control, Second Class [Navy rating] (DNAB) FTB2
Fire Control Technician, Ballistic Missile Fire Control, Third Class [Navy rating] (DNAB) FTB3
Fire Control Technician, Chief [Navy rating] .... FTC
Fire Control Technician, First Class [Navy rating] FT1
Fire Control Technician, Gun [Navy rating] .... FTG
Fire Control Technician, Gun Fire Control, Chief [Navy rating] (DNAB) .... FTGC
Fire Control Technician, Gun Fire Control, First Class [Navy rating] (DNAB) FTG1
Fire Control Technician, Gun Fire Control, Seaman [Navy rating] (DNAB) .... FTGSN
Fire Control Technician, Gun Fire Control, Seaman Apprentice [Navy rating] (DNAB) .... FTGSA
Fire Control Technician, Gun Fire Control, Second Class [Navy rating] (DNAB) FTG2
Fire Control Technician, Gun Fire Control, Third Class [Navy rating] (DNAB) FTG3
Fire Control Technician, Master Chief [Navy rating] .... FTCM
Fire Control Technician, Missile Fire Control, Chief [Navy rating] (DNAB) .... FTMC
Fire Control Technician, Missile Fire Control, First Class [Navy rating] (DNAB) FTM1
Fire Control Technician, Missile Fire Control, Seaman [Navy rating] (DNAB) .... FTMSN
Fire Control Technician, Missile Fire Control, Seaman Apprentice [Navy rating] (DNAB) .... FTMSA
Fire Control Technician, Missile Fire Control, Second Class [Navy rating] (DNAB) FTM2
Fire Control Technician, Missile Fire Control, Third Class [Navy rating] (DNAB) FTM3
Fire Control Technician, Second Class [Navy rating] FT2
Fire Control Technician, Senior Chief [Navy rating] .... FTCS
Fire Control Technician, Surface Missile [Navy rating] .... FTM
Fire Control Technician, Third Class [Navy rating] FT3
Fire Control Test Equipment .... FCTE
Fire Control Test Package .... FCTP
Fire Control Test Set .... FCTS
Fire Control Trainer .... FCT
Fire Control Unit .... FCU
Fire Control Workshop .... FCW
Fire Controlman [Navy rating Obsolete] .... FC
Fire Controlman, Range-Finder Operator [Navy rating Obsolete] .... FCR
Fire Controlman, Submarine [Navy rating Obsolete] .... FCS
Fire Coordination Exercise [Military] (ADDR) .... FCX
Fire Coordination Line [Military] (AABC) .... FCL
Fire Damper (OA) .... FD

Fire Department ... FD
Fire Department Access Point [*NFPA planning symbol*] (NFPA) ... FD
Fire Department Instructors Conference (EA) ... FDIC
Fire Detection Center ... FDC
Fire Detection Operation Center ... FDOC
Fire Detection System ... FDS
Fire Detector ... FD
Fire Detector Control Unit (MCD) ... FDCU
Fire Direction ... FD
Fire Direction Center [*Military*] ... FDC
Fire Direction Officer [*Army*] (AABC) ... FDO
Fire Distribution System ... FDS
Fire Door (AAG) ... FDR
Fire Drop (AABC) ... FD
Fire Emergency Equipment Dispatch System ... FEEDS
Fire Equipment Manufacturers Association (EA) ... FEMA
Fire Escape (DAC) ... FE
Fire Experimental Unit [*British Fire Service*] (IRUK) ... FEU
Fire Extinguisher (AAG) ... FE
Fire Extinguisher ... FEXT
Fire Extinguisher Cabinet [*Technical drawings*] ... FEC
Fire Extinguisher [*or Extinguishing*] **System** (AAG) ... FIREX
Fire Extinguisher Trades Association [*British*] (BI) ... FETA
Fire Fighting (MSA) ... FF
Fire Fighting Enterprises (Australia) Ltd. [*Commercial firm*] ... FFE(A)
Fire Fighting Vehicles Manufacturers Association [*British*] (DBA) ... FFVMA
Fire for Effect [*Army*] (INF) ... FFE
Fire Guardsman [*British World War II*] ... FG
Fire Hose (AAG) ... FH
Fire Hose Cabinet (KSC) ... FHC
Fire Hose Rack ... FHR
Fire Hose Reel ... FHR
Fire Hose Station [*Technical drawings*] ... FHS
Fire Hydrant ... FH
Fire Hydrant ... FHY
Fire Indicator Board ... FIB
Fire Industry Council [*British*] (DBA) ... FIC
Fire Information Retrieval System Technique ... FIRST
Fire Insurance Policy [*Legal shorthand*] (LWAP) ... FIP
Fire Insurance Research and Actuarial Association [*Later, ISO*] (EA) ... FIRAA
Fire Integration Support Team ... FIST
Fire Island [*Alaska*] [*Seismograph station code, US Geological Survey Closed*] (SEIS) ... FIS
Fire, Lightning, and Explosion [*Insurance*] (AIA) ... FLE
Fire Location RADAR (NG) ... FLORA
Fire Main (AAG) ... FM
Fire Mark Circle [*Liverpool, England*] (EAIO) ... FMC
Fire Mark Circle of the Americas (EA) ... FMCA
Fire Marshal of Ontario, Toronto, ON, Canada [*Library symbol Library of Congress*] (LCLS) ... CaOTFM
Fire Marshal of Ontario, Toronto, Ontario [*Library symbol National Library of Canada*] (NLC) ... OTFM
Fire Marshals Association of North America (EA) ... FMANA
Fire, Mildew, Water, and Weather Resistant (MCD) ... FMWWR
Fire Movement Range (MCD) ... FMR
Fire Offices Committee [*British*] (AIA) ... FOC
Fire Operational Characteristics Using Simulation [*System for comparing organizations for wildland fire protection services in cost-effective terms*] [*Department of Agriculture, Forest Services*] ... FOCUS
Fire Philatelic Group (EA) ... FPG
Fire Plug ... FP
Fire Plug (AAG) ... FPL
Fire Policy [*Insurance*] ... F/P
Fire Policy [*Insurance*] (DCTA) ... F/POL
Fire Prevention Canada Association ... FIPRECAN
Fire Prevention Officer [*British*] ... FPO
Fire Protection Association [*Australia*] ... FPA
Fire Protection Association [*British*] ... FPA
Fire Protection Equipment [*Nuclear energy*] (NRCH) ... FP
Fire Protection Industry Association of Australia (EERA) ... FPIAA
Fire Protection Pumphouse [*Nuclear energy*] (NRCH) ... FPPH
Fire Protection System [*Nuclear energy*] (NRCH) ... FPS
Fire Protection System ... FPS
Fire Protection Water Tank (IEEE) ... FPWT
Fire Pump Control (IEEE) ... FPC
Fire Pump Engine [*Auto racing engine model designation*] [*British*] ... FPE
Fire Pump Room [*NFPA pre-fire planning symbol*] (NFPA) ... FP
Fire Rescue Air Pack [*NASA*] ... FRAP
Fire Research Information Services [*National Institute of Standards and Technology*] (IID) ... FRIS
Fire Research Station [*Research center British*] (IRC) ... FRS
Fire Resistance Level ... FRL
Fire Resistant [*or Retardant*] ... FR
Fire Resistant ... FRES
Fire Resistant Materials Engineering (PDAA) ... FIREMEN
Fire Resistive ... FR
Fire Resistive Protected [*Insurance classification*] ... XP
Fire Resistive Unprotected [*Insurance classification*] ... XU
Fire Retardant [*Technical drawings*] ... FRT
Fire Retardant Chemicals Association (EA) ... FRCA
Fire Retarding Additive ... FRA
Fire Risk on Freight [*Insurance*] ... FROF
Fire Room ... FRM
Fire Safety Evaluation System [*National Institute of Standards and Technology*] ... FSES
Fire Safety Technology (SSD) ... FST
Fire Safety Toxicity ... FST
Fire Science Abstracts [*Department of the Environment*] [*Information service or system*] (IID) ... FSA
Fire Sensor Control Panel (MCD) ... FSCP
Fire Service ... FS
Fire Service College [*British*] ... FSC
Fire Service in Philately [*An association*] ... FSIP
Fire Service Inspectorate [*British*] ... FSI
Fire Service Instructors ... FSI
Fire Service Valve (IEEE) ... FSV
Fire Site Assembly (MCD) ... FSA
Fire Station [*Maps and charts*] ... FS
Fire Support ... FS
Fire Support Aerial System ... FAS
Fire Support and Target Acquisition Division [*Human Engineering Laboratory*] [*Army*] ... FSTAD
Fire Support Area [*Military*] ... FSA
Fire Support Armament Center [*Dover, NJ*] [*Army*] (GRD) ... FSAC
Fire Support Base [*Army*] (AABC) ... FSB
Fire Support Center [*Army*] (DOMA) ... FSC
Fire Support Combat Vehicle (MCD) ... FSCV
Fire Support Combined Arms Tactical Trainer [*Army*] (RDA) ... FSCATT
Fire Support Combined Arms Tactical Trainer [*Army*] ... FSCATT
Fire Support Coordination [*Military*] ... FSC
Fire Support Coordination Center [*Military*] ... FSCC
Fire Support Coordination Element [*Military*] ... FSCE
Fire Support Coordination Line [*Military*] (AABC) ... FSCL
Fire Support Coordination Measure [*Military*] (INF) ... FSCM
Fire Support Coordination Section [*Military*] ... FSCS
Fire Support Coordination Team Trainer (DOMA) ... FSCTT
Fire Support Coordinator [*Military*] (AABC) ... FSCOORD
Fire Support Element [*Military*] (AABC) ... FSE
Fire Support Modeling and Simulations Institute ... FSMSI
Fire Support Officer [*Military*] ... FSO
Fire Support Primary Base (DNAB) ... FSPB
Fire Support Ship ... FSS
Fire Support Station [*Navy*] (NVT) ... FSS
Fire Support Surveillance Base [*Military*] (VNW) ... FSSB
Fire Support Team [*Military*] (INF) ... FIST
Fire Support Team (MCD) ... FST
Fire Support Team and Combat Observation Lasing System [*Army*] ... FS/COLS
Fire Support Team Vehicle [*Army*] (RDA) ... FISTV
Fire Support Vehicle [*Military*] (MCD) ... FSV
Fire Suppression (MCD) ... FS
Fire Suppression System (MCD) ... FSS
Fire Suppression Systems Association (EA) ... FSSA
Fire Survivability for Ground Combat Vehicles (MCD) ... FIS-COV
Fire Switch (KSC) ... FS
Fire Team [*Marine Corps*] ... FT
Fire Team Support Weapon (MCD) ... FSW
Fire Technology Division [*National Institute of Standards and Technology*] ... FTD
Fire Thermostat (AAG) ... FT
Fire Unit Analyzer [*Military*] ... FUA
Fire Unit Deployed ... FUD
Fire Unit Effectiveness (MCD) ... FUE
Fire Unit Integration Facility [*Military*] ... FUIF
Fire Until Touchdown [*Apollo*] [*NASA*] ... FUT
Fire Up Decoder ... FUD
Fire Vent (BARN) ... fv
Fire Wall [*Technical drawings*] ... FW
Fire Warning (FAAC) ... FWRNG
Fire Water Service ... FWS
Fire, Water, Weather, Mildew Resistant (MCD) ... FWWMR
Fire Zone [*Bulkhead*] (DNAB) ... FZ
Fire-and-Forget (MCD) ... F & F
Firearm ... FRARM
Firearm and Security Trainers Management Association (EA) ... FSTMA
Firearms Acquisition Certificate [*Canada*] ... FAC
Firearms and Individual Rights [*A California organization*] ... FAIR
Firearms Consultative Committee [*Australia*] ... FCC
Firearms Lobby of America [*Later, CCRKBA*] (EA) ... FLA
Firearms Owners' Protection Act ... FOPA
Firearms Research and Identification Association (EA) ... FRIA
Firearms Training Systems, Inc. ... FATS
Fireball International [*Axminster, Devonshire, England*] (EAIO) ... FI
Fireball Mode of Combustion [*Combustion in engines*] ... FMC
Fireball Radius [*Military*] (AABC) ... FBR
Fireball Resources [*Vancouver Stock Exchange symbol*] ... FRB
Firebaugh, CA [*FM radio station call letters*] (RBYB) ... KAJP
Firebrick ... FBCK
Fireclay Grate Back Association [*British*] (BI) ... FGBA
Firecracker Alternative Book [*Award Program*] ... FAB
Fired (MSA) ... FIR
Fired (VRA) ... frd
Fired Vessel [*Insurance*] ... FV
Fire-Department Connection [*Technical drawings*] ... FDC
Firefighter [*Army*] (AABC) ... FFGT
Firefighter (AFM) ... FFTR
Firefighter Breathing System [*NASA*] ... FBS
Firefighting [*Army*] (AABC) ... FFTG
Fire-Fighting Equipment (AAG) ... FFE
Firefinder ... FF
Firefinder Intermediate Maintenance Trainer (DWSG) ... FIMT
Firefox Communications [*NASDAQ symbol*] (TTSB) ... FFOX

Firefox Communications, Inc. [*NASDAQ symbol*] (SAG) .... FFOX
Firefox Communications, Inc. [*Associated Press*] (SAG) .... Firefox
Firegreen Ltd. [*Food-processing and distributing company*] [*British*] .... FG
Fire-in-the-Hole [*Burn*] [*NASA*] .... FITH
Fireman [*Navy rating*] .... F
Fireman .... FIRMN
Fireman [*Nonrated enlisted man*] [*Navy*] .... FN
Fireman Apprentice [*Navy rating*] .... FA
Fireman Apprentice, Boilermaker, Striker [*Navy rating*] .... BRFA
Fireman Apprentice, Boilerman, Striker [*Navy rating*] .... BTFA
Fireman Apprentice, Engineman, Striker [*Navy rating*] .... ENFA
Fireman Apprentice, Interior Communications Electrician, Striker [*Navy rating*] .... ICFA
Fireman Apprentice, Machinery Repairman, Striker [*Navy rating*] .... MRFA
Fireman Apprentice, Machinist's Mate, Striker [*Navy rating*] .... MMFA
Fireman Apprentice, Molder, Striker [*Navy rating*] .... MLFA
Fireman Apprentice, Patternmaker, Striker [*Navy rating*] .... PMFA
Fireman Apprentice, Shipfitter [*Navy rating*] .... SFFA
Fireman, Boilermaker, Striker [*Navy rating*] .... BRFN
Fireman, Boilerman, Striker [*Navy rating*] .... BTFN
Fireman, Engineman, Striker [*Navy rating*] .... ENFN
Fireman, Interior Communications Electrician, Striker [*Navy rating*] .... ICFN
Fireman, Machinery Repairman, Striker [*Navy rating*] .... MRFN
Fireman, Machinist's Mate, Striker [*Navy rating*] .... MMFN
Fireman, Molder, Striker [*Navy rating*] .... MLFN
Fireman, Patternmaker, Striker [*Navy rating*] .... PMFN
Fireman Recruit [*Navy rating*] .... FR
Fireman, Shipfitter, Striker [*Navy rating*] .... SFFN
Firemen and Deckhands' Union of New South Wales [*Australia*] .... FDUNSW
Firemont Genl [*NYSE symbol*] (TTSB) .... FMT
Firenze [*Italy ICAO location identifier*] (ICLI) .... LIRQ
Firenze Ximeniano [*Florence*] [*Italy*] [*Seismograph station code, US Geological Survey*] (SEIS) .... FIR
Fireplace [*Real estate*] .... FP
Fireplace [*Real estate*] .... FPL
Fireplace [*Real estate*] .... fpla
Fireplace [*Real estate*] (WDAA) .... FPLCE
Fireplace [*Real estate*] (WGA) .... FRPL
Fireplace Association of America [*Later, WHA*] .... FAA
Firepower and Maneuver [*Army*] (AABC) .... FIRMA
Firepower Potential (AABC) .... FPP
Fireproof (DAS) .... Fp
Fireproof (AABC) .... FPRF
Fire-Resistant Brick [*Technical drawings*] .... FRB
Fire-Resistant Fuels (RDA) .... FRF
Fire-Retardant and Smoke-Suppressant [*Chemicals*] .... FRSS
Fire-Retardant Treated .... FRT
Firestone Firehawk Endurance Championship [*Auto racing*] .... FFEC
Firestone Indy Lights [*Auto racing*] .... FIL
Firestone Plastics Co. .... FPC
Firestone Polyvinyl Chloride .... FPC
Firestone Tire & Rubber Co., Akron, OH [*Library symbol Library of Congress*] (LCLS) .... OAkF
Firetector, Inc. [*Associated Press*] (SAG) .... Firetct
Firetector, Inc. [*NASDAQ symbol*] (NQ) .... FTEC
Fire-Tube Boiler .... FT
Fire-Tube Boiler (DS) .... FTB
Fire-Tube Boiler Survey (DS) .... FTBS
Fire-Weather Mobile Unit [*National Weather Service*] (NOAA) .... FWMU
Fire-Weather Office [*National Weather Service*] (NOAA) .... FWO
Firewood Cutters' Protective Society [*A union*] [*British*] .... FCPS
Firework .... FRWRK
FIREX [*Fire Extinguisher*] **and Launch Coolant Control Unit** [*Aerospace*] (AAG) .... FLCCU
Fir-Fast [*Forestry*] .... FF
Firing (FAAC) .... FIRG
Firing .... FRNG
Firing Attachment Blank Ammunition (MCD) .... FABA
Firing Battery (AABC) .... FB
Firing Channel [*Military*] (CAAL) .... FC
Firing Circuit Test Set .... FCTS
Firing Device Test Set [*Military*] (CAAL) .... FDTS
Firing Effectiveness Indicator [*Military*] (CAAL) .... FEI
Firing Error Indicator .... FEI
Firing Error Trajectory Recorder and Computer .... FIRETRAC
Firing Exercise (NVT) .... FIREX
Firing Field Equipment Service [*French Acronym is based on foreign phrase*] .... SECT
Firing in Extension [*Missiles*] .... FIX
Firing/Observation Port .... F/OP
Firing Order .... FO
Firing Out/Consolidate Operability Tests (MCD) .... FO/COT
Firing Out of Battery [*Military*] (PDAA) .... FOOB
Firing Point [*Military*] (INF) .... FP
Firing Port Weapon .... FPW
Firing Position [*Army*] (DOMA) .... FP
Firing Pulse Generator (IAA) .... FPG
Firing Research Investigation, Navy .... FRIN
Firing Room [*NASA*] (KSC) .... FR
Firing Set (NG) .... FS
Firing Set Maintenance Spares (NG) .... FSMS
Firing Site Command Post [*Army*] (AABC) .... FSCP
Firing Squad Synchronization, Simulation and Solution System .... F^S5
Firing Station (MUGU) .... FS
Firing Tables [*Military*] .... FT
Firing Temperature [*Military*] (IAA) .... FT
Firing Unit [*Military*] .... FU
Firing Unit Simulator .... FUS
Firing Unit Test Set .... FUTS
Firing Velocity .... FV
Firkin .... FIR
Firkin of Ale [*Unit of measurement*] (DAS) .... Afir
Firland Correctional Center, Resident Library, Seattle, WA [*Library symbol Library of Congress*] (LCLS) .... WaSFC-R
Firland Correctional Center, Staff Library, Seattle, WA [*Library symbol Library of Congress*] (LCLS) .... WaSFC
Firm .... F
Firm [*Horse racing*] .... FM
Firm and Midline [*Uterus*] [*Gynecology and obstetrics*] (DAVI) .... F & M
Firm Contract Cost Proposal (NASA) .... FCCP
Firm Cost Proposal (NASA) .... FCP
Firm Engineering Change Memo (SAA) .... FECM
Firm Fan Club [*Defunct*] (EA) .... FFC
Firm Fixed Incentive Price [*Government contracting*] .... FFIP
Firm Fixed Price with Economic Price Adjustment [*Government contracts*] .... FFPEPA
Firm Offer [*Business term*] .... FO
Firm Order [*Business term*] .... FO
Firm Time in Commission (DNAB) .... FTIC
Firma [*Legal term*] (DLA) .... Fa
Firma Conseta/Cirrus, Saabrucken [*Germany*] [*FAA designator*] (FAAC) .... COC
Firmen- und Marktinformationen [*Company and Market Information Data Base*] [*Society for Business Information*] [*Information service or system*] (IID) .... FINF
Firm-Fixed Price [*Government contracting*] .... FFP
Firm-Fixed Price Contract .... FFPC
Firm-Fixed Price Letter [*Government contracting*] (MCD) .... FFPLE
Firm-Fixed-Price Level of Effort [*Type of contract*] (AAGC) .... FFPLOE
Firmware [*Computer science*] .... FW
Firmware Control Memory .... FCM
Firmware Design Specification .... FDS
Firmware Development Plan .... FDP
Firmware Expansion Model [*Hewlett Packard*] (NITA) .... FEM
Firmware Requirement Specification .... FRS
Firmware Support Manual .... FSM
Firmware Test Plan [*Military*] .... FTP
Firouzabad [*Iran*] [*ICAO location identifier*] (ICLI) .... OISZ
Firouzkouh [*Iran*] [*ICAO location identifier*] (ICLI) .... OIIF
Firq [*Oman*] [*ICAO location identifier*] (ICLI) .... OOFQ
First .... FST
First a Friend, Then a Host [*Safety slogan encouraging partygivers to prevent guests' overindulgence in alcohol*] .... FAFTAH
First Access .... FA
First Advertising Agency Group .... FAAG
First Advertising Agency Network [*Later, First Network of Affiliated Advertising Agencies*] [*Defunct*] (EA) .... FAAN
First Aerodynamic Flight (NASA) .... FAF
First Aid [*Medicine*] .... FA
First Aid Mechanical Transport Outfit [*A vehicle standard pack for immediate repairs*] [*Military British*] .... FAMTO
First Aid Nursing Yeomanry Service [*British military*] (DMA) .... FANYS
First Aid Technical Stores Outfit [*Military British*] .... FATSO
First Air [*ICAO designator*] (AD) .... HF
First Air [*British ICAO designator*] (FAAC) .... HLE
First Air (Bradley Schedules) Ltd. [*Canada ICAO designator*] (FAAC) .... FAB
First Air Courier, Inc. [*ICAO designator*] (FAAC) .... FAC
First Alabama Bancshares, Inc. [*NASDAQ symbol*] (NQ) .... FABC
First Alabama Bank of Huntsville, Huntsville, AL [*Library symbol*] [*Library of Congress*] (LCLS) .... AHAB
First Alarm Code (SAA) .... FAC
First Alarm Register .... FAR
First Albany Companies, Inc. [*NASDAQ symbol*] (NQ) .... FACT
First Albany Companies, Inc. [*Associated Press*] (SAG) .... FAlban
First Albany Cos. [*NASDAQ symbol*] (TTSB) .... FACT
First Alert [*NASDAQ symbol*] (TTSB) .... ALRT
First Alert Capability [*Military*] .... FAC
First Alert, Inc. [*NASDAQ symbol*] (SAG) .... ALRT
First Alert, Inc. [*Associated Press*] (SAG) .... FstAlert
First Alliance Bancorp (GA) [*NASDAQ symbol*] (TTSB) .... FABC
First Alliance Bancorp, Inc. [*Associated Press*] (SAG) .... FAllian
First Alliance Corp. [*NASDAQ symbol*] (SAG) .... FACO
First Alliance Corp. [*Associated Press*] (SAG) .... FrstAll
First Alliance Premier Bancshares, Inc. [*Associated Press*] (SAG) .... FAlliPB
First Allied Airborne Army [*World War II*] .... FAAA
First Allied Resources Corp. [*Vancouver Stock Exchange symbol*] .... FDR
First Amendment Congress (EA) .... FAC
First Amendment Consumer and Trade Society (EA) .... FACTS
First Amendment Lawyers Association (EA) .... FALA
First Amendment Research Institute [*Defunct*] (EA) .... FARI
First Amer Finl [*NYSE symbol*] (TTSB) .... FAF
First Amer Hlth Concepts [*NASDAQ symbol*] (TTSB) .... FAHC
First Amer (Tenn) [*NASDAQ symbol*] (TTSB) .... FATN
First America Mining Corp. [*Vancouver Stock Exchange symbol*] .... FRM
First American Congress of Theater .... FACT
First American Corp. [*NASDAQ symbol*] (NQ) .... FATN
First American Corp. [*Associated Press*] (SAG) .... FtAT
First American Corp. [*Associated Press*] (SAG) .... FtATn
First American Financial Corp. [*NYSE symbol*] (SPSG) .... FAF
First American Financial Corp. [*Associated Press*] (SAG) .... FAFnc
First American Health Concepts [*Associated Press*] (SAG) .... FAmHlt

First American Health Concepts, Inc. [*NASDAQ symbol*] (NQ) ... FAHC
First American Railways, Inc. [*Associated Press*] (SAG) ... FstARwy
First American Railways, Inc. [*NASDAQ symbol*] (SAG) ... FTRN
First and Second Violins [*Music*] (ROG) ... VV
First Announcement ... FA
First Appearance Datum [*Geology*] ... FAD
First Approach and Landing [*Test*] [*NASA*] (NASA) ... FAL
First Article ... FA
First Article Acceptance Test (MCD) ... FAAT
First Article Approval [*or Audit*] ... FAA
First Article Capability Assessment Test (MCD) ... FACAT
First Article Configuration Inspection [*Gemini*] [*NASA*] (AFM) ... FACI
First Article Configuration Review [*Army*] (AABC) ... FACR
First Article Demonstration ... FAD
First Article Factory Tests (NATG) ... FAFT
First Article Flight Test ... FAFT
First Article/Initial Production Testing [*Army's Combat System Test Activity*] (INF) ... FA/IPT
First Article Inspection [*NASA*] (KSC) ... FAI
First Article Inspection Notice [*NASA*] (SAA) ... FAIN
First Article Inspection Notice Status Report [*NASA*] (SAA) ... FAIN/SR
First Article Inspection Tag [*NASA*] (SAA) ... FAIT
First Article Master Schedule (MCD) ... FAMS
First Article Preproduction Sample [*DoD*] ... FAPPS
First Article - Preproduction Test (MCD) ... FA-PPT
First Article Production Inspection (MCD) ... FAPI
First Article Test ... FAT
First Article Test/Limited Operational Test ... FAT/LOT
First Artillery Ammunition Resupply Vehicle [*Army*] (RDA) ... FASTV
First Ashland Financial [*NASDAQ symbol*] (TTSB) ... FSBS
First Ashland Financial Corp. [*NASDAQ symbol*] (SAG) ... FSBS
First Ashland Financial Corp. [*Associated Press*] (SAG) ... FtAshld
First Assessment Report (EERA) ... FAR
First Assistant Secretary (ADA) ... FAS
First Atomic Power Industry Group [*Japan*] ... FAPIG
First Atomic Ship Transport, Inc. ... FAST
First Attack [*Men's lacrosse position*] ... FA
First Australia Fund [*AMEX symbol*] (TTSB) ... IAF
First Australia Fund, Inc. [*Associated Press*] ... FtAust
First Australia Fund, Inc. [*AMEX symbol*] (SPSG) ... IAF
First Australia Prime [*AMEX symbol*] (TTSB) ... FAX
First Australia Prime Income Fund [*Associated Press*] ... FAusPr
First Australia Prime Income Fund [*AMEX symbol*] (SPSG) ... FAX
First Automotive Short-Term Bonds and Certificates [*Drexel Burnham Lambert, Inc.*] [*Finance*] ... FASTBAC's
First Automotive Works [*Chinese manufacturer*] ... FAW
First Available [*Military*] ... FIRAV
First Available Air Transportation ... FAIRTRANS
First Available Government Air Transportation [*Navy*] ... FAGAIRTRANS
First Available Government Transportation ... FAGT
First Available Government Transportation ... FAGTRANS
First Available Transportation ... FATRANS
First Bancorp (IN) [*Associated Press*] (SAG) ... FtBcIN
First Bancorp (Indiana) [*NASDAQ symbol*] (NQ) ... FBCV
First Bancorp (North Carolina) [*NASDAQ symbol*] (NQ) ... FBNC
First Bancorp North Carolina [*Associated Press*] (SAG) ... FtBNC
First Bancorp of Indiana, Inc. [*Associated Press*] (SAG) ... FtBcIN
First Bank of Philadelphia [*NASDAQ symbol*] (NQ) ... FBKP
First Bank of Philadelphia [*Associated Press*] (SAG) ... FBkPhila
First Bank of Philadelphia [*Associated Press*] (SAG) ... FBkPhl
First Bank Sys Wrrt [*NASDAQ symbol*] (TTSB) ... FBSWW
First Bank System [*Associated Press*] (SAG) ... FBkS
First Bank System [*NYSE symbol*] (TTSB) ... FBS
First Bank System [*NASDAQ symbol*] (SAG) ... FBSW
First Bank System, Inc. [*Associated Press*] (SAG) ... FBkS
First Bank System, Inc. [*NYSE symbol*] (SPSG) ... FBS
First Bank System, Inc. [*Associated Press*] (SAG) ... FtBkSy
First Banking Co. Southeast Georgia [*NASDAQ symbol*] (SAG) ... FBCG
First Banking Co. Southeast Georgia [*Associated Press*] (SAG) ... FBSoGA
First Banking S.E. Georgia [*NASDAQ symbol*] (TTSB) ... FBCG
First Banks 9% Incr Rt'C'Pfd [*NASDAQ symbol*] (TTSB) ... FBNKP
First Banks America [*NYSE symbol*] (TTSB) ... FBA
First Banks America, Inc. [*NYSE symbol*] (SAG) ... FBA
First Banks America, Inc. [*Associated Press*] (SAG) ... FBksAm
First Banks, Inc. [*NASDAQ symbol*] (SAG) ... FBNK
First Banks, Inc. [*Associated Press*] (SAG) ... FstBks
First Bankshares [*NASDAQ symbol*] (TTSB) ... FBSI
First Bankshares (GA) [*NASDAQ symbol*] (TTSB) ... FBGA
First Bankshares, Inc. (GA) [*NASDAQ symbol*] (SAG) ... FBGA
First Bankshares, Inc. (Georgia) [*Associated Press*] (SAG) ... FBkGA
First Bankshares of Missouri, Inc. [*NASDAQ symbol*] (SAG) ... FBSI
First Bankshares of Missouri, Inc. [*Associated Press*] (SAG) ... FstBkshs
First Base [*or Baseman*] [*Baseball*] ... 1B
First Battle: Battalion through Corps [*DoD*] ... FB:BC
First Bell Bancorp [*NASDAQ symbol*] (TTSB) ... FBBC
First Bell Bancorp, Inc. [*NASDAQ symbol*] (SAG) ... FBBC
First Bell Bancorp, Inc. [*Associated Press*] (SAG) ... FstBell
First Bergen Bancorp, Inc. [*NASDAQ symbol*] (SAG) ... FBER
First Bergen Bancorp, Inc. [*Associated Press*] (SAG) ... FBergen
First Bk Philadelphia PA [*NASDAQ symbol*] (TTSB) ... FBKP
First Bk Sys $3.5625 Cv91A Pfd [*NYSE symbol*] (TTSB) ... FBSPrX
First Book of Judgments [*1655*] [*England*] [*A publication*] (DLA) ... First Bk Judg
First Book of Judgments [*1655*] [*England*] [*A publication*] (DLA) ... First Book Judg
First Boston Corporation, New York, NY [*Library symbol Library of Congress*] (LCLS) ... NNFBC
First Boston Corp., New York, NY [*OCLC symbol*] (OCLC) ... YFB
First Boston Income Fund, Inc. [*Later, CS First Income Fund*] [*NYSE symbol*] (SPSG) ... FBF
First Boston Strategic [*Later, CS First Boston Strategic*] [*NYSE symbol NYSE symbol*] (SPSG) ... FBI
First Brands Corp. [*NYSE symbol*] (SPSG) ... FBR
First Brands Corp. [*Associated Press*] (SAG) ... FstBrnd
First Brands Corp. [*Associated Press*] (SAG) ... FtBrnd
First Brillouin Zone [*Physics*] ... FBZ
First Brochure ... FB
First Calgary Petroleums Ltd. [*Toronto Stock Exchange symbol*] ... FCP
First Canadian Destroyer Flotilla ... CANDESFLOT 1
First Canadian Energy Corp. [*Vancouver Stock Exchange symbol*] ... FEG
First Captive Flight [*NASA*] (NASA) ... FCF
First Cash [*NASDAQ symbol*] (TTSB) ... PAWN
First Cash, Inc. [*Associated Press*] (SAG) ... FstCsh
First Cash, Inc. [*NASDAQ symbol*] (SAG) ... PAWN
First Cash Wrrt [*NASDAQ symbol*] (TTSB) ... PAWNW
First Catholic Slovak Ladies Association (EA) ... FCSLA
First Catholic Slovak Ladies Union [*Later, FCSLA*] (EA) ... FCSLU
First Catholic Slovak Union of the USA and Canada (EA) ... FCSU
First Cavalry Division Association (EA) ... FCDA
First Central Financial Corp. [*AMEX symbol*] (SPSG) ... FCC
First Central Financial Corp. [*Associated Press*] (SAG) ... FtCntrl
First Central Finl [*AMEX symbol*] (TTSB) ... FCC
First Certificate in English [*Cambridge University*] [*British*] (AIE) ... FCE
First Cervical Nerve [*Second cervical nerve is C-2, etc., through C-7*] [*Medicine*] (DAVI) ... C-1
First Cervical Vertebra [*Second cervical vertebra is C-2 , etc., through C-7*] [*Medicine*] ... C-1
First Chair of America [*Defunct*] (EA) ... FCA
First Charter Bank NA [*NASDAQ symbol*] (SAG) ... FCBK
First Charter Bank NA [*Associated Press*] (SAG) ... FtChrtBk
First Charter Corp. [*NASDAQ symbol*] (NQ) ... FCTR
First Charter Corp. [*Associated Press*] (SAG) ... FtChrt
First Check Character Flip Flop [*Computer science*] (MHDI) ... FCCFF
First Chi NBD 5 3/4% Cv Dep Pfd [*NYSE symbol*] (TTSB) ... FCNPrV
First Chi NBD 7.5%PfdPurUnits [*NYSE symbol*] (TTSB) ... FCNPrU
First Chi NBD 5.50% 'DECS'97 [*NYSE symbol*] (TTSB) ... FND
First Chi NBD 8.45% Dep Pfd [*NYSE symbol*] (TTSB) ... FCNPrE
First Chi NBD Adj Div B Pfd [*NYSE symbol*] (TTSB) ... FCNPrB
First Chi NBD Adj Div C Pfd [*NYSE symbol*] (TTSB) ... FCNPrC
First Chicago Corp. [*NYSE symbol*] (SPSG) ... FNB
First Chicago Corp. [*NYSE symbol*] (SAG) ... FND
First Chicago Corp. [*Associated Press*] (SAG) ... FstChi97
First Chicago Corp. [*Associated Press*] (SAG) ... FstChic
First Chicago NBD [*NYSE symbol*] (TTSB) ... FCN
First Chicago NBD Corp. [*Associated Press*] (SAG) ... FChiNBD
First Chicago NBD Corp. [*NYSE symbol*] (SAG) ... FCN
First Chicago NBD Corp. [*Associated Press*] (SAG) ... FtChi
First China Investment Corp. [*Vancouver Stock Exchange symbol*] ... FCI
First Church of Christ, Scientist, Montreal, PQ, Canada [*Library symbol Library of Congress*] (LCLS) ... CaQMFC
First Church of Christ, Scientist, Montreal, Quebec [*Library symbol National Library of Canada*] (NLC) ... QMFC
First Citizens Bancshares [*Associated Press*] (SAG) ... FCtzBA
First Citizens Bancshares, Inc. [*NASDAQ symbol*] (NQ) ... FCNC
First Citizens BancShares'A' [*NASDAQ symbol*] (TTSB) ... FCNCA
First Citizens BancStock (SPSG) ... FIR
First Citizens Bank Stock [*Associated Press*] (SAG) ... FCtzBstk
First Citizens Bank Stock [*AMEX symbol*] (SAG) ... FIR
First Citizens Corp. [*Associated Press*] (SAG) ... FrstCtz
First Citizens Corp. [*NASDAQ symbol*] (SAG) ... FSTC
First Citizens Financial Corp. [*NASDAQ symbol*] (NQ) ... FCIT
First Citizens Financial Corp. [*Associated Press*] (SAG) ... FstCtzF
First Citizens Finl [*NASDAQ symbol*] (TTSB) ... FCIT
First City Bancorp, Inc. [*AMEX symbol*] (SPSG) ... FCT
First City Bancorp, Inc. [*Associated Press*] (SAG) ... FstCity
First City Financial Corp. [*NASDAQ symbol*] (SAG) ... FCFC
First City Financial Corp. [*Associated Press*] (SAG) ... FstCity
First City Financial Corp. Ltd. [*Toronto Stock Exchange symbol Vancouver Stock Exchange symbol*] ... FCY
First City Merchant Bank Ltd. ... FCMB
First City Trust Co. [*Toronto Stock Exchange symbol*] ... FCT
First City Trustco, Inc. [*Vancouver Stock Exchange symbol*] ... FIR
First Class [*or First Quality*] ... A1
First Class [*Airline fare code*] ... F
First Class Commission (HGAA) ... FCC
First Class Diver Badge [*Military decoration*] (AABC) ... FCDivBad
First Class or Saloon Passengers [*Shipping*] [*British*] ... FST
First Class Post Office ... FCPO
First Coast Guard District [*Boston, MA*] [*USCG*] (TAG) ... D1
First Coastal Corp. [*NASDAQ symbol*] (SAG) ... FCME
First Coastal Corp. [*Associated Press*] (SAG) ... FrstCstl
First Colonial Group [*Associated Press*] (SAG) ... FColnGp
First Colonial Group [*NASDAQ symbol*] (SAG) ... FTCG
First Colony [*NYSE symbol*] (SPSG) ... FCL
First Colony Corp. [*Associated Press*] (SAG) ... FColony
First Colorado Bancorp [*NASDAQ symbol*] (TTSB) ... FFBA
First Colorado Bancorp, Inc. [*NASDAQ symbol*] (SAG) ... FFBA
First Colorado Bancorp, Inc. [*Associated Press*] (SAG) ... FtColoBcp
First Come, First Served [*Computer science*] ... FCFS
First Comm Bancshares 'B' [*NASDAQ symbol*] (TTSB) ... FCBIB
First Commerce [*NASDAQ symbol*] (TTSB) ... FCOM
First Commerce 7.25% Cv Pfd '92 [*NASDAQ symbol*] (TTSB) ... FCOMP

First Commerce Bancshares [*Associated Press*] (SAG) ... FCmcBB
First Commerce Bancshares, Inc. [*NASDAQ symbol*] (NQ) ... FCBI
First Commerce Bancshares, Inc. [*Associated Press*] (SAG) ... FCmcBA
First Commerce Bancshares'A' [*NASDAQ symbol*] (TTSB) ... FCBIA
First Commerce Corp. [*Associated Press*] (SAG) ... FCmcC
First Commerce Corp. [*NASDAQ symbol*] (NQ) ... FCOM
First Commerce Corp. [*Associated Press*] (SAG) ... FComceC
First Commercial Bancorp [*NASDAQ symbol*] (NQ) ... FCOB
First Commercial Bancorp, Inc. [*Associated Press*] (SAG) ... FCmlBcp
First Commercial Bank [*Taiwan*] ... FCB
First Commercial Corp. [*NASDAQ symbol*] (NQ) ... FCLR
First Commericial Corp. [*Associated Press*] (SAG) ... FCmclCp
First Comml Bancorp, Inc. [*NASDAQ symbol*] (TTSB) ... FCOB
First Commonwealth [*NASDAQ symbol*] (TTSB) ... FCWI
First Commonwealth Financial Corp. [*Associated Press*] (SAG) ... FstCwlth
First Commonwealth Finl [*NYSE symbol*] (TTSB) ... FCF
First Commonwealth Fund [*NYSE symbol*] (TTSB) ... FCO
First Commonwealth Fund, Inc. [*Associated Press*] (SAG) ... FCmwF
First Commonwealth Fund, Inc. [*NYSE symbol*] (SPSG) ... FCO
First Commonwealth, Inc. [*NASDAQ symbol*] (SAG) ... FCWI
First Commonwealth, Inc. [*Associated Press*] (SAG) ... FstCom
First Communications Group, Inc. [*Coral Gables, FL*] (TSSD) ... FCG
First Communications, Inc. [*Atlanta, GA*] (TSSD) ... FCI
First Computer Interface Tester (MCD) ... FIT
First Cranial Nerve [*Anatomy*] (DMAA) ... CI
First Customer Shipment [*IBM Corp.*] [*Computer science*] ... FCS
First Czechoslovak Philatelic Club of North America (EA) ... FCPCNA
First Data [*NYSE symbol*] (SPSG) ... FDC
First Data Corp. [*Associated Press*] (SAG) ... FstData
First Day [*Philately*] ... FD
First Day Cover Collectors Club (EA) ... FDCCC
First Day of Issue [*Philately*] ... FDI
First Day of Issue [*Philately*] ... FDOI
First Day of Last Menstrual Period [*Gynecology and obstetrics*] (DAVI) ... FDLMP
First Defense [*Men's lacrosse position*] ... FD
First Defiance Financial Corp. [*NASDAQ symbol*] (SAG) ... FDEF
First Defiance Financial Corp. [*Associated Press*] (SAG) ... FstDefiFn
First Defiance Financial Corp. [*Associated Press*] (SAG) ... FtDefFn
First Defiance Fin'l [*NASDAQ symbol*] (TTSB) ... FDEF
First Degree Relatives ... FDR
First Derivation of Left Ventricular Pressure [*Cardiology*] (DAVI) ... LV dp/dt
First Destination Transportation [*Military*] (AFM) ... FDT
First Development System (MCD) ... FDS
First Devonian Explorations [*Vancouver Stock Exchange symbol*] ... FDI
First Division Association [*British*] ... FDA
First Dorsal Interosseous Muscle [*Myology*] ... FDI
First Dorsal Nerve [*Second dorsal nerve is D_2, etc., through D_{12}*] [*Medicine*] (DAVI) ... D_1
First Dorsal Vertebra [*Second dorsal vertebra is D_2, etc.*] [*Medicine*] ... D_1
First Down [*Football*] ... FD
First Dynasty Mines [*NASDAQ symbol*] (SAG) ... FDYM
First Dynasty Mines [*Associated Press*] (SAG) ... FtDynM
First Edition (ADA) ... FE
First Edition Club (NTCM) ... FEC
First Element Launch (SSD) ... FEL
First Empire State [*AMEX symbol*] (TTSB) ... FES
First Empire State Corp. [*AMEX symbol*] (SPSG) ... FES
First Empire State Corp. [*Associated Press*] (SAG) ... FtEmp
First Engine to Test ... FETT
First Enterprise Financial Group [*NASDAQ symbol*] (SAG) ... FENT
First Enterprise Financial Group [*Associated Press*] (SAG) ... FEntFn
First Entertainment [*NASDAQ symbol*] (TTSB) ... FTETD
First Entertainment, Inc. [*Associated Press*] (SAG) ... FstEnter
First Entertainment, Inc. [*Associated Press*] (SAG) ... FstEntr
First Entertainment, Inc. [*NASDAQ symbol*] (SAG) ... FTET
First Entry [*British military*] (DMA) ... FE
First Essex Bancorp [*NASDAQ symbol*] (TTSB) ... FESX
First Essex Bancorp, Inc. [*NASDAQ symbol*] (NQ) ... FESX
First Essex Bancorp, Inc. [*Associated Press*] (SAG) ... FtEsex
First European Airways Ltd. [*British ICAO designator*] (FAAC) ... FEL
First Failure Data Capture [*IBM Corp.*] [*Computer science*] (PCM) ... FFDC
First Families [*i.e., the aristocracy*] [*Slang*] ... FF
First Families of Carolina [*See also FFV*] ... FFC
First Families of Georgia 1733-1797 (EA) ... FFG
First Families of Virginia (BARN) ... FFV
First Families of Virginia [*Supposedly elite society*] [*Slang*] ... FFV's
First Family Bank Florida [*NASDAQ symbol*] (SAG) ... FFML
First Family Financial Corp. [*Associated Press*] (SAG) ... FtFamFL
First Family Finl [*NASDAQ symbol*] (TTSB) ... FFML
First Family Group, Inc. (MHDW) ... FFAM
First Fandom (EA) ... FF
First Fed Bancorp [*NASDAQ symbol*] (TTSB) ... FFBZ
First Fed Bancorp(MN) [*NASDAQ symbol*] (TTSB) ... BDJI
First Fed Bancshares (AR) [*NASDAQ symbol*] (TTSB) ... FFBH
First Fed Finl (KY) [*NASDAQ symbol*] (TTSB) ... FFKY
First Fed of Eau Clair [*NASDAQ symbol*] (TTSB) ... FFEC
First Fed S & L (CT) [*NASDAQ symbol*] (TTSB) ... FFES
First Fed Svg (GA) [*NASDAQ symbol*] (TTSB) ... FFBG
First Fed Svgs & Ln Assn [*NASDAQ symbol*] (TTSB) ... FSSB
First Fed Svgs Bk Siouxland [*NASDAQ symbol*] (TTSB) ... FFSX
First Federal Bancorp [*Associated Press*] (SAG) ... FtFdBcp
First Federal Bancorp, Inc. [*NASDAQ symbol*] (SAG) ... FFBZ
First Federal Bancorp, Inc. [*Associated Press*] (SAG) ... FtFdBc
First Federal Bancorp. MN [*Associated Press*] (SAG) ... FFdMN
First Federal Bancorporation Minnesota [*Associated Press*] (SAG) ... FFcMN
First Federal Bancorporation MN [*NASDAQ symbol*] (SAG) ... BDJI
First Federal Bancshares of Arkansas, Inc. [*Associated Press*] (SAG) ... FFBArk
First Federal Bancshares of Arkansas, Inc. [*NASDAQ symbol*] (SAG) ... FFBH
First Federal Bancshares of Eau Claire, Inc. [*Associated Press*] (SAG) ... FF EauCl
First Federal Bancshares of Eau Claire, Inc. [*NASDAQ symbol*] (SAG) ... FFEC
First Federal Capital [*NASDAQ symbol*] (TTSB) ... FTFC
First Federal Capital Corp. [*NASDAQ symbol*] (NQ) ... FTFC
First Federal Capital Corp. [*Associated Press*] (SAG) ... FtFCap
First Federal Financial Corp. [*Associated Press*] (SAG) ... FFedKY
First Federal Financial Corp. [*NASDAQ symbol*] (SAG) ... FFKY
First Federal Financial Services [*Associated Press*] (SAG) ... FFFS
First Federal of Alabama FSB [*Jasper, AL*] [*Associated Press*] (SAG) ... FtFAla
First Federal of Alabama FSB Jasper [*AMEX symbol*] (SPSG) ... FAB
First Federal Savings & Loan Association, East Hartford [*Associated Press*] (SAG) ... FFdEH
First Federal Savings & Loan Association, East Hartford [*NASDAQ symbol*] (SAG) ... FFES
First Federal Savings & Loan Association, San Bernardino [*Associated Press*] (SAG) ... FFSBern
First Federal Savings & Loan Association, San Bernardino [*NASDAQ symbol*] (SAG) ... FSSB
First Federal Savings & Loan of Ohio [*NASDAQ symbol*] (SAG) ... FDEF
First Federal Savings Bank Colorado [*NASDAQ symbol*] (SAG) ... FFBA
First Federal Savings Bank Colorado [*Associated Press*] (SAG) ... FtFedCO
First Federal Savings Bank Fort Dodge [*Iowa*] [*NASDAQ symbol*] (SAG) ... FFFD
First Federal Savings Bank Fort Dodge IA [*Associated Press*] (SAG) ... FFSvFD
First Federal Savings Bank of Brunswick [*NASDAQ symbol*] (SAG) ... FFBG
First Federal Savings Bank of Brunswick [*Associated Press*] (SAG) ... FFdBrun
First Federal Savings Bank Siouxland [*Associated Press*] (SAG) ... FFSSiou
First Federal Savings Bank Siouxland [*NASDAQ symbol*] (SAG) ... FFSX
First Fidelity Bancorp. [*NYSE symbol*] (SPSG) ... FFB
First Fidelity Bancorp, Inc. [*Associated Press*] (SAG) ... FFB
First Financial [*NASDAQ symbol*] (TTSB) ... FTFN
First Financial Bancorp [*NASDAQ symbol*] (NQ) ... FFBC
First Financial Bancorp [*Associated Press*] (SAG) ... FtFnBcp
First Financial Bancorp, Inc. [*NASDAQ symbol*] (SAG) ... FFBI
First Financial Bancorp, Inc. [*FL*] [*Associated Press*] (SAG) ... FFnBcp
First Financial Bancorp, Inc. Florida [*NASDAQ symbol*] (SAG) ... FPRY
First Financial Bancorp OH [*NASDAQ symbol*] (SAG) ... FFBC
First Financial Bancorp Ohio [*Associated Press*] (SAG) ... FFncOH
First Financial Bancshares Polk County [*NASDAQ symbol*] (SAG) ... FBPC
First Financial Bancshares Polk County [*Associated Press*] (SAG) ... FtFnPlk
First Financial Bankshares [*NASDAQ symbol*] (SAG) ... FFIN
First Financial Bankshares [*Associated Press*] (SAG) ... FtFnBk
First Financial Caribbean [*NASDAQ symbol*] (TTSB) ... FRCC
First Financial Caribbean Corp. [*NASDAQ symbol*] (CTT) ... FRCC
First Financial Caribbean Corp. [*Associated Press*] (SAG) ... FtFCrb
First Financial Caribbean Corp. [*Associated Press*] (SAG) ... FtFnCrb
First Financial Corp. [*NASDAQ symbol*] (NQ) ... FFHC
First Financial Corp. [*Associated Press*] (SAG) ... FstFnIN
First Financial Corp. [*Associated Press*] (SAG) ... FtFnCp
First Financial Corp. [*NASDAQ symbol*] (SAG) ... THFF
First Financial Corp. (Providence, RI) [*Associated Press*] (SAG) ... FFnCpRI
First Financial Corp. (Providence, RI) [*NASDAQ symbol*] (SAG) ... FTFN
First Financial Corporation Western Maryland [*Associated Press*] (SAG) ... FFinWM
First Financial Corp., Western Maryland [*NASDAQ symbol*] (SAG) ... FFWM
First Financial Fund [*NYSE symbol*] (TTSB) ... FF
First Financial Fund, Inc. [*NYSE symbol*] (SPSG) ... FF
First Financial Fund, Inc. [*Associated Press*] (SAG) ... FFinFd
First Financial Holdings, Inc. [*NASDAQ symbol*] (NQ) ... FFCH
First Financial Holdings, Inc. [*Associated Press*] (SAG) ... FstFnHld
First Financial Language [*Computer science*] ... FFL
First Financial Management Corp. [*NYSE symbol*] (SPSG) ... FFM
First Finl Bancorp [*NASDAQ symbol*] (TTSB) ... FFBI
First Finl Bancorp [*NASDAQ symbol*] (TTSB) ... FPRY
First Finl Bancorp(OH) [*NASDAQ symbol*] (TTSB) ... FFBC
First Finl Corp Wis [*NASDAQ symbol*] (TTSB) ... FFHC
First Finl Corp. Ind [*NASDAQ symbol*] (TTSB) ... THFF
First Finl Hldgs [*NASDAQ symbol*] (TTSB) ... FFCH
First Finl (MD) [*NASDAQ symbol*] (TTSB) ... FFWM
First Fit Algorithm (IAA) ... FF
First Fix Not Converted ... FFNC
First Fleet [*Pacific*] [*Navy*] ... FIRFLT
First Flight Cover [*Philately*] ... FFC
First Flight Readiness Review (SSD) ... FFRR
First Flight Society (EA) ... FFS
First Flowering Date [*Botany*] ... FFD
First Focal Distance [*Symbol*] [*Optics*] (ROG) ... F'
First Folio Edition [*1623*] [*Shakespearean work*] ... F1
FIRST - Foundation for Ichthyosis and Related Skin Types (EA) ... FIRST
First Franklin Corp. [*NASDAQ symbol*] (NQ) ... FFHS
First Franklin Corp. [*Associated Press*] (SAG) ... FtFrnk
First GARP [*Global Atmospheric Research Program*] **Global Experiment** [*National Academy of Sciences*] ... FGGE
First General Mine Management & Gold Corp. [*Vancouver Stock Exchange symbol*] ... FGM
First General Resources Co. [*Vancouver Stock Exchange symbol*] ... FGA
First Generation Non-English-Speaking Background ... NESB1
First Generation Resources Ltd. [*Vancouver Stock Exchange symbol*] ... FGN
First Georgia Holding [*NASDAQ symbol*] (TTSB) ... FGHC
First Georgia Holding, Inc. [*NASDAQ symbol*] (NQ) ... FGHC
First Georgia Holding, Inc. [*Associated Press*] (SAG) ... FtGaHd
First Grade Screening Test [*To detect learning disabilities*] ... FGST
First Greatwest Corp. [*NASDAQ symbol*] ... FGWC

First Guardian [*Vancouver Stock Exchange symbol*] ... FGP
First Half [*of month*] (DCTA) ... FH
First Harmonic Distortion [*Electronics*] (IAA) ... FHD
First Harrisburg Bancor, Inc. [*Associated Press*] (SAG) ... FHarBc
First Harrisburg Bancorp, Inc. [*NASDAQ symbol*] (NQ) ... FFHP
First Hawaiian [*NASDAQ symbol*] (TTSB) ... FHWN
First Hawaiian, Inc. [*NASDAQ symbol*] (NQ) ... FHWN
First Hawaiian, Inc. [*Associated Press*] (SAG) ... FtHaw
First Home Bancorp, Inc. [*NASDAQ symbol*] (SAG) ... FSPG
First Home Bancorp, Inc. [*Associated Press*] (SAG) ... FstHmBcp
First Home Savings Bank [*NASDAQ symbol*] (NQ) ... FSPG
First Home Savings Bank SLA [*Associated Press*] (SAG) ... FstHmSv
First Home Savings Bk [*NASDAQ symbol*] (TTSB) ... FSPG
First Horizontal Flight [*NASA*] (KSC) ... FHF
First Hospitality [*Vancouver Stock Exchange symbol*] ... FHC
First Hungarian Literary Society (EA) ... FHLS
First Iberian Fund [*AMEX symbol*] (TTSB) ... IBF
First Iberian Fund, Inc. [*Associated Press*] ... FtIber
First Iberian Fund, Inc. [*AMEX symbol*] (SPSG) ... IBF
First Idaho Resources [*Vancouver Stock Exchange symbol*] ... FI
First In, First Out [*Accounting*] ... FIFO
First In, Last Out [*Accounting*] ... FILO
First In Not Used First Out [*Processing procedure*] (NITA) ... FINFO
First Independence Corp. [*NASDAQ symbol*] (SAG) ... FFSL
First Independence Corp. [*Associated Press*] (SAG) ... FtIndp
First Independence Del [*NASDAQ symbol*] (TTSB) ... FFSL
First Independent Political Success [*Political campaigning*] ... FIPS
First Independent Research Support and Transition Award [*National Institutes of Health*] ... FIRST
First Indiana Corp. [*NASDAQ symbol*] (NQ) ... FISB
First Indiana Corp. [*Associated Press*] (SAG) ... FstIn Cp
First Indication of Trouble ... FIT
First Indl Rlty Tr 9.50% Pfd [*NYSE symbol*] (TTSB) ... FRPrA
First Industrial Realty Trust, Inc. [*NYSE symbol*] (SAG) ... FR
First Industrial Realty Trust, Inc. [*Associated Press*] (SAG) ... FstInRt
First Industrial Realty Trust, Inc. [*Associated Press*] (SAG) ... FtInRt
First Industrial Rlty Tr [*NYSE symbol*] (TTSB) ... FR
First Installed Article, Tests [*NATO*] (NATG) ... FIAT
First International Bank of Israel Ltd. (BJA) ... FIBI
First International BIOMASS Experiment [*ICSU*] (MSC) ... FIBEX
First International Radiation Experiment [*Climatology*] ... FIRE
First Interstate Bancorp [*Associated Press*] (SAG) ... FInt
First Interstate Bancorp [*Associated Press*] (SAG) ... FIntste
First Interstate Bancorp [*Associated Press*] (SAG) ... FtIn
First Interstate Bancorp. [*NYSE symbol*] (SPSG) ... I
First Investors Financial Services Group, Inc. [*NASDAQ symbol*] (SAG) ... FIFS
First Investors Financil Services Group, Inc. [*Associated Press*] (SAG) ... FirstInv
First Investors Finl Svcs Grp [*NASDAQ symbol*] (TTSB) ... FIFS
First Ionization Potential [*Physical chemistry*] ... FIP
First Irish Families ... FIF
First ISCCP [*International Satellite Cloud Climatology Project*] **Regional Experiment** [*National Oceanic and Atmospheric Administration*] ... FIRE
First ISLSCP [*International Satellite Land Surface Climatology Project*] **Field Experiment** [*NASA*] ... FIFE
First Israel Fund [*NYSE symbol*] (TTSB) ... ISL
First Israel Fund Corp. [*Associated Press*] (SAG) ... FtIsrl
First Jersey Securities ... FJS
First Judge [*Legal term*] (DLA) ... FJ
First Kent Financial Corp. [*NASDAQ symbol*] (SAG) ... FKFC
First Kent Financial Corp. [*Associated Press*] (SAG) ... FstKent
First Keystone Financial [*NASDAQ symbol*] (TTSB) ... FKES
First Keystone Financial, Inc. [*NASDAQ symbol*] (SAG) ... FKFS
First Keystone Financial, Inc. [*Associated Press*] (SAG) ... FtKeyst
First Knox Bancorp [*NASDAQ symbol*] (SAG) ... FKBC
First Knox Bancorp [*Associated Press*] (SAG) ... FtKnox
First Ladies' International Racing Team [*Group of women racing at Le Mans, France*] ... FLIRT
First Lady [*Imelda Marcos of The Philippines*] ... FL
First Lady of the United States ... FLOTUS
First Lancaster Bancshares, Inc. [*NASDAQ symbol*] (SAG) ... FLKY
First Lancaster Bancshares, Inc. [*Associated Press*] (SAG) ... FrstLanc
First Language (ADA) ... L1
First Leesport Bancorp [*NASDAQ symbol*] (SAG) ... FLPB
First Leesport Bancorp [*Associated Press*] (SAG) ... FtLesprt
First Level Adaptive Program ... FLAP
First Level Interrupt Handler [*Computer science*] ... FLIH
First Liberty Financial Corp. [*NASDAQ symbol*] (NQ) ... FLFC
First Liberty Financial Corp. [*Associated Press*] (SAG) ... FtLbty
First Liberty Fin'l 6% Cv Pfd [*NASDAQ symbol*] (TTSB) ... FLFCO
First Lieutenant [*Army*] ... 1LT
First Lieutenant [*Air Force, Army, Marine Corps*] ... O2
First Line Check ... FLC
First Line Unit (MCD) ... FLU
First Long Island [*NASDAQ symbol*] (TTSB) ... FLIC
First Lord of the Admiralty [*British*] ... FLA
First Lot Procurement Status (AAG) ... FLPS
First Lumbar Nerve [*Second lumbar nerve is L_2, etc., through L_5*] [*Medicine*] (DAVI) ... L_1
First Lumbar Vertebra [*Second lumbar vertebra is L_2, etc., through L_5*] [*Medicine*] ... L_1
First M & F Corp. [*NASDAQ symbol*] (SAG) ... FMFC
First M & F Corp. [*Associated Press*] (SAG) ... FrstMF
First Main [*Firefighting*] (ROG) ... FM
First Main Watch ... FMW
First Manned Captive Flight [*NASA*] (NASA) ... FMCF
First Manned Orbital Flight [*NASA*] ... FMOF
First Manned Orbital Flight with EVA [*Extravehicular Activity*] (MCD) ... FMOFEV
First Manned Orbital Flight with Payload (MCD) ... FMOFPL
First Marathon, Inc. [*Toronto Stock Exchange symbol*] ... FMS
First Marine Aircraft Wing ... FMAW
First Mariner Bancorp [*NASDAQ symbol*] (SAG) ... FMAR
First Mariner Bancorp [*Associated Press*] (SAG) ... FrstMar
First Maritime Mining Corp. Ltd. [*Toronto Stock Exchange symbol*] ... FMM
First Market Intelligence Ltd. [*Information service or system*] (IID) ... FMI
First Maryland Banc 7.875% Pfd [*NYSE symbol*] (TTSB) ... FMBPr
First Maryland Bancorp [*NYSE symbol*] (SPSG) ... FMB
First Maryland Bancorp [*Associated Press*] (SAG) ... FtMD
First Material Processing Test [*Japan*] ... FMPT
First Medical Management [*Vancouver Stock Exchange symbol*] ... FMA
First Menstrual Period [*Medicine*] ... FMP
First Mercantile Currency Fund, Inc. [*Toronto Stock Exchange symbol*] ... FMF
First Merchants Acceptance [*NASDAQ symbol*] (TTSB) ... FMAC
First Merchants Acceptance Corp. [*NASDAQ symbol*] (SAG) ... FMAC
First Merchants Acceptance Corp. [*Associated Press*] (SAG) ... FMerAcc
First Merchants Corp. [*NASDAQ symbol*] (NQ) ... FRME
First Merchants Corp. [*Associated Press*] (SAG) ... FtMerc
First Michigan Bank [*NASDAQ symbol*] (TTSB) ... FMBC
First Michigan Bank Corp. [*NASDAQ symbol*] (NQ) ... FMBC
First Michigan Bank Corp. [*Associated Press*] (SAG) ... FtMchBk
First Michigan Bank Corp. [*Associated Press*] (SAG) ... FtMichBk
First Midwest Bancorp [*NASDAQ symbol*] (TTSB) ... FMBI
First Midwest Bancorp [*Associated Press*] (SAG) ... FMidBc
First Midwest Bancorp, Inc. [*NASDAQ symbol*] (NQ) ... FMBI
First Midwest Financial [*NASDAQ symbol*] (SAG) ... CASH
First Midwest Financial [*Associated Press*] (SAG) ... FtMdwF
First Ministers' Conference [*Canada*] ... FMC
First Mississippi [*NYSE symbol*] (TTSB) ... FRM
First Mississippi Corp. [*NYSE symbol*] (SPSG) ... FRM
First Mississippi Corp. [*Associated Press*] (SAG) ... FtMiss
First Monthly Payment ... FP
First Mortagage Corp. [*Associated Press*] (SAG) ... FstMtge
First Mortgage [*NASDAQ symbol*] (TTSB) ... FMOR
First Mortgage Corp. [*NASDAQ symbol*] (SAG) ... FMOR
First Motion (KSC) ... F/M
First Multiyear Contract [*Military*] (RDA) ... MY I
First Mutual Bancorp [*NASDAQ symbol*] (TTSB) ... FMBD
First Mutual Bancorp, Inc. [*NASDAQ symbol*] (SAG) ... FMBD
First Mutual Bancorp, Inc. [*Associated Press*] (SAG) ... FstMutl
First Mutual Savings Bank [*NASDAQ symbol*] (NQ) ... FMSB
First Mutual Savings Bank of Washington [*Associated Press*] (SAG) ... FMWA
First Mutual Svgs (WA) [*NASDAQ symbol*] (TTSB) ... FMSB
First Name ... FN
First Name Unknown ... FNU
First National Bancorp of Gainesville [*NASDAQ symbol*] (NQ) ... FBAC
First National Bancorp of Gainesville [*Associated Press*] (SAG) ... FNtGa
First National Bank, Essex, IA [*Library symbol Library of Congress*] (LCLS) ... IaEsxFN
First National Bank Library, Phoenix, AZ [*Library symbol Library of Congress*] (LCLS) ... AzPhF
First National Bank of Chicago, Chicago, IL [*Library symbol Library of Congress*] (LCLS) ... ICFNB
First National Bankshares, Inc. [*AMEX symbol*] (SAG) ... FNH
First National Bankshares, Inc. [*Associated Press*] (SAG) ... FNtBsh
First National City Bank [*Later, Citibank*] [*New York City*] ... FNCB
First National Entertainment Corp. [*NASDAQ symbol*] (SAG) ... FNAT
First National Entertainment Corp. [*Associated Press*] (SAG) ... FtNatEnt
First National Entmt [*NASDAQ symbol*] (TTSB) ... FNAT
First National Financial Co. [*British*] ... FNFC
First National Group of Independent Real Estate Agents Ltd. [*Australia*] ... FNGIREA
First National Stores, Inc. ... FINAST
First Nations Financial Project (EA) ... FNFP
First Nationwide Bank A Federal Savings Bank [*NYSE symbol*] (SAG) ... FNW
First Nationwide Bank A Federal Savings Bank [*Associated Press*] (SAG) ... FstNtw
First Nationwide Bk 11.50% Pfd [*NYSE symbol*] (TTSB) ... FNWPr
First Natl Bankshares(LA) [*AMEX symbol*] (TTSB) ... FNH
First Normal Form (MHDB) ... FNF
First Northen Capital [*NASDAQ symbol*] (TTSB) ... FNGB
First Northern Capital Corp. [*NASDAQ symbol*] (SAG) ... FNGB
First Northern Capital Corp. [*Associated Press*] (SAG) ... FNthCap
First Northern Savings Bank SA [*NASDAQ symbol*] (NQ) ... FNGB
First Northern Savings Bank SA [*Associated Press*] (SAG) ... FNthSB
First Oak Brook Bancshares [*Associated Press*] (SAG) ... FtOakBrk
First Oak Brook Bancshares, Inc. [*NASDAQ symbol*] (NQ) ... FOBB
First Oak Brook Bancshrs'A' [*NASDAQ symbol*] (TTSB) ... FOBBA
First of America Bank [*NYSE symbol*] (SPSG) ... FOA
First of America Bank Corp. [*Associated Press*] (SAG) ... FstAm
First of America Bk [*NYSE symbol*] (TTSB) ... FOA
First of Class (DOMA) ... FOC
[*The*] **First of Long Island Corp.** [*NASDAQ symbol*] (NQ) ... FLIC
First of Long Island Corp. [*Associated Press*] (SAG) ... FstLI
First Officer [*Women's Royal Naval Service*] [*British*] ... 1/O
First Officer (ADA) ... FO
First Open [*First class train compartment*] (DCTA) ... FO
First Open Water [*Shipping*] ... FOW
First Operational Computer Installation (IAA) ... FOCI
First Operational Flight (MCD) ... FOF
First Orbit Penetration System (MCD) ... FOPS
First Orbital Flight [*NASA*] (NASA) ... FOF
First Orbital Vehicle [*NASA*] (NASA) ... FOV

First Order Gradient Technique ... FOGT
First Order Logic ... FOL
First Order Predicate Calculus (MHDB) ... FOPC
First, Outer, Inner, Last [*Mathematical term used in factoring second degree trinomials*] ... FOIL
First Overtone Band ... FOB
First Pacific Networks [*NASDAQ symbol*] (TTSB) ... FPNX
First Pacific Networks, Inc. [*NASDAQ symbol*] (SAG) ... FPNX
First Pacific Networks, Inc. [*Associated Press*] (SAG) ... FtPcNtw
First Palm Beach Bancorp [*NASDAQ symbol*] (TTSB) ... FFPB
First Palm Beach Bancorp, Inc. [*NASDAQ symbol*] (SAG) ... FFPB
First Palm Beach Bancorp, Inc. [*Associated Press*] (SAG) ... FstPalm
First Past the Post [*Electoral system*] [*British*] (ECON) ... FPTP
First Patriot Bankshares [*NASDAQ symbol*] (SAG) ... FPBK
First Patriot Bankshares [*Associated Press*] (SAG) ... FtPatBn
First Performance [*Music*] ... FP
First Periodic Inspection (AAG) ... FPI
First Philippine Civic Action Group [*Deployed in 1964 to assist South Vietnam*] (VNW) ... PHILCAG
First Philippine Fund, Inc. [*NYSE symbol*] (SAG) ... FPF
First Philippine Fund, Inc. [*Associated Press*] (SAG) ... FtPhil
First Phillipine Fund [*NYSE symbol*] (TTSB) ... FPF
First Phone of New England [*Telecommunications service*] (TSSD) ... FPNE
First Point of Aries [*Navigation*] ... FPA
First Port of Entry (AFM) ... FPOE
First Portuguese Canadian Club ... FPCC
First Preferred Stock [*Investment term*] ... FPS
First Preferred Trust [*Vancouver Stock Exchange symbol*] ... FPT
First Printings of American Authors [*A publication*] ... FPAA
First Production Article (MCD) ... FPA
First Production Unit ... FPU
First Proof (ADA) ... FP
First Quarter [*Moon phase*] ... FQ
First Quarto [*The earliest publication of the plays of William Shakespeare*] (WDMC) ... Q1
First Rank Symptoms [*Medicine*] (MEDA) ... FRS
First Rate Investments (DICI) ... FRI
First Reader ... FR
First Readiness State (AAG) ... FRS
First Recorded Appearance Time (SAA) ... FRAT
First Regional Bancorp [*Associated Press*] (SAG) ... FRegBc
First Regional Bancorp [*NASDAQ symbol*] (NQ) ... FRGB
First Regional Library, Hernando, MS [*Library symbol Library of Congress*] (LCLS) ... MsHe
First Renewal ... FR
First Republic Bancorp [*NASDAQ symbol*] (SAG) ... FRBK
First Republic Bancorp [*NYSE symbol*] (TTSB) ... FRC
First Republic Bancorp [*Associated Press*] (SAG) ... FRepBcp
First Republic Bancorp, Inc. [*NYSE symbol*] (SAG) ... FRC
First Republic Bancorp, Inc. [*Associated Press*] (SAG) ... FtRpBc
First Republic of Korea Army ... FROKA
First Savings Bancorp [*NASDAQ symbol*] (TTSB) ... SOPN
First Savings Bank [*NASDAQ symbol*] (NQ) ... FSBC
First Savings Bank [*Associated Press*] (SAG) ... FSNM
First Savings Bank FSLA Perth Amboy NJ [*Associated Press*] (SAG) ... FSBkNJ
First Savings Bank FSLA Perth Amboy NJ [*NASDAQ symbol*] (SAG) ... FSLA
First Savings Bank FSLA Perth Amboy NJ [*Associated Press*] (SAG) ... FSvBkNJ
First Savings Bank of Moore County [*Associated Press*] (SAG) ... FtSvBanc
First Savings Bank of Moore County [*NASDAQ symbol*] (SAG) ... SOPN
First Savings Bank of New Jersey [*NASDAQ symbol*] (SAG) ... FSLA
First Savings Bank of New Jersey [*NASDAQ symbol*] (SAG) ... FSNJ
First Savings Bank of New Jersy [*Associated Press*] (SAG) ... FstSvNJ
First Savings Bank Washington Bancorp, Inc. [*Associated Press*] (SAG) ... FSBWA
First Savings Bank Washington Bancorp, Inc. [*NASDAQ symbol*] (SAG) ... FWWB
First Savings Bank(N.J.) [*NASDAQ symbol*] (TTSB) ... FSNJ
First Savings Bk(Perth Amboy) [*NASDAQ symbol*] (TTSB) ... FSLA
First SB Clovis N Mex [*NASDAQ symbol*] (TTSB) ... FSBC
First Sea Level Test [*NASA*] (NASA) ... FSLT
First Sea Lord [*British*] (DI) ... FSL
First Security [*NASDAQ symbol*] (TTSB) ... FSCO
First Security Corp. [*NASDAQ symbol*] (NQ) ... FSCO
First Security Corp. [*Associated Press*] (SAG) ... FSecCp
First Sergeant [*Army*] ... 1SG
First Sergeant [*Army, Marine Corps*] ... E8
First Sergeant [*Army skill qualification identifier*] (INF) ... M
First Shenango Bancorp [*NASDAQ symbol*] (TTSB) ... SHEN
First Shenango Bancorp, Inc. [*Associated Press*] (SAG) ... FtShengo
First Shenango Bancorp, Inc. [*NASDAQ symbol*] (SAG) ... SHEN
First Ship Configuration Review [*Navy*] ... FSCR
First Ship Delivered (DNAB) ... FSD
First Society of Whale Watchers [*Defunct*] (EA) ... FSWW
First Soprano, Second Soprano, and Alto [*in all-women choral groups*] ... SSA
First Source Corp. [*Associated Press*] (SAG) ... 1stSrc
First Source Corp. [*NASDAQ symbol*] (NQ) ... SRCE
First South Africa [*NASDAQ symbol*] (TTSB) ... FSACF
First South Africa Corp. Ltd. [*NASDAQ symbol*] (SAG) ... FSAC
First South Africa Corp. Ltd. [*NASDAQ symbol*] (SAG) ... FSAU
First South Africa Corp. Ltd. [*NASDAQ symbol*] (SAG) ... FSAW
First South Africa Corp. Ltd. [*NASDAQ symbol*] (SAG) ... FSAZ
First South Africa Corp. Ltd. [*Associated Press*] (SAG) ... FSouth
First South Africa Corp. Ltd. [*Associated Press*] (SAG) ... FSth
First South Africa Corp. Ltd. [*Associated Press*] (SAG) ... FstSouth
First South Africa Unit [*NASDAQ symbol*] (TTSB) ... FSAUF
First South Africa Wrrt'A' [*NASDAQ symbol*] (TTSB) ... FSAWF
First South Africa Wrrt'B' [*NASDAQ symbol*] (TTSB) ... FSAZF
First Southeast Financial Corp. [*NASDAQ symbol*] (SAG) ... FSFC
First Southeast Financial Corp. [*Associated Press*] (SAG) ... FtSouest
First Southeast Finl [*NASDAQ symbol*] (TTSB) ... FSFC
First Southern Bancshares [*NASDAQ symbol*] (TTSB) ... FSTH
First Southern Bancshares, Inc. [*NASDAQ symbol*] (SAG) ... FSTH
First Southern Bancshares, Inc. [*Associated Press*] (SAG) ... FtSthnB
First Soviet Reactor ... FSR
First Spacelab Payload [*NASA*] ... FSLP
First Spanish Investment Trust [*London Stock Exchange*] ... FSIT
First Special Operations Command (DOMA) ... FSOCOM
First Special Service Force (MCD) ... FSSF
First Special Service Force Association (EA) ... FSSFA
First Stage [*Aerospace*] ... FS
First Stage Graphitization (PDAA) ... FSG
First Standard Mining Ltd. [*Vancouver Stock Exchange symbol*] ... FSL
First Star Energy [*Vancouver Stock Exchange symbol*] ... FSE
First State [*NASDAQ symbol*] (TTSB) ... FSBT
First State Bancorp [*NASDAQ symbol*] (SAG) ... FSNM
First State Bancorp (NM) [*Associated Press*] (SAG) ... FstStBc
First State Bancorporation [*NASDAQ symbol*] (TTSB) ... FSNM
First State Corp. [*NASDAQ symbol*] (SAG) ... FSBT
First State Corp. [*Associated Press*] (SAG) ... FtStateCp
First State Corp. [*Associated Press*] (SAG) ... FtSteCp
First State Financial Services, Inc. [*NASDAQ symbol*] (NQ) ... FSFI
First State Financial Services, Inc. [*Associated Press*] (SAG) ... FtStFin
First State Finl Svcs [*NASDAQ symbol*] (TTSB) ... FSFL
First Static Firing (MCD) ... FSF
First Step (MUGU) ... FS
First Sunday (EA) ... FS
First Surface Mirror ... FSM
First Surrey Rifles [*Military unit*] [*British*] ... FSR
First Svgs Bk Wash Bancorp [*NASDAQ symbol*] (TTSB) ... FWWB
First Task Fleet ... FIRSTASKFLT
First Team Sports [*NASDAQ symbol*] (TTSB) ... FTSP
First Team Sports, Inc. [*NASDAQ symbol*] (NQ) ... FTSP
First Team Sports, Inc. [*Associated Press*] (SAG) ... FtTeam
First Telecast (DOAD) ... FT
First Tenn Natl [*NASDAQ symbol*] (TTSB) ... FTEN
First Tennessee National Corp. [*Associated Press*] (SAG) ... FstTenn
First Tennessee National Corp. [*NASDAQ symbol*] (NQ) ... FTEN
First Tenor, Second Tenor, First Bass, and Second Bass [*in all-male choral groups*] ... TTBB
First Thoracic Nerve [*T2 Second Thoracic Nerve, etc., through T12*] [*Anatomy*] (DAVI) ... T1
First Thoracic Vertebra [*T2 Second thoracic vertebra, etc., through T12*] [*Anatomy*] (DAVI) ... T1
First Tier Debt [*Economics*] ... FTD
First Time Use ... FTU
First Toronto Capital Corp. [*Toronto Stock Exchange symbol*] ... FTO
First Training Unit ... FTU
First Transcript [*Genetics*] ... T1
First Tridon Industry [*Vancouver Stock Exchange symbol*] ... FTD
First Union $2.15 Cv B Pfd [*NYSE symbol*] (TTSB) ... FTUPrB
First Union 10.64% Dep Pfd [*NYSE symbol*] (TTSB) ... FTUPrF
First Union Adj D Pfd [*NYSE symbol*] (TTSB) ... FTUPrD
First Union Corp. [*Associated Press*] (SAG) ... FstUC
First Union Corp. [*NYSE symbol*] (SPSG) ... FTU
First Union RE EqSBI [*NYSE symbol*] (TTSB) ... FUR
First Union Real Estate Equity & Mortgage Investments [*Associated Press*] (SAG) ... FUnRl
First Unit Equipped (MCD) ... FUE
First Unit Equipped Date (MCD) ... FUED
First Unit Loading Cost ... FULC
First United Bancorp [*Associated Press*] (SAG) ... FtUtdBcp
First United Bancorp [*NASDAQ symbol*] (SAG) ... FUBC
First United Bancorp [*NASDAQ symbol*] (SAG) ... FUSC
First United Bancorporation [*Associated Press*] (SAG) ... FUtdBcp
First United Bancshares [*Associated Press*] (SAG) ... FtUtdBs
First United Bancshares, Inc. [*Associated Press*] (SAG) ... FtUtd
First United Bancshares, Inc. [*El Dorado, AR*] [*NASDAQ symbol*] (NQ) ... UNTD
First United Bancshrs [*NASDAQ symbol*] (TTSB) ... UNTD
First United Corp. [*Associated Press*] (SAG) ... FstUtdCp
First United Corp. [*NASDAQ symbol*] (SAG) ... FUNC
First United States Army ... FUSA
First United States Army Group ... FUSAG
First (United States Army Reserve) Company Chaplain Office ... FUCCO
First USA [*NYSE symbol*] (SPSG) ... FUS
First USA 6.25% 'PRIDES' [*NYSE symbol*] (TTSB) ... FUSPr
First USA, Inc. [*Associated Press*] (SAG) ... Fst USA
First USA, Inc. [*Associated Press*] (SAG) ... FtUSA
First USA Paymentech [*NYSE symbol*] (TTSB) ... PTI
First USA Paymentech, Inc. [*Associated Press*] (SAG) ... FUS Pay
First USA Paymentech, Inc. [*NYSE symbol*] (SAG) ... PTI
First Use Date [*NASA*] (NASA) ... FUD
First Utd SB Greencastle Ind [*NASDAQ symbol*] (TTSB) ... FUSB
First Vertical Flight [*NASA*] (NASA) ... FVF
First Victoria National Bank [*Associated Press*] (SAG) ... FstVict
First Victoria National Bank [*NASDAQ symbol*] (SAG) ... FVNB
First Victoria Natl Bank [*NASDAQ symbol*] (TTSB) ... FVNB
First Virginia Banks [*NYSE symbol*] (TTSB) ... FVB
First Virginia Banks, Inc. [*Associated Press*] (SAG) ... FtVaBks
First Virginia Bankshares Corp. [*NYSE symbol*] (SPSG) ... FVB
First Virtual Holdings, Inc. [*Associated Press*] (SAG) ... FrstVrtl
First Virtual Holdings, Inc. [*NASDAQ symbol*] (SAG) ... FVHI

First Voided Urine [*Medicine*] (CPH) .... FVU
First Volar Interosseous Muscle [*Myology*] .... FVI
First Wash Realty Trust [*NASDAQ symbol*] (TTSB) .... FWSH
First Wash Rlty 9.75% Cv Pfd [*NASDAQ symbol*] (TTSB) .... FWSHP
First Washingtn Bancorp, Inc. [*Associated Press*] (SAG) .... FstWash
First Washington Realty Trust [*AMEX symbol*] (SAG) .... FWR
First Washington Realty Trust [*NASDAQ symbol*] (SAG) .... FWSH
First Washington Realty Trust [*Associated Press*] (SAG) .... FWshR
First Washington Realty Trust [*Associated Press*] (SAG) .... FWshRT
First West Virginia Bancorp [*AMEX symbol*] (TTSB) .... FWV
First West Virginia Bancorp, Inc. [*Associated Press*] (SAG) .... FstWV
First West Virginia Bancorp, Inc. [*AMEX symbol*] (SAG) .... FWV
First Western Bancorp [*Associated Press*] (SAG) .... FtWBc
First Western Bancorp [*Associated Press*] (SAG) .... FtWstnBc
First Western Bancorp, Inc. [*NASDAQ symbol*] (NQ) .... FWBI
First Western Communications Corp. [*Vancouver Stock Exchange symbol*] .... FWW
First Woman on the Supreme Court [*Sandra Day O'Connor*] .... FWOTSC
First Women's Bank [*New York City*] .... FWB
First Word .... FW
First Word Address [*Computer science*] .... FWA
First Word Pointer [*Computer science*] (MHDB) .... FWP
First World War (DMA) .... FWW
First Yars Inc. (The) [*NASDAQ symbol*] (SAG) .... KIDD
First Years [*NASDAQ symbol*] (TTSB) .... KIDD
[*The*] First Years, Inc. [*Associated Press*] (SAG) .... FstYears
First Zen Institute of America (EA) .... FZIA
First-Aid and Water Safety [*Red Cross*] .... FAWS
First-Aid Box (AAG) .... FAB
First-Aid Instructor [*Red Cross*] .... FAI
First-Aid Instructor Trainer [*Red Cross*] .... FAIT
First-Aid Nursing Yeomanry [*British women's organization formed to do medical transport work for the army; later did general transport work*] .... FANY
First-Aid Post .... FAP
First-Aid, Small Craft, and Water Safety [*Red Cross*] .... FASCWS
First-Airborne Telescopic and Spectrographic Observatory (DNAB) .... FATSO
Firstar Corp. [*Associated Press*] (SAG) .... Firstar
Firstar Corp. [*NYSE symbol*] (SPSG) .... FSR
Firstar Corp. [*NASDAQ symbol*] (SAG) .... FSRP
Firstar Corp. $1.75 Cv Dep Pfd [*NASDAQ symbol*] (TTSB) .... FSRPZ
Firstbank of Illinois [*NASDAQ symbol*] (TTSB) .... FBIC
Firstbank of Illinois Co. [*NASDAQ symbol*] (NQ) .... FBIC
Firstbank of Illinois Co. [*Associated Press*] (SAG) .... FstbkIll
FirstBank Puerto Rico [*NYSE symbol*] (TTSB) .... FBP
Firstbank Puerto Rico [*Associated Press*] (SAG) .... FstbkPR
Firstcity Financial [*NASDAQ symbol*] (TTSB) .... FCFC
Firstcity Finl 'B' Pfd [*NASDAQ symbol*] (TTSB) .... FCFCP
First-Class Certificate .... FCC
First-Class Mail [*Postal Service*] .... FCM
Firstcorp, Inc. (MHDW) .... Fstcrp
First-Day Cover [*Philately*] .... FDC
First-Degree Stochastic Dominance [*Statistics*] .... FSD
First-Ended, First-Out [*Computer science*] .... FEFO
Firstfed American Bancorp, Inc. [*AMEX symbol*] (SAG) .... FAB
Firstfed Bancshares [*NASDAQ symbol*] (TTSB) .... FFDP
FirstFed Bancshares, Inc. [*NASDAQ symbol*] (SAG) .... FFDP
FirstFed Bancshares, Inc. [*Associated Press*] (SAG) .... FtFedBn
FirstFed Financial [*NYSE symbol*] (TTSB) .... FED
FirstFed Financial [*Associated Press*] (SAG) .... FstFed
Firstfed Finl Svcs [*NASDAQ symbol*] (TTSB) .... FFSW
FirstFederal Financial Services [*NASDAQ symbol*] (SAG) .... FFSW
FirstFederal Financial Services [*Associated Press*] (SAG) .... FstFedFn
FirstFederal Financial Services Corp. [*Associated Press*] (SAG) .... FFFn
FirstFederal Finl 7% Cv'A'Pfd [*NASDAQ symbol*] (TTSB) .... FFSWP
FirstFederal Finl 6.5% Cv'B' Pfd [*NASDAQ symbol*] (TTSB) .... FFSWO
Firstfund Capital Corp. [*Vancouver Stock Exchange symbol*] .... FFC
First-Hand Distribution .... FHD
FirsTier Finance, Inc. [*NASDAQ symbol*] (NQ) .... FRST
FirsTier Financial, Inc. [*Associated Press*] (SAG) .... Firstier
First-In/Not-Used/First-Out [*Replacement algorithm*] [*Computer science*] (BYTE) .... FINUFO
First-In, Still-Here [*Facetious extension of FIFO definition*] [*Accounting*] .... FISH
First-In, Still-There [*Facetious extension of FIFO definition*] [*Accounting*] .... FIST
First-in-Chain [*Computer science*] .... FIC
First-in-the-Hole (MCD) .... FITH
First-Knox Banc Corp. [*NASDAQ symbol*] (TTSB) .... FKBC
First-Light-Readiness [*Military alert*] (VNW) .... FLR
Firstmark Corp. [*NASDAQ symbol*] (SAG) .... FIRM
Firstmark Corp. [*Associated Press*] (SAG) .... Fstmark
FirstMerit Corp. [*NASDAQ symbol*] (SAG) .... FMER
FirstMerit Corp. [*Associated Press*] (SAG) .... FstMerit
FirstMiss Gold [*NASDAQ symbol*] (TTSB) .... FRMG
FirstMiss Gold, Inc. [*NASDAQ symbol*] (NQ) .... FRMG
FirstMiss Gold, Inc. [*Associated Press*] (SAG) .... FtMissG
First-Order Interpolator (IAA) .... FOI
First-Order Polarization Propagator Approach [*Physics*] .... FOPPA
First-Order Polynomial Interpolator .... FOPI
First-Order Polynomial Predictor .... FOPP
First-Order Predicate Logic (IAA) .... FOPL
First-Order Predictor (IAA) .... FOP
First-Pass Nuclear Angiocardiography [*Cardiology*] (DAVI) .... FPNA
First-Pass Radionuclide Angiogram [*Medicine*] .... FPRA
Firsts and Seconds [*Lumber trade*] .... FAS
FirstService Corp. [*NASDAQ symbol*] (SAG) .... FSRV
FirstService Corp. [*Associated Press*] (SAG) .... FstSvc

FirstService Corp.(Mfg) [*NASDAQ symbol*] (TTSB) .... FSRVF
First-Stage Conduit [*Aerospace*] .... FSC
First-Stage Conduit Container [*Aerospace*] .... FSCC
First-Stage Engine Cutoff [*Aerospace*] .... FSECO
First-Stage Hydraulics [*Aerospace*] .... FSH
First-Stage Ignition System [*Aerospace*] (MCD) .... FSIS
First-Stage Motor [*Aerospace*] .... FSM
First-Stage Motor Container [*Aerospace*] .... FSMC
First-Stage Rocket Motor [*Aerospace*] .... FSRM
First-Stage Separation [*Aerospace*] .... FSS
First-Stage Separation Device [*Aerospace*] .... FSSD
First-Time-Buy (MCD) .... FTB
First-Year Algebra [*National Science Foundation project*] .... FYA
Firth of Forth (DAS) .... F of F
Firwood (VRA) .... firwd
FIS [*Foreign Instrumentation Signals*] Intelligence (MCD) .... FISINT
Fisantekraal [*South Africa*] [*ICAO location identifier*] (ICLI) .... FAFK
Fiscal (AFIT) .... FI
Fiscal .... FIS
Fiscal (MUGU) .... FISC
Fiscal .... FISC
Fiscal Activities Guide [*Department of Labor*] (OICC) .... FAG
Fiscal Advisory Committee [*American Occupational Therapy Association*] .... FAC
Fiscal and Force Capability Guidance (DNAB) .... FFG
Fiscal Director of the Marine Corps .... FDMC
Fiscal Guidance (AABC) .... FG
Fiscal Guidance Category [*Military*] (CAAL) .... FGC
Fiscal Guidance Memorandum [*Navy*] .... FGM
Fiscal Information System .... FIS
Fiscal Intermediary (DNAB) .... FI
Fiscal Letter (OICC) .... FL
Fiscal Management Information System .... FMIS
Fiscal Operations Report and Application to Participate [*Department of Education*] (GFGA) .... FISAP
Fiscal Pay Services of Armies [*World War II*] .... FPS
Fiscal Policy Council (EA) .... FPC
Fiscal Quarter (AFM) .... FQ
Fiscal Service (IEEE) .... FS
Fiscal Station Number [*Military*] .... FSN
Fiscal Week [*Business term*] (IAA) .... FW
Fiscal Year [*Business term*] .... FY
Fiscal Year Data Summary .... FYDS
Fiscal Year Design Objective .... FYDO
Fiscal Year Development Plan (MCD) .... FYDP
Fiscal Year End (NFD) .... FYE
Fiscal Year Ending .... FYE
Fiscal Year Month .... FYM
Fiscal Year Option .... FYO
Fiscal Year Transition Quarter .... FYTQ
Fischer [*Rat strain*] .... F
Fischer Imaging [*NASDAQ symbol*] (TTSB) .... FIMG
Fischer Imaging Corp. [*Associated Press*] (SAG) .... FischIm
Fischer Rat Embryo [*Medicine*] (DMAA) .... FRE
Fischerei-Geraete-Station .... FGS
Fischer-Tropsch Synthesis [*Organic chemistry*] .... FT
Fischer-Tropsch Synthesis [*Organic chemistry*] .... FTS
Fischer-Tropsch Type [*Class of chemical reaction*] .... FTT
Fiserv, Inc. [*Associated Press*] (SAG) .... Fiserv
Fiserv, Inc. [*NASDAQ symbol*] (NQ) .... FISV
Fish Aggregating Device [*Pisciculture*] .... FAD
Fish Aggregating Device [*Marine science*] (OSRA) .... FAD
Fish Aggregation Device (EERA) .... FAD
Fish and Game Code [*A publication*] (DLA) .... Fish & GC
Fish & Game Library, Boise, ID [*Library symbol*] [*Library of Congress*] (LCLS) .... IdBFG
Fish and Meat Spreadable Products Association [*British*] (DBA) .... FMSPA
Fish and Shellfish Immunology [*A publication*] .... FSI
Fish and Wildlife Coordination Act (GFGA) .... FWCA
Fish and Wildlife Reference Service [*Fish and Wildlife Service*] [*Information service or system*] (MSC) .... FWRS
Fish and Wildlife Service [*Department of the Interior*] .... F & WS
Fish and Wildlife Service [*Department of the Interior*] .... FWS
Fish and Wildlife Service/Office of Biological Services [*Department of the Interior*] .... FWS/OBS
Fish Creek, AK [*Location identifier FAA*] (FAAL) .... FHC
Fish Culture Research Laboratory [*Kearneysville, WV*] [*Fish and Wildlife Service*] [*Department of the Interior*] (GRD) .... FCRL
Fish Culture Section [*American Fisheries Society*] (EA) .... FCS
Fish Disease Leaflet .... FDL
Fish Epidermal Keratocyte [*Marine science*] .... FEK
Fish Exports Inspector .... FEI
Fish Lake [*Pisciculture*] .... FL
Fish Meal .... FM
Fish Oil Film .... FOF
Fish Oil Restenosis Trial [*Cardiology*] .... FORT
Fish Pesticide Research Laboratory [*Department of the Interior*] .... FPRL
Fish Promotional Fund [*National Oceanic and Atmospheric Administration*] (GFGA) .... FPF
Fish Protein Concentrate [*For use in antistarvation programs*] .... FPC
Fish Protein Hydrolysate .... FPH
FishAmerica Foundation (EA) .... F/AF
Fisher and Lightwood on Mortgages [*9th ed.*] [*1977*] [*A publication*] (DLA) .... Fish & L Mort
Fisher and Lightwood on Mortgages [*9th ed.*] [*1977*] [*A publication*] (DLA) .... Fisher & Lightwood

Fisher Branch, MB [*Television station call letters*] ... CBWGT
Fisher Elementary School, Pasadena, TX [*Library symbol*] [*Library of Congress*] (LCLS) ... TxPFE
Fisher, IL [*FM radio station call letters*] (RBYB) ... WGNN-FM
Fisher Imaging Corp. [*NASDAQ symbol*] (SPSG) ... FIMG
Fisher Institute [*Dallas, TX*] (EA) ... FI
Fisher Institute of Applied Arts and Technology, Corner Brook, Newfoundland [*Library symbol National Library of Canada*] (NLC) ... NFCBFT
Fisher Junior College [*Boston, MA*] ... FJC
Fisher on Copyrights [*A publication*] (DLA) ... Fish Cop
Fisher on Mortgages [*A publication*] (DLA) ... Fish Mort
Fisher on Mortgages [*A publication*] (DLA) ... Fish Mortg
Fisher on Mortgages [*A publication*] (DLA) ... Fisher
Fisher on the United States Constitution [*A publication*] (DLA) ... Fish Const
Fisher on the Will Act [*A publication*] (DLA) ... Fish WA
Fisher. Pennsylvania Prize Cases [*A publication*] (DLA) ... Fisher Pr Cas (PA)
Fisher Public School, Fisher, MN [*Library symbol*] [*Library of Congress*] (LCLS) ... MnFisS
Fisher Scientific International [*Associated Press*] (SAG) ... FishrSci
Fisher Scientific International [*NYSE symbol*] (SPSG) ... FSH
Fisher Scientific Intl. [*NYSE symbol*] (TTSB) ... FSH
Fisher Significant Difference (PDAA) ... FSD
Fisher, WV [*AM radio station call letters*] ... WELD
Fisher, WV [*FM radio station call letters*] (RBYB) ... WJBQ
Fisher-Hirschfelder-Taylor [*Molecular model*] ... FHT
Fisheries ... FISH
Fisheries Advisory Committee of the South Pacific Commission ... FAC/SPC
Fisheries and Oceans Canada [*Peches et Oceans Canada*] **Halifax, Nova Scotia** [*Library symbol National Library of Canada*] (NLC) ... NSHF
Fisheries and Oceans Canada, Maurice Lamontagne Institute, Mont-Joli, PQ, Canada [*Library symbol*] [*Library of Congress*] (LCLS) ... CaQMJFM
Fisheries and Oceans Canada, Moncton, NB, Canada [*Library symbol*] [*Library of Congress*] (LCLS) ... CaNBMoF
Fisheries and Oceans Canada [*Peches et Oceans Canada*] **Moncton, New Brunswick** [*Library symbol National Library of Canada*] (NLC) ... NBMOF
Fisheries and Oceans Canada [*Peches et Oceans Canada*] **Ottawa, Ontario** [*Library symbol National Library of Canada*] (NLC) ... OOFI
Fisheries Conservation Zone ... FCS
Fisheries Department [*Western Australia*] ... FD
Fisheries Development Trust Account (EERA) ... FDTA
Fisheries Engineering Laboratory [*Marine science*] (MSC) ... FEL
Fisheries Licensing Panel [*Victoria, Australia*] ... FLP
Fisheries Loan Fund [*National Oceanic and Atmospheric Administration*] ... FLF
Fisheries Management Committee [*Victoria, Australia*] ... FMC
Fisheries Management Plan [*Marine science*] (OSRA) ... FMP
Fisheries Management Regional Library, Fisheries and Oceans Canada [*Bibliotheque Regionale de la Gestion des Pecheries, Peches et Oceans Canada*] **Vancouver, British Columbia** [*Library symbol National Library of Canada*] (NLC) ... BVAFI
Fisheries Museum of the Atlantic, Lunenburg, Nova Scotia [*Library symbol National Library of Canada*] (NLC) ... NSLFM
Fisheries Museum of the Atlantic, Lunenburg, NS, Canada [*Library symbol*] [*Library of Congress*] (LCLS) ... CaNSLuFM
Fisheries Oceanography Cooperative Users System (USDC) ... FOCUS
Fisheries Oceanography Cooperative Users System [*Marine science*] (OSRA) ... FOCUS
Fisheries Patrols [*Canadian Navy*] ... FISHPATS
Fisheries Products International [*Canada*] ... FPI
Fisheries Radiobiological Laboratory [*British*] (NUCP) ... FRL
Fisheries Research and Development Corporation [*Commonwealth*] (EERA) ... FRDC
Fisheries Research Board of Canada [*Marine science*] (MSC) ... FRB
Fisheries Research Institute [*University of Washington*] [*Research center*] ... FRI
Fisheries Research Institute [*Australia*] ... FRI
Fisheries Research Station [*British*] ... FRS
Fisheries Society of the British Isles ... FSBI
Fisheries-Oceanography Cooperative Investigations [*National Oceanic and Atmospheric Administration*] (USDC) ... FOCI
Fisheries-Oceanography Cooperative Investigations Biophysical Platform [*Marine science*] (OSRA) ... FOCI BP
Fisheries-Oceanography Cooperative Users System [*Marine science*] (OSRA) ... FOCI
Fisher-Johns [*Melting point method*] ... FJ
Fisher-Logemann Test of Articular Competence [*Speech and language therapy*] (DAVI) ... FLTAC
Fisherman's Information Bureau [*Chicago, IL*] ... FIB
Fishermen's Compensation Fund [*National Oceanic and Atmospheric Administration*] ... FCF
Fishermen's Guarantee Fund [*National Oceanic and Atmospheric Administration*] ... FGF
Fisher-Price Toys, East Aurora, NY [*Library symbol Library of Congress*] (LCLS) ... NEAuF
Fisher-Race Notation [*Medicine*] (MAE) ... FR
Fisher's Cases, United States District Courts [*A publication*] (DLA) ... Fish Cas
Fisher's Digest of English Common Law Reports [*A publication*] (DLA) ... Fish CL Dig
Fisher's Digest of English Common Law Reports [*A publication*] (DLA) ... Fish Dig
Fisher's Digest of English Criminal Law [*A publication*] (DLA) ... Fish Crim Dig
Fisher's Digest of Patent Law [*A publication*] (DLA) ... Fish Pat Dig
Fishers Island Library Association, Fishers Island, NY [*Library symbol Library of Congress*] (LCLS) ... NFisi
Fisher's United States Patent Cases [*A publication*] (DLA) ... Fish
Fisher's United States Patent Cases [*A publication*] (DLA) ... Fish Pat
Fisher's United States Patent Cases [*A publication*] (DLA) ... Fish Pat Cas
Fisher's United States Patent Cases [*A publication*] (DLA) ... Fisher Pat Cas (F)
Fisher's United States Patent Cases [*A publication*] (DLA) ... Fisher's Pat Cas
Fisher's United States Patent Reports [*A publication*] (DLA) ... Fish Pat R
Fisher's United States Patent Reports [*A publication*] (DLA) ... Fish Pat Rep
Fisher's United States Prize Cases [*A publication*] (DLA) ... Fish
Fisher's United States Prize Cases [*A publication*] (DLA) ... Fish Pr Cas
Fisher's United States Prize Cases [*A publication*] (DLA) ... Fish Prize
Fisher's United States Prize Cases [*A publication*] (DLA) ... Fish Prize Cas
Fisher's United States Prize Cases [*A publication*] (DLA) ... Fisher
Fisher's United States Prize Cases [*A publication*] (DLA) ... Fisher Pr Cas (F)
Fishery ... FSHRY
Fishery Board ... FB
Fishery Committee for the Eastern Central Atlantic [*See also COPACE*] ... CECAF
Fishery Conservation and Management Act [*1976*] [*Also, MFCMA*] ... FCMA
Fishery Conservation Zone ... FCZ
Fishery Council (EA) ... FC
Fishery Data Center [*FAO*] (MSC) ... FDC
Fishery Flag [*Navy British*] ... FY
Fishery Information, Data and Statistics Service [*Marine science*] (OSRA) ... FIDI
Fishery Management Council [*National Oceanic and Atmospheric Administration*] (GFGA) ... FMC
Fishery Management Information System [*Marine science*] (OSRA) ... FIMIS
Fishery Management Plan ... FMP
Fishery Officer [*Ministry of Agriculture, Fisheries, and Food*] [*British*] ... FO
Fishery Project Information System [*FAO*] [*United Nations*] (DUND) ... FIPIS
Fishery Protection Vessel ... FPV
Fishery Research Craft ... FRC
Fishery Statistics Data Base [*National Marine Fisheries Service*] [*Information service or system*] (CRD) ... FISHSTATS
Fishery Statistics Data Base [*National Marine Fisheries Service*] [*Information service or system*] (MSC) ... FSDB
Fishery-Oceanography Experiment [*Marine science*] (OSRA) ... FOX
Fishery-Oceanography Experiment (USDC) ... FOX
Fishguard [*Goodwick*] [*British depot code*] ... FGD
Fishing ... FSHNG
Fishing Boat Builders Association [*British*] (BI) ... FBBA
Fishing Clubs of Australia ... FCA
Fishing/Fisheries/Vessel Obligation Guarantee (USDC) ... FOG
Fishing Industry Advisory Committee [*Australia*] ... FIAC
Fishing Industry Appeals Tribunal [*Australia*] ... FIAT
Fishing Industry Grants [*Marine science*] (OSRA) ... FIG
Fishing Industry Grants (USDC) ... FIG
Fishing Industry Policy Council [*Australia*] ... FIPC
Fishing Industry Research and Development Council (EERA) ... FIRDC
Fishing Industry Research Council (EERA) ... FIRC
Fishing Industry Research Trust Account (EERA) ... FIRTA
Fishing Industry Training Board of Tasmania [*Australia*] ... FITBT
Fishing Research Vessel ... FRV
Fishing Stakes [*Nautical charts*] ... Fsh stks
Fishing Vessel ... FV
Fishing Vessel and Gear Damage Compensation Fund [*National Oceanic and Atmospheric Administration*] ... FVGDCF
Fishing Vessel Insurance Plan [*Canada*] ... FVIP
Fishing Vessel Obligation Guarantee [*Program*] [*Marine science*] (OSRA) ... FVOG
Fishing Vessel Obligation Guarantee [*Program*] (USDC) ... FVOG
Fishing Vessel Transmit Terminal (PDAA) ... FVTT
Fishpaper [*Insulation*] ... FPPR
Fisk University (GAGS) ... Fisk U
Fisk University, Nashville, TN [*OCLC symbol*] (OCLC) ... FSK
Fisk University, Nashville, TN [*Library symbol Library of Congress*] (LCLS) ... TNF
Fiske Free Library, Claremont, NH [*Library symbol Library of Congress*] (LCLS) ... NhCla
Fiskeridirektoratet [*Directorate of Fisheries*], Bergen-Nordens, Norway [*Library symbol Library of Congress*] (LCLS) ... NoBeFi
Fiske-Subbarow Positive Phosphorus [*Analytical chemistry*] ... FSPP
Fisk's Analysis of Coke on Littleton [*1824*] [*A publication*] (DLA) ... Fisk Anal
Fisons Corp. Ltd., Markham, Ontario [*Library symbol National Library of Canada*] (NLC) ... OTFP
Fisons Ltd. [*NASDAQ symbol*] (NQ) ... FISN
Fisons Ltd. [*Associated Press*] (SAG) ... Fisons
Fisons Pharmaceuticals Ltd. ... FPL
Fissile Material ... FM
Fission (MSA) ... FSSN
Fission Activated LASER Concept [*Sandia National Laboratories*] ... FALCON
Fission Fragment-Induced Ionization - Mass Spectroscopy ... FFII-MS
Fission Gas (NRCH) ... FG
Fission Gas Monitor (NRCH) ... FGM
Fission Initial Metal Atom [*Nuclear energy*] (NRCH) ... FIMA
Fission Product ... FP
Fission Product Control Screening Test Loop [*Nuclear energy*] (NRCH) ... FPCSTL
Fission Product Release [*Nuclear energy*] (NUCP) ... FPR
Fission Product Screening Loop [*Nuclear energy*] (NRCH) ... FPSL
Fission Products Conversion and Encapsulation [*Plant*] [*Nuclear energy*] ... FPCE
Fission Products Development Laboratory [*ORNL*] ... FPDL
Fission Track [*Geological age dating*] ... FT
Fission Yield Curve ... FYC
Fission-Fusion Ratio ... FFR
Fission-Fusion-Fission [*Bomb*] (DEN) ... FFF
Fissions per Initial Fissile Atom [*Nuclear energy*] ... FIFA
Fissions per Minute ... FPM
Fistful of Prisms [*Opthalmology*] (DAVI) ... FFP
Fistula ... FIST

Fistula Armata [Clyster-Pipe and Bladder Fitted for Use] [Pharmacy] (ROG) .... FIST ARM
Fit and Independent Traveler (TAG) .... FIT
Fit Anything to Anything You Like (MHDB) .... FATAL
Fit Check [NASA] (NASA) .... FC
Fit for Issue [Navy] .... FFI
Fit for Role [Military British] .... FFR
Fit for Service Everywhere [British military] (DMA) .... FE
Fit to Be Detained [Medicine] .... FTBD
Fitch on Real Estate Agency [A publication] (DLA) .... Fitch RE Ag
Fitchburg [Massachusetts] [Airport symbol] (AD) .... FIT
Fitchburg, MA [Location identifier FAA] (FAAL) .... FIT
Fitchburg, MA [AM radio station call letters] .... WEIM
Fitchburg, MA [AM radio station call letters] .... WFGL
Fitchburg, MA [FM radio station call letters] .... WXLO
Fitchburg, MA [FM radio station call letters] .... WXPL
Fitchburg Public Library and Regional Center for Central Massachusetts, RegionalLibrary System, Fitchburg, MA [Library symbol Library of Congress] (LCLS) .... MFi
Fitchburg Railroad .... FRR
Fitchburg State College (GAGS) .... Fitchburg St C
Fitchburg State College, Fitchburg, MA [OCLC symbol] (OCLC) .... FTB
Fitchburg State College, Fitchburg, MA [Library symbol Library of Congress] (LCLS) .... MFiT
Fitness .... FITNS
Fitness and Arthritis in Seniors Trial .... FAST
Fitness for Life (EA) .... FFL
Fitness for the Future [Nursing Services Course] [Red Cross] .... FFF
Fitness Institute of Victoria [Australia] .... FIV
Fitness, Intensity, Time [Exercise] .... FIT
Fitness Motivation Institute of America Association (EA) .... FMIAA
Fitness Reports Branch [BUPERS] .... FRB
Fitted (MSA) .... FTD
Fitted as Flagship [Suffix to plane designation] .... F
Fitted for Oil Fuel [Ships] .... OF
Fitted for Radio [Military British] .... FFR
Fitted for Wireless [British military] (DMA) .... FFW
Fitted Parts Tag (SAA) .... FPT
Fitted With Radio .... FWR
Fitter [Navy rating British] .... F
Fitter and Turner [Navy rating British] .... FT
Fitting (MSA) .... FTG
Fitting Out [Navy] (NG) .... FO
Fitting Out Availability [Navy] .... FOA
Fitting Out Management Information System [Navy] (CAAL) .... FOMIS
Fitting Out Supply Assistance Team [Navy] .... FOSAT
Fitting Out Supply Assistance Team, Atlantic [Navy] .... FOSATLANT
Fitting Out Supply Assistance Team, Pacific [Navy] .... FOSATPAC
Fitting Shop Trade Society [A union] [British] .... FSTS
Fitting-Out of Leased Premises .... FOLP
Fittings (ADA) .... FITTS
Fittings and Fixtures (ADA) .... F & F
Fitzadams on the Judicature Act [A publication] (DLA) .... Fitzad Jud Act
Fitzgerald, GA [Location identifier FAA] (FAAL) .... FZG
Fitzgerald, GA [AM radio station call letters] .... WBHB
Fitzgerald, GA [FM radio station call letters] .... WRDO
Fitzgerald on the Public Health [A publication] (DLA) .... Fitzg Pub H
Fitzgibbon's Irish Land Reports [A publication] (DLA) .... Fitzg
Fitzgibbon's Irish Land Reports [A publication] (DLA) .... Fitzg Land R
Fitzgibbon's Irish Land Reports [A publication] (DLA) .... Qly Land R
Fitzgibbon's Irish Local Government Decisions [A publication] (DLA) .... Fitz LG Dec
Fitzgibbon's Irish Local Government Decisions [A publication] (DLA) .... Fitzg LG Dec
Fitzgibbon's Irish Registration Appeals [A publication] (DLA) .... Fitzg
Fitzgibbon's Irish Registration Appeals [A publication] (DLA) .... Fitzg Reg Ca
Fitzgibbon's King's Bench Reports [England] [A publication] (DLA) .... Fitz
Fitzgibbon's King's Bench Reports [England] [A publication] (DLA) .... Fitzg
Fitzherbert's Abridgment [1516] [A publication] (DSA) .... F
Fitzherbert's Abridgment [1516] [A publication] (DLA) .... F Abr
Fitzherbert's Abridgment [1516] [A publication] (DSA) .... Fitz
Fitzherbert's Abridgment [1516] [A publication] (DLA) .... Fitz Abridg
Fitzherbert's Abridgment [1516] [A publication] (DLA) .... Fitzh
Fitzherbert's Abridgment [1516] [A publication] (DLA) .... Fitzh Abr
Fitzherbert's Justice, Enlarged by Crompton [A publication] (DLA) .... Cromp & F
Fitzherbert's Natura Brevium [A publication] (DLA) .... Fitz Nat Brev
Fitzherbert's Natura Brevium [A publication] (DLA) .... Fitzh N Br
Fitzherbert's Natura Brevium [A publication] (DLA) .... Fitzh Nat Brev
Fitzherbert's Natura Brevium [A publication] (DLA) .... Fitzh NB
Fitzherbert's Natura Brevium [A publication] (DLA) .... FNB
Fitzherbert's Natura Brevium [A publication] (DLA) .... Nat Brev
Fitzsimons Army Medical Center (AABC) .... FAMC
Fitzsimons General Hospital, Medical Technical Library, Denver, CO [Library symbol Library of Congress] (LCLS) .... CoDFG-M
Fitzwilliam Virginal Book .... FVB
Fiume Study Group (EA) .... FSG
Five [Roman numeral] V
Five Associated University Libraries [State University of New York at Buffalo and Binghamton, Cornell University, Syracuse University, University of Rochester] .... FAUL
Five Associated University Libraries, Rochester, NY [OCLC symbol] (OCLC) .... TPD
Five Associated University Libraries, Rochester, NY [OCLC symbol] (OCLC) .... TPE
Five Basic Exercises [British military] (DMA) 5BX

Five Civilized Tribes Foundation [Defunct] (EA) .... FCTF
Five College Radio Astronomy Observatory .... FCRAO
Five Dollars [Slang] V
Five Hundred [Roman numeral] .... D
Five International Associations Coordinating Committee [Hungary] (EAIO) .... FIACC
Five New Laender [Lands] [Name given to former East German territory after unification] .... FNL
Five Points, FL [FM radio station call letters] .... WCJX
Five Task Test [Psychology] .... FTT
Five Towns College, Merrick, NY [Library symbol Library of Congress] (LCLS) .... NMerkF
Five Year Intelligence Program [Military] .... FYIP
Five Year Master Construction Plan [DoD] .... FYMCP
Five Year Master Objectives Plan Program [Military] .... FYMOPP
Five-Hour Glucose Tolerance Test [Medicine] (DMAA) GLU-5
Five-Inch Evasion Device (MCD) .... FED
Five-Lipoxygenase Activating Protein [Biochemistry] .... FLAP
Five-Mile Camp, AK [Location identifier FAA] (FAAL) .... FVM
Five-Soldier Crew Tent .... FSCT
Five-Year Defense Plan [or Program] [Military] .... FYDP
Five-Year Defense Standardization Plan (MCD) .... FYDSP
Five-Year Design Objective .... FYDO
Five-Year Force Structure and Financial Program [Navy] (AFIT) .... FFS & FP
Five-Year Force Structure and Financial Program [Navy] .... FYFS & FP
Five-Year Force Structure and Financial Program [Navy] (KSC) .... FYFSFP
Five-Year Materiel Program [Military] .... FYMP
Five-Year Plan [Military] .... FYP
Five-Year Planning Base [Military] (AABC) .... FYPB
Five-Year Procurement Program [Military] (AABC) .... FYPP
Five-Year Program Plan .... FYPP
Five-Year Sentence [Criminal slang] V
Five-Year Test Program [Military] (AABC) .... FYTP
Five-Year Training Development Plan [Army] .... FYTDP
Fiwila [Zambia] [ICAO location identifier] (ICLI) .... FLFW
Fix [Navigation] .... FX
Fix Dump Reducer (SAA) .... FDR
Fix or Repair Daily [Reference to the alleged defects of Ford automobiles] .... FORD
Fix Up on Printer [Have technician add or change an effect by means of optical printing] [Motion-picture production] .... FUOP
Fixation .... FIXN
Fixation and Transfer [of text] (DNAB) .... FT
Fixation Fluid [Medicine] (DMAA) .... FF
Fixation in Glass of Active Liquid [British] (NUCP) .... FINGAL
Fixation Optokinetic Nystagmus [Eye movement] .... FOKN
Fixative (VRA) .... fxt
Fixed [JETDS nomenclature] .... F
Fixed (AAG) .... FXD
Fixed Abrasive Slicing [Semiconductor technology] .... FAST
Fixed Account Number (EPA) .... FAN
Fixed Acoustic Range .... FAR
Fixed Action Button (NVT) .... FAB
Fixed Action Pattern .... FAP
Fixed Air Capacitor .... FAC
Fixed Airlock Shroud [NASA] .... FAS
Fixed Allowance Management Monitoring System (MCD) .... FAMMS
Fixed Amount Reimbursement [Agency for International Development] .... FAR
Fixed and Dilated [Neurology and ophthalmology] (DAVI) .... F & D
Fixed and Exchangeable Disc Storage (NITA) .... FEDS
Fixed and Flashing Light [Navigation signal] .... FFL
Fixed and Group Flashing Light [Navigation signal] .... FGPFL
Fixed Area [of magnetic disk] .... FX
Fixed Area Scanning Alarm .... FASA
Fixed Array RADAR .... FAR
Fixed Asset [Business term] .... FA
Fixed Asset Accounting Package [Computer science] .... FAAP
Fixed Asset Depreciation System (PDAA) .... FADS
Fixed Asset System Control Information and Accounting [Computer science] (MHDI) .... FASCIA
Fixed Asset Transfer [Business term] .... FAT
Fixed Asset Utilization [Business term] (ADA) .... FAU
Fixed Asset Valuation Adjustment [Business term] (ADA) .... FAVA
Fixed Auto Transfer (MCD) .... FATR
Fixed Autotransformer .... FATR
Fixed Axial Weapon [Military] (VNW) .... FAW
Fixed Base Aft Station (MCD) .... FBAS
Fixed Bathtub Capacitor .... FBC
Fixed Binary (DEN) .... FXBIN
Fixed Block .... FB
Fixed Block Architecture .... FBA
Fixed Blocked [Computer science] (MHDB) .... FIXBLK
Fixed Camera (KSC) .... FC
Fixed Capital [Business term] .... FC
Fixed Center Drive .... FCD
Fixed Ceramic Capacitor .... FCC
Fixed Ceramic Disk Capacitor .... FCDC
Fixed Change Rate .... FCR
Fixed Charge [Business term] .... FC
Fixed Coaxial Attenuator .... FCA
Fixed Code Processor .... FCP
Fixed Communications Cabinet (MCD) .... FCC
Fixed Control Storage .... FCS
Fixed Control Storage (NITA) .... FCS
Fixed Cost [Economics] .... FC
Fixed Cost, Fixed Time (IEEE) .... FCFT

Fixed Cycle Operation ... FCO
Fixed Decade Capacitor ... FDC
Fixed Delay Line ... FDL
Fixed Disc Stores (NITA) ... FDS
Fixed Distributed Subsystem [*Antisubmarine warfare*] (MCD) ... FDS
Fixed Distribution System [*Acoustic antisubmarine warfare sensor*] (DOMA) ... FDS
Fixed Dose Procedure [*Proposed toxicological standard*] ... FDP
Fixed Dynamical Heating [*Climatology*] ... FDH
Fixed Echo Suppressor [*Electronics*] (IAA) ... FES
Fixed Electrolytic Capacitor ... FEC
Fixed Erythrocyte Turnover [*Hematology*] (DAVI) ... FET
Fixed/Exchangeable Disk Store ... FEDS
Fixed Federal Monitoring Network (FAAC) ... FFMN
Fixed Fee [*Business term*] (AAG) ... FF
Fixed Fee Incentive (SSD) ... FFI
Fixed Feed Through Capacitor ... FFTC
Fixed Film Capacitor ... FFC
Fixed Flexion Contracture [*Neurology and orthopedics*] (DAVI) ... FFC
Fixed Flexion Deformity of the Knee [*Orthopedics*] ... FFDK
Fixed Focus [*Photography*] ... FF
Fixed Format (IAA) ... f
Fixed Format Display (MCD) ... FFD
Fixed Former Message Entry Device (MCD) ... FFMED
Fixed Frequency Pulse (IAA) ... FFP
Fixed Frequency Receiver ... FFR
Fixed Frequency Sampling [*for water quality assessment*] ... FFS
Fixed Frequency Topside Sounder (SAA) ... FFTS
Fixed Function Key [*Computer science*] (ECII) ... FFK
Fixed Function Keyboard (MCD) ... FFK
Fixed Gain Control ... FGC
Fixed Gas-Filled Capacitor ... FGFC
Fixed Glass Capacitor ... FGC
Fixed Ground Radio Installations ... FGRI
Fixed Head (NITA) ... F
Fixed Head [*Computer science*] (MHDB) ... FH
Fixed Head Disk / Drum Store [*Computer science*] (MHDI) ... FHDS
Fixed Head File [*Computer science*] (MHDB) ... FHF
Fixed High-Temperature Capacitor ... FHTC
Fixed High-Volt Capacitor ... FHVC
Fixed Hub [*Rotary piston meter*] ... FH
Fixed Income Account ... FIA
Fixed Income Consumer Counseling [*ACTION*] ... FICC
Fixed Interim Baseline ... FIB
Fixed Internal (MAE) ... FI
Fixed Interval [*Reinforcement schedule*] ... FI
Fixed Interval Timer ... FIT
Fixed Jack [*Electronics*] (IAA) ... FJ
Fixed Laboratory Standard Capacitor ... FLSC
Fixed Leading Edge (MCD) ... FLE
Fixed Length Cavity Resonance ... FLCR
Fixed Light [*Navigation signal*] ... F
Fixed Light [*USCG*] (TAG) ... LT
Fixed Line of Sight (KSC) ... FLOS
Fixed Link Aerospace to Ground (SAA) ... FLAG
Fixed Loan Rate [*Business term*] ... FLR
Fixed Message Cycle [*Telecommunications*] (TEL) ... FMC
Fixed Mica Capacitor ... FMC
Fixed Mirror Concentrator ... FMC
Fixed Mobile Experiment (MCD) ... FME
Fixed Motor Run Capacitor ... FMRC
Fixed Motor Starting Capacitor ... FMSC
Fixed Mylar Capacitor ... FMC
Fixed Mylar Metallized Capacitor ... FMMC
Fixed Niobium Capacitor ... FNC
Fixed Nozzle Slow [*or Short*] **Landing** (MCD) ... FNSL
Fixed Oil ... FO
Fixed Oil Capacitor ... FOC
Fixed Orifice Sound Attenuator (DNAB) ... FOSA
Fixed Paper Capacitor ... FPC
Fixed Paper Metallized Capacitor ... FPMC
Fixed Parenchymal Turnover [*Physiology*] (DAVI) ... FPT
Fixed Partial Charge [*Physical chemistry*] ... FPC
Fixed Partial Denture [*Dentistry*] (DAVI) ... FPD
Fixed Path of Operation ... FPO
Fixed Pattern Noise [*Electronics*] (OA) ... FPN
Fixed Pattern Signal [*Optics*] ... FPS
Fixed Photoflash Capacitor ... FPC
Fixed Photoflash Capacitor ... FPFC
Fixed Plant Adapter (DWSG) ... FPA
Fixed Plasma Sheath ... FPS
Fixed Platform Supply Vessel ... FPSV
Fixed Point (MCD) ... FP
Fixed Point ... FXP
Fixed Point Address Arithmetic Logic Unit [*Computer science*] (MHDB) ... FXPALU
Fixed Point Calculation ... FPC
Fixed Point Operation ... FPO
Fixed Point Protocol (NITA) ... FPP
Fixed Point Representation ... FPR
Fixed Point Station [*RADAR*] ... FPS
Fixed Point System ... FPS
Fixed Point Test Site [*Military*] (CAAL) ... FPTS
Fixed Polycarbonate Capacitor ... FPC
Fixed Polycarbonate Capacitor ... FPCC
Fixed Porcelain Enamel Capacitor ... FPEC
Fixed Portion Queue Area [*Computer science*] ... FPQA
Fixed Position Keyboard ... FPK
Fixed Potential Electrode [*Electrochemistry*] ... FPE
Fixed Precision Capacitor ... FPC
Fixed Price ... FP
Fixed Price Award Fee [*Contract*] ... FPAF
Fixed Price Basis ... FPB
Fixed Price Call ... FPC
Fixed Price Contracts ... FPC
Fixed Price Firm (AFM) ... FPF
Fixed Price Incentive ... FPI
Fixed Price Incentive Contract ... FPIC
Fixed Price Incentive Fee ... FPIF
Fixed Price Incentive Firm [*Award*] [*Government contracting*] ... FPIF
Fixed Price Incentive Force (AFM) ... FPIF
Fixed Price Incentive Successive Targets ... FPIS
Fixed Price Incentive with Delay Firm Target (SAA) ... FPID
Fixed Price Open ... FPO
Fixed Price, Price Redetermination [*or Revision*] ... FPPR
Fixed Price Redeterminable (NG) ... FPR
Fixed Price Redeterminable Article ... FPRA
Fixed Price Redetermination Contract ... FPRC
Fixed Price Supply ... FPS
Fixed Price Tenders [*Commerce*] (BARN) ... FPT
Fixed Price with Escalation ... FPE
Fixed Principal Axes [*Hypothesis describing forces in a sand-pile*] ... FPA
Fixed Printed Circuit Capacitor ... FPCC
Fixed Priority Oriented Demand Assignment [*Telecommunications*] (OSI) ... FPODA
Fixed Problem Report (MCD) ... FPR
Fixed Program Computer ... FPC
Fixed Radial Shield [*Nuclear energy*] (NRCH) ... FRS
Fixed Radiation Pattern Antenna ... FRPA
Fixed Radio Communication ... FRC
Fixed Radio Transmission Facility ... FRTF
Fixed Rate Mortgage ... FRM
Fixed Ratio ... FR
Fixed Reserve Deposit Ratio [*Finance*] ... FRDR
Fixed Response (WDAA) ... F/R
Fixed Roof Tank [*Engineering*] ... FRT
Fixed Safety Level ... FSL
Fixed Sample Rate ... FSR
Fixed Sample-Size Procedure ... FSP
Fixed Satellite Communications (DNAB) ... FSC
Fixed Satellite Service ... FSS
Fixed Sequence Format ... FSF
Fixed Service Structure (MCD) ... FSS
Fixed Service Tower ... FST
Fixed Silicon Capacitor ... FSC
Fixed Silo Price [*Wheat*] ... FSP
Fixed Silver Mica Capacitor ... FSMC
Fixed Slot Acknowledgement [*Telecommunications*] (OSI) ... FSA
Fixed Stand-Off Capacitor ... FSOC
Fixed Station [*ITU designation*] (CET) ... FX
Fixed Station (IAA) ... FXSTA
Fixed Step Size Random Search (IAA) ... FSSRS
Fixed Systems Test Equipment (SAA) ... FSTE
Fixed Tantalum Capacitor ... FTC
Fixed Target Information [*Army*] (AABC) ... FTI
Fixed Target Rejection [*Military*] (IAA) ... FTR
Fixed Target Track (MCD) ... FTT
Fixed Temperature Compensating Capacitor ... FTCC
Fixed Term Agreement ... FTA
Fixed Term Lease Plan [*Business term*] (IAA) ... FTLP
Fixed Term Plan (BUR) ... FTP
Fixed Throttle Point [*NASA*] ... FTP
Fixed Time Call [*Telecommunications*] (NITA) ... FXT
Fixed Time Interval (PDAA) ... FTI
Fixed Time of Arrival [*Aviation*] ... FTA
Fixed Time Printing Mode [*Photography*] ... FTPM
Fixed Tissue Turnover [*Laboratory and physiology*] (DAVI) ... FTT
Fixed Tone ... FT
Fixed Transom (AAG) ... FTR
Fixed Treatment Unit [*Engineering*] ... FTU
Fixed Unblocked [*Computer science*] (MHDB) ... FIXUNB
Fixed Vacuum Capacitor ... FVC
Fixed VLF Station (MCD) ... FVLF
Fixed Wavelength [*Electronics*] ... FW
Fixed Wing [*Aircraft*] ... FW
Fixed Wireless Station (IAA) ... FWS
Fixed Word Address [*Computer science*] (IAA) ... FWA
Fixed Word Length [*Computer science*] ... FWL
Fixed-Angle Variable ... FAV
Fixed-Base Crew Station [*NASA*] (NASA) ... FBCS
Fixed-Base Operator [*Provider of nonairline aviation services to users of airports*] ... FBO
Fixed-Based Simulator (PDAA) ... FBS
Fixed-Bed Loop [*Chemical engineering*] ... FBL
Fixed-Fee-plus-Incentive [*Business term*] (MCD) ... FFPI
Fixed-Field Alternating Gradient [*Accelerator*] [*Nuclear energy*] ... FFAG
Fixed-Film Biological [*Process for wastewater treatment*] ... FFB
Fixed-Head Coupe [*Automobile design*] ... FHC
Fixed-Head Disk [*Computer science*] ... FHD
Fixed-Head Storage Facility [*Computer science*] ... FHSF
Fixed-Length Distinguishing Sequence [*Computer science*] (IAA) ... FLDS

Fixed-Length Field [*Computer science*] (BUR) .... FLF
Fixed-Length Word [*Computer science*] (IAA) .... FW
Fixed-Path Protocol [*Telecommunications*] .... FPP
Fixed-Payment Mortgage (DFIT) .... FPM
Fixed-Pitch Propeller (PDAA) .... FPP
Fixed-Point Unit .... FXU
Fixed-Price Incentive Fee Contract Value Engineering (AAGC) .... FPIFV
Fixed-Price Level of Effort Term (AAGC) .... FPLET
Fixed-Price Material Reimbursable (AAGC) .... FPMR
Fixed-Price with Economic Price Adjustment [*Type of contract*] (AAGC) .... FPEPA
Fixed-Price-Redeterminable-Prospective (MCD) .... FPRP
Fixed-Price-Redeterminable-Retroactive (MCD) .... FPRR
Fixed-Weight Indexes .... FWI
Fixed-Wing Aircraft [*Navy symbol*] V
Fixed-Wing Evaluation Exercise [*Aviation*] .... FIXWEX
Fixed-Wing Multiengine Qualification Course [*Aviation*] .... FWMQC
Fixed-Wing Special Instrument Flight Rules [*Aviation*] .... FW/SIFR
Fixed-Wing Special Visual Flight Rules [*Aviation*] .... FW/SVFR
Fixed-Wing Tactical Transport [*Aviation*] (MUGU) .... FWIT
Fixed-Wing Tactical Transport [*Aviation*] (MCD) .... FWTT
Fixed-Wing Transport Company, [*Army aviation company*] (VNW) .... FWT
Fixed-Wing Utility Company, [*Army aircraft company*] (VNW) .... FWU
Fixer [*Photography*] (DGA) .... F
Fixing (ADA) .... FXG
Fixing Fluid [*Histology*] .... FF
Fixity of Tenure, Fair Rents, and Free Sale [*Phrase used in Parliamentary discussions of Irish affairs, 1880-1882; opposition translated the initials as Fraud, Force, and Folly*] .... 3F's
Fixture .... FIX
Fixture .... FIX
Fixture .... FIXT
Fixture (MSA) .... FXTR
Fixture Data Processor .... FDP
Fixtures (ROG) .... FIXRES
Fixtures Manufacturers and Dealers (EA) .... FMD
[*The*] **Fixx Fan Club** (EA) .... TFFC
Fizean Toothed Wheel .... FTW
Fjord [*Maps and charts*] .... Fd
Fjord (WDAA) .... FJ
Fla Pwr&Lt $2 Pfd'A' [*NYSE symbol*] (TTSB) .... FPLPrA
Flaccid .... FLAC
Fladden Ground Experiment [*Oceanography*] (MSC) .... FLEX
Flag [*Computer science*] .... F
Flag [*British naval signaling*] .... FL
Flag [*Computer science*] (MDG) .... FLG
Flag Administrative Unit .... FAU
Flag Allowance (CINC) .... FA
Flag Cancel Society (EA) .... FCS
Flag Communications Officer [*Navy*] .... FCO
Flag Correlation Facility (MCD) .... FCF
FLAG [*FORTRAN Load and Go*] **Data Display System** (MCD) .... FDDS
Flag Engineering Officer [*British*] .... FEO
Flag Financial [*NASDAQ symbol*] (SAG) .... FLAG
Flag Financial [*Associated Press*] (SAG) .... FlagFncl
Flag Flange (MCD) .... FLG
Flag Gunnery Officer .... FGO
Flag Hoist .... FH
Flag Lieutenant [*Navy*] .... FL
Flag of Convenience .... FOC
Flag Officer [*Navy*] .... FO
Flag Officer, Admiralty Interview Board [*Navy British*] .... FOAIB
Flag Officer, Aircraft Carriers (NATG) .... FOAC
Flag Officer, Atlantic Coast [*Canada*] .... CANFLAGLANT
Flag Officer, Atlantic Coast [*Canada*] .... FOAC
Flag Officer, British Assault Area .... FOBAA
Flag Officer, Carrier Training [*British military*] (DMA) .... FOCT
Flag Officer, Carriers and Amphibious Ships [*Navy British*] .... FOCAS
Flag Officer, Central Europe .... FLAGCENT
Flag Officer Commanding .... FOC
Flag Officer Commanding, North Atlantic Station [*British military*] (DMA) .... FOCNAS
Flag Officer Commanding, Royal Indian Navy [*British military*] (DMA) .... FOCRIN
Flag Officer Commanding West Africa [*British*] .... FOCWA
Flag Officer, Denmark (NATG) .... FOD
Flag Officer, Flotilla [*British military*] (DMA) .... FOF
Flag Officer, Germany (NATG) .... FOG
Flag Officer, Gibraltar Mediterranean Area [*British*] .... FOGMA
Flag Officer, Levant and Eastern Mediterranean [*British Marines*] [*World War II*] .... FOLEM
Flag Officer, Naval Air Command [*British*] .... FONAC
Flag Officer, Naval Air, Pacific [*British*] .... FONAP
Flag Officer, Naval Air Stations [*British military*] (DMA) .... FONAS
Flag Officer, Newfoundland [*British*] .... FONF
Flag Officer, Pacific Coast [*Canada*] .... CANFLAGPAC
Flag Officer, Pacific Coast [*Canada*] .... FOPC
Flag Officer, Royal Yachts [*Navy British*] .... FORY
Flag Officer, Sea Training [*Navy British*] .... FOST
Flag Officer, Soviet Middle East Forces .... FOSMEF
Flag Officer, Submarines [*Navy British*] .... FOSM
Flag Officer, Taranto and Adriatic and for Liaison .... FOTALI
Flag Officer, Western Area, British Pacific Fleet .... FOWABPF
Flag Officer-in-Charge [*British-controlled port*] .... FOIC
Flag Officer's Newsletter [*A publication*] (DNAB) .... FONL
Flag Plot .... FP
Flag Post (MCD) .... FP
Flag Register Processing .... FRP
Flag Research Center (EA) .... FRC
Flag Tactical Data System (MUGU) .... FTDS
Flag Tower [*Maps and charts*] .... FTR
Flag Word (MCD) .... FW
Flageolet [*Music*] .... FLAG
Flagg Township Library, Rochelle, IL [*Library symbol*] [*Library of Congress*] (LCLS) .... IRocL
Flagler Beach, FL [*FM radio station call letters*] (RBYB) .... WJLH
Flagler College, St. Augustine, FL [*OCLC symbol*] (OCLC) .... FFC
Flagler College, St. Augustine, FL [*Library symbol Library of Congress*] (LCLS) .... FSaF
Flagler Community Library, Flagler, CO [*Library symbol Library of Congress*] (LCLS) .... CoFla
Flagler Memorial Library, Miami, FL [*Library symbol Library of Congress*] (LCLS) .... FMF
Flag-Lieutenant-Commander [*Navy British*] .... FLC
Flagon and Trencher (EA) .... FT
Flagpole .... FP
Flagship [*Navy*] (NVT) .... FLG
Flagship Data System (MCD) .... FSDS
Flagship Express Services, Inc. [*ICAO designator*] (FAAC) .... FSX
Flagship International Sports Television [*Phony TV station used as bait to capture fugitives*] [*Canada*] .... FIST
Flagstaff [*Arizona*] [*Seismograph station code, US Geological Survey Closed*] (SEIS) .... FLG
Flagstaff [*Arizona*] [*Airport symbol*] (OAG) .... FLG
Flagstaff .... FLGSTF
Flagstaff .... FS
Flagstaff, AZ [*Location identifier FAA*] (FAAL) .... FLG
Flagstaff, AZ [*AM radio station call letters*] .... KAFF
Flagstaff, AZ [*FM radio station call letters*] .... KAFF-FM
Flagstaff, AZ [*AM radio station call letters*] .... KCLS
Flagstaff, AZ [*FM radio station call letters*] .... KJTA
Flagstaff, AZ [*FM radio station call letters*] .... KMGN
Flagstaff, AZ [*FM radio station call letters*] (RBYB) .... KNAQ
Flagstaff, AZ [*FM radio station call letters*] .... KNAU
Flagstaff, AZ [*Television station call letters*] .... KNAZ
Flagstaff, AZ [*AM radio station call letters*] .... KVNA
Flagstaff, AZ [*FM radio station call letters*] .... KVNA-FM
Flagstaff, AZ [*Television station call letters*] (RBYB) .... KWBF
Flagstaff, AZ [*Television station call letters*] .... KZJC
Flagstaff City-Coconino County Public Library, Flagstaff, AZ [*Library symbol Library of Congress*] (LCLS) .... AzF
Flagstaff National Park Service Group .... FLAG
Flagstar Companies [*NASDAQ symbol*] (TTSB) .... FLST
Flagstar Companies, Inc. [*Associated Press*] (SAG) .... Flagstar
Flagstar Companies, Inc. [*Associated Press*] (SAG) .... Flgstr
Flagstar Companies, Inc. [*NASDAQ symbol*] (SAG) .... FLST
Flagstar Cos $2.25 Cv Ptd [*NASDAQ symbol*] (TTSB) .... FLSTP
Flagstone .... FLGSTN
Flak RADAR Automatic Kanon .... FRAK
Flakmessgerat [*Antiaircraft, gun-laying RADAR*] [*German*] .... FMG
Flamboyance (ABBR) .... FLMNC
Flamboyant (VRA) .... flamby
Flamboyant (ABBR) .... FLMNT
Flamboyantly (ABBR) .... FLMNTY
Flame (AAG) .... FL
Flame (MSA) .... FLM
Flame Absorption Spectroscopy .... FAS
Flame and Incendiary Technology Program [*Chemical Research, Development, and Engineering Center*] [*Army*] (INF) .... FIT
Flame Atomic Absorption Spectrometry .... FAAS
Flame Atomic Emission Spectrometry .... FAES
Flame Atomic Fluorescence Spectrometry .... FAFS
Flame Control System .... FCS
Flame Deflector .... FD
Flame Deflector Firex .... FDF
Flame Emission .... FE
Flame Emission Spectrometry .... FES
Flame Emission Spectroscopy .... FEM
Flame Fluorescence Spectroscopy .... FFS
Flame/Furnace Autosampling Technique with Automatic Calibration [*Spectroscopy*] .... FASTAC
Flame Hardness Standard (MCD) .... FHS
Flame Infrared Emission .... FIRE
Flame Ionization Analyzer and Detector .... FIAD
Flame Ionization Detector .... FID
Flame Ionization Method (PDAA) .... FIM
Flame Launched Assault Shoulder or Hip-Fired Weapon [*Army*] .... FLASH
Flame Leak Proof .... FLP
Flame Photometric Detector .... FPD
Flame Resistant (MSA) .... FLM RES
Flame Retardant (MSA) .... FLM RTD
Flame Retardant .... FR
Flame Retardant Phosphonitratic Polymer .... FRPP
Flame Shielding .... FS
Flame Smoke Toxicity .... FST
Flame Spraying [*Welding*] .... FLSP
Flame Spread Classification [*For polymers*] .... FSC
Flame Thermionic Ionization Detector [*Instrumentation*] .... FTID
Flame Tight .... FLMTT
Flame Tight .... FT
Flame Tight .... MT
Flame Traversing the Charge .... FTC

Flamel Technologies [*Associated Press*] (SAG) .... FlamelT
Flamel Technologies [*NASDAQ symbol*] (SAG) .... FLML
Flame-Launched Advance Material Experiment (DNAB) .... FLAME
Flameless Alkali Sensitized Detector [*Instrumentation*] .... FASD
Flameless Atomic Absorption .... FAA
Flameless Atomic Absorption Spectrophotometry .... FAAS
Flameless Gas Heater .... FGH
Flameless Ration Heater [*Army*] (RDA) .... FRH
Flameless, Smokeless [*Gunpowder*] .... FS
[*The*] Flamemaster Corp. [*NASDAQ symbol*] (NQ) .... FAME
Flamemaster Corp. [*Associated Press*] (SAG) .... Flamst
Flamenco Airlines [*ICAO designator*] (AD) .... FK
Flamenco Airways, Inc. [*ICAO designator*] (FAAC) .... WAF
Flamengo [*Costa Rica*] [*ICAO location identifier*] (ICLI) .... MRFL
Flameproof (MSA) .... FLMPRF
Flameproof (IAA) .... FLPRF
Flameproof (AAG) .... FP
Flamethrower (AABC) .... FLMTHR
Flamethrower [*Engineering*] (IAA) .... FT
Flaming Gorge [*Utah*] [*Seismograph station code, US Geological Survey
    Closed*] (SEIS) .... FGU
Flamingly (ABBR) .... FLMNGY
Flamingo Air, Inc. [*FAA designator*] (FAAC) .... FMR
Flamininus [*of Plutarch*] [*Classical studies*] (OCD) .... Flam
Flammable .... FL
Flammable (DNAB) .... FLAM
Flammable (MSA) .... FLMB
Flammable and Combustible Liquids Appeal and Variations Panel
    [*Queensland, Australia*] .... FCLAVP
Flammable Fabric Accident Case and Testing System [*National Institute of
    Standards and Technology*] .... FFACTS
Flammable Fabrics Act [*1953*] .... FFA
Flammable Liquids [*Fire classification*] .... B
Flanagan and Kelly's Irish Rolls Court Reports [*1840-42*] [*A publication*]
    (DLA) .... Fl & K
Flanagan and Kelly's Irish Rolls Court Reports [*1840-42*] [*A publication*]
    (DLA) .... Fla & K
Flanagan and Kelly's Irish Rolls Court Reports [*1840-42*] [*A publication*]
    (DLA) .... Flan & K
Flanagan and Kelly's Irish Rolls Court Reports [*1840-42*] [*A publication*]
    (DLA) .... Flan & Ke
Flanagan and Kelly's Irish Rolls Court Reports [*1840-42*] [*A publication*]
    (DLA) .... Flan & Kel
Flanagan Aptitude Classification Test [*Psychology*] .... FACT
Flanagan Industrial Tests [*Aptitude and skills test*] .... FIT
Flanagan McAdam Resources, Inc. [*Toronto Stock Exchange symbol*] .... FMR
Flanders [*Belgium*] (WDAA) .... FL
Flanders (VRA) .... Fland
Flanders Airlines [*Belgium ICAO designator*] (FAAC) .... FLN
Flanders Corp. [*Associated Press*] (SAG) .... Flanders
Flanders Corp. [*NASDAQ symbol*] (SAG) .... FLDR
Flanders Corp. [*NASDAQ symbol*] (TTSB) .... FLDR
Flanders Interaction Analysis Categories (EDAC) .... FIAC
Flanders Interaction Analysis System (EDAC) .... FIAS
Flanders' Lives of the Chief Justices of the United States [*A publication*]
    (DLA) .... Fland Ch J
Flanders' Maritime Law [*A publication*] (DLA) .... Fland Mar L
Flanders on Fire Insurance [*A publication*] (DLA) .... Fland Fire Ins
Flanders on Shipping [*A publication*] (DLA) .... Fland Sh
Flanders on the United States Constitution [*A publication*] (DLA) .... Fland Const
Flanders Technology International [*European technology fair*] .... FTI
Flandre Air [*ICAO designator*] (AD) IX
Flandre Air International [*France ICAO designator*] (FAAC) .... FRI
Flandre Air Service [*France ICAO designator*] (FAAC) .... FRS
Flange (WGA) .... FL
Flange (MSA) .... FLG
Flange Focal Distance (IEEE) .... FD
Flange Focal Distance (MCD) .... FFD
Flanged Connection [*Piping*] .... FC
Flanged Joint (DNAB) .... F
Flanged Tongue Terminal .... FTT
Flanging Tube .... FT
Flanigan's Enterprises [*AMEX symbol*] (TTSB) .... BDL
Flanigan's Enterprises, Inc. [*Formerly, Big Daddy's Lounges, Inc.*] [*AMEX
    symbol*] (SPSG) .... BDL
Flanigan's Enterprises, Inc. [*Associated Press*] (SAG) .... Flanign
Flank (ABBR) .... FLNK
Flanked (ABBR) .... FLNKD
Flanker [*Football*] .... FL
Flanker (ABBR) .... FLNKR
Flanker Back [*Football*] (IIA) .... FB
Flanking (ABBR) .... FLNKG
Flanks and Upper Quadrants [*Anatomy*] (DAVI) .... F & U
Flannel (VRA) .... flan
Flap (NASA) .... FLP
Flap Retraction Altitude (GAVI) .... FRA
Flapped (ABBR) .... FLPD
Flapper .... FLPR
Flapping (ABBR) .... FLPG
Flaps-Down Speed [*Aviation*] .... VF
Flap-Slat-Spoiler [*Aviation*] (MCD) .... FSS
Flare and Cells [*Ophthalmology*] (DAVI) .... F+C
Flare Build-Up Study [*Meteorology*] .... FBS
Flare Detection System (KSC) .... FDS
Flare Die .... FLDI

Flare Dispenser Pod .... FDP
Flare Exercises [*Navy*] .... FLAREX
Flare/Shallow Glide Slope (MCD) .... FSGS
Flare-Activated Radiobiological Observatory .... FARO
Flared .... FLRD
Flared Rudder (NASA) .... F/R
Flared Slot Antenna .... FSA
Flared Tube Fitting .... FTF
Flared Tube Fitting Gasket Seal (MSA) .... FTFGS
Flareout and Terminal Glide Beam Guidance [*Aerospace*] (AAG) .... FTGBG
Flares .... FLR
Flarescan Instrument Landing System .... FILS
Flaring .... FLRG
Flash [*Precedence*] [*Telecommunications*] (TEL) .... F
Flash (DAS) .... FI
Flash .... FLH
Flash (ABBR) .... FLSH
Flash Advisory [*Meteorology*] (FAAC) .... FL
Flash Airline Ltd. [*Nigeria*] [*ICAO designator*] (FAAC) .... FSH
Flash/Bang/Smoke (MCD) .... FBS
Flash Electrically Erasable Programmable Read Only Memory
    [*Electronics*] .... FEEPROM
Flash Evaporation (OA) .... FE
Flash Evaporator Plant .... FEP
Flash Evaporator System (MCD) .... FES
Flash Evoked Potential [*Behavioral science*] .... FEP
Flash Financial Report [*for prospective overruns*] [*Navy*] .... FLASH FIRE
Flash Flood Alarm System [*National Weather Service*] .... FFAS
Flash Format Program (SAA) .... FFR
Flash Lamp .... FL
Flash Lights and Send Help [*Florida highway driving aid*] .... FLASH
Flash Mass Thermal Analysis (KSC) .... FMTA
Flash Operate Relay .... FO
Flash Override [*Telecommunications*] (TEL) .... FO
Flash Pack Ltd. [*Vancouver Stock Exchange symbol*] .... FPK
Flash Photolysis [*Chemical kinetics*] .... FP
Flash Photolysis System .... FPS
Flash Photolysis-Resonance Fluorescence Technique [*Physics*] .... FP-RF
Flash Photolysis-Shock Tube Experiment [*For study of chemical
    kinetics*] .... FP-ST
Flash Point [*Graphic arts*] (DGA) .... FL PT
Flash Point [*Chemistry*] (IAA) .... FLPT
Flash Point .... FP
Flash RADAR Order of Battle (SAA) .... FROB
Flash Ranging .... FLRNG
Flash Ranging .... FR
Flash Ranging System .... FRS
Flash Temperature Parameter (IAA) .... FTP
Flash to Bang Time [*Army*] .... FBT
Flash Triangulation Reduction .... FTR
Flash Welding [*Metallurgy*] .... FL/W
Flash Welding [*Metallurgy*] .... FW
Flash/Wink Signal [*Telecommunications*] (TEL) .... FLINK
Flash X-Ray .... FXR
Flash X-Ray Device .... FXD
Flash X-Ray Facility .... FXF
Flash-Back (ABBR) .... FLSH-BK
Flashblindness Orientation Device .... FOD
Flashbulb [*Photography*] .... FB
Flashed (ABBR) .... FLSHD
Flashehood (ABBR) .... FLSHD
Flasher (ABBR) .... FLSHR
Flashes per Second (IAA) .... FPS
Flashes per Second [*Telecommunications*] (IAA) .... FS
Flashgun [*Photography*] .... FG
Flashier (ABBR) .... FLSHR
Flashier (ABBR) .... FLSHYR
Flashiest (ABBR) .... FLSHYST
Flashily (ABBR) .... FLSHLY
Flashily (ABBR) .... FLSHYY
Flashiness (ABBR) .... FLSHNS
Flashiness (ABBR) .... FLSHYNS
Flashing (DAC) .... FL
Flashing .... FLG
Flashing (ABBR) .... FLSHG
Flashing Light [*Navigation signal*] .... FL
Flashing Light System (AAG) .... FLS
Flashing Lights and/or Scotoma [*Neurology and ophthalmology*] (DAVI) .... FLS
Flashing Rear End Device .... FRED
Flashlamp-Pumped Dye LASER .... FPDL
Flashless [*NASA*] (KSC) .... FLHLS
Flashless .... FLHS
Flashless .... FLS
Flashless Nonhygroscopic [*Gunpowder*] .... FNH
Flashlight (ABBR) .... FLSHLT
Flashlight (MSA) .... FLT
Flash-Nitrogen Supply .... FNS
Flashpoint (GNE) .... FLP
Flash-Vacuum Pyrolysis .... FVP
Flash-Vacuum Thermolysis .... FVT
Flashy (ABBR) .... FLSHY
Flat .... FL
Flat (MSA) .... FL
Flat [*Commonly used*] (OPSA) .... FLAT
Flat .... FLT

Flat [*Alaska*] [*Airport symbol*] (OAG) ... FLT
Flat [*Paper*] ... FT
Flat, AK [*Location identifier FAA*] (FAAL) ... FLT
Flat Back [*Bookbinding*] (DGA) ... F/B
Flat Back ... FBK
Flat Band Metallic Armor (AAG) ... F
Flat Bar [*Technical drawings*] ... FB
Flat Board Reach [*Test*] [*Occupational therapy*] ... FBR
Flat Bottom (OA) ... FB
Flat Cable Stripping Tool ... FCST
Flat Cars [*Freight*] ... FL CRS
Flat Concurrent PROLOG [*Programming in Logic*] [*Language for fifth generation computer research*] (NITA) ... FCP
Flat Conductor Cable ... FCC
Flat Data Wing ... FDW
Flat Earth Research Society International (EA) ... FERSI
Flat/Exponential Filter ... FEF
Flat Face [*Diamonds*] ... FF
Flat Feet ... FF
Flat Field Conjugate (IAA) ... FFC
Flat Fillister Head [*Screws*] ... FFILH
Flat Gain Amplifier (IAA) ... FA
Flat Glass Council [*British*] (DBA) ... FGC
Flat Glass Jobbers Association [*Later, FGMA*] ... FGJA
Flat Glass Manufacturers Association [*British*] (DBA) ... FGMA
Flat Glass Marketing Association (EA) ... FGMA
Flat Grain [*Lumber*] ... FG
Flat Head [*Screw*] ... FH
Flat Head (MSA) ... FLH
Flat Head Brass [*Screw*] (IAA) ... FHB
Flat Head Galvanized [*Screw*] (IAA) ... FHG
Flat Head Machine Screw [*Technical drawings*] ... FHMS
Flat Head Steel [*Screw*] (IAA) ... FHS
Flat Head Wood Screw [*Technical drawings*] ... FHWS
Flat Keel [*Shipbuilding*] ... FK
Flat Load Cell ... FLC
Flat Moving Target Screen [*Weaponry*] (INF) ... FMTS
Flat Nose [*Projectile*] ... FN
Flat or Folded Flat [*Freight*] ... FFF
Flat or Nested [*Freight*] ... FN
Flat Oval [*Technical drawings*] ... FO
Flat Pack (IAA) ... FP
Flat Pack Diode ... FPD
Flat Pack Welder ... FPW
Flat Pack Welder System ... FPWS
Flat Pad ... FP
Flat Panel [*Computer science*] ... FP
Flat Paper (DAVI) ... FP
Flat Pattern ... F/P
Flat Plate [*Medicine*] ... FP
Flat Plate Collector [*Engineering*] (BARN) ... FPC
Flat Point [*Technical drawings*] ... FP
Flat Proof [*Graphic arts*] (DGA) ... FL PF
Flat Rack Container [*Shipping*] (DS) ... FR
Flat Response Audio Pickup ... FRAP
Flat River [*Missouri*] [*Seismograph station code, US Geological Survey Closed*] (SEIS) ... FRM
Flat Rock Consultants, Inc. [*Information service or system*] (IID) ... FRC
Flat Rock, VA [*Location identifier FAA*] (FAAL) ... FAK
Flat Roofing Contractors Advisory Board [*British*] (DBA) ... FRCAB
Flat Salary Payroll (AAG) ... FSP
Flat Screen Image Tube [*Computer science*] (IAA) ... FSIT
Flat Seam (DNAB) ... FS
Flat Slip (OA) ... FS
Flat Slip on Bottom (OA) ... FSB
Flat Slip on Top (OA) ... FST
Flat Slips All Around (OA) ... FSAA
Flat Square Tube [*IBM Corp.*] (PCM) ... FST
Flat Technology Monitor [*Zenith*] ... FTM
Flat Template ... FT
Flat Trim Template (MSA) ... FTT
Flat Washer ... FLW
Flat Work ... FLWK
Flat-Blade Turbine [*Engineering*] ... FBT
Flatbush Public Library, Alberta [*Library symbol National Library of Canada*] (NLC) ... AFL
Flat-Car (ABBR) ... FLT-CR
Flat-Coated Retriever Society of America (EA) ... FCRSA
Flateyri [*Iceland*] [*Airport symbol*] (OAG) ... FLI
Flat-Foot (ABBR) ... FLT-FT
Flathead County Free Library, Kalispell, MT [*Library symbol Library of Congress*] (LCLS) ... MtK
Flathead Senior High School, Kalispell, MT [*Library symbol*] [*Library of Congress*] (LCLS) ... MtKFH
Flathead Valley Community College, Kalispell, MT [*Library symbol Library of Congress*] (LCLS) ... MtKF
Flather's New Bankrupt Act [*A publication*] (DLA) ... Fla NBA
Flatland Atmospheric Observatory [*Marine science*] (OSRA) ... FAO
Flatland Atmospheric Observatory (USDC) ... FAO
Flatland Meteorological Observatory (USDC) ... FMO
Flatland Meteorological Observatory [*Marine science*] (OSRA) ... FMO
Flatly (ABBR) ... FLTY
Flatness (ABBR) ... FLTNES
Flatness (ABBR) ... FLTNS
Flat-Panel Display [*Instrumentation*] ... FPD
Flat-Plate Antenna [*or Array*] ... FPA
Flat-Plate Array Antenna ... FPAA
Flat-Plate Radiometer ... FPR
Flat-Plate Solar Array ... FSA
Flats [*Utah*] [*Seismograph station code, US Geological Survey Closed*] (SEIS) ... FLA
Flats [*Commonly used*] (OPSA) ... FLATS
Flats ... FLT
Flats [*Postal Service standard*] (OPSA) ... FLTS
Flats ... FLTS
Flat-Spectrum Radio Quasar [*Galaxy*] ... FSRQ
Flat-Tainers [*British*] (DCTA) ... F
Flatted (ABBR) ... FLTD
Flatten (MSA) ... FLN
Flatten (ABBR) ... FLTN
Flattened (ABBR) ... FLTND
Flattener (ABBR) ... FLTRNR
Flattening (ABBR) ... FLTNG
Flat-Tension Mask Screen (PCM) ... FTM
Flatter (ABBR) ... FLTR
Flatter, Squarer Tube [*Television picture tube*] ... FST
Flattered (ABBR) ... FLTRD
Flattered (ABBR) ... FLTRR
Flattering (ABBR) ... FLTRG
Flatteringly (ABBR) ... FLTRGY
Flattery (ABBR) ... FLTRY
Flattest (ABBR) ... FLTST
Flat-Tile Roof (AAG) ... FTR
Flatting (ABBR) ... FLTG
Flat-Topped [*Frames*] [*Optometry*] ... FT
Flatware (ABBR) ... FLTWR
Flatware Importers Association [*Defunct*] ... FIA
Flauntiest (ABBR) ... FLNTEST
Flautist (ABBR) ... FLST
Flautist (ABBR) ... FLTST
Flauto [*Flute*] [*Music*] (ROG) ... FL
Flavex Industries Ltd. [*Vancouver Stock Exchange symbol*] ... FLX
Flavin Mononucleotide [*Biochemistry*] (AAMN) ... FM
Flavin Mononucleotide [*Biochemistry*] ... FMN
Flavin Mononucleotide [*Reduced*] [*Biochemistry*] ... FMNH
Flavin Phosphate [*Biochemistry*] ... FP
Flavin Phosphate, Reduced [*Biochemistry*] (MAE) ... FPH_2
Flavin-Adenine Dinucleotide [*Biochemistry*] ... FAD
Flavin-Adenine Dinucleotide [*Reduced*] [*Biochemistry*] ... $FADH_2$
Flavin-Adenine Dinucleotide [*Biochemistry*] (MAE) ... FADN
Flavocytochrome C Sulfide Dehydrogenase [*An enzyme*] ... FCSD
Flavoprotein [*Biochemistry*] ... FP
Flavoprotein Disulfide Oxidoreductase [*An enzyme*] ... FDOR
Flavor (ABBR) ... FLVR
Flavor ... FLVR
Flavor and Extract Manufacturers Association of the USA (EA) ... FEMA
Flavor Profile [*Sensory test method developed by A. D. Little, Inc.*] ... FP
Flavor-by-Mouth [*Sensory testing*] ... FBM
Flavor-Changing Neutral Currents ... FCNC
Flavored (ABBR) ... FLVRD
Flavorer (ABBR) ... FLVRR
Flavorful (ABBR) ... FLVRFL
Flavorfully (ABBR) ... FLVRFLY
Flavoring (ABBR) ... FLVRG
Flavorless (ABBR) ... FLVRLS
Flavorous (ABBR) ... FLVRUS
Flavorsome (ABBR) ... FLVRSM
Flavour and Fragrance Association of Australia ... FFAA
Flavus [*Yellow*] [*Pharmacy*] ... FLAV
Flaw Detection Equipment ... FDE
Flaw Locating and Imaging Computer (PDAA) ... FLIC
Flawless [*Diamond clarity grade*] ... FL
Flax Institute of the United States [*Defunct*] (EA) ... FIUS
Flaxman Island, AK [*Location identifier FAA*] (FAAL) ... FXM
Flaxman's Registration of Births and Deaths [*1875*] [*A publication*] (DLA) ... Flax Reg
F-Layer Irregularity Zone [*Geophysics*] ... FLIZ
Flea Allergy Dermatitis [*Medicine*] ... FAD
Flebile [*Pensive*] [*Music*] (ROG) ... FLEB
Flechette Area Neutralizing Gun ... FANG
Fleck Resources Ltd. [*Vancouver Stock Exchange symbol*] ... FLK
Fleet ... F
Fleet [*Navy*] ... FLE
Fleet (CINC) ... FLT
Fleet ... FLT
Fleet Accountant Officer [*British*] ... FAO
Fleet Accounting and Disbursing Center [*Navy*] (NVT) ... FAADC
Fleet Accounting and Disbursing Center, Atlantic [*Navy*] (DNAB) ... FAADCLANT
Fleet Accounting and Disbursing Center, Atlantic Branch Office [*Navy*] (DNAB) ... FAADCLANT BRO
Fleet Accounting and Disbursing Center, Pacific [*Navy*] (DNAB) ... FAADCPAC
Fleet Activities ... FLEACT
Fleet Activities ... FLTACT
Fleet Activities Command [*Navy*] ... FAC
Fleet Activities, Yokosuka Naval Base (DNAB) ... FAY
Fleet Administration Office ... FAO
Fleet Admiral ... FADM
Fleet Admiral [*Navy*] (WDAA) ... FLT ADM
Fleet Aerospace Corp. [*Toronto Stock Exchange symbol*] ... FLT
Fleet Air [*Wing*] ... FAIR

Fleet Air Arm [*British*] ... FAA
Fleet Air Arm Service Trials Unit [*British*] ... FAASTU
Fleet Air Base ... FAB
Fleet Air Base Unit ... FABU
Fleet Air Broadcast (NATG) ... FAB
Fleet Air Control and Surveillance Facility (MCD) ... FACSFAX
Fleet Air Control and Survey Facility ... FACSFAC
Fleet Air Defense (MCD) ... FAD
Fleet Air Defense Exercise [*Navy*] (NG) ... FAIRDEX
Fleet Air Detachment [*Navy*] ... FAD
Fleet Air Eastern Atlantic and Mediterranean (NATG) ... FAIRELM
Fleet Air Gunnery Unit ... FAGU
Fleet Air Gunnery Unit, Pacific (MUGU) ... FAGUPAC
Fleet Air Intelligence Augmenting Unit (CINC) ... FAIAU
Fleet Air Mediterranean Repair Area (MCD) ... FAMRA
Fleet Air Photo Squadron ... FAPRON
Fleet Air Photographic Group ... FAPG
Fleet Air Photographic Laboratory (DNAB) ... FAPL
Fleet Air Reconnaissance Squadron ... FAIRECONRON
Fleet Air Reconnaissance Squadron [*Navy symbol*] (CINC) ... VQ
Fleet Air [*or Aircraft*] **Service Squadron** [*Obsolete*] ... FASRON
Fleet Air Tactical Unit ... FATU
Fleet Air Western Pacific Repair Area (MCD) ... FAWPRA
Fleet Air Wing ... FAIRWING
Fleet Air Wing [*Navy*] ... FAW
Fleet Air Wing, Atlantic Fleet (MCD) ... FAWAF
Fleet Air Wing, Western Pacific Area ... FAIRWESTPAC
Fleet Airborne Electronic Training Unit [*Navy*] ... FAETU
Fleet Airborne Electronic Training Unit, Atlantic ... FAETUA
Fleet Airborne Electronic Training Unit, Atlantic ... FAETULANT
Fleet Airborne Electronic Training Unit Detachment ... FAETUDET
Fleet Airborne Electronic Training Unit, Pacific (IEEE) ... FAETUP
Fleet Airborne Electronic Training Unit, Pacific [*Later, FASOTRAGRUPAC, F ASOTRAGRUPACFLT*] ... FAETUPAC
Fleet Aircraft Assessment for Navy Testing and Analysis for EMP Limitations (MCD) ... FAANTAEL
Fleet Aircraft Direction Officer [*Navy British*] ... FDO
Fleet Aircraft Maintenance Unit ... FAMU
Fleet Aircraft Service Squadron (MUGU) ... FASTRON
Fleet Airship Wing ... FAIRSHIPWING
Fleet Airships ... FAIRSHIPS
Fleet Airships, Atlantic ... FASA
Fleet Airships, Pacific ... FASP
Fleet All Weather ... FAW
Fleet All-Source Tactical Terminal (DOMA) ... FASTT
Fleet All-Weather Training Unit ... FAWTU
Fleet All-Weather Training Unit, Atlantic ... FAWTULANT
Fleet All-Weather Training Unit, Pacific ... FAWTUPAC
Fleet Amenities Fund [*Navy British*] ... FAF
Fleet Ammunition Ship Training Unit (DNAB) ... FASTU
Fleet Ammunition Ship Training Unit, Atlantic ... FASTULANT
Fleet Ammunition Ship Training Unit, Pacific ... FASTUPAC
Fleet Analysis and Cost Trends (PDAA) ... FACT
Fleet Analysis and Reconstruction of Exercise [*Navy*] (MCD) ... FAREX
Fleet Analysis Center [*Corona, CA*] [*Navy*] ... FAC
Fleet Analysis Center [*Navy*] (CAAL) ... FLTAC
Fleet Analysis Center Field Office [*Navy*] (DNAB) ... FLTACFO
Fleet Analysis Center Representative [*Navy*] (DNAB) ... FLTACREP
Fleet and Industrial Supply Center [*Formerly, Naval Supply Center, Norfolk, VA.; changed in 1993*] (DOMA) ... FISC
Fleet Antiair Warfare Coordinator [*Navy*] (CAAL) ... FAAWC
Fleet Antiair Warfare Training Center ... FAAWTC
Fleet Antiair Warfare Training Center ... FAAWTRACEN
Fleet Antisubmarine Data Analysis Program ... FADAP
Fleet Antisubmarine Warfare Command (IEEE) ... FASWC
Fleet Antisubmarine Warfare School ... FASWSCHOOL
Fleet Antisubmarine Warfare School (MUGU) ... FLEASWSCOL
Fleet Antisubmarine Warfare Tactical School ... FLEASWTACSCOL
Fleet Antisubmarine Warfare Training Center, Atlantic (DNAB) ... FLEASWTRACENLANT
Fleet Antisubmarine Warfare Training Center, Pacific (DNAB) ... FLEASWTRACENLPAC
Fleet Antisubmarine Warfare Training Group (DNAB) ... FLEASWTRAGRU
Fleet Antiterrorist Security Team [*Marine Corps*] (DOMA) ... FAST
Fleet Antiwarfare Training Center (MUGU) ... FAWTC
Fleet Application of Meteorological Observations from Satellites (IEEE) ... FAMOS
Fleet Area Control and Surveillance Facility [*Navy*] (DOMA) ... FACS
Fleet Area Telecommunications Center [*Navy*] (MCD) ... FATC
Fleet Assistance Group ... FAG
Fleet Assistance Group, Atlantic [*Navy*] ... FAGLANT
Fleet Assistance Group, Pacific [*Navy*] ... FAGPAC
Fleet ASW [*Antisubmarine Warfare*] **Training Center** [*Navy*] ... FLTASWTRACEN
Fleet Attack Submarine [*Navy*] (CAAL) ... FAS
Fleet Attitude Status (DNAB) ... FAST
Fleet Audio-Visual Center (DNAB) ... FAVC
Fleet Audio-Visual Center (DNAB) ... FLTAVCEN
Fleet Audio-Visual Center, Atlantic (DNAB) ... FLTAVCENLANT
Fleet Audio-Visual Center, Europe (DNAB) ... FLTAVCENEUR
Fleet Audio-Visual Center, Pacific (DNAB) ... FLTAVCENPAC
Fleet Audio-Visual Command, Atlantic (DNAB) ... FLTAVCOMLANT
Fleet Audio-Visual Command, Atlantic Detachment (DNAB) ... FLTAVCOMLANTDET
Fleet Audio-Visual Command, Pacific (DNAB) ... FLTAVCOMPAC
Fleet Audio-Visual Command, Pacific Detachment (DNAB) ... FLTAVCOMPACDET
Fleet Audio-Visual Facility (DNAB) ... FAVF
Fleet Audio-Visual Facility (DNAB) ... FLTAVFAC
Fleet Audio-Visual Facility, Atlantic (DNAB) ... FLTAVFACLANT
Fleet Audio-Visual Facility, Pacific (DNAB) ... FLTAVFACPAC
Fleet Augmentation Component ... FAC
Fleet Automatic Reconstruction and Opportunity Evaluation System [*Navy*] (CAAL) ... FAROES
Fleet Auxiliary [*British*] ... FA
Fleet Aviation Accounting Office ... FAAO
Fleet Aviation Accounting Office (DNAB) ... FLEAVNACCTO
Fleet Aviation Accounting Office, Atlantic (DNAB) ... FAAOLANT
Fleet Aviation Accounting Office, Atlantic (DNAB) ... FLEAVNACCTOLANT
Fleet Aviation Accounting Office, Pacific (DNAB) ... FAAOP
Fleet Aviation Accounting Office, Pacific (DNAB) ... FAAOPAC
Fleet Aviation Accounting Office, Pacific (DNAB) ... FLEAVNACCTOPAC
Fleet Aviation Material Office, Pacific (DNAB) ... FLEAVNMATOPAC
Fleet Aviation Material Support List [*Navy*] (AFIT) ... FAMSL
Fleet Aviation Officer [*British*] ... FAVO
Fleet Aviation Specialized Operational Training Group [*Navy*] (MCD) ... FASOTRAGR
Fleet Aviation Specialized Operational Training Group, Atlantic [*Navy*] (DNAB) ... FASOTRAGRULANT
Fleet Aviation Specialized Operational Training Group, Atlantic Detachment [*Navy*] (DNAB) ... FASOTRAGRULANTDET
Fleet Aviation Specialized Operational Training Group, Pacific [*Formerly, FAETUPAC*] [*Later, FASOTRAGRUPACFLT*] [*Navy*] ... FASOTRAGRUPAC
Fleet Aviation Specialized Operational Training Group, Pacific Detachment [*Navy*] (DNAB) ... FASOTRAGRUPACDET
Fleet Aviation Specialized Operational Training Group, Pacific Fleet [*Formerly, FASOTRAGRUPAC, FAETUPAC*] [*Navy*] ... FASOTRAGRUPACFLT
Fleet Aviation Support Unit (MCD) ... FASU
Fleet Ballistic Missile ... FBM
Fleet Ballistic Missile Program ... FBMP
Fleet Ballistic Missile Requisition [*Navy*] (AFIT) ... FBMR
Fleet Ballistic Missile Submarine (IAA) ... FBMS
Fleet Ballistic Missile Submarine (Nuclear powered) [*Navy symbol*] ... SSBN
Fleet Ballistic Missile Submarine Tender Load List ... FBMSTLL
Fleet Ballistic Missile Submarine Training Center ... FLEBALMISUBTRACEN
Fleet Ballistic Missile Submarine Training Center, Atlantic (DNAB) ... FBMSTCLANT
Fleet Ballistic Missile Submarine Training Center, Atlantic (DNAB) ... FLEBALMISUBTRACENLANT
Fleet Ballistic Missile Submarine Training Center, Pacific (DNAB) ... FBMSTCPAC
Fleet Ballistic Missile Submarine Training Center, Pacific (DNAB) ... FLEBALMISUBTRACENPAC
Fleet Ballistic Missile System ... FBMS
Fleet Ballistic Missile Tender Load List (DNAB) ... FBMTLL
Fleet Ballistic Missile Training Center (DNAB) ... FBMTC
Fleet Ballistic Missile Training Center (DNAB) ... FLEBALMISTRACEN
Fleet Ballistic Missile Weapon System ... FBMWS
Fleet Ballistic Missile Weapons Support System (DNAB) ... FBMWSS
Fleet Ballistic Submarine [*Navy symbol*] ... SSB
Fleet Boat Pool ... FBP
Fleet Broadcast [*Navy*] (NVT) ... FLTBCST
Fleet Broadcast [*Navy*] (NVT) ... FLTBDCST
Fleet Broadcast Receive Subsystem [*Navy*] (CAAL) ... FBRS
Fleet Carrier Qualification (DOMA) ... FLT CQ
Fleet Chief Air Fitter [*British military*] (DMA) ... FCAF
Fleet Chief Aircraft Artificer [*British military*] (DMA) ... FCAA
Fleet Chief Aircraft Mechanician [*British military*] (DMA) ... FACMN
Fleet Chief Aircrewman [*British military*] (DMA) ... FCACMN
Fleet Chief Armourer [*British military*] (DMA) ... FCA
Fleet Chief Caterer [*British military*] (DMA) ... FCCA
Fleet Chief Communication Yeoman [*British military*] (DMA) ... FCCY
Fleet Chief Control Electrical Artificer [*British military*] (DMA) ... FCCEA
Fleet Chief Control Electrical Mechanician [*British military*] (DMA) ... FCCEMN
Fleet Chief Control Electrician [*British military*] (DMA) ... FCCEL
Fleet Chief Cook [*British military*] (DMA) ... FCCK
Fleet Chief Electrical Artificer [*British military*] (DMA) ... FCEA
Fleet Chief Electrical Mechanician (Air) [*British military*] (DMA) ... FCELMN(A)
Fleet Chief Electrical Mechanician (Air Weapon) [*British military*] (DMA) ... FCELMN(AW)
Fleet Chief Electrician (Air) [*British military*] (DMA) ... FCEL(A)
Fleet Chief Electrician (Air Weapon) [*British military*] (DMA) ... FCEL(AW)
Fleet Chief Marine Engineering Artificer [*British military*] (DMA) ... FCMEA
Fleet Chief Marine Engineering Mechanic [*British military*] (DMA) ... FCMEM
Fleet Chief Medical Assistant [*British military*] (DMA) ... FCMA
Fleet Chief Medical Technician [*British military*] (DMA) ... FCMT
Fleet Chief Ordnance Electrical Artificer [*British military*] (DMA) ... FCOEA
Fleet Chief Ordnance Electrical Mechanician [*British military*] (DMA) ... FCOEMN
Fleet Chief Ordnance Electrician [*British military*] (DMA) ... FCOEL
Fleet Chief Petty Officer [*Navy British*] ... FCPO
Fleet Chief Physical Trainer [*British military*] (DMA) ... FCPT
Fleet Chief Radio Electrical Artificer [*British military*] (DMA) ... FCREA
Fleet Chief Radio Electrical Mechanician [*British military*] (DMA) ... FCREMN
Fleet Chief Radio Electrician (Air) [*British military*] (DMA) ... FCREL(A)
Fleet Chief Radio Supervisor (Special) [*British military*] (DMA) ... FCRS(S)
Fleet Chief Radio Supervisor (Warfare) [*British military*] (DMA) ... FCRS(W)
Fleet Chief Steward [*British military*] (DMA) ... FCSTD
Fleet Chief Stores Accountant [*British military*] (DMA) ... FCSA
Fleet Chief WREN [*Women's Royal Naval Service*] **Air Fitter** [*British military*] (DMA) ... FCWRENAF
Fleet Chief WREN [*Women's Royal Naval Service*] **Cinema Operator** [*British military*] (DMA) ... FCWRENCINE
Fleet Chief WREN [*Women's Royal Naval Service*] **Cook** [*British military*] (DMA) ... FCWRENCK

Fleet Chief WREN [*Women's Royal Naval Service*] **Dental Hygienist** [*British military*] (DMA) .... FCWRENDHYG

Fleet Chief WREN [*Women's Royal Naval Service*] **Dental Surgery Assistant** [*British military*] (DMA) .... FCWRENDSA

Fleet Chief WREN [*Women's Royal Naval Service*] **Education Assistant** [*British military*] (DMA) .... FCWRENEDUC

Fleet Chief WREN [*Women's Royal Naval Service*] **Meteorological Observer** [*British military*] (DMA) .... FCWRENMET

Fleet Chief WREN [*Women's Royal Naval Service*] **Photographer** [*British military*] (DMA) .... FCWRENPHOT

Fleet Chief WREN [*Women's Royal Naval Service*] **Quarters Assistant** [*British military*] (DMA) .... FCWRENQA

Fleet Chief WREN [*Women's Royal Naval Service*] **(RADAR)** [*British military*] (DMA) .... FCWREN(R)

Fleet Chief WREN [*Women's Royal Naval Service*] **Radio Electrician** [*British military*] (DMA) .... FCWRENREL

Fleet Chief WREN [*Women's Royal Naval Service*] **Radio Supervisor (Morse)** [*British military*] (DMA) .... FCWRENRS(M)

Fleet Chief WREN [*Women's Royal Naval Service*] **Regulating** [*British military*] (DMA) .... FCWRENREG

Fleet Chief WREN [*Women's Royal Naval Service*] **Steward** [*British military*] (DMA) .... FCWRENSTD

Fleet Chief WREN [*Women's Royal Naval Service*] **Stores Accountant** [*British military*] (DMA) .... FCWRENSA

Fleet Chief WREN [*Women's Royal Naval Service*] **Telephonist** [*British military*] (DMA) .... FCWRENTEL

Fleet Chief WREN [*Women's Royal Naval Service*] **Training Support Assistant** [*British military*] (DMA) .... FCWRENTSA

Fleet Chief WREN [*Women's Royal Naval Service*] **Weapon Analyst** [*British military*] (DMA) .... FCWRENWA

Fleet Chief WREN [*Women's Royal Naval Service*] **Welfare Worker** [*British military*] (DMA) .... FCWRENWW

Fleet Chief WREN [*Women's Royal Naval Service*] **Writer (General)** [*British military*] (DMA) .... FCWRENWTR(G)

Fleet Chief WREN [*Women's Royal Naval Service*] **Writer (Pay)** [*British military*] (DMA) .... FCWRENWTR(P)

Fleet Civil Engineer .... FCE

Fleet Combat Direction System Training Center [*Navy*] (CAAL) .... FCDSTC

Fleet Combat Direction System Training Center [*Navy*] (DNAB) .... FLECOMBDIRSYSTRACEN

Fleet Combat Direction System Training Center, Atlantic [*Navy*] (MCD) .... FCDSTCL

Fleet Combat Direction System Training Center, Atlantic [*Navy*] (DNAB) .... FCDSTCLANT

Fleet Combat Direction System Training Center, Atlantic [*Navy*] (DNAB) .... FLECOMBDIRSYSTRACENLANT

Fleet Combat Direction System Training Center, Pacific [*Navy*] (DNAB) .... FCDSTCP

Fleet Combat Direction System Training Center, Pacific [*Navy*] (DNAB) .... FCDSTCPAC

Fleet Combat Direction System Training Center, Pacific [*Navy*] (DNAB) .... FLECOMBDIRSYSTRACENPAC

Fleet Combat Direction Systems Support Activity [*Navy*] (MCD) .... FCDSSA

Fleet Combat Direction Systems Support Activity, San Diego [*California*] [*Navy*] .... FCDSSA/SD

Fleet Combat Training Center [*Navy*] (NVT) .... FCTC

Fleet Command Center [*Navy*] (CAAL) .... FCC

Fleet Command Support Center [*Navy*] (CAAL) .... FCSC

Fleet Command Support Center Development Group [*Navy*] (MCD) .... FCSCDG

Fleet Command Support Center Watch Officer [*Navy*] (MCD) .... FCSCWO

Fleet Commander in Chief [*Military*] (DOMA) .... FLTCINC

Fleet Commander-in-Chief [*Navy*] (MCD) .... FLTCINC

Fleet Communications Officer [*Navy British*] .... FCO

Fleet Communications Satellite [*Navy*] (MCD) .... FLEETSAT

Fleet Composite Group [*Navy*] (CAAL) .... FCG

Fleet Composite Operational Readiness Group [*Navy*] (CAAL) .... FLTCORGRU

Fleet Composite Squadron [*Navy*] .... FLECOMPRON

Fleet Composite Squadron Detachment [*Navy*] (DNAB) .... FLECOMPRONDET

Fleet Computer Programming Center [*Navy*] (MUGU) .... FCPC

Fleet Computer Programming Center [*Navy*] (MCD) .... FLECOMPUT

Fleet Computer Programming Center [*Navy*] (MCD) .... FLECOMPUTPROGCEN

Fleet Computer Programming Center, Atlantic [*Navy*] .... FCPCL

Fleet Computer Programming Center, Atlantic [*Navy*] .... FCPCLANT

Fleet Computer Programming Center, Atlantic [*Navy*] .... FLECOMPUTPROGCENLANT

Fleet Computer Programming Center, Pacific [*Navy*] .... FCPCP

Fleet Computer Programming Center, Pacific [*Navy*] (MCD) .... FCPCPAC

Fleet Computer Programming Center, Pacific [*Navy*] (DNAB) .... FLECOMPUTPROGCENPAC

Fleet Control .... FLTCON

Fleet Control List [*Navy*] (AFIT) .... FCL

Fleet Coordinating Group (DNAB) .... FLTCOORDGRU

Fleet Data Base [*Navy*] (CAAL) .... FDB

Fleet Database Production System [*Navy*] (MCD) .... FDBPS

Fleet Demonstration [*Navy*] (NVT) .... FLTDEMO

Fleet Dental Officer .... FDO

Fleet Dental Surgeon [*Navy British*] .... FDS

Fleet Digital System (MCD) .... FDS

Fleet Diving Unit (Atlantic) [*Canadian Navy*] .... FDU(A)

Fleet Diving Unit (Pacific) [*Canadian Navy*] .... FDU(P)

Fleet Duties [*British military*] (DMA) .... FD

Fleet Electrical Officer [*British military*] (DMA) .... FLO

Fleet Electromagnetic Radiation [*Team*] [*Navy*] (NVT) .... FEMR

Fleet Electronic Warfare Support Group .... FEWSG

Fleet Electronics Calibration Laboratory .... FECL

Fleet Employment Reports (MCD) .... FER

Fleet Engineer [*Navy British*] (ROG) .... FE

Fleet Engineer Officer [*Obsolete British*] .... FEO

Fleet Environmental Support System [*Navy*] .... FESS

Fleet Evaluation Trial [*Navy*] (NG) .... FET

Fleet Exercise [*Navy*] .... FEX

Fleet Exercise [*Navy*] (NVT) .... FLEETEX

Fleet Exercise [*Navy British*] .... FLEX

Fleet Exercise [*Navy*] (NVT) .... FLTEX

Fleet Exercise Publication [*Navy*] .... FXP

Fleet Expansion Unit (DNAB) .... FEU

Fleet [*Satellite Communications*] **Extremely** [*High Frequency*] **Package** (DOMA) .... FEP

Fleet Fighter [*Air Force*] .... FF

Fleet Fighter Acoustic Countermeasures Readiness Program [*Navy*] (MCD) .... FFARP

Fleet Fighter Air [*Combat*] Readiness Program [*Navy*] (DOMA) .... FFARP

Fleet Fighter Reconnaissance [*Air Force*] .... FFR

Fleet Financial Group [*Associated Press*] (SAG) .... FleetFnc

Fleet Financial Group [*Later, FNG*] [*NYSE symbol*] (SPSG) .... FLT

Fleet Financial Group [*Associated Press*] (SAG) .... FltFn

Fleet Fin'l 6.75% Dep Pfd [*NYSE symbol*] (TTSB) .... FLTPrG

Fleet Fin'l 7.25% Dep Pfd [*NYSE symbol*] (TTSB) .... FLTPrF

Fleet Fin'l 9.30% Dep Pfd [*NYSE symbol*] (TTSB) .... FLTPrD

Fleet Fin'l 10.12% Dep Pfd [*NYSE symbol*] (TTSB) .... FLTPrB

Fleet Fin'l 9.375% Dep Pfd [*NYSE symbol*] (TTSB) .... FLTPrC

Fleet Fin'l9.35% Dep Pfd [*NYSE symbol*] (TTSB) .... FLTPrE

Fleet Flag Data System [*Navy*] (MCD) .... FFDS

Fleet Flagship .... FF

Fleet Flash Network [*Navy*] .... FFN

Fleet Frequency Plans .... FFP

Fleet Gunnery Officer [*Obsolete British*] .... FGO

Fleet Gunnery School .... FLTGUNSCH

Fleet Gunnery School .... FLTGUNSCOL

Fleet Headquarters [*Australia*] .... FHQ

Fleet Home Town News Center .... FHTNC

Fleet Hospital Support Office (DNAB) .... FLEHOSPSUPPOFF

Fleet Hurricane Forecast Facility .... FHFF

Fleet Identification Number [*Automobile sales*] .... FIN

Fleet Imagery Satellite Terminal [*Navy*] (ANA) .... FIST

Fleet Improved Readiness by Expediting Procurement, Logistics, and Negotiations [*Navy*] (NG) .... FIRE PLAN

Fleet Improvement Program [*Navy*] .... FIP

Fleet In and Out (DNAB) .... FIO

Fleet Indoctrination Program [*Navy*] (MCD) .... FIP

Fleet Indoctrination Site [*Navy*] .... FIS

Fleet Indoctrination Team (MCD) .... FIT

Fleet Induction Replacement Model [*Navy*] .... FIRM

Fleet Information Exchange System [*Navy*] (MCD) .... FLIXS

Fleet Information Program [*Navy*] .... FIP

Fleet Information Service [*Navy*] .... FIS

Fleet Information Storage and Retrieval [*Navy*] .... FISAR

Fleet Input and Reserve Support Training .... FIRST

Fleet Installation Budget [*Navy*] .... FIB

Fleet Instruction Officer [*Navy British*] .... FIO

Fleet Integrated Logistics Support (DNAB) .... FILS

Fleet Intelligence Center [*Navy*] (NVT) .... FIC

Fleet Intelligence Center Computer-Aided Tactical Information System [*Navy*] (DNAB) .... FIC CATIS

Fleet Intelligence Center, Europe [*Navy*] .... FICEUR

Fleet Intelligence Center, Europe and Atlantic [*Navy*] (MCD) .... FICEURLANT

Fleet Intelligence Center, Pacific [*Navy*] (CINC) .... FICPAC

Fleet Intelligence Center, Pacific Facility [*Navy*] .... FICPACFAC

Fleet Intelligence Collection Manual (MCD) .... FICM

Fleet Intelligence Officer .... FIO

Fleet Intelligence Support Center [*Navy*] (DNAB) .... FLTINTSUPPCEN

Fleet Intelligence Training Center [*Navy*] (DNAB) .... FITC

Fleet Intelligence Training Center, Atlantic [*Navy*] (DNAB) .... FITCLANT

Fleet Intelligence Training Center, Pacific [*Navy*] (DNAB) .... FITCPAC

Fleet Intensified Repairables Management (DNAB) .... FIRM

Fleet Introduction Program [*Navy*] .... FIP

Fleet Introduction Team [*Navy*] (NVT) .... FIT

Fleet Introduction Team [*Navy*] (DNAB) .... FLEINTROTM

Fleet Issue Control [*Navy*] (NVT) .... FIC

Fleet Issue Load List [*Navy*] .... FILL

Fleet Issue Requirements List [*Navy*] .... FIRL

Fleet Issue Requirements List/Shopping Guide [*Navy*] (MCD) .... FIRL/SG

Fleet Issue Ship Shopping Guide [*Navy*] (NVT) .... FISSG

Fleet Issue Unit Load (DNAB) .... FIUL

Fleet Liaison Officer (DNAB) .... FLELO

Fleet Liaison Officer, Supreme Commander Allied Powers [*World War II*] .... FLTLOSCAP

Fleet Life Extension (MCD) .... FLEX

Fleet Loading Center .... FLC

Fleet Location and Information Reporting [*Police term*] .... FLAIR

Fleet Logistic Air Wing .... FLAW

Fleet Logistic Support Improvement Program [*Navy*] (NG) .... FLSIP

Fleet Logistic Support Wing [*Navy*] .... FLSW

Fleet Logistics .... FLOG

Fleet Logistics Air Wing [*Navy*] .... FLOGAIR

Fleet Logistics Air Wing [*Obsolete Navy*] .... FLOGWING

Fleet Logistics Air Wing, Atlantic [*Navy*] .... FLOGWINGLANT

Fleet Logistics Air Wing, Pacific [*Navy*] .... FLOGWINGPAC

Fleet Logistics Support Department [*Naval Weapons Support Center*] .... FLS

Fleet Logistics Support Department/Crane, IN [*Naval Ammunition Depot*] .... FLS/C

Fleet Logistics Support Detachment [*Naval Weapons Support Center*] (DNAB) .... FLSD
Fleet Logistics Support Improvement Program Consolidated Stock Allowance List (DNAB) .... FLSIP-COSAL
Fleet Logistics Support Squadron (DNAB) .... FLELOGSUPPRON
Fleet Logistics Support Squadron Detachment (DNAB) .... FLELOGSUPPRONDET
Fleet Logistics Wing [*Navy*] .... FLW
Fleet Mail Office [*British*] .... FMO
Fleet Maintenance and Logistics Support (DNAB) .... FMLS
Fleet Maintenance Assistance Group [*Navy*] (NVT) .... FMAG
Fleet Maintenance Assistance Group for Cruiser-Destroyer Force, Atlantic, Charleston, South Carolina [*Navy*] (DNAB) .... FMAG CRUDESLANT CHAR
Fleet Maintenance Assistance Group for Cruiser-Destroyer Force, Atlantic, Mayport, Florida [*Navy*] (DNAB) .... FMAG CRUDESLANT MPT
Fleet Maintenance Assistance Group for Cruiser-Destroyer Force, Atlantic, Norfolk, Virginia [*Navy*] (DNAB) .... FMAG CRUDESLANT NORVA
Fleet Maintenance Assistance Group for Service Forces, Atlantic, Norfolk, Virginia [*Navy*] (DNAB) .... FMAG SERVLANT NORVA
Fleet Maintenance Data Collection System (DNAB) .... FMDCS
Fleet Maintenance Group (Atlantic) [*Canada*] .... FMG(A)
Fleet Maintenance Group (Pacific) [*Canada*] .... FMG(P)
Fleet Maintenance Office [*or Officer*] .... FMO
Fleet Management Center (DNAB) .... FMC
Fleet Management Center Detachment (DNAB) .... FMCDET
Fleet Management Control Systems, Inc. [*Software*] .... FMCS
Fleet Management Information System [*Software*] .... FMIS
Fleet Management System [*Arrencross Ltd.*] [*Software package*] (NCC) .... FMS
Fleet Marine Air Wing .... FMAW
Fleet Marine Corps Reserve .... FMCR
Fleet Marine Engineering Officer [*Navy British*] .... FMEO
Fleet Marine Force [*Navy*] (DNAB) .... FLEMARFOR
Fleet Marine Force [*Navy*] .... FMF
Fleet Marine Force, Atlantic [*Navy*] (DNAB) .... FLEMARFORLANT
Fleet Marine Force, Atlantic [*Navy*] (MCD) .... FMFLANT
Fleet Marine Force Manual [*Marine Corps*] (MCD) .... FMFM
Fleet Marine Force, Pacific [*Navy*] (DNAB) .... FLEMARFORPAC
Fleet Marine Force, Pacific Fleet [*Navy*] .... FMFPAC
Fleet Marine Force, Western Pacific [*Navy*] .... FMFWESTPAC
Fleet Master-at-Arms [*British military*] (DMA) .... FMAA
Fleet Material Support [*Navy*] .... FMS
Fleet Material Support Office [*Navy*] .... FLEMATSUPPO
Fleet Material Support Office [*Navy*] .... FMSO
Fleet Material Support Office Detachment [*Navy*] (DNAB) .... FLEMATSUPPODET
Fleet Material Support Office, Fleet Assistance Group, Atlantic [*Navy*] .... FLEMATSUPPOFAGLANT
Fleet Material Support Office, Fleet Assistance Group, Pacific [*Navy*] .... FLEMATSUPPOFAGPAC
Fleet Mechanical Calibration Laboratory .... FMCL
Fleet Medical Officer .... FMO
Fleet Medical School (DOMA) .... FMS
Fleet Medical Service School (DNAB) .... FMSS
Fleet Meteorological Officer [*Navy British*] .... FMETO
Fleet Mine Warfare Training Center (DNAB) .... FLEMINWARTRACEN
Fleet Mine Warfare Training Center (DOMA) .... FLTMINWARTRACEN
Fleet Mine Warfare Training Center (DNAB) .... FMWTC
Fleet Minelayer [*Navy symbol*] .... MMF
Fleet Minesweeper (Steel-Hulled) [*Navy symbol*] .... MFS
Fleet Missile Systems Analysis and Evaluation Group [*Navy*] .... FMSAEG
Fleet Missile Systems Analysis and Evaluation Group Annex [*Navy*] (MCD) .... FMSAEGA
Fleet Missile Systems Analysis and Evaluation Group Annex [*Navy*] (DNAB) .... FMSAEGANX
Fleet Missile Systems Analysis and Evaluation Laboratory (MCD) .... FMSAEL
Fleet Mobile Operations Command Center (DOMA) .... FMOCC
Fleet Modernization [*Navy*] (DNAB) .... FLTMOD
Fleet Modernization and Repair Program [*Navy*] .... FRAM
Fleet Modernization Plan [*Navy*] .... FMP
Fleet Modernization Program (MCD) .... FMP
Fleet Modernization Program Management Information System [*Navy*] (GFGA) .... FMPMIS
Fleet Music School .... FMS
Fleet Naval Ordnance Inspecting Officer .... FNOIO
Fleet/Norstar Financial Group, Inc. (MHDW) .... FLT
Fleet Numerical Oceanography Center (DNAB) .... FLENUMOCEANCEN
Fleet Numerical Oceanography Center (MSC) .... FNOC
Fleet Numerical Weather Center [*Monterey, CA*] [*Navy*] .... FNWC
Fleet Numerical Weather Facility (MUGU) .... FLENUMWEAFAC
Fleet Numerical Weather Facility .... FNWF
Fleet Observation of Oceanographic Data [*Navy*] .... FLOOD
Fleet Ocean Surveillance Information Center [*Navy*] (CAAL) .... FOSIC
Fleet Ocean Surveillance Information Center, Pacific [*Navy*] (DNAB) .... FOSICPAC
Fleet Ocean Surveillance Information Facilities [*Navy*] .... FOSIF
Fleet Ocean Surveillance Information Facility, Western Pacific [*Navy*] (DNAB) .... FOSIFWESTPAC
Fleet Ocean Tug [*Navy symbol*] .... ATF
Fleet Operational Intelligence Training Center [*Navy*] .... FLEOPINTRACEN
Fleet Operational Intelligence Training Center [*Navy*] (DNAB) .... FOINTRACEN
Fleet Operational Intelligence Training Center [*Navy*] .... FOITC
Fleet Operational Intelligence Training Center, Atlantic [*Navy*] (DNAB) .... FLEOPINTRACENLANT
Fleet Operational Intelligence Training Center, Atlantic [*Navy*] (DNAB) .... FOINTRACENLANT
Fleet Operational Intelligence Training Center, Atlantic [*Navy*] (DNAB) .... FOITCL
Fleet Operational Intelligence Training Center, Atlantic [*Navy*] (DNAB) .... FOPINTRACENLANT
Fleet Operational Intelligence Training Center, Pacific [*Navy*] (DNAB) .... FLEOPINTRACENPAC
Fleet Operational Intelligence Training Center, Pacific [*Navy*] (DNAB) .... FOINTRACENPAC
Fleet Operational Intelligence Training Center, Pacific [*Navy*] (DNAB) .... FOITCP
Fleet Operational Intelligence Training Center, Pacific [*Navy*] (DNAB) .... FOPINTRACENPAC
Fleet Operational Investigation [*NOO*] .... FOI
Fleet Operational Readiness Accuracy Check Sites [*Navy*] .... FORACS
Fleet Operational Telecommunications Program (DNAB) .... FOTP
Fleet Operational Training Command, Atlantic [*Usually, COTCLANT*] .... OTCLANT
Fleet Operational Training Command, Pacific [*Usually, COTCPAC*] .... OTCPAC
Fleet Operations [*Navy*] (MCD) .... FO
Fleet Operations and Readiness .... FO & R
Fleet Operations Control Center [*Navy*] .... FOCC
Fleet Operations Control Center, Atlantic [*Navy*] (DNAB) .... FOCCLANT
Fleet Operations Control Center, Europe [*Navy*] .... FOCCEUR
Fleet Operations Control Center, Pacific Fleet [*Navy*] .... FOCCPAC
Fleet Operations Officer [*Navy British*] .... FOO
Fleet Optimum Inventory Level [*Navy*] .... FOIL
Fleet Oriented Consolidated Stock List [*Navy*] .... FOCSL
Fleet Paymaster [*Navy British*] (ROG) .... FP
Fleet Post Office [*Navy*] .... FPO
Fleet Probe Data System [*Navy*] (NG) .... FPDS
Fleet Program Support Material .... FPSM
Fleet Programming Center, Atlantic .... FPCLANT
Fleet Project Team (DNAB) .... FPT
Fleet Radio Unit .... FRU
Fleet Radio Unit, Melbourne [*World War II*] .... FRUMEL
Fleet Radio Unit, Pacific .... FRUPAC
Fleet Readiness [*Navy*] (AFIT) .... FR
Fleet Readiness Aircraft Maintenance Personnel [*Navy*] (MCD) .... FRAMP
Fleet Readiness Analysis [*NORRS*] .... FRAN
Fleet Readiness Assistance Program (MCD) .... FRAP
Fleet Readiness Aviation Maintenance Personnel [*Navy*] .... FRAMP
Fleet Readiness Enlisted Maintenance [*Trainees*] [*Navy*] .... FREM
Fleet Readiness Improvement Plan .... FRIP
Fleet Readiness Representative [*Navy*] (AFIT) .... FLEREADREP
Fleet Readiness Representative [*Navy*] (MCD) .... FLTREADREP
Fleet Readiness Squadron [*Navy*] (NVT) .... FRS
Fleet Records Office [*Navy*] .... FRO
Fleet Recreation Officer [*British*] .... FRO
Fleet Rehabilitation and Maintenance .... FRAM
Fleet Rehabilitation and Modernization [*Navy*] (MCD) .... FRAM
Fleet Rehabilitation and Modernization Program [*Navy*] .... FRAMP
Fleet Reliability Assessment Program [*Navy*] (MCD) .... FRAP
Fleet Religious Support Activity (DNAB) .... FLTRELSUPPACT
Fleet Religious Support Activity, Atlantic (DNAB) .... FLTRELSUPPACTLANT
Fleet Religious Support Activity, Pacific (DNAB) .... FLTRELSUPPACTPAC
Fleet Repair Service [*Navy*] (NVT) .... FRS
Fleet Repairables Assistance Agent (MCD) .... FRAA
Fleet Replacement and Modernization [*Marine science*] (OSRA) .... FRAM
Fleet Replacement Pilot [*Navy*] (NVT) .... FRP
Fleet Replacement Pilot Training [*Navy*] (NVT) .... FRPTNG
Fleet Replacement RADAR Intercept Officer [*Navy*] (NVT) .... FRRIO
Fleet Requirement Air Direction Unit [*British ICAO designator*] (FAAC) .... BWY
Fleet Requirements and Aircraft Direction Unit [*Navy*] (MCD) .... FRADU
Fleet Requirements and Aircraft Training Unit [*British military*] (DMA) .... FRATU
Fleet Requirements Units [*Aircraft*] .... FRU
Fleet Requirements Working Group (DOMA) .... FRWG
Fleet Reserve [*Navy*] .... FR
Fleet Reserve Association (EA) .... FRA
Fleet Reserve Association Auxiliary .... FRAA
Fleet Resources Office .... FRO
Fleet Resources Office Subsystem (MCD) .... FROS
Fleet Return Evaluation Program .... FREP
Fleet Royal Marines Officer [*Navy British*] .... FRMO
Fleet Satellite [*Navy*] (MCD) .... FLTSAT
Fleet Satellite (DOMA) .... FLTSAT
Fleet Satellite Broadcasting [*Navy*] (MCD) .... FSB
Fleet Satellite Communications [*System*] (DOMA) .... FLTSATCOM
Fleet Satellite Communications [*DoD*] .... FSC
Fleet Satellite Communications System [*DoD*] .... FLEETSATCOM
Fleet Satellite Communications System [*DoD*] .... FLTSATCOM
Fleet Satellite Communications System [*DoD*] (DNAB) .... FLTSATCOMSYS
Fleet Satellite Communications System [*DoD*] (DNAB) .... FSCS
Fleet Satellite Secure Voice Communications (MCD) .... FLTSATSEVCOM
Fleet Scheduling Program [*DoD*] (IAA) .... FSP
Fleet Secure Voice Communications [*Navy*] (NVT) .... FLTSEVOCOM
Fleet Security Officer [*Navy British*] .... FSYO
Fleet Service Mine Test [*Navy*] (NG) .... FSMT
Fleet Service School [*Navy*] .... FLTSERVSCOL
Fleet Service School [*Navy*] .... FSS
Fleet Service Support Group [*Military*] .... FSSG
Fleet Signals Officer [*Navy*] .... FSO
Fleet SONAR School [*Navy*] .... FLESONARSCOL
Fleet Sound School .... FLTSOUNDSCOL
Fleet Special Test and Checkout Equipment .... FSTACOE
Fleet Spotter Reconnaissance [*British military*] (DMA) .... FSR
Fleet Staff/Unit Expansion Group (DNAB) .... FS/UEG
Fleet Status [*Navy*] (MCD) .... F/S
Fleet Street Reports of Patent Cases [*England*] [*A publication*] (DLA) .... FSR
Fleet Submarine [*Navy symbol Obsolete*] .... SF
Fleet Submarine Training Facility [*Navy*] .... FLESUBTRAFAC
Fleet Supply Officer [*Navy*] .... FSO

Fleet Support [*Navy*] ... FS
Fleet Support Improvement Program [*Navy*] (DNAB) ... FLTSIP
Fleet Support Material List [*Navy*] ... FSML
Fleet Support Office [*Navy*] (DNAB) ... FLTSUPPO
Fleet Support Operations (NVT) ... FSO
Fleet Supportability Evaluation (MCD) ... FSE
Fleet Surgeon ... FS
Fleet Systems Capable (NVT) ... FSC
Fleet Tactical Field Office (DNAB) ... FLETAC
Fleet Tactical Support [*Navy symbol*] (NVT) ... VR
Fleet Tactical Support Squadron [*Navy*] ... FLETACSUPPRON
Fleet Tactical Support Squadron Carrier [*Navy symbol*] (CINC) ... VRC
Fleet Tactical Training Course (DOMA) ... FTTC
Fleet Technical Support Center Detachment (DNAB) ... FLETECHSUPPCENDET
Fleet Technical Support Center Detachment (DNAB) ... FTSCDET
Fleet Torpedo Bomber ... FTB
Fleet Torpedo Officer [*British*] ... FTO
Fleet Tracking Center [*Navy*] ... FLTRACKCEN
Fleet Training Base ... FLETRABASE
Fleet Training Center [*Navy*] ... FLETRACEN
Fleet Training Center [*Navy*] ... FLTTRACEN
Fleet Training Center [*Navy*] ... FTC
Fleet Training Command, Atlantic [*Navy*] ... TRALANT
Fleet Training Command, Pacific [*Navy*] ... TRAPAC
Fleet Training Exercise ... FTX
Fleet Training Group [*Navy*] ... FLTTRAGRU
Fleet Training Group [*Navy*] ... FTG
Fleet Training Group and Underway Training Element ... FLETRAGRUWATE
Fleet Training Group Detachment [*Navy*] (DNAB) ... FLETRAGRUDET
Fleet Training Group Services (NVT) ... FTGSVC
Fleet Training Group, Western Pacific [*Navy*] (DNAB) ... FLETRAGRUWESTPAC
Fleet Training Group, Western Pacific [*Navy*] (DNAB) ... FTGWP
Fleet Training Missile (MUGU) ... FTM
Fleet Training Publication [*Navy*] ... FTP
Fleet Training Squadron [*Navy*] ... FTS
Fleet Training Support Squadron (DNAB) ... FLTRASUPPRON
Fleet Training Unit (DNAB) ... FLETRAN
Fleet Training Unit ... FTU
Fleet Tug [*Navy symbol*] (MCD) ... ATFX
Fleet Undersea Surveillance System [*CIA terminology*] ... FUSS
Fleet Utility [*Navy*] ... FUT
Fleet Weapon Armament Maintenance [*Navy*] (MCD) ... FWAM
Fleet Weapons Center [*Navy*] ... FLTWEPCEN
Fleet Weapons Center [*Navy*] (MCD) ... FWC
Fleet Weapons Engineering Department (DNAB) ... FWED
Fleet Weapons Engineering Officer [*Navy British*] ... FWEO
Fleet Weather Center [*or Central*] [*NATO*] (NATG) ... FLEWEACEN
Fleet Weather Center [*Navy*] (NVT) ... FWC
Fleet Weather Facility [*NATO*] (NATG) ... FLEWEAFAC
Fleet Weather Facility [*Navy*] ... FWF
Fleet Wireless Officer [*British*] ... FWO
Fleet Work Study [*Navy*] (NG) ... FWS
Fleet Work Study Group [*Navy*] ... FWSG
Fleet Work Study Group, Atlantic [*Navy*] ... FLEWORKSTUDYGRULANT
Fleet Work Study Group Atlantic [*Norfolk, VA*] [*Navy*] ... FWSGLANT
Fleet Work Study Group Pacific [*San Diego, CA*] [*Navy*] ... FWSGPAC
Fleeting (ABBR) ... FLTG
Fleetingly (ABBR) ... FLTGY
Fleetingness (ABBR) ... FLTGNS
Fleetly (ABBR) ... FLTY
Fleetness (ABBR) ... FLTNS
Fleet-Sizing Analysis and Sensitivity Technique [*Bell System*] ... FAST
Fleetwood [*Alabama*] [*Seismograph station code, US Geological Survey*] (SEIS) ... FLT
Fleetwood Enterpr [*NYSE symbol*] (TTSB) ... FLE
Fleetwood Enterprises, Inc. [*NYSE symbol*] (SPSG) ... FLE
Fleetwood Enterprises, Inc. [*Associated Press*] (SAG) ... FleetEn
Fleetwood Petroleum [*Vancouver Stock Exchange symbol*] ... FED
Fleischner Society (EA) ... FS
Fleming Branch, Lincoln Public Library, Beamsville, Ontario [*Library symbol National Library of Canada*] (BIB) ... OBELF
Fleming Community Library, Fleming, CO [*Library symbol Library of Congress*] (LCLS) ... CoFle
Fleming Companies, Inc. [*Associated Press*] (SAG) ... Flemng
Fleming Companies, Inc. [*NYSE symbol*] (SPSG) ... FLM
Fleming Cos. [*NYSE symbol*] (TTSB) ... FLM
Fleming H. Revell Co., Old Tappan, NJ [*Library symbol Library of Congress*] (LCLS) ... NjOtR
Fleming International Airways, Inc. [*Air carrier designation symbol*] ... FLAX
Flemings in the World Development Cooperation [*Belgium*] (EAIO) ... FWDC
Flemingsburg, KY [*Location identifier FAA*] (FAAL) ... FGX
Flemingsburg, KY [*AM radio station call letters*] ... WFLE
Flemington, KY [*FM radio station call letters*] ... WFLE-FM
[*The*] **Flemington National Bank & Trust** [*Associated Press*] (SAG) ... FlemgBT
[*The*] **Flemington National Bank & Trust** [*NASDAQ symbol*] (SAG) ... FLNB
Flemington, NJ [*FM radio station call letters*] ... WCVH
Flemington, NJ [*AM radio station call letters*] ... WJHR
Flemish [*Language, etc.*] (ROG) ... FL
Flemish ... FLEM
Flemish (VRA) ... Flem
Flemish Ell [*Unit of length*] (ROG) ... FE
Flemish Giant Rabbit [*Medicine*] (DMAA) ... FG
Flendist [*England*] ... FLEND
Flensburg [*Germany ICAO location identifier*] (ICLI) ... EDZL
Flensburg/Schaferhaus [*Germany ICAO location identifier*] (ICLI) ... EDXF
Flers/Saint-Paul [*France ICAO location identifier*] (ICLI) ... LFOG
Flesh Public Library, Piqua, OH [*Library symbol Library of Congress*] (LCLS) ... OPi
Flesherton Public Library, Flesherton, ON, Canada [*Library symbol Library of Congress*] (LCLS) ... CaOFl
Flesherton Public Library, Ontario [*Library symbol National Library of Canada*] (NLC) ... OFL
Fleshiest (ABBR) ... FLSHST
Fleshly (ABBR) ... FLSHY
Fleshpots (ABBR) ... FLSH-PTS
Fletch on Trustees of Estates [*A publication*] (DLA) ... Fletch Tr
Fletcher [*Vermont*] [*Seismograph station code, US Geological Survey*] (SEIS) ... FLE
Fletcher Aviation Corp. ... FAC
Fletcher Challenge ADR ORD [*Associated Press*] (SAG) ... FletFD
Fletcher Challenge ADR ORD [*Associated Press*] (SAG) ... FletOD
Fletcher Challenge Bldg ADS [*NYSE symbol*] (TTSB) ... FLB
Fletcher Challenge Building [*NYSE symbol*] (SAG) ... FLB
Fletcher Challenge Building [*Associated Press*] (SAG) ... FletBld
Fletcher Challenge Canada Ltd. [*Toronto Stock Exchange symbol Vancouver Stock Exchange symbol*] ... FCC
Fletcher Challenge Ener.ADS [*NYSE symbol*] (TTSB) ... FEG
Fletcher Challenge Energy [*NYSE symbol*] (SAG) ... FEG
Fletcher Challenge Energy [*Associated Press*] (SAG) ... FletEgy
Fletcher Challenge Finance Canada, Inc. [*Toronto Stock Exchange symbol*] ... FRC
Fletcher Challenge Forest [*NYSE symbol*] (SPSG) ... FFS
Fletcher Challenge Forest ADS [*NYSE symbol*] (TTSB) ... FFS
Fletcher Challenge Investments II [*Toronto Stock Exchange symbol Vancouver Stock Exchange symbol*] ... FII
Fletcher Challenge Investments, Inc. [*Toronto Stock Exchange symbol Vancouver Stock Exchange symbol*] ... F
Fletcher Challenge ORD [*NYSE symbol*] (SPSG) ... FLC
Fletcher Challenge Paper [*Associated Press*] (SAG) ... FletPap
Fletcher Challenge Paper [*NYSE symbol*] (SAG) ... FLP
Fletcher Challenge Paper ADS [*NYSE symbol*] (TTSB) ... FLP
Fletcher Free Library, Burlington, VT [*Library symbol Library of Congress*] (LCLS) ... VtB
Fletcher Leisure Group, Inc. [*Toronto Stock Exchange symbol*] ... FLG
Fletcher School of Law and Diplomacy, Tufts University, Medford, MA [*OCLC symbol*] (OCLC) ... TFF
Fletcher Sutcliffe Wild [*Commercial firm British*] ... FSW
Fletcher's Cyclopedia of Corporations [*A publication*] (DLA) ... Cyc Corp
Fletcher's Cyclopedia of Corporations [*A publication*] (DLA) ... Fletcher Corporations
Fletcher's Cyclopedia of Corporations [*A publication*] (DLA) ... Fletcher Cyc Corp
Fletchers Fine Foods Ltd. [*NASDAQ symbol*] (SAG) ... FLCH
Fletchers Fione Foods Ltd. [*Associated Press*] (SAG) ... FltchFF
Fletronics International [*Associated Press*] (SAG) ... Flextrn
Flettner Aircraft Corp. (MCD) ... FAC
Fleur de Coin [*Mint state*] [*Numismatics*] ... FDC
Fleur-de-Lys [*Heraldry*] ... FDL
Fleurs [*Flowers*] [*Pharmacy*] ... ff
Fleurs Synthesis Telescope ... FST
Fleury's History of the Origin of French Laws [*1724*] [*A publication*] (DLA) ... Fleury Hist
Flex Hose (MCD) ... FH
Flex Multiplexer/Demultiplexer (MCD) ... FMDM
Flexair BV [*Netherlands ICAO designator*] (FAAC) ... FXY
Flexair Ltd. [*British ICAO designator*] (FAAC) ... CFX
Flexible (AABC) ... FLEX
Flexible (BARN) ... FLEXBL
Flexible [*Technical drawings*] ... FLX
Flexible Accelerator Path [*Economic theory*] ... FAP
Flexible Access System ... FAS
Flexible Accounting Control System [*Computer science*] (BUR) ... FACS
Flexible Ada Simulation Tool (SSD) ... FAST
Flexible Adaptive RADAR (MCD) ... FLEXAR
Flexible Air Data System ... FADS
Flexible Aircraft Takeoff and Landing Analysis (MCD) ... FATOLA
Flexible Algebraic Scientific Translator [*NCR Corp.*] ... FAST
Flexible and Selective Targeting Options [*DoD*] ... FTO
Flexible Automatic Circuit Tester ... FACT
Flexible Automatic Circuit Tester - Automatic Interconnection Device ... FACT-AID
Flexible Automatic Circuit Tester - Low Insertion Force Technique ... FACT-LIFT
Flexible Automatic Circuit Tester - Quick Universal Interface Connector ... FACT-QUIC
Flexible Automatic Depot ... FAD
Flexible Automation for Robotic Analysis ... FARA
Flexible Benefit Account [*Business term*] ... FBA
Flexible Benefits [*Health insurance*] (GHCT) ... FB
Flexible Benefits Program [*Human resources*] (WYGK) ... FBP
Flexible Binding (DGA) ... FL BDG
Flexible Central Processing Unit [*Computer science*] (MHDB) ... FCPU
Flexible Computer-Integrated Manufacturing Program [*Army*] (RDA) ... FCIM
Flexible Connection (OA) ... FC
Flexible Critical Experiment ... FCE
Flexible Digital Receiving Terminal ... FDRT
Flexible Digital Terminal ... FDT
Flexible Disc Unit (NITA) ... FDU
Flexible Disk ... FD
Flexible Disk Drive ... FDD
Flexible Disk System ... FDS
Flexible Display System ... FDS

Flexible Drive Shaft ..... FDS
Flexible Energy Management (MCD) ..... FLEXEM
Flexible Factory Automation ..... FFA
Flexible Fiber-Optic Borescope ..... FFOB
Flexible Fiber-Optic Bronchoscopy [*Medicine*] ..... FFB
Flexible File Finder [*Computer science*] (PCM) ..... FFF
Flexible Guidance Software System (MCD) ..... FGSS
Flexible Gyro Header ..... FGH
Flexible Gyro Header Assembly ..... FGHA
Flexible Header Assembly ..... FHA
Flexible Hours Action Group [*British*] ..... FLAG
Flexible Ideal Format for Information ..... FIFI
Flexible Image Transport System [*Computer science*] ..... FITS
Flexible Information Exploitation Interpretive Transfer [*Software engineering tool*] (NITA) ..... FIXIT
Flexible Infrared Transmission ..... FIT
Flexible Inspection System ..... FIS
Flexible Integrated Solar Cell Assembly ..... FISCA
Flexible Interface Technique (PDAA) ..... FIT
Flexible Intermediate Bulk Container [*Shipping*] ..... FIBC
Flexible Intermediate Bulk Container Association (EA) ..... FIBCA
Flexible Lightweight Agile-Guided Experiment Missile [*Military*] (SDI) ..... FLAGE
Flexible Linear Shaped Charge ..... FLSC
Flexible Loan Insurance Program ..... FLIP
Flexible Machine System [*Industrial engineering*] ..... FMS
Flexible Machining Center [*Manufacturing technology*] ..... FMC
Flexible Machining Network [*Automotive engineering*] ..... FMN
Flexible Machining System (DOMA) ..... FMS
Flexible Management Information System (DNAB) ..... FLEMIS
Flexible Management Information System (MHDI) ..... FLEXIMIS
Flexible Manufacturing Cell [*Industrial engineering*] ..... FMC
Flexible Manufacturing Cell / Flexible Manufacturing [*Industrial engineering*] (BTTJ) ..... FMC/FMS
Flexible Manufacturing System ..... FMS
Flexible Membrane Liner [*For waste containment*] ..... FML
Flexible Mild Steel Wire Rope ..... FMSWR
Flexible Modular Interface ..... FMI
Flexible Modular Scheduling (EDAC) ..... FMS
Flexible Monte Carlo [*Computer science*] ..... FMC
Flexible Motor Coupling ..... FMC
Flexible Multipipeline Processor ..... FMPP
Flexible Numerical Control [*Manufacturing engineering*] [*Computer science*] ..... FNC
Flexible Nylon Coupling ..... FNC
Flexible Operational Resolution for Combat Air Support [*Model*] (MCD) ..... FORCAST
Flexible Operations (DNAB) ..... FLEXOPS
Flexible Packaging Association (EA) ..... FPA
Flexible Parts Repair Material [*Automotive engineering*] ..... FPRM
Flexible Pavements (EA) ..... FPI
Flexible Payment Mortgage ..... FPM
Flexible Plastic Reactor (NRCH) ..... FPR
Flexible Polyurethane Foam ..... FPF
Flexible Polyvinyl Chloride [*Plastics*] ..... FPVC
Flexible Premium Annuity (PDAA) ..... FPA
Flexible Printed Circuit ..... FPC
Flexible Real Estate Loan Plan ..... FRELP
Flexible Reconfigurable Interconnected Multiprocessor ..... FRIMP
Flexible Regional Emissions Data System (GNE) ..... FREDS
Flexible Response Options (MCD) ..... FRO
Flexible Reusable Surface Insulation (MCD) ..... FRSI
Flexible Reworkable Chip Attachment Process (IAA) ..... FREWCAP
Flexible Rolled-Up Solar Array [*Air Force*] ..... FRUSA
Flexible Shielded Cable ..... FSC
Flexible Sigmoidoscopy [*Gastroenterology*] (DAVI) ..... flex sig
Flexible Sigmoidoscopy [*Proctoscopy*] ..... FS
Flexible Signal Collection and Processing (DNAB) ..... FLESCOP
Flexible Solar Array ..... FSA
Flexible Space Garment ..... FSG
Flexible Spending Account [*Employer distribution of nontaxable income to employees*] ..... FSA
Flexible Steel Wire ..... FSW
Flexible Steel Wire Rope ..... FSWR
Flexible Test Station ..... FTS
Flexible Test Station Test Procedure ..... FTSTP
Flexible Theatre Missile (AFM) ..... FTM
Flexible Track System [*Aviation*] (DA) ..... FTS
Flexible Trunk [*Hovercraft*] ..... FT
Flexible Turret System (MCD) ..... FTS
Flexible Waveguide ..... FWG
Flexible Wing Recovery System [*Aerospace*] (AAG) ..... FWRS
Flexible Working Hours ..... FWH
Flexible-Fuel Engine [*Automotive engineering*] ..... FFE
Flexible-Fuel Vehicle [*Operable by either gasoline or methanol*] [*Ford Motor Co.*] ..... FFV
Flexible-Fueled [*Automotive engineering*] ..... FF
Flexicore Manufacturers Association (EA) ..... FMA
Flexi-Filament ..... FF
Flexion [*Medicine*] ..... FL
Flexion [*Medicine*] ..... FLEX
Flexion, Abduction, External Rotation, Extension [*Orthopedics*] ..... FABERE
Flexion, Adduction, Internal Rotation [*Orthopedics*] ..... FADIR
Flexion/Extension [*Orthopedics*] ..... F/E
Flexion in Abduction and External Rotation [*Neurology and orthopedics*] (DAVI) ..... FABER
Flexion Producing Interneuron [*Neurology*] ..... FPI
Flexion-Extension Motion [*Orthopedics*] ..... FEM
Flex-Lead Torque ..... FLT
Flexographic Technical Association (EA) ..... FTA
Flexor [*Anatomy*] (DAVI) ..... flex
Flexor Carpi Radialis [*Anatomy*] (DMAA) ..... FCR
Flexor Carpi Radialis Brevis [*Anatomy*] (DAVI) ..... FCRB
Flexor Carpi Ulnaris [*Anatomy*] (DMAA) ..... FCU
Flexor Digiti Quinti Brevis [*Muscle or nerve*] [*Anatomy*] (DAVI) ..... FDQB
Flexor Digitorum Longus [*Muscle or nerve*] [*Anatomy*] (DAVI) ..... FDL
Flexor Digitorum Profundus [*Anatomy*] ..... FDP
Flexor Digitorum Sublimis [*Muscle or nerve*] [*Anatomy*] (DAVI) ..... FDS
Flexor Digitorum Superficialis [*Anatomy*] ..... FDS
Flexor Distal Phalanx [*Anatomy*] (DAVI) ..... FDP
Flexor Exciter [*Neurology*] ..... FE
Flexor Pollicis Brevis [*Anatomy*] ..... FPB
Flexor Pollicis Longus [*Anatomy*] ..... FPL
Flexowriter Equipment (AABC) ..... FLEX
Flexowriter Interrogation Tape ..... FLIT
Flexsteel Indus [*NASDAQ symbol*] (TTSB) ..... FLXS
Flexsteel Industries, Inc. [*Associated Press*] (SAG) ..... Flexstl
Flexsteel Industries, Inc. [*NASDAQ symbol*] (NQ) ..... FLXS
Flextronics International [*NASDAQ symbol*] (SAG) ..... FLEXF
Flextronics International [*Associated Press*] (SAG) ..... Flextrn
Flextronics Intl [*NASDAQ symbol*] (TTSB) ..... FLEXF
Flexure [*Mechanics*] ..... FLEX
Flexure Monitor Mounting Fixture ..... FMMF
Flick [*A motion-video format*] ..... FLI
Flicker Fusion Frequency [*Ophthalmology*] ..... FFF
Flicker Fusion Threshold [*Cardiology*] (DAVI) ..... FFT
Flicker Fusion Threshold [*Ophthalmology*] ..... FFT
Flickinger Foundation for American Studies (EA) ..... FFAS
Flied Out [*Baseball*] ..... F
Fliegerabwehrkanone [*German word for antiaircraft gun; acronym used in English for antiaircraft fire and as a slang term for dissension*] ..... FLAK
Flies-Odors-Ducts [*Veterinary science*] (OA) ..... FOD
Flight ..... FLGT
Flight (AFM) ..... FLT
Flight Acceleration Monitor Only System (NASA) ..... FAMOS
Flight Acceleration Safety Cutoff System (MCD) ..... FASCOS
Flight Acceptance ..... FA
Flight Acceptance Composite Test [*NASA*] ..... FACT
Flight Acceptance Meeting (SAA) ..... FAM
Flight Acceptance Profile (KSC) ..... FAP
Flight Acceptance Review (MCD) ..... FAR
Flight Acceptance Test ..... FAT
Flight Accrual Payment Action [*Air Force*] ..... FAPA
Flight Activities Officer [*NASA*] ..... FAO
Flight Activities Scheduling System [*NASA*] ..... FASS
Flight Advisory Service [*FAA*] ..... FAS
Flight Advisory Service Test [*FAA*] ..... FAST
Flight Advisory Weather Service ..... FAWS
Flight Aft (NASA) ..... FA
Flight Analysis Section ..... FAS
Flight and Laboratory Development (MCD) ..... F & LD
Flight and Weapons Simulator (MCD) ..... FWS
Flight Anomalies Reporting (KSC) ..... FLARE
Flight Anomaly Investigation [*NASA*] (KSC) ..... FAI
Flight Application Software [*NASA*] (NASA) ..... FLAP
Flight Application Software [*NASA*] (NASA) ..... FLAPS
Flight Aptitude Rating ..... FAR
Flight Aptitude Selection Test [*Army*] ..... FAST
Flight Article [*Army*] (AABC) ..... FLA
Flight Assignment Working Group [*NASA*] (NASA) ..... FAWG
Flight Assistance Service ..... FAS
Flight Attendant ..... FA
Flight Attendant in Training (DNAB) ..... FA-T
Flight Attendant Volunteer Corps (EA) ..... FAVC
Flight Attendants' Association of Australia ..... FAAA
Flight Attitude Table [*NASA*] (NASA) ..... FAT
Flight Augmentation Control System [*Aviation*] ..... FACS
Flight Calibration Procedure [*Aviation*] (DA) ..... FLTCAL
Flight Capsule ..... FC
Flight Cargo Implementation Plan (MCD) ..... FCIP
Flight Centre Victoria [*Canada ICAO designator*] (FAAC) ..... FCV
Flight Certificate ..... F/C
Flight Certificate ..... FLTCERT
Flight Change Control Order ..... FCCO
Flight Charts ..... FC
Flight Check [*Aviation*] ..... FLTCK
Flight Checkout Vehicle ..... FCV
Flight Circuit Tester (DNAB) ..... FCT
Flight Clearance Office ..... FCO
Flight Combat Instructor ..... FCI
Flight Combustion Facility Monitor (MCD) ..... FCFM
Flight Combustion Monitor [*NASA*] (KSC) ..... FCM
Flight Combustion-Stability Monitor [*Apollo*] [*NASA*] ..... FCSM
Flight Command Indicator (MCD) ..... FCI
Flight Command School ..... FCS
Flight Command Subsystem [*Spacecraft*] ..... FCS
Flight Commander (DAS) ..... Flt Comdr
Flight Communications Center ..... FCC
Flight Communications Operator ..... FCO
Flight Communications Operator in Training ..... FCO-T
Flight Composite Acceptance Test ..... FCAT
Flight Computer [*NASA*] (NASA) ..... FC

Flight Computer Operating System [*NASA*] (NASA)	FCOS
Flight Condition Recognition [*Army aviation*]	FCR
Flight Configuration Mode Test [*Gemini*] [*NASA*]	FCMT
Flight Configuration Review (MCD)	FCR
Flight Control	FC
Flight Control [*or Controller*]	FLICON
Flight Control	FLTCON
Flight Control [*Aerospace*] (IAA)	FLTCONT
Flight Control	FLYCON
Flight Control Applications Program [*NASA*] (NASA)	FCAP
Flight Control Assemblies	FCA
Flight Control Center	FCC
Flight Control Computer (KSC)	FCC
Flight Control Console	FCC
Flight Control Container	FCC
Flight Control Data Bus (MCD)	FCDB
Flight Control Division [*Johnson Space Center*] [*NASA*] (NASA)	FCD
Flight Control Electrical Package Container	FCEPC
Flight Control Electronic Set (MCD)	FCES
Flight Control Electronics	FCE
Flight Control Electronics Unit	FCEU
Flight Control Equipment [*NASA*] (NASA)	FCE
Flight Control Group (MCD)	FCG
Flight Control Group Electronic System (SAA)	FCGES
Flight Control Gyro Container	FCGC
Flight Control Gyro Package Container	FCGPC
Flight Control Hydraulics Laboratory [*NASA*] (NASA)	FCHL
Flight Control Indicator (MCD)	FCI
Flight Control Integration [*Apollo*] [*NASA*]	FCI
Flight Control Interface Module (MCD)	FCIM
Flight Control Laboratory	FCL
Flight Control Operating System [*NASA*] (NASA)	FCOS
Flight Control Operational Software (MCD)	FCOS
Flight Control Operations Branch [*NASA*] (MCD)	FCOB
Flight Control Panel (MCD)	FCP
Flight Control Programmer	FCP
Flight Control Ready Light System	FCRL
Flight Control Ready Light System	FCRLS
Flight Control Ready Light System (IAA)	FCRLSYS
Flight Control Room	FCR
Flight Control Sensor Group	FCSG
Flight Control Servo Assembly	FCSA
Flight Control Set	FCS
Flight Control System (AAG)	F/CS
Flight Control System Electronics (MCD)	FCSE
Flight Control System Proximity Unity (MCD)	FCSPU
Flight Control Systems Section	FCSS
Flight Control Team (MCD)	FCT
Flight Control Test Stand [*Aviation*]	FCTS
Flight Control Unit	FCU
Flight Controller (NASA)	F/C
Flight Controller Confidence Test (KSC)	FCCT
Flight Controllers Handbook	FCH
Flight Controllers Operations Handbook [*NASA*] (KSC)	FCOH
Flight Controls Electronics System (MCD)	FCES
Flight Coordination Center (AFM)	FCC
Flight Coordination Control Central	FCCC
Flight Corp. [*New Zealand*] [*ICAO designator*] (FAAC)	FCP
Flight Correction Proposal (MCD)	FCP
Flight Crew	FC
Flight Crew (KSC)	FLC
Flight Crew Accommodations Facility (MCD)	FCAF
Flight Crew and Crew Equipment	FC & CE
Flight Crew Compartment (MCD)	FCC
Flight Crew Equipment [*NASA*] (NASA)	FCE
Flight Crew Equipment Facility [*NASA*] (NASA)	FCEF
Flight Crew Information File (AFM)	FCIF
Flight Crew Mission Simulator [*NASA*] (KSC)	FCMS
Flight Crew Operating Manual (MCD)	FCOM
Flight Crew Operations [*NASA*]	FCO
Flight Crew Operations Directorate [*NASA*] (KSC)	FCOD
Flight Crew Plane Captain [*Navy*] (DNAB)	FCPC
Flight Crew Support Division [*NASA*] (KSC)	FCSD
Flight Crew System [*NASA*] (NASA)	FCS
Flight Crew Trainer [*NASA*] (KSC)	FCT
Flight Crew Trainer Simulator [*NASA*] (KSC)	FCTS
Flight Crew Training Building [*NASA*] (KSC)	FCTB
Flight Crew Workload [*Navy*]	FCW
Flight Critical (MCD)	FC
Flight Critical Forward (NASA)	FCF
Flight Critical Items (MCD)	FCI
Flight Data Acquisition and Management System (GAVI)	FDAMS
Flight Data Acquisition System	FDAS
Flight Data Acquisition Unit	FDAU
Flight Data and Flow Management Group [*ICAO*] (DA)	FDFM
Flight Data Company (GAVI)	FDC
Flight Data Distribution System	FDDS
Flight Data Entry [*Device*] [*SAGE*]	FLIDEN
Flight Data Entry Device (IAA)	FDE
Flight Data Entry Panel	FDEP
Flight Data Entry System (SAA)	FDDL
Flight Data File [*NASA*] (NASA)	FDF
Flight Data Input/Output [*Aviation*] (FAAC)	FDIO
Flight Data Input/Output Repeater [*Aviation*] (FAAC)	FDIOR
Flight Data Management and Communications Network (MCD)	FDMCN

Flight Data Management System [*Air Force*] (AFM)	FDMS
Flight Data Manager (MCD)	FDM
Flight Data Position	FLIDAP
Flight Data Processing (KSC)	FDP
Flight Data Processing System (DA)	FDPS
Flight Data Recorder	FDR
Flight Data Recorder and Fault Analyzer [*Military*]	FDRFA
Flight Data Recording System	FDRS
Flight Data Replay and Analysis System (GAVI)	FLIDRAS
Flight Data Storage Unit	FDSU
Flight Data System [*NASA*]	FDS
Flight Day (MCD)	FD
Flight Deck (MCD)	FD
Flight Deck	FLDK
Flight Deck Assembly (MCD)	FDA
Flight Deck Communication System [*Navy*] (CAAL)	FDCS
Flight Deck Debarkation Control [*Navy*] (CAAL)	FDDC
Flight Deck Hazardous Duty Billet [*Navy*]	FDHDB
Flight Deck Hazardous Duty Pay [*Navy*]	FDHDP
Flight Deck Officer [*British military*] (DMA)	FDO
Flight Deck Status Signaling System (MCD)	FDSSS
Flight Deck System Integration Simulator	FDSIS
Flight Delay	FD
Flight Demonstration Program (MCD)	FDP
Flight Demonstration Team (MCD)	FDT
Flight Design and Scheduling (MCD)	FDS
Flight Design Gross Weight	FLTDESGW
Flight Design Operations Review (MCD)	FDOR
Flight Design System (NASA)	FDS
Flight Detection and Annunciation (MCD)	FDA
Flight Determination Laboratory [*WSMR*]	FDL
Flight Determination Laboratory, Holloman Air Force Base	FDLH
Flight Development Engineering Order (MCD)	FDEO
Flight Development Quality Assurance (MCD)	FDQA
Flight Development Unit (MCD)	FDU
Flight Direction and Altitude Indicator	FDAI
Flight Direction Indicator	FDI
Flight Direction Instrument (SAA)	FDI
Flight Director [*NASA*] (KSC)	FD
Flight Director Attitude Indicator [*NASA*] (NASA)	FDAI
Flight Director Bombing Computer (MCD)	FDBC
Flight Director Computer (MCD)	FDC
Flight Director Group (MCD)	FDG
Flight Director Loop (MCD)	FDL
Flight Director Rate Indicator (KSC)	FDRI
Flight Director System (NATG)	FDS
Flight Display Cathode-Ray Tube (NASA)	FCRT
Flight Display Keyboard [*NASA*] (NASA)	FKB
Flight Display Research System	FDRS
Flight Displays and Interface System (NVT)	FDIS
Flight [*Control*] Division-Control Criteria [*Air Force*]	FDCC
Flight Duty Officer [*Air Force*] (AFM)	FDO
Flight Dynamic Laboratory [*Air Force*]	FDL
Flight Dynamics Branch [*NASA*] (KSC)	FDB
Flight Dynamics Division [*NASA*] (SSD)	FDD
Flight Dynamics Engineer (SSD)	FDE
Flight Dynamics Facility (SSD)	FDF
Flight Dynamics Group [*NASA*] (KSC)	FDG
Flight Dynamics Officer [*NASA*] (KSC)	FDO
Flight Dynamics Officer [*NASA*]	FIDO
Flight Dynamics Simulation Complex (MCD)	FDSC
Flight Dynamics Simulator (MCD)	FDS
Flight Dynamics Situation Complex (NASA)	FDSC
Flight Dynamics Software [*or System*] (MCD)	FDS
Flight Dynamics Staff Support Room [*Apollo*] [*NASA*]	FDSSR
Flight Elapsed Time (MCD)	FET
Flight Element Set (MCD)	FES
Flight Engine Test Facility	FETF
Flight Engineer (AIA)	F/Eng
Flight Engineer [*or Engineering*]	FE
Flight Engineer (IAA)	FENG
Flight Engineer in Training	FET
Flight Engineering Facility (MCD)	FEF
Flight Engineers Fault Isolation [*Aviation*]	FEFI
Flight Engineers' International Association (EA)	FEIA
Flight Engineer's Licence [*British*] (AIA)	FEL
Flight Envelope Protection System [*Aviation*]	FEPS
Flight Equipment Interface Device [*NASA*] (NASA)	FEID
Flight Error Instrumentation [*Aerospace*] (IAA)	FEI
Flight Evaluation Working Group (MCD)	FEWG
Flight Events Demonstration [*NASA*] (KSC)	FED
Flight Examiner [*Aeromedical evacuation*]	FE
Flight Experiment Shielding Satellite	FESS
Flight Express, Inc. [*ICAO designator*] (FAAC)	EXR
Flight Facilities Flight	FFF
Flight Ferry [*Navy*] (ANA)	FF
Flight Following Service [*FAA*]	FFS
Flight Forward (MCD)	FF
Flight Freedoms Foundation (EA)	FFF
Flight Guidance and Control Systems	FGCS
Flight Guidance System (MCD)	FGS
Flight Guidance System/Computer (GAVI)	FGS/C
Flight Half Coupling (MCD)	FHC
Flight Hardware Test Equipment [*Aviation*] (IAA)	FHTE
Flight Hour	FH

Flight Idle (DNAB) ... FI
Flight Implementation Directive (MCD) ... FID
Flight in a Radiation Environment ... FIRE
Flight Incident Recorder and Aircraft Monitoring System (MCD) ... FIRAMS
Flight Incident Recorder/Crash Position Locator [*Navy*] (RDA) ... FIR/CPL
Flight Information ... FLIFO
Flight Information Advisory Committee [*Terminated, 1977*] [*FAA*] ... FIAC
Flight Information and Control of Operations ... FICO
Flight Information Area ... FIA
Flight Information Billing System (DA) ... FIBS
Flight Information Bulletin (AABC) ... FIB
Flight Information Center ... FIC
Flight Information Center [*ICAO designator*] (ICDA) ... ZI
Flight Information Center [*FAA designator*] (FAAC) ... ZIZ
Flight information Data Base [*FAA designator*] (FAAC) ... ZEZ
Flight Information Data System [*United Airlines*] ... FIDS
Flight Information Database [*ICAO designator*] (ICDA) ... ZE
Flight Information Display ... FIND
Flight Information Display System [*Information service or system*] (IID) ... FIDS
Flight Information Manual ... FIM
Flight Information Plan ... FLIP
Flight Information Publication [*Air Force*] (NVT) ... FIPUB
Flight Information Publication [*Air Force*] ... FLIP
Flight Information Publication, Alaska Supplement [*Air Force*] (DNAB) ... FIPAS
Flight Information Region [*FAA*] ... FIR
Flight Information Region Boundary (FAAC) ... FIRB
Flight Information Report ... FIR
Flight Information Requirement (NVT) ... FIR
Flight Information Scheduling and Tracking System (MCD) ... FIST
Flight Information Service (AFM) ... FIS
Flight Input Workstation (DA) ... FIW
Flight Inspection Center [*Military*] (DOMA) ... FIC
Flight Inspection District Office [*FAA*] ... FIDO
Flight Inspection Field Office [*FAA*] ... FIFO
Flight Inspection Field Office High Altitude (FAAC) ... FIFO-H
Flight Inspection Field Office, Intermediate Altitude [*FAA*] (SAA) ... FIFO-I
Flight Inspection Group [*FAA*] ... FIG
Flight Inspection National Field Office [*FAA*] ... FINFO
Flight Inspection Positioning System ... FIPS
Flight Inspection Report (NG) ... FIR
Flight Inspector in Charge ... FIIC
Flight Instruction Program [*Air Force*] (AFM) ... FIP
Flight Instructor ... FI
Flight Instructor Training Course [*Navy*] (DNAB) ... FITC
Flight Instrument Signal Converter (MCD) ... FISC
Flight Instrument Trainer (AFM) ... FIT
Flight Instrumentation (MCD) ... FI
Flight Instrumentation Division [*Langley*] ... FID
Flight Instrumentation Engineer (MCD) ... FIE
Flight Integrity Management (MCD) ... FIM
Flight Interneuron [*Zoology*] ... FIN
Flight Investigation of Apollo Reentry Environment (MUGU) ... FIARE
Flight Investigation of the Reentry Environment ... FIRE
Flight Launched Infrared Probe ... FLIP
Flight Leader Identity [*RADAR*] ... FLI
Flight Level ... FL
Flight Level Change (GAVI) ... FLCH
Flight Level Pressure Altitude ... FLPA
Flight Level Sensing System [*or Subsystem*] (MCD) ... FLSS
Flight Lieutenant (ADA) ... F/LT
Flight Lieutenant ... FL
Flight Lieutenant [*British military*] (DMA) ... Flt Lieut
Flight Line ... FLTL
Flight Line Bunker (NATG) ... FLB
Flight Line Detection and Isolation Techniques ... FLIDIT
Flight Line, Inc. [*ICAO designator*] (FAAC) ... ACT
Flight Line, Inc. [*ICAO designator*] (FAAC) ... SOU
Flight Line Maintenance ... FLM
Flight Line Printer ... FLP
Flight Line Reference (NVT) ... FLR
Flight Line Taxi ... FLT
Flight Line Test Set [*Military*] (CAAL) ... FLTS
Flight Line Tester ... FLT
Flight Load Preparation System [*NASA*] (NASA) ... FLPS
Flight Load Recorder ... FLR
Flight Loads Unit (MCD) ... FLU
Flight Low-Level Image Receiver ... FLIR
Flight Management and Guidance System (DA) ... FMGS
Flight Management Computer ... FMC
Flight Management Computer System ... FMCS
Flight Management Guidance Computer (GAVI) ... FMGC
Flight Management Module (MCD) ... FMM
Flight Management Office [*Air Force*] (AFM) ... FMO
Flight Management System ... FMS
Flight Management Team [*Skylab*] [*NASA*] ... FMT
Flight Manifest and Hardware Tracking System (MCD) ... FMAHTS
Flight Manual (MCD) ... FM
Flight Manual Allowance ... FMA
Flight Manual Interim Changes ... FMIC
Flight Mechanic ... FM
Flight Mechanics, Dynamics, and Control (KSC) ... FMD & C
Flight Mechanics Laboratory [*Texas A & M University*] [*Research center*] (RCD) ... FML
Flight Mechanic's Panel ... FMP
Flight Medical Officer [*Air Force*] ... FMO
Flight Medicine Clinic ... FMC
Flight Mission Assignments Document (KSC) ... FMAD
Flight Mission Rules Document [*NASA*] (KSC) ... FMRD
Flight Mission Simulation Test (MCD) ... FMS
Flight Mode Annunciator (MCD) ... FMA
Flight Mode Panel [*Aviation*] ... FMP
Flight Model ... FM
Flight Model Discharge System (BARN) ... FMDS
Flight Monitor ... FM
Flight Motion Simulator ... FMS
Flight Motor Neuron [*Entomology*] ... FMN
Flight Navigator (AIA) ... F/Nav
Flight Navigator's Licence [*British*] (AIA) ... FNL
Flight Not Operating [*Travel industry*] ... NO-OP
Flight Nurse ... FN
Flight of Ideas [*Psychiatry*] (DAVI) ... FOI
Flight Officer (WDAA) ... FL O
Flight Officer [*Air Force*] (AFM) ... FLTO
Flight Officer [*Air Force*] ... FO
Flight Operating Costs ... FOC
Flight Operational/Fail Safe (MCD) ... FO/FS
Flight Operations and Air Traffic Management Integration [*FAA*] (TAG) ... FTMI
Flight Operations and Planning Scheduling (MCD) ... FOPS
Flight Operations Building [*NASA*] (KSC) ... FOB
Flight Operations Center ... FOC
Flight Operations Center/Flight Coordination Center (MCD) ... FOC/FCC
Flight Operations Directorate [*or Division*] [*Apollo*] [*NASA*] ... FOD
Flight Operations Engineer (MCD) ... FOE
Flight Operations Facility ... FOF
Flight Operations Group ... FOG
Flight Operations Integration Handbook (MCD) ... FOIH
Flight Operations Management Room [*NASA*] (KSC) ... FOMR
Flight Operations Panel ... FOP
Flight Operations Plan (MCD) ... FOP
Flight Operations Planner ... FLIOP
Flight Operations Planning Group [*NASA*] (NASA) ... FOPG
Flight Operations Quality Assurance [*FAA*] (TAG) ... FOQA
Flight Operations Quality Assurance (GAVI) ... FOQA
Flight Operations Review (MCD) ... FOR
Flight Operations Scheduling Office [*NASA*] (MCD) ... FOSO
Flight Operations Scheduling Officer [*NASA*] (NASA) ... FOSO
Flight Operations Support (KSC) ... FOS
Flight Operations Support Annex (SSD) ... FOSA
Flight Operations Support Personnel (MCD) ... FOSP
Flight Operations Support Team (MCD) ... FOST
Flight Operations Team (MCD) ... FOT
Flight Ops International [*FAA designator*] (FAAC) ... FOI
Flight Order ... FO
Flight Orderly ... FO
Flight Orders [*Aviation*] (FAAC) ... FLTO
Flight Path Accelerometer ... FPA
Flight Path Analysis ... FPA
Flight Path Analysis and Command [*Team*] [*NASA*] ... FPAC
Flight Path Analysis Area [*Space Flight Operations Facility, NASA*] ... FPAA
Flight Path Angle (MCD) ... FPA
Flight Path Control ... FPC
Flight Path Design Program ... FPDP
Flight Path Deviation Indicator [*Navigation*] ... DI
Flight Path Deviation Indicator [*Navigation*] ... FPDI
Flight Path Indicator [*Aviation*] (AIA) ... FPI
Flight Path Marker ... FPM
Flight Path Stabilization (MCD) ... FPS
Flight Patrol Fan Club (EA) ... FPFC
Flight Pay ... FP
Flight per Second (NASA) ... FPS
Flight Performance Propellant Reserve (MCD) ... FPR
Flight Performance Reserve ... FPR
Flight Plan (MSA) ... FLT PLN
Flight Plan [*Aviation*] ... FP
Flight Plan [*Aviation code*] ... PLN
Flight Plan Aided Tracking [*Aviation*] (IAA) ... FLAT
Flight Plan Approval [*Aviation*] (AFM) ... FPA
Flight Plan Area [*Aviation*] (FAAC) ... FPA
Flight Plan Filed in the Air [*Aviation code*] ... AFIL
Flight Plan Gas Load [*Air Force*] ... FPGL
Flight Plan Processing Center [*Aviation*] (IAA) ... FPPC
Flight Plan Processing System [*British*] ... FPPS
Flight Plan Progressing System (OA) ... FPPS
Flight Plan Support Specialist [*NASA*] ... FLASP
Flight Plan Talker [*Aviation*] (SAA) ... FPT
Flight Planning and Cruise Control Manual (MCD) ... FPCCM
Flight Position [*Aerospace*] (IAA) ... FP
Flight Power Subsystem ... FPS
Flight Preparation Ltd. [*British ICAO designator*] (FAAC) ... FPP
Flight Preparation Sheet (MCD) ... FPS
Flight Procedures Handbook (MCD) ... FPHB
Flight Programmer (AAG) ... F/P
Flight Programmer (AAG) ... FLT/PG
Flight Programmer Computer ... FPC
Flight Progress (KSC) ... FP
Flight Progress Board [*Aviation*] ... FPB
Flight Progress Strip [*Aviation*] ... FPS
Flight Project Support Office [*Jet Propulsion Laboratory*] ... FPSO
Flight Proof Test Plan (AAG) ... FPTP
Flight/Propulsion Control Coupling [*Air Force*] ... FPCC

Flight Propulsion Laboratory .... FPL
Flight Purpose Code (DNAB) .... FPC
Flight Qualification .... FQ
Flight Qualification Instrumentation (MCD) .... FQI
Flight Qualification Recorder (KSC) .... FQR
Flight Qualification Reviews (MCD) .... FQR
Flight Qualification Tape Recorder [*NASA*] (KSC) .... FQTR
Flight Qualified System (MCD) .... FQS
Flight Qualities and Performance .... FQ & P
Flight Quality Photomultiplier Assembly .... FQPA
Flight Radio Officer [*Aviation*] .... FRO
Flight Radio Subsystem .... FRS
Flight Radio Telephony Operator (DA) .... FRTO
Flight Range and Endurance Data Indicator .... FREDI
Flight Rated Bioinstrumentation .... FRB
Flight Rating Test .... FRT
Flight Readiness .... FR
Flight Readiness Demonstration .... FRD
Flight Readiness Evaluation Data System (MCD) .... FREDS
Flight Readiness Firing [*NASA*] (NASA) .... FRF
Flight Readiness Firing Test [*NASA*] (AFM) .... FRF
Flight Readiness Firing Test (MCD) .... FRFT
Flight Readiness Review (KSC) .... FRR
Flight Readiness Review Item Description [*NASA*] (NASA) .... FRRID
Flight Readiness Review Item Disposition [*NASA*] (NASA) .... FRRID
Flight Readiness Test .... FRT
Flight Readiness Training (MCD) .... FRT
Flight Readiness Vehicle .... FRV
Flight Recorder (MCD) .... FR
Flight Reference Stabilization Systems (KSC) .... FRSS
Flight Refueling (MCD) .... FR
Flight Refueling, Inc. .... FRI
Flight Related Element (MCD) .... FRE
Flight Reliability (MCD) .... FR
Flight Requirements Document (MCD) .... FRD
Flight Research and Development Instrumentation (KSC) .... FRDI
Flight Research Center [*Later, DFRC*] [*NASA*] .... FRC
Flight Research Institute, M. Gromov [*Former USSR*] [*FAA designator*] (FAAC) LII
Flight Research Laboratory [*University of Kansas*] [*Research center*] (RCD) .... FRL
Flight Rule (MCD) .... FR
Flight Rule Computer [*Aviation*] (IAA) .... FRC
Flight Safety (AFM) .... FS
Flight Safety Foundation (EA) .... FSF
Flight Safety Information Bulletin [*NASA*] .... FSIB
Flight Safety Ltd. [*British ICAO designator*] (FAAC) .... FSL
Flight Safety Officer (MCD) .... FSO
Flight Safety Research .... FSR
Flight Safety Review Board .... FSRB
Flight Safety Rules (MCD) .... FSR
Flight Safety System .... FSS
Flight Safety Training and Test Center .... FSTTC
Flight Scheduling Precedence .... FSP
Flight Security Controller [*Military*] .... FSC
Flight Security Supervisor [*Military*] .... FSS
Flight Sergeant [*RAF*] [*British*] (DMA) .... F/Sgt
Flight Sergeant [*RAF*] [*British*] .... FS
Flight Service .... FS
Flight Service Automation System [*FAA*] (TAG) .... FSAS
Flight Service Center .... FSC
Flight Service Center .... FSCEN
Flight Service Communications System .... FSCS
Flight Service Data Processing System [*FAA*] (TAG) .... FSDPS
Flight Service Station [*FAA*] .... FSS
Flight Service Unit (ADA) .... FSU
Flight Services Handbook .... FSH
Flight Services Officer (ADA) .... FSO
Flight Services Station Operations and Procedures Committee (FAAC) .... FSSCOM
Flight Simulated Training System [*Military*] .... FSTS
Flight Simulation Division [*Johnson Space Center*] [*NASA*] (NASA) .... FSD
Flight Simulation Engineer (MCD) .... FSE
Flight Simulation Laboratory [*NASA*] (NASA) .... FSL
Flight Simulation Monitor [*FAA*] (TAG) .... FSM
Flight Simulation Report .... FSR
Flight Simulation Test Data .... FSTD
Flight Simulator (AFM) .... FS
Flight Simulator for Advanced Aircraft [*NASA*] .... FSAA
Flight Software (MCD) .... FSW
Flight Software Readiness Review (MCD) .... FSRR
Flight Solar Reflectometer .... FSR
Flight Space .... FLSP
Flight Specific Requirements (MCD) .... FSR
Flight Standards and Qualification [*Army*] .... FS/Q
Flight Standards District Office [*FAA*] .... FISDO
Flight Standards District Office [*FAA*] .... FSDO
Flight Standards Service [*FAA*] (MCD) .... FSS
Flight Status Selection Board (DNAB) .... FSSB
Flight Steward .... FLTST
Flight Strip Generator (IAA) .... FSG
Flight Strip Printer [*Aviation*] (FAAC) .... FSP
Flight Strip Printer Control Module (MCD) .... FSPCM
Flight Suit with Integrated Flotation .... FSIF
Flight Support Equipment (KSC) .... FSE
Flight Support Operations Handbook (MCD) .... FSOH
Flight Support Request (KSC) .... FSR
Flight Support Station [*For manned maneuvering unit*] (NASA) .... FSS
Flight Support Structure (MCD) .... FSS
Flight Support System (MCD) .... FSS
Flight Support Tapes .... FST
Flight Surgeon (MCD) .... FLS
Flight Surgeon .... FLTSURG
Flight Surgeon .... FS
Flight Surgeon Badge [*Military decoration*] [*Army*] .... FLTSURBAD
Flight Surgeon Badge [*Military decoration Army*] (AABC) .... FltSurgBad
Flight System (MCD) .... FS
Flight System Interface Working Group .... FSISWG
Flight System Interface Working Group (MCD) .... FSIWG
Flight System Mockup .... FSM
Flight System Readiness Review (NASA) .... FSRR
Flight System Recording System (MCD) .... FSRS
Flight Systems Engineering Order (MCD) .... FSEO
Flight Systems Laboratory (MCD) .... FSL
Flight Systems Redundancy Test (MCD) .... FSRT
Flight Systems Simulator [*NASA*] (NASA) .... FSS
Flight Systems Software Requirement (MCD) .... FSSR
Flight Taxiing and Ingestion Risks [*Insurance*] (AIA) .... FT & IR
Flight Team (MCD) .... FT
Flight Team Operations Handbook (NASA) .... FTOH
Flight Technical Error [*Aviation*] (DA) .... FTE
Flight Technical Tolerance [*Aviation*] (DA) .... FIT
Flight Telemetry Subsystem [*Spacecraft*] .... FTS
Flight Telerobotic Servicer [*NASA*] .... FTS
Flight Television [*NASA*] (KSC) .... FTV
Flight Termination .... FT
Flight Termination Ordnance System [*Small intercontinental ballistic missile*] (DWSG) .... FTOS
Flight Termination System (AFM) .... FTS
Flight Test (KSC) .... F/T
Flight Test and Engineering Group [*Navy*] (DOMA) .... FTEG
Flight Test Article (KSC) .... FTA
Flight [*or Flying*] **Test Bed** .... FTB
Flight Test Center .... FTC
Flight Test Change Proposal (MCD) .... FTCP
Flight Test Conductor (NASA) .... FTC
Flight Test Coordinating Committee [*Air Force*] .... FTCC
Flight Test Data Recorder (MCD) .... FTDR
Flight Test Direction [*or Directive*] (AAG) .... FTD
Flight Test Division, Internal Project [*Navy*] (MCD) .... FTDIP
Flight Test Drawing (MCD) .... FTD
Flight Test Encoder .... FTE
Flight Test Engineer (MCD) .... FTE
Flight Test Engineering Order .... FTEO
Flight Test Equipment .... FTE
Flight Test Evaluation .... FTE
Flight Test Information Drawing (MCD) .... FTID
Flight Test Instrumentation System (NASA) .... FTIS
Flight Test Manual .... FTM
Flight Test Matrix (MCD) .... FTM
Flight Test Missile [*Air Force*] .... FTM
Flight Test Objective (KSC) .... FTO
Flight Test Operations .... FTO
Flight Test Operations Handbook (NASA) .... FTOH
Flight Test Plan [*or Procedure or Program*] .... FTP
Flight Test Planning and Evaluation .... FTP & E
Flight Test Release Ticket (MCD) .... FTRT
Flight Test Report .... FTR
Flight Test Report Guide (MCD) .... FTRG
Flight Test Reports Writer (MUGU) .... FTRW
Flight Test Request Memorandum (MCD) .... FTRM
Flight Test Requirements [*NASA*] (NASA) .... FTR
Flight Test Requirements Document [*NASA*] (NASA) .... FTRD
Flight Test Review Board (MCD) .... FTRB
Flight Test Rocket Facilities Mechanical Engineering (AAG) .... FTRFME
Flight Test Sketch (MCD) .... FTS
Flight Test Standard .... FTS
Flight Test Station [*ITU designation*] (CET) .... FAT
Flight Test Station (MCD) .... FTS
Flight Test Support .... FTS
Flight Test System (NASA) .... FTS
Flight Test Unit (KSC) .... FTU
Flight Test Vehicle [*Air Force*] .... FTV
Flight Test Vehicle Safety Plan [*Air Force*] (MCD) .... FTVSP
Flight Test Work Order (MCD) .... FTWO
Flight Test Working Group .... FTWG
Flight Time Constant .... FTC
Flight Time/Flight Hour (MCD) .... FT/FH
Flight Time Limitation [*Aviation*] (DA) .... FTL
Flight Trac, Inc. [*FAA designator*] (FAAC) .... CCK
Flight Trace Contaminant Sensor System [*NASA*] (KSC) .... FTCSS
Flight Traffic Specialist (SAA) .... FTS
Flight Training Device [*Aviation*] (DA) .... FTD
Flight Training Mission (MCD) .... FTM
Flight Unit (MCD) .... FU
Flight Vehicle .... FV
Flight Vehicle Power Branch .... FVPB
Flight Vehicles Systems (MCD) .... FVS
Flight Verification Vehicle (KSC) .... FVV
Flight Version (MCD) .... FV

Flight Warning Computer (MCD) .... FWC
Flight Warning System (MCD) .... FWS
Flight Watch Outlet [*Aviation*] (FAAC) .... FLTWO
Flight Watch Point [*Aviation*] (FAAC) .... FWP
Flight Watch Specialist [*Aviation*] (FAAC) .... FWS
Flight Watch Unit [*Aviation*] (FAAC) .... FWu
Flight Weight .... FW
Flight West Airlines [*Australia ICAO designator*] (FAAC) .... FWQ
Flight Work Orders - Ships Records (MCD) .... FWOSR
Flight Worthiness Demonstration Test (KSC) .... FWDT
Flight-by-Light [*OST*] (TAG) .... FBL
Flight-Chernobyl Association [*Russian Federation*] [*ICAO designator*] (FAAC) .... FCH
Flightcrew Licensing (DA) .... FCL
Flightcrew Record System (DA) .... FCRS
Flightexec Ltd. [*Canada ICAO designator*] (FAAC) .... FEX
Flightline [*British ICAO designator*] (FAAC) .... FLT
Flightline [*Spain*] [*FAA designator*] (FAAC) .... FTL
Flightline Support Unit (MCD) .... FSU
Flight-Plane-Aid Tracking (MCD) .... FLAT
Flightsafety International, Inc. [*Associated Press*] (SAG) .... FlghtSf
Flightsafety International, Inc. [*Aerospace NYSE symbol*] (SPSG) .... FSI
Flightsafety Intl. [*NYSE symbol*] (TTSB) .... FSI
Flimsier (ABBR) .... FLMSR
Flimsiest (ABBR) .... FLMSST
Flimsily (ABBR) .... FLMSY
Flimsiness (ABBR) .... FLMSNS
Flimsy (ABBR) .... FLMSY
Flin Flon [*Manitoba*] [*Seismograph station code, US Geological Survey*] (SEIS) .... FFC
Flin Flon [*Canada*] [*Airport symbol*] (OAG) .... YFO
Flin Flon General Hospital, Manitoba [*Library symbol National Library of Canada*] (NLC) .... MFFGH
Flin Flon, MB [*Television station call letters*] .... CBWBT
Flin Flon, MB [*AM radio station call letters*] .... CFAR
Flin Flon, MB [*ICAO location identifier*] (ICLI) .... CYFO
Flin Flon Mines [*Vancouver Stock Exchange symbol*] .... FLF
Flin Flon Public Library, Flin Flon, MB, Canada [*Library symbol Library of Congress*] (LCLS) .... CaMFF
Flin Flon Public Library, Manitoba [*Library symbol National Library of Canada*] (NLC) .... MFF
Flinch (ABBR) .... FLNH
Flincher (ABBR) .... FLNHR
Flinchingly (ABBR) .... FLNHGY
Flinders Institute for Atmospheric and Marine Sciences [*Australia*] [*Marine science*] (OSRA) .... FIAMS
Flinders Island [*Australia Airport symbol*] (OAG) .... FLS
Flinders Medical Centre [*Australia*] .... FMC
Flinders University of South Australia, Bedford Park, SA, Australia [*Library symbol Library of Congress*] (LCLS) .... AuBpF
Flinging (ABBR) .... FLNGG
Flint (AAG) .... F
Flint (ABBR) .... FLNT
Flint [*Michigan*] [*Airport symbol*] (OAG) .... FNT
Flint & Pere Marquette Railroad .... F & PM
Flint Aviation Services, Inc. [*FAA designator*] (FAAC) .... FAZ
Flint Glazed [*Paper*] (DGA) .... FG
Flint Junior College [*Michigan*] .... FJC
Flint, MI [*Location identifier FAA*] (FAAL) .... BIQ
Flint, MI [*Location identifier FAA*] (FAAL) .... FNT
Flint, MI [*Location identifier FAA*] (FAAL) .... TUN
Flint, MI [*FM radio station call letters*] .... WCRZ
Flint, MI [*FM radio station call letters*] .... WDZZ
Flint, MI [*FM radio station call letters*] .... WFBE
Flint, MI [*AM radio station call letters*] .... WFDF
Flint, MI [*AM radio station call letters*] .... WFLT
Flint, MI [*AM radio station call letters*] .... WFNT
Flint, MI [*FM radio station call letters*] .... WFUM
Flint, MI [*Television station call letters*] .... WFUM-TV
Flint, MI [*Television station call letters*] .... WJRT
Flint, MI [*Television station call letters*] .... WSMH
Flint, MI [*AM radio station call letters*] .... WTAC
Flint, MI [*AM radio station call letters*] .... WTRX
Flint, MI [*AM radio station call letters*] .... WWCK
Flint, MI [*FM radio station call letters*] .... WWCK-FM
Flint Public Library, Flint, MI [*Library symbol Library of Congress*] (LCLS) .... MiFli
Flint Rock Mines [*Vancouver Stock Exchange symbol*] .... FLI
Flintier (ABBR) .... FLNTR
Flintiest (ABBR) .... FLNTST
Flintily (ABBR) .... FLNTYY
Flintiness (ABBR) .... FLNTNS
Flintiness (ABBR) .... FLNTYNS
Flintlock [*British military*] (DMA) .... F/L
Flintoff's Introduction to Conveyancing [*A publication*] (DLA) .... Flint Conv
Flintoff's Real Property [*1839-40*] [*A publication*] (DLA) .... Flint R Pr
Flintshire [*Former county in Wales*] (WGA) .... Flint
Flintshire [*Former county in Wales*] .... FLINTS
Flinty (ABBR) .... FLNTY
Flinty [*Quality of the bottom*] [*Nautical charts*] .... fly
Flip-Flop [*Computer science*] .... F-F
Flip-Flop (IDOE) .... FF
Flip-Flop [*Computer science*] (DEN) .... FLF
Flip-Flop Circuit [*Computer science*] .... JK
Flip-Flop Complementary [*Computer science*] (MSA) .... FFC
Flip-Flop Latch [*Computer science*] (MSA) .... FFL

Flip-Flop - National Module [*Computer science*] (AAG) .... FF-NM
Flip-Flop Position Indicator [*Computer science*] .... FFPI
Flip-Flop Relay Driver [*Computer science*] .... FFRD
Flippancy (ABBR) .... FLPNC
Flippant (ABBR) .... FLPNT
Flippantly (ABBR) .... FLPNTY
Flippin, AR [*Location identifier FAA*] (FAAL) .... FLP
Flippin's Circuit Court Reports [*United States*] [*A publication*] (DLA) .... Flipp
Flippin's Circuit Court Reports [*United States*] [*A publication*] (DLA) .... Flipp (F)
FLIR [*Forward-Looking Infrared RADAR*] Augmented Cobra TOW Sight [*Tube-Launched, Optically-Tracked, Wire-Guided Weapon*] .... FACTS
FLIR Systems [*NASDAQ symbol*] (TTSB) .... FLIR
FLIR Systems, Inc. [*NASDAQ symbol*] (SAG) .... FLIR
Flirtation (ABBR) .... FLRTN
Flirtatious (ABBR) .... FLRTU
Float (IAA) .... FL
Float (ABBR) .... FLOT
Float (MSA) .... FLT
Float Bridge .... FLTBRG
Float On/Float Off .... FLO/FLO
Float Switch [*Aerospace*] (AAG) .... FS
Float Switch [*Aerospace*] (IAA) .... FTS
Float Trend Chart (PDAA) .... FTC
Float Zone [*Crystallization process*] .... FZ
Float Zone Crystal Growth (SSD) .... FZCG
Float Zone Experiment System .... FZES
Floatable (ABBR) .... FLTB
Floatage (ABBR) .... FLOTGE
Floatation (ABBR) .... FLTN
Floatation Tank Association (EA) .... TANK
Floated (ABBR) .... FLOTD
Floated Gyro [*Aerospace*] (AAG) .... FG
Floated Inertial Measurement Ball .... FLIMBAL
Floated Integrating Gyro [*Aerospace*] (AAG) .... FIG
Floated Lightweight Inertial Platform .... FLIP
Floated Rate Gyro [*Aerospace*] (AAG) .... FRG
Floater (ABBR) .... FLOTR
Floater (ABBR) .... FLTR
Floating (ABBR) .... FLOTG
Floating (AABC) .... FLTG
Floating Accumulator .... FAC
Floating Add [*Computer science*] (IAA) .... FA
Floating Add [*Computer science*] (IEEE) .... FAD
Floating Add Magnitude [*Computer science*] (IAA) .... FAM
Floating Aircraft Maintenance Facility [*Army*] (AABC) .... FAMF
Floating Airfields [*British World War II*] .... FA
Floating Arm Graphic Recorder (PDAA) .... FAGR
Floating Asset [*Business term*] .... FA
Floating Capital [*Business term*] .... FC
Floating Causeway .... FC
Floating Commutator .... FLOCOM
Floating Container (PDAA) .... FLOCON
Floating Control Regulator .... FCR
Floating Crane [*Non-self-propelled*] [*Navy symbol*] .... YD
Floating Crane [*Non-self-propelled*] [*Navy symbol*] (DNAB) .... YWN
Floating Decimal Abstract Coding System .... FACS
Floating Derrick [*Navy*] .... YD
Floating Digital Drive .... FDD
Floating Divide (IAA) .... FD
Floating Divide or Halt .... FDH
Floating Divide or Proceed (SAA) .... FDP
Floating Dollar Sign [*Computer science*] (IAA) .... FD
Floating Drift Tube Klystron .... FDTK
Floating Dry Dock [*Navy*] .... FDD
Floating Dry Dock Workshop (Hull) [*Non-self-propelled*] [*Navy symbol*] .... YRDH
Floating Dry Dock Workshop (Machine) [*Non-self-propelled*] [*Navy symbol*] .... YRDM
Floating Electronic Maintenance Facility (MCD) .... FEMF
Floating Error Code [*Digital Equipment Corp.*] .... FEC
Floating Foundation of Photography .... FFP
Floating Gate Tunnel Oxide [*Electronics*] (EECA) .... FLOTOX
Floating Homes Association (EA) .... FHA
Floating Hospital (EA) .... FH
Floating Indexed Point Arithmetic [*Computer science*] .... FLIP
Floating Input Distortion .... FID
Floating Input - Floating Output [*Computer science*] .... FIFO
Floating Input to Ground Output .... FITGO
Floating Input Transistor [*Electronics*] .... FIT
Floating Instrument Platform [*Navy*] (NG) .... FLIP
Floating Interpretative Automatic Translator (IAA) .... FIAT
Floating Interpretive Language [*Princeton University*] .... FLINT
Floating Laboratory Instrument Platform [*Movable oceanographic research station*] .... FLIP
Floating Landing (ROG) .... FL
Floating Machine Shop .... FMS
Floating Maintenance Shop (MCD) .... FMS
Floating Multiply (IAA) .... FM
Floating Nuclear Plant [*or Powerplant*] [*ERDA*] .... FNP
Floating Nuclear Power Plant Study [*Marine science*] (MSC) .... FNPP
Floating Ocean Research and Development [*Station*] .... FORD
Floating Ocean Research and Development Station .... FORDS
Floating Octal Point [*IBM Corp.*] .... FLOP
Floating Open Marine Policy [*Insurance*] (DS) .... FP
Floating Pile Driver [*Non-self-propelled*] [*Navy symbol*] .... YPD
Floating Pile Driver [*Non-self-propelled*] [*Navy symbol*] (DNAB) .... YWN

Floating Platform No. 1 [*English bilingual film made in Germany with actor Conrad Veidt, 1933*] FP1
Floating Point [*Electronics*] (ECII) .... FLOP
Floating Point [*Computer science*] .... FLP
Floating Point [*Computer science*] (BUR) .... FP
Floating Point Arithmetic System (NITA) .... FAP
Floating Point Co-Processor [*Motorola*] (NITA) .... FPCP
Floating Point Operation [*Computer science*] .... FLOP
Floating Point Operations Per Second (NITA) .... FLOP
Floating Point Process (NITA) .... FPP
Floating Point Register [*Computer science*] .... FBR
Floating Point Systems, Inc., Beaverton, OR [*Library symbol Library of Congress*] (LCLS) .... OrBFP
Floating Policy [*Insurance*] .... FP
Floating Power Barge [*Non-self-propelled*] [*Navy symbol*] .... YFP
Floating Power Platform (PDAA) .... FLOPP
Floating Production Facility .... FPF
Floating Production, Storage, and Offloading System [*Petroleum technology*] .... FPSO
Floating Production Vessel/System (DS) .... FPV/S
Floating Rate Certificate of Deposit .... FRCD
Floating Rate Enhanced Debt Securities (TDOB) .... FRENDS
Floating Rate Note .... FRN
Floating Rate Notes (TDOB) .... FRN
Floating Repair and Oil Storage Terminal .... FROST
Floating Round .... FRN
Floating Shuttle Tape Transport (PDAA) .... FSTT
Floating Si-Gate Channel Corner Avalanche Transition (MCD) .... FCAT
Floating Sign .... FS
Floating Spherical Gaussian Orbitals [*Atomic physics*] .... FSGO
Floating Stock Platform (DNAB) .... FSP
Floating Storage (DNAB) .... FLOT STOR
Floating Subtract (IAA) .... FS
Floating Subtract [*Computer science*] (IAA) .... FSB
Floating Subtract Magnitude [*Computer science*] (IAA) .... FSM
Floating Supply Base [*Military*] (PDAA) .... FSB
Floating Units Division [*Coast Guard*] .... OFU
Floating Workship [*Coast Guard symbol*] (DNAB) .... WYTM
Floating Workshop [*Non-self-propelled*] [*Navy symbol*] .... YR
Floating Zone Melting .... FZM
Floating-Gate Amplifier (PDAA) .... FGA
Floating-Gate Avalanche-Injection Metal-Oxide Semiconductor [*Computer science*] .... FAMOS
Floating-Gate Avalanche-Injection Metal-Oxide Silicon Transistor (IAA) .... FAMOST
Floating-Gate Reset (IAA) .... FGR
Floating-In Rates .... FIR
Floating-Interest-Rate Short-Term Securities [*Shearson Lehman Brothers, Inc.*] .... FIRSTS
Floating-Point Accelerator [*Computer science*] (BYTE) .... FPA
Floating-Point Arithmetic .... FPA
Floating-Point Arithmetic Library [*Computer science*] (MHDI) .... FPAL
Floating-Point Arithmetic Package [*Computer science*] .... FAP
Floating-Point Arithmetic Unit .... FLPAU
Floating-Point Array Processor [*Computer science*] .... FPAP
Floating-Point Binary [*Computer science*] .... FLBIN
Floating-Point Board [*Computer science*] (MHDI) .... FPB
Floating-Point C Extension [*Computer science*] .... FPCE
Floating-Point Calculation .... FPC
Floating-Point Decimal [*Computer science*] .... FLDEC
Floating-Point Hardware [*Computer science*] .... FPH
Floating-Point Instruction Address [*Computer science*] .... FIA
Floating-Point Instruction Set [*Computer science*] (MSA) .... FIS
Floating-Point Interpretive Program [*Computer science*] .... FLIP
Floating-Point Means and Variance [*Biochemistry, genetics*] .... FMEVA
Floating-Point Operations per Second [*Computer science*] .... FLOPS
Floating-Point Processor [*Computer science*] .... FPP
Floating-Point Register .... FPR
Floating-Point Root Isolation [*Computer science*] (MDG) .... FRTISO
Floating-Point Routine .... FPR
Floating-Point Systems, Inc. .... FPS
Floating-Point Unit [*Computer science*] (MCD) .... FPU
Floating-Point Wait [*Computer science*] .... FWAIT
Flocculation .... FLOCC
Flocculation Reaction [*Obsolete test for liver function*] .... FR
Flocculation Speed in Antigen-Antibody Reactions [*Immunology*] (DAVI) .... kf
Floccule (ABBR) .... FLOC
Flocculent (ABBR) .... FLOC
Flocculus Target Neuron [*Neuroanatomy*] .... FTN
Floccus (ABBR) .... FLOC
Flock .... FLCK
Flocked (VRA) .... flok
Flockhouse Virus .... FHV
Flong [*Printing*] (DGA) .... FLG
Flood (MSA) .... FL
Flood (MCD) .... FLD
Flood (ABBR) .... FLOD
Flood Control .... FC
Flood Control District [*Florida*] .... FCD
Flood Damage Prevention [*Type of water project*] .... FDP
Flood. Equitable Doctrine of Election [*1880*] [*A publication*] (DLA) .... Flood El Eq
Flood Insurance [*HUD*] .... FI
Flood Insurance Rate Map .... FIRM
Flood on Wills of Personal Property [*A publication*] (DLA) .... Flood Wills
Flood Plain Management Services [*Army*] .... FPMS

Flood Relief Punt [*Coast Guard*] .... FR
Flood. Slander and Libel [*1880*] [*A publication*] (DLA) .... Flood Lib
Flood Stage [*NWS*] (FAAC) .... FLDST
Flood Stage .... FS
Flood Warnings Issued .... FLWIS
Flooded (ABBR) .... FLODD
Flooding .... FLDNG
Flooding (ABBR) .... FLODG
Floodlight .... FLDT
Floodlight (DA) .... Flo
Floodplain and River Management Working Group [*Australia*] .... FRMWG
Floods .... F
Floor .... FL
Floor (DD) .... fl
Floor .... FL
Floor (VRA) .... flr
Floor .... FLR
Floor and Vacuum Machinery Manufacturers' Association [*Defunct*] (EA) .... FVMMA
Floor Area Ratio [*in office buildings*] .... FAR
Floor Ataxia Test Battery .... FATB
Floor Board [*Automotive engineering*] .... F/BRD
Floor Cleanout [*Technical drawings*] .... FLCO
Floor Covering (ADA) .... F/COV
Floor Covering Contractors' Association [*British*] (BI) .... FCCA
Floor Covering Installation Contractors Association (EA) .... FCICA
Floor Coverings Association of New South Wales [*Australia*] .... FCANSW
Floor Drain [*Technical drawings*] .... FD
Floor Drain Tank [*Nuclear energy*] (NRCH) .... FDT
Floor Drain Treatment System [*Nuclear energy*] (NRCH) .... FDTS
Floor Line (MSA) .... FL
Floor Machine Manufacturers Association .... FMMA
Floor Manager (DEN) .... FM
Floor Plate [*Technical drawings*] .... FPL
Floor Proximity Emergency Escape Path Marking [*Aviation*] (DA) .... FPEEPM
Floor Rug Manufacturers' Association [*British*] (BI) .... FRMA
Floor Service Stations (NRCH) .... FSS
Floor Space Ratio .... FSR
Floor Valve (NRCH) .... FV
Floor Valve Adapter (NRCH) .... FVA
Floor Waste .... FW
Floor-Ceiling Sandwich .... FCS
Floorcovering .... FLRCVG
Floored (ABBR) .... FLRD
Flooring (KSC) .... FLG
Flooring (ABBR) .... FLORG
Flooring (ABBR) .... FLRG
Flooring .... FLRNG
Flooring .... FLRNG
Flooring Division, Rubber Manufacturers Association (EA) .... FDRMA
Floor-to-Floor Time [*Engineering*] .... FFT
Floorwalker (ABBR) .... FLOR-WKR
Flopped (ABBR) .... FLOPD
Flopper (ABBR) .... FLOPR
Floppier (ABBR) .... FLOPR
Floppier (ABBR) .... FLOPYR
Floppiest (ABBR) .... FLOPST
Floppiest (ABBR) .... FLOPYST
Floppily (ABBR) .... FLOPLY
Floppiness (ABBR) .... FLOPNS
Flopping (ABBR) .... FLOPG
Floppy (ABBR) .... FLOPY
Floppy Disc Controller (NITA) .... FLPDC
Floppy Disc Management System (NITA) .... FDMS
Floppy Disc Memory (NITA) .... FLMEM
Floppy Disc Processor Module [*Transdata*] (NITA) .... FPM
Floppy Disk [*Computer science*] (BUR) .... FD
Floppy Disk Controller [*Computer science*] (MDG) .... FDC
Floppy Disk Drive [*Computer science*] .... FDD
Floppy Disk High-Density [*Computer science*] .... FDHD
Floppy Disk Operating System [*Computer science*] (IEEE) .... FDOS
Floppy Disk Send/Receive [*Computer science*] .... FDSR
Floppy Disk System [*Computer science*] .... FDS
Floppy Drive High Density [*Computer science*] .... FDHD
Floppy Operating System [*Computer science*] (IAA) .... FOS
Flora .... FLRA
Flora and Fauna Guarantee Act 1988 [*Victoria*] [*State Act*] (EERA) .... FFG
Flora and Fauna Preservation Society (EERA) .... FFPS
Flora and Fauna Protection Board (EERA) .... FFPB
Flora Carnegie Library, Flora, IL [*Library symbol Library of Congress*] (LCLS) .... IFL
Flora Europaea Organization [*British*] .... FEO
Flora, IL [*Location identifier FAA*] (FAAL) .... FOA
Flora, IL [*FM radio station call letters*] .... WNOI
Flora North America Program [*Defunct*] (EA) .... FNA
Flora of Australia [*Commonwealth*] (EERA) .... FA
Flora Reserve [*State*] (EERA) .... FLR
Florac-Sainte-Enimie [*France ICAO location identifier*] (ICLI) .... LFNO
Floral (ABBR) .... FLRAL
Floral .... FLRL
Floral Art Society of Victoria [*Australia*] .... FASV
Floral Ethel Propane (DLA) .... FEP
Floral Park Memorial High School, Floral Park, NY [*Library symbol*] [*Library of Congress*] (LCLS) .... NFlpMH

Floral Park Public Library, Floral Park, NY [*Library symbol Library of Congress*] (LCLS) ... NFlp
Floral Park-Bellerose Elementary School, Floral Park, NY [*Library symbol*] [*Library of Congress*] (LCLS) ... NFlpBE
Florala, AL [*AM radio station call letters*] ... WKWL
Flora-Monroe Public Library, Flora, IN [*Library symbol Library of Congress*] (LCLS) ... InFl
Flore Pleno [*With Double Flowers*] [*Botany*] [*Latin*] (BARN) ... flpl
Florence [*South Carolina*] [*Airport symbol*] (OAG) ... FLO
Florence [*Italy*] (ROG) ... FLOR
Florence [*Italy*] [*Airport symbol*] (OAG) ... FLR
Florence A. Smith School, Oceanside, NY [*Library symbol*] [*Library of Congress*] (LCLS) ... NOcSE
Florence, AL [*AM radio station call letters*] ... WBCF
Florence, AL [*FM radio station call letters*] ... WBHL
Florence, AL [*Television station call letters*] ... WFIQ
Florence, AL [*Television station call letters*] ... WOWL
Florence, AL [*FM radio station call letters*] ... WQLT
Florence, AL [*AM radio station call letters*] ... WSBM
Florence, AL [*FM radio station call letters*] ... WXFL
Florence, AL [*Television station call letters*] ... WYLE
Florence Atkinson Elementary School, Barnesville, MN [*Library symbol*] [*Library of Congress*] (LCLS) ... MnBarFe
Florence Babylonian Collection (BJA) ... FBC
Florence Ballard Fan Club (EA) ... FBFC
Florence County Library, Florence, SC [*OCLC symbol*] (OCLC) ... SCF
Florence County Library, Florence, SC [*Library symbol Library of Congress*] (LCLS) ... ScFl
Florence Crittenton Association of America [*Later, CWLA*] (EA) ... FCAA
Florence G. Heller - JWB [*Jewish Welfare Board*] **Research Center** [*Research center*] (RCD) ... FGH-JWB
Florence Griffith Joyner [*American track athlete and Olympic gold medalist*] ... Flojo
Florence, KY [*AM radio station call letters*] (RBYB) ... WKYN
Florence MacDougall Community School, High Level, Alberta [*Library symbol National Library of Canada*] (BIB) ... AHLFS
Florence/Municipal [*South Carolina*] [*ICAO location identifier*] (ICLI) ... KFLO
Florence Nightingale International Foundation [*Defunct*] (EA) ... FNIF
Florence, NJ [*AM radio station call letters*] ... WIFI
Florence, OR [*AM radio station call letters*] ... KCST
Florence, OR [*FM radio station call letters*] ... KCST-FM
Florence, OR [*FM radio station call letters*] ... KDUK
Florence Public Library, Florence, CO [*Library symbol Library of Congress*] (LCLS) ... CoFlo
Florence Public Library, Florence, OR [*Library symbol Library of Congress*] (LCLS) ... OrFl
Florence, SC [*Location identifier FAA*] (FAAL) ... FLO
Florence, SC [*Location identifier FAA*] (FAAL) ... GKF
Florence, SC [*Television station call letters*] ... WBTW
Florence, SC [*AM radio station call letters*] ... WJMX
Florence, SC [*Television station call letters*] ... WJPM
Florence, SC [*FM radio station call letters*] ... WLPG
Florence, SC [*AM radio station call letters*] ... WOLS
Florence, SC [*Television station call letters*] ... WPDE
Florence, SC [*FM radio station call letters*] ... WWMB
Florence, SC [*AM radio station call letters*] ... WYNN
Florence, SC [*FM radio station call letters*] ... WYNN-FM
Florence, SD [*Television station call letters*] ... KDLO-TV
Florence Williams Public Library, Christiansted, St. Croix, VI [*Library symbol Library of Congress*] (LCLS) ... VnSc
Florence-Darlington Technical College Library, Florence, SC [*Library symbol Library of Congress*] (LCLS) ... ScFIT
Florence-Darlington Technical College Library, Florence, SC [*OCLC symbol*] (OCLC) ... SFD
Florencia [*Colombia*] [*Airport symbol*] (OAG) ... FLA
Florencia/Capitolio [*Colorado ICAO location identifier*] (ICLI) ... SKFL
Florennes [*Belgium ICAO location identifier*] (ICLI) ... EBFS
Florentia [*Florence*] [*Latin*] (ROG) ... FLORENT
Florentinus [*Flourished, 2nd century*] [*Authority cited in pre-1607 legal work*] (DSA) ... Flo
Florentinus [*Flourished, 2nd century*] [*Authority cited in pre-1607 legal work*] (DSA) ... Flore
Florenville, LA [*Location identifier FAA*] (FAAL) ... FNA
Flores [*Flowers*] [*Latin*] ... FL
Flores [*Flowers*] [*Latin*] (ROG) ... FLOR
Flores [*Guatemala*] [*Airport symbol*] (OAG) ... FRS
Flores [*Guatemala*] [*ICAO location identifier*] (ICLI) ... MGFL
Flores & Rucks [*NYSE symbol*] (TTSB) ... FNR
Flores & Rucks, Inc. [*Associated Press*] (SAG) ... FloresRk
Flores & Rucks, Inc. [*NYSE symbol*] (SAG) ... FNR
Flores & Rucks, Inc. [*NASDAQ symbol*] (SAG) ... FNRI
Flores Assembly Program [*Computer science*] ... FLAP
Flores, Flores Island [*Portugal ICAO location identifier*] (ICLI) ... LPFL
Floresville, TX [*FM radio station call letters*] ... KRIO
Floresville, TX [*FM radio station call letters*] ... KWCB
Floret (ABBR) ... FLRT
Florham Park Community News, Florham Park, NJ [*Library symbol Library of Congress*] (LCLS) ... NjFpN
Florham Park Public Library, Florham Park, NJ [*Library symbol Library of Congress*] (LCLS) ... NjFp
Floriano [*Brazil*] [*Airport symbol*] (AD) ... FLB
Florianopolis [*Brazil*] [*Airport symbol*] (OAG) ... FLN
Florianopolis/Hercilioluz [*Brazil ICAO location identifier*] (ICLI) ... SBFL
Florian's Own Statistically Oriented Language [*Computer science*] (CSR) ... FOSOL
Florianus de Sancto Petro [*Deceased, 1441*] [*Authority cited in pre-1607 legal work*] (DSA) ... Flo
Florianus de Sancto Petro [*Deceased, 1441*] [*Authority cited in pre-1607 legal work*] (DSA) ... Flor
Florianus de Sancto Petro [*Deceased, 1441*] [*Authority cited in pre-1607 legal work*] (DSA) ... Flori
Florianus de Sancto Petro [*Deceased, 1441*] [*Authority cited in pre-1607 legal work*] (DSA) ... Floria
Floricultural (ABBR) ... FLRCLTRL
Floricultural Industry Council of Western Australia ... FICWA
Floriculturalist (ABBR) ... FLRCLTRST
Floriculture ... FLOR
Floriculture (ABBR) ... FLRCLTR
Florid (ABBR) ... FLRID
Florid Papillomatosis [*Medicine*] ... FP
Florida (ROG) ... FA
Florida [*Postal code*] ... FL
Florida (AFM) ... FLA
Florida (ODBW) ... Fla
Florida [*of Apuleius*] [*Classical studies*] (OCD) ... Flor
Florida [*MARC country of publication code Library of Congress*] (LCCP) ... flu
Florida [*Cuba ICAO location identifier*] (ICLI) ... MUFL
Florida [*MARC geographic area code Library of Congress*] (LCCP) ... n-us-fl
Florida A & M University, Tallahassee, FL [*Library symbol Library of Congress*] (LCLS) ... FTaFA
Florida Administrative Code [*A publication*] (DLA) ... Fla Admin Code
Florida Administrative Code Annotated (AAGC) ... FACA
Florida Administrative Code Weekly [*A publication*] (AAGC) ... Fla Admin Code Weekly
Florida Administrative Law Reports [*A publication*] ... FALR
Florida Administrative Weekly [*A publication*] (AAGC) ... FAW
Florida Agricultural and Mechanical University [*Tallahasse, FL*] ... FAMU
Florida Agricultural and Mechanical University (GAGS) ... Fla A&M U
Florida Agricultural and Mechanical University, Tallahassee, FL [*OCLC symbol*] (OCLC) ... FCM
Florida Air, Inc. [*ICAO designator*] (FAAC) ... OJY
Florida Airlines and Air South [*ICAO designator*] (AD) ... FE
Florida Aquanaut Research Expedition [*National Oceanic and Atmospheric Administration*] ... FLARE
Florida Architecture and Building Research Center [*University of Florida*] [*Research center*] (RCD) ... FABRIC
Florida Area Cumulus Experiment [*National Science Foundation*] ... FACE
Florida Association for Media in Education (SRA) ... FAME
Florida Association of Insurance Agents (SRA) ... FAIA
Florida Association of Life Underwriters (SRA) ... FALU
Florida Association of Livestock Markets (SRA) ... FALM
Florida Association of Marine Explorers ... FAME
Florida Association of Plumbing, Heating, and Cooling Contractors (SRA) ... FAPHCC
Florida Association of Science Teachers (EDAC) ... FAST
Florida Atlantic Coast Transport Study [*Marine science*] (OSRA) ... FACTS
Florida Atlantic Coast Transport Study (USDC) ... FACTS
Florida Atlantic University [*Boca Raton*] ... FAU
Florida Atlantic University (GAGS) ... Fla Atlantic U
Florida Atlantic University, Boca Raton, FL [*Library symbol Library of Congress*] (LCLS) ... FBoU
Florida Atlantic University, Boca Raton, FL [*OCLC symbol*] (OCLC) ... FGM
Florida Automatic Computer [*Air Force*] ... FLAC
Florida Automotive Industry Association (SRA) ... FAIA
Florida Bandmasters Association (SRA) ... FBA
Florida Center for Library Automation [*Florida State University System*] [*Information service or system*] (IID) ... FCLA
Florida Center for Library Automation, Gainesville, FL [*Library symbol*] [*Library of Congress*] (LCLS) ... FGCL
Florida Christian College ... FCC
Florida Citrus Commission [*Later, Florida Department of Citrus*] ... FCC
Florida Citrus Mutual (EA) ... FCM
Florida Citrus Nurserymen's Association (EA) ... FCNA
Florida Citrus Packers (EA) ... FCP
Florida Citrus Processors Association (SRA) ... FCPA
Florida College, Tampa, FL [*Library symbol Library of Congress*] (LCLS) ... FTFC
Florida College, Temple Terrace, FL [*Library symbol Library of Congress*] (LCLS) ... FTtF
Florida Commercial Fisheries Association (EA) ... FCFA
Florida Commuter [*ICAO designator*] (AD) ... PG
Florida Computer Catalog of Monographic Holdings [*Library network*] ... FLORIDA COMCAT
Florida Computer, Inc. [*Information service or system*] (IID) ... FCI
Florida Cooperative Fish and Wildlife Research Unit [*University of Florida*] [*Research center*] (RCD) ... CFWRU
Florida Customs Brokers and Forwarders Association (SRA) ... FCBF
Florida Defense Lawyers Association (SRA) ... FDLA
Florida Dental Laboratory Association (SRA) ... FDLA
Florida Department of Agriculture and Consumer Services, Division of Forestry [*FAA designator*] (FAAC) ... FFS
Florida Department of Citrus (EA) ... FDC
Florida Department of Environmental Regulations ... FDER
Florida Department of Environmental Regulations (DOGT) ... FDER
Florida East Coast Indus [*NYSE symbol*] (TTSB) ... FLA
Florida East Coast Industries, Inc. [*NYSE symbol*] (SPSG) ... FLA
Florida East Coast Industries, Inc. [*Associated Press*] (SAG) ... FlaEC
Florida East Coast Railway Co. [*AAR code*] ... FEC
Florida Education Computing Project (EDAC) ... FECP
Florida Employers Exchange (SRA) ... FEE
Florida Environmental Health Association (SRA) ... FEHA

Florida Express, Inc. [*ICAO designator*] (FAAC) ... FLX
Florida Facility [*NASA*] (KSC) ... FF
Florida First Bancorp [*NASDAQ symbol*] (TTSB) ... FFPC
Florida First Bancorp, Inc. [*NASDAQ symbol*] (SAG) ... FFPC
Florida First Bancorp, Inc. [*Associated Press*] (SAG) ... FlaFst
Florida First Federal Savings Bank [*NASDAQ symbol*] (NQ) ... FFPC
Florida First Federal Savings Bank [*Associated Press*] (SAG) ... FlaFst
Florida Foliage Association (EA) ... FFA
Florida Fresh Citrus Shippers Association [*Later, FCP*] (EA) ... FFCSA
Florida Fruit and Vegetable Association (EA) ... FFVA
Florida Gaming [*NASDAQ symbol*] (TTSB) ... BETS
Florida Gaming Corp. [*NASDAQ symbol*] (SAG) ... BETS
Florida Gaming Corp. [*Associated Press*] (SAG) ... FlaGam
Florida Gift Fruit Shippers Association (EA) ... FGFSA
Florida Group [*Navy*] ... FLAGRP
Florida High School Athletics Association (EDAC) ... FHSAA
Florida Historical Society, University of South Florida, Tampa, FL [*Library symbol Library of Congress*] (LCLS) ... FHi
Florida Hotel and Motel Association (SRA) ... FH&MA
Florida Industries Exposition ... FIE
Florida Information Resource Network (EDAC) ... FIRN
Florida Institute for Law Enforcement [*St. Petersburg Junior College*] [*Research center*] (RCD) ... FILE
Florida Institute of Oceanography ... FIO
Florida Institute of Phosphate Research, FIPR Library & Information Clearinghouse, Bartow, FL [*Library symbol*] [*Library of Congress*] (LCLS) ... FBIP
Florida Institute of Technology [*Melbourne*] ... FIT
Florida Institute of Technology (GAGS) ... Fla Inst Tech
Florida Institute of Technology, Jensen Beach Campus, Jenson Beach, FL [*Library symbol*] [*Library of Congress*] (LCLS) ... FJbF
Florida Institute of Technology, Melbourne, FL [*OCLC symbol*] (OCLC) ... FLT
Florida Institute of Technology, Melbourne, FL [*Library symbol Library of Congress*] (LCLS) ... FMeF
Florida Instructional League [*Baseball*] ... FIL
Florida International Agricultural Trade Council (SRA) ... FIATC
Florida International University [*Miami*] ... FIU
Florida International University, Miami, FL [*Library symbol Library of Congress*] (LCLS) ... FMFIU
Florida International University, Miami, FL [*OCLC symbol*] (OCLC) ... FXG
Florida International University, North Campus, North Miami, FL [*OCLC symbol*] (OCLC) ... FXN
Florida Junior College at Jacksonville, DTC, Jacksonville, FL [*OCLC symbol*] (OCLC) ... FJD
Florida Junior College at Jacksonville, Jacksonville, FL [*Library symbol Library of Congress*] (LCLS) ... FJF
Florida Junior College at Jacksonville, Kent, Jacksonville, FL [*OCLC symbol*] (OCLC) ... FJK
Florida Junior College at Jacksonville, North, Jacksonville, FL [*OCLC symbol*] (OCLC) ... FJN
Florida Junior College at Jacksonville, South, Jacksonville, FL [*OCLC symbol*] (OCLC) ... FJS
Florida Jurisprudence [*A publication*] (DLA) ... Fla Jur
Florida Keys Community College, Key West, FL [*Library symbol*] [*Library of Congress*] (LCLS) ... FKwC
Florida Keys National Marine Sanctuary ... FKNMS
Florida Keys National Marine Sanctuary [*USA*] [*Marine science*] (OSRA) ... FKNMS
Florida Keys Wild Bird Rehabilitation Center (EA) ... FKWBRC
Florida Language, Speech, and Hearing Association (SRA) ... FLASHA
Florida Law and Practice [*A publication*] (DLA) ... FLP
Florida Law Journal [*A publication*] (DLA) ... Fla LJ
Florida Law Review [*A publication*] (DLA) ... Fla L Rev
Florida Leader Active in Research ... FLAIR
Florida Library Information Network [*Florida State Library*] [*Tallahassee, FL*] [*Library network*] ... FLIN
Florida Lime and Avocado Administrative Committee (EA) ... FLAAC
Florida Lychee Growers Association (EA) ... FLGA
Florida Mango Forum (EA) ... FMF
Florida Marine Aquarium Society ... FMAS
Florida Medical Entomology Laboratory, Vero Beach, FL [*Library symbol Library of Congress*] (LCLS) ... FVbF
Florida Memorial College, Miami, FL [*OCLC symbol*] (OCLC) ... FMC
Florida Memorial College, Miami, FL [*Library symbol Library of Congress*] (LCLS) ... FMFM
Florida Mental Health Institute, Tampa, FL [*Library symbol*] [*Library of Congress*] (LCLS) ... FTFM
Florida Missile Test Range (MUGU) ... FMTR
Florida Movers and Warehousemen's Association (SRA) ... FMWA
Florida Municipal Electric Association (SRA) ... FMEA
Florida Music Educators Association (SRA) ... FMEA
Florida Natural Areas Inventory [*Information service or system*] (IID) ... FNAI
Florida Network of Youth and Family Services (SRA) ... FNYFS
Florida P&L 8.75% 'QUIDS' [*NYSE symbol*] (TTSB) ... FPD
Florida Panthers Holdings, Inc. [*Associated Press*] (SAG) ... FLPanth
Florida Panthers Holdings, Inc. [*NASDAQ symbol*] (SAG) ... PUCK
Florida Peace Officers Association (SRA) ... FPOA
Florida Pool and Spa Association (SRA) ... FPSA
Florida Power & Light [*Associated Press*] (SAG) ... FLPw25
Florida Power & Light [*NYSE symbol*] (SAG) ... FPD
Florida Power & Light Co. [*Associated Press*] (SAG) ... FLPw
Florida Power & Light Co. [*NYSE symbol*] (SPSG) ... FPL
Florida Power Corp., St. Petersburg, FL [*Library symbol*] [*Library of Congress*] (LCLS) ... FSpFP
Florida Presbyterian College [*Later, Eckerd College*] ... FPC
Florida Progress [*NYSE symbol*] (TTSB) ... FPC
Florida Progress Corp. [*Formerly, Florida Power Corp.*] [*Associated Press*] (SAG) ... FlaProg
Florida Progress Corp. [*Formerly, Florida Power Corp.*] [*NYSE symbol*] (SPSG) ... FPC
Florida Public Relations Association (SRA) ... FPRA
Florida Public Utilities [*AMEX symbol*] (TTSB) ... FPU
Florida Public Utilities Co. [*Associated Press*] (SAG) ... FlaPUt
Florida Public Utilities Co. [*AMEX symbol*] (SPSG) ... FPU
Florida Redevelopment Association (SRA) ... FRA
Florida Reports [*A publication*] (DLA) ... Fla
Florida Reports [*A publication*] (DLA) ... Fla R
Florida Reports [*A publication*] (DLA) ... Fla Rep
Florida Reports [*A publication*] (DLA) ... Flo R
Florida Reports [*A publication*] (DLA) ... Flor
Florida Reports [*A publication*] (DLA) ... Florida
Florida Reports [*A publication*] (DLA) ... Florida R
Florida Reports [*A publication*] (DLA) ... Florida Rep
Florida Retail Federation (SRA) ... FRF
Florida Rock Indus [*AMEX symbol*] (TTSB) ... FRK
Florida Rock Industries, Inc. [*Associated Press*] (SAG) ... FlaRck
Florida Rock Industries, Inc. [*AMEX symbol*] (SPSG) ... FRK
Florida Sea Grant College [*University of Florida*] [*Research center*] (RCD) ... FSG
Florida Session Law Service (West) [*A publication*] (DLA) ... Fla Sess Law Serv
Florida Society of Ophthalmology (SRA) ... FSO
Florida Society of Otolaryngology-Head and Neck Surgery (SRA) ... FSOHNS
Florida Solar Energy Center [*University of Central Florida*] [*Research center*] (RCD) ... FSEC
Florida Solar Energy Center, Cape Canaveral, FL [*Library symbol Library of Congress*] (LCLS) ... FCaF
Florida Solar Energy Center, Cape Canaveral, FL [*OCLC symbol*] (OCLC) ... FSE
Florida Southern College [*Lakeland*] ... FSC
Florida Southern College, Lakeland, FL [*Library symbol Library of Congress*] (LCLS) ... FLIS
Florida Southern College, Lakeland, FL [*OCLC symbol*] (OCLC) ... FSC
Florida Space Coast Writers Conference (EA) ... FSCWC
Florida Specialized Carriers Rate Conference, Inc., Jacksonville FL [*STAC*] ... FLS
Florida State Bar Association. Journal [*A publication*] (DLA) ... Fla SBA Jo
Florida State Bar Association. Law Journal [*A publication*] (DLA) ... Fla SBALJ
Florida State Hospital, Chattahoochee, FL [*Library symbol Library of Congress*] (LCLS) ... FChH
Florida State Law Journal [*A publication*] (DLA) ... Fla State LJ
Florida State League [*Baseball*] ... FSL
Florida State Library, Bureau of Book Processing, Tallahassee, FL [*Library symbol Library of Congress*] (LCLS) ... F-B
Florida State Library, Tallahassee, FL [*Library symbol Library of Congress*] (LCLS) ... F
Florida State University (GAGS) ... Fla St U
Florida State University [*Tallahassee*] ... FSU
Florida State University, Law Library, Tallahassee, FL [*OCLC symbol*] (OCLC) ... FSL
Florida State University, Law Library, Tallahassee, FL [*Library symbol Library of Congress*] (LCLS) ... FTaSU-L
Florida State University, School of Library Science, Tallahassee, FL [*OCLC symbol*] (OCLC) ... FLS
Florida State University, Tallahassee, FL [*OCLC symbol*] (OCLC) ... FDA
Florida State University, Tallahassee, FL [*Library symbol Library of Congress*] (LCLS) ... FTaSU
Florida Statutes [*A publication*] (DLA) ... Fla Stat
Florida Statutes, Annotated [*A publication*] (DLA) ... Fla Stat Ann
Florida Statutes, Annotated [*A publication*] (DLA) ... FSA
Florida Supplement [*A publication*] (DLA) ... Fla Supp
Florida Supplement [*A publication*] (DLA) ... FLS
Florida Supreme Court, Tallahassee, FL [*Library symbol Library of Congress*] (LCLS) ... F-SC
Florida Teacher Certification Examination (EDAC) ... FTCE
Florida Technical Advisory Committee on Citrus Canker (EA) ... FTACCC
Florida Technological University, Orlando, FL [*Library symbol Library of Congress*] (LCLS) ... FOFT
Florida Technology University (DAVI) ... FTU
Florida Telecommunications Industry Association (SRA) ... FTIA
Florida Test Center [*NASA*] (KSC) ... FTC
Florida Test Procedure [*Aerospace*] (AAG) ... FTP
Florida Tomato Exchange (EA) ... FTE
Florida Trail Association (EA) ... FTA
Florida Transit Association (SRA) ... FTA
Florida Tropical Fish Farms Association (EA) ... FTFFA
Florida Trucking Association (SRA) ... FTA
Florida Turfgrass Association (SRA) ... FTGA
Florida Union List of Serials ... FULS
Florida Union List of Serials, Gainesville, FL [*Library symbol Library of Congress*] (LCLS) ... FGULS
Florida Union List of Serials, Gainesville, FL [*Inactive*] [*OCLC symbol*] (OCLC) ... FUL
Florida West Airlines [*ICAO designator*] (FAAC) ... FWL
Florida West Coast Nuclear Group ... FWCNG
Florida-Alabama-Georgia League [*Old baseball league*] ... FLAG
Floridablanca Air Base, Pampanga [*Philippines*] [*ICAO location identifier*] (ICLI) ... RPUF
Floridity (ABBR) ... FLRIDT
Floridly (ABBR) ... FLRIDY
Floridness (ABBR) ... FLRIDNS
Florilege [*Record label*] [*France*] ... Flo
Florilegium. A Miscellany from Qumran. Cave Four (BJA) ... 4QFlor

Florin [*Monetary unit*] [*Netherlands*] .... F
Florin [*Monetary unit*] [*Netherlands*] .... FL
Florin [*Monetary unit*] [*Netherlands*] (ROG) .... FLO
Florin [*Monetary unit*] [*Netherlands*] .... FLR
Florissant [*Missouri*] [*Seismograph station code, US Geological Survey Closed*] (SEIS) .... FLO
Florissant, MO [*FM radio station call letters*] .... KXOK
Florist (ROG) .... FLOR
Florist (ABBR) .... FLRST
Florist .... FLRST
Florists' Transworld [*formerly, Telegraph*] Delivery [*Trademark*] .... FTD
Florists' Transworld Delivery Association (EA) .... FTDA
Floro [*Norway ICAO location identifier*] (ICLI) .... ENFL
Floro [*Norway*] [*Airport symbol*] (OAG) .... FRO
Florsheim Group [*Associated Press*] (SAG) .... FlorshGp
Florsheim Shoe [*NASDAQ symbol*] (TTSB) .... FLSC
[*The*] Florsheim Shoe Co. [*Associated Press*] (SAG) .... FlorshSh
[*The*] Florsheim Shoe Co. [*NASDAQ symbol*] (SAG) .... FLSC
Floruit [*He Flourished*] [*Latin*] .... FL
Floruit [*He Flourished*] [*Latin*] .... FLOR
Floryn [*Florin*] [*Monetary unit*] [*Afrikaans*] .... F
Flos-Elmvale Public Library, Elmvale, Ontario [*Library symbol National Library of Canada*] (BIB) .... OEFE
Flossier (ABBR) .... FLSR
Flossiest (ABBR) .... FLSST
Flossing, Brushing, and Irrigation [*Dentistry*] .... FBI
Flossmoor, IL [*FM radio station call letters*] .... WHFH
Flossmoor Public Library, Flossmoor, IL [*Library symbol Library of Congress*] (LCLS) .... IFlo
Flossy (ABBR) .... FLSY
Flota Aerea Mercane Argentina .... FAMA
Flota Argentina Navegacion Ultramar [*Argentine Ship Line*] .... FANU
Flotation (KSC) .... FLOT
Flotation (ABBR) .... FLOTN
Flotation (ABBR) .... FLTAN
Flotilla (AABC) .... FLOT
Flotilla (ABBR) .... FLOTL
Flotilla (ABBR) .... FLTLA
Flotilla Leader [*British*] .... FL
Flotilla or Squadron Commander (DNAB) .... FLOTRONCOM
Flotsam (ABBR) .... FLOT
Flotsam (ABBR) .... FLOTM
Flotsam (ABBR) .... FLTSM
Flounced (ABBR) .... FLNCD
Flouncing (ABBR) .... FLNCG
Flounder (ABBR) .... FLNDR
Floundered (ABBR) .... FLNDRD
Floundering (ABBR) .... FLNDRG
Flour (WGA) .... FL
Flour Millers Council of Australia .... FMCA
Flour Millers Export Association (EA) .... FMEA
Flour Milling (OA) .... FM
Flour Milling and Baking Research Association [*British*] (IRUK) .... FMBRA
Flourescence (ABBR) .... FLRSNC
Flourescent (VRA) .... flour
Flourescent (ABBR) .... FLRSNT
Flourescent Discharge Tube [*Technology*] .... FDT
Flouridate (ABBR) .... FLRDA
Flouridated (ABBR) .... FLRDAD
Flouridating (ABBR) .... FLRDAG
Flouridation (ABBR) .... FLRDN
Flourier (ABBR) .... FLORR
Flouriest (ABBR) .... FLORST
Flourish (WGA) .... FLOU
Flourish (ABBR) .... FLRH
Flourished (VRA) .... fl
Flourishing (ABBR) .... FLRHG
Flour-Milling Technology (OA) .... FMT
Flouroscope (ABBR) .... FLSCP
Flourous Biphase System [*For chemical catalysis*] .... FBS
Floury (ABBR) .... FLORY
Flouter (ABBR) .... FLUTR
Flow [*of blood*] [*Medicine*] .... F
Flow (NFPA) .... F
Flow (MSA) .... FL
Flow Actuated Sediment Trap [*Marine science*] (OSRA) .... FAST
Flow Actuated Sediment Trap (USDC) .... FAST
Flow Analysis Program [*Computer science*] .... FLAP
Flow and Temperature Removable Instrument Assembly [*Nuclear energy*] (NRCH) .... FTRIA
Flow Bias Functional Test (IEEE) .... FBFT
Flow Block .... FB
Flow Block Diagram .... FBD
Flow Blue International Collectors Club (EA) .... FBICC
Flow Brazing .... FLB
Flow Coating .... FC
Flow Control Assembly (MCD) .... FCA
Flow Control Decision Message (DA) .... FCDM
Flow Control Execution Message (DA) .... FCEM
Flow Control Time of Arrival [*Aviation*] (FAAC) .... FCTA
Flow Control Valve .... FCV
Flow Controller [*Nuclear energy*] (NRCH) .... FC
Flow Cytometry [*Analytical biochemistry*] .... FCM
Flow Diagram [*Engineering*] (IAA) .... FD
Flow Element [*Nuclear energy*] (NRCH) .... FE

Flow Gauge .... FG
Flow Generator [*Air Force*] (DOMA) .... FLOGEN
Flow Indicator .... FI
Flow Indicator Controller [*Electronics*] (ECII) .... FIC
Flow Indicator Recorder [*Electronics*] (ECII) .... FIR
Flow Indicator Recorder Controller [*Electronics*] (ECII) .... FIRC
Flow Indicator Transmitter [*Nuclear energy*] (NRCH) .... FIT
Flow Information Display .... FIND
Flow Injection [*Chemical processing*] .... FI
Flow Injection Analyzer [*Chemical analyses*] .... FIA
Flow International [*NASDAQ symbol*] (TTSB) .... FLOW
Flow International Corp. [*NASDAQ symbol*] (NQ) .... FLOW
Flow International Corp. [*Associated Press*] (SAG) .... FlowInt
Flow Line [*Technical drawings*] .... FL
Flow Line .... FLL
Flow Management Position [*ICAO*] (DA) .... FMP
Flow Management Unit [*Aviation*] (FAAC) .... FMU
Flow Measurement and Indication (DEN) .... FMI
Flow Measuring System .... FMS
Flow Meter (AAG) .... FL/MTR
Flow Meter (KSC) .... FM
Flow Microfluorometer [*Instrumentation*] .... FMF
Flow of Gold .... FOG
Flow Path Selector Valve (MCD) .... FPSV
Flow Proportioning Value (MCD) .... FPV
Flow Rate (AAG) .... FL/RT
Flow Rate (AAG) .... FLR
Flow Rate .... FR
Flow Rate [*Heat transmission symbol*] .... w
Flow Rate of Sample .... FR(s)
Flow Rate of Sparge Gas .... FR(g)
Flow Reactor Mass Spectroscopy (MCD) .... FRMS
Flow Recorder .... FR
Flow Recorder and Alarm [*Nuclear energy*] (NRCH) .... FRA
Flow Recorder Controller .... FRC
Flow Recording Controller Switch [*Nuclear energy*] (NRCH) .... FRCS
Flow Recording Ratio Controller (IAA) .... FRRC
Flow Recording Transmitter .... FRT
Flow Regulator [*Nuclear energy*] (NRCH) .... FR
Flow Resources Ltd. [*Vancouver Stock Exchange symbol*] .... FLW
Flow Switch .... FLS
Flow Switch .... FLSW
Flow Switch .... FS
Flow Through .... FT
Flow Totalizer .... FL/TOT
Flow Transducer [*Instrumentation*] .... FT
Flow Transmitter [*Nuclear energy*] (NRCH) .... FT
Flow Velocity Integral [*Cardiology*] .... FVI
Flow Volume [*Measurement*] [*Cardiology*] (DAVI) .... F-V
Flow Volume Loop [*Hemodialysis*] .... FVL
Flow-Assisted, Short-Term [*Balloon catheter*] [*Cardiology*] (DAVI) .... FAST
Flowchart [*Engineering*] (IAA) .... FC
Flowcharting FORTRAN [*Computer science*] (IEEE) .... FLOTRAN
Flow-Diversion Valve .... FDV
Flower .... F
Flower [*Botany*] .... fl
Flower .... FLR
Flower .... FLWR
Flower .... FLWR
Flower Essence Society (EA) .... FES
Flower Gardens Ocean Research Center [*Marine Biomedical Institute, University of Texas*] (PDAA) .... FGORC
Flower Growers' Association of New South Wales [*Australia*] .... FGANSW
Flower Hill Elementary School, Huntington, NY [*Library symbol*] [*Library of Congress*] (LCLS) .... NHuFE
Flower Length [*Botany*] .... FLWL
Flower of Friendship and Development of Macau [*Political party*] (EY) .... FADEM
Flowered [*Botany*] .... fld
Flowers and Plants Association [*British*] (DBA) .... FPA
Flowers Auditory Test of Selective Attention .... FATSA
Flowers Indus [*NYSE symbol*] (TTSB) .... FLO
Flowers Industries, Inc. [*NYSE symbol*] (SPSG) .... FLO
Flowers Industries, Inc. [*Associated Press*] (SAG) .... Flower
Flowers Publicity Council Ltd. [*British*] (BI) .... FPC
Flowers' Roguish Cultivator .... FRC
Flowers-Costello Test of Central Auditory Abilities .... FCTCAA
Flowing Afterglow [*Chemical kinetic*] .... FA
Flowing Gas Detonation Tube .... FDT
Flowing Gas Stream .... FGS
Flowmeter Calibration Stand .... FCS
Flowmeter Ordering and Indicating Unit .... FOIU
Flown .... FLN
Flowood, MS [*AM radio station call letters*] .... WPBQ
Flowrate Alarm [*Engineering*] .... FA
Flowrate Indicating [*Engineering*] .... FI
Flowrate Indicating Alarm [*Engineering*] .... FIA
Flowrate Indicating Controlling Alarm [*Engineering*] .... FICA
Flowrate Recording Alarm [*Engineering*] .... FRA
Flow-Through Aquatic Toxicology Exposure System [*Evaluation of sediment contaminants*] .... FATES
Flow-Through Tube Sampler [*Nuclear energy*] (NRCH) .... FTTS
Flow-Through Ventilation .... FTV
Floyd B. Watson School, Rockville Centre, NY [*Library symbol*] [*Library of Congress*] (LCLS) .... NRockWS
Floyd Satellite Communications Terminal .... FSCT

Floyd, VA [*AM radio station call letters*] .... WGFC
Floydada, TX [*AM radio station call letters*] .... KAWA
Floydada, TX [*FM radio station call letters*] .... KFLL
Floydada, TX [*AM radio station call letters*] (RBYB) .... KFLP-AM
Floyer's Proctors' Practice [*A publication*] (DLA) .... Floy Proct Pr
Fluctuant (ABBR) .... FLUCNT
Fluctuate .... FLUC
Fluctuated (ABBR) .... FLUCD
Fluctuating (ABBR) .... FLUCG
Fluctuating Asymmetry [*Embryology*] .... FA
Fluctuation (FAAC) .... FLCTN
Fluctuation (ABBR) .... FLUCN
Fluctuation-Dissipation [*Theorem*] [*Statistical mechanics*] .... FD
Flue Gas Recirculation [*Combustion engineering*] .... FGR
Flue-Cured Tobacco Cooperative Stabilization Corp. (EA) .... FCTCSC
Flue-Cured Tobacco Growers Association (EA) .... FCTGA
Flue-Gas Desulfurization .... FGD
Flue-Gas Treatment .... FGT
Flue-Gas-through-the-Tubes [*Incinerator*] .... FGTT
Fluency [*A factor ability*] [*Psychology*] .... F
Fluency (ABBR) .... FLUNC
Fluent (ABBR) .... FLUNT
Fluently (ABBR) .... FLUNTY
Fluffed (ABBR) .... FLUFD
Fluffier (ABBR) .... FLUFYR
Fluffiest (ABBR) .... FLUFYST
Fluffily (ABBR) .... FLUFYY
Fluffiness (ABBR) .... FLUFYNS
Fluffing (ABBR) .... FLUFG
Fluffy (ABBR) .... FLUFY
Fluffy Opaque Inclusions [*In a meteorite*] .... FOI
Flug & Fahrzeugwerke AG Altenrhein [*Switzerland ICAO aircraft manufacturer identifier*] (ICAO) .... AF
Flugbetriebsstoff-Kesselkraftwagen .... FBKKW
Flugdienst Fehlhaber GmbH [*Germany ICAO designator*] (FAAC) .... FFG
Flugfelag Austerlands Ltd. Egilsstadir [*Iceland*] [*ICAO designator*] (FAAC) .... EST
Flugfelag Islands H.F. [*Iceland Airways Ltd.*] .... FLUG
Flugfelag Nordurlands [*Iceland*] [*ICAO designator*] (FAAC) .... FNA
Flugfelag Nordurlands [*Northlands Air*] [*ICAO designator*] (AD) .... UI
Flugfelag-Icelandair [*ICAO designator*] (AD) .... FI
Flugzeug [*Airplane*] [*German military*] .... F
Fluharty Preschool Speech and Language Screening Test (DAVI) .... FPSLST
Fluid .... F
Fluid (KSC) .... FL
Fluid (AAG) .... FLD
Fluid .... FLUD
Fluid Air Ride [*Automotive engineering*] .... FAR
Fluid Amplifier Control Engine Test .... FACET
Fluid Amplifier Control System .... FACS
Fluid Analogies Research Group .... FARG
Fluid Analysis Spectrometer (MCD) .... FAS
Fluid and Chemical Processing (SSD) .... FCP
Fluid Bed Heat Exchanger (PDAA) .... FBHX
Fluid Catalytic Converter [*Environmental Protection Agency*] (GFGA) .... FCC
Fluid Catalytic Cracking [*Fuel technology*] .... FCC
Fluid Catalytic Cracking Unit [*Fuel technology*] .... FCCU
Fluid Checkout Unit (MCD) .... FCU
Fluid Circulation Storage Battery [*Automotive engineering*] .... FCSB
Fluid Conductivity Indicator .... FCI
Fluid Controls Institute (EA) .... FCI
Fluid Convection Cathode .... FCC
Fluid Coupling [*Automotive engineering*] .... F/CPLG
Fluid Digital Computer .... FDC
Fluid Distribution System (KSC) .... FDS
Fluid Distribution Unit (MCD) .... FDU
Fluid Dram .... FLDR
Fluid Dynamics (SSD) .... FLD
Fluid Dynamics Analysis Package [*Computer-assisted engineering*] .... FIDAP
Fluid Dynamics Research Group [*MIT*] (MCD) .... FDRG
Fluid Dynamics Research Laboratory [*MIT*] (MCD) .... FDRL
Fluid, Electrolytes, and Nutrition [*Dietetics*] [*Pharmacology*] (DAVI) .... FEN
Fluid Encapsulated Launch Technique (PDAA) .... FELT
Fluid Energy Mill (MCD) .... FEM
Fluid Extract [*Pharmacology*] (DAVI) .... Ext Fl
Fluid Extract [*Pharmacy*] .... FE
Fluid Extract [*Pharmacology*] (DAVI) .... fld ext
Fluid Film Bearing .... FFB
Fluid Flow .... FDFL
Fluid Flow Indicator .... FFI
Fluid Induction System [*Automotive engineering*] .... FIS
Fluid Inertial Balance (MCD) .... FLINBAL
Fluid Inject Valve Actuator .... FIVA
Fluid Jet Amplifier .... FJA
Fluid Level Sensor [*Engineering*] .... FLS
Fluid Levitation Accelerometer .... FLA
Fluid Logic Industrial Control Relay .... FLICR
Fluid Management and Distribution (SSD) .... FMAD
Fluid Management System (SSD) .... FMS
Fluid Mechanical (MCD) .... FLMECH
Fluid Mechanics Laboratory [*MIT*] [*Research center*] .... FML
Fluid Metering, Inc. .... FMI
Fluid Modeling Facility [*Environmental Protection Agency*] (GRD) .... FMF
Fluid Momentum Controller (SSD) .... FMC
Fluid Motion Panel [*of the British Aeronautical Research Council*] (MCD) .... FMP
Fluid Ounce .... F

Fluid Ounce .... FLOZ
Fluid Phase Marker .... FPM
Fluid Physics/Dynamics Facility (SSD) .... FP/DF
Fluid Physics Facility (SSD) .... FPF
Fluid Pint (WDAA) .... FL PT
Fluid/Plasma Ratio [*Biochemistry*] (DAVI) .... F/P
Fluid Poison Control Reactor (IAA) .... FPCR
Fluid Power Centre [*University of Bath*] [*British*] (CB) .... FPC
Fluid Power Consultants International (EA) .... FPCI
Fluid Power Distributors Association (EA) .... FPDA
Fluid Power Laboratory [*Ohio State University*] [*Research center*] (RCD) .... FPL
Fluid Power Research Center [*Oklahoma State University*] [*Research center*] (RCD) .... FPRC
Fluid Power Society (EA) .... FPS
Fluid Power Supply .... FPS
Fluid Power System .... FPS
Fluid Power Take-Off [*Hydraulic transmissions*] .... FPTO
Fluid Pressure [*Spinal fluid pressure*] [*Medicine*] (DAVI) .... FP
Fluid Pressure Line (MSA) .... FDPL
Fluid Properties Research, Inc. .... FPR
Fluid Purification System .... FPS
Fluid Rate Damper .... FRD
Fluid Regenerative Air Heater (PDAA) .... FRAH
Fluid Resistant .... FR
Fluid Restriction [*Dietetics*] (DAVI) .... fld rest
Fluid Sealing Association (EA) .... FSA
Fluid Shaft Encoder .... FSE
Fluid Storage Container .... FSC
Fluid Structure Interaction [*Nuclear energy*] (NRCH) .... FSI
Fluid Supply System (MCD) .... FSS
Fluid Switch .... FS
Fluid Thioglycolate [*Medium*] [*Microbiology*] .... FTG
Fluid Thioglycolate Medium [*Microbiology*] .... FTM
Fluid to Electric Switch .... FES
Fluid Transfer Management System (SSD) .... FTMS
Fluid Transpiration Arc .... FTA
Fluid Vacancy Model .... FVM
Fluid Velocity Potential .... FVP
Fluid Volume .... FV
Fluid Volume Measurement System (MCD) .... FVMS
Fluid Wetting and Spreading [*Lubrication*] .... FWS
Fluid-Bed Thermal Cracking [*A chemical process developed by the Institute of Gas Technology*] .... FTC
Fluidextractum [*Fluidextract*] [*Pharmacy*] .... FLDEXT
Fluidextractum [*Fluidextract*] [*Pharmacy*] .... FLDXT
Fluidextractum [*Fluidextract*] [*Pharmacy*] (ROG) .... FLUIDEXTER
Fluidextractum [*Fluidextract*] [*Pharmacy*] (ROG) .... FLUIDEXTR
Fluidic Emergency Thruster [*Aviation*] .... FET
Fluidic Environmental Sensor (RDA) .... FES
Fluidic Explosive Initiator (PDAA) .... FEI
Fluidic Industrial Control Module (IAA) .... FICM
Fluidic Logic Module .... FLM
Fluidic Output Device .... FOD
Fluidic Proportional Thruster .... FPT
Fluidic Rate Sensor (MCD) .... FRS
Fluidic Setting Device .... FSD
Fluidic Stability Augmentation System [*for helicopters*] .... FSAS
Fluidic Valve Operator .... FVO
Fluidics Inertial Bomb .... FIB
Fluidity (ABBR) .... FLT
Fluidized Bed .... FB
Fluidized Bed Electrode [*Electrochemistry*] .... FBE
Fluidized Bed Incinerator (DOGT) .... FBI
Fluidized Combustor Ash (OA) .... FCA
Fluidized-Bed Combustion (NASA) .... FBC
Fluidized-Bed Control Rod (PDAA) .... FBCR
Fluidized-Bed Film Reactor [*For water purification*] .... FBFR
Fluidized-Bed Gasifier [*Coal gasification*] .... FBG
Fluidized-Bed Hydrogenator [*Chemical engineering reactor*] .... FBH
Fluidized-Bed Process .... FBP
Fluidized-Bed Reactor (MCD) .... FBR
Fluidness (ABBR) .... FLNS
Fluid-Operated Digital Automatic Computer [*Sperry UNIVAC*] .... FLODAC
Fluids, Aeration, Nutrition, Communication, Activity, and Pain [*Medicine*] .... FANCAP
Fluids, Aeration, Nutrition, Communication, Activity, and Stimulation [*Medicine*] .... FANCAS
Fluids Control Assembly (NASA) .... FCA
Fluids Pressure Control (NASA) .... FPC
Fluidus [*Fluid*] [*Pharmacy*] .... FL
Fluidyne Engineering Corp. (KSC) .... FDEC
Fluke (ABBR) .... FLUK
Fluke Corp. [*NYSE symbol*] (SAG) .... FLK
Fluke Corp. [*Associated Press*] (SAG) .... Fluke
Fluked [*Naval architecture*] .... FLKD
Flummery (ABBR) .... FLMRY
Flunitrazepam [*A hypnotic*] .... FLU
Flunitrazepam [*A hypnotic*] .... FNZP
Flunk (CDAI) .... F
Flunky (ABBR) .... FLNKY
Fluocortin Butyl [*Pharmacology*] .... FCB
Fluor Canada Ltd., Calgary, AB, Canada [*Library symbol*] [*Library of Congress*] (LCLS) .... CaACFC
Fluor Canada Ltd., Calgary, Alberta [*Library symbol National Library of Canada*] (NLC) .... ACFC

Fluor Chrome Arsenate Phenol [*Wood preservative*] ... FCAP
Fluor Corp. [*NYSE symbol*] (SPSG) ... FLR
Fluor Corp. [*Associated Press*] (SAG) ... Fluor
Fluor Daniel/GTI [*NASDAQ symbol*] (TTSB) ... FDGT
Fluor Daniel GTI, Inc. [*NASDAQ symbol*] (SAG) ... FDGT
Fluor Daniel GTI, Inc. [*Associated Press*] (SAG) ... FlrDnlGTI
Fluor Engineers & Constructors, Fluor Houston Library, Houston, TX [*Library symbol Library of Congress*] (LCLS) ... TxHFE
Fluor Ocean Services, Engineering Library, Houston, TX [*Library symbol Library of Congress*] (LCLS) ... TxHFO
Fluor Power Services, Inc. (NRCH) ... FPS
Fluorenamine [*Also, AF*] [*Carcinogen*] ... FA
Fluorene [*Biochemistry*] ... Fln
Fluorenylacetamide [*Also, AAF, AcNHFln*] [*Organic chemistry*] ... FAA
Fluorenylmethyloxycarbonyl [*Organic chemistry*] ... FMOC
Fluorescamine [*Biochemical analysis*] [*Acronym is trademark of Roche Diagnostics*] ... FLURAM
Fluorescein Angiography [*Cardiology*] (DAVI) ... Fl Ang
Fluorescein Diacetate [*Organic chemistry*] ... FDA
Fluorescein Di(galactopyranoside) [*Organic chemistry*] ... FDG
Fluorescein Fundus Angiogram [*Ophthalmology*] (CPH) ... FFA
Fluorescein Isothiocyanate [*Organic chemistry*] (DAVI) ... FIT
Fluorescein Isothiocyanate [*Organic chemistry*] ... FITC
Fluorescein Isothiocyanate Conjugated Goat Antiserum to Rabbit Gamma Globulin [*Immunology*] ... FITC-gARGG
Fluorescein Mercury Acetate [*Analytical chemistry*] ... FMA
Fluorescein Mono(galactopyranoside) [*Organic chemistry*] ... FMG
Fluorescein Thiourea [*Organic chemistry*] ... FTU
Fluoresceinated Estrogen [*Clinical chemistry*] ... FE
Fluoresceinated Zymosan [*Clinical chemistry*] ... FZ
Fluorescein-Labeled Serum Protein [*Clinical chemistry*] ... FLSP
Fluorescence [*or Fluorescent*] ... FL
Fluorescence ... FR
Fluorescence Assay with Gas Expansion [*Analytical chemistry*] ... FAGE
Fluorescence Capillary Fill Device [*Instrumentation*] ... FCFD
Fluorescence Correlation Spectroscopy ... FCS
Fluorescence Detection [*Spectrometry*] ... FD
Fluorescence Digital Imaging Microscopy ... F-DIM
Fluorescence Energy Transfer [*Physics*] ... FET
Fluorescence Energy Transfer Immunoassay [*Analytical biochemistry*] ... FETI
Fluorescence Excitation Spectrum ... FES
Fluorescence In Situ Hybridization [*Analytical biochemistry*] ... FISH
Fluorescence Indicator Analysis ... FIA
Fluorescence Indicator Panel (IAA) ... FIP
Fluorescence Line-Narrowing Spectroscopy ... FLNS
Fluorescence Loss in Photobleaching [*Analytical biochemistry*] ... FLIP
Fluorescence Microphotolysis ... FM
Fluorescence Pattern Photobleaching Recovery [*for study of surfaces*] ... FPPR
Fluorescence Photobleaching Recovery ... FPR
Fluorescence plus Giemsa [*Cell-staining technique*] ... FPG
Fluorescence Polarization ... FP
Fluorescence Polarization Immunoassay ... FPIA
Fluorescence Recovery [*or Redistribution*] **after Photobleaching** [*Analytical biochemistry*] ... FRAP
Fluorescence Resonance [*or Resonant*] **Energy Transfer** [*Analytical biochemistry*] ... FRET
Fluorescence Spectroscopy ... FS
Fluorescence Thiourea [*Organic chemistry*] (DAVI) ... FTU
Fluorescence-Activated Cell Sorter [*Becton, Dickinson Electronics Laboratory*] [*Instrumentation*] ... FACS
Fluorescence-Activated Display (IAA) ... FLAD
Fluorescence-Detected Circular Dichroism [*Spectroscopy*] ... FDCD
Fluorescence-Detected Magnetic Resonance [*Physics*] ... FDMR
Fluorescence-Imaged Microdeformation [*Analytical chemistry*] ... FIMD
Fluorescence-Line Imager [*Instrumentation*] ... FLI
Fluorescence-Line Narrowed [*Spectrometry*] ... FLN
Fluorescene-Activated Display (PDAA) ... FLAD
Fluorescent [*Freight*] ... FLORSENT
Fluorescent [*or Fluoresces or Fluorescence*] (KSC) ... FLUOR
Fluorescent (ABBR) ... FLUORES
Fluorescent [*Technical drawings*] ... FLUR
Fluorescent Allergosorbent Test [*Medicine*] (CPH) ... FAST
Fluorescent Analog Cytochemistry [*Microscopic technique*] ... FAC
Fluorescent Angiography ... FA
Fluorescent Antibody [*Clinical chemistry*] ... FA
Fluorescent Antibody [*Biochemistry*] (DAVI) ... Fl Ant
Fluorescent Antibody Dark Field [*Clinical chemistry*] (MAE) ... FADF
Fluorescent Antibody Staining Technique [*Clinical chemistry*] ... FAST
Fluorescent Antibody Technique [*Immunology*] (DAVI) ... FAT
Fluorescent Antibody Test [*Clinical medicine*] ... FAT
Fluorescent Antibody-Membrane Antigen [*Immunochemistry*] ... FAMA
Fluorescent Antinuclear Antibody Test [*Serology*] ... FANA
Fluorescent Brightening Agent (PDAA) ... FBA
Fluorescent Discharge Tube [*Panasonic*] ... FDT
Fluorescent Focus Inhibition Test [*Medicine*] (BABM) ... FFIT
Fluorescent Gonorrhea Test [*Medicine*] (DMAA) ... FGT
Fluorescent Immunoassay [*Analytical biochemistry*] ... FIA
Fluorescent In Situ End-Labelling [*Analytical biochemistry*] ... FISEL
Fluorescent Ionic Resin (MCD) ... FIR
Fluorescent Lighting Association (EA) ... FLA
Fluorescent Microscopy [*Biochemistry*] (DAVI) ... FM
Fluorescent Particle ... FP
Fluorescent Penetrant Inspection (MSA) ... FPI
Fluorescent Pseudomonad ... Flp
Fluorescent Pseudomonad spp. ... FP
Fluorescent Rabies Antibody [*Immunology*] ... FRA
Fluorescent Runway Lighting ... FLORL
Fluorescent Tagging of Infiltrator [*Surveillance system*] ... FTI
Fluorescent Target ... FT
Fluorescent Titer Antibody [*Clinical chemistry*] ... FTA
Fluorescent Treponemal Antibody [*Clinical chemistry*] ... FTA
Fluorescent Treponemal Antibody - Absorption [*Test for syphilis*] ... FTA-ABS
Fluorescent Treponemal Antibody Test [*for syphilis*] ... FTAT
Fluorescent Treponemal Antibody-Absorption Syphilis Test [*Medicine*] (MAH) ... FTA-AB
Fluorescent Whitening Agent [*Detergent*] ... FWA
Fluorescent-Antibody Virus Neutralization Test [*Immunology*] ... FAVN
Fluorescently Labelled Bacteria [*Microbiology*] ... FLB
Fluoridation Committee [*Tasmania, Australia*] ... FC
Fluoridation of Public Water Supplies Advisory Committee [*New South Wales, Australia*] ... FPWSAC
Fluoride ... F
Fluoride [*or Fluoridation*] (WDAA) ... FLUOR
Fluoride Ion Electrode (PDAA) ... FIE
Fluoride Number (MAE) ... FN
Fluoride-Resistant Acid Phosphatase [*An enzyme*] ... FRAP
Fluorimetric Determination of Plasma Cortisol [*Clinical chemistry*] ... FDPC
Fluorinated Ethylene-Propylene [*Copolymer*] ... FEP
Fluorinator Off-Gas Recycle Compressor [*Nuclear energy*] (NRCH) ... FORC
Fluorine [*Chemical element*] ... F
Fluorine [*Symbol is F*] [*Chemical element*] (ROG) ... FL
Fluorine Facility [*Nuclear energy*] (NRCH) ... FF
Fluorine One-Stage Orbital Space Truck (KSC) ... FLOSOST
Fluorine, Refrigerant [*and the suffix-On*] [*Trademarked name of a gaseous inert chlorofluorocarbon used in refrigerants, aerosol propellants, and plastic foams*] ... Freon
Fluorine-Liquid Oxygen ... FLOX
Fluoriodocarbon [*Fire extinguishing compound*] ... FIC
Fluorite [*Mineral*] ... FL
Fluorite [*CIPW classification*] [*Geology*] ... fr
Fluoro [*As substituent on nucleoside*] [*Biochemistry*] ... fl
Fluoroactinomycin D [*Antineoplastic drug*] ... FACMD
Fluoroalanine [*Organic chemistry*] ... FA
Fluoroaldehyde Pyridylhydrazone [*Organic chemistry*] ... FAPH
Fluoro-Allergo Sorbent Test [*Biochemistry*] (DAVI) ... FAST
Fluorobenzyl(methylaminopurine) [*Biochemistry*] ... FBM
Fluorocarbon (ERG) ... FC
Fluorocarbon Co. (MHDW) ... FCBN
Fluorocarbon elastomer [*Plastics technology*] ... FPM
Fluorocarbon without Chlorine (ECON) ... HCF
Fluorocarbons [*Organic chemistry*] ... FC
Fluorocarbons Technical Panel [*of Manufacturing Chemists Association*] ... FTP
Fluorochlorocarbon [*Organic chemistry*] ... FCC
Fluorocytosine [*or Flucytosine*] [*Antineoplastic drug*] ... FC
Fluorocytosine Arabinoside [*Also, ara-FC*] [*Antitumor compound*] ... FCA
Fluorodeoxyglucose [*Organic chemistry*] ... FDG
Fluorodeoxyiodoara-C [*An antiviral compound*] ... FIAC
Fluorodeoxyiodoara-U [*An antiviral compound*] ... FIAU
Fluorodeoxythymidine [*Antiviral*] ... FLT
Fluorodeoxyuridine [*Floxuridine*] [*Also, FUDR Antineoplastic drug*] ... FldUrd
Fluorodeoxyuridine [*Floxuridine*] [*Also, FldUrd*] [*Antineoplastic drug*] ... FUDR
Fluorodinitrobenzene [*Also, DFB, DNFB*] [*Organic chemistry*] ... FDNB
Fluoro(dinitro)diethylaniline [*Organic chemistry*] ... FDNDEA
Fluoro(ethyl)arabinosyluracil [*Biochemistry*] ... FEAU
Fluoroethyl(deoxyuridine) [*Biochemistry*] ... FEDU
Fluoro(ethyl)norprogesterone [*Endocrinology*] ... FENP
(Fluoroethyl)spiperone [*Biochemistry*] ... FESP
Fluorogenic Drug Reagent [*Clinical chemistry*] ... FDR
Fluorogenic Enzyme-Linked Immunosorbent Assay [*Biochemistry*] ... FELISA
Fluoroimmunosensor [*Analytical chemistry*] ... FIS
Fluoroiodoarabinosylcytosine ... FIAC
Fluoro-meta-tyrosine [*Organic chemistry*] ... FMT
Fluorometholone [*Anti-inflammatory drug*] ... FML
Fluoro(methyl)arabinosyluracil [*Biochemistry*] ... FMAU
Fluoromethylhistidine [*Biochemistry*] ... FMH
Fluorometric [*or Fluorometry*] ... Fl
Fluorometry (DAVI) ... fluor
Fluoroorotate [*Organic chemistry*] ... FO
Fluoroorotic Acid [*Organic chemistry*] ... FOA
Fluorophenylalanine [*Biochemistry*] ... FPA
Fluoropolymers [*Organic chemistry*] ... FP
(Fluoropropyl)spiperone [*Organic chemistry*] ... FPSP
FluoroScan Imaging Sys [*NASDAQ symbol*] (TTSB) ... FLRO
Fluoroscan Imaging Sys Wrrt [*NASDAQ symbol*] (TTSB) ... FLROW
FluoroScan Imaging Systems, Inc. [*NASDAQ symbol*] (SAG) ... FLRO
FluoroScan Imaging Systems, Inc. [*Associated Press*] (SAG) ... FluroS
FluoroScan Imaging Systems, Inc. [*Associated Press*] (SAG) ... FluroScn
Fluoroscopy ... FLUOR
Fluoroscopy [*Radiology*] (DAVI) ... FLUORO
Fluoroscopy [*Medicine*] (DMAA) ... FX
Fluorospar International Technical Bureau (EAIO) ... FITB
Fluorosulfonylbenzoyl Adenosine [*Biochemistry*] ... FSBA
Fluorothermoplastic ... FTP
Fluorouracil [*Also, FU*] [*Antineoplastic drug*] ... F
Fluorouracil [*Also, F*] [*Antineoplastic drug*] ... FU
Fluorouracil, Adriamycin, Cisplatin [*Antineoplastic drug regimen*] (DAVI) ... FAP
Fluorouracil, Adriamycin, Cyclophosphamide [*Antineoplastic drug regimen*] ... FAC
Fluorouracil, Adriamycin, Cyclophosphamide, Levamisole [*Antineoplastic drug regimen*] ... FAC-LEV

Fluorouracil, Adriamycin, Cyclophosphamide, VP-16 [*Antineoplastic drug regimen*] (DAVI) .... FACVP
Fluorouracil, Adriamycin (Doxorubicin), Mitomycin C, and Streptozotocin [*Antineoplastic drug regimen*] .... FAM-S
Fluorouracil, Adriamycin, MeCCNU [*Semustine*] [*Antineoplastic drug regimen*] .... FAME
Fluorouracil, Adriamycin, Methyl-CCNU [*Antineoplastic drug*] (CDI) .... FAME
Fluorouracil, Adriamycin, Mitomycin [*Antineoplastic drug regimen*] .... FAM
Fluorouracil, Adriamycin, Mitomycin C, MeCCNU [*Semustine*] [*Antineoplastic drug regimen*] .... FAMMe
Fluorouracil, Adriamycin, Mitomycin-C [*Antineoplastic drug*] (CDI) .... FAM
Fluorouracil, Adriamycin, Mitomycin-C [*Antineoplastic drug regimen*] (DAVI) .... FAM-C
Fluorouracil and Adriamycin [*Antineoplastic drug regimen*] (DAVI) .... FA
Fluorouracil, Cisplatin, Etoposide [*Antineoplastic drug*] (CDI) .... FCE
Fluorouracil, Cyclophosphamide, Prednisone [*Antineoplastic drug regimen*] .... FCP
Fluorouracil, Doxorubicin [*Adriamycin*], Mitomycin, Triazinate [*Antineoplastic drug regimen*] .... FAM-T
Fluorouracil, ICRF-159 [*Razoxane*], MeCCNU [*Semustine*] [*Antineoplastic drug regimen*] .... FIME
Fluorouracil, Leucovorin Calcium [*Antineoplastic drug*] (CDI) .... F-CL
Fluorouracil, Methotrexate [*Antineoplastic drug regimen*] .... FUM
Fluorouracil, Methotrexate, Cyclophosphamide, Prednisone [*Antineoplastic drug regimen*] (DAVI) .... FEMED
Fluorouracil, Methyl-CCNU, Vincristine [*Antineoplastic drug*] (CDI) .... FMV
Fluorouracil, Mutamycin, Streotozocin [*Antineoplastic drug*] (CDI) .... FMS
Fluorouracil, Oncovin [*Vincristine*], Adriamycin, Mitomycin C [*Antineoplastic drug regimen*] .... FOAM
Fluorouracil, Oncovin [*Vincristine*], Mitomycin C [*Antineoplastic drug regimen*] .... FOMi
fluorouracil, Oncovin [*Vincristine*], Mitomycin-C [*Antineoplastic drug regimen*] (DAVI) .... FOM
Fluorouracil, Oncovin, Mitomycin-C, Cytoxan, Adriamycin, Platinol [*Antineoplastic drug*] (CDI) .... FOMi/CAP
Fluorouracil, Riboside [*Antineoplastic drug regimen*] (MAE) .... FUR
Fluor's Analytical Scheduling Technique (SAA) .... FAST
Fluothane, Oxygen, and Gas [*Nitrous oxide*] [*Anesthesiology*] (DAVI) .... FOG
Fluphenazine [*Tranquilizer*] .... FPZ
Fluphenazine Decanoate [*Tranquilizer*] (DAVI) .... FPZ-D
Flurazepam [*Organic chemistry*] .... FZ
Flurouracil, Adriamycin, Cyclophosphamide, Streptozocin [*Antineoplastic drug regimen*] (DAVI) .... FACS
Flurried (ABBR) .... FLRD
Flurry [*NWS*] (FAAC) .... FLRY
Flurrying (ABBR) .... FLRG
Flush (MSA) .... FL
Flush Armor Balance Watertight Hatch .... FABWH
Flush Deck Nose Gear Launch (MCD) .... FDNGL
Flush Door Fastener .... FDF
Flush Fitting .... FF
Flush Joint [*Diamond drilling*] .... FJ
Flush Joint [*Technical drawings*] .... FJT
Flush Left [*Graphic arts*] (DGA) .... FL
Flush Left [*Typography*] (WDMC) .... fl
Flush Metal Threshold [*Technical drawings*] .... FMT
Flush Mount .... FLMT
Flush Oiltight Ventilation Hole .... FLOVTH
Flush Oiltight Ventilation Hole (MSA) .... FOVH
Flush Plate Diode (PDAA) .... FPD
Flush Plate Dipole (PDAA) .... FPD
Flush Threshold [*Technical drawings*] .... FT
Flush Type .... FLTP
Flush Valve [*Technical drawings*] .... FV
Flushing Cistern Makers' Association [*British*] (BI) .... FCMA
Flushing Financial [*NASDAQ symbol*] (TTSB) .... FFIC
Flushing Financial Corp. [*NASDAQ symbol*] (SAG) .... FFIC
Flushing Financial Corp. [*Associated Press*] (SAG) .... FlushF
Flushing, NY (ABBR) .... FLS
Flushometer Tank .... FT
Fluster (ABBR) .... FLSTR
Flute .... FL
Flute (ABBR) .... FLUT
Flute Lead (MSA) .... FL
Fluted (MSA) .... FLTD
Fluted (ABBR) .... FLUTD
Fluted Socket .... FLUSOC
Fluted Socket Head .... FLUSOCH
Fluting (ABBR) .... FLUTG
Flutist (ABBR) .... FLST
Flutist (ABBR) .... FLUTST
Flutter (ABBR) .... FLTR
Flutter (MSA) .... FLUT
Flutter (ABBR) .... FLUTR
Flutter and Matrix Algebra System [*Computer science*] .... FAMAS
Flutter and Strength Optimization Program for Lifting Surface Structures (MCD) .... FASTOP
Flutter Exciter Control Unit (MCD) .... FECU
Flutter Mode Control [*Aviation*] .... FMC
Flutter Speed Index [*Aerodynamics*] .... FSI
Flutter Suppression System [*Aviation*] .... FSS
Flutter Wave (MEDA) .... F
Fluttered (ABBR) .... FLUTRD
Flutterer (ABBR) .... FLUTRR
Flutterier (ABBR) .... FLTRIR

Flutteriest (ABBR) .... FLTRIST
Fluttering (ABBR) .... FLTRG
Fluttering (ABBR) .... FLUTRG
Flutteringly (ABBR) .... FLTRGY
Fluttery (ABBR) .... FLTRY
Fluttery (ABBR) .... FLUTRY
Fluvio-Lacustrine Sandstone [*Geology*] .... FL
Flux (ABBR) .... FLUX
Flux [*Symbol*] [*IUPAC*] .... J
Flux Changes per Inch [*Computer science*] .... FCI
Flux Changes per Inch [*Computer science*] .... FCPI
Flux Changes per Millimeter [*Computer science*] (IAA) .... FCMM
Flux Controlled Negative Inductance (IAA) .... FCNI
Flux Cored Arc Welding .... FCAW
Flux Current Loop .... FCL
Flux Delta (IAA) .... FD
Flux Delta/Flux Flow (IEEE) .... FD/FF
Flux Density Versus Magnetizing Force [*Symbol*] (MCD) .... BH
Flux Flow (IAA) .... FF
Flux Lattice Dislocation (PDAA) .... FLD
Flux Logic Element Array .... FLEA
Flux Monitoring System [*Nuclear energy*] (NRCH) .... FMS
Flux Reversals/Inch [*Magnetic storage measure*] (NITA) .... FRI
Flux Reversals Per Second (NITA) .... FRPS
Flux Sensitive Resistor .... FSR
Flux Switch Alternator .... FSA
Flux Transfer Event [*Planetary physics*] .... FTE
Flux Transitions per Inch .... FTPI
Flux Transitions per Millimeter (IAA) .... FTPMM
Flux Valve .... FV
Flux-Asbestos Backing (PDAA) .... FAB
Flux-Cored Welding Wire (PDAA) .... FCW
Flux-Corrected Transport [*Algorithm*] .... FCT
Fluxed (ABBR) .... FLUXD
Fluxgate Magnetometer .... FGM
Fluxgate Magnetometer (MCD) .... FMAG
Fluxing (ABBR) .... FLUXG
Fluxion (ABBR) .... FLUXN
Flux-Line Lattice [*Superconductivity*] [*Physics*] .... FLL
Flxible Historic Association [*Defunct*] (EA) .... FLX
Fly America's Supersonic Transport [*Student group*] .... FASST
Fly Around Saturated Sectors and Terminals [*National Business Aircraft Association*] [*Database*] .... FASST
Fly as Is (MCD) .... FAI
Fly Before You Buy [*Aerospace industry slogan*] .... FBYB
Fly by Wire .... FBW
Fly by Wire System (IAA) .... FBWS
Fly Dressers Guild [*Pinner, Middlesex, England*] (EAIO) .... FDG
Fly Runway Heading [*Aviation*] (FAAC) .... FRH
Fly Wire Screen (ADA) .... FWS
Fly without Fear [*Commercial firm*] (EA) .... FWF
Flyable Engineering Model (KSC) .... FEM
Flyable Orbital Vehicle .... FOV
Flyair [*Spain*] [*FAA designator*] (FAAC) .... FLR
Fly-Along Infrared Program [*Army*] (RDA) .... FAIR
Flyaway Factory .... FAF
Fly-Away Kit (MCD) .... FAK
Flyback Transformer [*Electronics*] (IAA) .... FBT
Flyball Dog .... FD
Flyball Dog Champion .... FDCH
Flyball Dog Excellent .... FDX
Flyball Grand Champion .... FGDCh
Flyball Master .... FM
Flyball Master Champion .... FMCh
Flyball Master Excellent .... FMX
Flyby-Landing Excursion Mode [*Aviation*] .... FLEM
Fly-by-Light .... FBL
Flyer Coil Winder .... FCW
Fly-Fishing Network [*Information service or system*] .... FFN
Flygaktiebolaget Gota Vingar [*Sweden*] [*FAA designator*] (FAAC) .... GVG
Fly-In Echelon [*Navy*] (ANA) .... FIE
Flying [*Officer qualified as both pilot and observer*] [*British*] .... F
Flying (AABC) .... FLG
Flying .... FLY
Flying [*A publication*] (BRI) .... Fly
Flying .... FLY
Flying Activity Category (AFM) .... FAC
Flying Apache Association (EA) .... FAA
Flying Boat [*British military*] (DMA) .... F/Bt
Flying Boat .... FB
Flying Boat [*Russian aircraft symbol*] .... GST
Flying Boat [*Russian aircraft symbol*] .... N
Flying Boat Alighting Area .... FBAA
Flying Boat, Inc. [*ICAO designator*] (FAAC) .... CHK
Flying Boat Repair Depot [*British military*] (DMA) .... FBRD
Flying Buttress (VRA) .... fly butr
Flying Cargo Private Ltd. [*Maldives*] [*ICAO designator*] (FAAC) .... FCM
Flying Chiropractors Association (EA) .... FCA
Flying Colonels [*Delta Air Lines' club for frequent flyers*] (EA) .... FC
Flying Control [*Position*] [*British*] .... FLYCO
Flying Control Officer [*Navy*] .... FCO
Flying Days per Inspection Cycle [*Air Force*] (AFIT) .... FDIC
Flying Dentists Association (EA) .... FDA
Flying Disc Collectors Association (EA) .... FDCA
Flying Division Air Training Command .... FDATC

Flying Dutchman [*Racing dinghy*] ... FD
Flying Duty Period (DA) ... FDP
Flying Eagle and Indian Head Cent Collectors Society (EA) ... FEIHCCS
Flying Enterprise AB [*Sweden*] [*FAA designator*] (FAAC) ... FLY
Flying Evaluation Board ... FEB
Flying Fifteen International (EA) ... FFI
Flying Funeral Directors of America (EA) ... FFDA
Flying Hour ... FH
Flying Hour Program [*Army*] ... FHP
Flying Hours per Inspection Cycle [*Air Force*] (AFIT) ... FHIC
Flying Infantrymen with Naval Knowledge (SAA) ... FINK
Flying Infrared Signature Technology Aircraft [*Air Force*] ... FISTA II
Flying Instructor Course (DA) ... FIC
Flying Instrument School [*British military*] (DMA) ... FIS
Flying Junior [*Boating*] (DICI) ... FJ
Flying Lunar Excursion Experimental Platform [*NASA*] ... FLEEP
Flying Needle [*A publication*] (BRI) ... Fly Needle
Flying Object Report [*Air Force*] ... FLYOBRPT
Flying Officer [*British military*] (DMA) ... Fg Off
Flying Officer [*British*] (DMA) ... Fl/O
Flying Officer [*British*] (DMA) ... Fl Offr
Flying Officer [*British*] ... FO
Flying Optometrists Association of America (EA) ... FOAA
Flying Personnel Research Committee [*British*] (MCD) ... FPRC
Flying Pharmacists of America [*Defunct*] (EA) ... FPA
Flying Physicians Association (EA) ... FPA
Flying Psychologists [*Defunct*] (EA) ... FP
Flying Relay Station ... FRS
Flying Safety Officer [*Air Force*] (AFM) ... FSO
Flying Scholarship [*British military*] (DMA) ... FS
Flying Scot Sailing Association (EA) ... FSSA
Flying Scot Scanner Tube (PDAA) ... FSST
Flying Senior Citizens of United States of America [*Defunct*] (EA) ... FSCUSA
Flying Spot Digitizer ... FSD
Flying Spot Microscope (ADA) ... FSM
Flying Spot Scanner [*Optical character recognition*] ... FSS
Flying Spot Scanner System [*Optical character recognition*] (IAA) ... FSSS
Flying Squadron ... FSq
Flying Status [*Military*] ... fly stat
Flying Status ... FS
Flying Status Code (AFM) ... FSC
Flying Swiss Ambulance Maldives (Pvt) Ltd. [*ICAO designator*] (FAAC) ... SRM
Flying Thread Loom ... FTL
Flying Tiger Line, Inc. [*ICAO designator*] ... FT
Flying Tiger Line, Inc. ... FTL
Flying Tiger Line, Inc. [*Air carrier designation symbol*] ... FTLX
Flying Training Air Force ... FLYTAF
Flying Training Air Force ... FTAF
Flying Training Command [*Air Force*] ... FTC
Flying Training School ... FTS
Flying Training Squadron [*Air Force*] ... FTS
Flying Training Squadron [*Air Force*] ... FTSq
Flying Training Student Management System [*Air Force*] ... FTSMS
Flying Training Wing [*Air Force*] ... FTW
Flying Veterinarians Association (EA) ... FVA
Flying Wheel Casting [*Metallurgy*] ... FWC
Flying-Deck Cruiser [*Navy symbol Obsolete*] ... CF
Flyout ... F/O
Fly-to-Point (NVT) ... FTP
Fly-Under, Fly-Out (MCD) ... FUFO
Flyweight [*Boxing*] ... FLYWT
Flywheel [*Automotive engineering*] ... FLY
Flywheel ... FLYWHL
Flywheel Energy Storage System ... FESS
FM Broadcast Translator [*FCC*] (NTCM) ... FT
FM Broadcasting Station [*ITU designation*] (CET) ... BCF
FM Development Association [*Later, NRBA*] ... FMDA
FM Properties [*NASDAQ symbol*] (TTSB) ... FMPO
FM Properties, Inc. [*Associated Press*] (SAG) ... FM Prop
FM Properties, Inc. [*NASDAQ symbol*] (SAG) ... FMPO
FM Resources Ltd. [*Vancouver Stock Exchange symbol*] ... FML
FMC Corp. [*Formerly, Food Machinery Corp.*] [*Associated Press*] (SAG) ... FMC
FMC Corp. [*Formerly, Food Machinery Corp.*] [*NYSE symbol*] (SPSG) ... FMC
FMC Corp., Chicago, IL [*Library symbol Library of Congress*] (LCLS) ... ICFMC
FMC Corp., Niagara Chemical Division, R and D Library, Middleport, NY [*Library symbol Library of Congress*] (LCLS) ... NMidpF
FMC Corp., Princeton, NJ [*OCLC symbol*] (OCLC) ... FMN
FMC Corp., Princeton, NJ [*Library symbol Library of Congress*] (LCLS) ... NjPF
FMC Corp., Santa Clara, CA [*Library symbol Library of Congress*] (LCLS) ... CStclF
FMC [*Flight Management Computer*] **Fail** (GAVI) ... FAIL
FMC Gold [*NYSE symbol*] (SPSG) ... FGL
FMC Gold Co. [*Associated Press*] (SAG) ... FMC Gd
FMS Financial [*NASDAQ symbol*] (TTSB) ... FMCO
FMS Financial Corp. [*NASDAQ symbol*] (CTT) ... FMCO
FMS Financial Corp. [*Associated Press*] (SAG) ... FMS Fn
FNB Corp. [*NASDAQ symbol*] (NQ) ... FBAN
FNB Corp. [*Associated Press*] (SAG) ... FNB
FNB Corp. [*North Carolina*] [*NASDAQ symbol*] (SAG) ... FNBN
FNB Corp. 7.5% Cv'B' Pfd [*NASDAQ symbol*] (TTSB) ... FBANP
FNB Corp. (Pennsylvania) [*Associated Press*] (SAG) ... FNB PA
FNB Financial Services Corp. [*Associated Press*] (SAG) ... FNB FS
FNB Financial Services Corp. [*NASDAQ symbol*] (SAG) ... FNBF
FNB Financial Svcs [*NASDAQ symbol*] (TTSB) ... FNBF
FNB Rochester Corp. [*NASDAQ symbol*] (SAG) ... FNBR
FNB Rochester Corp. [*Associated Press*] (SAG) ... FNBRo
FNI Fashion, Inc. [*Vancouver Stock Exchange symbol*] ... FNI
Foam (VRA) ... fm
Foam and Condom [*Birth control methods*] (DAVI) ... F & C
Foam in System ... FIS
Foam Inhibiting Conjugate [*Chemical engineering*] ... FIC
Foam Laminators Association (EA) ... FLA
Foam Liquid ... FOLQ
Foam Monitor (DS) ... FM
Foam Stability Index [*Chemistry*] ... FSI
Foam Stability Test ... FST
Foam System [*NFPA pre-fire planning symbol*] (NFPA) ... FO
Foam Tape ... FT
Foam Upholstery Must End [*Royal Society for the Prevention of Accidents*] [*British*] (DI) ... FUME
Foam-Breaking Apparatus with a Rotating Disk [*Chemical engineering*] ... FARD
Foamed-in-Place [*Plastics technology*] ... FIP
Foamex International [*NASDAQ symbol*] (SAG) ... FMXI
Foamex International [*Associated Press*] (SAG) ... Foamex
Foam-Filled Honeycomb Core ... FFHC
Foaming Capacity [*Food technology*] ... FC
Foaming Stability [*Food technology*] ... FS
Foard on Merchant Shipping [*A publication*] (DLA) ... Foard Mer Sh
FOB Airport [*"INCOTERM," International Chamber of Commerce official code*] ... FOA
Focal (MSA) ... FOC
Focal Adhesion Kinase [*An enzyme*] ... FAK
Focal and Segmental Glomerulosclerosis [*Nephrology*] (DAVI) ... FSG
Focal Diameter ... FD
Focal Distance ... FD
Focal Glomerulosclerosis [*Medicine*] ... FGS
Focal Length [*Photography*] ... F
Focal Length [*Photography*] (WDMC) ... f
Focal Length [*Photography*] ... FL
Focal Length [*Photography*] (IAA) ... FLG
Focal Nodular Hyperplasia [*Medicine*] ... FNH
Focal Plane [*Photography*] ... FP
Focal Plane Camera (ROG) ... FPC
Focal Proliferative Glomerulonephritis [*Medicine*] (DMAA) ... FPG
Focal Proliferative Glomerulonephritis [*Medicine*] ... FPGN
Focal Region Investigation ... FRI
Focal Segmental Glomerular Hyalinosis and Sclerosis [*Medicine*] (DMAA) ... FSGHS
Focal Segmental Glomerulosclerosis [*Nephrology*] ... FSGS
Focal Skin Distance [*Radiology*] ... FSD
Focal Vascular Headache [*Cardiology and neurology*] (DAVI) ... FVH
Focal Zone [*Medicine*] (MAE) ... FZ
Focal-Plane Array (MCD) ... FPA
Focal-Plane Crystal Spectrometer ... FPCS
FOCI [*Fisheries-Oceanography Cooperative Investigations*] **Biophysical Platform** (USDC) ... FOCI BP
FOCI [*Fisheries-Oceanography Cooperative Investigations*] **Interactive Network** (USDC) ... FIN
FOCI [*Fisheries-Oceanography Cooperative Investigations*] **Interactive Network** [*Marine science*] (OSRA) ... FIN
Focke-Wulf [*A German fighter plane*] ... FW
Focke-Wulf GmbH [*Germany ICAO aircraft manufacturer identifier*] (ICAO) ... FW
Focolare Movement (EA) ... FM
Focsani [*Romania*] [*Seismograph station code, US Geological Survey*] (SEIS) ... FOC
Focus ... FCS
Focus (KSC) ... FOC
Focus, Aperture, Shutter, Tachometer [*Cinematography*] (NTCM) ... FAST
Focus Broadcast Satellite Corporation (NITA) ... FBS
Focus Control Block [*Computer science*] ... FCB
Focus Enhancements [*NASDAQ symbol*] (TTSB) ... FCSE
Focus Enhancements, Inc. [*NASDAQ symbol*] (SAG) ... FCSE
Focus Enhancements, Inc. [*Associated Press*] (SAG) ... Focus
Focus Enhancements, Inc. [*Associated Press*] (SAG) ... FocusEn
Focus Enhancements Wrrt [*NASDAQ symbol*] (TTSB) ... FCSEW
Focus Film Distance [*Radiology*] ... FFD
Focus National Mortgage Corp. [*Toronto Stock Exchange symbol*] ... FNC
Focus of Contraction [*Motion perception*] ... FOC
Focus of Expansion [*Motion perception*] ... FOE
Focus on Arms Information and Reassurance ... FAIR
Focus on Micronesia Coalition [*Later, MC*] (EA) ... FMC
Focus on the Family [*An association*] (EA) ... FF
Focus, Organize, Understand, Rehearse, and Simplify [*Business Term*] ... FOURS
Focus Policy Study Group [*British*] ... FPSG
Focus Projection and Scanning ... FPS
Focused Appendix Computed Tomography [*Medicine*] ... FACT
Focused Information Network (EERA) ... FIN
Focused Ion Beam [*Photonics*] ... FIB
Focused LASER Lithographic System ... FLLS
Focused Ultrasonic Surgery ... FUS
Focused What If [*Method for hazard analysis*] ... FWI
Focus-Forming Unit [*Medical/biochemical research*] ... FFU
Focus-Inducing Cell [*Population*] [*Immunochemistry*] ... FIC
Focusing ... FCSG
Focusing Array Study ... FAS
Focusing Mount [*Photography*] ... FM
Foderation der Europaischen Parkettindustrieverbande [*European Federation of the Parquet Floor Industry Associations*] [*EC*] (ECED) ... FEP
Foederalistische Union [*Federal Union*] [*Germany Political party*] (PPE) ... FU
Foederalistische Union Europaeischer Volksgruppen [*Federal Union of European Nationalities*] ... FUEV

Foelix. Droit International Prive [*A publication*] (DLA) ... Foel Dr Int
Foeniculum [*Fennel*] [*Pharmacy*] (ROG) ... FOENIC
Foeroe Islands (BARN) ... Faer
Fog [*Meteorology*] ... F
Fog ... FG
Fog Bell [*Navigation charts*] ... FB
Fog Detector Light [*Nautical charts*] ... Fog Det Lt
Fog Diaphone [*Navigation charts*] ... FD
Fog Factor ... FF
Fog Foam ... FOFM
Fog Gong [*Navigation charts*] ... FG
Fog Gun [*Navigation charts*] ... FG
Fog Horn [*Navigation charts*] ... FH
Fog, Intense, Dispersal Of [*NASA*] ... FIDO
FOG [*First Osborne Group*] **International Computer Users Group** (EA) ... FOG
Fog Investigation and Dispersal Operation [*System used on airfield landing strips*] [*World War II*] ... FIDO
Fog Nautophone [*Navigation charts*] ... FN
Fog Oil Smoke Generator ... FOSGEN
Fog Signal [*Station*] [*Maps and charts*] ... FS
Fog Signal Station [*Nautical charts*] ... FOGSIG
Fog Signal Station [*Coast Guard*] ... FSS
Fog Siren [*Navigation charts*] ... FS
Fog Trumpet [*Navigation charts*] ... FT
Fog Whistle [*Navigation charts*] ... FW
Foggia [*Italy*] [*Airport symbol*] (AD) ... FOG
Foggia [*Italy ICAO location identifier*] (ICLI) ... LIBF
Fogg's Reports [*32-35 New Hampshire*] [*A publication*] (DLA) ... Fogg
Foggy (MSA) ... FGY
Foggy River Boys Fan Club (EA) ... FRBFC
Fogo Public Library, Fogo, NF, Canada [*Library symbol Library of Congress*] (LCLS) ... CaNfF
Fogo Public Library, Newfoundland [*Library symbol National Library of Canada*] (NLC) ... NFF
FOI [*Freedom of Information*] **Digest** [*A publication*] (DLA) ... FOI Dig
Foika Systems Services, Inc., Moscow, PA [*Library symbol*] [*Library of Congress*] (LCLS) ... FoiS
Foil [*Dentistry*] ... F
Foil Research Supercavitating Hydrofoil ... FRESH
Foil Wound Coil ... FWC
Foilborne Water Line ... FWL
Foilmark, Inc. [*NASDAQ symbol*] (SAG) ... FLMK
Foilmark, Inc. [*Associated Press*] (SAG) ... Foilmark
Fokes Sentence Builder [*Speech and language therapy*] (DAVI) ... FBS
Fokker 50 [*Airplane code*] ... F50
Fokker Flight Operations [*Netherlands ICAO designator*] (FAAC) ... FOP
Fokker-Planck Equation [*Mathematics*] ... FP
Fokker-VFW BV [*Netherlands ICAO aircraft manufacturer identifier*] (ICAO) ... FK
Folatebinding Protein [*Medicine*] (DMAA) ... FABP
Folate-Binding Protein [*Biochemistry*] ... FBP
Fold ... FD
Foldable Elastic Tube [*Satellite hinge*] ... FET
Foldback [*Genetics*] ... FB
Folded and Gathered Sheets [*Printing*] ... F & G
Folded And Gathered Sheets [*Publishing*] (WDMC) ... f & g's
Folded Dipole Antenna ... FDA
Folded File ... FF
Folded Flat [*Freight*] ... FF
Folded Flat or Nested [*Freight*] ... FFN
Folded Flow Reactor ... FFR
Folded Other Than Flat [*Freight*] ... FOTF
Folded Sheets Mesoporous-Material [*Inorganic chemistry*] ... FSM
Folded Sideband Modulation ... FSM
Folded Triangular Dipole [*Electronics*] (OA) ... FTD
Folded Triangular Monopole [*Electronics*] (OA) ... FTM
Folded, Trimmed, Packed [*Books*] ... FTP
Folded-Tape Meander Line (IAA) ... FTML
Folding ... FG
Folding (MSA) ... FLDG
Folding Boat Equipment [*British military*] (DMA) ... FBE
Folding Boxboard (DGA) ... FB
Folding Boxboard (DGA) ... FBB
Folding Chair Rental Association of America [*Later, RSA*] ... FCRAA
Folding Fin (SAA) ... FF
Folding Fin Aircraft Rocket ... FFAR
Folding Float Bridge [*Military*] (RDA) ... FFB
Folding Light Acoustic Sonar for Helicopters (DOMA) ... FLASH
Folding Map [*Publishing*] ... FLDGM
Folding Paper Box Association (DGA) ... FPBA
Folding Paper Box Association of America [*Later, PPC*] (EA) ... FPBAA
Folding Platform Mechanism (MCD) ... FPM
Folding Pocket Kodak [*Photography*] (ROG) ... FPK
Foldout (MSA) ... FO
Foley, AL [*AM radio station call letters*] ... WHEP
Foley Catheter [*Urology*] ... FC
Foley Catheter [*Urology*] ... Fcath
Foley Community Library, Foley, MN [*Library symbol*] [*Library of Congress*] (LCLS) ... MnFo
Foley Elementary School, Foley, MN [*Library symbol*] [*Library of Congress*] (LCLS) ... MnFoE
Foley High School, Foley, MN [*Library symbol*] [*Library of Congress*] (LCLS) ... MnFoH
Foleyet Community Library, Ontario [*Library symbol National Library of Canada*] (NLC) ... OFC
Foley's English Poor Law Cases [*1556-1730*] [*A publication*] (DLA) ... Fol
Foley's English Poor Law Cases [*1556-1730*] [*A publication*] (DLA) ... Fol PL Cas
Foley's English Poor Law Cases [*1556-1730*] [*A publication*] (DLA) ... Fol PLC
Folge [*Series*] [*Publishing*] [*German*] ... F
Folgende [*And the Following Pages, Verses, etc.*] [*German*] (ROG) ... FF
Folger Shakespeare Library, Washington, DC [*Library symbol Library of Congress*] (LCLS) ... DFo
Folia [*Leaves*] ... FOL
Foliage Penetration [*RADAR*] (MCD) ... FOLPEN
Foliage Penetration [*RADAR*] (MCD) ... FOPEN
Foliage Penetration RADAR ... FPR
Foliage Penetration System [*Military*] ... FOLPES
Foliage-Gleaning Bat [*Zoology*] ... FGB
Folic Acid [*Also, PGA, PteGlu*] [*Biochemistry*] ... FA
Folicular Basal Lamina [*Medicine*] ... FBL
Foligno [*Italy*] [*Seismograph station code, US Geological Survey Closed*] (SEIS) ... FOL
Folin and Wu's Method [*Medicine*] (MAE) ... FW
Folin Phenol Reagent [*For protein assay*] ... FPR
Folin-Ciocalteau [*Clinical chemistry*] ... FC
Folin-Denis [*Analytical chemistry*] ... FD
Folin-Wu Reaction [*Medicine*] (DMAA) ... FW
Folin-Wu Reaction [*Medicine*] (DMAA) ... FWR
Folio [*Book 30 centimeters and over in height*] ... F
Folio [*On the Following Page*] [*Latin*] ... f
Folio ... FO
Folio ... FOL
Folio Recto [*Right-Hand Page*] [*Latin*] ... FR
Folio Recto [*Right-hand page number*] [*Right-hand page*] [*Publishing*] (WDMC) ... fr
Folio Society [*British*] (EAIO) ... FS
Folio Verso [*On the Back of the Page*] [*Latin*] ... FV
Folio Verso [*The left-hand page number*] [*The left-hand page*] [*Publishing*] (WDMC) ... fv
Folios [*Leaves*] ... FF
Folium [*or Foliorum*] [*Leaf (or Leaves)*] [*Pharmacy*] (ROG) ... FOL
Folk Artists Bibliographical Index [*A publication*] ... FABI
Folk Arts for Communication and Education ... FACE
Folk Education Association of America (EA) ... FEAA
Folk Heritage Institute (EA) ... FHI
Folk Lore Council of Australia ... FLCA
Folk Music Society of Ireland (EAIO) ... FMSI
Folkard's Edition of Starkie on Slander and Libel [*A publication*] (DLA) ... Folk St Sl
Folkard's Loans and Pledges [*2nd ed.*] [*1876*] [*A publication*] (DLA) ... Folk Pl
Folkebibliotekernes Automation System [*Denmark*] [*Public libraries automation system*] (NITA) ... FAUST
Folkepartiets Ungdomsforbund [*Liberal Youth*] [*Political party*] (EAIO) ... FPU
Folkestone-Boulogne Ferries [*English Channel ferry-boat service*] [*British*] (ECON) ... FBF
Folklore [*A publication*] (BRI) ... Folkl
Folklore Americas [*A publication*] ... FA
Folklore Canada International [*An association*] (EAIO) ... FCI
Folklore of American Holidays [*A publication*] ... FAH
Folklore of World Holidays [*A publication*] ... FWH
Folklore Studies Association of Canada ... FCAC
Folk-School Association of America [*Later, FEAA*] (EA) ... FSAA
Folkston, GA [*FM radio station call letters*] ... WOKF
Folkstone Resources Ltd. [*Vancouver Stock Exchange symbol*] ... FRK
Folkuniversitetet ... FU
Folkways (Ethnic Folkways Library) [*Record label*] ... EFL
Follett Library Book Co., Crystal Lake, IL [*Library symbol*] [*Library of Congress*] (LCLS) ... ICrlF
Follett Software Co., McHenry, IL [*Library symbol*] [*Library of Congress*] (LCLS) ... IMchF
Follett, TX [*Location identifier FAA*] (FAAL) ... FTE
Follicle Development Index [*Gynecology*] ... FDI
Follicle Regulatory Protein [*Endocrinology*] ... FRP
Follicle-Associated Epithelium [*Immunology*] ... FAE
Follicle-Stimulating Hormone [*Endocrinology*] ... FSH
Follicle-Stimulating Hormone and Luteinizing Hormone-Releasing Hormone [*Endocrinology*] (MAE) ... FSH/LH-RH
Follicle-Stimulating Hormone Beta Subunit [*Endocrinology*] ... FSHB
Follicle-Stimulating Hormone Receptor Binding Inhibitor [*Endocrinology*] ... FSHRBI
Follicle-Stimulating Hormone Releasing Factor [*Also, FSH-RF, FSH-RH*] [*Endocrinology*] ... FRF
Follicle-Stimulating Hormone Releasing Factor [*Also, FRF, FSH-RH*] [*Endocrinology*] ... FSH-RF
Follicle-Stimulating Hormone Releasing Hormone [*Also, FRF, FSH-RF*] [*Endocrinology*] ... FSH-RH
Follicle-Stimulating Hormone-Luteinizing Hormone [*Endocrinology*] (DAVI) ... FSH-LH
Follicle-Stimulating Hormone-Releasing Hormone [*Endocrinology*] (DAVI) ... FRH
Follicular Center Cell [*Cytology*] ... FCC
Follicular Dendritic Cell ... FDC
Follicular Diameter [*Medicine*] (DMAA) ... FD
Follicular Lymphoma [*Oncology*] ... FL
Follicular Lymphosarcoma [*Oncology*] ... FLSA
Follicular-Variant-Translocation [*Medicine*] (DMAA) ... FVT
Follow ... FLW
Follow (AFM) ... FOL
Follow Copy [*Printing*] ... FC
Follow Copy [*Typesetting*] [*Also, Folo Copy*] (WDMC) ... fc
Follow Sender [*Telecommunications*] (TEL) ... FS
Follow Shot [*Photography*] (NTCM) ... FS

Follow Through .... F-T
Follow Up (WDAA) .... F/UP
Following [*Pages*] [*Also, FF*] (MUGU) .... F
Following (WDMC) .... f
Following [*Copyediting*] (WDMC) .... ff
Following [*Pages*] [*Also, F*] .... FF
Following .... FLG
Following .... FLWG
Following [*Business term*] .... FOL
Following (ROG) .... FOLG
Following .... FOLL
Following (ROG) .... FOLLG
Following Amendment Authorized Effective (FAAC) ..... FAMAE
Following Individual Reported This Station [*Army*] (AABC) ..... FIRTS
Following Information Is Submitted [*Army*] (AABC) .... FOLIS
Following Items Not Available .... FINA
Following Items Not Available .... FOLNOAVAL
Following Landing Numbers [*Shipping*] .... FLN
Following Named Airmen .... FNA
Following Named Enlisted Member Organization Indicated ..... FNEORID
Following Named Enlisted Members Are Relieved Assignment ..... FNERAS
Following Named Enlisted Personnel .... FNE
Following Named Individuals .... FNI
Following Named Officers .... FNO
Following Named Officers and Airmen .... FNOA
Follow-On Contract .... FOC
Follow-On Development Test and Evaluation (MCD) ..... FD & E
Follow-on Early Warning System [*Satellite*] (DOMA) ..... FEWS
Follow-On Evaluation .... FOE
Follow-On Evaluation Test .... FOET
Follow-On Forces Attack .... FOFA
Follow-On In-Plant [*Test*] (MCD) .... FOIP
Follow-On Interceptor [*Military*] .... FOI
Follow-On Operational Test .... FOOT
Follow-On Operational Test (AFM) .... FOT
Follow-On Operational Test and Evaluation .... FOTE
Follow-On Parts Production (NASA) .... FOPP
Follow-On Production (NASA) .... FOP
Follow-On Program Development Plan (SAA) .... FPDP
Follow-On Soviet Tank [*In FST-1, model name of a Russian "supertank" having improved armor and a 135-mm gun*] [*Introduced in the late 1980's*] .... FST
Follow-On Spare Parts Selection List (MCD) .... FOSPSL
Follow-On Spares (AFM) .... FOS
Follow-On Spares Support List (AFIT) .... FOSSL
Follow-On Tactical Reconnaissance System [*Air Force*] (DOMA) ..... FOTRS
Follow-On Test .... FT
Follow-On Test and Evaluation (MCD) .... FOT & E
Follow-On Test and Evaluation (MCD) .... FT & E
Follow-On to Lance [*Army*] .... FOTL
Follow-On Wild Weasel [*Aircraft*] [*Air Force*] (DOMA) ..... FWW
Follows (NVT) .... FOLS
Follow-the-Leader Feedback [*Circuit theory*] (IEEE) ..... FLF
Follow-Up .... F
Follow-Up .... FLWP
Follow-Up .... FOLUP
Follow-Up .... FU
Follow-Up Alarm System .... FAS
Follow-Up Amplifier .... FUA
Follow-up and Evaluation Section (EERA) .... FUES
Follow-Up Error Alarm .... FEA
Follow-Up Note [*Medical records*] (DAVI) .... FUN
Follow-Up on Supply Action Taken .... FUPOSAT
Follow-Up Output (NASA) .... FUO
Follow-Up Report .... FUR
Follow-Up Reporting System (MCD) .... FURS
Folly Beach, SC [*FM radio station call letters*] .... WYBB
Folsom, CA [*AM radio station call letters*] .... KIOQ
Folsom, LA [*FM radio station call letters*] .... KGZC
Folsom, LA [*FM radio station call letters*] (RBYB) ..... WYLK-FM
Folsom, PA [*FM radio station call letters*] .... WRSD
Fomant Synthesis [*Speech synthesis*] (NITA) .... FS
Fomentation [*Pharmacology*] (DAVI) .... fo
Fomento Industrial do Piani, SA .... FOMINPI
Fon [*MARC language code Library of Congress*] (LCCP) ..... fon
Fonar Corp. [*Associated Press*] (SAG) .... Fonar
Fonar Corp. [*NASDAQ symbol*] (NQ) .... FONR
Fonblanque on Medical Jurisprudence [*A publication*] (DLA) ..... Fonbl
Fonblanque on Medical Jurisprudence [*A publication*] (DLA) ..... Fonbl Med Jur
Fonblanque on Medical Jurisprudence [*A publication*] (DLA) ..... Fonbl NR
Fonblanque's Bankruptcy Cases [*1849-52*] [*A publication*] (DLA) ..... FBC
Fonblanque's Bankruptcy Cases [*1849-52*] [*A publication*] (DLA) ..... Fon BC
Fonblanque's Bankruptcy Cases (or New Reports) [*1849-52*] [*A publication*] (DLA) ..... Fonbl R
Fonblanque's English Cases in Chancery [*A publication*] (DLA) ..... Fonbl NR
Fonblanque's Equity [*England*] [*A publication*] (DLA) ..... Fonb Eq
Fonblanque's Equity [*England*] [*A publication*] (DLA) ..... Fonbl
Fonblanque's Equity [*England*] [*A publication*] (DLA) ..... Fonbl (Eng)
Fonblanque's Equity [*England*] [*A publication*] (DLA) ..... Fonbl Eq (Eng)
Fonblanque's Equity [*England*] [*A publication*] (DLA) ..... Fonbl NR
Fonblanque's New Reports, English Bankruptcy [*1849-52*] [*A publication*] (DLA) ..... Fonbl
Fonblanque's New Reports, English Bankruptcy [*1849-52*] [*A publication*] (DLA) ..... Fonbl NR
Fonblanque's Rights and Wrongs [*1860*] [*A publication*] (DLA) ..... Fonbl R & Wr

Fonblanque's Treatise of Equity [*A publication*] (DLA) ..... Tr Eq
Fond du Lac Ojibway School, Cloquet, MN [*Library symbol*] [*Library of Congress*] (LCLS) ..... MnClOS
Fond Du Lac Public Library, Fond Du Lac, WI [*Library symbol Library of Congress*] (LCLS) ..... WFon
Fond Du Lac, WI [*Location identifier FAA*] (FAAL) .... FLD
Fond du Lac, WI [*AM radio station call letters*] .... KFIZ
Fond du Lac, WI [*FM radio station call letters*] (RBYB) ..... KFIZ-FM
Fond du Lac, WI [*Television station call letters*] .... WMMF
Fonda, Johnstown & Gloversville Railroad Co. [*AAR code*] ..... FJG
Fonda Public Library, Fonda, IA [*Library symbol Library of Congress*] (LCLS) ..... IaFon
Fonda Times, Fonda, IA [*Library symbol Library of Congress*] (LCLS) ..... IaFonT
Fondation Aga Khan [*Aga Khan Foundation*] (EAIO) ..... FAK
Fondation Canadienne de la Fibrose Kystique [*Canadian Cystic Fibrosis Foundation*] ..... FCFK
Fondation Canadienne d'Orientation et de Consultation (AC) ..... FCOG
Fondation Canadienne pour la Verification Integree (AC) ..... FCVI
Fondation Canadienne sur l'Alcohol et la Dependance aux Drogues [*Canadian Foundation on Alcohol and Drug Dependencies - CFADD*] ..... FCADD
Fondation de Bellerive [*Bellerive Foundation - BF*] (EAIO) ..... FB
Fondation de la Sante et des Droits de l'Homme [*Foundation for Health and Human Rights*] (EA) ..... FSDH
Fondation de l'Enseignement Superieur en Afrique Centrale ..... FESAC
Fondation de Recherches sur les Blessures de la Route au Canada (EAIO) ..... FRBRC
Fondation Denis de Rougemont pour l'Europe [*Switzerland*] (EAIO) ..... FDRE
Fondation d'Etudes du Canada [*Canada Studies Foundation - CSF*] ..... FEC
Fondation Europeenne de la Culture [*European Cultural Foundation - ECF*] [*Netherlands*] ..... FEC
Fondation Europeenne pour le Management [*European Foundation for Management Development*] [*Belgium*] (EAIO) ..... FEM
Fondation Europeenne pour l'Economie .... FEE
Fondation Europeenne "Pro Venetia Viva" [*European Foundation "Pro Venetia Viva"*] (EAIO) ..... PVV
Fondation Internationale Jacques Brel [*International Jacques Brel Foundation - IJBF*] (EA) ..... FIJB
Fondation Internationale Lelio Basso pour le Droit et la Liberation des Peuples [*International Lelio Basso Foundation for the Rights and Liberation of Peoples - ILBFRLP*] (EA) ..... FILBDLP
Fondation Internationale Penale et Penitentiaire [*International Penal and Penitentiary Foundation - IPPF*] [*Bonn, Federal Republic of Germany*] (EAIO) ..... FIPP
Fondation Internationale pour la Sauvegarde du Gibier [*International Foundation for the Conservation of Game*] (EAIO) ..... IGF
Fondation Internationale pour la Science [*International Foundation for Science - IFS*] (EAIO) ..... FIS
Fondation Internationale pour le Saumon de l'Atlantique [*International Atlantic Salmon Foundation*] [*Canada*] ..... FISA
Fondation Internationale pour l'Enseignement du Droit des Affaires [*Canada*] ..... FIEDA
Fondation Internationale pour un Autre Developpement [*International Foundation for Development Alternatives - IFDA*] [*Nyon, Switzerland*] (EAIO) ..... FIPAD
Fondation pour l'Assistance Mutuelle en Afrique au Sud du Sahara [*Foundation for Mutual Assistance in Africa South of the Sahara*] ..... FAMA
Fondation pour le Developpement de la Psychotherapie Medicale [*Foundation for t he Development of Medical Psychotherapy*] [*Switzerland*] (EAIO) ..... FDPM
Fondation pour le Progres de l'Homme [*France*] (EERA) ..... FPH
Fondation Vietnam-Canada [*Vietnam-Canada Foundation*] ..... FVNC
Fondest Love and Kisses [*Correspondence*] .... FLAK
Fondo Colombiano de Investigaciones Cientificas y Proyectos Especiales [*Colombian Fund for Scientific Research and Special Projects*] [*Colombia*] [*Information service or system*] (IID) ..... COLCIENCIAS
Fondo de Poblacion de las Naciones Unidas [*United Nations Population Fund*] [*Spanish*] (DUND) ..... FNUAP
Fondo Especial de Asistencia para el Desarrollo (de la OEA) [*Organizacion de Estados Americanos*] [*Washington, DC*] ..... FEAD
Fondo Financiero para el Desarrollo de la Cuenca del Plata [*Financial Fund for the Development of the Plata Basin*] (EAIO) ..... FONPLATA
Fondo Internacional de Desarrollo Agricola [*International Fund for Agricultural Development*] [*Spanish United Nations*] (DUND) ..... FIDA
Fondo Monetario Internacional [*International Monetary Fund*] [*Spanish United Nations*] (DUND) ..... FMI
Fonds Africain de Developpement [*African Development Fund*] ..... FAD
Fonds d'Action et d'Education Juridiques pour les Femmes [*Women's Legal Education and Action Fund - LEAF*] [*Canada*] ..... FAEJ
Fonds d'Activites Internationales [*International Activities Fund*] [*Canadian Labour Congress*] ..... FAI
Fonds de Recherches et de Developpement Forestier [*Forest Research and Development Foundation*] [*Canada*] ..... FRDF
Fonds des Nations Unies pour la Population [*United Nations Population Fund*] [*French*] (DUND) ..... FNUAP
Fonds des Nations Unies pour l'Enfance [*United Nations Children's Fund*] (EAIO) ..... FNUE
Fonds des Nations Unies pour les Refugies [*United Nations Funds for Refugees*] ..... FNUR
Fonds d'Investissement pour le Developpement Economique et Social [*Investment Fund for Economic and Social Development*] [*United Nations*] (AF) ..... FIDES
Fonds European d'Orientation et de Garantie Agriculturel [*European Agricultural Guidance and Guarantee Fund*] ..... FEOGA
Fonds Europeen de Cooperation Monetaire [*European Monetary Cooperation Fund*] ..... FECOM

Fonds Europeen de Developpement pour les Pays et Territoires d'Outre-Mer [*European Development Fund for Overseas Countries and Territories*] ... FEDOM
Fonds Europeen de Developpement Regional [*European Regional Development Fund - ERDF*] [*Belgium*] (EAIO) ... FEDER
Fonds Europeen d'Orientation et de Garantie Agricole [*Also known as EAGGF*] ... FEOGA
Fonds International de Developpement Agricole [*International Fund for Agricultural Development*] [*French United Nations*] (DUND) ... FIDA
Fonds International de Secours a l'Enfance [*Also known as Fonds des Nations Unies pour l'Enfance*] [*Canada*] ... FISE
Fonds International d'Indemnisation pour les Dommages dus a la Pollution par lesHydrocarbures [*International Oil Pollution Compensation Fund*] (EAIO) ... FIPOL
Fonds Internationale de Cooperation Universitaire [*International Fund for University Cooperation*] [*Canada*] (EAIO) ... FICU
Fonds Monetaire Andin [*Andean Monetary Fund*] (PDAA) ... FMA
Fonds Monetaire International [*International Monetary Fund*] ... FMI
Fonds National de Developpement [*Mauritania*] (EY) ... FND
Fonds Special pour la Jeunesse de l'UNESCO [*UNESCO Special Fund for Youth*] (EAIO) ... FPJU
Fonds un Pour Cent pour le Developpement [*One Percent for Development Fund*] (EAIO) ... FUPCD
Fondulac District Library, East Peoria, IL [*Library symbol Library of Congress*] (LCLS) ... IEp
Fondulac Public Library District, East Peoria, IL [*OCLC symbol*] (OCLC) ... IDY
Fonetic English [*for spelling words the way they sound*] ... FE
Fonetic English Spelling Association ... FESA
Fonit [*Record label*] [*Italy*] ... Fnt
Fonnafly AS [*Norway ICAO designator*] (FAAC) ... NOF
Fonni [*Italy ICAO location identifier*] (ICLI) ... LIEN
Fonodan [*Record label*] [*Denmark*] ... Fdn
Font ... F
Font (DNAB) ... FO
Font Change [*Computer science*] (BUR) ... FC
Font Change [*Typesetting*] (WDMC) ... fc
Font Graphics Accelerator [*Toshiba*] ... FGA
Font Object Content Architecture (CDE) ... FOCA
Fontana Corrosion Center [*Ohio State University*] [*Research center*] (RCD) ... FCC
Fontana Public Library, Fontana, WI [*Library symbol Library of Congress*] (LCLS) ... WFont
Fontana Regional Library, Bryson City, NC [*Library symbol Library of Congress*] (LCLS) ... NcBcF
Fontanelle Observer, Anita, IA [*Library symbol Library of Congress*] (LCLS) ... IaAniF
Fontanelle Observer, Fontanelle, IA [*Library symbol Library of Congress*] (LCLS) ... IaFontO
Fontbonne College, St. Louis, MO [*OCLC symbol*] (OCLC) ... MOF
Fontbonne College, St. Louis, MO [*Library symbol Library of Congress*] (LCLS) ... MoSF
Fonte Boa [*Brazil*] [*Airport symbol*] (AD) ... FBA
Fontenay-Le-Conte [*France ICAO location identifier*] (ICLI) ... LFFK
Fontenay-Tresigny [*France ICAO location identifier*] (ICLI) ... LFPQ
Fontes Iuris Romani ante Iustiniani [*A publication*] (OCD) ... FIRA
Fontes Iuris Romani Antiqui [*A publication*] (OCD) ... Font
Food ... FD
Food Additive ... FA
Food Additive Campaign Team [*British*] ... FACT
Food Additive Petition ... FAP
Food Additive Suppliers and Traders [*Database from Food Association*] [*British*] (NITA) ... FAST
Food Additives and Contaminants Committee [*British*] ... FACC
Food Advisory Committee [*New South Wales, Australia*] ... FAC
Food, Agriculture, and Nutrition Inventory [*Department of Agriculture*] [*Discontinued*] ... FANI
Food, Agriculture, Conservation and Trade Act of 1990 ... FACTA
Food Aid Committee (EAIO) ... FAC
Food and Agricultural Legislation [*A publication*] ... FAL
Food and Agricultural Organization of the United Nations, North American Regional Office, Washington, DC [*Library symbol Library of Congress*] (LCLS) ... DFAO
Food and Agricultural Policy Research Institute [*Iowa State University*] (RCD) ... FAPRI
Food and Agricultural Policy Simulator ... FAPSIM
Food and Agriculture (NATG) ... FA
Food and Agriculture Branch [*US Military Government, Germany*] ... F & ABR
Food and Agriculture Organization [*United Nations Italy Information service or system*] (IID) ... FAO
Food and Agriculture Organization Agricultural Information Storage and RetrievalSystem [*Operated by FAO*] (NITA) ... FAIRS
Food and Agriculture Organization Geographic Information System [*United Nations*] (DUND) ... FAOGIS
Food and Agriculture Organization Statistical Division Information System (GFGA) ... AGROSTAT
Food and Agriculture Planning Committee [*NATO*] (NATG) ... FAPC
Food and Allied Service Trades Department [*of AFL-CIO*] (EA) ... FAST
Food and Beverage ... F & B
Food and Beverage Importers' Association [*Australia*] ... FBIA
Food and Beverage Managers Association [*British*] (DBA) ... FBMA
Food and Beverage Trades Department [*of AFL-CIO*] (EA) ... FBTD
Food and Container Institute ... F & CI
Food and Disarmament International [*Belgium*] (EAIO) ... FDI
Food and Drink Federation [*England and Belgium*] ... FDF
Food and Drink Industries Council [*British*] ... FDIC
Food and Drug Administration [*Rockville, MD*] [*Department of Health and Human Services*] ... FDA
Food and Drug Administration Medical Library, Rockville, MD [*OCLC symbol*] (OCLC) ... DDF
Food and Drug Administration, Notices of Judgment [*A publication*] (DLA) ... DDNJ FDC
Food and Drug Administration, Notices of Judgment: Cosmetics [*A publication*] (DLA) ... CNJFDC
Food and Drug Administration, Office of Executive Director of Regional Operations (NRCH) ... FDA-EDRO
Food and Drug Directorate [*Canada*] ... FDD
Food and Drug Law Institute ... FDLI
Food and Energy Council (EA) ... FEC
Food and Feed Grain Institute [*Kansas State University*] [*Research center*] (RCD) ... FFGI
Food and Fertilizer Technology Center for the Asian and Pacific Region (EAIO) ... FFTC/ASPAC
Food and Libations Association of Virginia (SRA) ... FLAVA
Food and Nutrition Board (EA) ... FNB
Food and Nutrition Information Center [*Department of Agriculture*] (IID) ... FNIC
Food and Nutrition Research and Engineering Board [*Military*] (RDA) ... FNREB
Food and Nutrition Science Alliance ... FANSA
Food and Nutrition Service [*Department of Agriculture*] ... FNS
Food and Nutrition Service Regional Office [*Department of Agriculture*] (GFGA) ... FNSRO
Food and Nutritional System [*Military*] (AABC) ... FANS
Food and Service Workers of Canada ... FASWOC
Food Animal Concerns Trust (EA) ... FACT
Food Awareness Training ... FAT
Food Brokers Ltd. [*British*] ... FB
Food Brokers Ltd. [*Canada ICAO designator*] (FAAC) ... FBL
Food Business Network [*Information service or system*] (IID) ... FBN
Food Casings Association [*British*] (DBA) ... FCA
Food Chain Research Group [*University of California*] [*Research center*] (RCD) ... FCRG
Food Chemicals Codex [*National Academy of Sciences*] [*A publication*] ... FCC
Food, Clothing, Maintenance [*Red Cross*] ... FCM
Food Composition Table ... FCT
Food Containment System ... FCS
Food Control Diet ... FCD
Food Controller [*British World War II*] ... FC
Food Court Enter Wrrt 'A' [*NASDAQ symbol*] (TTSB) ... FCENW
Food Court Enter Wrrt 'B' [*NASDAQ symbol*] (TTSB) ... FCENZ
Food Court Entertain Unit [*NASDAQ symbol*] (TTSB) ... FCENU
Food Court Entertainment Network, Inc. [*NASDAQ symbol*] (SAG) ... FCENA
Food Court Entertainment Network, Inc. [*Associated Press*] (SAG) ... FdCrtE
Food Court Entertainment Network, Inc. [*Associated Press*] (SAG) ... FdCt
Food Court Entertainment Network, Inc. [*Associated Press*] (SAG) ... FdCtE
Food Court Entmt Network'A' [*NASDAQ symbol*] (TTSB) ... FCENA
Food Defense Fund (EA) ... FDF
Food Distribution Administration [*Terminated, 1945*] ... FDA
Food Distribution Division [*of AMS, Department of Agriculture*] ... FD
Food Distribution Order ... FDO
Food Distribution Program [*Department of Agriculture*] ... FDP
Food Distribution Program on Indian Reservations [*Department of Agriculture*] (GFGA) ... FDPIR
Food Distribution Research Society (EA) ... FDRS
Food Division [*Army Natick Laboratories, MA*] ... FD
Food, Drink, Tobacco [*Department of Employment*] [*British*] ... FDT
Food, Drug, and Consumer Product Agency [*Proposed successor to FDA*] [*HEW*] ... FDCPA
Food, Drug, and Cosmetic [*Act*] ... FDC
Food, Drug, and Cosmetic Act ... FD & C
Food, Drug, and Cosmetic Act (EG) ... FD & CA
Food, Drug, Cosmetic Law Reporter [*Commerce Clearing House*] [*A publication*] (DLA) ... FD Cosm L Rep
Food, Drug, Cosmetic Law Reporter [*Commerce Clearing House*] [*A publication*] (DLA) ... Food Drug Cos L Rep
Food, Drug, Cosmetic Law Reporter (Commerce Clearing House) [*A publication*] (DLA) ... Food Drug Cosm L Rep (CCH)
Food Education and Service Training ... FEAST
Food Education Society [*British*] ... FES
Food Engineering Laboratory [*Army*] ... FEL
Food Equipment and Additives Suppliers and Traders [*Leatherhead Food Research Association*] [*Information service or system*] (CRD) ... FEAST
Food Equipment Manufacturers Association (EA) ... FEMA
Food Equipment Manufacturers' Association of Australia ... FEMAA
Food Executives Club of Florida (EA) ... FECF
Food Facilities Consultants Society [*Later, FCSI*] (EA) ... FFCS
Food Facilities Engineering Society [*Later, FFCS*] (EA) ... FFES
Food for Peace [*Overseas food donation program*] ... FFP
Food for Poland [*Later, Food for Peace*] (EA) ... FFP
Food for the Hungry, Inc. (EA) ... FHI
Food from Britain ... FFB
Food Industries Center [*Ohio State University*] [*Research center*] (RCD) ... FIC
Food Industries Suppliers Association (EA) ... FISA
Food Industry Association Executives (EA) ... FIAE
Food Industry Association of Tasmania [*Australia*] ... FIAT
Food Industry Council of Australia ... FICA
Food Industry Institute [*Michigan State University*] [*Research center*] (RCD) ... FII
Food Information and Early Warning System [*FAO*] [*United Nations*] ... FIEWS
Food Integrated Tech, Inc. [*NASDAQ symbol*] (SAG) ... FITT
Food Integrated Tech, Inc. [*Associated Press*] (SAG) ... FoodIn
Food Integrated Tech, Inc. [*Associated Press*] (SAG) ... FoodIntg
Food Intolerance Testing (MEDA) ... FIT

Food Irradiation Reactor ... FIR
Food Laboratory [*Army*] ... FL
Food Launch Awareness in the Retail Sector [*Leatherhead Food Research Association*] [*Information service or system*] (CRD) ... FLAIRS
Food Law Institute [*Later, FDLI*] (EA) ... FLI
Food Linked Agro-Industrial Research (MHDB) ... FLAIR
Food Lion, Inc. [*Associated Press*] (SAG) ... FdLio
Food Lion, Inc. [*Associated Press*] (SAG) ... FdLioA
Food Lion, Inc. [*Associated Press*] (SAG) ... FdLioB
Food Lion Inc. Cl'A' [*NASDAQ symbol*] (TTSB) ... FDLNA
Food Lion Inc. Cl'B' [*NASDAQ symbol*] (TTSB) ... FDLNB
Food Machinery Association [*British*] (BI) ... FMA
Food Machinery Group [*British*] (DBA) ... FMG
Food Machinery Service Institute (EA) ... FMSI
Food Management Area (MCD) ... FMA
Food Management Assistance Team [*Army*] (INF) ... FMAT
Food Management Compartment (MCD) ... FMC
Food Management System [*or Subsystem*] (MCD) ... FMS
Food Manufacturers' Federation [*British*] ... FMF
Food Market Awareness Databank [*Leatherhead Food Research Association*] [*Information service or system*] (CRD) ... FOMAD
Food Marketing Institute (EA) ... FMI
Food Media Club [*Australia*] ... FMC
Food Merchandisers of America (EA) ... FMA
Food News Scanning Database [*Leatherhead Food Research Association*] [*Information service or system*] (CRD) ... FOSCAN
Food Operations Reference Manual (DNAB) ... FORM
Food Packaging Council (EA) ... FPC
Food Poisoning [*Medicine*] ... FP
Food Policy [*British*] ... FP
Food Preservers' Union of Australia ... FPUA
Food Preservers' Union of Western Australia ... FPUWA
Food Prices Review Board ... FPRB
Food Processing and Packaging (IMH) ... FPP
Food Processing Development Center, Leduc, Alberta [*Library symbol National Library of Canada*] (NLC) ... ALEF
Food Processing Development Irradiator ... FPDI
Food Processing Industry Training Council [*Australia*] ... FPITC
Food Processing Machinery and Supplies Association (EA) ... FPM & SA
Food Processors and Suppliers Group (EAIO) ... FPSG
Food Processors Institute (EA) ... FPI
Food Production [*British*] ... FP
Food Production Administration [*World War II*] ... FPA
Food Products and Equipment [*A publication*] ... FP & E
Food Protein Concentrate (PDAA) ... FPC
Food Protein Council [*Later, SPC*] (EA) ... FPC
Food Protein Research and Development Center [*Texas A & M University*] ... FPRDC
Food RA Online Scientific and Technical Information [*Leatherhead Food Research Association*] [*Information service or system*] (CRD) ... FROSTI
Food Ratio ... FR
Food Rationing Order [*British*] ... FRO
Food Regulation Enquiries [*Leatherhead Food Research Association*] [*Information service or system*] (CRD) ... FOREGE
Food Research and Action Center (EA) ... FRAC
Food Research Association Computerized Information Service [*Food Research Association*] [*Database*] (NITA) ... FRANCIS
Food Research Centre, Agriculture Canada [*Centre de Recherches sur les Aliments,Agriculture Canada*], Ottawa, Ontario [*Library symbol National Library of Canada*] (BIB) ... OOAGFR
Food Research Institute [*Australia*] ... FRI
[*The*] **Food Research Institute** [*Agricultural Research Council*] [*British*] ... FRI
Food Research Institute [*Canada*] (ARC) ... FRI
Food Research Institute [*University of Wisconsin - Madison*] [*Research center*] (RCD) ... FRI
Food Reserves on Space Trips ... FROST
Food Retailers' Association of New South Wales [*Australia*] ... FRANSW
Food Safety and Inspection Service [*Formerly, FSQS*] [*Department of Agriculture*] ... FSIS
Food Safety and Quality Service [*Later, FSIS*] [*Department of Agriculture*] ... FSQS
Food Safety Council [*Defunct*] (EA) ... FSC
Food Sanitation Institute (EA) ... FSI
Food Scan [*Database from Food Research Association*] [*British*] (NITA) ... FOSCAN
Food Science (DD) ... FoodSc
Food Science and Technology Abstracts [*Database*] (NITA) ... FSTA
Food Security Act [*of 1985*] ... FSA
Food Service (MSA) ... FDSVC
Food Service Brokers of America [*Defunct*] (EA) ... FSBA
Food Service Equipment Industry [*Later, FEDA*] (EA) ... FSEI
Food Service Executives' Association [*Later, IFSEA*] (EA) ... FSEA
Food Service/Lodging ... FS/L
Food Service Marketing Institute (EA) ... FSMI
Food Stamp ... FS
Food Stamp Employment and Training Program [*Department of Agriculture*] (GFGA) ... FSETP
Food Stamp Program ... FSP
Food Standards Code [*Australia*] ... FSC
Food Standards Committee [*British*] ... FSC
Food Storage Cell ... FSC
Food Supplement Co. [*British*] ... FSC
Food Supply Board [*Ministry of Food*] [*British World War II*] ... FSB
Food Surplus Commodities Corp. ... FSCC
Food Technology Association of Western Australia ... FTAWA
Food Technology Service, Inc. [*Associated Press*] (SAG) ... FoodTch
Food Technology Service, Inc. [*NASDAQ symbol*] (SAG) ... VIFL
Food Technology Svc [*NASDAQ symbol*] (TTSB) ... VIFL
Food to Microorganism Ratio (EPA) ... F/M
Food Trades Protection Society Ltd. [*British*] (BI) ... FTPS
Food Tray and Board Association [*Later, SSI*] ... FTBA
Food Tray Association [*Defunct*] ... FTA
Food Warmer (NASA) ... FD WMR
Food, Water, and Waste [*NASA*] (MCD) ... FWW
Food, Water, and Waste Management [*NASA*] (NASA) ... FWWM
Food, Water, and Waste Management Subsystem [*NASA*] (NASA) ... FWWMS
Foodarama Suermkts [*AMEX symbol*] (TTSB) ... FSM
Foodarama Supermarkets, Inc. [*Associated Press*] (SAG) ... Foodrm
Foodarama Supermarkets, Inc. [*AMEX symbol*] (SPSG) ... FSM
Foodbanking, Inc. [*An association*] (EA) ... FI
Foodbrands America [*NYSE symbol*] (TTSB) ... FDB
Foodbrands America, Inc. [*NASDAQ symbol*] (SAG) ... FBAI
Foodbrands America, Inc. [*Associated Press*] (SAG) ... Foodbrnd
Foodex, Inc. [*Toronto Stock Exchange symbol*] ... FDX
Foodland Associates Ltd. ... FAL
Food-Linked Agricultural Industrial Research [*EC*] (ECED) ... FLAIR
Foodmaker, Inc. [*NYSE symbol*] (SPSG) ... FM
Foodmaker, Inc. [*Associated Press*] (SAG) ... Foodmk
Foodquest, Inc. [*Associated Press*] (SAG) ... Foodq
Foodquest, Inc. [*Associated Press*] (SAG) ... Foodqust
Foodquest, Inc. [*NASDAQ symbol*] (SAG) ... FOOQ
Foodquest Inc. Wrrt [*NASDAQ symbol*] (TTSB) ... FOOQW
Foodservice and Lodging Institute (EA) ... FLI
Foodservice and Packaging Institute (EA) ... FPI
Foodservice Consultants Society International (EA) ... FCSI
Foodservice Equipment Distributors Association (EA) ... FEDA
Foodservice Group [*Atlanta, GA*] (EA) ... FG
Foodservice Organization of Distributors (EA) ... FOOD
Foodweek [*A publication*] ... Food
[*A*] **Fool and His Money Are Soon Parted** (ROG) ... FMSP
Foolish Rear End Device [*Electronic caboose replacement*] [*Bowdlerized version*] ... FRED
Foolproof Auditing and Sale of Tickets [*in motion picture theaters*] ... FAST
Foolproof Identification [*System*] ... FID
Foolscap [*Paper*] (ROG) ... CAP
Foolscap (NTCM) ... FC
Foolscap [*Paper*] ... FCAP
Foolscap [*Paper*] ... FCP
Foolscap (ABBR) ... FLS-CP
Foolscap (NTCM) ... FSC
Foolscap [*Paper*] (ROG) ... FSCP
Foord's Cape Of Good Hope Reports [*South Africa*] [*A publication*] (DLA) ... F
Foord's Supreme Court Reports [*Cape Colony, South Africa*] [*A publication*] (DLA) ... F
Foord's Supreme Court Reports [*Cape Colony, South Africa*] [*A publication*] (DLA) ... Foord
Foot (AAMN) ... ft
Foot Board Measure (MSA) ... FBM
Foot Drape [*Medicine*] ... FD
Foot Groove ... FG
Foot Guards [*British*] ... FG
Foot of Bed (CPH) ... FOB
Foot Orthosis [*Medicine*] ... FO
Foot Patrol (AFM) ... FP
Foot Shock [*Biometrics*] ... FS
Foot Shock-Induced Analgesia [*Neurology*] (DAVI) ... FSIA
Foot Switch [*Industrial control*] (IEEE) ... FTS
Foot Wide ... FW
Footage Dives [*Military*] (AABC) ... FTGDV
Foot-and-Mouth Disease [*Veterinary medicine*] ... FMD
Foot-and-Mouth Disease Virus [*Veterinary medicine*] ... FMDV
Football [*Freight*] ... FT BAL
Football ... FTBLL
Football Association [*Controlling body of British soccer*] ... FA
Football Association Coaching Tactics Skills [*British*] (DI) ... FACTS
Football Association of Ireland (DI) ... FAI
Football Club [*British*] ... FC
Football Committee [*British*] ... FC
Football Grounds [*Public-performance tariff class*] [*British*] ... FG
Football Hall of Shame [*Defunct*] (EA) ... FHS
Football Officials Association ... FOA
Football Writers Association of America (EA) ... FWAA
Foot-Candela [*Foot-Candle*] [*Illumination*] (ADA) ... FT CD
Foot-Candle [*Illumination*] ... FC
Foot-Candle (IDOE) ... fc
Foot-Candle [*Illumination*] ... FT-C
Foot-Controlled Maneuvering Unit [*Skylab*] [*NASA*] ... FCMU
Foote and Everett's Law of Incorporated Companies Operating under Municipal Franchises [*A publication*] (DLA) ... Foote & E Incorp Co
Foote, Cone & Belding Advertising, Inc., Corporate Inforamtion Center, Chicago, IL [*Library symbol*] [*Library of Congress*] (LCLS) ... ICFCB
Foote, Cone & Belding Communications [*Advertising*] [*Communications*] [*Chicago, IL*] (WDMC) ... FCB
Foote on Private International Jurisprudence [*A publication*] (DLA) ... Foote Int Jur
Foote's Bench and Bar of the South and Southwest [*A publication*] (DLA) ... Foote B & B
Foote's Law of Highways [*A publication*] (DLA) ... Foote Highw
Foothill College, Los Altos, CA [*Library symbol Library of Congress*] (LCLS) ... CLahF
Foothill Independent Banc [*NASDAQ symbol*] (TTSB) ... FOOT
Foothill Independent Bancorp [*NASDAQ symbol*] (NQ) ... FOOT
Foothill Independent Bancorp [*Associated Press*] (SAG) ... FootInd

Foothills Area Mental Health, North Carolina School for the Deaf, Morganton, NC [*Library symbol*] [*Library of Congress*] (LCLS) .... NcMoFM
Foothills Christian College, Calgary, Alberta [*Library symbol Obsolete National Library of Canada*] (NLC) .... ACBB
Foothills Hospital, Calgary, AB, Canada [*Library symbol*] [*Library of Congress*] (LCLS) .... CaACFH
Foothills Hospital, Calgary, Alberta [*Library symbol National Library of Canada*] (NLC) .... ACFH
Foothills Pipe Lines (Yukon) Ltd., Calgary, AB, Canada [*Library symbol Library of Congress*] (LCLS) .... CaACF
Foothills Pipe Lines (Yukon) Ltd., Calgary, Alberta [*Library symbol National Library of Canada*] (NLC) .... ACF
Footing (KSC) .... FTG
Foot-Lambert [*Illumination*] .... FL
Foot-Lambert (IDOE) .... fL
Foot-Lambert [*Illumination*] .... FT-L
Foot-Lambert [*Illumination*] (IAA) .... FTLA
Footnote .... FN
Footnote (WDMC) .... fn
Footnote (DLA) .... n
Footnote in Cross-Reference (DLA) .... note
Footnotes (DLA) .... nn
Footpath (ADA) .... FP
Foot-Pound [*Unit of work*] .... FP
Foot-Pound [*Unit of work*] (AAG) .... FT-LB
Foot-Pound Force .... FT LBF
Foot-Poundal [*Unit of work*] .... FT PDL
Foot-Pounds of Energy .... FPE
Foot-Pounds per Hour .... FT LB/H
Foot-Pounds per Minute .... FT LB/MIN
Foot-Pounds per Second .... FT LB/S
Foot-Pound-Second [*System*] .... FPS
Foot-Pound-Second (IDOE) .... fps
Foot-Pound-Second Magnetic System (IAA) .... FPSM
Foot-Second (ADA) .... FS
Footstar, Inc. [*Associated Press*] (SAG) .... Footstr
Footstar, Inc. [*NYSE symbol*] (SAG) .... FTS
Footwall Exploration [*Vancouver Stock Exchange symbol*] .... FTW
Footwear .... FTWR
Footwear and Accessories Council [*Defunct*] (EA) .... FAC
Footwear Caucus (EA) .... FC
Footwear Components Association Ltd. [*British*] (BI) .... FCA
Footwear Components Federation [*British*] (DBA) .... FCF
Footwear Council [*Defunct*] (EA) .... FC
Footwear Distributors and Retailers of America (EA) .... FDRA
Footwear Distributors Federation [*British*] (BI) .... FDF
Footwear Industries of America (EA) .... FIA
Footwear Industry Traffic and Distribution Council (EA) .... FITDC
Footwear Manufacturers' Association of Australia .... FMAA
Footwear Repairers' Association of New South Wales [*Australia*] .... FRANSW
Footwear Repairers' Association of Queensland [*Australia*] .... FRAQ
Footwear Repairers' Association of South Australia .... FRASA
Footwear Repairers' Association of Victoria [*Australia*] .... FRAV
Footwear Repairers' Association of Western Australia .... FRAWA
Footwear Retailers of America [*Later, FDRA*] (EA) .... FRA
For .... F
For [*Telecommunications*] (ADDR) .... FR
For a Separate Peace Before Carter [*Refers to Israeli-Egyptian agreements of 1978*] .... FSPBC
For Action .... FORAC
For Address, Write To .... FAWT
For Better Living [*NASDAQ symbol*] (TTSB) .... FBTR
For Better Living, Inc. [*NASDAQ symbol*] (NQ) .... FBTR
For Better Living, Inc. [*Associated Press*] (SAG) .... ForBetr
For Carter Before Camp David [*Refers to Israeli-Egyptian agreements of 1978*] .... FCBCD
For Colouring of Food [*British*] .... FCF
For Credit Of (WDAA) .... F/O
For Duration of [*Hospital*] **Stay** (CPH) .... FDS
For Duty [*Military*] .... FORDU
For Duty or Such Other Duty as [*Command or Activity Indicated*] **May Assign** [*Military*] .... DUSODA
For Each (DAVI) .... PER
For Early Domestic Dissemination (MCD) .... FEDD
For Engineering Information (AAG) .... FEI
For Examination Purposes Only [*Education*] .... FEPO
For Example [*Exempli Gratia*] [*Latin*] (WDMC) .... eg
For Example (ROG) .... FE
For External Use Only [*Pharmacy*] (DAVI) .... FEUO
For Further Assignment .... FFA
For Further Assignment .... FURAS
For Further Assignment by the Commander Naval Military Personnel Command to (Duty Indicated) (DNAB) .... FURASPERS
For Further Assignment to Duty in Submarine [*Navy*] (DNAB) .... FURASUB
For Further Clearance [*Aviation*] (FAAC) .... FFC
For Further Headings (DA) .... FFH
For Further Information .... FFI
For Further Instructions (DS) .... FFI
For Further Study (ACRL) .... FFS
For Further Transfer [*to*] [*Military*] .... FFT
For Illustrating Legal Methods [*Student legal action organization*] (EA) .... FILM
For Improved Labeling to Terminate Hazards [*Student legal action organization*] .... FILTH
For Information Only (AAG) .... FIO
For Instance .... FI
For Internal Use Only (KSC) .... FIUO
For Kids Entertainment, Inc. [*Associated Press*] (SAG) 4KidsEnt
For Kids Entertainment, Inc. [*NASDAQ symbol*] (SAG) .... KIDE
For Life [*An association*] (EA) .... FL
For Love of Children .... FLOC
For NASA Personnel Only (KSC) .... FNPO
For Necessary Action (ADA) .... FNA
For Official Use Only [*Army*] .... FOUO
For Official Use Only [*Army*] .... OFLUSE
For Oily Hair Only [*Trademark of The Gillette Co.*] .... FOHO
For Orders .... FO
For Our Children's Unpaid Support [*Defunct*] (EA) .... FOCUS
For Our Christian Understanding [*Program*] .... FOCUS
For Personal Use Only .... FPUO
For Position Only (WDAA) .... FPO
For Possible Reclearance [*Aviation*] (FAAC) .... FPRC
For Private Circulation .... FPC
For Private Use (ROG) .... FP
For Sale by Owner [*Real estate ads*] [*Pronounced "fizz-bo"*] .... FSBO
For Task Force [*Military*] (AABC) .... FORTSK
For the Benefit Of .... FBO
For the Birds [*Slang*] (IAA) .... FTB
For the Heart Elvis Presley Fan Club (EA) .... FHEPFC
For the Purpose Of .... FPUR
For the Record (DAVI) .... FTR
For Their Respective Rights and Interests [*Insurance*] (AIA) .... FTRR & I
For Ultraviolet .... FUV
For Valuation Only [*Business term*] .... FVO
For What It's Worth .... FWIW
For Your Amusement [*Computer hacker terminology*] (NHD) .... FYA
For Your Attention [*Business term*] .... FYA
For Your Eyes (BARN) .... FYE
For Your Files .... FYF
For Your Information .... FYI
For Your Information and Guidance .... FYIG
For Your Interest [*Internet language*] [*Computer science*] .... FYI
Forage Acre .... FA
Forage Corps [*British military*] (DMA) .... FC
Forage Crop [*Agriculture*] .... FC
Forage Value Index [*Agriculture*] .... FVI
Foragers of America (EA) .... FA
Foraging [*Ornithology*] .... F
Foramen [*Anatomy*] (MAE) .... F
Foramen of Labial Palpus [*Arthropod anatomy*] .... PLP FOR
Foramen Ovale [*Anatomy*] .... FO
Foramen Spinosum [*Neuroanatomy*] .... FS
Foraminifera [*Quality of the bottom*] [*Nautical charts*] .... Fr
Foraminiferal [*Geology*] .... FORAM
Foran. Code of Civil Procedure of Quebec [*A publication*] (DLA) .... For Pr
Forari [*Vanuatu*] [*ICAO location identifier*] (ICLI) .... NVVJ
Foras Ciseanna Saothair (ACII) .... FAS
Forasol-Foramer NV [*NASDAQ symbol*] (TTSB) .... FSOLF
Forbes [*Australia Airport symbol*] (OAG) .... FRB
Forbes Air Force Base [*Kansas*] (AAG) .... FOAFB
Forbes' Cases in St. Andrews Bishop's Court [*A publication*] (DLA) .... Forb
Forbes' Court of Session Decisions [*Scotland*] [*A publication*] (DLA) .... Forb
Forbes' Institutes of the Law of Scotland [*A publication*] (DLA) .... Forb Inst
Forbes' Journal of the Session [*1705-13*] [*Scotland*] [*A publication*] (DLA) .... Forb
Forbes' Journal of the Session [*1705-13*] [*Scotland*] [*A publication*] (DLA) .... Forbes
Forbes Library, Northampton, MA [*Library symbol Library of Congress*] (LCLS) .... MNF
Forbes Magazine, Inc., New York, NY [*Library symbol Library of Congress*] (LCLS) .... NNFoM
Forbes on Bills of Exchange [*A publication*] (DLA) .... Forb Bills
Forbes on Trustees and Post Office Savings Banks [*A publication*] (DLA) .... Forb Tr
Forbidden Combination Check .... FCC
Forbidden Planet [*Bookstore chain*] [*British*] .... FP
Forbush Decrease [*Geophysics*] .... FD
Forby Family Historical Society (EA) .... FFHS
Forca Aerea Brasileira [*Brazilian Air Force*] .... FAB
Forca de Unidade Popular [*Terrorist group*] [*Portugal*] (EY) .... FUP
Forca Expedicionaria Brasileira [*Brazilian Expeditionary Force, 1944-1955*] .... FEB
Force [*Symbol*] [*IUPAC*] .... F
Force (NVT) .... FOR
Force .... FRC
Force 5 Class Association (EA) F5CA
Force Accounting Structure .... FAS
Force Accounting System [*Army*] (AABC) .... FAS
Force Accounting System Track [*Army*] (MCD) .... FASTRACK
Force Accuracy Standards .... FORACS
Force/Activity Designator [*Military*] .... F/AD
Force Administration Data System [*Bell System*] .... FADS
Force Aerienne Belge [*Belgium ICAO designator*] (FAAC) .... AFB
Force Air Intelligence Study [*Air Force*] .... FAIS
Force Alignment Plan [*Military*] (INF) .... FAP
Force Analysis Simulation of Theater Administrative and Logistics Support [*Military*] .... FASTALS
Force and Financial Plan .... FAFP
Force and Financial Program (AFM) .... F & FP
Force and Mission .... F & M
Force and Rhythm [*of Pulse*] [*Medicine*] .... F & R
Force and Weapon Analysis System (AABC) .... FOREWAS
Force Application Processor (MCD) .... FORCAP

Force Application Tactics Evaluation (SAA) ... FATE
Force Assessment in the Central Region [*NATO*] (NATG) ... FACR
Force Associated Control Communications [*Military*] (AFM) ... FACC
Force Augmentation Planning and Execution System (DOMA) ... FAPES
Force Automation and Communications [*Military*] ... FACS
Force [*XXI*] **Battle Command Brigade and Below** [*Army*] ... FBCB2
Force Beachhead Line [*Navy*] ... FBHDL
Force Beachhead Line [*Navy*] (NVT) ... FBHL
[*Naval*] **Force Capabilities Planning Effort** (DOMA) ... FCPE
Force Capability Management System [*Military*] ... FCMS
Force Combat Air Patrol [*Military*] (NVT) ... FORCAP
Force Command Standards Activity ... FORMSA
Force Control (MCD) ... FC
Force Control Unit ... FCU
Force Cost Assessor (MCD) ... FCA
Force Cost Information System (MCD) ... FCIS
Force de Liberation Nationale Kamerunaise [*National Cameroonian Liberation Force*] [*Political party*] ... FLNK
Force de l'Union National Cambodge [*Cambodia*] [*Political party*] ... FUNC
Force Description [*Military*] (DOMA) ... FDESC
Force Design Update [*Army*] ... FDU
Force Designator ... FD
Force Development ... FD
Force Development Experimentation Testing (MCD) ... FDET
Force Development Integrated Management System [*Military*] ... FORDIMS
Force Development Management Information System [*Army*] ... FDMIS
Force Development Management Information System [*Army*] (MCD) ... FDMS
Force Development System Agency [*DoD*] ... FDSA
Force Development Testing and Experimentation [*Military*] (AABC) ... FDTE
Force Displacement [*Sports medicine*] ... FD
Force d'Urgence des Nations Unies ... FUNU
Force Effectiveness Indicator [*COEA*] (MCD) ... FEI
Force Electronic Warfare Coordinator (NVT) ... FEWC
Force Electronic Warfare/Tactical SIGINT ... FEWTS
Force Engineer Battalion [*Marine Corps*] (VNW) ... FEB
Force Evaluation Model [*Army*] (RDA) ... FORCEM
Force Exchange Ratio (MCD) ... FER
Force Feed (MSA) ... FF
Force Field ... FF
Force Fighter Director Officer ... FFDO
Force Flagship ... FF
Force (Fleet) High-Level Terminal [*Navy*] (CAAL) ... FHLT
Force Flow [*Model*] [*Army*] ... FORCEFLO
Force [*or Forced*] **Fluid** [*Medicine*] ... FF
Force Generation [*Military*] (SAA) ... FORGEN
Force Generation Levels [*Military*] (NVT) ... FGLS
Force Headquarters [*Allied forces*] [*World War II*] ... FH
Force Headquarters, Adjutant General [*World War II*] ... FHAG
Force Headquarters, Adjutant General, Executive [*World War II*] ... FHAGG
Force Headquarters, Adjutant General, Mail and Records [*World War II*] ... FHAGR
Force Headquarters, Adjutant General, Miscellaneous [*World War II*] ... FHAGM
Force Headquarters, Adjutant General, Personnel [*World War II*] ... FHAGP
Force Headquarters, Air Commander-in-Chief, Mediterranean [*World War II*] ... FHAIR
Force Headquarters, Antiaircraft [*World War II*] ... FHAAO
Force Headquarters, Chemical Warfare [*World War II*] ... FHCWS
Force Headquarters, Chief Administrative Officer [*World War II*] ... FHCAO
Force Headquarters, Chief of Staff [*World War II*] ... FHCOS
Force Headquarters, Civil Affairs [*World War II*] ... FHCIV
Force Headquarters, Claims and Hirings [*World War II*] ... FHCCH
Force Headquarters, Commander-in-Chief [*World War II*] ... FHCIC
Force Headquarters, Commander-in-Chief, Mediterranean [*World War II*] ... FHRNA
Force Headquarters, Deputy Allied Commander-in-Chief [*World War II*] ... FHDCC
Force Headquarters, Deputy Chief of Staff [*World War II*] ... FHDSC
Force Headquarters, Director of Harbor Craft [*World War II*] ... FHDHC
Force Headquarters, Engineer [*World War II*] ... FHENG
Force Headquarters, Expeditionary Forces Institute [*World War II*] ... FHEFI
Force Headquarters, Field Artillery Section [*World War II*] ... FHFLD
Force Headquarters, Headquarters Commandant [*World War II*] ... FHHDC
Force Headquarters, Information and Censorship [*World War II*] ... FHINC
Force Headquarters, Liaison [*World War II*] ... FHLIA
Force Headquarters, Military Government Section [*World War II*] ... FHMGS
Force Headquarters, Military Secretary Section [*World War II*] ... FHDMS
Force Headquarters, Movements and Transportation [*World War II*] ... FHGDM
Force Headquarters, North African Economic Board [*World War II*] ... FHAEB
Force Headquarters, Ordnance [*World War II*] ... FHORD
Force Headquarters, Petroleum [*World War II*] ... FHPET
Force Headquarters, Psychological Warfare Office [*World War II*] ... FHPWO
Force Headquarters, Public Relations [*World War II*] ... FHPRO
Force Headquarters, "Q" Army Equipment Branch [*World War II*] ... FHQAE
Force Headquarters, "Q" Maintenance [*World War II*] ... FHGDQ
Force Headquarters, Quartermaster [*World War II*] ... FHSUP
Force Headquarters, Secretary General Staff [*World War II*] ... FHSGS
Force Headquarters, Signal [*World War II*] ... FHSIG
Force Headquarters, Supply and Transport [*World War II*] ... FHGDT
Force Headquarters, Surgeon [*World War II*] ... FHMED
Force Headquarters, United States Naval Staff [*World War II*] ... FHUSN
Force Headquarters, Works [*World War II*] ... FHENW
Force Identification [*Military*] (NVT) ... FID
Force Identification Code [*Military*] ... FICOD
Force Improvement Plan (MCD) ... FIP
Force Indicator Code (MCD) ... FIC
Force Information Service [*Military*] (NVT) ... FIS
Force Integration Analysis [*DoD*] ... FIA
Force Integration Staff Officer [*Army*] (RDA) ... FISO
Force Integrator [*DoD*] ... FI
Force Level Control System ... FLCS
Force Logistics Command [*Marine Corps*] (NVT) ... FLC
Force Logistics Command [*Marine Corps*] (NVT) ... FORLOGMD
Force Logistics Support Group [*Marine Corps*] (NVT) ... FLSG
Force Logistics Support Unit [*Marine Corps*] (NVT) ... FLSU
Force Management and Personnel (DOMA) ... FM & P
Force Management System [*Air Force*] (GFGA) ... FMS
FORCE, Mass, Length, and Time [*Rocket dynamics*] (BARN) ... FMLT
Force Measurement Unit ... FMU
Force Measuring System (KSC) ... FMS
Force Missile Coordinator [*Navy*] (CAAL) ... FMC
Force Mobile (Canadian Forces) ... FMC
Force Mobilization Review and Evaluation Committee [*Military*] (MCD) ... FMREC
Force Mobilization Steering Committee [*Army*] (MCD) ... FORMOST
Force Modernization Division [*Military*] (MCD) ... FMD
Force Modernization Information System (MCD) ... FMIS
Force Modernization Integrated Logistics Support ... FMILS
Force Modernization Master Plan (MCD) ... FMMP
Force Modernization Milestone Reporting System [*Army*] (RDA) ... FMMRS
Force Modernization Office [*Army*] (RDA) ... FMO
Force Modernization Program ... FMP
Force Modernization Training [*Military*] ... FMT
Force Module Identifier (DOMA) ... FMI
Force Module Library (DOMA) ... FML
Force Module Logistics Sustainability Model (DOMA) ... FMLSM
Force Module Subsystem (DOMA) ... FMS
Force Movement Control Center [*Marines*] (ANA) ... FMCC
Force, Net Propulsive ... FNP
Force Objective (CINC) ... F/O
Force of Concentrated Load ... P
Force Out [*Baseball*] ... FO
Force Out of Service [*Telecommunications*] (TEL) ... FOOS
Force Over-the-Horizon Targeting Coordinator [*Navy*] (ANA) ... FOTC
Force Packaging Methodology [*Military*] ... FPM
Force Packaging Report [*Military*] ... FOPREP
Force Planning Analysis [*Army*] (AABC) ... FPA
Force Planning Estimate (MCD) ... FPE
Force Planning Guide [*Army*] (AABC) ... FPG
Force Planning Package [*Military*] (RDA) ... FPP
Force Planning System ... FORPA
Force Program Review [*DoD*] ... FPR
Force Reaction Motor ... FRM
Force Readiness Report [*DoD*] ... FRR
Force Recon Association (EA) ... FRA
Force Reconnaissance Company [*Marine Corps*] ... FORECONCO
Force Record Extract File [*Military*] (DOMA) ... FREF
Force Release [*Telecommunications*] (TEL) ... FR
Force Rendezvous Point [*Military*] (AFM) ... FRP
Force Requirement Number [*Army*] (AABC) ... FRN
Force Requirement Troop List Reporting System (AABC) ... FORTL
Force Requirements and Methodology [*Military*] ... FOREM
Force Requirements Expert System [*Navy*] ... FRESH
Force Requirements Generator ... FRG
Force Resources Ltd. [*Vancouver Stock Exchange symbol*] ... FOR
Force Sensing Probe ... FSP
Force Sensing Resistor [*Maxell*] [*Electronics*] ... FSR
Force Service Regiment [*Marine Corps*] (NVT) ... FSR
Force Service Support Group [*Military*] (DNAB) ... FORSERVSUPPGRU
Force Service Support Group [*Military*] (NVT) ... FSSG
Force Service Support Group Detachment [*Military*] (DNAB) ... FORSERVSUPPGRUDET
Force Service Support Group Detachment [*Military*] (DNAB) ... FSSGDET
Force Sizing Exercise [*Military*] ... FORSIZE
Force Spectral Density ... FSD
Force Status and Identity Report ... FORSTAR
Force Status Identity Report (MCD) ... FSIR
Force Status Report [*Military*] ... FORSTAT
Force Stratification System ... FSS
Force Structure Allowance [*DoD*] ... FSA
Force Structure Assessment System [*Model*] [*Army*] ... FSAS
Force Structure Committee (AFM) ... FSC
Force Structure Increase [*Military*] ... FSI
Force Structure Planning Group [*Marine Corps*] (DOMA) ... FSPG
Force Structure Planning Objective (MUGU) ... FSPO
Force Structure Requirements Study [*Military*] ... FSRS
Force Structure Subsystem [*Military*] ... FSS
Force Structure Trade-Off Analysis (MCD) ... FSTA
Force Structuring (MCD) ... FS
Force Supply Officer ... FSO
Force Terrestre Belge [*Belgium*] [*FAA designator*] (FAAC) ... AYB
Force/Torque Module [*NASA*] ... FTM
Force Track Coordinator [*Navy*] (NVT) ... FTC
Force Troops ... FORTRPS
Force, Type, District Code (DNAB) ... FTD
Force Weapons Coordinator [*Navy*] (NVT) ... FORWEPCORD
Force Weapons Coordinator [*Navy*] (NVT) ... FWC
Force XXI, Battle Command, Brigade and Below [*Army*] (RDA) ... FBCB2
Forced (WGA) ... FD
Forced Air (MSA) ... FA
Forced Answer (HGAA) ... FA
Forced Beachhead [*Navy*] (DNAB) ... FBH
Forced Circulation (DICI) ... FC

Forced Draft ... FD
Forced End of Volume (IAA) ... FEOV
Forced Equilibrating Expiration [*Physiology*] ... FEE
Forced Expiratory Capacity [*Medicine*] (DMAA) ... FEC
Forced Expiratory Flow [*Physiology*] ... FEF
Forced Expiratory Flow (GNE) ... FExF
Forced Expiratory Flow Maximal [*Achieved during a forced vital capacity*] [*Medicine*] (DAVI) ... FEFmax
Forced Expiratory Spirogram [*Medicine*] ... FES
Forced Expiratory Time [*Physiology*] ... FET
Forced Expiratory Time, in Seconds [*Physiology*] ... FETS
Forced Expiratory Volume [*Physiology*] ... FEV
Forced Expiratory Volume (In One Second)/Vital Capacity [*Physiology*] (MAE) ... FEV_1/VC
Forced Expiratory Volume (Timed) [*Medicine*] (DAVI) ... FEVt
Forced Expiratory Volume (Timed) to Forced Vital Capacity Ratio [*Expressed as a percentage*] [*Medicine*] (DAVI) ... FEVt/FVC
Forced Fault Entry [*Computer science*] ... FFE
Forced Incident Destiny Testing (IAA) ... FIDT
Forced Inspiration [*Medicine*] (MAE) ... FI
Forced Inspiratory Flow [*Physiology*] ... FIF
Forced Inspiratory Oxygen [*Physiology*] ... FIO_2
Forced Inspiratory Vital Capacity [*Medicine*] ... FIVC
Forced Landing (IAA) ... FDLDG
Forced Landing Incidents - Ground Accidents ... FLIGA
Forced Longitudinal Wave (MCD) ... FLW
Forced Mandatory Intermittent Ventilation [*Medicine*] (DAVI) ... FMIV
Forced Midexpiratory Flow [*Medicine*] (DAVI) ... FMF
Forced Oil and Air (MSA) ... FOA
Forced Oil Injection ... FOI
Forced Oscillation in a Tightening Oscillator [*Chemical kinetics*] ... FOTO
Forced Oscillation Program [*Military*] ... FOP
Forced Out by a Reduction in Force ... RIFFED
Forced Outage Hours [*Electronics*] (IEEE) ... FOH
Forced Outage Rate [*Electronics*] (IEEE) ... FOR
Forced Pair Copulation [*Sociobiology*] ... FPC
Forced Perfect Termination [*Computer science*] ... FPT
Forced Removal ... FR
Forced Response Simulation [*Computer science*] ... FRS
Forced Test End (NASA) ... FTE
Forced Vital Capacity [*Physiology*] ... FVC
Forced Volume, Expiratory [*Physiology*] ... FVE
Forced Whisper [*Medicine*] ... FW
Forced-Air-Cooled [*Transformer*] (IEEE) ... FA
Forced-Choice Preferential Looking ... FPL
Forced-Draft Blower ... FDB
Forced-Draft, Low-Nitrogen Oxide [*Combustion engineering*] ... FDLN
Forced-Flow Chemical Vapor Infiltration [*Materials science*] ... FCVI
Force-in-Being (ADA) ... FIB
Forcenergy Gas Exploration, Inc. [*NASDAQ symbol*] (SAG) ... FGAS
Forcenergy Gas Exploration, Inc. [*Associated Press*] (SAG) ... Forcen
Forcenergy Inc. [*NASDAQ symbol*] (TTSB) ... FGAS
Force-on-Force Trainer ... FOFT
Force-Optimized Recoil Control (MCD) ... FORC
Forceps Delivery [*Obstetrics*] ... FD
Forceps to After-Coming Head [*Obstetrics*] ... FACH
Forces Aeriennes Alliees Centre-Europe [*Allied Air Forces Central Europe*] [*NATO*] (NATG) ... FAACE
Forces Aeriennes Alliees Nord-Europe [*Allied Air Forces Northern Europe*] [*NATO*] (NATG) ... FAANE
Forces Aeriennes Alliees Sud-Europe [*Allied Air Forces Southern Europe*] [*NATO*] (NATG) ... FAASE
Forces Aeriennes Francaises [*France ICAO designator*] (FAAC) ... FAF
Forces Afloat Repair Procedures (DNAB) ... FARP
Forces and Weapons ... FOREWON
Forces Armees Laotiannes [*Federated Army of Laos*] ... FAL
Forces Armees Nationales Khmeres [*Cambodian National Armed Forces*] [*Replaced Royal Cambodian Armed Forces*] ... FANK
Forces Armees Nationales Tchadiennes [*Chad*] (PD) ... FANT
Forces Armees Neutralistes [*Neutralist Armed Forces*] [*Laos*] ... FAN
Forces Armees Royales [*Royal Armed Forces*] [*Laos*] ... FAR
Forces Armees Royales Khmeres [*Royal Cambodian Armed Forces*] [*Replaced by FANK*] ... FARK
Forces Armees Tchadiennes [*Chad Armed Forces*] (PD) ... FAT
Forces Command [*Formerly, CONARC*] [*Army*] ... FORSCOM
Forces Command [*Army*] (DOMA) ... FORSCOM
Forces Correspondence Courses Scheme [*Military British*] ... FCCS
Forces Courier Services [*Military British*] ... FCS
Forces de Liberation Africaine de Mauritanie [*Political party*] (EY) ... FLAM
Forces des Nations Unies [*United Nations Forces*] ... FNU
Forces Francaises de l'Interieur [*French Forces of the Interior*] [*World War II*] ... FFI
Forces Francaises de l'Ouest ... FFO
Forces Francaises en Allemagne [*French Forces in Germany*] ... FFA
Forces Francaises Libres [*Free French Forces*] ... FFL
Forces Help Society [*British*] (BI) ... FHS
Forces Intelligence Center (AABC) ... FORSIC
Forces Mobile Command [*Canada*] (DD) ... FMC
Forces Motoring Club [*British military*] (DMA) ... FMC
Forces Navales Francaises Libres [*Free French Naval Forces*] [*World War II*] ... FNFL
Forces Organized Ready for War and Able to Rapidly Deploy (MCD) ... FORWARD
Forces Post Office [*Military British*] ... FPO
Forces Postal Service [*British*] ... FPS
Forces to Eliminate No-Deposit/No-Return ... FENDRE
Forcible Entry and Detainer [*Legal term*] (DLA) ... FORC ENT
Ford (ROG) ... FD
Ford [*Commonly used*] (OPSA) ... FORD
Ford [*Postal Service standard*] (OPSA) ... FRD
Ford ... FRD
Ford Aerospace and Communications Corp. (MCD) ... FACC
Ford Aerospace Satellite Services Corp. [*Arlington, VA*] [*Telecommunications*] (TSSD) ... FASSC
Ford Aerosports Club (EA) ... FAC
Ford, Bacon & Davis, Inc., New York, NY [*Library symbol Library of Congress*] (LCLS) ... NNFB
Ford Central Community Unit Shool District, Piper City, IL [*Library symbol*] [*Library of Congress*] (LCLS) ... IPipSD
Ford City, CA [*FM radio station call letters*] ... KZPE
Ford Combustion Process [*Automotive engineering*] ... FCP
Ford County Film Cooperative, Melvin, IL [*Library symbol*] [*Library of Congress*] (LCLS) ... IMelF
Ford Forestry Center [*Michigan Technological University*] [*Research center*] (RCD) ... FFC
Ford Foundation ... FF
Ford Foundation, Ford Foundation Library, New York, NY [*Library symbol Library of Congress*] (LCLS) ... NNFF-FL
Ford Foundation Library, New York, NY [*OCLC symbol*] (OCLC) ... FOR
Ford Foundation, New York, NY [*Library symbol Library of Congress*] (LCLS) ... NNFF
Ford Four Car Club [*Australia*] ... FFCC
Ford Galaxie Club of America (EA) ... FGCA
Ford Holdings, Inc. [*NYSE symbol*] (SPSG) ... FHI
Ford Holdings, Inc. [*Associated Press*] (SAG) ... FrdH
Ford Instrument Co. (MCD) ... FICO
Ford International Business Development [*Ford Motor Co.*] ... FIBD
Ford Marketing Institute ... FMI
Ford Mercury Club of America [*Defunct*] (EA) ... FMCA
Ford Motor [*NYSE symbol*] (TTSB) ... F
Ford Motor 8.40% Cv Dep Pfd [*NYSE symbol*] (TTSB) ... FPr
Ford Motor Co. [*Wall Street slang names: "Tin Lizzy" or "Flivver"*] [*NYSE symbol*] (SPSG) ... F
Ford Motor Co. [*Toronto Stock Exchange symbol*] ... FM
Ford Motor Co. (MCD) ... FOMOCO
Ford Motor Co. [*Detroit, MI*] [*Associated Press*] (SAG) ... Ford
Ford Motor Co. [*Associated Press*] (SAG) ... FordM
Ford Motor Co. [*ICAO designator*] (FAAC) ... FRD
Ford Motor Co., Dearborn, MI [*Library symbol Library of Congress*] (LCLS) ... MiDbF
Ford Motor Co., Engineering and Research Library, Dearborn, MI [*OCLC symbol*] (OCLC) ... EEF
Ford Motor Co. Ltd. [*ICAO designator*] (FAAC) ... FOB
Ford Motor Co. of Canada Ltd. [*Toronto Stock Exchange symbol*] ... FMC
Ford Motor Credit Co. ... FMCC
Ford Motor Dep'B'Pfd [*NYSE symbol*] (TTSB) ... FPrB
Ford Nuclear Reactor ... FNR
Ford of Britain [*Corporate subsidiary*] ... FOB
Ford of Europe, Inc. [*British ICAO designator*] (ICDA) ... FD
Ford on Oaths [*8th ed.*] [*1903*] [*A publication*] (DLA) ... Ford Oa
Ford [*Automobile*] **Operating Cost Analysis System** ... FOCAS
Ford Philpot Evangelistic Association (EA) ... FPEA
Ford Satellite Plan [*Telecommunications*] ... FSP
FORDAC [*FORTRAN Data Acquisition and Control*] **Conversational System** [*Computer science*] (IAA) ... FOCOS
Forde [*Norway ICAO location identifier*] (ICLI) ... ENFD
Forde [*Norway*] [*Airport symbol*] (OAG) ... FDE
Forde/Bringeland [*Norway ICAO location identifier*] (ICLI) ... ENBL
Forderung der Wissenschaftlichen Forschung [*Austrian science foundation*] ... FWF
Fordham [*New York*] [*Seismograph station code, US Geological Survey Closed*] (SEIS) ... FOR
Fordham [*England*] ... FORD
Fordham University (GAGS) ... Fordham U
Fordham University, Bronx, NY [*OCLC symbol*] (OCLC) ... VYF
Fordham University, Institute of Contemporary Russian Studies, New York, NY [*Library symbol Library of Congress*] (LCLS) ... NNF-RS
Fordham University, Law Library, New York, NY [*Library symbol Library of Congress*] (LCLS) ... NNF-L
Fordham University, Library at Lincoln Center, New York, NY [*Library symbol Library of Congress*] (LCLS) ... NNF-LC
Fordham University, New York, NY [*Library symbol Library of Congress*] (LCLS) ... NNF
Fordham University School of Law, Corporate Law Institute (DLA) ... FCLI
Fordham Urban Solar Eco-System ... FUSES
Fords [*Commonly used*] (OPSA) ... FORDS
Fords [*Postal Service standard*] (OPSA) ... FRDS
Fords ... FRDS
Ford's Theatre Society (EA) ... FTS
Fordson Tractor Club (EA) ... FTC
Fordyce & Princeton Railroad Co. [*AAR code*] ... FP
Fordyce, AR [*AM radio station call letters*] ... KBJT
Fordyce, AR [*FM radio station call letters*] ... KQEW
Fore and Aft ... F & A
Fore and Aft Scanner System (PDAA) ... FASS
Fore Edges Painted [*Paper*] ... FEP
Fore Hatch [*Shipping*] ... FH
Fore Perpendicular ... FP
Fore River Railroad Corp. [*AAR code*] ... FOR
FORE Systems [*NASDAQ symbol*] (TTSB) ... FORE

Fore Systems, Inc. [*NASDAQ symbol*] (SAG) .... FORE
Fore Systems, Inc. [*Associated Press*] (SAG) .... ForeSys
Fore-Aft Scanning Technique [*Marine science*] (OSRA) .... FAST
Fore-Aft Scanning Technique (USDC) .... FAST
Forearm [*Anatomy*] .... FA
Forearm Blood Flow [*Medicine*] .... FBF
Forearm Flow [*Cardiology*] (DAVI) .... FF
Forearm Glucose Uptake [*Clinical chemistry*] .... FGU
Forearm Pronated [*Medicine*] .... fp
Forearm Supinated [*Medicine*] .... FS
Forearm Vascular Resistance [*Medicine*] .... FVR
Forebody .... FB
Forecast (AFM) .... FCST
Forecast and Control Technique (IAA) .... FACT
Forecast Center Station [*Telecommunications*] (TEL) .... FC
Forecast Office Facsimile [*National Weather Service*] .... FOFAX
Forecast Research Division [*Marine science*] (OSRA) .... FRD
Forecast Research Division [*Forecast Systems Laboratory*] (USDC) .... FRD
Forecast Sailing Report [*Navy*] (NVT) .... PRESAILEDREP
Forecast Support Date .... FSD
Forecast/Surface (NATG) .... FS
Forecast Systems Laboratory [*Marine science*] (OSRA) .... FSL
Forecast Systems Laboratory [*Environmental Research Laboratories*] (USDC) .... FSL
Forecast Unit .... FU
Forecast Upper Air (NATG) .... FU
Forecast Upper Wind and Temperature for Aviation [*ICAO*] (FAAC) .... WINTEM
Forecast Wind Factor [*NWS*] (FAAC) .... FRWF
Forecaster Aid [*Military*] .... FA
Forecaster's Intelligent Discussion Experiment System [*Marine science*] (OSRA) .... FIDES
Forecaster's Intelligent Discussion Experiment System (USDC) .... FIDES
Forecasting .... FRCSTNG
Forecasting and Assessment in Science and Technology [*Commission of the European Communities program, 1978-1983*] .... FAST
Forecasting and Inventory Control System .... FICS
Forecasting and Modeling System [*Computer science*] (BUR) .... FAMS
Forecasting and Scheduling Technique .... FAST
Forecasting Control and Updating Schedule (MCD) .... FOCUS
Forecasting Information Retrieval of Management System (IEEE) .... FIRMS
Forecasting International Ltd. [*Information service or system*] (IID) .... FI
Forecasting, Order Administration, and Master Scheduling (PDAA) .... FOAMS
Forecasting Passenger and Cargo (MCD) .... FORPAC
Forecastle .... F
Forecastle (KSC) .... FCSLE
Forecastle .... FOCSL
Forecastle (ROG) .... FO'C'SLE
Forecastle [*Navy British*] .... FX
Forecastle .... FXLE
Forecastle Deck (IAA) .... FCLE
Forecastle Deck [*Naval engineering*] .... FDK
Forecasts, Appraisals, and Management Evaluations (MCD) .... FAME
Forecasts-in-Depth (MHDB) .... FID
Foreclose [*Legal shorthand*] (LWAP) .... FORC
Foreclosure [*Legal shorthand*] (LWAP) .... FORCL
ForeFront Group [*NASDAQ symbol*] (TTSB) .... FFGI
ForeFront Group, Inc. [*NASDAQ symbol*] (SAG) .... FFGI
ForeFront Group, Inc. [*Associated Press*] (SAG) .... ForeFrt
Foregoing (ROG) .... FGOG
Foregoing (ROG) .... FOREG
Foreground [*Computer science*] (IAA) .... f
Foreground [*Film arts*] .... FG
Foreground [*Computer science*] .... FG
Foreground (VRA) .... forgr
Foreground and Background Monitor .... FBM
Foreground Initiated Batch [*Computer science*] .... FIB
Foreground Program [*Computer science*] (IAA) .... FGP
Foreground Table (MHDB) .... FGT
Foreign (AFM) .... FGN
Foreign .... FOR
Foreign .... FORGN
Foreign [*Searchable field*] (NITA) .... FR
Foreign .... FRGN
Foreign .... FRGN
Foreign Access to Computer Technology [*USIA*] .... FACT
Foreign Adoption Center [*Later, FCVN*] (EA) .... FAC
Foreign Aerospace Material Production (MCD) .... FOAMP
Foreign Aerospace Science and Technology Center [*Air Force*] .... FASTC
Foreign Affairs [*A publication*] (BRI) .... For Aff
Foreign Affairs Administrative Support System [*Department of State*] .... FAAS
Foreign Affairs Executive Seminar [*Department of State*] .... FAES
Foreign Affairs Information Management Effort [*Computer*] [*Department of State*] .... FAIME
Foreign Affairs Information System [*Department of State*] (GFGA) .... FAIS
Foreign Affairs Interdepartmental Seminar [*Military*] .... FAIS
Foreign Affairs Manual Circular [*Department of State*] [*A publication*] .... FAMC
Foreign Affairs Programming System (CINC) .... FAPS
Foreign Affairs Recreation Association (EA) .... FARA
Foreign Affairs Research Documentation Center [*Department of State*] .... FAR
Foreign Affairs Specialist Corps [*Department of State*] .... FASC
Foreign Affairs Theory, Operations, and Monitoring (DNAB) .... FATHOM
Foreign Agents Compulsory Ethics in Trade Act [*Proposed*] .... FACE IT
Foreign Agents Registration Act of 1938 .... FARA
Foreign Agricultural Club (EA) .... FAC
Foreign Agricultural Economic Reports .... FAER

Foreign Agricultural Organization .... FAO
Foreign Agricultural Relations Office .... FAR
Foreign Agricultural Service [*Department of Agriculture*] [*Washington, DC*] .... FAS
Foreign Agricultural Service Club [*Later, Foreign Agricultural Club*] (EA) .... FASC
Foreign Agriculture Including Foreign Crops and Markets [*A publication*] .... FA
Foreign Agriculture Report [*Department of Agriculture*] .... FAR
Foreign Aid Society [*British*] .... FAS
Foreign Air Carrier [*FAA*] (TAG) .... FAC
Foreign Air Mail .... FAM
Foreign Air Program .... FAP
Foreign Aircraft Production (MCD) .... FOAP
Foreign Allowable Catch [*Fishery management*] (MSC) .... FAC
Foreign & Colonial Emerging Middle East Fund, Inc. [*NYSE symbol*] (SAG) .... EME
Foreign & Colonial Emerging Middle East Fund, Inc. [*Associated Press*] (SAG) .... FCMidE
Foreign and Commonwealth Office [*British*] .... FCO
Foreign and Domestic Teachers' Bureau [*Defunct*] (EA) .... FDTB
Foreign Applied Sciences Assessment Center .... FASAC
Foreign Area and Language Study .... FALS
Foreign Area Consumer Dialing [*Telecommunications*] .... FACD
Foreign Area Fellowship Program [*Later, SSRC*] .... FAFP
Foreign Area Officer [*Army*] (INF) .... FAO
Foreign Area Officer Management System [*Army*] .... FAOMS
Foreign Area Officer Program [*Army*] (MCD) .... FAOP
Foreign Area Research Coordination Group [*Department of State*] .... FAR
Foreign Area Research Documentation Center [*Department of State*] (AEBS) .... FAR
Foreign Area Specialist [*Army*] .... FAS
Foreign Area Specialist Training [*Army*] .... FAST
Foreign Area Specialist Training Program [*Army*] .... FASTP
Foreign Area Toll [*Telecommunications*] (TEL) .... FAT
Foreign Area Translation [*Telecommunications*] (TEL) .... FAT
Foreign Army Material Production (MCD) .... FAMP
Foreign Assignment Resources Employees [*FAA*] .... FARE
Foreign Assistance Act [*1961*] (DOMA) .... FAA
Foreign Assistance Program (WDAA) .... FAP
Foreign Bank Supervision Enhancement Act [*1991*] (ECON) .... FBSEA
Foreign Bases Project (EA) .... FBP
Foreign Bird League [*British*] (BI) .... FBL
Foreign Body [*Medicine*] .... FB
Foreign Body Cornea Left Eye [*Medicine*] .... FBCOS
Foreign Body Cornea Right Eye [*Medicine*] .... FBCOD
Foreign Body Ingestion [*Medicine*] .... FBI
Foreign Bond (MHDW) .... FB
Foreign Bondholders Protective Council [*Defunct*] (EA) .... FBPC
Foreign [*or French*] Brandy [*British*] (ROG) .... FB
Foreign Broadcast Information System .... FBIS
Foreign Broadcast Intelligence Service [*FCC World War II*] .... FBIS
Foreign Building Office [*Department of State*] .... FBO
Foreign Car Haters Club of America (EA) .... FCHCA
Foreign Claims Commission [*Canada*] .... FGNCC
Foreign Claims Settlement Commission .... FCSC
Foreign Claims Settlement Commission. Annual Report [*A publication*] (DLA) .... FCSC Ann Rep
Foreign Claims Settlement Commission. Decisions and Annotations [*A publication*] (DLA) .... FCSC Dec & Ann
Foreign Classics [*A publication*] .... FC
Foreign Clearance Base (AFM) .... FCB
Foreign Clearance Guide (AFM) .... FCG
Foreign/Colon'l Eng MidEast Fd [*NYSE symbol*] (TTSB) .... EME
Foreign Commerce Bank [*Switzerland*] .... FOCOBANK
Foreign Commerce Club of New York (EA) .... FCC
Foreign Commercial Service [*International Trade Administration*] .... FCS
Foreign Comparative Testing [*DoD*] (RDA) .... FCT
Foreign Consul (ROG) .... FC
Foreign Corp. [*Legal term*] (DLA) .... FOR CORP
Foreign Corporation Project [*IRS*] .... FCP
Foreign Correspondents' Association of Australia .... FCAA
Foreign Correspondents Club of Japan (NTCM) .... FCC
Foreign Correspondents' Club of Japan .... FCCJ
Foreign Corrupt Practices Act [*1977*] .... FCPA
Foreign Corrupt Practices Act (AAGC) .... FCPR
Foreign Counterintelligence .... FCI
Foreign Counterintelligence Program [*DoD*] .... FCIP
Foreign Counterintelligence System [*Federal Bureau of Investigation*] .... FCIS
Foreign Countries and British Colonies [*A publication*] .... FCBC
Foreign Credit Insurance Association [*New York, NY*] (EA) .... FCIA
Foreign Credit Insurance Corp. [*Business term*] .... FCIC
Foreign Credit Interchange Bureau (EA) .... FCIB
Foreign Criminal Jurisdiction (AABC) .... FCJ
Foreign Currency .... FC
Foreign Currency Agriculture Research Program [*Department of Agriculture*] .... FCAR
Foreign Currency Banking Unit (WDAA) .... FCBU
Foreign Currency Deposit Units .... FCDU
Foreign Currency Exchange (MHDW) .... FCE
Foreign Currency Loan .... FCL
Foreign Currency Translation .... FCT
Foreign Demographic Analysis Division [*Census*] (OICC) .... FDA
Foreign Direct Investment .... FDI
Foreign Directory Name [*Telecommunications*] (TEL) .... FDN
Foreign Disclosure and Technical Information System .... FORDTIS
Foreign Disclosure Automated Data [*System*] .... FORDAD
Foreign Disclosure Policy Office [*Military*] (AFIT) .... FDPO

Foreign Disclosure Review Board (AAGC) ... FDRB
Foreign Disclosure Technology Security Plan [*Army*] ... FDTSP
Foreign Document Division [*of CIA*] ... FDD
Foreign Duty (DNAB) ... FORNDY
Foreign Duty Pay ... FDP
Foreign Earned Income Act [*1978*] ... FEIA
Foreign Economic Administration [*World War II*] ... FEA
Foreign Economic Development Service [*Abolished 1972, functions transferred to the Economic Research Service*] [*Department of Agriculture*] ... FEDS
Foreign Editor (NTCM) ... FE
Foreign Electromotive Force (TEL) ... FEMF
Foreign Enterprise Service Corp. [*China*] ... FESCO
Foreign Escorted Tour [*Travel*] ... FET
Foreign Excess Personal Property ... FEPP
Foreign Exchange [*Investment term*] ... FE
Foreign Exchange [*Telecommunications*] (TEL) ... FEX
Foreign Exchange [*Investment term*] ... FOREX
Foreign Exchange [*Investment term*] ... FX
Foreign Exchange [*ADP Network Services, Inc.*] [*Information service or system*] ... FX
Foreign Exchange Accounting and Management Information System ... FEAMIS
Foreign Exchange and Currency Deposit Brokers Association (MHDW) ... FECDBA
Foreign Exchange Brokers Association [*British*] ... FEBA
Foreign Exchange Brokers of New York City (EA) ... FEBNYC
Foreign Exchange Bulletin [*A publication*] (DLA) ... For Exch Bull
Foreign Exchange Certificate [*Special currency notes sold to foreigners*] [*People's Republic of China*] (ECON) ... FEC
Foreign Exchange Cost (AFM) ... FEC
Foreign Exchange Counselling System (NITA) ... FECS
Foreign Exchange Encashments Receipts [*Finance*] ... FXER
Foreign Exchange, Eurodollar, and Branch Accounting (PDAA) ... FEEDBAC
Foreign Exchange Gains and Losses ... FXGL
Foreign Exchange Operations Fund ... FEOF
Foreign Exchange Rate Service [*Refco, Inc.*] [*Information service or system*] (IID) ... FX
Foreign Exchange Rates Database [*Databank produced by Conticurrency*] (NITA) ... FX Database
Foreign Exchange Sale Receipts [*Finance*] ... FXSR
Foreign Fd Australia Index'WEBS' [*AMEX symbol*] (TTSB) ... EWA
Foreign Fd Austria Index'WEBS' [*AMEX symbol*] (TTSB) ... EWO
Foreign Fd Belgium Index'WEBS' [*AMEX symbol*] (TTSB) ... EWK
Foreign Fd Canada Index'WEBS' [*AMEX symbol*] (TTSB) ... EWC
Foreign Fd France Index 'WEBS' [*AMEX symbol*] (TTSB) ... EWQ
Foreign Fd Germany Index'WEBS' [*AMEX symbol*] (TTSB) ... EWG
Foreign Fd Hong Kong Index'WEBS' [*AMEX symbol*] (TTSB) ... EWH
Foreign Fd Italy Index'WEBS' [*AMEX symbol*] (TTSB) ... EWI
Foreign Fd Japan Index'WEBS' [*AMEX symbol*] (TTSB) ... EWJ
Foreign Fd Malaysia Index'WEBS' [*AMEX symbol*] (TTSB) ... EWM
Foreign Fd Mexico Index'WEBS' [*AMEX symbol*] (TTSB) ... EWW
Foreign Fd Netherl'ds Index'WEBS' [*AMEX symbol*] (TTSB) ... EWN
Foreign Fd Singapore Index 'WEBS' [*AMEX symbol*] (TTSB) ... EWS
Foreign Fd Spain Index 'WEBS' [*AMEX symbol*] (TTSB) ... EWP
Foreign Fd Sweden Index'WEBS' [*AMEX symbol*] (TTSB) ... EWD
Foreign Fd Switzer'd Index'WEBS' [*AMEX symbol*] (TTSB) ... EWL
Foreign Fd U.K. Index'WEBS' [*AMEX symbol*] (TTSB) ... EWU
Foreign Fishing Observer Fund [*National Oceanic and Atmospheric Administration*] ... FFOF
Foreign Fishing Vessel ... FFV
Foreign Fishing Vessel Licensing and Surveillance Hierarchical Information System [*Canada*] (MSC) ... FLASH
Foreign Flag ... FF
Foreign Force Reduction (NATG) ... FFR
Foreign Free World (MCD) ... FFW
Foreign Freight Agent ... FFA
Foreign Funds Control ... FFC
Foreign General Agent [*Insurance*] ... FGA
Foreign General Average [*Insurance*] ... FGA
Foreign Geneva [*Alcohol*] (ROG) ... FG
Foreign Government (AAGC) ... FG
Foreign Government (AFIT) ... FORGOV
Foreign Governments or Their Authorized Representatives (MCD) ... FGAR
Foreign Independent [*or Individual*] **Travel** [*Air travel term*] ... FIT
Foreign Instrumentation Signals (MCD) ... FIS
Foreign Intelligence (MCD) ... FI
Foreign Intelligence Advisory Board (CINC) ... FIAB
Foreign Intelligence and Security Service (MCD) ... FI & SS
Foreign Intelligence Office ... FIO
Foreign Intelligence Production Requirement [*Army*] (RDA) ... FIPR
Foreign Intelligence Relations Management System (MCD) ... FIRMS
Foreign Intelligence Special Security Office (MCD) ... FISSO
Foreign Intelligence Surveillance Act of 1978 ... FISA
Foreign Interest Payment Security [*Investment term*] ... FIPS
Foreign Internal Defense ... FID
Foreign Internal Defense Plan (MCD) ... FIDP
Foreign Investment [*Business term*] ... FI
Foreign Investment Fund ... FIF
Foreign Investment in Real Property Tax Act of 1980 ... FIRPTA
Foreign Investment Law ... FIL
Foreign Investment Review Act [*1973*] [*Canada*] (IMH) ... FIRA
Foreign Investment Review Act [*Canada*] (AAGC) ... FIRA
Foreign Investment Review Agency [*Canada*] ... FIRA
Foreign Investors Tax Act of 1966 ... FITA
Foreign Key [*Computer science*] (PCM) ... FK
Foreign Labor Trends [*Department of Labor*] [*A publication*] ... FLT
Foreign Language ... FL
Foreign Language (WDAA) ... FOR LANG
Foreign Language Aptitude Test ... FLAT
Foreign Language Arts in the Grades (EDAC) ... FLAG
Foreign Language Associates ... FLA
Foreign Language Bulletin ... FLB
Foreign Language Entrance and Degree Requirements (EDAC) ... FLEDR
Foreign Language Innovative Curricula Study [*University of Michigan*] (AEBS) ... FLICS
Foreign Language Press of America ... FLPA
Foreign Language Proficiency Pay [*Army*] (INF) ... FLPP
Foreign Language Program ... FLP
Foreign Language Training Program [*Air Force*] ... FLTP
Foreign Language Use in Northern Commerce and Industry (AIE) ... FLUNCI
Foreign Languages at Work (AIE) ... FLAW
Foreign Languages for Industry and Commerce [*British*] (DBQ) ... FLIC
Foreign Languages for Lower Attaining Pupils [*Project*] (AIE) ... FLLAP
Foreign Languages in Elementary Schools ... FLES
Foreign Leave [*Military*] (AABC) ... FLV
Foreign Liaison Office [*Military*] (AABC) ... FLO
Foreign Liaison Officer Program ... FLOP
Foreign Liquidation Commission ... FLC
Foreign Listing [*Telecommunications*] (TEL) ... FL
Foreign Market Value [*Business term*] ... FMV
Foreign Material (MCD) ... FM
Foreign Material (MCD) ... FORMAT
Foreign Material Catalog ... FOMCAT
Foreign Material Exploitation Tactical Air [*Military*] (CAAL) ... FMETA
Foreign Material for Training (MCD) ... FMT
Foreign Materiel Branch [*Military*] ... FMB
Foreign Materiel Exploitation (RDA) ... FME
Foreign Materiel Number [*Weapons*] (INF) ... FOM
Foreign Materiel Program [*Military*] (RDA) ... FMP
Foreign Media Representatives Association ... FMRA
Foreign Medical Graduate [*doing residency in US hospital*] ... FMG
Foreign Medical Graduate Examination in Medical Sciences ... FMGEMS
Foreign Member of the Royal Society [*British*] (BARN) ... FMRS
Foreign Military ... FM
Foreign Military Assistance (MCD) ... FOMA
Foreign Military Assistance Coordinating Committee [*Department of State*] [*Terminated, 1950*] ... FMACC
Foreign Military Assistance Steering Committee ... FMASC
Foreign Military Financing (DOMA) ... FMF
Foreign Military Financing Program [*DoD*] ... FMFP
Foreign Military Intelligence Collection Activities [*Navy*] (ANA) ... FORMICA
Foreign Military Sales (AFM) ... FMS
Foreign Military Sales Act (AFIT) ... FMSA
Foreign Military Sales Consolidated Support Equipment List (MCD) ... FMSCSEL
Foreign Military Sales Credit [*Financing*] ... FMSCR
Foreign Military Sales Financial Management Improvement Program (MCD) ... FFMIP
Foreign Military Sales Financing ... FMSF
Foreign Military Sales Management Plan (AFIT) ... FMSMP
Foreign Military Sales Order [*Army*] (AABC) ... FMSO
Foreign Military Sales Program [*Army*] (AABC) ... FMSP
Foreign Military Sales Training ... FMST
Foreign Military Service (MCD) ... FMS
Foreign Military Training (CINC) ... FMT
Foreign Military Training Affairs Group ... FMTAG
Foreign Military Training Board (AAGC) ... FMTB
Foreign Military Training Management Flight ... FMTMF
Foreign Minister [*or Ministry*] ... FM
Foreign Minister (CINC) ... FOMIN
Foreign Missile Production (MCD) ... FOMP
Foreign Mission ... FM
Foreign Mission Section [*Diocesan abbreviation*] (TOCD) ... FgM
Foreign Missons of Yarumal [*Colorado*] (EAIO) ... FMY
Foreign National Direct Hire [*Military*] ... FNDH
Foreign National Indirect (NVT) ... FNI
Foreign National Weather Agency ... FNWA
Foreign Newspaper Microfilm Project, Association of Research Libraries, Center for Research Libraries, Chicago, IL [*Library symbol Library of Congress*] (LCLS) ... ICRL(ARL)
Foreign Numbering Plan Area [*AT & T*] [*Telecommunications*] (TEL) ... FNPA
Foreign Object ... FO
Foreign Object Check (MCD) ... FOC
Foreign Object Damage ... FOD
Foreign Object Inspection [*or Investigation*] (MCD) ... FOI
Foreign Object Investigation ... FOI
Foreign Office ... FO
Foreign Office ... FONOFF
Foreign Office Research Department [*British*] ... FORD
Foreign Officer Supply Corps (DNAB) ... FOSCO
Foreign Operating Committee [*World War II*] ... FOC
Foreign Operating Group (LAIN) ... FOG
Foreign Operations Administration [*Later, ICA*] ... FOA
Foreign Order (ADA) ... FO
Foreign Organizations' Employees Union ... FOEU
Foreign Organizations Korean Employees' Union [*South Korea*] ... FOKEU
Foreign Ownership, Control, or Influence ... FOCI
Foreign Ownership Land Register [*Queensland*] [*State*] (EERA) ... FOLR
Foreign Patent Number (NITA) ... FN
Foreign Personal Holding Co. ... FPHC
Foreign Petroleum Supply Committee [*Terminated, 1976*] ... FPSC

Foreign Pharmacy Graduate Equivalency Examination ... FPGEE
Foreign Pharmacy Graduate Examination Commission (EA) ... FPGEC
Foreign Policy ... FP
Foreign Policy Association (EA) ... FPA
Foreign Policy Briefs ... FPB
Foreign Policy Clearing House [*Defunct*] ... FPCH
Foreign Policy Discussion Group (EA) ... FPDG
Foreign Press Association (EA) ... FPA
Foreign Program [*FCC*] (NTCM) ... FP
Foreign Rations Not Available (AABC) ... FRNA
Foreign Receiving Report (MCD) ... FRR
Foreign Relations (DLA) ... FR
Foreign Relations Committee [*US Senate*] ... FR
Foreign Requirements ... FR
Foreign Research Reactor (GAAI) ... FRR
Foreign Resources Associates ... FRA
Foreign Rights (WDAA) ... FOR RTS
Foreign Rights Marketing Assistance Program [*Australia*] ... FRMAP
Foreign Salable Technology and Licence [*South Korea Information service or system*] (IID) ... FSTL
Foreign Sales Corp. [*See also Domestic International Sales Corp. - DISC*] ... FSC
Foreign Science and Technology Center [*Army*] ... FSTC
Foreign Science Bulletin ... FSB
Foreign Science Information Program (SAA) ... FSI
Foreign Sea Duty ... FSD
Foreign Separate Rations (AABC) ... FSR
Foreign Service (DD) ... ForServ
Foreign Service [*Department of State*] ... FS
Foreign Service Act ... FSA
Foreign Service Allowances [*British*] ... FSA
Foreign Service Availability [*Military*] ... FSA
Foreign Service Credits [*Military*] ... FSC
Foreign Service Grievance Board [*Department of State*] ... FSGB
Foreign Service Information Officer [*Department of State*] ... FSIO
Foreign Service Inspection Corps [*Department of State*] ... FSIC
Foreign Service Institute [*Department of State*] ... FSI
Foreign Service Leave [*British military*] (DMA) ... FSL
Foreign Service Local (CINC) ... FSL
Foreign Service Officer [*Department of State*] ... FSO
Foreign Service Officers' Training School ... FSOTS
Foreign Service Pay ... FSP
Foreign Service Reserve (Unlimited) [*Department of State*] ... FSRU
Foreign Service Reservists (MUGU) ... FSR
Foreign Service Sales Expense ... FSSE
Foreign Service Selection Date ... FSSD
Foreign Service Tour [*Military*] ... FST
Foreign Service Tour Extension (INF) ... FSTE
Foreign Services Group [*British*] ... FSG
Foreign Services Institute [*Australia*] ... FSI
Foreign Services Research Institute (EA) ... FSRI
Foreign Ship Construction and Shipyards (MCD) ... FOSCAS
Foreign Shore Service ... FSS
Foreign Sovereign Immunities Act of 1976 (AAGC) ... FSIA
Foreign Staff College [*British*] ... FSC
Foreign State National ... FSN
Foreign Statesmen [*A publication*] ... FSA
Foreign Student Service Council (EA) ... FSSC
Foreign Systems Acquisition [*Army*] ... FSA
Foreign Systems Research Center ... FSRC
Foreign Tax Credit ... FTC
Foreign Tax Credit System ... FTCS
Foreign Tax Law Bi-Weekly Bulletin [*A publication*] (DLA) ... For Tax Bull
Foreign Tax Law Semi-Weekly Bulletin [*A publication*] (DLA) ... For Tax L S-W Bull
Foreign Tax Law Semi-Weekly Bulletin [*A publication*] (DLA) ... For Tax LS Weekly Bull
Foreign Tax Law Weekly Bulletin [*A publication*] (DLA) ... For Tax LW Bull
Foreign Technical Department [*Navy*] (NVT) ... FTD
Foreign Technology Activity Office [*or Officer*] (AFM) ... FTAO
Foreign Technology Directorate (DOMA) ... FTD
Foreign Technology Division [*Wright-Patterson Air Force Base, Ohio*] [*Air Force*] ... FTD
Foreign Technology Office [*Army Tank-Automotive Command*] ... FTO
Foreign Telecommunications Systems (MCD) ... FOTELSYS
Foreign Theater ... FT
Foreign Theological Library [*A publication*] ... FTL
Foreign to Occupation [*Insurance*] ... FO
Foreign Trade Association [*Cologne, Federal Republic of Germany*] (EAIO) ... FTA
Foreign Trade Division [*Census*] (OICC) ... FTD
Foreign Trade Institute [*Mexico*] ... FTI
Foreign Trade Reports ... FTR
Foreign Trade Statistics [*Bureau of Census*] ... FTS
Foreign Trade Statistics Regulations ... FTSR
Foreign Trade Zone [*New York City docks area*] ... FTZ
Foreign Trade Zone Board ... FTZB
Foreign Traders Index [*Department of Commerce*] [*Washington, DC Information service or system*] (IID) ... FTI
Foreign Training Officer [*Military*] ... FTO
Foreign Transaction (AFM) ... FT
Foreign Vehicle Resource Center [*Tank-Automotive Command*] [*Army*] ... FVRC
Foreign Weapon Development Program (NG) ... FWDP
Foreign Weapons, Equipment, and Technology Evaluation (MCD) ... FWETE
Foreign Weapons Evaluation ... FWE
Foreign-Born Irish ... FBI
Foreign-Object Elimination [*Manufacturing*] ... FOE
Foreign-Owned or Affiliated [*Business term*] ... FOA
Forel Parchment [*Bookbinding*] (ROG) ... FOR
Foreland ... FRLD
Foreland Corp. [*Associated Press*] (SAG) ... Foreld
Foreland Corp. [*Associated Press*] (SAG) ... Forelnd
Foreland Corp. [*NASDAQ symbol*] (NQ) ... FORL
Foreland Corp.Wrrt 'L' [*NASDAQ symbol*] (TTSB) ... FORLL
Foreman (AABC) ... FMAN
Foreman (WDAA) ... FORMN
Foreman ... FORMN
Foreman of Signals [*Military British*] ... F of S
Foreman's Association of America [*Defunct*] (EA) ... FAA
Foremanship Foundation [*Defunct*] (EA) ... FF
Foremost Aviation Ltd. [*Nigeria*] [*ICAO designator*] (FAAC) ... FMA
Foremost Corp.Amer [*NYSE symbol*] (TTSB) ... FOM
Foremost Corp. of America [*NASDAQ symbol*] (NQ) ... FCOA
Foremost Corp. of America [*Associated Press*] (SAG) ... ForAm
Foremost Dairies, Inc., San Francisco, CA [*Library symbol Library of Congress*] (LCLS) ... CSfFD
Foremost [*or Forward*] **Defended Localities** [*or Locations*] [*British*] ... FDL
Foremost Energy Corp. [*Vancouver Stock Exchange symbol*] ... FMT
Foremost Municipal Library, Alberta [*Library symbol National Library of Canada*] (NLC) ... AFOM
Foreningen Nordiska Pappershistoriker [*Association of Nordic Paper Historians - NPH*] [*Stockholm, Sweden*] (EAIO) ... FNPH
Forenoon (FAAC) ... FORNN
Forensic Medicine (DAVI) ... FM
[*The*] **Forensic Medicine Consultant-Advisor** [*Program*] ... FMCA
Forensic Pathology [*Medicine*] (DHSM) ... FOP
Forensic Pathology [*Medicine*] ... FOR
Forensic Science Database [*British Home Office Forensic Science Service*] [*Reading, Berkshire, England*] [*Information service or system*] (IID) ... FORS
Forensic Science Service [*British*] ... FSS
Forensic Science Society (EAIO) ... FSS
Forensic Sciences Foundation (EA) ... FSF
Forensic Technologies International Corp. [*Associated Press*] (SAG) ... ForeTch
Forensic Technologies International Corp. [*NASDAQ symbol*] (SAG) ... FTIC
Forensic Technologies Intl [*NASDAQ symbol*] (TTSB) ... FTIC
Forensic Urine Drug Testing [*Analytical chemistry*] ... FUDT
Forensically Informative Nucleotide Sequencing [*Technique for tracing genetic origin*] ... FINS
Forepeak [*Naval architecture*] ... FP
Forer Sentence Completion Test [*Psychology*] (DAVI) ... FSC
Forer Structured Sentence Completion Test [*Psychology*] ... FSSCT
Forer Vocational Survey [*Psychology*] ... FVS
Foreshorten (VRA) ... foresh
Foresight ... FORSGHT
Foresight (AAG) ... FS
Foresight Institute (EA) ... FI
Foresight Sierra Communications System (MCD) ... FSCS
Forest ... FOR
Forest [*Commonly used*] (OPSA) ... FOREST
Forest [*Commonly used*] (OPSA) ... FORESTS
Forest [*Postal Service standard*] (OPSA) ... FRST
Forest ... FRST
Forest ... FRST
Forest, Agriculture, Industry, and Research ... FAIR
Forest Airline South Africa [*ICAO designator*] (FAAC) ... FOL
Forest and Forest Products Policy Advisory Forum (EERA) ... FFPAF
Forest and Trees for Windows [*Channel Computing, Inc.*] [*Computer science*] (PCM) ... F & T/W
Forest and Wildlands Conservation Information System [*FAO*] [*United Nations*] (DUND) ... FOWCIS
Forest and Wood Products Research and Development Corporation (EERA) ... FWPRDC
Forest City Enterprises, Inc. [*AMEX symbol*] (SPSG) ... FCE
Forest City Enterprises, Inc. [*Associated Press*] (SAG) ... ForstC
Forest City, IA [*Location identifier FAA*] (FAAL) ... FXY
Forest City, IA [*FM radio station call letters*] (RBYB) ... KAMK-FM
Forest City, IA [*FM radio station call letters*] ... KIOW
Forest City, NC [*AM radio station call letters*] ... WAGY
Forest City, NC [*FM radio station call letters*] (RBYB) ... WFNQ
Forest City, NC [*AM radio station call letters*] ... WWOL
Forest City Summit, Forest City, IA [*Library symbol Library of Congress*] (LCLS) ... IaFcS
Forest Conservation Society of America ... FCSA
Forest Elementary School, Valley Stream, NY [*Library symbol Library of Congress*] (LCLS) ... NVsFE
Forest Engineer ... F Eng
Forest Engineer ... FE
Forest Engineering Research Institute of Canada [*Vancouver, BC*] ... FERIC
Forest Engineering Research Institute of Canada, Pointe-Claire, PQ, Canada [*Library symbol Library of Congress*] (LCLS) ... CaQMFER
Forest Engineering Research Institute of Canada [*Institut Canadien de Recherches en Genie Forestier*] **Pointe-Claire, Quebec** [*Library symbol National Library of Canada*] (NLC) ... QMFER
Forest Environment and Resources Information System [*Queensland*] [*State*] (EERA) ... FERIS
Forest Environment Research [*Department of Agriculture*] (GRD) ... FER
Forest Farmers Association (EA) ... FFA
Forest Genetics Research Foundation (EA) ... FGRF
Forest Hill Public Library, Toronto, ON, Canada [*Library symbol Library of Congress*] (LCLS) ... CaOTFH
Forest Hill Public Library, Toronto, Ontario [*Library symbol National Library of Canada*] (NLC) ... OTFH
Forest History Society (EA) ... FHS

Forest History Society, Inc., Durham, NC [*Library symbol*] [*Library of Congress*] (LCLS) .... NcDurF
Forest History Society, Santa Cruz, CA [*Library symbol Library of Congress*] (LCLS) .... CStcrF
Forest Hydrology Laboratory [*Forest Service*] .... FHL
Forest Industries Association of Tasmania (EERA) .... FIAT
Forest Industries Campaign Association (EERA) .... FICA
Forest Industries Council (EA) .... FIC
Forest Industries Federation [*Australia*] .... FIF
Forest Industries Federation, Western Australia .... FIF(WA)
Forest Industries Radio Communications [*Later, FIT*] (EA) .... FIRC
Forest Industries Telecommunications [*Eugene, OR*] (EA) .... FIT
Forest Industry Energy Program (HGAA) .... FIEP
Forest Industry Research and Development Corp. [*Commercial firm Australia*] .... FIRDC
Forest Industry Strategy (EERA) .... FIS
Forest Inventory and Regeneration System .... FIRS
Forest Laboratories, Inc. [*Associated Press*] (SAG) .... ForstLb
Forest Laboratories, Inc. [*AMEX symbol*] (SPSG) .... FRX
Forest Labs [*AMEX symbol*] (TTSB) .... FRX
Forest Lake Elementary School, Wantagh, NY [*Library symbol Library of Congress*] (LCLS) .... NWanFLE
Forest Lake, MN [*FM radio station call letters*] .... WLKX
Forest Land and Resource Management Plan [*US Forest Service*] .... FLRMP
Forest Lawn Museum, Glendale, CA [*Library symbol Library of Congress*] (LCLS) .... CGIF
Forest, MS [*Location identifier FAA*] (FAAL) .... FVS
Forest, MS [*FM radio station call letters*] .... WMBU
Forest, MS [*AM radio station call letters*] .... WQST
Forest, MS [*FM radio station call letters*] .... WQST-FM
Forest Oil [*NASDAQ symbol*] (TTSB) .... FOIL
Forest Oil $0.75 Cv Pfd [*NASDAQ symbol*] (TTSB) .... FOILO
Forest Oil Corp. [*NASDAQ symbol*] (NQ) .... FOIL
Forest Oil Corp. [*Associated Press*] (SAG) .... ForestO
Forest Oil Corp. [*Associated Press*] (SAG) .... ForstO
Forest Oil Wrrt [*NASDAQ symbol*] (TTSB) .... FOILW
Forest Park [*State*] (EERA) .... FP
Forest Park Elementary School, Dix Hills, NY [*Library symbol*] [*Library of Congress*] (LCLS) .... NDxhFE
Forest Park Public Library, Forest Park, IL [*Library symbol Library of Congress*] (LCLS) .... IFop
Forest Patrol [*Activity of Civil Air Patrol*] .... FP
Forest Pest Leaflets .... FPL
Forest Pest Management [*Program*] [*Forest Service*] .... FPM
Forest Pest Management Institute [*Environment Canada*] [*Research center*] (RCD) .... FPMI
Forest Pest Management Institute, Canadian Forestry Service [*Institut pour laRepression des Ravageurs Forestiers, Service Canadien des Forets*], Sault-Ste .-Marie, Ontario [*Library symbol National Library of Canada*] (NLC) .... OSTMFF
Forest Practices Act [*Tasmania*] [*State legislation*] (EERA) .... FPA
Forest Product Laboratory, Madison, WI [*OCLC symbol*] (OCLC) .... AGF
Forest Products Abstract Information Digest Service [*Database*] [*Germany*] (NITA) .... Forest AIDS
Forest Products Abstracts [*Oxford, England*] [*A publication*] .... FPA
Forest Products Accident Prevention Association .... FRAPA
Forest Products Association (EERA) .... FPA
Forest Products Council [*Western Australia*] .... FPC
Forest Products Industry .... FPI
Forest Products Laboratory [*Department of Agriculture*] .... FPL
Forest Products Marketing Laboratory [*Forest Service*] .... FPML
Forest Products Radio Service .... FPRS
Forest Products Research and Industries Development Commission .... FORPRIDECOM
Forest Products Research Laboratory [*British*] .... FPRL
Forest Products Research Society (EA) .... FPRS
Forest Products Safety Conference (EA) .... FPSC
Forest Products Traffic Association (EA) .... FPTA
Forest Products Trucking Council (EA) .... FPTC
Forest, Range, and Watershed Laboratory [*Laramie, WY*] [*Department of Agriculture*] (GRD) .... FRWL
Forest Range Environmental Production Analytical System (MCD) .... FREPAS
Forest Range Environmental Study (GNE) .... FRES
Forest Rangers [*British military*] (DMA) .... FR
Forest Research and Development Foundation [*Canada*] .... FRDF
Forest Research Institute [*Commonwealth*] (EERA) .... FRI
Forest Research Institute .... FRI
Forest Research Laboratory [*Oregon State University*] [*Research center*] (RCD) .... FRL
Forest Reserve [*State*] (EERA) .... FR
Forest Resource Survey [*Australia*] .... FRS
Forest Resources and Environment Collective (EERA) .... FRECoII
Forest Resources Committee [*Australia*] .... FRC
Forest Resources Information System [*Global Environmental Monitoring System*] .... FORIS
Forest Resources Laboratory [*Pennsylvania State University*] [*Research center*] (RCD) .... FRL
Forest Response Program [*USA*] (EERA) .... FRP
Forest Response to Anthropogenic Stress (GNE) .... FORAST
Forest Responses to Anthropogenic Stress [*Project sponsored by university and governmental research groups*] .... FORAST
Forest/Savanna Soils [*Agronomy*] .... F/S
Forest Service [*Later, Department of Natural Resources*] [*Department of Agriculture*] .... FS
Forest Service Acquisition Regulation [*A publication*] (AAGC) .... FSAR
Forest Service Handbook [*Department of Agriculture, Forest Service*] [*A publication*] .... FSH
Forest Service Information Network - Forestry Online [*US Forest Service*] [*Information service or system*] (IID) .... FS-INFO
Forest Service Information Network Northwest, University of Washington Campus, Seattle, WA [*Library symbol*] [*Library of Congress*] (LCLS) .... WaSFSI
Forest Service Research Notes .... FSRN
Forest Service Research Paper .... FSRP
Forest Tent Caterpillars .... FTC
Forest Trust [*An association*] (EA) .... FT
Forest Use Working Group [*Australia*] .... FUWG
Forest, Wildlife, and Range Experiment Station [*University of Idaho*] [*Research center*] (RCD) .... FWR
Forest Wildlife Population and Research Group, Grand Rapids, MN [*Library symbol*] [*Library of Congress*] (LCLS) .... MnGrFW
Forest Workers Association of Tasmania (EERA) .... FWAT
Forestburg Public Library, Alberta [*Library symbol National Library of Canada*] (NLC) .... AF
Forester Resources, Inc. [*Vancouver Stock Exchange symbol*] .... FRR
Forester Sisters Fan Club (EA) .... FSFC
Foresters of America .... FOA
Forestry .... FOR
Forestry .... FOR
Forestry .... FORS
Forestry .... FORSTRY
Forestry Abstracts [*Oxford, England*] [*A publication*] .... FA
Forestry Act [*Town planning*] [*British*] .... FA
Forestry and Forest Products Industry Council (EERA) .... FAFPIC
Forestry and Forest Products Industry Council [*Australia*] .... FFPIC
Forestry Branch, Saskatchewan Department of Natural Resources, Prince Albert, Saskatchewan [*Library symbol National Library of Canada*] (NLC) .... SPAF
Forestry Canada [*Forets Canada*], Ste.-Foy, Quebec [*Library symbol National Library of Canada*] (NLC) .... QQMC
Forestry Commission [*British*] .... FC
Forestry Commission [*New SouthWales*] [*State*] (EERA) .... FC
Forestry Commission of New South Wales [*State*] (EERA) .... FCNSW
Forestry Commission of Tasmania [*Australia*] .... FCT
Forestry, Conservation Communications Association (EA) .... FCCA
Forestry/Fuel-wood Research and Development Project (GNE) .... F/FRED
Forestry Incentive Program [*US Forest Service*] .... FIP
Forestry Management, Evaluation, and Co-Ordinating Unit [*Nigeria*] [*World Bank Assisted Project Federal Department of Rural Development*] .... FORMECU
Forestry Remote Sensing Laboratory .... FRSL
Forestry Science Laboratory, Juneau, AK [*Library symbol Library of Congress*] (LCLS) .... AkJFS
Forestry Sciences Laboratory [*US Forest Service*] [*Research center*] (RCD) .... FSL
Forestry Training Council (AIE) .... FTC
Forests and Forest Industries Strategy (EERA) .... FFIS
Forests Production Association [*Australia*] .... FPA
Forestville [*Canada*] [*Airport symbol*] (OAG) .... YFE
Forestville, PQ [*AM radio station call letters*] .... CFRP
Forestville, PQ [*ICAO location identifier*] (ICLI) .... CYFE
Foret Quality Class (EERA) .... FQC
Foretop [*Obsolete*] .... FT
Forever .... FORVR
Forever Nonstatic (IAA) .... FNS
Forever Yours .... FEY
Foreword .... FRWD
Foreword (BJA) .... fwd
Forex Association of North America (EA) .... FANA
Forfar Artillery Volunteers [*British military*] (DMA) .... FAV
Forfeiture (AFM) .... FORF
Forfeiture and Penalties [*Legal term*] (DLA) .... FORF & P
Forfeiture Endangers American Rights (EA) .... FEAR
Forfeiture of Pay (DNAB) .... FORFTR
Forfeiture of Pay .... FP
Forge [*Commonly used*] (OPSA) .... FORG
Forge .... FRG
Forge .... FRG
Forge Welding .... FOW
Forged .... FGD
Forged (VRA) .... forg
Forged Carbon Steel .... FCS
Forged Chrom-Moly .... FCM
Forged Eye Bolt Manufacturers Association [*Inactive*] (EA) .... FEBMA
Forged Steel .... FS
Forged Steel [*Technical drawings*] .... FST
Forger [*MARC relator code*] [*Library of Congress*] (LCCP) .... frg
Forgery [*Business term*] .... FORG
Forges [*Commonly used*] (OPSA) .... FORGES
Forges [*Postal Service standard*] (OPSA) .... FRGS
Forges .... FRGS
Forget It, I've Got My Orders [*Bowdlerized version*] [*Military slang*] .... FIIGMO
Forging (MSA) .... FORG
Forging Die [*Tool*] (AAG) .... FGDI
Forging Industry Association (EA) .... FIA
Forging Industry Educational and Research Foundation (EA) .... FIERF
Forging Ingot Makers' Association [*British*] (BI) .... FIMA
Forging Manufacturers Association [*Later, ODFI*] .... FMA
Forgoing .... FORGNG
Forgotten Americans Need Support (EA) .... FANS
Forgotten Boys of Iceland [*Nickname for US soldiers in Iceland*] [*World War II*] .... FBI's

Forgotten Generation (EA) .... FG
Forint [*Monetary unit*] [*Hungary*] .... F
Forint [*Florin*] [*Monetary unit*] [*Hungary*] (GPO) .... Ft
Forintek Canada Corp., Ottawa, Ontario [*Library symbol National Library of Canada*] (NLC) .... OOFP
Forintek Canada Corp., Vancouver, British Columbia [*Library symbol National Library of Canada*] (NLC) .... BVAFP
Foristell, MO [*Location identifier FAA*] (FAAL) .... FTZ
Fork (MSA) .... FK
Fork [*Commonly used*] (OPSA) .... FORK
Fork .... FRK
Fork .... FRK
Fork Elementary School, Hicksville, NY [*Library symbol Library of Congress*] (LCLS) .... NHickFE
Fork Lift Truck (DS) .... FLTx
Fork Truck Hire Association [*British*] (DBA) .... FTHA
Forked .... FKD
Forked River Generating Station [*Nuclear energy*] (NRCH) .... FRGS
Forklift (AABC) .... FLFT
Forklift .... FRKLFT
Forklift Truck .... FLT
Forklift Truck (DCTA) .... FT
Forks [*Commonly used*] (OPSA) .... FORKS
Forks [*Postal Service standard*] (OPSA) .... FRKS
Forks .... FRKS
Forks, WA [*FM radio station call letters*] .... KLLM
Forks, WA [*AM radio station call letters*] .... KVAC
Forli [*Italy*] [*Airport symbol*] (AD) .... FRL
Forli [*Italy ICAO location identifier*] (ICLI) .... LIPK
Form [*of*] .... F
Form [*Rorschach*] [*Psychology*] .... F
Form [*Letter*] [*Computer science*] [*Telecommunications*] .... F
Form .... FM
Form (VRA) .... form
Form and Finish Grinding .... FFG
Form and Structure of Corporate Headings [*Cataloguing*] [*Association for Library Collections and Technical Services*] .... FSCH
Form Block (MCD) .... FB
Form Block Check Template (MCD) .... FBCT
Form Block Line (MCD) .... FBL
Form Block Template (MSA) .... FBT
Form Block Template Set (MCD) .... FBTS
Form Clearance [*Manufacturing term*] .... cF
Form Cutter .... FMCU
Form Definition Component (IAA) .... FDC
Form Definition Language [*Xerox*] (NITA) .... FDL
Form Die .... FMDI
Form Die Bulge (MCD) .... FDB
Form Die Forge (MCD) .... FDF
Form Die Impact (MCD) .... FDI
Form Die Press (MCD) .... FDP
Form Die-Swage .... FDS
Form Factor (IAA) .... FF
Form Factor Brassboard .... FFBB
Form Feed [*Computer science*] .... FF
Form, Fit, and Function (MCD) .... FFF
Form/Genre .... f/g
Form In-Mold Surfacing [*Plastics technology*] .... FIMS
Form Letter .... FL
Form Mandrel [*Tool*] (AAG) .... FMMD
Form Molding Die (MCD) .... FMD
Form of Control Users System (MCD) .... FOCUS
Form Pads [*Tool*] (AAG) .... FMPS
Form Retrieval and Manipulation Language .... FOREMAN
Form Roll .... FMRL
Form Separator [*Computer science*] (PCM) .... FS
Form Tool .... FMTO
Forma [*Form*] [*Latin*] .... F
Forma Orbis Romanae. Carte Archeologique de la Gaule Romaine [*A publication*] (OCD) .... FOR
Forma Specialis [*Special Form*] [*Biology*] .... f sp
Forma Urbis Romae [*Rome*] [*A publication*] (OCD) .... FUR
Formable Metallized Plastics [*Industrial technology*] .... FMP
Formal .... FRML
Formal Advertising (MCD) .... FA
Formal Auto-Indexing of Scientific Texts [*Computer science*] (IEEE) .... FAST
Formal Change (MCD) .... FCHG
Formal Change Draft (SAA) .... FCD
Formal Configuration Audit (MCD) .... FCA
Formal Decorative [*Horticulture*] .... FD
Formal Description Technique [*Telecommunications*] (OSI) .... FDT
Formal Design Review .... FDR
Formal Development Method [*Computer science*] .... FDM
Formal Documents Issued [*Federal Power Commission*] .... FDI
Formal Engineering Change Proposal (MSA) .... FECP
Formal Environmental Assessment (MCD) .... FEA
Formal Evaluation Acceptance Test [*Apollo*] [*NASA*] .... FEAT
Formal Executor (IAA) .... FORMEX
Formal Functional Description (LAIN) .... FFD
Formal Inspection (MCD) .... FI
Formal Integrate Long Range Planning (PDAA) .... FILRAP
Formal Officer Career Utilization Structure [*Military*] .... FOCUS
Formal On-the-Job .... FOTJ
Formal On-the-Job Training .... FOJT
Formal Operational Reasoning Test (EDAC) .... FORT
Formal Qualification .... FQ
Formal Qualification Reviews (MCD) .... FQR
Formal Qualification Test (KSC) .... FQT
Formal Query Language (NITA) .... FQL
Formal Reading Inventory [*Educational test*] .... FRI
Formal Reliability Analysis Including Normal Testing, Inspection and Checking .... FRANTIC
Formal Semantic Language [*Computer science*] .... FSL
Formal Space Planning Language [*Computer science*] (PDAA) .... FOSPLAN
Formal Syntax Definition [*Aviation*] .... FSD
Formal Technical Documents .... FTD
Formal Technical Literature .... FTL
Formal Toxoid [*Medicine*] .... FT
Formal Training [*Military*] (AFM) .... FT
Formal Training and Certification (MCD) .... FT & C
Formal Training Data System (NVT) .... FTDS
Formal Validation .... FV
Formal Validation Test Program [*Military*] .... FVTP
Formaldehyde (GNE) .... CH_2O
Formaldehyde (GNE) .... HCHO
Formaldehyde [*Organic chemistry*] (DAVI) .... HCHO
Formaldehyde Institute (EA) .... FI
Formaldehyde Task Force Fund [*Defunct*] (EA) .... FTFF
Formaldehyde-Glutaraldehyde-Dichromate [*Fixative*] .... FGD
Formaldehyde-Induced Fluorescence .... FIF
Formalin, Acetic, Alcohol Solution [*Medicine*] (BABM) .... FAA SOL
Formalin, Acetic, and Alcohol Solution [*A fixative*] [*Organic chemistry*] (DAVI) .... FAA sol
Formalin-Acetic Acid-Alcohol [*Fixative*] [*Botany*] .... FAA
Formalin-Ammonium Bromide [*Fixative*] .... FAB
Formalin-Propionic Acid-Alcohol [*Fixative*] [*Botany*] .... FPA
Formalin-Treated Pyruvaldehyde-Stabilized Human Erythrocytes [*Immunology*] .... FPHE
Formality .... F
Formamidonitrofurylthiazole [*Organic chemistry*] .... FANFT
Forman Co., Monmouth, IL [*Library symbol Library of Congress*] (LCLS) .... FmC
Forman's Reports [*1 Scammon, 2 Illinois*] [*A publication*] (DLA) .... Form
Forman's Reports [*1 Scammon, 2 Illinois*] [*A publication*] (DLA) .... Forman
Forman's Reports [*1 Scammon, 2 Illinois*] [*A publication*] (DLA) .... Forman (Ill)
Format .... FMT
Format .... FRMT
Format and Protocol Language [*IBM*] (NITA) .... FAPL
Format Code [*Computer science*] .... F/C
Format Control Language .... FCL
Format Control Word (NASA) .... FCW
Format Conversion Unit [*Computer science*] .... FCU
Format Deficiency Document (MCD) .... FDD
Format Directed List Processor [*Computer science*] (IAA) .... FLIP
Format Effector [*Computer science*] .... FE
Format Element Descriptor (IAA) .... FED
Format Handling System (IAA) .... FHS
Format Identification [*Computer science*] (IBMDP) .... FID
Format Request Element (MCD) .... FRE
Format Statement (IAA) .... FS
Formate Dehydrogenase [*An enzyme*] .... FDH
Formation [*Lithology*] .... FM
Formation .... FMN
Formation (MSA) .... FORM
Formation .... FORMN
Formation (FAAC) .... FRMN
Formation .... FRMTN
Formation Drone Control [*Navy*] (NG) .... FDC
Formation Flight Display .... FFD
Formation Flight Operation .... FFO
Formation Flight Trainer [*Air Force*] .... FFT
Formation Flying (MCD) .... FF
Formation Flying Simulator .... FFS
Formation Ordnance Workshop [*British military*] (DMA) .... FOW
Formation Pennant [*Navy British*] .... FR
Formation Temperature Ratio (PDAA) .... FTR
Formative Evaluation Research Associates [*Research center*] (RCD) .... FERA
Formatted Data Entry Program [*Mohawk Data Systems*] .... FDEP
Formatted Data: Object Content Architecture (CDE) .... FD:OCA
Formatted Data Tapes .... FDT
Formatted File System [*Computer science*] .... FFS
Formatted File System Commercial Users' Group [*Computer science*] .... FFSCUG
Formatted Teletypewriter (CET) .... FORTEL
Formatter (MCD) .... FMTR
Formatter (MCD) .... FOMTR
Formatter Sense Amplifier (IAA) .... FSA
Formatting Output Specification Instance [*Computer science*] .... FOSI
Formazin Turbidity Unit [*Analytical chemistry*] .... FTU
Formed .... F
Formed .... FRMD
Formed Lines Using Interactive Data (MCD) .... FLUID
Formed Steel Institute .... FSI
Formed Steel Tube Institute [*Later, WSTI*] .... FSTI
Formed-in-Place .... FIP
Formed-in-Place Gasket [*Automotive engineering*] .... FIPG
Formed-in-Place Plastic Gasket [*Automotive engineering*] .... FIPG
Former .... FMR
Former (MSA) .... FRMR
Former Live-In .... FLI
Former Members of Congress [*US*] [*Later, AFMC*] .... FMC

Former name of the National Society of Fund Rainsing Executives Foundation (NFD) .... NSFRE Institute
Former Owner [*MARC relator code*] [*Library of Congress*] (LCCP) .... fmo
Former Priest .... FP
Former Pupil [*Alumnus*] [*British*] .... FP
Former Soviet Union (RDA) .... FSU
Former Spouse Protection Act .... FSPA
Former Yugoslav Republic of Macedonia .... FYRM
Former Yugoslav Republic of Macedonia [*Temporary name*] (ECON) .... FYROM
Former Yugoslav Republic of Macedonia .... Fyrom
Formerly .... FMLY
Formerly (EY) .... FMRLY
Formerly (ROG) .... FORM
Formerly Employed Mothers at the Leading Edge [*Previous name, Formerly Employed Mothers at Loose Ends*] .... FEMALE
Formerly Fat Housewife [*Weight Watchers, International; advertising*] .... FFH
Formerly Married .... FM
Formerly Restricted Data [*Military*] .... FORESDAT
Formerly Restricted Data [*Military*] .... FRD
Formerly Socialist Economy (ECON) .... FSE
Formerly Used Defense Site [*DoD*] .... FUDS
Formerly Utilized Sites Remedial Action Program [*Department of Energy*] .... FUSRAP
Form-Fit-Function [*Pronounced "f-cubed"*] .... F^3
Formimino-L-glutamic Acid [*Organic chemistry*] .... FIGLU
Forming (FAAC) .... FRMG
Forming Limit Curve [*Steel sheet fabrication*] .... FLC
Forming Limit Diagram [*Manufacturing term*] .... FLD
Forming Rolls (MCD) .... FR
Forming Up Place (MCD) .... FUP
Formosa [*MARC geographic area code Library of Congress*] (LCCP) .... a-ch--
Formosa [*Argentina*] [*Airport symbol*] (OAG) .... FMA
Formosa [*Guinea-Bissau*] [*ICAO location identifier*] (ICLI) .... GGFO
Formosa [*Argentina ICAO location identifier*] (ICLI) .... SARF
Formosa Patrol Force, US Pacific Fleet .... FORMPATPAC
Formosa Resources Corp. [*Vancouver Stock Exchange symbol*] .... FSA
Formosan Association for Human Rights (EA) .... FAHR
Formosan Association for Public Affairs (EA) .... FAPA
Forms and Publications Supply Office [*Military*] (CINC) .... FPSO
Forms Control Buffer [*Computer science*] (IBMDP) .... FCB
Forms Control Center (OICC) .... FCC
Forms Control Officer (GFGA) .... FCO
Forms Description Language [*Computer science*] (MHDB) .... FDL
Forms Entry System .... FES
Forms Management .... FM
Forms Management Officer [*Army*] (AABC) .... FMO
Forms Management System [*Computer science*] .... FMS
Forms Manufacturers Credit Interchange (EA) .... FMCI
Formula .... F
Formula .... FORM
Formula Algebraic Processor [*Computer science*] (CSR) .... FLAP
Formula and Statement Translator [*Computer science*] (MCD) .... FAST
Formula Assembler Translator [*Computer science*] (BUR) .... FAT
Formula Assembler Translator [*Computer science*] .... FORAST
Formula Atlantic [*Class of racing cars*] .... FA
Formula Calculation [*Pharmacology*] (DAVI) .... FOCAL
Formula Calculator [*Digital Equipment Corp.*] (CSR) .... FOCAL
Formula Coder [*Computer science*] .... FORC
Formula Continental [*Class of racing cars*] .... FC
Formula for Optimizing through Real-Time Utilization of Multiprogramming .... FORUM
Formula Ford [*Class of racing cars*] .... FF
Formula Grants [*Vocational education*] (OICC) .... FG
Formula Index [*Molecular formula indexing*] .... FORDEX
Formula Internationale [*Agreement of Unification of Formulae*] [*Medicine*] (ROG) .... FI
Formula Junior [*Class of racing cars*] .... FJ
Formula Libre [*Automotive competition*] .... FL
Formula Manipulation Compiler [*Programming language*] [*1962*] [*Computer science*] .... FORMAC
Formula Manipulation Language [*1970*] [*Computer science*] (MDG) .... FORMAL
Formula One [*Auto racing*] F1
Formula One Spectators Association (EA) .... FOSA
Formula Pricing Agreement (AAGC) .... FPA
Formula Super Volkswagen [*Class of racing cars*] .... FSV
Formula Translating System [*Programming language*] [*1953-54*] (CSR) .... FORTRAN
Formula Translation [*A computer programming language*] (WDMC) .... Fortran
Formula Translation Computer Language (IDOE) .... FORTRAN
Formula Vee [*Class of racing cars*] .... FV
Formula Volkswagen [*Class of racing cars*] .... FV
Formula Weight [*Chemistry*] .... FW
Formularorientiertes Interaktives Datenbanksystem [*Forms-Oriented Interactive Database System*] [*Germany*] .... FIDAS
Formulary .... FORMUL
Formulating Analytical and Technical Estimate (PDAA) .... FATE
Formulating Online Calculations in Algebraic Language [*Computer science*] (IAA) .... FOCAL
Formulating On-Line Calculations in Algebraic Language Simulator Language (PDAA) .... FOSIL
Formulation and Verification .... F & V
Formyl [*As substituent on nucleoside*] [*Biochemistry*] .... f
Formylaminoacyl [*As substituent on nucleoside*] [*Biochemistry*] .... fa
Formylglycinamide Ribonucleotide (MAE) .... FGAR
Formyliminodiacetic Acid [*Organic chemistry*] .... FIDA
Formylmethionyl [*Biochemistry*] .... fMet
Formylmethionyl (sulfonyl) Methyl Phosphate [*Biochemistry*] .... FMMP
Formyl(methionyl)(leucyl)phenylalanine [*Biochemistry*] .... FMLP
Formyl(norleucyl)(leucyl)phenylalanine [*Biochemistry*] .... FNLLP
Formyltetrahydrofolate [*Biochemistry*] .... FTHF
Fornax [*Constellation*] .... For
Fornax [*Constellation*] .... Forn
Forney Army Airfield [*Fort Leonard Wood, MO*] .... FAAF
Fornication [*FBI standardized term*] .... FORN
Fornix [*Neuroanatomy*] .... F
Fornix [*Medicine*] (DMAA) .... FX
Foro Napoletano [*A publication*] (ILCA) .... Foro Nap
Forouz Island [*Iran*] [*ICAO location identifier*] (ICLI) .... OIBF
Forrest [*Australia ICAO location identifier*] (ICLI) .... APFT
Forrest City, AR [*Location identifier FAA*] (FAAL) .... FCY
Forrest City, AR [*FM radio station call letters*] .... KBFC
Forrest City, AR [*AM radio station call letters*] .... KXJK
Forrest Lake School, Grand Rapids, MN [*Library symbol*] [*Library of Congress*] (LCLS) .... MnGrFLS
Forrester's English Chancery Cases Tempore Talbot [*A publication*] (DLA) .... For
Forrester's English Chancery Cases Tempore Talbot [*A publication*] (DLA) .... Forr
Forrester's English Chancery Cases Tempore Talbot [*A publication*] (DLA) .... Forrester
Forrest's English Exchequer Reports [*A publication*] (DLA) .... For
Forrest's English Exchequer Reports [*A publication*] (DLA) .... Forr
Forrest's English Exchequer Reports [*A publication*] (DLA) .... Forrest
[*The*] **Forschner Group, Inc.** [*Associated Press*] (SAG) .... Forsch
[*The*] **Forschner Group, Inc.** [*NASDAQ symbol*] (NQ) .... FSNR
Forschungsberichte Bundesrepublik Deutschland [*Fachinformationszentrum Karlsruhe GmbH*] [*Germany Information service or system*] (CRD) .... FBR
Forschungsdokumentation zur Arbeitsmarkt- und Berufsforschung [*Deutsche Bundesanstalt fuer Arbeit*] [*Germany Information service or system*] (CRD) .... FoDokAB
Forschungsinformationssystem Sozialwissenschaften [*Informationszentrum Sozialwissenschaften*] [*Database*] .... FORIS
Forschungsprojekte, Raumordnung, Stadtebau, Wohnungswesen [*Regional Planning, Town Planning, Housing, Research Projects Database*] [*Fraunhofer Society*] (IID) .... FORS
Forschungs-Reaktor Berlin .... FRB
Forschungsund Dokumentationszentrum Chile-Lateinamerika [*Germany*] .... FDCL
FORSCOM [*Forces Command*] **Automated Intelligence Support System, Enhan ced** [*Army*] (DOMA) .... FAISS-E
FORSCOM [*Forces Command*] **Automatic Program and Budget System** [*Army*] (MCD) .... FAPABS
FORSCOM [*Forces Command*] **Information System** [*DoD*] (GFGA) .... FIS
FORSCOM [*Forces Command*] **Intelligence Group** [*Army*] .... FORSIG
FORSCOM [*Forces Command*] **Mobilization and Deployment Planning System** (MCD) .... FORMDEPS
FORSCOM [*Forces Command*] **Mobilization Plan** [*DoD*] .... FMP
FORSCOM [*Forces Command*] **Redistribution Center** [*Army*] .... FRC
Forskningsbiblioteksradet [*Swedish council for research libraries*] (NITA) .... FBR
Forskolin [*Also, FSK*] [*Organic chemistry*] .... FOR
Forskolin [*Also, FOR*] [*Organic chemistry*] .... FSK
Forssa [*Finland ICAO location identifier*] (ICLI) .... EFFO
Forster [*Airport symbol*] .... FOT
Forsterite [*CIPW classification*] [*Geology*] .... fo
Forsterite-Anorthite-Silica [*Lunar geology*] .... Fo-An-Si
Forsterite-Silica [*Lunar geology*] .... Fo-Si
Forsterite-Spinel-Cordierite-Plagioclase [*Lunar geology*] .... Fo-Sp-Crd-Pl
Forster's Digest of the Laws of Customs [*A publication*] (DLA) .... Forst Cust
Forsvarets Forskningsanstalt [*Research Institute of National Defense*] [*Information service or system*] (IID) .... FOA
Forsyth County Defense League (EA) .... FCDL
Forsyth County Public Library, Clemmons Branch Library, Clemmons, NC [*Library symbol Library of Congress*] (LCLS) .... NcWs-C
Forsyth County Public Library, East Winston Branch, Winston-Salem, NC [*Library symbol Library of Congress*] (LCLS) .... NcWs-E
Forsyth County Public Library, Kernersville Branch Library, Kernersville, NC [*Library symbol Library of Congress*] (LCLS) .... NcWs-K
Forsyth County Public Library, Reynolda Manor Branch, Winston-Salem, NC [*Library symbol Library of Congress*] (LCLS) .... NcWs-R
Forsyth County Public Library, Rural Hall/Stanleyville Branch Library, Rural Hall, NC [*Library symbol Library of Congress*] (LCLS) .... NcWs-RS
Forsyth County Public Library, Southside Branch, Winston-Salem, NC [*Library symbol Library of Congress*] (LCLS) .... NcWs-S
Forsyth County Public Library System, Winston-Salem, NC [*Library symbol Library of Congress*] (LCLS) .... NcWs
Forsyth County Public Library, Thruway Branch, Winston-Salem, NC [*Library symbol*] [*Library of Congress*] (LCLS) .... NcWs-T
Forsyth Dental Center, Boston, MA [*Library symbol Library of Congress*] (LCLS) .... MBFo
Forsyth, GA [*FM radio station call letters*] .... WFXM
Forsyth, MT [*Location identifier FAA*] (FAAL) .... FOR
Forsyth, MT [*AM radio station call letters*] .... KIKC
Forsyth, MT [*FM radio station call letters*] .... KIKC-FM
Forsyth on Composition with Creditors [*A publication*] (DLA) .... For Comp
Forsyth on Composition with Creditors [*A publication*] (DLA) .... Fors Comp
Forsyth on Trusts and Trustees in Scotland [*A publication*] (DLA) .... Fors Tr
Forsyth Technical Institute, Winston-Salem, NC [*Library symbol Library of Congress*] (LCLS) .... NcWsF
Forsythe Township Public Library, Gwinn, MI [*Library symbol Library of Congress*] (LCLS) .... MiGw

Forsyth's Cases and Opinions on Constitutional Law [*A publication*] (DLA) ... For Cas & Op
Forsyth's Cases and Opinions on Constitutional Law [*A publication*] (DLA) ... For Cons Law
Forsyth's Cases and Opinions on Constitutional Law [*A publication*] (DLA) ... Fors Cas & Op
Forsyth's Custody of Infants [*A publication*] (DLA) ... For Inf
Forsyth's Custody of Infants [*A publication*] (DLA) ... Fors Inf
Forsyth's History of Trial by Jury [*A publication*] (DLA) ... Fors Tr Jur
Forsyth's Hortensius [*A publication*] (DLA) ... For Hort
Forsyth's Hortensius [*A publication*] (DLA) ... Fors Hor
Forsyth's Trial by Jury [*A publication*] (DLA) ... For Jury Tr
Forsyth-Stokes Area Mental Health Center, Winston-Salem, NC [*Library symbol*] [*Library of Congress*] (LCLS) ... NcWsFM
Fort (ROG) ... F
Fort [*Commonly used*] (OPSA) ... FORT
Fort (ROG) ... FR
Fort [*Commonly used*] (OPSA) ... FRT
Fort ... FT
Fort (AFM) ... FT
Fort Albany [*Canada*] [*Airport symbol*] (OAG) ... YFA
Fort Albany Band Library, Fort Albany, ON, Canada [*Library symbol*] [*Library of Congress*] (LCLS) ... CaOFtaB
Fort Albany Band Library, Ontario [*Library symbol National Library of Canada*] (BIB) ... OFAB
Fort Ann, NY [*FM radio station call letters*] ... WNGX
Fort Anne Museum, Annapolis Royal, Nova Scotia [*Library symbol National Library of Canada*] (NLC) ... NSARF
Fort Anne Museum, Annapolis Royal, NS, Canada [*Library symbol*] [*Library of Congress*] (LCLS) ... CaNSARF
Fort Assiniboine Public Library, Alberta [*Library symbol National Library of Canada*] (NLC) ... AFA
Fort Atkinson, WI [*AM radio station call letters*] ... WFAW
Fort Atkinson, WI [*FM radio station call letters*] ... WSJY
Fort Battleford National Historic Park, Parks Canada [*Parc Historique National Fort Battleford, Parcs Canada*] **Battleford, Saskatchewan** [*Library symbol National Library of Canada*] (NLC) ... SBIN
Fort Beausejour Museum, Sackville, NB, Canada [*Library symbol Library of Congress*] (LCLS) ... CaNBSaB
Fort Beausejour Museum, Sackville, New Brunswick [*Library symbol National Library of Canada*] (NLC) ... NBSAB
Fort Belknap Agency, MT [*FM radio station call letters*] (RBYB) ... KGVA
Fort Belknap College, Harlem, MT [*Library symbol*] [*Library of Congress*] (LCLS) ... MtHarC
Fort Belknap Community College, Harlem, MT [*Library symbol*] [*Library of Congress*] (LCLS) ... MtHarlF
Fort Belvoir, VA [*Location identifier FAA*] (FAAL) ... DAA
Fort Bend County Library System, George Memorial Library, Richmond, TX [*Library symbol*] [*Library of Congress*] (LCLS) ... TxRic
Fort Bend Hldg [*NASDAQ symbol*] (TTSB) ... FBHC
Fort Bend Holding Corp. [*NASDAQ symbol*] (SAG) ... FBHC
Fort Bend Holding Corp. [*Associated Press*] (SAG) ... FtBend
Fort Benning (Columbus), GA [*Location identifier FAA*] (FAAL) ... LSF
Fort Benning Officers' Open Mess [*Pronounced "fuhboom"*] ... FBOOM
Fort Bowie National Historic Site ... FOBO
Fort Bragg, CA [*AM radio station call letters*] ... KDAC
Fort Bragg, CA [*Television station call letters*] ... KFWU
Fort Bragg, CA [*FM radio station call letters*] ... KLLK
Fort Bragg, CA [*FM radio station call letters*] ... KOZT
Fort Bragg, CA [*FM radio station call letters*] ... KSAY
Fort Bragg, NC [*Location identifier FAA*] (FAAL) ... DOH
Fort Bragg Public Library, Fort Bragg, CA [*Library symbol Library of Congress*] (LCLS) ... CFb
Fort Bragg/Simons Auxiliary Air Base [*North Carolina*] [*ICAO location identifier*] (ICLI) ... KFBG
Fort Branch, IN [*FM radio station call letters*] ... WBGW
Fort Branch Public Library, Fort Branch, IN [*Library symbol Library of Congress*] (LCLS) ... InFb
Fort Branch Times, Fort Branch, IN [*Library symbol Library of Congress*] (LCLS) ... InFbT
Fort Bridger, WY [*Location identifier FAA*] (FAAL) ... FBR
Fort Calhoun Station [*Nuclear energy*] (NRCH) ... FCS
Fort Campbell, KY [*AM radio station call letters*] ... WABD
Fort Campbell, KY [*FM radio station call letters*] ... WCVQ
Fort Campbell, KY [*Location identifier FAA*] (FAAL) ... XRW
Fort Campbell Post Library, Fort Campbell, KY [*OCLC symbol*] (OCLC) ... APK
Fort Caroline National Memorial ... FOCA
Fort Carson, CO [*Location identifier FAA*] (FAAL) ... FCS
Fort Carson, CO [*Location identifier FAA*] (FAAL) ... IHS
Fort Carson Hospital, Medical Library, Colorado Springs, CO [*Library symbol Library of Congress*] (LCLS) ... CoCFc-M
Fort Carson Library, Colorado Springs, CO [*Library symbol Library of Congress*] (LCLS) ... CoCFc
Fort Chaffee, AR [*Location identifier FAA*] (FAAL) ... CCA
Fort Chimo [*Canada*] [*Airport symbol*] (OAG) ... YVP
Fort Chipewyan [*Canada*] [*Airport symbol*] (OAG) ... YPY
Fort Chipewyan, AB [*ICAO location identifier*] (ICLI) ... CYPY
Fort Churchill [*Manitoba*] [*Seismograph station code, US Geological Survey*] (SEIS) ... FCC
Fort Clatsop National Memorial ... FOCL
Fort Collins [*Colorado*] [*Airport symbol*] (OAG) ... FTC
Fort Collins, CO [*Location identifier FAA*] (FAAL) ... FCL
Fort Collins, CO [*AM radio station call letters*] ... KCOL
Fort Collins, CO [*FM radio station call letters*] ... KCSU
Fort Collins, CO [*FM radio station call letters*] ... KFCT
Fort Collins, CO [*FM radio station call letters*] ... KIMN
Fort Collins, CO [*FM radio station call letters*] (RBYB) ... KPAW
Fort Collins, CO [*FM radio station call letters*] ... KTCL
Fort Collins, CO [*Location identifier FAA*] (FAAL) ... LQP
Fort Collins/Loveland, CO [*Location identifier FAA*] (FAAL) ... FNL
Fort Collins Public Library, Fort Collins, CO [*Library symbol Library of Congress*] (LCLS) ... CoF
Fort Coulonge, PQ [*FM radio station call letters*] ... CHIP
Fort Dauphin [*Madagascar*] [*Airport symbol*] (OAG) ... FTU
Fort Davis National Historic Site ... FODA
Fort Dearborn Income Securities, Inc. [*NYSE symbol*] (SPSG) ... FTD
Fort Dearborn Income Securities, Inc. [*Associated Press*] (SAG) ... FtDear
Fort Dearborn Inc.Sec [*NYSE symbol*] (TTSB) ... FTD
Ft. Derik [*Mauritania*] [*Airport symbol*] (AD) ... FGD
Fort Detrick [*Maryland*] [*Army*] (MCD) ... FD
Fort Detrick Technical Library, Frederick, MD [*Library symbol Library of Congress*] (LCLS) ... MdFreD
Fort Devens (Ayer), MA [*Location identifier FAA*] (FAAL) ... AYE
Fort Dodge [*Iowa*] [*Airport symbol*] (OAG) ... FOD
Fort Dodge, Des Moines & Southern Railway Co. [*AAR code*] ... FDDM
Fort Dodge, Des Moines & Southern Railway Co. ... FDDM & S
Fort Dodge, IA [*Location identifier FAA*] (FAAL) ... FOD
Fort Dodge, IA [*FM radio station call letters*] ... KICB
Fort Dodge, IA [*FM radio station call letters*] ... KKEZ
Fort Dodge, IA [*Television station call letters*] ... KTIN
Fort Dodge, IA [*FM radio station call letters*] ... KTPR
Fort Dodge, IA [*FM radio station call letters*] ... KUEL
Fort Dodge, IA [*AM radio station call letters*] ... KVFD
Fort Dodge, IA [*AM radio station call letters*] ... KWMT
Fort Dodge Messenger, Fort Dodge, IA [*Library symbol Library of Congress*] (LCLS) ... IaFdM
Fort Dodge Public Library, Fort Dodge, IA [*Library symbol Library of Congress*] (LCLS) ... IaFd
Fort Donelson National Military Park ... FODO
Fort Drum, NY [*Location identifier FAA*] (FAAL) ... GTB
Fort Erie Historical Museum, Ontario [*Library symbol National Library of Canada*] (BIB) ... OFEHM
Fort Erie, ON [*FM radio station call letters*] ... CKEY
Fort Erie Public Library, Ontario [*Library symbol National Library of Canada*] (NLC) ... OFEP
Fort Eustis, VA [*Location identifier FAA*] (FAAL) ... FAF
Fort Frances [*Canada*] [*Airport symbol*] (OAG) ... YAG
Fort Frances Museum and Cultural Centre, Fort Frances, ON, Canada [*Library symbol*] [*Library of Congress*] (LCLS) ... CaOFFM
Fort Frances Museum and Cultural Centre, Ontario [*Library symbol National Library of Canada*] (BIB) ... OFFM
Fort Frances, ON [*Television station call letters*] ... CBWCT
Fort Frances, ON [*AM radio station call letters*] ... CFOB
Fort Frances Public Library, Fort Frances, ON, Canada [*Library symbol Library of Congress*] (LCLS) ... CaOFF
Fort Frances Public Library, Ontario [*Library symbol National Library of Canada*] (NLC) ... OFF
Fort Frederica National Monument ... FOFR
Fort Frontenac Library, Canada Department of National Defence [*Bibliotheque Fort Frontenac, Ministere de la Defense Nationale*] **Kingston, Ontario** [*Library symbol National Library of Canada*] (NLC) ... OKF
Fort Gaines, GA [*FM radio station call letters*] ... WJWV
Fort Garland, CO [*Location identifier FAA*] (FAAL) ... FGA
Fort Garry Horse [*Military unit*] [*World War I*] [*Canada*] ... FGH
Fort Garry Public Library, Winnipeg, Manitoba [*Library symbol National Library of Canada*] (NLC) ... MWFG
Fort Gay, WV [*FM radio station call letters*] ... WFGH
Fort George [*Canada*] [*Airport symbol*] (OAG) ... YKU
Fort George G. Meade [*Maryland*] ... FGGM
Fort Gordon, GA [*Location identifier FAA*] (FAAL) ... FNJ
Fort Greely Station (SAA) ... FGS
Fort Hamilton Post Library, Morale Support Activities, Brooklyn, NY [*OCLC symbol*] (OCLC) ... TSK
Fort Hays State University (GAGS) ... Fort Hays St U
Fort Hays State University, Hays, KS [*OCLC symbol*] (OCLC) ... KFH
Fort Hays State University, Hays, KS [*Library symbol Library of Congress*] (LCLS) ... KHayF
Fort Holabird Post Library, Baltimore, MD [*Library symbol Library of Congress*] (LCLS) ... MdBFH
Fort Hood Post Library, Library Service Center, Fort Hood, TX [*OCLC symbol*] (OCLC) ... APH
Fort Hope Band Library, Eabamet Lake, Ontario [*Library symbol National Library of Canada*] (BIB) ... OELF
Fort Howard [*NASDAQ symbol*] (TTSB) ... FORT
Fort Howard Corp. [*NASDAQ symbol*] (SAG) ... FORT
Fort Howard Corp. [*Associated Press*] (SAG) ... FtHwrd
Fort Huachuca, AZ [*Location identifier FAA*] (FAAL) ... DAO
Fort Huachuca/Sierra Vista [*Arizona*] [*Airport symbol*] (OAG) ... FHU
Fort Huachuca/Sierra Vista, AZ [*Location identifier FAA*] (FAAL) ... FHU
Fort Hunter-Liggett (Jolon), CA [*Location identifier FAA*] (FAAL) ... HGT
Fort Ikoma [*Tanzania*] [*ICAO location identifier*] (ICLI) ... HTFI
Fort Indiantown Gap [*Army*] (AABC) ... FTIG
Fort Indiantown Gap (Annville), PA [*Location identifier FAA*] (FAAL) ... MUI
Fort Jay, NY [*Location identifier FAA*] (FAAL) ... GNY
Fort Jefferson National Monument ... FOJE
Ft. Johnson [*Malawi*] [*Airport symbol*] (AD) ... FJO
Fort Jones, CA [*Location identifier FAA*] (FAAL) ... FJS
Fort Kent, ME [*AM radio station call letters*] ... WLVC
Fort Kent, ME [*FM radio station call letters*] ... WMEF
Fort Kent, ME [*FM radio station call letters*] ... WUFK

Fort Kent Public Library, Alberta [*Library symbol National Library of Canada*] (NLC) .... AFK
Fort Kent Public Library, Fort Kent, AB, Canada [*Library symbol Library of Congress*] (LCLS) .... CaAFk
Fort Keogh Livestock and Range Research Laboratory [*Miles City, MT*] [*Department of Agriculture*] (GRD) .... LARRL
Fort Knox Gold Resources, Inc. [*Toronto Stock Exchange symbol*] .... FNX
Fort Knox, KY [*Location identifier FAA*] (FAAL) .... FTK
Fort Knox, KY [*Location identifier FAA*] (FAAL) .... GOI
Fort Knox, KY [*FM radio station call letters*] (RBYB) .... WLVK
Fort Knox Minerals Ltd. [*Vancouver Stock Exchange symbol*] .... FKM
Fort Langley National Historic Park, Parks Canada [*Parc Historique National de Fort Langley, Parcs Canada*] **British Columbia** [*Library symbol National Library of Canada*] (NLC) .... BFLPC
Fort Laramie Historic Site, Fort Laramie, WY [*Library symbol Library of Congress*] (LCLS) .... WyFIL
Fort Laramie National Historic Site .... FOLA
Fort Larned National Historic Site .... FOLS
Fort Lauderdale [*Florida*] [*Airport symbol*] (OAG) .... FLL
Fort Lauderdale/Executive [*Florida*] [*ICAO location identifier*] (ICLI) .... KFXE
Fort Lauderdale, FL [*Location identifier FAA*] (FAAL) .... FXE
Fort Lauderdale, FL [*Location identifier FAA*] (FAAL) .... LHI
Fort Lauderdale, FL [*Location identifier FAA*] (FAAL) .... PJN
Fort Lauderdale, FL [*FM radio station call letters*] .... WAFG
Fort Lauderdale, FL [*FM radio station call letters*] .... WBGG
Fort Lauderdale, FL [*AM radio station call letters*] .... WFTL
Fort Lauderdale, FL [*FM radio station call letters*] .... WHYI
Fort Lauderdale, FL [*FM radio station call letters*] (RBYB) .... WPLL-FM
Fort Lauderdale, FL [*FM radio station call letters*] .... WRMA
Fort Lauderdale, FL [*Television station call letters*] .... WSCV
Fort Lauderdale, FL [*FM radio station call letters*] .... WSHE
Fort Lauderdale, FL [*AM radio station call letters*] .... WSRF
Fort Lauderdale/Fort Lauderdale-Hollywood International [*Florida*] [*ICAO location identifier*] (ICLI) .... KFLL
Fort Lauderdale Public Library, Fort Lauderdale, FL [*Library symbol Library of Congress*] (LCLS) .... FFl
Fort Lauderdale Public Library, Fort Lauderdale, FL [*Library symbol*] [*Library of Congress*] (LCLS) .... FFl
Fort Leonard Wood [*Missouri*] [*Airport symbol*] (OAG) .... TBN
Fort Leonard Wood Facilities Engineer Activity .... FLWFEA
Fort Leonard Wood, MO [*Location identifier FAA*] (FAAL) .... BHN
Fort Lewis College, Durango, CO [*Library symbol Library of Congress*] (LCLS) .... CoDuF
Fort Lewis, WA [*Location identifier FAA*] (FAAL) .... LAC
Fort Liard [*Canada*] [*Airport symbol*] (OAG) .... YJF
Fort Logan Mental Health Center, Children's Library, Denver, CO [*Library symbol Library of Congress*] (LCLS) .... CoDFC
Fort Logan Mental Health Center, Denver, CO [*Library symbol Library of Congress*] (LCLS) .... CoDF
Fort Lupton Public Library, Fort Lupton, CO [*Library symbol Library of Congress*] (LCLS) .... CoFlu
Fort Macleod Public Library, Alberta [*Library symbol National Library of Canada*] (NLC) .... AFMA
Fort Madison Democrat, Fort Madison, IA [*Library symbol Library of Congress*] (LCLS) .... IaFmD
Fort Madison, IA [*AM radio station call letters*] .... KBKB
Fort Madison, IA [*FM radio station call letters*] .... KBKB-FM
Fort Magsaysay, Nueva Ecija [*Philippines*] [*ICAO location identifier*] (ICLI) .... RPXM
Fort Major [*British*] (ROG) .... FM
Fort Malden National Historic Park, Amherstburg, ON, Canada [*Library symbol Library of Congress*] (LCLS) .... CaOAmF
Fort Malden National Historic Park, Amherstburg, Ontario [*Library symbol National Library of Canada*] (NLC) .... OAMF
Fort Matanzas National Monument .... FOMA
Fort McHenry National Monument .... FOMC
Fort McKay School, Alberta [*Library symbol National Library of Canada*] (BIB) .... AFMKS
Fort McMurray [*Canada*] [*Airport symbol*] (OAG) .... YMM
Fort McMurray, AB [*Television station call letters*] CBXFT-6
Fort McMurray, AB [*AM radio station call letters*] .... CJOK
Fort McMurray, AB [*FM radio station call letters*] .... CKYX
Fort McMurray, AB [*ICAO location identifier*] (ICLI) .... CYMM
Fort McMurray Public Library, Alberta [*Library symbol National Library of Canada*] (NLC) .... AFM
Fort McMurray Regional Hospital, Alberta [*Library symbol National Library of Canada*] (NLC) .... AFMH
Fort McMurray Regional Hospital, Fort McMurray, AB, Canada [*Library symbol*] [*Library of Congress*] (LCLS) .... CaAFmH
Fort McPherson [*Canada*] [*Airport symbol*] (OAG) .... ZFM
Fort McPherson Library System, Fort McPherson, GA [*OCLC symbol*] (OCLC) .... APP
Fort McPherson, NT [*ICAO location identifier*] (ICLI) .... CZFM
Fort Meade, MD [*Location identifier FAA*] (FAAL) .... FME
Fort Meade, MD [*Location identifier FAA*] (FAAL) .... ONN
Fort Meade, MD [*Location identifier FAA*] (FAAL) .... TAU
Fort Mill, SC [*Location identifier FAA*] (FAAL) .... FML
Fort Mitchell, AL [*FM radio station call letters*] .... WAGH
Fort Monmouth Procurement Division .... FMPD
Fort Monmouth Procurement Office .... FMPO
Fort Monmouth Signal Laboratory [*Army*] .... FMSL
Fort Morgan Carnegie Public Library, Fort Morgan, CO [*Library symbol Library of Congress*] (LCLS) .... CoFtm
Fort Morgan, CO [*Location identifier FAA*] (FAAL) .... FMM
Fort Morgan, CO [*FM radio station call letters*] .... KBRU
Fort Morgan, CO [*AM radio station call letters*] .... KFTM
Fort Myer Library System and Fort McNair Post Library, Fort Myer, VA [*OCLC symbol*] (OCLC) .... MDW
Fort Myers [*Florida*] [*Airport symbol*] (OAG) .... FMY
Fort Myers [*Florida*] [*Airport symbol*] (OAG) .... RSW
Fort Myers Beach, FL [*FM radio station call letters*] .... WJBX
Fort Myers, FL [*Location identifier FAA*] (FAAL) .... FMY
Fort Myers, FL [*Location identifier FAA*] (FAAL) .... RSW
Fort Myers, FL [*FM radio station call letters*] .... WAYJ
Fort Myers, FL [*Television station call letters*] .... WBBH
Fort Myers, FL [*AM radio station call letters*] .... WCRM
Fort Myers, FL [*TV station call letters*] (RBYB) .... WGCU-TV
Fort Myers, FL [*AM radio station call letters*] .... WINK
Fort Myers, FL [*FM radio station call letters*] .... WINK-FM
Fort Myers, FL [*Television station call letters*] .... WINK-TV
Fort Myers, FL [*FM radio station call letters*] .... WJYO
Fort Myers, FL [*AM radio station call letters*] .... WMYR
Fort Myers, FL [*FM radio station call letters*] .... WOLZ
Fort Myers, FL [*FM radio station call letters*] .... WSFP
Fort Myers, FL [*Television station call letters*] .... WSFP-TV
Fort Myers, FL [*FM radio station call letters*] .... WWGR
Fort Myers/Page Field [*Florida*] [*ICAO location identifier*] (ICLI) .... KFMY
Fort Myers Southern Railroad Co. [*AAR code*] .... FMS
Fort Myers Villas, FL [*FM radio station call letters*] (RBYB) .... WJST
Fort Necessity National Battlefield .... FONE
Fort Necessity National Battlefield, Farmington, PA [*OCLC symbol*] (OCLC) .... FNB
Fort Nelson [*Hobart*] [*Tasmania*] [*Seismograph station code, US Geological Survey*] [*Closed*] (SEIS) .... FNT
Fort Nelson [*Canada*] [*Airport symbol*] (OAG) .... YYE
Fort Nelson, BC [*AM radio station call letters*] .... CFNL
Fort Nelson, BC [*ICAO location identifier*] (ICLI) .... CYYE
Fort Nelson Public Library, British Columbia [*Library symbol National Library of Canada*] (NLC) .... BFN
Fort Payne, AL [*AM radio station call letters*] .... WFPA
Fort Payne, AL [*AM radio station call letters*] .... WZOB
Fort Peck Community College, Poplar, MT [*Library symbol*] [*Library of Congress*] (LCLS) .... MtPoF
Fort Pierce, FL [*Location identifier FAA*] (FAAL) .... FPR
Fort Pierce, FL [*FM radio station call letters*] (RBYB) .... WCLB-FM
Fort Pierce, FL [*AM radio station call letters*] .... WIRA
Fort Pierce, FL [*FM radio station call letters*] .... WJFP
Fort Pierce, FL [*AM radio station call letters*] .... WJNX
Fort Pierce, FL [*FM radio station call letters*] .... WKGR
Fort Pierce, FL [*FM radio station call letters*] .... WQCS
Fort Pierce, FL [*Television station call letters*] .... WTCE
Fort Pierce, FL [*Television station call letters*] .... WTVX
Fort Plain, NY [*FM radio station call letters*] .... WBUG
Fort Point Museum, La Have, Nova Scotia [*Library symbol National Library of Canada*] (NLC) .... NSLFP
Fort Point Museum, La Have, NS, Canada [*Library symbol*] [*Library of Congress*] (LCLS) .... CaNSLhFP
Fort Polk [*Louisiana*] [*Airport symbol*] (OAG) .... POE
Fort Polk Army Airfield [*Fort Polk, LA*] .... FPAA
Fort Polk, LA [*Location identifier FAA*] (FAAL) .... POE
Fort Portal [*Uganda*] [*ICAO location identifier*] (ICLI) .... HUFP
Fort Pulaski National Monument .... FOPU
Fort Raleigh National Historic Site .... FORA
Fort Reie Historical Museum, Fort Erie, ON, Canada [*Library symbol*] [*Library of Congress*] (LCLS) .... CaOFeHM
Fort Reliance, NT [*ICAO location identifier*] (ICLI) .... CYFL
Fort Resolution, NT [*ICAO location identifier*] (ICLI) .... CYFR
Fort Richardson, AK [*Location identifier FAA*] (FAAL) .... FRN
Fort Richardson/Bryant Army Air Field [*Alaska*] [*ICAO location identifier*] (ICLI) .... PAFR
Fort Riley, KS [*Location identifier FAA*] (FAAL) .... CVY
Fort Riley, KS [*Location identifier FAA*] (FAAL) .... FRI
Fort Riley, KS [*Location identifier FAA*] (FAAL) .... FTX
Fort Riley, KS [*Location identifier FAA*] (FAAL) .... ITY
Ft. Rousset [*Congo*] [*Airport symbol*] (AD) .... FTX
Fort Rucker, AL [*FM radio station call letters*] .... WXUS
Fort St. James [*British Columbia*] [*Seismograph station code, US Geological Survey*] (SEIS) .... FSJ
Fort St. James National Historic Site [*Parc Historique National Fort St.-James*], British Columbia [*Library symbol National Library of Canada*] (NLC) .... BFSJHS
Fort St. James National Historic Site, Fort St. James, BC, Canada [*Library symbol*] [*Library of Congress*] (LCLS) .... CaBFSJHS
Fort St. James Public Library, British Columbia [*Library symbol National Library of Canada*] (NLC) .... BFSJA
Fort St. James Public Library, Fort St. James, BC, Canada [*Library symbol*] [*Library of Congress*] (LCLS) .... CaBFSJA
Fort St. John [*Canada*] [*Airport symbol*] (OAG) .... YXJ
Fort St. John, BC [*AM radio station call letters*] .... CKNL
Fort St. John, BC [*ICAO location identifier*] (ICLI) .... CYXJ
Fort St. John Public Library, British Columbia [*Library symbol National Library of Canada*] (NLC) .... BFSJ
Fort St. Vrain [*Nuclear plant*] (NRCH) .... FSV
Fort St. Vrain Nuclear Generating Station (NRCH) .... FSVNGS
Fort St. Vrain Reactor [*Platteville, CO*] (GAAI) .... FSVR
Fort Sam Houston Morale Support Library, Fort Sam Houston, TX [*OCLC symbol*] (OCLC) .... APX
Fort Sanders Regional Medical Center, Knoxville, TN [*Library symbol Library of Congress*] (LCLS) .... TKFSM

Fort Saskatchewan Municipal Library, Alberta [*Library symbol National Library of Canada*] (NLC) ..... AFSM
Fort Saskatchewan Municipal Library, Fort Saskatchewan, AB, Canada [*Library symbol Library of Congress*] (LCLS) ..... CaAFSM
Fort Scott Junior College [*Kansas*] ..... FSJC
Fort Scott, KS [*Location identifier FAA*] (FAAL) ..... FSK
Fort Scott, KS [*AM radio station call letters*] ..... KMDO
Fort Scott, KS [*FM radio station call letters*] ..... KOMB
Fort Scott, KS [*FM radio station call letters*] ..... KVCY
Fort Severn [*Canada*] [*Airport symbol*] (OAG) ..... ZFV
Fort Severn Band Library, Fort Severn, ON, Canada [*Library symbol*] [*Library of Congress*] (LCLS) ..... CaOFsB
Fort Severn Band Library, Ontario [*Library symbol National Library of Canada*] (BIB) ..... OFSB
Fort Shawnee, OH [*FM radio station call letters*] ..... WBUK
Fort Sill, OK [*Location identifier FAA*] (FAAL) ..... FSI
Fort Sill, OK [*Location identifier FAA*] (FAAL) ..... OFZ
Fort Sill, OK [*Location identifier FAA*] (FAAL) ..... PFL
Fort Sill, OK [*Location identifier FAA*] (FAAL) ..... XFS
Fort Simpson [*Canada*] [*Airport symbol*] (OAG) ..... YFS
Fort Simpson, NT [*ICAO location identifier*] (ICLI) ..... CYFS
Fort Smith [*Arkansas*] [*Airport symbol*] (OAG) ..... FSM
Fort Smith [*Canada*] [*Airport symbol*] (OAG) ..... YSM
Fort Smith & Van Buren Railway Co. [*AAR code*] ..... FSVB
Fort Smith, AR [*Location identifier FAA*] (FAAL) ..... AFT
Fort Smith, AR [*Location identifier FAA*] (FAAL) ..... FSM
Fort Smith, AR [*FM radio station call letters*] (RBYB) ..... KAOW-FM
Fort Smith, AR [*FM radio station call letters*] ..... KBBQ
Fort Smith, AR [*AM radio station call letters*] ..... KFPW
Fort Smith, AR [*AM radio station call letters*] ..... KFSA
Fort Smith, AR [*Television station call letters*] ..... KFSM
Fort Smith, AR [*Television station call letters*] ..... KHBS
Fort Smith, AR [*FM radio station call letters*] ..... KISR
Fort Smith, AR [*FM radio station call letters*] ..... KMAG
Fort Smith, AR [*Television station call letters*] ..... KPOM
Fort Smith, AR [*AM radio station call letters*] ..... KTCS
Fort Smith, AR [*FM radio station call letters*] ..... KTCS-FM
Fort Smith, AR [*AM radio station call letters*] ..... KWHN
Fort Smith Carnegie City Library, Fort Smith, AR [*Library symbol Library of Congress*] (LCLS) ..... ArFs
Fort Smith Junior College [*Arkansas*] ..... FSJC
Fort Smith/Municipal [*Arkansas*] [*ICAO location identifier*] (ICLI) ..... KFSM
Fort Smith National Historic Site ..... FOSM
Fort Smith, NT [*ICAO location identifier*] (ICLI) ..... CYSM
Fort Steele Provincial Historic Park, British Columbia [*Library symbol National Library of Canada*] (NLC) ..... BFSPHP
Fort Steele Provincial Historic Park, Fort Steele, BC, Canada [*Library symbol*] [*Library of Congress*] (LCLS) ..... CABFSPHP
Fort Steilacoom Community College, Tacoma, WA [*Library symbol Library of Congress*] (LCLS) ..... WaTFS
Fort Stewart (Hinesville), GA [*Location identifier FAA*] (FAAL) ..... MOQ
Fort Stewart/Hunter AAF Library System, Fort Stewart, GA [*OCLC symbol*] (OCLC) ..... APT
Fort Stockton, TX [*Location identifier FAA*] (FAAL) ..... FST
Fort Stockton, TX [*AM radio station call letters*] ..... KFST
Fort Stockton, TX [*FM radio station call letters*] ..... KFST-FM
Fort Street Union Depot Co. [*AAR code*] ..... FSUD
Fort Sumner, NM [*Location identifier FAA*] (FAAL) ..... FSU
Fort Sumner Public Library, Fort Sumner, NM [*Library symbol Library of Congress*] (LCLS) ..... NmFs
Fort Sumter National Monument ..... FOSU
Fort Tejon [*California*] [*Seismograph station code, US Geological Survey Closed*] (SEIS) ..... FTC
Fort Thomas Financial Corp. [*NASDAQ symbol*] (SAG) ..... FTSB
Fort Thomas Financial Corp. [*Associated Press*] (SAG) ..... FtThom
Fort Thomas Finl [*NASDAQ symbol*] (TTSB) ..... FTSB
Fort Ticonderoga Association Museum and Library, Fort Ticonderoga, NY [*Library symbol Library of Congress*] (LCLS) ..... NFtT
Fort Totten, ND [*FM radio station call letters*] (RBYB) ..... KABU-FM
Fort Union National Monument ..... FOUN
Fort Union Trading Post National Historic Site ..... FOUS
Fort Valley, GA [*FM radio station call letters*] ..... WIBB
Fort Valley, GA [*FM radio station call letters*] ..... WJTG
Fort Valley, GA [*FM radio station call letters*] ..... WQBZ
Fort Valley, GA [*AM radio station call letters*] ..... WXKO
Fort Valley State College (GAGS) ..... Fort Valley St C
Fort Valley State College [*Georgia*] ..... FVSC
Fort Valley State College, Fort Valley, GA [*Library symbol Library of Congress*] (LCLS) ..... GFoF
Fort Valley State College, Fort Valley, GA [*OCLC symbol*] (OCLC) ..... GFV
Fort Vancouver National Historic Site ..... FOVA
Fort Vancouver Regional Library, Vancouver, WA [*Library symbol Library of Congress*] (LCLS) ..... WaV
Fort Vermilion Community Library, Alberta [*Library symbol National Library of Canada*] (NLC) ..... AFVC
Fort Vermilion Community Library, Fort Vermilion, AB, Canada [*Library symbol*] [*Library of Congress*] (LCLS) ..... CaAFvC
Fort Vermilion Public School, Alberta [*Library symbol National Library of Canada*] (BIB) ..... AFVPS
Fort Walsh National Historic Park, Parks Canada [*Parc Historique National Fort Walsh, Parcs Canada*] **Maple Creek, Saskatchewan** [*Library symbol National Library of Canada*] (NLC) ..... SMCPCF
Fort Walton Beach [*Florida*] [*Airport symbol*] (OAG) ..... VPS
Fort Walton Beach, FL [*Television station call letters*] ..... WAWD
Fort Walton Beach, FL [*AM radio station call letters*] ..... WFAV
Fort Walton Beach, FL [*Television station call letters*] ..... WFGX
Fort Walton Beach, FL [*AM radio station call letters*] ..... WFTW
Fort Walton Beach, FL [*FM radio station call letters*] ..... WJUS
Fort Walton Beach, FL [*FM radio station call letters*] ..... WKSM
Fort Walton Beach, FL [*Television station call letters*] ..... WPAN
Fort Walton Beach, FL [*FM radio station call letters*] ..... WPSM
Fort Wayne [*Indiana*] [*Airport symbol*] (OAG) ..... FWA
Fort Wayne Bible College [*Indiana*] ..... FWBC
Fort Wayne Bible College, Fort Wayne, IN [*OCLC symbol*] (OCLC) ..... IFB
Fort Wayne Bible College, Fort Wayne, IN [*Library symbol Library of Congress*] (LCLS) ..... InFwB
Fort Wayne Community Schools, Fort Wayne, IN [*Library symbol*] [*Library of Congress*] (LCLS) ..... InFwCS
Fort Wayne, IN [*Location identifier FAA*] (FAAL) ..... CHN
Fort Wayne, IN [*Location identifier FAA*] (FAAL) ..... FWA
Fort Wayne, IN [*Location identifier FAA*] (FAAL) ..... SMD
Fort Wayne, IN [*FM radio station call letters*] ..... WAJI
Fort Wayne, IN [*Television station call letters*] ..... WANE
Fort Wayne, IN [*FM radio station call letters*] ..... WBCL
Fort Wayne, IN [*FM radio station call letters*] ..... WBNI
Fort Wayne, IN [*AM radio station call letters*] ..... WFCV
Fort Wayne, IN [*Television station call letters*] ..... WFFT
Fort Wayne, IN [*Television station call letters*] ..... WFWA
Fort Wayne, IN [*FM radio station call letters*] ..... WFWI
Fort Wayne, IN [*AM radio station call letters*] ..... WGL
Fort Wayne, IN [*AM radio station call letters*] (RBYB) ..... WHWD-AM
Fort Wayne, IN [*Television station call letters*] ..... WKJG
Fort Wayne, IN [*FM radio station call letters*] ..... WLAB
Fort Wayne, IN [*FM radio station call letters*] ..... WLDE
Fort Wayne, IN [*AM radio station call letters*] ..... WLYV
Fort Wayne, IN [*FM radio station call letters*] ..... WMEE
Fort Wayne, IN [*AM radio station call letters*] ..... WOWO
Fort Wayne, IN [*Television station call letters*] ..... WPTA
Fort Wayne, IN [*AM radio station call letters*] ..... WQHK
Fort Wayne, IN [*FM radio station call letters*] ..... WXKE
Fort Wayne, IN [*Location identifier FAA*] (FAAL) ..... XBF
Fort Wayne Journal-Gazette, Fort Wayne, IN [*Library symbol Library of Congress*] (LCLS) ..... InFwJG
Fort Wayne National Corp. [*Associated Press*] (SAG) ..... FtWayne
Fort Wayne National Corp. [*NASDAQ symbol*] (NQ) ..... FWNC
Fort Wayne Union [*AAR code*] ..... FWU
Fort Wayne-South Bend [*Diocesan abbreviation*] [*Indiana*] (TOCD) ..... FTW
Fort William [*Scotland*] [*Airport symbol*] (OAG) ..... FWM
Fort Wingate Army Depot [*New Mexico*] ..... FTWIAD
Fort Wingate Army Depot [*New Mexico*] (AABC) ..... FWAD
Fort Wingate Depot Activity [*New Mexico*] [*Army*] ..... FWDA
Fort Worth [*Texas*] [*ICAO location identifier*] (ICLI) ..... KCNF
Fort Worth [*Texas*] [*ICAO location identifier*] (ICLI) ..... KRFW
Fort Worth & Denver City Railway Co. ..... FW & DC
Fort Worth & Denver Railway Co. [*AAR code*] ..... FWD
Fort Worth Army Depot [*Texas*] ..... FTWOAD
Fort Worth Art Museum, Fort Worth, TX [*Library symbol Library of Congress*] (LCLS) ..... TxFF
Fort Worth Belt Railway Co. [*AAR code*] ..... FWB
Fort Worth/Carswell Air Force Base [*Texas*] [*ICAO location identifier*] (ICLI) ..... KFWH
Fort Worth Christian College, Fort Worth, TX [*Library symbol Library of Congress*] (LCLS) ..... TxFCC
Fort Worth, Euless [*Texas*] [*ICAO location identifier*] (ICLI) ..... KZFW
Fort Worth Grain Exchange (EA) ..... FWGE
Fort Worth/Meacham [*Texas*] [*ICAO location identifier*] (ICLI) ..... KFTW
Fort Worth Museum of Science and History, Fort Worth, TX [*Library symbol Library of Congress*] (LCLS) ..... TxFM
Fort Worth Public Library, Fort Worth, TX [*OCLC symbol*] (OCLC) ..... IFA
Fort Worth Public Library, Fort Worth, TX [*Library symbol Library of Congress*] (LCLS) ..... TxF
Fort Worth Qualified Material List [*NASA*] (KSC) ..... FQML
Fort Worth, TX [*Location identifier FAA*] (FAAL) ..... CNF
Fort Worth, TX [*Location identifier FAA*] (FAAL) ..... FEX
Fort Worth, TX [*Location identifier FAA*] (FAAL) ..... FTW
Fort Worth, TX [*Location identifier FAA*] (FAAL) ..... FWH
Fort Worth, TX [*AM radio station call letters*] ..... KAHZ
Fort Worth, TX [*FM radio station call letters*] ..... KEGL
Fort Worth, TX [*AM radio station call letters*] ..... KESS
Fort Worth, TX [*AM radio station call letters*] ..... KFJZ
Fort Worth, TX [*Television station call letters*] ..... KFWD
Fort Worth, TX [*AM radio station call letters*] ..... KHVN
Fort Worth, TX [*FM radio station call letters*] ..... KLTY
Fort Worth, TX [*FM radio station call letters*] ..... KOAI
Fort Worth, TX [*FM radio station call letters*] ..... KPLX
Fort Worth, TX [*FM radio station call letters*] ..... KSCS
Fort Worth, TX [*FM radio station call letters*] ..... KTCU
Fort Worth, TX [*AM radio station call letters*] ..... KTNO
Fort Worth, TX [*Television station call letters*] ..... KTVT
Fort Worth, TX [*FM radio station call letters*] ..... KTXQ
Fort Worth, TX [*Television station call letters*] ..... KXAS
Fort Worth, TX [*Location identifier FAA*] (FAAL) ..... TCB
Fort Worth, TX [*AM radio station call letters*] ..... WBAP
Fort Worth, TX [*Location identifier FAA*] (FAAL) ..... ZFW
Fort Wright College, Spokane, WA [*Library symbol Library of Congress*] (LCLS) ..... WaSpN
Fort Yukon [*Alaska*] [*Seismograph station code, US Geological Survey*] ..... FY
Fort Yukon [*Alaska*] [*Airport symbol*] (OAG) ..... FYU
Fort Yukon [*Alaska*] [*Seismograph station code, US Geological Survey*] (SEIS) ..... FYU

Fort Yukon, AK [*Location identifier FAA*] (FAAL) .... FTO
Fort Yukon, AK [*Location identifier FAA*] (FAAL) .... FYU
Fort Yukon, AK [*AM radio station call letters*] .... KZPA
Fort Yukon Community/School Library, Fort Yukon, AK [*Library symbol Library of Congress*] (LCLS) .... AkFy
Fortaleza [*Brazil*] [*Airport symbol*] (OAG) .... FOR
Fortaleza/Pinto Martins [*Brazil ICAO location identifier*] (ICLI) .... SBFZ
Fortasse [*Perhaps*] [*Latin*] .... F
Fort-De-France [*Martinique*] [*Seismograph station code, US Geological Survey*] (SEIS) .... FDF
Fort-De-France [*Martinique*] [*Airport symbol*] (OAG) .... FDF
Fort-De-France/Le Lamentin, Martinique [*French Antilles*] [*ICAO location identifier*] (ICLI) .... TFFF
Fort-De-France, Martinique [*French Antilles*] [*ICAO location identifier*] (ICLI) .... TFFD
Forte [*Loud*] [*Music*] .... F
Forte [*Loud*] [*Music*] .... FOR
Forte Piano [*Loud, then Soft*] [*Music*] .... FFP
Forte Piano [*Loud, then Soft*] [*Music*] .... FP
Forte Princip [*Brazil*] [*Airport symbol*] (AD) .... FDB
Forte Software [*NASDAQ symbol*] (TTSB) .... FRTE
Forte Software, Inc. [*Associated Press*] (SAG) .... ForteSft
Forte Software, Inc. [*NASDAQ symbol*] (SAG) .... FRTE
Fortean Times [*A publication*] .... FT
Fortescue's English Courts Reports [*A publication*] (DLA) .... Fortes
Fortescue's English King's Bench Reports [*92 English Reprint*] [*1695-1738*] [*A publication*] (DLA) .... Fort
Fortescue's English King's Bench Reports [*92 English Reprint*] [*1695-1738*] [*A publication*] (DLA) .... Fortes Rep
Fortescue's English King's Bench Reports [*92 English Reprint*] [*1695-1738*] [*A publication*] (DLA) .... Fortesc
Fortescue's English King's Bench Reports [*92 English Reprint*] [*1695-1738*] [*A publication*] (DLA) .... Fortescue
Fortescue's English King's Bench Reports [*92 English Reprint*] [*1695-1738*] [*A publication*] (DLA) .... Fortescue (Eng)
FORTH Interest Group (EA) .... FIG
Fortification .... FORT
Fortification (ROG) .... FT
Fortification (VRA) .... ft
Fortification (AABC) .... FTN
Fortified [*Nutrition*] .... fort
Fortified .... FTD
Fortified Aqueous [*Pharmacology*] .... FA
Fortified Barrier System (MCD) .... FBS
Fortified Benzene Hexachloride [*Insecticide*] .... FBHC
Fortis [*Strong*] [*Pharmacy*] .... FORT
Fortis AMEV [*AM Symbol*] (TTSB) .... AMEVN
Fortis, Inc. [*Toronto Stock Exchange symbol*] .... FTS
Fortis Securities [*Formerly, AMEV Securities*] [*NYSE symbol*] (SPSG) .... FOR
Fortis Securities [*Associated Press*] (SAG) .... FortisSc
Fortissimo [*Very Loud*] [*Music*] .... FF
Fortissimo [*Very Loud*] [*Music*] (ROG) .... FO
Fortissimo [*Very Loud*] [*Music*] .... FORTIS
Fortissimo [*Very Loud*] [*Music*] (ROG) .... FORTISS
Fortissimus [*Strongest*] [*Pharmacy*] (ROG) .... FORTISS
Fortississimo [*As Loud as Possible*] [*Music*] .... FFF
Fortitudo Eius Rhodum Tenuit [*His Strength Keeps Rhodes*] [*Motto of Lodovico family. Initials were used on gold coin struck by Duke Lodovico (1439-1465)*] .... FERT
Fortnight .... FRT
Fortnightly .... FORTN
Fortnightly Law Journal [*A publication*] (DLA) .... Fort LJ
Fortnightly Law Journal [*A publication*] (DLA) .... Fortn LJ
Fortnightly Law Journal [*A publication*] (DLA) .... Fortnightly LJ
Fortnightly Law Journal (Canada) [*A publication*] (ILCA) .... FLJ (Can)
FORTRAN [*Formula Translating System*] Analytical Cross Reference TabulationSystem [*Computer science*] .... FACTS
FORTRAN [*Formula Translating System*] and Internal Translator System [*Computer science*] (IEEE) .... FORTRANSIT
FORTRAN [*Formula Translating System*] Assembly Program [*Computer science*] .... FAP
FORTRAN [*Formula Translating System*] Automatic Code Evaluation System [*NASA Computer science*] .... FACES
FORTRAN [*Formula Translating System*] Automatic Debugging System [*Computer science*] .... FADS
FORTRAN [*Formula Translating System*] Automatic Timing System [*Computer science*] .... FATS
FORTRAN [*Formula Translating System*] Compiled Block-Oriented Simulation Language [*Computer science*] (IEEE) .... FORBLOC
FORTRAN [*Formula Translating System*] Compiler [*Computer science*] (SAA) .... FORTOCOM
FORTRAN [*Formula Translating System*] Compiler Validation System [*Computer science*] .... FCVS
FORTRAN [*Formula Translating System*] Conversational Environment [*Computer science*] .... FORCE
FORTRAN [*Formula Translating System*] Debugging Aid Program [*Computer science*] .... FORDAP
FORTRAN [*Formula Translating System*] Deductive System [*Computer science*] (IAA) .... FDS
FORTRAN Enhancement Package (NITA) .... FEP
FORTRAN [*Formula Translating System*] Executive Assembly Program [*Computer science*] (IAA) .... FEAP
FORTRAN [*Formula Translating System*] Extended Graph Algorithmic Language [*1972*] [*Computer science*] (CSR) .... FGRAAL

FORTRAN [*Formula Translating System*] Information Bulletin [*Computer science*] (IEEE) .... FIB
FORTRAN [*Formula Translating System*] Input-Output Package [*Computer science*] (IEEE) .... FIOP
FORTRAN [*Formula Translating System*] Interactive Subroutine Library [*Computer science*] .... FISLIB
FORTRAN [*Formula Translation*] Language in Core Rapid Translator [*Xerox*] (NITA) .... FLAIR
FORTRAN [*Formula Translating System*] List Processing Language [*Computer science*] (IEEE) .... FLPL
FORTRAN [*Formula Translating System*] Load and Go [*Xerox Corp.*] [*Computer science*] .... FLAG
FORTRAN [*Formula Translating System*] Load and Go System [*University of Wisconsin*] [*Computer science*] (IEEE) .... FORGO
FORTRAN [*Formula Translating System*] Logical Information Retrieval Technique [*Computer science*] .... FLIRT
FORTRAN [*Formula Translating System*] Mathematical Programming System [*Computer science*] (IEEE) .... FMPS
FORTRAN [*Formula Translating System*] Matrix Abstraction Technique [*Computer science*] (MCD) .... FORMAT
FORTRAN [*Formula Translating System*] Matrix Abstraction Technique-FORTRAN [*Computer science*] (CSR) .... FORMAT-FORTRAN
FORTRAN [*Formula Translating System*] Matrix Analysis [*Computer science*] .... FORMA
FORTRAN [*Formula Translating System*] Monitor System [*Computer science*] .... FMS
FORTRAN [*Formula Translating System*] Operating System [*Computer science*] .... FOS
FORTRAN [*Formula Translating System*]-Oriented Information Management System [*Computer science*] .... FORIMS
FORTRAN [*Formula Translating System*] Programming Environment [*Computer science*] (HGAA) .... FPE
FORTRAN [*Formula Translating System*] Rules Used as a General Applications Language [*Computer science*] .... FRUGAL
FORTRAN [*Formula Translating System*] Style Runcible [*Computer science*] .... FORTRUNCIBLE
FORTRAN [*Formula Translating System*]-to-ALGOL Translator [*Algorithmic language*] [*Computer science*] (IEEE) .... FALTRAN
FORTRAN [*Formula Translating System*] Tuner [*Computer science*] .... FORTUNE
FORTRAN [*Formula Translating System*] Utility System [*Computer science*] .... FUS
Fortress Group [*NASDAQ symbol*] (TTSB) .... FRTG
Fortress Group, Inc. (The) [*Associated Press*] (SAG) .... FortGrp
Fortress Group, Inc. (The) [*NASDAQ symbol*] (SAG) .... FRTG
Fortress of Louisbourg, Canada Department of Indian Affairs and Northern Development, Fortress of Louisbourg, NS, Canada [*Library symbol Library of Congress*] (LCLS) .... CaNSLF
Fortress of Louisbourg, Canada National Historic Park [*Forteresse de Louisbourg, Parc Historique National*] Nova Scotia [*Library symbol National Library of Canada*] .... NSLF
Fortress Resources [*Vancouver Stock Exchange symbol*] .... FRS
Fortress Study Group (EAIO) .... FSG
Fortschrittliche Buergerpartei [*Progressive Citizens' Party*] [*Liechtenstein*] (PPW) .... FBP
Fortsetzung und Schluss Folgen [*To Be Continued and Concluded*] [*German*] .... FUSF
Fortuna, CA [*Location identifier FAA*] (FAAL) .... FOT
Fortuna, CA [*AM radio station call letters*] .... KAJK
Fortuna, CA [*FM radio station call letters*] .... KQEX
Fortunair Canada [*FAA designator*] (FAAC) .... FXC
Fortune .... FRTN
Fortune Petroleum [*AMEX symbol*] (TTSB) .... FPX
Fortune Petroleum Corp. [*Associated Press*] (SAG) .... FortPet
Fortune Petroleum Corp. [*Associated Press*] (SAG) .... FortPt
Fortune Petroleum Corp. [*AMEX symbol*] (SPSG) .... FPX
Fortune Public Library, Fortune, NF, Canada [*Library symbol Library of Congress*] (LCLS) .... CaNfFo
Fortune Public Library, Newfoundland [*Library symbol National Library of Canada*] (NLC) .... NFFO
Fortune Society (EA) .... FS
Fortune SRL [*Italy ICAO designator*] (FAAC) .... FOR
Fortunius Garcia de Erzila [*Flourished, 16th century*] [*Authority cited in pre-1607 legal work*] (DSA) .... Fortu
Fortville Tribune, Fortville, IN [*Library symbol Library of Congress*] (LCLS) .... InFtvT
Forty Automatic Report Generating Operation (MCD) .... FARGO
Forty Pound Charge (SAA) .... FPC
Forty Upward Network [*Defunct*] (EA) .... FUN
Forty-Eight Item Counseling Evaluation Test [*Psychology*] .... ICET
Fortyeightmo [*A 96-page, 48-leaf book*] (WDMC) 48mo
Forty-Foot [*Container*] Equivalent Unit (DOMA) .... FEU
Forty-Mile Air [*ICAO designator*] (FAAC) .... MLA
[*The*] Forum (AAGC) .... F
Forum [*Record label*] .... For
Forum .... FRUM
[*The*] FORUM [*Foundation of Research for Understanding Man*] (EA) .... TF
Forum Africain pour la Reconstruction [*Gabon*] [*Political party*] (EY) .... FAR
Forum Atomique Europeen [*Association of European Atomic Forums*] (EAIO) .... FORATOM
Forum: Bench and Bar Review [*A publication*] (DLA) .... Forum
Forum Democratico Angolana [*Political party*] (EY) .... FDA
Forum, Denver, IA [*Library symbol Library of Congress*] (LCLS) .... IaDvF
Forum. Dickinson School of Law [*A publication*] (DLA) .... Forum
Forum Europeen de l'Orientation Academique (AIE) .... FEDORA
Forum Fisheries Committee [*Australia*] .... FFC
Forum for Death Education and Counseling [*Later, ADEC*] (EA) .... FDEC

Forum for European Bio-industry Coordination [*Brussels-based umbrella group*] .... FEBC
Forum for Medical Affairs [*Formerly, CPOSMA*] (EA) .... FMA
Forum for the Advancement of Educational Therapy (AIE) .... FAET
Forum for the Advancement of Toxicology in Colleges of Pharmacy (EA) .... FATCP
Forum for the Restoration of Democracy [*Kenya*] [*Political party*] (ECON).... FORD
Forum for Women in Bridge [*Defunct*] (EA) .... FWB
Forum Group [*NASDAQ symbol*] (TTSB) .... FOUR
Forum Group, Inc. [*Associated Press*] (SAG) .... Forum
Forum Group, Inc. [*NASDAQ symbol*] (NQ) .... FOUR
Forum Institute [*Defunct*] (EA) .... FI
Forum International de Liaison des Forces de la Paix [*International Liaison Forum of Peace Forces - ILF*] [*Moscow, USSR*] (EAIO) .... FILFP
Forum International de Liaison des Forces de la Paix [*International Liaison Forum of Peace Forces - ILF*] (EA) .... ILFP
Forum International: International Ecosystems University (EA) .... IEU
Forum Jeunesse des Communautes Europeennes [*Youth Forum of the European Communities - YFEC*] (EAIO) .... FJCE
Forum Law Review [*A publication*] (DLA) .... Forum
Forum Law Review [*A publication*] (DLA) .... Forum LR
Forum Law Review [*A publication*] (ILCA) .... Forum Rev
Forum of African Voluntary Development Organizations .... FAVDO
Forum of Control Data Users [*Later, VIM, Inc.*] .... FOCUS
Forum of Environmental Journalists of Bangladesh (EERA) .... FEJB
Forum of National Hispanic Organizations (EA) .... FNHO
Forum of Private Business [*British*] .... FPB
Forum on Allied Health Data [*American Occupational Therapy Association*] .... FAHD
Forum on Information Resources and Microcomputers (NITA) .... FIRM
Forum on State and Tribal Toxics Action [*Environmental Protection Agency*] (EGAO) .... FOSTTA
Forum Public Speaking Clubs [*Australia*] .... FPSC
Forum (Public Speaking) Group [*Australia*] .... F(PS)G
Forum Resources Ltd. [*Vancouver Stock Exchange symbol*] .... FOM
Forum Retirement Partners Ltd. [*Associated Press*] (SAG) .... ForumR
Forum Retirement Partnership Ltd. [*AMEX symbol*] (SPSG) .... FRL
Forum Retirem't Ptnrs [*AMEX symbol*] (TTSB) .... FRL
Forum Romanum [*The Roman Forum*] .... FR
Forus [*Norway ICAO location identifier*] (ICLI) .... ENFO
Forval Turbo Interface [*Computer science*] .... FTI
Forward .... F
Forward (ADA) .... FD
Forward [*Business term*] .... FOR
Forward .... FORD
Forward [*Publishing*] (WDMC) .... fore
Forward (AFM) .... FWD
Forward Acquisition RADAR .... FAR
Forward Acquisition Sensor .... FAS
Forward Acquisition Sensor (IEEE) .... FASS
Forward Acquisition System .... FAS
Forward Acting Linear Combiner (IAA) .... FALC
Forward Acting Shift Register (MHDB) .... FASR
Forward Addition Algorithm Using the Nearest-Neighbor Distance Error Criteria [*Algorithm*] .... FANNDE
Forward/Aft (KSC) .... F/A
Forward Aid Station [*Army*] (INF) .... FAS
Forward Air Control [*or Controller*] [*Air Force*] .... FAC
Forward Air Control Party [*Military*] (CAAL) .... FACP
Forward Air Control Party Training [*Navy*] (ANA) .... FACPTNG
Forward Air Control Post (AFM) .... FACP
Forward Air Control / Self-Contained Airborne Reconnaissance [*Air Force*] (PDAA) .... FAC/SCAR
Forward Air Controller (Airborne) (NVT) .... FAC(A)
Forward Air Controller Terminal .... FACTER
Forward Air Freight (WDAA) .... FAF
Forward Air Guide (NVT) .... FAG
Forward Air Strike Evaluation .... FAST-VAL
Forward Air Strike Task (CINC) .... FAST
Forward Air Support Operations Center (NATG) .... FASOC
Forward Airborne Surveillance and Tracking .... FAST
Forward Airfield Maintenance Organization .... FAMO
Forward Airfield Supply Organization .... FASO
Forward Airhead Maintenance Area [*Military British*] .... FAMA
Forward America [*Defunct*] (EA) .... FA
Forward Angle Light Scattering [*Analytical biochemistry*] .... FALS
Forward Area Aiming and Refueling Point [*Military*] (MCD) .... FAARP
Forward Area Air Defense .... FAAD
Forward Area Air Defense Battery (DNAB) .... FAADBTY
Forward Area Air Defense Command and Control [*Military*] .... FAAD C2
Forward Area Air Defense Command and Control Intelligence System [*Army*] .... FAADC²I
Forward Area Air Defense Engagement Zone [*Army*] .... FAADEZ
Forward Area Air Defense Ground-Based Sensor [*Army*] .... FAAD-GBS
Forward Area Air Defense System .... FAADS
Forward Area Air Defense Weapon .... FAADW
Forward Area Alerting RADAR .... FAAR
Forward Area Alerting System (AABC) .... FAAS
Forward Area Antiballistic Missile System [*Military*] (IAA) .... FAABMS
Forward Area Ballistic Missile Intercept System (PDAA) .... FABMIS
Forward Area Collection and ECM [*Electronic Countermeasures*] .... FACE
Forward Area Collection Equipment (MCD) .... FACE
Forward Area Defense (DOMA) .... FAD
Forward Area Demagnetizing Range [*Military*] (DOMA) .... FADR
Forward Area Deployment, Spain .... FADS

Forward Area Ground Control (IAA) .... FAGC
Forward Area LASER Systems - Tactical and Fiscal [*Military*] .... FALSTAF
Forward Area LASER Weapon .... FALW
Forward Area Limited Observing Program (MCD) .... FALOP
Forward Area RAWINSONDE [*RADAR Wind Sounding and Radiosonde*] Set [*Army*] .... FARS
Forward Area Rearm and Refuel Point .... FARRP
Forward Area Rearm and Refuel Site (MCD) .... FARRS
Forward Area Rearm/Refuel Point [*Army*] (INF) .... FARP
Forward Area Refueling Equipment [*Army*] .... FARE
Forward Area Refuelling and Rearming .... FARR
Forward Area Resupply Point .... FARP
Forward Area Signal Center (MCD) .... FASC
Forward Area SONAR Research [*Navy*] .... FASOR
Forward Area Support Center (MCD) .... FASC
Forward Area Support Company [*Military*] .... FASCO
Forward Area Support Coordination Officer [*Army*] (AABC) .... FASCO
Forward Area Support Helicopter .... FASH
Forward Area Support Team [*Military*] (INF) .... FAST
Forward Area Tactical Teletype (MCD) .... FATT
Forward Area Tactical Teletypewriter Set .... FATTS
Forward Area Tactical Typewriter .... FATTY
Forward Area Trace (MCD) .... FAT
Forward Area Warning (IAA) .... FAW
Forward Area Water Point Supply System .... FAWPSS
Forward Area Weapons [*Military*] .... FAW
Forward Armored Mortar System (MCD) .... FAMS
Forward Artillery Observer [*Liaison officer*] [*Army*] (VNW) .... FAO
Forward Assembly Area [*Army*] (DOMA) .... FAA
Forward Avionics Bay .... FAB
Forward Ballast Tank (MSA) .... FBT
Forward Battle Zone [*British*] .... FBZ
Forward Body .... FB
Forward Bomb Line .... FWDBL
Forward Brigade Administrative Area [*British*] .... FWDBAA
Forward Brigade Maintenance Area [*Army*] .... FBMA
Forward Cab [*Automotive engineering*] .... FC
Forward Calculation Request .... FCR
Forward Chaining [*Psychology*] .... FC
Forward Channel [*Telecommunications*] .... FOCH
Forward Collect (FAAC) .... FWDC
Forward Combat Zone (NATG) .... FCZ
Forward Command Element (DOMA) .... FCE
Forward Command Post (NATG) .... FCP
Forward Compartment .... F
Forward Contactor (IAA) .... FCR
Forward Control [*Automotive engineering*] .... FC
Forward Control and Analysis Center (MCD) .... FCAC
Forward Copy of Orders with Endorsements to Administrative Office, Executive Office of the Secretary of the Navy (DNAB) .... FORCOPEXOS
Forward Crash Avoidance Systems [*NHTSA*] (TAG) .... FOCAS
Forward Defended Locality [*Military British*] .... FDL
Forward Defense Post (NATG) .... FDP
Forward Delivery Squadron [*British military*] (DMA) .... FDS
Forward Direction Center [*Air Force*] .... FDC
Forward Director Post .... FDP
Forward Distribution Point [*Military*] .... FDP
Forward Dressing Station [*Military British*] .... FDS
Forward Echelon [*Army*] .... Fwd Ech
Forward Echelon, Communications Zone [*Europe*] [*Army*] .... FECOMZ
Forward Echelon, Communications Zone [*Europe*] [*Army*] .... FECZ
Forward Edge of the Battle Area [*Army*] (AABC) .... FEBA
Forward End Cap .... FEC
Forward Engine Room .... FER
Forward Engineering Operating Station [*Navy*] (CAAL) .... FEOS
Forward Entry Device [*Army*] (DOMA) .... FED
Forward Environmental Protection Device (MCD) .... FEPD
Forward Equipment Bay (MCD) .... FEB
Forward Error Control Electronics System (IAA) .... FECES
Forward Error Correction [*Computer code*] .... FEC
Forward Error Detection and Correction .... FEDAC
Forward Events Controller (MCD) .... FEC
Forward Fighting Aircraft Rocket .... FFAR
Forward Fighting Operating Base [*Military*] (AFM) .... FFOB
Forward Firing Aircraft .... FFAR
Forward Firing Ordnance (MCD) .... FFO
Forward Floating Depot [*Army*] .... FFD
Forward Forces Command-Army (DOMA) .... FFC-A
Forward Forward Air Controller [*Military*] .... FFAC
Forward Fuel Ballast Tank .... FFBT
Forward Fuselage .... FF
Forward Gate .... FG
Forward Half-Line [*Feed*] .... FHL
Forward Headquarters Element .... FHE
Forward Heat Shield [*NASA*] (KSC) .... FHS
Forward Heat Shield (MCD) .... FWDHTSHLD
Forward Heat-Shield Separation [*NASA*] (KSC) .... FHSS
Forward Indicator BIT [*Binary Digit*] (TEL) .... FIB
Forward Industries [*NASDAQ symbol*] (SAG) .... FORD
Forward Industries, Inc. [*Associated Press*] (SAG) .... Forward
Forward Industries, Inc. [*Associated Press*] (SAG) .... Forwrd
Forward Industries(NY) [*NASDAQ symbol*] (TTSB) .... FORD
Forward Inspection Team [*Military*] .... FIT
Forward Interpretation Unit [*Military*] .... FIU
Forward Interworking Telephony Event [*Telecommunications*] (TEL) .... FITE

Forward Launched Aerodynamic Missiles ... FLAM
Forward Light Scatter ... FLS
Forward Line of Own Troops (MCD) ... FLOT
Forward Load Control (MCD) ... FLC
Forward Load Control Assembly (MCD) ... FLCA
Forward Logistical Element [*Military*] ... FLE
Forward Logistics Site [*Navy*] ... FLS
Forward Look SONAR ... FLS
Forward Looking Infrared RADAR [*Military*] (INF) ... FLIR
Forward Looking Strategy ... fls
Forward Maintenance Area (NATG) ... FMA
Forward Master Events Controller [*NASA*] (NASA) ... FMEC
Forward Medical Equipment Depot [*Military British*] ... FMED
Forward Medical Treatment Team [*Army*] (INF) ... FMTT
Forward Mobile Base Stockage (MCD) ... FMBS
Forward Mobile Support Unit ... FMSU
Forward Motion ... FM
Forward Motion Compensation ... FMC
Forward Oblique (CAAL) ... FO
Forward Observation Officer [*Military*] ... FOO
Forward Observation Post [*Military*] ... FOP
Forward Observer [*Military*] ... FO
Forward Observer [*Military*] ... FOBSR
Forward Observer Bombardment [*Military*] ... FOB
Forward Observer COLIDAR [*Coherent Light Detecting and Ranging*] ... FOC
Forward Observer - Forward Air Controller [*Military*] (INF) ... FO/FAC
Forward Observer LASER Range-Finder ... FOLR
Forward Observer Target Survey Unit [*Military*] ... FOBTSU
Forward Observer Team Equipped with Ground LASER Locator Designator (MCD) ... FOTEGLLD
Forward Observer Training Center [*Army*] (INF) ... FOTC
Forward Observer Vehicle [*Military*] (MCD) ... FOV
Forward of the FEBA [*Forward Edge of the Battle Area*] [*Military*] ... FOFEBA
Forward of Wing [*Aerospace*] (AAG) ... FW
Forward Operating Base [*Air Force*] (AFM) ... FOB
Forward Operating Location [*Military*] ... FOL
Forward Peak (DNAB) ... FP
Forward Peak Tank [*On ships*] ... FPT
Forward Perpendicular ... FP
Forward Pitch Amplifier (MCD) ... FPA
Forward Port Capabilities [*Navy*] ... FORPORT
Forward Power Control Assembly (MCD) ... FPCA
Forward Power Controller (MCD) ... FPC
Forward Power Supply (MCD) ... FPS
Forward Pricing Rate Agreement ... FPRA
Forward Propagation by Ionospheric Scatter [*Radio communications technique*] ... FPIS
Forward Propagation by Tropospheric Scatter [*Radio communications technique*] ... FPTS
Forward RADAR Enhancement Device ... FRED
Forward Rate Agreement [*Banking*] ... FRA
Forward Reaction Control Subsystem [*NASA*] (NASA) ... FRCS
Forward Reaction Jet Driver (MCD) ... FRJD
Forward Ready Signal [*Telecommunications*] (TEL) ... FRS
Forward Rearm and Refuel Point [*Military*] (VNW) ... FREARF
Forward Recoil Spectrometry [*Measurement method*] ... FRES
Forward Reconnaissance (NVT) ... FORECON
Forward Refueling Area ... FRA
Forward Refueling Point ... FRP
Forward Repair Team [*Military British*] ... FRT
Forward Sale Agreement [*EXFINCO*] ... FSA
Forward Scatter ... FS
Forward Scatter (NATG) ... FSC
Forward Scatter System (NATG) ... FSS
Forward Scattering Spectroscopy ... FSS
Forward Security Element [*Soviet military force*] ... FSE
Forward Sensor Interface Control [*Army*] (RDA) ... FSIC
Forward Sequence Number [*Telecommunications*] (TEL) ... FSN
Forward Service Support Element (AABC) ... FSSE
Forward Skirt Adapter ... FSA
Forward Sortation Area [*Mailing technique*] ... FSA
Forward Space Block (CMD) ... FSB
Forward Space File (CMD) ... FSF
Forward Space Record ... FSR
Forward Supply Point [*Military*] (AFM) ... FSP
Forward Supply Support ... FSS
Forward Support ... FS
Forward Support Area [*Military*] ... FSA
Forward Support Base ... FSB
Forward Support Battalion [*Army*] (INF) ... FSB
Forward Support Element ... FSE
Forward Support Medical Company [*Military*] (INF) ... FSMC
Forward Support Patrol Base ... FSPB
Forward Support Team (MCD) ... FST
Forward Support Unit (DOMA) ... FUS
Forward Swept Wing ... FSW
Forward Toward the Bow [*Stowage*] (DNAB) ... FW/B
Forward Transfer [*Telecommunications*] (TEL) ... FOT
Forward Transfer [*Telecommunications*] (TEL) ... FT
Forward Transfer Admittance ... FTA
Forward Transfer Function [*Telecommunications*] (IAA) ... FTF
Forward Traveling Wave ... FTW
Forward Unconventional Warfare Operations Base (MCD) ... FUWOB
Forward Unity Periscope ... FUP
Forward Utility Bridge (NASA) ... FUB
Forward Visibility ... FV
Forward Visibility More than ___ Miles [*Aviation*] (FAAC) ... MFV
Forward Volume Wave [*Telecommunications*] (TEL) ... FVW
Forward Wave [*Electronics*] (IAA) ... FW
Forward Wave Amplifier ... FWA
Forward Wave Tube ... FWT
Forward Weapons Controller [*Military*] (NVT) ... FORWEPCON
Forward-Area Armored Logistics System [*Military*] ... FAALS
Forward-Based Systems [*US aircraft based outside the US and capable of carrying nuclear weapons to the USSR*] ... FBS
Forwarded ... FWDD
Forwarder ... FWDR
Forwarder Air Waybill [*Shipping*] (DS) ... FAB
Forwarders Certificate of Receipt [*Shipping*] ... FCR
Forward-Explicit Congestion Notification [*Computer science*] ... FECN
Forward-Firing Aerial Rocket (IAA) ... FEAR
Forwarding ... FWDG
Forwarding ... FWDG
Forwarding Agents Commission [*Shipping*] (DS) ... fac
Forwarding Indian Resposibility in Education [*Bureau of Indian Affairs*] [*Department of the Interior*] (AEBS) ... FIRE
Forward-Loading Infrared (RDA) ... FLIR
Forward-Looking Advanced Multimode RADAR ... FLAMR
Forward-Looking Airborne Moving Target Indication (NG) ... FLAMTI
Forward-Looking Airborne RADAR ... FLAR
Forward-Looking Infrared ... FLI
Forward-Looking Infrared (AFM) ... FLIR
Forward-Looking Infrared Attack Set ... FLIRAS
Forward-Looking Infrared Sensor (VNW) ... FLIR
Forward-Looking Infrared System ... FLIRS
Forward-Looking Infrared Thermovision System (MCD) ... FLIRTS
Forward-Looking RADAR ... FLR
Forward-Looking RADAR Set (NVT) ... FLRS
Forward-Scattering Spectrometer Probe [*Aerosol measurement device*] ... FSSP
Forzando [*or Forzato*] [*Strongly Accented Music*] ... Fz
Forzatissimo [*Extremely Loud*] [*Music*] (ROG) ... FFZ
Forzato [*Strongly Accented*] [*Music*] ... FORZ
Fos-Associated Protein [*Biochemistry*] ... FAP
FOSIC [*Fleet Ocean Surveillance Information Center*] **Communications Processing Subsystem** (MCD) ... FCPS
Fos-Related Antigens [*Biochemistry*] ... FRA
Foss Launch & Tug [*AAR code*] ... FLT
Fossil (VRA) ... fsl
Fossil Energy Information Center [*ORNL*] (GRD) ... FEIC
Fossil Energy Information Group [*Department of Energy*] [*Information service or system*] (IID) ... FEIG
Fossil Energy Update [*A publication*] ... FEU
Fossil Fired Steam Plant (IEEE) ... FFSP
Fossil Fuel Fired Steam Generator (GNE) ... FFFSG
Fossil Fuel Resources Committee ... FFRC
Fossil Fuels ... FF
Fossil, Inc. [*NASDAQ symbol*] (SAG) ... FOSL
Fossil, Inc. [*Associated Press*] (SAG) ... Fossil
Fossil Operations and Maintenance Information Service (IID) ... FOMIS
Fossil Record ... FR
Fossil Stromgen Sphere (PDAA) ... FSS
Fosston High School, Fosston, MN [*Library symbol*] [*Library of Congress*] (LCLS) ... MnFtH
Fosston, MN [*Location identifier FAA*] (FAAL) ... FSE
Fosston, MN [*AM radio station call letters*] ... KKCQ
Fosston, MN [*FM radio station call letters*] ... KKCQ-FM
Fosston, MN [*FM radio station call letters*] (RBYB) ... KKEQ-FM
Fosston Public Library, Fosston,MN [*Library symbol*] [*Library of Congress*] (LCLS) ... MnFt
Foster ... FSTR
Foster and Finlason's English Nisi Prius Reports [*175, 176 English Reprint*] [*A publication*] (DLA) ... F & F
Foster and Finlason's English Nisi Prius Reports [*175, 176 English Reprint*] [*A publication*] (DLA) ... Fost & F
Foster and Finlason's English Nisi Prius Reports [*175, 176 English Reprint*] [*A publication*] (DLA) ... Fost & F (Eng)
Foster and Finlason's English Nisi Prius Reports [*175, 176 English Reprint*] [*A publication*] (DLA) ... Fost & Fin
Foster Aviation [*ICAO designator*] (FAAC) ... FSA
Foster [*L. B.*] **Co.** [*Associated Press*] (SAG) ... Foster
Foster [*L.B.*] **Co.** [*NASDAQ symbol*] (NQ) ... FSTR
Foster Father ... FF
Foster Grandparents Program (EA) ... FGP
Foster (LB)Cl'A' [*NASDAQ symbol*] (TTSB) ... FSTRA
Foster Mother ... FM
Foster on Doctors' Commons [*A publication*] (DLA) ... Fost Doct Com
Foster on Federal Practice [*A publication*] (DLA) ... Foster Fed Pr
Foster on Joint Ownership and Partition [*A publication*] (DLA) ... Fost Jt Own
Foster on the Writ of Scire Facias [*1851*] [*A publication*] (DLA) ... Fost on Sci Fa
Foster on the Writ of Scire Facias [*1851*] [*A publication*] (DLA) ... Fost Sci Fa
Foster Parents' Plan (EA) ... FPP
Foster Parents Plan of Australia ... FPPA
Foster, Pepper & Shefelman, Law Library, Seattle, WA [*Library symbol*] [*Library of Congress*] (LCLS) ... WaSFP
Foster Wheeler [*NYSE symbol*] (TTSB) ... FWC
Foster Wheeler Corp. [*Associated Press*] (SAG) ... FostWh
Foster Wheeler Corp. (MCD) ... FW
Foster Wheeler Corp. [*NYSE symbol*] (SPSG) ... FWC
Foster Wheeler-Bergbau Forschung [*Flue gas treatment*] ... FW-BF
Foster Yeoman Ltd. [*British ICAO designator*] (FAAC) ... JFY

Fostering and Assistance for Wildlife Needing Aid [*Australia*] ... FAWNA
Fostering, or Fighting, Innovations and Experiment in Teaching [*Game*] ... FIXIT
Fosterlaendska Folkroerelsen [*Patriotic People's Movement*] [*Finland*] (PPE) ... FFR
Fosters Brewing Group [*Australia Commercial firm*] ... FBG
Foster's Elements of Jurisprudence [*1853*] [*A publication*] (DLA) ... Fost El Jur
Foster's English Crown Law Cases [*168 English Reprint*] [*1743-61*] [*A publication*] (DLA) ... Fost
Foster's English Crown Law Cases [*168 English Reprint*] [*1743-61*] [*A publication*] (DLA) ... Fost CL
Foster's English Crown Law Cases [*168 English Reprint*] [*1743-61*] [*A publication*] (DLA) ... Fost CL (Eng)
Foster's English Crown Law Cases [*168 English Reprint*] [*1743-61*] [*A publication*] (DLA) ... Fost Cr Law
Foster's English Crown Law Cases [*168 English Reprint*] [*1743-61*] [*A publication*] (DLA) ... Foster
Foster's Legal Chronicle Reports [*Pennsylvania*] [*A publication*] (DLA) ... Fost
Foster's Legal Chronicle Reports [*Pennsylvania*] [*A publication*] (DLA) ... Foster (PA)
Foster's New Hampshire Reports [*A publication*] (DLA) ... Fost
Foster's New Hampshire Reports [*A publication*] (DLA) ... Fost (NH)
Foster's New Hampshire Reports [*A publication*] (DLA) ... Foster
Foster's Reports [*5, 6, and 8 Hawaii*] [*A publication*] (DLA) ... Fost
Foster's Reports [*5, 6, and 8 Hawaii*] [*A publication*] (DLA) ... Fost (Haw)
Foster's Treatise on Pleading and Practice in Equity in Courts of the United States [*A publication*] (DLA) ... Fost Fed Prac
Foster-Seeley Discriminator ... FSD
Fostoria Glass Society of America (EA) ... FGSA
Fostoria, OH [*Location identifier FAA*] (FAAL) ... FZI
Fostoria, OH [*FM radio station call letters*] ... WBVI
Fostoria, OH [*AM radio station call letters*] ... WFOB
Foto File Systems, Inc., Kansas City, KS [*Library symbol Library of Congress*] (LCLS) ... FoF
Fotoball USA, Inc. [*Associated Press*] (SAG) ... Fotoball
Fotoball USA, Inc. [*Associated Press*] (SAG) ... Fotobl
Fotoball USA, Inc. [*NASDAQ symbol*] (SAG) ... FUSA
Fotoball USA Wrrt [*NASDAQ symbol*] (TTSB) ... FUSAW
Fotografia F3 SA [*Spain ICAO designator*] (FAAC) ... FTE
Fotus [*A Fermentation*] [*A publication*] (ROG) ... FOTU
Foucault Rotating Mirror [*Physics*] ... FRM
Fougamou [*Gabon*] [*ICAO location identifier*] (ICLI) ... FOGF
Fougamou [*Gabon*] [*Airport symbol*] (OAG) ... FOU
Foul ... F
Foul Bottom [*Navigation signal*] ... fb
Foul Fly [*Baseball*] ... FF
Fouled Out [*Sports*] (IIA) ... FO
Fouled Up [*To describe a confused, mixed-up situation, person, or action*] [*Bowdlerized version*] ... FU
Fouled Up Beyond All Recognition [*Military slang*] [*Bowdlerized version*] ... FUBAR
Fouled Up Beyond Belief [*Military slang*] [*Bowdlerized version*] ... FUBB
Fouled Up More Than Usual [*See FU*] [*Bowdlerized version*] ... FUMTU
Foulke's Action at Law [*A publication*] (DLA) ... Foulk Act
Foulwind [*New Zealand*] [*Seismograph station code, US Geological Survey Closed*] (SEIS) ... FLW
Fouman [*Iran*] [*ICAO location identifier*] (ICLI) ... OIGF
Foumban [*Cameroon*] [*Airport symbol*] (AD) ... FOM
Foumban/Nkounja [*Cameroon*] [*ICAO location identifier*] (ICLI) ... FKKM
Found (MSA) ... FD
Found ... FND
Found ... FND
Found Abandoned ... FA
Found Brothers Aviation Ltd. [*Canada ICAO aircraft manufacturer identifier*] (ICAO) ... FB
Found Object (VRA) ... fndobj
Found on Road Dead [*Reference to the alleged defects of Ford automobiles*] ... FORD
Foundation (KSC) ... FDN
Foundation (VRA) ... fdtn
Foundation [*Technical drawings*] ... FND
Foundation ... FNDN
Foundation ... FNDTN
Foundation (AAGC) ... Found
Foundation ... FOUND
Foundation ... FOUNDN
Foundation Beefmaster Association (EA) ... FBA
Foundation Canadienne de Recherche en Publicite (AC) ... FCRP
Foundation Center (EA) ... FC
Foundation Center Library, New York, NY [*Library symbol Library of Congress*] (LCLS) ... NNFoC
Foundation City [*Dialog*] [*Searchable field*] [*Information service or system*] (NITA) ... FC
Foundation Code [*IRS*] ... FC
Foundation Europalia International (EAIO) ... FEI
Foundation Faith of God (EA) ... FFG
Foundation for a Christian Civilization (EA) ... FCC
Foundation for a Course in Miracles (EA) ... FACIM
Foundation for a Future [*Defunct*] (EA) ... FFF
Foundation for Accounting Education (EA) ... FAE
Foundation for Accredited Chiropractic Education [*Later, FCER*] (EA) ... FACE
Foundation for Administrative Research (MCD) ... FAR
Foundation for Advanced Computer Technology ... FACT
Foundation for Advancement in Cancer Therapy (EA) ... FACT
Foundation for Advances in Clinical Medicine and Science [*Later, FAMS*] (EA) ... FACMS
Foundation for Advances in Medicine and Science (EA) ... FAMS
Foundation for Aggregate Studies ... FAS
Foundation for Agronomic Research [*University of Pittsburgh*] [*Research center*] (RCD) ... FAR
Foundation for American Agriculture [*Later, FAAPFF*] (EA) ... FAA
Foundation for American Agriculture Program of the Farm Foundation [*Formerly, FAA*] (EA) ... FAAPFF
Foundation for American Communications (EA) ... FACS
Foundation for America's Sexually Exploited Children [*Defunct*] (EA) ... FASEC
Foundation for Anglican Traditions [*Defunct*] (EA) ... FAT
Foundation for Applied Science and Technology [*University of Pittsburgh*] [*Research center*] (RCD) ... FAST
Foundation for Basic Research [*Russia*] ... FBR
Foundation for Better Living (EA) ... FBL
Foundation for Biomedical Research (EA) ... FBR
Foundation for Blood Irradiation (EA) ... FFBI
Foundation for Blood Research [*Research center*] (RCD) ... FBR
Foundation for Books to China (EA) ... FBC
Foundation for Business Responsibilities [*British*] ... FBR
Foundation for Character Education (EA) ... FCE
Foundation for Child Development (EA) ... FCD
Foundation for Child Mental Welfare (EA) ... FCMW
Foundation for Children with Learning Disabilities [*Later, NCLD*] (EA) ... FCLD
Foundation for Chiropractic Education and Research (EA) ... FCER
Foundation for Christian Living (EA) ... FCL
Foundation for Christian Theology (EA) ... FCT
Foundation for Citizens Against Waste (EA) ... FCAW
Foundation for Commercial Banks (EA) ... FCB
Foundation for Community Creativity (EA) ... FCC
Foundation for Continuing Veterinary Education [*Murdoch University, Australia*] ... FCVE
Foundation for Cooperative Housing [*Later, CHF*] ... FCH
Foundation for Cotton Research and Education [*Later, The Cotton Foundation*] (EA) ... FCRE
Foundation for Creative Philosophy (EA) ... FCP
Foundation for Credit Education [*Nazareth, PA*] (EA) ... FCE
Foundation for Cure [*Defunct*] (EA) ... FFC
Foundation for Depression and Manic Depression (EA) ... FDMD
Foundation for Economic Education (EA) ... FEE
Foundation for Economic Education (Australia) ... FEE(A)
Foundation for Education and Research in Vision (EA) ... FERV
Foundation for Education Business Partnerships (AIE) ... FEBP
Foundation for Education with Production (EA) ... FEP
Foundation for Educational Futures (EA) ... FEF
Foundation for Elective Mutism, Inc. (EA) ... FEM
Foundation for Ethnic Dance (EA) ... FED
Foundation for European Language and Educational Centres (EA) ... EUROCENTRES
Foundation for Exceptional Children (EA) ... FEC
Foundation for Extension and Development of the American Professional Theatre (EA) ... FEDAPT
Foundation for Field Research (EA) ... FFR
Foundation for Financial Institutions Research [*Defunct*] (EA) ... FFIR
Foundation for Fire Safety [*Defunct*] (EA) ... FFS
Foundation for Fluency (EA) ... FFI
Foundation for Foreign Affairs (EA) ... FFA
Foundation for Future Generations (EA) ... FFG
Foundation for Gifted and Creative Children [*Defunct*] (EA) ... FGCC
Foundation for Giraffe Rescue ... FGR
Foundation for Glaucoma Research (EA) ... FGR
Foundation for Global Broadcasting (EA) ... FGB
Foundation for Grandparenting (EA) ... FG
Foundation for Hand Research (EA) ... FHR
Foundation for Handgun Education [*Later, EFEHV*] (EA) ... FHE
Foundation for Health (EA) ... FFH
Foundation for Health (EA) ... FH
Foundation for Health Care Evaluation (EA) ... FHCE
Foundation for Health Services Research (EA) ... FHSR
Foundation for Homeopathic Research [*Defunct*] (EA) ... FHR
Foundation for Hospice and Homecare (EA) ... FHH
Foundation for Human Development [*Australia*] ... FHD
Foundation for Human Rights and Democracy in China (EA) ... FHRDC
Foundation for Humanities Adulthood [*Australia*] ... FHA
Foundation for Ichthyosis and Related Skin Types (PAZ) ... FIRST
Foundation for Independent Higher Education (EA) ... FIHE
Foundation for Indiana University of Pennsylvania [*Research center*] (RCD) ... FIUP
Foundation for Information Technology in Local Government (AIE) ... FITLOG
Foundation for Innovation in Medicine (EA) ... FIM
Foundation for Instrumentation Education and Research [*Defunct*] ... FIER
Foundation for Insurance Reform and Education ... FIRE
Foundation for Integrative Education (EA) ... FIE
Foundation for Interior Design Education Research (EA) ... FIDER
Foundation for International Community Assistance (EA) ... FINCA
Foundation for International Cooperation (EA) ... FIC
Foundation for International Economic Policy (EA) ... FIEP
Foundation for International Human Relations (EA) ... FIHR
Foundation for International Meetings (EA) ... FIM
Foundation for International Potash Research [*Later, PI*] (EA) ... FIPR
Foundation for International Scientific Co-Ordination [*Paris, France*] (EAIO) ... FISC
Foundation for International Technological Cooperation (DICI) ... FITC
Foundation for International Trade Research (EA) ... FITR
Foundation for Latin American Anthropological Research (EA) ... FLAAR
Foundation for Latino-American Economic Research [*Argentina*] (EAIO) ... FLAER

Foundation for Law and Government [*Organization on television series "Knight Rider"*] ... FLAG
Foundation for Life Sciences [*Australia*] ... FLS
Foundation for Management Education [*British*] ... FME
Foundation for Medical Care [*Generic term*] (DHSM) ... FMC
Foundation for Medical Technology (EA) ... FMT
Foundation for Microbiology (EA) ... FFM
Foundation for Middle East Peace (EA) ... FMEP
Foundation for Mideast Communication [*Later, FMEC*] (EA) ... FMC
Foundation for Mideast Communication (EA) ... FMEC
Foundation for Moral Restoration (EA) ... FMR
Foundation for National Progress (EA) ... FNP
Foundation for Non-Lethal Warfare [*Defunct*] (EA) ... FNLW
Foundation for North American Wild Sheep (EA) ... FNAWS
Foundation for Oceanographic Research and Education ... FORE
Foundation for Oregon Research and Education (EDAC) ... FORE
Foundation for Peace (EA) ... FFP
Foundation for Philosophy of Creativity (EA) ... FPC
Foundation for Physical Therapy (EA) ... FPT
Foundation for Preservation of the Archeological Heritage (EA) ... FPAH
Foundation for Public Affairs (EA) ... FPA
Foundation for Public Relations Research and Education (EA) ... FPRRE
Foundation for Rational Economics and Education (EA) ... FREE
Foundation for Reformation Research, St. Louis, MO [*Library symbol Library of Congress Obsolete*] (LCLS) ... MoSFRR
Foundation for Religious Action in the Social and Civil Order (EA) ... FRASCO
[*The*] **Foundation for Research and Technology Hellas** [*Greece*] ... FORTH
Foundation for Research Development [*South Africa*] ... FRD
Foundation for Research in the Afro-American Creative Arts (EA) ... FRAACA
Foundation for Research on Economics and the Environment [*Research center*] (RCD) ... FREE
Foundation for Research on Human Behavior (EA) ... FRHB
Foundation for Research on the Nature of Man (EA) ... FRNM
Foundation for Savings Institutions [*Defunct*] (EA) ... FSI
Foundation for Science and Disability (PAZ) ... FSD
Foundation for Science and the Handicapped (EA) ... FSH
Foundation for Scientific Relaxation ... FSR
Foundation for Shamanic Studies (EA) ... FSS
Foundation for Student Communication [*Princeton, NJ*] (EA) ... FSC
Foundation for Teaching Economics (EA) ... FTE
Foundation for the Advancement of Artists (EA) ... FAA
Foundation for the Advancement of Chiropractic Tenets and Science (EA) ... FACTS
Foundation for the Arts of Peace [*Defunct*] (EA) ... FAP
Foundation for the Community of Artists (EA) ... FCA
Foundation for the Development of Medical Psychotherapy [*Switzerland*] (EAIO) ... FDMP
Foundation for the Establishment of an International Criminal Court (EA) ... FEICC
Foundation for the Jewish National Fund (EA) ... FJNF
Foundation for the New Freeman (EA) ... FNF
Foundation for the Peoples of the South Pacific (EA) ... FSP
Foundation for the Preservation and Protection of the Przewalski Horse (EA) ... FPPPH
Foundation for the Preservation of Antique and Contemporary Cup Plates (EA) ... FPACCP
Foundation for the President's Private Sector Survey on Cost Control (EA) ... PPSS
Foundation for the President's Private Sector Survey on Cost Control (EA) ... PPSSCC
Foundation for the Private Sector [*San Diego, CA*] (EA) ... FPS
Foundation for the Study of Cycles (EA) ... FSC
Foundation for the Study of Independent Social Ideas (EA) ... FSISI
Foundation for the Study of Infant Deaths [*British*] (DBA) ... FSID
Foundation for the Study of Plural Societies (EA) ... FSPS
Foundation for the Study of Presidential and Congressional Terms (EA) ... FSPCT
Foundation for the Study of Primitive Culture ... FSPC
Foundation for the Study of Wilson's Disease [*Later, NCSWD*] (EA) ... FSWD
Foundation for the Support of International Medical Training (EA) ... FSIMT
Foundation for Traffic Safety ... FTS
Foundation for World Literacy [*Defunct*] ... FWL
Foundation for Youth and Student Affairs [*Defunct*] (EA) ... FYSA
Foundation Health [*NYSE symbol*] (TTSB) ... FH
Foundation Health Corp. [*NYSE symbol*] (SPSG) ... FH
Foundation Health Corp. [*Associated Press*] (SAG) ... FoundH
Foundation Health Federal Services ... FHFS
Foundation Law Review [*A publication*] (DLA) ... Found L Rev
Foundation Member ... FM
Foundation Name [*Dialog*] [*Searchable fields*] [*Information service or system*] (NITA) ... FN
Foundation of America (EA) ... FA
Foundation of American College of Health Care Administrators (EA) ... FACHCA
Foundation of American College of Nursing Home Administrators [*Later, FACHCA*] (EA) ... FACNHA
Foundation of Automation and Employment Ltd. [*British*] (BI) ... FAE
Foundation of California State University, Sacramento [*Research center*] (RCD) ... FCSUS
Foundation of Human Understanding (EA) ... FHU
Foundation of Law and Society [*Defunct*] (EA) ... FLS
Foundation of Light and Metaphysical Education [*Defunct*] (EA) ... FLAME
Foundation of Motion Picture Pioneers (EA) ... FMPP
Foundation of Rehabilitation with Aboriginal Alcohol Related Difficulties [*Australia*] ... FORWAARD
Foundation of Thanatology (EA) ... FT
Foundation of the American Economic Council (EA) ... FAEC
Foundation of the Federal Bar Association (EA) ... FFBA
Foundation of the Flexographic Technical Association [*Later, FTA*] (EA) ... FFTA
Foundation of the Twelve Apostles (EA) ... FTA
Foundation of the Wall and Ceiling Industry (EA) ... FWCI
Foundation of Universal Unity (EA) ... FUU
Foundation on Economic Trends (EA) ... FET
Foundation Research Service ... FRS
Foundation State [*Dialog*] [*Searchable field*] [*Information service or system*] (NITA) ... FS
Foundation to Assist Canadian Talent on Records ... FACTOR
Foundation to Assist Scientific Research in Africa (EAIO) ... FASRA
Foundation to Improve Television (EA) ... FIT
Foundation Type [*Dialog*] [*Searchable field*] [*Telecommunications*] (NITA) ... FT
Foundations and Donors Interested in Catholic Activities (EA) ... FADICA
Foundations and Donors Interested in Catholic Activities (EA) ... FDICA
Foundations of Communication and Language (AIE) ... FOCAL
Foundations of Information Science [*American Society for Information Science*] ... FIS
Foundations Resources [*Vancouver Stock Exchange symbol*] ... FNR
Founded (EY) ... F
Founded ... FNDD
Founder ... FDR
Founder ... FNDR
Founders Financial Corp. [*NASDAQ symbol*] (SAG) ... FFCP
Founders Financial Corp. [*Associated Press*] (SAG) ... FndrFn
Founding ... FNDG
Founding Fathers Papers (EA) ... FFP
Foundry (KSC) ... FDRY
Foundry ... FNDRY
Foundry (BARN) ... Fndry
Foundry Business System [*Foundry Business Systems*] [*Software package*] (NCC) ... FBS
Foundry Educational Foundation [*Defunct*] (EA) ... FEF
Foundry Equipment and Materials Association [*Later, CISA*] (EA) ... FEMA
Foundry Equipment and Supplies Association [*British*] (DBA) ... FESA
Foundry Facings Manufacturers Group [*Later, FSMG*] (EA) ... FFMG
Foundry Industry Training Committee [*British*] (BI) ... FITC
Foundry Supply Manufacturers Group (EA) ... FSMG
Fount Description Random Access Memory (NITA) ... FDRAM
Fountain (VRA) ... fount
Fountain ... FTN
Fountain ... FTN
Fountain, CO [*FM radio station call letters*] ... KBIQ
Fountain, CO [*FM radio station call letters*] (RBYB) ... KPRZ-FM
Fountain County Star, Covington, IN [*Library symbol Library of Congress*] (LCLS) ... InCovFS
Fountain Inn, SC [*AM radio station call letters*] ... WFIS
Fountain Oil [*NASDAQ symbol*] (TTSB) ... GUSH
Fountain Oil, Inc. [*Associated Press*] (SAG) ... FountO
Fountain Oil, Inc. [*NASDAQ symbol*] (SAG) ... GUSH
Fountain Powerboat Ind [*AMEX symbol*] (TTSB) ... FPI
Fountain Powerboat Industries, Inc. [*Associated Press*] (SAG) ... FountPw
Fountain Powerboat Industries, Inc. [*AMEX symbol*] (SPSG) ... FPI
Fountain Powerboats [*NASDAQ symbol*] (SAG) ... FPWR
Fountainhall's Decisions, Scotch Court of Session [*1678-1712*] [*A publication*] (DLA) ... Fount
Fountainhall's Decisions, Scotch Court of Session [*1678-1712*] [*A publication*] (DLA) ... Fount Dec
Fountainhall's Session Cases [*1678-1712*] [*Scotland*] [*A publication*] (DLA) ... Lauder
Four Arrows (EA) ... FA
Four Bears, ND [*FM radio station call letters*] ... KMHA
Four by Five Inches (VRA) ... FRFV
Four Color [*Printing*] ... 4C
Four Conductor, Heat, Oil, and Flame Resistant [*Cable*] (IAA) ... FHOF
Four Corners Regional Commission [*Department of Commerce*] ... FCRC
Four County Library System, Binghamton, NY [*Library symbol Library of Congress*] (LCLS) ... NBiF
Four County Library System, Binghamton, NY [*OCLC symbol*] (OCLC) ... YXF
Four Cylinder Club of America ... FCCA
Four Factor Theory Questionnaire (EDAC) ... FFTQ
Four Island Air Ltd. [*Antigua and Barbuda*] [*ICAO designator*] (FAAC) ... FIA
Four London Airport Group [*British*] ... FLAG
Four Lucky Fellows [*In company name, FLF Associates*] [*Investment group comprised of four sons of Lawrence Tisch*] ... FLF
Four Mile Canyon [*Oregon*] [*Seismograph station code, US Geological Survey*] (SEIS) ... FMC
Four Party Joint Military Team [*Established March, 1973 as part of the Paris Peace Accords*] (VNW) ... FPJMT
Four Picture Test [*Psychology*] ... FPT
Four Plus Edema [*Medicine*] (DAVI) ... 4E
Four Power Joint Military Commission (AABC) ... FPJMC
Four Rivers Area Library Services Authority [*Library network*] ... ALSA
Four Seasons Hotels, Inc. [*Toronto Stock Exchange symbol*] ... FSH
Four Seasons Resources Ltd. [*Vancouver Stock Exchange symbol*] ... FSR
Four Sigma Society (EA) ... FSS
Four Star Aviation, Inc. [*Virgin Islands*] [*ICAO designator*] (FAAC) ... FSC
Four Stroke-Direct Injection [*Engine*] (RDA) ... 4SDI
Four Valve Type A [*Cosworth racing engines*] ... FVA
Four Winds Aviation Ltd. [*ICAO designator*] (FAAC) ... WDS
Four-Address to SOAP [*Self-Optimizing Automatic Pilot*] **Translator** [*Computer science*] (IEEE) ... FAST
Four-Ball Machine [*Engineering*] (IAA) ... FBM
Four-Bar Cutter Device ... FCD

Four-BIT [*Binary Digit*] **Interface Logic Unit** ..... FILU
Four-Coil Differential Transformer ..... FCDT
Four-Conductor [*Wire or cable*] 4/C
Four-Conductor Cables [*JETDS nomenclature*] [*Military*] (CET) ..... WF
Four-Conductor, Combination, Special Purpose, Flexible Cable (IAA) ..... FCSF
Four-Conductor, Heat and Flame Resistant, Thin Walled, Armored [*Cable*] (IAA) ..... FHFTA
Four-Conductor, Heat-and-Flame-Resistant, Armor [*Cable*] ..... FHFA
Four-Conductor, Lighting, Armor [*Cable*] (IAA) ..... FLA
Four-Dimensional (MSA) 4-D
Four-Dimensional Data Assimilation [*Scheme*] [*Marine science*] (OSRA) 4DDA
Four-Dimensional Data Assimilation [*Scheme*] (USDC) 4DDA
Fourdrinier Kraft Board Institute [*Later, CKPG*] (EA) ..... FKBI
Fourdrinier Wire Council (EA) ..... FWC
Fourgon ..... FORGN
FourHealth, Inc. [*Associated Press*] (SAG) 4Health
FourHealth, Inc. [*NASDAQ symbol*] (SAG) ..... HHHH
Four-Horse Club [*British*] ..... FHC
Fourier Coefficient Harmonic Analyzer ..... FOCOHANA
Fourier Color Hologram ..... FCH
Fourier Infrared Software Tools ..... FIRST
Fourier Integral Estimate ..... FIE
Fourier Integral Transform [*Physics*] ..... FIT
Fourier Interferometric Stimulation [*Instrumentation*] ..... FIS
Fourier Ion Resonance Mass Spectrometer ..... FIRMS
Fourier Number [*IUPAC*] ..... Fo
Fourier Transform ..... FT
Fourier Transform Holographic ..... FTH
Fourier Transform Inductively-Coupled Plasma [*Spectrometry*] ..... FT-ICP
Fourier Transform Infrared [*Spectroscopy*] ..... FT-IR
Fourier Transform Infrared Photoacoustic Spectroscopy ..... FTIR-PAS
Fourier Transform Infrared Radiometer [*Marine science*] (OSRA) ..... FTIR
Fourier Transform Infrared Radiometer (USDC) ..... FTIR
Fourier Transform Infrared Reflection Absorption Spectroscopy ..... FTIR-RAS
Fourier Transform Infrared Spectroscopy (EERA) ..... FTIR
Fourier Transform Ion Cyclotron Resonance Mass Spectrometry ..... FT-ICRMS
Fourier Transform/Mass Spectrometry ..... FT/MS
Fourier Transform Operator ..... FTO
Fourier Transform Spectrometer [*or Spectroscopy*] ..... FTS
Fourier Transform System ..... FTS
Fourier Transform-Faradic Admittance Measurements [*Spectrometry*] ..... FT-FAM
Fourier Transform-Ion Cyclotron Resonance [*Spectrometry*] ..... FT-ICR
Fourier Transform-Microwave [*Spectroscopy*] ..... FT-MW
Fourier Transform-Nuclear Magnetic Resonance [*Spectrometry*] ..... FT-NMR
Fourier-Transform Ultraviolet/Visible [*Spectrophotometer*] ..... FT-UV/Vis
Four-Impinging-Stream Reactor [*Chemical engineering*] ..... FIS
Fournier [*France ICAO aircraft manufacturer identifier*] (ICAO) ..... RF
Four-Pole [*Switch*] 4P
Four-Pole, Double-Throw [*Switch*] 4PDT
Four-Pole, Single-Throw [*Switch*] 4PST
Four-Pole Switch 4PSW
Four-Quadrant Multiplier ..... FQM
Fourteen-O-One Automatically-Controlled Test Optimizing Routine [*Military*] (SAA) ..... FACTOR
Fourteen-O-One Input-Output Tape System [*Military*] (SAA) ..... FITS
Fourteen-O-One Statistical Program [*Military*] (SAA) ..... FOOSP
Fourteenth Coast Guard District [*Honolulu, HI*] [*USCG*] (TAG) D14
Four-Terminal Field-Effect Transistor (IEEE) ..... FTFET
Fourth Allied Tactical Air Force, Central Europe ..... FOURATAF
Fourth Armored Division Association (EA) ..... FADA
Fourth Canadian Destroyer Squadron [*Canadian Navy*] ..... CANDESRON 4
Fourth Cranial Nerve [*Anatomy*] (DMAA) CIV
Fourth Day (IIA) ..... FD
Fourth Dimension [*Time*] (AAG) ..... FD
Fourth Dimension Software [*NASDAQ symbol*] (SAG) ..... DDDD
Fourth Financial Corp. [*NASDAQ symbol*] (NQ) ..... FRTH
Fourth Financial Corp. [*Associated Press*] (SAG) ..... FrthF
Fourth Financial Corp. [*Associated Press*] (SAG) ..... FrthFn
Fourth of July Road ..... F of JR
Fourth Section [*of Interstate Commerce Act*] ..... FS
Fourth Shift [*NASDAQ symbol*] (TTSB) ..... FSFT
Fourth Shift Corp. [*Associated Press*] (SAG) ..... FrthShift
Fourth Shift Corp. [*NASDAQ symbol*] (SAG) ..... FSFT
Fourth Stowage Adapter Container ..... FSAC
Fourth World Educational and Research Association Trust (EA) ..... FWERAT
Fourth World Movement [*Later, NI/FWM*] (EA) ..... FWM
Fourth-Generation Language [*Computer language*] 4GL
Fourth-Generation Language [*Programming language created by Charles Moore*] (CDE) ..... FORTH
Fourth-Year Medical Student (DMAA) ..... FYMS
Four-Way RADAR Surveillance ..... QUADRADAR
Four-Wheel Brake ..... FWB
Four-Wheel Drive [*Vehicle*] 4WD
Four-Wheel Drive [*Vehicle*] ..... FWD
Four-Wheel Independent Suspension [*Automotive engineering*] 4IS
Four-Wheel Steering [*Automotive engineering*] 4WS
Four-Wheeler of the Year [*Automotive promotion*] ..... FWOTY
Four-Wire 4W
Four-Wire, Shipboard, General Use, Armored [*Cable*] ..... FSGA
Four-Wire Terminating Set [*Telecommunications*] (TEL) 4WTS
Four-Year Plan ..... FYP
Foveantur [*Let Them Be Fermented*] [*Pharmacy*] (ROG) ..... FOVEANT
Foward Neutral Reverse ..... FNR
Fowl Antimouse Lymphocyte Globulin [*Immunochemistry*] ..... FALG
Fowl Plague Virus ..... FPV
Fowler [*Rick*] [*ICAO designator*] (FAAC) ..... WTV
Fowler, A. R., Saint Paul MN [*STAC*] ..... FAR
Fowler, CA [*FM radio station call letters*] ..... KEZL
Fowler, CA [*AM radio station call letters*] (RBYB) ..... KQEQ
Fowler, CA [*AM radio station call letters*] ..... KRGO
Fowler. Collieries and Colliers [*4th ed.*] [*1884*] [*A publication*] (DLA) ..... Fowl Col
Fowler on Church Pews [*A publication*] (DLA) ..... Fowl Pews
Fowler Public Library, Fowler, CO [*Library symbol Library of Congress*] (LCLS) ..... CoFow
Fowler Single Breath Test [*Medicine*] (DMAA) ..... FSBT
Fowler's Exchequer Practice [*A publication*] (DLA) ..... Fowl Pr
Fowler's Leading Cases on Collieries [*A publication*] (DLA) ..... Fowl L Cas
Fowlerville Public Library, Fowlerville, MI [*Library symbol Library of Congress*] (LCLS) ..... MiFow
Fox [*Phonetic alphabet*] [*World War II*] (DSUE) ..... F
Fox, AK [*Location identifier FAA*] (FAAL) ..... FOX
Fox and Smith's Irish King's Bench Reports [*1822-24*] [*A publication*] (DLA) ..... F & S
Fox and Smith's Irish King's Bench Reports [*1822-24*] [*A publication*] (DLA) ..... Fox & S
Fox and Smith's Irish King's Bench Reports [*1822-24*] [*A publication*] (DLA) ..... Fox & S (Ir)
Fox and Smith's Irish King's Bench Reports [*1822-24*] [*A publication*] (DLA) ..... Fox & Sm
Fox and Smith's Registration Cases [*1886-95*] [*A publication*] (DLA) ..... F & S
Fox and Smith's Registration Cases [*1886-95*] [*A publication*] (DLA) ..... Fox & S Reg
Fox and Smith's Registration Cases [*1886-95*] [*A publication*] (DLA) ..... Fox & Sm
Fox and Smith's Registration Cases [*1886-95*] [*A publication*] (DLA) ..... Fox & Sm RC
Fox Broadcasting Co. ..... FBC
Fox Creek Municipal Library, Alberta [*Library symbol National Library of Canada*] (NLC) ..... AFCM
Fox Creek Municipal Library, Fox Creek, AB, Canada [*Library symbol*] [*Library of Congress*] (LCLS) ..... CaAFcM
Fox Creek School, Alberta [*Library symbol National Library of Canada*] (BIB) ..... AFCS
Fox Editor Enhancement Library (PCM) ..... FEEL
Fox Glacier [*New Zealand*] [*Airport symbol*] (AD) ..... FGL
Fox Harbour Public Library, Fox Harbour, NF, Canada [*Library symbol Library of Congress*] (LCLS) ..... CaNfFH
Fox Harbour Public Library, Newfoundland [*Library symbol National Library of Canada*] (NLC) ..... NFFH
Fox News Channel ..... FNC
Fox Programming Language ..... FPL
Fox Resources Ltd. [*Vancouver Stock Exchange symbol*] ..... FXR
Fox Sparrow [*Ornithology*] ..... FXS
Foxair Ltd. [*British ICAO designator*] (FAAC) ..... FXR
Foxboro Control Package (NITA) ..... FCP
Foxboro Display Packages (NITA) ..... FDP
Foxbro Programming Language (OA) ..... FPL
Foxed (WGA) ..... FX
Foxer [*Navy British*] ..... FXR
Foxmeyer Corp. [*NYSE symbol*] (SPSG) ..... FOX
FoxMeyer Health [*NYSE symbol*] (TTSB) ..... FOX
FoxMeyer Health $5 Cv Pfd [*NYSE symbol*] (TTSB) ..... FOXPr
Foxmeyer Health Corp. [*Associated Press*] (SAG) ..... Foxm
FoxMeyer Health Corp. [*Formerly, National Intergroup*] [*Associated Press*] (SAG) ..... FoxMHlt
FoxMeyer Hlth $4.20 Ex'A'Pfd [*NYSE symbol*] (TTSB) ..... FOXPrA
Foxmoor Inds Ltd [*NASDAQ symbol*] (TTSB) ..... FOXI
Foxmoor Industries Ltd. [*NASDAQ symbol*] (SAG) ..... FOXI
Foxmoor Industries Ltd. [*Associated Press*] (SAG) ..... Foxmor
Foxon-Maddocks Associates (IID) ..... FMA
FoxPro Link Library [*Microsoft Corp.*] [*Computer science*] (PCM) ..... FLL
Fox's Circuit and District Court Decisions [*United States*] [*A publication*] (DLA) ..... Fox
Fox's Digest of the Law of Partnership [*A publication*] (DLA) ..... Fox Dig Part
Fox's Patent, Trade Mark, Design, and Copyright Cases [*Canada*] [*A publication*] (DLA) ..... Fox
Fox's Patent, Trade Mark, Design, and Copyright Cases [*Canada*] [*A publication*] (DLA) ..... Fox Pat C
Fox's Patent, Trade Mark, Design, and Copyright Cases [*Canada*] [*A publication*] (DLA) ..... Fox Pat Cas
Fox's Patent, Trade Mark, Design, and Copyright Cases [*Canada*] [*A publication*] (DLA) ..... Fox PC
Fox's Registration Cases [*England*] [*A publication*] (DLA) ..... Fox
Fox's Registration Cases [*England*] [*A publication*] (DLA) ..... Fox Reg Ca
Foxtail Mosaic Virus [*Plant pathology*] ..... FOMV
Foxtail Mosaic Virus ..... FTV
Foxtrot [*Phonetic alphabet*] [*International*] (DSUE) ..... F
Foxwarren, MB [*Television station call letters*] CKX-TV-1
Foxx Industry, Inc. [*Vancouver Stock Exchange symbol*] ..... FXX
Foya [*Liberia*] [*Airport symbol*] (OAG) ..... FOY
Foyer (MSA) ..... FOY
Foz Do Iguacu/Cataratas [*Brazil ICAO location identifier*] (ICLI) ..... SBFI
FP Bancorp [*NASDAQ symbol*] (TTSB) ..... FPBN
FP Bancorp, Inc. [*Associated Press*] (SAG) ..... FP Bcp
FP Bancorp, Inc. [*NASDAQ symbol*] (SAG) ..... FPBN
FPA Corp. [*Associated Press*] (SAG) ..... FPA
FPA Corp. [*AMEX symbol*] (SPSG) ..... FPO
FPA Medical Management [*Associated Press*] (SAG) ..... FPA Md
FPA Medical Management [*NASDAQ symbol*] (SAG) ..... FPAM
FPA Medical Mgmt [*NASDAQ symbol*] (TTSB) ..... FPAM
FPI Ltd. [*Toronto Stock Exchange symbol*] ..... FPL

FPIC Insurance Group, Inc. [*NASDAQ symbol*] (SAG) .... FPIC
FPIC Insurance Group, Inc. [*Associated Press*] (SAG) .... FPIC Ins
FPL Group [*NYSE symbol*] (TTSB) .... FPL
FPL Group, Inc. [*NYSE symbol*] (SPSG) .... FPL
FPL Group, Inc. [*Associated Press*] (SAG) .... FPL Gp
FR Aviation Ltd. [*British ICAO designator*] (FAAC) .... FRA
Fractal Design [*NASDAQ symbol*] (TTSB) .... FRAC
Fractal Design Corp. [*NASDAQ symbol*] (SAG) .... FRAC
Fractal Design Corp. [*Associated Press*] (SAG) .... Fractal
Fractal Image Format [*Computer graphics*] (PCM) .... FIF
Fractal Representation of Sets [*Genetics*] .... FRS
Fracti Dosi [*In Divided Doses*] [*Pharmacy*] .... FRACT DOS
Fraction (IAA) .... f
Fraction .... FRACT
Fraction Collector [*Chromatography*] .... FC
Fraction Inspired Oxygen [*Physiology*] .... FIO
Fraction of Inspired Carbon Dioxide [*Medicine*] (DAVI) .... $FICO_2$
Fraction of Labeled Mitoses [*Measurement of cell labeling*] .... FLM
Fraction of Rated Power (IEEE) .... FRTP
Fraction Optimizing .... FO
Fraction Reliability Deviation .... FRD
Fraction Thereof .... FCT
Fractional (MAE) .... F
Fractional (MSA) .... FRAC
Fractional (WGA) .... FRL
Fractional Allelic Loss [*Genetics*] .... FAL
Fractional and Unknown Nuclear [*Material in meteorites*] .... FUN
Fractional Area Concentration [*Radiation therapy*] (DAVI) .... FAC
Fractional Brownian Motion [*Mathematics*] .... fBm
Fractional Catabolic Rate [*Clinical chemistry*] .... FCR
Fractional Concentration [*in dry gas phase*] (AAMN) .... F
Fractional Concentration of Inspired Oxygen [*Physiology*] (DAVI) .... FIO_2
Fractional Destraction [*Supercritical distillation*] .... FD
Fractional Doppler Gate .... FDG
Fractional Extraction of Sodium [*Organic chemistry*] (DAVI) .... FE_{Na}
Fractional Horsepower (MSA) .... FHP
Fractional Loss Exchange Ratio (MCD) .... FLER
Fractional Orbital Bombardment (MCD) .... FOB
Fractional Orbital Bombardment System .... FOBS
Fractional Orbiting Missile (SAA) .... FOM
Fractional Proximal Resorption [*Medicine*] (DMAA) .... FPR
Fractional Quantum Hall Effect [*Solid-state physics*] .... FQHE
Fractional Reabsorption [*Biochemistry*] (DAVI) .... FR
Fractional Shortening [*Cardiology*] .... FS
Fractional Test Meal [*Medicine*] .... FTM
Fractional Urinalysis [*Medicine*] .... FU
Fractional Urine [*Biochemistry*] (DAVI) .... Fx
Fractionally Rapid Electronic Device .... FRED
Fractionator Reflux Analog Computer .... FRAC
Fraction-Optimizing X-Y Collector [*Spectroscopy*] .... FOXY
Fractions Armees Revolutionnaires Libanaise [*Lebanese Armed Revolutionary Faction*] .... FARL
Fractocumulus [*Meteorology*] .... FC
Fractocumulus [*Meteorology*] .... FRCU
Fractographic Examination [*Metallurgy*] .... FGE
Fractostratus [*Meteorology*] .... FS
Fracture .... F
Fracture [*Orthopedics*] (DAVI) .... fr
Fracture [*Medicine*] .... FRAC
Fracture [*Medicine*] .... FRACT
Fracture [*Medicine*] .... FX
Fracture [*Orthopedics*] (DAVI) .... FXR
Fracture Analysis Diagram (PDAA) .... FAD
Fracture Appearance Transition Temperature .... FATT
Fracture, Compound and Comminuted [*Orthopedics*] (DAVI) .... FCC
Fracture Frequency per Meter [*Mining technology*] .... FF/M
Fracture Frozen Section [*Medicine*] (DMAA) .... FX
Fracture Gradient .... FG
Fracture of Both Bones [*Medicine*] (MAE) .... Fr BB
Fracture of Both Bones [*Medicine*] .... Fx BB
Fracture, Simple [*Medicine*] .... FS
Fracture, Simple Comminuted [*Orthopedics*] (DAVI) .... FSC
Fracture Toughness Parameter .... FTP
Fracture Transition Elastic Temperature (MCD) .... FTE
Fracture Zone [*Geophysics*] .... FZ
Fracture-Dislocation [*Orthopedics*] (DAVI) .... Fx-Dis
Fracture-Dislocation [*Medicine*] (DMAA) .... Fx-dis
Fraeulein [*Miss*] [*German*] .... FRL
Fragile .... F
Fragile .... FRAG
Fragile Mental Retardation [*A gene*] (PAZ) FMR-1
Fragile Site [*Medicine*] (DMAA) .... FS
Fragile X [*Chromosome*] [*Genetics*] (DAVI) .... fra(X)
Fragile X Syndrome [*Genetics*] .... FXS
Fragility Response Spectrum (IEEE) .... FRS
Fragility Response System (IAA) .... FRS
Fragment (BJA) .... f
Fragment [*Military*] (AFM) .... FRAG
Fragment [*Used in correcting manuscripts, etc.*] .... FRAG
Fragment (VRA) .... frag
Fragment, Antigen, and Complement Binding [*Medicine*] (DMAA) .... Facb
Fragment, Antigen-Binding [*Immunochemistry*] .... Fab
Fragment Antigen-Binding of an Antigen [*Immunology*] (DAVI) .... Fab
Fragment Connection Table [*Chemistry*] .... FCT
Fragment, Crystallizable [*Immunochemistry*] .... Fc
Fragment of an Antibody (DAVI) .... F
Fragment Wound [*Medicine*] (DAVI) .... FW
Fragmenta [*of Aristotle*] [*Classical studies*] (OCD) .... Fr
Fragmenta Comicorum Graecorum [*A publication*] (OCD) .... FCG
Fragmenta Historica [*of Aristoxenus*] [*Classical studies*] (OCD) .... Fr Hist
Fragmenta Historicorum Graecorum [*A publication*] (OCD) .... FHG
Fragmenta Philosophorum Graecorum [*A publication*] (OCD) .... FPG
Fragmenta Poetarum Latinorum Epicorum et Lyricorum [*A publication*] (OCD) .... FPL
Fragmenta Poetarum Romanorum [*A publication*] (OCD) .... FPR
Fragmentary Order [*Military*] .... FRAGO
Fragmentation .... F
Fragmentation [*Weapon*] (DOMA) .... Frag
Fragmentation Bomb .... FRAGBOMB
Fragmentation Bomb, Parachute .... FRP
Fragmentation Protocol [*Telecommunications*] (ACRL) .... FRP
Fragmente der Griechischen Historiker [*A publication*] (OCD) .... FGrH
Fragmente der Vorsokratiker [*A publication*] (OCD) .... Vorsokr
Fragmented Coronoid Process [*Medicine*] .... FCP
Fragmented Network (MCD) .... FRAGNET
Fragmented Order [*Military*] (VNW) .... FO
Fragmenting Offensive Aerial Mine (MCD) .... FOAM
Fragmenting Warhead Rocket .... FRAGROC
Fragments .... FRAGM
Fragments of Attic Comedy [*A publication*] (OCD) .... FAC
Fragmentum [*Fragment*] [*Latin*] (ROG) .... FR
Fragrance .... FRGNC
Fragrance Foundation (EA) .... FF
Fragrance Materials Association of the US (EA) .... FMA
Fragrance Research Fund (EA) .... FRF
FRAM [*Ferroelectric RAM*]-Oriented Real-Time Environment .... FORTE
Framatome Connectors International [*Commercial firm*] (ECON) .... FCI
Frame (IAA) .... FM
Frame (MSA) .... FR
Frame (WDMC) .... fr
Frame (VRA) .... fra
Frame .... FRM
Frame Acquisition and Synchronization (LAIN) .... FAS
Frame Alignment Sequence [*Telecommunications*] (ACRL) .... FAS
Frame Alignment Signal [*Telecommunications*] (TEL) .... FAS
Frame Analysis System [*IBM UK Ltd.*] [*Software package*] (NCC) .... FAS
Frame Analyzer (MCD) .... FA
Frame and Grillage Analysis [*Modray Ltd.*] [*Software package*] (NCC) .... F & GA
Frame Antenna (IAA) .... FA
Frame by Frame .... FBF
Frame Check Character (NITA) .... FCC
Frame Check Sequence [*Computer science*] (IBMDP) .... FCS
Frame Construction .... F
Frame Control [*Computer science*] (TNIG) .... FC
Frame Counter (SAA) .... FRMC
Frame Difference .... FD
Frame Difference Signal .... FDS
Frame Ground [*Computer science*] (BUR) .... FG
Frame Ground [*Computer science*] (HGAA) .... FGND
Frame Handler [*Telecommunications*] (ACRL) .... FH
Frame Network Server [*Tylink Corp.*] .... FNS
Frame Orientated System for Spectroscopic Inductive Learning [*Data analysis*] .... FOSSIL
Frame per Second (IDOE) .... fps
Frame Period [*Computer science*] (IAA) .... FP
Frame Pointer [*Computer science*] .... FP
Frame Protected [*Insurance classification*] .... FP
Frame Recognition-Data Link Processor (NITA) .... FR-DLP
Frame Reference Line (MCD) .... FRL
Frame Reject .... FRMR
Frame Relay (ACRL) .... FR
Frame Relay Access Device [*Plantronics Futurecomms, Inc.*] .... FRAD
Frame Relay and Mux Expander [*Computer science*] .... FRAME
Frame Relay Bearer Service (ACRL) .... FRBS
Frame Relay Forum (ACRL) .... FRF
Frame Relay Service (ACRL) .... FRS
Frame Relay Switch [*Newbridge Networks Corp.*] .... FRS
Frame Representation Language [*Computer science*] .... FRL
Frame Reset [*Telecommunications*] (TEL) .... FR
Frame Scan (DEN) .... FS
Frame Space Bandwidth Product (IAA) .... FSBW
Frame Status (ACRL) .... FS
Frame Storage System [*Television*] .... FSS
Frame Structure Analysis (IAA) .... FRAN
Frame Synchronization Indication .... FSI
Frame Synchronization Word (MSA) .... FSW
Frame Synchronization Word (MUGU) .... FW
Frame Table Entry [*Computer science*] (IBMDP) .... FTE
Frame Time for Extrapolation (SAA) .... FEXT
Frame Unprotected [*Insurance classification*] .... FU
Frame User-to-Network Interface [*Telecommunications*] (ACRL) .... FUNI
Framed [*Construction*] .... FD
Framed (BARN) .... frd
Framed .... FRMD
Frames Per Foot of Film (WDMC) .... FPF
Frames per Inch [*Computer science*] .... FPI
Frames per Minute [*Telecommunications*] (IAA) .... FPM
Frames per Second (NTCM) .... F/S
Frames per Second [*Computer science*] .... FPS
Frames Per Second [*Electronics*] .... fps

Frames Per Second (WDMC) .... fps
Frames per Second [*Telecommunications*] (IAA) .... FRSEC
Frames to Come [*Optometry*] .... FTC
Frame-Scanning Mode [*Microscopy*] .... FSM
Frame-Supported Tension Structure [*Tent*] [*Navy*] .... FTS
Framework .... FRMWRK
Framework [*Also, FR*] [*Genetics*] (MSA) .... FRWK
Framework .... FW
Framework .... FWK
Framework Convention on Climate Change (EERA) .... FCCC
Framework Density [*Crystallography*] .... FD
Framework for Achieving Managerial Excellence (EPA) .... FAME
Framework for Distributed Application [*Telecommunications*] (OSI) .... DAF
Framework for the Development of Environmental Statistics [*Australia*] .... FDES
Framework Molecular Models .... FMM
Framework Region [*Genetics*] .... FR
Framework-Determining Region [*Immunogenetics*] .... FDR
Framing .... FRAMG
Framing [*of a ship*] (DS) .... FRMG
Framing Bit (ACRL) .... FB
Framing Camera Mopper .... FCM
Framing Error (HGAA) .... FE
Framingham Historical society, Framingham, MA [*Library symbol*] [*Library of Congress*] (LCLS) .... MFmHi
Framingham, MA [*FM radio station call letters*] .... WDJM
Framingham, MA [*FM radio station call letters*] (RBYB) .... WKLB-FM
Framingham, MA [*AM radio station call letters*] .... WKOX
Framingham, MA [*FM radio station call letters*] (RBYB) .... WROR-FM
Framingham Public Library, Framingham, MA [*OCLC symbol*] (OCLC) .... FRM
Framingham Relative Weight Index [*Cardiology*] .... FRWI
Framingham Savings Bank [*Associated Press*] (SAG) .... FramS
Framingham Savings Bank [*Associated Press*] (SAG) .... FramSv
Framingham Savings Bank [*NASDAQ symbol*] (SAG) .... FSBX
Framingham State College (GAGS) .... Framingham St C
Framingham State College, Framingham, MA [*OCLC symbol*] (OCLC) .... FST
Framingham State College, Framingham, MA [*Library symbol Library of Congress*] (LCLS) .... MFmT
Framingham Svgs Bank (MA) [*NASDAQ symbol*] (TTSB) .... FSBX
Framingham Town Library, Framingham, MA [*Library symbol Library of Congress*] (LCLS) .... MFm
Frammenti della Commedia Greca e del Mimo nella Sicilia e nella Magna Grecia [*A publication*] (OCD) .... FCGM
Frampton [*England*] .... FRAMP
Framycetin [*Neomycin B*] [*Antibacterial compound*] .... FRA
Framycetin [*Neomycin B*], Colistin [*Antineoplastic drug regimen*] .... FRACO
Framycetin [*Neomycin B*], Colistin, Nystatin [*Antineoplastic drug regimen*] .... FRACON
Fran Lee Foundation (EA) .... FLF
Franc [*Monetary unit*] [*Belgium*] .... BF
Franc [*Monetary unit*] [*Burundi*] .... BFU
Franc [*Monetary unit*] [*France*] .... F
Franc [*Monetary unit*] [*France*] (ROG) .... FC
Franc [*Monetary unit*] [*French Somaliland*] .... FD
Franc [*Monetary unit*] [*Malagasy Republic*] .... FMG
Franc [*Monetary unit*] [*France*] (EY) .... FR
Franc [*Monetary unit*] [*Luxembourg*] .... L FR
Franc [*Monetary unit*] [*Rwanda*] .... RF
Franc d'Avarie Particuliere [*Free of Particular Average*] [*Business term French*] .... FAP
Franc de Droits [*Free of Charge*] [*Shipping*] [*French*] .... FDD
Franc Macon [*Freemasonry*] [*French*] (ROG) .... FM
Franc Mali [*Monetary unit*] [*Mali*] .... FM
Franca [*Brazil*] [*Airport symbol*] (OAG) .... FRC
Franca [*Brazil ICAO location identifier*] (ICLI) .... SBFC
Francais [*French*] .... F
France [*MARC geographic area code Library of Congress*] (LCCP) .... e-fr--
France [*IYRU nationality code*] .... F
France [*ANSI two-letter standard code*] (CNC) .... FR
France [*MARC country of publication code Library of Congress*] (LCCP) .... fr
France (VRA) .... Fr
France [*ANSI three-letter standard code*] (CNC) .... FRA
France Amerique Latine [*France Latin America*] [*An association*] (EAIO) .... FAL
France and Colonies Philatelic Society (EA) .... FCPS
France, BENELUX .... FBX
France Cables & Radio Co. [*France Telecommunications*] .... FCR
France Europe Avia Jet [*ICAO designator*] (FAAC) .... FEJ
France Growth Fund [*Associated Press*] (SAG) .... France
France Growth Fund [*NYSE symbol*] (SPSG) .... FRF
France Info [*Radio France*] .... FI
France, Italy, Netherlands, Allemagne, Belgium, Luxembourg [*Army Chiefs of Staff Joint Committee*] (PDAA) .... FINABEL
France, Italy, Netherlands, Belgium, and Luxembourg [*Economic agreement*] .... FINEBEL
France Latin America [*An association*] (EAIO) .... FLA
France Marine Nationale [*ICAO designator*] (FAAC) .... FMN
France Telecom International, Inc. [*Telecommunications service*] (TSSD) .... FTI
France-Europe International [*An association*] (EAIO) .... FEI
France-Louisiane [*Later, FLFADDFA*] [*France*] (EAIO) .... FL
France-Louisiane/Franco-Americaine - Defense et Developpement de la FrancophonieAmericaine (EAIO) .... FLFADDFA
France-Reunion-Avenir [*Political party*] (EY) .... FRA
Frances L. Folks Memorial Library (Loogootee Public Library), Loogootee, IN [*Library symbol Library of Congress*] (LCLS) .... InLoo
France's Reports [*3-11 Colorado*] [*A publication*] (DLA) .... France
France's Reports [*3-11 Colorado*] [*A publication*] (DLA) .... France (Colo)
Francesville Tribune, Francesville, IN [*Library symbol Library of Congress*] (LCLS) .... InFrvT
Francesville-Salem Township Public Library, Francesville, IN [*Library symbol Library of Congress*] (LCLS) .... InFrv
Franceville/Mvengue [*Gabon*] [*ICAO location identifier*] (ICLI) .... FOON
Franchise .... Fchse
Franchise .... FRNCHS
Franchise Advice and Consultancy Trade Organization [*British*] (DBA) .... FACTO
Franchise Consultants International Association (EA) .... FCIA
Franchise Finance Corp. of America [*NYSE symbol*] (SAG) .... FFA
Franchise Finance Corp. of America [*Associated Press*] (SAG) .... FranFin
Franchise Finance Cp Amer [*NYSE symbol*] (TTSB) .... FFA
Franchise Industry Training [*High school dropout program*] [*Department of Labor*] .... FIT
Franchise Law Journal [*A publication*] (DLA) .... Franchise LJ
Franchise of Americans Needing Sports (EA) .... FANS
Franchise Operations Team [*Automobile sales and marketing*] .... FOT
Franchising .... FRNCHSNG
Francia Kommunista Part [*French Communist Party*] [*Political party*] .... FKP
Francillon's County Court Judgments [*England*] [*A publication*] (DLA) .... Franc Judg
Francillon's Lectures on English Law [*1860-61*] [*A publication*] (DLA) .... Fran Eng Law
Francis Bacon Foundation (EA) .... FBF
Francis Bacon Foundation, Inc., Claremont, CA [*Library symbol Library of Congress*] (LCLS) .... CCFB
Francis Bacon Research Trust [*British*] .... FBRT
Francis Bacon Society (EA) .... FBS
Francis Bitter National Magnet Laboratory [*MIT*] .... FBNML
Francis' Common Law Precedents [*A publication*] (DLA) .... Fran Prec
FRANCIS: Documentation Automatisee en Gestion des Entreprises [*Database*] .... FRANCIS: DOGE
Francis Drake Fellowship [*British*] (BI) .... FDF
Francis Grose Society [*Defunct*] (EA) .... FGS
Francis' Law of Charities [*2nd ed.*] [*1855*] [*A publication*] (DLA) .... Fran Char
Francis Marion College, Florence, SC [*Library symbol Library of Congress*] (LCLS) .... ScFlM
Francis Marion College, Florence, SC [*OCLC symbol*] (OCLC) .... SFM
Francis Marion National Forest [*South Carolina*] [*Seismograph station code, US Geological Survey Closed*] (SEIS) .... FMF
Francis' Maxims of Equity [*1722-46*] [*A publication*] (DLA) .... Fr M
Francis' Maxims of Equity [*1722-46*] [*A publication*] (DLA) .... Fra
Francis' Maxims of Equity [*1722-46*] [*A publication*] (DLA) .... Fra M
Francis' Maxims of Equity [*1722-46*] [*A publication*] (DLA) .... Fran Max
Francis' Maxims of Equity [*1722-46*] [*A publication*] (DLA) .... Francis Max
Francis Peak [*Utah*] [*Seismograph station code, US Geological Survey*] (SEIS) .... FPU
FRANCIS: Reseau Documentaire en Sciences Humaines de la Sante [*Database*] [*French*] .... FRANCIS: RESHUS
Francis X. Curzio [*In company name FXC Investors Corp.*] .... FXC
Francis X. Hegarty Elementary School, Island Park, NY [*Library symbol*] [*Library of Congress*] (LCLS) .... NIpHE
Franciscan [*Religious order*] (WDAA) .... FRANC
Franciscan .... FRANS
Franciscan Apostolate of the Way of the Cross (EA) .... FAWC
Franciscan Apostolic Sisters (TOCD) .... FAS
Franciscan Brothers of Christ the King (TOCD) .... OSF
Franciscan Brothers of Christ the King (TOCD) .... osf
Franciscan Brothers of the Holy Cross [*See also FFSC*] [*Germany*] (EAIO) .... FBHC
Franciscan Brothers of the Holy Cross (TOCD) .... FFSC
Franciscan Brothers of the Holy Cross (TOCD) .... ffsc
Franciscan Brothers of the Third Order Regular (TOCD) .... osf
Franciscan Education Center, Lake Geneva, WI [*Library symbol Library of Congress*] (LCLS) .... WLagF
Franciscan Educational Conference [*Defunct*] .... FEC
Franciscan Friars (TOCD) .... OFM
Franciscan Friars of the Atonement (TOCD) .... SA
Franciscan Friars of the Atonement (TOCD) .... sa
Franciscan Friars of the Immaculate (TOCD) .... FFI
Franciscan Friars of the Immaculate (TOCD) .... ffi
Franciscan Friars of the Renewal (TOCD) .... CFR
Franciscan Friars of the Renewal (TOCD) .... cfr
Franciscan Friars, Order of Friars Minor (TOCD) .... ofm
Franciscan Handmaids of the Most Pure Heart of Mary [*Roman Catholic religious order*] .... FHM
Franciscan Hospitaller Sisters of the Immaculate Conception [*Roman Catholic religious order*] .... FHIC
Franciscan Missionaries of Mary [*Roman Catholic women's religious order*] .... FMM
Franciscan Missionaries of Our Lady (TOCD) .... OSF
Franciscan Missionaries of St. Joseph [*Mill Hill Sisters*] [*Roman Catholic religious order*] .... FMSJ
Franciscan Missionaries of the Divine Child (TOCD) .... FMDC
Franciscan Missionaries of the Divine Motherhood [*Roman Catholic religious order*] .... FMDM
Franciscan Missionaries of the Infant Jesus (TOCD) .... FMIJ
Franciscan Missionaries Our Lady of Peace (TOCD) .... MFP
Franciscan Missionary Brothers of the Sacred Heart of Jesus (TOCD) .... OSF
Franciscan Missionary Brothers of the Sacred Heart of Jesus (TOCD) .... osf
Franciscan Missionary Sisters for Africa (TOCD) .... OSF
Franciscan Missionary Sisters of Assisi (TOCD) .... SFMA
Franciscan Missionary Sisters of Assisi [*Roman Catholic religious order*] .... SFMG
Franciscan Missionary Sisters of Our Lady of Sorrows (TOCD) .... OSF

Franciscan Missionary Sisters of the Divine Child [*Roman Catholic religious order*] .... FMDC
Franciscan Missionary Sisters of the Immaculate Conception (TOCD) .... OSF
Franciscan Missionary Sisters of the Sacred Heart [*Roman Catholic religious order*] .... FMSC
Franciscan Monastery, Washington, DC [*Library symbol Library of Congress*] (LCLS) .... DFM
Franciscan Preparatory Seminary .... FPS
Franciscan Sister, Daughters of the Sacred Hearts of Jesus and Mary (TOCD) .... OSF
Franciscan Sisters Daughters of Mercy (TOCD) .... FHM
Franciscan Sisters of Allegany, New York (TOCD) .... OSF
[*The*] Franciscan Sisters of Baltimore (TOCD) .... OSF
Franciscan Sisters of Chicago (TOCD) .... OSF
Franciscan Sisters of Christ the Divine Teacher (TOCD) .... OSF
Franciscan Sisters of Christian Charity (TOCD) .... OSF
Franciscan Sisters of Little Falls, Minnesota (TOCD) .... OSF
Franciscan Sisters of Mary (TOCD) .... FSM
Franciscan Sisters of Mary Immaculate of the Third Order of St. Francis of Assisi [*Roman Catholic religious order*] .... FMI
Franciscan Sisters of Our Lady (TOCD) .... FSOL
Franciscan Sisters of Our Lady of Grace (TOCD) .... FLG
Franciscan Sisters of Our Lady of Perpetual Help (TOCD) .... OSF
Franciscan Sisters of Our Lady of the Sacred Heart (TOCD) .... FNSSC
Franciscan Sisters of Peace (TOCD) .... FSP
Franciscan Sisters of Ringwood [*Roman Catholic religious order*] .... FSR
Franciscan Sisters of St. Clare (Pious Union) (TOCD) .... FSSC
Franciscan Sisters of St. Elizabeth [*Roman Catholic religious order*] .... FSSE
Franciscan Sisters of St. Joseph [*Roman Catholic religious order*] .... FSSJ
Franciscan Sisters of St. Joseph (Mexico City) (TOCD) .... HFdeSJ
Franciscan Sisters of St. Paul (TOCD) .... OSF
Franciscan Sisters of the Atonement (TOCD) .... SA
Franciscan Sisters of the Immaculate Conception (TOCD) .... OSF
Franciscan Sisters of the Immaculate Conception and St. Joseph for the Dying (TOCD) .... OSF
Franciscan Sisters of the Poor [*Roman Catholic religious order*] .... SFP
Franciscan Sisters of the Sacred Heart (TOCD) .... OSF
Franciscan Sisters of the Sorrowful Mother (TOCD) .... FSSM
Franciscan Sisters of the Spirit of Jesus (TOCD) .... FSSpJ
Franciscan Sisters of the Third Order of the Immaculate Conception [*Roman Catholic religious order*] .... FSIC
Franciscan Vocation Conference [*Formerly, AFSV*] [*Defunct*] (EA) .... FVC
Francisco Mendes, Santiago Island [*Cape Verde*] [*ICAO location identifier*] (ICLI) .... GVFM
Francisco Morazan Frente Constitucional [*Honduras*] [*Political party*] (EY) .... FMFC
Franciscus Anzolellus [*Authority cited in pre-1607 legal work*] (DSA) .... Fran Anz
Franciscus Anzolellus [*Authority cited in pre-1607 legal work*] (DSA) ...... Fran Anzol
Franciscus Anzolellus [*Authority cited in pre-1607 legal work*] (DSA) ...... Franc Anz
Franciscus Balduinus [*Deceased, 1572*] [*Authority cited in pre-1607 legal work*] (DSA) .... Fr Baldui
Franciscus Balduinus [*Deceased, 1572*] [*Authority cited in pre-1607 legal work*] (DSA) .... Francis Bald
Franciscus Connanus [*Deceased, 1551*] [*Authority cited in pre-1607 legal work*] (DSA) .... Franc Conn
Franciscus Coscius [*Deceased, 1556*] [*Authority cited in pre-1607 legal work*] (DSA) .... Fr Cosci
Franciscus de Accoltis de Aretio [*Deceased, 1486*] [*Authority cited in pre-1607 legal work*] (DSA) .... Fran Aret
Franciscus de Accoltis de Aretio [*Deceased, 1486*] [*Authority cited in pre-1607 legal work*] (DSA) .... Fran de Are
Franciscus de Accoltis de Aretio [*Deceased, 1486*] [*Authority cited in pre-1607 legal work*] (DSA) .... Franc de Are
Franciscus de Accursio [*Deceased, 1293*] [*Authority cited in pre-1607 legal work*] (DSA) .... F de Ac
Franciscus de Accursio [*Deceased, 1293*] [*Authority cited in pre-1607 legal work*] (DSA) .... Franc Ac
Franciscus de Accursio (Filius) [*Deceased, 1293*] [*Authority cited in pre-1607 legal work*] (DSA) .... Fra Ac F
Franciscus de Ramponibus [*Deceased, 1401*] [*Authority cited in pre-1607 legal work*] (DSA) .... F de Ramp
Franciscus de Ramponibus [*Deceased, 1401*] [*Authority cited in pre-1607 legal work*] (DSA) .... Fran de Rampo
Franciscus de Ramponibus [*Deceased, 1401*] [*Authority cited in pre-1607 legal work*] (DSA) .... Franc de Rampo
Franciscus de Saxolinis [*Flourished, 13th century*] [*Authority cited in pre-1607 legal work*] (DSA) .... Fra de Sax
Franciscus de Saxolinis [*Flourished, 13th century*] [*Authority cited in pre-1607 legal work*] (DSA) .... Fra de Saxolis
Franciscus de Telese [*Flourished, 1270-82*] [*Authority cited in pre-1607 legal work*] (DSA) .... Fr
Franciscus de Telese [*Flourished, 1270-82*] [*Authority cited in pre-1607 legal work*] (DSA) .... Fr de T
Franciscus de Telese [*Flourished, 1270-82*] [*Authority cited in pre-1607 legal work*] (DSA) .... Fra
Franciscus de Telese [*Flourished, 1270-82*] [*Authority cited in pre-1607 legal work*] (DSA) .... Fra de Te
Franciscus de Telese [*Flourished, 1270-82*] [*Authority cited in pre-1607 legal work*] (DSA) .... Fra de Tels
Franciscus de Telese [*Flourished, 1270-82*] [*Authority cited in pre-1607 legal work*] (DSA) .... Fran
Franciscus de Telese [*Flourished, 1270-82*] [*Authority cited in pre-1607 legal work*] (DSA) .... Franc
Franciscus de Telese [*Flourished, 1270-82*] [*Authority cited in pre-1607 legal work*] (DSA) .... Franc de T

Franciscus de Telese [*Flourished, 1270-82*] [*Authority cited in pre-1607 legal work*] (DSA) .... Franc de Tel
Franciscus Duarenus [*Deceased, 1559*] [*Authority cited in pre-1607 legal work*] (DSA) .... Fran Duar
Franciscus Duarenus [*Deceased, 1559*] [*Authority cited in pre-1607 legal work*] (DSA) .... Francis Duar
Franciscus Gonzaga [*Authority cited in pre-1607 legal work*] (DSA) .... Fr Gon
Franciscus Gonzaga [*Authority cited in pre-1607 legal work*] (DSA) .... Fra Gon
Franciscus Sonsbeccius [*Flourished, 16th century*] [*Authority cited in pre-1607 legal work*] (DSA) .... Francis Sonsb
Franciscus Tigrini de Pisis [*Flourished, 13th-14th century*] [*Authority cited in pre-1607 legal work*] (DSA) .... FT
Franciscus Vercellensis [*Flourished, 13th century*] [*Authority cited in pre-1607 legal work*] (DSA) .... Fran
Franciscus Vercellensis [*Flourished, 13th century*] [*Authority cited in pre-1607 legal work*] (DSA) .... Fran Vercell
Franciscus Vivius [*Flourished, 16th century*] [*Authority cited in pre-1607 legal work*] (DSA) .... Franc Viv
Franciscus Zabarella [*Deceased, 1417*] [*Authority cited in pre-1607 legal work*] (DSA) .... Fr Zabar
Franciscus Zabarella [*Deceased, 1417*] [*Authority cited in pre-1607 legal work*] (DSA) .... Fra Za
Franciscus Zabarella [*Deceased, 1417*] [*Authority cited in pre-1607 legal work*] (DSA) .... Fran
Franciscus Zoannettus [*Deceased, 1586*] [*Authority cited in pre-1607 legal work*] (DSA) .... Franc Zoannet
Franciso College Law Journal [*A publication*] (DLA) .... Fran Coll LJ
Francistown [*Botswana*] [*ICAO location identifier*] (ICLI) .... FBFT
Francistown [*Botswana*] [*Airport symbol*] (OAG) .... FRW
Francium [*Chemical element*] .... Fr
Franck Drawing Completion Test [*Psychology*] .... FDCT
Franco [*Free of Charge*] [*Shipping*] [*Spanish*] .... FCO
Franco [*Free of Charge*] [*Shipping*] [*French*] .... fco
Franco [*Free of Charge*] [*Shipping*] [*Italian*] .... FCO
Franco American Committee for Educational Travel and Studies [*Later, FACETS Tour France*] .... FACETS
Franco d'Avaria Particolare [*Free of Particular Average*] [*Business term Italian*] .... FAP
Franco Domicile [*Shipping*] (DS) .... FD
Franco-American Historical Society (EA) .... FAHS
Franco-Australian Friendly Society of Victoria [*Australia*] .... FAFSV
Francofortium [*Frankfort*] [*Imprint*] [*Latin*] (ROG) .... FRANCOF
Francofurtum Ad Moenum [*Frankfort-On-The-Main*] [*Imprint*] [*Latin*] (ROG) .... FRANC AD MOEN
Franco-Nevada Mining Corp. [*Toronto Stock Exchange symbol*] .... FN
Franconi Anemia [*Medicine*] (AAMN) .... FA
Franconia Notch [*New Hampshire*] [*Seismograph station code, US Geological Survey Closed*] (SEIS) .... FNN
Francophone Primatological Society [*See also SFDP*] [*Plelan Le Grand, France*] (EAIO) .... FPS
Franco-Scottish Society (ROG) .... FSS
Francs [*Monetary units*] (ROG) .... FRCS
Francs Francais [*French Francs*] [*Monetary unit*] .... FF
Francs-Tireurs et Partisans Corses [*Corsican Guerrillas and Partisans*] (PD) .... FTPC
Frangipani Mosaic Virus [*Plant pathology*] .... FMV
Frank Gasperro [*Designer's mark, when appearing on US coins*] .... FG
Frank J. Seiler Research Laboratory [*US Air Force Academy, CO*] .... FJSRL
Frank L. Weyenberg Library, Mequon, WI [*Library symbol Library of Congress*] (LCLS) .... WMeq
Frank Lloyd Wright [*American architect*] (IIA) .... FLW
Frank Lloyd Wright Association [*Later, FLWN*] (EA) .... FLWA
Frank Lloyd Wright Foundation (EA) .... FLWF
Frank Lloyd Wright Home and Studio Foundation (EA) .... FLWHSF
Frank Lloyd Wright Newsletter (EA) .... FLWN
Frank Nelson Doubleday [*American publisher*] .... FND
Frank on the United States Bankrupt Act of 1867 [*A publication*] (DLA) ..... Fr Bank
Frank Phillips College [*Texas*] .... FPC
Frank Phillips College, Borger, TX [*Library symbol Library of Congress*] (LCLS) .... TxBorF
Frank Porter Graham Child Development Center [*University of North Carolina at Chapel Hill*] [*Research center*] (RCD) .... FPG
Frank W. Horner Ltd. [*Research code symbol*] [*Canada*] .... FWH
Frank W. Horner Ltd., Montreal, PQ, Canada [*Library symbol Library of Congress*] (LCLS) .... CaQMFH
Frank W. Horner Ltd., Montreal, Quebec [*Library symbol National Library of Canada*] (NLC) .... QMFH
Frank White Elementary School, Park Rapids, MN [*Library symbol*] [*Library of Congress*] (LCLS) .... MnParFE
Frank Williams [*Racing car model designation prefix, indicating principal of company*] [*British*] .... FW
Franked Investment Income [*Accounting*] .... FII
Frankenmuth, MI [*AM radio station call letters*] .... WKNX
Frankford Arsenal [*Pennsylvania*] [*Closed*] [*Army*] .... FA
Frankford Arsenal [*Pennsylvania*] [*Army Closed*] (AABC) .... FFA
Frankford Public Library, Frankford, PA [*Library symbol Library of Congress*] (LCLS) .... PF
Frankford Public Library, Ontario [*Library symbol National Library of Canada*] (BIB) .... OF
Frankfort [*South Africa*] [*ICAO location identifier*] (ICLI) .... FAFF
Frankfort & Cincinnati Railroad Co. [*AAR code*] .... FCIN
Frankfort City Library, Frankfort, MI [*Library symbol Library of Congress*] (LCLS) .... MiFra
Frankfort Community Public Library, Frankfort, IL [*Library symbol Library of Congress*] (LCLS) .... InFrf

Frankfort First Bancorp [*NASDAQ symbol*] (TTSB) .... FKKY
Frankfort First Bancorp, Inc. [*NASDAQ symbol*] (SAG) .... FKKY
Frankfort First Bankcorp, Inc. [*Associated Press*] (SAG) .... FrankF
Frankfort Horizontal [*Eye-ear plane*] [*Anatomy*] .... FH
Frankfort, IN [*Location identifier FAA*] (FAAL) .... FKR
Frankfort, IN [*AM radio station call letters*] .... WILO
Frankfort, IN [*FM radio station call letters*] .... WSHW
Frankfort, KY [*Location identifier FAA*] (FAAL) .... FFT
Frankfort, KY [*Location identifier FAA*] (FAAL) .... JET
Frankfort, KY [*AM radio station call letters*] .... WFKY
Frankfort, KY [*AM radio station call letters*] .... WKED
Frankfort, KY [*FM radio station call letters*] .... WKED-FM
Frankfort, KY [*FM radio station call letters*] .... WKYW
Frankfort, MI [*FM radio station call letters*] .... WBNZ
Frankfort, NY [*FM radio station call letters*] .... WKLL
Frankfort Public Library District, Frankfort, IL [*Library symbol Library of Congress*] (LCLS) .... IFf
Frankfort-Mandibular Plane Angle [*Medicine*] (DMAA) .... FMA
Frankfurt [*Germany ICAO location identifier*] (ICLI) .... EDFF
Frankfurt [*Kentucky*] [*Airport symbol*] (AD) .... FFT
Frankfurt [*Germany Airport symbol*] (OAG) .... FRA
Frankfurt Am Main [*Germany ICAO location identifier*] (ICLI) .... EDDD
Frankfurt Am Main [*Germany ICAO location identifier*] (ICLI) .... EDDF
Frankfurt Am Main [*Germany ICAO location identifier*] (ICLI) .... EDDZ
Frankfurt Am Main, USAFE [*United States Air Force in Europe*] [*Germany ICAO location identifier*] (ICLI) .... EDAA
Frankfurt Army Regional Medical Center [*US Army 97th General Hospital*] [*Germany*] .... FARMC
Frankfurt City [*Germany ICAO location identifier*] (ICLI) .... EDOL
Frankfurt-North [*Germany ICAO location identifier*] (ICLI) .... EDOK
Frankie Laine Society of America (EA) .... FLSA
Frankie Laine Society of America (EA) .... FLSOA
Franklin [*Pennsylvania*] [*Airport symbol*] (OAG) .... FKL
Franklin [*Also, sC, statC*] [*Unit of electric charge*] .... Fr
Franklin Advantage Real Estate, Inc. [*AMEX symbol*] (SPSG) .... FAD
Franklin Advantage Real Estate, Inc. [*Associated Press*] (SAG) .... FrnkAdv
Franklin and Marshall College [*Pennsylvania*] .... F and M
Franklin and Marshall College [*Pennsylvania*] .... FMC
Franklin and Marshall College, Lancaster, PA [*OCLC symbol*] (OCLC) .... LFM
Franklin and Marshall College, Lancaster, PA [*Library symbol Library of Congress*] (LCLS) .... PLF
Franklin Bancorp [*NASDAQ symbol*] (SAG) .... FNBC
Franklin Bancorp [*Associated Press*] (SAG) .... FrkBncp
Franklin Bancorporation [*NASDAQ symbol*] (TTSB) .... FNBC
Franklin Bank NA [*Associated Press*] (SAG) .... FrnkBk
Franklin Bank NA [*NASDAQ symbol*] (SAG) .... FSVB
Franklin Bluffs, AK [*Location identifier FAA*] (FAAL) .... FKF
Franklin City Schools, Franklin, OH [*Library symbol Library of Congress*] (LCLS) .... OFrS
Franklin College of Indiana .... FCI
Franklin College of Indiana, Franklin, IN [*OCLC symbol*] (OCLC) .... IFC
Franklin College of Indiana, Franklin, IN [*Library symbol Library of Congress*] (LCLS) .... InFrlC
Franklin Computer Corp. (MHDW) .... FDOS
Franklin Cons Mng [*NASDAQ symbol*] (TTSB) .... FKCM
Franklin Consolidated Mining Co., Inc. [*NASDAQ symbol*] (NQ) .... FKCM
Franklin Consolidated Mining Co., Inc. [*Associated Press*] (SAG) .... FrkCon
Franklin Corp. [*AMEX symbol*] (SPSG) .... FKL
Franklin Corp. [*Associated Press*] (SAG) .... Frnkln
Franklin County Courthouse, Hampton, IA [*Library symbol Library of Congress*] (LCLS) .... IaHampCoC
Franklin County Courthouse, Hampton, IA [*Library symbol*] [*Library of Congress*] (LCLS) .... IaHampFC
Franklin County District Library, Franklin, ID [*Library symbol*] [*Library of Congress*] (LCLS) .... IdFr
Franklin County Historical Society, Hampton, IA [*Library symbol Library of Congress*] (LCLS) .... IaHampHi
Franklin County Library, Bunn Branch Library, Bunn, NC [*Library symbol*] [*Library of Congress*] (LCLS) .... NcLo-B
Franklin County Library, Louisburg, NC [*Library symbol Library of Congress*] (LCLS) .... NcLo
Franklin County Recorder's Office, Brookville, IN [*Library symbol Library of Congress*] (LCLS) .... InBrkvCR
Franklin D. Roosevelt Library .... FDRL
Franklin D. Roosevelt Library, Hyde Park, NY [*Library symbol Library of Congress Obsolete*] (LCLS) .... NHpR
Franklin D. Roosevelt Philatelic Society [*Defunct*] (EA) .... FDRPS
Franklin Daily Journal, Franklin, IN [*Library symbol Library of Congress*] (LCLS) .... InFrlJ
Franklin Delano Roosevelt [*US president, 1882-1945*] .... FDR
Franklin Electric [*NYSE symbol*] (TTSB) .... FELE
Franklin Electric Co., Inc. [*NASDAQ symbol*] (NQ) .... FELE
Franklin Electric Co., Inc. [*Associated Press*] (SAG) .... FrnkEl
Franklin Electronic Pub [*NYSE symbol*] (TTSB) .... FEP
Franklin Electronic Publishers, Inc. [*NYSE symbol*] (SAG) .... FEP
Franklin Electronic Publishers, Inc. [*Associated Press*] (SAG) .... FrkEPb
Franklin Elementary School, Eveleth, MN [*Library symbol*] [*Library of Congress*] (LCLS) .... MnEvIFE
Franklin Elementary School, Hewlett, NY [*Library symbol Library of Congress*] (LCLS) .... NHewFE
Franklin Furnace (EA) .... FF
Franklin Furnance Archives, New York, NY [*Library symbol*] [*Library of Congress*] (LCLS) .... NNFFu
Franklin General Hospital, Valley Stream, NY [*Library symbol Library of Congress*] (LCLS) .... NVsFH
Franklin Hldg Corp. [*AMEX symbol*] (TTSB) .... FKL
Franklin, IN [*FM radio station call letters*] .... WFCI
Franklin, IN [*FM radio station call letters*] .... WPZZ
Franklin Institute Laboratories (MUGU) .... FIL
Franklin Institute Laboratories Universal Pulser (KSC) .... FILUP
Franklin Institute, Philadelphia, PA [*Library symbol Library of Congress OCLC symbol*] (LCLS) .... PPF
Franklin Institute Research Laboratories .... FIRL
Franklin Junior High School, Brainerd, MN [*Library symbol*] [*Library of Congress*] (LCLS) .... MnBrFJ
Franklin, KY [*AM radio station call letters*] .... WFKN
Franklin, LA [*FM radio station call letters*] .... KFMV
Franklin, LA [*AM radio station call letters*] .... KFRA
Franklin Lakes, NJ [*FM radio station call letters*] (RBYB) .... WNJW
Franklin, MA [*FM radio station call letters*] .... WGAO
Franklin McLean Memorial Research Institute [*University of Chicago*] [*Research center*] (RCD) .... FMI
Franklin McLean Memorial Research Institute [*University of Chicago*] [*Research center*] .... FMMRI
Franklin Middle School, Thief River Falls, MN [*Library symbol*] [*Library of Congress*] (LCLS) .... MnTFM
Franklin Mint Collector's Society (EA) .... FMCS
Franklin Multi-Income Tr [*NYSE symbol*] (TTSB) .... FMI
Franklin Multi-Income Trust [*NYSE symbol*] (SPSG) .... FMI
Franklin Multi-Income Trust [*Associated Press*] (SAG) .... FrkMul
Franklin, NC [*FM radio station call letters*] .... WFQS
Franklin, NC [*AM radio station call letters*] .... WFSC
Franklin, NC [*AM radio station call letters*] .... WPFJ
Franklin, NC [*FM radio station call letters*] .... WRFR
Franklin, NH [*AM radio station call letters*] .... WFTN
Franklin, NH [*FM radio station call letters*] .... WFTN-FM
Franklin, NJ [*FM radio station call letters*] .... WSUS
Franklin Ophthalmic Instruments [*NASDAQ symbol*] (TTSB) .... FKLN
Franklin, PA [*Location identifier FAA*] (FAAL) .... FKL
Franklin, PA [*AM radio station call letters*] .... WFRA
Franklin, PA [*FM radio station call letters*] .... WFRA-FM
Franklin Parish Library, Winnsboro, LA [*Library symbol Library of Congress*] (LCLS) .... LWinF
Franklin Pierce [*US president, 1804-1869*] .... FP
Franklin Pierce Adams [*1881-1960*] [*American newspaper columnist*] .... FPA
Franklin Pierce Law School (GAGS) .... Franklin Pierce Law Sch
Franklin Planner [*Annual organizer*] .... FP
Franklin Principal Maturity [*NYSE symbol*] (SPSG) .... FPT
Franklin Principal Maturity Trust [*Associated Press*] (SAG) .... FrkPr
Franklin Public Library, Franklin, IN [*Library symbol Library of Congress*] (LCLS) .... InFrl
Franklin Public Library, Franklin, NH [*Library symbol Library of Congress*] (LCLS) .... NhFr
Franklin Public Library, Franklin, OH [*Library symbol Library of Congress*] (LCLS) .... OFr
Franklin Public Library, Franklin, PA [*Library symbol Library of Congress*] (LCLS) .... PFr
Franklin Quest [*NYSE symbol*] (TTSB) .... FNQ
Franklin Quest Co. [*NYSE symbol*] (SAG) .... FNQ
Franklin Quest Co. [*Associated Press*] (SAG) .... FrkQst
Franklin Real Estate Income Fund [*AMEX symbol*] (SPSG) .... FIN
Franklin Real Estate Income Fund [*Associated Press*] (SAG) .... FrnkRE
Franklin Research Center [*Research center*] (RCD) .... FRC
Franklin Resources [*NYSE symbol*] (TTSB) .... BEN
Franklin Resources, Inc. [*NYSE symbol*] (SPSG) .... BEN
Franklin Resources, Inc. [*Associated Press*] (SAG) .... FrnkRs
Franklin School, Hempstead, NY [*Library symbol*] [*Library of Congress*] (LCLS) .... NHemFE
Franklin Select R.E. Inc.Fd'A' [*AMEX symbol*] (TTSB) .... FSN
Franklin Select Real Estate Income Fund [*Associated Press*] (SAG) .... FrnkSel
Franklin Select Real Estate Income Fund [*AMEX symbol*] (SPSG) .... FSN
Franklin Simon & Co. [*Retail clothing stores*] .... FS
Franklin Square Public Library, Franklin Square, NY [*Library symbol Library of Congress*] (LCLS) .... NFs
Franklin Supply Co. Ltd. [*Associated Press*] (SAG) .... FrnkSup
Franklin Supply Co. Ltd. [*AMEX symbol*] (SPSG) .... FSL
Franklin, TN [*AM radio station call letters*] .... WAKM
Franklin, TN [*AM radio station call letters*] (RBYB) .... WHEW-AM
Franklin, TN [*AM radio station call letters*] .... WIZO
Franklin, TN [*FM radio station call letters*] .... WRLT
Franklin Township Historical Society, Indianapolis, IN [*Library symbol Library of Congress*] (LCLS) .... InIFHi
Franklin Township Public Library, Malaga, NJ [*Library symbol Library of Congress*] (LCLS) .... NjMal
Franklin, TX [*FM radio station call letters*] .... KLTR
Franklin, TX [*FM radio station call letters*] (RBYB) .... KLTR
Franklin Universal Tr [*NASDAQ symbol*] (TTSB) .... FT
Franklin Universal Trust [*Associated Press*] (SAG) .... FrkUnv
Franklin Universal Trust [*NYSE symbol*] (CTT) .... FT
Franklin University, Columbus, OH [*Library symbol Library of Congress*] (LCLS) .... OCoF
Franklin University, Columbus, OH [*OCLC symbol*] (OCLC) .... OFU
Franklin, VA [*Location identifier FAA*] (FAAL) .... FKN
Franklin, VA [*AM radio station call letters*] .... WLQM
Franklin, VA [*FM radio station call letters*] .... WLQM-FM
Franklin Watts Group [*Publishers*] [*British*] .... FW
Frankline (IDOE) .... fr
Franklin-Johnson County Public Library, Franklin, IN [*OCLC symbol*] (OCLC) .... IFJ
Franklinton, LA [*AM radio station call letters*] .... WFCG

Franklinton Public Library, Franklinton, NC [*Library symbol Library of Congress*] (LCLS) .... NcFrt

Franlin Early Childhood Center, Hewlett, NY [*Library symbol*] [*Library of Congress*] (LCLS) .... NHewFC

Fransciscan Brothers of the Third Order Regular (TOCD) .... OSF

Frantisek Kmoch Czech Bands Society [*British*] (DBA) .... FKCBS

Franz Rosenzweig Society (EA) .... FRS

Frascali-Ispra-Naples Torus (MCD) .... FINTOR

Fraser [*James E.*] [*Designer's mark, when appearing on US coins*] .... F

Fraser Culture Centre, Tatamagouche, Nova Scotia [*Library symbol National Library of Canada*] (NLC) .... NSTF

Fraser Culture Centre, Tatamagouche, NS, Canada [*Library symbol*] [*Library of Congress*] (LCLS) .... CaNSTaF

Fraser Fort George Regional Museum, Prince George, BC, Canada [*Library symbol*] [*Library of Congress*] (LCLS) .... CaBPGRM

Fraser - Fort George Regional Museum, Prince George, British Columbia [*Library symbol National Library of Canada*] (NLC) .... BPGRM

Fraser, Inc. [*Toronto Stock Exchange symbol*] .... F

Fraser Island Association [*Australia*] .... FIA

Fraser Island Environmental Inquiry [*Australia*] .... FIEI

Fraser Lake Public Library, British Columbia [*Library symbol National Library of Canada*] (NLC) .... BFRL

Fraser on Master and Servant in Scotland [*A publication*] (DLA) .... Fras M & S

Fraser on Personal and Domestic Relations [*Scotland*] [*A publication*] (DLA) .... Fras Dom Rel

Fraser Public Library, Fraser, CO [*Library symbol Library of Congress*] (LCLS) .... CoFra

Fraser Public Library, Fraser, MI [*Library symbol Library of Congress*] (LCLS) .... MiFras

Fraser Valley Antique Farm Machinery Association, Cleabrook, BC, Canada [*Library symbol*] [*Library of Congress*] (LCLS) .... CaBCFVA

Fraser Valley Antique Farm Machinery Association, Clearbrook, British Columbia [*Library symbol National Library of Canada*] (NLC) .... BCFVA

Fraser Valley College, Abbotsford, BC, Canada [*Library symbol Library of Congress*] (LCLS) .... CaBAbFV

Fraser Valley College, Abbotsford, British Columbia [*Library symbol National Library of Canada*] (NLC) .... BCLF

Fraser Valley College, Chilliwack, British Columbia [*Library symbol National Library of Canada*] (NLC) .... BCHF

Fraser Valley College, Clearbrook, BC, Canada [*Library symbol Library of Congress*] (LCLS) .... CaBCIF

Fraser Valley College Learning Resources Centre [*UTLAS symbol*] .... FVC

Fraser Valley College, Library Technician Program, Abbotsford, BC, Canada [*Library symbol*] [*Library of Congress*] (LCLS) .... CaBAbFVL

Fraser Valley Regional Library, Abbotsford, British Columbia [*Library symbol National Library of Canada*] (NLC) .... BABF

Fraser Valley Union Library, Abbotsford, BC, Canada [*Library symbol Library of Congress*] (LCLS) .... CaBAbF

Fraser Videotex Services [*Information service or system*] (IID) .... FVS

Fraserburg [*South Africa*] [*ICAO location identifier*] (ICLI) .... FAFR

Fraserfund Venture Capital Corp. [*Vancouver Stock Exchange symbol*] .... FZV

Fraser-Hickson Institute, Montreal, PQ, Canada [*Library symbol Library of Congress*] (LCLS) .... CaQMF

Fraser-Hickson Institute, Montreal, Quebec [*Library symbol National Library of Canada*] (NLC) .... QMF

Fraser's Conflict of Laws in Cases of Divorce [*A publication*] (DLA) .... Fras Div

Fraser's English Cases of Controverted Elections [*1776-77*] [*A publication*] (DLA) .... Fraser

Fraser's English Cases of Controverted Elections [*1776-77*] [*A publication*] (DLA) .... Fraser (Scot)

Fraser's English Election Cases [*1776-77*] [*A publication*] (DLA) .... Fr EC

Fraser's English Election Cases [*1776-77*] [*A publication*] (DLA) .... Fras

Fraser's English Election Cases [*1776-77*] [*A publication*] (DLA) .... Fras Elec Cas

Fraser's House of Lords Reports [*Scotland*] [*A publication*] (DLA) .... FHL

Fraser's Husband and Wife [*1876-78*] [*Scotland*] [*A publication*] (DLA) .... Fraser

Fraser's Parent and Child [*Scotland*] [*A publication*] (DLA) .... Fras Par & Ch

Fraser's Reports, Justiciary Court [*Scotland*] [*A publication*] (DLA) .... FJC

Fraser's Scotch Court of Sessions Cases [*A publication*] (DLA) .... F Ct Sess

Fraser's Scotch Court of Sessions Cases, Fifth Series [*A publication*] (DLA) .... F

Fraser's Scotch Court of Sessions Cases, Fifth Series [*A publication*] (DLA) .... Fraser

Frasnian-Famennian [*Boundary*] [*Geophysics*] .... F-F

Frater [*Brother*] [*Latin*] .... F

Frater [*Brother*] [*Latin*] .... FR

Frater Anselm [*Pseudonym used by Anselm Baker*] .... FA

(Frater) Johannes de Freiburg [*Deceased, 1314*] [*Authority cited in pre-1607 legal work*] (DSA) .... F Fr

Fraternal .... FRTRNL

Fraternal Actuarial Association [*Defunct*] (EA) .... FAA

Fraternal and Military Club Managers Association [*Defunct*] (EA) .... FMCMA

Fraternal Association of Steel Haulers [*Defunct*] (EA) .... FASH

Fraternal Field Managers' Association [*Appleton, WI*] (EA) .... FFMA

Fraternal Insurance Counsellors Association [*Later, NAFIC*] (EA) .... FICA

Fraternal Insurance Counselor [*Fraternal Field Managers' Association*] [*Designation awarded by*] .... FIC

Fraternal Order of Air Mail Pilots [*Defunct*] (EA) .... FOAMP

Fraternal Order of Eagles (BARN) .... FOE

Fraternal Order of Orioles (EA) .... FOO

Fraternal Order of Police, Grand Lodge (EA) .... FOP

Fraternitatis Regiae Socius [*Fellow of the Royal Society*] [*Latin*] .... FRS

Fraternitatis Regiae Socius et Associatus [*Fellow and Associate of the Royal Society*] [*Latin*] (ROG) .... FRS et AS

Fraternite des Commis de Chemins de Fer, de Lignes Aeriennes, et de Navigation, Manutentionaires de Fret, Employes de Messageries et de Gares [*Brotherhood of Railway, Airline, and Steamship Clerks, Freight Handlers, Express and Station Employees*] [*Canada*] .... FCCFA

Fraternite Internationale des Ouvriers en Electricite [*International Brotherhood of Electrical Workers - IBEW*] [*Canada*] .... FIOE

Fraternite Mondiale [*World Brotherhood*] .... FM

Fraternite Sacerdotale Saint Pie X [*International Sacerdotal Society Saint Pius X - ISSSP*] (EAIO) .... FSSP

Fraternity .... FRAT

Fraternity .... FRTRNTY

Fraternity Executives Association (EA) .... FEA

Fraternity of Canadian Astrologers .... FCA

Fraternity of Recording Executives (EA) .... FORE

Fraternity of the Wooden Leg [*Inactive*] (EA) .... FWL

Fraternity Scholarship Association [*Later, College Fraternity Scholarship Officers Association*] (EA) .... FSA

Fraternize (DSUE) .... FRAT

Fratres [*Brothers*] [*Latin*] .... FF

Fratres Maristae Scholarum [*Marist Brothers of the Schools*] [*Also known as Little Brothers of Mary*] (EAIO) .... FMS

Fratres Presentationis Mariae [*Presentation Brothers - PB*] (EAIO) .... FPM

Fratres Sancti Joseph [*Brothers of St. Joseph*] [*Roman Catholic religious order*] .... FSJ

Fratres Scholarum Christianarum [*Institute of the Brothers of the Christian Schools*] [*Also known as Christian Brothers*] (EAIO) .... FSC

Fratrum [*Of the Brothers*] [*Latin*] (ADA) .... FRUM

Fratrum Instructionis Christianae [*Brothers of Christian Instruction*] [*La Mennais Brothers*] [*Roman Catholic religious order*] .... FIC

Fratsuzskaia Kommunisticheskaia Partija [*Political party*] .... FKP

Fraud [*Legal shorthand*] (LWAP) .... FR

Fraud [*FBI standardized term*] .... FRD

Fraud Against the Government .... FAG

Fraud and Abuse Clearinghouse for Effective Technology Sharing [*Department of Health and Human Services*] .... FACETS

Fraud and Overservicing Detection System (ADA) .... FODS

Fraud Control Institute [*Communications Fraud Control Association*] (TSSD) .... FCI

Fraud Control Plan .... FCP

Fraud Investigation Group [*Serious Fraud Office*] [*British*] .... FIG

Fraud, Waste, and Abuse .... FWA

Fraudulent (MSA) .... FRAUD

Fraudulent (ROG) .... FRDLT

Fraudulent Enlistment .... F/E

Fraudulent Enlistment (DNAB) .... FRDENL

Frauendienst der Evangelisch-Methodistischen Kirche in der Schwiez und in Frankreich [*United Methodist Women in Switzerland and in France*] (EAIO) .... FEMKSF

Fraunhofer Line (PDAA) .... FL

Fraunhofer Line Discriminator [*Physics*] .... FLD

Frayed [*Bookselling*] (DGA) .... FYD

Frazee Elementary School, Frazee, MN [*Library symbol*] [*Library of Congress*] (LCLS) .... MnFraE

Frazee-Vergas High School, Frazee, MN [*Library symbol*] [*Library of Congress*] (LCLS) .... MnFraHS

Frazer Island Defenders Organisation (EERA) .... FIDO

Frazer Nash [*Automobile manufacturer*] [*British*] .... FN

Frazer's Admiralty Cases, Etc. [*Scotland*] [*A publication*] (DLA) .... Fraz

Frazer's Admiralty Cases, Etc. [*Scotland*] [*A publication*] (DLA) .... Fraz Adm

Frazier Elementary School, Houston, TX [*Library symbol*] [*Library of Congress*] (LCLS) .... TxHFzE

Frazier Park, CA [*AM radio station call letters*] .... KKGO

Frazier Park, CA [*AM radio station call letters*] (RBYB) .... KTRJ-AM

Freaks, Irregulars, Defects, and Oddities [*Numismatics*] .... FIDO

Fred Astaire Performing Arts Association .... FAPA

Fred B. Rothman & Co., South Hackensack, NJ [*Library symbol Library of Congress*] (LCLS) .... FbR

Fred Bear Sports Club (EA) .... FBSC

Fred Douglas Lodge Nursing Home, Winnipeg, Manitoba [*Library symbol National Library of Canada*] (NLC) .... MWFD

Fred Douglas Lodge Nursing Home, Winnipeg, MB, Canada [*Library symbol Library of Congress*] (LCLS) .... CaMWFD

Fred Hutchinson Cancer Research Center [*University of Washington*] [*Research center*] (RCD) .... FHCRC

Fred Hutchinson Cancer Research Center, Seattle, WA [*Library symbol Library of Congress*] (LCLS) .... WaSHCR

Fred Lawrence Whipple Observatory [*Amado, AZ*] [*Smithsonian Institution*] (GRD) .... FLWO

Fred Olsen Flyselskap AS [*Norway*] [*FAA designator*] (FAAC) .... FOF

Fred Society (EA) .... FS

Freddie [*Phonetic alphabet*] [*Pre-World War II*] (DSUE) .... F

Freddy [*Phonetic alphabet*] [*Royal Navy World War I*] (DSUE) .... F

Freddy Fender Fan Club (EA) .... FFFC

Frederic Burk Foundation, Inc. [*San Francisco State University*] [*Research center*] (RCD) .... FBFI

Frederic Chopin Society [*Later, IFCF*] (EA) .... FCS

Frederic R. Harris, Inc., Lake Success, NY [*Library symbol Library of Congress*] (LCLS) .... NLsH

Frederick A. Cook Society (EA) .... FACS

Frederick A. Praeger (AD) .... Praeger

Frederick Brewing [*NASDAQ symbol*] (TTSB) .... BLUE

Frederick Brewing Co. [*NASDAQ symbol*] (SAG) .... BLUE

Frederick Brewing Co. [*Associated Press*] (SAG) .... FredBrw

Frederick Burk Foundation Research Center .... FBRC

Frederick Cancer Research Center (RDA) .... FCRC

Frederick Cancer Research Center, Frederick, MD [*OCLC symbol*] (OCLC) .... FCR

Frederick Cancer Research Center, Frederick, MD [*Library symbol Library of Congress*] (LCLS) .... MdFreCR
Frederick Cancer Research Facility [*Frederick, MD*] [*Department of Health and Human Services*] (GRD) .... FCRF
Frederick Community College, Frederick, MD [*OCLC symbol*] (OCLC) .... FRE
Frederick Community College, Frederick, MD [*Library symbol Library of Congress*] (LCLS) .... MdFreFC
Frederick County Public Library, Frederick, MD [*Library symbol*] [*Library of Congress*] (LCLS) .... MdFre
Frederick Douglass Memorial and Historical Association (EA) .... FDMHA
Frederick Engineering's Dataline Monitor/Protocol Analyzer [*Computer science*] .... FELINE
Frederick Eugene Lykes, Jr., Memorial County Library, Brooksville, FL [*Library symbol Library of Congress*] (LCLS) .... FBro
Frederick Law Olmsted [*American landscape architect, 1822-1903*] .... FLO
Frederick Law Olmsted Association (EA) .... FLOA
Frederick, MD [*Location identifier FAA*] (FAAL) .... FDK
Frederick, MD [*AM radio station call letters*] .... WFMD
Frederick, MD [*Television station call letters*] .... WFPT
Frederick, MD [*FM radio station call letters*] .... WFRE
Frederick, MD [*FM radio station call letters*] .... WJTM
Frederick, MD [*AM radio station call letters*] .... WQSI
Frederick, MD [*AM radio station call letters*] (RBYB) .... WXTR-AM
Frederick, OK [*Location identifier FAA*] (FAAL) .... FDR
Frederick, OK [*FM radio station call letters*] .... KSYE
Frederick, OK [*AM radio station call letters*] .... KTAT
Frederick, OK [*FM radio station call letters*] .... KYBE
Frederick Point, AK [*Location identifier FAA*] (FAAL) .... FPN
Frederick Post Drafting Equipment (AD) .... POST
Frederick Research Center (KSC) .... FRC
Frederick Ungar [*Publisher*] .... FU
Frederick's of Hollywood, Inc. [*Associated Press*] (SAG) .... FdHly
Frederick's of Hollywood, Inc. [*NYSE symbol*] (SPSG) .... FOH
Fredericks Place Holdings [*British*] .... FPH
Fredericksburg [*Virginia*] [*Geomagnetic observatory code*] .... FRD
Fredericksburg and Spotsylvania County Battlefield Memorial National Military Park .... FRSP
Fredericksburg News, Fredericksburg, IA [*Library symbol Library of Congress*] (LCLS) .... IaFreN
Fredericksburg Review, Fredericksburg, IA [*Library symbol*] [*Library of Congress*] (LCLS) .... IaFreR
Fredericksburg, TX [*Location identifier FAA*] (FAAL) .... FKB
Fredericksburg, VA [*AM radio station call letters*] .... WFLS
Fredericksburg, VA [*FM radio station call letters*] .... WFLS-FM
Fredericksburg, VA [*AM radio station call letters*] .... WFVA
Fredericksburg, VA [*FM radio station call letters*] .... WJYJ
Fredericktown, MO [*AM radio station call letters*] .... KFTW
Fredericktown, OH [*FM radio station call letters*] .... WWBK
Fredericton [*City in Canada*] (ROG) .... FRED
Fredericton [*New Brunswick*] [*Seismograph station code, US Geological Survey*] (SEIS) .... UNB
Fredericton [*Canada*] [*Airport symbol*] (OAG) .... YFC
Fredericton, NB [*AM radio station call letters*] .... CBZ
Fredericton, NB [*FM radio station call letters*] .... CBZ-FM
Fredericton, NB [*AM radio station call letters*] .... CFNB
Fredericton, NB [*FM radio station call letters*] .... CHSR
Fredericton, NB [*FM radio station call letters*] (RBYB) .... CIBX-FM
Fredericton, NB [*AM radio station call letters*] .... CIHI
Fredericton, NB [*FM radio station call letters*] .... CKHJ
Fredericton, NB [*ICAO location identifier*] (ICLI) .... CYFC
Fredericton-St. John, NB [*FM radio station call letters*] .... CBZF
Frederiksdal [*Greenland*] [*ICAO location identifier*] (ICLI) .... BGFD
Frederikshab [*Greenland*] [*ICAO location identifier*] (ICLI) .... BGFH
Frederiksted, VI [*AM radio station call letters*] .... WRRA
Fredonia [*Record label*] .... Fred
Fredonia, KS [*FM radio station call letters*] (RBYB) .... KJGM
Fredonia, NY [*AM radio station call letters*] .... WCQA
Fredonia, NY [*FM radio station call letters*] .... WCVF
Fredonia Oil & Gas [*Vancouver Stock Exchange symbol*] .... FRN
Fredonia Veterans Association (EA) .... FVA
Fredricksburg, TX [*AM radio station call letters*] .... KNAF
Fredricksburg, TX [*FM radio station call letters*] .... KONO-FM
Fredricksburg, VA [*FM radio station call letters*] .... WBQB
Fred's Fan Club - Burstein's Buffalos [*Defunct*] (EA) .... FFCBB
Freds, Inc. [*NASDAQ symbol*] (SAG) .... FRED
Freds, Inc. [*Associated Press*] (SAG) .... Freds
Fred's Inc.'A' [*NASDAQ symbol*] (TTSB) .... FRED
Fredspolitisk Folkeparti [*People's Peace Policy Party*] [*Denmark*] (PPE) .... FF
Free .... F
Free [*Rate*] [*Value of the English pound*] .... F
Free (ADA) .... FR
Free Acid [*Medicine*] (MAE) .... FA
Free Air Delivered .... FAD
Free Air Facility Track [*Edwards Air Force Base*] (AAG) .... FAFT
Free Air Suspension System .... FASS
Free Air Temperature (NG) .... FAT
Free Air Test Facility .... FATF
Free Albania Organization (EA) .... FAO
Free Alongside [*Shipping*] .... FA
Free Alongside [*Insurance*] .... FAS
Free Alongside Carrier [*Business term*] .... FAC
Free Alongside Ship [*"INCOTERM," International Chamber of Commerce official code*] .... FAS
Free America [*In the movie "Red Dawn"*] .... FA
Free Amino Acid [*Biochemistry*] .... FAA

Free Amino Nitrogen (PDAA) .... FAN
Free and Accepted [*Freemasonry*] (ROG) .... F & A
Free and Accepted Masons .... F & AM
Free and Accepted Masons .... FAM
Free and Accepted Masons of Pennsylvania, Grand Lodge Library, Philadelphia, PA [*Library symbol Library of Congress*] (LCLS) .... PPPFM
Free and Clear (WDAA) .... F/C
Free and Independent Traveller (EERA) .... FIT
Free and Open Church Association [*British*] .... FOCA
Free and-Independent Travelers (BARN) .... FIT
Free Aperture [*Technical drawings*] .... FA
Free Application for Federal Student Aid (GAGS) .... FAFSA
Free Appropriate Public Education .... FAPE
Free Area (OA) .... FA
Free Asia Foundation (EA) .... FAF
Free Association [*Psychology*] (BARN) .... FA
Free Association Books [*Publisher*] [*British*] .... FAB
Free Astray .... FA
Free at Factory [*Business term*] .... FAF
Free at Mill [*Business term*] .... FAM
Free at Quay [*Business term*] .... FAQ
Free Available Chlorine [*Analytical chemistry*] .... FAC
Free Available Chlorine Test with Syringaldazine [*Analytical chemistry*] ..... FACTS
Free Balloon [*Navy symbol*] .... ZF
Free Baptist .... FB
Free Beaches Information Center [*Later, The Naturists*] (EA) .... FBIC
Free Board .... FBD
Free Body Diagram .... FBD
Free by Servitude (ADA) .... FS
Free Carrier [*Followed by a named point*] [*"INCOTERM," International Chamber of Commerce official code*] .... FRC
Free Cash Flow [*Finance*] (PDAA) .... FCF
Free Catecholamines Column Test .... FreeCATS
Free China Assistance (EA) .... FCA
Free China Fund for Medical and Refugee Aid .... FCF
Free Choice [*Psychology*] .... FC
Free Cholesterol [*Clinical chemistry*] .... FC
Free Church .... FC
Free Church (ROG) .... FR CH
Free Church Council [*British*] (DAS) .... FCC
Free Church Federal Council .... FCFC
Free Conducting Particle (PDAA) .... FCP
Free Congress Political Action Committee (EA) .... FCPAC
Free Congress Research and Education Foundation (EA) .... FCREF
Free Crystalline Silica .... FCS
Free Cuba Patriotic Movement (EA) .... FCPM
Free Cursor (NITA) .... FC
Free Cutting Brass .... FCB
Free Cytoprophyrin in Erythrocytes [*Hematology*] (DAVI) .... ECP
Free Delivery .... FD
Free Democrat Party [*Turkey Political party*] .... FDP
Free Democratic Union of Roma [*Political party*] .... FDUR
Free Diffusion Junction [*Electrochemistry*] .... FDJ
Free Discharge .... FD
Free Dispatch .... FD
Free Dock [*Business term*] .... FD
Free Drop .... FD
Free Electron LASER .... FEL
Free Electron Model [*Physical chemistry*] .... FEM
Free End [*Dentistry*] .... FE
Free Energy [*Physics*] (BARN) .... F
Free Energy Change .... FEC
Free Energy Function .... FEF
Free Energy Minimization Procedure [*Computer science*] .... FEMP
Free Enterprise Awards Association (EA) .... FEAA
Free Enterprise Legal Defense Fund [*Bellevue, WA*] (EA) .... FELDF
Free Enterprise Personnel (MCD) .... FEP
Free Erythrocyte Coproporphyria [*Hematology*] (MAE) .... FECP
Free Erythrocyte Coproporphyrin [*Hematology*] (MAE) .... FEC
Free Erythrocyte Protoporphyrin [*Hematology*] .... FEP
Free Erythrocyte Protoporphyrin [*Hematoloy*] (MAH) .... FEPP
Free Estimated Time of Overflight [*Aviation*] (DA) .... FETO
Free Europe Committee [*Later, RFE/RL*] (EA) .... FEC
Free Europe Committee, New York, NY [*Library symbol Library of Congress*] (LCLS) .... NNFE
Free Europe, Inc. [*Later, RFE/RL*] .... FEI
Free Fat [*Biochemistry*] (DAVI) .... FF
Free Fat Graft [*Medicine*] (DMAA) .... FFG
Free Fatty Acid [*Biochemistry*] .... FFA
Free Fatty Acid Phase [*Biochemistry*] (DAVI) .... FFAP
Free Field Analysis .... FFA
Free Field Room .... FFR
Free Field Voltage Sensitivity .... FFVS
Free Fire Area (AABC) .... FFA
Free Fire Zone [*Army*] (AABC) .... FFZ
Free Flight .... FF
Free Flight Aerial Rocket [*Military*] (INF) .... FFAR
Free Flight Analysis Section .... FFAS
Free Flight Data .... FFD
Free Flight Facility (MCD) .... FFF
Free Flight Plan [*Northwest Airlines, Inc.*] .... FFP
Free Flight Rocket (NATG) .... FFR
Free Flight Test Vehicle .... FFTV
Free Float Facility (SSD) .... FFF
Free Flood .... FF

Free Flow Electrophoresis [*Analytical biochemistry*] .... FFE
Free Flyaround (SAA) .... FF
Free Flyer (MCD) .... FF
Free Foil Switching Device .... FFSD
Free Foreign Agency [*or Agent*] [*Business term*] .... FFA
Free Form [*Automotive engineering*] .... FF
Free Fraction .... FF
Free French [*World War II*] .... FF
Free French [*World War II*] .... FFR
Free French [*World War II*] .... FRF
Free French Forces [*World War II*] .... FFF
Free from Alongside [*Shipping*] .... FFA
Free from Average [*Insurance*] .... FFA
Free from Chlorine .... FFC
Free from Foreign Capture (ROG) .... FFC
Free from Infection [*Medicine*] .... FFI
Free from Prussic Acid .... FFPA
Free from Tax, Affordable, Insured Rewarding [*Savings certificate*] [*Savings and Loan Association*] .... FAIR
Free Front Endpapers (DGA) .... FFE
Free Gas Volume .... FGV
Free Gyroscope (SAA) .... FG
Free Harbor .... FH
Free Height .... FRHGT
Free Hepatic Venous Pressure [*Medicine*] .... FHP
Free Hepatic Venous Pressure [*Medicine*] .... FHVP
Free In [*Shipping*] (ADA) .... FI
Free In and Out [*Shipping*] .... FIO
Free In and Out and Stowed [*Shipping*] .... FIOS
Free In and Out and Trimmed [*Shipping*] .... FIOT
Free In and Out of Trucks [*Business term*] .... FIOT
Free in and Stowed [*Shipping*] (DS) .... Fias
Free in Harbor [*Navigation*] .... FIH
Free in Store [*Business term*] .... FIS
Free in Truck [*Business term*] .... FIT
Free in Wagon [*Business term*] .... FIW
Free Indian Socially-Traditionally [*India*] [*Political party*] .... FIST
Free Indirect Discourse .... FID
Free Induction Decay [*Physics*] .... FID
Free Induction Delay .... FID
Free Instrument Package .... FIP
Free Insurance and Carriage [*Shipping*] (DS) .... FIC
Free Interstitial Atom .... FIA
Free into Barge [*Shipping*] .... FIB
Free into Bunker .... FIB
Free into Container Depot [*Business term*] .... FID
Free Jet Expansion .... FJE
Free Jet Test .... FJT
Free Kindergarten Association of Victoria [*Australia*] .... FKAV
Free Lance .... F/L
Free Lance Exchange .... FLEX
Free Lance Finders Network (EA) .... FLFN
Free Language Indexing [*Information retrieval*] (NITA) .... FLI
Free Language Information Retrieval Tool [*Netherlands*] (NITA) .... FLIRT
Free Learning Exchange [*An association Defunct*] (EA) .... FLEX
Free Library of Philadelphia, Carson Collection, Philadelphia, PA [*Library symbol Library of Congress*] (LCLS) .... PP-C
Free Library of Philadelphia, H. Josephine Widener Memorial Branch, Philadelphia, PA [*Library symbol Library of Congress Obsolete*] (LCLS) .... PP-W
Free Library of Philadelphia, Library for the Blind and Physically Handicapped, Philadelphia, PA [*Library symbol Library of Congress*] (LCLS) .... PP-DPH
Free Library of Philadelphia, Philadelphia, PA [*OCLC symbol*] (OCLC) .... PLF
Free Library of Philadelphia, Philadelphia, PA [*Library symbol Library of Congress*] (LCLS) .... PP
Free Library, Pittsfield, VT [*Library symbol Library of Congress*] (LCLS) .... VtPifi
Free Limiting Internal Truss [*Nuclear energy*] (NRCH) .... FLIT
Free Line Signal [*Telecommunications*] (TEL) .... FLS
Free Magnesium .... Mgf
Free Man of Color [*Term of reference for blacks after the Civil War*] .... FMC
Free Men [*Defunct*] (EA) .... FM
Free Methodist Historical Center, Winona Lake, IN [*Library symbol Library of Congress*] (LCLS) .... InWinFM
Free Methodist World Fellowship (EA) .... FMWF
Free Minds [*An association*] (EA) .... FM
Free Molecular Flow .... FMF
Free Motion Impedance .... FMI
Free National Movement [*Bahamas*] [*Political party*] (PPW) .... FNM
Free Nerve Ending [*Anatomy*] .... FNE
Free Oceanographic Instrument Float .... FOIF
Free of All Average [*Insurance*] .... FA
Free of All Average [*Insurance*] .... FAA
Free of Capture and Seizure [*Insurance*] .... FC & S
Free of Capture and Seizure [*Insurance*] .... FCS
Free of Capture, Seizure, Arrest, and Detainment [*Insurance*] .... FCSAD
Free of Capture, Seizure, Riots, and Civil Commotions [*Insurance*] .... FCSRCC
Free of Cells [*Medicine*] .... FC
Free of Charge [*Business term*] .... FOC
Free of Claim for Accident Reported [*Shipping*] (DS) .... FCAR
Free of Damage [*Business term*] .... FOD
Free of Disease [*Medicine*] .... FOD
Free of General Average .... FGA
Free of Heart Center (DAC) .... FOHC
Free of Income Tax .... FIT
Free of Interest [*Business term*] .... FOI
Free of Knots .... FOK
Free of Particular Average [*Insurance*] .... FPA
Free of Particular Average, American Conditions [*Insurance*] .... FPAAC
Free of Particular Average, English Conditions [*Insurance*] .... FPAEC
Free of Poundage Money Order .... FPMO
Free of Riots and Civil Commotions [*Insurance*] .... FR & CC
Free of Riots and Civil Commotions [*Insurance*] .... FRCC
Free of Tax .... FOT
Free on Aircraft [*Cargo delivery term for export traffic*] (DCTA) .... FOA
Free on Board [*"INCOTERM," International Chamber of Commerce official code*] [*Shipping*] .... FOB
Free on Board Airport [*Business term*] .... FOBA
Free on Board in Harbor [*Business term*] .... FBH
Free on Car [*Shipping*] .... FOC
Free on Quay [*Business term*] .... FOQ
Free on Quay [*Business term*] (ODBW) .... foq
Free on Rail/Free on Truck [*"INCOTERM," International Chamber of Commerce official code*] .... FOR
Free on Rail/Free on Truck [*Business term*] .... FOR/FOT
Free on Ship [*or Steamer*] [*Shipping*] .... FOS
Free on Station .... FOS
Free on Truck [*See also FOR*] [*Business term*] .... FOT
Free on Wagon [*Business term*] .... FOW
Free on Water [*Business term*] .... FOW
Free on Wharf [*Business term*] (ROG) .... FOW
Free Out [*Shipping*] .... FO
Free Overside .... FO
Free Pacific Association (EA) .... FPA
Free Papau Movement [*Indonesia*] [*Political party*] .... FPM
Free Pardon (ADA) .... FP
Free Patellar Tendon Graft [*Sports medicine*] .... FPTG
Free Piston [*Machinery*] (DS) .... FP
Free Piston Vessel (GFGA) .... FPV
Free Plasma Trytophan (PDAA) .... FPT
Free Play [*Military*] (CAAL) .... FP
Free Play Scenario Generator (MCD) .... FREPSOG
Free Polar Corticosteroids [*Endocrinology*] .... FPCS
Free Polymer-Derived Carbon [*Chemistry*] .... FPC
Free Port [*Shipping*] .... FP
Free Port Zone [*Shipping*] (DS) .... FPZ
Free Press Association (EA) .... FPA
Free Press, Phillipsburg, NJ [*Library symbol Library of Congress*] (LCLS) .... NjPhP
Free Progressive Wave .... FPW
Free Propellers (AAG) .... FP
Free Public Library, Chariton, IA [*Library symbol Library of Congress*] (LCLS) .... IaCh
Free Public Library, Mattapoisett, MA [*Library symbol Library of Congress*] (LCLS) .... MMat
Free Public Library, Metuchen, NJ [*Library symbol Library of Congress*] (LCLS) .... NjMe
Free Public Library of Irvington, Irvington, NJ [*Library symbol Library of Congress*] (LCLS) .... NjI
Free Public Library of Livingston, Livingston, NJ [*Library symbol Library of Congress*] (LCLS) .... NjLi
Free Public Library of Newark, Newark, NJ [*OCLC symbol*] (OCLC) .... NPL
Free Public Library of the Borough of Madison, Madison, NJ [*Library symbol Library of Congress*] (LCLS) .... NjM
Free Public Library of the City of Orange, Orange, NJ [*Library symbol Library of Congress*] (LCLS) .... NjO
Free Public Library of the Township of Mahwah, Mahwah, NJ [*Library symbol Library of Congress*] (LCLS) .... NjMah
Free Public Library of Woodbridge, Woodbridge, NJ [*Library symbol Library of Congress*] (LCLS) .... NjWoo
Free Public Library, West Liberty, IA [*Library symbol Library of Congress*] (LCLS) .... IaWl
Free Queue Element (IAA) .... FQE
Free Radical Assay Technique [*Clinical chemistry*] .... FRAT
Free Radical Photography .... FRP
Free Radical Retrograde Precipitation Polymerization [*Organic chemistry*] .... FRRPP
Free Ranging on Grid [*Computer-controlled transport system*] .... FROG
Free Reaction Sphere Satellite Attitude Control System (DNAB) .... FRSSACS
Free Recall Learning (PDAA) .... FRL
Free Recall-Controlled Recall Test [*Psychology*] (AEBS) .... FRCR
Free Representation Unit [*Legal term*] (DLA) .... FRU
Free Residual Chlorine .... FRC
Free Response .... FR
Free Ribosomes [*Cytology*] .... FR
Free Rocket over Ground [*USSR missile*] .... FROG
Free Romanian Press [*British*] .... FRP
Free Running Frequency .... FRF
Free Running Multivibrator (PDAA) .... FRMV
Free Rural Delivery [*British*] .... FRD
Free Safety [*Football*] .... FS
Free Search Terminal Interface [*Telecommunications*] .... FSTI
Free Secreting Component [*Immunology*] .... FSC
Free Serbian Orthodox Church [*Australia*] .... FSOC
Free Shear Layer .... FSL
Free Software Foundation (EA) .... SFS
Free Sons of Israel (EA) .... FSI
Free South Africa Movement (EA) .... FSAM
Free Southern Theater .... FST
Free Space Microwave Interferometer .... FSMWI
Free Space Transfer (MCD) .... FST

Free Spectral Range .... FSR
Free Speech Movement [*University of California, Berkeley*] .... FSM
Free St Con Gld Mines ADR [*NASDAQ symbol*] (TTSB) .... FSCNY
Free Standing (ADA) .... FS
Free State Consolidated Gold [*NASDAQ symbol*] (SAG) .... FSCN
Free State Consolidated Gold Mines Ltd. [*Associated Press*] (SAG) .... FreSCn
Free Sterol [*Biochemistry*] (OA) .... FS
Free Storage Block [*Computer science*] (IAA) .... FSB
Free Storage Block Pointer (HGAA) .... FSBPRT
Free Storage Block Semaphore [*Computer science*] (IAA) .... FSBSEM
Free Store/Food Bank (EA) .... FS/FB
Free Supersonic Jet .... FSJ
Free Support Area (MUGU) .... FSA
Free Surface Water Tunnel .... FSWT
Free System Resource [*Computer science*] (PCM) .... FSR
Free Territory of Ely-Chatelaine [*An association*] (EA) .... FTEC
Free Territory of Trieste .... FTT
Free Testosterone Index [*Endocrinology*] .... FTI
Free Text Retrieval (NITA) .... FTX
Free the Army [*Barracks graffiti; also, title of antimilitary play*] [*Bowdlerized version*] .... FTA
Free the Battery Hen Association [*Australia*] .... FBHA
Free the Eagle [*Washington, DC*] (EA) .... FTE
Free the Fathers (EA) .... FF
Free Thought Association (EA) .... FTA
Free Throw [*Basketball*] .... FT
Free Throwers Boomerang Society (EA) .... FTBS
Free Throws Attempted [*Basketball*] .... FTA
Free Throws Made [*Basketball*] .... FTM
Free Thyroxine [*Also, FT_4*] [*Endocrinology*] .... FT
Free [*Unbound*] **Thyroxine** [*Endocrinology*] (DAVI) .... FT_4
Free Thyroxine Equivalent [*Endocrinology*] .... FTE
Free Thyroxine Fraction [*Endocrinology*] (DAVI) .... FTF
Free Thyroxine Index [*Endocrinology*] FT4IX
Free Thyroxine Index [*Endocrinology*] .... FTI
Free to Member .... FTM
Free Trade Agreement [*or Arrangement*] .... FTA
Free Trade Agreement of the Americas [*Proposed*] .... FTAA
Free Trade Area .... FTA
Free Trade Area of the Americas [*NAFTA*] (ECON) .... FTAA
Free Trade Association [*European*] .... FTA
Free Trade Unions of Burma .... FTUB
Free Trade Unions of the Philippines .... FTUP
Free Trade Wharf .... FTW
Free Trade Zone (IMH) .... FTZ
Free Trader (ROG) .... FT
Free Triiodothyronine [*Endocrinology*] (DAVI) .... FT_3
Free Triiodothyronine Index .... FT_3IX
Free Turbine (AAG) .... FT
Free Turn .... FT
Free University Network [*Later, LERN*] (EA) .... FUN
Free University of New York .... FUNY
Free University, Washington-Paris-Moscow [*An association*] (EA) .... FUWPM
Free Vehicle Grab Respirometer (NUCP) .... FVGR
Free Visayan Workers' Union [*Philippines*] .... FVWU
Free Wallenberg Committee (EA) .... FWC
Free Water Damage (ADA) .... FWD
Free Water Reabsorption (DAVI) .... TH_2O
Free Wheel (ADA) .... FW
Free Wheeling Diode (IAA) .... FWD
Free Will Baptist Press Association (EA) .... FWBPA
Free Will Offering Scheme (ROG) .... FWOS
Free Workers' Trade Union Congress [*Aden*] .... FWTUC
Free World Air Intelligence Study (MCD) .... FWAIS
Free World Air Order of Battle (MCD) .... FWAOB
Free World Armed Forces .... FWAF
FREE [*Federated Republics of Earth and Its Environs*] **World Government** (EA) .... FWGE
Free World Military Assistance (CINC) .... FWMA
Free World Military Assistance Council .... FWMAC
Free World Military Assistance Forces [*Vietnam*] .... FWMAF
Free World Military Assistance Organization (MCD) .... FWMAO
Free World Military Forces [*Group of countries which provided military aid to South Vietnam*] [*Also, FWMF*] (VNW) .... FWF
Free World Military Forces [*Group of countries which provided military aid to South Vietnam*] [*Also, FWF*] (VNW) .... FWMF
Free Zone Authority (EA) .... FZA
Free-Agent Market Simulator [*Computer programmed to calculate the market value of free agents in the National Basketball Association*] .... FAMS
Free-Air Gradient [*Geophysics*] .... FAG
Free-Association Strength [*Psychometrics*] .... FAS
Free-Binding Capacity [*Serology*] .... FBC
Freeboard (KSC) .... FREEBD
Freeboard Measure (IAA) .... FBM
Freeburg Community High School 77, Freeburg, IL [*Library symbol Library of Congress*] (LCLS) .... IFrHS
Freed-Hardeman College [*Tennessee*] .... FHC
Freed-Hardeman College, Loden-Daniel Library, Henderson, TN [*Library symbol*] [*Library of Congress*] (LCLS) .... THenF
Freedom Airlines, Inc. [*ICAO designator*] (FAAC) .... FDM
Freedom and Justice for Cyprus Trust (EA) .... FJCT
Freedom, CA [*FM radio station call letters*] .... KPIG
Freedom Communications International News Agency (EAIO) .... FCI
Freedom Community Unit, School District 245, Earlville, IL [*Library symbol Library of Congress*] (LCLS) .... IEarFSD
[*The*] **Freedom Council** [*Defunct*] (EA) .... TFC
Freedom Defence Committee [*National Council for Civil Liberties*] [*British*] .... FDC
Freedom Democratic Party [*in Mississippi*] .... FDP
Freedom Federation [*Defunct*] (EA) .... FF
Freedom from Hunger Campaign [*UN Food and Agriculture Organization*] .... FFHC
Freedom from Hunger Campaign - Action for Development [*UN Food and Agriculture Organization*] .... FFHC/AD
Freedom from Hunger Foundation [*UN Food and Agriculture Organization*] (EA) .... FFH
Freedom from Religion Foundation (EA) .... FFRF
Freedom Fund [*An association Defunct*] (EA) .... FF
Freedom House (EA) .... FH
Freedom in Advertising [*British*] (DI) .... FIA
Freedom in Sport International Committee and Lobby [*British*] (DI) .... FISICAL
Freedom, Independence, God, Honor, Today (IIA) .... FIGHT
Freedom Information Service (EA) .... FIS
Freedom Leadership Foundation (EA) .... FLF
Freedom League (EA) .... FL
Freedom of Access to Clinic Entrances Act [*1994*] .... FACE
Freedom of Choice Act [*Abortion-rights bill*] (ECON) .... FOCA
Freedom of Expression Foundation (EA) .... FEF
Freedom of Faith: A Christian Committee for Religious Rights (EA) .... FFACCRR
Freedom of Information [*Army*] .... FOI
Freedom of Information Act [*1966*] (AFM) .... FIA
Freedom of Information Act .... FOI
Freedom of Information Act [*1966*] .... FOIA
Freedom of Information Act (TDOB) .... FOIO
Freedom of Information and Privacy Act .... FOIPA
Freedom of Information Center (EA) .... FOI
Freedom of Information Center. Reports [*A publication*] (DLA) .... FOICR
Freedom of Information Clearinghouse [*An association*] (EA) .... FIC
Freedom of Information Clearinghouse (EA) .... FOIC
Freedom of Information Reform Act of 1986 .... FIRA
Freedom of Navigation (DOMA) .... FON
Freedom of Ocean Science Task Group [*NAS-NRC*] (NOAA) .... FOSTG
Freedom Organisation for the Right to Enjoy Smoking Tobacco [*British*] (DI) .... FOREST
Freedom Socialist Party (EA) .... FSP
Freedom through Truth Foundation (EA) .... FTTF
Freedom to Advertise Coalition (EA) .... FAC
Freedom to Read Foundation .... FRF
Freedom to Read Foundation (EA) .... FTRF
Freedoms Foundation at Valley Forge (EA) .... FFVF
Freedom's Friends (EA) .... FF
Free-Fall .... FF
Free-Fall Bomb (SAA) .... FFB
Free-Fall Grab [*Marine geology*] .... FFG
Free-Fall Pop-Up Ocean Bottom Seismometer [*Marine science*] (MSC) .... POPS
Free-Fall Sensor .... FFS
Free-Fall Test (SAA) .... FFT
Free-Floating Thrombus [*Medicine*] .... FFT
Free-Flying Imagine RADAR Experiment/Soviet-American Microwave Experiment (MCD) .... FIREX/SAMEX
Free-Flying [*Experiment*] **Module** [*NASA*] (NASA) .... FFM
Free-Flying Teleoperator [*Program*] [*Electronics*] .... FFTO
Free-for-All (ADA) .... FFA
Free-Form Fabrication (ECON) .... FFF
Free-Form Language for Image Processing (PDAA) .... FLIP
Free-Heave Amplitude .... FHA
Free-Heave Test .... FHT
Freehold [*Legal term*] (ROG) .... F
Freehold [*Legal term*] .... FHLD
Freehold Ground Rent (ROG) .... FGR
Freehold Public Library, Freehold, NJ [*Library symbol Library of Congress*] (LCLS) .... NjFr
Freeholder [*Real estate*] (BARN) .... FH
Freelance Editors' Association of Canada .... FEAC
FreeLance Finders Network (EA) .... FFN
Freelance Journalist (DGA) .... FLJ
Freelance Network (EA) .... FLN
Freelance Network [*Defunct*] (EA) .... FN
Freelance Research Service, Houston, TX [*OCLC symbol*] (OCLC) .... THF
Freelance Research Service, Houston, TX [*Library symbol Library of Congress*] (LCLS) .... TxHFR
Freelance Syndicate, Inc. (EA) .... FSI
Freeland League for Jewish Territorial Colonization [*Later, LYI*] (EA) .... FLJTC
Freeland, PA [*FM radio station call letters*] .... WQEQ
Freeland, PA [*FM radio station call letters*] (RBYB) .... WWFH-FM
Freely Jointed Chain [*Model of a polymer*] [*Organic chemistry*] .... FJC
Freely Moving Human Subject .... FMHS
Free-Machining Steel .... FMS
Freeman Anxiety, Neurosis, and Psychosomatic Test [*Psychology*] .... FANPT
Freeman. Comparative Politics [*A publication*] (DLA) .... Freem Compar Politics
Freeman Elementary School, Houston, TX [*Library symbol*] [*Library of Congress*] (LCLS) .... TxHFrE
Freeman Fox International [*Commercial firm British*] .... FFI
Freeman Junior College [*South Dakota*] .... FJC
Freeman on Cotenancy and Partition [*A publication*] (DLA) .... Freem Cot
Freeman on Executors [*A publication*] (DLA) .... Freem Ex
Freeman on Judgments [*A publication*] (DLA) .... Freem Judgm
Freeman Public Library, Freeman, SD [*Library symbol Library of Congress*] (LCLS) .... SdFr
Freeman Time Unit [*Psychology*] .... FTU
Freeman Time Unit [*Psychology*] .... FU

Freeman-Journal, Webster City, IA [*Library symbol Library of Congress*] (LCLS) .... IaWecF
Freeman's English Chancery Cases [*A publication*] (DLA) .... Freem CC
Freeman's English Chancery Reports [*A publication*] (DLA) ...... Fr Ch
Freeman's English Chancery Reports [*A publication*] (DLA) .... Fr Chy
Freeman's English Chancery Reports [*A publication*] (DLA) .... Free
Freeman's English Chancery Reports [*A publication*] (ILCA) ...... Free CC
Freeman's English Chancery Reports [*A publication*] (DLA) ...... Free Ch
Freeman's English Chancery Reports [*A publication*] (DLA) ...... Freem
Freeman's English Chancery Reports [*A publication*] (DLA) ...... Freem Ch
Freeman's English Chancery Reports [*A publication*] (DLA) .... Freem Ch (Eng)
Freeman's English King's Bench and Chancery Reports [*A publication*] (DLA) .... Fr
Freeman's English King's Bench and Common Pleas Reports [*89 English Reprint*] [*A publication*] (DLA) ... Freem KB
Freeman's English King's Bench Reports [*89 English Reprint*] [*1670-1704*] [*A publication*] (DLA) ... Free
Freeman's English King's Bench Reports [*89 English Reprint*] [*1670-1704*] [*A publication*] (DLA) ... Free KB
Freeman's Growth of the English Constitution [*3rd ed.*] [*1876*] [*A publication*] (DLA) ... Freem Eng Const
Freeman's Journal [*A publication*] .... FJ
Freeman's Mississippi Chancery Reports [*A publication*] (DLA) ... Fr Ch
Freeman's Mississippi Chancery Reports [*A publication*] (DLA) ... Fr Chy
Freeman's Mississippi Chancery Reports [*A publication*] (DLA) ... Free Ch
Freeman's Mississippi Chancery Reports [*A publication*] (DLA) ... Freem
Freeman's Mississippi Chancery Reports [*A publication*] (DLA) ... Freem Ch (Miss)
Freeman's Mississippi Chancery Reports [*A publication*] (DLA) ... Freem Ch R
Freeman's Mississippi Chancery Reports [*A publication*] (DLA) ... Freem Chan
Freeman's Mississippi Chancery Reports [*A publication*] (DLA) ... Freem (Miss)
Freeman's Mississippi Chancery Reports [*A publication*] (DLA) ... Freeman Ch R
Freeman's Mississippi Chancery Reports [*A publication*] (DLA) ... Freeman's (Miss) Rep
Freeman's Practice [*Illinois*] [*A publication*] (DLA) ... Freem Pr
Freeman's Reports [*31-96 Illinois*] [*A publication*] (DLA) ... Free
Freeman's Reports [*31-96 Illinois*] [*A publication*] (DLA) ... Freem (Ill)
Freeman-Sheldon Parent Support Group (EA) ... FSPSG
Freemason (ROG) ... FM
Freemasons' Club of Western Australia ... FCWA
Freemasons' Hall [*Freemasonry*] (ROG) ... FMH
Freemasons Tavern [*Freemasonry*] (ROG) ... FMT
Freemen Institute (EA) ... FI
Freemont Gold [*Vancouver Stock Exchange symbol*] ... FGC
Free-Net Erlangen Nurnberg [*Information service or system*] (IID) ... FEN
Freephone Supplementary Service [*Telecommunications*] (DOM) ... FPH
Freeport [*Bahamas*] [*Airport symbol*] (OAG) ... FPO
Freeport, FL [*AM radio station call letters*] (RBYB) ... WGTX-AM
Freeport High School, Freeport, NY [*Library symbol Library of Congress*] (LCLS) ... NFreeHS
Freeport Hospital, Freeport, NY [*Library symbol Library of Congress*] (LCLS) ... NFreeH
Freeport, IL [*Location identifier FAA*] (FAAL) ... FEP
Freeport, IL [*FM radio station call letters*] ... WFPS
Freeport, IL [*AM radio station call letters*] ... WFRL
Freeport, IL [*Television station call letters*] ... WIFR
Freeport, IL [*AM radio station call letters*] (RBYB) ... WNIE-FM
Freeport, IL [*FM radio station call letters*] ... WXXQ
Freeport/International, Grand Bahama Island [*Bahamas*] [*ICAO location identifier*] (ICLI) ... MYGF
Freeport McMoRan Copper & Gold [*NYSE symbol*] (SPSG) ... FCX
Freeport McMoRan Copper & Gold [*Associated Press*] (SAG) ... FMCG
Freeport McMoRan, Inc. [*Associated Press*] (SAG) ... FrptMc
Freeport McMoRan O/G Rlty [*NYSE symbol*] (TTSB) ... FMR
Freeport McmoRan Res LP [*NYSE symbol*] (TTSB) ... FRP
Freeport McMoRan Resource Partners Ltd. [*Associated Press*] (SAG) ... FMRP
Freeport McMoRan(New) [*NYSE symbol*] (TTSB) ... FTX
Freeport Memorial Library, Freeport, NY [*Library symbol Library of Congress*] (LCLS) ... NFree
Freeport, NY [*AM radio station call letters*] ... WGBB
Freeport Resources, Inc. [*Vancouver Stock Exchange symbol*] ... FRI
Freeport, TX [*AM radio station call letters*] ... KBRZ
Freeport, TX [*FM radio station call letters*] ... KJOJ-FM
Freeport-McMoRan, Inc. [*NYSE symbol*] (SPSG) ... FTX
Freeport-McMoran Oil & Gas Royalty Trust [*Associated Press*] (SAG) ... FM RoyT
Freeport-McMoran Oil & Gas Royalty Trust [*NYSE symbol*] (SPSG) ... FMR
Freeport-McMoRan Resource Partnership LP [*NYSE symbol*] (SPSG) ... FRP
Freept McMoRan Copper&Gold'B' [*NYSE symbol*] (TTSB) ... FCX
Freept McMoRan Cp/Gld7%CvPref [*NYSE symbol*] (TTSB) ... FCXPr
Freept-McMo Cp/Gld'A'Dep Pfd [*NYSE symbol*] (TTSB) ... FCXPrA
Freept-McMo Cp/Gld'B'Dep Pfd [*NYSE symbol*] (TTSB) ... FCXPrB
Freept-McMo Cp/Gld'C'Dep Pfd [*NYSE symbol*] (TTSB) ... FCXPrC
Freept-McMo Cp/Slvr'D'Dep Pfd [*NYSE symbol*] (TTSB) ... FCXPrD
Freer Gallery of Art, Washington, DC [*Library symbol Library of Congress*] (LCLS) ... DFG
Free-Running Oscillator [*Instrumentation*] ... FRO
Free-Solution Capillary Electrophoresis [*Physical chemistry*] ... FSCE
Free-Standing Additional Voluntary Contribution [*Pension fund payment option*] [*British*] ... FSAVC
Freestanding Ambulatory Surgery Association (EA) ... FASA
Free-Standing Ambulatory Surgical Center ... FASC
Free-Standing Emergency Center ... FEC
Freestanding Emergency Clinic ... FEC
Freestanding Insert [*Advertising*] ... FSI
Free-Standing Operating System [*General Automation, Inc.*] ... FSOS
Free-Standing Surgical Outpatient Facility (HCT) ... FSOP

Freestone (ADA) ... FS
Freestyle Players Association ... FPA
Free-Text Retrieval [*Computer system alternative to Content-Addressable File Store*] ... FTR
Free-Thinker [*or Free-Thinking*] (ROG) ... FREE-TH
Free-Time System [*GE/PAC*] (IEEE) ... FTS
Freetown [*Sierra Leone*] [*Airport symbol*] (OAG) ... FNA
Freetown [*Sierra Leone*] **Hastings Airport** [*Airport symbol*] (OAG) ... HGS
Freetown/Lungi [*Sierra Leone*] [*ICAO location identifier*] (ICLI) ... GFLL
Freeway (ADA) ... F
Freeway [*Commonly used*] (OPSA) ... FREEWAY
Freeway [*Commonly used*] (OPSA) ... FREEWY
Freeway [*Commonly used*] (OPSA) ... FRWAY
Freeway ... FRWY
Freeway (MCD) ... FWY
Freeway (DD) ... Fwy
Freeway ... FWY
Freeway Air BV [*Netherlands ICAO designator*] (FAAC) ... FWC
Freeway and Arterial Management Effort [*FHWA*] (TAG) ... FAME
Freeway Driver Information System ... FDIS
Freeway Iberica SA [*Spain ICAO designator*] (FAAC) ... FIB
Freeway Management System ... FMS
Freeway Resources Ltd. [*Vancouver Stock Exchange symbol*] ... FEE
Free-Wheel Bicycle ... FWB
Free-Wheel Rectifier ... FWR
Free-Will Baptist Bible College, Nashville, TN [*Library symbol Library of Congress*] (LCLS) ... TNFB
Free-Will Baptists ... FWB
Freeze ... FREZ
Freeze [*NWS*] (FAAC) ... FRZ
Freeze Calculated Landing Time [*FAA*] (TAG) ... FCLT
Freeze Desalination Plant ... FDP
Freeze Speed Parameter [*FAA*] (TAG) ... FSPD
Freeze Substitution (OA) ... FS
Freeze Thaw Lysate [*Cytology*] ... FTL
Freeze Voter (EA) ... FV
Freeze-Dried ... FD
Freeze-Dried (Allogenic) Skin Graft [*Medicine*] ... FDSG
Freeze-Etch Technique ... FET
Freeze-Fracture Electron Microscopy ... FFEM
Freeze-Fracture Transmission Electron Microscopy ... FF-TEM
Freezer (DNAB) ... FRZER
Freezer (MSA) ... FRZR
Freezer ... FRZR
Freezing ... FRZG
Freezing ... FZ
Freezing Drizzle [*Meteorology*] ... FZDZ
Freezing Fog [*Meteorology*] ... FZFG
Freezing Gas Jet ... FGJ
Freezing Level [*NWS*] (FAAC) ... FRZLVL
Freezing Point ... FP
Freezing Point Calibration Standard ... FPCS
Freezing Point Osmometer ... FPO
Freezing Rain [*Meteorology*] ... FZRA
Freezing Rain [*Meterology*] (BARN) ... ZR
Freezing Rain Endurance Test [*Aviation*] (DA) ... FRET
Freezing Rain Information Not Available [*NWS*] (FAAC) ... ZRNO
Fregate Island [*Seychelles Islands*] [*Airport symbol*] (OAG) ... FRK
Frei aber Einsam [*Free but Lonely*] [*Motto of Joseph Joachim, 19th century German violinist*] (ECON) ... FAE
Freiburg/Breisgau [*Germany ICAO location identifier*] (ICLI) ... EDTF
Freie Demokratische Partei [*Free Democratic Party*] [*Germany Political party*] (EAIO) ... FDP
Freie Deutsche Jugend [*Free German Youth*] [*Germany Political party*] (PPE) ... FDJ
Freie Liste [*Free List*] [*Liechtenstein*] [*Political party*] (EY) ... FL
Freie und Angenommene Maurer [*Free and Accepted Mason*] [*Freemasonry*] [*German*] ... FUAM
Freie Union in Niedersachsen [*Free Union in Lower Saxony*] [*Germany Political party*] (PPW) ... FU
Freie Universitaet (Berlin) [*Free University (Berlin)*] [*Information retrieval Germany*] ... FU
Freie Universitaet (Berlin), Fachbereich Politische Wissenschaft, Bibliothek, Berlin, Germany [*Library symbol Library of Congress*] (LCLS) ... GyBFU-P
Freie Universitaet (Berlin), Garystrasse, Berlin, Germany [*Library symbol Library of Congress*] (LCLS) ... GyBFU
Freie Volkspartei [*Free People's Party*] [*Germany Political party*] (PPE) ... FVP
Freie-Buerger-Union [*Free Citizens' Union*] [*Germany*] (PPW) ... FBU
Freie-Koerper-Kultur [*Nudism, a pre-NAZI fad in Germany*] ... FKK
Freier Deutscher Gewerkschaftsbund [*Free German Trade Union Federation*] [*Germany Political party*] (PPE) ... FDGB
Freight ... FGT
Freight ... FRGHT
Freight (WDAA) ... FRGT
Freight (AFM) ... FRT
Freight Accounting Shipment Tracing System (MCD) ... FAST
Freight Agent ... FA
Freight, All Kinds [*Railroad*] ... FAK
Freight Allowal ... FA
Freight and Demurrage [*Shipping*] ... F & D
Freight and Equipment Reporting System for Transportation [*IBM Corp.*] ... FERST
Freight and Equipment Reporting System for Transportation/Virtual Storage [*IBM Corp.*] ... FERST/VS

Freight and Passenger Vessels [*Army*] .... FP
Freight Assurance Storage, United States .... FASUS
Freight Astray .... FA
Freight Auditor .... FA
Freight Automated System for Traffic Management (AABC) .... FAST
Freight Bill [*Business term*] .... FB
Freight Claim Agent .... FCA
Freight Claim Association .... FCA
Freight Classification Guide System .... FCGS
Freight Classification Packaging Data List (AFIT) .... FC/PDL
Freight Container Bureau [*AAR*] .... FCB
Freight, Demurrage, and Defense [*Shipping*] (DS) .... FD & D
Freight Department .... FD
Freight Equipment Environmental Sampling Test Program [*RSPA*]
    (TAG) .... FEEST
Freight Forward [*Shipping*] (DS) .... Frt Fwd
Freight Forwarder .... FF
Freight Forwarder (MCD) .... FRT FWDR
Freight Forwarder Location Code (AAGC) .... FFLC
Freight Forwarders Certificate of Receipt [*Shipping*] (DS) .... FFCR
Freight Forwarders Institute [*Defunct*] (EA) .... FFI
Freight Forwarders Tariff Bureau [*Defunct*] (EA) .... FFTB
Freight Forwarders Tariff Bureau, Inc., New York NY [*STAC*] .... FFT
Freight Information System [*BTS*] (TAG) .... FINS
Freight, Insurance, and Shipping Charges [*Business term*] .... FIS
Freight, Insurance, Carriage .... FIC
Freight Liner [*British Railways Board*] (DS) .... F/L
Freight/Luggage Panniers [*Hovercraft*] .... F/LP
Freight Movement Control System [*MTMC*] (TAG) .... FMCS
Freight Office .... FROF
Freight on Board (AAG) .... FOB
Freight Operation Control System (PDAA) .... FOCS
Freight or Carriage and Insurance Paid To _____ [*"INCOTERM," International
    Chamber of Commerce official code*] .... CIP
Freight or Carriage Paid To _____ [*"INCOTERM," International Chamber of
    Commerce official code*] .... DCP
Freight Pass-Through [*Publishing*] .... FPT
Freight Payable at Destination [*Business term*] .... FPAD
Freight Prepaid [*Business term*] (MHDW) .... Frt Ppd
Freight Receiving and Redistribution Unit .... FRRU
Freight Release .... FR
Freight Runners Express, Inc. [*ICAO designator*] (FAAC) .... FRG
Freight Ship .... FS
Freight Ship [*Coast Guard symbol*] (DNAB) .... WYTM
Freight Station Accounting Code [*Railroad term*] .... FSAC
Freight Supply Vessel [*Obsolete Navy*] .... FS
Freight Tariff Bureau .... FTB
Freight Ton .... FT
Freight Traffic Bureau .... FTB
Freight Traffic Committee - Trunk Line Territory Railroads .... FTC-TLTR
Freight Traffic Concurrence .... FX
Freight Traffic Department .... FTD
Freight Traffic Division [*Army*] .... FTD
Freight Traffic Division - Export [*MTMC*] (TAG) .... FTD-E
Freight Traffic Division - Import [*MTMC*] (TAG) .... FTD-I
Freight Traffic Division - Inspection [*MTMC*] (TAG) .... FTD-S
Freight Traffic Manager .... FTM
Freight Transport .... FT
Freight Transport Association [*British*] .... FTA
Freighter Travel Club of America (EA) .... FTC
Freightliner Advanced Concept Truck [*Experimental vehicle*] .... FACT
Freiheitlich Soziale Deutsche Volkspartei [*Liberal Social German People's
    Party*] [*Germany Political party*] (PPW) .... FSDVP
Freiheitliche Partei Oesterreichs [*Liberal Party of Austria (or Austrian
    Freedom Party)*] [*Political party*] (PPW) .... FPO
Freimaurer [*Freemason*] [*German*] (ROG) .... FM
Freisinnig-Demokratische Partei der Schweiz [*Radical Democratic Party of
    Switzerland*] (PPW) .... FDP
Freisoziale Union - Demokratische Mitte [*Free Social Union - Democratic
    Center*] [*Germany Political party*] (PPW) .... FSU
Frejus [*France*] [*Airport symbol*] (AD) .... FRJ
Frejus/Saint-Raphael [*France ICAO location identifier*] (ICLI) .... LFTU
Fremantle Arts Review [*A publication*] .... FAR
Fremantle Arts Review [*A publication*] .... Fr Ar Rev
Fremington [*England*] .... FREM
Fremitus Vocalis [*Vocal Fremitus*] [*Medicine*] .... FREM
Fremont, CA [*FM radio station call letters*] .... KBRG
Fremont, CA [*FM radio station call letters*] .... KOHL
Fremont County Courthouse, Sidney, IA [*Library symbol*] [*Library of
    Congress*] (LCLS) .... IaSidCoC
Fremont County District Library, St. Anthony, ID [*Library symbol*] [*Library of
    Congress*] (LCLS) .... IdSaF
Fremont County Library, Lander, WY [*Library symbol Library of Congress*]
    (LCLS) .... WyLan
Fremont County Library, Riverton Branch, Riverton, WY [*Library symbol
    Library of Congress*] (LCLS) .... WyRi
Fremont, Elkhorn & Missouri Valley Railroad .... FE & MV
Fremont Gazette, Fremont, IA [*Library symbol Library of Congress*]
    (LCLS) .... IaFremG
Fremont General Corp. [*NYSE symbol*] (SPSG) .... FMT
Fremont General Corp. [*Associated Press*] (SAG) .... Fremnt
Fremont General Corp. [*Associated Press*] (SAG) .... Fremont
Fremont Genl Fin 1 9%'TOPrS' [*NYSE symbol*] (TTSB) .... FMTPr
Fremont, MI [*Location identifier FAA*] (FAAL) .... FOJ
Fremont, MI [*AM radio station call letters*] .... WSHN

Fremont, MI [*FM radio station call letters*] .... WSHN-FM
Fremont, NE [*Location identifier FAA*] (FAAL) .... FET
Fremont, NE [*FM radio station call letters*] .... KFMT
Fremont, NE [*AM radio station call letters*] .... KHUB
Fremont, OH [*AM radio station call letters*] .... WFRO
Fremont, OH [*FM radio station call letters*] .... WFRO-FM
Fremont Peak [*California*] [*Seismograph station code, US Geological Survey*]
    (SEIS) .... FRP
Fremont Public Library, Fremont, IN [*Library symbol Library of Congress*]
    (LCLS) .... InFrem
Fremont Public Library, Fremont, MI [*Library symbol Library of Congress*]
    (LCLS) .... MiFrem
Fremont Public Library, Fremont, NE [*Library symbol Library of Congress*]
    (LCLS) .... NbFr
Fremont Township Library, Winn, MI [*Library symbol Library of Congress*]
    (LCLS) .... MiWin
Fremskridtspartiet [*Progress Party*] [*Denmark Political party*] (PPE) .... F
Fremskrittspartiet [*Progress Party*] [*Norway Political party*] (PPE) .... FP
French [*Catheter size*] [*Medicine*] (DAVI) .... F
French .... F
French [*Catheter gauge*] [*Medicine*] (DAVI) .... Fr
French .... FR
French .... FRE
French [*MARC language code Library of Congress*] (LCCP) .... fre
French (DNAB) .... FREN
French .... FRNCH
French Air Force .... FAF
French American Ridge Atlantic [*Program*] (USDC) .... FARA
French Antarctic Expedition [*1903-05,1908-10,1948-*] .... FrAE
French Army (NATG) .... FA
French Association for American Studies (EAIO) .... FAAS
French Atmospheric Nuclear Test (MCD) .... FANT
French Benevolent Society of New South Wales [*Australia*] .... FBSNSW
French Bulldog Club of America (EA) .... FBDCA
French Capitol [*Record label*] .... FCap
French Catheter Gauge (MAE) .... FCG
French Cetra-Soria [*Record label*] .... FSor
French Chamber of Commerce (DCTA) .... FCC
French Chamber of Commerce and Industry in Australia .... FCCIA
French Chamber of Commerce of the United States [*Later, French-American
    Chamber of Commerce*] .... FCCUS
French Chemical Society [*See also SFC*] (EAIO) .... FCS
French Commander-in-Chief, Atlantic [*NATO*] .... CECLANT
French Commander-in-Chief, Mediterranean [*NATO*] .... CECMED
French Committee of National Liberation [*World War II*] .... FCNL
French Communist Party .... FCP
French Communist Party [*Political party*] .... FKP
French Computing Association .... FCA
French Engineers in the United States (EA) .... FEUS
French Equatorial Africa .... FEA
French Expeditionary Corps .... FEC
French Expeditionary Force .... FEF
French Family Association (EA) .... FFO
French Fourragere [*Military decoration*] .... FF
French Fourragere [*Military decoration*] .... FRFOURRA
French Fragrances [*NASDAQ symbol*] (TTSB) .... FRAG
French Fragrances, Inc. [*NASDAQ symbol*] (SAG) .... FRAG
French Fragrances, Inc. [*Associated Press*] (SAG) .... FrenchF
French Franc [*Monetary unit*] .... FF
French Franc [*Monetary unit*] .... FFr
French Fried .... FF
French Frigate Shoals, HI [*Location identifier FAA*] (FAAL) .... HFS
French Government Tourist Office .... FGTO
French Guiana [*MARC country of publication code Library of Congress*]
    (LCCP) .... fg
French Guiana [*ANSI two-letter standard code*] (CNC) .... GF
French Guiana [*ANSI three-letter standard code*] (CNC) .... GUF
French Guiana [*MARC geographic area code Library of Congress*] (LCCP) .... s-fg--
French Guiana Space Center .... GUY
French Horn .... FH
French Institute/Alliance Francaise (EA) .... FIAF
French Institute/Alliance Francaise Library [*UTLAS symbol*] .... AFL
French Institute/Alliance Francaise, New York, NY [*Library symbol Library of
    Congress*] (LCLS) .... NNFi
French Institute in the United States [*Later, FIAF*] (EA) .... FIUS
French Language Intensive Program [*Illinois*] (EDAC) .... FLIP
French Library [*L'Alliance Francaise*], San Francisco, CA [*Library symbol
    Library of Congress*] (LCLS) .... CSfFL
French Lick, IN [*Location identifier FAA*] (FAAL) .... FRH
French Lick, IN [*Location identifier FAA*] (FAAL) .... JIF
French Lick, IN [*FM radio station call letters*] .... WFLQ
French Men of Letters [*A publication*] .... FML
French Mercury [*Record label*] .... FMer
French MGM [*Record label*] .... FMGM
French, Middle [*MARC language code Library of Congress*] (LCCP) .... frm
French Military Liaison Mission [*World War II*] .... FMLM
French Military Mission (NATG) .... FMM
French Naval Liaison Officer (NATG) .... FNLO
French Naval War College .... FRNWC
French Navy (NATG) .... FN
French Navy .... FNY
French North Africa .... FNA
French Ocean-Climat Atlantique Equatorial [*Program*] [*Marine science*]
    (OSRA) .... FOCAL
French, Old [*MARC language code Library of Congress*] (LCCP) .... fro

French Ordinances [*A publication*] (DLA) ... FR ORD
French Patent ... FP
French Polishers' Federation of Great Britain and Ireland [*A union*] ... FPFGBI
French Polydor Variable Micrograde [*Record label*] ... FPV
French Polynesia [*MARC country of publication code Library of Congress*] (LCCP) ... fp
French Polynesia [*ANSI two-letter standard code*] (CNC) ... PF
French Polynesia [*MARC geographic area code Library of Congress*] (LCCP) ... pofp
French Polynesia [*ANSI three-letter standard code*] (CNC) ... PYF
French Pressure Cell ... FPC
French Program Ocean-Climat Atlantique Equatorial (USDC) ... FOCAL
French RCA (Victor) [*Record label*] ... FV
French Research [*Satellite*] ... FR
French Review [*A publication*] (BRI) ... FR
French Rite [*Freemasonry*] (ROG) ... FR
French Sign Language ... FSL
French Socialist Party ... FSP
French Society of Acoustics [*Formerly, Group of French-Speaking Acousticians*] (EA) ... FSA
French Somaliland (VRA) ... Fr Soma
French Southern and Antarctic Lands [*ANSI three-letter standard code*] (CNC) ... ATF
French Southern and Antarctic Lands [*MARC country of publication code Library of Congress*] (LCCP) ... fs
French Southern and Antarctic Lands [*MARC geographic area code Library of Congress*] (LCCP) ... i-fs--
French Steel Sound [*Medicine*] (DMAA) ... FSS
French Telefunken [*Record label*] ... FT
French Territory of the Afars and Issas [*Djibouti*] [*MARC geographic area code Library of Congress*] (LCCP) ... f-ft--
French Territory of the Afars and Issas [*Djibouti*] [*MARC country of publication code Library of Congress*] (LCCP) ... ft
French Title [*Online database field identifier*] ... FT
French Togoland ... FRTO
French Training Mission [*Military*] (CINC) ... FTM
French Underground Nuclear Test (MCD) ... FUNT
French Union [*MARC geographic area code Library of Congress*] (LCCP) ... h-----
French Union Forces (VNW) ... FUF
French Urania [*Record label*] ... FUra
French Village [*Missouri*] [*Seismograph station code, US Geological Survey*] (SEIS) ... FVM
French West Africa ... FrWAfr
French West Africa ... FWA
French West Indies ... FWI
French Wire Gage (IAA) ... FWG
French-American Aid for Children (EA) ... FAAC
French-American Chamber of Commerce (EA) ... FACC
French-American Committee for the Statue of Liberty [*Defunct*] (EA) ... FAC
French-American Foundation (EA) ... FAF
French-American Mid-Ocean Undersea Study [*Joint undersea program*] ... FAMOUS
French-American-British [*Classification system for leukemia*] ... FAB
French-Anglo-United States Supersonic Transport ... FAUSST
Frenchay Dysarthria Assessment [*Speech and language therapy*] (DAVI) ... FDA
French-Canadian (WDAA) ... FR CAN
French-Language Association of Work Psychology [*Viroflay, France*] (EAIO) ... FLAWP
French-Language Infant Pneumology and Phthisiology Group [*Yerres, France*] (EAIO) ... FLIPPG
French-Language Society of Medical Psychology (EA) ... FLSMP
French's Reports [*6 New Hampshire*] [*A publication*] (DLA) ... French (NH)
French-Speaking Comparative Education Association [*See also AFEC*] [*Sevres, France*] (EAIO) ... FSCEA
French-Speaking Nations [*NATO*] ... FSN
French-Speaking Neuropsychological Society [*Paris, France*] (EAIO) ... FSNS
Frenchtown High School, Frenchtown, MT [*Library symbol*] [*Library of Congress*] (LCLS) ... MtFrHS
Frenchville [*Maine*] [*Airport symbol*] (OAG) ... WFK
Frenchville, ME [*Location identifier FAA*] (FAAL) ... FVE
Frend and Ware's Precedents of Instruments Relating to the Transfer of Land to Railway Companies [*2nd ed.*] [*1866*] [*A publication*] (DLA) ... F & W Pr
Frend and Ware's Precedents of Instruments Relating to the Transfer of Land to Railway Companies [*2nd ed.*] [*1866*] [*A publication*] (DLA) ... Fr & W Prec
Frend and Ware's Precedents of Instruments Relating to the Transfer of Land to Railway Companies [*2nd ed.*] [*1866*] [*A publication*] (DLA) ... Frend & W Prec
Frente Amplio [*Broad Front*] [*Uruguay*] [*Political party*] (PD) ... FA
Frente Amplio Popular [*Broad Popular Front*] [*Panama*] [*Political party*] (PPW) ... FRAMPO
Frente Anti-Comunista de Defensa Nacional [*Anti-Communist Front for National Defense*] [*Ecuador*] ... FADN
Frente Anticomunista del Nororiente [*Northeastern Anticommunist Front*] [*Guatemala*] (PD) ... FANO
Frente Anti-Imperialista de Liberacion [*Peruvian guerrilla group*] (EY) ... FAL
Frente Central de Resistencia-Partido Guatemalteco del Trabajo [*Political party*] (EY) ... FCR-PGT
Frente Civico Democratico [*Civilian Democratic Front*] [*Guatemala*] [*Political party*] (PPW) ... FCD
Frente da Libertacao de Mocambique [*Mozambique Liberation Front*] [*Political party*] (PPW) ... FRELIMO
Frente da Luta pela Independencia Nacional da Guine "Portuguesa" [*Front for the Fight for Guinea-Bissau's National Independence*] (PD) ... FLING
Frente de Accion Popular [*Popular Action Front*] [*Chile*] ... FRAP
Frente de Avance Nacional [*National Advancement Front*] [*Guatemala*] [*Political party*] ... FAN
Frente de Integracion Nacional [*Front for National Integration*] [*Guatemala*] ... FIN
Frente de Izquierda Popular [*Popular Left Front*] [*Argentina Political party*] (PPW) ... FIP
Frente de Izquierda Revolucionaria [*Peru*] ... FIR
Frente de Liberacion de los Pobres [*Liberation Front of the Poor*] [*Ecuador*] [*Political party*] (PD) ... FLP
Frente de Liberacion Nacional [*National Liberation Front*] [*Venezuela Political party*] (PD) ... FLN
Frente de Liberacion Nacional [*National Liberation Front*] [*Chile*] [*Political party*] ... FLN
Frente de Liberacion Nacional [*National Liberation Front*] [*Peru*] [*Political party*] ... FLN
Frente de Liberacion Nacional [*National Liberation Front*] [*El Salvador*] [*Political party*] ... FLN
Frente de Libertacao do Enclave de Cabinda [*Front for the Liberation of the Cabinda Enclave*] [*Angola*] (PD) ... FLEC
Frente de Reconstruccion Nacional [*Ecuador*] [*Political party*] (EY) ... FRN
Frente de Unidad Liberal [*Honduras*] [*Political party*] (EY) ... FUL
Frente de Unidad Nacional [*National Unity Front*] [*Guatemala*] [*Political party*] (PPW) ... FUN
Frente del Pueblo Unido [*Bolivia*] [*Political party*] (EY) ... FPU
Frente Democratica [*Democratic Front*] [*Guinea-Bissau*] [*Political party*] (EY) ... FD
Frente Democratica Social [*Democratic Social Front*] [*Guinea-Bissau*] [*Political party*] (EY) ... FDS
Frente Democratico [*Peru*] [*Political party*] (EY) ... FREDEMO
Frente Democratico contra la Represion [*Guatemala*] [*Political party*] (EY) ... FDCR
Frente Democratico Contra la Represion [*Democratic Front Against Repression*] [*Guatemala*] [*Political party*] (PD) ... FDR
Frente Democratico Eleitoral [*Democratic Electoral Front*] [*Portugal Political party*] (PPE) ... FDE
Frente Democratico Nacional [*Electoral Alliance*] [*Mexico*] (EY) ... FDN
Frente Democratico Oriental de Mexico Emiliano Zapata [*Political party*] (EY) ... FDOMEZ
Frente Democratico Revolucionario - Farabundo Marti de Liberacion Nacional [*Democratic Revolutionary Front/Farabundo Marti National Liberation Front*] [*El Salvador*] [*Political party*] (EY) ... FDR-FMLN
Frente Democratico Revolucionario / Farabundo Marti para la Liberacion Nacional [*Democratic Revolutionary Front/Farabundo Marti National Liberation Front*] [*Guatemala*] [*Political party*] ... FDR/FMLN
Frente Eleitoral do Povo Unido [*United People's Electoral Front*] [*Portugal Political party*] (PPE) ... FEPU
Frente Farabundo Marti de Liberacion Nacional [*Farabundo Marti National Liberation Front*] [*El Salvador*] (ECON) ... FMLN
Frente Juventil Lautaro [*Chile*] [*Political party*] (EY) ... FJL
Frente Morazanista de Liberacion Nacional [*Morazanista National Liberation Front*] [*Honduras*] [*Political party*] (PD) ... FMLN
Frente Morazanista de Liberacion Nacional de Honduras [*Honduran Morazanist National Front*] [*Political party*] ... FMLNH
Frente Morazanista para la Liberacion de Honduras [*Guerrilla forces*] (EY) ... FMLH
Frente Nacional Constitucionalista [*National Constitutionalist Front*] [*Ecuador*] [*Political party*] (PPW) ... FNC
Frente Nacional de Oposicion [*National Opposition Front*] [*Guatemala*] [*Political party*] ... FNO
Frente Nacional de Oposicion [*National Opposition Front*] [*Venezuela Political party*] ... FNO
Frente Nacional de Panama [*Panamanian National Front*] [*Political party*] (PD) ... FNP
Frente Nacional de Trabajadores y Campesinos [*National Workers' and Peasants' Front*] [*Peru*] [*Political party*] (PPW) ... FNTC
Frente Nacional de Trabajadores y Campesinos [*National Workers' and Peasants' Front*] [*Peru*] [*Political party*] (PD) ... FRENATRACA
Frente Nacional de Unidad [*National Unity Front*] [*Guatemala*] [*Political party*] (PPW) ... FRENU
Frente Nacional Democratico Popular [*Popular National Democratic Front*] [*Mexico*] (PD) ... FNDP
Frente Nacional Opositora [*National Opposition Front*] [*Panama*] [*Political party*] (PPW) ... FNC
Frente Nacional Opositora [*National Opposition Front*] [*Panama*] [*Political party*] (PPW) ... Freno
Frente Nacional Socialista Argentino [*Argentinian National Socialist Front*] [*Political party*] (PD) ... FNSA
Frente Obrero [*Workers' Front*] [*of the Carlists in the Workers Commissions*] [*Spain*] [*Political party*] ... FO
Frente Obrero [*Workers' Front*] [*Nicaragua*] [*Political party*] (PD) ... FO
Frente Obrero de Liberacion [*Workers' Liberation Front*] [*Netherlands Antilles*] [*Political party*] (PPW) ... FOL
Frente Patriotica de Libertacao Nacional [*Portugal*] ... FPLN
Frente Patriotico de Libertacao de Portugal [*Patriotic Front for the Liberation of Portugal*] [*Political party*] (PPE) ... FPLP
Frente Patriotico Hondureno [*Honduran Patriotic Front*] [*Political party*] (PD) ... FPH
Frente Patriotico Manuel Rodriguez [*Manuel Rodriguez Patriotic Front*] [*Chile*] [*Political party*] ... FPMR
Frente Patriotico Nacional [*National Patriotic Front*] [*Nicaragua*] [*Political party*] (PPW) ... FPN
Frente Patriotico para la Revolucion [*Patriotic Front for the Revolution*] [*Nicaragua*] [*Political party*] (PPW) ... FPR
Frente Popular 31 de Enero [*31st January Popular Front*] [*Guatemala*] (PD) ... FP-31
Frente Popular Contra la Represion [*Popular Front Against Repression*] [*Honduras*] [*Political party*] (PD) ... FPR

Frente Popular Costarricense [*Costa Rican Popular Front*] [*Political party*] (PPW) .... FPC
Frente Popular de Liberacion, Nueve de Mayo [*Honduras*] [*Political party*] (EY) .... FPL
Frente por la Unidad del Pueblo [*United Popular Front*] [*Colorado Political party*] (PPW) .... FUP
Frente Radical Alfarista [*Radical Alfarista Front*] [*Ecuador*] [*Political party*] (PPW) .... FRA
Frente Republicana e Socialista [*Republican and Socialist Front*] [*Portugal Political party*] (PPW) .... FRS
Frente Republicano Guatemalteco [*Political party*] (EY) .... FRG
Frente Revolucionaria de Izquierda [*Left Revolutionary Front*] [*Bolivia*] [*Political party*] (PPW) .... FRI
Frente Revolucionaria Sandinista [*Nicaragua*] [*Political party*] (EY) .... FRS
Frente Revolucionario Antifascista Patriotica [*Anti-Fascist and Patriotic Revolutionary Front*] [*Spain*] .... FRAP
Frente Revolucionario Nacionalista [*Chile*] [*Political party*] (EY) .... FREN
Frente Sandinista de Liberacion Nacional [*Sandinista National Liberation Front*] [*Nicaragua*] [*Political party*] (PPW) .... FSLN
Frente Social Progresista [*Progressive Social Front*] [*Ecuador*] [*Political party*] (PPW) .... FSP
Frente Socialista Popular [*Portugal*] .... FSP
Frente Unido de la Revolucion [*United Revolutionary Front*] [*Guatemala*] [*Political party*] (PPW) .... FUR
Frente Unido Nacionalista [*Nationalist United Front*] [*Venezuela Political party*] (PPW) .... FUN
Frente Unita Angolana [*Angolan United Front*] .... FUA
Frente Universitario Revolucionario 30 de Julio [*30th July Revolutionary University Front*] [*El Salvador*] FUR-30
Frente Urbana Zapatista [*Mexico*] .... FUZ
Frente Voluntario de Defensa [*Voluntary Defense Front*] [*Guatemala*] (PD) .... FUD
Freon Coolant Line [*NASA*] (NASA) .... FCL
Freon Coolant Loop [*Space shuttle*] [*NASA*] .... FCL
Freon Coolant Servicing Unit (MCD) .... FCSU
Freon Pump Package (MCD) .... FPP
Freon Servicer (MCD) .... FS
Freon Servicing Unit (NASA) .... FSU
Freon Tank Container .... FTC
Frequence Optimum de Travail [*Optimum Working Frequency*] (NTCM) .... FOT
Frequence Optimum de Travail [*Optimum traffic frequency*] [*Telecommunications*] (NITA) .... FOT
Frequencies and Mode-Shapes of Non-Union Beams (PDAA) .... FAMSNUB
Frequencies of Occurrence of Binary Words [*Computer science*] (PDAA) .... FOBW
Frequency .... F
Frequency [*Symbol*] [*IUPAC*] .... f
Frequency [*Online database field identifier*] .... FQ
Frequency (WGA) .... FQCY
Frequency .... FRE
Frequency [*or Frequent*] (AFM) .... FREQ
Frequency (WDMC) .... freq
Frequency (IAA) .... FREQN
Frequency [*Spectroscopy*] V
Frequency Adjusting Rheostat .... FAR
Frequency Adjustment (IAA) .... FA
Frequency Agile Search and Track Seeker .... FAST
Frequency Agility .... FA
Frequency Agility RADAR Modifications to Existing RADAR Systems [*DoD*] .... FARMERS
Frequency Allocation and Uses .... FAU
Frequency Allocation and Wave Propagation Subcommittee (NATG) ..... FAWPSC
Frequency Allocation Committee .... FAC
Frequency Allocation Coordinating Subcommittee [*Canada*] .... FACSC
Frequency Allocation List .... FAL
Frequency Allocation Multiplex (IAA) .... FAM
Frequency Allocation Panel .... FAP
Frequency Allocation Panel, United States (NVT) .... FAPUS
Frequency Allocation Panel, United States Military Communications Electronics Board .... FAPUSMCEB
Frequency Allocation Request .... FAR
Frequency Allocation [*or Assignment*] Subcommittee (AFM) .... FAS
Frequency Amplitude Modulation (IAA) .... FAM
Frequency Analog-to-Digital Converter (IAA) .... FADC
Frequency Analysis and Control .... FAC
Frequency Analysis and Synthesis [*Computer program*] .... FANSY
Frequency Analysis of System Program [*NASA*] .... FASP
Frequency and Amplitude (IAA) .... FRENA
Frequency and Amplitude Coded (IAA) .... FRENAC
Frequency and Load Control Box (MCD) .... FLCB
Frequency and Load Controller .... FLC
Frequency and Phase Shift Keying .... FPSK
Frequency and Time (IEEE) .... FT
Frequency and Time Circuit Analysis Technique [*NASA*] .... FATCAT
Frequency and Time Interval Meter (DNAB) .... FTIM
Frequency and Time Measurement Counter .... FTMC
Frequency and Time-Division Data Link .... FATDL
Frequency and Time-Division Multiple Access (MCD) .... FTDMA
Frequency and Timing Subsystem [*Deep Space Instrumentation Facility, NASA*] .... FTS
Frequency Angle Scanning, Tracking, and Ranging .... FASTAR
Frequency Application Index .... FAI
Frequency Assignment by Reference to Interference Charts (MCD) .... FABRIC
Frequency Assignment Model (SAA) .... FAM
Frequency Band of Emission (CET) .... FBOE
Frequency Change Approved [*Aviation*] (FAAC) .... FCA

Frequency Changer (IAA) .... FC
Frequency Changer (IAA) .... FREQCH
Frequency Clock Trigger (IAA) .... FCT
Frequency Coded Armaments System .... FCAS
Frequency Coded Firing System (MCD) .... FCFS
Frequency Coded System (MCD) .... FCS
Frequency Compression Demodulator .... FCD
Frequency Compressive Feedback .... FCF
Frequency Control Analysis Facility .... FCAF
Frequency Control Analysis Subsystem (MCD) .... FCAS
Frequency Control and Analysis .... FCA
Frequency Control and Analysis (IAA) .... FCAA
Frequency Control Board [*British*] (AIA) .... FCB
Frequency Control Division (SAA) .... FCD
Frequency Control Officer (MUGU) .... FCO
Frequency Control Panel (MCD) .... FCP
Frequency Converter .... FC
Frequency Converter (MCD) .... FREQCONV
Frequency Converter Excitation .... FCE
Frequency Converter Excitation, Saturable Reactor (IAA) .... FCESR
Frequency Converter Unit .... FCU
Frequency Coordinating Body .... FCB
Frequency Coordination System Association [*Ottawa, ON*] [*Telecommunications service*] (TSSD) .... FCSA
Frequency Coordination Working Group (MUGU) .... FCWG
Frequency Data Multiplexer (NASA) .... FDM
Frequency Demodulator .... FD
Frequency Dependent Negative Conductance [*Physics*] .... FDNC
Frequency Dependent Negative Resistance [*Physics*] .... FDNR
Frequency Dependent Rejection [*Telecommunications*] (TEL) .... FDR
Frequency Determining Unit .... FDU
Frequency Deviation Meter .... FDM
Frequency Difference Detector (IAA) .... FDD
Frequency Discrimination [*Neurophysiology*] .... FD
Frequency Distance [*Telecommunications*] (TEL) .... FD
Frequency Distortion Analyzer .... FDA
Frequency Distribution [*Mathematics*] (IAA) .... FD
Frequency Distribution Analysis Sheet .... FDAS
Frequency Diversity .... FD
Frequency Diversity RADAR .... FDR
Frequency Divider [*Electronics*] (IAA) .... FD
Frequency Divider (MCD) .... FREQDIV
Frequency Divider Unit [*Electronics*] (IAA) .... FDU
Frequency Division .... FD
Frequency Division Duplex [*Telecommunications*] (ACRL) .... FDD
Frequency Division Duplex .... FDD
Frequency Division Multiple Access [*Telecommunications*] (MCD) .... FDMA
Frequency Division Multiplex/Frequency Modulation [*Telecommunications*] (TEL) .... FDM/FM
Frequency Division Multiplexed Analogue Components [*Colour TV broadcasting method*] (NITA) .... FMAC
Frequency Division Separator [*Multiplexing*] .... FDS
Frequency Division Switching [*Radio and television broadcasting*] .... FDS
Frequency Domain Coding .... FDC
Frequency Domain Coding Technique .... FDCT
Frequency Domain Interferometer (MCD) .... FDI
Frequency Domain Optical Storage System [*Computer science*] .... FDOS
Frequency Domain Reflectometry .... FDR
Frequency Double LASER .... FDL
Frequency Doubler .... FD
Frequency Doubler (MSA) .... FDBLR
Frequency Doubling LASER Device .... FDLD
Frequency Doubling Unit .... FDU
Frequency Drift .... FD
Frequency Electronics, Inc. [*AMEX symbol*] (SPSG) .... FEI
Frequency Electronics, Inc. [*Associated Press*] (SAG) .... FreqEL
Frequency Electrs [*AMEX symbol*] (TTSB) .... FEI
Frequency Emitted [*On Doppler study*] [*Cardiology*] (DAVI) .... F_o
Frequency Engineering Laboratory (MCD) .... FEL
Frequency Exchange Keying .... FEK
Frequency Hopping [*Modulation*] .... FH
Frequency Hopping Signal .... FHS
Frequency Identification Unit (IAA) .... FIU
Frequency Indicator (IAA) .... FREQIND
Frequency, Intensity, and Time [*Exercise formula*] [*Army*] .... FIT
Frequency, Intensity, Time, and Type [*Exercise formula*] [*Army*] (INF) .... FITT
Frequency Interference Control .... FIC
Frequency Interference Control Center [*Air Force*] .... FICC
Frequency Jumper Identification .... FJI
Frequency Jumper Identification .... FREJID
Frequency Line Tracker [*Military*] (CAAL) .... FLIT
Frequency Locked Loop (IAA) .... FLL
Frequency Management [*Aviation*] (DA) .... FM
Frequency Management Advisory Council [*Department of Commerce*] [*Washington, DC*] (EGAO) .... FMAC
Frequency Management Branch [*White Sands Missile Range*] .... FMB
Frequency Management Division [*White Sands Missile Range*] .... FMD
Frequency Management Office (DOMA) .... FMO
Frequency Management System [*ITU*] [*United Nations*] (DUND) .... FMS
Frequency Mass Spectrometer Tube .... FMST
Frequency Measuring Devices [*JETDS nomenclature*] [*Military*] (CET) .... FR
Frequency Meter .... FM
Frequency Meter .... FREQM
Frequency Meter .... FRM
Frequency Mixer Stage .... FMS

Frequency Modulated Carrier Wave Radar (NITA) ... FMCWR
Frequency Modulation [*Radio*] ... FM
Frequency Modulation Altimeter (IAA) ... FMA
Frequency Modulation - Amplitude Modulation (IAA) ... FMAM
Frequency Modulation and Advanced Memory [*Yamaha International Corp.*] ... FAM
Frequency Modulation and Narrowband Noise Analyzer (MCD) ... FMNBNA
Frequency Modulation Broadcasters ... FMB
Frequency Modulation Deviation Meter ... FMDM
Frequency Modulation Discriminator ... FMD
Frequency Modulation Feed Forward (PDAA) ... FMFF
Frequency Modulation Feedback Discriminator ... FMFD
Frequency Modulation - Frequency Modulation ... FM-FM
Frequency Modulation Generator ... FMG
Frequency Modulation Intercity Relay Broadcasting ... FMI
Frequency Modulation on the Pulse (NG) ... FMOP
Frequency Modulation - Phase Modulation [*RADAR*] ... FM-PM
Frequency Modulation Signal Processor (NASA) ... FMSP
Frequency Modulation Team (IAA) ... FMTM
Frequency Modulation with Feedback ... FMFB
Frequency Monitoring and Interference Control [*Radio*] ... FMIC
Frequency Multiplex ... FM
Frequency Multiplier (KSC) ... FREQMULT
Frequency Multiplier (KSC) ... FRQMULT
Frequency Multiplier Oscillator (IAA) ... FMO
Frequency Multiplier Storer ... FMS
Frequency Network Analyzer ... FNA
Frequency of Dividing Cells [*Bacteriology*] ... FDC
Frequency of Every Allowable Term [*Computer science*] ... FEAT
Frequency of Fading [*Broadcasting*] ... F
Frequency of Minimum Delay ... FMD
Frequency of Optimum Operation (SAA) ... FOO
Frequency of Optimum Operation (MCD) ... FOT
Frequency of Signal Generator (IAA) ... FSG
Frequency of the Rarer Allele of a Pair [*Genetics*] (DAVI) ... q
Frequency Offset Generator ... FOG
Frequency on Target ... FOT
Frequency Optimum Traffic ... FOT
Frequency Phase Lock ... FPL
Frequency Plane Correlator (IAA) ... FPC
Frequency Planning Organisation [*Telecommunications British*] ... FPO
Frequency Position Modulation [*Telecommunications*] (IEEE) ... FPM
Frequency Programmer (IEEE) ... FQPR
Frequency Range ... FR
Frequency Rate (WDAA) ... FR
Frequency Received [*On Doppler study*] [*Cardiology*] (DAVI) ... F_1
Frequency, Recency, Amount and Type [*Direct marketing*] (WDMC) ... FRATS
Frequency Reference Protection ... FRP
Frequency Regulation and Network Keying (IEEE) ... FRANK
Frequency Regulation and Network Keying [*Computer science*] (IAA) ... FRNK
Frequency Resource Records System ... FRRS
Frequency Response ... FR
Frequency Response Curve ... FRC
Frequency Response Function [*Statistics*] ... FRF
Frequency Response Histogram [*Biometrics*] ... FRH
Frequency Response Measuring Equipment (PDAA) ... FRME
Frequency Response Plotter ... FRP
Frequency Response Survey (CET) ... FRS
Frequency Response Test (MCD) ... FRT
Frequency Scan [*Radar*] (DOMA) ... FRESSCAN
Frequency Scan RADAR (MCD) ... FREQSCANRA
Frequency Scan RADAR ... FSR
Frequency Scanning ... FRESCAN
Frequency Scanning RADAR ... FRESCANNAR
Frequency Select Control Unit (MCD) ... FSCU
Frequency Selective Amplifier (IAA) ... FSA
Frequency Selective Limiter (IAA) ... FSL
Frequency Selective Receiver System (MCD) ... FSRS
Frequency Selective Relay ... FSR
Frequency Selective Voltmeter ... FSV
Frequency Selective Voltmeter (IAA) ... FSVM
Frequency Shift (BUR) ... FS
Frequency Shift Audio Frequency [*Telecommunications*] (IAA) ... FSAF
Frequency Shift Communications System ... FSCS
Frequency Shift Converter ... FSC
Frequency Shift Keying [*Telecommunications*] ... FSK
Frequency Shift Keying Low-Frequency [*Converter*] (NATG) ... FSKLF
Frequency Shift Modulation [*Radio*] ... FSM
Frequency Shift Pulsing ... FSP
Frequency Shift Receiver ... FSR
Frequency Shift Reflector ... FSR
Frequency Shift Telegraphy ... FST
Frequency Shift Transmission ... FST
Frequency Ship Demodulator (DNAB) ... FSD
Frequency Space Characteristic Impedance ... FSCI
Frequency Spectral Density Analysis (PDAA) ... FSDA
Frequency Stability ... FS
Frequency Stability Analyzer ... FSA
Frequency Stability Code (PDAA) ... FRESCO
Frequency Standard ... FS
Frequency Standard, Primary ... FSP
Frequency Sweep Oscillator ... FSO
Frequency Synthesizer [*Electronics*] (OA) ... FS
Frequency Threshold Curve ... FTC
Frequency Time Base (DEN) ... FTB
Frequency Time Control ... FTC
Frequency Time Indicator [*RADAR*] ... FTI
Frequency Time Intensity [*RADAR*] ... FTI
Frequency Time Modulation (DEN) ... FTM
Frequency Time Schedule (NVT) ... FTS
Frequency Time Standard ... FTS
Frequency Time-Hopping Multiple Access [*Electronics*] (OA) ... FTHMA
Frequency to Voltage (IEEE) ... F/V
Frequency Tolerance ... FT
Frequency Tracker (MSA) ... FT
Frequency Transfer Control ... FTC
Frequency Transfer Unit ... FTU
Frequency Translation Distortion ... FTD
Frequency Translator ... FRELATOR
Frequency Translator/Recursive Filter (CAAL) ... FT/RF
Frequency Tuned Bandpass Filter ... FTBF
Frequency-Agile Solid-State High-Frequency Power Amplifier Coupler [*Army*] ... FSHPAC
Frequency-Azimuth Intensity [*RADAR*] ... FAI
Frequency-Differential/Phase-Shift Keyed System [*Computer science*] (TEL) ... FD/PSK
Frequency-Division Data Link [*Radio*] ... FDDL
Frequency-Division Modulation [*Telecommunications*] (IAA) ... FDM
Frequency-Division Multiplex [*or Multiplexing*] [*Telecommunications*] ... FDM
Frequency-Division Multiplex Voice Communication ... FDMVC
Frequency-Division Multiplexing System [*Radio*] (MCD) ... FDMS
Frequency-Domain Oscilloscope (PDAA) ... FDO
Frequency-Emphasizing Network (IEEE) ... FEN
Frequency-Following Response [*Neurophysiology*] ... FFR
Frequency-Hopping Multiple Access (IAA) ... FHMA
Frequency-Hopping Multiplexer (DWSG) ... FHMUX
Frequency-Hopping Spread Spectrum [*Computer science*] (PCM) ... FHSS
Frequency-Locked Automatic Computing Transfer Oscillator (PDAA) ... FLACTO
Frequency-Locked-Looped ... FLL
Frequency-Measuring Equipment ... FME
Frequency-Modulated Continuous-Wave [*RADAR*] (KSC) ... FMCW
Frequency-Modulated Cyclotron ... FMC
Frequency-Modulated Demodulator [*Telecommunications*] (IAA) ... FMD
Frequency-Modulated Intermittent Continuous Wave [*Electronics*] (OA) ... FMICW
Frequency-Modulated Quartz ... FMQ
Frequency-Modulated RADAR ... FMR
Frequency-Modulated Ranging (MCD) ... FMR
Frequency-Modulated Receiver [*Telecommunications*] ... FMR
Frequency-Modulated Transmitter [*Telecommunications*] ... FMT
Frequency-Modulated Transmitter [*Telecommunications*] (KSC) ... FMX
Frequency-Multiplexed Subcarrier ... FMS
Frequency-Referenced Scanning Beam [*Aviation*] (OA) ... FRSB
Frequency-Shift Keying (IDOE) ... FI
Frequency-to-Current Converter (IAA) ... FCC
Frequent [*In mention of occurrence of species*] ... F
Frequent ... FQT
Frequent ... FR
Frequent (ROG) ... FREQT
Frequent ... FRQ
Frequent Asked Question List [*Computer science*] (NHD) ... FAQL
Frequent Flier Bonus (BARN) ... FFB
Frequent Flier Program (BARN) ... FFP
Frequent Independent Traveler ... FIT
Frequent Traveler [*on airlines*] ... FT
Frequent Traveller's Medical Card [*British*] ... FREMEC
Frequenter Occurrit [*It Occurs Frequently*] [*Latin*] (ROG) ... FREQ OCC
Frequenting House of Ill Fame ... FHIF
Frequently (DAVI) ... f
Frequently (WDMC) ... freq
Frequently (ROG) ... FREQLY
Frequently Asked Question ... FAQ
Frequently Asked Questions (ACRL) ... FAQ
Frequently Sampled Intravenous Glucose Tolerance (Test) [*Clinical chemistry*] ... FSIGT
Frequently-Called-Numbers List [*Bell System*] ... FCNL
Freres [*Brothers*] [*French*] ... FRES
Freres de la Charite [*Brothers of Charity*] (EAIO) ... FC
Freres de l'Instruction Chretienne de Ploermel [*Brothers of Christian Instruction of Ploermel*] [*Rome, Italy*] (EAIO) ... FICP
Freres de Saint Gabriel [*Brothers of Christian Instruction of St. Gabriel*] [*Rome, Italy*] (EAIO) ... FSG
Fresco (VRA) ... frsc
Fresenius Medical Care AG [*NYSE symbol*] (SAG) ... FMS
Fresenius Medical Care AG [*Associated Press*] (SAG) ... FresenM
Fresenius USA [*AMEX symbol*] (TTSB) ... FRN
Fresenius USA, Inc. [*Associated Press*] (SAG) ... Fresenius
Fresenius USA, Inc. [*AMEX symbol*] (SAG) ... FRN
Fresh ... FR
Fresh ... FRSH
Fresh Acid Add [*Nuclear energy*] (NRCH) ... FAA
Fresh Air (OA) ... FA
Fresh Air Inlet (MSA) ... FAI
Fresh Air Input ... FAI
Fresh America [*NASDAQ symbol*] (TTSB) ... FRES
Fresh America Corp. [*NASDAQ symbol*] (SAG) ... FRES
Fresh America Corp. [*Associated Press*] (SAG) ... FreshAm
Fresh Cell Weight [*Biochemistry*] ... FCW
Fresh Choice [*NASDAQ symbol*] (TTSB) ... SALD
Fresh Choice, Inc. [*Associated Press*] (SAG) ... FrshChc
Fresh Choice, Inc. [*NASDAQ symbol*] (SAG) ... SALD

Fresh Frozen .... FF
Fresh Frozen Plasma [*Medicine*] .... FFP
Fresh Fruit and Vegetable Information Bureau [*British*] (CB) .... FFVIB
Fresh Fruits and Vegetables .... FF & V
Fresh Garlic Association [*Defunct*] (EA) .... FGA
Fresh Gas Flow .... FGF
[*The*] **Fresh Juice Co., Inc.** [*Associated Press*] (SAG) .... FrJuice
[*The*] **Fresh Juice Co., Inc.** [*NASDAQ symbol*] (NQ) .... FRSH
Fresh Juice Inc. [*NASDAQ symbol*] (TTSB) .... FRSH
Fresh Off the Boat .... FOB
Fresh Paragraph (ADA) .... FP
Fresh Water [*Technical drawings*] .... FW
Fresh Water Allowance (DS) .... FWA
Fresh Water Ballasting .... FWB
Fresh Water Bay [*Alaska*] [*Airport symbol*] (OAG) .... FRP
Fresh Water Damage .... FWD
Fresh Water Drain Collecting Tank .... FWDCT
Fresh Water Fish Wholesalers Association (EA) .... FWFWA
Fresh Water Institute [*Rensselaer Polytechnic Institute*] [*Research center*] (RCD) .... FWI
Fresh Water Institute, Canada Fisheries Research Board, Winnipeg, MB, Canada [*Library symbol Library of Congress*] (LCLS) .... CaMWFW
Fresh Water Pump (MSA) .... FWP
Fresh Water Supply Header [*Nuclear energy*] (NRCH) .... FWSH
Fresh Weight [*of fruit*] [*Botany*] .... FW
Freshbake Foods Group [*British*] .... FFG
Freshman [*or Freshmen*] (WDAA) .... FRESH
Freshman Issues and Concerns Survey (EDAC) .... FICS
Freshstart Venture Capital Corp. [*Associated Press*] (SAG) .... Freshst
Freshstart Venture Capital Corp. [*NASDAQ symbol*] (SAG) .... FSVC
Freshwater [*Load line mark*] .... F
Freshwater [*Load line mark*] .... FW
Freshwater Biological Association [*British*] (ARC) .... FBA
Freshwater Biological Investigation Unit [*Department of Agriculture for Northern Ireland*] [*British*] (IRUK) .... FBIU
Freshwater Cooling .... FWC
Freshwater Fish Marketing Corp. [*See also OCPED*] .... FFMC
Freshwater Institute [*Federal Department of Fisheries and Oceans*] [*Canada*] (IRC) .... FWI
Freshwater Institute, Fisheries and Oceans Canada [*Institut des Eaux Douces, Peches et Oceans Canada*] **Winnipeg, Manitoba** [*Library symbol National Library of Canada*] (NLC) .... MWFW
Freshwater Institute Report [*United Nations*] .... FIR
Freshwater Public Library, Freshwater, NF, Canada [*Library symbol Library of Congress*] (LCLS) .... CaNfFr
Freshwater Public Library, Newfoundland [*Library symbol National Library of Canada*] (NLC) .... NFFR
Freshwell [*England*] .... FRESHW
Fresnel Lens Optical Landing System [*Navy*] .... FLOLS
Fresnel Lens Optical Practice [*Navy*] .... FLOP
Fresnel Lens Optical Practice, Fleet [*Navy*] .... FLOPF
Fresnel Reflection Coefficient [*Optics*] .... FRC
Fresnel Zone Plate (PDAA) .... FZP
Fresno [*California*] [*Airport symbol*] (OAG) .... FAT
Fresno [*California*] [*Seismograph station code, US Geological Survey Closed*] (SEIS) .... FRE
Fresno [*Diocesan abbreviation*] [*California*] (TOCD) .... FRS
Fresno, CA [*Location identifier FAA*] (FAAL) .... FCH
Fresno, CA [*Television station call letters*] .... KAIL
Fresno, CA [*AM radio station call letters*] .... KBIF
Fresno, CA [*AM radio station call letters*] .... KEYQ
Fresno, CA [*FM radio station call letters*] .... KFCF
Fresno, CA [*AM radio station call letters*] .... KFIG
Fresno, CA [*FM radio station call letters*] .... KFNO
Fresno, CA [*AM radio station call letters*] .... KFRE
Fresno, CA [*Television station call letters*] .... KFSN
Fresno, CA [*FM radio station call letters*] .... KFSR
Fresno, CA [*AM radio station call letters*] .... KGST
Fresno, CA [*AM radio station call letters*] .... KIRV
Fresno, CA [*Television station call letters*] .... KJEO
Fresno, CA [*FM radio station call letters*] .... KJFX
Fresno, CA [*FM radio station call letters*] .... KJWL
Fresno, CA [*FM radio station call letters*] .... KKDJ
Fresno, CA [*AM radio station call letters*] .... KKTR
Fresno, CA [*AM radio station call letters*] .... KMJ
Fresno, CA [*FM radio station call letters*] .... KNAX
Fresno, CA [*FM radio station call letters*] .... KOQO
Fresno, CA [*FM radio station call letters*] .... KRBT
Fresno, CA [*Television station call letters*] .... KSEE
Fresno, CA [*FM radio station call letters*] .... KSJV
Fresno, CA [*FM radio station call letters*] .... KSKS
Fresno, CA [*FM radio station call letters*] .... KTHT
Fresno, CA [*FM radio station call letters*] .... KVPR
Fresno, CA [*Television station call letters*] .... KVPT
Fresno, CA [*AM radio station call letters*] .... KXEX
Fresno, CA [*AM radio station call letters*] .... KYNO
Fresno City College, Fresno, CA [*Library symbol Library of Congress*] (LCLS) .... CFC
Fresno Community Hospital, Fresno, CA [*Library symbol Library of Congress*] (LCLS) .... CFH
Fresno County Department of Health, Fresno, CA [*Library symbol Library of Congress*] (LCLS) .... CFDH
Fresno County Department of Mental Health Services, Fresno, CA [*Library symbol Library of Congress*] (LCLS) .... CFDMH
Fresno County Free Library, Fresno, CA [*Library symbol Library of Congress*] (LCLS) .... CF
Fresno/Fresno Air Terminal [*California*] [*ICAO location identifier*] (ICLI) .... KFAT
Fresno Pacific College, Center for Mennonite Brethren Studies, Fresno, CA [*Library symbol*] [*Library of Congress*] (LCLS) .... CFP-MB
Fresno Service Center [*IRS*] .... FSC
Fresno State College [*Later, California State University, Fresno*] .... FSC
Fret Payable a Destination [*Freight Payable at Destination*] [*French Business term*] .... FPAD
Fretted Instrument Guild of America (EA) .... FIGA
Fretter, Inc. [*Associated Press*] (SAG) .... Fretter
Fretter, Inc. [*NASDAQ symbol*] (SAG) .... FTTR
Freunde Guter Musik Club [*Record label*] [*Germany*] .... FGM
Freund's Adjuvant [*Immunology*] .... FA
Freund's Complete Adjuvant [*Immunology*] .... FCA
Freund's Incomplete Adjuvant [*Immunology*] .... FIA
Freustrum Location Addition .... FLA
Frevag Airlines [*Belgium ICAO designator*] (FAAC) .... FVG
Freymiller Trucking, Inc. [*NASDAQ symbol*] (NQ) .... FRML
Fria [*Guinea*] [*Airport symbol*] (AD) .... FIG
Fria [*Guinea*] [*ICAO location identifier*] (ICLI) .... GUFA
Friable Asbestos-Containing Material (GNE) .... FACM
Friable Asbestos-Containing Material (GNE) .... FAM
Friable Insulation Material (GNE) .... FIM
Friable Material (GNE) .... FM
Friant [*California*] [*Seismograph station code, US Geological Survey*] (SEIS) .... FRI
Friant, CA [*Location identifier FAA*] (FAAL) .... FRA
Friar .... F
Friar .... FR
Friars Club (EA) .... FC
Friary .... FRY
Fricandus [*To Be Rubbed*] [*Pharmacy*] (ROG) .... FRICAND
Fricative (BARN) .... fric
Fricentur [*Let Them Be Rubbed*] [*Pharmacy*] (ROG) .... FRICENT
Frick Art Reference Library, New York, NY [*Library symbol Library of Congress*] (LCLS) .... NNFr
Frick Chemical Laboratory (KSC) .... FCL
Fricktal-Schupfart [*Switzerland ICAO location identifier*] (ICLI) .... LSZI
Friction .... F
Friction .... FRCTN
Friction [*or Frictional*] (WDAA) .... FRIC
Friction .... FRICT
Friction Assessment Screening Test [*for brake linings*] .... FAST
Friction Braked Landing [*Aviation*] (IAA) .... FBL
Friction Cam Gear .... FCG
Friction Force Microscope .... FFM
Friction Glaze .... FG
Friction Horsepower .... FHP
Friction Materials Standards Institute (EA) .... FMSI
Friction Materials Test Machine .... FMTM
Friction Mean Effective Pressure [*Automotive engineering*] .... FMEP
Friction Measurement Test .... FMT
Friction Pendulum System [*for earthquake protection*] .... FPS
Friction Pressure Drop .... FPD
Friction Reducing Agent [*Chemicals*] .... FRA
Friction Volume Damper (OA) .... FVD
Friction Welding .... FRW
Frictional Force (DA) .... F_r
Friday .... F
Friday .... FR
Friday (EY) .... FRI
Friday (ODBW) .... Fri
Friday (ADA) .... FRID
Friday Harbor [*Washington*] [*Airport symbol*] (OAG) .... FRD
Friday Morning Quarterback [*In title FMQB Album Report*] .... FMQB
Fridays and Holidays Excepted .... F & HE
Fridays and Holidays Excepted (DS) .... FHEx
Fridays Only [*British railroad term*] .... FO
Frie Folkevalgte [*Freely Elected Representatives*] [*Norway*] (PPE) .... FF
Fried .... FRD
Friedberg [*Germany ICAO location identifier*] (ICLI) .... EDEV
Friedensengel [*Angel of Peace*] [*Torpedo auxiliary equipment*] [*German military - World War II*] .... FE
Friedenwald Archives (BJA) .... FA
Friedl Expert Committee (EA) .... FEC
Friedland [*Germany ICAO location identifier*] (ICLI) .... ETFL
Friedman and Koven, Library, Chicago, IL [*Library symbol Library of Congress*] (LCLS) .... ICFK
Friedman Indus [*AMEX symbol*] (TTSB) .... FRD
Friedman Industries, Inc. [*AMEX symbol*] (SPSG) .... FRD
Friedman Industries, Inc. [*Associated Press*] (SAG) .... Friedm
Friedman, John M., Hurricane WV [*STAC*] .... FJM
Friedman Library (Hugo Friedman Memorial), Tuscaloosa, AL [*Library symbol Library of Congress*] (LCLS) .... ATu
Friedman Test [*for pregnancy*] [*Obstetrics*] .... FRIED
Friedman-Robertson-Walker Theory [*Cosmology*] .... FRW
Friedmans, Inc. [*NASDAQ symbol*] (SAG) .... FRDM
Friedmans, Inc. [*Associated Press*] (SAG) .... Friedmn
Friedman's Inc.'A' [*NASDAQ symbol*] (TTSB) .... FRDM
Friedreich's Ataxia [*Medicine*] .... FA
Friedreich's Ataxia [*Medicine*] .... FRDA
Friedreich's Ataxia Group (EAIO) .... FAX
Friedreich's Ataxia Group in America [*Defunct*] (EA) .... FAGA
Friedreich's Ataxia Society of Ireland (EAIO) .... FASI
Friedrich Miescher Institute [*Switzerland*] .... FMI

Friedrich Technologies, Inc. [*Vancouver Stock Exchange symbol*] .... FHT
Friedrich-Alexander-Universitat zu Erlangen-Nurnberg, Abteilung fur Wirtschafts-und Socialwissenschaften, Nurnberg, Germany [*Library symbol Library of Congress*] (LCLS) .... GyNU
Friedrich-Alexander-Universitat zu Erlangen-Nurnberg, Erlangen, Germany [*Library symbol Library of Congress*] (LCLS) .... GyEU
Friedrich-Ebert-Stiftung, Archiv der Sozialen Demokratie, Bonn, Germany [*Library symbol Library of Congress*] (LCLS) .... GyBoFE
Friedrich-Naumann-Stiftung, Bonn, Germany [*Library symbol Library of Congress*] (LCLS) .... GyBoFN
Friedrichshafen [*Germany Airport symbol*] (OAG) .... FDH
Friedrichshafen-Lowental [*Germany ICAO location identifier*] (ICLI) .... EDTY
Friend (AABC) .... FRD
Friend .... FRND
Friend .... FRND
Friend Disease Virus [*Also, FLV, FV*] .... FDV
Friend Erythroleukemia Cell [*Medicine*] (DMAA) .... FEC
Friend Erythroleukemia Cell [*Oncology*] .... FEL
Friend Finders International [*Defunct*] (EA) .... FFI
Friend, Foe, or Neutral (MCD) .... FFN
Friend Leukemia [*Cytology*] (DMAA) .... FL
Friend Leukemia Cells [*Cytology*] .... FLC
Friend Leukemia Virus [*Also, FDV, FV*] .... FLV
Friend Murine Erythroleukaemia [*Cell line*] .... F-MEL
Friend Murine Leukemia Virus .... F-MuLV
Friend of a Friend [*Urban folklore term coined by Rodney Dale*] .... FOAF
Friend of a Friend .... FOAF
Friend of a Resistor-in-the-Army [*Peace movement slang during the Vietnam War*] (VNW) .... FRITA
Friend Virus [*Also, FDV, FLV*] .... FV
Friend Virus Anemia [*Medicine*] (DMAA) .... FVA
Friend Virus Polycythemia [*Medicine*] (DMAA) .... FVP
Friendless, Isolated, Needy, Disabled [*Project of National Council on the Aging - acronym used as name of New York City coffeehouse*] .... FIND
Friendly .... FRNDLY
Friendly Aircraft .... FA
Friendly Capabilities (MCD) .... FC
Friendly Contacts Associates [*Defunct*] (EA) .... FCA
Friendly Forces Information Requirements [*Military*] (INF) .... FFIR
Friendly Foreign Government .... FFG
Friendly Forward Disposition .... FFD
Friendly Hand Foundation (EA) .... FHF
Friendly Information System [*Military*] (RDA) .... FIS
Friendly Initiated [*Incident*] [*Vietnam*] .... FRI
Friendly Iron Moulders Society [*A union*] [*British*] .... FIMS
Friendly Laotian Forces (CINC) .... FLF
Friendly Peersuasion [*Girls Club of America*] (EA) .... FP
Friendly Query System [*IBM*] (NITA) .... FQS
Friendly Recoton Entertainment Decoder [*Television stereo adapter*] .... FRED
Friendly Robot Educational Device [*Androbot, Inc.*] .... FRED
Friendly, Round Robin, Special, Bee and Yoke Tracks (SAA) .... FRSBY
Friendly Situation (MCD) .... FRENSIT
Friendly Societies Act [*British*] (ILCA) .... FSA
Friendly Societies', Dispensaries, and Pharmacies Association of New South Wales [*Australia*] .... FSDPANSW
Friendly Society [*British*] (ILCA) .... FS
Friendly Society of Carpenters and Joiners [*A union*] [*British*] .... FSCJ
Friendly Society of Engravers and Sketchmakers [*Later, MPEA*] .... FSES
Friendly Society of Ironfounders of England, Ireland, and Wales [*A union*] .... FSIF
Friendly Society of Mechanics [*A union*] [*British*] .... FSM
Friendly Society of Operative Bricklayers [*A union*] [*British*] .... FSOB
Friendly Society of Operative Cabinet Makers [*A union*] [*British*] .... FSOCM
Friendly Society of Operative Stonemasons of England, Ireland, and Wales [*A union*] .... FSOSEIW
Friendly Society of Operative Tobacconists [*A union*] [*British*] .... FSOT
Friendly Society of Spade Tree Makers of the United Kingdom [*A union*] .... FSSTMUK
Friendly Society of Tin Plate Workers [*A union*] [*British*] .... FSTPW
Friendly Society of United Journeymen Platers and Moulders [*A union*] [*British*] .... FSUJPM
Friendly Society of Watermen [*A union*] [*British*] .... FSW
Friendly Status (MCD) .... FS
Friendly Strike or Support [*Military*] (NVT) .... FSTK/SUP
Friendly Union of Mechanics [*British*] .... FUM
Friendly United Society of Operative Brickmakers [*A union*] [*British*] .... FUSOB
Friend-Moloney-Rauscher [*Virus*] (AAMN) .... FMR
Friends Academy, Lower School, Glen Cove, NY [*Library symbol*] [*Library of Congress*] (LCLS) .... NGlcF-L
Friends Academy, Upper School, Glen Cove, NY [*Library symbol*] [*Library of Congress*] (LCLS) .... NGlcF-U
Friends Ambulance Unit [*British military*] (DMA) .... FAU
Friends and Associates for Yaddo (EA) .... FAY
Friends and Buddies of the Hour Glass Association (EA) .... FBHGA
Friends and Buddies of the Hour Glass Division Association [*Later, FBHGA*] (EA) .... FBHDA
Friends Around the World [*An association*] (EA) .... FAW
Friends Association for Higher Education (EA) .... FAHE
Friends Bible College [*Haviland, KS*] .... FBC
Friends Committee on National Legislation (EA) .... FCNL
Friends Committee on War Tax Concerns [*Defunct*] (EA) .... FCWTC
Friends Coordinating Committee on Peace [*Defunct*] (EA) .... FCCP
Friends Council on Education (EA) .... FCE
Friends Disaster Service (EA) .... FDS
Friends for Education [*Later, FFE*] (EA) .... FE
Friends for Education (EA) .... FFE
Friends for Free Enterprise (EA) .... FFFE
Friends for Jamaica (EA) .... FFJ
Friends for Jamaica [*An association*] (EA) .... FJ
Friends for Lesbian and Gay Concerns (EA) .... FLGC
Friends' Free Library of Germantown, Philadelphia, PA [*Library symbol Library of Congress*] (LCLS) .... PPFr
Friends General Conference (EA) .... FGC
Friends Historical Association (EA) .... FHA
Friends Historical Library of Swarthmore College, Swarthmore, PA [*Library symbol Library of Congress*] (LCLS) .... PSC-Hi
Friends Historical Library of Swarthmore College, Swarthmore, PA [*OCLC symbol*] (OCLC) .... PSH
Friends in Art of American Council of the Blind (EA) .... FAACB
Friends in Deed [*An association*] .... FID
Friends in Service Here .... FISH
Friends Involved in Sportfishing Heritage .... FISH
Friends Meeting House [*Quakers*] .... FMH
Friends Meeting, Stony Run, Baltimore, MD [*Library symbol Library of Congress*] (LCLS) .... MdBFr
Friends of Aerospace Supporting Science and Technology [*An association*] .... FASST
Friends of Africa in America [*Defunct*] (EA) .... FAA
Friends of American Art in Religion (EA) .... FAAR
Friends of American Writers (EA) .... FAW
Friends of Animals (EA) .... FOA
Friends of Ann Jillian (EA) .... FAJ
Friends of Appropriate Technology (EA) .... FAT
Friends of Astrology (EA) .... FA
Friends of Bill [*Political network built by President Bill Clinton*] .... FOB
Friends of Blue [*British*] [*An association*] (DBA) .... FOB
Friends of Bobby Vee (EA) .... FBV
Friends of Books and Comics (EA) .... FBC
Friends of Brain Injured Children of New South Wales [*Australia*] .... FBICNSW
Friends of Buddhism [*Defunct*] (EA) .... FB
Friends of Cast Iron Architecture (EA) .... FCIA
Friends of Cathedral Music (EA) .... FCM
Friends of Children of Vietnam (EA) .... FCVN
Friends of Clara Barton (EA) .... FCB
Friends of Community (EA) .... FC
Friends of Community (EA) .... FOC
Friends of Creation Spirituality (EA) .... FCS
Friends of David Cassidy [*Defunct*] (EA) .... FODC
Friends of Debbie Reynolds Fan Club (EA) .... FDRFC
Friends of Dennis Wilson (EA) .... FODW
Friends of Dromkeen Children's Literature Foundation [*Australia*] .... FDCLF
Friends of Eye Research [*Formerly, FERRAT*] [*Defunct*] (EA) .... FER
Friends of Eye Research, Rehabilitation, and Treatment [*Later, FER*] (EA) .... FERRAT
Friends of Families [*Defunct*] (EA) .... FOF
Friends of Family Planning (EA) .... FFP
Friends of Frank Ashmore [*Defunct*] (EA) .... FFA
Friends of Freddy (EA) .... FOF
Friends of Free Asia [*Defunct*] .... FOFA
Friends of Free China (EA) .... FOFC
Friends of French Art (EA) .... FFA
Friends of Fritz Busch [*Record label*] .... FFB
Friends of George Sand (EA) .... FGS
Friends of Georges Sadoul (EAIO) .... FGS
Friends of Guy Clark (EA) .... FGC
Friends of Haiti (EA) .... FOH
Friends of Haitian Refugees [*Defunct*] (EA) .... FHR
Friends of Helix Club (EA) .... FOHC
Friends of Hibakusha (EA) .... FH
Friends of Historical Pharmacy (EA) .... FHP
Friends of Holly Dunn (EA) .... FHD
Friends of Imperial Cancer [*British*] .... FIC
Friends of India Society International (EA) .... FISI
Friends of International Education [*An association*] (EA) .... FIE
Friends of Internet in Greece [*Discussion list*] .... FIG
Friends of Iris Society [*An association*] .... FOIS
Friends of Israel Association [*British*] (DBA) .... FIA
Friends of Israel Gospel Ministry (EA) .... FIGM
Friends of Jackie Wilson (EA) .... FJW
Friends of James Rogers (EA) .... FJR
Friends of Johnny Mathis [*Defunct*] (EA) .... FJM
Friends of Julio International (EA) .... FJI
Friends of Karen (EA) .... FK
Friends of Kate Smith [*Later, Kate Smith/God Bless America Foundation*] (EA) .... FKS
Friends of Kristoffer Tabori [*Defunct Defunct*] (EA) .... FKT
Friends of Libraries Australia .... FOLA
Friends of Libraries Charitable Trust [*British*] .... FLCT
Friends of Libraries USA (EA) .... FOL USA
Friends of Libraries USA [*American Library Association*] .... FOLUSA
Friends of Little Gidding (EA) .... FLG
Friends of Luna Park [*Sydney, New South Wales, Australia*] .... FLP
Friends of Medieval Dublin [*Irish*] .... FMD
Friends of National Public Radio [*Defunct*] (EA) .... FNPR
Friends of Nature (EA) .... FN
Friends of Neil Diamond (EA) .... FND
Friends of Nicaraguan Culture (EA) .... FNC
Friends of Old St. Ferdinand (EA) .... FOSF
Friends of Old-Time Music [*Later, Society for Traditional Music*] (EA) .... FOTM
Friends of Old-Time Radio (EA) .... FOTR

Friends of Opera in Victoria [*Australia*] .... FOV
Friends of Palestinian Prisoners (EA) .... FPP
Friends of Patrick Henry (EA) .... FPH
Friends of Peace Now (EA) .... FPN
Friends of Peace Pilgrim (EA) .... FPP
Friends of Photography (EA) .... FOP
Friends of Pioneering Israel .... FPI
Friends of R. [*Ralph*] **Emery** (EA) .... FRE
Friends of Radio for Peace International (EA) .... FRFPI
Friends of Shaun Cassidy Fan Club (EA) .... FSCFC
Friends of Solidarity (EA) .... FS
Friends of Terra Cotta (EA) .... FOTC
Friends of the American Museum in Britain (EA) .... FAMB
Friends of the Australian National University Library .... FANUL
Friends of the Conservative Party [*Defunct*] (EA) .... FCP
Friends of the Earth (EA) .... FOE
Friends of the Earth Foundation (EA) .... FEF
Friends of the Earth International .... FOEI
Friends of the Everglades (EA) .... FE
Friends of the Farm [*An association*] (EA) .... FF
Friends of the FBI (EA) .... FOF
Friends of the Filipino People (EA) .... FFP
Friends of the Golden State .... FGS
Friends of the Hop Marketing Order [*Defunct*] (EA) .... FHMO
Friends of the Jessup [*An association*] (EA) .... FOJ
Friends of the Kennedy Center (EA) .... FKC
Friends of the Lake District (EERA) .... FLD
Friends of the Land [*Later, IWLA*] .... FOL
Friends of the Library of Hawaii, Honolulu, HI [*Library symbol Library of Congress*] (LCLS) .... HHF
Friends of the Louvre Museum (EA) .... FLM
Friends of the National Libraries [*British*] .... FNL
Friends of the National Zoo (EA) .... FNZ
Friends of the National Zoo .... FONZ
Friends of the Origami Center of America (EA) .... FOCA
Friends of the Peaceful Alternatives [*Defunct*] (EA) .... FPA
Friends of the Prisoners [*Australia*] .... FOTP
Friends of the River (EA) .... FOR
Friends of the River (EA) .... FOTR
Friends of the Sea Lion Marine Mammal Center (EA) .... FSLMMC
Friends of the Sea Otter (EA) .... FSO
Friends of the Shakers (EA) .... FS
Friends of the Superior Court (EA) .... FSC
Friends of the Tango (EA) .... FT
Friends of the Third World (EA) .... FTW
Friends of the United States of Latin America (EA) .... FUSLA
Friends of the US National Arboretum (EA) .... FONA
Friends of the Vietnam Veterans Memorial (EA) .... FVVM
Friends of the Western Buddhist Order (EA) .... FWBO
Friends of the Wilderness [*Defunct*] (EA) .... FOW
Friends of the World Council of Churches (EA) .... FWCC
[*The*] **Friends of Tom Baker** (EA) .... TFOTB
Friends of Vieilles Maisons Francaises (EA) .... FVMF
Friends of Waycross Express [*Defunct*] (EA) .... FWE
Friends of Workshop Way (EA) .... FWW
Friends of Yesh Gvul (EA) .... FYG
Friends Outside (EA) .... FO
Friends Peace Committee (EA) .... FPC
Friends Peace Exchange (EA) .... FPE
[*The*] **Friends Program** (EA) .... FP
[*The*] **Friends Program** (EA) .... TFP
Friends' Provident Life Office [*Insurance*] [*British*] .... FP
Friends Reference Library, London, United Kingdom [*Library symbol Library of Congress*] (LCLS) .... UkLQ
Friends Service Council [*Quakers*] .... FSC
Friends United Meeting .... FUM
Friends United Press (DGA) .... FUP
Friends United through Astronomy [*Defunct*] (EA) .... FUTA
Friends United Toward Understanding, Rights, and Equality .... FUTURE
Friends University, Wichita, KS [*OCLC symbol*] (OCLC) .... KFU
Friends University, Wichita, KS [*Library symbol Library of Congress*] (LCLS) .... KWiF
Friends Vegetarian Society of North America (EA) .... FVSNA
Friends' Work Camp Committee [*British*] (BI) .... FWCC
Friends World College [*Huntington, NY*] (EA) .... FWC
Friends World Committee for Consultation [*British*] (EAIO) .... FWCC
Friendship Air Alaska [*ICAO designator*] (FAAC) .... FAL
Friendship Ambassadors Foundation (EA) .... FA
Friendship [*Airport*] **Annex** [*National Security Agency*] .... FANX
Friendship Association of Chinese Students and Scholars (EA) .... FACS
Friendship Book [*Address list circulated by Beatles fans*] .... FB
Friendship Facilities, Ottawa, IL [*Library symbol Library of Congress*] (LCLS) .... IOtF
Friendship Force (EA) .... FF
Friendship House (EA) .... FH
Friendship Junior College [*South Carolina*] .... FJC
Friendship Loans to Latin American Endeavors, Inc. .... FLAME
Friendship, NY [*FM radio station call letters*] .... WCID
Friendship Oil Pipeline [*Eastern Europe*] .... FOP
Friesian [*Language, etc.*] (ROG) .... FRIES
Friesland [*County in the Netherlands*] (ROG) .... FRIS
Frieze (VRA) .... frz
Frifly SpA [*Italy ICAO designator*] (FAAC) .... FIF
Frigate [*Navy symbol*] .... DL
Frigate [*Navy symbol*] .... FF
Frigate .... FR
Frigate LAMPS [*Light Airborne Multipurpose System*] **Integrated Team Training** [*Navy*] (ANA) .... FLITT
Frigg [*Norway ICAO location identifier*] (ICLI) .... ENFR
Frightened Little Man .... FLM
Frigid Zone (ROG) .... FZ
Frigidus [*Cold*] [*Pharmacy*] .... FRIG
Frigorie [*Unit of rate of extraction of heat*] [*Thermodynamics*] .... fr
Frijoles Canyon [*New Mexico*] [*Seismograph station code, US Geological Survey Closed*] (SEIS) .... FCN
Fringe (MSA) .... FRNG
Fringe Benefits (WDAA) .... FB
Fringe Benefits Tax .... FBT
Fringe Festival of Independent Dance Artists [*Canada*] .... fFIDA
Fringes of Equal Chromatic Order [*Optics*] .... FECO
Friona, TX [*FM radio station call letters*] .... KGRW
Frisch's Restaurants [*AMEX symbol*] (TTSB) .... FRS
Frisch's Restaurants, Inc. [*Associated Press*] (SAG) .... Frischs
Frisch's Restaurants, Inc. [*AMEX symbol*] (SPSG) .... FRS
Frisco Bay Industries [*NASDAQ symbol*] (SAG) .... FBAY
Frisco Bay Industries [*NASDAQ symbol*] (TTSB) .... FBAYF
Frisco Bay Industries [*Associated Press*] (SAG) .... FrisBay
Frisco, CO [*FM radio station call letters*] .... KYSL
Frisia Luftverkehr [*ICAO designator*] (AD) .... FV
Frisian [*MARC language code Library of Congress*] (LCCP) .... fri
Frisian [*Language, etc.*] .... FRIS
Frisian [*or Frisic*] [*Language, etc.*] .... FRS
Frisker-Monitor [*Radiation detection*] .... FM
Fritz Companies [*NASDAQ symbol*] (TTSB) .... FRTZ
Fritz Companies, Inc. [*Associated Press*] (SAG) .... Fritz
Fritz Companies, Inc. [*NASDAQ symbol*] (SAG) .... FRTZ
Fritz Engineering Laboratory [*Lehigh University*] .... FEL
Fritzlar [*Germany ICAO location identifier*] (ICLI) .... EDPF
Fritzoe [*Norway ICAO location identifier*] (ICLI) .... ENFZ
Frivolities [*Slang*] (DSUE) .... FRIVOLS
Frivolous (DSUE) .... FRIVOL
Froberg Elementary School, Rockford, IL [*Library symbol*] [*Library of Congress*] (LCLS) .... IRoFE
Frobisher [*Northwest Territories*] [*Seismograph station code, US Geological Survey*] (SEIS) .... FRB
Frobisher Bay [*Northwest Territories*] [*Seismograph station code, US Geological Survey Closed*] (SEIS) .... FBC
Frobisher Bay [*Canada*] [*Airport symbol*] (OAG) .... YFB
Frobisher, NT [*ICAO location identifier*] (ICLI) .... CYFB
Frobisher NV (European Airlines) [*Belgium ICAO designator*] (FAAC) .... FRO
Frobisher Resources Ltd. [*Vancouver Stock Exchange symbol*] .... FBR
Frog [*Engineering*] .... FG
Frog Adenovirus .... FAV
Frog Embryo Teratogenesis Assay - Xenopus [*Toxicology*] .... FETAX
Frog Otolith Experiment Package [*NASA*] .... FOEP
Frog Pond - Frog Collectors Club (EA) .... FP
Frogerius [*Rogerius Beneventanus*] [*Flourished, 12th century*] [*Authority cited in pre-1607 legal work*] (DSA) .... F
Frogerius [*Rogerius Beneventanus*] [*Flourished, 12th century*] [*Authority cited in pre-1607 legal work*] (DSA) .... Frog
Frolunda [*Sweden ICAO location identifier*] (ICLI) .... ESVF
From .... F
From (MUGU) .... FM
From (AFM) .... FR
From (VRA) .... fr
From (WDMC) .... fr
From .... FRM
From Other Service Centers [*IRS*] .... FOSC
From Own Correspondent .... FOC
From the Stone Age to Christianity [*A publication*] (BJA) .... FSAC
Front (KSC) .... F
Front (VRA) .... fnt
Front (WDMC) .... fore
Front .... FR
Front .... FRNT
Front .... FRO
Front [*Telecommunications*] (TEL) .... FRT
Front [*Automotive engineering*] .... FRT
Front [*Deltiology*] .... FT
Front Autonomiste et Socialiste Autogestionnaire Bretonne [*Breton Autonomist and Socialist Self-Rule Front*] [*France Political party*] (PPE) .... FASAB
Front Axle [*Automotive engineering*] .... FA
Front [*End*]/Back [*End*] .... FORBAK
Front Commun pour le Respect de la Vie [*Common Front for the Respect of Life*] [*Canada*] .... FCRV
Front Communiste Revolutionnaire [*France*] .... FCR
Front Congolais pour le Restauration de la Democratie [*Belgium Political party*] (EY) .... FCD
Front Congolais pour le Retablissement de la Democratie [*Zaire*] [*Political party*] (EY) .... FCD
Front d'Action Politique .... FRAP
Front d'Action Populaire en Reamenagement Urbain [*Canada*] .... FRAPRU
Front d'Alliberament Catala [*Spain*] .... FAC
Front de la Lutte pour l'Independence du Dahomey [*Battle Front for the Independence of Dahomey*] .... FLID
Front de Liberation de la Bretagne - Armee Republicaine Bretonne [*Liberation Front of Brittany - Breton Republican Army*] [*France*] (PD) .... FLB-ARB

Front de Liberation de la Bretagne pour la Liberation Nationale et le Socialisme [*Liberation Front of Brittany for National Liberation and Socialism*] [*France*] (PD) ... FLB-LNS
Front de Liberation de la Cote des Somalis [*Front for the Liberation of the Somali Coast*] [*Djibouti*] ... FLCS
Front de Liberation de la Polynesie [*Political party*] (EY) ... FLP
Front de Liberation de Quebec [*Quebec Liberation Front*] [*Separatist group*] ... FLQ
Front de Liberation et de Rehabilitation du Dahomey [*Dahomey Liberation and Rehabilitation Front*] [*Benin*] [*Political party*] (PD) ... FLRD
Front de Liberation Nationale [*National Liberation Front*] [*South Vietnam Use NFLSV*] [*Political party*] ... FLN
Front de Liberation Nationale [*National Liberation Front*] [*France Political party*] ... FLN
Front de Liberation Nationale [*National Liberation Front*] [*Algeria*] [*Political party*] (PPW) ... FLN
Front de Liberation Nationale [*Chad*] ... FROLINAT
Front de Liberation Nationale Congolais [*Congolese National Liberation Front*] [*Zaire*] [*Political party*] (PD) ... FLNC
Front de Liberation Nationale de la Corse [*Corsican National Liberation Front*] [*Political party*] (PD) ... FLNC
Front de Liberation Nationale Francaise [*French National Liberation Front*] (PD) ... FLNF
Front de Liberation Nationale Kanake Socialiste [*National Liberation Front ofSocialist Kanakes*] [*New Caledonia*] [*Political party*] ... FLINKS
Front de Liberation Populaire [*Quebec separatist group*] ... FLP
Front de Libertacao de Guinee [*Guinean Liberation Front*] [*Portuguese Guinea*] ... FLG
Front de l'Opposition Democratique [*Togo*] [*Political party*] (EY) ... FOD
Front de l'Unite Bangala [*Bangala United Front*] ... FUB
Front Democratique [*Democratic Front*] [*The Comoros*] [*Political party*] (EY) ... FD
Front Democratique Camerounais [*Cameroon*] [*Political party*] (EY) ... FDC
Front Democratique des Bruxellois Francophones [*French-Speaking Democratic Front*] [*Belgium Political party*] (PPW) ... FDF
Front Democratique des Patriotes Maliens [*Mali*] [*Political party*] (EY) ... FDPM
Front des Artistes Canadiens [*Canadian Artists' Representation - CAR*] ... FAC
Front des Forces Socialistes [*Front of Socialist Forces*] [*Algeria*] [*Political party*] (PD) ... FFS
Front des Jeunes Nationalistes Africains [*National African Youth Front*] ... FJNA
Front Door [*Automotive engineering*] ... F/DR
Front Door [*Shipping*] ... FD
Front du Quebec Francais ... FQF
Front d'Union Nationale de l'Angola [*National Union Front of Angola*] ... FUNA
Front End (ADA) ... FE
Front End ... FRTN
Front End Accessory Drive [*Automotive engineering*] ... FEAD
Front End Analysis ... FEA
Front End Communications Processor ... FECP
Front End Control Program (IAA) ... FEC
Front End for Databases [*GTE usage*] ... FRED
Front End Loader (ADA) ... FEL
Front End Package (OA) ... FEP
Front End Volatility Index [*Environmental Protection Agency*] (GFGA) ... FEVI
Front Engine, Front and Rear Drive [*Automotive engineering*] ... FFR
Front Engine, Front Drive [*Automotive engineering*] ... FF
Front Engine Power-Take-Off [*Automotive engineering*] ... FEPTO
Front Engine, Rear Drive [*Automotive engineering*] ... FR
Front Face of Block [*Automotive engineering*] ... FFOB
Front Focal Length [*Optics*] ... FF
Front Focal Length [*Optics*] ... FFL
Front for Democracy and Development [*Surinam*] [*Political party*] ... FDD
Front for Liberation and Unity [*Western Sahara*] ... FLU
Front for National Salvation [*Uganda*] ... FRONASA
Front for Popular Armed Struggle [*Iraq*] ... FPAS
Front for the Advancement and Progress of Haiti [*Political party*] ... FRAPH
Front for the Advancement and Progress of Haiti ... FRAPH
Front for the Liberation of Occupied South Yemen (PD) ... FLOSY
Front for the Liberation of Zimbabwe ... FROLIZI
Front Independantiste [*Independence Front*] [*New Caledonia*] [*Political party*] (PPW) ... FI
Front Interface Module [*Computer science*] ... FIM
Front Islamique de Salut [*Algeria*] [*Political party*] ... FIS
Front Jednosci Narodowej [*Polish Front of National Unity*] ... FJN
Front Lay [*Printing*] (DGA) ... FL
Front Line [*Revolutionary group*] [*Italy*] ... PL
Front Lower Control Arm ... FLCA
Front Luminous Vacuum Fluorescence Display (IAA) ... FLVFD
Front Malaysian Islamic Council [*Political party*] (FEA) ... FMIC
Front Matter [*Publishing*] ... FM
Front Militant Autonome [*Autonomous Militant Front*] [*French*] (PD) ... MAF
Front Militant Departementaliste [*Militant Departmentalist Front*] [*Reunion*] (PD) ... FMD
Front Mounting Light ... FML
Front National [*France Political party*] (PPW) ... FN
Front National [*Belgium Political party*] (EY) ... FN
Front National [*Gabon*] [*Political party*] (EY) ... FN
Front National de Concertation [*Haiti*] [*Political party*] (EY) ... FNC
Front National de la Jeunesse [*National Youth Front*] [*France*] (PD) ... FNJ
Front National de Liberation de Bretagne [*National Liberation Front of Brittany*] [*France*] (PD) ... FNLB
Front National de Liberation de l'Angola [*Angolan National Liberation Front*] (PD) ... FNLA
Front National de Liberation Guyanais [*Guiana National Liberation Front*] [*French Guiana*] (PD) ... FNLG
Front National de Renouvellement [*Algeria*] [*Political party*] (EY) ... FNR
Front National Martiniquais pour l'Autonomie [*Martinique National Front for Autonomy*] [*Political party*] (PPW) ... FNMA
Front National pour l'Algerie Francaise [*National Front for French Algeria*] [*Political party*] ... FNAF
Front National pour le Changement et la Democratie [*Haiti*] [*Political party*] (EY) ... FNCD
Front National Uni [*United National Front*] [*The Comoros*] ... FNU
Front National Uni des Komores [*National United Front of the Comoros*] [*Political party*] (PD) ... FNUK
Front Nationaliste Progressiste pour la Liberation de la Tunisie [*Progressive Nationalist Front for the Liberation of Tunisia*] [*Political party*] (PD) ... FNPLT
Front of Board (MSA) ... FOB
Front of Dash [*Technical drawings*] ... FD
Front of Escott Public Library, Mallorytown, Ontario [*Library symbol National Library of Canada*] (NLC) ... OMFE
Front of House (ADA) ... FOH
Front of House Spot [*Theatrical lighting*] (NTCM) ... FOH
Front of Leeds and Lansdowne Public Library, Lansdowne, Ontario [*Library symbol National Library of Canada*] (NLC) ... OLAFL
Front of Yonge Township Public Library, Mallorytown, Ontario [*Library symbol National Library of Canada*] (BIB) ... OMFY
Front Oubangais Patriotique - Parti du Travail [*Oubangian Patriotic Front - Party of Labor*] [*Central Africa*] (PD) ... FOP-PT
Front Paisanu di Liberazione [*Corsica*] ... FPCL
Front Panel [*Navy Navigation Satellite System*] (DNAB) ... FP
Front Panel Control ... FPC
Front Populaire [*Burkina Faso*] [*Political party*] (EY) ... FP
Front Populaire Ivoirien [*Ivorian Popular Front*] [*The Ivory Coast*] [*Political party*] (EY) ... FPI
Front Populaire Soudanais [*Sudanese Popular Front*] ... FPS
Front pour la Restauration de l'Unite et de la Democratie [*Djibouti*] [*Political party*] (EY) ... FRUD
Front Progressiste Voltaique [*Upper Volta Progressive Front*] [*Political party*] (PPW) ... FPV
Front Projection (NTCM) ... FP
Front/Rear ... F/R
Front Revolutionnaire Africain pour l'Independence Nationale des Colonies Portugaises [*African Revolutionary Front for the National Independence of Portuguese Colonies*] ... FRAIN
Front Revolutionnaire d'Action Proletarienne [*Terrorist organization*] [*Belgium*] (EY) ... FRAP
Front Royal, VA [*Location identifier FAA*] (FAAL) ... FRR
Front Royal, VA [*FM radio station call letters*] ... WFQX
Front Royal, VA [*AM radio station call letters*] ... WFTR
Front Royal, VA [*FM radio station call letters*] ... WFTR-FM
Front Royal, VA [*TV station call letters*] (RBYB) ... WVPY-TV
Front Striker Bulletin [*An association*] (EA) ... FSB
Front Supply Base Sections (MCD) ... FSBS
Front Suspension Arm ... FSA
Front Uni de Liberation Kanake [*New Caledonia*] [*Political party*] (FEA) ... FULK
Front Uni Liberateur de la Guinee Portuguesa et des Isles du Cap Vert [*United Liberation Front of Portuguese Guinea and Cape Verde*] [*Political party*] ... FUL
Front Uni National pour Cambodge Independant, Neutre, Pacifique et Cooperatif [*National United Front for an Independent National, Peaceful, and Cooperative Cambodia*] [*Political party*] (PD) ... FUNCINPEC
Front Uni pour l'Autonomie Interne [*United Front for Internal Autonomy*] [*French Polynesia*] [*Political party*] (PPW) ... FUAI
Front Unifie de la Lutte de la Race Opprime [*United Front for the Struggle of Oppressed Races*] (CINC) ... FULRO
Front Upper Control Arm ... FUCA
Front Upset Jaw (MSA) ... FUJ
Front Vertex Back Focal Distance ... FVD
Front View (MSA) ... FV
Front Wheel Drive ... FWD
Front Wheel Walker [*Rehabilitation*] (DAVI) ... FWW
Frontal [*Medicine*] (DAVI) ... F
Frontal Air-Sea Interaction Experiment [*Marine science*] (OSRA) ... FASINEX
Frontal Air-Sea Interaction Experiment (USDC) ... FASINEX
Frontal and Atlantic Storm-Track Experiment [*Planned Experiment*] [*Marine science*] (OSRA) ... FASTEX
Frontal Area [*Automotive engineering*] ... Af
Frontal Aviation [*Soviet tactical air force*] [*World War II*] ... FA
Frontal Bovine Serum [*Medicine*] (BARN) ... FBS
Frontal Cortex [*Neuroanatomy*] ... FCx
Frontal Eye Field [*Neuroanatomy*] ... FEF
Frontal Groove of Pinnule ... FGP
Frontal, Intermittent Delta Activity [*Medicine*] (DMAA) ... FIRDA
Frontal Lobe [*Brain anatomy*] ... FL
Frontal Passage [*NWS*] (FAAC) ... FROPA
Frontal Sinus [*Otorhinolaryngology*] (DAVI) ... F
Frontal Surface [*NWS*] (FAAC) ... FROSFC
Front-Connected ... FC
Fronte dell'Uomo Qualunque; Uomo Qualunque [*Common Man Front*] [*Italy Political party*] (PPE) ... UQ
Fronte Democratica Liberale dell'Uomo Qualunque [*Liberal Democratic Front of the Common Man*] [*Italy Political party*] (PPE) ... FDLUQ
Fronteer Directory [*NASDAQ symbol*] (TTSB) ... FDIR
Fronteer Directory Co., Inc. [*NASDAQ symbol*] (NQ) ... FDIR
Fronteer Directory Co., Inc. [*Associated Press*] (SAG) ... FrntDir
Fronteer Financial Holdings Ltd. [*NASDAQ symbol*] (SAG) ... FDIR
Fronteer Financial Holdings Ltd. [*Associated Press*] (SAG) ... FrntrFin
Fronteira [*Brazil ICAO location identifier*] (ICLI) ... SBFT

Frontenac County Library, Cloyne Branch, Cloyne, ON, Canada [*Library symbol*] [*Library of Congress*] (LCLS) .... CaOCIFC
Frontenac County Library, Kingston, ON, Canada [*Library symbol Library of Congress*] (LCLS) .... CaOKFC
Frontenac County Library, Kingston, Ontario [*Library symbol National Library of Canada*] (NLC) .... OKFC
Frontenac County Library, Sydenham Branch, Sydenham, ON, Canada [*Library symbol*] [*Library of Congress*] (LCLS) .... CaOSyFC
Frontenac County Public Library, Barriefield, ON, Canada [*Library symbol Library of Congress*] (LCLS) .... CaOBarF
Frontenac County Schools Museum Association, Kingston, Ontario [*Library symbol National Library of Canada*] (BIB) .... OKFCSM
Frontenac County Schools Museum Association, ON, Canada [*Library symbol*] [*Library of Congress*] (LCLS) .... CaOKFCSM
Front-End Computer .... FEC
Frontend International Technologies, Inc. [*Vancouver Stock Exchange symbol*] .... FEI
Front-End Network Processor .... FNP
Front-End Processor [*Computer*] (NASA) .... FEP
Front-End Purification [*Engineering*] .... FEP
Front-End Screening [*DoD*] .... FES
Front-End Sheet Metal .... FESM
Frontier .... FRNTR
Frontier .... FRON
Frontier Adjusters of Amer [*AMEX symbol*] (TTSB) .... FAJ
Frontier Adjusters of America, Inc. [*AMEX symbol*] (SAG) .... FAJ
Frontier Adjusters of America, Inc. [*Associated Press*] (SAG) .... FrontAdj
Frontier Airlines [*NASDAQ symbol*] (TTSB) .... FRNT
Frontier Airlines, Inc. [*Air carrier designation symbol*] .... FAL
Frontier Airlines, Inc. [*FAA designator*] (FAAC) .... FFT
Frontier Airlines, Inc. [*ICAO designator*] .... FL
Frontier Airlines, Inc. [*NASDAQ symbol*] (SAG) .... FRNT
Frontier Airlines, Inc. [*Associated Press*] (SAG) .... FrontA
Frontier Airlines, Inc. [*Associated Press*] (SAG) .... FrontrAir
Frontier Airlines Wrrt [*NASDAQ symbol*] (TTSB) .... FRNTW
Frontier Armed and Mounted Police [*British government*] .... FAMP
Frontier Corp. [*Formerly, Rochester Telephone*] [*NYSE symbol*] (SAG) .... FRO
Frontier Corp. [*Associated Press*] (SAG) .... FrontrCp
Frontier Corp. [*Formerly, Rochester Telephone*] [*Associated Press*] (SAG) .... FrtrCp
Frontier Flying Service, Inc. [*ICAO designator*] (FAAC) .... FTA
Frontier Force .... FF
Frontier Force Rifles [*British military*] (DMA) .... FFR
Frontier Guard, Finland [*FAA designator*] (FAAC) .... FNG
Frontier Insurance Gr [*NYSE symbol*] (TTSB) .... FTR
Frontier Insurance Group [*Associated Press*] (SAG) .... FrntrIns
Frontier Insurance Group, Inc. [*Associated Press*] (SAG) .... FrtrIns
Frontier Insurance Group, Inc. [*NYSE symbol*] (SPSG) .... FTR
Frontier Molecular Orbital Theory [*Physical chemistry*] .... FMO
Frontier Mounted Rifles [*British military*] (DMA) .... FMR
Frontier Nat Gas $1.20 Cv Ptd [*NASDAQ symbol*] (TTSB) .... FNGCP
Frontier Natural Gas [*NASDAQ symbol*] (SAG) .... FNGC
Frontier Natural Gas [*Associated Press*] (SAG) .... FrntN
Frontier Natural Gas [*Commercial firm Associated Press*] (SAG) .... FrntNat
Frontier Natural Gas [*Commercial firm Associated Press*] (SAG) .... FrntNt
Frontier Natural Gas [*Commercial firm Associated Press*] (SAG) .... FrtNt
Frontier Natural Gas Wrrt [*NASDAQ symbol*] (TTSB) .... FNGCW
Frontier Nursing Service (EA) .... FNS
Frontier School Division, Winnipeg, Manitoba [*Library symbol National Library of Canada*] (NLC) .... MWFSD
Frontiers Foundation Operation Beaver [*Canada*] (EAIO) .... FFOB
Frontiers International (EA) .... FI
Frontinus [*First century AD*] [*Classical studies*] (OCD) .... Frontin
Frontispiece (VRA) .... fntpc
Frontispiece (NTCM) .... Fp
Frontispiece [*Publishing*] (ROG) .... FPIECE
Frontispiece [*Publishing*] .... FR
Frontispiece [*Publishing*] .... FRONT
Frontispiece [*Publishing*] .... FRONTIS
Frontispiece [*Publishing*] (WGA) .... FSPC
Frontline Ambulance [*Army*] (INF) .... FLA
Fronto-Dextra Anterior [*A fetal position*] [*Obstetrics*] .... FDA
Fronto-Dextra Posterior [*A fetal position*] [*Obstetrics*] .... FDP
Fronto-Dextra Transversa [*A fetal position*] [*Obstetrics*] .... FDT
Frontogenesis [*NWS*] (FAAC) .... FNTGNS
Fronto-Laeva Anterior [*A fetal position*] [*Obstetrics*] (MAE) .... FLA
Fronto-Laeva Posterior [*A fetal position*] [*Obstetrics*] (MAE) .... FLP
Fronto-Laeva Transversa [*A fetal position*] [*Obstetrics*] (MAE) .... FLT
Frontolysis [*NWS*] (FAAC) .... FNTLYS
Frontone [*Italy ICAO location identifier*] (ICLI) .... LIVF
Fronto-Occipital [*Anatomy*] .... FO
Fronto-Parietal [*Anatomy*] (MAE) .... FP
Front-Panel Operation [*Computer science*] (PCM) .... FRPO
Front-Range Consortium [*Marine science*] (OSRA) .... FRC
Front-Range Consortium (USDC) .... FRC
Frontul Democratic Popular [*Democratic Popular Front*] [*Romania*] [*Political party*] (PPE) .... FDP
Frontul National Democratic [*National Democratic Front*] [*Romania*] [*Political party*] (PPE) .... FND
Frontul Renasterii Nationala [*Front of National Rebirth*] [*Romania*] [*Political party*] (PPE) .... FRN
Frontul Unitatii Socialiste [*Front of Socialist Unity*] [*Romania*] [*Political party*] (PPE) .... FUS
Frosinone [*Italy ICAO location identifier*] (ICLI) .... LIRH
Frost [*Meteorology*] (DA) .... FRST
Frost X
Frost & Sullivan, Inc. [*Information service or system*] (IID) .... F & S
Frost Campus Library, Sir Sandford Fleming College, Lindsay, Ontario [*Library symbol National Library of Canada*] (NLC) .... OLISF
Frost, Cog, and Screwmakers' Society [*A union*] [*British*] .... FCSS
Frost Warnings Issued (NOAA) .... FRWIS
Frost, WV [*AM radio station call letters*] .... WVMR
Frostburg, MD [*AM radio station call letters*] .... WFRB
Frostburg, MD [*FM radio station call letters*] .... WFRB-FM
Frostburg, MD [*FM radio station call letters*] .... WFWM
Frostburg, MD [*FM radio station call letters*] .... WLIC
Frostburg State College, Frostburg, MD [*Library symbol Library of Congress*] (LCLS) .... MdFroS
Frostburg State College, Library, Frostburg, MD [*OCLC symbol*] (OCLC) .... MFS
Frostburg State University (GAGS) .... Frostburg St U
Frostig Developmental Test of Visual Perception [*Psychiatry*] (DAVI) .... FDTVP
Frostig Developmental Test of Visual-Motor Perception [*Psychiatry*] (DAVI) .... FDTVMP
Frostig Program for the Development of Visual Perception [*Psychiatry*] (DAVI) .... FPDVP
Froude Number [*IUPAC*] .... F
Frozen .... FRZ
Frozen .... FRZN
Frozen Animal Procedure [*Medicine*] (DMAA) .... FAP
Frozen Asset [*Business term*] .... FA
Frozen Cell .... FC
Frozen Concentrated Orange Juice .... FCOJ
Frozen Embryo [*Medicine*] (HCT) .... FE
Frozen Equilibrium Flow .... FEF
Frozen Fish Trades Association (EA) .... FFTA
Frozen Food Action Communications Team (DICI) .... FACT
Frozen Food Association of Delaware Valley (SRA) .... FFADV
Frozen Food Association of New England (SRA) .... FFANE
Frozen Food Express [*NASDAQ symbol*] (TTSB) .... FFEX
Frozen Food Express [*Associated Press*] (SAG) .... FrozenFd
Frozen Food Express [*Associated Press*] (SAG) .... FrozFd
Frozen Food Express Industries, Inc. [*NASDAQ symbol*] (SAG) .... FFEX
Frozen Food Institute .... FFI
Frozen Foods Action Communications Team (EA) .... FFACT
Frozen Granular Snow [*Skiing condition*] .... FRGR
Frozen Onion Ring Packers Council [*AFFI*] [*Absorbed by*] (EA) .... FORPC
Frozen Pea Council [*Defunct*] .... FPC
Frozen Plasma [*Medicine*] .... FP
Frozen Potato Products Institute (EA) .... FPPI
Frozen Red Blood Cells [*Hematology*] (DAVI) .... FZRC
Frozen Red Cells [*Medicine*] .... FRC
Frozen Section [*Medicine*] .... FS
Frozen Section [*Medicine*] (MAE) .... fx
Frozen Storage .... FZSTO
Frozen Vegetable Council (EA) .... FVC
Frozya Industries [*Vancouver Stock Exchange symbol*] .... FRO
FRP Properties [*NASDAQ symbol*] (TTSB) .... FRPP
FRP Properties, Inc. [*Associated Press*] (SAG) .... FRP Pr
FRP Properties, Inc. [*NASDAQ symbol*] (NQ) .... FRPP
Fructose [*A sugar*] .... Fru
Fructose bisphosphatase [*An enzyme*] .... FBPase
Fructose bisphosphate [*Also, FDP*] [*Biochemistry*] .... FBP
Fructose Diphosphatase [*An enzyme*] .... FDPase
Fructose Diphosphate [*Biochemistry*] .... FDP
Fructose Monophosphate [*Biochemistry*] .... FMP
Fructus [*Fruit*] [*Latin*] (ROG) .... FR
Fructus [*Fruit*] [*Latin*] (ROG) .... FRUCT
Fruehauf Canada, Inc. [*Toronto Stock Exchange symbol*] .... FRH
Fruehauf Trailer [*NYSE symbol*] (SPSG) .... FTC
Fruehauf Trailer Corp. [*Associated Press*] (SAG) .... FruTrail
Frugal Responsible Unpretentious Mature Persons .... FRUMPS
Fruit .... fr
Fruit .... FRT
Fruit .... FRU
Fruit and Vegetable Division [*of Agricultural Research Service*] [*Department of Agriculture*] .... FV
Fruit and Vegetable Insects Research Laboratory [*Closed 1985*] [*Vincennes, IN*] [*Department of Agriculture*] (GRD) .... FVIRL
Fruit Color (Greenish Red to Dark Red) [*Botany*] .... FRCOB
Fruit Color (No Green to Mostly Green) [*Botany*] .... FRCOA
Fruit Frost (NOAA) .... FF
Fruit Growers' Group [*Australia*] .... FGG
Fruit Importers Association [*British*] (DBA) .... FIA
Fruit of the Loom, Inc. [*Associated Press*] (SAG) .... FruitL
Fruit of the Loom, Inc. [*NYSE symbol*] (SPSG) .... FTL
Fruit of The Loom'A' [*NYSE symbol*] (TTSB) .... FTL
Fruit Pressure Tester .... FPT
Fruit Width [*Botany*] .... FRWID
Fruita, CO [*FM radio station call letters*] .... KEKB
Fruita Elementary School, Fruita, CO [*Library symbol Library of Congress*] (LCLS) .... CoFruFE
Fruita Junior High School, Fruita, CO [*Library symbol Library of Congress*] (LCLS) .... CoFruFJ
Fruita Monument High School, Fruita, CO [*Library symbol Library of Congress*] (LCLS) .... CoFruFM
Fruita Public Library, Fruita, CO [*Library symbol Library of Congress*] (LCLS) .... CoFru
Fruitarian Network (EA) .... FN
Fruithurst, AL [*FM radio station call letters*] .... WCKS
Fruition Project (EA) .... FP

Fruitland, ID [*FM radio station call letters*] (RBYB) .... KWEI-FM
Fruitlet Core Rot [*of pineapple*] .... FCR
Fruits Agro-Industrie Regions Chaudes [*Institut de Recherches sur les Fruits et Agrumes*] [*Database*] .... FAIREC
Fruits or Vegetables [*Freight*] .... FRU VEG
Fruitvale Elementary School, Grand Junction, CO [*Library symbol Library of Congress*] (LCLS) .... CoGjFE
Fruitwood (VRA) .... frutwd
Frunze [*Former USSR Seismograph station code, US Geological Survey*] (SEIS) .... FRU
Frunze [*Former USSR Airport symbol*] (OAG) .... FRU
Frunze [*Former USSR ICAO location identifier*] (ICLI) .... UAFF
Frustillatim [*In Little Pieces*] [*Pharmacy*] (ROG) .... FRUST
Frustrated Multiple Internal Reflectance .... FMIR
Frustrated Total Internal Reflection .... FTIR
Frustrated Total Reflection .... FTR
Frustration, Anxiety, and Tension .... FAT
Frustration Tolerance Index [*Psychology*] .... FTI
Frustum Lifting Lug Kit (MCD) .... FLLK
Fry on Lunacy [*A publication*] (DLA) .... Fry Lun
Fry on Specific Performance of Contracts [*A publication*] (DLA) .... Fry
Fry on Specific Performance of Contracts [*A publication*] (DLA) .... Fry Sp Per
Fry on the Vaccination Acts [*A publication*] (DLA) .... Fry Vac
Frye Utilities for Network [*Frye Computer Systems*] [*Telecommunications*] (PCM) .... FUN
Fryeburg, ME [*Location identifier FAA*] (FAAL) .... FRY
FSB Fiancial Corp. [*Associated Press*] (SAG) .... FSB Fin
FSB Financial Corp. [*NASDAQ symbol*] (SAG) .... FSBF
FSF Financial [*NASDAQ symbol*] (TTSB) .... FFHH
FSF Financial Corp. [*NASDAQ symbol*] (SAG) .... FFHH
FSF Financial Corp. [*Associated Press*] (SAG) .... FSF Fin
FSI International [*NASDAQ symbol*] (TTSB) .... FSII
FSI International, Inc. [*Associated Press*] (SAG) .... FSI Int
FSI International, Inc. [*NASDAQ symbol*] (CTT) .... FSII
FSIS [*Food Safety and Inspection Service*] **Management and Communication System** [*Department of Agriculture*] (GFGA) .... FMCS
FSL [*Forecast Systems Laboratory*] **X-Window AWIPS-Like Prototype for Hydrometeorological Applications** (USDC) .... FX-ALPHA
FSLIC [*Federal Savings and Loan Insurance Corp.*] **Resolution Fund** [*Administ ered by the Federal Deposit Insurance Corp.*] .... FRF
FSS [*Flight Service Station*] **Assumes Flight-Plan Area** [*Aviation*] (FAAC) .... FAFAB
FSS [*Flight Service Station*] **Returns Flight-Plan Area and Service B** [*Aviation*] (FAAC) .... FRFAB
FSS [*Flight Service Station*] **Returns Service B** [*Aviation*] (FAAC) .... FRSB
FTAM [*File Transfer, Access, and Management*] **Protocol Data Unit** [*Telecommunications*] (OSI) .... FPDU
FTC Communications, Inc. [*New York, NY*] (TSSD) .... FTCC
FTI Foodtech International, Inc. [*Vancouver Stock Exchange symbol*] .... FTI
FTM Resources, Inc. [*Vancouver Stock Exchange symbol*] .... FTM
Ftorafur [*Analog of 5-fluorourical deoxyribose*] [*Soviet anticancer drug*] .... FT
Ftorafur, Adriamycin, Cyclophosphamide, Bacille Calmette-Guerin [*Antineoplastic drug regimen*] (DAVI) .... FAC-BCG
Ftorafur, Adriamycin, Cyclophosphamide, Bacille Calmette-Guerin [*Antineoplastic drug regimen*] (DAVI) .... FTOR-MIM-BCG
Ftorafur [*Tegafur*], Adriamycin, Cyclophosphamide, Platinol [*Cisplatin*] [*Antineoplastic drug regimen*] .... FACP
Ftorafur [*Tegafur*], Adriamycin, Mitomycin C [*Antineoplastic drug regimen*] .... FURAM
FTP Software [*Commercial firm Associated Press*] (SAG) .... FTP Sft
FTP Software [*Commercial firm NASDAQ symbol*] (SAG) .... FTPS
Fube [*Japan*] [*Seismograph station code, US Geological Survey*] (SEIS) .... FUB
Fuch's Heterochromic Iridocyclitis [*Ophthalmology*] (DAVI) .... FHI
Fuchsia [*Genotype of Phlox paniculata*] .... F
Fuchsin, Amido Black, and Naphthol Yellow [*Medicine*] (MAE) .... FAN
Fuchu [*Japan ICAO location identifier*] (ICLI) .... RJTZ
Fuchu Air Force Weather Central (CINC) .... FAFWC
Fucus [*Quality of the bottom*] [*Nautical charts*] .... Fu
Fudan Museum Foundation (EA) .... FMF
Fudger Medical Library, Toronto General Hospital, Ontario [*Library symbol National Library of Canada*] (NLC) .... OTGH
Fueggetlen Kisgazda-, Foeldmunkas- es Polgari Part [*Independent Smallholders' Party*] [*Hungary Political party*] (EY) .... FKgP
Fueggetlen Kisgazda Part [*Independent Smallholders' Party*] [*Hungary*] (PPE) .... FKP
Fuego [*Guatemala*] [*Seismograph station code, US Geological Survey*] (SEIS) .... FGO
Fuehrer der Luft [*Air liaison officer with Navy*] [*German military - World War II*] .... FDL
Fuel .... F
Fuel (KSC) .... FL
Fuel (NASA) .... FU
Fuel Additive Blender Unit .... FABU
Fuel Additive Mixture Unit .... FAMU
Fuel Adjustment Clause .... FAC
Fuel Advisory Departure [*Aviation*] (FAAC) .... FAD
Fuel Aerosol Simulation Test [*Nuclear energy*] (NRCH) .... FAST
Fuel Air Explosive (MCD) .... FAE
Fuel Air Explosive .... FAX
Fuel Air Explosive System Helicopter Delivered .... FAESHED
Fuel Air Incendiary Concussion Bomb (MCD) .... FAI
Fuel and Altitude Control System (DWSG) .... F & ACS
Fuel and Ammunition Resupply Study .... FARS
Fuel and Defueling (MSA) .... F & DF
Fuel and Electricity Survey [*Australia*] .... FES
Fuel and Fuel Additive Registration [*Environmental Protection Agency*] (GFGA) .... FFAR
Fuel and Fuel Additives [*Gasoline*] [*Automotive emissions*] .... F/FA
Fuel and Oil Metering Pump [*Engine design*] .... FOMP
Fuel and Power Industries Committee [*British*] (DCTA) .... FPIC
Fuel and Purchased Power Cost Adjustment .... FPPCA
Fuel and Sensor, Tactical (MCD) .... FAST
Fuel and Sensor Tactical Package (MCD) .... FASTPACK
Fuel and Transportation [*Navy*] .... F & T
Fuel and Transportation [*Navy*] .... FANDT
Fuel and Transportation (IAA) .... FAT
Fuel Assembly (NRCH) .... F/A
Fuel Assembly Stability Test (NRCH) .... FAST
Fuel Availability System (NITA) .... FAS
Fuel Bleed Valve (NASA) .... FBV
Fuel Booster Pump .... FBP
Fuel Building Filter System [*Nuclear energy*] (NRCH) .... FBFS
Fuel Building Ventilation [*Nuclear energy*] (NRCH) .... FBV
Fuel Capsule [*or Cell*] **Assembly** (MCD) .... FCA
Fuel Cell (KSC) .... FC
Fuel Cell (KSC) .... FCL
Fuel Cell Association (EA) .... FCA
Fuel Cell Battery .... FCB
Fuel Cell Catalyst .... FCC
Fuel Cell Module .... FCM
Fuel Cell Power Plant .... FCP
Fuel Cell Power Plant System (KSC) .... FCPPS
Fuel Cell Power System [*or Subsystem*] .... FCPS
Fuel Cell Servicing System (MCD) .... FCSS
Fuel Cell Test (MCD) .... FCT
Fuel Cell Test Facility (MCD) .... FCTF
Fuel Cells Display (SAA) .... FCD
Fuel Charge Kit .... FCK
Fuel Cladding Mechanical Interaction [*Nuclear energy*] (NUCP) .... FCMI
Fuel Cladding Transient Tester [*Nuclear energy*] (NRCH) .... FCTT
Fuel Composition Sensor [*Automotive engineering*] .... FCS
Fuel Computer System (MCD) .... FCS
Fuel Consuming Motor Vehicle .... FCMV
Fuel Consumption Projection (SSD) .... FCP
Fuel Consumption Unit (NATG) .... FCU
Fuel Contents Gauge (MSA) .... FCG
Fuel Control Computer .... FCC
Fuel Control Diaphragm Assembly .... FCDA
Fuel Controller (DAS) .... FC
Fuel Coolant Interaction [*Nuclear energy*] (NRCH) .... FCI
Fuel Core Reserve [*Nuclear energy*] .... FCR
Fuel Cut Defenser [*Automotive engineering*] .... FCD
Fuel Cycle (NRCH) .... FC
Fuel Cycle Facility [*Nuclear energy*] .... FCF
Fuel Deceleration Valve [*Automotive engineering*] .... FDV
Fuel Desulphurization, Inc. .... FDI
Fuel Dragster [*Class of racing cars*] .... FD
Fuel Economist (1925-1936) [*A publication*] .... Fuel Econ 1925-1936
Fuel Economy [*In automobile model name "Honda Civic 1300 FE"*] .... FE
Fuel Efficiency Automobile Test (PS) .... FEAT
Fuel Element Department (SAA) .... FED
Fuel Element Failure Propagation [*Nuclear energy*] .... FEFP
Fuel Element Failure Propagation Loop [*Nuclear energy*] (NRCH) .... FEFPL
Fuel Element Rupture Detection [*Nuclear energy*] (NRCH) .... FERD
Fuel Energy Ratio [*Petroleum refining*] .... FER
Fuel Equivalent Unit .... FEU
Fuel Examination Facility [*Nuclear energy*] (NRCH) .... FEF
Fuel Fabrication Plant [*Nuclear energy*] (NRCH) .... FFP
Fuel Failure Detection .... FFD
Fuel Failure Fraction [*Nuclear energy*] (NRCH) .... FFF
Fuel Failure Mock-Up [*Nuclear energy*] .... FFM
Fuel Fill Line (AAG) .... FFL
Fuel Fill to Fuel Prefab (AAG) .... FFP
Fuel Fill to Missile [*Aerospace*] (AAG) .... FFM
Fuel Filter [*Automotive engineering*] .... F/FILT
Fuel Filtration-Additive Unit .... FAV
Fuel Flow (AAG) .... FF
Fuel Flow Indicator .... FFI
Fuel Flow Totalizer [*Aerospace*] (AAG) .... FF/TOT
Fuel Flow Totalizer [*Aerospace*] .... FFT
Fuel Gage [*Automotive engineering*] .... F/GA
Fuel Gage (SAA) .... FG
Fuel Gas .... FG
Fuel Gas Desulfurization .... FGD
Fuel Handling and Radioactive Maintenance (NRCH) .... FH & RM
Fuel Handling and Radioactive Maintenance (IAA) .... FHARM
Fuel Handling Procedure [*Nuclear energy*] (NRCH) .... FHP
Fuel High Pressure (NASA) .... FHP
Fuel Indicator Reading .... FIR
Fuel Injection [*Automotive engineering*] .... F/INJ
Fuel Injection [*Automotive engineering*] .... FI
Fuel Injection Equipment [*Diesel engines*] .... FIE
Fuel Injection Line (MSA) .... FIL
Fuel Injection Pressure (KSC) .... FIP
Fuel Injection Pump (MSA) .... FIP
Fuel Injection System [*Automotive engineering*] .... FIS
Fuel Injector Driver [*Automotive engineering*] .... FID
Fuel Insolation Valves (MCD) .... FIV
Fuel Inspection and Sampling Cell [*Nuclear energy*] (NRCH) .... FISC
Fuel Line .... FLN

Fuel Loading Data [*Nuclear energy*] (NRCH)	FLD
Fuel Low Level Sensor (IAA)	FLLS
Fuel Lube Oil	FLO
Fuel Maintenance Panel (AAG)	FMP
Fuel Management Computer (NG)	FMC
Fuel Manufacturing Facility	FMF
Fuel Melt Fraction [*Nuclear energy*] (NRCH)	FMF
Fuel Oil	FO
Fuel, Oil, and Lubricants (PDAA)	FOL
Fuel Oil and Water Heater Manufacturers Association (EA)	FOWHM
Fuel Oil Barge [*Self-propelled*] [*Navy symbol*]	YO
Fuel Oil Barge [*Non-self-propelled*] [*Navy symbol*]	YON
Fuel Oil Cooler	FOC
Fuel Oil Equivalent (BARN)	FOE
Fuel Oil Equivalent Barrel	FOEB
Fuel Oil Pump (MSA)	FOP
Fuel Oil Quick Closing Valve (NVT)	FOQCV
Fuel Oil Return (AAG)	FOR
Fuel Oil Route Delivery and Control System [*Computer-based system*]	FORDACS
Fuel Oil Tank (MSA)	FOT
Fuel Oil Transfer	FOT
Fuel on Board [*Aviation*]	FOB
Fuel Packaging Facility [*Nuclear energy*]	FPF
Fuel Performance Test Facility (IAA)	FPTF
Fuel (Petroleum) (DA)	FP
Fuel Pool Cooling [*Nuclear energy*] (NRCH)	FPC
Fuel Pool Cooling and Cleanup [*Nuclear energy*] (NRCH)	FPCC
Fuel Pool Cooling and Cleanup System [*Nuclear energy*] (NRCH)	FPCCS
Fuel Pool Cooling System [*Nuclear energy*] (IEEE)	FPCS
Fuel Pool Exhaust Blower [*Nuclear energy*] (NRCH)	FPEB
Fuel Pool Pump Ventilation System [*Nuclear energy*] (NRCH)	FPPVS
Fuel Pool Water Treatment [*Nuclear energy*] (NRCH)	FPWT
Fuel Preburner (KSC)	FPB
Fuel Preburner and Oxidizer Valve (NASA)	FPBOV
Fuel Preburner and Oxidizer Valve (MCD)	FPOV
Fuel Pressure (NASA)	FP
Fuel Pressure Indicator	FPI
Fuel Pressure Out	FPO
Fuel Pump Control Unit (MCD)	FPCU
Fuel Pump Gasket [*Automotive engineering*]	FP
Fuel Pump Monitor [*Automotive engineering*]	FPM
Fuel Pump Relay [*Automotive engineering*]	FPR
Fuel Purification Unit [*Aerospace*] (AAG)	FPU
Fuel Quantity Indicating System [*Aviation*]	FQIS
Fuel Quantity Indicator	FQI
Fuel Receiving Air Blowers [*Nuclear energy*] (NRCH)	FRAB
Fuel Receiving Air Filters [*Nuclear energy*] (NRCH)	FRAF
Fuel Receiving and Storage Facility [*Nuclear energy*] (NRCH)	FRSF
Fuel Receiving Station [*Nuclear energy*] (NRCH)	FRS
Fuel Remaining [*Aviation*]	FR
Fuel Reprocessing Facility [*Nuclear energy*] (NRCH)	FRF
Fuel Reprocessing Plant [*Nuclear energy*] (NRCH)	FRP
Fuel Restoration Project	FRP
Fuel Rod Analysis Program [*Nuclear energy*] (NRCH)	FRAP
Fuel Rod Analysis Program - Steady-State [*Nuclear energy*] (NRCH)	FRAP-S
Fuel Rod Analysis Program - Transient [*Nuclear energy*] (NRCH)	FRAP-T
Fuel Saver [*Automotive engineering*]	FS
Fuel Savings Advisory System	FSAS
Fuel Savings Advisory System / Inertial Navigation System [*Air Force*]	FSAS/INS
Fuel Scheduling Computer (MCD)	FSC
Fuel Service Nozzle (MSA)	FSN
Fuel Storage Area (AAG)	FSA
Fuel Storage Basin [*Nuclear energy*]	FSB
Fuel Storage Cable Spread [*Nuclear energy*] (NRCH)	FSCS
Fuel Storage Control Room [*Nuclear energy*] (NRCH)	FSCR
Fuel Storage Exhaust Blower [*Nuclear energy*] (NRCH)	FSEB
Fuel Storage Facility [*Nuclear energy*] (NRCH)	FSF
Fuel Storage Personnel Area [*Nuclear energy*] (NRCH)	FSPA
Fuel Storage Pool [*Nuclear energy*] (NRCH)	FSP
Fuel Storage Processing Building [*Nuclear energy*] (NRCH)	FSPB
Fuel Storage Subsystem (MCD)	FS
Fuel Supply Depot [*Military*]	FSD
Fuel Supply Exhausted [*Aviation*] (FAAC)	FEXHA
Fuel Supply Module (MCD)	FSM
Fuel Supply Office [*Military*]	FSO
Fuel Supply Unknown [*Aviation*] (FAAC)	FENKN
Fuel Supply Until [*Aviation*] (FAAC)	FENTL
Fuel System Icing Inhibitor [*Aviation*] (AFIT)	FSII
Fuel System Supply Point	FSSP
Fuel Systems Analysis Report (SAA)	FSAR
Fuel Systems Capability (MCD)	FSC
Fuel Tank	FTK
Fuel Tank Helicopter	FTH
Fuel Tanking [*Aerospace*] (AAG)	FT
Fuel Tanking Panel [*Aerospace*] (AAG)	FTP
Fuel Tech [*NASDAQ symbol*] (SAG)	FTEKF
Fuel Tech [*Commercial firm Associated Press*] (SAG)	FuelTch
Fuel Tech N.V. [*NASDAQ symbol*] (TTSB)	FTEKF
Fuel Terms (DS)	FT
Fuel to Oxidizer [*Ratio*]	F/O
Fuel Transfer and Storage Assembly [*Nuclear energy*] (NRCH)	FT & SA
Fuel Transfer Canal [*Nuclear energy*] (NRCH)	FTC
Fuel Transfer Pool [*Nuclear energy*] (NRCH)	FTP

Fuel Transfer Port [*Nuclear energy*] (NRCH)	FTP
Fuel Transfer Pump (MSA)	FTP
Fuel Transfer System [*Nuclear energy*] (NRCH)	FTS
Fuel Transfer Tool	FTT
Fuel Transfer Unit [*NASA*] (KSC)	FTU
Fuel Treatment Apparatus	FTA
Fuel Use Act	FUA
Fuel Users Emergency Line [*Pennsylvania*]	FUEL
Fuel Valve (AAG)	FV
Fuel Vapor Detector	FVD
Fuel Wasting (MCD)	FW
Fuel-Air [*Ratio*]	F/A
Fuel-Air Cluster Bomb Unit [*Military*] (VNW)	FA-CBU
Fuel-Bound Nitrogen	FBN
Fuel-Critical, Unspecified Area	FCUA
Fueled Prototype Mock-Up System	FPMS
Fuel-Efficient Oil	FEO
Fueler [*Aircraft designation*]	F
Fuel-Fusing Option [*Nuclear energy*] (GFGA)	FUFO
Fuel-Handling and Preparation Cell [*Nuclear energy*] (NRCH)	FHPC
Fuel-Handling Building [*Nuclear energy*] (NRCH)	FHB
Fuel-Handling Building Ventilation Isolation [*Nuclear energy*] (NRCH)	FHBVI
Fuel-Handling Cell [*Nuclear energy*] (NRCH)	FHC
Fuel-Handling Equipment [*Nuclear energy*] (NRCH)	FHE
Fuel-Handling Equipment System [*Nuclear energy*] (NRCH)	FHES
Fuel-Handling System [*Nuclear energy*] (NRCH)	FHS
Fueling	FLNG
Fueling Barge [*Navy symbol Obsolete*]	YCD
Fueling-at-Sea [*Navy*] (MSA)	FAS
Fuel-Jet (DA)	FJ
Fuel-Monitoring System [*Cheshire County Council*] [*Software package*] (NCC)	FMS
Fuel-Oxygen Scrap (PDAA)	FOS
Fuels and Materials Examination Facility [*Department of Energy*]	FMEF
Fuels and Mining Practice Division [*Department of Mines and Technical Surveys*] [*Canada*]	FMP
Fuels Automated Management System [*Air Force*] (GFGA)	FAMS
Fuels Control Center (AFIT)	FCC
Fuels Management Officer [*Air Force*] (AFIT)	FMO
Fuels Open Test Assembly [*Nuclear energy*] (NRCH)	FOTA
Fuels Operating Instruction (AFIT)	FOI
Fuels Research Council [*Defunct*]	FRC
Fuels Research Laboratory [*MIT*] (MCD)	FRL
Fuel-Specific Nitrogen Oxide Emissions [*Air pollution*]	FSNOx
Fuerstenfeldbruck [*Germany ICAO location identifier*] (ICLI)	EDSF
Fuerstenfeldbruck [*Germany ICAO location identifier*] (ICLI)	EDZF
Fuerstenfeldbruck [*Germany*] [*Seismograph station code, US Geological Survey*] (SEIS)	FUR
Fuerstenzell Bei Passau [*Germany ICAO location identifier*] (ICLI)	EDMF
Fuerte Gral Roca [*Argentina ICAO location identifier*] (ICLI)	SAHR
Fuerte Sherman [*Panama*] [*ICAO location identifier*] (ICLI)	MPFS
Fuerteventura [*Canary Islands*] [*Airport symbol*] (OAG)	FUE
Fuerth [*Germany ICAO location identifier*] (ICLI)	EDEW
Fuerza Aerea Argentina [*ICAO designator*] (FAAC)	FAG
Fuerza Aerea del Peru [*ICAO designator*] (FAAC)	FPR
Fuerza de Guerrilleros de los Pobres [*Guerrilla group*] [*Guatemala*] (EY)	FGP
Fuerza Democratica Nicaraguense [*Nicaraguan Democratic Force*] (PD)	FDN
Fuerza Popular Organizada [*Organized Popular Force*] [*Guatemala*] [*Political party*] (PPW)	FPO
Fuerza Republicana [*Argentina Political party*] (EY)	FR
Fuerzas Aereas Espanolas [*Spain ICAO designator*] (FAAC)	AME
Fuerzas Armadas Anticomunistas [*Anti-Communist Armed Forces*] [*Nicaragua*] (PD)	FARAC
Fuerzas Armadas de Liberacio [*Argentina*]	FAL
Fuerzas Armadas de Liberacion Nacional [*Armed Forces of National Liberation*] [*Venezuela*] (PD)	FALN
Fuerzas Armadas de Liberacion Nacional Puertorriquena [*Armed Forces of Puerto Rican National Liberation*] (EA)	FALN
Fuerzas Armadas de Resistencia Nacional [*Armed Forces of National Resistance*] [*El Salvador*] (PD)	FARN
Fuerzas Armadas Democraticas [*Democratic Armed Forces*] [*Nicaragua*] (PD)	FAD
Fuerzas Armadas Peronistas [*Argentina*]	FAP
Fuerzas Armadas Rebeldes [*Rebel Armed Forces*] [*Guatemala*] (PD)	FAR
Fuerzas Armadas Revolucionarias Nicaraguenses [*Nicaraguan Armed Revolutionary Forces*] (PD)	FARN
Fuerzas de Accion Armada [*Armed Action Forces*] [*Guatemala*] (PD)	FADA
Fuerzas Populares de Liberacion Farabundo Marti [*Farabundo Marti Popular Liberation Forces*] [*El Salvador*] (PD)	FPL
Fuerzas Populares Revolucionarias [*Guerrilla forces*] [*Honduras*] (EY)	FRP
Fuerzas Populares Revolucionarias Lorenzo Zelaya [*Lorenzo Zelaya Popular Revolutionary Forces*] [*Honduras*] [*Political party*] (EY)	FPR
Fuerzas Rebeldes y Populares Lautaro [*Chile*] [*Political party*] (EY)	FRPL
Fuerzas Revolucionarias Armadas Populares [*People's Revolutionary Armed Forces*] [*Mexico*] (PD)	FRAP
Fugacity [*Thermodynamics*]	f
Fugitive Assessment Sampling Train [*Environmental Protection Agency*] (GFGA)	FAST
Fugitive Emissions [*Environmental Protection Agency*] (GFGA)	FE
Fugitive Emissions Information System [*Environmental Protection Agency*] (GFGA)	FEIS
Fugitive Information Data Organizer [*Database*]	FIDO
Fugitive Intercept Net Deployment [*Philadelphia police program*]	FIND
Fugitive Investigative Strike Team [*Operation conducted jointly by the US Marshals Service and local police*]	FIST

Fugitive Other Authorities [*FBI standardized term*] ... FOA
Fuiloro [*East Timor*] [*ICAO location identifier*] (ICLI) ... WPFL
Fuisz Technologies [*Associated Press*] (SAG) ... FuiszT
Fuisz Technologies [*NASDAQ symbol*] (SAG) ... FUSE
Fuisz Technologies [*NASDAQ symbol*] (TTSB) ... FUSE
Fujairah Aviation Centre [*United Arab Emirates*] [*ICAO designator*] (FAAC) ... FUJ
Fujeirah/International [*United Arab Emirates*] [*ICAO location identifier*] (ICLI) ... OMFJ
Fuji Heavy Industries Ltd. [*Japan ICAO aircraft manufacturer identifier*] (ICAO) ... FH
Fuji International Speedway Co. [*Automobile racing*] ... FISCO
Fuji Juken, Ogisaka, Kawabe, Asahi Juken and Sueno Kosan [*Group of Japanese development companies located in Osaka, Japan*] (ECON) ... FOCAS
Fuji Photo Film ADR [*NASDAQ symbol*] (TTSB) ... FUJIY
Fuji Photo Film Co. Ltd. [*NASDAQ symbol*] (NQ) ... FUJI
Fuji Photo Film Co. Ltd. [*Associated Press*] (SAG) ... FujiPh
Fujian Airlines [*China*] [*FAA designator*] (FAAC) ... CFJ
Fujinami Sarcoma Virus ... FSV
Fujisawa Pharmaceutical Co. [*Japan*] [*Research code symbol*] ... FK
Fujisawa Pharmaceutical Co. [*Japan*] [*Research code symbol*] ... NF
Fujisawa Pharmaceutical Co. [*Japan*] [*Research code symbol*] ... NTA
Fujitsu [*Japan*] (NITA) ... FUJ
Fujitsu Access and Transport System [*Computer science*] (ACRL) ... FACTR
Fujitsu America, Inc. [*Hillsboro, OR*] ... FAI
Fujitsu Network Architecture [*Fujitsu Ltd.*] [*Japan*] ... FNA
Fukien Province [*China, Mainland*] [*MARC geographic area code Library of Congress*] (LCCP) ... a-cc-fu
Fukue [*Japan*] [*Seismograph station code, US Geological Survey*] (SEIS) ... FKJ
Fukue [*Japan*] [*Airport symbol*] (OAG) ... FUJ
Fukue [*Japan ICAO location identifier*] (ICLI) ... RJFE
Fukui [*Japan*] [*Seismograph station code, US Geological Survey*] (SEIS) ... FUK
Fukui [*Japan ICAO location identifier*] (ICLI) ... RJNF
Fukui University, Fukui-shi, Japan [*Library symbol Library of Congress*] (LCLS) ... JFuU
Fukuoka [*Japan*] [*Seismograph station code, US Geological Survey*] (SEIS) ... FKK
Fukuoka [*Japan*] [*Airport symbol*] (OAG) ... FUK
Fukuoka [*Japan ICAO location identifier*] (ICLI) ... RJDG
Fukuoka [*Japan ICAO location identifier*] (ICLI) ... RJFF
Fukuoka Occupation Force ... FOF
Fukushima [*Japan*] [*Seismograph station code, US Geological Survey*] (SEIS) ... FKS
Fukuyama Type Congenital Muscular Dystrophy [*Medicine*] (DMAA) ... FCMD
Fulacunda [*Guinea-Bissau*] [*ICAO location identifier*] (ICLI) ... GGFU
Fulbeck's Parallel [*A publication*] (DLA) ... Fulb Par
Fulbeck's Study of the Law [*A publication*] (DLA) ... Fulb St Law
Fulbright Alumni Association [*Later, Fulbright Association*] (EAIO) ... FAA
Fulbright Association (EAIO) ... FA
Fulbright Association of Alumni of International Educational and Cultural Exchange (EA) ... FAAIECE
Fulbright Scholarship ... FSCH
Fulcrum (MSA) ... FUL
Fulcrum Development Ltd. [*Vancouver Stock Exchange symbol*] ... FMD
Fulcrum Tech, Inc. [*NASDAQ symbol*] (SAG) ... FULC
Fulcrum Tech, Inc. [*Associated Press*] (SAG) ... Fulcrum
Fulcrum Technologies [*NASDAQ symbol*] (TTSB) ... FULCF
Fulcrum, Weight, Power ... FWP
Fulda [*Germany ICAO location identifier*] (ICLI) ... EDEX
Fulda Elementary School, Fulda, MN [*Library symbol*] [*Library of Congress*] (LCLS) ... MnFuES
Fulda Junior-Senior High School, Fulda, MN [*Library symbol*] [*Library of Congress*] (LCLS) ... MnFuJSH
Fulda Public Library, Fulda, MN [*Library symbol*] [*Library of Congress*] (LCLS) ... MnFu
Fuldatal [*Germany ICAO location identifier*] (ICLI) ... EDFX
Fulfillment Management Association (EA) ... FMA
Fulguration [*Medicine*] (DAVI) ... fulg
Full ... F
Full Above the Eaves (ROG) ... FV
Full Access and Rights to Education Coalition ... FARE
Full Action ... FA
Full Adder [*Computer science*] ... FA
Full American Plan [*Hotel room rate*] ... FAP
Full Ammo [*Navy*] (DOMA) ... FAMMO
Full Analog Video ... FAV
Full and Change (ADA) ... F & C
Full and Open Competition [*Government contracting*] ... FOC
Full and Soft [*Dietetics*] ... FS
Full Aperture [*Photography*] (NTCM) ... FA
Full Arc (NRCH) ... FA
Full Army Mobilization War Reserves (AABC) ... FAM
Full Authority Digital Engine Control ... FADEC
Full Authority Electronic Control (MCD) ... FAEC
Full Bench ... FB
Full Bench Decisions [*India*] [*A publication*] (DLA) ... FBI
Full Bench Rulings [*Bengal, India*] [*A publication*] (DLA) ... FBR
Full Bench Rulings [*Calcutta*] [*A publication*] (DLA) ... Suth Sp N
Full Bench Rulings, Edited by Goodeve and Woodman [*Bengal*] [*A publication*] (DLA) ... Good & Wood
Full Bench Rulings, High Court [*Fort William, Bengal*] [*A publication*] (DLA) ... Ben FB
Full Bench Rulings, Northwest Provinces [*India*] [*A publication*] (DLA) ... FBRNWP
Full Berth Terms [*Shipping*] ... FBT
Full Bibliographic Record (NITA) ... FBR
Full Blood Count [*Medicine*] (ADA) ... FBC
Full Blood Examination [*Medicine*] (MAE) ... FBE
Full Boiling-Range [*Fuel technology*] (PDAA) ... FBR
Full Boiling-Range Fuel (PDAA) ... FBRE
Full Business Day (TEL) ... FBD
Full Career Seaman Officer [*Navy British*] ... FCSO
Full Charge [*Accounting*] ... FC
Full Circle Associates (EA) ... FCA
Full Cleanliness Training ... FCT
Full Cold Rolled [*Steel*] ... FCR
Full Commission ... F Comm
Full Common Intermediate Format (ACRL) ... FCIF
Full Configuration-Interaction [*Quantum chemistry*] (MCD) ... FCI
Full Container Load [*Shipping*] ... FCL
Full Corner [*Philately*] ... FC
Full Court (ADA) ... FC
Full Court Judgments [*Ghana*] [*A publication*] (DLA) ... FC
Full Court Judgments [*1922*] [*Ghana*] [*A publication*] (DLA) ... FC '22
Full Court Judgments [*1920-21*] [*Ghana*] [*A publication*] (DLA) ... FC '20-1
Full Couterpoise Procedure [*Physical chemistry*] ... FCP
Full Cycle Left (SAA) ... FCL
Full Cycling File Organization ... FCFO
Full Data Block (KSC) ... FDB
Full Descriptive Method ... FDM
Full Digital Arts Display [*FAA*] (TAG) ... FDAD
Full Dog Point (MSA) ... FDP
Full Dress [*Colloquial reference to formal dress*] ... FD
Full Duplex [*Telecommunications*] ... FD
Full Duplex [*Computer science*] (TNIG) ... FDUX
Full Duplex [*Telecommunications*] ... FDX
Full Duplex Teletype ... FDT
Full Duplex VOCODER [*Voice Coder*] ... FDV
Full Duration Half Maximum [*Mathematics*] ... FDHM
Full Employment [*Economics*] ... FN
Full Employment Act [*1946*] (OICC) ... FEA
Full Employment Action Council [*Defunct*] (EA) ... FEAC
Full Employment and National Purposes Budget (OICC) ... FENPB
Full Employment and Production Program (OICC) ... FEPP
Full Employment League ... FEL
Full Empty (NASA) ... F/E
Full Energy Peak Efficiency [*Nuclear science*] (OA) ... FEPE
Full Extraocular Motion [*or Movement*] [*Ophthalmology*] (DAVI) ... FEOM
Full Face [*Photography*] ... FF
Full Face Mask [*Military*] (CAAL) ... FFM
Full Faith and Credit [*Finance*] ... FFC
Full Fat Soy Flour (OA) ... FFSF
Full Field ... FF
Full Field Investigation (NRCH) ... FFI
Full Flight Regime Auto Throttle System (ADA) ... FFRATS
Full Floating [*Automotive engineering*] ... FF
Full Free Triple [*Lift truck*] ... FFT
Full Freight Allowed ... FFA
Full Frontal Area Impact Switch (MCD) ... FFAIS
Full Function Node (MHDB) ... FFN
Full Funding Grant Agreement (AAGC) ... FFGA
Full Funding Limit (AAGC) ... FFL
Full Fuzing Option [*Air Force*] ... FUFO
Full General-Emergency Striking Force Exercise [*Navy*] (NVT) ... FLTSTRIKEX
Full Gilt [*Bookbinding*] (ADA) ... FG
Full Gospel Business Men's Fellowship International (EA) ... FGBMFI
Full Gospel Evangelistic Association (EA) ... FGEA
Full Gospel Student Fellowship (EA) ... FGSF
Full Hard (MSA) ... FH
Full House Resorts [*NASDAQ symbol*] (SAG) ... FHRI
Full House Resorts [*Associated Press*] (SAG) ... FullHs
Full House Resorts [*Associated Press*] (SAG) ... FullHse
Full House Resorts Wrrt [*NASDAQ symbol*] (TTSB) ... FHRIW
Full Indicator Movement (MSA) ... FIM
Full Indicator Reading ... FIR
Full Inspection Report (MCD) ... FIR
Full Integral Simulation Test [*Nuclear energy*] (NRCH) ... FIST
Full Integrity Instrument Landing System ... FIILS
Full Interest Admitted ... FIA
Full Joint Range of Movement [*Orthopedics*] ... FJRM
Full Length Emergency Cooling Heat Transfer [*Nuclear energy*] (NRCH) ... FLECHT
Full Level Light Aircraft System Hardware (MCD) ... FLLASH
Full Lift (KSC) ... FL
Full Liquid [*Medicine*] ... FL
Full Load [*Displacement*] ... F
Full Load (KSC) ... F/L
Full Load ... FLLD
Full Load Amperes (MSA) ... FLA
Full Load Frame Time [*Term used in SAGE operations*] ... FLFT
Full Load Motor Current [*Kraus & Naimer Microelectronics*] ... FLMC
Full Marching Order [*British military*] (DMA) ... FMO
Full Marching Pack [*Military*] ... FMP
Full Maternal Behavior [*Physiology*] ... FMB
Full Matrix Least Square (IAA) ... FMLS
Full Metal Case [*Ammunition*] (DICI) ... FMC
Full Metal Jacket [*Ammunition*] (DICI) ... FMJ
Full Metal Jacket Boat Tail [*Weaponry*] [*Military*] (INF) ... FMJBT
Full Mission Engineering Simulator (KSC) ... FMES
Full Mission Fighter Simulator [*Air Force*] (PDAA) ... FMFS
Full Moon [*Astronomy*] (ROG) ... F MN
Full Moon [*Astronomy*] ... FM
Full Motion Video (BARN) ... FMV

Full Mouth Extraction [*Dentistry*] ... FME
Full Mouth Series [*Dentistry*] ... FMS
Full Mouth X-Ray [*Dentistry*] ... FMX
Full Normal Plot [*Computer science*] ... FUNOP
Full Octave Filter ... FOF
Full of Brooklyns [*Coined by baseball broadcaster Red Barber, initialism refers to bases loaded with Brooklyn Dodgers*] [*Obsolete*] ... FOB
Full Operational Capability (NASA) ... FOC
Full Operational Capability Program [*Navy*] (NVT) ... FOC
Full Operational Status ... FOS
Full Organ [*Music*] ... F ORG
Full Organ [*Music*] ... FO
Full Out [*Typesetting*] ... FO
Full Out Rye Terms [*Grain trade*] ... FORT
Full Out Terms [*Business term British*] (ROG) ... F/O
Full Outpatient Rate (AFM) ... FOPR
Full Overlap Slotted Container [*Packaging*] ... FOSC
Full Page Display (BYTE) ... FPD
Full Paid [*Stock exchange term*] (SPSG) ... FPD
Full Pay [*Military British*] (ROG) ... FP
Full Pension [*Hotel rate*] ... FP
Full Performance Level [*Aviation*] (FAAC) ... FPL
Full Period ... FP
Full Period Termination (CAAL) ... FPT
Full Power ... FP
Full Power Days [*Nuclear energy*] (NRCH) ... FPD
Full Power Frequency ... FPF
Full Power Hours [*Nuclear energy*] (DEN) ... FPH
Full Power Level [*NASA*] (NASA) ... FPL
Full Power Load (NASA) ... FPL
Full Power Response ... FPR
Full Power Trial ... FPT
Full Premium If Lost [*Insurance*] (MHDW) ... FPIL
Full Pressure Suit [*Aerospace*] ... FPS
Full Pressure Suit Training Unit [*Military*] ... FPSTU
Full Price (ADA) ... FP
Full Propellant Requirement ... FPR
Full Range (MCD) ... FR
Full Range Joint Movement [*Occupational therapy*] ... FRJM
Full Range of Motion [*Orthopedics*] (DAVI) ... FRM
Full Range of Motion [*or Movement*] [*Occupational therapy*] ... FROM
Full Recovery Time [*Medicine*] ... FRT
Full Reimbursement Rate (AFM) ... FRR
Full Remaining Radiation Service [*Unit*] [*Military*] ... FRRS
Full Scale [*Analog computers*] ... FS
Full Scale ... FSC
Full Screen Editor [*Computer science*] (IAA) ... FSE
Full Service History [*Automotive retailing*] ... FSH
Full Service Network [*Television broadcasting*] ... FSN
Full Shear Energy Absorption (PDAA) ... FSEA
Full Shot [*Photography*] (NTCM) ... FS
Full Size (MSA) ... FS
Full Stop (ADA) ... FS
Full Stop Landing [*Aviation*] ... FSL
Full Straps Roosevelt Dime Club (EA) ... FSRDC
Full Sun ... FS
Full Supply Level (ADA) ... FSL
Full Systems Capable [*Military*] (CAAL) ... FSC
Full Systems Ready (DNAB) ... FSR
Full Technological Certificate [*British*] ... FTC
Full Term [*Pregnancy*] [*Medicine*] ... FT
Full Term Born Dead [*Medicine*] ... FTBD
Full Term License [*For nuclear power plant*] (NRCH) ... FTL
Full Term Living Birth [*Medicine*] (MAE) ... FTLB
Full Term Normal Delivery [*Medicine*] ... FTND
Full Term Operating License (NRCH) ... FTOL
Full Text Retrieval (NITA) ... FTR
Full Thickness Graft [*Medicine*] ... FTG
Full Thickness Skin Graft [*Medicine*] (DMAA) ... FTSG
Full Throttle Position (KSC) ... FTP
Full Tilt Container (DCTA) ... FT
Full Time [*Employment, education*] ... FT
Full Time Equivalent (EERA) ... FTE
Full to Bursting [*Reply to question, "Have you had enough to eat"*] ... FTB
Full Transport Pack [*Military*] ... FTP
Full Travel Membrane (PDAA) ... FTM
Full Truck Loads ... FTL
Full Utilization of Rural Program Opportunities (EA) ... FURPO
Full Voltage (MSA) ... FV
Full Voltage Non-Reversing Motor (DICI) ... FVNR
Full Wave ... FW
Full Weight (IAA) ... FW
Full Weight Bearing [*Medicine*] ... FWB
Full Well Capacity (MCD) ... FWC
Full Width at Half Maximum [*Spectroscopy*] ... FWHM
Full Width at Half Peak [*Spectroscopy*] (DEN) ... FWHP
Full Width at Tenth Maximum (IEEE) ... FWTM
Full Width at Zero Intensity [*Spectroscopy*] ... FWZI
Full Width Attack Mine ... FWAM
Full Year ... FY
Full Year Equivalent (EERA) ... FYE
Fullam Family Organization (EA) ... FFO
Full-Aperture Kicker [*Synchrotron*] ... FAK
Fullback [*Football*] ... FB
Full-Boiling Range High-Sensitivity Unleaded [*Motor fuel*] ... FBRSU
Full-Boiling Range Unleaded [*Motor fuel*] ... FBRU
Full-Coverage Area [*Radio and TV*] ... FCA
Full-Coverage Film Cooling ... FCFC
Full-Duplex Switched Ethernet (CDE) ... FDSE
Fulleborn [*Papua New Guinea*] [*Airport symbol*] (OAG) ... FUB
Fuller [*H.B.*] **Co.** [*NASDAQ symbol*] (NQ) ... FULL
Fuller [*H. B.*] **Co.** [*Associated Press*] (SAG) ... FulrHB
Fuller (HB) [*NASDAQ symbol*] (TTSB) ... FULL
Fuller, R. H., Los Angeles CA [*STAC*] ... FRH
Fuller Theological Seminary, Pasadena, CA [*OCLC symbol*] (OCLC) ... CFT
Fuller Theological Seminary, Pasadena, CA [*Library symbol Library of Congress*] (LCLS) ... CPFT
Fuller's Church History [*A publication*] (DLA) ... Full Ch Hist
Fuller's Reports [*59-105 Michigan*] [*A publication*] (DLA) ... Fuller
Fuller's Reports [*59-105 Michigan*] [*A publication*] (DLA) ... Fuller (Mich)
Fullerton [*California*] [*Airport symbol*] (OAG) ... FUL
Fullerton, CA [*Location identifier FAA*] (FAAL) ... FUL
Fullerton Junior College [*Later, Fullerton College*] [*California*] ... FJC
Fullerton Junior College, Fullerton, CA [*Library symbol Library of Congress*] (LCLS) ... CFIJ
Fullerton Junior College Library, Fullerton, CA [*OCLC symbol*] (OCLC) ... CFU
Fullerton Language Test for Adolescents (DAVI) ... FLTA
Fullerton Public Library, Fullerton, CA [*Library symbol Library of Congress*] (LCLS) ... CFI
Full-Face Fire-Fighters' Mask (MCD) ... FFFFM
Full-Fashioned ... FF
Full-Frequency Range Recording ... FFRR
Full-Frequency Stereophonic Sound (DEN) ... FFSS
Full-Information Maximum Likelihood [*Econometrics*] ... FIML
Full-Matrix Least Squares [*Statistics*] (PDAA) ... FMLS
Full-Page Composition System [*Computer science*] ... FPCS
Full-Page Phototypesetting System (DGA) ... FPPS
Full-Potential Linear Augmented Plane Wave [*Physical chemistry*] ... FLAPW
Fullrack System ... FS
Full-Range Picture Vocabulary Test [*Intelligence test*] ... FRPV
Full-Range Picture Vocabulary Test [*Education*] ... FRPVT
Full-Rate [*Telegrams and cables*] ... FR
Full-Rate Production (DOMA) ... FRP
Full-Resolution Basic Image Data Record [*RADAR mapping*] ... F-BIDR
Full-Round Nose [*Diamond drilling*] ... FRN
Fullscale (ABBR) ... FLSCL
Full-Scale [*Intelligence quotient*] [*Psychology*] (DAVI) ... FS
Full-Scale Accuracy (IAA) ... FSA
Full-Scale Aerial [*or Afterburning*] **Target** ... FSAT
Full-Scale Deflection [*Instrumentation*] ... FSD
Full-Scale Development (MCD) ... FSD
Full-Scale Development Model (MCD) ... FSDM
Full-Scale Development Phase (MCD) ... FSDP
Full-Scale Engineering Development (MCD) ... FSED
Full-Scale Hydrodynamic Vehicle (MCD) ... FSHV
Full-Scale Output ... FSO
Full-Scale Production ... FSP
Full-Scale Prototype [*Military*] (CAAL) ... FSP
Full-Scale Range [*Military*] (IAA) ... FSR
Full-Scale Record [*Instrumentation*] ... FSR
Full-Scale Review ... FSR
Full-Scale Section (DNAB) ... FSS
Full-Scale Subsonic Wind Tunnel ... FSSWT
Full-Scale Test Vehicle [*NASA*] ... FSTV
Full-Scale Tunnel [*Aerospace*] ... FST
Full-Scale Unit (KSC) ... FSU
Full-Scale Weapons Delivery [*Military*] ... FSWD
Full-Screen Processing [*Computer science*] ... FSP
Full-State Assumption [*Education*] (AEE) ... FSA
Full-Strength Breast Milk [*Neonatology*] (DAVI) ... FSBM
Full-Term Deliveries, Premature [*Preterm*] **Deliveries, Abortions, and Living Children** [*Gynecology and obstetrics*] (DAVI) ... FPAL
Full-Term Living Female Child [*Obstetrics*] (DAVI) ... FTLFC
Full-Term Living Male Child [*Obstetrics*] (DAVI) ... FTLMC
Full-Term Nursery [*Neonatology*] (DAVI) ... FTN
Fulltext Sources Online [*Information service or system*] (IID) ... FULL
Fulltext Sources Outline [*A publication*] ... FSO
Full-Time Attendance (GFGA) ... FTA
Full-Time Care [*Pet-adoption terminology*] ... FTC
Full-Time Duty (ADA) ... FTD
Full-Time Education ... FTE
Full-Time Employee ... FTE
Full-Time Equivalency Enrollment [*Education*] ... FTEE
Full-Time Equivalent ... FTE
Full-Time Equivalent Software Personnel ... FSP
Full-Time Equivalent Staff (TDOB) ... FTE
Full-Time Equivalent Terminals [*Computer science*] ... FTET
Full-Time Manning (MCD) ... FTM
Full-Time Officer [*of an organization*] ... FTO
Full-Time Permanent [*Employment*] ... FTP
Full-Time Personnel [*Employment*] ... FTP
Full-Time Recruiting Force [*DoD*] ... FTRF
Full-Time Regular [*Civil Service employee category*] ... FTR
Full-Time Support ... FTS
Full-Time Support Management Center [*Army*] (INF) ... FTSMC
Full-Time Temporary [*Civil Service employee category*] ... FTT
Full-Time Temporary Personnel [*Employment*] ... FTTP
Full-Time Training Duty [*Army*] (AABC) ... FTTD
Full-Time Unit Support [*Army Reserve*] (INF) ... FTUS
Full-Tracked Vehicle ... FTRAC

Full-Up/Fit-to-Bust [*Slang British*] (DI) .... FUFTB
Full-Up Powerpack [*Military*] .... FUPP
Full-Up System Test (RDA) .... FUST
Full-Wave Alternating Current .... FWAC
Full-Wave Amplifier .... FWA
Full-Wave Balanced Amplifier .... FWBA
Full-Wave Bridge Rectifier .... FWBR
Full-Wave Direct Current .... FWDC
Full-Wave Rectified Unfiltered .... FWRU
Full-Wave Rectifier [*or Rectification*] .... FWR
Fully [*Expand*] [*Computer science*] [*Telecommunications*] .... f
Fully Accessible (IAA) .... FA
Fully Atomized Stratified Turbulence .... FAST
Fully Automated Accounting Computer System (MCD) .... FAACS
Fully Automated Computer Program (AAG) .... FACP
Fully Automated Information Retrieval System (NITA) .... FAIRS
Fully Automated Pilot Monitored, Air Traffic Control [*Aviation*] .... FAPMATC
Fully Automated Scoring Target [*System*] (MCD) .... FAST
Fully Automated Switched Telecommunications Network (PDAA) .... FASTNeT
Fully Automatic (KSC) .... FA
Fully Automatic Calibration Technology [*Analytical balances*] .... FACT
Fully Automatic Cataloging Technique [*Computer science*] (MCD) .... FACT
Fully Automatic Compiler [*or Computer*]-Translator [*Computer science*] .... FACT
Fully Automatic Compiling System .... FACS
Fully Automatic Compiling Technique [*Computer science*] .... FACT
Fully Automatic High-Quality Machine Translation [*Computer science*]
     (DIT) .... FAHQMT
Fully Automatic High-Quality Translation [*Computer science*] .... FAHQT
Fully Automatic Information Retrievel System [*Computer science*]
     (EECA) .... FAIRS
Fully Automatic Reperforator Transmitter Distributor [*Telecommunications*]
     (TEL) .... FRXD
Fully Automatic Sort and Test [*Computer science*] (IAA) .... FAST
Fully Automatically Controlled Train [*British*] .... FACT
Fully Buffered Channel .... FBC
Fully Built-Up [*Manufacturing*] .... FBU
Fully Cellular Containership (DS) .... FCC
Fully Diluted Earnings Per Share (TDOB) .... FDEPS
Fully Distributed Cost .... FDC
Fully Distributed Costs [*Finance*] (MHDB) .... FDC
Fully Documented History [*Automotive retailing*] .... FDH
Fully Enclosed Covered Area (ADA) .... FECA
Fully Engineered Prototype [*Automotive engineering*] .... FEP
Fully Furnished (ADA) .... F/FURN
Fully Good .... FG
Fully Good, Fair [*Business term*] .... FGF
Fully Heat Treated (IEEE) .... FHT
Fully Hydrogenated Menhaden Oil [*Food science*] .... FHMO
Fully Independent Traveller .... FIT
Fully Informed Jury Association (EA) .... FIJA
Fully Instrumented Submersible Housing [*An oceanographic instrument*] ..... FISH
Fully Integrated Discovery Organization [*Business term*] .... FIDO
Fully Integrated Pharmaceutical Company [*Business term*] .... FIPCO
Fully Integrated Road Safety Technology [*Automotive safety*] .... FIRST
Fully Integrated Robotized Engine [*FIAT*] .... FIRE
Fully Loaded Weight and Capacity [*Shipping*] .... FWC
Fully Mission Capable (MCD) .... FMC
Fully Optimized Reaction Space .... FORS
Fully Paid [*Business term*] .... FP
Fully Proceduralized Job Performance Aid (MCD) .... FPJPA
Fully Proceduralized Troubleshooting Aids [*Military*] .... FPTA
Fully Qualified Generic Identifier .... FQGI
Fully Qualified Procedure Correlation Identifier (ACRL) .... FQPCID
Fully Read Index [*Publishing*] .... FRI
Fully Refined Paraffinic Wax [*Petroleum technology*] .... FRP
Fully Registered .... FR
Fully Self-Contained (ADA) .... FSC
Fully Separated Subsidiary .... FSS
Fully Submerged Foil [*Hydrofoil craft*] .... FSF
Fully Tracked (NATG) .... FT
Fully-Qualified Domain Name [*Internet*] .... FQDN
Fulmer Research Institute (AAG) .... FRI
Fulmer Technical Services [*Research center British*] (IRC) .... FTS
Fulminant Hepatic Failure [*Medicine*] .... FHF
Fulminant Hepatitis [*Medicine*] .... FH
Fulminant [*or Fulminating*] Viral Hepatitis [*Medicine*] .... FVH
Fulminating (ABBR) .... FLMNAG
Fulmination (ABBR) .... FLMNAN
Fulsome (ABBR) .... FLSM
Fulsomely (ABBR) .... FLSMY
Fulsomeness (ABBR) .... FLSMNS
Fulton County Court House, Atlanta, GA [*Library symbol Library of
     Congress*] (LCLS) .... GAFC
Fulton County Historical Society, Rochester, IN [*Library symbol Library of
     Congress*] (LCLS) .... InRocFHi
Fulton County Law Library, Atlanta, GA [*Library symbol Library of
     Congress*] (LCLS) .... GAFL
Fulton County Medical Society, Atlanta, GA [*Library symbol Library of
     Congress*] (LCLS) .... GAFM
Fulton County Public Library, Rochester, IN [*Library symbol Library of
     Congress*] (LCLS) .... InRoc
Fulton County Recorder's Office, Rochester, IN [*Library symbol Library of
     Congress*] (LCLS) .... InRocCR
Fulton Financial [*NASDAQ symbol*] (TTSB) .... FULT
Fulton Financial Corp. [*NASDAQ symbol*] (NQ) .... FULT

Fulton Financial Corp. [*Associated Press*] (SAG) .... Fulton
Fulton Generating Station [*Nuclear energy*] (NRCH) .... FGS
Fulton, KY [*AM radio station call letters*] .... WKZT
Fulton, KY [*FM radio station call letters*] .... WWKF
Fulton, MO [*Location identifier FAA*] (FAAL) .... FTT
Fulton, MO [*AM radio station call letters*] .... KFAL
Fulton, MO [*FM radio station call letters*] .... KKCA
Fulton, MS [*FM radio station call letters*] .... WFTA
Fulton, MS [*AM radio station call letters*] .... WFTO
Fulton, NY [*FM radio station call letters*] .... WBBS
Fulton, NY [*AM radio station call letters*] .... WZZZ
Fulton School, Hempstead, NY [*Library symbol*] [*Library of Congress*]
     (LCLS) .... NHemFuE
Fulton-Montgomery Community College, Johnstown, NY [*Library symbol
     Library of Congress*] (LCLS) .... NJostF
Fulton-Montgomery Community College, Johnstown, NY [*OCLC symbol*]
     (OCLC) .... YJM
Fulton's Supreme Court Reports, Bengal [*1842-44*] [*India*] [*A publication*]
     (DLA) .... Fult
Fulton's Supreme Court Reports, Bengal [*1842-44*] [*India*] [*A publication*]
     (DLA) .... Fulton
Fulvic Acid [*Organic chemistry*] .... FA
Fumaramido Oripavine [*Biochemistry*] .... FAO
Fumarate .... FUM
Fumarate Concentration (OA) .... FU
Fumarate Hydratase [*An enzyme*] .... FH
Fumel/Montayral [*France ICAO location identifier*] (ICLI) .... LFDX
Fumeless In-Line Degassing (PDAA) .... FILD
Fume-Tight [*Technical drawings*] .... FT
Fumigacion Aerea Andalusa SA [*Spain ICAO designator*] (FAAC) .... FAM
Fumigate [*or Fumigation*] (AABC) .... FUM
Fumigation and Bath [*Military*] .... F & B
Fumigation and Bath [*Military*] .... FB
Fuming Nitric Acid (KSC) .... FNA
Fun Fairs [*Public-performance tariff class*] [*British*] .... S
Fun, Travel, Adventure [*Sarcastic alternate to FTA - Free the Army*] .... FTA
Funafuti [*Tuvalu*] [*ICAO location identifier*] (ICLI) .... NGFF
Funafuti Atol [*Tuvalu*] [*Airport symbol*] (OAG) .... FUN
Funafuti Atoll [*Ellice Islands*] [*Airport symbol*] (AD) .... FUN
Funafuti/International [*Tuvalu*] [*ICAO location identifier*] (ICLI) .... NGFU
Funatsu [*Kawaguchuko*] [*Japan*] [*Seismograph station code, US Geological
     Survey*] (SEIS) .... FUN
Funchal [*Portugal*] [*Airport symbol*] (OAG) .... FNC
Funchal [*Madeira Island*] [*Seismograph station code, US Geological Survey*]
     (SEIS) .... FUL
Funchal, Madeira Island [*Portugal ICAO location identifier*] (ICLI) .... LPFU
Funco, Inc. [*NASDAQ symbol*] (SAG) .... FNCO
Funco, Inc. [*Associated Press*] (SAG) .... Funco
Function .... F
Function (IDOE) .... f
Function (NASA) .... FCN
Function (MSA) .... FCT
Function (MSA) .... FCTN
Function (AAMN) .... fn
Function (FAAC) .... FNCTN
Function (MDG) .... FUN
Function (AABC) .... FUNC
Function (KSC) .... FUNCT
Function (DAVI) .... FXN
Function Bits Sent to Periphere for Control [*Computer science*] (ECII) .... FUN
Function Block Logic (ACII) .... FBD
Function Button [*Computer science*] .... FB
Function Cable Access Kit (DWSG) .... FCAK
Function Call (IAA) .... FC
Function Circuit Diagram .... FCD
Function Code (NITA) .... FC
Function Control Block [*Computer science*] (IBMDP) .... FCB
Function Control Package [*Computer science*] .... FCP
Function Designator (NASA) .... FD
Function Designator Database (MCD) .... FDDB
Function Generating Digital-to-Analog Converter [*Computer science*]
     (IAA) .... FGDAC
Function Generator [*Computer science*] (IEEE) .... FG
Function Key (MCD) .... FK
Function Key (CDE) .... Fkey
Function Key (CDE) .... Fn key
Function Key Button (IAA) .... FKB
Function Language One FL1
Function Management (ACRL) .... FM
Function Management Data (IBMDP) .... FMD
Function Management Header (ACRL) .... FMH
Function Maximum Rate (NASA) .... FMR
Function Memory Unit .... FMU
Function of a Quantity [*Mathematics*] (ROG) .... FF
Function of Astronaut Location [*NASA*] (KSC) .... FAL
Function Processor (NITA) .... FP
Function Return [*Computer science*] .... FRETURN
Function Safe-Release Panel [*Aerospace*] (AAG) .... FS/RPNL
Function Select (NITA) .... FS
Function Set .... FS
Function Status Review (MCD) .... FSR
Function Study [*Medicine*] (MAE) .... FS
Function Symbol (IAA) .... FS
Function Test Procedure [*or Progress*] (NASA) .... FTP
Function Timeline .... FCNTL

Function Timing Generator (IAA) .... FTG
Functional (NASA) .... FUNCT
Functional .... FUNCTL
Functional Acquisition Specialist [*Army*] (RDA) .... FAS
Functional Activity [*Medicine*] (MAE) .... FA
Functional Address Symbol [*Military*] (AFIT) .... FAS
Functional Adhesive Bonding .... FAB
Functional Administration (HCT) .... FA
Functional Aerobic Impairment [*Medicine*] (AAMN) .... FAI
Functional Analysis .... FA
Functional Analysis Sheet .... FAS
Functional Analysis System Technique .... FAST
Functional and Performance Requirements (MCD) .... FPR
Functional Area .... FA
Functional Area Assessment .... FAA
Functional Area Breakdown .... FAB
Functional Area Code .... FAC
Functional Area Description .... FAD
Functional Area Documentation Manager [*Air Force*] (AFM) .... FADM
Functional Area Management and Development Division [*US Army Personnel Command*] (RDA) .... FAMDD
Functional Area Review [*Military*] .... FAR
Functional Arm Brace [*Medicine*] .... FAB
Functional Assembly (MCD) .... FA
Functional Assessment Inventory [*Medicine*] (DAVI) .... FAI
Functional Assignment Control Panel (MCD) .... FACP
Functional Baseline (AAGC) .... FBL
Functional Block Diagram [*Telecommunications*] (TEL) .... FBD
Functional Bowel Disorder [*Medicine*] (MAE) .... FBD
Functional Breadboard System [*Skylab*] [*NASA*] .... FBB
Functional Capabilities List [*Computer science*] (MHDB) .... FCL
Functional Capacities Evaluation [*Test*] [*Occupational therapy*] .... FCE
Functional Capacity Index [*NHTSA*] (TAG) .... FCI
Functional Capacity (Residual Functional Capacity) [*Social Security Administration*] (OICC) .... FC (RFC)
Functional Check Flight [*Air Force*] (AFM) .... FCF
Functional Checkout .... FCO
Functional Checkout Set (IAA) .... FCS
Functional Chief [*of a civilian career program*] [*Military*] .... FC
Functional Chief's Representative [*Of a civilian career program*] [*Army*] (RDA) .... FCR
Functional Class [*Rehabilitation*] [*Medicine*] (DAVI) .... FC
Functional Code .... FC
Functional Communication Profile .... FCP
Functional Companion Standard (ACII) .... FCS
Functional Compatibility Analysis (MCD) .... FCA
Functional Configuration Audit .... FCA
Functional Configuration Documentation (AAGC) .... FCD
Functional Configuration Identification (KSC) .... FCI
Functional Configuration Management [*Air Force*] (GFGA) .... FCMS
Functional Configuration Review (MCD) .... FCR
Functional Context Training (DNAB) .... FCT
Functional Control Diagram (NRCH) .... FCD
Functional Cost Hour Report (MCD) .... FCHR
Functional Data Coordinator (MCD) .... FDC
Functional Demonstration and Acceptance (AAG) .... FDA
Functional Demonstration Requirement (AAG) .... FDR
Functional Description .... FD
Functional Description Block [*Telecommunications*] (TEL) .... FDB
Functional Description Document (DOMA) .... FDD
Functional Description Requirements Specification [*Army*] .... FDRS
Functional Description Table .... FDT
Functional Design Activity [*Army*] .... FDA
Functional Design Agency (MCD) .... FDA
Functional Design Criteria (NRCH) .... FDC
Functional Design Requirements (NRCH) .... FDR
Functional Design Review (MCD) .... FDR
Functional Design Specifications (MCD) .... FDS
Functional Development Model (MCD) .... FDM
Functional Diagram [*Implementation dependant*] (ACII) .... FD
Functional Differential Equation .... FDE
Functional Economic Area .... FEA
Functional Electrical Stimulation .... FES
Functional Electronic Block .... FEB
Functional Element Test .... FET
Functional Engineering Interface Device [*NASA*] (NASA) .... FEID
Functional Entity [*Telecommunications*] (TEL) .... FE
Functional Equipment Withholding Tab [*Obsolete*] .... FEWT
Functional Exploration of Bone .... FEB
Functional Extracellular Fluid Volume [*Medicine*] (MAE) .... FECV
Functional Feeding Groups [*Ecology*] .... FFG
Functional Flow Block .... FFB
Functional Flow Block Diagram .... FFBD
Functional Flow Diagram .... FFD
Functional Group Code (MCD) .... FGC
Functional Independence Measure [*Occupational therapy*] .... FIM
Functional Individual Training System [*Navy*] (NVT) .... FITS
Functional Input Report (MCD) .... FIR
Functional, Integrated, Designating, and Referencing (MCD) .... FINDER
Functional Integrated Systems Trainer (MCD) .... FIST
Functional Integration Test .... FIT
Functional Interface Specification [*Telecommunications*] (TEL) .... FIS
Functional Interpolating Transform System [*Computer science*] .... FITS
Functional Interpolating Transformational System [*HSC Software Co.*] (PCM) .... FITS

Functional Inventory of Cognitive Communication Strategies (EDAC) .... FICCS
Functional Item Replacement [*Program*] [*Navy*] (NG) .... FIR
Functional Item Replacement Program [*Navy*] .... FIRP
Functional Job Analysis .... FJA
Functional Language Survey (EDAC) .... FLS
Functional Level Management .... FLM
Functional Line Diagram (KSC) .... FLD
Functional Line Diagram (MCD) .... FUNCTLINE
Functional Line Organization .... FLO
Functional Listing and Interconnection Wiring Record .... FLIWR
Functional Literacy [*Program to provide marginally literate soldiers with minimal literacy skills*] [*Army*] (RDA) .... FLIT
Functional Machine Representation Language [*Computer science*] (CSR) .... FMRL
Functional Magnetic Resonance Imaging .... fMRI
Functional Magnetic Resonance Imaging .... FMRI
Functional Maintenance Procedure .... FMP
Functional Management Inspection [*Military*] .... FMI
Functional Manager (MCD) .... FM
Functional Mathematical Programming System [*Computer science*] (MCD) .... FM
Functional Mathematical Programming System [*Computer science*] .... FMPS
Functional Megaspore [*Botany*] .... FM
Functional Message Type [*Communications*] .... FMT
Functional Mock-Up (KSC) .... FMU
Functional Name Addresses .... FNA
Functional Network .... FN
Functional Neuromuscular Stimulation [*Physiotherapy*] .... FNS
Functional Nomenclature Signal .... FNS
Functional Objective (KSC) .... FO
Functional Observational Battery [*Toxicology*] .... FOB
Functional Operating Instruction .... FOI
Functional Operation Simulation System .... FOSS
Functional Operational Design .... FOD
Functional Operational Sequence Diagram .... FOSD
Functional Operational Specification [*Military*] (CAAL) .... FOS
Functional Path (NASA) .... FP
Functional Performance Time .... FPT
Functional Plan Block Diagram (DOMA) .... FPBD
Functional Planning Matrices (IEEE) .... FPM
Functional Problem Log [*Computer science*] (OA) .... FPL
Functional Program Elements [*NASA*] .... FPE
Functional Program Translator [*Computer science*] .... FPT
Functional Programming and Prolog .... FUNLOG
Functional Programming Language [*Computer science*] .... FPL
Functional Progression Chart [*Telecommunications*] (TEL) .... FPC
Functional Proofing Vehicle .... FPV
Functional Proponent .... FP
Functional Qualification Review .... FQR
Functional Query Language [*1978*] [*Computer science*] (CSR) .... FQL
Functional Recovery Routine [*Computer science*] (BUR) .... FRR
Functional Redundancy Check [*Computer science*] .... FRC
Functional Reference Device (IEEE) .... FRD
Functional Refractory Period [*Neurophysiology*] .... FRP
Functional Renal Failure [*Medicine*] .... FRF
Functional Requirement Diagram [*Implementation dependant*] (ACII) .... FRD
Functional Requirement Specification (AAG) .... FRS
Functional Requirements .... FR
Functional Requirements Document (SSD) .... FRD
Functional Requirements Envelope (SSD) .... FRE
Functional Requirements Summary .... FRS
Functional Reserve [*or Residual*] Capacity [*of the lungs*] [*Physiology*] .... FRC
Functional Residual Air (ADA) .... FRA
Functional Schedules (MCD) .... FS
Functional Schematic .... FS
Functional Selector .... FS
Functional Sequence Diagram [*Computer science*] .... FSD
Functional Simulator (NASA) .... FSIM
Functional Simulator and Translator [*Computer science*] (CSR) .... FST
Functional Specification [*Telecommunications*] (TEL) .... FS
Functional Specification Block [*Telecommunications*] (TEL) .... FSB
Functional Specification Package [*Computer science*] .... FSP
Functional Standard Conformance Statement [*Telecommunications*] .... FSCS
Functional Stretch Reflex [*of muscles*] .... FSR
Functional Subsystem Software Requirements (NASA) .... FSSR
Functional Supplementary Objective (MCD) .... FSO
Functional System Plan [*Military*] .... FSP
Functional Technical Validation (SDI) .... FTV
Functional Technology Vehicle [*Army*] .... FTV
Functional Terminal Innervation Ratio [*Psychiatry*] .... FTIR
Functional Test [*Computer science*] .... FT
Functional Test and Calibration (IEEE) .... FT & C
Functional Test and Calibration (IAA) .... FTAC
Functional Test Bulletin [*Computer science*] (IAA) .... FTB
Functional Test Change Request .... FTCR
Functional Test Data .... FTD
Functional Test Equipment .... FTE
Functional Test Flight (AFM) .... FTF
Functional Test Flight Checklist .... FTFC
Functional Test Manager [*Hewlett-Packard Co.*] .... FTM
Functional Test Objective (KSC) .... FTO
Functional Test Procedure [*or Program*] .... FTP
Functional Test Report .... FTR
Functional Test Requirement (IEEE) .... FTR
Functional Test Requirements Document (NASA) .... FTRD
Functional Test Specification (KSC) .... FTS

Functional Test Unit [*Computer science*] (IAA) .... FTU
Functional Tester [*Mars Electronics*] (NITA) .... FT
Functional Training Branch [*BUPERS*] .... FTB
Functional Unit [*Computer science*] .... FU
Functional Uptake of Carbon Monoxide [*Medicine*] (DAVI) .... FU_{co}
Functional User's Manual (AABC) .... FUM
Functional Uterine Bleeding [*Medicine*] .... FUB
Functional Validation Test [*Army*] .... FVT
Functional Verification Unit [*Photography*] .... FVU
Functional Vestibular Reserve [*Orientation*] .... FVR
Functional Workload Demonstration (AAGC) .... FWD
Functionalized Monolayers on Mesoporous Supports [*Organic chemistry*] .... FMMS
Functionally Distributed Computing System .... FDCS
Functionally Gradient Material [*Materials science and technology*] .... FGM
Functionally Related Observable Difference [*between weapons*] .... FROD
Functionally Significant Items (MCD) .... FSI
Functionally Terminated (MCD) .... FT
Functionally-Identifiable Maintenance System [*Computer science*] (EECA) .... FIMS
Functional-Oriented Maintenance Manual (MCD) .... FOMM
Functionary .... FUUNCTRY
Functioning of the GATT [*General Agreement on Tariffs and Trade*] **System** .... FOGS
Function-on-Generator-Stop (RDA) .... FOGS
Function-Oriented Organizational Structure (AAG) .... FOOS
Function-Oriented Symbolic Macromodelling Algorithm (PDAA) .... FOSMA
Functions and Responsibilities .... F & R
Functions/Parameters/Characteristics (MCD) .... FPC's
Fund (ROG) .... FD
Fund Amer Enterpr Hldgs [*NYSE symbol*] (TTSB) .... FFC
Fund American Enterprise Holdings [*Formerly, Fireman's Fund Corp.*] [*NYSE symbol*] (SPSG) .... FFC
Fund American Enterprises Holdings, Inc. [*Associated Press*] (SAG) .... FundA
Fund American Enterprises Holdings, Inc. [*Formerly, Fireman's Fund Corp.*] [*Associated Press*] (SAG) .... FundAm
Fund Availability Report (MCD) .... FAR
Fund Campaign [*Red Cross*] .... FC
Fund Classification Reference Number [*Military*] (AFIT) .... FCRN
Fund Code (AABC) .... FC
Fund Control Code .... FCC
Fund for a Conservative Majority (EA) .... FCM
Fund for a Democratic Majority (EA) .... FDM
Fund for Advancement of Camping (EA) .... FAC
Fund for American Studies (EA) .... FAS
Fund for America's Future [*Defunct*] (EA) .... FAF
Fund for an American Renaissance (EA) .... FAR
Fund for an Open Society (EA) .... OPEN
Fund for Animals Ltd. Australia .... FALA
Fund For Animals Ltd. Australia [*Commercial firm*] .... FFALA
Fund for Artists' Colonies [*Defunct*] (EA) .... FAC
Fund for Assuring an Independent Retirement (EA) .... FAIR
Fund for Constitutional Government (EA) .... FCG
Fund for Education in World Order [*Later, FFP*] (EA) .... FEWO
Fund for Human Dignity (EA) .... FHD
Fund for Human Need [*British*] .... FHN
Fund for Human Rights [*Later, WDL*] (EA) .... FHR
Fund for Integrative Biomedical Research .... FIBER
Fund for Investigative Journalism (EA) .... FIJ
Fund for Labor Defense (EA) .... FLD
Fund for Modern Courts (EA) .... FMC
Fund for Multinational Management Education (EA) .... FMME
Fund for New Leadership [*Defunct*] (EA) .... FNL
Fund for New Priorities in America (EA) .... FFNPA
Fund for Objective News Reporting (EA) .... FONR
Fund for Open Information and Accountability [*Defunct*] (EA) .... FOIA
[*The*] **Fund for Peace** [*An association*] (EA) .... FFP
[*The*] **Fund for Peace** [*An association*] (EA) .... TFP
Fund for Peaceful Atomic Development [*Defunct*] .... FPAD
Fund for Renewable Energy and the Environment (EA) .... FREE
Fund for Rural Economic Development [*Canada*] .... FRED
Fund for Special Operations [*Inter-American Development Bank*] .... FSO
Fund for Stockowners Rights (EA) .... FFSR
Fund for Stockowners Rights [*Later, FFSR*] (EA) .... FSR
Fund for the Advancement of Education [*Defunct*] (EA) .... FAE
Fund for the Advancement of Music Education [*Defunct*] (EA) .... FAME
Fund for the Feminist Majority (EA) .... FFM
Fund for the Future Committee (EA) .... FFC
Fund for the Improvement and Reform of Schools and Teaching [*Department of Education*] (GFGA) .... FIRST
Fund for the Improvement and Reform of Schools and Teaching Act [*1988*] .... FIRSTA
Fund for the Improvement of Postsecondary Education [*Department of Education*] (EGAO) .... FIPE
Fund for the Improvement of Postsecondary Education [*Department of Education*] .... FIPSE
Fund for the Preservation of the Mahyana Tradition [*An association*] .... FPMT
Fund for the Relief of Russian Writers and Scientists in Exile (EA) .... LITFUND
Fund for the Replacement of Animals in Medical Experiments .... FRAME
Fund for the Republic [*Later, Robert Maynard Hutchins Center for the Study of Democratic Institutions*] (EA) .... FR
Fund for the United Nations for the Development of West Irian .... FUNDWI
Fund for Theological Education (EA) .... FTE
Fund for UFO [*Unidentified Flying Object*] **Research** (EA) .... FUFOR
Fund Management Identification Code [*Military*] (AFM) .... FMIC
Fund of Funds .... FOF
Fund Raising [*Red Cross*] .... FR
Fund Raising and Financial Development Section [*Library Administration and Management Association*] .... FRFDS
Fund Raising Institute of New Zealand (NFD) .... FINZ
Fund Raising Organization Graphics Service .... FROGS
Fund Summary Record [*Military*] (AFIT) .... FSR
Fund to Restore an Educated Electorate [*Defunct*] (EA) .... FREE
Fund Type [*Military*] (AFIT) .... FT
Fundacao Casa de Rui Barbosa, Rio De Janeiro, Brazil [*Library symbol Library of Congress*] (LCLS) .... BrRF
Fundacion [*Colombia*] [*Airport symbol*] (AD) .... FDA
Fundacion Arte por Uruguay [*Formerly, Relatives Committee for Uruguay*] [*Sweden*] (EAIO) .... FAU
Fundacion de la Red de Informacion Cientifica Automatizada [*Spain*] (NITA) .... FUINCA
Fundacion para el Desarrollo de la Funcion Social de las Comunicaciones (IID) .... FUNDESCO
Fundacion para el Fomento de la Informacion Automatizada [*Foundation for the Promotion of Automated Information*] [*Information service or system*] (IID) .... FUINCA
Fundal Height [*Obstetrics*] (DAVI) .... FH
Fundal Pressure (MAE) .... FP
Fundament [*Slang British*] (DSUE) .... FUN
Fundamental (MSA) .... FUND
Fundamental Design Method .... FDM
Fundamental Electrical Standard (IAA) .... FES
Fundamental Equilibrium Exchange Rate [*Economics*] .... FEER
Fundamental Frequency (IAA) .... FUNDFREQ
Fundamental Frequency Indicator [*Medicine*] (DMAA) .... FFI
Fundamental Interpersonal Relations Orientation [*Psychology*] .... FIRO
Fundamental Interpersonal Relations Orientation - Behavior .... FIRO-B
Fundamental Interpersonal Relations Orientation - Behavior Characteristics [*Personality development test*] [*Psychology*] .... FIRO-BC
Fundamental Interpersonal Relations Orientation - Feelings [*Personality development test*] [*Psychology*] .... FIRO-F
Fundamental Land-Air Integrated Research (SAA) .... FLAIR
Fundamental Material Controls .... FMC
Fundamental Mode Asynchronous (IAA) .... FMA
Fundamental Order of Operation [*Mathematics game*] .... FOO
Fundamental Parameters Technique .... FPT
Fundamental Phenomena Experimentation (SSD) .... FPE
Fundamental Planning Analysis (MCD) .... FPA
Fundamental Questions Program (EERA) .... FQP
Fundamental Resonance (MCD) .... FR
Fundamental Standard Data Link Working Group [*NATO*] (NATG) .... FSDLWG
Fundamental Train Frequency [*Machinery*] .... FTF
Fundamentalist .... FNDMNTLST
Fundamentalist (WDAA) .... FUND
Fundamentalists Anonymous (EA) .... FA
Fundamentally Analyzable Simplified English [*Computer science*] .... FASE
Fundamentally Different Factors [*Environmental Protection Agency*] .... FDF
Fundamentals Graduate .... FG
Fundamentals of Application and System Training [*Course*] [*Computer science*] .... FAST
Fundamentals of Engineering [*Exam*] .... FE
Fundamentals of Library and Information Science [*Drexel University*] (NITA) .... FUNLIS
Fundamentals of Machine Operation [*John Deere Service Publications*] [*Moline, IL*] [*A publication*] .... FMO
Funded (ROG) .... FNDD
Funded Delivery Period [*DoD*] .... FDP
Funded Environmental and Morale Leave Program [*Military*] (DOMA) .... FEML
Funded Reimburseable Authority (MCD) .... FRA
Funder/Sponsor [*MARC relator code*] [*Library of Congress*] (LCCP) .... fnd
Funders Committee for Voter Registration and Education (EA) .... FCVRE
Fundic Gland Polyposis [*Medicine*] .... FGP
Fundic Type [*of epithelium*] [*Medicine*] .... FT
Funding .... FDG
Funding (KSC) .... FNDG
Funding .... FNDNG
Funding (NITA) .... FU
Funding (NITA) .... FUND
Funding Authorization Document (AABC) .... FAD
Funding Cycle (OICC) .... FC
Funding Exchange (EA) .... FE
Funding Greater Than [*Dialog*] [*Searchable field*] (NITA) .... FG
Funding Information Center [*Spokane Public Library*] [*Information service or system*] (IID) .... FIC
Funding Program Advice [*Military*] (AABC) .... FPA
Funding Request .... FR
Funding Sources Clearinghouse, Inc. (IID) .... FSC
Fundraising Institute-Australia, Inc. (NFD) .... FI-A
Funds Allocation Control System .... FACS
Funds Flow Analysis .... FFA
Funds Management Audit List (AFIT) .... FMAL
Funds Management Record [*Military*] (AFM) .... FMR
Funds Transfer [*Banking*] (MHDW) .... FTR
Funds Transfer System .... FTS
Funds Will Not Be Entrusted to Others for Any Purpose [*Army*] (AABC) .... FWNEOFAP
Fundus at Umbilicus [*Obstetrics*] (DAVI) .... F/U
Fundus Firm [*Obstetrics*] (DAVI) .... FF
Fundy Group Publications, Yarmouth, Nova Scotia [*Library symbol National Library of Canada*] (NLC) .... NSYFG

Fundy Group Publications, Yarmouth, NS, Canada [*Library symbol*] [*Library of Congress*] (LCLS) ... CaNSYFG
Funeral ... FNRL
Funeral and Bereavement Educators Association ... FBEA
Funeral Director's Diploma [*British*] (DI) ... FDDip
Funeral Home Public Service Group International [*Defunct*] (EA) ... FHPSGI
Funeral Telegraph Service ... FTS
Fungicide ... FUNGIC
Fungurume [*Zaire*] [*ICAO location identifier*] (ICLI) ... FZQF
Fungus Proof ... FP
Funk Aircraft Owners Association (EA) ... FAOA
Funk & Scott Publishing Co. [*Detroit, MI*] ... F & S
Funkstelle [*Radio Station*] [*German military - World War II*] ... FST
Funkstown, MD [*AM radio station call letters*] ... WPVG
Fun-Loving Youth En Route to Success [*Title of book by Lawrence Graham an d Lawrence Hamdan*] [*Lifestyle classification*] ... Flyers
Funnel (MSA) ... FUNL
Funnel Cloud ... FC
Funnel Length ... FL
Funnel Length Index ... FLI
Funnel-Web Spider Toxin ... FTX
Funnel-Web Spider Venom ... FWSV
Funny Car [*Class of racing cars*] ... FC
Funny Little Man [*Recognizable graphic type*] ... FLM
Funny Looking Beat [*Cardiology*] ... FLB
Funny Looking Child [*Medical slang*] ... FLC
Funny Looking Kid [*Syndrome*] [*Medical slang*] ... FLK
Funter Bay [*Alaska*] [*Airport symbol*] (OAG) ... FNR
Funter Bay, AK [*Location identifier FAA*] (FAAL) ... FNR
Funtshi Aviation Service [*Zaire*] [*ICAO designator*] (FAAC) ... FUN
Fuqua Enterprises [*NYSE symbol*] (SAG) ... FQE
Fuqua Enterprises [*Associated Press*] (SAG) ... FuquaEn
Fuquay Varina, NC [*FM radio station call letters*] ... WNND
Fuquay-Varina, NC [*AM radio station call letters*] ... WCRY
Fuquene [*Colombia*] [*Seismograph station code, US Geological Survey*] (SEIS) ... FUQ
Fur Breeders Association of the United Kingdom [*British*] ... FBA
Fur Brokers Association of America (EA) ... FBAA
Fur Buyers Association, Coat and Suit Industry (EA) ... FBACSI
Fur Council of Australia ... FCA
Fur Dressers Guild (EA) ... FDG
Fur Farm Animal Welfare Coalition (EA) ... FFAWC
Fur Garment Traveling Salesmen's Association ... FGTSA
Fur Industry Salvage Commission [*New Deal*] ... FISC
Fur Information and Fashion Council (EA) ... FIFC
Fur Institute of Canada ... FIC
Fur, Leather and Machine Workers Unions - Furriers Joint Council (EA) ... FLM-FJC
Fur Merchants Employers Council (EA) ... FMEC
Fur Skin Dressers' Union [*British*] ... FSDU
Fur Takers of America (EA) ... FTA
Fur Vault, Inc. (MHDW) ... FRV
Fur Wholesalers Association of America (EA) ... FWAA
Furancungo [*Mozambique*] [*ICAO location identifier*] (ICLI) ... FQFU
Furanose [*One-letter symbol*] [*Biochemistry*] ... f
Furazolidone [*Antimicrobial drug*] ... FZ
Furfuryl Alcohol [*Organic chemistry*] ... FA
(Furfurylamino)purine [*Plant hormone*] [*Organic chemistry*] ... FAP
Furioso [*Furiously*] [*Music*] (ROG) ... FURO
Furlong [*Unit of distance*] ... F
Furlong [*Unit of distance*] ... FUR
Furlong on the Irish Law of Landlord and Tenant [*A publication*] (DLA) ... Furl L & T
Furlough [*Military*] (ADA) ... F
Furlough [*Military*] (WGA) ... FUR
Furlough [*Military*] (ROG) ... FURL
Furlough Rations [*Army*] ... FR
Furloughed without Pay ... FWOP
Furman University (GAGS) ... Furman U
Furman University, Greenville, SC [*Library symbol Library of Congress*] (LCLS) ... ScGF
Furman University, Greenville, SC [*OCLC symbol*] (OCLC) ... SFU
Furman University Press (DGA) ... FUP
Furnace ... FRNC
Furnace (MSA) ... FUR
Furnace ... FURN
Furnace Atomic Absorption Spectrophotometry (PDAA) ... FAAS
Furnace Atomic Nonthermal Excitation Spectrometry ... FANES
Furnace Brazing ... FB
Furnace Cooled [*Engineering*] (IAA) ... FC
Furnace Exit Gas Temperature ... FEGT
Furnace Explosion [*Insurance*] ... FE
Furnace Fuel Oil (NATG) ... FFO
Furnace Sensitize (PDAA) ... FS
Furnace Soldering ... FS
Furness Railway [*Scotland*] ... FR
Furness Warren Line [*Steamship*] (MHDW) ... FWL
Furness, Withy & Co. [*Steamship line*] (MHDW) ... FW
Furnish (AFM) ... FURN
Furnish Assignment Instructions without Delay ... FAWOD
Furnish Copies of Orders to Appropriate Commanders ... FCOAC
Furnish, Deliver and Install (IAA) ... FDI
Furnish Full Names, Rates, and Social Security Numbers of Men Transferred in Accordance with This Directive (DNAB) ... FURNASER
Furnished ... FUR
Furnished and Installed (KSC) ... F & I
Furnished and Installed by Others (MCD) ... FIO
Furnished by Others [*Technical drawings*] ... FBO
Furnished Hardware and Services List (MCD) ... FH & SL
Furnished Recurring Intelligence File (MCD) ... FRIF
Furnished This Station [*Army*] (AABC) ... FURTS
Furnishing ... FURNG
Furnishing Springmakers Federation [*British*] (BI) ... FSMF
Furnishing Trades Society of New South Wales [*Australia*] ... FTSNSW
Furniture (ROG) ... FTURE
Furniture ... FURN
Furniture (VRA) ... furn
Furniture ... FURN
Furniture and Bedding Publicity Association Ltd. [*British*] (BI) ... FABPA
Furniture and Bedding Spring Institute [*Defunct*] (EA) ... FBSI
Furniture and Fixtures [*Insurance*] ... F & F
Furniture and Fixtures (DFIT) ... F&F
Furniture and Timber Industry Training Board [*British*] (BI) ... FTITB
Furniture Brands Intl [*NYSE symbol*] (TTSB) ... FBN
Furniture Brands Intl., Inc. [*NYSE symbol*] (SAG) ... FBN
Furniture Brands Intl., Inc. [*Associated Press*] (SAG) ... FurnBrds
Furniture Deliverers' Association ... FDA
Furniture Development Council [*British*] (BI) ... FDC
Furniture Factories' Marketing Association of the South [*Later, IHFMA*] (EA) ... FFMAS
Furniture, Fixtures, and Equipment [*Insurance*] ... FF & E
Furniture History Society (EA) ... FHS
Furniture Industry Consumer Advisory Panel [*Defunct*] (EA) ... FICAP
Furniture Industry Research Association [*Research center British*] (IRC) ... FIRA
Furniture Manufacturers' Association of Australia (EERA) ... FMAA
Furniture Manufacturers Association of Grand Rapids [*Later, GRAFMA*] (EA) ... FMAGR
Furniture Parts [*Freight*] ... FURN PTS
Furniture Rental Association of America (EA) ... FRAA
Furniture Retailers Council of South Australia ... FRCSA
Furniture Retailers' Council of Victoria [*Australia*] ... FRCV
Furniture, Timber, and Allied Trades Union [*British*] ... FTAT
Furniture, Timber, and Allied Trades Union [*British*] ... FTATU
Furniture Trades Benevolent Association [*British*] (BI) ... FTBA
Furon Co. [*NYSE symbol*] (SAG) ... FCY
Furon Co. [*Associated Press*] (SAG) ... Furon
Furon Formaldehyde [*Organic chemistry*] ... FF
Furosemide [*Pharmacology*] (DAVI) ... FRS
Furred [*Technical drawings*] ... FUR
Furrier ... FUR
Furrier ... FURR
Furriers Joint Council of New York (EA) ... FJCNY
Furrs Bishops [*Associated Press*] (SAG) ... FurBsh
Furr's/Bishop's Cafeteria Ltd. [*Associated Press*] (SAG) ... FurB
Furr's/Bishop's Cafeteria Ltd. [*Associated Press*] (SAG) ... FurBish
Furr's/Bishop's, Inc. [*NYSE symbol*] (SPSG) ... CHI
Further ... FHR
Further (AABC) ... FUR
Further ... FURR
Further ... FURTH
Further and Adult Council for Art and Design Education (AIE) ... FACADE
Further Assembly (IAA) ... FA
Further Assignment to Duty (DNAB) ... FASDU
Further Care [*Medicine*] ... FURTH C
Further Differentiated Fibroblast [*Cytology*] ... FDF
Further Education ... FE
Further Education Information Service (AIE) ... FEIS
Further Education Marketing Unit (AIE) ... FEMU
Further Education Research Association [*British*] (DBA) ... FERA
Further Education Revenue Account Survey (AIE) ... FERAS
Further Education Staff College (AIE) ... FESC
Further Education Statistical Record [*Department of Education and Science*] [*British*] ... FESR
Further Education Unit [*British*] ... FEU
Further Education Work Experience Co-Ordinator (AIE) ... FEWEC
Further Finished Than Primed [*Freight*] ... FHR FNSHD T PRMD
Further Finished Than Rough [*Freight*] ... FHR FNSHD T RGH
Further Flexion [*Neurology and orthopedics*] (DAVI) ... FF
Further Particulars When Available ... FPWA
Further Review (DNAB) ... F REV
Furthest-On Circle [*Navy*] (ANA) ... FOC
Furtwangen [*Schwarzwald*] [*Federal Republic of Germany*] [*Seismograph station code, US Geological Survey*] (SEIS) ... FWS
Fury Exploration Ltd. [*Vancouver Stock Exchange symbol*] ... FUY
Furylacryloylglycylleucine Amide [*Biochemistry*] ... FAGLA
Fusa [*Let It Be Fused*] [*Pharmacy*] (ROG) ... FUS
Fusable Read-Only Memory [*Computer science*] (MDG) ... FROM
Fusaric Acid (MEDA) ... FA
Fusarium Multiformis [*A fungus*] ... FM
Fusarium Wilt [*Plant pathology*] ... F
Fuscaldo [*Italy*] [*Seismograph station code, US Geological Survey*] (SEIS) ... FSC
Fuse (DEN) ... F
Fuse ... FS
Fuse (MSA) ... FU
Fuse (VRA) ... fus
Fuse Alarm (TEL) ... FA
Fuse Block (KSC) ... FB
Fuse Box (IAA) ... FB
Fuse Box ... FUBX
Fuse Chamber (TEL) ... FC

Fuse Current Rating ..... FCR
Fuse Enclosure Package (IEEE) ..... FEP
Fuse Holder ..... FUHLR
Fuse on Jam (MCD) ..... FOJ
Fuse Safe/Arm ..... FSA
Fuse Set Subsystem ..... FSSS
Fuse Voltage Rating ..... FVR
Fused Junction ..... FJ
Fused Polyethylene Aluminium ..... FPA
Fused Quartz ..... FQ
Fused Quartz Incandescent Lamp ..... FQIL
Fused Quartz Tubing ..... FQT
Fused to Metal [Dentistry] ..... FM
Fuselage [Aviation] (AABC) ..... FUS
Fuselage [Aviation] (MSA) ..... FUSLG
Fuselage Analysis and Design Synthesis ..... FADES
Fuselage, Lower Forward (MCD) ..... FUS/LF
Fuselage Reference Line [Aviation] ..... FRL
Fuselage Reference Plane [Aviation] (MCD) ..... FRP
Fuselage Station [Aviation] ..... FS
Fuselage, Upper Forward (MCD) ..... FUS/UF
Fushi Tarazu [Not Enough Segments] [Genetics] [Japan] ..... FTZ
Fusible (MSA) ..... FSBL
Fusible (DAC) ..... Fus
Fusible Link (EECA) ..... FL
Fusible Link-Bottom Register (OA) ..... FLBR
Fusible Link-Top Register (OA) ..... FLTR
Fusible Plug [Engineering] (IAA) ..... FP
Fusible Random Access Memory [Computer science] (PDAA) ..... FRAM
Fusiform Skin Revision [Medicine] (MAE) ..... FSR
Fusiformis [Microbiology] (MAE) ..... F
Fusil ..... FUSL
Fusilier ..... FUS
Fusing Point ..... FP
Fusion (WGA) ..... FN
Fusion ..... FUSN
Fusion at the Inferred Threshold [Test] [Medicine] ..... FIT
Fusion Bonded Coaters Association [CRSI] [Absorbed by] (EA) ..... FBCA
Fusion Energy Advisory Committee ..... FEAC
Fusion Energy Design Center (MCD) ..... FEDC
Fusion Energy Foundation (EA) ..... FEF
Fusion Engineering Device [Nuclear energy] ..... FED
Fusion Engineering Reactor [Japan] ..... FER
Fusion Materials Irradiation Test Facility [Proposed] ..... FMIT
Fusion Medical Technologies, Inc. [NASDAQ symbol] (SAG) ..... FSON
Fusion Medical Technologies, Inc. [Associated Press] (SAG) ..... FusnMed
Fusion Plasma Research Facility [Department of Energy] ..... FPRF
Fusion Point ..... FNP
Fusion Point ..... FNPT
Fusion Point ..... FUP
Fusion Policy Advisory Committee [Department of Energy] ..... FPAC
Fusion Power Associates (EA) ..... FPA
Fusion Power Systems (MCD) ..... FPS
Fusion Splicer Unit [Telecommunications] (NITA) ..... FSU
Fusion Systems [NASDAQ symbol] (TTSB) ..... FUSN
Fusion Systems Corp. [Associated Press] (SAG) ..... FusionSy
Fusion Systems Corp. [NASDAQ symbol] (SAG) ..... FUSN
Fusion Treaty [European Communities] [1965] (ILCA) ..... F Tr
Fusion-Fission Hybrid Reactor ..... FFHR
Fusobacteria [or Fusobacterium] Micro-Organism [Medicine] ..... FM
Fusobacterium [Microbiology] (MAE) ..... F
Fuss [Feet of organ stops] ..... F
Futaleufu [Chile] [Airport symbol] (AD) ..... FFU
Futaleufu/Futaleufu [Chile] [ICAO location identifier] (ICLI) ..... SCFT
Futbol Internacional [Ministerio de Cultura] [Spain Information service or
  system] (CRD) ..... FUTB
Futema [Ryukyu Islands] [ICAO location identifier] (ICLI) ..... ROTM
Futon Association of North America (EA) ..... FANA
Futuna [Vanuatu] [ICAO location identifier] (ICLI) ..... NVVF
Futuna/Pointe Vele [Wallis and Futuna Islands] [ICAO location identifier]
  (ICLI) ..... NLWF
Future ..... FUT
Future Age [A publication] (ADA) ..... FAGE
Future Air Navigation Systems [Aviation] ..... FANS
Future Airborne Communications Equipment and Technology (MCD) ..... FACET
Future Aircraft Technology Enhancement ..... FATE
Future Airline Pilots of America [BTS] (TAG) ..... FAPA
Future American Magical Entertainers ..... FAME
Future Anti-Air Concepts Experimental Technology Seeker [Military aircraft
  research program] [British] ..... FACETS
Future Armament Systems Technology (RDA) ..... FAST
Future Armored Combat System [Military] ..... FACS
Future Armored Resupply Vehicle [Army] ..... FARV
Future Armored Resupply Vehicle-Ammunition [Army] (RDA) ..... FARV-A
Future Aviation Professionals of America (EA) ..... FAPA
Future Battle Laboratory (RDA) ..... FBL
Future Budget Year (AFM) ..... FBY
Future Business Leaders of America [Washington, DC] (AEBS) ..... FBLA
Future Business Leaders of America - Phi Beta Lambda [Washington, DC]
  (EA) ..... FBLA-PBL
Future Characteristics Change [Military] (CAAL) ..... FCC
Future Close Combat Vehicle ..... FCCV
Future Close Combat Vehicle Program ..... FCCVP
Future Close Combat Vehicle System (MCD) ..... FCCVS
Future Command and Control Vehicle ..... FC²V

Future Concept Vehicle ..... FCV
Future Data Processor (IAA) ..... FDP
Future Digital Network (MCD) ..... FDN
Future Digital Radio [Army] ..... FDR
Future Electric Vehicle [Nissan Corp.] (PS) ..... FEV
Future Engineers of America (EA) ..... FEA
Future European Air Traffic System (GAVI) ..... FEATS
Future European Fighter Aircraft (PDAA) ..... FEFA
Future Experimental Vehicle [Toyota Motor Co.] ..... FXV
Future Farm Experts of the Junior Woodchucks of the World [Subgroup of
  Junior Woodchucks organization mentioned in Donald Duck comic by Carl
  Barks] ..... FFEJWW
Future Farmers of America [Later, NFFAO] (EA) ..... FFA
Future Farmers of Australia ..... FFA
Future Fisherman Foundation (EA) ..... FFF
Future Generation Computer Systems (NITA) ..... FGCS
Future Generations [An association] (EA) ..... FG
Future Global Maritime Distress and Safety System ..... FGMDSS
Future Homemakers of America (EA) ..... FHA
Future Homemakers of America (Home Economics Related Occupations)
  (OICC) ..... FHA (HERO)
Future Horsemen of America ..... FHA
Future Identification and Location Experiment [NASA] (NASA) ..... FILE
Future Impact Point (MCD) ..... FIP
Future Income Growth Security [Finance] ..... FIGS
Future Infantry Fighting Vehicle [Army] (RDA) ..... FIFV
Future Infantry Vehicle [Army] (INF) ..... FIV
Future Interest [Legal shorthand] (LWAP) ..... FI
Future International Military/Civil Airfighter [British] ..... FIMA
Future Issue Requirement ..... FIR
Future Journalists of America [Defunct] (EA) ..... FJA
Future Land Mobile Personal Telephone Service ..... FLMPTS
Future Language Information Processing System (BUR) ..... FLIPS
Future Large Aircraft [Cooperative manufacturing effort of France, Germany,
  Britain, Italy, Portugal, Spain and Turkey] (ECON) ..... FLA
Future Large Aircraft [Development] [Europe] ..... FLA
Future Launching System [Space flight] ..... FLS
Future Lawyers Investigating Transportation Employment [Student legal
  action organization] (EA) ..... FLITE
Future Mailing Address ..... FMA
Future Main Battle Tank (NATG) ..... FMBT
Future Management Services [A Lebanese arms company] (ECON) ..... FMS
Future Manned Interceptor [Military] ..... FMI
Future Military Systems Authority ..... FMSA
[The] Future Now, Inc. [NASDAQ symbol] (SPSG) ..... FNOW
Future Nurses Clubs [National League for Nursing] (AEBS) ..... FNC
Future of Freedom Foundation (EA) ..... FFF
Future of Scientific Ocean Drilling [Marine science] (MSC) ..... FUSOD
Future Operational Microwave Sounder (MCD) ..... FOMS
Future Physicians Clubs (EA) ..... FPC
Future Problem Solving Program (EA) ..... FPSP
Future Production (MCD) ..... FUPRO
Future Projects Office [NASA] ..... FPO
Future Public Land Mobile Telecommunications System ..... FPLMTS
Future Publication Uncertain ..... FPU
Future Reconnaissance Vehicle [Army] ..... FRV
Future Safety Research [Honda experimental vehicle] ..... FSR
Future Scientists of America [Defunct] (EA) ..... FSA
Future Scientists of America Foundation [Defunct] ..... FSAF
Future Scout Vehicle [Military] ..... FSV
Future Scout Vehicle [Army] (DOMA) ..... FSV
Future Secure Voice System (LAIN) ..... FSVS
Future Series (IAA) ..... FS
Future Shock Experimental [Mountain bike] (PS) ..... FSX
Future Space Transportation System ..... FSTS
Future Sports-Sedan Experimental [Concept car] ..... FS-X
Future Strategic Strategy Study [Military] (SDI) ..... FS³
Future Strategic Target List ..... FSTL
Future Strategic Targets (MCD) ..... FST
Future Studies Centre [British] (CB) ..... FSC
Future System [IBM Corp.] [Computer science] ..... FS
Future Teachers of America [Later, SAE] (EA) ..... FTA
Future Technology Communications [Distributor and networking specialist]
  [British] (NITA) ..... FTC
Future Technology Systems (NITA) ..... FTS
Future Time Perspective Inventory [Psychology] ..... FTPI
Future Value [Finance] ..... FV
Future Value Interest Factor [Finance] ..... FVIF
Future Villain Band [Evil rock music group in 1978 film "Sgt. Pepper's Lonely
  Hearts Club Band"] ..... FVB
Future Weapons Agency [Army] ..... FWA
Future Years Defence Plan (ECON) ..... FYDP
Futurebiotics, Inc. [Associated Press] (SAG) ..... Futrbi
Futurebiotics, Inc. [Associated Press] (SAG) ..... Futurbio
Futurebiotics, Inc. [Associated Press] (SAG) ..... Futurebio
Futurebiotics, Inc. [NASDAQ symbol] (SAG) ..... VITK
Futurebiotics Inc. Wrrt [NASDAQ symbol] (TTSB) ..... VITKW
Futuremedia Ltd. [NASDAQ symbol] (SAG) ..... FMDA
Futuremedia Ltd. [NASDAQ symbol] (SAG) ..... FMDY
Futuremedia Ltd. [Associated Press] (SAG) ..... Futmd
Futuremedia Ltd. [Associated Press] (SAG) ..... Futrmdia
Futuremedia PLC ADS [NASDAQ symbol] (TTSB) ..... FMDAY
Futuremedia PLC Wrrt [NASDAQ symbol] (TTSB) ..... FMDYW
Futures [Finance] (ODBW) ..... fut
Futures and Options Exchange [British] ..... FOX

Futures and Options Fund [*Investment term*] (ECON) .... FOF
Futures Commission Merchant .... FCM
Futures Contract [*Investment term*] .... FC
Futures Exchange [*Investment term*] .... FE
Futures for Children (EA) .... FFC
[*The*] **Futures Group** [*Commercial firm*] (EA) .... TFG
Futures Industry Association (EA) .... FIA
Futures Information Network [*Defunct*] (EA) .... FIN
Futures Information Retrieval System [*Congressional Research Service*] .... FIRST
Futures Information Service [*Institute for Futures Studies*] [*Information service
or system Defunct*] .... FUTU
Futures Network [*Ormskirk, Lancashire, England*] [*Defunct*] (EA) .... FN
Futures Spread [*Investment term*] .... FS
Futures World News [*Information service or system*] (CRD) .... FWN
Futures World News Network [*Information service or system*] (IID) .... FWN
Futurism (VRA) .... futr
Futurist [*A publication*] (BRI) .... Fut
Futurity Oils Ltd. [*Vancouver Stock Exchange symbol*] .... FTY
Futurtek Communications, Inc. [*Toronto Stock Exchange symbol*] .... FTK
Fuyang [*China*] [*Airport symbol*] (OAG) .... FUG
Fuyun [*China*] [*Airport symbol*] (OAG) .... FYN
Fuze (MSA) .... FZ
Fuze Arming Test Experiment .... FATE
Fuze Cavity Liner [*Projectile*] (NG) .... FCL
Fuze Committee [*Military*] .... FC
Fuze Control Device (MCD) .... FCD
Fuze Delay .... FD

Fuze Engineering Standardization Working Group [*Military*] (RDA) .... FESWG
Fuze Firing Circuit (RDA) .... FFC
Fuze Function Control (DNAB) .... FFC
Fuze Maintenance Spares (NG) .... FMS
Fuze Management Board [*Army*] .... FMB
Fuze Management Organization [*Army*] .... FMO
Fuze Set Test Set .... FSTS
Fuze-Activating Static Target (MCD) .... FAST
Fuzed Alloy .... FA
Fuzed Silica Tube .... FST
Fuze-Triggering Device (MCD) .... FTD
Fuzhou [*China*] [*Airport symbol*] (OAG) .... FOC
Fuzhou [*China*] [*ICAO location identifier*] (ICLI) .... ZSFZ
Fuzing, Arming, and Firing .... FAF
Fuzing, Arming, Test and Evaluation (PDAA) .... FATE
Fuzzy BIT [*Binary Digit*] **Map** [*Computer science*] .... FBM
Fuzzy Cluster Analysis [*Mathematics*] .... FCA
Fuzzy Cognitive Map [*Logic*] .... FCM
Fuzzy Inference Development Environment [*Computer science*] .... FIDE
Fuzzy Logic Adaptive Controller - Helicoptor [*Army*] (RDA) .... FLAC-H
Fuzzy Logic Inferences per Second [*Computer chip technology*] .... FLIP
Fuzzy Logical Inferences per Second [*Computer chip technology*] .... FLIPS
Fuzzy Network (PDAA) .... FNET
Fuzzy Relational Inference Language (NITA) .... FRIL
Fuzzy-Logic Controller [*Engineering*] .... FLC
FX Energy, Inc. [*Associated Press*] (SAG) .... FX Ener
FX Energy, Inc. [*NASDAQ symbol*] (SAG) .... FXEN
Fyresdal [*Norway ICAO location identifier*] (ICLI) .... ENFY